（修訂第二版）

英華大詞典

A NEW ENGLISH-CHINESE DICTIONARY

(Second Revised Edition)

First edited by Zheng Yi Li and Cao Cheng Xiu

SECOND REVISED EDITION
edited by Zheng Yi Li, Dang Feng De,
Xu Shi Gu, Hu Xue Yuan,
Liu Bang Shen, Shen Feng Wei
Executive editor: Xu Shi Gu
Managing editor: Dang Feng De

The Commercial Press
Beijing · Hong Kong
and
John Wiley and Sons, Inc.
New York · Chichester · Brisbane · Toronto

The Commercial Press Limited
4/F., Kiu Ying Bldg.
2D, Finnie St., Quarry Bay, Hong Kong

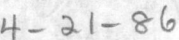

John Wiley & Sons, Inc.
605 Third Avenue
New York, NY 10158, USA

ISBN 0-471-80896-2 John Wiley & Sons, Inc.
(Worldwide with exception of Hong Kong
Japan, and SE Asia)

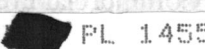

Printed by
C & C Joint Printing Co., (H.K.) Ltd.
75, Pau Chung Street,
Kowloon, Hong Kong

目　　次

Contents

前　言

Preface to the Second Revised Edition

《英华大词典》（修订第二版）是在1957年修订第一版的基础上，先经原编者作初步修订，后又由商务印书馆编辑部组织馆内外力量再作加工，於1981年初完成初稿陆续发排的。在发排过程中，又对初稿作了一次全面的修改和增补。现将新版增补修订的内容以及修订过程分别简述如下。

一、新版《英华大词典》增补修订的内容

增收大量新词：新版《英华大词典》在收词上，除保留旧版百科性条目和俚俗语词较多的优点外，并对旧版作了大量补充。新版增收了《英语新词词典》（商务印书馆，1978）的全部三万词条，又参照国内外同类型的词典，另行增补一批新词，并特别注意补收了旧版所忽视的“构词成分”(combining form)。这样，本词典的词目，包括缩略语、复合词和派生词在内，在删除旧版中个别过于冷僻的词目后，总数已达到十二万条以上，总字数约六百万字。

词目划分音节：新版的全部词目和绝大部分派生词都划分音节，以利于读者掌握读音和移行规则，这也是目前国外大部分英语词典的通行做法。

调整异源同形词：旧版中词源不同而拼写形式相同的词目，均放在一个条目词内处理，往往造成词义混淆和例证张冠李戴；新版中的这些词均分立条目。

更新、补充注音：新版在注音方面采用国际音标，按丹尼尔·琼斯的《正音词典》第十三版作了一定的更新，如以标音符号 əu 代替 ou 等。同时，旧版在处理条目词的注音时，凡认为与上条词目有相同的，该相同部分就略而不标；新版则全部标音，读者查阅时可以一目了然。

释义有较大的修订、补充：新版注意保持旧版释义译文表达方式丰富和生动活泼的特色，但对释义的义项作了大量修订和补充，若干重点词全部改写。旧版时常将动词的及物与不及物释义混杂在一起，有碍于读者辨别和理解词义，新版则力求区别处理。旧版对介词与形容词和动词的搭配关系未加注意，新版则尽量在汉语释义后用圆括号注明搭配的介词。旧版中某些词的多项释义含糊地并列，新版则尽量用①②③……符号加以分隔，按不同意义分项归并。此外，新版还有选择地在某些释义之后举出其反义词（置于圆括号内），以利于读者从对照中加深理解。

对例证、习语和复合词作一定的增补与调整：新版对例证、习语和复合词均有所补充，对习语的增补尤为注意，放宽界限，力求多收，以利于读者查阅。对旧版中例证、习语和复合词三者相互混淆的缺点，新版尽可能予以分类归并，务使界限分明，便于检索。

此外，在编排方式和规格体例方面，新版也作了一些方便读者的改动，详见“用法说明”。

二、新版《英华大词典》的修订过程

《英华大词典》原系郑易里、曹成修所编，1950年由三联书店在上海出版。1957年，由当时的时代出版社约请尚永清、张景明和陈羽纶就原纸型进行过挖改的修订工作。六十年代我馆委托原编者郑易里根据国外同类型的词典做过一番修订工作，但由于种种原因，未能付排问世。1978年，

我馆编辑部根据少量增补、小规模修订的原则，又请郑易里、胡学元、刘邦琛、沈凤威在郑的修订稿的基础上分别负责A－D字母、E－L字母、M－R字母和S－Z字母四个部分的增补修订工作。1980年初，我馆重新组织力量，对该稿进行增补、审订和加工整理工作，至1981年初完成初稿后陆续发排。在发排过程中，考虑到国内外英语词典发展的新形势，又由党凤德、徐式谷对校样作了一次全面的修改和增补。

这几年中，先后参加过本词典稿部分审订加工和整理定稿工作的，有王白石、刘邦琛、刘秀英、任永长、沈凤威、李华驹、陈少衡、陈羽纶、陈作卿、林光、费致德、姚乃强、欧阳达、徐式谷、党凤德、曹丽顺、戴钢等（姓名按汉字笔划顺序排列）。

本词典的责任编辑是徐式谷。

本词典修订、审读、定稿的总负责人是党凤德。

商务印书馆编辑部
一九八四年九月·香港

用 法 说 明

Guide to the Use of the Dictionary

一、词目

(1) 一般词目排黑正体；外来语词目排黑斜体。

(2) 同一词而拼法不同的，合并为一个词目，中以逗号分开，例如：**mac·ca·boy, mac·ca·baw.**

(3) 语源不同而拼法相同的词分立词目，例如：**lay·er**[1]，**lay·er**[2].

(4) 词目一律划分音节。

二、读音

(1) 国际音标套以方括号。重音和次重音符号打在重读音节之前，例如：**ab·o·li·tion** [ˌæbəˈliʃən]

(2) 同一词目有两个或两个以上读音时，音标相同的部分用“-”符号省略，例如：**mac·ca·boy, mac·ca·baw** [ˈmækəbɔi, -bɔː]

(3) 可不发音的音标用斜体字表示，例如：**na·tion** [ˈneiʃ*ə*n]。元音的长音符号可有可无时，用圆括号表示，例如：**cross** [krɔ(ː)s]

三、词类 词类按名词、代词、形容词、冠词、数词、动词、副词、连接词、前置词和感叹词划分为十类，在释义时使用各自的英语略语词，如 *n.* 指替名词，*a.* 指替形容词等(详见“缩略语表”)。

四、词形变化

(1) 名词，代词，形容词，副词和动词等的不规则词形变化排黑斜体，套以圆括号，并视需要加注读音。

(2) 变形词同一级别而拼法不同的，用逗号“，”分开；级别不同的，用分号“；”分开。例如：**gnaw** 的，词形变化为：(~***ed***; ~***ed***, ***gnawn*** [nɔːn])

五、释义

(1) 词类不同并需要分开释义时，在第二个和以后的词类变换前加“—”符号。

(2) 同词类有多项释义时，用 ①，②，③，……分开。某分义项需要再往下分时，用 a)，b)，c)，… 分开。

(3) 同一义项用一个以上汉语对等词释义时，凡意思相近的，用逗号分开，意思较远的，用分号分开，例如：**a·bout** *ad.* … ①大约，差不多；前后，左右。

(4) 释义之后所列搭配用词排白斜体，套以圆括号，例如：**look** *vi.* … ①看，注视 *(at)*.

(5) 可以互相替换用的词，不论英语或汉语，一律用方括号表示，例如：***a bird in the hand [bush]*** 现实[不现实]的、有[无]把握的事物。

(6) 释义时所用各种门类词缩略语见“缩略语表”。

(7) 释义中有关词目词的用法套以六角括号，例如：**a·ware** …〔用作表语〕知道。

(8) 释义时需要进一步注明用法和注意事项时，前面冠以“★”符号。

六、例证

(1) 例词例句基本上按不同词类分列，一律排白斜体。

(2) 词目词的例证不套括号；复合词和派生词的例证套以圆括号。

七、成语词组

(1) 成语词组集中在释义之后，基本上按其中心词的不同词类分列，其先后次序以成语首词的字母次序为准。

(2) 成语词组排黑斜体。

八、复合词

(1) 复合词排黑正体。

(2) 复合词需要分词类释义时，用 ①，②，… 分开，例如：**mad** 的复合词 **~cap** ① *n.* 狂妄的人，… ② *a.* 鲁莽的，…。

九、派生词

(1) 不立词条的简单派生词排黑正体，放在词条最后，并划分音节，酌情注音。

(2) 派生词前一律冠以“-”符号。此处“-”符号可代表本词目的全部拼法，例如：**-ly**，**-ness**；也可代表本词目的部分拼法，例如：**mac·ro·cyte** 的派生词写成 **-cyt·ic.**

十、其他符号

(1) “~”符号代表词目词的全部拼法。

(2) “-”符号代表词目词的部分拼法，但在简单派生词中也可代表词目词的全部。

缩 略 语 表

Abbreviations Used in the Dictionary

a. …… adjective（形容词）
ad. …… adverb（副词）
art. …… article（冠词）
c.f. …… confer（参看）
comb. f. …… combining form（构词成分）
conj. …… conjunction（连接词）
fem. …… feminine（阴性）
int. …… interjection（感叹词）
mas. …… masculine（阳性）
n. …… noun（名词）
neg. …… negative（否定词）
nom. …… nominative（主格）
num. …… numeral（数词）
obj. …… objective（宾格）
p. …… past（过去）
pl. …… plural（复数）
poss. …… possessive（所有格）
p. p. …… past participle（过去分词）
pref. …… prefix（前缀）
prep. …… preposition（前置词）
pres. …… present（现在）
pres. p. …… present participle（现在分词）
pro. …… pronoun（代词）
rel. pro. …… relative pronoun（关系代词）
sing. …… singular（单数）
suf. …… suffix（后缀）
v. …… verb（动词）
v. aux. …… auxiliary verb（助动词）
vi. …… intransitive verb（不及物动词）
vt. …… transitive verb（及物动词）

• • • • •

〔Am.〕…… 美国英语
〔Ar.〕…… 阿拉伯语
〔Aus.〕…… 澳大利亚英语
〔Ban.〕…… 班图语
〔Can.〕…… 加拿大用语
〔Chin.〕…… 汉语
〔D.〕…… 荷兰语
〔Egy.〕…… 埃及语
〔Eng.〕…… 英语
〔F.〕…… 法语
〔G.〕…… 德语
〔Gr.〕…… 希腊语
〔Haw.〕…… 夏威夷语
〔Heb.〕…… 希伯来语
〔Hind.〕…… 印地语
〔Ind.〕…… 印度用语
〔Ir.〕…… 爱尔兰语
〔It.〕…… 意大利语
〔Jap.〕…… 日语
〔Jav.〕…… 爪哇语
〔Kor.〕…… 朝鲜语
〔L.〕…… 拉丁语
〔Ma.〕…… 马来语
〔Maor.〕…… 毛利语
〔Per.〕…… 波斯语
〔Pg.〕…… 葡萄牙语
〔Phil.〕…… 菲律宾用语
〔Pol.〕…… 波兰语
〔Russ.〕…… 俄语
〔S.Afr.〕…… 南非用语
〔Sans.〕…… 梵语
〔Scot.〕…… 苏格兰语
〔Slav.〕…… 斯拉夫语
〔Sp.〕…… 西班牙语
〔Teut.〕…… 条顿语
〔Thai〕…… 泰语
〔Turk〕…… 土耳其语

• • • • •

(照笔画次序)
〔大洋〕……大洋洲
〔中〕……中国
〔日〕……日本
〔印〕……印度
〔希〕……希腊
〔英〕……英国
〔拉美〕……拉丁美洲
〔欧〕……欧洲
〔非〕……非洲
〔法〕……法国
〔美〕……美国
〔秘〕……秘鲁
〔爱〕……爱尔兰
〔意〕……意大利
〔德〕……德国
〔澳〕……澳大利亚

• • • • •

(照笔画次序)

〔儿〕……儿语
〔口〕……口语
〔反〕……反意语
〔方〕……方言
〔书〕……书面语
〔古〕……古语
〔旧〕……旧用
〔讽〕……讽刺语
〔罕〕……罕用语
〔卑〕……下流话
〔贬〕……贬义
〔废〕……废话
〔学〕……学生话
〔诗〕……诗歌
〔俚〕……俚语
〔弱〕……弱音
〔谑〕……玩笑话
〔谚〕……谚语
〔婉〕……委婉语
〔喻〕……比喻
〔强〕……强音
〔蔑〕……蔑称
〔缩〕……缩略语

• • • • •

(照笔画次序)

【工】……工业
【无】……无线电
【天】……天文学
【天主】……天主教
【贝】……贝类
【化】……化学
【化纤】……化学纤维
【气】……气象学
【计】……计算机
【心】……心理学
【水】……水利；水文
【占】……占星术
【古生】……古生物学
【电】……电工；电学
【史】……历史
【印】……印刷
【生】……生物学
【生化】……生物化学
【鸟】……鸟类
【乐】……音乐
【讯】……电讯
【圣】……圣经
【动】……动物；动物学
【地】……地质学；地理学
【机】……机械工程
【光】……光学
【虫】……虫类
【伦】……伦理学
【自】……自动化
【交】……交通
【宇】……宇宙空间技术
【军】……军事
【农】……农业
【医】……医学
【体】……体育
【邮】……邮政
【犹】……犹太教
【犹神】……犹太神话
【佛】……佛教
【希神】……希腊神话
【冶】……冶金
【社】……社会学
【纹】……纹章
【纺】……纺织；印染
【林】……林业
【矿】……矿物；采矿
【罗神】……罗马神话
【物】……物理
【股】……股票
【鱼】……鱼类
【法】……法律
【宗】……宗教
【空】……航空
【建】……建筑
【经】……经济学
【政】……政治学
【药】……药学
【修】……修辞学
【剑】……击剑
【胚】……胚胎学
【美】……美术
【语】……语言学
【神】……神学
【绘】……绘画
【统】……统计学
【原】……原子能
【哲】……哲学
【畜】……畜牧
【病】……病理学
【海】……航海
【拳】……拳击
【剧】……戏剧
【教】……教育
【基督】……基督教
【逻】……逻辑学
【船】……造船
【商】……商业
【猎】……打猎
【植】……植物；植物学
【牌】……牌戏
【摄】……摄影
【微】……微生物学
【解】……解剖学
【数】……数学
【精】……精神病学
【影】……电影
【雕】……雕刻
【韵】……音韵学
【徽】……徽章

主要参考书目

Bibliography

1. Webster's New World Dictionary of the American Language Second College Edition
2. Webster's Third New International Dictionary of the English Language Unabridged
3. Concise Oxford Dictionary of Current English (Sixth Edition)
4. Shorter Oxford English Dictionary
5. Shogakukan Random House English-Japanese Dictionary
6. Longman Dictionary of Contemporary English (1978)
7. Daniel Jones: Everyman's English Pronouncing Dictionary (Thirteenth Edition)
8. 6,000 Words, A Supplement to Webster's Third New International Dictionary
9. Webster's New Collegiate Dictionary
10. 新英汉词典(上海人民出版社)
11. 英语成语词典(厦门大学外文系编)
12. 英汉技术词典(清华大学编)
13. 简明英汉科技词典(西安交通大学编)
14. 国内出版的其他英汉专业词汇词典(科学出版社等出版社出版)
15. 综合英汉大辞典(商务印书馆)

A

A, a [ei] *(pl.* ***A's, a's*** [eiz]*)* ①英语字母表第一字母. ②A形物. ③【乐】A音; A调. ④【数】第一已知数. ⑤〔美〕(学业成绩的)优等, 五分. ⑥表示"第一"的符号. *A 1 = A one* [ˈei ˈwʌn] 头等的, 极好的. *A major [minor]* A大调[小调]. *straight A's* 全优. *A (No.)1. tea* 一级茶. *an A tent* A字形帐篷. *He is A (No.)1.* 他是头号人物. ***from A to Z*** 自始至终, 完全. ***not know A from B*** 一字不识.

a [强 ei; 弱 ə], **an** [强 æn; 弱 ən]〔an 用在以元音音素开始的词前〕 *indefinite art.* ①〔普通可数名词第一次提到时, 冠以不定冠词主要表示类别, 有时则兼含"一"的概念〕: *This is a transformer.* 这是变压器. *Ours is a socialist country.* 我国是个社会主义国家. *a house* 一所住宅. *an army* 一支军队. ②〔在数量概念上, 说明表示时间、距离、重量及数目的名词〕一. *a thousand* 一千. *an hour* 一小时. *a mile* 一英里. *a pound* 一磅. ③〔与数量形容词、数词等连用而表示一个整体单位〕: *a dozen times* 十二次. *a great many years* 许多年. *A ten years is not so long.* 十年的时间并不算怎么长. ④〔与某些复数名词连用而仍表示一个单位〕: *a glassworks* (一家)玻璃厂. *a falls in the river* 河中的瀑布. ⑤〔与序数词或形容词最高级结合共同限定所修饰的名词〕: *He tried to jump up a third time.* 他试图作第三次的跳高动作. *It was a most beautiful sight.* 这是一个最美丽的景致. ⑥〔表示同类事物中的代表〕任何一个〔种〕. *A horse is useful.* 马是有用的. ⑦同一的, 相同的. *We are all of a mind.* 我们大家一条心. *of a size* (属于)同一大小. *birds of a feather* 同一毛色的鸟. ⑧〔两件成套的东西, 用 and 连接, 仍视为一个单位〕一(副). *a cup and saucer* 带茶托的茶杯. ⑨〔抽象名词用作普通名词, 表示类别、例证〕: *Would you do me a kindness?* 你能帮我一下忙吗? *a virtue* 一种美德. ⑩〔用于专有名词前, 以整体概括个体, 表示类似的一个或某一个〕: *a Mr. Smith* 一个叫史密斯的人. *a Newton* 象牛顿那样的人. *a Ford* 一辆福特汽车. ⑪〔与强义词 how, what, such, too, so, quite, rather 以及 half 等搭配使用时, 常置于各该词的后面〕: *So beautiful a jewel!* 多么好看的宝石! *How great a man he is!* 他真是伟人! *rather a queer fellow* 十分古怪的家伙. *half an hour* 半小时. ⑫〔在习惯用法上, 相当于介词 in, for, on 的作用〕每(…), 在…内, 按(…而论), 换(得). *three times a day* 每天三回. *five dollors a catty* 五元美金(买)一斤. *twice a year* 一年内两次. ⑬〔口〕一客: *an ice* 一客冰淇淋.

A. = ①【化】argon 氩. ②【物】angstrom (unit) 埃(Å).

A. = ①absolute (temperature). ②Academy. ③Admiral. ④adult (=for adults only). ⑤America(n).

a. = ①about. ②accepted. ③acre. ④active. ⑤acting. ⑥adjective. ⑦after. ⑧afternoon. ⑨aged. ⑩alto. ⑪ampere. ⑫*anno* (= in the year of). ⑬answer. ⑭*ante* (= before). ⑮approved.

a- *pref.* ①表示加强: *a*bide, *a*rise, *a*wake. ②表示"on", "in", "to". "into" 的意思: *a*foot = on foot. *a*side = to one side. *a*back = backward. *a*bed = in bed. *a*sunder = into pieces. *a*sleep = in sleep. ③表示"of" 的意思: *a*kin (of kin); *a*new (of new). ④表示"from" 的意思: *a*bridge. ⑤表示 "out" 的意思: *a*mend. ⑥表示 "not" 的意思: *a*chromatic, *a*moral, *a*sexual.

A. A., AA = ①antiaircraft: *an A. A. artillery unit* 高射炮部队. ②ack-ack.

AAAL = American Academy of Arts and Letters 美国艺术和文学学会.

AAAS = ①American Association for the Advancement of Science 美国科学促进会. ②American Academy of Arts and Sciences 美国艺术和科学研究院.

AAF = Army Air Forces〔美〕陆军航空队.

AAJA = Afro-Asian Journalists' Association 亚非新闻工作者协会.

AAM = air-to-air missile 空对空导弹.

aard·vark [ˈɑːdvɑːk] *n.*【动】土豚〔南非食蚁兽〕.

aard·wolf [ˈɑːdwulf] *n.*【动】土狼〔南非产〕.

Aar·hus [ˈɔːhuːs] *n.* 奥尔胡斯〔丹麦港市〕.

Aar·on [ˈɛərən] *n.* ①艾伦〔男子名〕. ②亚伦〔基督教《圣经》中人物, 摩西之兄, 犹太教第一祭司长〕. **~'s beard**【植】黄栌, 虎耳草(之类). **~'s rod** ①【植】麒麟草. ②【圣】(缠有蛇的)亚伦魔杖. ③【建】缠蛇杆式装饰.

AAS = American Academy of Sciences 美国科学院.

AAUP = American Association of University Professors 美国大学教授联合会.

AAWB = Afro-Asian Writers' Bureau 亚非作家常设局.

A. B., AB = ①able-bodied seaman〔英军〕二等水兵;【海】一等水兵. ②〔L.〕*Artium Baccalaureus* (= Bachelor of Arts) 文学士. ③airborne. ④Atomic Bomb 原子弹.

ab. = ①abbreviation. ②about. ③absent. ④absolute. ⑤(-times) at bat【棒球】打球的次数.

ab- [æb-, əb-] *pref.* ①= away,(away) from, off, apart: *ab*normal; *ab*duct 等. ②【物】= absolute. ★在 c, t 前作 abs-, 如: *abs*cond, *abs*tract; 在 m, p, v 前作 a-, 如: *a*mentia *a*perient, *a*vert.

ab [æb] *prep.*〔L.〕从(= from, away). **~ *extra*** [ˈekstrə] 自外, 从外部, 外来. **~ *initio*** [iˈniʃiəu] 从开头, 从开始〔略 ab init〕. **~ *intra*** [ˈintrə] 从内部. **~ *origine*** [əuˈridʒiniː] 从起源. **~ *ovo*** [ˈəuvəu] 从开始. **~ *uno disce omnes*** [ˈjuːnəu ˈdisiː ˈɔmniːz] 由一斑而知全豹, 闻一而知十. **~ *urbe condita*** [ˈəːbi ˈkɔnditə] 由罗马建都(公元前 753 年)起算〔略 A.U.C.〕.

a·ba [ˈæbə] *n.* ①驼毛〔山羊毛等〕原色粗呢; 粗厚农民呢. ②阿拉伯式斗篷.

ab·a·ca [ˌɑːbəˈkɑː] *n.* 马尼拉麻; 麻蕉.

ab·a·ci [ˈæbəsai] abacus 的复数.

a·back [əˈbæk] *ad.* 向后;【海】逆帆. ***be taken*** **~** ①(突遇逆风)成逆帆. ②吓了一跳 *(He was taken ~ by the news.* 他被这消息吓了一跳*)*.

ab·a·cus [ˈæbəkəs] *n.* *(pl.* ***~es, -ci*** [-sai]*)* ①算盘. ②【建】(圆柱顶部的)顶板, 冠板. *learn to use [work] an ~* 学打算盘.

A·ba·dan [ˌæbəˈdɑːn] *n.* ①阿巴丹岛〔伊朗〕. ②阿巴丹〔伊朗港市〕.

A·bad·don [əˈbædən] *n.* ①无底洞, 地狱. ②地狱恶魔 (= Apollyon).

a·baft [əˈbɑːft] *ad., prep.*【海】在船尾, 向船尾; 在…后面. *~ the beam* 在船的横梁之后.

ab·a·lo·ne [ˌæbəˈləuni] *n.*【动】石决明〔旧称鲍鱼〕.

ab·am·pere [æbˈæmpɛə] *n.* 【物】绝对安培，电磁安培．
a·ban·don [əˈbændən] *vt.* ①扔弃(地位等)，离弃（家园)；断绝(念头等)，戒除(恶习等)．②【法】遗弃(妻子)，放弃（权利等)．③【保险】投保（货物等)．～ ***oneself to*** 恣意，沉迷（酒，色)（～ *oneself to pleasure(s)* 恣意享乐．～ *oneself to despair* 悲观失望．～ *oneself to emotion* 感情用事)．— *n.* 放肆；任性 (*opp.* restraint, constraint). ***with*** ～ 尽情地(唱等)．**-er** *n.* 放弃者，遗弃者；【保险】投保人．
a·ban·doned [əˈbændənd] *a.* ①被放弃[扔弃、遗弃]了的．②心灰意懒的，自暴自弃的；放荡的，堕落的，无耻的．*an* ～ *character* 荡子；无赖；无可救药的人．*an* ～ *child* 弃儿．
a·ban·don·ee [əˌbændəˈniː] *n.* ①【保险】承保人．②【法】被遗弃人．
a·ban·don·ment [əˈbændənment] *n.* ①放弃，断念．②放肆．③【保险】投保；遗弃．～ *of an action*【法】放弃诉讼．～ *of a right* 弃权．
à bas [ɑː ˈbɑː]〔F.〕打倒…（=down with).
a·base [əˈbeis] *vt.* 贬，降低(地位、价值、身分)．～ *oneself* 自贬，自卑．**-ment** *n.* 失意；屈辱；败落．
a·bash [əˈbæʃ] *vt.* 使…羞愧，使…脸红．*Nothing can* ～ *him.* 什么也不会使他脸红［羞愧]，他的脸皮很厚．*be [feel]* ～*ed* 侷促不安．**-ment** *n.*
a·bask [əˈbɑːsk] *ad.* 晒着太阳，靠近炉火(取暖)．
a·bate [əˈbeit] *vt.* ①减少，减轻（痛苦等)；降低，减(价)；缓和．②【法】取消(法令)，中止(诉讼)；排除（障碍)．③除掉；夺去．～ *a tax* 减税．～ *sb.'s pain* 减轻某人的痛苦．～ *sb. of sth.* 夺取某人的东西．～ *a nuisance* 排除骚扰．— *vi.* ①(洪水、风暴、病痛等）减少，减轻，减退．*The storm has* ～*d.* 风暴减弱了．②【法】中止，作废．
a·bate·ment [əˈbeitmənt] *n.* ①减少，减轻，减退．②【法】(遗产的)非法占有；中断；失效．～ *of penalty* 减刑．～ *of taxes* 减税．***plea in*** ～【法】妨诉抗辩．
ab·a·t(t)is [ˈæbətis] *n.* *(pl.* ～ [ˈæbətiːz])【军】鹿砦，拒木，障碍物．
ab·at·toir [ˈæbətwɑː] *n.*〔F.〕屠宰场．
ab·ax·i·al [æbˈæksiəl] *a.*【植】背轴的，远轴的 *(opp. adaxial).*
abb [æb] *n.* ①粗羊毛．②粗毛线．③纬纱（= woof; *opp.* warp).
Abb. = ①Abbess. ②Abbey. ③Abbot.
Ab·ba [ˈæbə] *n.* ①圣父〔东正教冠于主教和大主教名字前的尊称〕．②天父〔基督教祈祷时用于称呼上帝〕．
ab·ba·cy [ˈæbəsi] *n.* 修道院院长的职位[管区、任期]．
Ab·bas·sid [əˈbæsid, ˈæbəsid] *n.* (阿拉伯帝国)阿巴斯王朝(750–1258)的统治者．— *a.* 阿巴斯王朝的．
ab·ba·tial [əˈbeiʃəl] *a.* 男［女］修道院院长的；修道院的．
ab·bé [ˈæbei; F. abei] *n.*〔F.〕*(pl.* ～*s)* 修道院院长；神父．
ab·bess [ˈæbis] *n.* 女修道院院长．
Ab·be·vil·li·an [ˌæbiˈviliən, -ljən] *a.*【考古】阿贝维尔期的〔阿贝维尔为法国城市名，阿贝维尔期指旧石器时代晚期文化，特点是使用石手斧〕．
Ab·bey [ˈæbi] *n.* 阿比〔姓氏〕．
ab·bey [ˈæbi] *n.* ①修道院，大教堂，大寺院．②全院修道士[修道女]．*the Abbey* 伦敦威斯敏斯特 (Westminster) 大教堂．
Ab·bot(t) [ˈæbət] *n.* 阿博特〔姓氏〕．
ab·bot [ˈæbət] *n.* 男修道院院长．***the Abbot of Misrule [Unreason]***（英国指十五、十六世纪时）圣诞节狂欢会的主持人．
abbr(ev). = ①abbreviated. ②abbreviation.
ab·bre·vi·ate [əˈbriːvieit] *vt.* ①节略，省略，缩写．②缩短(行期等)．③【数】约分．*New York is* ～*d to N.Y.* New York 缩写为 N.Y.
ab·bre·vi·a·tion [əˌbriːviˈeiʃən] *n.* ①省略，缩写．②缩写词，略语．③【数】约分．④【乐】略号．
ab·bre·vi·a·tor [əˈbriːviˌeitə] *n.* 缩写者；节略者．
Abby [ˈæbi] *n.* 阿比〔女子名，Abigai 的昵称〕．
ABC [ˈeibiːˈsiː] *n. (pl. ABC's)* 字母表；初步，入门；基础知识．*the* ～ *of finance* 财政初步．～ *book* 初学书，入门书．～ *method*（由字母教起的）初级语文教授法．***as easy as*** ～ 极其容易．***the*** ～ ***(guide)***〔英〕(按字母顺序编排的)铁路旅行指南．
ABC = ①American Broadcasting Company 美国广播公司．②Australian Broadcasting Corporation 澳大利亚广播公司．③Asian Badminton Confederation 亚洲羽毛球联合会．
ABC warfare = atomic, biological, chemical warfare 原子、生物、化学战．
ab·cou·lomb [æbˈkuːlɔm] *n.*【物】绝对库伦；电磁制库伦．
ABD = All But Dissertation (已完成课程及考试但尚缺论文的)准博士．
ab·di·cate [ˈæbdikeit] *vt.* ①弃，放弃(权利)．②退(位)；让(位)；辞(职)；【法】废(嫡)．— *vi.* (国王)退位．～ ***the throne in sb.'s favour[in favour of sb.]*** 让位给某人．
ab·di·ca·tion [ˌæbdiˈkeiʃən] *n.* ①弃权；让位；辞职．②【法】废嫡．
ab·di·ca·tor [ˈæbdikeitə] *n.* 弃权人；让位者．
ab·do·men [ˈæbdəmen, æbˈdəumen] *n.* 腹，下腹部；【虫】腹部．
ab·dom·i·nal [æbˈdɔminl] *a.* ①腹部的，腹腔的．②【鱼】有腹鳍的．～ **breathing** 腹式呼吸．～ **catarrh** 肠炎．～ **cavity** 肠腔．～ **dropsy** 腹水病．～ **operation** 剖腹手术．～ **region** 腹部．～ **typhus** 肠伤寒．
ab·dom·i·nous [æbˈdɔminəs] *a.* 大肚皮的，肥胖的．
ab·duce [æbˈdjuːs] *vt.*【解】使外展．
ab·du·cent [æbˈdjuːsnt] *a.*【解、动】外展的 (*opp.* adducent). ～ **muscles** 外展肌．
ab·duct [æbˈdʌkt] *vt.* ①诱拐，拐走．②【生理】外展 (*opp.* adduct).
ab·duc·tion [æbˈdʌkʃən] *n.* ①诱拐．②外展(作用)．
ab·duc·tor [æbˈdʌktə] *n.* ①诱拐者，拐子．②【解】外展肌 (*opp.* adductor).
Abe [eib] *n.* 埃布〔男子名，Abraham 的昵称〕．
a·beam [əˈbiːm] *ad.* 正横〔与船的龙骨或飞机机身成直角〕．
a·be·ce·dar·i·an [ˌeibi(ː)si(ː)ˈdɛəriən] *a.* ①照ABC顺序的．②初学的；初步的，基本的．— *n.*〔美〕①初学者．②启蒙老师．
a·bed [əˈbed] *ad.*〔古〕在床上．*be ill [sick]* ～ 病倒床上．*lie* ～ 躺在床上；坐月子．
A·bel [ˈeibəl] *n.* ①埃布尔〔姓氏，男子名〕．②【圣】亚伯〔亚当和夏娃的次子〕．
a·bele [əˈbiːl, ˈeibl] *n.*【植】银白杨．
a·be·lian [əˈbiːljən] *a.*【数】能成立可换定律的．*an A-group*【数】可换群．
Ab·er·crom·bie, Ab·er·crom·by [ˈæbəkrʌmbi] *n.* 阿伯克龙比〔姓氏〕．
Ab·er·deen [ˌæbəˈdiːn] *n.* ①阿伯丁〔英国港市〕．②阿伯丁郡〔英国郡名〕(= ～shire). ③苏格兰粗毛猎狐狗 (= ～ terrier). ～ **Angus** [ˈæŋgəs] *n.*（苏格兰肉用）无角黑牛．
ab·er·de·vine [ˌæbədəˈvain] *n.*【鸟】金雀类．
a·ber·glau·be [ˌɑːbəˈglaubə] *n.*〔G.〕迷信．
ab·er·rance [æˈberəns], **-ran·cy** [-si] *n.* 离开正道，越轨．
ab·er·rant [æˈberənt] *a.* ①离开正路的，脱离常规的．②【生】畸变的，异常的．～ **form**【生】畸变型．
ab·er·ra·tion [ˌæbəˈreiʃən] *n.* ①偏差，越轨；错乱；一

时的记错；【法】过失．②【医】乖常，失常；【生】畸变；变型．③【物】象差；【天】光行差．*mental* ～ 精神失常．

a·bet [ə'bet] *vt.* 唆使，鼓动，怂恿，助长 (*opp.* hinder). ***aid and*** ～【法】教唆，煽动．***to*** ～ ***an ill-doer*** 助桀为虐．**-ment** *n.* 煽动，教唆．

a·bet·ter, -tor [ə'betə] *n.* 煽动者，教唆者．

a·bey·ance [ə'beiəns] *n.* 中止，暂搁，保留，缓议，缓办，停止；未定；【法】(所有权等的)未定．***be in*** ～ 暂停；未定．***fall into*** ～ (世袭爵位等)即行中止；(法规等)暂时失效．***hold [leave] in*** ～ 暂搁．

ab·hor [əb'hɔː] *vt.* ***(-hor·red; -hor·ring)*** 憎恶，厌恶，嫌弃．

ab·hor·rence [əb'hɔrəns] *n.* 嫌恶；厌恶，痛恨；极其讨厌的人[物]．***have an*** ～ ***of = hold in*** ～ 厌恶，痛恨．

ab·hor·rent [əb'hɔrənt] *a.* ①可恶的，讨厌的．②不相容的，跟…不(投)合的 ***(to; from)***；〔古〕嫌厌 ***(of)***. ***be*** ～ ***to*** ***(sb.; his idea)*** 和(某人)不相投；和(某人意见)不合．

ab·hor·rer [əb'hɔːrə] *n.* 嫌恶者；反对者．

a·bid·ance [ə'baidəns] *n.* ①继续．②留在 ***(in)***. ③遵守．～ *by rules [terms]* 遵守规章[条例]．

a·bide [ə'baid] *vi.* ***(a·bode*** [ə'bəud]***, a·bid·ed; a·bode, a·bid·ed)*** ①〔古〕住，居住；逗留．②保持，继续．③遵守．～ *at Paris* 住在巴黎．～ *in one's father's house* 住在自己父亲家里．～ *in sin* 怙恶不悛．～ *with one's father* 和父亲同住．— *vt.* ①等待．②忍受，忍耐〔用于否定和疑问〕：*I can not* ～ *him.* 我对他忍无可忍．～ ***by*** 坚持；遵守(法律、契约、诺言等)；依从，服从 (～ *by one's opinion* 固执己见．～ *by the inevitable* 迫于不得已)．

a·bid·ing [ə'baidiŋ] *a.* 〔书〕持久的，不变的．～ *friendship* 持久的友谊．～ *place* 住宅，家．

Ab·i·djan [ˌæbi'dʒɑːn] *n.* 阿比让〔象牙海岸首都〕．

Ab·i·gail ['æbigeil] *n.* ①阿比盖尔〔女子名〕．②[a-] (贵妇人的)使女．

a·bil·i·ty [ə'biliti] *n.* 能，能力，本领，技能；〔*pl.*〕才，才能，才干．*financial abilities* 财力．*a man of* ～ 有本事的人．***to the best of one's*** ～ 竭力，尽力，尽量．

-a·bil·i·ty *suf.* 由 -able 转成的名词后缀，表示"可能性"：cur*ability*.

ab ini·tio [ˌæbi'niʃiəu]〔L.〕从开始起．

a·bi·o·gen·e·sis [ˌeibaiəu'dʒenisis] *n.*【生】自然发生(论)；无生源说．

ab·i·o·ge·net·ic [ˌeibaiəudʒi'netik] *a.* 自然发生(论)的；无生源(说)的．

ab·i·og·e·nist [ˌeibai'ɔdʒinist] *n.* 自然发生论者，偶发论者，无生源说者．

a·bi·o·sis ['eibai'əusis] *n.*【医】生活力缺失．

abi·ot·ic [ˌeibai'ɔtik] *a.* 无生命的；非生物的．

ab·ject ['æbdʒekt] *a.* ①卑鄙的，下贱的，下流的．②不幸的，悲惨的．*an* ～ *time-server* 卑鄙的趋炎附势者．*make an* ～ *apology* 告饶．～ *poverty* 赤贫．— *n.*〔古〕小人，下流人．**-ly** *ad.* **-ness** *n.*

ab·jec·tion [əb'dʒekʃən] *n.* ①落魄．②卑劣．

ab·ju·ra·tion [ˌæbdʒuə'reiʃən] *n.* 发誓断绝；公开放弃．

ab·jure [əb'dʒuə] *vt.* 发誓弃绝(信仰等)；公开放弃(国籍、权利等)．～ *the realm* 宣誓离开本国．

ab·lac·ta·tion [ˌæblæk'teiʃən] *n.* 断奶．

ab·late [æb'leit] *vt., vi.* 切除；融化；消散；腐蚀．

ab·la·tion [æb'leiʃən] *n.* ①【医】部分切除(术)；【医】脱落．②【地】消融，冰面融化；【化】烧蚀．

ab·la·ti·val [ˌæblə'taivəl] *a.*【语法】夺格的．

ab·la·tive[1] ['æblətiv] *a., n.*【语法】(拉丁语的)夺格(的)．～ **absolute** 独立夺格(结构)．

ab·la·tive[2] ['æblətiv] *a.* 易切除的；易烧蚀的．～ *plastics* 烧蚀性塑料．

ab·la·tor [æb'leitə] *n.* 防烧蚀材料．

ab·laut ['æblaut; G. 'æplaut] *n.*【语音】元音交替〔*cf.* gradation〕．(例：sing — sang — sung)．

a·blaze [ə'bleiz] *a.*〔常用作表语〕, *ad.* ①燃烧，着火．②发光，烧起，炽燃，(东西)闪耀．③(人心)激昂．***be*** ～ ***with anger*** 发火，动怒．***set*** ～烧起，燃起．

a·ble ['eibl] *a.* ***(a·bler; a·blest)*** ①〔接不定式〕能；会．②(人)有才能的，有本事的，能干的 (*opp.* incompetent). ③(行为等)显示出才华的．④【法】有法定资格的．*be* ～ *to swim* 会游泳．*an* ～ *man* 能干人．*an* ～ *speech* 漂亮的演说．★ can 没有不定式，也没有将来式、过去式等变化，故必要时可说作 shall [will, may] be ～ to 或 have [has, had] been ～ to. **～-bodied** *a.* 强壮的，健全的 (*an* ～*-bodied seaman* 一级水手，二等水兵．*an* ～*-bodied man [woman]* 男子[女子]全劳动力)．**～-minded** *a.* 能干的，能力强的．

-a·ble *suf.*〔附在动词或名词后构成形容词〕①能…的，适于…的：bear*able*, sal*able*. ②易…的：change*able*. ★以 -ate 结尾的、三音节以上的拉丁系动词，应先略去 -ate 再加用 -able: educ*ate* — educ*able*. 与 -able 相对应的副词后缀是 -ably: not*able* — not*ably*.

a·blings ['eibliŋz], **a·blins** ['eiblinz] *ad.*〔Scot.〕多半，大概，也许．

a·bloom [ə'bluːm] *a.*〔多作表语〕, *ad.* (花)盛开；开着花．

ab·lu·ent ['æbluənt] *a.* 洗涤的．— *n.* 洗涤剂．

a·blush [ə'blʌʃ] *a.*〔常作表语〕, *ad.* (因羞愧而)脸红．

ab·lu·tion [ə'bluːʃən] *n.* ①洗净，沐浴．②〔主 *pl.*〕【宗】斋戒沐浴，洗礼．③净水，洗净液．④〔*pl.*〕〔英〕〔用作复数〕兵营内的洗浴设备；〔用作单数〕有洗浴设备的房间〔建筑〕．**-a·ry** [-əri] *a.*

a·bly ['eibli] *ad.* 巧妙地，适宜地，能干地．

-a·bly *suf.* 可…地．

ABM = ①antiballistic missile 反弹道导弹．②Atomic Bomb Mission〔美〕原子弹爆炸调查团．

Ab·na·ki [æb'nɑːki] *n.*〔*pl.*〕阿布纳基人〔早先聚居在美国缅因州的阿尔衮琴部落联盟的一支印第安人〕．

ab·ne·gate ['æbnigeit] *vt.* ①放弃(权利等)．②克制．

ab·ne·ga·tion [ˌæbni'geiʃən] *n.* ①放弃．②克制．

ab·ne·ga·tor ['æbnigeitə] *n.* ①克制者．②弃权者．

ab·nor·mal [æb'nɔːməl] *a.* 反常的；变态的；不规则的．～ *condition* 非常状态．～ *psychology* 变态心理学．**-ly** *ad.*

ab·nor·mal·i·ty [ˌæbnɔː'mæliti] *n.* ①反常，变态，不规则．②变体，畸形；反常事物．

ab·nor·mi·ty [æb'nɔːmiti] *n.* 反常，不规则；畸形．

abo ['æbəu] *n.*〔Aus.〕〔蔑〕土人，土著．

a·board [ə'bɔːd] *ad.* ①在船[飞机、车]上，上船[飞机、车]．②靠船边．*climb* ～ *a train [plane]* 上车[飞机]．*keep the land* ～ (船)靠岸开．— *prep.* 在船[飞机、车]上．*go home* ～ *a train* 坐火车回家．***All*** ～***!*** 各位上船！〔美〕各位上车[飞机]！***close [hard]*** ～ 紧靠船边．***fall*** ～ ***(of)*** *(another ship)* 与(他船)船边相撞．***go*** ～ ***(of) a ship*** 乘船．***lay*** *(enemy's ship)* ～ 靠近(敌船)．***step*** ～ 上(船、飞机等)．***take*** ～ 装入．

a·bode[1] [ə'bəud] abide 的过去式及过去分词．

a·bode[2] [ə'bəud] *n.* ①住所．②居住，寄住．***make one's*** ～ 居住．***take up one's*** ～ 住到，住进．

ab·ohm [æ'bəum] *n.*【物】绝对欧姆．

a·boi·deau [ˌɑːbwɑː'dəu] *n.*〔Can.〕堰．

a·boil [ə'bɔil] *ad., a.* 沸腾，滚(水)．

a·bol·ish [ə'bɔliʃ] *vt.* 取消，废除(制度等) (*opp.* establish). **-able** *a.* 可废除的．**-er** *n.* 取消者，废除者．**-ment** *n.* 取消，废除．

ab·o·li·tion [ˌæbə'liʃən] *n.* 废除，废弃，取消 (*opp.* establishment)；废除死刑；〔美〕废除黑奴制度．**-ism** *n.* 奴隶制度[死刑]废除论．**-ist** *n.* (奴隶制度)废除论者．

ab·o·ma·sum [ˌæbə'meisəm], **-sus** [-səs] *n.* 皱胃〔反

乌动物的第四胃〕.

A-bomb [ˈeibɔm] *n.* 原子弹. — *vt.* 用原子弹轰炸.

a·bom·i·na·ble [əˈbɔminəbl] *a.* 讨厌的,可恶的,可鄙的;〔口〕(天气等)极坏的. *an ~ affair* 丑事. **A- Snowman** (喜马拉雅山的)雪人. **-bly** *ad.* ①讨厌,可恶,可鄙. ②〔口〕极坏,丑.

a·bom·i·nate [əˈbɔmineit] *vt.* 厌恶,痛恨,憎恨,嫌恶.

a·bom·i·na·tion [əˌbɔmiˈneiʃən] *n.* 厌恶,憎恨,可恶,令人憎恶的[讨厌的]事物[行为]. ***hold … in ~*** 厌恶…,憎恶….

a·bom·i·na·tor [əˈbɔmineitə] *n.* 嫌恶者.

à bon mar·ché [a bɔːŋ marʃéi] 〔F.〕 廉价,便宜.

ab·o·rig·i·nal [ˌæbəˈridʒənl] *a.* 原来的;土著的;原住,原生. — *n.* 土著住民,土生动[植]物. **-ly** *ad.* 原来,本来,从最初. **-i·ty** [-ˈnæliti] *n.* 原生状态;原始性.

ab·o·rig·i·nes [ˌæbəˈridʒiniːz] *n.* 〔*pl.*〕 土著住民;土生动[植]物.

a·born·ing [əˈbɔːniŋ] *ad.* 在诞生[产生]过程中. — *a.* 〔用作表语〕诞生[产生]过程中的.

a·bort [əˈbɔːt] *vi.* ①流产,小产,堕胎. ②(计划等)失败. ③【生理】发育不全;退化. ④【空俚】飞行中断. — *vt.* ①使流产. ②抑止(将发之病). ③使(计划)夭折.

a·bor·ti·cide [əˈbɔːtisaid] *n.* 堕胎;堕胎药.

a·bor·ti·fa·cient [əˌbɔːtiˈfeiʃənt] *a.* 引起流产的. — *n.* 堕胎药或器械.

a·bor·tion [əˈbɔːʃən] *n.* ①流产,小产. ②流产的胎儿,不足月婴儿. ③【生】发育不全;畸形;败育. ④失败,夭折. *an induced ~* 人工流产. *have an ~* 流产,打胎. *prove an ~* (事情)结果流产[失败]. **-ist** *n.* 为人进行人工流产者.

a·bor·tive [əˈbɔːtiv] *a.* ①流产的. ②(药)打胎的. ③【生】发育不全的,败育的. ④【医】使病程中断的. ⑤失败的,夭折的. *an ~ egg* 败育卵. *prove ~* 归于失败. *apply ~ treatment to a disease* 对疾病采取预防措施. — *n.* ①早产婴儿. ②堕胎药. **-ly** *ad.*

ABO system [ˌei ˌbiː ˈəu ˈsistim] ABO 血型制.

a·bou·li·a [əˈbuːliə] *n.* = abulia.

a·bound [əˈbaund] *vi.* ①大量存在. ②充满,富有 *(in, with)*. *Wild animals ~s in this park.* 这个公园里野兽很多. *He ~s in courage.* 他很有胆量. *This country ~s with tigers.* 这里老虎很多.

a·bout [əˈbaut] *ad.* ①大约,差不多;前后,左右. *~ a mile* 大约一英里. *That's ~ right.* 大致不差. *That's ~ (the size of) it.* 就是那么一回事;大概如此. *It is ~ finished* 差不多要完成[终结]. ②周围,四面;到处. *look ~* 四顾. ③活动;盛行,到处散布,传布. *The news is going ~.* 消息正在传开. ④绕着,围着;倒转,掉转,*round ~* 掉转,回头,倒过来. *face ~* (使)转过来. *put the ship ~* 把船倒过头来. *the wrong way ~* 相反,倒转过来. ⑤附近;〔古〕周围. *Is the manager ~?* 经理在吗? *There is no one ~.* 附近无人. *a mile ~* 周围一英里. ⑥〔接带 to 的不定式〕将要. — *prep.* ①在周围. *~ the neck* 绕着脖子,围在颈上. ②在附近,在身边,手头. *somewhere ~ here* 在此地附近. *I have no money ~ me.* 我身边无钱. ③前后,左右;大概. *~ noon* 正午前后. ④对于,关于. *talk ~ sb.* 谈论某人. *He is most particular ~ being conscientious.* 他最讲究认真. ⑤从事于. *What are you ~?* 你在干什么? — *a.* 〔用作表语〕传播,流行. *Rumour is ~.* 谣言纷纷. ***~ and ~*** 〔美俚〕差不多,大致相同. ***(Right) ~ face*** 〔美〕向后转! ***~ turn*** 〔英〕向后转. ***be ~*** ①起来;活动;动手,做事 *(Butterflies are ~ early this year.* 今年蝴蝶活动得早. *He is not yet (up and) ~.* 他还没有起来;还未动手. *Mind what you are ~!* 当心! 注意!)②散布,传播,流行. ***be ~ to*** 准备,将要,正打算 *(He is ~ to speak.* 他正打算说话.) ***go ~*** ①正要,将要. ②使(船)掉头. ***go a long way ~*** 绕很多路. ***much ~*** 几乎. ***out and ~*** 从事日常工作,(病后等)起来做事. ***set ~*** 动手,着手. ***take turns ~*** 轮流. ***turn and turn ~*** 交互. **~-face** ① *n.* 【美军】向后转(的命令);改变观点[立场、主意]. ② *vi.* 改变立场[态度]. **~-ship** *vi.* 【海】改变航向. **~-sledge** *n.* 大铁锤. **~-turn** *n., vi.* = **~-face**.

a·bove [əˈbʌv] *ad.* ①在上面;在头上;【宗】在天上. *in the room ~* 在楼上房间里. ②上级;(河)上流;以上. *appeal to the court ~* 告到上级法院. *persons of fifty and ~* 五十岁以上的人们. ③上述,上文. *as is stated ~* 如上所说. — *prep.* ①在…之上,在上面. ②所不及,难于. ③超过,高过,多过,以上,以外. *500 feet ~ sea level* 海拔500英尺. *He is ~ doing such things.* 他不是做这种事的人. *I am not ~ asking questions.* 我不以发问为耻. *It is ~ comprehension.* 那是难于理解的. *persons ~ fifty* 五十岁以上的人们. *to rise ~ self* 不为私利所蔽. *to tower ~ the rest* 高过其他,超群,出类拔萃. ***~ all*** 尤其是,最重要的是. ***~ all things*** 第一是. ***~ oneself*** 〔口〕趾高气扬,得意忘形. ***~ price*** 无价之(宝). ***~ the rest*** 特别,格外. — *a.* 上记,前述. *the ~ facts* 上述事实. — *n.* ①上;天,天上. ②上记,前述. *The ~ shows a loss.* 以上表示亏损. *from ~* 从天上. **~board** *ad., a.* 公开,光明正大,光明磊落 *(open and ~* 光明正大). **~ground** *ad., a.* ①在地上;在世,活着(的),未死(的). ②正统的;官方的. **~-mentioned** *a.* 上述的.

abr. = abridged; abridg(e)ment.

ab·ra·ca·dab·ra [ˌæbrəkəˈdæbrə] *n.* ①三角形驱病符〔用 **ABRACADABRA** 一字每行递减末尾一字母排成的三角形[符箓;咒文]〕. ②胡言乱语.

a·brad·ant [əˈbreidənt] *a.* 磨损的. — *n.* 研磨料,腐蚀剂,研磨剂.

ab·rade [əˈbreid] *vt., vi.* 刮擦,擦伤,磨损. **-r** *n.* 研磨器.

A·bra·ham [ˈeibrəhæm, ˈeibrəhəm] *n.* ①亚伯拉罕〔男子名〕. ②亚伯拉罕〔基督教《圣经》中犹太人的始祖〕. ***in ~'s bosom*** ①同死去的祖先一道安息. ②处于极乐境界. ***sham ~*** 装病. **~ man** *n.* (十六、七世纪时流浪英国各地的)疯癫乞丐.

a·bran·chi·al [æˈbræŋkiəl] *a.* 【动】无鳃的.

ab·rase [əˈbreiz] *vt.* = abrade.

ab·ra·sion [əˈbreiʒən] *n.* ①磨去;擦去. ②擦伤;磨损. ③磨蚀;【地】冲蚀,海蚀. **~ resistance** 耐磨度.

ab·ra·sive [əˈbreisiv] *a.* ①有磨损力的,有剥蚀作用的. ②引起摩擦的,招人讨厌的. — *n.* 琢料,磨料,金刚砂. **~ fabric** 金刚砂布.

a·bra·zo [ɑːˈbrɑːðəu] *n.* (*pl.* *~s* [-ðəus]) 〔Sp.〕 拥抱〔尤指欢迎某人时的拥抱〕.

ab·re·act [ˌæbri(ː)ˈækt] *vt.* 【精】对…使用精神发泄疗法;发泄(受压抑的感情).

ab·re·ac·tion [æbriˈækʃən] *n.* 【精】精神发泄疗法.

a·breast [əˈbrest] *ad.* 相并,并肩;并列. ***keep ~ of [with]*** *(the times)* 跟着(时代)跑. ***line ~*** (舰队)横排成一线. ***walk*** *(three)* ***~*** (三人)并排着走.

a·bridge [əˈbridʒ] *vt.* ①省略,摘要,节略 *(opp.* lengthen);缩短(寿命). ②削,夺,剥夺. *an ~d edition* 节略版,节本. *~d notation* 【数】简记法. *~ (sb.) of (his liberty)* 剥夺(某人)(自由).

a·bridge·ment, a·bridg·ment [əˈbridʒmənt] *n.* ①概略,节略,摘要;节本. ②削减,剥夺.

abrim [əˈbrim] *ad.* 满满地,满边儿.

a·broach [əˈbrəutʃ] *a.* 〔常用作表语〕, *ad.* ①(酒桶)开着口(使酒可以流出). ②传播. ***set ~*** ①开(桶)口. ②发泄(感情);发表,吐露;倡导,传播.

a·broad [əˈbrɔːd] *ad.* ①到处,四处传开,流行. ②到国外,在海外. *He's never been ~ in his life.* 他有生以来没有出过国. *A lion at home, a mouse ~.* 在家如狮,在外如鼠. *He was sent ~.* 他被派到海外. ***at home and ~*** 在国内外. ***be all ~*** ①〔口〕〔常作表语〕满不是这么回事,离题万里,猜错. ②〔口〕简直莫名其妙. ***be all ~ to***

do anything with 对…一窍不通. *from* ～ 从国外,从海外; 舶来的. *get* ～ ①出去,出门. ②(谣言)传出去,传开. *go [travel]* ～ 到外国,出洋.

ab·ro·gate [ˈæbrəugeit] *vt.* 废除(法令等);取消,结束. **-ga·tion** [-ˈgeiʃən] *n.*

ab·ro·ga·tor [ˈæbrəugeitə] *n.* 废除者.

ab·rupt [əˈbrʌpt] *a.* ①突然的,猝然的. ②粗暴的,没礼貌的,(态度)生硬的. ③陡的, 险峭的; 急转的. ④(讲话、文章等)不连贯的,支离的. ⑤【地】断裂的; 【植】裂状的. *an* ～ *turn* 急转弯. *in an* ～ *manner* 无礼的态度. *an* ～ *entrance* 闯入. **-ly** *ad.* **-ness** *n.*

ab·rup·tion [əˈbrʌpʃən] *n.* 突然分离,分裂,断裂.

A. B. S. = ①American Bible Society【宗】美国圣经学会. ②American Bureau of Shipping 美国船舶局.

abs. = ①absent. ②absolutely. ③abstract.

abs- *pref.* 〔与 ab- 同,用于字母 c, t 前〕.

Ab·sa·lom [ˈæbsələm] *n.* ①押沙龙〔基督教《圣经》中人物,大卫王之宠儿,后因反叛其父被杀〕. ②阿布萨洛姆〔男子名〕.

ab·scess [ˈæbsis] *n.* 脓肿.

ab·scind [æbˈsind] *vt.* 切断,切开.

ab·scise [æbˈsaiz] *vt.* 切除,割断. — *n.*【植】脱落.

ab·scis·sa [æbˈsisə] *n.* (*pl.* ～*s*, *-sae* [-siː])【数】横座标,横轴.

ab·scis·sion [æbˈsiʒən] *n.* ①【医】切除;【植】脱离,(幼果)脱落. ②【修】顿断法.

ab·scond [əbˈskɔnd] *vi.* 潜逃, 隐匿; 失踪; 潜伏. ～ *with the money* 卷款潜逃.

ab·scond·ence [əbˈskɔndəns] *n.* 逃亡, 逃走; 失踪; 潜伏.

ab·sence [ˈæbsəns] *n.* ①不在,缺席,缺勤 (*opp.* presence). ②缺乏,缺少,无. ③心不在焉,不注意. *～from (school, office)* 缺(课),缺(席),缺(工),缺(勤),不在. ～ *in (London)* 暂离某地而在 (伦敦). ～ *of mind* 心不在焉,心神不定. ～ *of reason* 发狂. *in sb.'s* ～ 当某人不在时,背地里. *in the* ～ *of* 无…时, 缺少…时. *leave of* ～ 请假,准假. ～ *without leave* 擅离职守.

ab·sent [ˈæbsənt] *a.* ①不在的,缺席的,缺勤的 (*opp.* present). ②缺少的,无. ③不在意的,茫然的,恍惚的. *He is* ～ *on business.* 他因事外出. *to be* ～ *from a friend* 和朋友分离. *Long* ～ *soon forgotten.* 离久情疏. *an* ～ *air* 发呆,茫然,恍惚. *He was* ～ *in his mind then.* 当时他心不在焉. ～ *treatment* 〔美口〕顾客少,卖座少. *be* ～ *from (home, school, office)* 不在,缺(课),缺(席),缺(勤),缺(工). *be* ～ *in (Paris)* 不在某地而在(巴黎). *be* ～ *without excuse [leave]* 擅自缺席. *in an* ～ *sort of way* 心不在焉地,茫然. — [æbˈsent] *vt.* 使缺席. ～ *oneself from* 不在,不到,缺席,缺勤;擅自离开. **-ly** *ad.* 心不在焉地,茫然,心神不定地.

ab·sen·tee [ˌæbsənˈtiː] *n.* ①不在者; 缺席者, 缺勤者. ②在外者,外住者;(不居于产权所在地的)不在地主. ③【讯】空号. *an* ～ *without leave* 擅自缺席[外出]者. ～ **ballot** 缺席选举人票〔指缺席者预先交给选举机构的票〕. ～ **vote** 缺席投票〔因病等而通过邮寄投票〕. **-ism** *n.* ①不在外出地主的身分. ②旷工,旷课;缺勤. ～ **over leave**【军】超假不归.

ab·sen·te reo [æbˈsentiˈriːəu] *ad.* 〔L.〕【法】被告缺席.

ab·sent-mind·ed [ˌæbsəntˈmaindid] *a.* 心不在焉的,茫然的,心神恍惚的 (*opp.* attentive). **-ly** *ad.* **-ness** *n.*

ab·sinth(e) [ˈæbsinθ] *n.* ①苦艾酒. ②【植】苦艾;〔美〕山艾树(= sagebrush). **-ism** *n.* 苦艾酒中毒.

ab·sit o·men [ˌæbsitˈəumən] 〔L.〕大吉大利〔迷信语,原意是愿无不祥的征兆!〕.

ab·so·lute [ˈæbsəljuːt] *a.* ①绝对的 (*opp.* relative, comparative); 完全的, 纯粹的. ②无条件的, 无限制的. ③专制的,独裁的,独行的,独断的. ④确实的,肯定的. ⑤【语法】独立的,游离的. ～ *truth* 绝对真理. ～ *liberty* 无限自由. *an* ～ *ruler* 专制君主. ～ *proofs* 确实的证据. ～ *refusal* 断然拒绝. *by* ～ *necessity* 万不得已. *the A-* ①【哲】绝对. ②上帝,神. ～ **adjective** 独立形容词〔略去后续的名词,如: the rich, the poor〕. ～ **alcohol**【化】无水酒精, 纯酒精. ～ **altitude**【空】(由地面起算的)绝对高度,离地高度. ～ **ceiling** 理论升限;绝对升限. ～ **construction**【语法】独立结构. ～ **dry wood**【林】全干材. ～ **magnitude**【天】绝对星等. ～ **majority** 〔英〕绝对多数. ～ **monarchy** 君主专制国[政体]. ～ **music** 纯音乐,无标题音乐. ～ **pitch** ①绝对音高,标准音高;绝对音调. ②音高辨音力. ～ **temperature** 绝对温度〔用 K 或 R 为记号〕. ～ **value**【数】绝对值. ～ **verb** 省去宾语的动词. (例: He *gives* largely to hospitals. 他向医院大量捐钱). ～ **zero**【物】绝对零度〔−273.18°C〕. **-ness** *n.* 绝对;完全;专制.

ab·so·lute·ly [ˈæbsəljuːtli] *ad.* ①绝对地; 完全地. ②确实地. ③专制地,独裁地. ④【语】独立地. *an adjective used* ～ 略去后续名词而独立使用的形容词 (例: The blind cannot see. 盲人不能看东西.) — *interj.* 〔表示完全同意、赞成〕〔口〕是,是那样,当然. *"Do you think it will work well?" "A-!"* "这样做行不行?""当然行!"

ab·so·lu·tion [ˌæbsəˈljuːʃən] *n.* ①免取 (罪责); 解除(责任); 赦免 (*from; of*). ②【宗】忏悔式, 赦罪文. *pronounce the* ～ 宣读赦罪文.

ab·so·lut·ism [ˈæbsəljuːtizm] *n.* ①专制主义. ②绝对主义,绝对论.

ab·so·lut·ist [ˈæbsəljuːtist] *n.* ①专制主义者. ②绝对主义者,绝对论者.

ab·sol·u·to·ry [əbˈsɔljutəri] *a.* 免罪的,赦免的.

ab·solve [əbˈzɔlv] *vt.* ①免除, 解除. ② 赦免, 宽恕 (*opp.* blame). ③某学科考试及格取得(学分). ～ *(sb.) from (a promise; blame).* ①解 (约). ②替…开脱 (罪责). ～ *(sb.) of (sin)* 赦免(罪状).

ab·so·nant [ˈæbsənənt] *a.* ①不合拍的,不谐和的. ②不合理的,背理的,悖理的. ～ *from [to] (nature)* 违反(自然).

ab·sorb [əbˈsɔːb, -ˈzɔːb] *vt.* ①吸收. ②并吞; 合并; 同化. ③吸引(注意),使(精神)贯注. ④忍受; 承担 (费用). ⑤占用(时间). ⑥理解(含义). *A blotter* ～*s ink.* 吸墨纸吸收墨水. ～ *sb.'s attention* 吸引某人注意. *be* ～*ed by* 被…并吞; 为…所吸收. *be*～*ed in [with]* 全神贯注在…,一心从事,热衷于 (*be* ～*ed in the pursuit of knowledge* 一心研究学问). **-a·bil·i·ty** [-əˈbiliti] *n.* 吸收性. **-a·ble** [-ˈsɔːbəbl] *a.* 可吸收的,易吸收的.

ab·sorbed [əbˈsɔːbd] *a.* 注意集中的,一心一意的. *with* ～ *interest* 充满兴趣地. **-ly** *ad.* 一心, 专心一意地,一心不乱地.

ab·sor·be·fa·cient [əbˌsɔːbiˈfeiʃənt] *a.* 吸收性的. — *n.*【医】吸收剂.

ab·sorb·en·cy [əbˈsɔːbənsi] *n.* 吸收力.

ab·sorb·ent [əbˈsɔːbənt] *a.* 吸收的,有吸收力的,吸收性的. — *n.* ①吸收质,吸收体;【医】吸收剂,解酸剂,中和剂. ②【解】淋巴管;吸收管. ～ *cotton* 脱脂棉,药棉. ～ *of (heat)* 能吸收(热).

ab·sorb·er [əbˈsɔːbə] *n.* ①吸收者,吸收器, 吸收装置. ②减震器. *acoustic* ～ 消声器.

ab·sorb·ing [əbˈsɔːbiŋ] *a.* ①吸收的. ②非常有趣的,引人入胜的. *a shock-*～ *device* 减震装置. *an* ～ *well* 吸水井,渗井.

ab·sorp·tance [əbˈsɔːptəns] *n.*【物】吸收比.

ab·sorp·tion [əbˈsɔːpʃən] *n.* ①吸收,合并. ②专心,一心不乱, 热中 (*in*). ③〔口〕饮食. ～ *in one's work* 埋头工作. ～ *of heat* 吸收热量. ～ *of nourishment* 吸收营养. *the*～ *of smaller tribes* 兼并[吸收]小部落.

ab·sorp·tive [əbˈsɔːptiv] *a.* 有吸收力的, 吸收性的. **-ness** *n.*

ab·sorp·tiv·i·ty [ˌæbsɔːpˈtiviti] *n.* 吸收性, 吸收率〔系

数],吸收能力.

ab·squat·u·late [əbˈskwɔtjuleit] *vi.* 〔美俚〕逃走,逃跑,〔谑〕溜掉.

ab·stain [əbˈstein] *vi.* ①戒,断(烟等),慎(行). ②弃权. ~ **from** *(wine) [luxury, doing, voting]* 戒(酒)[避免奢华,不做,放弃投票].

ab·stain·er [əbˈsteinə] *n.* ①戒酒的人. ②弃权者. *a total* ~ 绝对戒酒的人.

ab·ste·mi·ous [æbˈsti:mjəs] *a.* ①有节制的;饮食有度的. ②节俭的. *an* ~ *diet* 适度的饮食. *an* ~ *meal [life]* 简朴的馔食[生活]. **-ly** *ad.* 有节制地,适度. **-ness** *n.* 饮食有度,节制.

ab·sten·tion [æbˈstenʃən] *n.* ①戒绝;克制;回避. ②弃权;投票弃权者. ~ *from exerting pressures on* 不对…施加压力. ~ *from voting* 弃权不投票. ~ *from smoking* 戒烟.

ab·sterge [æbˈstə:dʒ] *vt.* 揩去,洗净;使净化.

ab·ster·gent [æbˈstə:dʒənt] *a.* ①洗去的,洗净的,去垢的. ②清泻的. — *n.* ①去垢剂,洗涤剂(肥皂、洗衣粉等);去污粉. ②【医】洗涤药;泻药.

ab·ster·sion [æbˈstə:ʃən] *n.* 洗净,净化.

ab·ster·sive [æbˈstə:siv] *a.* 去垢的;使清洁的.

ab·sti·nence [ˈæbstinəns] *n.* ①禁欲;节制;戒酒. ②【经】节约.

ab·sti·nen·cy [ˈæbstinənsi] *n.* 节制;禁欲.

ab·sti·nent [ˈæbstinənt] *a.* 禁欲的;有节制的. **-ly** *ad.* 有节制地;适度地.

ab·stract [ˈæbstrækt] *a.* ①抽象的 *(opp.* concrete*)*;理论上的 *(opp.* applied*)*;观念的,空想的 *(opp.* practical*)*. ②难解的,深奥的. ③茫然的,恍恍惚惚的. ④【数】不名的. ⑤【美】抽象派的 *(opp.* representational*)*. ~ *expressionism* 抽象表现主义(派). ~ *mathematics* 理论数学. ~ *noun* 抽象名词. ~ *number* 不名数. — *n.* ①抽象;【逻】抽象概念,抽象名词. ②【化】萃取物,提出物;提要,摘要. ~ *of title* 财产权归属说明书. **in the** ~ 抽象地,观念上,理论上. **make an** ~ **of** 把…的要点摘录下来. — [æbˈstrækt] *vt.* ①提取,抽取;析离,分离;转移(注意等). ②〔婉〕偷窃. ③概括,摘录. ④使(概念等)抽象化. ~ *(somewhat) from sb.'s enjoyment* 使某人扫兴. ~ *sb.'s attention from* 从…上转移开某人的注意. **-ly** *ad.* 抽象地,理论上,观念上. **-ness** *n.* 抽象性.

ab·stract·ed [æbˈstræktid] *a.* ①分了心的. ②分离了的,脱离了的. ③抽象了的. **with an** ~ **air** 出神地,茫然,心不在焉. **-ly** *ad.* 呆呆地,茫然;抽象地. **-ness** *n.* 出神,发呆.

ab·strac·tion [æbˈstrækʃən] *n.* ①抽象(作用);抽象概念;提取,抽出. ②出神,发呆. ③〔婉〕偷窃. ④不切实际的观念. **with an air of** ~ 茫然,呆呆地,心不在焉. **-ism** *n.* 【美】抽象主义;抽象派艺术. **-ist** *n.* 抽象派画家[艺术家].

ab·strac·tive [æbˈstræktiv] *a.* ①有提取力的. ②抽象的. ③摘要的. **-ly** *ad.*

ab·strict [æbˈstrikt] *vt., vi.* 【植】分离,脱落.

ab·stric·tion [æbˈstrikʃən] *n.* 【植】分离,脱落.

ab·struse [æbˈstru:s] *a.* 难解的;深奥的. **-ly** *ad.* **-ness** *n.*

ab·surd [əbˈsə:d] *a.* 不合理的;荒谬的,荒诞的,荒唐无稽的;荒唐可笑的. *Don't be* ~不要胡闹[搞,说]. **-ly** *ad.* **-ness** *n.*

ab·surd·ism [əbˈsə:dizəm] *n.* (哲学和文艺方面的)荒诞主义.

ab·surd·ist [əbˈsə:dist] *n.* 荒诞主义者;荒诞派作家. — *a.* 荒诞主义的,荒诞派的. ~ *theatre* 荒诞派戏剧.

ab·surd·i·ty [əbˈsə:diti] *n.* 荒谬;谬论;荒唐事[话等]. *the height of* ~ 荒唐透顶.

abt., abt = about.

ABU = Asian Broadcasting Union 亚洲广播联盟.

A·bu Dha·bi [ˈæbu: ðæbi:] ①阿布扎比〔组成阿拉伯联合酋长国的酋长国之一〕. ②阿布扎比〔阿拉伯联合酋长国首都〕.

a·bu·li·a [əˈbju:liə] *n.* 【心、医】意志力丧失.

a·bun·dance [əˈbʌndəns] *n.* 丰富,充裕,富裕 *(opp.* scarcity*)*. *a year of* ~ 丰年. ~ **of** 丰富,充裕,富足. *(A- of instances are cited.* 引用了大量例子. *He has* ~ *of time to himself.* 他时间充裕.*)* **in** ~ 丰富,充裕,(生活)优裕.

a·bun·dant [əˈbʌndənt] *a.* 丰富的,大量的. *an* ~ *harvest* 丰收. *an* ~ *year* 丰年. **be** ~ **in** *(minerals)* 富有(矿物),(矿产)丰富. **-ly** *ad.* 丰富地,多.

a·buse [əˈbju:z] *vt.* ①滥用(职权等),妄用,误用(才能等). ②骂;讲…坏话,污蔑. ③虐待,酷待;凌辱;〔古〕欺骗. ~ *one's privilege* 滥用特权. — [əˈbju:s] *n.* ①滥用,妄用,乱用,误用. ②骂,讲坏话. ③〔常 *pl.*〕弊病,弊端,恶习. ④虐待,侮辱. *a crying* ~ 急应革除的恶习或弊病. *a word of* ~ 骂人话.

a·bu·sive [əˈbju:siv] *a.* ①骂人的,说人坏话的. ②滥用的,妄用的,误用的. ~ *language* 骂人话. *become* ~ 嘴变坏. **-ly** *ad.* 滥,妄;刻薄;侮辱地,无礼地. **-ness** *n.* 滥用;骂詈;虐待;弊害.

a·but [əˈbʌt] *vi., vt.* 邻接,毗连;贴近,靠紧,接近. ~ **against** 紧靠着. ~ **on [upon]** 接连,邻接;靠在…上.

a·bu·ti·lon [əˈbju:tilən] *n.* 【植】苘麻属;苘麻,白麻(等).

a·but·ment [əˈbʌtmənt] *n.* ①邻接,接界;接合(点). ②【建】桥台,桥座,支柱.

a·but·tal [əˈbʌtl] *n.* ①接界,邻接. ②〔常 *pl.*〕地界.

a·but·ter [əˈbʌtə] *n.* 〔美〕接邻房地产的业主.

a·buzz [əˈbʌz] *a.* 〔作表语〕①嗡嗡叫的. ②嘈杂,扰嚷;活跃,热闹. *The class is* ~ *with discussion.* 课堂讨论很热烈.

ab·volt [æbˈvəult] *n.* 【物】绝对伏特;电磁制伏特.

aby(e) [əˈbai] *vt.* *(a·bought* [əˈbɔ:t]*; a·bought)* 〔古〕偿,赔,赎(罪).

a·bysm [əˈbizəm] *n.* 〔诗〕= abyss.

a·bys·mal [əˈbizməl] *a.* ①深不可测的,无底的,地狱(似)的. ②极度悲惨[恶劣,卑下]的. ~ *ignorance* 绝端愚昧. ~ *poverty* 赤贫.

a·byss [əˈbis] *n.* ①深渊;无底洞. ②〔古〕地狱,阴间;浑沌. *an* ~ *of disgrace [ignominy]* 丢脸已极. *an* ~ *of despair* 绝望. *the* ~ *of time* 无限之时,永远. *the horror of an* ~ 看深渊时引起的恐怖心.

a·bys·sal [əˈbisəl] *a.* 深海的;深渊的. ~ **rock** 【地】深成岩. ~ **zone** 深海地带.

Ab·ys·sin·i·a [ˌæbiˈsinjə] *n.* 阿比西尼亚〔埃塞俄比亚 Ethiopia 旧名〕〔非洲〕.

AC, A. C. = ① air controlman 美海军航空兵的空中交通管制员. ②alternating current【电】交变电流,交流电. ③aircraft(s)man 空军士兵. ④〔L.〕*Ante Christum* (=before Christ) 公元前.

a/c, A/C = ①account. ②account current, current account 往来帐户;活期存款帐户.

-ac *suf.* 〔用以构成形容词,由此构成的形容词常用作名词〕①表示"有…性质的": elegi*ac*, demoni*ac*. ②表示"关于…的": cardi*ac*, coeli*ac*, ili*ac*. ③表示"有…病的": mani*ac*.

A·ca·cia [əˈkeiʃə] *n.* 【植】金合欢属;〔a-〕金合欢,银叶相思树;洋槐,刺槐;阿拉伯树胶.

Acad. = ① Academic. ② Academy.

ac·a·deme [ˌækəˈdi:m] *n.* 〔诗〕= academy.

ac·a·de·mia [ˌækəˈdi:mjə] *n.* ①学术界. ②学术生活和兴趣;学术环境.

ac·a·dem·ic [ˌækəˈdemik] *a.* ①学院的;大学的;学会的,(学术、文艺)协会的. ②学究的;学理上的;空谈的,非实用的. ③〔A-〕柏拉图学派的. ④〔美〕文科的,文学的. *an* ～ *curriculum* 大学课程. *an* ～ *degree* 学位. ～ *interests* 校董. *an* ～ *discussion* 学术讨论. ～ *freedom* 学术自由. ～ *front* 学术战线. ～ *rank* 学衔. ～ *research* 学术研究. — *n.* ①大学教师,大学生;学会会员. ②〔*pl.*〕纸上空论,空论. ③〔A-〕柏拉图学派的人.

ac·a·dem·i·cal [ˌækəˈdemikəl] *a.* = academic. *an* ～ *clique* 学阀. *an* ～ *year* 学年. — *n.*〔*pl.*〕大学礼服. ***in full*** ～*s* 穿着大学礼服. **-ly** *ad.* 学问上;理论上;用学究态度.

a·cad·e·mi·cian [əˌkædəˈmiʃən] *n.* 学会会员,院士.

ac·a·dem·i·cism [ˌækəˈdemisizəm] *n.* 学院风气. (= academism [əˈkædəmizəm]).

a·cad·e·my [əˈkædəmi] *n.* ①学会,研究院,学术协会,文艺协会. ②中等学校;专科院校. ③〔A-〕柏拉图学园;柏拉图哲学. *an* ～ *of music* 音乐学校. *a military* ～〔美〕军事学院. *the Military Academy* 陆军军官学校;〔英〕陆军炮工兵军官学校. *the naval* ～ 海军学校. *the Royal Academy of Arts*〔英〕皇家美术院. *the Royal Military Academy* 英国陆军军官学校. ～ **board** 油画纸.

ac·a·jou [ˈækəʒuː] *n.* = cashew.

-acal *suf.*〔用以构成形容词;特别在由 -ac 构成的形容词转为名词时,用以代替 -ac, 再构成形容词〕: demoniacal, maniacal.

ac·a·leph [ˈækəlef], **ac·a·lephe** [ˈækəliːf] *n.*【动】水母.

a·can·thine [əˈkænθin] *a.*【植】(似)老鼠簕属植物的.

a·can·tho·ceph·a·lan [əˌkænθəˈsefələn] *n.*【动】棘头纲动物.

a·can·thoid [əˈkænθɔid] *a.* 多刺的,棘状的 (= acanthous).

ac·an·thop·ter·yg·i·an [ˌækənˌθɔptəˈridʒiən] *n.*【动】棘鳍类鱼. — *a.* 棘鳍类的.

A·can·thus [əˈkænθəs] *n.* (*pl.* ～*es, -thi* [-θai]) ①【植】老鼠簕属植物. ②〔a-〕莨苕;【建】(柱头上)莨苕叶形装饰,叶板.

a cap·pel·la [ˌɑːkəˈpelə] *a.*〔It.〕【乐】无伴奏的〔指合唱〕.

a ca·pric·cio [ˌɑːkɑːˈpriːtʃɔː] *n.*〔It.〕【乐】随想曲.

ac·a·ri·a·sis [ˌækəˈraiəsis] *n.*【医】螨病(壁虱病).

a·car·i·cide [əˈkærisaid] *n.*【药】杀螨剂.

ac·a·rid [ˈækərid] *n.*【动】螨.

ac·a·roid [ˈækərɔid] *a.*【动】螨类的,螨状的.

ac·a·rol·o·gy [ˌækəˈrɔlədʒi] *n.* 螨虫学. **-gist** *n.* 螨虫研究专家.

a·car·pel·ous, a·car·pel·lous [æˈkɑːpələs] *a.*【植】无心皮的;无果爿的.

a·car·pous [æˈkɑːpəs] *a.*【植】不结果实的.

a·cat·a·lec·tic [eiˌkætəˈlektik] *a.*〔诗〕(音节数)完全的. — *n.* 完整的诗行.

a·cau·dal [eiˈkɔːdəl] *a.*【动】无尾的 (= acaudate).

a·cau·les·cent [ˌeikɔːˈlesənt] *a.*【植】无茎的;短茎的.

acc. = ①acceptance. ②according. ③account(ant). ④accusative.

ac·cede [ækˈsiːd] *vi.* ①同意,依从,答应,允诺. ②即(位),就(职),继承. ③加入,参加. ～ *to a request* 答应要求. ～ *to a party* 加入政党. ～ *to the throne* 继承王位.

ac·cel·er·an·do [ækˌseləˈrændəu] *ad.*〔It.〕【乐】渐快.

ac·cel·er·ant [ækˈselərənt] *n.* 促进物;【化】触媒,促进剂,催化剂;【冶】捕集剂.

ac·cel·er·ate [ækˈseləreit] *vt.* 加速;催促,促进. ～ *measure [the pace]* 加速步调. — *vi.* 速度增加. — *n.* 接受速成教育的学生. **-d** *a.*【物】加速的.

ac·cel·er·a·tion [ækˌseləˈreiʃən] *n.* ①加速;促进. ②【物】加速度;变速. ③【教】加速升级. *uniform [variable]* ～ 等[不等]加速度. *lightning* ～【汽车】瞬间加速度. *brief* ～ 瞬时有效加速度. ～ *of gravity* 重力加速度.

ac·cel·er·a·tive [ækˈselərətiv] *a.* 加速的,催促的.

ac·cel·er·a·tor [ækˈseləreitə] *n.* ①加速者;加速器;催速剂. ②【汽车】加速踏板. ③【摄】催显剂.

ac·cel·er·o·graph [ækˈselərəgrɑːf]【空】自动加速仪.

ac·cel·er·om·e·ter [ækˌseləˈrɔmitə] *n.* 加速表,加速计,加速仪;过荷指示器.

ac·cent [ˈæksənt] *n.* ①重音,扬音,强音;重音符号;韵符;抑扬. ②强调(*on*). ③音调,声调,口音,腔,土腔. ④特征,特色. ⑤〔*pl.*〕〔诗〕词句. *a primary [secondary]* ～ 第一[第二]重音,主[次]强音. *an acute* ～ 重音[扬音]符号 (ʹ). *a grave* ～ 抑音符号 (ˋ). *a circumflex* ～ 抑扬音符号 (^). *an Irish* ～ 爱尔兰腔调. ～ *of grief* 悲调. *in tender* ～*s* 用柔和的声调. — [ækˈsent] *vt.* ①重读;给…加上重音符号. ②〔美〕着重说,强调.

ac·cen·tu·al [ækˈsentjuəl] *a.* ①重音的,强音的. ②〔诗〕按照音节抑扬作成的 (*opp.* quantitative). **-ly** *ad.*

ac·cen·tu·ate [ækˈsentjueit] *vt.* ①着重说,着重指出,强调. ②重读;给…加上重音符号.

ac·cen·tu·a·tion [ækˌsentjuˈeiʃən] *n.* ①重读;重音符号. ②(音的)抑扬. ③强调;加重.

ac·cept [əkˈsept] *vt.* ①受,接受,收(礼等),领(情等). ②承担(职位等),答应,应(聘等);顺应(形势). ③同意,承认;信(教等),容纳;理解. ④【商】承兑,认付(汇票等). *She did not* ～ *his hand in marriage.* 她不肯和他结婚. ～ *the situation* 听天由命. ～ *…(as) true* 信…以为真. *the* ～*ed meaning* 普通意义,众所公认的意义. ～ ***of***〔古〕= accept ★ 目前在商业上、法律上均不接用 of. ～ ***the person [face] of***〔古〕偏袒,偏爱,宠. **-er** *n.* 领受人;接受者.

ac·cept·a·bil·i·ty [əkˌseptəˈbiliti] *n.* 接受;承诺;适意,合意.

ac·cept·a·ble [əkˈseptəbl] *a.* 可接受的;合意的,(礼物等)令人满意的.

ac·cept·ance [əkˈseptəns] *n.* ①接受;验收. ②答应,承认;(政党候选人)接受提名. ③【商】承兑,认付(期票). ～ ***for honour*** 参加承兑. ***find*** ～ ***with [in]*** 得…答应. ～ **house** 期票承兑行. ～ **market** 证券市场. ～ **supraprotest** 参加承兑. ～ **speech** 受命演说. ～ **test** 验收试验.

ac·cept·ant [əkˈseptənt] *a.* 容易接受的.

ac·cep·ta·tion [ˌæksepˈteiʃən] *n.* ①(字、句的)意义;通义. ②〔古〕承认. *formal* ～【逻】第一义,意义. *material* ～ 字义.

ac·cept·ed [əkˈseptid] *a.* 常规的;认可的;公认为真实的;有效的;正常的.

ac·cep·tor [əkˈseptə] *n.* ①领受人,接受者;承兑(票据)人. ②【生】受体. ③【无】接收器,接受体;受主;谐振电路. *electron* ～ 电子接受体.

ac·cess [ˈækses] *n.* ①接近;会面. ②捷径,门路〔指方法、手段〕;检查孔;进路,入口;【自】(存贮器的)存取. ③(病的)发作;(怒气等的)爆发. ④增加. *a man of difficult* ～ 难接近的人,难会见的人. ～ *and recess* (病的)发作和静止. *an* ～ *of anger* 发怒,动怒. *an* ～ *of fever* 发热. *an* ～ *of territory* 领土的增加. ～ *to books* 接触书籍的机会. ***be easy [hard, difficult] of*** ～ 容易[难]接近的;容易[难]进去的;容易[难]会见的. ***gain*** ～ ***to*** 接近;会见,谒见;接通(计算机). ***give*** ～ ***to*** 接见;准许出入. ***have*** ～ ***to*** 得接近;得会见;得进入. ***within easy*** ～ ***of*** *(Shanghai)* 容易去到(上海)的地方. ～ **clerk** 贵重物品保管员. ～ **time**【自】存取时间.

ac·ces·sa·ry [əkˈsesəri] *n.* = accessory.

ac·ces·si·bil·i·ty [ækˌsesiˈbiliti] *n.* ①可近,易接近,可亲. ③易受影响.

ac·ces·si·ble [əkˈsesəbl] *a.* ①能接近的,容易会见的. ②可以进入的;容易理解的. ③易受影响的. ④好相处的. *an* ～ *path* 通路. *an* ～ *person* 温和的人. *minds* ～ *to reason* 通情达理的人们. **-bly** *ad.*

A

ac·ces·sion [æk'seʃən] *n.* ①能接近,接近,到达. ②就任;继承. ③增加;增加物. ④〔美〕新添的图书〔作品〕. ⑤参加(某团体). ⑥【法】财产自然增益的所有权. ⑦【医】发作. ⑧同意. *a list of ~s to a library* 图书馆的新书目录. *the ~(s) book [number]* 新书登记簿〔号码〕. ***~ to manhood*** 成年. ***~ to the throne*** 即位. ***~ to a treaty*** 加盟,加入条约. — *vt.* 〔美〕把(新书)编入目录.

ac·ces·so·ry [æk'sesəri] *a.* ①附属的,附带的,辅助的. ②从犯的,同谋的. *an ~ bud [shoot]* 副芽. *~ fruits* 假果. — *n.* ①零件,附件,附属品. ②〔*pl.*〕(妇女)全套衣饰中的小配件. ③〔美〕从犯 (*opp.* principal). *the accessories (of a motor-car)* 【汽车】附件,零件. ***~ before [after] the fact*** 事前〔后〕从犯.

ac·ci·dence ['æksidəns] *n.* ①【语法】词法;词形变化(的研究). ②初步,入门.

ac·ci·dent ['æksidənt] *n.* ①故障,事故,偶发事件;偶然. ②灾难,灾害,不幸,不测,意外,事故,横祸. ③附带事件,附属品. ④【哲】偶然性 (*opp.* necessity). ⑤【地】褶皱;起伏,高低. *a happy ~* 巧事. *a chapter of ~s* 许多不幸;命途多舛. *an aeroplane ~* 飞机失事. *a tram ~* 电车事故. *~s of the ground* 【地】地表的高低起伏. ***by ~*** 偶然 (*opp.* on purpose). ***have an ~*** 遭受意外. ***meet with an ~*** 遭不测. ***without ~*** 平安,无恙. **~ insurance** 伤亡保险. **~-prone** *a.* (因粗枝大叶而)特别易出事故的.

ac·ci·den·tal [ˌæksi'dentl] *a.* ①偶然的,不测的,意外的 (*opp.* planned). ②非本质的 (*opp.* essential). ③附带的,附属的. *~ death* 意外死亡. — *n.* ①偶然事;偶然;附带事物. ②【乐】临时符. **~ colours** 【物】偶生色. **~ notation** 【乐】升降符号.

ac·ci·den·tal·ly [ˌæksi'dentəli] *ad.* 偶然,意外;附带. *to meet ~* 偶然碰到.

ac·ci·die ['æksidi:] *n.* = acedia.

Ac·cip·i·ter [æk'sipitə] *n.* (*pl.* ***-tres*** [-tri:z]) ①【动】鹰属. ②〔a-〕鹰.

ac·cipi·tral [æk'sipitrəl], **ac·cip·i·trine** [-train] *a.* 鹰(样)的;眼光敏锐的;贪婪的.

ac·claim [ə'kleim] *n.* 〔诗〕喝采,欢呼. — *vt., vi.* (为…)喝采,欢呼着欢迎(某人),欢呼着同意(某事).

ac·cla·ma·tion [ˌæklə'meiʃən] *n.* ①喝采,称赞,欢呼;鼓掌通过. *amidst the loud ~ of* 在欢声雷动中. *carry (a motion) by ~* 鼓掌通过(议案).

ac·clam·a·to·ry [ə'klæmətəri] *a.* 喝采的,欢呼的,全场一致的.

ac·cli·mate [ə'klaimit] *v.* 〔美〕= acclimatize.

ac·cli·ma·tion [ˌæklai'meiʃən] *n.* 〔美〕= acclimatization.

ac·cli·ma·ti·za·tion [əˌklaimətai'zeiʃən] *n.* 服水土,适应气候. **~ fever** 水土病.

ac·cli·ma·tize [ək'laimətaiz] *vt., vi.* (使)服水土,(使)适应新环境. *~ oneself to* 适应(新环境).

ac·cliv·i·ty [ə'kliviti] *n.* 倾斜,斜坡,上斜 (*opp.* declivity).

ac·cli·vous [ə'klaivəs] *a.* 向上倾斜的.

ac·co·lade ['ækəleid] *n.* ①武士爵位的授与(礼). ②嘉奖,表扬;(见面问好的)接吻〔拥抱〕. ③【乐】连谱号.

ac·com·mo·date [ə'kəmədeit] *vt.* ①适应,顺应,调节;迁就,迎合. ②劝息,调停,调解,排解. ③供应,供给,通融,借给,贷. ④留宿;收容(病人),装载(乘客);照应,招待. *The hotel is well ~d.* 这旅馆设备周全. *~ (sb.) for the night* 留(某人)住一夜. *The guests are well ~d.* 招待周到. ***~ oneself to*** *(circumstances)* 适应(环境),随遇而安. *~ (sb.)* ***with*** *(money, lodging)* 通融(某人款项),招待(某人住宿).

ac·com·mo·dat·ing [ə'kəmədeitiŋ] *a.* 亲切的,爽气的;易打交道的. *an ~ person* 爽快人,好人. **-ly** *ad.*

ac·com·mo·da·tion [əˌkəmə'deiʃən] *n.* ①适应(性),顺应,迁就;调节(作用). ②和解,调解,排解,调停. ③〔美,常 *pl.*〕供应,供给,通融;将就;便利;设备;膳宿;接待. ④【商】贷款;通融资金. *~s at a hotel* 旅馆设备. ***as a matter of ~*** 为…便利计. **~ bill** 〔英〕通融票据. **~ bridge** 专用〔特设〕桥梁. **~ ladder** 舷梯. **~ road** 专用道路. **~ sale** 【商】转批. **~ train** 〔美〕慢车 (*opp.* express train). **-ism** *n.* 迁就主义.

ac·com·mo·da·tor [ə'kəmədeitə] *n.* ①调节者. ②调解人. ③贷款人. ④临时的用人.

ac·com·pa·ni·ment [ə'kʌmpənimənt] *n.* ①伴随物,附属物. ②【乐】伴奏,和奏,助音. *to the ~ of* 伴和着,随着. *~ of the scale* 【乐】陪音. *play an ~* 伴奏.

ac·com·pa·nist [ə'kʌmpənist] *n.* 【乐】伴奏者,伴唱者.

ac·com·pa·ny [ə'kʌmpəni] *vt.* ①陪,伴,陪着;陪衬,衬,兼带. ②给…伴奏,与…和奏. *~ one's word with a blow* 边说边打. *an ~ing letter* 附函. *Accompanied by Miss X.* 由某某小姐伴奏. ***be accompanied by*** 有(某人)陪伴;伴有,附有,带着. ***be accompanied with*** *(a thing)* 带着,带有,兼有. — *vi.* 伴奏.

ac·com·plice [ə'kəmplis] *n.* 同谋,同犯;帮凶.

ac·com·plish [ə'kəmpliʃ] *vt.* 成就,完成,贯彻(计划等),达到(目的);实行. *~ one's object* 达到目的. *~ one's mission* 完成使命.

ac·com·plished [ə'kəmpliʃt] *a.* ①已完成的. ②有教养的,有才能的,学识渊博的. *~ facts* 既成事实. *an ~ villain* 臭名昭彰的坏蛋. *an ~ lady* 才女. ***be ~ in*** 专长,擅长,精通.

ac·com·plish·ment [ə'kəmpliʃmənt] *n.* ①成就,完成,履行,贯彻,实行. ②〔*pl.*〕才能,技能,教养. *difficult of ~* 实行起来困难的. *a girl of many ~s* 多才多艺的姑娘.

ac·cord [ə'kɔ:d] *vi.* 一致,与…符合(*with*). *His actions ~ with his words.* 他言行一致. — *vt.* ①使一致. ②给予(礼遇等). *They ~ed a warm welcome to me.* 他们对我热烈欢迎. — *n.* ①一致,调和;和谐;和解,协定. ②自愿,自动. ③【乐】和音,和弦 (*opp.* discord). ***be in ~ with*** 与…一致的,符合…的. ***be of one ~*** 一致. ***full ~ with*** 完全同意. ***of its own ~*** 自然,自行,自动. ***of one's own ~*** 自愿地,主动地. (*They won't do it of their own ~.* 他们不会自动去干这事的) ***out of ~ with***不符合…的,同…不一致. ***with one ~*** 一致地.

ac·cord·ance [ə'kɔ:dəns] *n.* ①一致,协调. ②给予. ***in ~ with*** 照,据,依照;与…一致,合乎 (*in ~ with the form provided* 照格式).

ac·cord·ant [ə'kɔ:dənt] *a.* 一致的,相合的;成谐音的;调和的 *(with; to)*.

ac·cord·ing [ə'kɔ:diŋ] *ad.* 照,依,据,按. ***~ as*** 照,依照,据,随. ***~ to*** 照,依照,据,据…所说 (*~ to his account* 照他的话. *~ to all accounts* 照大家的话. *act ~ to circumstances* 随机应变. *from each ~ to his ability, to each ~ to his work* 各尽所能,按劳分配).

ac·cord·ing·ly [ə'kɔ:diŋli] *ad.* ①因此,于是,所以. ②随着;相应地. *You may arrange ~.* 你可以权宜处理. ***~ as*** = according as.

ac·cor·di·on [ə'kɔ:djən] *n.* 手风琴. — *a.* (如手风琴般)可折迭的. **-ist** [-ist] *n.* 手风琴演奏者.

ac·cost [ə'kəst] *vt.* ①(接近…)搭话;招呼(不认识的人). ②(娼妓等)引诱,勾引.

ac·couche·ment [ə'ku:ʃmɑ̃:ŋ] *n.* 〔F.〕分娩,生产.

ac·cou·cheur [ˌæku:'ʃə:] *n.* 〔F.〕(男)产科医士.

ac·cou·cheuse [ˌæku:'ʃə:z] *n.* 〔F.〕女助产士.

ac·count [ə'kaunt] *n.* ①计算;帐,帐目;帐户;计算书,帐单;报告书,报表. ②说明,解释;记事,故事. ③理由,原因. ④重要性;考虑;价值;利益. *an open ~* 来往帐目,未结算帐目. *Bad things can be turned to good* ~. 坏事可以变成好事. ***Accounts differ.*** 言各不同. ***ask an*** ~ 请求付帐;请求回答. ***balance*** **~*s with*** 与…结清各帐. ***bring [call] to*** ~ 责问,质问,要求说明. ***by all*** **~*s*** 据大家所说. ***cast*** ~ 计算. ***charge*** *(a sum)* ***to sb.'s*** ~ 记某人帐. ***close an*** ~ ***with*** 与…停止交易. ***find no*** ~ ***in*** 不合算. ***find one's*** ~ ***in*** 因…得利(好处). ***for*** ~ ***of*** 为…代销. ***from all*** **~*s*** 从各种说法来估计. ***give a bad [poor]*** ~ ***of*** 〔俚〕贬责. ***give a good*** ~ ***of*** ①夸奖. ②〔口〕打败;【猎】打死. ***give a good [bad]*** ~ ***of oneself*** ①(未)付清欠账. ②表现好[糟],做成功[失败] *(He has not given a good ~ of himself in battle.* 他在战场上表现得不英勇). ***give an*** ~ ***of*** 报告,叙述,记述,说明. ***go to one's (long)*** ~ 死. ***hand in one's*** **~*s*** 死. ***hold ... in great*** ~ 极重视. ***hold ... of much*** ~ 看重,重视. ***hold ... of no*** ~ 看轻,藐视. ***in*** ~ ***with*** 与…有生意来往. ***joint*** ~ 共同计算. ***keep*** **~*s*** ①记帐,入帐,登帐. ②做会计员. ***keep*** ~ ***with*** 与…继续交易. ***lay one's*** ~ ***with*** 预期,期望;考虑,斟酌. ***leave (it) out of*** ~ 不把…打在数内,不顾,不考虑. ***make (much)*** ~ ***of*** 重视,看重. ***make little [no]*** ~ ***of*** 轻视,看轻. ***of (much)*** ~ 重要的 *(man of ~*要人). ***of no*** ~ 不重要的,无价值的. ***on*** ~ 先付,暂付 *(pay five pounds on ~* 先付五镑). ***on*** ~ ***of*** 因为,因. ***on all*** **~*s*** = ***on every*** ~ 无论如何,总之. ***on any*** ~ 无论如何. ***on no*** ~ = ***not ... on any*** ~决不,总不. ***on a person's [one's]*** ~ ①以某人[自己]费用. ② 为了某人[自己]. ***on one's own*** ~ ①为自己(利益)打算. ②依靠自己;自行负责. ***on this [that]*** ~ 因此,于是. ***open an*** ~ ***with*** 与…开一往来户头;开了…的头. ***pay ... on*** ~ 把…付作定钱. ***place [pass] to the*** ~ ***of*** 并入…帐内. ***render an*** ~ ①分辩,辩解. ②决算报告. ***sale on*** ~ 赊销. ***send in an*** ~ 报帐. ***send in*** **~*s*** 报销. ***settle [square]*** **~*s*** 结算,清算. ***Short*** **~*s make long friends.*** 帐目常清,友谊长存. ***take*** ~ ***of*** = ***take into*** ~ 考虑,斟酌,计及 *(take the interests of the whole into ~* 顾全大局. *take the whole situation into ~* 统筹全局). ***take no*** ~ ***of*** 不考虑,不计及,无视. ***the great [last]*** ~ 最后的审判. ***turn ... to (good)*** ~ 利用. — *vt.* 认为 …如何〔后接宾语及补足语〕. *be much [little] ~ed of* 被重[轻]视. *He ~s himself well paid.* 他认为自己的报酬不坏. *~ oneself happy* 自以为幸福. —*vi.* 说明. ~ ***for*** ①证明,说明;由于 *(How do you ~ for it?* 你如何说明它呢? *There is no ~ing for taste(s).* 人各有所好). ②说明(银钱等的)用途. ③打死,打落(敌机);【体】得(几)分. ~ **book** 帐簿. ~ **current** = **current** ~ 往来帐户〔略 a/c〕. ~ **executive** (广告公司等的)客户业务经理. ~ **note** 帐单. ~**s payable [receivable]** 应付[应收]帐. ~ **purchase** 赊买. ~ **rendered** (贷方交给借方审查和清算的) 借贷细帐. ~ **sales** ①销货帐. ②赊销. ~ **settled** 决算,清算. ~ **stated** (借贷双方都认可的)细帐.

ac·count·a·bil·i·ty [əˌkauntəˈbiliti] *n.* 有责任,有义务.

ac·count·a·ble [əˈkauntəbl] *a.* 有责任的,有解说义务的;可说明的. *Every person is ~ for his own work.* 每个人都要对自己的工作负责.

ac·count·an·cy [əˈkauntənsi] *n.* 会计工作,会计的职位.

ac·count·ant [əˈkauntənt] *n.* 会计员,帐房,出纳. ~ *general* 会计主任. *a chartered ~* 会计师.

ac·count·ing [əˈkauntiŋ] *n.* ①会计;会计学. ②帐;记帐;清算帐目. *business ~ at different levels* 分级核算.

ac·cou·ple·ment [əˈkʌplmənt] *n.* ①拼凑. ②【建】圆柱成对密立. ③拼凑在一起的木材.

ac·cou·tre, -ter [əˈkuːtə] *vt.* 穿;【军】装备. ***be ~d with [in]*** 穿着. **-ment** *n.* ①衣服. ②〔*pl.*〕(武器,军服以外的)装备,配备.

Ac·cra [əˈkrɑː] *n.* 阿克拉〔加纳首都〕.

ac·cred·it [əˈkredit] *vt.* ①相信,听信;认可. ②授权,委派,任命. ③认(某事)为(某人所为),归在 *(to, with)*. ④鉴定…为合格. *an ~ed journalist* 特派记者. *an ~ed school* 立案学校. *They ~ these remarks to him = He is ~ed with these remarks.* 他们认为那些话是他说的.

ac·crete [æˈkriːt] *vi.* ①增大,生长. ②合生;连生. — *vt.* 使附着,使与…相联合. — *a.*【植】合生的.

ac·cre·tion [æˈkriːʃən] *n.* ①增大. ②【地】冲积层. ③增加物;生长. ④连生,合生. ⑤【法】(财产的)自然增加. ~ ***cutting*** = ~ ***thinning***【林】促进生长的采伐. ~ ***of population*** 人口增加率.

ac·cru·al [əˈkruːəl] *n.* 增加,增殖;增加物;增加额.

ac·crue [əˈkruː] *vi.* ①增长. ②(利息等)自然增殖. ③【法】(诉讼)发生. *A profit ~s to the government from…* 政府由…得到利益. *pay the interest ~d* 支付所生利息. *Knowledge will ~s to you from reading.* 读书能增智.

acct. = account(ant).

ac·cul·tu·rate [əˈkʌltʃəˌreit] *vi., vt.* (使)受同化,(使)受融化.

ac·cul·tu·ra·tion [əˌkʌltʃəˈreiʃən] *n.* 文化移入;文化适应;文化交流.

ac·cum·bent [əˈkʌmbənt] *a.* ①依着的,横卧的. ②【植】依伏的.

ac·cu·mu·late [əˈkjuːmjuleit] *vt.* ①积累,存储,蓄积(财产等),堆积. ②〔英大学〕同时取得(高的和低的学位). — *vi.* ①积,贮,累积,积聚. ②〔英大学〕同时取得高的和低的学位. *~ed funds* 积累的资金.

ac·cu·mu·la·tion [əˌkjuːmjuˈleiʃən] *n.* ①积累,堆积;累积物. ②〔英大学〕高低学位的同时获得. *the ~ of knowledge* 知识的积累.

ac·cu·mu·la·tive [əˈkjuːmjulətiv] *a.* ①积累的,堆积的. ②热心贮蓄的. **-ly** *ad.*

ac·cu·mu·la·tor [əˈkjuːmjuleitə] *n.* ①累积者;积聚者. ②【机】蓄力器;【电】蓄电池;【计】累加器,记存器;【无】贮能电路;缓冲器. *a binary ~* 二进位累加器.

ac·cu·ra·cy [ˈækjurəsi] *n.* 正确,准确(度);精确. *firing ~* 命中率. ***with*** ~ 正确地.

ac·cu·rate [ˈækjurit] *a.* 准确的,精密的. **-ly** *ad.*

ac·curs·ed [əˈkəːsid], **ac·curst** [əˈkəːst] *a.* ①被咒的,不幸的,倒楣的. ②可恶的,讨厌的. **-ly** *ad.* **-ness** *n.*

ac·cus·a·ble [əˈkjuːzəbl] *a.* 可指责的;可指控的.

ac·cus·al [əˈkjuːzəl] *n.* = accusation.

ac·cus·ant [əˈkjuːzənt] *n.* 指责者;控诉者.

ac·cu·sa·tion [ækju(ː)ˈzeiʃən] *n.* ①非难,谴责. ②告发,控告. ③(被指控的)罪状,罪名. *a false ~* 诬告. ***be under an*** ~ 受指责,被控告. ***bring an*** ~ ***against*** 对…起诉,控告;指责;攻击(某人).

ac·cu·sa·ti·val [əˌkjuːzəˈtaivəl] *a.*【语法】直接宾格的.

ac·cu·sa·tive [əˈkjuːzətiv] *n., a.*【语法】直接宾格(的). ★ objective 较此词更常用.

ac·cu·sa·to·ri·al [əˌkjuːzəˈtɔːriəl] *a.* ①弹劾性的;非难的;声讨性的. ②公诉人的;告发人的.

ac·cu·sa·to·ry [əˈkjuːzətəri] *a.* ①非难的,责问的,问罪的. ②控告的,告发的.

ac·cuse [əˈkjuːz] *vt.* ①非难,谴责. ②因某事而谴责[指控]某人 *(for)*;把某事归罪于某人 *(for)*. ③控告[告发]某人犯某罪 *(of)*. *~ the times* 说时世不好. *Man often ~s nature for his own misfortunes.* 人类常把自身的不幸归咎于天. *They ~d him of taking bribes.* 他们控告他受贿. ***the ~ed***【法】被告,刑事被告. —*vi.* 控诉;起诉.

A

ac·cus·er [əˈkju:zə] *n.* 上诉人,原告;责难者.

ac·cus·ing [əˈkju:ziŋ] *a.* 非难的,谴责的. *point an ~ finger at a person* 指着某人责骂. **-ly** *ad.*

ac·cus·tom [əˈkʌstəm] *vt.* 使习惯. *one's ~ed hour* 惯常的时间. *~* ***oneself to*** 使自己惯于. ***be ~ed to*** *(hard work, early rising)* 惯于(苦干,早起).

ac·cu·tron [ˈækjutrɔn] *n.* 电子手表.

ace [eis] *n.* ①(纸牌、骰子等的)么,一 (*cf.* deuce 二, trey 三, cater 四, cinq 五, sice 六). ②同花色中最大的牌. ③(网球赛等的)发球得分. ④少许,毫厘. ⑤(击落五架以上敌机的)飞行勇士,空中英雄; (棒球等的)优秀选手,能手,专家. ⑥〔美口〕一元的钞票. ***~ in the hole*** 暗藏的"A"牌; 备用的论点或手段. ***~ of ~s*** 〔美〕空中英雄之英雄,能手中之能手,强中之强. ***have [keep] an ~ up one's sleeve*** 持有最重要的情报,手中有大牌〔良策〕. ***not an ~*** 毫无. ***within an ~ of ...*** 差点儿,几乎,险些儿 (*He came within an ~ of winning.* 他差点儿获胜). — *a.* 第一流的; 能干的. — *vt.* ①(网球赛等)以发球赢(对方)一分. ②在(考试)中得满分. ~**-high** *a.* 〔口〕①极好的(*feel ~ high* (身体) 顶好). ②有威望的; 受敬重的(*He is ~ high with me* 我尊敬他).

a·ce·di·a [əˈsi:diə] *n.* ①懒惰; 麻痹,不关心. ②【医】淡漠忧郁症.

A·cel·da·ma [əˈkeldəmə, əˈseldəmə] *n.* ①【圣】血田〔以出卖耶稣所得之钱购买的土地〕. ②流血之地.

a·cel·lu·lar [eiˈseljulə] *a.* 非细胞组成的.

ace·naph·thene [ˌæsəˈnæpθi:n] *n.*【化】苊.

a·cen·tric [æˈsentrik] *a.* 无中心的;偏心的,离心的.

-a·ce·ous *suf.*【生】…类的,…科的: crust*aceous* 甲壳类的; ros*aceous* 蔷薇科的.

a·ceph·a·lous [æˈsefələs] *a.* ①无头的. ②没有首领的. ③〔诗〕一行诗中缺少第一音步的.

a·ce·qui·a [əˈseikjə, -ˈseikiə] *n.* 水沟,水渠.

ac·er·ate [ˈæsərit] *a.*【植】针状的.

a·cerb [əˈsə:b] *a.* ①酸(味)的. ②(性情,言语等)尖刻的,厉害的,粗暴的.

ac·er·bate [ˈæsəbeit] *vt.* ①使变酸;使变苦. ②激怒;使不痛快.

a·cer·bic [əˈsə:bik] *a.* = acerb.

a·cer·bi·ty [əˈsə:biti] *n.* ①苦酸,苦涩. ②(语言等的)刻薄,辛辣.

ac·er·ose [ˈæsərəus] *a.*【植】针状的.

a·cer·vate [əˈsə:vit] *a.*【植】成堆生长的,丛生的,簇生的. **-ly** *ad.*

a·ces·cent [əˈsesnt] *a.* 容易变酸的;有酸味的,发酸的,微酸的.

a·cet- *comb.f.*= aceto-〔acet- 用于元音前〕: *acet*aldehyde, *acet*amide.

ac·e·tab·u·lum [ˌæsəˈtæbjuləm] *n.* (*pl.* ***-la*** [-lə]) ①(古罗马餐桌上用的)醋罐. ②【解】髋臼. ③【动】吸盘,碟状体.

ac·e·tal [ˈæsitæl] *n.* 乙缩醛,乙醛缩二乙醇.

ac·et·al·de·hyde [æsiˈtældəhaid] *n.*【化】乙醛.

ac·etam·ide [ˌæsiˈtæmaid] *n.*【化】乙酰胺.

ac·et·an·i·lide, ac·et·an·i·lid [ˌæsiˈtænilaid, -lid] *n.*【化】乙酰(替)苯胺;退热冰.

ac·e·tar·i·ous [ˌæsiˈtεəriəs] *a.* 拌生菜用的,拌色拉(salad) 用的;(蔬菜等)凉拌用的.

ac·e·tate [ˈæsitit] *n.*【化】醋酸盐;醋酸酯;醋酸根,醋酸基;醋酸纤维素.

a·ce·tic [əˈsi:tik, əˈsetik] *a.* 醋的; 酸的. *~* **acid** 醋酸,乙酸.

a·cet·i·fi·ca·tion [əˌsetifiˈkeiʃən] *n.*【化】醋化(作用).

a·cet·i·fy [əˈsetifai] *vt., vi.* (使)醋化,(使)变酸.

ac·e·tim·e·ter [ˌæsiˈtimitə] *n.* 醋酸(比重)计 (= acetometer).

ac·e·tin [ˈæsitn] *n.* 醋精,甘油醋酸酯.

aceto- *comb. f.* 乙酰,乙川〔用于辅音前〕: *aceto*benzoic.

ac·e·tom·e·ter [ˌæsiˈtɔmitə] *n.* 醋酸(比重)计.

ac·e·tone [ˈæsitəun] *n.*【化】丙酮.

ac·e·tose [ˈæsitəus] *a.* = acetous.

ac·e·tous [ˈæsitəs] *a.* 醋(一样)的,酸的;醋酸的.

a·ce·tum [əˈsi:təm] *n.*【药】醋.

ac·e·tyl [ˈæsitil] *n.*【化】乙酰(基).

a·cet·y·lene [əˈsetili:n] *n.*【化】乙炔; 电石气. *~* **lamp** 电石气灯,矿灯.

achar·ne·ment [F. aʃarnəmɑ̃] *n.* 〔F.〕凶猛,残暴.

A·cha·tes [əˈkeiti:z] *n.* 忠实的朋友〔Achates 原为 Virgil 所著史诗中忠于友情的英雄〕.

ache [eik] *vi.* ①痛,疼痛. ②〔口〕渴望 (*to* do). 怀想,想念 (*for*). *His heart ~s.* 他心口痛. *I am aching to join in the game.* 渴望参加比赛. — *n.* 痛,疼痛.

a·chene [æˈki:n] *n.* (*pl.* ***-nia*** [-niə])【植】瘦果.

Ach·er·on [ˈækərɔn] *n.*【希、罗神】冥河;阴间,地狱.

Acheson [ˈætʃisn] *n.* 艾奇逊〔姓氏〕.

à che·val [F. a ʃəˈval]〔F.〕①在马上;跨. ②(对一场争论所持的)骑墙态度.

a·chiev·a·ble [əˈtʃi:vəbl] *a.* 做得成的,可完成的.

a·chieve [əˈtʃi:v] *vt.* 完成,做到;获得(胜利等); 达到(目的),实现. *to ~ a great deal in one's work* 工作很有成绩. — *vi.* 取得预期效果.

a·chieve·ment [əˈtʃi:vmənt] *n.* ①完成; 达到. ②成绩,成就; 功绩; 造诣. ③【徽】纹章. *~* **age** 智力成就年龄. *~* **quotient**【心】造诣指数〔受教育年限与智力发展年限的比值〕.

Ach·il·le·an [ˌækiˈli:ən] *a.* 阿基里斯 (一样)的; 勇敢的; 刀枪不入的.

A·chil·les [əˈkili:z] *n.*【希神】阿基里斯. ***~(') heel*** 唯一致命的弱点〔传说 阿基里斯 除脚踵外全身刀枪不入〕.

aching [ˈeikiŋ] *a.* 痛的,疼痛的;心痛的. *an ~ tooth* 作痛的牙齿. *an ~ void* 悲痛空虚的感觉.

ach·la·myd·e·ous [ˌækləˈmidiəs] *a.*【植】无被的; 裸花的.

a·chlor·hy·dri·a [ˌeiklɔ:ˈhaidriə] *n.*【医】胃酸缺乏. **-hy·dric** [-haidrik] *a.*

a·chon·drite [eiˈkɔndrait] *n.* 无球粒陨石. **-drit·ic** [-draitik] *a.*

a·chon·dro·pla·sia [eikɔndrəˈpleiʒə] *n.*【医】软骨发育不全. **-plas·tic** [-ˈplæstik] *a.*

a·chro·mate [ˈækrəumeit] *n.* 全色盲者,色盲患者.

ach·ro·mat·ic [ˌækrəuˈmætik] *a.* 无色的;【生】非染色质的;【物】消色差的; 非彩色的 (指黑、白、灰色的). *~* **lens** 消色差透镜. *~* **vision** 全色盲.

a·chro·ma·tic·i·ty, a·chro·ma·tism [əˌkrəuməˈtisiti, -izəm] *n.*【物】无色; 消色差.

a·chro·ma·tin [əˈkrəumətin] *n.*【生】(细胞核内的)非染色质.

a·chro·ma·tize [əˈkrəumətaiz] *vt.* 使无色,灭色;【物】消…色差; 使成非彩色.

a·chro·ma·top·sia [əˌkrəuməˈtɔpsiə] *n.*【医】色盲,全色盲.

a·chro·ma·tous [əˈkrəumətəs] *a.* 无色的,颜色不足的.

a·chro·mic [əˈkrəumik] *a.* 无色的.

A·chro·my·cin [ˌækrəuˈmaisin; Am. ˌeikrəˈmaisin] *n.*【药】阿克洛密辛四环素〔tetracycline 的商标名〕;〔a-〕四环素.

a·cic·u·la [əˈsikjulə] *n.* (*pl.* ***-lae*** [-i:]) *n.*【生】针,刺;【地】针状结晶.

ac·id [ˈæsid] *a.* ①酸味的. ②【化】酸的,酸性的. ③〔喻〕尖酸刻薄的,易怒的. — *n.* ①酸味物. ②【化】酸. ③〔美俚〕麻醉药物 LSD (麦角酸二乙基酰胺). **~-head**

经常服用 LSD 的人. ~ **looks** 苦脸,易怒的面孔. ~ **number [value]** 酸值. ~**-proof** *a.* 耐酸的. ~ **radical** 酸根[基]. ~ **reaction** 酸性反应. ~**-resistant** ①耐酸的,抗酸的. ②耐酸物,抗酸物. ~ **rock** (引起吸毒幻觉似的)疯狂摇摆舞歌曲. ~ **test** 酸性试验;〔喻〕严峻的考验. ~ **trip** 〔俚〕因吸毒而引起的幻觉经历. **-ly** *ad.* -ness *n.*

ac·i·d(a)emia [ˌæsiˈdiːmiə] *n.*【医】酸血症.

ac·id-fast [ˈæsid-fɑːst] *a.* 抗酸的. ~ *bacteria* 抗酸细菌.

ac·id-form·ing [ˈæsidˌfɔːmiŋ] *a.* ①成酸的; 酸的. ②(食物)消化时产生大量酸性物质的.

a·cid·ic [əˈsidik] *a.* ①【化】酸性的. ②【矿】硅石多的.

ac·i·dif·er·ous [ˌæsiˈdifərəs] *a.* 生酸的,含酸的.

a·cid·i·fi·ca·tion [əˌsidifiˈkeiʃən] *n.* 酸化(作用), 成酸性,发酸.

a·cid·i·fi·er [əˈsidifaiə] *n.* ①酸化器. ②酸化剂.

a·cid·i·fy [əˈsidifai] *vt., vi.* (使)变酸,(使)酸化.

ac·i·dim·e·ter [ˌæsiˈdimitə] *n.*【化】酸(液)比重计,酸度计.

a·cid·i·ty [əˈsiditi] *n.* 酸味;酸性,酸度.

ac·id·ize [ˈæsidaiz] *vt.* 酸处理,酸化.

ac·i·doid [ˈæsidɔid] *a.* (土壤等) 似酸的; 有变酸倾向的. — *n.* 可能变酸的物质.

ac·i·dom·e·tre, -ter [æˈsidɔmitə] *n.* 酸度计; *p*H 计.

a·cid·o·phil [əˈsidəfil] *n.* 嗜酸细胞;嗜酸物.

ac·i·doph·i·lus milk [ˌæsiˈdɔfiləs milk] 酸(牛)奶.

ac·i·do·sis [ˌæsiˈdəusis] *n.*【医】酸中毒.

a·cid·u·late [əˈsidjuleit] *vt.* 使带酸性,酸化.

a·cid·u·lat·ed [əˈsidjuleitid] *a.* ①带酸味的. ②易怒的,尖刻的.

a·cid·u·lous [əˈsidjuləs] *a.* ①有酸味的,带酸的. ②脾气坏的,别扭的.

ac·i·er·ate [ˈæsiəreit] *vt.* 化(铁)为钢.

ac·i·form [ˈæsifɔːm] *a.* 针状的;锐利的.

ac·i·nac·i·form [ˌæsiˈnæsifɔːm] *a.*【植】短剑状的.

a·cin·i·form [əˈsinifɔːm] *a.* 腺泡状的,葡萄状的; 多核的.

ac·i·nus [ˈæsinəs] *n.* (*pl.* **-ni** [-nai])【植】小果; 葡萄核;【动】腺泡;粒体.

-a·cious *suf.* 有…倾向的,爱…的,…多的: loqu*acious*, pugn*acious*.

-ac·i·ty *suf.* 有…倾向: loqu*acity*, pugn*acity*.

ack-ack [ˈæk ˈæk] *a.*〔俚〕防空炮火的,高射炮的. — *n.* 高射炮,防空炮火.

ack em·ma [ˈæk ˈemə] ①〔英口〕午前〔报务员间通用〕. ②〔英军俚〕飞机修理工人. *at 10* ~ 上午十时.

Ackerman(n) [ˈækəmən] *n.* 阿克曼〔姓氏〕.

ac·knowl·edge [əkˈnɔlidʒ] *vt.* ①认,承认;供认. ②感谢,答谢. ③告知收到(信等). ④对(人)打招呼. ⑤【法】公证. ~ *one's defeat* 认输. ~ *one's fault* 认错,赔不是,道歉. ~ *a man as [to be] one's superior* 自认不如某人. ~ *(the receipt of) a letter* 表示收到来信. ~ *a statement* 声明已经注意到. ~ *a deed* 公证一项契约. ~ ***oneself to be*** 自认是. ~ ***the applause*** 谢幕.

ac·knowl·edged [əkˈnɔlidʒid] *a.* 世所公认的,已有定评的. *the ~ leader* 公认的领袖.

ac·knowl·edge·ment, ac·knowl·edg·ment [əkˈnɔlidʒmənt] *n.* ①承认;自认,供认. ②感谢;谢意. ③收条. ④【法】承认书. *bow one's ~s (of applause)* (对欢呼)点头答礼. ***in ~ of*** 领谢,答谢.

a·clin·ic [æˈklinik] *a.*【物】无倾角的. ~ **line**【物】无倾线,(地)磁赤道(线).

A.C.M. = Air Chief Marshal 空军上将.

ac·me [ˈækmi] *n.* 顶点,极点;极致. ~ *of science* 科学尖端. ***be the ~ of perfection*** 十全十美.

ac·ne [ˈækni] *n.*【医】脂肪腺炎;痤疮; 粉刺,酒刺. ~ **rosacea** 酒槽鼻. ~ **sebacea** 皮脂溢.

a·cock [əˈkɔk] *ad.* (帽边) 反卷. *set one's hat* ~ 反卷着帽边.

AC of S = Assistant Chief of Staff.〔美〕助理参谋长.

ac·o·lyte [ˈækəlait] *n.* ①侍僧. ②【天主】侍祭. ③侍者;助手.【天】陪星、卫星.

ac·o·nite [ˈækənait] *n.*【植】附子,草乌,乌头. **-nit·ic** [ˌækəˈnitik] *a.*

a·con·i·tine [əˈkɔnitiːn] *n.*【药】乌头碱.

a·corn [ˈeikɔːn] *n.* 栎子,橡子,槲果. ***come to the ~s*** 〔美〕处境困难. ~ **cup** 壳斗. ~ **shell** ①橡子壳. ②【贝】藤壶. ~ **tube,**〔英〕~ **valve**【无】橡实形(电子)管.

a·cot·y·le·don [æˌkɔtiˈliːdən] *n.*【植】无子叶植物. **-ous** [-əs] *a.*【植】无子叶的.

a·cou·me·tre, -ter [əˈkuːmitə] *n.* 测听计,听力计,测声器.

a·cous·tic(al) [əˈkuːstik(əl)] *a.* ①听觉的;声学的. ②助听的; 传音的. ③原声的,不经过电子设备传声的. ~ **phonogram** 传音相片. ~**(magnetic) mine** 感音(磁性)水雷. ~ **meter** 比声计. ~ **nerves** 听神经. ~ **wave** 声波. **-ti·cal·ly** *ad.* 在听觉上;在声学上.

ac·ous·ti·cian [ˌækuːsˈtiʃən] *n.* 声学家.

a·cous·ti·con [əˈkuːstikən] *n.* 助听器.

a·cous·tics [əˈkuːstiks] *n.* ①〔用作 *sing.*〕声学. ②〔用作*pl.*〕(剧院等的)音响装置,音响效果. *The ~ of this theater are faulty [admirable].* 这个剧院的音响效果不好[很好].

a·cous·to-e·lec·tron·ics [ˌækuːstəuiˈlektrɔniks]*n.* 电子声学.

à cou·vert [ɑːkuːˈvɛə]〔F.〕安全;受庇护.

ac·quaint [əˈkweint] *vt.* ①使熟悉,了解 *(with)*〔多用被动语态〕. ②把某事告知[通知,介绍]给某人 *I am already ~ed with the facts.* 我已经了解这些事实. *Let me ~ you with the facts.* 让我把事实告诉你. *She ~ed her roommates with my husband.* = *She made my husband ~ed with her roommates.* 她把我丈夫介绍给她的同室伙伴. ~ *each other with their views* 互通声气. ~ ***(sb.) with (a fact)*** 把(事实)告知(某人). ~ ***oneself with*** 知道,通晓. ***be [get] ~ed with*** ①了解,熟知. ②与…相识 (*We are ~ed with eath other.* 我们互相认识,彼此是熟人). ***make (sb.) ~ed with*** ①把…通知[告知](某人). ②把…介绍给(某人).

ac·quaint·ance [əˈkweintəns] *n.* ①相识,相熟;熟人. ②知识,心得. *a nodding ~* 点头朋友. *a speaking ~* 搭话朋友,初交. *He is not a friend, only an ~.* 他不是朋友,只是相识. *have a large circle of ~s* 交游甚广. *He has a slight ~ with astronomy.* 他懂一点儿天文学. ***cut [drop] sb.'s ~*** 和某人绝交. ***have [no] ~ with*** 和…[不]认识. ***make ~ with [of]*** 接近,结识. ***pick ~ with*** 结识,和…相识. ***scrape ~ with*** 设法结识. **-ship** *n.* 相识,相熟;认识.

ac·quest [əˈkwest] *n.* ①取得物. ②【法】继承方法以外取得的财产.

ac·qui·esce [ˌækwiˈes] *vi.* 默许,默认,勉强同意. (*opp.* protest). ~ ***in*** *(a plan; proposal)* 勉强同意(计划;提议).

ac·qui·es·cence [ˌækwiˈesns] *n.* 默认,默许. *He smiled ~.* 他笑了一笑表示同意.

ac·qui·es·cent [ˌækwiˈesnt] *a.* 默许的,默认的,勉强顺从的. **-ly** *ad.*

ac·quire [əˈkwaiə] *vt.* ①得,取得,获得;招致. ②学得(知识等),养成(习惯等). ③(在探测器上)捕捉住(目标). ~ *a bad habit* 养成不良习惯. *~ed a good reputation* 得了好名. ~ *currency* 流传,散布. **-ment** *n.* 取得,获得;学得;〔*pl.*〕学识,技艺.

ac·quired [əˈkwaiəd] *a.* ①已得到的,已获得的. ②已成习惯的. ③【生】习得的,后天的 (*opp.* natural). *an ~*

taste 学会的嗜好. ~ **character**【生】获得性. ~ **immunity** 后天免疫(性).

ac·qui·si·tion [ˌækwiˈziʃən] *n.* ①取得,获得;习得. ②取得物,获得物[人]. ③【无】探测.

ac·quis·i·tive [əˈkwizitiv] *a.* 可以得到的,可以学得的;想获得的 *(of)*; 贪得无厌的. *an ~ mind* 好学心,利欲心(等). **-ly** *ad.* **-ness** *n.*

ac·quit [əˈkwit] *vt.* ①使(某人)卸去(责任、义务等) *(of)*. ②宣判无罪 (*opp.* convict). ③表现 *(oneself)*; 完成,履行 *(oneself of)*. ④〔古〕付清,还清. ~ *a person of his responsibility [duty]* 解除某人的责任[义务]. *She ~ted herself well of [in] her promise.* 她很好地履行了自己的诺言. ~ **oneself** *(bravely)* 表现(勇敢),行动(勇敢). ~ **oneself of** *(one's duty)* 尽(责). **be ~ted of** *(a crime)* 被宣告无罪. **~tal** [-l] *n.* ①宣告无罪. ②付清,还清. ③尽责. **~tance** [-təns] *n.* ①免除,解除. ②还清;(清欠)收据.

ac·quitt·al, ac·quit·ment [əˈkwitəl,-mənt] *n.* ①宣判无罪. ②(义务的)履行. ③(债务的)清偿.

a·cre [ˈeikə] *n.* ①英亩(= 40.4687 ares)〔约中国六亩〕. ②〔*pl.*〕土地,耕地. ③〔*pl.*〕〔口〕大量. *broad ~s* 宽广的土地. *a lord of broad ~s* 大地主. *a library with ~s of books.* 有大量藏书的图书馆. **God's ~** 墓地.

a·cre·age [ˈeikəridʒ] *n.* ①英亩数; 面积. ②按亩出售[分配]的土地. *the ~ under cultivation* 耕地面积.

a·cred [ˈeikəd] *a.* ①英亩的. ②拥有许多地产的. *a many-~ estate* 许多英亩的地产.

ac·rid [ˈækrid] *a.* ①辣的,苦的; 腐蚀性的. ②毒辣的,刻毒的;泼辣的. **-ness** *n.* = acridity.

a·crid·i·ty [æˈkriditi] *n.* ①辣,苦. ②狠毒,刻毒.

ac·ri·dine [ˈækridin] *n.*【化】吖啶,氮蒽,氮杂蒽,夹氮蒽.

ac·ri·fla·vine [ˈækriˈfleiviːn] *n.*【化】吖啶黄.

ac·ri·mo·ni·ous [ˌækriˈməunjəs] *a.* ①恶毒的,毒辣的. ②剧烈的,厉害的. **-ly** *ad.* **-ness** *n.*

ac·ri·mo·ny [ˈækriməni] *n.* (态度、语言等的)毒辣,激烈,刻毒.

a·crit·i·cal [eiˈkritikəl] *a.* ①不批评的,不吹毛求疵的;不打算批评或品评的. ②【医】没有危险征兆的.

ac·ro- *comb. f.* 肢端,尖端;最高,顶上: *acrophobia.*

ac·ro·bat [ˈækrəbæt] *n.* ①杂技演员,走钢丝的演员. ②(主张、政见等的)善变者,翻云覆雨者.

ac·ro·bat·ic [ˌækrəuˈbætik] *a.* 杂技的;走钢丝的. ~ **feats** 杂技. ~ **flight** 特技飞行. **-i·cal·ly** *ad.*

ac·ro·bat·ics [ˌækrəuˈbætiks] *n. pl.* 〔用作单或复〕杂技;【军】特技飞行.

ac·ro·bat·ism [ˈækrəubætizəm] *n.* 杂技.

ac·ro·car·pous [ˌækrəuˈkɑːpəs] *a.* 【植】茎端结实的〔如某些藓苔〕;顶(生)蒴的.

ac·ro·gen [ˈækrəudʒen] *n.*【植】顶生植物.

ac·ro·le·in [əˈkrəuliːin] *n.*【化】丙烯醛.

ac·ro·lect [ˈækrəulekt] *n.* (流行于一个社区内最体面的)标准方言.

ac·ro·lith [ˈækrəuliθ] *n.* 石首石肢木身像.

ac·ro·meg·a·ly [ˌækrəuˈmegəli] *n.*【医】肢端肥大症. **-me·gal·ic** [-məˈgælik] *a., n.* 有肢端肥大症的(人).

a·cron·y·c(h)al [əˈkrɔnikəl] *a.*【天】日落后出现的〔指天体〕.

ac·ro·nym [ˈækrənim] *n.* 首字母缩略词〔如 loran = *lo*ng-*ra*nge *n*avigation〕.

a·crop·e·tal [əˈkrɔpitl] *a.*【植】向顶的. **-ly** *ad.*

ac·ro·pho·bi·a [ˌækrəuˈfəubiə] *n.*【医】高处恐怖(症).

ac·rop·o·lis [əˈkrɔpəlis] *n.* ①(古希腊都城的)卫城. ②〔the A-〕雅典的卫城.

across [əˈkrɔs] *ad.* ①横切,横断,越过,横过;(走)过. ②交叉,成十字地;对过,斜对面. ③宽,阔. *What is the distance ~?* 到对面有多少距离? *come ~ in a steamer* 乘船渡过(河等). *The channel is 20 miles ~.* 海峡宽20英里. *stand with two arms ~* 叉手站立着. — *prep.* ①横过,横断,越过;(走)过. ②与…交叉,与…成十字;在横过…处,在…对面. ③经过(一段时间). *walk ~ the street* 穿过街道. *He lives ~ the road.* 他住在马路对面. *lay (two sticks) ~ each other* 把(二棍)交叉放置. ~ *the nineteenth century* 在十九世纪整整一百年间. *all ~ China* 全中国. ~ **from**〔美口〕在…的正对面. ~ **(the) country** 全国各地. **be ~ a horse's back** 骑马. **come [run] ~** 发现;碰见 (*I came ~ an old friend.* 我碰见了一个老朋友. *I have come ~ a curious plant.* 我发现一种珍奇植物). **come ~ (one's) mind** 忽然想起. **get ~** ①使了解 (*get the idea ~ to the class* 使学生了解这一思想). ②与(人)冲突. ③(计划)成功. **go ~** ①渡过,越过. ②不顺 (*go ~ a bridge* 过桥. *Things go ~* 诸事不顺). **It's ~ to you.**〔口〕那是你的事了. **put** *(a business deal)* **~** 使生意成交. **put it ~ a person**〔口〕向某人报仇;欺骗某人. **~-the-board** *a.* ①全面的(*an ~-the-board tax cut* 普遍减税). ②定时播送的.

a·cros·tic [əˈkrɔstik] *a.* 藏头诗的;离合体的. — *n.* (各行首词首字母能联成句子的)藏头诗,(各行首词末字母能联成句子的)离合体诗.

a·cryl·ic [əˈkrilik] *a.*【化】丙烯酸的. ~ **acid** 丙烯酸. ~ **fibre** 丙烯酸系纤维. ~ **plastic** 丙烯酸塑料. ~ **resin** 丙烯酸(类)树脂.

act [ækt] *n.* ①行为;举动;动作. ②决议,决议书;法令,条例. ③(戏剧的)幕,段;简短的节目. ④(牛津、剑桥等大学的)学位论文答辩. *an ~ of hostility*【法】敌对行为. *Act III, Scene ii* 第三幕,第二场. ~ *and deed* 有约束力的契约;文据. ~ *of God [Providence, Nature]*【法】不可抗力,天灾; ~ *of grace* 恩典,特典;〔A-〕大赦令. ~ *of Parliament [Congress]* 法令. *The Acts (of the Apostles)* (基督教《圣经·新约全书》中的)《使徒行传》. **get into the ~** 插手,参加. **have ~ or part in** 参与,是…的同谋犯. **in the (very) ~ (of),** 正在动作时;当场 (*be caught in the ~* 当场被捕). **put on an ~**〔口〕装腔;炫耀自己. **to be in ~ to**〔古〕将要. — *vt.* ①演(戏);扮演(角色). ②学,仿效,装. ~ *the lord* 装阔. *He ~ed his part well.* 他演得不错;他做得不错. — *vi.* ①作,干,实行,举止. ②生效,发生作用. ③当演员;充当,装作. ~ *the fool* 做傻事情;出洋相. *How ought I to ~?* 我应该怎么办呢? *The medicine ~s well.* 药效不错. *The brake did not ~.* 煞车不灵了. ~ **against** 违反(法律等);作不利于…的事. ~ **a part** 扮演;装作,做戏. ~ **as** *(guide)* 做(向导). ~ **for** 代理. ~ **on** ①遵行,奉行,按照…行动. ②作用于,对…起作用[反应],影响到,有效验 (*Mind ~s upon mind.* 心心相印). ~ **one's age**〔美口〕行为聪明有礼,有大人气了,不再顽皮了. ~ **the part of** *(Hamlet; benefactor)*, 演(哈姆雷特);做(保护人). ~ **towards** *(a person)* 待人. ~ **up**〔美口〕①开玩笑,调皮. ②(机器等)出毛病. ~ **up to** 实行,遵守,遵照. ~ **upon** = ~ on (*We must heed the correct views, and ~ upon them.* 对正确的意见必须听,并且照它做). **~ing in the spirit of** 本着…的精神.

act·a·ble [ˈæktəbl] *a.* (剧本、角色等)可上演的,可扮演的.

Ac·ta Sanc·to·rum [ˈɑːktɑː sɑːŋkˈtəurəm]〔L.〕【宗】圣徒行传〔圣徒和殉教言行录集〕.

ac·tin [ˈæktin] *n.*【生】肌动朊,肌纤朊.

act·ing [ˈæktiŋ] *n.* ①行为. ②演技,演出. ③装假,做戏. *a play suitable for ~* 适合上演的剧本. — *a.* ①活动着的. ②代理的,临时的. ③(供)演出的. *an ~ principal* 代理校长. *an ~ copy [script]*【剧】台本,脚本. *an ~ volcano* 活火山.

Ac·tin·i·a [ækˈtiniə] *n.* (*pl.* **~s, -ae** [-iː])【动】红海葵属;〔a-〕红海葵.

ac·tin·ic [ækˈtinik] *a.*【化】(有)光化(性)的. ~ **ray**

光化射线.
ac·ti·nide ['æktinaid] **series** 锕系.
ac·tin·ism ['æktinizəm] *n.* 【化】射线作用, 光化作用, 光化度, 光化性.
ac·tin·i·um [æk'tiniəm] *n.* 【化】锕. 〔元素名, 符号为Ac〕
ac·ti·no- *comb. f.* 【物】放射线的, 【动】放射状的.
ac·tin·o·graph [æk'tinəugrɑːf] *n.* 【摄】曝光计; 【物】辐射仪, 日射计.
ac·ti·noid ['æktinɔid] *a.* 射线状的.
ac·ti·nol·o·gy [ˌækti'nɔlədʒi] *n.* 放射线学.
ac·ti·nom·e·ter [ˌækti'nɔmitə] *n.* 光量计; 露光仪; 光化线强度记录器, 曝光计.
ac·ti·no·mor·phic [ˌæktinəu'mɔːfik] *a.* 【生】辐射对称的.
ac·ti·no·my·ces [ˌæktinəu'maisiːz] *n.* 【微】放线菌.
ac·ti·no·my·cin [ˌæktinəu'maisin] *n.* 【微】放线菌素.
ac·ti·no·my·co·sis [ˌæktinəumai'kəusis] *n.* 【微】放线菌病.
ac·ti·non ['æktinɔn] *n.* 【化】锕射气 〔An〕.
ac·ti·no·ther·a·py ['æktinəu'θerəpi] *n.* 【医】(放射线、紫外线的)射线疗法.
ac·ti·no·u·ra·ni·um [ˌæktinəujuə'reinjəm] *n.* 【化】锕铀 〔AcU, 即铀235〕.
ac·tion ['ækʃən] *n.* ①动作, 活动; 行为, 行动. ★ act 指一次所作的行为; action 虽与 act 同义, 但多半指某一期间内出现数次的行动; 累积而成的 action 叫做 conduct. ②举动, 态度, 姿势. ③主动力, 作用, 机能. ④(机械装置中)有动作的部分; 机械装置[作用]. ⑤措施, 手段. ⑥(演员的)表演; (小说等中的)情节. ⑦【法】诉讼. ⑧【军】战斗, 战事. ⑨某一地区[场合]内最热闹盛行的活动. ⑩〔美口〕刺激性的活动; 赌博. *a chemical* ~ 化学作用 [反应]. *take (prompt)* ~ 采取 (快速) 措施. *accept* ~ 应战. *an encounter* ~ 遭遇战. *a defensive [an offensive]* ~ 防御 [攻击] 战. ***A-!*** 【影】开演! ***~ of the bowels*** 【医】通便 (作用). ***~ of the first impression*** 【法】新诉 〔无以前判例可循的诉讼〕. ***be in*** ~ 行动中. ***be put out of*** ~ 失掉战斗力; (机械等) 出毛病, 不灵. ***break off an*** ~ 停战. ***bring [take] an ~ against*** 对…提起诉讼, 控告. ***bring [come] into*** ~ 使…参加战斗, 参战, 使开始战斗, 开战. ***by [under] the ~ of*** 在…作用下. ***clear (a ship, or the decks) for*** ~ (军舰) 准备战斗. ***go into*** ~ 开始行动; 投入战斗. ***line of*** ~ 【物】作用线; 〔喻〕活动的形式[方针]. ***man of*** ~ 活动家, 实行家. ***out of*** ~ 损坏; 有故障. ***put into [in]*** ~ 实行, 实施; 开动. ***see*** ~ 加入战斗. ***suit the ~ to the word*** 见 suit 条. ***take ~ (in)*** ①着手, 动手, 开始. ②提起诉讼 *(against)*. — *vt.* 〔古〕对… 提起诉讼. ~ **committee** 行动委员会. ~ **group** 行动小组. ~ **painting** 洒泼画 〔抽象派画, 以乱洒颜料等为特征〕. ~ **radius** 【军】行动半径. ~ **shot** 动态照片. ~ **stations** (投入战斗前的) 作战岗位.
ac·tion·a·ble ['ækʃənəbl] *a.* 可控告的.
ac·ti·va·ble ['æktivəbl] *a.* 【化】能被活化的.
ac·ti·vate ['æktiveit] *vt.* ①使活动, 开动, 起动, 触发创设, 成立(机构等). ②【化】激活; 活化. ③【物】赋能; 使产生放射性. ④使(阴沟)产生微生物(而加以净化). *~d charcoal* 活性炭. *~d sludge process* 用活性污泥加速阴沟污物的分解. ~ *analysis* 活化[激活]分析. **-va·tion** [-'veiʃən] 激动, 激活, 活化(作用).
ac·ti·va·tor ['æktiveitə] *n.* 【化】活化剂; 催化剂.
ac·tive ['æktiv] *a.* ①活动的, 有活动力的; 【生】活性的; 【电】有功的; 【无】有源的. 【物】放射性的. ②有生气的, 活泼的, 灵敏的, 敏捷的; 主动的, 能动的, 积极的; 有力的, 勤勉的; 【医】有特效的. ③现行的, 活动中的, 【军】现役的. *an ~ demand* 畅销. *an ~ volcano* 活火山. *The market is* ~. 市场活跃. ~ *measures* 积极手段. ***on ~ service*** 【军】现役, 现役中的. ***take an ~ part [interest] in*** 积极参加. ~ **antenna** 有源天线. ~ **capital** 流动资本. ~ **carbon** 【化】活性碳. ~ **current** 【物】有功电流. ~ **defense** 【军】积极防御. ~ **duty** 现役. ~ **immunity** 自动免疫性. ~ **list** 【军】现役名册. ~ **voice** 【语法】主动语态, ~ **weapon** 【军】在编(制)武器. **-ly** *ad.* 活跃地; 积极地, 能动地; 【语法】主动地. **-ness** *n.* 活跃, 积极性.
ac·tiv·ism ['æktivizəm] *n.* ①积极精神. ②【哲】能动性. ③积极行动主义.
ac·tiv·ist ['æktivist] *n.* 积极分子; 积极行动者; 行动主义分子.
ac·tiv·i·ty [æk'tiviti] *n.* ①活动; 活跃; 动作; 活动力; 能动性. ②活性; 放射性. ③机能, 功能. ④〔美〕机构. ⑤〔*pl.*〕活动范围. *conscious* ~ 主观能动性. *recreational activities* 文娱活动. ***be in*** ~ (火山等) 在活动中. ***with*** ~ 精神充沛地.
ac·tiv·ize ['æktiˌvaiz] *vt.* 使活动, 使行动, 激起.
ac·to·my·o·sin [ˌæktəu'maiəsin] *n.* 【生化】肌纤凝蛋白.
Ac·ton ['æktən] *n.* 阿克顿〔姓氏〕.
ac·ton ['æktən] *n.* 锁子甲, 衬甲的衣服, 铠衣.
ac·tor ['æktə] *n.* ①男演员. ②行动者, 行为者. ③原告. ④【化】原动质. *a bad* ~ 〔美〕坏蛋 *(He's a bad ~ when he's drunk.* 他喝醉时, 行为不检点).
ac·tress ['æktris] *n.* 女演员.
ac·tu·al ['æktjuəl] *a.* 现实的, 实际的, 真实的, 现行的, 现在的. the ~ state 现状. ~ **cost** 实际成本. ~ **range** 【军】实际投弹距离; (火炮) 实际射程. ~ **sin** 【神】自罪. (*opp.* original sin). ***in ~ existence*** 现存. ***in ~ life*** 在现实生活中. **-ist** *n.* 实际家, 现实家; 现实论者. **-i·ty** [ˌæktju'æliti] *n.* 现实, 现存; 现实性; 〔*pl.*〕现状. **-i·za·tion** [ˌæktjuəlai'zeiʃən] *n.* 实现, 现实化. **-ize** ['æktjuəlaiz] *vt.* 使现实化, 实行, 实现. **-ly** *ad.* ①现在, 如今; 实际上; 真. ②竟然 *(Believe it or not, he ~ won.* 信不信由你, 他居然胜利了.)
ac·tu·ar·i·al [ˌæktju'ɛəriəl] *a.* ①〔古〕(法院) 记录员的. ②保险统计师的; 保险统计的.
ac·tu·ar·y ['æktjuəri] *n.* ①〔古〕(法院的) 记录员; 登记官. ②保险统计师; 计算员.
ac·tu·ate ['æktjueit] *vt.* 开动 (机械等); 驱使, 激励 (人等). ***be ~d by*** *(love)* 为(爱情)所驱使.
ac·tu·a·tion [ˌæktju'eiʃən] *n.* 开动; 驱使, 激励.
ac·tu·a·tor ['æktʃueitə] *n.* 【机】促动器; 【电】(电磁铁) 螺线管; 【自】执行元件; 激励器.
ac·u·ate ['ækjuit] *a.* 尖锐的.
a·cu·i·ty [ə'kju(ː)iti] *n.* ①尖锐. ②(思想、视力的) 敏锐. ③(疾病的) 剧烈. ~ *of wit* 才思敏锐.
a·cu·le·ate [ə'kjuːliit] *a.* ①【虫】有螫刺的. ②【植】有皮刺的. ③(语言) 尖锐的.
a·cu·le·us [ə'kjuːliəs] *n.* (*pl.* ***-le·i*** [-ai]) ①【植】皮刺. ②【动】螫针; 螫刺; 刺状产卵器.
a·cu·men [ə'kjuːmen] *n.* ①敏锐, 聪明. ②【植】尖头 [如叶子的尖端]. *political* ~ 政治才干. *business* ~ 业务手腕.
a·cu·mi·nate [ə'kjuːminit] *a.* 尖的; 有尖头的. — [ə'kjuːmineit] *vt., vi.* (使) 变尖.
a·cu·mi·na·tion [əˌkjuːmi'neiʃən] *n.* 尖锐; 尖头.
ac·u·punc·ture ['ækjupʌŋktʃə] *n.* 针刺 (法). ~ *and moxibustion* 针灸. ~ *points* 穴位. — *vt.* 对…施行针刺疗法.
acush·la [ə'kuʃlə] *n.* 〔爱〕爱人, 意中人.
a·cute [ə'kjuːt] *a.* ①锐, 尖 (*opp.* blunt; obtuse); 【植】急尖的. ②敏锐的, 精明的, 深刻的. ③剧烈的, 厉害的. ④【乐】尖锐的, 高音的; 【语音】锐音的; 【医】急性的 (*opp.* chronic). ~ *pain* 剧痛. ~ **accent** 撇形重音符号. ~ **angle** 锐角. ~ **appendicitis** 急性阑尾炎. **-ly** *ad.* 尖锐地; 剧烈地. **-ness** *n.* 锐利; 敏锐; 剧烈.

A

ACV=Air Cushion Vehicle 气垫运载工具.
-acy *suf.* 〔构成抽象名词〕表示"性质"、"状态"、"职位": accur*acy*, fall*acy*, magistr*acy*.
a·cy·clic [ei'saiklik] *a.* 非周期性的;【化】非环式的;【植】非轮生的.
ac·yl ['æsil] *n.*【化】酰(基).
AD, A. D. = ①active duty 现役. ②assembly district (美国某些州的)选区. ③〔L.〕*Anno Domini* 公元.
ad. = add; adverb; advertisement.
a.d. = 〔L.〕*ante diem* (= before the day).
ad[1] [æd] *n.*〔美俚〕*an* ~ *balloon* 广告气球.
ad[2] [æd] *n.*【网球】打成平局后得分 = advantage. ~ *in* (打成平局后)发球人得分. ~ *out* (打成平局后)接球人得分.
ad- *pref.* 向…;接近〔表示运动、方向、变化、添加等意义〕. ★ 在元音或在 b, d, h, m, v 之前,仍为 ad- 不变;在 c, f, g, l, n, p, q, r, s, t 之前, ad- 的 d 因受同化而变为 ac-, af-, ag-, al-, an-, ap-, ac〔在 q 前〕-, ar-, as-at-.
-ad *suf.* ① (a)集合名词的后缀: mon*ad* 一价元素, dy*ad* 二价元素, tri*ad* 三价元素, chili*ad* 一千, myri*ad* 一万. (b)女妖名: Dry*ad* 树精. (c) 诗名: Illi*ad*, Dunci*ad*. (d)植物科名: lili*ad* 百合花科. ②= -ade: ball*ad*, sal*ad*, etc.
ad [æd] *prep.* 〔L.〕①达,到(= *to; towards*). ②根据(= *up to; according to*). ~ ***ar·bi·tri·um***[ɑː'bitriəm]随意. ~ ***cap·tan·dum*** [kæp'tændəm]***(vul·gus)*** ['vʌlgəs] 讨好众人的. ~ ***e·un·dem*** [iː'ʌndəm] 按同等学历. ~ ***fi·nem*** ['fainem] 到[在] 最后. ~ ***hoc*** ['hɔk] 特定,特别 (*an* ~ *hoc committee* 特设委员会). ~ ***in·fi·ni·tum*** [ˌinfi'naitəm] 永远,无限,无穷(略 *ad inf.*) ~ ***i·ni·ti·um***[ini'ʃiːəm]在开始. ~ ***in·te·rim*** ['intərim] 暂时的,临时的〔略 *ad int.*〕 (*chargé d'affaires* ~ *interim* 临时代办). ~ ***lib·i·tum*** ['libitəm] 随意,任意(略 *ad lib.*);【乐】自由演唱. ~ ***loc·um*** ['lɔkəm] 在这里. ~ ***nau·se·am*** ['nɔːsiæm] 令人作呕,讨厌. ~ ***ref·er·en·dum*** [refə'redəm] 还要斟酌,尚须考虑 (~ *referendum contract* 暂定契约书, 草约). ~ ***rem*** [rem] 得要领, 中肯, 适宜. ~ ***un·guem (factus)*** ['ʌŋgwem] ('fæktəs) 完善. ~ ***va·lor·em*** [və'lɔrem] 按价 (~ *valorem duty* 按价收税). ~ ***ver·bum*** ['vəːbəm] 逐字.
A·da ['eidə] *n.* 埃达〔女子名〕.
a·dac·ty·lous [ə'dæktiləs] *a.* 生来无指缺趾的.
ad·age ['ædidʒ] *n.* 格言,箴言;古话,谚语.
a·da·gio [ə'dɑːdʒiəu] *ad., a.* 〔It.〕【乐】缓慢地(的),悠闲地(的). —*n.* ①【乐】柔板. ②悠闲的双人芭蕾舞.
Ad·am[1] ['ædəm] *n.* 亚当〔姓氏,男子名〕.
Ad·am[2] ['ædəm] *n.*【圣】亚当;最初的人. ***(as) old as*** ~ 古老;陈旧. ***from*** ~ ***on down*** 自从开天辟地以来. ***not know*** *(a person)* ***from*** ~ 全然不知,从未见过. ***the old*** ~【宗】人类本性之恶, 原罪. ~ **and Eve** 〔美口〕两个鸡蛋 (~ *and Eve on a raft*〔美口〕烤面包上两个鸡蛋). ~**'s ale [wine]**〔口〕水. ~**'s apple** ①【解】喉结, 喉核. ②【植】车前属; 柚; 冠状狗牙花. ~**'s needle**【植】丝兰属.
Ad·am[3] ['ædəm] *a.* (家具和建筑)亚当式的〔亚当是指十八世纪英国建筑师 Robert 和 James Adam 兄弟〕.
ad·a·mant ['ædəmənt] *n.* 坚硬无比的东西;【地】硬石(指金刚石等).—*a.* ①坚硬的. ②坚决的. *Once he had made his decision, he was* ~ *and would not change his mind.* 他一旦做出决定,就坚决不改变主意.
ad·a·man·tine [ˌædə'mæntain] *a.* ①金刚石似的; 坚硬无比的. ②(牙齿) 珐琅质的. ③坚决的, 断然的. ~ *chains* 极坚固的铁链. ~ **lustre** 金刚光泽. ~ **spar**【地】刚玉.
Ad·am·ite ['ædəmait] *n.* ① 亚当的后裔, 人. ②裸体的人;【宗】裸体生活宗派. — *a.* 亚当后裔的,人的.
Ad·ams ['ædəmz] *n.* 亚当斯〔姓氏〕.
ad·ams·ite ['ædəmzait] *n.* ①【化】二苯胺氯胂(毒气). ②【矿】暗绿云母.
Ad·ams·town ['ædəmz'təun] *n.* 亚当斯敦〔皮特凯恩岛(英)首府〕.
a·dapt [ə'dæpt] *vt.* ①使适应,使适合,使适于. ②改,修改,改编,改写(剧本等). ~ *(one's behaviour) to (the company)* 使(自己行动) 配合 (同伴). ~ *oneself to (circumstances)* 适应(环境),随遇而安, 通权达变. ~**ed** *a.* 适合…的; 改编成…的. *This book is* ~*ed to children.* 这书是为适合儿童需要而改写的. *The novel was* ~*ed for the stage.* 这部小说改编成剧本了. *The play is* ~*ed from a novel.* 这是一部由小说改编成的戏剧. — *vi.* 适应不同环境〔情况等〕.
a·dapt·a·bil·i·ty [əˌdæptə'biliti] *n.* 适应性,顺应性.
a·dapt·a·ble [ə'dæptəbl] *a.* ①可以适应的. ②能改编的.
ad·ap·ta·tion [ˌædæp'teiʃən] *n.* ①适合, 适应,顺应 *(to)*. ②改编(的作品) *(from)*. ③【生】适应性的改变;感官适应性调节. ④同化. *the principle of* ~ *to local conditions* 因地制宜的原则.
a·dapt·er, -or [ə'dæptə] *n.* ①改编者. ②【机】转接器,接头;插座;衬套. ③【无】拾音器.
a·dap·tion [ə'dæpʃən] *n.* 〔美〕 = adaptation.
a·dap·tive [ə'dæptiv] *a.* 适合的,适应的.
A·dar [ɑː'dɑː] *n.* 〔Heb.〕(犹太历)六月.
ad·ax·i·al [æ'dæksiəl] *a.*【植】近轴的.
ADB = Asian Development Bank 亚洲开发银行.
ADC = 〔F.〕*aide-de-camp*.
ad·col·umn ['ædkələm] *n.* 〔美口〕广告栏.
ad-craft ['ædkrɑːft] *n.* 〔美口〕广告业.
add [æd] *vt.* ①加,增,添,追加,附加;获得. ②又说;补充说. ③加算, 累积. ~ *some water to the tea* 给茶里加些开水. ~ *one thing to another* 加一物于另一物. *Add three and seven and you will have ten.* 7加3等于10. —*vi.* ①增加. ②作加法. ③加算, 合计. *learn to* ~ 学做加法. ~ **in** 算入. ~ **it on** 〔口〕浮报, 虚报. ~ **to** 增加 (*This* ~*ed to our difficulties.* 这增加了我们不少困难). ~ **up** 合计; 符合预期的数目 (*The figures don't* ~ *up right.* 这些数字加起来不对). ~ **up to** 总计共达;〔口〕总之就是!*(The evidence* ~*s up to a case of theft.* 证据显示出是一起盗窃案). **to** ~ **to** 更加, 又加 (*To* ~ *to the danger, darkness fell upon the water.* 更加危险的是,夜幕又降临水面). **-ed** *a.* 附加的;增加的;更多的.
add·a·ble, add·i·ble ['ædəbl] *a.* ①可加上的. ②被加上的.
add. = addenda; addendum; addition(al); address.
ad·dax ['ædæks] *n.*【动】曲角羚羊.
ad·dend ['ædend, ə'dend] *n.*【数】加数.
ad·den·dum [ə'dendəm] *n.* *(pl. -da)* ①附录, 补遗. ②追加物,附加物. ③(齿轮的)齿头高度,齿顶高.
ad·der[1] ['ædə] *n.* 加法器;加法电路.
ad·der[2] ['ædə] *n.* 小毒蛇, 蝰蛇. ***deaf as an*** ~ 完全耳聋.
ad·der's-mouth ['ædəzmauθ] *n.* 沼兰属植物.
ad·der's-tongue ['ædəzˌtʌŋ]【植】①山慈菇 (= dog-tooth violet). ②瓶尔小草属植物.
ad·dict [ə'dikt] *vt.* ①使沉溺,使嗜好; 热中于. ②使吸毒成瘾. ~ ***oneself to*** 沉溺于, 热中于, 一心在. ***be*** ~***ed to*** 嗜好,嗜爱. — *vi.* 使人上瘾. *Drugs are* ~*ing.* 麻醉品会使人上瘾. — ['ædikt] *n.* 〔俚〕有(毒)瘾的人. *a drug* ~ 吸毒成瘾者.
ad·dic·tion [ə'dikʃən] *n.* 热中,沉溺,嗜好;吸毒成瘾.
ad·dic·tive [ə'diktiv] *a.* 沉溺的;使成瘾的;上瘾的.
adding ['ædiŋ] *n.* 计算, 加算. ~ *machine* 计算器, 加算器.
Ad·dis ['ædis] *n.* 阿迪斯〔姓氏〕.

Ad·dis A·ba·ba [ˈædis ˈæbəbə] 亚的斯亚贝巴〔埃塞俄比亚首都〕.
Ad·di·son [ˈædisn] *n.* 阿迪森〔姓氏〕. **~'s disease** 阿迪森氏病,(肾上腺性)青铜色皮病,类青铜色皮病.
ad·dit·a·ment [əˈditəmənt] *n.* 增加物,附加物.
ad·di·tion [əˈdiʃən] *n.* ①附加,追加;附加物. ②【数】加法,加算. ③【法】(加在姓名后的)头衔,官衔;称号. ④(建筑物的)附加部分. *have an ~ (to one's family)* 生孩子,添人口. ***in*** ~ 加之,又,另外. ***in ~ to*** 加之,除…外又. ~ **compound**【化】加成化合物.
ad·di·tion·al [əˈdiʃənl] *a.* 附加的,追加的,另外的. *an ~ tax* 附加税. *the ~ regulation* 补充规定. **-ly** [əˈdiʃənəli] *ad.* 加之,另外,又.
ad·di·tive [ˈæditiv] *a.* ①附加的;增加的. ②【化】加成的,加和的. ③【数】加法的;加性的. —*n.* ①添加剂;添加物. ②【数】加法. ~ **group**【数】加法群. ~ **reaction**【化】加成反应.
ad·dle [ˈædl] *a.* ①变质腐败的,坏的;混乱的. ②(思想)糊涂的,空虚的. ~ *eggs* 臭蛋. — *vt., vi.* ①(使)腐坏. ②(使)变混乱. ~ *one's brain over figures* 给数字弄昏头脑. ~**brained,** ~**headed,** ~**pated** *a.* 思想糊涂的,昏头昏脑的. ~**head,** ~**pate** 昏愦的人,糊涂虫.
ad·dled [ˈædld] *a.* ①腐败了的,坏了的. ②(头脑等)混乱的;昏愦的.
ad·do·me·ter [əˈdɔmitə] *n.* 加算器.
add-on [ˈædˈɔn] *n.* 〔口〕分期付款方式.
ad·dress [əˈdres, *Am.* ˈædres] *n.* ①(信上的)称呼,姓名;地址. ②致辞;寒暄;演说;正式请愿. ③谈吐,风度. ④〔*pl.*〕求爱,献殷勤. ⑤灵巧,娴熟. *change one's ~* 改变住址. *an inside ~* 信纸左上角的收信人姓名、地址. *an inaugural ~* 就任致辞[演说]. *a man of pleasing [good] ~* 谈吐流利的人. *an ~ of thanks* 谢辞. *show great ~ in (doing sth.)* 在(做某事上)显出有本领. *pay one's ~es to a lady* 向某女士大献殷勤. ***opening [closing]*** ~ 开[闭]幕辞. ***the A-*** ①〔英〕议院答辞;〔美〕总统咨文. ②【法】撤职请求. ***with*** ~ 巧妙地. —*vt.* ①在…上写姓名住址;称呼;向…致意. ②【商】交,委托. ③给…讲话;向…演说,向…求爱,向…献殷勤. ④【法】(立法部门)请求撤消(不适任法官的)职务. ⑤引导,引见. ⑥【高尔夫球】瞄准. ~ *a letter to sb.* 写信给某人. ~ *an audience* 对听众演说. ~ *sb.* 跟人攀谈. ~ *a meeting* 向会众演说. ~ *a protest to sb.* 对某人提抗议. ~ *the ball*【高尔夫球】用棒碰球作瞄准准备. ~ ***oneself to*** ①专心(工作). ②向…讲话,和…通信. ③(在演说时)述及,讲到. ~ **book** 通讯花名册. ~**ing machine** 姓名住址印刷机.
ad·dress·ee [ˌædreˈsiː] *n.* 收信人,收件人.
ad·dress·er, -or [əˈdresə] *n.* ①发言人,陈述人. ②发信人;署名人.
ad·dress·o·graph [əˈdresəgrɑːf] *n.* 姓名住址印刷机〔原商标名〕.
ad·duce [əˈdjuːs] *vt.* 引用,引证,举出. ~ *reasons in support of one's case.* 提出理由来支持自己的论证.
ad·du·cent [əˈdjuːsnt] *a.*【生理】内转的;(肌肉)内收的.
ad·duc·i·ble [əˈdjuːsibl] *a.* 可以引用的.
ad·duct [əˈdʌkt] *vt.*【生理】使内收 (*opp.* abduct). —[ˈædʌkt] *n.*【化】加合物.
ad·duc·tion [əˈdʌkʃən] *n.* ①引用,引证. ②【解】内收(作用).
ad·duc·tor [əˈdʌktə] *n.*【解】内收肌 (*opp.* abductor);【动】闭壳肌.
Ade [eid] *n.* 埃德〔姓氏〕.
ade [eid] *n.* 〔美〕果汁水. *grape ~* 葡萄水.
-ade *suf.* 〔构成表示下列意义的各词〕①动作: block*ade* 堵塞. ②行动中的集团: caval*cade* 马队; ③动作的结果或成品: masquer*ade* 化装舞会, pom*ade* 发油. ④某些饮料: lemon*ade* 柠檬水.
Ad·e·la [ˈædilə] *n.* 阿迪拉〔姓氏,女子名〕.
Ad·e·laide[1] [ˈædəleid] *n.* 阿德莱德〔女子名〕.
Ad·e·laide[2] [ˈædəleid] *n.* 阿德莱德〔澳大利亚港市〕.
A·dele [əˈdel] *n.* 阿黛尔〔女子名〕.
Ad·e·li·ne [ˈædəliːn, ˈædiliːn] *n.* 阿德琳〔女子名〕.
a·demp·tion [əˈdempʃən] *n.*【法】(遗产的)取消;〔因立遗嘱人亡故时,遗产产权已非其所有〕.
A·den [eidn] *n.* 亚丁〔民主也门首都〕.
ad·e·nine [ˈædiniːn] *n.*【生化】腺嘌呤.
ad·e·ni·tis [ˌædiˈnaitis] *n.*【医】(淋巴)腺炎.
ad·e·no·car·ci·no·ma [ˈædinəuˌkɑːsiˈnəumə] *n.*【医】腺癌.
ad·e·noid [ˈædinɔid] *a.*【医】腺样(的). — *n.* ①【植】腺状物. ②〔*pl.*〕【医】腺样增殖(症). ③〔美俚〕声音微弱的电台歌手. ~ **growth** 腺样增殖(体).
ad·e·noi·dal [ˈædinɔidl] = adenoid *(a.)*.
ad·e·nol·o·gy [ˌædiˈnɔlədʒi] *n.*【医】腺学.
ad·e·no·ma [ˌædiˈnəumə] *n.*【医】腺瘤.
a·den·o·sine [əˈdenəsiːn] *n.*【生化】腺甙.
ad·e·no·vi·rus [ˌædinəuˈvaiərəs] *n.* 呼吸系统病毒.
ad·ept [ˈædept, əˈdept] *a.* 熟练的;内行的. *be ~ in [at]* 善于,擅长,精通. — *n.* 内行,熟手. *an ~ in philosophy* 哲学大家. *a musical ~* 音乐名手. **-ly** *ad.* **-ness** *n.*
ad·ep·tism [əˈdeptizm] *n.* 重用专家的作风,用人唯贤 (*opp.* nepotism).
ad·e·qua·cy [ˈædikwəsi] *n.* 适当,恰当;足够.
ad·e·quate [ˈædikwit] *a.* ①适当的;足够的,充分的. ②恰当,胜任的. ③尚可的,差强人意的. ~ **for** 适合;足够. ~ **to** *(one's needs)* 敷(用),够(用). ~ *to (one's post)* 胜(任). *The supply is not ~ to the demand.* 供不应求. *give only an ~ performance* 演出仅差强人意. **-ly** *ad.* **-ness** *n.*
a·der·min [əˈdəːmin] *n.* 维生素 B_6 (= pyridoxine).
à deux [F. a dø] 〔F.〕〔介词短语〕两人一起;两人之间.
A.D.F. = automatic direction finder【无】自动测向器.
ad·here [ədˈhiə] *vi.* ①粘附;固着 *(to)*. ②追随;依附. ③遵循;坚持 *(to)*. *the mud adhering to our shoes* 粘在鞋子上的泥. ~ *to neutrality* 严守中立. —*vt.* 使粘附.
ad·her·ence [ədˈhiərəns] *n.* ①粘附. ②固执;坚持,依附〔指精神方面的; adhesion 则是物质上的〕.
ad·her·ent [ədˈhiərənt] *a.* ①粘附…的,依附…的. ②【植】骈生的,连生的 *(to)*. ③【语法】(在名词之前的)修饰语的. — *n.* 追随者,支持者,拥护者,信徒〔其后通常接 of, 偶尔也接 to〕. *an enthusiastic ~ of the theory* 该学说的热情支持者.
ad·he·sion [ədˈhiːʒən] *n.* ①粘附,附着,胶着. ②粘附力;粘附(现象). ③追随;皈依;信奉;同意,加入. ④【医】粘连(物). ***give in one's*** ~ 表示同意,声明加入.
ad·he·sive [ədˈhiːsiv] *a.* 粘附性的,胶粘的. — *n.* 胶合剂,粘合剂. ~ **disc**【植】吸盘. ~ **envelope** 胶口信封. ~ **plaster** 橡皮膏. ~ **stamp** 带胶邮票. ~ **tape** 胶带. **-ly** *ad.* **-ness** *n.*
ad·hib·it [ædˈhibit] *vt.* ①贴,粘. ②〔古〕用,服(药等). ③容许(进入).
ad hoc [ædˈhɔk] 〔L.〕①〔介词短语〕特别是. ②〔用作定语〕特别的. *an ~ commission of inquiry* 特别调查委员会.
ad ho·mi·nem [ˌædˈhɔmiˌnem] 〔L.〕〔介词短语〕①怀有偏见地;感情用事地. ②矛头指向个人地.
ad·i·a·bat [ˈædiəbæt] *n.*【物】绝热线.
ad·i·a·bat·ic [ˌædiəˈbætik] *a.*【物】绝热的;不传热的. *an ~ curve* 绝热曲线.
Ad·i·an·tum [ˌædiˈæntəm] *n.*【植】①石长生属. ②〔a-〕= maidenhair.
ad·i·aph·o·re·sis [ˌædaiˈæfəriːsis] *n.*【医】无汗症.
ad·i·aph·o·ret·i·c [ˌædiˈæfəretik] *a.* 无汗的. — *n.*

A

止汗剂.

ad·i·aph·o·rous [ˌædiˈæfərəs] *a.* ①不偏不倚,中立,无可无不可. ②【医】无反应的,无活动的.

adi·a·ther·man·cy [ˌædiəˈθəːmənsi] *n.*【物】不透红外线性. **-ma·nous** *a.*

a·dieu [əˈdjuː] *int.* 再会, 一路平安. — *n.* *(pl.* **~s,** ***a·dieux*** [əˈdjuːz]*)* 告别, 辞别. ***bid ~ to (sb.)*** 向某人告别. ***make [take] one's ~*** 辞行.

ad·i·os [ɑːˈdjəus] 〔Sp.〕 *int.* 再见.

a·dip·ic [əˈdipik] *a.* ~ **acid**【化】已二酸.

ad·i·po·cere [ˌædipəuˈsiə] *n.* 尸蜡,尸油.

ad·i·pose [ˈædipəus] *a.* 脂肪质的,脂肪多的. — *n.* 动物脂肪.

ad·i·pos·i·ty [ˌædiˈpɔsiti] *n.* 多脂,肥胖.

ad·it [ˈædit] *n.* ①入口. ②【矿】横坑,平峒.

ADIZ = air defence identification zone【空】防空识别区.

adj. = adjacent; adjective; adjunct; adjustment.

ad·ja·cen·cy [əˈdʒeisənsi] *n.* ①接近,毗邻. ②邻接物. ③紧接在某一节目之前或之后的电视[广播]节目.

ad·ja·cent [əˈdʒeisənt] *a.* ①毗邻的, 邻近的. ②(时间上)紧接着的. ~ *angle* 邻角. ~ *towns and villages* 附近的城市和乡村. ***be ~ to*** 接近….

ad·jec·ti·val [ˌædʒekˈtaivəl] *a.*【语法】形容词的,形容词型的. **-ly** *ad.*

ad·jec·tive [ˈædʒiktiv] *n.*【语法】形容词. — *a.* ①形容词(性)的. ②附属的. ③【法】有关程序的. ~ **clause [phrase]** 定语从句[短语]. ~ **colours** 间接色素, 媒染染料. ~ **law**【法】附属法, 程序法 (*opp.* substantive law*)*.

ad·join [əˈdʒɔin] *vi.* 接,贴连,毗连,邻接;临. *The two houses ~.*这两座房子相连. — *vt.* ①接,邻;临. ②附上,加上,使结合. *Canada ~s the United States.* 加拿大与美国接壤.

ad·join·ing [əˈdʒɔiniŋ] *a.* 邻,邻接的,隔壁. *an ~ room* 邻室. ~ **rock** 围岩.

ad·journ [əˈdʒəːn] *vt.* 使延期; 使中止,休(会). ~ *the debate* 暂停辩论. — *vi.* ①延会,休会,散会. ②〔俚〕搬会场,移坐位. ~ *without day [sine die]* 无限期休会. ~ *to the dining room* 移到餐室. **-ment** *n.* ①延期,闭会,休会,延会. ②休会时期.

Adjt. = Adjutant.

ad·judge [əˈdʒʌdʒ] *vt.* ①判决,宣判;裁定. ②判给, 断与. ③断定,认为. ~ *a man (to be) guilty* 判决某人有罪. *be ~d wise to do sth.* 去做某事被视为明智.

ad·judge·ment, ad·judg·ment [əˈdʒʌdʒmənt] *n.* 判决;宣告;判定;定罪;判归.

ad·ju·di·cate [əˈdʒuːdikeit] *vt.* 判决, 裁断, 裁定. — *vi.* 审断,判决 *(on; upon)*. ~ *in a case [on a matter]* 判决案子[事件].

ad·ju·di·ca·tion [əˌdʒuːdiˈkeiʃən] *n.* ①判决, 宣告. ②破产宣告.

ad·ju·di·ca·tive [əˈdʒuːdikeitiv] *a.* 判决的.

ad·ju·di·ca·tor [əˈdʒuːdikeitə] *n.* 判决者, 裁定者, 审判者,评判人.

ad·junct [ˈædʒʌŋkt] *n.* ①附属物,附件. ②助手, 副手. ③【语法】附加语,修饰语. ④【逻】附属性质, 非本质属性. — *a.* 附属的 *(to; of)*. ~ **professor** 〔美〕副教授.

ad·junc·tion [æˈdʒʌŋkʃən] *n.* ①【数】附益, 附加. ②【语法】偏正语结〔叶斯伯森用语〕.

ad·junc·tive [əˈdʒʌŋktiv] *a.* 附属的;附加语的. **-ly** *ad.*

ad·ju·ra·tion [ˌædʒuəˈreiʃən] *n.* ①严令. ②恳请.

ad·jure [əˈdʒuə] *vt.* ①(以发誓或咒诅威迫的方式) 严令. ②恳求,恳请. ③ ~ *sb. to tell the truth* 要某人务必说实话.

ad·just [əˈdʒʌst] *vt.* ①调准(望远镜等), 对准, 校正,校准(机械等). ②调整; 整理, 整顿. ③核算(盈亏). ④【保险】评定(赔偿要求). ⑤调停,排解(纠纷等). ⑥使适应(环境). ~ *a camera* 校准镜头. ~ *accounts* 清理帐目; 核算. ~ *one's clothes* 整顿装束. ~ *differences* 调解分歧. ~ *oneself* 整装. ~ *oneself to one's environment* 使自己适应环境. —*vi.* ①获得校准. ②适应于 *(to)*. **~ing plane**【空】调节翼. **~ing points** (炮兵的试射点).

ad·just·a·ble [əˈdʒʌstəbl] *a.* 可校准的, 可调整的. *an ~ wrench* 活动扳手.

ad·just·er [əˈdʒʌstə] *n.* ①调整者; 调解者. ②【机】调整器. ③(赔偿财产损失等的)核算人.

ad·just·ment [əˈdʒʌstmənt] *n.* ①调整; 调节 (装置); 校正. ②调解. ③(赔偿损失的)清算.

ad·ju·tage [ˈædʒutidʒ] *n.* 喷射管.

ad·ju·tan·cy [ˈædʒutənsi] *n.* 副官职位.

ad·ju·tant [ˈædʒutənt] *a.* 补助的. — *n.* ①【军】副官. ②【鸟】鹳 (= ~ bird [crane, stork]). ~ **general** 〔*pl.* ~s **general**〕 副官长;〔the A- General〕〔美〕陆军副官; 副官署署长. **A- General's Department**【美陆军】军务局.

ad·ju·vant [ˈædʒuvənt] *a.* 辅佐的. — *n.* ①助理员, 助手. ②【医】辅药,佐药.

Ad·ler [ˈædlə] *n.* 阿德勒〔姓氏〕.

ad-lib [ædˈlib] *vt., vi.* ***(ad-lib·bed; ad-lib·bing)*** 〔美口〕 ①(演奏时)临时穿插;即兴撰造(词句、乐曲等). ②临时拼凑. — *n.* ①即兴[即席] 演奏, 临时穿插. ②权宜措施.— *a., ad.* ① 临时穿插的[地],临时拼凑的[地]. ③随意的[地]. *an ~ organization* 临时拼凑的组织. **-lib-ber** *n.* 即兴表演的人;即兴讲演者.

ad loc *ad.* 〔L.〕 在那地方;去那地方 (=ad locum).

adm. = administration; administrative; administrator; administratrix.

Adm. = Admiral; Admiralty.

ad·man [ˈædmæn] *n.* (*pl.* ***-men*** [-men]) 〔美俚〕 ①广告员. ②写广告的人.

ad·mass [ˈædmæs] *n.* ①(依靠各种宣传工具企图影响广大消费者的) 广告推销制度. ②受广告影响的社会. — *a.* ①广告推销性质的;受广告推销影响的.

ad·meas·ure [ædˈmeʒə] *vt.* 分配,配给. **-ment** *n.* ①分配,配给. ②测量;尺寸.

ad·min·i·cle [ædˈminikl] *n.* ①补助物. ②【法】副证, 补充证据.

ad·mi·nic·u·lar [ˌædmiˈnikjulə] *a.* 补助的;补充的.

ad·min·is·ter [ədˈministə] *vt.* ①管理, 管制, 掌管, 统制;处理,支配;治理. ②施行, 实施. ③给与, 供给; 下药, 使…吃药. ④使…发誓, 使…保证. ~ *justice* 执行法律,审判. ~ *medicine to sb.* 给某人吃药,下药. ~ *a rebuke* 责备. ~ *fuel to the fire of* ...煽动, 使…火上加油. ~ *sb. a box on the ear.* 给某人一个耳光. ~ *an oath to sb.* 使某人发誓. — *vi.* ①管理;承办,代办;【法】管理遗产. ②补助, 辅助. ~ **to** 有助于 (*Health ~s to peace of mind.* 健康有助于身心的安宁).

ad·min·is·trate [ədˈministreit] *vt.* 〔美〕管理,支配.

ad·min·is·tra·tion [ədˌminisˈtreiʃən] *n.* ①管理,掌管, 经营;〔英〕行政,施政. ②行政机关,局[处、署]; 〔A-主美〕政府. ③给与;施行. ④给药, (药的) 服法. ⑤【军】后方勤务. ⑥【法】遗产管理. ⑦(官员的) 任职期. *an ~ journal* 〔美〕当权派报纸. *an ~ senator* 〔美〕 支持政府的参议院议员. *a board of ~* 董事会. *Fewer and better troops and simple ~* 精兵简政. ~ *chief* 行政处长,总务处长. *civil ~* 民政. *military ~* 军政. ~ *of justice* 处罚. *oral ~*【医】口服.

ad·min·is·tra·tive [ədˈministrətiv] *a.* ①管理的;行政的. ②非战斗性行政勤务的. *the Broadcasting A- Bureau* 广播事业局. ~ *ability* 行政手腕; 管理[经营]才能. *an ~ district* 行政区划. ~ **services** ①非战斗性行政勤务. ②行政勤务部队.

ad·min·is·tra·tor [ədˈministreitə] *n.* ①管理人;理事;

行政官员. ②【法】遗产管理人. ③给药人. ④代管教区的牧师. **-ship** [-ʃip] *n.* 管理人[行政官等]之职.

ad·min·is·tra·trix [əd'ministreitriks] *n.* (*pl.* *~es; -trices* [-trisi:z]) ①女管理员. ②【法】女遗产管理人.

ad·mi·ra·ble ['ædmərəbl] *a.* ①可钦佩的, 可佩服的, 可惊叹的. ②美妙的,极好的. **-bly** *ad.* 可赞叹地,美妙地. **-ness** *n.* 美妙.

ad·mi·ral ['ædmərəl] *n.* ①海军上将; 海军将官; 舰队司令. ②(海军上将所乘的)旗舰. ③渔船队长,商船队长. ④【虫】红[白]纹蝶. *an ~ of the fleet* 〔英〕海军元帅. *a fleet ~* (美海军)五星上将. *an ~ of the navy* 〔苏联〕海军元帅. *a full ~* 海军大将. *a vice ~* 海军中将. *a rear ~* 海军少将. ***~'s watch*** 〔美俚〕熟睡一晚 (的机会); 充分的休息. **-ship** 海军上将[将官]之职.

ad·mi·ral·ty ['ædmərəlti] *n.* ①海军大将之职. ②〔A-〕〔英〕海军部. ③海事法; 海事法(庭). ④制海权. *the Board of A-* 〔英〕海军部委员会. *First Lord of the A-* 〔英〕海军大臣. *Lords Commissioners of the A-* 〔英〕海军部委员. *~* **cloth** 海军呢. *~* **council** 海军将官会议. **A- Court** 〔英〕海事法庭. *~* **creeper** 探海锚. *~* **mile** 〔英〕海里 = nautical mile. *~* **port** 海军要塞.

ad·mi·ra·tion [,ædmə'reiʃən] *n.* ①赞美, 钦佩, 羡慕, 佩服 *(for)*. ②人人赞美的人[物]. *a note of ~* 感叹号(!). ***be struck with ~*** 惊叹,赞叹. ***do sth. to ~*** 把某事做得极好. ***in ~ of*** 赞美,赏识. ***to ~*** 美满地 (*He has succeeded to ~.* 他已美满地成功了). ***with ~*** 用惊叹[羡慕]的神气.

ad·mire [əd'maiə] *vt.* ①赞美, 称赞, 钦佩, 羡慕; 崇拜. ②〔口〕夸奖,褒奖. ③〔美口〕想要,喜欢; 欣赏. *I'd ~ to go.* 我很想去. *He ~s her for her finished manner.* 他羡慕她的文明礼貌. *I ~ his impudence.* 〔反〕我佩服他的脸厚. —*vi.* 〔古〕惊异*(at)*.

ad·mir·er [əd'maiərə] *n.* 赞美者,敬慕者; 情人.

ad·mir·ing [əd'maiəriŋ] *a.* 赞美的,羡慕的. **-ly** *ad.*

ad·mis·si·bil·i·ty [əd,misə'biliti] *n.* ①许入; 许进. ②准许; 可接受.

ad·mis·si·ble [əd'misəbl] *a.* ①许进的. ②可采纳的, 可接受的. ③有资格加入的 *(to)*. *an ~ piece of evidence* 可接受的证据. *~ to an office* 有资格担任某职务. **-bly** *ad.*

ad·mis·sion [əd'miʃən] *n.* ①允许进入, 许可入场[入学、入会]; 入场[入会]费. ②承认; 招认, 坦白; 首肯. *A- by ticket only.* 凭票入场. *grant sb. ~* 允许某人进入. *~ of blame* 承认罪过. ***by [on] sb.'s own ~*** 据某人自己承认[供认]. ***gain [obtain] ~ to [into]*** 获准进入. ***grant sb. ~*** 准许进入. ***~ free*** 免费入场, 自由入场. ***A- Day*** 〔美〕加邦节〔各州加入联邦的纪念日〕. *~* **tickets** 入场券. *~* **valves** 进气阀.

ad·mis·sive [əd'misiv] *a.* 许入的,入场的; 容许有…的. *(of)*.

ad·mit [əd'mit] *vt.* *(-mit·ted; -mit·ting)* ①接受; 许可入场[入会、入学、入院]. ②承认,容许(辩解). ③收容, 容纳. *~ sb. to the third year class* 许某人入三年级. *I ~ that I was wrong.* 我承认我错了. *To ~ one.* (门票)只许一人入场. — *vi.* ①容许 *(of)*. ②通向, 通到*(to)*. ③承认 *(to)*. *This, I ~, is true.* 这的确是的. *This key ~s to the house.* 这把钥匙能进这间屋子. ***~ of*** 容许, 有…可能, 容有…的余地 (*~ of improvement* 有改良的余地. *~ of no reply* 无从答复. *~ of no excuse* 无可推诿, 无可宽恕). ***be admitted to bail*** 【法】准许保释. ***be admitted to the bar*** 〔美〕取得律师资格. ***(while) admitting that ...,*** 虽说, 即使.

ad·mit·ta·ble [əd'mitəbl] *a.* 可接受的; 可容许的.

ad·mit·tance [əd'mitəns] *n.* ①许可入场[入校等]. ②【建】通道. ③【物】导纳. *have free ~ to the theatre* 可免费进入剧场. ***gain [get] ~ to*** 准入…, 进入…. ***No ~ (except on business)*** (闲人)免进, (非公)莫入. *~* function【物】导纳函数.

ad·mit·ted [əd'mitid] *a.* 被承认了的; (事实)公认的,明白的. **-ly** *ad.* 明白地 (*I am admittedly afraid.* 我公开表示害怕了).

ad·mix [əd'miks] *vt., vi.* 掺合,混合 *(with)*.

ad·mix·ture [əd'mikstʃə] *n.* ①混合, 掺合. ②混合物, 掺合料[剂]; 外加物.

ad·mon·ish [əd'moniʃ] *vt.* ①忠告[劝告](某人做某事)〔后接不定式; 劝告不做某事后接 not 加不定式或接 against 加动名词〕. ②为某事 *(for, of)* 告诫某人. ③警告某人(有危险等) *(of)*. ④敦促、提醒某人(尽义务等) *(of, about)*. ⑤要求、催办(某事). *The teacher ~ed the students against being late.* 老师劝告学生不要迟到. *~ sb. of a danger* 警告某人注意危险. *~ silence* 叫静默点. **-ment** *n.*

ad·mo·ni·tion [,ædməu'niʃən] *n.* ①训戒, 忠告. ②温和的责备. **-mon·i·to·ry** [-'monitəri] *a.*

ad·mon·i·tor [əd'monitə] *n.* 劝告者,忠告者, 训诫者.

ad·mon·i·to·ry [əd'monitəri] *a.* ①劝告的,忠告的. ②责备的.

A.D.M.S. = Assistant Director of Medical Services 〔英〕助理军医局长.

ADN = 〔G.〕 *Allgemeine Deutsche Nachrichtendienst* 德意志通讯社[德意志民主共和国].

ad·noun ['ædnaun] *n.* 【语法】作名词用的形容词〔例: *The new* supersedes *the old.* 新陈代谢〕.

a·do [ə'du:] *n.* 骚扰, 无谓的纷扰, 忙乱; 费力, 艰难. ***make [have] much ~*** 大忙一阵, 费尽心力 (*He had much ~ in finding out his lodging.* 他费尽力气才找到住处). ***make much ~ about nothing*** 无事生非,小题大作. ***once for ~*** 只一次,一劳永逸. ***with much ~*** 煞费苦心,费尽心血,好容易才. ***without more [future] ~*** 以后毫不费力,以后立即 (*He paid up without any more ~.* 他不再啰嗦就付了钱).

-a·do *suf.* 来自西班牙语的名词的后缀: brav*ado*, desper*ado*.

a·do·be [ə'dəubi] *n.* ①砖坯. ②土砖砌成的房子〔土墙〕. ③(制)砖(粘)土. — *a.* ①用砖坯砌的. *~* **dollar** 〔口〕墨西哥银币. *~* **soil** 龟裂土.

ad·o·les·cence [,ædəu'lesns], **-cen·cy** [-si] *n.* 青年期, 青春期,青春.

ad·o·les·cent [,ædəu'lesnt] *a.* 青年期的,青春期的. — *n.* 少年,少女.

Ad·olf, Ad·olph ['ædolf] *n.* 阿道夫[男子名].

Ad·olphus [ə'dolfəs] *n.* 阿道弗斯[男子名].

ad·o·nai [,ædəu'neii] 〔Heb.〕上帝,天主〔在希伯来语的著述中为"耶和华"的代用词〕.

A·don·is [ə'dəunis] *n.* ①【希神】阿多尼斯; 爱神〔Venus 钟爱的美貌猎人〕; 美男子. ②【植】侧金盏花. ③〔英〕一种蝶.

ad·o·nize ['ædənaiz] *vt., vi.* 打扮, 装饰[指男人]. *~ oneself* (男子)打扮,装扮.

a·dopt [ə'dopt] *vt.* ①采用,采纳; 正式通过. ②选定(道路、职业等); 采取(立场等). ③【语】沿用, 借用(别国语言等). ④收养,立嗣,过继. *~ a proposal* 采纳提议. *words ~ed from a foreign language* 外来语. **-a·ble** *a.* 可采用的; 可沿用的; 可收养的. **-er** *n.* 采纳者; 接受器.

a·dopt·ed [ə'doptid] *a.* 收养的, 过继的. *an ~ son [daughter]* 养子[女],义子[女]. *my ~ country* 我所入籍的国家. *~ words* 外来语.

a·dop·tion [ə'dopʃən] *n.* ①接受, 采用. ②继嗣,过继. ③(外国语的)借用. ④(候选人的)指定.

a·dop·tive [ə'doptiv] *a.* ①采用的. ②收养的, 继嗣的, 过继的. ③倾向于采用的. ④假冒的. *an ~ father [son]* 养父[子],义父[子]. *an ~ disposition* 耳朵根子软的人. *an ~ courage* 假充勇敢.

a·dor·a·ble [ə'do:rəbl] *a.* 值得崇拜的, 值得敬慕的;

A

〔口〕可爱的. **-a·bly** [-bli] *ad.* 崇拜,敬重;可爱.
ad·o·ra·tion [ˌædɔːˈreiʃən] *n.* ①崇拜,崇敬;礼拜. ②敬爱,爱慕. ***in*** ~ 赞叹着,崇拜着,颂扬着.
a·dore [əˈdɔː] *vt.* ①崇拜,崇敬. ②敬慕,爱慕;〔口〕很欢喜.
a·dor·er [əˈdɔːrə] *n.* 崇拜者;爱慕者.
a·dor·ing [əˈdɔriŋ] *a.* 崇拜的;敬慕的,爱慕的. **-ly** *ad.*
a·dorn [əˈdɔːn] *vt.* 装饰,修饰,佩戴. ~ *(a room)* ***with*** *(flowers)* 用(花)装饰(屋子). ~ ***oneself with*** *(jewels)* 佩戴(宝石).
adorn·ment [əˈdɔːnmənt] *n.* ①装饰. ②〔有时可用 *pl.*〕装饰品. *personal* ~ 装饰.
ad·os·cu·la·tion [əˌdɔskjuˈleiʃən] *n.*【医】体外受精.
a·down [əˈdaun] *ad., prep.* 〔诗〕= down.
ADP =【化】Adenosine diphosphate 二磷酸腺苷.
ADPS = automatic data-processing system 自动数据处理系统.
ad·re·nal [əˈdriːnl] *n.* 肾上腺. — *a.* 肾脏附近的;肾上腺的. ~ **gland** 肾上腺.
ad·ren·al·in(e) [əˈdrenəlin] *n.*【生】肾上腺素.
ad·ren·er·gic [ˌædriˈnəːdʒik] *a.*【医】肾上腺素能的.
ad·re·no·cor·ti·cal [əˌdriːnəuˈkɔːtikl] *a.* 肾上腺皮质的.
ad·re·no·cor·ti·co·tro·phic [əˌdriːnəuˌkɔːtikəuˈtrɔfik] **-tro·pic** [-pik] *a.*【医】促肾上腺皮质的.
A·dri·an [ˈeidriən] *n.* 埃德里安〔姓氏,男子名〕.
A·dri·at·ic [eidriˈætik] *a.* 亚得里亚海的. ***the*** ~ ***(sea)*** 亚德里亚海.
A·dri·enne [ˈeidrien] *n.* 埃德里安娜〔女子名〕.
a·drift [əˈdrift] *a.*〔作表语用〕, *ad.*①飘浮,漂流无定〔指船〕. ②〔喻〕飘泊(无定);无定职. ③〔口〕孤陋寡闻. ***be all*** ~ 莫名其妙的;茫然失措的. ***get*** ~ (随风)漂流. ***go*** ~ 漂流;〔喻〕脱节. ***set*** ~ 使(船)随风飘流. ***turn*** *(sb.)* ~ 逐出(某人),使漂泊无依,免职,辞退.
a·droit [əˈdrɔit] *a.* 熟练的,灵巧的,敏捷的,机灵的. ~ *handling of an awkward situation* 巧妙地处理尴尬的局面. ***be*** ~ ***in [at]*** 善于. **-ly** *ad.* **-ness** *n.*
a·dry [əˈdrai] *a., ad.* 〔古〕干;渴.
ad·sci·ti·tious [ˌædsiˈtiʃəs] *a.* 追加的,附加的,补充的;外来的. *an* ~ *habit* 后天的习性. ~ *remarks* 补充发言.
ad·script [ˈædskript] *a.* 〔L.〕书写于后的.
ad·scrip·tion [ædˈskripʃn] *n.* 隶属(= ascription).
ad·scrip·tus gle·bae [ædsˈkriptəs ˈgliːbi] 〔L.〕(农奴)附属在土地上的.
ad·smith [ˈædsmiθ] *n.* 〔美谑〕广告写作者.
ad·sorb [ædˈsɔːb] *vt.*【化】吸附.
ad·sor·bate [ædˈsɔːbeit] *n.*【化】被吸附物.
ad·sor·bent [ædˈsɔːbənt] *a.* 有吸附力的. — *n.* 吸附剂.
ad·sorp·tion [ædˈsɔːpʃən] *n.*【化】吸附(作用).
ad·su·ki bean [ædˈzuːki biːn] *n.* 小豆,赤石(=adzuki bean).
ad·sum [ˈædsʌm] *int.* 〔L.〕到,有〔点名时的回答〕.
ad·u·lar·i·a [ˌædjuˈlɛəriə] *n.*【地】冰长石.
ad·u·late [ˈædjuleit] *vt.* 谄媚,奉承,拍…的马屁. **ad·u·la·tion** [ˌædjuˈleiʃən] *n.*
ad·u·la·tor [ˈædjuleitə] *n.* 拍马屁的人. **-y** [-ri] *a.* 奉承的.
A·dul·lam·ite [əˈdʌləmait] *n.*【英史】转党党员;退党议员〔指1886年英国下议院中因议会改革问题而退出自由党并加入保守党的议员〕.
a·dult [ˈædʌlt] *a.* ①已成人的,成年人的. ②老成的,已成熟的. ③适合成年人阅读〔观看〕的. — *n.* ①成年人. ②【生】成体;成虫. ~ **education** 成人教育. ~ **tooth** 固齿. **-hood** *n.* 成年. **-ly** *ad.*
a·dul·ter·ant [əˈdʌltərənt] *a.* 搀杂用的. — *n.* 搀杂物,搀杂剂.
a·dul·ter·ate [əˈdʌltəreit] *vt.* 搀,兑,搀杂. ~ *milk with water* 奶中兑水. — *a.* ①私通的,通奸的. ②搀假的;伪的,假的. ~ *coin* 伪币.
a·dul·ter·a·tion [əˌdʌltəˈreiʃən] *n.* 搀杂;伪造;冒牌货.
a·dul·ter·at·or [əˈdʌltəreitə] *n.* 搀假人;伪造人.
a·dul·ter·er [əˈdʌltərə] *n.* 奸夫.
a·dul·ter·ess [əˈdʌltəris] *n.* 奸妇.
a·dul·ter·ine [əˈdʌltərain] *a.* ①苟合的,通奸的;通奸所生的. ②不正当的,非法的. ③伪造的;不纯的. *an* ~ *child* 私生子. ~ *drugs* 伪劣药品. — *n.* 私生子.
a·dul·ter·ous [əˈdʌltərəs] *a.* ①私通的,通奸的;不正当的. ②〔古〕搀过假的.
a·dul·ter·y [əˈdʌltəri] *n.* 通奸,私通.
a·dul·toid [ˈædʌltɔid] *n.*【生】未熟成虫〔体〕.
ad·um·bral [æˈdʌmbrəl] *a.* 荫蔽的;在阴影里的,在暗处的.
ad·um·brate [ˈædʌmbreit] *vt.* ①画…的轮廓,勾画. ②暗示;预示. ③遮蔽,遮暗,在…上投下阴影.
ad·um·bra·tion [ˌædʌmˈbreiʃən] *n.* ①勾画;草图,轮廓. ②阴影. ③预示,预兆.
ad·um·bra·tive [æˈdʌmbrətiv] *a.* 轻描淡写的;暗示的;投影的.
a·dunc [əˈdʌŋk] *a.* 向内弯曲的〔如鹦鹉嘴〕.
a·dust [əˈdʌst] *a.* ①烘焦了的;晒黑了的. ②忧郁的,阴沉的.
adv. = *ad valorem* (= according to the price); advance; adverb; adverbial; advertisement; advocate.
ad·vance [ədˈvɑːns] *vt.* ①进,推进;促进(生长),助长;拨进(时针),增进;提早,提前. ②使升级,提升. ③提高,抬高,涨,加(价等). ④提出(意见等),提倡. ⑤预付,预支;借贷. ⑥前去(某地)做先遣工作. ~ *the hour hand* 向前拨动时针. ~ *sb. to the rank of colonel* 提升某人为上校. ~ *sb. a month's salary* 预支给某人一个月的薪水. — *vi.* ①推进,上进,前进,向前发展,进步. ②提高;晋升. ③涨价,腾贵. ④【军】前进,进攻 *(against; on; upon)*. ⑤从事先遣工作. ⑥(颜色等)醒目. ~ *in price* 涨价. ~ *in knowledge* 增进知识. ~ *in rank* 升级. *Deep colours* ~ 深的颜色醒目. ~ ***by rushes*** 突飞猛进. ~ ***in the world*** 发迹,出头. ~ ***on [toward] a place*** 向某地推进. — *n.* ①前进,进展;增进,进步;向上,晋升 *(in rank)*. ②腾贵,昂贵,上涨. ③预付;垫款,贷出款项. ④〔常 *pl.*〕接近;友好的表示;求爱. ⑤【军】前进,进攻. ⑥事先写好的新闻报导. *encourage [repel] sb.'s* ~*s.* 鼓励〔阻碍〕某人接近自己. *academic* ~*s* 学术成就. *an* ~ *sample* 订货小样. *His* ~*s were rejected.* 他的友好的表示被拒绝了. *Sound the* ~. 奏进行曲,吹前进号. *a temporary* ~ 暂垫款. ***be in*** ~ ***of*** 在…之前;比…进步;高出,优于,胜过 (*He is far in* ~ *of his class.* 他在班上是尖子). ***be on the*** ~ 渐涨. ***in*** ~ ①预先,事先. ②在先头,在前面 (*pay in* ~ 预付. *receive in* ~ 预收). ***make*** ~ ①垫款,先付,预付. ②接近(某人);表示友好;求爱 *(to)*. ***with the*** ~ ***of*** 与…俱进地,因(年)老而,因(夜)深而. — *a.*〔只作定语〕前进的;先头的;预先的. ~ **copy** (征求意见的)新书样本. ~ **guard**【军】前卫,先锋. ~ **man** (为政界候选人到某地前进行联系和做好安排的)先遣人员;〔美〕(剧团等的)先遣宣传员. ~ **sheets** 样本,样页,样张.
ad·vanced [ədˈvɑːnst] *a.* ①前进的,先驱的;高等的,高深的. ②先进的. ③(年纪)老的,(夜)深的. *most* ~ *branches of science and technology* 尖端科学技术. *rather an* ~ *young woman* 较先进的妇女. *a man* ~ *in years* 老年人. ~ *age* 高龄. ~ *grammar* 高等语法. ~ *ideas* 进步思想. ~ *post* 前哨. ~ *studies* 高等〔先进〕的学术研究. *a culturally* ~ *country* 高度文明的国家.
ad·vance·ment [ədˈvɑːnsmənt] *n.* ①前进;促进;进步,发达. ②升级;发迹,出头. ③预付;垫付.

ad·vance-trenches [əd'vɑːnstrentʃiz] *n.* 〔*pl.*〕火线上的战壕，前哨壕沟.

ad·van·tage [əd'vɑːntidʒ] *n.* ①利益，裨益；好处. ②优点，长处，优越性，有利方面；优胜，优势. ③【网球】打成平手 (deuce) 而延长比赛后一方先得的一分 (= vantage). *personal* ~*s* 美貌. ***be of great [no]*** ~ ***to*** 对…大大有利[毫无裨益]. ***gain [get, have, win] an*** ~ ***over [of]*** 胜过，优于. ***have the*** ~ 有…的利益；比…强，胜过；占上风，较…有利 (*You have the* ~ *of me.* ①你比我强；②您还认识我，我不认识您了，您是哪一位？) ***take*** ~ ***of*** ①乘，趁；利用. ②欺骗；引诱(女人). ***take (sb.) at*** ~ 乘(人)不备，乘(人之)虚而抢先. ***to*** ~ (因比较或衬托而)更加，越发 (*Her dress showed her beautiful figure to* ~. 她的衣服使她显得更加苗条). ***to sb.'s*** ~ = ***to the*** ~ ***of*** 对…有利地. ***turn out to sb.'s*** ~ 变得对某人有利. ***turn to*** ~ 使转化为有利. ***with*** ~ 有利地，有效地. — *vt.* 有利于，有益于，有助于. *Such action will* ~ *our cause.* 这样的行动有益于我们的事业. **-d** *a.* 占优势的，处于有利地位的.

ad·van·ta·geous [ˌædvən'teidʒəs] *a.* 有利的. **-ly** *ad.* **-ness** *n.*

ad·vec·tion [əd'vekʃən] *n.* (热的)对流；(空气的)平流. **-vec·tive** [-tiv] *a.*

ad·vent ['ædvənt] *n.* ①(季节、事件等的)到来，出现. ②〔A-〕耶稣降临；降临节. ***since the*** ~ ***of*** 自…出现以来. **Ad·vent·ism** *n.* 耶稣再生论. **Ad·ven·tist** *n.* 耶稣再生论者.

ad·ven·ti·tia [ˌædven'tiʃjə, -ʃiə, -ʃə] *n.*【解】外膜.

ad·ven·ti·tious [ˌædven'tiʃəs] *a.* ①偶然的；外来的. ②【生】不定的，偶生的；获得的，非遗传的. ③【医】偶发的. ~ **buds** 不定芽. ~ **root** 不定根. ~ **plants** 新引种植物，外来植物. **-ly** *ad.*

ad·ven·tive [æd'ventiv] *a.* 非本土的，外来的，引进的. — *n.* (动植物的)非本地生物，引进品种.

ad·ven·ture [əd'ventʃə] *n.* ①冒险. ②奇遇. ③【商】投机. ④冒险性格. *What an* ~! 啊呀，真了不得. *a singular* ~ 怪事. *go through strange* ~*s* 遍历奇险. — *vt.* ①以…冒险. ②大胆提出，大胆进行. ~ *one's life on it* 拼着性命去干. ~ *a proposal* 大胆提出建议. — *vi.* 冒险. **-tur·er** *n.* 冒险家；投机分子. **-tur·ism** *n.* 冒险主义.

ad·ven·ture·some [əd'ventʃəsəm] *a.* 冒险的.

ad·ven·tur·ess [əd'ventʃəris] *n.* 女冒险家，女投机分子.

ad·ven·tur·ous [əd'ventʃərəs] *a.* ①爱冒险的；胆大的. ②冒险的；危险的. **-ly** *ad.* **-ness** *n.*

ad·verb ['ædvəːb] *n.*【语法】副词. *a relative [interrogative]* ~ 关系[疑问]副词.

ad·ver·bi·al [əd'vəːbjəl] *a.* 副词的；状语的. *an* ~ *clause [phrase]* 状语从句[短语]. ~ *equivalents* 副词同等词. — *n.* 状语. **-ly** *ad.*

ad·ver·sar·y ['ædvəsəri] *n.* ①敌手，对手，反对者. ②〔*the A-*〕魔鬼. *an imaginary* ~ 假想敌.

ad·ver·sa·tive [əd'vəːsətiv] *a.* (词等)意义相反的. — *n.*【语法】反意语〔如 but, yet 等〕. **-ly** *ad.*

ad·verse ['ædvəːs] *a.* ①逆的；反对的，相反的. ②不利的，有害的，不幸的. ③对面的. ④【植】对生的. ~ *circumstances* 逆境. ~ *criticisms* 恶评，非难. ~ *fate [fortune]* 倒霉. *the* ~ *page* 对面的一页. ~ *trade balance* 入超. ~ *wind* 逆风. ***be*** ~ ***to*** 反对；不利于. **-ly** *ad.* 逆，反对地，相反地；不利，不幸 (*act to sb.'s interests* 举动对某人不利). **-ness** *n.* 逆，反对；不利，不幸.

ad·ver·si·ty [əd'vəːsiti] *n.* 逆境，苦难，不幸. *Sweet are the uses of* ~. 常常是苦尽甘来. *the prosperities and adversities of this life* 人生的荣辱盛衰. ***in [under]*** ~ 在艰难中，在患难中，倒霉时候.

ad·vert[1] [əd'vəːt] *vi.* 留意，注意；提到，谈到 (*to*). *He* ~*ed briefly to the news of the day.* 他简短地谈到当天的消息.

advert[2] ['ædvəːt] *n.*〔英口〕= advertisement.

ad·ver·tise ['ædvətaiz; Am. ˌædvə'taiz] *vt.* ①为…做广告. ②通告，通知 (*of*). ③宣扬. ~ *a reward* 登悬赏广告. ~ *(sth.) by posters* 用招贴为某物做广告. — *vi.* 登广告，做广告. ~ ***for*** 登招请[待聘等]广告. ~ ***oneself (as)*** 自吹(是).

ad·ver·tise·ment [əd'vəːtismənt; Am. ˌædvəː'taizmənt] *n.* ①做广告，登广告. ②广告，公告；告示.

ad·ver·tis·er ['ædvətaizə] *n.* ①登广告的人，广告客户. ②〔A-〕(以广告为主的)…报. *the Japan A-*《日本广告报》.

ad·ver·tis·ing ['ædvətaiziŋ] *a.* 广告(业)的. *an* ~ *agency* 广告公司. *the* ~ *pages* (报上的)广告版. — *n.* ①〔集合词〕广告. ②做广告，登广告. ③广告业〔技术〕. ~ **man** = adman.

ad·ver·tize = advertise.

ad·vice [əd'vais] *n.* ①忠告，劝告；建议；指教. ②(医生等的)诊察，意见. ③〔常 *pl.*〕(政治、外交上的)报导，报告. ④【商】通知. *an* ~ *note* 通知单. *a remittance* ~ 汇款通知. ~*s from foreign countries* 来自国外的报导. *a written* ~ 劝告书. ***act on*** ~ 依劝. ***ask*** ~ ***of*** 向…征求意见，请教，领教. ***by [on] sb.'s*** ~ 依某人劝告. ***follow sb.'s*** ~ 接受某人意见. ***give [tender]*** ~ 劝告，忠告. ***take*** ~ 征求意见，请教，领教 (*take medical* ~ 请医生诊视). ***take sb.'s*** ~ = follow sb.'s ~.

ad·vis·a·bil·i·ty [ədˌvaizə'biliti] *n.* 可劝告；适当，得当.

ad·vis·a·ble [əd'vaizəbl] *a.* 能劝告的，适当的，可取的. *an* ~ *course* 可取的方针. *Is it* ~ *for me to write to him?* 我给他写信合适吗？ **-ness** *n.*

ad·vis·a·bly [əd'vaizəbli] *ad.* 得当，适当.

ad·vise [əd'vaiz] *vt.* ①忠告，劝告，建议. ②【商】通告，通知. ~ *sb. against smoking* = ~ *sb. not to smoke* 劝告某人不要吸烟. — *vi.* ①商量. ②提出劝告. ~ ***each other*** 互提意见. ~ ***(sb.) of (sth.)*** 把(某事)通知[报告](某人). ~ ***with (sb.) on [about] (sth.)*** 和(某人)商量(某事). ***A- with your pillow.*** 好好考虑一宵.

ad·vised [əd'vaizd] *a.* ①考虑过的，细想过的〔今多用于构成复合词〕. ②消息灵通的. *well-*~ 深思熟虑的，明智的. *ill-*~ 失策的，愚蠢的. *be kept thoroughly* ~ 消息十分灵通.

ad·vis·ed·ly [əd'vaizidli] *ad.* 深思熟虑地；故意地.

ad·vise·ment [əd'vaizmənt] *n.* ①劝告，意见，忠告. ②考虑，深思熟虑. *take the application under* ~ 仔细考虑该项申请.

ad·vis·er, ad·vi·sor [əd'vaizə] *n.* ①劝告者，顾问. ②(美大学)指导教授，导师. *a legal* ~ 法律顾问. *an* ~ *to the President* 总统顾问.

ad·vi·so·ry [əd'vaizəri] *a.* ①劝告的，忠告的. ②顾问的，咨询的. *an* ~ *body* 咨询机关；顾问团. *an* ~ *committee* 咨询委员会. *He accompanied the President in an* ~ *capacity.* 他以顾问身份做总统随行人员.

ad·vo·ca·cy ['ædvəkəsi] *n.* 拥护；鼓吹；主张，辩护. *speak in* ~ *of* 为…辩护.

ad·vo·cate ['ædvəkit] *n.* ①拥护者，鼓吹者，提倡者. ②律师. *an* ~ *of [for] peace* 和平的鼓吹者. ~*s of military gambles* 军事冒险分子. ***the devil's*** ~ ①〔罗马天主教会〕负责指出加入圣列的死者的缺点的教吏. ②明知不对而争论不休的人. ***the Judge A-***【陆军】军法官. ***the Lord A-***〔Scot.〕检察长. — ['ædvəkeit] *vt.* 拥护；鼓吹，提倡；主张；辩护.

ad·vo·ca·tion [ˌædvə'keiʃən] *n.* ①〔废〕辩护. ②(苏格兰和罗马教庭)高级法院从初级法院提取自行审理的悬案.

ad·vo·ca·tor ['ædvəkeitə] *n.* 拥护者，鼓吹者，提倡者，

A

辩护者.
ad·voc·a·to·ry [ædˈvɔkəˌtəri] *a.* ①辩护士的. ②辩护的;鼓吹的.
ad·vo·ca·tus di·a·bo·li [ˌædvəˈkeitəs daiˈæbəlai] 〔L.〕 = devil's advocate.
ad·y·na·mia [ˌædiˈneimiə] *n.*【医】虚弱,无力,衰竭.
ad·y·nam·ic [ˌædaiˈnæmik] *a.* 衰弱的,虚弱的.
ad·y·tum [ˈæditəm] *n.* (*pl.* **-ta** [tə]) (古代庙宇中的)内殿,内院;密室,私室.
adz, adze [ædz] *n.* 手斧,锛子. — *vt.* 用锛子锛,用手斧劈.
ad·zu·ki bean [ædˈzuːki biːn] *n.* 小豆,赤豆.
æ 拉丁语和拉丁化了的希腊语中常见的连体字 (ligature);英语中,除固有名词(如 Cæsar, Æsop) 而外,常写作 ae, 有时略为 e.
ae. = *aetatis.*
ae [ei] *a.* 〔Scot.〕 一.
A.E.A. = Atomic Energy Authority 〔英〕原子能管理局.
A.E. and P. = Ambassador Extraordinary and Plenipotentiary 特命全权大使.
AEC = Atomic Energy Commission 〔美〕原子能委员会.
ae·cid·i·um [iːˈsidiəm] *n.* (*pl.* **-cid·i·a** [-ˈsidiə])【植】锈孢子器. **-cid·i·al** *a.*
ae·ci·o·stage [ˈiːsiəsteidʒ] *n.* 锈孢子器产生期.
ae·ci·um [ˈiːsiəm] *n.* (*pl.* **-ci·a** [-iə])【植】锈孢子器. **ae·ci·al** *a.*
a·ë·des [eiˈiːdiːz] *n.* (*pl.* ~) 伊蚊属蚊子, 〔尤指埃及伊蚊〕.
aeg. = 〔L.〕 *aeger* (= ill).
Ae·ge·an [i(ː)ˈdʒiːən] *a.* 爱琴海的. ***the ~ sea*** 爱琴海.
ae·ger [ˈiːdʒə] *n.* (若干英国与加拿大大学证明学生因病不能考试的)诊断证明书.
ae·gis [ˈiːdʒis] *n.* ①保护,掩护,庇护. ②【希神】(Zeus 神的) 神盾. ③赞助,主办. ***under the ~ of*** 在…保佑[掩护]下.
A.E.I. = Atomic Energy Institute. 〔英〕原子能学会.
-aemia *suf.* 〔构成名词〕表示"血的状态", "血质": *anaemia.*
Ae·ne·id [ˈiːniid] *n.* 《埃涅伊德》〔罗马诗人 Virgil 所著史诗〕.
a·ë·ne·ous [eiˈiːniəs] *a.* 青铜色泽的.
A-en·er·gy [ˈeienədʒi] *n.* 〔美俚〕原子能 (= atomic energy).
ae·o·li·an [i(ː)ˈəuljən] *a.* ①风神伊俄勒斯 (Aeolus) 的. ②【地】风成的 (= eolian). ③飕飕作响的. ~ **harp [lyre]** 风奏琴〔风吹自鸣之琴〕. ~ **rock** 风成岩.
Ae·ol·ic [iːˈɔlik] *a.* 伊奥里斯地方的;伊奥里斯人的. — *n.* 伊奥里斯语.
Ae·o·lis [ˈiːəlis] *n.* 伊奥里斯〔古希腊在小亚细亚西北海岸地区的殖民地〕.
ae·o·lo·trop·ic [ˌiːələuˈtrɔpik] *a.*【物】各向异性的.
ae·o·lot·ro·py [ˌiːəˈlɔtrəpi] *n.*【物】各向异性,偏等性.
Ae·o·lus [ˈi(ː)əuləs] *n.*【希神】伊俄勒斯〔风神〕.
ae·on [ˈiːən] = eon.
ae·o·ni·an [iːˈəunjən] = eonian.
ae·py·or·nis [ˌiːpiːˈɔːnis] *n.* (古时栖于马达加斯加岛的)隆鸟.
aer- *pref.* = aero-
a·er·ate [ˈeiəreit] *vt.* ①使暴露空气中, 使通气. ②使充以空气,打进空气[碳酸气等];向(血液等)供氧. ~*d breads* 用二氧化碳发的面包. ~*d waters* 汽水.
aer·a·tion [ˌeiəˈreiʃən] *n.* ①通风,通气. ②(饮料等的)充气,吹风. ③(肺中)换气.
a·era·tor [ˈeiəreitə] *n.* ①充气器,充气装置. ②【植】熏蒸(杀虫)装置.
aeri- *pref.* 表示"空气": *aeri*form.
aer·i·al [ˈɛəriəl] *a.* ①空气的,大气的,气体的. ②航空的,空中的. ③空气一样的,空气一样轻的;无形的,空想的. ④高耸空中的;生存在空中的,【植】气生的. ~ *music* 梦幻般的音乐. ~ *spires* 高耸入云的塔尖. — *n.* ①【无】天线. ②救火云梯. ~ **attack** 空袭. ~ **barrage** 气球空防. ~ **blitz(krieg)** 空中闪击战. ~ **bomb** 空投炸弹. ~ **cable** 架空电缆. ~**-cable way** 索道. ~ **camera** 空中摄影照相机. ~ **car** 气球吊篮;高架铁道车. ~ **cascade** 大气瀑流,急风. ~ **chart** 航空图. ~ **current** 气流;天线电流. ~ **defence** 防空. ~ **Derby** 飞行竞赛. ~ **farming** 飞机播种〔喷药(等)〕. ~ **fight** 空战. ~ **flare** 照明弹. ~ **fleet** 空中舰队,航空机队. ~ **ladder** 天梯,消防梯. ~ **light-house** 航空灯塔. ~ **line** 航空线. ~ **liner** 定期民航机. ~ **mail [post]** 航空邮寄. ~ **manoeuvre** 空中演习. ~ **mine** (用降落伞投下的)空雷. ~ **mosaic** 航空照片镶嵌图. ~ **navigation** 航空术. ~ **navigator** 飞机师,飞行员. ~ **parts**【植】地上部分. ~ **perspective** 浓淡远近透视法. ~ **plant** 气生植物. ~ **potato** 土豆叶瘤. ~ **railway** 架空铁道. ~ **root**【植】气生根. ~ **ropeway** (架空)索道. ~ **route** 空中航线. ~ **scout** 空中侦察(者). ~ **sickness** 航空病,晕机. ~ **telegraphy** 无线电信术. ~ **survey** 航空测量. ~ **torpedo** 空投鱼雷. ~ **train** 空中列车. ~ **transport** 空运. ~ **unit** 飞行部队. ~ **wire**【无】天线.
aer·i·al·ist [ˈɛəriəlist] *n.* 空中飞人,(走钢丝等)高空杂技演员.
aer·i·al·i·ty [ˌɛəriˈæliti] *n.* 空气的性质[状态],空虚.
aeri·ally [ˈɛəriəli] *ad.* 在空中;空气似地;空想地.
aer·ie [ˈɛəri, ˈiəri] *n.* ①(鹰等的)巢. ②巢中的雏群. ③高山住屋〔城堡等〕. ④〔古〕孩子.
aer·if·er·ous [ˌɛəˈrifərəs] *a.* 通气的.
aer·i·fi·ca·tion [ˌɛərifiˈkeiʃən] *n.* ①气(体)化. ②充满气体,充气状态.
a·er·i·form [ˈɛərifɔːm] *a.* ①气态的;气体的. ②无形的,无实体的;难捉摸的.
aeri·fy [ˈɛərifai] *vt.* ①在…中充注空气(= aerate). ②使气体化,使与空气化合.
aer·o [ˈɛərəu] *a.* 飞机的;航空的,飞行的. *an ~ club* 飞行俱乐部. — *n.* 〔口〕飞机;飞船;飞行. ~ **lens** (空中照相机所用)航空透镜.
aer·o- *pref.* 表示"空气","空中";"航空","飞机","飞船"等,如: *aero*lite, *aero*batics, *aero*dynamics.
aer·o·am·phib·i·ous [ˈɛərəuæmˈfibiəs] *a.* 海陆空(联合)的.
aer·o·bac·ter [ˌɛərəuˈbæktə] *n.*【生】气杆菌.
aer·o·bal·lis·tics [ˌɛərəubəˈlistiks] *n.* 〔*pl.*〕航空弹道学.
aer·o·bat·ic [ˌɛərəuˈbætik] *a.*【空】特技的. *an ~ flight* 特技飞行.
aer·o·bat·ics [ɛərəuˈbætiks] *n.* 特技飞行,特技飞行术;特技飞行表演.
aer·obe [ˈeiərəub] *n.* 好气生物,需氧菌,需氧(气)微生物.
aer·o·bic [ˌeiəˈrəubik] *a.* ①需氧的,需气的. ②需氧菌的;需氧菌产生的.
aer·o·bi·ol·o·gy [ˌɛərəubaiˈɔlədʒi] *n.* 大气生物学. **-bi·o·log·ic(al)** [-ˌbiəˈlɔdʒik(əl)] *a.*
aer·o·bi·um [ˌeiəˈrəubiəm] *n.* (*pl.* **-bi·a** [-biə]) 需氧菌.
aer·o·boat [ˈɛərəubəut] *n.* 水上飞机.
aer·o·bus [ˈɛərəubʌs] *n.* 客机,班机.
aer·o·cade [ɛərəuˈkeid] *n.* 飞行队,飞机队.
aero·cam·er·a [ˈɛərəukæmərə] *n.* 航空照相机.
aer·o·craft [ˈɛərəkrɑːft] *n.* 航空器,飞行器,飞机 (= aircraft).
aero·curve [ˈɛərəukəːv] *n.*【空】曲翼面.
aero·done [ˈɛərəudəun] *n.* 滑翔机.

aer·o·do·net·ics [ˌɛərəudəˈnetiks] *n.* 滑翔力学.
aer·o·drome [ˈɛərədrəum] *n.* 〔英〕飞机场 (= airdrome).
aer·o·drom·ics [ˈɛərəudrɔmiks] *n.* = aerodonetics.
aer·o·dro·mo·me·tre [ˌɛərəudrəuˈmɔmitə] *n.* 气流速度表.
aer·o·dy·nam·ic [ˌɛərəudaiˈnæmik] *a.* 空气动力学的. *an* ~ *missile* 飞航式导弹,有翼导弹. **-s** *n.* 空气动力学,气体力学.
aer·o·dyne [ˈɛərəudain] *n.* 重航空器,重于空气的飞行器.
aer·o·em·bol·ism [ˌɛərəuˈembəlizm] *n.* 【医】①航空气(泡)栓(塞)症. ②高空病.
aer·o·foil [ˈɛərəufɔil] *n.* 【空】机翼;翼型;翼剖面.
aer·o·gel [ˈɛərədʒəl] *n.* 气凝胶.
aer·o·gram(me) [ˈɛərəgræm] *n.* ①航空信件. ②无线电报. ③高空图解.
aer·o·graph [ˈɛərəgrɑːf] *n.* 高空气象计.
aer·og·raph·er [ɛəˈrɔgrəfə] *n.* 【军】高空气象侦察员.
aer·og·ra·phy [ɛəˈrɔgrəfi] *n.* 高空气象学.
aero·lite [ˈɛərəlait], **aer·o·lith** [ˈɛərəliθ] *n.* 陨石.
aer·ol·o·gist [ɛəˈrɔlədʒist] *n.* 高空气象学家.
aer·ol·o·gy [ɛəˈrɔlədʒi] *n.* ①(高空)气象学. ②【美海军】= meteorology.
aer·o·man·cy [ˈɛərəmænsi] *n.* 天气预报.
aer·o·ma·rine [ˌɛərəuməˈriːn] *a.* 海上飞行的.
aer·o·me·chan·ic [ˈɛərəumiˈkænik] *a.* 空气力学的. — *n.* 航空机械士. **-s** *n.* 空气力学,航空力学.
aer·o·med·i·cal [ˈɛərəuˈmedikəl] *a.* 航空医学的.
aer·o·med·i·cine [ˈɛərəˈmedsin] *n.* 航空医学.
aer·o·me·te·or·o·graph [ˌɛərəuˌmiːtiˈɔrəgrɑːf] *n.* 高空气象计.
aer·om·e·ter [ɛəˈrɔmitə] *n.* 气体比重计.
aer·om·e·try [ɛəˈrɔmitri] *n.* 气体测量.
aer·o·mo·bile [ˈɛərəuməbiːl] *n.* 气垫汽车.
aer·o·naut [ˈɛərənɔːt] *n.* 气球〔飞艇〕驾驶员;气球〔飞艇〕乘客.
aer·o·nau·tic, -i·cal [ˌɛərəˈnɔːtik, -əl] *a.* 航空的. *an* ~ *station* 航空无线电站.
aer·o·naut·ics [ˌɛərəˈnɔːtiks] *n.* 航空学,航空术. *the space* ~宇宙航行术,航天术.
aer·o·neu·ro·sis [ˈɛərəunjuəˈrəusis] *n.* (飞行员的)神经机能病.
ae·ron·o·my [ɛəˈrɔnəmi] *n.* 高层大气物理与化学研究.
aer·o·pause [ˈɛərəupɔːz] *n.* 大气的航空边界,大气上界.
aer·o·pha·gi·a [ˌɛərəuˈfeidʒiə] *n.* 【医】吞气症.
aer·o·phare [ˈɛərəfɛə] *n.* (空中导航用的)无线电信标.
aer·o·pho·bi·a [ɛərəuˈfəubiə] *n.* 【医】高空恐怖;气流恐怖.
aer·o·phone [ˈɛərəfəun] *n.* ①管乐器. ②助听器. ③(空袭时用的)探音机. ④(空中)无线电话机. ~ *listening device* 空中听音机.
aer·o·phore [ˈɛərəfɔː] *n.* 呼吸器〔供停止呼吸的初生婴儿或矿井、水下工人使用〕.
aer·o·pho·tog·ra·phy [ˌɛərəufəˈtɔgrəfi] *n.* 空中照相术,航空摄影术.
aero·phyte [ˈɛərɔfait, ˈɛːr-] *n.* 气生植物 (= epiphyte).
aer·o·plane [ˈɛərəplein] *n.* 〔英〕飞机. *a ship* ~ 舰上飞机. *a tractor* ~ 牵引式飞机. ***by*** ~ 乘飞机;用飞机. ***take*** ~ 坐飞机. ~ **carrier** 航空母舰. ~ **hangar** 飞机库. ~ **spotting** 飞机着弹观测.
aer·o·plank·ton [ˌɛərəuˈplæŋktən] *n.* 空中浮游微生物.
aer·o·pulse [ˈɛərəpʌls] *n.* 脉动式空气喷气发动机 (= pulsejet).
aer·o·scope [ˈɛərəskəup] *n.* 空气纯度检查器;细菌灰尘收检器. **-scop·ic** [-ˈskɔpik] *a.*

aer·o·sid·er·ite [ˌɛərəuˈsidərait] *n.* 【天】陨铁.
aer·o·sid·er·o·lite [ˌɛərəuˈsidərəlait] *n.* 【天】陨铁石.
aer·o·si·nus·i·tis [ˌɛərəusainəˈsaitis] *n.* 【医】高空鼻窦炎,飞行员鼻窦炎.
aer·o·sol [ˈɛərəsɔl] ①【化】气溶胶;烟雾剂. ②悬浮微粒. ~ **bomb** 喷射烟雾剂的小容器. ~ **insecticide** 喷雾杀虫剂. ~ **shaving cream** 喷雾刮脸膏.
aer·o·space [ˈɛərəuspeis] *n.* 大气圈及其以外的宇宙空间. — *a.* 宇宙空间的,宇宙航行的.
aer·o·sphere [ˈɛərəusfiə] *n.* (地球周围的)大气,气圈.
aer·o·stat [ˈɛərəustæt] *n.* ①浮空器,高空气球. ②【虫】气囊.
aer·o·stat·ic [ˌɛərəuˈstætik] *a.* 空气静力学的;航空术的;空中平衡的.
aer·o·stat·ics [ˌɛərəuˈstætiks] *n.* 空气静力学,气体静力学.
aer·o·sta·tion [ˌɛərəuˈsteiʃən] *n.* 气球〔飞船〕操纵术〔学〕.
aer·o·ther·a·peu·tics [ˌɛərəuˌθerəˈpjuːtiks] *n.* 〔*pl.*〕空气疗法.
aer·o·ther·mo·dy·nam·ics [ˌɛərəuˈθəːməuˈdainæmiks] *n.* 〔*pl.*〕空气热力学.
aer·o·tow [ˈɛərətəu] *vt.* 空中牵引(飞机). — *n.* 空中牵引.
aer·o·train [ˈɛərəutrein] *n.* 悬浮火车,单轨气垫火车.
aer·o·trans·port [ˈɛərəuˈtrænspɔːt] *n.* 运输机.
aer·ugi·nous [iəˈruːdʒinəs] *a.* 铜绿(色)的.
aer·y[1] [ˈeiəri] *a.* 〔诗〕= aerial.
aer·y[2] [ˈɛəri, ˈiəri] *n.* = aerie.
AES = Army Exchange Service 〔美〕陆军商品零售部.
AESC = American Engineering Standards Committee 美国工程标准委员会.
Aes·cu·la·pi·an [ˌiːskjuˈleipjən] *a.* ①医神艾斯库累普(Aesculapius)的. ②医术的;药的.
Aes·cu·la·pi·us [ˌiːskjuˈleipjəs] *n.* ①【罗神】艾斯库累普〔医神〕. ②〔喻〕医师.
Ae·sop [ˈiːsɔp] *n.* 伊索〔希腊寓言作者,公元前620?—560?〕. ~***'s Fables*** 《伊索寓言》. **-i·an** [iːˈsəupiən] *a.* 伊索寓言式的,伊索的.
aes·the·si·a [iːsˈθiːziə] *n.* 知觉;感觉;感觉力,知觉性(= esthesia).
aes·thete [ˈiːsθiːt, Am. ˈesθiːt] *n.* ①审美家. ②唯美主义者.
aes·thet·ic(al) [iːsˈθetik(əl), Am. es-] *a.* ①审美的. ②美的,艺术的. ③美学的.
aes·thet·i·cal·ly [iːsˈθetikəli, Am. es-] *ad.* ①审美地. ②从美学观点上.
aes·the·ti·cian [ˌiːsθiˈtiʃən, Am. es-] *n.* 审美学者;审美学家.
aes·thet·i·cism [iːsˈθetisizəm, Am. es-] *n.* ①唯美主义. ②艺术感,美感;艺术感的培养.
aes·thet·ics [iːsˈθetiks, Am. es-] *n. pl.* 〔动词用单数〕美学;审美学;美的哲学.
aes·tho·phys·i·ol·ogy [ˈiːsθəuˌfiziˈɔlədʒi; Am. ˈesθəuˌfiziˈɔlədʒi] *n.* 感觉生理学.
aes·ti·val [iːsˈtaivəl] *a.* 夏天的,适于夏季的. ~ *diseases* 夏天的疾病.
aesti·vate [ˈiːstiveit] *vi.* ①过夏,消夏. ②【动】(蜗牛等)夏眠,夏蛰.
aes·ti·va·tion [ˌiːstiˈveiʃən] *n.* ①消夏. ②【动】夏蛰,夏眠 (*opp.* hibernation). ③【植】花被卷叠式.
aet., aetat. = 〔L.〕*aetatis.*
ae·ta·tis [iːˈteitis] *a.* 〔L.〕…岁的;在…岁时. (=at the age of) 〔一般多用其缩略形式. 例: *aet.* [*aetat.*] 30 年龄为 30 岁〕.
ae·ther [ˈiːθə] = ether. **-the·re·al** [iˈθiəriəl] *a.* =

etherial.

ae·ti·ol·o·gi·cal [ˌiːtiəˈlɔdʒikəl] *a.* ①原因论的. ②病原学的,病因论的.

ae·ti·olo·gy [ˌiːtiˈɔlədʒi] *n.* ①原因论. ②病原学,病因论. *the* ～ *of a folkway* 民间习俗的起因. *a headache of unknown* ～ 原因不明的头痛.

AEW = airborne early warning【军】空中预先警报.

Af. = ①Africa. ②African.

AF = ① Air France 法国航空公司. ②air force 空军. ③Admiral of the Fleet〔英〕海军元帅. ④audio frequency【无】音频. ⑤automatic following【无】自动跟踪. ⑥Allied Forces 盟军.

af- *pref.* = ad-.〔用于 f 前〕: *af*fect.

A.F.A.C. = Air Force Armament Centre〔美〕空军军械中心.

a·far [əˈfɑː] *ad.* 由远方; 在远处; 到远方; 遥远. ～ ***off*** 遥远地,在远方. ***from*** ～ 从远方(来等).

AFB = Air Force Base〔美〕空军基地.

AFBMC = Air Force Ballistic Missile Committe〔美〕空军弹道导弹委员会.

AFC, A.F.C. = automatic frequency [flight] control 自动频率[飞行]控制.

A.F.C.E. = automatic flight control equipment 飞行自动控制设备.

a·feard, a·feared [əˈfiəd] *a.*〔方、古〕恐惧的; 担忧的.

a·fe·brile [əˈfiːbrəl, -ˈfebrəl] *a.*【医】不发烧的, 无热的.

aff. = ①affectionate. ②affirmative. ③affirming.

af·fa·bil·i·ty [ˌæfəˈbiliti] *n.* 殷勤,温柔,和蔼.

af·fa·ble [ˈæfəbl] *a.* ①殷勤的, 和蔼的,友好的. ②(天气等)宜人的. *an* ～ *smile* 笑容可掬. **-bly** *ad.*

af·fair [əˈfɛə] *n.* ①事,事情,事件. ②〔常 *pl.*〕事务; 事态. ③不正当的恋爱事件, 男女间的暧昧关系. ④〔口〕东西, 物品. *Mind your own* ～! [*That is none of your* ～. *That's my own* ～.] 莫管闲事. *a got-up* ～ 预谋事件,圈套. *one's private* ～*s* 私事. *public* ～*s* 公事,公务. *family* ～*s* 家务,家事. *material* ～ 物质生活. *political* ～*s* 政治事务. *the* ～*s of state* 国事,政务. *a man of* ～*s* 事务家. *the state of* ～*s* 形势,事态. *a wonderful* ～ 奇异物品,珍品. ***an*** ～ ***of honour*** 决斗. ***be at the head of*** ～***s*** 总理政务. ***have an*** ～ ***with*** …与…搞不正当的恋爱. ***wind up one's*** ～***s*** 料理事务,了结事务.

af·faire d'a·mour [aˈfɛːr daˈmuːr], ***af·faire de cœur*** [aˈfɛːr də ˈkəːr]〔F.〕恋爱事件,桃色事件.

af·faire d'hon·neur [afɛːr dɔˈnəː]〔F.〕决斗.

af·fect[1] [əˈfekt] *vt.* ①影响, 作用; 感受, 感染. ②害(病),伤(风),中(暑). ③感动. *be* ～*ed by heat* [*cold*] 中暑[着凉]. *His lungs are* ～*ed.* 他患肺病了. *His death* ～*ed us deeply.* 他的死使我们深为感伤. — *n.* [ˈæfekt] ①【心】情感,感情. ②【数】偏差.

af·fect[2] [əˈfekt] *vt.* ①假装,佯装,假冒,冒充. ②爱,好,爱用, 爱穿. ③成(某种形状). ④常去, 常在(某处). ～ *composure* 假充沉着. ～ *ignorance* 假装不知. ～ *the scholar* 冒充学者. ～ *loud neckties* 爱用花哨的领带. *Drops of water* ～ *roundness.* 滴水成珠. *Moss* ～*s the northern slopes.* 北坡常长青苔.

af·fec·ta·tion [ˌæfekˈteiʃən] *n.* 假装; 做作, 矫揉造作, 装模作样(的态度). *an* ～ *of kindness* 假慈悲. ***without*** ～ 老老实实地,直率地.

af·fect·ed[1] [əˈfektid] *a.* ①受了影响的,感染了的. ②感动的. *the* ～ *part* 患部.

af·fect·ed[2] [əˈfektid] *a.* ①装模作样的, 做作的. ②觉得…的. *His manners are* ～. 他的态度不自然. *How is he* ～ *towards us?* 他觉得我们怎么样? ***ill*** ～ *(to)*对…不友好的. ***well*** ～ *(to)* 对…怀好意的. ～ ***airs***装模作样. ～ ***laugh*** 装笑, 假笑. **-ly** *ad.* 装模作样地, 不自然地.

af·fect·ing [əˈfektiŋ] *a.* 令人感动的,动人的,引起同情的. *an* ～ *scene*惨状. *an* ～ *sight* 动人的情景. **-ly** *ad.*

af·fec·tion [əˈfekʃən] *n.* ①爱; 〔*pl.*〕爱慕. ②心情;【心】感情. ③〔古〕性情. ④作用, 影响. ⑤疾病. *the object of one's* ～*s* 所钟爱的人[物], 意中人. ～ *of the skin* 皮肤病. *the reciprocal* ～ *of moving bodies* 运动物体的相互作用. ***have an*** ～ ***for [towards]*** 深爱着. ***set one's*** ～***s on [upon]*** 钟爱.

af·fec·tion·al [əˈfekʃənl] *a.* 爱情的; 感情的.

af·fec·tion·ate [əˈfekʃənit] *a.* 感情深厚的; 有感情的,慈爱的. *He is* ～ *to me.* 他爱我. *an* ～ *mother* 慈母. *be on* ～ *terms with* 和…交情极好. **-ness** *n.*

af·fec·tion·ate·ly [əˈfekʃənitli] *ad. Yours* ～ = *A- yours* 你的亲爱的〔写家信时结尾用语〕.

af·fec·tive [əˈfektiv] *a.* 感动的,感情的. *an* ～ *state* 激动状态.

af·fer·ent [ˈæfərənt] *a.*【生理】传入的,输入的. ～ **nerve** 传入神经.

af·fet·tu·o·so [əˌfetjuˈəuzəu] *a., ad.*〔It.〕【乐】哀婉动人的[地].

af·fi·ance [əˈfaiəns] *n.*〔古〕①信用,信托 *(in)*. ②婚约; 誓约. — *vt.*〔古〕订婚. *one's* ～*d husband*[*wife*] 某人的未婚夫[妻]. ***be*** ～***d to*** 是…的未婚夫[妻], 和…订婚.

af·fi·ant [əˈfaiənt] *n.*【法】宣誓作证者; 写口供书者.

af·fiche [æˈfiːʃ] *n.*〔F.〕布告,招贴.

af·fi·da·vit [ˌæfiˈdeivit] *n.*【法】宣誓口供,宣誓书.

af·fil·i·ate [əˈfilieit] *vt.* ①把…收作会员; 使隶属于,使成为…的分支机构. ②〔～ oneself〕使加入. ③把…收为养子;【法】认定(私生子的)父亲为(某人). *(to, upon).* ④源自 *(to)*,来自 *(upon)*. *the* ～*d middle school* 附属中学. ～*d societies* 支部,分会. ～ *sth. to* [*upon*] *its author* 认定某事为某人所为. ～ ***oneself with*** 加入. ***be*** ～***d with*** 与…有关系; 与…结合; 和…来往; 加入. — *vi.* 参加; 与…密切联系 *(with)*. *She* ～*s with an academic society.* 她是某学术团体的成员. — [əˈfiliit, -eit] *n.* ①〔美〕分支机构,分会. ②会员.

af·fil·i·a·tion [əˌfiliˈeiʃən] *n.* ①加入,入会. ②〔美〕亲密关系. ③【法】私生子父亲的认定. ④追溯由来, 溯源. *democrats with no party* ～ 无党派民主人士. *a sister city* ～ 姐妹城市的亲善关系.

af·fine [əˈfain] *a.*【数】远交的,仿射的.

af·fined [əˈfaind] *a.* ①有密切关系的, 姻亲的. ②有义务约束的.

af·fin·i·ty [əˈfiniti] *n.* ①姻亲关系 *(cf.* consanguinity*)*; 密切关系. ②(语言等的)类似,近似. ③(男女之间的)吸引力,吸引人的异性. ④【数】仿射性. ⑤【化】亲和力. ⑥【生】类缘, 亲缘, 类同. *have an* ～ *for children* 喜欢小孩. *the close* ～ *of German with English* 德语与英语的密切近似.

af·firm [əˈfəːm] *vt.* ①断言,肯定. ②使(法律等)生效,批准. ③【法】不经宣誓而庄严宣布; 证实. ④(上级法院)维持(下级法院的判决). ～ *one's loyalty to one's country* 声言忠于祖国. ～ *a judgement of the lower court* 维持下级法庭的判决. —*vi.* 证明,证实(事实等) *(to)*.

af·firm·a·ble [əˈfəːməbl] *a.* 可断言的,可确定的.

af·firm·ance [əˈfəːməns] *n.* 断言; 确认.

af·firm·ant [əˈfəːmənt] *n.* 断言者; 确认者.

af·fir·ma·tion [ˌæfəːˈmeiʃən] *n.* ①断言; 肯定. ②证实; 批准. ③【法】不经宣誓而作出的证词. *The desirability of peace needs no* ～. 和平的可取无容赘言.

af·firm·a·tive [əˈfəːmətiv] *a.* 确言的; 肯定的,正面的; 赞成的. *an* ～ *answer* 肯定的答复. *an* ～ *approach to the problem* 正面解决问题. *an* ～ *vote* 赞成投票. — *n.* ①确言; 赞成. ②肯定词,肯定语. ③【逻】肯定; 肯定命题. *an* ～ *proposition* 肯定命题. *Two negatives make an* ～. 两个否定构成肯定. *an* ～ *sign*【数】正号. ***answer***

[reply] in the ~ 肯定答复. **-ly** *ad.* 肯定地;断然.

af·fix [ə'fiks] *vt.* ①附加上. ②贴上,粘上. ③签署;盖(章). ~ *a label to a bottle* 给瓶子贴上标签. ~ *one's signature* 署名,签名. ~ *a seal* 打上图章. — ['æfiks] *n.* ①附加物,附件. ②【语法】词缀〔前缀、后缀、中缀〕.

af·fix·a·tion [ˌæfik'seiʃən] *n.* ①附加物. ②【语】缀合法〔加前缀或后缀〕.

af·fix·ture [ə'fikstʃə] *n.* 附加物,附添;贴.

af·fla·tus [ə'fleitəs] *n.* 〔诗〕神感;(诗人等的)灵感.

af·flict [ə'flikt] *vt.* 使苦恼,折磨. ***be ~ed with*** 患(病),为…所苦 (*be ~ed with gout* 害痛风病. *be ~ed with a conscience* 受良心的呵责).

af·flic·tion [ə'flikʃən] *n.* 痛苦 (*opp.* relief); 哀伤,忧伤;苦恼;困苦,不幸. ***to bear up under*** ~ 忍受苦难,不屈不挠.

af·flic·tive [ə'fliktiv] *a.* 苦恼的,悲伤的;悲惨的.

af·flu·ence ['æfluəns] *n.* ①丰富;富裕,富足. ②流入;汇集. *live in* ~ 生活优裕. *an* ~ *of youths* 青年汇集.

af·flu·ent ['æfluənt] *a.* ①丰富的;富足的. ②流入的;畅流的,滔滔的. *the* ~ *society* 富足的社会. *land* ~ *in natural resources* 自然资源丰富的土地. *an* ~ *fountain* 滔滔不断的泉水. — *n.* 支流. **-ly** *ad.*

af·flux ['æflʌks] *n.* ①流入,汇集. ②充血. *an* ~ *of blood to the head* 脑充血.

af·ford [ə'fɔːd] *vt.* ①(财力、时间等)足以承担(损失、后果等),花费得起,经受得住. 〔与 *can, may* 连用〕. ②给与,供给;产,生产,出产. *I cannot* ~ *the expense [time].* 我花不起这笔费用[腾不出工夫来]. *I cannot* ~ *to be critical.* 我不能苛求. ~ *sb. an opportunity* 给与某人(…)机会. *The earth* ~*s grain.* 土地出产粮食.

af·for·est [æ'fɔrist] *vt.* 在…植树造林.

af·for·est·a·tion [æˌfɔris'teiʃən] *n.* 造林,绿化. *reclamative* ~ 农业造林. *an* ~ *plan* 绿化规划.

af·fran·chise [ə'fræntʃaiz] *vt.* 使(某人)摆脱奴役状态[义务等] (*cf.* enfranchise).

af·fray [ə'frei] *n.* (在公共场所)吵架,打架;纷争,闹事,骚扰,滋扰. — *vt.* 〔古〕吓唬.

af·freight [ə'freit] *vt.* 租用(船只)〔由船主负责行驶〕,包租(船只).

af·freight·ment [ə'freitmənt] *n.* 租船(运货).

af·fri·cate ['æfrikit] *n.*【语】破擦音〔如 churoh 中的 ch〕 — [-keit] *vt.* 使发破擦音.

af·fri·ca·tion [ˌæfri'keiʃən] *n.* 【语】(音的)破擦,塞擦.

af·fright [ə'frait] *vt.* 〔古、诗〕恐吓,吓. — *n.* 恐怖,惊吓.

af·front [ə'frʌnt] *vt.* ①侮辱,冒犯. ②毅然对抗,泰然面对. *look ~ed* (受辱后)愤愤不平. ~ *death* 临死不惧. — *n.* 当众侮辱. ***offer an ~ to [upon] = put an ~ to [upon]*** 侮辱.

af·fron·tive [ə'frʌntiv] *a.* 〔古〕侮辱的;公然冒犯的.

af·fu·sion [ə'fjuːʒən] *n.* ①【宗】洗礼时的浇水. ②【医】泼水疗法. *cold* ~ 冷泼疗法〔降发热病人的体温〕.

Af·ghan ['æfgæn] *a.* 阿富汗的;阿富汗人的;阿富汗语的. — *n.* ①阿富汗人;阿富汗语. ②〔a-〕一种针织软毛毯,一种针织羊毛头巾.

Af·ghan·i·stan [æf'gænistæn] *n.* 阿富汗〔亚洲〕.

Afgh. = Afghanistan.

a·fi·cio·na·do [ɑːˌfiːsjə'nɑːdəu] *n.* (*fem.* ***a·fi·cio·na·da*** [-də]) 〔Sp.〕热爱者,迷. *a football* ~ 足球迷.

a·field [ə'fiːld] *ad.* ①在野外,在田中. ②在战场上. ③远离(家园、常道). ***far*** ~ 远离;迷路 (*His remarks are far* ~. 他的话离题太远了). ***go [lead] too far*** ~ 走入[使走入]歧途.

a·fire [ə'faiə] *a.* 〔多作表语〕, *ad.* ①燃着,燃烧. ②大为激动. *with heart* ~ 热血沸腾,大为激动. *set a house* ~ 放火烧房.

a·flame [ə'fleim] *a.* 〔多作表语〕, *ad.* ①燃烧着,冒火焰. ②涨红了脸;发亮. ③大为激动. *His face is* ~ *with blushes.* 他的脸羞得通红. *I was* ~ *with curiosity.* 我好奇得要命.

af·la·tox·in [ˌæflə'tɔksin] *n.* 黄曲霉毒素〔尤指花生所含者〕.

AFL-CIO = American Federation of Labor and Congress of Industrial Organizations 美国劳工联合会-产业工会联合会〔略作劳联-产联〕.

a·float [ə'fləut] *a.* 〔多作表语〕, *ad.* ①浮,漂浮. ②在海上;在船上. ③(甲板等)浸在水中. ④流行,传播,散播. ⑤【商】(票据)流通,(经济上)不困难. ⑥(计划等)尚未定案. *all the shipping* ~ 航行中的所有船只. *cargo* ~ 海上货物. *life* ~ 海上生活. ***get*** (*a newspaper*) ~ 发行(一份报纸). ***keep*** ~ 使…漂浮不沉;使…流通;使…不致负债. ***set*** (*rumours*) ~ 散布(谣言).

a·flut·ter [ə'flʌtə] *a.* 〔多作表语〕, *ad.* ①(旗等)飘扬;(翅膀)鼓动. ②激动. ③有动静. *All are* ~ *at the thought of his return.* 想到他的归来,大家都很激动. *The woods were* ~ *with unknown birds.* 树林里因有不知名的小鸟而有动静.

AFMTC = Air Force Missile Test Centre 〔美〕空军导弹试验中心.

A.F.of L. = AFL.

à fond [ɑː'fɔ̃ːŋ] 〔F.〕完全,彻底. *supporting their party's principles* ~ 完全支持他们的党的原则.

a·foot [ə'fut] *a.* 〔多作表语〕, *ad.* ①徒步,步行. ②进行中,活动中. *go* ~ 走路去. *A plot is* ~. 阴谋在酝酿中. *be early* ~ 早在进行. ***get*** ~ 要走,会走;开始,实施. ***set*** ~ 建立,建设;引起;施行.

a·fore [ə'fɔː, ə'fɔə] *ad., prep., conj.* 〔古、方〕①在…之前(= before). ②以前,早先. *serve* ~ *the mast* 做普通水手. ~**cited** *a.* 上述,前举. ~**hand** *a., ad.* 〔古〕事先,预先. ~**mentioned** *a.* 前述,该. ~**named** *a.* 前举,上举. ~**said** *a.* 前述的,该. ~**thought** *a.* 〔多用于被修饰的名词之后〕预谋的,故意的 (*malice* ~*-thought*【法】预谋). ~**time** *ad.* 从前;早先.

a for·ti·o·ri ['ei ˌfɔːti'ɔːrai] 〔L.〕更不必说,更加,何况. *If no major country has the resources for the enterprise,* ~ *neither has any lesser power.* 如果大国没有人力物力来进行这项事业,小国就更加没有了.

a·foul [ə'faul] *ad.* 〔美〕碰撞,冲突;缠住. ***run [fall]*** ~ ***of*** 和…碰撞[冲突、纠缠] (*run* ~ *of the law* 和法律抵触. *The ship ran* ~ *of the floating seaweed.* 船只和漂浮的海草纠缠在一起).

AFP = 〔F.〕*Agence France Presse* (= French Press Agency) 法国新闻社,法新社.

Afr. = ①Africa. ②African.

a·fraid[ə'freid] *a.* 〔常用作表语〕①畏惧,害怕. ②恐怕,担心,愁着,担忧. *Who's* ~? 谁怕?一点不怕. *Don't be* ~. 别怕,不要怕. *This is nothing to be* ~ *of.* 这没有什么了不起. *He is* ~ *for [about] his own safety [what will happen].* 他担心自己的安全[将来发生的事]. ***be afraid of [to (do), that]*** 怕,害怕 (*He is not* ~ *of anything.* 他肆无忌惮. *He is* ~ *of his own shadow.* 他提心吊胆,连自己的影子都害怕). ***I'm*** ~ … 〔口〕恐怕(是),我看(是): *I'm* ~ *we can't go on Monday.* 星期一恐怕去不了. ***I am*** ~ ***that*** … 不瞒你说,我看是这样.

A-frame ['eiˌfreim] *a.* A 字形架的;(屋顶)A 字形结构的. — *n.* A 字形屋顶,A 形架.

Afr·a·mer·i·can [ˌæfrə'merikən] *n., a.* 美国黑人(的)(= Afro- American).

AFRASEC = Afro-Asian Organization for Economic Cooperation 亚非经济合作组织.

af·reet, af·rit(e) ['æfriːt] *n.*【阿神】恶魔.

a·fresh [ə'freʃ] *ad.* 从新,重行,再,另外. ***start*** ~ 再从

头开始。

Af·ric [æ'frik] *a.* 〔诗〕= African.

Af·ri·ca ['æfrikə] *n.* 非洲.

Af·ri·can ['æfrikən] *a.* 非洲的; 非洲人的. — *n.* 非洲人. ~ **golf** 〔美〕掷双骰儿.

Af·ri·can·der [ˌæfri'kændə] *n.* (一种)南非牛.

Af·ri·can·ist ['æfrikənist] *n.* ①研究非洲文化语言的学者〔专门家〕. ②主张新兴的非洲国家独立的人; 泛非主义者.

Af·ri·can·ize ['æfrikənaiz] *vt.* ①使非洲化. ②使…带有非洲观点、性质等. **-i·za·tion** [ˌæfrikənai'zeiʃən] *n.*

Af·ri·kaans [ˌæfri'kɑːns] *n.* 布尔语〔南非通用的荷兰语〕.

Af·ri·kan·der [ˌæfri'kændə] *n.* ①南非生长大的白人. ②南非牛; 南非羊.

Af·ri·ka·ner [ˌæfri'kɑːnə] *n.* 〔D.〕祖籍欧洲(尤其是荷兰)的南非人; 布尔人.

Af·ro ['æfrəu] *a.* ①(仿效黑人留的)蓬松发型的. ②〔口〕美洲黑人的. — *n.* 蓬松发型.

Afro- *comb. f.* 表示"非洲(的)".

Af·ro-A·mer·i·can ['æfrəuə'merikən] *n., a.* = Afra-merican.

Af·ro-A·sian [ˌæfrəu'eiʃən] *a.* 亚非的. *an ~ conference* 亚非会议.

Af·ro-A·si·at·ic [ˌæfrəuˌeiʃi'ætik] *a.* (包括柏柏尔语、埃塞俄比亚语、闪语、乍得语和古埃及语的)亚非语系的.

a·front [ə'frʌnt] *ad.* 在前面,在对面.

A.F.S. = Auxiliary Fire Service〔英〕辅助消防队.

AFSWC = Air Force Special Weapons Centre〔美〕空军特种武器中心.

aft [ɑːft] *a., ad.*【海】在船尾,近船尾,向船尾. ***fore and ~*** 从船头到船尾. ***right ~*** 正在(船)后.

aft. = after(noon).

af·ter ['ɑːftə] *ad.* 在后; 继后; 后来. *follow ~* 跟着. *look before and ~* 瞻前顾后, 前思后想. *soon ~* 不久. *three days ~* 三日后. — *prep.* ①〔表示时间关系〕在…以后; (*opp.* before); 〔美〕(…点)过(…分)〔= past〕. ②〔位置地点〕在…后面(*opp.* before). ③〔表示次第顺序〕位于…之后; (地位、规模、重要性等)次于; (仅)低于. ④〔表示事件或时间的连续性〕紧挨着; (一个)接(一个); 相继. ⑤〔原因〕由于,因为; 既然. ⑥〔表示让步关系,介词宾语前常冠以强义限定词 all〕虽然,尽管. ⑦追求, 寻找; 追捕〔常与 be, go, run 等词连用〕. ⑧仿照, 模仿; 依据…(而改写、命名等). ⑨符合, 一致; (很)象. ⑩关注,关照. *~ four days* 四天以后. *~ supper* 晚饭后. *~ school* 放学后. *It's twenty ~ six.* 〔美〕现在是六点二十分. *Shut the door ~ you when you leave the room.* 离开房间时请随手关门. *A- you, please!* 请您先走. *A-you!* 您先走!〔回答前一礼让语时的用语, you 应重读〕. *A- you with the paper, please.* 您看过这报纸后给我看看. *the largest city ~ Beijing* 仅次于北京的一个大城市. *A colonel comes ~ a general.* 上校的地位低于将军的地位. *Please line up one ~ another.* 请按顺序排队. *day ~ day* 一天又一天. *time ~ time* 再三, 常常. *She was very hungry ~ her long morning walk.* 她因为早晨散步很久,所以感到饿得很. *I shall never speak to him ~ what has happened.* 既然发生了这样的情况, 我就永远不再跟他说话了. *A- all warnings, he presisted.* 尽管有各方警告,他仍坚持到底. *A- all my care in packing it the clock arrived broken.* 尽管我把这座时钟小心包装, 可是运来时它还是被损坏了. *John is ~ you.* 约翰在找你. *He is much run ~.* 他是众所欢迎的人. *I don't go ~ fame or money.* 我不追名逐利. *The police ran ~ the burglars.* 警察追捕抢劫犯. *long ~ home* 怀恋家乡. *hunt ~ novelty* 猎奇. *He was named ~ his uncle.* 他是依照叔父的名来命名的. *a play ~ Shakespeare.* 模仿莎士比亚的剧作编写成的剧本. *He takes ~ his mother.* 他的长相和母亲一模一样. *You are a man ~ my heart.* 你这人很合我的心意. *look ~ one's child* 照料孩子. *Somebody asked ~ you this morning.* 今天上午有人打听你来着. ***~ all*** 毕竟; 终于(*He succeeded ~ all* 他终于胜利了). ***be ~ doing*** 〔英方〕刚…了(*I am ~ having my dinner.* 我刚刚吃了晚饭). ***one ~ another*** 陆续,相继,换次. ***one ~ the other*** 轮流. — *conj.* 在后, 后. *He arrived ~ I did.* 他在我到后就到了. ***~ all is said and done*** 终归. — *a.* 后,后来的; 后面的. *the ~ results* 后果. ***in ~ years*** 在后来的年月里. ***in ~ life*** 晚年. — *n.*〔英俚〕正餐的最后一道食品(如点心、水果等). **~birth**【医】胞衣, 胎胞; 遗腹子的生产. ~ **body** 船体后部. **~brain**【解】后脑. **~burner**【空】补燃器, 加力燃烧室. ~ **cabin** 后舱. **~care** 病后调养; 罪犯释放后的安置. **~clap** 意外变动,意外结果. **~cooler**【机】后冷却机. **~crop** 第二次收获. **~culture** 补种. **~damp** 矿山爆炸后的毒气. **~deck** 后甲板. **~-dinner** *a.* 餐后的. **~effect**【物】后效应, 后效; 副作用; 余功. **~glow** 晚霞; 余辉. **~grass** 再生草. **~heat**【物】余热. ~ **hours** *a.* 公余的, 业余的. **~image**【心】遗像; 余像; 余味; 余音. **~life** ①后世, 来世. ②后半生, 晚年. **~light** ①夕照. ②事后的领悟. **~-market** (汽车)零件市场. **~math** ①(牧草的)第二次刈割; 再生草. ②余波, 余殃, 余累; 结果, 后果(*the ~math of war* 战后余殃). **~most** *a.* ①最后头的. ②【船】靠近船尾的. **~pains**〔*pl.*〕【医】产后痛. **~piece** ①【剧】剧终余兴. ②【船】舵盘脚. **~-product** 副产物. **~ripening** 后熟. **~sales** *a.* 出售以后的(*~sales services* 售后服务). ~ **sensation**【心】后觉. **~shock** (地震的)余震. **~taste** 回味, 余味; 余韵. **~thought** ①事后的想法. ②计划外的加添物. **~-treatment** (印染物品等的)第二次处理. **~wit** 事后聪明. **~word** 跋, 编后记. **~years** *n.* 事后的岁月.

af·ter·noon ['ɑːftə'nuːn] *n.* ①下午, 午后. ②〔书〕后半期, 后半. *this ~* 今天下午. *Good ~!* ①您好〔下午见面时招呼语〕. ②再见〔下午分手时用语〕. *an ~ farmer* 懒人. *of an ~* 常常在下午. *the ~ of life* 后半生, 晚年. **-s** *ad.* 〔美〕每天下午(*He slept late and worked afternoons.* 他每天睡得晚, 总在午后工作).

af·ter·wardz ['ɑːftəwədz], 美 **-ward** [-wəd] *ad.* 其后, 后来, 继后, 然后, 以后. *I left there ~.* 后来我就离开那里了.

A.G., AG = ① adjutant general. ② air gunner. ③ attorney general.

Ag【化】元素 argentum (银) 的符号.

Ag. = August.

ag. = agriculture.

ag [æg] *a.* 农业的, 农用的.

ag- *pref.* = ad-〔在 g 前用 ag-: *agglutinate*〕.

a·ga ['ɑːgə] *n.* (奥托曼帝国时代穆斯林国家的)统帅.

a·gain [ə'gein] *ad.* ①又, 再; 再一次; 加一倍. ②此外, 另外; 而且, 加之. ③(信息等)返回来. ④而, 但, 抑或. *Come ~.* 请再来. *be home ~* 回到家. *Bring us word ~.* 带回音来. *A- we must remember that …* 而且我们得考虑考虑…. *This is better, but then ~ it costs much.* 这个好些, 就是太贵. *Then ~, why did he go?* 那么, 他为什么要走呢? ***~ and ~*** 再三再四, 一再, 三番五次. ***as large ~ as …*** 之两倍大的. ***as many [much] ~ as*** 多一倍, 加倍, 二倍于. ***back ~*** 复原, 照旧, 照样. ***be oneself ~*** 病好了, 复原了. ***echo [ring] ~*** 反响, 响应. ***ever and ~ = now and ~*** 时时. ***once ~*** 再一次. ***once and ~ = ~ and ~.*** ***over ~*** 再一次. ***over and (over) ~*** 翻来复去, 多次. ***time and ~*** 好几次.

a·gainst [ə'geinst] *prep.* ①对, 对着, 冒着; 反对, 敌对, 逆; 相反, 不利于; 违反, 违背, 犯. ②撞着, 碰, 触; 靠近; 靠, 倚. ③防, 御, 以防, 以备. ④以…为背景; 对照. ⑤

〔表示方向,常同 over 连用〕在…的对面. ⑥〔表示对比关系,有时可同 as 连用〕…而…. ⑦〔表示交换关系〕以…抵付;凭…换取. *Are you for or* ~ *the plan?* 那个计划你是赞同呢还是反对? *Her age is* ~ *her.* 她的年龄不行了. *Luck is* ~ *him.* 他运气不好. *talk* ~ *sb.* 说(人)坏话. ~ *rule* 犯规. *fight for the weak* ~ *the strong* 扶弱抑强. *inform* ~ *sb.* 告发(某人). *set a chair* ~ *the wall* 把椅子靠在墙上. *Caution* ~ *fire.* 小心火烛. ~ *the famine* 防饥荒. ~ *the evening sky* 以黄昏的天空为背景. *a matter of reason as* ~ *emotion* 与感情相对立的理智问题. *The park opens five hours a day this year* ~ *three hours a day last year.* 这公园今年每天开放五小时,而去年每天开放三小时. *Document* ~ *Acceptance.* 承兑后交单. *the rates* ~ *pounds sterling* 英镑兑换率. ~ ***a rainy day*** 未雨绸缪,以备不时之需. ~ ***all chances*** 无望. ~ ***one's will*** 无可奈何地,无奈. ~ ***the stream*** 逆流;(在逆境中)奋斗. ~ ***time [the clock]*** 准时,按时,尽快;加油,使劲儿. ***be*** ~ 反对. ***be up*** ~ ***(it)*** 遇到(经济上的)巨大困难. ***over*** ~ *(the cinema)* 在(电影院)正对面,正对电影院. ***run up*** ~ 忽然碰上〔碰到〕. — *conj.* 〔古、方〕在…之时,在…之前.

ag·a·lite [ˈægəlait] *n.*【矿】纤滑石.

ag·a·ma [ˈægəmə] *n.* (欧洲)蜥蜴.

Ag·a·mem·non [ˌægəˈmemnən] *n.*【希神】阿加迈农〔围攻 Troy 城的联军统帅〕.

a·ga·mete [ˈeigəmiːt, əˈgæmiːt] *n.* 非配偶子.

ag·a·mi [ˈægəmi] *n.*【鸟】鸨类.

a·gam·ic [əˈgæmik] *a.* ①【生】无配子的; 无性生殖的 (= asexual). ②【植】隐花的 (= agamous).

ag·a·mo·gen·e·sis [ˌægəməuˈdʒenisis] *n.*【生】无配生殖;出芽生殖;单性生殖.

ag·a·mous [ˈægəməs] *a.*【生】无性 (生殖)的.【植】隐花的.

A·ga·ña [ɑːˈgɑːnjə] *n.* 阿加尼亚〔关岛(美)首府〕.

ag·a·pan·thus [ˌægəˈpænθəs] *n.*【植】百子莲(= African lily).

a·gape[1] [əˈgeip] *a.* 〔用作表语〕, *ad.* 目瞪口呆,哑然;大开着,张着. *The wind set the window agape.* 风把窗吹开.

ag·a·pe[2] [ˈægəpiː] *n.* (*pl.* ***-pae*** [-piː])①神对人的爱;教友之爱; 自发之爱. ②早期基督教徒的会餐 (*cf.* love feast).

ag·a·pe·mo·ne [ˌægəˈpiːməni] *n.* 温柔角〔搞自由恋爱的地方,常有贬意〕.

a·gar [ˈeigɑː] *n.* ①洋菜,琼脂,石花菜. ②细菌培养基.

a·gar-agar [ˈeigɑːˈreigɑː] = agar ①.

ag·a·ric [ˈægərik, əˈgærik] *n.*【植】伞菌,蘑菇;木耳. ~ **mineral** 岩乳 (= rock milk).

Ag·ate [ˈeigət] *n.* 埃格特〔姓氏〕.

ag·ate [ˈægət] *n.* ①玛瑙;〔美〕$5\frac{1}{2}$ 点铅字〔英国叫 ruby〕;〔美〕(小孩玩的)石子. ② [ˈægit]〔喻〕矮子. ~ **jasper** 碧玉玛瑙. ~ **line** 报纸上一栏宽、十四分之一英寸长的广告面积.

ag·ate·ware [ˈægətˌwεə] *n.* ①玛瑙彩釉的铁器皿. ②玛瑙纹彩的陶器.

Ag·a·tha [ˈægəθə] *n.* 阿格莎〔女子名〕.

A·ga·ve [əˈgeivi] *n.*【植】龙舌兰属;〔a-〕龙舌兰.

a·gaze [əˈgeiz] *ad.* 注视,凝视.

age [eidʒ] *n.* ①年龄. ②成年〔满廿一岁〕. ③老年,晚年. ④寿命;终生,一生. ⑤时代,时期,年代. ⑥〔口〕很长的时间 *a man in his green old* ~ 童颜老者. *full* ~ 成年. *A- before honesty.* 小孩必须礼让老人. *the* ~ *to come* 后世. *of the* ~ 现代的. *the present* ~ 现代. *It is* ~*s since I saw you last.* 好久不见了. ~***s ago*** 从前;〔口〕老早,早就. ***an*** ~ ***ago*** 一代人以前,多年以前. ***at the*** ~ ***of*** 在…岁时. ***be of*** ~ 成年. ***be over [under]*** ~ 超过〔未达〕适龄年限. ***come of*** ~ 达成人年龄. ***from*** ~ = with ~. ***from*** ~ ***to*** ~ 世世,代代. ***from an*** ~ = ***for*** ~***s*** 久远,长久. ***(in) all*** ~***s*** 今昔(皆然). ***in one's*** ~ 在老年. ***of all*** ~***s*** 古往今来的(事情);老老少少的(人). ***to all*** ~***s*** 直到千秋万代. ***with*** ~ 因年老而…. — *vi.* ①上年纪,显老,变老,苍老. ②【化】老化,陈化. — *vt.* ①催人老,使人老. ②【化】使老化,使陈化. *Grief* ~*s us.* 忧伤逼人老.

-age *suf.* 〔名词后缀〕①集体: cellar*age*, bagg*age*. ②地位、身分、状态: baron*age*, bond*age*. ③动作: break*age*, pass*age*. ④费用、租金: cart*age*, post*age*.

a·ged [ˈeidʒid] *a.* ①老,老年的 (*opp.* young); 陈年的. *an* ~ *man* 老人. *the* ~ 老人,老者. ~ *wine* 陈年老酒. ②【物】被老化的. ③ [eidʒd] …岁的,(动物)达到几岁龄的〔通常,马7岁龄,牛 3 岁龄,猪 2 岁龄,羊 1 岁龄〕. *a man* ~ *forty (years)* 四十岁的人. **-ness** *n.* 老年,高龄.

age·ing [ˈeidʒiŋ] *n.* ①变陈; 成熟;【化】老化. ②【冶】时效.

age·ism [ˈeidʒizəm] *n.* 对老年人的歧视.

age·less [ˈeidʒlis] *a.* 不会老的,长生不老的; 永远的.

a·gen·cy [ˈeidʒənsi] *n.* ①动作,作用;行为;动力,力量;媒介. ②经办,代理,代办;代销处. ③机构; (党、政)机关,厅. ④〔美〕印第安人事务局(= Indian ~). *the free* ~ *of the citizens* 市民的自由行动. *the* ~ *of the wind* 风力. *a detective* ~ 秘密侦察所. *a general* ~ 总代理店. *an employment* ~ 职业介绍所. *the Xinhua News A-* 新华通讯社. *A- for International Development* 国际开发署. ***through [by] the*** ~ ***of*** (某人)经手,经(某人)斡旋.

a·gen·da [əˈdʒendə] *n.* 〔*pl.*〕(*sing.* ***-dum*** [-dəm]) ①议事日程,会议事项. ②记事册. ③【神学】实际行为〔相对于信仰而言〕. *the first item on the* ~ 议程的第一项. ***place [put] sth. on the*** ~. 把某事提到日程上来.

a·gen·dum [əˈdʒendəm] *n.* agenda 的单数〔一般用其复数形式〕.

a·gen·e·sis [əˈdʒenisis] *n.* 发育不全;阳萎,无生殖力.

a·gent [ˈeidʒənt] *n.* ①行为者,动作者;【语法】主动者. ②原因;动因; 作用物,(作用)药剂. ③代理人,代办人;代理商,经理人. ④事务官,总办,总管;〔美〕印第安人事务官(= *Indian* agent). ⑤〔美口〕行商. ⑥〔英〕选举干事. ⑦间谍,密探,特务. *advance* ~ (剧团等的)先遣人员. *biological [chemical]* ~ 生物〔化学〕制剂. *a commercial* ~ 商务总管. *a consular* ~ 代理领事. *enemy* ~*s* 奸细,敌特. *a forwarding* ~ 运输商,运输行. *a general* ~ 总代理. *a house [land]* ~ 房屋〔地产〕经理人. *natural* ~*s* 自然力. *a road* ~ 〔美〕(驿站道路的)拦路强盗. *a secret* ~ 特务,侦探. *a sole* ~ 包销人. *a station* ~ 〔美〕站长. *a ticket* ~ 〔美〕售票员.

a·gen·tial [eiˈdʒenʃəl] *a.* ① 代理人的. ②【语法】主动者的.

a·gen·tive [ˈeidʒintiv] *a.* 【语法】 表示动作主体的词尾的. — *n.* 动作主体词尾〔如 *defendant* 的 *-ant*〕. **-tiv·al** [-ˈtaivl] *a.*

a·gent pro·vo·ca·teur [aʒɑ̃ prɔvɔkaˈtəː] ***(pl. agents provocateurs)*** 〔F.〕(打入革命组织等内部、并故意诱使其成员触犯刑律而被捕的)密探,内奸,坐探.

ag·er·a·tum [ˌædʒəˈreitəm] *n.*【植】藿香,藿香蓟.

ag·gie [ˈægi] *n.* ①〔美俚〕农科(大学)学生;农业学校〔大学〕. ②(小孩玩的)弹球.

ag·gior·na·men·to [ɑːˌdʒɔːnɑːˈmentɔː] *n.* 〔It.〕(使罗马天主教的教义、制度等)现代化.

ag·glom·er·ate [əˈglɔməreit] *vt., vi.* (使)成团,(使)成块,(使) 凝聚. — [əˈglɔmərit] *a.* ①团集的, 凝聚的,成块的. ②【植】群生的, 密集的. — *n.* ①附聚物, 凝聚物;团块. ②集块岩;烧结矿,烧结块.

ag·glom·er·a·tion [əˌglɔməˈreiʃən] *n.* 团聚作用, 凝聚;团块. ***be an*** ~ ***of*** 是集…之大成.

ag·glom·er·a·tive [əˈglɔməreitiv] *a.* 凝聚的，附聚的；烧结的．

ag·glu·ti·nant [əˈgluːtinənt] *a.* 粘聚的；凝集的．— *n.* 粘聚物；凝集物；烧结剂；凝集剂．

ag·glu·ti·nate [əˈgluːtineit] *vt., vi.* ①胶合，粘上；粘合，接合．②(使)胶质[胶状]化．③(使)(细菌)凝聚．—[-nit] *a.* 胶合的；胶着性的．— *n.*【矿】粘合集块岩．

ag·glu·ti·na·tion [əˌgluːtiˈneiʃən] *n.* ①胶合，粘合．②(伤口)愈合．③凝集(作用，现象)．

ag·glu·ti·na·tive [əˈgluːtinətiv] *a.* 粘着的，胶合的．

ag·glu·ti·nin [əˈgluːtinin] *n.*【微、医】(使细菌、血球等起凝结作用的)凝集素．

ag·glu·tin·o·gen [ˌægluˈtinədʒən] *n.*【微、医】(产生凝集素的)凝集原．**-ic** *a.*

ag·grade [əˈgreid] *vt.* 使(河床或河谷)填积，加积．**-gra·da·tion** *n.*

ag·gran·dize [əˈgrændaiz] *vt.* ① 加大，扩大 (*opp.* reduce)．②提高(权利、地位)．③夸张 (*opp.* minimize)．*The king sought to ~ himself at the expense of his people.* 国王以牺牲百姓为代价来扩大自己的权势．**-ment** *n.*

ag·gra·vate [ˈægrəveit] *vt.* ①加重(病情等)；使恶化．②〔口〕惹恼，激怒．

ag·gra·vat·ing [ˈægrəveitiŋ] *a.* ①使…恶化的．②〔口〕可恼的，可厌的，惹人生气的．*How ~!* 多令人生气呀!

ag·gra·va·tion [ˌægrəˈveiʃən] *n.* ①加重；恶化．②〔口〕激怒，惹恼．

ag·gre·gate [ˈægrigeit] *vt.* ①集合，(使)聚集．②总计，共计，合计．*The sum will ~ a thousand dollars.* 总额共计一千元．— [ˈægrigit] *a.* ①聚合的；(花)聚生的．②【地】聚成岩的．③合计的，总．*an ~ flower* 聚生花．— *n.* ①聚合，集合．②总数．③聚合体；凝聚体；团粒．④【建】混凝料．***in the ~*** 总计，合计．**~ animals** 群体动物．**~ motion** 集成运动．**~ power** 总力．**~ tonnage** (船的)总吨位．**~ unit** 联合机组；联动装置[机构]．

ag·gre·ga·tion [ˌægriˈgeiʃən] *n.* ①聚合，集合，凝聚，集成．②【植】族聚；【动】群聚．③集团，集合体，集成体．**-ga·tive** [ˈægrigeitiv] *a.*

ag·gress [əˈgres] *vi.* 攻击；侵略，挑衅 *(on, upon, against)*．*~ upon the public property* 侵占公共财产．

ag·gres·sion [əˈgreʃən] *n.* 攻击；侵略，侵犯．*cultural ~* 文化侵略．*economic ~* 经济侵略．***commit ~ against*** (对…)进行侵略．

ag·gres·sive [əˈgresiv] *a.* ①侵略的，侵犯的；攻势的．②借故生端的；爱打架的，要打架的．③〔美〕有进取心的，积极行动的 *(opp.* retiring*)*．*an ~ policy* 侵略政策．***assume [take] the ~*** 挑战，取攻势．**-ly** *ad.*

ag·gres·sor [əˈgresə] *n.* 攻击者，侵略者；侵略国(= *~ nation*)．

ag·grieve [əˈgriːv] *vt.* ①〔常用被动语态〕使烦恼；使悲伤．②侵害，使受委屈．***feel [be] ~d at [by]*** 感到受屈．

ag·gro [ˈægrəu] *n.* 〔英俚〕挑衅(性)．

a·gha [ˈɑːgə, ˈægə] *n.* 大人；统帅；老总〔土耳其和其他穆斯林国家对大官吏的尊称〕(= aga)．

a·ghast [əˈgɑːst] *a.* 〔常用作表语〕吃惊的，吓呆的．***stand ~ at*** 被…吓一跳；被…吓呆．

ag·ile [ˈædʒail] *a.* 轻快的，灵便的，敏捷的，灵活的．*an ~ mind [wit]* 头脑灵活[才思敏捷]．**-ly** *ad.*

a·gil·i·ty [əˈdʒiliti] *n.* 轻快，敏捷；机敏．

a·gin [əˈgin] 〔方〕= again, against.

ag·ing [ˈeidʒiŋ] age 的现在分词．— *n.* ①陈酿．②熟化．

ag·io [ˈædʒiəu] *n.* *(pl.* ~*s)* ①【商】贴水，扣头，折扣．②汇兑，兑换．

ag·io·tage [ˈædʒətidʒ] *n.* ①汇兑(业务)；兑换．②〔罕〕股票买卖．

ag·ism [ˈeidʒizəm] *n.* = ageism.

ag·i·tate [ˈædʒiteit] *vt.* ①搅动，摇动．②激励，鼓动，煽动．③搅乱(人心)，使不安，使焦虑．④热烈讨论．⑤思考．⑥(通过演说或文章)使人注意．*The wind ~d the sea.* 风使海浪翻滚．*~ a fan* 摇扇．*be ~d by the bad news* 为听到坏消息而不安．*~ a question* 热烈讨论问题．— *vi.* 鼓吹，游说．***~ for*** *(reform)* 倡导(改革)，鼓吹(改革)运动．**-d** *a.* ①表现出不安的．②颤抖的．③(问题等)被热烈讨论的，被激烈辩论的．

ag·i·ta·tion [ˌædʒiˈteiʃən] *n.* ①搅动，搅拌．②激动；焦虑．③议论；鼓动．④(民众的)骚动．⑤【医】兴奋．*an anti-slavery ~* 废除奴隶运动．***be all ~*** 异常焦虑．**-al** *a.* 鼓动性的．

a·gi·ta·to [ˌædʒiˈtɑːtəu] *ad.* 〔It.〕【乐】快速而又激动地．

ag·i·ta·tor [ˈædʒiteitə] *n.* ①鼓动者，鼓吹者．②搅拌器．

ag·it·prop [ˈædʒitprɔp] *a.* (戏剧、传单等)宣传鼓动性的．— *n.* ①宣传鼓动．②宣传鼓动机关；宣传鼓动者．

a·gleam [əˈgliːm] *a.* 〔用作表语〕, *ad.* 发光地；发光的．*a city ~ with lights* 灯火辉煌的城市．

ag·let [ˈæglit] *n.* ①(带端)金属箍，带扣．②(服装上装饰用的)挂襻[饰钮、带子、别针]．

a·gley [əˈgliː, əˈglai] *ad.* 〔Scot.〕斜，歪．

a·glit·ter [əˈglitə] *a.* 〔用作表语〕, *ad.* 闪耀的[地]．

a·glow [əˈgləu] *a.* 〔用作表语〕, *ad.* 发亮，发红；兴奋．***be ~ with*** (点)得通红，(烧)得发红 (*He is ~ with health.* 他气色好，他容光焕发．*The garden is ~ with many flowers.* 园中百花盛开)．

ag·nail [ˈægneil] *n.* ①(指甲旁的)倒刺．②甲沟炎．③(脚趾上的)鸡眼．

ag·nate [ˈægneit] *a.* ① 父方的，男系的 (*cf.* cognate)．②同族的，同种族的．— *n.* ①男系亲属．②同族；同种．

ag·nat·ic [ægˈnætik] *a.* 男系亲属的．

ag·na·tion [ægˈneiʃən] *n.* 男系亲属，宗族关系．

Ag·nes [ˈægnis] 阿格尼丝〔女子名〕．

ag·no·men [ægˈnəumen] *n.* *(pl.* ***~s, ag·nom·i·na*** [ægˈnɔminə]*)* ①〔古罗马〕(因功授与的)附名，第四名〔如 *P. Cornelius Scipio Africanus* 即因出征阿非利加有功而被授与第四名 *Africanus*〕．②浑名，绰号．

ag·nos·tic [ægˈnɔstik] *a.* 【哲】不可知论的．— *n.* 不可知论者．

ag·nos·ti·cism [ægˈnɔstisizəm] *n.*【哲】不可知论．

Ag·nus De·i [ˈɑːgnusˈdeiiː] 〔L.〕神羔；神羔像；神羔诵；神羔祈祷式．

a·go [əˈgəu] *ad.* 以前，前．*ten years ~* 十年前．*How long ~ did you saw him?* 你多久以前见过他．***long ~*** 很久以前，从前．***not long ~*** 前不久．***some time ~*** 不久前．

a·gog [əˈgɔg] *a.* 〔常用作表语〕, *ad.* ①急着要，渴望．②极度兴奋．*set the whole town ~* 轰动全城．***all ~ for*** 热望，急待．***all ~ to (do)*** 急着要，急待．

ago·go [əˈgəugəu] *a.* ①活泼的，精力充沛的．②最时髦的．③摇摆舞的，跳摇摆舞者的，摇摆舞音乐唱片的，摇摆舞厅的．

a·gon [ˈɑːgɔn] *n.* *(pl.* ***~s, a·go·nes*** [əˈgəuniːz]*)* ①(古希腊的运动、文学等的)锦标赛．②(古希腊戏剧中的)人物之间的冲突．

ag·o·nal [ˈægənl] *a.* 垂死痛楚的；呻吟待毙的；濒死的．

a·gone [əˈgɔn] *a., ad.* 〔古〕以前，过去，往昔．

a·gon·ic [əˈgɔnik] *a.* 不成角的；【物】无偏差的．**~ line** 【物】零磁偏线．

ag·o·nist [ˈægənist] *n.*【解】主动肌．

ag·o·nis·tic [ˌægəuˈnistik] *a.* ①〔古希腊〕运动比赛的．②争辩的，论战的．③紧张的，不自然的．*~ poses* 做作的姿态．**-s** *n.* 运动比赛学．

ag·o·nize [ˈægənaiz] *vi.* 苦闷；挣扎．— *vt.* 使烦恼，使

苦恼. *an ~d look* 愁眉苦脸,苦相. **-d** *a.* 烦恼的,痛苦的.
ag·o·niz·ing [ˈægənaiziŋ] *a.* 使人苦恼的. *an ~ pain [feeling]* 令人坐卧不安的痛苦[感觉]. **-ly** *ad.*
ag·o·ny [ˈægəni] *n.* ①苦恼,烦闷. ②死的痛苦. ③(感情的)迸发. ④挣扎. *~ **of mind*** 苦闷,苦恼. ***in ~*** 在苦恼中. ***in an ~ of joy*** 喜极,乐极. *~* **column** (寻物、寻人、离婚等的)广告栏.
ag·o·ra[1] [ˈægərə] *n.* (*pl.* ***-rae*** [-riː], *~s* [-rəz]) 古希腊的大会场〔尤指集市〕.
a·go·ra[2] [ɑːgəuˈrɑː] *n.* (*pl.* ***-rot*** [-rəut]) 阿高拉〔以色列货币名,等于一(以色列)镑的 1/100〕.
ag·o·ra·pho·bi·a [ˌægərəˈfəubiə] *n.* 【医】广场恐怖;旷野恐怖.
a·gou·ti [əˈguːti] *n.* (*pl.*) 【动】刺鼠.
a·gou·ty [əˈguːti] *n.* (*pl.* ***-ties***) = agouti.
a·graffe [əˈgræf] *n.* 钩钮,搭扣;搭钩.
a·gran·u·lo·cy·to·sis [əˌgrænjuˌləusaiˈtəusis] *n.*【医】粒性白血球缺乏症.
ag·ra·pha [ˈægrəfə] *n. pl.* 〔Gr.〕 未载于福音书中的耶稣的言论.
a·graph·i·a [æˈgræfiə] *n.* 【医】(因脑受损而不能写字的)失写症. **-ic** *a.*
a·grar·i·an [əˈgreəriən] *a.* ①土地的,耕地的. ②农民的;农业的. ③生于田野间的,野生的. *an ~ outrage* 农民暴动. *~ reforms* 土地改革. *~ revolution* 土地革命. *~ plants* 野生植物. — *n.* 土地均分论者. **-ism** *n.* 土地均分论,土地均分运动.
a·grav·ic [əˈgrævik] *n.* 【宇】无重力区,无重力状况.
a·gree [əˈgriː] *vi.* ①同意,赞成,承认,答应. ②意见相合[相投];(气候、饮食等)适合,合适,合;调和. ③约定,商定. ④符合;【语法】(人称、数、格、性等前后)一致, *I ~.* 好,我赞成. *Brothers and sisters should ~.* 兄弟姐妹应当和好相处. — *vt.* 同意(某事);使…达到一致;认为正确无误. *We are all agreed that the plan is a good one.* 我们一致认为这个计划很好. *~ **in** (opinion; thinking)* (意见)相合;(想法)一致. *~ **like cats and dogs*** 象猫狗一样处不好. *~ **on [upon, as to]*** 对…意见一致. *~ **to** (a proposal; terms)* 答应,承认(提议;条件). *~ **to differ [to disagree]*** 彼此同意保留不同意见. *~ **with*** ①赞同,与…意见相同,与…符合,与…相投. ②与…一致. ③适合,合(口胃),相宜.
a·gree·a·ble [əˈgriəbl] *a.* ①适意的,愉快的. ②有礼貌的,会处人的. ③欣然赞同的,可答应的. ④适合…的,一致的. *I am quite ~.* 〔口,俚〕很好,我很同意. *~ to the taste* 可口,味道好. *be ~ to ear* 动听. *be ~ to a proposal* 欣然赞同一项建议. *be ~ to reason* 合乎道理. *~ **to*** 依,从,遵,照,如 (*A- to my promise, I have come.* 如约而来). ***do the ~*** 亲切款待. ***make oneself ~ to*** 尽量迎合,亲切待人. **-ness** *n.* 适合,一致;适意,愉快.
a·gree·a·bly [əˈgriəbli] *ad.* ①欢然,欣然. ②依照,一致,一样. *~ **to*** 照,应,依 (*~ to your request* 遵照您的要求).
a·greed [əˈgriːd] *a.* 已一致〔同意〕的. *(It is) ~!* 好!行! *They met at the ~ time.* 他们按约定时间见面.
a·gree·ment [əˈgriːmənt] *n.* ①一致,同意. ②契约;协约,协定. ③【语法】一致,呼应. ***a gentleman's [gentlemen's]*** *~* 君子协定. ***by ~*** 同意,依约. ***arrive at [come to] an ~*** 达成协议. ***bring about an ~*** 商妥. ***conclude [enter into] an ~*** 订约. ***in ~ with*** 符合…,照…. ***make an ~ with*** 与…达成协议.
a·gré·ment [agremã] *n.* 〔F.〕①(驻在国政府对派遣外交使节的)同意. ②〔*pl.*〕(环境的)舒适,惬意. ③〔*pl.*〕【乐】装饰音. *the ~ of social life* 社交生活上令人愉快的礼仪举止.
a·gres·tic [əˈgrestik] *a.* ①乡土(气)的. ②粗野的.
ag·ri·bar·on [ˈægribærən] *n.* 〔美〕农业综合企业界巨头.
ag·ri·busi·ness [ˈægriˌbiznis] *n.* (美国垄断资本的)农业综合企业〔其业务包括农产品的加工、农业机械的制造以及化肥的生产等〕.
agric. = ① agricultural. ② agriculture. ③ agriculturist.
ag·ri·cul·tur·al [ˌægriˈkʌltʃurəl] *a.* 农业的,耕种的,农学(上)的. *an ~ experimental station* 农业试验场. *~ products* 农产物. *an ~ school* 农业学校. *an ~ show* 农业展览会.
ag·ri·cul·ture [ˈægrikʌltʃə] *n.* 农业,农耕;农业生产;农学.
ag·ri·cul·tur·ist [ˌægriˈkʌltʃərist] ***-tur·al·ist*** [-tʃurəlist] *n.* 农民,农场经营者;农学家.
ag·ri·mo·ny [ˈægriməni] *n.* 【植】龙芽草.
ag·ri·mo·tor [ˈægriməutə] *n.* 农用拖拉机.
ag·ri·ol·o·gy [ˌægriˈɔlədʒi] *n.* 无文字民族的风俗研究.
ag·ro [ˈægrəu] *n.* = aggro.
ag·ro- *comb. f.* 土地,田地;农业.
ag·ro·bi·ol·o·gy [ˌægrəubaiˈɔlədʒi] *n.* 农业生物学.
ag·ro·chem·i·cal [ˌægrəuˈkemikl] *n.* ①农业化学制品;农业化学药品. ②从农产品中提取的化学药品(如糠醛).
ag·rol·o·gy [əgˈrɔlədʒi] *n.* 农业土壤学.
ag·ro·nom·ic,-i·cal [ˌægrəuˈnɔmik(əl)] *a.* 农业的,农艺的. *~ practices* 农业技术. *~ characters* 农艺性状.
ag·ro·nom·ics [ˌægrəuˈnɔmiks] *n.* 耕作学,农学;农业经营.
ag·ron·o·mist [æˈgrɔnəmist] *n.* 耕作学家,农学家.
ag·ron·o·my [əgˈrɔnəmi] *n.* 农学;作物学.
ag·rost·olo·gy [ˌægrəusˈtɔlədʒi] *n.* 【植】草本学.
ag·ro·tech·nic·al [ˈægrəuˈteknikəl] *a.* 农业技术的.
ag·ro·tech·nic·i·an [ˈægrəutekˈniʃən] *n.* 农业技术员,农技师.
ag·ro·tech·nique [ˈægrəutekˈniːk] *n.* 农业技术.
ag·ro·tech·ny [ˈægrəutekni] *n.* 农产品加工学.
ag·ro·town [ˈægrəutaun] *n.* 农业地区的城镇.
ag·ro·type [ˈægrəutaip] *n.* ①农田类型. ②作物类型.
a·ground [əˈgraund] *a.* 〔用作表语〕, *ad.* ①在地上. ②搁浅,触礁. ***get [go, run, strike] ~*** (船)搁浅,触礁.
a·guar·dien·te [ɑːgwɑːdiˈentei] *n.* 〔Sp.〕 次白兰地酒;〔美西部〕甘蔗做的酒.
a·gue [ˈeigjuː] *n.* ①疟疾. ②打冷颤,发冷.
a·gued [ˈeigjuːd] *a.* 患冷热病的,害疟疾的.
a·gue·weed [ˈeigjuːwiːd] *n.* ①五叶龙胆. ②贯叶泽兰 (= boneset).
a·gu·ish [ˈeigju(ː)iʃ] *a.* ①容易产生疟疾的;易患疟疾的;疟疾引起的. ②打冷颤的,发冷的.
a·gu·ti [əˈguːti] *n.* = agouti.
ah [ɑː] *int.* 啊!呀!嗳!〔表现痛苦、惊奇、怜惜、厌弃、欢喜等〕 *Ah me!* 嗳呀!
A.H. = 〔L.〕 *anno Hegirae* (= in the year of the Hegira) 穆罕默德纪元.
a.h. = ampere-hour 安培小时,安时.
aha [ɑ(ː)ˈhɑː, əˈhɑː] *int.* 嗳呀!哎嘿!〔表现喜悦、轻蔑、惊愕等〕.
à haute voix [ɑːˈəutˈvwɑ] 〔F.〕 高声地.
a·head [əˈhed] *a.* 〔常作表语〕, *ad.* ①在前;向前;提前. ②〔美〕赢得;领先. *set the clock ~* 把钟朝前拨. *He is ~ of his times.* 他走在时代前面. *be ~ of the other students in the class* 在班上名列前茅. *~ **of*** 在…前面;比…进步;优于;胜于 (*walk ~ of sb.* 走在某人前面). ***be ~*** 〔口〕赢;赚. ***be ~ of*** …比…好. ***Breakers ~!*** 前面有碎浪[暗礁]!前途危险! ***Full speed ~!*** 全速前进. ***get ~*** 前进;抢先. ***get ~ in the world*** 出头,发迹. ***go ~*** 上前;前进,继续下去;进步 (*Things were going ~.* 事事顺畅). ***Go ~!*** ①【海】前进!冲啊!

(opp. go astern!*)*；开呀！〔美国对火车的口令〕；动手！干呀！〔工作口令〕. ②那末，还有呢〔提话口气〕 ***Right [straight]*** ～ ① 就在眼前. ②勇往直前（*They saw it right* ～. 他们看见那东西就在眼前. *galloping straight* ～ 驰骋向前）. ***wind*** ～ 顶头风，迎面风.

a·heap [əˈhiːp] *ad.* 〔英〕重叠，堆积.

a·hem [əˈhem, hm] *int.* ①阿嗨！〔引起注意〕. ②嗯〔语塞时发音〕.

a·him·sa [əˈhimsə] *n.* 【佛】不伤生；杀戒.

a·his·tor·ic(al) [ˌeihisˈtɔːrik(əl)] *a.* 稗史的；与历史无关的；无历史记载的. **-al·ly** *ad.*

A.H.M.S. = American Home Missionary Society 美国国内传教会.

A-ho·ri·zon [ˈeihəˈraizn] *n.* 【地】表土，上层（甲层）土壤（腐植土）.

a·hoy [əˈhɔi] *int.* 【海】喂！ 啊嗬！ 〔呼叫他船之声〕. *Ship* ～*!* 船呀，喂！

AHQ = army headquarters 集团军司令部.

Ah·ri·man [ˈɑːrimən] *n.* 【袄教】鬼，邪神.

à huis clos [ɑːˈwiːˈkləu] 〔F.〕 关着门；秘密.

a·hull [əˈhʌl] *ad.* 【海】卷帆并转舵于下风.

A·hu·ra Maz·da [ˈɑːhurəˈmæzdə] 【袄教】最高的神，创世主，善灵（= Ormazd）.

Ahwaz [ɑːˈwɑːz] *n.* 阿瓦士〔伊朗城市〕.

a·i[1] [ˈɑːiː] *n.* 【动】三趾树獭〔南美产〕.

ai[2] [ai] *int.* 唉！〔痛苦、悲伤、怜悯等的感叹词〕.

AIAA = ①American Institute of Aeronautics and Astronautics 美国航空和星际航空协会. ② Aircraft Industries Association of America 美国飞机工业协会.

AIC = ammunition identification code 弹药识别代字.

AICE = ① American Institute of Chemical Engineers 美国化学工程师协会. ② American Institute of Consulting Engineers 美国顾问工程师协会.

AIChE = American Institute of Chemical Engineers 美国化学工程师协会.

AID = Agency for International Development 〔美〕国际开发署.

aid [eid] *n.* ①帮助，援助. ②帮助者，助手. ③辅助设备. ④【海】航标. ⑤〔美〕副官（= aide-de-camp）. ⑥【英史】（国会允许的）国王特享税. *a deaf* ～ 助听器. *audio-visual* ～*s* 直观教具. *short-range* ～*s* 【无】近程导航设备. ***by [with] the*** ～ ***of*** 借…的帮助. ***call in sb.'s*** ～ 求某人援助. ***call (sb.) to one's*** ～ 求助于（人），向（人）求援. ***give first*** ～ 急救. ***go to sb.'s*** ～ 援助（某人）. ***in*** ～ ***of*** 以助…，来帮助…. ***What's (all) this in*** ～ ***of?*** 〔口〕你的用意何在？— *vt., vi.* 助，帮助，援助；协助；接济. ～ ***and abet*** 【法】同谋，教唆. ～ *(sb.) in (doing; one's work)* 帮助（某人做），帮忙. ～**man** 战地医务急救员. ～**post,** ～**station** 救护所.

A·i·da [ɑːˈiːdə] 《阿伊达》〔意大利歌剧家威尔第的一部歌剧〕.

aid-de-camp [ˈeiddəˈkæmp] *n.* (*pl.* ***aids-*** [ˈeidz-]) 〔美〕 = aide-de-camp.

aide [eid] *n.* ①= aide-de-camp. ②助手.

aide-de-camp [eidəˈkɑ̃ːŋ] *n.* (*pl.* ***aides-*** [ˈeidz-]) 〔F.〕【军】随从武官〔参谋〕；副官；幕僚.

aide-mé·moire [ˈeidˈmemwɑː] *n.* 〔F.〕（外交上的）备忘录.

aid·man [ˈeidmən] *n.* (*pl.* ***-men*** [-men]) 【军】战斗部队医务员.

AIEE = American Institute of Electrical Engineers 美国电气工程师协会.

ai·glet [ˈeiglit] *n.* = aglet.

ai·grette [ˈeigret, eiˈgret] *n.* ①【鸟】白鹭. ②【植】冠毛. ③鹭鸶毛帽饰. ④（宝石的）枝状饰.

ai·guille [ˈeigwiːl, ˈeigwiː] *n.* ①尖峰，锥岩. ②（岩石的）钻孔器.

ai·guil·lette [ˌeigwiˈlet] *n.* 【军】饰带，肩带.

AIIE = American Institute of Industrial Engineers 美国工业工程师协会.

Ai·ken [ˈeikin] *n.* 艾肯〔姓氏〕.

ai·ki·do [aiˈkiːdəu] *n.* 〔Jap.〕合气道〔一种自卫角斗术〕.

ail [eil] *vt.* 使苦恼，使烦恼. *What* ～*s you?* 你怎么啦？哪里不舒服？— *vi.* 不舒服，生病（= ill）. *The child is* ～*ing.* 小孩生病了.

ai·lan·thus [eiˈlenθəs] *n.* (*pl.* ～*es*) 臭椿属植物，樗树属植物. **-lanth·ic** [-θik] *a.*

Ai·leen [ˈeiliːn] *n.* 艾琳〔女子名，Helen 的异体〕.

ai·ler·on [ˈeilərɔn] *n.* 〔常 *pl.*〕【空】副翼，辅（助）翼.

ail·ing [ˈeiliŋ] *a.* 不舒服的，害病的.

ail·ment [ˈeilmənt] *n.* 小病，失调.

ai·lu·ro·pho·bi·a [aiˌluərəˈfəubiə] *n.* 恐猫病，畏猫. **-phobe** *n.*

AIM = ① American Indian Movement 美国印第安人运动. ② air intercept missile 空中截击导弹.

aim [eim] *vi.* ①瞄准，针对. ②指望，企图，旨在 *(at)*. ～ *at a mark* 瞄准目标. ～ *at success* 指望成功. ★英国说 ～ at doing，美国则说 ～ to do. ～ ***at the moon*** 〔口〕妄想. ～ ***high*** 胸怀大志，有志气，力争上游. ～ ***too low*** 胸无大志. — *vt.* 把…瞄准，把…指向；把…掷向 *(at)*. ～ *a pistol at sb.* 以手枪瞄准某人. ～ *a book at sb.'s head* 拿起一本书向某人的头上扔去. — *n.* ①照准，瞄准；靶子，目标. ②目的，志向；宗旨. *achieve [attain] one's* ～ 达到目的. *miss one's* ～ 瞄歪；(希望）落空，失败. *the* ～ *and end of art* 艺术的终极目的. ***take*** ～ ***(at)*** （对…）瞄准. ***without*** ～ 无目的地，乱，瞎.

aim·less [ˈeimlis] *a.* 无目的的，无目标的. **-ly** *ad.* **-ness** *n.*

ain [ein] *a.* 〔英方〕自己的.

aî·né [eˈnei] *a.* 〔F.〕 长子的，兄的〔*cf.* cadet〕.

aî·née [eˈnei] *a.* 〔F.〕 姊的.

Ai·no [ˈainəu] *a.* 〔日〕阿伊努族的，虾夷人的. — *n.* (*pl.* ～*(s)*) 〔日〕阿伊努人，虾夷人.

ain't [eint] 〔口〕 = am not, are not, is not, has not, have not. *A- we got fun?* 〔美〕不愉快吗？

A Int = Air Intelligence 航空情报.

Ai·nu [ˈainuː] *n.* (*pl.* ～ *(s)*) =Aino *(n.)* — *a.* = Aino *(a.)*.

air [εə] *n.* ①空气，大气. ②天空，空中. ③微风，和风. ④态度，样子，风度，气派；〔*pl.*〕 高傲的架子. ⑤传播，公开. ⑥【乐】曲调，主调. *fresh [foul]* ～ 新鲜的〔污浊的〕空气. *open* ～ 户外. *(a) change of* ～ 转地（疗养）. *noxious* ～ 毒气. *a slight* ～ 微风. *a vernal* ～ 春风. *a national* ～ 国歌. *sing an* ～ 唱一曲. *have an* ～ *of importance* 摆架子. ～***s and graces*** 装腔作势. ***assume*** ～***s*** = put on ～s. ***be on the*** ～ 正在广播. ***beat the*** ～ 徒劳，白劳. ***by*** ～ 用〔坐〕飞机；用无线电. ***clear the*** ～ 通通空气；澄清事实；消除误会. ***fan the*** ～ 打空，扑空. ***fish in the*** ～ = plough the ～. ***get the*** ～ 〔美俚〕被辞退，被解聘；被朋友〔情人等〕抛弃. ***give*** ～ ***to one's view*** 说出自己意见. ***give oneself*** ～***s***充气派，自大，摆架子. ***give (sb.) the*** ～ 〔美俚〕辞退，解聘，撵走（某人）；抛弃朋友〔情人等〕. ***go off the*** ～ 【无】停止播送. ***go on the*** ～ 【无】开始播送. ***go up in the*** ～ 〔美俚〕①忿激，突然生气. ②（演员）突然忘记台词. ***hot*** ～ 〔口〕吹牛，夸夸其谈. ***in the*** ～ ①在空中. ②（谣言等）流传. ③（计划等）悬着，未决，渺茫 *(His plans are still in the* ～. 他的计划还很渺茫). ④【军】无掩护的，未设防的. ***live on*** ～ 靠喝风过日子. ***make the*** ～ ***blue*** 诅咒. ***on the*** ～ 广播中，播送中. ***out of thin*** ～ 无中生有地. ***plough the*** ～ 白费气力. ***put on*** ～***s*** 傲慢，摆架子，装气派. ***put [sent] (sb.) on***

the ~〔口〕传播，宣扬. *speak on the* ~ 发表广播演说. *take* ~ 传开，泄漏. *take the* ~ ①出外兜风，散步. ②【空】离地，腾空，飞起来. ③【无】开始播送. ④〔俚〕离开，走开. *take to the* ~ 做飞行家. *tread (up) on* ~ 扬扬得意. *up in the* ~ (计划等) 未决，渺茫. *walk on* ~ 扬扬得意. *with word and* ~ 演唱皆备. — *vt.* ①晾，吹吹，使通风；烘干，烤干；风干. ②宣扬，显示；夸示. ③播送. ~ *one's clothes on the roof* 在屋顶晾衣服. ~ *the dog* 牵着狗散步. ~ *a room* 让房间通通风. ~ *oneself* 出外兜风，散步. ~ *costly jewels* 夸示贵重宝石. ~ *one's opinion* 发表己见. *The game was* ~*ed to all parts of the country.* 比赛实况向全国广播. — *vi.* ①散步，兜风. ②晾着. ③播送. ~ **action** 空战. ~ **alarm** 空袭警报. ~ **alert** ①空袭警报 (期间). ②【军】空中待机. ~ **attack** 空中攻击，空袭. ~ **base** 航空〔空军〕基地. ~ **bath** 空气浴(装置)；空气干燥器. ~ **battery** (可以再充电的)空气电池. ~ **bearing** 空气轴承. ~ **bed** 气垫，气床. ~ **bladder**【动】气泡；鳔. ~ **blast** 鼓风，空气喷射. ~**boat** 用在空气中旋转的螺旋桨推进的平底船. **Air Board** 航空局. ~**borne** *a.* 空运的，机载的；空降的；空中传播的；用空气运送的；通过无线电〔电视〕播送的. (~*borne bacteria* 空气传播的细菌. ~*borne troops* 空运部队). ~ **brake** 空气制动器；减速板. ~**breather** 以吸入的大气助燃推进的导弹. ~**brick** 多孔砖，空心砖. ~-**bridge** 空运线. ~**brush** ①*n.* 喷枪. ②*vt.* 用喷枪喷. ~**bus**〔口〕(短程或中程) 大型客机. ~ **cast** ①*n.*〔美〕无线电广播. ②*vt.* 用无线电广播. ~ **caster**〔美〕无线电广播员. ~ **castle** 空中楼阁，妄想. ~ **cell**【解】气胞，气囊. ~ **chamber** 气胞；气腔；气室. ~ **coach** 二等客机. ~**cock** 气旋塞. **Air Commodore**〔英〕空军中将. ~ **compressor** 空气压缩机. ~ **condenser** 空气冷却机. ~-**condition** *vt.*〔美〕在…装设空气调节器；调节…的空气湿度和温度. ~-**conditioned** *a.* 装有空气调节器的. ~ **conditioner** 空气调节器. ~-**conditioning** 空气调节. ~ **control** 空中交通管制. ~-**cooled** *a.* 气冷 (式). ~ **cooler** 空气冷却器，气冷装置，气冷机. ~ **corps**〔美〕(陆军中的) 飞行大队. ~ **corridor** 空中走廊. **Air Council**〔英〕空军最高会议. ~ **cover** = ~ umbrella. ~**craft** 航空器，飞行器，飞机. ~**craft(s)man**〔英〕空军地勤技师. ~**craftwoman** 空军地勤女技师. ~**crew** 飞机乘务员，空勤人员. ~-**cure** *vt.* 晾，用空气处理. ~ **current** 气流. ~ **cushion** 气垫；气褥；气枕；气室. ~-**cushioned** *a.* 气垫的(~*-cushioned vehicle* 气垫运载工具). ~ **defence** 防空. ~**dent** 气喷磨牙机. ~ **division**〔美〕空军师. ~ **drain** 气眼，气门，通气管，气道；防湿沟. ~ **drill** 风钻. ~**drome**〔美〕飞机场. ~**drop** *n., vt.* 空投. ~-**dry** *vt.* 风干. ~ **engine** 空气发动机. ~ **express** 空运包裹. ~**field** 飞机场. ~ **fight** *n.* 空战. ~ **fleet** 航空机队. ~**flow** 气流. ~-**flue** 气道，风道，烟道. ~**foil**【空】机翼；翼形，翼剖面. ~ **force** 空军. ~**frame** 机架；导弹弹体；(火箭等的)构架. **Air France** 法国航空公司. ~ **freight** 空中货运 (费). ~ **freighter** 货机. ~ **ga(u)ge** 气压计. ~**glow**【气】气辉. ~**graph**〔英〕缩印航空邮件. ~-**ground** *a.* 陆空的. ~ **group** 空军大队. ~ **gun** 气枪. ~ **hammer** 气锤. ~ **harbour** 航空港. ~-**head** (伞兵的) 着陆阵地. ~ **hole** 通气孔，风眼；气门，(船舱等的)风窗；冰孔，不冻水面；【空】= airpocket. ~**hop** ①*n.* 短程空中旅行. ②*vi.* 经常作空中短程旅行. ~ **hostess** 客机女服务员，空中小姐. ~ **jacket** 空气救生衣 (= life belt)；气套. ~**land** *vt.*【军】空降. ~ **lane**【空】空中航线. ~-**launch** *vt.* 空中发射. ~ **letter** 航空信；航空邮笺. ~**lift** ①*vt.* 空运. ②*n.* 空运；空中补给线；空气升液器. ~**line**〔美〕直路，近路；空中航线；定期航空，定期航空公司；最短距离；(潜水用) 送气管. ~-**line** ①*a.* 直 (*an* ~*-line road* 直路)；飞行的；直线的. ②两点间的直线；航线；航空系统；航空公司. ~ **liner** 客机，班机. ~ **lock** 气塞，气闸. ~-**mail** 航空邮件，航空信. ~**man** 飞行员，飞机师；空军士兵. ~**manship** 飞行术. ~ **map** 空摄地图. **Air Marshal**〔英〕空军中将. ~ **mass** 气团. ~-**minded** *a.* 热心航空的. ~**ometer** 风速计；气流计. ~ **park** 小型飞机场. ~ **patrol** 空中侦察；侦察飞行队. *vi.* ~ **pipe** 通风管，通气管. ~ **piracy** 空中劫持，劫机. ~ **pirate** 空中劫机者. ~**plane** ①*n.*〔美〕飞机〔英国说 aeroplane〕. ②*vi.* 坐飞机. ~ **play** (电台)播放唱片. ~ **pocket**【空】空中陷阱，垂直气流. ~ **pollution** 大气污染. ~**port** 飞机场，航空站. ~ **post** = air-mail. ~ **power** 空军威力；制空权；空军部. ~**pressure** 风压；气压. ~**proof** ①*a.* 不透气的，密封的，气密的. ②*vt.* 使不透气. ~ **propeller** 扇风机. ~ **pump** 气泵. ~-**raid** 空袭 (*an* ~*-raid alarm* 空袭紧急警报. *an* ~*-raid precaution* 空袭预备警报. *an* ~*-raid shelter* 防空洞，防空壕. *an* ~*-raid warning* 空袭警报). ~ **raider** 空袭机，空袭兵. ~ **rifle** 气枪. ~ **route** 航空路线. ~ **sac**【生】气囊. ~**scape** 空瞰图. ~ **scoop**【空】进气口. ~ **scout**【空】侦察机. ~**screw** 飞机螺旋桨. ~-**sea** *a.* 海空的. ~ **shaft**【矿】通风井. ~**shed** 飞机仓库. ~**ship** 飞船. ~**shipper** 空运企业. ~**sickness** 航空病，晕机. ~-**slaked** *a.* 风化了的. ~ **sleeve**, ~ **sock** 锥形风标. ~**space** ①空域，领空. ②广播时间. ~ **speed** (飞机与空气相对的) 飞行速度，空速 (*cf. ground speed*). ~ **speedometer** 空速表. ~ **spring** 气褥，气垫(= ~ cushion). ~ **station** 航空站. ~**stop** 直升飞机航空站. ~ **stream** 气流. ~**strip** (速成) 机场跑道，简易机场. ~-**taxi** (来往于无固定航线小城镇之间的)短程飞机. ~ **thread** 游丝；蜘蛛丝；〔*pl.*〕= gossamer. ~**tight** *a.* 不透气的，密闭的；严密的；无懈可击的 (*an* ~ *tight test* 气密试验). ~**time** (电台或电视台的)广播时间. ~-**to-air** *a.* 空对空的. ~ **turbulence** 晴空湍流颠簸. ~ **umbrella** 空中掩护. ~ **vehicle** 空中运载工具. ~**waves**〔美俚〕无线电广播. ~**way** ①【矿】通风道. ②空中航线；航空公司. ③〔*pl.*〕(电视台的)频道. ~-**wise** *a.* 熟悉航空的. ~**woman** 女飞行员，女飞机师. ~**worthiness** 航空适宜性，耐飞性. ~**worthy** *a.* 耐飞的，适宜飞行的. -**er** *n.*〔英口〕晒衣架.

AIRBM = Anti-intermediate range ballistic missile 反中远程弹道导弹.

Air·cav [ˈɛəkæv] *n.*〔美〕空降部队.

Aire·dale [ˈɛədeil] *n.* ①硬毛杂种猎犬 (= ~ terrier). ②〔a-〕〔美〕飞机师；飞机机务员；航空母舰飞机管理员.

air·i·ly [ˈɛərili] *ad.* 轻快地；活泼地，快活地.

air·i·ness [ˈɛərinis] *n.* ①通风. ②空虚. ③轻快，快活.

airing [ˈɛəriŋ] *n.* ①晾，晒；烘干. ②散步；(用汽车) 兜风. ③表态. ④广播. *give the clothes an* ~ 晾干衣服. *give a scandal an* ~ 把丑事传开. *take an* ~ 散步.

air·less [ˈɛəlis] *a.* ①空气不流通的，缺少新鲜空气的. ②没有风的.

air·tel [ˈɛətel] *n.* 机场饭店.

air·y [ˈɛəri] *a.* (*-i·er; -i·est*) ①空气 (一样) 的，无形的. ②航空的. ③空中的，耸立空中的. ④通风的. ⑤空虚的；空想的. ⑥轻浮的，轻佻的. ⑦袅娜的，优美的；轻柔的. ⑧快活的，轻快的. ⑨〔口〕装阔的，做作的. ~ *dreams* 幻梦. *an* ~ *tone* 做作的声调.

AIS = Artillery Intelligence Service 炮兵情报勤务，炮兵情报勤务处.

aisle [ail] *n.* ①(教堂的) 走廊；耳堂. ②〔美〕(戏院、客车等内的) 过道，通道. ③任何狭长的通路. *down the* ~ 走向神坛去举行婚礼. *(roll) in the* ~ (观众) 捧腹大笑.

ait [eit] *n.*〔英方〕(河、湖中的)小岛.

aitch [eitʃ] *n.* H(h) 字； h 音. *drop one's ~es* 漏发 h 音 (如把 ham [hæm] 读作 'am [æm] 等). — *a.* H 形的. ~ **bone**〔英〕牛的臀骨；牛臀部净肉.

Ait·ken [ˈeitkin] *n.* 艾特肯〔姓氏〕.

a·jar[1] [əˈdʒɑː] *a.* 〔多作表语〕,*ad.* (门)微开，半开. *The door stood ~.* 门半开半掩.

ajar[2] [əˈdʒɑː] *a.* 〔常用作表语〕, *ad.* 不协调. *He is ~ with the world.* 他与人处事总是格格不入.

a·kim·bo [əˈkimbəu] *a.* 〔多作表语〕, *ad.* 两手叉腰. *with arms ~* 两手叉腰.

a·kin [əˈkin] *a.* 〔常用作表语〕①血族的，同族的. ②同种的,同样的,类似的. **be ~ to** 是…的同族〔近亲〕；类似,近似 (*Pity is ~ to love.* 怜悯生爱情).

Ak·kad [ˈækæd] *n.* ①古巴比伦阿卡德区. ②古巴比伦首都阿卡德；古巴比伦的阿卡德人. ③= Akkadian.

Ak·ka·di·an [əˈkeidiən, -ˈkɑː-] *a.* 古阿卡德的；古阿卡德人的；古阿卡德语的. — *n.* 古阿卡德语〔美索不达米亚地区已消亡的闪语〕.

ak·va·vit [ˈɑːkvəvit, ˈæk-] *n.* 阿瓜维特酒〔北欧出产的一种粮食酒，有香菜子味，通常作开胃酒饮用〕 (= aquavit).

AL = ① Arab League 阿拉伯联盟. ② American Legion 美国军团.

al- *pref.* 〔用于 l 前〕 = ad-: *al*lude.

-al[1] *suf.* ①造成"…的,有…性质的,…特有的"等意义的形容词: post*al*, sensation*al*, tropic*al*. ②由动词造成表示该动作的名词: arriv*al*, refus*al*.

-al[2] *suf.* 【化】醛: acet*al* 乙缩醛, chlor*al* 氯醛.

à la [ɑː lɑː] *prep.* 〔F.〕 ①…派的，…式的. ②【烹】…风味的. *chou à la crème* 奶油馅包.

ala [ˈeilə] (*pl.* ***a·lae*** [ˈeili]) *n.* 【生】翼,翅；翼状部.

Ala. = Alabama.

Al·a·bam·a [ˌæləˈbæmə] *n.* 亚拉巴马〔美国州名〕. **-bam·an** ①*a.* 阿拉巴马州的. ②*n.* 阿拉巴马州人.

al·a·bam·ine [ˌæləˈbæmin] *n.* 【化】砹〔署作 Ab,元素砹 (astatine) 的旧名〕.

al·a·bas·ter [ˈæləbɑːstə] *n.* 雪花石膏. — *a.* 雪花石膏制的；雪花石膏一样的，雪白的. ~ *glass* 乳色玻璃.

à la bonne heure [ˌɑːlɑːˈbɔˈnəː] 〔F.〕 好极了！ 巧极了！ 做得好！ 好！

à la carte [ɑː lɑːˈkɑːt]〔F.〕照菜单点的. *à la carte meal* 点菜〔*cf.* table d'hôte meal 客饭,份菜〕.

a·lack [əˈlæk], **a·lack·a·day** [əˈlækədei] *int.* 〔古〕呜呼！ 哀哉！

a·lac·ri·ty [əˈlækriti] *n.* ①乐意. ②敏捷. ***with ~*** 快；敏捷,踊跃,欣然. *He accepted my invitation with ~.* 他欣然接受我的邀请.

Aladdin [əˈlædin] *n.* 阿拉丁〔《天方夜谭》(*Arabian Nights*) 中获得神灯的青年名〕. ***~'s lamp***如意灯,神灯；〔喻〕能满足一切愿望的东西.

a·lae [ˈeiliː] ala 的复数.

à la fran·çaise [a la frɑ̃ˈsez] 〔F.〕 法国式(的).

à la king [ˌɑːləˈkiŋ] 〔F.〕【烹】切成小粒泡在有蘑菇、胡椒和青椒的奶油汁内的. *chicken ~* 奶油鸡丁.

a·la·li·a [əˈleiliə] *n.* 【医】语言不清,哑.

al·a·meda [ˌæləˈmeidə,-miːdə] *n.* 〔美〕林荫走道.

al·a·mo [ˈɑːləməu, ˈælə-] *n.* ***(pl. ~s)*** 杨树，三角叶杨〔美国西南部产〕.

al·a·mode [ˈæləməud] *n.* 阿拉莫德薄黑绸 〔又名 ~ silk〕. — *ad., a.* = *à la mode.*

à la mode [ɑːləːˈməud] *ad.* 时髦地. — *a.* 〔F.〕 ①流行的，时新的. ②加奶油〔冰淇淋(等)〕的. ***beef ~*** 蔬菜炖牛肉. ***pie ~*** 奶油馅饼.

à la mort [ˌæləˈmɔːr] 〔F.〕 ①病危. 濒死. ②无精打采；忧郁. ③致命地.

Al·an [ˈælən] *n.* 阿伦〔男子名〕.

à l'an·glaise [alɑ̃ŋˈlez] 〔F.〕 英国式(的).

al·a·nine [ˈæləni(ː)n] *n.* 【化】丙氨酸.

à la page [ɑː lɑː paʒ] 〔F.〕时髦的，跟上时代的，新式的.

alar [ˈeilə] *a.* ①(有) 翼的，(有)翅的. ②【植】腋生的. ③【解】腋下的.

a·larm [əˈlɑːm] *n.* ①惊慌，恐慌. ②警报，急报. ③警报器,警铃. *The fire caused much ~.* 火灾引起很大恐慌. *a fire ~* 火警. *a false ~* 虚惊一场. ***give the ~ = raise an ~*** 发警报，向…告急. ***in ~*** 惊慌；担心. ***sound the ~*** 响警报,吹警号〔笛〕. ***take (the) ~ at*** 对…感到吃惊. — *vt.* ①向…告急,向…报警；警戒. ②吓,惊动；使放心不下. *Don't ~ yourself.* 不要惊慌. ***be ~ed at*** *(the news)* 被 (那消息) 吓一跳. ***be ~ed for*** *(the safety of ...)* 放心不下，担心 (…的安全). ~ **bell** 警钟；警铃. ~ **clock** 闹钟 *(set the ~ clock for half past seven* 把闹钟拨到七点半). ~ **gauge** (锅炉上的) 气压报警器. ~ **gun** 信号炮. ~ **post**【军】紧急集合处. ~ **signal** 警报信号. ~ **whistle** 警笛. **~-word** 暗号,口令. **-ing** *a.* 可惊的；使人惊慌的；恐慌的.

a·larm·ing [əˈlɑːmiŋ] *a.* 使人惊慌的；引起惊慌的；告急的,危言耸听的.

a·larm·ism [əˈlɑːmizm] *n.* 危言耸听；慌报军情.

a·larm·ist [əˈlɑːmist] *n.* 危言耸听者；慌报情况夸大事实者.

a·lar·um [əˈlɛərəm] *n.* 〔古，诗〕 = alarm.

a·la·ry [ˈeiləri] *a.* 翼的，翅的；翅状的.

Alas. = Alaska.

a·las [əˈlɑːs] *int.* 哎呀！哎哟！〔表示悲痛、遗憾等〕. ***Alas the day!*** 〔古〕嗳呀！ 天哪！

A·las·ka [əˈlæskə] *n.* 阿拉斯加〔美国州名〕.

A·las·kan [əˈlæskən] *a.* 阿拉斯加州的. — *n.* 阿拉斯加州人.

alate [ˈeileit], **alat·ed** [-id] *a.* 有翼(状物)的.

alb [ælb] *n.* (牧师、神父穿的)白麻布长袍.

Alb. = ① Albania(n). ② Albany. ③ Albert. ④ Alberta.

al·ba [ˈɑːlbə, ˈæl-] *n.* (法国普罗旺斯人的)晨歌；朝曲.

al·ba·core [ˈælbəkɔː] *n.* ***(pl. ~(s))*** 长鳍金枪鱼.

Al·ba·ni·a [ælˈbeinjə] *n.* 阿尔巴尼亚〔欧洲〕.

Al·ba·ni·an [ælˈbeinjən] *a.* 阿尔巴尼亚的；阿尔巴尼亚人的；阿尔巴尼亚语的. — *n.* ①阿尔巴尼亚人. ②阿尔巴尼亚语.

Al·ba·ny [ˈɔːlbəni] *n.* ①美国纽约州州城. ②(加拿大) 阿尔巴尼河.

al·bata [ælˈbeitə] *n.* 洋银 (= German silver).

al·ba·tross [ˈælbətrɔs] *n.* ***(pl. ~es)*** ①【动】信天翁. ②〔喻〕引起忧虑的事物〔源出英国诗人柯勒律治(Coleridge)所著长诗《老水手》，该诗叙述水手误杀信天翁以致全船遭难〕.

al·be·do [ælˈbiːdəu] *n.* ①【天】反照率. ②【物】反射率,反照率.

al·be·it [ɔːlˈbiːit] *conj.* 〔古〕纵令,虽然.

Al·bert [ˈælbət] *n.* 艾伯特〔男子名〕.

al·bert [ˈælbət] *n.* 挂在背心上的表链(=~ chain). ***The A- Hall*** (伦敦) 阿尔伯特纪念堂〔常作音乐会和其他集会的会场〕.

Al·ber·ta [ælˈbəːtə] *n.* 艾伯塔〔男子名〕.

al·bert·ite [ˈælbəˈtait] *n.* (加拿大 Albert 矿所出的)一种黑沥青.

al·bes·cent [ælˈbesənt] *a.* 发白的,正在变白的.

Al·bi·gen·ses [ˌælbiˈdʒensiːz] *n.* 〔*pl.*〕 阿尔比教派〔大约在公元 1020—1250 年在法国南部兴盛的教派,后被视为异端而被镇压〕. **-gen·si·an** *a., n.*

Al·bin [ˈælbin] *n.* 阿尔宾〔男子名〕.

al·bi·nism [ˈælbinizəm] *n.* 【医】白化病.

al·bi·no [ælˈbiːnəu] *n.* ***(pl. ~s)*** ①患白化病的人〔动植物〕. ②【生】白化体,白变种. ~ **rat** (生物试验用的)天

竺鼠.

Al·bi·on [ˈælbjən] *n.* ①〔诗〕英格兰. ②【希神】阿尔比安〔海神之子〕.

al·bite [ˈælbait] *n.* 【矿】钠长石.

al·biz·zi·a [ælˈbiziə] *n.* 【植】合欢属植物.

ALBM = Air-launched ballistic missile 空中发射的弹道导弹.

al·bo·my·cin [ˌælbəˈmaisin] *n.* 【药】白霉素.

al·bu·gin·e·ous [ˌælbjuˈdʒiniəs] *a.* 眼白的; 似眼白的.

al·bum [ˈælbəm] *n.* ①相片簿, 邮票簿. ②〔古〕来宾签名簿 (= visitor's book). ③文集; 歌曲集. ④唱片套; 唱片集.

al·bu·men [ˈælbjumin] *n.* ①蛋白. ②【生化】白朊, 白蛋白(= albumin). ③【植】胚乳.

al·bu·men·ize [ælˈbjuːmənaiz] *vt.* ①使蛋白质化. ②【摄】在…上涂蛋白. ~**d paper** 蛋白感光纸.

al·bu·min [ælˈbjumin] *n.* 【生化】白朊, 白蛋白.

al·bu·mi·nate [ælˈbjuːmineit] *n.* 清蛋白盐.

al·bu·mi·noid [ælˈbjuːminɔid] *a.* 硬朊的, 硬蛋白的. — *n.* 【生化】硬朊, 硬蛋白质.

al·bu·mi·nose [ælˈbjuːminəus], **-nous** [-nəs] *a.* (含)蛋白质的; 多胚乳的.

al·bu·mi·nu·ri·a [ælˌbjuːmiˈnjuəriə] *n.* 【医】蛋白尿(病).

al·bu·mose [ˈælbjuməus] *n.* 【生化】(蛋白)脲.

al·bur·num [ælˈbəːnəm] *n.* 边材, 白木质 (= sapwood).

al·ca·hest [ˈælkəhest] *n.* = alkahest.

al·cai·de, al·cay·de [ɑːlˈkaidi] *n.* ①(西班牙等地)要塞司令; 督军. ②(西班牙等地监狱的)看守; 监狱长.

al·cal·de [ɑːlˈkɑːldei] *n.* (西班牙等地的)市长, 镇长, 村长.

al·caz·ar [ælˈkæzə] *n.* (西班牙等地的)宫殿, 堡垒.

al·chem·ic, al·chem·i·cal [ælˈkemik(əl)] *a.* 炼金术的.

al·che·mist [ælˈkemist] *n.* 炼金术士.

al·che·mis·tic, al·che·mist·i·cal [ˌælkiˈmistik(əl)] *a.* 炼金术的; 炼金术士的. **-i·cal·ly** *ad.*

al·che·my [ˈælkimi] *n.* ①炼金术; (中国古代的)炼丹术. ②魔力, 秘法. *convince the public of one's innocence by alchemies of eloquence* 用雄辩的口才让人相信自己无罪.

al·ci·dine [ˈælsidain] *a.* 【动】海雀科的.

ALCM = air-launched cruise missile 空中发射的巡航导弹.

al·co·hol [ˈælkəhɔl] *n.* ①【化】醇; 乙醇, 酒精. ②含酒精饮料. *absolute* ~ 无水酒精. *He does not touch* ~. 他不喝酒.

al·co·hol·ic [ˌælkəˈhɔlik] *a.* ①酒精的, 含酒精的. ②酒精中毒的. ~ *drinks* 含酒精的饮料. — *n.* 酒鬼. **Alcoholics Anonymous** 嗜酒者互诫协会〔美国的戒酒团体, 略作 AA, A.A.〕. ~ **poisoning** 酒精中毒.

al·co·hol·ism [ˈælkəhɔlizəm] *n.* 酒精中毒.

al·co·hol·ize [ˈælkəhɔlaiz] *vt.* ①用酒精泡[浸、渍]. ②【化】醇化. ③使醉.

al·co·hol·om·e·ter [ˌælkəhɔˈlɔmitə] *n.* 酒精比重计.

Al·co·ran [ælkɔˈrɑːn, -ˈræn] *n.* 〔古〕(伊斯兰教的)《古兰经》(= Koran).

Al·cott [ˈɔːlkət] *n.* 奥尔科特〔姓氏〕.

al·cove [ˈælkəuv] *n.* ①壁橱; 壁龛; 凹室; 洞穴中凹处. ②林中空地; 园中凉亭. *dining* ~ (客厅或起居室一部分凹入的)餐室. *coat* ~ 衣帽间.

Al·cuin [ˈælkwin] *n.* 阿尔昆〔姓氏〕.

Al·cy·o·ne [ælˈsaiəni] 【天】昴宿六〔金牛座〕.

Ald., aldm. = Alderman.

al·de·hyde [ˈældihaid] *n.* 【化】乙醛; 醛.

Al·den [ˈɔːldən] *n.* 奥尔登〔男子名〕.

al den·te [ælˈdentiː] 〔It.〕 咬起来硬的; 耐嚼.

alder [ˈɔːldə] *n.* 【植】桤木. *the black* ~ 冬青. *the red [white]* ~ 赤[白]杨.

al·der·man [ˈɔːldəmən] *n.* *(pl. -men)* ①〔美〕市参议员. ②〔英〕(仅次于市长的)高级市政官; 副市长. ③【英史】郡长. **-ic** *a.* (象) alderman 的.

Al·dine [ˈɔːldain, -diːn] *a.* 阿尔杜斯版的〔指 Aldus Manutius 及其家人于 1494—1597 年在威尼斯和罗马印行的精装古籍〕; 精装本的.

Al·ding·ton [ˈɔːldiŋtən] *n.* 奥尔丁顿〔姓氏〕.

al·dol [ˈældɔːl] *n.* 【化】丁间醇醛.

al·dose [ˈældəus] *n.* 【化】醛(式)糖.

al·do·ste·rone [ælˈdɔstəˈrəun, ˈældəus-] *n.* 【生化】醛甾酮.

al·do·ste·ron·ism [ˈældɔstərəunizm] *n.* 【医】醛甾酮增多症.

Al·dous [ˈɔːldəs, ˈældəs] *n.* 奥尔德斯〔男子名〕.

Al·dridge [ˈɔːldridʒ] *n.* 奥尔德里奇〔姓氏〕.

al·drin [ˈɔːldrin] *n.* 【化】艾氏剂; 氯甲桥萘; 爱耳德萘〔一种杀虫剂〕.

ale [eil] *n.* ①(淡色)浓啤酒. ②乡下啤酒节. ★ ale 与 beer 同义, 但较高级. *Good* ~ *will make a cat speak.* 好酒能使人说真话. *small* ~ 淡啤酒. *Adam's* ~ 水. ~**house** 酒馆; 啤酒店. ~**wife** ①啤酒店老板娘. ②〔美〕鲱白鱼类.

a·le·a·to·ric [ˌeiliəˈtɔrik] *a.* ①碰运气的. ②(音乐)胡乱凑成的, 噪乐的. ~ *music* (信手胡乱演来的)任意音乐.

a·le·a·to·ry [ˈeiliətəri] *a.* 碰运气的, 侥幸的. *the* ~ *element in life* 人生中不可预测的因素.

Alec(k) [ˈælik] *n.* 亚历克〔男子名, Alexander 的昵称〕.

ale·con·ner [ˈeilkɔnə] *n.* 【英史】酒类检查官; 市镇挂名官员.

a·lee [əˈliː] *a.* 〔常用作表语〕, *ad.* 【海】在背风处; 向下风 (*opp.* aweather).

ale·gar [ˈeiligə] *n.* 〔英方〕发酸的啤酒; 啤酒醋.

Al·e·man·ni [ˌæliˈmænai] *n.* 〔*pl.*〕 阿勒曼尼人〔公元五世纪初侵入阿尔萨斯和瑞士部分领土, 并在该地区定居, 后于 496 年被克洛维斯所征服〕.

Al·e·man·nic [ˌæliˈmænik] *n.* 阿勒曼尼语〔在德国西南部、阿尔萨斯和瑞士所讲的任何一种日耳曼方言〕. — *a.* 阿勒曼尼的.

a·lem·bic [əˈlembik] *n.* ①蒸馏器, (古代炼金术士用的)昇华锅. ②任何起净化作用的事物.

A·len·çon [əˈlensən] *n.* 阿郎松针绣花边.

a·leph [ˈɑːlif] *n.* 希伯来语字母表的第一个字母.

a·leph·null [ˈɑːlifˈnʌl] *n.* 【数】阿列夫零.

A·lep·po [əˈlepəu] *n.* 阿勒颇〔叙利亚城市〕.

a·lert [əˈləːt] *a.* ①警惕的; 警觉的. ②机警的, 机灵的. — *n.* ①警戒; 警报. ②警戒期间. ③【军】紧急待命. *No. one* ~ 一级战备. **on the** ~ 警惕, 提防. —*vt.* 使警戒. *The troops were* ~*ed.* 部队在待命中. **-ly** *ad.* **-ness** *n.*

a·leu·k(a)e·mi·a [ˌeiljuˈkiːmiə] *n.* 【医】白血球缺乏症. **-mic** [mik] *a.*

a·leu·rone [əˈljuərɔn, -rəun] *n.* 【化】糊粉. **-ron·ic** [-ˈrɔnik] *a.*

Al·eut [ˈæliuːt] *n.* ①阿留申岛人. ②阿留申语.

A·leu·tian [əˈluːʃjən] *a.* ①阿留申群岛的. ②阿留申群岛人的. — *n.* ①阿留申人. ②〔*pl.*〕 阿留申群岛(=~ Islands).

Alex [ˈæliks] *n.* 亚历克斯〔男子名, Alexander 的昵称〕.

Al·ex·an·der [ˌæligˈzɑːndə], **the Great** 亚历山大大帝〔古马其顿国王, 公元前 356—323〕.

Al·ex·an·dra [ˌæligˈzɑːndrə] *n.* 亚历山德拉〔女子名〕.

Al·ex·an·dri·a [ˌæligˈzɑːndriə] *n.* 亚历山大〔埃及港市〕.

Al·ex·an·dri·an [ˌælig'zɑːndriən] *a.* ① 亚历山大港(Alexandria) 的. ②古代亚历山大文化时期的〔指古代亚历山大地区发展的古希腊文化，亦称古希腊后期文化〕. ③(马其顿) 亚历山大大帝的. ④(诗歌) 亚历山大格式的 (= Alexandrine).

Al·ex·an·drine [ˌælig'zændrain] *n.* 亚历山大格式(的诗)，英雄体(的诗)〔指六音步十二音节为一行抑扬格式诗〕.

al·ex·an·drite [ˌælig'zɑːndrait] *n.* 变色宝石〔日光下呈深绿色,灯光下呈深红色〕.

a·lex·i·a [ə'leksiə] *n.*【医】失读症；无读字能力.

a·lex·in [ə'leksin] *n.*【医】(体液内的) 补体，杀菌素.

A·lex·is [ə'leksis] *n.* 亚历克西斯〔男子名〕.

a·lex·i·phar·mic [əˌleksi'fɑːmik] *a.* 消毒的，解毒的. — *n.* 解毒剂.

Alf. = Alfonso; Alfred.

'alf = half.

al·fal·fa [æl'fælfə] *n.*【植】紫花苜蓿.

Al Fatah [ɑːl'fɑːtɑː] 阿法塔〔巴勒斯坦人的一个战斗组织〕.

al·fil·a·ri·a, al·fil·e·ri·a [ælˌfilə'riə] *n.*【植】芹叶太阳花.

al fine [ɑːl'fiːnei]〔It.〕【乐】复唱〔奏〕到头.

Al·fon·so [æl'fɔnsəu] *n.* 阿方索〔男子名〕.

al·for·ja [æl'fɔːhə] *n.* 帆布鞍囊，皮鞍囊.

Al·fred ['ælfrid] *n.* 阿尔弗雷德〔男子名〕.

al·fres·co [æl'freskəu] *ad., a.* 在户外，户外的. *dine* ~ 吃野餐. *an* ~ *luncheon* 野餐. ★ 作副词用时常分写作 al fresco.

Alg. = ① Algeria(n). ② Algernon. ③ Algiers.

alg. = ① algebra. ② algebraical.

al·ga ['ælgə] *n.* (*pl.* **-gae** [-dʒi])【植】〔常 *pl.*〕藻；藻类.

al·gae·cide ['ældʒiːsaid] *n.* (游泳池等处用的)除藻剂.

al·gar·ro·ba, al·ga·ro·ba [ˌælgə'rəubə] *n.* ①角豆树，角豆荚. ②牧豆树，牧豆荚.

al·ge·bra ['ældʒibrə] *n.* 代数学.

al·ge·bra·ic, -i·cal [ˌældʒi'breiik(əl)] *a.* 代数的，代数学(上)的. **-i·cal·ly** *ad.* 代数学上.

al·ge·bra·ist [ˌældʒi'breiist], **al·ge·brist** ['ældʒibrist] *n.* 代数学家.

Al·ger ['ældʒə] *n.* 阿尔杰〔姓氏〕.

Al·ge·ria [æl'dʒiəriə] *n.* 阿尔及利亚〔非洲〕.

Al·ge·ri·an [æl'dʒiəriən] *a.* ①阿尔及利亚的；阿尔及利亚人的. ②阿尔及利亚语的. — *n.* ① 阿尔及利亚人. ②阿尔及利亚语.

Al·ge·rine [ˌældʒi'riːn] *a.* 阿尔及利亚的. — *n.* ①阿尔及利亚人(尤指柏柏尔人的后裔). ②〔a-〕阿尔及利亚横条纹毛呢〔薄的做头巾，厚的做帐篷〕. ③古代的北非海盗.

Al·ger·non ['ældʒənən] *n.* 阿尔杰农〔男子名〕.

-al·gi·a *suf.*〔L.〕痛: neur*algia*.

al·gid ['ældʒid] *a.* 寒冷的，打寒颤的.

al·gid·i·ty [æl'dʒiditi] *n.* 寒冷，严寒.

Al·giers [æl'dʒiəz] *n.* 阿尔及尔〔阿尔及利亚首都〕.

al·gin ['ældʒin] *n.*【化】藻朊(酸).

al·gin·ic [æl'dʒinik] *a.* ~ **acid**【化】藻朊酸.

al·goid ['ælgɔid] *a.* 藻的，藻质的.

Al·gol ['ælgɔl] *n.*【天】大陵五〔英仙座β〕.

ALGOL = ①algebraic-oriented language【计】代数排列语言. ②algorithmic language【计】算法语言.

al·go·lag·ni·a [ˌælgə'lægniə] *n.*【精】变态淫乐；性(被)虐待狂.

al·gol·o·gist [æl'gɔlədʒist] *n.* 藻类学家.

al·gol·o·gy [æl'gɔlədʒi] *n.* 藻类学.

al·gom·e·ter [æl'gɔmitə] *n.* 痛觉计. **-met·ric, -met·ri·cal** *a.* **-me·try** *n.* 痛觉测验.

Al·gon·ki·an [æl'gɔŋkiən] *a.*【地】元古代的 (= Late Precambrian).

Al·gon·quin, Al·gon·kin [æl'gɔŋkwin] *n.* 北美阿尔公金族印第安人〔语〕.

al·go·pho·bi·a [ˌælgə'fəubiə] *n.* 疼痛恐怖.

al·go·rism ['ælgərizəm] *n.* ①十进制，十进位计数法. ②算法；算术. ③阿拉伯数字系统. ***a cipher in ~*** "0"(零)；有名无实的人，傀儡.

al·go·rithm ['ælgəriðəm] *n.*【数】算法；规则系统；演段.

al·gua·zil, al·gua·cil [ˌælgwə'ziːl] *n.* (西班牙)警官.

al·gum ['ælgəm] *n.*【植】檀香树.

Al·ham·bra [æl'hæmbrə] *n.* 中古西班牙摩尔人 (Moor) 诸王的宫殿〔以装饰豪华著称〕.

Al·ham·bresque [ˌælhæm'bresk] *a.* (中古西班牙) 摩尔诸王所建宫殿式的.

a·li·as ['eiliæs, 'eiliəs] *ad.* 别名. *Smith* ~ *Simpson* 史密斯别名普逊. — *n.* 化名，别名. *go by the* ~ *Johnson* 化名约翰逊.

al·i·bi ['ælibai] *n.* (*pl.* ~**s** [-z]) ①【法】不在犯罪现场的抗辩〔事实〕. ②〔美口〕辩解，托辞. ***set up [prove] an ~*** 证明被告当时不在犯罪现场所. — *vi.*〔美口〕辩解，托词闪避. — *vt.* 为(某人)提供不在现场的证词.

al·i·ble ['ælibl] *a.* 有营养价值的.

Al·ice ['ælis] *n.* 艾丽斯〔女子名，Adelaide 的异体〕.

A·li·ci·a [ə'liʃə] *n.* 艾丽西亚〔女子名，Adelaide 的异体〕.

Alick ['ælik] *n.* 亚历克〔男子名，Alexander 的昵称〕.

al·i·cy·clic [ˌæli'saiklik] *a.*【化】脂环(族)的.

al·i·dad(e) ['ælideid] *n.* 旋标装置；测高仪；照准仪.

al·ien ['eiljən] *a.* ①外国(人)的；异已的. ②(与…)相异 *(from)*；(与…) 相反，不合 *(to)*. *an* ~ *enemy* 敌侨. ~ *friends* 友邦侨民. ***~ to the subject*** 不合题目. — *n.* 外国人；外侨；外来人. — *vt.* ①〔诗〕疏远；离间. ②【法】(所有权的)让渡，转让.

a·lien·a·bil·i·ty [ˌeiljənə'biliti] *n.* ①让渡的可能性. ②疏远的可能性.

al·ien·a·ble ['eiljənəbl] *a.* ①可让渡的. ②能疏远的.

al·ien·age ['eiljənidʒ] *n.* 外侨的法律地位.

al·ien·ate ['eiljəneit, -liən-] *vt.* ①疏远；离间，挑拨，使…不和. ②【法】让渡，转让(所有权). ③把(资金等)移作他用 *(from)*. ~ *him from his friend* 离间他和他的朋友. ~ *lands to another* 把土地转让给别人. ***~ oneself from*** 使自已脱离. ***be ~d from*** 与…不和.

al·ien·a·tion [ˌeiljə'neiʃən] *n.* ①疏远；离间. ②让渡，转让. ③精神错乱. ④【哲】异化. ~ *of affection* 爱情的转移. ~ *of mind* 精神错乱.

al·ien·a·tor ['eiljəneitə] *n.* 让渡人；离间者.

a·lien·ee [ˌeiljə'niː] *n.*【法】受让人.

al·ien·ism ['eiljənizəm] *n.* ①外侨身分. ②异国情调. ③精神病学；精神病治疗；神经错乱.

alien·ist ['eiljənist] *n.* 精神病学家，精神病医生.

al·ien·or ['eiljəˌnə] *n.* (财产)转让者.

a·lif ['ɑːlif] *n.* 阿拉伯语的第一个字母.

ali·form ['ælifɔːm] *a.* 翼状的，翅状的.

a·light[1] [ə'lait] *vi.* (~**ed**,〔罕〕**a·lit** [ə'lit]) ①降；下车〔马〕*(from)*；【空】降落；(鸟)飞落(在树上) *(on)*. ②偶然发现，碰见，遇见 *(on, upon)*. ~ *at Shanghai* 在上海下车. ***~ on one's feet*** 跳下站住；没有受伤. **-ing deck** (航空母舰上的)降落甲板.

alight[2] [ə'lait] *a.*〔常作表语〕①烧着，烧起. ②照亮，照着. ***be ~ with*** 给…烧起来〔烧着〕；给…照着 *(The room was ~ with lamps.* 房间里灯光明亮). ***get [set] ~*** 使烧着…，把…烧起来 *(get the wood ~* 把木柴点燃).

a·lign [ə'lain] *vt.* ①使排成一线〔一行〕；校直. ②使结盟，使密切合作. ③【物】匹配；调准. *He ~ed himself with the liberals.* 他与自由党人结成联盟. ~ *the television receiver* 调整电视机. — *vi.* ①成一行，成一线；校直.

②结盟,参加. *The troops* ～*ed.* 士兵们排成一行. **-er** *n.* 校准器.

a·lign·ment [əˈlainmənt] *n.* ①列队，成直线. ②校直;调整，调准. ③【工】准线. ④【政】结盟. (公路或铁路的)线路平面图. *class* ～*s* 阶级阵线.

a·like [əˈlaik] *a.* 〔常作表语〕相同，一样，相似. *The two brothers look very much* ～. 兄弟俩长得一模一样. — *ad.* 一样，相等，相似. *We think* ～. 我们想法一样. ***share and share*** ～ 等分. ***young and old*** ～ 老少一样.

al·i·ment [ˈælimənt] *n.* ①食物；滋养品. ②生活必需品. ③抚养(费). — [-ment] *vt.* ①给与…食物[养料]. ②抚养.

al·i·men·tal [ˌæliˈmentəl] *a.* 食物的，营养的；富有养分的.

al·i·men·ta·ry [ˌæliˈmentəri] *a.* ①有关食物的，有关营养的. ②富有养分的. ～ *canal* 消化管. ③给予资助的,抚养的. *an* ～ *endowment* 资助金. ～ **canal** 消化道.

al·i·men·ta·tion [ˌælimenˈteiʃən] *n.* ①供给食物；营养. ②扶养.

al·i·men·to·ther·a·py [ˌæliˈmentəuˈθerəpi] *n.* 食物疗法.

ali·mo·ny [ˈæliməni] *n.* 【法】赡养费；抚养费；生活费.

A-line [ˈeiˈlain] *a.* (服装)A 字型的，上窄下宽的.

a·line [əˈlain] = align. **-ment** = alignment.

Al·i·oth [ˈæliːɔθ] *n.* 【天】玉衡，北斗五〔大熊座 ε〕.

al·i·ped [ˈæliped] *a.* 有翼肢的. — *n.* 翼肢动物.

al·i·phat·ic [ˌæliˈfætik] *a.*【化】脂肪的，脂(肪)族的.

al·i·quant [ˈælikwənt] *a.* 【数】除不尽的. — *n.* 除不尽的数.

al·i·quot [ˈælikwɔt] *a.* 【数】除得尽的. — *n.* 除得尽的数.

Al·i·son [ˈælisn] *n.* 艾丽森〔女子名，Alice 的昵称〕.

a·lit [əˈlit] alight[1] 的过去式及过去分词.

-al·i·ty *suf.* 〔构成名词〕表示"性质": gener*ality*, speci*ality*, mor*ality*.

a·li·un·de [ˌeiliːˈʌndiː] *ad.*, *a.* 〔多置于被修饰语之后〕【法】出于别的来源地[的]，非由本文引证地[的]. *evidence* ～ 引自别处的证据.

a·live [əˈlaiv] *a.* 〔多作表语〕①活着的；活动的，活泼的，精神抖擞的. ②热闹的 *(with)*. ③注意到的，敏感的 *(to)*. ④〔口〕生满（虱子等）的. ⑤【电】通有电流的，加有电压的. *be caught* ～ 被活捉，被生擒. *the happiest man* ～ 世上最幸福的人. ～ ***and kicking*** 生气勃勃，活蹦乱跳. ***all*** ～〔口〕活蹦乱跳；精神抖擞. ***any man*** ～ 任何人. ***as sure as I am*** ～ 极确实地. ***be*** ～ ***to*** 注意，对…有敏感 (*He is* ～ *to his own interests.* 他斤斤计较自己利益). ***be*** ～ ***with*** 勃勃，洋洋，兴旺，拥挤，(热情)洋溢 (*He is* ～ *with ambition.* 他雄心勃勃. *The hive is* ～ *with bees.* 蜂房里蜜蜂闹闹嚷嚷). ***bury*** ～ 活埋. ***come*** ～ 活跃起来；觉悟起来；显得象真的一样. ***Heart*** ～***!*** 什么！哎呀！〔强烈的感叹句〕. ***keep*** ～ 使活着，把(鱼)养着；让(火)烧着；使继续下去 (*keep old memories* ～ 永志不忘). ***Look*** ～***!*** 〔口〕赶快！加油！***Man*** ～***!*** = ***Sakes*** ～***!*** = ***Heart*** ～***!*** ***skin*** ～ 活活剥去…的皮；〔口〕严厉谴责；〔口〕彻底击败.

a·li·yah [ˌɑːliːˈjɑː] *n.* 〔Hebr.〕犹太人往以色列移民.

a·liz·a·rin(e) [əˈlizərin] *n.* 茜(草色)素，茜草红.

alk. = alkali.

al·ka·hest [ˈælkəhest] *n.* 〔古〕(炼金术师探求的) 万能溶剂.

al·ka·les·cence [ˌælkəˈlesns] *n.* 微碱性.

al·ka·les·cent [ˌælkəˈlesnt] *a.* 微碱性的.

al·ka·li [ˈælkəlai] *n.* *(pl.* ～*(e)s)*【化】碱；强碱. ～ **blue** 碱性蓝. ～ **metals** 碱金属. ～ **rock** 【矿】碱性(火成)岩. ～ **soil** 碱土.

al·kal·ic [ælˈkælik] *a.* 【地】①碱性的；强碱性的. ②(岩石)含大量钠和钾盐的.

al·ka·li·fy [ˈælkælifai] *vt.* 使碱化；给…加碱.

al·ka·lim·e·ter [ˌælkəˈlimitə] *n.* 碱量计；碳酸定量计.

al·ka·line [ˈælkəlain] *a.* 碱的，含碱的，碱性的；强碱的. — *n.* 碱性. ～ **earth**【化】碱土. ～ **soil** 含碱土壤. ～ **reaction**【化】碱性反应.

al·ka·line-earth metals [ˈælkəlinˈəːθ, -lain- ˈmetlz]【化】碱土金属.

al·ka·lin·i·ty [ˌælkəˈliniti] *n.* 碱性，碱度.

al·ka·lin·ize [ˈælkəliˌnaiz] *vt.* 使碱化. **-i·za·tion** *n.*

al·ka·lize [ˈælkəˌlaiz] *vt.* 碱化. **-li·za·tion** *n.*

al·ka·loid [ˈælkəlɔid] *a.* 碱的，碱一样的，含碱的. — *n.* 生物碱，植物盐基.

al·ka·loid·al [ˌælkəˈlɔidəl] *a.* 生物碱的.

al·ka·lo·sis [ˌælkəˈləusis] *n.* 碱中毒.

al·kane [ˈælkein] *n.* 【化】链烷，烷(属)烃.

al·ka·net [ˈælkənet] *n.* 【植】朱草；朱草染料.

al·kene [ˈælkiːn] *n.*【化】链烯，烯烃.

al·kine [ˈælkain] *n.* = alkyne.

Al·ko·ran [ælkɔˈrɑːn, -ˈræn] *n.* (伊斯兰教的) 古兰经 (= Koran).

al·ky [ˈælki] *n.* 〔美俚〕酒精.

al·kyd [ˈælkid] *n.* 醇酸树脂.

al·kyl [ˈælkil] *n.* 【化】烷基；烃基 (= alkyl radical). **-lic** *a.*

al·ky·la·tion [ˌælkiˈleiʃ(ə)n] *n.* 烷基取代，烷化. **-late** [-ˌleit] *n.*, *vt.*

al·kyne [ˈælkain] *n.* 【化】炔.

all [ɔːl] *a.* ①所有的，全部的，整个的，一切的. ②非常的，极度的，尽可能的. ③〔口〕用尽，用完. ～ *night* 终夜，一夜. ～ *place* 处处，到处. ～ *one's life* 终生，毕生. ～ *round* 周围. ～ *the world over* 世界各地. ～ *the year (round)* 一年到头. *He is* ～ *eyes.* 他只是看. *She is* ～ *smiles.* 她只管笑. *What is* ～ *this noise?* 这么吵嚷究竟是怎么回事？*The storm raged in* ～ *its fury.* 暴风雨猛烈极了. *Life is not* ～ *pleasure.* 生活不光是享乐. *The bread is* ～. 面包吃完了. *All men cannot be masters.* = *We cannot* ～ *be masters.* 并非人人都能当头头. ***All Fools' Day*** 愚人节〔4月1日〕. ～ ***fours*** ①(兽的)四足，(人的)手足. ②一种纸牌玩法 (*go [run] on* ～ *fours* 爬着走. *be on* ～ *fours with* 〔英方〕与…相一致［吻合］). ***All Hallows*** 〔古〕= ***All Saints' Day.*** ～ ***hours*** 有便的时候；深夜. ～ ***jolly fine*** 极好的，极漂亮的. ～ ***kind(s) of*** 种种. ***All Saints' Day*** 万圣节. ～ ***sort(s) of*** 种种. ～ ***the go[mode, rage]*** 〔美〕非常流行. ～ ***the world and his wife*** 〔谑〕谁都，人人都. ～ ***things to*** ～ ***men*** 八面玲珑. ～ ***this*** 这一切. ～ ***wool and a yard wide*** 〔美〕顶好的；真的；靠得住的. ***and*** ～ ***that*** 及其他各物，…等等. ***at*** ～ ***events*** 总之. ***at*** ～ ***times*** 时时. ***by*** ～ ***means*** 一定. ***for*** ～ 虽有［无论］…仍然 (*For* ～ *you say, I still like him.* 虽然你说了这一番话，我还是喜欢他). ***for*** ～ ***that*** = ***for all.*** ***in*** ～ ***directions*** 四面八方. ***in*** ～ ***its splendour [glory]*** 荣耀之极，趾高气扬. ***of*** ～ 有的是… (*Why go to Norway, of* ～ *countries?* 有的是国家，为什么偏要去挪威呢？) ***not*** ～ 不一定都 (*Not* ～ *men are wise.* 人不一定都聪明). ***with*** ～ = ***for*** ～. ***with*** ～ ***speed*** 尽快，赶快. — *n.*, *pro.* 全部；全体；一切. *All are agreed.* 全体赞成. *All is still.* 万籁俱寂. *He lost his* ～. 他已倾家荡产. *He's* ～ *we got to go on.* 他是我们探寻的唯一线索. *That is* ～ *that there is to it.* 不过如此. *That's* ～. 就只这些，没有了，只此而已. ～ ***in*** ～ ①完全 (*trust me not at* ～, *or* ～ *in* ～. 毫不信任我或完全信任我). ②全部，一切. ③最心爱的，第一 (*Study is* ～ *in* ～ *to me.* 在我是学习第一). ***All is lost [over]*** 已无望，全完了. ***A- is not gold that glitters.*** 发光的东西并不都是金子. ～ ***of*** … 全体，大家，一齐，都，各自；〔美〕足足，整整 (～ *of 100 dollars* 整整一百元). ～ ***of a doodah***

[ˈduːdə]〔美俚〕兴奋，神经过敏． ***All's well*** 都好了． ***All's well that ends well.***〔谚〕结果好就一切都好． **~ *told*** 合计，总计． ***above ~*** 尤其，最，最主要的． ***and ~*** 及其他一切；等等；连…都 (*He ate it, bone and ~.* 他连骨头都吃掉了)． ***at ~*** 全然；既然，究竟 (*No danger at ~.* 毫无危险． *Do you know at ~?* 你究竟知不知道？ *If you do it at ~, do it well.* 既做就得好好地做． *very little, if any at ~* 就是有也很有限)． ***after ~*** 终归，到底． ***be ~ one*** 全是一样；怎么都好 (*to*)． ***for ~ I care*** 与我何干． ***for ~ I know*** 也未可知． ***for good and ~*** 永远． ***in ~*** 总计． ***not at ~*** 毫不，毫无 (*He is not at ~ stupid.* 他一点不傻． *Oh, not at ~.* 啊，一点也不． *Thank you so much. — Not at ~.* 多谢多谢．— 不谢不谢)． ***once for ~*** 只此一次；断然． ***one and ~*** = ***~ and sundry*** 全都，尽都，无论谁都． ***That's ~.*** 没有了，完了；全有了． ***when ~ comes to ~***〔古〕结果． ***when ~ is said (and done)*** 毕竟，到底，终于． — *ad.* ①完全，全然，都；〔口〕极；简直． ②〔诗〕正当，正在． ③【体】各，彼此． **~** *as the day began to break* 正当破晓时． *The score is two ~.* 比赛成绩彼此两分． *love ~* 彼此零分． **~ *alone*** 仅仅一个人；独力． **~ *along*** 始终，一直都；一路，沿途． **~ *around*** 遍处；一一． **~ *at once*** 突然． **~ *but*** 简直是，几乎跟…一样 (*He is ~ but dead.* 他简直是死人[行尸走肉])． **~ *gone***〔口〕完了，没有了． **~ *in*** 疲倦极了 (*I'm ~ in.* 我疲倦极了)． **~ *out*** 竭尽全力 (*go ~ out* 全力以赴)． **~ *over*** ①遍身；〔美〕到处，处处． ②全完了 (*The meeting was ~ over.* 会开完了)． ③〔口〕完全，完全象 (*He is his father ~ over.* 他完全象他父亲)． **~ *over with*** 全完了，不行了 (*It is ~ over with him.* 他完全完了[无希望了])． **~ *quiet*** 十分平静，无问题． **~ *ready*** 一切就绪． **~ *right***〔俚〕不错；好，行；没关系，没有什么 (*All right!* 可以可以！ 晓得了；好！〔反〕好！ 看！ *All right! You shall repent this.* 好！ 以后不要懊悔)． **~ *square***〔美俚〕①付清款项，完成应做的工作． ②（运动）比分拉平． **~ *the better [more]*** 反而更（好），却更． **~ *the farther***〔美俚〕尽…所有，尽…所能 (*That is ~ the farther I got.* 那是尽我所有了)． **~ *the same*** 依然． **~ *there*** 头脑清醒 (*He is not ~ there.* 他头脑不清)． **~ *too*** 总是太，过． **~ *too often*** 再三再四． **~ *too soon*** 总是太早． **~ *up* (*with*)** 全完了[无望、失败]． **~ *very fine [well]***〔口、反〕很好，顶好 (~ *very well, but …* 固然很好，但是…)． **~ *wet***〔美俚〕完全弄错． **All-American** *n., a.* 全美代表选手；全美（国）的． **~-around** *a.*〔美〕= all-round. **~ clear** 解除警报． **~-fired** *a., ad.* 非常的（地） (*Don't be so ~-fired sure of yourself.* 不要过分自信)． **~-important** *a.* 最重要的，重大的． **~-in** *a.*〔英〕①包含全部的 (*an ~-in 10-day tour* 包括一切的十日游)． ②竭尽全力的 (*an ~-in effort* 全力以赴)． ③【摔交】自由式的，无限制的． **~-inclusive** *a.* 包括一切的． **~-in-one**（妇女胸罩和腰带连在一起的）紧身胸衣． **~-mains** *a.*（收音机等）适应各种电压的〔仅作表语〕． **~-night** *a.* 通宵的，整夜营业的． **~-or-none** *a.* 全有或没有的． **~-or-nothing**〔*a.* 获得一切或一无所有的，不全则无的，孤注一掷的．〕**~-out** *a.*〔俚〕全力的；全面的；彻底的 (*an ~-out conflict* 全面战争． *an ~-out effort* 全力以赴． *an ~-out reform* 彻底改革)． **~ over** ① *a.* 全，满． ② *n.* 全花织物． **~-overish** *a.*〔俚〕浑身难过的；说不出地不舒服的 (*feel ~-overish* 觉得不舒服)． **~-possessed**〔美俚〕着了魔的，入了迷的 (*like ~-possessed* 仿佛中了邪)． **~-powerful** *a.* 全能的，力量无限的． **~-purpose** *a.* 通用的，可作各种用途的． **~-red [All-Red]** *a.*（航线等）在全英国的，英联邦范围内的． **~-round** *a.* 广博的，多方面的；万能的，多才多艺的 (*an ~-round athlete* 全能运动选手． *~-round education* 圆满的教育． *an ~-round magazine* 综合杂志． *an ~-round price* 各费在内的价钱)． **~-rounder** 多面手；全能运动员． **~seed** 多种子植物． **~-sided** *a.* 全面的． **~spice**【植】多香果． **~-star** *a.* 名角全体的 (*an ~-star cast [team]* 名角会演，一流选手［队］)． **~-time** *a.* 一时不闲的；专职的，全时工作的；空前的 (*an ~-time record* 空前的纪录)． **~-up weight** 空中总重量［包括飞机和机载客货在内］． **~-way** *a.*（飞机场）具有各向跑道的． **~ways fuze** 不论落地角度如何均可引爆的炸弹触爆雷管)． **~-weather** *a.* 全天候的；任何天候皆能应用[适应]的． **~-year** *a.* 全年的．

Al·lah [ˈælə, ˈælɑː] *n.*（伊斯兰教的）真主． **~ *is* ~.** 真主之外无真主．

Al·lan [ˈælən] *n.* 阿伦〔男子名，Alan 的异体〕．

al·lan·to·ic [ˌælənˈtəuik] *a.* 尿囊的；有尿囊的．

al·lan·toid [əˈlæntɔid] *a.* 尿囊的；尿囊状的；腊肠状的．

al·lan·to·in [æˈlæntɔin] *n.* 尿囊素．

al·lan·to·is [æˈlæntəuis] *n.*【解】尿囊．

al·lar·gan·do [ˌɑːllɑːˈgɑːndəu] *a., ad.*【乐】渐慢和渐强．

al·lay [əˈlei] *vt.* 减轻，压（惊），止（渴），消（痛），解（忧）．

al·lée [əˈlei] *n.*〔林荫〕小径．

al·le·ga·tion [ˌæliˈgeiʃən] *n.* 断言，主张；陈述，辩解．

al·lege [əˈledʒ] *vt.* ①断言，宣称． ②提出… 作为理由． *It is ~d that …* 据说．

al·leg·ed [əˈledʒd] *a.* ①被提出而尚未证实的；有嫌疑的． ②声称的，宣称的． ③作为理由[辩解等]的． *the ~ thief* 嫌疑盗窃犯． *the ~ reason* 举出来的理由．

al·le·giance [əˈliːdʒəns] *n.* ①忠诚，归顺，忠心 (*opp.* treason)． ②（封建）臣道，忠节． *in ~ to science* 献身科学．

al·le·gor·ic, -i·cal [ˌæliˈgɔrik, -ikəl] *a.* 比喻的，寓言的． **-i·cal·ly** *ad.*

al·le·go·rist [ˈæligərist] *n.* 讽喻家，寓言作者．

al·le·go·rize [ˈæligəraiz] *vt.* 用比喻讽喻的方式说；以讽喻的含义解释． — *vi.* 作寓言；使用讽寓．

al·le·go·ry [ˈæligəri] *n.* 比喻；寓言；象征．

al·le·gret·to [ˌæliˈgretəu] *ad.*〔It.〕【乐】稍快，稍急． — *n.* 小快板．

al·le·gro [əˈleigrəu] *ad.*〔It.〕【乐】轻快地，活泼地． — *n., a.* 快板（的）．

al·lel(e) [əˈliːl], **al·lelo·morph** [əˈliːləmɔːf] *n.*【遗】等位基因．

al·le·lu·ia [ˌæliˈluːjə] *n., int.* = hallelujah.

al·le·mande [ˌæliˈmɑːnd] *n.* ①阿列曼达舞〔德国十六—十八世纪的一种舞蹈〕． ②阿列曼达舞曲． ③方形舞的一个舞姿．

Al·len [ˈælin, ˈælən] *n.* 阿伦〔姓氏，男子名〕．

Al·len·by [ˈælənbi] *n.* 阿伦比〔姓氏〕．

al·ler·gen [ˈælədʒən], **-gin** [-dʒin] *n.*【医】变应素，变应原，过敏原［如药物、食物、花粉等］．

al·ler·gic [əˈləːdʒik] *a.* ①过敏症的，变（态反）应性的． ②〔俚〕神经过敏的，敏感的；憎恶的． *an ~ reaction to wool* 对羊毛的过敏反应． *~ to studying* 不喜欢念书．

al·ler·gist [ˈælədʒist] *n.* 治疗过敏症专家，变态反应症专家．

al·ler·gy [ˈælədʒi] *n.* ①【医】变（态反）应性，过敏． ②憎恶，反感． *have an ~ to hard work* 厌恶做辛苦的工作，好逸恶劳．

al·le·thrin [ˈæliθrin] *n.* 丙烯拟除虫菊酯．

al·le·vi·ate [əˈliːvieit] *vt.* 减轻（痛苦等），缓和（愁苦等）．

al·le·vi·a·tion [əˌliːviˈeiʃən] *n.* ①减轻，缓和． ②起缓和作用的东西，解痛物，慰藉物．

al·le·vi·a·tive [əˈliːviətiv], **-to·ry** [-təri] *a.* 减轻的，缓和的，解痛的，解忧的．

al·le·vi·a·tor [əˈliːvieitə] *n.* 减轻者，安慰者，缓和物，解痛品．

al·ley [ˈæli] *n.* ①小街，小巷，胡同，弄堂． ②公园[庭园]中的小径． ③【网球】双打时球场两边留出的空地． *an ~ off Fleet Str.* 从弗利特街分出的小巷． *a blind ~* 死巷，死胡同；无发展前途的职业. ***down [up] one's ~*** 〔俚〕拿手，专长. ~ **way** *n.* 〔美〕窄街，通道.
alley-oop [ˌæliˈuːp] *int.* 杭育〔劳动呼声[号子]〕.
All·fa·ther [ˈɔːlˈfɑːðə] *n.* 神，上帝.
all hail [ˈɔːlˈheil] 〔古〕身体好；〔招呼语〕.
All·hal·low·mas [ˈɔːlˈhæləuməs] = All hallows.
All·hal·low·tide [ˌɔlˈhæləutaid] *n.* 〔古〕万圣节日.
al·li·a·ceous [ˌæliˈeiʃəs] *a.* ①葱属的，葱的，韭的，大蒜的. ②有葱味[蒜味等]的.
al·li·ance [əˈlaiəns] *n.* ①同盟，联盟. ②联姻. ③同盟条约. ④同盟者. ⑤近似，共同点. ⑥【植】群落属. *a dual [triple, quadruple]* ~ 二国[三国、四国]同盟. *an offensive and defensive* ~ 攻守同盟. *worker-peasant* ~ 工农联盟. ***enter into [form an]* ~ *with*** 与…联盟[结盟]. ***in* ~ *with*** 与…联合.
al·li·cin [ˈælisin] *n.* 蒜素.
al·lied [əˈlaid, ˈælaid] *a.* ①同盟的，同盟国的. ②姻亲的. ③同源的；类似的. ④[A-]（第一次世界大战中）协约国的；（第二次世界大战中）同盟国的. *the A- and Associated Powers*（第一次世界大战的）协约国. *the A-Military Government*（第二次世界大战中的）联合国军政府〔略 AMG〕.
Al·lies [ˈælaiz, əˈlaiz] *n.* 〔*pl.*〕①（第一次世界大战的）协约国. ②（第二次世界大战的）同盟国.
al·li·ga·tor [ˈæligeitə] *n.* ①短鼻鳄鱼. ②鳄皮. ③水陆两用平底军用车. ④鳄式碎石机. ⑤摇摆舞音乐爱好者. ~ **bait** 〔美口〕鳄饵；难吃之物. ~ **ring** 齿环. ~ **tortoise** 甲鱼，水鱼，团鱼. ~ **wrench** 鳄式扳手.
al·lit·er·ate [əˈlitəreit] *vi.* ①押头韵 *(with)*. ②用头韵体作诗. — *vt.* 使成头韵体.
al·lit·er·a·tion [əˌlitəˈreiʃən] *n.* 头韵(法).
al·lit·er·a·tive [əˈlitərətiv] *a.* 头韵法的，头韵体的.
al·li·um [ˈæliəm] *n.* 葱属植物.
al·lo [ˈæləu] *a.* 紧密相联的；【化】同分异构的.
allo- *comb. f.* 异，他: *allonym, allomorph.*
al·lo·cate [ˈæləukeit] *vt.* ①分派，配给. ②配置；部署. ③划拨(经费等). ~ *funds for housing* 拨款盖房子. ~ *sb. to a certain duty* 派某人担任某任务.
al·lo·ca·tion [ˌæləuˈkeiʃən] *n.* ①(原料等的)分配，配给. ②配给物，配给量. ③定位置，部署. ④【会】(经费、收入等的)分配法. ***be under* ~** 作为配售品. ***put on* ~** 实行配销.
al·lo·chro·ic [ˌæləˈkrəuik] *a.* 【医】变色的.
al·loch·tho·nous [əˈlɔkθənəs] *a.* 外来的；非本土的.
al·lo·cu·tion [ˌæləuˈkjuːʃən] *n.* (罗马教皇、将军等的)训谕，面谕.
al·lod [ˈælɔd] *n.* 封建地产，自主地产.
al·lo·di·al [əˈləudjəl] *a.* 自主地产的.
al·lo·di·um [əˈləudjəm] *n.* (*pl.* **-dia** [-diə])【法】(封建时代的)自主地产.
al·log·a·my [əˈlɔgəmi] *n.* 【植】异花受粉；【动】异体受精.
al·lom·er·ism [əˈlɔmərizm] *n.* 【化】异质同晶(现象).
al·lom·e·try [əˈlɔmitri] *n.* 【生】体形变异(学).
al·lo·morph [ˈæləmɔːf] *n.* ①【矿】同质异晶. ②【语】同词素的异形词. **-ic** [ˌæləˈmɔːfik], **-ous** [ˌæləˈmɔːfəs] *a.* **-ism** [ˌæləˈmɔːfizəm] *n.* 同质异晶(现象).
al·lo·nym [ˈælənim] *n.* ①(著作者假托的)别名、假名. ②假托伪名的著作.
al·lo·path, al·lop·a·thist [ˈæləupæθ, æˈlɔpəθist] *n.* 对抗疗法医师. **-path·ic** [-ˈpæθik] *a.*
al·lop·a·thy [æˈlɔpəθi] *n.* 对抗疗法(说).
al·lo·pat·ric [ˌæləˈpætrik] *a.* 【生】在各区生长的；分布区不重迭的；孤立地发生的. **-cal·ly** *ad.* **-lop·a·try** *n.*
al·lo·phane [ˈæləfein] *n.* 【矿】水铝英石.
al·lo·phone [ˈæləfəun] *n.* 【语音】音素的变形. *The relatively short (æ) of mat and the relatively long (æ) of mad are ~s.* 单词 mat 中较短的 æ 和单词 mad 中较长的 æ 是音素的变形.
al·lo·plasm [ˈæləplæzm] *n.* 【生】异质. **-plas·mic** [ˌæləˈplæzmik], **-plas·mat·ic** [ˌæləplæzˈmætik] *a.*
al·lo·pol·y·ploi·dy [ˌæləˈpɔliˌplɔidi] *n.* 【生】异源多倍性. **-poly·ploid** [-ˌplɔid] *n., a.* 异源多倍体(的).
al·lo·sau·rus [ˌæləˈsɔːrəs] *n.* 侏罗纪的恐龙.
al·lot [əˈlɔt] *vt.* ①分配，摊派给，发给；把…拨给 *(to)*. ②指定[拨出](款项等)作某种用途 *(for)*. ③规定，派定. ~ *the profits* 分配红利. ~ *shares* 分摊股分. ~ *money for a school* 拨款办学. *Each speaker is ~ted five minutes.* 每个发言人规定发言五分钟. ***~ upon ...*** 〔美俚〕打算，正想.
al·lo·the·ism [ˈæləθiːizəm] *n.* 异神崇拜；异神教.
al·lot·ment [əˈlɔtmənt] *n.* ①分配，分派；份额. ②〔英〕(划成小块出租的)副业生产地. ③【美军】从工资中扣除的费用(如扣除亲属赡养费，人寿保险费). ④命运，天命.
al·lo·trope [ˈælətrəup] *n.* 【化】同素异形体.
al·lo·trop·ic, al·lo·trop·i·cal [ˌæləˈtrɔpik, -ikəl] *a.* 【化】同素异形的. **-i·cal·ly** *ad.*
al·lot·ro·pism [əˈlɔtrəpizəm], **al·lot·ro·py** [əˈlɔtrəpi] *n.* 【化】同素异形(现象)，同素异性(作用).
all' ot·ta·va [ˌɑːləˈtɑːvə; It. ˌɑːlloˈttɑːvɑː] 【乐】高或低八度演奏.
al·lot·tee [ˌəlɔˈtiː] *n.* 接受配给的人.
al·low [əˈlau] *vt.* ①准许(做某事)，许可(某现象存在). ②容许，听任，任，由，允许，让(某人做某事)〔接不定式〕. ③承认(某事) *(that)*；承认(某人如何)〔接不定式〕. ④给予…以，让…得到. ⑤沉溺，放纵〔用反身代词〕. ⑥酌量；酌情增[减]. ⑦〔美口〕想要〔接不定式〕. ⑧(由于不小心而)让(某事)得以发生. *Allow me to introduce to you my friend Johnson.* 请允许我把我的朋友约翰逊介绍给您. ~ *a free passage* 准许自由通行. *Dogs are not ~ed in the park.* 不许带狗进入公园. *No smoking (~ed).* 禁止吸烟. *We ~ that we are wrong.* 我们承认自己错了. *They all ~ him to be a good football player.* 他们都承认他是一位优秀足球运动员. ~ *three percent of our profits for tear and wear* 少算百分之三的利润作为损耗费. ~ *a bread to burn* (不小心)让面包烤焦. — *vi.* ①承认 *(of)*. ②容许 *(of)*. ③原谅，体谅；考虑到，酌量 *(for)*. ④为…酌留余地，以防 *(for)*. *The question ~s of no dispute.* 问题无争论余地. ~ *of sb's authority* 承认某人的权威. *We must ~ for his youth.* 我们得体谅他年轻. ~ *for the circumstances* 考虑到具体情况. ***~ oneself in*** 耽溺. ***~ing that*** 即令是…也〔仍〕.
al·low·a·ble [əˈlau-əbl] *a.* 可容许的，可承认的，不碍事的，正当的. *Two mistakes are ~ in this game.* 这种游戏允许犯规两次. **-bly** *ad.*
al·low·ance [əˈlau-əns] *n.* ①允给物，给与额，津贴，补助. ②【机】(加工)留量；配合公差. ③斟酌，酌量；预留；容差；【商】折扣. ④默许，默认；承认. ⑤【体】给对方的让步. *an ~ of rice* 给予一份大米. *a clothing [traveling] ~* 服装[旅]费. *short ~* 给予量不足. *a time ~* (给对方的)时间的宽限. *By your ~ I'd like to leave before you.* 对不起，我要先走了. ***at no ~*** 无限制，尽性 (*plunder at no ~* 大肆掠夺). ***make ~ for*** ①留有余地；斟酌，酌量，估量. ②原谅，体谅. ③扣除 (*make an ~ of 10% for cash payment* 现款九折). — *vt.* ①给…发津贴. ②按定量供给.
al·low·ed·ly [əˈlauidli] *ad.* ①被许可. ②当然，肯定.
al·loy [ˈælɔi] *n.* ①合金，齐. ②(合金中的)劣等金属. ③(金银的)成色，成份. ④〔喻〕掺杂品. *Brass is an ~ of copper and zinc.* 黄铜是铜和锌的合金. *pleasure without ~* 玩得痛快. — [əˈlɔi] *vt.* ①合铸，熔合(金属). ②在…中搀以杂质；使(金属)减低成色. ③减损(兴趣

等). — *vi*. 熔合,掺. ~ **steel** 合金钢,特种钢.

all·spice [ˈɔːlˌspais] *n*. 牙买加胡椒.

al·lude [əˈljuːd] *vi*. 暗指,暗示;(婉转)提到;指…说 *(to)*. *Were you alluding to me?* 是指我说吗?

al·lure [əˈljuə] *vt*. 引诱,勾引,诱惑. *Rewards ~ men to brave danger.* 重赏之下必有勇夫. *~**d by hopes*** 被希望引诱着. ~ *(sb.)* ***from*** 诱使(某人)离开…. ~ *(sb.)* ***into [to]*** 把(某人)诱进,骗入. — *n*. 诱惑力,魅力.

al·lure·ment [əˈljuəmənt] *n*. 引诱,诱惑;诱惑力,诱惑物.

al·lur·ing [əˈljuəriŋ] *a*. 诱惑的,迷人的,引人的,媚人的. *Circuses are ~ both to children and to adults.* 马戏既吸引小孩,也吸引大人. **-ly** *ad*. 诱人地,妩媚地.

al·lu·sion [əˈljuːʒən] *n*. 暗示,暗指,提及,引喻. ***in ~ to*** 暗指. ***make ~ to*** 提及.

al·lu·sive [əˈljuːsiv] *a*. ①暗指的. ②(文章、谈话等)多用典故的,引喻的. *a story ~ to her history* 影射她的身世的故事.

al·lu·vi·al [əˈljuːvjəl] *a*.【地】冲积的. ~ *deposits* 冲积物. ~ *gold* 沙金. —*n*. 冲积土[层,矿床],淤积土.

al·lu·vi·on [əˈljuːvjən] *n*. ①波浪的冲击. ②泛滥,洪水. ③【法】(冲积造成的)土地增加. ④沙滩,沙洲,冲积地;冲积物.

al·lu·vi·um [əˈljuːvjəm] *n*. (*pl*. ***~s, -vi·a*** [-viə])【地】冲积层;冲积土.

Al·ly [ˈæli] *n*. 艾丽〔女子名,Alice 的昵称〕.

al·ly[1] [əˈlai, æˈlai] *vt., vi*. (使)结盟;(使)联姻. ~ ***oneself with [to]*** 与…结盟[联合];与…联姻. ***be allied to*** 类似,与…是同类. — [ˈælai,əˈlai] *n*. ①同盟者,同盟国. ②伙伴;助手. ③同类的动植物. *the Allies* ①(第一次世界大战中的)协约国. ②(第二次世界大战中的)同盟国.

al·l(e)y[2] [ˈæli] *n*. 弹球〔游戏用〕.

al·lyl [ˈælil] *n*.【化】烯丙基.

alm [ælm] *n*. 捐赠,施舍.

Al·ma [ˈælmə] *n*. 阿尔玛〔女子名〕.

Al·ma-A·ta [ˈɑːlməˈɑːtə] *n*. 阿拉木图〔苏联城市〕.

al·ma(h) [ˈælmə] *n*. 埃及舞女.

Al·ma·gest [ˈælmədʒest] *n*. ①天文学大成〔公元二世纪时普托勒密作的天文学数学名著〕. ②〔a-〕(中古时代)占星学书;点金术书.

Al·ma Ma·ter [ˈælmə ˈmeitə]〔L.〕①母校. ②〔美〕校歌.

al·ma·nac [ˈɔːlmənæk] *n*. 历书,日历,月份牌;年鉴.

alman·dine [ˈælməndain], **al·man·dite** [ˈælməndait] *n*.【矿】铁铝榴石,贵榴石.

al·might·i·ness [ɔːlˈmaitinis] *n*. 全能.

al·might·y [ɔːlˈmaiti] *a*. ①全能的. ②〔口〕非常的,无比的,可怕的. — *ad*. 非常;…得够呛[要命]. *It's ~ hot.* 热得要命. ***A- God*** = ***God A-*** = ***the A-*** 全能之神. *in an ~ fix* 处境万分狼狈.

al·mond [ˈɑːmənd] *n*. ①巴旦杏,扁桃;杏仁. ②〔古〕扁桃腺. ~ ***oil*** 杏仁油. ***~-eyed*** *a*. 杏眼的.

al·mon·er [ˈɑːmənə] *n*. ①救济品分发员,施赈人员. ②〔英〕医院的社会服务员.

al·mon·ry [ˈɑːmənri] *n*. 救济品分发处,施赈所.

al·most [ˈɔːlməust, ˈɔːlməst] *ad*. 差不多,几乎,将近,快要. *It's ~ two o'clocks now.* 现在快两点了. ~ *never [no, nothing]*〔美〕难得,几乎从不[没有]. — *a*.〔罕〕近似的. *his ~ impudence* 他的近似无礼的态度.

alms [ɑːmz] *n*.〔*sing., pl*.〕①施舍. ②施舍物,救济品. *ask for ~* 募捐. ~ **deed** 乐善好施的行为. **~giver** 慈善家,施主. **~giving** 施舍,赈济. **~house** 济贫院. **~man** 受救济的人.

al·mu·can·tar [ˌælmjuːˈkæntə] *n*.【天】(地)平纬圈,高度方位仪.

al·muce [ˈælmjuːs] *n*. 皮兜帽〔原为牧师帽〕.

al·mug [ˈælməg] *n*. = algum.

al·ni·co [ˈælnikəu] *n*.【冶】铝镍钴合金.

al·od [ˈælɔd] *n*. (封建时代的)自主地产,自由地产.

a·lo·di·um [əˈləudiəm] *n*. 封建地产,自主地产. **a·lo·di·al** *a*.

al·oe [ˈæləu] *n*. ①【植】芦荟;沉香,茄楠香. ②〔*pl*.〕芦荟油〔泻药〕. ③〔美〕龙舌兰〔亦作 American ~〕. **~swood** [-zwud] 伽罗木,沉香.

A·lo·fi [əˈlɔfi] *n*. 阿洛菲〔纽埃岛(新)首府〕.

a·loft [əˈlɔft] *ad*. ①高高地;在上面. ②在空中. ③【海】桅上,桅杆高处,帆索高处. *be sent ~ to bed* 被打发上楼睡觉. *climb ~* 爬到桅杆高处. ***go ~***〔俚〕升天,死.

a·lo·ha [əˈləuə, ɑːˈləuhɑː, əˈləuə] *int*.〔Haw.〕阿洛哈〔问候或告别时用语〕. ~ **shirt** 夏威夷式的运动衫. **A-State** 美国夏威夷州的别名.

al·o·in [ˈæləuin] *n*.【化】芦荟素.

a·lone [əˈləun] *ad*. ①单独地;独自;孤独地. ②〔用在名词或代词后,起限定的作用〕只,只有;仅仅. *He walked on ~ to the book store.* 他一个人走着到书店去. *She ~ can speak French.* 只有她会讲法语. — *a*.〔用作表语〕单独的;独一无二的. *I want to be ~.* 我愿意一个人生活. *I am not ~ in this opinion.* 不单是我意见这样. *He was all ~.* 他只一个人. ***leave ~*** 不要管,不要动 *(Leave my book ~.* 不要动我的书). ***let ~*** ①听,由,任随 (*Let me ~ to do it.* 由我做吧). ②莫说…(连) *(I know the whole tune, let ~ the words.* 莫说歌词,连整个歌曲我都知道的. *let-alone policy* 放任政策). ***let well enough ~*** 满足于现状. ***not ~ ... but*** 不仅…又.

a·long [əˈlɔŋ] *ad*. ①成一行地,纵长地;沿,循. ②一块儿,一道(去). ③上前,在前. ④〔美口〕(时间)晚,一直到,过去. ⑤在手头. *All the cars parked ~ by the station.* 所有的汽车都沿着车站停放成一行. *Come ~.* 跟我来. *walk ~* 向前走. *~ toward evening* 一直到傍晚. *The afternoon was well ~.* 下午又快过去[快完]了. ***all ~*** ①始终;一直;一贯. ②从左到右;从上到下. ~ ***about*** 大约在 (*~ about two o'clock* 接近两点钟时). ~ ***back***〔美口〕刚才,近来. ***(all) ~ of***〔俚〕因,由于. ~ ***with*** 与…一道;以外 (*~ with other advantages* 其他利益以外). ***be ~***〔俚〕来到;赶上 (*He will be ~ soon.* 他一会儿就来). ***Get [Go] ~!***〔俚〕向前走,走开. ***get ~*** ①生活,过日子. ②上年纪 ***get ~ with*** (工作)进行,进步. ***right ~***〔口〕不停,不断,一直,始终. — *prep*. 沿着. *The road runs ~ the river.* 公路与河并行. **~-shore** ①*ad., a*. 沿海,沿岸. ②*n*. 岸;码头.

a·long·side [əˈlɔŋˈsaid] *ad*. 在…的侧面;与…并排. *The two ships lay ~ of each other.* 两条船并排靠着. *sit ~ of sb.* 和某人并肩坐着. — *prep*. 横靠,傍着. *The ship lies ~ the pier.* 船横靠着码头停泊.

a·loof [əˈluːf] *ad*. ①离开,避开,隔开. ②【海】向上风方向. ***keep [hold, stand] ~ (from)*** 离开(…);对(…)敬而远之. ***stand ~ over*** 对…采取超然态度. — *a*. 〔多作表语〕①冷淡的. ②孤零零的. *an ~ church* 一座孤零零的教堂. *The girl's manner was ~.* 姑娘的态度是冷淡的. **-ness** *n*.【医】超然,冷淡.

al·o·pe·ci·a [ˌæləuˈpiːsiə] *n*. 脱发(症).

a·lors [æˈlɔː] *int*.〔F.〕那么;那就〔一般化的口头语〕.

a·loud [əˈlaud] *ad*. 高声,响亮. *shout ~* 大叫. **It reeks ~.**〔俚〕臭极了. **think ~** 自言自语.

a·low [əˈləu] *ad*. 向下,在下;在船内. *~ and aloft* 上上下下都;无处不.

A.L.P. = American Labor Party 美国劳工党.

alp [ælp] *n*. ①高山,高峰. ②(阿尔卑斯)山地牧场. ***~s on ~s*** 重重高山;重重难关.

al·pac·a [ælˈpækə] *n*. ①【动】(南美)羊驼. ②羊驼毛;羊驼呢.

al·pen·glow [ˈælpingləu] *n*. (高山上见到的)早霞,晚霞.

al·pen·horn ['ælpinhɔ:n] *n.* (瑞士阿尔卑斯牧民用的)长柄木号角.
al·pen·stock ['ælpinstɔk] *n.* 登山杖.
al·pes·trine [æl'pestrin] *a.* ①阿尔卑斯山脉和山区的. ②【植】生长于亚高山区的.
al·pha ['ælfə] *n.* ①阿尔法[希腊语字母表首字母 α, 相当于英语的 a]. ②最初. ③【天】α 星, 主星. ~ ***and omega*** 首尾, 始终; 全体. ~ **plus** 最高级的, 最好的. ~ **decay**【原】α 衰变. ~ **rays**【物】α 射线. ~**rhythm** ***[wave]*** 脑中每秒钟约十下的波动. ~**scope** 计算机屏幕显示器.
al·pha·bet ['ælfəbit] *n.* ①字母表. ②初步. *a phonetic* ~ 音标文字. *the* ~ *of law* 法学入门.
al·pha·bet·ic, -i·cal [ˌælfə'betik(əl)] *a.* ABC 的, 字母的; 照字母表次序的. *in* ~ *order* 按照字母顺序. **-i·cal·ly** *ad.* 用字母表, 照字母次序.
al·pha·bet·ize ['ælfəbitaiz] *vt.* ①照字母表次序排列. ②用字母标记, 使拼音化.
al·pha·nu·mer·ic [ˌælfənju:'merik] *a.* 字母数字式的.
al·pha·tron ['ælfətrɔn] *n.*【空】α 粒子电离压强计.
Al·phon·so [æl'fɔnzəu] *n.* 阿方索[男子名].
alp·horn ['ælphɔ:n] *n.* 长柄木号角 (= alpenhorn).
al·pho·sis [æl'fəusis] *n.* 白化症状.
al·pine ['ælpain] *a.* ①高山(性)的. ②[A-]阿尔卑斯山的; 阿尔卑斯山区居民的. — *n.* ①高山植物. ②高山型的白种人[不同于地中海型和北欧型的白种人]. ~ **club** 登山俱乐部. ~ **garden** 奇石园. ~ **hat** 登山帽. ~ **light** 紫外线. ~ **plants** 高山植物.
al·pin·ism ['ælpinizm] *n.* 登山.
al·pin·ist ['ælpinist] *n.* [常 A-]登山运动员, 登山家.
Alps [ælps] *n.* [the ~]阿尔卑斯山脉.
al·read·y [ɔ:l'redi] *ad.* ①[表示现在或过去某时发生的事实]已经, 早已. ②[问句或否定句中表示惊愕、意外时]还(没有吗?), 已经…(吗?). *I have* ~ *met him.* 我已经同他会面了. *When we came in, we found they had* ~ *arrived.* 我们来时, 发现他们已经到了. *Have you finished supper* ~? 吃完晚饭了吗? *You haven't* ~ *done your washing, have you?* 你的衣服还没有洗完吗?
al·right [ɔ:l'rait] *ad.* [俚] = all right.
a.l.s. = autograph letter signed 亲笔签署的信.
Al·sace ['ælsæs] *n.* 阿尔萨斯[法国一地区].
Al·sa·tia [æl'seiʃjə] *n.* ①法国 Alsace 地区的旧名. ②阿尔塞西区[伦敦市中央的一区, 昔为债务人和罪犯的藏匿地]. ③[喻]避难所.
al·sike (clover) ['ɔ:lsaik (klauvə)] *n.*【植】杂三叶草.
Al Si·rat [ˌælsi'rɑ:t] ①《古兰经》的真谛. ②【穆斯林】(架于地狱火上)通向天堂的窄桥.
Al·sop(p) ['ɔ:lsəp] *n.* 奥尔索普[姓氏].
al·so ['ɔ:lsəu] *ad.* 亦, 也, 同样; [口]而且, 还. *Tom has been to Canada. Harry has* ~ *been to Canada.* 汤姆去过加拿大, 哈里也去过. ★在口语中, 多用 *as well* 或 *too*; 在否定句中, 则用 *either*. — *conj.* = and. *She was noble,* ~ *beautiful.* 她很高尚, 而且长得美. ***not only … but*** ~ … 不但…并且…. ~**-ran** *n.* ①【赛马】落选的马. ②(比赛、竞争、竞选等的)失败者. ③无足轻重的人.
alt [ælt] *n., a.*【乐】中高音(的). ***in*** ~ ①高音的. ②[俚]得意洋洋, 趾高气扬.
alt. = alternate; altitude.
Al·ta ['æltə] *n.* 阿尔塔[女子名].
Al·tai [æl'teiai] *n.* [the ~] 阿尔泰山.
Al·tai·an [æl'teiən] *a., n.* 阿尔泰山 (Altai) 的(人).
Al·ta·ic [æl'teiik] *a.* ①阿尔泰山脉的; 阿尔泰山人的. ②阿尔泰语系的. — *n.* 阿尔泰语系[包括突厥语, 蒙语和通古斯语].
Al·ta·ir [æl'tεə] *n.*【天】河鼓二, 牛郎星.
al·tar ['ɔ:ltə] *n.* ①祭坛; 圣餐台; 圣坛. ②(干船坞的)台阶. ***lead (a woman) to the*** ~ 娶(某女), 与(某女)结婚. ~ **boy** 祭坛小厮, 祭坛侍者. ~ **cloth** 祭坛罩. ~ **piece** 祭坛背后的绘画[雕刻, 屏风].
alt·az·i·muth [ælt'æzimәθ] *n.*【天】(地平)经纬仪.
al·ter ['ɔ:ltə] *vt.* ①变更; 改变, 改换; 改建(房屋), 改做(衣服). ②[美方]阉割, 给(雄性动物)去势, 给(雌性动物)割去卵巢. — *vi.* 变, 改; (人)变老. ~ ***for the better [worse]*** 改好[坏], 变好[坏]. **-a·bil·i·ty** 可变性. *n.* **-a·ble** *a.* 可改变的. **-a·bly** *ad.*
al·ter·ant ['ɔ:ltərənt] *a.* 引起变化的. — *n.* 引起变化的东西; 变质[色]剂.
al·ter·a·tion [ˌɔ:ltə'reiʃən] *n.* ①变更, 改变, 变化. ②【地】蚀变. ③[美方]阉割.
al·ter·a·tive ['ɔ:ltərətiv] *a.* ①引起改变的. ②【医】增强体质的. — *n.*【医】体质改变药; 体质改变疗法.
al·ter·cate ['ɔ:ltə:keit] *vi.* 争辩; 口角, 吵嘴. ~ *with sb. about a trifle* 与某人因细故口角.
al·ter·ca·tion [ˌɔ:ltə:'keiʃən] *n.* 争辩, 吵嘴, 口角.
al·ter e·go ['æltər 'egəu] [L.] ①他我, 另一个我; 个性中的另一面. ②心腹朋友, 知己.
al·ter·nant [ɔ:l'tə:nənt] *a.* ①交替的, 互换的. ②【地】(砂与泥等的)互隔层的. — *n.*【数】交替函数.
al·ter·nate [ɔ:l'tə:nit] *a.* ①交替的, 轮流的. ②隔一的, 间隔的. ③备用的, 补充的; 预备的, 候补的. ④【植】交错的, 互生的. ⑤[美俚]副, 代理的. *an* ~ *member of the committee* 候补委员. ~ *angles*【数】(一对)错角. ~ *hope and fear* 一喜一忧. ~ *layout* 另一方案. ~ *leaves*【植】互生叶. ***each*** ~ ***day*** 每隔一日. ***in*** ~ ***lines*** 隔一行. ***on*** ~ ***days*** 隔日. — *n.* ①替换物. ②[美](委员)代理人. *delegates and* ~*s* 代表们和代理人们. — ['ɔ:ltə:neit] *vt.* ①使交替, 使轮流. *The sentries* ~*d their watch.* 哨兵轮流站岗. *He* ~*s joy with grief.* 他时喜时忧. — *vi.* ①交替, 轮流. ②【电】交流. ~ *between joy and grief* 悲喜交集. *alternating current*【电】交流(电流). **alternating personality**【心】多重人格. *alterating series*【数】交错级数. *alternating temperature* 变温.
al·ter·na·tion [ˌɔ:ltə:'neiʃən] *n.* ①交替, 更迭, 变换; 间隔. ②【数】错列. ③【植】交错. ④【农】轮种. *the* ~ *of crops* 作物的轮种. *the* ~ *of the seasons* 四季的循环. ~ ***of generations***【生】世代交替.
al·ter·na·tive [ɔ:l'tə:nətiv] *a.* 随便一个的, 二中择一的, 交替的. ~ *conjunctions* 选择连接词 (如: *or, nor*). ~ *courses* (或死或降的)两条路. *an* ~ *question* 选择疑问句(如: Is the baby a boy or a girl?) — *n.* 二者之一, 二中选一; 交替; 可采用的方法; 替换物. *That's the only* ~. 那是唯一可取的办法. *There are three* ~*s.* 如上[如下]三者任择其一. *There is no other* ~. 别无他法. *The* ~*s are death and submission* 或死或降, 任选其一. ***no*** ~ ***but*** … 除…外别无他法(无可奈何, 只好…). **-ly** *ad.* 二中择一地; 替换着.
al·ter·na·tor ['ɔ:ltə(:)neitə] *n.* 交流发电机. *a radio frequency* ~ 射频振荡器; 高频发生器.
al·th(a)e·a [æl'θi:ə] *n.*【植】①蜀葵属. ②木槿(= rose of sharon).
al·tho [ɔ:l'ðəu] *conj.* [美] = although.
alt·horn ['æltho:n] *n.*【乐】中音萨克号.
al·though [ɔ:l'ðəu] *conj.* 尽管, 虽然[引导让步状语从句, 主句中不用 but, 可用yet]. *A- I believe it, yet I must consider.* 我虽然相信, 但还要考虑一下. *A- many difficulties and obstacles are still ahead, nevertheless, we are certain to make still greater achievements.* 尽管在前进道路上还存在着许多困难和障碍, 但是, 我们一定能够取得更加伟大的成就.
al·ti·graph ['æltigrɑ:f] *n.* 高度自记仪, 高度记录器; 气压计.
al·tim·e·ter ['æltimi:tə] *n.* 测高计, 高度表.
al·tim·e·try [æl'timitri] *n.* 高度测量术.

al·ti·tude [ˈæltitjuːd] *n.* ①高，高度；海拔(高度)．②【天】地平纬度．③〔常 *pl.*〕高处．④高位，高等．⑤【数】顶垂线，高线．*the ceiling* ～ 升限．*high [low]* ～【空】高[低]空．*(an)* ～ *sickness* 高空病．*grabbing for* ～ (空战中) 抢占高度；〔喻〕渐渐发怒．*In these* ～*s, snow never melts.* 在这么高的地方，积雪终年不化．～ **flight** 高空飞行．

al·to [ˈæltəu] *n.* 〔It.〕①【乐】男声最高音；中高音，女低音．②中提琴 (= viola)．③唱男声最高音[中高音，女低音]的歌手．

al·to·cu·mu·lus [ˈæltəuˈkjuːmjuləs] (*pl.* ***al·to·cu·mu·li*** [ˈæltəuˈkjuːmjulai]) *n.* 【气】高积云〔略 Ac〕．

al·to·geth·er [ˌɔːltəˈgeðə] *ad.* ①全然，全，完全．②一共．③总之．*not* ～ *wrong* 不完全错．*He wrote six books* ～．他一共写了六本书．*A-, it's a great success* 总的说来是巨大的成功．**taken** ～ 总而言之．— *n.* 〔口〕〔the ～〕裸体．**in the** ～〔口〕赤身露体．

Al·ton [ˈɔːltən] *n.* 奥尔顿〔姓氏，男子名〕．

al·to-re·lie·vo [ˈæltəuriˈliːvəu] *n.* 高凸浮雕〔*cf.* basso-relievo〕．

al·to-ri·lie·vo [ˈɑːltɔːriˈljevɔː] *n.* (*pl.* ***alti-rilievi*** [ˈɑːltiriˈljɛvi]) 〔It.〕= alto-relievo.

al·to·stra·tus [ˈæltəuˈstreitəs] *n.*【气】高层云〔略 As〕．

al·tri·cial [ælˈtriʃəl] *a.* 守窠的，守雏的〔指某些幼鸟出生时眼盲，需双亲照料〕．

al·tru·ism [ˈæltruizəm] *n.* 利他主义，爱他主义．

al·tru·ist [ˈæltruist] *n.* 利他主义者，爱他主义者．

al·tru·is·tic [ˌæltruˈistik] *a.* 利他的，利他主义的．**-ti·cal·ly** *ad.*

al·u·del [ˈæljudel] *n.* 【化】梨状升华器〔回收升华物时使用的陶制或玻璃制的梨状器皿，使用时打开上下口并按次序接上管子的插口〕．

al·u·la [ˈæljulə] *n.* (*pl.* ***-lae*** [-liː]) ①【动】角翼，小翼．②(昆虫的)翼膜，翅瓣．

al·um[1] [ˈæləm] *n.* 明矾．*basic [cubic]* ～ 明矾石．

a·lum[2] [əˈlʌm] *n.* 〔口〕校友 (= alumnus 或 alumna)．

a·lu·mi·na [əˈljuːminə] *n.* 【化】矾土，铝氧土．

a·lu·mi·nate [əˈluːmineit] *n.* 铝酸盐．

a·lu·mi·ni·fer·ous [əˌljuːmiˈnifərəs] *a.* 含铝的；含铝土的；含矾的．

a·lu·min·ium [ˌæljuˈminjəm] *n.* 【化】铝．～ **acetate** 醋酸铝．～ **bronze** 铝铜，矾铜．～ **foil** 铝箔．～**ware** 铝制厨房用具，铝制器皿．

a·lu·mi·nize [əˈluːminaiz] *vt.* 给…镀铝；在…涂铝；对…进行铝处理．

a·lu·mi·no·ther·my [əˈluːminəuˌθəːmi] *n.* 铝热(法)．

a·lu·mi·nous [əˈljuːminəs] *a.* ①明矾的，含明矾的．②矾土的，含矾土的．③铝的，含铝的．

a·lu·mi·num [əˈljuːminəm] *n.* 〔美〕= aluminium.

a·lum·na [əˈlʌmnə] *n.* (*pl.* ***-nae*** [-niː]) 〔L.〕女毕业生；女校友．

a·lum·nus [əˈlʌmnəs] *n.* (*pl.* ***-ni*** [-nai]) 〔L.〕男毕业生，男校友．*an alumni association* 〔美〕校友会，同学会 (= old boys' association)．

al·um·root [ˈæləmruːt] *n.* 【植】矾根草〔虎耳草属〕．

A·lun·dum [əˈlʌndəm] *n.* ①【商标】钢铝石，钢玉石，人造磨石．②〔a-〕铝氧粉．

al·u·nite [ˈæljunait] *n.* 明矾石．

Al·va [ˈælvə] *n.* 阿尔瓦〔男子名，女子名〕．

alve·o·lar [ælˈviələ, ˌælviˈəulə] *a.* ①【解】齿槽的．②【解】肺泡的，气泡的．③【语音】齿龈的．— *n.* 【语音】齿龈音 (如 t, d, s 等)．

alve·o·late [ælˈviəlit] *a.* ①蜂窝状的，有小窝的；【动】具有气泡的．

alve·o·lus [ælˈviələs] *n.* (*pl.* ***-li*** [-lai]) ①蜂窝；小窝．②【解】齿槽．③【解】肺泡，【动】气泡．

Al·vin [ˈælvin] *n.* 阿尔文〔男子名〕．

al·vine [ˈælvain] *a.* ①小肠的；肠的．②腹部的．

al·way [ˈɔːlwei] *ad.* 〔古、诗〕= always.

al·ways [ˈɔːlwəz, ˈɔːlweiz] *ad.* ①永远，始终．②经常，老是，总是，一直．③不断地．*She is* ～ *busy.* 她总是忙．*You must* ～ *bear this in mind.* 这一点你要经常记在心里．*Near,* ～ *near, he came.* 他一步步走过来，愈来愈近了．***almost*** ～ 通常．**not** ～ 未必，不一定．

a·lys·sum [əˈlisʌm] *n.* 【植】庭芥属植物．*sweet* ～ 香雪球．

AM = amplitude modulation 调辐．

Am 【化】元素镅 (amercium) 的符号．

Am. = ①America. ②American. ③Ammunition.

am = ①ampere-meter. ②ammeter.

a.m. = 〔L〕*anno mundi* (= in the year of the world)．

A.M. = ①*Artium Magister* 文学硕士 (= Master of Arts)．

a.m., A.M. [ˈeiˈem] ①=〔L.〕ante meridiem 午前，上午 (= before noon)．②由午夜至中午．★此词常为小写，但在时间表中或作标题时则为大写．*from 8 to 10 a.m.* 上午 8 时至 10 时．

am [强 æm; 弱 əm] be 的第一人称、单数、直陈式、现在时．

Am·a·bel [ˈæməbel] *n.* 阿玛贝尔〔女子名〕．

am·a·da·vat [ˌæmədəˈvæt] *n.* 【动】莓莺〔印度的一种观赏鸣禽〕．

am·a·dou [ˈæmæduː] *n.* (止血和引火用的) 火绒〔取自树上菌类的一种海绵状物质〕．

a·mah [ˈɑːmə] *n.* (东方国家的) 保姆，女仆，阿妈．

a·main [əˈmein] *ad.* 〔古、诗〕①全力地．②全速地．③突然地，急忙地．④非常地．

a·mal·gam [əˈmælgəm] *n.* ①【冶】汞合金，汞齐．②混合物．

a·mal·gam·a·ble [əˈmælgəməbl] *a.* 可汞合的；可汞齐化的．

a·mal·ga·mate [əˈmælgəmeit] *vt., vi.* ①【冶】使 (金属) 与水银混合，使(金属)汞齐化．②混合；合并；融合．～*d union* 联合工会．

a·mal·ga·ma·tion [əˌmælgəˈmeiʃən] *n.* ①【冶】汞合，汞齐化．②混，合并．③〔美〕(种族等的) 融合．**-tive** *a.*

a·mal·ga·mat·or [əˈmælgəmeitə] *n.* ①混汞机．②混合物；合并者．③【冶】(混汞) 提金器．

A·man·da [əˈmændə] *n.* 阿曼达〔女子名〕．

am·a·ni·ta [ˌæməˈnaitə] *n.* 【植】蛤蟆菌属菌类．

a·man·u·en·sis [əˌmænjuˈensis] *n.* (*pl.* ***-ses*** [-siːz]) 抄写员，听写员，秘书．

am·a·ranth [ˈæməræn θ] *n.* ①(传说中的) 不凋花．②【植】苋；〔A-〕苋属．③苋菜红，深紫红．

am·a·ran·thine [ˌæməˈrænθain] *a.* ①不凋的．②似苋的．③深紫红的．

am·a·relle [ˌæməˈrel] *n.* 酸樱桃．

Am·a·ryl·lis [ˌæməˈrilis] *n.* ①〔诗〕女牧羊人．②孤挺花属；〔a-〕孤挺花．

a·mass [əˈmæs] *vt.* 积累，积聚；收集．～ *great fortunes* 发大财．— *vi.* 集合．**-er** *n.* 积聚者．

a·mass·ment [əˈmæsmənt] *n.* 积聚，积累，收集．

am·a·teur [ˈæmətə(ː), ˈæmətjuə] *a.* 爱好…的，业余的．*an* ～ *performance* 游艺会．*an* ～ *dramatic club* 业余剧社．— *n.* 业余者，爱好者 (*opp.* professional)．*an* ～ *in boxing* 业余拳击爱好者．*a radio* ～ 业余无线电爱好者．

am·a·teur·ish [ˌæməˈtəːriʃ, -ˈtjuər-] *a.* ①业余的．②不熟练的．

am·a·teur·ism [ˈæmətəːrizəm, -tjuər-] *n.* 业余活动，业余性质[方式、身分、技艺]．

am·a·tive [ˈæmətiv] *a.* 恋爱的；色情的．

am·a·tol [ˈæmətɔl] *n.* 硝铵、三硝基甲苯炸药，阿马图炸药．

am·a·to·ri·al [ˌæməˈtɔːriəl], **am·a·to·ry** [ˈæmətəri] *a.* 恋爱的；色情的. ～ *poems* 情诗.
am·au·ro·sis [ˌæmɔːˈrəusis] *n.* 【医】黑内障，黑矇，青光瞎. **-rot·ic** [-ˈrɔtik] *a.*
a·maze [əˈmeiz] *vt.* 使惊奇，使吃惊. ***be ～d at [by]*** 对…大为惊异. ***be ～ to see [hear, find]*** 看到[听到，发现]…大为吃惊. — *n.* [诗] = amazement.
a·mazed·ly [əˈmeizidli] *ad.* 愕然.
a·maze·ment [əˈmeizmənt] *n.* 惊奇，诧异，惊异. ***be filled with ～*** 大为惊异. ***in ～*** 骇然. ***to sb.'s ～*** 使某人惊异的是….
a·maz·ing [əˈmeiziŋ] *a.* 令人惊异的. **-ly** *ad.* 可惊地，非常.
Am·a·zon¹ [ˈæməzən] *n.* [the ～] [南美] 亚马孙河.
Am·a·zon² [ˈæməzən] *n.* ①【希神】亚马孙族女战士. ②[a-]女战士. ③[a-] 彪形妇女. ④[a-]中美和南美产的绿色小鹦鹉. ⑤[a-]【动】悍蚁[这种蚂蚁奴役其他的蚂蚁]. ⑥[a-] 亚马孙毛呢.
A·ma·zo·nas [ˌæməˈzəunəs] *n.* 亚马孙[巴西州名].
Am·a·zo·ni·an¹ [ˌæməˈzəunjən] *a.* [南美]亚马逊河流域的. — *n.* 亚马逊河区的印第安人.
Am·a·zo·ni·an² [ˌæməˈzəunjən] *a.* ①亚马孙族女战士一样的. ②[常 a-] 刚勇的（女人）.
am·a·zon·ite [ˈæməzənait] *n.*【矿】天河石，微斜长石.
am·bag·es [æmˈbeidʒiːz] *n.* [古] [*pl.*] ①迂回的道路. ②转弯抹角的说法[做法]. ③诡秘行为.
am·ba·gious [æmˈbeidʒəs] *a.* [古] 迂回曲折的. ～ *reasoning* 迂回曲折的推理.
am·ba·ri, -ry [æmˈbɑːri] *n.* ①洋麻，槿麻. ②洋麻[槿麻]纤维(= kenaf).
am·bas·sa·dor [æmˈbæsədə] *n.* ①大使；使节. ②专使，特使. ③代表. *an ～-at-large* 巡回大使，无任所大使. *an ～ extraordinary* 特派大使. *A tourist abroad can be an ～ of good-will for his country.* 国外旅游者可以做本国的亲善代表. *an ～ plenipotentiary* 全权大使. ***The ～ to the court of St. James's*** 驻英大使.
am·bas·sa·do·ri·al [æmˌbæsəˈdɔːriəl] *a.* 大使的. *an ～-level meeting* 大使级会议.
am·bas·sa·dress [æmˈbæsədris] *n.* 女大使；大使夫人.
am·ber [ˈæmbə] *n.* ①琥珀. ②琥珀色. ③【军】线状无烟火药(弹). — *a.* ①琥珀制的. ②琥珀色的. — *vt.* 使成琥珀色.
am·ber·gris [ˈæmbəgri(ː)s] *n.* 龙涎香.
am·ber·jack [ˈæmbədʒæk] *n.* 【鱼】①环带鰤. ②杜氏鰤. ③长背鰤.
Am·ber·ite [ˈæmbərait] *n.* 琥珀炸弹[一种无烟炸药.]
Am·ber·lite [ˈæmbəlait] 安珀莱特[离子交换树脂的商标名称]；[a-] 离子交换树脂.
am·ber·oid [ˈæmbərɔid] *n.* 人造琥珀；安伯罗合成琥珀.
am·bi- *comb.f.* 表示"二"，"二者"：*ambi*dextrous.
am·bi·ance [ˈæmbiəns] *n.* 环境；气氛 (=ambience).
am·bi·dex·ter [ˈæmbiˈdekstə] *n.* ①两只手都很灵巧的人. ②两面讨好的人，怀二心的人. — *a.* ①两只手都很灵巧的. ②有二心的，口是心非的，表里不同的.
am·bi·dex·trous [ˈæmbiˈdekstrəs] *a.* ①两只手都很灵巧的. ②表里不同的，怀有二心的. ③非常熟练的. *A- tennis players are rare.* 能用左右手打网球的人很少.
am·bi·ence [ˈæmbiəns] *n.* = ambiance.
am·bi·ent [ˈæmbiənt] *a.* 包围着的；周围的. ～ *temperature* 室温.
am·bi·gu·i·ty [ˌæmbiˈgjuːiti] *n.* ①可作两种或多种解释；含糊；意义不明确. ②模棱两可的话，含糊的话.
am·big·u·ous [æmˈbigjuəs] *a.* ①有两种或多种意思的. ②含糊的，不明确的. *an ～ answer* 模棱两可的答复. *an ～ future* 前途未卜. ～ **case**【数】歧例. **-ly** *ad.* 含糊地. **-ness** *n.* 含糊.
am·bi·sin·is·ter [ˌæmbiˈsinistə] *a.* 两只手都很笨拙的.
am·bi·syl·lab·ic [ˌæmbisiˈlæbik] *a.* (辅音)与前后元音都有关系的[如 cynic 中的 n].
am·bit [ˈæmbit] *n.* 界限；范围；周围.
am·bi·tend·en·cy [ˌæmbiˈtendənsi] *n.* 【心】自我矛盾倾向.
am·bi·tion [æmˈbiʃən] *n.* ①抱负，志气，雄心. ②野心，奢望. ③[俚]锐气，精力. *Until all is over ～ never dies.* 不到黄河心不死. *burns with an ～* 野心勃勃. *the height of one's ～* 最高志向. — *vt.* 热望，想望得到.
am·bi·tious [æmˈbiʃəs] *a.* ①野心勃勃的，有雄心的，抱负不凡的；心怀奢望的. ②热望的. ③炫耀的，矫饰的. ***be ～ of*** 热望着，渴望着. *an ～ style* 矫饰的文体. **-ly** *ad.* **-ness** *n.*
am·biv·a·lence [ˈæmbiˈveiləns] *n.* (对同一人、物、事的)矛盾心理(如又爱又憎).
am·biv·a·lent [ˈæmbiˈveilənt] *a.* (对人或事务) 有矛盾感情的. — *n.* 两性人. **-ly** *ad.*
am·bi·ver·sion [ˌæmbiˈvəːʃən] *n.*【心】中向性格.
am·bi·vert [ˈæmbivəːt] *n.* 【心】具有合乎内向和外向之间性格的人；具有中向性格的人.
am·ble [ˈæmbl] *n.* ①(马的)慢步，溜蹄. ②(人的)漫步，缓步. — *vi.* (马)溜花蹄；(人)慢慢走.
am·blyg·o·nite [æmˈbligənait] *n.*【矿】磷铝石.
am·bly·o·pi·a [ˌæmbliˈəupiə] *n.* 【医】弱视，视力不足. **-op·ic** *a.*
am·bo [ˈæmbəu] *n.* (*pl.* ***～s, ～nes*** [-ˈbəuniːz]) (早期教堂的)读经台，讲道台.
am·bo·cep·tor [ˈæmbəˌseptə, -bəu-] *n.*【微】介体.
Am·boi·na (wood) [æmˈbɔinə] 青龙木，蔷薇木，黄柏木[产于亚洲，为家具用材].
am·broid [ˈæmbrɔid] *n.* = amberoid.
Am·brose [ˈæmbrəuz] *n.* 安布罗斯[男子名].
am·bro·sia [æmˈbrəuzjə] *n.* ①【希、罗神】 神仙的食物. ②美味芳香的食品 [饮料]. ③蜜蜂的食料. ～ **beetle** 粉蠹虫.
am·bro·sial [æmˈbrəuzjəl], **am·bro·sian** [-zjən] *a.* ①上天诸神食用的. ②美味的. ③芬芳的. ④美妙的.
am·bro·type [ˈæmbrətaip] *n.* (老式的)玻璃版照相.
am·bry [ˈæmbri] *n.* ①[古]橱柜，壁橱；神器柜；食品柜. ②教堂内的壁龛.
ambs·ace [ˈeimzeis] *n.* ①(骰子的)双幺，最低的点数. ②厄运，倒霉. ③最无价值的东西，最不重要的东西. ***within ～ of*** [古]快要，濒于，差点儿… (= within an ace of).
am·bu·la·crum [ˌæmbjuˈleikrəm] *n.* (*pl.* ***-cra*** [-krə]) 【动】(昆虫的)步行足；步带. **-la·cral** *a.*
am·bu·lance [ˈæmbjuləns] *n.* ①野战医院. ②救护车[船、飞机]，红十字车. ③(旧时美国西部)旅客乘坐的旅行车. ～ **chaser [lawyer]** [美俚](交通)事故律师[指鼓动(交通)事故受害者起诉要求赔偿的律师]. ～ **corps** 野战卫生队. ～**man** 救护车[船、飞机]上的救护人员.
am·bu·lant [ˈæmbjulənt] *a.* ①走动的，移动的. ②【医】能走动的，不卧床的. *an ～ radio station* 流动电台. *an ～ blacksmith* 走街串巷的铁匠.
am·bu·late [ˈæmbjuleit] *vi.* 步行，走动，移动. *The patient was allowed to ～ in his room.* 病人被允许在屋里走动. **-tion** *n.*
am·bu·la·to·ry [ˈæmbjulətəri] *a.* ①步行的，(适于)走动的. ②流动的. ③【医】= ambulant. ④【法】可变更的，未确定的. *an ～ court* 流动法庭. *an ～ will* 可变更的遗嘱. — *n.* (有顶的)回廊，走廊.
am·bu·let [ˈæmbjulit] *n.* (长途)救护车.
am·bur·y [ˈæmbəri] *n.* ①(牛马的)软瘤. ②【植】根肿病(= anbury).
am·bus·cade [ˌæmbəsˈkeid] *n.* ①伏击. ②埋伏地点. ③伏兵. — *vt.* 伏击. — *vi.* 打埋伏.

am•bush ['æmbuʃ] *n.* 伏击；埋伏(处)；伏兵. ***fall into an*** ~ 中埋伏. ***lay [make] an*** ~ ***(for)*** 打埋伏，埋伏着等…；设置伏兵. ***lie [hide] in*** ~ 打埋伏，埋伏着等. — *vt.* ①自埋伏处出击. ②伏(兵)于(隐处等)*(in)*. *We were* ~*ed.* 我们遭到伏击. ~ *troops in the woods* 设伏兵于林中. — *vi.* 设置伏兵；埋伏；伏击. **-ment** *n.*

a•me•ba [ə'mi:bə], **a•me•boid** [-bɔid] *n.* = amoeba, amoeboid.

am•e•bi•a•sis [ˌæmi'baiəsis] *n.* 变形虫病，内变形虫病.

a•me•bo•cyte [ə'mi:bəˌsait] *n.* 变形细胞 (= amoebocyte).

âme dam•née [ɑm dɑ:'nei] *n.* 〔F.〕 (*pl.* ***âmes damnées***) 甘心当工具的人；奴才.

a•meer [ə'miə] *n.* (伊斯兰教国家的)亲王，贵族；司令官；元首 = amir, emir. **-ate** *n.* = amirate, emirate.

A•me•lia [ə'mi:ljə] *n.* 阿米莉亚〔女子名〕.

a•mel•io•rant [ə'mi:ljərənt] *n.* 起改良作用的东西；土壤改良剂.

a•mel•io•rate [ə'mi:ljəreit] *vt.* 改善，改良. ~ *housing conditions* 改善住房条件. — *vi.* 改良，变好. *The situation has* ~*ed.* 情况好转. **-tion** *n.* **-tive** *a.* **-tor** *n.* 改良者，改良物.

A•men ['ɑ:mən] *n.* (古埃及的)太阳神〔生命与生殖之神〕.

a•men ['ɑ:'men, 'ei'men] *int.* 阿门〔= So be it. 但愿如此，基督教祈祷结尾语〕. — *n.* 〔美口〕认可，批准(的表示). ***give one's [say]*** ~ ***to*** 核准. —*vt.* 〔美口〕①批准，核准. ②完成. ~ ['ei-] **corner** 〔美〕教堂前座〔领着说阿门的人的座位〕. ~ **seat** 〔美〕教堂前座的座位.

a•me•na•ble [ə'mi:nəbl] *a.* ①有服从义务的，应服从(法律等)的. ②可依照的；顺从的，肯听话的，(人)服理的. ③经得起检验的，可以由…处理的*(to)*. *a person easily* ~ *to flattery* 易为谗言所动的人，耳朵软的人. *be* ~ *to law* 服从(法律)，*be* ~ *to reason* 讲(理)；通达(情理). *He is* ~ *to counsel.* 他这人听劝. *an* ~ *servant* 俯首贴耳的奴仆. *These data are*~ *to checking.* 这些资料经得起检查. **-bil•i•ty** [əˌmi:nə'biliti] *n.* **-ness** *n.* **-bly** *ad.*

a•mend [ə'mend] *vt.* ①订正，改正，修正(议案等). ②改变(行为等). — *vi.* 改良；改过. *an* ~*ed bill* 修正案. ~ *one's ways* 改过自新. **-able** *a.* **-er** *n.* 订正者，改正者，修正者.

a•mend•a•ble [ə'mendəbl] *a.* 能改正的.

a•mend•a•to•ry [ə'mendətəri] *a.* 〔美〕改正的；修正的；矫正的，纠正的.

a•mende [æ'mɑ̃:nd; F. amɑ̃:d] *n.* 〔F.〕罚款；道歉；赔偿. ~ ***honorable*** [〔F.〕 amɑ:ŋ dɔ:nɔ:'rabl] 正式道歉，赔偿.

a•mend•ment [ə'mendmənt] *n.* ①改善，改进. ②改正，修正. ③修正草案，修正建议. ④改良土壤的物质(如石灰). *propose [move] an* ~ 提修改建议.

a•mends [ə'mendz] *n.* ①赔偿；赎罪. ②〔古〕(健康的)恢复，复元. ***make*** ~ ***(for)*** 赔偿(损失)；道歉；赎罪. ★原为复数形，现作单数用.

A•men•ho•tep [ˌɑ:mən'həutep] 阿孟和蒂〔公元前十六至十四世纪古埃及四法老中的任何一个〕.

a•men•i•ty [ə'mi:niti] *n.* ①(环境、房屋等的)适意，舒适，快感. ②优雅，温厚. ③〔*pl.*〕愉快，快事，乐事；(社交上令人愉快的)举止，礼仪. *amenities of home life* 家庭乐趣. *an exchange of amenities* 相互问好，寒暄.

a•men•or•rhe•a, a•men•or•rhoe•a [eiˌmenə'ri:ə] *n.* 月经不调，经闭.

A•men-Ra ['ɑ:mən'rɑ:] 古埃及太阳神 (= Amon-Re)

a men•sa et tho•ro [ei 'mensei et 'θɔ:rəu] 〔L.〕【法】夫妻未解除婚约但不共寝食的分居(关系).

am•ent[1] ['æmənt] *n.*【植】葇荑花序.

a•ment[2] ['eimənt] *n.* 〔英〕智力欠缺的人；呆子，白痴.

am•en•ta•ceous [ˌæmən'teiʃəs] *a.* 葇荑花的，葇荑花状的，象葇荑花的.

a•men•tia [ei'menʃiə] *n.*【医】智力缺陷，精神错乱.

am•en•tif•er•ous [ˌæmən'tifərəs] *a.*【植】柔荑花的；柔荑花序的.

a•merce [ə'mə:s] *vt.* ①对罚款. ②惩罚. ~ *the crimial in the sum of eighty dollors* 对该犯课以罚金八十元. ~ *sb. of a month's salary* 罚某人扣薪一个月. **-ment** *n.* 罚金，罚款.

a•mer•ci•a•ble [ə'mə:siəbl] *a.* 应罚款的.

A•mer•i•ca [ə'merikə] *n.* ①美洲. ②美国. ③〔*pl.*〕南北美洲，西半球. *North [South]* ~ 北〔南〕美洲. *Central* ~ 中美洲. *Latin* ~ 拉丁美洲. *the United States of* ~ 美利坚合众国〔略作 U.S.A.〕.

A•mer•i•can [ə'merikən] *a.* ①美洲的. ②美国的. *an* ~ *citizen* 美国公民. *Amazon and other* ~ *rivers* 亚马逊河和美洲的其他河流. — *n.* ①美洲人；美国人. ②美国英语. ③美洲印第安人. ~ **Beauty**【植】美国月月红. ~ **cheese** = cheddar. ~ **cloth [leather]** (做桌布用的) 漆布. ~ **crawl** 自由式游泳法. ~ **English** 美国英语. ~ **Indians** 美洲印第安人. ~ **organ** 小风琴. ~ **plan** (旅馆的)供膳制〔不供膳的叫 European plan〕. ~ **Revolution** 美国独立战争.

A•mer•i•ca•na [əˌmeri'kɑ:nə] *n.* 〔*pl.*〕美国志书；有关美国〔美洲〕的史料〔文物〕.

A•mer•i•can•ese [əˌmerikə'ni:z] *n.* 〔贬〕美国英语.

A•mer•i•can•ism [ə'merikənizəm] *n.* ①美国英语，美国腔；美国语法. ②美国派，美式；美国习惯〔想法〕. ③崇尚美国，效忠美国.

A•mer•i•can•ist [ə'merikənist] *n.* ①美国〔美洲〕事务〔史地等〕的研究者〔生〕. ②研究美洲印第安人及其文化的人类学者. ③亲美国者.

A•mer•i•can•i•za•tion [əˌmerikənai'zeiʃən] *n.* 美国化.

A•mer•i•can•ize [ə'merikənaiz] *vt., vi.* ①(使) 美国化. ②(使)带美国腔.

am•er•ic•i•um [ˌæmə'risiəm] *n.*【化】镅〔1944 年美国发现超铀新元素之一，符号 Am，因发现地取名〕.

Am•er•ind ['æmərind] *n.* 美洲印第安人；爱斯基摩人.

Am•er•indi•an [ˌæmər'indjən] ① *n.* = Amerind. ② *a.* 美洲印第安人(文化)的，爱斯基摩人(文化)的.

a•mes•ace ['eimzeis] *n.* = ambsace.

a•met•a•bol•ic [ˌeimetə'bɔ:lik], **a•me•tab•o•lous** [ˌeimə'tæbələs] *a.*【动】(昆虫在发育中)无变态的.

am•e•thyst ['æmiθist] *n.* ①【矿】紫石英，紫晶；紫兰色青玉. ②紫色.

am•e•thys•tine [ˌæmi'θistain] *a.* 紫晶质，紫色的.

am•e•tro•pi•a [ˌæmi'trəupiə] *n.* 屈光不正；变常眼. **-trop•ic** [-'trəupik, -'trɔpik] *a.*

Am•ex ['æmeks] *n.* ①美国股票交易所 (= American Stock Exchange). ②(第一次世界大战中派赴欧洲的)美国远征军 (= American Expeditionary Force).

AMG = Allied Military Government 盟国军政府.

Am•ha•ra [ɑ:m'hɑ:rɑ:] *n.* ①阿姆哈拉〔埃塞俄比亚一地区〕. ②阿姆哈拉族；阿姆哈拉人.

Am•har•ic [æm'hærik] *n., a.* ①阿姆哈拉(人)的. ②阿姆哈拉语的. — *n.* 阿姆哈拉语〔一种闪族语，旧时为埃塞俄比亚宫廷贵族语言〕.

Am•herst ['æməst, 'æmhə:st] *n.* 阿默斯特〔姓氏〕.

a•mi [a'mi:] *n.* (*pl.* ~*s* [æ'mi:]) 〔F.〕①男朋友 *(opp. amie)*. ②〔欧洲人口语〕美国人.

a•mi•a•bil•i•ty [ˌeimjə'biliti] *n.* 亲切，和蔼；温和，和气；可爱.

a•mi•a•ble ['eimjəbl] *a.* 可爱的，和蔼可亲的，亲切的；温和的. **-ness** *n.* **-a•bly** *ad.*

am•i•an•thus [ˌæmi'ænθəs], **-an•tus** [-'æntəs] *n.*【矿】(优质)细丝型石棉，石麻，石绒.

am·i·ca·bil·i·ty [ˌæmikəˈbiliti] *n.* 友好,和睦,亲善;温和.

am·i·ca·ble [ˈæmikəbl] *a.* 亲切的,和蔼的,友好的,和睦的. ~ *relations* 友好关系. ~ *settlement* 和解. ~ **number**【数】互满数. **-ness** *n.* **-bly** *ad.*

am·ice[1] [ˈæmis] *n.*【天主】①(僧侣做弥撒时围在颈后肩头上的)长方形白麻布. ②僧侣带头巾的披肩.

am·ice[2] [ˈæmis] *n.* 皮头巾;皮帽;(连在外套上的)兜帽.

ami·cron [eiˈmaiˌkrɔn] *n.*【化】次微(胶)粒,超微粒〔超倍显微镜不可见的,直径小于 10^{-7} 厘米〕.

a·mi·cus cu·ri·ae [əˈmaikəsˈkjuəriiː]【法】法庭之友〔审理某些案件时前往提供或被传去提供情况、或提醒法庭在审理时加以注意的人〕.

a·mid [əˈmid] *prep.* = amidst.

am·ide [ˈæmaid] *n.*【化】①酰胺. ②氨化物.

am·i·din [ˈæmidin] *n.*【化】淀粉在水中的透明溶液.

am·i·dine [ˈæmiˌdiːn] *n.*【化】脒.

a·mi·do·gen [əˈmiːdədʒən, əˈmidədʒən] *n.*【化】(酰)胺基;氨基.

am·i·dol [ˈæmidɔl] *n.*【摄】二氨酚显影剂.

am·i·done [ˈæmidəun] *n.*【化】阿米酮,美沙酮 (= methadone).

a·mid·ship(s) [əˈmidʃip(s)] *ad.* 在船中部,在船腹.

a·midst [əˈmidst] *prep.* 在…的当中,在…的包围中. ~ *enemies [dangers]* 在敌人[危险]包围中.

a·mie [aˈmiː] *n.* (*pl.* ~*s* [aˈmiː])〔F.〕女朋友.

a·mi·go [əˈmiːgəu] *n.* (*pl.* ~*s* [-gəuz])〔Sp.〕①朋友. ②对美国人友好的西班牙语系人.

amil [ˈɑːmil] *n.*【史】(印度)收税员;税款包收员. **-ar** *n.* =amil.

am·i·nate [ˈæmineit] *vt.*【化】使胺化.

am·i·na·tion [ˌæmiˈneiʃən] *n.*【化】胺化作用.

a·mine [ˈæmiːn] *n.*【化】胺.

a·mi·no [ˈæminəu, əˈmiːnəu]【化】氨基的. ~ **acid** 氨基酸;氨酸.

a·mi·no·bu·tone [əˌmiːnəuˈbjuːtiːn] *n.*【化】氨基丁烯〔一种解痛剂〕.

a·mi·no·phe·nol [əˌmiːnəuˈfiːnəul] *n.*【化】氨基(苯)酚〔用作染料、显影剂〕.

a·mi·no·plast [əˈmiːnəuplæst] *n.* 氨基塑料.

a·mi·no·py·rine [əˌmiːnəuˈpairiːn, æmənəu-] *n.* 氨基比林;匹拉米董〔用做退烧剂、减痛剂〕.

a·mi·no·tri·a·zole [əˌmiːnəuˈtraiəˌzəul] *n.* 氨基三唑〔除草药〕.

a·mir [əˈmiə] *n.* = ameer. **-ate** *n.* 酋长国(= emeerate).

A·mis [ˈeimis] *n.* 埃米斯〔姓氏〕.

Am·ish [ˈɑːmiʃ, ˈæmiʃ] *n.*〔*pl.*〕【宗】阿门宗派〔十七世纪成立的一个教规严格的孟诺教派,因创此教派的雅可布·阿门而得名〕. — *a.* 阿门宗派的.

a·miss [əˈmis] *ad.* ①差错,错. ②不顺当,不合,不适当. *Nothing happened* ~. 没有错,无不顺当. *speak* ~ 说错. ***come*** ~ 不称心,有妨碍(*Nothing comes* ~ *to him.* 他事事顺当. *Nothing comes* ~ *to a hungry man.* 饥不择食). ***do*** ~ 做错,犯错误. ***go*** ~ 不顺当,别扭 (*all went* ~ 事事别扭). ***take*** (*sth.*) ~ 见怪,见责;生气;误会(*Don't take my words* ~. 请不要介意我的话). — *a.* 不顺当,别扭,有毛病. *What's* ~ *with it?* 那怎么啦? *There is something* ~ *with him.* 他有点失常;他有点不对头. ***not*** ~ 不错,不坏 (*It is not* ~ *to ask advice.* 求教总没错,不妨商量. *She is not* ~. 她(容貌)不坏).

A·mi·ta·bha [ˌʌmiˈtɑːbə] *n.*〔Sans.〕阿弥陀佛.

a·mi·to·sis [ˌæmiˈtəusis] *n.*【生】无丝分裂.

am·i·trol [ˈæmitrɔːl] *n.* 氨基三唑〔一种除草药〕(= aminotriazole).

am·i·ty [ˈæmiti] *n.* 亲睦,友好,和好. *a treaty of* ~ *and peace* 友好和平条约. *live [be] in* ~ *with* 和…友好相处.

AMM = antimissile missile 反导弹导弹.

Am·man [əˈmɑːn] *n.* 安曼〔约旦首都〕.

am·me·ter [ˈæmitə] *n.* 电流表,安培计.

am·mine [ˈæmiːn] *n.*【化】氨(络);氨络物.

am·mo [ˈæməu] *n.* 〔军俚〕弹药〔由 ammunition 一词缩成〕.

Am·mon [ˈæmən] *n.* (古埃及的)太阳神.

am·mo·nal [ˈæmənæl] *n.* 阿芒拿〔硝铵、铝、炭炸药〕.

am·mo·nia [əˈməunjə] *n.*【化】氨 〔NH_3〕;氨水.

am·mo·ni·ac [əˈməuniæk] *a.* 氨(性)的,含氨的. — *n.* 氨草胶 (= gum ~). ~ *nitrogen* 氨态氮. *sal* ~ 硇砂.

am·mo·ni·a·cal [ˌæməuˈnaiəkəl] *a.* = ammoniac.

am·mo·ni·ated [əˈməunieitid] *a.* 充氨的,含氨的.

am·mo·nic [əˈməunik] *a.* 氨的,铵的.

am·mo·ni·fi·ca·tion [əˌməunifiˈkeiʃən] *n.* ①加氨(作用). ②(分解)成氨(作用).

am·mo·ni·fy [əˈməunifai] *vt.* 使生氨;给…加氨. — *vi.* 进行氨处理,成氨.

am·mo·nite [ˈæmənait] *n.* ①【古生】菊石,鹦鹉螺化石. ②硝石炸药. ③干肉粉〔作肥料用〕.

am·mo·ni·um [əˈməunjəm] *n.*【化】铵. ~ **chloride** 氯化铵. ~ **nitrate** 硝酸铵. ~ **sulphate** 硫酸铵.

am·mo·no [ˈæmənəu] *a.* ①氨的,含氨的. ②氨衍生的.

am·mo·no·tel·ic [ˌæmənəuˈtelik] *a.* 排氨代谢的. **-not·el·ism** [-ˈnɔtlizm] *n.*

am·mu·ni·tion [ˌæmjuˈniʃən] *n.* ①弹药. ②〔废〕军需品. ③〔喻〕战斗手段. ~ **boots**〔英〕军用鞋. ~ **box [chest]** 弹药箱. ~ **clip** 子弹夹. ~ **depot**, ~ **dump** 军火库. ~ **industry** 军需工业. ~ **wagon** 弹药车. — *vt.* 供给…弹药,给…装弹药.

am·ne·sia [æmˈniːzjə] *n.*【医】健忘症.

am·nes·tic [æmˈnestik] *a.* 引起遗忘(症)的.

am·nes·ty [ˈæmnesti] *n.* ①大赦,特赦. ②〔古〕故意忽视(某人的过失). — *vt.* 大赦,赦免.

am·ni·on [ˈæmniən] *n.* (*pl.* **-nia** [-niə])【解】羊膜.

am·ni·o·tin [æmˈniːətin] *n.*【药】安尼奥廷〔含雌性激素物质的油剂,用如雌酮〕.

am·o·bar·bi·tal [ˌæməuˈbɑːbitɔːl] *n.*【药】异戊巴比妥〔一种镇静剂和安眠药〕.

am·o·di·a·quin [ˌæməuˈdaiəkwin] *n.*【药】安双喹〔疟疾药〕.

a·moe·ba [əˈmiːbə] *n.* (*pl.* **-bae** [-biː], ~*s*) 阿米巴,变形虫.

amoe·b(a)e·an [ˌæmiˈbiːən] *a.* (诗歌等)对话体的,应答的. ~ **strains** 对话体的诗歌.

am·oe·bi·a·sis [ˌæmiˈbaiəsis] *n.* 变形虫病,内变形虫病 (= amebiasis).

a·moe·bic [əˈmiːbik] *a.* 阿米巴的,阿米巴性的.

a·moe·bo·cyte [əˈmiːbəsait] *n.* 变形细胞.

a·moe·boid [əˈmiːbɔid] *n.*【医】阿米巴状的,变形虫似的.

a·mok [əˈmɔk] *ad.* = amuck.

a·mo·le [əˈməulei] *n.* ①(产生美国西南部和墨西哥的)代皂植物的根. ②代皂植物.

A·mon [ˈɑːmən] 亚蒙神〔原义司生殖力的神〕;埃及主神 (= Ammon).

a·mong [əˈmʌŋ] *prep.* 在(多数)之中,在…中间. ★ between 一般指"在两者之间",among 一般指"在三者或三者以上之中". ~ *us Chinese* 在我们中国人中间. ~ *the Greeks* 在希腊时代. *life* ~ *the Arabs* (别国人的)阿拉伯生活. *a house* ~ *the trees* 树木环绕着的屋子. *fall* ~ *thieves* 沦落到与盗贼为伍. *quarrel* ~ *themselves* 内部相互争吵. *be* ~ *the best books* 是最优秀的作品之一. ~ ***others [other things]*** 其中,就中,尤其,格外,加上[以及]其他种种事实[问题]. ~ ***the missing***〔美〕

失踪中,下落不明. ~ ***themselves [ourselves, yourselves]*** 在自已人中间. ~ ***the rest*** 其中之一;也在其中 (*myself* ~ *the rest* 我也是其中的一个). ***from*** ~ 从…中. ***one*** ~ ***a thousand*** 千中挑一的人,奇人.

a·mongst [ə'mʌŋst] *prep.* 〔书〕 = among.

A·mon-Re ['ɑːmən'rei], **Amon-Ra** [-'rɑː] *n.* 古埃及太阳神.

a·mon·til·la·do [əˌmɔnti'lɑːdəu] *n.* (*pl.* ~*s*) (西班牙产的)白葡萄酒. 〔喻〕平淡无味,态度冷淡.

a·mor·al [ei'mɔrəl] *a.* 非道德的,超道德的,与道德无关的,没有道德意识的. *Infants are* ~. 婴儿没有道德意识.

a·morce [ə'mɔːs] *n.* 起爆剂.

am·o·ret·to ['ɑːmə'retəu] *n.* (*pl.* ***-ret·ti*** [-reti]) (意大利十六世纪艺术作品中的)小爱神.

am·o·rist ['æmərist] *n.* ①情人;好色之徒. ②恋爱文学作家.

am·o·rous ['æmərəs] *a.* ①好色的;色情的. ②多情的,脉脉含情的. ②恋爱的;有关爱情的. ~ *songs* 恋歌,情歌. ~ *glances* (女人传情的)眼神,秋波. *be* ~ *of* 爱慕. **-ly** *ad.* 好色地;情意脉脉地. **-ness** *n.* 好色.

a·mor pa·tri·ae ['eimɔː 'peitriiː] 〔L.〕 爱国心.

a·mor·phism [ə'mɔːfizəm] *n.* ①无定形(现象). ②【化】无晶形,非晶性. ③无组织;无定向;虚无主义. ④乱七八糟,杂乱无章. **-phous** [ə'mɔːfəs] *a.* **-phous·ly** *ad.*

a·mort [ə'mɔːt] *a.* 死了似的,死气沉沉的,意气消沉的.

am·or·tise, -tize [ə'mɔːtaiz] *vt.* ①【法】把(不动产)转让(尤指让与教会永久管理);把(不动产)让与法人. ②分期偿还(债务等);分期注销(费用等),摊提(资产).

am·or·ti·za·tion [əˌmɔːti'zeiʃən] *n.* ①【法】不动产的让渡[捐赠]. ②分期偿还,摊提(资产等).

A·mos ['eimɔs] *n.* ①【圣】阿摩司〔公元前八世纪的希伯来先知〕. ②【圣】(旧约中的)《阿摩司书》. ③埃莫斯〔男子名〕.

am·o·site ['æməsait] *n.* 铁石棉.

a·mount [ə'maunt] *vi.* ①总计,共计,合计 (*to*). ②相当于,等于. ③成为 (*to*). *Their expences* ~ *to fifty dollars.* 他们的花销共计五十元. *His answer* ~*s to a threat.* 他的回答等于恐吓. *What, after all, does it* ~ *to?* 结果怎么样? ~ ***to little*** = ***not*** ~ ***to much*** 没有什么了不起,有限得很,无多大道理. ~ ***to much*** 大起来,变伟大. ~ ***to something*** (人)成器,成才. — *n.* ①总和,总额. ②数值,量,金额. ③结果,效果;要旨. *a lethal* ~ 致死剂量. *a trace* ~ 微量,痕量. *the gross* ~ 约计,概数. *the net* ~ 细数. *the* ~ 总数. *What is the* ~*?* 一共多少? *a large* ~ *of money* 巨额的钱. *This is the* ~ *of what he said.* 这是他所说的要点. ***an*** ~ ***of (work)*** 相当数量的(工作),适量[度]的. ***any*** ~ ***(of)*** 任何数量(的);大量(的). ***in*** ~ 总之,结局;总计.

a·mour [ə'muə] *n.* 〔F.〕 私通;不正当的恋爱事件. *have an* ~ *with ...* 同…有不正当的男女关系.

a·mour-pro·pre ['æmuə 'prɔpr] *n.* 〔F.〕 自尊,自负.

Amoy [ə'mɔi] *n.* 厦门〔中国〕.

amp. = ampere; amperage.

AMP = ①adenosine monophosphate 腺苷酸. ②amplification 放大. ③amplifier 放大器.

AMPAS = Academy of Motion Picture Arts and Sciences 〔美〕电影艺术和科学研究院.

am·pe·lop·sis [ˌæmpə'lɔpsis] *n.* 【植】①〔A-〕白蔹属. ②蛇葡萄科植物.

am·per·age ['æmpɛəridʒ] *n.* 安培数,电流量.

Am·père ['æmpɛə] **A.M.** 安培〔1775—1836, 法国物理学家〕.

am·pere, am·père ['æmpɛə] *n.* 【电】安培. **~-hour** 安培时. **~meter** [-miːtə] 电流表,安培表. **~'s law** 【物】安培定律. **~ turn** 安匝(数).

am·per·sand ['æmpəsænd] *n.* '&' (= and) 的名称〔原为 *and per se and*〕.

am·phet·a·mine [æm'fetəmiːn] *n.* 【药】氨基丙苯,苯基丙胺,安非他明〔解除忧郁、疲劳的药〕.

am·phi- *comb. f.* 〔Gr.〕 ①两侧,两端: *amphi*stylar. ②周围. ③两类: *amphi*biotic.

am·phi·ar·thro·sis [ˌæmfiɑː'θrəusis] *n.* 【解】微动关节.

am·phi·as·ter ['æmfiˌæstə] *n.* 【医】双星体.

Am·phib·i·a [æm'fibiə] *n.* 〔*pl.*〕【动】两栖纲.

am·phib·i·an [æm'fibiən] *a.* 两栖类的. — *n.* ①两栖动物[植物]. ②水陆两用飞机[战车]. ③双重性格的人.

am·phi·bi·ot·ic [ˌæmfibai'ɔtik] *a.* 【动】(一成长阶段在水,一成长阶段在陆的)水陆先后两栖的;水生陆栖的;水陆两生的.

am·phib·i·ous [æm'fibiəs] *a.* ①两栖的. ②水陆两用的. ③有双重性格的. ~ *forces* 海陆空军. ~ *operations* 海陆空军协同作战. **-ly** *ad.*

am·phi·bole ['æmfibəul] *n.* 【矿】闪石.

am·phib·o·lite [æm'fibəlait] *n.* 【矿】闪岩.

am·phi·bol·o·gy [ˌæmfi'bɔlədʒi] *n.* 含糊语句;意义含糊,文意不明.

am·phib·o·lous [æm'fibələs] *a.* 含糊的,模棱两可的.

am·phi·brach ['æmfibræk] *n.* 〔古诗〕抑扬抑格〔弱强弱的三音节诗格〕.

am·phi·chro·ic [ˌæmfi'krəuik] *a.* 【化】两变色的.

am·phi·coe·lous [ˌæmfi'siːləs] *a.* 【解】两凹形的;两边内陷的.

am·phic·tyon [æm'fiktiən] *n.* ①(古希腊的近邻同盟会议)代表. ②〔*pl.*〕(古希腊)近邻同盟会议.

am·phic·ty·o·ny [æm'fiktiəni] *n.* (*pl.* ***-nies***) 邻邦同盟〔古希腊近邻诸邦以保护神庙为名而结成的联盟〕. **-o·nic** [-'ɔnik] *a.*

am·phi·go·ry, am·phi·gou·ri ['æmfigəri] *n.* 打油诗;胡乱诌成的诗文.

am·phim·a·cer [æm'fiməsə] *n.* 〔古诗〕扬抑扬格〔强弱强的三音节诗格〕.

am·phi·mix·is [ˌæmfi'miksis] *n.* 【生】两性融合;杂交繁育.

am·phi·ox·us [ˌæmfi'ɔksəs] *n.* 【动】蛞蝓鱼,文昌鱼.

am·phi·pod ['æmfipɔd] *n.* 【动】片脚动物. — *a.* 【动】片脚类的.

am·phi·pro·style [æm'fiprəustail] *n.* 【建】两向拜式〔前后有排柱而两傍无柱的建筑〕.

am·phis·bae·na [ˌæmfis'biːnə] *n.* ①【希、罗神】两头蛇. ②【动】无足蜥蜴. ③〔A-〕蜥蜴属.

am·phis·bae·ni·an [ˌæmfis'biːniən] *n.* 蚓蜥属动物.

am·phi·sty·lar [ˌæmfi'stailə] *a.* 【建】两侧或前后有圆柱的.

am·phi·the·a·tral [ˌæmfi'θiətrəl] *a.* = amphitheatrical.

am·phi·the·a·tre, am·phi·the·a·ter ['æmfiˌθiətə] *n.* ①(古罗马时代的)圆形剧场,竞技场. ②阶式剧场[教室]. ③盆状地形. **-the·at·ric** [ˌæmfiθi'ætrik]

am·pho·ra ['æmfərə] *n.* (*pl.* ***-rae*** [-riː], ~***s***) (古希腊的)双耳酒罐[油罐].

am·phor·ic [æm'fɔrik] *a.* 【医】瓮音的,空瓮性的.

am·pho·ter·ic [ˌæmfə'terik] *a.* 有酸碱两性的.

am·pho·ter·i·cin B [ˌæmfə'terəsin] 两性霉素乙.

am·ple ['æmpl] *a.* (***-pler; -plest***) ①(房屋)广大的,宽敞的. ②丰富的,充足的,富裕的. (*opp.* scanty, meager). ~ *evidences* 充足的证据. *of* ~ *means* 富有的. *do* ~ *justice to a meal* 大吃,饱餐. **-ness** *n.* 广大;丰富,充足.

am·plex·i·caul [æm'pleksikɔːl] *a.* 【植】抱茎的.

am·pli·a·tion [ˌæmpli'eiʃən] *n.* 〔古〕扩大,扩张;(加某

物以)增大.

am·pli·a·tive [ˈæmplieitiv] *a.* 【逻】扩充的,扩张(性)的.

am·pli·dyne [ˈæmplidain] *n.* (微场)电机放大器,交磁放大机.

am·pli·fi·ca·tion [ˌæmplifiˈkeiʃən] *n.* ①扩大;扩充. ②【电】增幅,放大(率). ③(声明等的)补充材料.

am·pli·fi·er [ˈæmplifaiə] *n.* ①【电】扩大器;扩音器. ②放大镜;放大器. *a sight* ~ 雷达瞄准放大器. *speech* ~ 音频放大器.

am·pli·fy [ˈæmplifai] *vt.* ①扩大,放大. ②引伸,详述. ③【电】增强(电流等). ④夸大. — *vi.* 引伸,详说,作进一步阐述 *(on)*. *There is no need to* ~. 无详述之必要. ~ *on a certain subject* 详细阐述某一问题.

am·pli·tude [ˈæmplitjuːd] *n.* ①广阔,广大. ②丰富,充足. ③(思想的)广度. ④(天体出没时偏离正东或正西的)角度距离. ⑤【物、电】振幅. ~ **modulation**【无】振幅调制.

am·ply [ˈæmpli] *ad.* 广大地,广泛地;充足地;详细地. *He apologized* ~ *for his error.* 他因自己的过失而大为抱歉. *They were* ~ *supplied with food.* 他们有充足的食物供应.

am·poule, am·pul(e) [ˈæmpuːl] *n.* ①(装针药水的)小玻璃管,安瓿. ② = ampulla.

am·pul·la [æmˈpulə] *n.* (*pl.* **-lae** [-liː]) ①(古罗马的)细颈坛. ②神酒瓶;圣油瓶. ③【解】壶腹. ④【生】坛状体.

am·pul·la·ceous [ˌæmpəˈleiʃəs] *a.* 细颈坛状的,坛形的.

am·pu·tate [ˈæmpjuteit] *vt.* 切断,截除,截(肢).

am·pu·ta·tion [ˌæmpjuˈteiʃən] *n.* 【医】截肢(术).

am·pu·ta·tor [ˈæmpjuteitə] *n.* 施行截肢手术者.

am·pu·tee [ˌæmpjuˈtiː] *n.* 被截肢者.

am·ri·ta [əmˈriːtə] *n.* 【印度神】①长生不老酒. ②长生不老.

Am·ster·dam [ˈæmstəˈdæm] *n.* 阿姆斯特丹〔荷兰首都,海牙为政府所在地〕.

amt. = amount.

am·trac [æmˈtræk], **am·track** [ˈæmtræk] *n.* (第二次世界大战中使用的)小型水陆两用登陆车.

amu, AMU = atomic mass unit 原子质量单位.

a·muck [əˈmʌk] *ad., a.* 狂暴;狂怒;杀气腾腾. ***run*** ~乱斩乱杀,横行霸道;乱窜. ***run*** ~ ***at society*** 胡作非为. — *n.* (马来人常患的)神经错乱.

am·u·let [ˈæmjulit] *n.* 护身符,驱邪符.

A·mur [əˈmuə] *n.* 阿穆尔河〔即黑龙江〕.

a·muse [əˈmjuːz] *vt.* 娱乐,使…喜欢〔高兴〕,逗…笑. *You* ~ *me!* 傻气! 多好笑! ~ ***oneself by [with]*** 以…自娱〔消遣〕. ***be*** ~***d at [by, with]*** 觉得…有趣〔好笑〕;以…为乐. **a·musa·ble** *a.* **-r** *n.*

a·muse·ment [əˈmjuːzmənt] *n.* ①娱乐,消遣;乐趣. ②娱乐品;娱乐活动. *an* ~ *park* 露天游艺场. *find much* ~ *in* 最爱…,对…最有兴趣. ~ **tax** 娱乐捐.

a·mu·si·a [ˌəˈmjuːziə] *n.* 【医】(失去唱歌能力的)失歌症.

a·mus·ing [əˈmjuːziŋ] *a.* 有趣的;好笑的. *How* ~*!* 多有趣! 多好笑! **-ly** *ad.*

a·mu·sive [əˈmjuːziv, əˈmjuːsiv] *a.* 有趣的;引人发笑的.

AMVETS = American Veterans of World War II 美国第二次世界大战退伍军人协会.

Am·vets [ˈæmvets] *n. pl.* = AMVETS.

A·my [ˈeimi] *n.* 埃米〔女子名〕.

a·myg·da·la [əˈmigdələ] *n.* (*pl.* **-lae** [-liː]) ①杏仁. ②【解】扁桃(腺).

a·myg·da·la·ceous [əˌmigdəˈleiʃəs] *a.* 樱属植物的〔如桃、杏、樱桃等多肉的坚果植物〕.

a·myg·da·late [əˈmigdəlit] *a.* ①杏仁(似)的. ②扁桃(腺)的.

a·myg·dale [əˈmigdeil] **a·myg·dule** [-duːl, -djuːl] *n.* 【矿】杏仁石;杏仁孔.

a·myg·da·lin [əˈmigdəlin] *n.* 【化、药】苦杏仁苷,苦扁桃仁苷〔用作祛痰药或调味剂〕.

a·myg·da·loid [əˈmigdəˌlɔid] *n.* 【矿】杏仁岩. — *a.* ①杏仁状的. ②杏仁岩的. ③扁桃状的.

a·myg·da·loid·al [əˌmigdəˈlɔidl] *a.* 杏仁状的 (= amygdaloid).

am·yl [ˈæmil] *n.* 【化】戊基,戊烷基.

am·y·la·ceous [ˌæmiˈleiʃəs] *a.* 淀粉(状)的,淀粉质的.

am·yl·ase [ˈæmileis] *n.* 【生化】淀粉(糖化)酶.

am·yl·ene [ˈæmiˌliːn] *n.* 【化】戊烯.

a·myl·ic [əˈmilik] *a.* 淀粉的.

amyl(o)- *comb.f.* = amyl, amylum.

a·myl·o·gen [əˈmilədʒən] *n.* 可溶性淀粉.

am·y·loid [ˈæmilɔid] *a.* 淀粉状的,淀粉质的. — *n.* ①【生化】淀粉状朊. ②【造纸】(硫酸)胶化纤维素.

am·y·lol·y·sis [ˌæmiˈlɔlisis] *n.* 【生化】淀粉分解. **a-my·lo·ly·tic** [ˌæmiləuˈlitik] *a.*

am·y·lo·pec·tin [ˌæmiləuˈpektin] *n.* 【生化】支链淀粉;胶淀粉.

am·y·lop·sin [ˌæmiˈlɔpsin] *n.* 【生化】胰淀粉酶.

am·y·lose [ˈæmiləus] *n.* 【生化】直链淀粉;糖淀粉.

am·y·lum [ˈæmiləm] *n.* 【化】淀粉 (starch) 的拉丁名称.

a·my·o·to·ni·a [eiˌmaiəˈtəuniə] *n.* 【医】肌弛缓.

Am·y·tal [ˈæmitəl, -tæl] *n.* 【药】阿米他;异戊巴比妥〔用作镇静剂、安眠药〕(= amobarbital).

an[1] [强 æn; 弱 ən, n] *indef. art.* 见 **a.** 条.

an[2], **an'** [强 æn; 弱ən] *conj.* ①〔方、口〕= and. ②〔古、方〕= (and) if.

an. = ①*anno.* ②anonymous. ③answer. ④*ante.*

an- *pref.* ① = 〔L.〕*ad-*: *an*nex. ② = 〔Gr.〕*a-*: *an*archy (*cf.* a-[3]). ③ = 〔Gr.〕*ana-*: *an*ode.

-an *suf.* ①〔构成形容词〕表示"…的,有…性质;属于…的;【动】…纲〔类〕的": Mahomet*an*, Elizabeth*an*, Mammali*an*. ②〔常构成与形容词同形的名词〕表示"…地方的人;精通…的人;信奉…的人": histori*an*, Americ*an*.

A.N., A-N = Anglo-Norman 英格兰和诺曼底的;英格兰诺曼底人(的);英格兰诺曼底语(的).

ANA = ①All Nippon Airways 全日本航空公司. ②American Nurse Association 全美护士协会.

a·na[1] [ˈɑːnə] *n.* (*pl.* ~*(s)*)丛谈,语录;轶事谈;回忆录.

an·a[2] [ˈænə] *ad.* 【处方】= āā等量;各. *wine and honey* ~ *two ounces* 酒和蜂蜜各二两.

ana- *pref.* ①表示"向上": *ana*dromous. ②表示"向后": *ana*gram. ③表示"再一次": *ana*baptist. ④表示"贯穿": *ana*lysis. ⑤表示"类似": *ana*logy.

-ana *suf.* 〔附在人名地名后〕表示"语录,逸话,杂记,集": Shakespeari*ana* 莎士比亚轶事集.

an·a·bae·na [ˌænəˈbiːnə] *n.* 【植】①念珠藻科的水藻〔常生于蓄水池,可使水发腥味〕. ②念珠藻团.

an·a·bap·tism [ˌænəˈbæptizəm] *n.* ①【宗】再洗礼;再浸礼论. ②〔A-〕再浸礼教. **-tist** *n.* 再浸礼教徒.

an·a·bas [ˈænəbæs] *n.* 【动】攀鲈亚目鱼;攀鲈属〔因此种鱼有攀登习性,故名〕.

a·nab·a·sis [əˈnæbəsis] *n.* (*pl.* **-ses** [siːz]) ①进军,远征. ②〔A-〕(色诺芬 (Xenophon) 所写的)《希腊远征波斯记》. ③【医】病加重(期). ④艰险撤军.

an·a·bat·ic [ˌænəˈbætik] *a.* 【气】(风、气流等)上升的.

an·a·bi·osis [ˌænəbaiˈəusis] *n.* 【医】复苏,回生.

a·nab·o·lism [əˈnæbəlizəm] *n.* ①(食物的)吸收和同化. ②【生】组成〔合成〕代谢.

an·a·branch [ˈænəbrɑːntʃ] *n.* 【地】再会流侧流;再流入主流的支流.

a·nach·ro·nism [əˈnækrənizəm] *n.* ①时代错误,弄错

年代．②与时代不合的事物．*Contemporary monarchy is an* ～．现代的君主政体是不合时宜的事物．**-nis·tic, -nis·ti·cal** [əˌnækrəˈnistik(əl)], **-nous** [əˈnækrənəs] *a.*

an·a·clas·tic [ˌænəˈklæstik] *a.*【光】屈折的；由折射引起的．

an·a·cli·nal [ˌænəˈklainl] *a.*【地】正倾型的；逆地层下倾的方向而活动的．

an·a·clit·ic [ˌænəˈklitik] *a.* ①依靠的，依赖的．②【心】情感依附的．

an·a·co·lu·thon [ˌænəkəuˈlu:θən] *n.* (*pl.*-*tha* [-θə]) ①句中由一种结构改为另一种结构的错格现象．②错格句〔如：As a regular reader of your papers — Why does it give so little space to science? 作为贵报的一名忠实读者——(我想提的意见是)贵报给予科学问题的版面为什么这样少？

an·a·con·da [ˌænəˈkɔndə] *n.*【动】(南美产的)蟒蛇．

A·nac·re·on [əˈnækriən] *n.* 安纳克里昂〔纪元前约570—480年间希腊抒情诗人，特嗜歌颂爱情和欢宴〕．

a·nac·re·on·tic [əˌnækriˈɔntik] *a.* (古希腊抒情诗人)安纳克里昂(Anacreon)派的；歌颂爱情和欢宴的；酒色的．— *n.*〔*pl.*〕安纳克里昂风格的诗，专写醇酒妇人的诗．

an·a·cru·sis [ˌænəˈkru:sis] *n.* 行首额外音节〔以重音开始的诗句前额外加上的轻音节，但不作为该诗句的第一音步〕．

an·a·cul·ture [ˈænəkʌltʃə] *n.*【微】细菌的混合培养(尤指为生产自体疫苗用的)．

an·a·dem [ˈænədem] *n.*〔诗〕花冠，花环．

an·a·di·plo·sis [ˌænədiˈpləusis] *n.*【修】反复法，蝉联法〔为了强调反复使用句中关键性字眼，特别是把末一词用于下句之首：*He gave his life; life was all he could give*〕．

a·nad·ro·mous [əˈnædrəməs] *a.* (海鱼)溯河产卵的，溯河(性)的．～ **fish** 溯河性海鱼．～ **migration** 溯河回游．

a·nae·mi·a [əˈni:mjə] *n.*【医】贫血症(= anemia)．

a·nae·mic [əˈni:mik] *a.* 贫血(症)的(= anemic)．

an·aer·obe [əˈneiərəub] *n.*【微】厌氧微生物，厌气微生物(*opp.* aerobe)．**-bic** [əˌneiəˈrɔbik] *a.*【微】厌气性的．

an·aer·o·bi·um [ˌænəˈrəubiəm] *n.* (*pl.* **-bia** [-biə]) 厌氧菌．

an·aes·the·si·a [ˌænisˈθi:zjə] *n.*【医】①感觉缺失，麻木．②麻醉．*local* ～ 局部麻醉．*general* ～ 全身麻醉．

an·aes·thet·ic [ˌænisˈθetik] *a.* 麻醉的．— *n.* 麻醉药〔剂〕．

an·aes·the·tist [æˈni:sθitist] *n.* 麻醉医师．

an·aes·the·ti·za·tion [æˌni:sθitaiˈzeiʃən] *n.* 麻醉；麻木．

an·aes·the·tize [æˈni:sθitaiz] *vt.* 使麻醉；使麻木．

an·a·glyph [ˈænəglif] *n.* ①浅浮雕．②立体照片〔影片〕．

an·a·glyph·ic [ˌænəˈglifik] *a.* ①浮雕(装饰)的．②立体照片的．

an·ag·no·ri·sis [ˌænægˈnɔ:risis] *n.* (戏剧的)大团圆〔如：剧中人终于认出自己的亲人或自己的真实处境〕．

an·a·go·ge [ˌænəˈgəudʒi] *n.* (对圣经的)神秘解释〔旨在揭示隐晦的含义〕．

an·a·gog·ic, -i·cal [ˌænəˈgɔdʒik(əl)] *a.* (对《圣经》的解释)神秘的．*an* ～ *interpretation* 神秘的解释．

an·a·gram [ˈænəgræm] *n.* ①颠倒字母而成的词句〔如 *emit* 作 *mite*, lived 作 devil 等〕．②〔*pl.* 作单数用〕字谜游戏．**-mat·ic, -mat·i·cal** *a.* **-ma·tism** *n.* 字谜作法．**-mat·ize** *vt.* 把…作字谜．

a·nal [ˈeinəl] *a.* 肛门的，直肠的；【昆】臀的，尾端的．～ **fistula** 痔瘘．～ **length** (鱼的)吻至肛门长度．

anal. = ①analogy. ②analysis. ③analytic.

an·al·cite [əˈnælsait], **an·al·cime** [-saim, -si:m] *n.*【矿】方沸石．

an·a·lec·ta [ˌænəˈlektə] *n. pl.* = analects.

an·a·lec·tic [ˌænəˈlektik] *a.* 选集的，拔萃的．

an·a·lects [ˈænəlekts] *n. pl.* 文选，选集，言论集．*the A- of Confucius* 《论语》．

an·a·lem·ma [ˌænəˈlemə] *n.* (地球仪上表示)太阳的日倾斜度的刻度〔通常穿过赤道，呈延长了的8字形〕．

an·a·lep·tic [ˌænəˈleptik] *a.* 提神的；强身的．— *n.* ①回苏剂，兴奋剂．②强壮剂，复原剂．

an·al·ge·si·a [ˌænælˈdʒi:zjə] *n.*【医】①痛觉缺失．②无痛法，止痛法．

an·al·ge·sic [ˌænælˈdʒesik] **an·al·get·ic** [-ˈdʒetik] *a.* 止痛的．— *n.* 止痛药．

an·a·log [ˈænəlɔg] *n.* = analogue.

an·a·log·ic, -i·cal [ˌænəˈlɔdʒik(əl)] *a.* ①类似的，相似的．②类推的，对比的．**-i·cal·ly** *ad.*

a·nal·o·gism [əˈnælədʒizəm] *n.*【逻】推论，类推．

a·nal·o·gist [əˈnælədʒist] *n.* 进行类推的人；类比推理者．

a·nal·o·gize [əˈnælədʒaiz] *vt.* 用类推法说明，类推，推论．— *vi.* 使用类推法作推理．

a·nal·o·gous [əˈnæləgəs] *a.* ①类似的，相似的．②【生】同功的，功能相同的．**be** ～ **to** 类似．～ **organ** 同功器官．～ **pole** 热正极．**-ly** *ad.* **-ness** *n.*

an·a·logue [ˈænəlɔg] *n.* ①类似物．②同源语．③【生】相似体．③相对应的人；对手方．*The gill of a fish is the* ～ *of the lung of a cat.* 鱼的鳃和猫的肺是类似物．～ **computer** 模拟计算机．

a·nal·o·gy [əˈnælədʒi] *n.* ①类似，相似 *(between; to; with)*．②【逻】类推．③【语】类同．④【生】异体同功，同功器官〔*cf.* homology〕．⑤模拟，比拟．*a false* ～ 似是而非的对比．*a forced* ～ 勉强的类推，牵强附会．**by** ～ 照此类推．**by** ～ **with** 由…类推．**by way of** ～ 比方．**have [bear]** ～ **to [with]** 类似．**on the** ～ **of** = by ～ with. **trace an** ～ **between** 在(二者)间寻求类似点．

an·al·pha·bet·ic [ænˌælfəˈbetik] *a.* ①不按字母顺序的．②不识字的，文盲的．③非字母注音的．

an·a·lys·a·ble [ˈænəlaizəbl] *a.* 可以分析的，分解得了的．

a·nal·y·sand [əˈnælisænd] *n.* 精神分析对象〔正在接受精神分析疗法治疗的患者〕．

an·a·lyse [ˈænəlaiz] *vt.* ①分解；分析；解析．②〔美〕= psychoanalyse. ～ ... **into** 把…分解成．

a·nal·y·sis [əˈnælisis] *n.* (*pl.* **-ses** [-si:z]) ①分解，分析；【数】解析．②梗概，要略．③〔美〕用精神分析法治疗(= psychoanalysis)．**in the last** ～ = **on (the last)** ～ 归根结底，总之．**under** ～ 在精神分析治疗下．～ **situs**【数】拓朴(学)．

an·a·lyst [ˈænəlist] *n.* ①分解者，分析者；化验员．②〔美〕精神病医师(= psychoanalyst)．

an·a·lyt·ic, -i·cal [ˌænəˈlitik(əl)] *a.* 分解的，分析的．*The analytical method is dialectical.* 分析的方法就是辩证的方法．～ **balance** 分析天平〔一种极精密的天平，供化学分析用〕．～ **chemistry** 分析化学．～ **geometry** 解析几何学．**-i·cal·ly** *ad.*

an·a·lyt·ics [ˌænəˈlitiks] *n. pl.*〔用作单或复〕分析学，解析学．

an·a·lyze [ˈænəlaiz] *vt.*〔美〕= analyse.

an·am·ne·sis [ˌænæmˈni:sis] *n.* ①回想，回忆(尤指对假想的前世生活的回忆)．②【医】既往症；既往病历．

an·a·mor·phism [ˌænəˈmɔ:fizəm] *n.*【地】合成变质．

an·a·mor·pho·scope [ˌænəˈmɔ:fəskəup] *n.* 歪像(变正)镜〔一种改变歪像为正像的曲面镜〕．

an·a·mor·pho·sis [ˌænəˈmɔ:fəsis] *n.* ①歪像，畸态．②【植】畸形，变体．③【生】渐进变化，渐变．④【虫】增

节变态.

a·na·nas [əˈnɑːnəs] *n.* 〔罕〕【植】凤梨 (= pineapple).

an·an·drous [æˈnændrəs] *a.* 【植】无雄蕊的,隐花的.

An·a·ni·us [ænəˈnaiəs] *n.* ①【圣】亚拿尼亚〔把应该献给使徒的钱私藏了一部分的信士,见《圣经》使徒行传第五章〕.②〔转义〕〔a-〕撒谎的人.

an·a·nym [ˈænənim] *n.* 倒拼的名字〔如将 Smiles 写作 Selims〕.

an·a·paest [ˈænəpiːst] *n.* 〔诗〕①抑抑扬 [短短长] 格. ②抑抑扬格的诗句 〔如: And the ˈsheen of their ˈspears was like ˈstars on the ˈsea〕.**-ic** [ˌænəˈpiːst] *a.*

an·a·phase [ˈænəfeiz] *n.* 【生】(细胞分裂的)后期.

a·naph·o·ra [əˈnæfərə] *n.* ①【语】首语重复 (法) (*opp.* epistrophe) 〔指一个单词或短语出现在连续数句的开头〕.②指代法〔使用代替词来指代前面的语词,如: Mary dances better than June does 中,用 does 代替 dances〕.

an·aph·ro·dis·i·ac [ænˌæfrəˈdiziæk] *a.* 平性欲的,制性欲的. — *n.* 平性欲剂,制性欲剂.

an·a·phy·lac·tic [ˌænəfiˈlæktik] *a.* 【医】过敏反应的.

an·a·phy·lac·tin [ˌænəfiˈlæktin] *n.* 【医】过敏素.

an·a·phy·lax·is [ˌænəfiˈlæksis] *n.* 【医】过敏性(反应).

an·a·plas·tic [ˌænəˈplæstik] *a.* ①【医】整形手术的;整形的. ②(细胞)退化的;(肿疱)恶性的.

an·a·plas·ty [ˈænəplæsti] *n.* 【医】整形(外科)术.

an·ap·tyx·is [ˌænæpˈtiksis] *n.* (*pl.* **-tyx·es** [-tiksiːz]) 【语】加元音现象 〔为发音的方便而外加一元音,如 athlete 读成 [ˈæθəliːt]〕. **an·ap·tyc·tic** [ˌænæpˈtiktik] *a.*

an·arch [ˈænɑːk] *n.* = anarchist.

an·ar·chic, -i·cal [æˈnɑːkik(əl)] *a.* 无政府(主义)的.

an·ar·chism [ˈænəkizəm] *n.* 无政府主义; 无政府(状态).

an·ar·chist [ˈænəkist] *n.* 无政府主义者.

an·ar·cho- *comb. f.* 表示"无政府主义的": *anarcho*-socialist.

an·ar·cho·so·cial·ist [ˈænəkəuˈsəuʃəlist] *n.* 无政府社会主义者.

an·na·cho·syn·dic·a·lism [ˈænəkəuˈsindikəlizəm] *n.* 无政府工团主义.

an·ar·chy [ˈænəki] *n.* 无政府(状态);混乱.

an·ar·thri·a [æˈnɑːθriə] *n.* 【医】(因大脑受伤引起的)口齿不清,口吃.

an·a·sar·ca [ˌænəˈsɑːkə] *n.* 【医】全身水肿,普遍性水肿.

An·a·sta·sia [ˌænəˈsteizjə] *n.* 阿纳斯塔西娅〔女子名〕.

an·a·stat·ic [ˌænəˈstætik] *a.* 【印】凸版的. **~ printing** 凸版印刷.

an·as·tig·mat [æˈnæstigmæt] *n.* 【摄】去像散透镜. **-ic** [æˌnæstigˈmætik] *a.* 去像散的.

an·as·to·mose [əˈnæstəməuz] *vt., vi.* ①(使)(血管)吻合. ②(使)(河流)汇合.

an·as·to·mo·sis [ˌænəstəˈməusis] *n.* (*pl.* **-ses** [-siːz]) *n.* ①(筋脉等的)吻合(术). ②(运河等的)交叉合流.

a·nas·tro·phe [əˈnæstrəfi] *n.* 【修】倒装法〔如 Homeward directly he went〕.

anat. = ①anatomical. ②anatomist. ③anatomy.

an·a·tase [ˈænəteiz] *n.* 【矿】八面石(锐钛矿).

a·nath·e·ma [əˈnæθimə] *n.* ①咒,诅咒. ②【宗】咒逐〔用诅咒逐出教会〕. ③被诅咒的人[物]. ④极其讨厌的人[物].

An·a·to·li·a [ˌænəˈtəuljə] *n.* ①小亚细亚古名. ②安纳托利亚〔土耳其的亚洲部分〕.

an·a·tom·ic, -i·cal [ˌænəˈtɔmik(əl)] *a.* ①解剖的,解剖(学)上的. ②组织的,构造上的. **~** *terms* 解剖学术语. **-i·cal·ly** *ad.* 解剖地;在解剖上.

a·nat·o·mist [əˈnætəmist] *n.* 解剖学者.

a·nat·o·mize [əˈnætəmaiz] *vt.* ①解剖. ②分析,解析.

a·nat·o·my [əˈnætəmi] *n.* ①解剖术;解剖学. ②解剖体;组织,构造. ③解剖,分解,分析. ④〔俚、古〕骨骼. ⑤瘦得仅剩皮包骨头的人. *human* ~ 人体解剖学. *morbid* ~ 病理解剖学.

a·nat·ro·pous [əˈnætrəpəs] *a.* 【植】(胚珠)倒生的.

a·nat·to [ɑˈnɑːtəu] *n.* 胭脂树红,果红〔用来给食品着色〕.

an·bur·y [ˈænbəri] *n.* ①(牛马的)软瘤,血痣. ②(植物的)根瘤病.

-ance *suf.* ①表示行动、状态、性质等的名词后缀〔相对应的形容词后缀为 -ant〕: brilli*ance*, dist*ance*. ②附于动词后形成名词: assist*ance*.

an·ces·tor [ˈænsistə] *n.* ①祖先,祖宗. ②【生】先祖,原种. ③【法】被继承人.

an·ces·tral [ænˈsestrəl] *a.* 祖先的;祖传的. ~ *forms of life* 生物的原始形态. ~ *features* 遗传性状.

an·ces·tress [ˈænsistris] *n.* 女祖先〔*cf.* ancestor〕.

an·ces·try [ˈænsistri] *n.* ①〔集合词〕祖先. ②家世,世系. ③世家,名门. ④【生】系谱. *He is of good* ~. 他出身名门.

an·chi·there [ˈæŋkiθiə] *n.* 【古生】化石马.

an·chor [ˈæŋkə] *n.* ①锚;锚状物. ②桩,支架. ③〔喻〕依靠. ④【体】一队运动员中最后参加比赛的人;殿后的人〔如接力赛中跑最后一棒的人〕. ⑤〔美俚〕(卡车的)紧急煞车器. *a bower [kedge]* ~ 中[小]锚. *a sheet* ~ ①〔古〕主锚. ②〔喻〕希望,靠山. ***be [lie, ride] at*** ~ 停泊着,抛着锚. ***back an*** ~ 抛副锚. ***cast [drop]*** ~ 抛锚. ***cat the*** ~ 挂锚. ***come to (an)*** ~抛锚;〔喻〕住下来,住定. ***lay out an*** ~ ***to windward*** 为安全打算. ***Stand by the*** ~! 〔命令〕准备抛锚! ***swallow the*** ~ 摆脱航海生活. ***The*** ~ ***comes home.*** ①脱锚了. ②事情失败了. ***weigh*** ~ 起锚,开船. — *vi.* ①抛锚. ②停泊; 固定. — *vt.* ①抛锚泊(船). ②把…固定住. ~ ***one's hope in [on]*** 把希望寄托在…上. ~ **and collar** (门上的)铰链. ~ **escapement** (钟表的)卡摆擒纵机. ~ **gear** 【海】抛[起]锚设备. ~ **ground** 【海】锚地. ~ **ice** 【海】底冰. ~ **light** 船首夜间指示灯. **~-man** ①(电台或电视台新闻节目中的)现场报导员. ②(电台或电视台讨论节目中的)主持人. ~ **ring** 【数】环面. ~ **watch** 【海】锚更.

An·chor·age [ˈæŋkəridʒ] *n.* 安克雷奇〔美国阿拉斯加州港市〕.

an·chor·age [ˈæŋkəridʒ] *n.* ①抛锚;停泊. ②抛锚地. ③停泊税. ④〔喻〕寄托.

an·cho·ress [ˈæŋkəris] *n.* 女隐士;女修道者.

an·cho·ret [ˈæŋkərit], **-rite** [-rait] *n.* 隐士.

an·cho·ret·ic [ˌæŋkəˈretik] *a.* 隐士的,隐居的.

an·cho·vy [ˈæntʃəvi] *n.* (*pl.* **~(s)**) 【鱼】鳀. ~ *sauce* 鳀制酱油,鳍鱼汁.

an·chu·sa [ænˈkjuːzə] *n.* 【园艺】毛茎植物,阿看草.

an·chu·sin [æŋˈkjuːsn, -zn] *n.* 阿看草染料.

an·chy·lose [ˈæŋkiləuz] *vt., vi.* ①(使)(关节)僵硬(起来). ②(使)(骨与骨)胶合,粘连. **-d** [-zd] *a.* 关节僵硬的.

an·chy·lo·sis [ˌæŋkaiˈləusis] *n.* ①关节僵硬. ②骨骼胶合.

an·cien ré·gime [ɑ̃ːnˈsjɛ̃ːŋ reiˈʒiːm] 〔F.〕(特指法国 1789 年革命前的)旧制度.

an·cient[1] [ˈeinʃənt] *a.* ①已往的,古代的. ②古来的,古老的,旧式的. ③〔古〕年老的. *an* ~ *city* 古城. ~*relics* 古代遗物. — *n.* ①古(代的)人. ②〔古〕高龄老人,老者. ③〔the ~s〕古文明国的国民;(希腊、罗马时代的)古典作家〔艺术家〕. ***A- of Days*** 上帝,神. ~ **lights** 【法】(他人无权遮蔽其光线的)二十年以上的老窗户. ~ **regime** = *ancien régime*. **-ly** *ad.* 从前,古时候,在古代. **-ness** *n.* 旧;古代.

ancient² [ˈeinʃənt] *n.* 〔古〕旗；旗手.

an·cient·ry [ˈeinʃəntri] *n.* ①古旧；古风. ②古代. ③〔废〕世家.

an·cil·lar·y [ænˈsiləri] *a.* 辅助的，附属的，副 *(to)*. *an ~ science* 辅助科学. — *n.* 〔英〕助手，随从.

an·cip·i·tal [ænˈsipitl] **an·cip·i·tous** [-təs] *a.* 【植】(茎)有两棱的.

an·cle [ˈæŋkl] *n.* = ankle.

an·con [ˈæŋkɔn] *n.* ①肘. ②【建】肘托. **A- sheep** 长身短腿羊.

an·cress [ˈæŋkris] *n.* = anchoress.

-ancy *suf.* = -ance: ascend*ancy*.

an·cy·los·to·mi·a·sis [ˌænsiˌlɔstəˈmaiəsis] *n.* 钩虫病.

and [强 ænd; 弱 ənd, nd] *conj.* ①〔表示并列或对称关系〕及，和，与，同；又，兼. *a statesman ~ writer* 政治家兼作家. *I went to his house, ~ he came to mine.* 我去他家，他也来我家. ②〔表示配合，整体〕*a carriage ~ four* 四马马车. *a cup ~ saucer* 连碟茶杯. *brandy ~ water* 兑水的白兰地. ③〔表示连续、反复〕*They walked two ~ two* 一双一双地走. *many ~ many a time* 屡次，多次. *talked ~ talked* 说了又说. ④〔表示种种不一〕*There are books ~ books [men ~ men]* 书[人]有种种，好坏不一. ⑤〔表示结果〕那么；就会；一…就…. *The sun came out ~ the glasses dried.* 日出草干. *He spoke ~ all was still.* 他一讲话，全体立即肃静无声. ⑥〔用于祈使语气引导出条件句〕假如…那就…. *Stir ~ you are a dead man.* 你要动就要你的命. *Speak the truth [If you speak the truth], ~ you need have no shame.* (假如)你说真话，就不必害羞. ⑦〔口〕〔用于 go, come, try 等动词间〕*Try ~ (= try to) do* 试着做一做. *Go ~ (= go to) see* 去看看吧. ⑧〔连接数词〕*one ~ twenty is [are] 21. two hundred ~ twenty-three is [are] 223* 〔百位数之后美国常不加用 and〕. *seven ~ six* 〔英币〕7先令6辨士〔略作 7/6〕. ⑨〔表示转折〕但，却 *So able, ~ he is very modest.* 他这样能干，但很谦虚. ⑩〔强调进一步，加重语气〕而且，又 *He did it, ~ did it well.* 他做了，而且做得很好. ⑪〔用于二形容词之间，使前一形容词带有副词性质〕*nice ~ warm* 暖和得舒服. *fine ~ thin* 纤细的. *rare ~ hungry* 饥肠辘辘. *fine ~ startled = extremely startled* 大吃一惊. ⑫〔惊异，得知真情时〕*A- are you really going?* 嘿，你真要走吗？ ⑬〔表示动作的连续〕于是，然后. *She read for half an hour ~ went to bed.* 她读了半小时书，然后就睡觉了. ⑭〔表示同时〕又. *eat ~ drink* 又吃又喝. ⑮〔表示目的〕*Go ~ tell her the news.* 去把消息告诉她. ⑯〔用于句首起承接作用〕于是，因此，接着. *A- he said unto Moses.* 接着他对摩西说. *A- you may now tell us all about it.* 因此，现在你可以把这件事情的原委讲给我们听了. ⑰〔连接两个名词使后一名词具有形容词意义的特殊用法〕*dance ~ delight = delightful dance* 愉快的跳舞. *~ all* ①〔口〕连…都一齐 (*He ate the fish, bone ~ all.* 他吃鱼连骨头都一齐吃了). ②〔方〕此外；的确. *~ all that* = ~ so on. *~ all this* = ~ that. *~ as well* 以及，又. *~ … at that* 而且. *~ Co.* [ən ˈkəu] = *& Co.* … 公司. *~ how* 〔美〕非常，很，真 (*He was a miser —~ how!* 他是吝啬鬼——可不是吗！). *~ no wonder* 也难怪. *~ now* 那么. *~/or* [ænd ɔː] 及(或) (*Contributions in money ~/or garments are welcome.* 欢迎捐助现金及(或)衣服). *~ others* 其他等等. *~ so* 所以. *~ so forth* = *~ so on* 等等，云云. *~ that* 而且 (*You must tell him, ~ that at once.* 你必须告诉他，而且要立刻告诉他). *~ the like* 等等，云云. *~ the rise* 〔美〕还多 (*a hundred ~ the rise* 一百以上). *~ then* 其次，然后，于是就. *~ what not* 等等，云云. *~ with reason* 也难怪. *~ yet* 然而，但. *by twos ~ threes* 三两成群. — *n.* ①附加条件. ②〔常 *pl.*〕附加细节. *He accepted the job, no ~ about it.* 他接受了这项工作，没有附加条件. *It was a long story, with many ~s.* 这故事说来话长，有许多细节. **"and" gate** 【计】"与"门.

and. = **an·dan·te** [ænˈdænti] *ad.* 〔It.〕【乐】缓慢地，温和地，用行板. — *n.* 【乐】行板.

An·da·lu·sia [ˌændəˈluːzjə] *n.* 安达卢西亚〔西班牙南部一区域〕.

An·da·lu·sian [ˌændəˈluːziən] *n.* 安达卢西亚；安达卢西亚人；安达卢西亚鸡. — *a.* 安达卢西亚(人)的.

an·da·lu·site [ˌændəˈluːsait] *n.* 【矿】红柱石.

An·da·man(s) [ˈændəmæn(z)] *n.* 安达曼群岛〔印度〕(= Andaman Islands). **-ese** [ˌændəmænˈniːz] *n.* ①安达曼群岛上的当地居民. ②安达曼语.

an·dan·ti·no [ˌændænˈtiːnəu] *ad.* 〔It.〕【乐】用小行板. — *n.* 【乐】小行板.

An·de·an [ˈændiən, ænˈdiːən] *a.* (南美)安第斯山脉的. — *n.* 安第斯山人.

An·der·son [ˈændəsn] *n.* ①安德森〔姓氏〕. ②**H. C.** ~ 安徒生〔1805—1875，丹麦童话作家〕. ③**C. D.** ~ 安德森〔1905— ，美国物理学家，positron 的发现者〕.

Anderson shelter 〔英〕家庭防空壕.

An·des [ˈændiːz] *n. pl.* 〔the ~〕安第斯山脉〔南美〕.

an·des·ite [ˈændizait] *n.* 【矿】安山岩.

and·i·ron [ˈændaiən] *n.* (壁炉的)柴架.

An·dor·ra [ænˈdɔrə] *n.* 安道尔〔欧洲〕. ~ *La Vella* 安道尔(市)〔安道尔首都〕.

an·dr- *comb.f.* 〔用于元音前〕= andro-.

an·dra·dite [ˈændrədait] *n.* 【矿】钙铁榴石.

An·dre [ˈændri, ˈɑːndrei] *n.* 安德烈〔男子名，Andrew 的异体〕.

An·drew [ˈændruː] *n.* 安德鲁〔男子名〕.

An·drews [ˈændruːz] *n.* 安德鲁斯〔姓氏〕.

an·dro- *comb. f.* 表示"男性的"，"雄性的"：*andro*gynous, *andro*sphinx.

an·droe·ci·um [ænˈdriːʃiəm] *n.* 【植】雄蕊.

an·droc·ra·cy [ænˈdrɔkrəsi] *n.* 男性中心社会.

an·dro·gen [ˈændrədʒən] *n.* 雄性激素.

an·drog·e·nous [ænˈdrɔdʒinəs] *a.* 【生】产雄的.

an·dro·gyne [ˈændrɔdʒain] *n.* 雌雄同序植物.

an·drog·y·nous [ænˈdrɔdʒinəs] *a.* ①兼两性的，雌雄同体的. ②【植】雌雄同丝的；雌雄同序的.

an·drog·y·ny [ænˈdrɔdʒini] *n.* 【植】雌雄同体.

an·droid [ˈændrɔid] *n.* (科学幻想小说中的)机器人；似人自动机 (*cf.* robot).

An·drom·e·da [ænˈdrɔmidə] *n.* ①【希神】安德罗米达〔埃塞俄比亚公主，其母夸其美貌而得罪海神，致使全国遭殃〕. ②〔the ~〕【天】仙女座.

an·dro·sphinx [ˈændrɔsfiŋks] *n.* 男面狮身像.

an·dros·ter·one [ænˈdrɔstərəun] *n.* 【化】(雄)甾酮.

An·dy [ˈændi] *n.* 安迪〔男子名，Andrew 的昵称〕.

ane [ein] *a., n.* 〔Scot.〕= one.

-ane *suf.* ①-an 的变体，但所表意义与 -an 不同：hum*ane* — hum*an*. ②【化】烷：meth*ane* (甲烷)，eth*ane* (乙烷).

a·near [əˈniə] *ad., prep.* 〔方、诗〕近，在近旁；接近.

an·ec·dot·age [ˈænikdəutidʒ] *n.* ①轶事集，逸话集. ②〔谑〕好谈逸事的老年时代. *Grandfather is in his ~.* 爷爷年老话多，爱谈往事.

an·ec·dot·al [ˌænekˈdəutl] *a.* 逸事(多)的.

an·ec·dote [ˈænikdəut] *n.* 逸话，轶事，掌故，奇闻；〔*pl.*〕秘史.

an·ec·dot·ic, -i·cal [ˌænekˈdɔtik(əl)] *a.* 逸事(多)的，爱讲逸事的.

an·e·cho·ic [ˌæneˈkəuik] *a.* 无回声的；无反响的. ~ **chamber** 隔音室.

a·nele [əˈniːl] *vt.* 〔古〕给…行；临终涂油礼.

a·ne·mi·a [əˈniːmiə] *n.* = anaemia.

a·ne·mic [əˈniːmik] *a.* = anaemic.

a·nem·o·graph [ə'neməgrɑːf] *n.* 风速计. **-ic** [əˌneməˈgrɑːfik] *a.*
an·e·mol·o·gy [ˌænəˈmɔlədʒi] *n.* 测风学.
an·e·mom·e·ter [ˌæniˈmɔmitə] *n.* 风速表.
an·e·mo·met·ric(al) [ˌænimə*u*ˈmetrik(*ə*l)] *a.* 测定风速和风向的.
an·e·mom·e·try [ˌæniˈmɔmitri] *n.* 风速测定(法).
a·nem·o·ne [əˈneməni] *n.* ①【植】银莲花,白头翁. ②【动】海葵 (= sea ～).
an·e·moph·i·lous [ˌæniˈmɔfiləs] *a.* 【植】风媒的〔*cf.* entomophilous〕. ～ **flower** 风媒花.
a·nem·o·scope [əˈneməskəup] *n.* 风向仪.
an·e·mo·sis [ˌæniˈməusis] *n.* (树木因风吹而在年轮之间发生的)轮裂.
a·nent [əˈnent] *prep.* 〔古〕关于,论及;在…方面.
-a·neous *suf.* 属于…的: extr*aneous*.
an·er·gy [ˈænədʒi] *n.* 【医】①能力缺失,精力缺乏. ②缺乏免疫性;对抗原注射无反应;无变应性. **-er·gic** *a.*
an·er·oid [ˈænərɔid] *a.* (晴雨表等)不用液体的,不装水银的. — *n.* 无液〔空盒〕气压表,无液晴雨表 (= ～ barometer).
an·es·the·sia [ˌænisˈθiːzjə] *n.* = anaesthesia.
an·es·the·si·ol·o·gist [ˌænisˌθiziˈɔlədʒist] *n.* 麻醉学医师,麻醉学专家.
an·es·the·si·ol·o·gy [ˌænisθiziˈɔlədʒi] *n.* 麻醉学.
an·es·thet·ic [ˌænisˈθetik] *a.* = anaesthetic.
an·es·the·tist [æˈniːsθətist] *n.* = anaesthetist.
an·es·the·tize [æˈnisθətaiz] *a.* = anaesthetize.
a·nes·trus [æˈnestrəs] *n.* 【动】乏情期,不动情期.
an·e·thole [ˈænəθəul] *n.* 【化】茴香脑.
An·eu·rin [əˈnaiərin] *n.* 阿奈林〔男子名〕.
an·eu·rin [ˈænjuərin] *n.* 【化】维生素 B_1, 盐酸硫胺素;抗神经炎素.
an·eu·rism, an·eu·rysm [ˈænjuərizəm] *n.* 【医】动脉瘤. **-ris·mal, -rys·mal** [-ˈrizməl] *a.*
a·new [əˈnjuː] *ad.* 重新,再,另. *begin one's life* ～ 重新做人. *edit* ～ 改订.
an·frac·tu·os·i·ty [ænˌfræktjuˈɔsiti] *n.* ①弯曲;曲折,错综. ②〔*pl.*〕弯曲的路〔沟渠等〕.
an·frac·tu·ous [ænˈfræktjuəs] *a.* 弯曲的,迂回的;错综的.
ANG = Air National Guard 空中国民警卫队.
A.N.G. = American Newspapers Guild 美国报业公会.
an·ga·kok [ˈæŋgəkɔk] = angekok.
an·ga·ry [ˈæŋgəri] *n.* 【国际法】战时征用权〔指交战国征用或毁坏中立国财产的权利,但负有赔偿义务〕.
an·ge·kok [ˈæŋgəkɔk] *n.* Eskimo 巫医.
an·gel [ˈeind*ʒ*əl] *n.* ①天使;守护神. ②安琪儿,可爱的人. ③英国古金币名. ④〔美口〕后台老板. *an* ～ *of a child* 天使一样的小孩. *an evil [a fallen]* ～ 恶魔,凶神. *a good [guardian]* ～ 吉神,守护神. ～*'s vist* 不常有的事. ***entertain an*** ～ ***unawares*** 无意中接待了要人〔名人〕而不知其身分,无意中有恩惠于微服私行的要人〔名人〕. ***Speak of*** ～***s, and you will hear their wings.*** 说到某人,某人就到. ～ **cake [food]** 〔美〕(面粉、糖、蛋白做的)白蛋糕. ～**fish** *n.*【鱼】辐乌鲂. ～**-on-horse-back** 薰肉夹牡蛎. ～**puss** *n.* 〔美俚〕天使面孔. ～**-shark** *n.* 扁鲨. — *vt.* 〔美口〕做…的后台老板;出钱资助(演出等).
An·ge·la [ˈænd*ʒ*ilə] *n.* 安吉拉〔女子名〕.
An·gel·e·no [ˌændʒiˈliːn*əu*] *n.* (*pl.* ～*s*) 洛杉矶人.
an·gel·ic, -i·cal [ænˈdʒelik(*ə*l)] *a.* 天使(似)的,有天使性质的.
an·gel·i·ca [ænˈdʒelikə] *n.* ①【植】白芷. ②〔A-〕白芷属;白芷味白葡萄酒. ～ **tree** *n.*【植】楤木.
An·ge·li·na [ˌændʒiˈliːnə] *n.* 安吉利娜〔女子名,Angela 的昵称〕.
An·gell [ˈeindʒəl] *n.* 安吉尔〔姓氏〕.
An·ge·lo [ˈændʒiləu] *n.* 安吉洛〔男子名〕.
an·ge·lus [ˈændʒiləs] *n.* ①【天主】(早晨、中午、晚上为纪念耶稣降临人世而做的)祈祷. ②祈祷钟 (= Angelus bell).
an·ger [ˈæŋgə] *n.* ①怒,忿怒. ②〔方〕(伤口处的)发炎,炎症. *He is easily moved to* ～. 他动辄发怒. *be furious [filled] with* ～ 满腔怒火. ***in a fit of*** ～ 勃然大怒. ***in a moment of*** ～ 一时之气,一阵气恼. ***in*** ～ 动怒,生气. — *vt.* 激怒,触怒,使发怒,使生气. *He was* ～*ed at the insult.* 他因受辱而恼怒. — *vi.* 发怒,恼火. *She* ～*s with little or no provocation.* 她无缘无故就发怒.
an·gi·na [ænˈdʒainə] *n.* 【医】①咽喉痛,咽峡炎. ②心绞痛 (= ～ pectoris).
an·gi·og·ra·phy [ˌændʒiˈɔgrəfi] *n.* ①血管照相术. ②血管学.
an·gi·ol·o·gy [ˌændʒiˈɔlədʒi] *n.* 血管学,血管淋巴管学.
an·gi·o·ma [ˌændʒiˈəumə] *n.* (*pl.* ***-ma·ta*** [-mətə], ～*s*) 血管瘤. **-tous** [-ˈɔmətəs, -ˈəumətəs] *a.*
an·gi·o·sperm [ˈændʒiəuspəːm] *n.* 被子植物.
Ang·kor [ˈæŋkɔː] *n.* 吴哥〔柬埔寨古城〕. ～ **Wat [Vat]** 吴哥窟,吴哥庙〔古高棉王朝庞大的宫殿遗址〕.
Angl. = ①Anglican. ②Anglice.
An·gle [ˈæŋgl] *n.*【英史】盎格鲁人〔*cf.* Angles〕.
an·gle[1] [ˈæŋgl] *n.* ①角,隅,角落;棱,棱角. ②【数】角,角位,角的度数. ③【机】角铁. ④见地,观点. ⑤(事物的)方面,角度. ⑥〔口〕隐蔽的个人动机;诡计. ⑦〔口〕(新闻报道的)偏见,歪曲. *an auxiliary [subsidiary, suplementary]* ～ 补角. *an external [exterior]* ～ 外角. *an internal [interior]* ～ 内角. *an obtuse* ～ 钝角. *a vertical* ～ 对顶角. *a right* ～ 直角. *a straight* ～ 平角. *an optical [a visual]* ～ 视角;〔矿〕光轴角. ～ *of attack* 【空】气压角,迎角. ～ *of bank [roll]* 【空】转角. ***meet at right*** ～***s*** 相交成直角. ***take the*** ～ 测角度. ***view from various*** ～***s*** 由各方面观察. — *vt.* ①使(摄影机等)偏成〔转向〕某一角度. ②使(新闻报道等)带上色彩〔倾向性〕. *She* ～*d her column of chitchat towards teen-agers.* 她的闲话专栏着眼于青少年. ～ *one's camara* (摄影时)对角度. ～ *a report* 使报告掺杂偏见. — *vi.* ①转变角度;突然朝某方向转去. ②以一个角度移动. ～**-dozer** 铲土机,侧铲推土机. ～**iron [bar]** 角铁, L 形铁. ～**-site** 硫酸铅矿. ～**-table**【建】托架,斜撑铁.
an·gle[2] [ˈæŋgl] *n.* 〔古〕钓钩;钓具. *a brother of the* ～ 钓鱼者. — *vi.* ①钓鱼. ②〔美俚〕钓(誉),贪图,图谋. ～ *for carp* 钓鲤鱼. ～ *for praise* 沽名钓誉. — *vt.* 在…钓鱼. ～**worm** *n.* 蚯蚓 (= earthworm).
an·gled [ˈæŋgld] *a.* 有角的;成角度的.
an·gle·pod [ˈæŋglpɔd] *n.* 萝藦科属植物.
an·gler [ˈæŋglə] *n.* ①钓鱼者. ②沽名钓誉者,追逐(名利等)的人 (*for*). ③【鱼】鮟鱇.
An·gles [ˈæŋglz] *n.* 〔*pl.*〕盎格鲁族〔五世纪由 Schleswig (今德国北部)移住英国的条顿族的一支,其居住地即称 Angle-land, 后转为今名 England〕.
An·gli·a [ˈæŋgljə] 〔L.〕= England.
An·gli·an [ˈæŋgljən] *a.* 盎格鲁的,盎格鲁人的. — *n.* 盎格鲁人〔语〕.
An·glic [ˈæŋglik] *n.* (瑞典语言学家 R. E. Zachrisson 氏创制的)简易英语.
An·gli·can [ˈæŋglikən] *a.* ①英国国教的,英国圣公会的. ②〔美〕英国的. *the* ～ *Church* 英国国教. — *n.* 英国国教徒,英国圣公会教徒. **-ism** *n.* ①英国国教(教义),英国圣公会(教义). ②英国风度;英国方式.
An·gli·ce [æŋˈglɔsi] *ad.* 〔L.〕用英语,照英语说.
An·gli·cism [ˈæŋglisizəm] *n.* ①英国风格. ②英国说法〔语法、语义〕,英国惯用语. ③〔美〕英国语法. **-gli·cist** *n.* 英国语言和文学的研究者.
An·gli·cize [ˈæŋglisaiz], **An·gli·fy** [-fai] *vt., vi.* (使)

变为英国派；（在语言习惯等方面）(使…)英语化. ★亦可作 a-.
an·gling [ˈæŋgliŋ] *n.* 钓鱼(术).
An·glist [ˈæŋglist] *n.* 英国通.
An·glis·tics [ˌæŋˈglistiks] *n.* 英语学.
An·glo [ˈæŋgləu] *n.* *(pl. ~s)* （住美洲西南地区讲英语的)北欧裔美国人.
An·glo-[ˈæŋgləu-] *comb. f.* 〔English 一词的构词形式〕表示"英国,英裔;英国的: *Anglo-African*.
An·glo-Af·ri·can [ˈæŋgləuˈæfrikən] *n., a.* 英裔非洲人的.
An·glo-A·mer·i·can [ˈæŋgləuəˈmerikən] ① *n.* 英裔美国人；住在美国的英国人. ② *a.* 英美的；英裔美国人的.
An·glo-Cath·o·lic [ˈæŋgləuˈkæθəlik] *n., a.* 英国国教高教会派的.
An·glo-French [ˈæŋgləu ˈfrentʃ] *n.* ①英法的； 英国法语的. ②英国法语.
An·glo·ma·ni·a [ˈæŋgləuˈmeiniə] *n.* 英国狂，亲英. **-c** [-niæk] *n.* 醉心英国的人,亲英分子.
An·glo-Nor·man [ˈæŋgləuˈnɔːmən] ① *a.* 英格兰和诺尔曼(人、语)的；诺尔曼系英国人的. ② *n.* 诺尔曼系英国人；盎格鲁诺尔曼语.
An·glo·phil(e) [ˈæŋgləufail] ① *a.* 亲英派的. ② *n.* 亲英分子,亲英派.
An·glo·phobe [ˈægləufəub] 反对[憎恶]英国者，恐英者. **-pho·bia** [-ˈfəubiə] *n.* 反对.
An·glo·pho·bi·a [ˌægləuˈfəubiə] *n.* 反对[憎恶]英国；恐英病.
An·glo·phone [ˈæŋgləufəun] *n.* （在有包括英语在内的多种语言的国家中)以英语为母语的人.
An·glo-Sax·on [ˈægləu ˈsæksən] ① *n.* 五世纪左右移居英国的日耳曼族人民；〔*pl.*〕盎格鲁撒克逊族；盎格鲁撒克逊语〔又名 Old English〕；简易英语；英国人. ② *a.* 盎格鲁撒克逊族[语]的；古代英语的；英国的. **-ism** 盎格鲁撒克逊风格[腔调]；英人气质.
An·go·la [æŋˈgəulə] *n.* 安哥拉〔非洲〕；〔a-〕= Angora. **-lan** [-lən] *n.* 安哥拉人.
an·gor [ˈæŋgəː] *n.* ①剧痛. ②心绞痛 (= angina pectoris).
An·go·ra [æŋˈgɔːrə] *n.* ①安哥拉棉毛呢. ②安哥拉猫 (= ~ cat). ③安哥拉兔 (= ~ rabbit). ④= Ankara. ~ **cloth** 安哥拉绣花布；马海毛呢. ~ **goat** 安哥拉山羊.
an·gos·tu·ra [ˌæŋgɔsˈtjuərə] *n.* ①(南美) 安哥斯图拉苦味树皮〔可解热滋补〕.
an·gri·ly [ˈæŋgrili] *ad.* 怒,忿然.
an·gry [ˈæŋgri] *a.* ①发怒的，忿怒的. ②(风雨等)凶猛的. ③(颜色等)刺目的. ④(伤口等)肿痛的,发炎的. ~ *waves* 怒涛. ~ *winds* 烈风. *an* ~ *wound* 发炎的伤口. ~ **red** 鲜红. ***be [get]*** ~ ***at (about)*** 因…而发怒，生…的气. ***be [get]*** ~ ***with*** *(sb.)* 生(某人)的气. ***have*** ~ ***words with*** … 和…吵嘴. ***make*** *(sb.)* ~ 惹(某人)发火[发怒,生气].
angst [aːŋst] *n.* 担心；焦虑；苦恼.
Ang·strom [ˈæŋstrəm] *n.*【物】埃〔一亿分之一厘米，用做测量波长的单位〕.
an·guine [ˈæŋgwin] *a.* (象)蛇的.
an·guish [ˈæŋgwiʃ] *n.* （极度)痛苦，苦闷，烦恼. *in* ~ 极度痛苦. — *vt., vi.* (使)痛苦；(使)苦恼. **-ed** *a.* 痛苦的.
an·gu·lar [ˈæŋgjulə] *a.* ①有角的，角形的；尖锐的. ②用角度量的；角的. ③瘦骨嶙峋的. ④不灵活的，生硬的. ***in an*** ~ ***manner*** (态度)生硬. ~ **bone** 隅骨. ~ **leaf spot** 叶角斑病. ~ **process** 隅骨突起. **-ly** *ad.*
an·gu·lar·i·ty [ˌæŋgjuˈlæriti] *n.* ①有角；角弯曲度. ②〔*pl.*〕角状部分，棱角. ③(样子、衣着等)难看,生硬. ④【机】斜度. *soften down [round off] awkward angularities* 磨去笨拙的棱角.
an·gu·late [ˈæŋgjuleit] *a.* 有角的,成角的. — *vt., vi.* (使)具棱角.
an·gu·la·tion [ˌæŋgjuˈleiʃən] *n.* ①作角,作成角度. ②角的形状、部分或位置.
An·gus [ˈæŋgəs] *n.* ①安格斯〔男子名〕. ②苏格兰东部州名.
ang·wan·ti·bo [æŋˈgwaːntibəu] *n.* *(pl. ~s)*【动】金熊猴.
an·har·mon·ic [ˌænhaːˈmɔːnik] *a.*【物】非谐的. ~ **force** 非谐力. ~ **ratio**【物】交比,非调和比.
an·hin·ga [ænˈhiŋgə] *n.*【动】蛇鸟.
an·hy·drid(e) [ænˈhaidraid] *n.*【化】酐.
an·hy·drite [ænˈhaidrait] *n.*【矿】硬石膏,无水石膏.
an·hy·drous [ænˈhaidrəs] *a.*【化】无水的.
an·i·co·nic [ˌænaiˈkɔnik] *a.* 不把崇拜的神做成人形[兽形]的,不使用偶像(作崇拜对象)的；反对偶像的；只崇拜象征性的神的.
a·nigh [əˈnai] *ad., prep.*〔英方〕近.
an·il [ˈænil] *n.* ①【植】木兰. ②靛蓝.
an·ile [ˈeinail] *a.* ①衰老的；老太婆似的. ②糊涂的.
an·i·lin(e) [ˈæniliːn] *n.*【化】苯胺. ~ **printing** 曲面双色印刷,阿尼林印刷 (= flexographic printing).
an·il·i·ty [æˈniliti] *n.* ①衰老,老年昏瞆. ②〔常 *pl.*〕糊涂言行.
an·i·ma [ˈænimə] *n.*〔L.〕人生之本；灵魂.
an·i·mad·vert [ˌænimædˈvəːt] *vi.* 谴责，责备，苛责 *(on, upon)*. ~ ***on sb.'s shortcomings*** 揭人缺点[疮疤]. **-ver·sion** [-ˈvəːʃən] *n.*
an·i·mal [ˈæniməl] *n.* ①动物；兽；牲畜. ②〔俚〕家畜，牲口. ③〔俚〕畜生(一般的人)〔骂人语〕. *domestic ~s* 家畜. *wild ~s* 野兽. — *a.* 动物的；肉欲的. ~ *appetites [desires]* 兽欲. ~ *courage* 蛮勇. ~ *food* 肉食. ~ *heat* 体温. ~ *husbandry* 畜牧业,家畜学. ~ *kingdom* 动物界. ~ *life* 动物的生态. ~ *magnetism* 魅力. ~ *passion* 肉欲,兽欲. ~ *spirits* 血气,元气. **-ly** *ad.* 肉体上.
an·i·mal·cule [ˌæniˈmælkjuːl] *n.* 微动物；微生物.
an·i·mal·cu·lum [ˌæniˈmælkjuləm] *n.* (*pl.* **-la** [-lə]) 极微动物 (= animalcule).
an·i·mal·ism [ˈænimәlizәm] *n.* ①动物的生活[活动、性状]. ②兽性；兽欲. ③人即动物的学说.
an·i·mal·ist [ˈæniməlist] *n.* ①兽欲主义者. ②动物画家[雕刻家].
an·i·mal·i·ty [ˌæniˈmæliti] *n.* ①兽性. ②动物生态. ③动物界.
an·i·mal·i·za·tion [ˌæniməlaiˈzeiʃən] *n.* ①动物化,兽性化. ②(食物等)动物质化.
an·i·mal·ize [ˈæniməlaiz] *vt.* ①使动物化；使象野兽一样. ②使耽于兽欲. ③使变成动物质. *to ~ food through digestion* 通过消化使食物变成动物质. *men that were ~d by war* 由于战争而变得和野兽一样的人.
an·i·mate [ˈænimeit] *vt.* ①使活起来，赋与…以生命. ②给与…以生气；使有生气；使活泼. ③鼓舞，激励，激发. ④绘制(动画片). — *a.* [ˈænimit] ①有生命的；有生气的. ②生气蓬勃的，活泼的. ~ *nature* 生物界,动物界.
an·i·mat·ed [ˈænimeitid] *a.* ①精力旺盛的,生气蓬勃的. ②栩栩如生的. ③热闹的,热烈的. *an* ~ *bust* 栩栩如生的胸像. *an* ~ *cartoon [drawing]* 动画片. *an* ~ *description* 生动的描写. *an* ~ *discussion* 热烈的讨论. ~ *pictures* 走马灯；〔古〕电影. *an* ~ *talk* 畅谈.
an·i·mat·er [ˈæniˌmeitə] *n.* ①赋予生气者,鼓舞者. ②【影】画动画片的人.
an·i·mat·ing [ˈænimeitiŋ] *a.* 使有生气的,令人兴奋的,活泼的.
an·i·ma·tion [ˌæniˈmeiʃən] *n.* ①生气；生机. ②生动,活

泼. ③动画片(制作). *a face devoid of* ~ 死人(一样的)面孔. *suspended* ~ 假死,晕厥. ***with*** ~ 活泼地,生动地.
an·i·ma·tism [ˈænimətizəm] *n.* 物活论〔指非生物的东西具有意识或个性〕.
an·i·ma·tor [ˈænimeitə] *n.* = animater.
an·i·mé [ˈænimei] *n.* 〔F.〕 芳香树脂. — *a.* 有生命的.
an·i·mism [ˈænimizəm] *n.* 万物有灵论; 泛灵论; 精灵崇拜. **an·i·mist** *n.* 泛灵论者; 精灵崇拜者.
an·i·mos·i·ty [ˌæniˈmɔsiti] *n.* 怨恨,仇恨,敌视,憎恶. *animosities between classes* 阶级间的仇恨. ***have*** ~ ***against [towards]*** 仇视,敌视.
an·i·mus [ˈæniməs] *n.* ①意图,宗旨,主导思想. ②敌意,恶意.
an·i·on [ˈænaiən] *n.*【化】阴离子,阳向离子.
an·ise [ˈænis] *n.*【植】大茴香.
an·i·seed [ˈænisiːd] *n.* 大茴香子,八角子.
an·i·sei·ko·ni·a [ˈæˌnaisəˈkəunjə] *n.* (眼睛的)左右异像症;【医】(两眼)物像不等.
an·i·sette [ˌæniˈzet] *n.* 〔F.〕 大茴香酒.
aniso- *comb. f.* 不等的; 不同的,异 (*opp.* iso-):*aniso*tropic.
an·i·sole [ˈænisəul] *n.*【化】茴香醚,苯甲醚,甲氧基苯.
an·i·so·mer·ic [æˌnaisəuˈmerik] *a.*【化】非异构的.
an·i·som·er·ous [ˈænaiˈsɔmərəs] *a.*【植】(花部的)不齐数的.
an·i·so·met·ric [əˌnaisəuˈmetrik] *a.* 不等轴的.
an·i·so·me·tro·pi·a [əˌnaisəumiˈtrəupiə] *n.*【医】屈光参差. **-trop·ic** [-trɔpik] *a.*
an·i·so·trop·ic [əˈnaisəuˈtrɔpik] *a.* ①【植】对外界刺激有不同反应的. ②【物】各向异性的. **an·i·sot·ro·py** [ˌænaiˈsɔtrəpi], **an·i·sot·ro·pism** [-pizm] *n.* **an·i·so·trop·i·cal·ly** *ad.*
A·ni·ta [əˈniːtə] *n.* 安妮塔〔女子名, Ann 的昵称〕.
An·ka·ra [ˈæŋkərə] *n.* 安卡拉〔土耳其首都〕.
an·ker [ˈæŋkə] *n.* 安克〔荷兰液量名,约 10 加仑〕.
an·ker·ite [ˈæŋkərait] *n.*【矿】铁白云石.
ankh [æŋk] *n.* T 型十字(章)〔古埃及生命的象征〕.
an·kle [ˈæŋkl] *n.* 踝; 踝节部,脚脖子. — *vi.* 〔美俚〕走,走路. ~ **bone** 踝骨. ~ **boot** 高帮鞋. **~-deep** *a., ad.* 深及踝部地.
an·klet [ˈæŋklit] *n.* ①踝环,脚镯. ②〔*pl.*〕翻口短袜,套袜. ③带踝襻的女鞋.
an·kus [ˈæŋkəs] *n.* (有尖钉和钩的)驱象刺棒.
an·ky·lo·saur [ˈæŋkələuˌsɔː] *n.* 甲龙亚目动物.
an·ky·lose [ˈæŋkiləus] *vt.* ①使(骨)长合. ②使(关节)僵硬. — *vi.* ①(骨与骨)长合. ②(关节)变僵硬.
an·ky·lo·sis [ˌæŋkaiˈləusis] *n.* = anchylosis.
an·ky·los·to·mi·a·sis [ˌæŋkaiˌlɔstəˈmaiəsis] *n.* 钩虫病.
an·lace [ˈænlis] *n.* (中世纪的)双刃短剑.
an·la·ge [ˈɑːnlɑːgə] *n.* (*pl.* **-gen** [-gən], ~*s* [-gəz]) ①后期发展的基础; 基础. ②【胚】原基.
Ann [æn] *n.* 安〔女子名〕.
ann. = ①〔L.〕 *anni* (= years). ②annals. ③annuities. ④annuity.
An·na [ˈænə] *n.* 安娜〔女子名, Ann 的异体〕.
an·na [ˈænə] *n.* 安那〔印度旧币名, 一卢比(rupee) 的十六分之一〕. *have eight* ~*s of dark blood* 〔口〕对半混血.
An·na·bel·la [ˌænəˈbelə] *n.* 安娜贝拉〔女子名〕.
an·na·berg·ite [ˈænəˈbəːgait] *n.* 镍华.
an·nal·ist [ˈænəlist] *n.* 编年史作者,年表编者.
an·nal·ist·ic [ˌænəˈlistik] *a.* 编年史的; 按年代编辑的.
annal [ˈænəl] *n.* 〔古〕 纪要,纪事录.
an·nals [ˈænəlz] *n.pl.* ①编年史. ②年代记,年表,年鉴,年刊. ③历史记载. *the* ~ *of war* 战史. *the* ~ *of the publisher's association* 出版家协会的年刊.
An·nap·o·lis [əˈnæpəlis] *n.* 安纳波利斯〔美国港市〕.
an·nat·to [əˈnɑːtəu] *n.* 胭脂树红, 果红〔用做食品着色剂〕.
Anne [æn] *n.* ①安妮〔女子名〕. ②英国女王〔1702—14 年在位〕. *Queen* ~ *is dead.* 〔古〕陈旧的消息.
an·neal [əˈniːl] *vt.* ①【冶】使韧化,使退火,使焖火. ②〔喻〕锻炼(意志). ③〔古〕(在窑里)烧,给…上釉.
an·nec·tent, an·nec·tant [əˈnektənt] *n.*【生】连接的.
an·ne·lid [ˈænəlid] *n.*【动】环虫,蠕虫,环节动物.
An·nel·i·da [əˈnelidə] *n. pl.*【动】环节动物门.
an·nel·i·dan [əˈnelidən] *n., a.* 环节动物(的).
An·netta [əˈnetə] *n.* 安妮塔〔女子名, Ann 的昵称〕.
An·nette [əˈnet] *n.* 安妮特〔女子名, Ann 的昵称〕.
an·nex [əˈneks] *vt.* ①附加,添加,追加; 附带(条件) *(to)*. ②签署,盖(印). ③合并,并吞,兼并(领土) *(to)*. ④获得,得到. ⑤擅自拿走,偷. *a protocol* ~*ed to the treaty* 附加于条约的议定书. *The manager* ~*ed his seal to the document.* 经理在文件上盖印. ~ ***the honors [laurels]*** 〔美〕竞赛获胜,得锦标. — [ˈæneks] *n.* ①附录,附件; 附属品. ②附属建筑. *an* ~ *to a hotel* 旅馆的增建部分.
an·nex·a·tion [ˌænekˈseiʃən] *n.* ①附加. ②合并,归并,吞并. ③附加物,吞并物.
An·nie [ˈæni] *n.* 安妮〔女子名, Ann 的昵称〕. ~ **Oakley** [ˈəukli] 〔口〕优待券,免费入场券.
an·ni·hi·la·ble [əˈnaiələbl] *a.* 可歼灭的; 可消灭的.
an·ni·hi·late [əˈnaiəleit] *vt.* ①消灭,歼灭. ②废止(法律). ③彻底打败. ③【物】使(一个核粒子及另一反粒子)湮灭. *annihilating operation* 歼灭战. *The home basketball team* ~*d the visiting team.* 本地篮球队大败客队.
an·ni·hi·la·tion [əˌnaiəˈleiʃən] *n.* ①绝灭,消灭,歼灭. ②【物】湮灭. ③【神学】灵魂与肉体的毁灭. **-ism**【宗】灵魂寂灭论〔认为作恶者死后灵魂必归毁灭〕.
an·ni·hi·la·tor [əˈnaiəleitə] *n.* ①消灭者,歼灭者. ②灭火器. ③【数】零化子. ④【空】减震器,阻尼器.
an·ni·ver·sa·ry [ˌæniˈvəːsəri] *a.* ①年年的,每年的. ②周年的; 周年纪念的. *The celebration is an* ~ *affair.* 庆祝会年年举行. *an* ~ *gift* 周年纪念礼物. — *n.* 周年纪念(日). *a wedding* ~ 结婚周年纪念. ~ ***of sb.'s birth*** 生日. ~ ***of sb.'s death*** 忌日,逝世纪念日.
An·no Do·mi·ni [ˈænəu ˈdɔminai] 〔L.〕 ①公元〔略 A.D.〕〔*cf.* B.C.〕. ②〔口, 谑〕衰龄,老年. *A.D. is his trouble.* 他衰老了. ***the Anno Domini clause*** 〔谑〕年老退职制度.
An·no Hegirae [ˈænəu hiˈdʒairiː] 〔L.〕 伊斯兰教纪元.
an·no mun·di [ˈænəu ˈmʌndai] 〔L.〕 开天辟地以来,世界纪元〔略 A.M.〕.
an·no·tate [ˈænəuteit] *vt., vi.* 注解,注释. *an* ~*d edition* 注释版. **-ta·tion** [-ˈteiʃən] *n.* **-ta·tor** *n.* 注释者.
an·nounce [əˈnauns] *vt.* ①告知,报知,通告. ②宣布,宣告,发表; 唱名报(客等)通知(开宴等). ③预告; 显示. ④当(节目的)报幕员[广播员]. ~ *a call* (长途电话)接通通知. ~ *a new edition* 登新书广告. ~ *a visitor* 通报有客. *It has been semiofficially* ~*d that* ... 据半官方消息. ~ *a lecture series* 宣告有一系列讲演. *The servant* ~*d Mr. and Mrs. Smith.* 仆人唱名报告"史密斯先生和夫人到". ~ *dinner* 通知开宴[饭]. *He* ~*s three programmes a week.* 他每星期播送三个节目. — *vi.* ①做报幕员[广播员]. ② 宣布参加竞选 *(for)*. ③ 宣布支持某人 *(for)*. *He* ~*ed for governor.* 他宣布竞选州长.
an·nounce·ment [əˈnaunsmənt] *n.* ①通告,布告,宣告,预告,声明. ②宣布的行动[过程]. ③言谈. *Every new* ~ *of hers was greeted with shouts of laughter.* 她说的每一句话都引起哄堂大笑. *an* ~ *of marriage* 结婚通告.
an·nounc·er [əˈnaunsə] *n.* ①宣告者. ②(电视、电台)播音员; (戏剧等的)报幕员; (比赛等的)解说员.
an·noy [əˈnɔi] *vt.* 惹恼, 打搅; 使烦恼. *A fly keeps* ~*ing me.* 一个苍蝇老在打搅我. *I was much* ~*ed with him.* 我被那家伙缠死了. — *n.* 〔诗、罕〕= annoyance.

an·noy·ance [ə'nɔiəns] *n.* ①烦恼,为难;麻烦. ②烦恼的事情. ***put (sb.) to ~*** 使(人)烦恼,为难,打搅. ***to one's ~*** 为难的是,烦恼的是.

an·noy·ing [ə'nɔiiŋ] *a.* 令人烦恼的;令人厌烦的,令人讨厌的. *How ~!* 多讨厌! 真讨厌! **-ly** *ad.*

an·nu·al ['ænjuəl] *a.* ①每年的;年度的;一年(一次)的. ②(植物)一年一生的,一季生的. *an ~ report* 年报. — *n.* ①一年生[一季生]植物. ②年刊,年报,年鉴. ~ **expenditure [revenue]** 岁出[入]. ~ **ring**【植】年轮. ~ **plant**一年生植物. **-ly** *ad.* 年年,每年.

an·nu·i·tant [ə'nju(:)itənt] *n.* 领年金者.

an·nu·i·ty [ə'nju(:)iti] *n.* 年金. *a contingent [life, terminable] ~* 临时[终身、定期]年金.

an·nul [ə'nʌl] *vt.* 取消(命令),废除,注销. *The treaty was annulled.* 条约废除了.

an·nu·lar ['ænjulə] *a.* 环的;环状的,轮状的,有环纹的. ~ **eclipse**【天】环食. ~ **saw** 圆锯,钢丝锯. **-ly** *ad.* 环状地.

an·nu·late, an·nu·lat·ed ['ænjuleit(id)] *a.* ①有环的,有环纹的. ②由环构成的.

an·nu·la·tion [ˌænju'leiʃən] *n.* ①成环,成环状. ②环,环状物.

an·nu·let ['ænjulit] *n.* ①小环. ②【动】小节. ③【建】圆箍线.

an·nul·ment [ə'nʌlmənt] *n.* 取消,废止,作废,注销.

an·nu·loid ['ænjulɔid], **an·nu·lose** ['ænjuləus] *a.* 有环的,有环节的.

an·nu·lus ['ænjuləs] *n.* (*pl.* **-li** [-lai], *~es*) ①环(带),环节,环轮. ②【动】体环;菌环. ③【天】环食带. ④【数】圆环域.

an·num ['ænəm] *n.* [L.] 年. *per ~* 每年.

an·nun·ci·ate [ə'nʌnʃieit] *vt.* [罕]公布,通告.

an·nun·ci·a·tion [əˌnʌnsi'eiʃən] *n.* ①通告,公布. ②[the A-]【宗】天使报喜[指天使加布里埃尔通知圣母玛丽,她将生育耶稣]. ③天使报喜节[三月二十五日]. ~ **lily** 白色百合花.

an·nun·ci·a·tor [ə'nʌnʃieitə] *n.* ①通告者. ②[美]信号器. *alarm ~* 警报信号器.

anoa [ə'nəuə] *n.* (印度尼西亚西里伯岛上的)小野牛.

an·ode ['ænəud] *n.*【电】阳极,正极,板极. **a·nod·ic** [ə'nɔdik] *a.*

an·o·dize ['ænəudaiz] *vt.* 对…作阳极化处理,阳极电镀.

an·o·dyne ['ænəudain] *a.* 止痛的. — *n.* 止痛药[剂].

an·o·e·sis [ˌænəu'i:sis] *n.* 纯被动的意识.

an·oes·trum [æn'estrəm] *n.*【动】非发情期间 (*opp.* oestrum).

a·noint [ə'nɔint] *vt.* ①给…涂油,在(伤口上)涂油. ②【宗】涂油使神圣化. ③照天意选定. ***the (Lord's) Anointed*** ①救世主,基督. ②神权国王,古犹太王. **-ment** *n.* 涂油.

an·o·lyte ['ænəlait] *n.* 阳极电解液.

a·nom·a·lism [ə'nɔməlizəm] *n.* [罕] = anomaly.

a·nom·a·lis·tic [əˌnɔmə'listik] *a.* ①异常的,不规则的. ②【天】近点的. ~ **month**【天】近点月[约$27\frac{1}{2}$日]. ~ **year**【天】近点年[365日6时13分53秒]. **-cal·ly** *ad.*

a·nom·a·lous [ə'nɔmələs] *a.* 不规则的,异常的,反常的. ~ **(finite) verb**【语法】特殊既定式动词[指 am, ought, dare, can, shall 等在否定句和疑问句中用法与助动词相同的二十四个动词形式]. **-ly** *ad.* **-ness** *n.*

a·nom·a·lure [ə'nɔməljuə] *n.*【动】鳞尾松鼠 (=scale-tailed squirrel).

a·nom·a·ly [ə'nɔməli] *n.* ①不规则,反常(现象),异常,破格. ②畸形物. ③【天】近点角[指行星偏离近日点的角度距离]. *the ~ of English spelling* 英语拼写法的不规则. *gravity ~*【物】重力异常. *A harelipped monkey is an ~.* 豁嘴的猴子是异常的东西.

an·o·mie, an·o·my ['ænəmi] (社会)反常状态;混乱;(不顾准则和法纪的)无法无天行为.

an·o·mite ['ænəmait] *n.*【矿】褐云母.

anomo- *comb. f.* 表示"不规则的".

a·non [ə'nɔn] *ad.* [古]①即刻,立即. ②不久. ③下次再. *and ~* 时或. *ever and ~* 时时. *About that, more ~* 关于此事,容当他日言及.

anon. = anonymous.

an·o·nym ['ænənim] *n.* ①匿名(作)者,无名氏. ②假名.

an·o·nym·i·ty [ˌænə'nimiti] *n.* 匿名,无名. *men hiding behind ~* 隐姓埋名的人.

a·non·y·mous [ə'nɔniməs] *a.* ①匿名的;无名的;假名的. ②无个性特征的. *an ~ author* 无名氏作者. *an ~ letter* 匿名信. *an ~ placard* 无名告示. *~ faces* 生面孔. **-ly** *ad.* **-ness** *n.*

a·noph·e·les [ə'nɔfili:z] *n.*【动】疟蚊属. ~ **mosquito** 疟蚊.

a·no·rak ['ɑ:nərɑ:k] *n.* (严寒地带人所穿)带风帽的厚茄克,皮猴.

an·o·rex·i·a [ˌænəu'reksiə] *n.*【医】食欲缺乏,厌食. ~ **nervosa** 神经性食欲缺乏.

an·or·thite [ə'nɔ:θait] *n.* 钙长石. **-thit·ic** [-'θitik] *a.*

an·os·mi·a [æ'nɔsmiə] *n.*【医】嗅觉缺失.

an·oth·er [ə'nʌðə] *a.* ①又一,另一. ②别的,另外的. ③类似的. *Will you take ~ cup?* 再来一杯好吗? *One man's meat is ~ man's poison.* [谚]利于甲者(可能)不利于乙. *I'll come to see you at ~ time.* 改日再来看你. *He may be ~ Edison.* 他可能成为爱迪逊那样的人物. — *pron.* ①另一件东西,另一个人. ②别的东西,别的人. ③那样的人[东西],同样的人[东西]. *X versus Y and ~*【法】某甲对某乙及另外一人的案件[不指出第三者真名时的说法]. *Have ~, please.* 请再吃一个. *Liar! — You're ~!* 撒谎的家伙! ——你就是这种人! ***~ day*** 他日,改天. ***~ day or two*** 再过一两天. ***~ place*** 别处,另外一处[[英]在下院时是指上院、在上院时是指下院而言]. ***~ thing [question]*** 另一回事,另一个(问题). ***~ time*** 下次. ***~ world*** 来世;天国. ***in ~ moment*** 过一会儿. ***one after ~*** 相继,顺次. ***one ~*** 相互. ***one way and ~*** 用种种方法. ***one way or ~*** 设法,无论如何. ***such ~*** (另一个)那样的人或东西;无独有偶的人[事、物] (*You will never see such ~.* 那样的人恐怕再看不到了. *It's just such ~.* 这真是无独有偶). ***taken one with ~*** 从大体上说,大体上,总的看来.

an·our·ous, an·u·rous [ə'nuərəs] *a.*【动】无尾的.

an·ox·e·mi·a [ˌænɔk'si:miə] *n.*【医】血缺氧,缺氧血症. **-mic** [-mik] *a.*

an·ox·i·a [æ'nɔksiə] *n.*【医】缺氧症.

an·ox·ic [æ'nɔksik] *a.*【医】缺氧的.

ans. = answer.

ANSA = [It.] *Agenzia Nazionale Stampa Associata* [意]安莎通讯社 (= Associated National Press Agency).

an·sa ['ænsə] *n.* (*pl.* ***an·sae*** [-si:])【解】襻,脊神经.

an·sate ['ænseit] *a.* 有柄的,有把手的.

An·schluss ['ɑ:nʃlus] *n.* [G.] ①(政治或经济的)联合,结合. ②(1938年纳粹德国对奥地利的)吞并.

An·selm ['ænselm] *n.* 安塞尔姆[男子名].

an·ser·ine ['ænsərain], **an·ser·ous** ['ænsərəs] *a.* ①鹅(似)的. ②愚蠢的. — *n.*【化】鹅肌肽.

an·swer ['ɑ:nsə] *n.* ①回答,答复. ②解答,答案. ③答辩,抗辩. ④报复. *an ~ to a problem* 某问题的解答. *have no ~ to (sb.'s letter)* 无回音[回信]. ***in ~ to*** …以回答,为答复(抗议等)而. ***one who knows all the ~s*** [美俚]万事通;老世故. ***The ~'s a lemon.*** [回答荒唐提问时用语]你这个(可笑的)问题,无法回答;废话! — *vt.* ①答,回答,答复;答应. ②解答,答辩. ③报复. ④适合;符合. ⑤尽(责),偿(债). ⑥响应. *~ a* *charge* 对控告做出答辩. ~ *a debt* 偿还债务. ~ *a letter* 回信. ~ *a riddle* 解谜. ~ *blows with blows* 以眼还眼,以牙还牙. ~ *the bell [door]* 应声开门. — *vi.* ①回答;答辩,辩解. ②负责,保证;抵偿. ③适合,符合,一致. ④见效,成功. ~ *(to) the purpose of* ...可用作.... *Gypsum* ~*s as manure* 石膏可作肥料. *Everything* ~*ed.* 事事顺利[如愿]. ~ **back** 〔卑〕顶嘴,还口. ~ **for** 负…的责任,保证;偿(罪),负责(受处分);代(被问人)回答 (*I'll* ~ *for her safety.* 我将为她的安全负责. ~ *for a crime* 负罪责. *I won't* ~ *for what I'll be doing.* 我就老实不客气了). ~ **to** 回答;符合. ~ **to the name of** 叫做,名叫 (*The dog* ~*s to the name of John.* 这只狗叫做约翰). ~ **up** 应答快 (~ *up to a question* 立刻回答问题).

an·swer·a·ble ['ɑːnsərəbl] *a.* ①可答复的;应答辩的. ②应负责的;应抵偿的. ③适合的,相当的. ~ *for an act* 为某行为负责. ~ *for damages* 有赔偿损害的责任; ~ **to** 对(某人)有责任,适合(目的) (*the government* ~ *to the people* 对人民负责的政府. *achievements* ~ *to expectation* 与希望相符的收获).

an·swer·ing ['ɑːnsəriŋ] *a.* 回答的;适当的;符合…的. *a person* ~ *to this description* 和相貌说明书相符的人. *an* ~ *pennant* 应答旗〔国际船舶用以表示已收到信号〕. — *n.* 回答. ~ **service** 代客接听电话服务.

ant [ænt] *n.* 蚂蚁. ***have*** ~***s in one's pants*** (因焦急、气愤等而)坐立不安,急于采取行动. ~ **bear**【动】大食蚁兽. ~ **cow** 蚜虫. ~**eater** 食蚁兽 (*the scaly* ~*eater* 穿山甲). ~ **hill** 蚁冢;人口稠密的地方. ~ **lion**【虫】沙挼子,蚁狮〔蛟蜻蛉科幼虫〕.

ant- *pref.* 用于元音前, = anti-.

an't [ɑːnt] ①〔口〕= are not. ②〔英口〕am not. ③〔方、卑〕= is not, has not, have not.

ant. = ①antenna. ②antiquarian. ③antiquities. ④antonym.

-ant *suf.* ①…性的: stimul*ant*. ②…的人[物]: serv*ant* stimul*ant*.

an·ta ['æntə] *n.* (*pl.* ***-tae*** [-tiː], ~*s*) 〔L.〕【建】壁端柱.

ant·ac·id ['ænt'æsid] *a.* 中和酸的,解酸的. — *n.*【医】解酸剂;抗酸剂.

An·tae·us [æn'tiəs]【希神】安泰〔大力士,大地之子,只要不离开其母大地就不可战胜〕. **-tae·an** *a.*

an·tag·o·nism [æn'tægənizəm] *n.* ①敌对,对立. ②相克作用,对抗(作用),对抗性. ~ *of the oppressed against [to] the oppressor* 被压迫者对压迫者的敌视[仇视]. *the* ~ *between Capital and Labour* 劳资间的对立. ***be brought into*** ~ ***with*** = ***come into*** ~ ***with*** 和…闹翻脸. ***in*** ~ ***to*** 反对,对抗.

an·tag·o·nist [æn'tægənist] *n.* ①敌手,反对者;对抗者. ②【解】对抗肌,拮抗肌. ③【医】对抗剂. ④【解】对合牙. ⑤(戏剧、小说等的)反面人物 (*opp.* protagonist).

an·tag·o·nis·tic, -ti·cal [æn,tægə'nistik, -tikəl] *a.* 对抗(性)的,敌对的,相反的,不相容的. *Cats and dogs are* ~. 狗和猫是敌对的. 对抗性矛盾. **-ti·cal·ly** *ad.* 反对地,敌对地,翻起脸来.

an·tag·o·nize [æn'tægənaiz] *vt.* ①反抗,对抗. ②引起…的对抗. ③中和,抵销. ④招…的怨. *His speech* ~*d many voters.* 他的发言引起许多投票者的反抗. ~ *a bill* 反对某项议案. — *vi.* 引起对抗,招怨.

ant·al·ka·li [ænt'ælkəlai] *n.* (*pl.* ***-li(e)s***) 解碱剂.

ant·aph·ro·dis·i·ac [,æntæfrə'diziæk] *a.* 抑制性欲的,制欲的. — *n.*【医】制欲药.

ant·arc·tic [ænt'tɑːktik] *a.* 南极(地方)的. — *n.* 南极(地带). *the A- Circle* 南极圈. *the A- Ocean* 南冰洋. *the A- Zone* 南极地带.

Ant·arc·ti·ca [æn'tɑːktikə] *n.* 南极洲.

An·ta·res [æn'tɛəriːz]【天】心宿二,大火〔天蝎座 α〕.

an·te ['ænti] *n.* ①【牌】预下的赌注. ②〔口〕(应摊的)份子. — *vt.* (***-ted, -teed; -te·ing***) ①预下(赌注). ②〔口〕拿出(钱、意见等);出(份子) (*up*). *He* ~*d up his half of the* ***bill***. 他付了该他分担的一半帐单. ~ *up ideas* 提出想法.

an·te- *pref.* …前的,较…前的: *antecedent, anteroom.*

an·te·bel·lum [,ænti'beləm] *a.* 〔L.〕 战前的;〔美〕南北战争前的. ~ *days* 战前时代. *the status quo* ~ 战前状况.

an·te·cede [,ænti'siːd] *vt.* 在…之前;居…之先. *Shakespeare* ~*s Milton.* 莎士比亚在密尔顿之前.

an·te·ced·ence [,ænti'siːdəns] *n.* ①先行,居先. ②【天】逆行.

an·te·ced·ent [,ænti'siːdənt] *a.* ①先行的,先前的. ②【逻】假定的,前提的. ③【地】先成的. — *n.* ①先例,前例. ②〔*pl.*〕经历,履历,学历. ③〔*pl.*〕祖先. ④【语法】先行词. ⑤【逻】前提,前件. ⑥【数】(比例的) 前项〔如 a:b 中的 a〕. *inquire into sb.'s* ~*s* 调查某人履历. *a man of shady* ~*s* 来历可疑的人. ~*s and consequences of the war* 战争的前因和后果. *of English* ~*s* 祖籍英国. **-ly** *ad.* 在前,在先.

an·te·ces·sor [,ænti'sesə] *n.* ①先行者,先驱者,前任. ②〔罕〕祖先.

an·te·cham·ber ['ænti,tʃeimbə] *n.* 接待室;前堂,前厅.

an·te·chap·el ['ænti,tʃæpəl] *n.* 教堂门厅.

an·te·choir ['ænti,kwaiə] *n.* (教堂的)唱诗台.

an·te·date ['ænti'deit, 'æntideit] *n.* 比实际早些的日期. — *vt.* ①把…上的日期填早(若干时间). ②把…说早;使提前. ③前于,先于. ~ *a letter by a week* 把信上日期填早一星期. *The cold weather* ~*ed their departure.* 寒冷的天气使他们提前离开. *His death* ~*ed his brother's.* 他去世先于他的兄弟.

an·te·di·lu·vi·an [æntidi'ljuːvjən] *a.* ①(《圣经》所说的)大洪水以前的. ②上古的;古风的,古老的,原始的. *an* ~ *automobile* 古老的汽车. — *n.* ①大洪水以前的人. ②老朽,时代落伍者.

an·te·fix ['æntifiks] *n.* (*pl.* ~*es*)【建】檐口饰. **-al** *a.*

an·te·lope ['æntiləup] *n.* (*pl.* ~*(s)*) ①羚羊. ②羚羊皮. ③〔美〕叉角羚 (= pronghorn).

an·te·me·rid·i·an ['æntimə'ridiən] *a.* 午前的.

an·te me·ri·di·em ['ænti me'ridiem] 〔L.〕 午前, 上午〔略 A.M. 或 a.m.〕〔*cf.* P.M.〕.

an·te·mor·tem ['ænti'mɔːtəm] *a.* 〔L.〕 死前的. *an* ~ *confession* 临终忏悔.

an·te·mun·dane [,ænti'mʌndein] *a.* 世界创造前的,开天辟地以前的.

an·te·na·tal ['ænti'neitl] *a.* 胎儿的, 出生前的, 产前的. ~ *training* 胎教. *an* ~ *life* 母胎内的生命.

an·ten·na [æn'tenə] *n.* (*pl.* ***-nae*** [-niː], ~*s*) ①【动】触角. ②【无】天线〔英国常用aerial〕. ~ **array**【无】天线阵. **-l** [-nəl], **-ry** [-ri] *a.*

an·te·nup·tial ['ænti'nʌpʃəl] *a.* 结婚前的.

an·te·pen·di·um [,ænti'pendiəm] *n.* ①(教堂祭坛前的)帷幔,缎帐. ②(教堂布道讲坛上的)桌布.

an·te·pe·nult ['æntipi'nʌlt] *n., a.* 倒数第三音节(的)〔如 accumulate 中的 cu〕.

an·te·pe·nul·ti·mate ['æntipi'nʌltimit] *n., a.* ①倒数第三音节(的). ②倒数第三个(的).

an·te·pran·di·al ['ænti'prændjəl] *a.* 正餐前的, 饭前的.

an·te·ri·or [æn'tiəriə] *a.* (*opp.* posterior) ①以前的,先前的,先存在的 (*to*). ②前面的,前部的 (*to*). *an* ~ *age* 早期. *age* ~ *to the flood* 洪水以前的时期. **-i·ty** [æn,tiəri'ɔriti] *n.* 先前;原先; **-ly** *ad.* 在以前;在前面.

an·te·room ['æntirum] *n.* 接待室,休息室,前室.

an·te·ty·pe ['æntitaip] *n.* 前型,原型.

an·te·ver·sion [æntiˈvəːʃən, -ʒən] *n.* 【医】子宫前倾.
an·te·vert [ˌæntiˈvəːt] *vt.* 【医】引起…前倾.
ant·he·li·on [æntˈhiːljən] *n.* 【气】反假日,幻日.
ant·hel·min·tic [ænθelˈmintik] *a.* 驱肠虫的. — *n.* 驱肠虫剂.
an·them [ˈænθəm] *n.* ①圣歌,赞歌. ②国歌. ③校歌. *a national* ~ 国歌. *the Royal Anthem* 英国国歌.
an·the·mi·on [ænˈθiːmiən] *n.* (*pl.* **-mi·a** [-ə]) 花状平纹,叶状平纹〔绘画,雕刻中的装饰〕.
an·ther [ˈænθə] *n.* 【植】药,花粉囊. ~ **dust** 花粉. ~ **sac** 花粉囊. ~ **stalk** 花丝.
an·ther·id·i·um [ˌænθəˈridiəm] *n.* (*pl.* **-idi·a** [-ə]) 【植】(隐花植物如苔、蕨等的)精子囊,雄器;精子器. **-id·i·al** *a.*
an·ther·o·zo·id [ˌænθərəˈzəuid] *n.* 【植】(隐花植物如苔、蕨等的)游动精子.
an·the·sis [ænˈθiːsis] *n.* 开花;开花期.
an·tho·car·pous [ˌænθəˈkɑːpəs] *a.* 【植】副生的;掺花果的.
an·tho·cy·a·nin [ˌænθəˈsaiənin], **an·tho·cy·an** [-ˈsaiən] *n.* 【化】花青甙,花色甙.
an·tho·di·um [ænˈθəudiəm] *n.* (*pl.* **-di·a** [-ə]) 【植】集合花.
an·thol·o·gist [ænˈθɔlədʒist] *n.* 文集编者;文选编者.
an·thol·o·gy [ænˈθɔlədʒi] *n.* (诗、文、曲、画等的)选集.
An·tho·ny [ˈæntəni, Am. -θəni] *n.* 安东尼〔男子名〕. ***St.*** ~ 圣安东尼〔猪倌的保护神〕. ***St.*** ~***'s fire*** 【医】丹毒. ~ **pig** 一胎中最小的仔猪.
an·thoph·i·lous [ænˈθɔfiləs] *a.* (虫等)爱花的,栖息花上的,以花为食的.
an·tho·phore [ˈænθəˈfɔː] *n.* 【植】花冠柄.
An·tho·zo·a [ˌænθəˈzəuə] *n.* 〔*pl.*〕【动】珊瑚虫纲.
an·tho·zo·an [ˌænθəˈzəuən] *n.* 【动】珊瑚虫〔包括珊瑚、海葵、海团扇等〕. — *a.* 珊瑚虫的. ~ **polyp** 珊瑚虫〔珊瑚水螅〕.
an·thra·cene [ˈænθrəsiːn] *n.* 【化】蒽.
an·thra·cite [ˈænθrəsait] *n.* 无烟煤,硬煤.
an·thra·cit·ic [ˌænθrəˈsitik] *a.* 无烟煤的;无烟煤似的.
an·thra·cit·ous [ˈænθrəsaitəs] *a.* 含无烟煤的.
an·thrac·nose [ænˈθræknəus] *n.* 【植】炭疽病.
an·thra·coid [ˈænθrəkɔid] *a.* 似炭疽的.
an·thrax [ˈænθræks] *n.* (*pl.* ***an·thra·ces*** [ˈænθrəsiːz]) 【医】炭疽(病). ~ **bacillus** 炭疽杆菌.
an·thro·p(o)- *comb. f.* 表示"人,人类,人类学": *anthropogeny.*
an·thro·po·cen·tric [ˌænθrəpəuˈsentrik] *a.* ①以人类为宇宙中心的. ②按人类标准判断宇宙万物的. **-trism** [-trizəm] *n.* 人类中心说,人类本位说.
an·thro·po·gen·e·sis [ˌænθrəpəuˈdʒenisis] *n.* 人类起源和发展学.
an·thro·pog·e·ny [ˌænθrəˈpɔdʒini] *n.* = anthropogenesis.
An·thro·pog·ra·phy [ˌænθrəˈpɔgrəfi] *n.* 人类地理分布学.
an·thro·poid [ˈænθrəupɔid] *a.* (猿等)似人类的. —*n.* 类人猿.
an·thro·po·log·ic, an·thro·po·log·i·cal [ænθrəpəˈlɔdʒik(əl)] *a.* 人类学(上)的. **-i·cal·ly** *ad.* 人类学上.
an·thro·pol·o·gist [ˌænθrəˈpɔlədʒist] *n.* 人类学者.
an·thro·pol·o·gy [ˌænθrəˈpɔlədʒi] *n.* 人类学.
an·thro·pom·e·try [ˌænθrəˈpɔmitri] *n.* 人体测量(学).
an·thro·po·mor·phism [ˌænθrəupəuˈmɔːfizəm] *n.* 拟人说,人格化〔使神仙、动物、非生物具有人的形状或特点〕. **-phic, -phic·al** *a.*
an·thro·po·mor·phize [ˌænθrəupəuˈmɔːfaiz] *vt., vi.* 赋与(…)人性〔人形〕,(使)人格化.
an·thro·po·mor·phous [ˌænθrəupəuˈmɔːfəs] *a.* 有人形的,似人的.
an·thro·pop·a·thy [ˈænθrəuˈpɔpəθi] *n.* 神人同感论;神人同情说;上帝有人情之说.
an·thro·poph·a·gi [ˌænθrəuˈpɔfədʒai] *n. pl.* (*sing.* ***-agus*** [-əgəs]) 食人肉的人.
an·thro·poph·a·gite [ˌænθrəuˈpɔfədʒait] *n.* 吃人肉者;吃同类之肉的动物.
an·thro·poph·a·gous [ˌænθrəuˈpɔfəgəs] *a.* 吃人肉的.
an·thro·poph·a·gus [ˌænθrəuˈpɔfəgəs] *n.* (*pl.* ***-gi*** [-dʒai]) 食人肉的人〔此词一般多用其复数形式〕.
an·thro·poph·a·gy [ˌænθrəuˈpɔfədʒi] *n.* 嗜吃人肉,吃人习俗.
an·thro·po·so·ci·ol·o·gy [ˈænθrəuˌpəuˌsəusiˈɔlədʒi] *n.* 人类社会学.
an·thro·pot·o·my [ˌænθrəuˈpɔtəmi] *n.* 人体解剖学.
an·thu·ri·um [ænˈθjuriəm] *n.* 天南星科安修里昂属植物.
an·ti [ˈænti,ˈæntai] *n.* (*pl.* ~*s*) 〔口〕反对者,反对派. *pros and* ~*s* 赞成派和反对派. *the* ~ *group* 反对派. — *a.* 唱反调,反对. *He is terribly* ~. 他爱唱反调. — *prep.* 反对. *He was* ~ *all that.* 凡此种种他都反对.
anti- *pref.* ①反,排: *anti*alien, *anti*militarism. ②伪,假: *anti*pope ③对: *anti*type, *anti*thesis. ④非: *anti*grammatical. ⑤抗,阻,防: *anti*toxin, *anti*aircraft. ⑥逆,正反对: *anti*cyclone, *anti*pole.
an·ti·air [ˈæntiˈeə] *a.* 〔口〕= antiaircraft.
an·ti·air·craft [ˈæntiˈeəkrɑːft] *a.* 防空(用)的. — *n.* ①高射炮. ②高射炮部队. ③高射炮炮火. ~ **artillery** 高射炮队〔略 AAA〕. ~ **control** 防空管制. ~ **devices** 防空设备. ~ **dug-out** 防空壕. ~ **gun** 高射炮.
an·ti-alien [ˈæntiˈeiljen] *a.* 排外的.
an·ti·a·part·heid [ˈæntiəˈpɑːthaid] *a.* 反(南非)种族隔离的.
an·ti·ar [ˈæntiɑː] *n.* ①见血封喉〔爪哇产植物〕. ②见血封喉毒汁〔用来涂在箭头上〕.
an·ti·aux·in [ˈæntiˈɔːksin] *n.* 【生】抗生长素.
an·ti·bac·te·ri·al [ˈæntibækˈtiəriəl] *a.* 抗细菌的. — *n.* 抗菌剂,抗菌物.
an·ti·bal·lis·tic [ˈæntibəˈlistik] *a.* 反弹道的. ~ **missile** 反弹道导弹.
an·ti·bar·y·on [ˈæntiˈbæriən] *n.* 【物】反重子.
an·ti·bil·ious [ˈæntiˈbiljəs] *a.* 【医】抗胆病的.
an·ti·bi·ont [ˈæntiˈbaiɔnt] *n.* 【生】对抗生物,相克生物.
an·ti·bi·o·sis [ˈæntibaiˈəusis] *n.* (*pl.* ***-ses*** [-siːz]) 【生】抗菌,抗生(现象).
an·ti·bi·ot·ic [ˈæntibaiˈɔtik] *a.* ①破坏〔伤害〕生命的. ②抗生的,抗菌的. — *n.* 抗菌素.
an·ti·bod·y [ˈæntiˌbɔdi] *n.* 【医】抗体.
an·tic [ˈæntik] *a.* ①滑稽的,诙谐的. ②〔古〕奇异的,古怪的. — *n.* 〔常 *pl.*〕①滑稽动作,古怪行径. ②〔古〕小丑. — *vi.* (***-ticked; -ticking***) 做滑稽动作.
an·ti·cat·a·lyst [ˈæntiˈkætəlist] *n.* 【化】反催化剂.
an·ti·ca·thode [ˈæntiˈkæθəud] *n.* 【物】对阴极.
an·ti·christ [ˈæntikraist] *n.* ①反对基督者. ②〔the A-〕假耶稣.
an·ti·chris·tian [ˈæntiˈkristjən] *a., n.* 反对基督(教)的(人). **-ism** *n.* 反基督(教).
an·tic·i·pant [ænˈtisipənt] *a.* 预期的,期望的 (*of*). *We were eagerly* ~ *of her arrival.* 我们热切地期望她的到来. — *n.* 期待者.
an·tic·i·pate [ænˈtisipeit] *vt.* ①预期,预料,预测;指望,期待. ②预行讨论〔考虑,处置〕;预先挪用;预支,预付. ③抢先于,占…之先. ④促进,提早,使提前发生. *I* ~

(that there will be) trouble. 我预料会有麻烦. ～ *a story* 为某个故事埋下伏笔. ～ *one's wages* 预支工资. ～ *the enemy* 先发制敌. ～ *the question* 预先估定问题. ～ *one's ruin* 促其灭亡. *Did the Vikings* ～ *Columbus in discovering America?* 北欧海盗是在哥伦布之前发现美洲的吗? —*vi.* 预测,预言,预感.

an·tic·i·pa·tion [æn͵tisiˈpeiʃən] *n.* ①预期,预测,预料;期待. ②预先挪用,预支. ③预感;预言. ④占先;抢先. ⑤【法】提前提取信托金的收益. ⑥【医】提前出现. ⑦【乐】先取音. ⑧【修】预期描写法,预辩法 (= prolepsis). *The children waited with eager* ～ *for Christmas.* 孩子们热切期待圣诞节的到来. **by** ～ = **in** ～ 先,预先 (*Thanking you in* ～. 预先致谢). **in** ～ **of** 期待 (*in* ～ *of an increase in salary* 期待加薪).

an·tic·i·pa·tive [ænˈtisipeitiv] *a.* ①预期的,预想的. ②抢先的,先发制人的. **-ly** *ad.*

an·tic·i·pa·tor [ænˈtisipeitə] *n.* ①先见者,预想者;期望者. ②抢先者,占先者,先发制人者. ③【无】预感器,预测器.

an·tic·i·pa·to·ry [ænˈtisipeitəri] *a.* ①预期的,期望着的. ②提前发生的. ③因预想将来而有所表示的. ④【语法】先行的. **-to·ri·ly** *ad.*

an·ti·cler·i·cal [ˈæntiˈklerikəl] *a.* 反教权的.

an·ti·cli·max [ˈæntiˈklaimæks] *n.* ①【修】突降法 (*opp.* climax). ②(重要性、兴趣等的)突降;(命运等的)突然衰败,虎头蛇尾.

an·ti·cli·nal [ˈæntiˈklainəl] *a.* 【地】逆斜的,背斜的〔*cf.* synclinal〕.

an·ti·cline [ˈæntiˈklain] *n.* 【地】背斜.

an·ti·cli·no·ri·um [ˈæntiklaiˈnɔːriəm] *n.* 【地】复背斜.

an·ti·clock·wise [ˈæntiˈklɔkwaiz] *a., ad.* 逆时针方向的[地],反时针方向旋转的[地] (= counterclockwise).

an·ti·co·ag·u·lant [ˈæntikəuˈægjulənt] *n.* 抗凝(血)剂.

an·ti·co·ag·u·late [͵æntikəuˈægjuleit] *vt.* (用抗凝剂)抗(血凝).

an·ti·co·don [æntik] *n.* 【生】反密码子.

an·ti·co·her·er [ˈæntikəuˈhiərə] *n.* 【电】散屑器.

an·ti·cy·clone [ˈæntiˈsaikləun] *n.* 【气】反气旋;高气压.

an·ti·de·pres·sant [ˈæntidiˈpresənt] *a.* 【精】抗抑郁症(药物)的. — *n.* 抗抑郁症药.

an·ti·diph·the·rit·ic [ˈænti͵difθəˈritik] *a.* 预防白喉的. — *n.* 抗白喉血清.

an·ti·dot·al [ˈæntidəutl] *a.* 解毒的.

an·ti·dote [ˈæntidəut] *n.* ①解毒剂 (*for; against; to*). ②〔喻〕矫正法,防止法. ～ *against arsenic* 解砷毒剂. *Hard work is the best* ～ *to mischief.* 繁忙的工作是防止为非作歹的最好方法.

an·ti·draft [ˈæntiˈdrɑːft] *a.* 反征兵的. — *n.* 反征兵,抗拒征兵.

an·ti·drom·ic [͵æntiˈdrɔmik] *a.* 【生理】(神经作用)逆向的,逆行的.

an·ti·dump·ing [ˈæntiˈdʌmpiŋ] *a.* 反倾销政策的.

an·ti·e·lec·tron [ˈænti-iˈlektrɔn] *n.* 阳电子,正电子,正子.

an·ti·e·met·ic [ˈæntiiˈmetik] *n.* 止呕剂,抗吐剂. — *a.* 止呕的,抗吐的.

an·ti·fat [ˈæntiˈfæt] *a.* 减肥的.

an·ti·fe·brile [ˈæntiˈfiːbrail] *a.* 退热的. — *n.* 退热剂.

an·ti·fe·brin(e) [͵æntiˈfebrin] *n.* 【药】退热冰,乙酰苯胺.

an·ti·fed·er·al [ˈæntiˈfedərəl] *a.* 【美史】反联邦制度的. **-ism** *n.* 反联邦制度. **-ist** *n.* 反联邦制度者.

an·ti·fer·til·i·ty [ˈæntifəːˈtiliti] *a.* 避孕的,防止生殖的.

an·ti·for·eign [ˈæntiˈfɔrin] *a.* 排外的.

an·ti·freeze [ˈæntiˈfriːz] *n.* 防冻剂,防冻液,抗凝剂〔用于汽车散热器的水中或坦克的汽油中〕.

an·ti·fric·tion [ˈæntiˈfrikʃən] *a.* 减少摩擦的. — *n.* 减摩剂,润滑剂. ～ *bearing* 滚动轴承.

an·ti·fun·gal [ˈæntiˈfʌngəl] *a.* 杀真菌的.

an·ti·gas [ˈæntiˈgæs] *a.* 防毒(气)的. *an* ～ *kit* 单人防毒装备. *an* ～ *mask* 防毒面具.

an·ti·gen [ˈæntidʒən] *n.* 【医】抗原.

an·ti·gen·i·ci·ty [ˈæntidʒəˈnisiti] *n.* 抗原性.

an·ti·grop·e·los [ˈæntiˈgrɔpiləuz] *n.* 〔单复同〕〔谑〕防水绑腿.

an·ti-G suit [ˈæntidʒiːsjuːt] (飞行员穿的)加压服.

An·ti·gua [ænˈtigə] *n.* 安提瓜(岛)〔拉丁美洲〕.

an·ti·he·lix [ˈæntiˈhiːliks] *n.* (*pl.* **-hel·i·ces** [-ˈhelisiːz], ～**es** [-siz]) 【解】对耳轮.

an·ti·he·ro [ˈæntiˈhiərəu] *n.* (小说等)不按传统主角品格塑造的主角,非正统派主角.

an·ti·his·ta·mine [ˈæntiˈhistəmi(ː)n] *n.* 【药】抗组胺剂〔用以治疗过敏反应〕. **-his·ta·min·ic** [-͵histəˈminik] *a.*

an·ti·hy·per·on [͵æntiˈhaipərɔn] *n.* 【物】反超子.

an·ti-ic·er [ˈæntiˈaisə] *n.* 【空】防冰[防冻]装置.

an·ti·il·lit·er·a·cy [ˈæntiiˈlitərəsi] *n.* 扫除文盲. ～ *campaign* 扫盲运动.

an·ti-im·pe·ri·al·ism [ˈæntiimˈpiəriəlizəm] *n.* 反帝国主义.

an·ti·knock [ˈæntiˈnɔk] *n.* 减震,消震;(内燃机减低燃料爆音的)减震剂. — *a.* 减震的.

an·ti·la·bor [͵æntiˈleibə] *a.* 反工会的,反工人利益的.

an·ti·lep·ton [͵æntiˈleptən] *n.* 【物】反轻子.

an·ti·leu·ke·mic [ˈæntiljuːˈkemik] *a.* 抗白血病的.

an·ti·lith·ic [ˈæntiˈliθik] *n.* 【医】(泌尿器的)抗结石剂. — *a.* 【医】抗结石的.

An·til·les [ænˈtiliːz] *n. pl.* 安的列斯群岛〔西印度群岛的组成部分〕. **Greater and Lesser** ～ 大、小安的列斯群岛.

an·ti·log·a·rithm [ˈæntiˈlɔgəriθəm] *n.* 【数】逆对数,真数.

an·til·o·gy [ænˈtilədʒi] *n.* (观念、言语等的)前后矛盾,自相矛盾.

an·ti·ly·sin [ˈæntiˈlaisin] *n.* 【医】抗溶素.

an·ti·lys·sic [ˈæntiˈlisik] *a.* 【医】抗狂犬病的,防治狂犬病的.

an·ti·ma·cas·sar [ˈæntiməˈkæsə] *n.* (椅子或沙发等的)背套,扶手套.

an·ti·mag·net·ic [͵æntimægˈnetik] *a.* (手表)防磁的. *an* ～ *watch* 防磁手表.

an·ti·ma·lar·i·al [͵æntiməˈlɛəriəl] *a* 抗疟的. — *n.* 抗疟药.

an·ti·masque, an·ti·mask [ˈæntimɑːsk] *n.* (假面戏幕间的)滑稽穿插.

an·ti·mat·ter [͵æntiˈmætə] *n.* 【物】反物质.

an·ti·merch·a·nized [ˈæntiˈmekənaizd] *a.* 【军】反装甲的. ～ *weapons* 反装甲武器.

an·ti·mere [ˈæntimiə] *n.* 【动】体辐. **-mer·ic** [-ˈmerik] *a.* 体辐的.

an·ti·me·tab·o·lite [ˈænti͵meˈtæbəlait] *n.* 【生化】抗代谢物.

an·ti·mil·i·ta·rism [͵æntiˈmilitərizəm] *n.* 反军国主义,反黩武主义.

an·ti·mis·sile [ˈæntiˈmisail] *a.* 反导弹的.

an·ti·mo·nar·chi·cal [ˈæntiməˈnɑːkikəl] *a.* 反君主政体的,反君主制的. **-chist** *n.* 反君主政体者.

an·ti·mo·ni·al [͵æntiˈməunjəl] *a.* 锑的,含锑的. — *n.* 含锑药剂.

an·ti·mon·ic [͵æntiˈməunik] *a.* ①锑的,含锑的. ②【化】五价锑的,五价锑的化合物的.

an·ti·mo·nous [ˈæntiməunəs], **an·ti·mo·ni·ous** [-ˈməuniəs] *a.* ①有锑的,似锑的. ②【化】亚锑的,三价锑

的；含锑的.
an·ti·mon·soon [ˌæntimɔnˈsuːn] *n.*【气】反季风.
an·ti·mo·ny [ˈæntiməni] *n.*【化】锑.
an·ti·morph [ˈæntimɔːf] *n.*【生】反效等位基因.
an·ti·my·cin [ˈæntiˈmaisin] *n.*【药】抗霉素.
an·ti·neu·tri·no [ˈæntinjuːˈtriːnəu] *n.*【物】反中微子.
an·ti·neu·tron [ˈæntiˈnjuːtrɔn] *n.*【物】反中子.
an·ti·node [ˈæntinəud] *n.*【物】(波)腹、腹点.
an·ti·noise [ˈæntiˈnɔiz] *a.* 抗噪音的，减少噪音的.
an·ti·no·mi·an [ˌæntiˈnəumiən] *a.*【宗】反对遵从道德律的，唯信仰论的〔指单纯依靠信仰而不必遵从道德法规就能得到拯救〕. — *n.* 道德律废弃论者，唯信仰论者. **-ism** *n.*【宗】唯信仰主义.
an·tin·o·my [ænˈtinəmi] *n.* ①(某一法律与另一法律的)对立. ②(两个显然都合理的原则或法律之间的)矛盾，不一致. ③【哲】二律背反.
an·ti·nov·el [ˈæntiˈnɔvəl] *n.* (不按传统格式写成的)非传统小说(如不以情节为主，运用意识流手法等)小说.
an·ti·nu·cle·on [ˈæntiˈnjuːkliɔn] *n.*【物】反核子.
an·ti·ox·i·dant [ˌæntiˈɔksidənt] *n.* 防氧化剂，抗氧化剂〔用做食物防腐剂〕. — *a.* 防氧化的.
an·ti·par·ti·cle [ˈæntiˈpɑːtikl] *n.*【物】反粒子.
an·ti·pas·to [ˌæntiˈpɑːstəu] *n.* (*pl.* ~*s*)〔It.〕饭前小菜，开胃食物.
an·ti·pa·thet·ic, -i·cal [ænˌtipəˈθetik(əl)] *a.* ①生来厌恶的，不合天性的，格格不入的. ②引起反感的. *He was ~ to any change.* 他素来厌恶任何变革.
an·ti·path·ic [ˌæntiˈpæθik] *a.* ①不相容的，反对的. ②【医】相克症状的.
an·tip·a·thy [ænˈtipəθi] *n.* ①嫌忌；厌恶；反感，憎恶；不相容性. ②被人厌恶的事物. ***have an ~ to*** 对…有反感，生性不爱…(*Some people have an ~ to cats.* 有的人讨厌猫).
an·ti·pe·ri·od·ic [ˈæntiˌpiəriˈɔdik] *a.* 抗周期性病的. — *n.* 抗疟剂.
an·ti·per·i·stal·sis [ˈæntiˌperiˈstælsis] *n.*【生理】(肠壁的)逆蠕动.
an·ti·per·se·cu·tion [ˈæntiˌpəːsiˈkjuːʃən] *a.* 反迫害的.
an·ti·per·son·nel [ˈæntiˌpəːsəˈnel] *a.* 杀伤(性)的〔旨在杀伤人而不在摧毁物资〕. ~ *bombs* 杀伤炸弹.
an·ti·per·spir·ant [ˈæntiˈpəːspirənt] *n.* 止汗药.
an·ti·phlo·gis·tic [ˈæntiflɔuˈdʒistik] *a.*【医】消炎的. — *n.* 消炎剂.
an·ti·phlo·gis·tine [ˈæntifləuˈdʒistin] *n.*【医】消炎膏，消肿膏.
an·ti·phon, an·tiph·o·ny [ˈæntifən(i)] *n.* ①唱和的诗歌. ②应答轮唱的赞美诗. ③在唱赞歌前(或后)朗读的诗句.
an·tiph·o·nal [ænˈtifənl] *a.* 应答轮唱的，对唱的. — *n.* 唱和歌集.
an·tiph·o·nar·y [ænˈtifənəri] *n.* 唱和歌集.
an·tiph·ra·sis [ænˈtifrəsis] *n.* 词义反用法；反语，反话〔表示幽默或讽刺，如：a giant of three feet, four inches 中的 giant〕.
an·tip·o·dal [ænˈtipdl], **an·tip·o·de·an** [ænˌtipəˈdi(ː)ən] *a.* ①【地】对跖的，在地球上正相反面的. ②恰恰相反的. ③【生】反足的. *twin brothers with ~ personalities* 性格恰恰相反的孪生兄弟.
an·ti·pode [ˈæntipəud] *n.* ①恰恰相反的事务. ②【化】对映体. ③【无】对蹠点.
an·tip·o·de·an [ænˌtipəˈdiːən] *a.* = antipodal.
an·tip·o·des [ænˈtipədiːz] *n. pl.* ①对蹠地，地球上相反的地区. ②〔英〕〔A-〕新西兰和澳大利亚. ③〔罕〕对蹠人. ④〔也用作单数〕恰恰相反的事物. *The South Pole is the antipode of the North Pole.* 南极是北极的对蹠地. *Our ~ sleep while we wake.* 我们醒着的时候，我们地球背面的人却在睡觉. *The ~ of love is hatred.* 爱的反面是恨.
an·ti·pole [ˈæntipəul] *n.* ①相反极. ②恰恰相反的事物(*of, to*).
an·ti·pol·lu·tion [ˈæntipəˈljuːʃən] *n., a.* 反污染(的).
an·ti·pope [ˈæntipəup] *n.* 伪教皇.
an·ti·pro·ton [ˈæntiprəutən] *n.*【物】反质子.
an·ti·py·ret·ic [ˈæntipaiˈretik] *a.* 退热的. —*n.* 退热药.
an·ti·py·rin(e) [ˌæntiˈpaiərin] *n.*【药】安替必灵〔退热药〕.
Antiqua-Barbuda [ˈɑːntikwæ-ˈbɑːbuːdæ] *n.* 安提瓜和巴布达〔加勒比海国家名〕.
an·ti·quar·i·an [ˌæntiˈkwɛəriən] *a.* ①古物的，文物的. ②研究文物的，搜集古物的. ③搜集古籍的. — *n.* ①文物工作者，古物收藏者. ②古籍商，古玩商. ③大幅图画纸〔31×53 英寸〕. **-ism** *n.* 古物癖，好古癖；对古物的研究.
an·ti·quar·i·um [ˌæntiˈkwɛəriəm] *n.* 古物陈列馆.
an·ti·quark [ˈæntiˈkwɑːk] *n.*【物】反夸克.
an·ti·quar·y [ˈæntikwəri] *n.* 文物工作者，古物收藏者.
an·ti·quate [ˈæntikwit] *vt.* ①使变旧；使过时. ②使具有古风，把…设计得古色古香. ~ *a building* 设计一座古代风格的建筑物.
an·ti·quat·ed [ˈæntikwitid] *a.* ①陈旧的，旧式的，过时的. ②古色古香的，有古风的. ③年老的.
an·tique [ænˈtiːk] *a.* ①古代的；古风的. ②旧式的，过时的. — *n.* ①古物，古董. ③古(代)式(样)，古风. ③一种黑体字. *an ~ dealer* 古董商. — *vi.* 购买古玩. **an·tiqu·er** *n.* 古物收藏家. **-ly** *ad.* **-ness** *n.*
an·tiq·ui·ty [ænˈtikwiti] *n.* ①古旧. ②古代. ③〔集合词〕古人. ④〔*pl.*〕古代的风习〔制度等〕. ⑤〔*pl.*〕古物，古迹，古代文物. ***of ~*** 太古的.
an·ti·rab·ic [ˈæntiˈræbik] *a.* 抗狂犬病的.
an·ti·rac·ism [ˈæntiˈreisizəm] *n.* 反种族主义，反种族歧视.
an·ti·rat·tler [ˈæntiˈrætlə] *n.* (车辆等的)防震音装置.
an·tir·rhi·num [ˌæntiˈrainəm] *n.*【植】金鱼草；〔A-〕金鱼草属.
an·ti·sab·ba·tar·ian [ˈæntisæbəˈtɛəriən] *a.* 反对安息日的. — *n.* 不守安息日的人，反对安息日者.
an·ti·sa·loon [ˈæntisəˈluːn] *a.*〔美〕反对卖酒的. *A-League* 主张关闭酒店的同盟〔成立于 1893 年〕.
an·ti·scor·bu·tic [ˈænti-skɔːˈbjuːtik] *a.* 抗坏血病的. — *n.* 抗坏血病药.
an·ti·scrip·tur·al [æntiˈskriptʃərəl] *a.* 反对圣经的，违反圣经的.
an·ti-seis·mic [ˈæntiˈsaizmik] *a.* 抗地震的.
an·ti-Sem·ite [ˈæntiˈsiːmait] *n.* 排犹(太)分子，反犹分子.
an·ti-Se·mit·ic [ˈæntisiˈmitik] *a.* 反犹太人的.
an·ti-Sem·i·tism [ˈæntiˈsemitizəm] *n.* 排犹主义，反犹太主义.
an·ti·sep·sis [ˌæntiˈsepsis] *n.* 防腐(法)，消毒(法)，灭菌(法).
an·ti·sep·tic [ˌæntiˈseptik] *a.* ①防腐的，有消毒力的. ②消过毒的，无菌的. ③异常整洁的. ④冷静的；客观的. — *n.* 防腐剂；杀菌剂〔如碘酒、酒精、硼酸等〕. ~ **finish** 防腐加工. ~ **gauze** 消毒纱布. **-ti·cal·ly** *ad.*
an·ti·sep·ti·cize [ˌæntiˈseptisaiz] *vt.* 使起防腐作用，以防腐剂处理.
an·ti·se·rum [ˈæntiˈsiərəm] *n.*【医】抗血清.
an·ti·skid [ˈæntiˈskid] *a.* 防滑的.
an·ti·slav·er·y [ˈæntiˈsleivəri] *n., a.* 反对奴隶制度(的).
an·ti·smut [ˈæntismʌt] *a.* 禁淫秽书报的.

an·ti·so·cial [ˈæntiˈsəuʃəl] *a.* ①厌恶社交的. ②反社会(组织)的，反社会福利的. **-ist** *n.* ①厌恶社交的人. ②反社会主义者.

an·ti·spas·mod·ic [ˈæntispæzˈmɔdik] *a.* 治痉挛的，防痉挛的. — *n.* 镇痉药.

an·ti·stat·ic [ˌæntiˈstætik] *a.* 抗静电的.

an·tis·tro·phe [ænˈtistrəfi] *n.* ①(古希腊戏剧中) 歌咏队在舞台上从左向右的舞动；从左向右舞动时唱的歌. ②【乐】对照乐节；对唱乐节. ③【修】同语溯用法〔如: the glory of success and the success of glory〕；反唇相讥〔用对方原语反击对方〕. **-stroph·ic** [-ˈstrɔfik] *a.*

an·ti·sub·mar·ine [ˈæntiˌsʌbməˈriːn] *a.* 反潜(艇)的，防潜(艇)的. ~ **bomb** 深水炸弹. ~ **gun** 反潜艇炮.

an·ti·tank [ˈæntiˈtæŋk] *a.* 反坦克的〔略 A. T. 或 AT〕. *an* ~ *gun* 反坦克炮.

an·ti·tech·nol·o·gy [ˈæntiˌtekˈnɔlədʒi] *n.* 反技术化〔一种出于所谓人道主义考虑而反对进行技术研究的观点〕.

an·ti·the·ism [ˈæntiˈθiːizəm] *n.* 无神论.

an·ti·the·ist [ˈæntiˈθiːist] *n.* 无神论者.

an·tith·e·sis [ænˈtiθisis] *n.* (*pl.* **-ses** [-siːz]) ①【修】对语，对句〔如: Man proposes, God disposes〕. ②对语的后半部. ③对照，对立(面). ④【乐】对应乐节. *Joy is the* ~ *of sorrow.* 欢乐是苦恼的对立面.

an·ti·thet·ic, an·ti·thet·i·cal [ˌæntiˈθetik(əl)] *a.* ①对立的，对照的. ②正相反的. **-i·cal·ly** *ad.*

an·ti·tox·ic [ˌæntiˈtɔksik] *a.* 抗毒(性)的.

an·ti·tox·in(e) [ˈæntiˈtɔksin] *n.* 【生】抗毒素.

an·ti·trade [ˈæntiˈtreid] *n.* 〔*pl.*〕反贸易风，反信风.

an·ti·tra·gus [ænˈtitrəgəs] *n.* (*pl.* **-gi** [-dʒai]) 【解】对耳屏.

an·ti-Trin·i·tar·i·an [ˈæntitriniˈtɛəriən] *a.* 【神】反对三位一体说的. —*n.* 反三位一体论者. **-ism** [-izm] *n.* 反三位一体说.

an·ti·trust [ˈæntiˈtrʌst] *a.* 反托拉斯的，反垄断的.

an·ti·tus·sive [ˈæntiˈtʌsiv] *a.* 镇咳的. — *n.* 镇咳药.

an·ti·type [ˈæntitaip] *n.* ①模型〔典型〕所代表的原型，象征所代表的事物. ②【神学】《圣经》《旧约》中所预示的《新约》中的事物.

an·ti·u·ni·verse [ˈæntiˈjuːnivəːs] *n.* 【物】反宇宙.

an·ti·ven·in [ˈæntiˈvenin] *n.* 抗蛇毒素.

an·ti·vi·ral [ˈæntiˈvairəl] *a.* 【医】抗病毒的.

an·ti·viv·i·sec·tion [ˈæntiˌviviˈsekʃən] *n.* 反对活体实验〔反对在活的动物身上作医学实验的主张〕. **-ist** *n.*, *a.*

an·ti·war [ˈæntiˈwɔː] *a.* 反战的.

an·ti·world [ˈæntiˈwəːld] *n.* 反物质世界〔由所谓反物质组成的假想世界〕.

an·ti·yan·kee·ism [ˈæntiˈjæŋkizəm] *n.* ①反美国佬主义. ②反美国腔，反美国式.

ant·ler [ˈæntlə] *n.* 多叉鹿角.

An·toi·nette [ˌæntwɑːˈnet] *n.* 安托万内特〔女子名，Antonia 的昵称〕.

An·ton [ˈæntən] *n.* 安东〔男子名，Ant(h)ony 的异体〕.

An·to·ni·a [ænˈtəunjə] *n.* 安东尼娅〔女子名〕.

An·to·nio [ænˈtəuniəu] *n.* 安东尼奥〔男子名，Ant(h)ony 的异体〕.

an·to·no·ma·sia [ˌæntənəuˈmeiziə] *n.*【修】代称，换称〔如: 称法官为 his honor, 称 a wise man 为 a Solomon〕.

an·to·nym [ˈæntəunim] *n.* 反义词 (*opp.* synonym). *'Bad' is the* ~ *of 'good'.* "坏"是"好"的反义词.

an·ton·y·mous [ænˈtɔniməs] *a.* 反义的，反义词的.

an·tre [ˈæntə] *n.* 〔诗〕洞窟.

an·trorse [ænˈtrɔːs] *a.* 【生】向上的，向前的. **-ly** *ad.*

an·trum [ˈæntrəm] *n.* (*pl.* **-tra** [-rə]) 【解】窦，房. *dental* ~ 牙窦.

AN·TU, an·tu [ˈæntuː] *n.* 安妥〔杀鼠药 alpha-naphthyl-thiourea 的商标名称〕.

Ant·werp [ˈænt-wəːp] *n.* 安特卫普〔比利时港市〕.

A·nu·bis [əˈnjuːbis, -ˈnuː-] 亡灵接引神〔埃及的豺面神，引领亡灵前去接受审判〕.

a·nu·cle·ar [eiˈnuːkliə, -njuː-] *a.* 【生】无细胞核的.

an·u·ran [əˈnjurən] *n.*, *a.* 【动】无尾目动物(的)〔包括青蛙、癞蛤蟆等〕.

an·u·re·sis [ˌænjuˈriːsis] *n.* 尿闭，无尿症. **-ret·ic** [-ˈretik] *a.*

an·u·ri·a [əˈnjuəriə] *n.* 无尿(症). **an·ur·ic** [-rik] *a.*

an·u·rous [əˈnjuərəs] *a.* (蛙，蟾蜍等)无尾的.

anus [ˈeinəs] *n.* (*pl.* ~(*es*)) 〔L.〕【解】肛门.

an·vil [ˈænvil] *n.* ①(铁)砧. ②【解】(耳朵里的)砧骨. ③(电键的)下接点. ④砧琴〔一种敲击乐器〕. ***on the*** ~ 在讨论中，在制作中，在编辑中. (*We have now another scheme on the* ~. 我们正在准备另一个计划).

anx·i·e·ty [æŋˈzaiəti] *n.* ①悬念，挂虑，忧虑. ②切望，渴望. ③【病】(精神)不安，苦闷. *cause sb. much* ~ 使人极不放心. ***be all [in great]*** ~ 担忧. ***feel no*** ~ ***about*** 对…不愁，不着急〔关心〕. ***give*** ~ ***to*** 使…担心. ***with great*** ~ 非常担忧、焦急. ~**-ridden** *a.* 忧心忡忡的.

anx·ious [ˈæŋkʃəs] *a.* ①忧虑的，担心的；挂念的，焦急的. ②切望的，渴望的；急想. ③使人不安的. *He is* ~ *to see you.* 他急想见你. ~ ***seat [bench]*** 〔美〕忏悔者座位 (*on the* ~ *seat* 坐立不安). ***be*** ~ ***about*** (*sb.'s health; the consequences*) 担忧(某人健康)；害怕(结果). ***be*** ~ ***for*** 切望，急欲，急着，愁着. (*The boy was* ~ *for a radio.* 那孩子渴望有一个收音机. *be* ~ *for sb.'s safety* 为某人的安全担心). **-ly** *ad.*

an·y [ˈeni] *a.* ①〔用于疑问句、否定句、条件从句中，或用于肯定句但与含有疑问、否定意义的词连用〕什么，一些，一点. *Have you* ~ *book to read?* 你有什么可读的书吗？*If there arise* ~ *difficulty, send for me.* 有什么麻烦找我好了. *I cannot see* ~ *difference.* 我一点差别也看不出. ②〔通常重读，多用于肯定句〕任何，随便哪一个，每一个. *Any child knows that* .... 任何孩子都知道…. *You may call* ~ *day you please.* 随便哪天来都可以. ③一般的，普通的. *We don't accept just* ~ *students.* 我们并不收一般的学生〔只收高材生〕. *You are not just* ~ *girl.* 你和一般女子就是不一样. ④〔与单数名词连用，代替 a, an, one〕一个. *This buckle is useless — it hasn't* ~ *handle.* 这桶没啥用场——它没有桶柄. —*pron.* 〔*sing.*, *pl.*〕哪个，无论哪个，任何，(无论)多少. *Choose* ~ *of these books.* 这些书随便挑哪本好了. *Do* ~ *of you know?* 你们当中，有谁知道吗？*Keep the apple, I don't want* ~. 把苹果收起来，我不要吃. *A- is better than none.* 有总比没有好. — *ad.* 一些，少许，略微，稍微. 〔常与比较级连用〕. *Is he* ~ *better today?* 他今天好些吗？*Did she cry* ~*?* 她一点没有哭吗？~ ***and every*** 统统，全体 (~ *and every book in this library* 这个图书馆里的全部藏书). ~ ***amount [number]*** 许多，很多 (*"Have you* ~ *salt?"* 你有盐吗？*"Any amount."* 啊，有的是). ~ ***longer*** 再 (*I don't drink* ~ *longer.* 我不再喝酒了). ~ ***more*** 再；更 (*I won't smoke* ~ *more.* 我不再抽烟了). ~ ***old*** 任何…都 (*A- old colour will do.* 任何颜色都好). ~ ***one*** 随便哪一个 (*You may take* ~ *one of these.* 任择其一). ~ ***time*** 无论何时，随便什么时候 (*You are welcome* ~ *time.* 无论何时，你都受欢迎). ***at*** ~ ***cost*** 无论如何，必得，非要 (*The stolen painting must be recovered at* ~ *cost.* 无论如何要把被盗的画找回来). ***at*** ~ ***rate*** 好歹，总之，无论如何；至少 (*The firm has done much better this year than last; at* ~ *rate, so I am told by one of the staff.* 这家公司今年比去年好，至少我是听一位职工这样说的). ***if*** ~ 若有；即使有也(极少) (*there is little (water), if* ~. (水吗) 大概没有). ***in*** ~ ***case*** 横竖，总之 (*In* ~ *case you* *had better hear what your wife has to say.* 总之,你最好听你妻子的话). **of ~** 在所有的…之中(*the biggest war of ~ since 1946* 1946 年以来最大的一次战争). ***scarcely [hardly]*** ~ 几乎没有,少有.

an·y·bod·y [ˈeniˌbɔdi] *pron.* ①〔用于疑问句、否定句、条件从句中〕任何人. *Is ~ here?* 有人吗? *I haven't seen ~.* 我没有看到任何人. ②〔用于肯定句中〕随便哪一个人. *You may ask ~ here for help.* 这里随便哪一个人都可以为你效劳. *He doesn't lend his book to ~.* 他不借书给任何人;〔但 anybody 用降调读,则 anybody 便等于 everybody〕他的书不一定谁都借. ***~ else*** 别人 (*Does ~ else want it?* 还有别人要吗?) ***~'s game*** 〔美〕输赢不能预测的比赛. ***~'s guess*** 谁也预料不到的事情〔问题〕. ***if ~*** 如果有人的话 (*She can do it if ~.* 要是有人能做的话,她就能). — *n.* ①有声名的人,重要人物. ②平常人. *Is he ~?* 他是要人吗? *If you wish to be ~.* 你要是想出名的话. *Everybody was invited who is ~.* 重要人物都被邀请了. *two or three anybodies* 两三个普通人.

an·y·how [ˈenihau] *ad.* ①总之,无论如何,不管怎样 (= in any case). ②无论用什么方法 (= in any possible way). ③马马虎虎,随随便便. *A-, let us try.* 好歹试试看. *The door was locked; We couldn't get into the room ~.* 门锁着,我们不论用什么办法也进不了房间. ***all ~*** 〔美口〕草率,潦草,马虎(*Things are all ~.* 事事都很马虎). ***feel ~*** (身体)不舒服.

an·y·more [ˈeniˈmɔː] *ad.* 再也(不),(不)再〔用于含有否定意义的结构〕. *He doesn't live here ~.* 他(现在)不再住在这里了. *That's hard to get ~.* 那个已经难弄到了.

an·y·one [ˈeniwʌn] *pron.* 任何人 (= anybody).

an·y·place [ˈenipleis] *ad.* 〔美口〕在任何地方,无论哪里 (= anywhere).

an·y·thing [ˈeniθiŋ] *pron.* ①〔用于疑问句、否定句、条件从句中,或用于肯定句但与含有疑问、否定意义的词连用〕任何事〔物〕,什么事〔物〕. ②〔用于肯定句〕随便哪件事〔东西〕. *Is there ~ for me?* 有东西给我吗? *Tell me if there is ~ wrong with this watch.* 请告诉我这块表有什么毛病. *A- will do.* 什么东西都可以. *I can't do ~.* 我什么也不能做;〔anything 用降升调读时〕我不是什么事都能做. ***~ but*** ①决不是 (*He is ~ but a Marxist.* 他决不是马克思主义者). ②除…外什么都,只不,单单不(*I will do ~ but that.* 除那个而外,我什么都干). ***~ like*** ①象…那样的. ②全然(没有) (*Can the student use his dictionary with ~ like efficiency.* 这个学生能多多少少有效地使用字典吗? *I have not ~ like finished it.* 我还一点都没完成呢). ***~ of*** ①很少,一点,多少. ②有…气派 (*Do you see ~ of him?* 你不常看见他吗? *Is he ~ of a scholar?* 他有学者气派吗?). ***as ... as ~*** 〔口〕无比地,非常 (*He is as proud as ~.* 他非常骄傲). ***for ~*** 给什么都(不干),决(不) (*I would not do it for ~.* 我绝对不干). ***for ~ I care*** 管不着,与我无关 (*He may die for ~ I care.* 他死关我屁事〔我管不着〕). ***for ~ I know [to the contrary]*** 据我所知,总之,大概 (*He may be a good man for ~ I know.* 据我所知,他可能是好人). ***if ~*** 要说呢,只是…罢了 (*He is, if ~, a little taller than I.* 要说呢,只是他比我高一点罢了). ***like ~*** 〔口〕极,非常 (*He worked like ~.* 他非常勤勉). ***not come to ~*** 落空了 (*His plan did not come to ~.* 他的计划落空了). ***unable to do ~ with*** 对…无可奈何.

an·y·time [ˈenitaim] *ad.* ①在任何时候. ②总是,无例外地,一定. *You can get a job ~.* 你无论什么时候都能找到工作. *I can do better than that ~.* 我一定会做得比这还好〔如果去做的话〕.

an·y·way [ˈeniwei] *ad.* = anyhow.

an·y·ways [ˈeniweiz] *ad.* 〔口〕从任何观点来看,不管怎样. *It doesn't see ~ good for him.* 不论从哪个方面看,这对他都没有好处.

an·y·where [ˈenihwɛə] *ad.* ①无论何处,任何地方. ②〔口〕(用于否定句)根本(不). ③〔表示数字的不能确定〕大概在…之间. *You can go ~ you like.* 你爱到什么地方去都可以. *She never came ~ near to knowing the value of life.* 她根本不懂得人生的意义. *~ from 800 to 1200 men* 大致是八百至一千二百人. ***~ you go*** 到处. ***get ~*** 〔口〕吃得开,成功 (*You'll never get ~ with that attitude!* 你那种态度可不行). ***not [never] go ~*** 哪里也不去,隐居.

an·y·wise [ˈeniwaiz] *ad.* 无论如何,决(不),总(不). *He couldn't finish reading it ~.* 他无论如何也读不完.

Anzus, ANZUS [ˈænzəs] = Australia, New Zealand and the United States (Mutual Security Pact) 澳美新(安全条约): the ~ Council 澳美新理事会.

A.O. = Army Order 军令.

a/o, A/O = account of ... 帐上.

A.O.C., AOC = Air Officer Commanding 〔英〕空军指挥官.

A.O.D. = Army Ordnance Department 〔美〕陆军军械部.

A. of F. = Admiral of the Fleet 〔英〕海军元帅.

A-OK [ˌeiəuˈkei] *a.* 〔口〕极好,妙. *an A-OK rocket launching* 一次完美的火箭发射. — *int.* 妥了,一切就绪.

AOL = absent over leave 逾假未归.

Aomori [ˈaumәri] *n.* 青森〔日本港市〕.

A one [ˈei ˈwʌn] *a.* 〔口〕第一流的. *The meals there are ~.* 那里的饭菜是第一流的.

aor. = aorist.

a·o·rist [ˈeərist] *n.* (希腊动词的)不定过去式.

a·or·ta [eiˈɔːtə] *n.* (*pl.* ***-tae*** [-tiː]) 【解】主动脉; 【虫】大血管. **aor·tic** [-tik] *a.*

a·ou·dad [ˈaudæd] *n.* 【动】鬣羊.

à out·rance [ɑː uːˈtrɑ̃ːns] 〔F.〕(战斗)至死. *a war waged à outrance* 一场打到底的战争.

AP, A.P. = ①Associated Press 〔美〕联合通讯社〔简称美联社〕. ②airplane.

Ap. = ①April. ②Apostle.

ap- *pref.* ①〔用于p前〕 = ad-: *ap*pear. ② = apo-.

a·pace [əˈpeis] *ad.* 飞快地,迅速地. *Old age comes on ~.* 老来日子快. *Ill news runs ~.* 恶事传千里.

A·pach·e [əˈpætʃi] *n.* 阿帕切人〔美国西南部印第安人的一族〕.

a·pache [əˈpæʃ] *n.* (巴黎等地的)流氓. *~ dance* 巴黎下层社会狂乱的双人舞.

ap·a·nage [ˈæpənidʒ] *n.* ①王子的封地〔封禄〕. ②合法的额外收入. ③属性,附属物. ④属地.

a·pa·re·jo [ˌæpəˈreihəu] *n.* (*pl.* ***~s***) 〔Sp.〕皮驮鞍.

a·part [əˈpɑːt] *ad.* ①分,离. ②分别,各别. ③相距,相隔. ④撇开,除去. ⑤拆开,卸开. *fall ~ from decay* 因腐朽而崩溃. *New York and Tokyo are thousands of miles ~.* 纽约和东京相距几千英里. *Consider a question ~ from the others.* 撇开其他问题而单独考虑某一问题. ***~ from*** 且莫说,除了…以外. ***come ~*** (精神)错乱,涣散. ***jesting [joking] ~*** 笑话且莫讲,说正经的. ***lay [put, set] (sth.) ~ for*** 把(某物)留给…. ***take (the machine) ~*** 把(机械等)拆开. — *a.* 〔置于名词后〕(与众)不同的. *a race ~* 与众不同的人种.

a·part·heid [əˈpɑːtheit, əˈpɑːthaid] *n.* ①(南非的)种族隔离(政策). ②孤傲.

a·part·ment [əˈpɑːtmənt] *n.* ①〔美〕(一座房屋隔成数家的)公寓住宅. ★英国称 block of flats; (公寓住宅一家分得的)一套房间. ②〔*pl.*〕〔英〕(备有傢俱的)出租房间. ③(宫殿等的)房间. ***He's got ~s to let.*** 〔俚〕他脑筋有点差〔傻〕. **~ complex** 〔美〕公寓大楼. **hotel** 〔美〕公寓饭店. **~ house [building]** 〔美〕公寓,公共住宅.

a·part·o·tel [ə͵pɑːtəˈtel] *n.* = apart hotel.
ap·a·tet·ic [͵æpəˈtetik] *a.*【动】保护色的,保护形态的. *the ~ coloration or form of some animals* 某些动物的保护色或保护形态.
ap·a·thet·ic(al) [͵æpəˈθetik(əl)] *a.* ①无动于衷的,麻木不仁的,感觉迟钝的 *(opp.* emotional*)*. ②无表情的,冷淡的 *(opp.* concerned*)*. *~ airs* 暮气. **-i·cal·ly** *ad.*
ap·a·thy [ˈæpəθi] *n.* 无感情,冷淡,漠不关心 *(opp.* ardor, fervor*)*. ***have an ~ to*** 对…冷淡.
ap·a·tite [ˈæpətait] *n.*【矿】磷灰石.
APC = ①aspirin, phenacetin, and caffeine compound【药】复方阿司匹林. ②automatic phase control【无】自动相位控制.
A.P.D. = Army Pay Department. 陆军军饷署.
ape [eip] *n.* ①猿;无尾猿,短尾猿,类人猿. ②学人的人. ③无教养的人,粗笨的人. ④失去自制,狂热. ***an ~ leader*** 老处女. ***a God's ~*** 生来的傻子. ***lead ~s in hell***〔谑〕终身不嫁. ***play the ~*** 模仿,学样. ***say an ~'s paternoster*** (吓得,冷得)牙齿打战. ***go ~*** 失去自制,变狂热. ***go ~ over [for]***〔美口〕热衷于,迷住,爱上. — *vt.* 仿效. ***~ it*** 仿效. ~ **hanger**〔美〕(自行车的)高把手;(电车等的)高扶手. ~**man** 猿人.
a·peak [əˈpiːk] *a.*〔用作表语〕, *ad.*【海】(锚、桨等)竖着.
Ap·en·nine [ˈæpinain] *a.* 亚平宁山的.
Ap·en·nines [ˈæpinainz] *n. pl.* (意大利的)亚平宁山脉.
a·pep·sia [əˈpepsiə], **a·pep·sy** [-si] *n.*【医】消化停止,不消化.
a·per·çu [͵æpəːˈsjuː] *n.*〔F.〕①一瞥,一瞥的印象. ②洞察,敏悟. ③摘要,梗概.
a·per·i·ent [əˈpiəriənt] *a.*【医】轻泻的.— *n.* 轻泻剂.
a·pe·ri·od·ic [͵eipiəriˈɔdik] *a.* ①非周期的. ②【物】非周期性(振动)的. **-o·dic·i·ty** [-ˈdisiti] *n.* 无周期性.
a·pé·ri·tif [ə͵periˈtiːf] *n.*〔F.〕开胃酒.
a·per·i·tive [əˈperitiv] *a., n.* = aperient; apéritif.
ap·er·ture [ˈæpətjuə] *n.* ①孔,隙缝. ②(照相机的)光圈;孔径,口径. ~ **card** 穿孔卡片;(镶有缩微胶片的)窗孔卡片.
ap·er·y [ˈeipəri] *n.* ①学样,摹仿. ②猴房. ③愚蠢的行为,恶作剧的行为.
a·pet·a·lous [eiˈpetələs] *a.*【植】无花瓣的.
a·pex [ˈeipeks] *n. (pl. ~es* [-iz], ***a·pi·ces*** [ˈeipisiːz]*)* ①(山)顶;尖端;顶点,绝顶. ②【天】奔赴点,向点. ③【无】(电波由电离层反射时的)反射点. ④【矿】矿脉顶〔指离地面最近的矿脉〕. *the ~ of a mountain* 山顶. *His election to the presidency was the ~ of his career.* 当选总统是他一生事业的顶峰.
aph- *pref.* = apo-.
aph·a·nite [ˈæfənait] *n.*【矿】隐晶岩,非显晶岩.
a·ph(a)er·e·sis [əˈfiərisis] *n.*【语法】头音节省略〔advantage 转变为 vantage; It is 转变为 'tis 等〕. **-ret·ic** [-ˈretik] *a.*
a·pha·si·a [æˈfeizjə] *n.*【医】无语言能力,失语(症).
a·phe·li·on [æˈfiːljən] *n. (pl. -lia* [-liə]*)*【天】远日点〔指星体轨道上离日最远的点, *opp.* perihelion〕.
a·phe·li·ot·ro·pism [ə͵fiːliˈɔtrəpizəm] *n.* (植物的)背光性,背日性. **-o·trop·ic** [-əuˈtrɔpik] *a.*
aph·e·sis [ˈæfisis] *n.*【语】词首元音脱落〔esquire 转变为 squire 等〕.
aph·i·cide [ˈæfisaid] *n.*〔农〕杀蚜虫剂.
a·phid [ˈeifid] *n.* = aphis.
a·phis [ˈeifis] *n. (pl.* ***a·phides*** [eifidiːz]*)* 蚜虫;〔A-〕蚜虫属.
a·pho·ni·a [æˈfəunjə] *n.*【医】失音(症),无发音能力.
a·phon·ic [͵eiˈfɔnik] *a.* ①无发音能力的,失音的; ②【语音】不发音的;无声的. — *n.* 失音症患者.
aph·o·rism [ˈæfərizəm] *n.* 格言,警句.
aph·o·rist [ˈæfərist] *n.* 警句家.
aph·o·ris·tic(al) [͵æfəˈristik(əl)] *a.* ①格言式的. ②富于警句的;爱引用格言的.
a·pho·tic [eiˈfəutik] *a.* 无光的〔尤指 aphotic zone (无光带)和 aphotic region (无光区),即海洋中三百英尺以下的地方〕. *~ depths* 无光的深处.
aph·ro·dis·i·a [͵æfrəuˈdiziə] *n.* 性欲.
aph·ro·dis·i·ac [͵æfrəuˈdiziæk] *a.* 刺激性欲的. — *n.* 催欲剂,春药.
Aph·ro·di·te [͵æfrəuˈdaiti] *n.* ①【希神】阿芙罗狄蒂〔爱与美的女神,相当于 Venus〕. ②〔a-〕黑斑褐色蝴蝶.
aph·tha [ˈæfθə] *n. (pl. -thae* [-θiː]*)*【医】①口疮. ②小溃疡.
a·phyl·lous [eiˈfiləs] *a.*【植】无叶(性)的.
Apia [ɑːˈpi(ː)ə] *n.* 阿皮亚〔西萨摩亚首都〕.
a·pi·an [ˈeipjən] *a.* 关于蜜蜂的.
a·pi·ar·i·an [͵eipiˈɛəriən] *a.* 蜜蜂的;养蜂的. — *n.* 养蜂人.
a·pi·a·rist [ˈeipiərist] *n.* 养蜂家,养蜂人.
a·pi·ar·y [ˈeipjəri] *n.* 养蜂场;蜂房.
ap·i·cal [ˈæpikəl] *a.* ①顶点的,顶端的. ②【语】用舌尖发音的. — *n.* 舌尖音〔如 t, d, s, l 等〕.
ap·i·ces [ˈeipisiːz] apex 的复数.
a·pi·cul·ture [ˈeipikʌltʃə] *n.* 养蜂(学).
a·pi·cul·tur·ist [͵eipiˈkʌltʃərist] *n.* 养蜂家.
a·piece [əˈpiːs] *ad.* 每人,每个,各. *The cakes cost a dollar apiece.* 蛋糕每块一元. ★主语是单数名词时应作 The *cake* cost a dollar *a piece.*
à pied [aˈpjei]〔F.〕徒步,步行.
A·pis [ˈeipis] 神牛〔古埃及人信奉为神的化身的公牛〕.
ap·ish [ˈeipiʃ] *a.* ①猿一样的. ②学人样的;乱模仿的. ③傻里傻气的.
a·piv·o·rous [eiˈpivərəs] *a.* 食蜂的〔如某些鸟类〕.
a·pla·cen·tal [͵eipləˈsentl] *a.* 无胎盘的〔如袋鼠〕.
ap·la·nat [ˈæplənæt] *n.*【光】消球差透镜;齐明镜. **-ic** [͵æpləˈnætik] *a.* 消球差的. **-ism** *n.* 消球差;等光程.
a·plen·ty [əˈplenti] *ad.*〔美口〕①丰富,很多. ②极. *There's water ~ there.* 那里水很多. *be scared ~* 吓得要死. — *a.* 丰富的〔多置于被修饰的名词之后〕. *money ~ for one's needs* 足够花的钱. — *n.*〔美〕丰富,大量 (= a plenty).
ap·lite [ˈæplait] *n.* 细晶岩,半花岗岩.
a·plomb [ˈæplɔ̃ːŋ] *n.*〔F.〕①垂直. ②冷静,沉着;自信,自恃. *with ~* 沉着地.
ap·neu·sis [æpˈnjuːsis] *n.*【医】长吸呼吸.
ap·n(o)e·a [æpˈniːə] *n.*【医】呼吸暂停,窒息.
apo. = apogee.
APO = Army Post Office 军用邮局.
Apoc. = Apocalypse; Apocrypha ①.
a·poc·a·lypse [əˈpɔkəlips] *n.*【基督教】天启,启示;〔the A-〕【圣】启示录. **-lyp·tic, -lyp·ti·cal** [-ˈliptik(l), -tikəl] *a.* ①天启的,启示的. ②《圣经》启示录中恐怖场景的,预示世界末日情景的.
a·po·car·pous [͵æpəˈkɑːpəs] *a.*【植】离心皮的.
apo·chro·mat [ˈæpəkrəumæt] *n.*【光】复消色差透镜.
a·po·chro·mat·ic [͵æpəkrəuˈmætik] *a.* 消多色差的.
a·poc·o·pate [əˈpɔkəpeit] *vt.* 删除(词尾字母或音节)〔如: mos' 代替 most〕. **-pa·tion** *n.*
a·poc·o·pe [əˈpɔkəpi] *n.*【语法】词尾省略,词尾消失〔例 mine 变化为 my; cinematograph 变化为 cinema〕.
a·poc·ry·pha [əˈpɔkrifə] *n.*〔*sing., pl.*〕①〔A-〕【宗】伪经,经外书. ②不足凭信的书;著者不明的书. **-phal** [-fəl] *a.*
a·poc·y·na·ceous [ə͵pɔsiˈneiʃəs] *a.*【植】夹竹桃科的.
a·poc·y·num [əˈpɔsinəm] *n.* 罗布麻,红野麻.
ap·od [ˈæpəd] *n.* ①无足动物. ②无腹鳍鱼. — *a.* ①无

足的. ②无腹鳍的. **-al** *a.*

ap·o·deic·tic [ˌæpəuˈdaiktik], **ap·o·dic·tic** [-ˈdiktik] *a.* ①可以明确表示[证实]的. ②绝对肯定的; 必然真实的. ③【逻】具有[表达]必然真理的;【哲】必然的.

a·pod·o·sis [əˈpɔdəsis] *n.* *(pl. -ses* [-siːz]*)* 【语法】条件句的结论句〔如: If I could go, I would go. 里的 I would go〕.

ap·o·en·zyme [ˌæpəuˈenzaim] *n.* 【生化】酶朊.

a·pog·a·my [əˈpɔgəmi] *n.* 【植】无配子生殖.

ap·o·gee [ˈæpəudʒiː] *n.* ①【天】远地点〔指月亮、人造卫星轨道上离地球最远的点, *opp.* perigee〕. ②最高点, 最远点; 极点. *the ~ of Renaissance art* 文艺复兴时代艺术的最高峰. **-ge·an** [ˌæpəuˈdʒiːən] *a.*

ap·o·ge·ot·ro·pism [ˌæpəudʒiˈɔtrəpizm] *n.* 【植】(植物器官的)背地性; 负向地性.

ap·o·laus·tic [ˌæpəˈlɔːstik] *a.* 恣意享乐的; 放纵的.

a·po·lit·i·cal [ˌæpəˈlitikəl] *a.* ①非政治的, 无关政治的. ②不关心政治的. **-ly** *ad.*

A·pol·lo [əˈpɔləu] *n.* ①【希神】阿波罗〔太阳、音乐、诗、健康等的守护神〕. ②〔诗〕太阳. ③美男子. ~ **Program** 阿波罗计划〔包括登月行动的美国宇航计划〕.

A·pol·lyon [əˈpɔljən] *n.* (地狱中的)魔王.

a·pol·o·get·ic, a·pol·o·get·i·cal [əˌpɔləˈdʒetik(əl)] *a.* ①辩护的, 辩解的. ②谢罪的, 道歉的, 认错的. *He was very ~.* 他已表示十分道歉了. — *n.* 〔常 *pl.*〕辩解; 辩护; 护教学〔指神学中为基督教教条进行辩护的一个分支〕. **-i·cal·ly** *ad.* 辩解, 道歉, 认错.

ap·o·lo·gi·a [ˌæpəˈləudʒiə] *n.* ①(口头或书面的) 正式辩解, 辩解书. ②道歉.

a·pol·o·gist [əˈpɔlədʒist] *n.* ①辩解者, 辩护者. ②护教学专家(指为基督教信仰进行辩护的人).

a·pol·o·gize [əˈpɔlədʒaiz] *vi.* ①辩解, 辩护. ②道歉, 认错, 赔不是. *A- to him for your rudeness.* 你对人不礼貌, 向他赔个不是. *~ for oneself.* 替自己辩护.

ap·o·logue [ˈæpəlɔg] *n.* 寓言, 富有教育意义的故事.

a·pol·o·gy [əˈpɔlədʒi] *n.* ①辩解, 辩护. ②道歉, 赔不是. ③〔口〕临时凑合的代用品. *a lame ~* 蹩脚的辩解. *a letter of ~* 道歉信. ***an [a mere] ~ for*** *(a dinner)* 勉强充作(正餐)的(食物). ***in ~ for*** 为…辩解, 为…赔不是. ***make an ~ for*** 为…道歉. ***owe someone an ~*** 得向某人道歉.

a·po·lune [ˈæpəuljuːn] *n.* 月(球)轨(道)最远点, 远月点.

ap·o·mict [ˈæpəumikt] *n.* 无配偶生殖植物. **-ic** *a.*

ap·o·mix·is [ˌæpəuˈmiksis] *n.* 无融合生殖, 无性生殖.

ap·o·mor·phine [ˌæpəuˈmɔːfiːn] *n.* 阿朴吗啡〔用做呕吐剂、祛痰剂的缩水吗啡〕.

ap·o·neu·ro·sis [ˌæpəunuˈrəusis] *n.* *(pl. -ses* [-siːz]*)* 腱膜. **-rot·ic** [-ˈrɔtik] *a.*

ap·o·pemp·tic [ˈæpəuˈpemptik] *a.* 〔古〕告别的, 送别的; 临别所言的. *an ~ song* 离歌.

ap·o·phthegm [ˈæpəuθem] *n.* 格言, 箴言 (= apothegm). **-atic** [ˌæpəuθegˈmætik] *a.*

a·poph·y·ge [əˈpɔfidʒiː] *n.* (古典建筑物的) 蜗牛形柱墩.

a·poph·yl·lite [əˈpɔfilait] *n.* 【矿】鱼眼石.

a·poph·y·sis [əˈpɔfisis] *n.* *(pl. -ses* [-siːz]*)* ①【解】骨突; 表皮层. ②【植】蒴托; 鳞质〔指球果鳞片〕. **-y·se·al** [-ˈsiəl] *a.*

ap·o·plec·tic, ap·o·plec·ti·cal [ˌæpəuˈplektik(əl)] *a.* 中风的, 易患中风病的. *an ~ fit [stroke]* 中风.

ap·o·plex·y [ˈæpəupleksi] *n.* 【医】中风, 卒中. *cerebral ~* 脑溢血. *be seized with ~* 中风.

a·port [əˈpɔːt] *ad.* 【海】在左舷. *put the helm ~* 使舵柄靠左. ***Hard ~!*** 尽力使舵柄靠左! 左满舵!

ap·o·se·mat·ic [ˌæpəusiˈmætik] *a.* 【动】警戒色的. **-i·cal·ly** *ad.*

ap·o·si·o·pe·sis [ˌæpəuˌsaiəuˈpiːsis] *n.* 【修】说话中断法〔如: The first thing I saw — but I dare not describe the dreadful sight. 我一眼看到的是——啊, 太可怕了, 我简直不敢去形容〕.

a·po·spor·y [ˈæpəuˌspɔːri] *n.* 无孢子生殖.

a·pos·ta·sy [əˈpɔstəsi] *n.* 背教; 脱党; 变节; 放弃信仰.

a·pos·tate [əˈpɔstit] *a.* 背教的; 脱党的; 变节的, 放弃信仰的. — *n.* 背教者, 脱党者; 背信者, 变节者, 叛徒. **-ta·tic** [ˌæpəuˈstætik] *a.*

a·pos·ta·tize [əˈpɔstətaiz] *vi.* 弃教; 脱党; 变节.

a pos·te·ri·o·ri [ˈei pɔsˌteriˈɔːrai] *a.* 〔L.〕【逻】①由结果追溯到原因的; 由特殊推论出一般的; 归纳的. ②凭经验的 *(opp.* a priori*).* *~ **reasoning*** 归纳推理.

a·pos·til(le) [əˈpɔstil] *n.* 旁注, 注.

a·pos·tle [əˈpɔsl] *n.* ①〔A-〕【基督教】(《圣经》中所讲的)使徒. ②最初的传教士. ③(主义、政策等的) 提倡者, 鼓吹者. ④【海】船头系缆柱. ~ **spoon** (柄端刻成使徒像的)使徒匙. **-ship** *n.* 使徒的职位[身分].

a·pos·to·late [əˈpɔstəulit] *n.* 使徒的职务[身分、任期].

ap·os·tol·ic [ˌæpəsˈtɔlik] *a.* ①使徒的. ②适合使徒教义的. ③使徒传来的. ④罗马教皇的. ~ **age** 使徒时代〔即基督教创立的最初时期〕. ~ **delegate** 教皇代表〔教皇派往与梵蒂冈无外交关系的国家的代表〕. ~ **indulgence** 教皇的赦免. ~ **succession** 使徒传统〔指耶稣交给圣彼得等使徒的宗教权力, 由各代主教相传下来〕.

a·pos·tro·phe[1] [əˈpɔstrəfi] *n.* ①撇号, 省字号〔例 can't (= can not), '55 (=1955)〕. ②所有格符号〔例 boy's, boys'〕. ③复数符号〔例 many M.P.'s〕. ④表示一字中的某一音不发〔如: 'lectric (= electric)〕. **-troph·ic** [ˌæpəsˈtrɔfik] *a.* 使用撇号的.

a·pos·tro·phe[2] [əˈpɔstrəfi] *n.* 【修】顿呼法〔叙述中忽然对不在场的第三者所发出的直接呼语; 或对无生命物发出呼唤, 如: Frailty, thy name is woman. 脆弱啊, 你的名字就是女人〕. **-troph·ic** [ˌæpəsˈtrɔfik] *a.* 使用顿呼法的.

a·pos·tro·phize[1] [əˈpɔstrəfaiz] *vt., vi.* 加省字号以缩短(单词的拼写形式); (给…) 记上省字符号〔所有格符号〕.

a·pos·tro·phize[2] [əˈpɔstrəfaiz] *vt., vi.* (对…) 发出呼语.

a·poth·e·car·y [əˈpɔθikəri] *n.* ①药剂师; 药房老板. ②药房. *apothecaries' measure.* 药用容量单位. *apothecaries' weight* 药用重量单位.

ap·o·the·ci·um [ˌæpəˈθisiəm] *n.* *(pl. -cia* [-siə]*)* 【植】子囊盘. **-the·ci·al** [-siəl] *a.*

ap·o·thegm [ˈæpəuθem] *n.* 格言. **-at·ic** *a.*

ap·o·them [ˈæpəuˌθem] *n.* 【数】边心距, 垂幅.

a·poth·e·o·sis [əˌpɔθiˈəusis] *n.* *(pl. -ses* [-siːz]*)* ①尊为神, 封为神, 神化. ②礼赞, 崇拜. ③极点, 顶峰.

a·poth·e·o·size [əˈpɔθiəusaiz] *vt.* ①把…尊为神, 神化. ②尊崇, 崇拜, 颂扬.

app. = apparatus; apparent(ly); appended; appendix; appointed; apprentice; approved; approximate.

Ap·pa·la·chi·an [ˌæpəˈleitʃiən] *a.* 阿巴拉契亚山脉的.

Ap·pa·la·chi·ans [ˌæpəˈleitʃjənz] *n.pl.* 〔the ~〕阿巴拉契亚山脉〔北美洲〕.

ap·pal(l) [əˈpɔːl] *vt.* 吓坏, 使惊骇, 使胆寒. *be ~ed at* 被…吓坏, 弄得毛骨悚然.

ap·pal·ling [əˈpɔːliŋ] *a.* ①骇人的, 可惊的. ②〔口〕(愚笨等)过分的. *an ~ accident* 骇人听闻的事故. *~ ignorance* 过分愚蠢. **-ly** *ad.* 可惊地.

ap·pa·loo·sa [ˌæpəˈluːsə] *n.* 阿巴鲁萨马〔北美西部骑用马〕.

ap·pa·nage [ˈæpənidʒ] *n.* = apanage.

ap·pa·rat [ˌɑːpɑːˈrɑːt] *n.* 〔Russ.〕= apparatus③.

ap·pa·ra·tus [ˌæpəˈreitəs] *n.* *(pl. ~(es))* ①器具, 装

置,设备,机器,器械,仪器. ②(身体上的)器官. ③政治机构,机关,政党的基层组织,地下活动组织. ④(学术著作中的)注释(或索引等). *a chemical* ~ 化学仪器. *a feeding* ~ 给水装置. *a fire* ~ 灭火器. *a radio [wireless]* ~ 无线电信机,无线电装置. *the respiratory* ~ 呼吸器官. *the state* ~ 国家机构. ~ ***criticus*** 书中所附的参考资料.

ap·par·el(l) [əˈpærəl] *vt.* 〔书〕使穿衣;装饰. *a girl gaily* ~*ed* 衣着漂亮的少女. *a book tastefully* ~*ed* 装饰雅致的书. —*n.* ①服装. ②(衣服上的)装饰. ③法衣的长方形绣花装饰. ④外表,外观. ⑤船具〔如:桅、帆、索具和锚〕. *the queen's* ~ 女王的服饰. *the gay* ~ *of spring* 明媚的春光.

ap·par·ent [əˈpærənt] *a.* ①明显的,显而易见的 *(to)*. ②貌似的;表面的,外观上的. ③【物】表观的;视在的,外显的. *His reluctance was only* ~. 他不过是表面上不愿意罢了. *The solution to the problem was* ~ *to all.* 问题的解决方法是显而易见的. ~ **angle**【地】视角. ~ **dip**【地】视倾角. ~ **expansion**【物】表观膨胀. ~ **load**【物】视载荷. ~ **solar time**【天】视太阳时. **-ly** *ad.* 显然地,表面上.

ap·pa·ri·tion [ˌæpəˈriʃən] *n.* ①鬼,幽灵,妖怪. ②幻象,幻影. ②(星等的)出现.

ap·par·i·tor [əˈpæritɔː] *n.* ①(古罗马行政官的)执行吏. ②(宗教裁判所的)命令送达官.

ap·pas·si·o·na·ta [əˌpɑːsiəˈnɑːtə] *a.* 〔It.〕【乐】热情的.

ap·peal [əˈpiːl] *vi.* ①呼吁;要求. ②诉诸于;向…求助 *(to)*. ③投合…心意,对…有吸引力 *(to)*. ④【法】控诉,上诉 *(to)*. ~ *for aid* 请求援助. ~ *for sympathy* 呼请同情. *They* ~*ed to the public to help the distressed children.* 他们呼吁公众帮助那些受难的儿童. ~ *to a higher court* 上诉. ~ *against the judge's decision* 不服判决而上诉. *These pictures do not* ~ *to me.* 这些画不合我意[我不欣赏]. ~ ***to the country*** (解散议会)请国民公断. ~ ***to force*** 诉诸武力. ~ ***to reason*** 讲理. — *n.* ①呼吁(书),恳求. ②控诉;起诉;上诉. ③魅力,吸引力. *an* ~ *for help to the public* 向公众求援的呼吁. *a court of* ~上级法院. ***lodge [enter] an*** ~ 提出上诉. ***make an*** ~ ***to*** 诉诸.

ap·peal·ing [əˈpiːliŋ] *a.* ①恳求的,哀求的. ②有感染力的,吸引人的. *an* ~ *smile* 动人心弦的微笑. **-ly** *ad.* **-ness** *n.*

ap·pear [əˈpiə] *vi.* ①出现,露出,显现. ②出庭,出场,演出,(在公开场合)露面. ③(书等)出版;发表. ④变得明显. ⑤显得,好象. ~ *in public* 露面. ~ *in court* 出庭,到案. *for reasons that do not* ~ 用含糊的理由. ~ *on the stage* 上台,演出. *He* ~*s to have caught cold.* 他似乎是受凉了. *He* ~*s (to be) very young.* 他显得很年轻. *It* ~*s to me that you are right.* 我觉得你是对的. ***It*** ~***s that*** … 似乎是…. ***strange as it may*** ~ 虽似奇怪〔插入语〕.

ap·pear·ance [əˈpiərəns] *n.* ①出现;露面,出场,登台. ②出版,刊行. ③外貌,外观;〔*pl.*〕表面的迹象〔征兆〕. ④〔古〕幻像;幽灵. ⑤【法】出庭. ⑥【哲】现象 *(opp.* essence). *Appearances are deceptive.* 外表是靠不住的. *Never judge by* ~. 不要以貌取人. *personal* ~ 容貌,风采. ***at first*** ~ 乍一看,初看起来. ***at the*** ~ ***of*** 看见…而,与…的出现同时,…公布后即. ***enter an*** ~出庭,出面. ***for*** ~ ***sake*** 为了装门面,为了体面. ***give the*** ~ ***of*** *(honesty)* 假装(老实). ***in*** ~ 看上去,外表上. ***keep up*** ~***s*** 装场面,保全体面,维持面子. ***make a good [an ill]*** ~ 以壮[有碍]观瞻. ***make an*** ~ 出面,出庭,到案. ***make its first*** ~ (书)初版,(杂志)创刊. ***make one's*** ~ 露面. ***make one's first [last]*** ~ ***on the stage.*** 初次[末次]登台. ***put in an*** ~ 出面,出庭. ***put on the*** ~ ***of*** *(innocence)* 假装(清白). ***save*** ~***s*** = keep up ~. ***There is every*** ~ ***of*** 无一处不象…. ***There is no*** ~ ***of*** *(him; rain)* 简直不见(他的影子);一点没有(下雨的样子). ***to all*** ~ 显然;没有不象…的,看着都….

ap·peas·a·ble [əˈpiːzəbl] *a.* 平息得了的;缓和得了的,劝解得了的.

ap·pease [əˈpiːz] *vt.* ①平息(愤怒),缓和(情绪),劝慰,抚慰. ②对…让步,安抚,姑息;绥靖. ③充(饥),果(腹),解(渴),满足(欲望). ~ *the king's anger* = ~ *the angry king* 劝使国王息怒. ~ *one's hunger with cake* 吃饼充饥. ~ *sb's curiosity* 满足某人的好奇心. *Hitler was* ~*d at Munich.* 在慕尼黑对希特勒实行了绥靖政策.

ap·pease·ment [əˈpiːzmənt] *n.* 姑息,迁就;抚慰;缓和,绥靖;满足. ~ **policy** 绥靖政策,姑息政策.

ap·pel [əˈpel] *n.*【剑】垫步.

ap·pel·lant [əˈpelənt] *n.*【法】控诉人;上诉人,请求人. —*a.*【法】有关上诉的,上诉的.

ap·pel·late [əˈpelit] *a.*【法】受理上诉的. *an* ~ *court* 受理上诉的法院.

ap·pel·la·tion [ˌæpeˈleiʃən] *n.* ①称呼. ②名称,称号.

ap·pel·la·tive [əˈpelətiv] *a.* ①命名的;名称的. ②【语法】通称的 *(opp.* proper);普通名词的. — *n.* ①称号,名称;通称. ②【语法】普通名词.

ap·pel·lee [ˌæpəˈliː] *n.* 被告.

ap·pel·lor [əˈpelə] *n.* 控诉人,上诉人,原告.

ap·pend [əˈpend] *vt.* ①(用线等)挂上. ②附上,添上,加上;追加,增补. ~ *a label to a trunk* 给行李挂上标签. ~ *an index to a book* 给书籍加上索引. ~ *one's signature* 签名,署名. ~ *a seal to a contract* 在合同上盖章.

ap·pend·age [əˈpendidʒ] *n.* ①附属物,配件. ②【生】附器;附肢〔如:树的枝,狗的尾等〕.

ap·pend·ant [əˈpendənt] *a.* 附加的,附属的 *(to)*. *the salary* ~ *to a position* 随着职务而来的薪水. — *n.* ①附属物. ②【法】附带的遗产(或权利).

ap·pen·dec·to·my [ˌæpənˈdektəmi] *n.*【医】阑尾截除术.

ap·pen·di·ci·tis [əˌpendiˈsaitis] *n.*【医】阑尾炎.

ap·pen·di·cle [əˈpendikl] *n.* 小附属物.

ap·pen·dic·u·lar [ˌæpənˈdikjulə] *a.* 附属物的,有附属物的(尤指脊椎动物的四肢).

ap·pen·dix [əˈpendiks] *n.* *(pl.* ~***es; -dices*** [-disiːz]). ①附属物;附庸. ②附录,附言,补遗. ③【解】阑尾(= vermiform ~). ③(飞船充气和放气用的)气量调节管. —*vt.* 附加于.

ap·pen·tice [əˈpentis] *n.*【建】厢房;耳房.

ap·per·ceive [ˌæpə(ː)ˈsiːv] *vt.* ①【心】(借助老经验来)阐明(新概念). ②【哲】统觉,明觉. ③〔废〕领悟,知觉.

ap·per·cep·tion [ˌæpə(ː)ˈsepʃən] *n.* ①【哲】统觉;明觉(作用). ②【心】借助老经验来理解新概念;触类旁通.

ap·per·tain [ˌæpə(ː)ˈtein] *vi.* 属于;和…有关 *(to)*. *a house and everything* ~*ing to it.* 房屋及其附属物. *Forestry* ~*s to agriculture.* 森林学和农学有关.

ap·pe·tence, ap·pe·ten·cy [ˈæpitəns(i)] *n.* ①强烈的欲望. ②本能的倾向,习性. ③【化】亲和力 *(for)*. *an* ~ *for [after] knowledge* 强烈的求知欲. **-tent** *a.*

ap·pe·tite [ˈæpitait] *n.* ①欲望,(特指)胃口,食欲. ②嗜好,爱好. *the sexual* ~ 性欲. *Fit the* ~ *to the dishes and dress to the figure.* 看菜吃饭,量体裁衣. ***A good*** ~ ***is a good sauce.*** 〔谚〕饥不择食. ***give*** ~ 促进食欲. ***have a good [poor]*** ~ 食欲旺盛[不振]. ***have an*** ~ ***for*** *(music)* 爱好(音乐). ***to one's*** ~ 合口味,正合…胃口. ***with a good*** ~ 胃口好,大大(吃了一顿).

ap·pe·ti·tive [əˈpetitiv] *a.* 食欲上的;增进食欲的;开胃的.

ap·pe·tiz·er, -tis·er [ˈæpitaizə] *n.* ①开胃菜,开胃酒. ②刺激欲望的事物. *Hunger [Exercise] is a good* ~. 饥

饿[运动]是最好的开胃物.

ap·pe·tiz·ing, -tis·ing [ˈæpitaiziŋ] *a.* ①刺激食欲的. ②美味的. *the ~ smell of cakes* 蛋糕那令人馋涎欲滴的香味.

Ap·pi·an [ˈæpiən] **way** 阿庇乌大道〔古罗马皇帝 Appius 所建军用大道,从罗马经过加普亚通到布朗迪西恩(今布林迪西),长 350 英里〕.

ap·plaud [əˈplɔːd] *vt., vi.* ①鼓掌欢迎[喝采],欢呼. ②赞美,夸奖,称赞. *I ~ (you for) your decision.* 我赞佩你的决心. *~ (sb.) for (his courage)* 夸奖(某人勇敢).

ap·plause [əˈplɔːz] *n.* ①喝采,热烈鼓掌. ②夸奖,称赞. *a storm of ~* 掌声雷动,暴风雨般的掌声. *unanimous ~* 全场鼓掌. *win ~* 博得喝采,受到赞扬. **ap·plaus·ive** *a.*

ap·ple [ˈæpl] *n.* ①苹果,苹果树. ②苹果状的东西. ③〔美俚〕(棒球的)球;炸弹;手榴弹. ④〔美俚〕人,家伙. *a cherry ~* 棠梨. *a mad ~* 茄子. *a Persian ~* 枸橼. ***Adam's ~*** 喉结. ***~ of discord***【希神】(各女神争夺的、作为最美丽者象征的)金苹果,纷争之果;〔喻〕争端,祸根. ***~ of love*** 番茄. ***~ of Sodom = Dead Sea ~*** (传说中的)一摘就冒烟成灰的美丽的苹果;〔喻〕华而不实的事物. ***~ of the [one's] eye*** 瞳孔,眼珠;珍爱之物,掌中珠. ***throw away the ~ because of the core*** 因噎废食. ***upset the [或 sb.'s] ~ cart*** 打破(某人)计划. ~ **jack**〔美〕苹果白兰地. ~ **knocker**〔美口〕①苹果采摘人. ②农夫,庄稼汉. ③生手. **~-pie** ① *n.* 苹果馅饼. ② *a.* 典型美国式的. **~-pie bed** (学生恶作剧)故意把被褥叠得使人睡下伸不直脚的卧铺. **~pie order**〔口〕井然有序 (*in [into] ~-pie order* 秩序井然,整整齐齐. *put things into ~-pie order* 把东西收拾得整整齐齐). ~ **polisher**〔美俚〕拍马屁的人(尤指学生). ~ **polishing**〔美俚〕巴结(教授). ~ **sauce** ①苹果酱. ②不诚恳的奉承. ③胡说. **~wife, ~woman** 卖苹果的女人. **~wood** 苹果木.

Ap·ple·ton [ˈæpltən] *n.* 阿普尔顿[姓氏].

ap·pli·ance [əˈplaiəns] *n.* ①器具,用具;器械;装置,设备. ②适用,应用. *Stoves, irons, etc. are household ~s.* 炉子、熨斗等是家庭用具. *~ of (a principle) to ...* 把(原理)应用到…上.

ap·pli·ca·bil·i·ty [ˌæplikəˈbiliti] *n.* 适用性,应用性;适当.

ap·pli·ca·ble [ˈæplikəbl] *a.* ①(规则)可适用的,能应用的. ②合适的,适当的 *(to)*. *an ~ rule* 切实可行的规则. *a solution that is ~ to the problem* 适合于这个问题的解决方法. **-bly** *ad.* 适当. **-ness** *n.* 适切,剀切.

ap·pli·cant [ˈæplikənt] *n.* 请求人,申请人. *an ~ for a situation* 找事的,求职者. *an ~ for admission to a school* 入学申请者.

ap·pli·ca·tion [ˌæpliˈkeiʃən] *n.* ①适用,应用;运用. ②申请,请求;申请表格. ③勤勉,用功. ④敷用;敷用药. *a written ~* 申请书. *an ~ for admission (to a school)* 入学申请. *fill out an ~* 填写申请表. *He shows very little ~ to his study.* 他不用功,不勤学. *a man of close ~* 勤奋的人,专心一意的人. *a point of ~* 作用点,施力点. *for external [internal] ~* 外用[内用](药). ***make an ~ for (help) to (sb.)*** 请求(某人)(帮助). ***on ~ (to)*** (向…)提出要求 (*A list of new books will be sent on ~ to the publisher.* 新书目录,可向出版者函索). ~ **blank [form]** 空白申请书.

ap·pli·ca·tive [ˈæplikeitiv] *a.* 可适用的,合用的;实用的.

ap·pli·ca·tor [ˈæplikeitə] *n.* (耳鼻科用的)棒状涂药器,棉棍.

ap·pli·ca·to·ry [ˈæplikətəri] *a.* 可适用的,适宜的;实用的.

ap·plied [əˈplaid] *a.* 适用的,应用的,实用的 *(opp.* pure, abstract, theoretical*)*. ~ **art** 实用美术. ~ **chemistry** 应用化学. ~ **mathmatics** 应用数学.

ap·pli·qué [æˈpliːkei] *a.* 〔F.〕(花纹)缝上的;贴补的. *~ lace* 补贴的花边. — *n.* (服装等的)补花,贴花,嵌花. — *vt.* ***(-quéd; -quéing)*** 缝饰,镶饰在…上贴花. *~ a satin blouse with wool of the same colour* 用同色毛线在一件缎衫上贴花.

ap·ply [əˈplai] *vt.* ①运用,应用(原则),把…运用于. ②用(药)敷,搽;用(火)点(灯); 用(…)做(…). ③专心,致力. —*vi* ①适合,适用. ②申请,请求. *~ scientific discoveries to the industrial production* 把科学发现应用于工业生产. *~ heat to a retort* 给甑加热. *~ a plaster to a wound* 用膏药贴伤口. *A- at the office.* 请在办事处接洽. *~ paint to a house* 油漆房屋. — *vi.* ①适合;适用. ②申请,请求. ③专心,努力. *~ to the Danish Consul for a visa.* 向丹麦领事馆申请签证. *For particulars ~ to the office.* 详情请问办事处. *~ for a position* 求职. ***~ oneself to*** 专心(做事). ***~ one's mind to*** *(one's lessons)* 专心致志于,热心于(学习). ***~ to*** *(a person)* ***for*** *(help)* 向(某人)求(援).

ap·pog·gia·tu·ra [əˌpɔdʒəˈturə] *n.* 〔It.〕【乐】倚音,花音.

ap·point [əˈpɔint] *vt.* ①委派,任命 *(opp.* dismiss*)*. ②指定,约定(时间、地点等). ③给…提供装备[设备]. ④【法】处置(财产). ⑤命令. ⑥规定. *He was ~ed ambassador.* 他已被任命为大使. *~ a new secretary* 委派一名新秘书. *~ a time for a meeting* 约定开会的时间. *The house is well ~ed.* 这房子设备齐全. *The law was ~ed by the king.* 这项法律是由国王规定的.

ap·point·ed [əˈpɔintid] *a.* ①指定的,约定的. ②设备…的. *at the ~ time* 在约定的时间. *one's ~ lot* 宿命. *one's ~ task* 指定的工作,本职工作. *a well [poorly] ~ guest-room* 设备完美的[简陋的]客房.

ap·point·ee [æpɔinˈtiː] *n.* ①被任命者,被指定者. ②【法】被指定为财产的受益者. **ap·point·er** *n.* 任命者.

ap·point·ive [əˈpɔintiv] *a.* ①(官职等)委任的,任命的. ②有任命[指定]权的. *an ~ office* 委任的职务. *the president's ~ power* 总统的委任权.

ap·point·ment [əˈpɔintmənt] *n.* ①任命,委派,任用. ②任职,官职,职位. ③法令,命令;天意. ④指定;约定,约会;【医】(门诊)预约. ⑤〔*pl.*〕设备;家具. ⑥【法】指定(财产受益人). *obtain a good ~* 获得一项好差事. *an ~ for [to meet at] six o'clock* 六点钟的约会. ***by a natural ~*** 由于自然的巧合. ***by ~*** 照章,按约. ***have an ~ with sb.*** 和某人有约会. ***keep [break] one's ~*** 守[违]约. ***make an ~ with sb.*** 和某人定下约会时间. ***take up an ~*** 就职,上任. ~ **call**【讯】定人定时呼叫.

ap·point·or [əˈpɔintə] *n.* ① = appointer. ②【法】指定人[有权用证书或遗嘱指定财产归属的人].

ap·port [əˈpɔːt] *n.* 幻姿〔指在招魂会或降神会上用幻术来产生有形的东西〕. — *vt.* 使生幻姿.

ap·por·tion [əˈpɔːʃən] *vt.* 分派,分摊;分配 *(among)*. *an ~ed task* 所分担的工作. *~ time among various employments* 为做各项不同的工作分配时间. **-ment** *n.* 分配,分摊.

ap·pos·a·ble [əˈpəuzəbl] *a.* 可并置的,可置于附近的. *The human thumb is ~.* 人类的拇指与其他四指对置.

ap·pose [əˈpəuz] *vt.* ***(-posed; -posing)*** ①并列;把…置于对面或附近. ②〔古〕把某物置于[应用于]他物上. *~ food before a guest* 把食物放在客人面前. *~ a seal to a document* 在文件上盖章.

ap·po·site [ˈæpəzit] *a.* ①适当的,合适的. ②【植】并生的;附着的. *an ~ answer* 得当的答复. *be ~ to the case* 切合实情的. **-ly** *ad.* **-ness** *n.*

ap·po·si·tion [ˌæpəˈziʃən] *n.* ①并置;并列. ②【植】敷着,附着生长. ③【语法】同格,同位. *growth by ~* (细胞膜的)附着生长. *the ~ of thumb and forefinger* 大拇

指与食指并列. *a noun in* ~ 同格名词. ***in ~ to*** 与…同格. **-al** *a.*

ap·pos·i·tive [əˈpɔzitiv] *a.*【语法】同位的,同格的. —*n.*【语法】同位语. ~ **adjective** 同位形容词. ~ **construction** 同位结构. ~ **noun** 同位名词. **-ly** *ad.*

ap·prais·a·ble [əˈpreizəbl] *a.* 可估价的,可评价的.

ap·prais·al [əˈpreizəl] *n.* 评价, 估价, 估计, 鉴定. *make [give] an objective ~ of* 对…作出客观的评价.

ap·praise [əˈpreiz] *vt.* ①评价, 估价. ②鉴定, 品定. *Property is ~d for taxation.* 估产定税. **-ment** *n.* 评价; 估价,估计价额;鉴定,评定.

ap·prais·er [əˈpreizə] *n.* 估价人,评价人,鉴定人.

ap·pre·ci·a·ble [əˈpriːʃiəbl] *a.* ①可估价的. ②可察觉的. *There is no ~ difference.* 大致相同.

ap·pre·ci·ate [əˈpriːʃieit] *vt.* ①估价,评价,鉴别. ②体会;了解,意识到,懂得. ③欣赏,鉴赏,赏识. ④感激,感谢. ⑤使提价. ~ *the difficulties of the situation* 意识到局势困难. *I ~ your kindness.* 多谢厚意. ~ *good food* 欣赏美味. ~ *sb.'s friendship* 珍视某人的友谊. *New buildings ~s the value of land.* 新建筑物提高了土地的价值. —*vi.* 涨价,腾贵 (*opp.* depreciate). *Things ~ as time goes on.* 货物逐日腾贵.

ap·pre·ci·a·tion [əˌpriːʃiˈeiʃən] *n.* ①评价, 鉴别. ②知道,了解. ③鉴赏, 欣赏. ④感谢; 感激. ⑤(地价等的)上涨,腾贵(*opp.* depreciation). ~ *of literature* 文学鉴赏. *She has an ~ of art and music.* 她对于美术和音乐有了解. *in ~ of* 因赏识…而,因感激…而. *We offer this small token by way of ~.* 我们赠送这个小纪念品作为酬谢.

ap·pre·ci·a·tive [əˈpriːʃjətiv] *a.* ①能评价的; 有鉴别力的,有眼力的;有欣赏力的. ②感谢的. *an ~ audience* 有欣赏力的观众. *I am very ~ of your kindness.* 我很感激你的厚意.

ap·pre·ci·a·tor [əˈpriʃiˌeitə] *n.* 鉴别者; 赏识者; 鉴赏者.

ap·pre·ci·a·to·ry [əˈpriːʃjətəri] *a.* = appreciative.

ap·pre·hend [ˌæpriˈhend] *vt.* ①理解, 领悟. ②逮捕, 捉拿; 拘押. ③怕, 忧虑. *I don't ~ his meaning.* 我不理解他的意思. ~ *danger in every sound* 风声鹤唳, 草木皆兵. *It is ~ed that ...* 恐怕会…. ~ *a hot summer* 担心会有一个炎热的夏季. ~ *a criminal* 捕捉罪犯. —*vi.* ①理解,领悟. ②忧虑,害怕.

ap·pre·hen·si·bil·i·ty [ˈæpriˌhensiˈbiliti] *n.* 可理解.

ap·pre·hen·si·ble [ˌæpriˈhensəbl] *a.* 可理解的. *not ~ even to professional men* 连专门家都难以理解的(东西).

ap·pre·hen·sion [ˌæpriˈhenʃən] *n.* ①理解(力); 领悟. ②见解. ③逮捕(*opp.* release); 拘押. ④〔常 *pl.*〕不安, 忧虑. ***be dull [quick] of ~*** 头脑敏捷[迟钝]. ***entertain [have] some ~s for [of]*** 恐怕,深怕. ***in my ~*** 我以为,在我想来. ***under the ~ that...*** 唯恐,就怕.

ap·pre·hen·sive [ˌæpriˈhensiv] *a.* ①忧虑的, 担心的. ②有理解力的,善于领会的,聪明的,敏捷的. *an ~ mind* 敏捷的头脑. ③有关理解力的. ④意识到…的 (*of*). *be ~ for sb.'s safety* 担心某人的安全. *be ~ of danger* 害怕有危险. *be ~ of one's folly* 意识到自己的愚蠢. ***be ~ that ... may*** 怕…会. **-ly** *ad.*

ap·pren·tice [əˈprentis] *n.* ①徒弟,学徒;学徒工. ②见习生,生手,初学者. *an ~'s indenture* 学徒契约. *an ~s' school* 艺徒学校. ***be bound ~ to*** 做…的学徒. ***go ~*** 做学徒. —*vt.* 使做学徒. ~ ***oneself to*** *(a tailor)* 做(裁缝)学徒. ***be ~ to*** 做…的学徒[徒弟]. **-ship** 徒弟的身分 [年限] (*the period of apprenticeship* 见习期限,学徒年限. *serve one's apprenticeship at ... [with sb.]* 在…[跟某人]做学徒). ~ **seaman** 〔美〕三等水手.

ap·pressed [əˈprest, æ-] *a.* 紧贴的; 紧靠的; 平贴着的.

ap·prise [əˈpraiz] *vt.* 〔书〕报告, 通知,告知. ~ ***sb. of (sth.)*** 告知某人某事 (~ *him of my arrival* 通知他我已到达).

ap·prize [əˈpraiz] *vt.* = appraise.

appro. = approval.

app·ro [ˈæprəu] *n.* 〔仅用于下列成语〕: ***on ~*** 〔俚〕(商品)供试用的,包退包换的.

ap·proach [əˈprəutʃ] *vt.* ①向…接近, 走近; 使接近. ②探讨;看待,对待,处理. ③向…接洽[提议]. ④〔美〕企图收买. ~ *one's home* 快到家. ~ *completion* 将近完成. *It is wrong to ~ a problem from a metaphysical point of view.* 用形而上学的观点来看待问题是错误的. ~ *Shakespeare as a poet* 诗才堪与莎士比亚相比拟. ~ *the manager with a suggestion* 向经理提出建议. ~ *the manager on a business* 为一项事务与经理接洽. ~ *a government officer* 企图向政府官员行贿. —*vi.* 临近,靠近; 近似. *Winter ~es.* 冬天快到了. —*n.* ①走近, 接近, 逼近. ②近似,类似. ③进路,入口;门径,接近[处理]的方法,手段. ④探索,探讨. ⑤看法,观点. ⑥〔*pl.*〕亲近;打交道. ⑦【军】(为逼近敌方工事而挖的)战壕. ⑧【空】进场(飞行),进入(投弹点). ⑨【军】战斗前进. ⑩〔*pl.*〕提议,建议. *the best ~ to study a foreign language* 学习外国语的最佳方法. *the blind ~*【空】盲目(按仪表)进场. *the instrument ~*【空】按仪表进场. *a scientific ~* 科学态度. *his nearest ~ to a smile* 他的似笑非笑的笑容. *an ~ to the bridge* 桥畔,引桥. *the ~ to the village* 到村庄去的路. ***make ~es to (sb.)*** 同(某人)亲近; 和(某人)打交道. ~ **light**【空】着陆信号灯.

ap·proach·a·bil·i·ty [əˌprəutʃəˈbiliti] *n.* 可接近, 易接近.

ap·proach·a·ble [əˈprəutʃəbl] *a.* ①可进入的. ②易接近的;易交谈的,平易近人的.

ap·pro·bate [ˈæprəubeit] *vt.* 〔美〕认可,批准. ~ *an act* 通过议案. ~ *the applicant to keep a shop* 批准申请人开业.

ap·pro·ba·tion [ˌæprəˈbeiʃən] *n.* ①认可, 批准. ②嘉奖,称赞. *meet with one's ~* 得某人同意. ***on ~*** (略 *appro.*) (商品)供试用的 〔*cf.* on approval〕.

ap·pro·ba·to·ry [ˈæprəbeitəri] *a.* 表示赞许的, 表示同意的.

ap·pro·pri·a·ble [əˈprəupriəbl] *a.* ①可作专用的. ②可挪用的,可盗取的. ③可拨作…经费的.

ap·pro·pri·ate [əˈprəuprieit] *vt.* ①擅用, 挪用, 占用, 盗用. ②〔美口〕盗取(少量公物). ③充用,充当,拨作…费用. ④〔美〕(州议会)认可(某项)经费. ~ *money for the navy* 拨款作海军费用. ~ *the building for storage* 拨房子当仓库. ~ *public funds for one's own private use* 挪用公款. ~ *public property to oneself* 私拿公物. —[-priit] *a.* ①适当的,合适的 (*to*). ②特定的, 专属的. *an ~ example* 适当的例子. *Each played his ~ part.* 每个人都起了他所特有的作用[各得其所]. ***be ~ for [to]*** 适于,合乎. **-ly** *ad.* 适当地. **-ness** *n.* 适当.

ap·pro·pri·a·tion [əˌprəupriˈeiʃən] *n.* ①专用. ②私用;挪用,擅用,盗用. ③充当,充用. ④经费. ⑤【宗】圣俸的转让;转让的圣俸;拨款;拨款的立法行动. *The ~ of the land made it possible to have a new building.* 该块土地的拨用使得建造新楼成为可能. ~ *of public fund* 盗用公共基金. *a large ~ for aid to the homeless children* 用来抚养无家可归儿童的巨额拨款. ***the Appropriations Committee*** 〔美〕岁出委员会;拨款委员会. ~ **bill** 〔美〕(提交议会的)岁出预算案,拨款预算案.

ap·pro·pri·a·tive [əˈprəupriətiv] *a.* ①专用[私用]的. ②盗用的,挪用的,占用的. ③充作…用的,政府支出的.

ap·pro·pri·a·tor [əˈprəuprieitə] *n.* ①拨给者. ②专用者. ③擅用者;盗用者.

ap·prov·a·ble [əˈpruːvəbl] *a.* 可批准的; 可赞同的.

ap·prov·al [əˈpruːvəl] *n.* ①赞成,同意. ②批准; 认可. *Do not lightly express your ~ or disapproval.* 不可轻易表示赞成或反对. *meet with sb.'s ~* 得某人赞成. ***for (sb.'s)***

～ 提请(某人)批准[承认];求(某人)指正. ***on*** ～〔俚〕(商品)供试用的,包退包换的. ***with ～ of the authorities*** 经当局批准.

ap·prove [əˈpruːv] *vt.* ①批准,认可(*opp.* reject). ②赞成,满意. ③[～ oneself]〔古〕显示,证明,证实. ～ *the work of a student* (老师)赞许学生的作业. *Congress ～d the bill.* 国会批准了该项法案. *The plan ～d itself to me.* 我认为这个计划已证实是好的. *the most ～d method* 最好的办法. — *vi.* 赞成,满意(*of*). ～ ***of*** 赞成 (*I quite ～ of your plan.* 我十分赞成你的计划). ～ ***oneself*** 证实自己是…(*He ～d himself ripe for the military command.* 他显现得已经可以做司令官了. *He ～d himself a good man.* 他证实自己是好人). ***be ～d for distribution*** 批转,批发.

ap·proved [əˈpruːvd] *a.* 已被承认的;良好的;有效的. *an ～ tenderer* 指定投标人. ～ **school**〔英〕少年罪犯教养院,工读学校.

ap·prov·er [əˈpruːvə] *n.* ①赞成者,批准者. ②【法】自首告发同犯的人.

approx. = approximate(ly).

ap·prox·i·mal [əˈprɔksiməl] *a.*【解】邻近的;邻接的.

ap·prox·i·mate [əˈprɔksimeit] *vt.* ①使接近. ②接近;走近. ③近似,约计. ④模拟. ⑤估计. ～ *a solution to a problem* 使问题近于解决. ～ *sth.* ～ *something to perfection* 使某物臻于完善. *The total income this year ～s 10,000 dollors.* 今年总收入接近一万元. ～ *the motions of the stars in a planetarium* 在天文馆中模拟行星的运行情况. *We ～d the distance at 100 miles.* 我们估计行程距离为 100 英里. — *vi.* 近于. *His income this year ～s to 8,000 dollars.* 他今年的收入接近八千美元. — [əˈprɔksimit] *a.* 近似的,大概的. *an ～ account* 简要的说明. *an ～ date* 大约的日期. *the ～ estimate* 大概的估计. *an ～ number* 概数. *an ～ value* 近似值. **-ly** *ad.* 大体,大致.

ap·prox·i·ma·tion [əˌprɔksiˈmeiʃən] *n.* ①接近;近似. ②【数】近似值. ③概算,略计. *successive ～s* 逐次近似计算法. ***be a very close ～ to*** 很接近于….

ap·pur·te·nance [əˈpəːtinəns] *n.* ①[常 *pl.*]附属物,从属物. ②【法】(财产上的)附属[附带]权利[如:道路通行权、果园所有权等]. ③[*pl.*](附属)装置,设备. *a house and all its ～s* 房子及其一切附属物.

ap·pur·te·nant [əˈpəːtinənt] *a.* ①附属的,从属的 (*to*). ②贴切的,恰当的. *a right-of-way ～ to land [buildings]* 随着土地[房子]而来的道路通行权. *a note ～ to the subject* 切合主题的注解. — *n.* 附属物.

Apr.＝April.

a·prax·i·a [əˈpræksiə] *n.*【医】(精神性)失用症.

a·prax·ic [əˈpræksik], **a·prac·tic** [-ˈpræktik] *a.*【医】患精神性失用症的.

a·près [æprei] *prep.*〔F.〕在…之后;[用在带连字符的复合词中]在…之后的: ～ *moi le déluge* 死后闹大水,与我何干,身后事与我何干. *an ～-ski party* 滑雪运动后举行的茶会.

a·pri·cot [ˈeiprikɔt] *n.* ①【植】杏,杏树. ②杏黄色. ③[A-]【植】李属. ～ *plum* 红李. *Japanese* ～ 梅.

A·pril [ˈeiprəl] *n.* ①四月. ②埃普丽尔〔女子名〕. ～ **fool** 四月傻瓜[愚人节中受愚弄的人]. **～-fool day** 愚人节[每年 4 月 1 日]. **～shower** 忽下忽停的春雨.

a pri·o·ri [ˈei praiˈɔːrai] *a.*〔L.〕由原因推及结果的;演绎的;先验的;推测的 (*opp.* a posteriori). *an ～ judgment* 忆测的判断. — *ad.* 演绎地,先验地.

a·pri·o·rism [ˌei-praiˈɔːrizəm] *n.* 先验论,先验的原理;演绎推理.

a·pri·or·i·ty [ˌei-praiˈɔriti] *n.* ①演绎性,推论性,先验性. ②演绎推论法的运用.

a·pron [ˈeiprən] *n.* ①围裙. ②(炮的)旋转保护罩. ③【船】(船头的)护船木. ④【机】(防护)挡板;(机床刀座下的)拖板箱. ⑤【地】冰川沉积堆. ⑥【剧】舞台幕前的突出部分,台口 (= ～ *stage*). ⑦【空】(飞机的)库前跑道,停机坪. ⑧〔美口〕铁丝网;伪装天幕. — *vt.* 用围裙围住. ～ **stage** 台口. ～ **string** 围裙带 (*be tied to one's mother's [wife's] ～ string* 为母亲[妻子]所左右,受裙带影响). **-ful** *n.* 满满一围裙(的)东西 (*an apronful of hazelnuts*) 满满一围裙的榛子.

ap·ro·pos [ˈæprəpəu] *a.,ad.* ①适当的[地],恰好,凑巧. ②顺便说一说. (= by the way). *Your telegram comes ～.* 你的电报来得正是时候. *A-, I have something to tell you.* 顺便跟你说个事. — *prep.*〔口〕关于. ～ ***of*** 关于,就…说,至于,说到. ～ ***of nothing*** 突然地;毫无理由地.

APS, A.P.S. = ①American Peace Society 美国和平协会. ②American Philosophical Society 美国哲学学会. ③American Physical Society 美国物理学会.

apse [æps] *n.* (*pl.* ***ap·ses*** [ˈæpsəz, -siz]) ①(教堂东端的)半圆室. ②【天】拱点 (= apsis).

ap·si·dal [ˈæpsidl] *a.* ①【天】拱点的. ②【建】半圆室的. ～ **motion** 拱线运动. ～ **surface**【数】长短径曲面.

ap·sis [ˈæpsis] *n.* (*pl.* ***apsi·des*** [æpˈsaidiːz]) ①【天】近日点 (= lower ～),远日点 (= higher ～),拱点. ②【建】= apse.

AP star [ˈeipiː stɑː]【天】特一级星[光度属一级而光谱自具特点的星].

apt [æpt] *a.* ①易于…的,有…倾向的,好…的[后接不定式][美]有…可能的. ②适当的,恰当的. ③灵敏的,灵巧的;擅长的;(学生等)有希望的. *He is ～ at teaching.* 他善于教书. *He is ～ to succeed.* 他很可能成功. *We are ～ to think ill of others.* 我们往往从坏的方面考虑人. *Iron is ～ to rust.* 铁易生锈. *an ～ comment* 恰当的评论.

apt(s) = apartment(s).

ap·ter·al [ˈæptərəl] *a.* ①【动】无翅的. ②【建】无侧柱的.

ap·ter·ous [ˈæptərəs] *a.*【动】无翅的,无翼的.

ap·ter·yg·i·al [ˌæptəˈridʒiəl] *a.*【动】缺少对鳍或对肢的.

ap·ti·tude [ˈæptitjuːd] *n.* ①适合性. ②倾向. ③天资;才能. ④颖悟,聪颖. *an ～ test* 智能测验 (*cf.* intelligence test). *a boy of remarkable ～* 神童. ***have an ～ for*** 有…的才能. ***have an ～ to*** (*vices*) 易染(恶习).

apt·ly [ˈæptli] *ad.* 适当地,善,巧. *It has ～ been said that….* 说得对[好].

apt·ness [ˈæptnis] *n.* ①适合性. ②性情,倾向. ③才能.

A·pus [ˈeipəs] *n.*【天】天燕(星)座.

a·py·ret·ic [ˌeipaiˈretik] *a.*【医】无热的,不发热的.

AQ, A.Q. = achievement quotient.

aq. =〔L.〕*aqua* (= water).

aq·ua [ˈækwə] *n.*〔L.〕水;溶液. ～ ***ammoniae*** [əˈməuniiː]【化】氨水. ～***fortis*** [ˈfɔːtis]【化】硝酸. ～ ***pura*** [ˈpjuərə] 纯水,,蒸馏水. ～ ***regia*** [ˈriːdʒiə]【化】王水. ～ ***vitae*** [ˈvaitiː] 烧酒;酒精.

aq·ua·cade [ˈækwəkeid] *n.*〔美〕水技会演大会.

aq·ua·cul·ture [ˈækwəkʌltʃə] *n.* 水产养殖. **-tur·al** *a.*

aq·ua·fer [ˈækwəfə] *n.* 含水层 (= aquifer).

aq·ua·gun [ˈækwəgʌn] *n.* (潜水员用的)水枪.

aq·ua-lung [ˈækwəlʌŋ] *n.* (潜水员用的)水中呼吸器.

aq·ua·ma·rine [ˌækwəməˈriːn] *n.* ①【矿】海蓝宝石,蓝晶. ②海蓝色.

aq·ua·naut [ˈækwənɔːt] *n.* ①海底科学工作者,深水操作人员. ②穿紧身潜水服的潜泳者.

aq·ua·plane [ˈækwəplein] *n.* (由小汽艇拖行的)滑水板. — *vi.* 站在滑水板上滑行.

aq·ua·relle [ˌækwəˈrel] *n.*〔F.〕透明水彩画(法);套色版画(法).

A·quar·i·an [əˈkwɛəriən] *a.* 宝瓶座时代的;太空时代

的.

a·quar·ist [əˈkwɛərist] *n.* ①(室内)养鱼爱好者,爱养水生动植物者. ②水族馆馆长,水族馆的领导人.

a·quar·i·um [əˈkwɛəriəm] *n. (pl. ~s, ~ria* [-riə]*)* ①水族馆. ②水族槽;养鱼缸;玻璃鱼池.

A·quar·i·us [əˈkwɛəriəs] *n.* ①【天】宝瓶(星)座. ②【天】宝瓶宫(黄道第十一宫).

a·qua·tel [ˌækəˈtel] *n.* 〔英口〕水上旅店〔供应住宿设备的系船池〕.

a·quat·ic [əˈkwætik] *a.* ①水的;水生的,水栖的. ②水上的,水中的. *an ~ bird* 水鸟. *~ plant* 水生植物. *~ products* 水产物. *~ sports* 水上运动. — *n.* ①水生动植物. ②〔*pl.*〕水上运动.

aq·ua·tint [ˈækwətint] *n.* 蚀刻凹板(画).

aq·ua·vit [ˈækwəvit] *n.* 阿瓜维特酒〔北欧产开胃酒〕.

aq·ue·duct [ˈækwidʌkt] *n.* ①渠道;渡槽,导水管. ②【解】导管.

a·que·ous [ˈeikwiəs] *a.* ①水的;水样的;水多的. ②水成的. ~ **solution** 水溶液. ~ **humor**【解】(眼球水晶体的)水状液. ~ **rock** 水成岩. ~ **tint** 水彩,水色. ~ **tissue**【植】储水组织.

aq·ui·cul·ture [ˈækwikʌltʃə] *n.* 水产养殖;(植物的)溶液培养. **-tur·al** *a.*

aq·ui·fer [ˈækwifə] *n.* (其含水量足可成为泉或井的)蓄水层.

Aq·ui·la [ˈækwilə] *n.*【天】天鹰(星)座.

aq·ui·le·gi·a [ˌækwiˈlidʒiə] *n.* 毛茛科耧斗菜属植物.

aq·ui·line [ˈækwilain] *a.* ①鹰的,似鹰的. ②(象鹰嘴那样)弯曲的. *an ~ nose* 鹰钩鼻.

a quo [ei kwəu] 〔L.〕从此.

AR = ①account receivable 应收帐. ②annual return 年度报告.

A.R. = ①all risks【保险】综合险. ②〔L.〕*anno regni* (= in the year of the reign) …朝代.

AR. = 〔美〕Army Regulations 军政法规汇编.

Ar【化】= ① 元素氩 (argon) 的符号. ②aryl radical.【化】芳基.

Ar. = ①Arabic. ②Aramaic. ③argentum.

ar. = ① argent. ②aromatic. ③arrive. ④arrival.

ar- *pref.* 〔用于 r 前〕= ad-: *ar*rest.

-ar *suf.* ①…的,…性的,…似的: famili*ar*, simil*ar*. ②…的人[物]: schol*ar*, alt*ar*. ③= -er, -or: begg*ar*, li*ar*.

A.R.A. = ①American Railway Association 美国铁路协会. ②Associate of the Royal Academy 〔英〕皇家艺术院准会员.

Ar·ab [ˈærəb] *n.* ①阿拉伯人. ②阿拉伯马. ③街头流浪儿 (= street ~). — *a.* 阿拉伯的,阿拉伯人的. **-dom** *n.* 阿拉伯世界.

Arab. =Arabia; Arabian; Arabic.

Ar·a·bel·(l)a [ˌærəˈbelə] *n.* 阿拉贝拉〔女子名〕.

ar·a·besque [ˌærəˈbesk] *a.* ①阿拉伯式的. ②精致的;奇异的. ③蔓藤花纹的. ④(文句)复杂难懂的. — *n.* ①蔓藤花纹. ②芭蕾舞的一种姿势〔身体向前,一足落地,一足后伸,两手前后平伸〕. ③轻松的狂想乐曲. ④复杂难懂的文句.

A·ra·bi·a [əˈreibjə] *n.* 阿拉伯半岛〔亚洲〕.

A·ra·bi·an [əˈreibjən] *a.* 阿拉伯(半岛)的;阿拉伯人的. ***the ~ bird*** 凤凰. ***the A- Nights' Entertainments*** = *the Thousand and One Nights* 《一千零一夜》〔旧译《天方夜谭》,古代阿拉伯民间故事集〕. — *n.* 阿拉伯人.

Ar·a·bic [ˈærəbik] *a.* 阿拉伯的;阿拉伯人[语]的. — *n.* 阿拉伯语. ~ **figures [numerals]** 阿拉伯数字.

Ar·ab·ist [ˈærəbist] *n.* 阿拉伯(语)学者,阿拉伯研究专家.

A·rab·i·za·tion [ˌærəbaiˈzeiʃən] *n.* 阿拉伯化.

A·rab·i·ze [ˈærəbaiz] *vt.* 使阿拉伯化.

ar·a·ble [ˈærəbl] *a.* ①适于耕种的,可耕的. ②〔英〕从事农作物栽培的. — *n.* (可)耕地(= ~ land). ~ *farming* 作物栽培. ~ *soil* 适于耕种的土壤.

Ar·a·by [ˈærəbi] *n.* 〔诗〕= Arabia.

a·rach·nid [əˈræknid] *n.* 蜘蛛纲动物〔包括蝎子、蜘蛛、虱子等〕.

a·rach·noid [əˈræknɔid] *a.* ①蛛网状的. ②【解】蛛网膜的. — *n.*【解】蛛网膜. ~ *of brain* 脑蛛网膜.

a·rae·o·style [əˈriːəstail] *n.*【建】疎柱式建筑物. — *a.*【建】疏柱式的.

a·rae·o·sys·tyle [əˌriːəˈsistail] *n.*【建】对柱式建筑物. — *a.*【建】对柱式的.

A·ra·gon [ˈærəgən] *n.* 阿拉贡〔西班牙东北部地名,古为一王国〕.

Ar·a·go·nese [ˌærəgəˈniːz] *a.* 阿拉贡的;阿拉贡人的;阿拉贡语的. — *n.* ①*(pl. ~)* 阿拉贡人. ②阿拉贡西班牙方言.

a·rag·o·nite [əˈrægənait,ˈærəgə-] *n.*【矿】霰石,文石.

ar·ak, ar·rack[ˈærək] *n.* 亚力酒〔椰子、大米、糖汁等酿成的一种烧酒〕(= arrack).

Ar·al [ˈɑːrəl] *n.* **Lake** ~ 咸海〔苏联〕〔亦作 ~ **Sea**〕.

Ar·am [ˈɛərəm] *n.* 阿拉姆〔姓氏〕.

Ar·a·mae·an, Ar·a·me·an [ˌærəˈmiən] *n.* ①阿拉姆人〔古叙利亚和美索不达米亚人〕. ②= Aramaic. — *a.* ①阿拉姆人的. ②阿拉姆语的.

Ar·a·ma·ic [ˌærəˈmeiik] *n.* 阿拉姆语〔古代西南亚的通用语言〕(略 **Aram.**).

a·ra·ne·id [əˈreiniid] *n.*【动】真蜘蛛类动物,蜘蛛.

A·rap·a·ho [əˈræpəhəu] *n. (pl. ~)* ①阿拉帕荷人〔原住北美北普拉特和阿肯色河,现住怀俄明和俄克拉荷马的一支印第安人部落〕.

ar·a·pai·ma [ˌærəˈpaimə] *n.* 巨骨舌鱼〔产于南美长达 3.5 m. 的一种大淡水鱼〕.

ar·a·ro·ba [ˌærəˈrəubə] *n.* ①柯桠粉〔来自柯桠树,用以制药〕. ②柯桠树〔巴西的一种树〕.

Ar·au·ca·ni·an [ˌærɔːˈkeiniən], **A·rau·can** [əˈrɔːkən] *n.* ①阿洛柯人〔智利和阿根廷的一支印第安人〕. ②阿洛柯语. — *a.* 阿洛柯人的;阿洛柯语的.

Ar·au·car·i·a [ˌærɔːˈkɛəriə] *n.*【植】①南洋杉属. ②〔a-〕南洋杉.

A·ra·wak [ˈɑːrɑːˌwɑːk,ˈærəˌwæk] *n.* 阿拉瓦人〔南美洲的一支印第安人〕.

A·ra·wa·kan [ˌɑːrɑːˈwɑːkən] *a.* 阿拉瓦语系的. — *n.* ①阿拉瓦部落人. ②阿拉瓦语系.

ar·ba·lest, ar·ba·list [ˈɑːbəlist] *n.* (中世纪的)劲弩.

ar·bi·ter [ˈɑːbitə] *n.* ①仲裁人,调停人,公断人. ②裁决者,决定者.

ar·bi·tra·ble [ˈɑːbitrəbl] *a.* 可调停的,可仲裁的;委诸仲裁的.

ar·bi·trage [ˈɑːbitridʒ] *n.* ①〔古〕裁判;仲裁. ②[ˌɑːbiˈtrɑːʒ]【商】套利,套汇〔指在一个市场购进汇票、股票,而在另一市场卖出,以赚取价格的差额〕. *an ~ house* 套利公司.

ar·bi·tral [ˈɑːbitrəl] *a.* 仲裁(人)的,公断(人)的.

ar·bit·ra·ment [ɑːˈbitrəmənt] *n.* ①仲裁. ②仲裁做出的决定,裁决. ③仲裁的权力.

ar·bi·trar·i·ly [ˈɑːbitrərili; Am.ˌɑːbiˈtrerili] *ad.* ①任意;恣意,擅自. ②专横地.

ar·bi·trar·i·ness [ˈɑːbitrərinis] *n.* ①任意;任性. ②霸道;专横,独断,武断. *In criticism, it is essential to guard against subjectivism and ~.* 批评要防止主观武断.

ar·bi·trar·y [ˈɑːbitrəri] *a.* ①任意的;任性的,随心所欲的. ②霸道的,专横的,独断独行的. *~ and unreasonable* 蛮横无理. *~ arguments* 强词夺理的议论.

ar·bi·trate [ˈɑːbitreit] *vt.* ①仲裁;公断. ②把…交付仲裁,使…听任公断. *~ quarrels* 仲裁争端. — *vi.* 进行仲裁. *~ between two parties* 在双方间进行仲裁. *~ in a dispute* 就某争端进行仲裁.

ar·bi·tra·tion [ˌɑːbiˈtreiʃən] *n.* 仲裁，公断，调解．～ ***of exchange*** 汇兑的套利〔指在两个或两个以上的市场上，同时买进和卖出外汇，以赚取价格的差额〕．***refer [submit] to*** ～ 交付公断．

ar·bi·tra·tor [ˈɑːbitreitə] *n.* 仲裁人，裁决者．

ar·bi·tress [ˈɑːbitris] *n.* 女仲裁人．

ar·bor[1] [ˈɑːbə] *n.*【机】轴；(机床的)心轴，刀轴．

ar·bor[2] [ˈɑːbɔː] *n.* *(pl.* ～*es* [ˈɑːbəriːz]*)* 树木，乔木．**A- Day** 〔美〕植树节．

ar·bor[3] [ˈɑːbə] *n.* 〔美〕＝ arbour.

ar·bo·ra·ceous [ˌɑːbəˈreiʃəs] *a.* ①树状的．②树木繁茂的．

ar·bo·re·al [ɑːˈbɔːriəl] *a.* ①树的，乔木的；木本的．②栖息在树上的，生活在树上的．

ar·bo·re·ous [ɑːˈbɔːriəs] *a.* ①树木繁茂的，森林多的．②树木的．③树状的．

ar·bo·res·cence [ˌɑːbəˈresns] *n.* ①树状．②(矿物等的)枝状．

ar·bo·res·cent [ˌɑːbəˈresnt] *a.* ①树状的．②树枝状的．

ar·bo·re·tum [ˌɑːbəˈriːtəm] *n.* *(pl.* ～*s, -ta* [-tə]*)* 树木园，植物园．

ar·bor·i·cul·tur·al [ˌɑːbəriˈkʌltʃərəl] *a.* 培植树木的；树木栽培学的，林学的．

ar·bor·i·cul·ture [ˈɑːbərikʌltʃə] *n.* 栽树，造林；林学，树木栽培学．

ar·bor·i·cul·tur·ist [ˌɑːbəriˈkʌltʃərist] *n.* 造林专家，树木栽培家．

ar·bor·ist [ˈɑːbɔːrist] *n.* 树艺家，树木栽培家，树木研究者．

ar·bor·i·za·tion [ˌɑːbəraiˈzeiʃən] *n.* (结晶、血管等的)树枝状．

ar·bor·ize [ˈɑːbəraiz] *vt., vi.* (使)(血管等)形成树枝状，(使)分叉．

ar·bor·ous [ˈɑːbərəs] *a.* 树的，乔木的；由树木组成的．

ar·bor·vi·tae [ˈɑːbəvaiti] *n.* ①【植】侧柏；〔A-〕金钟柏属．②【解】(小脑)活树．

ar·bour [ˈɑːbə] *n.* ①(树枝交叉形成的)棚架，藤架，凉亭．②〔废〕草地；花园．

ar·bo·vi·rus [ˈɑːbəˈvaiərəs] *n.*【微】树木病毒．

Ar·buth·not [ɑːˈbʌθnət] *n.* ①阿巴斯诺特〔姓氏〕．② **John** ～ 阿巴斯诺特(1667—1735)，苏格兰讽刺作家，医生．★英国人绰号 John Bull 即出自其所著 *The History of John Bull* 一书．

Ar·bu·tus [ɑːˈbjuːtəs] *n.*【植】杨梅属〔石南科〕；〔a-〕杨梅树；岩梨．

ARC, A.R.C. ＝ American Red Cross. 美国红十字会．

arc [ɑːk] *n.* ①弧；弓形，拱(洞)．②电弧，弧光．～ **de triomphe** 凯旋门．～ **furnace** 电弧炉．～ **lamp** 弧光灯．～ **light** ①弧光．②弧光灯．～**-over** *n.*【物】电弧放电．～ **welding** (电)弧焊．

ar·cade [ɑːˈkeid] *n.* ①【建】拱廊，连拱廊．②有拱廊〔骑楼〕的街道〔两边多有店铺〕．

ar·cad·ed [ɑːˈkeidid] *a.* 连拱式的；拱廊式的，有骑楼的．

Ar·ca·di·a [ɑːˈkeidjə] *n.* ①阿卡狄亚〔古希腊一山地牧区，以境内居民生活淳朴与宁静著称〕．②〔喻〕世外桃源．

Ar·ca·di·an [ɑːˈkeidjən] *a.* ①阿卡狄亚的．②田园的；淳朴的；牧歌的．—*n.* ①阿卡狄亚人．②淳朴的人．**-ism** *n.* 淳朴的田园风趣，牧歌似的情调．

Ar·ca·dy [ˈɑːkədi] *n.* 〔诗〕＝ Arcadia.

ar·ca·num [ɑːˈkeinəm] *n.* *(pl.* ～*s, -na* [-nə]*)* ①秘密的知识．②秘密，神秘．③秘方，秘药．

ar·ca·ture [ˈɑːkətʃə] *a.*【建】①小拱廊，小连环拱廊．②封闭式拱廊，假拱廊〔作为装饰用〕．

arc-bou·tant [ˌɑːbuːˈtɑːn] *n.* *(pl. -tants* [-ˈtɑːn]*)* 〔F.〕【建】飞拱．

arch[1] [ɑːtʃ] *n.* ①【建】弓架结构；拱廊，拱门；弓形门；穹窿，拱洞，拱顶．②弓形，半圆形．*a memorial* ～ 纪念门，牌坊．*a triumphal* ～ 凯旋门．～ *of the foot* 足底弓．*the* ～ *of the heavens* 苍穹．***the Court of Arches*** (坎特伯雷的)宗教裁判上诉院．—*vi.* ①【建】作(成)拱．②成弓形，弓着．—*vt.* ①【建】把…作成拱形；使弯作弓形．②用拱连接，用拱覆盖．*The rainbow* ～*es the heaven.* 虹在天上成弓形．*A cat* ～*es its back.* 猫弓着背．

arch[2] [ɑːtʃ] *a.* 首要的；总的．*the* ～ *villain* 流氓头子．

arch[3] [ɑːtʃ] *a.* 诡诈的；淘气的．*an* ～ *smile* 顽皮的微笑．

arch. ＝ archaic; archaism; archery; archipelago; architect; architecture.

arch- *pref.* 首位的，主要的，最高的：*arch*duke, *arch*bishop.

-arch *n. suf.* 统治者，王，皇帝：matri*arch*, mon*arch*.

Ar·chae·an [ɑːˈki(ː)ən] *n., a.*【地】太古代(的)；太古代岩石(的)．

ar·chae·o-, ar·che·o- *comb. f.* 古代的，原始的：*archaeo*logy.

ar·chae·o·log·i·cal [ˌɑːkiəˈlɔdʒikəl] *a.* 考古学(上)的．**-ly** *ad.*

ar·chae·ol·o·gist [ˌɑːkiˈɔlədʒist] *n.* 考古学家．

ar·chae·ol·o·gy [ˌɑːkiˈɔlədʒi] *n.* ①考古学，古物学．②〔罕〕古代史．③文化遗物．

ar·chae·op·ter·yx [ˌɑːkiˈɔptəriks] *n.*【古生】始祖鸟．

Ar·chae·o·zo·ic [ˌɑːkiəˈzəuik] *a.* 太古代的．—*n.* 〔the ～〕太古代(＝ the ～ era).

ar·cha·ic [ɑːˈkeiik] *a.* ①古代的，古风的．②(语言等)古体的，陈旧的．*the* ～ 古代；古物．*Thou is an* ～ *form of you.* "Thou" 是 "you" 的古体．**-al·ly** *ad.*

ar·cha·ism [ˈɑːkeiizəm] *n.* ①古语，古体，古风．②(语言等的)拟古主义．

ar·cha·ist [ˈɑːkeiist] *n.* ①拟古主义者，摹仿古风的人．②古物研究家．

ar·cha·is·tic [ˌɑːkeiˈistik] *a.* 古风的，拟古的．

ar·cha·ize [ˈɑːkeiaiz] *vt.* ①使(文章等)有古风．②用古词古语；仿古．

arch·an·gel [ˈɑːkˌeindʒəl] *n.* ①天使长，大天使．②【植】白芷属 *(＝ angelica)*.

ar·chan·thro·pine [ɑːˈkænθrəpain] *n.* 猿人．

arch·bish·op [ˈɑːtʃˈbiʃəp] *n.* 大主教．**-ric** *n.* 大主教的职位〔任期、管区〕．

arch·dea·con [ˈɑːtʃˈdiːkən] *n.* 副主教．**-ry** *n.* 副主教的职权〔地位、管区、宅邸〕．

arch·di·o·cese [ˈɑːtʃˈdaiəsis] *n.* 大主教管区．

arch-dove [ˈɑːtʃˈdʌv] *n.* (政治上的)鸽派首脑．

arch·du·cal [ˈɑːtʃˈdjuːkəl] *a.* ①大公的．②大公领地的，大公国的．

arch·duch·ess [ˈɑːtʃˈdʌtʃis] *n.* ①大公夫人．②(从前奥地利皇家的)公主．

arch·duch·y [ˈɑːtʃˈdʌtʃi] *n.* 大公领地，大公国．

arch·duke [ˈɑːtʃˈdjuːk] *n.* 大公〔1918年前奥国皇太子的称呼〕．

Ar·che·an [ɑːˈkiən] *a.* ＝ Archaean.

arched [ɑːtʃt] *a.* 拱形的，半圆形的；弓架结构的．*an* ～ *bridge* 拱桥．

arch·en·e·my [ˈɑːtʃˈenimi] *n.* ①【基督教】(魔王)撒旦．②主敌，大敌．

Arch·er [ˈɑːtʃə] *n.* 阿彻〔姓氏〕．

arch·er [ˈɑːtʃə] *n.* ①射手，弓箭手．②〔A-〕【天】射手座；人马宫．～**-fish** 射水鱼〔东南亚淡水鱼，嘴能喷水〕．

arch·er·y [ˈɑːtʃəri] *n.* ①射箭，箭术．②(弓、箭等)射箭用具．③〔集合词〕弓箭手；射箭运动员．

ar·che·typ·al [ˈɑːkitaipəl] *a.* ①原始模型的．②典范的．

ar·che·type [ˈɑːkitaip] *n.* ①原始模型．②典型．

arch•fiend [ˈɑːtʃˈfiːnd] *n.* 魔王；【基督教】撒旦.

ar•chi- *pref.* ①= arch-. ②【生】原；*archi*plasm.

Ar•chi•bald [ˈɑːtʃibəld, ˈɑːtʃibɔːld] *n.* 阿奇博尔德〔男子名〕.

ar•chi•bald [ˌɑːtʃibəld,ˈɑːtʃbɔːld] *n.* 〔俚〕高射炮.

ar•chi•cer•e•brum [ˈɑːkiˈseribrəm] *n.* 【动】原脑.

ar•chi•di•ac•o•nal [ˌɑːkidaiˈækənəl] *a.* 副主教的.

Ar•chie [ˈɑːtʃi] *n.* 阿奇〔男子名，Archibald 的昵称〕.

ar•chie [ˈɑːtʃi] *n.* 〔俚〕高射炮.

ar•chi•e•pis•co•pal [ˌɑːkiiˈpiskəpəl] *a.* 大主教的.

ar•chil [ˈɑːkil] *n.* ①紫色地衣染料；苔色素. ②石蕊地衣，海石蕊.

ar•chi•mage [ˈɑːkiˌmeidʒ] *n.* 大魔法师，大巫师.

Ar•chi•me•des [ɑːkiˈmiːdiːz] *n.* 阿基米得〔古希腊数学家287?— 212 B.C.〕. **-me•de•an** [-ˈmiːdjən] *a.*

ar•chin, ar•chine [ɑːˈʃiːn] *n.* 〔苏联〕俄尺〔等于 28 英寸〕.

ar•chi•pel•a•go [ˌɑːkiˈpeligəu] *n.* *(pl. ~es, ~s)* ①多岛海. ②群岛. ③〔the A-〕爱琴海及其岛屿. **-lag•ic** *a.*

ar•chi•plasm [ˈɑːkiplæzəm] *n.* 【生化】原形质.

ar•chi•tect [ˈɑːkitekt] *n.* ①建筑师，设计师；创制者. ②〔A-〕造物主. *a naval ~* 造船技师. *the ~ of one's own fortunes* 掌握自己命运的人. *the ~s of the Constitution* 宪法起草者. ***the Great A- (of the Universe)*** 造物主，上帝.

ar•chi•tec•ton•ic(al) [ˌɑːkitekˈtɔnik(əl)] *a.* ①建筑术的. ②构造的，结构的. ③(知识)成体系的，系统化的. **~s** *n. pl.* 〔用作 *sing.*〕①建筑学. ②建筑设计；结构设计. ③【哲】(认识)体系论，(知识)系统化. *the ~s of a symphony* 交响音乐的结构设计.

ar•chi•tec•tur•al [ˌɑːkiˈtektʃərəl] *a.* 建筑学的；建筑上的. **-ly** *ad.* 建筑(学)上.

ar•chi•tec•ture [ˈɑːkitektʃə] *n.* ①建筑学. ②建筑（样式、风格）；建筑物. ③构造，结构. *civil ~* 民用建筑. *domestic ~* 住宅建筑. *naval ~* 造船术，造船学. *the ~ of a beehive* 蜂窝的结构.

ar•chi•trave [ˈɑːkitreiv] *n.* 【建】①框缘. ②(柱的)下楣. ③(窗等的)嵌线. ④额枋.

ar•chi•val [ɑːˈkaivəl] *a.* 档案的；档案里的；包括有档案的.

ar•chives [ˈɑːkaivz] *n. pl.* ①档案馆〔室〕，档案处. ②档案. *the State A- Bureau* 国家档案局. *family ~* 家谱.

ar•chi•vist [ˈɑːkivist] *n.* 档案保管人.

ar•chi•volt [ˈɑːkivəult] *n.* 【建】①拱门饰〔拱门沿边的嵌线或其他饰物〕. ②拱门内侧的穹窿.

ar•chon [ˈɑːkən] *n.* ①古希腊雅典九人执政官之一；执政官. ②主要官员.

ar•cho•saur [ˈɑːəsɔ] *n.* 【考古】祖龙.

arch•priest [ˈɑːtʃˈpriːst] *n.* ①【宗】(原义为主教的)主助祭；副主教. ②主祭.

arch•way [ˈɑːtʃwei] *n.* 拱道；拱洞.

arch•wise [ˈɑːtʃwaiz] *ad.* 拱状地；拱廊似地；成弓形.

-ar•chy *suf.* 政治，政体：matri*archy*, mon*archy*.

ar•ci•form [ˈɑːsifɔːm] *a.* 拱形的，弓状的.

arc•o•graph [ˈɑːkəgrɑːf] *n.* (不用中心点画圆的)圆弧规.

arc•ol•o•gy [ɑːˈkɔlədʒi] *n.* 生态建筑〔在单一建筑内达到完整的计划城市或环境〕.

arc•tic [ˈɑːktik] *a.* ①北极的；寒带的 (*opp.* antarctic). ②极冷的；(态度等)冷淡的. —*n.* ①北极圈；北极地方. ②〔*pl.*〕〔美〕橡皮套靴. *the A- Circle* 北极圈. *an ~ expedition* 北极探险. *the A- pole* 北极 (= North Pole). *the A- Ocean* 北冰洋. *an ~ smile* 冷笑.

Arc•tu•rus [ɑːkˈtjuərəs] *n.* 【天】大角(牧夫座 α).

ar•cu•ate [ˈɑːkjuit], **ar•cu•at•ed** [ˈɑːkjueitid] *a.* ①弓形的. ②【建】拱式的. *~ islands* 弓形列岛.

-ard *suf.* 做…的人，…的人，沉湎…的人：drunk*ard*, Spani*ard*, slugg*ard*.

ar•deb [ˈɑːdeb] *n.* 阿德布〔埃及干品容量单位，等于 5.6189 (美制蒲式耳〕.

Ar•dell(e) [ɑːˈdel] *n.* 阿黛尔〔女子名，Adele 的异体〕.

Ar•den [ˈɑːdn] *n.* ①阿登〔姓氏，男子名〕. ②阿尔丁〔英国沃里克郡的小林区，原系大森林. 莎士比亚以该地作为《皆大欢喜》一剧的背景〕.

ar•den•cy [ˈɑːdənsi] *n.* 热心，热情；热烈.

ar•dent [ˈɑːdənt] *a.* ①热心的；热烈的. ②炽热的. ③强烈的. *an ~ admirer* 热烈的赞美者. *~ passion* 热情. *an ~ protest* 强烈的抗议. *~ hate* 愤恨. *~ spirits* 烧酒. **-ly** *ad.* **-ness** *n.*

Ar•dis [ˈɑːdis] *n.* 阿迪丝〔女子名〕.

ar•do•me•ter [ɑːˈdɔmitə] *n.* 光测高温计.

ar•dour, 〔美〕**ar•dor** [ˈɑːdə] *n.* ①热情，热心. ②〔罕〕灼热. *patriotic ~* 爱国热情. *with ~* 热心地. *with enthusiastic ~* 轰轰烈烈地.

ar•du•ous [ˈɑːdjuəs] *a.* ①费力的，艰巨的. ②奋斗的，努力的. ③险峻的. *~ paths* 陡峭的道路. *an ~ task* 艰难的工作. *an ~ winter* 严冬. *an ~ worker* 勤奋的工人. **-ly** *ad.* 艰苦地. **-ness** 艰难，艰苦，奋斗.

are[1] 〔强 ɑː; 弱 ɑ,ə〕be 的第二人称单数. 第一、三人称复数现在陈述语气. *Are you there?* (电话用语)喂！喂！

are[2] [ɑː] *n.* 公亩〔等于 100 平方米〕.

ar•e•a [ˈɛəriə] *n.* ①面积；平地；地面. ②空地；〔英〕地下室前的空地. ③地区，地方；〔喻〕区域；范围. *a vast uncultivated ~* 广阔的未开垦地. *a mountainous ~* 山区. *a fortified ~* 要塞地带. *an ~ of investigation* 研究范围. *the liberated ~s* 解放区. *an ~ of fire* 【军】射界. *This room is 16 square metres in ~.* 这个房间的面积为16平方米. ~ **bombing** 【军】(无特定目标的全区性) 区域轰炸. ~ **bell** 地下室门铃. ~ **bombing** 大面积轰炸 (= carpet bombing). ~ **code** (美国、加拿大)电话分区的三位数代号. ~ **rug** (房间内只遮住部分地面的) 小地毯. ~**way** ①〔英〕地下室前的空地. ②(建筑物之间的通道).

Ar•e•ca [ˈærikə] *n.* ①【植】槟榔属. ②〔a-〕槟榔；槟榔树〔又称 betel palm〕. ~ **nut** 槟榔果. ~ **palm** 槟榔树.

a•re•na [əˈriːnə] *n.* ①古罗马圆形剧场中央的竞技场；(一般的)竞技场所. ②活动场所，竞争场所. *an ~ of warfare* 战场. *the ~ of politics.* 政治舞台. *a boxing ~* 拳击比赛场地. *a circus ~* 马戏场. ~ **theater** 舞台设在观众座席中央的剧场，圆形剧场.

ar•e•na•ceous [ˌæriˈneiʃəs] *a.* ①砂(质)的，多砂的. ②似砂的，枯燥无味的. ③(植物)砂中生长的.

ar•e•nic•o•lous [ˌæriˈnikələs] *a.* 生活在沙中的，生长在沙中的.

ar•e•nite [ˈærinait] *n.* 【矿】粗屑岩.

aren't [ɑːnt] ①= are not. ②〔英口〕= an't, am not: *I am good, ~ I* (= am I not)?

a•re•o•la [æˈriələ] *n.* *(pl. ~s, -lae* [-liː]) ①小空隙. ②【生】(叶脉间、翅脉间的)网隙. ③【解】乳头晕. ④【植】果脐. **-r** *a.*

ar•e•om•e•ter [ˌæriˈɔmitə] *n.* 液体比重计，浮秤.

Ar•e•op•a•gite [ˌæriˈɔpəgait] *n.* 古希腊雅典最高法院的法官.

Ar•e•op•a•gus [ˌæriˈɔpəgəs] *n.* ①雅典一小丘名〔雅典最高法院在该处断案〕. ②(古希腊)雅典最高法院.

A•re•qui•pa [ˌæriˈkiːpə] *n.* 阿雷基帕〔秘鲁城市〕.

Ar•es [ˈɛəriːz] *n.* 【希神】阿瑞斯〔战神，相当于罗马神话中的 Mars〕.

a•rête [æˈreit] *n.* 〔F.〕险峻的山脊；【地】刃岭.

arg. = ①argent. ②argentum.

ar•gal, ar•gol [ˈɑːgɔl] *n.* 粗酒石〔酒桶里酒变陈时的沉淀〕.

ar·ga·la [ˈɑːgələ] *n.*【鸟】(印度)鹳类.

ar·ga·li [ˈɑːgəli] *n.*【动】(亚洲)大角野羊.

ar·gand [ˈɑːgænd] *n.* 管状灯芯的灯.

ar·gent [ˈɑːdʒənt] *n.* ①〔古、诗〕银. ②〔诗〕银白色. ③〔废〕银币; 货币. —*a.* ①银的; 银似的. ②银制的. ③银色的.

ar·gen·tic [ɑːˈdʒentik] *a.* 银的,含银的〔尤指含二价银的化合物而言〕.

ar·gen·tif·er·ous [ˌɑːdʒənˈtifərəs] *a.* (矿砂等)含银的; 产银的,有银的.

Ar·gen·ti·na [ˈɑːdʒənˈtiːnə] *n.* 阿根廷〔拉丁美洲〕.

ar·gen·tine [ˈɑːdʒəntain] *a.* 银的; 象银的; 银色的. —*n.* ①银,银色金属. ②【矿】珠光石,银白色页状方解石. ③银色素〔取自鱼鳞,用来做人造珍珠〕.

Ar·gen·tine [ˈɑːdʒəntain] *a.* 阿根廷的; 阿根廷人的. —*n.* ①阿根廷人. ②〔the ～〕阿根廷.

Ar·gen·tine·an [ˌɑːdʒənˈtiniən] *n.* 阿根廷人. —*a.* 阿根廷的; 阿根廷人的.

ar·gen·tite [ˈɑːdʒənˌtait] *n.* 辉银矿.

ar·gen·tous [ɑːˈdʒentəs] *a.*【化】亚银的,含亚银的〔指含一价银的化合物而言〕.

ar·gil [ˈɑːdʒil] *n.* ①白粘土,陶土. ②矾土.

ar·gil·la·ceous [ˌɑːdʒiˈleiʃəs] *a.* ①粘土的. ②含粘土的. ③粘土似的.

ar·gil·lite [ˈɑːdʒilait] *n.*【地】①厚层泥岩. ②泥质板岩.

ar·gi·nase [ˈɑːdʒineis] *n.*【生化】(肝脏里的)精氨酸酶; 胍基戊氨酸酶.

ar·gi·nine [ˈɑːdʒini(ː)n] *n.*【生化】精氨酸.

Ar·give [ˈɑːgaiv] *n., a.*〔诗〕希腊人(的).

ar·gle-bar·gle [ˈɑːglˈbɑːgl] *n., vi.*〔英口〕①争论,辩论,热烈讨论. ②讨价还价.

Ar·go [ˈɑːgəu] *n.* ①【希神】亚尔古舟〔贾森找金羊毛所乘的船〕. ②【天】南船座.

ar·gol [ˈɑːgɔl] *n.* 粗酒石〔酒桶里酒变陈时的沉淀〕.

ar·gon [ˈɑːgɔn] *n.*【化】氩〔元素名,符号为 A〕.

Ar·go·naut [ˈɑːgənɔːt] *n.* ①【希神】亚尔古英雄〔随同贾森乘亚尔古舟,去海外寻找金羊毛的英雄〕. ②【美史】1849 年左右到加利福尼亚去淘金的人. ③〔a-〕船鱼(= paper nautilus). **-ic** [-tik] *a.* 亚尔古船上人的,乘亚尔古船远行的.

ar·go·sy [ˈɑːgəsi] *n.*〔诗〕①大商船. ②大商船队. ③丰富的贮藏,丰富的供应.

ar·got [ˈɑːgəu] *n.*〔F.〕①(某一职业或团体惯用的)行话. ②(盗贼等的)暗语,黑话.

ar·gu·a·ble [ˈɑːgjuəbl] *a.* 可论证的,可争辩的,有疑义的.

ar·gue [ˈɑːgju] *vt.* ①辩论,争论,争辩(某事,某论点等),为(某事、某论点等)作辩解,(找理由)把(某事等)辩解[搪塞]过去 *(away, off)*. ②说服,劝说,劝服(某人)做[不做]某事 *(into [out of])*. ③主张,认为; 论证 *(that)*. ④(事实、行为等)证明,表明. ～ *a point [a matter]* 就一个论点[问题]进行辩论. *He ～d me into joining the party.* 他说服我参加舞会. *She ～d herself into going back.* 她经过多次反复考虑后决定返回去了. *Columbus ～s that the world is round.* 哥伦布提出地球是圆的. *Her clothes ～ poverty.* 她的服装表明她家境清寒. *It ～s him to be a rogue.* 那证明他是一个无赖. —*vi.* 争论,辩论. ～ ***against*** 反对…,成为…的反证. ～ ***down*** 说服(某人). ～ ***for*** 赞成,力主,为…作争辩. ～ *(sb.)* ***into*** *(consent)* ***[out of*** *(his opinion)]* 劝(某人)使其(答应)[放弃(其意见)]. ～ ***it away [off]*** 用话把它搪塞过去. ～ ***on*** [***upon***] 论及. ～ ***with*** *(sb.)* ***about [on]*** 与(某人)讨论,议论(某事).

ar·gu·er [ˈɑːgjuə] *n.* 辩论者,争论者.

ar·gu·fy [ˈɑːgjufai] *vi., vt.*〔美俚〕啰哩啰嗦地辩论; 纠缠不休地争论.

ar·gu·ment [ˈɑːgjumənt] *n.* ①争论,辩论,论证. ②论据,论点. ③(书籍等的)梗概,摘要,大纲; (剧本等的)情节. ④【数】幅角; 宗量,宗数,自变数. ⑤【逻】(三段论中的)中项,中词. ⑥〔废〕证据. *an artificial* ～ 巧辩,诡辩. *start [put forward] an* ～ 开始[挑起]争论. ～ ***against [for, in favour of]*** 反对[赞成]…的论点. ***get [fall] into an*** ～ ***with*** 与…发生争论. ***ram an*** ～ ***home*** 反复说明论点使对方接受. ***without*** ～ 无异议.

ar·gu·men·ta·tion [ˌɑːgjumenˈteiʃən] *n.* ①立论,推论,论证. ②辩论,争论. ③(有别于描写、叙述和说明的)论说; 论说文; 辩论性的演说.

ar·gu·men·ta·tive [ˌɑːgjuˈmentətiv] *a.* ①争辩的,辩论的. ②好争辩的. **-ly** *ad.* **-ness** *n.*

ar·gu·men·tum [ˌɑːgjuˈmentən] *n.*〔L.〕= argument. ～ ***ad hominem*** (= to the man) ①向辩论对手作人身攻击而不回答其论点. ②辩论时以迎合听众特殊的情绪、偏见或利益取胜,使用哗众取宠的手法.

Ar·gus [ˈɑːgəs] *n.* ①【希神】百眼巨人. ②机警的看守(人). **～-eyed** [aid] *a.* 眼光锐利的; 机警的.

ar·gute [ɑːˈgjuːt] *a.* ①锐利的; 伶俐的,机警的. ②(声音)尖锐的. ③(叶边等)锯齿形的.

ar·gy-bar·gy [ˈɑːgiˈbɑːgi] *n.*〔方、口〕争争吵吵,抬杠,讨价还价.

ar·gyle [ˈɑːgail] *a.* 阿盖尔(图案)的〔阿盖尔图案是不同颜色的斜方形或菱形拼成的图案,用于针织品〕. —*n.* ①针织品的多角菱形图案,阿盖尔图案. ②〔*pl.*〕花格短袜.

Ar·gyll [ɑːˈgail] *n.* 阿盖尔〔苏格兰郡名〕.

ar·gyr·i·a [ɑːˈdʒiriə] *n.* 银中毒,银质沉着病.

ar·gyr·o·dite [ɑːˈdʒirədait] *n.* 硫银锗矿.

a·ri·a [ˈɑːriə] *n.*〔It.〕【乐】咏叹调; 唱腔; 唱段.

-aria *suf.*【动】…目: actini*aria* 海葵目.

-arian *suf.* …派的(人),…岁的(人): veget*arian* sexagen*arian*.

Ar·i·an[1] [ˈɛəriən] *a.* 阿里乌斯(教)的. —*n.* 阿里乌斯教徒. **-ism** *n.* 阿里乌斯教〔亚历山大神学家阿里乌斯(Arius)的教义,认为耶稣不是神,但比凡人高超〕.

Ar·i·an[2] [ˈɛəriən] *a., n.* = Aryan.

ar·id [ˈærid] *a.* ①干旱的; 贫瘠的,荒芜的. ②枯燥无味的. *an* ～ *land* 旱地. **-ly** *ad.*

a·rid·i·ty [æˈriditi] *n.* ①干旱; 贫瘠,荒芜. ②枯燥,乏味.

ar·i·el [ˈɛəriəl] *n.*【动】(阿拉伯)羚羊.

Ar·i·el [ˈɛəriəl] *n.* ①(莎士比亚剧本《暴风雨》中的)空气般的精灵. ②【天】天王星的第一卫星,天(王)卫一.

Ar·i·es [ˈɛəriːz] *n.*【天】白羊(星)座.

ar·i·et·ta [ˌæriˈetə] *n.*〔It.〕【乐】小咏叹调.

a·ri·ga·to [ˌɑːriːˈgɑːtəu] *n.*〔Jap.〕谢谢.

a·right [əˈrait] *ad.*〔书〕正确地,不错. ***if I*** *remember* ～ 如果我没记错. *He guessed* ～. 他猜对了. —*vt.*〔书〕改正,纠正.

A·ri·ka·ra [əˈriːkərə] *n.* ①阿里卡拉人〔美国密苏里河平原的一支印第安人〕. ②阿里卡拉人讲的卡多恩语.

ar·il [ˈæril] *n.*【植】假种皮,子衣,子壳.

ar·i·ose [ˈæriəus, ˌɛəriˈəus] *a.* 如歌的; 旋律的.

a·ri·o·so [ˌɑːriəˈəuzəu] *a.*〔It.〕悦耳的,宛如咏叹调的. —*ad.* 悦耳地,宛如咏叹调地. —*n.* 咏叹调.

-arious *suf.* …性的: greg*arious*.

a·rise [əˈraiz] *vi.* ***(a·rose*** [əˈrəuz]***; a·ris·en*** [əˈrizn]***)*** ①起,兴起; 出现; 发生. ②(人早上)起来,起身. ③(太阳)上升. ④产生于,起因于,出身于 *(～ from, ～ out of)*. *Questions arose.* 问题发生了. *Accidents ～ from carelessness.* 事故往往起因于疏忽.

a·ris·ta [əˈristə] *n.* *(pl.* ***-tae*** [-tiː]*)* (谷)芒; (蝇类的)口刺; 触角芒.

a·ris·tate [əˈristeit] *a.* 有芒的,有刺的; 有触角芒的.

ar·is·toc·ra·cy [ˌærisˈtɔkrəsi] *n.* ①贵族政治〔政府〕,

贵族统治的国家. ②〔the ~〕(集合词)贵族,贵族阶层,上层阶级,第一流人物. ③贵族的派头. *the ~ of wealth* 富豪. *an ~ of scientists* 科学家的佼佼者.

a·ris·to·crat [ˈæristəkræt] *n.* ①贵族. ②贵族政治论者. ③有贵族派头的人. *a struggle between the ~s and the plebeians* 贵族与平民之间的斗争.

a·ris·to·crat·ic, a·ris·to·crat·i·cal [ˌæristəˈkrætik(əl)] *a.* ①贵族的,(主张)贵族掌政的. ②贵族气派的. *~ bearing* 贵族派头. *~ snobbishness* 媚上骄下. **-i·cal·ly** *ad.*

ar·is·toc·rat·ism [ˌærisˈtɔkrətizəm] *n.* 贵族主义; 贵族气派〔作风〕.

Ar·is·tot·le [ˈæristɔtl] *n.* 亚里士多德〔公元前 384—322 年,古希腊哲学家〕. **~'s lantern** (海胆的)咀嚼器.

Ar·is·to·te·li·an (亦作 **Ar·is·to·te·le·an**) [ˌæristɔˈtiːljən, -tiˈliːən] *a.* ①亚里士多德的. ②亚里士多德学派的. — *n.* ①亚里士多德学派的人. ②求实者〔思想上倾向于注重经验和实际的人〕.

a·rith·me·tic [əˈriθmətik] *n.* ①算术,算法; 计算. ②算术书. *I challenge your ~.* 你的算法靠不住. *mental ~* 心算. *~ device* 运算装置,运算器. *~ speed* 运算速度.

ar·ith·met·i·cal [ˌæriθˈmetikəl] *a.* 算术(上)的. ~ **complement** 余数. ~ **progression** 算术级数,等差级数. **-ly** *ad.* 用算术,算术上.

a·rith·me·ti·cian [əˌriθməˈtiʃən] *n.* 算术家.

ar·ith·mom·e·ter [ˌæriθˈmɔmitə] *n.* (初期的)加算器,四则计算机.

-arium 〔L.〕 *n. suf.* 关于…的物, …的场所: aqu*arium*, honor*arium*.

a ri·ve·der·ci [ɑːriveiˈdeətʃi] 〔It.〕〔古〕回头见; 再见〔暂时分别时用语〕.

Ariz. = Arizona.

Ar·i·zo·na [ˌæriˈzəunə] *n.* 亚利桑那〔美国州名〕.

Ark. = Arkansas [ˈɑːkənsɔː; Am. ˈɑrkənsɔ, ɑrˈkænzəs] *n.* 阿肯色〔美国州名〕.

ark [ɑːk] *n.* ①【圣】方舟;〔喻〕避难所. ②〔方、诗〕箱,柜;【圣】约柜. ③犹太教堂中贮存圣经和犹太教法典卷轴的地方. ④〔美〕大平底船,河船. ***Noah's ~*** 挪亚方舟〔《圣经》中挪亚为避洪水而造的方舟,舟中载有成对的各类动物〕; 装有各种动物的玩具船. ***~ of the covenant*** 约柜〔装有两块十诫碑的箱子〕.

Ar·kan·sas [ˈɑːkənsɔː; Am. ˈɑrkənsɔ, ɑrˈkænzəs] *n.* ①阿肯色〔美国州名〕. ②〔the ~〕阿肯色河〔美国〕.

Ar·kan·san [ɑːˈkænzən], **Ar·kan·si·an** [ɑːˈkænziən] ① *a.* 阿肯色州(人)的. ② *n.* 阿肯色州人.

Ar·kan·saw·yer [ˌɑːkənˈsɔːjə] *n.* 〔美〕阿肯色州人〔用做绰号〕.

Ar·kie [ˈɑːkiː] *n.* 〔美〕(从阿肯色州来的)临时雇农.

ar·kose [ˈɑːkəus] *n.* 〔F.〕长石砂岩.

Ark·wright [ˈɑːkrait] *n.* ①阿克赖特〔姓氏〕. ②**Sir Richard ~** 阿克赖特〔1732—1792, 英国纺织机发明人〕. ③〔a-〕(能制箱、柜等的)木匠.

Ar·len [ˈɑːlən] *n.* 阿伦〔姓氏,男子名〕.

Ar·lene [ɑːˈliːn] *n.* 阿琳〔女子名〕.

arles [ɑːlz] *n. pl.* 〔用作单〕〔Scot.〕定钱(尤指雇用仆人时先付的钱).

Ar·lo [ˈɑːləu] *n.* 阿洛〔男子名〕.

arm[1] [ɑːm] *n.* ①臂,【动】前肢. ②【机】(轮)辐;【电】线担,支路,支架. ③臂状物; 衣袖; 电唱头臂; (椅子)扶手. ④树枝,枝干. ⑤港湾,海湾. ⑥力,权力. ⑦【棒球】投球能力. *the right ~* 右臂; 得力的助手. *Justice has long ~s.* 天网恢恢,疏而不漏. *an ~ of the sea* 海湾; 河口. *the ~ of the government* 政府的分支机构. *the strong ~ of the law* 法律的威力. *the ~ of a record player* 唱机的唱头臂. *lose one's ~* 【棒球】失去投球能力. ***~ in ~*** 臂挽着臂. ***by the strong ~*** 强制地. ***chance one's ~*** 〔英口〕冒险一试. ***child in ~s*** 怀抱中的婴儿. ***cost (sb.) an ~ and a leg*** 〔俚〕使付出一大笔钱. ***give one's ~*** 伸手臂给(同行女人挽);〔喻〕提携. ***in the ~s of Morpheus*** 进入梦乡. ***keep (sb.) at ~'s length*** 疏远,不使接近. ***make a long ~*** 伸臂(攫取). ***offer one's ~*** = give one's ~. ***put the ~ on sb.*** 向某人讨钱; 抢劫某人. ***take (sb.'s) ~s*** 拉伸出之臂. ***take (a child) in one's ~s*** 抱(孩子). ***talk sb.'s ~ off*** 〔俚〕对某人唠叨个没完. ***the ~ of flesh*** 人力,人的努力. ***twist sb.'s ~*** 倒扭某人手臂; 向某人施加压力. ***throw one's ~s around another's neck*** 搂住脖子. ***under the ~*** 挟在腋下. ***with folded ~s*** 两臂交叉于胸前 (*look on with folded ~s* 袖手旁观). ***within ~'s reach*** 在左近,近在咫尺. ***with open ~s*** 伸开双手,真心诚意地(欢迎). ***would give one's right ~ for*** 〔口〕愿意为…付出巨大代价. **~band** 臂章. **~hole** 袖孔. **~pad** 椅子扶手上的小垫子. **~pit** 腋窝. **~rest** (靠椅、拐杖等的)扶手. **~'s-length** *a.* 不友好的,不亲密的. **~-twisting** *n., a.* 强大压力(的). **~ wrestling** 臂力,拗手腕.

arm[2] [ɑːm] *n.* ①〔*pl.*, 罕 *sing.*〕军械,武器. ②〔喻〕军事. ③(步、骑等的)兵种. ④〔*pl.*〕(盾、旗等上的)纹章. *a man at ~s* 战士. *a passage of [at] ~s* 比武,两人对打. *a stand of ~s* (一名士兵的)全副武装. *deed of ~s* 战功. *force of ~s* 武力,兵力. *small ~s* 轻兵器(指手枪、步枪、机枪等). *the suspension of ~s* 休战. ***appeal to ~s*** 诉诸武力. ***bear ~s*** 服兵役. ***bred to ~s*** 自幼习武. ***by ~*** 用武力. ***carry ~s*** 携带武器; 服兵役. ***go to ~s*** 诉诸武力. ***lay down ~s*** 缴械; 投降. ***Order ~s!*** 枪放下! ***Pile ~s!*** 架枪! ***Present ~s!*** 举枪(敬礼)! ***rest on one's ~s*** (战斗中的)暂时休息. ***rise in ~s*** 动武,起兵. ***Shoulder ~s!*** 枪上肩! ***take up ~s*** 拿起武器. ***To ~s!*** 快拿武器! 准备战斗! ***turn one's ~s against*** 攻击. ***under ~s*** ①备战. ②在服兵役期间. ***up in ~s*** 武装反抗. — *vt.* ①供给…武器,武装(军队等). ②供给; 发给 (*with*). ③打开(雷等)的保险; 给…装上导火线. ④给…装甲. *an ~ed mediation* 武装调解. *I ~ed my men with guns.* 我发枪给部下. *be ~ed at all points* 全身武装,周身披甲; 戒备严密. *be ~ed to the teeth* 全副武装,武装到牙齿. *be ~ed with* 用…武装着; 装备着 *be ~ed with a letter of introduction* 带着介绍信. — *vi.* 拿起武器,武装起来.

ar·ma·da [ɑːˈmɑːdə] *n.* ①舰队. ②(飞机、汽车等的)大队. ③〔the A-〕(1588 年西班牙进攻英国时的)无敌舰队 (= the Invincible [Spanish] Armada). *an ~ of planes* 飞机机群. *an ~ of buses* 汽车队.

ar·ma·dil·lo [ˌɑːməˈdiləu] *n.* 【动】犰狳.

Ar·ma·ged·don [ˌɑːməˈgedn] *n.* ①【圣】世界末日善恶决战的战场. ②(国际间的)大决战.

Ar·ma·gnac [ˈɑːmənjæk] *n.* 〔有时作 a-〕阿马涅克白兰地〔法国加斯柯尼的阿马涅克所产的一种酒〕.

ar·ma·ment [ˈɑːməmənt] *n.* ①军队. ②(一国的)武装力量. ③(军舰、要塞等的)火炮; 一个作战单位的武器,装备. ④武装(过程). ⑤(动植物的)防护器官. ⑥战斗部〔指导弹的弹头、引信和保险装置系统的结合部〕. *the reduction of ~s* 裁(减)军(备). *an anti-torpedo ~* 水雷防御炮. *a main [secondary] ~* 主[副]炮. *the vast ~ sent by the Rome emperor* 罗马皇帝派遣的大批军队. *planes with the newest ~* 配备有最新武器的飞机. *The country's ~ will take years.* 国家的武装过程需要几年.

ar·ma·men·tar·i·um [ˌɑːməmənˈteəriəm] *n.* (*pl.* ~*s*, **-ia**[-ə]) 物资、器械装备(尤指医疗物资和器械).

Ar·mand [ˈɑːmənd] *n.* 阿曼德〔男子名, Herman(n) 的异体〕.

ar·ma·ture [ˈɑːmətjuə] *n.* ①【电】转子,电枢; 衔铁; 引铁. ②甲胄. ③【生】防御器官;【虫】体刺. ④【建】加强料; 钢筋. ⑤(塑像的)骨架. *a small animal having sharp teeth for its ~* 有利齿当武器的小动物.

arm·chair [ˈɑːmˈtʃɛə] *n.* 扶手椅子. ①安逸的,舒适的. ②理论性的,不切实际的. *an* ~ *travel* 舒适的旅行. *an* ~ *soldier* 不上前线的士兵. *an* ~ *strategist* 纸上谈兵者.

arme blanche [ɑːm ˈblɑːŋʃ] 〔F.〕①(骑兵用的)大刀,标枪. ②骑兵.

armed [ɑːmd] *a.* ①武装了的. ②【动、植】有(刺、齿等)护身器官的. ③(炮弹等)装上导火线的. ④有准备的. ⑤装甲的. *an* ~ *merchantman* 武装商船. ~ *neutrality* 武装中立. ~ *peace* 武装和平. ~ *robbery* 武装抢劫,持械抢劫. ~ *forces [services]* 军队;海陆空三军. ~ *eyes* 戴着眼镜的眼睛 (*cf.* naked eye). ~ *glass* 铁丝网夹心玻璃. *long* ~ 长胳膊的.

Ar·me·ni·a [ɑːˈmiːnjə] *n.* 亚美尼亚〔苏联加盟共和国名〕.

Ar·me·ni·an [ɑːˈmiːnjən] *a.* 亚美尼亚(人)的. — *n.* 亚美尼亚人〔语〕.

ar·met [ˈɑːmet] *n.* (中世纪的)铁盔.

arm·ful [ˈɑːmful] *n.* 一抱. *an* ~ *of wood* 一抱柴.

ar·mi·ger [ˈɑːmidʒə] *n.* *(pl.* ***-ge·ri*** *[-ri])* (中世纪)骑士的扈从;(骑士与自由民之间的)乡绅.

ar·mil·lar·y [ɑːˈmiləri] *a.* 环的,手镯的;环形的. ~ **sphere** 浑天仪.

ar·mip·o·tent [ɑːˈmipətənt] *a.* 〔罕〕兵力强大的.

ar·mi·stice [ˈɑːmistis] *n.* ①停战,休战. ②休战条约,停战协定. **A- Day** 第一次世界大战的停战纪念日〔11月11日〕.

arm·less [ˈɑːmlis] *a.* ①无臂的. ②无武装[战备]的. ③(动植物)无防护器官的.

arm·let [ˈɑːmˈlit] *n.* ①小海湾. ②臂饰,臂环,臂章.

arm·load [ˈɑːmləud] *n.* 〔美口〕一抱(量).

arm·lock [ˈɑːmˌlɔk] *n.* 【摔交】锁臂勾腿.

ar·moire [ɑːˈmwɑːr] *n.* 〔F.〕大型衣橱.

ar·mor [ˈɑːmə] *n.* 〔美〕= armour.

ar·mo·ri·al [ɑːˈmɔːriəl] *a.* 纹章的,盾徽的. — *n.* 纹章集. ~ **bearings** 纹章.

Ar·mor·ic, Ar·mor·i·can [ɑːˈmɔrik, ɑːˈmɔrikən] *a.* 阿莫里卡(法国布列塔尼之旧名)的,阿莫里卡人的,阿莫里卡语的. — *n.* ①阿莫里卡人,布列塔尼人. ②阿莫里卡语;布列塔尼语.

ar·mor·y [ˈɑːməri] *n.* 〔美〕= armoury.

ar·mour [ˈɑːmə] *n.* ①甲胄,盔甲. ②铠板;装甲用钢板. ③(动植物的)防护器官. ④潜水服. ⑤装甲部队. ⑥(覆盖在电线外的)铠装. *~-piercing projectile* 穿甲弹. ***be clad in*** ~ 穿着盔甲的,武装着的;装甲的. — *vt.* 为…装甲;为…穿上铠甲. **~-bearer** 武士的扈从. **~-clad** ① *a.* 武装的,装甲的. ②*n.* 装甲舰. **~plate** 装甲用钢板. **-ing** *n.* 武装;铠装.

ar·mo(u)red [ˈɑːməd] *a.* ①武装的;装甲的. ②穿戴铠甲的;(电缆等)铠装的. ~ *cable* 铠装电缆. ~ *concrete* 钢筋混凝土. *an* ~ *cruiser* 装甲巡洋舰. ~ *forces* 装甲部队. *an* ~ *seat* 【空】装甲座位. *an* ~ *train* 铁甲列车.

ar·mo(u)r·er [ˈɑːmərə] *n.* ①(从前的)盔甲、兵器制造者. ②武器制造者. ③(部队里、战舰上维修武器的)军械士.

ar·mo(u)r·y [ˈɑːməri] *n.* ①军械库. ②〔美〕国民警卫队训练场. ③〔美〕兵工厂. ④〔集合词〕武器,军械. ⑤〔古〕纹章. ⑥纹章学.

arms [ɑːmz] *n.* 〔*pl.*〕①见 arm² 条. ②(手枪等)小武器. ③纹章 (= coat of arms).

Arm·strong [ˈɑːmstrɔŋ] *n.* 阿姆斯特朗〔姓氏〕.

ar·mure [ˈɑːmjuə] *n.* ①小卵石纹织物. ②〔废〕盔甲.

ar·my [ˈɑːmi] *n.* ①陆军;军队. ②军;集团军;兵团;野战军. ③大群;团体. ~ *and navy* 陆海军. *a regular* ~ 正规军. *a reserve* ~ 后备军. *a standing [conventional]* ~ 常备军. *the Chinese People's Liberation A-* 中国人民解放军. *an* ~ *of ants* 大群蚂蚁. *the* ~ *of the unemployed* 失业大军. ~ ***act*** 陆军刑法,军法. ***A- Air Forces*** 〔美〕陆军航空部队. ***A- and Navy Store*** 〔英〕军人消费合作社. ~ ***of operation*** 野战军. ***A- Service Corps*** 辎重队. ***join the*** ~ 入伍,参军. ***raise an*** ~ 招兵,募兵. ***serve in the*** ~ 服兵役,在军队中工作. ~ **act** 陆军刑法,军法. ~ **bral** 〔美俚〕(随营长大的)陆军官或士兵的儿子. ~ **brow** 军服黄色. ~ **corps** 军. ~ **coups commander** 军长. **A- Day** 陆军节. ~ **group** 集团军. **~-list** 陆军 军官名册. ~ **register** = **~-list.** ~ **surplus** 陆军剩余物资. ~ **worm** (成群结队毁坏庄稼的)粘虫.

Arne [ɑːn] *n.* 阿恩〔姓氏,男子名〕.

ar·ni·ca [ˈɑːnikə] *n.* ①【植】山金车花. ②【药】阿尼卡酊剂〔用以治疗扭伤〕.

Ar·nold [ˈɑːnld] *n.* 阿诺德〔姓氏,男子名〕.

ar·oid [ˈærɔid,ˈɛər-] *n.* 天南星科植物.

a·roint [əˈrɔint] *int.* 〔古〕去! *A- thee!* 去!滚!

a·ro·ma [əˈrəumə] *n.* ①芳香,香味. ②气派,风格,风味. *a city with the* ~ *of Paris* 具有巴黎风格的城市.

ar·o·mat·ic [ˌærəuˈmætik] *a.* ①香气浓的,芳香的. ②【化】芳香族的. — *n.* ①芳香植物. ②〔常 *pl.*〕香料,芳香剂. ~ **crops** 香料作物. ~ **compounds** 芳香族化合物.

a·ro·ma·tize [əˈrəumətaiz] *vt.* ①使芳香;在…中加香味. ②【化】使芳构化.

a·rose [əˈrəuz] arise 的过去式.

a·round [əˈraund] *ad.* ①周围,四面. ②〔美口〕各处,四处. ③左近,在附近. ③围着,环绕. ④向相反方向. ⑤循环重现;旋转. ⑥恢复知觉. ⑦活跃着. ⑧到(谈话双方都熟悉的)某地. *Travel* ~ *from place to place* 周游. *look* ~ 环视,四顾. *sit* ~ *a table* 围着桌子坐. *a car circling* ~ 一辆在兜着圈子的车. *Will you please wait* ~ *for me?* 请在附近等我好吗? *Turn* ~! *You're going the wrong way.* 转回来,你走错路了! *The column measures two feet* ~. 这根柱子周长 2 英尺. *She hasn't been* ~ *lately.* 她最近不活跃了. *He came* ~ *to see me.* 他到这里来看我. *bring sb.* ~ 使某人恢复知觉. ***all*** ~ 四处,到处;都,一一 (*shook hands all* ~ 一一握手). ***all the year*** ~ 整年 (*mild all the year* ~ 一年四季都很温暖). ***be*** ~ 〔美口〕起床;走动 (*He's up and* ~ *now.* 他起来走动了). ***fool*** ~ 〔口〕吊儿郎当. ***hang*** ~ 在附近徘徊. ***have been*** ~ ***(a lot)*** 〔口〕见识(很)多;世故(很)深. ***the other way*** ~ 〔美〕从相反方向;用相反方式. — *prep.* ①在周围,围着;绕过. ②〔美口〕在近处,在附近;前后,左右,差不多. ③〔美口〕到处. ④在那边. ⑤朝着各个方向. ⑥在(某人)身边. ~ *here* 在这边. ~ *the corner* 〔美〕在拐角那里 (=〔英〕*round the corner*). *roam* ~ *the country* 漫游全国. *stay* ~ *the house* 总不离家. ~ *four o'clock* 四点前后. *travel* ~ *the world* 作环球旅行. *leave the books* ~ *the house* 在房子里到处乱丢书. *the few men* ~ *the despot* 暴君身边寥寥可数的几个人. ***get*** ~ 绕过(障碍),解决(困难),回避(事实). **~-the-clock** *a.* 连续二十四小时的;连续不停的 (*an ~-the-clock operation* 连续二十四小时的作业).

a·rous·al [əˈrauzəl] *n.* 〔罕、古〕觉醒;激励,唤起.

a·rouse [əˈrauz] *vt.* ①唤醒. ②唤起,引起. ③鼓励,激发. ~ *suspicion* 引起猜疑. ~ *sb. from sleep* 唤醒某人. — *vi.* 睡醒.

a·row [əˈrəu] *ad.* 〔诗〕一列,一排.

A.R.P., ARP = air raid precautions 空袭预防措施. **ARP post** 防空哨. **ARP shelter** 防空洞. ~ **warden** 防空监视员.

ar·peg·gio [ɑːˈpedʒiəu] *n.* 〔It.〕*(pl.~s)* 【乐】琶音,急速和弦.

ar·pent [ˈɑːpənt] *n.* 阿邦〔法国旧地积度量单位,现仍在加拿大的魁北克和美国的路易西安纳部分地区使用,约等于5/6英亩〕.

ar·que·bus [ˈɑːkwibəs] *n.* 火绳钩枪.

ar·rack [ˈærək] *n.* (大米、糖蜜或椰汁制成的) 烧酒 (=arak).

ar·rah [ˈærə] *int.* 啊呀〔表示惊愕、愤怒等的声音〕.

ar·raign [əˈrein] *vt.* ①【法】传讯,提审,审问. ②弹劾,责难,控告. **-ment** *n.*

ar·range [əˈreindʒ] *vt.* ①整理,整顿;布置. ②商定,商妥. ③准备,安排. ④调停(纠纷). ⑤【乐】改编. ~ *one's collections* 整理搜集品. *The meeting is ~d for Saturday afternoon.* 会议安排在星期六下午. *Everything is so far ~d.* 样样都准备好了. ~ *a dispute* 调解纠纷. ~ *a novel for the stage* 改编小说为剧本. —*vi.* ①商定,商妥. ②准备,设法,安排. *I will ~ somehow.* 我终归想好办法了. *We have ~d for him to live near us.* 我们已安排他住在附近. ~ **for** *(an appointment)* 约(会面时间). ~ *(things)* **in order** 整顿(东西). ~ **with** *(sb.)* **about** *(sth.)* 与(某人)商定(某事).

ar·range·ment [əˈreindʒmənt] *n.* ①整顿,整理;排列,布置,分类. ②〔*pl.*〕安排,料理,筹备,预备. ③商定,约定. ④调解,和解. ⑤改作,改编;改编的乐曲. *Arrangements have been made for the party.* 为聚会做了安排. ***come to an*** ~ 谈妥. ***make ~s for*** 为…做准备. ***make ~s with*** 与…达成协议. ***make business*** ~ 接洽事务. ~ **committee** 筹备委员(会).

ar·rant [ˈærənt] *a.* 彻头彻尾的;臭名远扬的. *an ~ fool* 大傻瓜. *an ~ hypocrite* 彻头彻尾的伪君子. *an ~ lie* 弥天大谎. **-ly** *ad.*

ar·ras [ˈærəs] *n.* (壁上装饰的)挂毯.

ar·ray [əˈrei] *vt.* ①打扮,装饰. ②使…列队,排列. ③提出(陪审官)名单,使(陪审官)列席,召集(陪审官). *The general ~ed his troops for battle.* 将军使军队列队准备战斗. *The girl ~ed herself in her finest clothes.* 这姑娘打扮得花枝招展. *The count and his men ~ed themselves against the king.* 伯爵举兵对抗国王. — *n.* ①整列,队列,阵(列);阵容. ②〔诗〕衣裳,装扮,打扮. ③陪审官名单. ④一大批,一大群,一连串. ⑤【数】排列. *a battle ~* 战斗队形,列阵. *holiday ~* 节日盛装. *be in fine ~* 盛装. *an ~ of actors* 演员的阵容. *a window ~* 橱窗陈列品. ***an ~ of*** *(umbrellas)* 一排(伞). ***in battle*** ~ 列阵,严阵. ***in proud*** ~ 堂堂正正.

ar·ray·al [əˈreiəl] *n.* ①列阵,军容. ②排列.

ar·rear [əˈriə] *n.* ①〔*pl.*〕欠款,尾数;欠工,尾活. ②(工作的)耽搁,延误,落后. ③剩余品. ***~s of stock*** 滞销货. *~s of rent* 欠租,拖欠未交的租金. *~s of correspondence* 待复的信件. ***in ~(s)*** 拖欠,下欠 *(fall in(to) ~(s)* 拖欠款项). ***in ~ of*** 赶不上,不及. ***in ~(s) with*** *(payments)* 拖延(交款). ***work off ~s*** 补做尾活;陆续补还欠款.

ar·rear·age [əˈriəridʒ] *n.* ①〔*pl.*〕欠款. ②落后,拖延,延误. ③备用品.

ar·rect [əˈrekt] *a.* ①(耳朵)竖着的. ②仔细听着的,警觉的. *a rabbit with ears ~* 竖着耳朵的兔子.

ar·rest [əˈrest] *vt.* ①逮捕,拘捕,扣留. ②止住,阻止,抑制. ③吸引(注意). *The policeman ~ed the thief.* 警察逮捕了窃贼. *The doctor ~ed the growth of the disease.* 医生止住了病情的恶化. *The bright colours of the flowers ~ed the girl's attention.* 花的艳丽色彩引起了姑娘的注意. *She ~ed herself in the act of sitting.* 她要坐而没坐下来. ~ *(sb.)* **for** *(a crime)* 因(罪嫌)逮捕(某人). ~ ***sb.'s eye*** 惹人注目. — *n.* ①停止,阻止,抑制;制动(装置). ②逮捕;拘留,收押. ~ ***of judgement*** 暂缓判决〔陪审团宣布有罪或无罪后;法官因某种法律的原因而暂不作判决〕. ***be put [held, placed] under*** ~ 在拘留中. ***under house*** ~ 软禁.

ar·rest·er [əˈrestə] *n.* ①逮捕者. ②防止装置. ③避雷器. *a lightning ~* 避雷针. *a spark ~* 火花制止器〔防止火花外射的装置〕.

ar·rest·ing [əˈrestiŋ] *a.* ①引人注意的,显著的. ②制动的. *an ~ work of art* 引人注意的艺术品.

ar·rest·ment [əˈrestmənt] *n.* ①阻止;制动. ②逮捕,拘捕;扣押,扣留.

ar·ret [ərei] *n.* 〔F.〕①命令. ②裁判,判决. ③逮捕;扣押.

ar·rhyth·mi·a [əˈriðmiə, əˈriθ-] *n.* 【医】心律不齐. **ar·ryth·mic, -rhyth·mi·cal** [əˈriðmik(əl), əˈriθ-] *a.* **-rhyth·mi·cal·ly** *ad.*

ar·ride [əˈraid] *vt.* 〔古〕使喜欢,使满足.

ar·rière-ban [æriεəˈbæn] *n.* 〔F.〕①【史】(中世纪法国国王召集臣下的)总动员令. ②对国王有应召服军役义务的诸侯.

ar·rière-pen·sée [ˈæriεəpɑ̃ːnˈsei] *n.* 〔F.〕心事,心思;隐蔽的意图.

ar·ris [ˈæris] *n.* 【建】棱(角). ~ **gutter** V形檐槽.

ar·ri·val [əˈraivəl] *n.* ①到达,抵达. ②到达者;到达物. ③出现,登场. ④新生婴儿. *The new ~ was a daughter.* 新生婴儿是一个女孩. *a new ~* 新来者;新到货;新生儿. ~ *at a conclusion* 得出结论. *on his ~ at sixty* 年满六十. ***cash on*** ~【商】货到付款. ***delivery on*** ~【商】货到即交. ~ **list** 抵埠乘客名单. ~ **station** 末站,终点站.

ar·rive [əˈraiv] *vi.* ①到达,抵,到,达. ②(时间、事件等)到来,发生. ③达到(结果),得出(结论等) *(at)*. ④(艺术家等)成功,成名. ~ *at a place* 到达某地. ~ *in England* 到英国. ~ *at a conclusion* 得到结论. ~ *at manhood* 达成年. ~ *upon the scene* 到场. *The time has ~d for action.* 采取行动的时刻到来了. *He has ~d professionally.* 他在职业上功成名就. ★指到达的时间或地点用 at, 到某大都会时用 in.

ar·ri·ve·der·ci [ɑːˌriveˈdeətʃiː] *int.* 〔It.〕回头见! 再见! 〔暂时分别时用语〕.

ar·ri·viste [ˌæriːˈvist] *n.* 〔F.〕暴发户,野心家,钻营者,名利狂.

ar·ro·ba [əˈrɔːbə] *n.* 〔Sp.〕阿罗瓦〔①西班牙重量单位,用于南美某些国家,合 25.36 磅. ②葡萄牙重量单位,用于巴西,合 32.38 磅. ③液量单位用于某些操西班牙语的国家,相当于 13 到 17 夸脱〕.

ar·ro·gance, ar·ro·gan·cy [ˈærəgəns, -si] *n.* 自大,傲慢 *(opp.* humility*)*. ~ ***of power*** (大国的)炫耀武力.

ar·ro·gant [ˈærəgənt] *a.* 自大的,傲慢的,妄自尊大的. ~ *airs* 骄气. ~ *and unreasonable demands* 蛮横无理的要求. **-ly** *ad.*

ar·ro·gate [ˈærəugeit] *vt.* ①僭称,冒称;霸占,擅取. ②不当地把…归于 *(to)*. ~ *the right to make decisions* 冒称有权做出决定. ~ *to oneself some importance* 妄自尊大. ~ *bad motives to sb.* 无根据地认为某人别有用心.

ar·ro·ga·tion [ˌærəuˈgeiʃən] *n.* 僭称;霸占;僭越.

ar·ron·disse·ment [ˌærɔnˈdiːsˈmɑ̃ːŋ] *n.* 〔F.〕县,(大城市的)区.

ar·row [ˈærəu] *n.* ①矢,箭. ②箭状物;箭头记号〔→〕. ③〔the A-〕【天】天箭座. *shoot an ~* 射箭. *a spent ~* 强弩之末. *a traffic ~* 交通箭头标志. ***a broad*** ~ 宽矢形戳记〔标明英国政府财产的官印〕. ***as straight as an*** ~ 笔直. ***have an ~ left in one's quiver*** 还有资本;还有对策. **~head** [ˈærəuhed] *n.* ①箭头镞. ②=broad arrow. ③【植】慈姑. **~-headed** *a.* 箭头形的,镞状的. **~-headed characters** 楔形文字. **~root** [ˈærəuruːt] *n.* 【植】①竹芋,葛. ②竹芋粉,葛粉. **~wood** [ˈærəuwud] *n.* 【植】弓木,荚蒾〔北美印第安人用以制箭〕.

ar·row·worm [ˈærəuˌwəːm] *n.* 【虫】箭虫.

ar·row·y [ˈærəui] *a.* ①矢的,箭一样的;笔直的. ②象箭一样迅速的.

ar·roy·o [əˈrɔiəu] *n.* *(pl.* ~*s)* 〔美〕①小河,小溪. ②旱谷,干涸的沟壑.

ARS = ①American Rocket Society 美国火箭学会．②Agricultural Research Service 农业研究服务处〔美国农业部一机构〕．

arse [ɑːs] *n.* 〔卑〕屁股．

ar·se·nal [ˈɑːsinl] *n.* ①军械库，武器库．②兵工厂．③〔喻〕(思想等的)武库．*a naval* ～ 海军军工厂．

ar·se·nate [ˈɑːsinit] *n.* 【化】砷酸盐．

ar·se·nic [ˈɑːsnik] *n.* 【化】砷，信石，砒霜．— *a.* 砷的．～ *acid* 砷酸．*white* ～ 砒霜．

ar·sen·i·cal [ɑːˈsenikəl] *a.* 砷的，含信石的．～ *poisoning* 砷中毒．— *n.* 砷化物．

ar·se·nide [ˈɑːsinaid] *n.* 砷化物．

ar·se·ni·ous, -nous [ɑːˈsiːnjəs] *a.* (含)砷的；亚砷的．～ **acid** 亚砷酸．

ar·se·nism [ˈɑːsinizəm] *n.* 慢性砷中毒．

ar·se·nite [ˈɑːsinait] *n.* 【化】砷华，亚砷酸盐．

ar·se·niu·ret·ed, ar·se·niu·ret·ted [ɑːˈsiːnjəˈretid, -ˈsen-] *a.* 砷化的．

ar·se·no·py·rite [ˌɑːsinəuˈpairait] *n.* 【矿】含砷黄铁矿，毒砂．

ars gra·ti·a ar·tis [ˈɑːzˈgreiʃjəˈɑːtis] 〔L.〕 为艺术而艺术．

ar·shin [ɑːˈʃiːn] *n.* 〔苏联〕俄尺〔＝28 英寸〕．

ar·sine [ɑːˈsiːn, ˈɑːsiːn] *n.* ①胂．②砷化三氢．

arsis [ˈɑːsis] *n.* *(pl. -ses* [-siːz]*)* ①(古典诗的)弱音节．②(英国诗的)强音节〔因误解 arsis 的希腊文原义，而讹传为强音节〕．③【乐】弱拍．

ar·son [ˈɑːsn] *n.* (故意)放火，纵火(罪)．

ars·phen·a·mine [ˌɑːsfenəˈmiːn, ɑːsˈfenəmiːn] *n.* 【药】胂凡纳明，六〇六(药)〔用以治疗梅毒〕．

art[1] [ɑːt] *n.* ①艺术，美术．②〔*pl.*〕(中世纪大学的)文科 (= liberal arts)．③技术；技巧；技艺．④策略，诡计，奸计．⑤〔美口〕(新闻、杂志上的)插图．⑥〔古〕学问．⑦做作，装模作样．*the* ～ *for* ～ *school* 艺术至上派，唯美派，*an* ～ *gallery* 美术馆；画廊．*the* ～ *of agriculture* 农艺．*the* ～ *preservative of all* ～*s* 印刷术．*the black* ～ 魔术．*the fine* ～*s* 美术〔包括绘画、雕塑、建筑、文学、音乐、戏剧等〕．*the industrial* ～*s* 工艺．*the healing [benevolent]* ～ 医术．*the liberal* ～*s* 文科〔包括文学、音乐、哲学等〕．*the manly [noble, self-defence]* ～ 拳术．*the mechanical [useful]* ～*s* 手工工艺．*a bachelor of* ～*s* 文学学士．*a master of* ～*s* 文学硕士．*a smile without* ～ 自然的〔天真的〕微笑．～ *of strategy* 战略．～ ***and part*** 策划并参与 (*He is* ～ *and part in the crime.* 他是这个罪案的共犯；他策划并参与犯罪活动)．～ ***for*** ～***'s sake*** 为艺术而艺术．— *vt.* 使艺术化〔仅用于下列成语〕．～ ***up*** 使艺术化．～ **deco [A- D-]** 装饰艺术．～ **director** ①(电影、电视的)美术设计人．②美术编辑．～ **form** 艺术形式．～ **glass** 彩色艺术玻璃；艺术玻璃花瓶〔灯等〕．～ **store** 艺术用品商店．～ **ware** 工艺品．～ **work** 书刊、杂志上的图片．

art[2] [ɑːt] *vi.* 〔古、诗〕〔主语为 thou 时〕be 的第二人称、单数、现在、陈述语气．

art. = ①article．②artist．③artillery．④artificial．

-art *suf.* = -ard: braggart.

ar·tal [ˈɑːtɑːl] *n.* 〔rotl 的复数形〕穆斯林地区的重量名〔相当于 1—5 磅不等〕．

ar·te·fact [ˈɑːtifækt] *n.* = artifact.

ar·tel [ɑːˈtel] *n.* (旧俄时代的)劳动组合，(生产)合作社．

Ar·te·mis [ˈɑːtimis] *n.* 【希神】阿特米丝〔月亮女神〕．

ar·te·mis·i·a [ˌɑːtiˈmiziə] *n.* 【植】艾属；艾．

ar·te·ri·al [ɑːˈtiəriəl] *a.* ①动脉的，动脉状的．②干线的．*an* ～ *road [highway]* 公路干线．

arteri·al·ize [ɑːˈtiəriəlaiz] *vt.* 使(静脉血)转变为动脉血．

ar·te·ri·og·ra·phy [ɑːˌtiəriˈɔgrəfi] *n.* ①动脉搏描记法．②动脉照相术．

ar·te·ri·ole [ɑːˈtiəriəul] *n.* 小动脉．**-ri·o·lar** [-ˈəulə] *a.*

ar·te·ri·ol·o·gy [ɑːtiːriˈɔlədʒi] *n.* 【医】动脉学．

ar·te·ri·o·scle·ro·sis [ɑːˌtiəriəuskliəˈrəusis] *n.* 【医】动脉硬化(症)．

ar·te·ri·ot·o·my [ɑːˌtiəriˈɔtəmi] *n.* 【医】动脉切开术．

ar·te·ri·o·ve·nous [ɑːˌtiəriəuˈviːnəs] *a.* 动静脉的．

ar·te·ri·tis [ˌɑːtəˈraitis] *n.* 【医】动脉炎．

ar·ter·y [ˈɑːtəri] *n.* ①【解】动脉．②干线，要道；中枢．*the brachial [carotid, pulmonary]* ～ 上膊〔颈、肺〕动脉．*the main* ～ 大动脉．*a traffic* ～ 交通干线．

ar·te·sian [ɑːˈtiːzjən] *a.* 自流的．～ **well** 自流井，喷水井．

art·ful [ˈɑːtful] *a.* ①狡猾的．②有手腕的；机灵的，巧妙的．③〔古〕不自然的，人为的．*an* ～ *swindle* 诈骗．*an* ～ *trick* 妙计．**-ly** *ad.* **-ness** *n.* 狡猾，巧妙．

ar·thral·gia [ɑːˈθrældʒiə] *n.* 关节痛．

ar·thrit·ic [ɑːˈθritik] *a.* 关节炎的．— *n.* 关节炎患者．

ar·thri·tis [ɑːˈθraitis] *n.* 【医】关节炎．

Ar·thro·gastra [ˌɑːθrəˈgæstrə] *n.* 〔*pl.*〕【动】腹节类〔如蝎子等〕．

ar·throp·a·thy [ɑːˈθrɔpəθi] *n.* 关节病．

ar·thro·pod [ˈɑːθrəpɔd] *a.* 节肢动物的．— *n.* 节肢动物．

Ar·throp·o·da [ɑːˈθrɔpədə] *n.* 〔*pl.*〕【动】节肢动物门．

ar·thro·sis [ɑːˈθrəusis] *n.* ①关节．②关节病．

ar·thro·spore [ˈɑːθrəspɔː] *n.* 【生】分节孢子．

Ar·thros·tra·ca [ɑːˈθrɔstrəkə] *n.* 〔*pl.*〕【动】节甲类．

Ar·thur [ˈɑːθə] *n.* 亚瑟〔男子名〕．***King*** ～ 亚瑟王〔传说中的六世纪前后英国国王〕．

Ar·thuri·an [ɑːˈθjuəriən] *a.* 亚瑟王的，有关亚瑟王及其圆桌骑士的传奇的．

Ar·ti·choke [ˈɑːtitʃəuk] *n.* 【植】①朝鲜蓟，洋蓟．②菊芋 (= Jerusalem ～)．*Chinese* ～【植】甘露子，宝塔菜．

ar·ti·cle [ˈɑːtikl] *n.* ①物品；制品，商品．②项目，条款．③【动】节．④(报章杂志中的)文章，论文．⑤【语法】冠词．⑥〔古〕(之)际，刹那．⑦〔俚〕人，家伙．*an* ～ *of food* 一种食品．*a smooth* ～ 圆滑的人．～*s of trade* 商品．～*s of luxury* 奢侈品．*And the next* ～*?* 〔店员用语〕还要别的吗？～*s and clauses* 条款．*an editorial* ～〔美〕= *a leading* ～〔英〕社论．～*s of apprenticeship* 学徒合同．*the definite [indefinite]* ～ 定〔不定〕冠词．～ ***by*** ～ 逐条．～***s of association*** 公司章程．***Articles of Confederation*** 美国建国初期十三州的第一部宪法．～***s of war*** 陆军法规．***in the*** ～ ***of death*** 临终，弥留之际．— *vt.* ①把…逐条登载，分条解释．②列举(罪状)；控告．③用条款约束；定契约把…收为学徒．～ *an apprentice* 收学徒．*be* ～*d to a printer* 在印刷厂当学徒．*an* ～*d clerk* 〔美〕定有年限契约的店员．*an* ～*d apprentice* 定有年限契约的徒弟．— *vi.* ①订契约．②约定 *(with)*．

ar·tic·u·lar [ɑːˈtikjulə] *a.* 关节的．*an* ～ *inflammation* 关节炎．

ar·tic·u·late [ɑːˈtikjulit] *a.* ①明了的，明白的；发音清晰的，音节分明的．②能说话的；口齿清晰〔伶俐〕的．③有关节的；有节的；接合起来的．*an* ～ *system of philosophy* 一套说得头头是道的哲学体系．*A baby can not use* ～ *speech.* 婴儿说话口齿不清．*The backbone is an* ～ *structure.* 脊椎骨是一种关节相连的结构．— *n.* 节体动物．— [-leit] *vt., vi.* ①发音清晰地说，清晰认真地发音．②【语】形成(声音)．③表现(思想)．④(用关节)接合．*A- your words carefully.* 请仔细咬清字眼说吧．*a full* ～*d system* 完整的体系．～ *distinctly* 发音清晰．*The injured bone didn't* ～ *well.* 受伤的骨头没有连接好．

ar·tic·u·la·tion [ɑːˌtikjuˈleiʃən] *n.* ①发音；发音的方法．②发出的音，辅音．③接合，连接．④(骨头的)关节，(植物的)节．⑤【无】清晰度．⑥(假牙的)咬合．

ar·tic·u·la·tor [ɑːˈtikjuleitə] *n.* ①发音清楚的人．②发

音器官. ③(假牙的)咬合器. ④接骨的人.

ar·tic·u·la·to·ry [ɑːˈtikjuleitəri] *a.* 有音节的; 关节的.

ar·ti·fact [ˈɑːtifækt] *n.* ①人工制品〔尤指原始工具〕. ②【生】(组织结构的)人为现象. ③脑电波图中不是来源于人脑的电波.

ar·ti·fice [ˈɑːtifis] *n.* ①技巧,技能. ②诡计,巧计; 策略,谋略,手段. *by* ~ 用手段,用计.

ar·tif·i·cer [ˈɑːtifisə] *n.* ①技工; 工匠. ②【军】技术兵. ③设计者,发明家. *the A- of the Universe = the Great A-* 造物主.

ar·ti·fi·cial [ˌɑːtiˈfiʃəl] *a.* ①人工的, 人造的; 人为的 (*opp.* natural). ②摹拟的 (*opp.* genuine, real); 不自然的,矫揉造作的, 虚假的. ③武断的, 随意决定的. ~ *rules for dormitory residents* (不考虑居住者实际情况的)武断的宿舍管理规则. *an* ~ *system of classification* 人为的分类系统. ~ *daylight* 太阳灯. *an* ~ *eye* 人造眼,假眼. *an* ~ *tooth* 假牙. ~ *flowers* 假花. ~ *ice* 人造冰. *an* ~ *smile* 假笑. —*n.* 人造肥料; 〔美〕假花. ~ **aids** 骐. ~ **daylight** 太阳灯. ~ **fertilizer** 化肥. ~ **horizon** 飞行水平差. ~**inoculation** 人工接种. ~ **intelligence** 人工智能. ~ **person**【法】法人〔团体、学校、公司等〕. ~ **respiration** 人工呼吸. ~ **satellite** 人造卫星. ~ **selection**【生】人为淘汰. **-i·ty** [-ˈæliti] *n.* 人工,人造,人为; 人造物,人为之事; 不自然. **-ly** *ad.* 人工地,人为地; 不自然地,虚伪地. **-ness** *n.* 人工, 人为,矫揉造作,不自然.

ar·til·ler·ist [ɑːˈtilərist] *n.* ①炮兵, 炮手. ②炮术家.

ar·til·ler·y [ɑːˈtiləri] *n.* ①大炮. ②〔the ~〕炮兵, 炮队. ③炮术; 炮学. ④〔美俚〕防身武器. ⑤〔美俚〕(注射麻醉剂的)皮下注射器. ⑥〔喻〕口才,辩才. ~ **duel** 炮战. ~ **escort** 炮兵掩护. ~ **fire** 炮火,炮击. ~**man** 炮兵, 炮手. ~ **park** 放炮场地. ~ **preparation** 准备炮击. ~ **train** 炮兵纵列.

ar·ti·o·dac·tyl [ˌɑːtiəuˈdæktil] *n.* 偶蹄动物〔如骆驼、鹿〕.

Ar·ti·o·dac·tyla [ˌɑːtiəuˈdæktillə] *n.* 〔*pl.*〕【动】偶蹄目.

ar·ti·san [ˌɑːtiˈzæn] *n.* 工匠,手工业工人.

art·ist [ˈɑːtist] *n.* ①美术家,艺术家. ②能手. *a commercial* ~ 商业美术家. *He is an* ~ *with cards.* 他是打牌能手.

ar·tiste [ɑːˈtiːst] *n.* 〔F.〕 职业艺术家,艺人; 〔谑〕大师.

ar·tis·tic, -ti·cal [ɑːˈtistik(əl)] *a.* ①美术(家)的, 艺术(家)的. ②(爱好)艺术的,风雅的. **-ti·cal·ly** *ad.*

art·ist·ry [ˈɑːtistri] *n.* ①艺术的手腕〔技巧, 才干〕. ②艺术效果,艺术性. ③艺术作品; 艺术(工作).

art·i·zan [ˌɑːtiˈzæn] *n.* = artisan.

art·less [ˈɑːtlis] *a.* ①无虚饰的, 天真的, 朴实的 (*opp.* cunning). ②粗笨的, 拙劣的. **-ly** *ad.* **-ness** *n.* 朴质, 率直; 拙劣.

art·mo·bile [ˈɑːtməbiːl] *n.* 流动艺术展览; 巡回画廊; 流动艺术展览车.

ar·to·type [ˈɑːtəutaip] *n.*【印】= collotype.

art·sy [ˈɑːtsi] *a.* ①对艺术有一知半解的兴趣的. ②过分装饰的,浮华的.

art·sy-craft·sy [ˌɑːtsiˈkrɑːftsi] *a.* 〔口〕①(家具等)装饰浮华而不切实用的. ②冒充懂艺术的,附庸风雅的. *an* ~ *chair* 华而不实的椅子. *an* ~ *person* 冒充懂艺术的人.

art·y [ˈɑːti] *a.* 〔口〕冒充艺术品的; 自命艺术家的. ~-*and-crafty* 〔口、谑〕华而不实的.

a·ru·gu·la [əˈruːgələ] *n.*【植】芝麻菜.

Ar·um [ˈɛərəm] *n.*【植】白星海芋属. **arum lily**【植】白星海芋.

a·rundi·na·ceous [əˌrʌndiˈneiʃəs] *a.* 芦苇的, 芦苇一样的.

a·rus·pex [əˈrʌspeks] *n.* (*pl.* **-pi·ces** [-pəsiːz]) 肠卜祭司〔古罗马从事以肠祭品卜吉凶的迷信活动的低级祭司〕.

Ar·vee [ɑːˈviː] *n.* 游乐汽车.

Ar·vid [ˈɑːvid] *n.* 阿维德〔男子名〕.

-ary *suf.* ①…的,有关…的: element*ary*, milit*ary*. ②…的人[物、场所]: advers*ary*, diction*ary*, gran*ary*.

Ar·y·an [ˈɛəriən] *a.* ①亚利安语系的〔或指印欧语系, 或指印度波斯语系〕. ②亚利安人种的. — *n.* ①亚利安语. ②亚利安人.

ar·yl [ˈærəl] *n.*【化】芳基.

ar·y·te·noid [ˌæriˈtiːnɔid, əˈritnɔid] *a.*【解】杓状的. — *n.* (咽喉的)杓状软骨或杓状肌.

as[1] [强 æz; 弱 əz, z] *ad.* (同…)一样…; 同样〔在此是指 as ... as... 结构中的第一个 as, 它在主句中为指示副词, 第二个 as (在从句中)和第一个 as 相关联, 故转为连接词(见 *conj.* 各条). 第二个 as 引导的从句, 可省略一部或全部,包括 as 本身〕. *It is* ~ *white* ~ *snow (is white).* 它白得象雪一样. *She is* ~ *wise* ~ *(she is) fair.* 她的聪明比得上她的美貌. *He is* ~ *clever (~ you).* 他(跟你)一样聪明. *I can do it* ~ *well (~ they).* (跟他们一样)这件事我也能做. *I have* ~ *many [much].* 我也有这许多. *He did the work in two hours, but it took me* ~ *many days.* 他两小时做完这件工作, 可是我要两天功夫才做完. — *conj.* ①〔此处指 as...as 结构中的第二个 as, 它与第一个 as 相关而表示比较〕同…(一样…). *I am* ~ *tall* ~ *you.* 我和你一般高. *Mother loves her* ~ *dearly* ~ *(she loves) him.* 母亲对她和他都一样疼爱. *Mother loves her* ~ *dearly* ~ *he.* 母亲和他都同样疼爱她. ②〔反面比较时现在常说作 not so ... as 而少说 not as ... as, 但在 n't 后仍常说 as...as〕不如…那样…. *Belgium is not so large* ~ *France.* 比利时没有法国那么大. *He doesn't work* ~ *hard* ~ *you.* 他工作没有你那样努力. ③〔表示方式、程度、情况等〕如同; 象; 按照. *I work* ~ *others do.* 我跟别人一样工作. *Do* ~ *(= according* ~*) you are told.* 叫你怎样做就怎样做. *They will improve* ~ *they grow older.* 他们年纪大一些, 进步也就快一些. *I remember it* ~ *it were but yesterday.* 我想起这件事就仿佛是昨天发生的事一样. *Two is to three* ~ *(= what) four is to six.* 二比三等于四比六. *Parks are to the city* ~ *lungs are to the body.* 公园对于都市正如肺脏对于身体一样. *China* ~ *she was fifty years ago.* 五十年前的中国. ④〔as ..., so ... 的结构, 也表示同等程度的对比关系,但书面语色彩比较浓厚〕正如…一样. *As you like music, so I like poetry.* 正象你喜欢音乐一样,我喜欢诗歌. *As two is to three, (so) four is to six.* 四比六等于二比三. *As a man lives, so he dies.* 人有生也就有死. ⑤〔时间〕当…时; 一边…一边…. *He came up* ~ *I was speaking.* 我正在说话,他就来了. *I read the book* ~ *I went along.* 我边走边读. ⑥〔原因〕因为〔语气比 because 或 for 轻〕; 既然〔语气比 since 轻〕. *As I am ill, I won't go.* 我有病,不去了. ⑦〔让步〕虽然,尽管〔词序倒装,语气比 though 强〕. *Successful* ~ *he is, he is not proud.* 他虽成功, 却不骄傲. ⑧〔结果、目的〕以致,以便. *He so arranged matters* ~ *to suit everyone.* 他把事情安排得人人满意. — *prep.* ①作为; 以…身分. *language,* ~ *a means of intercourse* 作为交际工具的语言. *All hearts beat* ~ *one.* 大家一条心. *I have come here* ~ *a journalist.* 我是以记者身分到这里来的. ②当作〔用在某些及物动词之后〕*I look upon him* ~ *a guest.* 我把他当作客人看待. *He treats me* ~ *a child.* 他把我当作小孩对待. ③例如 (= for instance). *Some birds,* ~ *the parrot, can imitate human voice.* 有些鸟儿,如鹦鹉,能模仿人的声音. — *rel. pron.* ①〔与 such, the same, as 连用〕. *such men* ~ *do you harm* 危害你的那些人们. *the same book* ~ *you have* 象你所有的同样书籍. ~ *many children* ~ *came* 所有来的孩子们. ②那是(由)…(知道)的. *He was a foreigner,* ~ *I knew from his accent.* 他是外国人,那

是由他口音知道的. ***and ... ~ well*** 也. ~ ***a general thing [rule]*** 通常,通例,概. ~ ***above*** 如上. ~ ***against*** 比〔对〕… (*The business done this year amounts to 50,000 dollars ~ against 30,000 dollars last year.* 今年交易总额为五万元,而去年则为三万元). ~ ***(bright)*** ~ ***any*** *(in the class)* (班级) 中最 (聪明) 的. ~ ***...*** ~ ***as ever*** 依旧. ~ ***(fast)*** ~ ***possible [one can]*** 尽(快). ~ ***far*** ~ ①〔限度〕尽…所… (*As far ~ I know ...* 尽我所知. *All right ~ far ~ it goes* 目前的状况还好). ②〔距离〕(一直) 到. ~ ***for*** 就…而论, 至于, 说到. ~ ***from*** 由…日〔契约生效日〕起. ~ ***good*** ~ 见 good 条. ~ ***if*** 仿佛, 恰象…一样 (*As if you didn't know!* 别装蒜啦! *It isn't ~ if he were poor.* 他不见得穷). ~ ***is*** 〔美口〕原样, 照原来样子. ~ ***it is*** ①〔在句尾时〕原样, 照原来样子, 照事实 (*leave it ~ it is* 听其自然). ②原样的, 现在的 (*the world ~ it is* 现在的世界). ③〔在句头时〕但事实上 (*As it is, I cannot pay you.* (能付的话当然要付) 但事实上我现在不能付给你). ~ ***it stands*** = as it is ①②. ~ ***it was*** 其实是…. ~ ***it were*** 可谓, 好象. ~ ***large*** ~ ***life*** 按实物大小. ~ ***many*** (与…) 同样多的, (与…) 数量相同的. ~ ***matters [the case] stand(s)*** 在现状下. ~ ***much*** 同量的; 同样地 (*I thought ~ much.* 我也同样想). ~ ***of*** (某月某日) 的, 当前的, 现在的; 到…时候为止的 (*the U.S. Cabinet ~ of Sep. 1, 1964.* 一九六四年九月一日的美国内阁). ~ ***per*** 【商】照, 按 (~ *per advice* 照通知). ~ ***regards*** 至于, 提到. ~ ***soon*** ~ 见 soon 条. ~ ***such*** 见 such 条. ~ ***the world goes*** 照习惯说. ~ ***things are*** 在现状下, 照现况说. ~ ***though*** = as if. ~ ***to*** = for. ~ ***well (as)*** 见 well 条. ~ ***who should say*** 〔古〕象要说…似的 (*He smiled ~ who should say 'well done!'* 他象要说'做得好!'似的笑了). ~ ***yet*** 尚, 还, 至今还. ***As you were!*** 〔口令〕复原! ***Be so kind [good]*** ~ ***to*** *(let me know)*. 务必请 (通知我). ***not so [~]*** *(white)* ~ *(snow)* 不及 (雪白). ***so*** ~ ***to*** *(do)* (= *in order to*) 以便, 为要…才…, 为的是. **~-maintained** *a.* 〔美〕(按照国家标准局等所定度量衡制) 规定的. **~-told-to** *a.* 〔美〕口述笔录式的.

as² [æs] *n.* *(pl.* ***as·ses*** ['æsiz]*)* 阿斯 (①古罗马铜币. ②古罗马重量单位, 约 327.4 克).

as- *pref.* 〔用于 s 前〕= ad-: assert.

as·a·fet·i·da, as·a·foet·i·da [ˌæsə'fetidə] *n.* 【植】阿魏〔伞形科植物〕; 阿魏胶.

As·a·rum ['æsərəm] *n.* 【植】细辛.

as·bes·tic [æz'bestik] *a.* = asbestine *(a.)*

as·bes·tine [æz'bestain] *a.* 石棉 (状) 的; 不燃性的. — *n.* 滑石棉.

as·bes·tos, as·bes·tus [æz'bestɔs, -təs] *n.* 石棉.

as·bes·to·sis [ˌæzbes'təusis] *n.* 【医】石棉沉着病.

ASC = ①Air Service Command 〔美〕空军后勤司令部. ②Army Service Corps 〔英旧〕陆军后勤部队.

ASCAP = American Society of Composers, Authors and Publishers 美国作曲家、作家与出版者协会.

as·ca·ri·a·sis [ˌæskə'raiəsis] *n.* 【医】蛔虫病.

as·ca·rid ['æskərid] *n.* 【动】蛔虫.

as·cend [ə'send] *vi.* ①上升, 登高 *(opp.* descend*)*. ②追溯. *The path ~s here.* 由此上坡. ~ *to a height* 登高. ~ *to a former century* 追溯到前一世纪. — *vt.* 攀登; 登上. ~ *the throne* 登上王位.

as·cend·ance, as·cend·ence [ə'sendəns] *n.* = ascendancy.

as·cend·an·cy, as·cend·en·cy [ə'sendənsi] *n.* 优势; 权势; 主权. *have an ~ over* 优于, 胜过. *get the ~* 占上风, 揽权. *attain the highest ~* 鼎盛, 全盛; 登峰造极.

as·cend·ant, as·cend·ent [ə'sendənt] *a.* ①向上的, 上升的 *(opp.* descendant*)*. ②占优势的; 占支配地位的. ③【天】向天顶上升的. — *n.* ①优势地位, 支配地位. ②祖先. ③【卜】星位; (诞生时的) 运星. *be in the ~* 在优越地位上, 有旭日初升之势, 福星高照. *lineal ~* 直系尊属. *the lord of ~* 首座星.

as·cend·ing [ə'sendiŋ] *a.* ①上升的; 向上的. ②【植】上向的; 【解】上行的. *an ~ slope* 上坡. ~ **inflorescence** 【植】上升花序. ~ **powers** 【数】升幂.

As·cen·sion [ə'senʃən] *r.* 阿森松〔南大西洋岛屿〕.

as·cen·sion [ə'senʃən] *n.* ①上升, 升腾. ②登位. ③〔the A-〕(耶稣) 升天. **A- day** 耶稣升天节〔复活节后的第四十天〕. **~tide** *n.* 从耶稣升天节至圣灵降临节间的十日. **-al** *a.*

as·cen·sive [ə'sensiv] *a.* ①上升的. ②【语法】强调的, 加强语意的 (= intensive).

as·cent [ə'sent] *n.* ①(地位等的) 上升, 晋升. ②登高, 攀登. ③追溯, 上溯. ④上坡; 斜坡; 坡度; 阶梯. *the ~ of a mountain* 登山. *a rapid [gentle] ~* 陡〔缓〕坡. ***make an ~ of*** 登.

as·cer·tain [ˌæsə'tein] *vt.* ①确定, 查明, 弄清. ②〔罕〕确定, 把…弄实在. ~ *what really happened* 查明究竟发生了什么事. **-able** *a.* 可确定的; 可查明的. **-ment** *n.* 确定; 查明; 探知.

as·cet·ic [ə'setik] *n.* 禁欲主义者, 苦行者. — *a.* 苦行的, 禁欲主义的. **-i·cal** *a.* **-i·cal·ly** *ad.*

as·cet·i·cism [ə'setisizəm] *n.* 苦行, 禁欲主义.

as·cid·i·an [ə'sidiən] *n.* 【动】海鞘类动物.

as·cid·i·um [ə'sidiəm] *n.* *(pl.* ***-cid·i·a*** [-ə]*)* 【植】瓶状体; 瓶状叶.

as·ci·tes [ə'saiti:z] *n.* 【医】腹水 (肿).

as·cle·pi·a·da·ceous [æsˌkli:piə'deiʃəs] *a.* 【植】(属于或类于) 萝藦科的.

As·cle·pi·a·de·an [æsˌkli:piə'diən] *a.* 希腊诗人埃斯克里庇亚德斯 (Asclepiades) 散文诗格的. — *n.* 上述诗格的诗.

As·cle·pi·us [æs'kli:piəs] *n.* 【希神】阿斯克勒庇俄斯〔医生的始祖〕.

as·co·carp ['æskəukɑ:p] *n.* 【植】子囊果. **-ous** [-'kɑ:pəs] *a.*

as·co·go·ni·um [ˌæskəu'gəuniəm] *n.* *(pl.* ***-ni·a*** [-ə]*)* 【植】产囊体.

as·co·my·ce·tes [ˌæskəumai'si:ti:z] *n. pl.* 【植】子囊菌.

a·scor·bate [ə'skɔ:beit] *n.* 抗坏血酸盐.

as·cor·bic [əs'kɔ:bik] *a.* 治〔防〕坏血症的. ~ **acid** 抗坏血酸〔维生素 C〕.

as·co·spore ['æskəuspɔ:] *n.* 【植】子囊孢子.

As·cot ['æskət] *n.* ①英国爱斯科赛马场; 爱斯科赛马会. ②〔a-〕爱斯科式领带.

as·crib·a·ble [əs'kraibəbl] *a.* 可归于…的, 起因于…的. *His failure is ~ to innocence.* 他的失败可归咎于无知.

as·cribe [əs'kraib] *vt.* 把…归于, 把…推诿到…上, …说是 (某人) 所… *(to)*. *He ~s his failure to fate.* 他把失败归咎于命运. *The alphabet is usually ~d to the Phoenicians.* 人们一般都说字母表是腓尼基人发明的.

as·crip·tion [əs'kripʃən] *n.* ①归与; 归因; 推诿. ②【宗】(牧师在布道后所说"把荣耀归于上帝"等的) 赞美词.

as·cue ['æskəs] *n.* *(pl.* ***as·ci*** [-sai]*)* 【植】子囊.

as·dic ['æzdik] *n.* (英国早期的) 潜艇探测器.

-ase *suf.* 【化】…酶: lactase.

ASEAN = Association of Southeast Asian Nations 东南亚国家联盟.

a·seis·mat·ic [ˌæsaiz'mætik] *a.* 耐震的.

a·sep·sis [æ'sepsis] *n.* 【医】无菌 (法); 防腐 (法).

a·sep·tic [æ'septik] *a.* ①无菌的, 防腐的. ②无生气的, 冷漠的; 超然的, 客观的. ③使清洁的, 起净化作用的. ~ *surgery* 无菌手术. — *n.* 防腐药. **-al·ly** *ad.*

a·sex·u·al [æˈseksjuəl] *a.*【生】无性的；无性器官的. ~ *reproduction* 无性生殖. **-ly** *ad.*

a·sex·u·al·i·ty [æˌseksjuˈæliti] *n.*【生】无性别，无性.

As·gard [ˈæsgɑːd] *n.* (北欧神话中的)天堂，仙境.

ash[1] [æʃ] *n.* ①〔常 *pl.*〕灰. ②〔*pl.*〕灰烬；废墟. ③〔*pl.*〕骨灰，遗骨；〔诗〕遗骸. ④灰色，苍白. ⑤炭酸钠 (= sodium carbonate). *soda* ~ 纯碱. *the* ~*es of an ancient empire* 古帝国的废墟. ***be reduced [burnt] to*** ~***es*** 烧成灰烬，化为乌有. ***bring back the*** ~***es*** 〔英板球〕雪耻，转败为胜. ***in dust and*** ~***es***【宗】悲切忏悔. ***lay…in*** ~***es*** 使化为灰烬，烧光. ***turn to dust and*** ~***es*** 消失，(希望等)幻灭，化为尘埃. **~-bin** 垃圾桶，煤灰桶. **~cake** 焙制玉米饼. **~ can** ① *n.* 〔美〕= ash-bin (*into the* ~ *can* 丢脸). ②〔美口〕深水炸弹. **~can** *a.* (绘画等)如实地描写城市生活(阴暗面)的. **~ cart** 垃圾车. **~ fire** 灰火，余烬. **~ heap** 灰堆 (*on the* ~ *heap* 被抛弃). **~man** 〔美〕除灰工人 (= cinderman). **~tray** 灰盘，烟灰缸. **A-Wednesday** 四旬节的第一天〔罗马天主教在这一天向忏悔者头上撒灰〕.

ash[2] [æʃ] *n.* ①【植】梣，秦皮. ②梣木. *a chinese* ~ 梣，白蜡树. *a red* ~ 洋白蜡树. — *a.* = ashen. **~ key** 梣的翅果.

a·shamed [əˈʃeimd]〔常用作表语〕*a.* 羞耻，惭愧，害臊. ***be*** ~ ***of*** 以为…是耻辱. ***be*** ~ ***of oneself for*** 害羞，因…而害羞[惭愧]. ***be*** ~ ***to*** *(tell)* 不好意思(说). ***feel*** ~ ***for sb.*** 替某人感到羞愧.

A·shan·ti [əˈʃænti] *n.* ①*(pl.* ~*(s))* 非洲西部阿散蒂地区的人. ②阿散蒂语.

ash·en[1] [ˈæʃn] *a.* 灰的，灰色的. *turn* ~ 变苍白.

ash·en[2] [ˈæʃn] *a.* 梣的，梣木的.

ash·er·y [ˈæʃəri] *n.* 钾碱厂；草碱制作场.

Ash·ke·naz·im [ˌæʃkiˈnæzəm; ˌɑːʃkiˈnɑːzəm] *n. pl.* *(sing.* ***-naz, -nazi*****)**. 北欧的犹太人〔区别于 sephardim(西班牙或葡萄牙的犹太人)〕. **-naz·ic** *a.*

Ash·kha·bad [ˌɑːʃkɑˈbɑːd] *n.* 阿什哈巴德〔苏联城市〕.

ash·lar [ˈæʃlə] *n.* ①【建】方石，琢石. ②【建】墙面石板.

ash·lar·ing [ˈæʃləriŋ] *n.* 砌[贴]方石墙面.

ash·ler [ˈæʃlə] *a.* = ashlar.

a·shore [əˈʃɔː] *ad.* ①上岸，上陆. ②岸上，陆上. ~ *and adrift* 陆上和海上. *be driven* ~ = *run* ~ 搁浅. *go* ~ 上岸，登陆. *life* ~ 陆上生活.

ash·ram [ˈæʃrəm] *n.* ①阿什拉姆〔印度教徒的一个团体隐居之地〕. ②〔美〕嬉皮士群居村.

ash·y [ˈæʃi] *a.* ①灰的；覆盖着灰的. ②灰色的，苍白的. *His face went* ~. 他脸色苍白.

A·sia [ˈeiʃə] *n.* 亚洲. ~ *Minor* 小亚细亚.

A·si·an [ˈeiʃən], **A·si·at·ic** [ˌeiʃiˈætik] *a.* 亚洲的；亚洲人的. — *n.* 亚洲人. ★ 现多用 Asian，如用 Asiatic 则带有贬意.

a·side [əˈsaid] *ad.* ①在旁边，在一边；到旁边，到一边. ②【剧】独(白)，旁(白). ③撇开(…暂且不谈). *draw the curtain* ~ 把幕布拉到一边. *It is* ~ *from the question.* 那是问题以外的事. *jesting* ~ 笑话不提(且说…). ***~ from*** 〔美〕且别说，暂置不论；加之；除…外 (*A- from a fright, he was uninjured.* 除了吓一跳以外，他没受伤). ***lay*** ~ 停止，抛弃；留着；打消；撇开 (*lay the proposal* ~ *temporarily* 把建议暂时放在一边). ***put*** ~ 收拾起；暂搁；除外；停止，撇开 (*Put your cares* ~. 请莫挂心. *put some money* ~ 贮存一些钱). ***set*** ~ = put aside (*He set* ~ *that night to finish a paper.* 他留出一天晚上把论文写完). ***speak*** ~ 独语，暗暗说；【剧】(背朝着其他剧中人物而向观众)独白，旁白. ***stand*** ~ 站开，让开路. ***take [draw]*** *(a person)* ~ *(to speak to him)* 拉(某人)到一边(对他说). ***turn*** ~ 转向一边. — *n.* ①【剧】旁白；独白. ②离题的话. *a novelist's* ~ *to the reader* 作者致读者的话.

as·i·nine [ˈæsinain] *a.* ①驴的，驴子一样的. ②愚蠢的，固执的.

as·i·nin·i·ty [ˌæsiˈniniti] *n.* 愚蠢；蠢话，蠢事.

-asis *suf.* …病：elephantiasis 象皮病，psoriasis 牛皮癣.

ask [ɑːsk] *vt.* ①问，质问，询问. ②求，请求，祈求. ③需要. ④讨(价). ⑤约，请，邀请. ⑥〔古〕公布(结婚预告). ~ *the way* 问路. ~ *the doctor to come* 请医生来. ~ *sb. to a party* 邀人赴会. *He was* ~*ed out (to dinner).* 他被请去(吃饭). *The matter* ~*s haste.* 事不宜迟. *The affair* ~*s secrecy.* 事要机密. "*This is the first time of* ~*ing.*" "这是第一次宣读结婚预告"〔询问是否有人提出异议〕. —*vi.* 请求，问. ~*(sb.)* ***about*** 问某人…. ***~ after*** 问安，问候. ***~ again [back]*** 反问. ***~ for*** ①征求，请求，请(某人)给…，要(价) (~ *20 dollars for the book* 该书要价 20 元). ②来找(*Did anybody* ~ *for me?* 有人来找没有?) ③要 (~ *for money* 要钱). ***~ for it*** 〔口〕= ~ ***for trouble*** 自找麻烦，自找苦吃. ~ *(sb.)* ***in*** 叫(某人)进来. ***~ … of*** *(sb.)* 向(某人)问[求] (~ *the reason of him* 向他问理由). ***~ out*** 〔美〕辞职，引退. ***be*** ~***ed in church*** 请教堂预告结婚〔*cf.* banns〕. ***if you*** ~ ***me*** 你若不见怪，不瞒你说，要说呢就是… (*How do you like my hat?* 你喜欢我的帽子吗? *A little old-fashioned, if you* ~ *me.* 要说呢就是样子有点旧了.)

a·skance, a·skant [esˈkæns,-t] *ad.* 横；斜；斜视. *The kids were eyeing him* ~. 孩子们斜眼看他. ***look*** ~ ***at*** (因愤恨、嫉妒等而)斜楞着眼睛看，瞟.

as·kar·i [ˈɑːskɑːri, əˈskɑːri] *n.* 非洲兵，非洲人警察〔尤指受雇用于殖民当局者〕.

ask·er [ˈɑːskə] *n.* 请求者；发问者；乞丐.

a·skew [əsˈkjuː] *ad.* 斜，歪. *hang a picture* ~ 把图画挂歪. *look* ~ *at the dinner* 对饭菜不屑地一瞥. *wear one's hat* ~ 歪戴帽子.

ask·ing [ˈɑːskiŋ] *n.* 问；请求. **~ price** (讨价还价的)要价. ***for the*** ~ 只要索取，就免费供给 (*You may have it [It is yours] for the* ~. 承索即赠).

a·slant [əˈslɑːnt] *ad., prep.* ①斜，倾. ②斜跨. *walk with head* ~ 歪着头走路. ***run*** ~ 和…抵触 (*run* ~ *laws and regulations* 与法令抵触).

a·sleep [əˈsliːp] *a.*〔用作表语〕, *ad.* ①睡着，睡熟. ②长眠，已死. ③发呆，不活泼. ④(四肢)麻木，发麻. ⑤(陀螺)转得稳，(风帆鼓得)饱满不动. *The cat is* ~. 猫睡着了. *My arm is* ~. 我的胳膊发麻. ***~ at the switch*** 玩忽职守；坐失良机.

a·slope [əˈsləup] *a.*〔用作表语〕, *ad.* 斜，倾斜. *lean* ~ *against the wall* 斜靠着墙.

ASM = air-to-surface missile 空对地导弹.

As·ma·ra [æzˈmɑːrə] *n.* 阿斯马拉〔埃塞俄比亚城市〕.

ASME = American Society of Mechanical Engineers 美国机械工程师学会.

As·mo·de·us [æsˈməudjəs]【犹神】恶魔，魔王. ★在弥尔顿 (Milton) 的长诗《失落园》(Paradise Lost) iv. 168 行中，须读作 [æsməuˈdiːəs].

a·so·cial [eiˈsəuʃəl] *a.* ①不与人往来的，不合群的. ②(对别人利益)漠不关心的；自私的.

asp[1] [æsp] *n.* 小毒蛇，蝮蛇.

asp[2] [æsp] *n., a.* 〔诗〕= aspen.

ASP = American Selling Price 美国售价.

ASP [æsp] = Anglo-Saxon Protestant 英国新教徒.

ASPAC = Asian and Pacific Council 亚洲太平洋地区理事会；亚太理事会.

as·par·a·gine [əˈspærədʒiːn] *n.*【生化】天冬酰胺.

as·par·a·gus [əsˈpærəgəs] *n.*【植】文竹，石刁柏，天门冬；龙须菜.

as·par·tame [əsˈpɑːteim] *n.* 阿斯巴特〔一种糖精〕.

as·par·tic [æsˈpɑːtik] *a.* **~ acid**【化】天冬氨酸.

as·pect [ˈæspekt] *n.* ①样子，光景；容貌，神色. ②(房屋

等的)方向,方位. ③局势,形势,局面. ④(问题的)方面;见地. ⑤【语法】体,态. *a beautiful* ~ 好景;美观. *a thing in its true* ~ 事物的真相. *The house has a southern* ~. 那间房子朝南. *the physical* ~ *of China* 中国的地势. *consider a question in all its* ~*s* 由各方面考虑问题. ***assume [take on] a new*** ~ 面目一新,呈新局面. ~ **ratio** (电视影象的)纵横比;【空】展弦比.

asp·en [ˈæspən] *n.* 【植】白杨属;欧洲山杨. *the Chinese* ~ 响叶杨. *tremble like an* ~ *leaf* 飕飕飕地颤抖. —*a.* ①白杨的. ②(象白杨树叶)飕飕地颤抖的.

as·per [ˈæspə] *n.* 阿斯皮尔〔土耳其和埃及从前的银币名,后来作为钱币的单位,等于 1/120 皮阿斯特〕.

as·per·ges [əsˈpəːdʒiːz] *n.* 【天主】①(作大弥撒前的)洒圣水仪式. ②洒圣水仪式上唱的赞美诗.

As·per·gil·lin [ˌæspəˈdʒilin] *n.* 【药】曲霉素.

as·per·gil·lo·sis [ˌæspədʒiˈləusis] *n.* 【医】曲霉病,曲菌病.

as·per·gil·lum [ˌæspəˈdʒiləm] *n.* ***(pl. -gil·la*** [ˈ-dʒilə]) (洒圣水仪式用的)洒水器〔如刷子、带孔容器〕.

as·per·gil·lus [ˌæspəˈdʒiləs] *n.* ***(pl. -gilli*** [-lai]) 【微】曲霉菌.

as·per·i·ty [æsˈperiti] *n.* ①(表面)粗糙;(气候)严酷;(声音)刺耳. ②(性格)刻薄;(语言)粗暴. *speak with* ~ 粗暴地说. *the asperities of a winter campaign* 冬季作战的艰苦.

as·per·mous [æˈspəːməs] *a.* 【植】无种子的;【医】无精液的. *an* ~ *watermelon* 无子西瓜.

as·perse [əsˈpəːs] *vt.* ①辱骂;诬蔑,中伤. ②【天主】对…洒洗礼水;撒. ~ *a fish with salt* 用盐撒在鱼上. ~ *sb.'s character [honor]* 毁谤人格[名誉].

as·per·sion [əsˈpəːʃən] *n.* ①诬蔑,中伤. ②【天主】洒圣水. *cast* ~ *on (sb.)* 中伤(某人). *baptize by* ~ 洒圣水洗礼.

as·per·so·ri·um [ˌæspəˈsɔːriəm] *n.* ***(pl. -ri·a*** [-ə], ***-ri·ums*** [-əmz]) ①【宗】圣水盂. ②(洒圣水仪式用的)洒水器.

as·phalt [ˈæsfælt] *n.* 沥青,柏油. ~ *concrete* 柏油混凝土. *an* ~ *pavement* 柏油路. —*vt.* 涂柏油,用柏油铺(路). ~ **cloud** 沥青云〔一种由反弹道导弹喷射出的沥青微粒,用以毁灭敌方导弹的隔热屏〕. ~ **jungle** 沥青森林〔大城市或大城市中犯罪猖獗的某一区〕.

as·phal·tic [æsˈfæltik] *a.* 柏油(质)的.

as·phal·tite [ˈæsfəltait] *n.* 沥青岩.

as·phal·tum [æsˈfæltəm] *n.* = asphalt.

as·pho·del [ˈæsfədəl] *n.* ①【植】日光兰;水仙. ②【希神】(乐园中的)常春花.

as·phyx·i·a [æsˈfiksiə] *n.* 【医】窒息. **as·phyx·i·al** *a.*

as·phyx·i·ant [æsˈfiksiənt] *a.* 窒息的;使气绝的;致假死的. —*n.* 窒息剂,绝气药;致窒息的环境或条件.

as·phyx·i·ate [æsˈfiksieit] *vt.* 使窒息. *an asphyxiating gas* 窒息性气体.

as·phyx·i·a·tion [æsˌfiksiˈeiʃən] *n.* 窒息.

as·phyx·i·a·tor [æsˈfiksieitə] *n.* ①窒息剂. ②动物窒息试验器.

as·phyx·y [æsˈfiksi] *n.* = asphyxia.

as·pic[1] [ˈæspik] *n.* 〔诗〕= asp[1].

aspic[2] [ˈæspik] *n.* 肉冻.

aspic[3] [ˈæspik] *n.* 【植】熏衣草.

as·pi·dis·tra [ˌæspiˈdistrə] *n.* 【植】蜘蛛抱蛋.

as·pir·ant [əsˈpaiərənt] *a.* 有志愿的,抱负不凡的,努力向上的. —*n.* ①有志者;(名誉、地位的)追求者. ②候补者,考生. *an* ~ *after [for, to] honors* 追求名誉者.

as·pi·rate [ˈæspəreit] *vt.* ①【语音】把…发成送气音. ②【医】用吸管吸出. ③吸入(空气等). *aspirating dust into the lung* 把灰尘吸入肺里. —[ˈæspərit] *n.* 【语音】送气音,h 音. —*a.* 【语音】送气音的,h 音的 (= aspirated).

as·pi·rated [ˈæspəreitid] *a.* 【语音】送气音的,h 音的.

as·pi·ra·tion [ˌæspəˈreiʃən] *n.* ①热望,切望,渴望;志愿,愿望,抱负 (*for; after*). ②【医】(从体腔中)吸出. ③吸入. ④【语音】发送气音,送气音. *She had* ~*s to be an actress.* 她想做女演员.

as·pi·ra·tor [ˈæspəreitə] *n.* ①吸气器 (= respirator). ②【医】吸引器.

as·pir·a·to·ry [əˈspairətəri] *a.* 呼吸的,吸气的;适于呼吸或吸气的.

as·pire [əsˈpaiə] *vi.* ①热望,渴望;有志于,立志要. 〔与介词 *after, at, to, toward* 连用或接不定式〕. ②〔诗、古〕登,升;高耸. ~ *after wealth* 追求金钱. ~ *to be a hero* 渴望成为英雄.

as·pir·er [əsˈpaiərə] *n.* 热望者,渴望者,追求者.

as·pi·rin [ˈæspərin] *n.* 阿司匹林〔退热药〕.

as·pir·ing [əsˈpaiəriŋ] *a.* ①有大志的,抱负不凡的;热望的. ②巍然高耸的. *an* ~ *writer* 胸怀大志的作家. *an* ~ *tower* 巍然屹立的塔.

a·squint [əˈskwint] *a.* 〔多作表语〕, *ad.* 横目,侧目,斜视〔一般指眼睛有生理缺陷所致〕.

ass [æs] *n.* ①驴子. ②〔常 ɑːs〕傻子,笨蛋;老顽固. ③〔美俚〕屁股;〔卑〕性交. *You silly* ~*!* 你这笨蛋! ***an*** ~ ***with two panniers*** 两臂各挽一女人招摇过市的男子. ~***es' bridge*** 笨人难过的桥〔命题'三角形两边相等,两底角亦相等'的别名〕,初学者难解的问题. ***make an*** ~ ***of sb.*** 愚弄某人. ***make an*** ~ ***of oneself*** 做傻事;出洋相. ***not ... until the*** ~ ***ascends the ladder*** 万不能,决不能. ***on one's*** ~ 〔美俚〕处境恶劣;破产. ***play the*** ~ 作糊涂事,胡闹. ~**-kisser** 〔美俚〕无耻已极的马屁精.

ass. = ①assembly. ②assistant. ③association.

Assab [ˈæsəb] *n.* 阿萨布〔埃塞俄比亚港市〕.

as·sa·fet·i·da, as·sa·foet·ida [ˌæsəˈfetidə] *n.* 阿魏;阿魏胶.

as·sa·gai, as·se·gai [ˈæsəgai] *n.* ①(南非人用的)标枪. ②【植】南非茱萸. —*vt.* 用标枪刺.

as·sa·i [əˈsɑːi] *ad.* 〔It.〕【乐】最,非常. *adagio* ~ 非常慢. *allegro* ~ 非常快.

as·sail [əˈseil] *vt.* ①攻击,袭击. ②(用言论)指责. ③毅然应付(难局、工作等). *Shouts* ~*ed our ears.* 呼叫声逼近了. ~ *a task* 着手解决一项任务. ***be*** ~***ed by*** *(fears)* 被(恐怖)袭击. ***be*** ~***ed with*** *(questions)* 受到质问. **-able** *a.* 可攻击的;有弱点的,有隙可乘的.

as·sail·ant [əˈseilənt] *n.* 攻击者,加害者. —*a.* 攻击的.

As·sam [ˈæsæm] *n.* 阿萨姆〔印度邦名〕.

As·sa·mese [ˌæsəˈmiːz, -ˈmiːs] *a.* (印度)阿萨姆邦的;阿萨姆人的;阿萨姆语的 —*n.* ①***(pl.*** ~) 阿萨姆人. ②阿萨姆语.

as·sart [æˈsɑːt] *n.* 【法】(灌丛地、林地的)开垦;开垦地. —*vt., vi.* 【法】开垦.

as·sas·sin [əˈsæsin] *n.* 刺客,凶手. ***the Assassins*** 【史】十字军东征时,暗杀基督教徒的穆斯林秘密团体成员.

as·sas·si·nate [əˈsæsineit] *vt.* ①暗杀,行刺. ②中伤,破坏(名誉等). ~ *sb.'s character* 进行人身攻击.

as·sas·si·na·tion [əˌsæsiˈneiʃən] *n.* 暗杀.

as·sas·si·na·tor [əˈsæsineitə] *n.* 凶手,刺客,暗杀犯.

as·sault [əˈsɔːlt] *n.* ①(动手或动口的)攻击. ②【军】猛袭,袭击,突击. ③【法】威胁;殴打. ④〔婉〕强奸. ~ ***and battery*** 【法】口头威胁和动手殴打. ~ ***at [of] arms*** ①剑术比赛. ②拼刺. ***by*** ~ 用猛袭(攻克). ***make an*** ~ ***on*** 猛袭. —*vt.* ①攻击,袭击. ②殴打;威胁. ③〔古〕非议. ~ **boat** 登陆艇. ~ **carrier** (可以发动空降突击或提供空中支援的)航空母舰. ~ **troops** 突击队. **-able** *a.* 可攻击的;可袭击的. **-er** *n.* 攻击者;殴打者.

as·say [əˈsei] *n.* ①化验;分析;鉴定,测定,验定. ②被分析物,被化验物. ③化验结果,化验报告. ④〔古〕企图,尝试. ⑤〔古〕(把食品给贵人以前预先)尝味. ***do one's* ~** 竭力,尽力. — *vt.* ①化验;试,试验. ②企图. *~ one's strength* 检验自己的力量. *~ an alloy* 化验合金. —*vi.* 经验明含有. *The ore ~s high in silver.* 这种矿石验明含银量很高. ~ **bar** (政府铸造来做为标准的)纯金[银]条. ~ **master** 化验官. ~ **ton** 化验吨〔29.166克〕.

as·say·er [ə'seiə] *n.* 试金者;化验者.

assd. = ①assessed. ②assigned. ③assured.

as·se·gai ['æsiˌgai] *n.* ①(南非部族人所用的)细木柄标枪. ②【植】南非茱萸. — *vt.* 用标枪刺.

as·sem·blage [ə'semblidʒ] *n.* ①集合,会合,集会. ②会众;集合物. ③(机器的)装配. ④集合艺术,集合艺术品〔由布料、木料、金属、废品或其他东西的碎片组成〕. *an ~ of colours* 五彩缤纷.

as·sem·blag·ist [ə'semblist] *n.* 集合艺术家.

as·sem·ble [ə'sembl] *vt.* ①收集,集合 (*opp.* disperse). ②装配(机器等). *an assembling plant* 装配厂. *~ information for a report* 为写报告收集资料. *The workers were ~d in the hall.* 工人们在会议厅集合开会. *~ a watch* 装配手表. — *vi.* 集合;聚集. **-er** *n.* ①装配工,做装配工作的人[机器]. ②【计】汇编程序.

as·sem·bly [ə'sembli] *n.* ①集合. ②集会. ③会众. ④〔A-〕立法会议,议院,(特指)下院〔美国州议会通常称作 General Assembly,有许多州将其下院称作 Assembly〕. ⑤【军】集合号,集合鼓;集合. ⑥【机】装配;装配车间;供装配的零件. ⑦(统计力学中的)系集. ***the National A-*** ①【法史】国民议会. ②国民代表大会. ~ **district**〔美〕可选一名州议会议员的选区. ~ **hall** 会场;会馆. ~ **line** 装配线,流水作业线. ~ **plant** 装配厂. ~ **program**【计】汇编程序,组合程序. ~ **room** ①会场;会议室;跳舞会场. ②(机械等的)装配室. **General A-** ①〔美〕最高宗教裁判会议. ②州议会. ③联合国大会.

As·sem·bly·man [ə'semblimən] *n.* ①〔美〕州议会议员. ②装配工.

as·sent [ə'sənt] *n.* 同意,赞成 *(to)*. *the Imperial [Royal] ~* (君主对议会议案的)批准. *~ and consent* (对预算案)赞成,通过. *by common ~* 一致同意. *give one's ~ to* 同意,赞成. *with one ~* 无异议,一致赞成. —*vi.* 同意. *~ to (a proposal)* 赞同(提议).

as·sen·ta·tion [ˌæsen'teiʃən] *n.* (特指盲从式的)同意,赞成;听从,附和.

as·sen·tient [ə'senʃiənt] *a.* 同意的,赞成的. — *n.* 同意者,赞成者.

as·sen·tor [ə'sentə] *n.* 同意者;赞成者;附和者.

as·sert [ə'sə:t] *vt.* ①主张,硬说;断言,声明. ②维护(权利),闹. *They ~ed that the man was innocent.* 他们断言那人无罪. *~ one's rights* 维护自己权利. ***~ oneself*** 坚持自己的权利;表现自己(*Justice will ~ itself.* 正义必将伸张;公道自在人心).

as·ser·tion [ə'sə:ʃən] *n.* ①主张,断言,确言. ②维护,坚持. ***stand to one's ~*** 坚持己见.

as·ser·tive [ə'sə:tiv] *a.* 断言的,肯定的;武断的. **-ly** *ad.* **-ness** *n.*

as·ser·tor [ə'sə:tə] *n.* 主张者;断言者;维护者.

as·sess [ə'ses] *vt.* ①估定,评定(财产价值等). ②确定(税款、罚款、赔款的)数额. ③征收,摊派(税款、会费等). ④评价(人物、工作等). *His annual income was ~ed at ten thousand dollars.* 他的年收入估定为一万美元. *~ a tax on sb.'s property* 对某人的财产课税. *~ sb.'s efforts* 评价某人的工作.

as·sess·a·ble [ə'sesəbl] *a.* 可估定的,可估价的;可征税的,应抽税的.

as·sess·ment [ə'sesmənt] *n.* ①(价格的)评定,(税额的)估定,(损害额的)查定. ②税额,摊派额. ③【商】应缴股款. ④(功过的)评价. *a standard of ~* 课税标准. *~ of the work done* 计工.

as·ses·sor [ə'sesə] *n.* ①财产估价人;估税员. ②陪审法官;助理行政官.

as·set ['æset] *n.* ①资产;财产. ②有用的资源,宝贵的人[物]. *Good health is a great ~.* 健康就是财富. *He is a most valuable ~ to the firm.* 他是公司的宝贵人材. *~s and liabilities* 资产与负债.

as·sev·er·ate [ə'severeit] *vt.* 确言,断言,坚持说. *He ~d that he had seen a flying saucer.* 他坚持说,他看见了飞碟.

as·sev·er·a·tion [əˌsevə'reiʃən] *n.* 确言,断言.

as·sib·i·late [ə'sibileit] *vt.*【语音】把…发成咝擦音,使齿音化. *~ the t of bastion* ['bæstʃən] 把 bastion 里的 t 发成咝擦音.

as·si·du·i·ty [ˌæsi'dju(:)iti] *n.* ①刻苦,勤勉. ②〔*pl.*〕(对人的)关心,照顾,殷勤. ***with ~*** 孜孜不倦,兢兢业业.

as·sid·u·ous [ə'sidjuəs] *a.* ①刻苦的,勤勉的;百折不挠的. ②殷勤的. *He is ~ in his studies.* 他学习勤奋. *He is ~ over his visitor.* 他对来访者很殷勤.

ass·ify ['æsifai] *vt.* 愚弄.

as·sign [ə'sain] *vt.* ①分配,派给. ②指定,选定,定. ③把…归因于. ④【法】把(财产、权利等)转让,让与,过户给. *They ~ed me a small room.* 他们分给我一个小房间. *The rooms were ~ed to the workers.* 把房间分配给工人. *The teacher ~ed ten problems for today.* 老师今天指定十个问题. *The event is ~ed to various causes.* 这一事件被归因于各种原因. *detectives ~ed to the case* 负责侦破该案的刑警. *~ property to another* 把财产转让给别人. — *vi.*【法】转让财产. — *n.*【法】受让人. *heirs and ~s* 继承人和受让人. **-able** *a.*

as·sig·nat [æsi'njɑ:] *n.* 〔F.〕法国革命时发行的纸币.

as·sig·na·tion [ˌæsig'neiʃən] *n.* ①分配. ②(会场、时间的)指定,选定. ③〔美〕约会,幽会,约定. ④转让. ⑤归因.

as·sign·ee [ˌæsi'ni:] *n.*【法】①受托者,代理人. ②受让人 (*opp.* assignor).

as·sign·ment [ə'sainmənt] *n.* ①分给,分配. ②指定,委派. ③(理由等的)陈述;(错误等的)指出. ④(财产、权利的)转让,让与. ⑤让与证书,委托证书. ⑥〔美〕任命;任务,工作;(课外)作业. *give students ~s* 给学生留作业. *He left for his ~ in the Middle East.* 他去中东赴任.

as·sign·or [əsai'nɔ:] *n.* ①分配者;委派者. ②(权利的)转让人,让与人 (*opp.* assignee).

as·sim·i·late [ə'simileit] *vt.* ①同化. ②使相似,使相同,使成一样. ③将(甲)比作(乙) *(to, with)*. ④消化,吸收. ⑤使(语言等)融合. *The community ~d persons of many nationalities.* 这个社会同化了许多不同国籍的人. *~ life to a dream* 把人生比作梦. — *vi.* ①变得相似,变得相同. ②被吸收,被同化. *Some foods ~ more readily than others* 有些食物比别的食物容易吸收. ③【语音】因同化而改变. **-able** *a.* 可同化的;可吸收的.

as·sim·i·la·tion [əˌsimi'leiʃən] *n.* ①吸收(作用). ②同化(作用). *The p in cupboard has been lost by ~ to b.* cupboard 里的 p 由于和 b 同化而失去读音.

as·sim·i·la·tive, as·sim·i·la·to·ry [ə'similətiv, -təri] *a.* ①吸收的. ②同化的.

as·sim·i·la·tor [ə'simileitə] *n.* 吸收者;同化者.

as·sist [ə'sist] *vt.* ①(在某方面)帮助,援助,协助 *(in, with)*. ②帮助某人做某事 *(in doing sth; to do sth)*. ③搀扶(某人)上[下]车 *(in) [out of]*;扶(某人)站起 *(to his foot)*;给(小孩)喂食 *(to)*. *~ an architect in project* 帮助设计师搞设计. *She ~ed him in correcting [to correct] the proof.* 她帮助他做改校样的工作. *I ~ed my son with homework.* 我帮助儿子做作业. *~ a child to food* 给小孩喂食. — *vi.* ①援助,帮助 *(in)*. ②出席,

参加 *(in, at)*. ~ *in a store* 在店里帮忙. ~ *at a ceremony* 参加仪式. — *n.* ①援助,帮助;协助. ②机器助手,辅助装置. *a financial* ~ 财政援助.

as·sis·tance [əˈsistəns] *n.* ①援助,帮助. ②〔古〕出席;出席者. ***come to sb.'s*** ~ 援助某人. ***give [render]*** ~ ***(to)*** 给以援助.

as·sis·tant [əˈsistənt] *a.* 帮助的,副的. *an* ~ *engineer* 副工程师. *an* ~ *manager* 协理,副理. *an* ~ *professor* 助理教授〔高于讲师,低于副教授 (associate professor)〕. — *n.* ①助手;帮手,助理. ②助教. ③店员,伙计. ④辅助物;(染色的)辅助剂;起辅助作用的东西. *a shop* ~ 店员. *an* ~ *to memory* 帮助记忆的辅助物. ~**ship** (大学)研究生奖学金〔该研究生同时任助教〕.

as·size [əˈsaiz] *n.* ①〔常 *pl.*〕〔英〕巡回裁判(开庭期,开庭地). ②〔古〕(度量衡的)法定标准;(面包、啤酒的)法定价格. ③条例,条令. ***the Great A-***【神】最后审判(日).

as·so·ci·a·bil·i·ty [əˌsəuʃjəˈbiliti] *n.* ①可联合性. ②可联想性. ③【医】交感性. ④社交性.

as·so·ci·a·ble [əˈsəuʃjəbl] *a.* ①可以联想的,联想得到的. ②可联合的. ③社交性的. ④【医】交感性的.

as·so·ci·ate [əˈsəuʃieit] *vt.* ①使联合 *(opp.* dissociate*)*;使加入〔参加〕. ②由…联想到…;把…同…联系起来 *(with)*. *be* ~*d with sb. in an enterprise* 与某人联合从事一项企业. *It was impossible to* ~ *failure with him.* 想不到他会失败. — *vi.* 交往,结交. *Never* ~ *with bad companions.* 勿与恶友交往. ~ ***oneself in*** 参加,加入. ~ ***oneself with*** 赞同,支持;与…交往. — [-ʃiit] *a.* ①同伙的,同伴的. ②准…,副的. ③伴随的;有关的. — *n.* ①伙伴,朋友;同事,同人. ②准会员,准社员,准校友. ③联想观念,联想物. ④相伴物. ~ **degree** 〔美〕(大学上完两年的)肄业证书. ~ **editor** 〔美〕副主笔. ~ **judge** 陪审法官. ~ **member** 准会员. ~ **number**【数】联带数,相伴数. ~ **professor** 〔美〕副教授〔低于正教授 (full professor), 而高于助理教授 (assistant professor)〕.

as·so·ci·at·ed [əˈsəuʃieitid] *a.* ①联合的. ②联想的. *an* ~ *university* 联合大学. ***the A- Press*** (略作 A.P.) 美国联合通讯社〔简称美联社〕. ~ **mineral** 伴生矿物.

as·so·ci·a·tion [əˈsəusiˈeiʃən] *n.* ①联合;联系;联盟;合伙;交际,交往. ②社团,协会;学会. ③【生】群落,社会. ④联想. ⑤【化】缔合. ⑥英式足球. *an* ~ *of banks and bankers* 银行公会. ~ *of ideas* 联想. ***in*** ~ ***with*** 与…联合. ~ **book [copy]** 因与名人有关而受珍视的书〔如有作者本人签字、加注,或曾为名人所有等〕. ~ **football** 英式足球 (= soccer). **-ism** *n.* 联想论;联想心理学. **-ist** ①联想论者. ②协会会员.

as·so·ci·a·tive [əˈsəuʃjətiv] *a.* ①联合的,连带的. ②联想的. ③【数】结合的. *an* ~ *responsibility* 连带的责任.

as·soil [əˈsɔil] *vt.* 〔古〕①赦免,释放. ②补偿,赎. ~ *sb. of [from] sin* 赦免某人的罪过. ~ *one's fault* 赎罪.

as·so·nance [ˈæsənəns] *n.* ①声音的相似,协音〔如: penitent, reticence〕. ②只押元音的韵,半谐音〔如: late, make〕.

as·so·nant [ˈæsənənt] *a.* 协音的,半韵的. — *n.* 与另一个字合成半韵的字.

as·sort [əˈsɔːt] *vt.* ①把…分级,把…分类. ②配备;配齐(花色). ~ *apples for market* 把苹果分类出售. — *vi.* ①相配,相称,调和. ②相交,交际 *(with)*. *It ill [well]* ~*s with his character.* 这和他的性格不协调〔很调和〕.

as·sort·ed [əˈsɔːtid] *a.* ①配合的,相称的. ②各色俱备的,什锦的. ~ *biscuits* 什锦饼干. *an ill-*~ *pair* 不相称的配偶. *well-*~ *goods* 各色俱全的货物.

as·sort·ment [əˈsɔːtmənt] *n.* ①分类,搭配. ②种类,花色品种;一套〔全套〕物品. *an* ~ *of tools* 一套工具.

ASSR, A.S.S.R. = Autonomous Soviet Socialist Republic 苏维埃社会主义自治共和国.

asst. = assistant.

as·suage [əˈsweidʒ] *vt.* ①缓和,减轻(痛苦). ②宽慰(人心);平息(怒气). ③满足(食欲),充(饥),解(渴). ~ *sorrow* 解忧. ~ *thirst* 止渴. **-ment** *n.*

as·sua·sive [əˈsweisiv] *a.* 缓和的,使镇静的,安慰的. — *n.* 缓和剂.

as·sum·a·ble [əˈsjuːməbl] *a.* ①可假定的. ②可采取的;可承担的. ③可假装的.

as·sum·a·bly [əˈsjuːməbli] *ad.* 假想地,多半,大概,恐.

as·sume [əˈsjuːm] *vt.* ①执掌;接受,承担,担任. ②假装,装作…的样子,采取(…态度). ③僭取,擅取;冒称. ④假定,想象,设想;以…为先决条件. ⑤表现为,呈. ⑥穿…在身上. ⑦承担(别人的)债务. ⑧采用. ~ *office* 就职,上任. ~ *responsibility* 负责. ~ *the reins of government* 执政,掌握政权. ~ *the air of cheerfulness* 假装高兴. ~ *a haughty mien* 采取傲然态度. ~ *the offensive* 采取攻势. *The problem has* ~*d a new form.* 问题已经以一种新的方式出现. ~ *the chair* 就议长席. *I* ~ *that you know.* 我以为你是知道的. ~ *a new name* 用一个新名字. ~ ***airs of*** 摆…的架子. ***assuming that ...*** 假定…,若.

as·sumed [əˈsjuːmd] *a.* ①假装的,装做…的,假的. ②假定的;想象的. ③(债务)保付的,承付的. ④僭越的. ~ *ignorance* 假装不知道(的样子). *an* ~ *name* 假名. *an* ~ *voice* 假装的声调,摹拟的声音. *hearing evidence in an* ~ *capacity* 以僭越的身分听取证词. ~ **bonds**【商】保付证券〔由一公司发行、由另一公司保付的证券〕.

as·sum·ed·ly [əˈsjuːmidli] *ad.* 大概,也许.

as·sum·ing [əˈsjuːmiŋ] *a.* 僭越的,傲慢的.

as·sump·tion [əˈsʌmpʃən] *n.* ①采取,承担. ②假设,假定;臆说;想当然. ③傲慢,僭越. ④假装. ⑤〔A-〕圣母升天(节)〔8月15日〕. ⑥【逻】小前提. *the* ~ *of an office* 就任. *the* ~ *of power* 掌权. *an air of* ~ 傲慢的态度. ***on the*** ~ ***that*** 假定.

as·sump·tive [əˈsʌmptiv] *a.* ①假定的,假设的. ②傲慢的,僭越的. ③假装的.

as·sur·a·ble [əˈʃuərəbl] *a.* 可保证的.

as·sur·ance [əˈʃuərəns] *n.* ①保证,担保. ②确信,自信;断言. ③狂妄;厚脸皮,无耻. ④〔英〕(人寿)保险. ⑤【法】财产转让(书). *an easy* ~ *of manner* 悠然自信的态度. *an A- Co.* 保险公司. *give an* ~ *that ...* 保证…. *have (every)* ~ *of* 有(一切)把握取得. *have the* ~ *to (do)* 厚着脸皮(做)…. *make* ~ *doubly [double] sure* 加倍小心. *with* ~ 凭自信.

as·sure [əˈʃuə] *vt.* ①保证,担保,确告,郑重宣告. ②使安心,让…放心,包. ③使确信. ④给…保险. *I* ~ *you of his honesty.* (那人)包你老实可靠. ~ *one's life* 保人寿险. ~ ***oneself of*** 弄清楚,查明 *(I must* ~ *myself of the real situation.* 我必须查明真实情况*)*. ***I*** ~ ***you that ...*** 包你….

as·sured [əˈʃuəd] *a.* ①有保证的,确实的. ②自信的;狂妄的,胆大妄为的. ③保着险的. *an* ~ *position* 有保证的职务. *His success is* ~. 他取得成功是无疑的. *You may rest* ~ *that ...* 对…你尽可放心. ***be*** ~ ***of*** 确信,坚信. ***the*** ~ 被保险人. **-ly** *ad.* ①的确,无疑地. ②自信;大胆. **-ness** *n.* ①确实,确信. ②狂妄.

as·sur·er, -or [əˈʃuərə] *n.* 保证者;〔英〕保险商.

as·sur·gent [əˈsəːdʒənt] *a.* ①上升的. ②【植】倾斜向上的. ③【徽】由海中出来的. *a sea horse* ~ 从海中出来的海马.

as·sur·ing [əˈʃuəriŋ] *a.* 确实的;使人放心的,使人有信心的. **-ly** *ad.* 一定,无疑地.

As·syr·i·a [əˈsiriə] *n.* 亚西利亚〔亚洲西部古国,即亚述〕.

As·syr·i·an [əˈsiriən] *a.* 亚述的; 亚述人[语]的. — *n.* 亚述人[语].
As·syr·i·ol·o·gy [æˌsiriˈɔlədʒi] *n.* 亚述研究.
A.S.T. = Atlantic Standard Time. 大西洋标准时间.
as·ta·cene, as·ta·cin [ˈæstəsiːn, -sin] *n.* 【生化】虾红素.
a·stat·ic [æˈstætik] *a.* ①【物】无定向的. ②不安定的. ~ **galvanometer** 无定向电流计. ~ **needle** 无定向(磁)针.
as·ta·tine [ˈæstətiːn] *n.*【化】砹〔元素名,符号为 At〕.
as·ter [ˈæstə] *n.* ①【植】紫苑; 〔A-〕紫苑属. ②【动】星(状)体. *the China* ~ 翠菊.
-aster *suf.* 〔蔑〕小,臭,丑等: poet*aster* 烂诗人.
aster- *comb.f.* 表示"星": *aster*oid.
as·ter·isk [ˈæstərisk] *n.* ①星号〔即*〕. ②星状物. — *vt.* 给…注上星号. ~ *a word that requires a foot note* 给一个需加注释的词打上星号.
as·ter·ism [ˈæstərizəm] *n.* ①【印】三星标记〔即⁂〕. ②【天】星群. ③【矿】星状光彩,星芒.
a·stern [əsˈtəːn] *ad.* ①【海】在船[机]尾,向船[机]尾. ②在后,向后. *ship next* ~ 后续舰. ~ ***of*** 在…的后面. ***back*** ~ 倒驶. ***drop [fall]*** ~ 落在别船后头, 被赶过. ***Go*** ~*!* 后退!〔口令〕.
a·ster·nal [əˈstəːnl] *a.* 【解,动】①不连胸骨的. ②无胸骨的.
as·ter·oid [ˈæstərɔid] *a.* 星状的. — *n.* ①【天】(火星及木星轨道间的)小行星. ②【动】海星(= starfish). ③【物】星状曲线. **-al** *a.*
as·the·ni·a [æsˈθiːnjə] *n.*【医】虚弱.
as·then·ic [æsˈθenik] *a.*【医】虚弱的.
as·the·no·pi·a [ˌæsθiˈnəupiə] *n.* 眼疲劳, 视力衰弱. **-nop·ic** [-ˈnɔpik] *a.*
asth·ma [ˈæsmə] *n.*【医】气喘(病).
asth·mat·ic [æsˈmætik] *a.* 气喘的; 患气喘病的. — *n.* 气喘患者.
as·thore [əsˈθɔː] *n.* 〔Ir.〕〔呼唤用语〕= darling.
as·tig·mat·ic [ˌæstigˈmætik] *a.* ①散光的;【物】象散的. ②矫正散光的. ③不正视事实的. ~ *eyes* 散光眼. ~ *lenses* 散光眼镜. — *n.* 眼睛散光的人. ~ **pencil** 【物】散象光束. **-i·cal·ly** *ad.*
a·stig·ma·tism [æsˈtigmətizəm] *n.* ①散光,乱视. ②【物】散象性,散象现象.
a·stir [əˈstəː] *a.* 〔多作表语〕, *ad.* ①活动; 哄动. ②起床,行动. ***be*** ~ ***with*** 因…而哄动(*The whole town was* ~ *with the news.* 因某消息而全城哄动). ***be early*** ~ 早起.
ASTM, A.S.T.M. = American Society for Testing Materials 美国材料试验学会.
a·stom·a·tous [əˈstɔmətəs, -ˈstəumə-] *a.*【生】无口的, 无呼吸孔的.
As·ton [ˈæstən] *n.* 阿斯顿〔姓氏〕.
as·ton·ied [əsˈtɔnid] *a.* 〔古〕大吃一惊的, 惊奇的; 困惑的.
as·ton·ish [əsˈtɔniʃ] *vt.* 使吃惊, 使惊讶. *be* ~*ed at* 对…感到惊讶. *be* ~*ed to see* 见到…感觉惊讶.
as·ton·ish·ing [əsˈtɔniʃiŋ] *a.* 令人惊讶的. **-ly** *ad.*
as·ton·ish·ment [əsˈtɔniʃmənt] *n.* ①惊奇, 惊讶. ②令人惊讶的事物. ***in [with]*** ~ 愕然, 吃惊地 (*stare in* ~ 惊得目瞪口呆). ***to one's*** ~ 令…惊讶的是(*To my* ~*, she were so politeless.* 使我惊讶的是, 她竟这样没有礼貌).
As·tor [ˈæstə, ˈæstɔː] *n.* 阿斯特〔姓氏〕.
as·tound [əsˈtaund] *vt.* 使…大吃一惊,使惊奇.
as·tound·ing [əsˈtaundiŋ] *a.* 可惊的; 使人震惊的. **-ly** *ad.*
as·tra·chan [ˌæstrəˈkæn] *n.* 俄国羔皮 (= astrakhan).
as·trad·dle [əsˈtrædl] *a.* 〔多作表语〕, *ad.* 跨. *stand* ~ 两脚分开站着. — *prep.* 跨着. *sit* ~ *a horse* 跨在马上.
as·tra·gal [ˈæstrəgəl] *n.* ①【建】半圆饰. ②【解】距骨.
as·trag·a·lus [æsˈtrægələs] *n. (pl.* ***-li*** [-lai]*)* ①【解】距骨. ②〔A-〕【植】黄芪属,黄耆属.
As·tra·khan [ˌæstrəˈkæn] *n.* ①阿斯特拉罕〔苏联一城市〕. ②〔a-〕俄国羔皮; 充羔皮; 充羔皮织物.
as·tral [ˈæstrəl] *a.* ①星的; 星状的;【生】星状体的. ②星界的,星际的. ~ **body** (迷信传说的)魂灵,魂魄. ~ **hatch** (飞机上的)圆形天窗. ~ **lamp** 无影灯〔一种没有投影的油灯〕. ~ **spirits** (迷信传说的) 星星上的鬼魂.
a·stray [əsˈtrei] *ad.* 迷路; 堕落. *go* ~ 走错路; 堕落,误入歧途. *lead (sb.)* ~ 误人; 带坏,使人堕落, 把人引入歧途. — *a.* 〔多作表语〕出正轨的,迷途的. *We are all* ~. 我们都迷路了.
as·trict [əsˈtrikt] *vt.* ①束缚, 限制. ②(在道德和法律上)约束. ③使收缩,使便秘. *In the old society, peasants were* ~*ed to the soil.* 在旧社会,农民被束缚在土地上.
as·tric·tion [əsˈtrikʃən] *n.* ①限制; 收缩; 束缚. ②【医】收敛(作用); 便秘.
as·tric·tive [əsˈtriktiv] *a.* 收敛的. — *n.*【药】收敛剂.
A·strid [ˈæstrid] *n.* 阿斯特丽德〔女子名〕.
a·stride [əsˈtraid] *a.* 〔多作表语〕, *ad.* 两脚分开,跨. ***be*** ~ ***of a river*** (军队)跨河布阵. ***sit*** ~ ***of a horse*** 骑(马). — *prep.* ①跨骑. ②在两边. ③占压倒性地位. *ride* ~ *a horse* 骑着马. *The city lay* ~ *the river.* 城市横跨河的两岸. *stand* ~ *the whole country* 统治全国.
as·tringe [əsˈtrindʒ] *vt.* ①束缚; 使收敛. ②收缩,压缩.
as·trin·gen·cy [əsˈtrindʒənsi] ①*n.* 收敛性. ②严肃性, 严峻,严格.
as·trin·gent [əsˈtrindʒənt] *a.* ①【医】收敛的, 止血的. ②严厉的,严格的. ~ *taste* 涩味. *an* ~ *style of writing* 犀利的文风. *Green persimmons are strongly* ~. 绿柿子非常涩. — *n.*【药】收敛剂; 止血药. **-ly** *ad.*
as·tri·on·ics [ˌæstriˈɔniks] *n.* 天文电子学.
astro- *comb. f.* 表示"外太空,宇宙,天体,天文,星": *astro*logy, *astro*metry.
as·tro·bi·ol·o·gy [ˌæstrəubaiˈɔlədʒi] *n.* 宇宙生物学.
as·tro·bleme [ˌæstrəuˈbliːm] *n.* 陨石坑,太空疤痕.
as·tro·com·pass [ˈæstrəuˌkʌmpəs] *n.* 星象罗盘.
as·tro·cyte [ˈæstrəuˌsait] *n.* 星形 (胶质) 细胞. **-cytic** [-ˈsitik] *a.*
as·tro·dome [ˈæstrəudəum] *n.*【空】(飞机机身顶部透明的半圆形)天文观测窗[室].
as·tro·dy·nam·ics [ˌæstəudaiˈnæmiks] *n.* 天文动力学,星际[宇宙]飞行力学.
as·tro·gate [ˈæstrəugeit] *vt.* 驾驶 (宇宙飞船); 导引(火箭)在宇宙空间飞行. — *vi.* 作宇宙航行. **as·tro·ga·tion** [ˌæstrəuˈgeiʃən] *n.* 宇宙航行学,航天学. **as·tro·ga·tor** *n.* 宇宙航行者,宇航员.
as·tro·graph [ˈæstrəugrɑːf] *n.* 天体照相仪, 天文定位器.
as·troid [ˈæstrɔid] *a.* 星状的, 星形的. — *n.*【数】星形线.
astrol. = ① astrologer. ②astrological. ③astrology.
as·tro·labe [ˈæstrouleib] *n.*【天】(旧时天文学者用以测定天体位置的)星盘.
as·trol·o·ger [əsˈtrɔlədʒə] *n.* ①星体研究者. ②占星学家.
as·tro·log·ic, as·tro·log·i·cal [æstrəuˈlɔdʒik(əl)] *a.* 占星术的,占星学的. **-cal·ly** *ad.*
as·trol·o·gy [əsˈtrɔlədʒi] *n.* ①占星术. ②原始天文学.
as·tro·me·te·or·ol·o·gy [ˈæstrəuˌmiːtjəˈrɔlədʒi] *n.* 天体气象学.
as·trom·e·try [æsˈtrɔmitri] *n.* 天体测量(学).
astron. = ①astronomer. ②astronomical. ③astronomy.
as·tro·naut [ˈæstrəunɔːt] *n.* 宇(宙)航(行)员. **-ess** 女

宇航员.

as·tro·nau·tic,-ti·cal [ˌæstrəuˈnɔːtik(əl)] *a.* 宇宙航行(员)的. **-tically** *ad.*

as·tro·nau·tics [ˌæstrəuˈnɔːtiks] *n.* 宇宙航行学.

as·tro·nav·i·ga·tion [ˌæstrəuˌnæviˈgeiʃən] *n.* 宇宙航行;天文导航.

as·tron·o·mer [əsˈtrɔnəmə] *n.* 天文学家,星学家. **A- Royal** 格林威治[爱丁堡]天文台台长.

as·tro·nom·ic [ˌæstrəuˈnɔmik] *a.* = astronomical.

as·tro·nom·i·cal [ˌæstrəuˈnɔmikəl] *a.* ①天文学(上)的. ②〔口〕(数字等)庞大的. ~ *figures* 〔美口〕庞大的数字;天文数字. ~ **day** 天文日,平均太阳日. ~ **observatory** 天文台. ~ **time** 天文时. ~ **unit** 天文单位[地球至太阳间的平均距离]. ~ **year** 回归年. **-ly** *ad.*

as·tron·o·my [əsˈtrɔnəmi] *n.* 天文学. *gravitational* ~ 天体力学. *radio* ~ 射电天文学.

as·tro·pho·tog·ra·phy [ˌæstrəufəˈtɔgrəfi] *n.* 天体照相(术).

as·tro·phys·ics [ˈæstrəuˈfiziks] *n. pl.* 〔用作单或复〕天体物理学.

as·tro·space [ˈæstrəuspeis] *n.* 外太空,宇宙空间.

as·tro·sphere [ˈæstrəsfiə] *n.* ①【生】中心球,细胞的摄引球. ②【地】地心圈,地核.

a·strut [əsˈtrʌt] *a.* 〔用作表语〕, *ad.* 大摇大摆,趾高气扬.

as·tu·cious [æsˈtuːʃəs, -ˈtjuː-] *a.* = astute.

as·tute [əsˈtjuːt; Am. əsˈtjuːt] *a.* 机敏的,伶俐的;狡猾的. **-ly** *ad.* **-ness** *n.*

a·sty·lar [æˈstailə] *a.*【建】无柱式的.

A·sun·ción [əˌsunsiˈəun] *n.* 亚松森[巴拉圭首都].

a·sun·der [əˈsʌndə] *a.* 〔多作表语〕, *ad.* ①(分)开,(折)断,(扯)碎. ②散;分离,隔离. *We are as wide* ~ *as the poles.* = We are whole worlds ~. 我们天南地北相隔极远. *break* ~ 折断. *come* ~ 离开,散开. *fall* ~ 崩散. *fly* ~ 逃散. *pull* ~ 拉开. *take* ~ 拆开,隔开. *tear* ~ 扯碎.

ASW = ①antisatellite weapon 反卫星武器. ②antisubmarine warfare 反潜(艇)战. ③Association of scientific workers 科学工作者协会.

As·wan [ɑːsˈwɑːn] *n.* 阿斯旺[埃及城市]. **the** ~ **dam** 阿斯旺大水坝.

a·swarm [əˈswɔːm] *a.* 〔多作表语〕充满的,拥挤的,麇集的. *The square was* ~ *with people.* 广场上人山人海的.

a·syl·lab·ic [ˌeisiˈlæbik] *a.*【语音】非音节的,不成音节的.

a·sy·lum [əˈsailəm] *n.* ①(孤儿等的)收容所,养育院. ②避难所. ③【国际法】庇护(权). *a lunatic* ~ 精神病院. *a blind and dumb* ~ 盲哑院. *a foundling [an orphan]* ~ 孤儿院,育婴堂. *an* ~ *for lepers* 麻风院. ~ *for the aged* 养老院. *He sought* ~ *in the church.* 他到教堂去避难. *grant* ~ *to* 给予庇护.

a·sym·met·ric, a·sym·met·ri·cal [ˌæsiˈmetrik(əl)] *a.* 不对称的.

a·sym·me·try [æˈsimitri] *n.* 不对称(现象).

a·symp·to·mat·ic [æˌsimptəˈmætik] *a.*【医】无症状的.

as·ymp·tote [ˈæsimptəut] *n.*【数】渐近线.

a·syn·chro·nism [æˈsiŋkrənizəm] *n.* ①时间不一致,非同时性. ②【电】异步.

a·syn·chro·nous [æˈsiŋkrənəs] *a.* ①时间不一致的,不同时的. ②【电】异步的.

a·syn·de·ton [æˈsinditən] *n.* ①【修】(并列复合句中)连接词的省略[如: smile, shake hands, part]. ②【图书馆学】目录中对照参考资料的省略.

a·syn·tac·tic [ˌæsinˈtæktik] *a.*【语法】结构松散的,不合语法的.

AT, A.T. = ①Air Transport(ation). ②【电】ampere turn. ③Antitank. ④Atlantic Time.

at 〔强 æt; 弱 ət〕 *prep.* ①〔位置、地点、场合〕在,于,到;经由. ~ *the foot [top] of the hill* 在山脚[顶]. *stand* ~ *the door* 站在门口. *live* ~ *Oxford* 住在牛津. *be (present)* ~ *the meeting* 出席会议. *be present* ~ *the funeral [wedding]* 参加葬仪[婚礼]. *arrive* ~ *one's destination* 到达目的地. *Smoke came out at the chimney.* 烟经过烟囱逸出. ②〔时刻、年节、年龄〕在…. ~ *five o'clock* 在5点. ~ *noon* 在中午. ~ *Christmas* 在圣诞节. ~ *(the age of) forty* 年四十. ③〔动作的一次〕 ~ *a bound* 一跳就. ~ *a gallop* 飞奔;(骑马)奔驰. ~ *a [one] sitting* 一口气. ~ *a mouthful* 一口. ④从事. *at work* 做着,正在工作. ~ *dinner* 正在吃饭. ⑤〔表示性能〕在…方面 *be quick [slow]* ~ *learning* 记性好[坏]. ⑥〔状态〕处于…中. ~ *war* 在战争中. ~ *will* 随意,任意. ⑦〔动作的目标、方向〕向,对. *Up and* ~ *them, boys!* 弟兄们,向他们进攻吧! *aim* ~ *the target* 对准目标. *laugh at sb.* 嘲笑某人. ⑧〔动作、感情的原因〕应,照,见…而,闻…而;一…(就). *I did it* ~ *your request.* 照你请求的办了. *be surprised* ~ *the sight* 看见那光景就吓了一跳. ⑨〔程度、比例、价格高低、距离等〕以、用、有. *sell* ~ *six dollars* 以六美元(价格)出售. *estimate a crowd* ~ *ten thousand* 群众估计有一万人. ⑩从…. *The prisoners got good treatment* ~ *the hands of his captors.* 这些俘虏从捕获者那里受到良好的待遇. ★ (1) *at auction, at retail, at whole sale* 等的 at 系美式用法,英国则用 by. (2)美国俚语中常喜应用本可不用的 at. 例: *I want to know where it is* ~. ***and…*** ~ ***that*** 而且;此外还,又 (*He lost an arm, and the right arm* ~ *that.* 他失去了一只手臂,而且又是一只右臂). ~ ***that*** 就照那样 (*I will take it* ~ *that.* 就照(你说)那样好了). **be** ~ 从事,做 (*What are you* ~ *now?* 你现在是做什么? *Be up and* ~ *it before sunrise.* 日出前起来做吧). **where …** ~〔美俚〕身居何处 (*He doesn't know where he is* ~. 他不知道他自己的立场)〔英语不用 *at*〕.

At =【化】astatine.

at- *pref.* 为前缀 ad 的同化形式,用在 t 字母前.

at. = ①airtight. ②atmosphere(s). ③atomic.

at·a·bal [ˈætəˌbæl] *n.* (摩尔人的)铜鼓,手鼓.

At·a·brine [ˈætəbrin] *n.*【药】阿的平〔治疟药〕.

at·a·ghan [ˈætəgæn] *n.* 土耳其剑〔穆斯林战士所用的一种长剑或弯刀〕.

at·a·man [ˈætəmən] *n.* ***(pl.*** ~***s)*** (帝俄哥萨克军的)首领,长官.

at·a·mas·co lily [ˌætəˈmæskəuˈlili] 孤挺花科葱莲属植物.

a·tap [ˈætæp] *n.* ①(马来亚茅屋的)聂帕榈屋顶. ②聂帕榈;聂帕果;聂帕果汁.

at·a·rac·tic, ata·ra·xic [ˌætəˈræktik,-ˈræksik] *n.* 镇静剂,安定药. — *a.* 镇静剂的,镇静作用的.

at·a·rax·i·a, at·a·rax·y [ˌætəˈræksiə, -si] *n.* 不激动,不动心;心平气和.

ataunt, a·taun·to [əˈtɔːnt, -əu] *ad.*【海】扯着所有风帆. ***all*** ~ 万事齐备.

at·a·vism [ˈætəvizəm] *n.* ①【医】隔代遗传,返祖(现象),返祖性. ②呈现返祖现象的人. **-vis·tic** [-ˈvistik] *a.*

a·tax·i·a [əˈtæksiə] *n.* ①混乱,无秩序. ②【医】(肌肉的)运动失调,动作机能不协调.

a·tax·ic [əˈtæksik] *a.* ①混乱的,无秩序的. ②运动失调的. — *n.*【医】运动机能失调者. ~ **deposit** 不成层矿床.

a·tax·y [əˈtæksi] *n.* = ataxia.

ATC = ①Air Training Corps〔英〕航空训练团. ②Air Training Command〔美〕空军训练部. ③Air Transport Command 空运勤务部. ④ Air Traffic Control 空中

交通管制.

ate [et; Am. eit] eat 的过去式.

-ate[1] *suf.* 〔构成名词〕①官位,职位: consul*ate*. ②【化】…酸盐: sulf*ate*. ③动作涉及的对象: leg*ate*, mand*ate*. ④产品: condens*ate*. ⑤团体: elector*ate*.

-ate[2] *suf.* 〔构成形容词〕①充满…的: foli*ate*. ②有…特征的: collegi*ate*. ③相当于以 -ed 结尾的过去分词: anim*ate* (= animated).

-ate[3] *suf.* 〔构成动词〕①成为…: evapor*ate*. ②使化合;处理: oxygen*ate*, vaccin*ate*. ③原取自拉丁语的过去分词与其他词干的结合: actu*ate*, agit*ate*.

at·e·brin [ˈætəbrin] *n.* = atabrine.

at·e·lec·ta·sis [ˌætiˈlektəsis] *n.* 【医】肺膨胀不全.

at·el·ier [ˈætəliei] *n.* 〔F.〕①工作室; 画室. ②制作室〔车间〕.

a tem·po [ɑːˈtempəu] 〔It.〕【乐】照原速.

ath·a·na·si·a [ˌæθəˈneizə] *n.* 不死,不灭.

Ath·a·na·sian [ˌæθəˈneiʃən] *a.* 阿他那修斯的〔Saint Athanasius 为希腊亚历山大城主教, 296?—373〕. ~ **Creed** 阿他那修斯信条〔主张三位一体〕.

ath·an·a·sy [əˈθænəsi] *n.* = athanasia.

Ath·a·pas·can, Ath·a·paskan [ˌæθəˈpæskən, -kæn] *a.* 阿萨巴斯加人的〔包括纳瓦霍,阿帕斯部落在内的北美印第安人〕,阿萨巴斯加语族的. — *n.* 阿萨巴斯加人〔语〕.

a·the·ism [ˈeiθiizəm] *n.* 无神论 *(opp.* theism); 不信神.

a·the·ist [ˈeiθiist] *n.* 无神论者;不信神的人. **a·the·is·tic, -ti·cal** [ˌeiθiˈistik, -tikəl]*a.*

ath·el·ing [ˈæθəliŋ] *n.* (盎格鲁撒克逊的) 太子,皇子,贵族,公子.

A·the·na, A·the·ne [əˈθiːnə, əˈθiːni(ː)] *n.* 【希神】雅典娜〔智慧、技术、学问、战争的女神〕.

Ath·e·nae·um, Ath·e·ne·um [ˌæθiˈni(ː)əm] *n.* ①雅典娜神殿〔古希腊文人学者集会处〕. ②〔a-〕古罗马法律〔文艺〕学校. ③〔a-〕文艺〔科学〕协会. ④〔a-〕图书馆,阅览室.

A·the·nai [əˈθiːne] *n.* Athens 的希腊名.

A·the·ni·an [əˈθiːnjən] *a., n.* 雅典的(人).

Ath·ens [ˈæθinz] *n.* ①雅典〔希腊首都〕. ②【史】雅典〔古希腊雅典城邦的首府〕. ③〔喻〕作为文学艺术中心的城市.

a·ther·man·cy [əˈθəːmənsi] *n.* 【物】不透辐射热(性),不透红外线性质. **a·ther·mic** [-mik] *a.*

ath·er·o·ma [ˌæθiəˈrəumə] *n.* *(pl.* ***~s, -ma·ta*** [-mətə]) 【医】①动脉粥样化. ②粉瘤. **-tous** [-təs] *a.*

ath·er·o·scle·ro·sis [ˌæθərəuskliəˈrəusis] *n.* 【医】动脉粥样硬化. **-scle·rot·ic** [-ˈrɔtik] *a.*

Ath·er·ton [ˈæθətən] *n.* 阿瑟顿〔姓氏〕.

a·thirst [əˈθəːst] *a.* 〔仅作表语〕①〔诗〕渴. ②渴望. *be ~ for fame* 追求名誉.

ath·lete [ˈæθliːt] *n.* 运动员,体育家; 强壮的人. **~'s foot** 【医】脚气,脚癣. **~'s heart** 【医】心脏肥大.

ath·let·ic [æθˈletik] *a.* ①运动的,体育的. ②有膂力的,强壮的;活跃的. *an ~ meet(ing)* 运动会. *~ sports* 体育运动. *the ~ type* 运动员体型. **-i·cal·ly** *ad.*

ath·let·i·cism [æθˈletisizəm] *n.* ①运动练习;运动比赛迷. ②运动员气质.

ath·let·ics [æθˈletiks] *n.* ①〔用作 *sing.* 或 *pl.*〕体育(运动);竞技;〔英〕田径运动. ②〔用作 *sing.*〕体育(课); 运动法;健身术.

ath·o·dyd [ˈæθədid] 冲压式喷气发动机 (= aero-thermo-dynamic-duct).

at-home [ətˈhəum] *n.* (家庭)招待会.

a·thwart [əˈθwɔːt] *ad.* ①横穿过,横过,斜. ②【海】船侧朝风. ③〔罕〕逆,不顺,不便. *Everything goes ~ (with me).* 事事违愿. — *pep.* ①横过. ②逆,相反. ③【海】横越(航向). ***go ~ one's purpose*** 不如意,事与愿违.

-atic *suf.* …的: Asi*atic*, dram*atic*.

a·tilt [əˈtilt] *ad.* ①挺着枪,摆着冲刺姿势. ②倾斜着. *run [ride] ~ at [against]* 向…挺枪冲过去. *Hold the bottle slightly.* ~ 使瓶子微微倾斜.

-ation *suf.* ①表示动作: alter*ation*. ②表示状态: gratific*ation*. ③表示结果 compil*ation*.

-ative *a. suf.* 表示关系、倾向、性质等: demonstr*ative*, inform*ative*, talk*ative*.

At·kins [ˈætkinz] *n.* 阿特金斯〔姓氏〕.

A.T.L. = Atlantic Transport Line 大西洋轮船运输公司.

Atl. = Atlantic.

At·lan·ta [ətˈlæntə] *n.* 亚特兰大〔美国城市〕.

At·lan·te·an [ˌætlænˈtiən; ətˈlæntiən] *a.* ①巨人阿特拉斯(Atlas)神的;强有力的. ②阿特兰提斯洲〔岛〕的.

at·lan·tes [ətˈlæntiːz] *n. pl.* 【建】男像柱.

At·lan·tic [ətˈlæntik] *a.* ①大西洋的. ②巨人阿特拉斯(Atlas)的. — *n.* 大西洋. *an ~ flight* 横越大西洋飞行. *an ~ liner* 大西洋航线定期船. *~ states* 美国大西洋沿岸各州. *the ~ Ocean* 大西洋. ~ **Charter** 大西洋宪章. ~ **Pact** 北大西洋公约.

At·lan·tis [ətˈlæntis, æt-] 阿特兰提斯洲〔岛〕〔传说史前位于大西洋直布罗陀以西的一个洲或岛. 古代著作家认为它是经地震而沉入大洋的〕.

At·las [ˈætləs] *n.* ①【希神】阿特拉斯〔双肩掮天巨神〕;〔喻〕身负重担的人. ②非洲阿特拉斯山. ③〔a-〕地图集;图表集. ④〔a-〕大张绘图纸. ⑤〔a-〕【解】寰椎. ⑥〔a-〕【建】男像柱. ⑦大力神导弹〔美〕. ~ **beetle** 印度大甲虫. ~ **cedar** 小亚细亚雪松. ~ **folio** 最大版本〔16×25 英寸〕. ~ **moss** 东亚大蛾. ~ **silk** 樗蚕丝.

at·man [ˈɑːtmən] *n.* 〔Sans.〕①灵魂,自我. ②〔A-〕宇宙的灵魂.

atmo- *comb. f.* 表示"气,蒸气": *atmo*meter.

at·mol·y·sis [ætˈmɔlisis] *n.* 【化】微孔分气法.

at·mom·e·ter [ætˈmɔmitə] *n.* (测定水的蒸发速度的) 蒸发计,汽化计.

at·mos·phere [ˈætməsfiə] *n.* ①大气;大气层,气圈; 空气. ②四围情况,环境,气氛. ③(艺术品的)基调;风格. ④气压. ⑤【化】雾. *a tense ~ at a meeting* 会场中的紧张空气. *a tiny inn full of ~* 一个十分别致的小酒馆. *ion ~* 离子雾. *electron ~* 电子云. ***clear the ~*** 消除误会;缓和紧张空气.

at·mos·pher·ic [ˌætməsˈferik] *a.* ①大气(中)的. ②大气所致的. ③空气的. ④气压的. ⑤有…气氛的. *high (low) ~ pressure* 高〔低〕气压. ~ **depression** 低气压. ~ **discharge** 【电】天电放电. ~ **disturbance** 【无】天电干扰. **-i·cal** *a.* **-i·cal·ly** *ad.* 在大气影响下;气压上.

at·mos·pher·ics [ˈætməsˈferiks] *n.* 【无】天电,天电扰乱;大气干扰.

at·mos·pher·i·um [ˌætməsˈferiəm] *n.* (用以模拟大气现象的)大气馆.

ATO rocket = assisted takeoff rocket 助飞火箭.

at·oll [æˈtɔl] *n.* 【地】环状珊瑚岛,环礁. ~ **lake** 环礁湖.

at·om [ˈætəm] *n.* ①原子. ②微粒;微量. *chemical ~s* 原子. *physical ~s* 分子. ***have [there is] not an ~ of*** 一点也没有. ***break to ~s*** 粉碎 (*The vase was broken to ~s.* 花瓶敲得粉碎). **~-blitz** *n., vt.* 用原子弹进行闪电空袭. **~-bomb** *n., vt.* (用)原子弹(轰炸). **~-free** *a.* 无原子武器的. ~ **gun** 回旋加速器. ~ **mania** 原子弹狂. ~ **probe** 原子探测器. ~ **smasher** 核粒子加速器. **~-stricken** *a.* 受原子爆炸污染的. **~-tipped** *a.* 装有原子弹头的.

at·o·mar·i·um [ˌætəˈmɑːriəm] *n.* (显示原子结构等的)原子馆.

a·tom·ic [əˈtɔmik] *a.* ①原子的. ②极微的. ③强大的. ~ **age** 原子时代. ~ **blackmail** 原子讹诈. ~ **bomb**

原子弹. ~ **cocktail**〔俚〕放射性治癌吞服剂. ~ **energy**【化】原子能. ~**fission** 原子核裂变. ~ **formula**【化】原子式, 结构式. ~ **group**【化】原子团. ~ **intimidation** 原子恫吓. ~ **model**【化】原子模型. ~ **nucleus**【化】原子核. ~ **number**【化】原子序数. ~ **pile** 原子堆. ~ **reaction** 原子反应. ~ **reactor** 原子反应堆. ~ **rocket** 原子火箭. ~ **structure** 原子构造. ~ **value**【化】原子价. ~ **volume**【化】原子体积. ~ **warhead** 核弹头. ~ **weight**【化】原子量. **-bearing** *a.* 携带原子弹的. **-cosmic** *a.* 掌握原子能和空间宇宙技术的. ~ **proof** *a.* 防原子的. ~ **tipped** *a.* 装有原子弹头的.

a·tom·i·cal [əˈtɔmikəl] *a.* = atomic. **-ly** *ad.*

at·o·mic·i·ty [ˌætəˈmisiti] *n.* ①【化】(气体分子中的)原子数. ②原子价.

a·tom·ics [əˈtɔmiks] *n.* 原子学,原子工艺学,核工艺学.

at·om·ism [ˈætəmizəm] *n.* 原子说,原子论.

at·om·ist [ˈætəmist] *n.* 原子论者;原子学家.

at·om·is·tic [ˌætəˈmistik] *a.* 原子的;原子论的;原子学家的.

at·om·i·za·tion [ˌætəmaiˈzeiʃən] *n.* ①原子化,化成微粒. ②喷雾;雾化(法).

at·om·ize [ˈætəmaiz] *vt.* ①使化为原子,使成原子. ②把…喷成雾,使雾化,使粉化. ③〔俚〕用原子弹轰炸.

at·omi·zer [ˈætəmaizə] *n.* (药品或香水的)喷雾器.

at·o·my[1] [ˈætəmi] *n.* 〔古〕①原子;微粒;尘埃. ②矮子.

at·o·my[2] [ˈætəmi] *n.* 〔古〕①骸骨. ②瘦人.

a·ton·a·ble [əˈtounəbl] *a.* (罪等)可赎回的;(过失等)可补偿的.

a·ton·al [eiˈtounl] *a.* 无调的,不成调的. **-ism** *n.* **-ist** *n.* **-ist·ic** *a.* **-ly** *ad.*

a·to·nal·i·ty [ˌætouˈnæliti] *n.*【乐】无调性,无调主义.

a·tone [əˈtoun] *vi.* 补偿(过失),赎(罪). — *vt.* 〔古〕①偿. ②〔废〕和解,调解. ~ ***for*** 偿,抵,赎 (*Blood must ~ for blood* 以命抵命;血债要用血来还).

a·tone·ment [əˈtounmənt] *n.* 补偿; 赎罪. ***make ~ for*** 偿,赎(罪).

a·ton·ic [æˈtɔnik] *a.* ①【语音】(词或音节) 非重读的. ②【语法】平音的. ③【医】(肌肉)缺乏张力的, 弛缓的. — *n.* ①【语音】无重读音的词[音节]. ②【语法】平音.

at·o·ny [ˈætəni] *n.* ①无重读音;缺乏声调. ②【医】(肌肉)弛缓,张力缺乏.

a·top [əˈtɔp] *ad., prep.* 在(…)顶上.

-a·tor *suf.* …的人[物]: aviator.

-a·to·ry *suf.* 表示"具有…特征的";"由…产生的": laud*atory*.

ATP = adenosine triphosphate【生化】三磷酸腺苷.

at·ra·bil·ious [ˌætrəˈbiljəs] *a.* ①忧郁的; 沉闷的. ②乖张的;有疑心病的. **-ness** *n.*

a·trem·ble [əˈtrembl] *ad.* 〔诗〕发着抖,战栗着.

at·ri·cho·sis [ˌætriˈkəusis] *n.*【医】(先天性) 无毛症,毛发缺乏.

a·trip [əˈtrip] *a.* 〔用作表语〕①起锚. ②扬帆.

a·tri·um [ˈɑːtriəm] *n.* ***(pl.* -tria** [-triə]***)*** ①(罗马建筑内部的)中庭. ②【建】门廊. ③【解】心房; (耳的) 鼓室. ④【动】口前腔;气门室.

a·tro·cious [əˈtrouʃəs] *a.* ①凶暴的, 残忍的, 万恶的. ②〔口〕糟透的. *an ~ pun* 恶毒的俏皮话. ~ *weather* 恶劣的天气. **-ly** *ad.* **-ness** *n.*

a·troc·i·ty [əˈtrɔsiti] *n.* ①凶恶, 残忍; 暴虐. ②暴行. ③〔口〕令人不愉快的事物. *Her ~ is an ~.* 她打扮得俗不可耐.

a·troph·ic [æˈtrɔfik] *a.* 萎缩(性)的,衰退的.

at·ro·phy [ˈætrəfi] *n.* ①【医】萎缩症,虚脱. ②【生】衰退, 退化, 退缩. — *vt., vi.* ①(使)萎缩. ②(使)虚脱. *muscular ~* 肌肉萎缩.

at·ro·pin(e) [ˈætrəpi(ː)n] *n.*【化】颠茄碱,阿托品.

at·ro·pism [ˈætrəpizəm] *n.* 颠茄碱中毒,阿托品中毒.

ATS = ①Air Training School 空军训练学校. ②American Technical Society 美国技术学会. ③American Television Society 美国电视学会. ④applications techsnology satellite 应用技术卫星. ⑤Army Transport Service 陆军水上运输部队〔美国〕.

att., atty. = attorney.

at·ta·bal, a·ta·bal [ˈætəbæl] *n.* (摩尔人的) 铜鼓或手鼓.

at·ta·boy [ˈætəbɔi] *int.* 〔美〕顶好! 痛快痛快! 好样的! 〔That's the boy! 的转讹,表示赞赏〕.

at·tach [əˈtætʃ] *vt.* ①附上, 加上(条件等). ②贴上,系上,缚上. ③使附属,使隶属. ④使依恋,使执着. ⑤逮捕;拘留;扣留;查封. ⑥【军】临时委派, 指派. ⑦签署. ~ *a wire to a radio* 给收音机接线. *No blame is ~ed to his act.* 他的行为无可非议. *The tourist ~ed labels to all his bags.* 旅游者把他的行李都系上标签. ~ *a horse to a tree* 把马系到树上. *The hospital is ~ed to that university.* 这医院附属于那所大学. ~ *part of sb.'s salary* 扣下某人部分薪金. ~ ***importance to*** 把重点放在, 重视. ~ ***oneself to*** ①附着于;属于加入(政党等). ②依恋. ***be ~ed to*** ①爱上,爱慕,依恋. ②隶属于 (*She is deeply ~ed to him.* 她很爱慕他). — *vi.* 附着, 附属; 相连,相伴 *(to, upon). No blame ~s to him.* 他无可责备. **-a·ble** *a.*

at·ta·ché [əˈtæʃei; Am. ˌætəˈʃei] *n.* (大使、公使的) 随员,专员;使馆职员. *a commercial ~* 商务专员[参赞]. *a military [naval] ~* 使馆陆[海]军武官. ~ **case** (公文)手提皮箱.

at·tach·ment [əˈtætʃmənt] *n.* ①附着,附着物;附属物,附件. ②爱慕,依恋;依附 *(for; to)*. ③【法】逮捕; 扣押 (人、财产). ④扣押证. *~s to a sewing machine* 缝纫机的附件. *form a profound ~ for sb.* 对某人大为倾倒.

at·tack [əˈtæk] *vt.* ①攻击 *(opp.* defend*)*. ②非难, 抨击. ③着手,动手,投入. ④(疾病)侵袭. ⑤【化】腐蚀. *We will not ~ unless we are ~ed; if we are ~ed, we will certainly counter-~.* 人不犯我, 我不犯人; 人若犯我, 我必犯人. ~ *a task* 动手工作. ~ *a problem* 着手解决问题. *Strong acids ~ metals.* 强酸对金属有腐蚀作用. ***be ~ed with*** *(a disease)* 害 (病). — *n.* ①攻击 *(opp.* defense*)*,袭击. ②抨击. ③【空】迎角,冲角,攻角. ④着手,动手. ⑤发作,发病. ⑥(表演或竞赛中的)主动. *A- is the best defense.* 进攻是最好的防御. ~ *formation* 攻击队形. *have an ~ of* 为…所侵袭; 害, 患(病). *make an ~ on* 攻击. **-er** *n.* 攻击者.

at·tain [əˈtein] *vt.* ①达到,获得 *(opp.* miss*)*; 遂 (愿). ②到达. ~ *one's object* 达到目的. ~ *one's end* 得遂所愿; 如愿以偿. ~ *the opposite shore* 到达彼岸. — *vi.* 达到; 获得 *(to)*. ~ *to man's estate* 达到成年. ~ *to power* 得掌大权. **-a·ble** *a.* **-a·bil·i·ty, -a·ble·ness** *n.*

at·tain·der [əˈteində] *n.* ①【法】(对判处死刑者、逃犯) 褫夺公权,剥夺财产. ②〔古〕耻辱.

at·tain·ment [əˈteinmənt] *n.* ①达到,到达. ②〔*pl.*〕成就,造诣;学识,才能. *a man of varied ~s* 多才多艺的人. *a scholar of high ~s* 博学之士. ~ **age** 学业成绩年龄(=achievement age).

at·taint [əˈteint] *vt.* ①【法】使被褫夺公权; 使被剥夺财产. ②污损(名誉); 污辱. ③〔罕〕使感染. — *n.* ①公民权利(或财产)的剥夺. ②〔古〕污辱;污名.

at·tain·ture [əˈteintʃə] *n.* 〔废〕①民权剥夺, 公权丧失. ②玷辱,凌辱.

at·tar [ˈætə] *n.* 香精;玫瑰油.

at·tem·per [əˈtempə] *vt.* ①使缓和. ②冲淡. ③和匀; 调和,调匀. ④使适合. ⑤调节 (温度). ⑥【冶】使回火. ★现今各义通例均用 temper.

at·tempt [əˈtem pt] *vt.* ①试,企图. ②窥伺, 觊觎,意欲夺取;袭击. ③〔古〕诱惑. ④〔古〕企图杀害. ~ *a diffi-*

cult task 想完成一件艰难工作. ~ *a fortress* 欲夺取要塞. ~ *too much* 不自量力地做;纵欲过度. ~ *sb.'s life [the life of sb.]* 想杀某人. — *n.* ①企图;努力. ②〔古〕攻击,袭击. ③【法】未遂(罪). *an ~ at an offence* 未遂罪. *a poor ~ at a smile* 强笑未成的笑脸. ***in a vain ~*** 妄图. ***make an ~ (at)*** 企图,尽力. ***make an ~ on*** *(sb.'s life; a fortress)* 想结果(某人性命);欲夺取(要塞). **-a·ble** *a.* 可以尝试的.

at·tend [əˈtend] *vt.* ①出席,到场,参加;上,到. ②随侍,服侍;随行. ③陪,伴,伴随. ④看护,照料. ⑤〔古〕注意. ⑥〔古〕期待. ~ *school* 上学. ~ *(a course of) lectures* 听讲. *an ~ing physician* 主治医生. *The meeting was well ~ed.* 到会人数众多. ~ *church* 上教堂(做礼拜). *be ~ed by a doctor* 由医生照料. *be ~ed with difficulties [good results]* 遇到困难,收效良好. — *vi.* ①注意,留意;倾听 *(to)*. ②照顾,办理 *(to)*. ③侍奉,服侍;陪,伴随 *(on, upon)*. ④出席. ~ ***to*** *(one's work; health)* 照料(工作),注意(健康). ~ ***upon*** *(sb.; sb.'s wishes)* 侍奉(某人);听候(某人差遣).

at·tend·ance [əˈtendəns] *n.* ①出席,到场,参加 *(at)*. ②陪从,看护;照料. ③出席者,参加者. ④出勤率. *a large ~* 会众[观众]不少. *medical ~* 医疗护理. ***be in ~ on*** 服侍;随侍. ***dance ~ on*** 奉承,献殷勤. ~ **book** 签到簿. ~ **area** (到公学上学的)就学地区. ~ **officer** (检查学生出勤情况的)校纪检查官 (= truant officer).

at·tend·ant [əˈtendənt] *a.* ①随行的,跟随的 *(on, upon)*. ②出席的. ③伴随的,附随的 *(on, upon)*. ~ *circumstances* 附带情况. ~ *questions* 伴随而来的问题. ~ *crowd* 在场群众. — *n.* ①陪从,随员. ②服务员;值班员. ③出席人,参加人. ④伴随物,附属品.

at·tent [əˈtent] *a.* 〔古〕注意的,留意的.

at·ten·tat [ətɑːnˈtɑ] *n.* 〔F.〕谋刺(尤指未遂的政治上的谋杀).

at·ten·tion [əˈtenʃən] *n.* ①注意,注目;留心专心;注意力. ②【军】立正. ③〔*pl.*〕殷勤,厚待. ④关照;礼貌. *He was all ~.* 他十分专心. ~ *to a stranger* 对一个陌生人的礼貌. *A- please!* 请注意. *Your application will have ~.* 你的申请会得到考虑. ***arrest [attract] sb.'s ~*** 惹起某人注意. ***Attention!*** (略 'shun[ʃʌn]) 立正!〔口令〕. ***call away the ~*** 转移开注意. ***call sb.'s ~ to*** 促使某人注意. ***come to ~*** 【军】(采取)立正(姿势). ***devote one's ~ to*** 热中于,专心于. ***fix one's ~ on*** 留意. ***pay sb. ~s*** 殷勤招待某人. ***pay one's ~s to*** ①注意. ②(对女人)献殷勤. ***stand at ~*** = come to ~. ***turn one's ~ to*** 注意. ***with ~*** 注意,郑重. **~-getting** *a.* 引起注意的. ~ **span** 一个人能集中注意力于某事的时间. **-al** *a.*

at·ten·tive [əˈtentiv] *a.* ①注意的,留心的. ②周到的;殷勤的. ***be ~ to*** 注意;敬重;倾听 (*be ~ to one's duty* 忠于职守). **-ly** *ad.* **-ness** *n.*

at·ten·u·ant [əˈtenjuənt] *a.* 使变稀薄的. — *n.* 稀释剂.

at·ten·u·ate [əˈtenjueit] *vt.* ①使变稀薄,使淡,稀释. ②弄细,弄薄. ③使减弱. ④使病毒毒性减弱. — *vi.* ①变稀薄. ②变细,变薄. ③减弱,变弱;衰减,衰耗. — [əˈtenjuit] *a.* ①稀薄的. ②细的,薄的. ③减弱的. ④【植】渐尖的.

at·ten·u·a·tion [əˌtenjuˈeiʃən] *n.* ①变薄,变细. ②减少,减弱. ③稀释. ④【物】衰减.

at·ten·u·a·tor [əˈtenjueitə] *n.* 【物】衰减器.

at·test [əˈtest] *vt.* ①证明,证实. ②表明. ③使发誓. ④使服兵役. ~ *the truth of a statement* 证明供词属实. *His works ~ his industry.* 他的工作表明他的勤奋. *an ~ed herd* 经过检疫证明无病的牲口. *The recruits were ~ed.* 新兵应征入伍. —*vi.* 证明,证实 *(to)*. *The expert ~ed to the genuineness of the document.* 专家证明该文件系真品.

at·tes·ta·tion [ˌætesˈteiʃən] *n.* ①证实,证明. ②证据,证言;证明书. ③宣誓.

at·tes·tor [əˈtestə] *n.* 证人,证明者.

Att. Gen. = Attorney General.

At·tic [ˈætik] *a.* ①古希腊阿蒂卡 (Attica) [雅典]的;雅典派的. ②文雅的,古雅的. — *n.* ①雅典人. ②雅典城邦的希腊语. ~ **faith** 坚定的信念. ~ **order** 【建】角柱式. ~ **salt [wit]** 文雅的机智,文雅的俏皮话. ~ **taste** 雅兴.

at·tic [ˈætik] *n.* 屋顶室,楼顶间,顶楼.

At·ti·ca [ˈætikə] *n.* 阿蒂卡〔古希腊以雅典为统治中心的地区,在今希腊东南部〕.

at·ti·cism [ˈætisizəm] *n.* ①雅典派[式]. ②文雅的言辞[表现]. ③对雅典的爱慕.

At·ti·la [ˈætilə] *n.* 阿提拉〔侵入罗马帝国的匈奴王(406?—453)〕.

at·tire [əˈtaiə] *n.* ①服装,装束. ②(纹章上的)多叉鹿角. *the ~ of spring* 春(天的服)装. — *vt.* 打扮,装饰. *The girl was ~d in pink.* 这姑娘一身粉红色打扮.

at·ti·tude [ˈætitjuːd] *n.* ①姿势,身段. ②态度,看法. ③【军】飞行姿态. ④芭蕾舞的一个姿势. *the ~ of flight* 【空】飞行姿势. *the ~ of mind* 心情. *level ~* 【空】水平位置. ***strike an ~*** 装腔作势,摆架子. ***take [assumed] an ~ of*** 取…态度.

at·ti·tu·di·nize [ˌætiˈtjuːdinaiz] *vi.* ①采取某种姿态. ②(在谈话、写作、行动中)装腔作势.

Att·lee [ˈætli] *n.* 阿特利〔姓氏〕(艾德礼).

attn. 〔美〕= attention.

atto- *comb. f.* 渺,微微微 ($=10^{-18}$).

at·torn [əˈtəːn] *vi.* ①〔古〕改换门庭(投靠新领主). ②(佃户)承认新地主〔即同意在新地主门下继续当佃户〕.

at·tor·ney [əˈtəːni] *n.* ①〔美〕辩护律师;〔英古〕事务律师〔现在用 solicitor〕. ②代理人;代言人. *a letter [power, warrant] of ~* 委任状. *an ~ at law* 〔美〕律师. *an ~ in fact* 代理人. *by ~* 凭代理人. *a circuit [district] ~* 〔美〕地方检查官. ~ **general** 首席检查官. **A- General** 〔美〕司法部长. **-ship** *n.* 代理人的身分[职务];代理,代言.

at·tract [əˈtrækt] *vt.* ①吸引 *(opp.* repel*)*. ②引诱,诱惑. *A magnet ~s steel.* 磁石吸引钢铁. ~ *a large audience* 吸引了很多观众,叫座. ~ *(sb.'s) attention* 引(人)注意,惹眼. — *vi.* ①有吸力. ②引人注意. *It's a property of matter to ~.* 物质有引力. *be intended to ~* 旨在引人注目. **-or** *n.* 引人注意的人;有吸引力的人. **-a·ble** *a.* 可被吸引的. **-a·bil·i·ty** *n.* 吸引性.

at·tract·ant [æˈtræktənt] *n.* 引诱物;【虫】引诱剂.

at·trac·tion [əˈtrækʃən] *n.* ①引,吸引;【物】引力. ②魅力. ③引人注意的东西;有趣的东西;精彩节目. ④【语法】形态同化. *the ~ of gravity* 重力. *magnetic ~* 磁力. *the chief ~ of the night* 今晚最精彩的节目.

at·trac·tive [əˈtræktiv] *a.* ①有吸引力的. ②引人注目的. ③媚人的;俏的,标致的. **-ly** *ad.* **-ness** *n.*

at·trib. = ①attribute. ②attributive(ly).

at·trib·ut·a·ble [əˈtribjutəbl] *a.* 可归因于…的,由…引起的 *(to)*. *a disease ~ to alcoholism* 酒精中毒引起的疾病.

at·trib·ute [əˈtribju(ː)t] *vt.* ①把(某事)归因于…. ②认为…系某人所为. ~ *(one's success)* **to** *(hard work)* 认为(成功)是(努力)的结果. ***be ~d to*** 被认为是…所为 *(The play is ~d to Shakespeare.* 这剧本被认为是莎士比亚写的*)*. — [ˈætribjuːt] *n.* ①属性,特质. ②(人物、官职等的)标志,表征. ③【语法】定语. *A scepter is the ~ of power.* 权杖是权力的标志.

at·tri·bu·tion [ˌætriˈbjuːʃən] *n.* ①归属,归因. ②属性. ③〔古〕职权,权限.

at·trib·u·tive [əˈtribjutiv] *a.* ①属性的,归属的. ②【语法】定语的,修饰语的 *(opp.* predicative*)*. — *n.* 定语,修饰语. **-ly** *ad.*

at·trit [əˈtrit] *vt.* 〔美军俚〕①消耗. ②(以辱骂)降低(士气).

at·trite [əˈtrait] *vt.* (通过摩擦)使…消耗,磨损,削弱.

at·trit·ed [əˈtraitid] *a.* 磨损的,磨坏的.

at·tri·tion [əˈtriʃən] *n.* ①摩擦. ②磨损,磨灭;消耗. ③缩员,缩减人员. ④【神】不彻底的忏悔. *a war of* ~ 消耗战.

ATTU = Asian Table Tennis Union 亚洲乒乓球联盟,亚乒联盟.

at·tune [əˈtjuːn] *vt.* ①调(音). ②使调和,使协调. ~ *a violin to a piano* 使提琴与钢琴合调.

atty. = attorney.

Atty. Gen. = Attorney General 〔英〕检察总长;〔美〕司法部长.

ATV = ①Associated Television 〔英〕联合电视公司. ②All-Terrain Vehicle 全地形交通工具.

a·twain [əˈtwein] *ad.* 〔古〕分为二. *cut* ~ 切成两份.

a·tween [əˈtwiːn] *prep., ad.* 〔古〕在两者之间.

a·twit·ter [əˈtwitə] *a.* 〔用作表语〕〔俚〕高兴;兴奋.

at.wt. = atomic weight【化】原子量.

a·typ·ic, a·typ·i·cal [æˈtipik(əl)] *a.* 非典型的;不规则的.

au [əu; F. o] *prep.* 〔F.〕= to the; at the; with the. ***au contraire*** [əu kɔːŋˈtrer] 反之. ***au courant*** [əu kurã] ①熟悉,通晓*(with)*. ②跟上时代. ***au fait*** [əu ˈfɛ] 熟练,精通 *(in; at)*;熟悉 *(with)* (*Put me au fait of*… 请教给我…). ***au fond*** [əu ˈfɔ̃] 根本上,实质上;彻底地. ***au grand sérieux*** [əuˈgrɑːŋ seirjˈəː] 极其认真地. ***au lait*** [əu lei] 掺有牛奶的 (café au *lait* 牛奶咖啡). ***au naturel*** [əu natyrɛl] ①原样. ②裸体. ③供生吃的,略加烹调的. ***au pied de la lettre*** [əu pjei d la ˈlɛtr] 照字面意义. ***au revoir*** [əu rəˈvwɑːr] 再会.

Au =【化】aurum (= gold).

A.U., AU = astronomical unit.

Au. = August.

au·bade [əuˈbɑːd] *n.* 〔F.〕晨歌;朝乐〔*cf.* serenade〕.

au·berge [əuˈbɛəʒ] *n.* 〔F.〕旅馆.

au·ber·gine [ˌəubəˈʒiːn, ˌəubɛəˈʒiːn] *n.* ①茄子. ②紫红色.

Au·brey [ˈɔːbri] *n.* 奥布里〔姓氏,男子名〕.

au·burn [ˈɔːbən] *a.* 红褐色的. — *n.* 红褐色.

Au·bus·son [əubʌˈsəun] *n.* 奥布松〔法国城市〕. ~ **rug** (奥布松出产的)精细的华丽地毯.

A.U.C. = ab urbe condita 从(罗马)城市建立以来.

Au·chin·leck [ˌɔːkinˈlek] *n.* 奥金莱克〔姓氏〕.

Auck·land [ˈɔːklənd] *n.* 奥克兰〔新西兰港市〕.

auc·tion [ˈɔːkʃən] *n.* ①拍卖,标售. ②(桥牌)拍卖玩法 (= ~ bridge). *a public* ~ 拍卖. ***a Dutch*** ~ 喊价逐步减低的拍卖. ***put up to [at]*** ~ 交付拍卖. ***sell (a thing) by*** [〔美〕***at***] ~ 拍卖. — *vt.* 拍卖.

auc·tion·eer [ˌɔːkʃəˈniə] *n.* 拍卖人. *a* ~ *hammer* 拍卖槌. — *vt.* 拍卖.

auc·to·ri·al [ɔːkˈtɔːriəl] *a.* 著者的,作家的;作者(著)的.

au·cu·ba [ˈɔːkjubə] *n.* 桃叶珊瑚属植物.

aud. = audit; auditor.

au·da·cious [ɔːˈdeiʃəs] *a.* ①大胆的. ②厚颜无耻的;鲁莽的,蛮横无礼的. **-ly** *ad.* **-ness** *n.*

au·dac·i·ty [ɔːˈdæsiti] *a.* ①大胆. ②厚脸,无耻;无礼,鲁莽. ***have the ~ to (do)*** 有脸(做)…,竟然敢(做)…,厚颜无耻地….

Au·den [ˈɔːdn] *n.* 奥登〔姓氏〕.

au·di·bil·i·ty [ˌɔːdiˈbiliti] *n.* ①听得见,可听性. ②【物】可闻度.

au·di·ble [ˈɔːdəbl] *a.* 听得见的. ~ **frequency**【无】(成)声频(率). **-ness** *n.* **au·di·bly** [ˈɔːdəbli] *ad.*

au·di·ence [ˈɔːdjəns] *n.* ①听众;观众;读者. ②谒见;接见. ③倾听;听取. *a large [small]* ~ 大量〔少数〕观众. *a farewell* ~ 告别谒见. ***be given an*** ~ 得到发言机会. ***be received in*** ~ 蒙召见,赐见. ***give ~ to*** 听取;接见,召见. ***grand (sb.) an*** ~接见(某人),召见(某人). ***have ~ of*** 拜谒,拜会. ***in general [open]*** ~ 当众,公然. ***in sb.'s*** ~ 当着某人面前,据某人所闻. ~ **chamber** 接见室. ~ *pictures* 〔俚〕受观众欢迎的影片. ~**-proof** *a.* (戏剧)肯定卖座的.

au·di·ent [ˈɔːdiənt] *a.* 倾听的;注意的.

audi(o)- *comb. f.* 听: *audio*meter.

au·dile [ˈɔːdail] *a.* 听觉的;听得到的 — *n.*【心】对听觉印象特别敏感的人;听象型.

au·di·o [ˈɔːdiəu] *a.*【无】听觉的,声音的,音频的;成音的. ~ **frequency**【无】(成)声频(率).

au·di·o·gram [ˈɔːdiəˌgræm] *n.* 听力敏度图.

au·di·ol·o·gy [ˌɔːdiˈɔlədʒi] *n.* 听觉学,听觉病矫治学. **-o·log·i·cal** [ˌɔːdiəˈlɔdʒikl] *a.* **-ol·o·gist** *n.* 听觉病矫治专家.

au·di·om·e·ter [ˌɔːdiˈɔmitə] *n.* 听度计,听力计.

au·di·om·e·try [ˌɔːdiˈɔmitri] *n.*【物】测听术;听力测定.

au·di·on [ˈɔːdiən] *n.*【无】三极(真空)管.

au·di·o·phile [ˈɔːdiəufail] *n.* 高保真度录音(唱片)的爱好者;讲究音质者,HI-FI 迷.

au·di·o·tape [ˈɔːdiəuteip] *n.* 录音磁带.

au·di·o·typ·ing [ˌɔːdiəuˈtaipiŋ] *n.* 录音打字.

au·di·o-vis·u·al [ˌɔːdiəuˈvizjuəl] *a.* ①视觉听觉的. ②视听(教学法)的〔书本之外,借助电影、幻灯、录音、无线电等〕. ~ **aids** 视听教具.

au·di·phone [ˈɔːdifəun] *n.* 助听器.

au·dit [ˈɔːdit] *n.* ①会计检查,查帐. ②(地主与佃户间的)决算. — *vt., vi.* ①检查,查(帐). ②〔美〕(大学生)旁听(课程). *commissioners of* ~ 会计检查官.

au·di·tion [ɔːˈdiʃən] *n.* ①听,听觉. ②(招收演员时的的)试听,声量检查. — *vt.* 试听(演员的发声). — *vi.* (演员)试音.

au·di·tor [ˈɔːditə] *n.* ①会计检查官,查帐员,审计员. ②听者. ③〔美〕旁听生.

au·di·to·ri·al [ˌɔːdiˈtɔːriəl] *a.* 会计检查(官)的;审计的;审计员的.

au·di·to·ri·um [ˌɔːdiˈtɔːriəm] *n.* *(pl.* ~*s, -ria* [-riə]*)* ①听众席,观众席. ②〔美〕讲堂,教室;会厅,大会堂,大礼堂.

au·di·to·ry [ˈɔːditəri] *a.* 耳的,听觉的. — *n.* ①听众. ②听众席. ③礼堂,讲堂. ~ **nerves** 听神经. ~ **meatus** 耳道. ~ **localization** 声源定位.

au·di·tress [ˈɔːditris] *n.* ①女查帐员. ②女听者〔*cf.* auditor〕.

Au·drey [ˈɔːdri] *n.* 奥德丽〔女子名〕.

Au·du·bon [ˈɔːdəbɔn], **J.J.** 奥特朋〔1785—1851,美国鸟类学家〕.

Auf·klä·rung [G. ˈaufklɛːruŋ] *n.* 〔G.〕启蒙;(十八世纪的)启蒙思潮〔运动〕.

auf wie·der·se·hen [G. auf ˈviːdərzeiən] 〔G.〕再会,再见.

Aug. = August.

Au·ge·an [ɔːˈdʒi(ː)ən] *a.*【希神】①奥吉亚斯王 (Augeas) 的. ②极脏的. ~ **stables** 奥吉亚斯王的牛厩〔相传养牛三千头,三十年未扫,后为 *Hercules* 用河水在一日内扫清〕,藏垢纳污的地方.

au·ger [ˈɔgə] *n.* 螺(丝)钻,钻孔器;钻孔机.—*vt.* 钻(孔).

aught¹ [ɔːt] *n.* 任何事物 (= anything). ***(He may starve) for ~ I care.*** (他饿死也罢)我才不管呢. ***(He may be rich) for ~ I know.*** (他也许有钱)但我不大知道. — *ad.* 〔古〕一点也. ***if ~ there be*** 〔古〕即使有也,就有也(极有限).

aught² [ɔːt] *n.* 〔俚〕零〔naught 的转讹〕;〔古〕无,乌有.

au·gite [ˈɔːdʒait] *n.*【矿】(普通)辉石.

aug·ment [ɔːgˈment] *vt., vi.* ①(使)扩张, 扩大;【军】扩编; (使)增大,增加. ②【语法】(希腊文和梵文)(在…上)附加接头元音字母. ③【乐】(在…上)增音. ④【纹章】(在…上)加添新徽章. — [ˈɔːgmənt] *n.* ①增大. ②【语法】接头元音字母〔希腊文或梵文加在动词过去式字首的母音〕.

aug·men·ta·tion [ˌɔːgmenˈteiʃən] *n.* ①扩大, 增加. ②增加物. ③【乐】增音. ④【军】扩编. ⑤【徽】名誉副徽.

aug·ment·a·tive [ɔːgˈmentətiv] *a.* ①增大性的, 增加的. ②【语法】扩大[增强]词义的. — *n.*【语法】增强语, 扩张语〔指增强词义的前缀、后缀或构词成分, 如: *per*durable, eat *up*〕.

aug·ment·er [ɔːgˈmentə] *n.*【机】助力器;增压器.

aug·ment·or [ɔːgˈmentə] *n.* ①= augmenter. ②(代替人在极危险环境中工作的)替身机器人.

au·gur [ˈɔːgə] *n.* ①(古罗马的)卜占官;卜占师. ②预言者. — *vt., vi.* ①占卜;预卜,预言. ②成为(…的)预兆, 预示. *I ~ ill of his success.* 我看他的成功有问题. *~ **well [ill]*** 兆头好[不好].

au·gu·ral [ˈɔːgjurəl] *a.* ①占卜的. ②预言的; 预兆性的.

au·gu·ry [ˈɔːgjuri] *n.* ①占卜, 占卜仪式. ②征兆, 预兆. *a happy ~* 吉兆.

Au·gust [ˈɔːgəst] *n.* ①奥古斯特〔男子名〕. ②八月.

au·gust [ɔːˈgʌst] *a.* ①尊严的, 威严的. ②威风凛凛的, 堂堂的,雄赳赳的. *your ~ father* 令尊. **-ly** *ad.* **-ness** *n.* 庄严,威严.

Au·gus·tan [ɔːˈgʌstən] *a.* ①古罗马皇帝奥古斯都·恺撒的; 奥古斯都时代的. ②文艺全盛期的; 古典的. ③【英史】安妮女王时代的. — *n.* 奥古斯都时代的作家; 文艺全盛时期的作家. ~ **age** 文学的黄金时代.

Au·gus·tine [ɔːˈgʌstin] *n.* ①奥古斯廷〔姓氏〕. ②**Saint ~** 奥古斯丁〔354—430,古罗马基督教神父〕.

Au·gus·tin·i·an [ˌɔːgəsˈtiniən] *n., a.* ①奥古斯丁教义(的),奥古斯丁教团教士(的).

Au·gus·tus [ɔːˈgʌstəs] *n.* ①奥古斯塔斯〔男子名, 爱称是 Gus, Gustus〕. ②奥古斯都〔罗马帝国第一代皇帝 Octavianus Caesar 的尊称〕.

au jus [əuˈʒuː, əuˈdʒuːs]〔F.〕(肉)带原汁的.

auk [ɔːk] *n.*【动】海雀.

auk·let [ˈɔːklit] *n.* 小海雀.

auld [ɔːld] *a.*〔Scot.〕= old.

auld lang syne [ˈɔːld læŋ ˈsain] (= old long since, days gone by)〔Scot.〕过去的日子,令人怀念的往日.

au·lic [ˈɔːlik] *a.* 宫廷的. **Aulic Council**【史】①神圣罗马帝国枢密院. ②旧德帝国的枢密院会议.

AUM = air-to-underwater missile 空对水下导弹.

a.u.n. = absque ulla nota (〔L.〕= unmarked). 无任何标记.

aunt [ɑːnt] *n.* ①伯母,婶娘; 姨母, 姑母; 舅母. ②阿姨, 大妈〔对一般年长妇女的爱称〕. ***Aunt Sally*** [sæli] ①掷棒击落女像口中所含烟斗的游戏. ②〔英俚〕代人受过者; 易遭批评的对象. ③〔a- s-〕〔英俚〕任何无聊的娱乐节目. ***My (sainted) ~!*** 嗳呀! 啃! ***go and see one's ~***〔俚〕去大便.

aunt·ie[1] [ˈɑːnti] *(pl. ~s) n.* 伯母, 阿姨〔aunt 的亲热称呼〕.

aunt·ie[2] [ˈɑːnti] *n.*〔口〕反导弹导弹.

aunt·y [ˈɑːnti] *n. (pl.* ***aun·ties*** [-tiz]*)*= auntie!

au pair [əu pɛə]〔F.〕换工的. *She was an ~ girl who helped with the housework in return for room and board.* 她是换工的女孩,以帮助料理家务换取食宿.

au·ra [ˈɔːrə] *n. (pl. ~s, -rae* [-riː]*)* ①(人[物]的) 气味; 气氛,氛围. ②【电】电风,辉光. ③【医】(中风等的) 先兆,预感. *a blue ~* 蓝辉〔电子管中的辉光〕. *an ~ of culture* 文化气氛.

au·ral[1] [ˈɔːrəl] *a.* ①气味的,香味的; 气氛的. ②【电】电风的,辉光的. ③【医】预兆的.

au·ral[2] [ˈɔːrəl] *a.* 耳的,听觉的; 听到的.

au·ra·min(e) [ˌɔːrəˈmiːn] *n.*【化】金胺; (碱性) 槐黄.

au·rar [ˈaurɑː] *n. pl. (sing.* ***ey·rir*** [ˈeiriə]*)* 艾利尔〔冰岛货币单位,相当于 1/100 克朗〕.

au·re·ate [ˈɔːriit] *a.* ①镀金的; 金色的. ②灿烂的.

au·re·li·an [ɔːˈriːljən] *a.* 蝶蛹的. — *n.* 鳞翅目昆虫研究专家; 昆虫采集家.

Au·re·li·us [ɔːˈriːljəs] *n.* 奥里留斯〔121—180, 罗马皇帝兼哲学家〕.

au·re·o·la [ɔːˈriələ], **au·re·ole** [ˈɔːrəul] *n.* ①(神像画中头部或身体周围的)圆光,光环,光轮. ②(日、月等的)晕.

au·re·o·my·cin [ˌɔːriəuˈmaisin] *n.*【药】金霉素 (chlortetracycline 的商标名).

au re·voir [ˌəuriˈvwɑː, ˈəuri-]〔F.〕再见!

au·ric [ˈɔːrik] *a.* ①金的; 含金的. ②【化】三价金的.

au·ri·cle [ˈɔːrikl] *n.* ①【解】外耳,耳廓. ②(心脏的)心房,心耳. ③【解】耳形突; 耳状骨. ④【植】叶耳.

au·ric·u·la [əˈrikjulə] *n. (pl. -lae* [-liː], *~s)* ①【植】报春花. *~ primrose* 耳状报春花. ②= auricle.

au·ric·u·lar [ɔːˈrikjulə] *a.* ①耳的. ②听觉的; 耳语的. ③耳状的. ④【解】心耳的; 耳廓的. *~ confession* 秘密忏悔. *an ~ finger* 小指. *an ~ tube*【医】听诊器. **-ly** *ad.* 用耳; 用耳语. — *n.*〔*pl.*〕(鸟类的)耳羽.

au·ric·u·late [ɔːˈrikjulit] *a.* 有耳的; 耳形的.

au·rif·er·ous [ɔːˈrifərəs] *a.* 产金的; 含金的.

au·ri·form [ˈɔːrifɔːm] *a.* 耳形的.

Au·ri·ga [ɔːˈraigə] *n.*【天】御夫座.

Au·rig·na·cian [ˌɔːriˈnjeiʃən, -rigˈnei-] *a.* 奥里尼雅克期的〔指法国旧石器时代前期〕.

au·ris [ˈɔːris] *n.*〔L.〕耳. *~* ***externa*** 外耳. *~* ***interna*** 内耳. *~* ***media*** 中耳.

au·ris·cope [ˈɔːriskəup] *n.* 耳镜.

au·rist [ˈɔːrist] *n.* 耳科医生,耳科学家.

au·rochs [ˈɔːrɔks] *n. (pl. ~(es))*【考古】西欧野牛.

au·ro·ra [ɔːˈrɔːrə] *n.* ①极光; 曙光, 晓光. ②〔A-〕【罗神】曙光女神. ~ **australis** [ɔːsˈtreilis] 南极光. ~ **borealis** [bɔːriˈeilis] 北极光. ~ **polaris** [pəuˈlɛəris] 极光. ~ **yellow** 镉黄色.

au·ro·ral [ɔːˈrɔːrəl] *a.* ①极光的; 曙光的. ②玫瑰红的.

au·rous [ˈɔːrəs] *a.* ①金的,含金的. ②【化】亚金的.

au·rum [ˈɔːrəm] *n.*〔L.〕【化】金.

AUS = Army of the United States 美国陆军.

Aus. = ①Australia. ②Austria. ③Austriian.

aus·cul·tate [ˈɔːskəlteit] *vt., vi.*【医】听诊. **-ta·tion** *n.* [ˌɔːskəlˈteiʃən] 听诊. **-ta·tor** *n.* 听诊者; 听诊器.

aus·pex [ˈɔːspeks] *n. (pl.* ***aus·pic·es*** [-pəsiːz]*)* (古代罗马的)鸟兽声迹占卜者.

aus·pi·cate [ˈɔːspikeit] *vt.* 创始, 开张, 举行…开幕礼. — *vi.*〔废〕占卜, 预言.

aus·pice [ˈɔːspis] *n.* ①前兆,吉兆. ②(根据鸟的飞行而进行的)占卜. ③〔常 *pl.*〕保护, 赞助; 主办. ***take ~s*** 卜吉凶. ***under favourable ~s*** 吉利, 顺遂. ***under the ~s of*** 由…主办(主持); 在…保护[赞助]下.

aus·pi·cial [ɔːsˈpiʃəl] *a.* ①预言的; 占卜的. ②吉兆的, 幸运的.

aus·pi·cious [ɔːsˈpiʃəs] *a.* ①吉兆的, 吉利的, 吉祥的. ②幸运的,顺利的. **-ly** *ad.* 吉祥如意地; 幸而. **-ness** *n.* 吉兆,吉祥.

Aus·sie [ˈɔːsi] *n.*〔俚〕澳大利亚人[军人].

Aus·ten [ˈɔstin] *n.* 奥斯汀〔姓氏〕.

aus·ten·ite [ˈɔːstənait] *n.*【冶】奥氏体〔钢的结构〕. ~ **steel** 奥氏体钢.

Aus·ter [ˈɔːstə]〔L.〕〔诗〕南风〔拟人化的说法〕.

aus·tere [ɔsˈtiə] *a.* ①严格的,严厉的. ②严肃的;自我克制的;苦行的. ③朴素的;质朴的. ④苦涩的. **-ly** *ad.* **-ness** *n.*
aus·ter·i·ty [ɔsˈteriti] *n.* ①严格;严肃. ②简朴,朴素. ③苦涩味. ④〔常 *pl.*〕苦行. ⑤(经济的)紧缩. ~ **program** 经济紧缩方案〔如减少消费,增加出口〕.
Aus·tin [ˈɔstin] *n.* 奥斯汀〔姓氏〕.
aus·tral [ˈɔːstrəl] *a.* ①南方的;向南的,偏南的. ②〔A-〕= Australian.
Aus·tral. = ①Australasia. ②Australia.
Aus·tral·a·si·a [ˌɔstrəˈleiʒjə] *n.* 澳大利西亚〔澳大利亚大陆、新西兰和新西兰附近各岛的总称,连南太平洋诸岛全部包括在内时,统称 Oceania〕.
Aus·tral·a·sian [ˌɔstrəˈleiʒjən] *a.* 澳大利西亚的. — *n.* 澳大利西亚人.
Aus·tral·ia [ɔsˈtreiljə] *n.* 澳大利亚〔大洋洲〕.
Aus·tral·ian [ɔsˈtreiljən] *a.* 澳大利亚的;澳大利亚人的. — *n.* 澳大利亚人. ~ **ballot** (上有全部候选人名单的)圈选选票.
Aus·tra·loid [ˈɔːstrəlɔid] *a.* 澳大利亚土著居民的. —*n.* 澳大利亚土著居民.
Aus·tra·sia [ɔːsˈtreiʒə; ɔːsˈtreiʃə] 奥斯特拉西亚〔六至八世纪法兰克墨洛温王国的极东部,包括现在法国东北部,比利时和西德〕.
Aus·tri·a [ˈɔstriə] *n.* 奥地利〔欧洲〕.
Aus·tri·a-Hun·ga·ry [ˈɔːstriəˈhʌŋgəri] *n.* (第一次世界大战前的)奥匈帝国.
Aus·tri·an [ˈɔstriən] *a.* 奥地利的;奥地利人的. — *n.* 奥地利人.
Aus·tro- *comb. f.* = Austria. *Austro*-German 德奥的.
Aus·tro-As·i·at·ic [ˌɔːstrəuˌeiʒiˈætik] *a.* 奥亚语系的,东南亚语言的. — *n.* 流行于东南亚的语言〔包括越南语等〕.
aut- *pref.* 〔用于元音前〕= auto-.
au·ta·coid [ˈɔːtəkɔid] *n.* 【生】激素.
au·tar·chy [ˈɔːtɑːki] *n.* ①绝对主权;专制. ② = autarky. **-chi·cal** *a.* **-chi·cal·ly** *ad.*
au·tar·ky [ˈɔːtɑːki] *n.* 自给自足(政策).
au·te·cious [ɔːˈtiːʃəs] *a.* 单主寄生的;(雌雄)异苞同株的;单寄主的.
aut·e·col·o·gy [ˌɔːtiˈkɔlədʒi] *n.* 【生】个体生态学.
au·teur [əuˈtəː] *n.* (*pl.* ~*s*) 〔F.〕*n.* 表现自我的电影导演,性格导演. **-ism** *n.* ①在电影导演中表现的个人风格. ②性格导演主持拍摄的影片.
auth. = ①authentic. ②author(ess). ③authorized.
au·then·tic [ɔːˈθentik] *a.* ①可信的;可靠的,确实的;有根据的. ②真的,真正的. ③【法】认证了的,正式的. ~ *news* 可靠消息. ~ *signature* 真正手迹的签字. *an* ~ *deed* 手续完备的地契.
au·then·tic·ate [ɔːˈθentikeit] *vt.* 为…出立证据,证实;鉴定;认证. *The document was* ~*d by a seal.* 文件有印鉴为凭.
au·then·ti·ca·tion [ɔːˌθentiˈkeiʃən] *n.* 确定,鉴定,证明;认证. **-ti·ca·tor** *n.* 确定者,认证者.
au·then·tic·i·ty [ˌɔːθenˈtisiti] *n.* 确实,确实性;真伪.
au·thor [ˈɔːθə] *n.* ①著者,作家. ②著作物,作品. ③创造者;发起人. *Scott is his favorite* ~. 他喜欢读司各脱(的作品). *the* ~ *of mischief* 祸首;为非作歹者. ***the A- of all being*** 造物主,上帝,神. — *vt.* 〔美〕①写,写作. ②创造,创始. ~ *a book* 写一本书. ~ *a design* 设计一个图样. ~ **catalog** (图书馆中)按作(译)者编排的图书目录.
au·thor·ess [ˈɔːθəris] *n.* 女作家〔通常仍用 author〕.
au·tho·ri·al [ɔːˈθɔːriəl] *a.* 著者的,作者的.
au·thor·ise [ˈɔːθəraiz] *vt.* = authorize.
au·tho·ri·tar·i·an [ɔːˌθɔriˈteəriən] *a.* 权力主义的,命令〔独裁〕主义的. — *n.* 独裁主义者,命令主义者. **-ism** *n.* 命令主义.
au·thor·i·ta·tive [ɔːˈθɔritetiv] *a.* ①有权威的,可靠的. ②靠权力的;命令式的. ③当局的,官方的. *an* ~ *opinion* 权威意见. *an* ~ *person* 权威人士. ~ *information* 官方消息. **-ly** *ad.* **-ness** *n.*
au·thor·i·ty [ɔːˈθɔriti] *n.* ①权威,威信;权力,权柄;权限,职权,权能. ②工程管理处〔局、委员会等〕;〔*pl.*〕当局,官方. ③根据,凭据. ④权威者,泰斗,大家. ⑤【法】判决例,先例. ⑥代理权. *an organ of* ~ 权力机关. *the Yangtze Valley Authority* 三峡水库工程处. *the local authorities* 地方当局. *That is no* ~. 那不能做证据. *an academic* ~ 学术权威. ***the authorities concerned = the proper authorities*** 有关方面,当局. ***by the* ~ *of*** 以…的权力;得…许可. ***on good* ~** 由可靠方面,由确实根据. ***on one's own* ~**据一己之见,凭独断. ***On whose* ~?** 得何人许可? ***those in* ~** 有权有势的人们,当权者. ***with* ~** 凭威信,有权威.
au·thor·i·za·tion [ˌɔːθəraiˈzeiʃən] *n.* ①授权,委任. ②认可,核准. ***without* ~** 擅自.
au·thor·ize [ˈɔːθəraiz] *vt.* ①授权,委托,委任. ②批准,认可,允许. ③正式承认,公认. *The city* ~*d a housing project.* 市政当局批准了盖房计划. *an expression* ~*d by custom* 约定俗成的用语. *be* ~*d to act for sb.* 被授权充当某人的代理人. **-iz·a·ble** *a.* 可授权的;可批准的;可认定的.
au·thor·ized [ˈɔːθəraizd] *a.* 公认的,审定的,核准的. *an* ~ *agent* 指定的代理人. ~ *capital* (公司被批准发放的)股额. *an* ~ *text-book* 审定的教科书. *an* ~ *translation* 经原著人认可的翻译. ***Authorized version*** 钦定圣经译本〔1611 年英王 James 一世核定发行的英译圣经,亦称 King James Version〕.
au·thor·ship [ˈɔːθəʃip] *n.* ①作者的身分〔资格、职业〕. ②原作者. ③(谣言等的)来源. *a poem of unknown* ~ 作者不详的诗.
au·tism [ˈɔːtizəm] *n.* 【心】孤独性;自我中心. **au·tistic** [-ˈtistik] *a.*
au·to [ˈɔːtəu] *n.* (*pl.* ~*s*) 〔美口〕汽车. ~ **court** 汽车旅馆. ~ **parts** 汽车零件. ~ **road** 汽车路. — *vi.* 坐汽车.
auto- *comb. f.* ①自,自己,自身: *auto*biography. ②自动: *auto*alarm. ③汽车: *auto*cade.
au·to·a·larm [ˈɔːtəuəˌlɑːm] *n.* 自动报警器.
au·to·bahn [ˈɔːtəubɑːn] *n.* (*pl.* ***-en*** [-ən]) 〔G.〕高速公路,汽车干路.
au·to·bike [ˈɔːtəubaik] *n.* 〔美口〕机器脚踏车.
au·to·bi·og·ra·pher [ˌɔːtəubaiˈɔgrəfə] *n.* 自传作者.
au·to·bi·o·graph·ic, au·to·bi·o·graph·i·cal [ˈɔtəuˌbaiəuˈgræfik(əl)] *a.* 自传(式)的.
au·to·bi·og·ra·phy [ˌɔːtəubaiˈɔgrəfi] *n.* 自传;自传文学.
au·to·boat [ˈɔːtəubəut] *n.* 汽艇.
au·to·bus [ˈɔːtəubʌs] *n.* 〔美俚〕公共汽车.
au·to·cade [ˈɔːtəukeid] *n.* 〔美〕(汽)车队(伍).
au·to·car [ˈɔːtəukɑː] *n.* 汽车.
au·to·ca·tal·y·sis [ˌɔːtəukəˈtælisis] *n.* 【化】自动催化(作用).
au·to·ceph·a·lous [ɔːtəuˈsefələs] *a.* (教会等)独立的,自治的.
au·to·chang·er [ˈɔːtəuˌtʃeindʒə] *n.* (电唱机的)自动换片器.
au·to·chrome [ˈɔːtəukrəum] *n.* 彩色照片;彩色底片.
au·toch·thon [ɔːˈtɔkθən] *n.* (*pl.* ~*(e)s* [-θəˌniːz]) ①土著,原居民. ②土生土长的动植物. ③【地】原地岩.
au·toch·tho·nal [ɔːˈtɔkθənəl], **au·toch·tho·nous** [ɔːˈtɔkθənəs] *a.* ①土生的,本地的. ②【地】原地(生成)的.
au·to·cide[1] [ˈɔːtəsaid] *n.* 自我毁灭.

au·to·cide² [ˈɔːtəusaid] *n.* 撞车自毁，用撞车方式自杀。
au·to·clave [ˈɔːtəukleiv] *n.* 压热器，高压消毒锅，高压蒸锅。— *vt.* 用高压锅消毒[烹煮等]。～ **treatment** 压热法。
au·to·cod·er [ˌɔːtəuˈkəudə] *n.*【自】自动编码器。
au·to·co·her·er [ɔːtəukəˈhiərə] *n.*【无】自动粉末检波器〔又作 autodetector〕。
au·to·coids [ˈɔːtəukɔidz] *n.* 内分泌物。
au·to·col·li·ma·tion [ˌɔːtəuˌkɔləˈmeiʃən] *n.*【物】自准直。
au·to·cor·re·la·tion [ˌɔːtəuˌkɔrəˈleiʃən] *n.*【自】自相关。
au·toc·ra·cy [ɔːˈtɔkrəsi] *n.* ①独裁政治，专制政治。②独裁权。③独裁政府，专制国家。
au·to·crat [ˈɔːtəukræt] *n.* ①独裁君主，专制君主；独裁者。②专横霸道的人。
au·to·crat·ic, au·to·crat·i·cal [ˌɔːtəuˈkrætik(əl)] *a.* 独裁的，专制的。**-i·cal·ly** *ad.*
au·to·crat·rix [ɔːˈtɔkrətriks] *n.* (旧俄的)专制女皇。
au·to·crit·i·cism [ˌɔːtəuˈkritisizəm] *n.* 自我评定；自我反省，自我批评。
au·to·cy·cle [ˈɔːtəusaikl] *n.* 机器脚踏车；摩托车。
au·to-da-fé [ˈɔːtəudɑːfei] *n.* (*pl.* ***au·tos-*** [ˈɔːtəuz]) 〔Sp.〕【宗】(中世纪宗教裁判所对异教徒的)死刑宣告[处决](特指火刑)。
au·to·di·dact [ˈɔːtəudiˌdækt] *n.* 自修者。
au·to·dom [ˈɔːtəudəm] *n.* 汽车制造与推销界。
au·to·drome [ˈɔːtəudrəum] *n.* 赛车跑道。
au·to·dyne [ˈɔːtəudain] *a., n.* ①【无】自拍(的)，自差(的)。②自差接收机；自激振荡电路。
au·to·fin·ing [ˈɔːtəufainiŋ] *n.*【化】(石油)自动精炼，氢自供精炼。
au·tog·a·mous [ɔːˈtɔgəməs] *a.*【植】自花受粉的；【动】自配的，自体受精的。
au·tog·a·my [ɔːˈtɔgəmi] *n.*【动】自体受精；【植】自花受粉。
au·to·gen·e·sis [ˌɔːtəuˈdʒenisis] *n.*【生】自然发生。
au·tog·e·nous [ɔːˈtɔdʒinəs] *a.* ①【生】自生的；自体的。②气焊的。～ **soldering** 气焊法。～ **vaccine** 自体菌苗。
au·tog·e·ny [ɔːˈtɔdʒini] *n.*【生】自然发生；单性生殖。
au·to·gi·ro [ɔːtəuˈdʒaiərəu] *n.* = autogyro.
au·to·graft [ˈɔːtəugrɑːft] *n.*【医】自体移植。
au·to·graph [ˈɔːtəugrɑːf] *n.* ①亲笔，自署。②手稿。③真迹石版复制品。— *a.* 亲笔的，自署的。*an* ～ *album* 请人题字的纪念册。*an* ～ *fiend*〔美俚〕爱用纪念册请人题字的人。— *vt.* ①亲笔写，自书，自署；署名。②用石版术复制。
au·to·graph·ic, au·to·graph·i·cal [ɔːtəuˈgræfik(əl)] *a.* ①亲笔写成的。②亲笔签名的。③用石版复制的。
au·tog·ra·ph·o·me·ter [ˌɔːtəugrəˈfɔmitə] *n.* 自动图示仪。
au·tog·ra·phy [ɔːˈtɔgrəfi] *n.* ①亲笔书写。②亲笔写的字。③【印】石版复制术。
au·to·gra·vure [ˌɔːtəugræˈvjuə] *n.*【印】照相版雕刻法。
au·to·gy·ro [ˈɔːtəuˈdʒaiərəu] *n.* 自转旋翼飞机〔现已为直升飞机取代〕。
au·to·harp [ˈɔːtəuˌhɑːp] *n.* 自鸣筝〔一种古琴〕。
au·to·hyp·no·sis, au·to·hyp·no·tism [ˈɔːtəuhipnəusis, -nətizəm] *n.*【医】自我催眠。
au·to·im·mune [ˌɔːtəuiˈmjuːn] *a.* 自体免疫的。**au·to·im·mu·i·ty** [-niti] *n.* 自我免疫性。
au·to·in·fec·tion [ˈɔːtəuinˈfekʃən] *n.*【医】自体感染。
au·to·in·oc·u·la·tion [ˈɔːtəu-iˌnɔkjuˈleiʃən] *n.*【医】自体接种。
au·to·in·tox·i·ca·tion [ˈɔːtəuinˌtɔksiˈkeiʃən] *n.*【医】自体中毒。
au·to·ist [ˈɔːtəuist] *n.*〔美口〕开汽车的人；开车旅行的人(= motorist)。
au·to·ki·net·ic [ˌɔːtəukaiˈnetik] *a.* 自动运动的。
au·tol·o·gous [ɔːˈtɔləgəs] *a.* 自体同源的，自体固有的。
au·tol·y·sate [ˌɔːtəuˈlaiseit, ɔːˈtɔliseit] *n.* 自溶产物。
au·to·ly·sin [ˌɔːtəuˈlaisin] *n.*【生化】自溶素。
au·toly·sis [ɔːˈtɔlisis] *n.*【生化】自溶，自体溶解。
au·to·lyze [ˈɔːtəlaiz] *vt., vi.* (使)自溶，(使)自体分解。
au·to·man [ˈɔːtəumən] *n.* 汽车制造商(=～ maker)。
au·to·mat [ˈɔːtəumæt] *n.* ①(食物的)自动售货机。②自动售货饮食店，自助食堂。③自动装置；自动开关。④自动枪[炮]。自动照相机。
au·tom·a·ta [ˈɔːˈtɔmətə] *n.* automaton 的复数。
au·to·mate [ˈɔːtəmeit] *vt.* ①使(工厂、工序等)自动化。②使用自动化技术于(某方面)。～*d teaching* 自动控制教学，自动化教学。— *vi.* 自动化。*Many plants have begun to* ～. 许多工厂已开始实行自动化生产。
au·to·mat·ic [ˌɔːtəˈmætik] *a.* ①自动的；机械的。②【生理】自动性的，无意识的。— *n.* ①自动机械；自动装置。②自动手枪。～ **cashier** 现金自动出纳机。～ **following** 自动跟踪 ～ **numbering machine** 自动号码机。～ **pilot**【空】自动驾驶仪。～ **spotter**【空】自动侦示机。～ **sprinkler** 自动灭火器；撒水装置。
au·to·ma·tic·i·ty [ˌɔːtəməˈtisiti] *n.* ①自动，自动性。②自动化程度。
au·to·ma·tion [ˌɔːtəˈmeiʃən] *n.* 自动化，自动操作。
au·tom·a·tism [ɔːˈtɔmətizəm] *n.* ①自动，自动作用。②【生理】自动性；无意识行为。
au·tom·a·tize [ɔːˈtɔmətaiz] *vt.* ①使自动化。②使用自动化技术于…。**-ti·za·tion** *n.*
au·to·mat·o·graph [ˌɔːtəuˈmætəgrɑːf] *n.* (人体无意识行动的)自动纪录器(= autoscope)。
au·tom·a·ton [ɔːˈtɔmətən] *n.* (*pl.* ～***s***, ***-ta*** [-tə]) ①自动物；自动玩具；自动开关；自动装置。②机械式工作的人。
au·to·mo·bile [ˈɔːtəməubiːl, Am. ˌɔːtəməuˈbiːl] *n.*〔主美〕汽车。— *vi.* 开汽车；坐汽车。— *a.* 自动的。*an* ～ *torpedo* 自动鱼雷。
au·to·mo·bil·ism [ˌɔːtəˈməubilizəm] *n.*〔美〕汽车使用法[开法]。
au·to·mo·bil·ist [ˌɔːtəˈməubilist] *n.*〔美〕开汽车的人。
au·to·mor·phic [ˌɔːtəuˈmɔːfik] *adj.* ①【地】自形的。②【数】自守的，自同构的。
au·to·mo·tive [ˌɔːtəuˈməutiv] *a.* ①自动的；自动机的。②汽车的。*the* ～ *industry* 汽车制造业。
au·to·nom·ic [ˌɔːtəuˈnɔmik] *a.* ①自治的。②【解】自主的。③【植】自发的。
au·ton·o·mist [ɔːˈtɔnəmist] *n.* 主张自治的人。
au·ton·o·mous [ɔːˈtɔnəməs] *a.* ①自治的，自主的。②【植、生】自发的。*an* ～ *republic* 自治共和国。～ *tariffs* 国定税率，自主关税。
au·ton·o·my [ɔːˈtɔnəmi] *n.* ①自治；自治权。②自治州；自治团体。③人身自由。④【哲】自律，意志自由。⑤【生】自发性。
au·to·nym [ˈɔːtəunim] *n.* ①真名，本名〔*oppo.* pseudonym〕。②署名作品，以真名发表的作品。
au·to·phyte [ˈɔːtəufait] *n.*【植】自养植物。**-phyt·ic** [-ˈfitik] *a.* **-phyt·i·cal·ly** *ad.*
au·to·pi·a [ˈɔːtəupiə] *n.* 汽车专用区。
au·to·pi·lot [ˈɔːtəupailət] *n.*【空】自动驾驶仪。
au·to·plas·ty [ˈɔːtəuplæsti] *n.*【医】自体移植[成形]术。
au·top·sy [ˈɔːtəpsi] *n.* ①尸体解剖[剖检]。②(事后的)分析，检查。

au·top·tic, au·topt·i·cal [ɔːˈtɔptik(əl)] *a.* 以实地考察为根据的. *an ~ report* 实地考察报告.

au·to·ra·di·o·graph [ˈɔːtəuˈreidiəgrɑːf] *n.* 自动射线照相. **-y** *n.* 自动射线照相术.

au·to·ro·ta·tion [ˌɔtəurəuˈteiʃən] *n.* 自动旋转; 自转.

au·to·route [ˈɔːtəuruːt] *n.* (法语国家的)高速公路.

au·to·scope [ˈɔːtəuskəup] *n.* ①【医】自检器. ②【机】点火检查示波器.

au·to·some [ˈɔːtəusəum] *n.* 常染色体. **-so·mal** [-ˈsəuməl] *a.*

au·to·sta·bil·i·ty [ˌɔːtəustəˈbiliti] *n.* 【物】固有安定性; 自动稳定性; 内在稳定性.

au·to·stra·da [ˌautəuˈstrɑːdɑː] *(pl. **-strade*** [ˌautəuˈstrɑːdei]*)* *n.* 〔It.〕(汽车的)高速公路.

au·to·sug·ges·tion [ˈɔːtəusəˈdʒestʃən] *n.* 【心】自我暗示.

au·to·tel·ic [ˌɔːtəuˈtelik] *a.* 自有其目的的; 为其本身的. **-tel·ism** *n.* 艺术创作有其自身的目的.

au·to·tim·er [ˈɔːtəutaimə] *n.* 自动定时器.

au·tot·o·mize [ɔːˈtɔtəmaiz] *vi., vt.* 【动】(使)自割; (使)自行分裂〔如螃蟹受到袭击时,自行把钳子卸掉〕.

au·tot·o·my [ɔːˈtɔtəmi] *n.* 【动】自割,自截,自切. **-tom·ic** [ˌɔːtəuˈtɔmik] *a.*

au·to·tox·e·mi·a, au·to·tox·ae·mi·a [ˌɔːtəutɔkˈsiːmiə] *n.* 自体中毒.

au·to·tox·in [ˌɔːtəuˈtɔksin] *n.* 自体毒素.

au·to·trans·form·er [ˌɔːtəutrænsˈfɔːmə] *n.* 【电】自耦变压器.

au·to·troph [ˈɔːtəutrɔf] *n.* 自养生物.

au·to·troph·ic [ˌɔːtəuˈtrɔfik] *n.* 【生】自养的〔指植物通过光合作用,细菌通过化学合成作用自行制造食物〕.

au·to·truck [ˈɔːtəutrʌk] *n.* 运货汽车,卡车 (= motor truck).

au·to·type [ˈɔːtəutaip] *n.* ①【印】单色印相法. ②复印品,复制品. — *vt.* 用单色印相法复印; 影印; 复制.

au·to·work·er [ˈɔːtəuwəːkə] *n.* 汽车厂工人.

au·tox·i·da·tion [ɔːˌtɔksiˈdeiʃən] *n.* 自动氧化. **-da·tive** [-tiv] *a.*

au·tumn [ˈɔːtəm] *n.* ①秋,秋季〔英国为八、九、十月; 美国普通称 fall, 指九、十、十一月〕. ②成熟期; 凋落期; 晚年. *~ harvesting* 秋收. ***the ~ of life*** 中年,初老.

au·tum·nal [ɔːˈtʌmnəl] *a.* ①秋的. ②秋天开花的,秋天结实的,秋熟的. ③已过壮年的,中年的,近衰老的. **~ equinox** 秋分. **~ tints** (树叶的)秋色,红叶,霜叶.

au·tun·ite [ˈɔːtənait] *n.* 钙铀云母.

aux. = auxiliary.

au·xa·nom·e·ter [ˌɔːksəˈnɔmitə] *n.* 植物生长计〔用以测定植物生长速度〕.

aux·e·sis [ɔːgˈziːsis] *n.* 【生】细胞增大性生长. **aux·et·ic** [-ˈzetik] *a.*

aux·il·ia·ry [ɔːgˈziljəri] *a.* ①辅助的. ②补充的,备用的. ③副的. *~ coins* 辅币. *~ troops* 援军. *an ~ vessel* 辅助舰. *an ~ verb* 【语法】助动词. — *n.* ①辅助者. ②辅助设备; 辅助装置. ③补助舰〔如油船、供应船〕. ④〔*pl.*〕(外国来的)援军. ⑤【语法】助动词. ⑥附属机构,附属团体. *This club has a women's ~.* 这个俱乐部有妇女的附属机构.

aux·i·mone [ˈɔːksiməun] *n.* 植物激长素.

aux·in [ˈɔːksin] *n.* (植物)生长素.

aux·o·chrome [ˈɔːksəkrəum] *n.* 助色团〔用以使染料固着在织物上〕.

aux·o·troph [ˈɔːksətrɔf] *n.* 【生】营养缺陷型,营养缺陷体.

A.V. = Authorized Version.

av. = avenue; average; avoirdupois.

a.v., A/V = according to value.

a·vail [əˈveil] *vi.* 〔多用否定结构〕有益于,有利于,有助于. *Nothing ~ed against the flood.* 什么都无助于防治这次洪峰. *No words ~ed to pacify him.* 说什么都不能使他平静下来. —*vt.* 使对某人有利〔有益〕. *It ~ed him nothing.* 这对他毫无用处. *~ **oneself of** (an opportunity)* 利用时机,趁(机会) (*He ~ed himself of every opportunity.* 他利用了一切机会). — *n.* ①效用〔现多用于成语中〕. ②〔*pl.*〕〔古〕利益,收益. *a weapon of little ~* 用处很少的武器. *the ~s of the sale* 销货收益. ***be of ~*** 有用,有益 (*Of what ~ is it?* 那有什么益处?) ***be of no (little) ~*** 完全无用,全然无益; 不怎样有用. ***to little ~*** 不大有用. ***to no ~ = without ~*** 无益,徒劳,无效.

a·vail·a·bil·i·ty [əˌveiləˈbiliti] *n.* ①有效,有益,可利用,可得到. ②可得到的东西〔人员〕. ③(候选人的)当选可能性. *local availabilities* 可从当地获得的东西. *the ~ of a candidate* 候选人的当选可能性.

a·vail·a·ble [əˈveiləbl] *a.* ①有用的,可利用的. ②可以得到的,可以买到的. ③有效的. ④有当选希望的; 愿意参加竞选的. *He is not ~ for the job.* 他不适宜做这个工作. *~ water* 有效水分. *employ all ~ means* 用尽一切方法. *ticket ~ on day of issue only* 限当日通用〔有效〕的票子. *This book is not ~ here.* 这里没有这本书. *The doctor is ~ now.* 医生现在有空了. **-bly** *ad.* 有效地. **-ness** *n.* 有利,有效; 效用,利用.

av·a·lanche [ˈævəlɑːnʃ] *n.* ①雪崩,崩落,崩坠. ②蜂拥而来,纷至沓来; 雪崩式打击. ③【物】离子雪崩. *with the momentum of an ~* 以排山倒海之势. *an ~ of mail* 邮件的纷至沓来. *an ~ of blows* 劈头盖脸的打击. — *vi.* 雪崩; 雪崩似地落下. — *vt.* 大量涌进(市场等).

a·vant-cou·ri·er [ˈævɑ̃ːŋˈkuriə] *n.* 〔F.〕①先驱. ②〔*pl.*〕前锋,先锋.

a·vant-garde [ˈævɑ̃ːŋˈgɑːrd] *n.* 〔F.〕①先锋,先驱. ②(艺术的)先锋派. — *a.* ①先锋的,先驱的. ②先锋派的,标新立异的. *~ writers* 先锋派作家. **-ism** *n.* (文学艺术上的)先锋派主义.

av·a·rice [ˈævəris] *n.* 贪心,贪婪.

av·a·ri·cious [ˌævəˈriʃəs] *a.* 贪心的,贪婪的. *~ of wealth* 贪财. **-ly** *ad.* **-ness** *n.*

A·va·ru·a [ˌɑːvəˈruə] *n.* 阿瓦鲁阿〔库克群岛(新)首府〕.

a·vast [əˈvɑːst] *int.* 【海】停住! ***A- heaving.*** 停止曳绳!

av·a·tar [ˌævəˈtɑː] *n.* ①(印度教中神的)下凡. ②化身; 体现,具体化. *the divinest ~ of common sense* 常识的最佳体现.

a·vaunt [əˈvɔːnt] *int.* 〔古〕去! 走开!

AVC = American Veterans Committee 美国退伍军人委员会.

avdp. = avoirdupois.

a·ve [ˈɑːvi] *int.* ①欢迎! ②一路平安! 再会! — *n.* ①欢迎; 一路平安. ②〔A-〕= Ave Maria 【天主】万福马利亚〔追念圣母马利亚的祈祷〕. **~ bell** 祈祷报时钟.

Ave. = Avenue.

A·ve·ling [ˈeivli] *n.* 埃夫林〔姓氏〕.

a·venge [əˈvendʒ] *vt.* 为…报仇,替…雪耻; 为…对…报复. *~ one's father [father's wrongs]* 报父仇. *I will ~ you.* 我一定为你复仇. *He ~d himself on the his enemies.* 他对仇人实行报复. *She ~d her mother's death upon the Nazi soldier.* 她惩处了纳粹士兵以报母仇. — *vi.* 报复,复仇.

a·veng·er [əˈvendʒə] *n.* 报仇者.

av·ens [ˈævinz] *n.* 【植】水杨梅属.

a·ven·tu·rine [əˈventjurin] *n.* ①金星玻璃〔含有金色细粒的不透明玻璃,作装饰用〕. ②【矿】砂金石.

av·e·nue [ˈævinjuː] *n.* ①林荫路; 道路; 通路. ②〔美〕(南北向)街道〔东西向者称 street〕. ③〔喻〕手段,途径. ***an ~ to success*** 成功之道 *an ~ of escape* 逃路.

a·ver [əˈvəː] *vt.* ①宣告(某事)千真万确,断言 *(that)*.

②【法】证明. *I ~ that I have spoken the truth.* 我断言,我说了真话. *as he ~s* 如他所说.

av·er·age [ˈævəridʒ] *n.* ①平均,平均数. ②一般水平,平均标准. ③【商】海损;海损费用;(给领航的)报酬. *arithmetical [geometrical] ~*【数】相加[相乘]平均数,算术[几何]平均数. *general [particular] ~* 共同[单独]海损. *petty [accustomed] ~s* (支付给领航、港口等的)小额[例行]酬劳费. ***above [below] the ~*** 平常以上[以下]. ***on an [the] ~*** 平均;一般说来. ***take [strike] an ~*** 平均起来,折衷,扯平算. ***up to the ~*** 合一般标准. — *a.* ①平均的. ②普通的,一般的. ③【商】按海损估价的. *The ~ age of the boys here is ten.* 这些孩子的平均年龄是十岁. *students of ~ intelligence* 智力水平一般的学生. — *vt.* ①平均,均分. ②平均是. *I ~ six hours a day.* 我每天平均工作六小时. *If you ~ 4 and 6, you get 5.* 4和6均分得5. — *vi.* ①平均. ②(为得到更有利的平均价格而)买进(或)卖出(更多的股票、货物等). ***~ down [up]*** 以低于平均价格买进[以高于平均价格卖出]. ***~ out*** ①最终达到平衡. ②达到平均数,平均为 *(to)* (*The gain ~d out to 30 percent* 利润平均为百分之三十).

a·ver·ment [əˈvəːmənt] *n.* ①断言,确定. ②【法】事实的陈述.

A·ver·nus [əˈvəːnəs] *n.* ①意大利一臭水湖〔在那不勒斯附近,传说湖边有一通道通往地狱〕. ②地狱的入口,地狱.

a·verse [əˈvəːs] *a.* ①嫌恶的,反对的,不乐意的. ②【植】与茎方向相反的. ***be ~ to*** 〔后接名词、动名词或动词〕不喜欢,不爱,不愿意,讨厌. **-ness** *n.* 讨厌,嫌恶.

a·ver·sion [əˈvəːʃən] *n.* ①嫌恶;反感. ②讨厌的人[东西]. ③【生】排斥. *one's pet ~* 最厌恶的东西. ***have an ~ to [for]*** 讨厌,不爱,不喜欢.

a·vert [əˈvəːt] *vt.* ①防止,避免. ②避开,转移,把(脸、眼睛)转过去 *(from)*. *~ one's glance from sth.* 避而不看某物. *He apologized to ~ trouble.* 他道歉以避免麻烦.

a·vert·i·ble [əˈvəːtəbl] *a.* 可避开的,可防止的.

A·ver·tin [əˈvəːtin] *n.* 阿佛丁〔一种口服麻醉剂的商标名,学名为 tribro-moethanol〕.

A·ves [ˈeiviːz] *n.* 〔*pl.*〕〔L.〕【动】鸟纲.

A·ves·ta [əˈvestə] *n.* 祆教经典.

A·ves·tan [əˈvestən] *a.* ①祆教经典的. ②用以写成祆教经典的印欧语、伊朗语. — *n.* 与古波斯语很接近的上述语言.

avg. = average.

av·gas [ˈævgæs] *n.* 航空汽油〔*av*iation *gas*oline 的缩略词〕.

a·vi·an [ˈeiviən] *a.* 鸟类的;鸟纲的. — *n.* 鸟.

a·vi·a·rist [ˈeivjərist] *n.* 飞禽饲养家;鸟类饲养家.

a·vi·ar·y [ˈeivjəri] *n.* 鸟舍,飞禽饲养所.

a·vi·ate [ˈeivieit] *vi.* 飞行,驾驶飞机;航空.

a·vi·a·tion [ˌeiviˈeiʃən] *n.* ①飞行,航空. ②飞行术,航空学. ③〔集合词〕飞机,军用飞机. ④飞机制造业. ~ **goggles** 航空眼镜. ~ **ground** 飞机场. ~ **meet** 飞行比赛会. ~**'s spirit** 汽油.

a·vi·at·or [ˈeivieitə] *n.* 飞行员,飞机师. *a civilian ~* 民航飞机师. *a lady ~* 〔美〕女飞行员. ~ **glasses** 飞机师眼镜,金属框茶色镜片眼镜. ~**'s ear** 〔口〕高空中耳炎.

avi·a·to·ri·al [ˌeiviəˈtɔːriəl] *a.* ①航空的. ②飞行员的.

a·vi·a·tress, a·vi·a·trix [ˈeivieitris, -triks] *n.* 女飞行员.

a·vi·cul·ture [ˈeivikʌltʃə] *n.* 养鸟;养鸟法;鸟类饲养.

av·id [ˈævid] *a.* ①渴望的;贪婪的. ②热心的. *~ for food* 渴想食物. *be ~ of (money)* 贪(财). *an ~ reader of books* 热心的读者.

av·i·din [ˈævidin] *n.*【生化】抗生物素蛋白.

a·vid·i·ty [əˈviditi] *n.* ①贪婪;饥渴;热望. ②【化】亲合力,活动性. ***with ~*** 贪(*eat with ~* 贪婪地吃).

a·vi·e·tte [ˌeiviˈet] *n.* 小型滑翔机.

a·vi·fau·na [ˌeiviˈfɔːnə] *n.* (一地方或一国的)鸟类.

av·i·ga·tion [ˌæviˈgeiʃən] *n.* 航空(术);空中导航.

av·i·ga·tor [ˈeivigeitə] *n.* 〔美〕飞机师;【空】领航员.

A·vi·gnon [əˈviːnjɔːŋ] *n.* 阿维尼翁〔法国城市〕.

a·vi·on [æˈvjɔ̃ːŋ] *n.* 〔F.〕军用飞机. ***~ de chasse*** [dəʃæs] 驱逐机. ***par*** [pɑːr] *~* 航空邮寄.

a·vi·on·ics [ˌeiviˈɔniks] *n.* 航空电子学;航空控制系统.

a·vir·u·lent [æˈvirjulənt] *a.* 无毒性的.

a·vi·so [əˈvaizəu] *n.* (*pl.* *~s*) 〔Sp.〕①急件,急送公文. ②通信艇.

a·vi·ta·min·o·sis [æˌvaitəmiˈnəusis] *n.*【医】维生素缺乏症.

avn. = aviation.

av·o·ca·do [ˌɑːvəˈkɑːdəu] *n.*【植】鳄梨,鳄梨树.

av·o·ca·tion [ˌævəuˈkeiʃən] *n.* ①副业,兼差. ②〔罕〕正业,本职. ③〔古〕消遣,娱乐. *He is a doctor by profession and a novelist by ~.* 他的职业是医生,副业是作家.

a·voc·a·to·ry [əˈvɔkətəri] *a.* 召回的,撤销的. *an ~ letter* 召回书.

av·o·cet [ˈævəuset] *n.*【鸟】反嘴长脚鹬.

a·void [əˈvɔid] *vt.* ①避,回避,避免,逃避;防止. ②【法】使无效;撤销,废止. ③〔废〕驱逐,逐出. *~ bad company* 避免和坏人来往. *I cannot ~ seeing him.* 我不能不会见他. *~ a purchase* 撤销一项购货. **-a·ble** [-əbl] *a.*

a·void·ance [əˈvɔidəns] *n.* ①回避,逃避. ②(牧师职位的)空缺. ③【法】无效;废止.

avoir. = avoirdupois.

av·oir·du·pois [ˌævədəˈpɔiz] *n.* ①常衡〔16 ounces = 1 pound〕. ②重量,体重. ③〔美口〕肥胖. *5 lb. ~* 常衡五磅. *a woman of much ~* 异常肥胖的女人. ~ **weight** 常衡.

a·vo·me·ter [əˈvɔmitə] *n.*【电】安伏欧计,万用电表.

à vo·tre san·té [ə ˌvɔtr sɑːnˈtei] 〔F.〕〔祝酒词〕祝你健康!为您的健康干杯!

a·vouch [əˈvautʃ] *vt.* ①声言,断言. ②保证,担保. ③公开承认. — *vi.* 保证,担保 *(for)*;断言. **-ment** *n.* 声言;断言;保证.

a·vow [əˈvau] *vt.* ①声言,声明,承认. ②【法】供认. *~ one's guilt* 认罪. *~ oneself (to be) in the wrong* 自认错误. ***~ oneself*** 自称为…(*He ~ed himself a patriot* 他自称是爱国者).

a·vow·al [əˈvau-əl] *n.* 声明,供认,承认.

a·vowed [əˈvaud] *a.* 公然承认的,明言的. *an ~ work* 署名作品. *an ~ neutralist* 公开宣布中立的人. **-ly** *ad.*

a·vul·sion [əˈvʌlʃən] *n.* ①扯离,撕开. ②【医】撕脱法,抽出术. ③【法】河水改道后土地的转移〔指转入他人地产内〕. ④撕裂开的部分.

a·vun·cu·lar [əˈvʌŋkjulə] *a.* ①叔伯的,似叔伯的. ②〔废〕当铺的〔俚语当铺叫 uncle〕.

aw [ɔː, ɔ] *int.* 哦!噢!〔表示抗议,厌恶,讨厌,怜悯等的感叹词〕.

a.w. = atomic weight.

a·wa [əˈwɑː, -ˈwɔː] *ad.* 〔Scot.〕离开,远,那边(= away).

a·wait [əˈweit] *vt.* 〔书〕等,等待;期待. *~ sb.* 等人. *~ a decision* 等待决定. *Awaiting the favor of your prompt attention.* 火速赐复为盼〔信尾语〕.

a·wake [əˈweik] *vt.* ***(awoke*** [əˈwəuk]***; awoke, awaked)*** ①唤起,叫醒,唤醒;提醒. ②激起,激发,启发. *~ sb. from ignorance* 启人蒙昧. *~ (sb.)* ***to*** *(a sense of sin)* 激起(某人)(悔罪念头). — *vi.* ①醒. ②觉醒,觉悟,奋起 *(to)*. ***~ to a fact*** 开始发觉[领悟](某事). ***~ to find***

… 醒过来才知道[发现]. — *a.* 〔用作表语〕醒着，注意着，警戒着. *He tried to keep* ~. 他尽力醒着不睡. *He lay* ~. 他醒着躺在那里. *I was wide* ~. 我完全没有睡着. ~ *or asleep* 无论醒着睡着. ***be*** ~ ***to*** 不疏忽，深知. ***be full*** ~ ***to*** 对…十分注意. ***be wide*** ~ ***to*** 对…十分清醒.

a·wak·en [əˈweikən] *vt.* 使觉醒，唤醒 *the* ~*ed people* 觉醒了的人民 ~ *sb.'s sympathy* 唤起某人的同情心. — *vi.* 醒悟到，认识到 *(to)*. ~ *to the importance of* 认识到…的重要性.

a·wak·en·ing [əˈweikəniŋ] *n.* ①醒，觉醒. ②激励，启发. — *a.* 唤醒的；惊醒的.

a·ward [əˈwɔːd] *vt.* ①授与，给与；奖与. ②断与，判归. ~ *a prize to sb.* 授奖品给某人. ~ *a damage of 1,000 dollars* 判定赔偿损失一千美元. — *n.* ①审判，裁定. ②裁定书；裁定额. ③奖品.

a·ware [əˈwɛə] *a.* 〔用作表语〕知道，晓得，发觉，觉得. ***be*** ~ ***of (that)*** 知道，觉得. ***become*** ~ ***of*** 发觉，注意到. ***make sb.*** ~ ***that*** 提醒某人注意….

a·wash [əˈwɔʃ] *a., ad.* ①(暗礁等)与水面齐平；被水覆盖着. ②被波浪冲击[打湿]. ③喝醉了的[地].

a·way [əˈwei] *ad.* ①离开. ②…去，…掉. ③不在. ④不断，继续，…下去. ⑤到完，到底，完. ⑥立刻. ⑦【棒球】退场(= out). ⑧〔美〕远. ★用于其他副词如 back, behind, down, off, up 等之前加强其义；常略作 'way, way. *go* ~ 去，走开. *run* ~ 逃掉. *work* ~ 做下去. *put (or lay)* ~ 收拾，放在一边. *fade* ~ 消失；褪色. ~ *below the average* 远在平均以下，远在中等以下. ~ *(to the) east* 远在东方. *turn* ~ 掉转身去. *He let the water boil* ~. 他听任水烧干. *Keep* ~ *from the fire.* 别靠近火. *give* ~ 放弃. *The sounds died* ~. 声音逐渐消逝了. ***A-!*** 走开！ ~ ***back*** 〔美口〕老早以前 (~ *back in February* 早在二月里). ***A- with*** …! 扫除掉，赶掉，拿开〔用于无动词的命令句或感叹句〕. ***A- with him!*** 赶他出去！ ***A- with it!*** 停止！ 挪开！ ***A- with you!*** 让开！滚开！ ***be*** ~ 不在，缺席；…去了(*She is* ~ *(from home) today.* 她今天不在(家). *He is* ~ *on journey [for the summer].* 他旅行[避暑]去了). ***cannot*** ~ ***with*** 〔古〕不能忍耐[忍受]. ***do*** ~ ***with*** 废除；干掉，杀死. ***far and*** ~ …得多，最 (*far and* ~ *the best* 好得多). ***far*** ~ 很远，在很远地方. ***Fire*** ~！ 立刻开火！ ***from*** ~ 〔美〕从远方. ***make*** ~ ***with*** 废除 (*He made* ~ *with himself* 他自杀了). ***once and*** ~ 只一次，偶尔，间或. ***out and*** ~ 远，甚，无比 (*out and* ~ *the best* 远为好；好得多). ***right [straight]*** ~ 马上，即刻. ***Where*** ~? (船上所见物)是在什么方向[哪里]？ — *a.* (运动)在对方场地上比赛的.

awe [ɔː] *n.* ①畏惧，敬畏. ②〔古〕(使人敬畏的)威风. ③怕. ***be in*** ~ ***of*** 敬畏，怕. ***be struck with*** ~ 懔然敬畏. ***keep (sb.) in*** ~ 使(人)敬畏. ***stand in*** ~ ***of*** 敬畏，怕. — *vt.* 使害怕，使敬畏. *be* ~*ed into obedience [silence]* 吓得乖乖服从[哑口无言].

a·wear·y [əˈwiəri] *a.* 〔诗〕= weary.

a·weath·er [əˈweðə] *ad.* 【海】迎风，向风，向上风 (*opp.* alee). ***Helm*** ~! 迎风使舵！

a·weigh [əwei] *a.* 〔用作表语〕，*ad.* 【海】(锚) 快要离开水底，就要被拉上来. *with anchor* ~ 起锚.

awe·less [ˈɔːlis] *a.* ①〔古〕无威仪的，不会使人害怕的. ②无畏惧的，大胆的.

awe·some [ˈɔːsəm] *a.* ①可怕的；有威严的，使人敬畏的. ②表示敬畏的. *an* ~ *sight* 可怕的场面. *an* ~ *expression* 敬畏的表情.

awe-strick·en, awe-struck [ˈɔːstrikən, ˈɔːstrʌk] *a.* 畏惧的，恐惧的，害怕的.

aw·ful [ˈɔːful] *a.* ①可怕的. ②威风懔懔的，严肃的. ③ [ˈɔːfl] 〔口〕丑陋的，极坏的；厉害的；非常的，异常的；很大的. *die an* ~ *death* 死得可怕，死于非命. *an* ~ *miser* 极吝啬的人. — *ad.* 〔口〕非常，极其. *I'm* ~ *glad you came.* 你来了，我非常高兴.

aw·ful·ly [ˈɔːfulli] *ad.* ①令人畏惧地；令人敬畏地. ②〔口〕糟糕地. ③[ˈɔːfli] 〔口〕非常，很，了不得. ~ *good* 好得了不得. *It is* ~ *good of you.* 您真好. *to behave* ~ 表现得很糟糕.

aw·ful·ness [ˈɔːfulnis] *n.* ①威严，庄严. ② [ˈɔːflnis] 〔口〕不快，不愉快；丑态，卑鄙无耻，丢脸的行为.

a·while [əˈhwail] *ad.* 暂时，片刻. *After dinner sit* ~, *after supper walk a mile.* 午饭后歇一歇，晚饭后走一走.

a·whirl [əˈhwəːl] *a.* 〔用作表语〕旋转着. — *ad.* 旋转地.

awk·ward [ˈɔːkwəd] *a.* ①(机器等)有毛病的，难使用的，不称手的，(衣裳)不合身的. ②(质问，事情等) 棘手的；为难的，麻烦的. ③笨拙的，不灵活的，不雅观的；粗劣的. *be in* ~ *situation,* 处境困难. *He is* ~ *in his movements.* 他动作笨拙. *I felt* ~. 我觉得局促不安，真尴尬，真别扭. ~ *customer* 难对付的家伙. *an* ~ *instrument* 不顺手的工具. ~*position* 狼狈处境. *an* ~ *remark* 不得体的话. ~ **age** 将近成年的时期. **-ly** *ad.* **-ness** *n.*

awl [ɔːl] *n.* (绱鞋用的)锥子.

AWL, A.W.L., a.w.l. = absent(or absence) with leave 准假离职.

aw·less = aweless.

awn [ˈɔːn] *n.* 【植】芒. **-ed** *a.* 有芒的. **-less** *a.* 无芒的.

awn·ing [ˈɔːniŋ] *n.* 布篷；船篷；凉篷；雨篷.

a·woke [əˈwəuk] awake 的过去式及过去分词.

AWOL, a.w.o.l. [ˈeiwɔːl] = absent without leave; absence with out official leave 擅离职守，开小差.

AWOL·ism [ˈeiwɔːlizəm] *n.* 擅离职守的行为.

AWRE = Atomic Weapons Research Establishment 〔英〕原子武器研究所.

a·wry [əˈrai] *a.* 〔常作表语〕*ad.* ①曲，歪，斜，拗，扭. ②错误. ***be*** ~ ***from*** 违反. ***go*** ~ 失败，弄错. ***look*** ~ 斜视，瞟. ***run*** ~ = ***tread*** ~ = go ~. ***tread the shoe*** ~ ①通奸. ②失足.

AWS = Air Weather Service 〔美〕航空气象处.

axe, 〔美〕**ax** [æks] *n.* (*pl.* ***ax·es*** [ˈæksiz]) ①斧. ②战斧；(刽子手的)砍头斧. ③〔美俚〕任何一种乐器. ***get the*** ~ ①被解雇；被开除(学籍). ②(求爱等)被拒绝. ③被杀头. ***hang up one's*** ~ ①放弃无益的计划. ②洗手不干；退休. ***have an*** ~ ***to grind*** 〔美〕别有企图，有私心. ***lay the*** ~ ***to the root of*** 动手消灭…. ***put the*** ~ ***in the helve*** 解谜，大刀阔斧解决难题. ***send the*** ~ ***after the helve [hatchet]*** 吃了亏还要做，坚持做没有指望的事. ***set the*** ~ ***to*** 动手砍倒[破坏]. ***the*** ~ (经费的)大削减，彻底减少. — *vt.* ①用斧砍. ②大刀阔斧地削减(经费等). ~ **man** 用斧(伐木)的人. ~ **hammer** 斧槌. ~ **stone** 斧形软玉石.

ax·es *n.* ① [ˈæksiz] ax(e) 的复数. ②[ˈæksiːz] axis 的复数.

ax·i·al [ˈæksiəl] *a.* ①轴的. ②成轴的. ③轴周围的，轴向的. ~ **elements** 结晶常数. ~ **pencil** 【数】平面束. ~ **root** 【植】主根，直根. ~ **symmetry** 【数】轴对称. **-ly** *ad.* 在轴的方向，与轴平行地.

ax·il [ˈæksil] *n.* 【植】腋〔叶子、枝子同茎之间的角度〕.

ax·ile [ˈæksail, ˈæksil] *a.* 【植】轴的，轴上的.

ax·il·la [ækˈsilə] *n.* (*pl.* ~*s*, ***-lae*** [-liː]) ①【解】胳肢窝，腋. ②【植】腋 (= axil).

ax·il·la·ry [ækˈsiləri] *a.* ①【解】腋下的. ②【植】腋的，腋生的. — *n.* (鸟类的)腋羽.

axi·nite [ˈæksinait] *n.* 【矿】斧石.

ax·i·ol·o·gy [ˌæksiˈɔlədʒi] *n.* 【哲】价值论〔唯心主义的道德观、美学观、宗教观流派〕. **-log·i·cal** [-əlˈdʒikl] *a.* **-log·i·cal·ly** *ad.*

axi·om ['æksiəm] *n.* ①自明之理. ②【逻、数】公理; 原理,原则,通则. ③格言.

ax·i·o·mat·ic, ax·i·o·mat·i·cal [ˌæksiə'mætik(əl)] *a.* ①公理的,自明的. ②格言(多)的. **-i·cal·ly** *ad.* 照公理,公理上,自明地. **-ics** *n.* 公理体系〔系统〕; 公理学.

ax·is ['æksis] *n.* (*pl.* **ax·es** ['æksi:z]) ①轴,轴线. ②【植】茎轴. ③【解】第二颈椎,第二脊骨. ④【政】轴心〔国家间的联盟,特指第二次大战中德意日等国的联盟〕. ⑤【化】晶轴,【物】光轴. *the ~ of the eye* 视轴. *the major ~* (椭圆的)长径,长轴. *the minor ~* (椭圆的)短径,短轴. ***A- powers*** 轴心国. ***the A-*** (第二次世界大战中的)德意日轴心.

ax·le ['æksl] *n.* 心棒,轴,车轴.

ax·le·tree ['æksltri:] *n.* ①轮轴. ②【机】心棒.

Ax·min·ster ['æksminstə] *n.* (英国的)一种以黄麻为底的)羊毛织花地毯.

ax·o·lotl [ˌæksə'lɔtl] *n.* 【动】(墨西哥)蝾螈.

ax·on ['æksɔn] *n.* 【动】(神经细胞的)轴突. ~ **reflex** 轴突反射.

ax·o·no·me·try [ˌæksə'nɔmitri] *n.* ①轴线测定; 轴量法. ②均角投影图法.

ax·seed ['ækssi:d] *n.* 多变小冠花.

ay[1], **aye** [ai] *int.* 是,行,赞成! *Aye, ~, sir!* 是,是,官长!〔海员对长官的回答〕. — *n.* 赞成票; 赞成者. *the ayes and noes* 赞成票与反对票. *The ayes have it.* 赞成者占多数.

ay[2] [ei] *int.* 〔古、方〕唉! 呜呼!〔表惊愕、悔恨等〕. *Ay me!* 哀哉!

ay[3], **aye** [ei] *ad.* 〔诗、方〕常,永久. ***for (ever and) ~*** 永久,永远.

aye-aye ['aiai] *n.* 【动】指猴.

a·yin ['ɑ:jin] *n.* 希伯来语第十六个字母.

Ay·ma·ra [ˌaimə'rɑ:] *n.* ① (*pl.* ~(*s*)) 艾马拉人〔南美的一支印第安人〕. ②艾马拉语. **-n** *a., n.*

Ayr·shire ['ɛəʃiə] *n.* ①(苏格兰)额尔郡. ②额尔郡乳牛.

a·yun·ta·mien·to [əˌjuntə'mjentəu] *n.* (*pl.* ~*s*) 〔Sp.〕(西班牙、南美的)市政府,市议会.

a·zal·ea [ə'zeiljə] *n.* 【植】杜鹃花.

a·zan [ɑ:'zɑ:n] *n.* 伊斯兰教的祷告会〔由伊斯兰教寺院报祈祷时刻的人在尖塔上呼报召集,每日五次〕.

A·za·zel [ə'zeizl, 'æzəzel] 亚撒色〔英国诗人弥尔敦(Milton) 所作《失乐园》中和撒旦一起反抗上帝的天使〕.

a·zed·a·rach [ə'zedəræk] *n.* ①楝树. ②(苦)楝皮〔用以制泻药和呕吐剂〕.

a·ze·o·trope [ei'ziətrəup] *n.* 【化】共沸混合物. **-trop·ic** [-trɔpik] *a.*

Az·er·bai·jan [ˌæzəbai'dʒɑ:n] *n.* 阿塞拜疆. *the ~ Soviet Socialist Republic* 阿塞拜疆苏维埃社会主义共和国.

A·zer·bai·ja·ni [ˌæzəbai'dʒɑ:ni] *n.* (*pl.* ~(*s*)) ①阿塞拜疆人. ②阿塞拜疆语.

az·ide ['eizid] *n.* 【化】叠氮化物.

A·zil·ian [ə'ziljən] *a.* 阿济尔期的〔指法国旧石器时代最后期与新石器时代之间的史前文化〕, 阿济尔期文化的.

az·i·muth ['æziməθ] *n.* ①方位(角). ②【天】地平经度. ~ **angle** 方位角. ~ **circle** 方位圈. ~ **compass** 方位罗盘. ~ **stabilizer** 【空】纵舵机,方位稳定器.

az·i·muth·al [ˌæzi'mʌθəl] *a.* ①方位角的. ②【天】(地)平经(度)的.

az·ine ['æzi:n] *n.* 【化】连氮; 吖嗪.

az·lon ['æzlɔn] *n.* 人造蛋白质纤维,再生蛋白质纤维.

az·o ['æzəu] *a.* 【化】偶氮的. ~ **compound** 偶氮化合物. ~ **dyes** 偶氮染料.

azo- *comb. f.* 表示"偶氮": *azo*benzene.

az·o·ben·zene [ˌæzəu'benzi:n] *n.* 【化】偶氮苯.

a·zo·ic [ə'zəuik] *a.* ①〔有时作A-〕【地】无生物时代的. ② 无生命的. ~ **era** 无生物时代. ~ **group** 无生界.

az·ole ['æzəul] *n.* 【化】氮杂茂,唑.

az·on ['æzɔn] *n.* 方向可变炸弹 (= azon bomb).

a·zon·al [ei'zəunl] *a.* 【地】不分地带的.

a·zon·ic [æ'zɔnik] *a.* 非局部地区的,非本地的.

A·zores [ə'zɔ:z] *n.* (大西洋北部的)亚速尔群岛.

az·ote [ə'zəut] *n.* 【化】氮〔旧名〕. **a·zot·ic** [-tik] *a.* (含)氮的.

az·o·te·mi·a [ˌæzə'ti:miə] *n.* 【医】氮血(症).

az·oth ['æzɔθ] *n.* ①(炼金术的)水银. ②(传说为瑞士炼金家及医生巴拉塞尔斯所炼的)金丹〔万灵药〕.

az·o·tize ['æzətaiz] *vt.* 【化】使氮化.

a·zo·to·bac·ter [ə'zəutəˌbæktə] *n.* 【微】(土壤中的)固氮(细)菌.

az·o·tom·e·ter [ə'zəutəmi:tə] *n.* 氮素计.

a·zo·to·my·cin [ə'zəutə'maisin] *n.* 【药】含氮霉素.

A·zov ['ɑ:zɔf] *n.* (黑海北面的)亚速海. *The Sea of ~* 亚速海.

Az·ra·el ['æzreiəl] *n.* (犹太教和穆斯林信仰中使灵魂离开躯体的)死神.

Az·tec ['æztek] *n.* ①阿兹台克人〔墨西哥原始居民〕. ②阿兹台克语. — *a.* ①阿兹台克人的. ②阿兹台克语的.

az·ure ['æʒə] *a.* 天蓝色的,淡青的,蔚蓝的; 青天的. — *n.* ①天蓝色,浅蓝色. ②〔诗〕苍天,青空. ~ *eyes* 碧眼. — *vt.* 使成天蓝色. ~ **stone** 琉璃; 青金石,天青石.

az·u·rite ['æʒərait] *n.* 【矿】石青,蓝铜矿.

az·y·gous ['æzəgəs] *a.* 【解】非双生的,单一的,不成对的.

az·ym(e) ['æzaim] *n.* 无酵母面包.

B

B, b [bi:] (*pl.* ***B's, b's*** [bi:z]) ①英语字母表第二字母. ②【数】(顺序)第二,乙; 第二已知数. ③【乐】B 调, B 音. ④B形物; 〔B〕表示铅笔芯软硬的符号. ⑤〔美〕〔B〕(学业成绩)良好. ⑥〔B〕B 级,第二流. ⑦B 血型. *a B picture* 第二流影片. *a B student* 成绩乙等的学生. *B battery* 【无】B 电池组. *B flat* 【乐】降 B 调〔记号 B♭〕. *B major [minor]* 【乐】B 大调〔小调〕. ***not know B from bull's foot*** 见牛脚而不识 B 字; 目不识丁; 文盲〔英语字母 B 源于腓尼基象形文字"牛". 牛为偶蹄类,脚趾形似字母 B. 见牛趾而不识 B 字,喻文盲极其无知,故有此说〕.

B., b. = ①bachelor. ②【乐】bass; basso. ③battery. ④bay. ⑤book. ⑥born. ⑦brother. ⑧Bible. ⑨Boston. ⑩British.

B.A., BA = Bachelor of Arts 文学士.
Ba =【化】barium.
ba [bɑː] *n.*【埃神】魂灵〔被古埃及人描述成人头鸟身,死时飞离肉体,以后又要飞回,所以要保存尸体〕.
baa [bɑː] *n.* 咩咩〔羊叫声〕. — *vi.* (羊等)咩咩叫. **~-lamb** *n.* 羊咩咩〔儿语羊的名称〕.
Ba·al [ˈbeiəl] *n.* (*pl.* **~s, Ba·al·im** [ˈbeiəlim]) ①(古代腓尼基人等崇拜的)太阳神,山神,丰产之神. ②邪神,神;偶像. **-ism** *n.* 太阳神崇拜;偶象崇拜.
baas [bɑːs] *n.* 〔南非〕老板;先生〔旧时黑人对白人的称呼〕.
baas·kaap [ˈbɑːskɑːp] *n.* 〔S.Afr.〕(南非种族主义的)白人绝对统治方针.
Bab [bæb] *n.* ①Barbara〔女子名〕的通称. ②波斯巴比教祖的称号.
ba·ba au rhum [ˈbɑːbɑːəuˈrʌm] *n.* 〔F.〕 甜酒浸蛋糕.
ba·bas·su [ˌbɑːbɑːˈsuː] *n.*【植】巴西棕榈(= *Orbignya speciosa* 或 *Orbignya martiana*);巴西棕榈油.
Bab·bitt [ˈbæbit] *n.* 白璧特〔典型的粗俗实业家,得名于美国作家Sinclair Lewis 的同名小说〕;粗俗的市侩.
bab·bitt [ˈbæbit] *n.*【冶】①巴比特合金,巴氏合金,轴承合金〔锡、锑、铜合金〕. ②巴氏合金轴承衬. — *vt.* 给…浇巴氏合金. **~ metal** 巴氏〔轴承〕合金.
Bab·bitt·ry [ˈbæbitri] *n.* 〔常作 b-〕〔美〕庸俗的实业家性格,市侩作风;低级趣味.
bab·ble [bæbl] *vi.* ①(婴儿等)呀呀学语. ②胡言乱语;喋喋不休,唠叨 (*about*). ③(流水)潺潺作声. — *vt.* ①喋喋不休地讲. ②(因多说话而)泄漏 (*out*). — *n.* ①呀呀学语声;听不清楚的话;胡话;空话. ②潺潺(水声);【无】多路感应的复杂失真;(电话)串线杂音.
bab·bler [ˈbæblə] *n.* ①呀呀学语的婴儿. ②胡言乱语〔说话不清楚〕的人;碎嘴子;(因多说话而)泄漏秘密的人. ③【鸟】莺类小鸟.
babe [beib] *n.* ①〔诗〕赤子,婴孩;孩子气的人,不知世故的人. ②〔美俚〕(美丽的)姑娘;宝贝〔对亲爱女人的称呼〕. **~ *in the wood(s)*** 容易受骗的老好人. **~ *of love*** 非婚生子,私生子. ***~s and sucklings*** 年轻小伙子们,娃娃们;太天真的人,没经验的人.
Ba·bel [ˈbeibəl] *n.* ①【圣】(古巴比伦人建筑未成的)通天塔〔见创世纪十一章〕. ②〔b-〕〔喻〕摩天楼;空想的计划. ③〔b-〕喧哗,混乱声. *raise a ~ of criticism* 引起纷纷议论. **-ism** *n.* 〔有时作 b-〕(思想、语言等的)混乱. **-ize** *vt.* 使(习俗、语言等)混杂.
Ba·bi [ˈbɑːbiː] *n.* (= Babism) 巴比教徒〔1844 年在波斯兴起〕.
ba·biche [bɑːˈbiːʃ] *n.* 〔加拿大〕皮条,皮带.
Ba·bing·ton [ˈbæbiŋtən] *n.* 巴宾顿〔姓氏〕.
bab·i·ru·sa, bab·i·rou·sa [ˌbæbəˈruːsə] *n.*【动】马来野猪.
bab·ka [ˈbɑːbkə] *n.* 老妈妈饼〔一种加有葡萄干的甜酒味发面糕〕.
ba·boo [ˈbɑːbuː] *n.* ①〔印尊称〕先生;印度绅士. ②〔蔑〕半英化印度人〔多指会写点英文的印度职员〕. **~ English** 矫揉造作不合习惯用法的英语.
ba·boon [bəˈbuːn] *n.*【动】狒狒.
ba·bou·che [bəˈbuːʃ] *n.* 土耳其式拖鞋.
ba·bu [ˈbɑːbu] = baboo.
ba·bul [bəˈbuːl] *n.* 巴布尔橡胶树;巴布尔橡胶树皮〔树胶〕.
ba·bush·ka [baˈbuʃkə] *n.* 〔美〕(只露面部的女用)三角头巾〔源出俄语,其本义为老太婆〕.
ba·by [ˈbeibi] *n.* ①婴儿,赤子,奶娃娃. ②孩子气的人;幼小动物;小东西;一个集体〔家庭〕中最年幼的人. ③〔常作定语〕小型,微型. ④〔美俚〕姑娘;(美丽动人的)女人;爱人;(任何)人;(任何)物〔东西〕;得意杰作. ⑤〔口〕容易的〔讨厌的〕差事〔任务〕. *a regular ~* 十足的娃娃. *It's your ~, not mine.* 那是你的任务,不是我的. ***carry [hold] the ~*** ①受束缚,不能自由行动. ②担负讨厌的职务,做不愿意做的事;背包袱. — *vt.* 把…当婴儿看待,对…娇生惯养. **~ act** 幼稚行为 (*plead the ~ act* 〔美〕以幼稚无经验为口实). **~ alps** 〔美〕重量级拳击选手. **~ blue** 淡蓝色. **~ bond** 票面百元以下的债券. **~-bound** *a.* 〔美〕有孕的. **~ car** 童车;微型汽车. **~ carrier** 轻航空母舰. **~ carriage [buggy]** 〔美〕童车. **~-face** 孩儿脸(的人). **~ farm** 育婴院. **~ farmer** 代人育婴者. **~ firm** 〔美〕托儿所. **~-sitter** (论时计酬的)代人照看孩子的人. **~-hood** *n.* 婴孩期;幼小时代,幼稚;〔集合词〕婴儿. **~ kisser** 〔美俚〕为拉选票到处笼络人心的政治家.
ba·by·ish [ˈbeibiiʃ] *a.* 婴孩一样的,孩子气的.
Bab·y·lon [ˈbæbilən] *n.* ①巴比伦〔古代巴比伦王国首都〕. ②奢华淫靡的大都市. ***the Modern ~*** 现代巴比伦〔伦敦的别称〕.
Bab·y·lo·ni·a [ˌbæbiˈləunjə] *n.* (古代)巴比伦帝国.
Bab·y·lo·ni·an [ˌbæbiˈləunjən] *a.* ①巴比伦的,巴比伦帝国的. ②邪恶的;奢华堕落的. — *n.* 巴比伦人;迦勒底(Chaldea)人;占星家.
ba·by's breath [ˈbeibiz breθ]【植】①满天星,线形瞿麦,锥花丝石竹. ②茜草科猪殃殃属植物.
ba·by-sit [ˈbeibiˌsit] *vi.* (**-sat; -sitting**) (临时代人)照管孩子,照看婴儿.
ba·by-watch [ˈbeibiˌwɔtʃ] *vi.* = baby-sit.
bac·ca [ˈbækə] (*pl.* ***bac·cae*** [-ksiː]) *n.* 浆果(=berry).
bac·ca·lau·re·ate [ˌbækəˈlɔːriit] *n.* ①学士学位. ②〔美〕(对大学毕业生的)训辞.
bac·ca·ra(t) [ˈbækərɑː] *n.* 〔F.〕【牌】比九点〔一种用三张牌拼凑九、十九、二十九点的玩牌法〕.
bac·cate [ˈbækeit] *a.*【植】结浆果的;浆果状的.
bac·cha·nal [ˈbækənl] *a.* ①酒神的;酒神节的. ②狂欢闹饮的,发酒疯的. — *n.* ①酒神崇拜者;发酒疯的人,酒徒. ②〔B-〕〔*pl.*〕酒神节.
Bac·cha·na·li·a [ˌbækəˈneiljə] *n.* ①古罗马酒神节. ②〔b-〕大酒宴;狂闹乱饮;狂饮的闹宴.
bac·cha·na·li·an [ˌbækəˈneiljən] *a.*, *n.* = bacchanal.
bac·chant [ˈbækənt] *n.* ①酒神祭司. ②信奉酒神的人. ③爱酗酒胡闹的人. — *a.* = bacchanal (*a.*).
bac·chan·te [bəˈkænt(i)] *n.* ①酒神女祭司. ②信奉酒神的女人. ③爱酗酒胡闹的女人.
Bac·chic [ˈbækik] *a.* ①酒神 Bacchus 的. ②〔b-〕热闹的;狂饮乱闹的;闹宴的.
Bac·chus [ˈbækəs] *n.*【罗神】酒神 (=【希神】Dionysus). ***a son of ~*** 大酒鬼.
bacci- *comb. f.* 表示"浆果".
bac·cif·er·ous [bækˈsifərəs] *a.* 有浆果的,结浆果的.
bac·ci·form [ˈbæksifɔːm] *a.* 浆果状的.
bac·civ·or·ous [bækˈsivərəs] *a.* 以浆果为食的.
bac·co [ˈbækəu], **bac·cy** [ˈbæki] *n.* (*pl.* **-cies**) 〔英口〕烟草(= tabacco).
Bach [bɑːx, bɑːk], **Johann Sebastian** 巴赫〔1685-1750, 德国作曲家〕.
bach [bætʃ] *vi.* 〔美俚〕过独身〔鳏夫〕生活〔多用于短语 to bach it〕. — *n.* 独身男子,单身汉.
Bach(e) [beitʃ] *n.* 贝奇〔姓氏〕.
bach·e·lor [ˈbætʃələ] *n.* ①单身汉,独身男子;未交配的雄兽〔尤指海豹〕. ②学士. ③【史】青年〔下级〕骑士〔武士〕(= bachelor at arms). **~ *girl*** 自食其力的未婚独身女子. ***B- of Arts*** 文学士〔略作 B.A. 或 A.B.〕. ***B- of Science*** 理学士〔略作 B.S. 或 B. Sc.〕. ***~'s buttons*** ①花形似钮扣的植物〔矢车菊等〕. ②杏仁小饼干. ***~'s baby*** 私生子. ***~'s hall*** 单身男子的住处. **-dom, -hood** 男子独身(身分),独身,独身时代. **-ism** (男子)独身,独身主义. **-ship** ①(男子)独身. ②学士学位.
bach·e·lor·ette [ˌbætʃələˈret] *n.* 年轻未婚女子.
bacill- *comb. f.* 〔L.〕表示"小杆": *bacillin.*

bac·il·lar·(y) [bəˈsiləri; Am. ˈbæsileri] *a.* 小杆的；杆状的；(杆状)细菌(性)的 (= bacilliform).
ba·cil·li [bəˈsilai] *n.* bacillus 的复数.
ba·cil·li·form [bəˈsilifɔːm] *a.* 杆状的；杆菌状的.
ba·cil·lin [bəˈsilin] *n.*【药】杆菌素.
ba·cil·lo·my·cin [bəˌsiləuˈmaisin] *n.* 【药】杆菌抗霉素.
ba·cil·los·po·rin [bəˌsiləuˈspɔːrin] *n.*【药】多粘菌素.
ba·cil·lus [bəˈsiləs] *n.* (*pl.* ***ba·cil·li*** [bəˈsilai])【微】牙孢杆菌，杆菌；细菌，病菌. **Bacillus Cal·mette-Gué·rin** [kælˈmetgeiˈrɛ̃ːn]【药】卡介苗. ～ **carrier** 杆菌载体.
ba·cil·y·sin [ˌbæsiˈlaisin] *n.*【药】杆菌溶素.
bac·i·tra·cin [ˌbæsiˈtreisn] *n.*【药】杆菌肽 (*bacillus subtillis*)，杆菌肽素，枯草杆菌抗生素.
back [bæk] *n.* ①背，背部；背脊；背面，反面；背后；后部，后面，里面. ②(指)甲；(刀)背；(手)背；(书)背；(椅子)靠背；(山)脊；(船的)龙骨；衬垫，底座. ③体力；力气. ④【摔交】仰面倒下. ⑤【剧】(舞台的) 背景. ⑥足球后卫. ⑦【语】舌根音〔软口盖音〕. ⑧〔*pl.* **-s**〕〔美〕假钞票. *at the ～ of a house* 房屋背后. *the ～ of the mouth* 口腔深处. *full ～* (足球的) 后卫. *half ～* 中卫. *lazy ～* 椅子的靠背. ***at sb.'s ～*** 做某人的靠山. ***at the ～ of*** 在…之后，在…背后 (*at the ～ of one's mind* 在心里，内心上；下意识). ～ ***and belly*** 背与腹；衣食；腹背(都). ～ ***and edge*** 尽力，拼命. ～ ***to*** ～ ***(with)*** 背对背. ***behind sb.'s*** ～ 在某人背后；背地里，暗中. ***break one's*** ～ 折断脊背骨；负担过重，承受不住. ***break the*** ～ ***of*** ①毁坏；伤其要害. ②克服某事最艰巨的部分；度过最困难的时刻. ***cast sth. behind one's*** ～把某事置之脑后. ***get off sb.'s*** ～ 停止对某人攻击〔责难〕. ***get one's*** ～ ***up*** 发怒. ***get [put, set] sb.'s*** ～ ***up***〔口〕触怒某人，惹恼〔由猫怒弓背而来〕. ***get the*** ～ ***of*** 绕至…的背后. ***give [make] a*** ～ (游戏) 弯背作马状供人跳过. ***give the*** ～ ***to*** (转过身子) 背向着；遗弃. ***have [with] one's*** ～ ***to the wall*** 陷入绝境. ***have sb. at one's*** ～ 以某人作靠山. ***in*** ～ ***of***〔美口〕在…之后，在…的背面. ***on one's*** ～ 仰向，朝天 (*lie on one's* ～ 仰卧. *fall on one's* ～ 仰面倒下；背，驮；逼近背后). ***on [upon] the*** ～ ***of*** 由…背后，紧靠…的后面，继续；此外，加之. ***one's*** ～ ***is up*** (象猫发怒一样)耸着背 (*His* ～ *was up.* 他发怒了). ***put one's*** ～ ***into (sth.)*** 努力干(某事). ***see the*** ～ ***of*** 赶走，撵走；摆脱某人. ***set one's*** ～ ***against the wall*** 以寡敌众，负隅顽抗. ***show the*** ～ ***to*** 逃出，逃离. ***slap sb. on the*** ～ 拍拍(某人)脊背〔表示赞成、鼓励〕. ***the Backs***〔英口〕(Cambridge 大学的) 校后校园. ***the*** ～ ***of beyond*** 偏僻之地，遥远的地方. ***to the*** ～ 到骨髓，完全. ***turn the*** ～ 逃亡，败走. ***turn the [one's]*** ～ ***on*** 不理睬；丢弃；逃出. 一 *a.* ①后部的，背部的，后面的 (*opp.* front)；内地的，偏僻的；〔美〕边远的，边陲的. ②(货物等)回程的；向后动的，逆的. ③(思想) 落后的. ④〔美〕未缴的，拖欠下的，未付的. ⑤(杂志等)过了期的. ⑥【语】舌根的. *a* ～ *street*〔美〕背街. *a* ～ *door* 后门. ～ *teeth* 大牙，槽牙. *a* ～ *settler* 边疆居民，边疆移住民. ～ *cargo* 归程(载运的)货物. *a* ～ *current* 逆流. *a* ～ *salary [rent]* 欠薪[租]. *give a* ～ *answer* 回嘴；顶撞. ***take a*** ～ ***seat*** 坐末位，坐下席；谦下. ***take the*** ～ ***track***〔美〕回去，退去. 一 *ad.* ①向后，退，在后面，向背面，倒，回头，返，归，复；离开；隐匿. ②压制着，勒，扣，阻碍. ③以前，过去；从前. *answer* ～ 回嘴. *pay* ～ 付还. *send* ～ 送回. *What is the fare to London and* ～*?* 去伦敦来回要多少钱？ *a few pages* ～ 两三页前. *for some time* ～ 前些时以来. *two years* ～ 二年前. ***B-!*** 回去！ ～ ***and forth***〔美〕①来来去去. ②翻来复去. ～ ***of***〔美口〕在…的后部，在…的背后. ***be*** ～〔口〕回家；回来 (*I'll be* ～ *in a minute* 马上就回). ***come*** ～ ＝ ***go*** ～ 回，归. ***go*** ～ ***from [(up)on]*** 抛弃、辜负、出卖(朋友) (*He went* ～ *on his friends.* 他背叛了朋友). ***go*** ～ ***from one's word*** 违约，食言. ***keep*** ～***!*** 不要过来！不要前进！ ***keep*** ～ ***(sth.)*** 阻止向前；忍住；勒住；扣下；隐匿〔瞒〕(*keep* ～ *the truth* 隐瞒真相). ***look*** ～ 回顾. ***talk*** ～ 回嘴，还嘴；反复重说. ***there and*** ～ ＝***to and*** ～ 往返；来回. 一 *vt.* ①裱(画)；给…装背衬；装上(椅)背；作(风景等)的背景. ②给…做后援，支持，资助；怂恿；下赌注于. ③背书(支票等)，落名(信后等). ④使后退，使折回. ⑤乘、骑(马)；〔口〕背，驮. ⑥〔美〕位于…的背后. ～ *an automobile* 倒车，退车. ～ *a picture* 裱画. ～ *a check* 背书支票，在支票背面签字. 一 *vi.* 退后，倒退，逆行；(风向) 反(时针)转. ～ ***a sail***【海】转帆使船缓进. ～ ***and fill***【海】(风向紊乱时)看风使舵因势前进；〔美〕逡巡，踌躇. ～ ***down*** 放弃权利等，撒手；打退堂鼓，取消前言. ～ ***off*** 退避；后退. ～ ***on to***〔美〕背靠着. ～ ***out (of)*** 缩手(放弃某事)，取消；扭松，旋出；逃避(责任等). ～ ***the wrong horse***〔美口〕估计错；选错. ～ ***up*** 支持，为…撑腰；堵塞，拦(水)；【棒球】抢救后方. ～**ache** 背痛，腰痛. ～**-alley** ① *n.* 街后窄巷. ② *a.* 陋巷的；穷困的. ～**-bencher** 后座议员〔英国下院普通议员〕. ～ **benches** 后座议员席. ～ **bend** 桥形〔向后弯腰至头着地的杂技动作〕，～**bite** ①*vt.*〔口〕暗骂，背地里骂. ②*vi.*〔口〕背后骂人. ～**biter** 背地骂人的人. ～ **blocks**〔澳〕偏僻的牧场；(都市中)贫民窟. ～ **board** 后板，背板；(篮球架上的)篮板；脊椎矫正板. ～**bone** 脊骨，脊椎；分水岭，主要山脉；主要成分；中枢；中坚，骨干；主力；刚毅，骨气；书脊 (*the* ～*bone of a defence* 防御主力. *to the* ～*-bone* 完完全全，纯粹，十足，彻头彻尾. *an Englishman to the* ～*bone* 道地的英国人). ～**boned** *a.* 有脊骨的，有脊椎的；有骨气的. ～**breaking** *a.* 极费力气的；累坏人的；极讨厌的. ～**-burner** *a.* 不重要的. ～ **cap** *n.*〔美俚〕揭别人阴私 (*give sb. a* ～ *cap* 诽谤人，说人坏话). ～**-cap** *vt.*〔美俚〕说…的坏话；毁谤. ～**chat**〔口〕闲聊；回嘴；反唇相讥；(喜剧中)用俏皮话互相逗引〔挖苦〕. ～ **cloth**【剧】背景幕布；印花衬布. ～**cross**【生】①回交，逆代杂交(的产物)，回交种[品]. ②*vt., vi.* (使) 回交，(使)逆代杂交. ～ **country**〔美〕穷乡僻壤，边远地区. ～**date** *vt.* ①把发生的日期说成〔写成〕比实际的更早. ②追溯至 (过去某时) ～ *the salary increase three months* 加薪自三个月前起算). ～**door** *a.* 后门的，二门的；私下的，秘密的 (～*door methods* 秘密[非法]途径，阴谋). ～**down**〔口〕原先要求〔主张、态度、声明〕的改变；让步；退却. ～**drop**〔美〕背景；背景幕布. ～**-field**〔美〕(足球场的)中圈. ～**fill** ①*n.* (坑洞等的) 回填土，回填料. ②*vt.* 回填(坑洞等). ～**fire** ①*n.* (故意引燃以阻止野火蔓延的)迎火；逆火，回火〔内燃机因点火过早发生的不时爆发〕；(摩托车的)放气声. ② *vi.* 发生回火；放迎火；发生意外；产生适得其反的恶果 (*The plot* ～*ed.* 这一阴谋招来了相反的结果). ～**-formation**【语】逆构词；反成法〔如由 typewriter 逆构成 typewrite〕. ～**-ground** *n.* ①后景，背景；基本情况；(纺织品等的)底子；出身；经历. ②隐蔽的[不引人注目的]地位；幕后. ③衬托音乐，伴音；【无】干扰杂音 (*students of workers'* ～*-ground.* 工人出身的学生. *in the* ～*ground* 背地下，背后，在幕后(活动)). ～**grounder** 提供背景资料的记者招待会〔尤指政府为说明官方所采取的行动或方针政策而举行的非正式记者招待会〕. ～**hand** ①*n.* 反向；【网球】反手拍；(书法)左斜体. ②*vt.* 用反手击. ③*a., ad.* ＝ ～**handed.** ～**handed.** ①*a.* 反手的；逆的；(书法)左斜体的；间接的，转弯抹角的，暧昧的，讽刺的；(绳子)反搓的 (*a* ～*handed compliment* 挖苦的恭维话). ②*ad.* 反手地. ～**hander** ①反手打，反拍；间接攻击；(反手倒给右座人的)第二杯酒. ②〔俚〕贿赂. ～**house** 后屋，户外厕所. ～**lash** ① *n.* 后冲；后座；(政治等方面)强烈的反响；(任何)对抗性的反应；【机】轮齿隙；齿隙游移；钓丝缠结. ② *vi.* 发生后冲，产生对抗性的反

应. ~**lining**【建】背衬;【印】(加固书脊的)背衬料. ~**list** ①*n.* 多年未绝版书书目;旧版书存货目录. ②*vt.*把…列入旧版书书目. ~**log** 〔美〕①*n.* (加置炉膛深处的)垫薪圆柴;〔口〕存货;储备金;应急预备用物;积压的工作;未交付的订货. ②*vi.,vt.* 积压. ~ **matter** (正文后的)附加资料. ~**most** *a.* 最后部的,顶后面的. ~ **number** 过期杂志;落后于时代的人,老古董. ~**order**【商】留待将来交付的订货. ~**page** *a.*(报纸的)最后几版的;没有多大新闻价值的. ~**pedal** *vi.* 倒踏脚踏板;(拳击)向后躲闪;变卦,收回意见〔立场、主张〕. ~ **resistance** 反向电阻. ~**rest** (座椅等的)靠背. ~**road** 便道;村间道路〔尤指未铺过的道路〕. ~ **room** 里屋;密室. ~**room** *a.* 在密室中(工作)的. ~**room boy** 〔英口〕幕后策划人,智囊. ~ **seat** 〔口〕后座;低下的职位,无聊的工作 (*won't take a ~ seat to anyone* 不愿屈居人下). ~**-seat driver** 〔美口〕坐在后座乱指点司机的人;多管闲事的人;政治评论家. ~**-seat driving**〔美〕管闲事;政治评论. ~**set** 倒流;后退,倒退,挫折;(疾病的)复发;逆水;涡流. ~**sheesh,** ~**-shish** = baksheesh. ~**side** ①后部. ②〔常*pl.*〕屁股. ~**sight** 反视;【测】后视;照尺;【军】反觇;瞄准孔;表尺缺口. ~ **slang** 倒读隐语〔如 pig 读作 gip〕. ~**slap** *vt., vi.* 拍(某人的)背以示亲热. ~**slapper** 〔口〕(对人)过于推心置腹的人;热情太过的人. ~**slide** *vi.*, *n.*倒退;退步;故态复萌;堕落;违背(宗旨等). ~ **slum** 贫民窟. ~**space** *vi.*(按打字机退格键)使倒退一格,倒格. ~**spin**反旋转. ~**stage** ①*a.* 后台的,幕后的;关于戏剧界人物私生活的. ②*ad.* 在后台;在幕后;私下,秘密地. ~**stair(s)** ①*n.*后楼梯;厨房门. ②*a.* 见不得人的;肮脏的;暗地里的,秘密的(*~stair(s) influence* 潜势力,有权势的后台). ~**stay**【机】后支条〔撑条〕,背撑;【海】后支索,后索〔自桅至后舷侧的绳索〕. ~**stitch** ①*n.* 扣针脚,倒缝. ②*vt., vi.* 倒缝. ~**-stop** ①*n.* 托架;后障;【机】棘爪;【棒球】档球网;(击球手后的)接球手. ② *vt.* 挡住;支持. ~**-street** *a.* 偷偷摸摸干的〔做成的〕;秘密的,暗中的. ~**stroke** ①*n., vi.* 回击;反手击球;仰泳. ② *vt.* 用反手击. ~**swept** *a.* 后掠(角)的. ~**sword** 单刃剑;大砍刀;木剑. ~ **talk** 回嘴还口;顶嘴,对吵. ~**track** *vi.* 走回头路;改变过去的意见〔主张〕. ~**up** = ~**-up**①*n.* 后补物,替代物,备用物;支持;阻塞. ②*a.* 后补的,副(手)的,替代的,备用的;支持性的;伴奏的 (*a ~ pilot* 副领航员,助航员). ~ **vowel** (舌)后元音. ~**wash** 回浪;逆流;反动;反响;余波. ~**water** ①*n.* (被阻退回的)回水,回流;逆流;循环水,再用水;死水,滞水;〔喻〕停滞;文化落后的地方 (*live in a ~water* 蛰居乡间). ②*vt.* 倒划,倒开船;〔美口〕放弃原来的立场,食言. ~**woods** 〔*pl.*〕〔美〕偏僻的森林地带;落后的边远地区. ~**woodsman** 林区〔边远区〕居民;〔讽〕蛰居乡间的人;〔英〕不〔很少〕参加上议院活动的贵族. ~**woodsy** *a.* 〔美〕乡下气的;粗野的. ~**yard** ①*n.* 〔美〕后院. ②*a.* 本地的,私人的. ~**yardism** 〔美〕排外主义.

backed [bækt] *a.* ①有后援的,有支持的. ②有后衬的;以…作背面的〔常用作带连字符的复合词后缀,意为有某种后援或后衬的: *well-~* 后台硬的. *canvas-~* 帆布背衬的〕.

back·er [ˈbækə] *n.* ①(期票的)背书人;主持人,后台老板,后援者;支持物. ②(打字机的)垫纸. ③(赛马等的)赌客. ~**-up** 支持者;指示轰炸目标的飞机.

back·gam·mon [bækˈgæmən, ˈbækgæmən] *n.* (二人各持十五子,掷骰行棋的)十五子棋.

back·ing [ˈbækiŋ] *n.* ①后退,倒退,逆行. ②支持物;支援;(一群)支持人. ③衬垫物;(书的)背衬,衬里;照相底板. ④【建】隔板,衬板,底板;内墙. ⑤(法官等)对令状的签署批准. ⑥〔俚〕音乐伴奏. ~ **light** (舞台)背景灯光;(汽车尾部)后退灯.

back·less [ˈbæklis] 无(靠)背的;无背部的.

back·ward¹, back·wards [ˈbækwəd, ˈbækwədz] *ad.* 向后;在后,在后方;倒,逆;回向原处. *lean ~s* 往后靠. *spell ~s* 倒拼;误解,曲解. *~(s) and forward(s)* 忽前忽后;来回地. *go ~s* 倒退,退步,堕落. *say ~s* 倒说.

back·ward² [ˈbækwəd] *a.* ①向后方的,向后的. ②倒的;反的,相反的. ③落后的,晚的;迟缓的,慢的;进步慢的. ④愚钝的;畏缩的,迟疑的,怕羞的. *a ~ child* 智力差(落于人后)的孩子. *The country is in a ~ state.* 那个国家是落后的. *Summer is ~ this year.* 今年夏天来得晚. *be ~ in (preparations, duty)* (准备)迟缓;忽视(责任). ~ **blessing** 诅咒. ~ **process** 相反的程序. **-ly** *ad.* **-ness** *n.* 落后,迟疑.

back·ward·a·tion [bækwəˈdeiʃən] *n.*〔英〕(证券)交割延期(费).

ba·con [ˈbeikən] *n.* ①(用背或肋部肉加工的)熏猪肉,咸肉. ②〔美口〕报酬,利益,奖品. *bring home the ~* ①成功;得胜. ②谋生. *save one's [sb.'s] ~* 使自己〔某人〕免于死亡〔受害〕. *sell one's ~* 卖身.

Ba·con [ˈbeikən] *n.* ①培根〔姓氏〕. ②**Francis** ~ 培根〔1561—1626, 英国经验论哲学家〕. ③**Roger** ~ 培根〔1214—1294,英国自然科学、哲学家〕.

Ba·co·ni·an [beiˈkəunjən] *a.* 培根的,培根派哲学的. — *n.* 培根派哲学家. ~ **method** 归纳法. ~ **theory** "培根写剧说"〔英国文学史研究中的一家之言,认为莎士比亚戏剧实际上全为培根所写〕.

ba·con·y [ˈbeikəni] *n.* 咸猪肉一样的;脂肪质的,多油的.

bact. = ①bacteriology. ②bacteriological.

bac·te·re·mi·a [ˌbæktəˈri:miə] *n.*【医】细菌血症.

bac·te·ri- *comb. f.* 表示"细菌(的)".

bac·te·ri·a [bækˈtiəriə] *n. pl. (sing. bac·te·ri·um)* ①细菌. ②〔美俚〕拳击迷. *acid fast ~* 抗酸细菌. ~**-free** *a.* 无菌的.

bac·te·ri·al [bækˈtiəriəl] *a.* 细菌的. ~ **fertilizer** 细菌肥料.

bac·te·ri·cide [bækˈtiərisaid] *n.* 杀菌剂. **-cid·al** *a.* 杀菌的.

bac·te·ri·o·chlo·ro·phyll [bækˌtiəriəˈklɔ(:)rəfil] *n.* 细菌叶绿素.

bac·te·ri·o·cin [bækˈtiəriəsin] *n.* = bacillin.

bac·te·ri·o·log·i·cal [bəkˌtiəriəˈlɔdʒikəl] *a.* 细菌学(上)的;使用细菌的. ~ **warfare** 细菌战. ~ **weapon** 细菌武器.

bac·te·ri·ol·o·gist [bækˌtiəriˈɔlədʒist] *n.* 细菌学家.

bac·te·ri·ol·o·gy [bækˌtiəriˈɔlədʒi] *n.* 细菌学.

bac·te·ri·ol·y·sin [bæktiəriˈɔlisin] *n.*【微】溶菌素.

bac·te·ri·ol·y·sis [bækˌtiəriˈɔləsis] *n.*【微】溶菌(作用). **-ri·o·lyt·ic** *a.* [-ˌtiəriəˈlitik].

bac·te·ri·o·phage [bækˈtiəriəfeidʒ] *n.*【生】噬菌体.

bac·te·ri·os·co·py [bækˌtiəriˈɔskəpi] *n.* 细菌镜检法.

bac·te·ri·o·sta·sis, bac·te·ri·o·stat [ˌbæktiəriəˈsteisis, -əˈstæt] *n.*【生】制菌作用. **-o·stat·ic** [-əˈstætik] *a.*

bac·te·ri·o·ther·a·py [bækˌtiəriəuˈθerəpi] *n.*【医】细菌疗法.

bac·te·ri·um [bækˈtiəriəm] *n. (pl. bac·te·ri·a* [bækˈtiəriə]) 细菌〔单数不常用〕.

bac·te·rize [ˈbæktiraiz] *vt.* 使受细菌作用. **-ri·za·tion** *n.*

bac·te·roid [ˈbæktirɔid] *n.* 假菌体,变形细菌. — *a.* 细菌状的.

bac·te·roid·al [ˌbæktəˈrɔidl] *a.* 细菌状的.

Bac·tri·a [ˈbæktriə] *n.*【史】大夏〔即巴克特里亚王国,亚洲西部阿姆河与兴都库什山之间一古国〕.

Bac·tri·an [ˈbæktriən] *n., a.* 大夏〔巴克特里亚〕人(的). ~ **camel** 双峰骆驼.

ba·cu·li·form [bæˈkju:lifɔ:m] *a.* 杆状的,直的.

bac·u·line [ˈbækjulain] *a.* 棍棒的;笞刑的.

bac·u·lum [ˈbækjələm] *n. (pl. ~s, bac·u·la* [ˈbækjələ])

(哺乳动物的)阴茎骨.

bad[1] [bæd] *a.* ***(worse*** [wəːs]; ***worst*** [wəːst]***)*** ①坏的,恶的,歹的,不好的,不道德的. ②不正确的,错误的. ③不中用的;低劣的;拙劣的. ④不利的;有害的. ⑤腐败的;臭的. ⑥痛的,病的,不舒服的. ⑦使人不愉快的;懊恼的. ⑧严重的,厉害的. ⑨【法】不成立的;空名的. *a ~ blunder* 大错. *a ~ conductor* 不良导体. *a ~ conscience* (做坏事后的)内疚. *a ~ guess* 猜错. *a ~ light* 不充足的亮度,不适当的见解. *a ~ year* 不景气的一年. *~ for the health* 损害健康的. *~ for the stomach* 伤胃的. *~ habits* 坏习惯. *~ pains* 剧痛. *Bad drives cause ~ accidents.* 技术差的司机往往造成严重事故. *That's too ~.* 那太糟了;那太可惜了;那真过意不去. *~* ***actor*** 〔口〕坏人;难对付的动物;惯犯. *~* ***blood*** 恨,恶感;敌对情绪. *~* ***coin*** 劣币. *~* ***check*** 空头支票. *~* ***debts*** 倒帐,收不回来的债. *~* ***egg*** 坏蛋;〔俚〕混蛋,坏人. *~* ***hat*** 〔俚〕混蛋,坏蛋,歹徒. *~* ***language*** 骂人的话;下流话. *~* ***law*** 错误的定律. *~* ***lot*** (一个或一帮)坏家伙. *~* ***news*** 凶报,恶耗;〔美俚〕困难;麻烦的事[人];期票. *~* ***time*** 苦境. *~* ***trip*** 〔美俚〕(吸毒者的)恶性迷幻〔引起痛苦、恐怖的幻觉等〕. *~* ***woman*** 不正经的女人. ***be [be taken] ~*** 有病[生病] *(be ~ with gout* 患痛风病). ***be ~ at*** 不善于,…不行 (*be ~ at figures* 不擅长计算). ***be ~ for*** 对…有害,不适宜于 (*Smoking is ~ for health.* 吸烟对身体有害). ***feel ~*** 觉得不舒服;有病. ***feel ~ about*** 为…感到懊悔,为…觉得遗憾 (*feel ~ about an error* 为做错事感到懊悔). ***go ~*** (食物)变坏,腐败. ***have a ~ time (of it)*** 遭遇困难,倒霉,吃苦头. ***in a ~ way*** 〔口〕情况很不好;不景气;(健康)可虑. ***not (so,half) ~*** 不坏;不错 (*Not (so) ~.* 还不错,还好. *The boy is not half ~.* 这个男孩子还不错). — *n.* 恶劣状态,恶;不幸,倒霉. ***be in ~*** 〔美口〕倒霉;失宠 ***(with)*** (*He is in ~ with his father.* 他爸爸不喜欢他了). ***(go) from ~ to worse*** 越来越坏;每况愈下, 变本加厉. ***go to the ~*** ①变坏,堕落. ②衰败;落魄,一筹莫展. ③得病 (*She wept at seeing her son go to the ~.* 她为儿子的堕落痛哭流涕). ***to the ~*** 亏空,亏损,亏欠 (*I am six pounds to the ~.* 我亏损了六镑). ***with a ~ grace*** 勉强地,风度不佳地 *(He took his defeat with a ~ grace.* 他对自己的失败表现得不够有风度). —*ad.* 〔美口〕笨拙 (*Do you need money that ~?* 你那么缺钱用吗?). **~land** 邪恶横行地区[赌风猖獗、盗匪横行的地区]. **~lands** 〔*pl.*〕〔美〕荒原,荒瘠不毛地带. **~man** 偷牲口的贼;亡命徒;(美国早期西部)受雇用的带枪歹徒. **~mouth** *vt.* 诋毁,贬低;给…脸上黑;严厉批评. **~-neighbour policy** 恶邻政策,与邻国为敌的政策. **~-tempered** *a.* 脾气坏的,易怒的,暴躁的.

bad[2] [bæd] *v.* 〔古〕bid 的过去式.

Ba·da·ri·an [bɑːˈdɑːriən] *a.* 巴达里期的〔指上埃及新石器时代文化,特点是开始驯养家畜,制作精美陶器和品种繁多的装饰品〕.

Ba·der [ˈbɑːdə] *n.* 巴德〔姓氏〕.

bad·der·locks [ˈbædəˌlɔks] *n.*【植】翅菜.

bad·die [ˈbædi] *n.* 〔美口〕坏蛋〔尤指电影或小说中与主角为敌的恶人〕.

bad·dish [ˈbædiʃ] *a.* 次的,不甚好的;相当坏的.

bade [beid, bæd] bid 的过去式.

BADGE = Base Air Defense Ground Environment【美空军】基地防空地面警备系统.

badge [bædʒ] *n.* ①徽章,像章,奖章. ②标记;象征. *a ~ for rank* 军阶章[肩章,领章]. *a merit ~* 奖章. *a school ~* 校徽. *The pine is a ~ of constancy.* 松树是节操的象征.

badg·er[1] [ˈbædʒə] *n.* ①【动】獾,穴熊;獾皮,獾毛. ②〔美〕〔-B〕威斯康星州人. ***the B- State*** 〔美〕威斯康星州. *~* **game** 〔美口〕美人计. **~-legged** 两腿一长一短的.

badg·er[2] [ˈbædʒə] *n.* 〔方〕(卖食品的)小贩.

badg·er[3] [ˈbædʒə] *vt.* (一半开玩笑地)欺负,惹,撩;纠缠,使困恼;还(价). *Stop badgering me!* 别再缠我了!

bad·i·nage [ˈbædinɑːʒ] *n., vt.* 〔F.〕打趣,开玩笑,嘲弄.

bad·ly [ˈbædli] *ad.* ***(worse*** [wəːs]; ***worst*** [wəːst]***)*** ①坏,恶劣地. ②笨,拙劣地;不正确地. ③有害地. ④〔口〕严重地,厉害,非常. *He was ~ wounded.* 他受了重伤. *We need money ~ now.* 我们现在非常需要钱. ***be ~ off*** 景况不好,没钱,困穷;(感到)缺少. ★也作形容词用. ***feel ~*** 感到不舒服,有病. ***feel ~ about*** 对…感到遗憾[懊恼] (*I feel ~ about your leaving so soon.* 我对你这么早就走感到遗憾).

bad·min·ton [ˈbædmintən] *n.* ①羽毛球. ②(英国的一种)葡萄酒苏打水.

bad·ness [ˈbædnis] *n.* 坏,恶劣,不良,不正;不吉;严重.

Bae·de·ker [ˈbeidikə] *n.* (德国人 Karl ~ 于十九世纪出版的)旅行指南;(一般的)导游手册. *~* **raids** (1942 年)德军对英国一些历史名城的空袭.

baff [bæf] *n., vi.*【高尔夫球】刮地打(使球高飞).

baf·fle [ˈbæfl] *vt.* ①使受挫折,挫败,破坏,阻碍(计划、努力等). ②使困惑;使人为难;使迷惑. ③用隔音板隔(音). ④挡住(水流等). *These questions ~ me.* 这些问题使我无法回答. *~ description* 难以形容. *~ enemy's plan* 挫败敌方计划. *~ inquiry* 问不出,追究不出. *~ one's pursuer* 使追赶者扑空. — *vi.* 折腾;徒作挣扎. — *n.* ①迷惑. ②缓冲板;折流板;挡板,隔板;障板;栅极;反射板. ③遮护物;阻碍体.【军】迷彩. **~-board** (扬声器的)反射板;隔音板. **~gab** 〔美口〕冗长难解的谈话[文章]. *~* **painting** 〔美〕船舶的保护色.

baf·fling [ˈbæfliŋ] *a.* 起阻碍作用的;使…为难的;不能理解的,原因不明的. *a ~ man* 难以理解的人. *a detective's most ~ case* 难侦破的案件. *~* **wind** 方向无定的弱风.

baff·y [ˈbæfi] *n.* 木制短高尔夫球棒.

baft [bæft] *n.* 一种粗棉布. *~* **ribbon** (全由经纱胶粘成的)胶纱带.

bag [bæg] *n.* ①袋,囊;枕套. ②钱包;手提皮包;〔*pl.*〕财富. ③猎囊;猎获物. ④囊状物;【棒球】垒囊;(母牛、母羊等的)乳房;肿眼泡. ⑤〔美俚〕丑姑娘;妓女. ⑥〔*pl.*〕〔英俚〕大量,很多 ***(of)***;裤子;肚子,内脏;〔美〕阴囊. ⑦〔俚〕啤酒壶. ⑧〔口〕专长,爱好. ⑨〔口〕情绪;境遇. ⑩个人特有的生活方式[习惯]. ⑪〔美俚〕(一包)毒品. *~* ***and baggage*** ①全部所有物. ②总的,整个地. (*The equipment had disappeared ~ and baggage.* 那台设备全部失踪了). *~* ***of bones*** 瘦骨嶙峋的人[动物]. ***a ~ of wind*** 夸夸其谈的人. *~* ***worm***【动】袋虫. ***~s of*** 〔俚〕许多. ***bear the ~*** 掌管银钱,握经济权. ***empty the ~*** 倒空袋子;〔口〕和盘托出;把话说完说尽. ***get the ~*** 〔口〕被解雇[辞退]. ***give sb. the ~*** 解雇[辞退]某人;给(求婚人)碰钉子. ***give [leave] sb. the ~ to hold*** 困难时丢弃别人,使别人承担责任[背黑锅]. ***green [blue] ~*** (英国)律师用的公事包. ***hold the ~*** 〔美口〕分得最差的一份;独自一人承担本应与他人共同承担的全部责任. ***in the ~*** 〔俚〕已是囊中物;拿在手里,掌握着;十拿九稳的;〔俚〕喝醉了的. ***in the bottom of the ~*** 最后一手. ***make a ~ of*** 捕获,消灭. ***put sb. in a ~*** 占某人上风,制胜某人. ***set one's ~ for*** 〔美〕对…抱有野心;追逐某人[某物]. ***the whole ~ of tricks*** 一切手段;一肚皮的诡计. — *vt.* ①把…装进袋里,偷窃;私吞,吞没. ②捕获;击落,杀. ③使成袋状,使膨胀. — *vi.* ①膨胀[下垂]如囊. ②怀孕. *~* ***a title*** 〔美俚〕获得锦标. *~* ***a win*** 〔美俚〕竞赛得胜. — *int.* 〔说作 Bags!〕〔英口〕是我的;该我先来[先得等]! *Bags, I go first!* 是我的,我先来. *Bags I (first drink)!* 我先(喝)! *Bags I the corner!* (小孩玩抢位游戏时)这个角落是我的! *~* **fox** 用袋装带到猎场放出使猎狗追逐的狐狸. *~* **guy** 〔美〕卖气球的. *~* **job** (对间谍活动证据的)非法搜查.

~**play** *vt.* 巴结，拍…的马屁．~**wig**（十八世纪流行的）袋装假发．

B. Ag. = Bachelor of Agriculture 农学士．

ba·gasse [bəˈgæs] *n.*〔F.〕蔗渣．

bag·a·telle [ˌbægəˈtel] *n.*〔F.〕①琐事；小玩艺儿．②短小的乐曲，短钢琴曲．③九穴台球〔一种类似桌上高尔夫球的球戏〕．*To him money is a* ~．金钱对他来说不算一回事．

Bag·dad, Bagh·dad [bægˈdæd] *n.* 巴格达〔伊拉克首都〕．

ba·gel [ˈbeigl] *n.* 过水面包圈〔发面圈经滚开的水煮然后烤成〕．

bag·ful [ˈbægful] *n.* ①满口袋，一袋．②相当多．

bag·gage [ˈbægidʒ] *n.* ①〔美〕（手提）行李〔英国叫 luggage〕；【军】军用行李，辎重．②精神包袱；多余的东西；过时货．③〔口、旧〕荡妇，淫妇；妓女；〔现指〕轻佻的女人〔又叫 impudent ~〕．**excess** ~ 超重行李．*a large amount of* ~ 一大堆行李．*a piece of* ~ 一件行李．~ **allowance**〔美〕行李重量限度．~ **car**〔美〕行李车厢；【军】辎重车．~ **check**〔美〕行李票，行李上的牌子．~**man**〔美〕行李房办事人员．~**master**〔美〕行李处处长；辎重队长．~ **office** 行李房．~**-smasher**〔美俚〕（车站的）行李搬运员〔乱摔行李者之意〕．~ **stock**〔美〕搬运马戏团行李等的驮马．

bagged [bægd] *a.*〔俚〕①喝醉酒的；沉醉的．②松弛下垂的．

bag·ger [ˈbægə] *n.* ①装袋人；装袋器．②【棒球】…垒打．③泥斗，掘泥机．*two [three]* ~ 二[三]垒打．

bag·ging [ˈbægiŋ] *n.* ①袋布，袋料．②装袋，装包．

bag·gy [ˈbægi] *a.* ***(-gi·er; -gi·est)*** 膨胀如袋的；宽大的，松弛下垂的．

Bagh·dad = Bagdad.

bag·man [ˈbægmən] *n.*〔英〕小贩，行商；〔美〕检信员；〔美俚〕舞弊者；行贿、赌博等的钱财收送经手人；诈骗钱财的小流氓．

bagn·io [ˈbɑːnjəu] *n.* ***(pl. ~s)*** ①（意大利、土耳其的）澡堂．②〔古〕（土耳其等的）牢狱．③妓院．

bag·pipe(s) [ˈbægpaip(s)] *n.* ①风笛．②【无】人为干扰发射机．

bag·pip·er [ˈbægpaipə] *n.* 吹风笛的人．

ba·guet(te) [bæˈget] *n.* ①狭长方形钻石[宝石]．②狭长方形．③【建】小凸圆体花饰．

bah [bɑː] *int.* 呸！〔表示轻蔑、厌恶等〕．— *vt.* 嘲笑．

ba·ha·dur [bəˈhɑːdə] *n.*〔印〕阁下〔印度人加在姓名或官职前的尊称〕．

Ba·hai [ˈbəhai, bəˈhɑːi] *n.* ***(pl. ~s)*** ①巴哈派教徒．②= Bahaism. — *a.* 巴哈派教义的．

Ba·ha·ism [bəˈhɑːizəm] *n.*【宗】巴哈派教义〔源出伊朗十九世纪的一个穆斯林教派，主张四海之内皆兄弟、社会平等等〕．**Ba·ha·ist** *n., a.* 巴哈派信徒(的)．

Ba·ha·ma(s) [bəˈhɑːmə(z)] *n.* 巴哈马〔拉丁美洲〕．

Ba·ha·mi·an [bəˈhɑːmiən] *a.* 巴哈马群岛的．— *n.* 巴哈马群岛的本地居民．

Bah·rein, Bah·rain [bɑːˈrein] *n.* 巴林〔亚洲〕．

baht [bɑːt] *n.* ***(pl. ~(s))*** ①铢〔泰国的货币名称〕．②铢的硬币．

Ba·hu·tu [bəhuːˈtuː] *n.* ***(pl. ~(s))*** ①布隆迪和卢旺达农民．②班图语．

bai·gnoire [ˈbeinwɑː] *n.*〔F.〕（戏院中与厅座同一层的）大厅包厢．

Bai·kal [baiˈkɑːl] **Lake** 贝加尔湖〔苏联〕．

bail[1] [beil] *n.*【法】保释金；保释人；保释．***accept [allow, take]*** ~准许保释．***admit [let] (sb.) to*** ~ 准许（某人）保释．***give*** ~（被告）缴保释金．***give leg*** ~ (= take leg ~)．***go*** ~ ***for*** 做（某人）的保释人；〔喻〕保证，担保．***I'll go*** ~ ***that*** ...〔口〕我肯定…．***jump*** ~ = skip ~．***offer*** ~ = give ~．***on*** ~, ***out on*** ~ 在保释中．***refuse*** ~（法官）不准保释．***save [forfeit] one's*** ~ 保释后如期出庭[不出庭]．***skip*** ~ 保释中逃跑．***take*** ~ 允许保释．***take leg*** ~〔口、谑〕逃走；溜掉．— *vt.* ①【法】准许保释；为…做保释人；救出．②帮助…摆脱困境．③将（财物）委托给…．~ ***out*** 保释（被告）；委托（货物）．~ **bond** 保释保证书．~ **jumper** 从保释中逃亡的嫌疑犯．

bail[2] [beil] *n.* 水斗〔戽出船肚水用〕．— *vt., vi.* 舀（水），从（船中）戽出水．~ *water out of a boat* = ~ *out a boat.* 戽出船肚里的水．~ ***out***〔俚〕（从飞机上）跳伞．

bail[3] [beil] *n.*【板球】三柱门上的横木；【史】（欧洲中世纪）城堡的外围工事；城堡的内院；（马厩的）栅栏；【无】轨，排．

bail[4] [beil] *n.*（篷帐的）半圆形支撑箍；（桶、壶等的）半圆形拎环；（打字机上把纸张压在滚筒上的）夹紧箍．

bail·a·ble [ˈbeiləbl] *a.*【法】可保释的．

bail·ee [beiˈliː] *n.*【法】（财物的）受委托人．

bail·er [ˈbeilə] *n.* ①掏船肚水的人；水斗；泥浆泵．②【板球】打中三柱门横木的球．

Bai·ley [ˈbeili] *n.* 贝利〔姓氏，男子名〕．***(the) Old*** ~ 伦敦中央刑事法院．~ **bridge**【军】活动便桥，军用轻便桥．

bai·ley [ˈbeili] *n.* ①城郭，外栅．②（欧洲中世纪）城堡外墙．

bai·lie [ˈbeili] *n.* ①〔Scot.〕市高级行政官．②〔方〕= bailiff.

bai·liff [ˈbeilif] *n.* ①法警；执行官；监守者．②〔英〕地主管家．③【英史】镇长，低级地区行政官．*a water* ~ 取缔秘密打鱼的水上巡警．

bai·li·wick [ˈbeiliwik] *n.* ①执行官的职权范围〔管辖区〕．②〔美〕个人活动〔兴趣、职权〕范围；最擅长的范围，专长．

bail·ment [ˈbeilmənt] *n.*【法】（财物的）委托；保释．*a contract of* ~ 委托契约．

bail·or [ˈbeilə] *n.*【法】（财物的）委托人．

bail·out [ˈbeilaut] *n.* 紧急跳伞．— *a.* 应付紧急状况的．

bails·man [ˈbeilzmən] *n.* 保释人．

Bain [bein] *n.* 贝恩〔姓氏〕．

bain·ite [ˈbeinait] *n.*【冶】贝菌体，贝氏体．

bain-ma·rie [bænməˈriː] *n.* ***(pl. bains-ma·rie)*** 隔水炖锅；水浴器．

Bai·ram [baiˈrɑːm] *n.* 拜兰节〔伊斯兰教节日，一年两次〕．

bairn [bɛən] *n.*〔Scot.〕幼儿，小孩．

bait [beit] *n.* ①饵；引诱物；诱惑．②（路上的）休息（或进食）．*jump at the* ~ 轻易上当．*poison* ~ 毒饵．*rise to a* ~（鱼）上钩；（人）上当．*swallow the* ~ 吞饵上钩；落进圈套．*a white* ~ 银鱼．— *vt.* ①把饵装到…上；引诱．②（在路上）喂（马）．③使狗逗（熊等）；欺负（人）；作弄（人）．~ *a hook* 给钓钩装饵．— *vi.*（在路上）休息（或吃东西）．~ **advertizing**〔美口〕诱售广告〔在广告上刊登实际上并不出售的廉价商品，以招徕顾客至本店购买昂贵商品〕．~**-and-switch**〔美口〕*a.* 诱售法的．

baize [beiz] *n.* 桌面呢．— *vt.* 用桌面呢做…的衬底；在…上铺桌面呢．

bake [beik] *vt.* ①烘，焙，烤，烧．②焙干，烧硬，烧固．~ *pottery in a kiln* 在窑内烧陶器．— *vi.* 烤面包[饼等]；烤熟；烘干；（砖等）在焙干中．— *n.* 烘，焙，烤；烘烤的成品；〔美〕烧烤会餐．

Bak·er [ˈbeikə] *n.* 贝克〔姓氏〕．

bak·er [ˈbeikə] *n.* ①面包师傅．②〔美〕轻便烤箱．~***'s*** *dozen* 十三．~***'s*** *salt* 碳酸铵〔制面包用〕．~***'s*** *yeast* 面包酵母．***spell*** ~〔美俚〕做难事．~**-kneed** *a.* 膝头内曲的，对鸡脚的．~**-legged** *a.* (=~-kneed)．

bak·er·y [ˈbeikəri] *n.* 面包糕点饼干厂[铺]．

bake·house [ˈbeikhaus] *n.* 面包厂；面包店．

ba·ke·lite [ˈbeikəlait] *n.*【商标】酚醛塑料[树脂]，电木，胶木．~ **varnish** 胶木漆．

bake-shop [ˈbeikʃɔp] *n.* 〔美〕面包铺；面包烘房（= bakery）.

bak·ing [ˈbeikiŋ] *n.* 烘烤（面包等），焙烘. — *a.* 烘烤的，灼热的. ～ *heat* 炎热. ～ **powder** 发（酵）粉，焙粉〔化学膨松剂〕. ～ **soda** 小苏打，碳酸氢钠.

bak·la·va [ˌbɑːkləˈvɑː] *n.* （希腊、土耳其的）果仁蜜馅点心.

bak·sheesh, bak·shish [ˈbækʃiːʃ] *n.* ①（土耳其、埃及等地的）小费，酒钱，小帐，赏金. ②〔美空军俚〕（不遇敌机时的）容易差事.

Ba·ku [bɑːˈkuː] *n.* 巴库〔苏联城市〕.

Ba·ku·nin [bɑːˈkuːnin], **Mi·kha·il A·le·ksan·dro·vich** [mixɑːˈiːl ˌɑːlekˈsɑːndrɑvitʃ] 巴枯宁〔1814—1876，俄国无政府主义者，作家〕.

ba·laam [ˈbeilæm] *n.* ①〔B-〕【圣】遭驴子责备的先知. ②不可靠的预言者〔伙伴〕. ③〔英俚〕（报章杂志上的）补白备用资料；作废或不用的稿件. ～ **box** 废稿箱.

Bal·a·kla·va, Bal·a·cla·va [ˌbæləˈklɑːvə] *n.* ①巴拉克拉瓦〔苏联黑海一港口〕. ②〔b-〕大绒帽. ～ **helmet** 〔英〕大毡盔.

bal·a·lai·ka [ˌbæləˈlaikə] *n.* 俄国巴拉拉伊卡琴〔三角琴〕.

bal·ance [ˈbæləns] *n.* ①〔常作 a pair of ～s〕天平，秤. ②平衡，均衡，对称；抵销；比较，对照，对比. ③（钟表的）平衡轮，摆轮. ④平衡块，平衡力. ⑤【商】收付平衡〔差额〕；余额；找头，尾数. ⑥〔B-〕【天】天平座，天平宫. ⑦（情绪的）稳定，镇静. ⑧（艺术作品中）布局和比例的协调. ⑨〔美口〕〔the ～〕剩余部分. *You may keep the* ～. 尾数〔找头等〕你收下好了. *The* ～ *of the account is against me.* 两抵下来是我欠人. *a favorable* 〔*an unfavorable*〕 ～ *of trade* 顺〔逆〕差；贸易出〔入〕超. ～ ***due*** 帐簿中贷方超过借方的数. ～ ***on hand*** 帐簿中借方超过贷方的数. ～ ***of accounts*** 对帐. ～ ***of clearing*** 汇划结算余额. ～ ***of (international) payment*** 国际收支差额，国际收支. ～ ***of power*** 力量对比；力量均势. ～ ***of trade*** 贸易〔输出入〕差额. ***be (thrown) off one's*** ～ 失去平衡；摔倒；张皇失措；烦恼. ***be out of*** ～ 在不平衡状态下. ***hang in the*** ～ = tremble in the ～. ***hold in*** ～ 悬置未决. ***hold the*** ～ 掌握决定权；举足轻重. ***in*** 〔***on***〕 ～ 总的来说. ***in the*** ～ 犹豫未决，忐忑不安. ***keep one's*** ～ 保持身体平衡；镇定. ***lose one's*** ～ 身体失去平衡，摔倒；慌乱. ***on (the)*** ～ 两抵，结果. ***redress the*** ～ 公平处理〔调整〕. ***strike a*** ～ 结帐；衡量得失，作出结论. ***throw sb. off his*** ～ 使（某人）失去身体平衡，使摔倒；扰乱，使（某人）狼狈不堪. ***tremble in the*** ～ 处于紧要关头，吉凶未决. — *vt.* ①（用天平等）秤. ②使均等，使平衡. ③比较，对照；权衡，斟酌. ④和…相抵；两抵；抵销. ⑤结算，清（帐）. — *vi.* ①平衡，均等. ②收支平衡. ③踌躇；摇摆不定. ④（舞蹈）作摇摆动作. *a* ～*d criticism* 实事求是的批评. *a balancing plane* 【空】安定翼面；平衡翼. *a balancing test* 【空】平衡试验. ～ *accounts* 使收支平衡；结帐. ～ *the book* 结清各帐. ～ ***oneself*** 保持身体平衡. ～ ***out*** 【物】衡消. ～ **account** 【商】差额账. ～ **beam** 【体】平衡木. ～ **bridge** 开启桥. ～ **sheet** 【商】资产负债表，资金平衡表. ～ **wheel** 平衡轮，轮摆；均衡轮.

bal·ance·a·ble [ˈbælənsəbl] *a.* 可秤的；可平均的，可使平衡的.

bal·anced [ˈbælənst] *a.* ①平衡的；稳定的. ②和谐的；有条不紊的. ～ **diet** （营养）均衡的食谱. ～ **sentence** 【语法】平衡句〔由两个平行的从句构成〕. ～ **yarn** 【纺】不卷缩纱线.

bal·anc·er [ˈbælənsə] *n.* ①权衡者；平衡物. ②走钢丝演员. ③（双翅类昆虫的）平衡器.

bal·as [ˈbæləs] *n.* 【矿】玫瑰红尖晶石，浅红晶石.

bal·a·ta [ˈbælətə] *n.* ①（西印度）巴拉塔树. ②（能在热水中软化的）无弹性树胶（= ～ gum）.

Bal·bo·a [bælˈbəuə] *n.* ①V.N.de ～ 巴波亚（1475?—1517），西班牙探险家，西方太平洋发现人. ②巴波亚〔巴拿马运河西端港口〕. ③〔b-〕巴波亚〔巴拿马的一种硬币〕.

bal·brig·gan [bælˈbrigən] *n.* ①巴尔布里根棉织品〔爱尔兰织品名，用以做袜子、内衣等〕. ②〔*pl.*〕巴尔布里根织品服装. — *a.* 巴尔布里根织品制的.

bal·co·nied [ˈbælkənid] *a.* 有阳台的.

bal·co·ny [ˈbælkəni] *n.* ①露台，阳台. ②（剧场二楼）楼座〔gallery 之下，dress circle 之上〕. ③舰尾望台.

bald [bɔːld] *a.* ①秃（头）的；【动】白头的. ②无毛的；无叶的；无树的；无芒的. ③无装饰的；单调的，枯燥的. ④赤裸裸的，毫无掩饰的. *the* ～ *wheat* 裸麦. *the* ～ *eagle* 【动】（北美）白头海雕. *a* ～ *mountain* 童山，秃山. *a* ～ *lie* 睁着眼睛说瞎话. ～ **coot** （= baldicoot）. ～ **cypress** 【植】落羽杉. ～**face** 〔美俚〕劣等威士忌酒. ～**-faced** *a.* （动物）脸上有白斑的；厚颜无耻的. ～**head** ①秃头的人. ②一种家鸽. ～**-headed** ①*a.* 秃头的，秃顶的. （*go* ～*headed for* 〔*at, into*〕 冒险向…突进）. ②*ad.* 〔口〕鲁莽地. ～**pate** ①秃头的人. ②赤颈凫（=widgeon）.

bal·da·chin, bal·da·quin [ˈbɔːldəkin] *n.* ①锦缎. ②（祭坛或宝座上的）华盖. ③【建】龛室.

bal·der·dash [ˈbɔːldədæʃ] *n.* ①梦呓，胡言乱语，妄语. ②〔废〕劣酒.

bal·d(i)·coot [ˈbɔːld(i)kuːt] *n.* ①【鸟】骨顶鸟，大鹞. ②秃子；和尚.

bald·ing [ˈbɔːldiŋ] *a.* 〔口〕变秃的. *a* ～ *head* 头发日稀.

bald·ish [ˈbɔːldiʃ] *a.* 快秃的，略秃的.

bald·ly [ˈbɔːldli] *ad.* 直言不讳地，坦率地. ***put it*** ～ 直言不讳地写〔讲〕；直截了当地说.

bald·ness [ˈbɔːldnis] *n.* ①秃，秃头. ②毫无掩饰；露骨.

bal·dric [ˈbɔːldrik] *n.* （悬挂剑、号角等的）饰带，肩带；胸绶.

Bald·win [ˈbɔːldwin] *n.* 鲍德温〔姓氏〕.

bal·dy [ˈbɔːldi] *n.* 〔美俚〕秃子.

bale[1] [beil] *n.* ①大包，大捆；多量. ②〔*pl.*〕货物. ③龟群. *a* ～ *of cotton* 一包棉花. *a* ～ *of hay* 一捆干草. — *vt.* 把…打包. *a baling press* 打包机.

bale[2] [beil] *n.* 〔古、诗〕祸，灾害；不幸；痛苦；悲叹.

bale[3] [beil] *vt.,vi.* = bail[2].

ba·leen [bəˈliːn] *n.* 【动】鲸须.

bale·fire [ˈbeilfaiə] *n.* （户外的）大火堆，大篝火；焚尸火；烽火.

bale·ful [ˈbeilful] *a.* ①有害的，破坏性的；恶毒的. ②〔古〕悲惨的.

Bal·four [ˈbælfuə] *n.* 巴尔弗〔姓氏〕.

Ba·li [ˈbɑːli] *n.* 巴厘（岛）〔印度尼西亚〕.

Ba·li·nese [ˌbɑːliˈniːz, ˌbæliˈniːz] *a.* 巴厘（岛）的；巴厘人的；巴厘语的；巴厘文化的. — *n.* ①（*pl.* ～）巴厘人. ②巴厘语.

balk, baulk [bɔːk] *n.* ①障碍，阻碍，妨碍. ②失败；错误，过失，挫折. ③田埂. ④【体】波克〔运动员跑过起跳线以后又退回另跳〕；【棒球】（投球员的）假投；【台球】波克线与台边之间的部分. ⑤【建】圆方料，梁木；【机】（多臂机的）摆动杆；【军】浮桥长梁；【矿】煤层中的岩石包裹体. *a* ～ *to traffic* 交通妨碍. *make a* ～ *of good ground* 失去好机会. — *vt.* ①使受挫折；阻碍. ②〔古〕忽视；避免；逃避. — *vi.* ①突然停止，急止. ②（马等）逡巡不前；畏缩不前. ***be*** ～***ed of*** （希望等）受挫折，为…所阻，打破. ***do not*** ～ ***at*** 不惜，不避. ***never*** ～ ***at*** 对…在所不惜. ～ **back** 绒背呢. ～**line** ①【体】波克线，田赛起点线，起跳线. ②【台球】发球线；波克线〔与台边平行的四条井字线〕.

Bal·kan [ˈbɔːlkən] *n.* 巴尔干（半岛）. ***the*** ～***s*** ①巴尔干山脉. ②巴尔干国家（= the ～ states） — *a.* 巴尔干半岛（山脉）的；巴尔干各国（人）的. ～ **frame** （医治骨折的）吊架. **-ite** *n.* 巴尔干人.

Bal·kan·ize [ˈbɔːlkənaiz] *vt.* 使巴尔干化；使割据；使分裂成互相敌对的小国. **-za·tion** *n.* 巴尔干化.

balk·y [ˈbɔːki] *a.* 〔美〕执拗的，顽劣的，不愿意干的；逡巡不前的；(马)爱突然站住不走的.

Ball [bɔːl] *n.* 鲍尔〔姓氏〕.

ball[1] [bɔːl] *n.* ①球；球状物. ②球戏，(特指)棒球；【棒球】坏球 (*opp.* strike). ③【军】子弹，炮弹. ④(人体上的)圆形突出部分. ⑤眼球. ⑥〔俚〕〔*pl.*〕睾丸，〔喻〕胡说. ⑦【兽医】丸剂，丸药. ⑧【烹】肉〔鱼等〕丸子；面(粉)团. ⑨【天】星球，天体；(特指)地球. ⑩〔the ～〕(企业等的)管理权. ⑪〔俚〕人，家伙. *a ～ of string* 一团绳子. *the earthly ～* 地球. *The ～ is with you.* 该你发球了；轮到你了. *an advance ～* (录音机里的)滑动滚珠. *a spent ～* 死弹〔冲力已尽的子弹〕. ***a ～ of fire*** 一团火；〔美〕精力奋发的学生〔实干家〕；〔美俚〕特别快车. ***a ～ of fortune*** 命途多舛的人. ***～ of the eye*** 眼球. ***～ of the foot [thumb]*** 拇趾〔拇指〕底部的肉球. ***be on the ～*** 〔美俚〕精力奋发地干；熟习内情. ***carry the ～*** 〔口〕负责. ***catch [take] the ～ before the bound*** 抢接飞球；先发制人. ***Get on the ～!*** 〔美俚〕灵敏一些! ***have nothing on the ～*** 〔美俚〕毫无本领. ***have something [a lot, much] on the ～*** 〔美俚〕有点本事. ***have the ～ at one's feet [before one]*** 机会就在眼前. ***keep the ～ rolling [up]*** 不使(谈话)中断，不使(事业)中辍. ***make a ～ of*** 把…弄糟. ***no ～*** 【板球】犯规的球. ***on the ～*** 机灵，灵敏. ***play at ～*** 打球. ***play ～*** 打球，开始赛球；开始活动；合作，共事；行事公道. ***put [leave] the ～ in sb.'s court*** 把球踢到某人场地上〔逼他作出反应〕. ***take up the ～*** 接下来讲；轮到，接替. ***three golden [brass] ～*** 三个金〔铜〕球〔当铺的标识〕. — *vt.* 使成球；把…抟成丸. — *vi.* ①成球形. ***be (all) ～ed up*** 〔美俚〕混乱；着慌，不知所措，说不出话来. ～ ***and chain*** 〔美〕附有铁球的脚镣，束缚. 〔喻〕妻，老婆. ～ ***and socket*** 球窝关节. ～ **bearings** 滚珠轴承. ～ **firing** 实弹射击. ～ **game** ①球戏〔尤指棒球〕. ②〔美俚〕活动中心〔领域〕；情况，形势. ～ **cartridge** 实弹. ～ **cock** 浮球活栓. ～ **control** (篮球、足球比赛中拖延时间的)终场控球战术. ～**-flower**【建】球心花饰，花球. ～ **lightning** 球状电闪，电火球. ～ **park** 棒球〔垒球〕场. ～ **player** 棒球〔垒球〕手. ～ **pen**, ～**-point pen** 圆珠笔. ～**proof** *a.* 避弹的. ～ **turret** (战斗机枪手的)球形座位. ～ **valve** (浮)球阀，球闸门，漂子门.

ball[2] [bɔːl] *n.* 跳舞会；〔俚〕狂欢会. *give a ～* 开跳舞会(招待宾客). ***have a ～*** 〔美俚〕狂欢作乐. ***lead the ～*** 领导跳舞；开始行动. ***open the ～*** 开始舞；领头做，取攻势. — *vi.* 〔美俚〕狂欢，尽情作乐；与…发生性关系 (*with*). ～**room** 舞厅 (*～room dancing* 交际舞).

bal·lad [ˈbæləd] *n.* ①民谣，歌谣，小调. ②【乐】叙事曲. ～ **metre**【韵】民谣调. ～**-monger** 民谣作者；民谣歌本叫卖人；〔蔑〕蹩脚诗人，打油诗作者. ～ **stanza** 歌谣的诗节〔通常为4行，押 abcb 韵〕.

bal·lade [bæˈlɑːd] *n.* 〔F.〕①【韵】三解韵格〔由八行句三节及四行跋词形成的法国诗体〕. ②配乐民谣. ③【乐】(为钢琴等独奏谱写的)拟叙事乐曲. ～ *royal* 各行由十音节形成的七〔八〕行诗体.

bal·lad·eer [bæləˈdiə] *n.* 民谣歌手；民谣作者.

bal·lad·rom·ic [ˌbæləˈdrɔmik] *a.* (火箭、导弹的)准确飞向目标的.

bal·lad·ry [ˈbælədri] *n.* ①〔集合词〕民谣. ②民谣创作.

bal·last [ˈbæləst] *n.* ①镇重物，压载物，压舱物，底货(石、沙等)；(轻气球的)沙囊. ②【铁路】道碴，道床. ③【电】镇流电阻，镇流器. ④使(性格)坚定的经验〔道德等〕，稳定因素；〔喻〕沉着，稳定. ***in ～*** 【海】只装底货；只装(沙、石等)压舱物. — *vt.* 在…上装压舱物〔沙囊〕；为(铁路等)铺道碴；使稳定，使沉着. **-ing** *n.* ①装底货，铺道碴. ②压舱材料；道碴材料.

bal·le·ri·na [ˌbæləˈriːnə] *n.* (*pl.* ***bal·le·ri·ne*** [ˌbæləˈriːni]) 〔It.〕(芭蕾舞)女演员〔尤指女主角〕.

bal·let [ˈbælei; Am. bæˈlei] *n.* ①芭蕾舞，舞剧. ②芭蕾舞剧团. ③芭蕾舞音乐. ～ **blan** (女演员穿白色裙的)白裙芭蕾. ～ **dancer** 芭蕾舞女演员，舞剧演员. ～**-skirt** 芭蕾舞裙.

bal·let·o·mane [bæˈletəmein] *n.* 芭蕾舞迷.

bal·let·o·ma·ni·a [bæˌletəˈmeinjə] *n.* 芭蕾舞狂.

bal·lism [ˈbælizm] *n.* 【医】颤搐 (=ballismus).

bal·lis·mus [bæˈlizməs] *n.* 【医】舞蹈病，颤搐.

bal·lis·ta [bəˈlistə] *n.* (*pl.* ***bal·lis·tae*** [bəˈlistiː]) 〔L.〕(古代的)弩炮，投石器.

bal·lis·tic [bəˈlistik] *a.* 弹道(学)的；发射(技术)的. ～ **curve** 弹道曲线. ～ **missile** 弹道导弹. ～ **pendulum**【物】冲击摆. ～ **rocket** 弹道火箭. ～ **trajectory** (火箭的)放射弹道.

bal·lis·ti·cian [ˌbælisˈtiʃən] *n.* 弹道学家；发射体设计家.

bal·lis·tics [bəˈlistiks] *n.* ①【军】弹道学；(谋求最远飞行距离的)发射体设计学〔技术〕. ②(火器、弹药等的)发射特性. *rocket ～* 火箭〔导弹〕弹道学.

bal·lis·tite [ˈbælistait] *n.* 混合无烟火药〔原为商标名〕.

bal·lis·to·car·di·o·graph [bəˌlistəuˈkɑːdiəugrɑːf] *n.* 【医】投影心搏计.

bal·lon d'es·sai [balɔ̃ desɛ] 〔F.〕试风向的小气球；〔喻〕(对舆论等的)试探.

bal·lo·net [ˌbæləˈnet] *n.* 〔F.〕①小气球. ②小气囊，(飞船的)气室.

bal·loon [bəˈluːn] *n.* ①轻气球，气球；气罐. ②【纺】气圈. ③【建】球饰. ④【化】球形大烧瓶. ⑤(漫画中人物的)讲话引线. *a captive ～* 系留气球. *a dirigible ～* 可操纵气球，飞船. *an observation ～* (射弹)观测用气球. *a sounding ～* 探测气球. — *vi.* ①用〔坐〕气球上升. ②膨胀如气球. ③激增. ④〔美〕(演员)忘记台词. — *vt.* 使充气，使膨胀如气球. *a ～ing eye* 【纺】导纱钩. — *a.* ①气球状的. ②(货物等)分量轻而体积大的. ③(分期付款)最后一笔大数目的. ～ **barrage** 气球防空网. ～ **construction** 轻捷型构造. ～**fish** 河豚. ～ **score** 〔美〕运动比赛的高分. ～ **tire** 低压(汽车)轮胎；〔美俚〕(演员)下眼皮松弛. **-ing** 气球驾驶；气泡上升；【军】飞机拉飘；【商】股票上涨. **-ist** *n.* 气球驾驶人.

bal·lot [ˈbælət] *n.* ①投票用纸，选票；投票用小球. ②无记名投票. ③投票；投票权. ④投票总数. ⑤抽签. ⑥候选人名单. ⑦〔美〕决定总统候选人的选举. *take a secret ～* 举行无记名投票. *vote by ～* 投票表决. *elected by ～* 投票选举. ***cast a single ～*** 〔美〕造成一致通过的现象. — *vi.* ①投票，投票表决 (*for; against*). ②拈阄，抽签. — *vt.* ①通过投票〔抽签〕选出. ②向…拉票. ～**box** 投票箱. ～**paper** 投票用纸.

bal·lot·age [balɔtaːʒ] 〔F.〕决选投票〔对得票最多而又均未达到决定多数的几名候选人再次投票决选〕.

bal·lotte·ment [bəˈlɔtmənt] *n.* 【医】①反击触诊. ②按胎法. ③摸腹壁检查浮肾法.

bal·lute [bəˈluːt] *n.* (宇宙飞船的)减速气球，气球式降落伞.

bal·ly [ˈbæli] *a., ad.* 〔英俚〕讨厌，非常，极，究竟. ★这是 bloody 的代用语，语气较委婉. *too ～ tired* 疲倦极了. *Whose ～ fault is that?* 究竟是谁不好?

bal·ly·hack [ˈbælihæk] *n.* 〔美俚〕毁灭，灭亡，地狱. ***go to ～*** 滚蛋! 去他的!

bal·ly·hoo [ˈbælihuː] *n.* 〔美俚〕①哗众取宠、大吹大擂的广告〔文章，演说〕. ②喧闹，吵吵嚷嚷，宣传. *a ～ artist* 善于自吹的人. *～ in the street* 街头的喧闹声. — [bæliˈhu] *vi.* 大肆宣传. — *vt.* 为…大吹大擂.

bal·ly·rag [ˈbæliræg] *vt., vi.* 〔俚〕虐待，欺负，折磨，戏弄，骂.

balm [bɑːm] *n.* ①香油，香脂，香膏. ②芳香，香味. ③止

痛药，镇痛剂；〔喻〕安慰物．④【植】滇荆芥；白壳杨．— *vt.* ①在…上搽香油．②安抚，安慰．③止(痛)．～ **cricket** 蝉．

bal·ma·caan [ˌbælməˈkɑːn] *n.* 粗呢套袖大衣．

Bal·mor·al [bælˈmɔrəl] *n.* ①巴莫拉尔宫〔英国 Victoria 女皇在苏格兰的离宫〕．②斜纹呢衬裙．③苏格兰厚呢无边便帽．④〔b-〕一种镶花边的靴子[鞋子]．

balm·y [ˈbɑːmi] *a.* ①芬芳的，有香气的；香脂味的．②止痛的，安慰的．③(气候等)温和的．④〔俚〕笨的，愚鲁的；〔英〕轻狂的．

bal·ne·al [ˈbælniəl] *a.* 关于洗澡的；关于浴室的．

bal·ne·ol·o·gy [ˌbæniˈɔlədʒi] *n.* 【医】浴疗学，矿泉疗养学．

bal·neo·therapy [ˌbælniəˈθerəpi] *n.* 【医】浴疗法．

Ba·lo·ney Bou·le·vard [bəˈləuni ˈbuːlivɑː] *n.* 美国纽约 Broadway 的别名．

ba·lo·ney [bəˈləuni] *n.* ①〔口〕大香肠．②＝boloney．～**dollar** 〔美口〕劣质金元．

bal·sa [ˈbɔːlsə] *n.* 〔Sp.〕①西印度轻木 *(Ochroma lagopus)*．②轻木材．③救生筏．

bal·sam [ˈbɔːlsəm] *n.* ①香液，香脂，香膏；枞胶．②镇痛剂；安慰物．③产香脂的植物．④【植】香脂冷杉；凤仙花；凤仙花属植物．⑤〔美俚〕金钱．*the garden* ～ 凤仙花．— *vt.* 在…上搽香膏；安慰，止(痛)．～ **fir** 胶枞；胶冷杉．～ **pear [apple]** 苦瓜．

bal·sam·ic [bɔːlˈsæmik] *a.* ①香膏质的，香脂一样的．②止痛的；安慰的．

bal·sam·if·er·ous [ˌbɔːlsəˈmifərəs] *a.* 产生香液〔香脂〕的．

bal·sam·ine [ˈbɔːsəmin] *n.* 【植】凤仙花．

Bal·tic [ˈbɔːltik] *a.* 波罗的海的．*the* ～ *Sea* 波罗的海．

Bal·ti·more [ˈbɔːltimɔː] *n.* 巴尔的摩〔美国马里兰州一港口〕．

Bal·to-Sla·vic [ˈbɔːltəuˈslɑːvik, -ˈslæv-] *n.* 波罗的—斯拉夫语族．— *a.* 波罗的—斯拉夫语族的．

Ba·lu·chi [bəˈluːtʃiː] *n.* *(pl.* ～*(s))* 俾路支人．

bal·un [ˈbælən] *n.* 【无】平衡—不平衡变换器．

bal·us·ter [ˈbæləstə] *n.* ①【建】栏干柱；〔*pl.*〕栏干．②椅背支柱．

bal·us·trade [ˌbæləsˈtreid] *n.* 栏干，扶栏，回栏，扶手．

Bal·zac [ˈbælzæk], **Honoréde** 巴尔扎克〔1799—1850，法国小说家〕．**-ian** [bælˈzeiʃən] *a.* 巴尔扎克的，巴尔扎克文风的．

bam[1] [bæm] *vt., n.* 〔俚〕哄，诱骗．

bam[2] [bæm] *vt.* 〔美俚〕打，揍．

Ba·ma·ko [ˈbɑːməkəu] *n.* 巴马科〔马里首都〕．

bam·bi·no [bæmˈbiːnəu] *(pl.* **～s,** ***bam·bi·ni*** [bæmˈbiːniː]) 〔It.〕①婴孩，幼儿．②幼年耶稣像．

bam·boo [bæmˈbuː] *n.* ①竹．②竹杆，竹棍．～ *grove [thicket]* 竹林．～ *shoots [sprouts]* 竹笋．*a* ～ *chair* 兜子，竹轿．*a* ～ *ware* 精致竹器．*the sacred* ～ 南天竹．

bam·boo·zle [bæmˈbuːzl] *vt.* 〔俚〕①哄，骗，欺骗，愚弄．②迷惑，使困惑．～ *(sb.)* ***into*** *(doing)*．哄(某人)做…．～ *(sb.)* ***out of*** 骗取(某人的)…．—*vi.* 哄，骗．**-ment** *n.*

ban[1] [bæn] *n.* ①禁止，禁令．②(社会上的)禁忌，(舆论上的)谴责．③【宗】诅咒，逐出教门．***lift [remore] the*** ～ 开禁，解禁．***place [put] under a*** ～ 禁止．***under the*** ～ 被禁止；被逐出教门；被放逐．— *vt.* ①禁止，取缔 (*opp.* allow)．②把…逐出教门；— *vi.* 〔古〕诅咒．

ban[2] [bæn] *n.* ①布告．②〔*pl.*〕＝ banns．③【史】(中世纪封建君主征召家臣从军的)召集令；被召集来的家臣．

ban[3] [bɑːn] *n.* *(pl.* ***ba·ni*** [ˈbɑːni]) 巴恩〔罗马尼亚货币名，等于 1/100 列伊〕．

Ban·a·gher [ˈbænəgə] *n.* 巴纳格〔爱尔兰一地名〕．***beat [bang]*** ～ 超过一切；极其，非常．

ba·nal [bəˈnɑːl] *a.* 平庸的，陈腐的．

ba·nal·i·ty [bəˈnæliti] *n.* 平庸，陈腐；陈词滥调．

ba·nal·ize [ˈbeinəlaiz] *vt.* 使陈腐；使庸俗．

ba·nan·a [bəˈnɑːnə] *n.* ①【植】香蕉；芭蕉树．②〔美俚〕喜剧演员．③〔美俚〕大鼻子．*a hand of* ～*s* 一串香蕉．～ **oil** ①【化】香蕉油，醋酸戊酯．②〔美俚〕圆滑，伪善．～ **republic** "香蕉国"〔指只有单一经济作物的拉丁美洲小国〕．～ **seat** (自行车)细长而后部翘起的车座．**-s** *a.* 〔美俚〕令人发疯的 *(go bananas* 发疯，发狂*)*．

ba·naus·ic [bəˈnɔːsik] *a.* 仅以实用为目的的，实利的；机械的；通俗的．

Ban·bur·y cake [ˈbænbəri ˈkeik] *n.* (英国 Banbury 地方特产的)加料果馅饼．

banc [bæŋk], **ban·co** [ˈbæŋkəu] *n.* 法官席．***in*** ～ 全体法官列席，在大法庭上 (*a hearing in* ～ 由大法庭审理)．

Ban·croft [ˈbænkrɔft] *n.* 班克罗夫特〔姓氏〕．

band[1] [bænd] *n.* ①带，绳，带形物；箍；箍条；嵌条；镶边；锯条；〔*pl.*〕(法官等的)宽领带．②束缚，羁绊；义务；〔古〕缧绁，枷，镣，铐(等)．③【建】带形装饰，带花；【生】横纹．④【物】频带，波段；光带；【机】调带；【地】夹层；【无】波段．⑤(装订)钉书线，缀线．*an iron* ～ 铁箍．*a legal [moral]* ～ 法律[道义]上的义务．*a rubber* ～ 橡皮筋，橡皮圈．— *vt.* ①用带捆扎．②在…上加条饰〔镶边〕．③〔后接复数反身代词或用被动语态〕团结，联合．*They are* ～*ed together closely.* 他们紧密团结．*We* ～ *ourselves closely against the invaders.* 我们紧密地团结起来抗击入侵者．— *vi.* 团结，联合 *(with)*．～**-aid** *a.* 急忙拼凑的．～ **house** 〔美口〕监狱．～ **mill** 带锯制材厂．～**-pass filter** 选带滤波器．～ **saw** 带锯．～ **switching**【无】波段转换．～ **wheel**【机】带轮．

band[2] [bænd] *n.* ①队，团，群；(盗贼等的)帮，伙．②(吹奏)乐队．*a* ～ *of robbers* 一伙强盗．*a* ～ *of stray dogs* 一群野狗．*a dance* ～ 跳舞的伴奏乐队．*a military [marine]* ～ 陆军[海军]军乐队．***the B- of Hope*** 〔英〕少年禁酒团．***beat the*** ～ 〔美〕显眼，出众；猛烈地；非常 *(It rained all day to beat the* ～*.* 大雨倾盆，终日不止．*Business fell off to beat the* ～*.* 生意一落千丈)．***when the*** ～ ***begins to play*** 事态变严重时．～**master** 乐队指挥．～ **moll** 乐队女郎〔和摇摆舞乐队演员鬼混的少女〕．～ **razor** 装有单面刀刃卷带的安全剃刀．～**sman** 乐队队员．～**-stand** *n.* (户外的)音乐台．～**wagon** 〔美〕领头的乐队车；某一时期流行的思想［政策］*(jump [be, hop, climb, get] on [aboard] the* ～*wagon* 赶浪头)．

band·age [ˈbændidʒ] *n.* 绷带，包带；带．*a triangular* ～ 三角形绷带．— *vt.* 包扎，用绷带缚上．— *vi.* 给…上绷带．～ **roller** *n.*【军】看护兵．

Band-Aid, bandaid [ˈbænˌdeid] *n.* 〔B-〕【商标】急救带〔一种急救包扎绷带〕；〔b-〕急救绷带．

ban·dan·(n)a [bænˈdænə] *n.* (印度)班丹纳花绸 (大手帕，大头巾)．

ban·dar [ˈbʌndɑː] *n.* 【动】印度狭鼻猴．～**-log** 胡说乱讲的人．

Ban·dar Abbas [bænˈdɑː əˈbɑːs] 阿巴斯港〔伊朗港市〕．

Ban·dar Seri Begawan [bænˈdɑː ˈsiəriː bəˈgɑːwæn] 斯里巴加湾港〔文莱首府〕．

band·box [ˈbændbɔks] *n.* ①(装衣帽等的) 硬纸盒．②〔口〕纸盒式小建筑．***look as if one had just come out of a*** ～ 衣着整洁．

ban·deau [ˈbændəu] *n.* *(pl.* **-x** [-z]) 〔F.〕①(妇女用的)发带，头带；细带．②奶罩．

ban·de·ril·la [ˌbɑːndeˈriːljɑː] *n.* (西班牙斗牛的) 短扎枪．

ban·de·ril·le·ro [ˌbɑːnderiːˈljerɔː] *n.* 〔Sp.〕斗牛士，斗牛者．

ban·de·rol(e) [ˈbændərəul] *n.* ①小旗，旒旗，枪旗；葬旗；墓旗．②【建】刻扁．③(有铭文的)绶带．

ban·di·coot [ˈbændikuːt] *n.*【动】①印度大鼠. ②澳大利亚袋狸.
ban·dit [ˈbændit] *n.* *(pl. ~s, -ti* [bænˈditi(ː)]*)* ①恶棍,暴徒;盗贼,土匪,匪. ②〔英空军俚〕敌机. *a banditti = a set of ~s* 一队土匪. *mounted ~s* 马贼. *a ~ gang* 匪帮. **-ry** *n.* 盗匪活动 (*commit banditry* 抢劫).
B and O = Band and Orchestra〔美〕乐队.
ban·dog [ˈbændɔg] *n.* (用铁链拴着的)看门狗,猛犬.
ban·do·leer, ban·do·lier [ˌbændəˈliə] *n.*【军】子弹带.
ban·do·le·ro [ˌbændəˈliərrəu] *n.* 〔Sp.〕路劫强盗.
ban·do·line [ˈbændəliːn] *n.* 发油,头油. —*vt., vi.* (给…)涂发油.
ban·dore [bænˈdɔː, ˈbændɔː] *n.* 班多拉琴〔略似吉他的古琴〕.
B and S = brandy and soda 掺苏打水的白兰地酒.
Ban·dung, Ban·doeng [ˈbɑːnduŋ] *n.* 万隆〔印度尼西亚城市〕.
ban·dy[1] [ˈbændi] *vt.* ①把(球)打来打去,丢来丢去;来回摆弄. ②交换,互换,受授. ③议论,谈论,传播. *~ blows with sb.* 与某人对打. *~ compliments with sb.* 互道寒喧,互相问候. *~ a rumour about* 散布谣言. ***~ words with*** 与(人)对吵[顶嘴]. —*n.* ①〔废〕旧式网球. ②曲棍球 (= hockey);简化式曲棍球 (=shinny).
ban·dy[2] [ˈbændi] *a.* 膝向外曲的. ***~-legged*** *a.* 罗圈腿的.
ban·dy[3] [ˈbændi] *n.* 印度马车,(特指)牛车.
bane [bein] *n.* ①巨毒. ★此义现仅用于 ratsbane, henbane 等复合词. ②毁灭者,害人精;祸害. ③死,毁灭.
bane·ber·ry [ˈbeinberi] *n.* ①类叶升麻属植物. ②类叶升麻属植物的浆果.
bane·ful [ˈbeinful] *a.* ①有害的. ②有毒的. ③致死的,导致毁灭的. *a ~ superstition* 有害的迷信. *~ herbs* 毒草.
bang[1] [bæŋ] *vt.* ①咚地敲(鼓等);哨地撞(钟等);轰地开(炮等);砰地关上(门等). ②粗手粗脚地摆弄. ③〔俚〕痛打,重打. ④〔俚〕胜过,超过. —*vi.* ①(钟等)哨哨响;(炮等)轰地放;(门等)砰地关上 *(to)*. ②砰砰作响. ***~ (oneself) against*** 砰地撞上,碰在…上. ***~ away at*** ①专心致志地做 (*students ~ing away at their homework* 学生专心做功课). ②攻击,向…发动猛攻. ***~ in the arm*** 〔美〕打(吗啡等)麻醉针. ***~ (sth.) into sb. [sb.'s head]*** 硬把(某事物)灌输进某人头脑. ***~ low*** 〔美〕(拳击)打腰带以下;犯规. ***~ off*** 轰然开炮;(织机)碰撞关车;立即. ***~ on*** 〔英口〕好,要得 *(That cap is exactly ~ on.* 那顶帽子正好). ***~ out [up]*** 〔美口〕好!好货色! ***~ up*** ①砰地摔上. ②弄伤,弄坏. —*n.* ①棒打,重打;冲击. ②爆炸声;咚咚声,哨哨声,轰隆声,砰砰声. ③〔美口〕猛冲,突然跃起. ④热情,精力. ⑤〔美俚〕刺激,快感;服用(麻醉品). *a sonic ~* 音速冲响. ***in a ~*** 赶紧,急忙. ***with a ~*** ①砰地一声,轰然. ②剧烈而突然地. ③成功地. —*ad.* ①砰然,轰然. ②蓦地,突然. ③〔口〕正巧;全然. *~ in the middle* 正当中. *Bang went the gun.* 砰地响了一枪. *Bang went sixpence.* 六便士大洋完蛋了〔对吝啬鬼的讽刺〕. *go ~* 砰地关上;咔嚓破裂. **~-bang** 战争影片. **~ zone** (飞机)声爆(影响所及)区.
bang[2] [bæŋ] *n.* 前刘海(发式). —*vt.* 把(前额头发)剪成刘海式〔剪短〕. **~tail** 〔美俚〕比赛用的马.
bang[3] [bæŋ] = bhang.
ban·ga·lore [ˌbæŋgəˈlɔː] *n.* 爆破筒 (= ~ torpedo).
bang·er [ˈbæŋə] *n.* 〔英俚〕①香肠. ②爆竹. ③噪音大的破旧汽车,老爷车.
Bang·kok [bæŋˈkɔk] *n.* 曼谷〔泰国首都〕.
Ban·gla·desh [ˌbɑːŋgləˈdeʃ] *n.* 孟加拉国〔亚洲〕. **-de·shi** [-ˈdeʃi] *n.* 孟加拉人.
ban·gle [ˈbæŋgl] *n.* 手镯;脚镯.
Ban·gui [bɑːŋˈgiː] *n.* 班吉〔中非共和国首都〕.
bang-up [ˈbæŋˈʌp] *a.* 〔美俚〕上等的,顶好的. *a really ~ fur coat* 顶刮刮的一件皮大衣.
ban·gy [ˈbæŋgi] *a.* 〔美俚〕= bang-up.
ba·ni [ˈbɑːni] *n. pl.* (*sing.* **ban** [bɑːn]) 巴尼〔罗马尼亚货币名〕.
ban·ian, ban·yan [ˈbæniən] *n.* ①【植】(印度)榕树. ②(印度人的)法兰绒宽衬衣. **~ day**【海】素餐日.
ban·ish [ˈbæniʃ] *vt.* ①把…充军,处…以流刑,流放,放逐. ②消除,排除(恐惧等). *~ sb. from [out of] the country* 把某人流放国外. *~ (sth.) from memory* 完全忘记. *~ care* 打消忧虑.
ban·ish·ment [ˈbæniʃmənt] *n.* ①充军,放逐,流刑,流放. ②驱逐;排除.
ban·is·ter [ˈbænistə] *n.* ①栏干小柱. ②〔*pl.*〕栏干,楼梯扶手.
ban·jo [ˈbændʒəu] *n.* *(pl. ~(e)s)* 班卓琴. **-ist** *n.* 班卓琴奏者.
Ban·jul [ˈbændʒuːl] *n.* 班珠尔〔冈比亚首都〕.
bank[1] [bæŋk] *n.* ①堤,堤防;岸,河畔. ②埂,垄,堆. ③(海中水下的)沙洲,滩. ④斜坡,边坡,坡度;转弯.【空】(飞机转弯时的)倾斜状态,倾斜. ⑤【矿】采煤工作面地区[通道],井口区;【台球】(球台的)橡皮边. *the right [left] ~* (顺流方向的)右[左]岸. *a sand ~* 沙洲. *the angle of ~* (飞行中的)倾角. *~ of clouds* 云峰,云层. ***from ~ to ~*** (矿工)由下井到出井(的时间). —*vt.* ①在…旁筑堤;堆积;围;封(火). ②【空】使倾斜;【台球】使(球)碰边(入袋). ③使(公路、铁路转弯处)外侧比内侧超高. *~ a fire* 封火. —*vi.* ①形成堤;(云)拥积. ②【空】倾斜;倾斜着飞行;(汽车)倾斜着行驶. ***~ up*** 堵截(河流等);封(火);【冶】封炉;成堤状,(重叠)成层 (*Clouds began to ~ up.* 云层开始重叠起来).
bank[2] [bæŋk] *n.* ①银行,金库. ②庄家;庄家面前的赌本;赌场主. ③库,贮藏所,贮备. *a blood ~* 血库. *a savings ~* 储蓄银行. ***break the ~*** 耗尽资源;(赌博)下庄,把庄上的钱全部赢来. ***in ~*** 存入银行;准备着,储蓄着. ***safe as the ~*** 十分安全. ***the Bank = the Bank of England*** 英格兰银行. —*vt.* ①把(钱)存入银行. ②资助,为…提供资金. —*vi.* ①开银行. ②在银行里存款;与银行往来*(with)*. ③(赌博)做庄家. ***~ on [upon]*** 〔口〕信赖,依赖,指望,依靠. ***~ with*** 和(银行)有往来. **~ acceptance** 银行承兑[背书]支票. **~ account** 银行往来帐,活期存款. **~ annuities** 英国统一公债. **~ balance** 银行存款余额. **~ bill** 〔美〕钞票;〔英〕转帐票据. **~book** 银行存折. **~ cable transfer** 银行电汇. **~ card** (赊帐用的)银行信用卡. **~ clearing** 票据交换. **~ credit** 银行担保(书). **~ demand** *n.* (国外汇兑的)银行即期支付. **~ deposit** 银行存款. **~ discount** 银行贴现. **~ draft** 银行汇票. **B- for International Settlement** 国际清算银行. **~ holiday** 〔美〕(星期日以外的)银行假日;〔英〕(银行)公假日〔一年六次,即 Good Friday, Easter Monday, Whitmonday, 8 月的第一个星期一, Christmas Day, Boxing Day〕. **~ money** 银行票据[本票,汇票等]. **~ night** 〔美俚〕电影院举行观众抽奖的夜晚. **~ note** 纸币. **~ of circulation [issue]** 发钞银行. **~ paper** 钞票;(银行)承兑票据. **~ rags** 〔美俚〕钞票. **~-rate** 银行贴现率,银行日息. **~ reserve** 银行准备金. **~ returns** 银行营业报告. **~roll** ①*n.* 〔Am.〕一卷钞票;货币储备;有效资金. ②*vt.* 〔口〕为…提供资金,对…通融资金. **~ sneak** 银行贼. **~ year** 银行会计年度.
bank[3] [bæŋk] *n.* ①排,列,组,系列;【电】触排,线弧;组合. ②【乐】键座. ③〔美〕一排电梯. ④桨手(座位);【法】法官席位. ⑤报纸小标题. *transformer ~s* 变压器组. ***~s of*** 成排[组]的. ***in ~s*** 成排[组]地. —*vt.* 把…排成一列. *~ the seats* 把座位摆成一排.
bank·a·ble [ˈbæŋkəbl] *a.* 银行肯保的,(证券等)银行可承兑的.
bank·er[1] [ˈbæŋkə] *n.* ①银行家;财东. ②(赌博)庄家;

赌场帐房. ③一种(赌博性)纸牌戏. ④〔美口〕付帐人. *Let me be your* ~.我借钱给你. *a* ~*'s clearing house* 票据交换所. *Let him be the* ~ *this time.* 这回让他给钱好了. ~**'s bill** 银行对外国银行开出的汇票.

bank·er[2] [ˈbæŋkə] *n.* ①堤防工人;〔英方〕挖沟工人. ②(纽芬兰近海的)捕鳕人[船]. ③【猎】跳过堤埂的猎马.

bank·er[3] [ˈbæŋkə] *n.* (雕石像、砌砖等用的)造型台,工作台.

bank·ing[1] [ˈbæŋkiŋ] *n.* ①筑堤,堤防. ②(纽芬兰的)近海渔业. ③【空】横倾斜.

bank·ing[2] [ˈbæŋkiŋ] *n.* 银行业;银行学;金融. ~ **centre** 金融中心. ~ **holiday** (周转不灵等时的)银行休业[搁浅]. ~ **hours** 银行营业时间. ~ **house** 银行. ~ **power** 贷出能力. ~ **reserve** = bank reserve.

bank·roll·er [ˈbæŋkrəulə] *n.* ①提供资金者,资助者,财东. ②〔美俚〕红演员,红角,红播音员.

bank·rupt [ˈbæŋkrəpt] *n.* ①破产者,无力偿还债务者. ②丧失(名誉、智力等)的人. *a moral* ~ 道德沦丧的人. — *a.* ①破了产的;无支付力的,无力偿还债务的. ②(名誉)扫地的,(智力等)完全丧失的. ③垮了的,枯竭的. *be declared* ~ 宣告破产. ~ ***of [in]*** 完全丧失,完全缺乏 *(be* ~ *in reputation* 声誉扫地). ***go*** ~ 破产. ***play the*** ~ 破产;(用破产方式)骗钱;〔喻〕失信用. — *vt.* 使破产,使无力偿付.

bank·rupt·cy [ˈbæŋkrəptsi] *n.* ①破产,倒闭,倒帐,无偿付能力. ②(勇气、智力等的)完全丧失 *(of; in)*. ***go into*** ~ 破产. ~ **administrator** 【法】破产管理人.

Banks [bæŋks] *n.* 班克斯〔姓氏〕.

bank·si·a [ˈbæŋksiə] *n.* 【植】山茂樫.

banks·man [ˈbæŋksmən] *n.* (煤矿的)井外监工.

ban·lieue [bɑːnˈljə] *n.* 〔F.〕郊区;市郊住宅区.

ban·ner [ˈbænə] *n.* ①旗,国旗,军旗;标识,旗帜;横幅标语. ②〔美〕(报上横贯全页的)大字标题〔又称 ~ head 或 ~ line〕. ③〔中〕(内蒙古行政区划的)旗〔相当于县〕;【史】(满清军事组织的)旗. ***carry the*** ~ 〔美俚〕(没有地方睡)在街上走一夜;流浪街头. ***follow [join] the*** ~ ***of*** 投入…旗帜下. ***under the ... of*** 在…旗帜下. ***unfurl one's*** ~ 使旗帜鲜明,表明主张. — *a.* ①杰出的,第一流的,为首的. ②〔美〕突出地支持(某一政党)的. *a* ~ *year for crop* 丰年. *a* ~ *Democratic county* 一个突出支持民主党的县. ~ **bearer** 旗手. ~**man**① 旗手. ②(满清的)旗人. ~ **screen** (吊在炉前的) 防火隔屏. ~ **state** 美国的主要州.

ban·ner·et(te) [ˌbænəˈret] *n.* ①小旗. ②【英史】小旗骑士〔能在自己的旗下率领部下上阵的骑士〕; 小旗骑士爵位〔在 baron 之下〕.

ban·ner·ol(e) [ˈbænərəul] *n.* = banderol(e).

ban·nis·ter [ˈbænistə] *n.* = banister.

ban·nock [ˈbænək] *n.* (苏格兰的)燕麦[大麦]烤饼.

banns [bænz] *n.* 〔*pl.*〕结婚预告〔于教堂中结婚前预告婚事〕. ***ask [call, publish, put up] the*** ~ (在教堂中结婚前)预告婚事以防异议. ***forbid the*** ~ 对别人婚事提出异议. ***have one's*** ~ ***asked*** 请教堂公布结婚预告.

ban·quet [ˈbæŋkwit] *n.* (通常指正式的) 宴会,请客;酒席. *give [hold] a* ~ 举行宴会. *a state* ~ 国宴. *a regular* ~ 豪华的酒席. — *vt.* 宴请,设宴招待. — *vi.* 饮宴,参加宴会;大吃大喝.

ban·quette [bæŋˈket] *n.* ①【军】(战壕内的)射击踏垛. ②弃土堆;填土;护坡道. ③〔美〕人行道. ④(公共马车等的)长凳. ⑤【建】窗口凳.

Ban·quo [ˈbæŋkwəu,ˈbæn-] 班戈〔莎士比亚戏剧《麦克佩斯》中的苏格兰勇将〕.

bans [bænz] *n.* = banns.

ban·shee, ban·shie [bænˈʃiː, ˈbænʃiː] *n.* (英国古代民间传说中的)报丧女妖.

bant [bænt] *vi.* 〔谑〕实行蔬食减胖法.

ban·tam [ˈbæntəm] *n.* ①〔B-〕【动】矮脚鸡. ②矮小好斗的人;〔美俚〕不够征兵标准高度的矮子. ③轻量级拳师. ④〔*pl.*〕(欧战时的)矮子大队. — *a.* ①矮小好斗的. ②小型的. ~**weight** *n.* 【拳】最轻级〔体重 116 (英), 118 (美)磅以下〕.

ban·ter [ˈbæntə] *n.* ①(没有恶意的) 开玩笑,逗乐. ②〔美方〕挑战. — *vt.* (没有恶意地)取笑;〔美方〕挑,逗. — *vi.* 开玩笑. **-ing** *a.* 开玩笑的. **-ly** *ad.*

Bant·ing·ism [ˈbæntiŋizəm] *n.* 蔬食减胖疗法〔英国医生 W. Banting 所倡导〕.

bant·ling [ˈbæntliŋ] *n.* 〔蔑〕乳臭小儿.

Ban·tu [ˈbænˈtuː] *n.* (南非的)班图语;班图人.

ban·yan [ˈbæniən] *n.* = banian.

ban·zai [ˈbɑːnˈzɑːi] *int.* 〔日〕万岁! 冲呀! — *a.* 拼死的,自杀式的. ~ **attack [charge]** 敢死队的进攻〔冲锋〕.

ba·o·bab [beiəbæb] *n.* 【植】猢狲面包树〔非洲产,又名 monkey-bread tree, 所产果实可供食用〕.

bap [bæp] *n.* 〔Scot.〕小面包(卷儿).

bap·ti·si·a [bæpˈtiziə, -ˈtiʒə] *n.* 【植】赝靛属植物.

bap·tism [ˈbæptizəm] *n.* ①【基督】洗礼,浸礼. ②命名(式). ~ ***of blood*** 殉教. ~ ***of fire*** ①(圣经中)圣灵的洗礼. ②炮火的洗礼,初经战场,第一次战斗经验〔严重经验〕. ***the clinic*** ~ 病床洗礼,临终洗礼.

bap·tis·mal [bæpˈtizməl] *a.* 洗礼的,浸礼的. *a* ~ *name* 洗礼名,教名.

Bap·tist [ˈbæptist] *n.* ①【基督】(主张全身浸水的)浸礼教徒. ②圣徒约翰 (= St. John the ~). ③〔b-〕施浸礼者. *the* ~ *Church [the* ~*]* (基督教新教)浸礼会.

bap·tis·t(e)r·y [ˈbæptist(ə)ri] *n.* ①洗礼所,洗礼堂. ②洗礼盘.

bap·tize, bap·tise [bæpˈtaiz] *vt.* ①【基督】给…施行洗礼. ②给…命名. ③(精神上)洗涤,使净化. — *vi.* 举行洗礼.

BAR = Browning automatic rifle 白朗宁自动步枪.

Bar [bɑː] *n.* 巴尔〔南斯拉夫港市〕.

bar [bɑː] *n.* ①棒,杆,条;棒状物. ②横木,闩. ③栅栏;关卡,城门. ④障碍,妨碍 *(to)*. ⑤(河口的) 沙洲. ⑥(法庭上的)围栏;法庭;刑事被告席;〔喻〕审判台; 制裁;谴责;律师团;律师业; 停止诉讼〔权利要求〕的申请. ⑦(酒吧等的)卖酒柜台;酒吧. ⑧(光、色等的)线,条,带. ⑨【乐】节线〔节间纵线〕;小节;【徽】盾的横线;【军】(领章上的)军阶线;【生】棒眼;【数】横; 杆件;【物】巴〔压强单位〕. ⑩〔美〕蚊帐 (= mosquito ~). *prison* ~*s* 监牢. *the color* ~ 对有色人种的歧视〔差别待遇〕. *a tie* ~ 连岛沙洲. ***at the*** ~ 受到公开审问. ***be a*** ~ ***to*** 成…的障碍. ***be admitted to the*** ~〔美〕= ***be called to [before] the B-*** 得到(法院所属) 律师的资格. ***be called within the*** ~ 被任命为皇室律师. ***behind (the)*** ~***s*** 在监狱〔禁闭室〕中. ***behind bolt and*** ~ 被关在监牢里. ***cross the*** ~ 死,去世. ***go to the*** ~ 当律师. ***in*** ~ ***of*** 【法】为禁止,为防止;除…之外的. ***let down the*** ~***s*** 撤除障碍. ***play a few*** ~***s*** 奏几小节 (曲子). ***practise at the B-*** 以律师为职业. ***trial at*** ~ 【法】(全体法官) 列席审判. ***the*** ~ ***of conscience [public opinion]*** 良心〔舆论〕的制裁. ***the*** ~ ***of the house*** 英下院的惩罚法庭. — *vt.* ①闩,闩上. ②阻挡,拦住,阻挠;防止,禁止;排斥;除去;【法】(用法律手段)阻止诉讼. ③〔俚〕反对,讨厌,不准. ④在…上划线,在…上划出颜色线条,用色线配上 *(with)*. ~ **in** 关在里面. ~ **out** 关在外头,阻在外面. — *prep.* 除,除…之外 (= barring). ~ *a few names* 除开四、五名. ~ *none* 无例外. ~**bell** 【体】杠铃. ~**-chart** (统计用的)条线图. ~ **fly** 〔美〕酒徒,酒鬼. ~ **girl** 常去酒吧间的妓女,酒吧女郎. ~**graph** = ~**chart.** ~**hop** ① *n.* 〔美俚〕酒吧女侍. ② *vi.* 一家又一家地逛酒店. ~ **iron** 铁条,棒状铁. ~**keep(er)** 〔美〕酒店主; 酒吧服务员. ~ **magnet** 磁棒,条形磁铁. ~**maid** 酒吧女侍. ~**man** 〔英〕酒吧服务员. ~**room** 酒吧间. ~**tend** *vi.*

做酒店侍者. ~**tender** 〔Am.〕(= ~man).
Ba·rab·bas [bəˈræbəs] *n.*【圣】巴拉巴〔因耶稣替死而得释放的强盗〕.
bar·a·the·a [ˌbεərəˈθiə] *n.* 巴拉瑟亚领带绸; 巴拉瑟亚毛葛; 巴拉瑟亚军服呢.
barb[1] [bɑːb] *n.* ①倒钩,倒刺; 毛刺,芒刺;〔喻〕刺耳之言. ②【动】(鸟毛的)羽支; (鱼口边的)触须. ③(女修道士的)遮喉白布. ④〔美俚〕不加入学生会的大学生. ⑤【动】石首鱼. — *vt.* 在…上装倒钩; 用刺耳之言伤(人). — *a.* 具倒刺的; (话)带刺的. ~ **words** 伤人之言. ~**ed wire** 有刺铁丝. ~**ed wire entanglement**【军】倒刺铁丝网.
barb[2] [bɑːb] *n.* (由非洲 Babary 输入西班牙的)巴巴利马; 巴巴利鸽.
Bar·ba·dos [bɑːˈbeidəuz] *n.* 巴巴多斯〔拉丁美洲〕. **Bar·ba·di·an** [bɑːˈbeidiən] *n.* 巴巴多斯人.
Bar·ba·ra [ˈbɑːbərə] *n.* 巴巴拉〔女子名〕.
bar·bar·i·an [bɑːˈbεəriən] *a.* 野蛮(人)的(*opp.* civilized). — *n.* ①野蛮人,原始人. ②无教养的人,粗汉.
bar·bar·ic [bɑːˈbærik] *a.* 未开化的, 野蛮人一样的; 粗俗的,煞风景的.
bar·ba·rism [ˈbɑːbərizəm] *n.* ①野蛮(状况), 未开化; 暴虐. ②(语文的)不纯粹,不规范; 芜杂,芜杂的语句,鄙俗的语句.
bar·bar·i·ty [bɑːˈbæriti] *n.* ①野蛮行为,残忍,暴虐,凶猛,粗野. ②(语文的)不规范,芜杂.
bar·ba·ri·za·tion [ˌbɑːbəraiˈzeiʃən] *n.* ①野蛮化. ②(语文等)不规范化.
bar·ba·rize [ˈbɑːbəraiz] *vt., vi.* ①(使)(人等)变野蛮. ②(使)(语文)变得不规范,变芜杂.
bar·ba·rous [ˈbɑːbərəs] *a.* ①野蛮的, 未开化的; 粗野的; 凶猛的,暴虐的,残忍的. ②(语言等)芜杂的,不纯粹的,不规范的; 非希腊、拉丁语的; 异国语的; 无学识的,鄙俗的. **-ly** *ad.* **-ness** *n.*
Bar·ba·ry [ˈbɑːbəri] *n.* (除埃及外) 北非伊斯兰教国家的总称. ~ **Coast** 北非海岸. ~ **sheep** (北非)大角野绵羊.
bar·bas·co [bɑːˈbæskəu] *n.* (*pl.* ~*(e)s*)【植】多花薯蓣(*Dioscorea floribunda*).
bar·bate [ˈbɑːbeit] *a.*【动、植】有胡须[毛簇]的, 有长绒毛的.
bar·be·cue [ˈbɑːbikjuː] *n.* ①(猪、牛等的)烧烤全牲. ②〔美〕(吃烧烤全牲的)野外大宴会. ③野餐烤肉架. ④咖啡豆干燥场. — *vt.* 全烧,全烤(猪、牛等),红烧(肉块等).
bar·bel [ˈbɑːbəl] *n.* ①(鱼类唇边的) 触须. ②有触须的鱼〔白鱼之类〕. **-led** *a.* 有触须的.
bar·bel·late [ˈbɑːbileit, bɑːˈbelit] *a.*【植】有短硬毛的.
Bar·ber [ˈbɑːbə] *n.* 巴伯〔姓氏〕.
bar·ber [ˈbɑːbə] *n.* ①理发师〔多指为男子理发的人,为女子理发者多用 hair-dresser〕. ②〔美〕多嘴多舌的人. — *vt.* 为…理发剃须. — *vi.* 〔美〕多嘴. *a* ~*'s shop* =〔美〕*a* ~ *shop* 理发店. ~**'s itch [rash]** 须疮. ~**'s pole** 理发店的红白条纹圆筒招牌. **do a** ~〔美俚〕唠唠叨叨; 话很多. ~**shop** ①*n.* 理发店. ②*a.* 〔美口〕(伤感歌曲等)男声重唱的.
bar·ber·ry [ˈbɑːbəri] *n.*【植】伏牛花,伏牛花子.
bar·bet [ˈbɑːbit] *n.*【鸟】须䴕〔一种热带鸟〕.
bar·bette [bɑːˈbet] *n.* ①炮垛. ②(军舰的) 露天炮塔, 固定炮塔; 炮架.
bar·bi·can [ˈbɑːbikən] *n.* 外堡,碉楼.
bar·bi·cel [ˈbɑːbisel] *n.* (鸟的)羽纤支.
bar·bi·tal [ˈbɑːbitɔː], **bar·bi·tone** [ˈbɑːbitəun] *n.* 巴比妥,安眠药〔二乙基丙二酰脲〕.
bar·bi·tu·rate [bɑːˈbitjərit] *n.*【化】巴比妥酸盐.
bar·bi·tu·ric [ˌbɑːbiˈtjuərik] *a.* ~ **acid**【化】巴比土酸.
bar·bo·la [bɑːˈbəulə] *n.* 粘附装饰〔用塑料糊把小花、果等粘附于小物件上〕(= ~ work).
bar·bule [ˈbɑːbjuːl] *n.*【动】①羽小支. ②小倒刺.
bar·ca·rol(le) [ˈbɑːkərəul] *n.* (意大利威尼斯船工唱的)船歌.
Bar·ce·lo·na [ˌbɑːsiˈləunə] *n.* 巴塞罗那〔西班牙港市〕. ~ **chair** 钢架皮垫椅.
bar·chan [bɑːˈkɑːn, ˈbɑːkɑːn] *n.* 新月形沙丘.
Bar·clay [ˈbɑːkli] *n.* 巴克利〔姓氏,男子名〕.
bard[1] [bɑːd] *n.* ①吟游诗人,流浪乐人. ②(史诗等的)作者[吟诵者]. ③〔古〕(抒情)诗人. ④〔the B-〕= William Shakespeare. *a B- specialist* 〔美〕莎士比亚研究家. ***the B- of Avon*** 莎士比亚的别称.
bard[2] [bɑːd] *n.* (中世纪)马的铠甲.
bard·ic [ˈbɑːdik] *a.* 吟游诗人的.
Bar·dol·a·ter [bɑːˈdɔlətə] *n.* 〔美〕莎士比亚崇拜者.
Bar·dol·a·try [bɑːˈdɔlətri] *n.* 〔美〕莎士比亚崇拜.
bare[1] [bεə] *a.* ①裸的,裸体的; 无遮蔽的,赤裸裸的. ②空的,空虚的,无…的 (*of*). ③仅有的,极少的,勉勉强强的; 单,徒. ④无装饰的,朴质的; 坦率的; 煞风景的. ⑤(织物)穿旧了的. ~ *facts* 赤裸裸的事实, 明摆着的事实. ~ *feet* 赤脚. ~ *hands* 徒手,空手. ~ *sword* 出鞘的剑. *with one's* ~ *head* 不戴帽,光着头. *a* ~ *and barren land* 不毛之地. *a room* ~ *of furniture* 空无家具的屋子. *be* ~ *of credit* 缺乏信用. *a* ~ *contract*【法】无条件契约. ~ *necessities of life* 刚够维持生命的必需品. ~ *possibility* 仅有的(一点点)可能性[希望]. *a* ~ *majority* 勉勉强强的过半数. ***at the ~ thought [idea]*** 一想起…(就). ~ ***cloth*** 稀布; 方眼布. ~ ***livelihood*** 仅能糊口的生活. ~ ***navy*** 〔美俚〕(海军)光是罐头的食品. ***believe (sth.) on sb.'s ~ word*** 光听某人的话就相信(某事). ***lay*** ~ 露出,暴露, 揭发, 戳穿; 表白,说出. ***(escape) with ~ life*** 仅留性命(逃脱),仅以身免. — *vt.* ①剥去,剥开; 拔出(剑等). ②敞开,露出,暴露. ~ *one's head* 脱帽. ~ *one's heart [soul, thoughts]* 剖白[表明]心意. ~**back** *a., ad.* 无鞍(的); 用滑马 [裸马]. ~**boat** ①*a.* (租船业务中)只租空船的. *n.* 出租的空船(由客户负责配备人员、补给、保养等). ~**bone** 瘦人. ~**bones** 梗概. ~**faced** 不戴面罩的; 露骨的, 无耻的 (~*faced falsehood* 信口雌黄). ~**foot(ed)** *a., ad.* 赤脚 (的). ~**handed** *a., ad.* 未戴手套 (的); 空手 (的); 赤手空拳(的). ~**headed** *a., ad.* 未戴帽子 (的), 无帽(的); 光着头(的). ~**legged** *a.* 露着腿的. ~**necked** *a.* 露着脖子的. ~**sark** ① *n.* = berserker. ②*ad.* 不披挂甲胄地.
bare[2] [bεə] *v.* 〔古〕 bear 的过去式.
ba·rège, ba·rege [bəˈreʒ] *n.* 巴勒吉纱罗; 巴勒吉披巾.
bare·ly [ˈbεəli] *ad.* ①仅,好容易才; 几乎没有. ②赤裸裸地,无遮蔽地. ③公然地, 露骨地. *He* ~ *escaped.* 他好容易才逃了出来. *There was* ~ *enough for all.* 就全体(人数)来说算是勉强够了. *He is* ~ *of age.* 他刚成年.
barf [bɑːf] *vi., vt.* 〔美俚〕呕吐.
bar·gain [ˈbɑːgin] *n.* ①契约,合同,协定,成交条件; 交易,买卖. ②便宜货,廉价品; (通过讨价还价)成交的商品. *A* ~*'s a* ~. 契约终是契约(成议不可妄毁). *That's a* ~. 那已经决定了. *a bad [good]* ~ = *a losing [great]* ~ 买贵了[买得便宜]的东西. *a dead* ~ 买价极便宜的货物. ***a*** ~ 便宜 (*I got this a* ~. 买得便宜). ***beat a*** ~ 还价,讲价. ***close [conclude] a*** ~ 定契约[合同]. ***drive a*** ~ (不断) 磋商, 讲价. ***drive a hard*** ~ 乱讲价[还价]. ***in [into] the*** ~ 加之, 而且 (*He gave me 30 dollars into the* ~. 他另外又给我三十元). ***make a ~ with*** 与…订约 [约定]. ***make the best of a bad*** ~ 善处逆境. ***pick up ~s (at a sale)*** 找便宜货. ***sell sb. a*** ~ 戏弄, 愚弄; 使某人意外为难. ***strike a*** ~ 进行交易, 成交. — *vi.* 谈判, 订约; 约定; 〔口〕讨价还价. — *vt.* ①议(价); 约定. ②把…议价卖出; 通过讲条件去掉…. ③预料,预期. ~ *a new wage increase* (通过谈判)达成增

加工资的新协议. *I did not ~ for that.* 原来不是那样约定的，我料不到是那样的. ~ **away** 廉价售出. ~ **for** 期待；预计到. ~ **on** 指望. **Dutch** ~ 酒席上议定的生意. ~ **basement** (地下室)廉价部. ~**-basement** *a.* 便宜的，质量不佳的. ~ **day** 廉价日. ~ **counter** 〔美〕廉价柜台. ~ **hunter** 到处找便宜货的人. ~ **money** 定钱. ~ **sale** 大廉价.

bar·gain·ee [ˌbɑːgiˈniː] *n.* 买主.

bar·gain·er [ˈbɑːginə] *n.* 议价者，讨价还价者.

bar·gain·ing [ˈbɑːginiŋ] *n.* ①讨价还价，议价. ②交涉；契约. ~ **policy** 互惠通商政策. ~ **tariff** 互惠协定关税. ~ **unit** 集体交涉时代表工人的工会.

bar·gain·or [ˈbɑːginə] *n.* 【法】卖主.

barge [bɑːdʒ] *n.* ①大平底船，驳船；〔美〕(有楼)游船，彩船. ②游览汽车；(旅馆的)旅客接送车. ③【美海军】司令〔将官〕专用汽艇；(国王的)御船；(Oxford 大学的)艇库. ④〔俚〕争吵. — *vt.* 用驳船运，乘驳船去. — *vi.* ①蹒跚前进 *(along)*. ②〔口〕闯入 *(in; into)*. ③〔口〕相撞 *(against)*. ~ **about** 瞎跑瞎跳. ~ **around** 〔美口〕闲荡，闲逛. ~ **in** 闯入；〔美俚〕强行加入，干涉，管别人闲事. ~ **into** ①闯入. ②撞上. ~ **board** 【建】挡风板. ~ **couple** 【建】山墙上的椽；伸出山墙的檐. ~ **course** 山墙沿瓦；山墙沿石板. ~ **pole** 撑篙 *(I wouldn't touch it with a ~ pole.* 我很讨厌它；连碰也不想碰它).

bar·gee, barge·man [bɑːˈdʒiː, ˈbɑːdʒmən] *n.* 〔英〕驳船〔游船〕船夫. *a lucky ~* 〔口〕幸运的家伙.

bar·ghest, bar·guest [ˈbɑːgest] *n.* 〔Scot.〕〔北英〕(预告凶事的)犬形妖怪.

Bar·ham [ˈbærəm] *n.* 巴勒姆〔姓氏〕.

bar·i·at·rics [ˌbæriˈætriks] *n.* 【医】肥胖症治疗学.

bar·ic[1] [ˈbærik] *a.* 【化】钡的，含钡的.

bar·ic[2] [ˈbærik] *a.* 气压(计)的.

ba·ril·la [bəˈrilə] *n.* 【化】苏打灰，海草灰苏打.

bar·ite [ˈbeərait] *n.* 【矿】重晶石.

bar·i·tone [ˈbæritəun] *n.* 〔美〕【乐】①(tenor 与 bass 之间的)男中音；男中音歌手. ②萨克斯号. ③(歌剧中)供男中音唱的角色. — *a.* 男中音的.

bar·i·um [ˈbeəriəm] *n.* 【化】钡. ~ **chloride** 氯化钡. ~ **hydroxide** 氢氧化钡. ~ **peroxide** 过氧化钡. ~ **sulfate** 硫酸钡.

bark[1] [bɑːk] *vi.* ①(狗等)吠，叫；(枪等)响. ②咆哮，怒吼. ③〔美口〕喀喀地咳嗽. — *vt.* ①大声喊出，吼叫出. ②大声叫卖. — *n.* ①犬吠声. ②枪声. ③咳嗽声. *His ~ is worse than his bite.* 他嘴坏心不坏. ~*ing irons* 〔美俚〕手枪. ~ **at** 吠，咬. ~ *at the moon* 白嚷，空嚷，徒劳. ~ *away [back]* 喝走〔叫回〕. ~ *up the wrong tree* 〔美口〕认错目标，弄错，看错. *Go ~ up another tree!* 〔美口〕少管闲事，用不着你操心.

bark[2] [bɑːk] *n.* ①茎皮，树皮；规那皮；鞣酸皮. ②〔俚〕皮肤. — *vt.* ①剥(树皮). ②用(树皮)盖(屋顶)；用树皮鞣(革). ③擦破(膝盖等处的)皮. *between the ~ and the wood* 双方无得失〔损益〕. *come [go] between the ~ and the tree* 管闲事. *stick in [to] the ~* 〔美口〕不过分干预〔接近〕. *talk the ~ off a tree* 〔美口〕大嚷. *tighter than the ~ on a tree* 〔美口〕极吝啬的. *with the ~ on* 〔美口〕粗鲁 *(a man with the ~ on* 粗鲁的人). ~ **bed** 鞣皮的温床. ~ **beetles** 一种棘胫小蠹科甲虫〔森林害虫之一〕. ~ **borer** 蛀树皮虫. ~**bound** *a.* 被树皮紧箍因而生长受阻的. ~ **pine** 白皮松. ~ **stove** =~**bed**.

bark[3], **barque** [bɑːk] *n.* ①三桅帆船. ②〔诗〕帆船，小船.

bark·an·tine, bar·ken·tine [ˈbɑːkəntiːn] *n.* = barquentine.

bark·er[1] [ˈbɑːkə] *n.* ①动辄就嚷嚷的人，愤怒咆哮的人. ②吠叫的狗〔狐〕. ③〔美口〕(马戏场等门口的)叫客员；游览向导. ④〔俚〕大炮，手枪. *Great ~s are no biters.* 会叫的狗不会咬人.

bark·er[2] [ˈbɑːkə] *n.* ①剥树皮的人. ②剥树皮机.

bark·er·y [ˈbɑːkəri] *n.* 鞣皮场.

bark·ies [ˈbɑːkiz] *n.* 〔美口〕= talkies.

Bar·kley [ˈbɑːkli] *n.* 巴克利〔姓氏〕.

bar·ley[1] [ˈbɑːli] *n.* 大麦. ~**-break**, ~**-brake** (游戏)绕麦堆捉人. ~**-bree** 麦芽酒；(特指)威士忌酒. ~ **broth** 〔Scot.〕烈性啤酒. ~**corn** ①大麦粒. ②古尺度名(=1/3 英寸) *(John Barleycorn* (拟人语)啤酒，威士忌). ~**-mow** 大麦堆. ~ **sugar** 麦芽糖，麦精柠檬糖(=~candy). ~**-sugar** ① *n.* 把他人手臂反扭到背后的动作. ② *vt.* 反扭(他人手臂). ~ **water** (病人饮用的)大麦茶.

bar·ley[2] [ˈbɑːli] *n.* 〔Scot.〕(特指儿童游戏喊的)停止，停战；停战谈判. *cry ~* 喊停战.

bar·low (knife) [ˈbɑːləu] *n.* 单刃大刀.

barm [bɑːm] *n.* 〔英口〕(发酵时的)啤酒泡沫〔酵母〕〔现多用 yeast 或 leaven〕.

Bar·me·cide [ˈbɑːmisaid] *n.* 允许给人好处而不兑现的人，口惠而实不至的人. — *a.* 口惠而实不至的，欺骗性的，虚伪的. ~ **feast** 空想的利益，空头支票〔出自阿拉伯文学作品《一千零一夜》，Barmecide 用自称珍味而实系空杯空盘请客的酒席〕.

Bar·men [ˈbɑːmən] *n.* 巴门〔西德城市〕.

bar mitz·vah, bar miz·vah [bɑːˈmitsvə] *n.* 〔也作 B-M-〕①犹太受戒龄少年〔犹太男孩年至十三岁即承担宗教义务〕. ②【犹】受戒仪式. — *vt.* 【犹】使受戒.

barm·y [ˈbɑːmi] *a.* ①(含)酵母的；发泡沫的. ②〔英俚〕轻狂的；傻头傻脑的. *go ~* 发疯；发痴.

barn[1] [bɑːn] *n.* ①仓，谷仓，库房. ②〔美〕厩，马房；牛房. ③〔蔑〕空空洞洞的房子. *a car ~* 〔美〕电车车库. *between you and I and the ~* 〔美口〕仅有你知我知的，保密的. ~ **dance** 〔美〕谷仓舞. ~ **door** ①仓库大门. ②〔喻〕容易打中的目标. ③【无】挡光板 *(as big as a ~ door.* 又大又宽. *not be able to hit a ~ door* 枪法不好). ~**-door fowl** 鸡. ~**owl** 仓枭. ~ **swallow** 家燕. ~ **sash** 一种小窗框. ~**yard** ① *n.* 谷仓空场. ② *a.* 谷场近旁地区的；龌龊的. ~**yard grass [millet]** 稗. ~**-yard manure** 厩肥.

barn[2] [bɑːn] *n.* 【物】靶(恩)〔核反应截面单位，$=10^{-24}$ 厘米^2/核〕.

bar·na·cle [ˈbɑːnəkl] *n.* ①【贝】茗荷介，藤壶. ②北极黑雁. ③〔口〕(对职位等)恋栈的人；瞎纠缠的人.

bar·na·cles [ˈbɑːnəklz] *n.* 〔*pl.*〕(钉掌时制马用的)鼻钳. ②〔英方〕眼镜.

Bar·nard [ˈbɑːnəd] *n.* 巴纳德〔姓氏，男子名〕.

Barnes [bɑːnz] *n.* 巴恩斯〔姓氏〕.

Bar·net(t) [ˈbɑːnit] *n.* 巴尼特〔姓氏，男子名〕.

Bar·ney [ˈbɑːni] *n.* 巴尼〔男子名，Bernard 的昵称〕.

barn·storm [ˈbɑːnstɔːm] *vi.* ①(竞选中)四出游说. ②(演员)到各地巡回演出. ③飞行游览，作特技飞行表演. — *vt.* 在(某地)作巡回演出〔飞行游览〕，到(某地)进行游说. **-er** *n.* 游说者；飞行游览者；作巡回演出者.

baro- *comb. f.* 重力，气压.

bar·o·dy·nam·ics [ˌbærəudaiˈnæmiks] *n.* 【物】重结构力学，重(量)力学.

bar·o·gram [ˈbærəugræm] *n.* 【气】气压图，气压自计曲线.

bar·o·graph [ˈbærəugrɑːf] *n.* 【气】气压自记器；【空】自记高度计.

ba·rol·o·gy [bəˈrɔlədʒi] *n.* 【物】重力论.

ba·rom·e·ter [bəˈrɔmitə] *n.* ①晴雨表，气压计. ②〔喻〕(舆论等的)标记.

bar·o·met·ric [ˌbærəuˈmetrik] *a.* 气压计(上)的，测定气压的. ~ **gradient** 气压梯度. ~ **pressure** (大)气压(力). ~ **maximum [minimum]** 最高〔最低〕气压.

ba·ro·met·ri·cal [ˌbærəuˈmetrikəl] *a.* = barometric.

-ly *ad.* 用气压计.

ba·rom·e·try [bəˈrɔmitri] *n.* 气压测定法.

bar·on [ˈbærən] *n.* ①男爵〔和姓并用时, 英国男爵称 Lord X, 别国称 Baron X〕. ②【英史】贵族. ③〔美口〕富商, …大王. ④【法】有妇之夫(*opp.* feme). ⑤(牛、羊的)脊肉. *an oil* ～ 煤油大王. ～ ***and feme***【法】夫妇. ～ ***of beef*** (牛的)脊肉. **-age** 男爵阶级; 贵族阶级; 男爵勋位. **-ess** 男爵夫人; 女男爵. ★ 外国人称作 Barness, 英国人称作 lady.

bar·on·et [ˈbærənit] *a.* 准男爵. **-cy** [-ci] *n.* 准男爵的身份[勋位].

ba·rong [bəˈrɔːŋ, -ˈrɔŋ] *n.* (菲律宾摩洛族人的)重鞘刀.

ba·ro·ni·al [bəˈrəunjəl] *a.* ①男爵的, 象男爵的. ②男爵领有的. ③豪华的, 堂皇的.

ba·ronne [bɑːˈrɔːn] *n.* 〔F.〕男爵夫人.

bar·on·y [ˈbærəni] *n.* ①男爵领地. ②男爵勋位. ③〔美〕…财阀, …王国. ④〔Scot.〕大庄园; 〔爱尔兰〕郡的区划.

ba·roque [bəˈrəuk] *a.* ①怪异的; 矫揉造作的. ②【建】巴罗克式的, 建筑风格过分雕琢和怪诞的; 【乐】在音乐上表现奇异风格的. — *n.* ①新奇作品; 奇怪的样式, 怪异型. ②巴罗克建筑形式; 巴罗克艺术风格.

bar·o·scope [ˈbærəskəup] *n.* (一般的)验压器, 气压计, 大气浮力计.

bar·o·stat [ˈbærəstæt] *n.* 气压调节器, 恒压器.

bar·o·ther·mo·graph [ˈbærəuˈθəːməgrɑːf] *n.* 自记气压温度计; 气压温度记录器.

ba·rouche [bəˈruːʃ] *n.* 双马四轮大马车.

barque [bɑːk] *n.* = bark³.

bar·quen·tine [ˈbɑːkəntiːn] *n.* (只前桅有横帆的)三桅船.

bar·rack [ˈbærək] *n.* ①〔常 *pl.*〕兵营, 营盘, 兵舍. ②临时工房; 简陋敞房[收容所等]; 〔美〕临时干草棚. *an army* ～*s* 一座兵营. — *vt.* ①使驻扎兵营内. ②使住在棚屋内. — *vi.* 〔澳〕①嘲弄. ②(观众)起哄, 喝倒彩; 声援, 助威. ～**-square** 兵营附近操练场. ～**s bag** 战士行军袋, 士兵背囊.

bar·ra·coon [ˌbærəˈkuːn] *n.* 奴隶[罪犯]集中场所.

bar·ra·cu·da [ˌbærəˈkuːdə] *n.* (*pl.* ～*(s)*)【动】魣鱼, 梭鱼.

bar·rage [ˈbærɑːʒ, bæˈrɑːʒ] *n.* ①【军】掩护炮火, 阻击火网; 【无】阻塞, 遮断; (菌丝体生长)阻隔现象. ②〔英〕[ˈbɑːridʒ] 拦河坝, 堰. ③〔喻〕不断猛击, 倾泻. *a balloon* ～ (防空)气球阻击网. *a box* ～ 缘边射击. *a creeping* ～ 诱导弹幕. *a protective* [*covering*] ～ 掩护弹幕. *a* ～ *of questions* 连珠炮一样的质问. ～ **balloon** 阻塞气球. ～ **fire** 弹幕射击. ～ **jamming**【无】全波段干扰; 阻塞干扰. ～ **plan** 弹幕射击计划.

bar·ra·mun·da [ˈbærəˈmʌndə, ber-] *n.* (*pl.* ～*(s)*) 澳大利亚肺鱼 (*Neoceratodus forsteri*).

bar·ra·mun·di [ˈbærəˈmʌndi] *n.* (*pl.* ～, ～*(e)s*) 澳大利亚肺鱼 (= barramunda).

bar·ran·co, bar·ran·ca [bəˈræŋkəu, bəˈræŋkə] *n.* 〔Sp.〕绝壁, 深谷; 火山濑; 羊尾沟.

Bar·ran·quil·la [ˌbɑːrɑːŋˈkiːljɑː] *n.* 巴兰基利亚〔哥伦比亚城市〕.

bar·ra·tor, bar·ra·ter [ˈbærətə] *n.* ①诉讼教唆者. ②为非作歹的船员[船长]. ③受贿的法官; 卖官鬻爵者; (教会)出卖圣职者.

bar·ra·trous [ˈbærətrəs] *a.* ①教唆诉讼的. ②有受贿罪的; 出卖官职[圣职]的. ③为非作歹的.

bar·ra·try [ˈbærətri] *n.* ①【法】诉讼教唆, 无根据诉讼. ②船长[船员]的不法行为. ③法官的受贿罪. ④官职[教会圣职]的买卖.

barred [bɑːd] *a.* ①被堵塞[阻碍]了的; 上了闩的. ②被禁止的. ③划了线条的. ～ **fabrics** 横条花布.

bar·rel [ˈbærəl] *n.* ①桶, 大琵琶桶. ②装满的桶, 桶装. ③一琵琶桶(的分量)〔美国液量 = $31\frac{1}{2}$ gallons, 果蔬 = 105 dry quarts. 英国桶量有 36, 18 或 9 gallons 的, 大小不一〕. ④筒状物, 枪筒, 膛; 【机】圆筒. ⑤(钟表的)发条匣; (照相机的)镜头筒; 【火箭】燃烧室; 火箭发动机. ⑥(牛、马的)身腔. ⑦〔口〕许多. ⑧〔美〕选举经费. *a* ～ *of monkeys* 许多猴子. ～ *of the ear* 鼓室, 中耳. ～ *of fun* 〔美俚〕愉快的游玩. ***have sb. over a*** ～ 〔美俚〕(在经济上)勒住[掐住]某人. — *vt.* 把…装桶. — *vi.* 〔美俚〕高速行进. ～ **bulk** *n.* 五立方英尺容积. ～**-chested** *a.* 胸围特别宽阔的. ～ **drain** 筒形排水渠. ～ **goods** 〔美俚〕酒类. ～ **house** 〔美俚〕低级酒馆; (美国南部)妓院; (早期)下流吵闹的爵士音乐. ～ **house bum** 醉鬼. ～ **organ** 手摇风琴. ～ **roll**【空】(特技飞行中的)横滚; 桶滚. ～ **vault** 筒形穹窿.

bar·relled [ˈbærəld] *a.* ①桶装的. ②有躯干的; 有枪身的. *a double* ～ *gun* 双眼[双筒]枪. *a well* ～ *horse* 身躯发育壮美的马.

bar·ren [ˈbærən] *a.* ①不妊的, 不会生育的, 石女的. ②(植物)不结子的; 不毛的, (土地)荒芜的. (*opp.* fertile). ③无益的, 无效的, (计划)无结果的; (思想等)贫乏的, 无趣味的, 无聊的. ④空, 缺, 无 (*of*). *a* ～ *effort* 无效的努力. *be* ～ *of result* 无结果. — *n.* 〔常 *pl.*〕不毛之地, 荒地, 荒原. **-ness** *n.* 不妊; 秕粒; 不毛; 无趣味.

bar·ren·wort [ˈbærənwəːt] *n.* 【植】淫羊藿属; 高山淫羊藿.

bar·re·ra [bɑːˈreirɑː] *n.* 〔Sp.〕①斗牛场栅栏. ②〔*pl.*〕斗牛场第一排座位.

bar·ret [ˈbærit] *n.* 扁平便帽.

bar·re·try [ˈbærətri] *n.* = barratry.

Bar·rett [ˈbærət, ˈbærit] *n.* 巴雷特〔姓氏, 男子名〕.

bar·rette [bəˈret] *n.* 发夹.

bar·ri·cade [ˌbæriˈkeid], **bar·ri·ca·do** [ˌbæriˈkeidəu] *n.* ①防寨, 防栅; (阻断交通的)栅栏, 路障, 街垒. ②防御, 阻碍. — *vt.* ①在…筑防寨(设栅); 在…设路障; 用栅围住. ②阻塞, 遮住. *They* ～*d themselves in.* 他们设栅栏自卫.

Bar·rie [ˈbæri] *n.* 巴里〔姓氏, 男子名〕.

bar·ri·er [ˈbæriə] *n.* ①栅, 栅栏, 隔栏, 障壁, 隔板, 挡板; 赛马的出发栅. ②关口, (海关)关卡. ③障碍; 壁垒; 界线. ④(扩伸到海洋中的)南极洲冰层. *a moisture* ～ 防湿层. *a potential* ～【物】势垒, 位垒. *a* ～ *to progress* 进步的障碍. *set up a* ～ *between* 在…中间设置障碍. *the* ～*s of class* 阶级的壁垒. *the* ～ *physics* 边缘物理学. *the language* ～ 语言的隔阂. — *vt.* 用栅围住. ～ **bar** [**beach**] 滨外滩〔海浪造成的沙滩, 常与海滩平行, 中间为二者围成的湖〕. ～ **reef** 堡礁.

bar·ring [ˈbɑːriŋ] *prep.* 不包括, 除, 除…之外. *Barring accidents, I'll be there.* 若无意外我一定去.

bar·ri·o [ˈbɑːriəu] *n.* (*pl.* ～*s*) 〔Sp.〕①(说西班牙语国家的)城市行政区. ②(拉丁美洲和菲律宾的)村庄, 村镇, 郊区. ③美国城市(尤指西南部)说西班牙语居民的集居区.

bar·ris·ter [ˈbæristə] *n.* ①〔英〕(能出席高级法庭的)律师. ②〔美〕法律顾问, 律师.

bar·row¹ [ˈbærəu] *n.* ①独轮车; 〔英〕手推双轮车. ②担架. ③(鲨鱼等的)鱼子. ～**-boy** 〔英〕叫卖小贩. ～**-man** 〔英〕叫卖菜贩. ～ **pit** 路边开掘的沟渠; 采石坑; 手车运输的露天矿.

bar·row² [ˈbærəu] *n.* ①(史前人的)冢, 古坟. ②(兽)穴. ③…山〔仅用于英国山名前〕.

bar·row³ [ˈbærəu] *n.* 〔英方〕(阉过的)公猪.

bar·row⁴ [ˈbærəu] *n.* 〔英〕无袖婴儿绒衣.

Bar·ry [ˈbæri] *n.* 巴里〔男子名〕.

Bar·ry·more [ˈbærimɔː] *n.* 巴里莫尔〔姓氏〕.

Bart [bɑːt] *n.* 巴特〔男子名, Bartholomew 的昵称〕.

bar·ter [ˈbɑːtə] *vt.* 以…物物交换, 以(货)换(货). ～ *furs for powder* 用毛皮换火药. — *vi.* 作易货贸易, 作物

物交换. ~ *with natives* 与当地居民以货换货. ~ ***away*** (因不善交易而)吃亏卖出;(因贪图物质利益而)出卖(名誉等). —*n.* ①物物交换,换货,实物交易. ②用以换货的交易品,互换品. ③【数】换算法. ~ *system* 换货贸易制. *exchange and* ~ 以物易物. *expressed in* ~ *terms* 按实物交换比率来说. *on a* ~ *basis* 以易货方式. **-er** 进行易货贸易者.

Bar·thol·o·mew [bɑːˈθɔləmjuː] *n.* ①巴塞洛缪〔男子名〕. ②【圣】基督十二使徒之一. ~ **Fair** 〔英〕巴塞罗缪节大集市. **-tide** [-taid] *n.* 巴塞罗缪节(8月24日).

bar·ti·zan [ˌbɑːtiˈzæn] *n.*【建】小望楼,顶塔.

Bart·lett [ˈbɑːtlit] *n.* 巴特利特〔姓氏〕.

Bar·ton [ˈbɑːtn] *n.* 巴顿〔姓氏〕.

bar·ton [ˈbɑːtn] *n.*〔英方〕①(庄园中的)农场. ②农家场院.

Bart's [bɑːts] *n.* 伦敦 St. Bartholomew's Hospital (圣巴塞洛缪医院)的简称.

Bar·uch [ˈberək] *n.* ①【基督】巴録,巴鲁〔先知耶利米的书记员〕. ②巴鲁书〔上述人物的作品,新教教徒认为是伪经〕.

bar·y- *comb. f.* 重: *bary*tron.

bar·y·cen·tre, bar·y·cen·ter [ˈbærisentə] *n.*【物】重心,质(量中)心.

bar·y·on [ˈbæriɔn] *n.*【物】激(发核)子,重子. ~ **number**【物】重子数.

bar·y·sphere [ˈbærisfiə] *n.*【地】重圈,(地球)重核层,地核,地心圈.

ba·ry·ta [bəˈraitə] *n.*【化】重土〔氧化钡〕.

ba·ry·te(s) [bəˈrait(iːz)] *n.*【矿】重晶石.

bar·y·tone[1] [ˈbæritəun] *n.* = baritone.

bar·y·tone[2] [ˈbæritəun] *a., n.*【希语法】最后音节无重音的(词).

bar·y·tron [ˈbæritrɔn] *n.*【物】介子,重电子.

Bar·uch [bəˈruːk] *n.* 巴鲁克〔姓氏〕.

bas·al [ˈbeisl] *a.* ①基部的. ②基础的,基本的. *the* ~ *parts of a column* 柱的底部. —*n.*【地】基板. ~ **area** 底面积;基域. ~ **leaves**【植】基生叶. ~ **metabolism** 基础代谢. ~ **plane** 底(平)面,基面.

ba·salt [ˈbæsɔːlt] *n.* ①【地】玄武岩. ②一种黑色磁器.

ba·salt·ic [bəˈsɔːltik] *a.* (含)玄武岩的,似玄武岩的.

bas·an, baz·an [ˈbæzən] *n.* 栎鞣羊皮革,书面羊皮.

bas·a·nite [ˈbæsənait] *n.* ①试金石. ②【地】碧玄岩.

bas blcu [ˈbɑːˈbləː] *n.*〔F.〕女学者,女才子;学者气派的女人.

bas·cule [ˈbæskjuːl] *n.* 吊桥活动桁架. ~ **bridge** 开合吊桥,活动桥.

base[1] [beis] *n.* ①基底,基,根基,底座;底层,底子;(纪念碑等的)基址;(山)麓. ②【军】基地,根据地. ③根据,基础. ④【化】碱;【纺】(染色)固色剂;媒染剂;【药】主剂. ⑤【数】底,底面,底边,基点,基线;基数. ⑥【体】起点,出发线;【棒球】垒;目标. ⑦【语】语根;词干. *an air* ~ 空军基地. *the economic* ~ 经济基础. *first [second, third]* ~【棒球】一[二、三]垒. *a* ~ *angle* 底角. *a bayonet* ~ 卡口灯座. *a code* ~ (信息论)编码基数. *a prisoner's* ~ 捉迷藏. ~ *of operation* 作战根据地. ***at the*** ~ ***of*** 在…之麓;在…的基部. ***change one's*** ~〔口〕撤退. ***get to first*** ~ 取得成功的. ***off*** ~〔口〕①大错特错地. ②冷不防地. ③〔美俚〕傲慢的. —*vt.* 把…的基础放在(…)上 *(on; upon)*, 以(…)作为…的根据[基地]. ~ *one's arguments upon facts* 以事实作论辩根据. ~ *one's hopes on…* 把希望寄托在…上. ~**band**【无】基(本频)带. ~**board**【建】脚板;护壁板. ~**burner** 底燃火炉,自给暖炉. ~ **course**【建】底层. ~ **exchange** (海、空军)基地商店. ~ **fertilizer** 基肥. ~ **hospital**【军】后方医院. ~**-court** (城堡)外院;(农场)后院. ~ **level** 基面. ~ **line** 基线;【网球】界限线. ~**man**【棒球】守垒员. ~ **map**【地】工作草图. ~ **oil** 原油. ~ **pair**【生化】碱基对. ~ **paper** (造币)铜版币胚. ~ **pay** 基本工资. ~ **plate**【机】底板,支承板;【医】装假牙的底板. ~ **runner**【棒球】跑垒员. **-less** *a.* 无基础的,无根据的;无原由的.

base[2] [beis] *a.* ①贱的,劣的;卑下的,低级的;卑鄙的. ②(子女)庶出的;私生的. ③(语言)不纯正的,粗俗的. ④【乐】低音的. —*n.*【乐】低音;低音部. ~ **billon** 劣币. ~**born** *a.* 出身低微的;私生的. ~ **coin** 劣币;伪币. ~ **court** (城堡)外院;(农庄)后院;〔英〕下级法院. ~ **Latin** 拉丁俗语. ~ **metals** 普通金币,贱金属(锡,铅等). ~**-mined** *a.* 品质卑劣的,下贱的,卑鄙的. **-ness** *n.* (品质等的)恶劣;下贱,卑鄙.

base·ball [ˈbeisbɔːl] *n.* ①棒球. ②棒球运动. *play* ~ 打棒球. *a* ~ *team* 棒球队. ~ **classic** 〔美〕棒球大比赛. ~ **field [ground]** 棒球场. ~ **fiend**〔美〕棒球迷. **-er, -ist** *n.*〔美〕棒球员,棒球选手.

Ba·sel [ˈbɑːzəl] *n.* 巴塞尔〔瑞士城市〕.

base·ment [ˈbeismənt] *n.* ①建筑物的底部. ②【建】底层;地下室 (*cf.* cellar). ~ **complex**【地】基底杂岩. ~ **storey** 底层.

ba·sen·ji [bəˈsendʒi] *n.*〔Ban.〕猴面犬.

ba·ses[1] [ˈbeisiz] base 的复数.

bas·es[2] [ˈbeisiːz] basis 的复数.

bash [bæʃ] *vt.*〔英方、美俚〕猛击,痛击;打坏. —*vi.* 猛撞. —*n.* ①猛击,痛打. ②痛快的玩乐[消遣]. ③〔英方〕尝试. ~ *sb. on the head* 猛击某人的头. *give him* ~*es and kicks* 对他拳打脚踢. ***have a*** ~ ***at*** 〔英方〕试试看. ***on the*** ~〔英方〕做娼妓.

Ba·sham [ˈbæʃəm] *n.* 巴沙姆〔姓氏〕.

ba·shaw [bəˈʃɔː] *n.*〔古〕①= pasha. ②〔口〕傲慢的官僚.

bash·ful [ˈbæʃful] *a.* 害羞的,羞怯的,腼腆的. ~ *manner* 忸怩. **-ly** *ad.* **-ness** *n.*

bas·ic [ˈbeisik] *a.* ①基础的,基本的,根本的. ②【化】碱性的,碱式的. ③【矿】基性的,含少量硅酸的. ④【军】初步的;最下级的. ~ *data* 基本数据. ~ *industry* 基础工业. —*n.*〔常 *pl.*〕①基础,基本. ②基础训练. *work for the* ~*s* 为衣食住等操劳. ~ **credit line**【美商】(准备银行的)贷款限额. ~ **dye** 碱性染料. **B- English** 基本英语〔英国学者 C. K. Ogden 等人用 850 个英语基本词汇创制的一种国际辅助语〕. ~ **private** 〔美〕陆军三等兵. ~ **process**【冶】碱性炼钢法. ~ **slag** 碱性熔渣.

Basic = Basic English.

ba·sic·i·ty [bəˈsisiti] *n.*【化】碱度;碱性;【地】基性度.

ba·sid·io·my·cete [bəˌsidiəuˈmaisiːt] *n.*【植】担子菌.

ba·sid·i·o·spore [bəˈsidiːəuspɔː] *n.*【植】担子孢子. **-spor·ous** [-ˈspɔːrəs] *a.*

ba·sid·i·um [bəˈsidiəm] *n. (pl.* ***ba·sid·i·a*** [bəˈsidiə]*)*【植】担子. **ba·sidi·al** *a.*

ba·si·fi·ca·tion [ˌbeisifiˈkeiʃən] *n.*【化】碱化;【地】基性岩化.

bas·i·fixed [ˈbeisifikst] *a.*【植】底着的.

ba·sif·uge [ˈbeisifjuːdʒ] *n.*【植】避碱植物,嫌碱植物.

bas·i·fy [ˈbeisifai] *vt.*【化】使碱化.

Bas·il [ˈbæzl] *n.* 巴兹尔〔男子名〕.

bas·il [ˈbæzl] *n.*【植】罗勒;罗勒属植物.

bas·i·lar [ˈbæsilə] *a.* ①基底的,基础的. ②脑壳低部的. ③【植】基部的;(花柱)基生的.

bas·i·lect [ˈbæsilekt] *n.* 下层社会的语言.

ba·sil·ic(al) [bəˈsilik(əl)] *a.* ①帝王的,皇家的. ②王宫的;(古罗马)长方形大会堂[教堂]的. ③【解】主要的,重要的〔指静脉〕. ~ **vein**【解】上臂两头肌肉侧的大静脉.

ba·sil·i·ca [bəˈzilikə] *n.* ①王宫. ②(古罗马)长方形大会堂[教堂].

ba·sil·i·con [bəˈzilikən] *n.* 松脂蜡膏.

bas·i·lisk [ˈbæzilisk] *n.* ①【神】蛇怪〔传说出没于非洲沙漠,其目光或呼气均足以使人丧命〕. ②【动】(热带)蜥蝎．~ ***glance*** 使人见而遭殃的眼神．

ba·sin [ˈbeisn] *n.* ①面盆；水盆．②满盆，(一)盆．③盆地，流域．④水坑，地塘；(港湾)深度；内湾，小湾；【船】船坞．⑤【地】盘层，煤田．⑥【解】骨盘，骨盘腔．~ *irrigation* 小块灌溉．*the Thames* ~ 泰晤士河流域．*a* ~ *of water* 一盆水．*a river* ~ 流域．*a setting* ~ 澄水池．~ **stand** 洗脸架．**-ful** *n.* 一满盆．

bas·i·net, bas·net [ˈbæsinit, ˈbæsnit] *n.* ①(中世纪欧洲的)露面钢盔．②(盔下)衬帽．

ba·si·on [ˈbeisiən] *n.* 颅底骨．

ba·sip·e·tal [beiˈsipətl] *a.* 【植】向基的．

ba·sis [ˈbeisis] *n.* (*pl.* ***ba·ses*** [ˈbeisi:z]) ①基础；基底；台座；【地】坡基．②根据，基准．③主要成份；主药．④【数】基．*On a production* ~ 在大规模生产的基础上．*On what* ~？凭什么条件(雇佣等)？*on the war* ~ 按战时体制．*the* ~ *of argument* 论据．*the* ~ *of assessment* 课税标准．***on the*** ~ ***of*** 以…为基础．

bask [bɑ:sk] *vi.* ①晒太阳；取暖．②受宠，沐恩；〔喻〕感到舒适．— *vt.* 使(自身)受(暖)，使(自身)受(太阳晒)．~ *oneself in a sunny place* 晒太阳．~ ***in sb.'s smile [favor]*** 得某人欢心〔恩宠〕．~ ***in the sunshine*** 晒太阳．~**ing shark** 姥鲨．

Bas·ker [ˈbɑ:skə] *n.* 巴斯克〔姓氏〕．

bas·ket [ˈbɑ:skit] *n.* ①篮，笼，篓，筐．②一篮〔笼，篓，筐〕．③【空】(气球的)吊篮．④【建】花篮状柱头．⑤(篮球运动的)篮；一次投篮得分．⑥一组问题．*a* ~ *of apples* 一篮苹果．*a* ~ *of clips* 赏心乐事，愉快．***be left in the*** ~ 落选，卖剩．***make a*** ~ (篮球) 投中一球．***sneeze into a*** ~ 上断头台，被斩首．***the pick of the*** ~ 精品．— *vt.* 把…装入篮内，把…丢入字纸篓里．~**-ball** 【体】篮球．~ **carriage** 柳条车身的马车．~ **case** 四肢被截断的(病)人．~ **chair** 柳条椅．~ **cloth**绣花(用)十字布．~ **dinner**〔美〕(大规模的)野餐．~ **fish**，~**-handle arch** 【建】三心拱．~ **hilt** (刀剑的) 篮状柄．~**-of-gold** 【植】岩生庭荠．~ **star** 【动】星鱼〔海盘车类〕．~ **weave** 【纺】方平组织．~ **work** (篮子等)编织品．~ **worm** 【虫】结草虫．**-ful** *n.* 满篮，一篮．**-ry** (篮，篓，笼，筐等的)编织法；(篮子等)工艺品．

bas mitz·vah, bas miz·vah [bɑ:sˈmitsvə] *n.* ①犹太受戒龄女孩．②(犹太教)受戒仪式．

bas·net [ˈbæsnit] *n.* = basinet.

ba·son [ˈbeisn] *n.* = basin.

ba·so·phil·ic [ˈbeisəufilik], **ba·so·ph·i·lou** [beiˈsɔfiləs] *a.* (植物)适碱(性)的，喜碱(性)的．

Basque [bæsk, bɑ:sk] *n.* ①巴斯克人〔西班牙比利牛斯山西部居民〕．②巴斯克语．③〔b-〕巴斯克式妇女紧身衣，女人短裙．— *a.* 巴斯克地区的；巴斯克人的；巴斯克语的．

Bas·ra [ˈbæzrə] *n.* 巴士拉〔伊拉克港市〕．

bas-re·lief [ˈbæsrili:f] *n.* 半浮雕，浅浮雕．

bass[1] [beis] *n.* 【乐】①男低音；低音奏唱者．②低音部．③低音乐器．— *a.* 低音的．~ **clarinet** 低音单簧管．~ **viol** 低音提琴 (= violoncello).

bass[2] [bæs] *n.* (*pl.* ~***(es)***) 【鱼】欧洲鲈鱼．

bass[3] [bæs] *n.* ①【植】椴树；椴属树木，美洲椴木．②椴树韧皮．③〔*pl.*〕韧皮纤维制品〔如席子绳索等〕．

Bass [bæs] *n.* 巴斯(厂的)啤酒；一瓶巴斯啤酒．

bas·set[1] [ˈbæsit] *n.* 矮脚长耳猎狗．

bas·set[2] [ˈbæsit] *n.* 【矿、地】矿层露头．— *vi.* (矿脉) 露出．~ **horn** (tenor 音的)木管箫．

Basse-Terre [bɑ:ˈsteə] *n.* 巴斯特尔〔瓜德罗普岛(法)首府〕．

bas·si·net [ˌbæsiˈnet] *n.* (婴儿的)(柳条)摇篮，摇篮车．

bass·ist [ˈbeisist] *n.* 倍大提琴演奏者，倍大提琴家．

bas·so [ˈbæsəu] *n.* (*pl.* ~***s***, ***bas·si*** [ˈbæsi:]) 〔It.〕【乐】①低音(部)．②男低音，男低音歌手．~ **buffo** 歌剧中的低音滑稽歌手．~ **contante** 抒情低音．~ **profundo** 最低音；最低音歌手．

bas·soon [bəˈsu:n, bəˈzu:n] *n.* 【乐】①巴松管，大管．②风琴上的低音簧．*a contra* ~ 低音大管．**-ist** *n.* 巴松管吹奏者．

bas·so-ri·lie·vo [ˈbæsəuriˈli:vəu] *n.* 〔It.〕 = bas-relief.

bass·wood [ˈbæswud] *n.* (美洲)椴树；椴木．

bast [bæst] *n.* ①【植】韧皮部，韧皮(纤维)．②椴树的内皮．~ **fiber** 韧皮纤维．~ **fiber plants** 麻黄．~ **silk** 生丝．

bas·ta [ˈbɑ:stɑ:] *int.* 〔It.〕够了！罢了！足了！

bas·tard [ˈbæstəd] *n.* ①私生子．②【动、植】杂种．③代用品，假冒品；劣货；粗劣的糖．④〔俚〕坏蛋，讨厌鬼；〔俚〕家伙〔亲热的玩笑用语〕．— *a.* ①私生的．②杂种的；不纯粹的．③伪的，假的．④奇形怪状的，异常的．~ *charity* 伪善．~ **asbestos** 变种石棉．~ **file** 粗齿锉．~ **slip** 【植】吸枝．~ **stucco** 混毛泥灰．~ **title** 【印】简略标题．~ **wheat** 杂种小麦．~ **wing** (鸟类的)小翼羽．

bas·tard·ize [ˈbæstədaiz] *vt.* ①判定〔证明〕…为私生．②使不纯，使品质变坏．③乱用，误用(言语等)．— *vi.* 变坏，变为不纯．**-i·za·tion** *n.*

bas·tard·ly [ˈbæstədli] *a.* ①私生的，出身低贱的；杂交的．②伪造的，赝制的．③卑鄙的．

bas·tard·y [ˈbæstədi] *n.* 私生子身分；私生．

baste[1] [beist] *vt.* 用长针脚缝，疏缝，假缝．

baste[2] [beist] *vt.* ①〔口〕痛打，狠揍．②痛骂，说…的闲话．③〔美俚〕用枪打死，枪毙．

baste[3] [beist] *vt.* 在(烤肉、煎肉)上溜油〔涂油〕；撒上(粉等)．

Bas·til(l)e [bæsˈti:l] *n.* ①巴士底监狱〔创建于14世纪的法国城堡和国家监狱，位于巴黎，1789 年法国大革命中被攻破〕．②〔b-〕牢狱；〔古〕城砦；【建】堡塔．~ **Day** 巴士底日〔7 月 14 日，为法国国庆日，1789 年于该日攻破巴士底狱〕．

bas·ti·na·do [ˌbæstiˈneidəu] *n.* ①笞蹠，打脚掌．②笞蹠刑．③棍，杖．— *vt.* 打…的脚掌，对…处蹠刑．

bast·ing[1] [ˈbeistiŋ] *n.* ①疏缝，假缝．②〔*pl.*〕绷线，假缝用线．

bast·ing[2] [ˈbeistiŋ] *n.* (烤肉时的)涂油脂；涂在烤肉上的油脂．

bast·ing[3] [ˈbeistiŋ] *n.* 一顿狠揍；一顿痛骂．

bas·ti·on [ˈbæstiən, Am. ˈbæsʃən] *n.* ①棱堡．②设防地区，阵地工事．③〔喻〕堡垒．**-a·ry** *a.*

Ba·su·to [bəˈsu:təu] *n.* (*pl.* ~***s***) 巴苏陀人．

Ba·su·to·land [bəˈsu:təulænd] 巴苏陀兰〔莱索托的旧名〕．

bat[1] [bæt] *n.* ①短棍；(棒球等的)球棒，(网球等的)球拍．②(棒球等的)击球员；轮到击球．③砖块；(粘土等的)硬块．④〔常 *pl.*〕棉卷，棉胎．⑤〔口〕打击，猛击；(海上)导弹．⑥〔英俚〕步调，速度．⑦〔美俚〕喝闹酒，欢宴，狂欢．⑧〔美俚〕一块钱．⑨【矿】油页岩淀积．*a* ~ *breaker* 【美棒球】击球凶猛的人．*behind the* ~ (棒球)接球员的位置．*cross* ~*s with* 与…比赛(棒球)．*times at* ~ (棒球) 打数．***at*** ~ 【棒球】就击球员位置；握紧打棒．~ ***hides*** 〔美俚〕(总称)钞票．***carry one's*** ~ ①【板球】没有犯规退场．②〔口〕打赢，达到目的．***go full*** ~ 急走，全速前进．***go off at a rare*** ~ 飞快逃走．***go on a*** ~ 〔美俚〕喝闹酒．***go to*** ~ ***for*** 〔美俚〕替…辩护，主张．***hot [right] off the*** ~ 〔俚〕马上，立刻．***off one's own*** ~ 凭自己努力，独力，独立．***on one's own*** ~〔口〕独立，自力．***the side at*** ~ (棒球的) 攻方．— *vt.* ①用球棒〔球拍〕打(球)；打．②〔俚〕突击；(为主义等)战斗．③详细讨论，反复考虑．— *vi.* ①用球棒〔球拍〕打球．②轮到击球．*Which side is batting now?* 现在是哪一方进攻？~ ***out*** 粗制滥造．~ ***round*** ①到处寻乐．②探讨，琢磨．

bat[2] [bæt] *n.* ①蝙蝠．②〔俚〕妓女．***blind as a*** ~ 瞎的；

眼力不行的. ***have ~s in the belfry*** 发痴; 异想天开. **~-blind, ~-eyed** *a.* 眼力坏的, 半瞎的; 愚蠢的. **~wing** 蝙蝠翼战斗机.

bat[3] [bɑ:t,bæt] *n.* ①〔Ind.〕〔the ~〕(外国语中的) 白话,口语. ②〔英口〕口语,成语,俗话. ***sling the*** ~ 〔军俚〕说外国话.

bat[4] [bæt] *vt.* 〔方〕①眨(眼睛). ②拍(翅). *a bird batting its wings* 鸟拍翅. ***not ~ an eyelid [eye]*** 泰然不动.

Ba·ta [ˈbɑ:tɑ:] *n.* 巴塔〔赤道几内亚港市〕.

Ba·ta·vi·a [bəˈteiviə] *n.* 巴达维亚〔①美国 New York 州西北部城市. ②印尼首都和最大商港雅加达 (Djakarta) 之旧称〕. **-n** [-vjən] *a.* 巴达维亚的.

batch [bætʃ] *n.* ①(面包等的)一炉. ②一次投料量;一次生产量. ③一宗,一批,一束,一组,一群. ④【计】成批(工作). *the first ~ of goods* 第一批货物. ***in ~es*** 分批;成批. ~ **processing**【计】成批处理.

batch·y [ˈbætʃi] *a.* 〔俚〕疯狂的,狂妄的.

bate[1] [beit] *vt.* ①〔古〕减少;降低. ②减轻,抑制,削弱. *not ~ a penny of it* 一文不减让. ~ ***an ace*** 寸步不让. ***with ~d breath*** 屏息. — *vi.* 〔方〕减退;衰落,变弱.

bate[2] [beit] *n.* 〔英俚〕愤怒. *get in a ~* 发怒,生气.

bate[3] [beit] *n.* (使皮革软化的) 脱灰碱液. — *vt.* 把(皮革)浸入软化液,用脱灰碱液使(皮革)软化.

ba·teau [bæˈtəu] *n.* (*pl.* **~x** [-z]) ①(美国北部和加拿大的)平底河船. ②搭浮桥的船. ~ **bridge** 浮桥.

bate·ment-light [ˈbeitməntlait] *n.*【建】跛窗.

Bates [beits] *n.* 贝茨〔姓氏〕.

bat·fish [ˈbætfiʃ] *n.* (*pl.* ~,~*es*) ①蝙蝠鱼科的鱼. ②鷂鲼 (*Aetobatus californicus*). ③【鱼】豹鲂鮄 (= flying gurnard).

bat·fowl [ˈbætfaul] *vi.* 夜间点火捉巢中鸟.

bath [bɑ:θ] *n.* (*pl.* ***baths*** [bɑ:ðz]) ①沐浴,洗澡. ②浴缸;澡盆. ③浴室,(公共)澡堂. ④〔常 *pl.*〕(豪华的)大浴场;温泉浴场. ⑤浸,泡;洗澡水;(泡酸菜的)卤水;染液. ⑥【化】浴;浴器,液盘,电镀槽,电解槽;【冶】炉底;平炉铁浆;【摄】定影液. *a cold [hot] ~* 冷水[热水]浴. *a shower ~* 淋浴. *a sand ~* 砂浴. *a mud ~* 泥浴. *a steam [vapor] ~* 蒸气浴. *a succession ~* 冷温交替浴. *a sun ~* 日光浴. *a swimming ~* 游泳浴池〔附设室内游泳池〕. *a Turkish ~* 土耳其浴,蒸气浴. *a plating ~* 电镀槽. *a public ~* 公共浴场. *the Roman ~s* 古罗马公共浴场. ~ ***of blood*** 浴血,大屠杀,血洗. ***have [take] a ~*** 入浴,洗澡. ***take the ~s*** 洗温泉(治病). — *vt.* 给(孩子等)洗澡. ~ *a baby* 给孩子洗澡. — *vi.* 洗澡,入浴. **~house** 浴室,澡堂;(海水浴场等的)换衣处. ~ **mat** (浴室内的)防滑垫,揩脚垫. **~robe**〔美〕浴衣(=〔英〕dressing-gown). **~room** 浴室,沐浴间,洗澡间;盥洗室,〔书〕厕所. **~tub** ①澡盆,浴缸. ②〔美空军俚〕(战斗机中枪手的)球形坐位;〔美俚〕摩托车的边车. **~tub gin** 〔美俚〕私酿的杜松子酒.

Bath[1] [bɑ:θ] *n.* (英国的)巴斯勋位,巴斯勋章. ***Order of the ~*** 巴斯勋位[勋章].

Bath[2] [bɑ:θ] 巴斯〔英国 Somerset 州首邑,以温泉著名〕. ***go to ~!*** 滚蛋! 出去! ~ **brick** (研磨金属用的)巴斯研磨粉. ~ **chair** (病人用的)车椅. ~ **chap** 〔英〕(猪的)下颚肉. ~ ***stone*** 巴斯石灰石〔建筑用〕.

bathe [beið] *vt.* ①把…浸泡在液体中(*in*);给…洗澡. ②(光线、暖气等)充满于,笼罩,包覆(全身). ③(浪)冲刷(岸等). ④(用海绵等)洗,把…弄湿,润湿 (*in, with*). ~ *one's throat* (用水等)润喉. ~ *a wound* 洗伤口. *a morning fog bathing the city* 朝雾笼罩城市. *The Nile ~s Egypt.* 尼罗河灌溉埃及. ~ ***(oneself) in*** (*water; the sun*) 泡在(水中);浸在(日光中). — *vi.* ①洗澡. ②(在河、海等里) 游泳. ③沉浸, 沐浴 (*in*). — *n.* 〔英〕(在河、海中的) 游泳. ***go for a ~*** 去游泳. ***have [take] a ~*** 游泳, 洗(海水)澡. **-a·ble** *a.* 可洗浴的,适于游泳的.

bath·er [ˈbeiðə] *n.* 游泳者,洗澡的人;浴疗者.

ba·thet·ic [bəˈθetik] *a.* ①【修】顿降法的. ②平凡的,陈腐的. ③假作悲伤的,过分感伤的.

bath·i·nette [ˈbɑ:θiˈnet] *n.* 巴希奈小浴盆〔原为小儿浴盆商标名称;胶布制,轻便,可折叠〕;胶布小浴盆.

bath·ing [ˈbeiðiŋ] *n.* ①游泳;洗海[河、湖] 水澡. ②(海滨等的)游泳条件. *He's fond of ~.* 他喜欢(在海、河、湖中)游泳. *The ~ here is safe.* 这里洗海水澡很安全. ~ **cap** 女子游泳帽. ~ **clothes [costume, dress, suit]** 游泳衣. ~ **drawers** 游泳裤. ~ **machine** (浴场)换衣马车〔曳入水中,以便游泳者更衣〕. ~ **place** 海滨浴场,游泳场;浴疗场.

batho- *comb. f.* = deep.

bath·o·chrome [ˈbæθəkrəum] *n.*【化】向红团.

bath·o·lith [ˈbæθəliθ], **bath·o·lite** [-lait] *n.*【地】岩基.

ba·thom·e·ter [bəˈθɔmitə] *n.* =bathymeter.

bat·horse [ˈbæthɔ:s] *n.* (驮军官行李等的)驮马.

ba·thos [ˈbeiθɔs] *n.* ①【修】顿降法〔由庄重突转庸俗之法〕;虎头蛇尾. ②假悲哀; 过分的感伤, 感伤癖. ③陈腐,平凡.

Bath·urst [ˈbæθə(:)st] 巴瑟斯特 〔Banjul 班珠尔的旧称〕.

bath·y·al [ˈbæθiəl] *a.* 洋深的.

ba·thyb·ic [bæˈθibik] *a.* 深海性的.

ba·thym·e·ter [bæˈθimitə] *n.* 水深测量器,测深仪.

bathy·met·ric [ˌbæθiˈmetrik] *a.* ①深测法的. ②【地】等深的. ③关于深水生物分布的.

ba·thym·e·try [bæˈθimitri] *n.* ①海洋测深学[术]. ②海洋生物分布学.

bath·y·scaph(e) [ˈbæθiskæf] *n.* 深海潜测艇, 深海生物调查潜艇,深海潜艇.

bath·y·sphere [ˈbæθisfiə] *n.* 深海球形潜水器.

bath·y·ther·mo·graph [ˌbæθiˈθə:məgrɑ:f] *n.* 海水测温计,深海温度仪.

ba·tik [bætik] *n.* = battik.

bat·ing [ˈbeitiŋ] *prep.* 〔古〕除…之外.

ba·tiste [bæˈti:st] *n.* 细麻布,细棉布;麻纱.

bat·man [ˈbætmən] *n.* 〔英〕(军官的)马夫; 马弁; 勤务兵.

bat-mon·ey [ˈbætmʌni] *n.* 〔英〕(将校的)战地津贴.

ba·ton [ˈbætən] *n.* ①(表示军阶、官阶的)官杖; 司令杖. ②警棍. ③【乐】指挥棒. ④【体】接力棍. *the ~ of a field marshal* 陆军元帅的官杖. *an orchestra under the ~ of …* 某某人指挥的管弦乐队. ***carry [have] a Marshal's ~ in one's knapsack*** 有将帅器量. ***wield a good ~*** 指挥灵活. — *vt.* 用短棒打. ~ **charge** 警察的干涉. ~ **gun** (发射硬橡胶子弹的) 防暴枪. ~ **round** 防暴子弹. ~ **sinister**【徽】私生子的记号. **-ist** 指挥者.

bat·pay [ˈbætpei] *n.*〔英军俚〕战时特别津贴.

Ba·tra·chi·a [bəˈtreikjə] *n.* 〔*pl.*〕【动】(无尾)两栖类;蛙类.

ba·tra·chi·an [bəˈtreikjən] *n., a.* 两栖类(的), 无尾类(的),蛙类(的).

bats [bæts] *a.* 〔美口〕发狂的,发疯的. *He's gone ~.* 那家伙发疯了.

bats·man [ˈbætsmən] *n.* (棒球等的)击球员.

bat·tal·ion [bəˈtæljən] *n.* ①【军】营,大队;营部. ②〔*pl.*〕大军,部队; 一大群人, 一大批物品. *~s of bureaucrats* 一大群官僚.

Bat·tam·bang [ˈbætəm-bang] *n.* 马德望〔柬埔寨城市〕.

bat·tel [ˈbætl] *n.* ①(牛津大学的)膳宿杂费(学期末结算清单). ②〔*pl.*〕(牛津大学的)学费〔包括膳宿杂费〕.

bat·ten[1] [ˈbætn] *n.* ①【建】板条;挂瓦条,压缝条. ②小方材, 小圆材. ③【海】扣板, 压条,条板. ④(舞台)装灯光的横木条. ⑤万能曲线尺. ~ *door* 条板门. — *vt.*

装条板于；在…上钉扣板，把…用板条钉牢。～ *down (the hatches)*【海】(暴风雨或失火时)钉上扣板密闭舱口。

bat·ten[2] [ˈbætn] *n.*【纺】筘(座)。

bat·ten[3] [ˈbætn] *vi.* ①饱餐，大吃 *(on; upon)*。②养肥自己，长胖 *(on)*〔尤指损人利己〕；肥私囊。～ *on the poor* 靠盘剥穷人养肥自己。— *vt.* 养肥(猪、羊等)。

bat·ter[1] [ˈbætə] *n.*〔美〕(棒球等的)击球员。

bat·ter[2] [ˈbætə] *n.*【烹】(做糕饼时用粉、牛奶等调成的)奶油面糊。

bat·ter[3] [ˈbætə] *vt.* ①连续地猛打[捶，捣]。②炮击；攻击，乱轰。③打坏，敲碎，摧毁，捶薄；把…打得七凸八凹，打扁(帽子等)。④用坏(铅字等)，磨损(家具等)。*badly ～ed and mauled* 碰得头破血流。～ *the door down* 把门冲垮。— *vi.* ①作连续猛打；乱打，炮轰 *(at)*。②【建】(墙壁等的)内倾，倾斜。— *n.* (铅字的)磨损，毁损。*continue to ～ at the door* 不断地用力敲门。

bat·tered [ˈbætəd] *a.* ①打扁了的，打垮了的，敲碎了的。②用旧了的。③(因生活困难等)憔悴的，消瘦的。***the ～ baby [child] syndrome*** 儿童被摧残造成的综合症。

bat·ter·ing [ˈbætəriŋ] *n.* 连续猛击。～ **artillery**〔集合词〕攻城炮。～ **charge** 最大装(弹)药量。～ **ram** (古代的)破城槌，撞车；(铁匠的)大槌。～ **train** 攻城炮列。

bat·ter·y [ˈbætəri] *n.* ①炮兵连[营，中队]；(军舰上的)炮组，炮列；炮台；炮(兵)阵(地)；(炮的)待发射状态。②(金属器具的)一套，一组；(问题等的)一连串。③【法】殴打。④【电】电池(组)。⑤【纺】(自动织机的)纬管库。⑥【棒球】投球员与接球员。⑦(乐队的)一组打击乐器。⑧孵蛋箱组。*a ～ of questions* 一连串的质问。*a cooking ～* 一套烹调用具。*a local ～* 自给电池。*a solar ～* 太阳能电池。***change one's ～*** 变更攻击方向，换手攻击。***in ～*** 准备发射。***turn a sb.'s ～ against [upon] himself*** 抓住对方理论反击对方，以子之矛攻子之盾。～ **charger** 电池充电器。～ **eliminator** 电池组代用器。**bat·ter·ied** *a.* (装配有)电池的。

bat·tik [ˈbætik] *n.*【纺】①蜡染法，蜡防印花法。②蜡染花布。

bat·ting [ˈbætiŋ] *n.* ①(棒球等的)击球，击球法。②棉胎，棉絮，毛絮。～ **average** (棒球)击球平均得分数；〔口〕平均成功率；〔美〕能力。～ **eye** (棒球)击球的眼力。

bat·tle [ˈbætl] *n.* ①战，战斗(行动)，交战，会战，战役，(一般)战争。②斗争，竞争；〔美〕竞赛。③胜利，成功。*a ～ of words* 论战。*the disposition for a ～* 战术的部署。*the ～ of life* 生存斗争。*The battle is not always to the strong* 强者不一定常胜。*a naval ～* 海战。*a close ～* 近战，肉搏。*a decisive ～* 决战。*a general's ～* 战略和战术的较量，韬略战。*a soldier's ～* 勇气和力量的较量，兵力战。*a pitched ～ = a plain ～* 鏖战，酣战。*a sham ～*〔美〕模拟战，战斗演习。*a street ～* 巷战。***accept ～*** 应战，迎战。***be killed in ～*** 阵亡。***do ～ = fight a ～*** 挑战，开战，交战。***fall in ～*** 阵亡。***fight one's ～s over again*** 忆谈当年勇，反复叙述当年功绩[经历]。***gain a ～*** 打胜仗。***give ～ = do ～***。***give the ～*** 认输，战败。***go into ～*** 投入战斗。***half the ～*** 成功[胜利]的一半 *(Youth is half the ～.* 年轻气锐就是一半成功)。***have the ～*** 战胜。***join ～*** 参战。***lose a ～*** 打败仗。***lose the ～*** 战败。***offer ～*** 挑战。***refuse ～*** 拒绝应战。— *vi.* 作战，战斗，斗争，奋斗 *(against; with; for)*。*～ with poverty* 与贫困作斗争。—*vt.*〔美〕与…作战，与…斗争。*～ the storm* 与暴风雨作斗争。～ **array** 战斗队形，阵容。**～-ax(e)** (中古的)战斧，大斧；〔美俚〕硕大凶悍的女人。～ **bill** 战斗配置表。～ **bowler**〔军口〕钢盔。**～-clad** *a.* 全副武装的。～ **cruiser** 战列巡洋舰。～ **cry** ①(作战时的)呐喊，助攻声。②标语，(斗争)口号。～ **dress** 战地服装。～ **effectiveness** 战斗力。～ **fatigue** 战斗疲劳症。**～field** 战场，战地。～ **formation** 战斗队形。～ **front** 战线。**～ground** 战场；论争的主题。～ **group** 战斗群。～ **line** ①战线，前线。②(海军)作战队形。～ **painter** 军事题材画家。～ **piece** 战争画，战争记事。**～plane** 战斗机。**～-ready** *a.* 作好战斗准备的。～ **royal** ①(斗鸡)大战。②大混战，大论战。**～-scarred** *a.* 有战斗疤痕的；有战争痕迹的。**～ship** *n.* 战舰。～ **sky** 作战空域。**～-some** *a.* 爱争吵的，好口角的。～ **stations** 阵地，战斗岗位；紧急集结点。～ **trim** 战斗准备 ～ **wag(g)on**〔俚〕战舰。**～-wise** *a.* 有战斗经验的；身经百战的。**～-worth** *a.* (武器等)适合用于战斗的。**～-worthiness** 适合战斗的性能[状态]。

bat·tled [ˈbætld] *a.* 有城垛的，有雉堞的。

bat·tle·dore [ˈbætldɔː] *n.* ①板羽球球板；板羽球游戏。②(洗衣等用)杓状杵。***play ～ and shuttlecock*** 打板羽球。～ *the plan* 计划被推来推去。— *vt.* 把…扔来扔去。— *vi.* 互相间扔来扔去。

bat·tle·ment [ˈbætlmənt] *n.*〔常 *pl.*〕雉堞，城垛；有枪眼的防御墙。

bat·tue [bæˈtjuː] *n.*〔F.〕〔英〕①(向猎人埋伏处)赶兽，追猎。②追猎队，追猎猎获品。③大量捕杀，滥杀。

bat·ty [ˈbæti] *a.* ①蝙蝠(似)的。②〔美俚〕愚蠢的，疯狂的；反常的。*go ～* 发疯。

bat·wing [ˈbætˌwiŋ] *a.* 蝙蝠翼状的。— *n.* 蝙蝠翼战斗机。

bau·ble [ˈbɔːbl] *n.* ①美观的便宜货，小玩意，骗钱货。②骗孩子的东西，玩具。③【史】弄臣[丑角]的手杖。***A fool should never hold a ～ in his hand.*** 不要自己出乖露丑。

baud [bɔːd] *n.* ①波特〔发报速率单位〕。②计算机的秒速。

bau·de·kin, bal·da·chin [ˈbɔːdəkin, ˈbɔːldəkin] *n.* ①【纺】宝大锦。②祭坛华盖；宝座华盖。③【宗】祭坛上的华盖状大理石结构。

bau·drons [ˈbɔːdrənz] *n.*〔Scot.〕猫〔不加冠词〕。

Bau·er [ˈbauə] *n.* 鲍尔〔姓氏〕。

baulk [bɔːk, bɔːlk] *n., v.* = balk.

Bau·mé [bəuˈmei] *n.* 玻(美)度；玻美液体比重计。—*a.* 玻美标度的。～ **hydrometer** 玻美比[浮]重计，玻美表。～ **scale** 玻美比重标(度)，玻氏比重计。

baux·ite [ˈbɔːksait] *n.*【矿】铝矾土，铝土矿。

Ba·var·i·a [bəˈvɛəriə] *n.* 巴伐利亚〔西德州名〕。**-n** ① *a.* 巴伐利亚(人)的；巴伐利亚语的。② *n.* 巴伐利亚人[语]。

bav·in [ˈbævin] *n.* 柴，柴捆。～ *wood* 束材。

baw·bee [bɔːˈbiː] *n.*〔Scot.〕①半便士；小钱。②〔口〕小事。

baw·cock [ˈbɔːkɔk] *n.*〔古〕好人，好汉。

bawd [bɔːd] *n.* ①鸨母，妓院女老板。②妓女。③淫猥语，猥亵语。

bawd·ry [ˈbɔːdri] *n.* ①〔废〕开妓院；卖淫；私通，不贞。②〔古〕猥亵的言语[行为]。

bawd·y [ˈbɔːdi] *a.* 淫猥的，猥亵的。— *n.* 淫猥的言辞。～ **house** 妓院。

bawl [bɔːl] *vi.* ①喊，叫，咆哮。②〔口〕大哭。*She ～ed to me across the street.* 她在街对面大声叫我。— *vt.* ①大声喊出。②叫卖。③责骂。～ *one's wares in the street* 沿街叫卖。～ *one's dissatisfaction* 大嚷大叫地发泄不满。～ ***about*** 叫卖。～ ***and squall*** 怪喊怪叫。～ ***at [against]*** 叱责。～ ***out*** 喊叫；〔美〕大骂，痛责。— *n.* 叫喊(声)；〔口〕大哭。

baw·ley [ˈbɔːli] *n.*〔英方〕渔船。

Bax·ter [ˈbækstə] *n.* 巴克斯特〔姓氏〕。

bax·ter [ˈbækstə] *n.*〔Scot.〕做面包的人。

bay[1] [bei] *n.* ①(比 gulf 小、比 cove 大的)湾，海湾。②(山中的)凹地。③【火箭】凹槽；盘，舱。④【英军】战壕通路。*Hudson ～* 哈德逊湾。*the ～ of Bengal* 孟加拉湾。～ **salt** 粗盐。～ **state**〔美〕= Massachusetts 州。～ **Stater**〔美〕马萨诸塞州人。

bay[2] [bei] *n.* ①(猎犬等追捕猎物时的)吠声. ②绝境，穷途末路（尤指走投无路时反噬的状态）. ***be at*** ～ ①走投无路；被包围，被遏制. ②作困兽斗. ***bring [drive] to*** ～ ①穷追，使陷绝境. ②迫使…作困兽斗. ***come to*** ～ 陷入绝境；作困兽斗. ***keep [hold, have] at*** ～ ①围住，使走投无路. ②不使…接近，遏制 (*hold a stag at* ～ 围住一头鹿. *keep a danger at* ～ 竭力不使危险迫近). ***stand at*** ～ = be at ～. ***turn to*** ～ = come to ～. — *vi.*(猎犬追捕猎物时不断地)吠，叫，咆哮. — *vt.* ①向…吠叫. ②穷追；使陷入绝境. ③阻止(敌人)不使前进. ④用拉长的低沉声音说. ～ *a defiance* 大声反抗. ～ ***the moon*** (狂犬)吠月；无事空扰，空嚷，徒劳.

bay[3] [bei] *n.* ①【植】月桂树. ②〔*pl.*〕桂冠；荣誉，名誉. ～**berry** 月桂果；杨梅属植物. ～ **oil** 月桂油香精. ～ **rum** 月桂发油. **bull** ～ 洋玉兰.

bay[4] [bei] *n.* ①【建】架间(跨度)，格距；壁洞. ②【空】舱；【船】(军舰)中舱前部，船上救护室〔病房〕. ③浮桥桥节. ④(谷仓)堆干草处. ⑤(停车场的)支线终点. ⑥吊窗，凸窗. *a bomb* ～ 炸弹仓. *an engine* ～ 发动机仓. ～ *of joists* 堆搁栅(托梁)的房间. *the sick* ～ 甲板上挤满病号士兵的地方. ～**-line** (铁道的) 专用支线. ～ **window** (凸出墙外的)吊窗，凸窗；〔讽〕(胖子的) 罗汉肚.

bay[5] [bei] *a.* 赤褐色的，栗色的. — *n.* 栗色马，骝. *a* ～ *horse* 栗色马.

bay[6] [bei] *n.* 堤防，河堤. — *vt.* 筑堤遏(水). ～ *water up* 筑堤堵水.

ba·ya·dère [ˌbeijəˈdɛə] *n.* 〔F.〕①(印度)寺院舞蹈女. ②条花绸.

Bay·ard [ˈbeiɑːd] *n.* 贝阿德〔姓氏〕.

bay·o·net [ˈbeiənit] *n.* ①(枪上的)刺刀；〔喻〕武力. ②〔*pl.*〕步兵. *by the* ～*s* 用武力. *2,000* ～*s* 步兵二千. ***at the point of the*** ～ 用武力. ***Charge*** ～***s!*** 上刺刀! ***Fix [unfix]*** ～***s!*** 〔号令〕上〔下〕刺刀! — *vt.* 刺杀，用刺刀刺；用武力迫使 (*into*). ～ *the enemy into submission* 用武力迫使敌人投降. ～ **charge** 刺刀冲锋，白刃战. ～ **drill [practice]** 劈刺训练. ～ **fencing** 劈刺术. ～ **holder [socket]** 卡口灯头.

bay·ou [ˈbaijuː] *n.* (*pl.* ～*s*) ①(美国南部的)牛轭湖；长沼；(江，湖的) 沼泽出入口. ②河川的支流. ***the B-State*** = Mississippi 州.

bay·wood [ˈbeiˌwud] *n.* 洪都拉斯桃花心木 (*Swietenia macrophylla*).

ba·za(a)r [bəˈzɑː] *n.* ①(东方各国的)市场，集市. ②(英美等国的)廉价商店，百货店，小工艺品商店. ③义卖展销. *a charity* ～ 义卖市场. *hold a* ～ *in aid of…* 为支援…举行义卖.

ba·zoo [bəˈzuː] *n.* 〔美俚〕①嘴. ②鼻. ③大话，吹牛，浮夸.

ba·zoo·ka [bəˈzuːkə] *n.* ①火箭筒；反坦克火箭炮. ②(超高频) 由平衡到不平衡的变换装置. ～**man** 火箭〔筒，炮〕手.

BBC = British Broadcasting Corporation 英国广播公司.

BB gun 汽枪.

bbl., bbl = barrel(s).

BC, B.C. = Before Christ 公元前.

B.C. = ①Bachelor of Chemistry. ②Bachelor of Commerce.

BCD = binary coded decimal. 【计】二进制编码的十进制.

BCG = Bacillus Calmette-Guérin 【药】卡介苗.

B Complex 维生素 B 复合物，复合维生素 B.

BCU = big close-up (电视中)演员的特写镜头.

bdel·li·um [ˈdeliəm] *n.* ①芳香树脂. ②【圣】宝石，珍珠，琥珀.

B.E., BE, B/E, b.e. = bill of exchange 汇票.

Bé = Baumé.

be [强 biː; 弱 bi] 〔陈述语气现在时〕 *(I)* ***am;*** *(you)* ***are;*** 〔古〕 *(thou)* ***art;*** *(he, she, it)* ***is;*** *(we, you, they)* ***are.*** 陈述语气过去时 *(I)* ***was;*** *(you)* ***were,*** 〔古〕 *(thou)* ***wast*** or ***wert;*** *(he, she, it)* ***was;*** *(we, you, they)* ***were.*** 虚拟语气现在时(通称、通数) ***be;*** 虚拟语气过去时 (通称、通数) ***were,*** 但〔古〕 *(thou)* ***wert.*** 祈使语气 ***be.*** 过去分词 ***been.*** 现在分词 ***being.*** 缩写:〔口〕 ***'m*** (=am), ***'s*** (= is), ***'re*** (= are); 〔口俚〕 ***ain't*** (= am 〔is, are〕 not) 〔〔俚〕 ***be'nt*** (= be not)〕. *vi.* ①有；存在，生存. *Can such things be?* 会有这样的事吗？ *There is no water in the vase.* 瓶里没有水. *There are seven of us.* 我们有七个人. *I think, therefore I am.* 我思故我在〔唯心主义哲学的一种说法〕. *Churchill is no more.* 丘吉尔已经不在人世. *To* ～*, or not to* ～*: that is the question.* 活还是死，是个要考虑的问题. ②发生，产生，举行. *The accident was last week* 事故是上周发生的. *When is the wedding to* ～? 婚礼何时举行？③在；逗留；到达，来到. *The book is on the desk.* 书在桌子上. *He is in London.* 他在伦敦. *Will you* ～ *here long?* 你在这里呆得久吗？*Has anybody been here?* 有人来过吗？④听任(保持原状). *Let it* ～. 随它去. *Let her* ～. 由她去，不要管她. ⑤属于；伴随；降临〔用于祈使语气〕. *May good fortune* ～ *with you.* 祝你顺利. *Woe* ～ *to you!* 愿你倒霉〔诅咒语〕! ⑥是…〔表示性质、状态等〕. *Iron is hard.* 铁是硬的. *I am a pupil.* 我是小学生. ⑦是；值；等于〔表示时间、度量、价值等〕 *Today is Saturday.* 今天是星期六. *The station is two miles away.* 车站离这里两英里. *I am twenty (years old).* 我二十岁. *This book is five dollars.* 这本书价值五美元. *Twice four is eight.* 四乘二等于八. ★以上⑥⑦两项释义用于连接表语称为连系动词 (linking verb) 或系词 (copula). ⑧做；成为，变成. 〔多用命令语气或不定式〕 *Be prudent.* 要谨慎小心. *Be a pupil before you become a teacher.* 先做学生，然后再做先生. *To* ～ *subjective means not to look at problems objectively.* 所谓主观性，就是不知道客观地看问题. *John wants to* ～ *a poet.* 约翰想成为诗人. — *v. aux.* ①〔be + 及物动词的过去分词构成被动语态〕. *We were awarded the first prize.* 我们获得了一等奖. *I was scolded by father.* 我被父亲骂了. ②〔be + come, go 等不及物动词的过去分词构成完成时〕. *Spring is come.* 春天来了. *His health was broken.* 他的身体垮了. *I am finished.* 我完了. ③〔be + 现在分词构成进行时〕. *I was walking in the park at the time.* 当时我正在公园里散步. *The ship is being built.* 船正在建造中. ④〔be + 有 to 的不定式，表示约定、计划、职责、义务、愿望、可能、命运等〕. *He is to see me today.* 他今天要来看我. *The book is to come.* 书就会来的. *They are to* ～ *married in May.* 他们预定在五月结婚. *You are not to do that.* 你不该做那件事. *They knew that their love was to* ～ *eternal.* 他们深信彼此将永远相爱. *He was never to see his wife again.* 他此后就再没有和妻子见面了〔多用过去式〕. ⑤〔were + 带 to 的不定式，表示虚拟的假定〕. *If I were to be [were I to be] here tomorrow* … 假若我明天来这里的话…. ～ ***at*** 从事于，做 (*What are you at?* 你在干什么？). ～ ***for*** ①到…去. ②赞成，要 (*I am for Shanghai.* 我到上海去. *We are for just war.* 我们赞成正义的战争). ～ ***from*** ①从…来. ②生在(某处) (*She is from London.* 她从伦敦来〔她是伦敦人〕). ***Be gone!*** 走开! 去! ***Be it so!*** = ***So*** ～ ***it*** (= Let it ～ so). ①就这样吧；这样也好；算啦，别管它了. ②但愿如此；心诚所愿 (= amen!). ***Be it that*** 即使…，也得…. ***Be seated*** 请坐. ***be that as it may*** 即使如此，总得…. ***have been*** 〔口〕来过 (*Has anyone been?* 有人来过没有？) ***have been (and gone) and*** 〔口〕干下了…〔与过去分词并用表示抗议、惊愕等〕 (*And d'you know what she's been and gone and done?* 你知道她干了些什么吗？ *Who has been and moved my paper?* 是谁动了我的文件？ *You have been and bought a new pen.* 你买了一枝新笔啦). ***have been at [in, to]***

到过，去过 *(Have you ever been at [to] Beijing*? 你到过北京吗?). ***have been to*** 到 (某处) 去过了; 去过, 到过 *(I have been to Shanghai.* 我到上海去过了). ***if so*** ~ 真是那样的话, 如若是这样. *(Mrs. Smith)* ***that is [that was, that is to be]*** 现在的[原来的, 将来的] 史密斯夫人. ***the... to*** ~ 未来的… *(the bride to* ~ 未来的新娘). ***There is [was, are等]*** 有.

be- *pref.* ①be + *vt.* 表示"到处"、"全体"等意义, 如 *be*smear, *be*scorch. ②be + *vt.* 表示"充分", "过度"等意义, 如 *be*deck. ③使*vi.* 变为 *vt.*, 如 *be*moan. ④使形容词、名词成为带有"使之"、"叫做"等意义的及物动词: *be*fool, *be*madam. ⑤使名词成为带有"包围"、"看做"等意义的及物动词, 如 *be*cloud, *be*friend. ⑥变名词为以 -ed 结尾的形容词, 常有轻蔑或取笑的含义, 如 *be*spectacled. ⑦加强语气, 如 *be*labo(u)r.

BEA = British European Airways 英国欧洲航空公司 (后已与 British Overseas Airways Corporation 英国海外航空公司合并, 称 British Airways 英国航空公司).

beach [biːtʃ] *n.* ①(湖、河、海的)滨, 海滨. ②海滩, 沙滩. ③(水滨的)卵石, 细砾. *take a walk along the* ~ 沿海滨散步. ***on the*** ~ ①失业的; 穷愁潦倒的. ②【海】担任陆上职务. — *vt.* 使(船)冲上沙滩, 使 (船) 靠岸; 把(船)拖上海滩. ~ *the landing craft* 使登陆艇靠岸. *The storm ~ed half the fleet.* 风暴使舰队的半数舰只搁浅. — *vi.* 船搁浅. — *a.* 在海滨使用 [穿用] 的. ~ **ball** (在海滨和游泳池玩的)水皮球. ~ **coat** 游泳衣上披的衣服, 海滨服. ~**comb** *vi.* 在海滨或码头上捡破烂或求乞为生. ~**comber** *n.*〔美〕①海滨巨浪. ②(太平洋各岛码头上的)白人乞丐[游民]. ~ **flea** 沙蚤. ~ **grass** 海滨草. ~**head**【军】①滩头阵地. ②滩头堡. ~**-la-mar** [ˈbiːtʃləˈmɑː] 西南太平洋岛屿上流行的土腔英语. ~**master** 登陆指挥官, 陆战队指挥官. ~**-rescue** 海滨浴场救生员. ~ **ridge** 滩脊. ~**scape** 海滨风景. ~ **umbrella** (海滩或花园用的) 太阳伞. ~ **wagon** (原名 station wagon) 旅行汽车; 客货两用汽车. ~**wear** 海滩装.

beach·y [ˈbiːtʃi] *a.* 〔废、罕〕有沙滩的, 砂砾满地的. ***Beachy Head*** 英国 sussex 州高 565 英尺的海岬.

bea·con [ˈbiːkən] *n.* ①(作为信号的)烽火, 篝火. ②信号所, 望楼; 灯塔, 信标. ③警标, 界标. ④【交】指向标;【物】标向波;〔喻〕警告, 指南. *a home* ~ 归航信标. *a non-directional radio* ~ 全向无线电信标. *a radar* ~ 雷达指向标. *a tracking* ~ 雷达应答器. ~ **fire** 烽火, 信号篝火. ***Belisha*** ~ (马路横行道口的)黄色指示灯. ~ **light** 信标灯 (光). ~ **station** 指向电台. — *vi.* 象灯塔般照耀. — *vt.* ①为…装设指向标; 用灯引导. ②照亮;〔喻〕警告, 鼓励.

bead [biːd] *n.* ①有孔小珠, 玻璃球; 〔*pl.*〕(成串的) 念珠, 数珠. ②露珠, 滴; 水泡. ③(枪的)照星, 准星. ④【建】珠缘, 串珠线脚;【机】卷边, (轮)胎边, (车)轮(圆)缘. *a dielectric* ~ 绝缘垫圈, 电解质小球. *Baily's ~s* 【天】(全蚀时月边缘所显现的)粒状光. ~ *tree* 苦楝树. *~s of pesspiration [sweat]* 汗珠. ~ *fabric* 轮胎布. ***count [bid, tell, say] one's ~s*** 数念珠; (用念珠)祷告 [念佛]. ***draw [get] a ~ on*** 向…瞄准. ***pray without (one's) ~s*** 打错了算盘, 算计错了. — *vt.* 用小珠装饰, 把…连成一串. *a ~ed handbag* 饰有小珠的手提包. *~ed velvet* 提花丝绒. — *vi.* ①形成珠, 起泡. ②瞄准. *Sweat ~ed on his forehead* 他的头上冒出汗珠. ~ **house** 收容所, 救济院. ~ **roll** ①名单, 名册; 目录. ②一串念珠. ~**-ruby** 加拿大舞鹤草. ~**-work** 串珠状细工;【建】珠状花边, 串珠状缘饰.

bead·ing [ˈbiːdiŋ] *n.* ①(酒等的)起泡. ②【建】串珠状缘饰;【纺】经纱起球;【电】玻璃熔接.

Bea·dle [ˈbiːdl] *n.* 比德尔[姓氏].

bea·dle [ˈbiːdl] *n.* ①〔英〕教区事务员. ②(英国大学举行典礼时的)执权标领队者. ③(法院等处的) 差役. ④小官吏.

bea·dle·dom [ˈbiːdldəm] *n.* 小官僚性格; 小官僚作风; 愚蠢的官僚主义.

beads·man [ˈbiːdzmən] *n.* ①济贫院中的受济人. ②(受雇)为他人祈祷求福者. ③〔苏格兰〕官丐[官准接收公共施舍的行乞者].

bead·y [ˈbiːdi] *a.* ①珠子似的, 饰有珠子的. ②多泡沫的. ~ *eyes* 圆湛湛的眼睛.

bea·gle [ˈbiːgl] *n.* ①猎兔猎犬. ②警察, 密探. ③〔俚〕自动搜索干扰(电)台. ④执行官. ⑤〔美俚〕香肠, 红肠.

bea·gl·ing *n.* 用小猎兔犬猎兔.

beak[1] [biːk] *n.* ①(猛禽等的)嘴, 喙. ②钩形鼻; 〔美俚〕鼻子. ③鸟嘴状物; (茶壶等的)壶嘴; (古代战舰舰首冲敌的)铁嘴; 箭口. ④【建】柱尖; 壳尖;【地】喙形饰像. ⑤圆口灯. **-ed** *a.* 有钩形嘴的; 钩形的. **-y** *a.* ①=beaked. ②爱管闲事的.

beak[2] [biːk] *n.* ①〔英俚〕治安法官. ②〔学〕校长, 先生.

beak·er [ˈbiːkə] *n.* ①【化】烧杯. ②(有脚的)大酒杯; 一大酒杯的量. *a ~ of gin* 一大杯杜松子酒.

bea·kie [ˈbiːki] *n.* 〔美俚〕暗中监视工会会员的警察.

be-all [biːˈɔːl] *n.* 重要的东西. ***be-all and end-all*** ①主要原因; 要素; 一切的一切; 整体; 总体. ②不可救药的人; 无可补救的事. ③极点, 终极.

beam [biːm] *n.* ①梁, 栋梁, 桁条; (船的)横梁. ②船幅; (动物、人的)体幅. ③(秤)杆; 杠杆, (织机的)卷轴, 经轴; (鹿角的)主干; 车辕; 犁柄; 锄把. ④(光线的)束, 道, 柱;【物】波束, 射束. ⑤(笑容、表情等的)焕现. ⑥【无】有效播听范围. ⑦【空】信号电波, 指向电波. *a ~ of light* 一束光线. *the common* ~ 标准秤; 准则. ~ *and scales* 天平. *a ~ of delight* 高兴的表情, 笑逐颜开. *an erector* ~【火箭】(发射时调整导弹位置的)千斤顶. *radio* ~ 无线电领航信号. *a landing* ~【空】降落指示波. ***abaft the*** ~ = before the ~. ***a ~ in one's eye*** 自己本身的大缺点 [与他人目中之刺相比, 自己眼中有梁, 源出《圣经》马太福音]. ***before the*** ~【海】正横前. ***broad in the*** ~ 〔口〕臀部阔大. ***fly the*** ~【空】按指向电波飞行. ***fly the wet*** ~【空】顺着河流飞行. ***kick [strike] the*** ~ ①(秤一方)翘起; 过轻, 不足抗衡, 无足轻重. ②输, 遭受失败. ***off the*** ~ 脱离航向, 不顺利; 不对头; 做错. ***on the*** ~ ①【海】与龙骨垂直地, 正横地. ②在航向上; 对头, 做对. ***on the port [larboard]*** ~【海】左舷正横前. ***on the starboard*** ~【海】右舷正横前. ***on the weather*** ~【海】迎着正横风. ***ride the*** ~ = ***fly the*** ~. — *vi.* ①辐射, 发光, 闪光. ②微笑, 眉开眼笑. — *vt.* ①发射(光线、电波). ②向…放 [播] 送. ③(用雷达)探测. ④(用波束)导航(飞机等). ~ *the program at America* 向美国播送节目. *the sun ~ing overhead* 红日当头照. ~ **upon** 看着…微笑. ~ **with joy** 眉飞色舞, 笑逐颜开. ~ **antenna**【无】定向天线. ~ **compass**, 长脚圆规, 长径规. ~**-ends** 〔*pl.*〕【海】船梁末端 *(on her ~-ends* 船身快要倾覆. *on one's [the] ~-ends* 濒临危境; 计穷智尽; (经济)窘迫万分). ★ 亦可写作 *on the ~'s ends.* ~**cast** *vt.* 对…作定向无线电传真. ~ **sea**【海】横波. ~ **system**【无】定向制. ~ **weapon** 死光武器, 光束武器. ~**width**【无】射束宽度. ~ **wind** 【海】横风.

beam·ing [ˈbiːmiŋ] *a.* ①光闪闪的. ②喜气洋溢的, 眉飞色舞的. **-ly** *ad.*

beam·ish [ˈbiːmiʃ] *a.* ①放光的, 放射的. ②神采焕发的, 愉快的.

beam·y [ˈbiːmi] *a.* ①(船等)幅身广阔的. ②〔诗〕(枪、矛等)梁一样的, 粗大的. ③〔罕〕光闪闪的; 眉飞色舞的. ④【动】(雄鹿般)有叉角的.

bean [biːn] *n.* ①豆; 蚕豆; 菜豆属植物. ②豆形果实; 结豆形果实的植物. ③〔转义〕琐物; 无价值的东西;〔*pl.*〕少量. ④〔*pl.*〕〔俚〕申斥, 惩罚. ⑤〔*pl.*〕〔英俚〕钱; (特指)金币, 硬币;〔美俚〕一块钱. ⑥〔美俚〕头, 脑袋. ⑦

〔英俚〕家伙,人. *aspargus* ~ 豇豆. *small [red]* ~ 红豆,小豆. *broad [garden]* ~ 蚕豆. *French [kidney]* ~ 菜豆、扁豆. *mung* ~ 绿豆. *soy(a)* ~ 大豆. *sword* ~ 刀豆. *Egyptian* ~ 莲子. *string* ~ 豇豆. — *vt.* (投物)击…的头. ***Every ~ has its black.*** 各人有各人的缺点. ***full of ~s*** ①精力充沛,兴高采烈. ②〔美俚〕完全错误的. ***get ~s***〔俚〕被申斥,挨骂. ***give (sb.) ~s***〔俚〕惩罚,申斥(某人). ***have too much ~s*** 精神旺盛. ***haven't a ~*** 莫名一文. ***know how many ~s make five*** 精明,会算计. ***like ~s*** 猛烈地(*run like ~s* 猛跑). ***not care a ~*** 毫不介意,不关心. ***not know ~s***〔俚〕大傻瓜,什么也不懂. ***old ~***〔英俚〕老兄〔熟人间的称呼〕; ***spill the ~s***〔美〕①不慎泄密,说漏嘴. ②破坏计划. ③陷入窘境. **~bag** (扔子游戏的)豆子袋;扔子游戏. **~ ball**【棒球】投向击球手头部的球〔犯规行为〕. **~ beetle** 瓢虫. **~ cake** 豆饼,豆渣. **~ curd** 豆腐. **~ eater**〔美〕波斯顿人的别名. **~ feast** *n.*〔英〕东家请雇员的酒席;(一年一次的)村庄宴会;〔口〕愉快的宴会. **~-fed** *a.*〔口〕精力充沛的,兴高采烈的. **~ head** *n.*〔美〕蠢人,笨蛋. **~-noodle** *n.* 残粉,粉丝,粉条(*a ~-noodle mill* 粉坊). **~-paste** *n.* 豆腐. **~ pod** *n.* 豆荚. **~ pole** ①豆架. ②瘦长的人. **~ sheet**〔美〕职工工作成绩表. **~ shooter** 儿童豆子枪〔玩具〕. **~ sprout** 豆芽. **~ stalk** 豆茎. **~ town**〔美〕波斯顿市的别名. **~-tree** 豆荚树〔如梓等会结荚的树木〕. **~ weevil**【虫】豆象岬. (学生戴在头顶的)小帽.

bean·e·ry [ˈbiːnəri] *n.*〔美俚〕素饭馆,经济饭馆〔因供应烧豆为主菜而得名〕. **~ queen**〔美口〕女招待.

bean·ie [ˈbiːni] *n.*〔口〕(有花饰或羽饰的)小圆女帽;童帽.

bean·o [ˈbiːnəu] *n.* (*pl.* ~*s*)〔英俚〕= beanfeast.

bean tote [ˈbiːn təut]〔美〕立刻〔法语 *bientôt* 之讹〕.

bean·y[1] [ˈbiːni] *a.* (***bean·i·er; bean·i·est***)〔口〕精神旺盛的;狂妄的.

bean·y[2] [ˈbiːni] *n.* = beanie.

bear[1] [bɛə] (***bore*** [bɔː],〔古〕***bare*** [bɛə]; ***borne, born*** [bɔːn]) *vt.* ①支,支持;背,负担,负载,负荷;承担(责任等). ②携带;运,运走〔除成语外,现多用 carry〕;引导. ③具有(名声等),带有(特色等);(和…)有(关系,比率,比较等);佩有,佩戴(徽章等),载明,记有(日脚),标有,刻有(记号);怀有(感情),抱(怨),含(恨),挟(嫌),记(仇). ④举止,处身;表现〔~ oneself〕. ⑤堪,忍受,忍耐;容忍;经得起,耐得住〔主要用于否定句〕;适宜于;值得. ⑥生(儿女),结(果实),产生. ⑦挤压,推动,驱. ⑧行使,掌握(支配权等). ⑨提供(证据等). ⑩保持(某种姿势等). ⑪散布,传播(流言等). ~ *a loss* 承担损失. ~ *the weight of the roof* 承受屋顶的重量. ~ *tales (gossip, news)* 搬是非,扯闲话. ~ *a resemblance to it* 跟它相似. *a tree that ~s fruit* 一棵结果子的树. *His hands ~ the marks of toil.* 他手上有劳动标记[老茧]. *a ship ~ing the French colours* 挂着法国旗的船. *The letter ~s no date.* 这封信没注明日期. *We ~ him no grudge.* 我们对他无恶意. ~ *testimony (witness) to* 证明…,担保…. ~ *one's head high* 高高地昂起头. *I can't ~ being alone for long.* 我不堪长期孤独生活. *This cloth will ~ washing.* 这布经[耐]洗. *an expression that does not ~ translation* 无法翻译出来的语句. ~ *a child* 生孩子〔现在一般是说 have a child. 此义多用 bear 的过去分词: She has borne two children 她生了两个孩子了〕. *He was born of poor parentage.* 他出身贫苦〔作"生育"解时用 borne,作"出身"或"出生"解时用 born〕. — *vi.* ①支,支持得住,经得起,受得住;忍耐. ②靠;推,压迫 (*on; upon; against*). ③位,坐落;朝向;倾向于 (*to*). ④有关系〔影响〕(*on; upon*). ⑤结果实. ⑥开动,运动. *The discussion bore against the bill.* 讨论带有否决该法案的倾向. *The ice ~s.* 冰承受得住〔厚得能走人了〕. *We were borne backwards by the crowd.* 人群把我们挤到后面去了. ~ *comparison with* 可与…相匹敌. *All these ~ upon him with cruching weight.* 这些问题使他的负担极其沉重. *The trees ~ well.* 这些树结的果实多. *The island ~s east-ward.* 那个岛位于东面. *The ship ~s west.* 船向西开航. *Bear to the right.* 靠右边(走). ***~ a hand*** 帮忙,帮助;参加 (*in*). ***~ a part in*** 分担,参加;在…中有一份. ***~ and forbear*** 一忍再忍. ***~ a rein upon a horse*** 用缰绳勒住马. ***~ arms*** ①携带武器. ②从军,参军. ③武装反抗,对…作战 (*against*). ④饰有纹徽. ***~ away*** ①夺走,抢去. (赢)得(奖品等). ②【海】改变航向(驶向下风). ***~ (away) the prize [bell]*** 得奖,得锦标,优胜. ***~ back*** ①驱退(人群等). ②退. ***~ (sb.) company*** 和(某人)做伴. ***~ down*** ①压倒,压服(对方). ②加紧干;全力以赴. ***~ down on [upon]*** ①冲向,(船或人)向…逼近. ②强调. ③压迫,使承受负担. ***~ hard [heavily]*** 勉强忍受. ***~ in mind*** 记住,铭记不忘;注意. ***~ in with***【海】驶向陆地[他船]. ***~ no relation to*** 与…无关系. ***~ off*** ①夺得,夺走(奖赏等). ②使避开(相撞). ③【海】驶离(陆地等). ***~ on [upon]*** ①压迫,使困苦 (*The famine bore heavily [hard] on the farmers.* 灾荒使农民困苦不堪). ②靠,倚恃,压在…上. ③瞄准,朝向. ④与…有关系,对…有影响. ***~ oneself*** 举止,行为〔与 *well, bravely, nobly* 等副词并用〕(*She ~s herself gracefully.* 她举止文雅. *He ~s himself bravely.* 他行为勇敢). ***~ out*** 证明,证实 (*The facts ~ me out.* 事实为我作了证明). ***~ rule [sway]*** 统治,支配,掌权. ***~ the blame [punishment]*** 受责难[惩罚]. ***~ the test*** 经得起考验. ***~ up*** ①支持,拥护. ②咬紧牙关坚持. ③【海】驶向下风. ***~ up for [to]*** 走向…,接近…方面. ***~ upon*** = ~ on. ***~ with*** 宽恕,容忍. ***borne away by*** (*anger*) 被(愤怒)驱使着. ***borne in upon*** (*sb.*) (某人)确信,相信 (*It was borne in upon me that …,* 我相信…). ***born in the purple*** 生长王侯人家,出身显贵.

bear[2] [bɛə] *n.* ①【动】熊. ②【股】空头,卖方,看跌的人 (*opp.* bull). ③【机】打孔器. 小型冲(孔)机. ④粗暴的人,鲁莽汉. ⑤〔口〕有奇才的人,天才. *a ~ for physics* 物理学天才. *the black ~* 黑熊. *the brown ~* 罴. *the grizzly ~* 灰熊. *the polar ~* 北极熊. *~'s gall* 熊胆. ***as cross as a ~*** 脾气极坏. ***be a ~ for*** ①(工作等)有干劲. ②经得起,耐得住 (*be a ~ for punishment* 经得起折磨,顽强). ***loaded for ~*** 作好准备;〔美俚〕准备打架. ***play the ~ with***〔口〕糟踏,搞坏. ***Sell the skin before one has killed the ~.*** 熊未到手先卖皮,过早乐观. ***take a ~ by the tooth.*** 作不必要的冒险. ***the Great B-***【天】大熊座 (=Ursa Mayor). ***the Little B-***【天】小熊座 (=Ursa Minor). — *vt.* (以抛售等方法)使跌价. ~ *the market by selling* 以抛售压低市价. **~ baiting** 逗熊游戏〔嗾狗去咬绑着的熊,十六、十七世纪流行于英国,后被禁止〕. **~ berry** ①熊果. ②熊莓〔越桔、羊鼠李等植物的乡土名〕. **~ cat**〔美俚〕①勇猛的拳击选手;坚贞不屈的人,硬汉. ②有权势者. ③熊猫. ④非常好用的器具. **~ garden** ①养熊场. ②嘈杂喧闹的场所. **~hug** *vt.* 紧抱住,象熊一样把…紧抱住. **~ leader** ①要熊的人. ②〔谑〕带领学生旅行的人;家庭教师. **~ market** 跌风笼罩下的市场. **~-pit** 熊坑〔动物园中展出熊的场所,多为一凹坑〕. **~'s-breech**【植】老鼠簕属植物,莨苕. **~'s ear** 耳状报春花. **~'s foot**【植】斗蓬草. **~ skin** ①熊皮;熊皮制品. ②(英国近卫兵的)黑皮高帽. ③象熊皮的粗毛织品. **~ward** 饲熊者. **~ wood**【植】药鼠李.

bear·a·ble [ˈbɛərəbl] *a.* 堪,忍受得住的,忍耐力强的;支持得住的,承受得起的.

beard [biəd] *n.* ①(下巴上的)胡子. ②【虫】口鬃;【动】颌毛. ③(牡蛎等的)鳃. ④【植】芒. ⑤(箭、钓钩等的)倒钩;针钩. ⑥〔美俚〕广播错误;口齿不清的广播员;蓄胡须的人,"大胡子"〔尤指颓废派人物或大学生、教授等知识分子〕. *grow a ~* 生胡子. *He wears a ~.* 他(下巴上)留着胡子. *a heavy [light]* ~ 胡须浓[稀]. *a ~ hair* 刚毛. ***in spite of sb.'s*** ~ 违抗某人意志,蔑视某人. ***laugh at sb.'s*** ~愚弄(某人). ***laugh in one's*** ~ 偷偷嘲笑. ***meet [run] in one's*** ~ 公然反对某人. ***pluck [take] by the*** ~. 毅然反对,大胆攻击. ***seize sb.'s*** ~ 侮辱某人. ***speak in one's*** ~ 喃喃地说. ***to sb.'s*** ~ 当面. —*vt.* ①使有胡须[颌毛、芒刺]. ②抓[捋]住…的胡子; 拔…的胡子; 〔喻〕公然反抗. ~ ***a man [the lion] in his den*** 太岁头上动土,奋勇搏敌. ***the Old-Man's Beard*** 【植】〔俚〕女萎. ~ **tongue** 钓钟柳属植物; 草本象牙红属植物. **-ed** *a.* 有胡须的; 有倒钩的; 有颌毛的; 【植】有芒刺的. **-less** *a.* 无胡须的,年轻的,乳臭未干的; 无倒钩的; 无芒刺的.

Beard [biəd] *n.* 比尔德〔姓氏〕.

Beards·ley [ˈbiədzli] *n.* 比尔兹利〔姓氏〕.

bear·er [ˈbɛərə] *n.* ①(票据、支票等的)持票人; 送信人; 搬运工人; 抬棺人; 轿夫; 担架; 运载工具. ②【机】托架; 支座; 垫块; 承木. ③有官职[身分]的人. ④结子实的植物. ⑤【化】载体; 【物】受力体. *a good [poor]* ~ 结实多[少]的植物,高[低]产作物. *a ~ of ill tidings* 报凶信的人. ***payable to*** ~ 【商】付持票人,见票即付. ~ **battalion [company]** 【军】担架大[中]队. ~ **securities [cheque]** 不记名证券[票据].

bear·ing [ˈbɛəriŋ] *n.* ①忍耐,忍受. ②态度,举止,风采,姿态. ③关系,影响,方面,联系 *(on; upon)*; 意义. ④〔常 *pl.*〕方位,方位角,向位,(矿脉)走向,航向. ⑤【机】轴承,支座. ⑥〔常 *pl.*〕【纹】(盾上的)徽章,标记. ⑦产子; 结实; 结实期. *I fail to see the ~ of that remark.* 我不明白该批评真意何在. *the ability to find one's ~s independently* 独立工作的能力. *a man of dignified* ~ 举止庄重的人. *child* ~ 生育. *consider the matter in all its ~s* 从各个方面考虑问题. *a ball* ~ 滚珠轴承. *a plain* ~ 滑动轴承. *The pilot radioed his* ~ 驾驶员用无线电定位. *directional* ~ 定向探位. *a tree past* ~. 已不会结果实的树. ***be out of one's ~s=lose one's ~s.*** ~ ***strength*** 抗压强. ***beyond [past] all*** ~忍无可忍. ***bring sb. to his ~s*** 使(人)不致忘本,使(人)反省,使人清醒一些. ***have a ~ on*** 关系到. ***have no ~ on the question [subject]*** 和那个问题毫无关系. ***in all its ~s*** 从各方面. ***lose one's ~s*** 迷失方向; 不知所措,惶惑. ***take one's [the] ~s*** 判明自己位置,观望形势. ~ **bronze [metals]** 制造轴承的铜合金[金属]. ~ **rein** 【马术】支头短缰. ~ **sword** 交由随从携带的长剑.

bear·ish [ˈbɛəriʃ] *a.* ①熊一样的; 粗鲁的. ②【股】起跌风的,看跌的. **-ly** *ad.* 粗鲁地,笨拙地. **-ness** *n.* 粗鲁,笨拙.

beast [biːst] *n.* ①动物; (与鸟、鱼相对而说的)走兽〔普通说 animal〕; (与人相对而说的)畜牲. ②牛马,家畜; 〔英〕〔*pl.* ~〕菜牛. ③人面兽心的人,衣冠禽兽; 凶残的人; 举止粗鲁的人. ④〔俚、讽〕老顽固,坏蛋; 〔学〕严格的老师. *You* ~! 你这畜牲. *Don't be a* ~. 别那么顽固. ***a ~ of*** 恶劣; 粗野 (*Don't make a ~ of yourself.* 不要那副难看[馋]相. *It was a ~ of a day, bleak, cold, and rainy.* 冷风凄雨,天气恶劣). ~ ***of burden*** 役畜(牛、马等). ~ ***of prey*** 食肉兽,猛兽. ~ ***of the chase*** 可猎兽. ***the*** ~ (人的)兽性. ***the B-*** 【基督教】反对基督的人.

beast·ie [ˈbiːsti] *n.* 〔主苏格兰〕小动物.

beast·li·ness [ˈbiːstlinis] *n.* ①兽性; 残忍; 粗暴,凶恶; 污秽; 淫猥. ②贪食; 大醉; 令人作呕的食物.

beast·ly [ˈbiːstli] *a.* ①野兽(一样)的. ②肮脏的; 卑鄙的; 残忍的. ③〔英口〕恶劣的; 讨厌的. *a ~ headache* 剧烈的头痛. ~ *hours* 要命的[讨厌的]时刻〔如贪睡者指大清早等〕. ~ *pleasures [appetites]* 兽欲. ~ *weather* 恶劣的天气. —*ad.* 〔英口〕很,非常. *be ~ drunk* 烂醉. *It's ~ bad.* 糟透了. *It's ~ cold out.* (屋子)外面冷得很.

beat [biːt] *vt.* ***[beat; beat·en*** [biːtn], 〔古〕***beat]*** ①打,拍,敲,连打. ②打败(敌人等); 胜过,超过. ③锤薄; 锤平,敲平(金属). ④走出,踏出(道路); 挤入,挤出. ⑤在…中搜寻(猎物等). ⑥敲响,击(鼓),撞(钟); 【乐】打(拍子). ⑦扑打(翅膀),鼓(翼). ⑧搅(蛋等起泡),捣(蒜、药等). ⑨绕过,逃过(约束等); 缓和,减轻. ⑩〔俚〕使为难; 使摸不着头脑; 〔美俚〕欺骗. ~ *a man black and blue* 把人打得青一块紫一块. *The long tramp ~ him.* 长途跋涉使他筋疲力尽. *You won't easily ~ that record.* 你恐怕不容易打破那个记录. *That ~s me.* 那就叫人哑口无言[认输]了. *That ~s everything I have heard.* 还没有听见过这样的怪事. *I ~ the truth out of him.* 我从他那里探出了真情. ~ *swords into plowshares* 化剑为犁. *Princeton ~ Harvard at football.* 普林斯顿大学在橄榄球赛中胜了哈佛大学. *You ~ me in French.* 你法语比我强. *It ~s me how he got the job.* 我不明白他怎么找到那个工作的. *If you want rest and change, you can't ~ a sea trip.* 你要想换个环境散散心,再没有比作一次航海旅行更好的了. ~ *the woods for game* 在树林中搜寻猎物. *waves ~ing against the shore* 惊涛拍岸. —*vi.* ①连打,连敲 *(at)*. ②(风)吹,(浪)击,(雨)打 *(against)*,(日)晒,射 *(on; upon)*. ③(脉等)跳动,(心)悸动. ④(鼓)冬冬响. ⑤【海】迎风[逆流]斜驶,作锯齿形前进. ⑥(翅)扑打. ⑦(蛋等)打出泡沫. ⑧在树林[灌木丛]搜索 *(for)*. ⑨〔口〕胜,赢. *This cream won't* ~. 这种奶油打不出泡沫. ~ ***a charge*** 击鼓为号命令冲锋. ~ ***a path [track]*** 走成一条路. ~ ***sb. all hollow [all to sticks]*** 〔美俚〕使人大吃苦头. ~ ***a retreat*** 匆忙撤退; 打退堂鼓. ~ ***about*** 【海】迎风斜驶. ~ ***about for*** 搜索,找寻; 设法(解决等). ~ ***about [around] the bush*** 拨打草丛搜索猎物; 旁敲侧击地刺探人意. ~ ***all [anything, everything, creation, the band, the world]*** ①真是从来没有的怪事. ②压倒一切; 超过一切; 极其,非常 (*His impudence ~s everything.* 他的厚颜无耻简直令人难以置信. *It rained to ~ the band.* 大雨倾盆). ~ ***away*** ①连打; 打跑. ②【矿】凿开. ~ ***back*** 击退. ~ ***billy*** 猛烈地,拼命(跑等). ~ ***cock-fighting*** 瞎扯,胡说. ~ ***down*** ①打倒,推翻(制度、学说等); 镇压. ②使沮丧,使失望. ③〔口〕还(价),杀(价). ~ ***it*** 〔美俚〕①逃走,跑掉,匆匆走掉. ②出去! 静一静! 别管他. ~ ***off*** 击退,打退(进攻). ~ ***one's brains*** 绞脑汁. ~ ***one's breast [chest]*** 捶胸悲叹. ~ ***one's way*** ①挤出. ②〔美俚〕无票乘车,(无票)混进. ~ ***out*** ①凿出,敲出; 锤薄(金属等). ②弄明白,搞清楚(意义、真相等). ③击走,击退. ④使筋疲力尽. ~ ***sth. into sb.*** 向某人灌输 (*I'll ~ some sense into him.* 我要教他懂点道理). ~ ***the air [wind]*** 徒劳,白费力气. ~ ***the band*** 〔美俚〕迅猛地. ~ ***the devil around the bush*** 〔口〕转弯抹角地说,旁敲侧击. ~ ***the [a] drum*** 大肆宣传. ~ ***the Dutch*** 〔美俚〕从来没有的怪事,叫人吃惊. ~ ***the rap*** 逃脱刑事责任[处分]. ~ ***time*** 打拍子 *(to)*. ~ ***to*** 打成…. (~ *to death* 打死. ~ *to a mummy [jelly]* 打得半死). ~ ***(sb.) to it*** 〔美〕瞒; 占先,抢先一步. ~ ***up*** ①冷不防地,乘人不备 (~ *up the quarters of* 突然访问). ②打鼓召集. ③搅(蛋). ④(帆船)迎风斜驶. ⑤〔美俚〕殴打,虐待,杀. ~ ***up and down*** 上下奔走,左右奔逃. ~ ***up for*** 为募集…而奔走. ~ ***up on*** 〔美俚〕殴,打. —*n.* ①(连续的)敲打; 敲打声; 鼓声; (时钟等的)滴答声. ②(心脏、脉搏等的)跳动,悸动. ③(巡警等的)巡逻区域; 常去之地; 一次巡逻任务; 游猎区域. ④【乐】节拍,拍子; 【物】拍,差拍; 跳动; 脉冲; 〔诗〕(韵脚的)强音. ⑤(报馆发表新闻对同业的)占先,抢先; 胜过他人[他物]的优点. ⑥〔美俚〕忘恩负义的人; 骗子; 食客. ⑦【计】取字时间. ⑧〔美口〕= beatnik. *I've never seen his* ~. 我从来没有见过胜过他的. ~*s of fifth* 【乐】五分之一拍. *cross ~s* 【物】交叉跳动. *a dead* ~ 【物】无差拍; 不摆. ***on [out of] one's*** ~ 〔不〕是…的专长[本行,专业]; 〔不〕在职权内; (钟表声的)〔不〕匀整. ***off one's*** ~ ①不再作做惯的事. ②非本行; 超出自己熟悉的领域. ***off the***

~ 不合拍子. ***on the*** ~ ①合拍子. ②在巡逻中. ***out of one's*** ~ = off one's ~. — *a.* ①〔口〕疲乏的 (= beaten). ②颓废的;属于"垮掉的一代"的. *dead* ~ 疲倦已极, 筋疲力尽; 惨败. ~**-age** *a.* 颓废派的. ~**-beat** 一种利用雷达追踪导弹的系统. ~ **frequency**【物】拍频(率). ~ **generation** (美国)"垮掉的一代"〔五十年代末美国青年中的一个颓废派,以蓄长发、奇装异服、酗酒、吸毒、玩世不恭等为特征〕. ~**-out** *a.* 疲倦不堪的. ~**-up** *a.* 〔俚〕①衣衫褴褛的,破烂的,不体面的. ②用坏了的;击碎了的.

beat·en [ˈbiːtn] beat 的过去分词. — *a.* ①(接连)被打击的. ②打成的,(金属等)锤薄的,敲平的;(路等)踏平的,走出来的;〔喻〕陈腐的,平凡的. ③打败了的;被打伤的; 精疲力尽的; 精神颓丧的. ~ *gold* 金箔. *a* ~ *army* 败军. ~ *work* 打制成的工艺品. ***a*** ~ ***path [track]*** 走惯的路,常道,常轨,老路, 惯例. ***follow the*** ~ ***track*** 墨守陈规,照例. ***off the*** ~ ***track*** 不墨守陈规,破例,越轨,别开生面. ~**-up** *a.* 破旧的, 年久失修的. ~ **zone**【军】落弹地带.

beat·er [ˈbiːtə] *n.* ①打击者; 帮助猎人从隐蔽处赶出野兽的助手. ②杵,槌,锤,夯具;【造纸】打浆机,搅拌器;【纺】打手, 翼子板;弹(棉)花器. *an egg* ~ 打蛋器.

be·a·tif·ic [ˌbiːəˈtifik] *a.* ①赐福的,使极乐的. ②极乐的;有福的;天使般的. *a* ~ *smile* 恬淡的微笑. ~ *vision*【天主】至福直观(天使等).

be·at·i·fy [bi(ː)ˈætifai] *vt.* ①赐福于,使极乐. ②【天主】为…行宣福礼〔宣布死者已升天堂的仪式〕.

beat·ing [ˈbiːtiŋ] *n.* ①打, 敲; 搅打; 笞打. ②失败, 溃败. ③(心脏的)跳动,脉搏;(翅的)拍打. ④【造纸】打浆;(把金属)打扁〔锻伸〕,打制;【海】迎风斜驶. *deserve a* ~ 该打. *take [get] a* ~ 挨打, 受打击, 受谴责. *take the* ~ 吃败仗. ~ **degree**【造纸】浆度.

be·at·i·tude [bi(ː)ˈætitjuːd] *n.* 至福; 〔the Beatitudes〕【宗】耶稣登山训众所说的八种幸福.

Beatles [ˈbiːtlz] *n.* (英国)披头士四人爵士乐队. **Beatlemania** 披头士热〔崇拜"披头士"乐队的狂热〕.

beat·nik [ˈbiːtnːk] *n.* (美国)"垮掉的一代"派的成员〔借用俄语 *sputnik* 一词的语尾造出的新字〕.

Be·a·trice [ˈbiətris] *n.* 比阿特丽斯〔女子名〕.

Be·a·trix [ˈbiətriks] *n.* 比阿特丽克斯〔女子名〕.

beau [bəu] *n.* (*pl.* ~*s*, ~*x* [-z]) ①纨袴子弟, 花花公子. ②爱人,情人;(妇女的)伴侣,向妇女献殷勤的男子. — *vt.* 为(妇女)做伴侣〔指社交活动〕.

beau [bəu] *a.* 〔F.〕善,美. ~ ***geste*** [ˈʒest] ①善行;大度,雅量. ②漂亮话, 故作大方, 口惠而实不至的姿态. ~ ***ideal*** 理想的极致, 至美 (*He is my* ~ *ideal of a soldier.* 他是我理想中最好的战士). ~ ***monde*** [mɔnd] 〔旧〕社交界; 上流社会.

beau·coup [bəuˈkuː] *a.* 〔F.〕很多,大量. ~ *jack* 〔美俚〕充分.

Beaufort [ˈbəufət] *n.* 博福特〔蒲福〕(姓氏). ~ **Scale**【气】蒲福风级〔将风力分为 0,1,2,3,4,5,6,7,8,9, 10, 11,12 级,称为 calm, light airs, slight breeze, gentle breeze, moderate breeze, fresh breeze, strong breeze, moderate gale, fresh gale, strong gale, whole gale, storm, hurricane 等,即无风、软风、轻风、微风、和风、清风、强风、疾风、大风、烈风、狂风、暴风、飓风〕.

Beaumé [bəuˈmei] = Baumé.

Beau·mont [ˈbəumənt] *n.* 博蒙特〔姓氏〕.

Beaune [bəun] *n.* 波恩红葡萄酒.

beaut [bjuːt] *n.* 〔美俚〕美人〔beauty 的略语,常作反语用〕. *His excuse was a* ~. 他的借口可真冠冕堂皇.

beau·te·ous [ˈbjuːtjəs] *a.* 〔诗〕美, 美丽的. **-ly** *ad.* **-ness** *n.*

beau·ti·cian [bjuːˈtiʃən] *n.* ①美容术专家,美容师. ②美容用品制造者.

beau·ti·ful [ˈbjuːtəful, -ti-] *a.* ①美, 美丽的, 美好的; 漂亮的, 华丽的, 优美的. ②极好的. *a* ~ *girl* 美丽的少女. *a* ~ *speech* 精彩的演说. *a* ~ *character* 美好的人品. *have an eye for the* ~ 有审美眼光. *a* ~ *opportunity* 极好的机会,大好时机. *a* ~ *stratagem* 上策. *the true, the good, and the* ~ 真善美. ~ **people** 漂亮人士〔或作 B- P-, 指上层社会时髦人物,缩写为 BP〕. **-ly** *ad.* **-ness** *n.*

beau·t·i·fy [ˈbjuːtifai] *vt.* 使美丽,美化;修饰,装饰. —*vi.* 长美,变美. **-fi·ca·tion** *n.* 美化; 装饰. **-ti·fi·er** *n.* 美化者;装饰者.

beau·ty [ˈbjuːti] *n.* ①美,美丽,漂亮 (*opp.* ugliness); 美感. ②〔the ~〕〔集合词〕美丽的人们; 〔a ~〕美人,佳人. ③美好的东西〔事物〕,美景, 美貌〔俗语中常作反语用〕. ④美点, 妙处. ⑤〔*pl.*〕名句集,佳句集. *She is* ~ *itself.* 她美透了. *That's the* ~ *of it.* 这就是它的妙处〔优点〕. *a society* ~ 交际花. *the wits and* ~ *of the town* 城中的才子佳人. *Beauty is but skin-deep.* 美貌只是外表,人不可以貌相. *the beauties of nature* 大自然的美景. *She is a regular* ~. 她真是漂亮得吓人. *Well, you are a* ~, *you've lost me the game.* 好, 你真能干, 能干得给我输了〔反语〕. *Come along, my beauties!* (亲密地对人或动物,尤其是狗或马)来,来,一块儿来. ~ **art** 美容术. ~ **contest** 选美会. ~ **culture** 美容术;美容业. ~ **parlo(u)r**, ~ **salon**, ~ **shop** 美容院. ~**-shopped** *a.* 〔美俚〕用美容术打扮起来的. ~ **sleep** 前半夜的甜睡. ~ **specialist** 美容技师. ~ **spot** ①美人斑, 美斑〔妇女面颊上化妆的黑点〕. ②痣; 小疵瑕. ③美景, 名胜. ~ **wash** 化妆水. ~ **water** 化妆香水.

beaux [bəuz] beau 的复数. ~***arts*** [bəuˈzaːr] 美术. ~***esprits*** [ˈbəuzesˈpriː] 〔F.〕 *bel-esprit* 的复数. ~***yeux*** [ˈbəuzˈjəː] 〔F.〕明眸,漂亮的眼睛; 美貌; 美人 (*We didn't hire you for your* ~*yeux.* 我们不是因为你面孔漂亮才雇用你的).

bea·ver[1] [ˈbiːvə] *n.* ①海狸, 海獭. ②海狸皮; 獭皮帽; 礼貌,高帽; 獭皮手套. ③【纺】海狸呢;海狸绒布. ④〔美俚〕(下巴上的)大胡子; 蓄胡子的人. ⑤工作勤恳的人. ⑥〔俚〕干扰雷达的电台; 轻〔中〕型飞机加油装置. ⑦〔B-〕美国 Oregon 州人. *like a* ~ 极勤奋,孜孜不倦. ~ **board**一种人造纤维板. ~ **cloth** 海狸绒布. **B- State** 〔美〕Oregon 州的别名.

bea·ver[2] [ˈbiːvə] *n.* (头盔遮防颜面下部的)护面甲; 脸罩.

bea·ver[3] [ˈbiːvə] *n.* 〔美俚〕胡须; 留有漂亮胡须的人,美髯公.

Bea·ver·brook [ˈbiːvəbruk] *n.* 比弗布鲁克〔姓氏〕.

bea·ver·ette [ˈbiːvəret] *n.* ①獭皮一样的兔皮. ②〔军俚〕轻装甲车.

bea·ver·teen [ˈbiːvətiːn] *n.* 仿海狸皮绒布.

be·bee·rine [biˈbiriːn, -rin] *n.*【药】贝比碱; 卑比令碱.

be·bee·ru [biˈbiruː] *n.*【植】绿心树.

be-bop [ˈbiːbɔp] *n.* 〔美〕疯狂即兴爵士乐〔其特征为节奏疯狂急速〕. **-er** 疯狂即兴爵士乐演奏者.

be·call [biˈkɔːl] *vt.* 〔古、口〕骂.

be·calm [biˈkaːm] *vt.* ①【海】(因风停)使(帆船)不能前进〔常用被动语态〕. ②〔古〕使(海等)平静. *The ship was* ~*ed for three days.* 船遇风停航三天.

be·came [biˈkeim] become 的过去式.

be·cause [biˈkɔz, bəˈkɔz, biˈkəz] *conj.* 因为. *The boy was absent* ~ *he was ill.* 那个孩子因病缺席. *I love her all the more* ~ *she is poor.* 正因为她穷,我更爱她. *I respect him none the less* ~ *he is young.* 我并不因为他年轻而减少对他的尊重. —*ad.* 因. ~ ***of*** 因, 因为, 由于 (*The game was called off* ~ *of rain.* 比赛因雨停止).

★ (1) ~ of 已往是用 ~ that (*conj.*). (2) because 在口语中可代 that (*The reason I don't eat much is* ~ *[that] I've got indigestion.* 我吃得少是因为我消化不良). (3) 表示理由的从属连接词还有 since, as, 但其语气和

主从关系不如 because 那样强和那样直接，至于 for 一词则语气更弱，关系更加间接。

bec·ca·fi·co [ˌbekəˈfiːkəu] *n.* (*pl.* **~s, ~es**) (意大利人爱吃的)一种小鸟〔特指 garden warbler〕.

be·ch·a·mel [ˈbeiʃəmel] *n.* 贝夏美调味酱〔一种由奶油、面粉等制成的白色调味品，得名于路易十四时代的御膳官贝夏美〕.

be·chance [biˈtʃɑːns, biˈtʃæns] *vt., vi.* 〔罕〕发生；落到.

bêche-de-mer [ˌbeiʃdəˈmɛə] *n.* (*pl.* ***bêch-es-de-mer***) 〔F.〕①(中餐所吃的)海参. ②(太平洋西南的岛区本土人和白人所讲的)一种混杂着土语的英语 = beach-la-mar.

Be·cher [ˈbiːtʃə] *n.* 比彻〔姓氏〕.

be·chic [ˈbiːkik] *a.* 【医】治咳的.

Bech·u·a·na·land [ˌbetʃuˈɑːnəlænd] *n.* 贝专纳 (Botswana 博茨瓦纳的旧称)〔非洲〕.

Beck [bek] *n.* 贝克 〔女子名，Rebecca 的昵称〕.

beck[1] [bek] *n.* 点头；招手〔以示召唤〕. ***be at sb.'s ~ and call*** 惟…之命是从，听命于(某人). ***hang upon sb.'s ~*** 听从某人差遣〔安排〕. ***have (sb.) at one's ~*** 随心所欲地使唤(某人)，对(某人)颐指意使. — *vt., vi.* 〔古〕点头〔摇头、打手势等〕召唤，指使.

beck[2] [bek] *n.* 〔英〕小河，急流，山溪，溪流.

beck·et [ˈbekit] *n.* 【海】环索，把手索，绳环.

Beck·et(t) [ˈbekit] *n.* 贝克特〔姓氏〕.

beck·on [ˈbekən] *vt.* ①点头；招手，打手势；(用头、手等动作)指挥. ②引诱，吸引. *He ~ed me to come nearer.* 他招手叫我走过去. *Lush grasslands ~ed the herdsman.* 肥沃的草地吸引了牧人. — *vi.* ①表示召唤. ②有诱惑力. *The mountains ~.* 青山诱人. *He ~ed to me to come nearer.* 他示意要我走过去.

Be·cky [ˈbeki] *n.* 贝基 〔女子名，Rebecca 的昵称〕.

be·cloud [biˈklaud] *vt.* ①遮暗，使黑暗；使模糊不清. ②使混乱，使糊涂. *Angry words ~ed the issue.* 愤激的言辞使问题更加说不清了.

be·come [biˈkʌm] *vi.* (***became*** [biˈkeim]; ***become***) ①变成，成为，转为，变得〔后接名词、形容词和分词等表语〕. *He has ~ a sailor.* 他成为一名水手. *It has ~ warmer.* 天暖和起来了. *At last the truth became known to us.* 我们终于知道了真相. ②发生，产生. *It sometimes ~s that these accounts are misleading.* 这些说法有时会引起误解. — *vt.* 适宜，适合，适于；与…相称，与…相当. *Such words do not ~ a scholar.* 那样的话不象出自学者之口. *It would ill ~ you to praise yourself.* 你自夸自赞是很不得体的. *Your dress ~s you well.* 你的衣裳挺合身. ***~ of*** (人或事物的)情况，遭遇，结果，归属 (*What has ~ of him?* 他后来的情况怎样了？〔口〕他到哪里去了？ *I don't know what will ~ of the children if their father dies.* 我不知道这些孩子在他们的父亲死后会发生什么情况).

be·com·ing [biˈkʌmiŋ] *a.* 相合的，相称的；相当的，合适的. *a hairdo ~ to her* 适合她的发型. *~ conduct for a hero* 无愧于英雄称号的行为. — *n.* ①适合，适应. ②【哲】将然存在 (*opp.* being)；【心】生成，转成，转化. ③(礼仪等的)得体. ***being and ~*** 存在和生成〔发展的过程〕. **-ly** *ad.* **-ness** *n.*

Bec·que·rel [ˌbekəˈrel], **Henry** 昂利·贝克雷尔〔1852—1908，法国物理学家，1903年诺贝尔奖金获得者〕.

bed [bed] *n.* ①床，床铺；床位，铺；(动物的)窝；〔喻〕安乐窝，坟墓；床垫；睡眠；就宿. ②婚姻，夫妇关系. ③台，土台；苗床，圃，花坛；养殖场；河床；矿床；湖底，海底. ④【地】层，底；【火箭】试验台；基地；【机】底座；衬；机床床身；【建】地脚，地基；【铁路】路基；【印】版盘. ⑤一层；(树叶等的)一堆. *He is too fond of his bed.* 他太贪睡了. *a single [double] ~.* 单〔双〕人床. *a feather ~* 羽毛褥垫. *a cup of cocoa and then bed* 喝一杯可可再睡觉. *two yuan for bed* 宿费二元. *a flower ~* 花坛. *a ~ of clay* 粘土层. *an oyster ~* 牡蛎养殖场. *reeds ~* 苇地. ***~ ways*** 【机】床身导轨. ***be brought to ~*** (*of a child*) 生(孩子)，分娩，临产，坐蓐，临盆. ***be contained to one's ~*** 病倒床上，卧病. ***~ and board*** ①膳宿；兼包伙食的宿舍. ②夫妻关系，夫妻生活〔夫妻寝食与共〕；③〔美〕家. ***~ of down [roses, flowers]*** 安乐的生活，称心如意的处境；安乐窝. ***~ of dust*** 墓. ***~ of honour*** 阵亡将士墓. ***~s of guns*** 【军】备炮过多的兵舰. ***~-to-breakfast folks*** 〔美俚〕城市人〔一起来就吃的人们〕. ***die in (one's) ~*** 寿终正寝，病死，老死；善终. ***get out of ~*** 起床. ***get out of ~ on the right [wrong] side*** 心情好〔坏〕. ***go to ~*** ①睡，就寝；同床. ②〔卑〕不要吵了！③【印】付印 (*The paper went to ~ at three.* 报纸三点付印). ***go to ~ in one's boots*** 大醉. ***have one's ~*** 临产. ***in ~*** ①睡着. ②男女同床. ***keep the ~*** (因病)卧床. ***keep to one's ~*** 病倒床上，卧病. ***lie in ~*** 横躺在床上. ***lie in [on] the ~ one has made*** 自作自受. ***lie on a ~ of thorns*** 如坐针毡，坐卧不安. ***make a [the] ~*** 收拾床铺；铺床. ***make one's ~*** 〔口〕自作自受 (*As you make your ~, so you must lie upon it.* 自食其果). ***make up a ~*** 搭一临时床铺. ***(one's) narrow [lowly] ~*** 坟墓. ***put (child) to ~*** ①让(孩子等)睡觉；②【美印】上版(备印)；〔美俚〕(编辑)清稿(付排). ***put to ~ with a shove*** ①把…葬掉. ②〔美俚〕把(醉汉)扶上床. ***separate from ~ and board*** 夫妇分居〔但不离婚〕. ***take to one's ~*** (因病)睡倒，病倒床上. — *vt.* ①使睡；〔美〕为…提供住宿. ②栽种；造苗林，移植(幼苗等)于苗床内 (*out*). ③安顿，给人铺床，给(牲畜)等铺垫草 (*down*). ④把…铺平；固定，嵌入. ⑤把…分层. — *vi.* ①睡，就寝，住宿；同床，同居 (*with*)；睡下 (*down*). ②(金属物置于他物上)搁稳，摆稳. ③【地】分层. *early to ~ and early to rise* 早睡早起. *bedding in earth* 【植】假植. ***~ it*** 〔美俚〕病倒. ***~ well*** 搁得稳 (*The rail ~s well on the ballast.* 铁轨在道碴上搁得很稳). **~bug** 〔美〕臭虫. **~chair** 卧椅，躺椅. **~chamber** 〔古〕卧室；英国王室的寝室 (*Groom of the ~chamber* 〔英〕侍寝官〔王室卧房侍从的官职〕. *a lady of the ~chamber* 〔英〕宫女. *a lord of the ~chamber* 〔英〕侍从). **~clothes** *n. pl.* 寝具，铺盖〔被、褥等〕. **~cover** 床单，垫单. **~fast** *a.* 〔美、英方〕卧床不起的，缠绵病榻的. **~fellow** ①同床者；妻. ②〔喻〕伙伴；同事 (*an awkward ~-fellow* 难同住的人；难共事的人，难接近的人，难打交道的人. *make strange ~fellows.* 不择伙伴. *be ~fellow to* 和…同床；和…非常要好). **~gown** (女)睡衣；〔Scot.〕女短衣. **~-in** 露宿示威. **~jacket** 女睡衣短外套. **~lamp [light]** 床头灯. **~lift** 床靠〔病床的活动装置，可使病人坐起〕. **~linen** 床用织品〔床单、枕套等〕. **~load** 河床上被水流带来的沙石等. **~maker** ①制床工匠. ②(英牛津、剑桥大学)打扫寝室的工人. **~moulding** 【建】深凹饰. **~pan** 夜壶，(病人在床上用的)便盆；(暖床用的)汤婆子. **~piece, ~plate** 【机】底板，台板. **~post** 床柱 (*between you and me and the ~post* 暗地里，秘密〔莫对别人说〕. *in the twinkling of a ~post* 转瞬间，立即，马上). **~rail** 床栏. **~rock** ①【地】底岩，基岩；床岩. ②根本原理〔事实〕；根底，基础. ③最低点，最少量 (*~rock price* 〔美〕底价. *get down to ~rock* 穷根究底；到了底；〔俚〕用得一文不剩). **~roll** 铺盖. **~room** 寝室，卧室. **~room community [town]** 近郊居住区〔供在大城市工作的人居住〕. **~side** 床侧，枕边 (*be [sit, watch] at the ~side of* (守)在床边〔多指守望病人〕. *good ~side manner* 医生对待病人的和蔼态度；〔讽〕逢迎周到). **~sit** 〔口〕①*vi.* 居住一间坐卧两用的房间. ②*n.* = ~sitter. **~sitter** 〔英口〕坐卧两用的房间，寝室兼起居间. **~sitting-room** = ~sitter. **~sore** 【医】褥疮. **~space** (旅馆、医院、宿舍等的)床位(总数). **~spread** 床单，垫单. **~spring** 弹簧床座；床座弹簧. **~stead** 床架，床凳. **~straw** 【植】猪殃殃；

砧草〔可编草垫〕(*(Our) Lady's ~straw* 【植】蓬子菜). ~**table** 【医】诊察台. ~**tick** 褥布,褥套,垫褥套. ~**time** 就寝时间. ~**time story** 催眠故事;〔喻〕动听而不可信的解说. ~**-wetting** 尿床,遗尿症. **-ward(s)** *ad.* 上床,就寝.

be·dab·ble [biˈdæbl] *vt.* 泼(水等),泼脏,溅湿.

be·dad [biˈdæd] *int.* 〔爱〕= begad.

be·daub [biːˈdɔːb] *vt.* ①涂,乱涂. ②弄污;〔喻〕中伤,骂. ③恶俗地装饰.

be·daz·zle [biˈdæzl] *vt.* ①使眼花,使眩惑. ②使着魔. *be ~d by the lake and the green hills* 为湖光山色所迷. **-ment** *n.* 眼花缭乱.

bed·der [ˈbedə] *n.* ①(英国大学学生宿舍中)收拾寝室的人. ②苗圃[花坛]观赏植物.

bed·ding [ˈbediŋ] *n.* ①寝具,床上用品. ②(家畜的)垫草. ③基底;【建】基坑;【地】层理;【农】定植. ~ **plane** 【地】层面,顺层面. ~ **plant** 花坛草花.

bed·do [ˈbed-dəu] *n.* (日本人设计的)一种电子活动床.

bed·dy-bye [ˈbediˌbai] *n.* 床;上床〔就寝〕时间〔原为托儿所用语,现为幽默语〕.

Bede [biːd] *n.* 比德〔姓氏〕.

be·dead [biˈded] *vt.* 【医】使麻醉.

be·deck [biˈdek] *vt.* 装饰,修饰 *(with)*.

bede·house [ˈbiːdˌhaus] *n.* 收容所,救济院(= bead-house).

bedes·man [ˈbiːdzmən] *n.* *(pl. -men [-mən])* ①代人祈福者〔尤指被雇用代人祈福者〕. ②收容所里的被收容者. ③〔Scot.〕乞丐(=beadsman).

be·dev·il [biˈdevl] *vt.* ***(bedevil(l)ed; bedevil(l)ing)*** ①魅(人),迷惑,骗. ②虐待,折磨,纠缠. ③使糊涂. *He is ~ed by his mistaken ideas.* 他被错误思想弄糊涂了. **-ment** *n.* 着魔,迷惑;苦恼,懊恼.

be·dew [biˈdjuː] *vt.* 沾湿,濡. *a pillow ~ed with tears* 泪水打湿的枕头.

Bed·ford [ˈbedfəd] *n.* 贝德福德〔姓氏〕.

Bed·ford·shire [ˈbedfədʃiə] *n.* ①(英国)贝德福郡. ②〔儿〕= bed. ***go to ~*** 〔儿〕上床睏觉.

be·dight [biˈdait] *vt.* ***(~; ~, ~ed)*** 〔古〕装饰. ★常用过去分词.

be·dim [biˈdim] *vt.* 使阴暗,使朦胧;使(思想等)模糊.

be·di·z·en [biˈdaizn] *vt.* (俗里俗气地)装饰[打扮].

bed·lam [ˈbedləm] *n.* ①疯人院,精神病院. ②喧闹;吵闹的地方;疯狂状态. ③〔B-〕英国伦敦东南部圣母玛利亚疯人院的俗称. *a ~ of laughter* 乱哄哄的一阵大笑. ***Jack [Tom] o'Bedlam*** 〔古〕狂人. ***like Bedlam*** 〔英〕吵闹的,混乱的;精神错乱的.

bed·lam·ite [ˈbedləmait] *n.* 疯子,狂人;精神病院病人.

Bed·ou·in [ˈbeduin] *n.* 〔*pl.* ~〕①贝都因人〔沙漠地带从事游牧的阿拉伯人〕. ②流浪者;游牧民. — *a.* ①贝都因人的;游牧的. ②流浪的.

be·drab·bled [biˈdræbld] *a.* 被雨泥弄脏的,拖泥带水的.

be·drag·gle [biˈdrægl] *vt.* (在泥水中把衣服等)拖湿,拖脏.

bed·rid [ˈbedrid], **bed·rid·den** [ˈbedridn] *a.* 卧病在床的,长期卧床不起的;不自由的.

Beds. = Bedfordshire.

bee [biː] *n.* ①蜂,蜜蜂;〔喻〕诗人;勤勉工作者的人,忙忙碌碌的人. ②〔美〕(邻里朋友之间为互相帮忙、娱乐等举行的)聚会,游艺会. ③古怪的念头,奇想. ④〔英方〕蝇. *queen-right ~s* 有王蜂群. *a queen ~* 蜂王. *a working [worker] ~* 工蜂. *a swarm [cluster] of ~s* 蜂群. *a sewing ~* 缝纫会〔妇女们一道做针线活的一种聚会〕. *a spelling ~* (小学生等的)拼字比赛会. ***as busy as a ~*** 颇忙碌. ~ ***line*** = beeline. ***have a ~ in one's bonnet [head, brain]*** ①苦思冥想;对某事入了迷;具有某种难以更改的想法. ②胡思乱想;神经失常. ***keep ~s*** 养蜂. ***put the ~ on*** 〔口〕向…募捐[借钱]. ***swarm like ~s*** 云集,群集. ~**bird** 【鸟】食蜂鸟. ~**bread** 蜜蜂食料. ~**eater** 食蜂鸟〔产于热带,羽毛极美丽〕. ~**hive** ①蜂箱,蜂窝,蜂窠,蜂房. ②嘈杂的场所,熙熙攘攘的地方. ③蜂窠式发型. **Beehive State** 美国 Utah 州的别名. ~ **house** 养蜂场. ~**keeper** 养蜂人,养蜂家. ~**line** ①*n.* 捷径,最短距离,两点间的直线. ② *vi.* 走直线 (*in a ~line* 笔直,一直. *take [follow, make, strike] a ~line* 一直走,对直走,走近路). ~**martin** 〔美方〕 = kingbird ~**master** 养蜂家. ~**'s knees** 〔俚〕极好的东西.

Bee·be(e) [ˈbiːbi] *n.* 毕比〔姓氏〕.

beech [biːtʃ] *n.* 【植】山毛榉,椈.

Bee·cham [ˈbiːtʃəm] *n.* 比彻姆〔姓氏〕.

beech·drops[ˈbiːtʃˌdrɔps] *n. pl.* 【植】美国山毛榉寄生.

beech·en [ˈbiːtʃən] *a.* 山毛榉的,椈科的.

Bee·cher [ˈbiːtʃə] *n.* 比彻〔姓氏〕.

beech·mast [ˈbiːtʃmɑːst] *n.* (落在地上的)椈子.

beech·nut [ˈbiːtʃnʌt] *n.* ①椈子,山毛椈坚实. ②〔俚〕地空通信系统.

beech·wood [ˈbiːtʃˈwud] *n.* 【植】山毛榉木.

beef [biːf] *n.* (*pl. beeves* [biːvz], *~s*) ①牛肉;〔转义〕食用肉. ②〔常用 *pl.*〕食用牛,菜牛. ③〔口〕肌肉;体力,膂力,力量. ④〔口〕肥瘦(程度),体重. ⑤〔美口〕*(pl. ~s)* 不平,牢骚,诉苦;告发. *horse ~* 马肉. *a wrestler with a great deal of ~* 肌肉发达的摔跤选手. *The team was lacking in ~.* 该队体力不够. *I have my ~ about that.* 我对那件事很不满. ***after the ~*** 〔美口〕向警察局告发后. ***ahead of the ~*** 〔美口〕向警察局告发前. ~ ***to the heels [knees]*** 肥胖太过. ***dressed like Christmas ~*** 〔英口〕穿得漂亮. ***put on ~*** 体重增加,长膘. ***put some ~ into it!*** 〔英口〕加油干! —*vt.* ①使(菜牛等)长膘. ②〔美俚〕加强,充实 *(up)*. *~ up the army* 加强陆军. —*vi.* 〔美口〕①向警察局报告,告发. ②发牢骚. —*a.* ①牛类的. ②供食用的. ~ **cake** 〔美俚〕男性的健美. ~**cattle** 菜牛. ~**eater** ①吃牛肉者. ②身强力壮的人,大力士. ③英王的卫兵;伦敦塔守卫人;〔讽〕饱食终日无所事事的人,饭桶;〔美俚〕英国人. ~ **extract** 浓缩牛肉汁. ~ **squad** 打手队,大力士队. **Beef State** 〔美〕得克萨斯州的别名. ~ **steak** 牛肉块;牛排. ~ **tea** 牛肉茶. 二齿铁线子. ~**-witted** *a.* 愚笨的,験的. ~**wood** 【植】木麻黄.

beef·er [ˈbiːfə] *n.* ①肉用牛,菜牛. ②〔美口〕诉苦者,发牢骚者;告发者.

beef·y [ˈbiːfi] *a.* ①牛似的,肌肉发达的;结实的,粗壮的. ②愚钝的,戆.

Be·el·ze·bub [bi(ː)ˈelzibʌb] *n.* ①撒旦,魔王,恶魔,堕落的天使长. ②〔南美〕猴子. ***Call in ~ to cast out Satan.*** 叫魔王赶撒旦;召鬼驱鬼.

been [biːn, bin] be 的过去分词.

beep [biːp] *n.* ①(人造卫星等的)信号音. ②(汽车喇叭等的)嘟嘟声. ③〔美俚〕小型警用汽车;吉普车. — *vt.* ①使(汽车喇叭等)嘟嘟响. ②用嘟嘟声发出(警告等). *drivers ~ing their horns* 驾驶员嘟嘟鸣笛. *impatient drivers ~ing their annoyance* 等得不耐烦的驾驶员嘟嘟鸣笛表示不满. — *vi.* ①按喇叭. ②(汽车喇叭等)发嘟嘟声. **-er** *n.* ①给无人驾驶飞机发送信号的装置. ②〔美俚〕无人驾驶飞机的遥控人员.

beer[1] [biə] *n.* 啤酒,麦酒;(一般)发酵饮料. *black [dark] ~* 黑啤酒. *ginger ~* 姜汁啤酒. *nettle ~* 荨麻啤酒. *draught ~ = ~ on draught* 生啤酒,桶装啤酒. *bock [duck] ~ =double ~* 酒精含量高的啤酒. *a ~ place* 啤酒馆. ***a small ~*** ①酒精含量低的淡啤酒. ②〔喻〕琐事,微不足道的东西. ***in ~*** 啤酒喝醉. ~ ***and skittles*** 悠游的生活 (*Life is not all ~ and skittles.* 人生并不就是吃喝玩乐). ***think small ~ of*** 轻视,小视 (*thinks no small ~ of oneself* 妄自尊大,夜郎自大. *think no* *small* ~ *of* 珍视,重视). ~ **belly** 大肚子;肚子大的人. ~ **garden** 屋外花园酒店. ~ **house** 〔英〕啤酒铺. ~ **money** 〔英〕酒钱,小费.

beer[2] [biə] *n.* 【纺】比尔〔英制经纱单位〕.

Beer·bohm [ˈbiəbəum] *n.* 比尔博姆〔姓氏〕.

beer·y [ˈbiəri] *a.* *(-i·er; -i·est)* ①啤酒(一样)的. ②喝啤酒喝醉了的;有点儿醉的. *a* ~ *breath* 满嘴啤酒味.

beest·ings, beast·ings, biest·ings [ˈbi:stiŋz] *n.* 〔用作单数〕【畜】(哺乳动物、尤指母牛的)初乳.

bees·wax [ˈbi:zwæks] *n.* 蜜蜡,黄蜡. — *vt.* 涂蜜腊于,给…上蜜蜡.

bees·wing [ˈbi:zwiŋ] *n.* 酒膜;陈年葡萄酒.

beet[1] [bi:t] *n.* 【植】 恭菜, 甜菜; 〔*pl.*〕〔美〕亚麻捆(= beetroot). ~**-faced** *a.* 鲜红的,红色的. ~ **sugar** 甜菜糖. ~**root** 甜菜根.

beet[2] [bi:t] *vt.* 〔英方〕①悔(过); 改(过), 抵(罪). ②修理,改进. ③减轻;解(渴); 充(饥); 接济. ④点着(火),使燃.

Bee·tho·ven [ˈbeithəuvən], **Ludwigvan** 贝多芬(1770—1827),德国大作曲家. **-i·an** *a.*

bee·tle[1] [ˈbi:tl] *n.* ①甲虫. ②近视眼(的人);糊涂虫,笨虫〔笨人〕. ~ ***blind*** = ***blind as a*** ~ 非常近视的. ***deaf [dumb] as a*** ~ 全聋〔哑〕. — *vi.* 〔英〕(象甲虫一样)走来走去;匆匆忙忙地走,赶紧;瞎撞,乱撞. ~ ***off*** 〔英俚〕急忙离开,赶. ~**-crusher** 大靴子;大脚.

bee·tle[2] [ˈbi:tl] *n.* 大(木)槌; 夯; 杵; 槌布机; 搅打机. ***between the*** ~ ***and the block*** 介于槌砧之间, 上下交逼地,在危险中. — *vt.* 用大槌捶打〔打进、打碎〕; 用杵捣;捶(衣、布等).

bee·tle[3] [ˈbi:tl] *a.* 突出的;愁眉苦脸的. — *vi.* (眉、毛、绝壁等)突出,伸出,俯临 *(over)*. *a cliff that* ~*s over the sea* 俯临大海的悬崖. *The prospect of bankruptcy* ~*d over him.* 破产的前景威胁着他. *beetling walls* 绝壁. ~**-browed** *a.* 额头突出的;眉毛浓厚的;眉头紧皱的;怒目而视的. ~**-headed** *a.* 糊涂的, 呆笨的.

beeves [bi:vz] beef 的复数.

bee·zer [ˈbi:zə] *n.* 〔美俚〕鼻子.

be·fall [biˈfɔ:l] *vt.* *(**befell** [biˈfel]; **befall·en** [biˈfɔ:lən])* 落到…的身上, 降临于. *Evil befell him.* 灾祸落到他身上. — *vi.* 发生,降临. *What befell?* 发生什么事了?

be·fit [biˈfit] *vt.* 适合, 适宜, 与…相当, 对…合式; 为…的义务,对…为正常. *It ill* ~*s you to do so.* 你这样做是不适宜的. *His clothes* ~*s the occasion.* 他的服装适合那种场合.

be·fit·ting [biˈfitiŋ] *a.* 相宜的, 适当的, 合式的 *(opp.* improper*)*. ~ *words* 言词得体. **-ly** *ad.* 适当地.

be·fog [biˈfɔg] *vt.* ①把…笼罩在云雾中. ②使迷惑; 使含糊;使神秘莫测. *Low-hanging black clouds beforgged the city.* 黑云压城.

be·fool [biˈfu:l] *vt.* ①愚弄, 欺骗. ②〔古〕骂…是傻瓜.

be·fore [biˈfɔ:] *ad.* ①在前,在前方,在前头,在前面. ②在以前,从前,前此;较早. *run on* ~ 跑在前面. *look* ~ *and after* 瞻前顾后. *He is as happy as* ~. 他和从前一样幸福. *His garment buttoned* ~. 他的衣服前面扣上钮扣. *long* ~ 很久以前. *Begin at noon, not* ~. 正午开始, 不要提前. — *prep.* ①在…以前; 较…早〔先〕. *Lilacs come* ~ *the roses.* 紫丁香比蔷薇开得早. *the day* ~ *yesterday* 前天. *the night* ~ *last* 前晚. ②在…的前面;当着…的面;向…;〔转义〕借…的力,被…推着;有…等待着;向…开放,供…使用. *put [lay] the matter* ~ *sb.* 在某人面前提出〔汇报〕这件事. *the question* ~ *us* 当前的问题. *man and wife* ~ *Heaven* 正式夫妇. *Pride goes* ~ *a fall.* 骄必自败. *The ship sailed* ~ *the wind.* 船顺风行驶. *The golden age is* ~ *us.* 黄金时代就在我们前面,前途无限美好. *Our services are* ~ *you.* 我们乐于为您服务. ③先于,优于. *Ladies* ~ *gentlemen.* 女先男后. *A marquis is* ~ *a count.* 侯爵在伯爵之上. ④与其…(不如),宁可…(也不). *Death* ~ *dishonour!* 宁死不屈. *They would die* ~ *surrendering* 他们宁死也不投降. — *conj.* ①〔表示时间关系〕比…早些, 在…以前; 还没有…(就); 然后再,再;就;才. *They arrived* ~ *we expected.* 我们没有想到他们来得那么早. *I must finish my work* ~ *I go home.* 我必须把我的工作做完才回家. *It will not be long* ~ *father returns.* 父亲不久就要回来. *Do it now* ~ *you forget.* 现在就做,免得忘记. *The sun had scarcely risen before the fog began to disappear.* 太阳刚一升起,雾气就开始消散. ②〔表示选择关系〕与其…(不如); (宁愿); …也不. *He will die* ~ *he submit.* 他宁死不屈. ~ ***Christ*** 公元前〔B.C.〕. ~ ***everything*** 先要,第一要. ~ ***long*** 不久. ~ ***now*** 从前. ~ ***sb.'s very eyes*** 当某人面. ~ ***one knows where one is*** 马上就,转瞬之间就,突然一下就. ~ ***one's time*** 提前,过早;未出世〔死〕前. ~ ***the mast*** 在桅前;做普通水手. ~ ***the world*** 在全世界面前;公然,冒天下之大不韪. ~ ***you can say knife [Jack Robinson]*** 一刹那,很快就. ~**-mentioned** *a.* 上述的. ~**-tax** *a.* 未抽税前的.

be·fore·hand [biˈfɔ:hænd] *ad.* ①事先,预先. ②赶先,超前,提前. *Please let me know* ~. 请事先通知我. *He is always* ~ *with his report.* 他总是提前交出报告. ***be*** ~ ***with*** ①预先准备;先发制人. ②太早,提早. ***be*** ~ ***with the world*** 〔古〕手头有现款,手边宽裕.

be·fore·time [biˈfɔ:taim] *ad.* 〔古〕以前,从前,往昔.

be·foul [biˈfaul] *vt.* ①使污,弄脏. ②说…的坏话,污蔑,中伤. ~ ***one's own nest*** 说自家人坏话,家丑外扬.

be·friend [biˈfrend] *vt.* 友好对待,亲近;援助,帮助;照顾;扶助. **-er** *n.* 扶助者,恩人.

be·fud·dle [biˈfʌdl] *vt.* ①使烂醉. ②迷惑,蒙蔽.

beg [beg] *vt.* ①乞求, 请求; 恳请. ②讨(饭). ③(议论等)回避(问题). ④请(原谅); 请(允许)〔礼貌语〕. ~ *one's bread.* 讨饭. — *vi.* ①乞求,恳请 *(for)*. ②讨饭,行乞. *a begging letter* 借钱信. *I* ~ *to be excused.* 请原谅. ***Beg!*** 对(狗说)拜拜!〔让狗举起前脚作乞讨状〕 ~ ***for*** 乞,讨(~ *for mercy* 乞怜). ~ ***leave to*** *(do)* 很抱歉,对不起;〔商业信件用语〕敬启〔复〕者 (*I* ~ *leave to disagree* 恕不同意. *I* ~ *leave to say in reply* …敬复者. *I* ~ *leave to inform you that* …敬启者). ~ ***of*** *(sb.)*, 求(人),请(人);奉恳,拜托 (*I* ~ *of you not to run any risk.* 请你不要冒险. *I* ~ *a favour of you.* 我有一件事拜托您〔求您〕). ~ ***off*** (用作不及物短语动词) ①对不能出席约会等表示歉意. ②对不能出席约会等请求原谅后而不出席了 (*He promised to come and help but has since* ~*ged off.* 他答应来帮忙,但已表示歉意不能来). ~ *(sb.)* ***off*** 辞退;谢绝;请求原谅(某人); (*He begged the servant off.* 他辞退了佣人). ~ ***sb.'s pardon*** 求饶,赔不是,道歉 (*I* ~ *your pardon.* ①对不起〔抱歉语〕. ②(对不起) 请再说一遍〔重读后部, 用升调, 亦可只说 ~ pardon〕. ③非常遗憾〔提出异议前说的话〕). ~ ***the question*** (故意回避论点时) 以假定为论据的狡辩. ~ ***to do*** = ~ ***leave to do. B- your pudding [pudden]*** 〔英口〕= I beg your pardon. ***go begging*** ①去乞讨. ②没有买主,无销路.

be·gad [biˈgæd] *int.* 〔口〕天哪! 的确! 一定! 完了! 糟糕!〔by god 的委婉语〕.

be·gan [biˈgæn] begin 的过去式.

be·get [biˈget] *vt.* *(**be·got** [biˈgɔt]; **be·got·ten** [biˈgɔtn], **be·got**)* ①(父亲)生(子女). ②产生,引起,招致. *Abraham begot Issac.* 亚伯拉罕生以撒. *Money* ~*s money.* 金钱生息. ***Like*** ~***s like.*** 有其父必有其子.

be·get·ter [biˈgetə] *n.* 父.

beg·gar [ˈbegə] *n.* ①乞丐, 叫化子;穷人. ②募捐者. ③〔俚〕家伙〔对人的爱称、戏称〕. *a good* ~ 善于募捐;会讨东西. *Beggars must not be choosers.* 饥者难择食. *die a* ~ 穷死困死. *nice little* ~*s* 可爱的小家伙〔指幼儿、幼小动物说〕. *poor* ~*!* 可怜可怜! — *vt.* ①使做乞

丐,使变穷. ②使…无用,难以…. *Her beauty ~s description.* 她的美貌非笔墨所能形容. ***I'll be ~ed if …*** 〔口〕决不会;如果…,让我变叫化子好了〔赌咒口吻〕. **~-my-neighbo(u)r** ①*a.* (外交政策等)损人利益的. ②*n.*【牌】乞食成霸〔一种纸牌戏,以一人吃尽所有人的纸牌为止〕. **-liness** *n.* 贫穷,卑贱; 卑劣; 贫弱. **-ly** *a.* ①乞丐似的,赤贫的; 下贱的, 卑劣的. ②很少的, 起码的 (*a few beggarly dollars* 很少几元钱. *a beggarly amount of learning* 学识浅陋).

beg·gar's-lice [ˈbegəzˌlais] *n.* *(pl. ~)* ① 紫草科(如:倒提壶属植物;郝吉利草属植物;鹤虱属植物).②上述植物之实. (= beggar-lice).

beg·gar's-ticks [ˈbegəztiks] *n.* *(pl. ~)* ①山马蝗属植物.②山马蝗属植物荚果的细裂片.③鬼针草属植物(bur marigold); 鬼针草属植物的瘦果. ④ = beggar's-lice (亦作 beggar-ticks).

beg·gar·weed [ˈbegəwiːd] *n.* 生长于荒地的多种三叶植物〔例如:萹蓄、兔丝子、金鸡菊等;尤指扭曲山马蝗〕.

beg·gar·y [ˈbegəri] *n.* ①乞丐生活〔处境〕,赤贫. ②贫民窟. ③〔总称〕乞丐. *be reduced to ~* 变成赤穷, 沦为乞丐.

be·gin [biˈgin] *vi.* ***(be·gan*** [biˈgæn]***; be·gun*** [biˈgʌn]***)*** ①开始 *(opp.* end*)*; 着手,动手.②始于,源于 *(from)*. *School ~s on Monday.* 星期一开课. — *vt.* ①开始, 创始; 动手,着手. ②创建. *It has begun to be done.* = *It has been begun.* 工作开始了. *He began (to speak).* 他开口了. *a book I began (to read)* 开始读的书. *~ a dynasty* 开创一个朝代. *~* ***again*** 重做, 从头另做. *~* ***at*** 从…开始 (*~ at the wrong end* 开错了头. *~ at page 10* 从第 10 页开始). *~* ***by*** (doing …) 从 (做…) 开始, 先做…. *~* ***on [upon]*** 着手,动手 *(He has begun on a new book.* 他已开始读[写]另一本新书). *~* ***the world*** 开始为人[处世]; 开始独立生活. *~* ***with*** 从…开始,先做 (*A little caviar to begin with, madame?* 先吃一点鱼子酱怎么样,女士?). ***not ~ to (do)*** 〔口〕决不会,完全不 *(It does not ~ to meet the specifications.* 这完全不合规格. *I can't begin to tell you how grateful I am.* 我不知道怎样感激你才好). ***to ~ with*** 首先, 第一, 第一个理由是; 本来〔插入语〕 (*To ~ with, he is too young.* 首先[第一],他太年轻了).

be·gin·ner [biˈginə] *n.* ①初学者,生手. ②创立人, 鼻祖. *a book for ~s* 初学者的入门书. *~ of the Impressionist school.* 印象派绘画的创始人. ***~'s luck*** 初学者的幸运, 侥幸 *(Making a grand slam the first time you play bridge is simply ~'s luck.* 你第一次打桥牌就打满贯,这纯粹是侥幸).

be·gin·ning [biˈginiŋ] *n.* ①初,当初; 开始, 端绪, 发端; 出发点. ②本原,起源. ③〔常 *pl.*〕早期阶段. ④起头部分. *at the ~ of the month* 月初. *the ~ of a book* 书的开头部分. *the ~s of science* 科学的摇篮期. *rise from humble [modest] ~s* 出身微贱. *A misunderstanding was the ~ of their quarrel.* 他们的争吵起因于彼此误解. ***at the (very) ~*** 在当初; 首先. ***from ~ to end*** 自始至终,始终; 从头到尾. ***In every ~ think of the end.*** 凡事都要想到它的后果. ***in the ~*** 当初, 起初. ***make a ~*** 开一个头,动手. ***the ~ of the end*** 事变的前兆,一叶落而知天下秋.

be·gird [biˈgəːd] *vt.* ***(be·girt*** [biˈgəːt], ***begird·ed; be-girt)*** ①用带绕〔束〕. ②围绕, 包围. ★常用过去分词 begirt. *a castle begirt with a moat* 有壕沟围绕着的城堡.

be·gone [biˈgɔn] *int.* 出去! 去! 滚! — *vi.* 去, 走开. *Tell her to ~.* 叫她走开. *order sb. to ~* 喝令某人走开. ★作 *vi.* 时多用于此种句型.

Be·gon·ia [biˈgəunjə] *n.*【植】秋海棠属; 〔b-〕 秋海棠.

be·got [biˈgɔt] beget 的过去式及过去分词.

be·got·ten [biˈgɔtn] beget 的过去分词. *his only ~ son* 他的独生子.

be·grime [biˈgraim] *vt.* (灰尘等)弄脏,沾污. *~d streets* 灰尘遍地的街道.

be·grudge [biˈgrʌdʒ] *vt.* ①吝惜, 舍不得给. ②嫉妒. *She did not ~ the money spent on her children's education.* 她决不吝惜花在她子女身上的教育费. *No one ~s to help her.* 没有不乐意帮助她的. *She ~d her friend the award.* 她嫉妒她的朋友获奖.

be·guile [biˈgail] *vt.* ①骗,欺诈; 诱惑. ②解(闷), 消磨(时间); 哄慰(孩子). *~ sb. of [out of] sth.* 骗取某人的东西. *He ~d me into consenting.* 他甜言蜜语地使我答应了. *~ the long afternoon with a good book* 读一本好书消磨漫长的下午. *We ~d the children with fairy tales.* 我们讲童话故事哄孩子. **-ment** *n.*

be·guil·er [bigailə] *n.* ①欺骗者,骗子. ②诱惑品; 消遣的人; 消遣品.

be·guil·ing [biˈgailiŋ] *a.* 消遣性的. **-ly** *ad.*

be·guine [biˈgiːn] *n.* 贝津舞〔西印度群岛的马提尼克岛和圣卢西亚岛上的一种土风舞,略似伦巴〕.

Beg·uine [ˈbegiːn] *n.* 慈善修女〔12世纪以来荷兰等国的一种半世俗女修道会的成员〕.

be·gum [ˈbiːgəm, ˈbeigəm] *n.* (印度穆斯林)贵妇, 公主; (英国)英印混血贵妇; 〔B-〕夫人〔对穆斯林贵妇等的尊称〕.

be·gun [biˈgʌn] begin 的过去分词.

be·half [biˈhɑːf] *n.* 利益,维护,支持〔仅用于下列成语〕. ***in ~ of*** 为…,为…的利益〔现罕用〕. ***in [on] sb.'s ~*** 为,替,给,为了某人,代表某人 (*He interceded in my ~.* 他给我说情. *She gave evidence on her own behalf.* 她为自己提出证据). ***in [on] this (that) ~*** 关于这件[那件]事. ***on ~ of*** ①替、代表 (*on ~ of my colleagues, I address you tonight.* 今晚我仅代表我的同事对诸位讲话). ②为…的利益 (*He has returned safely from a mission on ~ of his country.* 他已经为国完成使命,安全归来).

be·have [biˈheiv] *vi.* ①处身,行为,做人,举止,表现. ②(机器等)开动,运转. ③行为得体, 讲礼貌, 守规矩. ④(对环境或刺激的)反应, 反作用, 显示特色. *He doesn't know how to ~.* 他不懂礼貌. *He ~d badly to me.* 他对我不好. *The ship ~s well.* 这条船走得不错. *Did the child ~?* 这孩子守规矩吗? *Do you notice how mysteriously the colors ~ here?* 你注意到这些色彩的情调在这里显得如何神秘吗? — *vt.* 〔用反身代词〕①使举止得当,使守规矩; 表现. ②使正常运转. *He ~d himself like a man.* 他做人有骨气. ***B- yourself!*** (对孩子) 安分点! 规矩点!

be·hav·iour, be·hav·ior [biˈheivjə] *n.* ①行为, 品行; 举止, 态度, 举动, 表现, 行动. ②(生物的)习性; (机器等的)特性, 性能, 状态; (药品等的)作用, 功效. *gallant ~* 英雄行为. *a bad ~ at meals* 吃饭的难看相. *aerodynamic ~* 空气动力特性. ***on [upon] one's good [best] ~*** ①善自检点,谨慎,规矩.②在见习中,在试用期间(*The child was on his good ~.* 这孩子很规矩). ***put sb. on his best ~.*** 劝告[警告]某人检点一些. **-al** *a.* 关于行为的 (*behavioural science* 人类活动学〔如社会学、人类学等〕). *~* **pattern**【社会学】行为模式. *~* **therapy**【医】行为疗法〔一种心理疗法〕. **-ism** *n.*【心】行为主义. **-ist** *n.*【心】行为主义心理学家.

be·head [biˈhed] *vt.* 把…斩首,砍…的头. —*a.* 被砍了头的;〔美俚〕被解雇的. *~ed* **river**【地】断头河, 夺流河, 被夺河. **-ing** *n.* 斩首; 斩罪;【地】断头.

be·held [biˈheld] behold 的过去式及过去分词.

be·he·moth [biˈhiːmɔθ] *n.* ①【圣】巨兽. ②〔美口〕庞然大物. — *a.* 巨大的.

be·hest [biˈhest] *n.* 〔书〕①命令, 谕令, 指示. ②紧急指示. *the pope's ~* 教皇谕令. *act at sb.'s ~* 按某人指示办事.

be·hind [biˈhaind] *ad.* ①在后,在后面,向后; 已成过去.

②背地,在幕后,在背后. ③迟,过(期),落后. *lag* ~ 落后. *My joy lies* ~. 我的欢乐已经消逝. *He came ten minutes* ~. 他迟到了十分钟. *glance [look]* ~回头(看). *The clock is more than five minutes* ~. 钟慢了不止五分. *Your watch runs* ~. 你的表慢了. *There is more* ~. 里头还有情况〔内幕〕. *The season is* ~. 季节拖迟了. — *n.* 〔口〕屁股. — *prep.* ①在…之后, 向…后面; 在…的那边. ②在…的背后; 作…的后盾; 在…的里面, 在…的幕后, 操纵. ③在…死后. ④落后于; 迟于; 劣于. *get* ~ *a tree* 躲在树后. *He left* ~ *him a great reputation.* 流芳后世. *His house is a few yards* ~ *the church.* 他的家在教堂过去几步远. *an argument with experience* ~ *it* 经验之谈, 有经验为证的论点. *He is* ~ *the plan.* 他是幕后策划人. *the person* ~ *the wheel of a car* 汽车驾驶人, 司机. *His apprenticeship was* ~ *him.* 他的学徒期已满. *I am* ~ *my class in mathematics.* 我的数学比同班同学差. ***be (far)*** ~ (非常)迟缓, 落后; (很)坏 (*Can spring be far* ~? 春天还会远吗?). ***be*** ~ ***in [with]*** (*payments; work*) (支付)误期; (工作)落后, 耽误. ~ ***the times*** 落后, 赶不上时代, 不合时宜. ~ ***time*** 误期, 过期, 过时, 迟. ***from*** ~ 从后. ***get*** ~ = ***go*** ~ 追究…的根源〔真相〕. ***leave*** ~ 留在后头; 忘记 (*He left his stick* ~ *him.* 他忘记拿手杖就走了). ***put*** ~ ***one*** 拒绝考虑(某事). **~hand** *a.* 〔只用作表语〕①落后, 迟延; 过期, 误期. ②入不敷出, 困窘 (*be [get]* ~*hand* 落后. *be* ~*hand in one's circumstances* 家境不好. *live* ~*-hand* 入不敷出. ~*hand with payments [work]* 支付误期〔耽误工作〕). **~-the-scene(s)** *a.* 幕后的 (*a* ~*-the-scene(s) master [boss]* 后台老板).

be·hold [biˈhəuld] *vt.* (***be·held*** [biˈheld]; ***be·held***) 〔书〕观看, 注视, 观察. — *vi.* 看〔用于祈使语气〕 — *int.* 看哪! *lo and*~ 嗨, 你瞧! **-er** *n.* 观看者.

be·hold·en [biˈhəuldən] *a.* 蒙恩, 见爱; 铭感〔作表语用〕. *I am greatly* ~ *to you for your kindness.* 承蒙厚爱, 十分感激.

be·hoof [biˈhu:f] *n.* 〔古〕利益〔仅用于介词片语 for sb.'s ~ 等中〕. ***for [in, on, to] sb.'s*** ~ = *for [in, on, to] the* ~ *of sb.* 为了某人, 为某人的利益 (*The money was spent for his own* ~. 那笔钱是为他自己花的. *For whose* ~ *is this done?* 做这件事为了谁?).

be·hove, be·hoove [biˈhəuv, biˈhu:v] *vt.* ①对…来说是应该的, 是…的义务. ②对…来说是必要的〔主语均用 it〕. *It* ~*s everyone to do his duty.* 尽本分人人应该. — *vi.* 〔古〕是责任, 是义务〔主语用 it〕. *It* ~*s that I be silent.* 我应该沉默. *It* ~*s to write to her.* 应该写信给她.

Beh·ring [ˈberiŋ] *n.* = Bering.

Behr·man [ˈbeəmən] *n.* 贝尔曼〔姓氏〕.

beige [beiʒ] *n.* ①原色哔叽; 混色线呢. ②米色. — *a.* 米色的.

be·in [ˈbi:in] *n.* (在公园等公共场所举行的)狂欢会.

be·ing [ˈbi:iŋ] be 的现在分词. ①〔用作独立短语中的系词〕*things* ~ *as they are.* 事情既然如此. *Dinner* ~ *over, they left the hall.* 他们吃完饭后离开了食堂. *B- a soldier, he has a strong sense of discipline.* 他是个士兵, 有很强的纪律性. ②〔构成被动语态进行式〕…着. *These countries are* ~ *swept by an economic crisis.* 这些国家正在受着一场经济危机的冲击. ③〔由 be 的"存在"、"现存"等意义转来的分词, 用作定语, 修饰少数表示时间概念的名词〕. *for the time* ~ 暂时; 一时; 临时. — *n.* ①实在, 存在. ②生存, 生命, 人生, 一生, 人间. ③物; 生物, 人; 实在物. ④本质, 特质, 本性. ⑤〔B-〕上帝, 神; 本体. *the aim of our* ~ 人生的目的. *actual* ~ 实在. *to the very depth of one's* ~ 灵魂深处. *a human* ~ 人, 人间. *animate [inanimate]* ~ 生〔无生〕物. *the Supreme B-* 上帝. ~ ***as [that]*** 〔口〕既然; 因为. ~ ***in itself***【哲】物自体. ***call [bring] into*** ~ 使产出, 使形成. ***come into*** ~ 发生, 诞生, 成立(*The European Common Market came into* ~ *in 1958.* 欧洲共同体成立于 1958 年). ***in*** ~ 现有的, 现存的, 存在的 (*the fleet in* ~ 现有的舰队. *the record in* ~ 现存的记录). **-less** *a.* 不存在的.

Bei·ra [ˈbaiərə] *n.* 贝拉〔莫桑比克港市〕.

Bei·rut [beiˈru:t] *n.* 贝鲁特〔黎巴嫩首都〕.

be·jab·bers [biˈdʒæbəz] *int.* 啊呀呀! 真糟糕! 〔表示惊奇、高兴、愤怒、烦恼等, 是 by Jesus 的委婉说法〕. — *n.* 鬼东西, 混帐家伙. ***beat [knock, scare] the*** ~ ***out of sb.*** 狠狠揍某人一顿.

be·jew·el [biˈdʒu:əl] *vt.* 给…饰以珠宝, 以宝石镶嵌.

Bel [bel] *n.* 贝尔〔女子名, Arabella, Isabel, Isabella 等的爱称〕.

Bel. = Belgian; Belgium.

bel [bel] *n.*【物】贝(尔)〔电平单位〕.

be·la·bour, be·la·bor [biˈleibə] *vt.* ①猛烈攻击; 狠狠责备, 痛骂. ②啰啰嗦嗦地说明. ③〔古〕痛打. ~ *an endless argument* 啰啰嗦嗦地议论不休.

be·lat·ed [biˈleitid] *a.* ①落后了的, 过了期的; 过时的; 已经迟了的; 旧式的. ②天已暗了的, (旅客等)天色已晚还在赶路的. ~ ***efforts*** 为时已晚的努力. *a* ~ *view of world politics* 对世界政治的过时看法. ~ *travelers* 天色已晚还在赶路的行旅.

be·laud [biˈlɔ:d] *vt.* 褒扬; 〔讽〕过分吹捧.

be·lay [biˈlei] *vt.* ①【海】把绳子作 S[8] 形拴在(套索桩等上); 停止. ②把(绳)拴在身体〔物体〕上. ③(登山运动)把(人)系在绳端. — *vi.* ①用绳系住. ②【海】停住〔用于命令句〕. — *n.* ①(登山时的)系绳处. ②【海】S 形挽桩. ***Belay there!*** 〔海俚〕停止!

be·lay·ing pin [biˈleiŋ pin] *n.*【船】缠索栓, 套索桩, 缆耳.

bel can·to [bel ˈkɑ:ntəu] *n.* 〔It.〕【乐】美声唱法〔一种以发声洪亮圆润为特点的传统唱法〕.

belch [beltʃ] *vi.* ①打嗝, 呃逆. ②态度蛮横地发出(叱咤等). ③(火山等)猛烈喷射, 爆发. ④〔美俚〕发牢骚; 〔罕〕讲, 谈. — *vt.* ①(火山、大炮等)喷, 冒(烟、火焰等). ②猛烈地发出. *an air shaft* ~*ing fire and smoke* 喷出烟火的烟囱. *Factories* ~ *furth clouds of smoke.* 工厂喷出团团烟雾. — *n.* ①打嗝. ②喷射, 爆发(声). ③劣质啤酒.

bel·ch·er [ˈbeltʃə] *n.* ①(英国)蓝白花围巾〔常作 ~ handkerchief〕. ②〔美俚〕爱发牢骚的人; 碎嘴子.

bel·dam(e) [ˈbeldəm] *n.* 老太婆; 泼妇, 丑妇.

be·lea·guer [biˈli:gə] *vt.* ①围攻, 围困, 包围. ②使烦恼. ~ *a town* 围攻一座城市. ~*d with troubles* 诸事多烦恼.

bel·em·nite [ˈbeləmnait] *n.*【古生】箭石〔乌贼类化石〕.

bel-es·prit [ˈbelesˈpri:] *n.* (*pl.* ***beaux es·prits*** [ˈbəuzes-ˈpri:]) 〔F.〕才子.

Bel·fast [belˈfɑ:st] *n.* 贝尔法斯特〔英国港市〕.

bel·fried [ˈbelfrid] *a.* 有钟楼的; 有钟塔的.

bel·fry [ˈbelfri] *n.* ①(教堂等的)钟楼; 钟塔; 钟架. ②〔口〕头脑, 脑筋. *a* ~ *full of curious notions* 满脑子古怪思想. ***have bats in the [one's]*** ~ 脑筋有点怪, 有点神经失常.

Bel·gian [ˈbeldʒən] *n.* 比利时人. — *a.* 比利时的; 比利时人的.

Bel·gic [ˈbeldʒik] *a.* ①古比利时族 (Belgae)人的. ②比利时(人)的. ③古荷兰的.

Bel·gium [ˈbeldʒəm] *n.* 比利时〔欧洲〕.

Bel·grade [belˈgreid] *n.* 贝尔格莱德〔南斯拉夫首都〕.

Bel·gra·vi·a [belˈgreivjə] *n.* ①贝尔格莱维亚区〔伦敦海德公园附近的高级住宅区〕. ②典型的上层阶级; 贵族. ③中上阶层的人.

Bel·gra·vi·an [belˈgreivjən] *a.* 贝尔格莱维亚区的; 中上阶层的. — *n.* 高级住宅区居民; 中上阶层分子.

Be·li·al [ˈbiːljəl] *n.* ①【圣】恶魔，魔鬼〔出自《新约》〕. ②【圣】邪恶〔出自《旧约》〕. *daughters of* ～ 不正经的女子. *sons [men] of* ～ 堕落者，浪子，无赖.

be·lie [biˈlai] *vt.* (～*d*; *-ly·ing*) ①歪曲…的真相，伪装，使人误解. ②证明…是假的；与…相背[相反，相左]. ③辜负(希望等)，违背(约言等). ④〔美〕责备…虚假. *His clothes* ～ *his station.* 他的衣服掩饰了他的身分. *His acts* ～ *his words.* 他言行不一. *His trembling hands* ～*d his calm voice.* 他颤抖的双手戳穿了他平静的语调. *Summer* ～*s its name.* 今年夏天一点也不热. *The results* ～*d his father's expectations.* 后来的情形使他父亲的希望落空了.

be·lief [biˈliːf] *n.* ①信，信任；相信 (*in*)；信仰，信心. ②信念；意见. ③【基督新教】信条；教义；[the B-] 使徒信条. *He has no great* ～ *in religion* 他不大相信宗教. *a man worthy of* ～ 可以信得过的人. *a person light of* ～ 轻信的人. *My* ～ *is that ...* 我相信，在我看来. ***beyond*** ～ 难以置信；非常，想象以外地. ***in the*** ～ ***that ...*** 相信…. ***to the best of my*** ～ 我相信，以我看来.

be·liev·a·ble [biˈliːvəbl] *a.* 可信(任)的. **-a·bil·i·ty, -ness** *n.* 可信任性. **-a·bly** *ad.*

be·lieve [biˈliːv] *vt.* ①信，相信，确信. ②想，以为，认为. *I* ～ *him.* = *I* ～ *what he says.* 我相信他(的话). *I* ～ *him to be honest.* 我认为他是诚实的. *I don't* ～ *I know him.* 我想我不认识他. *The fugitive is* ～*d to be headed for the border.* 逃犯被认为在向国境线逃窜. *I* ～ *so.* 我认为如此；我想是这样. — *vi.* ①相信. ②信任，信赖. ③信奉，信仰 (*in*). *I* ～ *not.* 我认为不是这样. *Seeing is* ～*ing.* 百闻不如一见，眼见心服. *I* ～ *in you.* 我相信你，我对你有信心. ～ *in Zoroastrianism* 信奉祆教. *I* ～ *in early rising.* 我相信早起是好的. *I don't* ～ *in marrying young.* 我不赞成早婚. ～ ***it or not*** 〔美口〕信不信由你，我说的是真的. ***B- me.*** 真的，是真的呀. ***make*** ～ 假装 (*She make* ～ *not to hear me.* 她假装没有听到我的话). ***You'd better*** ～ 〔美口〕的确，无疑.

be·liev·er [biˈliːvə] *n.* 相信的人；信仰者，信徒 (*in*). *a* ～ *in Buddhism* 佛教信徒.

be·liev·ing [biˈliːviŋ] *a.* 有信仰的，有信心的. **-ly** *ad.*

be·like [biˈlaik] *ad.* 〔古〕或者，多半.

Be·lin·da [biˈlində] *n.* 比琳达〔女子名〕.

be·lit·tle [biˈlitl] *vt.* 〔美〕①(相形之下)使显得微小，缩小. ②小视，轻视，贬损，贬低. *The bulk of the warehouse* ～*s the houses around it.* 货栈的庞大使周围的房屋显得矮小了. ～ *oneself* 自卑.

Be·lize [beˈliːz] *n.* ①伯利兹〔拉丁美洲〕. ②伯利兹〔伯利兹原首府〕.

Bell [bel] *n.* ①贝尔〔姓氏〕. ②**Alexander Graham** ～ 〔1847—1922，生于苏格兰的美国人，电话发明者〕.

bell[1] [bel] *n.* ①钟，铃；门铃；〔常 *pl.*〕【海】船钟；雾钟；轮班钟〔$4\frac{1}{2}$、$8\frac{1}{2}$、$12\frac{1}{2}$时各一击，其后每 $\frac{1}{2}$ 时递增一击〕〔*cf.* eight bells〕. ②钟声. ③(铁管的)承口；扩散管，漏斗；〔*pl.*〕喇叭裤；【建】圆屋顶；【动】(水母等的)伞膜；【植】钟状花冠. ④〔美俚〕拳赛终了. *electric* ～*s* 电铃. *a hand* ～ 手摇铃. *a door* ～ 门铃. *answer the* ～ 听到铃声去开门. *There's the* ～. 有客来了. *marriage* ～*s* 婚钟. *passing* ～*s* 丧钟. *rise at the* ～ 鸣钟即起. *a set of* ～*s* 一组钟. ***(as) sound [clear] as a*** ～ 极健康〔清楚〕. ***bear [carry away] the*** ～ ①站在前头. ②获胜，得奖品. ～, ***book and candle*** 【宗】驱逐出教的威胁，教会的威权. ***by*** ～ ***and book*** 凭着钟声和圣经起誓〔中世纪起誓用语〕. ***gain the*** ～ 得胜. ***hang all one's*** ～***s on one horse*** 把所有的财产遗留给独生子. ***hang the*** ～ ***about the cat's neck.*** 敢于冒险；敢于在危险中挺身而出. ***lose the*** ～ 战败，败北. ***ring a*** ～ 引起反应，使人想起某事 (*That rings a* ～. 〔口〕那使人回想起某事来了). ***ring the*** ～ ①敲钟，摇铃. ②〔美俚〕使如愿以偿；使满意〔欢迎，成功〕. ***ring the*** ～***s backward*** 报警，告急. ***saved by the*** ～ (拳击手)因铃响宣告一个回合结束而免于被击倒；(人)因偶发事件而避开灾难. ***That rings a*** ～. 那是一个提醒. ***with*** ～***s on*** 〔口〕热切希望，很想，很喜爱. — *vt.* ①系铃于，给…装上铃. ②使成铃状. ③鸣钟[按铃]召(人). ④把…放在钟形罩内. ～ *the man to come up* 鸣钟[按铃]叫人来. ～ ***the cat*** 给猫系铃，想办难事. ～ **bird** 钟声鸟. ～**-bottom trousers** 喇叭裤. ～ **boy** 〔美〕①旅馆侍者. ②随身电话装置，无线电话机. ～ **buoy**【海】(设在暗礁上的)打钟浮标. ～ **button** 电铃的揿钮. ～ **captain** 旅馆服务员领班. ～ **flower** 【植】〔口〕风铃草属 (*Campanula*) (*the Chinese* ～*flower* 桔梗). ～ **founder** 铸钟匠. ～ **foundry** 铸钟厂. ～ **glass** (钟形)玻璃罩. ～ **hanger** (旧时的)装铃匠. ～ **hop** 〔美口〕= bellboy. ～ **jar** (钟状)玻璃罩. ～**man** (教堂)打钟人；管誉报钟的人；上街鸣钟向公众报事的人；更夫. ～ **metal** 钟铜〔铜锡合金，即青铜〕. ～**mouthed** *a.* 钟口状的，钟口的. ～**-pull** 钟〔门铃〕的拉索；铃扣. ～ **polisher** 〔美俚〕事情谈好还不回去的客人. ～ **push** 电铃按钮. ～ **ringer** 摇铃的人；敲钟的人，钟童. ～ **ringing** 鸣钟；鸣钟法. ～ **tent** 钟形帐篷. ～ **tower** 钟楼. ～ **wether** (做羊群领队的)系铃羊；前导.

bell[2] [bel] *n.* (交尾期的)雄鹿鸣声. — *vi.* (雄鹿)鸣，叫.

Bel·la [ˈbelə] *n.* = Bel.

bel·la·don·na [ˌbeləˈdɔnə] *n.* ①【植】颠茄. ②【药】颠茄制剂. ～ **lily** 孤挺花.

bel·la·fi·gu·ra [ˈbelɑːfiːˈguːrɑː] 〔It.〕 良好的印象；优雅的风度.

Bel·la·my [ˈbeləmi] *n.* 贝拉米〔姓氏〕.

belle [bel] *n.* 〔F.〕美女，第一美人，…花 ～ ***amie*** [ˈbeˈlæmiː] (美貌的)女朋友. ***the*** ～ ***of society*** 交际花. ***the*** ～ ***of the ball*** 舞会花魁〔第一美人〕.

belle époque, la [beleiˈpɔːk] 〔偶而作 B-E〕〔F.〕高雅风流年代〔指 1871 年普法战争结束至第一次世界大战前法国文学艺术大繁荣的时期〕.

Bel·ler·o·phon [bəˈleərəfən] *n.* 【希神】柏勒洛丰〔骑着天马 Pegasus 杀死喷火怪物 Chimera 的科林斯勇士〕. **-tic** *a.* (*Bellerophontic letter* 内容不利于送信者的信件).

belles-let·tres [ˈbelˈletr] *n.* 〔*pl.*〕〔F.〕 美文学；纯文学，纯文艺〔指诗歌、小说、戏剧等〕.

bel·let·rist [ˈbelˈletrist] *n.* ①美文学研究者. ②纯文学作者.

bel·le·tris·tic [ˈbelleˈtristik] *a.* 有关美文学研究的；纯文学的.

bel·li·cose [ˈbelikəus] *a.* 好战的，爱打架的，好斗的. **-ly** *ad.* **-ness** *n.*

bel·li·cos·i·ty [ˌbeliˈkɔsiti] *n.* 好战，好斗(性).

bel·lied [ˈbelid] *a.* 有腹的；膨胀的，鼓起的；凸起的；张满的. ②…腹的〔用以构成复合词〕. *big- [pot-]* ～ 大腹便便的，大肚皮的；有孕的. *empty-*～ 空着肚子的. *a* ～ *sail* 张满的风帆.

bel·lig·er·ence [biˈlidʒərəns, beˈlidʒərəns] *n.* ①好战性. ②交战，战争行为.

bel·lig·er·en·cy [biˈlidʒərənsi, beˈlidʒərənsi] *n.* ①(国与国等处于)交战中，交战状态. ②好战性.

bel·lig·er·ent [biˈlidʒərənt, beˈlidʒərənt] *a.* ①交战中的；交战国的. ②好战的，好斗的. ～ *powers* 交战国. *a* ～ *tone* 挑衅的语调. — *n.* 交战国；交战的一方. *the defeated* ～ 战败国；战败一方.

Bell·man [ˈbelmən] *n.* 贝尔曼〔姓氏〕.

Bel·loc [ˈbelɔk] *n.* 贝洛克〔姓氏〕.

Bel·lo·na [bəˈləunə] *n.* ①【罗神】女战神. ②(人格化的)战争. ③身高体壮的美女，颀长的美女.

bel·low [ˈbeləu] *vi.* ①(公牛、象等)吼，大声叫. ②(人)怒吼，咆哮；(风)怒号；(海)呼啸；(大炮、雷)轰轰地响、轰鸣. ～ *with rage* 怒吼. — *vt.* 大声喊〔发〕出. *He* ～*d his answer across the room.* 他从屋子那边大声地答复. ～

off 大声驱赶；喝使哑口无言．~ ***out [forth]*** 大声咆哮（~ *out [forth] a laugh* 放声大笑）．— *n.* ①(公牛等的)吼声．②咆哮；怒号．

Bel·low(s) [ˈbeləu(z)] *n.* 贝洛(斯)〔姓氏〕．

bel·lows [ˈbeləuz] *n.* 〔*sing., pl.*〕①手拉风箱，手用吹风器〔有两个把手的叫 a pair of ~，俗称皮老虎；固定的叫 (the) ~〕．②(管风琴等的)风箱；【机】波纹管；(真空)膜盒；(照相机的)蛇腹．③〔俚〕肺．*a ~ pocket* 褶裥的口袋．~ *type gun* 风箱嘴油枪；风箱型喷射器．***have ~ to mend*** 〔俚〕(马等)喘气，发喘．~**like** *a.*

bel·lum [ˈbeləm] *n.* (波斯湾的)小独木船．

bell·wort [ˈbelˌwəːt] *n.* ①颚花属植物．②〔主英〕风铃草属植物．

bel·ly [ˈbeli] *n.* ①肚子，腹，腹部 (*opp.* back)；胃；子宫．②(物件的)凸部，凹部；前部，下部，内部．③胃口，食欲；贪心．④腹状物；腹状部；炉腰；(飞机、轮船等的)舱内部；【海】被风张满的帆；【机】桁腹；【建】隆腹形．*The ~ has no ears.* 肚子会饿不会听，衣食足而后礼义兴．*the ~ of a sail* 帆的鼓起部分．*a pot ~* 大肚子．***back and*** ~ 背与腹；衣食．~ ***laugh*** 〔美口〕捧腹大笑；(戏剧中)叫人捧腹大笑的动作(等)．~ ***timber*** 食物．***full in the*** ~ 〔口〕大肚子〔怀孕〕．***have fire in one's*** ~ 肚里明亮，内心聪明．***lie on one's*** ~ 匍匐．***make a god of one's*** ~ 贪吃，嘴馋．— *vt.* 使鼓起，使张满；使胀．— *vi.* ①胀满，鼓起．②匍匐前进．~***in*** (飞机)以腹部触地降落．~ ***out*** (帆)迎风鼓起；(矿脉)突然增广．~**ache** ① *n.* 肚子痛，腹痛．② *vi.* 〔美俚〕哭诉，发牢骚，鸣不平．~**band** (马的)肚带．~**board** 冲浪运动中用的一种腹部贴卧的浮板．~**-bound** *a.* (肠)秘结，便秘．~**button** 〔美俚〕脐．~**fat** 〔美俚〕浪费或多余的东西．~**flop** 〔口〕腹部击水的拙劣跳水动作；(滑雪时)肚子贴着雪橇的下滑．~ **god** 贪吃的人；考究饮食的人．~**hold** 机腹货舱 ~**-land** *vi.* 【空】以机腹着陆．~**-pinched** *a.* 挨饿的．~ **tank** (用完就扔弃的)额外油筒．~**-up** *a.* ①死的．②破产的．~ **wash** 〔美口〕清凉饮料，冷饮品．~ **worm** 〔口〕蛔虫．~ **worship** 大吃大喝，暴饮暴食．**-ful** *n.* 满腹，充分 (*of*)．

Bel·mo·pan [ˈbelməpæn] *n.* 贝尔莫潘〔伯利兹首都〕．

be·long [biləŋ] *vi.* ①属，属(某人)所有，是(某人)的东西 (*to*)；应归入(某)部类 (*to, among, in, under, with*)．②〔美口〕是…的会员〔成员，附件〕(*to*)．③〔美口〕住，居住．④爱接近人，爱交际；适合于(某)环境．⑤〔俚〕拥有 (*to*)．⑥〔Scot.〕应该〔后接不定式〕．*This book ~s to me.* 这本书是我的．*This book ~s in every home.* 这本书家家需要．*Poetry ~s with music.* 诗歌与音乐相近．*He ~s here.* 他是此地人．*Where do you ~ (to)?* 你是哪里人？*The lid ~s to this jar.* 盖子是这把壶上的．*Where does these things ~?* 这些东西原来放在哪里？*You don't ~ in this club.* 你不是这个俱乐部的成员．*She is smart and jolly, but she just doesn't ~.* 她爽直快活，就是有些孤僻．*We all ~.* 我们彼此合得来．*He doesn't ~.* 他人缘不好．*Your objection doesn't ~ to this discussion.* 你的反对意见和这场讨论没有关系．*Who ~s to this dictionary?* 〔俚〕这本字典是谁的？*They ~ to come at o'clock.* 他们应该在七点钟来．

be·long·ing [biˈləŋiŋ] *n.* ①〔常 *pl.*〕附属品，附件．②〔*pl.*〕所有物；财产；行李．③〔*pl.*〕〔口〕家属．④亲密关系．**-ness** *n.* 有所归属；【心】相属关系．

Be·lo·rus·sia [ˌbjeləˈrʌʃə] *n.* 白俄罗斯．— *n., a.* 白俄罗斯人(的)．

be·lov·ed [biˈlʌvd, biˈlʌvid] *a.* ①[biˈlʌvd] 被…爱的〔用作表语，与 *by, of* 连用〕．②[biˈlʌvid]可爱的，亲爱的，被热爱的〔用作定语〕．*a ~ child* 爱儿．— *n.* [biˈlʌvd] 心爱的人，可爱的人．*My ~* 亲爱的 (= darling)．*The most ~* 最可爱的人．★本词作为古语 belove 的过去分词，现时只通用被动语态：She was ~ by [of] all who knew her. 凡是认识她的人都喜欢她．She is ~ of [by] John. 约翰喜欢她．

be·low [biˈləu] *ad.* ①在下面，向下；在下方．②在地上，在下界，在人世．③在地下，在地狱中．④在楼下；在甲板下，在舱面下，向船室〔*cf.* on deck〕；在下游．⑤(在)下级．⑥在(书的)页末，在下文，列后．⑦(动物)在下腹部；(舞台)台下．*B- there!* 喂，下面的人注意〔往下抛东西时叫人当心〕；*the vally ~* 下面的山谷．*see ~* 参见下文．*He was demoted to the class ~.* 他被降级．*the place ~* 地狱．*the court ~* 下级法院．— ***prep.*** ①在…之下．②低于；劣于．③在…的下游．④有失…的身分，无…的价值．⑤(温度)零下的．*six ~* 零下六度．*next ~ a colonel* 上校之下．*sink ~ the horizon* 沉落到地平面以下．*sell ~ cost* 亏本出售．*~ the average* 平均水平以下．*an action ~ his notice* 不值得他注意的一件事．*It is ~ a lady to do such a thing.* 一位女士做这种事是有失身分的．*He is ~ her in intelligence.* 他知识比她差．— *n.* 下面．*from ~* 从下面．~ ***the mark*** ①在标准以下(的)，劣等的．②身体不好．***down*** ~ 地狱中；坟墓中；海底下．***go*** ~ 【海】(由舱面)进舱内，下舱；下班．***here*** ~ 在地上，在这个世界上．**-decks** *adv.* 在船内．**-ground** *a.* ①地下的．②已经埋葬的．**-stairs** *adv., a.* 在楼下；在地下室．

belt [belt] *n.* ①带，皮带；绶带；线条；带状物．②【机】传动带；【天】云状带；【军】子弹带；腰皮带；单层铁丝网；(战舰)吃水线以下的装甲带；(飞机)保险带．③〔美〕产区；地带，区域．④〔美〕环行电车〔铁路〕线．⑤〔美俚〕抽打；〔美俚〕快感，刺激．*a leather ~* 皮带．*a waist ~* 腰带．*a sword ~* 剑带．*the cotton ~* 产棉地带．*a green ~* (都市)绿化区．*the marine ~* 领海．*He caught me a ~ on the ear.* 他用皮带抽了一下我的耳朵．*the Great [little] Belt* (由北海通至波罗的海的)大[小]海峡．*the Black Belt* ①美国南部黑土地带．②美国南方[城市]黑人多于白人的地区．***hit [strike] below the*** ~ 【拳】击对手腰带下部犯规行为；【口】卑劣行为，玩卑鄙手段，暗箭伤人．***hold the*** ~ (在拳击等比赛中) 夺得锦标．***tighten [pull in] one's*** ~ 〔讽〕勒紧肚带，饿着肚皮，含辛茹苦；紧缩开支．***under one's*** ~ 〔俚〕①在肚皮里．②已有经验．— *vt.* ①在…上系带子．②用带扎上．③佩带(剑等)．④环绕．⑤用皮带抽打；〔口〕痛打．⑥〔口〕大声唱．⑦〔美〕环(状)剥(树皮)．⑧喝(酒) ***(down)***；狂饮．*~ a sword on* 佩剑．— *vi.* 急走，快速移动．*~ along the road* 顺路急进．~ ***the ball*** 【美棒球】打，连续打出稳球．~ ***out*** 【美拳】打倒．~ ***up*** 〔口〕〔命令〕住口！别响！〔口〕系上座位安全带．~ **highway** 城市周围的环状公路．~ **line** (电车等的) 环行路线．~ **man** ①机器修理工．②(游泳池)救生员．

belt·ed [ˈbeltid] *a.* ①束带的，佩绶带的．②有条纹的．③装甲的．*a ~ dress* 有绶带的服装．*a ~ cow* 花条母牛．~**-bias tyre** 带束斜交轮胎．

belt·ing [ˈbeltiŋ] *n.* ①带料；带布．②〔集合词〕带，带类；【机】传动带(装置)．③〔口〕(用皮带等) 抽打．*Give him a ~.* 用皮带抽他一顿！

be·lu·ga [bəˈluːgə] *n.* (*pl.* ***~(s)***) ①欧洲鳇．②白鲸．

bel·ve·dere [ˈbelvidiə] *n.* 〔It.〕 ①【建】望楼，瞭望塔；亭子．② 〔the B-〕罗马梵蒂冈宫的绘画馆．

be·ly·ing [biˈlaiiŋ] belie 的现在分词．

B.E.M. = British Empire Medal 不列颠帝国勋章．

be·ma [ˈbiːmə] *n.* (*pl.* ***bemata*** [ˈbiːmətə], ***~s***) ①(教堂中高级教士的)高座．②讲坛．

be·mean [biˈmiːn] *vt.* 〔~ oneself〕 使变卑贱 (= demean)．

be·mire [biˈmaiə] *vt.* ①被泥弄脏，使沾上泥污．②使陷泥中．*The muddy road ~d the wagon.* 马车陷入了泥泞的道路．

be·moan [biˈməun] *vt.* ①悲叹，哀悼；惋惜．②对…不满．— *vi.* 悲叹，哀悼．~ *one's fate* 悲叹自己的命运．

be·mock [biˈmɔk] *vt.* 嘲弄，讥笑．

be·muse [bi'mju:z] *vt.* ①使迷迷糊糊,使昏头昏脑;使发呆. ②使着迷〔多用被动语态〕. *be ~d with drink* 喝酒喝得昏昏沉沉.

Ben [ben] *n.* 本〔男子名, Benjamin 的昵称〕.

ben[1] [ben] *n.* 〔Scot., Ir.〕…峰. ***Ben-Nevis*** (英国最高的)尼维思峰.

ben[2] [ben] *n.* 〔Scot.〕(相连二室的)内室. — *a., ad.* 在内部,在里面. *but and ~* 外室和内室. ***be but and ~ with*** 与…有亲密关系. ***far ~*** 在最里面一间;〔喻〕(和)…特别亲密 *(with)*.

ben·act·y·zine [bə'næktizi:n] *n.* 【药】苯乃静, 胃复康〔治精神病的一种镇定剂〕.

be·name [bi'neim] *vt.* *(-named, -nempt; -named, -nempted; -naming)* 〔古〕取名;叫做.

bench [bentʃ] *n.* ①长凳,条凳. ②船上的坐板;座,架,(木工、钳工等的)工作台;【矿】(煤矿的)台阶,(矿的)梯段;【地】阶地;【园艺】(温室中的)苗床;【机】拉丝机. ③(动物展览会的)陈列台;〔美〕畜犬展览会. ④法院;法官席;列席法官;(英议院的)议席;(运动员的)特别席,选手席,队员席;场外的全体候补队员. ⑤【宗】主教. *a park ~* 公园长凳. *an experimental ~* 试验架. *a carpenter's ~* 木工工作台. *front ~es* (英议会)政党领袖席,大臣席. *back ~es* (下院后座)一般议员席. *ministerial ~es* (议长右侧前方)政府部员席. *the Treasury ~* 财政大臣席. *A weak ~ hurt their chances for championship.* 他们因后备运动员力量不足而妨碍了夺魁. ***be raised to the ~*** 被任命为法官[主教]. ***~ and bar*** 法官和律师. ***on the ~*** ①做法官[主教]. ②(运动员)作为候补选手. ***sit on the Penniless B-.*** 一文不名,一贫如洗. ***take a seat on the ~*** 当法官[主教]. ***the free ~*** (英国法律上的)寡妇财产权. ***the King's [Queen's] Bench*** 〔英〕高等法院. ***the Upper Bench*** 【英史】皇家高等法院. — *vt.* ①在…安置凳子;使坐凳子上. ②使坐席位;使坐名誉席. ③(把狗等)摆上台展览. ④【体】使(比赛员)退场,把(队员)调下来. ⑤【矿】从下面掘(煤层). — *vi.* ①【地】形成台地. ~ **board**【无】控制盘,台式配电器. ~ **jockey** 喝对方倒采的运动员. ~ **land** 滩地,沙洲. ~ **lathe** 台式车床. ~**-made** *a.* 手工制的;定做的. ~ **man** 收音机[电视机]修理工. ~ **mark** ①【测】水准点. ②标准;规范. ③【计】标准检查程序. ~ **show** 〔美〕畜犬[家猫]展览会. ~ **warmer** 候补席上的运动员. ~ **warrant** 法院传票,逮捕证. ~ **worker** 钳(床)工(人).

bench·ed [bentʃt] *a.* 【美棒球】被调换下来的.

bench·er ['bentʃə] *n.* ①坐凳子的人. ②英国律师协会的主管委员. ③(小艇的)划手. ④〔俚〕欢喜坐酒馆的人.

Bench·ley ['bentʃli] *n.* 本奇利〔姓氏〕.

bend[1] [bend] *vt.* ***(bent*** [bent]***; bent,*** 〔古〕***~ed)*** ①弄弯,使弯曲,拗弯(棍子等);屈(膝);弯(弓). ②使屈服,压服. ③热中于,集中思想于. ④(耳、目等)转向;使(脚步等)改变方向. ⑤【海】系(绳索、帆等). *~ an iron rod into a hoop* 把铁条弯成箍. *~ a crooked thing straight* 把弯曲的东西扳直. *~ the (one's) brow* 皱眉. *~ing strength* 抗弯强度. *~ one's knees* 屈膝(行礼);跪. *~ the neck* 低头;屈服. *~ one's will* 使自己的意志屈从于他人. *~ sb. to one's will* 使别人屈从自己的意志. *~ one's eyes [gaze] on it* 把眼睛转向它. *~ one's way [steps] homeward* 往家里走. *~ one's energies to an end* 全力以赴地实现某个目的. *~ the cable* 把锚链系在锚环上. — *vi.* ①弯曲;转向;屈身. ②服从,屈服. ③倾注,集中力量于 *(to)*. *a bow that ~s easily* 一张易弯的弓. *~ down* 弯下身来. *~ to the east [left]* 向东(左)转. *~ toward the south* 向南转. *He will not ~.* 他断然不屈,不妥协. ***be bent on*** 尽想,一心要 (*He is bent on mischief.* 他尽想坏主意,他一心要捣蛋). ***~ one's efforts for*** 致力,为…贡献力量. ***~ one's mind to [on, upon]*** 一心向,专心致志于. ***~ oneself to*** 竭力要,致力于. ***~ over*** ①弯腰, 身子贴近,伏在…上 (*~ over and pick up a thing* 弯下身子拾起一件东西. *~ over desk* 伏案工作). ***~ over backward(s)*** *(to do sth.)* 〔贬〕拼命(做某事). ***~ to*** ①为…所屈;顺从(*~ to circumstances* 适应环境. *~ to fate* 屈服于命运). ②专心, 用全力 (*~ to the oars* 拼命划桨). —*n.* ①曲, 弯曲; 弯曲部, 曲处. ②弯管, 接头; 可曲波导管. ③(心的)归向, 倾向; 屈服. ④ [the ~s] 〔口〕沉箱病, 潜函病; 〔美口〕航空病. ⑤【海】结索(法);索结. ⑥ 〔*pl.*〕(木船的)外条板. ⑦【美军】特约酒馆. ***above one's ~*** 〔美〕为…力所不及的,是…办不了的. ***Get a ~ on you!*** 〔卑〕快点! 加油! ***go on the [a] ~*** 〔美口〕狂饮,闹饮. ***on the ~*** 用不法手段,用不正当的办法. ***round the ~*** 〔英口〕发狂,发昏.

bend[2] [bend] *n.* ①【徽】(盾上自右上至左下的)右斜线. ②〔*pl.*〕(妇女)头带. ③皮革的左[右]半张整皮. ***~ sinister*** 【徽】左斜线〔私生子的标志〕.

bend·ed ['bendid] *a.* ①弯着的,弯曲的. ②热心的. ***on [upon, with] ~ knees*** 跪着; 苦苦地. ***with ~ bow*** 〔书〕拉满弓.

bend·er ['bendə] *n.* ①弯曲者,弯曲物;【机】折弯机. ②〔英俚〕六便士银币;〔美俚〕狂饮;〔Scot.〕酒量大的人. ③【棒球】曲球;〔英方〕美妙的东西;〔美口〕两腿. *a ~ of a night* 美妙的一晚.

Ben·dix ['bendiks] *n.* 〔美口〕洗濯器.

Ben·dy ['bendi] *n.* 【植】秋葵.

bene- *comb. f.* = well (*opp.* male-): *bene*diction, *bene*factor.

be·neath [bi'ni:θ] *prep.* ①〔诗、古、书〕在…之下, 低于; 在…的(正)下方; 在…脚下, 在(或紧挨着)…的底下〔通常用 below, under〕. ②不值得, 不足取; 有失…的身分, 有损于(尊严等), 不称, 不配; 劣于, 比…不如. *live ~ the same roof* 同住一屋. *the first drawer ~ the top one* 顶档以下的第一个抽屉. *~ attention* 不值得注意. *~ contempt* 不齿, 极可鄙. *It would be ~ him to cheat.* 他去行骗未免有失身分. *marry ~ one* 和身分比自己低的人结婚. *be far ~ (sb.) in (attainments)* (造诣)远较(某人)为低. *~ one's breath* 低声. *~ one's dignity* 有损威严,不合身分. — *ad.* ①在下, 在下面, 在下方, 在下位. ②在地下. *The valley lay ~.* 山谷就在下面. *the heaven above and the earth ~.* 天上和地下.

Be·ne·di·ci·te [ˌbeni'daisiti] *n.* 【新教】万物颂(乐曲); 〔b-〕饭前祷告. — *int.* 天哪! 我的天哪!

ben·e·dict ['benidikt] *n.* (放弃多年独身主义而结婚的)新郎〔出自莎士比亚的喜剧《无事烦恼》〕.

Ben·e·dict ['benidikt] *n.* 本尼迪克特〔姓氏,男子名〕.

ben·e·dick ['benidik] *n.* = benedict.

Ben·e·dic·tine [ˌbeni'diktain] *a.* (五世纪意大利名僧)圣本尼迪克特 (St. Benedict) 的; 本尼迪克特教团的. — *n.* ①本尼迪克特教团的僧侣. ②〔b-〕[ˌbeni'dikti:n] (本尼迪克特教团僧侣所酿造的)法国费康 (Fécamp) 产的一种甜酒.

ben·e·dic·tion [ˌbeni'dikʃən] *n.* ①【基督】祝福,礼拜末尾的祝祷; (餐前餐后的)谢恩祷. ②【天主】(圣体)祝福式. ③祈福, 天恩. *give the ~* 举行祝福式. **-al, -dic·tive,-dic·to·ry** *a.* 祈福的,祝福的.

ben·e·fac·tion [ˌbeni'fækʃən] *n.* ①慈善,慈善行为. ②捐助,施舍;捐助物,捐款. *He is known for his many ~s.* 他以做了许多善事知名. *solicit ~s for earthquake victims* 为地震区灾民募捐.

ben·e·fac·tor ['benifæktə] *n.* *(fem.* ***-tress*** ['benifæktris]*)* 恩人;保护人;捐助人.

be·nef·ic [bi'nefik] *a.* 慈善的,行善的,仁慈的;仁爱的.

ben·e·fice ['benifis] *n.* ①教士的有俸圣职;教区牧师享有的教产. ②封地,采邑. — *vt.* 使获得有俸圣职.

be·nef·i·cence [bi'nefisəns] *n.* ①慈善; 善行. ②施舍物,捐款;救济品. *bestow many ~s* 捐赠许多救济品.

be·nef·i·cent [bi'nefisənt] *a.* 慈善的,行善的, 仁慈的;

仁爱的. *exert a ~ influence on* 施恩泽于. **-ly** *ad.*

ben·e·fi·cial [ˌbeniˈfiʃəl] *a.* 有利的,有益的 *(to)* *(opp.* injurious);【法】可享受利益的,有收入权益的. *~ birds [insects]* 益鸟[虫]. *a ~ association* 互助组合. ***a ~ legacy*** 一笔仅有收入权益的遗产〔可享受其收入,但无所有权和处理权〕.

ben·e·fi·ci·a·ry [ˌbeniˈfiʃəri] *a.* (封建制度下)受封的;采邑的;臣服的. — *n.* ①(遗嘱、保险等的)受益人;(退休金等的)领受人;〔美〕公费生;【邮】(国际汇兑的)收款人. ②〔原义〕封臣. ③受俸牧师.

ben·e·fit [ˈbenifit] *n.* ①利益,好处;利润. ②恩惠,恩泽;恩典,特典. ③(为赈灾等举行的)义演,义赛. ④退休金;(依照社会保险付给的)津贴,救济金,抚恤金. ⑤〔俚、反〕好机会,好差事. *a public ~* 公益. *for your special ~* 特为你(利益)打算. *a ~-match* 义赛. *a ~-night* 义演晚会. *medical [maternity] ~s* 医疗[产妇]津贴. *I had no end of a ~ getting things straight.* 我那收拾东西的好差事没完没了. *~ of clergy* 牧师的特权;(结婚时)教会的证明. *~ society [club]* 共济会,互济会. ***be of ~*** 有益,裨益. ***for sb.'s ~ = for the ~ of*** 为…(利益)打算;〔反〕为惩戒… (*Was he doing that for my ~?* 他那样做是为我好吗? *He wasn't really angry, that was just an act for his girl friend's ~.* 他不是真生气, 那是为了治治他那女朋友的). ***give (sb.) the ~ of the doubt*** 对(某人的过错等)作善意解释,(在证据不足的情况下)假定某人无辜,给(某人)"虽可疑但无罪"的处理. — *vt.* 对…有利,有益于…;使得利益. *a health program to ~ all mankind* 一项有益于全人类的卫生计划. —*vi.* 得益,受益 *(by; from)*. *a person who has never ~ed from experience* 一个从不吸取经验教训的人.

Be·ne·lux [ˈbenilʌks] *n.* 比(利时)、荷(兰)、卢(森堡)经济联盟. *the ~ countries* 比、荷、卢三国.

be·nempt [biˈnempt] 〔古〕 bename 的过去分词 (= benempted).

Be·nét [beˈnei] *n.* 贝内〔姓氏〕.

be·nev·o·lence [biˈnevələns] *n.* ①仁爱,亲切;厚道,慈善. ②善行,捐款;捐助. ③【英史】(英国国王征收的)王税.

be·nev·o·lent [biˈnevələnt] *a.* ①仁爱的,仁慈的. ②乐善好施的,慈善的. ③亲切的,善意的. *the ~ art* 仁术,医术. *her ~ smile* 她那亲切的微笑. **-ly** *ad.*

Ben·gal [beŋˈgɔːl] *n.* ①孟加拉〔亚洲〕. ②孟加拉生丝(织品). ***Bay of ~*** 孟加拉湾. *~* **light [fire]** 信号烟火. *~* **stripes** 条花棉布.

Ben·ga·lee, Ben·ga·lese [beŋgəˈliː, -z], **Ben·gal·i** [beŋˈgɔːli] *a.* 孟加拉的;孟加拉人的;孟加拉语的. — *n.* 〔*sing., pl.*〕 孟加拉人;孟加拉语.

ben·ga·line [ˈbeŋgəliːn] *n.*【纺】罗缎.

Ben·ge [bendʒ] *n.* 本奇〔姓氏〕.

Ben·g(h)a·zi, Ben·g(h)a·si [beŋˈgaːzi] *n.* 班加西〔利比亚港市〕.

be·night·ed [biˈnaitid] *a.* ①(旅客等)走到天黑的,赶路到黑的. ②愚昧的,蒙昧的,无知的. *a ~ traveler* 赶路到天黑的旅客. *~ ages of barbarism and superstition* 野蛮迷信的蒙昧时代.

be·nign [biˈnain] *a.* ①仁慈的,宽厚的;亲切的;温和的. ②(气候等)温和的,良好的,有益于健康的. ③吉祥的 *(opp.* sinister*)*. ④【医】良性的 *(opp.* malignant*)*. *~ rule* 仁政. *a ~ climate* 温和的气候. *a ~ tumor* 良性瘤. **-ly** *ad.*

be·nig·nan·cy [biˈnignənsi] *n.* ①仁慈,亲切;(气候)温和. ②【医】良性.

be·nig·nant [biˈnignənt] *a.* ①仁慈的,亲切的;宽厚的. ②(气候)温和的;【医】良性的.

be·nig·ni·ty [biˈnigniti] *n.* ①宽厚,亲切,仁慈. ②(气候)温和. ③善行. *benignities born of selfless devotion* 由无私的献身精神产生的宽厚胸怀.

Be·nin [beˈnin] *n.* 贝宁〔非洲〕.

ben·i·son [ˈbenizn] *n.* 〔古〕祝福 *(opp.* malison*)*;神恩.

Ben·ja·min [ˈbendʒəmin] *n.* ①本杰明〔男子名,希伯来语源,意为"幸运儿". 爱称 Ben, Benjie, Bennie〕. ②【圣】卞雅悯〔雅各的末子〕;〔喻〕老儿子,爱子,宠儿. ③〔b-〕〔美俚〕男紧身大衣. ***~'s mess*** (分东西时)特多的一份,头一份.

ben·ja·min = benzoin.

ben·(n)e [ˈbeni] *n.* 芝麻;芝麻籽;胡麻 (= sesame).

Ben·nett [ˈbenit] *n.* 贝内特〔姓氏,男子名,Benedict 的异体〕.

ben·nies [ˈbeniz] *n.* 〔美俚〕= Benny.

Ben·ny, Ben·nie [ˈbeni] *n.* 本尼〔男子名,Benjamin 的昵称〕.

ben·ny [ˈbeni] *n.* *(pl.* **-nies***)* 〔美俚〕安非他明药片 (= Benzendrine).

Ben·son [ˈbensn] *n.* 本森〔姓氏〕.

bent[1] [bent] bend 的过去式及过去分词. — *a.* ①弯,弯曲的. ②决心的;专心的. ③〔口〕偷来的,有偷癖的. ④〔口〕同性爱的. ⑤〔美俚〕喝醉的. *be ~ double with age* 年老背驼. ***be ~ on [upon]*** 决心要;专想,一心要 (*be ~ on buying a new car* 决心要买一辆新车. *be ~ on mischief [gain]* 专想捉弄人[赚钱]. *be ~ over one's work* 专心工作). — *n.* ①弯,曲,弯曲处. ②倾向,嗜好,癖性,性格. ③能力;耐力. ④【机】弯头,曲轴;【建】桥脚;脚柱;框架结构. *square ~* (水管的)直角弯头. *a young man with a literary ~* 爱好文学的青年. *She has a natural ~ for painting* 她生性爱绘画. ***follow one's ~*** 随心所好,凭爱好办事. ***to the top of one's ~*** 尽量;尽力;尽情地. **~wing** 后掠机翼,后掠翼飞机.

bent[2] [bent] *n.* ①【植】小糠草;深山糠草;苇草;(同上草类的)枯茎,枯草. ②〔Scot.〕(小糠草等繁生的)荒草地〔作为牧场、狩猎场等〕;荒野;沼泽地.

Ben·tham [ˈbentəm, ˈbenθəm] *n.* ①本瑟姆(边沁). 〔姓氏〕. ② **Jeremy ~** 杰·边沁 〔1748—1832, 英国法学家及哲学家〕.

Ben·tham·ism [ˈbentəmizəm] *n.* 功利主义,多数幸福说〔边沁鼓吹的一种伦理学说〕.

Ben·tham·ite [ˈbentəmait] *n.* 功利主义者;边沁主义者.

ben·thic [ˈbenθik], **ben·thal** [ˈbenθəl] *a.* 关于[发生于]水底[海底]的.

ben·thon [ˈbenθɔn] *n.*【生】生活于水底部分的生物.

ben·thos [ˈbenθɔs] *n.* ①(深海)海底,湖底. ②海底生物,水底生物.

ben·tho·scope [ˈbenθəskəup] *n.* (研究海底生物用的)球形深海潜水器.

Ben·ton [ˈbentən] *n.* 本顿〔姓氏,男子名〕.

ben·ton·ite [ˈbentəˌnait] *n.*【矿】膨润土,皂土,膨土岩,班脱岩.

bent·wood [ˈbentˌwud] *a.* 弯成木的〔指用弯成木做的家具〕. — *n.* (做家具用的)弯成木. *a ~ chair* 弯木椅.

be·numb [biˈnʌm] *vt.* ①使失去感觉,使麻木. ②使麻痹,使瘫痪,使僵化. *be ~ed with [by] cold* 冻麻木,冻僵. *~ the intellectual faculties* 失去智能,变呆. **-ed** *a.* ①失去感觉的,麻痹了的;冻僵的. ②吓呆了的.

ben·zal·de·hyde [benˈzældiˌhaid] *n.*【化】苯(甲)醛.

Ben·ze·drine [ˈbenzidri(ː)n] *n.*【药】苯齐巨林〔amphetamine (安非他明,苯异丙胺)的商品名〕.

ben·zene [ˈbenziːn, benˈziːn] *n.*【化】①苯. ② = benzine. *methyl ~* 甲苯. *ethyl ~* 乙苯.

ben·zi·dine [ˈbenziˌdiːn] *n.*【化】联苯胺.

ben·zine [ˈbenziːn, benˈziːn] *n.*【化】挥发油;〔澳〕汽油.

benzo- *comb. f.*【化】与苯有关的;安息香的.

ben·zo·ate [ˈbenzəuˌeit] *n.*【化】苯(甲)酸盐[酯].

ben·zo·caine [ˈbenzəˌkein, -zəu-] *n.*【化】苯坐卡因,对氨基苯酸乙酯.

ben·zo·ic [benˈzəuik] *a.* 安息香的. *~* **acid** 安息香酸,

苯(甲)酸.

ben·zo·in [ˈbenzəuin] *n.* ①【化】苯偶姻;二苯乙醇酮. ②安息香.

ben·zol [ˈbenzɔl] *n.* ①【化】= benzene. ②(工业用)粗制苯.

ben·zol·ine [ˈbenzəliːn] *n.* = benzine.

ben·zo·phe·none [ˌbenzəufiˈnəun, -ˈfiːnəun] *n.* 【化】二苯甲酮,苯酮,苯酰苯.

ben·zo·py·rene [ˌbenzəuˈpairiːn] *n.* 【化】苯并芘 (= benzpyrene).

ben·zo·sul·fi·mide [ˈbenzəuˈsʌlfimaid] *n.* 【化】糖精 (= saccharin).

ben·zo·yl [ˈbenzəuil] *n.* 【化】苯甲酰〔从苯甲酸衍生的一价基〕.

ben·zyl [ˈbenzil] *n.* 【化】苄基,苯甲基.

Be·o·wulf [ˈbeiəwulf] *n.* ①《贝奥伍尔夫》〔英国 8 世纪古代史诗〕. ②贝奥伍尔夫〔上述史诗中的主人公〕.

be·plas·ter [biˈplɑːstə] *vt.* 在…上厚厚地涂;覆满,布满. ~ *one's face with cosmetics* 把脸厚厚涂上一层脂粉,浓装艳抹. *a coat ~d with medals* 挂满勋章的上衣.

be·pow·der [biˈpaudə] *vt.* 用粉撒上;在…上搽厚香粉.

beqt. = bequest.

be·queath [biˈkwiːð] *vt.* 把…遗留给,把…传给(后代);【法】遗赠(动产). ~ *a large sum of money to one's daughter* 遗留一大笔钱给女儿. *a sword ~ed to the family by their forefathers* 祖传宝剑. **-ment, -al** *n.* 遗赠;遗产,遗物. **-er** 遗赠者.

be·quest [biˈkwest] *n.* ①【法】(动产)遗赠. ②遗产,遗物;让与物. *He left ~s of money to all his friends.* 他给所有的朋友都遗赠了一些钱.

Be·rat [beˈrɑːt] *n.* 培拉特〔阿尔巴尼亚城市〕.

be·rate [biˈreit] *vt.* 〔美〕责骂,训斥.

Ber·ber [ˈbəːbə] *n.* ①(北非)柏柏尔人. ②柏柏尔语. — *a.* ①柏柏尔人的. ②柏柏尔语〔文化〕的.

Ber·ber·a [ˈbəːbərə] *n.* 伯贝拉〔索马里港市〕.

ber·ceuse [bεəˈsəːz] *n.* 〔F.〕【音】摇篮曲; 音调柔和的乐曲.

be·reave [biˈriːv] *vt.* (*~d, be·reft* [biˈreft]; *-reav·ing*) 使丧失(家属等)〔过去式和过去分词一般用 ~d〕. ②使失去(希望、理智等)〔过去式和过去分词一般用 bereft〕. *Illness ~d her of her son.* 她死了孩子. *a man bereft of sense [reason]* 疯子. *Indignation bereft him of speech.* 他愤怒得说不出话来. **-ment** *n.* (亲人等的)丧失,死别,丧亲之痛,居丧.

be·reaved [biˈriːvd] *a.* 死了…的,丧…的;丧亡了家族的. *the ~* 遗族,孤儿. *the ~ family* 遗族. ***be ~ of** (one's husband; wife)* 丧(夫),丧(妻).

be·reft [biˈreft] *a.* 被夺去,失去. *He is utterly ~.* 他全完了. ***be ~ of** (hope; reason)* 失(望);失去(理智),发狂.

be·ret [ˈberei] *n.* 〔F.〕贝雷帽,荷叶帽,圆扁便帽;【英军】军帽. *the Green Berets* 〔美〕特种部队〔戴绿色贝雷帽〕.

berg[1] [bəːg] *n.* 大冰块,冰山〔iceberg 的缩略语〕.

berg[2] [bəːg] *n.* 〔南非〕山.

ber·ga·mot [ˈbəːgəmɔt] *n.* ①【植】佛手柑;香柠檬. ②佛手柑油,香柠檬油. ③【植】一种香梨. ④(意大利人 Bergamo 创制的)花毡.

Ber·gen [ˈbəːgən] *n.* 卑尔根〔挪威港市〕.

Ber·ger [ˈbəːdʒə] *n.* 伯杰〔姓氏〕.

ber·gère, ber·gere [bεəˈʒεə] *n.* 围手椅〔尤指十八世纪法国式藤条椅子〕.

berg·mehl [ˈbəːgmeil] *n.* 硅藻土.

berg·schrund [ˈbεəgʃrund] *n.* 〔G.〕【地】冰河上端的龟裂,悬岩与冰河间的罅隙.

Berg·son [ˈbəːgsən], **Henri** 柏格森〔1859—1941, 法国哲学家〕.

Berg·so·ni·an [bəːgˈsəunjən] *a.* 柏格森(哲学)的. — *n.* 柏格森派.

Berg·son·ism [ˈbəːgsənizəm] *n.* 柏格森哲学.

berg·y [ˈbəːgi] *a.* 大块冰多的,多冰山的.

be·rhyme, be·rime [biˈraim] *vt.* 作诗颂扬;作诗讽刺.

ber·i·ber·i [ˈberiˈberi] *n.* 【医】脚气(病).

Be·ring [ˈberiŋ] *n.* 白令〔1680—1741, 丹麦航海家〕. ~ **sea** 白令海. ~ **strait** 白令海峡. ~ **time** 白令时间.

Berke·lei·an [ˈbɑːkli(ː)ən] *n.* 【哲】贝克莱(主义)的. — *n.* 贝克莱主义者. **-ism** *n.* 贝克莱主义.

Berke·ley[1] [ˈbɑːkli, ˈbəːkli] *n.* ①伯克利〔姓氏〕(贝克莱). ② **George** ~ 贝克莱〔1685—1753, 爱尔兰主教及哲学家〕.

Berke·ley[2] [ˈbəːkli] *n.* 伯克利〔美国港市〕.

ber·ke·li·um [ˈbəːkliəm] *n.* 【化】锫〔人工放射性金属元素,略作 Bk〕.

Berks. = Berkshire.

Berk·shire [ˈbɑːkʃiə] *n.* 巴克夏〔英格兰南部郡名〕;巴克夏猪.

Ber·lin [bəːˈlin] *n.* 柏林. ~ **black [varnish]** 耐热漆. ~ **blue** 柏林蓝,普鲁士蓝. ~ **gloves** 毛线手套. ~ **warehouse** 毛线商店. ~ **wool** 细毛线. **-er** 柏林人,柏林居民.

ber·lin [bəːˈlin] *n.* ①二人乘四轮轿式马车. ②高级细绒线 (= Berlin wool).

berm(e) [bəːm] *n.* 【建】(城墙与外壕间的)狭道;〔美〕(马路两边的)边道,便道;小搁板.

Ber·mu·da(s) [bə(ː)ˈmjuːdə(z)] *n.* 百慕大 (群岛) (= the Bermuda Islands) 〔大西洋西北部〕. ~ **grass** 鸭茅. ~ **Triangle** 百慕大神秘三角〔百慕大群岛、弗罗里达和波多黎各之间的三角形地区,许多船只、飞机均曾神秘地于该地区失踪〕.

Ber·na·dette [ˌbəːnəˈdet] *n.* 伯纳黛特〔女子名〕.

Ber·na·dine [ˈbəːnədiːn] *n.* 伯纳丁〔女子名〕.

Ber·nal [ˈbəːnəl] *n.* 伯纳尔〔姓氏〕.

Ber·nard [bəːˈnɑːd, ˈbəːnəd] *n.* ①伯纳德〔姓氏〕. ② [ˈbəːnəd] 伯纳德〔男子名〕.

Bern(e) [bəːn, bεən] *n.* 伯尔尼〔瑞士首都〕.

Ber·nese [bəːˈniːz] *a.* (瑞士首都)伯尔尼的. — *n.* 〔*sing., pl.*〕伯尔尼人.

Ber·nice [ˈbəːnis, bəːˈniːs] *n.* ①伯尼斯〔姓氏〕. ② [ˈbəːnis] 伯妮斯〔女子名〕.

Ber·nie [ˈbəːni] *n.* 伯尼〔男子名, Bernard 的昵称〕.

Bern·stein [ˈbəːnstain] *n.* 伯恩斯坦〔姓氏〕.

be(r)·ret·ta [biˈretə] *n.* 【天主】四角帽,法冠 (= biretta).

ber·ried [ˈberid] *a.* ①有浆果的. ②(虾等)有子的.

ber·ry [ˈberi] *n.* ①浆果〔如草莓等〕. ②(咖啡等的)子,干种子,干果仁. ③(鱼等的)子,卵. ④〔美俚〕一块钱;〔*pl.*〕〔美俚〕钱,上等东西. *lobsters and shrimps in ~* 正在产子的龙虾和小虾. *barley berries* 大麦粒. *Coffee berries* 咖啡豆. *holy berries* 冬青果. *It's the berries.* 这个好极了. — *vi.* ①结出浆果. ②采集浆果. *go ~ing* 去采集浆果. *~ing shrubs* 结浆果的灌木.

ber·sa·glie·re [ˌbεəsɑːliˈεəri(ː)] *n.* (*pl. -ri* [-riː]) 〔It.〕【军】狙击兵.

ber·seem [bəˈsiːm] *n.* 【植】埃及车轴草,亚历山大车轴草.

ber·serk [bə(ː)ˈsəːk] *n.* = berserke. — *a.* 狂暴的. *with ~ fury* 狂怒. *go ~* 变狂暴.

ber·serk·er [bə(ː)ˈsəːkə] *n.* (北欧传说中战前喜饮酒的)狂暴战士;暴汉;流寇.

Bert, Burt [bəːt] *n.* 伯特〔男子名, Albert, Bertram, Herbert 的昵称〕.

berth [bəːθ] *n.* ①(车、船等的)卧铺. ②投锚处,停泊地;船台. ③(轮船上的)住舱;住处. ④〔英〕职位,地位;〔美〕队形,球员位置. ⑤(船与沙滩等之间留出的)安全距离. *a foul* ～ (常易撞碰他船的)不好的停泊地. *plenty room for ten* ～*s* 可停10条船而绰绰有余. *The ship shifted its* ～. 船转移了停泊地. *find a snug* ～ 找个轻松愉快的工作. ～ ***list*** 舱位分配表. ***give a wide*** ～ ***to*** = ***keep a wide*** ～ ***of*** ①远远离开…抛锚. ②避开[躲开](某人). ***on the*** ～ 停泊待货的船. ***take up a*** ～ 抛锚,停泊. — *vt.* ①使停泊,开到抛锚处. ②为…提供卧铺;(车库等)容纳. ③使就职. ～ *a plane in the hangar* 让一架飞机停进机库. — *vi.* ①停泊. ②占铺位. *The ship effortlessly* ～*ed*. 那条船顺利停泊. ～ *beside one's father* 在父亲旁边的铺位就寝.

Ber·tha [ˈbəːθə] *n.* 伯莎〔女子名〕.

ber·tha, berthe [ˈbəːθə, bəːθ] *n.* (妇女服装上披肩状的)花边领.

berth·age [ˈbəːθidʒ] *n.* ①停泊处,泊位. ②停泊税,泊费.

Ber·tie [ˈbɑːti, ˈbəːti] *n.* 伯蒂〔姓氏, Albert, Bertram, Bertha, Robbert 的昵称〕.

Ber·til·lon system [ˈbəːtilɔn] (通过指纹肤色等侦察犯罪的)柏提永氏人体测验法〔法国人类学者 A. ～ (1853—1914)发明〕.

Ber·tram [ˈbəːtrem] *n.* 伯特伦〔男子名〕.

Ber·ty = Bertie.

Ber·yl [ˈberil] *n.* 贝丽尔〔女子名〕.

ber·yl [ˈberil] *n.* ①【矿】绿柱石,绿玉. ②海绿色.

be·ryl·li·o·sis [bəriliːˈəusis] *n.* 【医】铍中毒.

be·ryl·li·um [bəˈriljəm] *n.* 【化】铍〔别名 glucin(i)um〕.

Ber·ze·li·us [bəˈziːliəs] J. 伯泽列厄斯〔1779—1848, 瑞典化学家,化学符号创制人〕.

B.E.S.A. = British Engineering Standards Association 〔旧〕英国工程标准协会.

be·seech [biˈsiːtʃ] *vt.* ***(be·sought*** [biˈsɔːt], ～***ed; be·sought,*** ～***ed)*** 恳求, 哀求. ～ *(sb.) for mercy [forgiveness, permission]* 求(人)怜悯[原谅、允许]. *They* ～*ed him to go at once.* 他们请他立即就去. ～ *sb.'s help* 请求某人帮助. —*vi.* 恳求,哀求. **-ing·ly** *ad.* 恳求地.

be·seem [biˈsiːm] *vi.* 〔书〕合式,适当. *such a style as well* ～*s* 合适的文体. — *vt.* 〔书〕对…适当,对…合式,对…相称〔仅用于无人称句〕. *It ill* ～*s you to be ungrateful.* 你不象是忘恩负义的人. **-ing·ly** *ad.* 适当地,适合地,相称地.

be·set [biˈset] *vt.* ***(be·set; be·set)*** ①包围,围绕;【海】被冰块包围. ②扰,攻,袭;缠扰,为(病)所苦. ③镶,嵌. *His life is* ～ *with hardships.* 他的生活充满艰辛. *be* ～ *by enemies* 遭到敌人攻击. *a man* ～ *with a sense of guilt* 自知犯罪而内心不安的人. *be* ～ *by (innumerable) difficulties* 困难重重. *a dense forest that* ～*s the village* 围绕着村庄的密林. ～ *a crown with pearls* 用珍珠镶嵌王冠. **-ting** *a.* ①不断侵袭的 (*besetting sin* 易犯的恶习). ②(念头等)缠绕人的. **-ment** *n.* ①(被)包围;(被)困扰;(被)围攻. ②烦恼.

be·show [biˈʃəu] *n.* 裸盖鱼 (= sablefish).

be·shrew [biˈʃruː] *vt.* 〔古〕咒. ***B- me!*** 讨厌! 可恶! ***B- you!*** 该死! ***B- him [it]!*** 讨厌的家伙 [东西]! 该死! 可恶!

be·side [biˈsaid] *prep.* ①在…旁边,在…一侧,在…附近. ②和…相比, 比起…来; 比得上. ③不中(目标), 不对(题),与…无关. ④除…之外. *the house* ～ *the river* 河边的房子. *B- Latin English is imperfect.* 比起拉丁语来,英语是不严谨的. *musical achievement that can be ranked* ～ *masters* 堪与大师们相媲美的音乐成就. *His argument is* ～ *the subject in hand.* 他的议论离开了讨论的问题. *I have no treasure* ～ *this.* 我此外再没有钱了. ***be*** ～ ***oneself*** 发狂,(乐极)忘形,失常(*He is* ～ *himself with rage.* 他愤怒得发狂). ～ ***the mark*** ①未射中目标. ②搞错,离题,不中肯 ***(=*** ～ ***the point [question])***. — *ad.* 〔古〕= besides.

be·sides [biˈsaidz] *ad.* 加之,更,又,还有,而且;另外. *I am too tired to go, (and)* ～*, it is late.* 我不去了,太累啦,而且时候又晚了. *They had a roof over their heads but not much* ～. 他们除了住房,此外就没有什么财产. — *prep.* ①在…之外(还有),…之余兼. ②除…外(不再有). *He speaks German* ～ *English.* 他懂英语而外还会说德语. *B-being a statesman, he was a painter.* 他是政治家,又是画家. *There is no one here* ～ *Bill and me.* 这里只有比尔和我,再没外人.

be·siege [biˈsiːdʒ] *vt.* ①围,包围,围困,围攻. ②拥挤在…周围. ③对…不断提出 (质问等). *The vacationers besieged the travel offices* 度假者挤满了旅游社. ～ *sb. with requests* 对某人提出一大堆要求. **-ment** *n.* (被)包围,(被)围攻;攻城.

be·sieg·er [biˈsiːdʒə] *n.* 围攻者;攻城兵,〔*pl.*〕围攻军.

be·sla·v·er [biˈsleivə] *vt.* = beslobber.

be·slob·ber [biˈslɔbə] *vt.* ①流涎于,用涎沾湿. ②肉麻地吹捧. ③乱吻. *The child* ～*ed his bib.* 这孩子的口水把围嘴都弄湿了.

be·smear [biˈsmiə] *vt.* ①涂搽,涂抹,涂满. ②抹脏,玷污;中伤. *faces* ～*ed with pigments* 脸上涂得花花绿绿. ～ *sb.'s reputation* 破坏某人的名誉.

be·smirch [biˈsməːtʃ] *vt.* ①抹脏,染污. ②丑化,糟塌(名誉等). *Her soul was horribly* ～*ed.* 她的心灵已经变得肮脏不堪.

be·som [ˈbiːzəm] *n.* ①长把帚,竹扫帚;〔喻〕扫除(坏风气等)的手段. ②【植】金雀花. ③〔英方〕女流氓, 女二流子;滥货. — *vt.* 扫除,扫.

be·sot [biˈsɔt] *vt.* 使醉;使糊涂;使沉迷〔此动词一般使用被动语态〕. *get* ～*ted* 吃醉酒. *a mind* ～*ted with fear* 害怕得六神无主. *He is* ～*ted by her youth and beauty.* 他被她的年轻美貌迷住了. **-tingly** *ad.*

be·sot·ted [biˈsɔtid] *a.* 变糊涂的,昏迷的;沉迷…的. *be* ～ *about [with] sb.* 迷恋某人. **-ly** *ad.* **-ness** *n.*

be·sought [biˈsɔːt] beseech 的过去式及过去分词.

be·span·gle [biˈspæŋgl] *vt.* ①饰以闪闪发光的东西;饰以[包以]金[银]箔. ②使灿烂发光. *the sky* ～*d with stars* 星光灿烂的天空. *poetry* ～*d with vivid imagery* 充满生动比喻的诗歌.

be·spat·ter [biˈspætə] *vt.* ①溅,溅污. ②诽谤,辱骂,诋毁. *The truck* ～*ed my new suit with mud.* 卡车把我的新衣服溅一身泥. *be* ～*ed by malicious gossip* 遭到流言蜚语的攻击.

be·speak [biˈspiːk] *vt.* ***(be·spoke*** [biˈspəuk]; ***be·spo·ken*** [biˈspəukən], ***be·spoke)*** ①〔英〕预约, 预定, 定(货). ②预先请求. ③表明, 证明. ④〔诗〕向…说. ⑤〔废〕预示,暗示.

be·speck·le [biˈspekl] *vt.* 使有斑点.

be·spec·ta·cled [biˈspektəkld] *a.* 戴眼镜的.

be·spice [biˈspais] *vt.* 用香料调(味),加香料于.

be·spoke [biˈspəuk] bespeak 的过去式及过去分词. — *a.* ①〔英〕定做的;专做定货的 (*opp.* ready-made). ②已预定出去的. ③〔方〕已订了婚的. *a* ～ *boot-maker [tailor]* 专接定货的靴匠 [成衣匠]. ～ *suits* 定做的衣服. ～ *a seat in a theatre* 预定戏票. ～ *a dress* 预定服装. ～ *the reader's patience* 预先请读者耐心. *This* ～*s a kindly heart.* 这种行为显示了一颗善良的心. — *n.* ①(为募捐、赈灾等义演向演员)预约,要求. ②〔英〕(借书)预约. ③预定的货.

be·spo·ken [biˈspəukən] bespeak 的过去分词.

be·spot [biˈspɔt] *vt.* 使有斑点.

be·spread [biˈspred] *vt.* ***(be·spread; be·spread)*** 铺,覆盖,铺满. *a paddy field* ～ *with young rice plants* 一块铺满秧苗的稻田. ～ *a table with fine linens* 给桌子铺上亚麻台布.

be·sprent [biˈsprent] *a.* 〔诗〕撒布,撒遍,洒满. *leaves* ～

with raindrops 洒满雨珠的树叶.

be·sprin·kle [bi'spriŋkl] *vt.* 洒，撒布. *grass ~d with dew* 洒满露珠的草. *~ one's food with salt* 在食物上撒盐.

Bess [bes] *n.* 贝丝〔女子名,Elizabeth 的昵称〕.

Bes·se·mer ['besimə] *n.* ①贝西默〔姓氏〕. ② **Sir Henry ~** 贝西默爵士〔1813—1898, 首创酸性转炉钢的英国人〕. **~ converter** 转炉. **~ process**【冶】酸性转炉法. **~ steel** 酸性转炉钢.

Bes·sie ['besi] *n.* 贝西〔女子名,Elizabeth 的昵称〕.

best[1] [best] *a.* 〔good 和 well 的最高级〕*(opp.* worst*)*. ①最好的. ②最合适的. ③最多的，大部分的. ④〔口〕最厉害的,彻头彻尾的. *the ~ painter of our day* 当代最优秀的画家. *the ~ thing to do* 最好的办法. *She feels ~ in the morning.* 她早上精神最好. *the ~ man for the job* 最适合做那项工作的人. *the ~ part of a day* 大半天. *the ~ liar* 吹牛大家. ***one's ~ boy [fellow]*** 〔俚〕男朋友们，情人. ***one's ~ days*** 全盛时代，得意时代. ***one's ~ girl***〔俚〕女朋友们，情人. ***put [set] one's ~ foot [leg] foremost [forward]*** ①〔英〕拼命走，赶快. ②〔美〕逞能,自夸；拼命造成好印象. — *ad.* 〔well 的最高级〕最好，第一；〔口〕极，厉害地，大大地. *Everything goes ~ with me.* 我一切顺利. *~-suited* 最适合的. *~ known* 最有名的. *the ~ hated man* 最可恨的人. *the ~ abused book* 被批评得一无是处的书. ***as ~ (as) one can [may]*** 尽可能，尽量. ***had ~*** 最好是；以…为最妙 (*You had ~ go with him.* 你最好是跟他去. *He had ~ have done so.* 他这样做了就最好了). — *n.* ①最佳，至上，最大努力. ②最好的人；最好的事物［部分、衣服、结果、服装等］. *The ~ is the enemy of the good.* 至上乃致善之敌，标准过高反于成功不利. *Bad is the ~.* 决无好事. *the second ~* 次好. *The ~ of us can make mistakes.* 我们当中最好的人也会做错事. *the ~ of it [the joke]* 最好的地方，最精采处［最好笑处］. *one's Sunday ~* 最漂亮的衣服，节日的服装. *That's the ~ I can do for you.* 我仅能帮你这么多忙了. ***at (the) ~*** 至多，充其量也不过 (*You look a fool at the ~, and a knave at worst.* 你呀，说好呢不过象个傻瓜，说坏呢不过象个流氓. *We can not arrive before Friday at ~.* 我们在最好的情况下也得星期五到达). ***at one's [its] ~*** 最美时期；最得意处；全盛时代，发挥最高的技术水平，处于最佳健康[精神]状态(*He is at his ~ in short lyrics.* 他最擅长的是写抒情短诗. *at one's creative ~* 在创作能力最旺盛时期. *cherry-blossoms at their ~* 樱桃花盛开时节. *Beer is at its ~ when it is cool.* 冷啤酒味道最美). ***at the very ~*** 〔强调语气〕= at best. ***~ of all*** 首先，第一；最. ***do one's ~*** 竭力，尽力. ***do one's level ~***〔俚、口〕竭尽个人最大可能，全力以赴. ***(all) for the ~*** ①出于好意. ②会[想]得到最好结果 (*Everything will turn out for the ~.* 一切到最后都会好的. *He did it all for the ~.* 他那样做全是好意. *Hope for the ~.* 切莫悲观. *It was at the time hard to realize how it could be all for the ~.* 当时很难想到怎么会有这么好的结果). ***get (have) the ~ of*** 获胜；胜过 (*His arthritis gets the ~ of him from time to time.* 关节炎时常把他压倒). ***give sb. ~*** 〔口〕向…屈服；向…认输（*All right, I give you ~.* 算了，我认输). ***give it ~*** 对（某事）罢念，想开. ***have the ~ of it*** = ***get the ~ of it.*** ***make the ~ of*** 尽量利用，善用，善处. ***make the ~ of a bad job [business, bargain]*** (处境不利时)尽量把损失减到最小，善处逆境. ***make the ~ of one's way*** 拼命快走. ***make the ~ of things*** 随遇而安. ***none of the ~*** 不甚好. ***of the ~*** 最好的；〔英口〕1 镑钞票 (*ten of the ~* 一镑钞票十张) ***to the ~ of one's*** *(power; knowledge)* 竭力，不遗余力；竭尽（所能，所知). ***try one's ~*** 尽全力. ***with the ~*** 不比任何人坏，不下于人. — *vt.* 〔口〕①超过，击败(某人). ②欺，骗，瞒. *He ~s me in the mathematics.* 他在数学方面超过我. ***~ the pistol*** 抢跑，枪未响即冲出起跑线. **~ bet**〔美〕看来最可靠的办法，最适当的措施. **~ bib and tucker**〔口〕漂亮衣服. **~ foot** 最吸引人的优点；拿手技术. **~ man** 男傧相. **~ seller** 畅销货；畅销书；畅销书作者. **~-selling author** 畅销书作者.

be·star [bi'stɑ:] *vt.* 用星遮蔽，用星装饰.

be·stead[1] [bi'sted] *vt.* *(~ed; ~ed, ~)* 帮助；援助；对…有所裨益，对…有用，有利于.

be·ste(a)d[2] [bi'sted] *a.* 〔古〕处境…的〔多与 ill, hard 等连用〕. ***be ill [sore] ~*** 处境极难. ***~ by*** 被…困住. ***~ with*** 在…中.

bes·ti·al ['bestjəl] *a.* ①兽类的；畜牲一样的. ②凶暴的；兽性的；兽欲的；下流的. *~ features* 狰狞面貌. *~ lust* 兽欲. *~ words* 下流言语，污言秽语. — *n.* [Scot.] 家畜；牛. **-ly** *ad.* 畜牲一样地，毫无人性地.

bes·ti·al·i·ty [ˌbesti'æliti] *n.* 兽性，兽心；兽行，兽欲；兽奸.

bes·tial·ize ['bestjəlaiz] *vt.* 使兽化，使行同禽兽.

bes·ti·ar·y ['bestjəri] *n.* 动物寓言(集).

be·stir [bi'stə:] *vt.* 使发奋，使振作. ***~ oneself*** 发奋；活跃，努力 (*You will fail unless you ~ yourself.* 你必须努力，否则就要失败).

be·stow [bi'stəu] *vt.* ①给与，授，赠，赐. ②放置，安置，贮藏. ③使用，用. ④〔口〕给…提供住宿，让…留宿. *~ a benefit on sb.* 施恩于某人. *~ the trophy upon the winner* 把奖品赠给获胜者. *Time spent in study is well ~ed.* 把时间用于学习是值得的. *~ sb. for the night* 留某人过夜. *He ~ed his life on science.* 他一生钻研科学.

be·stow·al [bi'stəuəl] *n.* ①赠与，授与；赠品. ②贮藏. *the ~ of Medals of Honor* 授与荣誉勋章. *God's ~ upon man* 天赋，才能.

be·strew [bi'stru:] *vt.* *(~ed; ~ed, ~n* [bi'stru:n]*)* 撒布，撒满，散布在…. *grounds ~n [~ed] with pieces of papers* 地上撒满碎纸片. *~ the path with flowers* 用花撒满道路. *flowers ~ing the meadow* 鲜花开满草原.

be·stride [bi'straid] *vt.* ***(be·strode*** [bi'strəud], ***be·strid*** [bi'strid]; ***be·strid·den*** [bi'stridn], ***be·strid)*** ①骑，跨. ②跨越，横跨于…上. ③威慑，支配，高距于…之上. *~ a horse [bikes]* 骑马[自行车]. *~ a groove* 跨过沟. *a bridge bestriding the raging river* 横跨湍流的桥.

bet [bet] *n.* ①赌，打赌. ②赌金，赌品，赌注，被打赌的对象. ③〔口〕意见. ④适于做某事的人；适宜的手段［事物］. *a two-dollar ~* 两元钱的赌注. *That horse looks like a good ~.* 那匹马看来值得下注. *He is the poorest ~ for the job.* 他是最不适合干那种事的人了. *Your best ~ is to sell them now.* 你现在最好的办法就是把它们卖掉. *My ~ is that he won't come.* 我看他不会来了. *a heavy [paltry] ~* 大[小]赌. ***an even ~*** ①互无输赢. ②一对一的赌注，见一赔一. ***lay sb. a bet*** 和某人打赌 (*I will lay you a ~.* 我要和你打个赌). ***make [place] a ~ with sb.*** 和某人打赌. ***take [accept] a ~*** 同意与人打赌［赌钱］. ***win [lose] a ~ with [against] sb.*** 和某人打赌赌赢[输]. — *vt.* ***(~, bet·ted*** ['betid]***)*** ①用…打赌；与…打赌. ②敢断定. *I will ~ ten dollars that he will fail.* 他必定失败，否则我愿输十元. *~ sb. on sth.* 与某人就某事打赌. *~ $ 30 on [upon] the horse race* 下赛马赌注 30 美元. *~ $ 10 against [on] his winning* 赌十美元断定他必输［必赢]. *I [I'll] ~ he doesn't come.* 我敢断定他没有来. — *vi.* 赌，赌钱；下赌注；打赌. *Do you ever ~?* 你和人家打过赌吗？ ***~ money***〔美俚〕认为可靠. ***~ one's boots [bottom dollar, life, soul] on*** ①对…孤注一掷. ②确信；可以断定 (*You can ~ your boots no one's going to praise her.* 你可以相信绝对不会有人去赞扬她的). ***B- you***〔口〕当然，的确 (*Bet you he meant it.* 他可不是说了玩的). ***I'll ~ my life*** 我敢用生命担保；当然，保管没错. ***I ~ you*** 一定，必定

(*I ~ you a shilling he has forgotten.* 他肯定忘掉了). ***You ~!*** 〔美俚〕当然,一定,必定,的确 ("*Is it in a safe place?*" "*You ~ it is.*" "那东西放的地方保险吗?""当然保险啦"). ***You ~?*** 〔口〕你敢肯定吗? 你有把握吗?

bet. = between.

be·ta [ˈbiːtə, ˈbeitə] *n.* ①希腊字母第二字〔B, β〕. ②第二位的东西. ③【天】β 星〔星座中第二等最亮的星〕. ~ **decay**【原】β 衰变. ~ **minus** 仅次于第二等. ~ **particle**【物】β 粒子, β 质子. ~ **plus** 略高于第二等. ~ **ray**【化】β 射线. ~ **test**【心】不用文字及口答的一种智力测验.

be·ta·fite [ˈbiːtəfait] *n.* 钶钛铀矿.

be·ta·ine [ˈbiːtiiːn] *n.*【化】①甜菜碱,三甲铵乙内酯. ②内酸盐,三甲(基)铵内酯.

be·take [biˈteik] *vt.* (***be·took*** [biˈtuk]; ***be·tak·en*** [biˈteikən]) ①〔书〕使用,诉诸于 (*to*). ②〔古〕去,往,投身于,专心于,致力于 (*to*). ★均用 ~ oneself 形式. ~ *oneself to a debate* 加入一场争论. ~ *oneself to one's heels* 一溜烟地逃走. ~ *oneself to town* 进城去.

be·ta·tron [ˈbiːtətrɔn, ˈbei-] *n.*【物】电子回旋〔感应〕加速器.

be·tel [ˈbiːtəl] *n.*【植】蒟酱 (= ~ pepper, 又名 piper ~) 〔用其叶包槟榔嚼之〕. ~ **nut** 槟榔子. ~ **palm** 槟榔(树).

bête noire [ˈbeit ˈnwɑː] 〔F.〕可怕的东西,极讨厌的东西〔人〕.

Beth [beθ] *n.* 贝丝〔女子名, Elizabeth 的昵称〕.

beth [beiθ, beθ] *n.* 希伯来语第二个字母.

beth·el [ˈbeθəl, beˈθel] *n.* ①圣地,圣所. ②〔美〕海员礼拜堂. ③〔英讽〕反国教派教堂〔通常叫 little ~〕.

be·think [biˈθiŋk] *vt.* (***be·thought*** [biˈθɔːt]) ①考虑, 细想. ②反省, 提醒自己. ③想起, 忆起, 想到 (*of; how; that*). ④决心. ⑤〔古〕铭记. *I bethought myself a moment.* 我想了一下. ~ *oneself of family obligations* 反省自己对家庭应负的责任. *She lives in the past now, ~ing herself of happier days.* 她现在整天回想过去,缅怀着往昔更美好的岁月. ~ *oneself of learning Latin* 决心学拉丁文. — *vi.* 〔古〕考虑,细想,冥想.

Beth·le·hem [ˈbeθlihem] *n.* ①伯利恒〔巴勒斯坦地名,在耶路撒冷南方六英里之处,相传为耶稣降生地〕. ②伯利恒〔美国一城市〕.

be·thought [biˈθɔːt] bethink 的过去式及过去分词.

Be·thune [ˈbiːtn, beˈθjuːn] *n.* 贝休恩(白求恩)〔姓氏〕.

be·tide [biˈtaid] *vi.* 〔书〕(事故等)发生,(祸)起. *Whate'er [may] ~, maintain your courage.* 无论有什么事发生,都不要惊慌失措. — *vt.* ①(灾难等)降临于〔多用于诅咒语〕. ②预示,预兆. *Woe ~ the villain!* 愿那个恶棍遭殃! *These things ~ evil.* 这些事都是不祥之兆.

be·times [biˈtaimz] *ad.* 〔书〕①及时,准时,合时. ②早. ③即刻,不久以后. *He started ~ in the morning.* 他一大早就上路了. *He was up ~ doing his lessons.* 他及时做功课. *We hope to repay your visit ~.* 希望不久以后能对您回访.

bê·tise [beiˈtiːz] *n.* 〔F.〕①愚钝,蠢笨. ②愚行; 蠢话,不合时宜的言行. ③荒谬的事物,无价值的事物.

be·to·ken [biˈtəukən] *vt.* ①表示,表白. ②预示,是…的预兆. *looks ~ing rage* 怒容. *a thunderclap that ~s foul weather* 预示着恶劣天气的雷声.

bét·on [ˈbetən; F. betɔ̃] *n.* 〔F.〕混凝土. ~ **armée** 钢筋混凝土.

bet·o·ny [ˈbetəni] *n.*【植】①水苏(属). ②石蚕(属).

be·took [biˈtuk] betake 的过去式.

be·tray [biˈtrei] *vt.* ①背叛,出卖,密告,陷害(朋友等). ②辜负. ③诱惑; 玩弄(女性). ④泄漏(秘密). ⑤不自觉地露出,暴露,表现. ~ *one's country to the enemy* 卖国,做卖国贼. *He ~ed his friend's confidence.* 他辜负了朋友的信任. *She was ~ed into a snare.* 她被诱入陷阱. ~ *a secret* 泄露秘密. *an unfeeling remark that ~s his lack of concern* 他那冷冷的话语表现出他的漠不关心. ***Confusion ~s the guilty.*** 慌张显出有罪,神色慌张必有鬼.

be·tray·al [biˈtreiəl] *n.* ①背叛; 背信; 告密. ②泄密; 欺瞒. ③引诱; 玩弄(女性).

be·tray·er [biˈtreiə] *n.* ①卖国贼; 叛徒; 内奸; 背信者; 告密人. ②欺骗者,诱惑者.

be·troth [biˈtrəuð] *vt.* ①〔书〕(女子)同…订婚 (*to*) 〔多用被动语态〕. ②〔古〕把(女儿)许配给… (*to*). *become [be] ~ed to (sb.)* (已)和…订婚. ~ *oneself to* 和…订婚. ~ *one's daughter to sb.* 把女儿许配给某人. *The couple was ~ed with the family's approval.* 那对男女经家庭同意订了婚.

be·troth·al [biˈtrəuðəl] *n.* 订婚(礼); 婚约. *enter into ~* 订婚. *a ~ party* 订婚宴. *break off a ~ with sb.* 同某人解除婚约.

be·trothed [biˈtrəuðd] *a.* 订过婚的. — *n.* 未婚夫〔妻〕. *the ~ pair* 未婚夫妻. *He introduced us to his ~.* 他介绍我们同他的未婚妻见面. *the ~* 已订婚的人,未婚夫〔妻〕.

Bets(e)y [ˈbetsi] *n.* 贝齐〔女子名, Elizabeth 的昵称〕.

bet·ta [ˈbetə] *n.* 〔L.〕【动】搏鱼 (= fighting fish).

bet·ter[1] [ˈbetə] *a.* 〔good, well 的比较级〕(*opp.* worse) ①较好的,更好的. ②大半的, 大部分的. ③更合适的. ④较有品德的. ⑤健康状态转好的,(疾病)渐愈的. *He has seen ~ days.* 他曾经阔过一个时候. ~ *people* 善良的人. *a ~ thing to do* 更合适的办法. *the ~ part of a lifetime* 大半生. *You'll feel ~ after a good sleep.* 你睡个好觉, 精神就会好一些了. — *ad.* 〔well 的比较级〕①更,更加,更好地. ②更多地,以上. *Do ~ another time.* 下次干好点. *I walked ~ than a mile to town.* 我步行一英里以上进城去. *He is ~ loved than ever.* 他更加受人爱了. ***all the ~*** 更好,更合式 (*I like her all the ~ for her simplicity.* 由于她单纯,我反而更喜欢她了). ***be ~ off*** 情况〔处境〕更好; 更加富有. ***be ~ than one's word*** 所做的超过所许诺的,比所许诺的更慷慨〔做得更多,表现得更好〕. ***be the ~ for it*** 对…反而好,反而更好 (*Give the child no money, he'll be the ~ for it.* 不要给孩子钱,那样反而会对他有好处). ~ ***bet*** 〔美〕更好〔聪明〕的选择. ***B- late than never.*** 迟干胜于不干,亡羊补牢不算晚. ***the ~ part of*** …的大部分 (*the ~ part of a month* 一个月的大部分时间,大半个月). ~ ***sort*** 长辈. ~ ***than nothing*** 聊胜于无; 不更坏就算运气. ***for ~ (or) for worse*** 有福同享, 有祸同当, 祸福与共, 同甘共苦, 不论变好变歹〔出自祈祷书,举行结婚仪式时的用语〕(*They have taken each other for ~ or for worse.* 他们已结为夫妇,今后同甘共苦). ***for the ~*** 转好 (*change for the ~* (处境)改善; (病)转好; (职位)升迁). ***get ~*** (病)渐愈,快好. ***get the ~ of*** 胜过,超出,占…的上风. ***go (sb.) ~*** 〔美俚〕胜过(某人),超过(某人),比(某人)体面. ***had ~*** 最好…,还是以…为好 (*You had ~ do so.* 你还是这样做好). ***know ~*** 知道是不好〔不对〕的,很懂得,很明白(而不致于…) (*I know ~.* 没有的事,我不信. *She said she didn't cheat, but I knew ~.* 她说她没有欺骗人,但我深知不是那么一回事. *I know ~ than to quarrel.* 我傻也不会傻到就吵架的. *ought to know ~ (to do sth.)* 不该傻到去(做某事),不该这样傻). ***little ~ than*** 比…好不了多少. ***no ~ than*** 并不比…好,简直就是; 顶多不过是 (*He is no ~ than a shop-keeper.* 他顶多不过是一个店老板罢了). ***no ~ than he should be*** 行为不正,不规矩,不正派. ***not ~ than*** 不比…更好; 顶好也不过是. ***one's ~ feelings*** 天良,优良的天性,高尚的感情. ***one's ~ half*** 〔谑〕妻子〔丈夫〕. ***one's ~ self*** 良心. ***so much the ~*** 这就更好〔更妙、好极〕了. ***think ~ of*** ①另行考虑,改变对…的想法,经考虑后决定不做(某事). ②对…有较高评价. — *n.* ①较好的东西〔事、条件、行为等〕. ②(知识、能力、财产等)较优的人; 〔*pl.*〕

上级,上司;长上,长辈,前辈. *the ~ of two choices* 两个选择物中的较优者. *You'll soon get a ~ than Willy.* 很快就派一个比威利更高明的人给你. *Respect your ~s.* 尊敬你的长辈. *Do not ape your ~s.* 不要效颦. 不要不自量力地模仿比你强的人. ***for want of a ~*** 因为没有更好的东西〔人,办法等〕. — *vt.* 改良,改善. ②优于,胜过,超出. *~ one's previous record* 刷新本人过去的记录. *~ oneself* 提高自己; 改善个人处境. — *vi.* (情况等)有改善, 变得有改进. **~-off** *a.* (经济) 情况较好的. **~-to-do** ①*a.* 较为富裕的. ②*n.* 〔*sing., pl.*〕较为富裕的人.

bet·ter[2] [ˈbetə] *n.* 打赌的人.

bet·ter·ment [ˈbetəmənt] *n.* ①改良,改善,改正. ②(不动产的)增值. ③〔常 *pl.*〕【法】(房屋等的)修缮,改建,扩建.

bet·ter·most [ˈbetəməust] *a.* ①最好的,上等的. ②大部分的. *the ~ part of the time* 这段时间的大部分.

bet·ting [ˈbetiŋ] *n.* 赌博,打赌. **~-book** 赌帐. **~-shop** ①私营赛马赌券经营所. ②政府许可开设的赌场.

bet·tor [ˈbetə] *n.* = better[2].

Bet·ty [ˈbeti] *n.* 贝蒂〔女子名,Elizabeth 的昵称〕.

bet·ty [ˈbeti] *n.* ①〔美〕长颈瓶. ②〔俚〕(盗贼撬门用的)铁杆. ③爱做家务的男子. ④一种奶油果馅糕点.

be·tween [biˈtwiːn] *prep.* ①位于…之间;处在…中间;介于…间. ②在…之间的时候. ③来往于…之间. ④比较;在…中任择其一. ⑤为…所共有. ⑥由…协力合作. ⑦由于…作用的结果. ⑧私下,暗中,私人之间. *~ three and four o'clock* 在三点到四点(钟)之间. *the sunshine ~ the leaves* 树叶间漏下的阳光. *with a cigarette ~ one's lips* 嘴上叼着烟卷. *choose ~ the two* 二中择一. *They are ~ jobs.* 他们正在失业. *a color ~ pink and red* 介乎粉红与红之间的颜色. *a passageway ~ two rooms* 连接两个房间的过道. *I have no preference ~ the two wines.* 我对这两种酒没有偏爱. *He couldn't see the difference ~ good and bad.* 他不识好歹〔不分善恶〕. *B- two stools one fall to the ground.* 脚踏两边船,两不落实. *We'll keep this matter ~ the two of us.* 这件事将只有我们两人知道. *B- sewing, cleaning, and raising her children, she was kept busy.* 缝啦,洗啦,带孩子啦,弄得她从来不得松闲. *The children had one room ~ them.* 孩子们共住一间屋. *We did not have ten dollars ~ us.* 我们凑不出十块钱. *Divide these apples ~ you two [three].* 你们俩〔三〕人分掉这些苹果吧. ★严格地讲,本来二者之间是用 between, 三者以上之间是用 among, 但前者亦可代替后者使用,尤其是当有三方发生关系而每两方之间须分别考虑时.例如: a treaty ~ three powers 三国条约. insert ~ the lines 插入行间. Have no quarrels ~ gentleman. 君子自重. ***~ the cup and the lip*** 正要成功的时候,正在重要关头. ***~ ourselves = ~ you and me and the gate-post [lamp-post]*** 你知我知,莫对人讲. ***~ two fires = ~ the devil and the deep sea*** 进退两难,进退维谷,左右为难. ***~ the lines*** 言外之意. ***~ whiles [times]*** 时时,偶尔. ***~ wind and water***【船】在吃水线间 (*be hit ~ wind and water* 被击中要害). ***(few and) far ~*** 很冷落,极少 (*In this part of Egypt houses are far ~.* 在埃及的这部分地区房屋极少,非常冷落. *visits that are far ~* 相隔时间很长的访问). — *ad.* 当中,中间. *two windows with a door ~.* 两扇窗户当中有一扇门. *We could not see the moon, for a cloud came ~.* 我们看不见月亮了,因为有云遮住. *the years ~* 这中间的年月. ***in ~*** ①在…期间;在中间;每隔… (*two houses and a yard in ~* 两所房屋中间的院子. *I don't care if she's black, white or in ~.* 我不管她是黑皮肤、白皮肤,还是半黑半白). ②挡路(*The dog got in ~.* 狗挡住了路). **~-decks** 【船】中舱. **~-maid** 〔英〕(在侍女和烧饭女仆之间) 两边打杂的女佣 = tweeny.

be·tween·brain [biˈtwiːnˌbrein] *n.* 【生】间脑 (= diencephalon).

be·tween·times [biˈtwiːnˌtaimz] *ad.* 有时;间或 (= between-whiles). *a part-time teacher who studied law ~* 一个有时攻读法律的兼课教师.

be·twixt [biˈtwikst] *prep., ad.* 〔古、诗、方〕= between. ***~ and between*** 介于二者之间;模棱两可 (*The child of Anglo-Indian parents, he felt somehow ~ and between.* 作为一个英印混血儿,他在感情上似乎摇摆于两国之间). ***There is many a slip ~ the cup and the lip*** 〔见 slip 条〕.

Beu·lah [ˈbjuːlə] *n.* ①【圣】以色列的别名. ②安息地〔生命行程的终点,出自英国作家班扬的《天路历程》〕. ③〔英〕反国教派的礼拜堂. ④比尤拉〔女子名〕.

Bev, BeV, bev = billion electron volts 十亿电子伏(特).

Be·van [ˈbevən] *n.* 贝文〔姓氏〕.

bev·a·tron [ˈbevətrɔn] *n.* 【物】高功率质子回旋加速器,高能质子同步稳相加速器.

bev·el [ˈbevəl] *n.* ①斜角;倾斜,斜面;【数】斜截,斜削. ②万能角尺,斜角规. ③【机】伞齿轮. — *a.* 斜的,倾斜的,斜角的;斜削的. — *vt.* 把…截成斜角形,斜切,斜截. — *vi.* 成斜角;倾斜,斜. ~ **gear** 【机】伞(形)齿轮. ~ **square** 角度尺,斜角规. ~ **wheel** 【机】斜齿轮,歪角齿轮.

bev·er·age [ˈbevəridʒ] *n.* ①饮料〔除水而外的饮料,如茶、酒、牛奶、汽水等〕. ②〔英方〕筵宴;餐费,酒费. *cooling ~s* 清凉饮料. ~ **room** 〔加〕(旅馆里的)酒吧.

Bev·er·idge [ˈbevəridʒ] *n.* 贝弗里奇〔姓氏〕.

Bev·er·l(e)y [ˈbevəli] *n.* 贝弗莉〔女子名〕.

Be·vin [ˈbevin] *n.* 贝文〔姓氏〕.

bev·y [ˈbevi] *n.* (鹌鹑等和妇女、姑娘等的)群. *a ~ of quails* 一群鹌鹑. *a ~ of young women* 一群年轻妇女.

BEW, B.E.W. = Board of Economic Warfare 〔英旧〕经济作战局.

be·wail [biˈweil] *vt.* 悲叹,叹惜;哀悼;痛哭. *~ one's bad luck* 悲叹自己的命途多舛. — *vi.* 哀悼;悲叹 (*over, for*). *~ over one's misfortune* 为自己的不幸而悲叹. *~ for sb.'s death* 哀悼某人的去世.

be·ware [biˈweə] *vi., vt.* 注意,当心,谨防. ★这一动词无词尾变化,仅能用不定式或祈使语气或与助动词must, should 等连用;其后接用 of(也有略去 of 的), lest, how, that, not 等. *I was told to ~ (of) pickpockets.* 人们告诉我要谨防扒手. *B- (of) fire.* 火烛小心,谨防引起火灾. *a man to ~ of* 一个要提防的人物. *B- lest you (should) fall [B- that you do not fall] into this mistake again.* 请注意不要再犯这种错误.

be·wil·der [biˈwildə] *vt.* ①使为难,使着慌;使手足无措;使变糊涂. ②〔古〕使迷路. **-ing** *a.* 令人为难的,使人手足无措的,使人狼狈的. **-ingly** *ad.* **-ment** *n.* ①为难,狼狈,慌张; 迷惑. ②混乱(状态) (*be thrown into ~ment* 被弄得不知所措; 被弄得迷惑不解. *We enter into a ~ment of smoke, noise and crowding people.* 我们进入了一个乌烟瘴气、吵吵闹闹和拥挤不堪的混乱环境中).

be·witch [biˈwitʃ] *vt.* ①迷,迷惑,蛊惑,(妖言)惑(众). ②令人心醉,(春色等)恼(人). *He felt as if ~ed by a fox.* 他觉得好象被一个狐狸精迷惑住了. *~ed by the glorious sunset* 被残阳如血的壮丽景色迷住了.

be·witch·ing [biˈwitʃiŋ] *a.* 迷人的,妖媚的;蛊惑的. **-ly** *ad.*

be·witch·ment [biˈwitʃmənt] *n.* 迷惑,蛊惑;魔力,妖术.

be·wray [biˈrei] *vt.* 〔古〕(无意之间)泄露;暴露(本性).

bey [bei] *n.* ①(土耳其帝国时代的) 省督〔有时用作敬称,加在显贵人物的名后,已于 1934 年废止, 如 *Ismet Bey* (伊斯迈特阁下)〕. ②突尼斯 (Turnis) 本地统治者的称号.

bey·lic [ˈbeilik] *n.* (土耳其帝国时代的)省督辖区,省.

be·yond [biˈjɔnd] *prep.* ①〔场所〕在〔向〕…的那边;离…以外,远于. ②〔时间〕过了…,迟于. ③〔程度等〕超过…的范围,在…所不及处. ④〔能力等〕在…以上,胜过,优于. ⑤除…以外〔多用于否定或疑问语气〕. *far* ~ *the sea* 远在大海那边. *B- those trees [green willows] you'll find his [my] house.* 在树林那边,你将找到他的家〔绿柳深处是我家〕. *a mile* ~ *the town* 离城一英里以外. *We saw peak* ~ *peak.* 我们眼前是重重山岭. ~ *the horizon* 在地平线以外. ~ *the tomb [grave]* 来世,死后. *I cannot go* ~ *a dollar.* 一元以上我就不买了. ~ *possibility* 不可能. *injured* ~ *help* 受了无法医治的重伤. ~ *endurance* 无法忍耐. *a skill* ~ *Raffael's* 拉斐尔〔意大利名画家〕之上的手法. *wise* ~ *all others* 比所有的人都聪明. *live* ~ *one's means* 生活支出超出收入,入不敷出. *B- this I know nothing.* 此外我全无所知. ~ *the usual hour* 较迟于平常,过了平常时间. ~ *the fixed time* 过了约定时间. ~ ***all hope*** 完全绝望. ~ ***all praise*** 夸奖不尽,好极. ~ ***all question*** 毫无疑问,当然. ~ ***all things*** 第一,首先. ~ ***comparison [compare]*** 无与伦比,不可相提并论. ~ ***comprehension*** 难于理解,难解. ~ ***dispute*** 无争论余地,无疑. ~ ***doubt*** 无可置疑,无疑. ~ ***expectation*** 超出预想地,意外地. ~ ***expression [description]*** 形容不出,非笔墨所能形容. ~ ***measure*** 非常,极度,无可估量地. ~ ***one [sb.]*** 某人能力所不及;某人所不能理解 (*The problem is* ~ *me [him].* 这个问题不是我〔他〕能解决得了的). ~ ***one's depth*** ①在脚不着底的深处,深到要没顶的地方. ②难以了解. ~ ***one's [sb.'s] power*** 力所不及,怎样都不能 (*It is* ~ *my [his] power to give it to her.* 我〔他〕无法把这件东西给她). ~ ***the seas*** 在海外,在国外. ***go*** ~ ***oneself*** 失度,忘形 (*He went* ~ *himself with joy.* 他欢喜得忘形了). — *ad.* ①在〔向〕很远的那边,在〔向〕远处;更远地. ②此外,以外. *as far as the house and* ~ 直到那间房的远处. *What is* ~? 再往前还有什么东西? *He gave me nothing* ~. 他此外再没给我什么东西. ***the life*** ~ 来世,彼岸. ***unable to see*** ~ 囿于,看不穿. — *n.* 那边. ***the back of*** ~〔口〕远方,穷乡僻壤;天涯海角. ***the (great)*** ~ 死后的世界;未知的世界(*go to the* ~ 死,去到另一个世界).

Bey·routh [ˈbeiruːt] *n.* = Beirut.

bez·ant [ˈbezənt] *n.* ①拜占庭币〔昔日拜占庭帝国的金币〕. ②【建】列圆饰;【徽】金黄小圆徽.

bez antler [ˈbezæntlə] *n.* (鹿角的)副枝,桠枝 (= bay-antler).

be·zazz [biˈzæz] *n.* 〔俚〕①力,活力,生气,精神. ②敏锐;风度;光采;鉴别力;闪光 (= pizazz).

bez·el [ˈbezəl] *n.* ①凿刃的斜面. ②宝石的斜面;(戒指)宝石座. ③(钟表等嵌玻璃的)沟缘.

be·zique [biˈziːk] *n.* 【牌】①比齐克牌戏〔64 张牌由二人或四人玩的一种纸牌戏,以赢墩数多寡计胜败〕. ②凑四十分〔在比齐克牌戏中用两张牌(如黑桃皇后与方块贾克)配合作成 40 分的一种打法〕.

be·zoar [ˈbiːzɔː] *n.* ①【药】毛粪石,胃石,牛黄,马宝〔一种解毒剂〕. ②〔废〕解毒剂.

be·zugs schein [beˈzugsʃaiin] *n.* 〔G.〕购物证,日用品配给证.

bf, b.f. = ① boldface【印】黑体,粗体. ② bloody fool〔讽〕大傻瓜. ③ board foot 板英尺.

B.F. = ①Bachelor of Finance 财政学学士. ②Bachelor of Forestry 森林学学士.

B/F, b.f. = brought forward【会计】结转.

BFRE【无】= before.

bg. = ① bag. ② bugler.

B-girl [ˈbiːgəːl] *n.* 〔美〕酒吧女郎.

bgs = bags.

bhak·ti [ˈbʌkti] *n.*【印度教】终身信奉一神,一神崇拜.

B'ham. = Birmingham.

bhang [bæŋ] *n.* ①印度大麻. ②用印度大麻制成的麻醉药.

bhees·ty, bhees·tie [ˈbiːsti] *n.* (*pl.* **-ties**) 担水者〔印度为军队担水的人〕.

b.h.p., bhp = brake horsepower【机】制动马力.

Bhu·tan [buːˈtaːn] *n.* 不丹〔亚洲〕.

Bhu·tan·ese [ˌbuːtəˈniːz] *n.* 〔*sing.*, *pl.*〕不丹人;不丹语. — *a.* 不丹的;不丹人的;不丹语的.

Bi【化】= bismuth.

bi [bai] *a.* 〔美俚〕(在性欲上)对男女两性都感兴趣的.

bi- *pref.* ①二,两,双,复. ②【化】二,重,双,联. ③(二)等分. ④每…二次的,每二…一次的.

Bi·a·fra [baiˈaːfrə] *n.* 比夫拉〔尼日利亚一地区〕. **-n** *a.* 比夫拉的.

bia·ly [biˈaːli] *n.* (*pl.* **bia·lys**) 葱花面筋薄饼卷(=biali).

bi·an·gu·lar [baiˈæŋgjulə] *a.* 有二角的,双角的.

bi·an·nu·al [baiˈænjuəl] *a.* ①一年二次的,半年一次的. ②〔废〕两年一次的. *a* ~ *meeting* 一年举行两次的会议. **-ly** [baiˈænjuəli] *ad.*

bi·an·nu·late [baiˈænjulit, -leit] *a.* 【动】有双环的;有双色带的.

bi·as¹ [ˈbaiəs] *n.* ①成见,先入之见,偏执,偏见 (*opp.* impartiality);倾向,嗜好,癖 (*towards*). ②(衣服等上面缝的)斜线,斜痕;【无】偏,偏压;偏置. ③【体】使球斜进的偏力〔偏重〕;(球的)歪圆形;不按直线前进的倾向;【电】偏压;【统】倾向统计值;【生】偏倚. *a racial* ~ 种族偏见. *a strong musical* ~ 对音乐的强烈爱好. *copper* ~【电】正偏压. *zinc* ~【电】负偏压. *cut on the* ~ 斜裁,斜切. ***be free from*** ~ 丝毫不受偏见左右. ***be under a*** ~ ***in favor of [against]*** 对…有偏爱〔偏见〕. ***have a*** ~ ***to [towards]*** 对…有偏心. ***without*** ~ ***and without favour*** 不偏不倚地,公公平平地. — *a.* 斜的;【电】偏动的. ~ *bands* 斜带. — *ad.* 斜,偏. *cut material* ~ 斜切料,斜开料,斜裁. ~**-ply tyre** 斜交薄布轮胎.

bias² [ˈbaiəs] *vt.* (**~ed, ~ing**;〔英〕**~sed, ~sing**) ①使有偏见,使偏重,使偏向一方. ②【电】加偏压于. *be bias(s)ed against* 对…抱有偏见. ~ … *into*【电】加偏压使进入…. *My ignorance* ~*ed me against my teacher.* 我由于无知而对老师抱有偏见. **-ed** *a.* 有偏见的.

bi·ath·lete [baiˈæθliːt] *n.* 滑雪射击运动员.

bi·ath·lon [baiˈæθlən, -lɔn] *n.* 【体】现代冬季两项〔包括滑雪和射击的冬季奥林匹克运动项目〕.

bi·aur·al [baiˈɔːrəl] *a.* 有两耳的,用两耳的(=binaural).

bi·au·ric·u·late [ˌbaiˈɔːrikjulit] *a.* 【解】有两耳的 (= biauricular).

bi·ax·i·al [baiˈæksiəl] *a.* 【光】二轴的.

Bib., bib., bibl. = Bible; Biblical.

bib [bib] *n.* (小儿)围涎,围嘴;围腰的上部. ~ ***and*** ~〔口〕衣服. ***one's best*** ~ ***and tucker***〔口〕漂亮衣裳. — *vi.*, *vt.* 〔古〕(经常地)喝(酒),慢慢地呷(烈酒). ~**-cock** 弯嘴龙头. **-ful** *a.*, *n.* 满涎布的(量) (*slobber a bibful* 〔美口〕大谈特谈,唠叨不休).

bi·bas·ic [baiˈbeisik] *a.* 【化】二元的;二盐基性的;二代的(指盐).

bibb [bib] *n.* ①弯管旋塞,龙头. ②【船】桅头用以支持棚木之旁木.

bib·ber [ˈbibə] *n.* 贪酒的人,酒鬼〔通例用于复合词: *a wine-*~ 大酒鬼〕.

bi·be·lot [ˈbibləu] *n.* 〔法〕室内装饰品;床饰;小件古玩;小玩意儿.

bi-bi·va·lent [ˌbaibaiˈveilənt] *a.* 【化】双二价的.

Bi·ble [ˈbaibl] *n.* ①【基督、犹】〔the ~〕圣经. ②经典. ③〔b-〕有权威的典籍;金科玉律. *The Mohammedan* ~ 伊斯兰教的圣经〔即古兰经,= the Koran〕. *The old sea captain regarded his Bowditch as his bible.* 老船长把他那本波迪奇航海手册奉为金科玉律. ***Douai*** ~, ***Douay*** ~ 多维

版《圣经》〔1582—1610年在多维地方由英国教士团将拉丁文《圣经》译为英语，并作修订，供天主教徒使用〕. ***King James*** ～ 钦译《圣经》〔由英国国王詹姆士一世于1604年倡议，完成于1611年，是讲英语国家新教徒使用最广泛的英译本，又称 Authorized Version〕. ***the Wicked [Adulterous]*** ～ 邪[秽]版《圣经》〔1631年版《圣经》，该版本将 Thou shalt not commit adultery 句中的 not 一词漏印，使"汝切勿通奸"一语变成"汝可通奸"〕. ～ **belt** 〔美〕美国南部和中西部正统主义派教徒多的几个州；〔转义〕教徒多的地方；〔讽〕伪君子多的地方. ～ **Christians** 圣经主义派〔19世纪新教中的一派〕. ～ **class** (主日学校的)读经班. ～**-clerk** 读经生〔牛津大学二、三个学院中负有诵读圣经义务的公费生〕. ～ **college** 培训宗教工作者的基督教大学. ～ **drink** 祷告会，礼拜会. ～ **oath** 吻《圣经》立的誓，庄严的誓言. ～ **paper** 圣经纸〔用于印刷《圣经》等的一种极薄的纸〕. ～ **pounder [puncher, ranter]** 〔美口〕牧师，传道师. ～ **punching** 〔美俚〕讲经布道. ～ **reader** 读经者〔挨门逐户向病人、穷人讲读《圣经》的人〕. ～ **school** (进行宗教教育的)主日学校. ～ **Society** 《圣经》出版协会，《圣经》公会.

Bib·li·cal [ˈbiblikəl] *a.* 圣经的；合圣经宗旨的. *the* ～ *style* 圣经文体. ～ *Stories* 圣经(上的)故事.

Bib·li·cist [ˈbiblisist] *n.* ①拘泥于圣经的人；圣经主义者. ②圣经通；圣经研究者.

bib·li·o- *comb. f.* 书籍的；圣经的.

bib·li·o·film [ˈbibliəufilm] *n.* (图书摄影用的)显微胶卷.

bib·li·og. = bibliography [-phic, -phical, -pher].

bib·li·o·graph [ˈbibliəuˌgræf] *vt.* ①(为书、文章)加书目提要，加书志，加书目. ②作…的书目提要.

bib·li·og·ra·pher [ˌbibliˈɔgrəfə] *n.* ①书目编者；书目提要编者. ②书志学家，目录学家，文献学家.

bib·li·o·graph·i·cal [ˌbibliəuˈgræfikəl] *a.* ①书目的；书目提要的. ②书志学的，文献学的.

bib·li·og·ra·phy [ˌbibliˈɔgrəfi] *n.* ①书目提要；书目，书志学，书志. ②文献，文献学.

bib·li·o·klept [ˈbibliəuklept] *n.* 书贼，窃书人.

bib·li·ol·a·ter [ˌbibliˈɔlətə] *n.* 书籍崇拜者. ②圣经崇拜者.

bib·li·ol·a·trous [ˌbibliˈɔlətrəs] *a.* ①崇拜书籍的. ②崇拜圣经的.

bib·li·ol·a·try [ˌbibliˈɔlətri] *n.* ①书籍崇拜. ②圣经崇拜.

bib·li·ol·o·gy [ˌbibliˈɔlədʒi] *n.* 书志学；版本学；目录学. ②〔常B-〕圣经学.

bib·li·o·man·cy [ˈbibliəumænsi] *n.* 圣经卦〔拿翻开圣经看到的句子占卜吉凶〕.

bib·li·o·ma·ni·a [ˌbibliəuˈmeinjə] *n.* 藏书癖；珍本书收集狂.

bib·li·o·ma·ni·ac [ˌbibliəuˈmeiniæk] *a.* 藏书癖的，书痴的. — *n.* 藏书家，书狂，书痴.

bib·li·op·e·gy [ˌbibliˈɔpidʒi] *n.* 书籍装订术.

bib·li·o·phil(e) [ˈbibliəufail], **bib·li·o·ph·i·list** [ˈbibliəufilist,-failist] *n.* 爱书家，藏书癖者〔尤指玩赏版式设计、装帧、印刷者〕.

bib·li·o·ph·i·lism [ˌbibliˈɔfilizəm] *n.* (爱)书癖，藏书癖.

bib·li·o·pole [ˈbibliəupəul] *n.* 书商，(特指)珍本书商.

bib·li·op·o·ly [ˌbibliˈɔpəli] *n.* 书籍买卖，珍本书买卖.

bib·li·o·the·ca [ˌbibliəuˈθiːkə] *n.* ①〔集合词〕文库，藏书. ②图书目录，(特指)书商售书目录. ③〔B-〕〔废〕圣经.

bib·li·ot·ic [ˌbibliˈɔtic] *a.* 文献鉴定学的；笔迹鉴定学的. **-s** *n.* 文献鉴定学，笔迹鉴定学.

bib·u·lous [ˈbibjuləs] *a.* 〔书〕①嗜酒的. ②非常能吸水的，吸湿性强的.

bi·cam·er·al [baiˈkæmərəl] *a.* 有上、下院的，二立法机构的，两院制的. ～ *system* 两院制. **-ism** 两院制主义者，主张两院制论者.

bi·cap·su·lar [baiˈkæpsələ, -sjulə] *a.*【植】有双蒴果的.

bi·carb [baiˈkɑːb] *n.* 〔美口〕= bicarbonate.

bi·car·bon·ate [baiˈkɑːbənit] *n.*【化】碳酸氢盐，重碳酸盐. ～ *of soda* 碳酸氢钠，小苏打.

bice [bais] *n.* ①蓝色，绿色. ②一种蓝色绘图颜料；绿色颜料.

bi·cen·te·nar·y [bai-senˈtiːnəri], **bi·cen·ten·ni·al** [bai-senˈtenjəl] *a.* ①二百周年的；二百周年纪念的. ②二百年间的，持续二百年的. ③每二百年(一次)的. *a* ～ *exposition* 二百周年纪念展览会. *a* ～ *return of a comet* 彗星二百年一次的回归. — *n.* ①二百周年(纪念). ②二百年间，持续二百年. ③每二百年(一次). *The town will have its* ～ *next year.* 该城的二百周年纪念日明年即将到来.

bi·ceph·a·lous [baiˈsefələs] *a.*【生】(畸胎等)(有)二头的.

bi·ceps [ˈbaiseps] *n.* ①【解】二头肌. ②膂力. *brachial* ～ *muscle* 上臂二头肌. *femoral* ～ *muscle* 大腿[下股]二头肌.

bi·chlo·ride [ˈbaiˈklɔːraid, -rid] *n.*【化】二氯化物. ～ ***of mercury*** 二氯化汞，升汞.

bi·chro·mate [ˈbaiˈkrəumit, -meit] *n.*【化】重铬酸盐. ***a*** ～ ***cell*** 重铬酸盐电池.

bi·chrome [ˈbaikrəum] *a.* 两色的.

bi·cip·i·tal [baiˈsipitəl] *a.* ①【生】(有)二头的. ②【解】二头肌的.

bick·er[1] [ˈbikə] *vi.* ①斗嘴，争吵. ②(雨等)哗啦哗啦地下；(溪水等)哗啦哗啦地流. ③(火焰、光等)一晃一晃地闪，闪烁. *They are forever* ～*ing and biting.* 他们常常拌嘴. *The raging stream* ～*ed down the valley.* 湍急的涧水哗啦哗啦地淌下山谷. *The afternoon sun* ～*ed through the leaves.* 午后的阳光闪烁于树叶之间. — *n.* ①斗嘴，口角. ②(流水等)哗啦哗啦的响声；(雨的)淅淅沥沥声；(鸟的)啭鸣. ③(火焰等的)摇晃，闪烁.

bick·er[2] [ˈbikə] *n.* 〔Scot.〕木碟，木钵，木盘.

bi·col·or [ˈbaiˌkʌlə] *a.* 双色的(= bicolored).

bi·con·cave [baiˈkɔnkeiv] *a.* 两面凹的，双凹的. *a* ～ *lens* 双凹面透镜.

bi·con·vex [ˈbaiˈkɔnveks] *a.* 两面凸的，双凸的.

bi·corn [ˈbaikɔːn] *a.* ①【动、植】有两角的，有两角状物的. ②新月形的. *a* ～ *rhinoceros* 两角犀. — *n.* 有双角的帽子[动物] (= bicornuate).

bi·cor·po·ral [baiˈkɔːpərəl, -prəl] *a.* ①有两体的，双身的. ②【天】有两个主部的〔黄道十二宫的某些标志〕(= bicorporeal).

bi·cron [ˈbaikrɔn] *n.* 10^{-9}米，毫微米〔一米的一千兆分之一，符号是 $\mu\mu$〕.

bi·crural [baiˈkruərəl] *a.* 双腿的.

bi·cul·tur·al [baiˈkʌltʃərəl] *a.* 两种文化的；有关〔包括〕两种文化的.

bi·cus·pid [baiˈkʌspid] *n.*【解】二尖齿，前臼齿. — *a.* 有二尖头的. ～ **valve**【解】二尖瓣.

bi·cy·cle [ˈbaisikl] *n.* ①自行车，脚踏车〔又名 push-～，系对 motor-～ 而言〕. ②〔美〕〔卡车驾驶员用语〕机器脚踏车. ③(学生作弊用的)夹带. *a lady's* ～ = *a* ～ *for ladies* 女用自行车，女车. *a racing* ～ 赛车，跑车. *a convertible* ～ 男女兼用型自行车. *a tandem* ～ 双座自行车. *ride (on) a* ～ 骑自行车. *go by [on a]* ～ 骑(自行)车去. *walk the* ～ 推着(自行)车. — *vi.* 骑自行车. ～ *to the office* 骑(自行)车上班.

bi·cy·cler [ˈbaisiklə], **bi·cy·clist** [ˈbaisiklist] *n.* 骑自行车的(人). *a professional* ～ 自行车运动员.

bi·cy·clic [baiˈsaiklik, -ˈsiklik] *a.* ①双环的，形成双环的；两个轮子的；自行车的. ②【植、化】二环的.

bid [bid] *vt.* ***(bade*** [beid], ***bid; bid·den*** [ˈbidn], ***bid)*** ①〔书〕命令，嘱，吩咐〔过去式多用 bade〕. ②〔书〕表示(欢迎)，告(别)，赠(言)；祝〔过去式多用 bade〕. ③出价，(拍卖时的)竞买，喊(价)〔过去式及过去分词多用 bid〕. ④〔古〕邀，请；发表(结婚预告等)，公告〔过去式多用 bade〕. ⑤【牌】叫(牌)〔过去式和过去分词多用 bid〕. ⑥〔美口〕接纳〔吸收〕…为会员〔成员〕. *Do as you are ~ [bidden]*. 请照吩咐去做. *Bid him go [to go]*. 叫他走开吧. *~ sb. good-night* 祝某人晚安. *~ farewell* 告别. *~ welcome [good-bye] to* 向…表示欢迎〔告别〕. *~ three spades* 叫牌打黑桃三. *a bidden guest* 邀来之客. — *vi.* ①出价；〔美〕投标. ②叫牌. ③〔书〕嘱咐，吩咐. ***~ against each other*** 竞相出价. ***~ defiance to*** 见 defiance 条. ***~ fair to*** 有…的可能，有…的希望(*This plan ~s fair to be a success*. 此项计划大有成功希望). ***~ for*** ①投标求包(工程). ②出价竞买(某物). ③争取得到(拥护等). ***~ in*** 拍卖人故意抬高售价使(拍卖物)落入自手. ***~ off*** ①使(拍卖物)卖出〔标落他手〕. ②给以拍卖处分. ***~ on*** *(some project)* 承包(某工程等的)投标；***~ up*** (拍卖中)竞出高价，哄价，抬价. — *n.* ①出价，喊价，投标. ②【牌】叫牌；有资格叫牌的一手牌. ③〔美俚〕邀请，提议. ④努力，企图. ***call for ~s on*** 招标. ***in a vain ~*** 妄图. ***make a [one's] ~ for*** ①投标争取承包；(拍卖中)出价竞买. ②企图得到(人望、恩宠等).

b.i.d., BID =〔L.〕*bis in die*【处方】一日两次(= twice a day).

bi·dar·ka [baiˈdɑːkə], **bi·dar·kee** [baiˈdɑːki] *n.* (爱斯基摩人)用海豹皮做的皮舟.

bid·da·ble [ˈbidəbl] *a.* ①柔顺的，驯良的〔尤指孩子〕. ②【牌】有叫牌资格的. *a ~ suit at bridge* 桥牌中有叫牌资格的一手牌.

bid·den [ˈbidn] bid 的过去分词.

bid·der [ˈbidə] *n.* ①(拍卖中的)出价人，竞买人；投标人. ②命令者，嘱咐者. ③【牌】叫牌人. ④〔美俚〕邀请.

bid·ding [ˈbidiŋ] *n.* ①出价，投标. ②命令，吩咐. ③邀请. ④公告. ⑤叫牌. ***at one's [sb.'s] ~*** 依嘱，遵命(*He seemed to have the whole world at his ~*. 他自以为全世界捏在他手里. *We went there at his ~*. 我们照他的吩咐去那里). ***do one's [sb.'s] ~*** 照…的命令做，照…的话办. ~ **block** 拍卖场. ~ **prayer**〔英〕讲道前的祷告.

Bid·dle [ˈbidl] *n.* 比德尔〔姓氏〕.

bid·dy[1] [ˈbidi] *n.* 〔美，英方〕小鸡，鸡.

bid·dy[2] [ˈbidi] *n.* 〔俚〕①大惊小怪〔小题大作〕的人. ②神经质的老太婆；长舌妇. ③女仆，女佣. ④〔俚〕女教师.

bide [baid] *vi.* ***(~d, bode*** [bəud]; ***~d)*** 〔古、诗、方〕①持续. ②等候，住，留. — *vt.* ①忍耐，经受. ②等待〔仅用于 ~ one's time 中〕. *~ a storm* 经受一场风暴. ***~ one's time*** 待机，等机会.

bi·dent [ˈbaidənt] *n.* 两尖器，两叉矛.

bi·den·tate [baiˈdenteit] *a.* 【生】有两齿的，两齿的；有两齿状的.

bi·det [bideː] *n.* 〔F.〕①小马. ②(房内洗身用的)脚盆.

bi·di·a·lec·tal [baiˈdaiəˌlektəl] *a., n.* 能流利地说同一语言中两种方言的(人).

bi·di·a·lec·tal·ism [baiˈdaiəlektəˌlizəm], **bi·di·a·lect·ism** [baiˈdaiəˌlektizəm] *n.* 对同一语言中两种方言的精通.

bi·don·ville [biːdɔ̃ˈviːl] *n.* 〔F.〕(北非的)市郊贫民区.

bie·ber·ite [ˈbiːbərait] *n.* 【矿】赤矾，钴矾.

bield [ˈbiːld] *n.* 〔Scot.〕避难所，避雨处. — *vt.* 隐避，掩护，寄身.

Bie·lo·rus·sia = Byelorussia.

bien en·ten·du [bjæn nɔntɔnˈdjuː] 〔F.〕那自然，不言而喻，必定.

bi·en·ni·al [baiˈeniəl] *a.* ①二年一次的；持续两年的. ②【植】二年生的. — *n.* 二年生植物；二年一次的事物；两年一次的试验. **-ly** *ad.* 两年一次地；一连两年地.

bi·en·ni·um [baiˈeniəm] *n.* ***(pl. bi·en·ni·a*** [baiˈenjə]***)*** 〔L.〕二年间，两年的时期.

bien·ve·nue [bjænvəˈnju] *a., n.* 〔F.〕受欢迎(的人)(= welcome).

bier[1] [biə] *n.* ①棺架，尸架. ②棺材.

bier[2] [biə] *n.* = beer[2].

biest·ings [ˈbiːstiŋz] *n.* (牛产后的)初乳(= beestings).

bi·fa·cial [baiˈfeiʃəl] *a.* ①(正反)两面一样的. ②【植】有两面的；(叶子等)正反两面不同的，异面的. *~ leaves* 异面叶.

bi·far·i·ous [baiˈfɛəriəs] *a.*【植】二重的；相背的. ②二纵列的.

bi·fer [ˈbaifə] *n.* 一年开花两次的植物.

biff [bif] *n.* 〔美俚〕梆地一打，啪地一击. — *vt.* (梆地)打，殴打. *give a ~ on the head* 对头上梆地一记. ***biffing brawl*** 〔美口〕拳击比赛.

bif·fin [ˈbifin] *n.* 〔英〕①深红色餐用苹果. ②苹果饼.

bi·fid [ˈbaifid] *a.* 【天】二叉的，叉形的(彗星尾等)；【植】两裂的.

bi·fi·lar [baiˈfailə] *a.* 双线的；涉及用两条线的. — *n.* 【机】双线千分尺. **-ly** *ad.*

bi·flag·el·late [baiˈflædʒilit, -ˌleit] *a.* 【生】有两纤毛枝的，双鞭毛的.

bi·flex [ˈbaifleks] *a.* 有双处弯曲的.

bi·fo·cal [baiˈfəukəl] *a.* ①【物】双焦点的. ②(望远镜等)远近两用的. ③有二重观点的. *a ~ view* 双重观点. — *n.* 〔*pl.*〕双光眼镜，远近视两用眼镜；双焦点透镜.

bi·fo·li·ate [baiˈfəuliit, baiˈfəulieit] *a.* 【植】有二叶的，双叶的.

bi·forked [ˈbaiˌfɔːkt] *a.* = bifurcate.

bi·form [ˈbaifɔːm] *a.* 有两形的〔如人鱼等〕，两种形体结合成的；把不同两体的特征合在一起的.

Bif·rost [ˈbiːfrɔst] *n.* 【北欧神】从地上通向天宫的彩虹桥.

bi·fur·cate [ˈbaifəːkeit, baiˈfəːkit] *a.* 【植】成叉的，两叉的，分为二枝的. — *vi.* 成叉状；分叉. — *vt.* 使分叉. **-ly** *ad.*

bi·fur·ca·tion [ˌbaifəːˈkeiʃən] *n.* 分枝，分叉. ②分叉点，分枝点.

big [big] *a.* ①大，巨大；大规模的；已长大的. ②〔口〕重要的，重大的；伟大的；出名的，极成功的，受欢迎的. ③骄傲的，傲慢的，自大的. ④怀着(孕)，有(身子)；〔喻〕充满着…的，洋溢着…的(*with*). ⑤宽大的，宽宏大量的. ⑥〔口〕(风等)剧烈的. *a ~ house* 大房子. *a ~ enterprise* 大企业. *a ~ pay* 高薪. *art with a ~ A* 具有特种暗含意义的艺术；抽象的艺术. *the ~ man of the town* 城中名人. *~ words* 豪言壮语，大话. *He looks ~*. 他神气活现. *That's very ~ of you*. 你真宽宏大量. *~ with (young, child)* 怀孕，有喜. *a question ~ with the fate of the Empire* 有关帝国生死存亡的问题. *eyes ~ with tears* 满眼泪水. *a ~ storm [earthquake]* 剧烈的风暴〔地震〕. *a ~ piece of news* 重要新闻. ***as ~ as life*** 和原物一样大. ***be ~ on*** 〔口〕热中；偏爱. ***be [get, grow] too ~ for one's boots [breeches, trousers]*** 妄自尊大，目中无人. ***go over ~*** 〔美口〕(演出等)大大成功；(演员等)大受欢迎. ***make ~*** 〔美俚〕飞黄腾达. — *ad.* ①〔口〕非常大量. ②〔口〕自大，夸大. ③宽宏大量地. ④成功地. *talk ~* 吹牛. *eat ~* 食量大. *a ~ busy day* 忙得不可开交的一天. *pay ~* 付给高薪〔高报酬〕. — *n.* 大亨，巨子；大公司. ~ **bad (wolf)** 〔美口〕市面萧条，不景气. **~-bang (theory)** 【天】(宇宙起源的)大爆炸(学说). ~ **beat** 摇摆音乐. ~ **beef** 〔美俚〕蠢汉. **B- Ben** 英国议会大厦上的大钟〔直径 2.8 米，重 13,500 公斤〕. **B- Bertha** 〔美俚〕德国巨型加农炮；大

型客机;【拳】猛击. **B- Board** 〔美〕纽约证券交易所(行情牌). ~ **board** 〔美〕热门股票. ~ **boy** 〔美俚〕好家伙,好一个大汉;大人物;大型野炮; 百元钞票;大学中特别突出的学生. ~ **bozo** [ˈbəuzəu] 〔美俚〕著名拳击选手. ~ **brother** 老大哥;〔B-B-〕专制国家[组织](的领导). ~ **brute**=~ **bozo.** ~ **bug** 〔美俚〕要人,名人.~ **business** 大企业,大财阀. ~ **butter-and-egg man** 〔美俚〕骄傲俗气的乡下富翁,土财主. ~ **cheese** 〔美俚〕大人物,大亨;有权力的人,官老爷;粗鲁的男子. ~ **coat** 〔Scot.〕 = overcoat. **B- Ditch** 〔美俚〕①大洋. ②〔the B- D-〕大西洋;巴拿马运河. ~ **dog** ①看门狗;保镖. ②〔美俚〕大物. ~ **dough** 〔美俚〕巨款,大笔款子. ~ **drink** 〔美俚〕①大洋. ②密西西比河. ~ **end** 【机】连杆头. ~ **eye** 大眼鲷科鱼. ~**-eyed** *a.* ①大眼的. ②惊讶的. **B- Five** 世界五强〔指第一次世界大战巴黎会议中的美、英、法、意、日,或指第二次大战后之中、美、英、法、苏〕. ~ **friend** 〔俚〕(己方的)轰炸机. ~ **game** 【猎】巨兽〔象、狮子等〕;(钓鱼)大鱼;〔俚〕(需冒危险获得的)特大奖赏[目标]. **B- Government** 实行高压统治的政府. ~ **gun** = ~ **bug.** ~ **guy** 〔美俚〕官吏;老板;暴徒头子;要人,名人;上帝. ~ **hand** 〔美俚〕大喝采. ~ **head** 〔美俚〕自大,自大的人;喝醉;(兽类)头部浮肿病. ~ **headed** *a.* 自大的. ~ **heart** (海一样)宽大的胸怀. ~ **house** 〔美俚〕州[联邦]监狱;村中首户;〔卑〕习艺所,济贫院. ~ **idea** 〔美〕计划,提议;意图,目的. **B- Inch**(二次大战中美国所筑)大输油管. ~ **jeep** 〔俚〕巨型轰炸机. ~ **John** 〔俚〕新兵. ~**-leagued** *a.* 〔美〕第一流的,头等的. ~ **mouth** 〔美俚〕多嘴多舌的人. ~ **name** 〔美俚〕名士. ~**-name** *a.* 大名鼎鼎的. ~ **noise** 〔美俚〕轰动一时的事实[声明];名人,要人;重磅炸弹. ~ **Navy** 【政】大海军主义. ~ **one** 〔美俚〕①千元钞票. ②大便. ③〔the〕重要节目. **B- pond [puddle]** 大西洋的别名. ~ **shot** 〔俚〕 = ~ **bug.** ~ **stick** 〔美〕 ①武力,实力,威吓,大棒政策. ②〔美口〕长梯,云梯. ③〔*pl.*〕大片森林带. ~**-ticket** *a.* 高价的. ~ **time** *n.*〔口〕①(杂技等的)大成功. ②最高水准;最重要的位置. ③欢乐愉快的时刻. ~ **time** *a.* 有名的;有钱的;成功的. ~ **toe** 拇趾. ~ **tree** 【植】巨杉. ~ **wheel** 〔美俚〕要人. ~ **wig** = ~ **bug.** **-ness** *n.* 大,巨大,庞大,重大;夸大(*bigness scale* 粗测).

big·a·lop·o·lis [ˌbigəˈlɔpis] *n.* 〔美口〕大都市.

bi·gam·ic [baiˈgæmik, biˈgæmik] *a.* 重婚的.

big·a·mist [ˈbigəmist] *n.* 重婚者,犯重婚罪者. **-ic** *a.* **-ti·cal·ly** *ad.*

big·a·mous [ˈbigəməs] *a.* 重婚的;犯重婚罪的.

big·a·my [ˈbigəmi] *n.* 重婚,重婚罪;【宗】违反教会诫律的婚姻.

big·ar·reau [ˌbigəˈrəu, ˈbigərəu] *n.* 〔B-〕 红白樱桃(= bigaroon).

bi·gem·i·nal [baiˈdʒeminl] *a.* 【解】二联的,成双的,成对的. ~ *pulse* 二联脉.

bi·gem·i·ny [baiˈdʒemini] *n.* 【生理】重发状态,两两连发〔比如心脏的律动一跳是两下〕.

bi·gen·er [ˈbaidʒinə] *n.* 【生】属间杂种.

bi·ge·ner·ic [ˌbaidʒiˈnerik] *a.* 【生】属间杂种的.

big·foot [ˈbigfut] *n.* 大脚毛人 (= sasquatch).

bigg [big] *n.* 〔Scot.〕四棱大麦.

big·ge·ty [ˈbigiti] *a.* 〔美〕傲慢的.

big·gie [ˈbigi] *n.* 〔口〕权贵,大亨,权要人物,名人,伟人,要人 (= bigwig).

big·gin [ˈbigin] *n.* ①〔英方〕童帽. ②睡帽.

big·ging, big·gin [ˈbigin] *n.* 〔英方〕大楼,建筑物.

big·gish [ˈbigiʃ] *a.* 稍大的.

big·horn [ˈbighɔːn] *n.* 巨角岩羊.

bight [bait] *n.* ①(海岸线或江岸等的)弯曲部;海湾. ②【海】绳耳,绳扣;一条松开的绳子中部. *the Great Australian B-* 澳大利亚大海湾. — *vt.* 把(绳子)结成扣;用绳扣缚住.

big·no·ni·a [bigˈnəuniə] *n.* 【植】比格诺藤属植物.

big·ot [ˈbigət] *n.* 顽固的迷信者,盲信者;执拗的人. **-ed** *a.* 顽固的,执迷不悟的,执拗的 (*She is bigoted to [in] her opinion.* 她固执己见).

big·ot·ry [ˈbigətri] *n.* ①固执,顽固,执拗;偏狭. ②固执的行为.

Bi·har [biˈhɑː] **State** 比哈尔邦〔印度邦名〕.

bi·jou [ˈbiːʒuː] *n.* (*pl.* ***-joux*** [ˈbiːʒuːz]) 〔F.〕①宝石,珠宝;玉石装饰品. ②小巧精致的物品. — *a.* (汽车、别墅等)小巧精致的. *a ~ villa* 小巧精致的别墅.

bi·jou·te·rie [biːˈʒuːtəri] *n.* 〔F.〕①宝石,珠宝. ②小巧精致的装饰品.

bi·ju·gate [ˈbaidʒugeit, baiˈdʒuːgit] *a.* 【植】二对的,二对小叶的(= bijugous).

bike[1] [baik] *n.* 〔口〕① = bicycle. ②电动自行车. ③摩托车. — *vi.* 骑自行车;骑摩托车. ~ **grind** 〔美〕自行车比赛. ~**way** 自行车道. **-r** *n.* 骑自行车的人.

bike[2] [baik] *n.* 〔Scot.〕①(蜂、蚁等的)群体,大群,窝. ②人群,群众.

Bi·ki·ni [biˈkiːni] *n.* ①比基尼岛〔1946 年美国原子弹实验地〕. ②〔b-〕(半裸体的)比基尼式女子游泳衣.

bi·la·bi·al[baiˈleibiəl]*a.* ①有两唇的,两唇的. ②【语音】唇音的,双唇音的(如 p, b, m 等). — *n.* 【语音】唇音.

bi·la·bi·ate [baiˈleibieit] *a.* 【植】二唇的,二唇形的.

bil·an·der [ˈbiləndə, ˈbailəndə] *n.* 双桅小船.

bi·lat·er·al [baiˈlætərəl] *a.* ①【动、植】两侧[左右]对称的. ②两侧的,两边的. ③双方的,双边的. ④双向(作用)的,双通的;对向的. ⑤双系的. *the ~ symmetry of the organs* 器官左右对称. ~ *affiliation* 双系亲属关系. ~ *circuit* 双向电路. ~ *switching* 双通开关. ~ *treaty* 双边条约. — *n.* 双边会议;双边会谈. **-ism** *n.* ①(贸易)互惠主义. ②(动植物器官)的左右对称.

Bil·ba·o [bilˈbɑːəu] *n.* 毕尔巴鄂〔西班牙港市〕.

bil·ber·ry [ˈbilbəri] *n.* 【植】欧洲越桔.

bil·bo[1] [ˈbilbəu] *n.* (*pl.* ~***s***, ~***es***) 〔诗〕剑;(西班牙 Bilbo 地方产)比尔波剑;精工冶制的剑.

bil·bo[2] [ˈbilbəu] *n.* (*pl.* ~***es***) 〔常 *pl.*〕足枷式脚镣.

bil·bo·ism [ˈbilbəizəm] *n.* 〔美〕种族仇视;顽固,偏执.

bile [bail] *n.* ①【生理】胆汁. ②愤怒,生气,坏脾气,乖戾. *black ~* 忧郁. ***rouse [stir] sb.'s ~*** 逗恼人,激怒人. ~ **acid** 【化】胆汁酸. ~ **stone** *n.* 【医】胆石.

bi·lec·tion [baiˈlekʃən] *n.*【建】凸出嵌线 (= bolection).

bi·lev·el [baiˈlevl] *n.* 两层平房〔第二层入口低于地面〕.

bilge [bildʒ] *n.* ①(桶等的)中腹,鼓起部分. ②【海】船底弯曲部(尤指船底和船侧间的弯曲部). ③舱底污水. ④〔口〕糊涂话,傻话;无聊文章. — *vi.* ①【海】舱底开口;舱底漏水. ②鼓胀,凸出. ③〔美俚〕考试不及格. — *vt.* 把(舱底)凿破,使(舱底)漏水. ~ **keel** 舭龙骨. ~ **pump** 舱底污水泵. ~ **water** 【海】舱水,舱底污水;〔俚〕废话.

bilg·y [ˈbildʒi] *a.* 有船肚水臭的.

bil·har·zi·a [bilˈhɑːziə] *n.* 裂体吸虫,住血吸虫;住血吸虫病.

bil·har·zi·a·sis [ˌbilhɑːˈzaiəsis] *n.* 裂体吸虫病,住血吸虫病.

bil·i·ar·y [ˈbiljəri] *a.* 胆汁的;输送胆汁的. *a ~ duct* 胆管. ~ **calculus** 胆石.

bi·lin·e·ar [baiˈliniə] *a.* 【数】双线性的,双一次性的. ~ *coordinates* 双一次座标.

bi·lin·gual [baiˈliŋgwəl] *a.* ①两国语言的. ②能讲两国话的. ③用两种语言书写[印刷]的. — *n.* 能讲两国话的人. **-ism** *n.* 使用[通]两种语言. **-ly** *ad.*

bi·lin·guist [baiˈliŋgwist] *n.* 通两国语言的人.

bil·ious [ˈbiljəs] *a.* ①胆汁(质)的;胆汁病(引起)的. ②易怒的,脾气大的. ~ **complaint** 胆汁病.

bil·i·ru·bin [ˌbiliˈruːbin] *n.* 【生理】胆红素.

bi·lit·er·al [baiˈlitərəl] *a.* ①由两个字母构成的. ②由两种字体构成的. *a* ~ *word* 两个字母构成的单词.

-bi·li·ty *comb. f.* 与 -ble, -able, -ible, -uble 相对应的名词后缀: a*bility*, possi*bility*.

bil·i·ver·din [ˌbiliˈvəːdn] *n.* 【生理】胆绿素.

bilk [bilk] *vt.* ①逃避付钱给…,赖掉(帐、债等). ②欺,骗,瞒. ③挫败,使受挫. ~ *a cabman* 蒙混坐车,白坐出租汽车. ~ *his creditors* 赖债. ~ *sb. out of his money* 骗取某人的钱. *She* ~*ed his efforts to discover her.* 她使他找寻她的努力落空. — *n.* ①赖帐,混骗. ②骗子. **-er** *n.* 骗子;坐车不买票的人;赖帐者.

Bill [bil] *n.* 比尔〔男子名, William 的昵称〕.

bill[1] [bil] *n.* ①帐单;清单. ②报单,贴条,招贴,告白,传单,广告;戏单,戏报. ③【商】证券;汇票,支票,票据;凭单. ④〔美〕纸币;〔美俚〕百元钞票. ⑤议案,法案;【法】起诉书,诉状. *a time* ~ 时间表. *a grocery* ~ 食品店(收款)帐单. *Post [Stick] no* ~*s.* 禁止招贴. *introduce [bring in] a* ~ 提出议案. *reject [throw out] a* ~ 否决议案. *a ten-dollar* ~ 一张十元钞票. ~ *at (3 day's) sight* 见票后(三天)照付的汇票(等). ~ *for collection* 代收[托收]票据. ~ *of clearance* 出港报表. ~ *of costs* 【法】讼费清单. ~ *of credit* 取款凭单; 付款通知书. ~ *of debt* 期票. ~ *of dishonour* 拒付支票. ~ *of entry* 入港报表, 报税通知单. ~ *of exchange* 汇票. ~ *of fare* 菜单;戏单,剧目. ~ *of health* (船员、船客)健康证书;检疫证. ~ *of lading* 运货证书,提单,提货凭单〔略作 B/L〕. ~ *of mortality* 死亡统计表. ~ *of parcels* 发票. ~ *of quantities* 〔英〕建筑细则. *pay a* ~ 付账.
— *vt.* ①填报; 填(表), 把…列成表. ② 开帐单给…. ③(以传单、广告等)宣布, 贴海报. ~ *goods* 开列商品清单[目录]. ~ *passengers* 填报乘客名单. *The store will* ~ *me.* 百货店要给我送帐单来了. *She is* ~*ed to lecture tonight.* 贴海报说她今晚演讲. ***a Bill of Oblivion*** 大赦令. ~ ***of sale*** 卖据;【法】抵押证券. ~ ***of sight*** (海关)临时起岸报单. ~ ***of store*** (海岸)船上用品免税单;再输入免税单. ~ ***payable* [receivable]** 应付[应取]票据. ~ ***to bearer [order]*** 不记名[记名]票据. ***fill the*** ~〔美口〕符合要求,解决问题. ***find a true*** ~ (陪审团认为)诉状应予受理. ***foot the*** ~〔口〕①负担费用, 会钞. ②承担责任. ***head the*** ~ (演员)挂头牌,领衔主演. ***ignore the*** ~ (陪审团认为)诉状不应受理. ***kill the*** ~ 否决议案,阻止议案通过. ***post (up) a*** ~ 贴标语(等). ***sell (sb.) a*** ~ ***of goods*** 〔美〕以花言巧语等骗得(某人)相信[同意]. **the B- of Rights** ①《权利法案》〔英国 1689 年颁布的确立君主立宪制的根本大法之一〕. ②《人权法案》〔美国宪法的第一次修正案, 1789 年通过〕. ~ **board** ①〔美〕广告牌, 揭示牌. ②【海】锚床. ~ **book** 支票簿,解款[送金]簿. ~ **broker** 证券经纪人. ~**discounter** 贴现业者. ~ **fold** 单据夹,票夹,钱夹. ~ **head** (印有招牌地址等的)空白单据[发票等]. ~ **poster,** ~ **sticker** ①贴广告(等)的人. ②〔美俚〕伪造票据者,伪造票据犯. ~ **stamp** 印花税票.

bill[2] [bil] *n.* ①(水禽等细长而扁平的)嘴〔猛禽的钩状嘴通例叫 beak〕. ②嘴状岬. ③锚爪. ④鹤嘴锄;钩镰;钩状戟. — *vi.* ①(鸽子似地)接嘴,亲嘴,接吻. ②亲热,爱抚. ~ ***and coo*** (鸽子)接嘴;〔喻〕(男女间)互相接吻,爱抚和喁喁情话.

bill[3] [bil] *n.* ①(欧洲中世纪步兵用的)长柄矛. ② = billhook. ~**-hook** (剪枝等用的)钩镰,钩刀.

bill·a·bong [ˈbiləˌbɔŋ] *n.* ①回水湖,回水池,死水潭. ②只有在一定季节才涨水的干涸河床.

bill·bug [ˈbilˌbʌg] *n.* 【虫】象岬.

bill·er [ˈbilə] *n.* ①开帐单的人;开清单的人. ②帐单机.

bil·let[1] [ˈbilit] *n.* ①【军】分配令〔军事当局发给户主指示提供军人住宿地的命令〕. ②(兵士分住民家或公共建筑物时的)营舍. ③〔英〕职位, 地位. ④便条; 短简. ⑤【海】船员宿舍. *a good* ~ 好差事. ***Every bullet has its*** ~. 颗颗子弹有归宿;天命难违. — *vt.* 为…指定宿营地,为…分配宿舍 (*on*). ~ *soldiers on a village* 把士兵安顿在一个村子里宿营. *We arrange with the townspeople to* ~ *the students.* 我们和镇上人协商给学生提供宿舍. — *vi.* 住屯. *They* ~*ed in Youth Hotel.* 他们在青年饭店住下来.

bil·let[2] [ˈbilit] *n.* ①木柴块. ②(金属的)坯段; 钢坯. ③【建】错齿饰. *steel* ~ 钢坯. *solid* ~ 整轧坯,实心坯. ~ **wood** 圆材.

bill., billds = billiards.

bil·let-doux [ˈbileiˈduː] *n.* (*pl.* ***bil·lets-doux*** [ˈbileiˈduːz]) 〔F.〕情书;〔反〕不愿收到的信〔催帐信等〕.

bill·fish [ˈbilfiʃ] *n.* (*pl.* ~, ~*es*) 长喙鱼〔有细长如鸟喙之颚的鱼,如针鱼〕,帆鱼,旗鱼,真旗鱼.

bil·liard [ˈbiljəd] *a.* 台球(用)的〔仅作定语〕. *a* ~ *cue* (台球)球棒. *a* ~ *marker* (台球)记分员. *a* ~ *room* 弹子房. *a* ~ *table* (台球)球桌,弹子台. — *n.* 〔美口〕= carom *n.*

bil·liards [ˈbiljədz] *n. pl.* 台球戏〔俗称"打弹子",常作单数用〕. *play (at)* ~ 打台球,打弹子. *have a game at* ~ 比赛台球,比赛打弹子. *B- isn't popular here.* 这里不流行玩台球.

Bil·lie [ˈbili] *n.* 比莉〔女子名〕.

Bil·li·ken [ˈbilikən] *n.* 〔美〕福神(神像).

bill·ing [ˈbiliŋ] *n.* ①(节目单、剧院门口华盖等上的)演员表. ②(演员表上的)演员名次.

Bil·lings·gate [ˈbiliŋzgit] *n.* ①(昔日的)伦敦鱼市场. ②〔b-〕猥亵话,下流话,骂人话.

bil·lion [ˈbiljən] *num.* ①〔法、美〕十亿 ($=10^9$). ②〔英、德〕万亿,兆 ($=10^{12}$). ③无数. *several* ~*s of people* 几十亿人. ~ *electron-volts* 十亿电子伏.

bil·lion·aire [biljəˈnɛə] *n.* 亿万富翁.

bil·lionth [ˈbiljənθ] *a.* ①第十亿(个)的〔美、法用法〕. ②第一万亿(个)的〔英、德用法〕. — *num.* ①第十亿,十亿分之一. ②第一万亿,万亿分之一.

bil·lon [ˈbilən] *n.* 金铜[银铜]铸币合金,金[银]与其他金属的合金.

bil·low [ˈbiləu] *n.* ①巨浪;〔诗〕波涛;滚滚烟尘(等). ②〔诗〕〔the ~s〕海. *angry* ~*s* 怒涛. ~*s of flames* 烈焰翻滚. ~ *cloud* 波状云. — *vi.* 起大浪,波涛汹涌;(烟尘)翻滚. *red flags* ~*ing in the breeze.* 红旗飘扬. — *vt.* 使翻腾.

bil·low·y [ˈbiləui] *a.* 巨浪的;巨浪似的;起巨浪的;波涛汹涌的,波浪滔天的. *a rough,* ~ *sea.* 翻江倒海卷巨澜.

Bil·ly, Billie [ˈbili] *n.* 比利〔男子名, William 的昵称〕.

bil·ly[1] [ˈbili] *n.* ①警棍;棍棒. ②〔Scot.〕伙伴,朋友,弟兄. ③【英纺】粗纱机. ~**boy** 〔英〕独桅平底船. ~ **club** 警棍,棍棒. ~**cock** 〔英〕(宽边低顶的)毡帽. ~**goat** 公山羊.

bil·ly[2] [ˈbili] *n.* 〔澳〕(野营烧水用的)洋铁罐,瓦罐.

billy-(h)o [ˈbili(h)əu] *n.* 〔英口〕极度〔仅与 like 连用〕. ***like*** ~ 猛烈地 (*roar like* ~ 狂吼,咆哮如雷. *It rained like* ~ 大雨倾盆).

bi·lo·bate [baiˈləubeit] *a.* 【植】二裂的,有二裂片的;有二叶的.

bi·loc·u·lar [baiˈlɔkjulə] *a.* 【植】具二室的.

bil·sted [ˈbilsted] *n.* 【植】①胶皮糖香树. ②胶皮糖香树木. ③苏合香 (= sweet gum).

bil·tong [ˈbiltɔŋ] *n.* (南非)干肉条.

bim [bim] *n.* 〔美俚〕女人〔尤指荡妇〕.

Bim·a·na [ˈbimənə] *n.* 〔*pl.*〕【动】两手类.

bim·a·nous [ˈbimənəs, baiˈmeinəs] *a.* 【动】有两手的.

bi·man·u·al [baiˈmænjuəl] *a.* 用两手的,须用两手的. *a machine designed for* ~ *operation* 须用双手操作的机器. **-ly** *ad.*

bim·bo [ˈbimbəu] *n.* ①柠檬汁葡萄酒. ②〔俚〕家伙;流

氓. ③〔卑〕轻浮女子；邋遢女人；妓女.

bi·mes·ter [bai'mestə] *n.* 两个月(期间). **-tri·al** [bai'mestriəl] *a.* 两月一次的；持续两月的.

bi·met·al ['bai'metl] *a.* ①双金属的. ②两本位制的；复本位制的 (= bimetallic). ～ *sheet* 双金属板. — *n.* 双金属物质，双金属片；复合钢材.

bi·me·tal·lic [ˌbaimi'tælik] *a.* 双金属的；(金银)两本位制的，复本位制的. ～ *standard* 复本位制.

bi·met·al·lism [bai'metəlizəm] *n.* (金银)两本位制；复本位制主义.

bi·met·al·list [bai'metəlist] *n.* 复本位制主义者.

bi·mod·al [bai'məudl] *a.*【统】(分布曲线)双峰的. **-i·ty** *n.*

bi·mo·lec·u·lar [ˌbaimə'lekjələ] *n.*【化】双分子.

bi·month·ly ['bai'mʌnθli] *a.* ①两月一次的，隔月的. ②每月两次的. — *ad.* ①隔月. ②每月两次. — *n.* ①双月刊. ②半月刊.

bi·morph ['baimɔːf] *n.*【电】双压电晶片.

bi·mor·phe·mic ['baimɔː'fiːmik] *a.*【语】涉及双词素的，包含双词素的.

bi·mo·tored [bai'məutəd] *a.* 双发动机的 (= twin-engined).

bin [bin] *n.* ①(放五谷、煤炭等的)有盖大箱. ②〔英〕收采酒花的帆布袋. ③(地下室)葡萄酒贮藏库. ④垃圾箱. ⑤〔口〕精神病院. ⑥〔英口〕裤子口袋. *a rubbish [dust]* ～ 垃圾箱. — *vt.* 把…装进贮藏库[大木箱].

bin- *comb. f.* 〔用于元音前〕= bi-: *bin*aural.

binac ['bainæk] *n.* = *bin*ary *a*utomatic *c*omputer (二进制自动计算机).

bi·nal ['bainl] *a.* 两倍的，两重的.

bi·na·ry ['bainəri] *a.* 二，双，复；【化】二元的；【数】二进制的. — *n.* 二，双，复；双体，复体；【天】双[联]星；【数】二进制. ～ **alloy**【冶】二元合金. ～ **compound**【化】二元化合物. ～ **computer** 二进制计算机. ～ **element**【无】双态元件. ～ **measure**【乐】二拍子. ～ **notation** 二进位符号，二进(位记数)法. ～ **scale**【数】二进法. ～ **star**【天】双[联]星. ～ **system** 二进制；二元系；双星系.

bi·nate ['baineit] *a.*【植】双生的，成对的.

bin·au·ral [bi'nɔːrəl] *a.* ①(用)双耳的. ②立体声的. ～ *broadcasting* 立体广播. *a* ～ *stethoscope* 双耳听诊器.

bind [baind] *vt.* ***(bound*** [baund]; ***bound,*** 〔古〕***bounden)*** ①缚，捆，扎，绑；束；裹，卷 *(about; around, round).* ②(用绷带)包扎*(up).* ③定，缔结. ④装订(书籍)；给…镶边；收边. ⑤使便秘. ⑥支配，牵制；(义务等)束缚(人)，使…受拘束，使…承担义务. ⑦(冰等)封住；(用水泥)粘固；使结合. ⑧〔英口〕使厌烦. ～ *up a wound* (用绷带)包扎伤口. ～ *a bargain* 定买卖契约. ～ *a book in morocco* 用摩洛哥皮装订书. *This food* ～*s the bowel.* 这种食物引起便秘. *Please* ～ *the carpet before cleaning it.* 请在清洗地毯以前把边收一收. *I am bound to warn you.* 我应该警告你. *All are bound to obey the laws.* 人人有服从法律的义务. *Ice bound the soil.* 地面被冻实了. *a shirt that* ～*s me* 一件过紧的衬衫. *He was bound (as an) apprentice to a shoe-maker.* 他做了鞋店的学徒. *The movie* ～ *me.* 这场电影太无聊. — *vi.* ①(门窗等)开关不灵便；(衣服等)紧身；(义务等)有约束力. ②土、沙、雪等凝固，变硬；(车轮)粘牢不动. ③〔英口〕发牢骚. ～ *about one's extraduties* 对做额外工作发牢骚. *Clay* ～*s to heat.* 粘土遇热变硬. *an obligation that* ～*s* 一项有约束力的义务. ***be bound for*** 船开往…. ***be bound to do sth.*** 有义务…，应该…，必须…，非…不可，决心要…. ***be bound to sth.*** 被束缚在…上. ***be bound up with*** 与…有密切联系；与…结合在一起. ～ ***oneself to (do sth.)*** 发誓(做某事). ～ ***(sb.) over to (do) sth.*** 使具结，要…发誓 (*I bound him over to good behaviour.* 我要他发誓改过自新). ～ ***up*** ①包扎. ②装订. — *n.* ①带子，索子；蔓，葛，藤. ②【乐】连线〔即⌒〕；【矿】(煤层间的)泥岩；〔英〕(鲑、毛皮等的)计数单位；【建】撑条，系杆. ***in a*** ～ 受很大压力，处于困境. ***safe [S-]*** ～ 见 safe 条.

bind. = binding.

bind·er[1] ['baində] *n.* ①缚者，绑者，包扎者；(书籍)装订工. ②包扎物，包扎工具，绳索，带子；缀合物；绷带，(产妇用)腹带；(草捆的)扎结处. ③【农】割捆机；(缝纫机)滚边器；【机】结合件；【建】接合料，系梁；连结石；【医】结合剂；【冶】粘合剂，胶合剂；胶合物；(书的)活页封面；装订机；【医】止泻药. ④临时契约；购买不动产的定金(收据). ⑤〔英口〕感到厌烦的人；发牢骚的人. ～ **board** 刨花板；纸板.

bin·der[2] ['bində] *n.* 〔英〕(食物的)大量，多量.

bind·er·y ['baindəri] *n.* 〔美〕书籍装订所.

bind·ing ['baindiŋ] *a.* ①缚[捆、绑]…的；粘合的；系连的，连结的. ②有束缚力的，有拘束力的，附有义务的. ③〔口〕引起便秘的. ④〔英口〕发牢骚的. ***be*** ～ ***on*** 对…有约束力；使承担义务 (*The statement is unofficial and not* ～ *on either country.* 本声明系非官方性的，对两国均不具有约束力. *This regulation is* ～ *on everybody.* 本规则人人皆须遵守). — *n.* ①捆绑，束缚；缀结，连接；粘合；【物】结合；键联. ②滚条；绷带；(书籍的)装钉，装帧；封面；边. ③【法】具结. ～ **agent** 粘合剂，接合剂. ～ **energy**【物】结合能. ～ **force** 结合[内聚]力. ～ **joists**【建】梁；小梁. ～ **musline** 书面布. ～ **post**【物】接线柱. ～ **screw**【电】接线螺钉；【机】紧固螺钉.

bin·dle ['bindl] *n.* 〔美俚〕流浪汉的小行李卷. ～ **stiff** (带着一个小行李卷的)乞丐，流浪汉；流动工人.

bind·weed ['baindwiːd] *n.*【植】旋花属植物；旋花.

bind·wood ['baindwud] *n.*【植】常春藤.

bine [bain] *n.* ①(爬藤或攀生植物的)蔓，葛. ②忽布〔酒花〕蔓.

bing [biŋ] *n.* 〔英方〕堆. *a* ～ *of potatoes* 一堆土豆.

binge [bindʒ] *n.* 〔俚〕①欢闹；喝闹酒. ②社交集会.

bin·gle[1] ['biŋgl] *n.*【棒球】稳打. — *vi.* 打出稳球.

bin·gle[2] ['biŋgl] *n.* 妇女剪的一种短发型.

bin·go ['biŋgəu] *n.* ①排五点〔一种赌博性游戏〕. ②〔口〕白兰地酒. — *int.* 瞧!

bin·na·cle ['binəkl] *n.*【海】罗经柜.

bin·o·cle ['binɔkl] *n.* 〔罕〕(双目)望远镜.

bi·nocs [bə'nɔks] *n.* 〔口〕= binoculars.

bin·oc·u·lar [bai'nɔkjulə, bi'n-] *a.* 双目的，双筒的. *a* ～ *telescope [microscope]* 双筒[目]望远镜[显微镜]. — *n.* 〔常 *pl.*〕双筒望远镜；双目显微镜.

bi·no·mi·al [bai'nəumiəl] *a.* ①【数】二项(式)的. ②【生】双名的，复名的. ～ *theorem*【数】二项式定理. ～ *nomenclature*【生】双名法. — *n.* ①【数】二项式. ②【生】二名法，双名法.

bi·nom·i·nal [bai'nɔminl] *a.* = binomial. ～ *system* (以属名、种名命名动植物的)双名制.

bin·tu·rong ['bintjurɔŋ] *n.*【动】麝猫.

bi·nu·cle·ate [bai'nuːkliːit] *a.* 二核的 (= binucleated, binuclear).

bio- *comb. f.* = life, living things (生命，生物).

bio[1] ['baiəu] *n.* = biography.

bio[2] ['baiəu] *n.* 个人经历，个人历史.

bi·o·as·say [ˌbaiəuˈæsei, -æ'sei] *n.*【生】生物鉴定，生物测定. — *vt.* 对…作生物鉴定.

bi·o·as·tro·nau·tics [ˌbaiəuˌæstrə'nɔːtiks] *n.* 〔*pl.*〕宇宙航行生物学.

bi·o·cat·a·lyst [ˌbaiəu'kætəlist] *n.* 生物触媒，生物催化剂. **-lyt·ic** *a.*

bi·oc·el·late [bai'ɔsəleit] *a.*【生】有两只普通眼睛的，有两点眼状标记的.

bi·o·ce·nol·o·gy [ˌbaiəusi'nɔlədʒi] *n.* 生物群落学.

bi·o·ce·no·sis [ˌbaiəusi'nəusis] *n.* 生物群落 (= biocoenosis, biocenose [-'siːnəus]).

bi·o·chem·i·cal [baiəuˈkemikl] *a.* 生物化学的. — *n.* 生物化学物质. **-ly** *ad.*
bi·o·chem·ics [ˈbaiəuˈkemiks], **bi·o·chem·is·try** [ˈbaiəuˈkemistri] *n.* 生物化学;生理化学.
bi·o·chem·y [ˈbaiəukemi] *n.* = biochemistry.
bi·o·cide [ˈbaiəsaid] *n.* 生物杀灭剂, 杀虫剂. **-cid·al** *a.*
bio·clean [ˈbaiəukli:n] *a.* 无菌的;十分清洁的.
bi·o·cli·ma·tol·o·gy [ˈbaiəuˌklaiməˈtɔlədʒi] *n.* 生物气候学. **bi·o·cli·mat·ic** [-klaiˈmætik] *a.*
bi·o·crat [ˈbaiəukræt] *n.* 生物主义者〔代表生物科学界的科技人员〕.
bi·o·cy·ber·net·ics [ˈbaiəuˌsaibə(:)ˈnetiks] *n.* 生物控制论.
bi·o·de·grad·a·ble [ˌbaiəudiˈgredəbl] *a.* (废纸、饭屑等)可以进行分解和还原处理的〔和铅制品、塑料制品等相对而言〕.
bi·o·dy·nam·ics [ˌbaiəudaiˈnæmiks] *n.* 生物动力学.
bi·o·e·col·o·gy [ˌbaiəui:ˈkɔlədʒi] *n.* (生物)生态学.
bi·o·e·lec·tric·i·ty [ˌbaiəuiˈlektrisiti] *n.* 生物电流.
bio·elec·tron·ics [ˈbaiəuˌilekˈtrɔniks] *n.* ①仿生电子学. ②生物电子学.
bi·o·en·gi·neer·ing [baiəuˌendʒiˈniəriŋ] *n.* 生物工程学.
bi·o·eth·ics [ˈbaiəueθiks] *n.* 生物伦理学〔探讨在器官移植、遗传工程、人工授精等科学研究中所涉及的伦理问题〕.
bi·o·feed·back [ˈbaiəuˌfi:dbæk] *n.* 机能反馈疗法〔利用机械医疗作用, 使病人自动控制和调整正常机能的医疗技术〕.
bi·o·fla·vo·noid [baiəuˈfleivənɔid, -ˈflævə-] *n.* 生物黄酮类.
biog. = biography, biographical, biographer.
bi·o·gen·e·sis [ˈbaiəuˈdʒenisis] *n.*【生】生源说.
bi·o·gen·ic [ˈbaiəuˈdʒenik] *a.* ①(发酵等)生物活动所产生的. ②(食物、水等)生物的生命活动所必需的.
bi·og·e·ny [baiˈɔdʒəni] *n.* ①生源说,生物续生说. ②生物续生(= biogenesis).
bi·o·ge·o·chem·i·cal [ˌbaiəuˌdʒiəu-ˈkemikl] **cycle** 生物地质化学循环,生物地理化学循环.
bi·o·ge·og·ra·phy [ˌbaiəudʒiˈɔgrəfi] *n.* 生物地理学.
bi·o·graph [ˈbaiəugrɑ:f] *n.* ①(初期的)电影放映机. ②〔罕〕小传.
bi·og·ra·phee [baiˌɔgrəˈfi:] *n.* 传记的主人公.
bi·og·ra·pher [baiˈɔgrəfə] *n.* 传记作者. *sb.'s* ~ 为某人写传的人.
bi·o·graph·ic [ˌbaiəuˈgræfik] *a.* = biographical.
bi·o·graph·i·cal [ˌbaiəuˈgræfikəl] *a.* 传记的,传记体的. ~ *data* 传记材料. *a* ~ *dictionary* 人名辞典. *a* ~ *novel* 传记体小说. **-ly** *ad.* 成传记体;传记上.
bi·og·ra·ph·ize [baiˈɔgrəfaiz] *vt.* 为…作传记.
bi·og·ra·phy [baiˈɔgrəfi] *n.* ①传,传记;(城市、团体等的)变迁史. ②传记体;传记文学. *the* ~ *of Byron* 拜伦传. *the* ~ *of the town [village]* 镇[村]史. — *vt.* 为…写传记.
bi·o·herm [ˈbaiəuˌhə:m] *n.* ①生物礁. ②珊瑚礁(= coral reef).
biol. = biologist; biological; biology.
bi·o·log·ic [ˌbaiəˈlɔdʒik] *a.* = biological. **-s** *n.*【药】生物制品.
bi·o·log·i·cal [baiəˈlɔdʒikəl] *a.* 生物学(上)的. *a* ~ *test* 生物学检验. — *n.*【药】生物制品, 生物制剂. ~ **agent** 生物制剂. ~ **clock**【生】生物钟〔生物体内自动调节对时间的反应的一种机能〕. ~ **control** 生物防治. ~ **engineering** 生物工程; 人工育种. ~**form** 生物小种;生物型. ~ **races** 生物宗,生物族;生理宗. ~ **sociology** 生物社会学. ~ **strain**【生】生物小种. ~ **warfare** 细菌战,生物战. **-ly** *ad.* 生物学地,生物学上.
bi·ol·o·gist [baiˈɔlədʒist] *n.* 生物学者.
bi·ol·o·gy [baiˈɔlədʒi] *n.* ①生物学. ②生态学. ③〔总称〕一个地区的生物. *the* ~ *of a worm* 一种虫子的生态学. *the* ~ *of Pennsylvania* 宾夕法尼亚州的生物.
bi·o·lu·mi·nes·cence [ˈbaiəuˌlu:miˈnesns] *n.* 生物(性)发光. **-es·cent** *a.*
bi·ol·y·sis [baiˈɔlisis] *n.*【生】生物分解. **bi·o·lyt·ic** [baiˈɔlitik] *a.*
bi·o·mass [ˈbaiəumæs] *n.*【生态】生物量〔某一地域或单位面积内存在的生物的总量〕.
bio·ma·te·ri·al [ˌbaiəuməˈtiəriəl] *n.*【医】(适用于修复术中与活组织接触的)生物材料.
bi·o·math·e·mat·ics [ˌbaiəuˌmæθiˈmætiks] *n.*〔*pl.*〕生物数学.
bi·ome [ˈbaiəum] *n.* 生物群落.
bi·o·me·chan·ics [ˌbaiəuməˈkæniks] *n.*〔*pl.*〕生命力学. **-me·chan·i·cal** *a.*
bi·o·med·i·cal [ˈbaiəuˈmedikəl] *a.* 生物(学和)医学的.
bi·o·med·i·cine [ˌbaiəuˈmedisn] *n.* 生物药剂学. **-med·ic·al** *a.*
bi·o·me·te·or·ol·o·gy [ˌbaiəuˌmi:tjəˈrɔlədʒi] *n.* 生物气象学,生物环境学.
bi·o·met·rics [ˌbaiəuˈmetriks] *n.* 生物统计学,生物测定学.
bi·om·e·try [baiˈɔmitri] *n.* ①人寿测定(法). ② = biometrics.
bi·o·mor·phi·sm [ˌbaiəuˈmɔ:fizm] *n.* (艺术上的)生物形态主义.
bi·on·ics [baiˈɔniks] *n.* 仿生学.
bi·o·nom·ics [ˌbaiəuˈnɔmik], **bi·on·o·my** [baiˈɔnəmi] *n.* (个体)生态学.
bi·on·o·my [baiˈɔnəmi] *n.* ①生理学. ②生态学.
bi·o·phore [ˈbaiəufɔ:] *n.*【生】最小生活体,生源体.
bi·o·phys·ics [baiəuˈfiziks] *n.*〔*pl.*〕生物物理学. **-si·cist** [-zisist] *n.* 生物物理学家.
bi·o·plasm [ˈbaiəuplæzəm] *n.*【生】活质,原生质.
bi·o·plast [ˈbaiəuplæst] *n.*【生】活粒.
bio·poly·mer [ˌbaiəuˈpɔlimə] *n.* 生物(高分子)聚合物.
bi·op·sy [ˌbaiˈɔpsi] *n.*【医】活组织检查.
bio·re·search [ˌbaiəuriˈsə:tʃ] *n.* 生物科学的研究.
bi·os [ˈbaiɔs] *n.*【生化】酵母促生物.
bi·o·sat·el·lite [ˌbaiəuˈsætlait] *n.* 生物实验卫星〔运载生物或人的人造卫星〕.
bi·o·sci·ence [ˈbaiəuˌsaiəns] *n.* 外太空生物学.
bi·o·scope [ˈbaiəskəup] *n.* ①(初期的)电影放映机. ②〔主英〕电影院.
bi·os·co·py [baiˈɔskəpi] *n.*【医】生死检定法.
bio·sen·sor [ˌbaiəuˈsensə] *n.* 生物传感器.
bi·o·sphere [ˈbaiəsfiə] *n.* ①生物圈,生命层,生物大气层. ②生物界.
bi·o·stat·ics [ˌbaiəuˈstætiks] *n.* 生物静力学.
bi·o·sta·tis·tics [ˌbaiəustəˈtistiks] *n.*〔*pl.*〕生物统计学. **-ti·cal** *a.* **-ti·cian** *n.*
bio·stra·te·gic [ˈbaiəustrəˈti:dʒik] *a.* 对动植物细菌病害用抗菌素疗法的.
bio·strat·e·gy [ˈbaiəuˈstrætidʒi] *n.*【生】动植物细菌病害的抗菌素疗法.
bi·o·strome [ˈbaiəuˌstrəum] *n.* 生物层.
bi·o·syn·the·sis [ˌbaiəuˈsinθisis] *n.* 生物合成. **-thet·ic** *a.* **-thet·i·cal·ly** *ad.*
bi·o·sys·te·mat·ics [baiəuˌsistiˈmætiks] *n.*〔*pl.*〕生物分类学. **-mat·ic** *a.* **-mat·i·cal·ly** *ad.*
bi·o·ta [baiˈəutə] *n.* 生物区;生物群.
bi·o·tech·nol·o·gy [ˌbaiəutekˈnɔlədʒi] *n.* 生物工艺学.
bi·o·te·lem·e·try [ˌbaiəutiˈlemitri] 生态遥测术〔宇宙飞船对地球〕.

bi·o·ther·a·py [ˌbaiəuˈθerəpi] *n.* 生物制剂疗法.

bi·ot·ic [baiˈɔtik] *a.* 生命的, 生物的; 生物引起的(= biotical).

bi·o·tin [ˈbaiətin] *n.* 【生化】生物素,促生素,酵母生长素,维生素 H.

bi·o·tite [ˈbaiətait] *n.* 【矿】黑云母.

bi·o·tope [ˈbaiətəup] *n.* 【生】群落生境; 生活小区.

bi·o·tron [ˈbaiəutrən] *n.* (密闭并可控制温度的)生物研究室.

bi·o·type [ˈbaiətaip] *n.* 同型小种; 生物型; 生活型. **-typic** [-ˈtipik] *a.*

bi·o·ty·pol·o·gy [ˌbaiəutaiˈpɔlədʒi] *n.* 体质类型学.

bi·pack [ˈbaipæk] *n.* 【摄】二重胶片〔用于彩色摄影〕.

bi·pa·ri·e·tal [ˌbaipəˈraiətl] *a.* 左右颅顶骨的.

bip·a·rous [ˈbipərəs] *a.* ①【动】产双胎的. ②【植】有二枝〔二轴〕的.

bi·par·ti·san [baiˌpɑːtiˈzæn], **bi·par·ti·zan** [baiˈpɑːtizən] *a.* 两党的; 代表两党的; 获得两党支持的. *a ~ foreign policy* 获得两党支持的外交政策. **-ship** 〔美〕两党合作.

bi·par·tite [baiˈpɑːtait] *a.* ①由两部分构成的. ②【法】一式两份的; (条约等)两方之间的. ③【植】有二深裂的(叶子等). ④【数】除两次的. *a ~ contract* 一式两份的合同. *a ~ pact* 两国协定. *~ rule* 共同支配. *a ~ leaf* 二裂叶.

bi·par·ti·tion [ˌbaipɑːˈtiʃən] *n.* 二分,双开,分为二.

bi·ped [ˈbaiped] *a.* 〔罕〕二足的. — *n.* 二足动物. *a feathered ~* 鸟.

bi·ped·al [ˈbaiˌpedl] *a.* 二足动物的; 二足的.

bi·pet·al·ous [baiˈpetələs] *a.* 有两花瓣的; 二叶的.

bi·phen·yl [baiˈfenl, -fiːnl] 【化】联(二)苯; 二苯基(= diphenyl).

bi·pin·nate [baiˈpineit] *a.* 【植】(复叶)二回羽状的,两羽状的.

bi·plane [ˈbaiplein] *n.* 双翼(飞)机.

bi·pod [ˈbaipɔd] *n.* 两足支架〔如自动步枪的支架〕.

bi·po·lar [baiˈpəulə] *a.* ①【电】两极的,双极的. ②有两种相反性质〔见解〕的. ③关于或涉及地球两极地区的. **-i·ty** [ˌbaipəuˈlæriti] *n.*

bi·pro·pel·lant [ˌbaiprəˈpelənt] *n.* 二元推进剂, 二元燃料.

bi·quad·rate [baiˈkwɔdrit, -reit] *n.* 【数】四乘方, 四次方, 双二次方.

bi·quad·rat·ic [ˌbaikwɔˈdrætik] *a.* 【数】四次的, 双二次的. — *n.* 【数】四次幂; 四次方程式.

bi·quar·ter·ly [baiˈkwɔːtəli] *a.* 每三个月二次的.

bi·ra·cial [baiˈreiʃəl] *a.* 含有两个种族的〔尤指黑人和白人〕,涉及两个种族的.

bi·ra·di·al [baiˈreidiəl] *a.* 【生】两辐对称的.

bi·ra·mous [baiˈreiməs] *a.* 二支的, 两岔的.

birch [bəːtʃ] *n.* ①【植】桦, 白桦; 桦属. ②桦木; (处罚学童用的) 桦枝, 桦条〔又名 ~-rod〕. ③桦皮船. *the black ~* 西方桦. *the white [silver, Japanese] ~* 白桦. — *vt.* 用桦条打. — *a.* 桦木的; 桦木制的.

birch·en [ˈbəːtʃən] *a.* 桦木的, 桦木制的. *~ furniture* 桦木家具.

bird [bəːd] *n.* ①鸟, 禽. ②猎鸟〔供猎食的鸟, 英国特指鹧鸪〕. ③〔俚〕少女, 姑娘; 人, 家伙, 东西; 〔讽〕非凡人物. ④〔口〕飞机; 〔美口〕火箭, 导弹. ⑤羽毛球. ⑥〔the ~〕(蔑视、起哄时的)嘘嘘声; 解雇. ⑦〔美俚〕(代表军阶的) 鹰徽. ⑧〔俚〕服徒刑, 刑期. *The early ~ gets [catches] the worm.* 捷足先得, 先下手为强. *Each ~ loves to hear himself sing.* 鸟都爱听自己唱, 人都以为自己棒. *It's an ill ~ that fouls its own nest.* 弄脏自己窝巢的不是好鸟〔家丑不可外扬〕. *a game ~* 供猎食的鸟, 猎鸟. *a queer ~* 怪人, 奇人. *a gay ~* 爽快的人. *a bonny ~* 俏姑娘. *an early ~* 早起者; 早来的人. *an old ~* 老练的人, 城府很深的人; 老混蛋. *my ~* 可爱的孩子. *The ~ is [has] flown.* 对手〔要捕捉的人, 囚徒〕逃走了. *A little ~ told me.* 有人告诉我了. ***a ~ in [the] hand [bush]*** 现实〔不现实〕的利益, 已经〔尚未〕到手的东西, 有〔无〕把握的事物(*A ~ in the hand is worth two in the bush.* 双鸟在林不如一鸟在手, 现得为上). ***a ~ of one's own brain*** 自己本身的想头. ***a little ~*** 〔口〕私下有人 (*A little ~ told me that....* 听说…). ***Arabian ~*** = ***~ of wonder*** 凤凰; 长生鸟; 唯一无二之物, 稀世之珍. ***~ in one's bosom*** 良心; 内心. ***~ of ill omen*** 凶鸟〔乌鸦、猫头鹰等〕; 报凶讯的人. ***~ of Jove*** 鹰; 鹫. ***~ of Juno*** 孔雀. ***~ of paradise*** 极乐鸟, 风鸟. ***~ of passage*** 渡鸟, 候鸟; 漂泊不定的人. ***~ of peace*** 鸽. ***~ of prey*** 猛禽(鹫、鹰、枭等). ***~s of a feather*** 同类的人; 一丘之貉 (*Birds of a feather flock together.* 物以类聚). ***eat like a ~*** 吃得很少. ***for the ~s*** 〔常作表语〕毫无意义; 荒唐可笑 (*Their opinions on art are for the ~s.* 他们对艺术的看法简直荒唐可笑). ***get a big ~; get the ~*** 〔俚〕①被嘘嘘地奚落, 被喝倒采. ②被解雇. ***give (sb.) the ~*** 〔俚〕①用嘘嘘声奚落; 嘘, 赶, 撵. ②解雇. ***hear a ~ sing*** 私下听人说, 得密报, 密闻. ***kill two ~s with one stone*** 一举两得, 一石两鸟, 一箭双雕. ***like a ~*** 毫无困难; 毫不犹豫 (*sing like a ~* 唱得好. *work like a ~* 干得麻利). ***the ~s and the bees*** (可对儿童解说的) 有关两性关系的基本常识. ***the secular ~*** 不死鸟, 凤凰. — *vi.* ①捕鸟, 打鸟. ②在野外观察识别野鸟. ~ **bath** (花园的)鸟(浴)池. ~ **brain** 〔美俚〕轻浮无知的人; 笨蛋. ~ **cage** 鸟笼; 鸟笼式房子〔牢房等〕; 〔美俚〕女子宿舍. ~ **call** ①哨子, 鸟笛. ②鸟叫声; 类似鸟叫的声音; 鸟求偶的叫声; 模仿鸟叫的声音. ~ **catcher** 捕鸟者, 捕鸟器. ~ **colonel** 〔美军俚〕陆军上校. ~ **dog** ①捕鸟猎犬. ②搜罗人才的人. ③〔美俚〕兜揽生意的人, 股票经纪人的囮子. ④〔美军俚〕战斗机, 歼击机. ~**-dog** *vt., vi.* ①(猎犬)注视(鸟). ②搜索, 网罗. ~**-eyed** *a.* 目光锐利的. ~**-fancier** 爱玩鸟的人; 经营小鸟的商人. ~**farm** 【海】〔口〕航空母舰. ~**-foot** *n.* 花或叶呈鸟足形的植物. ~**house** 鸟房, 鸟舍, 鸟馆. ~**lime** 未粘鸟胶; 陷捕物. ~**man** ①飞行员; 飞机乘客. ②捕鸟者; 鸟类学家, 鸟类研究者. ~**-minded** *a.* 〔美俚〕蠢, 笨; 轻浮的, 不负责任的. ~**seed** 喂鸟的谷粒. ~ **shot** 鸟枪子弹. ~ **strike** 鸟撞击〔飞机和一群鸟相撞, 可能造成失事〕. ~ **watching** (作为一种爱好的) 野鸟习性观察. ~ **woman** 女飞行家. **-dom** 〔美俚〕美女世界. **-er** *n.* ①捕鸟的人. ②玩鸟的人. ③野鸟研究家.

Bird [bəːd] *n.* 伯德〔姓氏〕.

bird·ie [ˈbəːdi] *n.* ①小鸟〔爱称, 多为儿语〕. ②【无】(一万赫左右的差拍引起的)尖叫声. ③【高尔夫球】得分少于标准分的一击. ④〔美俚〕女性化的男子. ***hear the ~s sing*** 〔美俚〕被打昏过去. ***Watch this ~!*** 照这边, 照相啦!

bird·ing [ˈbəːdiŋ] *n.* ①捕鸟, 打鸟; 玩鸟. ②观察野鸟习性. ~**-piece** 鸟枪.

bird's-eye [ˈbəːdzai] *a.* ①俯视的, 鸟瞰的; 概观的. ②鸟眼一样(有斑点)的; 【纺】鸟眼花纹的. — *n.* ①【植】一种有鲜艳小花的植物〔如粉报春等〕. ②【纺】鸟眼花纹(织物). ③(木材上的)鸟眼纹理. ~ **diamond** 鸟眼花纹精纺毛织品. ~ **view** 鸟瞰图; 概观 (*a ~ view of the city* 城市鸟瞰图. *a ~ view of ancient history* 古代史概观).

bird's-foot [ˈbəːdzfut] *n.* ①叶或花似鸟足的植物〔尤指某些豆科植物〕; 三叶草. ②形似鸟足的动物, 海盘车. ~ **violet** 鸟足堇菜 (*Viola pedata*) 〔美国 Wisconsin 州的州花〕.

bird's-nest [ˈbəːdznest] *n.* ①鸟巢; 燕窝. ②【植】野参, 野生胡萝卜. ③内含水果、坚果等的菜肴. ④【海】捕鲸船桅顶瞭望台.

bird's-nest·ing [ˈbəːdznestiŋ] *n.* ①摸鸟巢，掏鸟蛋. ②〔讽〕马左右摆头癖.
bird·y [ˈbəːdi] *a.* ①似鸟的. ②多鸟的.
bi·re·frin·gence [ˌbairiˈfrindʒins] *n.* 【物】双折射. **-gent** *a.*
bi·reme [ˈbairiːm] *n.* (古代的)对排桨海船.
bi·ret·ta [biˈretə] *n.* (天主教教士等戴的)四角帽，法冠.
Birk·beck [ˈbəːkbek] *n.* 伯克贝克〔姓氏〕.
birl [bəːl] *vt., vi.* ①呼呼旋转. ②踩着运转(浮木). ③〔口〕大把花钱；赌博. — *n.* 〔口〕①企图. ②赌博.
birle, birl [bəːl] *vt.* 〔主 Scot.〕注酒，劝酒. — *vi.* 〔主 Scot.〕痛饮，狂饮.
birl·ing [ˈbəːliŋ] *n.* (伐木工人的)滚筏木游戏〔站在筏木上滚动筏木而保持身体平衡〕.
Bir·ming·ham [ˈbəːmiŋəm] *n.* ①伯明翰〔英国城市〕. ②[ˈbəːmiŋhæm] 伯明翰〔美国城市〕.
bi·ro [ˈbaiərəu] *n.* (可以吸墨水的)圆珠笔.
bi·ro·ta·tion [ˌbairəuˈteiʃən] *n.* 【物】变异旋光.
birr [bəː] *n.* ①冲力，动力；强调. ②飕飕声，呼呼声. — *vi.* 作飕飕声；飕飕(声中)移动.
Bir·rell [ˈbirəl] *n.* 比勒尔〔姓氏〕.
birth [bəːθ] *n.* ①出生，诞生；生产，分娩. ②出身，家系；血统；门第，家世. ③起源，开始. ④〔古〕产物，产儿. *the date of one's* ~ 生日. *a still [difficult]* ~ 死〔难〕产. *five young at a* ~ 一胎产五仔. *a person of* ~ *[of no* ~*]* 出身高贵〔卑微〕的人. *of Grecian* ~ 希腊血统. *new* ~ 再生，更生，复活，新生. *B- is much, but breeding is more.* 教养比门第更重要. *kill the cases at* ~ 防微杜渐. *the* ~ *of Protestentism* 新教的起源. **by** ~ ①血统，出生于. ②生来，天生是 (*She is French by* ~ *and British by marriage.* 她原是法国人，嫁给英国人就入英国籍了. *a musician by* ~ 天生的音乐家. *be a Parisian by* ~ 生在巴黎). **give** ~ **to** 生，产生，引起，使发生 (*give* ~ *to twin girls* 生下一对女双胞胎. *give* ~ *to a controversy* 引起一场争论. *This town gave* ~ *to many great men.* 该城出了很多伟人). ~ **control** 节(制生)育. (*~-control pill* 女用口服避孕药). **~day** 生日，诞辰，成立纪念日 (*a ~day book* 生日登记簿. *keep [observe] a* ~ 过生日. *a ~day gift* 生日礼品). **~day honours** 在英国国王〔女王〕诞辰授与的勋爵. **~day suit** ①英国国王〔女王〕诞辰穿的礼服. ②〔讽〕生来的衣裳，自己的皮肤，裸体. ~ **mark** ①痣；黑斑胎记. ②某人的特征. ~ **pangs** ①(分娩时的)阵痛. ②任何变化带来的困难或混乱. ~ **place** 出生地，故乡；发祥地，发源地. ~ **rate** 人口出生率. **~-right** ①与生俱来的权利. ②继承权〔尤指长子继承权〕(*sell one's ~right for a mess of pottage* 一碗肉粥卖掉长子继承权，因小失大). **~stone** 诞生石〔迷信与诞生月星座有关系的宝石，常带身边可得幸福. 如二月是 amethyst 紫水晶，4 月是 diamond 金刚石，6 月是 pearl 珍珠等〕.
birth·root [ˈbəːθˌruːt, -rut] *n.* 【植】延龄草属植物〔尤指直立延龄草〕.
birth·wort [ˈbəːθˌwəːt] *n.* 【植】马兜铃属植物.
BIS = Bank for International Settlements 国际清算银行.
bis [bis] *ad.* 〔L.〕二度，二回，重，又；【乐】重叠，重复. *page* 5 ~ 第 5 页的副页. — *inter.* 再来一个！再演〔唱〕一次！
B.I.S. = ①British Information Services 英国情报服务社. ②British Interplanetary Society 英国星际航行学会.
bis. = bissextile；【化】bismuth.
bis- *pref.* = bi-〔多用于 c 或 s 前，复杂的化学名词之前亦常用：*bis*sextile〕.
Bi·sa·yan [biˈsɑːjən] *n., a.* ①(菲律宾)米沙鄢群岛(的). ②米沙鄢人(的). ③米沙鄢语(的)(= Visayan).
Bis·cayne [bisˈkein, ˈbiskein] *n.* 比斯坎湾〔美国〕(= ~ Bay).
bis·cuit [ˈbiskit] *n.* ①饼干〔美国叫 cracker〕；〔美〕热松饼. ②饼干色，淡褐色. ③本色陶〔瓷〕器，素坯. *a ship's* ~ 硬面包. *take the* ~ 〔英俚〕屈居末座. ~ **hooks** 〔美俚〕拳头，手. ~ **shooter** 〔美俚〕女招待. ~ **ware** 本色陶器；充瓷器.
bise [biːz] *n.* ①北寒风〔瑞士、意大利及法国南部对农作物有害的干冷的北风或东北风〕. ②〔转义〕不幸，灾害.
bi·sect [baiˈsekt] *vt.* ①把…一分为二，二分，两分；平分；对开，对截；【数】二等分. ②与…相交叉，横切. ~ *a right angle* 将一个直角二等分. *the spot where the railroad tracks* ~ *the highway* 铁道与公路的交叉点. — *vi.* (道路等)分开，分叉.
bi·sec·tion [baiˈsekʃən] *n.* ①两断，两分；二等分，折半. ②【数】平分点，平分线. ③平分的两部分之一. ~ **theorem** 二等分定理，电路中分定理. **-al** *a.*
bi·sec·tor, bisec·trix [baiˈsektə, baiˈsektriks] *n.* ①【数】二等分线；平分面. ②二等分物.
bi·ser·rate [baiˈsereit, -it] *a.* ①【植】重锯齿的. ②【动】具二锯齿的.
bi·sex·u·al [ˈbaiˈseksjuəl] *a.* ①两性的. ②雌雄同体〔同株〕的. ③〔美俚〕(在性欲上)对男女两性都有兴趣的. — *n.* 【生】两性体. **-ism, -ity** *n.* 雌雄同体〔同株〕.
bish·op [ˈbiʃəp] *n.* ①(基督教的)主教；(佛教的)住持. ②(国际象棋中的)象〔棋子为教士帽形〕. ③香甜葡萄酒. **~'s lawn** 轧光细薄平布. **~'s length** 画布尺寸〔107×70 英寸〕.
bish·op·ric [ˈbiʃəprik] *n.* 主教(等)的职位〔管区〕.
bish·op's-cap [ˈbiʃəpsˌkæp] *n.* 哨呐草属植物.
bisk [bisk] *n.* 贝鸟汤〔贝类、鸡等煮成的浓羹〕.
Bis·ley [ˈbizli] *n.* (英国 Surrey 地方的)比兹利打靶场；比兹利打靶比赛会.
Bis·marck [ˈbizmɑːk] *n.* ①**Ot·to von** ~ [ˈɔːtəu fən] 俾斯麦〔1815—1898，德国政治家，德意志帝国第一任首相〕. ②俾斯麦群岛〔在太平洋西南部，新几内亚东北〕.
Bis·mil·lah [bisˈmilə] *int.* 以真主的名义！〔穆斯林誓语〕.
bis·muth [ˈbizməθ] *n.* 【化】铋〔略作 Bi〕. ~ **ocher** 铋华，赭铋矿.
bis·mu·thic [ˈbizməθik, bizˈmjuːθik] *a.* 【化】含(五价)铋的.
bis·muth·ous [ˈbizməθəs] *a.* 【化】含(三价)铋的.
bi·son [ˈbaisn] *n.* (*pl.* ~) 【动】北美野牛，犎牛.
Bis·pham [ˈbisfəm] *n.* 比斯法姆〔姓氏〕.
bisque[1] [bisk] *n.* ①(人像等的)本色陶器，素瓷. ②黄褐色. — *a.* 黄褐色的.
bisque[2] [bisk] *n.* (网球等)比赛中让给弱方的 1 分.
bisque[3] [bisk] *n.* = bisk.
Bis·sau, Bissão [biˈsau] *n.* 比绍〔几内亚(比绍)首都〕.
bis·sex·tile [biˈsekstail] *n.* 【天】闰，闰年. — *a.* (有)闰年〔日〕的. *The years 1960 and 1964 were both* ~. 1960 和 1964 年都是闰年.
bi·sta·ble [baiˈsteibl] *n., a.* 【物】双稳定(的)，双稳态(的).
bis·ter [ˈbistə] *n.* 〔美〕= bistre.
bis·tort [ˈbistəːt] *n.* 【植】拳参.
bis·tou·ry [ˈbisturi] *n.* (外科用的)柳叶刀.
bis·tre [ˈbistə] *n.* ①(由木煤烟中提出、多作底色用的)褐色颜料. ②黄褐色. — *a.* 黄褐色的.
bis·tro [ˈbistrəu] *n.* 〔口〕小咖啡馆；小酒馆；小夜总会.
bi·sul·cate [baiˈsʌlkeit] *a.* ①有两沟的. ②【动】偶蹄的；分趾蹄的.
bi·sul·phate, bi·sul·fate [baiˈsʌlfeit] *n.* 【化】酸式硫酸盐，硫酸氢盐.
bi·sul·phide, bi·sul·fide [baiˈsʌlfaid] *n.* 【化】二硫化物.
bi·sul·phite, bi·sul·fite [baiˈsʌlfait] *n.* 【化】亚硫酸

氢盐；酸式亚硫酸盐．

bit [bit] *n.* ①少许，一点儿，一些；(食物的)一口，少量食物；〔*pl.*〕吃剩的食物；小片．②〔口〕一会儿，一转眼；短时间．③〔英〕小银币，小铜币；〔美口〕十二分半．④(戏里的)小角色；(电影、戏剧)一小段；(书)一小节．⑤〔俚〕小姑娘，少女；女人．⑥〔美〕表演，演奏；例行节目；〔转义〕老一套．⑦【计】毕特〔二进位制信息单位〕；位，数位；环节．⑧〔美俚〕刑期．*a ~ of chalk* 一点儿粉笔．*exchange ~s of gossip* 闲聊几句．*bite [tear] sth. into ~s* 咬[撕]碎．*wait a ~* 等一下，等一会儿．*I was in India for a ~* 我在印度作短期逗留．*six ~s* (美元)七角五分．*a twopenny ~* 一枚两便士铜币．*make a supper from the ~s* 把上顿剩下的菜又当晚饭．***a ~*** 有点儿〔作状语用〕(*I was a ~ impatient.* 我有点不耐烦了)．***a ~ and a sup*** 一点儿吃喝．***a ~ of*** 一点儿，少量的 (*a ~ of land* 一小块地．*Have a ~ of patience.* 请忍耐一下．*get a ~ of rest* 休息片刻)．***a ~ of a ...*** 有点儿…的味道，多少有些… (*a ~ of a girl* 有点儿象女孩子．*a ~ of a snob* 有点儿势利的味道．*I am a ~ of a reader myself.* 我自己好歹也是个读者)．***a ~ of all right*** 〔口〕无可挑剔的人[物]；美丽[可爱]的女人．***a ~ of blood*** 纯血种(的马)．***a dainty ~*** 一口好吃的东西．***a good ~*** 〔俚〕相当长久．***a long [short] ~*** 〔美俚〕一角五分 [一角]钱．***a nice ~ of*** (*money*)〔俚〕很多(钱)．***at the ~*** 〔Scot.〕适当其时．***~ by ~*** 一点一点地；渐次．***~ of business*** 〔俚〕人；家伙．***~ of stuff*** 〔俚〕(俗气的)女子．***~s and pieces*** 零星小玩意，杂物．***by ~s = ~ by ~***．***do one's ~*** 应尽一臂之力；尽自己本分．***every ~*** 由任何一点看；完全 (*He is every ~ a scholar of him.* = *He is a scholar, every ~ of him.* 他是一个地道的学者)．***give (sb.) a ~ of one's mind*** 直说；面责．***not a ~ (of it)*** 一点没有，一点也不 (*I don't mind a ~.* 毫无关系，我根本不放在心上．*O no, not a ~* 啊不，没关系〔对别人向自己道歉的回答〕)．***pull to ~s*** ①把…撕成碎片．②把…贬得一文不值．***quite a ~*** 〔美俚〕相当多，相当．

bit² [bit] *n.* ①马衔，(马的)咬嘴，嚼子．②约束，抑制．③(斧等的)刃口，(工具上的)切削刃；刀头，刀片；钻头；锥，凿子；钥匙齿．*jack ~* 岩心钻头．*finishing ~* (车工)光刀刀头．*a drill ~* 钻头(尖)．***draw ~*** 勒马；勒着，减缓速度．***take [get] the ~ between [in] the [one's] teeth*** (马)不服管；(人)不肯受约束，反抗．***take the ~s*** (马张嘴)接受上嚼子．— *vt.* ①给(马)上嚼子；使(马)习惯于上嚼子．②约束，抑制，勒着．③给(钥匙)锉齿．

bit³ [bit] bite 的过去式及过去分词．

bi·tar·trate [baiˈtɑːtreit] *n.*【化】酒石酸氢盐，酒石酸氢酯．

bitch [bitʃ] *n.* ①母狗 [母狼等]．②〔俚〕娼妇；淫妇；泼妇．③〔美俚〕【牌】黑桃女王．④牢骚；弯扭事．*a ~ fox* 雌狐．*The test was a ~.* 那个实验真弯扭．***make a ~ of*** 〔口〕弄糟，弄坏．***son of a ~*** 〔骂人语〕狗养的〔略作 s.o.b.〕— *vi.* 〔美俚〕发牢骚，埋怨．— *vt.* ①弄糟，弄坏．②对…不满．③欺骗．***~ up*** 〔俚〕弄糟，弄坏．**~ goddess** 发财，致富 (*worship the ~ goddess* 追求金钱)．**-y** *a.*

bite [bait] *vt.* (*bit* [bit]; *bit·ten* [bitn], *bit*) ①咬；咬住；咬掉 (*off*)；(蚊、蚤等)叮，螫，刺．②(胡椒等)辣(鼻)；(利器等)刺穿；(寒风等)刺痛；(霜等)把…冻伤．③(酸等)腐蚀，侵蚀．④(锚、齿轮等)吃住，咬住；紧抓住．⑤〔口〕欺骗；使恼怒；〔美俚〕偷．*A dog bit him on his arm.* 狗咬了他的手臂．*The file ~s the metal.* 锉刀锉得深．*Nitric acid ~s copper.* 硝酸能腐蚀铜．*The anchor ~s the ground.* 锚勾住海底．*an icy wind that ~s our face* 刺面的寒风．*She ~d me for a new coat.* 她骗我给她买件皮大衣．*I got bitten in a mail-order swindle.* 我在一场邮购骗局中上了当．*What's bitting you?* 什么事让你这么生气？— *vi.* ①咬，咬着；喜欢咬人．②刺痛；辣；腐蚀．③刺穿．④固着，咬住，把住，紧抓住．⑤(鱼)吞饵，上钩；受骗，上当．*This mustard does not ~ much.* 这种芥末不很辣．*The fish were biting well yesterday.* 昨天鱼上钩不少．*Does your parrot ~?* 你养的八哥啄人吗？*The dog may ~ at you.* 狗会咬你的．*The screw ~s.* 螺丝钉钉得牢．***be bitten with*** 感染，被沾染上，害(疮等)；迷上．***~ at*** ①要咬…，向…咬去．②对…叫骂．***~ back*** (咬住嘴唇)不说出来．***~ in [into]*** 腐蚀；侵入．***~ off [away]*** ①咬下，咬掉．②停止讲话．③(广播中)截断(节目)．***~ off a big chunk*** 〔美俚〕承担难事．***~ off more than one can chew*** 贪多嚼不烂，担任自己不胜任的事．***~ off one's own head*** 害人不到反害己．***~ one's lips*** 压制着感情，忍怒；保持沉默．***~ one's nails*** 咬指甲〔表示妒忌〕．***~ one's thumb at*** 向…挑战，侮辱．***~ on granite*** 做徒劳无益的事．***~ the bullet*** 硬着头皮；咬紧牙关；死撑硬顶．***~ the dust [ground]*** 倒在地上；阵亡，倒毙；败，一败涂地；〔美俚〕死，被杀，破产，失败．***~ the hand that feeds one*** 恩将仇报，以怨报德．***~ the tongue [off]*** 咬着舌头；保持沉默．***Once ~ [bitten], twice shy.*** 一朝被蛇咬，十年怕草绳．— *n.* ①咬，叮，螫；紧咬；穿透力．②一小口(食物)，少量(食物)；〔口〕便餐．③咬伤，螫伤；冻伤；腐蚀；伤口；(伤口等的)疼痛，刺痛，苦痛．④辛辣，刺激性．⑤受骗，上当；(鱼)上钩．⑥【机】啮合．⑦【医】上下齿的啮合情况；(锯、锉等的)齿；切削刀头．⑧〔美口〕(捐税等一次次收取的)一笔．*I have not taken a ~ all day.* 我整天没有吃一点东西．*a screw with a good ~* 螺丝咬得紧．*give a ~ at the bone* 啃骨头．*a deep ~* 很深的伤口．*The air had a frosty ~.* 寒气袭人．*The ~ of the original* 原作的强烈风味．*whisky with a ~ in it* 辣嘴的威士忌酒．***(a) ~ and (a) sup*** 饮食；便餐．***put the ~ on*** 〔美俚〕向…借钱；向…敲竹杠．***take [make] two ~s at [of] a cherry*** ①匀分微不足道的东西；零敲碎打地搞，把(原可一气做完的)小事情分数次做．②踌躇；拘谨．

bit·er [ˈbaitə] *n.* ①辣嘴的东西，咬人的动物；上钩的鱼．②骗子．*That monkey is a ~.* 那只猴子咬人．***The ~ (is) bit [bitten].*** 骗人者反被人骗，害人反害己．***Great barkers are no ~s.*** 会叫的狗不咬人．

bit·ing [ˈbaitiŋ] *a.* ①辛辣的，刺激性的；讥刺的．②锐利的，刺痛的；腐蚀性的．*~ cold* 刺骨的寒冷．*a ~ caricature* 辛辣的漫画．**-ly** *ad.*

bit·stock [ˈbitˌstɔk] *n.* 钻柄．

bitt [bit] *n.* 〔常 *pl.*〕【海】(系)缆柱．— *vt.* 把(缆)系在缆柱上．

bit·ten [ˈbitn] bite 的过去分词．

bit·ter [ˈbitə] *a.* ①(药等)苦．②严(寒)，烈(风)，厉害的；辛苦的，悲惨的．③怀恨的；抱怨的；讥刺的．*~ tincture* 苦味药酒．*~ tears* 辛酸的眼泪．*a ~ experience* 惨痛的经验．*a ~ winter* 严冬．*~ hatred* 刻骨仇恨．*have a ~ tongue* 刻薄嘴．*~ remarks* 刻薄话，恶毒的话．*~ discipline* 严格的训练．*~ enemy* 死敌，活冤家死对头．***be ~ against*** 激烈反对．***to the ~ end*** 坚持到底；拚命，直到死而后已 (*fight to the ~ end* 血战到底)．— *n.* ①苦，苦味；苦味物．②〔常 *pl.*〕苦味药；苦味大补酒；(某些鸡尾酒的)配料；〔英〕苦啤酒．*the sweets and ~s of life* 人世间的悲欢．***get one's ~s*** 〔美口〕遭天罚，报应．— *ad.* 非常，剧烈，厉害．*a ~ cold night* 酷寒的夜晚．— *vt.* 把…弄苦，使变苦．*herbs employed to ~ vermouth* 用于给苦艾酒加苦味的药草．— *vi.* 变苦．**~ cup** 苦木杯．**~ end**【海】①索端．②锚链末端．**~-ender** 〔美俚〕坚持不屈的人，顽抗到底的人．**~-enderism** 〔美俚〕顽抗主义．**~ lake** 盐湖．**~nut** 心果山核桃．**~root** 一种马齿苋．**~ rot** 植物炭疽病．**~-sweet** ① *a.* 又苦又甜的；稍带苦笑的 (*a ~-sweet memory* 甜蜜而又辛酸的回忆)．② *n.* 又苦又甜的东西；【植】南蛇藤．**~weed** 苦味植物〔如美洲豚草、堆心菊、珠

蓍等〕.

bit·ter·ish [ˈbitəriʃ] *a.* 微苦的,带苦味的.

bit·ter·ly [ˈbitəli] *ad.* ①苦,惨痛地. ②剧烈,酷,厉害地. *cry* ~ 痛哭.

bit·tern[1] [ˈbitə(:)n] *n.*【鸟】麻鳽.

bit·tern[2] [ˈbitə(:)n] *n.* ①盐卤,卤汁. ②(搀啤酒的)酒花汁.

bit·ter·ness [ˈbitənis] *n.* ①苦味. ②苦难;悲哀. ③酷烈. ④讥刺.

bitts [bits] *n.*〔*pl.*〕【船】系柱.

bit·ty [biti] *a.*〔谑、儿〕小.

bit·u·lith·ic [ˌbitjuˈliθik] *a.* 沥青混凝土的. — *n.* 沥青混凝土路.

bit·u·men [ˈbitjumin; Am. biˈtju:min] *n.* ①【矿】沥青,沥青质. ②〔澳口〕柏油路.

bi·tu·mi·nite [biˈtju:minait] *n.*【矿】①烟煤,沥青煤. ②(芽胞)油页岩.

bi·tu·mi·nize [biˈtju:minaiz] *vt.* ①使成沥青. ②使与沥青混合.

bi·tu·mi·nous [biˈtju:minəs] *a.* 沥青的,含沥青的. ~ *coal* 烟煤. ~ *grout* 含沥青溶液,水沥青.

bi·u·nique [ˈbaiju(:)ˌni:k] *a.*【数】一对一的(关系).

bi·u·ret [ˌbaijuˈret] *n.*【生化】缩二脲.

bi·va·lence [ˈbaiˌveiləns, ˈbivə-] *n.*【化】双化合价,双原子价,二价(= bivalency).

bi·va·lent [ˈbaiˌveilənt] *a.* ①【化】二价的. ②【生】二价染色体的. ~ *chromosome* 二价染色体. — *n.*【生】二价染色体.

bi·valve [ˈbaivælv] *a.*【植】有两瓣的;【动】有双壳的. — *n.*【动】双壳贝;牡蛎.

bi·valved [ˈbaivælvd], **bi·val·vu·lar** [baiˈvælvjulə] *a.* = bivalve.

bi·vi·nyl [baiˈvainil] *n.*【化】丁(间)二烯.

biv·ou·ac [ˈbivuæk] *n.* 露营,野营;露营地. — *vi.* (***biv·ou·acked; biv·ou·ack·ing***) 露营,露宿.

bi·week·ly [ˈbaiˈwi:kli] *a.* ①二周一次的. ②每二周的. — *ad.* ①二周一次. ②每周两次. — *n.* ①双周刊. ②半周刊.

bi·year·ly [baiˈjiəli] *a.* ①两年一次的. ②一年两次的. — *ad.* 两年一次. ②一年两次.

biz [biz] *n.*〔俚〕= business. ~ **confab**〔美俚〕商量.

bi·zad [ˈbizæd] *n.*〔美俚〕商业管理科;商业管理科学生.

bi·zarre [biˈzɑ:] *a.*〔F.〕希奇古怪的,不同寻常的. ~ *clothing* 奇装异服. *The story has a certain* ~ *interest.* 这个故事听起来别有风味.

bi·zar·re·rie [biˈzɑ:rəri] *n.*〔F.〕希奇古怪,奇异;奇怪的东西.

Bi·zer·te [biˈzə:t], **Bi·zer·ta** [biˈzə:tə] *n.* 比塞大〔突尼斯港市〕.

bi·zon·al [baiˈzəunl] *a.* 两国共管区的,与两国共管区有关的.

BK =【化】berkelium.

BK. =【棒球】balks.

bk. = bank; bark; block; book.

bkg. = banking.

bkrpt. = bankrupt.

bkry. = bakery.

bkt. = basket.

B.L. = Bachelor of laws.

B/L = bill of lading 提(货)单.

blaa [blɑ:] *int., n.* = blah.

blab [blæb] *vt.* 泄漏(秘密等). *She blabbed my confidences to everyone.* 她把我的隐私逢人便讲. — *vi.* 乱说乱讲. *Don't confide in him, because he* ~*s.* 不要对他推心置腹,他喜欢乱讲话. — *n.* ①泄漏秘密者;喜欢乱说乱讲的人,搬弄是非者. ②乱说乱讲. *These stories are false, just so much* ~. 那些故事都是假的,全是一派胡言.

blab·ber [ˈblæbə] *n.* 饶舌者;泄露秘密者.

blab·ber·mouth [ˈblæbəmauθ] *n.*〔口〕碎嘴子.

Black [blæk] *n.* 布莱克〔姓氏〕.

black [blæk] *a.* ①黑,黑色的. ②暗的;黑暗的. ③皮肤黑的;黑种人的,有关黑人的. ④(教士等)穿黑衣的. ⑤污染的,(手等)弄脏了的;丢脸的. ⑥阴郁的,忧郁的;发着脾气的,怒冲冲的. ⑦(前途)暗淡的,有凶兆的,不吉利的;邪恶的. ⑧黑市的,非法买卖的. ⑨(土地)被荒废的;(咖啡)不加糖的;(钢材等)未加工的. ⑩〔英〕被(罢工工人)抵制装卸的. ⑪〔美口〕纯粹的,完全的,极度的. ~ *clouds* 黑云. *The street was* ~ *with people.* 街上黑压压的一片人群. *the* ~ *knight* 黑衣骑士. *a* ~ *night* 黑夜. *Things look* ~. 事态险恶,趋势恶劣. *be* ~ *with rage* 愤怒得脸色发紫. *give sb. a* ~ *look* 对人板面孔. *He is not so* ~ *as he is painted.* 他不象传说的那样坏. *a* ~ *heart* 黑心肠(的人). *a* ~ *villian* 大坏蛋,恶棍. ~ *areas of drougt* 荒废的干旱地带. *half* ~ 半加工的,半处理的. ~ *in the face* 脸色发紫. *be beaten* ~ *and blue* 被打得青一块紫一块. ~ *darkness* 漆黑一团. ~ *day* 凶日. ~ *despair* 大失所望. ~ *diamond* 黑金刚石;〔*pl.*〕煤炭. ~ *earth* 黑钙土. *B- English* 黑人英语. ~ *flag* 海盗旗;(处决人犯时用的)死刑旗. ~ *frost* 严霜. ~ *gang*【海】火夫,轮机人员. ~ *ingratitude* 极端的忘恩负义. ~ *words* 不吉利的话. ~ **art** 魔术;妖术. ~ ***dog*** 忧郁,不开心 (*be under the* ~ *dog* 绷着脸,皱着眉头). ~ ***eye*** 眼珠乌黑的眼;眼眶周围被打伤的紫斑.〔喻〕耻辱. ***paint sb.*** ~把某人描写成坏人. ***say*** ~ ***in sb.'s eye*** 非难,谴责. — *n.* ①黑,黑色. ②黑色染料,黑色颜料,黑色墨水. ③黑人. ④黑衣;丧服. ⑤黑斑;污点;煤;(靶子等的)黑点. ⑥黑马. ~ ***or white*** 非此即彼的,不是黑就是白,走极端. ***in the*** ~ 出现黑字,赚钱 (*opp.* in the red). ***put the*** ~ ***on*** 〔卑〕输. ***talk*** ~ ***into white*** = ***prove that*** ~ ***is white*** 认黑作白,指鹿为马,诡辩. — *vt.* 把…弄黑;把(鞋等)搽黑;弄脏,染污. — *vi.* 变黑,成黑色. ~ ***down*** 用柏油涂黑船具. ~ ***out*** ①用墨涂掉,抹杀;使停刊;封锁(新闻). ②【剧】使舞台转暗;【空】(空袭时)熄灯;(战时)实行灯火管制. ③(飞机等急降时)眼睛发黑,头发昏;【无】干扰. ~ ***and tan*** *a.* ①脊黑.头足茶褐色的〔指一种犬〕. ②〔常 B- and T-〕拥护〔实行〕黑人和白人在政治上按比例选举代表的. ③(夜总会等)黑人和白人都常去的. *n.*④(脊黑,头足茶褐色的)猨犬. ⑤黑人和白人都常去的夜总会. ~ ***and white*** ①白纸黑字;书写品;印刷品,黑白版钢笔画 (*have (something down) in* ~ *and white* 写下来,印下来). ②用墨水(在白纸上)写的;黑白的,未着色的,印刷的. ③黑白电影. ~**ball** ①*vt.* 投黑球(反对). ②*vt.* 开除…的会籍,排斥. ③*n.* 黑球〔表示反对的投票〕. ~**beetle** 蟑螂,飞蠊. **B- Belt** (美国)黑人聚居地带;黑土带〔美国亚拉巴马及密西西比河沿岸棉花产区〕;(日本柔道协会标志)黑带. ~**berry** ①*n.*【植】黑莓. (*plentiful as* ~*berries* 俯拾即是). ②*vi.* 采黑莓 (*go* ~*berrying* 去采黑莓). ~**bird**〔英〕画眉;〔美〕燕八哥;〔澳〕(被诱卖异乡的)黑人. ~**birding**(殖民主义者的)贩奴活动. ~**board** 黑板. ~**board jungle** 黑板丛林〔秩序混乱、无法无天的市区学校〕;学校中混乱的状况. ~ **body**【物】黑体〔指能全部吸收电磁辐射而毫无反应的一种理想物体〕. ~ **book** ①黑名单. ②学生记过簿;黑皮书. ③巫术书 (*be in sb's* ~ *book* 得罪了某人). ~ **bottle** 黑药(尤指三氯乙醛). ~**-browed** *a.* 愁眉苦脸的,阴郁的,凄凉的. ~ **box**〔美俚〕①黑箱〔复杂电子仪器〕. ②律师. ③(装在飞机上记录飞行情况等的)密封仪器. ④【自】未知框〔指内部特性未输出的框图等〕. ⑤整体装拆自动电子元件. ~ **bourse** 黑市. ~**cap** ①【鸟】〔欧〕莺类;〔美〕白鹡鸟. ②【植】(美国)糙莓. ③〔英〕(宣判死刑时法官所戴的)黑色法官帽. ~ **capitalism**〔美〕黑人资本主义〔黑人资本家拥有和经营私人企业〕. ~ **cattle** (苏格兰及威尔士出产的)肉用牛. ~**coat**〔贬〕僧侣,牧师;〔英〕职员,领薪阶层. ~**cock**【鸟】黑色公松鸡. ~ **comedy** 黑色喜剧〔一种现代派剧作,其幽默源于荒唐、怪诞的场面〕. ~ **coffee**(不加牛奶和糖的)浓咖啡. ~ **crop** (对麦类而言的)豆类作物. ~ **copper**【冶】粗铜. **B- Country** 黑乡〔英国中部煤铁产区〕. ~ **damp** 矿井内的窒息性空气. ~ **death** 黑死病. ~ **draught** (泻叶与泻盐泡成的)泻药. ~**-eyed** *a.* 黑眼睛的;(被打得)眼圈发青的. ~**face** ①黑面羊;黑面兽. ②装扮成黑人的演员. ③【印】粗黑体活字. ~**-faced** *a.* ①脸黑的;愁眉苦脸的,忧郁的. ②【印】粗黑体的. ~**-fellow** 澳洲本地人. ~**fin** 黑鳍笛鲷;黑鳍白鲑. ~**-fish** 黑鱼类;巨头鲸;刚产卵后的鲑. ~ **fly** 蚋. ~**foot** ①〔Scot.〕中人,媒人. ②〔B-〕美洲印第安人的一族. **B- Forest** 黑林〔德国西南部森林地带〕. ~ **game**【鸟】(欧洲)松鸡. **B- Hand** 黑手党〔本世纪初纽约一个诈骗犯罪集团〕;秘密犯罪集团. ~**head**【鸟】黑头鸟;〔美〕黑头白胸鸭;【医】黑头面疱〔粉刺〕. ~**heart** ①心形黑樱桃. ②(植物的)黑心病. ~**-hearted** *a.* 黑心肠的,心毒的;罪大恶极的. ~ **hole** ①【天】黑洞〔假设存在于太空中的有巨大引力的洞穴,为天体坍陷所形成〕. ②土牢;(军营中的)禁闭室. ~ **humour** 黑色幽默〔采用荒谬、怪诞、可怕场面的幽默文艺形式〕. ~ **ink**〔美〕黑字,贷方. ~**jack** ①*n.*(外涂柏油的革制)大酒杯;海盗旗;〔美〕(铅头)皮棍棒;【矿】方锌矿;【植】槲属;【牌】二十一点. ②*vt.*〔美〕拿铅头皮棍棒打. ~ **law** 关于黑人的法律. ~ **lead**【矿】石墨,笔铅. ~**lead** *vt.* 在…上涂黑铅;用黑铅磨. ~**leg** ①假赌徒,骗子;(破坏罢工的)工贼. ②【兽医】炭疽热;【植】黑胫病,甜菜蛇眼病. **B- Legion** 黑党〔美国一恐怖团体〕. ~ **letter**【印】黑体字. ~**-letter** *a.* ①黑体字的. ②不吉利的,倒霉的(*a ~ letter day* 凶日,倒霉的日子). ~ **light**【物】不可见光. ~**list** ①*n.* 黑名单. ②*vt.* 把…记入黑名单. ~ **lung** 黑肺病. ~**mail** ①*n.* 勒索,敲诈,讹诈;〔古英〕(盗匪征收的)保护费,免抢税(*nuclear ~* 核讹诈). ②*vt.* 勒索,敲诈,讹诈. ~**mailer** 勒索者,敲诈钱财的人. **b-man** ①= negro. ②〔B- M-〕恶魔. **B- Maria** ①〔口〕警察局的囚车. ②〔俚〕黑烟榴弹. ~ **mark** 黑点〔学生品行不良的记载〕. ~ **market** 黑市. ~**market** ①*vi.* 做黑市交易. ②*vt.* 在黑市上卖. **B- Mass** ①(天主教的)安魂弥撒. ②(异教徒的)恶魔崇拜. **B- Monday** ①复活节后的第一个礼拜一. ②〔学俚〕开学后的第一个礼拜一. ~ **money** 黑钱〔没有报税的收入〕. **B-Muslim** (美国)黑人穆斯林运动的成员. ~ **nationalism** 黑人民族主义. ~**out** ①*n.*【剧】舞台转暗;关灯;闭火;断电;(战时的)灯火管制;【空】(急降等时)眼睛发黑,突然发昏;暂时失去知觉;删除;(新闻)封锁;(广播等)停止. ②*a.* 防空袭的,灯火管制的(*~ curtains* 遮灯防空窗帘). **B- Panther** (美国黑人)黑豹党的成员. ~**poll**【鸟】黑头森莺. ~ **power** (美国) 黑人权力. ~ **pudding** 血(香)肠. ~ **race** 黑种人. **B- Radio** (心理战中)一方冒充另一方的电台广播. **B- Rod** 黑仗侍卫〔英国上院的侍卫〕. ~ **rot**【植】黑斑病. ~ **rust**【植】黑锈病. ~ **sand** 黑砂〔含有砂金的砂〕. **B- Sea** 黑海. **B- Shirt** 黑衫党〔前意大利法西斯组织〕;希特勒警卫队;法西斯分子. ~ **sheep** 害群之马;败家子;恶棍. ~**smith** 铁匠,锻工. ~**snake** ①黑蛇. ②〔美〕重皮鞭. ~ **stem rust**【植】杆锈病. ~**strap** ①混合酒. ②〔俚〕劣质葡萄酒. ③糖渣. ④〔美俚〕咖啡. **B- Stream** 黑潮,日本海流. ~ **studies** (美国)黑人文化研究. ~ **tea** 红茶. ~ **terror** 黑人拳击选手. ~**thorn** ①【植】黑刺李,〔美〕山楂属. ②〔爱〕用刺李木材做的手杖(*the ~ thorn winter* 刺李花开的冬天〔吹西北风的寒冷天气〕). ~ **tie** ①(穿无燕尾礼服所戴的)黑蝴蝶领结. ②晚会男礼服. ~**-tie** *a.* (晚会)要求穿男礼服的. ~**top** ①*n.* 沥青路面. ②*vt.* 用沥青铺(路面). ~ **vomit** ①黄热病. ②黄热病末期的呕吐物. ~ **water**〔美〕黑水州〔尼布拉斯加州的别名〕. ~**water fever** 黑水热〔热带病〕. ~ **widow** ①(交媾后就吃掉雄性的)有毒黑蜘蛛. ②(美国)"黑寡妇"式夜间战斗机. ~ **wood** 黑木相思树;黑檀.

black-a-moor [ˈblækəmuə] *n.*〔蔑〕黑种人,黑色的人.

black·a·vised [ˈblækəvaist, ˈblækəvaizd] *a.*〔古〕脸黑的,黑色的.

black·en [ˈblækən] *vt.* ①使黑,使暗. ②中伤(名誉等),诽谤. — *vi.* 变黑,变暗.

black·en·ing [ˈblækəniŋ] *n.* ①变黑;上黑;致黑;【机】发黑处理;发黑度. ②黑色涂料〔染料〕;炭粉〔铸造用〕.

Black·ett [ˈblækit] *n.* 布莱基特〔姓氏〕.

black·guard [ˈblægɑːd] *n.* ①下流人,流氓,恶棍. ②满口脏话的人,爱骂人者. — *a.* 粗鄙的,下流的,嘴臭的. — *vt.* 用脏话骂(人). ***The pot is ~ing the kettle.***〔谚〕乌鸦笑猪黑,流氓骂恶棍. **-ism** *n.* ①粗鄙,下流,恶棍行为. ②说脏话;乱骂人. **-ly** *a.* 粗鄙的,下流的;恶棍式的(*use ~ language* 口出不逊,使用下流语言).

black·ing [ˈblækiŋ] *n.* 黑色涂料;黑鞋油;炭粉. *put shoe ~ on* 给…上黑鞋油.

black·ish [ˈblækiʃ] *a.* 稍黑的,带黑色的.

black·ly [ˈblækli] *ad.* ①黑;暗. ②阴郁地,愤怒地. ③阴险地,残忍地,邪恶地. *a plot ~ contrived to wreak vengeance* 一项阴险的复仇计划.

Black·more [ˈblækmɔː] *n.* 布莱克莫尔〔姓氏〕.

black·ness [ˈblæknis] *n.* ①黑,黑色. ②阴郁. ③阴险,凶恶.

Black·wood [ˈblækwud] *n.* 布莱克伍德〔姓氏〕.

black·y [ˈblæki] *n.*〔蔑〕黑人;黑鸟;黑兽.

blad·der [ˈblædə] *n.* ①【解】膀胱;泡;囊. ②(球等的)胆,救生圈,气球;囊状物. ③趾高气扬的人;吹牛的人. ~**nose**【动】冠海豹(= hooded seal). ~**nut**【植】省沽油属植物(的荚). ~ **worm** 囊尾蚴(= cysticercus). ~**-wort** *n.*【植】狸藻.

blad·der·y [ˈblædəri] *a.* ①膀胱状的,囊状的. ②有气泡的.

blade [bleid] *n.* ①(谷、草等的)叶片,叶身,叶. ②刀片;(安全)剃刀刀片(= razor ~);刀口,刃;刀,剑;击剑师,剑术家. ③桨叶;(推进器的)翼;击球板;肩胛骨;【语音】舌的前部,舌面. ④浮华少年;蛮横任性的人. *a single ~ of grass* 一片草叶,未吐穗. *a gay ~ from the nearly* 从邻区来的浮华子弟. *He is a good ~.* 他刀法〔剑术〕很高. ***in the ~*** 正在长叶子,尚未吐穗. ~**-bone**【解】肩胛骨. ~**smith** 刀剑匠.

blad·ed [ˈbleidid] *a.* 有…叶片的;有…刀〔剑〕身的.

blae·ber·ry [ˈbleibəri] *n.*〔北英〕= bilberry.

Blagoveshchensk [ˌblɑːgəˈveʃtʃensk] *n.* 布拉戈维申斯克〔即海兰泡,苏联城市〕.

blague [blɑːg] *n.*〔F.〕吹牛,撒谎;愚弄,恶作剧.

blah [blɑː] *int.*〔美俚〕瞎说!胡扯!废话! — *n.* 浮夸的文章,胡扯,瞎淡. — *a.* 无聊的,枯燥无味的. *That's ~.*〔美〕那是骗人的,靠不住的呀. *What they say is ~.* 他们说的全是废话.

blain [blein] *n.*【医】脓泡,水泡;【兽医】炭疽.

Blaine [blein] *n.* 布莱恩〔姓氏,男子名〕.

Blair [blɛə] *n.* 布莱尔〔姓氏,男子名〕.

Blake [bleik] *n.* ①布莱克〔姓氏〕. ② **William ~** 布莱克〔1757—1827,英国漫画家,诗人〕.

blam·a·ble [ˈbleiməble] *a.* 该责备的,有过失的.

blam·a·bly [ˈbleiməbli] *ad.* 该责备地,有过失地.

blame [bleim] *n.* ①责怪,责备,非难,指责;挑剔;谴责. ②过失,过错,罪,咎;责;责任. ***bear [take] the ~*** 负责,承担责任,背过. ***in ~ of*** 责备…. ***incur great ~ for*** 为…大受责备. ***lay the ~ at the door of another*** 把责任推到别人头上. ***lay [cast] the ~ on [upon] sb. for*** 把…推在某人身上,使某人负…之责. ***It is small ~ to sb. that*** … (发生了)…也不能多怪某人. —*vt.* ①责备,谴责,非难,挑剔. ②把…归咎于,把怪在…头上(*on; upon*). ③〔美俚〕〔诅咒语〕= damn. *B- it!*〔美俚〕

该死! 去你的! *You ~ it on society.* 这是社会的责任. *be ~d for ...* 为(某事)受责备. *B- if I do [don't] = I'm ~d if I do [don't].* 我决不…,死也不…[一定要…,非得…不可]. *B- my hide if I go.* 我决不去. ***be to ~*** 该负责,应受责 (*I am to ~ for it.* 我该负责,是我不对).

blamed [bleimd] *a.* 〔美俚〕该死的,可恶的,混蛋的. *(I'm) ~ if ...* 〔见 blame 条〕. *The ~ car won't start.* 这辆该死的车发动不起来. *I have a pain in every ~ joint.* 每一个讨厌的关节都有点儿痛. — *ad.* 〔美方〕非常,很. *The pistol looked so ~ dangerous.* 这支手枪看着挺危险. *It's ~ cold out tonight.* 今天晚上怪冷的.

blame·ful [ˈbleimful] *a.* 该责备的;有过错的. **-ly** *ad.*

blame·less [ˈbleimlis] *a.* 无可责难的,无罪的,无过失的. *a ~ child* 没有过失的乖孩子. *lead a ~ life* 生活正派. **-ly** *ad.* **-ness** *n.*

blame·wor·thy [ˈbleimˌwəːði] *a.* 该责备的,有罪的,有过失的. *a ~ administration* 弊政.

blanch [blɑːntʃ] *vt.* ①【化】漂白,使变白. ②遮断日光使(植物)变苍白. ③使(面色)变苍白;【烹】(用沸水)煮白;烫去(杏仁等的)皮. ④在(金属)上镀锡,酸洗(金属)使变白. — *vi.* 发白;变白;(面色)变苍白. ~ ***over*** 粉饰.

Blanche [blɑːntʃ] *n.* 布兰奇〔女子名〕.

blanc-mange [bləˈmɔnʒ] *n.* 牛奶冻〔用牛奶、蛋、糖、玉米粉等做成的胶状甜食〕.

bland [blænd] *a.* ①(态度等)温和的,柔和的. ②平淡无味的. ③(药等)刺激性少的,纯和的;(烟等)味醇的. ④不动感情的,无动于衷的. **-ly** *ad.* **-ness** *n.*

blan·dish [ˈblændiʃ] *vt., vi.* 谄媚,奉承,讨好. *~ sb. into ...* 奉承某人使做某事. **-ment** *n.* 〔常 *pl.*〕奉承,讨好卖乖(*threats and -ments* 又吓又哄).

blank [blæŋk] *a.* ①(表格等)空白的,(纸等)无字的;空着的;【商】(支票等)不记名的. ②(子弹等)空的,(精神等)空虚的;(努力等)无效果的;(年成等)饥荒的;无聊的,单调的;(诗等)没有韵的. ③苍白的,失色的;发呆的,呆呆的,无表情的,漠然的. ④无齿的,无槽的,无纹的. ⑤完全的,纯粹的. *a ~ space* 空白,空处;空地. *a ~ map* 轮廓地图,白地图. *a ~ wall* 无修饰的墙,空墙. *a ~ existence* 空虚的生活. *a ~ mind* 心不在焉. *~ efforts* 白忙,空忙. *He looked perfectly ~.* 他完全呆了. *You ~ idiot.* 你这个大傻瓜. *~ stupidity* 愚蠢透顶. *a ~ refusal* 断然拒绝. — *n.* ①空白;空白处,间隔;空地;白纸;〔美〕表格纸,空白表格〔英国叫 form〕. ②(精神上的)空虚;(个人生活中的)平淡时期,空签;【军】空弹;目标,靶心白点. ③【无】(阴极射线管的)底;熄灭脉冲. ④【机】胚(料),毛胚. ⑤〔古〕无韵诗. ⑥〔英〕(议案中用斜体字表示的)未决部分. ⑦(用横线"—"表示的)空白部分,某,某某. ⑧〔口、婉〕= damn〔用横线"—"作记号,读作 ~, ~y, ~ed, ~-ety 等〕;省略号"—"的读法. *a telegraph ~* 〔美〕电报空格纸. *I'm a ~ on the subject of Whiteman.* 我对惠特曼的作品没有作过研究. *B- him [it 等]!* 该死! *My mind became a complete ~.* 什么都忘了. *Mr. —* = Mr. Blank 某人. *— — Esq. of — Hall* = Blank Blank Esquire of Blank Hall 某宅某某先生. ***draw (a) ~*** 抽空签;〔口〕终于落空,失败. ***in ~*** 空白(待填). — *vt.* ①抹掉,使无效,作废,取消 *(out)*. ②〔美口〕(比赛等)使(对方)不能得分. ③使不能通行,封锁 *(off)*. ④【机】冲切,下料. *~ out an entry* 抹去一笔帐. *~ off a tunnel* 封锁隧道. — *vi.* ①消失,湮灭. ②失神. *The music ~d out.* 乐声逐渐消失. *His mind ~d out momentarily.* 他一时走神了. ~ **application** 空白申请书. ~ **book** 空白簿. ~ **cartridge [firing]** 空弹[空弹射击]. ~ **cheque** ①空白[不记名]支票. ②无限制的权力,自由处理权(*give a ~ cheque to sb.* 给与某人无限制的可动用金额或权力). ~ **credit**【商】信用票据. ~ **endorsement** (票据的)不记名背书. ~ **form** 空白表格. ~ **impossibilities** 完全不可能的事. ~ **verse** 无韵诗. ~ **wall** ①没有窗或门的墙. ②障碍 (*run into ~ wall* 遇到障碍).

blan·ket [ˈblæŋkit] *n.* ①毛毯,绒被;毛毡状物,层,垫. ②(火箭)表面层;(反应堆)再生区;(空气动力的)阴影. *a thermal insulation ~* 绝热层. *sand ~* 砂盖层,过滤层. *a ~ of snow* 一层雪,白雪皑皑. *a ~ of smoke* 烟幕. ***a wet ~*** 扫兴的人,败兴的事[物]. ***be born on the wrong side of the ~*** 是私生儿. ***split the ~***〔美口〕离婚. ***stretch the [one's] ~***〔美口〕夸张. ***throw a wet ~ on [over]*** 使扫兴,对…泼冷水,使锐气受挫折. ***toss in a ~*** 把…放在毯子上上下颠簸〔一种处罚〕. — *a.* 〔美〕一般的,总括的;无大差别的,(胜负等)不分上下的. — *vt.* ①用毛毯包[盖]. ②把(人)放在毯子上上下颠簸. ③遮掩(丑事等). ④【海】抢…的上风. ⑤〔美〕妨碍,干扰. ⑥(规则等)适用于. *the rates that ~ the whole region* (全区)通用运费. ~ **agreement** 一揽子协议. ~ **area** ①【无】广播受干扰地区. ②敷层面积. ~ **bombing** 地毯式轰炸,成片轰炸. ~ **drill** 〔美俚〕午觉,歇晌;睡眠. ~ **flower**【植】天人菊属. ~ **Indians** (用毯子裹身的)印第安人. ~ **insurance** 总括保险. ~ **policy** 总括保险单. ~ **roll**【军】背袋,背包. ~ **rules** 总则.

blan·ket·ing [ˈblæŋkitiŋ] *n.* ①〔集合词〕毛毯类的东西(= blankets). ②把人置毛毯上上下颠簸的处罚. ③【电视】熄灭,匿影;【无】通讯受干扰.

blan·ket·y-blank, blank·y [ˈblæŋkitiˈblæŋk, ˈblæŋki] *a., ad.* 该死〔诅咒语 damn, damned 的委婉说法〕. *the blankety-blank train* 该死的火车. *What the blankety-blank blue blazes went on!* 搞的什么鬼名堂!

blank·ly [ˈblæŋkli] *ad.* ①无表情地,茫然,惘然. ②完全地;斩钉截铁地.

blank·ness [ˈblæŋknis] *n.* ①空白;空虚. ②茫然;单调.

Blanqu·ism [ˈblɑːŋkizəm] *n.* 布朗基主义.

blare [blɛə] *vi.* 叫,吼,咆哮,怒号;(喇叭等)嘟嘟地大声响. *The trumpets ~d as the procession got under way.* 行列行进时,喇叭嘟嘟地响个不休. — *vt.* 高声发出(或奏出);高声宣布 *~ out the threat of the war* 发出战争叫嚣. — *n.* ①(喇叭等的)响声;巨响;吼叫. ②(颜色等)耀眼的光泽. ③大吹大擂.

blar·ney [ˈblɑːni] *n.* 奉承话;甜言蜜语. — *vt.* 巧言引诱,甘言哄骗. — *vi.* 说奉承话,拍马屁. **Blarney stone** 巧言石〔爱尔兰 Blarney 城上的石头,相传吻此石后即变得口齿伶俐〕.

bla·sé [ˈblɑːzei] *a.* 〔F.〕享乐过度而感到厌倦的,玩厌了的.

blas·pheme [blæsˈfiːm] *vt.* 亵渎(神祇等),骂(天等);中伤,侮慢. — *vi.* 骂天骂地;(语言)渎神. **~r** *n.*

blas·phe·mous [ˈblæsfiməs] *a.* 不敬的,骂神的,冒渎的;恶声的,侮慢的.

blas·phe·my [ˈblæsfimi] *n.* 不敬,亵渎,骂神;咒骂.

blast [blɑːst] *n.* ①(风)一阵,(气流等的)一股;疾风,强风;【冶】鼓风,送风;喷气,喷焰. ②管乐器声,汽笛声. ③爆炸声;爆炸;爆破;冲击波;一次用的炸药. ④毒气,瘟气;【农】稻瘟. ⑤【冶】鼓风机,喷砂器. ⑥【地】变晶. ⑦〔美口〕无线电广播;牢骚,怨言;〔美俚〕口头攻击;〔*pl.*〕〔美俚〕宣传文章. ⑧〔美俚〕热闹的聚会;闹宴;游艺会. *a ~ of wind* 一阵风. *wintry ~s* 寒风劲吹. *one ~ of siren* 汽笛一声长鸣. *a rocket ~*【火箭】火舌. *H-bomb ~* 氢弹爆炸. ***at [in] full ~*** ①(鼓风炉)开足,猛吹. ②〔口〕全速;竭尽全力;最强烈地. ***at one ~*** 一口气,一直. ***in [out of] ~*** (鼓风炉或人)在工作[在休息]. — *vt.* ①使爆炸,爆破,炸掉;摧毁. ②使枯萎,(霜等)冻死;摧残,损伤,毁坏. ③〔美俚〕骂倒,大肆攻击. ④〔美俚〕打,揍. *~ sb.'s reputation* 使某人声誉扫地. *~ sb.'s hope* 使某人的希望全成泡影. *~ the granite* 爆破花岗岩. *~ the evidence* 使该证据不能成立. — *vi.* ①发出尖响. ②进行爆破. ③吹牛,夸口. ④〔Scot.〕抽烟. ⑤枯萎,衰亡. ⑥〔美俚〕广播;公开批评;发牢骚;射击. ~ *away* 轰;【美体】拚命. *B- him [it]!* 该死! 活该! ~ *off* (使)(火箭等)发火起飞. ~ *out a homer* 【美棒球】打出还垒球. *B- the time!* 要命的时间〔表示时间紧迫〕! ~ **furnace** *n.* 高炉,鼓风炉. ~ **lamp** 风灯. ~**-off** (火箭)发射. ~ **pipe** 风管.

-blast *comb. f.*【生】胚;芽.

blast·ed [ˈblɑːstid] *a.* ①已枯萎的,被摧残掉的; 被毁的. ②〔婉〕该死的,讨厌的. *The ~ pen never did work properly.* 这支该死的笔总是出毛病.

blast·er [ˈblɑːstə] *n.* ①爆破工人; 爆裂药. ②〔美俚〕无线电广播员.

blas·te·ma [blæsˈtiːmə] *n. (pl.* ***blas·te·ma·ta*** [blæsˈtiːmətə]*)*【生】胚轴原,芽基.

blas·tie [ˈblɑːstiː, ˈblæstiː] *n.* 〔Scot.〕侏儒,矮子.

blasto- *comb. f.* "胚","芽".

blas·to·coele, blas·to·cele [ˈblæstəusiːl] *n.*【生】囊胚腔;分裂腔.

blas·to·cyst [ˈblæstəusist] *n.*【生】囊胚 (= blastula).

blas·to·derm [ˈblæstəudəːm] *n.*【生】胚盘,胚膜.

blas·to·disc, blas·to·disk [ˈblæstəudisk] *n.*【生】胚盘 (= germinal disc).

blas·to·gen·e·sis [ˌblæstəuˈdʒenisis] *n.*【生】①芽生. ②种质遗传.

blas·to·mere [ˈblæstəumiə] *n.*【生】胚节;分裂球;分沟细胞.

blas·to·my·cete [ˌblæstəumaiˈsiːt, -ˈmaisiːt] *n.*【生】芽生菌.

blas·to·my·co·sis [blæstəumaiˈkəusis] *n.*【病】芽生菌病,酵母病.

blas·to·pore [ˈblæstəupɔː] *n.*【生】原口,胚孔.

blas·to·sphere [ˈblæstəuˈsfiə] *n.*【生】囊胚(= blastula).

blast-pipe [ˈblɑːstpaip] *n.*【机】送风管,吹管.

blas·tu·la [ˈblæstjulə] *n. (pl.* ***-lae*** [-liː]*)*【生】囊胚.

blat [blɑːt] *vi.* 〔口〕(小牛小羊似地)叫;瞎说,胡说乱讲. — *vt.* 〔口〕大声地说出,不谨慎地说出.

bla·tan·cy [ˈbleitənsi] *n.* ①喧骚,吵闹. ②炫耀.

bla·tant [ˈbleitənt] *a.* ①露骨的. ②吼叫的,喧骚的. ③炫耀的. ~ *fraud* 无耻的欺诈. ~ *radios* 吵吵闹闹的收音机. *the ~ colors of her dress* 她的服装过于艳丽. **-ly** *ad.* 悍然,嚣然.

blath·er [ˈblæðə] *vi.* 胡说乱讲. — *vt.* 瞎扯(废话). — *n.* 胡说,废话. ~ **skite** *n.* 〔口〕①胡说八道的人,吹牛大王. ②无聊话,胡话.

blat·ter [ˈblætə] *vi.* 〔美方〕胡说;乱吹.

Blat·tner·phone [ˈblætnəfəun] *n.* 磁带录音机,钢丝录音机.

blau·bok [ˈblauˌbɔk] *n. (pl.* ~, ~*s)*【动】兰灰弯角羚.

blaw [blɔː] *vt., vi.* 〔英方,苏格兰〕吹.

blaze[1] [bleiz] *n.* ①火焰. ②闪光,光明,光辉. ③激发,爆发;(感情)昂扬. ④〔the ~s〕〔俚〕地狱. *the ~ of day* 光天化日. *the ~ of fame* 声名远扬. *the ~ of fury* 勃然大怒. *the ~ of publicity* 众所周知的事. ***Go to ~s!*** 该死! 活该! ***in a ~*** ①四面着火,烧做一团. ②激烈. ***in a ~ of passion*** 盛怒之下. ***like ~s*** 猛烈地. ***Old Blazes*** 〔口〕恶魔. ***What the ~s*** *(am I to do)?* (我)到底〔究竟〕(该怎么办)? — *vi.* ①燃烧, 冒火焰. ②发(强)光,闪闪生辉. ③激动,激昂. ~ ***away [off]*** ①连连开枪. ②猛干 *(at)*. ③扰嚷不已. ~ ***out*** ①燃烧;烧起来. ②大怒. ~ ***up*** ①燃烧起来. ②暴怒. — *vt.* ①燃烧着…. ②发出…光辉. ③明显表示.

blaze[2] [bleiz] *vt.* (大声) 宣布; 宣扬; 传播. ~ ***about [abroad]*** 传播,宣扬出去.

blaze[3] [bleiz] *n.* ①(马等脸上的)白斑. ②(树皮上的)指路刻痕. — *vt.* ①在(树皮)上刻记号. ②在树片上刻痕指示(道路等). ~ ***the trail*** 在树皮上刻路标; 〔转义〕领先,开路.

blaz·er[1] [ˈbleizə] *n.* ①燃烧物,发火焰物;大热天. ②(法兰绒的)运动上衣〔颜色多鲜艳夺目〕. ③大谎话.

blaz·er[2] [ˈbleizə] *n.* 传播者,宣传者.

blaz·ing [ˈbleiziŋ] *a.* ①炽烈燃烧的. ②灿烂的; 明显的, 显著的. ③【猎】(猎物遗臭) 浓烈的 *(opp.* cold*)*. *the ~ sun* 大热天, 烈日. *a ~ indiscretion* 过分轻率, 太不慎重. ***a ~ scent***【猎】(猎物) 浓烈的遗臭. ~ **star** ①彗星; 惹人注意的人物; 趣味中心. ②【植】(北美产)蓟属;矮百合.

bla·zon [ˈbleizn] *n.* ①徽, 纹章; 纹章解说, 徽章法. ②炫示,夸示;宣扬;表彰. *make a ~ of sb.'s error* 大肆宣扬某人的错误. — *vt.* ①画(纹章);专门解释(徽章);用徽章等装饰. ②把…公开, 宣扬, 表彰 *(forth; out; abroad)*. ~ *the event abroad* 把这件事公之于众.

bla·zon·ry [ˈbleizənri] *n.* ①纹章画法; 纹章解说法; 纹章. ②装饰,美化.

bldg., blg. = building.

-ble *suf.* 可, 能. ★通例带有被动意义,相应的副词后缀是 -bly, 名词后缀是 -bleness, -bility.

B.L.E. = Brotherhood of locomotive Engineers 〔美〕火车司机兄弟会.

bleach [bliːtʃ] *vt.* 漂白,漂; 晒白; 弄白. ~*ed goods* 漂白布匹. — *vi.* 变白; 脱色. — *n.* 漂白; 漂白法; 漂白剂; 漂白度. **bleach·a·bil·i·ty** *n.* 可漂白程度〔性〕. **-able** *a.* 可漂白的.

bleach·er [ˈbliːtʃə] *n.* ①漂布工人, 漂白业者. ②漂白器;漂白剂;漂白坯布. ③〔常 *pl.*〕〔美〕(棒球场等的)露天看台,廉价看台.

bleach·er·ite [ˈblitʃərait] *n.* 〔美〕露天看台的看客.

bleach·er·y [ˈbliːtʃəri] *n.* 漂白厂;漂白作坊.

bleach·ing [ˈbliːtʃiŋ] *n.* 漂白. —*a.* 漂白的. ~ **fastness** 漂白坚牢度. ~**-out** *a.* 褪色的. ~**-powder** 漂白粉. ~ **power** 漂白能力.

bleak[1] [bliːk] *a.* ①风吹雨打的,无遮蔽的. ②荒凉的,凄凉的,萧瑟的;阴冷的,寒冷的. ③苍白的; 暗淡的; 惨淡的,悲哀的. *a ~ wind* 寒风,风萧萧. *a ~ prospect* 前途暗淡. *a ~ plain* 荒原. **-ly** *ad.* **-ness** *n.*

bleak[2] [bliːk] *n.*【鱼】(淡水产)银鲤.

blear [bliə] *a.* ①(眼睛)花的; 湿的,烂的. ②〔诗〕朦胧的. *eyes ~ with tears* 泪眼模糊. — *vt.* ①使(眼)花〔湿、烂〕;使朦胧〔昏暗〕. ②使误入歧途,蒙蔽. *a biting wind that ~ed the vision* 寒风吹得人眼睛发花. — *n.* 视力模糊. ~**-eyed** *a.* 烂眼的; 朦胧眼的,目光不灵的;目光短浅的.

blear·y-eyed [ˈbliəriaid] *a.* ① = blear-eyed. ②〔美口〕醉眼惺松的. **-ness** *n.*

bleat [bliːt] *vi.* ①(羊、小牛等)叫,哞哞地叫. ②讲废话;哭诉.—*vt.*①声音颤抖地讲. ②以微弱的声音说.~ ***out*** 无力地〔愚蠢地〕说. — *n.* ①(羊、小牛等的)叫声. ②废话. ③哭诉. *the ~ of distant horns* 远处号角的悲鸣.

bleb [bleb] *n.* ①【医】起泡, 水肿; 泡疹. ②(水、玻璃等物中的)水泡,气泡. ~ *ingot* 有泡钢锭.

bleed [bliːd] *vi.* ***(bled*** [bled]***)*** ①流血,出血,内出血;受伤,死,战死. ②悲痛, 同情 *(for)*. ③【植】(伤口)流液汁,伤流;(树脂)分泌出;(油液等)渗出;(印染等)渗色,渗开. ④〔口〕掏腰包, 被敲诈, 被吸膏血. ⑤【印】被印成出血版,被切边. ~ *at [from] the nose.* 流鼻血. ~ *like a struck hog* 〔美口〕血流如注. *A nation ~s for its dead heroes.* 举国悼念为国死难的烈士. *fight and ~ for one's country* 为国流血,国殇,阵亡. *My heart ~s.* 忧思难忘, 痛心极了. *All the colors bled when the dress was washed.* 这件衣服一洗, 颜色都洇开了. — *vt.* ①使出血;【医】给…放血. ②榨取…的液汁; 放出(液、浆等); 把…的水抽干. ③【空】放(气); 从…抽气减压. ④〔口〕从…身上榨取钱财,敲…竹杠. ⑤【印】把…印成出血版,切去(超出开本的边). ~ *a patient* 给病人放血. ~ *one's family* 拚命向家里要钱花. *bled timber* 去脂材. ~ ***(sb.) white*** (使)流尽鲜血; 把…的血汗榨干;被榨干血

汗. — *n.*【印】出血版. — *a.*【印】出血版的.

bleed·er [ˈbliːdə] *n.* ①易出血的人, 血友病患者. ②放血人, 静脉切开放血术医师. ③泄水管, 放水闸;【船】泄水孔;【机】放油开关;【电】分压器; 分泄电阻, 旁漏. ④〔俚〕敲诈者; 寄生者, 食客; 〔英蔑〕家伙. ~ **cock** 放水龙头, 旋塞.

bleed·ing [ˈbliːdiŋ] *n.* ①出血; 放血; 静脉切开术. ②【植】伤流, 泌脂. ③〔美俚〕(车胎) 放气, 换油. ④【纺】渗化, 渗色, 化开. ⑤(沥青路面的) 泛油; (混凝土表面的) 泛浆. *the ~ pressure of roots*【植】根压. — *a.* ①流血的. ②悲痛的. ③渗色的. ④〔卑、婉〕= bloody. ~ **heart** ①【植】荷包牡丹. ②〔口〕软心肠的人; 〔蔑〕自夸同情[关心]人的人. ~**-off** *n.* 泄放, 排出; 除去, 取消.

bleep [bliːp] *n.* ①哔哔〔汽车喇叭或自行车铃声〕. ②嘟嘟〔电动警铃声〕. — *vi.* 发哔哔[嘟嘟]声. — *vt.* ①使发哔哔[嘟嘟]声. ②= blip.

bleep·er [ˈbliːpə] *n.* 无线电呼唤机.

blem·ish [ˈblemiʃ] *n.* 瑕疵, 缺点, 污点; 不名誉. *a ~ on his record* 历史污点. *without ~* 十分完美. — *vt.* 有损…的完美, 损害…的名誉; 玷污 *(opp.* purify*)*. *The novel is ~ed by those long descriptions.* 那些冗长的描写使小说大为减色.

blench[1] [blentʃ] *vi.* 退缩, 畏缩; 退避. — *vt.* 无视, 回避 (事实).

blench[2] [blentʃ] *vt.* 弄白, 使苍白. — *vi.* 变白, 变苍白.

blend [blend] *vt., vi.* *(~ed, blent* [blent]*)* 混合, 掺合, 混杂, 搀杂; 融合, 调和. ~ *the ingredients in a recipe* 按配方调料. *Sea and sky seemed to ~.* 海天一色. *The red sofa did not ~ with the purple wall.* 这种红色沙发和紫色墙壁不调和. ~ *whisky* 加料威士忌酒. — *n.* 混合; 混合种; 混合色; 合成语; 混纺纱. *tea of our own ~* 本店特有的配制茶. ~ **word** 混成语, 合成语〔如 brunch 由 breakfast 和 lunch 合成〕.

blende [blend] *n.* ①【矿】闪锌矿. ②(一般) 硫化物.

blend·er [ˈblendə] *n.* ①搅拌者, 混合物. ②搅拌器, 拌和器, 掺合机.

blend·ing [ˈblendiŋ] *n.* 混合; 融合; 配料; 折衷;【语】合成. ~ **inheritance**【生】融合遗传.

Blen·heim [ˈblenim] *n.* ① (spaniel 种) 小猎犬〔头小, 耳尖长〕. ②〔英〕布雷尼单翼轰炸机.

blen·nor·rhea [ˌblenəˈriːə] *n.*【医】脓性卡他, 脓性黏液溢.

blen·ny [ˈbleni] *n.*【鱼】鲇鱼, 鳚鱼.

blent [blent] blend 的过去分词.

bleph·a·ri·tis [ˌblefəˈraitis] *n.*【医】睑炎.

bles·bok [ˈblesbɔk] *n.* (南非) 大羚羊.

bless [bles] *vt.* *(~ed, blest* [blest]*)* *(opp.* curse*)* ①赐惠于, 赐福于, (上帝) 保佑. ②为…祈福, 为…祝福. ③感谢 (上帝); 赞美, 颂扬 (上帝). ④使神圣, 净化 (食物等). ⑤使幸福; 使有幸得到. ⑥〔反〕诅咒〔过去式和过去分词一般用 blest〕. ⑦对…划十字〔为…祈福〕. *greatly ~ed in one's children.* 大享儿女福气. *B- the name of the Lord.* 颂主之名〔基督教祈祷用语〕. *B- this house* 愿上帝给这一家赐福. *B- me (from all evils)!* 愿上帝保佑我 (消灾去祸)! *I am ~ed with a good appetite.* 我幸而胃口好. *Well, I'm ~ed [blest]* 奇怪! *I'm blest [Blest] if I do.* 我决不做. *I'm ~ed [blest] if I know.* 我一点儿也不知道; 我要是知道, 天诛地灭. **be ~ed** 受惠, 幸好, 有 *(with)*; 〔反〕折 (死), 遭天报. ***B- me! = God ~ me [you, him, her, them]! = B- the boy! = B- my soul! = Well, I'm blest!*** 哎呀; 天呀; 完了; 啧啧; 谢天谢地; 〔表惊愕、愤怒、庆幸等, 因人而异〕. ~ ***one's stars*** 庆幸, 运气好. ~ ***oneself*** 自祝, 庆幸; 画十字袚除 (*I ~ myself from such customers.* 不和这样一些顾客打交道真是谢天谢地). ***God ~ you!*** 愿上帝保佑你! 谢天谢地, 天呀!

bless·ed [ˈblesid] *a.* ①享福的, 受惠的; 有福的;【宗】死后已升天的; 幸运的, 令人愉快的. ②神圣的, 清净的. ③〔反〕遭殃的, 受祸的, 遭天罚的, 该死的〔damned, cursed 的委婉说法〕. ④用于加强语气〔*every ~ cent* 每一分大洋〕. *every ~ one* 每一个人, 人人, 大家. *not a ~ one* 一个也没有, 谁都没有. *the whole ~ lot* 全部, 统统. *the land of the ~* 天国. *B- are the pure in heart.* 清心的人有福了〔《圣经》马太福音中语〕. *the ~ assurance of a steady income* 有固定收入的可喜保障. *Those ~ bells!* 吵死人的鬼钟. *a ~ event* 〔美俚〕喜事, 福气〔指生孩子, 有时也指动物下崽〕. ***of ~ memory*** 前, 先, 已作古的 (*my mother of ~ memory* 先母). — *n.* 〔the ~〕有福者;【宗】死后已升天者. *the ~ in heaven* 天上诸圣. *[Isles] of the blest* 乐土. ***the B- Trinity***【基督】三位一体. ***the B- Virgin*** (基督教) 圣母马利亚. **-ly** *ad.* 幸福, 幸运地; 幸喜. **-ness** *n.* 幸福 (*a state of single blessedness* 〔谑〕快乐的独身生活).

bless·ing [ˈblesiŋ] *n.* ①赐福; 祝福. ②【宗】饭前[饭后]祷告. ③应允, 纵容. ④幸事. ⑤〔婉〕责备. *an unappropriated ~* 〔谑〕未婚女子. *give the ~* (神父等) 给教徒祝福. *ask [say] a ~* (教徒) 饭前[饭后]祷告. *the ~ of liberty* 自由的幸福. *by the ~ of God* 蒙天佑助. *a proposed law with the ~ of the governor* 经州长同意而提出的一项法律. *He got quite a ~ from his superier.* 他被上级训了一顿. ~ ***in disguise*** 祸中得福, 变相的幸福〔历尽千辛万苦而得到幸福结局或宝贵经验等〕. ***have the ~ of*** 得到…同意.

blest [blest] bless 的过去式及过去分词. — *a.* 〔诗〕= blessed. *the Islands [Isles] of the ~* 乐土, 极乐世界.

blet [blet] *n.* (水果熟透后的) 腐烂. — *vi.* (水果熟透后) 变腐烂.

bleth·er [ˈbleðə] *v., n.* = blather.

blew [bluː] blow 的过去式.

blew·it [ˈbluːit] *n.*【植】面口蘑〔蘑菇的一种〕.

Bligh [blai] *n.* 布莱〔姓氏〕.

blight [blait] *n.* ①(植物病理) 枯萎病, 火烧病; (对植物有大害的) 阴冷天气〔土壤条件〕; 虫害. ②(使士气崩溃, 希望计划等落空的) 破坏性因素; 扼杀, 打击. ③黑影, 阴影. ④坏影响. *early [later] ~* (植物的) 早[晚]疫病. *bactenial ~ of rice* 稻白叶枯病. *urban ~* 都市生活的恶劣影响. *Bankruptcy was the ~ of the family.* 破产毁了这一家. *His absence cast a ~ over the family.* 他的不在场使家庭笼罩上一层阴影. — *vt.* ①使 (植物) 有病, 使枯萎. ②妨害, 挫折, 摧残; 损伤. *Frost ~ed the crops* 霜冻使作物枯死. *Illness ~ed his hope.* 疾病摧毁了他的希望. *~ed being* 希望破灭的人〔尤指失恋的人〕. *~ed hopes* 希望化为泡影, 失望. *~ed love* 失恋. — *vi.* (植物) 生枯萎病.

blight·er [ˈblaitə] *n.* 〔俚〕①混蛋, 讨厌东西. ②家伙.

blight·y [ˈblaiti] *n.* 〔英军俚〕〔常 B-〕英国老家, 英国本土. ***a ~ (one)*** 需要送回英国本土治疗的伤〔第一次世界大战期间英军中的流行语〕. ***get one's ~*** (因负伤) 送归本国.

bli·mey [ˈblaimi] *int.* 〔英口〕啊呀!

blimp [blimp] *n.* ①〔俚〕小型软式飞艇. ②〔美俚〕可疑的 (不正派的) 女人. ③电影摄影机上的隔音装置. ④大胖子, 大块头. ***a Colonel B-*** (漫画中的) 顽固保守分子.

blind[1] [blaind] *a.* ①盲, 瞎, 失明的; 供盲人用的. ②盲目的, 轻率的, 鲁莽的; 胡来的; 蛮干的; 蒙昧的, 愚昧的, 无知的, 无先见的. ③无光的; 隐蔽的, 不显露的; 匿名的. ④堵死的; 一端不通的. ⑤未经眼见的;【空】单凭仪表操纵的. ⑥无结果的;【植】不开花的. ⑦难解的, 不易识别的. ⑧失去知觉的; 〔俚〕喝醉了的. ⑨(书籍装订) 不烫金的. *a ~ stupor* 完全昏迷. *a ~ passage in a book* 书中难懂的地方. *be ~ of [in] an eye* 一目失明. *He was ~ to all arguments.* 和他有理也讲不通. ~ *tenacity* 死顽固. ~ *chance* 纯出偶然. ~ *obedience* 盲从. ~

faith 迷信. ~ *quotation* 未经核实的引文. *a* ~ *asylum* 盲人收容所. ~ *education* 盲人教育. *a* ~ *ad* 匿名广告. ***be*** ~ ***to*** 不明,不看(事实),对…是盲目的. ***be*** ~ ***to the world*** 〔俚〕烂醉. ***be*** ~ ***with*** 被…弄得眼花[糊涂] (*His mind was* ~ *with weeping*. 他哭糊涂了). ***go*** ~ 失明 (*I'm going* ~ *in one eye*. 我一只眼快失明了). ***go in*** ~ 〔美口〕猜测. ***turn a [one's]*** ~ ***eye to*** 假装不见,熟视无睹. ***with*** ~ ***fury*** 猛烈地. — *ad.*〔口〕①＝blindly. ②厉害地. ***go it*** ~ ①胡来,蛮干. ②【空】单凭仪表操纵地. ***be*** ~ ***drunk*** 〔俚〕烂醉. — *vt.* ①弄瞎,使失明; 把…的眼睛弄花. ②蒙蔽,欺瞒; 使昏聩. ③使隐蔽,使变暗,遮暗,使相形失色. ④给(新路面)铺砂砾〔以填塞衔接处的空隙〕. *Her eyes were* ~*ed with the rain*. 雨水打得她的眼睛什么也看不见了. *The room was* ~*ed by the heavy curtains*. 厚窗帘把房间遮暗. *His resentment* ~*s his good sense*. 愤怒使他失去理智. *a radiance that* ~*s the sun* 使太阳黯然失色的强光. — *vi.* (驾驶员)瞎开车. — *n.* ①遮目物; 百叶窗; 簾子,屏风; 〔美〕(马的)眼罩. ②(猎人的)隐棚,埋伏地. ③障眼物,挡箭牌,搪塞话,口实. ④诱饵,囮子. ⑤〔口〕痛饮,发酒疯. *Venetian* ~ 软百叶窗. ***draw [pull down] the*** ~***(s)*** (日常或家中有事故时)拉下百叶窗. ~ **alley** 死胡同 (*a* ~ *alley occupation* 无出路的职业). ~ **baggage** 【美铁路】铁闷子车〔用作行李车、邮车等〕. ~ **bud** 叶芽,不开花结果的芽. ~ **car** 【铁路】行李车. ~ **coal** 无烟煤. ~ **date** 介绍会面〔由第三方介绍,为互不相识的男女安排的初次会见〕; 介绍会面赴约者〔参加这种会见的任何一方〕. ~ **ditch** 暗沟. ~ **door** 假门〔作成门形的外壁〕. ~ **fish** 【动】盲鳉属鱼. ~ **flying** 【空】盲目飞行〔全凭仪表操纵的飞行〕. ~ **god** 爱神,恋爱之神. ~ **gut** ①＝cecum. ②肠封闭; 肠梗阻. ~ **letter** 死信,姓名住址不明的信件. ~ **man** ①瞎子,盲人. ②(邮局中的)辨字员. ~ **nail** 暗钉. ~ **pig** 〔美〕(实行禁酒法时的)秘密酒店. ~ **radio** 〔美〕(邮局中的)辨字员. ~ **reader** 〔美口〕(相对电视而言的)普通广播. ~ **shell** 死弹,失效弹. ~ **side** 未防备的一面; 弱点 (*get sb. on his* ~ *side* 抓住某人弱点; 攻其不备). ~ **spot** 盲点〔眼神经无光感处〕; 个人不理解或不关心的方面; 【无】静区〔收音不清楚的地方〕. ~ **tiger** 〔美俚〕＝ ~ pig. ~ **trust** 绝对信任委托〔把管理钱财的事完全交给受托人代管,委托人完全不过问〕. ~ **wall** 闷墙,无窗墙. ~ **window** 假窗〔作成窗形的外壁〕. ~ **worm** 【动】蛇蜥蜴. ~ **zone** 盲区〔雷达波探测不到的区域〕.

blind·age [ˈblaindidʒ] *n.* 【军】盲障,掩体.

blind·er [ˈblaində] *n.* ①眩眼的人〔物〕. ②〔*pl.*〕〔美〕(马的)眼罩. ③〔*pl.*〕障眼物.

blind·fold [ˈblaind*f*əuld] *vt.* ①蒙住…的眼睛; 弄昏〔弄花〕…的眼睛. ②遮住…的视线. ③蒙骗,迷惑. — *a.* 蒙住眼睛的,盲目的. — *ad.* 瞎来,胡乱地. *act* ~ 胡来,蛮干. — *n.* 遮眼的蒙布; 障眼物.

blind·ing [ˈblaindiŋ] *a.* ①眩目的,晃眼的,使人眼花撩乱的. ②使盲的; 使人昏聩糊涂的. *a* ~ *day* 阳光刺眼的白天. ~ *anger* 使人丧失理智的愤怒,狂怒. ~ *tears* 泪眼模糊. — *n.* ①(新铺路面的)填塞; (填塞路面的)细砂,细石子. ②【纺】失光. ~ **tree** 土沉香.

blind·ly [ˈblaindli] *ad.* ①盲目地. ②没头没脑地; 妄自,胡来地,乱来地,蛮干地. ③一端不通地. *The passage ended* ~ *50 feet away*. 通道走下去五十英尺就不通了.

blind·man [ˈblaind*m*æn] *n.* 〔现多分写为 ~ man〕. ①盲人,瞎子. ②(邮局中的)辨字员. ~**'s buff** 捉迷藏. ~**'s holiday** 黄昏.

blind·ness [ˈblaind*n*is] *n.* ①视觉缺失,失明. ②愚昧,文盲. ③昏聩胡涂; 轻举妄动. *night* ~ 夜盲症. *taste* ~ 味盲,味觉失灵.

blin·i [bliˈniː] *n.* 〔*pl.*〕(*sing.* ***blin*** [blin])〔Russ.〕(中有鱼子酱和酸乳酪的)薄烤饼.

blink [bliŋk] *vi.* ①眨眼睛. ②(灯等)闪亮,闪烁. ③眯着眼看 *(at)*; 惊愕地看 *(at)*. ④无视,假装不见 *(at)*. *She* ~*ed to stop tears*. 她眨着眼止住眼泪. ~ *at the harsh light* 眯着眼看那刺目的光. ~ *at sb.'s sudden fury* 对某人的突然发脾气瞠目不知所措. ~ *at the law* 无视法律. — *vt.* ①眨(眼); 眨着眼挤掉(眼泪,眼中异物等). ②使闪烁. ③无视,闭眼不看(事实等). ④用闪光信号表示. ~ *one's eyes* 眨眼. ~ *the light* 打灯光信号. *There is no* ~*ing the possibility of a scandal*. 不能无视发生丑闻的可能性. — *n.* ①眨眼睛; 瞬间. ②瞥见; 一瞥. ③闪光; 灯光的明灭. ④冰映光; 水照云光. *the faithful* ~ *of the lighthouse* 灯塔定时的闪光. *not a* ~ *of light* 一点光亮也没有. ***in a*** ~ ＝ ***like a*** ~ 〔口〕立刻,马上. ***on the*** ~ 〔俚〕(机器等)出毛病,需要修理; (人)不舒服. ***without a*** ~ ***or qualm*** 不在乎,很镇静.

blink·ard [ˈbliŋkəd] *n.* 〔罕〕①老眨眼睛的人; 眯缝着眼睛看的人. ②不明事理的人,胡涂虫.

blink·er [ˈbliŋkə] *n.* ①眨眼睛的人; 瞥视者; 〔卑〕眼. ②闪光信号灯; 〔美〕(铁路栅口的)闪光警戒标. ③〔*pl.*〕护目镜,防尘眼镜; (马的)眼罩. ***be in*** ~***s*** 瞎,盲目,蒙住眼 (*run in* ~*s* 瞎跑). — *vt.* ①给…上眼罩. ②蒙蔽.

blink·ing [ˈbliŋkiŋ] *a.* ①眨眼的; 晃眼的. ②〔英俚〕眼不忍见的,可恶的,该死的〔代 bloody 用的委婉语〕. *Stop that* ~ *noise!* 别那么吵死人了! *You* ~ *idiot!* 你这个大傻瓜!

blintz [blints] *n.* (卷有乳酪、果品等的)薄烤饼.

blip [blip] *n.* ①【无】(显示器屏幕上的)尖头信号,标志,记号,(雷达的)可视信号. ②疾而尖的音响. ③(因抹音引起的)电视节目中的声音中断. ④〔美俚〕五分钱硬币. — *vi.* (*-pp-*) 发信号. — *vt.* 在录象磁带上抹去(所录的音).

Bliss [blis] *n.* 布利斯〔姓氏〕.

bliss [blis] *n.* ①无上幸福,至福. ②天福; 天堂; 极乐. ③狂喜; 满足. *wedded* ~ 美满姻缘. *the road to eternal* ~ 通向天国之路.

bliss·ful [ˈblisf*u*l] *a.* 至福的,极乐的,有造化的. **-ly** *ad.* **-ness** *n.*

blis·ter [ˈblistə] *n.* ①水疱,水肿,火肿,疱(病). ②(植物的)疱状突起. ③【医】起疱膏,发疱药. ④(钢,玻璃漆器等表面上的)气泡,砂眼. ⑤〔俚〕令人讨厌的人. ⑥【无】(雷达的)天线罩; 【船】附加外壳; (军舰的)附雷隔堵; (飞机上的)固定舱座. — *vt.* ①使起水疱,把…烫出疱. ②狠揍; 痛斥; 挖苦,责备,辱骂. — *vi.* 起疱,烫伤. ~ **beetle**【动】斑蝥. ~ **cloth** 泡泡呢. ~ **copper** 粗铜. ~ **gas** 糜烂性毒气.

blis·ter·ing [ˈblistəriŋ] *a.* ① 使起疱的. ②恶毒的; 激烈的. ③〔口〕可恶的,该死的. *a* ~ *tongue* 刻薄嘴. *a* ~ *sun* 灼热的阳光.

blithe [blaið] *a.* ①欢乐的,愉快的 *(opp.* joyless*)*. ②活泼的,爽快的. ③轻率的,冒失的; 不注意的. **-ly** *ad.*

blith·er [ˈbliðə] *n.* 〔美口〕废话,空谈. — *vi.* 瞎谈,噜噜苏苏地谈.

blith·er·ing [ˈbliðəriŋ] *a.* 〔口〕①噜噜苏苏的,唠叨没完的. ②绝顶的,无以复加的,头号的. *a* ~ *idiot* 大傻瓜.

blithe·some [ˈblaiðsəm] *a.* 欢乐的,快活的; 活泼的.

B. Lit(t)., **BLit(t)** ＝ Bachelor of Literature 文学(学)士 (＝ Bachelor of Letters).

blitz [blits] *n.* ①【军】闪电战,闪击战; 大规模空袭. ②(疾病,宣传等的)闪电式行动,突然袭击,闪电攻势. — *a.* 闪电战的,闪电式的. — *vt.* 〔口〕用闪电战攻击,用闪电战制服; 对…进行猛烈空袭.

blitz·krieg [ˈblitsˌkriːg] *n.* ＝ blitz.

bliz·zard [ˈblizəd] *n.* 〔美〕雪暴,暴风雪; 〔俚〕大打击.

bloat [bləut] *vt.* ①熏制(鲱鱼等). ②使肿起,使胀. ③使自负. — *vi.* ①肿起,胀. ②自负,得意忘形. — *n.* 〔美〕肿胀病人; (家畜的)气胀病; 〔美俚〕醉鬼.

bloat·ed [ˈbləutid] *a.* ①发胀的,肿起的,膨胀的; (因多

食而)病态发胖的. ②傲慢的,趾高气扬的. ③〔美俚〕喝醉的;(要求)过高的.

bloat·er [ˈbləutə] *n.* 熏鲱,熏鱼.

blob [blɔb] *n.* ①(墨水等的)一滴;(半流质物品的)一团;(颜料的)一抹;小斑点. ②(鱼)跳水声. ③【板球】零分. ④〔美俚〕错误. ***on the*** ~〔俚〕在口头上,用谈话方式. — *vt.* (墨水等)污染,弄脏. — *vi.* ①(鱼)跳水. ②〔美俚〕弄错.

blob·ber-lipped [ˈblɔbəlipt] *a.* 嘴唇厚而凸的.

bloc [blɔk] *n.* 〔F.〕①(国家、团体等的)集团. ②〔美〕跨党派议员集团. *a position "outside ~s"* "超集团"立场. *the Axis* ~ (第二次世界大战中的)轴心国集团. *the dollar [sterling]* ~ 美元〔英镑〕集团. *the farm* ~〔美〕农场主议员集团;农业区议员集团.

block [blɔk] *n.* ①片,块,大块;粗料,毛料;木料;石料;金属块;【建】块料,砌块;【地】地块. ②俎,砧板,(切肉等的)墩,台;断头台;骑马台(等);【印】(插图)衬版,版垫;(印花)模板;剪裁样板;(装订)钢模;帽模,帽楦;【船】船台;刹车;【计】部件. ③滑车,辘轳,滑轮组. ④一组,一套,一批;粘贴的帐;大宗股票. ⑤一排大建筑;〔英〕大楼,大厦;〔美〕街区〔四条街当中的地区〕;街段,地段;区,区组. ⑥(铁路)区段,区截;(戏院)座位区;(政府分配移民等的)划区;〔澳〕〔the ~〕热闹街道,闹市,繁华的大马路. ⑦(橱窗陈列帽、假发等用的)木制假头;〔美口〕头;挂表;名誉不好的人;木头人,笨汉;铁石心肠的人. ⑧障碍,阻碍;【无】停振;【医】阻滞;〔英〕(交通的)堵断;(对议案的)反对声明;【体】(合法)阻挡;【棒球】障碍球. ⑨集团(= bloc). *concret ~s* 水泥板. *paving ~s* 铺路石板. *a ~ of stone* 石料. *building ~ [~s]*【建】砌块〔儿童玩的积木〕. *a hat ~* 帽楦. *a single [double] ~* 单〔复〕滑车. *traffic ~* 交通堵塞. *a large ~ of tickets* 一大叠戏票. *He has a ~ when it comes to math.* 一碰上数学,他的脑子就木了. *an input [output] ~*【计】输入〔输出〕部件. *a swage ~*【机】花砧. *gauge ~*【机】块规. *screw ~* 千斤顶. ***as like as two ~s*** 象极了的. ***cut ~s with a razor*** 剃刀砍木头,用非其当. ***go [be sent, be brought] to the*** ~ (被送)上断头台;被提出拍卖. ***in [the]*** ~ 成批,成套. ***knock sb.'s ~ off*** 给某人吃苦头,痛揍某人. ***on the*** ~ 拿出拍卖;〔澳〕逛闹市. ***to do the*** ~ 散步,逛马路. — *vt.* ①妨碍,阻挠;堵塞,封锁;冻结(资金等);杜绝;〔英〕对(议案)事先作反对宣传. ②把…放置台上;用木片等塞牢;使…成块状;用帽模打(帽样);给(书籍)烫金;(球类运动中合法)阻挡. ③【铁路】以区截制管理(行车). ④【剧】排练(主要位置和动作). ⑤画出…的轮廓〔草图〕. *~ a hat* 打帽样. *~ed funds* 被冻结资金. *two-way ~ing positions* 两面阻击阵地. *a ~ing oscillator*【物】间歇振荡器. — *vi.* ①【剧】排练. ②【体】(合法)阻挡. ~ ***in*** ①画略图;设计. ②堵塞. ~ ***out*** 画略图;拟大纲,打草样. ~ ***up*** 堵塞,隔断,封锁;停用. ***Blocked!***〔揭示〕禁止通行! 此路不通! ~ **book** 木版书. ~ **booking** (电影院对影片的)整批承包. ~ **brush**【电】碳刷. ~ **chain** (自行车等的)车链. ~ **club**〔美〕互助委员会,地区居民保安联会. ~ **cutter** 木版师. ~ **diagram** 立体图,方块〔框〕图. ~ **effect**【无】体效应. ~ **head** 痴汉,木头人. ~ **house**【军】防舍;圆木小屋;碉堡. ~ **letter** 木版字;大型字体,大写印刷字体. ~ **movement**【地】地块运动. ~ **print** (木)版画. ~ **printing** 木版印刷(版本);雕刻版印刷;木版印染法. ~ **release** (欧洲国家企业界的)进修离职制. ~ **ship** 沉没的障碍船舰. ~ **signal**【交】区截信号. ~ **stream** 岩流,泥石流. ~ **structure**【地】块状结构. ~ ˈ**style** 大写印刷字体;商业文书格式. ~ **system**【铁路】闭塞制〔站与站间一次限行一车〕. ~ **tin** (提炼过的)锡锭〔块〕.

block·ade [blɔˈkeid] *n.* ①封锁,堵塞. ②实施封锁的武力〔部队〕. ③〔美〕(交通的)阻断. ***enforce a*** ~ 实行封锁. ***raise [lift] a*** ~ 解除封锁. ***run the*** ~ 偷越封锁线. — *vt.* 封,堵塞,封锁;妨止,阻止. *a ~d port* 被封锁的港口. *a ~ expedition* 执行封锁任务的远征军. ~ **runner** 偷过封锁线者;偷过封锁线的船.

block·ad·er [blɔˈkeidə] *n.* 封锁者,堵塞者;封港船,执行封锁任务的船.

block·age [ˈblɔkidʒ] *n.* ①封锁(状态). ②堵塞;障碍. ③【医】(心理)阻滞. *the ~ of the streets* 交通堵塞. *emotional ~* 感情阻滞症.

block·bust·er [ˈblɔkˌbʌstə] *n.*〔俚〕①高爆力巨型炸弹. ②特别神通广大的人;风靡一时的事物〔尤指被大吹大擂以招徕观众、读者的消耗巨资拍摄的影片或小说等〕. ③(从事唆卖房屋的)房地产掮客.

block·bust·ing [ˈblɔkˌbʌstiŋ] *n.* (房地产掮客的)房屋唆卖生意.

block·ette [blɔˈket] *n.*【自】数字组;子〔次〕字组;子群.

block·ish [ˈblɔkiʃ] *a.* ①木头一样的. ②愚钝的;顽固的. **-ly** *ad.* **-ness** *n.*

block·y [ˈblɔki] *a.* ①块状结构的,短而粗的,结实的. ②浓淡不匀的,斑驳的.

bloke [bləuk] *n.* ①〔俚〕家伙;〔伦敦隐语〕头子,首领. ②〔海军俚〕〔the ~〕舰长. ③醉鬼;笨蛋. *an old ~* 老糊涂.

Blom [blɔm] *n.* 布洛姆〔姓氏〕.

blond(e) [blɔnd] *a.* ①(头发)亚麻色的,金色的. ②美貌的;白肤金发碧眼的. ③(家具等)浅色的. *a ~ girl* 白肤金发碧眼的姑娘. — *n.* ①白肤金发碧眼人〔指女性时拼作 blonde〕. ②= ~ lace. ~ **lace** 丝带,丝花边.

blood [blʌd] *n.* ①血,血液;生命液. ②血族,血统;种族;家族(关系);家世;门第;名门,门阀;〔the ~〕贵族血统. ③生命,活力;元气. ④流血,杀戮,杀人(罪),牺牲. ⑤血气;气质,气性,脾气;热情;激怒;肉欲,兽欲. ⑥〔主英〕血气方刚的人;花花公子,纨袴子. ⑦〔集合词〕人员. ⑧(树木、果子等的)赤色汁液;〔美俚〕蕃茄酱. ⑨(马的)纯种. *the circulation of ~* 血液循环. *His ~ is up.* 他热情激昂〔动怒,发火〕. *They demand ~ for ~.* 他们要求以血还血. *avenge the ~ of one's father* 报杀父之仇. *be of mixed ~* 混血种. *a lady of ~* 贵妇人. *be related by ~* 有亲戚关系. *Blood is thicker than water.* 血比水浓;〔喻〕自己人总是自己人;近客不如远亲,疏不间亲. *My ~ be on your head!* 我若死其罪在你. *It made my ~ run cold.* 令人心惊胆寒,毛骨悚然. *We need fresh ~.* 我们需要新的人员. *the young ~s of Cambridge* 剑桥大学的少壮派. *a young ~* 血气方刚的少年. *a bit of ~* 纯种马. ***bad*** ~ 敌意;不和;仇恨;恶感 (*make bad ~ between the brothers* 使兄弟之间不睦). ~ ***and iron***【史】(德国宰相俾斯麦的)铁血政策;黩武政策. ~ ***in one's eyes***〔美〕期待必胜. ~ ***out of a stone*** (得到)冷酷人的同情. ~ ***transfusion*** 输血. ***blue*** ~ 贵族血统. ***for the ~ of me*** 拼命,无论如何. ***fresh*** ~ (社团、家庭的)新成员;新手. ***full [whole]*** ~ (同父母的)嫡亲关系. ***get in the [one's]*** ~ 动人,迷人 (*Golf is something that gets in the ~.* 高尔夫球是一项迷人的运动). ***get [have] one's ~ up*** (使)激动,(使)愤激. ***half*** ~ 异父〔异母〕关系. ***ill*** ~ = ***bad*** ~. ***in*** ~ 生命力旺盛;欣欣向荣. ***in cold*** ~ ①蓄意地(而非出于一时冲动地);残忍地. ②冷静地. ***in hot [warm]*** ~ 怒,愤激. ***in sb.'s [the]*** ~ 遗传的,生来的. ***man of*** ~ 凶险的人,残忍成性的人;凶手. ***make sb.'s ~ run cold*** 使人不寒而慄,毛骨悚然. ***out for sb.'s*** ~ 要某人的命. ***out of*** ~ 毫无生气. ***penny*** ~〔英俚〕(描写凶杀等惊险情节的)廉价小说〔刊物〕. ***princes [princesses] of the*** ~ 王子,亲王〔公主〕. ***shed*** ~ ①流血〔受伤或死〕. ②杀人. ***spill*** ~ 犯杀〔伤〕人罪. ***spill the ~ of*** 杀死…. ***sweat*** ~ ①没命地干,拼死拼活地干. ②忧虑万分. ***taste*** ~ (猎狗等)尝鲜血味;〔喻〕初识真味. ***to the last drop of one's*** ~ 只要一息尚存. — *vt.* ①使出血;抽…的血;〔古〕给…放

血．②使(猎狗等)先尝(猎物的)鲜血味；使(新手等)先取得经验；使(新兵)初战．③用血染(皮革等)；用血弄湿．~-and-thunder (小说、戏剧等) 充满凶杀打斗等刺激性情节的．~ **bank** 血库．~ **bath** 血洗，大屠杀．~ **brother** 亲兄弟；歃血结盟兄弟．~ **brotherhood** 兄弟[把兄弟]关系[情谊]．~ **cell** 血球．~-**and-thunder** *a.* (小说等) 惊险的．~ **corpuscle** 【生理】血球．~ **count** 【医】血球计数．~**curdling** *a.* 令人心惊胆寒的；令人毛骨悚然的．~ **donor** 供血者，献血者．~ **feud** 家族之间的宿仇，族仇．~**fin** 【动】红鳍脂鲤．~ **fluke** 【医】血吸虫，住血吸虫．~ **flux** 【医】赤痢．~ **group** 【医】血型．~ **grouping** 【医】血型鉴定．~ **guiltiness** 杀人罪．~**guilty** *a.* 杀过人的；犯杀人罪的．~ **heat** 血温〔摄氏 37 度，华氏 98.6 度〕．~ **horse** 纯种马．~**hound** ①(英国种) 警犬．②侦探．~ **lefting** 【医】抽血，放血；〔喻〕(战斗等的)流血．~ **line** 血统；世系．~ **lust** 杀戮欲．~-**mobile** 流动收血车．~ **money** ①血腥钱；损人而得到的利益．②偿付被杀者亲属的钱．~ **plasma** 【生理】血浆．~ **platelet** 【生理】血小板．~ **poisoning** 【医】败血症．~ **pressure** 血压．~ **pudding** 血肠．~ **purge** 血腥清洗．~-**red** *a.* ①血红的．②血迹斑斑的，染满血的(*a ~-red sunset* 残阳如血)．~ **relation** 血族，骨肉．~-**root** *n.* 【植】美洲血根草．~ **royal** 皇族．~ **serum** 【生理】血清．~**shed** *n.* 流血，虐杀 (*revenge for ~shed* 报仇)．~**shot** 充血的 (*see things ~shot* 红了眼，杀气腾腾)．~ **sport** 流血娱乐，见红消遣〔狩猎、斗牛等〕．~**stain** 血迹．~**stained** *a.* 血污的，血腥的，有血痕的；〔喻〕杀过人的．~**stock** 纯种马．~**stone** 【矿】血玉髓；血滴石．~ **stream** 【生理】血流．~**sucker** 吸血动物；蛭；凶汉；吸血鬼，高利贷者，剥削者．~ **test** 验血．~-**thirstiness** 嗜血，杀人狂；残忍，凶恶．~**thirsty** *a.* 嗜血的，以血充饥的；残忍的，凶恶的．~ **transfusion** 输血(法)．~ **type** = ~ group. ~ **typing** = ~ grouping. ~ **vessel** 血管．~**worm** 鱼虫；(做钓饵的)蚯蚓〔小红虫〕．~**wort** 【植】血红酸模．

blood·ed [ˈblʌdid] *a.* ①〔作复合词用〕…血的．②〔美〕(马、牛等)良种的，纯种的；(人)血统优良的，身世清白的．*warm-~ animals* 温血动物．*a cold-~ killer* 冷酷的杀人犯．

blood·i·ly [ˈblʌdili] *ad.* 血淋淋地；残忍地，惨酷地，凶恶地．

blood·i·ness [ˈblʌdinis] *n.* 血污；残忍，残酷．

blood·less [ˈblʌdlis] *a.* ①不流血的，无流血之惨的．②贫血的，无血色的，苍白的．③〔喻〕无生气的，无精打彩的，冷淡的．④冷血的，冷酷的．~ *surgery* 无血手术．*a ~ face* 苍白的面容．~ *data* 无情的数据．

blood·y [ˈblʌdi] *a.* ①血的；血一样的．②血糊糊的；血染的，血迹斑斑的．③嗜血的，好杀的．④血腥的，残忍的．⑤〔口〕过分的，不合情理的．⑥〔英俚〕= damned〔有时仅用以加强语气〕．*a ~ battle* 一场血战．~ *tissue* 血液组织．*a ~ king* 暴君．*not a ~ likely* 一点儿也不象．*It's a ~ shame* 真是太丢脸了．*not a ~ one* 就是一个也没有．— *ad.* ①〔英口〕过分，太，不顾死活地．②= damned. *be ~ drunk* 烂醉如泥．*It is ~ lucky.* 真是太走运了．★此词常略作 B-(d)y. — *vt.* 血污，血染．~ **mary** ①番茄汁掺伏特加酒．②〔B- M-〕杀星玛丽〔英国女王 Maria (1516—1558) 的绰号，因血腥迫害新教徒而得此名〕．~ **flux** 【医】赤痢．~ **hand** ①红手〔从男爵的纹章〕．②〔英，古法〕侵犯他人猎区的证据．~-**minded** *a.* ①残忍的，狠心的．②〔英口〕故意不合作的；无理作对的．~ **murder** ①血腥的谋杀．②〔美俚〕一败涂地 (*yell [scream] ~ murder* 大喊救命)．~ **shirt** ①(被杀者的)血衣．②煽起复仇心理的手段 (*wave the ~ shirt* 煽动复仇)．~ **work** 虐杀．

bloo·ey, bloo·ie [ˈbluːiː] *a.* 〔美俚〕不灵的，不能使用的〔主要用于 go ~ (出毛病)〕．

bloom[1] [bluːm] *n.* ①花〔特指观赏植物的花〕；开花(期)；(花)盛开．②〔*sing.*〕青春，风华正茂；最盛期．③(面颊的)红润；(外观的)艳美[新鲜]；(原棉的)光亮．④(叶面、虫体等的)粉被，粉，霜；【化】起霜(作用)．⑤【电视】刺眼的闪光．*the ~ of the cherry tree* 樱花．*The gardens are all in ~.* 鲜花满园，春色满园．*the ~ of Romanticism* 浪漫主义的鼎盛时期．*the ~ of the grape* 葡萄上的粉霜．***be out of ~*** 过了花期，花已落．***come into ~*** 开花．***in (full) ~*** (花)盛开；充分发挥．***take the ~ off*** 使…失去美貌；使…显得不新鲜．***the ~ of youth*** 青春，年富力强．— *vi.* ①开花；(花)盛开．②兴旺，繁盛．③进入青春时代．④发亮，闪烁生辉．*These plants ~ in spring.* 这些树春天开花．~ ***into*** 发育为，成长为．— *vt.* ①使繁盛．②使开花．③使艳丽．④使模糊．*Industry ~s his talents* 勤奋使他的才能发出光辉．*Their breath ~ed the frosty pane.* 他们的呼吸使冰冻的窗玻璃凝上一层雾气．

bloom[2] [bluːm] *n.* 【冶】大钢坯，钢锭；铁块，钢块，初轧坯．— *vt.* 【冶】把…轧成钢坯，初轧．

Bloom·er [ˈbluːmə] *n.* 布卢默〔姓氏〕．

bloom·er[1] [ˈbluːmə] *n.* ①〔古〕布鲁姆女服〔纽约 *Bloomer* 夫人创始的一种有短裙和灯笼裤的女服〕；穿布鲁姆女服的妇女．②〔*pl.*〕女灯笼裤．~ **boy** 〔美俚〕伞兵．

bloom·er[2] [ˈbluːmə] *n.* ①开花植物．②成年人，有作为的(年青)人．③〔英俚〕大错误，大失策；失败．*a night ~* 夜间开花的植物．*a late ~* 大器晚成．

bloom·ery, bloom·a·ry [ˈbluːməri] *n.* 【冶】土法〔木炭〕熟铁吹炼炉．

Bloom·field [ˈbluːmfiːld] *n.* 布卢姆菲尔德〔姓氏〕．

bloom·ing [ˈbluːmiŋ] *a.* ①正开花的，(花)盛开的．②青春正盛的，妙龄的．③旺盛的．④〔英口〕异常的，无比的，十足的．~ *cheeks* 红润的双颊．~ *business* 生意兴隆．*a ~ fool* 十足的大傻瓜．— *n.* 【物】敷霜，图象浮散；光学膜．

Blooms·bu·ry [ˈbluːmzbəri] *n.* 布卢姆茨伯里区〔包含大英博物馆(British Museum) 在内的伦敦地区名，从前是高级住宅区，今为学者、文人集中的文教区〕．

bloom·y [ˈbluːmi] *a.* ①开花的，盛开的．②有粉衣的．

bloop [bluːp] *n.* 【影】杂音；防杂音设备．— *vi.* 发出杂音．— *vt.* 消除…的杂音．

bloop·er [ˈbluːpə] *n.* 〔美俚〕①(在广播中或电视上出的)差错〔洋相〕．②【棒球】仅仅击出内场的飞球．③【无】发出射频电流 (对附近其他接收机起干扰作用的)接收机．

Bloor [bluː, bloə] *n.* 布卢尔〔姓氏〕．

blos·som [ˈblɔsəm] *n.* ①花〔特指果树花〕；群花．②开花时期；(发育的)初期．③兴旺时期．***in ~*** 开着花．***in full ~*** 盛开．— *vi.* 开花；繁荣；兴旺，茂盛；发展成，长成 *(into)*．~ *(out) into a statesman* 〔讽〕(眼看着) 变成政治家．③***nip in the ~*** 把…消灭于萌芽状态．

blot[1] [blɔt] *n.* ①墨污，墨渍，污点，污斑．②瑕疵；耻辱，污名．③〔古〕涂去，抹去．*a ~ on her past [her character]* 她历史[品格]上的污点．*drop an ink ~ on an envelope* 信封玷上了一块墨污．— *vt.* ①用 (墨水等) 弄脏，涂污．②涂去，抹掉 *(out)*．③用吸墨纸吸干．④遮蔽(风景等)，遮暗，使昏暗．⑤玷污，损害(名誉等)．⑥〔美俚〕杀死；乱涂，乱写；〔诗〕擦掉．*The sun was ~ted by the moon.* 月亮遮暗了太阳，日食．~ *the wet pane* 擦干潮湿的窗玻璃．~*ting pad* 吸墨水纸滚台．— *vi.* ①(墨水)渗开；造成污渍．②(纸等)玷上墨污；(吸墨纸)吸掉墨水．*This pen ~s.* 这支笔漏墨水．*This paper ~s easily.* 这种纸容易吸水．~ ***one's copybook*** 损坏自己名誉．~ ***out*** ①涂去(文字)．②遮掉(风景等)，遮暗．③〔美俚〕消灭，杀掉；毁掉．**blotting pad** 吸墨纸滚台．**blotting paper** 吸墨纸．

blot[2] [blɔt] *n.* ①(十五子棋中) 易被吃掉的孤立棋子．②弱点．***hit a ~*** 吃去弱子，突破弱点．

blotch [blɔtʃ] *n.* ①(皮肤上的)疱,疙瘩; (植物的)白斑,白斑病. ②(墨水等的)污点,斑污;印花色底. — *vt.* 弄脏,涂污.

blotch·y [ˈblɔtʃi] *a.* ***(-i·er; -i·est)*** 有疱的; 斑斑点点的; 布满污痕的.

blot·ter [ˈblɔtə] *n.* ①吸墨纸, 吸墨用具. ②弄脏东西的人; 笔迹潦草的人. ③【商】流水帐; 临时记录册; 〔美〕(警察等的)事故登记簿, 拘留记录簿.

blot·tesque [blɔˈtesk] *a.* (绘画)粗涂乱抹的.

blot·ting·pa·per [ˈblɔtiŋpeipə] *n.* 吸墨纸.

blot·to [ˈblɔtəu] *a.* 〔俚〕泥醉的,烂醉的.

blouse [blauz] *n.* ①〔F.〕宽阔的罩衫;【美军】(作为日常军服穿的)短上衣. ②女衬衫;〔法〕工装.

blous·on [ˈblu:sɔn] *a.* (衣裙)有长上衣式样的.

blow[1] [bləu] *vi.* ***(blew*** [blu:]; ***blown*** [bləun]***)*** ①(风)吹. ②(汽笛等)叫,鸣,响. ③喘气;吹气;(鲸等)喷水;喷气. ④(轮胎等)爆炸;〔俚〕发怒;〔美口〕炫弄, 夸口,吹牛. ⑤〔俚〕走掉, 逃掉. ⑥【电】(熔丝等)熔断,熔解,熔化. ⑦(苍蝇)产卵. ⑧〔美俚〕吸用麻醉品. ~ *on one's hands* 以手指吹口哨. *It* ~*s.* 刮风了. *The whistle was* ~*ing.* 汽笛长鸣. *We heard the burgles* ~*ing.* 我们听见号角声响. *The old man was puffing and* ~*ing.* 这老人气喘吁吁. *He* ~*s too much.* 他好吹牛. ~ *about one's medals* 炫弄自己的奖章. *The rear tire blew out.* 后胎炸了. — *vt.* ①吹, 吹动; 吹成, 吹制; 吹胀; 吹着(火等); 使通气. ②鸣(笛等); 吹奏(乐器等). ③使(马)喘气〔常用被动语态〕. ④传播, 发布, 宣扬. ⑤〔俚〕= damn, curse 〔诅咒用语, 此义过去分词用 ~ed〕. ⑥挥霍,浪费(钱财). ⑦使(轮胎等)爆炸;使(保险丝)熔断;毁坏. ⑧(蝇等) 下子于, 产卵于. ⑨〔俚〕使自负. ⑩〔俚〕背叛. ⑪【冶】 吹炼. ⑫〔美俚〕吸(毒). *Try* ~*ing your nose.* 把鼻子擤一擤. ~ *glass* 吹玻璃〔吹制玻璃器皿〕. ~ *out one's cheeks* 鼓起腮帮子. ~ *a tyre* 轮胎放炮. ~ *a fuse* 烧断保险丝. ~ *the rumor about* 传谣. ~ *an egg* 吸蛋〔开小孔吸食〕. *The horse is badly blown.* 马骑得喘极了. *the trees blown down by the storm* 被风暴吹折的树. *He has* ~*n (in) the whole sum.* 他把全部款项都花完了. *I'm* ~*ed if I know.* 〔俚〕畜牲才知道, 我知道不算人. *B- the cost!* 价钱真贵! ~ *town* 离开城市. ~ ***about [away]*** 吹散; 传播. ~ ***down*** ①吹倒; 吹落. ②(锅炉)喷出 (蒸汽). ~ ***great guns (and small arms)*** 刮大风, (风) 狂吹. ~ ***high,*** ~ ***low*** 在任何情况下, 不管发生什么事. ~ ***hot and cold*** 反复无常,忽褒忽贬,无定见. ~ ***in*** ①鼓风入(熔铁炉), (风)吹进来. ②〔美口〕忽然来访. ③〔美口〕乱花,浪费; 花光(或几乎用光). ***B- it!*** 混蛋! 讨厌! ~ ***itself out*** (风)停. ***B- me down!*** 〔美口〕真没料到! 一惊; 真不坏! ~ ***off*** ①*vi.* 刮掉,吹掉; 喷出(蒸汽);〔俚〕抱怨, 诉苦; 直言不讳. ②*vt.* 放出(锅炉中的水、蒸汽等); (以怒冲冲的谈话等) 发泄 (不满) 〔又作 ~ off steam〕. ~ ***one's bazoo*** [bəˈzu:] 〔美口〕吹牛, 夸口. ~ ***one's lines*** 说错(台词). ~ ***one's nose*** 擤鼻子. ~ ***one's own horn*** 〔美口〕自吹, 自夸. ~ ***one's own trumpet*** 自卖自夸, 自赞, 自大. ~ ***out*** ①停吹, 停止鼓风. ②(吹)胀; 吹破. ③(灯等)熄灭; 把(灯等)吹灭. ④〔美俚〕杀掉; (枪等)打穿(脑袋等); (保险丝)烧断. ~ ***over*** ①经过,走过. ②(云)吹散; (风)已定; 消灭. ③被淡忘. ~ ***sb. to a dinner*** 〔美俚〕请某人吃饭. ~ ***sb. up*** 责备某人. ~ ***the bellows [the coals, the fire]*** 〔古〕挑唆,煽动. ~ ***the show*** 〔美俚〕吹掉演出合同. ~ ***up*** ① *vi.* 炸,炸裂,被炸掉;〔俚〕失败, 被揭穿; 起(风), 来(风暴), (暴风雨等)更加厉害; 〔口〕发脾气 (~ *up at sb. over sth.* 在某事上对某人发脾气). ②*vt.* 炸掉, 炸破,爆破; 吹胀; 把(某人)捧上天,夸大; 毁掉,弄糟; 骂, 责备;【摄】〔口〕放大 (照相) (*A storm blew up.* 起风暴了. *The ship blew up.* 船爆炸了. ~ *up a bridge* 把桥炸掉. *He blew himself up importantly.* 他趾高气扬,不可一世). ~ ***upon*** ①*vt.* 害, 使倒霉; 使失信用; 使乏味; 告密,告发 (*His reputation is blown upon.* 他名誉扫地了). ②*n.* 吹风,一阵风; 暴风,疾风; 鼓风; 擤鼻涕; 吹奏(声); 大言不惭的人; (鲸的)喷水; (蝇的)产卵, 蝇卵; 〔口〕傲慢; (保险丝)熔断;【冶】吹炼 (*give the fire a* ~ 吹火. *clean the machinery with a* ~ 吹风打扫机器. *a few discordant* ~*s by bugler* 几声不协调的号声). ~**ball** (蒲公英等的)絮球. ~**-by** *n.* ①漏气; 漏液. ②(汽车的)废气燃烧器,尾气清理装置. ~**-by-**~ *a.* (讲述)极其详细的(*a* ~*-by-*~ *account of a debate* 对一次论战的极详细叙述). ~**-cock** 放泄旋塞. ~**-fish** ①吹气的人[物]. ②河豚; 黄麻鲈. ~**fly** 绿头大苍蝇. ~**gun** 吹箭筒. ~**hard** 〔美俚〕夸口大家, 吹牛大家. ~**hole** (鲸的)喷水孔; (铸件的) 气泡. ~**ing cat** 〔美俚〕爵士乐师. ~**iron** 吹管. ~**-job** 【空】〔口〕 喷气式飞机. ~**lamp** 喷灯. ~**mobile** 一种放在滑雪屐上以螺旋桨推动的车辆. ~ **moulding** (玻璃器皿等的) 吹气塑造法. ~**-of-cotton** (棉花)吐絮. ~**off** ①吹泄, 喷出. ②被吹掉之物. ③〔俚〕吹牛大家; 〔俚〕 绝顶, 顶点. ~**-off pipe [valve]** (汽锅的)安全排汽[水]管[阀]. ~**out** 喷出(口), 爆发;【电】熔解; 熄火,停炉; 车胎的爆裂[裂口], 沙丘的吹断;〔俚〕大宴会; 大事件. ~ **pipe** 吹管,吹火筒; 吹箭筒. ~**torch** 喷灯;〔美俚〕喷气战斗机. ~**tube** 玻璃吹制管. ~**up** ①爆炸; 崩溃; 破裂. ②(脾气等的)发作. ③(照片等的)放大; 放大了的照片等. **-er** *n.* ①吹玻璃工人,吹者,吹的东西. ②【机】鼓风机,风箱; 通风机; 增压器;【空】螺旋桨. ③【动】鲸; 河豚之类. ④〔美口〕夸口的人,吹牛家.

blow[2] [bləu] *vi.* ***(blew*** [blu:]; ***blown*** [bləun]***)*** (花)开放. — *vt.* 使开花; 开(花). — *n.* ①花; 开花(状态). ②绚丽多姿. *a rich, full* ~ *of color* 五彩缤纷. *in full* ~ (花)盛开.

blow[3] [bləu] *n.* ①打,打击,一击; 殴打. ②意外的灾害, 横祸,不幸. ③奇袭,猛攻. *a* ~ *to the head* 对头部的一击. *a* ~ *with the fist* 打来一拳. *a* ~ *to one's pride* 对自尊心的打击. ***at a (single)*** ~ ***[at one*** ~***]*** 一击就, 一举,一下子. ***at*** ~***s*** 在殴打[格斗]. ***come [fall] to*** ~***s*** 互相打起来; 开战. ***deal [give] a*** ~ ***at*** 打击, 给…一击. ***exchange*** ~***s*** 互殴,相打. ***strike a*** ~ ***against*** 抵抗, 抗击. ***strike a*** ~ ***for*** 为…斗争; 帮助, 支持. ***strike a*** ~ ***to*** 对…发起攻击,打击…. ***without striking a*** ~ 轻轻易易,坐享其成地,兵不血刃地.

blown[1] [bləun] *v.* blow[1] 的过去分词. —*a.* ①吹胀了的; 胀起的,鼓起的. ②(马等)累得喘气的; 疲劳极了的. ③满是蝇卵的. ④吹制的. ⑤被炸毁的; 坏了的; (食物等)走味的. ~ *stomachs* 胀鼓鼓的肚子, 大腹便便. *dispose of* ~ *canned goods* 对变质罐头食品的处理. ~**-moulded** *a.* 以吹气法塑造的. ~**-up** *a.* ①(照片等) 放大的. ②(因爆炸)损坏的. ③(气球等) 膨胀的. ④夸大的, 吹牛的.

blown[2] [bləun] *v.* blow[2] 的过去分词. — *a.* 开了花的, (花)盛开的.

blow·y [ˈbləui] *a.* ***(-i·er; -i·est)*** ①刮风的,风大的. ②风吹过的; 被风吹来吹去的,容易被风吹起的.

blowzed, blowz·y [blauzd, ˈblauzi] *a.* ①红脸的; 相貌粗俗的. ②邋遢的, 头发蓬乱的 (= blowsed, blowsy).

bls. = bales; barrels.

BLS = Bureau of Labour Statistics 〔美〕劳工统计局.

blub [blʌb] *vi.* 〔学俚〕哭.

blub·ber[1] [ˈblʌbə] *vt.* ①哭脏, 哭肿(脸). ②哭诉,哭着说. ~ *one's face* 哭肿(脏)脸. — *vi.* 哇哇地哭; 哭闹. — *n.* 哭泣,哭闹. *in a* ~ 哭泣,哭闹.

blub·ber[2] [ˈblʌbə] *a.* 肿大的; 肥厚的,(嘴唇)厚嘟嘟的. *thick,* ~ *lips* 肥厚的嘴唇.

blub·ber[3] [ˈblʌbə] *n.* ①鲸油, 鲸脂; 海兽脂. ②多余的脂肪.

blub·ber·y [ˈblʌbəri] *a.* ①哭泣的. ②脂肪多的,肥的;

脂肪一样的. ～ *lips* 厚嘴唇.

blu·chers [ˈbluːtʃə, -kə] *n.* 〔*pl.*〕①布柳彻半统靴〔因普鲁士元帅布柳彻而得名〕. ②(鞋舌与鞋面是一块皮,鞋帮皮在鞋面皮之上的)浅腰皮鞋.

bludg·eon [ˈblʌdʒən] *n.* 大头棒. — *vt.* ①用大头棒(不断地)打. ②威胁,强迫. *The boss finally ～ed him into accepting responsibility.* 上司强迫他负起责任. *the ～ of satire* 讽刺性的抨击.

blue [bluː] *a.* ①青,蓝,蓝色的,天蓝色的;(脸色)发灰[青]的,(皮毛等)青灰色的. ②阴郁的,忧郁的,沮丧的,悲观的;(气候)阴凉的;(希望等)暗淡的,无精打采的. ③穿蓝衣服的;以蓝色为标志的;〔美〕(南北战争中)北军的. ④〔英〕清教徒的,禁律严厉的. ⑤〔口〕(女子)有文艺趣味的,有学问的(女子). ⑥淫猥的,猥亵的,下流的;渎神的. ～ *smoke* 青烟. *feel* ～ 不高兴. ～ *from cold* 脸冻得发青. *look* ～ 愁眉不展;情绪不好;(形势)恶劣. *a* ～ *outlook* 悲观的见解. *Things look* ～. 事不称心,无希望. ～ *talk* 下流言论. *The air was* ～ *with oaths.* 到处是不堪入耳的咒骂. ***drink till all's*** ～ 大醉,烂醉,一醉方休. ***in a*** ～ ***funk*** 〔俚〕非常恐怖. ***like*** ～ ***murder*** 用全速力. ***once in a*** ～ ***moon*** 机会极少地,千载难逢地. ***till all is*** ～ 继续不断,长期地,彻底地,到最后. — *n.* ①青色,蓝色;〔the b-〕碧空,苍天,青天;海,苍海. ②蓝色颜料[染料](等);蓝布;穿蓝制服的人;〔美〕(南北战争中的)北军;(美国耶鲁 (Yale)、英国剑桥、牛津大学的)大学色标,大学体育队选手〔尤指上述三大学〕. ③英保守党员. ④女学者. ⑤〔the ～s〕一种感伤的黑人民歌;布鲁斯舞(曲)〔爵士音乐及舞步的一种〕. ⑥〔口〕〔the ～s〕忧郁,忧闷,不乐,沮丧. ***dark*** ～ 暗青色(此色又指 Oxford 大学和 Harrow 公学及其体育代表队选手而言). ***in*** ～ 穿蓝衣. ***in the*** ～. 在碧蓝的天空[海洋]里. ***light*** ～ 淡青色〔此色又指 Combridge 大学和 Eton 公学及其体育代表队选手而言〕. ***navy*** ～ 藏青,暗蓝. ***the Blues*** 英国的近卫骑兵. ***the men in*** ～ 警察;水兵;美国军队. ***be in the*** ～***s*** 没精打采;怏怏不乐,沮丧. ***have the*** ～***s*** = be in the ～s. ***out of the*** ～ 意外地,晴天霹雳,从天而降,突然. — *vt.* 把…染成天青色[蓝色],给…上蓝;〔口〕浪费,滥花(金钱). ～ **alert** 空袭警报;台风警报. ～ **baby** 有先天性心脏缺陷的婴儿. **Bluebeard** ①青髯公〔法国民间故事中一个连杀六妻的恶人的别号〕;〔喻〕残酷的丈夫;乱娶妻妾的男子. ②【植】蕕,蔺香草. ～**bell**【植】圆叶风铃草 *(the* ～*bell of Scotland* = *harebell)*. ～**-bellied Yankee** 〔美〕地道的新英格兰人. ～**belt**〔日〕蓝带〔授予受过三年训练的柔道家的带子〕. ～**berry**【植】乌饭树;乌饭树的紫黑浆果. ～**bill**〔美方〕美洲蓝嘴鸟. **B- Bird** 女童露营团. ～**bird**【鸟】(美国)蓝知更鸟. ～**-black** *a.* 深蓝色的. ～ **blood** 贵族,名门. ～**-blooded** *a.* ①出身贵族的,名门的. ②(马等)纯种的. ～ **bonnet** ①(苏格兰)蓝色便帽. ②【植】特克萨斯羽扇豆;(苏格兰)矢车菊. ～ **book** ①〔B- Book〕(英、美等国政府的)蓝皮书〔就某一专题发表的报告、外交文书等〕. ②〔美俚〕职工名册,名人录;(大学考试用)蓝皮白纸簿. ～**bottle** ①【植】矢车菊. ②〔俚〕青蝇. ③〔俚〕蓝衣警察. ～**-brick university**〔俚〕名牌大学(指牛津、剑桥等大学). ～ **chip** 热门的股票. ～**-chip** *a., n.* ①热门的(股票);靠得住的(财产). ②第一流的;值钱的. ～**coat** 蓝衣人〔水手、警察、美国南北战争中北军士兵等的别名〕(*a* ～ *coat boy* 慈善学校〔特指伦敦 B- School〕的学生;蓝衣侍者). ～**-collar** *a.* 穿蓝领工装的;体力劳动的. **B- Cross** ①〔美〕畜类保护协会. ②医疗服务救济协会. ③催嚏性毒气〔俗名〕. ～ **devils** ①忧郁;沮丧. ②惊险的幻想. ～**-eyed** *a.* ①蓝眼的. ②心爱的. ③〔美俚〕容易上当的. ～**fish**【鱼】(美洲大西洋海岸产的)青鱼. ～**-flag**〔美〕蓝鸢尾〔Tennessee 州州花〕. ～ **funk** ①〔美俚〕沮丧,为难. ②难以抑制的恐惧. ～ **gag** 下流话. ～**gill**【鱼】翻车鱼. ～**grass**〔美〕(盛产于肯塔基州中部的)蓝绿茎牧草. **B- grass state**〔美〕肯塔基州〔别名〕. ～ **grassers** ①肯塔基州人〔别名,又叫 ～ grass folks〕. ②〔美〕传统乡村音乐. ～**heart**【植】鬼羽箭属. ～ **helmet** 蓝盔军〔联合国武装部队〕的一员. ～ **hens**〔美〕特拉华人〔别名〕. ～**jack** ①硫酸铜. ②栎属植物. ～**jacket** 水兵. ～ **jeans** 蓝色工装裤. ～ **jersey** 水兵,水手. ～ **john**【矿】紫萤石. ～ **laws**〔美〕①清教徒法规. ②〔美史〕星期日法规〔殖民地时代新英格兰禁止星期日跳舞、宴会等〕. ～ **light(s)** 信号花火. ～ **line**【体】(冰球场的)蓝线. ～ **man**〔俚〕穿制服的警察. ～ **mass**〔美〕= blue-pill. ～**nose** ①青鼻子的人. ②清教徒,卫道士;〔B-〕〔加〕沿海各省〔尤指 Nova Scotia〕的居民[船、马铃薯]. ～ **Monday** 四旬节 (Lent) 前的星期一;〔美〕不开心的星期一. ～ **moon** 极长的一个时期. ～ **movie** 色情电影. ～ **murder** 恐怖的喊声. ～**nose**〔俚〕拘谨的人. ～ **ointment**【医】水银药膏. ～ **pig**〔美俚〕威士忌酒. ～**-pencil** *vt.* 用蓝铅笔校订(原稿等);〔美俚〕否决,不批准. ～ **pigeon**【海】测深锤. ～**-pill** ①【药】汞丸. ②〔美国〕子弹. ～**point**【贝】蓝点蛎. ～**print** ① *n.* 蓝色照相,蓝色版;蓝图,设计图;计划大纲;原本. ② *vt.* 为…制蓝图;晒(图);为…制订计划. ～ **revolution** ①(一些西方国家的所谓)"性解放". ②黄色读物的泛滥. ～**-ribbon** *a.* ①第一流的. ②(陪审用)特选的. ～**-ribbon jury [panel]**〔美俚〕(审理重大案件的)特选陪审团. ～ **ruin** 低级杜松子酒. ～**runner**【鱼】闪光鲹. ～**stem**(北美西部作干草用的)蓝茎草. ～**-sky** *a.* ①(股票)不可靠的;财务不健全的. ②纯理论性的. ③不切实际的. ～**-sky law**〔美〕无信用股票取缔法. ～**stocking** ①女学者,女才子,女文学家. ②(冒充)学者气派的女性. ～**stone**【矿】硫酸铜,胆矾;〔美〕(建筑或铺路用的)青石;黏土质砂岩. ～ **streak** ①连续的事物. ②极快的闪光,一闪即逝的东西. ③连珠炮似的谈话 (*talk a* ～ *streak* 讲话滔滔不绝. *like a* ～ *streak* 很快;极有成效地). ～ **Sunday Law** 星期日禁止劳动法. ～**throat** *n.*【动】蓝喉鸲. ～ **water** 深海,沧海. ～**weed**【植】蓝蓟. ～ **white finish** (织物的)上蓝整理. ～ **William**〔美俚〕五十元钞票. ～ **wool** 高级有光羊毛. **-ness** *n.* 蓝色,青蓝.

blueing [ˈblu(ː)iŋ] *n.* = bluing.

blueish [ˈblu(ː)iʃ] *a.* = bluish.

blues·rock [ˈbluːzrɔk] *n.* 布鲁斯摇摆乐〔以摇摆音乐为背景的一种黑人伤感音乐〕.

blu·et [ˈbluːit] *n.*【植】茵草科青花植物之名;矢车菊等.

blue·y [ˈbluːi] *a.* 带蓝色的.

bluff[1] [blʌf] *a.* ①绝壁的,壁立的,陡峭的. ②直率的,爽快的,坦率的;粗率的 (*opp.* subtle). ③【海】(船头等)前端平阔而垂直的. — *n.* ①峭壁,断崖. ②(船头等的)鼓起部分. *the B-* 高地. **-ly** *ad.* 率直地;粗率地. **-ness** *n.* ①陡壁. ②朴直.

bluff[2] [blʌf] *vt.* ①〔俚〕以假象欺骗;假装. ②(虚张声势地)恐吓,吓唬. ③【牌】(持弱牌时)下大注吓倒(对方). ～ *sb. into doing sth.* 欺骗某人使做某事. ～ *sb. out of doing sth.* 吓倒某人使不敢做某事. ～ *and deceive* 招摇撞骗. — *vi.* 虚张声势;装腔作势. — *n.* ①欺骗,吓唬. ②虚张声势的人,吓唬人的人. *make a* ～ = *play a game of* ～ 采取恐吓手段. ***call sb.'s*** ～【牌】(顶住某人的下大注威吓)叫某人摊牌;揭露某人的外强中干. (*He always said he would quit, so we finally called his* ～. 他常以辞职相要挟,我们终于让他另请高就). ***put on a good*** ～ ***(run a*** ～ ***on)*** 虚张声势地恐吓,吓唬;蒙蔽,欺骗.

bluff·er [ˈblʌfə] *n.* ①骗子,招摇撞骗的人. ②虚张声势的人,吓唬人的人.

blu·ing [ˈbluːiŋ] *n.*【化】上蓝剂,蓝色漂白剂〔用以防止白色织物洗染时变黄〕.

blu·ish [ˈblu(ː)iʃ] *a.* 带青色的,浅蓝色的. **-ness** *n.*

Blume [blu:m] *n.* 布卢姆〔姓氏〕.
blun·der [ˈblʌndə] *n.* 大错,失策,疏忽. *commit a* ~ 犯大错. — *vi.* ①犯大错;出漏子. ②跌跌撞撞地走〔跑〕;慌张地走〔跑〕*(along; on; into)*; 摔,拌交. *Without my glasses I ~ed into the wrong room.* 我因为没戴眼镜,跌跌撞撞地走错了房间. — *vt.* ①无意中说出,漏嘴说出. ②弄糟,弄错,做错,办错. ~ *the account* 算错帐. ~ ***against*** 碰着,撞着. ~ ***away*** 错失(良机等). ~ ***into*** *(sense)* 无意中得(妙解). ~ ***on [upon]*** 无意中发现,碰见. ~ ***out*** *(secret)* 不觉中泄漏出(秘密). ~ ***through*** *(one's lesson)* 胡乱做完(功课). ~**head** 傻瓜.
blun·der·buss [ˈblʌndəbʌs] *n.* ①老式大口径短程霰弹枪. ②(因粗卤、轻率而易做错事的)大笨蛋.
blun·der·er [ˈblʌndərə] *n.* 容易做错事的人; 犯大错的人.
blun·der·ing [ˈblʌndəriŋ] *a.* ①浮躁的; 粗笨的; 粗卤的. ②容易犯错误的;大错的. **-ly** *ad.*
blunge [blʌndʒ] *vt.* (烧窑时)将(胶泥)用水搅拌. ~**r** ①拌胶泥工. ②拌胶泥大桶;拌泥杵.
blunt [blʌnt] *a.* ①(刀等)钝,不快的,不锋利的,无锋刃的;(笔尖等)无尖锋的. ②(感觉等)迟钝的;愚钝的. ③粗卤的,直率的,干脆的; 骇板的. *short,* ~ *nose* 短小扁平的鼻子. ~ *about the feeling of others* 对别人的感情很少理解〔觉察、体会等〕. ***to be*** ~ 〔插入语〕老实说. — *n.* ①短粗的针〔雪茄烟等〕. ②钝器. ③〔俚〕现金,现钞. — *vt.* ①把…弄钝,使失锋刃. ②使变愚钝;使受挫,减弱. *a knife ~ed from use* 用钝的刀. *imagination ~ed by wine* 想象力因喝酒而受损害. ~ *the enemy's attack* 挫敌锋芒. **-ly** *ad.* *(to put it* ~〔插入语〕直截了当地说,(和你)直说吧). **-ness** *n.*
blur [blə:] *n.* ①污点,污斑;污名. ②暧昧不明,一片模糊,模糊不清的东西〔声音〕. *~s in one's life* 历史污点. *a book full of ~s* 满是污痕的书. *the foggy* ~ 雾气一片模糊. — *vt.* ①把…弄模糊. ②污损,涂污,弄脏. — *vi.* ①沾染污迹. ②变模糊. *Everything blurred as he ran.* 他奔跑的时候眼前一片模糊. ~ ***out*** ①使变模糊. ②抹掉,涂掉.
blurb [blə:b] *n.* 〔美口〕①新书推荐广告〔多印在书的护封上〕. ②大肆吹捧的广告. — *vt.* (通过护封简介)吹捧(作家); 为…大做广告. **-ing** *n.* 〔美口〕无线电广告. **-ist** *n.* 写护封书评者,吹捧者.
blurble [blə:bl] *vt.* 〔美口〕大捧特捧,极力夸奖.
blurt [blə:t] *vt.* 突然说出,失口说出, 漏出*(out)*. *He ~s out all he hears.* 他漏嘴说出了他听到的一切. — *n.* 漏嘴说出的话.
blush [blʌʃ] *vi.* ①脸红,惭愧. ②害臊,怕羞,忸怩 *(at, for)*. ③呈现红色. ~ *for sb.* 替某人脸红. ~ *to the roots of one's hair* 脸红到发根,极度羞愧. *He did not ~ to (do).* 他厚颜无耻地(做)…. — *vt.* ①把…弄红. ②因脸红而表露出(真实情感等). ~ *one's truth* 因脸红而表露出真情. — *n.* 红脸;红色;〔古〕一见,一瞥. ***at [on] (the) first*** ~ 猛一见,骤然看来. ~ ***at one's words*** 因失言而脸红. ~ ***for [with] shame*** 羞愧得脸红. ***put (sb.) to the*** ~ 使(某人)窘得脸红. ***Spare my ~es.*** 别让我脸红了〔不要过分夸赞我了〕. **-er** *n.* 胭脂. **-ful** *a.* (使人)脸红的. **-ingly** *ad.*
blus·ter [ˈblʌstə] *vi.* ①(风等)狂吹;(浪等)汹涌. ②(人)咆哮,嚷. *A typhoon ~ed over the land.* 飓风扫过大地. *He ~ed and swaggered like a conquering hero.* 他声势汹汹,不可一世. — *vt.* ①喝叱,恐吓. ②怒冲冲地说 *(out, forth)*. *He ~ed his way through the crowd.* 他吆喝着挤出人群. ~ *out [forth] threats* 大声威吓. ~ ***about*** 叫嚣. ~ ***at one's will*** 横行霸道. ~ ***oneself into anger*** 勃然大怒. — *n.* ①狂风声,惊涛骇浪声. ②骚音,大吵大闹,咆哮. ③恐吓;大话. **-ous** [-əs], **-y** *a.* = blustering.
blus·ter·er [ˈblʌstərə] *n.* 咆哮的人,狂暴的人; 吓唬人的人.
blus·ter·ing [ˈblʌstəriŋ] *a.* ①狂风大作的;(波涛)汹涌的. ②恐吓的,狂暴的. **-ly** *ad.*
blvd = boulevard.
BM, B.M. = ①Bachelor of Medicine 医学士. ②British Museum 不列颠博物馆(旧称大英博物馆). ③bowel movement〔口〕大便.
BMDS = ballistic missile defence system 防弹道导弹系统.
BMEWS = ballistic missile early warning system 反弹道导弹预报系统,弹道导弹远程预警系统.
BMOC = big man on campus〔美学俚〕校内大人物.
BO, B.O., b.o. = ①back order 暂时无法满足的订货. ②body odo(u)r 体臭,狐臭. ③box office 戏院票房,戏院售票处. ④branch office 分支机构,分支办公室.
bo [bəu] *n.* ①〔美口〕老兄,老弟,老朋友. ②〔美口〕浪子;流浪汉. ③小伙子. — *int.* = boh.
bo·a [ˈbəuə] *n.* ①圆筒形皮毛〔羽毛〕围巾. ②大蛇,蟒蛇. ~ **constrictor** *n.* 王蛇,蟒蛇.
B.O.A. = British Olympic Association 英国奥林匹克委员会.
BOAC = British Overseas Airways Corporation 英国海外航空公司〔现已与 British European Airways 英国欧洲航空公司合并,称 British Airways 英国航空公司〕.
Bo·a·ner·ges [ˌbəuəˈnə:dʒi:z] *n.* 雷子〔耶稣赐与其门徒 James 及 John 的别号〕;〔用作 *sing.*〕嗓子大的传教师〔雄辩家〕.
boar [bɔ:] *n.* ①(未阉的)公猪; 公猪肉. ②〔又作 wild boar〕公野猪.
board [bɔ:d] *n.* ①板〔通常指宽 4 英寸半以上厚 2 英寸半以下者〕,木板;纸板. ②(广告)牌;(棋)盘;〔口〕配电盘(等). ③〔*pl.*〕【剧】舞台. ④餐桌;食物;伙食,〔有时指〕膳宿. ⑤会议桌;会议;全体委员;委员会;部,厅,局,管理处. ⑥船的甲板;舷,舷侧;船内;车内. ⑦〔废〕边;海岸. *cloth ~s* (书籍的)布面精装. *a remote control* ~ 遥控盘,遥控台. *a* ~ *for checkers* 棋盘. *a piece of* ~ 一块板. *a groaning* ~ 盛宴,丰盛的饭菜. *a bulletin* ~ 布告牌. ~ *and lodging* 膳宿. ~ *of directors* 理事会,董事会. ***above*** ~ 光明正大. ~ ***and [by, on]*** ~ (船)并排. ***B- of Education***〔英〕教育部〔现改名 the Ministry of Education〕; ~ ***of education*** (一般的)教育委员会;〔美〕(各州、县、市管理中小学的)教育管理委员会. ~ ***of equalization***〔美〕税率调查委员会. ***B- of Trade***〔英〕商业部;〔b- of t-〕〔美〕商会;芝加哥市农产品交易所. ***by the*** ~ 在舷外,越过舷边,(由船上)向海中. ***come on*** ~ 回船. ***fall on*** ~ = run on ~. ***fall over*** ~ 从船上掉落水中. ***free on*** ~【商】船上交货,离岸价格(略作 FOB 或 f.o.b.). ***go by the*** ~ (桅杆)折断落于船外;破产;(努力等)落空;(计划)成泡影,失败. ***go on the ~s*** 当演员. ***have [take]*** … ***on*** ~ 载有,装有. ***lay a ship on*** ~ 使船靠拢(他船). ***make short ~s***【海】常常逆风斜进. ***on*** ~ ①在船上,在船〔飞机〕中 *(on ~ the plane* 在飞机上);〔美〕在车上 *(go [get] on* ~ 乘船,乘车). ②【棒球】〔口〕出垒. ***on the ~s*** 登台,做演员. ***on even*** ~ ***with*** 与…齐舷并进;在和…同条件下. ***run on*** ~ *(of another ship)* ①撞着(别船). ②攻击. ***sweep the*** ~ 赢得全部赌注,通吃;全胜. ***tread the ~s*** = ***walk the ~s*** = go on the ~s. — *vt.* ①用板铺〔盖、围、堵〕上. ②为…提供膳食〔包饭〕;使寄膳;〔美〕寄养(马). ③上(船),坐(船);〔美〕搭(车);乘(飞机). ④攻入(敌船等); 强行靠近(敌船等). ~ *over a well* 用木板做井栏. *They ~ed him for $ 40 a week.* 他们按每周收费 40 美元给他包伙. *The pirate ship ~ed the clipper.* 海盗船强行靠近快艇. — *vi.* ①寄膳,搭伙,包饭. ②【海】逆风斜进. ~ ***around***【美】轮餐〔教员轮流在学生家吃饭〕. ~ ***at*** *(so much a week)* (每周)给膳费(若干). ~ ***in*** 在寄宿处寄膳.

~ *out* 在外面寄膳. ~ *over* 用木板铺上(围住). ~ *up* 用板钉上[围上] (~ *up the door* 把门用板钉上). ~ **chairman** 董事长. ~ **foot** 板英尺〔木材计量单位，相当于厚一英寸、面积一平方英尺的木材〕. ~ **game** 需用棋盘的游戏〔如 Chess, checkers 等〕. ~ **money** = ~ wages. ~**-out** *vt.* 使因病退伍. ~ **room** (董事会等的)会议室. ~**-school** (英国的)公立小学校〔现在叫 county council school〕. ~ **wages** 〔*pl.*〕①(给仆人等的)膳费折合的津贴；代作工资的膳宿. ②仅够膳宿的工资. ~**walk** 〔美〕(海滨等的)木板(散步)路.

board·er [ˈbɔːdə] *n.* ①寄膳者，寄宿生. ②(车船、飞机等的)乘客. ③闯入敌船者，攻入敌船的队员. ④〔美〕寄养的马. *a day* ~ 寄膳不寄宿的人[学生].

board·ing [bɔːdiŋ] *n.* ①围板，隔板，地板〔总称〕，木板；(由几块板拼成的)大木板. ②寄膳，搭伙；寄膳宿. ③上船[车、飞机]. ④攻入[占领]敌船. *an uneventful* ~ 一次平安无事的乘船[车、飞机]旅行. ~**-card** (班机等的)客货单. ~**house** (供膳的)寄宿处，公寓. ~ **measure** 量木材的特用计量制. ~**-out** ①在外寄膳. ②(孤儿的)寄养. ~ **school** 寄宿学校〔*opp.* day school〕.

boar·fish [ˈbɔːˌfiʃ] *n.* (*pl.* ~*(es)*) 豚鼻鱼.

boar·hound [ˈbɔːhaund] *n.* 野猪猎犬.

boar·ish [ˈbɔːriʃ] *a.* 野猪一样的；卤莽的；凶猛的.

Bo·as [ˈbəuæz, ˈbəuəz] *n.* 博厄斯〔姓氏〕.

boast [bəust] *vi.* 夸，自夸，夸耀 (*of, about*). *She* ~*ed of her family's wealth.* 她自夸家里有钱. *We must never brag and* ~. 我们决不可自吹自擂. — *vt.* ①夸，夸耀，夸口说. ②以有…而自豪，有可以夸耀的…；自负有，自恃有. *The town* ~*s a fine park.* 该城以有一座漂亮的公园而自豪. *He* ~*s himself a genius.* 他自称是天才. ~ *of [about]* 夸耀，自夸，吹嘘. ~ *oneself of* 自夸，自负，自恃. *without* ~*ing* 并非夸口，不是自吹〔插入语〕(*Without* ~*ing, I may say* .... 并非夸口，我可以说…). — *n.* ①夸，夸口，自负. ②自负的事物，引为自傲的东西. *Talent is his* ~. 他自夸有才，他以才子自居. *great* ~*, small roast.* 夸夸其谈，所成无多；好大言者实行少. *make a* ~ *of* 自夸，夸耀.

boast·er [ˈbəustə] *n.* 自夸者，大言不惭的人.

boast·ful [ˈbəustful] *a.* 夸口的，自负的，傲慢的. *be* ~ *of* ... 自夸是…，以…自夸. **-ly** *ad.* **-ness** *n.*

boat [bəut] *n.* ①小舟，小船，(小)艇，(大船所载)救生艇；帆船，渔船. ②汽轮〔常指小汽轮〕；邮船，大轮船. ③船形物，船行器皿；【化】舟皿；【宗】舟形香炉. *a motor* ~ 机帆船. *a sailing* ~ 帆船. *an open* ~ 无甲板船. *a rowing* ~ 划艇. *a sauce* ~ 船形佐料碟. ~*'s length* 艇身 (*win by a* ~*'s length* 赛艇时领先一艇长的距离). *burn one's* ~*s* 布背水之阵，破釜沉舟. *by* ~ 乘船 (*go by* ~ 乘船去). *fasten [get out] a* ~ 系住船. *have an oar in every man's* ~ 多管闲事，乱管闲事. *in one [the same]* ~ 在同一状态下，处境相同；同舟共济，共患难. *man a* ~ 为船配备船员. *miss the* ~ ①失败；错过机会，坐失良机. ②未能抓住(问题的)要点. *push the* ~ *out* 〔口〕庆祝. *rock the* ~ 捣乱. *ship's* ~ 船上小艇；舰载救生艇. *take* ~ 乘船，坐船. *take to the* ~*s* ①乘船上小艇逃生. ②仓猝放弃所进行的事业. — *vt.* ①用船装运. ②把…装入船内. *They* ~*ed us across the bay.* 他们把我们用船运过[摆渡过]海湾. — *vi.* ①坐船去. ②划船；乘船(游玩). *We* ~*ed down the Thames.* 我们放舟直下太晤士河. ~ *it* ①坐船去；划船. ②顺风驶. *B- the oars!* 收桨! ~ **bill** 【鸟】(南美)阔啄苍鹭. ~**-billed heron** 【鸟】舟嘴鹭. ~ **chocks** 短艇架. ~**-deck** 救生艇甲板. ~ **drill** 【海】救生演习. ~ **fall** 短艇索. ~ **fly** 船蝇. ~ **hoist** 起艇机. ~**hook** 有钩的篙子. ~**house** 船库，艇库〔水边停放游艇的处所〕. ~ **line** 【海】(由母船丢给小艇的)系索. ~**load** *n.* ①一船货[旅客]. ②载一船之量. ~**man** ①船夫，船工；桨手. ②出租[出售]游艇者，租船老板. ~**manship** 划船术. ~ **race** 划船比赛. ~ **train** (与船运衔接的)联运列车. **-ful** *n.* 一船所载的量.

boat·a·ble [ˈbəutəbl] *a.* ①可用小船运输的. ②可通航小船的.

boat·age [ˈbəutidʒ] *n.* ①小船运输. ②小船运费. ③救生艇[船载小艇]容量.

boat·el [bəuˈtel] *n.* 〔美〕(附有停船设施的)汽艇游客旅馆.

boat·er [ˈbəutə] *n.* ①乘小船的人，游艇乘客. ②〔英口〕硬壳平顶草帽〔十九世纪英国人夏季划船时所戴〕.

boat·ing [ˈbəutiŋ] *n.* ①划船；乘船(游玩). *go* ~ 乘船〔尤指划船〕游玩.

boat·nik [ˈbəutnik] *n.* 〔口〕水上人家，船户.

boat·swain, bo's'n, bo'sun, bosun [ˈbəusn, 〔罕〕ˈbəutswein] *n.* ①(商船的)水手长. ②(军舰的)掌帆长；(掌帆缆的)准尉. ~**'s chair** (绳系吊板的)高空作业台. ~**'s mate** 掌帆长副手；副水手长.

bob¹ [bɔb] *n.* ①(女人、小孩的)短发；束发，髻；卷毛，卷毛假发；(马等)截短的尾巴. ②诗节落尾的迭句，歌曲的短迭句. —*vt.* 截短，剪短(发、尾等). *They bobbed their hair to be in style.* 她们剪了赶时髦的短发式. *wear one's hair bobbed* 剪短发. ~ **wig** 〔英〕法官戴的假发.

bob² [bɔb] *n.* ①【物】摆锤，称锤(等)；耳珰；(钓丝的)浮子，漂. ②一组钓钩；一串浮饵；一束叶子；一串花(葡萄等). ③急动；急牵；(点一点头)招呼；(快速一屈膝)行礼. ④摆，摆动；跳舞；浮动，振动. ⑤〔俚〕步兵. ⑥ = ~ sled. *a* ~ *of the head* 微微点一下头. *a plumb* ~ (测量用)铅锤. — *vi.* ①上下跳动；急动，急牵. ②行屈膝礼. ③浮动；用浮漂钓 (*for*). *The cork was bobbing on the water.* (钓丝的)浮子在水中上下跳动. — *vt.* ①轻敲；使敲(或撞). ②急速摆动. ~ *the head* 头微微点一点. ~ *a greeting.* 点头打招呼(= ~ *at sb.*) ~ *at [for] (apple)* 把(苹果)用线吊着用嘴去吃的游戏. ~ *up* 急忙浮上；突然出现；突然站起 (*The question often* ~*s up.* 那个问题常被提起). ~ *up like a cork* 挽回颓势，东山再起；恢复元气 (*He* ~*s up like a cork.* 他虽然屡经挫折，总是能东山再起). *dry* ~ 〔英〕板球组学生. *light* ~*s* 〔古〕轻装步兵. *wet* ~ 〔英〕划船组学生.

bob³ [bɔb] *n.* 〔*sing., pl.*〕〔英口〕= shilling.; 〔美口〕= dollar.

bob⁴ [bɔb] *n.* 未断奶的小牛.

bob⁵ [bɔb] *n.* 【动】(一群)沙蝎.

Bob, Bob·by [bɔb, ˈbɔbi] *n.* 鲍勃〔男子名，*Robert* 的昵称〕. ~**'s *your uncle*** 〔原英〕不要紧，没关系，放心好了，别着急 (~*'s your uncle when* ... 如果发生…的情况，请不必着急).

Bob·a·dil [ˈbɔbədil] *n.* 好夸口的人，吹牛大家〔作家 Ben Johnson 的作品 *Every Man in His Humour* 中的人物〕.

bo·ba·tor·i·um [bɔbəˈtɔːriəm] *n.* 〔美〕专剪短发型的理发店〔= bobber shop〕.

bobbed [bɔbd] *a.* 短毛的，短发的；截尾的.

bob·ber [ˈbɔbə] *n.* ①晃动的人或物. ②钓丝浮子.

bob·ber·y [ˈbɔbəri] *n.* 〔口〕吵闹，叫喊，骚动. *raise a* ~ 大吵大闹. — *a.* 吵闹的. *a* ~ *pack* 一群吵闹的猎狗.

Bob·bie [ˈbɔbi] *n.* 博比〔女子名，Roberta 的昵称〕.

bob·bin [ˈbɔbin] *n.* ①木管，纱管，绕线筒；鼓轮. ②(拴在插梢绳末端的)小木球；(门扣上的)吊带把手. ③【纺】(纺纱机的)筒管，筒子；亚麻捆；【电】绕丝管，线圈架，点火线圈. *a ribbon* ~ 色带盘. ~ *oil* 锭子油. ~ ***and fly frame*** 粗纺机.

bob·bi·net [ˌbɔbiˈnet, ˌbɑbəˈnet] *n.* 【纺】珠罗纱，六角网眼纱.

bob·bish [ˈbɔbiʃ] *a.* 〔俚〕高兴的，笑哈哈的，快活的，活泼的，精神抖擞的.

bob·ble [ˈbɔbl] *vi., n.* ①反复跳动；(篮球)在蓝圈上跳动. ②〔英口〕水波荡漾；微波荡漾的小港湾. ③(球)漏踢，漏接；〔美俚〕失误. — *vt.* 〔美俚〕失(球).

Bob·by [ˈbɔbi] *n.* 博比〔男子名，Robert 的昵称〕.

bob·by [ˈbɔbi] *n.* ①〔英俚〕警察. 初生之犊(=～ calf).

bob·by-dazz·lers [ˈbɔbiˌdæzləz] *n.* 〔英方〕引人注目的东西；华而不实的东西.

bobby pin [ˈbɔbi pin] *n.* 〔美〕(短发型)发夹.

bob·by·socks, bob·by·sox [ˈbɔbisɔks] *n.* 〔美口〕女孩短袜.

bob·by·sox·er, bob·by-sock·er [ˈbɔbisɔksə, ˈbɔbisɔkə] *n.* 〔美口〕赶时髦的少女.

bob·cat [ˈbɔbkæt] *n.* 【动】美国山猫.

bo·bèche [bəuˈbeʃ] *n.* 〔F.〕烛台托盘.

bob·o·link [ˈbɔbəliŋk] *n.* 【鸟】(北美洲的)食米鸟.

bob·sled, bob·sleigh [ˈbɔbsled, ˈbɔbslei] *n.* 〔美〕(滑雪和雪地运木材的)连橇. — *vi.* 乘双连雪橇.

bob·stay [ˈbɔbstei] *n.* 【海】船头斜桅支索.

bob·tail [ˈbɔbteil] *n.* ①截短的尾；截短尾的动物〔犬、马等〕. ②晚礼服. ③〔军俚〕罢免，革退. — *a.* 截尾的；截短了的. — *vt.* 截…的尾；截短.

bob·white [ˈbɔbˈhwait] *n.* 【鸟】北美鹑.

bo·ca·sin [bɔˈkæsin] *n.* 一种细麻布.

Boc·cac·cio [bəuˈkɑːtʃiəu], **Gio·van·ni** [ˈdʒiːəvɑːni] 薄加丘〔1313—1375，文艺复兴时期意大利作家，《十日谈》的作者〕.

boc·cle, boc·ce, boc·ci [ˈbɔtʃiː] *n.* 木球.

Boche, boche [bɔʃ] *n.* 〔俚、蔑〕①德国人；德国兵. ②暴民. ③傻瓜.

bock [bɔk] *vi.* 〔Scot.〕〔英方〕作呕，呕吐. — *n.* 烈性黑啤酒；一杯(黑)啤酒 (= ～ beer).

bod [bɔd] *n.* 〔英口〕人〔body 之略〕. ～ **biz** 〔美俚〕自我感觉训练 (=sensitivity training).

bo·da·cious [bəuˈdeiʃəs] *a.* 〔美俚〕胆大包天的〔由 bold 与 audacious 二词组合而成〕.

bode[1] [bəud] *vt., vi.* 预示，预兆；〔古〕预报. *The news ～s evil days for him.* 这个消息对他是不祥之兆. *The beginning of that summer ～ed ill.* 夏季一开始就来势不善. ～ ***ill [well]*** 主凶〔吉〕.

bode[2] [bəud] bide 的过去式及过去分词.

bode[3] [bəud] 〔废〕bid 的过去式及过去分词.

bode·ful [ˈbəudful] *a.* 预兆的；不祥的.

bo·de·ga [bəuˈdiːgə] *n.* 〔Sp.〕①酒窖，酒库. ②酒店；(特指西班牙籍美国人的)杂货店.

bode·ment [ˈbəudmənt] *n.* 前兆，预兆，预示；凶兆，不祥之兆.

bo·dhi [ˈbəudi] *n.* 【佛】大彻大悟.

bo·dhi·sat [ˈbəudisæt], **bo·dhi·satt·va** [ˌbəudiˈsætvə] *n.* 【佛】菩萨.

bod·ice [ˈbɔdis] *n.* ①(女人)紧身胸衣；女服的上部；妇女穿在衬衫外的背心. ②鲸骨褡，乳褡.

bod·ied [ˈbɔdid] *a.* ①有形体的，有躯体的. ②具有…躯体〔形体〕的〔用以构成复合词〕. *strong-～* 身体强壮的. *big-～* 身材魁梧的.

bod·i·less [ˈbɔdilis] *a.* 无体的，无形的，脱离形体的.

bod·i·ly [ˈbɔdili] *a.* ①躯体的，身体的，肉体的. ②有形的，具体的. ～ *organs* 身体各器官. ～ *defects* 身体缺陷. ～ *punishment* 体罚. ～ *and mental diseases* 肉体上和精神上的疾病. ***in ～ fear*** 害怕危及身体. — *ad.* ①肉体上. ②有形体地. ③亲身，自己. ④一切，全部，悉，整体. *The audience rose ～.* 听众全体起立. ～ **exercise** 体操.

bod·ing [ˈbəudiŋ] *a.* 凶兆的；预兆的. ～ ***care*** 不祥的忧虑，不吉利的念头. — *n.* 凶兆；前兆，预兆.

bod·kin [ˈbɔdkin] *n.* ①大针，粗针；锥子；串子. ②(束发)长别针. ③【印】活字铗. ④〔英口〕挤在两人当中的人. ⑤〔军〕短剑. ***sit ～*** 挤坐两人当中. ***ride ～*** 夹在两骑当中. **～-work** (女服)金线衣边.

Bod·ley [ˈbɔdli] *n.* 博德利〔姓氏〕.

bod·y [ˈbɔdi] *n.* ①身体，体躯，肉体；尸首；躯干；【林】立木. ②本体，主体；主力；本文，ˈ正文；部分. ③(衣服的)上身部；女胸衣. ④队，群，一团；团体，机关，机构. ⑤〔口〕人〔常用以构成复合词，如 anybody〕；(犯人、继承人等的)身份. ⑥物体，(液)体；实质；(酒等的)密度，浓度. ⑦车身；船身；【空】机身；(陶器等的)素胚；(乐器等的)共鸣部分；布身，布的厚薄软硬；【数】立体；【天】天体；【印】铅字身. *the human ～* 人体. *cremate the ～* 将尸体火化. *the ～ of a tree* 树的主干. *a regular ～* 正多面体. *a solid [liquid, gaseous] ～* 固〔液、气〕体. *the ～ of the population* 人口的主要成分. *a ～ of cavalry* 一队骑兵. *the ～ of the book* 本文. *the student ～* 学生会. *a diplomatic ～* 外交团. *a ～ of words* 一组单词. *a good sort of ～* 好人. *an heir of the ～* 直系继承人. *a ～ of facts* 一大堆事实. *heavenly bodies* 天体. *wine of good [full] ～* 醇厚的葡萄酒. ～ *corporate* 法人团体. ～ ***and soul*** 整个，全心全意 (*work night and day, ～ and soul* 日以继夜、全心全意地工作). ～ ***crash tactics*** (日本在第二次世界大战中以敢死飞机冲击军舰的)肉弹战术. ～ ***of Christ*** 圣餐面包. ～ ***politic*** 国家. ***give ～ to*** 使…具体化，实现；使有形体. ***heir of one's ～*** 直系继承人. ***in a ～*** 全体，整个 (*resign in a ～* 总辞职). ***in ～*** 亲身，自行. ***in the ～*** 生动；活着，神志清醒. ***keep ～ and soul together*** 勉强维持生活，苟延残喘. ***the main ～***【军】主力部队. ***the whole ～*** 全身；全体. — *vt.* ①赋与…以形体. ②使具体化，体现，实现；刻划；使呈现于心中 (*forth*). *Imaginations bodies forth the forms of things unknown* 想象力使未知事物的形象呈现于心中. ～ **bag** 口袋〔带拉链的橡皮袋〕. ～ **blow**【拳】向对手身体的打击. ～ **builder** ①车身制造者. ②滋补品. ③健身器械. ④健身者. **～-centreed** *a.*【物】体心的. ～ **check** ①*n.* (冰球赛等)用身体挡住对方. ②*vt.* 用身体阻挡. ～ **burden** 人体负担(指身体所吸入的辐射或有毒物质). ～ **clock** 人体时钟，生理节奏. ～ **colo(u)r** 不透明色. ～ **corporate**【律】法人团体. ～ **count** ①敌尸计数. ②(死亡)人数统计. **～guard** 保镖，卫兵，警卫员. ～ **language** ①身势语，体语. ②身不由己的举动. ～ **mike**〔美俚〕贴身步话机. ～ **paper**【造纸】铜版纸胚. ～ **plan**【船】正面图. ～ **shirt** 紧身衬衫〔背心〕. ～ **shop** 车身制造〔修理〕工场. ～ **snatcher** (为解剖等目的)盗尸的人；〔军俚〕担架兵. ～ **stocking** 紧身衣(裤). ～ **track** 调车场的车轨. ～ **type**【印】用以排印正文的铅字. ～ **wave** (从震心向各方辐射的)震波. ～ **wood** 无枝桠材. **～work** 车〔机、船〕身制造.

boehm·ite [ˈbeimait] *n.* 【矿】勃姆石；薄水铝矿.

Boe·o·tian [biˈəuʃjən] *a.* 粗野的；愚钝的. — *n.* 粗野的人；愚钝的人.

Boer [bəuə] *n.* 布尔人〔南非荷兰人后裔〕. — *a.* 布尔人的.

bœuf bour·gui·gnon [bif buːgiːˈnjəun] 〔F.〕勃艮第牛肉丁〔牛肉丁加洋葱、磨菇在红酒中煮沸〕.

boff [bɔf] *n.* 〔俚〕①尽情的大笑，狂笑；引起大笑的情节. ②(戏剧、电影、歌曲等)空前成功的表演.

bof·fin [ˈbɔfin] *n.* 〔英俚〕科学技术人员，科研工作者.

bof·fo [ˈbɔfəu] *a.* 〔俚〕受人欢迎的，很得人心的；非常成功的. — *n.* 〔俚〕尽情大笑.

bof·fo·la [bəˈfəulə] *n.* = boff ②.

Bo·fors [ˈbəufɔːz] (**gun**) *n.*【军】①博福斯式高射炮〔口径为 40 厘米的自动高射炮〕. ② 二弹连发高射炮.

bog [bɔg] *n.* ①泥炭地，泥塘，沼泽. ②潮湿地带，沼泽地带. ③〔常 *pl.*〕〔英口〕户外厕所. — *vi., vt.* (使)陷入沼泽，(使)沉入泥中 (*down*). ～ ***down*** 阻碍；(使)陷入困境，(使)不能活动 (*Things have bogged down.* 事情已陷于停顿. *We were bogged down by overwork.* 过分繁重的工作已经使我们陷入困境). ～ **bean** 睡菜 (=buckbean). ～ **berry** 酸果蔓属植物. ～ **brother** 〔蔑〕爱尔兰人. ～ **butter**【矿】沼油. ～ **head** 藻煤，烟煤.

~-house 〔俚〕厕所. ~ **iron [ore]** 沼铁,沼铁矿. ~-**land** 〔谑〕爱尔兰〔别名,因该地多沼泽〕. ~ **oak** 泥炭中的黑栎. ~ **wood** (泥炭地中的)埋木.

bo·gen·fah·ren [ˈbəugənfɑːrən] *n.* 〔G.〕【滑雪】制动滑降.

bo·gey [ˈbəugi] *n.* ①妖怪,妖魔;可怕的人;可怕的东西;【军】可疑的飞机;〔美俚〕不明飞行物(=UFO). ②坦克负重轮;【高尔夫球】每穴击球分数;比赛的标准分数. ~**man** (讲出来吓唬孩子的)妖怪;可怕的东西.

bog·gle[1] [ˈbɔgl] *n.* = bogle.

bog·gle[2] [ˈbɔgl] *vi.* ①(马等)惊跳. ②犹豫,踌躇,退缩 *(at; about)*. ③装糊涂,搪塞 *(at)*. ④乱搞,胡乱地干. — *vt.* ①搞坏(事情等). ②〔英口〕使吃惊. — *n.* ①(马的)惊跳;吃惊. ②犹豫;退缩. ③搪塞. ④胡乱干的工作.

bogg·trot·ter [ˈbɔgtrɔtə] *n.* ①住在沼泽地带的人. ②〔常蔑〕爱尔兰乡下人.

bog·gy [ˈbɔgi] *a.* ①沼泽多的;沼泽状态的. ②潮湿的. **-gi·ness** *n.*

bo·gie [ˈbəugi] *n.* ① = bogy. ②【铁路】转向架. ③〔美空军俚〕来路不明的飞机. ④〔英口〕(运石料等的)低座四轮卡车.

bo·gle [ˈbəugl] *n.* 妖怪.

Bo·gor [ˈbəugɔː] *n.* 茂物〔印度尼西亚城市〕.

Bo·go·tá [ˌbəugəˈtɑː] *n.* 波哥大〔哥伦比亚首都〕.

bog·trot·ter [ˈbɔgtrɔtə] *n.* ①住在沼泽地带的人. ②= bog brother.

bo·gus [ˈbəugəs] *a.* 〔美〕伪造的,假的. — *n.* 赝品,伪物. ~ **certificate** 伪造的证件. ~ **company** (骗人的)空头商行. ~ **money** 伪币. ~ **regime** 伪政权(组织).

bo·gy(-man) [ˈbəugi(mæn)] *n.* = bogey.

boh [bəu] *int.* = bo.

Boh. = Bohemia; Bohemian.

bo·hea [bəuˈhiː] *n.* 武夷茶.

Bo·he·mi·a [bəuˈhiːmjə] *n.* ①波希米亚〔吉卜赛人最多的捷克斯洛伐克西部地区〕. ②波希米亚式群落,放荡不羁的文化人〔主要指颓废派的文化人〕.

Bo·he·mi·an [bəuˈhiːmjən] *a.* ①波希米亚的;波希米亚语的. ②流浪的,漂泊的. ③放浪的,放荡不羁的,豪放的. — *n.* ①波希米亚人;波希米亚语. ②流浪者;吉卜赛人. ③放荡不羁的人〔尤指狂放的艺术家〕. **-ism** *n.* 放纵主义,放荡不羁;放荡生活.

Boho [bəuˈhəu] *a.* 波希米亚式的;颓废派文化人的,放荡不羁的.

Bohr [bɔr], **Niels Henrik David** 玻耳〔1885—1962,丹麦物理学家,获 1922 年诺贝尔物理奖金〕.

bo·hunk [bəuˈhʌŋk] *n.* 〔美俚〕外国劳工〔尤指从中欧移民来的工人〕.

boil[1] [bɔil] *vi.* ①沸腾,达到沸点,开,滚,煮滚;汽化. ②激昂,奋激,鼎沸;汹涌. ③被熬浓;可以压缩. *He ~s [is ~ing] with rage.* 他勃然大怒. *The sea ~ed in the storm.* 暴风雨中,大海波涛汹涌. ~ ***down to*** (被)归结起来是…;(审判等到最后)表明 *(I suppose it all ~s down to this.* 我看归结起来可以这样说). ~ ***forth*** 口沫四溅地说. ~ ***out*** 煮沸;试验. ~ ***over*** ①沸溢. ②发怒. ~ ***up*** 煮滚,烧开. ~***ing hot*** 沸腾;〔口〕酷热. ***keep the pot ~ing*** 糊口,维持生活;维持市面. — *vt.* ①煮,使沸腾;使激动. ②熬制(盐,糖等). ~ *eggs* 煮蛋. ~ *the salt off the water* 熬盐. ~ ***away*** 煮干. ~ ***down*** 熬稠;煮干. ~ ***sth. down to*** 把(文章等)压缩成;把(内容等)归结为. ~ ***off*** 煮去,使脱胶,退浆. — *n.* 煮沸;沸腾. ***be on [at] the ~*** 煮着,正在沸腾. ***bring to the ~*** 使沸腾,烧滚. ~**off** *n.* 蒸发损耗.

boil[2] [bɔil] *n.* 【医】疖肿,脓肿;〔*pl.*〕疔,疖子. *a blind ~* 无脓〔脓未出头的〕疮. ~ **smut** (玉米)黑粉病.

boiled [bɔild] *a.* ①煮沸的,烧滚的. ②〔美俚〕喝醉的. ~ *eggs* 煮熟的蛋. ~ ***as an owl*** 〔美俚〕喝得烂醉的. ~ **dinner** 〔美〕配上蔬菜的煮肉. ~ **linen** 脱胶亚麻布,精练亚麻布. ~ **oil** 熟炼油〔尤指熟炼胡麻子油〕. ~ **owl** 〔美俚〕喝醉的人. ~ **rag** 〔美俚〕刚洗好的衬衫. ~ **rice** 饭. ~ **shirt** 〔美俚〕硬胸衬衫;架子十足的家伙,不易亲近的人. ~ **sweet** 〔英〕硬糖果(= hard candy).

boil·er [ˈbɔilə] *n.* ①煮器(壶,锅等);熬煮东西的人. ②汽锅,锅炉;〔美俚〕酒类干馏器. ③〔俚〕导弹. *a once through ~* 直流锅炉. ***burst one's ~*** 〔美〕悲伤. ~ **iron** 锅炉钢板. ~**maker** ①锅炉修理工. ②〔口〕啤酒掺威士忌. ~ **plate** (做锅炉用的)钢板;〔美〕做成纸型送来的新闻稿. ~ **protector** 锅炉套. ~ **room** 锅炉房;〔口〕(证券经纪人专靠电话买卖的)营业室. ~ **scale** 锅垢. ~ **suit** 〔英〕外衣,罩衣;连衫裤工作服.

boil·ing [ˈbɔiliŋ] *a.* ①沸腾的;汹涌的. ②激昂的. — *ad.* 非常,达到沸腾程度地. ~ ***hot*** 〔口〕酷热 *(a ~ hot day* 要命的大热天). ***at hhe ~ point*** 大怒. — *n.* ①煮沸;沸腾,滚. ②一次烹煮量[物]. ③〔俚〕一群;全体. ***the whole ~*** 〔俚〕全体. ~-**point** ①【物】沸点. ②极度兴奋;激昂. ~ **stone** 放在沸水里以阻止水涌出的小石. ~ **water** 〔美俚〕麻烦事,乱子.

Boi·se [ˈbɔisi] *n.* 博伊西〔美国爱达荷州的首府〕.

bois·ter·ous [ˈbɔistərəs] *a.* ①狂暴的,狂风暴雨的. ②喧闹的,吵吵闹闹的,骚嚷的. *the ~ entertainment area* 喧闹的娱乐区. *a ~ wind* 狂风. **-ly** *ad.* **-ness** *n.*

boîte [bwat] *n.* 〔F.〕小夜总会,宵夜酒店,小酒馆;酒楼.

bo·ko [ˈbəukəu] *n.* 〔俚〕头,脑袋;鼻.

bo·koo [ˈbəukuː] *a., ad.* 〔美口〕很多;非常〔法语 *beaucoup* 的别字〕. ~ ***soused*** [sauzd] 〔美口〕大醉.

Bol. = Bolivia.

bo·la [ˈbəulə] *n.* 套牛绳球〔长绳或皮条末端系有重球体物,作驱赶和套牛用〕(= bolas).

bold [bəuld] *a.* ①大胆的,果敢的. ②不客气的,卤莽的,冒失的. ③狂放的,富有想象力的,雄浑的;显眼的,突出的. ④陡峭的,险峻的. ⑤【海】水深足够大船直接靠岸的. ⑥【印】用黑体铅字排的. *a ~ hand-writing* 粗笔划的字,笔法雄浑. *a ~ mathematician* 思路开阔的数学家. *~ lines* 粗线. *a ~ clifi* 悬崖绝壁. ***in ~ relief*** 轮廓鲜明地浮出. ***in ~ strokes*** (字写得)粗大. ***make [be] (so) bold (as) to (do)*** 冒昧,敢,擅自,恕…无礼 *(I make ~ to give you my opinion.* 不揣冒昧贡献您一点意见). ***put a ~ face on*** *(the matter)* 对…假装不在乎. ~ **face** ①*n.*【印】黑体,粗体. ②*vt.* 把…印成黑体. ~-**faced** *a.* ①厚颜无耻的,冒失的. ②卤莽的. ③【印】黑体的,粗体的. **-ly** *ad.* ①大胆地;冒失地,卤莽地. ②显然,醒目地,显著地. ③粗,黑体. **-ness** *n.* ①大胆,勇敢;冒失;厚脸皮;狂放,显著.

bole[1] [bəul] *n.* 【植】树干,干材.

bole[2] [bəul] *n.* ①【地】红玄武土,胶块土. ②红褐色颜料.

bo·lec·tion [bəuˈlekʃən] *n.* 【建】凸出嵌线.

bo·le·ro [bəˈlɛərəu] *n.* *(pl. ~s)* 〔Sp.〕①波莱罗舞(曲). ② [ˈbɔlərəu] (妇女)波莱罗短上衣.

bo·le·tus [bəˈliːtəs] *n.* 【植】牛肝菌属菌类.

Bol·eyn [ˈbulin] *n.* 博林〔姓氏〕.

bo·lide [ˈbəulaid] *n.* 【天】火流星,爆发流星,火球.

Bol·ing·broke [ˈbɔliŋbruk] *n.* 博灵布鲁克〔姓氏〕.

Bol·i·var [bɔˈliːvɑː, bɔˈlibar] *n.* 博利瓦〔姓氏〕.

Bo·liv·i·a [bəˈliviə] *n.* 玻利维亚〔拉丁美洲〕.

Bo·liv·i·an [bəˈliviən] *a.* ①玻利维亚的. ②玻利维亚人的. — *n.* 玻利维亚人.

boll [bəul] *n.* (棉,亚麻等的)圆荚,珠蒴. ~ **rot** 铃腐病. ~ **stainer** 棉椿象,污棉虫. **(pink) ~worm** (棉)红铃虫.

bol·lard [ˈbɔləd] *n.* ①【海】系缆柱,双系柱. ②〔英〕(保护花坛等的)矮栏;(行人安全岛的)护柱.

bol·lix [ˈbɔliks] *vt.* 〔俚〕弄糟,做坏;笨手笨脚地弄坏〔常与 up 连用〕. *His interference ~ed up the whole deal.* 他的插手把全部事情都弄糟了. — *n.* 乱糟糟的一团.

bolo[1] [ˈbəuləu] *n.* (菲律宾人用的)大砍刀.

bolo[2] [ˈbəuləu] *n.* 〔美陆军俚〕 枪法还不合格的士兵. — *vi.* 枪法还不够格.

Bo·lo·gna [bəˈləunjə] *n.* ①波洛尼亚〔意大利城市〕. ②〔b-〕大红肠〔意大利波洛尼亚大香肠〕(= ~ sausage).

bo·lo·graph [ˈbəuləgrɑːf] *n.* 【物】①测辐射热仪. ②测辐射热仪的记录.

bo·lom·e·ter [bəuˈlɔmitə] *n.* = bolograph ①.

bo·lo·ney [bəˈləuni] *n.* 〔美俚〕敷衍话;瞎扯. — *int.* 〔美口〕瞎扯! 胡说!

Bol·she·vik [ˈbɔlʃəvik] *n.* (*pl.* **~s, Bolsheviki** [ˈbɔlʃiviki]) 布尔什维克. — *a.* 布尔什维克的, 布尔什维主义的.

Bol·she·vism, bol·she·vism [ˈbɔlʃəvizəm] *n.* 布尔什维主义.

Bol·she·vist, bol·she·vist [ˈbɔlʃəvist] *n.* 布尔什维主义者,布尔什维克. — *a.* 布尔什维克的.

Bol·she·vize, bol·she·vize [ˈbɔlʃəvaiz] *vi., vt.* (使)布尔什维克化. **Bol·she·vi·za·tion, bol·she·vi·za·tion** [ˌbɔlʃivaiˈzeiʃən] *n.*

Bol·shie, Bol·shy [ˈbɔlʃi] *n., a.* 〔俚〕= Bolshevik.

bol·son [ˈbəulsən] *n.* 沙漠盆地,干湖地.

Bol·so·ver [ˈbɔlsəvə] *n.* 博尔索弗〔姓氏〕.

bol·ster [ˈbəulstə] *n.* ①枕垫,长枕; 枕状支持物〔枕梁、承板等〕. ②【机】软垫,垫木,枕; (车辆的)枕梁; 【纺】(纺机的)锭脚,锭管; 【建】承枕,托木; 横撑. — *vt.* ①(用支持物)支撑,垫. ②援助,帮助; 费力支持 *(up)*; 增强. *They ~ed their morale by singing.* 他们用唱歌来鼓舞士气.

bolt[1] [bəult] *n.* ①螺钉,螺栓. ②(门窗等的)插销;闩,锁簧. ③箭,矢;弩箭;【军】枪机,枪栓. ④电光,闪电. ⑤(水等的)喷射. ⑥(马等的)脱缰; 跑掉,逃走,逃亡; 缺课;〔美〕脱党,变节. ⑦(棉布等的)一匹; (纸等的)一卷. ⑧短(木)材. *a ~ and nut* 螺栓与螺母. *He has shot his last ~.* 他已作出最后努力〔弹尽矢绝〕. *stud ~* 柱〔双头〕螺栓. *anchor ~* 地脚螺栓. *a thunder ~* 雷电, 霹雳. *a ~ of linen* 一匹亚麻布. ***a ~ from the blue*** 晴天霹雳; 祸从天降,意外事件. ***A fool's ~ is soon shot.*** ①蠢兵乱射箭,箭筒很快空; 愚者易于智穷力竭. ②愚者喜挥霍,很难存下钱. ***do a ~*** 〔俚〕逃出. ***make a ~ of it = make one's ~*** 〔俚〕逃走. ***shoot one's ~*** 竭尽最大努力,使出浑身解数,尽其所能. — *vi.* ①射出, 窜出,冲出,跳出,(马等的)脱缰; 逃走,逃亡; 〔美俚〕缺课. ②〔美〕拒绝支持本党政策〔提名等〕,脱党,退出团体,变节. ③狼吞虎咽. *~ off to catch the train* 飞跑去赶火车. *~ into* 窜入. — *vt.* ①给(门窗等)上插销,闩(门); (用螺栓等)拴住. ②发射(矢、石等). ③囫囵吞下,仓促咽下. ④〔美〕拒绝支持(本党的政策等); 退出(党派、团体等). ⑤脱口说出 *(out)*. ⑥把(纸等)卷成一卷. *~ a political party* 脱离某政党. *~ one's breakfast* 三口两口地吃完早饭. ***~ (sb.) in*** 把(某人)关在屋内. ***~ (sb.) out*** 把(某人)关在门外. — *ad.* 象箭似地,突然. ***~ upright*** 僵直,笔直 (*sit ~ upright* 坐得笔直,僵直地坐着). **~-action** *a.* (步枪)有用手操作的枪机的. **~ boat** 适于在波涛汹涌的海上航行的船. **~-head** ①螺栓头. ②长颈烧瓶. ③(枪)机头. **~-hole** (动物的)避难穴;〔喻〕安全藏匿所,狡兔三窟. **~-on** *a.* (设计得)可上栓锁的. **~-rope** 【海】(帆的)栓索,缝在帆边的组绳.

bolt[2], **boult** [bəult] *n.* 筛子. — *vt.* ①筛. ②淘汰; 筛选. ③〔古〕细查. ***~ to the bran*** 筛到糠麸; 精细查勘. **~ing cloth** 作筛眼用的麻布〔纺织品〕.

bolt·er[1] [ˈbəultə] *n.* ①(经常)脱缰的马. ②跑开者; 逃亡者,出走者. ③〔美〕脱党者,变节者,背叛者.

bolt·er[2] [ˈbəultə] *n.* ①筛子; 筛选机. ②机筛工人.

bol·to·ni·a [bəulˈtəuniə, -jə] *n.* 【植】波菊属植物.

bo·lus [ˈbəuləs] *n.* ①【药】(给牛马服用的)大丸药. ②(嚼过的)食物团.

bomb [bɔm] *n.* ①【军】弹,炸弹. ②【地】火山弹〔火山喷出的球状熔岩〕. ③【医】(用于治疗的)放射源; 高压弹〔高压气体容器〕; (储藏放射性物质的)铅容器〔如钴炮等〕. ④惊人事件,(耸人听闻的)"炸弹"宣言;〔美俚〕(演出)大失败. ⑤〔美俚〕蛋; (足球)长传; (篮球)远投. ⑥〔the ~〕〔总称〕原子弹,原子武器; 核武器. ⑦〔美俚〕加有麻醉毒品的香烟. *an aerosol ~* 烟幕弹. *a flare ~* 照明弹. *a depth ~* 深水炸弹. *incendiary ~* 燃烧弹. *a time ~* 定时炸弹. *an atomic ~* 原子弹. *a hydrogen ~ [H ~]* 氢弹. *a guided [controlled] ~* 导弹. *a rocket ~* 火箭导弹,弹道导弹. *a hung ~* 挂弹〔发生故障未能投出的炸弹〕. — *vt.* ①向…投炸弹,轰炸. ②以巨大优势[比分等]压倒(对手). — *vi.* ①投弹. ②〔美俚〕惨败. ***~(s) away*** 投弹完毕. ***~ out*** ①炸毁; 被轰炸得由家里逃出. ②〔美俚〕惨败. ***~ up*** 给(飞机)装上炸弹. **~bay** (轰炸机的)炸弹舱. **~ carrier** ①轰炸机. ②炸弹架. **~ cluster** 集束炸弹,集束燃烧弹. **~ damage** 【军】轰炸效果. **~-disposal** 未爆弹处理. **~-dropping** 【空】投弹. **~gas** 钢瓶〔瓶装〕气体. **~ gear** 投弹器. **~-hatch** 【空】(飞机上的)投弹门. **~ line** (空中地图上划开敌我阵地的)轰炸分界线. **~load** 载弹量. **~proof** ① *a.* 避弹的,防弹的. ② *n.* 【军】防空洞,避弹房. ③ *vt.* 使有防弹能力. **~ rack** (轰炸机上的)炸弹架. **~-release** 【空】投弹器; 投弹. **~ run** (自看到目标至投下炸弹之间的)轰炸航程. **~shell** ①炸弹; 炮弹. ②爆炸性事件,突然轰动视听的事件〔人物〕(*a regular ~-shell* 大骚动,大惊吓). **~ shelter** 防空洞. **~ sight** 【空】轰炸瞄准器. **~site** 炸后遗迹〔废墟〕. **~ sniffer** 炸弹嗅探器. **~ thrower** 掷弹手; 炸弹发射炮; 掷弹筒.

bomb. = bombardment.

bom·bard[1] [ˈbɔmbɑːd] *n.* 射石炮〔古时的臼炮〕.

bom·bard[2] [bɔmˈbɑːd] *vt.* ①炮击; 轰炸. ②【原】(以中子等)轰击;对…进行粒子辐射. ③痛骂,攻击,痛斥,(连珠炮似地)质问. *~ a necleus* 轰击原子核. *~ sb. with questions [letters]* 象连珠炮似地对(某人)提出问题[信件象雪片一样地向(某人)飞来].

bom·bar·dier [ˌbɔmbəˈdiə] *n.* 炮击者;〔美〕轰炸员,投弹手;【史】炮手; 〔英〕炮兵伍长. **~ beetle** 放屁虫〔一种受惊后即放出难闻气体的甲虫〕.

bom·bard·ment [bɔmˈbɑːdmənt] *n.* ①炮击; 轰炸,轰击. ②痛斥,连珠炮似的提问.

bom·bar·don [bɔmˈbɑːdn] *n.* ①【乐】低音大号. ②【乐】(风琴的)簧舌塞子.

bom·ba·sine [ˈbɔmbəziːn] = bombazine.

bom·bast [ˈbɔmbæst] *n.* 夸大其词的话〔文章〕,豪言壮语. — *a.* 夸大的.

bom·bas·tic [bɔmˈbæstik] *a.* 夸大的,夸张的,过甚其词的,夸夸其谈的. **-ti·cal** *a.* **-al·ly** *ad.*

bom·bax [ˈbɔmbæks] *a.* 【植】木棉科植物的.

Bom·bay [bɔmˈbei] *n.* 孟买〔印度港口城市〕. **~ duck** 鰄鱼.

bom·ba·zine [ˈbɔmbəziːn, ˈbɔmbəˌziːn] *n.* 邦巴辛毛葛,丝经毛纬,细斜纹.

bom·bé [bəumˈbei] *a.* 〔F.〕(家具)突起的,隆起的. *a ~ china cabinet* 圆肚瓷器柜.

bombe [bəumb] *n.* 〔F.〕邦布冰果〔鸡蛋加糖等做成的冷冻点心〕.

bombed [bɔmd] *a.* ①遭到轰炸〔轰击〕的. ②〔俚〕喝醉了酒的; 吸毒麻醉了的. **~-out** *a.* ①被炸毁的. ②被炸得无家可归的.

bom·bee [bɔmˈiː] *n.* 被轰炸的人.

bomb·er [ˈbɔmə] *n.* ①投弹手. ②〔现今特指〕轰炸机. *a guided ~* 导航〔无人驾驶〕轰炸机,可操纵飞航导弹.

a jet ~ 喷气式轰炸机. *attack [dive]* ~ 攻击[俯冲]轰炸机. *heavy [light]* ~ 重[轻]型轰炸机. ~ **escort** 掩护轰炸机的战斗机(群).

bom·bi·nate [ˈbɔmbiˌneit] *vi.* (苍蝇似地)嗡鸣. **-nation** [ˌbɔmbiˈneiʃən] *n.*

bomb·ing [ˈbɔmiŋ] *n.* 轰炸, 投弹. ~ **plane** 轰炸机. ~ **run** 轰炸航程. ~ **sight** 轰炸瞄准器.

bomb·let [ˈbɔmlit] *n.* 小型炸弹.

bom·by·cid [ˈbɔmbisid] *n.* 【动】蚕蛾.

bon [bɔn; F. bɔ̃] *a.* 〔F.〕 = good. ~ ***ami*** [F. bɔ̃ami] 男朋友; 情人. ~ ***jour*** [bɔ̃ ˈʒuːr] 您好! 早安! 日安! ~ ***mot*** [bɔ̃ ˈmou] *(pl.* ***bons mots****)* 警句, 妙语, 名言. ~ ***sens*** [bɔ̃ sɛ̃] 良知. ~ ***soir*** [bɔ̃ swaːr] 晚安! ~ ***ton*** [bɔ̃ ˈtɔ̃ːŋ] 优雅; 礼让; 时髦; 上流社会. ~ ***vivant*** [bɔ̃ ˈviːvaːŋ] *(pl.* ***bons vivants****)* 考究饮食的人. ~ ***voyage*** [bɔ̃ vwajˈaːʒ] 一路平安!

bo·na [ˈbaunə] *a.* 〔L.〕 = good. ~ ***fide*** [ˈfaidi] 真正的, 真实的, 善意的, 照实, 真诚地, 以诚意. ~ ***fides*** [ˈfaidiːz] 真实, 诚意.

bo·nan·za [bəuˈnænzə] *n.* 【地】富矿脉. ②〔口〕发财, 走鸿运; 富源, 使人致富[走运]的东西. *a* ~ *business* 兴旺的事业. *a* ~ *year* 大丰年. *a* ~ *farm* 兴旺的大农场. ***B- State,*** 美国 Montana 州的别名. ***in*** ~ =***strike a*** ~ ①找到富矿脉. ②大走鸿运.

Bo·na·parte [ˈbəunəpaːt] *n.* 波拿巴 〔法国科西嘉岛上的家族〕. **Napoleon** ~ 拿破仑·波拿巴 〔1769—1821, 法国皇帝〕.

Bo·na·part·ism [ˈbəunəpaːtizəm] *n.* 【法史】波拿巴主义. **-ist** *n.* 【法史】波拿巴主义者.

bon·bon [ˈbɔnbɔn] *n.* 〔F.〕 糖果; 夹心糖.

bon·bon·nière [F. bɔ̃nbɔnjɛːə] *n.* 〔F.〕 糖果店; 糖果盒子.

bond[1] [bɔnd] *n.* ①结合(物), 结合力, 粘合(剂), 联结. ②束缚, 羁绊; 〔*pl.*〕 拘束; 镣, 铐. ③契约, 契约义务, 盟约; 同盟, 联盟. ④证券, 公债, 债券; 借据; 证券纸; (付款)保证书; 保证人; 【商】海关扣存(待完税). ⑤【化】键; 【电】耦合, 固定; 连结器, 接头; 【建】砌合; (砖等的)砌式; 【铁路】轨条接线; 【机】焊接. *the* ~*s of friendship [matrimony]* 友谊[婚姻]的纽带. *the* ~ *between nations* 国家间的同盟. *His word is as good as his* ~. 他的话是极可靠的[象契约一样可靠]. *My word is my* ~. 我是讲信用的. *a cross* ~ 【电】交叉扎线. *treasury* ~*s* 国库债券. *government* ~*s* 公债. *war* ~ 国防公债. *brick* ~ 砌砖法. *ionic* ~ 【化】离子键. *steel* ~ 铁粉结合器. *rail* ~ 导轨夹紧器. ***break [sever] a*** ~ 废除 〔中断〕契约. ***break the*** ~ ***of*** *(convention)* 打破(成规)的束缚. ***call a*** ~ 收兑 (债券). ***consolidated*** ~ (英国发行的) 统一公债. ***enter into a*** ~ ***(with)*** (与…)订约. ***give*** ~ ***for [to do sth.]*** 为…作担保[担保做某事]. ***(goods) in*** ~ (货物被海关) 扣存关栈以待完税. ***in*** ~***s*** 被束缚着; 被奴役; 在拘留中. ***take (the goods) out of*** ~ (完税后) 提出被海关扣存的(货物). — *vt.* ①以证券为(债务等)作保证抵押. ②把(进口货)存入关栈以待完税. ③【建】砌合(砖); 粘着(水泥等). 【化】以化学键使结合在分子[结晶体]内. ④使订契约. ~**holder** 债券持有者. ~**paper** 证券纸 〔一种上等道林纸, 用以印制证券、钞票、商业文书等〕. ~ **servent** 奴隶; 被奴役的人. ~**stone** 【建】束石. **B- Street** 证券街 〔伦敦最繁华的一条街, 有很多高级商店〕. **-er** *n.* ①【无】联接器, 结合器. ②发债券者. ③将货物存入关栈者. ④【建】束石. **-ing** *n.* ①粘合工艺; 搭接. ②【电】屏蔽接地; 压焊.

bond[2] [bɔnd] *n.* 〔废〕农奴; 奴隶. — *a.* 被奴役的; 奴隶的 〔多用作复合词, 如 ~*maid* 女奴, ~*(s)man* 奴隶, 农奴, ~*woman* 女奴, 等〕.

bond·age [ˈbɔndidʒ] *n.* ①奴隶处境, 奴役, 劳役. ②束缚; 监禁; 屈从. ③(英国古代的)农奴租地法. *in* ~ *to* 被…奴役. *hold sb. in* ~ 使某人被奴役[束缚, 监禁].

bond·ed [ˈbɔndid] *a.* ①有债券作保证的; 有抵押的, 有担保的. ②(货物)存入[关栈]待完税的. ③(织物)多层粘合的; 【化】化合的, 结合的. ~ **debt** 公债借款. ~ **goods [merchandise]** 存关待完税货物. ~ **store** = 〔美〕~ **warehouse** (海关扣存待完税货物的)关栈. ~ **whisky** 陈年威士忌酒.

bonds·man [ˈbɔndzmən] *n.* ①奴隶, 农奴 (= bondman). ②【法】保证人, 保人.

bonds·wo·man [ˈbɔndzwumən] *n.* ①女奴 (= bondwoman). ②【法】女保证人.

bon·duc [ˈbɔnˌdʌk] *n.* 【植】加拿大皂荚.

bone [bəun] *n.* ①骨(头); 骨状物〔象牙等〕; 骨制品; (食用的)肉骨头. ②〔*pl.*〕遗骸, 尸体; 骨骼; 身体. ③〔*pl.*〕〔口〕骰子; 【乐】响板; (乐队)打拍员; (妇女)胸衣张骨. ④【矿】黑矸子. ⑤〔美俚〕一块钱; 用功的学生. ⑥〔*pl.*〕〔口〕外科医生. ⑦争端. *the pubic* ~ 耻骨. *a ham* ~ 火腿. *His* ~*s are massive.* 他骨骼粗大. *my old* ~*s* 我这把老骨头. *His* ~*s was laid in Westminster.* 他的遗骸陈放在威斯敏斯脱大教堂. ***be upon the*** ~***s of*** 攻击. ~ ***in her teeth*** 【海】船头浪. ~ ***of contention*** 争执的原因[题目], 争端. ~ ***of one's*** ~ (=flesh of one's flesh) 关系非常密切[亲密]的. ~ ***top*** 〔美俚〕笨人. ***bred in the*** ~ 生来的, 改不了的. ***carry a*** ~ ***in the mouth [teeth]*** 【海】(船)破浪前进. ***cast (in) a*** ~ ***between*** 使…之间起争端, 离间. ***cut to the*** ~ 根除; 削减. ***feel [believe, know, think] in one's*** ~***s*** 深知, 深深感觉到, 确信. ***get into sb.'s*** ~***s*** 迷住. ***have a*** ~ ***in one's throat [leg]*** 难于启齿[行动]. ***have a*** ~ ***to pick with sb.*** 对某人有怨言, 要与某人争论. ***horse with plenty of*** ~ 骨骼[身段]良好的马. ***in one's*** ~***s*** 天生的. ***lay one's*** ~***s*** 死, 埋葬. ***make no*** ~***s of [about, to (do)]*** 率直; 对…毫不踌躇 (*He makes no* ~*s about helping his wife with dishes.* 他毫不踌躇地帮助妻子洗碗碟). ***make old*** ~***s*** 〔用于否定句〕 长寿 (*I'm afraid he will never make old* ~*s.* 我看他活不长). ***No*** ~***s broken!*** 没有什么! 没事没事! ***point [sing] a*** ~ ***at sb.*** (澳洲土著居民)以符咒咒人遭灾[死、病等]. ***roll the*** ~***s*** 吹牛、夸张; 闲谈. ***spare*** ~***s*** 不肯吃苦, 懒. ***the ten*** ~***s*** 十指. ***to the*** ~ 彻骨, 透骨, 入骨; 到极点, 深, 极端 (*cut expenses to the* ~ 把费用缩减到极限. *I'm tired to the* ~. 我累极了. *He worked his fingers to the* ~. 他拼命工作). ***without more*** ~***s*** 不再费力; 立刻. — *vt.* ①去…的骨, 剔掉…的骨. ②用鲸骨撑大(妇女上衣等). ③施骨肥于. ④〔俚〕盗, 偷, 抢去. ⑤测量…的高度. ~ *a turkey* 给火鸡剔骨. —*vi.* 〔美〕死用功, 用苦功 *(up)*. *She is boning up for her finals* 她在拼命用功, 准备大考. ~ *up on Latin* 下苦功学拉丁语. ~ **ash** 骨灰. ~**bed** 【地】骨层. ~ **bender** 〔美俚〕摔跤选手. ~**black** 骨炭 〔一种漂白剂〕. ~ **box** 〔美俚〕口, 嘴. ~ **china** 骨灰瓷〔一种含有骨灰的瓷器〕. ~**-dry** *a.* ①十分干的, 干透了的. ②〔美俚〕绝对禁酒的. ~ **dust** 骨粉. ~ **eater** 〔美俚〕 狗. ~**fish** 北梭鱼. ~ **grace** 【医】眼睑. ~**head** 〔美〕笨蛋, 傻子; 囚犯〔罪犯语〕; = boner. ~**idle,** ~**-lazy** *a.* 〔美俚〕懒透了的. ~**less** *a.* ①无骨的. ②(文章等)无风骨的. ~ **meal** 【农】骨粉. ~ **oil** 骨油. ~ **orchard** 〔美俚〕墓地. ~**-set** ①*vi.* 接骨, 正骨. ②*n.* 【美植】贯叶泽兰, 接骨草. ~**-setter** 接骨者, 正骨医生. ~**setting** 接骨术. ~**-shaker** ①(早期)无橡皮轮胎的自行车. ②〔俚〕破旧的车辆, 颠散骨头的车. ~ **top** 〔美俚〕笨人. ~**-weary** *a.* 十分疲倦的. ~**yard** ①〔美〕动物尸骨埋放地; 废马屠杀场. ②〔口〕墓地. ③〔口〕废车、船存放地.

boned [bəund] *a.* ①剔去骨头的. ②(女上衣等)撑上鲸骨的. ③骨头…的〔用以组成复合词, 如 *big-*~ 骨头粗大的. *beautifully-*~ 体型优美的 等〕. ④施过骨粉肥料的. ~ *land* 施过骨粉肥料的土地.

bon·er [ˈbəunə] *n.* 〔美俚〕(学生答卷里)可笑的错误; 大错.

bon·fire [ˈbɔnˌfaiə] *n.* 篝火,祝火,营火. ***make a ~ of*** *(rubbish)* 烧掉(垃圾).

bong [bɔŋ] *n.* (锣声)噹噹. — *vi.* 发噹噹声.

bon·go [ˈbɔŋgəu] *n.*【动】(非洲)大羚羊.

bon·ho·mie [ˈbɔnɔmiː] *n.* 〔F.〕温和,和蔼; 友好. **bon·ho·mous** [ˈbɔnɔməs] *a.*

Bon·i·face [ˈbɔnifeis] *n.* ①博尼费斯〔姓氏〕. ②〔b-〕旅馆老板.

Bo·nin [ˈbəunin] *n.* ~ **Islands** 小笠原群岛〔太平洋〕.

bon·i·ness [ˈbəuninis] *n.* 多骨,瘦骨嶙峋.

bon·ism [ˈbɔnizəm] *n.* (视现世为善,但尚未达到至善境地的)乐观主义,世善说 (*opp.* malism).

Bo·ni·ta [bəˈniːtə] *n.* 博妮塔〔女子名〕.

bo·ni·to [bəˈniːtəu] *n.*【鱼】东方狐鲣.

bon·kers [ˈbɔŋkəz] *a.* 〔俚〕神经错乱的; 疯狂的.

Bonn [bɔn] 波恩〔德意志联邦共和国首都〕.

bonne [bɔn] *n.* 〔F.〕 女仆; 保姆. — *a.* 好 (= good). ~ ***amie*** [bɔn ˈæmi] ①亲密的女友. ②爱人,情人.

bonne bouché [ˈbɔn ˈbuː] 〔F.〕(最后一口)美味; 一小块好吃的东西〔糖果等〕.

bonne nuit [ˈbɔn ˈnwiː] 〔F.〕晚安.

Bon·ner [ˈbɔnə] *n.* 邦纳〔姓氏〕.

bonnet [ˈbɔnit] *n.* ①(男用)无边苏格兰圆帽; (儿童或妇女戴的)有带户外软帽; (无边)矿工帽; (北美印地安人的)羽毛头饰. ②帽状物; 罩子;【机】阀帽,管帽,阀盖,烟囱帽; 机罩;〔英〕汽车罩. ③〔俚〕(赌场、拍卖场中的)囮子,合伙骗人者. ~ ***laird*** 〔Scot.〕小地主. ~ ***rouge*** [bɔneiˈruːʒ] 红帽子〔法国革命时革命派的标志〕; 革命党员. ***fill sb.'s ~*** 取而代之; 与人不相上下. ***have a bee in one's ~*** 发疯; 心神不宁. ***have a green ~*** 生意失败. — *vt.* ①给…戴帽子,给…加罩. ②把(某人)帽子拉下遮掉眼睛. ③〔俚〕合伙诱骗. — *vi.* 脱帽行礼.

Bon·nie [ˈbɔni] *n.* 邦妮〔女子名〕.

bon·ny, bon·nie [ˈbɔni] *a.* 〔主 Scot.〕①美丽的. ②健康的,强壮的; 活泼的. ③好的; (场所等)令人愉快的. — *ad.* 〔英方〕愉快; 好. — *n.* 〔Scot.〕〔古〕美女. **bon·ni·ly** *ad.*

bon·ny·clab·ber [ˈbɔniklæbə] *n.* 酸凝乳.

bon·sai [bɔnˈsai] *n.* 〔Jap.〕①盆景,盆栽植物. ②盆景树木.

bon·spiel [ˈbɔnspiːl, -spəl] *n.* 〔Scot.〕(两俱乐部或两城市之间举行的)冰上蹓石比赛.

bon·swar [bɔnˈswɑː] *int.*【美军】晚安〔法语的讹用〕.

bon·te·bok [ˈbɔntiˌbɔk] *n.* *(pl.* ~, ~*s)*【动】南非羚羊.

bo·nus [ˈbəunəs] *n.* ①奖金; 额外津贴. ②红利; 额外股息. ③退职金,退伍金;〔美〕出征奖金〔保险等〕. ④〔口〕意外的礼物; (购货时另外给顾客的)奉送品. *Every purchaser of a pound of coffee received a box of cookies as a ~.* 每买一磅咖啡,奉送顾客一盒小甜饼.

bon·y [ˈbəuni] *a.* ①骨的, 多骨的. ②骨骼粗大的. ③瘦的,憔悴的. *a ~ man* 骨骼粗大的人. *~ fingers* 瘦瘦的手指.

bonze [bɔnz] *n.* (中国、日本等的)和尚,僧.

bon·zer [ˈbɔnzə] *a.* 〔澳俚〕极好的,头等的.

boo[1] [buː] *int.* 呸〔表示厌恶、轻蔑等〕. ***can't say ~ to a goose*** 非常胆小, 怯懦. — *vi.* 发出"呸"的音. — *vt.* 对…发"呸"声(以示轻蔑等).

boo[2] [buː] *n.* 〔美俚〕大麻; 粉蓝烟草.

boob [buːb] *n.* 〔美俚〕①笨蛋, 蠢材. ②大错误, 大失策. ③〔*pl.*〕(妇女的)乳房. — *vi.* 犯荒唐大错. ~ **tube** 电视机; 电视.

boo-boo, boo·boo [ˈbuːbuː] *n.* *(pl.* ~*s)* ①〔俚〕愚蠢的错误; 大错. ②〔儿〕(皮肤的)微伤,擦伤,撞伤.

boo·by [ˈbuːbi] *n.* ①呆子,蠢材 ②【鸟】鲣鸟. ③得分最少的球队; 演出最差的歌舞队. ~ **hatch** ①【海】(甲板上的)小舱口. ②〔美俚〕精神病院. ~ **mine** 〔军〕饵雷,诡雷. ~ **prize** 末奖. ~ **trap** ①"门顶陷阱"(置物于微开门上以惊打来人的恶作剧). ②【军】伪装地雷〔炸弹〕; 陷阱,阴谋. **~-trap** *vt.* 在…设饵雷; 在…设陷阱.

boo·by·ish [ˈbuːbiiʃ] *a.* 呆,蠢.

boo·dle [ˈbuːdl] *n.* 〔美俚〕大笔现款〔尤指政治上的贿赂〕. ②不法利益; 赃品; 伪钞. ③一群人,一套〔一堆〕东西. *the whole (kit and) ~*全部,全套.

boo·dler [ˈbuːdlə] *n.* 〔美俚〕受贿者,贪赃枉法的政界人士.

boog·a·loo [ˌbuːgəˈluː] *n.* 波加洛舞〔一种两拍子节奏的摇摆舞〕.

boog·ie [ˈbu(ː)gi] *vi.* (随着摇摆舞音乐节奏)摆动身体. ~ **rock** 爵士摇摆乐.

boog·ie-woog·ie [ˈbu(ː)giˌwuːgi] *n.* 低音连奏爵士乐〔爵士乐中的一种钢琴奏法〕.

booh [buː] *int.* = boo.

boo·hoo [ˈbuːhuː] *vi.* 哭闹. — *n.* [ˈbuːhuː] *n.* 哭闹, 号哭.

book [buk] *n.* ①书,书籍; 著作; 〔the B-〕基督教《圣经》. ②〔常 *pl.*〕帐簿; 帐册; 名册. ③卷,篇,册,本; (烟叶等的)一捆,包,把. ④(歌剧等的)歌词,脚本. ⑤装订成册的车票〔支票等〕; (赛马赌博等的)赌注登记簿; 电话号码簿. ⑥〔美俚〕罪状的总和. ⑦给人教益的东西, (从事某项工作的)全部知识〔经验〕; (历史等的)记录. ⑧〔the ~〕惯例,常规. *~ of time* 历史. *~ of reference* 参考书. *examine the ~s* 查帐. *an account ~* 帐本. *an exercise ~* 练习本. *The petrified tree was a ~ of nature.* 树木化石是大自然的历史记录. ***a sealed ~*** 天书; 高深莫测的事. ***according to an open ~*** 人所共知的事物. ***at one's ~s*** 读书用功. ***be written in the ~ of life*** 【宗】列入死后获救者名单. ***bring (sb.) to ~*** ①诘问,盘问. ②法办,判罪. ***by (the) ~*** ①正式地; 有根据地,正确地. ②照章办事地; 按照惯例. ***close the ~s*** ①【会】结帐,决算. ②结束,终止. ***come to the ~*** 〔英口〕宣誓能做陪审员. ***do [get] the ~*** 〔美〕受最大处罚. ***enter in the ~s*** 把…记入帐内. ***hit the [one's] ~s*** 〔美〕用功. ***hold ~***【剧】做提词人. ***in one's ~*** 根据自己的判断. ***in sb.'s bad [good] ~s*** 失〔得〕宠于某人,给某人留下不好〔良好〕的印象. ***keep ~s*** 上帐,记帐. ***kiss the ~*** 吻《圣经》宣誓. ***know like a ~*** 熟手,通晓. ***like a ~*** ①一板一眼地,精确地. ②正确地,彻底地. ***make ~*** ①打赌; (赛马等)接受不同数目的赌注. ②以接受打赌为业 (*make ~ on it that* …就…打赌). ***off the ~s*** 除名,退会. ***on the ~s*** 列名簿上,做会员. ***one for the ~s*** 〔口〕意外事,惊人事. ***set ~s*** 指定的备考书. ***read sb. like a book*** 对某人的心思完全了解,看透某人. ***shut the ~s*** 停止交易〔来往〕. ***speak like a [by the] ~*** 确切地说话. ***suit sb.'s ~*** 适合某人目的,合某人意的; 对某人方便的. ***take a leaf out of another's ~*** 仿效别人行动,学某人的样子,效颦. ***take kindly to one's ~s*** 好学. ***the B- of B-s*** 《圣经》. ***the devil's ~(s)*** 纸牌. ***throw the ~ at*** 〔俚〕重罚,严罚. ***without ~*** ①无根据,任意,随意(乱说等). ②默诵,默记. — *vt.* ①登载,登记,记入,给…注册,给…挂号. ②预定, 定(戏位、车位等); 托运(行李等). ③(警察)记下(某人的)违法行为. ④代理…接受(赛马等的)赌注. ~ *one's order* 登记收到的订货单. ~ *cinema seats* 预定电影票. — *vi.* ①定座位; 定票. ②〔主英〕(旅客在旅馆)登记姓名. ***be ~ed*** 〔俚〕被捉住,逃不脱 (*I am ~ed (for it)* 我逃不脱了). ***be ~ed for [to]*** 买有往…去的票子; 非去不可,约好…,预定好…. ***be ~ed up*** 已经与人有约; (戏票等)已被预定一空;〔俚〕无丝毫闲空,太忙. ~ ***in*** 〔主英〕登记住入(旅馆等). ~ ***through*** *(to London)* 买(到伦敦的)直达

票. — *a.* ①书籍的. ②书本上的. ③帐面上的. *the ~ department downstairs* 楼下售书部. ~ *knowledge* 书本知识. ~ *profit* 帐面利润. ~ **account** 往来帐户. ~ **binder** 装订工人. ~ **bindery** 装订厂. ~ **binding** 装订,钉书. ~ **case** 书橱,书箱. ~ **club** 读书会. ~ **concern** 〔美〕出版社,发行所. ~ **credit** 帐面信用, 赊销金额. ~ **debt** 帐面负债, 赊购金额. ~**end** 书靠; 书立, 书挡. ~ **hunter** 猎书者, 珍本秘本书搜猎者. ~ **jacket** (书的)护封. ~ **keeper** ①簿记员, 帐房,管帐人, 记帐人. ②〔谑〕借书久借不还的人. ~**-keeping** 簿记. ~**land** 【英史】特许保有地. ~**-learned** *a.* 书上学到的, 书本知识的; 迷信书本的. ~ **learning** 书本知识;〔俚〕学问; 正规教育, 学校教育. ~**let** 小册子. ~ **lore** = ~ **learning.** ~**maker** 著作家; (以营利为本位的) 编书人; (赛马等的)登记赌注者. ~**making** ①著作. ②编辑. ③赛马赌博登记簿. ~**man** ①学者; 文人. ②书商. ~**mark** 书签. ~**mobile** 流动书车; 车上图书馆. ~ **nonsense** 〔美俚〕 纸上谈兵. ~**plate** ①书牌; (书面上的)贴头. ②书页铅版. ~ **post** 〔英〕 书籍邮件. ~ **rack** 书架; (书籍)借阅架; 书摊, 书亭, 书柜(台). ~ **rest** (置放摊开书本用的) 阅书架. ~ **review** 书评. ~**seller** 书商. ~**selling** 售书. ~**shelf** 书橱, 书架. ~**shop** 书店. ~ **slide** 活动书架. ~ **society** 读书会. ~ **stack** 分层书架. ~**stall** (旧)书摊; 书亭; 书店. ~ **stand** 书柜台; 书架; 旧书摊. ~**-store** 〔美〕 书店. ~ **value** ①帐面价值. ②买卖净值. ③股本净值. ④单股价值. ~**work** 理论研究, 钻研书本; 勤学. ~**worm** ①蠹鱼, 蛀书虫. ②读书迷, 书呆子. **-able** *a.* 〔英〕可预购〔约、定〕的.

book·ie [ˈbuki] *n.* ①〔英口〕(赛马等的) 赌注登记者. ②〔美口〕粗制滥造的作家.

book·ing [ˈbukiŋ] *n.* ①记帐; 登记. ②(邀请讲演者、演出者等的)预约, 演出契约. ③挂号; (座位等的)预定. ④售票. ~ **agent** ①代订机票、戏票的人. ②(演员等的)经纪人. ~ **clerk** ①售票员. ②负责安排与登记旅客、货物、行李等的服务员. ~ **hall,** 〔美〕 ~ **office** 售票处.

book·ish [ˈbukiʃ] *a.* ①书上的. ②嗜书的, 好读书的; 博览群书的. ③咬文嚼字的; 学究气的, 书本上的. *a ~ way of thinking* 书呆子的想法.

Bool·e·an [ˈbuːljən] **algebra** 布尔代数, 逻辑代数.

boom[1] [buːm] *n.* ①(雷、炮等的)隆隆声, 轰轰声; (波浪的)澎湃声; (鼓等的)咚咚声; (蜂等的)营营声; (鹭鸶等的)鸣叫; 有回响的声音. ②(市面的)忽然兴旺, 景气, 繁荣, 勃兴; (候选人等的)突然大得人心〔出名〕; (形势的)突然好转; (城市等的)急速发展; (物价等的)暴涨; (人口等的)激增. *the war* ~ 战争景气. *a building* ~ 建筑业的兴旺. — *vi.* ①(雷等)隆隆响; (波浪声)澎湃; (鼓等)咚咚地响; (蜂声)营营; (鹭鸶等)鸣叫. ②(市面等)突然兴隆, 繁荣; (物价等)暴涨; (人口等)激增; (城市等)急速发展; (形势等)突然好转; (候选人等)突然得人心〔出名〕. *Guns are ~ing.* 炮声隆隆. *Not far off the Pacific ~ed.* 不远处, 太平洋的涛声轰鸣. — *vt.* ①用隆隆声发出. ②(用广告等)推广销路; 捧(候选人等). ③使迅速发展, 使兴旺. *He ~ed out the verse.* 他用低沉的声音朗读诗句. — *a.* 〔美〕猛涨起来的, 忽然发展〔兴旺〕起来的. ~ *prices* 猛涨起来的物价. ~**-and-bust [slump]** *n.* 经济繁荣与萧条的交替循环. ~ **town** 新兴城市.

boom[2] [buːm] *n.* ①【船】帆的下桁, 帆杠, 横梁; 吊杆; 悬〔转、起重〕臂. ②横江铁索, (港口的)水栅; 栅栏; 水上航标; 【林】筏堰. — *vt.* (以下桁)张开帆脚. — *vi.* (船)以最高速航行. ~ *nets* 【军】栅栏网〔战时港口的水底铁丝网〕. *heavy* ~ 重吊杠. ***lower the ~ on*** 〔口〕①禁止. ②严惩.

boom·er [ˈbuːmə] *n.* ①〔美口〕走红运的人; 讨人喜欢的东西. ②〔美俚〕(往来无定的)短工; 赶往新兴地区安家者. ③〔澳〕 雄性大袋鼠; (北美)山狸. **B- State** 美国俄克拉何马州的别名.

boom·er·ang [ˈbuːməræŋ] *n.* 飞去来器〔澳大利亚土著居民扔出后能飞回的飞镖〕; 〔喻〕自食其果的言行. — *vi.* 象飞镖似地返回; 对自己的言行起反作用; 害人反害己, 自食其果.

boom·ing [ˈbuːmiŋ] *a.* ①突然兴旺的. ②大受欢迎的. ③暴涨的; 激增的. ④发轰隆声的.

boom·let [ˈbuːmlit] *n.* 〔美口〕小兴旺, 小景气, 暂时繁荣.

boom·ster [ˈbuːmstə] *n.* 〔美俗〕造成兴旺的东西〔人〕.

boon[1] [buːn] *n.* ①〔古〕恳求. ②赐物, 赠物; 恩惠, 恩典; 恩赐; 福利; 裨益, 照顾. ***ask a ~ (of sb.)*** 请求(某人) (*May I ask a ~ of you?* 我能请你帮个忙吗?). ***be [prove] a great ~ to [for]*** (成为) 对…极可感谢的〔有用的〕东西 (*The aid was a great ~ for the country.* 这项援助对该国有极大的好处).

boon[2] [buːn] *a.* ①愉快的, 快活的. ②〔古诗〕(气候等) 温和的; 仁厚的. *a ~ companion* 酒友, 好友.

boon·docks [ˈbuːndɔks] *n. pl.* 〔俚〕 ①孤立的森林; 荒野. ②偏僻的农村; 边省; 内地.

boon·dog·gle [ˈbuːndɔgl] *n.* 〔美俚〕 ①(童子军的)皮绳; (皮或柳条制的)手工品. ②无价值的琐事. — *vi.* (花钱费时间)做无价值的事〔尤指无价值的政府工程〕.

Boon(e) [buːn] *n.* 布恩〔姓氏〕.

boop·er [ˈbuːpə] *n.* 〔美俚〕 花腔舞剧歌手〔指常在歌词中穿插美妙音节的歌手〕.

boor [buə] *n.* 农民; 乡下人; 粗俗的男子; 〔B-〕 = Boer.

boor·ish [ˈbuəriʃ] *a.* 乡下气的, 粗俗的, 土俗的; 粗鲁的. **-ly** *ad.* **-ness** *n.*

boost [buːst] *vt.* ①〔美口〕(由下或由后)推, 升; 提. ②〔美俚〕吹捧(候选人等); 支援; 增加, 提高; 促进; 煽起(买风). ③【电】升(压); 助(爆). ~ *the output of cotton* 提高棉花产量. ~ *sb. into the wagon* 把某人推进马车. ~ *one's hometown* 吹嘘自己的家乡. ~ *prices* 提价. — *n.* ①升, 后推. ②帮助; 促进. ③提高, 增加. ④吹捧, 宣传. ⑤助推发动机, 加速〔助推〕器. ⑥〔美俚〕(假扮顾客的)店铺扒手. *give sb. a ~ into the wagon* 把某人推进马车. *a ~ in price* 提价.

boost·er [ˈbuːstə] *n.* ①【电】升降压器; 调压电阻; 【机】升压机〔泵〕; 【导弹】助推器; 多级火箭的第一级; 【无】(电视等的)放大器; 【原】增益棒; 【军】助爆药; 〔美〕辅助机车; 【药】辅助药剂; 转播站. ②〔美口〕援助者, 后援者; 煽动买风的人. ③〔美俚〕(假扮顾客行窃的)店铺扒手; 足球运动员. *a negative ~* 降压器; 减压机. ~**dose [shot]** 【药】促效剂, 辅药. ~ **station** 【无】升压电台, (电视的)中继台.

boot[1] [buːt] *n.* ①〔美〕长筒靴. ②〔英〕(马车、汽车后部的) 行李箱. ③马脚绊; 【史】靴状刑具, 夹足刑具. ④【机】进料斗; 接受器; 【电】引出罩; (汽车等的)保护罩; 〔空俚〕(飞机上)防结冰皮管. ⑤〔俚〕〔the ~〕解雇. ⑥〔美俚〕海军〔海军陆战队〕新兵. ⑦〔口〕愉快, 开心. ⑧〔英〕〔*pl.* 作 *sing.* 用〕(旅馆)擦靴侍者. *high ~s* 〔英〕长统靴. *elastic-side ~s* 长筒橡皮靴. *put on [off]* 穿〔脱〕靴. *a ~s*〔英〕旅馆的擦靴侍者〔兼管搬行李等〕. *laced ~s* 编带靴. *a ~ camp* 新兵宿舍. ***be in sb.'s ~s*** 站在某人立场上, 赞同某人. ***bet your ~s*** 有把握, 必然, 一定 (*You can bet your ~s I'll be there.* 我一定去). ***big for one's ~s*** 自大, 自骄 (*Don't get too big for your ~s.* 别太自大). ~ ***and saddle*** 〔美〕 (骑兵) 上马预备号. ***die in one's ~s = die with one's ~s on*** 不是死在床上, 暴死, 死于非命, 横死. ***get the ~*** 〔俚〕被解雇, 被开除. ***get [put] the ~ on the wrong leg*** 误释, 错解. ***give sb. a ~*** 使某人开心. ***give sb. the ~*** 解雇某人. ***go down in one's ~s*** 〔美口〕感到恐怖, 害怕. ***go to bed in one's ~s*** 烂醉如泥, 酩酊大醉. ***have one's heart in one's ~s*** 害怕; 提心吊胆. ***I'll eat my ~s if …*** 我决不…; 决无此事. ***in seven lea-***

gue ~s 飞速，极快. ***lick sb.'s ~s*** 向某人屈服，迁就；奉承某人. ***lick the ~s off*** 使惨败 (*He licked the ~s off me.* 他把我打得惨败). ***like old ~s*** 〔俚〕猛烈地，彻底地，可惊地 (*It's raining like old ~s.* 大雨倾盆，正下大雨). ***move one's ~s*** 〔美口〕出发. ***over shoes over ~s*** 将错就错，一不做二不休. ***put the ~ in*** ①猛踢. ②采取决定性行动. ***put the ~ on the wrong leg*** 错爱，错赏. ***rise out of one's ~s*** 飞快地起床，从床上飞快跳起. ***The ~ is on the other foot [leg].*** ①责任在其他方面[人等]. ②弄错人. ③事实恰恰相反. ***wipe one's ~s on sb.*** 侮辱某人. ***with one's heart [voice] in one's ~s*** 提心吊胆. — *vt.* ①穿(靴). ②〔美〕用靴踢；踢出，赶出，轰走，〔俚〕解雇 (*out*). ~**black** 〔美〕以擦皮鞋为业者. ~ **camp** 〔美〕(海军)新兵训练所. ~**jack** 脱靴器. ~ **lace** 靴带. ~ **last** 靴型，靴楦，靴衬. ~**leg** ① *vt.* 〔美俚〕偷卖[贩、酿、运](酒). ② *vi.* 违禁卖[贩、酿、运]酒. ③ *n.* 违禁的酒，私酒. ④ *a.* 违禁的，私酿的，私造的，私自贩运的. ~**lick** *vt., vi.* 〔美俚〕巴结，奉承，拍马屁. ~ **licker** 拍马者，奉承者. ~**maker** 制靴厂；靴匠. ~ **stage** 【植】抽穗期. ~**strap** ① *n.* 鞋袢 (*pull [lift, raise] oneself up by one's [own] ~straps* 凭自己的力量出人头地). ② *a.* 依靠自己力量的；自己做的 (*a ~strap operation* 独立进行的一次手术). ~ **training** (美国海军的)新兵训练(期). ~ **tree** = boot last.

boot[2] [buːt] *n.* 〔古诗〕利益；救济，援助. ***to ~*** 加之，而且 (*He is lame to ~.* 而且他又是跛子). — *vt.* 对…有利，对…有用. *It ~s (you) not to complain.* 怨天尤人(于你)毫无好处. *What ~s it to repeat how time is slipping underneath our feet?* 不断空喊光阴不待人又有何益?

boot·ed [ˈbuːtid] *a.* ①穿靴的. ②〔美俚〕失了业的，已被解雇的. *be ~ and spurred* 穿了马靴，上了靴刺〔准备上马〕.

boot·ee [ˈbuːtiː] *n.* ①【商】轻巧女鞋；小儿毛线鞋. ②〔美俚〕被解雇的人.

Bo·ö·tes [bəuˈəutiːz] *n.* 【天】牧夫座.

booth [buːð] *n.* ①小舍，棚，窝棚；货摊，摊子. ②隔开的小间，(餐馆的)火车座. ③(选举)投票站. *a telephone ~* 电话间. *an announcer ~* 播音员室. *a public telephone ~* 公用电话亭. *a polling ~* (用帐篷等搭的)投票处. *a motion picture projection ~* 电影放映室. ~ **man** *n.* 〔美〕电影放映员.

Booth [buːð] *n.* 布斯〔姓氏〕.

boot·less [ˈbuːtlis] *a.* 〔古〕无益的，无用的. **-ly** *ad.* 无益，徒然，徒劳，白白地. **-ness** *n.*

Boots [buːts] *n.* 布茨〔男子名〕.

boo·ty [ˈbuːti] *n.* ①缴获，战利品. ②赃物，掠夺物. ③奖品，赚头. *war ~* 战利品. ***play ~*** 通同作弊，相互勾结，朋比为奸.

booze [buːz] *vi.* 〔口〕①暴饮，痛饮，滥饮(酒). ②贪杯，经常饮酒. — *n.* ①酒. ②暴饮；酒宴. *go on the ~* 贪杯痛饮. *have a ~* 饮酒. *~ bourse* 〔美〕纽约 Brooklin 区的别名. *~ fighter* 酒徒. ***drive sb. to ~ or dope*** 使迷糊，使醉. ***hit the ~*** 〔美俚〕饮酒. ***on the ~*** 不停的喝酒，痛饮. ~**-hoisting** 〔美俚〕喝酒. ~**-up** 〔英俚〕狂欢作乐，纵酒狂欢.

booz·y [ˈbuːzi] *a.* 大醉的；爱酒如命的.

bop [bɔp] *n.* 〔美俚〕一击，一捆. — *vt.* (用拳、棍棒等)打，打击.

bo·peep [bəuˈpiːp] *n.* 躲猫〔一种躲在隐蔽处突然出现的逗小儿的游戏〕. ***play ~*** ①玩躲猫游戏. ②(政客等)圆滑，耍花腔，躲躲闪闪.

Bo-Peep [bəuˈpiːp] *n.* 〔英俚〕睡眠.

BOQ, B.O.Q. 【美军】= Bachelor Officer's Quarters. 单身军官宿舍.

BOR = British Other Ranks 英国兵.

bor. = boron; borough.

bo·ra [ˈbɔːrə] *n.* 【气】布拉风〔亚得里亚海北部干冷凶猛的东北风〕.

bo·rac·ic [bəˈræsik] *a.* = boric. ~ **ointment** 硼酸药膏.

bo·ra·cite [ˈbɔːrəˌsait] *n.* 【矿】方硼石.

bor·age [ˈbɔːridʒ] *n.* 【植】硫璃苣〔其叶可作调味料〕.

bo·ral [ˈbɔːrəl] *n.* 【药】硼酒石酸铝〔用作收敛剂〕.

bo·rane [ˈbəurein] *n.* 【化】甲硼烷；甲硼烷衍生物.

bo·rate [ˈbɔːreit] *n.* 【化】硼酸盐；硼酸酯. — *vt.* 使与硼砂[硼酸]混合.

bo·rax[1] [ˈbɔːræks] *n.* 【化】硼砂；月石.

bo·rax[2] [ˈbɔːræks] *n.* 〔俚〕好看的便宜货，〔特指〕式样繁多的便宜家具.

bo·ra·zon [ˈbɔːrəˌzɔn] *n.* 【化】一氮化硼结晶体.

Bor·deaux [bɔːˈdəu] *n.* ①波尔多〔法国西南部商港〕. ②波尔多白葡萄酒. ~ **mixture** 波尔多液〔加硫酸铜于石灰乳中所成的一种农用杀霉菌剂和杀虫剂〕.

bor·del [ˈbɔːdl] *n.* 〔古〕妓院.

bor·del·lo [bɔːˈdeləu] *n.* 妓院.

bor·der [ˈbɔːdə] *n.* ①边，缘，边沿，框. ②边界，国界，国境，边境；边地；领地. ③(女服的)滚边；布边；(印刷品等的)边饰. ④(庭园沿边或走道两旁的)花坛. *the ~ clashes* 边界冲突. *cross the ~* 越过国境线. *a ~ along the path* 沿路边的花坛. *the ~ of a lake* 湖畔. *the ~ army* 边防军. *the B- of B-s* 英格兰与苏格兰交界区. ***on the ~ of*** ①将要，正要. ②接近于，濒临于. ***on the ~s*** 在边界上，接近交界边. ***out of [within] ~s*** 在国境〔领地〕外〔内〕. ***over the ~*** 越过国境. — *vi.* ①接界，邻接 (*on, upon*). ②近似，相近 (*on, upon*). *His conduct ~s upon madness.* 他的行为近乎疯狂. *The U.S. ~s on Canada.* 美国与加拿大接壤. — *vt.* ①在(衣服等上)镶边[滚，加缘饰]. ②与…接壤，邻接；接近. *a park ~ed by modern buildings* 为现代化建筑所环绕的公园. *the countries that ~ the Danube* 以多瑙河分界的国家. ~**land** ①国境地带，边境，边陲；边缘地带. ②〔喻〕模糊不清的境界；梦境 (*lives on the ~ of society* 生活在社会的边缘地带. *the ~ between fantacy and reality* 幻想与现实之间的境地). ~ **line** ①国境线；分界线. ②两可之间. ~**line** *a.* ①在国界〔公界线〕上的. ②两可的，不明确的；语义暧昧的〔尤指近于下流的〕(*a ~line joke* 近于不雅的玩笑). **-er** *n.* 边境居民. **-ing** *n.* ①立界标. ②边，缘. **-ism** (英格兰与苏格兰)边境居民的特殊风习〔语言〕.

bor·de·reau [bɔːdəˈrəu] *n.* (*pl.* ***-reaux*** [-ˈrəuz]) 〔F.〕= invoice.

bor·dure [ˈbɔːdjuə] *n.* 【纹】盾边.

bore[1] [bɔː] *n.* ①膛；膛腔；孔，孔腔；眼，炮眼；枪膛，炮膛. ②膛径，孔径，口径，内径. ③钻[扩]孔器，锥，镗头. *basic ~* 【机】基孔. *~ bit* 钻孔钻头. *~ size* 内径. — *vt.* ①穿(孔)，钻(孔)，【机】镗(孔)；挖(洞)，在…上打眼，开凿(隧道等). ②挤入(人群)；【赛马】拨开(别的马). *~ a plank* 在木板上钻孔. *~ a tunnel through the Alps* 凿一条穿过阿尔卑斯山的隧道. *~ an oil well 3,000 feet deep* 钻一眼 3,000 英尺深的油井. — *vi.* ①打眼，钻孔；【机】镗孔；开凿，挖掘. ②钻入，挤入 (*through; into*). *Certain types of steel don't ~ well.* 有些品种的钢材不容易打眼. *~ for oil [coal]* 钻探石油[煤炭]. ***~ from within*** 从内部破坏. ***~ one's way through (the crowd)*** 挤入(人群). ~**-hole** 钻孔，镗孔；炮眼，井眼. ~**scope** 管道内孔探测镜；光学孔径仪. ~**-sight** ①瞄准线，视轴. ②炮膛舰视器，枪筒瞄准.

bore[2] [bɔː] bear 的过去式.

bore[3] [bɔː] *n.* 使人讨厌的人[物]，讨厌的工作；打扰. *The play was a ~.* 这出戏没意思. *I'm afraid that I'm a ~ to you.* 我恐怕打扰您了. — *vt.* 使厌烦，烦扰，打扰 (*with*). *be ~d to death* 厌烦得要死. *Am I boring you?*

我打扰您了吧？ *be ~d with the past* 对过去的事已不感兴趣。

bore[4] [bɔː] *n.* 高潮，怒潮；海啸。

bo·re·al [ˈbɔːriəl] *a.* ①北(方)的；北风的。②〔B-〕【希神】北风之神的。③〔B-〕(生长于)北半球北部山区的。

Bo·re·as [ˈbɔ(ː)riæs] *n.*【希神】北风之神；〔诗〕北风；朔风。

bore·cole [ˈbɔːkəul] *n.*【植】羽衣甘蓝。

bore·dom [ˈbɔːdəm] *n.* ①讨厌，无聊，无趣。②令人厌烦的事物。*in infinite ~* 极其无趣。

bor·er [ˈbɔːrə] *n.* ①穿孔者；镗工，钻工，打眼工。②钻孔器，钻头，钻机；凿岩机；錾；【机】镗床，镗孔刀具。③【动】凿船虫，钻蛀虫。*a jig ~* 座标镗床。*a collar ~* 象鼻虫。*a maize ~* 玉米螟。*a rice ~* 稻螟虫。

bore·some [ˈbɔːsəm] *a.* 令人厌烦的，令人厌倦的，讨厌的；无聊的。

bo·ric [ˈbɔːrik] *a.*【化】硼的，含硼的。**~ acid** 硼酸。

bo·ri·ckite [ˈbɔrikait] *n.*【矿】褐磷酸钙铁矿。

bo·ride [ˈbɔːraid] *n.*【化】硼化物。**~ cermet** 硼〔金属〕陶瓷。

bor·ing[1] [ˈbɔːriŋ] *n.* ①穿孔，钻孔；镗削；地质钻探。②〔*pl.*〕镗屑，钻屑。— *a.* 镗(钻)孔的。**~ machine** 钻孔机，镗床。**~ sample** 岩心取样。

bor·ing[2] [ˈbɔːriŋ] *a.* 令人厌烦的，无聊的，无趣的。*~people* 令人讨厌的人。

Bor·is [ˈbɔris] *n.* 鲍里斯〔男子名〕。

born [bɔːn] 作"产，生"解的 bear[1] 的过去分词。— *a.* ①出生的；出身于…的。②生来就…的，命中注定的。③天生的；有天才的。*one's first-~ child* 第一个孩子。*a newly-~ idea* 新产生的想法。*a Chicago-~ New Yorker* 出生在芝加哥的纽约人。*He was ~ to be hanged.* 他命中注定要上绞架。*a ~ musician* 天生的音乐家。*a ~ fool* 生下来就是白痴。***be ~ again*** 再生，自新，更生。***be ~ of*** *(rich parents)* 出身于(有钱人家)。***be ~ to*** *(wealth)* 生来(有钱)。***be ~ with a silver spoon in one's mouth*** 生在富贵人家。***~ and bred*** 在…生长大的；地地道道的，… 本地的 (*a ~ and bred Parisienne* 地地道道的巴黎妇女)。***~ of woman*** 同是娘养的。***~ yesterday*** 天真的，乳臭未干的，无经验的。***in all one's ~ days*** 有生以来，一生中，生平 (*In all my ~ days I've never seen such a fool as you are.* 我有生以来还从没有见过你这样的傻子)。

borne [bɔːn] 不作"产，生"解的 bear[1] 的过去分词。★在作"产，生"解时只限于生育(子女等)一义，有以下两种情况：一是用于完成时，置于助动词 have 之后；一是用于被动语态，置于介词 by 之前。*She has ~ two children. Two children were ~ by her.* 她生了两个孩子。

borné [ˈbɔːnei] *a.* 〔F.〕心地窄狭的，小心眼儿的，偏狭的；局限的。

Bor·ne·o [ˈbɔːniəu] *n.* 婆罗洲〔Kalimantan 加里曼丹的旧称〕。

bor·ne·ol [ˈbɔːniɔl] *n.*【化】龙脑；冰片。

born·ite [ˈbɔːnait] *n.*【矿】斑铜矿。

boro- *comb.f.* 硼：*borohide, boron.*

bo·ron [ˈbɔːrən] *n.*【化】硼。**~ oxide** 二氧化硼。**-ic** *a.* **-ization** *n.*【冶】渗硼。

bo·ro·sil·i·cate [ˌbɔːrəuˈsilikit] *n.*【化】硼硅酸盐。*~ glass* 光学玻璃。*hard ~ glass* 耐火玻璃。

bor·ough [ˈbʌrə] *n.* ①〔英〕(享有特权的)自治城市；有议员选举权的城市；〔美〕自治村镇；纽约市五个行政区之一。②〔古〕城，镇；〔美阿拉斯加〕县。***a close [pocket] ~*** ①为一人〔一家〕操纵的议员选区。②一人〔一家，一集团〕操纵的政治团体。***rotten ~***【英史】朽镇〔虽已衰落但仍有选举权的市镇，1832 年被废止〕。**~-English** *n.* 〔英〕末子继承制〔英国某些地区的一种习俗，规定由末子〔如无子嗣则由末弟〕继承财产〕。

bor·row [ˈbɔrəu] *vt.* ①借，借用。②模仿，剽窃。③【数】由上位借。*The neighbors ~ed my lawn mower.* 邻居们借用我的除草机。*~ a word from German* 借用一个德语词。*~ (money) from [of]* 由… 处借(钱)。*~ 1 from 4 in the number of 42 to add as 10 to 2* 在 42 这个数字中向 4 借 1 作 10 加给 2〔减法演算中的借位〕。***~ money on ...*** 以…抵借，押借。— *vi.* ①借钱，借用；【数】借位。②模仿，剽窃。③【海】迎风〔靠岸〕航行。④【高尔夫球】斟酌风向〔斜度〕打球。*Japanese has ~ed heavily from English.* 日语中借用了很多英语。***~ trouble*** 喜作无益的忧虑，自找麻烦，自寻烦恼 (*It was her nature to ~ trouble.* 她生来喜欢自寻烦恼)。***in ~ed plumes*** 穿着别人的漂亮衣裳；借用他人声望。— *n.* ①借，借用。②担保物，抵押。③【英史】什一税。**~ pit** (筑堤取土挖成的)土坑。**-ed** *a.* 借来的 (*borrowed light* 反射过来的光；内窗。*borrowed time* 奇迹般的获救，寿命的意外延长)。

Bor·row [ˈbɔrəu] *n.* 博罗〔姓氏〕。

bor·row·er [ˈbɔrəuə] *n.* 借钱人，借用人；剽窃者。*~'s card* 借书证。

bor·row·ing [ˈbɔrəuiŋ] *n.* 借，借用；借用的东西，借用的词〔譬喻等〕；模仿其他民族的风习。

borsch, borsht, borshtsh, bortsch [bɔːʃ, bɔːʃt, bɔːtʃ] *n.* 俄国菜汤。

Bor·stal [ˈbɔːstl] *n.* 〔英〕(青少年罪犯)教养院 (= ~ institution)。**~ boy** 〔英〕教养院的青少年罪犯。

bort, bortz [bɔːt, bɔːts] *n.* (仅用于切削或研磨的)不纯金刚石，金刚石粒；金刚石粉。*short ~* 劣等金刚石。

bor·zoi [ˈbɔːzɔi] *n.* 〔*pl.* ~*s*〕俄国大猎狗〔猎狼狗〕。

bos [bɔs] *n., vt., vi.* 〔英俚〕做错，看差；猜错；弄糟。

Bo·san·quet [ˈbəuznkit] *n.* 博桑基特〔姓氏〕。

bos·cage, bos·kage [ˈbɔskidʒ] *n.* 〔诗〕灌木丛；树丛。

bosch·bok, bosh·bok [ˈbɔʃbɔk] *n.* *(pl. ~, ~s)*【动】林羚 (= bushbuck)。

Bosche [bɔʃ] *n., a.* = Boche.

bosch·vark [ˈbɔʃvaːk] *n.*【动】非洲野猪。

bosh[1] [bɔʃ] *n.* 〔口〕胡说，空话，废话。— *vt.* 〔学俚〕愚弄，戏弄；欺负。— *int.* 胡说八道！瞎说！

bosh[2] [bɔʃ] *n.* ①(鼓风)炉腹。②【化】浴；锅，槽，桶。

bosk, bos·ket, bos·quet [bɔsk, ˈbɔskit] *n.* 树丛；(园内)小树林。

bosk·y [ˈbɔski] *a.* ①矮树丛生的；林木荫蔽的，有丛林的。②〔英俚〕喝醉了的。

bo's'n [ˈbəusn] *n.*【海】= boatswain.

Bos·ni·a [ˈbɔzniə] *n.* 波斯尼亚〔南斯拉夫一地区〕。**-n** ① *a.* 波斯尼亚(人)的。② *n.* 波斯尼亚人。

bos·om [ˈbuzəm] *n.* ①胸，胸膛；心胸，胸怀，内心。②里面，内部，当中；亲密关系。③(湖、海等的)宽阔的表面。④(衣类的)胸部；〔美〕衬衫胸部。⑤〔*pl.*〕(女人的)乳房；〔古〕怀抱。*the wife of one's ~* 〔古〕爱妻。*press sb. to one's ~* 搂抱某人。*put a baby to the ~* 给婴儿喂乳。*with panting ~* 情绪激动。*in the ~ of the earth* 地球内部。*the tranquil ~ of the Seine* 塞纳河宁静的水面。***in Abraham's ~*** 死，升天。***in the ~ of one's family*** 一家团聚；享天伦之乐。***keep in one's ~*** 秘藏胸中。***speak one's ~*** 倾吐衷曲。***take (sb.) to ~*** ①娶。②与…做心腹朋友。③重视。— *vt.* ①搂抱。②怀有；把…秘藏心中；隐匿，把…藏起来。**Abraham's ~** 天国。**~ chums** 〔美俚〕虱。**~ friend** 心腹朋友，知交，密友。**~ secret** 重要秘密。**~ sin** 深藏心中的罪恶。

bos·omed [ˈbuzəmd, ˈbuːzəmd] *a.* 有(某种)胸部的〔用以构成复合词〕。*small-~* 胸部狭小的。

bos·om·y [ˈbuzəmi] *a.* 胸部隆起的，乳房丰满的。

bos·on [ˈbəusɔn] *n.* 【物】玻色子〔遵从玻色统计法的粒子〕。

Bos·po·rus, Bos·pho·rus [ˈbɔspərəs, ˈbɔsfərəs] *n.* (黑海与马尔马拉海间的)博斯普鲁斯海峡。

bos·que [ˈbɔskei] *n.* 〔Sp.〕〔主美国西南部〕小林子，丛

林.

bos·quet [ˈbɔskit] *n.* 矮林,丛林 (= bosket).

boss[1] [bɔs] *n.* ①〔口〕头儿;老板;上司;经理;工头;工长. ②〔美〕(政党)领袖,首领;伟人;支柱. *a political* ~ 政界大亨. *He is my* ~. 他是我的头儿. *His wife's the* ~ *in his family.* 他的妻子是一家之主. *a straw* ~ 工头助手. — *a.* ①〔口〕管事的;掌权的. ②〔俚〕第一流的. ~ *shoemaker* 第一流的鞋匠. — *vt.* 当…的首领;支配,统率,指挥,把…呼来喝去. ~ *the house* 做一家之长. — *vi.* ①当头儿. ②摆出上司架子. ~ ***(sb.) about [around]*** 支配某人,把某人差来遣去. ~ ***it*** 摆架子. ~ ***the show*** 指挥,主持. ~ **rule** 政党领袖对选民的操纵. ~ **windjammer** 〔美俚〕乐队领班. **-dom** *n.* ①政治领袖的势力范围. ②政治领袖对政治的控制.

boss[2] [bɔs] *n.* ①(动、植物身上的)结疤,瘤;突起部. ②【地】岩瘤;【建】浮凸饰;(盾中心的)浮雕. ③【机】轴套;套筒;轮毂. *a* ~ *on an animal's horn* 动物角上的瘤. *a* ~ *of granite* 一块突出的花岗岩. — *vt.* ①用凸饰装饰. ②浮雕.

boss[3] [bɔs] *n., v.* = bos.

boss[4] [bɔs] *n.* 〔美〕①母牛,小牛. ②牛〔对母牛和小牛的呼唤用语〕.

bossed [bɔst] *a.* 有浮凸饰的,有结疤的.

bos(s)-eyed [ˈbɔsaid] *a.* ①〔俚〕独眼的;斜眼的. ②〔转义〕偏私的.

boss·ism [ˈbɔsizəm] *n.* 〔美俚〕头头控制〔首领对政党或政治机构的控制〕.

boss·y[1] [ˈbɔsi] *a.* 有浮凸饰的;有结疤的.

boss·y[2] [ˈbɔsi] *a.* 〔俚〕俏皮的,风流俊俏的.

boss·y[3] [ˈbɔsi] *a.* 〔美俚〕霸道的,专横的.

boss·y[4] [ˈbɔsi] *n.* 牛,牛宝宝〔对牛的一种爱称〕.

Bos·ton [ˈbɔstən] *n.* ①波士顿〔美国城市〕. ②〔b-〕波士顿纸牌戏〔四人用两副纸牌〕. ③〔b-〕波士顿圆舞. ~ **arm** 一种人造假手. ~ **bag** 一种手提包. ~ **rocker** 一种讲究的摇椅. ~ **Tea Party** 【美史】(1773 年波士顿居民抗议英国政府对殖民地进口茶叶征收苛税的)波士顿茶叶事件. **-i·an** *n.* 波士顿人.

bo·sun [ˈbəusn] *n.* = boatswain.

Bos·well [ˈbɔzwəl] *n.* ①博斯韦尔〔姓氏〕. ② **James** ~ 博斯韦尔〔1740—95, 英国杰出的传记作家,著有 *Samuel Johnson* 传〕.

Bos·well·ian [bɔzˈweliən] *a.* 博斯韦尔(体)的.

Bos·well·ism [bɔzˈwelizəm] *n.* 博斯韦尔体〔写传记时巨细无遗地记述被作传者的言行〕.

bot [bɔt] *n.* ①马蝇幼虫;马蝇. ②〔the ~s〕马蝇寄生病. ~**-fly** 马蝇.

bo·tan·ic [bəˈtænik] *a.* 植物(学)的. *the United States B- Garden* 美国植物园. ★本字仅用于植物园名称等.

bo·tan·i·cal [bəˈtænikəl] *a.* 植物(学)的. ~ **gardens** 植物园. ~ **survey** 植物学调查. — *n.* 植物性药材. **-ly** *ad.* 植物学上.

bot·a·nist [ˈbɔtənist] *n.* 植物学家,专门研究植物的人.

bot·a·nize, bot·a·nise [ˈbɔtənaiz] *vi.* ①采集植物. ②研究植物. — *vt.* 为研究植物品种而勘察(某地等).

bot·a·ny [ˈbɔtəni] *n.* ①植物学. ②〔总称〕一个地区的植物. ③植物生态. ④植物学书籍〔论著〕. *the* ~ *of Alaska* 阿拉斯加地区的植物生态. *the* ~ *of deciduous trees* 落叶树的生态.

Bot·a·ny [ˈbɔtəni] *n., a.* 澳洲细羊毛(的). ~ *(wool)* 澳洲细羊毛. ~ *yarn* 澳洲细毛线.

botch[1] [bɔtʃ] *vt., vi.* ①粗拙地补缀. ②笨手笨脚地弄坏. *He* ~*ed the job badly.* 他把活儿做得一塌糊涂. — *n.* ①拙劣的工作,笨活. ②粗拙的补缀. *make a complete* ~ *of one's work* 把事情干得一团糟.

botch[2] [bɔtʃ] *n.* 〔英方〕疮,瘤.

botch·er [ˈbɔtʃə] *n.* ①笨拙的工人〔鞋匠等〕. ②拙劣的写作者.

botch·y [ˈbɔtʃi] *a.* 工作拙劣的. **botch·i·ly** *ad.* **botch·i·ness** *n.*

bo·tel [bəuˈtel] = boatel.

both [bəuθ] *a.* 两,双,双方,两面,二者. ~ *times* 两次. ~ *sides* 双方. ~ *these books* 这两本书. ~ *(the) brothers* 兄弟二人. ~ *his hands* 两手. *B- girls are beautiful.* 两个姑娘都漂亮. *I don't want* ~ *books.* 我不是两本书都要〔只要其中一本〕. ***have it*** ~ ***ways*** (在议论中)忽左忽右〔以自相矛盾的观点作为论据〕. ***not*** ~ 一面,单独. — *pro.* 两者,二者,双方. *B- are dead.* 这两人都死了. ~ *of them* 他们双方,两者都. *B- of the girls are beautiful.* 两个姑娘都漂亮. *They were scientists* ~. 双方都是科学家〔both 与 they 同格〕. *I don't know* ~. 我不是两个人都认识〔只认识其中之一〕. — *ad.* 皆,哪个都;并且,兼,又〔用在有 and 连接的二个以上词句前,与 neither ... nor 正相反〕. *B- brother and sister are dead* 哥哥和妹妹都死了. *It is* ~ *good and cheap.* 它又便宜又好,它价廉物美. *She can* ~ *sing and dance.* 她又会唱歌又会跳舞,她能歌善舞. ~ *before the war and during the war.* 无论在战前还是在战时. ~ *Chaucer and Shakespeare and Milton* 无论是乔叟、莎士比亚还是密尔顿. ~ **hand·ed** *a.* 用两手的,两手都行的.

both·er [ˈbɔðə] *vt.* ①烦扰,打扰. ②使迷惑,使胡涂,使伤脑筋. ③〔口〕= damn, confound〔表示厌烦等〕. *Don't* ~ *me with such trifles.* 不要用这些小事打扰我. *His baby sister* ~*ed him for candy.* 小妹妹缠着他要糖吃. *His inability to understand her* ~*ed him.* 他不能理解她,这使他大伤脑筋. *B- it! [B- you!]* 讨厌! — *vi.* 烦恼;操心. *No one* ~*ed to visit him.* 没人想到去看他. ~ *with trifles* 为小事烦恼〔操心〕. ~ *with sb. about sth.* 为某事同某人发生纠纷. ~ ***about*** 为…操心 *(Don't* ~ *about getting dinner for me.* 别为我做饭麻烦了*)*. ~ ***one's head [brain] about*** 为…伤脑筋. ~ ***the record*** 〔美俚〕打破记录,创造新纪录. ***without*** ~***ing to reply*** 懒得回答. — *n.* ①麻烦,操心,累赘,烦扰;吵闹. ②讨厌的人,麻烦的事物. *What is all this* ~ *about?* 这闹的是什么呀! *Doing the laundry every week is a terrible* ~. 每星期洗衣服麻烦死了. *Hey, don't go to any* ~. 嗨,别麻烦了. — *int.* 讨厌! *Oh,* ~! 真讨厌!

both·er·a·tion [ˌbɔðəˈreiʃən] *n.* 〔俚〕烦恼;麻烦. — *int.* 讨厌! *Oh,* ~! 真讨厌!

both·er·some [ˈbɔðəsəm] *a.* 讨厌的,麻烦的,累赘的,为难的. *How* ~ *it is to forget names!* 忘掉人的名字真烦人!

Both·nia [ˈbɔθniə] *n.* 波士尼亚. ***Gulf of*** ~ (瑞典芬兰间的)波士尼亚湾.

both·y, both·ie [ˈbɔθi] *n.* 〔Scot.〕(农民等住的)茅屋;(独间)小屋,窝棚.

bo tree [ˈbəu triː] *n.* 菩提树.

bot·ry·oid(al) [ˌbɔtriˈɔid(əl)] *a.* 一串葡萄状的.

bot·ry·o·my·co·sis [ˌbɔtriəumaiˈkəusis] *n.* 葡萄菌病.

bots [bɔts] *n.* 蝇蛆病.

Bot·swa·na [bɔtˈswɑːnə] *n.* 博茨瓦纳〔非洲〕.

bott [bɔt] *n.* = bot.

bot·tine [bɔˈtiːn] *n.* 短筒女靴.

bot·tle[1] [ˈbɔtl] *n.* ①瓶;一瓶的量. ②〔the ~〕奶瓶;(瓶装)牛奶. ③〔the ~〕酒;饮酒. ④(装酒、油等的)皮囊. *a wine* ~ 酒瓶. *a* ~ *of wine* 一瓶酒. *a* ~ *messenger* (用作测定海流等试验的)海流瓶. *a three-* ~ *man* 酒量大的人. ***be fond of the*** ~ 好酒贪杯. ***bring up [raise] on the*** ~ 用奶瓶喂(婴儿),用牛奶把(婴儿)哺育大. ***crack a*** ~ 开瓶饮酒. ***hit the*** ~〔俚〕饮酒过多,酗酒. ***keep (sb.) from the*** ~ 不让(某人)喝酒. ***keep to the*** ~ 爱喝酒,嗜酒. ***(talk) over a*** ~ 一面喝酒一面(谈话等). ***pass*** ~ 传杯轮饮. ***take to the*** ~ 喝上酒,爱上酒. — *vt.* ①把(酒等)装瓶;把(水果等)装

罐贮藏. ②忍着，含着(不平、怒气等) *(up)*. ③〔英俚〕捕获(逃犯等)，使(逃犯、敌军等)陷入困境 *(up)*. ～ *grape juice* 把葡萄汁装瓶. ～ *up one's temper* 克制住自己的脾气. ***Bottle it!*** 〔美俚〕不要吵了！静一静！～ ***off*** 把…由桶中移装瓶内(～ *off a cask of wine* 把一桶酒分装进若干小瓶). ～ ***up*** ①把…封在瓶内；压住(感情)，隐匿(事实). ②封锁(交通等)；捕获(逃犯等)；使(逃犯等)陷入困境 (*keep things ～ed up* 把事情瞒起来. *Traffic was ～ed up in the tunnel.* 隧道停止通行). ～ **baby** 用奶瓶哺育的婴孩. ～**brush** ①洗瓶刷. ②【植】问荆，红千层属植物. ～ **chart**【海】(根据海流试验瓶画成的)漂瓶图，海流图. ～ **cap** 瓶盖. ～**-fed** *a.* 人工喂养的，(婴儿)以牛奶哺育的. ～**-feeding** (婴儿的)人工喂养. ～**glass** (深绿色的)瓶料玻璃. ～**gourd**【植】葫芦. ～ **green** 深绿色. ～ **holder** ①瓶托，瓶架. ②【拳】(拳击选手的)副手. ③后援(人). ～**neck** ① *n.* 瓶颈口；(交通易堵塞的)隘道，狭口；〔美〕(特指生产中的)妨碍进度的因素，薄弱环节. ② *vt.* 阻碍，限制. ③ *vi.* 交通堵塞. ④ *a.* (街道等)狭隘的. ～**nose** 酒糟鼻，红鼻子. ～ **opener** 开瓶起子，拔塞器. ～ **party** 各人自带酒的宴会. ～ **washer** 洗瓶工；杂役. **-d** *a.* ①瓶装的. ②〔俚〕醉醺醺的，喝醉了的 (～ *gas* 瓶装煤气，瓶装液化石油气).

bot·tle^{2} [ˈbɔtl] *n.* 〔英方〕(干草等的)束，堆. ***look for a needle in a ～ of hay*** 干草堆里找针，吃力不讨好，徒劳无益.

bot·tling [ˈbɔtliŋ] *n.* 装瓶；灌注. *a ～ machine* 装瓶机.

bot·tom [ˈbɔtəm] *n.* ①底，底部. ②地基，基础；根底；底细，真相，原因，根源. ③(树的)根干；(山)麓；〔方，常 *pl.*〕河边低地，谷，洼地；(页的)下端；(餐桌、班级等的)末席，(名单的)末尾；〔英〕(港湾、街道等的)尽头，末端，(庭院等的)顶里面；【纺】(织物的)地，底子，底色. ④水底，海底，湖底，河底. ⑤(吃水线以下的)船底(部)，舱底；货船，船舶. ⑥臀部，屁股；〔*pl.*〕睡裤；(椅子的)椅垫. ⑦精力，持久力，耐力. ⑧〔*pl.*〕底部沉积物，残渣，脚子. ⑨最低点；最坏的地步. ⑩【棒】下半局. *the ～ of the stairs* 楼梯下段. *the ～ of a page* 一页纸的下端. *the ～ of a flatiron* 熨斗的底. *the ～ of the street* 街的尽头处. *foreign ～s* 外国船. *sit at the ～ of the table* 坐末席. *a horse of good ～* 根底好的〔有耐久力的〕马. *Well, bless my fat ～.* 啊，我的天！ ***at (the)*** ～ 实际上，内心里；本质上 (*a good man at ～* 本质上是好人. *know at ～ that ...* 心里明白…). ***at the ～ of fortune's wheel*** 时乖命舛，倒霉透顶. ***be at the ～ of*** ①在…深处. ②是…的主动者〔主因〕，引起 (*at the ～ of one's heart* 内心深处. *at the ～ of all these crimes* 引起这一切犯罪现象的原因是…). ～ ***up*** 倒置，反转. ***Bottoms up!*** 〔美俚〕干杯！ ***from the ～ of one's [the] heart*** 发自内心深处，真心诚意. ***from the ～ up*** 从一开始；彻底地. ***get to the ～ of*** 走到…的尽头；彻底查明(问题等). ***go to the ～*** 沉，沉没；深究，探究. ***knock the ～ out of ...*** 证明…无价值，使…失去立足基础. ***on her own ～***【海】(商船、渔船等)无债，已付清应缴款项. ***reach the ～*** 达到水底. ***scrape the ～ of the barrel*** 刮桶底；〔美俚〕使出最后一招. ***send to the ～*** 弄沉；打沉，击沉. ***smell the ～ (ground)*** (船)擦泥缓行. ***stand on one's own ～*** 独立；自力更生. ***swim to the ～*** 〔谑〕下沉，沉下水. ***to the ～*** 到最底下，彻底 (*drink the cup to the ～* 饮干一杯. *search (sth.) to the ～* 彻底探究，追根穷源). ***touch ～*** ①(船)搁浅. ②(数值等)达到最低点. ③(研究等)接触根底，得到根据〔结论〕，理解. — *a.* ①底部的；最下层的，最低的. ②最后的；根本的. ③(鱼等)底栖的. *her ～ lips* 她的下嘴唇. ～ *fish* 栖于水底的鱼. *the ～ book in the stack* 书架最下面一层的书. *the ～ floor* 最底一层. *the ～ cause* 根本原因. ～ *dollar* 最后一块钱，所有的钱 (*bet one's ～ dollar* 孤注一掷；保证，确信). ～ *prices* 底价，最低价格. ～ *recessive*【生】隐性基因纯合体. ～ *rung* (社会阶梯的)底层. ***come out ～*** 考试成绩倒数第一名. — *vt.* ①给…上底；给(椅子)装面. ②给…打地基；给…打底；建立…的基础. ③着(海等的)底，达到…的底. ④测量(海底等)的深度；查明…的真相〔原因〕. ～ *a chair* 给椅子装面. *arguments ～ed on facts* 言之有据，有事实作依据的论点. ～ *sb.'s plan* 弄清某人的打算〔计划〕. ～ *the sub* 使潜水艇沉下水底. — *vi.* ①变得有基础，建立基础. ②达到底，停于底部. *The submarine ～ed on the ocean floor.* 潜水艇停在洋底. ～ **out** 降到最低点. ～ **board** (短艇的)底板. ～ **drawer** 〔英〕(妇女为结婚准备的)嫁衣. ～ **land** 〔美〕河边低地，洼地；河边野草. **-less** *a.* ①无底的；深不可测的. ②无限的. ③深奥难解的. ④无底板的(*a bottomless problem* 深奥的难题. *a bottomless abyss* 无底深渊). **-most** *a.* 最下面的；最低的；最深的；最根本的.

Bot·tome [bəˈtəum] *n.* 博托姆〔姓氏〕.

bot·tom·ry [ˈbɔtəmri] *n.* ①以船作抵押的借款. ②冒风险的放债.

bot·u·lin [ˈbɔtjulin] *n.*【生化】肉毒杆菌毒素.

bot·u·li·nus [ˌbɔtʃəˈlainəs] *n.*【生化】肉毒杆菌.

bot·u·lism [ˈbɔtjulizəm] *n.*【医】腊肠〔腐肉〕中毒；罐头食品中毒.

bou·clé, bou·cle [buːˈklei] *n.* 珠毛呢，仿羔皮呢.

bou·doir [ˈbuːdwɑː, buːˈdwɑː] *n.* 〔F.〕闺房.

bouf·fant [buːˈfɑ̃ːŋ] *a.* 〔F.〕鼓起的；(裙)膨鼓的；(发)蓬松的.

bouffe [buːf] *n.* 〔It.〕滑稽歌剧.

Bou·gain·vil·lae·a [ˌbuːgənˈviliə] *n.*【植】九重葛属，叶子花属.

bough [bau] *n.* ①大枝，树枝. ②〔古〕绞刑架. ～**pot** ①大花瓶. ②〔英方〕花束. **-ed** *a.* (树)长有大枝的.

bought [bɔːt] buy 的过去式及过去分词.

bought·en [ˈbɔːtn] *a.* 〔美方〕买来的 (*opp.* homemade).

bou·gie [ˈbuːʒiː] *n.* ①【医】探条. ②【药】栓剂. ③蜡烛.

bouil·la·baissé [ˌbuːljəˈbeis, ˌbuːjɑːˈbeis] *n.* 〔F.〕浓味燉鱼〔用两种以上的鱼加酒等烹调而成〕.

bouil·li [ˈbuːjiː] *n.* 〔F.〕白煮肉；燉肉.

bouil·lon [ˈbuːjɔ̃ːŋ] *n.* 〔F.〕①肉汁清汤〔用牛肉、鸡肉等作成〕. ②【兽医】蹄瘤. ③(衣服的)膨褶. ④一种细菌培养基. ～ **cube** (切成方块的)浓缩肉汤冻.

boul. = boulevard.

bou·lan·ger·ite [buːˈlændʒərait] *n.*【矿】硫锑铅矿.

boul·der [ˈbəuldə] *n.* 圆石，卵石；【地】冰砾，巨砾；漂砾. ～ **clay**【地】泥砾；冰砾泥. **B- Dam** 顽石坝〔美国科罗拉多河上的大坝，高 221 米，坝顶长约 360 米〕. ～ **setter** 砾石铺砌层.

Bou·le [ˈbuːliː] *n.* 〔希〕①(古希腊的)立法会议. ②(现代希腊的)议会〔尤指众议院〕.

bou·le·vard [ˈbuːlivɑːd] *n.* ①宽敞的步道，林荫路. ②〔美〕大马路，干道，大街.

boule·var·dier [buːlvaiːˈdje] *n.* 〔F.〕巴黎林荫大道咖啡店的主顾；〔转义〕活跃于社交界的男子，花花公子.

boule·ver·se·ment [buːlveəsˈmɔn] *n.* 〔F.〕颠倒；颠覆，推翻；混乱.

Bou·logne [buˈləun] *n.* 布伦〔法国北部一港口〕.

boult [bəult] *v.* = bolt^{2}.

boul·ter [ˈbəultə] *n.* 多钩粗钓丝.

bounce [bauns] *vi.* ①(球等)跳起，弹起，反跳，弹回；(人)跳跃，跳起 *(up)*，跳进 *(in)*，跳出 *(out)*，乱跳乱蹦 *(about)*，急促地动. ②夸口，吹牛，说大话；虚张声势. ③〔俚〕(支票)退票，拒付. *The ball ～ed off the wall.* 球从墙壁上反弹回来. ～ *out of the room* 冲出屋外. ～ *up and down on the seat* 在座位上前后颠簸. *His checks ～.* 他的支票被银行拒付. — *vt.* ①使弹回，使跳起；拍(球). ②〔口〕责骂. ③〔英〕威胁，逼使；诈骗.

④〔美俚〕赶出，撵走；解雇，辞退，开除，将…撤职．～ *a ball* 拍球．～ *sb. out of sth.* 骗走某人的东西．～ *sb. into [out of] doing sth.* 逼使某人做［不做］某事．～ ***a beauty***〔美、棒球〕打出好球．～ ***back***〔口〕很快挽回(颓势、败局)，立即恢复(元气等)．— *n.* ①跳，弹，(球等的)弹回；〔口〕弹力；〔俚〕活力．②夸口，吹牛，自大；鲁莽．③猛击；【军】(在较高高度对敌机的)突然袭击．④〔美俚〕赶出，解雇．*rise with a* ～ 猛地跳起．*contact* ～【物】接点颤动．*This tennis ball has no more* ～．这个网球已经失去弹力了．*get the (grand)* ～〔美俚〕被解雇［被辞退，撵走，斥退］．*give sb. the (grand)* ～ 解雇［辞退，撵走，斥退］某人．*There is* ～ *in his step.* 他步履轻捷［走路有精神］．— *ad.* ①猛跳．②猛然，突然，砰地．*come* ～ *into [against]* 与…砰地相撞．～**-back**【物】反冲，反射．～ **plate** 反跳板．

bounc·er [ˈbaunsə] *n.* ①(同类中特大的)巨人，巨物．②跳跃者．③大话，谎话；吹牛大家．④〔美俚〕戏院［旅馆］保镖．*That dog is a* ～．那条狗长得特别大．

bounc·ing [ˈbaunsiŋ] *a.* ①跳跃的．②(人)强壮的，生气勃勃的，精神饱满的．③巨大的，异常的．④吹牛的．*a* ～ *sum* 一笔巨款．*a* ～ *lie* 大吹其牛．***a* ～ *baby*** ①活蹦乱跳的孩子．②〔军俚〕榴散地雷．

boun·cy [ˈbaunsi] *a.* ***(-ci·er, -ci·est)*** ①生气勃勃的．②有弹力的．③自高自大的．

bound[1] [baund] *n.*〔*pl.*〕①界限，界线，限度．②边界，边境；边界线内的领土．③区域，领域，范围．*the* ～*s of space and time* 时空范围．*the farthest* ～*s of the ocean* 大洋最远的界限．***beyond the* ～*s of*** 越出…的范围以外，为…所不及．***break* ～*s*** 越轨；过度，逾限；【军】擅自进入军事禁区．***keep within* ～*s*** 使不过度；约束，守规；持中．***know no* ～*s*** 不知足，无餍，无限制．***out of* ～*s*** ①越界，越轨，越限．②禁止…入内 *(to)* (*The ball bounced out of* ～*s.* 球跳出界外．*The park is out of* ～*s to students.* 此公园不准学生入内)．***set [put]* ～*s to*** 限制．***within (the)* ～*s*** 在规定范围内，不越轨．— *vt.* ①限，限制．②形成…的界限［边界］，以…为界，邻接．③指出…的范围［界限］．～ *one's desires by reason* 以理性约束欲望．*The United States is* ～*ed on the north by Canada.* 美国北与加拿大接壤．*The students were asked to* ～ *their country.* 学生被要求指出本国的国界．— *vi.*〔古〕接界*(with)*．

bound[2] [baund] *n.* 跳，跳跃，跳起；弹跳，跃进．*a* ～ *forward* 向前跳跃．*hit a ball on the* ～ 在球跳起来的时候击球．***at a [with one]* ～** 一跃，一跳．***by leaps and* ～*s*** 连跑带跳地，飞快地 (*advance by leaps and* ～*s* 进步飞跃)．— *vt.* 使跳跃，使弹起．— *vi.* 跳跃，跳起，弹起；跳开．～ *to one's feet* 一跃而起．*The ball* ～*ed against the wall.* 球从墙上反弹回来．～ ***into fame [favor]*** 一举成名［受欢迎］．～ ***on [upon]*** 猛扑 (*The leopard* ～*ed on the prey.* 那只豹猛扑向猎物)．

bound[3] [baund] bind 的过去式及过去分词．— *a.* ①绑着的，被束缚的．②负有义务的，有责任的，理应…的；受(合同、法律等)约束的．③装订的，有封面的．④被…封锁的；秘结的，便秘的．⑤必定的，肯定的．⑥〔美俚〕下了决心的，决心要…．⑦密切关联的；【化、物】结合的；粘合的，耦合的．*a* ～ *prisoner* 被绑缚着的犯人．*She is* ～ *to her family.* 她被家庭束缚住了．*man-*～ 因人员不足不能开船的．*ice-*～ 冰封的．*desk-*～ 整日伏案工作的．*He is* ～ *by the terms of the contract.* 他受到合同条款的约束．*a book* ～ *in leather* 皮面精装书．～ *volume* 合订本．*It's* ～ *to happen.* 这件事必然要发生．*She is* ～ *to go.* 她决心要走．***be* ～ *up in*** 热中于，专心于，忙于 (～ *up in one's work* 专心工作)．***be* ～ *up with*** 和…有密切关系．***I'll be* ～**．一定，保证，我可以担保．～ **charge**【物】束缚电荷．～ **medium**【化】粘合介质．～ **pocket** 暗口袋．～ **vector**【数】束缚矢量．～ **water**【化】结合［束缚］水．

bound[4] [baund] *a.*〔作表语用〕①开往(某处)去的，要往(某处)去的．②〔古〕准备，打算．*Where are you* ～ *(for)?* 你到哪里去？***be* ～ *for*** 以…为目的地的 (*The train is* ～ *for Denver.* 列车开往丹弗)．

bound·a·ry [ˈbaundəri] *n.* 边界，疆界，限界 *(between)*；(球场)边线；界标；界限，范围，分野．*a* ～ *dispute* 边界纠纷．*the* ～ *between Canada and the United States* 美加国界．***boundaries on all sides*** 四方辐辏之所，四通八达．～ **condition**【数】边界条件．～ **effect**【物】边界效应．～ **layer**【物】边界层．～**-line** (边)界线．～ **rider**〔澳〕牧场巡边工．～ **science** 边缘科学．

bound·ed [ˈbaundid] *a.* ①有界限的，有限制的．②【数】有界的．～ **function**【数】有界函数，囿函数．～ **set**【数】有界集，囿集．**-ness** *n.*

bound·en [ˈbaundən] bind 的古体过去分词．— *a.* ①义不容辞的．②〔古〕受恩的．***be* ～ *to* … *for* …** 多亏…才，仗有…才 (*I'm* ～ *to him for my success.* 我的成功多亏了他)．***one's* ～ *duty*** 义不容辞的责任，职责所在．

bound·er [ˈbaundə] *n.* ①〔英俚〕鲁莽［粗俗］的人．②【棒球】定界员．

bound·less [ˈbaundlis] *a.* 无限的，无穷的，无边无际的．～ *ambition* 欲壑难填，无限大的野心．～ *energy* 无穷的精力．**-ly** *ad.* **-ness** *n.*

boun·te·ous [ˈbauntiəs] *a.*〔书〕①宽宏大量的，博爱的，慷慨的．②富裕的，丰富的，丰厚的．**-ly** *ad.* **-ness** *n.*

boun·ti·ful [ˈbauntiful] *a.* ①宽宏大量的，慷慨的．②丰富的 *(of)*．*a* ～ *giver* 慷慨解囊的人．*a* ～ *harvest* 丰收．**-ly** *ad.* **-ness** *n.*

boun·ty [ˈbaunti] *n.* ①慷慨，仁爱，博爱，宽大；恩惠．②赐物，赠物；赐金，赠金．③赏金；奖金 *(on; upon; for)*．*She depends on his* ～．她倚靠他的施舍生活．*There was a* ～ *on his head.* 悬赏买他的人头．*offer a* ～ *for dead wolves* 悬赏奖励打狼．***the* ～ *of nature*** 自然的恩赐．～ **hunter** 为获赏而追捕野兽［逃犯等］的人．～ **jumper** (美国南北战争时)领取入伍津贴后开小差的人，壮丁油子．～ **land** (军功)赐地．～ **money** (军功)赏金．

bou·quet [ˈbu(:)kei, buˈkei] *n.*〔F.〕①花束；一丛礼花，一束烟火．②恭维话．③ [buˈkei] (葡萄酒的)香，芳香；(文艺作品的)特殊风格．*a* ～ *of roses* 一束玫瑰花．～*s and brickbats* 褒贬之词．***throw* ～*s at*** 赞美，称赞．

Bour·bon [ˈbuəbən] *n.* ①【法史】波旁皇室的一员．②〔美〕最顽固的保守分子；极端保守的政治家．③〔b-〕波旁威士忌［美国 Kentucky 州 Bourbon 地方出产的烈性威士忌酒 = **b- whisky**］．**-ism** *n.* 对波旁皇室的拥护；保皇主义，顽固的保守主义．

bour·don [ˈbuədən] *n.* ①【乐】(风琴的)最低音簧；风笛的低音管．②嗡嗡的低音．③〔罕〕朝山香客的手杖．— *vi.* 发嗡嗡声．

bourg [buəg] *n.*〔F.〕①(中世纪筑有城堡的)村镇．②市镇．

bour·geois[1] [ˈbuəʒwɑ:] *(pl.* ～*)*〔F.〕①中产阶级的市民；中世纪城镇的自由民．②业主，店主，商人．③有产者；〔*pl.*〕资产阶级．— *a.* ①资产阶级的，中产阶级的．②商人根性的，市侩的；无教养的，鄙俗的；注意物质享受的．～ *taste* 庸俗趣味．

bour·geois[2] [bəːˈdʒɔis] *n.*〔古〕【印】九点活字［相当我国新五号铅字］．

bour·geoi·sie [ˌbuəʒwɑːˈziː] *n.* 商人阶级；中产阶级，资产阶级．*the bureaucrat-*～ 官僚资产阶级．*the comprador* ～ 买办资产阶级．*the national* ～ 民族资产阶级．*the petty* ～ 小资产阶级．

bour·geon [ˈbəːdʒən] *vi.* = burgeon.

bourn(e)[1] [buən] *n.*〔Scot.〕小河．

bourn(e)[2] [buən] *n.* ①〔古〕境界，界限．②〔诗〕目的地；目的．③领域．*the undiscover'd country from whose* ～ *no traveller returns* 那片渺渺茫茫的土地啊，走向那里的旅

客一去不复还〔莎士比亚剧本《哈姆雷特》中的诗句〕.

bour·rée [bu:ˈrei] *n.* ①布列舞〔十七世纪法国的一种舞蹈〕. ②布列舞曲.

bourse [buəs] *n.* 〔F.〕(证券)交易所; 〔B-〕巴黎证券交易所.

bouse[1] [bu:z, bauz] *vi., n.* = booze.

bouse[2] [bauz] *vt., vi.* 【海】用辘轳吊(某物).

bous·tro·phe·don [ˌbaustrəˈfi:dən] *n.* 一行由右而左一行由左而右的写法. — *a., ad.* 右行左行交互书写的〔地〕.

bout [baut] *n.* ①(工作、闹饮等的)一阵, 一回, 一转, 一次, 一番. ②(耕地等的)一个来回; (赌赛等的)一场, 一次较量, 一个回合. ③(绳的)一绕; 一缕; 一锄; 一犁; 一刈(等); (病的)发作(时期). *a ~ of work* 干一阵工作. *a ~ of illness* 病发作一阵. *a drinking ~* 一次宴会. *a wrestling ~* 一场摔跤. *play a ~ or two* (赌博等)玩一两回.

bou·tique [bu(:)ˈti:k] *n.* 〔F.〕①(妇女)时装用品小商店. ②镶嵌珠宝〔镀金〕的日用品.

bou·ton·nière [ˌbu:təˈnjɛə] 〔F.〕钮孔花〔别在钮扣眼上的一束〔朵〕花〕.

bouts ri·més [ˈbu:ˈri:mei] 〔F.〕和韵; 和韵诗.

bou·zou·ki [bu:ˈzu:ki] *n.* 布素奇琴〔一种希腊弦乐器, 似曼陀林琴〕.

Bo·vey [ˈbu:vi] *n.* 博维〔姓氏〕.

bo·vid [ˈbəuvid] *a.* 牛科的. — *n.* 牛科动物.

bo·vine [ˈbəuvain] *a.* ①牛科的; 牛的; 牛一样的. ②鲁钝的. *a ~ temperament* 鲁钝的性格. — *n.* 牛科动物. ~ **pest** 牛瘟.

bov·ril [ˈbɔvril] *n.* 〔英〕牛肉汁〔来源于商标名〕.

bov·ver [ˈbɔvə] *n.* 〔英俚〕(流氓等的)街头殴斗. — *vi.* 参加街头殴斗. ~ **boot** 街斗靴〔一种装上平头钉和钢鞋尖的重靴, 用以踢击伤人〕.

bow[1] [bəu] *n.* ①弓; 石弩; 弓形物〔饰〕; 弓形弯曲; 弧. ②【乐】琴弓; 【机】锯弓. ③虹. ④蝴蝶结, 蝴蝶结领带. ⑤〔美〕眼镜框〔脚〕. ⑥弓手. ⑦凸肚窗. ~ *compasses* 小两规; 外卡钳. *tie a ribbon in a ~* 把缎带打一个蝴蝶结. ~ *and arrow* 弓矢. *He is the best ~ in the country.* 他是国内最好的射手. ***bend [draw, pull] the [a] long ~*** 吹牛, 说大话. ***draw a ~ at a venture*** 瞎开弓; 胡搞. ***have two [many] strings to one's ~*** 作好两〔几〕手准备. — *vt.* ①把…弯作弓形; 弯. ②用弓拉奏. — *vi.* ①弯作弓形. ②用弓拉琴. ~**-backed** *a.* 驼背的, 弯腰屈背的. ~ **compass(es)** 两脚规, 圆规; 外卡钳. ~**drill** 弓钻. ~**fin** 弓鳍鱼. ~**-front** *a.* 弓背形的, 凸形的 (*a ~ front chest* 鸡胸). ~ **hand** ①持弓的手〔通常为左手〕. ②拉琴弓的手〔通常为右手〕. ~ **instrument** 弓弦乐器. ~ **knot** 滑结, 活结. ~**leg** 〔常 *pl.*〕弓形腿, 罗圈腿. ~**legged** *a.* 弓形腿的, 罗圈腿的. ~ **man** 弓手. ~**pen** 两脚规. ~ **saw** 弓锯. ~**shot** 箭的射程, 一箭之地〔约200—400英尺〕. ~**string** ① *n.* 弓弦; 绞索. ② *vt.* 给(弓)装弦; 绞死, 勒死. ~ **tie** 蝴蝶结领带. ~ **window** 【建】凸肚窗, 弓形窗; 〔卑〕罗汉肚. **-ing** *n.* (弦乐器)弓法; (音乐家的)演奏技巧.

bow[2] [bau] *n.* ①点头, 鞠躬. ②低头, 屈服. *with a low ~* 深深地鞠一躬. ***a ~ and a scrape*** 打躬作揖. ***make a ~ to*** 对…行礼. ***make one's ~*** (讲完演说等)鞠躬而退出〔进入〕, 退场, 退席, 退出(社会生活等). ***take a ~*** (在鼓掌声中)点头答礼; 答谢. — *vi.* ①鞠躬, 打躬, 点头; (树等)弯屈. ②屈服, 屈从 (*to*). ~ *to sb.* 向某人鞠躬〔点头招呼〕. ~ *from the waist* 弯腰鞠躬. ~ *one's thanks* 鞠躬致谢. ~ *to sb.'s knowledge* 对某人的学识表示敬意. *The pines ~ed low.* 松树深深地弯曲着身子. — *vt.* ①弯(腰等); 低(头等); (点头)指示, 表示. ②使屈从. ③压弯 (*down*) ***be ~ed with*** (*age; care*), (年老)腰弯; (因操心而)意气消沉. ~ ***and scrape*** 打躬作揖. ~ ***before [to] the inevitable*** 屈服于(必然的)命运之前. ~ ***down to*** 屈服于…之下; 给…行礼. ~ ***out*** 〔美〕辞职; 退出, 退场. ~ ***(sb.) in [out]*** 恭迎入内〔恭送出门〕. ~ ***the knees to*** 对…行屈膝礼, 对…表示敬意, 崇拜, 信奉. ~ ***the neck*** 屈服, 服从, 低头. ~***ing acquaintance*** 点头之交.

bow[3] [bau] *n.* 〔常 *pl.*〕①船首; 舰首; 机首. ②前桨手. ~***s on*** 船首向前; 勇往直前地. ~***s under*** (船头)被淹没; 困难地(前进); 张皇失措地. ***in ~s*** ①命令起桨开船. ②准备靠岸〔靠拢大船〕. ***on the ~*** 在船首方向〔船头前面左右45度弧内〕. ~ **chaser** 舰首炮. ~ **fast** 船首的铁链. ~ **grace** (保护船首的)保险杠〔垫〕. ~ **gun** 前枪, 前炮〔舰艇、坦克等前部的枪炮〕. ~ **mar** 前桨手. ~ **oar** 前桨; 前桨手. ~ **spirit** 第一斜桅; 牙樯. ~ **wave** 【海】(头)激波, 船首波, 顶头波.

Bo·wa·ter [ˈbəuˌwɔ:tə] *n.* 鲍沃特〔姓氏〕.

Bow bells [ˈbəuˈbelz] ①伦敦市区. ②道地的伦敦人〔源自伦敦 St. Mary-le-Bow 教堂的钟声所及处〕. ***within the sound of Bow bells*** 在伦敦市区内.

bowd·ler·ize [ˈbaudləraiz] *vt.* 删去(书中)不妥处〔尤指不适合青少年阅读处, 源出 Thomas Bowdler 1818年出版莎士比亚剧作删节本〕; 删改. **-i·za·tion** *n.*

bowed [bəud] *a.* ①弓一样弯曲的, 弓形的; 有弓的. ②(头等)低下的. *listen with a ~ head.* 低头恭听.

bow·el [ˈbauəl] *n.* ①〔常 *pl.*〕(人)肠〔作定语或医学术语时用单数〕. ②〔*pl.*〕内脏; 内部. ③〔*pl.*〕同情心, 怜悯心. *the large [small] ~s* 大〔小〕肠. *I have loose ~s.* 我泻肚了. *a ~ complain* 肠道疾病. *The ~s move [are open]* 要大便. *move [loosen, relax] the ~s* 大便. *relieve the ~s* 通便, 大便, 小便. *bind the ~s* 止痢. *the ~s of the earth* 地球内部, 地壳深处. *The cabins were in the ~s of the ship* 客舱在船的内部. *have no ~s* 无情, 残忍, 不通情理. ~ **movement** *n.* ①排便. ②粪便, 屎尿.

Bow·en [ˈbəuin] *n.* 鲍恩〔姓氏〕.

bow·er[1] [ˈbauə] *n.* ①亭子, 凉亭; 树荫处. ②〔诗〕卧室, 闺房. ③〔诗〕隐居处; 乡间茅舍, 村舍; 精舍. — *vt.* 荫蔽. ~**-bird** 园丁鸟. ~**-maid** 侍婢, 丫头.

bow·er[2] [ˈbauə] *n.* 优克立 (euchre) 牌戏中的王牌. *best ~* 百搭. *right ~* 王牌 jack. *left ~* 王牌 jack 和同花 jack.

bow·er[3] [ˈbauə] *n.* 【船】大锚, 主锚, 船首锚. ***the best [small] ~*** 右舷〔左舷〕主锚.

bow·er[4] [ˈbəuə] *n.* 用弓拉奏乐器的人.

bow·er·ed [ˈbauəd] *a.* = bowery.[1]

bow·ery[1] [ˈbauəri] *a.* ①有亭的, 凉亭似的. ②有树荫的. *Trees made the meadow a ~ maze.* 树木使草原成了绿荫处处的迷宫.

bow·er·y[2] [ˈbauəri] *n.* ①〔美〕(昔日南非、纽约等地的)荷兰移民农场. ②〔the B-〕(纽约市小饭馆和流浪者多的)波威里街. — *a.* 俗丽的, 漂亮而不值钱的.

bow·ie [ˈbəui] *n.* 〔美〕长猎刀 (= ~-knife). *Bowie State* 〔美〕Arkansas 州的别名.

bowl[1] [bəul] *n.* ①钵, 碗; 一钵〔碗〕的量; 〔美〕盘, 盆. ②〔诗〕饮器, 大杯; 〔喻〕烈酒; 欢宴, 狂饮. ③碗状物; (天平、秤等的)碗形等盘; 匙, 烟斗. ④盆地; 〔美〕圆形竞技场. *a rice ~* 饭碗. *a sugar ~* 糖钵. *a ~ of soup* 一碗汤. *the flowing ~* 满杯的酒. ***over the ~*** 在酒宴上; 一边喝酒一边(谈话等).

bowl[2] [bəul] *n.* ①(游戏用的)木球. ②〔*pl.*〕滚木球戏, 九柱戏 (ninepins), 〔美〕十柱戏 (tenpins). ③【机】(离心机等的)转筒, 转子; 浮筒, 辊筒. *play [at] ~s* 玩滚木球戏. *have a game of ~s* 玩一场滚木球戏. ~ *mill* 【机】球磨机. *float ~* 浮筒. ***at long ~s*** 远距离地(尤指军舰远程炮轰). — *vt.* ①滚转(球、环、轮等); 使稳捷地行驶; (用车等)运送. ②(滚木球戏中)完成(规定的回数); 得到…分; 【板球】投(球); 打倒. *He ~s a good game.* 他的滚(木)球玩得好. ~ *a 120 game*

(滚木球戏)得 120 分. ~*s 150* 得 150 分. — *vi.* ①转球,投球; 玩滚(木)球. ②(象木球样)轱辘轱辘地滚走; (车等)稳捷地行驶. ③【板球】投球给击球手. ~ *along* 稳捷地走[行驶]. ~ *down* ①(滚木球戏等)用球击倒. ②〔口〕打倒,撞倒,打败. ~ *off*【板球】打落. ~ *out* ①【板球】击中三柱门[击落三柱门横木]. ②〔俚〕戳穿(某人谎话). ③= ~ down. ~ *over* ①(九柱戏中)击倒; 撞倒. ②使狼狈,使慌张 (*He's ~ed over by a dashing horse.* 他被奔马撞倒. *~ed over by the evil news* 噩耗传来,不知所措).

bowl·der [ˈbəuldə] *n.* = boulder.

bowl·er[1] [ˈbəulə] *n.* ①玩滚木球戏[九柱戏、十柱戏]者, 滚木球的人. ②【板球】投球手.

bowl·er[2] [ˈbəulə] *n.* 〔英〕圆顶硬礼帽. ~ *hat* 〔英〕圆顶硬礼帽. ~**-hat** *vt.* 〔俚〕由(军队等处)退役, 退职.

Bowles [bəulz] *n.* 鲍尔斯[姓氏].

bowl·ful [ˈbəulˌful] *n.* 一满钵[碗、盘].

bow·line [ˈbəulin] *n.* ①【船】帆脚索. ②单套结 (= ~ knot). *on a* ~ 【海】趁风扬帆开行. *on an easy* ~ 【海】抢风满帆开行.

bowl·ing [ˈbəuliŋ] *n.* ①滚木球,玩滚木球戏; 玩九柱戏. ②(板球的)投球. ~**-alley** 滚球场. ~ **green** 木球草地,草地滚球场.

Bow·man [ˈbəumən] *n.* 鲍曼[姓氏].

bow·pot [ˈbaupɔt] *n.* ①大花瓶. ②花束.

bowse[1] [bu:z, bauz] *n., vi.* 〔古〕暴饮,狂饮,痛饮; 酒,酒宴 (= booze).

bowse[2] [bauz] *vt., vi.* 【海】= bouse[2].

bows·er [ˈbauzə] *n.* ①(机场等用的)加油车. ②加油艇 (= ~ boat).

Bow·street [ˈbəustri:t] (伦敦中央违警罪法庭所在地的)玻街. **the ~ Court** 伦敦违警罪法庭. ~ **officer [runner]** (19 世纪初期)伦敦违警罪管治科警官.

bow·wow [ˈbauˈwau] *int.* (模仿狗叫的)汪汪! — [ˈbauwau] *n.* ①狗吠声. ②〔儿〕汪汪狗 (= dog). — *vi.* ①(狗)汪汪叫. ②作狗叫声. ***go to the ~s*** 〔美俚〕堕落; 毁灭. ***the (big) ~ style*** 武断语调[笔调]. ~ **theory**【语】拟声说.

bow·yer [ˈbəujə] *n.* ①弓匠. ②弓商.

box[1] [bɔks] *n.* ①箱,柜,匣,盒; 罩壳; 钱柜; 〔美口〕保险箱; 邮箱,信箱; 〔英〕礼盒; 礼物; (旅行用)衣箱. ②一箱,一盒. ③(戏院等的)包厢; (饭店等的)分格座位; (马等的)格形厩; (法庭的)证人席; 陪审席; 被告席; 专席. ④哨房,岗亭,信号所,事务所; 〔英〕(猎人等的)小屋; 电话间; 〔美〕猎鸭小船. ⑤(马车等的)驭者座; (卡车的)车兜. ⑥(窗)框,壁橱; 【机】轴承箱,箱状部分; 箱状物. ⑦【棒球】投手位; 打手位. 〔俚〕(足球)禁区; (以线标出的)小区. ⑧〔美〕(树上挖的)取液孔. ⑨(报纸上的)花边读物. ⑩〔俚〕话匣子,留声机; 电唱机; 电视机. ⑪〔卑〕(女性的)外阴部; 〔俚〕弦乐器; 钢琴. *mail* ~ 邮箱. *money* ~ 钱匣. *a ~ of candy* 一盒糖果. *a press* ~ 记者席. *witness* ~ 证人席. *jury* ~ 陪审员席. *a shooting* ~ 狩猎小屋. *a call* ~ 电话室. *a police* ~ 岗亭. *black* ~ (探测地下核试验的)黑箱. *key* ~ 电键匣. *pull* ~ (电线)分线盒. *a gear* ~ 齿轮箱. *a fire-alarm* ~ 火警报警器. *an eternity* ~ 〔俚〕棺材. ***~ and needle***【航海】罗盘. ***in a ~ = in a bad [tight] ~*** 处逆境, 为难,困. ***in the same ~*** 处于同一地位, 处于同样的困境. ***in the wrong ~*** 搞错地方,不得其所; 处于窘境. — *vt.* ①把…装盒[装箱],给…装上罩壳; 包围. ②把…做成箱形[盒形]. ③分隔. ④【海】使(船)顺风转向. ⑤在树上挖孔采液汁. ⑥【气】沿 (风暴区) 边缘作箱形飞行. ⑦使挤在一处. ~ *the glassware* 把玻璃器皿装箱. ~ *a wheel hud* 给轮毂加罩壳. ~ *a storm*【气】在风暴区边沿作箱形飞行. *With no windows I felt ~ed in suffocating.* 由于没有窗户,我觉得关在屋子里很闷气. ~ ***a horse*** 把马系在格形厩栏里. ~ ***about***【海】使(船)转向. ~ ***in*** ① = ~ up. ②【赛马】阻拦(他马). ~ ***off*** ①把…隔成小房. ②使(船)微微调向. ~ ***the compass*** ①依次列举罗盘的三十二方位. ②屡变(议论、意见等)而终于采行原议. ~ ***up*** ①把…装箱. ②把…困在狭小区域内,使陷困境,使挤在一处. ③〔口〕弄乱; 弄错. ~ **barrage**【军】①缘边射击. ②高射炮火网. ~ **bed** ①四周围成箱形的床. ②可以折摺如箱的床. ~**board** (制盒、箱用的) 硬纸板. ~ **bridge**【电】电阻箱电桥. ~ **calf** (制靴的)小牛皮. ~ **car** 箱车; 〔美〕有盖货车; 〔*pl.*〕骰子的十二点[在双骰赌中掷出者为输]; 【物】矩形波串. ~ **cloth** (做驭者大衣的)茶黄色厚呢,缩绒厚呢. ~ **coat** 驭者外套; 连披肩厚外套. ~**cotton** 标准样棉. ~ **horn** 喇叭形天线. ~**iron** 熨斗. ~**keeper** 包厢管理员. ~ **kite** 箱形风筝[测气象用]. ~ **lunch** 午餐盒饭. ~ **number** 信箱号. ~ **office** 售票室. ~**-office** *a.* 卖座很好的; 受人欢迎的,流行的. ~**-office value** 票房价值. ~ **oyster** 精选大蠔,礼蠔. ~ **respirator** 箱形面具, 防毒面具. ~ **score**【棒球】比赛纪录表. ~ **seat** ①(马车)驭者座. ②(剧院)包厢, (运动场)正面看台座. ③便于观看的地方. ~ **spring** 弹簧床座. ~ **stall** (厩的)分格栏. ~ **wagon** 〔英〕有盖货车. ~ **wrench [key, spanner]**【机】套筒扳手.

box[2] [bɔks] *n.* 一掌,一拳. *He gave the boy a ~ on his ear.* 他打了那个男孩一记耳光. — *vt.* ①用手打,用拳头打. ②和…比拳. ~ *sb.'s ears* 打某人耳光. — *vi.* 打拳,从事拳击运动[比赛]. *He has ~ed since he was 16.* 他十六岁就参加拳击比赛了. ~ ***it out*** 打(拳)到胜负分晓.

box[3] [bɔks] *n.*【植】黄杨; 黄杨木. (=~wood).

Box and Cox [ˈbɔks ənd ˈkɔks] *n.* ①同室而难相见的人[住同一房间,但因轮流外出工作而总是不在一起的两个人, 出自 J. M. Morton 的笑剧]. ②轮流担任一事的人, 交替保持一地位的人. *to share a room in a ~ arrangement* 以两人轮流使用的安排方式同住一室. — *a., ad.* 轮流的[地],相互交替的[地].

box·ber·ry [ˈbɔksˌberi] *n.*【植】①平铺白珠树; 冬青油, 冬绿油; 白珠香料. ②蔓虎刺; 蔓虎刺果.

box·er[1] [ˈbɔksə] *n.* 拳击家; 拳师; 参加拳击运动的人. ***the Boxers***【史】义和团,义和拳. ***the Boxer Indemnity***【史】庚子赔款. ~ **shorts** (拳击运动服型)男短裤.

box·er[2] [ˈbɔksə] *n.* ①制箱[盒]者. ②装箱[盒]者.

box·haul [ˈbɔksˈhɔ:l] *vt.*【海】使船顺风微转.

box·ing[1] [ˈbɔksiŋ] *n.* ①装箱[盒]. ②制箱[盒]木料. ③窗箱,箱状罩壳.

box·ing[2] [ˈbɔksiŋ] *n.* 拳击, 拳术, 打拳. ~ **fiend** 〔美〕拳击迷. ~ **glove** 拳击手套. ~ **match** 拳击比赛. ~ **ring** 拳击比赛场. ~ **weights** 拳击体重等级.

Box·ing·day [ˈbɔksiŋdei] 〔英〕节礼日, 圣诞礼馈赠日[英国法定假日,是圣诞节的次日,如遇星期日则顺延一天,俗例于此日向雇员、邮递员等赠送礼品].

box·thorn [ˈbɔksˌθɔ:n] *n.*【植】宁夏枸杞 (=matrimony vine).

box·y [ˈbɔksi] *a.* 似盒子状的, 盒状的, 四四方方的. **box·i·ness** *n.*

boy [bɔi] *n.* ①少年,童子,男孩; 儿子. ②孩子气的男子; 活泼的男子,男子; 青年; 〔口〕小伙子; 〔蔑〕家伙. ③仆人,侍役,勤杂人员,服务员. ④练习生; 【海】见习水手. ⑤〔口〕情人, 男朋友; 〔美〕男学生. ⑥〔*pl.*〕〔美〕军人[尤指战斗人员]; 〔*pl.*〕〔美俚〕外勤记者 *a nice old ~* 这家伙不错. *I have two ~s and a girl.* 我有二男一女. *the ~s overseas* 海外的大兵们. *college ~s* 男大学生. ***a ~ in buttons*** 侍役. ***a slip of a ~*** 瘦长小伙子. ***my (old) ~*** 我的儿子; 喂[招呼自己的儿子]; 喂,老兄[招呼朋友]; 喂,小东西[招呼自己的狗]. ***old ~*** 见 old 条. ***one of the ~s*** 〔俚〕高等游民. ***the ~*** 〔俚〕香槟酒. ***the ~s*** 家中的男子. ***the old ~*** = the devil. ***yellow ~s*** 〔俚〕金币. — *int.* 〔美〕嘿! 噢! 真的, 当

然了!〔表示惊奇、承认、不愉快等，也可说作*Oh, boy!*〕 ~**friend** 要好的男朋友，爱人，未婚夫. ~ **husband [lover]** 年青的丈夫〔爱人〕. ~**s gun** 坦克炮. ~**'s play** 儿戏. ~ **scout** ①童子军(的一员). ②〔美俚〕〔蔑〕极天真的男子；女人气的男子；乐于助人的人. **the B-Scouts** 童子军.

bo·yar(d) [bəuˈjɑː(d)] *n.* ①沙俄特权贵族,大贵族. ②罗马尼亚旧时贵族.

boy·cott [ˈbɔikət] *vt.* ①联合抵制；抵制(货物等). ②一致与…绝交. ~ *a nation* 对某国实行抵制. ~ *a commercial product* 抵制某种商品. ~ *sb.* 一致不与某人往来. — *n.* 联合抵制；联合拒绝购买〔使用、经售等〕. *a class* ~ 罢课. *put sb. [shop, goods] under a* ~ 对某人〔商店、货物〕实行联合抵制.

Boyd [bɔid] *n.* 博伊德〔姓氏,男子名〕.

boy·hood [ˈbɔihud] *n.* ①少年期，少年时代. ②〔集合词〕少年们,男孩们. *B- is a happy time of life.* 少年时代是人生的一个幸福阶段. *one's* ~ 一个人的少年时代.

boy·ish [ˈbɔiiʃ] *a.* 少年的,(男)孩子气的；幼稚的. **-ly** *ad.* (男)孩子一样地. **-ness** *n.* (男)孩子气,幼稚.

Boyle[1] [bɔil] *n.* 博伊尔〔姓氏〕.

Boyle[2] [bɔil], **Robert** 波义耳〔(1627—1691),英国化学家、物理学家〕. ~**'s law**【物】波义耳定律.

boy·sen·ber·ry [ˈbɔisnbəri] *n.*【美植】波森莓.

bo·zo [ˈbəuzəu] *n.* (*pl.* ~*s*) 〔美俚〕家伙,男人,大汉.

B.P., BP = ① British Pharmacopoea 英国药典. ② British Petroleum Company 英国石油公司. ③ blood pressure 血压. ④ British Patent 英国专利. ⑤ Bachelor of Philosophy. ⑥Bachelor of Pharmacy.

BP = ①Beautiful People 风头人物. ②Black Panther 黑豹党员.

b.p. = boiling point 沸点.

B/P = ① bill(s) payable 应付票据. ② bill of parcel 发票. ③ blueprint. ④ board president 董事长.

bpi = bits [bytes] per inch【自】每英寸位数.

Br = bromine.

B/R = bill(s) receivable 应收票据.

bra [brɑː] *n.* 〔口〕奶罩 = brassiere. **-less** *a.* ①(女人)不戴奶罩的. ②主张不带奶罩的〔作为"妇女解放"的象征〕.

brab·ble [ˈbræbl] *n.* 〔古〕吵嘴,争执. — *vi.* 为小事争吵 *(with)*.

brace [breis] *n.* ①支柱,支持物,撑柱;【机】撑臂,拉条；曲柄,把;【医】支架;〔*pl.*〕(牙齿)矫正器;【矿】支撑;竖坑口,井口. ②【印】大括弧〔即 {}〕;【海】转帆索. ③〔*pl.*〕〔英〕(裤子)背带 (=〔美〕suspenders);(弓手等的)护腕带. ④〔*sing., pl.*〕(猎获物等的)一双,一对. ⑤〔口〕(新兵等的)生硬的立正姿势. *a pair of* ~*s* 一副背带. *a* ~ *of grouse* 一对松鸡. *a pole* ~ 电杆拉线. *a crank [hand]* ~手摇钻. ~ ***(and) bit*** 曲柄钻孔器，摇钻，弓钻. ***in a*** ~ ***of shakes*** 马上，立刻. ***splice the main*** ~ 〔俚〕喝酒. ***take a*** ~ 〔美〕鼓起勇气，奋力. — *vt.* ①撑牢,支住. ②给…装拉条;系紧;拉紧,张(弓),叉开(两腿). ③使(神经)紧张;激励,振作(精神);【海】以转帆索转(帆);【印】用大括弧括. ④〔美俚〕向…借钱;向…乞求. ~ ***oneself (up)*** = ~ ***one's energies*** 奋勇，鼓起精神,振作. ~ **game** 欺诈的牌局. ~ **jack** (舞台上放在背景后的)三角形支架.

brace·let [ˈbreislit] *n.* ①手镯，镯头. ②〔*pl.*〕〔谑〕手铐.

brac·er [ˈbreisə] *n.* ①支持物；索，带. ②(射箭时佩戴的)薄臂套，腕甲. ③〔美俚〕兴奋剂，刺激品；刺激性饮料,清晨喝的酒.

bra·ce·ro [brəˈserəu] *n.* (*pl.* ~*s*) 〔Sp.〕墨西哥短工〔到美国去当临时工的墨西哥人,尤指季节性农业工人〕.

brach [brætʃ] *n.* 〔古〕雌猎犬.

bra·chi·al [ˈbreikjəl] *a.*【解】臂(状)的,臂状部分的.

bra·chi·ate [ˈbreikiit] *a.*【植】交互对枝的,十字对生的. — *vi.* 双臂交互攀缘. **-a·tion** *n.*

bra·chi·o·pod [ˈbreikiəˌpɔd] *n.* 腕足类动物.

bra·chi·um [ˈbreikiəm, ˈbrækiəm] *n.* (*pl.* ***bra·chi·a*** [ˈbreikiə]) ①臂. ②【生】臂状部位. ③【动】肱;(上)臂;肘脉;前胫节.

brach·y·ce·phal·ic, brach·y·ce·pha·lous [ˌbrækiseˈfælik, ˌbrækiˈsefələs] *a.* (人类)短头的，短头颅的.

brach·y·cra·ni·al [brækiˈkreiniəl] *a.* (头指数在81以上的)宽颅的 (= brachycranic). **-crany** *n.*

brach·y·dac·tyl·ic [ˌbrækidækˈtilik] *a.*【解】短指〔趾〕的 (= brachydactylous [-ləs]). **-dac·ty·ly** *n.*

bra·chyl·o·gy [brəˈkilədʒi] *n.* ①【语】省略法〔*He looked out (of) the window*〕. ②(语言的)简洁;简化的表达法.

bra·chyp·ter·ous [bræˈkiptərəs] *a.*【动】(鸟类)短翅的.

brach·y·u·ran [ˌbrækiˈjurən] *a.*【动】十足甲壳类的 (= brachyurous). — *n.* 十足甲壳类动物.

brac·ing [ˈbreisiŋ] *a.* 使拉紧的；振奋精神的；爽快的. ~ *wire [cable]* 拉索. *a* ~ *breeze* 凉爽的清风. *the* ~ *mountain air* 山区的清新空气. — *n.* ①【建】拉条,联条；加强肘. ②背带. ③支柱，支撑物. ④刺激. *radial* ~ 径向支撑.

brack·en [ˈbrækən] *n.*【英植】欧洲蕨.

brack·et [ˈbrækit] *n.* ①【建】斗拱,托架,角撑架;【机】支架,悬臂,座;(墙上装的)煤气灯嘴〔电灯座〕. ②〔*pl.*〕【印】括弧〔(),[],{}〕. ③【数】(同一个括号内的)同类项. ④(按纳税额、收入、年龄等区分的)阶层,等级,类别. ⑤【军】(炮的)夹叉射击. *bearing* ~ 轴承座〔架〕. ~ *crane* 悬臂式起重机. *high [low, middle] income* ~ 高〔低、中等〕收入阶层. *the 18 to 22 age* ~ 18-22 岁这一档. *the $ 20,000 income* ~ 年收入二万美元的阶层. *a different social* ~ 不同的社会阶层. *square [angle]* ~*s* 方括弧〔圆括弧普通称 *round* ~ 或 *parentheses*, 大括弧可简称 ~〕. — *vt.* ①为…装托架. ②用(方)括弧括，把…括在括号内；不予考虑. ③把…分类. ④【军】夹叉射击(目标). ~ *into groups* 把…分成几类. *They* ~*ed discussion off for a moment.* 他们对问题暂停讨论. ~ ***up*** 把…列为同类. ~ **clock** 可摆设在托架上的小钟. ~ **foot** (方形家具下端将两边相连的)托脚. ~ **saw** 曲线锯.

brack·ish [ˈbrækiʃ] *a.* ①(水)略有咸味的，含盐的. ②不好吃的,味道不好的；讨厌的. ~ *tea* 味道不好的茶.

bract [brækt] *n.*【植】苞，托叶；苞片. ~**-scale** 苞鳞. **-let** 小苞片.

brac·te·al [ˈbræktiəl] *a.*【植】苞的，苞状的.

brac·te·ate [ˈbræktiit] *a.*【植】 有苞的.

brad [bræd] *n.* 曲头钉,无头钉，角钉，土钉. ~**awl** 打眼钻,锥钻;(钻皮革等用的)小锥子.

brad·bury [ˈbrædbəri] *n.* 〔英俚〕〔常 B-〕一镑(或十先令)钞票.

Brad·bury [ˈbrædbəri] *n.* 布拉德伯里〔姓氏〕.

Brad·ford [ˈbrædfəd] *n.* 布拉德福〔姓氏,男子名〕.

Brad·ley [ˈbrædii] *n.* 布拉德利〔姓氏，男子名〕.

brad·y- *comb. f.* 表示"缓慢": *brady*cardia, *brady*pepsia.

brad·y·car·di·a [ˌbrædiˈkɑːdiə] *n.*【医】心搏缓慢.

brad·y·pep·si·a [ˌbrædiˈpepsiə] *n.*【医】消化徐缓.

brae [brei] *n.* 〔Scot.〕急坡;斜堤;(沿河一带的)山坡.

brag [bræg] *n.* 自夸，自大；自夸之物;自夸的人. ***make*** ~ ***of*** 自夸 (*He made* ~ *of his skill.* 他自夸技术高超). — *vi.* 自大，自夸，吹嘘 *(of; about)*. *Many conceited people like to* ~. 许多骄傲的人都喜欢自吹自擂. — *vt.* 自夸,夸口说. *He bragged that he had won.* 他自夸打赢了. ~ ***and boast*** 自吹自擂. ***have the effrontery to*** ~ ***that*** 大言不惭地说. — *a.* 第一流的;极好的;〔罕〕活泼的. *a* ~ *crop* 丰收. *a* ~ *dancer* 第一流的舞蹈家,舞跳得极好的人.

Bragg [bræg] *n.* 布拉格〔姓氏〕.
brag·ga·do·ci·o [ˌbrægəˈdəutʃiəu] *n.* ①夸口,吹牛. ②吹牛大家,自夸的人.
brag·gart [ˈbrægət] *n.* 吹牛大家. — *a.* 吹牛的,自夸自大的.
Brah·ma [ˈbrɑːmə] *n.* 〔印度教〕婆罗吸摩,梵;梵天〔一切众生之父〕.
brah·ma [ˈbrɑːmə] *n.* 【动】婆罗吸摩鸡,印度大种鸡.
Brah·man [ˈbrɑːmən], **Brah·man·ic** [brɑːˈmænik], **Brah·man·ism** [ˈbrɑːmenizm] = Brahmin, Brahminic, Brahminism.
Brah·min [ˈbrɑːmin] *n.* ①婆罗门〔印度种姓 (caste) 四等级中的最高等级,即僧侣〕. ②〔美口〕名门贵族;文人雅士.
Brah·min·ee [ˌbrɑːmiˈniː] *n.* 女婆罗门. **b- (ox)** (印度的)圣牛.
Brah·min·ic, Brah·min·i·cal [brɑːˈminik, brɑːˈminikəl] *a.* 婆罗门的,婆罗门教的.
Brah·min·ism [brɑːˈminizm] *n.* 婆罗门教.
Brah·min·ist [brɑːˈminist] *n.* 婆罗门教徒.
Brah·mo·ism [ˈbrɑːməuizəm] *n.* 新印度教. **-mo(ist)** *n.* 新印度教徒.
Brahms [brɑːmz], **Johannes** 勃拉姆斯〔1833—1897,德国作曲家〕. **-i·an** *a.* ①勃拉姆斯(音乐作品)的. ②爱好勃拉姆斯音乐的.
braid [breid] *n.* ①缏子,条带,编带,编织物. ②发辫. ③束发带;(衣服上的)穗带. *an elastic* ～ 松紧带. *a straw* ～ 草帽缏. *wear one's hair in* ～*s* 把头发编成辫子,打辫子. — *vt.* ①编,把…打缏子. ②用缏装饰. ③把(头发)梳成辫子;给(衣服)镶穗带. ～ *a rope* 编绳. ～ *one's hair* 编头发辫. ～*ed fabric* 编织物. ～ ***St. Catharine's tresses*** 过处女生活,终生不嫁.
braid·er [ˈbreidə] *n.* ①打缏子的人,编织工. ②编织机,编结机,编带机.
braid·ing [ˈbreidiŋ] *n.* ①辫线类. ②辫线装饰. ③编结.
brail [breil] *n.* ①【船】卷帆索;斜撑,斜杆. ②(捕鱼用的)抄网. — *vt.* ①【海】卷(帆),卷起 *(up)*. ②用抄网拉(鱼). ～ *up the sail* 卷起帆.
braille [breil] *n.* (盲人用的)点字(法)〔法国人布雷尔 (Louis Braille) 为盲人创制的凸点符号文字〕. — *vt.* 用盲文印〔写〕.
brain [brein] *n.* ①脑,〔*pl.*〕脑髓;〔俚〕计算机;(导弹的)制导系统. ②〔常 *pl.*〕智力,智能,智慧,脑力;头脑. ③〔口〕聪明人;〔口〕〔*pl.*〕智囊,出谋划策者. ★当作器官时用单数,当作物质时用复数. *be full of* ～*s, have good [plenty of]* ～*s* 聪明,好脑筋. *man of* ～*s* 聪明人. *have no* ～*s* 没头脑,笨. *have a lucid* ～ 思路清晰,头脑清醒. *the* ～ *of the conspiracy* 阴谋的策划者. *electron* ～〔俚〕电脑,电子计算机. ***beat [cudgel, pound, puzzle, rack] one's*** ～***s*** 绞脑汁,苦思. ***beat one's*** ～***s out*** 拼命,竭力 (*She beat her* ～*s out studying.* 她拼命用功). ***blow sb.'s*** ～***s out*** 使某人脑袋开花. ***coin one's*** ～***s*** 想方设法挣钱. ***get [have](sth.)on the*** ～ 专心,全神贯注在(某事上). ***overtax one's*** ～***s*** 用脑过度. ***pick [suck] sb.'s*** ～***s*** 采用〔窃取〕某人的主张〔想法,知识,研究成果等〕. ***turn sb.'s*** ～ 冲昏某人头脑,使自以为了不起. ***water on the*** ～ 脑水肿. — *vt.* ①打破〔碎〕…的脑袋. ②打…的头部. ～ **case** 脑壳,头颅. ～**child** 智力产儿〔指计划、主意、想法、作品等脑力劳动的成果〕. ～**-derby**〔美〕学术竞争. ～ **drain** 人材流失(国外). ～**-drain** ①*vi.* 人才外流. ②*vt.* 使发生人才外流现象. ～**-drainer** *n.* 外流人才. ～**fag** 神经衰弱,用脑过度. ～ **fever**【医】脑(膜)炎. ～ **man** 谋士,参谋,军师. ～**-pan** 脑壳,头盖骨;〔美〕头. ～**power** ①智力. ②〔集合词〕智囊团,参谋团. ～**sick** *a.* 神经错乱的,疯狂的. ～**-stealer** 剽窃者. ～**storm** ①【医】脑猝变,脑猝病. ②〔美俚〕灵机一动,突如其来的好思想〔主意〕;(专家顾问对重大问题的)献策献计 (*a* ～*-storm specialist*〔美俚〕理论家). ～**-teaser,** ～**-twister** 动脑筋游戏,(供消遣的)待解难题. ～ **trust** ①〔美俚〕智囊团〔美国经济参谋本部的通称〕;(一般)专家顾问团. ②〔英〕〔Brains Trust〕(广播电台中给听众解答问题的)答问员. ～ **truster** 智囊团团员,顾问,参谋. ～**wash** ①*vt.* 对(人)实行洗脑,把某种思想强加于(人). ②通过宣传等说服. ③ *n.* 洗脑,强行灌输思想. ～ **wave** ①灵感,灵机,妙想. ②【心】脑波. ～**work** 脑力劳动. ～**worker** 脑力劳动者. **-less** *a.* 没有头脑的,愚钝的,笨的.
brain·y [ˈbreini] *a.* 〔美口〕多智的,聪明的.
braise, braize [breiz] *vt.* (用文火)炖,焖(肉).
brake[1] [breik] *n.* ①制动器,制动装置,闸,刹车;〔喻〕妨碍(因素);(闸式)测功器. ②麻梳,捶麻器;剥(柳条)皮器;榨汁机;揉面机. ③(碎土用的)大耙;唧筒柄. ④(金属板)压弯成形机. ⑤〔英〕大型四轮游览马车. ⑥〔古〕拷问架,行刑台. *a hydraulic* ～ 液压制动器,油煞车. *a hand* ～ 手闸. *an air* ～ 气闸. *a vacuum* ～ 真空闸. ～ *block* 闸瓦,制动片. *press* ～ 弯板机,弯边机. *a flex* ～ 剥麻机. ～ *horse-power* 制动马力,纯马力〔略作 B.H.P.〕. ～ *shoe* 闸瓦. *a shooting* ～〔俚〕电视车. ***apply [put on] the*** ～ ①关制动器,关闸. ②使停止进行,使停顿. ***ride the*** ～ 半制动〔指刹车不踩到底〕. ***take off the*** ～ 开闸,松闸. — *vt.* ①关(闸),刹(车),制动. ②剥(麻);用麻梳梳;用大耙碎(土);用揉面机揉(面);用榨汁机榨(汁). ～ *a car* 刹住车. — *vi.* (车)刹住,制动器起作用. *The car* ～*ed to a stop.* 车刹住不走了. ～ **band** 闸带. ～ **block** 闸块. ～ **drum** 闸轮. ～ **pedal** 刹车脚踏板. ～**(s)man**〔美〕司闸员,制动手. ～ **van**【铁路】缓急车,司闸车.
brake[2] [breik] *n.* 【植】大羊齿类,〔特指〕蕨.
brake[3] [breik] *n.* 灌木丛,荆棘.
brake[4] [breik] *v.* 〔古〕break 的过去式.
brake·age [ˈbreikidʒ] *n.* ①刹车,制动器,制动装置. ②制动作用,制动力.
brak·ie [ˈbreiki] *n.* 〔美俚〕司闸员,制动手 (= brake(s) man).
brak·y [ˈbreiki] *a.* 多蕨的;多荆棘的.
bram·ah [ˈbrɑːmə] *n.* (英国技师 Bramah 创制的)布拉马式机具. ～ **lock** 布氏锁. ～ **press** 布氏水压机.
bram·ble [ˈbræmbl] *n.* ①荆棘. ②【植】悬钩子属;欧洲黑莓.
bram·bling [ˈbræmbliŋ] *n.* 【鸟】花鸡.
bram·bly [ˈbræmbli] *a.* ①多荆棘的;多刺的. ②长满黑莓的.
Bra·min [ˈbrɑːmin] *n.* = Brahmin.
bran [bræn] *n.* 麸皮,糠. *shrimp* ～ 虾皮糠. ～ **disease** 麸皮病〔马驹吃多麸皮生的一种软骨病〕. ～**-pie** 摸彩盆〔盆中装糠,礼物藏于其中,让儿童摸取之〕. ～**-tub** 摸彩桶〔类似于摸彩盆〕.
branch [brɑːntʃ] *n.* ①(树)枝〔泛指大枝或小枝;bough 特指大枝,也指连花、果折下的枝;limb 指大枝,twig 指小枝〕. ②支脉;支派;支管;支线;(家族的)支系;【语】(语系的)支,族. ③(学科)分科;部门,支部,分部,分行,分店. ④〔美〕支流,小河,小川. ⑤【电】分流;【计】转移. *the* ～*s of a deer's antelers* 鹿角的岔枝. ～ *road* 岔道. *the various* ～*es of learning* 各门学科. *the executive* ～ *of the government* 政府的行政部门. *an overseas* ～ 海外分店. *the Germanic* ～ *of the Indo-European language family* 印欧语系的日尔曼语族. *a party* ～ 党支部. ***root and*** ～ 彻底的[地]. — *vi.* ①(树)出枝,开叉. ②分部,分门;分岔;分支. *The main road* ～*s off to the left.* 大道向左分出一条岔路. *Numerous lesser roads* ～*ed off from the main highway.* 从主要公路上分出无数小道. — *vt.* ①使分枝. ②用枝、叶、花等图案装饰(织物). ～ ***forth*** (树)扩展枝叶;(商店等)扩展分支机构. ～ ***off [away]*** (道路等)分叉,岔开. ～ ***out*** ①(树)发枝,长

出枝条；(话等)横生枝节．②(事业等)扩大规模．*His firm ~ed out to New York.* 他的公司把分支机构扩大到了纽约．~ **line** 支线．~ **litter** 枯枝层．~ **point**【物】支化点；【计】转移点．~ **water** ①小溪的水．②水〔尤指普通自来水，用作威士忌配用水〕．

branched [brɑːntʃt] *a.* 有枝的；分岔的．~ **chain**【化】支(碳)链．

bran·chi·(o)- [ˈbræŋki(əu)-] *comb. f.* 鳃：*branchia.*

bran·chi·a [ˈbræŋkiə] *n.* (*pl.* ***bran·chi·ae*** [ˈbræŋkiiː])〔用复数〕【动】*n.* 鳃．

bran·chi·al, bran·chi·ate [ˈbræŋkiəl, ˈbræŋkieit] *a.* 鳃的；鳃状的；有鳃的．~ *arch* 鳃弓．~ *cleft* 鳃孔．

branch·ing [ˈbrɑːntʃiŋ] *n.* ①分支；分流；分科；支线；支流；支脉．②【物】分支放射；【化】支化(作用)；【电】叉形接头，插销头；【计】转移．— *a.* 长枝的；分岔的．~ *program* 线路图．

bran·chi·o·pod [ˈbræŋkiəpɔd] *n.* 鳃足亚纲动物．

branch·y [ˈbrɑːntʃi] *a.* 枝多的，枝密的．*a* ~ *tree trunk* 桠叉多枝的树干．

brand [brænd] *n.* ①燃烧着的木头；〔诗〕火炬；〔诗、古〕刀，剑．②烙铁；(古时打在罪犯等身上的)烙印；〔喻〕污名，耻辱．③【商】火印；牌子，牌号，商标；〔喻〕品种，品质．④【植】枯死病．*a* ~ *name* 商标名称．*the best* ~ *of coffee* 最上等的咖啡．~ *mark* 商标(符号)．*the* ~ *of villainy* 罪恶的烙印．***the burning*** 因悔过[经大难]得救的人〔出自《圣经》《撒迦利亚书》〕．***the*** ~ ***of Cain*** 杀人罪〔*cf.* Cain〕．***the Jove's*** ~ 电光．***the Phoebus's*** ~ 一闪一闪的日光．— *vt.* ①在…上打火印[标记]；黥，在…身上刺字．②污辱，玷辱．③使铭记，使永志难忘．*be ~ed with infamy* 玷上污名．~ *the lesson on one's mind* 永远记住这个教训．~ *the scene in one's memory* 把这一景象铭刻在记忆中．~ *sb. (as) a heretic* 指某人为异教徒．~**ing iron** 烙铁，烙印．~ **iron** ① = ~ing iron．(烤肉的)铁丝网．②(烘炉等里面的)薪架；(烤肉的)铁丝网．

brand·er [ˈbrændə] *n.* ①打火印[烙印]的人．②〔Scot.〕烙器．

bran·died [ˈbrændid] *a.* 有白兰地酒味的，掺有白兰地酒的．

bran·dish [ˈbrændiʃ] *vt.* ①挥，舞(刀、剑等)．②炫耀地挥舞(武器)．~ *one's sword* 挥剑，舞刀．— *n.* (刀、剑等的)挥舞．

brand·ling [ˈbrændliŋ] *n.* (钓鱼时作饵用的)红纹蚯蚓．

bran(d)-new [ˈbræn(d)ˈnjuː] *a.* 崭新的，新制的．*a* ~ *wallet* 崭新的皮夹子．*her* ~ *baby* 她刚生下的婴儿．

bran·dreth [ˈbrændriθ] *n.* ①(堆干草等用的)三脚架．②井栏．

bran·dy [ˈbrændi] *n.* 白兰地酒．*a* ~ 一杯白兰地酒．— *vt.* ①在…中加白兰地酒．②把…在白兰地酒中浸泡．~ ***and soda*** 搀汽水的白兰地酒．~ ***and water*** =~-pawnee．~ **ball** (带酒味的)白兰地糖果．~**-pawnee** *n.* 搀水白兰地酒．~ **sling** 白兰地冷饮〔以白兰地酒、水、糖、柠檬汁等制成〕．~**-snap** (带酒味的)白兰地姜饼．

branks [bræŋks] *n.* ①〔*pl.*〕口钳〔古代一种铁制的钳口刑具〕；〔英方〕马嚼子．②〔英方〕【医】腮腺炎．

bran·ner·ite [ˈbrænərait] *n.*【矿】钛铀矿．

bran·ni·gan [ˈbrænigən] *n.*〔美俚〕①闹饮，喝酒乱闹．②放肆吵闹，大吵大闹．*go on a* ~ 闹饮一番；大吵大闹一番．

bran·ny [ˈbræni] *a.* (有)麸的，(有)糠的；似麸的，似糠的．

brant [brænt] *n.* = brent.

brash[1] [bræʃ] *n.* ①【医】胃灼热，反酸．②〔方〕(疾病的)发作．③〔英方〕骤雨，阵雨．

brash[2] [bræʃ] *n.* ①(岩石等的)碎片；碎冰块；碎冰群．②(修剪下的)碎树枝．**-y** *a.* 脆的，易脆的．

brash[3] [bræʃ] *a.*〔口〕①好发脾气的，性情急躁的．②轻率的；莽撞的．③脆的，易破的．④活跃的．⑤傲慢的，无礼的．**-ly** *ad.* **-ness** *n.*

bra·sier [ˈbreizjə] *n.* = brazier.

Bra·si·lia [brəˈziːljə] *n.* 巴西利亚〔巴西首都〕．

brass [brɑːs] *n.* ①黄铜．②〔主 *pl.*〕黄铜制品；铜管乐器；〔the ~〕(乐队的)铜管乐器部；〔俚〕(刻有肖像、纹章等)黄铜纪念牌．③〔俚〕金钱〔尤指现金〕；好看而不值钱的东西；〔俚〕妓女．④〔口〕厚脸皮；〔美俚〕高级将校，高级官员．⑤【机】黄铜轴承衬；〔*pl.*〕(煤层内的)黄铁矿；空弹壳．*clean [do] the ~es* 把黄铜器皿擦亮．*medical* ~ 医学界的名流．*have the* ~ *to do* 厚着面皮做(某事)．***as bold as*** ~ 老脸厚皮，厚颜无耻．***double in*** ~〔俚〕(在爵士乐队中)能演奏一种以上乐器的；多面手的．***pound*** ~〔俚〕按电键，发电报．— *a.* ①黄铜(制)的；含黄铜的．②(天空系)黄铜色的．③声音洪亮的．④铜管乐器的．~ *rods* 黄铜棒．*the* ~ *band* 吹奏乐团，管乐团，军乐队．— *vt.* ①【冶】把…包铜．②〔口〕无耻地胡搞〔常作 ~ it〕．③〔英〕付(款)．***be ~ed off***〔英俚〕厌烦，满腹怨气，消沉．~ ***up***〔俚〕付(钱)；付清．~**bound** *a.* ①包黄铜的．②顽固保守的．③不妥协的，不容变更的．④厚脸皮的 (*a* ~ *bound idealist* 不妥协的理想主义者．*a set of ~bound regulations* 不容变更的一套规定)．~ **check**〔美俚〕大财团暗中给报界人士的贿赂．~ **check sheets** 暗中接受财团贿赂的报纸．~ **farthing**〔口〕铜钱，小钱；无价值的东西；极少的数量 (*not care a ~ farthing* 毫不在乎)．~ **foundry** 黄铜铸造厂．~**hat**〔俚〕高级将校；大官；大亨．~ **knuckles** (打架用的)指节铜套．~ **plate** (钉在门上或棺木上的)黄铜名牌．~ **pounder**〔美俚〕电信技师．~ **rags** (水手、水兵等的)拖把，揩布 (*part* ~ *rags with someone*〔海俚〕与人绝交，和人闹翻)．~ **ring** ①铜戒指．②得奖[发财]的机会．~ **section** 管弦乐队中的铜管乐器部分．~**smith** 黄铜匠．~ **tacks** ①黄铜平头钉．②〔俚〕具体事实，主要事实，要点；当务之急 (*get down to* ~ *tacks* 谈实质性问题；谈重要问题)．~**-visaged** *a.* 厚脸的．~**ware** 黄铜器皿．~ **winds** 铜管乐器(部)．

bras·sage [ˈbræsidʒ] *n.* 铸币费．

bras·sard [bræˈsɑːd] *n.* ①臂章．②臂铠．

bras·se·rie [ˈbræsəriː] *n.* (兼卖小吃的)啤酒店．

brass·ie [ˈbrɑːsi] *n.*【高尔夫球】铜头球棒．

bras·sière [ˈbræsiə] *n.*〔F.〕奶罩．

brass·i·ly [ˈbrɑːsili] *ad.* 老脸厚皮地．

brass·i·ness [ˈbrɑːsinis] *n.* ①黄铜质；黄铜色．②厚颜无耻．

brass·y [ˈbrɑːsi] *a.* ①黄铜的；似黄铜的；(金属音)刺耳的．②(趣味等)庸俗的；厚颜无耻的．③吵闹的．— *n.*【高尔夫球】铜头球棒．

brat [bræt] *n.*〔蔑〕臭娃娃，小家伙〔尤指调皮捣乱的孩子〕．

Bra·ti·sla·va [ˌbrætiˈslɑːvə] *n.* 布拉迪斯拉发〔捷克斯洛伐克城市〕．

Brat·tain [ˈbrætən] *n.* 布拉顿〔姓氏〕．

brat·tice, brat·tic·ing [ˈbrætis, ˈbrætisiŋ] *n.* ①(矿井通气用的)间壁，风幛．②【建】临时木建筑，(保护机械等的)围板；〔古〕(守城时的)临时胸墙．

brat·tle [ˈbrætl] *n.*〔Scot.〕咕隆声；(脚步的)呱哒声．— *vi.* ①咕咕隆隆地响．②呱哒呱哒地跑．

brat·wurst [ˈbrætwəːst] *n.* 多味腊肠．

Braun [braun] *n.* 布劳恩〔男子名〕．~ **tube**【物】布劳恩管，阴极射线管，示波管．

braun·ite [ˈbraunait] *n.* 褐锰矿．

Braun·schwei·ger [ˈbraunʃwaigə] *n.*〔G.〕〔常 b-〕〔美〕五香肝肠．

bra·va [ˈbrɑːvɑː] *n., int.*〔It.〕= bravo.

bra·va·do [brəˈvɑːdəu] *n., vi.* (*pl.* ***~s, ~es***)〔Sp.〕恐吓，虚张声势．*He flourished the weapon in an attempt at* ~. 他挥舞武器意在恐吓．

brave [breiv] *a.* ①勇敢的. ②华丽的, 漂亮的. ③〔古〕极好的. *a ~ man [act]* 勇敢的人[行为]. *as ~ as lion* 狮子一样凶猛. *a girl decked out in a ~ dress* 浓装艳抹的姑娘. *O ~ new world,…!* 啊, 多么好的新世界〔莎士比亚诗句〕! — *vt.* ①冒(风雨、危险等), 拼, 抵抗; 不顾. ②敢于做(某事), 不把(强敌等)放在眼里, 向…挑战. *~ misfortunes [difficulties]* 勇敢地面对不幸[困难]. *~ blizzards* 迎着暴风雪前进. *She ~ed the journey to New York.* 她毅然踏上去纽约的旅途. *~ **it out*** 拼着干下去. *~ **the wind and dew*** 风餐露宿. — *n.* 勇士; 印第安人的战士. **-ness** *n.*

brave·ly [ˈbreivli] *ad.* ①勇敢地, 毅然. ②漂亮地, 华丽地. *fight ~ for a cause* 为事业英勇斗争. *a ~ decked house* 装饰华丽的房屋.

brav·er·y [ˈbreivəri] *n.* ①勇敢, 英勇, 大胆, 刚毅. ②华丽; 美装; 盛装. *girls in Sunday ~* 服装华丽的姑娘们.

bra·vis·si·mo [brɑːˈviːssiːmoː] *int.* 好极了! 妙极了!

bra·vo[1] [ˈbrɑːˈvəu] *n. (pl. ~s, ~es)* ①喝采声, 叫好声. ②【讯】代表 B 字的讯号. — *int.* 好! 好啊! 妙啊! — *vt.* 向…喝采叫好.

bra·vo[2] [ˈbrɑːvəu] *n.* 刺客〔尤指被人雇佣的行刺者〕; 歹徒; 亡命之徒.

bra·vu·ra [brəˈvjuərə] *n.* 〔It.〕 ①【乐】气势磅礴[雄壮华丽]的演奏[乐曲]; 要求演奏者毕竟其技的乐段. ②壮举.

braw [brɔː] *a.* 〔Scot.〕 ①衣着华丽的. ②美好的; 极好的. *a ~ new dress* 漂亮的新衣. *a ~ night* 美好的夜晚.

brawl [brɔːl] *vi.* ①吵闹, 口角; 互骂. ②(流水)哗哗地响. *the river ~ing by* 河水哗哗地流过. — *n.* ①吵闹, 口角. ②〔美俚〕闹宴; 喧闹的舞会; 乱哄哄的拳赛. *political ~s* 政治上的论战. *a ~ between husband and wife* 夫妇之间的争吵. **-er** *n.* 争吵者; 喧闹者. **-ing** *n., a.* 争吵(的); 喧闹(的). **-y** *a.* 好争吵的; 喧闹的.

brawn [brɔːn] *n.* ①肌肉. ②膂力, 体力. ③腌野猪肉; 咸猪头. *~* **drain** (劳动者、工人、运动员等的)体力外流.

brawn·y [ˈbrɔːni] *a.* 肌肉结实的, 强壮的. **brawn·i·ness** *n.*

brax·y [ˈbræksi] *n.* ①【兽医】羊炭疽. ②患羊炭疽病的羊. — *a.* 患羊炭疽的.

bray[1] [brei] *n.* ①驴叫声. ②(喇叭的)嘟嘟声. ③喧哗, 乱哄哄的抗议. — *vi.* ①(驴)叫. ②(喇叭)嘟嘟响. ③喧嚷, 刺耳地喊. *~ at the top of one's voice* 尽着嗓门喊叫. — *vt.* ①嚷出, 粗声粗气地说出. ②乱哄哄地演奏. *The gramophone ~ed out its vulgar tune.* 留声机闹哄哄地唱着庸俗的小调.

bray[2] [brei] *vt.* ①捣碎, 研碎. ②【印】薄涂(油墨等).

Bray [brei] *n.* 布雷〔姓氏〕.

bray·er [ˈbreiə] *n.*【印】(明)胶(墨)辊.

Braz. = Brazil(ian).

braze[1] [breiz] *vt.* ①用黄铜制造[镶饰, 镀]. ②〔古〕使坚如黄铜. ③〔诗〕使成黄铜色. *~* ***over*** 镀黄铜于.

braze[2] [breiz] *vt.*【机】(用锌铜合金)焊接, 铜焊, 硬焊. *~d joint*【机】黄铜接头, 硬钎焊接.

bra·zen [ˈbreizn] *a.* ①黄铜制的; 黄铜色的; (黄铜一样)坚硬的. ②(象破铜锣一样)声音响而刺耳的. ③厚颜无耻的. *a ~ image of Buddha* 一尊铜佛. *a ~ liar* 厚颜无耻的说谎者. — *vt.* 厚着脸皮干 *(out, through)*. *~* ***it out [through]*** 厚着脸皮干下去[混下去] *(He prefers to ~ it out rather admit defeat.* 他宁可厚着脸皮混下去, 也不愿承认失败). *~* ***law of wages*** 【经】工资铁律 (= iron law of wages). *~* **age** (希腊)黄铜时代, 混战时代. *~***-faced** *a.* 厚颜无耻的. **-ly** *ad.* 厚着脸皮, 粗暴地, 肆无忌惮地, 悍然.

bra·zier[1] [ˈbreizjə] *n.* 黄铜匠. **-y** *n.* 黄铜工艺制品厂; 黄铜细工.

bra·zier[2] [ˈbreizjə] *n.* ①(金属)火盆; 焊炉. ②(烤肉)火锅.

Bra·zier [ˈbreiʒə] *n.* 布雷热〔姓氏〕.

Bra·zil [brəˈzil] *n.* 巴西〔拉丁美洲〕. *~* **nut** 三角形巴西胡桃. *~***wood**【植】巴西苏木.

bra·zil [brəˈzil] = Brazilwood.

Bra·zil·ian [brəˈziljən] *a.* 巴西的; 巴西人的. — *n.* 巴西人.

Braz·za·ville [ˈbræzəvil, ˌbrɑːzəˈviːl] *n.* 布拉柴维尔〔刚果首都〕.

breach [briːtʃ] *n.* ①(对法律、义务等的)破坏, 违犯, 违背, 不履行; (对他人权利等的)侵害, 侵犯. ②(友好关系的)破裂, 绝交, 不和. ③(城堡、防御线等的)破口, 裂口, 缺口;【军】突破, 突破口. ④【海】碎浪, 冲击船[堤等]的波浪. ⑤鲸跳〔鲸的跳出水面〕. ⑥〔罕〕伤口. *a ~ of contract* 违约, 违反合同. *a ~ of duty* 失职; 不履行义务. *~ of trust* 背叛; 辜负信任. *~ of prison* 越狱. *It caused a lifelong ~ with his father.* 这使得他们父子终身失和. ***a clean ~***【海】冲走甲板上物件的波浪. ***a clear ~*** 冲过甲板的波浪. *~* ***of close***【法】非法侵入他人地界. *~* ***of promise*** 毁约;【法】毁弃婚约. *~* ***of the peace***【法】妨害治安(罪). ***heal the ~*** 调停. ***make a ~ in*** *(the wall)* 攻破(城墙); 在(墙)上打开缺口. ***slip one's ~*** 死. ***stand in [throw oneself into] the ~*** 独当难局, 首当其冲, 独力承受攻击. — *vt.* ①攻破, 突破, 使有缺口. ②违(约); 不履行(义务); 破坏(法律). *~ the city wall* 攻破城墙. *~ an agreement* 违反协议. — *vi.* (鲸鱼)跳出水面. *a whale ~ing* 跳出水面的鲸鱼.

bread [bred] *n.* ①面包. ②食物, 粮食; 〔喻〕生计, 生活必需品. ③【基督】(圣餐式上的)一块[份]面包. ④〔美俚〕钱. *a slice of ~* 一块面包. *black [brown] ~* 黑面包. *the ~ of life* 活命粮. *one's daily ~* 每天的食物. ***beg one's ~*** 讨饭, 行乞. *~* ***buttered on both sides*** 两面涂黄油的面包; 极幸福的境遇, 安乐的生活. ***break ~ with*** ①受…款待. ②与…共用圣餐. ***cast [throw] one's ~ upon the water(s)*** 甘尽义务, 施舍, 行善. ***eat the ~ of affliction [idleness]*** 受折磨, 遭遇坎坷[坐食, 游手好闲]. ***in good [bad] ~*** 〔俚〕生活安乐[困苦]. ***know (on) which side one's ~ is buttered*** 自知己利所在, 善于为个人利益打算. ***make [earn] one's ~*** 谋生. ***out of ~*** 〔口〕无职业, 失业. ***quarrel with one's ~ and butter*** 自砸饭碗, 与自己过不去. ***ship's ~***【海】硬饼干. ***take the ~ out of sb.'s mouth*** 抢人饭碗. *~* **and butter** ①涂奶油的面包. ②必需的食物; 生计. ③主要的收入来源. *~***-and-butter** *a.* ①有关生计的, 日常生活的; 提供最低(生活)需要的. ②实利的, 实用的. ③主要的. ④为所受款待表示谢意的. ⑤〔主英〕孩子气的, 不成熟的, 年轻的 *(a ~-and-butter account* 最低限度的经费. *~-and-butter products* 主要产品. *~-and-butter arguments* 讲求实际的议论. *a ~-and-butter letter* 给东道主的感谢信. *a ~-and-butter miss* 馋嘴的小姑娘, 女学生; 娇小姐. *a ~-and-butter item* 生活必需品). *~* **and cheese** 面包和干酪; 家常食品, 粗食, 糊口的方法. *~* **and circuses** 公共当局提供的饮食和娱乐. *~* **and milk** 牛奶泡面包. *~* **and salt** 面包和盐〔待客的象征〕 **(eat [share] sb. ~ and salt** 款待某人, 待某人如贵宾). *~* **and scrape** 黄油涂得不足的面包. *~* **and water** 面包和水, 最简单的食物, 粗粝之食. *~* **and wine**【基督教】圣餐. *~***basket** ①面包篮; 〔喻〕谷物产区. ②〔俚〕胃, 肚子. ③〔美俚〕一种爆炸燃烧弹. *(~-basket land* 产粮区). *~***board** ①揉面板; 切面包板. ②(手提式电子实验)线路板, 摸拟板, 实验模型. *~***box** 面包箱, 糕点储放箱. *~***crumb** ① *n.* 〔常 *pl.*〕面包屑〔尤指专为烹调而揉碎者〕; 面包心. ② *vt.* 把…裹上面包屑(煎、炸). *~***fruit** 面包果〔面包树的果实〕. *~* **knife** 面包刀〔通常有波浪形或锯齿形刀锋〕. *~* **line**

[queue]〔美〕排队领救济品的穷人队伍. ~ **mold**【植】黑根霉. ~ **riot** 饥饿[缺粮]骚动. ~ **root**【植】食用补骨脂(根)〔产于北美〕. ~ **salesman**〔美〕面包店的送货人. ~**stuffs**〔*pl.*〕制面包的原料,面包粉;面包类. ~ **ticket** 面包券,饭票. ~ **tree** 面包树. ~**winner** *n.* ①养家活口的人. ②生计;职业;谋生的工具[手艺]. **-less** *a.* 无面包的,缺粮的;失去生计的.

breadth [bredθ] *n.* ①宽度 (*opp.* length, depth), 幅,横幅,幅员;广度,宽广;(学识等的)广博. ②(布的)幅面;船幅. ③(性格、胸襟等的)宽宏大量,宽容;豪放,磊落. ④(绘画、作品等气势的)雄浑,恢弘. ⑤【逻】外延. *This room is nine feet in* ~. 这个房间宽九英尺. *a* ~ *of cloth* 一幅布. ~*s of grass* 辽阔的草地. ~ *of mind* 心胸开阔. *a man of intellectual* ~ 知识渊博的人. *There is too much* ~ *in his jokes [behaviour].* 他的笑话[行为]太过火了. **by a hair's** ~ 差一点儿,险些,几乎. **in** ~ 幅宽,阔. **to a hair's** ~ 精确地.

breadth·ways, breadth·wise [ˈbredθweiz, ˈbredθwaiz] *ad.* 横. *a course of bricks laid* ~ 一排横着放的砖.

break [breik] *vt.* (**broke** [brəuk]; **broken** [brəukən], 〔古〕**broke**) ①毁坏,弄坏,损坏,毁损. ~ *a doll* 弄坏洋囡囡. ~ *a sewing machine* 损坏缝纫机. ②打破,碰破,撞破;打碎;折断;擦破;撕开. ~ *a bottle [cup]* 打破瓶[杯]子. ~ *a vase to pieces* 把花瓶打得粉碎. ~ *an arm* 折断手臂. ~ *(off) a branch* 折断树枝. ~ *one's head* 撞破头. ~ *the skin* 擦破皮肤. ~ *cloth [paper]* 撕开布[纸]. ③犯,违犯,破坏,违,违背;破除;通过法律手续使(遗嘱)失效;取消,解除. ~ *a promise* 违反诺言,食言. ~ *the law* 违法,犯法. ~ *a law [rule]* 触犯某项法律[规定]. ~ *a contract* 违反合同. ~ *off an engagement* 解除婚约. ~ *a will* 取消遗嘱,使遗嘱失效. ~ *the chains* 砸开锁链. ④冲开(水面等), 开垦(土地等),翻(土),梳(麻);打开(门等), 挑开(水疱);破(门);闯入;冲破;越(狱),突(围),逃出,跳出;打开(局面等),开创(新路等). ~ *the door open* 冲开大门. ~ *jail [prison]* 越狱. ~ *ground* 破土(动工). ~ *fresh ground* 开辟新天地. *He broke the blister with a needle.* 他用针挑开水疱. ~ *a siege* 突围,冲破围困. ~ *a trail through the woods* 披荆斩棘在林中行进. ~ *the water* (鱼)跳出水面. ~ *surface [water]* (潜水艇)浮出水面. ⑤使中止;打断,切断,截断,遮断;妨碍;打搅,搅乱;戒除;破除. ~ *a journey* 中止旅程,中途下车. ~ *an electric circuit* 切断电流. ~ *the cigarette habit* 戒烟. ~ *the tie* 打破不分胜负的局面. ~ *the convention* 打破成规. ~ *a strike* 使罢工停止. ~ *sb.'s sleep* 打扰了某人的睡眠. ~ *the silence with a cry* 以喊声打破寂静. *The railway communication is broken.* 铁路交通断绝了. ⑥兑开(钞票);分开;拆开(整体),卸开(枪的)装弹和发射部. ~ *a dollar bill into change* 把一元钞票兑成零钱. *The prism broke the light into all the colors of the rainbow.* 棱镜把阳光分解成虹的所有色彩. ~ *a dining room set by buying a chair* 买走一把椅子使一套餐厅家具不再成套. ⑦制服;驯(兽),使驯服;制止;阻止;破获(案件),破解(密码);解决,解开(难题等);削减,减弱;挫败,压倒. ~ *a horse* 驯马. *The bushes will* ~ *his fall.* 灌木丛会减弱他摔下来的势头. ~ *the case* 破获案件. ~ *a cipher system* 破解开一套密码. *A stand of trees will* ~ *the wind.* 一排树会减弱风势. ~ *a man of his bad habit* 制止某人的恶习. ~ *the problem* 解决了问题. *He was broken by the threats.* 他被威胁压服了. ~ *sb.'s spirit* 挫折某人的锐气. ⑧暗示,泄漏,暴露(秘密等). ~ *secret plans to the enemy* 把秘密计划泄露给敌方. *He broke the good news to her at dinner.* 他吃饭时把好消息透露了给她. ⑨使衰败;使破产;免(职),降(职);葬送(前途). *He broke the bank at Monte Carlo.* 他在蒙特卡罗的豪赌使银行破产了. ~ *one's career* 毁掉了前途. *He was broken from sergeant to private.* 他从军士降为列兵. ⑩打破,超过(记录). ~ *all track records* 打破径赛项目的全部记录. ~ *a speed record* 创造一项速度新记录. ⑪驳倒,使(证据、辩辞等)不能成立. ~ *down a witness* 驳倒伪证. ~ *sb.'s alibi* 揭穿某人的辩词. ⑫发动(宣传等). ⑬【棒球】投(歪球),投(曲线球);【拳】制止(扭抱). ~ *a curve*【棒球】投出曲线球. ⑭【法】非法侵入. ~ *a house* 非法侵入他人住宅. ⑮使(股票等)猛跌价.

— *vi.* ①破裂,碎;损坏,发生故障;崩;断,折断;中断;受扰;挫折;(军队等)溃散;(疮)溃烂. *The glass broke.* 杯子打坏了. *A piece of china* ~*s easily.* 瓷器容易打碎. *The rope broke.* 绳子断了. *The TV set broke.* 电视机发生故障. *My heart will* ~. 我心要碎了. ②闯入 *(into)*; 逃出 *(from; out of)*; 摆脱,离开. ③突现,爆发,忽起;突变,【乐】变音;(霜、雾等)消散;(天)破晓,放晴. *The weather broke.* 天气变晴. *His face broke out into a smile.* 他变得笑逐颜开. *The day broke hot and sultry.* 天亮了,天气又热又闷. *Dawn began to* ~ 东方欲晓. *The storm broke.* 暴风雨突然来临. *The boy's voice has broken.* 这孩子发育变嗓音了. ④破产,倒闭;(信用、名誉等)扫地;(健康等)垮掉,变弱,衰;(抵抗等)崩溃;(在压力等之下)屈服. *The bank broke.* 这家银行破产了. *His health broke after years of hardship.* 多年的困苦生活使他的身体垮了. ⑤(花)发芽,打苞,长(蕾). ⑥(消息)传开,透露出. *The story broke in a morning paper.* 消息在一家晨报上透露出来了. ⑦(工作中)略事休息. ~ *for lunch* 暂停下工作吃顿饭. ⑧【棒球】(球)曲行,(球)投歪. ⑨〔美〕(证券)行市暴跌;(潜艇等)突现于水面;〔美〕突进,猛冲 *(for)*; (波浪)冲击 *(over; on; against)*. ⑩【拳】(从扭抱中)放开,分开;〔裁判员命令扭抱中的双方〕分开! ⑪发生,发展,进展. *For the team to succeed, everything has to* ~ *right.* 必须一切情况正常,该队才能打赢. ~ **a butterfly on the wheel** 小题大作,杀鸡用牛刀. ~ **a lance with** 与…交锋;与…争论. ~ **a leg**〔英俚〕演出成功(*I hope you* ~ *a leg.* 我希望你演出成功). ~**away** *(from)* ①逃走,脱逃,脱身. ②(柄等)脱离,离开. ③背弃,叛离. ④戒除(积习),摆脱(陈规等). ⑤(赛马时)抢先起步 (~ *away from a habit* 戒除某项习惯. *The prisoner broke away from his guards.* 犯人趁看守不备逃跑了). ~ **bounds** 见 bound 条. ~ **bulk**【海】开始全部[部分]卸货. ~ **camp** 拔营,起营. ~ **cover [covert]** (猎物)跳[飞]出躲藏处[树丛]. ~**down** ① *vt.* 破坏,打破,击破,粉碎;击穿;压倒;把(化合物)分解,把(机器等)拆散,把(总帐等)分成细目 *(into)*. ② *vi.* (机器)损坏,发生故障,(门等)坍陷;(计划)失败;(身体)变衰弱;(精神等)崩溃;(化合物)分解,(总帐等)细分,易于分成细目 *(into)*; (发言等)突然中断.【物】衰[蜕]变. ~ **even**〔美口〕①(球赛)不分胜负,打成和局. ②得失相当,不赚不赔,扯平. ~ **formation**【军】打乱队形,离开编队. ~ **forth** ①喷出,涌出;爆发. ②突然发出(欢呼、叫声等);开始滔滔不绝地讲 (~ *forth in cheers [into singing]* 突然爆发出欢呼声[歌声]). ~ **(free) from** 脱离;突然离开. ~ **ground** 动工,开工,【海】起锚 (~ *ground for a new housing development* 新住宅建设破土动工). ~ **hibernation** 从冬眠中苏醒;〔美〕上演(一季的)开炮戏. ~ **in** ①闯入;插嘴. ②驯(马);训练(人). ③使物件[鞋]逐渐合用[脚]. ④(人)开始工作;(机器等)开始运转[活动]. ~ *in a pony* 驯一匹小马. *The boss is* ~*ing in a new assistant.* 头儿正在训练一个新助手. *These shoes haven't been broken in.* 这鞋子还没有穿合脚. ~ **in on [upon]** ①突然袭击,突然出现,于…之前. ②拦阻;打断,打扰 (*The mob broke in on us.* 暴徒对我们突然袭击. ~ *in on one's thought* 忽然想起). ~ **into** ①闯进,侵入;拦(别人话头);侵占(别人时间等). ②突然…起来 (~ *into a talk* 插嘴. ~ *into tears* 哇地一声哭起来). ~ **into [to] pieces** 打碎. ~ **liberty** 回船迟到〔水手上岸超出许可时间〕. ~ **loose** ①脱出,摆脱,挣脱开 *(from)*. ②迸发出来. ~ ***(sb. [oneself])***

of a habit (自己)放弃某种习惯,(使某人)放弃某种习惯. ~ ***off*** ① *vt.* 折取,掐,摘;把…折断;使脱落;打断,断绝,解除(婚约);使突然停止. ② *vi.* 折,裂,分;突然中止,中断;【军】突然改变航向;暂停工作,稍事休息. (*He broke off a branch of the tree.* 他把一根树枝折断. *A branch of the tree broke off.* 一根树枝断了. ~ *off the negotiation* 中断谈判. *Let's* ~ *off for a minute.* 我们来歇一会儿). ~ ***on the scene*** 突然出场. ~ ***one's fast*** 停止绝食;〔古〕吃早餐〔早餐 breakfast 一词即源于此〕. ~ ***one's mind to (sb.)*** 向(某人)表白心事,剖明心迹. ~ ***open*** 砸开,打破;〔美〕现出,显出. ~ ***out*** ①起,发生;(战争等)突发,爆发. ②(囚犯等)逃脱,逃出. ③忽然叫出〔做出〕(*into*). ④倒空(容器);由(船舱)卸货. ⑤【海】起(锚). ⑥拖出,起出. ⑦取出备用,使处于备用状态. (*An epidemic broke out.* 发生了传染病. ~ *out the parachutes* 准备好降落伞. ~ *out one's best wine* 拿出家藏的上品佳酿. ~ *out a sled from the ice* 从冰中拖出雪橇. *He broke out into loud laughter.* 他忽然哈哈大笑起来). ~ ***(the) rank*** 【军】打乱队形. ~ ***short*** 使突然终止,中断. ~ ***step*** 【军】走乱步伐. ~ ***the back [neck] of*** (*an undertaking*) 办完(某事)的极困难〔重要〕部分,大体做完(某事). ~ ***the ice*** 带个头;打破沉默,使气氛活跃. ~ ***the ground*** ①犁(地),翻(地). ②动工,着手. ③【军】挖战壕. ~ ***through*** ①挤过去;突破;打(洞等);(太阳由云间)钻出. ②犯(规),违(章). ~ ***up*** ① *vt.* 弄破,打碎;拆散,拆开;剖割(兽体等);破坏;挖,垦(地);解散,驱散(人群等);终止,中断;分化;〔口〕使哄堂大笑;使苦恼. ② *vi.* (会)散,(队伍等)解散,(学校)放假;(家庭等)解体;(冰)熔,(雾等)消散;(身体)变衰弱,(士气)瓦解;细分为,分解为 (~*up the crowds* 驱散人群. (*school*) ~*s up for holidays* 学校放假. *They broke up into small groups.* 他们分散为各个小组. ~ *up a friendship* 绝交. ~ *up the audience* 使听众哄堂大笑. *The loss broke up the old man.* 这项损失使老人身心交瘁. ~ *up an old ship* 拆掉旧船. *B- it up!* 住手〔别吵了〕!). ~ ***upon*** 突然出现;显露. ~ ***well*** 〔美〕(赛马等)起跑得好. ~ ***wind*** 放屁. ~ ***(off) with*** 与…断绝关系,与…绝交,与…决裂;破除(恶习等) (~ *with one's family* 与家庭决裂).

—*n.* ①破,坏;损坏;裂,裂口,碎裂;折断 (*a* ~ *in the window* 玻璃窗上的裂缝. *a* ~ *in the clouds* 云朵间的一线青天). ②(天气的)突变;破晓,天亮 (*a* ~ *in the weather* 天气骤变. ~ *of day* 天亮). ③中止,停顿,断绝;(电视广播节目等的)暂停;休息(时间);决裂,绝交 (*a* ~ *for the commercial* 广告节目. *a* ~ *with convention* 与陈规决裂. *a* ~ *in one's conversation.* 谈话的暂停. *a lunch* ~ 午休. *a coffee* ~ 上下午的工间小休息,吃茶时间). ④【台球】连得分数;(球的)反跳,屈折;【乐】急剧变调,换声点;短促停顿;【电】切断,中断,断线,断路(器);【矿】断裂,断层;【海】船楼端部;【建】断面;【印】(一行最末一词过长需转行接写的)断开处;连接符号"-". 【拳】(从扭抱中)分开. ⑤逃走,跑出;(赛马等的)起跑;练马用马车,大型四轮马车 (*a jail* ~ 越狱. *a* ~ *for freedom* (从囚禁中)逃跑). ⑥〔口〕闯进,猛冲,奔,突破;(飞机失速后的)突然下降;〔古〕爆发,激发 (*The started deer made a* ~ *for the thicket.* 受惊的鹿奔向丛林). ⑦〔美俚〕错误,失策,失败;(市价等的)暴跌;语言无礼,举止不当 (*a bad* ~ 失礼,失仪,失礼的举动). ⑧〔俚〕运气,命运;〔口〕机会;分歧点 (*She's won too. What's a* ~*!* 她也赢了,真是好运气. *Give him a* ~. 给他一个改过的机会吧!). ⑨开垦地;(谷物的)春磨. ***a lucky [bad, rotten]*** ~ 好运气〔倒霉〕. ***a*** ~ ***in one's life*** 一生中的转机〔转折〕. ***an even*** ~ 〔美俚〕不相上下,(输赢)各半;均等的机会. ~ ***for the hungry*** 〔美俚〕穷困时突如其来的好差使. ~ ***the*** ~***s*** 【美体】碰到好运气,走运. ***get a*** ~ 交好运,时来运转. ***give (sb.) a*** ~ 给(某人)一个面子. ***make a (bad)*** ~ 失礼,失仪,出丑. ***make a*** ~ ***for*** 向…急跑. ***make a*** ~ ***for home*** ①往家跑. ②【棒球】跑回本垒. ***make a*** ~ ***of*** 【台球】连续得(分). ***without a*** ~ 连续地,不停顿地,不休息地. ~**away** ① *n.* 分离;【空】脱离队形;【美影】简易道具. ② *a.* 脱党的,分离派的;【戏剧】(道具)简易的. ~**bone (fever)** 【美医】断骨热,登革热. ~-**bulk** *a.* 零件〔小件〕装运的. ~-**even** *a.* 得失相当的,不赚不赔的. ~-**even point** 【商】损益两平点. ~**front** ① *a.* (橱柜等)中部凸出的. ② *n.* 中凸橱柜. ~**head** 船头破冰器. ~-**in** 闯入;【军】突破;插入,挤入,嵌入;【机】试车,试运转. ~**mark** 【纺】(绸缎等的)灰点,疵点. ~**neck** *a.* 极危险的 (*at* ~ *neck speed* 以危险的高速行驶). ~**out** 爆发;【军】突围;强行越狱;皮疹,皮炎. ~**over** (报刊上文章的)转页,转版. ~-**point** 【化】转效点;【电】断点,停止点. ~-**point order** 【自】返回指令. ~-**promise** 违约者,食言者. ~ **through** 【军】突破(点);(科技等的)重大发现,重大进展;关键问题的解决;(物价等的)暴涨. ~**up** 解散;瓦解,崩溃;分离,(夫妇)分居;分裂,脱离;停止,完结. ~**up value** 破产企业的财产清理价值. ~**water** 防波堤. ~**wind** 〔英〕幕;风障;防风林;挡风墙(篱). -**able** ① *a.* 容易破碎的. ② *n.* 〔常 *pl.*〕易破碎的东西.

break·age [ˈbreikidʒ] *n.* ①破坏,毁损;断裂;裂口,破损处;【电】断路,断线;【纺】断头率. ②破损物;损耗量,破损量;【商】损耗补偿(款额);【海】(舱内装货后的)剩余空位. *There was a great deal of* ~ *in that shipment of glassware.* 那批玻璃器皿损坏了很多. ~ **allowance**【商】破损折扣.

breakdown [ˈbreikdaun] *n.* ①崩溃,倒塌;破损,损耗;损伤;损坏,故障;失败,挫折;中断,停止. ②【空】下降;【电】击穿;【原】衰〔蜕〕变;【化】分解(作用),分析. ③(体力等的)衰弱,垮,衰退. ④分类;分成细目;分类帐. ⑤〔美〕(黑人首创的)一种喧嚣、急促的集体舞. ⑥〔*pl.*〕【机】粗轧板坯. *nervous* ~ 神经衰弱. *the* ~ *of communication* 交通中断. *the* ~ *current* 击穿电流. *a* ~ *in health* 身体垮下来. ~ *of food during digestion* 食物在消化过程中分解. *a* ~ *of data* 数据的分类. — *a.* 专门修理故障的. ~ **gang [van]** (火车等出事故时的)抢修队〔车〕. ~ **test** 耐久(力)试验,断裂试验,破坏试验,稳定性试验. ~ **voltage** 击穿电压.

break·er[1] [ˈbreikə] *n.* ①破坏者,破碎者;破碎装置,轧碎〔石、煤〕机;离解机;【纺】头道梳毛机. ②【海】(打在暗礁、海岸上的)碎浪花. ③驯兽者. ④【电】断路器;汽车的拥胎带. ⑤(垦荒用的)锄;开拓者. *a* ~ *of idols* 捣毁偶像者. *a coal* ~ 碎煤机. *a horse* ~ 驯马师,驯马者. ~***s ahead!*** 【海】注意暗礁!危险! ~ **fabric** 轮胎布. ~-**in** 训练牛、马的人.

break·er[2] [ˈbreikə] *n.* (救生艇上的)淡水桶,小水桶.

break·fast [ˈbrekfəst] *n.* 早餐;早餐食物. *at* ~ 早餐时;正吃早餐. *a* ~ *of bacon and eggs* 一顿咸肉加鸡蛋的早餐. — *vi.* 吃早餐. ~ *on eggs* 以鸡蛋作早餐. — *vt.* 为(某人)备早餐;请(某人)吃早餐. ~ *sb. in the restaurant* 请某人进饭馆早餐. ~ **food** 早餐食用的谷类食物. ~-**in-bed folks** 〔美〕懒鬼.

break·ing [ˈbreikiŋ] *n.* ①破坏;损伤;中断;折断;【电】断路. ②驯兽,训练. ③【语音】音的分裂. ④〔*pl.*〕亚麻下脚. ~ **and entering** 【法】破坏侵入. ~ **down** 【电】击穿;中断;冲淡(电池酸液). ~-**in** ①【电】插入;滚动,碾平. ②(工具等的)用熟,使惯;试车,试运转. ③开始生产〔使用〕(*This car needs no* ~-*in.* 这部车子一使用就称心). ~ **point** ①断裂点,破损点;破损程度. ②忍耐极限,自我抑制极限. ~ **strength** 【物】抗断强度.

bream[1] [briːm] *n.* 【鱼】①鲤科的淡水鱼,鳊. ②鲷科的海鱼;隆头鱼科的鱼.

bream[2] [briːm] *vt.* 【海】(以加热和刮擦的方法)清扫(船底).

breast [brest] *n.* ①乳房;〔喻〕营养的来源. ②胸; 胸脯,胸膛; 胸口; 胸怀,心情. ③(山)腹; (衣服的)胸部. ④(扶栏、梁等的)下侧; (器物的)侧面; 窗腰,窗下墙; 炉胸;【矿】工作面;【船】中央系索. *bare one's* ~ 袒开胸部. *Joy filled his* ~. 他满心欢喜. ***at the*** ~ 未断奶的 (*a child at the* ~ 奶娃娃,吃奶的婴儿). ***give (a child) the*** ~ 给(婴儿)喂奶. ***have a feeling heart in one's*** ~ 有同情心. ***make a clean*** ~ ***of*** 完全说出(秘密等),坦白. ***past the*** ~ 断了奶. — *vt.* ①挺胸面对,挺胸承当; (运动员)以胸部触(线); 挺进, 逆…而进, 冒着…前进; 毅然对抗, 慨然担起(难事等). ②吮吸(奶头); (鸟)用胸部护(小鸟). ③登, 爬(山等). *The sprinter* ~*ed.* 那个短跑运动员首先冲到终点. *The ship* ~*ed the waves.* 船破浪前进. ~ *a hill* 爬山. *The coach* ~*ed a slight incline.* 马车上一个缓坡. ~ ***it out*** 抵抗到底. ~ ***the tape*** (赛跑时)冲到终点线 (=〔美〕~ ***the yarn***). ~**-beating** 大声抗议, 捶胸顿足. ~**bone** 胸骨. ~**-deep** *a.* 深[高]及胸部的. ~ **drill**【机】胸压手摇钻. ~**-feed** *vt.* 自己奶养(婴孩); 给(婴儿)喂奶. ~ **harness** 不戴颈环、只系胸带的马具. ~**-high** *a.* 高与胸齐的. ~**hook**【海】尖蹼板; 船首甲板撑材. ~**-knot** 胸结. ~**pin** 领带夹针;〔美〕胸口饰针. ~**plate** ①胸甲; (使用胸压工具时佩挂的)胸垫. ②胸前送[受]话器. ③(龟的)腹甲. ④(马)鞅,胸带皮. ⑤(古时犹太教大祭司穿的)镶宝石法衣. ~**-pump** (奶胀时用的)吸奶器. ~**rail** (船侧、窗前的)栏杆. ~**-stroke**【体】俯泳〔蛙式、蝶式等〕. ~ **summer**【建】横楣. ~ **telephone** 挂胸(式)电话机. ~ **transmitter** 胸前送话器. ~**-wall** 胸壁, 防浪墙, 挡土墙. ~**work**【军】胸墙;【船】前后两甲板的栏杆. **-ed** *a.* 贴…胸的 (*a single [double] breasted coat* 钉有一[两]排纽扣的上衣).

Breas·ted [ˈbrestid] 布雷斯特德〔姓氏〕.

breath [breθ] *n.* ①气息, 呼吸. ②呼吸力; 生命. ③一息,一气,一口气; 微风; 声息,微音; 低语,喃喃; 气味; 香气(的漂动). ④一瞬间; 休止,小歇. ⑤迹象,表示. ⑥【语音】无声音, 气音. ⑦琐事, 小事. ⑧〔美俚〕洋葱. *be short of* ~喘气,上气不接下气. *have foul [bad]* ~ 口臭. *a hard and jerky* ~ 急促的呼吸. *the* ~ *of spring* 春天的气息. *She stopped to regain her* ~. 她停下来换一口气. *Give him a little* ~. 让他歇会儿. *She got a* ~ *of the perfectly chill night air.* 她吸了一口清凉的夜气. *In a* ~ *the street was empty.* 转眼之间,大街上就空无一人了. *The* ~ *of slander never touched him.* 从来没有人对他造谣中伤. *There is not a* ~ *of air.* 一丝风也没有. *a* ~ *of wind* 一阵微风. *the* ~ *of roses* 玫瑰花的香味. ***above one's*** ~ 大声,说出声. ***at a*** ~ 一气,一口气. ***below [under] one's*** ~ 小声,低声细语. ~ ***of air*** 微风. ~ ***of life [the nostrils]*** 生命,灵魂; 生活的必需品 (*Music is the* ~ *of life to him.* 音乐是他生活的必需品). ***catch one's*** ~ 歇一口气, 休息一下. ②憋着呼吸, 紧张起来. ***draw a*** ~ 吸一口气 (*draw a long [deep]* ~ 松一口气, 放下心). ***fetch one's*** ~ 苏醒过来,活转来. ***gather a*** ~ 透一口气. ***get [recover] one's*** ~ ***(again)*** 恢复正常(呼吸). ***give up [yield] the*** ~ 死. ***hold [keep] one's*** ~ 屏息. ***in a*** ~ ①一瞬间,一刹那. ②一口气,一举. ***in one*** ~ 立刻; 同时; 一口气 (*say yes and no in one* ~ 才说同意又说不同意). ***in the same*** ~ 同时 (*She lost her temper and apologized in the same* ~. 她刚一发火又表示道歉). ***keep [save, spare] one's*** ~ ***to cool one's porridge*** 不如沉默不言,何必白费口舌. ***knock the*** ~ ***out of*** 使吓一跳. ***lose one's*** ~ 透不过气来,呼吸困难. ***not a*** ~ ***of*** 一点儿没有 (*not a* ~ *of suspicion* 丝毫没有可疑的地方). ***out of*** ~ 大喘气,上气不接下气. ***pant for*** ~ 喘. ***put (sb.) out of*** ~ 弄死. ***save one's*** ~ 不必多说,不作声,闭口不言. ***spend [waste] one's*** ~ 徒费唇舌,说也无用,白说. ***stop sb.'s*** ~ 闷死某人. ***take*** ~ 歇一口气,歇一歇 (*without taking* ~ 不歇地,一口气地. *take a deep* ~ 长长地吸一口气,深呼吸). ***take sb.'s*** ~ ***(away)*** 使大吃一惊〔美语常省去 *away*〕. ***to the last*** ~ 至死 (*fight to the last* ~ 战斗到最后一息). ***with bated*** ~ 屏息地, 小声. ***with one's bad*** ~ 心怀恶意. ***with the last*** ~ 临终时; 最后. ~ **holding test**【医】屏息试验. ~ **test** 呼吸(测醉)分析. ~**-test** *vt.* 对…进行呼吸(测醉)分析. ~ **sounds** 呼吸声.

breath·a·lyse [ˈbreθəlaiz] *vt.* 对…的呼吸进行测醉试验.

breath·a·lys·er [ˈbreθəlaizə] *n.* (测醉用)呼吸试验器.

breathe [briːð] *vi.* ①呼吸. ②活着, 生存; (肖像等)栩栩如生. ③歇一口气, 休息一下. ④(风等)微微吹动; (人)低语; (香气)飘溢; (酒)开瓶后接触空气. ⑤(内燃机)以空气维持燃烧. *Hardly a man* ~*s who has not loved a woman.* 没有产生过爱情的男子几乎是没有的. *I can* ~ *easier now.* 我现在可以松一口气了. — *vt.* ①呼吸. ②使喘气, 使疲劳; 使(运动员)出力训练. ③使歇口气, 使休息. ④发散(香气等); 说出, 吐露出(心意等), 漏出(真相等); 表现出(感情等). ⑤低声说[唱]出;【语】发(气息音). ⑥向…注入(新内容等), 赋与…以(生气等) (*into*). ⑦喷(火); 吐(血). ~ *fresh air* 呼吸一下新鲜空气. ~ *a horse* 让马喘喘气,让马歇一歇. *He was so* ~*d that he could not walk.* 他累得走不动了. ~ *a prayer* 小声祈祷. *The novel* ~*s despair.* 这部小说表现出绝望的情绪. *She* ~*d life into the party.* 她给舞会带来了生气. ~ *blood* 吐血. *It's said that dragons* ~ *fire.* 据说龙能喷火. *She never* ~*d a word about it.* 她对这件事绝口不提. ~ ***a vein*** 〔古〕切开血管放血. ~ ***down one's neck*** 威吓,装着要追赶的样子. ~ ***freely [easy, easily, again]*** (紧张之后) 安下心, 放下心. ~ ***one's last (breath)*** 断气,死 (*He* ~*d his last.* 他死了.) ~ ***sober*** 〔美〕戒酒. ~ ***upon*** ①对…哈气; 使(玻璃等)失去光泽. ②中伤. ***(be) still breathing*** 还活着. ***not*** ~ ***a word [syllable] about [of]*** 对…严守秘密. **breath·a·ble, breathe·a·ble** *a.* **breathe·a·ble·ness** *n.*

breathed [breθt, briːðd] *a.* ①【语】气息音的. ②有…气息的〔用以构成复合词〕. *a long-*~ *speaker* 能一口气讲个不停的演说者.

breath·er [ˈbriːðə] *n.* ①呼吸者,生物. ②(使人大喘气的)激烈运动[费力的工作];〔美〕喘着气的拳击选手. ③片刻的休息, 使呼吸恢复正常的休息. ④通气孔[管、筒]; 呼吸阀[瓶]; (潜水服等的)送气装置;【电】(变压器用的)吸潮器. ~ *pipe* 通气管. *have [take] a* ~ *after a heavy work* 干完重活后休息一下. *a heavy* ~ 鼻息重的人,气粗的人. *go for a* ~ 作一会儿体育锻炼.

breath·ing [ˈbriːðiŋ] *a.* ①呼吸的,活的. ②(画像等)栩栩如生的. — *n.* ①呼吸; 通气,供氧. ②空气的微微流动,微风; (香气的)飘溢. ③愿望,向往; (意见的)发表,表示; 发言. ④【语】气息音,气音符号. ⑤歇息, 休息. ⑥【化】放气;【电】(变压器的)受潮; (送话器电阻的)周期性小变化. ~ *exercises* 呼吸运动. *It all happened in a* ~. 这都是一转瞬之间发生的. ~**-capacity** 肺活量. ~ **hole** 通气孔. ~**-mask** 口罩. ~ **pipe** 通气管. ~**-place** ①(歌唱、朗诵时的)停顿. ②休息场所; 空气清新的休养地. ~**-space** ①休息时间[场所]. ②喘息的机会,考虑问题的时间. ③起码的活动余地或空间 (*give the opponent no* ~*-space* 不给对手喘息的时间. *The bus was so crowded that there was hardly* ~*-space.* 公共汽车上挤得水泄不通).

breath·less [ˈbreθlis] *a.* ①气喘吁吁的; 透不过气来的. ②(紧张得)屏住气息的;〔诗〕已死的,气绝的. ③微风全无的,(空气等)静止的. *The blow left him* ~. 一拳打得他透不过气来. ~ *listeners of the mystery story* 屏息静听神怪故事的听众. *a* ~ *summer day* 没有一丝风的夏日. ***with*** ~ ***anxiety*** 提心吊胆地. ***with*** ~ ***interest*** 屏住气,紧张着. **-ly** *ad.* **-ness** *n.*

breath·tak·ing [ˈbreθˌteikiŋ] *a.* ①使人吃惊的，惊人的. ②令人透不过气来的. ③惊险的. *a* ~ *car race* 惊险的汽车比赛. *his* ~ *ignorance* 他那惊人的无知.
breath·y [ˈbreθi] *a.* 大声呼气的，带有喘息声的. **breath·i·ly** *ad.* **breath·i·ness** *n.*
b. rec., B. Rec. = bills receivable.
brec·ci·a [ˈbretʃə] *n.*【地】(断层)角砾岩.
brec·ci·ate [ˈbretʃiˌeit] *vt.* ①【地】(将岩石碎片)合成角砾岩. ②将(岩石)击成碎片. **-a·tion** *n.*
bred [bred] breed 的过去式及过去分词.
brede [bri:d] *n.*〔古〕= braid.
bree [bri:] *n.*〔Scot.〕清汤；肉汤.
breech [bri:tʃ] *n.* ①屁股，臀部. ②(枪、炮的)后膛，尾部. ③水平烟道；【机】滑车底部；【海】肘材. ④〔*pl.*〕= breeches. — *vt.* ①给…穿裤子. ②给(枪、炮)装枪尾[炮尾]. ③〔古〕打(屁股). ~ **birth** = ~ delivery. ~**block** 枪闩，炮闩；(枪机柄的)螺体. ~**bolt** 炮闩. ~**cloth**, ~**clout** 围腰布. ~ **delivery**【产科】(臀位、横位等)异常分娩. ~**-loader** 后膛枪，后膛炮. ~**loading** *a.* 后膛的，后装式的. ~**-sight** 瞄准器.
breech·es [ˈbritʃiz] *n. pl.* 马裤；宫廷礼裤；〔口〕裤子；短裤. *wear the* ~〔英〕压制丈夫，女人当家. **B- Bible** 1560年版英译圣经〔将《创世纪》中 apron 一词错作 breeches〕. ~ **buoy**【海】裤形救生圈. ~ **part**【剧】(女子扮演的)男角.
breech·ing [ˈbritʃiŋ] *n.* ①(挽马用的)尻带. ②(阻止炮身发射时倒退的)驻退索. ③烟道.
breed [bri:d] (*bred* [bred]; *bred*) *vi.* ①(动物)生产，生子，下崽，下蛋. ②怀胎. ③繁殖；育种. ④产生，引起，滋生. *Many animals* ~ *in the spring.* 许多动物都在春天繁殖. *Bacteria will not* ~ *in alcohol.* 细菌不能在酒精内繁殖. ~ *from a mare of good stock* 以一匹良种母马育种. *Militarism* ~*s in armies.* 军国主义造成穷兵黩武. — *vt.* ①产(子)，下(崽)，下(蛋). ②孵(卵)；怀(胎). ③繁殖，饲养. ④养育，抚养；教养，培育；训练. ⑤产生，滋生，使发生，酿成，惹起，引起. ⑥【原】再生，增殖. *Every mother breeds not sons alike.* 母别子异，一个娘养的儿子一个样. ~ *horse* 养马. *Stagnant water* ~*s mosquitoes.* 死水滋生蚊虫. *be bred to the law* 受法律教育. ~ *several strains of corn together to produce a new variety* 用几个品系的玉米育新种. ***bred and born*** = ***born and bred*** 道地的，…本地的. ~ ***in and in*** 同种繁殖；近亲结婚. ~ ***out*** 在人工繁殖过程中消除(品种的特性). ~ ***out and out*** 异种繁殖. ~ ***of cat(s)***〔俚〕种类 (*be a different* ~ *of cat from* … 和…是两回事). ~ ***true to type*** (杂种)形成定型〔生产同一特质的后代〕. ~ ***up*** 养育；教育，养成. ***ill [well] bred*** 有[没有]教养. ***what is bred in the bone*** 遗传的特质，本性 (*What is bred in the bone will come out in the flesh.* 本性难移，骨头里生的总要在肉里长). — *n.* ①【遗传】品种. ②种族，血统，家系. ③种类，群，集团. *He belongs to that* ~ *of pups.*〔美〕他是那一种人. *Scholars are a quiet* ~. 学者们大都沉默寡言. *fine* ~ 良种；高贵的血统.
breed·er [ˈbri:də] *n.* ①繁殖的动[植]物；种畜. ②饲养人；养育者；家畜繁殖家. ③发起人；起因. ④【原】增殖(反应)堆. *slow [rapid]* ~*s* 繁殖慢[快]的动物. ~ ***reactor***【原】增殖反应堆.
breed·ing [ˈbri:diŋ] *n.* ①孵化；饲养；繁育. ②选种，育种. ③繁殖，生育. ④熏陶；养育，教养，礼貌. ⑤【原】增殖，再生. *a man of fine* ~ 有教养的人. *cross [out-and-out]* ~ 杂交繁育. *close [in-and-in]* ~ 近亲繁育. *mass* ~ 混合育种. *cattle* ~ 养牛业. ~**cocoon**种茧. ~**ground** ①饲养场. ②(产生、培养某种思想的)温床. ~ **pond** 养鱼塘. ~ **plumage** (鸟的)婚羽. ~ **ratio** 增殖比. ~ **season** 繁殖期. ~ **station** 配种站.
breeks [bri:ks] *n.*〔*pl.*〕〔Scot.〕= breeches.
breen [bri:n] *n.* 褐绿色. — *a.* 褐绿色的.

breeze[1] [bri:z] *n.* ①微风；柔风，和风. ②〔俚〕吵闹，小风波，小纷争. ③〔俚〕流言，谣言. ④〔美俚〕轻而易举的事情. *a faint [gentle, light, moderate, fresh, strong]* ~ 微[柔，轻，和，疾，烈]风. *The horse won in a* ~. 这匹马轻而易举地就跑赢了. ***bat [shoot] the*** ~〔口〕①闲谈，聊天. ②吹牛，夸大. ***in a*** ~ 不费力地. ***kick up a*** ~ 惹乱子，引起风波. — *vi.* ①刮微风. ②〔美〕轻快地急走；闯入，冲进. ③逃走. ~ *through the book* 不费力地很快读完了全书. *It* ~*d from the west all day.* 整天吹微微的西风. ~ ***in***〔美〕①(比赛)轻易得胜. ② = ~ into. ~ ***into*** = ~ out. ~ ***off***〔美俚〕住嘴；走开. ~ ***out***〔俚〕毫不在乎，漫不经心地行动，飘然出现. ~ ***up*** 风渐渐大起来. — *vt.* 使全速飞跑. ~ *a horse around the track* 策马沿跑道飞奔. ~**way** (房屋与房屋之间的)有顶过道[走廊]. **-less** *a.* 无风的，平静的.
breeze[2] [bri:z] *n.*〔英〕煤渣，煤屑；煤粉. ~ *oven* 煤粉化铁炉. ~ *blocks* (煤渣与水泥制的)煤渣砖.
breeze[3] [bri:z] *n.*【虫】虻，牛蝇〔又名 ~**-fly**〕.
breez·i·ly [ˈbri:zili] *ad.* ①微风徐徐. ②轻快地. ③快活地.
breez·i·ness [ˈbri:zinis] *n.* ①微风的轻吹. ②轻快，活泼. ③快活.
breez·y [ˈbri:zi] *a.* ①有微风的，通风良好的. ②有生气的，活泼的，轻快的. ③〔美〕说说笑笑的；多嘴的，爱谈笑的；傲慢的. *a* ~ *slapstick*〔美〕妙透了的俏皮话. *talk in a* ~ *way.* 谈笑风生.
breg·ma [ˈbregmə] *n.* (*pl.* ***breg·ma·ta*** [-mətə])【解】前囟. **-tic** [bregˈmætik] *a.*
brek·ker [ˈbrekə] *n.*〔学生俚〕早餐.
Bre·men [ˈbreimən] *n.* 不来梅〔德意志联邦共和国港市〕.
brems·strah·lung [ˈbremsˈtrɑ:luŋ] *n.*【物】(原子弹)韧致辐射.
Bren [bren] *n.* (捷克造)布朗式轻机关枪 (= ~ gun, ~ machine gun). *a* ~ *carrier* 履带式小型装甲车.
Bren·da [ˈbrendə] *n.* 布伦达〔女子名〕.
Bren·nan [ˈbrenən] *n.* 布伦南〔姓氏〕.
Brent [brent] *n.* ①布伦特〔姓氏，男子名〕. ②〔b-〕【鸟】黑雁 (= ~-goose).
br'er [brə:] *n.*〔美方〕= brother.
bres·sum·mer [ˈbresəmə] *n.*【建】大木 (= breast-summer).
Brest [brest] *n.* ①布雷斯特〔法国港市〕. ②布列斯特〔苏联城市〕.
Bre·tagne [F. brətaɲ] *n.* = Brittany.
breth·ren [ˈbreðrin] *n. pl.*〔古〕同党，同会，会友；同业；〔古〕同胞.
Bre·ton [bretən] *n.* (法国)布列塔尼地区的人；布列塔尼地区的语言.
Bret·ton Woods [ˈbretən wudz] 布雷顿森林〔美国游览胜地〕.
breve [bri:v] *n.* ①【乐】二全音符 (‖0‖). ②【印】(元音上的)短音符号 (︶). ③(法律诉讼的)令状；(教皇的)训谕示；(国王的)敕令.
bre·vet [ˈbrevit] *n.*【军】(不提薪的)名誉晋级(令)，加衔(令). — *vt.* 予以加衔，予以名誉晋升. — *a.* 名誉晋升的，加衔的.
bre·vet·cy [briˈvetsi] *n.* 名誉级，名誉衔〔提职不提薪〕.
brevi- *comb. f.* 短: *brevi*ostrate.
bre·vi·ar·y [ˈbri:vjəri] *n.* ①【天主】每日祈祷；〔常 B-〕祈祷书. ②节略.
bre·vier [brəˈviə] *n.*【印】八点活字〔相当于六号铅字〕.
brev·i·ros·trate [ˌbreviˈrɔstreit] *a.*【动】短喙的.
brev·i·ty [ˈbreviti] *n.* ①(语言等的)简洁；简短. ②(时间等的)短促，短暂. *B- is the soul of wit.* 言以简洁为贵，简洁是智慧的真谛. *the* ~ *of human life* 短促的人生，人生如寄. *send a telegram in its* ~ 打一份文字简洁的

电报.

brew [bru:] *vt.* ①酿造(啤酒等); 调(饮料),泡(茶). ②酝酿,策划. *She ~ed a pot of soup from the leftovers.* 她用吃剩下的菜冲一盆汤. ~ *mischief* 策划恶作剧. ~ *trouble* 图谋捣乱. — *vi.* ①酿酒; (水等)煮沸. ②(暴风雨等)即将来临, (脾气等)行将发作; (阴谋等)成熟, 紧迫. *The tea ~s and we wait.* 茶泡上了, 我们等一会儿. *There is something ~ing.* 眼看就要出什么乱子. *A storm is ~ing in the west.* 暴风雨就要从西边过来. ***As you ~, so you must drink.*** 自酿苦酒自家喝,自作自受. — *n.* ①酿造; (一次)酿造量. ②(酿造出的)饮料; 热茶,热咖啡(等); 混合饮料. ③(酒等的)品味. *a good strong ~* 浓味佳酿. *the first ~ of tea* 刚泡的茶, 头道茶. *a witches' ~* 女巫调制的神秘药酒.

brew·age [ˈbru:idʒ] *n.* ①(酒的)酿造; (饮料的)调制. ②啤酒; 饮料. ③(阴谋等的)策划; (暴风雨等的)酝酿.

brew·er [ˈbru:ə] *n.* ①酿(啤)酒人, 酿(啤)酒商. ②阴谋家. **~'s grain** (啤)酒糟. **~'s yeast** ①啤酒酵母. ②(啤酒酿成后的)酵母副产品.

Brew·er [ˈbru(:)ə] *n.* 布鲁尔〔男子名〕.

brew·er·y, brew·house [ˈbruəri, ˈbru:haus] *n.* 啤酒厂,酿酒厂.

brew·ing [ˈbru:iŋ] *n.* ①酿造(啤酒); 一次酿造量; 酿酒法. ②混合, 搀合. ③(阴谋等的)策划; (暴风雨等的)酝酿.

brew·is [ˈbru:is] *n.* 〔方〕肉汁,肉汤; 泡在肉汤〔热奶〕中的面包.

Brew·ster [ˈbru:stə] *n.* 布鲁斯特〔姓氏〕.

Bri·an [ˈbraiən] *n.* 布赖恩〔姓氏,男子名〕.

bri·ar [ˈbraiə] *n.* = brier[1,2].

Bri·a·re·us [braiˈɛəriəs] *n.* 【希神】百手巨人. **Bri·ar·e·an** [braiˈɛəriən] *a.*

bri·ar·root [ˈbraiəˌru:t] *n.* = brierroot.

bri·ar·wood [ˈbraiəwud] *n.* = brierwood.

brib·a·bil·i·ty [ˌbraibəˈbiliti] *n.* 受贿〔被收买〕的可能性; 易受贿.

brib·a·ble [ˈbraibəbl] *a.* 能行贿的, 可收买的, 容易收买的.

bribe [braib] *n.* ①贿赂,私礼. ②诱惑物. *take [offer] a ~* 受〔行〕贿. *give [offer, handout] ~s to sb.* 向某人行贿. *The children were given candy as a ~ to be good.* 用糖果哄孩子们不要闹. — *vt.* ①用贿赂引诱; 向…行贿, 收买. ②用贿赂影响. ~ *sb. into silence* 用贿赂封住某人的嘴. — *vi.* 行贿.

brib·ee [braiˈbi:] *n.* 受贿人.

brib·er [ˈbraibə] *n.* 行贿人.

brib·er·y [ˈbraibəri] *n.* ①行贿,收买. ②受贿. *commit ~* 行〔受〕贿.

bric-à-brac [ˈbrikəbræk] *n.* 〔F.〕 *(sing; pl.)* ①古董,古玩,古物. ②装饰品; 小摆设.

Brice [brais] *n.* 布赖斯〔姓氏,男子名〕.

brick [brik] *n.* ①砖; 砖块. ②砖形物; 砖形面包; 茶砖; 方料,块料; 积木(玩具); 一砖的厚度. ③〔口〕好心人; 好汉. *a fire [stone] ~* 耐火砖. *a gold ~* 金砖; 坚固的东西. *bake [make, burn] ~s* 烧砖, *lay ~s* 砌砖. *one and a half ~s thick* 一砖半厚. *a Bath [Bristol] ~* 砖形砂石〔磨石〕. *as dry as a ~* 干得象砖头一样. *a regular~* 好汉,好人. *You've been a perfect ~ to me.* 你待我太好了. **~ by ~** 一点一点. ***drop a ~*** 〔口〕出丑, 出错,失言. ***have a ~ in one's hat*** 有醉意. ***hit the ~s*** 〔美俚〕①走上街头. ②罢工; 巡察. ③释放出狱. ***like a ~*** 〔口〕勇猛地,活泼地. ***like a hundred [thousand, a load, tons] of ~s*** 〔口〕勇敢地,猛烈地; 以压倒优势. ***make ~s without straw*** 徒劳,做吃力不讨好的事情. — *vt.* 用砖砌; 用砖镶填 *(up)*; 用砖围砌 *(in)*; 用砖铺筑,用砖建造. ~ *up a disused entrance* 用砖堵死不再需要的入口. — *a.* ①用砖砌〔铺〕的. ②砖似的. *a ~ pavement* 砖铺的人行道. *a ~ wall* 砖墙. — *vt.* 用砖砌; 用砖围起. *a garden ~ed in on three sides* 三面用砖围起的园子. ~ *up the opening* 用砖砌起豁口. **~bat** ① *n.* (扔人的)砖片, 碎砖; 贬责的话,严厉的批评. ② *vt.* 讽刺,攻击. ~ **clay** 砖土,(制砖的)粘土. **~dust** 砖粉,砖灰,砖屑. **~field** 砖厂. ~ **fielder** 〔澳〕燥热的北风. **~kiln** 砖窑. **~layer** 砌砖工. **~laying** 砌砖; 泥水业. ~ **nogging** 【建】木架砖壁. **~-on-edge** 侧(砌)砖. **~-on-end** 竖(砌)砖. ~ **red** 红砖色. **~-red** *a.* 红砖色的. ~ **tea** 砖茶. **~work** ①砌砖工程, 砖房. ②砖圬工. **~yard** 砖厂; 售砖处.

brick·le [brikl] *a.* 〔方〕易碎的,脆的. **-ness** *n.*

brick·y [ˈbriki] *a.* 砖的,砖一样的; 砖色的.

bri·cole [ˈbrikəl] *n.* ①〔古〕石弩. ②【台球】撞空; 【网球】(碰壁)弹回; 〔喻〕间接的一击. ③(拖炮用的)垫肩.

brid·al [ˈbraidl] *a.* ①新人的,新娘的. ②婚礼的. *a ~ suite* (旅馆等的)新婚夫妇房间. *a ~ couple* 新郎新娘. — *n.* ①婚礼,结婚仪式. ②〔古〕喜筵. ~ **chamber** 新房,洞房. ~ **veil** (新娘披的)面纱. ~ **wreath** 【植】笑靥花.

bride[1] [braid] *n.* ①新娘; 即将出嫁的女子. ②〔英俚〕十多岁的姑娘. *a ~-to-be* 未来的新娘. ***~ and groom on a raft*** 〔美俚〕鸡蛋烤面包片. ***lead one's ~ to the altar*** 娶某女为妻〔指在教堂内结婚〕. **~-cake** *n.* 喜饼,礼饼. **~-price** (婚前男方给女方的)聘金,财礼.

bride[2] [braid] *n.* 花边上连接花纹用的狭条; 妇女宽边帽上的系带.

bride·groom [ˈbraidgrum] *n.* 新郎.

brides·maid [ˈbraidzmeid] *n.* 女傧相.

brides·man [ˈbraidzmən] *n.* 男傧相.

bride·well [ˈbraidwəl] *n.* ①〔古〕监狱. ②〔美〕感化院.

bridge[1] [bridʒ] *n.* ①桥,桥梁; 【船】舰桥,船桥. ②鼻梁; (假牙上的)齿桥; 【乐】弦柱, 弦马; 【电】电桥; 【机】天车, 桥架; 【台球】球棒架. ③(文艺作品的)过渡性章节, 过场; 穿插,插曲. *a ~ of boats* 船桥. *a bascule ~* 活动桥. *a suspension [wire] ~* 吊桥,悬索桥. *Wheatstone ~* 【物】惠斯登电桥. *throw a ~ across [over] a river* 在河上架桥. ***~ of gold [silver] = golden [silver] ~*** 退路,逃路,易于突破难关的办法. ***burn one's ~s (behind one)*** 布背水阵,破釜沉舟. ***Don't cross the ~ until you come to it.*** 不要杞人忧天,不要预先自寻苦恼. ***in ~*** 【物】并联; 跨接; 加分路. — *vt.* ①在…之间架桥, 搭桥于, 用桥连接; 【电】跨接. ②〔喻〕越过, 跨过 *(over)*. *The road ~s the river.* 在河上架桥把路连接起来. ~ *over obstacles* 越过障碍. **~board** 【建】短梯基. **~builder** *n.* 搭桥人; 斡旋者, 调解人. ~ **crane** 桥式吊车. **~head** 【军】桥头堡. ~ **host** 【生】过渡寄主. ~ **house** 桥旁小屋,【海】桥楼, **~-opening** 桥孔. **~-pier** 桥墩. **~-toll** 过桥钱. ~ **train** 【军】架浮桥用具; 架桥中队. **~ward** 守桥人. **~work** 桥梁工事; (假牙的)齿桥.

bridge[2] [bridʒ] *n.* 【牌】桥牌戏,打桥牌. *auction ~* 拍卖式桥牌. *contract ~* (打不到预定墩数要受罚的)合约式桥牌.

Bridg·es [ˈbridʒiz] *n.* 布里奇斯〔姓氏〕.

Bridg·et [ˈbridʒit] *n.* 布丽奇特〔女子名〕.

Bridge·town [ˈbridʒtaun] *n.* 布里奇敦〔巴巴多斯首都〕.

Bridg·man [ˈbridʒmən] *n.* 布里奇曼〔姓氏〕.

bridg·ing [ˈbridʒiŋ] *n.* ①造桥, 架桥. ②【建】搁栅撑.

bri·dle [ˈbraidl] *n.* ①笼头〔缰、辔、口衔的总称〕; 拉手〔缰绳〕. ②约束物; 束缚, 抑制; 【机】束带, 限动物; 制动器; 【海】系船索(链); 【解】系带. ***give the ~ to*** 放松缰绳; 使…自由活动; 放纵. ***go well up to the ~*** (马)听从骑者的驾驭, 服从驾驭. ***lay the ~ on the neck of*** 放松,放纵. ***put [set] a ~ on*** 克制, 抑制. — *vt.* ①给(马)套笼头〔上辔头〕. ②抑制, 约束. ~ *one's passions [anger]* 克制欲望〔愤怒〕. — *vi.* 仰头,昂首(表示傲慢、轻侮、愤怒) *(up)*. ~ *up with anger* 气冲冲地昂起

头. ～ ***at*** 对…仰着头表示看不起. ～ **bridge** 通马不通车的狭桥. ～ **hand** 执缰绳的手〔左手〕. ～**-joint** (木工)啮接. ～ **path [road, way]** (不能通车的)马道. ～ **rein** 马缰. ～ **trail** 马踏成的路. ～**-wise** *a.* 〔美〕(马)养乖了的,有训练的,听从骑者指挥的.

bri•doon [briˈduːn] *n.* (军马的)缰绳口衔,小勒缰.

Brie [briː] *n.* (法国布里产的)咸味白乳酪.

brief [briːf] *a.* ①(时间)短暂的. ②(文体等)简洁的. ③(答复等)简短的. *a ～ stay in the country* 在该国小留数日. *a ～ life* 短暂的人生. *a ～ hope* 暂时的希望. *a ～ report* 简短的报告. *He is ～ of speech.* 他说话简单扼要. *a cold and ～ welcome* 寥寥几句冷淡的欢迎. *to be ～ with you* 简单地和你说吧. ***to be ～*** 简单地说,一句话. — *n.* ①概要,摘要;短文. ②【法】诉讼事实摘要,诉讼事件;(律师的)辩护状. ②(攻击开始前给飞行员等的)指令,简短命令. ③(罗马教皇的)敕书. ④〔*pl.*〕紧身裤,三角裤. ⑤【剧】〔英〕免费入场券. ⑥〔废〕信件. ***～ of title***【法】转让(财产等的)书面摘要. ***have plenty of ～s*** (律师)承办的案件多. ***hold a ～*** 当辩护律师. ***hold a ～ for*** 为…辩护,主张…,为…大声疾呼. ***in ～*** 简单地说,要言之. ***make ～ of*** 把…很快办完. ***take a ～*** (律师)接受诉讼案件. — *vt.* ①节略,作…的摘要〔提要〕. ②〔英〕向(律师)陈述诉讼事实摘要;委托…作辩护律师. ③向…下达简令;对(飞行员等)作最后指示;对…事先作简要指点. *He ～ed his salesmen on the coming campaign.* 他就即将开展的推销运动向推销员作简短指示. ～ **bag** 〔英〕= ～ **case.** 公文皮包. **-ing** *n.* ①下达简令; 情况简介〔汇报〕会. ②简令; 简要情况 (*a (news) ～ing officer* 〔美〕新闻发布官 *a briefing chart* 任务简要讲解图. *a briefing room* 简令下达室).

brief•less [ˈbriːflis] *a.* 无人委托诉讼的,无诉讼案件的.

brief•ly [ˈbriːfli] *ad.* 简短地,简单地,简略地. ***to put it ～*** 简单地说.

brief•ness [ˈbriːfnis] *n.* 简单,简略;简洁的风格.

bri•er[1], **bri•ar**[1] [ˈbraiə] *n.*【植】多刺的木质茎植物(丛);野蔷薇(丛). ***～s and brambles*** 茂盛的刺丛. ～ **grape** 刺葡萄. ～ **rose**【植】蔷薇莓. **-y** *a.* 荆棘丛生的,多刺的.

brier[2], **briar**[2] [ˈbraiə] *n.* ①【植】石南. ②欧石南根烟斗. ～**root**【植】欧石南根.

brig[1] [brig] *n.* ①横帆双桅船. ②〔美军俚〕舰上禁闭室;舰上警卫室. ③〔美俚〕监狱;警察局. — *vt.* 监禁.

brig[2] [brig] *n.*, *vt.* 〔Scot.〕= bridge[1].

brig. = brigade; brigadier.

bri•gade [briˈgeid] *n.* ①【军】旅;大部队. ②(从事一定活动的)队,组. — *vt.* ①【军】把…编成旅. ②把…编成队〔组〕. *a fire ～*消防队. *a rescue ～* 急救队. ～**-major** 〔英〕副旅长.

brig•a•dier [ˌbrigəˈdiə] *n.* ①旅长. ②〔英〕陆军〔海军陆战队〕准将. ③〔美〕=B- General. ***B- General***〔美〕陆军〔空军、海军陆战队〕准将,少将旅长.

brig•and [ˈbrigənd] *n.* 土匪,强盗. **-age, -ism** *n.* 抢劫;强盗行为. **-ish** *a.* 强盗般的.

brig•an•tine [ˈbrigəntain] *n.* ①(前桅为横帆,主桅为纵帆的)纵横帆双桅船. ② = brig[1].

Brig. Gen. = Brigadier General 〔美〕陆军〔空军、海军陆战队〕准将.

Briggs [brigz] *n.* 布里格斯〔姓氏〕.

bright [brait] *a.* ①光明的,明亮的; 辉煌的,闪烁的; 灿烂的;晴朗的. ②(水、酒等)透明的,晶莹的;(颜色)鲜艳的;(证据等)明白的;(声名)显赫的. ③聪明的,伶俐的,乖巧的; 细心的; 机灵的. ④活泼的; 欣喜的,快活的; 幸福的; 有希望的. ～ *coins* 亮闪闪的硬币. *a bright day* 大晴天. ～ *passages of prose* 漂亮的文章,有文采. *a ～ wine* 晶莹的美酒. *the ～ water* 清可见底的水. *the ～ pageantry* 宫廷的富丽堂皇. ～ *hope(s)* 光明的希望. *a ～ period* 辉煌的时期. *a ～ red dress* 鲜红的服装. *a ～ reputation* 声名显赫. ～ *silk* 熟丝. *a ～ boy* 聪明的小伙子. *a ～ idea* 好主意,妙想. *the bird's ～ song* 欢快的鸟鸣. *a ～ and happy child* 活泼快乐的孩子. ***～ and early*** 大清早. ***～ in the eye*** 〔口〕微醉,带醉. ***～ side of things*** 事物的光明面 (*look on [at] the ～ side of things* 对事物抱乐观态度). — *ad.* = brightly. *The sun was shining ～.* 阳光灿烂. — *n.* ①〔*pl.*〕(开行中的)车头灯 (*opp.* parking ～). ②烤得金黄的烟叶. ③方尖画笔. ④〔古〕光辉. ～**-eyed** *a.* 眼睛清莹的. ～ **field**【物】明视场. ～ **light districts,** ～ **lights**〔口〕市区娱乐场所. ～ **line**【物】明线. ～**work** (船、车等的)光亮的金属构件;【船】无漆木料构件. **-ly** *ad.* **-ness** *n.*

Bright [brait] *n.* 布赖特〔姓氏〕. **B-'s disease**【医】肾炎〔总称〕.

bright•en [ˈbraitn] *vt.* ①使发光辉,使发亮,擦光,磨亮. ②使活跃,使快活; 使有希望; 使聪明. *The new teacher ～ed the life of all his pupils.* 新来的老师使全体学生的生活变得活跃起来了. — *vi.* ①闪耀,发亮,发光. ②(天)晴; (人)露喜色,快活起来. ③(前途)有希望. *His face ～ed.* 他喜形于色. *B- up!* 拿出精神来! 别垂头丧气! **-ing**【纺】增艳处理.

Brigh•ton [ˈbraitn] *n.* 布赖顿〔英国城市〕.

Brig•id [ˈbridʒid] *n.* = Bridget.

Bri•gitte [ˈbridʒit] *n.* 布丽奇特〔女子名, Bridget 的异体〕.

brill [bril] *n.* (*pl.* ～, ～*s*)【鱼】滑菱鲆.

bril•liance [ˈbriljəns], **bril•lian•cy** [ˈbriljənsi] *n.* ①光彩,光辉,光泽. ②【光】辉度,亮度. ③漂亮;(名声)煊赫;文采;才气焕发,才华横溢. *the ～ of a fine diamond* 宝石的光辉. *the brilliancies of Congreve's wit* 康格里夫的出众才华.

bril•liant [ˈbriljənt] *a.* ①明亮的,辉煌的,灿烂的; 漂亮的. ②英明的; 卓越的; (声名)显赫的; 才气焕发的. ③声音嘹亮的; (色彩)鲜明的. *a ～ star* 亮晶晶的星. *a ～ record* 辉煌的记录. *a ～ mind* 头脑敏锐的人,有才华的人. — *n.* ①(琢成多角形而呈现异彩的)宝石. ②【印】$3\frac{1}{2}$ 点铅字. **-ly** *ad.* **-ness** *n.*

bril•lian•tine [ˌbriljənˈtiːn] *n.* ①润发油. ②【纺】亮光薄呢〔一种有光泽的棉毛交织品〕.

brim [brim] *n.* ①(杯,碗等容器的)缘,边;〔古〕水边,岸边. ②帽边. *fill a glass to the ～* 把杯子倒满. *the ～ of a cup* 茶杯边. *the ～ of a hat* 帽子的翻边. ***full to the ～*** 漫到边,满,溢. — *vt.* 把(容器)装满,注满,倒满. *～ the cup* 把茶杯倒满. — *vi.* 满,溢,漫出. *Tears ～ed in her eyes.* 她的眼中充满了泪水. ***～ over with*** (精神等)饱满;(才华等)横溢;漫出,充满 (*She is brimming over with health.* 她全身上下都焕发着健康的气息).

brim•ful [ˈbrimˈful] *a.* ①漫到边的. ②洋溢着…的. *her ～ eyes* 她那泪汪汪的眼睛. *a ～ cup* 满满的一杯(水、酒等). *be ～ of hope and health* 充满了健康和希望. **-ness** *n.*

brim•med [brimd] *a.* ①满,漫到边的. ②有(…)边的. *a broad-～ hat* 宽边帽.

brim•mer [brimə] *n.* 满杯.

brim•stone [ˈbrimstəun] *n.* ①〔古〕硫黄石;【圣】地狱之火的燃料. ②泼妇,悍妇. ***Fire and ～*** 硫磺烈火〔《圣经》中讲的地狱之火,用以惩罚有罪者〕. ～ **moth**【动】黄蛾.

brim•ston•y [ˈbrimstəuni] *a.* ①硫黄质〔色〕的,有硫黄臭味的. ②地狱般气氛的;恶魔的.

brin•ded [ˈbrindid] *a.* 〔古〕= brindled.

brin•dle [ˈbrindl] *n.* ①斑,斑纹. ②斑皮动物;〔特指〕花狗. — *a.* = brindled.

brin•dled [ˈbrindld] *a.* 斑驳的,有斑纹的,花的.

brine [brain] *n.* ①卤水;咸水,盐水;【化】盐溶液. ②海水;海. ③〔诗〕泪水. — *vt.* 用盐水泡,用盐水处理. ～ **pan** 盐灶;熬盐锅. ～**pit** 盐井. ～ **shrimp** 盐水褐虾.

bring [briŋ] ***(brought***[brɔːt]***; brought)*** *vt.* ①拿来,带来,携来,取来;引来;使(人)来到;〔方〕陪,护送. ②劝导,劝诱;迫使. ③招致,导致;使处于某种状态. ④生出,产生;(投资等)获得(利润). ⑤举出(论据等),提起(诉讼等),提出(议案等). ⑥(货物等)能卖(多少钱),能换(多少东西). *I have brought my umbrella with me.* 我带伞来了. *Her scream brought the police.* 她的叫声引来了警察. *I cannot ~ him to my point of view.* 我无法说服他同意我的观点. *I cannot ~ myself to do it.* 我实在不能干那件事. ~ *the car to a stop* 使车子停下来. ~ *sb. into the conversation* 使某人参加谈话. *The news brought him to his feet.* 这个消息使他惊得站了起来. *This car will ~ a good price.* 这汽车能卖大价钱. ~ *an action for damages* 提出为所受损害要求赔偿的诉讼. ~ ***about*** ①造成,带来,引起. ②【海】(使船)回转,掉头 (~ *about a war* 引起战争. *What brought the quarrel about?* 争吵是怎么引起的? ~ *the ship about* 使船掉头). ~ ***along*** ①带来. ②指导,教导 (*B- along your friend.* 请把你的朋友带来). ***~ around [round]*** ①说服,(某人)做某事(*to*). ②〔口〕使恢复知觉[等]. ③〔口〕把(某人)作为客人带来 (*We can ~ him around to agreeing with the plan.* 我们可以说服他同意该项计划. *The new medicine brought him around.* 服用新药使他恢复了健康. *They brought around a new employee this morning.* 他们今天早晨请来了一位新雇员). ~ ***back*** ①使回忆起. ②使恢复. ③送回,还回,拿回,带回(~ *sb. back to health*使某人恢复健康). ~ ***close to*** 引近,领来. ~ ***down*** ①贬低;〔口〕煞(某人)威风,使受挫;把(人)毁掉;打倒. ②使落下[跌落];射落,击落,打下;打伤,打死. ③削减;降低. ④致(祸),获(罪). ⑤放下,卸下(货物等). ⑥使浓缩. ⑦把(记录)记到(某时)为止. (~ *down the birds* 把鸟击落. ~ *down the price* 降价). ***~ down on oneself*** 招人恨[嫉妒、报复等]. ~ ***down the house*** 博得满场喝采. ~ ***forth*** ①生,产生,产(子),结(实),开(花),出(芽). ②显现,提出,发表. (~ *forth a son* 生儿子. ~ *forth a proposal* 提出建议). ~ ***forward [on]*** ①提出(计划等);提示;提前;公开;显出. ②【会计】把(帐目)结转(到次页). ③把…提前(*B- forward the prisoner.* 带犯人出庭! ~ *forward an opinion* 提出意见. ~ *forward a meeting* 把会议召开日期提前). ~ ***(sth.) home (to sb.)*** ①使(某人)清楚地认识到[痛切地感觉到了](某事). ②确凿证明(某人)犯(某罪). ~ ***home the bacon*** 〔口〕①成功;如愿以偿. ②谋生. ~ ***in*** ①生产,产出;生(利);收获(农作物等);挣得(报酬等). ②带来,引入,传进. ③提出(议案等);(陪审团)下(判决);【棒球】使跑回本垒. (*His extra job doesn't ~ in much.* 他的兼职工作挣不了多少钱. ~ ***sb. in guilty [not guilty]*** 宣判某人有罪[无罪]. ~ ***into effect*** 使生效;使起作用. ~ ***into play*** 使活动,使发挥作用. ~ ***off*** ①办完,圆满完成. ②(从失事船只上)救出. ~ ***on*** ①惹起,引起(议论等),导致. ②使发展;使出现. ③提出;介绍;使(演员)与观众见面. ④〔卑〕使(性欲)冲动. ~ *on a crisis* 引起一场危机. *His words brought on a storm.* 他的话使全场哗然. ~ ***out*** ①公布,发表;说出;出版;上演. ②显示出,揭示出,现出(颜色、性质等);显露(才华). ③使(女子)进入社交界 (*Peril ~s out unsuspected qualities.* 危难使人显示出真实的品质. *She brought the fact out with shame.* 她羞愧地讲出了事实. ~ *out a play* 上演一出戏. ~ *out a book* 出版一本书). ~ ***over*** ①把…带来;从外国运来;把…引渡. ②把…拉入(某组织等);使改变意见[信仰等],把…争取过来. ~ ***(sb.) through*** ①帮助(某人)脱离险境[克服困难,突破障碍]. ②救活 (~ *a patient through* 救活病人). ~ ***to*** ①使恢复知觉,使复苏. ②【海】使停船. (~ *him to by artificial respiration* 以人工呼吸法使他恢复知觉). ~ ***to an end [a close, a stand, a stop]*** 使终止,使停止,结束. ~ ***to bear*** ①施加(压力等),使受(影响等). ②瞄准,把(枪、炮)向…对准. ③集中(力量),竭尽(才智等). ④使成功,使(意见)被接受,完成,实现 (~ *a gun to bear on the mark* 把大炮对准目标). ~ ***together*** 集合,召集 (~ *together all kinds of talent* 把各种人才集合起来). ~ ***to light*** 暴露,公开,公布. ~ ***to mind*** 想起,回想. ~ ***to pass*** ①使发生,引起. ②做成,完成. ~ ***under*** ①压服,镇压. ②抑制;把…置于(权力、支配等)之下. ~ ***up*** ①抚养,养育,教育,培养. ②提出(问题等);派出(军队等),发出. ③把(某人)带上法庭;准许(议员)发言;结转,滚入(计算). ④使(车辆等)突然停止;【海】抛锚;(船等)到终点. ⑤呕吐 (*a well brought-up young man* 一个有教养的青年. ~ *up a new subject* 提出新问题. ~ *up blood* 吐血. ~ *up the car* 使车子猛然停住). ~ ***up the rear*** 殿后,压队,最后来.

bring·down [ˈbriŋdaun] *n.* 〔美俚〕①使人灰心丧气[不满]的东西. ②经常愁眉苦脸的人. — *a.* ①令人不满的;不能胜任的. ②使人沮丧的;阴沉的.

bring·ing-up [ˈbriŋiŋˈʌp] *n.* ①(儿童的)养育,抚养. ②教养.

brin·ja(u)l [ˈbrindʒɔːl] *n.* 【植】茄子.

brink[briŋk] *n.* ①边,界,涯,滨,岸. ②〔喻〕濒临;(战争)边缘. *the ~ of a precipice* 悬崖边沿. *a ~-of-war policy* 战争边缘政策. *beyond the ~ of our endurance* 超出了我们忍耐的限度. ***on the ~ of*** 即将要,濒临,在…的边缘 (*be on the ~ of doing* 即将要做. *on the ~ of starvation* 快要饿死). ~**(s)man** 奉行战争边缘政策的人.

brink(s)·man·ship [ˈbriŋk(s)mənʃip] *n.* ①(战争)边缘政策. ②玩弄(战争)边缘政策.

brin·y [ˈbraini] *a.* ①盐水的;咸的,腌的. ②海水的. ③〔诗〕泪水的. *a ~ taste* 咸味. ***the ~*** 〔俚〕海(水),大洋 (*a dip in the ~* 大海里的一滴水).

brio [ˈbriːəu] *n.* 〔It.〕【乐】活泼;愉快;兴奋. *an elderly woman whose ~ astounds everyone.* 一个活泼得使大家吃惊的上年纪的妇人.

bri·oche [ˈbri(ː)əuʃ] *n.* 奶油鸡蛋小面包.

bri·o·lette [ˌbriəˈlet] *n.* 棱面金刚石.

Bri·o·ni [briˈəuni] *n.* 布里俄尼(群岛)〔南斯拉夫〕.

bri·o·ny [ˈbraiəni] *n.* 【植】泻根属植物(= bryony).

bri·quet(te) [briˈket] *n.* 煤砖,煤球.

bri·sance [briˈzɑːns] *n.* 炸药震力. **-sant** *a.*

Bris·bane [ˈbrizbən] *n.* 布里斯班〔澳大利亚港市〕.

brise-bise [ˈbriːzˈbiːz] *n.* 半截式窗帘.

brisk [brisk] *a.* ①活泼的,轻快的,生气勃勃的 (*opp.* languid). ②(天气)清新的;(生意)兴旺的. ③(酒等)咝咝冒泡的,味浓的. ④(语调等)刻薄的,尖酸的. *a ~ walk* 轻快的步调. *a ~ trade* 活跃的行情. *a ~ wind* 凉爽的风. ~ *cider* 冒泡的苹果酒. — *vt.* 使活泼;使活跃;使兴旺. — *vi* 活泼起来;兴旺起来 (*up*) *Business ~ed up.* 生意兴旺起来了. **-ly** *ad.* **-ness** *n.*

bris·ket [ˈbriskit] *n.* (兽的)胸,胸部;胸肉.

bris·ling,bris·tling [ˈbrisliŋ] *n.* 【鱼】(北欧产)小鲱鱼.

bris·tle [ˈbrisl] *n.* ①(猪等的)鬃毛;(动、植物的)短硬毛. ②(刷子等的)毛. ③(人的)胡须茬;鬃毛状物. ***set up one's ~s*** 勃然大怒,怒发冲冠. ***set up sb.'s ~s*** 激怒某人. — *vt.* ①使(毛发等)竖起;把…弄粗糙. ②给(刷子等)安鬃毛. *The rooster ~d his crest.* 公鸡竖起了鸡冠. — *vi.* ①(毛发等)倒竖. ②发怒 (*up*). ③(树木等)密密地覆盖;(困难等)重重,充满 (*with*). *His hair ~d on his scalp with anger.* 他气得头发都竖起来了. *The hog ~d up* 公猪竖起了鬃毛. *The plain ~d with bayonet.* 平原上刀枪林立. ~**tail** 【虫】(双尾目和樱尾目中作鬃毛状的)无翼昆虫. **bris·tly** *a.* ①有硬毛的;硬毛般的. ②(毛发等)竖起的,直立的. ③林立的,丛生的. ④发怒的.

Bris·tol [ˈbristl] *n.* ①布里斯托尔〔英国港市〕. ②〔b-〕= B- board. ~ **alloy** 白铜. ~ **board [paper]** (绘图等用)上等板纸. ~ **cream [milk]** 芳醇的雪利酒. ~ **diamond [stone, gem]** 【矿】美晶石英. ~ **fashion**

【海】整洁的,有条不紊的. ~ **glaze** 窑釉.

brit(t) [brit] *n.* ①【鱼】小鱼群,小鲱. ②(鲸鱼吃的)小浮游生物.

Brit. = Britain; Britannia; British.

Brit·ain [ˈbritən] *n.* 英国, 不列颠〔英格兰、威尔士和苏格兰的总称〕: *The United Kingdom of Great ~ and Northern Ireland* 大不列颠及北爱尔兰联合王国〔英国的正式名称〕.

Bri·tan·ni·a [briˈtænjə] *n.* ①【史】布立吞里亚〔罗马人给不列颠岛起的名称〕. ②〔诗〕英国〔女性拟人名称〕. ~ **metal, britania metal** 不列颠金〔锡、铜、锑的银白色合金〕.

Bri·tan·nic [briˈtænik] *a.* 大不列颠的, 英国的〔主要用于对国王的尊称: *His [Her] ~ Majesty* 英国国王〔女王〕陛下〕.

britch·es [ˈbritʃiz] *n. pl.* 〔口〕裤子. ***too big for one's*** ~ 〔口〕过分自信的; 傲慢的.

Brit·(t)i·cism [ˈbritisizəm] *n.* 〔美〕英国语法〔英国人特有的语言现象,如一些特有的词、习语、表达方式等,美国不用〕.

Brit·ish [ˈbritiʃ] *a.* ①不列颠的, 英国的. ②不列颠人的,英国人的. ③英联邦的,英联邦人的. ④古英语的; 英国英语的. — *n.* ①〔the B-〕〔集合词〕英国人; 英联邦人. ②英国英语; 古英语. *the ~ Commonwealth of Nations* 英联邦. *the ~ Empire* 英帝国. *the ~ House of Lords [Commons]* 英国上〔下〕议院. *the ~ Isles* 英伦诸岛〔包括不列颠、爱尔兰和曼岛〕. ~ **Academy** 英国科学院. ~ **Association** 英国学术协会. ~ **Council** 英国(对外)文化协会. ~ **dollar** (香港、海峡殖民地通用的)英元. ~ **English** (与美国英语等相区别的)英国英语. ~ **lion** 英国国徽; 英国国民. ~ **meson**【物】介子. ~ **Museum** 大英博物馆. ~ **thermal unit** 〔略 B.T.U., BTU 或 Btu〕 英国热单位〔将一磅水升高摄氏一度的热量〕. ~ **warm** (军用)厚呢短大衣.

British Columbia [ˈbritiʃ kəˈlʌmbiə] *n.* 不列颠哥伦比亚〔加拿大省名〕.

Brit·ish·er [ˈbritiʃə] *n.* 〔美〕英国人.

Brit·ish·ism [ˈbritiʃizəm] *n.* = Brit(t)icism.

Brit·on [ˈbritən] *n.* ①布立吞人〔古代不列颠南部凯尔特人的一支〕. ②(大)不列颠人, 英国人. *a North ~* 苏格兰人.

Brit·ta·ny [ˈbritəni] 布列塔尼〔法国西北部一地区〕.

brit·tle[1] [ˈbritl] *a.* ①易碎的, 脆的; 脆弱的; 易损坏的. ②虚幻的,靠不住的. ③(声音等)尖利的; 容易生气的. ④(态度)冷淡的; 利己的,专为自己打算的. ~ *as glass* 象玻璃一样容易打碎. *a ~ fame* 浮名. *His promise turned out ~.* 他的诺言原来是靠不住的. *a ~ and selfish woman* 一个态度冷淡自私自利的女人. *a ~ personality* 容易生气的个性. — *vi.* 变脆. ~ **hand** *a.* 〔美〕(拳击选手)情况不妙的. **-ly, brittl·y** *ad.* **-ness** *n.* 脆弱, 脆性, 脆度.

brit·tle[2] [ˈbritl] *n.* 薄片脆糖. *peanut ~* 薄片花生糖.

britz·ka, brits·ka [ˈbritskə] *n.* (波兰的)四轮马车.

Br·no [ˈbəːnəu] *n.* 布尔诺〔捷克斯洛伐克城市〕.

bro. *n.* *(pl. ~s)* = brother.

broach [brəutʃ] *n.* ①铁叉, 烤肉叉. ②尖塔, (塔上)尖阁. ③【机】三角锥; 钻头; 扩孔器; 拉刀; (石工用的)宽凿. ④(女服)饰针. — *vt.* ①把(肉等)串在铁叉上. ②【建】粗刻;【机】拉削. ③在(桶等)上开孔〔打眼〕; 向(矿藏等)里面开采〔凿进〕; (用凿子)开(洞),把(眼子)弄大. ④说出, 提倡, 提议; 首次宣布. ⑤(风浪)使(船)横转. *a good time to ~ afresh the question* 重新提出问题的好时机. *~ a subject* 提出一个供讨论的题目. — *vi.* ①(船因风向改变而)横转〔有倾覆危险〕; 侧,横向. ②(鲸鱼、鱼雷等)冒出海面.

broach·er [ˈbrəutʃə] *n.* ①钻孔者; 钻孔器;【机】扩孔器; 拉刀. ②倡议者,提倡者.

broad [brɔːd] *a.* ①广,广大,广袤,宽阔的,辽阔的; 广泛的,普遍的;【纺】宽幅的. ②气量大的, 宽厚的, 豁达的. ③明朗的,明白的,显著的. ④主要的, 概括的, 一般的. ⑤露骨的; 粗俗的,淫猥的,下流的. ⑥地方音重的,口音重的;【语】(元音)成开音节的. ~ *shoulders* 宽肩. *three feet ~* 宽三英尺. *~ views* 开明的见解. *the ~ plains* 辽阔的原野. *a ~ daylight* 大白天. *~ accent* 十足的土腔. *~ humour* 下流的俏皮话. *~ words* 露骨的言词. *a ~ joke* 下流的笑话. *state one's views in ~ outline* 讲个概要, 说个大意. *a ~ hint* 明白的暗示. — *n.* ①〔英〕〔*pl.*〕河流的开阔部分, (由河流扩张成的)湖沼. ②手〔脚〕掌的宽阔部分. ③〔英古〕金币; (摄影场的)地灯. ④〔美俚〕女人; 娼妓. ⑤〔美俚〕〔*pl.*〕纸牌. *the (Norfolk) Broads* (英国东南部的) 湖沼地带. ***as ~ as it is long*** 宽长一样; 半斤和八两, 结果一样. ~ ***place [spot] in the road*** 〔美〕小都市. ~ ***on the beam*** 【海】 垂直于船中横梁到船头方向的. ~ **rule** 一般标准, 常规, 常例. ~ **Scotch** 显著的苏格兰土腔. — *ad.* ①宽广地, 充分地. ②土腔十足地. ~ *awake* 十分清醒. *speak ~* 土腔十足地说. ~ **arrow** ①有倒刺镞的箭. ②(英国官方物品上的)箭头标记〔尤指印在囚衣上的标记〕. ~**ax(e)** 钺. ~**band** *n.*【无】宽带; 宽波段. ~ **bean** 蚕豆. ~**bill** 阔嘴鸭,野鸭. ~**-blown** *a.* (花)满开的. ~**brim** ①宽边帽. ②〔口〕Quaker 教徒. ~**-brush** *a.* 粗线条的. **B- Church** (英国教会的)广教派. ~**cloth** ①【纺】(高级)绒面呢. ②〔美〕= poplin. ~**-goods** 阔幅绸缎. ~ **gauge** ①宽轨距〔4 英尺 8 英寸半以上〕. ②宽轨铁路; 宽轨(铁路上的)火车. ~**-gauge** *a.* ①(铁路)宽轨距的. ②〔口〕气量大的. ~ **hatchet** 阔斧. ~ **jump** 〔Am.〕 跳远〔正式作 Long jump〕. ~**-leaf** ① *n.* 宽叶烟草. ② *a.* 宽叶的. ~**-leaved** *a.* 宽叶的. ~**loom** *a.* 阔幅地毯〔绸缎〕的. ~**-minded** *a.* 气量大的. ~ **seal** 国玺; (政府的正式)印鉴, 公章. ~**-sheet** 【印】单面〔双面〕印刷的大幅印张〔印刷品〕. ~**-side** ① *n.* (水面以上的)舷侧; 舷侧炮; 偏舷(各炮)齐发;〔喻〕一连串的诽谤,排炮般的攻击; (建筑物的)侧面; 宽面; = ~ sheet. ② *ad.* (船、车等)侧向, 露出侧面; 齐射地; 无目标地 (*The truck hit the fence ~.* 卡车侧着撞到篱笆上了). ③ *vi.*【海】(船)侧着前进; 舷边排炮齐射. ~**-spectrum** *a.* 【物】宽谱的. ~**sword** 大砍刀, 腰刀; 带腰刀的人. ~**tail** 中亚大尾绵羊〔羔羊〕; 中亚大尾绵羊羔皮. ~**way** *ad.* 横着, 侧向着. ~**wife**【美史】(以主人家的男奴为夫的)有夫女奴. ~**wise,** ~**way(s)** *ad.* 横着,宽面朝前地.

Broad [brɔːd] *n.* 布罗德〔姓氏〕.

broad·cast [ˈbrɔːdkɑːst] *a.* ①撒播的; 广泛散布的. ②【无】播音的,广播的. ~ *rumors* 流传广泛的谣言. *a ~ sower* 撒播机. *seed sown ~* 撒播的种子. *a ~ program(me)* 广播节目. — *n.* ①(种子的)撒播. ②无线电广播, 播音; 广播节目. ~ *band* 广播波段. ~ *relaying* 广播转播〔中继〕. *simultaneous ~* (各电台)联播. *today's ~ program* 今天的广播节目. — *vt.* (~ 或 *~ed*) ①【无】广播. ②散布, 乱传(消息等). ③撒播(种子). *The President will ~ his message on all stations tonight.* 总统今晚将向全国广播咨文. *She ~(ed) the gossip all over the town.* 她把这个流言传遍了全镇. — *vi.* ①【无】广播. ②在广播节目上讲话〔演出〕. ③散布消息〔谣言等〕. ~ **on** 用…波长广播.

broad·cast·er [ˈbrɔːdkɑːstə] *n.* ①撒种机,撒播物. ②【无】广播者; 广播电台; 广播装置; 广播协会.

broad·cast·ing [ˈbrɔːdˌkɑːstiŋ] *n.* ①广播,播音. ②广播业. *chain ~* 联播. *relayed ~* 转播. *sound-sight [television, visual] ~* 电视广播. *a ~ station* 广播电台. *a ~ studio* 播音室. *a career in ~* 从事广播工作. *binaural ~* 立体声广播. *~ transmitter* 广播发射机.

broad·en [ˈbrɔːdn] *vt.* 加宽, 放阔, 使扩大. *Reading and traveling ~ the mind.* 读书和旅行使人开阔心胸. — *vi.*

变宽，变阔.

broad·ly [ˈbrɔːdli] *ad.* ①广，宽. ②明白；露骨. ③粗鲁. ④用土腔. ~ ***speaking*** 总而言之，概括地说.

broad·ness [ˈbrɔːdnis] *n.* ①广阔，宽. ②尺面，门面，幅. ③明白. ④粗鲁.

Broad·way [ˈbrɔːdwei] *n.* ①百老汇大街〔美国纽约的繁华街道，剧院、夜总会等多设于此〕. ②纽约的娱乐〔戏剧〕业. — *a.* ①百老汇的. ②纽约娱乐〔戏剧〕业的. ③花哨的. *a* ~ *star* 纽约的戏剧明星.

Brob·ding·nag [ˈbrɔbdiŋnæg] *n.* 大人国〔出自英国作家斯维夫特 (Swift) 所著《格列佛游记》〕.

Brob·ding·nag·i·an [ˌbrɔbdiŋˈnægiən] *a.* 大人国的，巨大的. — *n.* ①大人国的居民. ②巨人.

bro·cade [brəˈkeid] *n.* 锦缎，花缎；织锦. *gold [silver]* ~ 织金〔银〕锦缎. — *vt.* 在(织物上)织出花纹；把(花纹)织入织物.

bro·cad·ed [brəˈkeidid] *a.* ①锦缎(一样)的. ②穿着锦缎的，用锦缎装饰的.

broc·a·telle, broc·a·tel [ˌbrɔkəˈtel] *n.* ①花缎；缎纹塔夫绸；凸花厚缎；织花被褥布. ②彩色大理石.

broc·(c)o·li [ˈbrɔkəli] *n.* 【植】(仅茎可食用的) 嫩茎硬花球，花椰菜，花茎甘蓝.

bro·ché [brəuˈʃei] *a.* 〔F.〕(织物)有提花图案的，有浮纹的. — *n.* 提花绸缎，浮纹织物，绒头花纹织物. ~ *quilts* 提花床单布.

bro·chette [brəuˈʃet] *n.* 烤肉小铁签子.

bro·chure [brəuˈʃjuə] *n.* 假钉本，小册子.

brock [brɔk] *n.* ①【动】獾. ②〔英方〕卑鄙的家伙，脏东西.

brock·et [ˈbrɔkit] *n.* 二岁雄鹿；〔南美〕短角小鹿.

bro·die [ˈbrəudi] *n.* 〔美俚〕〔有时作 B-〕①失败，失策，大错. ②(从桥上投水)自杀. *do a* ~ (投水)自杀.

bro·gan [ˈbrəugən] *n.* = brogue².

brög·ger·ite [ˈbrɔːgərait] *n.* 【矿】钍铀矿.

brogue¹ [brəug] *n.* 土腔，〔特指〕爱尔兰土腔.

brogue² [brəug] *n.* ①生皮翻毛皮鞋. ②低跟镂花牛皮鞋.

broi·der, broi·der·y [ˈbrɔidə,ˈbrɔidəri] 〔诗〕= embroider, embroidery.

broil¹ [brɔil] *n.* 吵闹，争辩；骚动. *a violent* ~ *over who was at fault* 在谁办错了事的问题上发生的激烈争吵. — *vi.* 大声争吵. **-er** *n.* 爱吵闹的人.

broil² [brɔil] *vt.* ①(用火)烤〔焙，炙〕(肉等). ②(太阳等)灼(人)，(暑热等)蒸人；使直接受到灼热. ~ *a steak* 烤牛排. *a* ~*ing sun* 赤日炎炎. — *vi.* ①烤〔焙、炙〕肉. ②被烤焦. ③(因恼怒、忧虑等)激动，焦躁不安. ~ *with anger* 气得七窍生烟. — *n.* ①烤，焙，炙；灼热. ②被焙烤之物；烤肉. *a beef* ~ 一客烤牛肉. **-er** *n.* ①烤肉师傅；烤肉器. ②(适合焙烤的)童子鸡. ③〔口〕酷暑，大热天.

bro·kage [ˈbrəukidʒ] *n.* = brokerage.

broke [brəuk] break 的过去式；〔古〕break 的过去分词. — *a.* 〔口〕破了产的；〔俚〕分文不名的，一个钱也没有的〔仅用作表语〕. ***be*** ~ ***to the wide [world]*** 〔口〕完全破产的，一个钱也没有的. ***be clean [dead, flat, stone, stony]*** ~ 〔口〕完全破产. ***go*** ~ 〔俚〕破产. ***go for*** ~ 〔俚〕竭力，全力以赴；耗尽全部财力. — *n.* 破纸；〔*pl.*〕(头部、腹部剪下的)劣等羊毛.

bro·ken [ˈbrəukən] break 的过去分词. — *a.* ①破裂的，打碎了的，弄坏了的；(腿、臂等)已骨折的. ②(地面等)起伏不平的，(天气)忽阴忽晴的. ③灰了心的，已失望的，沮丧的，唉声叹气的；(身体)变衰弱的；【植】(花)染上碎斑病的. ④破了产的，倒闭的；(家庭等)遭破坏的；(诺言等)被违背的. ⑤(语言等)拙劣的，不合标准〔语法〕的，乱七八糟的. ⑥(线条)虚线的，断续的；零碎的，七零八落的，拆散了的；被打断的. ⑦(马等)养驯了的，有训练的. ⑧(方向)不断改变的. ⑨〔口〕降了级的. ⑩【印】不足一令(500 张)的. *a* ~ *vase* 打碎的花瓶. *a* ~ *leg* 打断的腿骨. *The fox ran in a* ~ *line.* 狐狸跑的时候不断地改变方向. ~ *meat* 碎肉. *a* ~ *promise* 言而无信，违背诺言. *a* ~ *man* 心灰意懒的人. ~ *health* 垮掉的身体. *a well-*~ *horse* 极驯服的马. *a* ~ *circle* 虚线圆. ~ *sobs* 抽泣. *a few* ~ *words* 断断续续的几句话. ~ *water* 波浪起伏的水面. ~ *country* 起伏不平的田野. *a* ~ *firm* 一家破产的公司. *the* ~ *fortunes of his family* 家道中落. ~ **bone** 〔美〕出事受伤的人. ~ **clouds** 遮掉大半个天空的乌云. ~ **colour** (绘画的)点描法；复色，配合色. ~**-down** *a.* ①毁坏了的，已被捣毁的. ②(健康) 衰弱已极的，垮掉的. ③(企业等)败落了的；(人)毁掉的，堕落了的. ④(马)累得〔衰弱得〕不能动的；(机器等)临时出了故障的. ~**-ends** (纱线的)断头. ~ **English** 拙劣的英语，洋泾浜英语，不合语法〔标准〕的英语. ~ **ground** ①【军】起伏不平的地面，崎岖地. ②新开垦地. ~ **heart** 失意，失恋. ~**-hearted** *a.* ①极度失望的，痛心的；心碎的. ②失恋的，忧伤的. ~ **home** 破裂的家庭〔夫妇分居或离婚所造成的〕. ~ **line** ①虚线. ②【数】折线. ③(马路上的)车道线. ~ **lot** 【商】零星股〔一百股以下〕. ~ **lots** 〔美〕特价品. ~ **money** 零钱. ~ **numbers** 【数】分数，余数，小数. ~ **reed** 不可信赖的人〔事物〕. ~ **sleep** 断断续续的睡眠，时醒时睡，不时被吵醒〔打扰〕的睡眠. ~ **soldier** 残废的伤兵. ~ **tea** 散茶，碎茶，茶叶末. ~ **time** (因经常被打扰而变得)零零散散的工作时间. ~ **weather** 阴晴不定的天气. ~ **wind** 【兽医】(马的)喘气病. ~**-winded** *a.* (马)呼吸急促的，喘气的；呼吸器官有病的.

bro·ker [ˈbrəukə] *n.* ①(股票等的)经纪人，掮客；(买卖的)中间人，代理人. ②〔英〕旧货商人；当铺主；(经官方批准对债务人被扣押财物的)估价员〔出售人〕. ③〔口〕婚姻介绍人. *a street [curbstone]* ~ 〔美〕场外经纪人.

broker·age [ˈbrəukəridʒ] *n.* ①经纪业，掮客业. ②佣金，回扣，经手费(= brokage).

bro·king [ˈbrəukiŋ] *n.* 经纪业. — *a.* 经纪(业)的；掮客(业)的，中间人的.

brol·ly [ˈbrɔli] *n.* ①〔口〕洋伞. ②〔英俚〕降落伞.

bro·ma [ˈbrəumə] *n.* ①去油可可粉. ②去油可可(饮料). ③【医】固体食物.

bro·mal [ˈbrəuməl] *n.* 【化】溴醛；三溴乙醛.

bro·mate [ˈbrəumeit] *vt.* 使与溴化合，用溴处理. — *n.* 【化】溴酸盐.

brome [brəum] *n.* 【植】雀麦属植物 (= brome grass).

brome [bruːm] *n.* 布罗姆〔姓氏〕.

bro·me·li·ad [brəuˈmiliˌæd] *n.* 【植】凤梨科植物.

Brom·field [ˈbrɔmfiːld] *n.* 布罗姆菲尔德〔姓氏〕.

bro·mic [ˈbrəumik] *a.* 溴的，含溴的；【化】五价溴的. ~ *acid* 溴酸.

bro·mide [ˈbrəumaid] *n.* ①【化】溴化物；溴化物乳剂. ②〔美俚〕平庸可厌的人，喜欢讲陈词滥调的人；陈词滥调. *silver* ~ 溴化银. ~ **paper** 溴素纸；相片纸.

bro·mid·ic [brəuˈmidik] *a.* ①平庸的，陈腐的；陈词滥调的. ②(人)总是讲陈词滥调的.

bro·mi·nate [ˈbrəumiˌneit] *vt.* 【化】溴化；溴化处理. **-nation** *n.*

bro·mine [ˈbrəumiːn] *n.* 【化】溴〔略作 Br.〕.

bro·mism [ˈbrəumizəm] *n.* 【医】溴中毒.

bro·mize [ˈbrəumaiz] *vt.* 【化】溴代；溴化(作用). **-zation** *n.*

bro·mo·selt·zer [ˈbrəuməuˌseltsə] 溴塞尔泽〔成药，一种治头痛的泡腾盐〕.

bro·my·rite [ˈbrəumirait] *n.* 【矿】溴银矿.

bronc [brɔŋk] *n.* = bronc(h)o.

bron·chi [ˈbrɔŋkai] *n.* bronchus 的复数.

bron·chi·al, bron·chic [ˈbrɔŋkiəl, ˈbrɔŋkik] *a.* 【解】支气管的. ~ **tubes** 支气管.

bron·chi·ole [ˈbrɔŋkiˌəul] *n.* 【解】细支气管.

bron·chi·tis [brɔŋ'kaitis] *n.* 【医】支气管炎. **-chi·tic** *a.*

bronch(o)- *comb. f.* 支气管: *broncho*scope.

bron·cho·cele ['brɔŋkəusi:l] *n.* 【医】支气管肥大;甲状腺肥大〔囊状肿〕.

bron·cho·pneu·mo·nia ['brɔŋkəunju:'məunjə] *n.* 【医】支气管肺炎.

bron·cho·scope ['brɔŋkəskəup] *n.* 【医】支气管窥镜.

bron·c(h)o ['brɔŋkəu] *n.* ①〔美〕(北美西部平原的)半野生的马. ②〔Can.〕英国人〔尤指英国移民〕.

bron·c(h)o·buster ['brɔŋkəuˌbʌstə] *n.* 驯马师,(美国西部的)驯马牧童,牛仔.

bron·chus ['brɔŋkəs] *n.* (*pl.* ***bron·chi*** ['brɔŋkai])【解】支气管,细支气管.

Bron·të ['brɔnti] *n.* ①布朗蒂〔姓氏〕. ②英国小说家三姐妹:〔**Anne** ～ (1820—1849),《阿格奈斯·格雷》的作者; **Charlotte** ～ (1816—1855),《简·爱》的作者; **Emily Jane** ～ (1818—1848),《呼啸山庄》的作者〕.

bron·tides ['brɔntaidz] *n.* 【地】(轻微地震引起的)短暂的震声.

bron·to·saur ['brɔntəˌsɔ:], **bron·to·saur·us** [ˌbrɔntə'sɔ:rəs] *n.* 【古生】雷龙.

Bronx [brɔŋks] *n.* ①〔the ～〕布朗克斯区〔美国纽约市一区名〕. ②布朗克斯鸡尾酒. ～ **cheer** 〔美口〕(表示嘲笑厌恶等的)嘘嘘声. ～ **vanilla** 〔美〕大蒜.

bronze [brɔnz] *n.* ①青铜,古铜. ②青铜制品;青铜艺术品;(半身)铜像;〔古〕青铜币. ③青铜色(颜料). *gear* ～ 齿轮[磷]青铜. *gun* ～ 炮铜. ～ *mica* 金云母. *a statue in* ～ 青铜像. ～*s and ivories* 青铜和象牙艺术品. — *vt.* ①在…上镀青铜;上青铜色于. ②使硬得象古铜. ③〔古〕使变冷酷. *The sun* ～*d his face.* 太阳把他的脸晒成古铜色. — *vi.* 变成青铜色;(皮肤)晒黑. — *a.* 青铜色的;青铜制的;青铜器的. **B- Age** ①青铜器时代. ②【希神】(人类的)青铜时代,战乱蜂起的时代. ～ **medal** 铜牌〔通常奖给比赛优胜的第三名〕. **B- Star Medal** 【美军】殊勋勋章〔不包括空战战功〕. **-d** *a.* 镀青铜的;青铜色的;晒黑的.

bronz·ite ['brɔnzait] *n.* 【矿】古铜辉石.

bronz·y ['brɔnzi] *a.* 青铜一样的;青铜色的,黄褐色的.

brooch [brəutʃ] *n.* 饰针,胸针.

brood [bru:d] *n.* ①(鸡雏等的)一窝;同窝幼雏;幼蜂;(昆虫等)一次产出的卵;(动物)一次下的崽. ②(动物的)种,属,群;种族;〔蔑〕(一家的)孩子们;同伙,同党,同胞;(事物的)一组. ～ *box* (蜂的)育卵箱,子箱. *a* ～ *of chickens* 一窝鸡雏. *a* ～ *of modern paintings* 一组现代画. — *vt.* ①孵(蛋),孵出. ②(鸟、母鸡等)用翅膀护(幼雏、小鸡等). ③盘算,仔细考虑. *He* ～*ed the problem.* 他仔细考虑这个问题. — *vi.* ①孵卵,伏窝般地静坐. ②焦急地考虑,郁闷地想 (*over; on*). ③(云、雾、忧愁等)低覆,笼罩 (*over; on*). ～*ing twilight* 苍茫的暮色. *a* ～*ing hate* 日益郁结的仇恨. ～ ***above [over]*** ①俯视. ②笼罩 (*The house on the hill* ～*ed above the village.* 山上的那间房子俯视着村庄. *Hate* ～*ed over the town.* 仇恨的情绪笼罩着全镇). ～ ***over [on]*** 焦急地考虑,郁闷地沉思 (～ *on one's difficulties* 焦急地考虑所处的困境). — *a.* ①传种用的,繁殖用的. ②(母鸡等)抱窝的;(昆虫等)产卵的. *a* ～ *mare* 传种母马. *a* ～ *hen* 抱窝的母鸡. ～ **body** 【生】繁殖体. ～ **cell** 【生】芽孢. ～ **gemma** 【生】芽孢体.

brooder ['bru:də] *n.* ①育雏器,孵卵器.(育雏的)炕坊. ②沉思的人. ③育雏的人,炕坊师傅;孵卵的鸡〔鸟,动物〕.

brood·y ['bru:di] *a.* ①要孵卵的,爱伏窝的;繁殖力强的. ②郁郁不乐的,沉闷的. *a* ～ *hen* 爱伏窝的母鸡.

brook[1] [bruk] *n.* 溪流,小河. **-like** *a.* 小溪般的.

brook[2] [bruk] *vt.* 忍,耐,捱,容忍,忍受〔用于否定结构〕. *A great man cannot* ～ *a rival.* 两雄不并立,一山难容两虎. *It* ～*s no delay.* 事情不容延误〔刻不容缓〕.

Brook(e) [bruk] *n.* 布鲁克〔姓氏〕.

brook·ite ['brukait] *n.* 【矿】板钛矿.

brook·let ['bruklit] *n.* 细流,小溪.

brook·lime ['bruklaim] *n.* 【植】(玄参科的)婆婆纳.

Brook·lyn ['bruklin] *n.* 布鲁克林区〔美国纽约市的一区,在长岛西部〕. **-ese** 布鲁克林腔〔布鲁克林区的人特有的语言风格〕.

Brooks [bruks] *n.* 布鲁克斯〔姓氏,男子名〕.

broom [bru:m] *n.* ①帚,扫帚. ②【无】自动搜索干扰振荡器. ③【植】金雀花,金雀花属植物. —*vt.* 扫除,用扫帚扫. ***New*** ～***s sweep clean.*** 〔谚〕新官上任三把火,新到职者办事热心认真. ～**corn** 【植】高粱〔可用来做扫帚〕. ～**pine** 【植】大王松. ～**rape** 【植】肉苁蓉. ～**-stick** 扫帚把 (*a witch on a* ～*stick* 乘扫帚柄飞行于空中的女巫〔一种民间传说〕. *a* ～*stick skirt* 〔美〕帚花裙〔西南部印第安人穿的一种服装〕. *marry [jump] over a* ～*stick [broom staff]* 做露水夫妻,野合).

broom·y ['bru:mi] *a.* ①扫帚的,帚状的. ②金雀花的,金雀花多的.

Bros. = brothers: *Smith Bros. & Co.* 史密斯兄弟公司.

brose [brəuz] *n.* 〔英〕麦片粥.

broth [brɔ(:)θ] *n.* (*pl.* ～*s* [brɔ(:)θs, brɔ:ðz]) 肉汁;肉汤;清汤;培养基. *chicken* ～ 鸡汤. *a* ～ *of a boy* 〔爱尔兰〕好汉,男子汉,好男儿.

broth·el ['brɔθl] *n.* 妓院,窑子.

broth·er ['brʌðə] *n.* (*pl.* ～*s*,〔古〕***breth·ren*** ['breðrin]) ①兄弟,同胞. ②〔*pl.* 多用 brethren〕同事,同僚,同业,社友,同志,会友. ③王兄〔帝王间相互的呼称〕. ④〔美国黑人用法〕黑人兄弟 (= soul brother);〔泛指〕(任何)黑人. ⑤〔口〕老兄. ⑥(不准备接受圣职的)男修士,不出家的修士. *an elder* ～ 兄,哥哥. *a younger* ～ 弟弟. *one's bigger [little]* ～ 兄[弟]. *a whole [full]* ～ 同父母弟兄. *a half* ～ 异父[异母]弟兄. *the* ～*s Smith, the Smith* ～*s* 史密斯兄弟们. *Smith B-s* 史密斯兄弟公司〔商店〕. *professional brethren* (医生等的)同行. *a fraternity* ～ 会友. ～*s in the trade* 同业. *a lay* ～ 不出家的修士. *All men are* ～*s.* 四海之内皆兄弟也. *a band of* ～*s* (利害关系相共的)一团体. *B-, can you spare a dime?* 老兄,能借给我一角钱吗? ～ ***of the brush*** 画工,油漆匠. ***Brothers of the Coast*** (16—17 世纪加勒比海的)海盗. ～ ***of quill*** (古代)著作家. ～ ***of the whip*** 马车夫,驭者. — *vt.* 和…结成弟兄,对…以兄弟相待,视…如兄弟. — *inter.* 真要命〔对别人厚脸皮的行为等表示厌恶、惊讶等〕; ～**-german** 同父母兄弟. ～**-in-arms** 战友. ～**-in-law** (*pl.* ～**s-in-law**) ①姐夫,妹夫. ②内兄,内弟. ③大伯,小叔. ④连襟〔广义用法〕. **B- Jonathan** 〔英〕①美国政府,美国. ②(典型的)美国人〔此为旧日用语,现在叫 Uncle Sam〕. ～ **officer** 袍泽,军官同僚. ～**-uterine** 同母异父兄弟. **-hood** *n.* ①兄弟关系,手足之亲,同胞. ②同事,会友;同业,同行. ③社,会,协会,公会;团体;会友;〔美〕兄弟会〔美国工会名称、大指铁路工会〕. ④四海一家,人类情谊 (*universal* ～ 四海同胞. *international* ～ 国际亲善).

broth·er·ly ['brʌðəli] *a.* 弟兄的,亲弟兄似的,友情深厚的. ～ *love* 手足之情. *in a most* ～ *manner* 态度极友善地. — *ad.* 〔古〕兄弟一样地;亲密地. **-li·ness** *n.* 弟兄之谊,友情,友爱,亲切.

brough·am ['bru(:)əm] *n.* ①四轮轿式马车. ②〔废〕布鲁姆式汽车.

brought [brɔ:t] bring 的过去式及过去分词.

brou·ha·ha [bru:'hɑ:ˌhɑ:] *n.* 〔F.〕①骚动,吵闹,暴动〔由较大事件引起的〕. ②喧嚣,嘈杂,起哄〔由较小事件引起〕.

brow [brau] *n.* ①〔常 *pl.*〕眉,眉毛. ②额. ③容貌;表情. ④悬岩;岩顶,山顶,坡顶;陡坡. ⑤〔口〕智力水平. ⑥【海】跳板. *bend [knit] one's* ～*s* 蹙眉,皱眉头. *the* *heavy ~s* 浓眉. *raise one's ~s* 扬眉. *by the sweat of one's ~s* 额头冒汗. *His ~ darkened.* 他沉下脸来. *She looked down over the ~ of the hill.* 她从山顶上望下去. ~ **ache** 偏头痛. ~ **tine** 眉叉〔鹿角〕. **-ed** *a.* 眉毛…的〔用以构成复合词〕(*dark-browed* 浓眉的).

brow·a·gue [ˈbraueigjuː] *n.*【医】偏头痛, 额部神经痛 (= brow ache).

brow·beat [ˈbraubiːt] *vt.* (~; *~en* [ˈbraubiːtn]) 吓, 威吓, 威逼; 对…扬眉怒目. *She ~ed him into agreeing.* 她威逼他同意自己的意见.

Brown [braun] *n.* 布朗(姓氏). *~, Jones, and Robinson* 张三李四, 普通人 (= *Tom, Dick, and Harry*).

brown [braun] *a.* ①褐色的, 棕色的. ②阴郁的. ③晒黑了的. ~ *shoes* 棕色鞋. — *n.* ①褐色, 棕色, 茶色. ②褐色颜料〔染料〕. ③黑皮肤的人. ④〔英俚〕铜币. ⑤〔the ~〕鸟群〔指飞行中黑鸦鸦一片的鸟群〕. *chestnut ~* 栗色. *Spanish ~* 羊肝色. *do ~* ①把(面包)烤成褐色. ②〔卑〕欺骗, 使…上当. *do it up ~* ①〔口〕彻底做好(某事), 把(事情)干得漂亮, 很好地完成. ②把(面包)烘焦. ***fire into the ~*** ①射击鸟群. ②〔喻〕向机群开炮〔发射火箭〕. ***in a ~ study*** ①沉思默想. ②幻想, 空想. — *vt.* ①上褐色于, 把…染成褐色. ②烘焦. ③晒黑. ④(向鸟群等)胡乱射击. *~ the onion* 把洋葱烘焦. — *vi.* ①变成褐色. ②(皮肤)晒黑. *~ off* 〔美俚〕出大错. ~ *out* 〔美〕使(灯光)暗淡〔为了防空或节约用电等〕. ~**-bag** *vt., vi.* ①自带牛皮纸袋(装饭食). ②自带牛皮纸袋(装一瓶酒去不售酒的饭店或俱乐部). ~ **belt** ①褐带〔三段柔道家佩戴的标志〕. ②褐带高手(指柔道家). **B- Beret** ①褐色贝雷帽. ②美籍墨西哥人争取自身权利的组织. ~ **betty** 苹果面包屑布丁〔亦作 B- Betty〕. ~ **bread** 黑面包. ~ **coal** 褐煤. ~**ed-off** *a.* ①厌烦透了的, 感到无聊的. ②不满的. ~ **fat** 棕色脂肪〔冬眠动物体内的生热脂肪〕. **B-George** 褐色大水缸. ~ **haematite [iron ore]**【矿】褐铁矿. ~ **goods** 褐色商品〔指收音机、电视机等电子产品, 因其外壳多漆成茶褐色〕. ~ **lace** 原色花边. ~**nose** 〔美〕① *vt.* 拍…的马屁. ② *vi.* 拍马屁, 献媚. ~**out** *n.* ①灯火〔部分〕管制; 节电. ②灯光暗淡; 电压不足. ~ **paper** 褐色打包纸, 牛皮纸. ~ **polish** 〔美〕黑白混血儿. **B- Power** "褐色权力"〔美籍墨西哥人提出的争取权利的口号〕. ~ **rice** 糙米. ~ **shirt** 〔常作 B- S-〕(纳粹德国)褐衫党党员; 纳粹党党员. ~**stone** ① *n.* 褐色沙石, 褐色沙石建筑物. ② *a.* 生活富裕的 (*~ district* 〔美〕高级住宅区). ~ **sugar** 红糖;【化】黄糖. ~ **ware** 陶器. **-ish, -y** *a.* 带褐色的. **-ness** *n.*

Brown(e) [braun] *n.* 布朗〔姓氏〕.

brown·ie [ˈbrauni] *n.* ①〔Scot.〕棕仙〔传说中夜间来帮助农家做家务事的仙童〕. ②(8—11岁的)幼年女童子军; 〔美〕小孩子. ③布朗尼照相机; 〔俚〕轻便雷达装置. ④〔美〕巧克力小方饼.

Brown·ing [ˈbrauniŋ] *n.* 布朗宁〔姓氏〕. ~ **automatic rifle** 〔美〕布朗宁自动步枪. ~ **machine gun** 〔美〕布朗宁机枪.

browse [brauz] *n.* ①(牲畜吃的)嫩草, 嫩叶, 嫩枝, 嫩芽. ②(牲畜的)吃嫩枝〔草等〕, 放牧. *the cattle at ~* 正在吃草的牛. — *vt.* ①(牲畜)吃(嫩枝, 草等). ②放牧. ③浏览(书刊), 随便翻阅(书刊). *a cow ~ing thistles* 正在吃蓟草的牛. *The deer are ~ing the hillside.* 鹿在吃山边的草. *~ cattle on twigs* 让牛吃嫩枝. *He is ~ing the shelves for something to read.* 他在书架上翻找可读的书. — *vi.* ①(牲畜)吃草; 吃(*on*). ②浏览, 翻阅. *~ on shoots* (牲畜)吃嫩芽. *~ through the newspaper* 浏览一下报纸. *~ about [around, among] the second-hand bookshops.* 逛旧书店. *~**ing by game*** (牧草地等的)兽害〔如野兔等的破坏牧草地〕. **browsing room** 图书浏览室.

Br.P. = British Patent 英国专利.

B.R.R.A. = British Rayon Research Association 英国人造丝研究会.

brt. for. = brought forward 结转, 转下.

Bruce [bruːs] *n.* 布鲁斯〔姓氏, 男子名〕.

bru·cel·lo·sis [ˌbruːsəˈləusis] *n.*【医】布鲁士菌病, 地中海热, 马耳他热 (= Malta fever).

bru·cine [ˈbruːsi(ː)n] *n.* 番木鳖碱; 二甲氧基马钱子碱.

Bru·in [ˈbru(ː)in] *n.* ①熊先生〔著名童话《列那狐的故事》中的拟人动物〕. ②〔b-〕熊〔尤指褐熊〕.

bruise [bruːz] *vt.* ①撞伤, 打伤(人), 使成瘀伤〔暗伤〕; 碰伤, 擦伤(水果、植物等). ②〔喻〕损害(感情). ③舂碎; 捣烂, 研碎. ④在(木料、金属等)上造成凹痕. ⑤〔古〕使成残废; 殴打, 争斗. *~ apples* 碰伤苹果. *She ~d herself against the car.* 她碰到车子上撞伤了. *~ sb.'s feeling* 伤害了某人的感情. — *vi.* ①撞伤, 碰伤, 擦伤; 变青肿, 产生瘀伤. ②(感情)受到损害. ③【猎】骑马瞎冲乱跑. *Peaches ~ easily.* 桃子容易碰伤. *Her feelings ~ easily.* 她很容易动气. — *n.* ①(人体、水果、植物等因碰撞, 跌压等造成的)伤痕, 青肿, 擦伤. ②(感情受到的)伤害. *cuts and ~s* 刀剑伤和跌打伤.

bruiser [ˈbruːzə] *n.* ①爱斗殴的人. ②职业拳击家. ③〔美口〕彪形大汉. ④捣碎机, 压碎〔扁〕机. ⑤骑马瞎冲的人.

bruit [bruːt] *n.* ①【医】(心)杂音, (听诊器听出的)异常音. ②〔古〕谣言, 传闻. ③〔古〕喧声, 吵嚷. — *vt.* 〔古〕〔美〕传播, 散布(谣言等) (*about; abroad*). *It is ~ed that* …谣传说…. *The report was ~ed through the village.* 消息传遍了全村.

Brum [bruːm] *n.* 〔英口〕伯明翰 (= Birmingham)〔英国城市〕. **-mie** 伯明翰人.

Bru·maire [bruːˈmɛə] *n.* 〔F.〕雾月〔法兰西共和历的第二月, 相当于公历10月22—23日至11月21—23日〕.

bru·mal [ˈbruːməl] *a.* 〔古〕冬季的; 冬天似的.

brum·by [ˈbrʌmbi] *n.* 〔澳俚〕野马.

brume [bruːm] *n.* 雾, 霭.

Brum·ma·gem [ˈbrʌmədʒəm] *a.* 〔口〕①(珠宝、钱币等)假的, 冒充的. ②(装饰品等)花哨而便宜的. — *n.* 便宜货; 假珠〔从擅长制造假珠宝等的城市 Birmingham 的转讹〕.

bru·mous [ˈbruːməs] *a.* 冬季的.

brunch [brʌntʃ] *n.* 〔俚〕(早点与午餐并作一顿吃的)晚早餐, 早中饭〔**br**(eakfast) + (l)**unch**〕. ~ **coat** (女用)长围裙.

Bru·nei [ˈbruːnai] *n.* ①文莱〔亚洲〕. ②文莱〔文莱首府〕.

bru·net [bruːˈnet] *a.* (白种人中男子)浅黑型的. — *n.* 浅黑型的男子.

bru·nette [bruːˈnet] — *a.* (白种人中女子)浅黑型的. — *n.* 浅黑型的女子.

bru·ni·zem [ˈbruːniˌzem] *n.* 黑(钙)土.

Bru·no [ˈbruːnəu] *n.* ①布鲁诺〔男子名〕. ② **Giordano** ~ 乔丹诺·布鲁诺〔1548?—1600, 意大利哲学家, 为维护太阳中心说被宗教法庭烧死〕.

Bruns·wick [ˈbrʌnzwik] *n.* ①不伦瑞克〔德国原中部州名, 市名〕. ②布伦斯威克〔澳、美、新西兰地名〕. ~ **black** 一种黑色清漆. ~ **line** 汉诺威王室世系 (= the House of Hanover).

brunt [brʌnt] *n.* ①(来自攻击一方的)主要力量〔冲势, 压力〕. ②〔废〕袭击, 突击, 强攻. *His arm took the ~ of the blow.* 他的手臂承受了狠狠的一击. *She had to bear the ~ of the criticisms.* 她不得不承当批评的压力. *These exhausted men carried the ~ of the war.* 这些疲倦的士兵承受了战场上的主要压力. ***bear the ~*** 首当其冲, 承担主要压力.

brush[1] [brʌʃ] *n.* ①刷子, 毛刷; 刷状物;【电】电刷; 刷形放电 (= ~ discharge). ②画笔, 毛笔; 绘画风格, 画法; 画家. ③(作帜饰的)羽毛; (动物)粗大的尾巴; 狐尾

〔犹指作打猎纪念保存的狐尾〕. ④【植】冠毛. ⑤(一)刷,擦,轻触,擦过. ⑥〔美〕小冲突,遭遇战,激烈的小战斗. ⑦(骑马)疾驰. ⑧〔美俚〕悍然拒绝. ⑨〔澳、新西兰俚〕姑娘,年轻女人. *Give your hat another* ~. 再把你的帽子刷一刷[擦一擦]. *a paint* ~ 画笔. *a laundry* ~ (洗衣) 板刷. *a writing* ~ 毛笔. *get a* ~ *from (sth.)* 被(某物) 擦了一下. *the* ~ *of Manet* 曼纳特的画风. *have a* ~ *with* …和…发生小冲突. *a narrow* ~ *with death* 差点送命. ***at a*** ~ 一举. ***at a [the] first*** ~ ①在最初的小冲突中. ②最初,首先,一开头; 立刻. ***be tarred with the same*** ~ 一丘之貉, 一路货色. ***give sb. the [a]*** ~ 把某人打发掉,不理睬某人. ***the*** ~ ①画家. ②画法, 绘画风格. — *vt.* ① (用刷子) 刷, 擦, 掸, 拂; 擦掉. ②轻擦, 轻触. ~ *the dirt off his coat* 刷去衣服上的尘土. *His lips* ~*ed her ear*. 他用嘴唇轻轻地碰了一下她的耳朵. — *vi.* ①擦过, 掠过 *(against, by, past, through)*. ②飞跑, 急奔. ③刷牙; 刷头发. *B- after meal*. 饭后刷牙. *He* ~*ed by without noticing me*. 他飞跑过去,没有注意到我. ~ ***aside*** ①刷去; 扫除. ②无视,不顾,漠视 (*Our complaints were simply* ~*ed aside*. 我们的意见根本没有被理睬). ~ ***away*** ①刷去,擦去. ②= ~ aside. ~ ***down*** 刷下来. ~ ***off*** ①刷去. ②〔美俚〕不客气地拒绝,打发走; 摒弃. ③〔美俚〕跑脱,逃掉. ④〔美俚〕走开〔常用于祈使句〕. ~ ***over*** ①轻轻上色. ②用刷子刷; 擦过. ③〔美口〕浅耕. ~ ***round*** 〔美俚〕活动一下(身体). ~ ***up (on)*** ①刷光,擦亮; 把…打扮整洁. ②重新学习,重温,复习. ③提高(技巧等),使完善 (*I must* ~ *up on my French*. 我得把法语复习一下. ~ *up one's acquaintance with another* 与人重温旧交). ~ ***up against*** 轻轻接触. ~ **ability** (画家) 运笔自如. ~ **burn** 擦伤. ~ **cut** 男子刷形发型. ~ **discharge** 【电】刷形放电,电晕放电. ~**-off** 〔美俚〕拒绝; 打发走, 断然解雇(免职), 摒弃 (*give sb. the* ~*-off* 把某人打发走, 根本不睬某人). ~ **pencil** 图画笔. ~**-stroke** ①刷子[画笔等]的一挥. ②绘画技巧. ~**-up** ①刷光,擦亮; 打扮. ②复习; 学好,练好. ③提高,改进,润色 (*have a wash and* ~*-up*. 梳洗打扮. *He gave his Spanish a* ~*-up*. 他温习了一下西班牙语). ~ **wheel** 【机】刷轮,刷车. ~**work** ①绘画. ②画风.

brush[2] [brʌʃ] *n.* ①灌木丛,杂木林. ②柴. ③〔the ~〕〔美〕尚未开拓的土地; 地广人稀的林区. ~ **fire** 灌木丛的火灾〔有别于森林大火〕. ~**-fire** *a.* 灌木林火式的, 局部的,小规模的. ~**fire war** *n.* 小规模[局部地区]的战争,灌木林火(式战争). ~**wood** ①砍下的树枝. ②密集的小树丛.

brushed [brʌʃt] *a.* (织物) 拉绒的. ~ *fabrics* 拉绒织物. ~ *goods* 拉绒针织品.

brush·ing [ˈbrʌʃiŋ] *a.* 飞跑过去的, 一闪而过的. — *n.* ①刷光,擦亮. ②刷布; 拉绒. ③〔*pl.*〕扫[刷]拢来的东西.

brush·y [ˈbrʌʃi] *a.* 矮林多的; 毛刷一样的; 毛厚的.

brusque, brusk [brusk] *a.* 粗暴的, 无礼的, 唐突的. *a* ~ *refusal* 粗暴地拒绝. **-ly** *ad.* **-ness** *n.*

brus·que·rie [ˌbru:skəˈri:] *n.* 〔F.〕粗暴,无礼,唐突.

Brus·sels [ˈbrʌslz] *n.* 布鲁塞尔〔比利时首都〕. ~ **carpet** 布鲁塞尔毛圈地毯. ~ **lace** 布鲁塞尔枕结花边; 机织花边. ~ **sprouts** (可食用的)球芽甘蓝.

brut [bryt] *a.* 〔F.〕(香槟酒)未加糖和香料的.

bru·tal [ˈbru:tl] *a.* ①兽(一样)的,兽性的,肉欲的; 残忍的; 不讲理的,粗暴的. ②〔俚〕讨厌的; (天气等)令人不愉快的. ~ *nature* 兽性. ~ *treatment* 野蛮拷打. ~ *weather* 恶劣的气候. *a* ~ *brodie* 〔美〕严重错误. **-ly** *ad.*

bru·tal·ism [ˈbru:təlizəm] *n.* ①兽行,残忍. ②〔美〕野兽派艺术〔尤指建筑方面使用夸张和畸形以造成效果的艺术风格〕. **-ist** *n., a.* 野兽派艺术家(的).

bru·tal·i·ty [bru(:)ˈtæliti] *n.* 兽性; 残忍; 蛮横.

bru·tal·ize [ˈbru:təlaiz] *vt.* ①把…弄成野兽一般; 使变残忍. ②把…当禽兽看待. *troops* ~*d by years of warfare* 因连年征战而变得野蛮了的士兵. *an accord not to* ~ *prisoners of war* 一项不得虐待战俘的协议. — *vi.* 变成野兽一样; 变残忍,变凶猛. **-i·za·tion** *n.*

brute [bru:t] *n.* ①动物,兽,畜生. ②人面兽心的人,残暴的人. ③〔the ~〕兽性,劣根性. ④〔口〕可恶的东西〔人〕. *a* ~ *of a husband* 残横的丈夫. *heartless* ~ 没心肝的畜生. *the* ~ *in him* 他身上的兽性. — *a.* ①畜生的,动物的. ②粗暴的,残忍的,凶恶的; 蛮横的. ③无感觉的,无理性的,盲目的; 无生物的. *the* ~ *creation* 兽类,畜生. *a* ~ *courage* 蛮勇,匹夫之勇. ~ *force [violence]* 暴力. ~ *matter* 非生物. ~ *powers of nature* 盲目的自然力. *a* ~ *struggle* 〔美〕拳击比赛. **the ~s** 兽类,畜生. **-hood** *n.* 兽性的特点.

bru·ti·fy [ˈbru:tifai] *vt., vi.* = brutalize.

brut·ish [ˈbru:tiʃ] *a.* ①兽的,畜生般的. ②粗暴的,残忍的; 野蛮的,肉欲的. ③粗鲁的,愚钝的. ~ *appetite* 兽欲. **-ly** *ad.* **-ness** *n.*

bru·tum ful·men [ˈbru:təm ˈfʌlmen] 〔L.〕吓唬,空口威胁,虚张声势.

Bry·an [ˈbraiən] *n.* 布赖恩〔姓氏,男子名〕.

Bry·ant [ˈbraiənt] *n.* 布赖恩特〔姓氏〕.

Bryce [brais] *n.* 布赖斯〔姓氏,男子名〕.

bry·ol·o·gy [braiˈɔlədʒi] *n.* 苔藓植物学.

bry·o·ny [ˈbraiəni] *n.* 【植】泻根草;【药】泻根〔吐剂或泻剂〕.

bry·o·phyte [ˈbraiəˌfait] *n.* 藓苔植物. **-phyt·ic** [-ˈfitik] *a.*

bry·o·zo·an [ˌbraiəˈzəuən] *n.* 藓苔虫 (= ectoproct).

Bryth·on [ˈbriθən] *n.* ①布立吞人〔从前居住在不列颠的凯尔特人〕. ②讲布立吞语的人.

Bry·thon·ic [briˈθɔnik] *a.* 布立吞人的; 布立吞语的. — *n.* (印欧语系的)布立吞语支.

BS, B.S. = ① Bachelor of Science 理学士. ② balance sheet 资产负债表. ③ British Standard 英国(工业)规格,英国(工业)标准.

b.s. = ① balance sheet 资产负债表. ②bill of sale 卖契.

B/S = bill of sale 卖契.

BSA = ①Birmingham Small Arms 〔英〕伯明翰轻武器公司. ②Boy Scouts of America 美国童子军.

B.Sc., B Sc = Bachelor of Science 理学士.

B-school [ˈbi:ˌsku:l] *n.* 〔口〕商业学校 (= business school). **-er** 商业学校学生.

B-station [ˈbi: ˈsteiʃən] 船上的无线电台.

Btu, B.t.u. = British thermal unit(s) 英国热单位.

bu. = ① bureau. ② bushel(s).

bub [bʌb] *n.* 〔美俚〕小兄弟, 小伙子〔对部下,晚辈称呼用〕.

bu·bal(e) [ˈbju:bəl], **bu·ba·lis** [ˈbju:bəlis] *n.* (北非)大羚羊.

bu·ba·line [ˈbju:bəlain] *a.* ①羚羊属的. ②野牛的,野牛状的.

bub·ble [bʌbl] *n.* ①泡,水泡; 气泡; 泡沫. ②幻想, 安想,泡影; 欺诈性的投机事业. ③冒泡,起泡,沸腾(声). ④泡泡发型. *soup* ~*s* 肥皂泡. ~*s in glass* 玻璃中的气泡. *the Florida real-estate* ~. 骗人的佛罗里达不动产投机公司. ***blow*** ~***s*** ①吹肥皂泡. ②空谈,空想. ~ ***and squeak*** 肉菜捲心菜〔有时加土豆等〕. ***prick a***~ 戳穿西洋镜,揭破真面目. ***South Sea B-*** 【史】南海泡影〔十八世纪初英国一些人组织南海公司声称在南美进行开拓活动的大骗局〕. — *vt.* ①使冒泡. ②滔滔不绝地讲(话). ③〔古〕骗, 欺哄. *He* ~*d the good news*. 他不停嘴地报告好消息. — *vi.* ①起泡,冒泡; 沸腾; 沸沸地响; (泉等)涌. ②(水)汩汩地流; 发噗噗声; (莺)啭; (人)格格地笑. ③兴奋, 欢闹. *The tea* ~*d in the* *pot.* 壶里的茶开了. *a bubbling stream* 汩汩流过的小溪. *The play ~d with songs and dances.* 这出戏载歌载舞,非常热闹. *Nationalism has been bubbling here.* 这里一直激荡着民族主义情绪. ~ ***out*** 勃突勃突地涌出. ~ ***off*** 形成气泡溢出. ~ ***over*** ①冒泡漫出,煮沸溢出 *(over)*. ②兴奋,欢闹. *She is bubbling over with enthusiasm.* 她情绪炽烈,激动不已. ~ ***up*** 冒泡,发出气泡. ~***with laughter [wrath]*** 哄堂大笑[怒气冲冲]. ~ **bath** ①(使浴水起泡的)芳香泡沫剂. ②(使用泡沫剂的)泡沫浴. ~ **car** 微型汽车. ~ **chamber**【原】泡沫室. ~ **company** 为行骗而虚设的公司. ~ **dance** 气球(虚掩的裸体)舞. ~ **gum** ①可吹成泡泡的口香糖. ②以青少年为主要对象的一种摇摆乐. ~**head**〔美俚〕笨蛋. ~-**top** ①(车后部的)透明防弹窗;透明防弹罩. ②圆顶透明伞.

bub·bler [ˈbʌblə] *n.* ①喷水式饮水口. ②【化】起泡器,扩散器;水浴瓶.

bub·bly [ˈbʌbli] *a.* 泡多的;发泡的. — *n.*〔英俚〕香槟酒. ~-**jock** *n.*〔Scot.〕雄火鸡.

bub·by[1] [ˈbʌbi] *n.*〔美〕= bub.

bub·by[2] *n.*〔俚〕女性的胸脯,乳房,奶子.

bu·bo [ˈbjuːbəu] *n.*【医】腹股沟腺炎.

bu·bonic [bju(ː)ˈbɔnik] *a.* 腹股沟腺炎性的. ~ **plague** 淋巴腺鼠疫.

bu·bon·o·cele [bju(ː)ˈbɔnəsiːl] *n.*【医】腹股沟不全疝.

buc·cal [ˈbʌkəl] *a.*【解】口的;颊的. *the ~ cavity* 口腔. *~ division* 口部;颊部.

buc·ca·neer [ˌbʌkəˈniə] *n.* ①海盗. ②无所顾忌的冒险家〔尤指在政治和商业方面〕. — *vi.* ①做海盗. ②从事(政治、商业等的)冒险活动. **-ish** *a.* 海盗似的.

buc·ci·na·tor [ˈbʌksineitə] *n.*【解】颊肌.

bu·cen·taur [bjuˈsentɔː] *n.* ①(神话中的)半牛半人形怪物. ②半牛半人形的船.

Bu·ceph·a·lus [bju(ː)ˈsefələs] *n.* ①亚历山大大帝的爱马. ②〔b-〕〔古〕马;悍马;〔谑〕乘用马.

Bu·cha·rest [ˈbjuːkərest] *n.* 布加勒斯特〔罗马尼亚首都〕.

Buch·en·wald [ˈbukənwɔːld; G. ˈbuːxənvalt] *n.* 布痕瓦尔德〔德意志民主共和国市镇,1934—45年德国法西斯曾在此设立集中营,残酷屠杀爱国者和战俘〕.

buck[1] [bʌk] *n.* *(pl. ~,~s)* ①雄鹿;公羊;公兔;雄鱼. ②〔南非〕羚羊;〔美〕公羊毛. ③纨绔子,花花公子;横冲直撞的年轻人. ④〔美俚,蔑〕男黑人 (= ~ nigger);男印第安人;最下级士兵. ⑤【体】鞍马. ⑥〔美,澳俚〕元. ⑦【牌】做庄家的标记. *fifty ~s of candles* 值五十块钱的蜡烛. ***cut the*** ~ ①有效地[很快地]做. ②干得漂亮. ***in the*** ~〔美俚〕手头有钱. ***make a*** ~ 挣钱,捞钞票. ***Old ~!*** 老伙计,老朋友〔熟人之间称呼用〕. ***pass the ~ to*** 把责任[工作]推给别人. — *vt.* ①(马)拱背猛跳使(骑者)摔下(*off*). ②〔美口〕(山羊等用头、角)觝,撞. ③猛烈反抗,反对;突破(困难等). ④(足球队员)带球冲入(敌阵). *~ off the rider* 马猛跳使骑者摔下. *The plane ~ed a strong head wind.* 飞机顶着强风飞行. *~ing a trend* 反对某种倾向. *~ the question on to someone else* 把问题推给别人. — *vi.* ①(马)猛然弓背跳起. ②(孤注一掷地)赌. ③〔美〕传递,把(问题)推给(别人). ④〔美口〕(羊等)觝;撞过去,冲过去;(机器)颤动,(车等)颠簸,猛然开动. ⑤〔美口〕抵抗;强烈反对 *(against)*. *The pony ~ed.* 小马弓背跳起. *~ against fate* 与命运抗争. *~ against the suggestion* 反对该项建议. *~ for vice-presidency* 拼命钻营副董事长的职位. ~ ***for***〔俚〕(不择手段地)争取(升级、利益)等. ~ ***up*** ①振作精神;鼓励. ②打起精神来!加油〔祈使语气〕;③〔俚〕打扮. ④匆忙. ~ ***up against***〔美俚〕反抗;不甘沉默. — *a.* ①雄的;〔美俚〕男的. ②〔美俚〕某一军衔等级中最低一级的. ~**bean**【植】睡菜. ~ **fever**〔美口〕①(猎物接近时初猎者的)兴奋,紧张. ②(新鲜的)体验,(从未有过的)兴奋. ~**horn** 鹿角. ~**hound** 猎鹿用的小猎狗. ~**jump** ① *vi.* (马)弯背猛跳. ② *vt.* (马)弯背猛跳使(骑者)摔下. ~**jumper** 劣马. ~ **lunch**〔俚〕男用盆餐. ~ **passer** 推诿家〔专把责任推诿给他人的人〕. ~ **private**〔美俚〕大兵. ~**saw** 木锯. ~**shot** 鹿弹〔大粒散弹〕. ~**skin** ①鹿皮. ②〔*pl.*〕鹿皮裤;鹿皮衣. ③〔美〕穿鹿皮色服装的人. ~ **slip** 为推卸责任而写的便条. ~**stick** 说大话的人,吹牛大王. ~**tooth** 獠牙,龅牙. ~**thorn**【植】鼠李. ~**wheat** 荞麦;荞麦粉. **-er** 猛然跳起把人摔下的马.

buck[2] [bʌk] *n.* (运货马车的)车身,车架;门框;〔美〕锯木架. ~-**board** 弹簧板四轮马车.

buck[3] [bʌk] *n.*〔英〕捕鳝鱼的竹笼.

buck[4] [bʌk] *ad.*〔方〕完全. ~ *naked* 全裸.

buck[5] [bʌk] *n.*〔古、方〕①洗衣碱水;起泡肥皂水. ②用碱水[肥皂水]浸洗过的衣服. — *vt.* 用碱水[肥皂水]浸[洗]衣服. ~ **basket**〔古〕洗衣筐.

buck. = buckram.

Buck [bʌk] *n.* 巴克〔姓氏〕.

buck·a·roo [ˈbʌkəruː], **buck·ay·ro** [bəkˈɛərəu] *n.*〔美西部〕牧童,牛仔;驯野马者.

buck·een [ˌbʌkˈiːn] *n.*〔英,方〕(穷而高傲的)贵族青年.

buck·et [ˈbʌkit] *n.* ①水桶,提桶;吊桶. ②(唧筒的)活塞;(水车循环运转的)戽斗;(挖土机等的)铲斗,勺斗;(汽轮机等的)叶片. ③一桶[勺斗],满桶[勺斗];大量. ④〔俚〕交通工具〔尤指行驶缓慢的旧船,旧汽车等〕. ⑤〔俚〕屁股. ⑥(篮球场的)篮下禁区. *a ~ of sand* 一勺斗黄沙. *shed ~s of tears* 泪如雨下. *skip ~* 翻斗. *turbine ~* 涡轮叶片. *flame ~* 火焰反射器. ***a drop in the ~*** 沧海一粟,九牛一毛. ***give sb. the ~***〔俚〕解雇. ***kick the ~***〔俚〕死,翘辫子. — *vt.* ①用桶装,用桶运;〔美〕用桶打(水). ②〔英口〕催(马)猛奔. ③〔美俚〕骗;利用(顾客的定钱、资金等)做投机生意. — *vi.*〔口〕急奔;猛开车;猛划船. ~ **brigade** ①(救火时为传递水等排成的)一字长蛇阵,人墙. ②应急突击队. ~ **seat** (飞机等的)凹背座椅〔坐板可以翻起〕. ~ **shop**〔美俚〕小交易所;小酒馆. **-ful** *n.* 一满桶[勺斗];一桶[勺斗]的量 (*a bucketful of water* 一桶水).

buck·eye [ˈbʌkai] *n.* ①(美国)橡树. ②〔B-〕〔俚〕美国俄亥俄州的人. ***the B- State*** 美国俄亥俄州〔别名〕. — *a.* (色彩等)奔放的,大胆的,花哨的.

Bucking·ham [ˈbʌkiŋəm] *n.* = Buckinghamshire. ***the ~ Palace*** (伦敦的)白金汉宫〔英国王宫〕.

Buck·ing·ham·shire [ˈbʌkiŋəmʃiə] *n.* 白金汉郡〔英国郡名〕.

buck·ish [ˈbʌkiʃ] *a.* ①爱时髦的,浮华的. ②性急的,浮躁的;莽撞的.

buck·le [ˈbʌkl] *n.* 扣子,带扣;(衣、鞋等的)扣形装饰品. ***hold [bring] ~ and thong together*** =〔美〕***make ~ and tongue meet*** 使收支相抵,量入为出. — *vt.* ①用带扣扣住,把…扣紧,扣上(皮带等) *(on, up)*;〔谑〕使…结婚. ②(加热或压力)使变弯曲,使翘棱;使起伏不平;使塌陷. ③努力从事于. *~ a belt* 扣上带子. *~ on a sword* (用带扣)挂上佩剑. ~ ***oneself to*** 专心从事于. — *vi.* ①扣住,扣紧. ②(由于受压、受热等)变弯曲,翘棱;弯成起伏不平;塌陷 *(up)*. ③屈服,屈从,屈降. ④专心做事. *His boot wouldn't ~.* 他的靴子扣不紧. *cornstalk ~ing in wind* 玉米秆被风吹得弯下来. *The supports ~d under the strain.* 支柱因为受力过重坍下来. *~ under press* 在压力下屈服. *~ up for safety* 把扣子扣紧以保安全. *He found it hard to ~ down.* 他很难专心做一样事情. ~ ***on (one's armour)*** (用带扣)穿戴上(铠甲). ~ ***(down) to*** 倾全力于 (*She ~d down to housework.* 她埋头家务). **-d** *a.* ①(鞋等)有带扣的. ②弯曲的,翘棱的.

Buck·le [ˈbʌkl] *n.* 巴克尔〔姓氏〕

buck·ler [ˈbʌklə] *n.* ①圆盾，孔盖板. ②防御，防御物，庇护者. ③【船】锚链孔盖. — *vt.* ①(持圆盾)防卫. ②防御，防护.

buck·mast [ˈbʌkmɑːst] *n.* = beechmast.

buck·o [ˈbʌkəu] *n.* ①〔海俚〕暴徒，恶霸，恶棍. ②〔英方〕小伙子〔称呼语〕. — *a.* ①残忍的，虐待狂的. ②粗鲁的，蛮横的.

buckra [ˈbʌkrə] *a.* 〔贬〕白种人的，白佬儿的〔美国南部、西印度群岛及非洲黑人用语〕. *a* ~ *house* 白佬儿的房子. *a* ~ *manner* 白佬儿的气派. — *n.* ①白种人. ②老板，先生.

buck·ram [ˈbʌkrəm] *n.* ①硬麻布，硬布. ②〔古〕古板；拘泥；生硬. ③色厉内荏，外强中干. *library* ~ 书面帆布. **men in** ~ = ~ men. — *a.* ①硬(麻)布制的. ②(态度)古板的；拘泥的；生硬的. ③外强中干的，色厉内荏的. — *vt.* ①(用硬麻布)衬硬. ②〔古〕使变古板[拘泥]. ③使摆出外强中干的架势. ~ **men** 稻草人.

buck·shee [ˈbʌkʃiː] *n.* ①〔英，军俚〕额外津贴，额外供应品. ②预料以外的赠与物. — *a.* ①额外获得的. ②免费的. — *ad.* 免费地.

bu·col·ic [bju(ː)ˈkɔlik] *a.* 农家风味的；田园生活的；牧羊生活的，牧歌式的. *a simple* ~ *life* 简朴的田园生活. — *n.* ①〔常 *pl.*〕牧歌；田园诗. ②〔古〕农民，乡下人.

bud[1] [bʌd] *n.* ①芽，萌芽，幼芽；蓓蕾，胥朵；【动】芽体，芽状凸起. ②未成熟的人[东西]；〔喻〕少女，少年；〔美〕刚进社交界的姑娘. *a tactile* ~ 触觉芽. *a gustatory* ~ 味蕾. ***in [the]*** ~ 含苞未放，发芽，尚在萌芽时期. ***nip in the*** ~ 把…消灭在萌芽状态，防患于未然 (*nip a rebellion in the* ~ 把叛乱扑灭于萌芽状态). — *vt.* ①使发芽. ②【植】使芽接. — *vi.* ①发芽，萌芽；含苞待放. ②开始发育[发展，成长]. ③【植】芽接. ④处于未成熟状态. ~ ***off from*** 变成芽体从(母体)分离出来；〔喻〕从…分离出来，建立新组织. ~ ***out*** 〔美俚〕打扮得漂漂亮亮. **-like** *a.* 芽似的，蓓蕾似的.

bud[2] [bʌd] *n.* 〔口〕伙伴，兄弟〔buddy 的缩写〕.

Bu·da·pest [ˈbjuːdəpest] *n.* 布达佩斯〔匈牙利首都〕.

bud·ded [ˈbʌdid] *a.* 发了芽的，有蓓蕾的，接了芽的.

Bud·dha [ˈbudə] *n.* 佛陀〔佛教徒对释迦牟尼的尊称〕，佛，如来佛.

Bud·dhism [ˈbudizəm] *n.* 佛教；佛法.

Bud·dhist [ˈbudist] *n.* 佛教徒. *a* ~ *monk* 僧，和尚. *a layman* ~ 居士. — *a.* 佛陀的；佛法的；佛教徒的.

Bud·dhis·tic, Bud·dhis·ti·cal [buˈdistik(əl)] *a.* 佛陀的；佛法的，佛教(徒)的.

bud·ding [ˈbʌdiŋ] *a.* ①正发芽的，含苞待放的. ②开始发育[发展]的. ③初露头角的. *a* ~ *beauty* 妙龄女郎. *a* ~ *lawyer* 初露头角的律师. *a* ~ *scientist* 正在成长中的科学家. — *n.* ①发芽；含苞. ②【植】芽接(法). (出)芽(繁)殖.

bud·dle [ˈbʌdl] *n.* 【矿】洗矿槽，淘汰盘. — *vt.* 用洗矿槽[淘汰盘]洗(矿石).

Bud·dle·ia [bʌdˈliːə] *n.* 【植】醉鱼草；醉鱼草属植物.

bud·dy [ˈbʌdi] *n.* 〔美军口〕伙伴；弟兄〔尤指士兵间的称呼〕；好朋友；小朋友〔称呼用〕. *a bosom* ~ 好朋友，密友. ~-~ *a.* 〔美俚〕亲热的.

Bud·dy [ˈbʌdi] *n.* 巴迪〔男子名〕.

budge[1] [bʌdʒ] *vt.* 〔通例用于否定句〕①微微一动，动. ②(立场等)动摇，让步. *The car won't* ~ *an inch.* 车子一动也不动. *She wouldn't* ~ *on the issue.* 她在这个问题上不肯让步. — *vt.* ①推动. ②使动摇，使让步. *The three of them couldn't* ~ *the rock.* 他们三个人都推不动那块石头. *Money can't* ~ *me.* 金钱不能使我改变立场.

budge[2] [bʌdʒ] *n.* ①羔皮. ②革囊. ③〔美方〕酒.

budg·er·i·gar [ˈbʌdʒəriˌgɑː] *n.* 【动】虎皮鹦鹉.

budg·et [ˈbʌdʒit] *n.* ①预算，预算案. ②经营费；生活费；(有限制的)供应，来源. ③〔古〕〔方〕小皮包；小皮包中的东西. ④〔喻〕(书信等的)一束，一捆；(要闻)汇编〔作报名用〕. *the Literary B-* 文艺汇编. *a* ~ *committee* 预算委员会. *the monthly* ~ *for a family of four* 一家四口的每月生活费. *His* ~ *of good will was running out.* 他的好心肠已经快没有了. ~ *estimate* 概算. ~ *statement* 预算书. ~ *making* 编预算. ***open [introduce] the*** ~ 向议会提出预算案. — *vt.* ①把…编入预算；按预算来安排(生活、工程等). ②安排，预定. ~ *a new hospital* 把建立一座新医院列入预算. ~ *manpower in a tight labor market* 在劳动力短缺的情况下安排人力. ~ *one's time* 安排自己的时间. — *vi.* ①编预算. ②作好安排. ~ *for a vacation* 安排好时间去度假. ~ *for the project* 为工程编制预算. ~ **plan** 分期付款. ~ **shoppers** 按照预算购物的顾客. **-ary** *a.* 预算上的. **-eer, -er** *n.*①预算编制人. ②受预算限制的人.

bud·let [ˈbʌdlit] *n.* 幼芽，小芽.

bue·nas no·ches [ˈbwenɑːs ˈnɔːtʃes] 〔Sp.〕再见！晚安！

Bue·nos Ai·res [ˈbwenəs ˈaiəriz] 布宜诺斯艾利斯〔阿根廷首都〕.

bue·nos di·as [ˈbwenɔːs ˈdiːɑːs] 〔Sp.〕 您好！早安！

buff[1] [bʌf] *n.* ①(水牛等淡黄色的)软皮；(擦镜头用的)麂皮；皮制军服；淡黄色印相纸. ②浅黄色，柔皮色. ③(人)裸露的皮肤. ④〔美〕爱好者，迷；热心人. ⑤〔口〕野牛. ⑥【机】磨轮，抛光轮. *Civil War* ~*s* 爱好钻研美国南北战争史的人. *a trolley car* ~ 喜欢乘电车的人. ***in*** ~ 赤身裸体. ***strip to the*** ~ 使一丝不挂，把…的衣服剥得精光. — *vt.* ①(用软皮等)擦亮，抛光，擦净. ②把(皮革)弄软；把(皮革)染成纯黄色. *a* ~*ing machine* 抛光机. ~ *shoes* 擦皮鞋. ~ *a waxed floor.* 把打蜡的地板擦亮. — *a.* ①软牛皮制的. ②浅黄色的. ~ **coat** ①麂皮制服. ②穿麂皮制服的军人.

buff[2] [bʌf] *vt.* 减低…的力量，缓冲. — *n.* 〔方〕打击.

buf·fa·lo [ˈbʌfələu] *n.* *(pl.* ~***es,*** ~***s,*** 〔集合词〕~*)* ①水牛；〔美〕野牛. ②〔军俚〕水陆两用坦克. — *vt.* 〔美俚〕①威吓. ②迷惑. *He was* ~*ed by the complexity of problem.* 他被复杂的问题弄得昏头昏脑. *He didn't let the older boys* ~ *him.* 他没有让大孩子们吓住. ~ **bird** 香羽鸟. ~ **chips** (做燃料用的)干牛粪. ~ **cloth** 长绒大衣呢. **B- Indians** 平原地区印第安人. ~ **range** 〔美〕原野.

Buf·fa·lo [ˈbʌfələu] *n.* 布法罗〔美国港市〕.

buff·er[1] [ˈbʌfə] *n.* ①【机】缓冲器，缓冲垫；阻尼器，减震器；消声器. ②【化】缓冲，缓冲剂. ③缓冲者；缓冲物；缓冲国〔= ~ state〕. ④【计】缓冲存储装置. *oil* ~【机】油压减震器. — *vt.* ①【化】用缓冲剂处理. ②缓和；缓冲；保护；使不利影响减少. ~ *economy by raising interest rates* 以提高利率来保护经济. *The drug* ~*ed his pain.* 这剂药减轻了他的病痛. ~ **computer** 缓冲型计算机. ~ **solution**【化】缓冲溶液. ~ **state** 缓冲国. ~ **zone** 缓冲地带.

buff·er[2] [ˈbʌfə] *n.* ①【机】抛(光)盘，抛光轮，抛光棒. ②抛光工人.

buff·er[3] [ˈbʌfə] *n.* ①〔英俚〕无能的人，老派人物. ②家伙，人. ③【海】水手[掌帆]长副手. *He was a bit of* ~. 他有点低能. ***an old*** ~ 老家伙，老糊涂，老朽.

buf·fet[1] [ˈbʌfit] *n.* ①打击，殴打；一巴掌，一拳. ②(风、波浪等的)冲击；(命运等的)折磨，蹂躏. ③【空】抖振. *give* ~*s to sb.* 殴打某人. *the* ~*s of the storm* 暴风雨的冲击. *recurrent* ~*s of fate* 命途多舛. — *vt.* ①用手打，用拳击，掴. ②(波浪等)冲击；(命运等)蹂躏，打击. ③(人与命运、波浪等)搏斗. *be* ~*ed by adversity* 处于逆境. *The wind* ~*ed the boats.* 风冲击着小船. *The ship* ~*ed her way through the waves.* 这艘船在浪涛中奋勇前行. — *vi.* ①(用手)打，殴打. ②(与风浪等)搏斗，奋勇前进.

buf·fet[2] *n.* ① [ˈbʌfit] 碗橱，餐具架. ② [ˈbufei] (车站，火车内的)餐室；小吃店，快餐柜台；小卖部. —*a.* 快

餐式的，自助式的〔无固定餐桌，就餐者自取食物〕. *cold* ～（菜单上的）冷肉. ～ **car**（火车上的）餐车. ～ **lunch [supper]** 简易午〔晚〕餐. ～ **service** 快餐部.

buf·fle·head [ˈbʌflˌhed] *n.*【动】巨头鹊鸭.

buf·fo [ˈbufəu] *n.* (*pl.* ***buf·fi*** [ˈbufiː]), *a.*〔It.〕滑稽歌手(的)，滑稽歌剧演员(的).

buf·foon [bʌˈfuːn] ①丑角；演滑稽戏的人. ②言谈诙谐的人. *play the* ～ 当小丑. — *vt.* 丑化. — *vi.* 当小丑. **-ish** *a.* 滑稽的，小丑似的.

buf·foon·er·y [bʌˈfuːnəri] *n.* 滑稽(表演)，插科打诨.

buf·fy [ˈbʌfi] *a.* ①淡黄色的. ②〔俚〕喝醉了的.

Bu·ford [ˈbjuːfəd] *n.* 比福德〔姓氏，男子名〕.

bu·fo·ten·ine [ˌbjuːfəˈteniːn] *n.*【药】蟾蜍特宁，蟾毒色胺.

bug [bʌg] *n.* ①〔英〕臭虫；〔美口〕虫，昆虫. ②〔口〕微生物，病菌. ③(机器、设计等的)小缺陷，瑕疵. ④癖，狂，迷，热衷于(某事)者. ⑤【电】故障，损坏；干扰；〔俚〕雷达位置测定〔指示〕器；半自动发报键，电键. ⑥窃听器；暗设报警器. ⑦〔古〕要人，名人. ⑧星号. ⑨小型汽车. *a lighting* ～〔美〕萤火虫. *an intestinal* ～ 肠菌. *a big* ～〔贬〕名人，要人. *The test flight was to discover the* ～*s in the new plane.* 试验飞行是要发现新飞机有何缺陷. *a sports car* ～ 赛车迷. *a* ～ *on education* 热衷于教育事业的人. ～ ***under the chip***〔美〕秘密. ***on*** ～给…迷上，热衷于…. ***put a*** ～ ***in sb.'s ear*** 事先警告某人. — *vt.* ①灭除(害虫). ②〔美俚〕在…暗设报警器〔窃听器〕；(通过窃听器)窃听. ③〔美俚〕烦恼，折磨，激怒. ④使(眼珠)凸出. ～ *the phone* 窃听电话. *Don't* ～ *me with petty details.* 不要讲那些琐碎的细节来烦我. — *vi.* ①捉臭虫. ②(眼珠)凸出. ③〔美俚〕离开；撤退. ～ ***off***〔美俚〕滚开，匆匆走开. ～ ***out*** ①〔美俚〕逃窜；逃避. ②眼珠暴突. ③无趣地走开. ～ ***up***〔美俚〕①激动起来. ②被弄糊涂. ～ **doctor**〔美俚〕(监狱等处的)精神病医师，心理学专家. ～ **eaters**〔美〕内布拉斯加州人. ～**-eyed** *a.*〔美〕眼球凸出的；惊得目瞪口呆的. ～ **hole**【地】晶穴. ～**juice**〔美〕①(劣等)酒，(低级)威士忌. ②合成饮料，着色清凉饮料. ～ **light** 小闪光灯；小灯塔. ～**out** ①〔军俚〕匆忙的撤退. ②〔俚〕擅离职守的人. ～ **test**〔美俚〕智力测验；心理测验.

bug·a·boo [ˈbʌgəbuː] *n.*〔美〕= bugbear.

bug·bane [ˈbʌgˌbein] *n.*【植】升麻属植物.

bug·bear [ˈbʌgbɛə] *n.* ①吓人的东西，妖怪. ②无端的惊恐. ③令人头痛的事.

bug·eye [ˈbʌgai] *n.*〔美，海〕中型帆船.

bug·ger [ˈbʌgə] *n.* ①鸡奸者. ②〔卑〕坏蛋，坏家伙；坏东西. ③家伙，小伙子〔多用于幽默、亲热的说法〕. *a cute little* ～ 一个聪敏伶俐的小家伙. — *vt.* ①鸡奸. ②使疲乏不堪. ③诅咒. — *vi.* ①搞鸡奸. ②诅咒. ～ ***about***〔英俚〕(人)追来追去. ～ ***off***〔英俚〕走开，离开. ～ ***up***〔俚〕搞坏，弄糟，搞乱（～ *things up* 把事情搞糟）. **-y** *n.* 鸡奸.

bug·gy[1] [ˈbʌgi] *a.* ①臭虫多的. ②神经有毛病的；古怪的；淘气的. *a* ～ *old lady who continually mutters to herself.* 一个不断自言自语的古怪老太婆.

bug·gy[2] [ˈbʌgi] *n.* ①〔英〕无盖二轮马车；〔美〕二轮〔四轮〕轻马车. ②儿童车，婴儿手推车. ③(短途运送金属、矿石等的)短途运输车. ④〔美俚〕汽车〔尤指旧汽车〕. *a*～ *bandit*〔美俚〕偷汽车的贼. ～ ***days***〔美俚〕从前.

bug·house [ˈbʌghaus] *n.*〔美口〕精神病院，疯人院. — *a.* ①癫狂的，发疯的. ②低能的. *a* ～ *fable* 荒唐无稽的故事〔事情〕. **B- Square** 疯人院广场〔美国纽约街头一广场，系一街头演说者聚集场所〕.

bug-hunt·er [ˈbʌghʌntə] *n.*〔英俚，讽〕昆虫学家. **-ing** *n.* 昆虫采集.

bu·gle[1] [ˈbjuːgl] *n.* ①军号，喇叭. ②〔古〕(狩猎时用的)号，角，笛. *blow [sound] a* ～ 吹号，鸣角. *a* ～ *call* 进军号，集合号. ***like a*** ～ ***call*** 突然. — *vi.* ①吹号. ②发出吼声. — *vt.* ①吹号集合. ②吹号表示(冲锋、撤退等). ～ *reveille* 吹起床号. ～**-horn** 号角；角笛；角杯. **-er** *n.* 号手；司号兵.

bu·gle[2] [ˈbjuːgl] *n.*〔常 *pl.*〕(妇女装饰衣服的)玻璃〔塑料〕珠〔小圆管〕. — *a.* (衣服)有玻璃〔塑料〕珠装饰的.

bu·gle[3] [ˈbjuːgl] *n.*【植】夏枯草，筋骨草属植物，匍匐筋骨草.

bu·gle[4] [ˈbjuːgl] *n.*〔英俚〕鼻子.

bu·glet [ˈbjuːglit] *n.* (汽车上的)小喇叭.

bu·gle·weed [ˈbjuːglˌwiːd] *n.*【植】①夏枯草. ②地笋属植物.

bu·gloss [ˈbjuːglɔs] *n.*【植】牛舌草.

bug·o·lo·gy [bʌˈgɔlədʒi] *n.*〔口〕昆虫学.

bugs [bʌgz] *a.*〔美俚〕疯狂的. ***go*** ～ 发疯.

bug·seed [ˈbʌgˌsiːd] *n.*【植】海索草叶虫实.

bug·shah [ˈbʌgʃə, -ʃɔː] *n.* (*pl.* ～, ～*s*) 布格席〔也门货币名，等于 1/40 里亚尔〕.

buhl [buːl], **buhlwork** [ˈbuːlwəːk] *n.* ①(龟壳、金银等的)镶嵌装饰. ②镶嵌工艺品.

buhr·stone [ˈbəːˌstəun] *n.* ①砂质多孔石灰岩. ②细砂质磨石 (= buhr). *a* ～ *mill* 石磨.

BUIC = backup interceptor control【军】后援截击机控制.

build [bild] *vt.* (***built*** [bilt],〔诗、古〕～***ed; built,*** ～***ed***) ①建，盖，建筑；建设，建造；筑，造. ②建立，创立，确立，树立；培养. ③抬高(身份)，捧(演员)；扩大(*up*). ～ *a house [bridge, ship]* 盖房子〔造桥，造船〕. ～ *a fire* 生火. ～ *an empire* 创立帝国. ～ *a fortune* 挣家私，治产. ～ *a gun* 造大炮. ～ *a pile of bricks into a factory* 用一堆砖头砌成厂房. *a novel built on four sections* 分成四部分的一部小说. ～ *a new kind of morality* 建立一种新的道德风尚. ～ *boys into men* 把少年培养成人. *He is very well built.* 他体魄健壮. *I am not built that way.*〔美〕我生来不是那样的人. *Don't* ～ *your future on dreams.* 不要把你的未来建立在空想上，不要好高骛远. — *vi.* ①被建造；从事营造业. ②逐渐达到高峰；逐步扩大范围. ～ *to a climax* 逐步发展到最高潮. *a line of people* ～*ing along the avenue* 沿着人行道越来人越多的队伍. ～ ***down*** 衰减，降低. ～ ***in*** ①加入，插进(用料)；埋入，装入. ②围以(房屋、围墙等)（～ *in bookcases between windows* 在窗户之间砌成嵌入式书架）. ～ ***on [upon]*** ①把…建筑于. ②依赖，靠，指望(*We* ～ *our hopes on our own efforts.* 我们把希望寄托在自己的努力上). ～ ***round*** 用建筑物包围. ～ ***up*** ①(用砖等)阻塞(门，窗等)；把(空场)盖满(房子). ②建立，确立，树立(名誉，人格，产业等)，组成机关等. ③增进(健康)，加强(体格)，振兴，扩大，复兴. ④【军】集结(部队)；聚集，积累. ⑤赞扬，吹捧（～*up a bank account* 开银行往来帐. ～ *up the body* 锻炼身体. ～ *up a library* 建立一座图书馆. *a salesman* ～*ing up his product* 宣扬本企业产品的推销员. *clouds* ～*ing up on the horizon* 在天边愈积愈浓的云层）. — *n.* ①构造，造型. ②骨格，体格，成形. ③〔俚〕优美的体型，肉体美. *The house was a modern* ～. 那座房子是现代式样. *He has a strong* ～. 他体格健壮. *She has some* ～. 她长得还不错. *of sturdy* ～ 体格健壮的.

build·er [ˈbildə] *n.* ①建筑工人；经营建筑业者. ②建设者；创建者. ③(增加洗涤剂清洁作用的)增洁剂；【化】组份；(计算机的)编码程序. *a master* ～ 营造大师. *a great empire* ～ 一个大帝国的创立者. ～**'s knot**【海】卷结，8 字形套结.

build·ing [ˈbildiŋ] *n.* ①建筑物，房屋，大楼，大厦. ②制造；营造，建筑；组合，组装；建筑术. *a public* ～ 公共建筑物. *the art of* ～ 建筑术. *car* ～ 汽车制造. *fabricated* ～ 装配式建筑. ～ **area** 建筑地积. ～ **berth [slip]** 造船台. ～ **block** ①(儿童玩的)积木. ②建筑砌块. ～ **lease** 租地造屋权，造屋租地的年限. ～ **line** 建筑

界限，房基线．～ **machine** 轮胎装配床，配套机．～ **material** 建筑材料．～ **method**（制造汽油的）合成法．～ **paper** 防潮纸，油毛毡．～ **room** 装配间．～ **sheet** 建筑钢板．～ **society**〔英〕＝～ **(and loan) association**〔美〕住宅互助协会〔会员集股投资以帮助买房造房的互助组织〕．

build-up [ˈbildʌp] *n.* ①组成，装配，组合，组装，安装．②上升，升高，增长，增强．③组成，结构，构造；（戏剧的）情节．④【军】（战斗部队的）集合，集结；蓄积，积累，堆积（现象）；结瘤，结垢．⑤捏造；吹嘘，宣传．⑥计算，作图．⑦形成，产生，出现．⑧用砖填塞（门窗）．⑨连续发生，连锁反应．⑩（事前）准备．⑪鼓舞，鼓励．*the ～ of the nation's industry* 国家的工业建设．*They spent a lot of money on her ～.* 他们为给她做广告花掉不少钱．*the ～ of the salt deposit* 岩盐的蓄积过程．*a lengthy ～* 长期的准备．

built [bilt] build 的过去式及过去分词．— *a.* ①建造成的，组合的，拼成的．②〔俚〕体型美的．～ *like a castle*（马）体格健壮．*a ～ mast*（几根木料拼成的）组合桅．～ *frame* 拼装框架．*a slimly ～ girl* 身材苗条的姑娘．*She sure is ～.* 她的体型的确不错．— *n.*〔俚〕体型美，肉体美．

built-in [ˈbiltˈin] *a.* ①（家具等）作为固定装置而建造的；固定的，不可分开的；嵌入的．②内在的；固有的．*a ～ bathtub* 固定浴盆．～ *cabinets* 固定壁橱．*a ～ trait of human nature* 人性的固有特征．— *n.* 嵌入式家具．

built-up [ˈbiltˈʌp] *a.* ①组合的，拼成的，合成的．②围建的，建筑物多的．～ *gear* 组合齿轮．*This shoe has a ～ heel.* 这种鞋子的后跟是拼装式的．*a ～ city* 按计划建设成的城市．～ **area** ①盖满房屋的街区，房屋密集区．②组合面积．

Bu·jum·bu·ra [ˌbuːdʒəmˈburə] *n.* 布琼布拉〔布隆迪首都〕．

Bu·kha·ra [buˈkɑːrɑ] *n.* 布哈拉〔苏联城市〕．

bulb [bʌlb] *n.* ①【植】球根；鳞茎．②球状物；（寒暑表的）水银球；灯泡；烧瓶；真空管；测温包．③【解】球；〔*pl.*〕扁桃腺．④（照相机的）快门．⑤（汽车的）圆形车壳；【海】球形船首．*a lily ～* 百合根．*an electric ～* 电灯泡．*the ～ of a hair* 毛根，发根．*the ～ of the eye* 眼球．*the ～ of the spinal cord*【解】延髓．— *vi.* ①生球茎．②肿[涨]成球，形成球状．～ ***up***（卷心菜等）打包，形成球状包．**-ed** *a.* ①有鳞[球]茎的．②鳞[球]茎形，圆形的．

bul·ba·ceous [bəlˈbeiʃəs] *a.*【植】①鳞茎的；鳞茎状的；有鳞茎的．②由鳞茎生长的．

bul·bar [ˈbʌlbə] *a.* ①鳞茎的，球的．②【解】延髓的．

bulb·if·er·ous [bʌlˈbifərəs] *a.* 有球茎的，有鳞茎的．

bulb·i·form [ˈbʌlbifɔːm] *a.* 球茎状的．

bul·bil, bul·bel [ˈbʌlbil, ˈbʌlbəl] *n.*【植】珠芽，零余子．

bul·bous [ˈbʌlbəs] *a.* 球茎状的，鳞茎状的；由球茎[鳞茎]长成的．*a ～ plant* 球茎[鳞茎]植物．

bul·bul [ˈbulbul] *n.* ①【鸟】夜莺．②歌手，诗人．

Bul·gar [ˈbʌlgɑː] *n.* = Bulgarian.

Bul·gar·i·a [bʌlˈgɛəriə] *n.* 保加利亚〔欧洲〕．

Bul·gar·i·an [bʌlˈgɛəriən] *a.* 保加利亚的；保加利亚人的；保加利亚语的．— *n.* 保加利亚人；保加利亚语．

bulge [bʌldʒ] *n.* ①膨胀；肿胀．②凸出部分；（桶等的）鼓出部，（身体的）发胖部位．③（体积、价格等的）暴涨．④【海】（军舰外侧的）鱼雷防护线；（船的）底边．⑤〔美俚〕优越，优势．*a ～ in a wall* 墙面的不平部分．*a ～ in the rug* 地毯的鼓胀处．*the ～ keel* 船腹．*the ～ in profits* 利润的突然增长．***get [have] the ～ on***〔美俚〕胜过，赛过，占…的上风．***the Battle of the B-*** 第二次大战中德军的最后攻势．— *vi.* ①膨胀，鼓起，凸出；装满（*with*）．②上涨，急增．③船底破漏．*His stomach ～d after the dinner.* 他吃过饭以后，肚子都鼓起来了．*The box ～d with cookies.* 盒子里装满了甜饼．*bulging eyes* 凸眼．— *vt.* 使膨胀，使鼓起，使凸出．*columns ～d a bit in the center* 中间被弄得有点鼓肚子的圆柱．

bulg·er [ˈbʌldʒə] *n.* ①凸面高尔夫球棒．②〔美〕巨物．

bulg·y [ˈbʌldʒi] *a.* 膨胀的，凸出的．

bu·lim·i·a [bjuːˈlimjə], **bu·li·my** [ˈbjuːlimi] *n.* ①【医】易饥症，食欲过盛．②贪欲．

bulk[1] [bʌlk] *n.* ①体积，容积，大小．②巨大；庞然大物；大块；大批，大量．③货舱；船货；散装货物．④〔the ～〕大半，大部分，大多数；主体．⑤【物】胀量；松密度．⑥〔书〕身体；胖人，大块头；〔诗〕巨人，巨兽．*a ship of great ～* 体积庞大的船．*The ～ of it!* 这东西真大！*The ～ of the debt was paid.* 大部分的债都还清了．*He lifted his huge ～ from the chair.* 他那庞大的身躯从椅子上站起来．～ *analysis*【化】总分析．～ *cargo* 散装货．***break ～*** 下货，卸货．***by ～*** 估堆，按堆（计算等）．***in ～*** ①不加包装，散装．②大批，大量（*load in ～* 散装入船，散运．*sell in ～* 原舱出售所装运的货，整批出售）．— *vi.* ①显得庞大；看上去重要．②增大，膨涨，胀大；堆积起来；形成大块；扩展；（重要性等）增加．*The problem ～s large in his mind.* 这个问题在他心目中显得很重要．— *vt.* ①使膨胀；使增大．②堆积（鱼等）．③用眼力估计，毛估（重量、容量等）．～ ***large [small] in one's eyes [minds]*** 在某人眼〔心目〕中显得巨大．～ ***up*** ①胀大．②形成大数目．**～-cheap** *a.* 薄利多销的．～ **density** 松密度．**～-grade**（羊毛等的）大致等级．**～head**【船】舱壁；【空】隔板；【矿】（坑内的）分壁；【建】挡土墙；堤岸；（通地下室的）盖板门．～ **modulus**【物】体积弹性率．～ **piling** 散（装容）积．～ **selection** 混合选择．

bulk·y [ˈbʌlki] *a.* 庞大的，笨重的，体积大的．*a ～ book* 一本大厚书．*a ～ cargo* 体积庞大的货物．～ **yarn** 膨体纱．**bulk·i·ness** *n.*

bull[1] [bul] *n.* ①公牛；雄象，雄鲸；雄性大动物．②躯体庞大的人，粗壮的人；〔美俚〕工头；农场监工；〔美俚〕火车头．③〔B-〕= John Bull；【天】金牛宫，金牛座．④（股票投机中的）买方，多头（*opp.* bear）．⑤〔美俚〕警察；侦探．⑥瞎话，大话．⑦〔英俚〕（旧制）五先令银币．*an elephant ～* 雄象．*He had a mother's soul in a body of ～* 他身体粗壮而心地善良．***a china-shop ～*** 动辄闯祸的粗人，磁器店里的大象．～ ***in the ring***（小孩子玩的）突围游戏．***like a ～ at a (five-barred) gate*** 狂怒地；猛烈地，凶猛地．***milk the ～*** 做徒劳无功的事，想从公牛身上挤奶．***take the ～ by the horns*** 挺身面对危险，毅然处理难局；（斗牛士）敢抓公牛角．***throw [shoot] the ～*** 吹牛，胡说八道．— *a.* ①雄的，公的；公牛一样的．②【商】买方的，哄抬证券价格的．～ *movement*（股票投机中）哄抬行情的活动，买方[多方]的策动．***a ～ head [neck; voice]*** 公牛一样的头[颈，嗓音]．***a ～ whale*** 公鲸．— *vi.* ①哄抬证券价格，做多头，做买方．②〔美俚〕排除困难前进，奋力前行．③〔美俚〕夸口，吹牛，自大；说空话．④〔俚〕配种，交尾．～ *through the crowd* 从人群中挤过去．— *vt.* ①哄抬（证券等的行情）．②强行通过（议案等），挤出（路等）．③【海】（以船首）猛撞．～ *stocks* 哄抬股票行情．～ *a bill through congress* 在议会中强行通过一项议案．～ *one's way through the crowd* 从人群中挤出一条路．**～baiting** 以狗逗牛戏〔现已废止〕．**～bat**【动】蚊母鸟．**～boat** 牛皮浅水船．**～calf** 小公牛；笨蛋．**～dog** ① *n.* 恶犬，斗犬；硬汉；〔学俚〕学监的随从；〔俚〕手枪，大炮；〔美〕晚报的第一版〔午前出版〕，晨报的第一版〔上半夜出版〕；〔美〕纸牌的老 K．② *a.* 勇猛的．③ *vt.*〔美西部〕抓住双角摔倒（小公牛）．～ **fiddle**〔美口〕低音提琴（= double bass）．**～-fight** 斗牛．**～-fighter** 斗牛士．**～finch** ①【鸟】红腹灰雀．②（旁边有沟的）树篱．**～frog** ①【动】牛蛙．②〔美俚〕声音低沉的电影演员．**～head** ①【鱼】大头鱼〔尤指杜父鱼、美洲鲴鱼〕．②小圆头．③〔美俚〕顽固的人，倔强的人．**～-hide**

厚灯芯布. ~**horn** ①手提式电子扩音器. ②〔美俚〕大号(= tuba). ~ **market** 〔商〕上涨行情. ~**necked** *a.* 头颈粗短的. ~**nose**【建】外圆角. ~**pen** ①牛栏. ②(候审犯人的)大拘留室. ③(棒球场内的)接替投手赛前练习室. ④【棒球】接替投手. ~**ring** ①斗牛场. ②〔美俚〕(监狱里的)犯人散步场;监狱的围墙. ~**roarer** ①牛吼器〔以铜锣等系上木片扔出的一种玩具〕. ②大嗓门的演说者. ~**-session** 〔美俚〕自由讨论. ~**'s-eye** ①靶心;【军】(射击取得的)十环. ②【海】(舷侧)圆窗;单眼木制滑车. ③圆天窗;【气】风暴眼. ④牛眼灯,凸透镜. ⑤圆形硬糖. ⑥〔美〕大怀表 (*make [score] the ~'s-eye* 打中靶心;取得大成功). ~**shit** 〔英俚〕胡说,废话. ~**shot** 掺汤鸡尾酒〔用杜松子酒或伏特加酒和肉汤制成〕. ~**-shooter** 〔美俚〕吹牛大家. ~**tewier** 虎斑猛犬〔英国种〕. ~ **tongue** (耕棉田用的)牛舌形犁片. ~ **trout** 〔英〕鳟鱼. ~**whack** ① *n.* 〔美〕牛鞭. ② *vt., vi.* 用牛鞭鞭打. ~**whacker** 〔美〕赶牛人. ~ **wheel** (齿轮组中的)大齿轮,牛轮. ~**whip** 长牛鞭. ~**'s wool** 〔口〕劣质粗呢. ~**work** 牛马活,苦活.

bull² [bul] *n.* (罗马教皇的)训谕,训令.

bull³ [bʌl] *n.* 滑稽的矛盾,可笑的错误(= Irish ~). ***make an Irish ~*** 说荒唐可笑的话.

bull(s). = bulletin(s).

bul·la [ˈbʌlə, ˈbulə] *n.* (*pl.* ***bullae*** [ˈbuliː]) 〔L.〕 ①垂饰;印玺. ②【医】水疱. ③气门片.

bul·lace [ˈbulis] *n.* 【植】紫野生李;野生李树.

bul·late [ˈbʌleit] *a.* ①【动、植】有疱的. ②水疱状的. ③【解】隆起的,肿胀的.

bull·doze [ˈbuldəuz] *vt.* ①〔美俚〕威胁,恐吓. ②用推土机推平,用压路机压平;排除(障碍). ~ *a building site* 用推土机把一处建筑工地推平. ~ *trees from a building site* 用推土机把建筑工地上的树推平.

bull·doz·er [ˈbuldəuzə] *n.* ①〔美俚〕威吓者. ②推土机,压路机.

bull·er [ˈbulə] *n.* 〔口〕代理人〔讼师,学监〕的助手.

bul·let [ˈbulit] ①子弹,弹头,弹丸;【矿】取心弹,射孔弹. ②(钓丝上的)铅锤;插塞;锥形体;【印】着重号〔加在文字下面表示强调的黑点〕. 〔*pl.*〕〔美俚〕豆〔尤指炒豆〕;钱;【牌】手中的A牌. *a stray ~* 流弹. *bite the ~* 忍辱负重,忍气吞声. ***Every ~ has its billet.*** 每颗子弹都有归宿,命中注定无法逃. ~ **alloy** 子弹合金〔含铅94%,锑6%〕. ~ **bait** 〔美俚〕无战斗经验的新兵;炮灰. ~**-drawer** 子弹钳. ~**-head** 圆头;圆头人;〔俚〕傻瓜. ~**-headed** *a.* ①似子弹头的,圆头的. ②愚笨的,执拗的. ~**proof** *a.* 防弹的 (*a ~proof jacket* 防弹衣. *It's ~proof.* 〔口〕我的话保险不错). ~ **train** (日本的)高速火车.

bul·le·tin [ˈbulitin] *n.* ①告示;公告,公报;(学术团体等定期出版的)会刊. ②(关于要人的)病情公报. ③新闻简报. — *vt.* 告示,揭示,用公报发表. ~**-board** 公告牌.

bul·lion [ˈbuljən] *n.* ①(造币用的)金〔银〕块;条金〔银〕. ②纯金,纯银. ③条形金属. ④粗金属锭;粗铅. ⑤金〔银〕丝缨缝〔花边〕. *lead ~* 铅锭. *copper ~* 粗铜锭. *gold ~ standard* (货币的)金本位制. **-ism** *n.* 硬币主义. **-ist** *n.* 硬币论者.

bull·ish [ˈbuliʃ] *a.* ①公牛一样的. ②顽固的;愚蠢的. ③【商】股票行情看涨的;做多头的;〔喻〕乐观的. *a ~ market* 看涨的行情. **-ly** *ad.* **-ness** *n.*

bull·ock [ˈbulək] *n.* ①(四岁以上的)小公牛. ②阉牛. — *vi.* 象小公牛一样乱闯. ~ ***one's ways*** 乱闯乱撞,横冲直撞. ~**cart** 牛车. **-y** *a.* 小公牛似的.

bul·ly¹ [ˈbuli] *n.* ①暴徒;欺侮弱者的人;(学校中)以大欺小的学生;〔古〕打手. ②(足球等的)争球. ③〔古〕妓女的保镖,妓院的拉客者. ④〔古〕情人;好朋友;好家伙. ***come the ~ over sb.*** 对…盛气凌人. ***play the ~*** 欺侮人,以强凌弱. — *a.* 〔美口〕①第一流的,顶好的. ②快活的. ③恶霸一样的,盛气凌人的. *feel ~* 心情很好. — *int.* 好,妙(= bravo). ***B- for you!*** 好极了!妙极了! — *vi.* 盛气凌人,以强凌弱. — *vt.* 威吓;欺侮,欺负. ~ ***sb. into [out of]*** 恐吓某人使做〔使停止做〕某事 (~ *sb. into working* 恐吓某人使他干活. *He bullied her into a car.* 他把她威逼进汽车). ~**boy** 摆臭架子的恶棍;职业流氓. **-able** *a.* 可威吓的.

bul·ly² [ˈbuli] *n.* 罐头牛肉(= ~ beef).

bul·ly·rag [ˈbuliræg] *v.* = ballyrag.

bul·rush [ˈbulrʌʃ] *n.* 【植】①藨草属植物. ②〔英〕宽叶香蒲;水烛. ③(《圣经》《旧约》中经常提及的)纸莎草. ④(美洲)灯心草.

bul·wark [ˈbulwə(ː)k] *n.* ①露天掩体;堡垒;寨,堡坞. ②防波堤. ③防御物,屏障,保障. ④〔*pl.*〕【船】舷墙. *The new dam was a ~ against future floods.* 新堤坝是抵御未来洪水的屏障. *the ~s of the State* 国之干城. — *vt.* ①用堡垒防护. ②防御;保护.

Bul·wer [ˈbulwə] *n.* 布尔沃〔姓氏〕.

bum¹ [bʌm] *n.* 〔俚〕屁股. ~**-sucker** 〔英俚〕谄媚者,马屁精.

bum² [bʌm] *n.* 〔美俚〕①(无业)游民;懒鬼;酒鬼,酒徒. ②寄食者;蹩脚运动员〔工作者〕;(沉缅于体育运动、娱乐等而不顾家庭和前途的)玩角. ③闹饮;放荡. *I called the umpire a ~.* 我认为裁判是个不中用的家伙. *ski ~s* 忘掉一切的滑雪迷. ~***'s comforter*** 报纸. ~***s on the plush*** 有钱的懒汉,富裕的玩角. ~***'s rush*** 强制驱逐出境;粗暴打发走. ***go on the ~*** 过流浪生活. ***on a ~*** 〔俚〕正在闹饮. ***on the ~*** 〔美〕①过流浪生活. ②游手好闲. ③〔口〕有毛病,失修 (*The oven is on the ~ again.* 炉子又有毛病了). — *a.* ①质量低劣的,无价值的. ②可怜的,不中用的. ③瘦弱的,残废的. ④假的;谬误的. ~ *advice* 错误的劝告. *a ~ trip* 不愉快的旅行. *a ~ knee* 残废了的膝盖. *a ~* ***hunch*** 〔美俚〕错误的念头,错误的想象. *a ~* ***rap*** 〔美俚〕虚构的罪名. *a ~* ***steer*** 〔美俚〕假报告;有害的劝告;错误的情报. — *vi.* 〔美口〕①流浪. ②做懒汉闲吃,寄食. ③闹饮. — *vt.* 乞讨,乞求. *He's always bumming cigarettes from me.* 他经常向我讨烟抽. ~**boat** ①(向港内或岸边大船兜售杂货等的)小卖艇. ②垃圾船.

bum·bail·iff [bʌmˈbeilif] *n.* 〔英蔑〕(地方上的)小执行吏.

bum·ber·shoot [ˈbʌmbəʃuːt] *n.* 〔美俚〕伞.

bum·ble¹ [ˈbʌmbl] *n.* 〔英〕骄横的小官吏〔出自狄更斯小说《大卫·科波菲尔》中的一教区小吏〕. **-dom** *n.* 妄自尊大,小官吏习性. **-bling** *a.* 官气十足的,妄自尊大的.

bum·ble² [ˈbʌmbl] *vi.* ①嗡嗡叫;营营响. ②结结巴巴地讲话. ③笨拙地〔错乱地〕行动;踉跄地前进. *He somehow ~d through two years of college.* 他胡乱地混过了两年大学生活. — *vt.* 弄糟,拙劣地做. **bum·bling** ① *a.* 经常出差错的,不称职的. ② *n.* 无能,失职.

bum·ble·bee [ˈbʌmblbiː] *n.* 【动】大黄蜂,土蜂,野蜂.

bum·ble·foot [ˈbʌmblfut] *n.* 【兽医】(家畜因扭伤或细菌感染造成的)肿蹄.

bum·bo [ˈbʌmbəu] *n.* 香甜酒.

bumf [bʌmf] *n.* ①〔英俚〕便纸,草纸. ②〔贬〕文件,公文. ③撒纸赛跑.

bum·kin [ˈbʌmkin] *n.* 〔贬〕乡下佬(= bumpkin).

bum·mer [ˈbʌmə] *n.* 〔美俚〕①懒汉,游手好闲的人. ②失败;令人失望的事〔人〕. ③(吸毒后)严重不愉快的幻觉.

bump¹ [bʌmp] *vi.* ①碰,撞,冲撞 (*against; into*). ②(笨重车子在坏路上)嘎噔嘎噔地走,颠簸 (*along*). ~ *against a wall* 撞到墙上. *The old car ~ed along the road.* 那部老爷车在路上颠簸着行驶. — *vt.* ①撞,打肿,撞伤(头等);【赛船】追撞. ②取消(旅行计划等);(依仗权势)排挤掉;解雇;否决. ③哄抬(物价等). ④〔美俚〕杀死,谋

杀. *The cat ~ed the vase off the shelf.* 猫把花瓶从架上撞下来. *His car ~ed a truck.* 他的小汽车撞到了一辆货车上. *He ~ed the price of corn.* 他哄抬谷价. *The senator was ~ed by the voters.* 那位参议员被选民抛弃了. ~ ***into*** 〔口〕偶然碰见. ~ ***off*** ①猛然推开,撞开. ②〔美俚〕干掉,杀死,谋杀. — *n.* ①碰撞,撞击,扑通一声. ②肿;瘤;(骨相家所说的)头骨隆起;(骨相家认为因头骨隆起而显示的)才能;〔口〕能力. ③【赛船】撞声,追撞. ④(车的)颠簸;【空】突变的气流,(气流突变造成的)突降,簸动. ⑤〔美俚〕降职. *fall with a ~* 扑通一声跌倒. ~ ***on a log*** 〔美〕麻烦的同伴. ***have no ~ of locality*** 记不牢地点,不熟习地理. — *ad.* ①突然地,猛烈地. ②扑通一声. *come ~ on the floor* 扑通一声跌倒在地板上.

bump^2 [bʌmp] *n.* 鹭鸶的叫声. — *vi.* 作鹭鸶叫.

bump·er^1 [ˈbʌmpə] *n.* ①冲撞物;防撞器,缓冲器,减震器. ②(汽车后部的)保险杆. ~ ***to*** ~ (汽车)拥塞,挤撞 (~ *to* ~ *traffic* 汽车一辆接一辆的交通拥挤). ~ **sticker,** ~ **strip** 汽车保险杆上的招贴.

bump·er^2 [ˈbʌmpə] *n.* ①(干杯时的)满杯. ②〔俚〕丰收;(剧场等的)满场,满座. ③〔口〕同类中的特大者,巨物. ~ ***book*** 内容空洞的大厚书. ~ ***crowd*** 〔美〕满场观众. —*a.* 丰富的;丰收的. *a ~ audience* 满座. ~ *crops* 大丰收. — *vt.* ①把(酒杯)斟满. ②撞(杯). — *vi.* 干杯.

bump·ing-race [ˈbʌmpiŋreis] *n.* 追撞船赛.

bump·kin [ˈbʌmpkin] *n.* 〔贬〕粗人,乡下佬. **-ly** *a.*

bump-supper [ˈbʌmpˈsʌpə] *n.* 追撞船赛祝捷晚餐会.

bump·tious [ˈbʌmpʃəs] *a.* 〔口〕傲慢的,狂妄的,唐突的. *be ~ over one's inferiors* 对下级态度傲慢.

bump·y [ˈbʌmpi] *a.* ①(路等)崎岖不平的. ②(车等)颠簸的. ③【空】气流变换不定的. *a ~ sidewalk* 崎岖不平的人行道. *have a ~ ride* 车子颠簸行驶. **-i·ly** *ad.*

bun^1 [bʌn] *n.* ①葡萄干甜面包,小圆面包. ②头;(小圆面包状的)圆髻. *She had her fair hair done up in a ~.* 她把自己漂亮的头发做成了个圆髻. ***take the*** ~ 〔俚〕得头名;占第一位;获胜;登峰造极. **~-fight** 茶会.

bun^2 [bʌn] *n.* 〔美俚〕①滥醉,酩酊大醉. ②酒宴,闹饮. ***have [get] a ~ on*** 〔美俚〕喝醉.

bun^3 [bʌn] *n.* ①〔英方〕尾巴〔尤指兔尾〕. ②〔英〕(童话中的)兔先生,〔美〕(童话中的)松鼠先生.

Buna, bu·na [ˈbjuːnə] *n.* 【化】(德国制)布纳(橡胶),丁(二烯)钠(聚)橡胶. ~*-N* 丁腈橡胶. ~*-S* 丁苯橡胶.

bunch [bʌntʃ] *n.* ①球,束,朵,串. ②瘤;隆起,突起;【矿】小矿巢;【物】(电子)聚束. ③〔美俚〕一群,一帮;一团;牛群,马群;伙伴;一群好友. ④亚麻纱小包〔每包 $1\frac{1}{2}$—12 绞〕;亚麻纱长度单位〔=180,000 码〕. *a ~ of bananas* 一串香蕉. *a ~ of papers* 一束纸. *a ~ of cattle* 一群牛. *The whole ~ of thieves was arrested.* 一伙窃贼全部被捕. *an ore ~* 矿巢,矿囊. ~ ***of calico*** 〔美俚〕女人. ~ ***of fives*** 〔俚〕拳头,手. ***the best [pick] of the*** ~ 精华,出类拔萃的人〔物〕(*In our party he is the best of the ~.* 在我们这群人当中他是尖子). — *vi.* ①捆成一束;穿成一串;(人)集拢. ②起褶. ③隆起. — *vt.* ①使成束〔串〕;集拢. ②使起褶. ~ *straw into sheaves* 把稻草打成把. **~backed** *a.* 驼背的. **~berry** 【植】御膳桔. **~flower** 【植】墨花. **~grass** (美国西部)簇生草,疏丛性牧草. ~ **planting** 【农艺】丛播,穴播. **-er** *n.* 【无】(电子)聚束栅,群象器.

Bunch(e) [bʌntʃ] *n.* 本奇〔姓氏〕.

bunch·y [ˈbʌntʃi] *a.* ①成束的,成球的. ②隆起的. *a round ~ face* 胖圆脸. ~ **top** 【植】簇顶病. ~ **yarn** 竹节纱.

bun·co [ˈbʌŋkəu] *n.* 〔美俚〕(赌博中的)骗局. — *vt.* 骗,骗取. ~ **game** 行骗的赌局. ~ **man,** ~ **steerer** 〔美俚〕骗子,(赌博的)囮子.

bun·combe [ˈbʌŋkəm] *n.* 〔口〕讨好(选民)的演说;空话,废话. *talk [speak] for [to] ~* 作讨好选民的演说.

Bund [bʌnd, G. bʌnt] *n.* (*pl.* ***Bünde*** [bʌndə])〔G.〕①(政治上的)同盟,联盟. ②(美国三十年代的亲纳粹的)德美协会. **-ist** *n.* (美国三十年代的)亲纳粹派.

bund [bund] *n.* (印度、日本、中国等的)堤岸,江〔海〕边大道;码头.

Bun·des·tag [ˈbundəstɑːk] *n.* (联邦德国)联邦议院〔下院〕.

bun·dle [ˈbʌndl] *n.* ①包袱,包裹. ②包,捆,扎,束,卷,把,丛. ③【植】维管束;【生】(神经等的)纤维束. ④〔俚〕一大笔钱,一大堆(东西);(人等的)群,组. ⑤【纺】〔Ir.〕亚麻纱单位〔每 6000 码重 10 磅〕. *a ~ of clothes* 一包衣服. *a ~ of personal belongings* 行李卷. *a ~ of sticks* 一捆棍棒. *a ~ of rascals* 一群坏蛋. *a ~ of problems* 一大堆问题. ***a ~ of nerves*** 动辄就紧张不安的神经过敏者. ***make one's*** ~ 〔美俚〕挣一大笔钱. — *vt.* ①包;捆,扎 (*up*). ②把…乱七八糟地扔进〔塞进〕(*in, into*);把…匆匆忙忙打发走 (*away, off, out*). ③〔美俚〕偷. ~ ***oneself up*** (用…)把自己身体裹裹暖,穿暖和些 (~ *oneself up in blanket* 用毯子裹住身体). ***~ (sb.) out [off, away]*** 把(某人)匆忙赶出,毫不留情地撵出. — *vi.* ①急急忙忙收拾行李. ②匆忙离去 (*off, out, away*). ③和衣而睡. ~ *clothes into a drawer* 把衣服乱七八糟塞进抽屉里. *They indignantly ~d out of the meeting.* 他们急匆匆地愤然离开会场. ~ ***in*** 蜂拥而来. ~ ***out [off, away]*** 仓皇离开. ***B- out of this place!*** 从这里走开!快走开! ~ **handkerchiefs** (英国)深蓝格子手帕.

bung^1 [bʌŋ] *n.* ①(桶口、瓶口等的)塞子. ②桶口,桶孔. ③家畜的盲肠〔肛门〕. ④〔俚〕撒谎,骗人的话. — *vt.* ①(用塞子)塞住(桶孔等). ②〔俚〕扔(石子等). ③使膨胀. ~ ***off*** 〔俚〕逃跑. ~ ***up*** 〔美俚〕①打伤,把…打肿〔打成青紫〕. ②使(鼻等)阻塞;塞满. ③打破,撞破 (*eyes ~ed up from fighting* 在斗殴中眼睛被打肿了. *My car was ~ed up from the accident.* 我的车子出事撞坏了). **-hole** 桶孔,桶口.

bung^2 [bʌŋ] *n.* 〔美俚〕①(机器等的)故障,损坏. ②破产. ③死. ***go*** ~ 〔美俚〕失败;破产;死 (*Many firms went ~ in the panic.* 许多商号在这场经济恐慌中破产了).

bun·ga·loid [ˈbʌŋgəlɔid] *a.* 平房式的〔多带贬意〕.

bun·ga·low [ˈbʌŋgələu] *n.* 有凉台的平房,平房.

bun·gee [ˈbʌndʒiː] *n.* ①橡皮筋,松紧绳,弹性束. ②【空】过度操纵防止器.

bun·gle [ˈbʌŋgl] *vt.* ①粗糙草率地修补;粗制滥造. ②搞坏(事情等),做坏(工作等). ~ *the job* 工作搞得一塌糊涂. — *vi.* 拙劣地工作. *He is a fool who ~s consistently.* 他是一个总把活儿做得很糟的傻瓜. — *n.* 粗制滥造,笨拙. *make a ~ of* 把…搞得一塌糊涂. **-r** *n.* 手艺笨拙的人,把工作做坏的人.

bun·ion [ˈbʌnjən] *n.* 【医】拇趾囊肿胀.

bunk^1 [bʌŋk] *n.* ①(火车等椅床两用的)床铺,铺位,卧铺. ②〔口〕床,卧处. ③牲口食槽;木材搬运车. — *vi.* 〔口〕①睡(在床铺上),去睡. ②与人同床睡 (*with*). ~ *in the attic* 睡在阁楼上. *I ~ed with him.* 我和他同睡一张床. ~ **bed** 双层床. **~mate** 住上下铺或邻铺的伙伴.

bunk^2 [bʌŋk] *n.* 〔美俚〕①骗人的话,废话. ②讨好选民的演说.

bunk^3 [bʌŋk] *vt.* 〔英俚〕从…缺席. ~ *a history class* 上历史课时缺席. — *vi.* 逃走,避开. ~ ***it*** 〔英俚〕逃掉,逃课. — *n.* 逃走〔仅用于 do a ~ 习语中〕. ***do a*** ~ 逃走,走开.

bunk·er [ˈbʌŋkə] *n.* ①(兼充坐椅的)箱子;煤柜,(船上的)煤库;燃料仓;贮槽. ②(进料用的)漏斗,煤斗,料斗. ③浅沟;障碍;【军】掩蔽壕,地堡;防护围墙;【高尔夫球】障碍洞. ④〔美俚〕同房囚犯,同房间的人,战友. *a coal ~* 煤箱,煤库. *a storage ~* 贮藏箱,贮藏库. — *vt.* ①把(煤等)堆入仓内. ②【高尔夫球】把(球)打入洼洞内;〔喻〕使遇到障碍;使陷入困境. *a vessel full ~ed* 上满煤仓的船. ~ **coal** 船用煤. ~ **capacity** (船的)载煤力. ~**-fatigue**〔美俚〕①午睡. ②病卧.
Bunk·er [ˈbʌŋkə] *n.* 邦克〔姓氏〕.
bunk·house [ˈbʌŋkhaus] *n.* (建筑工等的)简易工棚; (矿工等的)简易住屋.
bun·ko [ˈbʌŋkəu] *n.* = bunco.
bun·kum [ˈbʌŋkəm] *n.* = buncombe.
bun·ny [ˈbʌni] *n.* ①〔口〕小兔子〔儿童对兔子的爱称〕. ②〔美俚〕可爱的女郎. ~ **(girl)** 衣着象征兔子的夜总会女招待. ~ **hug** 一种美国交际舞.
Bun·sen [ˈbʌnsn], **R. W.** 本生〔1811—1899, 德国化学家〕. ~ **burner** 本生灯〔一种煤气灯〕.
bunt¹ [bʌnt] *n.* ①抵,撞. ②【棒球】短打; 以短打打出的球. — *vi., vt.* ①(以头、角等)抵,撞. ②【棒球】用短打打出(球). ~ *a curve* 用短打打出一个曲线球.
bunt² [bʌnt] *n.*【海】(帆等的)中央鼓起部分. ②(鱼网的)网身. — *vi.* (帆等)膨胀,鼓起.
bunt³ [bʌnt] *n.*【植】(小麦的)腥黑穗病; 腥黑穗病病菌.
bun·ting¹ [ˈbʌntiŋ] *n.*【鸟】白颊鸟,黄胸鹀.
bun·ting² [ˈbʌntiŋ] *n.* ①旗布; 幔幕. ②信号旗; 船旗; (节日装饰街、屋等的)彩旗〔美多用 *pl.* ~*s*〕. ~ **tosser**〔军俚〕信号兵.
bunt·line [ˈbʌntlin,-ˌlain] *n.*【海】帆脚索,篷缆.
bun·ya-bun·ya [ˈbʌnjəˈbʌnjə] *n.*【植】披针叶南美杉.
Bun·yan [ˈbʌnjən] *n.* 巴尼安〔姓氏〕. **John** ~ 约翰·班扬〔1628—1688, 英国著名宗教讽喻小说《天路历程》(Pilgrim's Progress) 的作者〕.
bun·yan [ˈbʌnjən] *n.* = bunion.
Bu. Ord. = Bureau of Ordnance〔美〕军器司.
bu·oy [bɔi] *n.* ①浮标, 浮子. ②浮圈, 救生圈. *an anchor* ~ 锚浮标. *a mooring* ~ 系船浮标. *a light* ~ 灯浮标. *a can [nun]* ~ 罐[锥]形浮标. — *vt.* ①使浮起 *(up)*; 〔喻〕支持, 鼓励. ②用浮标指示(礁、水道等) *(out)*. *The life jacket ~ed her up until help arrived.* 救生衣使她浮在水上直到获救. *Hopes ~ed her up.* 希望在支撑着她. ~ *a channel* 用浮标标出航道. — *vi.* 浮, 浮上. ~ **boat** 拖住已捕获的鲸鱼的小船.
bu·oy·age [bɔiidʒ] *n.* ①〔集合词〕浮标; 浮标装置. ②(系船)浮标使用费.
buoy·ance [ˈbɔiəns], **buoy·an·cy** [ˈbɔiənsi] *n.* ①浮力; 浮性. ②活泼,轻快; 开朗. ③【商】涨风, 上涨行情; (国家岁入的)增长趋势. *net [gross, reserve]* ~ 净[总,后备]浮力. *a* ~ *gauge* 浮力计. *the centre of* ~【物】浮力中心,浮心.
buoy·ant [ˈbɔiənt] *a.* ①有浮力的,易浮的,会浮的. ②轻快的; 活泼的; 开朗的; 使人振奋的. ③(价格等)上涨的; (国家岁入等)趋向增长的. ~ *matters* 浮体. ~ *force* 浮力. *a* ~ *mine* 浮游水雷,浮标水雷. ~ *spirits* 活泼开朗. ~ *steps* 轻快的步伐. ~ *news for the depressed* 使意气消沉者振作起来的消息.
BUP = British United Press, Ltd. 英国合众社.
bup·leu·rum [bjuːˈplurəm] *n.*【植】柴胡属.
bu·pres·tid [bjuːˈprestid] *n.*【动】吉丁虫科昆虫.
bur [bəː] *n.* ①栗刺,芒刺; 草籽; 带刺草屑. ②【植】(栗、苍耳、牛蒡等)刺果植物; 刺球状花序. ③粘附物, 钩着物; 难以摆脱的人,吃闲饭的人, 寄生虫(指人). ④【机】(铸件等的)毛口,毛头(=burr). ***a* ~ *in the throat*** 梗在喉咙里的东西,骨梗在喉. ***stick like a* ~** 如刺粘衣, 难以摆脱.
bu·ran [buˈrɑːn] *n.*【气】大风雪; 风搅雪,布拉风.
Bur·bage [ˈbəːbidʒ] *n.* 伯比奇〔姓氏〕.
Bur·bank [ˈbəːbæŋk] *n.* 伯班克〔姓氏〕.
Bur·ber·ry [ˈbəːbəri] *n.*〔商品名〕柏帛丽大衣呢; 柏帛丽防水布; 柏帛丽雨衣.
bur·ble [ˈbəːbl] *vi.* ①(水等)发出汩汩声;【空】起气泡; 产生涡流. ②嘟嘟囔囔地说话; 暗笑; 暗暗地生气. *a ~ing brook* 水声汩汩的溪流. — *n.* ①空谈. ②【空】气流分离; 旋涡. ~ **point**【空】临界角. **bur·bly** *a.*
bur·bot [ˈbəːbət] *n.*【鱼】江鳕.
burd [bəːd] *n.*〔Scot.〕女士; 少女,处女.
bur·den¹ [ˈbəːdn] *n.* ①担子,驮子; 负荷,装载量,载重吨数. ②负担,包袱,重累. ③责任,义务. *a beast of* ~ 驮兽. *a ship of* ~ 货船. *carry a* ~ *on one's back* 负重. *financial* ~ 财政上的负担. *the* ~ *of leadership* 领导者的重任. *a ship of a hundred tons* ~. 载重 100 吨的船. *Life has become a* ~ *to him.* 生活对他来说已经成了负担. *shoulder the* ~ *of responsibilities* 担起责任. ***bear the* ~ *and heat of the day*** 吃苦耐劳; 完成责任. ***lay down life's* ~**〔婉〕死. ***(the)* ~ *of proof***【法】举证责任. — *vt.* ①使负重担; 使烦恼,劳累 *(with)*. ②向(车、船等)上装货. ~ *a horse with a load* 让马驮东西. ~ *the people with heavy taxes* 使人民承担沉重的赋税. *a ship heavily ~ed* 装满货的船. **-ed** *a.* ①负荷的. ②有负担的,负担沉重的. ③(两船相遇时)有义务让路的.
bur·den² [ˈbəːdn] *n.* ①歌曲末尾的叠句[重唱句]. ②〔古〕(舞蹈的)伴唱. ②(诗歌、发言等的)重点, 要点,主旨. *the* ~ *of argument* 论点的要旨. ***like the* ~ *of a song*** 反反复复.
bur·den·some [ˈbəːdnsəm] *a.* ①沉重的,难于负担的; 累赘的; 令人烦恼的. ②〔美〕有输送能力的,(船)容积巨大的. *a* ~ *task* 一项艰巨的任务. **-ly** *a.* **-ness** *n.*
bur·dock [ˈbəːdɔk] *n.*【植】牛蒡,牛蒡属植物.
bu·reau [bjuəˈrəu, ˈbjuərəu] *n.* *(pl.* ~*s*, ***bureaux*** [bjuəˈrəuz]*)*〔英〕①(有抽屉的)办公桌,写字台;〔美〕梳妆台,有镜衣柜. ②〔美〕(政府机构的)局 (=〔英〕office); 司(=〔英〕department); 处,办公署. ③编辑部, 事务所,社,室. *an employment* ~ 职业介绍所. *a travel* ~ 旅行社; 旅行事务代办所. *an information* ~〔美〕问讯处, 传达室. *Information B- [B- of Information]* 新闻处. *Tourist Bureau* 旅游事业管理局. ***the B- of the Mint*** (美国财政部的)造币局. ***the B- of the Budget***〔美〕预算局. ***the B- of Customs***〔美〕关税局. ***~-scarf***〔美〕梳妆台罩布.
bu·reauc·ra·cy [bjuəˈrɔkrəsi] *n.* ①官僚主义; 官僚政治,官僚机构. ②〔集合词〕官僚.
bu·reau·crat [ˈbjuərəukræt] *n.* ①官僚主义者; 官僚派头的人. ②官僚,官吏. *the ~s* 官僚. **-ic, -ical** *a.* 官僚政治的,官僚主义的; 官僚派头的. **-ism** 官僚主义; 官僚派头. **-ist** *n.* 官僚主义者.
bu·reau·cra·tese [ˌbjuərəkrəˈtiːz] *n.* 官僚语言,官腔; 公文体.
bu·reau·cra·tize [bjuˈrɔkrətaiz] *vt., vi.* (使)变为官僚主义; (使) 官僚化. **-cra·ti·zation** [bjuˌrɔkrətaiˈzeiʃən] *n.*
bu·reaux [bjuəˈrəuz] *n.* bureau 的复数.
bu·ret(te) [bjuəˈret] *n.*【化】玻璃量管,滴定管.
burg [bəːg] *n.* ①【史】(中世纪的)城堡. ②〔英〕有权选举议员的城镇 (= borough). ③〔美口〕城市,城镇.
-burg, -burgh *comb. f.* 城,市.
bur·gage [ˈbəːgidʒ] *n.* (英国封建时代的)租地法,租地权.
bur·gee [ˈbəːdʒiː] *n.* (船的)燕尾旗; 三角旗.
bur·geon [ˈbəːdʒən] *n.* 嫩芽,蓓蕾. — *vi.* ①发芽. ②(突然)发展,急速成长. *Willows have ~ed forth.* 柳树已经发芽. *The town ~ed into a city.* 这个集镇很快发展成一座城市.
bur·ger [ˈbəːgə] *n.* 汉堡包,肉饼三明治 (=hamburger).
-burger *comb. f.* 构成类似汉堡包的各种肉类或肉类代用品的三明治: fish~ 鱼饼三明治; nut~ 碎果仁饼三明治.
bur·gess [ˈbəːdʒis] *n.* ①(英国自治市的)市民,有市民权的居民. ②【史】(自治市或大学选出的)议员;【美史】美国独立前的马里兰州和弗吉尼亚州议员.
Bur·gess [ˈbəːdʒiz] *n.* 伯吉斯〔姓氏〕.
burgh [ˈbʌrə] *n.*〔Scot.〕自治市.

burgh·er [ˈbəːgə] *n.* (自治市的)市民.
Burgh·ley [ˈbəːli] *n.* 伯利〔姓氏〕.
bur·glar [ˈbəːglə] *n.* (夜间闯入室内的)夜盗,夜间窃贼. ***a belly*** ～〔美俚〕伙食采购员,膳务员. ***a cat*** ～ (从屋顶潜入室内的) 飞贼. ～ **alarm** 防盗警报器. **-i·ous** *a.* 夜盗的,犯夜盗罪的 (*a* ～ *entry* 夜间入室盗窃).
bur·glar·ize [ˈbəːgləraiz] *vi.* 〔美〕夜间盗窃, 做夜盗. — *vt.* 夜间潜入(某处)盗窃. *Thieves* ～*d the warehouse.* 盗贼夜晚潜入仓库作案.
bur·gla·ry [ˈbəːgləri] *n.* 盗窃,夜盗罪. *commit [a]* ～ 夜间入室盗窃;犯夜盗罪.
bur·gle [ˈbəːgl] *vt., vi.* 〔美口〕 = burglarize.
bur·go·mas·ter [ˈbəːgəumɑːstə] *n.* (荷兰等国的)市长. **-ship** *n.*
bur·go·net [ˈbəːgənet] *n.* 【史】带面甲的头盔.
bur·goo [bəːˈguː] *n.* ①〔海俚〕燕麦牛奶粥. ②〔美方〕菜肉浓汤.
bur·grave [ˈbəːgreiv] *n.* 【史】①(中世纪的)城防统帅. ②(世袭的)守城官.
Bur·gun·dy, bur·gun·dy [ˈbəːgəndi] *n.* ①勃艮第〔法国东南部一地区〕. ②〔b-〕勃艮第(地区出产的)红[白]葡萄酒;仿勃艮第葡萄酒. ③〔b-〕暗红色. — *a.* 〔b-〕暗红色的.
bur·i·al [ˈberiəl] *n.* ①埋葬,葬礼. ②埋葬地,墓地. *a* ～ *at sea [on shore]* 海葬[陆葬]. ～ **case** 〔美〕棺材. ～ **ground,** ～ **place** 埋葬地,墓地. ～ **service** 葬礼,葬仪.
Bur·i·at [ˈbuːriæt] *n.* 布利亚特人〔贝加尔湖畔的蒙古人〕,布利亚特语.
bur·ied [ˈberid] bury 的过去式及过去分词.
bur·i·er [ˈberiə] *n.* ①殡葬者. ②殡具.
bu·rin [ˈbjuərin] *n.* ①金属雕刻刀,錾刀. ②雕刻风格. ③(史前人用的)燧石打火器. **-ist** *n.* (铜版)雕刻家.
burke [bəːk] *vt.* ①〔古〕勒死(某人)以出卖尸体(供解剖用). ②秘密镇压[取消,禁止]; 扣压(议案等). ③暗中消弭(争端等). *The proposal got* ～*d.* 提案被扣压了. ～ *an issue* 暗中解决争端.
Burk(e) [bəːk] *n.* 伯克〔姓氏,男子名〕.
burl [bəːl] *n.* ①(线、布等的)线头,粒节,疵点. ②(树的)节疤,瘿. — *vt.* 消除(布上的)疵点,修(布).
bur·lap [ˈbəːlæp] *n.* 〔美〕打包粗麻布;麻袋.
bur·lesque [bəːˈlesk] *a.* ①滑稽的,诙谐的. ②戏谑的,讽刺的. — *n.* ①打油诗,游戏笔墨;滑稽戏,笑剧;漫画. ②〔美俚〕杂耍;脱衣舞. — *vt.* (以夸张的模仿手法)讥笑;使滑稽化. ～ *old romances* 以夸张手法把古代传奇故事弄得滑稽可笑. **-r** *n.* 〔美〕滑稽戏演员.
bur·les·queen [ˌbəːlesˈkwiːn] *n.* 〔美俚〕滑稽戏女演员.
bur·let·ta [bəːˈletə] *n.* 小滑稽歌剧.
bur·ley, Bur·ley [ˈbəːli] *n.* (产于美国肯塔基州及其附近诸州的)茫叶浅色烟草.
bur·ley·cue [ˈbəːlikjuː] *n.* 〔美俚〕 = burlesque.
Bur·lin·game [ˈbəːliŋgeim] *n.* 伯林盖姆〔姓氏〕.
bur·ly [ˈbəːli] *a.* ①魁伟的,结实的,健壮的,粗鲁的. ②直率的,直截了当的. *a* ～ *oak* 高大的橡树. *a* ～*-set young man* 一个体格魁伟的青年. *a* ～ *way of speaking* 直截了当的讲话方式. — *n.* ①〔美俚〕身材魁伟的人. ②〔美〕滑稽戏. **-i·ly** *ad.* **-i·ness** *n.*
Bur·ma [ˈbəːmə] *n.* 缅甸〔亚洲〕.
Bur·man *n.* *(pl.* ～*s), a.* = Burmese.
Bur·mese [bəːˈmiːz] *n.* 〔*sing., pl.*〕 ①缅甸人. ②缅甸语. — *a.* 缅甸的;缅甸人的;缅甸语的.
burn[1] [bəːn] ***(burnt*** [bəːnt], ***～ed;burnt,～ed)*** *vt.* ①烧;点(烛、灯等). ②烧焦,烧坏;烧伤,烫伤;烧死;〔美〕用电椅处死,电毙;对…处火刑. ③烧制,焙烧(砖瓦等);烧穿,烧通. ④烙上(火印等);使铭感. ⑤(用烙铁、硫酸等)炙,烙,烧灼. ⑥【化】使燃烧,使氧化,利用(铀等的)核能. ⑦晒(黑等);晒干. ⑧使发烧;使(喉咙)辣得难受. ⑨激怒,挑动. ⑩消耗;浪费,挥霍. ⑪〔美俚〕欺骗;出售(劣质或假的麻醉药品). ⑫〔美俚〕使(火箭发动机等)点火. *This furnace* ～*s gas.* 这个炉子烧的是煤气. ～ *a torch* 点火把. ～ *(sb.) alive* 把(某人)活活烧死. ～ *clay to bricks* 把粘土烧成砖. ～ *charcoal* 烧炭. *She* ～*ed the roast again.* 她又把肉烤焦了. ～ *one's face in the sun* 晒黑面孔. ～ *a finger* 灼伤手指. ～ *a hole in his sleeve* 衣袖上烧了一个洞. *heretics* ～*ed at the stake* 在火刑架上被烧死的异教徒. ～ *one's money* 挥霍钱财. ～ *one's energy* 浪费精力. — *vi.* ①燃烧,烧着;点着. ②烧黑,烧焦,烧坏;烫痛;烫伤;晒黑. ③发热,发光,发红;(因患病等)发热;发烫. ④(因吃辛辣食物等)辣得发烧. ⑤激动,兴奋;〔美〕发火,发怒;渴望;(问题等)白热化. ⑥【化】氧化;热熔;【物】利用核能. ⑦〔俚〕坐电椅(被处死). ⑧〔美俚〕(火箭发动机等)点火. *a fireplace* ～*ing merrily* 炉火暖融融. ～ *briskly* 火旺. *a light* ～*ing in the house* 屋内灯光明亮. *the burning sand* 发烫的沙子. *ears* ～*ing from cold* 耳朵冻得发痛. *Iodine* ～*s so.* 碘酒给人一种热辣辣的感觉. ～*ing to tell the story* 急着要讲那个故事. ～ *with jealousy* 妒火中烧. *the potatoes* ～*ed to a crisp* 土豆烧焦了. *She* ～*s easily.* 她的皮肤容易晒黑. *murderer sentensed to* ～ 被判处上电椅的凶手. ～ *with fever* (患病)发烧. ～ ***away*** ①烧完;烧落;烧去. ②继续燃烧;(渐渐)消灭. ～ ***blue*** 烧得火光发青. ～ ***daylight*** 白昼点灯,徒劳无益. ～ ***down*** ①烧光,把…烧成平地. ②(蜡烛等)逐渐烧完;火力减弱 (*The barn was* ～*ed down.* 谷仓被烧掉了). ～ ***for*** 渴望,热中于. ～ ***into [in]*** ①烧进;(因氧化作用等)腐蚀. ②(在瓷器等上)烧上(装饰画等),烙上;留下(深刻印象等)(～ *into memory* 深刻地留在记忆里). ～ ***itself out [away]*** 烧完. ～ ***low*** 火头无气儿,火力弱. ～ ***off*** ①烧去;烫去(污点等). ②渐渐烧完 (*The sun* ～*ed off the mist.* 太阳驱散雾霭). ～ ***on*** 焚烧;焊接. ***～one's boats [bridges] (behind one)*** 破釜沉舟,自断退路. ～ ***one's fingers*** 由于管闲事[鲁莽]而吃苦头. ～ ***oneself out*** (人等因过度劳累而)精疲力尽;(机器等因使用过度而)出故障;(爱情等因过于炽烈而)耗完. ～ ***out*** ①烧起来;烧光;烧尽;烧坏,烧断. ②(精力等)耗尽;(炉子等因燃料耗完而)熄灭;(机器等因过度使用而)损坏. ③放火把(野兽)赶出. ④(因房子起火)烧得逃了出来〔多用被动语态〕(*They are burnt out.* 他们因失火而逃了出来. ～ *the rats out* 用火把老鼠赶出来). ～ ***the candle at both ends*** 过分耗费精力. ～ ***the earth [wind]*** 〔美〕飞快地去,开足马力去;走马观花地旅行. ～ ***the midnight oil*** 干到深夜,开夜车. ～ ***the water*** 用灯光等诱捕(蛙等). ～ ***together*** 熔接,烧焊. ～ ***to the ground*** 把…烧光,被烧成平地. ～ ***up*** ①烧完,燃尽. ②(炉火等)烧了起来,旺起来. ③使恼怒,激怒;〔美〕生气,发怒. ④使变狂热,使热衷于 (*The paper* ～*ed up in a minute.* 那张纸倾刻之间就烧掉了. *He was getting* ～*ed up about something* 他在为某件事生气). ～ ***up the cinders*** 〔美〕(赛跑时)拼命冲. ***Burn you!*** 该死的! ***have money [time] to*** ～ 〔美〕过分有钱[有时间]. ***money*** ～***s hole in one's pocket*** 爱花钱;钱烧口袋漏,一有就不留. ***One's [The] ears*** ～. 有人说(自已)闲话,耳根发烧. ***There you*** ～! ①(玩捉迷藏游戏快接近对方时喊叫)我可抓住你了! ②(快解决问题时说)答案快找到了! — *n.* ①烧伤,火伤;灼伤,电击伤,辐射伤;烧焦;烧痕. ②烧(制). ③怒火〔主要用于slow ～词组中〕. ④〔美〕(森林等着火烧出的)林间平地;烧山. ⑤〔口〕雪茄烟. ⑥〔美俚〕(宇宙飞行火箭发动机)在飞行中起动. ⑥〔*pl.*〕〔美俚〕短的连鬓胡子;鬓角. *a* ～ *on the hand* 手上的烧伤. *a* ～ *where fire ripped through the forest* 森林着火后烧出的林间平地. *first [second, third] degree* ～ 一度[二度,三度]烧伤. ***slow*** ～ 愈来愈上升的怒火. ～ **artist** 〔美俚〕出售假的或劣质毒品的人. **～-back** *n.* (焊接)烧结. **～bag** (装着随时可烧毁的机密文件的) 烧袋. **～-in** *n.* 烧上; 黄化,

预烧. ~-**off** *n.* (焊接)熔焊穿. ~-**on** *n.* 焊上, 焊补. ~-**out** *n.* ①燃完, 熄灭; (喷气发动机等的)歇火. ②大火灾; 烧毁, 烧光. ~-**up** ①【物】燃耗. ②耗尽. -**ed** *a.* ①烧焦的. ②〔美〕被处电刑的.

burn² [bə:n] *n.* 〔Scot.〕小溪, 小川, 小河.

burn·a·ble [ˈbə:nəbl] *a.* 可燃烧的. — *n.* 可燃物〔尤指废料〕.

Burne-Jones [ˈbə:nˈdʒəunz] *n.* 伯恩-琼斯〔姓氏〕.

burn·er [ˈbə:nə] *n.* ①烧…人; 气焊工, 气割工. ②燃烧物; 炉子; 灯; 灯头, 灯口; 喷烧器, 喷灯; 喷嘴; 燃烧室. ③火药柱. *a charcoal [brick]* ~ 烧炭〔砖〕工人. *a gas* ~ 煤气灯. *an U*²³⁵ ~ 铀²³⁵ 反应堆. *slow* ~ 缓燃剂.

bur·net [ˈbə:nit] *n.* 【植】(美洲)地榆.

Bur·nett [bə(:)ˈnet, ˈbə:nit] *n.* 伯内特〔姓氏〕.

Bur·ney [ˈbə:ni] *n.* 伯尼〔姓氏〕.

burn·ing [ˈbə:niŋ] *a.* ①燃烧的, 象燃烧一样的; 灼痛的; 辛辣的. ②猛烈的, 强烈的; 热烈的. ③议论纷纷的; 紧急的. ④极恶劣的; 明摆着的. *under a* ~ *sun* 酷日之下. *forests* ~ *with autumn tints* 满林秋叶红似火. *a* ~ *thirst* 渴得要命; 急切希望. *a* ~ *love* 热恋. *a* ~ *taste* 辣味. *a* ~ *situation* 紧急事态. *in* ~ *need of* 亟需. *a* ~ *mistake* 明摆着的错误. *a* ~ *shame* 奇耻大辱. — *n.* ①燃烧. ②烧制. ③炎症. ~ **glass** 凸透镜, 火镜. ~ **mountain** 火山. ~ **oil** 燃油, 灯油. ~ **point** 燃(烧)点.

bur·nish [ˈbə:niʃ] *vt.* ①磨, 打磨. ②【机】抛光, 轧光; 擦亮; 使光滑. — *vi.* (金属等经擦、磨等而)发亮. *The stone* ~*s well.* 这种石头容易磨亮. — *n.* 光泽, 光亮; 光滑. *a high* ~ 很亮的光泽. -**er** *n.* ①把…磨亮的人, 打磨工. ②磨擦抛光辊, 磨滑器, 磨棒; (牙科用的)研磨器. -**ing** *n.* 磨擦抛光.

bur·noose, bur·nous [bə:ˈnu:s], **bur·nouse** [bə:ˈnu:z] *n.* (阿拉伯人等穿的)带有包头巾的外衣.

Burns [bə:nz] *n.* 伯恩斯〔彭斯〕〔姓氏〕. **Robert** ~ 罗伯特·彭斯〔1759—1796, 苏格兰诗人〕.

Burn·side [ˈbə:nsaid] *n.* 伯恩赛德〔姓氏〕.

burn·sides [ˈbə:nsaidz] *n.* 〔*pl.*〕〔美口〕连鬓胡子.

burnt [bə:nt] burn 的过去式及过去分词. — *a.* ①烧过的; 烧伤的; 烧制成的. ②烧焦的; 赭色的. ③(谷物)受病害的. *a* ~ *taste* 焦臭味. *taste* ~ 焦臭. ~ *orange* 赭色的橘子. ***A [The]*** ~ ***child dreads the fire.*** 烧伤过的孩子怕火, 惊弓之鸟. ~ **ochre** 烧赭土. ~ **offering** 【宗】烧祭, 祭神的烧烤全牲. ~ **plaster** 焦石膏. ~ **sienna** ①富铁煅黄土. ②深褐色; 深褐色燃料. ~ **umber** 烧赭土; 赭色.

burp [bə:p] *n., vi.* 〔美俚〕打嗝. — *vt.* (用拍背或摩背的方法)使(婴儿)打嗝〔以排出胃中闷积的气体〕. ~ **gun** 〔美军俚〕手提机关枪〔冲锋枪〕.

burr¹ [bə:] *n.* ①(发"r"音时小舌颤动的)粗喉音〔多为英格兰北部和苏格兰的地方音〕; 粗浊的发音. ②嘎嘎声, 吓吓声. — *vt.* 用粗喉音说(话). — *vi.* 用粗喉音说话, 发音粗浊.

burr² [bə:] *n.* ①【机】垫圈; (冲孔机冲下的)金属小圆片. ②(月)晕, 光圈. ③(木材的)瘤部木纹; 【矿】坚硬石灰岩.

burr³ [bə:] *n.* ①(铜版等的)粗刻纹, 锯齿状刻纹. ②【机】毛口, 毛头. ③钻孔锥; (牙科用的)磨锥(=~ drill). ④ = bur. ~-**breast** 【纺】粗梳机. ~-**wire** 锯齿钢丝.

burr⁴ [bə:] *n.* 粗磨(刀)石.

Burr [bə:] *n.* 伯尔〔姓氏〕.

bur·ro [ˈbʌrəu] *n.* ①美国西部小毛驴. ②驴子.

Bur·rough(s) [ˈbʌrəu(z)] *n.* ①伯勒(斯)〔姓氏〕. ② **Edgar Rice** ~ 伯勒斯, 系列小说集《泰山》(Tarzan)的作者.

bur·row [ˈbʌrəu] *n.* ①(狐、兔等的)穴, 窟, 地洞. ②(地下)躲藏处, 避难所. — *vi.* ①掘穴, 打洞. ②穴居; 钻入洞里, 潜伏. ③钻研, 查阅 *(into)*. *Worms* ~ *into fruit.* 虫蛀水果. *a* ~*ing animal* 穴居动物. ~ *into archives* 埋头查阅文件. — *vt.* ①打(地洞), 掘(穴); 掘成. ②把(自己)藏入洞内, 让(自己)躲藏起来. ③埋藏. ~ *a hole* 打地洞. ~ *a path through the crowd* 从人群中钻出来.

burr·stone, bur·stone, buhr·stone [ˈbə:stəun] *n.* 磨石; 臼石.

bur·ry [ˈbə:ri] *a.* ①【机】毛刺多的. ②【纺】(布)疵点多的. ③(讲话时)喉音重的.

bur·sa [ˈbə:sə] *n.* *(pl.* ~*s,* ***bur·sae*** [ˈbə:si:]*)* ①【解】囊; 滑囊, 粘液囊; 翅囊. ②【植】交和缴. ③(中世纪的)大学宿舍.

bur·sar [ˈbə:sə] *n.* ①(英国大学等的)帐房, 会计〔出纳〕员. ②(中世纪)大学生; 〔Scot.〕大学生津贴〔奖学金〕, 领津贴大学生.

bur·sar·i·al [bəˈseriəl] *a.* ①(大学等)管帐的, 会计的. ②(大学生)津贴的, 奖学金的.

bur·sa·ry [ˈbə:səri] *n.* ①(大学或修道院的)财务处. ②〔英〕(大学)奖学金.

burse [bə:s] *n.* ①钱包. ②(大学生的)奖学金(= bursary); 奖学金基金. ③【天主】圣餐布箱.

bur·seed [ˈbə:ˌsi:d] *n.* 【植】鹤虱属植物(=stickseed).

bur·si·form [ˈbə:siˌfɔ:m] *a.* 【解、动】囊状的; 袋状的.

bur·si·tis [bə:ˈsaitis] *n.* 【医】粘液囊炎, 滑囊炎.

burst [bə:st] *(~; ~)* *vi.* ①破裂, 迸裂, 爆炸; 爆发出, 喷出; (花蕾等)绽开, (洪水等)溃决; 〔俚〕破产. ②突然发作, 忽然出现. ③胀破; 充满 *(with)*. *The shell* ~ *overhead.* 炸弹在头上爆炸. *The buds are* ~*ing.* 花蕾正在绽开. *The door* ~ *open.* 门猛然打开. *Oil* ~ *to the surface.* 石油喷出地面. ~ *on the eye* 突然出现在眼前. *The applause* ~ *from the crowd.* 人群中爆发出掌声. *I am* ~*ing to tell him the news.* 我恨不得马上就告诉他那个消息. — *vt.* ①使破裂, 使爆裂; 打开, 劈开, 撞开; 突破, 冲破. ②使充满, 使胀破. ~ *the baloon with a pin* 用针把气球戳破. *He became so excited that he almost* ~ *a blood vessel.* 他兴奋得几乎血管都要破裂了, 他万分兴奋. ~ *a door open* 把门撞开. ~ *a conspiracy* 破获一起阴谋. ~ *the restraints* 打破束缚. *banks* ~ *by flood* 被洪水冲破的堤防. ***be*** ~***ing to do (sth.)*** 忍不住〔急着〕要做(某事). ~ ***away*** ①破裂, 爆发. ②〔诗〕急忙逃走. ~ ***forth*** ①忽然跳出; 忽然出现; 突然爆发; (血等)喷出 *(A great epidemic* ~ *forth.* 突然发生了一场大瘟疫). ~ ***in*** ①扑进, 闯进; 打扰, 侵入. ②插嘴, 打断(别人谈话). ③突然出现 *(Sorry if we* ~ *in on you.* 突然来打扰您, 非常抱歉). ~ ***into*** ①闯进. ②突然发作, 突然…起来 *(*~ *into a room* 扑进房内. ~ *into fame* 忽然出名. ~ *into flames* 忽然烧起来. ~ *into laughter [tears]* 突然哈哈大笑〔哇地一声哭起来〕. ~ *into bloom* 开花. ~ *into speech* 急忙说起来). ~ ***one's sides (with laughing)*** 笑破肚皮. ~ ***oneself*** (过劳)伤身. ~ ***on the ear*** 忽然听见 *(A sound* ~ *on [upon] their ears.* 一个声音突然传进他们耳中). ~ ***open*** 推开; 忽然打开; (花)渐开, (板栗)裂开. ~ ***out*** ①冒出; 现出. ②突然发作; 突然发生; 突然…起来. ~ ***through*** 推开, 拨开. ~ ***up*** ①爆发. ②失败, 破产, 垮台. ③突然激动, 勃然大怒. ④使崩溃. ~ ***upon [on]*** 突然出现; 袭击 *(A splendid view* ~ *upon us.* 我们的眼前突然呈现一片壮丽的景色. *The real situation* ~ *upon me.* 我突然认清了真实的形势). ~ ***with*** 装满, 充满 *(He is* ~*ing with health.* 他极其健康. *a bag* ~*ing with gold* 装满金子的口袋. *a heart ready to* ~ *with indignation* 容易动怒). ***go*** ~ 〔口〕失败, 破产. — *n.* ①突然破裂, 炸裂, 爆炸. ②(油等的)喷出; (感情等的)爆发, (景物等的)突然出现. ③突进, 疾走; 【军】(自动武器的)连发射击, 扫射. ④一口气, 一阵, 一下子. ⑤【无】脉冲; 正弦波群; 〔口〕闹饮. *a* ~ *of tire* 轮胎爆裂. *a great* ~ *of light* 突然出现一大片亮光. *a* ~ *of passion* 激情的迸发. *a* ~ *of blood from the wound* 伤口喷血. *a* ~ *of mountain and plain* 突然展开的峰峦和平原的景色. *The* *car passed us with a ~ of speed.* 那辆车子突然加快速度超过我们. *a fine ~ of the countryside* 眼前突然呈现出一派秀丽的乡村景色. *a ~ in the dike* 决堤. *a ~ from the machine gun* 机枪的扫射. ***at a [one] ~*** 一阵;一口气;一举,一下 (*go up a hill at a ~* 一口气爬上山). ***go on the ~*** 〔俚〕闹饮. ***in sudden ~s*** 一阵一阵[忽冷忽热] 地工作 (*work in sudden ~s* 冷一阵热一阵地干工作). **~-up** 〔口〕垮台,破产.

Bur. St. = Bureau of Standards 国家标准局.

burst·er [ˈbəːstə] *n.* ① = buster. ②进行爆破的人,爆破工,爆破兵;爆炸物. ③炸药 (= bursting charge).

burst·ing [ˈbəːstiŋ] *n.* 爆裂,爆炸,爆发;突然发生. ~ **chamber** 爆炸室. ~ **charge** 炸药. ~ **layer** 爆破层;(防空洞上的)坚固覆盖层. ~ **point** 爆发点;(情绪等的)忍耐极限 (*His impatience was almost at its ~ point.* 他的不耐烦情绪几乎已经达到了顶点. *They habitually gorged to the ~ point on Sunday.* 他们每到星期天总要大吃大喝,直到快把肚子胀破). ~ **strength**【物】破裂强度.

bur·then [ˈbəːðən] *n., vt.* burden 的古体.

bur·ton [ˈbəːtn] *n.*【机】复滑车. ***go [knock] for a ~*** 〔俚〕无影无踪,消失,不再存在.

Bur·ton [ˈbəːtn] *n.* 伯顿[姓氏,男子名].

Bu·run·di [buˈrundi] *n.* 布隆迪〔非洲〕. **-an** *n.* 布隆迪人.

bur·weed [ˈbəːwiːd] *n.*【植】有刺壳果的植物[如牛蒡、狼把草、欧龙牙草等].

bur·y [ˈberi] *vt.* ①埋葬,葬;为…举行葬礼. ②埋藏,遮盖,掩蔽. ③专心致志于,埋头于 *(in)*. ④忘却,从记忆中排除. ⑤死去(家属). ⑥插入,刺入*(in, into)*. *~ treasure under the ground* 把宝物埋到地下. *~ sb. with military honors* 以军礼安葬某人. *She has buried two children.* 她已经死去两个孩子. *~ wrongs* 文过饰非. *~ one's face in one's hands* 以手遮面. *be buried in sloth* 懒散. *~ one's differences* 忘去(原有)争端. *~ oneself in the country* 隐退乡村. *be buried in oblivion* 被世人忘却. *be buried in thought [grief]* 沉思冥想[哀怨满腹]. *~ oneself in one's work* 埋头工作. ***be buried alive*** 被活埋;隐居,退隐. ***~ one's head in the sand*** 把头埋进沙里,避眼不看现实. ***~ the hatchet [tomahawk]*** 埋起战斧,讲和,化除干戈.

Bur·y [ˈbjuəri, ˈberi] *n.* 伯里[姓氏].

bur·y·ing [ˈberiiŋ] *n.* 埋,埋葬. *a ~ lot* 葬地. ~ **ground,** ~ **place** 墓地,坟场.

bus, 'bus [bʌs] *n. (pl. ~ses, ~es)* ①公共马车;公共汽车;客机. ②〔口〕汽车,机器脚踏车; 飞机. ③【电】信息转移通路;汇流条,母线. ④〔美俚〕(小餐馆等的)服务员 (= ~ boy). ⑤〔美俚〕火箭[导弹]的一级. *a double-decker ~* 双层公共汽车. *get a ~* 乘公共汽车. ***miss the ~*** ①失掉机会. ②事业失败. — *vi.* 〔美口〕①乘公共汽车. ②充当餐馆服务员的下手[打杂工]. *~ for one's meal* 以充当饭馆打杂工换取饭费. *We bussed to New York.* 我们乘公共汽车去纽约. — *vt.* 用公共汽车接送学童〔为抵制学校的种族隔离政策而采取的一种措施〕. ~ ***it*** 〔口〕乘公共汽车 (*~ it from New York to Washington* 从纽约乘公共汽车去华盛顿). **~-bar**【电】汇流条,母线. **~boy** 〔美俚〕餐馆服务员的下手,餐馆打杂工. **~-conductor** (公共汽车)售票员. ~ **driver** ①(公共汽车)驾驶员[有时兼售票员]. ②〔俚〕轰炸机驾驶员. ~ **girl** 〔美俚〕餐馆女打杂工,服务员的女下手. **~load** 公共汽车最大载容量. **~man** (公共汽车的)驾驶员[乘务员](*a ~man's holiday* 照常工作的假日). **~nod**【电】导(电)条. ~ **queue** 等候公共汽车的长队. **~-shelter** (公共汽车)候车棚. ~ **stop** 公共汽车站.

bus. = bushel; bushels; business.

bus·by [ˈbʌzbi] *n.* (英国陆军轻骑兵、近卫兵等戴的)熊皮鸟缨高顶帽.

bush[1] [buʃ] *n.* ①灌木;矮树丛;丛林. ② 〔the ~〕〔澳〕未开垦的丛林地. ③(从前酒店做招牌的)长春藤;〔古〕酒店. ④〔俚〕蓬头,蓬发;蓬松的尾巴;【猎】孤尾. ⑤〔*pl.*〕= ~ league. *trees and ~es* 高高矮矮的树木. *a clump of ~es* 一片灌木林. *Good wine needs no ~.* 酒好客自来(无需做广告). ***beat about [around] the ~*** 旁敲侧击. ***beat the ~es*** 到处搜寻 (*beat the ~es for engineers* 搜罗工程师). ***go ~*** 〔澳俚〕①(逃犯等)躲入丛林. ②(动物)变野 (*a pack of dogs that have gone ~* 一群变野了的狗). ***take to the ~*** 逃入丛林地带;做强盗,当绿林好汉.— *vi.* ①(毛发等)丛生.②形成灌木林. *His eyebrows ~ed together.* 他的眉毛浓密. — *vt.* ①用灌木围住,用灌木支持;在栽灌木. ②〔美俚〕使筋疲力尽. *a frozen lake ~ed where the ice is not safe* 在上冻的湖面冰薄的地方栽上灌木[作为危险标志]. ~ ***it*** 住入丛林地带. **~baby**【动】猩〔非洲森林中的一种小猿,其声似婴儿啼哭〕. **~buck** 南非羚羊. ~ **cat**【动】薮猫. **~craft** 丛林中生活的技能. **~fighter** 丛林游击兵. **~-fighting** 丛林战. **~fire** 灌木林火 (*~-fire war* 灌木林火式战争). ~ **hat** (澳大利亚军装的)阔边帽. **~hammer** ①凿石锤. ②(使混凝土路面不致过滑的)气动凿毛机. **~hog** (南非)野猪. **~hook** (剪修灌木用的)长柄大镰刀. ~ **jacket** 有腰带的棉布短上衣. **~land** 〔Can.〕原始森林区. ~ **league** ①(棒球等)次级竞赛联合会. ②外行;次等. **~-league** *a.* 次级的,不成熟的,二流的. **~man** ①新垦地移民;〔澳〕林居人;乡下人. ②〔B-〕(南非游牧民族) 布希曼人. **~manship** = ~craft. **~master** (南非) 大毒蛇. ~ **parole** 〔美俚〕越狱. ~ **pilot** 在无人区飞行的飞行员. **~ranger** 丛林居民;〔澳〕土匪. ~ **telegraph** 情报[谣言等]的迅速传播. **~-veld** 丛林地带;南非草原. ~ **warbler** 黄莺. **~whack** *vi., vt.* ①〔美〕开伐丛林. ②(利用丛林)伏击. **~whacker** ①〔美〕林中居民;开伐丛林的人. ②〔美史〕(南北战争中的)游击兵. ③(砍伐丛林的)大镰刀.

bush[2] [buʃ] *n.*【机】衬套,套管,套筒;轴衬,轴瓦. *insulating ~* 绝缘套管. *brake ~* 闸衬. — *vt.* 加(金属)衬套[轴衬]于.

Bush [buʃ] *n.* 布什〔姓氏〕.

bushed[1] [buʃt] *a.* ①〔澳口〕迷路在灌木林中的;不知所措的. ②〔美口〕疲劳不堪的. *get ~ without a guide* 因没有向导在丛林中迷路.

bushed[2] [buʃt] *a.*【机】加有衬套的.

bush·el[1] [ˈbuʃl] *n.* ①蒲式耳[谷物计量单位;美国 Winchester ~ = 35.238 升,英国 Imperial ~ = 36 升]. ②一蒲式耳的容器;容量相当于一蒲式耳的重量. ③ 大量. *~s of gems* 大量珠宝. *a ~ of lies* 一大堆谎言. ***hide one's light [candle] under a ~*** 不露锋芒. ***measure other people's corn by one's own ~*** 拿自己的标准衡量别人,以己度人. **~basket** 一蒲式耳筐〔一筐等于一蒲式耳〕. ~ **iron** 碎铁.

bush·el[2] [ˈbuʃl] *vi., vt.* (**-ll-**) 〔美〕改[翻新](衣服). **-(l)er** *n.* 改制衣服的人;补衣工〔尤指成衣工助手〕.

Bu·shi·do [ˈbuːʃidəu] *n.* 〔Jap.〕武士道.

bush·ing [ˈbuʃiŋ] *n.* = bush.[2]

bush·wa, bush·wah [ˈbuʃwɑː] *n.* 〔美俚〕胡话,胡扯;空话,废话.

bush·y [ˈbuʃi] *a.* ①灌木似的. ②灌木茂密的. ③(毛发等)浓密的. *~ eyebrows* 浓眉. **~-bearded** 胡须浓的. **-i·ly** *ad.* **-i·ness** *n.*

bus·i·ly [ˈbizili] *ad.* 忙,繁忙,忙碌. *wag one's tongue ~* 碎嘴,讲个不停. *study ~* 忙着做功课.

bus·i·ness [ˈbiznis] *n.* ①事务,业务;事,事业,行业,工作. ②实业;商业,营业,买卖,交易;营业额,交易量;商情. ③商店,企业,公司;事务所. ④职责,本分;权利. ⑤要事,要务;难事. ⑥【剧】动作,表情. ⑦(会议等的)议程. *~ as usual* 照常营业. *follow the ~ of* 以…为业. *What line of ~ is he in?* 他是干什么的? *His ~ is poultry farming.* 他从事养鸡业. *hours of ~ [~ hours]* 营业[办公]时间. *do good [a great] ~* 生意好,赚钱

[做大买卖]. *We shut up ~ at six.* 我们六点钟停止营业. *depression of ~* 商情不景气. *domestic [foreign] ~* 国内[对外]贸易. *open a ~* 开店[开业]. *build [set] up a ~* 开店,设商号. *His ~ is on the corner of Broadway and Elm street.* 他的商号设在百老汇和埃尔姆街拐角的地方. *~ centre* 商业中心. *What a ~ it is!* 实在麻烦! *an awkward ~* 麻烦事. *What is your ~ here?* 有什么事? *It is none of your ~.* 不干你事,别管闲事. *I have ~ with him.* 我跟他有要紧的事要谈. *It's your ~ to wash the dishes now.* 现在该你洗碗碟了. ***be doing good ~ with*** 和…关系不错. ***~ accounting unit*** 经济核算单位. ***B- before pleasure.*** 正事要紧. ***the ~ end*** 〔俚〕(工具等)起作用的部分,使用[锐利]的一头(*the ~ end of a scythe* 大镰刀的刀身. *the ~ end of a revolver* 手枪的枪身). ***B- is ~.*** 公事公办;生意是生意,交情归交情. ***come [get] to ~*** 动手做事;言归正传. ***do sb.'s ~ = do the ~ for sb.*** 〔口〕要某人的命(*That much will be enough to do his ~.* 那就足够要他的命了. *This will do the ~ for him.* 这会要他的命的). ***enter on [upon] ~*** 开业. ***Everybody's ~ is nobody's ~.*** 人人负责,结果无人负责. ***get down to ~*** 认真干起来. ***get [give] the ~*** 〔美俚〕(被)粗暴地对待;(被)作弄. ***go about one's ~*** 做自己的事;〔常作命令式〕(*Go about your ~.* 去你的,走开). ***go into ~*** 入实业界做生意. ***go out of ~*** 停业;改行. ***go to ~*** 上班. ***Good ~!*** 干得好! 妙极了! ***have no ~ to do [say] sth.*** 没有做[说]某事的权利[道理]. (*You have no ~ coming into this house.* 你没有进这个屋子的权利. *The weather has no ~ to be so warm in winter.* 冬天的气候不该这样暖和). ***know one's ~*** 精通本行. ***like nobody's ~*** 〔口〕特别地. ***make ~ of*** 以…为业. ***make a great ~ of it*** 觉得难办[棘手],甚觉麻烦. ***make the ~ for*** 了结. ***man of ~*** ①实业家;事务家. ②商业[法律]代理人(*He is a man of ~.* 他是一个实业家. *He is her man of ~.* 他是她的商业[法律]代理人). ***mean ~*** (行动、话等)是当真的(*I mean ~.* 我是当真的,不是说笑. *By the fire in his eyes we know that he meant ~.* 从他愤怒的眼神中,我们看出他不是说着玩的). ***Mind your own ~.*** 不要管闲事. ***monkey ~*** 〔美俚〕胡闹;欺骗. ***on ~*** 因公,有事,有要事(*No admittance except on ~.* 非公莫入,闲人免进). ***out of ~*** 破产,失业. ***send sb. about his ~*** 赶走某人;辞退[解聘]某人. ***stick to one's ~*** 专心做事. ***talk ~*** 说正经话,谈正经的. **~ card** 业务名片. **~ circle** 商界. **~ college** 商学院. **~ cycle** 经济危机周期;工商业循环. **~ English** 商业英语. **~ flying** (正常班次以外的)商务飞行. **~man** 实业家;商人. **~ office** 商业事务所. **~ school** 商业学校. **~ unionism** 工联主义. **~woman** 女实业家,女商人. **-like** *a.* ①事务式的;有条理的. ②有效的,讲究实际的(*a ~ administration* 有效的经营. *He did his work in a ~ way.* 他踏踏实实地工作).

busk [bʌsk] *n.* ①(妇女紧身衣胸部的)鲸骨架[铜片、木片等]. ②〔英方〕紧身衣.

busk·er [ˈbʌskə] *n.* 街头音乐师;巡回[街头]艺人.

bus·kin [ˈbʌskin] *n.* ①(半)高统靴. ②(古代希腊、罗马悲剧演员穿的)厚底长编扣凉鞋. ③悲剧. ***put on the ~s*** 写[演]悲剧.

bus·kin·ed [ˈbʌskind] *a.* ①穿(半)长统靴的. ②悲剧的;悲壮的,崇高的. *speak in a ~ language* 以悲壮激昂的语言讲话.

buss[1] [bʌs] *n.* (用于捕鲱鱼的一种)双桅渔船.

buss[2] [bʌs] *n., vt., vi.* 〔古、方〕接吻,吻.

bust[1] [bʌst] *n.* ①半身像,胸像. ②(妇女的)胸部[胸围]. **~ bodice** (妇女的)紧身围腰.

bust[2] [bʌst] *n.* 〔俚〕①欢闹,闹饮. ②失败;破产;经济萧条. ③殴打. *a beer ~* 吵吵闹闹地喝啤酒. *make ~s* 欢闹,闹饮. *give sb. ~s* 殴打某人. *He got a ~ in the nose.* 他鼻子上挨了一拳. — *vt.* ①〔口〕= burst. ②〔俚〕使破产[没落](*up*). ③〔口〕殴打. ④驯服(野马等). ⑤【军】贬降(士兵等的)军阶. *The financial panic ~ed many firms.* 经济恐慌使许多家公司倒闭. *be ~ed from sergeant to private* 从伍长降为列兵. — *vi.* ①爆裂;破裂. ②破产;(力争成功紧张过度时的)失败,崩溃. ***~ a gut*** 〔美〕拼命努力. ***~ loose*** 〔美〕脱离,脱出,离开;破戒. ***~ up*** 拆散;解散;(夫妻)分居;(友谊)破裂. — *a.* 破产的;一文不名的. *be clean [dead] ~* (穷得)一文不名. *The company went ~.* 该公司破产了. **~-up** ①(婚姻、友谊等的)破裂. ②盛大的招待会;闹宴.

bust[3] [bʌst] *vt.* 〔美俚〕①逮捕. ②(警察)突然搜查. *be ~ed on a narcotic charge* 以吸毒罪被捕. — *n.* ①逮捕. ②突击搜查.

bus·tard [ˈbʌstəd] *n.* 【鸟】鸨.

bust·er [ˈbʌstə] *n.* ①〔美口〕破坏者,扑灭者;爆破者,爆破物;(巨型)炸弹. ②〔美俚〕(同类中)特别巨大[漂亮]的东西,特别能干[漂亮]的人. ③〔俚〕闹饮,纵酒闹饮的人. ④〔美〕驯马人;(大洋洲)寒冷猛烈的西南风. ⑤〔美俚〕健壮的孩子;〔常 B-〕老兄〔称呼语〕. ⑥【机】钉头切断机;犁. *a tank ~* 反坦克炮. *crime ~s* (侦破罪案的)侦探,探员. *B-, come here* 老兄,到这边来. **~ slab** 【军】防弹墙.

bus·tle[1] [ˈbʌsl] *vi.* ①喧闹. ②忙乱,奔忙(*about; up*). *~ about cooking breakfast* 忙着做早饭. *~ in* 匆匆忙忙地跑进来. *The office ~d with people and activity.* 办公室里人来人往,忙忙碌碌. — *vt.* ①催促,使忙乱. ②使活跃. *He ~d her upstairs.* 他催着她跨上台阶. *~ the fire to make the kettle boil* 拨弄火使水壶快点烧开. ***~ up*** 拼命工作;急急忙忙(*Tell her to ~ up* 叫她快点儿). — *n.* ①奔走,奔忙,忙乱. ②喧闹,熙攘. *be in a ~* 忙乱;吵吵闹闹,乱哄哄. *the ~ of Christmas preparations* 乱哄哄地忙着准备过圣诞节. *the hustle and ~ in business quarters* 商业区一片闹哄哄的景象. *without hurry or ~* 不慌不忙. **bus·tling** *a.* **bus·tling·ly** *ad.*

bus·tle[2] [ˈbʌsl] *n.* (妇女撑裙褶的)腰垫,裙撑.

bustop [ˈbʌstɔp] *n.* (双层公共汽车的)车上层.

bus·y [ˈbizi] *a.* ①忙,繁忙的;无闲空的(*opp.* unoccupied),〔美〕(电话)线没空,占线. ②勤勉的(*opp.* indolent)孜孜不倦的,专心致志的. ③爱管闲事的(*in*). ④繁华的,热闹的. ⑤(花样)富丽的,繁杂的. *a ~ day* 忙碌的一天. *a ~ town* 热闹的城市. *~ idleness* 无事忙. *The place was ~ with passengers.* 那地方行人众多,非常热闹. *Line's ~.* (电话)占线! *get a ~ signal* 从(听筒中)听到占线的信号声. *be ~ in another's affair* 喜欢干涉别人的事. *a ~ floral wallpaper* 花纹图案复杂多变的糊壁纸. ***a ~ bee*** 埋头工作者. ***a ~ tongue*** 话多的人. ***be ~ at [about, over, with] sth.*** (人等)忙于做某事(*be ~ at one's work* 忙着自己的工作). ***be ~ doing (sth.)*** 忙着干(某事)(*be ~ preparing for ...* 忙着为…作准备). ***get ~*** 〔美口〕干起来,开始工作[奔走,活动]. — *vt.* 使忙于,使奔走,使经营. *be busied with studies* 忙于研究工作. *She busied herself about the house.* 她忙于家务. *I have busied the gardener for the afternoon.* 我让园丁忙了一下午. ***~ oneself with [at, in, doing (sth.)]*** 忙于,正在忙着做(某事)(*She busied herself imagining the worst possible.* 她不停地想着可能发生的最坏结果). — *n.* 〔英俚〕侦探,包打听. **~body** 好事的人,爱管闲事的人. **~ signal** (电话的)占线信号. **~work, ~-work** 外加作业〔使学生不致空闲而故意外加的作业〕. **-ness** *n.* 忙碌,繁忙.

but[1] [强 bʌt; 弱 bət] *conj.* ①但,但是,可是,然而,不过. *He is rich, ~ (he is) not happy.* 他有钱但是不幸福. *Lend me some novel, ~ an interesting one.* 借给我一本小说,不过得要有趣一点的. ②(不是…)而是,倒是,(非…)乃. *He is not a soldier ~ a sailor.* 他不是陆军而是海军. *It is not I ~ you who are to blame.* 该责备的是你而不

是我. *Not that I love Caesar less,* ~ *that I love Rome more.* 不是我不爱凯撒,而是我更爱罗马. ③(虽…)仍,(尽管…)还是,还没有到…的地步. *No enemy is so ferocious* ~ *[~ that,* ~ *what] we can defeat it.* 不管敌人多么强大,我们都能打败他. *He is not such a fool* ~ *he knows it.* 他尽管笨,这个还是懂的; 他还没有笨到连这个都不懂. *No one is so old* ~ *that he may learn.* 年纪再大也可以学习,活到老学到老. ④除非…否则不; 只有…(才能…). *Nothing would satisfy him* ~ *I come along.* 只有我来他才会满意. *Who knows anyman* ~ *he be his brother?* 除非是亲兄弟,否则谁了解谁? *It will go hard* ~ *I will get there.* 除非我到那里去,不然事情就难办了. ⑤若非,要不是. *B- that I saw it, I could not have believed it.* 要不是我亲眼看见,我是不会相信的. *She would have fallen* ~ *that he caught her.* 要不是他抓住她,她就跌下去了. ⑥(不…则已,一…)就会…,总会…. *It never rains* ~ *it pours.* 天不下雨则已,一下就是暴雨倾盆; 一倒霉就步步倒霉. *You cannot look into the index* ~ *you will find the word.* 你一查索引就会找到那个词. *There was never a new theory* ~ *some one objected to it.* 新理论一出现,总会有人反对. ⑦只能,仅能,不得不. *I could not choose* ~ *speak the truth.* 我只能讲出事实真相. *They had no other choice* ~ *[to] surrender.* 他们别无选择,只能投降. *I can't help* ~ *feel sorry for him.* 我只能为他感到难过. *I can not* ~ *admire his courage.* 我不得不佩服他的勇敢. ⑧〔用于否定词或疑问词之后,表示否定,相当于 that not〕. *Never fear* ~ *I'll go.* 不要担心我不走. *I don't know* ~ *it is all true.* 我可不能肯定这都不是真的. *Who knows* ~ *that everything will come out all right?* 谁能担保一切都不出差错呢? *There is no knowing* ~ *such an accident may happen?* 谁能说不会发生这种意外呢? *It was impossible* ~ *he should see it.* 他不可能没有看到它. *How is it possible* ~ *that we should be discontented?* 我们怎么会感到满意呢? 我们怎么能不感到不满呢? ⑨〔用于 deny, doubt, question 等词的否定语气之后,无实义,仅仅相当于 that〕. *I do not doubt* ~ *that you are surprised.* 我敢断定你是感到吃惊了. *I do not deny* ~ *that it is difficult.* 我不否认这是件困难的事. *I don't question* ~ *you are correct.* 我不怀疑你是正确的. *I shouldn't wonder* ~ *she wants to be a singer.* 她想当歌手,我不应该感到惊讶. *There is no doubt* ~ *(that) he was murdered.* 毫无疑问,他是被谋杀的. ⑩〔用于 odds, ten to one, a thousand to one 等表语之后,表示可能性,无实义,仅仅相当于 that〕. *It is odds [ten to one]* ~ *you lose.* 你十之八九要输. *It is a thousand to one* ~ *you'll succeed.* 你成功的机会只有千分之一,你几乎失败定了. ⑪〔用于加强语气〕*Good heavens,* ~ *she's beautiful!* 天哪,她多漂亮呀! *Heavens,* ~ *it rains!* 啊呀,下大雨了! *Beg pardon,* ~ *haven't you met my sister on the way?* 对不起,您在路上碰见我妹妹了吗? ⑫除(某人)以外,除了(某人). 见以下 *prep.* ②. — *rel. pro.* 没有不…的〔相当于 who not, that not〕. *There is no rule* ~ *has exceptions.* 没有无例外的规律,任何规律都有例外. *Nobody* ~ *has his faults.* 人孰无过,没有人身上不存在缺点. — *prep.* ①除了,除去,除…之外. *This letter is nothing* ~ *an insult.* 这封信完全是一种侮辱. *It's anything* ~ *modest.* 这绝不是谦虚. *owing nothing* ~ *his clothes* 除去身上的衣服,此外一无所有. *They live next door* ~ *one.* 他们的住处只有一户之隔. *He was the last* ~ *one to arrive.* 他是倒数第二个到的. *last* ~ *two [three]* 倒数第三[四]. ②除(某人)以外,除了(某人)〔此种用法与用作 *conj.* 很难分清〕. *All are wrong* ~ *he [him].* 除他以外,别人都错了. *No one* ~ *a fool would believe it.* 只有傻瓜才会相信它. *No one replied* ~ *me.* 除了我,没有别人回答. ③只…,仅仅…〔引进名词从句〕. *Nothing would please her* ~ *that we go along.* 只有我们一道去,她才会高兴. *I ask nothing from you* ~ *that you should come to see me once in a while.* 我只要求你有时候来看看我. — *ad.* ①〔书〕不过,只,仅仅; 只能,至少,好歹. ②刚刚,才. ③〔书〕然而,另一方面. *This took him* ~ *a few minutes.* 这仅仅花他几分钟时间. *She is* ~ *a child.* 她不过是一个孩子罢了. *I can* ~ *hear.* 我只能听听而已. *If I could* ~ *see him!* 我要是能见一见他就好了! *I can* ~ *try it.* 我好歹试试看. *He left* ~ *an hour ago.* 他一小时以前才离开. *It happened* ~ *yesterday.* 这件事昨天刚发生. *B- I did go there.* 然而我确实是去过那里了. — *vt.* 对(某人)讲"但是"(以示反对、拒绝等). — *vi.* (讲话时)总是"但是","但是"的. — *n.* ①(讲话时说的)"但是","不过". ②保留; 反对; 例外. *B- me no* ~*s.* 请你不要'但是,但是'的吧,请你别反对[拒绝、推诿]吧.〔前一个 but 是 *vt.* 后一个 but 是 *n.*〕. *Do as I tell you, no* ~ *about it.* 就照我说的办,不要有二话. ***all*** ~ ①几乎,差点〔but 作副词〕(*I all* ~ *fell into the well.* 我几乎跌下井去). ②除…而外的全部〔but 作介词〕(*He could find all* ~ *one of his books.* 他的书全能找到,只有一本除外). ~ ***definitely***〔美〕的确,不错. ~ ***for***〔书〕①除…而外. ②要不是,如果没有 (*B- for his footsteps, there was no other sound.* 除他的脚步声而外,再没有别的声音. *She would have fallen* ~ *for his sudden arm.* 要不是他一把抓住,她就摔倒了). ~ ***good***〔美俚〕完全; 毫无疑问; 狠狠地 (*I chewed him out* ~ *good — it won't happen again.* 我把他狠狠地训斥了一通,这样的事不会再发生了. ~ ***then [yet]*** 但是,然而,可是,不过,另一方面 (*She didn't want to go to Paris —* ~ *then she didn't want to be at home either.* 她不想去巴黎——但她也不想呆在家里). ~ ***what*** ①〔= ~ those which〕(*There are no events* ~ *what have meaning.* 但凡发生事件,都必有其意义). ②〔= ~ that, 表示不肯定〕. (*I don't know* ~ *what I will go.* 我不知道我是不是去). ***not*** ~ = ***not*** ~ ***that*** =〔方、口〕***not*** ~ ***what*** ... 虽不说不是,虽然 (*I cannot do it; not* ~ *that a stronger might.* 我干不了这件事,虽然不能说比我强的人也干不了).

but² [bʌt] *ad.* 〔Scot.〕向外; 向外室,向厨房. — *n.* (苏格兰两间一套房屋的)外室,厨房. ~ ***and ben with*** 与…亲密相处. (*apartments* ~ *and ben with each other* 外室相连的两套房间). ~**-and-ben** ① *n.* 两间一套的住所. ② *ad.* 一前一后地,一来一往地. ③ *ad.* 在相对两端.

bu·ta·di·ene [ˌbjuːtəˈdaiiːn] *n.*【化】丁二烯.

bu·tane [ˈbjuːtein] *n.*【化】丁烷.

bu·ta·no·ic [ˌbjuːtəˈnəuik] *a.* 丁烷的. ~ **acid**【化】丁酸.

bu·ta·nol [ˈbjuːtənəl,-ˌnəul] *n.*【化】丁醇 (= butal alcohol).

bu·ta·none [ˈbjuːtəˌnəun] *n.*【化】丁酮.

butch¹ [butʃ] *n.*〔俚〕①大老粗. ②男人似的女子. ③女性同性恋中充当男性的角色. — *a.* ①(男子发型)平头的. ②男人似的. ~**haircut**〔美〕(男子发型的)平头. ②(女子发型的)短发.

butch² [butʃ] *vt.*〔方〕①使崩溃,弄糟. ②惨杀,屠杀. ~ *a job* 弄坏事,做坏工作.

butch·er [ˈbutʃə] *n.* ①屠夫,屠户; 屠杀者,刽子手; 残酷的人. ②〔口〕笨工拙匠. ③〔美〕(在剧场、火车等处兜售糖果等杂物的)小贩. ④〔美〕拳击选手;〔美俚,贬〕军医,外科医生; 医生. ⑤肉铺. *a pork* ~ 猪肉铺. *Hitler was as great a* ~ *as the world has seen.* 希特勒是有史以来最大的杀人狂. ~***'s bill*** ①屠户的帐单. ②阵亡者名单. ③战费. ④【植】假叶树. ~***'s meat*** ①(猪、牛、羊等的)鲜肉; 剁肉,斩碎的肉. ②〔俚〕赊来的肉. ~***'s wool*** 皮板毛. ***the*** ~***, the baker, the candlestick-maker*** 各行各业(的人),七十二行. — *vt.* ①屠宰; 屠杀,虐杀; 把…处死刑. ②弄糟,做坏; (以粗暴的批评等)扼杀(作品等). ~ *hogs* 杀猪. ~ *the play beyond recognition* 把这个戏糟蹋得面目全非. ~ *a job* 做坏活儿. ~**bird**【鸟】百劳科的鸟,百劳. ~ **knife** 屠刀. ~ **shop** 肉店. **-ly** *a.* 屠夫一样的; 残忍的 (*a* ~*ly act* 一桩残酷的行为. *a* ~*ly* *ruffian* 残忍的暴徒).

butch·er·y [ˈbutʃəri] *n.* ①大屠杀,惨杀. ②屠场;肉店;屠宰业. ③弄糟,做糟. — *a.* 屠杀的;残忍的. ***make a ~ of*** 粗手笨脚地弄糟.

bu·tene [ˈbjuːtiːn] *n.* 【化】丁烯 (= butylene).

bu·te·o [ˈbjuːtiəˌəu] *n.* 【鸟】鵟属鸟.

but·le [ˈbʌtl] *vi.* 〔口〕当管事;管伙食.

but·ler [ˈbʌtlə] *n.* ①管事,男管家;(主管酒饭的)侍役长. ②【史】(皇宫中的)司膳官,王室酒类管理官. ***~'s pantry*** (厨房外餐厅后面的)配膳室.

But·ler [ˈbʌtlə] *n.* 巴特勒〔姓氏〕.

butler·y [ˈbʌtləri] *n.* = buttery.

butt[1] [bʌt] *n.* ①(钓竿、箭等的)粗端;(工具等的)柄,把,枪托;(树木等的)残端,根端;针脚;〔美俚〕屁股;〔美〕烟蒂;纸烟. ②残片;残余部分. ③(制革的)厚皮,背皮;(铸件的)锭,坯. *a cigar ~* 纸烟头,烟蒂. *a candle ~* 蜡烛头. **~ buffer** 枪托缓冲器. **~ cut** 【林】根端材. **~ end** ①枪托. ②残部. ③大头,粗端.

butt[2] [bʌt] *n.* ①大酒桶. ②桶〔英 = 108 加仑,美 = 129.7 加仑〕. ③澳洲小包羊毛〔净毛重 112 磅〕.

butt[3] [bʌt] *n.* ①〔常 *pl.*〕(练习箭术等的)靶子;射垛,箭靶垫;打靶场. ②目的,目标;笑柄,(批评等的)对象. ③【农】未犁的余地;〔古〕界限. ④【建】铰链;【机】平接(合),对接. *make sb. the ~ of contempt* 使某人成为被轻蔑的对象. *~ of dirty jokes* 下流笑话的对象. ***~ and ~*** 一头〔端〕接一头〔端〕. ***~s and bounds***【法】地界,地积的宽窄长短. — *vt.* 使邻接 *(on, upon, against)*;使两端对接;紧靠. *~ two strips of wallpaper* 把两张糊壁纸衔接起来. — *vi.* 邻接,毗连. *The house ~s to a cemetery.* 这所房子和墓地相连. *The lot ~s on a croft.* 这块地和农场毗连. **~joint** 【木工】对接. **~ welding** 【机】对头焊接.

butt[4] [bʌt] *vt.* ①(用头、角等)抵触,顶撞,冲. ②碰撞. *a couple of rams ~ing at each other* 两只正在用角互相抵触的羊. *~ a wall* 撞墙. *~ one's opponent heavily in the ribs* 猛撞对手的肋骨. — *vi.* ①抵触,顶撞 *(against; into)*. ②伸出,突出 *(into; out)*. ③〔口〕插手,干涉 *(in, into)*. *~ against a fense* 撞到篱笆上. *~ against [into] sb.* 撞到某人身上. *~ up against sb.'s policy* 与某人的方针相抵触. *a gallery ~ing out from the house* 从房屋伸出的走廊. — *n.* ①顶撞,冲撞,碰撞. ②(击剑中的)突刺. *give sb. a ~ in the stomach* 猛撞某人的腹部. — *ad.* 用头撞;猛撞. ***~ in [into]*** 〔俚〕插手,插嘴 (*Don't ~ into people's business* 不要管闲事). ***~ out*** 〔俚〕不干预;不多嘴 (*Nobody asked your opinion so ~ out.* 没有人征求你的意见,请你别多嘴). ***come (full) ~ against*** 猛撞在….

butte [bjuːt] *n.* (美国西部平原上孤立的)小尖山;孤山;地垛.

but·ter [ˈbʌtə] *n.* ①黄油,白脱油. ②(植物)脂;脂状物,酱;象黄油的东西. ③〔口〕奉承话,巴结话. ④焊膏. *fresh [rancid] ~* 新鲜[陈]黄油. *artificial ~* 人造黄油. *spread bread with ~ = spread ~ on bread* 在面包上涂黄油. *apple [peanut] ~* 苹果[花生]酱. *cocoa ~* 可可脂. *antimony ~*【化】锑酪,三氯化锑. *~ of zinc [tin]* 【化】氯化锌[锡]. *entice sb. with ~* 用奉承话勾引某人. ***B- to ~ is no relish.*** 黄油加黄油不成美味;千篇一律的东西令人生厌. ***lay on [spread] ~*** 奉承,巴结. ***look as if ~ would not melt in one's mouth*** 装出一付老实相,装得一本正经. — *vt.* ①在…上涂黄油[酱、黄油状物];用黄油煎[煮]食物. ②〔口〕巴结,讨好 *(up)*. ***~ one's bread on both sides*** 浪费,奢华. ***Fine words ~ no parsnips.*** 花言巧语是不顶用的. ***have one's bread ~ed for life*** 一辈子享福. ***know which side one's bread is ~ed (on)*** 对自己的利益很精明. **~-and-egger** = **~-and-egg man** 〔美俚〕外表阔气的假大亨,假公子哥儿. **~-and-eggs** 【鱼】抑穿鱼. **~ball** 〔美口〕胖子;【动】巨头鹊鸭. **~ bean** 肾形豆;利马豆;棉豆. **~boat** (船形)黄油碟. **~bur** 【植】菊科蜂斗叶属植物〔尤指紫蜂斗叶〕. **~ cooler** 黄油防融器〔内盛冷水储放黄油的器皿〕. **~cup** 【植】毛茛. **~fat** 乳脂 (*~fat content in milk* 牛奶中的乳脂含量). **~fingered** *a.* 手指柔弱的,拿不稳东西的;接到球容易掉落的;手笨的. **~fingers** 手指柔弱的人;不中用的人;拿不稳东西的人,容易失球的队员. **~fish** 【鱼】酪鱼〔尤指鲳科鱼〕. **~milk** 提去奶油的牛奶,脱脂乳,酪乳,酪酱 (*a ~milk cow* 〔美〕母牛). **~ nut** 【植】灰胡桃(树). **~-scotch** 黄油硬糖. **~-weed** 【植】加拿大苦苣 (= horseweed). **~wort** 【植】捕虫堇. **-ing** *n.* ①涂黄油. ②巴结,奉承. ③【建】(用镘)抹灰浆.

but·ter·fly [ˈbʌtəflai] *n.* ①蝴蝶;蝶式,蝶形. ②〔喻〕举止轻浮的人〔尤指轻浮的妇女〕;游手好闲的人. ③【机】蝶形阀;活动目标探测器;【雕】×形支柱. ④(可收起放小的)折板桌. ⑤〔*pl.*〕(由紧张等情绪引起的)欲呕的感觉. *a social ~* 轻浮的交际花. —*vt.* 【烹】(把鱼肉等)切开摊平. *a butterflied shrimp [steak].* 切开摊平的烹虾 [牛排]. ***break a ~ on the wheel*** 杀鸡用牛刀,小题大作. ***butterflies in the stomach*** 颤栗,害怕得发抖. **~ bomb** 蝶形炸弹. **~ dive** 【泳】蝶式〔大字式〕跳水. **~ net** 捕虫网. **~ nut** 蝶形螺母. **~ stroke** 【泳】蝶泳. **~ valve** 【机】蝶形阀〔活门〕.

but·ter·in(e) [ˈbʌtəri(ː)n] *n.* (动物质)人造黄油.

butter·is [ˈbʌtəris] *n.* (兽医等用的)削蹄刀.

but·ter·y[1] [ˈbʌtəri] *n.* ①饮食品库房;〔口〕配膳室;酒库. ②(牛津、剑桥等大学的)饮食服务处. **~ hatch** (食堂传递饮食品的)售货窗口.

but·ter·y[2] [ˈbʌtəri] *a.* ①黄油状的,涂有黄油的. ②〔口〕油滑的;谄媚的.

butt·in·sky, butt·in·ski [bʌˈtinski] *n.* 〔美口〕爱管闲事的人. *Don't be a ~.* 别管闲事. *Mr. ~* 爱管闲事的先生,好事佬.

but·tock [ˈbʌtək] *n.* ①半边屁股. ②〔常 *pl.*〕臀部,屁股. ③艄,船尾. ④【摔交】背摔. — *vt.* 【摔交】背摔. **~ line** 【船】船体纵剖线.

but·ton [ˈbʌtn] *n.* ①扣子;钮扣. ②揿钮,电钮,按钮(开关);(桨的)插扣. ③节,小球,(把手的)圆顶,(剑把上的)皮圆顶. ④扣状物;【植】芽,苞;【冶】金属小珠;〔美〕领扣;袖扣;圆形小徽章. ⑤〔*pl.*〕〔英口〕(穿有金色排扣制服的)侍者,服务员;服务员制服;警察. ⑥一点儿,少许;无价值的东西. ⑦〔*pl.*〕〔俚〕神经的健全. ⑧〔俚〕颏尖;钱. *a shell ~* 贝壳钮扣. *fasten [unfasten, undo] ~* 扣上[解开]钮扣. *war fought by pushing ~s* 按电钮的战争. *cobalt ~* 钴粒. ***a ~ short*** 〔英口〕脑子差点劲. ***boy in ~s*** 穿制服的侍者[服务员]. ***have a ~ [a few ~s] missing*** 〔俚〕神经失常. ***have a soul above ~s*** 觉得自己不称职[不胜任]. ***have all one's ~s*** 〔俚〕神经正常. ***hold [catch, take] sb. by the ~*** 留人长谈,拖住人谈话. ***not care a ~ (about)*** (对…)毫不介意. ***not have all one's ~s*** 〔俚〕神经反常,失常. ***not worth a ~*** 一文不值. ***on the ~*** 〔美俚〕①击中下颌. ②准确. ③准时. ***push [press, touch] the ~*** ①按(电铃等的)揿钮,按电钮. ②拍快照. ③〔俚〕慌忙发动(某事). ***push [press] the panic ~*** 〔俚〕惊慌失措,因一时慌乱而铸成大错. — *vt.* ①钉钮扣于,用钮扣装饰. ②(用钮扣)扣住,扣紧 *(up)*. *~ a glove* 给手套缝上钮扣. *He ~ed the top ~ of his shirt.* 他扣上衬衣的领扣. — *vi.* ①装有扣子. ②扣上钮扣;扣得住. *These shoes ~ easily.* 这种鞋子容易扣紧. *This coat ~s, but that one zips.* 这件外衣用钮扣,那件外衣用拉链. *~ the banknote into a pocket* 把钞票装进口袋扣好. *~ up one's pockets [purse]* 拒绝给钱. **~ up** 〔俚〕①别讲话. ②关闭(机器等). ③完全做好,完工;〔美军俚〕侥幸完成任务 (*B- it up.* 静一静,别讲话. *Everything on the submarine was ~ed up.* 潜水艇上的机器都关闭了. *~ed up to the chin* 把外套〔上

衣等]的钮扣一直扣到下巴；穿直领西装．*The report is all ~ed up.* 报告全部写出来了)．***B- up your face [lips]!***〔美俚〕别讲了！静下来！～**ball**〔美〕美国梧桐．～**boot** 带扣长统靴．～**bush**【植】风霜树．～**down**①活动衣领的．②圆通的；世故的；彬彬有礼的．③(衣着等)守旧的．～**ear** 前垂的狗耳．～**hold** *vt.*〔古〕硬留人长谈．～**holder** = ～ holer．～**hole** ① *n.* 钮扣服，饰孔；钮扣眼上插的花．② *vt.* 在…上开钮扣眼；抓住(某人的)钮扣；强留(客人)长谈．～**holer** 强留客人长谈的人．～**hook** (皮鞋等上的)绊钩，钮扣钩．～**man** (黑社会犯罪集团中的)爪牙．～**mold** 包钮．～**-on** *a.* 用纽扣扣上去的．～**stick** (擦亮金属纽扣时用以防止弄脏制服的)垫条．～**wood**〔美〕美国梧桐；使君子树．

but·tress [ˈbʌtris] *n.* ①【建】(前)扶垛，撑墙，扶壁；【矿】支壁．②支持物，支持人，后台老板．③扶壁状物；山的扶壁状凸出部；(植物根部的)根肿；(马蹄后根的角质)蹄突．*a flying* ～ 扶壁拱架．*the* ～ *of the home* 一家的台柱．*the* ～ *of public opinion* 舆论的支持．— *vt.* ①用扶壁支衬[支撑、加固]．②支持，鼓励*(up)*．～ *up an argument* 拥护某一论点．

but·ty [ˈbʌti] *n.*〔英方〕①同事，伙伴．②监工，工头．③采煤承包人．

bu·tyl [ˈbjuːtil] *n.* ①【化】丁基．②〔B-〕【商标】丁基橡胶．～**alcohol** 丁醇．～**rubber** 异丁(烯)橡胶．

bu·tyl·ene [ˈbjuːtiliːn] *n.*【化】丁烯．～**glycol**【化】丁二醇．

Bu·tyn [ˈbjuːtin] *n.* 菩他卡因的商标名；〔b-〕【药】菩他卡因麻醉剂．

bu·ty·ra·ceous [ˌbjuːtəˈreiʃəs] *a.* 油的，含油的；油性大的；油腻的．

bu·tyr·al·de·hyde [ˌbjuːtəˈrældiˌhaid] *n.*【化】丁醛．

bu·ty·rate [ˈbjuːtireit] *n.*【化】丁酸盐；丁酸酯．

bu·tyr·ic [bju(ː)ˈtirik] *a.* 黄油的；酪酸的．～ *acid*【化】酪酸；丁酸．

bu·ty·rin [ˈbjuːtərin] *n.*【化】三丁酸甘油酯．

bux·om [ˈbʌksəm] *a.* ①(女性)丰满的，有健康美的．②活泼的．*a* ～ *blonde* 胸部丰满的金发女郎．**-ly** *ad.* **-ness** *n.*

buy [bai] ***(bought*** [bɔːt]; ***bought)*** *vt.* ①买，购 (*opp.* sell)．②收买，雇用．③(付出代价)赢得，获得．④〔美俚〕采纳(他人意见)；接受…的宣传．⑤具有…的购买力；同意，赞成．～ *sth. from [of] sb.* 从某人处购买某物．～ *sth. for sb.* 为某人购某物．～ *favour with flattery* 以谄媚获得恩宠．～ *a new centre* 请来一位(足球)中锋．～ *sb. to silence* 贿赂某人保持沉默．*The dollar* ～*s less today* 美元的购买力下降了．*Okay, I'll* ～ *that.* 好，赞成．*He bought the whole story.* 他相信了那套鬼话．～***-and-sell shop*** (纽约的)旧货店．～ ***a pig in a poke*** 不看清货色就买．～ ***for cash*** 用现金买．～ ***in*** 买进(股票)；买回(自己送出拍卖的东西)；大宗买进．～ ***into***〔俚〕(出钱)做股东[会员]，买地位 (～ *into the club* 花钱买了个俱乐部会员资格)．～ ***it***〔俚〕①(解答不了谜语、问题等而)撒手，放手，放弃．认输 (*I'll* ～ *it.* 我答不出，我想不出来)．②阵亡(*He bought it at Dunkirk.* 他在敦克尔克阵亡了)．～ ***off*** (用贿赂)收买；用钱疏通[保护，救] (～ *off the police* 用钱疏通警察)．～ ***on credit*** 赊买．～ ***out*** 出钱使某人出让地位[产权等]；买下…的全部产权．～ ***over*** (用贿赂)收买．～ ***time*** 设法延迟作出决定[采取行动]．～ ***up*** ①囤积；整批收购，买尽．②购进(其他公司) (～ *up all the goods* 购进全部货物)．— *vi.* 买，购买，购物．— *n.* ①〔美〕购买．②买卖，交易．③〔俚〕便宜货，合算的买卖[交易等] (*It's a real* ～ *at that price.* 这是一笔价钱合算的买卖)．～**boat**〔美〕(鱼行等的)买鱼船，收购船．～**-in**〔美〕补偿购入〔证券交易中的一种程序〕．～**-out**〔美〕购空存货〔把某种商品的存货全部购入〕．**-able** *a.* ①可购买的．②可收买的．**-ing** *n.* 购买 (*buying power* 购买力)．

buy·er [ˈbaiə] *n.* ①买方；买主．②采购员，货物代办人．～**s' market** 跌风笼罩下的市场．～**s' strike** 罢购，消费者的抵制行动．

buzz [bʌz] *vi.* ①(蜂等)营营地叫[飞] *(about; over; in; out)*；(机器等)发嗡嗡音，发蜂音，用蜂音器传呼．②喊喊喳喳地讲；(谣言等)传开．③〔俚〕跑来跑去*(about)*；慌忙走开*(off; along)*．④【空】低飞过原野[城市]；(电话)发占线的信号声．*flies* ～*ing about* 嗡嗡乱飞的苍蝇．*The town was* ～*ing with the news.* 这个新闻传遍全城．*men* ～*ing about in a frantic activity* 跑来跑去忙得要命的人们．*B-off!* 快走开！— *vt.* ①使嗡嗡叫，使营营响．②喊喊喳喳地传播[散布](谣言等)；异口同声地说．③〔口〕给…打电话；用蜂音器传呼；〔军俚〕(用信号)传送．④〔美军俚〕(飞机低飞)掠过，向…俯冲；飞近(另一飞机)进行骚扰．⑤猛扔(石头等)．⑥〔英方〕倒干(酒瓶)，喝干(一瓶酒)．*The fly* ～*ed its wings.* 那只苍蝇振翅嗡嗡作响．～ *a rumor [gossip]* 散布谣言[流言蜚语]．*He* ～*ed his secretary.* 他用蜂音器传呼秘书．*planes* ～*ing the crowd* 飞机低飞掠过人群．～ ***away***〔俚〕慌忙走开．～ ***off*** ①搁断电话．②〔俚〕慌忙走开，溜掉．— *n.* ①营营声，嗡嗡声；【无】蜂音．②喊喊喳喳声，嘈杂声．③风声，流言，传闻；谣言．④蜂音器信号；〔俚〕电话；〔军俚〕电话兵．⑤〔美〕圆锯；〔口〕醉．*a* ～ *of conversation* 嗡嗡的谈话声．*My brain was in* ～. 我的脑袋嗡嗡响．*give sb. a* ～ 给某人打电话．***go with a*** ～ 进行得很成功，很顺利．— *int.* (消息)早过时了！老掉牙了！～**bomb**〔军口〕"嗡嗡弹"，"V"型飞弹，喷气推进式炸弹．～**box** = ～**wag(g)on**．～**-saw**〔美〕电动小圆锯．～**session** 非正式的小型座谈会．～**wag(g)on**〔美俚〕汽车．～**wig** ①假发；戴假发的人．②要人，伟人 (*a political* ～*wig* 政界要人)．～**word** (企业、政府、科技等方面的)流行词语[口号]．

buz·zard [ˈbʌzəd] *n.* ①【动】鹞鵰，美国秃鹰．②营营发声的昆虫．③〔俚〕无耻之徒；贪婪的人；乖僻的人；老头儿，老胡涂．

buzz·er [ˈbʌzə] *n.* ①营营发声的虫；(工厂的)汽笛；【无】蜂音器．②〔军俚〕信号兵，〔*pl.*〕信号部队．

BVDs = a pair of undershorts 短衬裤．

B.V.M. = Blessed Virgin Mary.

BW = ① bacteriological warfare 细菌战．② biological warfare 生物战．

bwa·na [ˈbwɑːnə] *n.*〔常作 B-〕老爷；先生〔非洲部分地区对人的尊称，原为斯瓦希里语〕．

BX = Base Exchanger.

by [bai] *prep.* ①在侧，在旁；贴近，挨近，靠近，(方向)偏于．～ *the fire* 炉旁．～ *the seaside* 海边．*north* ～ *east* 北偏东．*a path* ～ *the river* 滨河路．②顺，经，沿，由；经过…旁边．*enter* ～ *the back door* 由后门进来．*She went right* ～ *him.* 她从他身边走过．*travel* ～ *land [water]* 走陆[水]路．～ *the nearest road* 抄近道，走近路．③(交通，通讯等)坐，乘；以．～ *bus [train]* 乘公共汽车[火车]．*arrive* ～ *ship* 乘船到达．*tell sb. the news* ～ *letter [telegram]* 以书信[电报]将消息告知某人．*correspond* ～ *tape recorder* 以录音彼此通讯．④到，到…时为止，不晚于；到…已经．*He must be there* ～ *this time.* 他现在必定已经到那里了．*I usually finish work* ～ *five o'clock.* 我一般五点钟做完工作．～ *tomorrow* 到明天．⑤在(夜间、白天等)时间内．*walk* ～ *night* 夜行．*work* ～ *day* 白天工作．*lover's walk* ～ *moonlight* 恋人的月下散步．⑥被，由．*(written)* ～ *Marx* 马克思(写的)著作．*Who is this poem* ～? 这首诗是谁写的；*My brother has one child* ～ *his first wife.* 我兄弟有一个前妻生的孩子．*be bitten* ～ *a dog* 被狗咬．⑦靠，用，通过，借助于〔表示方法、手段等〕．～ *this means* 通过这种方法．*earn one's living* ～ *writing* 靠写作为生．*learn* ～ *heart* 记牢，熟记，背熟．*take* ～ *force* 用武力夺取．*teach* ～ *example* 以身作则．*die* ～ *poison [madness]* 中毒[发疯]死去．⑧由于，因．*We meet* ～ *chance* 我们偶然相遇．*I took his* *pen* ~ *mistake.* 我错拿了他的笔. ⑨照,凭,据,按. *judge* ~ *appearance* 凭外表判断. *This is a bad movie* ~ *any standard.* 不管根据什么标准来看, 这都是一部坏影片. *It's just five o'clock* ~ *my watch.* 我的表现在是五点. *sell* ~ *the yard [weight]* 按码[重量]卖. *work* ~ *the hour [day]* 按时[日]计工. *I'm paid* ~ *the week.* 我按周领薪. *live* ~ *faith* 遵照信仰生活. *He goes* ~ *the name of Nerville.* 他以尼维尔的名字进行活动. ⑩逐一; 连续. *one* ~ *one* 一个一个地. *drop* ~ *drop* 一滴一滴地. ~ *degrees* 渐次. *little* ~ *little* 一点一点地. ~ *two and threes* 三三两两. ⑪相差. *miss* ~ *a foot* 偏了一英尺左右. *miss the train* ~ *two minutes* 迟两分钟误了火车. *too many* ~ *one* 只多一个. *The production of food-stuff increased* ~ *50 percent.* 粮食产量增长50%. ⑫在…方面是, 就…来说是. *John* ~ *name* 名叫约翰. *They were peasants by occupation and Catholics* ~ *religion.* 他们的职业是务农,信仰上是天主教徒. *cousins* ~ *blood* 血统上是表弟兄. *a grocer* ~ *trade* 做杂货生意. ~ *nature* 从本性上说. ⑬对,比〔表示面积〕; 对待, 对于〔表示义务,态度等〕; 用…去乘[除]. *3 ft.* ~ *5 ft.* 〔= 3 ft. × 5 ft. = 3 ft. : 5ft.〕 3英尺宽5英尺长. *a room 10 feet* ~ *12 feet* 一间长12英尺宽10英尺的房间. *my duty* ~ *him* 我对他的义务. *do one's duty* ~ *one's friend* 尽朋友的责任. *He did well* ~ *his children.* 他对孩子很好. *Do as you would be done by.* 你想人怎样对你,你也要怎样对人. *multiply [Divide] 18* ~ *6.* 用6去乘[除]18. ⑭在…部位〔表示动作所及处〕. *catch a dog* ~ *a tail* 抓住狗尾巴. *hold a horse* ~ *the nose* 牵住马鼻子. *The water pulled the ship down* ~ *the stern.* 水从船尾使船沉没. ⑮(客人等)来(串门,访问). *Drop* ~ *my office this afternoon.* 下午到我办公室来谈谈. *She came* ~ *my house for a few minutes.* 她到我家坐了几分钟. ⑯指,当,凭,对(天)赌咒[发誓]. *swear* ~ *all that is sacred* 凭着神圣发誓. *By god, I never observed it.* 老天爷在上,我绝没有注意过它. *By Heavens, I will have his heart's blood.* 上天作证,我一定要杀死他. — *ad.* ①在侧,在旁,在附近. ②(搁)在一边,(放)到旁边,(存)在一旁; 收着. ③(由旁边)经过, 过去. ④(岁月等)流过. ⑤〔美口〕(请)来(访问,玩玩,谈谈等)〔与 call, come, stop 等连用〕. *No one was* ~. 没有人在旁边. *The school is close* ~. 学校就在近旁. *stand [sit]* ~ 站[坐]在一旁. *a store near* ~ 邻近的一家店铺. *pass* ~ 经过,走过,通过. *hurry* ~ 匆匆走过. *The car drove* ~. 汽车驶过. *The bird flew* ~. 鸟飞过. *Put your work* ~ *for a moment.* 把你的工作搁一搁. *These apples were put* ~ *for the winter.* 这些苹果储存起来冬天卖[吃]. *lay* ~ *enough money to retire* 储蓄足够的钱以便退休. *in days gone* ~ 往日. *Next time you're over this way, please come* ~. 下次路过这里,请来坐一坐. — *a.* ★ 通例用作 by(e)-. — *n.* =bye. ~ ***and again*** 〔美〕时时,常常. ~ ***and*** ~ 不久以后, 不一会儿 (*The clouds will disappear* ~ *and* ~. 云很快就要散了). ~ ***and large*** 全盘,总的来说,一般地说,大体上. ~ ***far*** 见 far 条. ~***half*** 见 half 条. ~ ***oneself [itself]*** 单独,独立; 独自. ~ ***the*** ~***(e)*** 顺便说到. ~ ***the way*** 见 way 条. ~**-and-**~ *n.* (不远的)将来 (*in the sweet* ~*-and-*~ 美好的未来). ~**-bidder** 抬价卖出者; 拍卖者. ~**-bidding** 抬价出卖; 拍卖者. ~**-blow** ①偶然的[间接的]一击. ②私生子. ~**-channel** 支渠. ~**-election** (英国国会的)补缺选举. ~**-end** ①私意,私心. ②(诗歌等的)片断. ~**-effect** 副作用. ~**-lane** 小巷,僻巷; 小路. ~**law** ①附则,细则. ②(英国地方自治单位的)地方法. ③(协会、团体等的)会章,社章. ~**-line** ① *n.* (新闻杂志标题下的)作者署名; (铁路干线的)支线. ②副业. ③ *vt.* 在(新闻、杂志文章等的)下面署名 (~*-line a magazine piece* 在一篇杂志文章下面署名). ~**-motive** 隐秘的动机,暗中的打算. ~**-mordant** 【化】辅助媒染剂. ~**name** ①浑名,绰号; 假名,伪名; 别名. ②姓,(古罗马人的)家名, 第三名. ~**pass** ① *n.* 【机】(煤气等的)旁(通)管; (为疏散交通而设的迂回的)旁路; 小道,间道; 【电】分路迂回. ② *vt.* 为…加设旁路[旁通管]; 绕过,越过,超过; 回避,忽视 (~*-pass a congested city* 加设旁路疏散拥挤的城市交通. *bright sunshine* ~*-passing the thin curtains* 强烈的阳光透过薄窗帘. ~*-pass congress* 绕过国会.) ~**-passer** = passer-by. ~**past** *a.* 过去的,以往的. ~**-path** 小路,旁路,侧道,僻径. ~**-place** 穷乡僻壤. ~**play** 【剧】(主题以外)穿插戏; 枝节故事. ~**-plot** (小说、戏剧的)从属情节, 次要情节. ~**-product** 副产品. ~**road** 小路,间道. ~**stander** 旁观者,看热闹的,局外人 (*a* ~*stander behavior* 局外人的态度). ~**street** 小街,背街. ~**-talk** 闲话; 杂谈. ~**-time** 余暇,闲空,空闲. ~**way** 小路, 间道, 侧道; 〔喻〕次要方面; (研究等方面的)冷门 (*highways and* ~*-ways* 大路和小路; 〔喻〕直接方面和间接方面,主要和次要方面. *a* ~*way of learning* 冷门学科). ~**word** ①俗话,谚语. ②笑柄. ③〔罕〕浑名, 绰号; 口头禅 (*the old* ~*word of lookers-on seeing most of the game* 旁观者清的老话). ~**work** 副业,兼职,业余工作. ~**-your-leave** 对不起〔因未获准许而作某事的道歉语〕.

by- *comb. f.* ①附随的,附属的; 枝节的,第二义的,副的. ②附近的,邻近的,旁边的,旁的; 偏的. ③秘密的, 私, 阴: *by*stander, *by*passer,*by*street, *by*path, *by*product.

bye [bai] *n.* ①枝节,小事,附属事物. ②【板球】球越过打手及守门者时所得的分数. ③【体】(抽签)轮空的选手[队]. ***by the*** ~ ***[by]*** 顺便说到, 就便提起 (*By the* ~, *how do you spell your name?* 顺便问一句,您的名字怎样拼写?). ***draw a*** ~ 抽签抽到轮空(不战而胜). ~ **team** (抽签轮空的)不战而胜队.

bye- *comb. f.* = by-.

bye-bye[1] [ˈbaibai] *n.* 〔儿〕瞌睡; 床. ***go to*** ~ 睡觉吧. — *ad.* 上床,睡觉. ***go*** ~ 去睡觉.

bye-bye[2] [ˈbaiˈbai] *int.* 再会! 回头见!

Bye·lo·rus·sia [ˌbjeləˈrʌʃə] *n.* 白俄罗斯〔苏联加盟共和国名〕(= White Russia). **-n** *n., a.* ①白俄罗斯人(的). ②白俄罗斯语(的).

bye-low [ˈbaiˌləu] *ad., int.* 〔儿〕嘘! 别响,静一静! 〔用于催眠曲和摇篮曲〕.

by·gone [ˈbaigɔ(:)n] *a.* 〔书〕①过去的,已往的. ②过时的,旧式的. *a* ~ *age* 昔日,往日. *in* ~ *years* 以往的年代. ~ *days* 逝去的岁月. *revivals of* ~ *styles* 旧时式样[风格]的复活. — *n.* 过去的事; 往事. *Let's not talk of* ~*s.* 我们不要谈旧事[翻老账]了. ***let*** ~***s be*** ~***s*** 过去的事就让它过去吧; 忘掉过去的冤仇; 捐弃前嫌; 既往不究 (*Let's let* ~*s be* ~*s and begin again.* 让我们忘却旧事重新开始).

byn·ocu·lar [baiˈnɔkjulə] *n.* = binocular.

BYOB = Bring Your Own Bottles. 请自带酒.

Byrd [bəːd] *n.* 伯德〔姓氏〕.

byre [baiə] *n.* 〔英〕牛栏,牛棚.

Byrne(s) [bəːn(z)] *n.* 伯恩(斯)〔姓氏〕.

byr·nie [ˈbəːni] *n.* (甲胄)锁子甲,连环铠甲.

By·ron [ˈbaiərən] 拜伦〔姓氏〕. **George Noel Gordono** ~ 乔·拜伦〔1788—1824 英国诗人〕.

By·ron·ic [baiˈrɔnik] *a.* 拜伦的; 拜伦诗风的; 慷慨悲歌式的. **By·ron·ism** 拜伦主义. **-ally** *ad.*

bys·si·no·sis [ˌbisiˈnəusis] *n.* 【医】棉屑沉着病.

bys·sus [ˈbisəs] *n.* ①古代的亚麻纤维. ②(古埃及用以裹扎木乃伊的)亚麻布[棉、丝织物等]. ③【动】(贝类等的)丝足足丝; 【植】菌丝.

byte [bait] *n.* 【计】二进位组,信息组,字节,位组.

By·zan·tine [biˈzæntain] *a.* ①【史】拜占廷的; 东罗马帝国的. ②【建】拜占廷式的. ③爱玩弄阴谋的, 诡计多端的. — *n.* ①拜占廷人. ②拜占廷式建筑,拜占廷风格的画家. ~ **Church** 东正教. ~ **Empire** 拜占廷帝国,东罗马帝国.

By·zan·tin·esque [bi͵zænti'nesk] *a.* 【建】拜占廷风格的.

By·zan·tin·ism [bi'zæntinizəm] *n.* ①(建筑、艺术等的)拜占廷风格. ②拜占廷主义[精神].

By·zan·ti·um [bi'zæntiəm] *n.* 【史】拜占廷〔古罗马城市，一度称为 Constantinople, 今名 Islanbul〕.

Bz. = benzene.

C

C, c [si:] *(pl. C's, c's* [si:z]*)* ①英语字母表第三字母. ② C 形物. ③【乐】C 调, C 音;【数】第三个已知数; 第三,丙. ④〔美〕〔C〕(学业成绩) 中. ⑤〔C〕罗马数字 100. ⑥〔C〕【化】元素碳 (carbon) 的符号. ⑦〔C〕[电] 库伦 (coulomb) 的符号. ⑧〔C〕〔美俚〕可卡因 (cocaine). *C major [minor]* C大[小]调. *a C-spring* C字形(承力)弹簧(= Cee-spring). CCCL = 350. *C*3 [读作 'si: θri:] 丙等(的),体格劣等(的) *(a C3 concert* 第三流音乐会*)*. ***C and A Pocket*** 〔美〕无业游民做在上衣里用来装多余粮食的口袋 (Chicago and Alton pocket). ***C and S*** 【美军】整洁而严肃的 (= clean and sober).

C., c. = ①candle. ②capacity. ③Catholic. ④cathode. ⑤Celtic. ⑥cent(s). ⑦centigrade. ⑧〔F.〕*centime.* ⑨centimetre. ⑩century. ⑪chapter. ⑫Chancellor. ⑬〔L.〕*circa.* ⑭copy; copyright. ⑮cost. ⑯cubic. ⑰Congress. ⑱Conservative. ⑲Corps. ⑳Court. ㉑city. ㉒cloudy. ㉓centre.

C/A = ①current account 往来帐户; 活期存款帐户. ②capital account 资本帐; 股本帐; 公积帐. ③cash account 现金帐户.

CA = chlormadinone 氯地孕酮〔避孕药〕.

Ca 【化】元素钙 (calcium) 的符号.

Caaba ['kɑ:bə] *n.* (= Kaaba) (穆斯林参拜的)麦加的黑石; 供有黑石的石造圣堂.

CAAC = General Administration of Civil Aviation of China 中国民用航空总局〔CAAC 是前译名 Civil Aviation Administration of China 的缩写,现仍沿用〕.

CAB = Civil Aeronautics Board〔美〕民用航空局.

cab[1] [kæb] *n.* ①出租马车; 出租汽车. ②(机车、卡车、拖拉机、起重机等的)司机室. *take a* ~ 坐马车[汽车]去. — *vi.* ***(cabbed; cabbing)*** 〔俚〕〔常说作 ~ it〕坐出租马车[汽车]. *They cabbed to the theatre.* 他们坐出租汽车去剧场. ~**driver** 出租汽车司机; 赶马车的人. **-getter** 出租汽车的乘客. ~**man** 出租马车驾驶人; 出租汽车司机. ~ **rank**〔英〕①等候出租的马车[汽车]行列. ②= ~stand. ~**stand** 出租马车[汽车]停车处.

cab[2] [kæb] *vi.* ***(cabbed; cabbing)*** 〔英学俚〕抄夹带; 作弊. — *n.* 夹带; 作弊.

cab[3] [kæb] *n.* 开普〔古希伯来粮食等干物的量具名, 容量相当二夸脱〕.

ca·bal [kə'bæl] *n.* ①(人数不多的)秘密组织; 阴谋. ②〔C-〕【英史】(查理二世时代)五大臣小组〔他们名字的开首字母恰巧是 C,A,B,A,L 五个字母〕. ③(美术、文艺中的)派系. ~ *system* 首字串联法〔把各词首字母连接成一词以记忆全文的方法〕. — *vi.* 玩弄阴谋; 结党(图谋).

cab·a·la [kə'bɑ:lə,'kæbələ] *n.* ①(对《圣经》作神秘主义解释的)犹太神秘哲学. ②神秘教义.

cab·a·lism ['kæbəlizəm] *n.* ①犹太神秘教义. ②(文字的)晦涩难解.

cab·a·list ['kæbəlist] *n.* 犹太神秘哲学家; 秘法家.

cab·a·lis·tic [͵kæbə'listik] *a.* 犹太神秘哲学的; 神秘的, 玄妙的.

ca·bal·ler [kə'bælə] *n.* 阴谋家.

ca·bal·le·ro [͵kæbə'ljeərəu] *n.* 〔Sp.〕①绅士; 骑士; 骑马的人. ②(美国西南部)骑马者; 妇女崇拜者.

ca·ba·ña [kə'bɑ:nə] *n.* 〔Sp.〕小房间, 私室; (海滨等处的)浴室.

ca·bane ['kæbən] *n.*【空】翼柱, 翼间架.

cab·a·ret ['kæbəret, 'kæbərei] *n.* ①(有舞蹈、音乐等表演的) 餐馆. ②餐馆里的歌舞表演 (亦作 ~ show). ~ **tax** 娱乐税.

cab·bage[1] ['kæbidʒ] *n.* ①【植】甘蓝, 卷心菜. ②〔美俚〕劣等雪茄烟, 粗烟. ③〔美俚〕〔指纸币〕钱. ④〔美俚〕少女. *Chinese* ~ 大白菜. ~ *white* = ~ *butterfly* 白蝶. ~ *rose* 洋蔷薇. — *vi.* 长 (菜) 头, 长成甘蓝状头. ~**head**〔美〕笨蛋, 呆子. ~ **palm**【植】槟榔子. ~**worm**【动】甘蓝虫.

cab·bage[2] ['kæbidʒ] *vt.* (裁缝) 偷 (布). — *vi.* (裁缝) 偷布, 偷. — *n.* 偷剪的布料; (裁剪剩下的) 碎料; 被偷的东西.

cab·ba·la ['kæbələ], **cab·ba·lism** [-lizəm] = cabala, cabalism.

cab·by, cab·bie ['kæbi] *n.* 〔美口〕出租汽车司机 (= cabman).

Cab·ell ['kæbəl] *n.* 卡贝尔〔姓氏〕.

ca·ber ['keibə] *n.* (苏格兰等地投棒比臂力游戏中所用的)松木棒. *tossing the* ~ 投松木棒(比臂力).

cab·e·zon ['kæbi͵zɔn] *n.* 【动】拟鲉鱼.

cab·in ['kæbin] *n.* ①小屋, 小室; 〔英〕(铁路等的)信号室. ②船室[舱], 头[二]等客舱;【空】座舱; 舰长室, 长官室, 军官室. ③卧室; 小房间, 私室. — *vt.* ①把…关在小屋内; 使受拘束. ②隔开(房间). — *vi.* 住在小屋内; 寄住. ~**boy** (船长室、舰长室、一二等客舱的) 服务员. ~ **class**头等舱. ~ **court** (公路旁为汽车游客服务的) 家庭式小旅馆. ~ **cruise** 带有住宿设备的汽艇. ~ **de luxe**贵宾室; 特等舱. ~**-officer** 有资格在军官餐室吃饭的军官. ~**-passenger** 头二等船客.

Ca·bin·da [kə'bində] *n.* ①卡宾达〔非洲〕. ②卡宾达〔卡宾达首府〕.

cab·ined ['kæbind] *a.* ①狭窄的, 被关进狭窄场所的. ②有船室的.

cab·i·net ['kæbinit] *n.* ①〔常作 C-〕内阁; 〔英〕内阁会议(室); 〔美〕总统[州长、市长]顾问团. ②小房间, 私室, 密议室. ③陈列室; (矿物、生物、古钱币等) 陈列品. ④饰架; 珍品橱, 柜, 箱, 盒; 【物】(机)箱. ⑤【摄】六英寸片. *a card* ~ 卡片箱; (公用电话) 收费箱. *a shadow* ~ (在野党领袖虚拟的) 影子内阁. — *a.* ①内阁的; 秘密的. ②小房间用的; 小巧的, 玲珑的. ③细木工做的. ④(相片)六英寸的. ~ **council** (内) 阁 (会) 议. ~ **crisis** 内阁(瓦解)危机. ~ **edition** (书籍装帧的) 中型版(式). ~**-maker** ①家具师, 桌椅匠. ②〔讽〕组阁者; 新任内阁总理. ~**making** ①家具制造, 家具业. ②〔讽〕组阁. **Cabinet Minister** = 〔美〕~ **member [officer]** 阁员. ~ **organ** 竖立式小风琴. ~ **photograph** 六英寸照片. ~ **piano** (竖式) 钢琴. ~ **pudding** 干果布丁. ~**work**

细木工家具；细木工。
cab·inet·eer [ˌkæbiniˈtiə] *n.* 〔美〕无能的〔名气不好的〕阁员。
Ca·ble [ˈkeibl] *n.* 凯布尔〔姓氏〕。
ca·ble [ˈkeibl] *n.*①【船】锚链，锚索，(周长 10 英寸以上的)左捻三根三股索；粗索，巨缆；钢丝绳。②电缆；海底电线；海底电报；【空】张索；绞线；【电】多心导线，被覆线。③锚链〔= cable's length 海上测距单位〕。④【纺】(针织)软轴。*by* ~ 用海底电报。*cut [slip] one's [the]* ~〔海俚〕死。— *vt.* ①(用锚链，缆索等)系住。②给…打海底电报；通过海底电缆发(电报)。— *vi.* 打海底电报，用海底电线通信。*a cabling machine* 搓绳机。*nothing to* ~ *home about* 〔Aus.〕无足轻重，无用，不重要。~ **address** (地址姓名等的) 海外电报挂号。~ **car** 缆车。~**cast** *vt.* 用有线电视〔公共天线〕播放。~**gram** 海底电报。~**-laid** *a.*【船】左捻三根三股的。~ **message** 海外电报。~**('s) length** 一锚链长〔185 米，即 1/10 浬〕。~ **railway** 缆车道。~ **station** 海底电报局；海底电报，水线电报。~**-knitting** 绞花编结。~ **TV** ①电缆〔有线〕电视。②公共天线。~**way** 索道。
ca·blese [keiˈbliːz] *n.* 电报用语〔如简省、缩写等〕。
ca·blet [ˈkeiblit] *n.*【船】(周长小于 10 英寸的) 左捻三根三股索。
ca·bling [ˈkeibliŋ] *n.*【建】①卷缆柱。②卷绳状雕饰。
ca·bob [kəˈbɔb] *n.* ①叉烧肉片洋葱〔西红柿〕。②叉烧肉(= kebab, kabab, kebob)。
ca·bo·chon [ˌkæbɔˈʃɔːŋ] *n.* 〔F.〕(顶部磨成圆形并不加刻面的) 圆顶平底宝石。*en* ~ (宝石的)圆顶平底式。
ca·bom·ba [kəˈbɔmbə] *n.*【植】水盾草属植物〔尤指鱼草 *Cabomba Caroliniana*〕。
ca·boo·dle [kəˈbuːdl] *n.* 〔美口〕群，团；捆，堆。*the whole (kit and)* ~ 全部，全体。
ca·boose [kəˈbuːs] *n.* ①(商船甲板上的) 厨房。②〔美〕(货车后部车务员坐的)公务车。③小房间，狭窄的地方。
Cabot [ˈkæbət] *n.* 卡伯特〔姓氏〕。**John** ~ 约翰·卡伯特〔1450—1498?，意大利航海家，1497 年发现北美大陆〕。
cab·o·tage [ˈkæbətidʒ] *n.* ①沿(海)岸航行(权)；沿(海)岸贸易。②【空】国内航空权。
ca·bret·ta [kəˈbretə] *a.* 巴西绵羊皮革的；软羊皮革的。
ca·bril·la [kəˈbrilə, kəˈbiːjə] *n.*【动】鲭科鱼。
cab·ri·ole [ˈkæbriəul] *n.* (英国老式家具特有的)狮爪形弯腿。
cab·ri·o·let [kæbriəˈlei] *n.* 〔F.〕单马篷车；活顶小轿车。
cab·rit [ˈkæbrit] *n.*【动】美洲羚羊。
ca'·can·ny [kɑːˈkæni, kɔː-] *vi.* ①〔Scot.〕(车辆)慢行。②〔英〕磨洋工，怠工。— *n.* 〔英〕怠工。
ca·ca·o [kəˈkɑːəu, kəˈkeiəu] *n.*【植】可可树；可可豆。
cac·ci·a·to·re [ˌkætʃiˈtɔːri] *a.* (用橄榄油、蕃茄、洋葱等)在砂锅里焖煮的。*Chicken* ~ 罐焖鸡。
cach·a·lot [ˈkæʃəlɔt] *n.*【动】抹香鲸。
cache [kæʃ] *n.* ①(探险者等贮藏粮食、器材等的)暗窖，密藏处。②贮藏物。— *vt.* 贮藏；密藏；窖藏。
ca·chec·tic [kəˈkektik] *a.*【医】(由慢性病等造成的) 恶病质的，极度瘦弱的。
cache·pot [ˈkæʃpɔt, -pəu] *n.* 花盆，花瓶。
ca·chet [ˈkæʃei] *n.* 〔F.〕①药包，胶囊。②(书信等的)封印；特征，标志。③纪念邮戳。④(得自名人的)称赞。⑤威信；(高贵的)身分。*lettre de* ~【法史】密令。
ca·chex·i·a, ca·chex·y [kəˈkeksiə, kəˈkeksi] *n.*【医】(由慢性病等造成的)恶病(体)质；极度瘦弱。
cach·in·nate [ˈkækineit] *vi.* 大笑，哄笑。
cach·in·na·tion [ˌkækiˈneiʃən] *n.* 大笑，高声狂笑，哄笑。
cach·in·na·to·ry [kəˈkinətəri] *a.* 大笑的，哄笑的。
cach·o·long [ˈkætʃəlɔŋ] *n.*【矿】美蛋白石。
ca·chou [kəˈʃuː, kæˈʃuː] *n.* 口香片(= catechu)。
ca·chu·cha [kəˈtʃuːtʃə] *n* 〔Sp.〕(西班牙的)客曲洽舞〔舞曲〕。
ca·cique [kæˈsiːk] *n.* ①(西印度群岛、墨西哥、秘鲁等地的)印第安人酋长；(菲律宾等地的)大地主。②〔美〕地方政治首领。
ca·ciquism [kəˈsiːkizəm] *n.* (由党魁等操纵的) 腐败的地方政治。
cack [kæk] *n.* 〔美〕小儿用平底靴。
cack·le [ˈkækl] *n.* ①(母鸡、鹅等的)咯咯叫声。②饶舌；〔美〕废话，空话。③尖声的笑。*cut the* ~ ①〔俚〕使不说废话而抓住要点。②(命令)住嘴，别响。— *vi.* ①(鸡等下蛋后)咯咯地叫。②唠唠叨叨地讲。③咯咯地笑。— *vt.* 唠唠叨叨地讲出。
cack·ler [ˈkæklə] *n.* ①饶舌家，碎嘴子。②〔美俚〕戏剧演员，艺人。③〔*pl.*〕〔美俚〕鸡蛋。
caco- *comb. f.* 恶，丑：*caco*logy.
cac·o·dae·mon, cac·o·de·mon [ˌkækəˈdiːmən] *n.* ①恶鬼；恶人。②恶梦，梦魇。
cac·o·dyl [ˈkækədil] *n.*【化】卡可基；二甲胂基；四甲二胂。**-ic** *a.*
cac·o·e·py [ˈkækəuepi] *n.* 发音不正。
cac·o·ë·thes [kækəuˈiːθiːz] *n.* 〔L.〕①恶习，恶癖；(某种)狂癖。②【医】恶性溃疡。~ ***scribendi*** [skriˈbendai] 〔L.〕著作狂。
cac·o·gen·e·sis [ˌkækəˈdʒenisis] *n.*【生】①构造异常。②畸形。
ca·cog·ra·pher [kæˈkɔgrəfə] *n.* ①别字大王。②书法不好的人。
ca·cog·ra·phy [kæˈkɔgrəfi] *n.* ①拼写错误，写别字。②拙劣的书法。**ca·c**o**g·ra·phic(al)** *a.*
ca·col·o·gy [kæˈkɔlədʒi] *n.* ①措词不当。②发音不正。
cac·o·mis·tle [ˈkækəˌmisl] *n.* ①【动】蓬尾浣熊。②蓬尾浣熊毛皮。
ca·coph·o·nous [kæˈkɔfənəs] *a.* 发音不和谐的，粗腔横调的。
ca·coph·o·ny [kæˈkɔfəni] *n.* ①不愉快的音调；杂音。②【医】声音异常，口齿不清。③【乐】噪音。
cac·ta·ceous [kækˈteiʃəs] *a.*【植】仙人掌类植物的。
cac·tus [ˈkæktəs] *n.* (*pl.* ~*es, cac·ti* [ˈkæktai]) ①【植】仙人掌类植物。②〔美俚〕沙漠。
ca·cu·mi·nal [kəˈkjuːminl] *a.*【语音】卷舌的。— *n.* 卷舌音。
cad [kæd] *n.* ①〔口〕下流人，粗鄙无礼的人。②〔英废〕车夫；仆人。
C.A.D., C/D = cash against documents 押汇证。
ca·das·tral [kəˈdæstrəl] *a.* 地籍的，课税地的。*a* ~ *survey* 地籍测量。
cad·as·tra·tion [kædəsˈtreiʃən] *n.* 地籍测量。
ca·das·tre, ca·das·ter [kəˈdæstə] *n.* 地籍图。
ca·da·ver [kəˈdeivə, -ˈdæ-] *n.* ①(解剖用的) 尸体。②〔美俚〕失败了的事业，破产事业。**-ic** [-rik] *a.*
ca·dav·er·ine [kəˈdævərin, -əˌriːn] *n.*【生化】尸胺；1,5-戊二胺。
ca·dav·er·ous [kəˈdævərəs] *a.* 尸体一样的；灰白色的，形容枯槁的。
cad·dice [ˈkædis] *n.*【动】毛翅目幼虫。~ *fly* 石蚕蛾。
cad·die [ˈkædi] *n.* ①【高尔夫球】(受雇做背球棒等杂事的)球童。②〔Scot.〕杂役。③(运物用的) 有轮手推车。— *vi.* 当球童。
cad·dis [ˈkædis] = caddice.
cad·dish [ˈkædiʃ] *a.* 下流的，粗鄙的。
Cad·do [ˈkædəu] *n.* (*pl.* ~*es,* ~*s,* ~) ①卡多族〔美国一印第安部落名〕。②卡多人。③卡多语。
Cad·do·an [ˈkædəuən] *a.* (印第安人)卡多语系的。—*n.* 卡多语系。
cad·dy[1] [ˈkædi] *n.* ①茶叶盒，茶叶罐。②柜，箱，(放唱片之类用的)盒。

cad·dy² [ˈkædi] = caddie.
Cade [ˈkeid] *n.* 凯德〔姓氏〕.
cade¹ [keid] *a.* 作为爱畜驯养的. *a ~ lamb* 驯羊.
cade² [keid] *n.* 【植】刺桧 *(Juniperus oxycedrus)*.
ca·delle [kəˈdel] *n.* 【动】大谷盗.
ca·dence [ˈkeidəns] *n.* ①音律;调子. ②声音的抑扬. ③节奏,拍子;(行军时的)步度. ④【乐】乐章的结尾. ⑤【电】步调信号. — *vt.* 使成节奏. **-d** *a.* 音调抑扬的.
ca·den·cy [ˈkeidənsi] *n.* ①= cadence. ②【纹】小辈分支家系.
ca·dent [ˈkeidnt] *a.* ①下降的. ②有韵律的,有节奏的,抑扬的.
ca·den·za [kəˈdenzə] *n.* 〔It.〕【乐】华彩乐段;终止.
ca·det [kəˈdet] *n.* ①(陆海军官学校的)学员〔英国通例叫 gentleman ~,美国 1902 年后正式叫 midshipman〕;商船学校学生. ②幼子,次子;弟弟. ③〔C-〕(旧俄)立宪民主党党员. ④〔新西兰〕牧羊学徒;少年店员. ⑤海蓝色,深蓝色. ~ **corps** 〔英〕学生军训队. **-ship** *n.* 军校学员的地位[级别,学习期限].
ca·det [kəˈdet] *n.* 〔F.〕 弟〔附加姓名后与兄相区别 *(opp.* aîné)〕.
cadge [kædʒ] *vi.* ①〔口〕行乞. ②〔方〕做叫卖小贩. —*vt.* ①〔口〕乞讨;敲诈,勒索(钱等). ②〔方〕叫卖(鱼、蛋等). ~ *a meal* 求食.
cadg·er [ˈkædʒə] *n.* ①乞丐;二流子;寄生虫. ②叫卖小贩.
cadg·y [ˈkædʒi] *a.* 〔Scot.〕①好色的;淫猥的;放荡的. ②风流的;快活的.
ca·di [ˈkɑːdi, ˈkei-] *n.* (*pl.* ~*s*)(穆斯林国家的)法官.
Cad·me·an [kædˈmiːən] *a.*【希神】勇士卡德摩斯 (Cadmus) 的. ~ **victory** 以巨大牺牲换得的胜利〔源出卡德摩斯种下龙牙,生成许多武士相互残杀殆尽的故事〕.
cad·mi·um [ˈkædmiəm] *n.* 【化】镉. ~ **spat** 菱镉矿. ~ **yellow** 镉黄(颜料).
Cadmus [ˈkædməs] *n.* 【希神】卡德摩斯〔曾杀一龙,种下龙牙,生成许多武士,相互残杀殆尽〕.
ca·dre [ˈkɑːdə, ˈkædri] *n.* ①骨干;干部. ②骨骼,架子. ~**man** 骨干.
ca·du·ce·us [kəˈdjuːsiəs] *n.* (*pl.* ***-ce·i*** [-siai]), (罗马神话中传信天使 Mercury 的)双蛇杖;(美国陆军军医部队的)双蛇杖标记.
ca·du·ci·ty [kəˈdjuːsiti] *n.* ①暂时,无常;老衰;短命. ②【植】早落[凋]性.
ca·du·cous [kəˈdjuːkəs] *a.* ①易散的;易脱落的;易衰老的;短命的. ②【植】早落的,早凋的;【动】脱落性的.
cae·cal, ce·cal [ˈsiːkəl] *a.* ①一端密闭的,袋形的. ②【解】盲孔的;盲肠的.
cae·cil·i·an [siːˈsiliən, -ˈsiljən] *n.* 【动】蚓螈科 *(Caeciliidae)* 动物;蚓螈目[无足目] *(Gymnophionia)*.
cae·ci·tis [siːˈsaitis] *n.* 【医】盲肠炎.
cae·cum, ce·cum [ˈsiːkəm] *n.* (*pl.* ***-ca*** [-kə])【解】盲孔;盲肠;盲囊.
Caes. = Caesar.
Cae·sar [ˈsiːzə] *n.* ①【史】凯撒;罗马皇帝. ②暴君,独裁者. *Julius* ~ 朱利乌斯·凯撒〔公元前 100—44,罗马将军,皇帝,政治家,历史家〕. ***Great*** ~! 啊呀! 天哪!
Cae·sar·e·an, Cae·sar·i·an [si(ː)ˈzɛəriən] *a.* ①凯撒的,(罗马)皇帝的. ②独裁的,专制的. — *n.* 罗马皇帝[帝国]崇拜者;主张独裁主义的人. ~ **birth** 【医】剖腹产. ~ **operation [section]** 【医】剖腹产 (手术)〔因 Julius Caesar 是剖腹生的,故名〕. ~ **salad** 凯撒色拉〔一种用长莴苣、大蒜、凤尾鱼、油泡面包片等拌成的色拉〕.
Cae·sar·ism [ˈsiːzərizəm] *n.* 独裁主义,专制政治,帝政.
Cae·si·ous [ˈsiːziəs] *a.* 青灰色的,苍白的.
cae·si·um, ce·si·um [ˈsiːziəm] *n.* 【化】铯.
caes·pi·tose [ˈsespitəus] *a.* 【植】(藓苔等)簇生的,丛生的.
cae·su·ra [si(ː)ˈzjuərə] *n.* 〔诗〕行内[句中]休止;【乐】中间休止. **-l** *a.*
ca·fard [kəˈfɑː] *n.* 〔F.〕苦闷;愁闷,忧郁;没精打采.
ca·fe [ˈkæfei, ˈkæfi] *n.* 〔英〕咖啡馆,(欧陆诸国的)餐馆;〔美〕酒馆;咖啡馆. ~ *society* 〔美〕经常上咖啡馆的人们. ~ *chantant* [ˈʃɑ̃ːntɑ̃ːŋ] 有音乐等表演的咖啡馆.
ca·fé [kəˈfei] *n.* 〔F.〕咖啡. ~ ***au lait*** [əuˈlei] 牛奶咖啡. ~**curtain** 半截窗帘. ~ ***filtre*** [filtr] 滴漏咖啡 ~ ***noir*** [ˈnwɑːr] (不加牛奶的)清咖啡.
caf·e·te·ri·a [ˌkæfiˈtiəriə] *n.* 〔美〕(自取菜饭的)自助食堂.
caf·e·to·ri·um [ˌkæfiˈtɔːriəm] *n.* (学校等的)兼作食堂的礼堂.
caff [kæf] *n.* 〔美口〕小吃店.
caf·fe·ic [kəˈfiːik] *a.* (取自)咖啡的. ~ **acid** 【化】咖啡酸.
caf·fe·ine [ˈkæfiːn] *n.* 咖啡硷,咖啡因.
Caf·fre [ˈkæfə] *n.* = Kaf(f)ir.
caf·fy [ˈkæfi] *n.* 〔美俚〕咖啡;咖啡馆.
caf·tan [ˈkæftən, kæfˈtɑːn] *n.* (中东的)束腰长袖长袍.
C.A.G. = Civil Air Guard 〔美〕民用航空警卫队.
cage [keidʒ] *n.* ①笼;槛;监牢;战俘营. ②电梯厢;(矿井内的)升降车. ③外壳;(建筑物的)钢骨结构. ④炮架,炮座. ⑤【棒球】练球场;篮球的球篮;冰球的球门. *reinforcement* ~*s* 钢筋骨架. ~ *gals* 〔美俚〕女售票员. — *vt.* 把…关进笼内;把…关入槛中;把(冰球等)打入球门. ~ *up* 把…收监. ~ **antenna** 【无】笼形天线. ~**-work** 透孔织物[制品].
cage·ling [ˈkeidʒliŋ] *n.* 笼鸟〔亦作 cagebird, 指鹦鹉等〕.
cag·er [ˈkeidʒə] *n.* 〔美俚〕篮球选手[运动员].
cage·y [ˈkeidʒi] *a.* 〔美口〕①狡猾的. ②谨慎小心的;当心的. *a ~ reply* 谨慎的回答.
Ca·glia·ri [kæˈljɑːri, ˌkæliˈɑːri] *n.* 卡利亚里〔意大利港市〕.
ca·gy [ˈkeidʒ] *n.* = cagey. **-gi·ly** *ad.* **-gi·ness** *n.*
ca·hier [kɑːˈjei] *n.* 〔F.〕①笔记本. ②政策报告;程序报告.
ca·hoot(s) [kəˈhuːt(s)] *n.* 〔美俚〕合伙,共同;共谋. ***in ~(s)*** 共同,共谋. ***go ~s = go in ~(s)*** 均分;分担.
CAI = computer-assisted [aided] instruction 用电子计算机辅助的教学.
cai·man [ˈkeimən] *n.* = cayman.
Cain [kein] *n.* ①该隐〔《圣经》中亚当的长子,曾杀害其弟 Abel〕. ②〔喻〕杀弟者;凶手;恶魔. ~ ***and Abel*** [ˈeibl] 〔美俚〕椅子和桌子. ***raise*** ~ 〔俚〕引起骚乱;制造麻烦.
Ca·ino·zo·ic [kainəˈzəuik, ˈkei-] *a.* =Cenozoic.
ca·ique [kaiˈiːk] *n.* ①(博斯普鲁斯海峡上的)划桨轻舟. ②(地中海东部的)小帆船.
caird [kɛəd] *n.* 〔Scot.〕①流动铜匠. ②流浪汉.
cairn [kɛən] *n.* ①石塚,累石堆;堆石标. ②(躯小、脚短的)㹴狗(=~ terrier).
cairn·gorm [ˈkɛənˈgɔːm] *n.* 【矿】(苏格兰 Cairngorm 山出产的)烟水晶.
Cai·ro [ˈkaiərəu] *n.* 开罗〔埃及首都〕.
cais·son [ˈkeisən] *n.* ①弹药箱;弹药车;地雷箱. ②(打捞沉船用的)潜函,沉箱;充气浮筒;(船坞等的)铁浮门;蓄气装置. ③【建】藻井. ~ **disease** 【医】潜函病,沉箱病.
cai·tiff [ˈkeitif] *a., n.* 〔古、诗〕卑鄙的(人).
caj·e·put [ˈkædʒipət] *n.* = cajuput.
ca·jole [kəˈdʒəul] *vt.* 勾引,哄骗. ~*(sb.)* ***into [out of] doing sth.*** 诱(人)做[停止做]某事. ~ ***(sth.) out of [from] sb.*** 花言巧语骗走某人的(某物). **-ment** *n.* 笼络,诱骗. **-r** *n.* 骗子.

ca·jol·er·y [kəˈdʒəuləri] *n.* 笼络,诱骗.
Ca·jun, Ca·jan [ˈkeidʒən] *n.* ①卡真人〔美国路易斯安那州的本地人,原系阿卡地亚法国移民后裔〕. ②卡真方言.
caj·u·put [ˈkædʒəpət] *n.* 【植】白千层 (*Melaleuca leucadendra*).
cake [keik] *n.* ①饼,糕;〔古〕扁形小面包;〔Scot.〕燕麦饼;〔美〕烧饼. ②(肥皂等)饼状物,(衣服等上的)硬泥块. ③〔美〕爱跟女学生厮混的男学生. ④〔美俚〕妖娆女子. *a sponge* ~ 松软蛋糕. *a* ~ *of soap* 一块肥皂. *I wish my* ~*s were dough again.* 我要是还没有结婚就好了. ***a piece of*** ~ 〔口〕容易事,快心事. ~***s and ale*** 欢宴,狂喝闹饮;优游的岁月;世俗的享乐. ***go off like hot*** ~***s*** 畅销;敏捷迅速地打发(处置等). ***Land of*** ~***s*** 苏格兰的别号. ***One's*** ~ ***is dough.*** 打算错误;计划失败(*My* ~ *is dough.* 〔美俚〕我(的计划)已经失败了). ***sell like hot*** ~ 畅销. ***take the*** ~ 得一等奖;超人一等 (*His arrogance takes the* ~. 他那份傲气可真不得了). ***You cannot eat your*** ~ ***and have it.*** 不能两全;不能(两种利益)兼得. —*vt.* ①使成扁平的硬块,使固结;使烧结,使胶凝. ②加块结物于…上. —*vi.* ①块结,胶凝. ②〔美俚〕跟女学生厮混. ~**-eater** 〔美俚〕(醉生梦死过悠闲岁月的)浪子. ~ **ink** 墨. ~**walk** (美国黑人的)步态舞;步态竞赛〔因当初是用蛋糕做奖品,故名〕.
cak·(e)y [ˈkeiki] *a.* 饼状的,凝固了的.
Cal. = ①California. ②large calorie(s)【物】大卡,千卡.
cal. = ①calendar. ②calibre. ③small calorie(s)【物】小卡.
Cal·a·bar [ˈkæləbɑː] *n.* 卡拉巴尔〔尼日利亚〕. ~ *bean* 【植】卡拉巴尔毒豆.
cal·a·bash [ˈkæləbæʃ] *n.* 【植】葫芦.
cal·a·boose [ˈkæləbuːs] *n.* 〔美口〕监狱;拘留所.
ca·la·di·um [kəˈleidiəm] *n.* 【植】杯芋 (*Caladium bicolor*).
Cal·ais [ˈkælei; F. kalɛ] *n.* 加来〔法国港市〕.
cal·a·man·co [ˌkæləˈmæŋkəu] *n.* (*pl.* ~*es*, ~*s*) 【纺】有光呢.
cal·a·man·der [ˌkæləˈmændə] *n.* 【植】柿属 (*Diospyros*) 植物.
cal·a·ma·ry [ˈkæləməri] *n.* 【动】枪鲗.
cal·a·mine [ˈkæləmain] *n.* ①【矿】异极矿;碳酸锌矿;菱锌矿. ②【药】炉甘石.
cal·a·mint [ˈkæləˌmint] *n.* 【植】塔花属植物〔尤指塔花 (*satureja calamintha*)〕.
cal·a·mite [ˈkæləmait] *n.* 【古生】芦木.
ca·lam·i·tous [kəˈlæmitəs] *a.* 多灾多难的;悲惨的;不幸的. **-ly** *ad.* **-ness** *n.*
ca·lam·ity [kəˈlæmiti] *n.* 灾难,灾害,困苦;不幸. ~ **howler** 〔美俚〕凶事预言者. ~ **issue** (选举时)对己党不利的灾难性问题. **C- Jane** 〔美〕(预示不祥的)杀星,凶星〔原为美国小说中边疆女英雄简·柏克的绰号,因为她枪法高明,一枪就能击毙对方〕.
cal·a·mon·din [ˌkæləˈmɔndin] *n.* 【植】加拉蒙地亚桔 (*Citrus mitis*).
cal·a·mus [ˈkæləməs] *n.* (*pl.* **-mi** [-mai]) ①【植】菖蒲;芦苇;芦笛;芦管笔. ②〔C-〕【植】省藤属. ③【鱼】鲷的一种. ④【鸟】羽,羽根.
ca·lan·do [kəˈlændəu] *a., ad.* 〔It.〕【乐】减少音量的[地];音量渐减和速度渐缓的[地].
ca·lan·dria [kəˈlændriə] *n.* ①【物】加热体,加热器. ②【化】排管式.
ca·lash [kəˈlæʃ] *n.* ①双马四轮马车;车篷. ②(十八世纪女人的)皱纹丝头巾[女帽].
cal·a·thus [ˈkæləθəs] *n.* (*pl.* **-thi** [-θai]) 古希腊水果篮(图案)〔象征丰产〕.
cal·a·ver·ite [ˌkæləˈveərait] *n.* 【矿】碲金矿.
calc. = calculate.
calc- *comb. f.* 〔用于元音前〕石灰,钙: *calc*tufa.
cal·ca·ne·us [kælˈkeiniəs] *n.* (*pl.* **-ne·i** [-niai]) ①【解】跟骨. ②空凹足. 亦作 **cal·ca·ne·um** [-əm], (*pl.* **-nea** [-niə]). **cal·ca·ne·al** *a.*
cal·car[1] [ˈkælkɑː] *n.* (*pl.* ***cal·cari·a*** [kælˈkeəriə]) ①【植】距管. ②【动】距. **-ca·rate** [-kəreit, -rit] *a.*
cal·car[2] [ˈkælkɑː] *n.* 【化】(熔化玻璃的)熔炉;煅烧炉.
cal·car·e·ous, cal·car·i·ous [kælˈkeəriəs] *a.* 含钙的,石灰质的.
cal·ced·o·ny [kælˈsedəni] *n.* 【矿】玉髓.
cal·ce·i·form [ˈkælsifɔːm] *a.* 【植】拖鞋状的.
cal·ce·o·lar·i·a [ˌkælsiəˈleəriə] *n.* 【植】蒲包花属的植物;〔C-〕蒲包花属.
cal·ce·o·late [ˈkælsiəleit] *a.* 【植】拖鞋状的〔如兰花瓣〕(= calceiform).
calces [ˈkælsiːz] *n.* calx 的复数.
calci- *comb. f.* 〔用于辅音前〕石灰,钙: *calci*ferol.
cal·cic [ˈkælsik] *a.* ①含钙的. ②石灰(质)的.
cal·ci·cole [ˈkælsikəul] *n.* 【植】钙生植物. **-cic·o·lous** [kælˈsikələs] *a.*
cal·cif·er·ol [kælˈsifərəul] *n.* 【生化】(麦角)钙化醇,骨化醇,维生素D_2.
cal·cif·er·ous [kælˈsifərəs] *a.* 含钙的.
cal·cif·ic [kælˈsifik] *a.* 石灰质的,钙化的.
cal·ci·fi·ca·tion [ˌkælsifiˈkeiʃən] *n.* ①【医】石灰性变,钙化(作用). ②骨化(作用). ③(意见、立场等的)硬化,僵化.
cal·ci·fuge [ˈkælsifjuːdʒ] *n.* 【植】避钙植物,嫌钙植物. **-cif·u·gous** [kælˈsifjugəs] *a.*
cal·ci·fy [ˈkælsifai] *vt., vi.* ①【医】(使)钙化,(使)石灰质化. ②(使)硬化,(使)僵化.
cal·ci·mine [ˈkælsimain, -min] *n.* (粉墙用的)白粉. —*vt.* 用白粉涂刷(墙等).
cal·ci·na·tion [ˌkælsiˈneiʃən] *n.* ①【化】煅烧,焙烧;(石灰的)烧成. ②【冶】氟化法;烧矿法;(铁矿的)整矿法.
cal·cine [ˈkælsain] *vt., vi.* 煅烧;焙烧. ~*d alum* 烧明矾,枯矾. ~*d lime* 生石灰. ~*d cocoon*僵蚕茧.
cal·cite [ˈkælsait] *n.* 【矿】方解石.
cal·ci·um [ˈkælsiəm] *n.* 【化】钙. ~ **carbonate** 碳酸钙. ~ **chloride** 氯化钙. ~ **cyanamide** 氰氨化钙,石灰氮. ~ **fluoride** 氟化钙,萤石. ~ **hydroxide** 氢氧化钙. ~ **light** 钙光;石灰光. ~ **phosphate** 磷酸钙. ~ **sulphate** 硫酸钙. ~ **superphosphate** 过磷酸钙.
calc-sin·ter [ˈkælksintə] *n.* 【化】钙华,石灰华.
calc·spar [ˈkælkspɑː] *n.* 【矿】方解石(= calcite).
calc-tu·fa [ˈkælktuːfə],**calc·tuff** [ˈkæltʌf] *n.* 【化】石灰华.
cal·cu·la·bil·i·ty [ˌkælkjuləˈbiliti] *n.* ①可计算性;可预见性. ②可靠性,可依赖程度.
cal·cu·la·ble [ˈkælkjuləbl] *a.* ①能计算的;预想得到的. ②可指望的,可依赖的.
cal·cu·la·graph [ˈkælkjuləgrɑːf] *n.* 【商标】(电话)记时器.
cal·cu·late [ˈkælkjuleit] *vt.* ①计算,核算. ②预测,推测. ③〔多用被动语态〕计划,筹划;使充作,使适合 (*for*). ④〔美口〕打算;想,以为;猜想. ~ *an eclipse* 预测日(月)蚀. ~ *the consequences of* 推测…的结果. ***be*** ~***d for*** 为了…(的目的),做成[制订]的. ***be*** ~***d to (do)*** 适于(做)…,计划(做)…. —*vi.* ①计算,考虑. ②预料;指望 (*on, upon*). ③〔美〕以为,认为. ~ *on the fine weather tomorrow* 预料明天天晴. ~ *on earing big money* 指望挣大钱.
cal·cu·lat·ed [ˈkælkjuleitid] *a.* ①有计划的,有意的,故意的. ②(预备)供…之用的,合于…之用的. ③算清了的;被预测出的. *a* ~ *risk* 有意进行的冒险.
cal·cu·lat·ing [ˈkælkjuleitiŋ] *a.* ①计算(用)的;有打算的,不落空的. ②精打细算的,慎重的;为自己打算的.

~ *machine* 计算机. ~ *scale [rule]* 计算尺. *a* ~ *man* 一个有心计的人.
cal·cu·la·tion [ˌkælkjuˈleiʃən] *n.* ①计算, 计算法. ②推定, 预测. ③深思熟虑, 精打细算; 慎重的计划; 算计. *checking* ~ 验算. *rough* ~ 概算. *careful and meticulous* 精打细算.
cal·cu·la·tive [ˈkælkjulətiv] *a.* ①(需要)计算的. ②有打算的, 不落空的.
cal·cu·la·tor [ˈkælkjuleitə] *n.* ①计算者. ②计算机; 计算机操纵者. ③(使计算方便的) 一览表. ④有打算的人, 不落空的人; 谋略家. *an electronic* ~ 电子计算机.
cal·cu·lous [ˈkælkjuləs] *a.* 石一样的;【医】结石(病)的.
cal·cu·lus [ˈkælkjuləs] *n.* (*pl.* ~*es*, *-li* [-lai]) ①【医】结石, 石; 积石; 牙垢. ②【数】运算, 演算; 微积分(学). ~ *of finite differences*【数】差分演算 (法), 差分学. ~ *of variation* 变分法[学]. *differential [integral]* ~ 微[积]分(学). *urinary* ~【医】尿结石.
Cal·cut·ta [kælˈkʌtə] *n.* 加尔各答〔印度港市〕. ~ **hemp** 黄麻. ~ **Tonnage Scale** 加尔各答运货吨数〔通常以 50 立方英尺或 20 英担为一吨〕.
cal·dar·ium [kælˈdɛəriəm] *n.* (*pl.* ***-ria*** [-riə]) 〔L.〕(古罗马的)高温浴室.
Cal·der [ˈkɔːldə] *n.* 考尔德〔姓氏〕.
cal·de·ra [kælˈdiərə] *n.* ①【地】破火山口. ②大锅 (= caldron).
cal·dron [ˈkɔːdrən] *n.* 釜, 大锅 (= cauldron).
Cald·well [ˈkɔːldwəl] *n.* 考德威尔〔姓氏〕.
ca·lèche, ca·leche [kəˈleʃ] *n.* = calash.
Cal·e·do·nia [ˌkæliˈdəunjə] *n.* ①〔诗〕苏格兰. ②卡列多尼亚〔女子名〕.
Cal·e·do·ni·an [ˌkæliˈdəuniən] *a.* ①古代苏格兰的;〔诗〕苏格兰的; 苏格兰人的. ②【地】加里东的. —*n.* 苏格兰人.
cal·e·fa·cient [ˌkæliˈfeiʃənt] *a.*【医】使温暖的, 发热的. —*n.*【医】发暖剂.
cal·e·fac·tion [ˌkæliˈfækʃən] *n.* ①暖, 发暖. ②【化】发暖作用. ③热污染.
cal·e·fac·tive [ˌkæliˈfæktiv] *a.* 暖, 热; 温热性的.
cal·e·fac·to·ry [ˌkæliˈfæktəri] *a.* 温暖的; 生热的. —*n.* (旧时常作起居室用的)修道院暖室.
cal·e·fy [ˈkælifai] *vt., vi.* (使)发暖, (使)变热, (使)发热.
cal·em·bour [ˈkæləmbuə] *n.* 〔F.〕俏皮话, 双关妙语.
cal·en·dar [ˈkælində] *n.* ①历, 历法. ②历书, 日历; 月历. ③日程表; 一览表; 总目录;【法】案件日程表;〔美〕议会日程. *a perpetual* ~ 万年历. *a wall* ~ 挂历. *the lunatic [solar]* ~ 阴[阳]历. —*vt.* ①把…记入日程表中; 把…列入表中. ②为(文件等) 作分类索引. ~ **art** 年历画. ~ **clock** 日历钟. ~ **day** (日)历日〔由午夜到午夜〕. ~ **month** (日)历月. ~ **watch** 日历表. ~ **year** (日)历年〔scholastic year (学年), fiscal year (会计年度)等之对〕.
cal·en·der¹ [ˈkælində] *n.*【纺, 造纸】轧光机, 砑光机; 压延机; 轮压机. ~ *printing* 辊筒印花. —*vt.* 用砑光机砑光; 把…上轮压机. **-er** 轧光机 [压延机、轮压机] 操作工.
cal·en·der² [ˈkælində] *n.* (伊斯兰教国家的一种)游方教士.
cal·en·dry [ˈkælindri] *n.* 砑光机操作场.
cal·ends [ˈkælindz] *n.* (古罗马历法的) 朔日, 初一. ***at [on] the Greek*** ~ 永远不会有[发生, 实现等]的那一天〔因希腊历法中没有 Calends〕.
ca·len·du·la [kəˈlendjulə] *n.*【植】①金盏花. ②〔C-〕金盏花属.
cal·en·ture [ˈkælintjuə] *n.* ①(热带的)热病. ②【医】中暑.
ca·les·cence [kəˈlesns] *n.* (逐渐)增热, (逐渐)增温.
ca·les·cent [kəˈlesnt] *a.* 渐暖的; 变热的. **ca·les·cence** *n.*
calf¹ [kɑːf] *n.* (*pl.* ***calves*** [kɑːvz]) ①小牛, 犊; (鲸、象等的)仔; 犊皮. ②〔口〕傻头傻脑的青年人. ③冰山崩落下来的漂流冰块. ④大岛附近的小岛. ~ ***round***〔美〕打转儿, 彷徨, 浪荡. ***cast her*** ~ (牛) 流产. ***golden*** ~ (古以色列人崇拜的) 金犊;〔喻〕黄金崇拜. ***in [with]*** ~ 怀着孕的(牛). ***kill the fatted*** ~ ***for*** 盛宴接待[庆祝]. ***slip the [her]*** ~ (牛)流产. ~**bound** *a.* (书) 用小牛皮装订的. ~**dozer** 小型推土机. ~ **love** 少年时代的恋爱. ~**skin** 小牛皮. ~**'s teeth** 乳齿.
calf² [kɑːf] *n.* (*pl.* ***calves*** [kɑːvz]) 腓, 腿肚子. ~ **knee**【医】膝关节内翻.
Ca·li [ˈkɑːli] *n.*〔美〕= California.
Cal·i·ban [ˈkælibæn] *n.* ①(莎士比亚戏剧《暴风雨》中的)半兽半人怪物. ②〔喻〕丑恶残忍的人.
cal·i·ber [ˈkælibə] *n.*〔美〕= calibre.
cal·i·brate [ˈkælibreit] *vt.* ①测定…的口径. ②在(尺、秤等上)刻度, 分度. ③校准. ④使标准化.
cal·i·bra·tion [ˌkælibˈreiʃən] *n.* ①测定口径. ②刻度, 标度, 划度数. ③校准; 标准化.
cal·i·bre [ˈkælibə] *n.* ①(枪、炮的)口径; (子弹、炮弹的)直径; 炮口, 枪口. ②圆柱径. ③能力, 才干; 器量; (价值的)等级, 水准. ④规, 卡钳, 测径器. ⑤【机】轧辊型缝. *a heavy [intermediate]* ~ 大[中]口径. *a man of excellent* ~ 才能出众的人. *books of this* ~ 这一等级的书籍.
ca·li·ces [ˈkeilisiːz] *n.* *calix* 的复数.
cal·i·che [kɑːˈliːtʃi] *n.* ①【化】生硝; 智利硝. ②(土壤的)钙质层.
cal·i·cle [ˈkælikl] *n.*【生】杯状窝, 杯状器官, 小杯状体.
cal·i·co [ˈkælikəu] *n.* (*pl.* ~*s*, ~*es*) ①〔英〕白布;〔美〕印花布. ②花斑动物〔如花狗、斑马等〕. ③〔美俚〕女学生, 女人. —*a.*〔美〕杂色的, 花的; 印花布一样的. ~ *horse* 花马. ~ **paper** 印花纸. ~ **printing**【纺】棉布印花.
cal·i·co·back [ˈkælikəuˌbæk] *n.*【动】菜蝽蟓 (harlequin bug).
ca·lic·u·lar [kəˈlikjulə] *a.* ①【生】杯状的. ②【植】副萼(性)的.
Calif. = California.
ca·lif [ˈkeilif, ˈkɑː-] *n.* = caliph.
Cal·i·for·nia [ˌkæliˈfɔːnjə] *n.* 加利福尼亚〔美国州名〕. ~ **moccasins**〔美〕御寒厚袜. ~ **pants**〔美〕条纹[格纹]羊毛裤. ~ **poppy**【植】花菱草〔加州州花〕.
Cal·i·for·ni·an [ˌkæliˈfɔːnjən] *a., n.* 加利福尼亚州的[人].
cal·i·for·ni·um [ˈkæliˈfɔːniəm] *n.*【化】锎.
ca·lig·i·nous [kəˈlidʒinəs] *a.*〔古〕黑暗的, 幽暗的.
ca·lig·ra·phy [kəˈligrəfi] *n.* = calligraphy.
cal·i·ol·o·gy [ˌkæliˈɔlədʒi] *n.* 鸟巢学.
cal·i·pash [ˈkælipæʃ] *n.* 龟背肉.
cal·i·pee [ˈkælipiː] *n.* 龟肚肉.
cal·i·pers [ˈkælipəz] *n. pl.* = callipers.
cal·iph [ˈkælif, ˈkɑː-] *n.* 哈里发〔伊斯兰教国家政教合一的领袖的尊号〕.
cal·i·ph·ate [ˈkælifeit, ˈkɑː-] *n.* 哈里发的地位[政权, 统治区].
cal·i·sa·y·a [ˌkæləˈseijə] *n.*【植】黄金鸡纳树 (Cinchona calisaya). ~ *bark* 黄金鸡纳树皮.
cal·is·then·ic [ˌkælisˈθenik] *a.* = callisthenic. ~**s** *n.* = callisthenics.
calix [ˈkeiliks] *n.* (*pl.* ***-lices*** [-lisiːz]) ①【解】杯状窝, 杯状器官; 肾盂. ②【植】萼.
calk¹ [kɔːk] *n.*〔美〕(鞋底上防滑的)尖铁. —*vt.* ①加尖铁于. ②用尖铁伤害.
calk² [kɔːk] *vt.* = caulk.
calk³ [kɔːk] *vt.* 摹画复制, 临, 拓.

cal·kin [ˈkɔːkin] *n.* = calk[1].

call [kɔːl] *vt.* ①大声念[说],喊,叫. ②召唤,叫来,请来;召集,征召;号召;唤醒. ③把…取名为,称呼,把…叫做. ④以为,认为,看做. ⑤命令;任命. ⑥对…打电话. ⑦要求,请求,催促;责备;【牌】要求(摊牌,出牌). ⑧〔美〕【体】停止(比赛);判定. ~ *sb. by name* 叫某人姓名. ~ *a halt* 喝令停止. ~ *a meeting* 召集会议. ~ *a roll* 点名. ~ *the roll* 〔美〕点名. ~ *sb. from sleep* 叫起某人. ~ *the bill so much* 估计帐款是这么多. *I* ~ *that mean.* 我以为那是小气的. *have nothing to* ~ *one's own* 什么也没有;一无所长. ~*ed game* 【棒球】评定胜负. *Call no man happy before he is dead.* 人未盖棺勿谓有福. — *vi.* ①高声念[说],呼喊,叫唤,鸣,啼. ②到,访问,拜望. ③鸣信号;命令,要求;打电话. ④【牌】叫牌;要求看牌. ~ ***after*** ①追喊. ②以…的名字命名. ~ ***a spade a spade*** 是什么说什么,直言. ~ ***at*** *(a house; a place)* 访问(某家),(车船)停靠(某地). ~ ***away*** 使转移开,排解(忧闷);叫走. ~ ***back*** ①喊回,叫转来,召唤. ②取消,收回(说错的话). ③回一个电话;再打一个电话来. ~ ***down*** ①祈求,呼求(天恩). ②招惹(灾祸等). ③〔美俚〕骂,申斥,谴责. ~ ***for*** ①请求,要求,要;提倡,号召;招募. ②去拿(物件);去接(某人). ③(批注信封上)留交. ④叫喊,(为喝采等)喊出(演员等) (*This disease* ~*s for prompt treatment.* 这病必须急救). ~ ***forth*** 唤起;提起,用出,拿出(精神,勇气等). ~ ***heaven to witness*** 指天发誓. ~ ***in*** ①回收(通货等). ②招,请,叫(医生等);叫进;引入,引起;调入. ③来访 (*Call in, or ring us up.* 你可以亲自来访,也可以打电话来). ④打电话到服务单位,请假. ~ ***in question*** 疑,怀疑,对…表示异议;非难. ~ ***into being [existence]*** 创造,产出,使成立. ~ ***into play*** 使动作,使活动,使抒发. ~ *(sb.)* ***names*** 咒骂,骂人. ~ ***off*** ①叫开;转移开(注意力等). ②〔口〕命令停止,宣告终止;丢手,放手;取消(婚约). ③〔美〕点(名),列举(数字). ~ ***on [upon]*** ①访问. ②指名要(某人)去干(某事);请求,要求;号召 (*He* ~*ed upon me to make a speech.* 他请我演说). ~ ***out*** ①向…挑战. ②动员;〔美口〕命令,号召(罢工);唤起. ③大声叫喊. ④诱出. ⑤〔美俚〕请…跳舞. ~ ***over to*** 打电话给. ~ ***sb.'s bluff*** 〔美〕接受挑战〔请求〕. ~ ***the time*** 指挥事件的进行,领导行动. ~ ***the tune [shots, turn]*** 〔美〕预定比赛结果;定调子;发号施令;操纵. ~ ***things by their names*** 摆明(事实)说,明明白白地说. ~ ***to account*** ①要求作出解释;要求认错;责备. ②与…结帐,向…送欠单. ~ ***to arms*** 命令武装. ~ ***to mind*** 想起. ~ ***to order*** (议长)要求遵守秩序;〔美〕宣布开会. ~ ***together*** 召集. ~ ***up*** ①召唤,传,叫出来;召集,动员. ②提起,提出. ③打电话给;【讯】呼唤. ④想出来,想起. ***what one*** ~*s* = ***what is*** ~*ed* 所谓. — *n.* ①呼声,叫声,鸣声. ②号声;角声. ③叫喊;传唤;点名;招请,召集,号召. ④(电话)通话. ⑤吸引力. ⑥天职;命;必要,要求,义务. ⑦访问,到来;停泊,停车. ⑧(旗、灯等的)信号. ⑨清求,要求;【商】催收(股款等);(股票的)限价买进 (*opp.* put);催付. ⑩(纸牌)叫牌,叫牌权,所叫的牌. *a* ~ *before the curtain* (闭幕后对演员)喝采要求谢幕. *a bugle* ~ 号声. *a telephone* ~ (打)一次电话. *a messenger* ~ (电话)传呼. *the* ~ *to battle* 战斗号召. *You have no* ~ *to interfere.* 用不着你来管闲事. *30 days after* ~ 见票后三十天照付. ***at*** ~ 随叫随…,随要随…. ***at sb.'s beck and*** ~ 随某人之意摆布;完全听命于某人. ~ ***of nature*** 要上厕所,要解手. ***close*** ~ 幸免,死里逃出,危险关头. ***get the*** ~ 【美体】当选;被雇用. ***have a*** ~ ***to*** 做…是天职. ***have the*** ~ ***of the market*** 市面繁荣,供需旺盛. ***house of*** ~ 客栈;酒馆. ***make [pay] a*** ~ 访问,到. ***money on*** ~ =call money. ***on*** ~ 〔美〕①随要随(付),承索即(寄). ②随时待命,时刻准备着. ***place of*** ~ 停泊地,所到地. ***receive a*** ~ 接待,接见. ***return*** ~ 答拜,回访. ***take a*** ~ 【剧】谢幕. ***within*** ~ 声音到达之处,附近. ~**-back** *n.* 〔美俚〕①召回(暂时停雇职工). ②收回 (待修产品). ③加班. ~ **bell** 电铃. ~**-bird** 媒鸟,囮子. ~**-board** (车站等地的)公告牌. ~ **box** ①公共电话间 (=〔美〕public telephone booth). ②(由用户到邮局领邮件的)留局信箱. ~**boy** (对出场演员的) 呼喊员;【海】传令员;侍者. ~**day** 报喜节〔法学院学生取得律师资格的日子〕;当日节目〔指听众用电话来提出的意见、问题或要求当日照办的广播或电视节目〕. ~ **girl** (用电话召唤的) 妓女. ~ **house** 〔美俚〕(妓女可应召外出的) 妓院. ~**-in** *n.* 〔美〕电话点播节目. ~ **loan** 【商】活期贷款〔贷主有权随时要求归还〕. ~ **money** 活期贷款的款子. ~ **number** 图书馆(图书的)书架号码,索书号. ~**-over** 点名 (= roll~). ~ **rate** 活期贷款利率. ~ **signal** 【无】呼号. ~**-up** *n.* 征集令;征兵数,召集人数.

cal·la [ˈkælə] *n.* 【植】水芋;〔C-〕荷兰海芋属.

call·a·ble [ˈkɔːləbl] *a.* 可随时支取的〔尤指要求下即支付的(如贷款);要求下即兑付的(如公债)〕.

Call-A-Mart [ˈkɔːləmɑːt] *n.* 电子计算机化的超级市场〔雇客可用电话订货〕.

cal·lan(t) [ˈkælən(t)] *n.* 〔Scot.〕少年.

Ca·lla·o [kɑːˈjɑːəu] *n.* 卡亚俄〔秘鲁港市〕.

callee [kɔːˈliː] *n.* 〔美〕受访问者;被呼唤人;电话受话人.

call·er[1] [ˈkɔːlə] *n.* 呼唤者;招请者;召集者;访问者,来访者;打电话者.

cal·ler[2] [ˈkælə] *a.* 〔Scot.〕①(鱼等)新鲜的. ②(天气等)凉爽的,舒适的.

cal·li·gram(me) [ˈkæligræm] *n.* 画诗〔将诗文排列成与诗的主题有关的图画的一种诗〕.

cal·li·graph [ˈkæligrɑf] *vt.* 手书,手抄.

cal·lig·ra·pher, cal·lig·ra·phist [kəˈligrəfə, -fist] *n.* 书法家,写字能手.

cal·li·gra·phy [kəˈligrəfi] *n.* 善于书写 (*opp.* cacography);书法;笔迹.

call·ing [ˈkɔːliŋ] *n.* ①呼,唤,叫喊;点名. ②招请,召集,号召;(神的)感召,天命;天职. ③职业. ④名称. ⑤访问,到来;停靠(口岸). ⑥欲望;雌猫的叫春(期). *(a carpenter)* ***by one's*** ~ 职业是(木匠). ~ **card** 〔美〕名片;〔美俚〕指纹.

Cal·li·o·pe [kəˈlaiəpi] *n.* 【希神】卡拉培〔雄辩和叙事诗的女神,缪斯九神之首〕.

cal·lio·pe [kəˈlaiəpiː] *n.* 汽笛风琴. **-an** *a.*

cal·li·op·sis [ˌkæliˈɔpsis] *n.* 【植】金鸡菊属植物,金鸡菊,波斯菊(= coreopsis).

cal·li·per [ˈkælipə] *n.* ①〔*pl.*〕【机】卡钳,两脚规,测径器,测圆器 (= ~ compasses). ②【机】(阻力)制动片[夹]. ③(纸板等的)厚度. *inside [outside]* ~*s* 内[外]卡钳. *vernier* ~*s* 【机】游标卡. — *vt.* 用卡钳测量.

cal·lis·then·ic [ˌkælisˈθenik] *a.* 柔软体操的;健美体操的. ~*s n.* ①〔作复数用〕(主指女子的)柔软体操(术). ②〔作单数用〕健美体操(术).

Cal·lis·to [kəˈlistəu] 【天】木卫四.

cal·li·thump [ˈkæliθʌmp] *n.* 吵吵闹闹的游行〔以吹号角、敲铁锅及其他噪音乐器为主,以示嘲笑或敌意〕.

cal·li·thum·pi·an [kæliˈθʌmpiən] *n., a.* 〔美俚〕吵吵闹闹的游行者(的).

cal·lose [ˈkæləus] *n.* 【生】胼胝质.

cal·los·i·ty [kæˈlɔsiti] *n.* ①(皮肤)硬结;胼胝,老茧. ②无情,无感觉,麻木.

cal·lous [ˈkæləs] *a.* ①已硬结的,起老茧的. ②无情的,硬心肠的;无感觉的 (*to*). — *vt.* ①使硬结. ②使无感觉;使无情. **-ly** *ad.* **-ness** *n.*

cal·low [ˈkæləu] *a.* ①羽毛未生的;幼小的;未发育的;无经验的. ②〔Ir.〕(草地)低湿的. — *n.* 〔Ir.〕低湿的牧场.

cal·lus [ˈkæləs] *n.* (*pl.* **-li** [-lai]) ①硬固部;硬瘤;【医】胼胝;骨痂;接骨质. ②【植】愈合组织,胼胝体;(禾本植

物的)颖托。

calm [kɑːm] *a.* ①(海洋、天气等) 安静的，平静的。②(人)平稳的；镇定的，沉着的。③〔俚〕恬不知耻的，若无其事的，脸皮厚的。— *n.* ①平静，镇定。②零级风，无风，风平浪静。*a ~ before the storm* 暴风雨来前的无风〔平静〕时期。— *vt., vi.* (使)平静下来，(使) 镇定，(使) 沉着，(使) 从容。*Calm yourself.* 请别激动。~ ***down*** 平静下来 (*The sea ~ed down.* 海上风平浪静)。~ **belt** 无风带。~ **day**【物】(地磁)平静日。**-ly** *ad.* **-ness** *n.*

cal·ma·tive [ˈkælmətiv, ˈkɑːm-] *a.*【医】镇静的。— *n.*【医】镇静剂。

cal·o·mel [ˈkæləməl] *n.*【化】甘汞，氯化亚汞。

calori- *comb. f.* 热，热的：*calori*meter.

ca·lor·ic [kəˈlɔrik] *n.* 热(量)；【化】热质。— *a.* 热(量)的；热质的；蒸气推动的；卡(路里)的。**-al·ly** *ad.*

cal·o·ric·i·ty [ˌkæləˈrisiti] *n.* ①【医】食物的热量，生热力。②【物】热值。

cal·o·ri·e [ˈkæləri] *n.* ①【物】卡(路里)〔热量单位〕。②〔C-〕大卡，千卡。③产生一千卡热量的食物量。*large [great]* ~ 大卡，千卡。*small* ~ 小卡。

cal·o·ri·fa·cient [kəˌlɔriˈfeiʃənt] *a.* (食物) (产)生热(量)的。

cal·o·rif·ic [ˌkæləˈrifik] *a.* ①发热的，生热的。②热(量)的。~ **power** 卡值，热值。

ca·lo·ri·fi·ca·tion [kəˌlɔrifiˈkeiʃən] *n.* (动物体内) 热的发生，生热；发热力。

cal·o·rif·ics [kæləˈrifiks] *n.* ①加热术。②【物】热学。

cal·o·rif·i·er [kəˈlɔriˌfaiə] *n.* (液体的一种)加热装置。

cal·o·ri·fy [kəˈlɔrifai] *vt.* 加热于。

cal·o·rim·e·ter [ˌkæləˈrimitə] *n.* 卡计，热量计。

cal·o·rim·e·try [ˌkæləˈrimitri] *n.* 量热法，量热学。

cal·o·rize [ˈkæləraiz] *vt.*【冶】热镀(铝)，使铝渗入(某物)。

cal·or·stat [ˈkælɔːstæt] *n.* 恒温器，恒温箱。

cal·o·ry [ˈkæləri] *n.* = calorie.

ca·lotte [kəˈlɔt] *n.* ①(无边)小帽。②帽状物。③【动】纤毛帽；帽罩；(苔藓虫的)回缩盘。

cal·o·yer [ˈkælɔiə] *n.* (东正教会的)修士。

cal·pac, cal·pack [ˈkælpæk] *n.* (中近东的)羊皮帽，黑毡帽。

calque [kælk] *n.*【语】①仿造词〔如英语 *masterpiece* 是德语 *meisterstück* 的仿造词〕。②加倍；重复，反复；音节或词的重复。

Cal State [ˈkælsteit]〔美俚〕加(利福尼亚)州(立)大学。

Caltech [ˈkæltek] *n.*〔美俚〕加(利福尼亚)州工学院。

CALTEX = California Texas Oil Company (美国)德士古石油公司。

cal·trop, cal·trap [ˈkæltrəp] *n.* ①三角钉；【军】铁蒺藜。②【植】蒺藜。**water** ~【植】菱。

cal·u·met [ˈkæljumet] *n.* (印第安人的)(长杆)旱烟袋；〔喻〕和平的象征。***smoke the ~ together*** 和睦相处。

ca·lum·ni·ate [kəˈlʌmnieit] *vt.* 诽谤，诬蔑。

ca·lum·ni·a·tion [kəˌlʌmniˈeiʃən] *n.* 诽谤，诬蔑；【法】诬告。

ca·lum·ni·a·tor [kəˈlʌmnieitə] *n.* 诽谤者，诬蔑者；诬告者。

ca·lum·ni·a·to·ry, ca·lum·ni·ous [kəˈlʌmniətəri, -niəs] *a.* 诽谤的，诬蔑的。

cal·um·ny [ˈkæləmni] *n.* 诽谤，诬蔑。

cal·u·tron [ˈkæljətrɔn] *n.*【物】电磁同位素分离器。

Cal·va·dos [ˈkælvəˌdəus, ˌkælvəˈdəus] *n.* 法国苹果白兰地。

cal·var·i·a [kælˈveiriə] *n.* = calvarium.

cal·var·i·um [kælˈveiriəm] *n.* (*pl.* ***-vari·a*** [-ə])【解】颅顶，颅盖。**-i·al, -i·an** *a.*

cal·va·ry [ˈkælvəri] *n.* ①(十字架上的)耶稣受难像。②大磨难，苦恼。③〔C-〕耶稣受难处。

calve [kɑːv] *vi.* ①(牛、鲸、鹿等)产(仔)。②(冰河、冰块等)分离，崩解。— *vt.* ①生(小牛、小鹿等)。②使(冰块)崩解。

calved [kɑːvd] *a.* 有腿肚子的。

Cal·ver·ley [ˈkælvəli] *n.* 卡尔弗利〔姓氏〕。

Cal·vert [ˈkælvə(ː)t, ˈkɔːlvət] *n.* 卡尔弗特〔姓氏〕。

calves [kɑːvz] calf 的复数。

Cal·vin [ˈkælvin] *n.* 卡尔文〔姓氏〕。**John** ~ 约翰·加尔文〔1509—1564，法国宗教改革家〕。

Cal·vin·ism [ˈkælvinizəm] *n.* 加尔文教，加尔文主义。

Cal·vin·ist [ˈkælvinist] *n.* 加尔文教徒。

Cal·vin·is·tic [kælviˈnistik], **Cal·vin·is·ti·cal** [-kəl] *a.* 加尔文的，加尔文教的。

cal·vi·ties [kælˈviʃiiːz] *n.* (*sing., pl.*)【医】秃头，脱发病。

calx [kælks] *n.* (*pl.* ***calces*** [ˈkælsiːz]) ①金属灰〔烧渣〕，矿灰。②〔古〕生石灰。

ca·ly·ce·al [ˌkæliˈsiːəl] *a.*【植】萼的，萼状的。

ca·ly·ces [ˈkeilisiːz, ˈkæ-] *n.* calyx 的复数。

cal·y·ci·form [ˈkælisifɔːm] *a.*【植】萼状的。

ca·lyc·i·nal [kəˈlisinl], **cal·y·cine** [ˈkælisain] *a.*【植】萼(一样)的。

cal·y·cle [ˈkælikl] *n.*【植】副萼。

ca·lyc·u·lus [kəˈlikjuləs] *n.* (*pl.* ***-li*** [-lai])【解】小萼；味蕾。

ca·lyp·so[1] [kəˈlipsəu] *n.*【植】匙唇兰。

ca·lyp·so[2] [kəˈlipsəu] *n.* (特里尼达等地居民临时编唱的一种)即兴小调。

ca·lyp·tra [kəˈliptrə] *n.*【植】藓帽；根冠；冠状部。

ca·lyp·tro·gen [kəˈliptrədʒən] *n.*【植】根冠原。

ca·lyx [ˈkeiliks] *n.* (*pl.* ***~es, ca·ly·ces*** [ˈkeilisiːz])【植】萼；【解】(肾)盂。

cam [kæm] *n.*【机】凸轮，偏心轮；靠模。~ **shaft** 凸轮轴。~**wood**【植】紫木。

Cam., Camb. = Cambridge.

cam. = camouflage.

Ca·ma·güey [ˌkɑːmɑːˈgwei] *n.* 卡马圭〔古巴城市〕。

ca·ma·ra·de·rie [ˌkɑːməˈrɑːdəriː] *n.* 〔F.〕同志间的感情；友谊；友爱。

ca·ma·ril·la [ˌkæməˈrilə] *n.* 〔Sp.〕①秘密顾问。②奸党。③秘密会议室。

cam·a·ron [ˈkæmərən] *n.*【动】(淡水)大斑节虾。

cam·ass, cam·as [ˈkæməs] *n.*【植】卡马夏属(*Camassia*)植物。

cam·ber [ˈkæmbə] *n.* ①向上弯曲，翘曲；弯度；中凸形。②小船坞，筏渠。③【空】(机翼的)弯曲，曲度弧。④【船】梁拱，拱高。— *vt.* 把(道路、甲板等)造成弧形〔上弯形〕。— *vi.* (梁、道路等)向上弯，翘起。~ **beam**【建】弓背梁。

cam·bist [ˈkæmbist] *n.* ①各国度量衡及货币比值表〔手册〕。②汇兑商；汇兑行家。

cam·bi·um [ˈkæmbiəm] *n.*【植】形成层，新生层。

cam·blet [ˈkæmblet] *n.* = camlet.

Cam·bo·di·a [kæmˈbəudiə] *n.* 柬埔寨〔亚州〕(=Kampuchea).

Cam·bo·di·an [kæmˈbəudjən] *a.* 柬埔寨的；柬埔寨人的；柬埔寨语的。— *n.* 柬埔寨人；柬埔寨语(=kampuchean).

cam·bo·gi·a [kæmˈbəudʒiə] *n.*【化】藤黄。

Cam·bri·a [ˈkæmbriə] *n.*〔古〕=Wales.

Cam·bri·an [ˈkæmbriən] *a.* ①〔诗〕威尔士的。②【地】寒武系〔纪〕的。— *n.* ①〔诗〕威尔士人。②【地】寒武纪。~ **system**【地】寒武系。

cam·bric [ˈkeimbrik] *n.* ①麻纱白葛布；麻纱手帕。②细漆布〔电工材料〕。~ **grass** 苎麻。~ **paper** 布纹纸。

Cam·bridge [ˈkeimbridʒ] *n.* ①剑桥〔英国城市，剑桥大学所在地〕。②坎布里奇〔美国马萨诸塞州城市，哈佛大学所在地〕.
Cambs. = Cambridgeshire 剑桥郡〔英国〕.
Cam·den [ˈkæmdən] *n.* 卡姆登〔姓氏〕.
came[1] [keim] come 的过去式.
came[2] [keim] *n.* (固定花格窗玻璃等用的)有槽铅条.
cam·el [ˈkæməl] *n.* ①骆驼. ②【船】起重浮箱, 打捞浮筒. *an Arabian [a Bactrian]* ~ 单峰[双峰]驼. ***break the ~'s back*** 受不了, 忍无可忍. ***swallow a ~*** 默忍难于置信[容忍]的事. ~**back** 驼背; 驼峰. ~**backed** *a.* 驼背的. ~ **bird** 驼鸟. ~ **cade** 〔美〕骆驼队. ~ **corps** 〔美俚〕步兵. ~**'s hair** 骆驼毛, 骆驼绒; 栗鼠尾毛画笔.
cam·el·eer [ˌkæmiˈliə] *n.* 赶骆驼的(人); 骆驼骑兵.
ca·mel·li·a [kəˈmiːljə, kəˈmel-] *n.*【植】山茶(花).
ca·mel·o·pard [ˈkæmiləpɑːd, kəˈmeləpɑːd] *n.* ①〔罕〕【动】长颈鹿〔一般称 giraffe〕; 〔C-〕【天】鹿豹座. ② [ˈkæmelepəd] 〔谑〕瘦长的女人.
Cam·e·lot [ˈkæmilɔt] *n.* 卡米洛特〔传说中英国亚瑟王宫廷所在地〕; 〔喻〕象征灿烂岁月或繁荣昌盛的地方.
cam·el·ry [ˈkæməlri] *n.* ①骆驼骑兵; 骆驼队. ②骆驼驮的货物.
cam·e·o [ˈkæmiəu] *n.* ①(玉石、贝壳上的)浮雕; 有浮雕的玉石[贝壳等]. ②【影, 剧】小品, 片断. — *a.* 小型的, 小规模的. ~ **role** (衬托名星演员的)小配角.
cam·er·a [ˈkæmərə] *n.* ①*(pl. ~s)*【摄】照相机; 电影摄影机; 电视摄像机; 暗箱; 暗房. ②*(pl. cam·er·ae* [-əriː]*)*【法】法官室. ③罗马教廷的财政部. *load a* ~ 装胶卷到照相机内. *a sound* ~ 录音器. ***in*** ~ 禁止旁听; 秘密地. ***on*** ~ 被电视机摄取; 出现在电视上. ~ **obscura** [əbsˈkjuərə] 暗箱. ~**cature** 〔美〕电影动画. ~ **gun**【军】(能自动拍摄空战射击情况的)照相枪. ~ **lucida** [ˈluːsidə] 显像描绘器. ~**man** 照相师, (电影)摄影师; 摄影记者. ~**plane** 摄影用飞机. ~**-shy** *a.* 不愿照相的. ~ **tube**【电视】析象管, 阴极射线管. ~ **work** 摄影技巧.
cam·er·al [ˈkæmərəl] *a.* 推事室的, 咨询委员会的.
cam·er·a·lis·tic [ˌkæmərəˈlistik] *a.* ①财政(上)的. ②机关事务学的. — *n.* 〔*pl.*〕〔用作单数〕财政学.
Cam·er·on [ˈkæmərən] *n.* 卡梅伦〔姓氏, 男子名〕.
Cam·e·roon [ˈkæməruːn] *n.* 喀麦隆〔非洲〕.
cam·i·knick·ers [ˌkæmiˈnikəz] *n.* 连裤女衬衣.
Ca·mil·(l)a [kəˈmilə] *n.* 卡米拉〔女子名〕.
cam·i·on [ˈkæmiən] *n.* 〔F.〕(军用)卡车.
cam·i·sade, cam·i·sado [ˌkæmiˈseid, ˌkæmiˈseidəu] *n.* 〔古〕【军】夜袭.
ca·mise [kəˈmiːs] *n.* 宽大的衬衣[罩衣; 袍子].
cam·i·sole [ˈkæmisəul] *n.* ①女人短袖衬衣, 贴身背心. ②宽女外套, (绣花)化妆衣. ③疯人紧身衣.
cam·let [ˈkæmlit] *n.*【纺】羽纱.
cam·o·mile [ˈkæməmail] *n.*【植】春黄菊.
cam·ou·flage [ˈkæmuflɑːʒ] *n.* ①【军】伪装. ②隐瞒, 掩饰. ③〔喻〕幌子. *under [behind] the ~ of* 在…的掩盖[伪装]下. — *vt.* 使改头换面, 伪装, 掩饰; 欺瞒.
ca·mou·flet [ˌkæmuˈflei] *n.* 〔F.〕①(炸弹、地雷等的)地下爆炸. ②地下爆炸的炸弹[地雷]. ③(地下爆炸造成的)弹坑.
cam·ou·fleur [ˈkæmufləː] *n.* 〔F.〕伪装技术员.
Camp [kæmp] *n.* 坎普〔姓氏〕.
camp [kæmp] *n.* ①野营, 露营地; 露营队, 出征军; 阵营, 阵地, 战场; 军队生活. ②露宿; 帐幕, 帐篷; 〔美〕山中小房; (牧场中)作住处用的马车. ③集团, 阵营; 〔美〕分会. ④〔美俚〕(原为同性爱圈子内行话)下流; 庸俗; 过分打扮[做作]. *a break* ~ 折叠帐篷. ***be in the same [enemy's]*** ~ 是同志[敌人]. ***go into*** ~ 布阵. ***strike [break up]*** ~ 撤营. ***the ~ eye*** 〔美〕守露营帐篷的. — *vt.* ①使扎营住宿. ②临时安顿. — *vi.* ①露营; 宿营; 露宿. ②住宿. ~ ***out*** 露宿. ~ **bed** 行军床. ~ **car** 野营车. ~ **chair** 折椅. ~**craft** 野营术. **C-David** 戴维营〔美国总统别墅所在地〕. ~ **fever** 露营病〔主指斑疹伤寒〕. ~**fire** 营火; 〔美〕营火会. ~ **fire girl** 美国营火少女团团员. ~ **follower** ①随营人员; 营妓. ②附和者, 依附者. ~ **ground** 野营地, 野营布道会场. ~**site** 营地. ~ **stool** 折凳. **-er** *n.* ①露营者. ② = ~ car.
Cam·pa·gna [kæmˈpɑːnjə] *n.* *(pl. -pa·gne* [-ˈpɑːnjei]*)* ①(罗马四郊的)罗马平原. ②〔c-〕(一般的)平原.
cam·paign [kæmˈpein] *n.* ①战役. ②竞选运动; 运动, 游说. ③【冶】开炉时间. *an advertising* ~ 大做广告. *a ~ against [for]* … 反对[赞成]…的运动. ***enter upon a*** ~ 走上征途; 发动运动. ***on*** ~ 从军, 出征. — *vi.* ①从军, 出征. ②参加[从事](某一)运动. ***go ~ing*** ①从军. ②参加(某一)运动. ~ **club** 〔美〕某候选人后援会. ~ **emblem** 〔美〕政党徽章.
cam·paign·er [kæmˈpeinə] *n.* ①运动参加者; 竞选者. ②从军者. ③老兵; 老练的人. *an old* ~ 老兵; 经验丰富的人, 老手.
cam·pa·ni·le [ˌkæmpəˈniːli] *n.* *(pl. -li* [-liː], *~s)* (靠近教堂的)钟楼, 钟塔.
cam·pa·nol·o·gy [ˌkæmpəˈnɔlədʒi] *n.* ①鸣钟术. ②铸钟术.
cam·pan·u·la [kəmˈpænjulə] *n.* ①【植】风铃草(属). ②【动】铃状部[结构].
cam·pan·u·late [kəmˈpænjuleit] *a.*【植】钟形的, 钟状的, 铃状的.
Camp·bell [ˈkæmbl] *n.* 坎贝尔〔姓氏〕.
camp·er [ˈkæmpə] *n.* ①露营者. ②(可随车携带、折叠的)活动住房, 野营帐篷.
cam·pe·si·no [ˌkɑːmpeˈsiːnə] *n.* *(pl. -nos* [-nɔs]*)* 〔Sp.〕农民, 农业工人.
cam·pes·tral [kæmˈpestrəl] *a.* 〔罕〕野外的; 乡村的.
cam·phene [ˈkæmfiːn] *n.*【化】莰烯.
cam·phire [ˈkæmfaiə] *n.* ①【植】散沫花. ②散沫花染料. ③棕色.
cam·phol [ˈkæmfɔl] *n.*【药】龙脑, 冰片.
cam·phor [ˈkæmfə] *n.* 樟脑; 【化】莰酮-〔2〕; 〔美〕樟脑水. ~ **ball** 樟脑丸. ~ **glass** (樟脑脂状的)乳白(不透明)玻璃. ~ **ice** 樟脑药膏. ~ **tree**【植】樟树. ~ **wood** 樟木.
cam·phor·ate [ˈkæmfəreit] *vt.* 使与樟脑化合, 在…中加入樟脑. **-d** *a.* 含樟脑的.
cam·phor·ic [kæmˈfɔrik] *a.* (含)樟脑的; 樟脑酸的. ~ **acid** 樟脑酸.
camp·ing [ˈkæmpiŋ] *n.* 野营, 露营; 帐幕生活, 露营生活.
cam·pi·on [ˈkæmpjən, -piən] *n.*【植】剪秋罗属, 狗筋蔓属.
cam·po [ˈkɑːmpəu] *n.* *(pl. ~s)* ①(巴西等地的)大草原. ②【植】坎普群落.
camp·o·ree [ˌkæmpəˈriː] *n.* 地区性童子军集会.
cam·po santo [ˈkæmpəu ˈsæntəu] 〔It.〕坟地; (特指)公墓.
camp·shed [ˈkæmpʃed] *vt.* 堆土[石]堆并铺木板于(河岸).
camp·shot [ˈkæmpʃɔt] *n.* (堆土[石]堆并铺以木板的)护岸, 河防.
cam·pus [ˈkæmpəs] *n.* 〔美〕校园, 学校范围内; 大学. ~ *activities* 校内活动. ~ *cave* 〔美〕学生消遣地. ***off*** ~ 在校外. ***on (the)*** ~ 在校内.
camp·y [ˈkæmpi] *a.* 〔美俚〕①同性恋爱的. ②下流的; 庸俗的; 过分打扮的; 矫揉做作的.
cam·py·lot·ro·pous [ˌkæmpiˈlɔtrəpəs] *a.*【植】弯生胚珠的.
can(i)- *comb.f.* 表示"狗""犬": canine.
can[1] [强 kæn; 弱 kən, kn] *v. aux.* ***(could*** [强 kud; 弱

kəd]) ①〔表示能力〕能,会. ②〔表示可能性〕(可)能,会得;(偶然,有时)会. ③〔口〕〔表示许可或请求〕可以…,行. ④〔表示轻微的命令语气,多与 not 连用〕(不)可以…,(不)能…. ⑤〔在疑问句中重读,表示惊异、不耐烦等〕怎么会,难道会;究竟. ⑥〔表示必须〕就得. ⑦〔与 see, hear, smell 等感觉动词连用,代替一般的现在式或过去式〕(看、听、嗅…)得到,(感觉)得出. *I ~ swim.* 我会游泳. *You ~ go.* 你可以去;去好了;去罢. *Curiosity ~ get you into trouble.* 好奇可能招引麻烦. *Do you think he ~ yet be living?* 你以为他还会活着吗? *How ~ you?* 你怎么能这样!你真做得出! *If you don't be quiet you ~ leave the room.* 你再不安静下来就得离开房间. *I ~ see her easily from here.* 我从这里很容易看到她. *I couldn't understand him.* 我听不懂他的话. **as ... as ~ be** 很 (*He is as happy as ~ be.* 他是很幸福的. 他(幸福得)不能再幸福了). **~ but** ... 只能…罢了 (*I ~ but speak.* 我只能说说罢了). **~ not but ...** ①不得不 (**= c ın not help**). ②不会不,不能不,必然 (*I ~ not but speak that ... = cannot help speaking that ...*我不得不说〔认为〕…. *One ~ not but be moved by his fate.* 人们不能不为他的命运所感动). **cannot too** 决不会…得太…,无论怎样…都不够 (*You cannot be too modest.* 人越谦虚越好〔无论怎样谦虚都不为过〕. *We cannot praise him too much.* 我们无论怎样称赞他都不为过分). **~-do** *a.* 有干劲的,勤奋的,热心的.

can² [kæn] *n.* ①〔美〕罐头,听头 (=〔英〕tin);(装液体的)铁罐,玻璃罐(等);一罐(之量);茶杯. ②〔美俚〕保险箱. ③〔美俚〕监牢;警察局. ④〔美俚〕浴室;厕所;屁股. ⑤〔军俚〕驱逐舰;飞机;(深水)炸弹. ⑥〔俚〕〔*pl.*〕头戴听筒,耳机. ⑥〔美俚〕一盎司大麻麻醉药. **~ *moocher*** 破落到拣垃圾箱里罐头盒的浪子,不可救药的败家子. **~ *of corn*** 【美棒球】容易接的飞球. **~ *of worms*** 问题成堆的地方,老大难的工作;一团糟. ***carry [take] the (back) ~*** 负责任,受责备;代人受过. ***in the ~*** (影片等)编成,制成,现成(可用). — *vt.* ①〔美〕把…装成罐头. ②〔美俚〕解雇,辞退;抛弃;开除(学生);停用;停止. ③〔俚〕录音(在磁带上). **~ *the ad lib*** 〔美剧俚〕请安静. **~ *the highbrow stuff*** 〔美俚〕停止夸口. **~ *the twit*** 〔美俚〕 停止说话. **~-box** 【纺】 条筒针梳机. **~carrier** 〔美俚〕为某事负责任的人. **~ opener** 开罐头用具.

Can. = Canada; Canadian.

can. = canceled; canon; canto.

Ca·naan [ˈkeinən] *n.* ①迦南〔《圣经》中所说上帝赐给亚伯拉罕的地方,现在的巴勒斯坦西部〕. ②〔喻〕希望之地;天国,乐土.

Ca·naan·ite [ˈkeinənait] *n.* 迦南人〔语〕.

Can·a·da [ˈkænədə] *n.* 加拿大〔北美洲〕.

Ca·na·di·an [kəˈneidjən] *a.* 加拿大的; 加拿大人的. — *n.* 加拿大人.

Ca·na·di·an·ism [kəˈneidiənizəm] *n.* ①加拿大习惯、特点、信仰. ②加拿大英语特有的词或短语.

ca·naille [kəˈnɑːi] *n.* 〔F.〕〔集合词〕愚民,下层社会;乌合之众.

cana·kin [ˈkænəkin] *n.* = cannikin.

ca·nal [kəˈnæl] *n.* ①运河;沟渠,水道. ②【建】沟;【解】管,道. ③【天】火星表面的运河状细长沟纹. *the alimentary ~* 消化道. *the Suez C-* 苏伊士运河. ***the C-Zone*** 巴拿马运河区. — *vt.* ***(-l(l)ed; -l(l)ing)*** 在…开运河;在…开沟;疏导. **~ boat** 运河船〔一种专门在运河中航行的大驳船〕. **~ rays** 【物】极隧射线,阳极射线.

ca·nal·age [kəˈnælidʒ] *n.* ①开运河. ②〔集合词〕运河,水道;运河运输. ③运河通行税.

can·al·ic·u·late, can·al·ic·u·lated [ˌkænəˈlikjulit, -leitid] *a.* 【解、植】有小管的,有小沟的.

can·al·icu·lus [ˌkænəˈlikjuləs] *n.* ***(pl. -li*** [-lai]***)*** 【解】小管;小沟.

ca·nal·i·za·tion [ˌkænəlaiˈzeiʃən] *n.* ①开挖运河. ②运河规划;渠道网;导管组织;堰闸法. ③【医】穿通;造管术. ④(思想等的)开导.

ca·nal·ize [ˈkænəlaiz] *vt.* ①在…上开运河〔沟〕;把(河道)改造成运河. ②使(水)流向一定方向;〔喻〕把(思想等)导向某一途径. — *vi.* 流入渠道. *~d development hypothesis* 【生】限向发育说.

ca·naller [kəˈnælə] *n.* 运河货船;运河船的船员.

can·a·pé [kænəˈpei] *n.* 〔F.〕(上加鱼、肉、乳酪等的)开胃饼干〔烤面包〕.

ca·nard [kæˈnɑːd] *n.* 〔F.〕 ①谣言,误传. ②【空】前置安定面飞机;前置安定面. ③【烹】鸭.

ca·nar·i·ensis [kənɛəriˈensis] *n.* 【植】金丝雀蔓草.

ca·nar·y [kəˈnɛəri] *n.* ①【鸟】金丝雀. ②(非洲)加那利群岛白葡萄酒〔又作 C- wine〕. ③鲜黄色,嫩黄色. ④〔美俚〕女歌手;女人;女学生. ⑤〔美俚〕告密者. ⑥〔*pl.*〕【美影】录音时刺耳的嘎嘎声. — *a.* ①加那利群岛的. ②鲜黄色的. **~ bird** 金丝雀;〔美俚〕 罪犯. **~-bird flower** 【植】金莲花. **~ creeper** 金丝雀蔓草. **~ grass** 【植】虉草. **~ stone** 黄石髓.

Canary Islands [kəˈnɛəriˈailəndz] *n.* 加那利群岛〔大西洋东北部〕.

ca·nas·ta [kəˈnæstə] *n.* 加纳斯塔牌〔一种二至六人玩的纸牌游戏〕.

ca·naster [kəˈnæstə] *n.* ①苇篮,蒲篮〔装烟叶用〕. ②(南美)板烟.

Can·ber·ra [ˈkænbərə] *n.* 堪培拉〔澳大利亚首都〕.

canc. = cancel, cancelled, cancellation.

can·can [ˈkãŋkãːŋ] *n.* 〔F.〕(妇女跳的一种多踢足动作的)康康舞.

can·cel [ˈkænsəl] *vt.* ***(-lled,*** 〔美〕 ***-led)*** ①划掉,略去,删去. ②注销,盖销;取消,把…作废. ③抵消,偿还. ④撤消,解除. ⑤【数】约去;消去(帐目或方程式两边的相等部分). *a cancelled cheque* 付讫的支票. *~ a contract* 取消合同. *~ each other* 互相抵消. *a cancelling stamp* 作废〔注销〕图章. — *vi.* 相消,互相抵消 *(out)*. *The pros and cons ~ out.* 正反两种意见互相抵消. — *n.* ①删略;取消;【数】(相)约,(相)消;盖销. ②〔常 *pl.*〕轧票机,打孔铁 ***(a pair of) ~s*** 作废打孔器;轧票机. **-(l)er** *n.* ①删略者,取消者. ②【无】消除器,补偿设备.

can·cel·late, can·cel·la·ted [ˈkænsəleit, -tid] *a.* 【动】格子状的,网眼状的.

can·cel·la·tion [ˌkænsəˈleiʃən] *n.* ①删除,勾消. ②取消,撤消,注销;(邮票等的)盖销,盖销记号;废除;解除. ③【数】(相)消,(相)约.

can·cel·lous [ˈkænsiləs] *a.* ①【解】网眼状的,多孔的;松质骨的. ②【植】(某些叶子的)细密网状脉的 (= cancellate).

can·cer [ˈkænsə] *n.* ①【医】癌症;癌(瘤),肿瘤. ②弊病;社会恶习. ③〔the C-〕【天】巨蟹座;巨蟹宫. *gastric ~* 胃癌. *lung ~* 肺癌. ***the Tropic of C-*** 夏至线,北回归线. **~ stick** 〔俚〕纸烟. **-d** *a.* 得了癌症的.

can·cer·o·gen·ic [ˈkænsərəuˈdʒenik] *a.* 产生癌的,致癌的. **~ substance** 【医】致癌物质.

can·cer·ol·o·gy [ˌkænsəˈrɔlədʒi] *n.* 癌学.

can·cer·ous [ˈkænsərəs] *a.* ①癌的,癌肿性的. ②得了癌症的;不治的.

can·croid [ˈkæŋkrɔid] *a.* ①【医】癌肿状的. ②蟹状的. — *n.* ①角化癌;皮癌. ②蟹状甲壳动物.

can·de·la [kænˈdiːlə] *n.* 【物】新烛光,堪(德拉)〔发光强度单位〕.

can·de·la·brum [ˌkændiˈlɑːbrəm] *n.* ***(pl. -bra*** [-brə], ***~s)*** ①枝状烛台,烛架. ②【建】华柱. ★也有以 candelabra 作单数,而以 candelabras 作复数的.

can·de·lil·la [ˈkændiˌlilə] *n.* 【植】蜡大戟,蜡拖鞋花.

can·dent [ˈkændənt] *a.* 〔古〕白热的,炽烈的.

can·des·cence [kænˈdesns] *n.* 白热.

can·des·cent [kænˈdesnt] *a.* 白热的.
C.&F.【商】= cost and freight 成本加运费.
can·did [ˈkændid] *a.* ①正直的,耿直的,公正的. ②率直的,坦白的,老实的,忠厚的. ③真实的,传真的;非排演的;【摄】趁人不备时偷拍的. ④(光等)白色的. ~ *camera* 趁人不备时快拍用的小照相机. ~ *friend* 坦率的朋友. *to be ~ (with you)* 老老实实讲,不瞒你说. **-ly** *ad.* **-ness** *n.*
can·di·da·cy [ˈkændidəsi] *n.* 候选(人)资格[身分];提名候选.
can·di·date [ˈkændidit] *n.* ①候选人;候补人 *(for)*. ②学位应考人,投考生. — *vi.* [-deit]〔美口〕提名候选.
can·di·da·ture [ˈkændiditʃə] *n.*〔英〕= candidacy.
can·died [ˈkændid] *a.* ①糖渍的,蜜饯的. ②冰糖一样坚硬的;亮晶晶的. ③甜蜜的. *have a ~ tongue* 会讲甜言蜜语,嘴甜. — *n.*【纺】浆斑.
Can·di·ot [ˈkændiˌɔt, -ət] *a.* 克里特岛(居民)的. — *n.* 克里特岛居民.
can·dle [ˈkændl] *n.* ①蜡烛. ②蜡烛状物. ③【物】烛光〔光强度单位〕. *the international ~* 国际标准烛光. *a lighted ~* 夜会;宴会. *burn the ~ at both ends* 滥费精力[财产](等). *cannot hold a ~ to* 远不如,不能与…相比. *hide one's ~ under a bushel* 不露锋芒. *hold a ~ to another* 为别人尽力. *hold a ~ to the devil* 助纣为虐,为虎作伥;离开正道. *hold a ~ to the sun* 白费,徒劳. *not fit to hold a ~ to ...* = *can not hold a ~ to ...* 远不如,不能与…相比. *not worth the ~* 不上算,值不得,得不偿失. *sell by the ~ [by inch of ~]* (以蜡烛点完来决定成交的)拍卖. — *vt.* 用亮光检查(鸡蛋的)好坏. **~berry** ①【植】杨梅属植物;月桂果. ②= **~nut**. **~ bomb** 照明弹. **~ ends**〔*pl.*〕蜡烛头;一点一点积蓄成的东西. **~fish** *n. (pl. ~es)*【动】太平洋烛鱼. **~foot** 烛光英尺(= foot-~). **~holder** 烛台. **~light** ①烛光,灯火. ②黄昏. **~nut**【植】石栗(树). **~pin** ①(一种游戏用的)烛形木柱. ②〔*pl.*〕烛柱戏. **~ power**【物】烛光 (*a burner of 50 ~ power* 五十支烛光的灯). **~stick** 烛台. **~wick** 烛芯;〔美〕织物上凸起的花纹. **~wood** ①【植】蜡烛木. ②有脂之树或灌木. ③(引火或作火炬用的)烛材.
Can·dle·mas [ˈkændlməs] *n.*【宗】圣烛节(二月二日). **~ Day**〔Scot.〕春季结帐日.
can·do(u)r [ˈkændə] *n.* ①公正,公平. ②率直,坦率. ③白色;光明.
C & R Sec = Courier and Runner Section【美军】传令组.
C & W, C-and-W = country and western〔美〕(用电吉他演奏的)仿西部乡土音乐.
can·dy [ˈkændi] *n.* ①冰糖;水果糖;〔美〕蜜饯,糖果(=〔英〕sweets). ②〔美俚〕可卡因(= cocaine). ③砂糖结晶冰糖. *He'd take a ~ from a baby.*〔美口〕他是一个贪鄙的小人. *sugar ~* 冰糖(=〔美〕rock ~). — *vt.* ①蜜饯,糖煮. ②使结晶成冰糖[块];把…煮成结晶. — *vi.* 结晶成糖. — *a.*〔美俚〕(服饰)花哨的. **~ bar** 方糖块. **~ butcher**〔美俚〕卖糖小贩. **~ floss**〔英俚〕①棉花糖. ②不切实际的主意[计划]. **~ pull** (备有糖果的青年人的)联欢会. **~ store**〔美〕糖果店(=〔英〕sweet shop). **~-stripe** (织物的)条纹图案,条子花.
can·dy·tuft [ˈkænditʌft] *n.*【植】屈曲花(属);伞形屈曲花.
cane [kein] *n.* ①(藤、竹等的)茎;藤料,竹料. ②甘蔗. ③杖,手杖,笞杖;〔美〕棍棒,棒. *take up the ~* 拿起藤条(处罚学生). — *vt.* ①用棍打. ②用藤做(椅背等). **~-brake** 藤丛,竹丛. **~ chair** 藤椅. **~ gun** 手杖形手枪. **~ land** 甘蔗地. **~ rush**〔美〕(校内)班级间的比赛. **~ sugar** 蔗糖. **~ work** 编藤细工. **-r** *n.* 藤椅编制工.

ca·nel·la [kəˈnelə] *n.* (做香料等用的)白桂皮.
ca·ne·pho·ros [keiˈni:fərəs, kəˈnef-] *n. (pl. -ri [-rai])* ①(古希腊)头顶盛有祭物篮子的少女. ②【建】(作建筑物装饰用的)顶篮童女雕塑(= canephor).
ca·nes·cent [kəˈnesnt] *a.* ①变成白色或微灰色的. ②【植】(某些叶子)披灰白毛的.
can·ful [ˈkænful] *n.* 一罐,满罐.
cang(ue) [kæŋ] *n.* 枷〔中国古时的一种刑具〕.
cani- *comb. f.* 表示"犬"(= can-).
Ca·nic·u·la [kəˈnikjulə]【天】天狼星.
ca·nic·u·lar [kəˈnikjulə] *a.* ①【天】天狼星的;根据天狼星升起来度量的. ②三伏天的,酷暑的.
ca·nine [ˈkeinain] *a.* ①犬的;似犬的. ②犬属的. ③[ˈkænain] 犬齿的. — *n.* ①犬. ②犬属动物. ③[ˈkænain]【解】犬齿. *a ~ laugh* 冷笑. *a ~ control officer* 搜捕无主野狗的公务员. **~ madness**【医】狂犬病. **~ species** 犬族. **~ tooth** 犬齿.
can·ing [ˈkeiniŋ] *n.* ①鞭打;笞刑. ②藤料编制作业,编藤细工. *He wants a sound ~.* 得重重鞭他一顿才行.
Ca·nis [ˈkeinis] *n.*【动】犬属. **~ Major [Minor]**【天】大[小]犬座.
can·is·ter [ˈkænistə] *n.* ①罐,茶筒. ②【化】滤毒罐;【军】榴霰弹筒. ③〔美俚〕挂表;手枪. **~ shot** 霰弹.
can·ker [ˈkæŋkə] *n.* ①【医】痈;溃疡;口疮. ②【兽医】口蹄疫;【植】黑腐病;(梨、茶等的)枝枯病;蛀孔. ③【虫】尺蠖;尺蠖类的害虫. ④【喻】腐败;弊害;烦恼,苦恼. — *vt., vi.* ①(使)害痈病;(使)腐蚀,(使)(植物)生黑腐病;(使)溃烂. ②(使)受毒害. ③(使)苦恼. **~ worm**【虫】尺蠖;尺蠖类害虫.
can·ker·ous [ˈkæŋkərəs] *a.* ①溃疡的,痈(似)的. ②有腐蚀性的,引起溃烂的.
can·na [ˈkænə] *n.*【植】美人蕉;〔C-〕美人蕉属.
can·na·bin [ˈkænəbin] *n.*【化】大麻甙,大麻脂.
can·na·bis [ˈkænəbis] *n.* ①【植】大麻. ②大麻雌花顶部.
canned [kænd] can[2] 的过去式及过去分词. — *a.* ①〔美〕罐装的. ②〔美俚〕酩酊大醉的. ③〔美俚〕被解雇的;被囚禁的. ④录音的. ⑤〔美〕(新闻稿等)同时供几家报刊[通讯社]发出的;千篇一律的,刻板的. ⑥〔美俚〕事先准备好的. **~ cow**〔美俚〕炼乳. **~ editorials.** 统一发出的社论. **~ goods**〔美俚〕罐头(食品). **~ heat**〔美俚〕①小罐装的化学燃料〔多作野餐用〕. ②烈酒. **~ music**〔美俚〕唱片音乐. **~ speech**〔美俚〕录音演说.
can·nel [ˈkænl] *n.*【矿】烛煤(= ~-coal).
can·nel·lo·ni [ˌkæniˈlouni] *n.*〔*pl.*〕〔集合词〕烤碎肉卷子.
can·ne·lure [ˈkænəljuə] *n.* ①(唱片等的)槽. ②【军】弹壳槽线.
can·ner [ˈkænə] *n.* ①〔美〕罐头制造业者. ②(只能制狗食罐头用的)肉质低劣的动物.
can·ner·y [ˈkænəri] *n.* ①〔美〕罐头工厂. ②〔俚〕监狱.
Cannes [kæn] *n.* 戛纳〔法国港市〕.
can·ni·bal [ˈkænibəl] *n.* 食人者;吃同类的动物. — *a.* 吃人(肉)的;吃同类的. **-ism** *n.* ①嗜食人肉的恶习;同类相残. ②残忍.
can·ni·bal·is·tic [ˌkænibəˈlistik] *a.* ①食人者的;同类相残的. ②灭绝人性的,野蛮的.
can·ni·bal·ize [ˈkænibəlaiz] *vt., vi.* ①吃(人);吃(同类). ②用拆下的零件修配(另一机器等),拆取(旧机器等的)零配件. ③调拨(某一单位等的)人员充实另一单位. ~ *a radio set from two old ones* 拆取两台旧收音机的零件修配一台新收音机. **-za·tion** *n.*
can·ni·kin [ˈkænikin] *n.* 小罐;小酒杯[水杯];小木桶.
Can·ning [ˈkæniŋ] *n.* 坎宁〔姓氏〕.
can·ning [ˈkæniŋ] *n.*〔美〕罐头制造业[法].
can·nist·er [ˈkænistə] = canister.
Can·non [ˈkænən] *n.* 坎农〔姓氏〕.

C

can·non [ˈkænən] *n.* *(pl.* ~*s,* 〔集合词〕~*)* ①大炮；榴弹炮；【空】机关炮. ②【机】(二重)套轴. ③【动】(有蹄类的) 管骨. ④【英台球】连撞二球. ⑤〔美口〕连珠枪，手枪；扒手，小偷. — *vi.* ①开炮，炮轰. ②【英台球】连撞二球，间接碰撞 *(against; into; with).* ~ *off the red* 【台球】连撞两个红球. — *vt.* ①炮轰. ②〔美俚〕对…偷窃. ~**ball** ①*n.* 炮弹；快车；【网球】炮弹式发球；〔美俚〕犯人间秘密传递的消息. ②*vi.* (象炮弹般)疾飞. ~-**bit** 圆辔. ~ **bone**【动】炮骨；马胫骨，管骨. ~ **cracker** 大型鞭炮. ~ **fodder** ①炮灰〔指兵士〕. ②待磨的谷物. ~**proof** *a.* 防炮弹的. ~ **shot** 炮弹；射程，弹程.

can·non·ade [ˌkænəˈneid] *n.* 连续炮击；轰隆声. ②〔口〕口头攻击. — *vt.* 炮击. — *vi.* 炮击；轰隆轰隆地响.

can·non·eer [ˌkænəˈniə] *n.* 炮手，炮兵.

can·non·ry [ˈkænənri] *n.* ①开炮；连续炮击. ②〔总称〕炮.

can·not [强 ˈkænɔt; 弱 ˈkænət] = can not.

can·nu·la [ˈkænjulə] *n.* *(pl.* **-lae** [-liː], ~*)* 【医】套管，插管.

can·nu·lar [ˈkænjulə] *a.* 管的，管状的，中空的 (= cannulate [-lit, -ˌleit]).

can·ny [ˈkæni] *a.* ①机警的，精明的，心细的；狡猾的. ②〔Scot.〕俭约的；安全的；安静的，稳定的，温和的；幸运的. ③〔英方〕悦目的，吸引人的. **-i·ly** *ad.* **-ni·ness** *n.*

ca·noe [kəˈnuː] *n.* 独木舟；小划子；小游艇；皮舟. *paddle one's own* ~(靠自己力量)独力进行. — *vi.* 划[乘]独木舟. — *vt.* 用独木舟载运.

ca·noe·ing [kəˈnuːiŋ] *n.* 〔美〕划独木舟.

ca·noe·ist [kəˈnuːist] *n.* 划独木舟的人.

can·on[1] [ˈkænən] *n.* ①教规，宗规；圣典，经典；圣徒名单. ②规则，规范，准则. ③真作；真传经典；(基督教圣经的)正经. ④【乐】轮唱法，轮唱曲. ⑤【印】48 磅大活字. ⑥【天主教】弥撒的主要部分. ~*s of taxation* 课税原则. ~ **law** 教会法，寺院法. ~ **sin** 死罪.

can·on[2] [ˈkænən] *n.* 大教堂教士会成员；(天主教)教团团员. **-ess** [-is] 修女会会员；修女.

ca·ñon [ˈkænjən] *n.* 〔Sp.〕= canyon.

ca·non·ic [kəˈnɔnik] *a.* ① = canonical. ②【乐】卡农的，轮唱曲的.

ca·non·i·cal[1] [kəˈnɔnikəl] *a.* ①(合乎)宗规的，以寺院法为准则的；《圣经》正经的，真作的. ②被认为正经的；规范的；典范的. ③【数】正则的，典型的. — *n.* 〔*pl.*〕(布道时应穿的)法衣. ~ **ensemble**【物】正则系综. ~ **hours** ①(上午 8 点至下午 3 点的)祈祷时间，教堂婚礼时间. ②合适的时间. ~ **dress** 教士法衣. **-ly** *ad.*

ca·non·i·cal[2] [kəˈnɔnikəl] *a.* 关于大教堂教士 (会)的.

ca·non·i·cate [kəˈnɔnikeit, -kit] *n.* 大教堂教士会成员的职位(= canonry).

can·on·ic·i·ty [ˌkænəˈnisiti] *n.* ①符合宗规. ②可作为正典的资格. ③合乎正规.

can·on·ist [ˈkænənist] *n.* 宗教[教会]法规学者.

can·on·ize, -ise [ˈkænənaiz] *vt.* ①追认[尊崇](某死者)为圣徒. ②承认…为正典 [正经]. **-za·tion** [kænənaiˈzeiʃən] *n.*

can·on·ry [ˈkænənri] *n.* 大教堂教士会成员的职位.

ca·noo·dle [kəˈnuːdl] *vi.* 〔美俚〕①搂抱. ②爱抚. — *vt.* 用爱抚[搂抱]来劝动(某人).

can·o·pied [ˈkænəpid] *a.* 有天篷的.

Ca·no·pus [kəˈnəupəs] *n.*【天】老人星〔船底座 α〕.

can·o·py [ˈkænəpi] *n.* ①天篷；罗伞，华盖. ②覆盖. ③(飞机的)座舱盖；(降落伞的)伞盖；【植】(树)冠；冠层. ④天空. ~ *of heaven* 苍穹. *under the* ~ 〔美〕究竟，到底 (*Where under the* ~ *did you come from?* 你究竟是从哪儿来的?). — *vt.* *(-pied; -py·ing)* 用天篷遮覆.

ca·no·rous [kəˈnɔːrəs] *a.* 音调[音色]优美的；共鸣的. **-ly** *ad.* **-ness** *n.*

canst [强 kænst, 弱 kənst] *v. aux.* 〔古〕= can[1] 〔用于主语为 thou 时〕.

cant[1] [kænt] *n.* ①行话；(盗贼的)黑话，隐语. ②(政党的)应时标语[口号]；时髦话. ③哀诉声. ④伪善的口吻[言语]. ~ *phrase* 时髦话；流行语；黑话. *in the* ~ *of the day* 用时髦话来说. — *vi.* ①用伪善口吻解释；侈谈；〔罕〕哀诉，苦求. ②讲时髦话，讲黑话. ③〔美俚〕瞎聊天. ~**ing heraldry** 象征本人名字的徽章〔如 Shakespeare 用挥枪的鹰代表 shake spear〕.

cant[2] [kænt] *n.* ①(晶体、河岸等的)斜面；斜角. ②有棱的木材；(船的)斜肋骨〔又作 ~ frame〕. ③斜撞，斜推. ④切角，斜切. — *vt.* ①使(船等)倾斜. ②投掷(球等). ③把…的棱角切掉. ④使 (网等) 倒转；突然改变…的方向. — *vi.* ①倾斜. ②倒转. ③(船) 改变方向. ~ *over* 翻倒. ~**-hook** 滚木钩. **-ed** *a.* 有角的；倾斜的.

cant[3] [kænt] *a.* 〔英方〕活泼有力的.

can't [kɑːnt; 〔Am.〕 kɑːnt] = cannot.

Cant. = Canterbury; Canticles; Cantonese.

Can·tab [ˈkæntæb], **Can·ta·brig·i·an** [ˌkæntəˈbridʒiən] *n.* ①(英国)剑桥市人，剑桥大学学生[毕业生，校友]. ②(美国)马萨诸塞州坎布里奇人，哈佛大学学生[毕业生，校友]. — *a.* ①(英国)剑桥市的；(美国)坎布里奇市的. ②剑桥大学的；哈佛大学的.

can·ta·bi·le [kænˈtɑːbili] *a., ad.* 〔It.〕【乐】象歌唱一样的[地]；流畅的[地]. — *n.* 歌唱般的音乐.

can·ta·la [kænˈtɑːlə] *n.* 【植】狭叶番麻 *(= Agave cantala).*

can·ta·le·ver, can·ta·li·ver [ˌkæntəˈlevə, -liːvə] *n.* = cantilever.

can·ta·loup(e) [ˈkæntəluːp] *n.* ①【植】(南欧)甜瓜，棱瓜. ②〔美俚〕棒球用球.

can·tan·ker·ous [kənˈtæŋkərəs] *a.* 脾气坏的，爱吵闹的. **-ly** *ad.* **-ness** *n.*

can·tar, kan·tar [kɑːnˈtɑː] *n.* 坎塔尔〔穆斯林国家的一种重量单位. 从 100 磅到 700 磅不等〕.

can·ta·ta [kænˈtɑːtə, kən-] *n.* 〔It.〕【乐】清唱剧；大合唱.

can·ta·trice [ˈkæntətriːs, It. ˌkæntaˈtriːtʃe] *n.* *(pl.* ~*s* [-tris], It. ***-tri·ci*** [-ˈtriːtʃi]*)* *n.* 〔It.〕(歌剧中的) 专业女歌唱家，女歌手.

can·teen [kænˈtiːn] *n.* ①(兵营等内部的)小卖部；小饭馆〔美国通常叫 Post Exchange (PX)〕；临时餐室. ②(军用)饭盒，水罐；炊具箱. ③(家用)餐具箱；小器皿箱. *a dry [wet]* ~ 不卖酒的[卖酒的]食品小卖部. *a public* ~ 公共小饭馆.

can·ter[1] [ˈkæntə] *n.*【马术】普通跑步；慢跑. ★马速共 5 种: walk, amble, trot, canter, gallop. *a preliminary* ~ 预备练习时的慢跑；〔喻〕预备动作. *win at [in] a* ~ (马)轻易赛赢. — *vt.* 使(马)慢跑. — *vi.* (马) 用普通慢跑前进 *(along)*；骑着马慢跑.

canter[2] [ˈkæntə] *n.* ①说黑话的人. ②哀诉者. ③伪善者. ④流浪者.

Can·ter·bu·ry [ˈkæntəbəri, -beri] *n.* ①坎特伯雷〔英格兰东南部大城市〕. ②〔c-〕乐谱架. *The C- Tales* (英国作家乔叟写的)《坎特伯雷故事集》. ~ **bell**【植】风铃草，吊钟花.

can·thar·i·des [kænˈθæridiːz] *n.* 〔*pl.*〕① cantharis 的复数. ②〔作 *sing.* 用〕【药】斑蝥〔指其干燥制剂〕.

can·tha·ris [ˈkænθəris] *n.* *(pl.* ***can·thar·i·des*** [kænˈθæriˌdiːz]*)*【动】斑蝥，花金龟 (= Spanish fly).

can·thus [ˈkænθəs] *n.* *(pl.* **-thi** [-θai]*)*【解】眼角，眦；【动】(昆虫眼的)刺突.

can·ti·cle [ˈkæntikl] *n.* ①(宗教)颂歌，赞歌. ②咏歌，小歌曲. ③〔the Canticles〕(旧约圣经的) 雅歌 (= The Song of Solomon).

can·ti·hook [ˈkæntihuk] *n.*【无】转杆器.

can·ti·le·na [ˌkæntiˈlinə] *n.*【乐】坎蒂列那〔优美动听的短歌〕.

can·ti·le·ver [ˈkæntiliːvə] *n.* ①(桥梁的)悬臂,肱梁;支架. ②电缆吊线夹板;纸条盘. ~ **bridge** 悬臂桥. ~ **crane** 伸臂起重机.
can·til·late [ˌkæntəˈleit] *vt.* (在犹太教礼拜仪式中)吟唱.
can·til·la·tion [ˌkæntəˈleiʃən] *n.* (犹太教礼拜仪式中的)吟唱.
can·ti·na [kænˈtiːnə] *n.* ①〔美方〕小酒馆,酒吧. ②鞍头挂袋.
can·tle [ˈkæntl] *n.* ①鞍子的后弓〔后部翘起部分〕. ②切下的一角;切头,残块.
cant·mould·ing [ˈkæntməuldiŋ] *n.*【建】斜状饰.
can·to [ˈkæntəu] *n.* ①(长诗的)篇章. ②【乐】最高音部;歌,旋律. ③〔美〕拳击的一局,比赛的一节.
Can·ton [ˈkænˈtɔn] *n.* (旧时欧美人所习称的)广州. ~ **crepe** 广绫〔做拷绸用〕;重双绉. ~ **linen** 夏布. ~ **River** (旧时欧美人所习称的)珠江.
can·ton [ˈkæntɔn] *n.* ①(瑞士的)州. ②(法国的)市区,镇,村. ③ [ˈkæntən]【徽】(徽章或旗子的)右上角的小方块部分. — *vt.* [kænˈtɔn] ①把…分成州〔区,村〕(*out*). ② [kənˈtuːn]【军】使驻扎;分配营房给(部队等). **-al** [ˈkæntənl] *a.* 州的,县的. **-al·ism** *n.* 州郡行政制.
Can·ton·ese [ˌkæntəˈniːz] *a.* 广州的. —*n.*〔*pl.*, *sing.*〕①广州人. ②广州话.
can·ton·ment [kænˈtuːnmənt] *n.*【军】〔常 *pl.*〕宿营地,(临时)兵营;冬营.
can·tor [ˈkæntɔː, -tə] *n.* (教会的)合唱指挥人,歌咏班领唱者.
can·to·rial [kænˈtɔːriəl] *a.* 歌咏班领唱人的,合唱指挥人的;教堂圣坛北边的.
can·trip [ˈkæntrip] *n.*〔主 Scot.〕①(魔法的)符咒. ②恶作剧.
Can·tuar. = Cantuaria (= Canterbury).
can·tus [ˈkæntəs] *n.* (*pl.* ~)〔L.〕【乐】= canto. ~ **firmus**【乐】定旋律.
cant·y [ˈkænti] *a.*〔英方〕活泼的,快活的.
Ca·nuck [kəˈnʌk] *n.* ①〔美口,常蔑〕法裔加拿大人〔语〕. ②〔美俚〕加拿大人;加拿大种的马.
can·vas(s) [ˈkænvəs] *n.* ①粗帆布. ②(一套)风帆. ③(一套)帐篷;天幕. ④(一块)油画布;(一幅)油画. ⑤【美拳】拳击场的地板. *single* ~ 绣花十字布. ***kiss the*** ~【美拳】被击倒. ***under*** ~ ①挂着风帆. ②(军队支起帐篷)露营. ~**back**〔美〕(北美)灰背野鸭. ~**boat** 帆布船. ~**-duck** 粗帆布. ~ **hotel**〔美俚〕帐篷. ~ **opera**〔美俚〕马戏. ~ **shoes**〔*pl.*〕帆布鞋. ~ **stretcher** 画布框.
can·vass [ˈkænvəs] *vt.* ①兜揽(生意);劝募;游说,运动(选票等). ②〔美〕详细检查,点(选票等). ③(详细)讨论(问题等);详细考查〔调查〕. ~ *a district* 在竞选区游说. ~ *the votes cast*〔美〕检点票数. — *vi.* 游说,运动,劝诱. ~ *for* (*insurance; subscription*) 兜揽(保险等),劝募(捐款等). ~ *for votes* 活动竞选. — *n.* ①(竞选)运动,活动;劝募. ②(详细)检查,检点;论究,讨论.
can·vass·er [ˈkænvəsə] *n.* 游说者,兜揽员,推销员;〔美〕检票员.
can·y [ˈkeini] *n.* ①藤(制)的. ②多藤的.
can·yon [ˈkænjən] *n.* 峡(谷). *the Grand C-* (美)科罗拉多大峡谷.
can·zo·ne [kænˈtsəuni] *n.* (*pl.* **-ni** [-niː]) ①歌曲. ②抒情诗;抒情歌曲(如牧歌)(= can·zona [-nɑː]).
can·zo·net [kænzəˈnet] *n.*【乐】(轻快优美的)短小歌曲,小歌.
caou·tchouc [ˈkautʃuk] *n.*【化】生橡胶;纯橡胶.
cap [kæp] *n.* ①无边帽,便帽;制服帽;军帽;头巾. ②鞘,(笔)套,盖,罩子;(鞋)尖. ③【建】柱头;【矿】顶板岩石;【船】桅尖;【解】膝盖骨;【植】根冠;菌盖;【军】(枪弹等的)雷管,火帽. ④【数】求交运算. ⑤脱帽礼. ⑥【猎】会费. ⑦〔英俚〕避孕药. ⑧〔美俚〕一胶囊毒品〔迷幻药等〕. *Where is your* ~? (对孩子说)脱帽行礼吧. *If the* ~ *fits, wear it.* 帽子合适就戴,批评合适就得接受. *a lamp* ~ 灯头. *the* ~ *of fools* 傻瓜大王. ***bear the*** ~ ***and bells*** 成为众人取笑的对象. ~ ***and bells*** (丑角戴的)系铃帽;小丑. ~ ***and gown*** (大学校的)方帽长袍正式校服;学者. ~ ***in hand*** 脱帽;谦恭地,恭敬地. ~ ***of liberty*** 自由帽〔古罗马获得自由后的奴隶所戴的圆锥帽〕;共和政体的标志. ~ ***of maintenance***〔英〕(英王、贵族等的)冠冕. ***fling*** [***throw***] ***one's*** ~ ***over the mill*** 不顾利害地干,冒身败名裂的危险. ***fuddle one's*** ~ 酩酊大醉. ***get one's*** ~〔英〕做选手. ***pull*** ~***s*** 争吵,扭打. ***put on one's considering*** [***thinking***] ~ 仔细考虑. ***send the*** ~ ***round*** 传帽子(收集捐款等). ***set one's*** ~ ***at*** [美 ***for***] (女子向男子)挑逗,追求. ***The*** ~ ***fits.*** 评论〔描写等〕得正合适,言之中肯. — *vt.* ①给…戴帽. ②〔Scot.〕授与…以学位;使做选手. ③在…上装雷管. ④覆盖于…顶上,包覆于…顶端. ⑤向…脱帽致意,向…行礼. ⑥胜过,凌驾. ⑦(行诗令中)接引(诗句等). — *vi.* 脱帽致意 (*to*). *be capped for* 做…的选手. ~ *an anecdote* 讲更有趣的话. ~ ***the climax*** 走极端,过度,出乎意料. ~ ***verses*** 行(诗句的)接尾令. ***to*** ~ (***it***) ***all*** 最后又加上;超群出众. ~**piece** 帽木. ~ **product**【数】卡积.
CAP = Civil Air Patrol〔美〕市民防空协会.
cap. = capital; capitalize; capital (letter); captain; *caput* (= chapter).
C.A.P. = chloro-aceto-phenone【化】苯氯乙酮(毒药).
ca·pa·bil·i·ty [ˌkeipəˈbiliti] *n.* ①能力,才能,本领. ②性能;容量;功率,生产率. ③〔*pl.*〕潜在能力. *first rate capabilities* 卓越的能力,过硬本领. *a man of great capabilities* 很有前途的人;可造之材.
ca·pa·ble [ˈkeipəbl] *a.* 有才能的,有手腕的,有技能的,有资格的 (*for*). *a* ~ *teacher* 能干的教师. ~ *of* ①(事物)可以…的;能…的;易…的 (*of*). ②(人)敢于…的,做得出…的;易于做出…的 (*He is* ~ *of doing anything.* 他什么事都干得出. *This statement is* ~ *of various interpretations.* 对这一声明可以作各式各样的理解. *The cask is* ~ *of holding 8 gallons.* 这个桶能装八加仑). **-ness** *n.* **ca·pa·bly** *ad.*
ca·pa·cious [kəˈpeiʃəs] *a.* ①广阔的;容积大的. ②气度宏大的. *a man of* ~ *mind* 心胸开阔的人. **-ness** *n.*
ca·pac·i·tance [kəˈpæsitəns] *n.*【电】电容;电容量.
ca·pac·i·tate [kəˈpæsiteit] *vt.* ①使能够,赋与…以能力;使适合于 (*for*). ②授予…资格,使合格;使法律上有权利. ③【生】使(精子)获得能育力〔突入卵子授胎的能力〕. **-ta·tion** [-teiʃən]【生】(精子)能育力获得(过程).
ca·pac·i·tive [kəˈpæsitiv] *a.*【电】电容的.
ca·pac·i·tiv·i·ty [kəˌpæsiˈtiviti] *n.*【电】电容率〔米-千克-秒单位介电常数〕.
ca·pac·i·tor [kəˈpæsitə] *n.*【电】电容器 (= condenser). *a* ~ *microphone* 电容传声器〔话筒,微音器〕.
ca·pac·i·tron [kəˈpæsitrɔn] *n.*【物】电容汞弧管;原子击破器.
ca·pac·i·ty [kəˈpæsiti] *n.* ①包容力,吸收力,收容力. ②容积,容量;【电】电容;负载量. ③能力,才干,本领;性能,机能. ④地位,资格,身分. ⑤【法】法定资格,权力,权能. ⑥生产额,(最大)产量〔生产力〕. *measures of* ~ 容积,容量. *a mind of great* ~ 度量大的人. *the crop* ~ 作物(最大)生产力〔单位面积产量〕. ~ *crowd*〔美〕满座的观众. *be filled to* ~ 客满. ~ *for heat* 热容量. ~ *to action*【法】诉讼能力. *be in* ~ 法律上有资格. ~ *tonnage* 载重量,吨位. ~ *house*〔美〕客满的戏院. *in a civil* ~ 以市民身分. *in my individual* ~ 以我个人身分. *in one's* ~ *as* (*a critic*) 以(批评家)的立场〔身分〕. *to the utmost of one's* ~ 尽自己所能.
cap-a-pie, cap-à-pie [kæpəˈpiː] *ad.*〔F.〕从头到脚,全身. *be armed* ~ 从头武装到脚,全副武装.

C

ca·par·i·son [kəˈpærisn] *n.* ①华丽的马衣；装饰性的鞍辔. ②(武士的)盛装；服装；行头. —*vt.* 给(马)穿马衣；使…着盛装.
Cap·com [ˈkæpkɔːm] *n.* 〔美口〕(宇宙航行中心的)地面通讯主任.
cape¹ [keip] *n.* 岬，崎，海角；〔C-〕好望角 (= The Cape of Good Hope). **C- boy** 黑白混血种的南非人. **C- cart** 有篷牛车. ~ *chisel* 狭凿. **C- Cod** 科德角〔美国〕. **C- doctor** 好望角的东南风. **C- Horn** 合恩角(智利). **C- Horn rainwater**糖酒. **C- smoke** 南非产白兰地.
cape² [keip] *n.* 披肩，短斗篷.
cap·e·lin [ˈkæpəlin] *n.* = caplin.
Ca·pel·la [kəˈpelə]【天】五车二(御夫座 α).
ca·per¹ [ˈkeipə] *n.* ①跳跃. ②嬉戏. ③〔俚〕(盗贼的)犯罪行为. —*vi.* ①跳跃，雀跃. ②嬉戏，开玩笑. *cut ~s* = *cut a ~* 雀跃；嬉戏.
ca·per² [ˈkeipə] *n.*【植】续随子，驴蹄草；〔*pl.*〕续随子的花芽.
cap·er·cail·lie, cap·er·cail·zie [ˌkæpəˈkeilji, -ˈkeilzi] *n.*【鸟】雷鸟，松鸡.
cape·skin [ˈkeipˌskin] *n.* 好望角羊皮〔一种精制羊皮革，常用来制手套〕.
Cape Town, Cape·town [ˈkeiptaun] 开普敦〔南非(阿扎尼亚)港市〕.
Cape Verde [ˈkeipˈvəːd] *n.* 佛得角〔非洲〕. **C- V- Islands** 佛得角群岛.
cap·ful [ˈkæpful] *n.* ①一帽子[瓶盖子](的数量)；少许，少量. ②一阵(轻风等). *a ~ of wind* 轻风. *a ~ of detergent* 一瓶盖子去垢粉. *a ~ of beans* 一帽子豆子.
caph [kɑːf] *n.* 希伯来文的第十一个字母，相当于拉丁字母k (= kaph).
ca·pi·as [ˈkeipiæs] *n.* 〔F.〕【法】拘票.
cap·il·la·ceous [ˌkæpiˈleiʃəs] *a.* ①毛状细丝的，毛状纤维的. ②发状的，线状的.
cap·il·lar·i·ty [ˌkæpiˈlæriti] *n.*【物】毛细管状态；毛细管作用[现象].
cap·il·lar·y [kəˈpiləri] *a.* ①毛发状的，细长的. ②毛细管作用[现象]的. ③表面张力的. —*n.*【物】毛细管，微管. ~ **action** 毛细管作用. ~ **tube** 毛细管.
ca·pi·ta [ˈkæpitə] *n.* caput 的复数.
cap·i·tal¹ [ˈkæpitəl] *a.* ①首位的，最重要的，主要的，基本的，根本的. ②〔口〕优秀的，上好的，第一流的. ③大写(字母)的. ④应处死刑的；致命的. ⑤资本的. *C-!* 好极了！~ *city* 首都. ~ *construction* 基本建设. ~ *crime* 死罪. ~ *letter* 大写. ~ *punishment* 死刑. ~ *ship* 主力舰. —*n.* ①首都；首府. ②大写(字母). ③资本；基金；股款，本钱；资源；资方，资产阶级. *circulating [floating] ~* 流动资本. *financial ~* 金融资本. *fixed ~* 固定资本. *foreign ~* 外资. *working ~* 周转资本. *the relations between labour and ~* 劳资关系. *~ and interest* 本金和利息. ***make ~ (out) of*** 利用，从中取利[捞一把]. ~ **account** 资本帐，股本帐. ~ **assets** 资本资产. ~ **bonus** 红利，股息. ~ **expenditure** 基本建设费用. ~ **goods** 资本货物. ~**-intensive** *a.* 资本大量投资的. ~ **levy** 资本课税. ~ **stock**股本. ~ **structure** 资本构成. ~ **sum** (给保险人的)最大保险金额.
cap·ital² [ˈkæpitəl] *n.*【建】柱头.
cap·i·tal·ism [ˈkæpitəlizəm] *n.* 资本主义(制度).
cap·i·tal·ist [ˈkæpitəlist] *n.* 资本家；资本主义者；〔口〕财主. —*a.* ①有资本的. ②资本主义的. *a ~ country* 资本主义国家.
cap·i·tal·is·tic [ˌkæpitəˈlistik] *a.* ①在资本主义下存在[经营]的；有资本主义特征的. ②赞成[推行]资本主义的. ~ *economy* 资本主义经济. **-ti·cal·ly** *ad.*
cap·i·tal·i·za·tion [kəˌpitəlaiˈzeiʃən] *n.* ①资本化；〔美〕投资. ②(收入等的)资本估价. ③作首都. ④〔美〕用大写.
cap·i·tal·ize [kəˈpitəlaiz] *vt.* ①把…资本化，使成为资本，用…作资本，把…估价为资本；认可[决定]资本为…股. ②〔美〕对…投资，给…提供资本. ③把(某一时期内的收益等)折合成当前价值. ④把…定为首都. ⑤〔美〕用大写字母写[印]. —*vi.* 利用 *(on; upon)*.
cap·i·tal·ly [ˈkæpitəli] *ad.* ①〔口〕极好；妙. ②按死刑(程序)办处.
cap·i·tate, cap·i·tated [ˈkæpiteit, -teitid] *a.*【植】头状的，锤形的.
cap·i·ta·tion [ˌkæpiˈteiʃən] *n.* ①按人计算. ②人头〔人口〕税. ~ **fee** 按人均摊的用费. ~ **grant** 按人计算的补助费.
Cap·i·tol [ˈkæpitəl] *n.* ①(古罗马的)朱庇特 (Jupiter) 神殿. ②〔美〕国会大厦；〔c-〕州议会会堂. ~ **Hill** 美国国会.
Cap·i·to·line [ˈkæpitəlain] *n.* 罗马的卡彼托山〔罗马七丘之一〕. —*a.* 有关卡彼托山的；朱庇特神殿的；古罗马神殿的.
ca·pit·u·lar [kəˈpitjulə] *a.* 教士会的. —*n.* 牧师会会员.
ca·pit·u·lar·y [kəˈpitjuləri] *n.* 教士会法规.
ca·pit·u·late [kəˈpitjuleit] *vi.* ①(在一定条件下)投降. ②停止抵抗.
ca·pit·u·la·tion [kəˌpitjuˈleiʃən] *n.* ①(有条件的)投降. ②投降条约；〔*pl.*〕协定. ③(声明、协议等载明的)条款，条件[项目，概要，一览表]. ***the C-s***【史】(给与住在本国的外国人的)治外法权条款. **-ism** 投降主义. **-ist** 投降主义者.
ca·pit·u·lum [kəˈpitʃələm] *n.* (*pl.* **-la** [-lə]) ①【解、动】小头，头端，假头. ②【植】头状花序，头状体.
cap·las·to·me·ter [ˌkæpləsˈtɔmitə] *n.*【物】粘度计.
cap·lin [ˈkæplin] *n.*【动】毛鳞鱼.
ca·po¹ [ˈkeipəu] *n.* (*pl.* **-pos**)【乐】(吉他等的)品柱.
ca·po² [ˈkɑːpəu] *n.* 〔美俚〕(黑手党等犯罪集团分支机构的)头目. ~**regime** (capo 之下的)副头目.
ca·pon [ˈkeipən] *n.* 阉鸡.
ca·pon·ize, -ise [ˈkeipənaiz] *vt.* 给(鸡)去势，阉(鸡).
cap·o·ral [ˌkæpəˈrɑːl] *n.* 〔F.〕一种法国粗烟丝.
cap·o·ral [ˌkæpəˈrɑːl] *n.* 〔美方〕(美国西南部的)大牧场主.
ca·pot [kəˈpɔt] *n.* (两人对玩的皮克 (piquet) 牌戏中的)全胜〔40 点〕. —*vt.* 全胜(对方).
ca·pote [kəˈpəut] *n.* ①连帽长外套；女式长袍；(斗牛士的)披肩. ②系有带子的无边女帽. ③(可调整的)活动车篷.
cap·per [ˈkæpə] *n.* ①制帽者. ②〔美〕(拍卖商的)假买手，竞买囮子；引诱者，骗子的搭档. ③(瓶罐等的)封口机，压盖机；封口[压盖]工人. ④〔美俚〕结局，结尾；高潮.
cap·ping [ˈkæpiŋ] *n.* 〔美〕(拍卖时)使用假买手诱骗哄抬.
cap·re·o·late [ˈkæpriəleit, kəˈpriəlit] *a.*【植】有卷须的.
cap·ric [ˈkæprik] *a.* 公山羊的. ~ **acid** 癸酸，羊蜡酸.
ca·pric·ci·o [kəˈpritʃiəu] *n.* (*pl.* **~s**) 〔It.〕①狂喜；怪想；异想天开. ②【乐】随想曲，狂想曲.
ca·pric·ci·o·so [kəˌpriːtʃiːˈəuzəu] *a., ad.*【乐】变化无常的[地]，任意的[地]，古怪的[地].
ca·price [kəˈpriːs] *n.* ①反复无常，任性. ②怪想，异想天开. ③古怪[随意空想]的作品[乐曲].
ca·pri·cious [kəˈpriʃəs] *a.* ①反复无常的，任性的. ②怪想的. **-ly** *ad.* **-ness** *n.*
Cap·ri·corn [ˈkæprikɔːn], **Cap·ri·cor·nus** [ˌkæpriˈkɔːnəs] *n.*【天】山羊座；摩羯宫. ***the Tropic of ~*** 冬至线，南回归线.
cap·ri·fi·ca·tion [ˌkæprifiˈkeiʃən] *n.* (使用虫媒传送

花粉的)无花果早熟法.

cap·ri·fig [ˈkæprifig] *n.* 【植】野生无花果.

cap·rine [ˈkæprain] *a.* 公山羊(一样)的.

cap·ri·ole [ˈkæpriəul] *n., vi.* 【马术】跳跃,跃起〔扬蹄而不前进的动作〕.

ca·pri pants [ˈkɑːpri pænts] 卡普里式〔山羊式〕紧身女裤.

ca·pris [kɑːpris] *n. pl.* = capri pants.

ca·pro·ic [kəˈprəuik] *a.* 山羊的. ~ **acid** 【化】己酸,羊油酸.

cap·ro·lac·tam [ˌkæprəuˈlæktəm] *n.* 【化】己内酰胺.

ca·pron(e) [ˈkæprəun] *n.* 【化、纺】卡普隆〔聚己内酰胺纤维的商品名〕.

ca·pryl [ˈkæpril] *n.* 【化】①癸酰. ②(现多指)辛基;辛酰.

ca·pryl·ic [kəˈprilik] *a.* 【化】辛酸的. ~ **acid** 【化】辛酸,羊脂酸.

caps. 【印】 = capital letters.

cap·sa·i·cin [kæpˈseiəsin] *n.* 【化】辣椒素.

Cap·si·an [ˈkæpsiən] *a.* 【考古】嘎普萨期的〔指北非旧石器时代文化〕.

Cap·si·cum [ˈkæpsikəm] *n.* 【植】①辣椒属. ②〔c-〕辣椒.

cap·size [kæpˈsaiz] *vt., vi.* (使)(船、车等)倾覆,(使)翻转. —*n.* 翻船,翻车.

cap·stan [ˈkæpstən] *n.* 起锚机,绞盘. ~ **bar** 绞盘棒.

cap·stone [ˈkæpstəun] *n.* ①拱顶石;顶(层)石. ②顶部;顶点. ③海胆化石.

cap·su·lar [ˈkæpsjulə] *a.* ①【植】蒴果(状)的. ②胶囊(状)的. ③雷管的.

cap·su·late, cap·su·lated [ˈkæpsjuleit, -leitid] *a.* ①【植】有蒴的. ②胶囊包裹的. ③装入雷管的.

cap·sule [ˈkæpsjuːl] *n.* ①【生理】荚膜,囊状物;【植】蒴,荚,种囊. ②【化】(蒸发用的)小碟;小皿,小盒. ③囊状器,帽状器,封瓶锡包,瓶帽;【药】胶囊. ④【物】膜盒,传感器. ⑤【宇】密闭舱. ⑥提要. —*a.* ①简略的. ②小而结实的. *a* ~ *biography* 简历. *a* ~ *review* 简评,短评. —*vt.* ①压缩,节略. ②以瓶帽密封.

cap·sul·i·form [ˈkæpsjulifɔːm] *a.* 囊形的.

cap·sul·ize [ˈkæpsjuˌlaiz] *vt.* ①把…装于(胶)囊内,把…装于小容器内. ②简明表达;使凝练,压缩.

Capt. = Captain.

cap·tain [ˈkæptin] *n.* ①首领;领队者,指挥者;魁首,头子. ②船长,舰长;机长. ③〔英〕(陆军及海军陆战队)上尉〔空军上尉为 flight lieutenant〕;〔美〕(陆、空军及海军陆战队)上尉;〔英、美〕(海军)上校;舰长. ④(工厂等的)管理员,监督员. ⑤(球队的)队长;(学校班级的)级长,(小组的)组长. ⑥名将,军事指挥家. ⑦〔美〕消防队队长;政党的地方领导人. ~ *of industry* 工业巨头,大企业家. *C- of the Fleet* 【英海军】舰队副官. *a copper* ~ 冒充有地位的人. —*vt.* 统率,指挥,做…的首领. **-cy, -ship** *n.* ①船长〔上尉等〕的地位〔职权、辖区〕. ②主将之才,统率之才,统帅资格.

cap·tion [ˈkæpʃən] *n.* ①〔美〕标题,题目;【影】字幕;(插图的)说明;目录,节目. ②【法】(法律文件等的)提要,标示. ③〔英〕逮捕. —*vt.* 在(文件等)上加标题;在(图片等)上加说明;在(电影)上加字幕.

cap·tious [ˈkæpʃəs] *a.* ①吹毛求疵的;(评论等)恶意的. ②强词夺理的,似是而非的;无理强辩的. ~ *criticism* 恶意的批评. **-ly** *n.*

cap·ti·vate [ˈkæptiveit] *vt.* ①(以某种感染力)吸住;迷惑住. ②〔古〕逮捕;征服.

capti·vat·ing [ˈkæptiveitiŋ] *a.* 使人神魂颠倒的,有魅力的.

cap·ti·va·tion [ˌkæptiˈveiʃən] *n.* ①迷惑,魅力. ②〔古〕逮捕.

cap·ti·va·tor [ˈkæptiˌveitə] *n.* 有吸引力的人〔物〕.

cap·tive [ˈkæptiv] *a.* ①被活捉到的;被监禁了的;被拴住的,被控制而不能独立行动的. ②被迷住的. *a* ~ *bird* 笼鸟. *a* ~ *shop* 职工商店,内部商店. *a* ~ *balloon* 系留气球. —*n.* 俘虏;被(爱情等)迷住的人. ***take [hold, lead]*** ~ 活捉,俘虏.

cap·tiv·i·ty [kæpˈtiviti] *n.* 囚禁;俘虏;束缚 (*opp.* freedom).

cap·tor [ˈkæptə] *n.* ①捕捉者,捕手;攻夺者;夺得者. ②捕捉船.

cap·tress [ˈkæptris] *n.* 女捕捉者,俘虏了(某人)的女人.

cap·ture [ˈkæptʃə] *n.* ①捕获,夺得;【原】俘获;掳掠,掠夺. ②俘虏;捕获品,战利品. —*vt.* ①俘获,捕获. ②攻夺;取,夺取,夺得(奖品等);赢得,引起(注意等). ③〔转义〕记录,接收,拍摄. ~*d river* 被截断的河流. **-r** [ˈkæptʃərə] *n.* 捕获者,俘获者.

cap·u·chin [ˈkæpjuʃin] *n.* ①〔C-〕(天主教的)圣方济会托钵僧. ②带风帽的女斗篷. ③【动】(南美的)卷尾猴. ~ **monkey** 戴帽猿. ~ **pigeon** 有风帽状冠毛的鸽子.

ca·put [ˈkæpət] *n.* (*pl.* ***ca·pi·ta*** [ˈkæpitə]) 【解】(骨等的)(瘤状)头.

ca·put mor·tu·um [ˈkæput ˈmɔːtjuəm] 〔L.〕①骷髅;头盖. ②(化石)废物,残渣.

cap·y·ba·ra [ˌkæpiˈbɑːrə] *n.* 【动】水豚(*Hydrochoerus capybara.*)

CAR = ① civil air regulations 民航条例. ② controlled avalanche rectifier 可控雪崩整流器.

car[1] [kɑː] *n.* ①车辆;(小)汽车;电车. ②(火车)车厢;〔英〕运货马车;〔诗〕战车,凯旋车;(飞艇,电梯等的)吊舱. *a dining* ~ (火车上的)餐车. *a freight* ~ 货车. *beat the* ~〔美〕非常地,厉害地. *by* ~ 乘电车;乘汽车. *take a* ~ 乘(电)车. *the* ~ *of the sun* 〔诗〕日轮,太阳. *the* ~*s* 〔美〕列车,火车. —*vi.* 坐汽车去. ~ *it* 〔美〕坐汽车旅行. ~ **bed** 携带式婴儿小床. ~ **catcher** 〔美〕(火车)制动手. ~ **coat** 短大衣. ~ **fare**〔美〕(市内)电车费;火车费,票价. ~**hand**〔美〕铁路员工. ~**hop**〔美〕① *n.* (把饭菜递给汽车乘客的)路边餐馆服务员. ② *vi.* 充当路边餐馆服务员. ~ **knock [whack]** 〔美〕火车修理工人. ~**load** 车辆荷载;一车皮货物;一车皮装载量. ~**loading**〔常 *pl.*〕(以铁路货车计算的)货物运入〔出〕量. ~ **lots** 【美商】货车到站数. ~**man** [ˈkɑːmən] ①赶马车的人. ②电车〔汽车等〕的驾驶员,货车驾驶员. ③(车辆上货物的)搬运工人;火车检修工,车辆制造工. ~ **park** 〔英〕停车场. ~ **pool** 〔美〕合伙使用汽车组织. ~**port** (无门户的)敞开式汽车间. ~**sick** *a.* 晕车的. ~ **sickness** 晕车. ~**topper** (可放在汽车顶上的)小汽艇. ~ **wash** 汽车擦洗处. **-ful** *n.* 一车之量. **-less** *a.* 没有汽车的.

car[2] [kɑː] *a.* 〔Scot.〕①惯用左手的. ②不吉利的;不自然的.

car. = carat; carpentry.

ca·ra·bao [ˌkɑːrəˈbɑːəu] *n.* (*pl.* ~*s*,~) 〔Phil.〕水牛.

car·a·bid [ˈkærəbid] *n.* 【动】步行虫 (= ground beetle).

car·a·bin, car·a·bine [ˈkærəbin, ˈkærəbain] *n.* 卡宾枪(=carbine).

car·a·bi·neer, -nier [ˌkærəbiˈniə] *n.* ①〔the C-〕〔英〕第六龙骑兵团. ②卡宾枪手 (= carbineer).

car·a·cal [ˈkærəkæl] *n.* 【动】狞猫,山猫;山猫皮.

ca·ra·ca·ra [ˌkɑːrəˈkɑːrə] *n.* (南美等地的)一种长脚鹰.

Ca·ra·cas [kəˈrækəs] *n.* 加拉加斯〔委内瑞拉首都〕.

car·a·col(e) [ˈkærəkəul] *n.* ①【马术】半旋转. ②旋转跳跃的动作. ③【建】螺旋形楼梯,盘梯. —*vi.* (马)作半旋转动作;(骑马)作半旋转.

car·a·cul [ˈkærəkəl] *n.* 〔苏联〕卡拉库尔〔阿拉斯特罕〕羔皮;仿羔皮. ~ **cloth** 仿羔皮呢.

Ca·rad·oc [kəˈrædək] *n.* ~ **stage** 【地】喀拉多克阶〔晚

C

奥陶世〕。

ca·rafe [kəˈrɑːf] *n.* (餐桌上的)玻璃水瓶,饮料瓶。

ca·ra·ga·na [ˌkærəˈgɑːnə] *n.* 【植】锦鸡儿(属)。

car·a·geen [ˈkærəˌgiːn] *n.* 【植】①角叉菜。②多乳头杉海苔。

ca·ram·ba [kɑːˈrɑːmbɑː] *int.* 啊! 〔表示惊愕、恐怖的感叹词〕。

ca·ram·bo·la [kræmˈbəulə] *n.* 【植】杨桃,五敛子〔产中国广东,东南亚及西印度群岛等地〕。

car·a·mel [ˈkærəmel] *n.* ①(着色或加味用的)焦糖。②(吃布丁用的)糖蜜;(果味)块糖。③淡褐色,酱色。

car·a·mel·ize [ˈkærəmelaiz, ˈkaimə-] *vt., vi.* (使…)变成焦糖。

ca·ran·gid [kəˈrændʒid] *n.* 【动】鲹科鱼。**-ran·goid** [-ˈræŋgɔid] *a.*

car·a·pace [ˈkærəpeis] *n.* 【动】甲壳;(龟等的)壳。

car·at [ˈkærət] *n.* ①克拉〔宝石重量单位 = 200 毫克〕。②开〔黄金纯度单位,纯金为 24 开〕(= karat)。

car·a·van [ˈkærəvæn] *n.* ①(沙漠地带的)商队;旅队;车马队。②〔美〕移民列车;(马戏团的)搬运车;(吉卜赛人等的)有篷马车,大篷车。③〔英〕活动住宅。— *vi.* 参加旅行队旅行。**-eer** 乘有篷马车旅行者。**-ner** 乘有篷马车旅行者;〔英〕用汽车活动住屋住在野外者。

car·a·van·sa·ry, car·a·van·se·rai [ˌkærəˈvænsəri, -sərai] *n.* (东方国家的)商队旅馆;大车客店。②〔美〕旅馆。

car·a·vel [ˈkærəvel] *n.* (16 世纪西班牙、葡萄牙人的)轻快帆船。

car·a·way [ˈkærəwei] *n.* 【植】芷茴香,贯蒿。

carb- *comb. f.* = carbo-。

car·ba·mate [ˈkɑːbəmeit] *n.* 【化】氨基甲酸酯。

car·bam·ide [ˈkɑːbəmaid] *n.* 【化】尿素,碳酰二胺。

car·ban·i·on [ˈkɑːbənaiən] *n.* 【化】碳酸根[基]离子,阴碳离子,负碳离子。

carbarn [ˈkɑːbɑːn] *n.* 〔美〕(电车、公共汽车的)车库。

car·baz·ole [ˈkɑːbəzəul] *n.* 【化】咔唑。

car·ba·zone [ˈkɑːbəzəun] *n.* 【药】卡巴肿。

car·ben·i·cil·lin [ˌkɑːbeniˈsilin] *n.* 【药】羧苄青霉素,卡比西林。

carb·he·mo·glo·bin [ˈkɑːbˌhiːməuˈgləubin] 【生化】碳酸血红朊。

car·bide [ˈkɑːbaid] *n.* 【化】碳化物;碳化钙;电石〔粗制 CaC_2〕。

car·bine [ˈkɑːbain] *n.* 马枪,卡宾枪。*a machine* ~ 冲锋枪,卡宾枪。

carbi·neer [ˌkɑːbiˈniə] *n.* 马枪手,卡宾枪手。

car·bi·nol [ˈkɑːbinəl] *n.* 【化】甲醇。

car·bo- *comb. f.* 碳;羰: *carbo*hydrate.

car·bo·cy·clic [ˌkɑːbəˈsaiklik] *a.* 【化】碳环型的。

car·bo·he·mo·glob·in [ˈkɑːbəuˌhiːməuˈgləubin] *n.* 【生化】碳酸血红蛋白 (= carbhemoglobin)。

car·bo·hy·drate [ˈkɑːbəuˈhaidreit] *n.* 【化】碳水化合物,糖类。

car·bo·lat·ed [ˈkɑːbəleitid] *a.* 【化】含酚盐(石炭酸盐)的。

car·bol·ic [kɑːˈbɔlik] *a.* 【化】①由炭和油中取得的。②煤焦油的。~ **acid** 石炭酸,苯酚。~ **oil** 酚油。~ **soap** 酚皂,石炭酸皂。

car·bo·lize [ˈkɑːbəlaiz] *vt.* 用石炭酸洗[处理];用酚处理,使与酚化合。

car·bo·my·cin [ˌkɑːbəuˈmaisin] *n.* 【药】碳霉素。

car·bon [ˈkɑːbən] *n.* ①【化】碳。②【电】碳精棒[片、粉];碳精电极。③(一张)复写纸。④复写的副本。*a* ~ *of a letter* 一封信的复本。~ **bisulfide** 二硫化碳。~ **black** 松烟;炭黑。~ **brush** 碳精刷。~ **copy** 复写[打字]的副本;〔口〕极相象的人[物]。~**copy** *vt.* 复制。~**date** *vt.* 【考古】用放射性碳素测定(年代)。~ **dating** 【考古】碳 14 年代测定(法)。~ **dioxide** 二氧化碳,碳酐 (*frozen* ~ *dioxide* 干冰)。~ **filament** (灯泡用)碳丝。~ **monoxide** 一氧化碳。~ **paper** 复写纸。~ **spot** (硬币上的)碳斑,黑斑。~ **star** 【天】碳星。

car·bo·na·ceous [ˌkɑːbəˈneiʃəs] *a.* 【化】碳的,碳质的,含碳的。

car·bo·na·do [kɑːbəˈneidəu] *n.* ①黑金刚石。②烤肉片,烤鱼片。— *vt.* ①烧,焙,烘,烤炙(肉片等)。②砍,在…上砍出深痕。

Car·bo·na·ri [ˌkɑːbəˈnɑːri] *n.* 〔*pl.*〕(*sing.* **-na·ro** [-ˈnɑːrəu]) 〔It.〕【史】烧炭党。

car·bon·ate [ˈkɑːbəneit] *vt.* ①使与碳酸化合;给…充碳酸气。②使碳化,使化合成碳酸盐[脂];把…烧成炭。③使活泼[活跃]。—*n.* [ˈkɑːbənit] 碳酸盐[脂];黑金刚石。**car·bon·a·tor** [ˈkɑːbəneitə] *n.* 碳酸化器。

car·bon·a·tion [kɑːbəˈneiʃən] *n.* 【化】①碳酸饱和。②碳酸盐法。③碳化(作用)。

car·bon-date [ˈkɑːbən-ˈdeit] *vt.* 以含碳量测定(化石等的)年代。

car·bon·ic [kɑːˈbɔnik] *a.* 【化】(含)碳的,由碳得到的。~ **acid** 碳酸。

car·bon·if·er·ous [ˌkɑːbəˈnifərəs] *a.* ①〔C-〕【地】石碳纪的。②含碳的。*C- Period [Strata]* 石碳纪[层]。

car·bon·ite [ˈkɑːbənait] *n.* 【化】碳质炸药;硝酸甘油,硝酸钾;锯屑炸药。

car·bon·i·um [kɑːˈbəuniəm] *n.* 【化】碳鎓,阳碳。

car·bon·i·za·tion [ˌkɑːbənaiˈzeiʃən] *n.* 【化】碳化(作用)。

car·bon·ize [ˈkɑːbənaiz] *vt.* 【化】使碳化,使焦化;使与碳化合。

car·bon·ous [ˈkɑːbənəs] *a.* 含碳的;似碳的。

car·bon·yl [ˈkɑːbənil] *n.* 【化】羰基;碳酰。

car·bo·run·dum [ˌkɑːbəˈrʌndəm] *n.* 【商标】金刚砂,碳化硅。~ **paper** (金刚)砂纸。

car·box·ide [kɑːˈbɔksaid] *n.* 【化】①羧基。②酮基。

carbox(y)- *comb. f.* 羧基。

car·box·yl [kɑːˈbɔksil] *n.* 【化】羧基。

car·box·yl·ase [kɑːˈbɔksileis] *n.* 【化】羧(基)酶,羧化酶。

car·box·yl·ate [kɑːˈbɔksileit] *n.* 【化】羧化物,羧酸盐[酯]。— *vt.* 使羧化。**-yl·a·tion** *n.*

car·box·yl·ic [ˌkɑːbɔkˈsilik] *a.* (含)羧基的。~ **acid** 羧酸。

car·boy [ˈkɑːbɔi] *n.* (用木箱或藤罩保护着、专装硫酸等腐蚀性液体的)大玻璃瓶,酸瓶,酸坛。

car·bun·cle [ˈkɑːbʌŋkl] *n.* ①【矿】红玉,红宝石。②【医】痈;疔;面皮包,酒刺。**-d, -bun·cu·lar** [-ˈbʌŋkjulə] *a.*

car·bu·ret [ˈkɑːbjuret] *n.* 【化】碳化物。— *vt.* (**~(t)ed; ~(t)ing**) ①使与碳化合;给…增碳。②使(气体)与碳氢化合物混合。③汽化,使(汽油等)与空气混合。*carburetted hydrogen* 碳化氢,矿坑气。*carburetted spring* 碳酸泉。

car·bu·ret·ant [ˈkɑːbəˌreitnt] *n.* 【化】碳化剂。

car·bu·ret·ter, car·bu·ret·or [ˈkɑːbjuretə] *n.* ①【机】汽化器,化油器。②【化】增碳器。

car·bu·rize [ˈkɑːbjuraiz] *vt.* ①【化】汽化;使汽油与空气混合。②【冶】使渗碳。**-ri·za·tion** [ˌkɑːbjuraiˈzeiʃən] *n.* 渗碳法[作用]。

car·bur·i·zer [ˈkɑːbjuraizə] *n.* 【冶】渗碳器。

car·byl [ˈkɑːbil] *n.* 【化】二价碳基。

car·byl·a·mine [ˌkɑːbiləˈmiːn] *n.* 【化】胩;乙胩。

car·ca·jou [ˈkɑːkəˌdʒuː] *n.* 【动】狼獾;狼獾毛皮。

car·ca·net [ˈkɑːkənet] *n.* (宝玉镶饰的)项圈,项链。

car·cass, car·case [ˈkɑːkəs] *n.* ①(兽类的)尸体。②〔蔑〕(人的)死尸;身躯。③(家畜屠宰后的)躯体。④(废屋、废船等的)骨架,遗骸。⑤(车胎的)外胎身。*to save one's* ~ 为保全身体[性命],怕送命[受伤]。~**-fabric**

轮胎织物. ~ **flooring**【建】毛地板. ~ **roofing**【建】毛屋顶.

carcin(o)- *comb. f.* 表示"肿瘤","癌": *carcino*ma.

car·cin·o·gen [kɑːˈsinədʒən] *n.*【医】致癌物(质),诱癌因素.

car·ci·no·ma [[ˌkɑːsiˈnəumə] *n. (pl. ~s, ~ta* [-tə]*)*【医】癌. ~ **hepatis** 肝癌. ~ **uteri** 子宫癌. ~ **ventriculi** 胃癌.

car·ci·no·ma·to·sis [ˌkɑːsiˌnəuməˈtəusis] *n.*【医】癌扩散,癌转移,并发癌.

car·ci·no·tron [kɑːˈsinəutrɔn] *n.*【电】回波管.

card[1] [kɑːd] *n.* ①纸牌; 〔*pl.*〕纸牌戏. ②卡片(纸); 明信片; 请柬; 入场券; 名片. ③节目单; 程序单; 戏单; 菜单; 广告; 个人启事[声明]. ④(磁石的)方位盘,罗盘面. ⑤某种措施; 手段; 策略; 办法; 〔口〕(正合适的)事物. ⑥〔口〕别有风趣的人,怪人. ⑦〔美俚〕(吸毒者吸的)一服麻醉剂. *play (at) ~s* 打纸牌. *a New Year ~* 贺年片. *a doubtful ~* 不可靠的办法. *a sure [safe] ~* 可靠的办法,安全的计划, 万全之策. *a great ~* 大名鼎鼎的人物. *a knowing ~* 精明的家伙. *a leading ~* 先例,榜样; 有力的论点. *That's the ~ for it.* 那就最好; 正是那个. ***be at ~s*** 在打牌. ***~s and spades*** (过分自信时)大幅度让与弱方的有利条件. ***count on one's ~*** 指望着自己的机会[措施]. ***(a) drawing ~*** 肯定叫座的人物[节目]. ***have one's ~ up one's sleeve*** 成竹在胸. ***have [hold] the ~s in one's hand*** 有把握. ***house [castle] of ~s*** 厚纸制的房子[城堡]; 空中楼阁,不可靠的计划. ***in the ~s*** 多半,可能. ***lay [place, put] one's ~s on the table*** 摊牌; 公开[公布]计划. ***make a ~*** (牌戏)打成一墩. ***leave one's ~ (on)*** (访人不遇)留名片而归. ***(It is) on the ~s*** 多半,可能. ***play one's best [trump] ~*** 打出王牌,采取最好办法. ***play one's ~s well [badly]*** 手腕高明[不高明],处理得好[不好]. ***play one's last ~*** 打出最后一张牌,采取最后手段. ***put all ~s on the table*** 把牌全亮出来,打开天窗说亮话. ***send up one's ~*** 递名片(给门房送进去). ***show one's ~s*** 摊牌; 公开自己计划. ***shuffle the ~s*** 洗牌; 进行人事大调动; 改变政策. ***speak by the ~*** 正确地说. ***stack the ~s*** 洗牌时作弊; 暗中设立陷阱(进行欺骗). ***tell sb.'s fortune from ~s*** 用纸牌给某人算命. ***the (proper) ~*** 正合适的东西[办法]. ***The ~s are in sb.'s hands.*** 某人已操胜券[一定成功]. ***throw up the ~s*** 放弃计划,罢手; 屈服. ***turn down one corner of the ~*** 把名片折一角(表示本人曾来访问). — *vt.* ①在…上附加卡片. ②把…记入卡片内; 把…制成卡片. ③〔美〕拟订(拳赛节目等); 把…列入时间表. **~-carrying** *a.* ①有党证的; (会员等)正式的. ②道地的,货真价实的; 典型的. ~ **case** 卡片盒; 名片盒. ~ **catalog** 卡片目录. ~ **index** 卡片式索引. **~man**〔美〕工会会员. **~room** 桥牌室. ~ **shark** ①玩纸牌老手. ② = card sharp(er). **~sharp(er)** 玩牌时经常作弊的人. ~ **system** 信用卡记帐法. ~ **vote** 凭卡投票〔某些欧洲工会选举时,卡上记明所代表的工人数〕.

card[2] [kɑːd] *n.*【纺】①梳理机,梳棉[毛、麻]机; (梳棉机)钢丝车. ②纹板, 花板. ③(梳牛马的)梳子. — *vt.* ①(用梳棉机等)梳,刷. ②使起绒毛. **~-cutter**【纺】纹板冲孔机. **~ing machine** 梳棉[毛、麻]机.

Card. = Cardinal.

car·da·mom, car·da·mum, car·damon [ˈkɑːdəməm,-mən] *n.*【植】小豆蔻.

Car·dan, car·dan [ˈkɑːdən]【机】万向节, 万向接头 (= ~joint). ~ **shaft** 万向轴.

card·board [ˈkɑːdbɔːd] *n.* 硬纸板,卡(片)纸板, 卡纸. *a sheet of ~* 一张硬纸板. —*a.* 纸板般的有名无实的. *a ~ prime minister* 有名无实的总理.

cardi- *comb. f.* = cardio-.

car·di·a [ˈkɑːdiə] *n.*【解】贲门.

car·di·ac [ˈkɑːdiæk] *a.*【医】①心脏(病)的. ②(胃的)贲门的. —*n.* ①心脏病患者. ②强心剂. ③健胃剂. ~ **cycle** 心搏周期. ~ **passion** 胃灼热[痛],心痛 (= cardialgia). ~ **symptoms** 心脏病症状.

car·di·al·gi·a [kɑːdiˈældʒiə] *n.*【医】胃灼痛,心痛.

Car·diff [ˈkɑːdif] *n.* 加的夫〔英国港市〕.

car·di·gan [ˈkɑːdigən] *n.* (开襟)羊毛衫,羊毛背心,开襟绒线衫.

car·di·nal[1] [ˈkɑːdinəl] *a.* ①主要的; 基本的. ②深红色的. —*n.* ①带头巾的女外套. ②深红色. ③(烫热的)红葡萄酒. ④〔常 *pl.*〕基数. ⑤【鸟】北美红雀 (= ~-bird). ~ **flower**【植】红花半边莲. ~ **number [numeral]**【数】基数,纯数. ~ **points** (罗盘的) 基本方位〔即东、南、西、北〕.

car·di·nal[2] [ˈkɑːdinəl] *n.*【天主】枢机主教〔亦称红衣主教,为梵蒂冈教廷枢密院成员〕. **-ship** *n.* = cardinalate.

car·di·nal·ate [ˈkɑːdinəleit] *n.* ①(天主教)枢机[红衣]主教的职位. ②枢机[红衣]主教团.

car·di·nes [ˈkɑːdiniːz] *n.* cardo 的复数.

cardio- *comb. f.* 表示"心脏": *cardio*gram.

car·di·o·dyn·i·a [ˌkɑːdiəuˈdiniə] *n.*【医】心痛,胸痛.

car·di·o·gram [ˈkɑːdiəgræm] *n.*【医】心电图,心动描记曲线.

car·di·o·graph [ˈkɑːdiəgrɑːf] *n.*【医】心动描记器.

car·di·oid [ˈkɑːdiɔid] *n.*【数】心脏线.

car·di·ol·o·gy [ˌkɑːdiˈɔlədʒi] *n.*【医】心脏病学. **-ol·o·gist** *n.* 心脏病学家.

car·di·om·e·ter [ˌkɑːdiˈɔmitə] *n.*【医】心能测量器,心力计.

car·dio·res·pi·ra·to·ry [ˈkɑːdiəurisˈpaiərətəri] *a.* 心和肺的.

car·di·o·scope [ˈkɑːdiəskəup] *n.*【医】心脏镜.

car·di·o·ta·chom·e·ter [ˌkɑːdiəutəˈkɔmitə] *n.*【医】心动计数器,心率计.

car·di·o·ton·ic [ˌkɑːdiəuˈtɔnik] *a.*【医】强心的. —*n.* 强心剂.

car·di·o·vas·cu·lar [ˌkɑːdiəuˈvæskjulə] *a.*【医】心血管性的. ~ **system** 循环系统.

car·di·tis [kɑːˈdaitis] *n.*【医】心脏炎. *internal ~* 心脏内膜炎.

car·do [ˈkɑːdəu] *n. (pl.* **car·di·nes** [ˈkɑːdiniːz]*)*【动】轴节; 阳(茎)基环.

car·doon [kɑːˈduːn] *n.*【植】刺菜蓟.

CARE = Cooperative for American Relief Everywhere 美国援外合作组织.

care [kɛə] *n.* ①忧烦,忧虑; 挂念,思念; 心事,牵累. ②关怀,爱护. ③管理,监督,维护,照料,看护,抚育. ④注意,留心,小心,当心; 〔*pl.*〕需要小心的事. *free medical ~* 免费[公费]医疗. *the ~s of state* 国事. *domestic [family] ~s* 家事. *worldly ~s.* 人世间的操劳. *My first ~ was ....* 我的第一件心事是…. ***be free from ~s*** 放心,安心,舒坦. ***bestow [give] great ~ upon*** 对…煞费苦心. ***C- killed the [a] cat.*** 久虑伤身. ~ ***committee***〔英〕贫民保护委员会. ***care of***〔信封上用语,略作 c/o〕烦…转交 (*Mr. A. c/o Mr. B.* 烦 B 先生转交 A 先生). ***have a ~ = take ~. in ~ of***〔美〕= ***~ of. in the ~ of = under the ~ of. take ~*** 留心,当心(*Take ~ what you say.* 说话要慎重). ***take ~ of*** 照看,看管;〔美〕收拾; 处理; 清除. ***take ~ of oneself*** 保重身体,注意健康. ***take ~ to (do so)*** 采取办法,设法,竭力(这样做). ***take good ~ of*** 爱护. ***under the ~ of*** 在…照看下,在…保护下,在…管教下 (*leave under the ~ of* 委托…照料). ***with ~*** 小心,注意, 慎重 (*Handle with ~!* 小心轻放[货运包装用语]). —*vi.* ①挂念,思念,忧虑,愁 *(for, about).* ②看管,照管,照应,看护,抚育,监督 *(for).* ③关怀; 关心 *(for)*; 介意,计较,(不)管,

(不)顾,(不)问 (*for, about*). ④〔与 for 连用〕爱好;愿意;望,欲. ~ *for her health* 挂念她的健康. *He ~s ~ for music.* 他喜欢音乐. *~for sb.'s education* 负责某人的教育. *Who ~s?* 管它呢? *a don't ~ condition* 【计】自由选取条件. *That's more than I ~ for.* 那我可无所谓[并不关心]. *vt.* 〔方〕介意,计较; 愿意 (后接不定式). *Nobody ~s what I do.* 没有人管我干什么. *I don't ~ a bit [a damn, a button, a fig, a straw, etc.].* 〔口〕一点儿也不在乎. *I don't ~ if I go.* 〔口〕去一去也好. *I should not ~ to be seen with him.* 我不喜欢给人家看见和他在一块儿. *Will he ~ to come with us.* 不晓得他愿不愿跟我们一块儿去. ***for all I ~*** ①我不管,不关我事 (*It may go to the devil for all I ~.* 无论如何我一概不管). ②也许,或者 (*It may be true for all I ~.* 那也许是真的).

ca·reen [kəˈriːn] *vt.* ①使(船)倾斜(以便修船底). ②在倾斜位置上修理(船). ③使倾斜. — *vi.* ①(船)倾斜;(车等)歪斜着行驶. ②修理倾侧着的船. — *n.* ①(船等的) 倾斜. ②【船】倾(船)修(理). ***on the ~*** 船身倾斜.

ca·reen·age [kəˈriːnidʒ] *n.* ①【船】倾船. ②船底修理费,倾修费. ③修船所.

ca·reer [kəˈriə] *n.* ①生涯;经历;履历;遭遇;(星球等的)轨迹. ②(外交官等的)职业;前途;成功,出头,发迹. ③飞跑,全速. ④〔古〕猛袭. *His ~ is run.* 他的一生[前途]完了. *a business ~* 从事实业,在商界. *a political ~* 从政. ***in full ~*** 用全速,极力飞跑. ***in mid ~*** 在中途. ***make [carve] a ~*** 追求名利,争取前途;向上爬. — *a.* 〔美〕职业性质的. — *vi.* 猛冲,飞跑 (*about*).

ca·reer·ism [kəˈriərizəm] *n.* 野心;追求名利. ~ **man** 〔美〕职业外交家,专业外交家. ~ **woman** 职业妇女;〔美〕(事业上)成功的女人;有事业心(而轻结婚)的女人.

ca·reer·ist [kəˈriərist] *n.* ①专业人员. ②投机分子,个人野心家.

care·free [ˈkeəfriː] *n.* 无忧无虑的,快活的.

care·ful [ˈkeəful] *a.* ①注意的,小心谨慎的,周到的. ②重视[关心]…的;细致的,精心的, 严密的. ③〔古〕忧虑的. *Be ~!* 小心点! *be ~ about* 注意,重视,关切;讲究. *be ~ for* 当心,挂虑,惦记. *be ~ of* 珍重,注意,留意. *~ painting* 精心的绘画. *~ reading* 精读,熟读. **-ly** *ad.* **-ness** *n.*

care·lad·en [ˈkeəˌleidn] *a.* 忧心忡忡的.

care·less [ˈkeəlis] *a.* ①不注意的,粗心大意的;由粗心引起的. ②漫不经心的,不介意的. ③轻率的,粗鲁的,草率的;拙劣的. ④〔古〕无忧无虑的. *a happy ~ youth* 快乐而轻率的青年. *a ~ life* 轻松随便的生活. *be ~ about* 不关心,不重视,不讲究,漠视. *be ~ of* 不放在心上,不关心. **-ly** *ad.* **-ness** *n.*

ca·ress [kəˈres] *n.* 爱抚[拥抱、接吻、抚弄等]. —*vt.* ①抚爱,抚摩;怜爱,宠爱. ②奉承;哄骗. ***~ the canvas [rosin]*** 〔美俚〕【拳】被击倒.

ca·ress·ing [kəˈresiŋ] *a.* 抚爱的,抚慰的. —*n.* 爱抚. **-ly** *ad.*

car·et [ˈkærət] *n.* 脱字号,补注号. 〔∧, ∨〕.

care·tak·er [ˈkeəteikə] *n.* ①看管者,管理人,看守(人);〔美〕看门的人. ②暂时代理(职务)者. ~ **cabinet [government]** (新内阁产生之前的)看守内阁[政府].

care·worn [ˈkeəwɔːn] *a.* 操心的,焦虑的.

Car·ey [ˈkeəri] *n.* 凯里〔姓氏〕.

car·fax [ˈkɑːfæks] *n.* (四条或更多条马路的)交叉路口.

car·go [ˈkɑːgəu] *n.* (*pl.* ~*s*, ~*es*) 船货;负荷,荷重. *ship [discharge] the ~* 装[卸]货. *a ~ boat [ship, vessel]* 货船. ~ **capacity** 载货能力[量]. ~**liner** 【空】大型货(运飞)机.

Carib, Caribbee [ˈkærib, ˈkæribiː] *n.* ①加勒比人. ②加勒比语.

ca·ri·be [kəˈriːbei] *n.* 【动】比拉鱼 (= piranha).

Car·ib·be·an [kæriˈbi(ː)ən] *a.* ①加勒比人的. ②(拉丁美洲)加勒比海的. ***the ~ Sea*** 加勒比海. —*n.* ①〔the ~〕加勒比海 (= the ~ Sea). ②加勒比人 (= Carib).

car·i·bou [ˈkæribuː] *n.* (*pl.* ~, ~*s*)【动】(北美)驯鹿.

car·i·ca·ture [ˌkærikəˈtjuə] *n.* ①漫画,讽刺画[文];漫画手法. ②滑稽可笑的模仿,丑化(可笑)的相似物;丑化. ***make a ~ of*** 画…的漫画,把…画成漫画;使滑稽化. — *vt.* 用漫画表现[讽刺],把…画成漫画;使滑稽化. **-tur·a·ble** [-ˈtjuərəbl] *a.* 适于被讽刺的;具有被讽刺的形态的. **-tur·al** [-ˈtjuərəl] *a.* 讽刺画[文]的,滑稽的.

car·i·ca·tur·ist [ˌkærikəˈtjuərist] *n.* 漫画家.

caries [ˈkeəriiːz] *n.* 〔L.〕【医】①骨疡. ②龋. ~ *of the teeth* 蛀牙.

car·il·lon [kəˈriljən] *n.* ①【乐】编钟;电子钟琴. ②钟乐曲. ③(风琴的)钟乐音栓. — *vi.* 用编钟演奏乐曲,奏钟乐.

car·il·lon·neur [kəˌriljəˈnəː] *n.* 〔F.〕钟琴演奏者.

Ca·ri·na [kəˈrainə] *n.* 〔L.〕【天】船底(星)座.

ca·ri·na [kəˈrainə] *n.* (*pl.* ~*s*, *-nae* [-niː])【生】①隆线,脊,突. ②峰板. ③(珊瑚)脊板. **-l** *a.*

car·i·nate [ˈkærineit] *a.* 【动】有龙骨的;龙船状的,具有隆线的.

car·i·ole [ˈkæriəul] *n.* = carriole.

car·i·ous [ˈkeəriəs] *a.* 【医】患骨疡的;(齿)龋的;腐烂了的. *a ~ tooth* 虫牙,龋齿.

cark [kɑːk] *vt., vi.* 〔古〕(使)烦恼,(使)焦虑. —*n.* 〔古〕痛苦,焦急.

cark·ing [ˈkɑːkiŋ] *a.* 忧虑的; 烦躁的. ~ *care(s)* 焦虑,操心.

Carl [kɑːl] *n.* 卡尔〔男子名, Karl 的异体〕.

carl(e) [kɑːl] *n.* ①(普通的)人. ②〔主 Scot.〕没有教养的人,粗野的人,傢伙.

carlet [ˈkɑːlit] *n.* 〔美〕小车子;小汽车.

Car·ley [ˈkɑːli] *n.* (船上的)橡皮救生艇 (= ~ float).

car·lin(e)[1] [ˈkɑːlin] *n.* 〔Scot.〕①老太婆. ②巫婆.

car·line[2], **car·ling** [ˈkɑːliŋ] *n.* 【船】短纵梁.

Car·lism [ˈkɑːlizəm] *n.* 【史】(拥护查理一世及其后裔继承王位的)西班牙王室正统论.

Car·list [ˈkɑːlist] *n.* ①西班牙王室正统派成员. ②法国王室正统派成员〔查理十世及波邦 (Bourbon) 王朝的支持者〕.

Car·los [ˈkɑːlɔs] *n.* 卡洛斯〔男子名, Charles 的异体〕.

Car·lo·vin·gi·an [ˌkɑːləuˈvindʒiən] *a., n.* = Carolingian.

Carlowi·tz [ˈkɑːləuwits] *n.* (南斯拉夫)卡罗威次红葡萄酒.

Carl·ton [ˈkɑːltən] *n.* 卡尔顿(姓氏,男子名). ***the ~ (Club)*** (英国保守党的)卡尔顿俱乐部. ~ **table** (带有抽屉、小柜的)卡尔顿式写字台.

Car·lyle [kɑːˈlail, ˈkɑːlai] *n.* ①卡莱尔〔姓氏,男子名〕. ② **Thomas** ~ 托马斯·卡莱尔〔1795—1881,英国作家,历史家,哲学家〕. **-ism** *n.* 卡莱尔的风格[信条].

car·ma·gnole [ˈkɑːmənjəul] *n.* 〔F.〕①(1789—1794 年法国革命派所着的、配以黑裤、红色小帽、三色腰带的)短上衣. ②(法国革命时代)伴唱革命歌曲的街头舞蹈(曲).

Car·mel·ite [ˈkɑːmilait] *n.* ①【天主】 (12 世纪创立于叙利亚卡迈尔山的)白袍修士,卡迈尔派男[女]修士. ②〔c-〕法国平纹薄呢.

Car·men [ˈkɑːmen] *n.* ①卡门〔女子名〕. ②法国作家梅里美同名短篇小说中的女主角.

car·min·a·tive [ˈkɑːminətiv] *a.* 【医】排除肠胃气胀[气体]的. —*n.* 【医】(医治肠胃气胀的)排气剂.

car·mine [ˈkɑːmain] *n.* ①洋红;胭脂红;卡红. ②洋红色. —*a.* 洋红色的.

car·nage [ˈkɑːnidʒ] *n.* ①大屠杀,残杀. ②〔古〕(战场上)狼藉的尸体.

car·nal [ˈkɑːnl] *a.* ①肉体的;肉欲的,淫欲的. ②世俗

的;现世的,物质的. ~ *ambition* 名利心,物质欲. ~ *appetite [desire, lust]* 肉欲. ~ *knowledge* 性经验;【法】性关系. ~ *pleasures* 淫乐. **-ism** *n.* 肉欲(主义),好色. **-ize** *vt.* 使耽于淫欲. **-ly** *ad.*

car·nal·i·ty [kɑːˈnæliti] *n.* 肉欲;淫荡,好色;(特指)性交.

car·nal·lite [ˈkɑːnəlait] *n.* 【矿】光卤石;杂盐.

car·nas·si·al [kɑːˈnæsiəl] *a.* 【动】肉食齿的. — *n.* 食肉齿,裂牙,裂齿.

car·na·tion [kɑːˈneiʃən] *n.* ①【植】麝香石竹〔美国俄亥俄州的州花〕. ②淡红色,肉色;〔*pl.*〕【绘】肉色部. —*a.* 肉色的. —*vt.* 使带肉色.

car·nau·ba [kɑːˈnaubə] *n.* 【植】巴西蜡棕(树) *(Copernica cerifera)*.

Car·ne·gie [kɑːˈnegi] *n.* 卡内基〔姓氏〕. ~ **Hall** 卡内基音乐堂〔美国纽约有名的演奏场所〕. ~ **unit** (美国中学内)课程的学年及格分数.

car·nel·ian [kəˈniːljən] *n.* 【矿】光玉髓,肉红玉髓.

car·net [kɑːˈnɛ] *n.* 〔F.〕 ①执照;(尤指欧洲边境地区通行所需的)海关文件, 通行证. ②(公共汽车等的)车票本. ③工作手册,笔记本.

car·ney, car·nie [ˈkɑːni] *vt., n.* = carny.

car·ni·fy [ˈkɑːnifai] *vt., vi.* 【生】(使)变成肉质.

cor·ni·tine [ˈkɑːnitiːn] *n.* 【生化】肉毒碱.

car·ni·val [ˈkɑːnivəl] *n.* ①群众饮宴作乐〔尤指天主教国家在四旬斋前一周内之狂欢,通常有化装游行〕; 嘉年华会,狂欢节. ②庆祝,欢宴, 狂欢. ③(巡回旅行的)杂技〔杂耍〕表演. ④节日表演节目; 〔美〕运动比赛,竞赛;博览会. ~ **glass** 狂欢节彩色玻璃〔一种虹彩色调的压制玻璃〕.

Car·ni·vo·ra [kɑːˈnivərə] *n.* 〔L.〕〔*pl.*〕【动】食肉目;〔c-〕食肉动物.

car·ni·vore [ˈkɑːnivɔː] *n.* 【生】食肉动物; 食虫植物.

car·niv·o·rous [kɑːˈnivərəs] *a.* 【动】食肉(目)的. ~ *animals* 肉食动物. ~ *plants* 食虫植物.

car·no·tite [ˈkɑːnətait] *n.* 【矿】矾酸钾铀矿.

car·ny [ˈkɑːni] *n.* 〔俚〕①巡回游艺团. ②巡回游艺团成员. — *vt.* (用甜言蜜语)哄骗.

car·ob [ˈkærəb] *n.* 【植】蝗卵豆槐,角豆树.

ca·roche [kəˈrautʃ,-ˈrauʃ] *n.* (十七世纪时隆重场合使用的)豪华马车; 花车.

Car·ol [ˈkærəl] *n.* 卡罗尔〔姓氏,女子名, Caroline 的昵称〕.

car·ol [ˈkærəl] *n.* 喜歌,颂歌;〔诗〕鸟的啼啭. *Christmas ~s* 圣诞颂歌. —*vi., vt.*(〔英〕*-ll-*) ①欢唱,唱颂歌(赞美). ②歌唱; 啼啭.

Car·o·li·na [ˌkærəˈlainə] *n.* (美国)卡罗来纳州. ***the ~s*** 南北卡罗来纳州 ***(= North ~ and South ~)***. ~ **all-spice** 【植】黑花腊梅. ~ **nine** 〔美〕(骰子)对九.

car·ol(l)er [ˈkærələ] *n.* 欢唱颂歌的人.

Car·o·line[1] [ˈkærəlain, -lin] *a.* 【英史】英王查理 *(Charles)* 一世〔二世〕的.

Car·o·line[2] [ˈkærəlain] *n.* 卡罗兰〔女子名〕.

Caroline Islands [ˈkærəlain ˈailəndz] 加罗林群岛〔西太平洋〕 (= Carolines).

Car·o·lin·gi·an [ˌkærəˈlindʒiən] *a.* (公元 751 年成立的法兰克王国第二个王朝)加洛林王朝的. —*n.* 第二法兰克王朝的君主〔人〕.

Car·o·lin·i·an [kærəˈliniən] ① *a., n.* 美国卡罗来纳州的(人). ② = Caroline.[1]

car·om [ˈkærəm] *n., vi.* = carrom.

car·o·tene [ˈkærətiːn] *n.* 【生化】胡萝卜素; 叶红素.

ca·rot·e·noid, ca·rot·i·noid [kəˈrɔtinɔid] *n.* 【生化】类胡萝卜素.

ca·rot·id [kəˈrɔtid] *n., a.* 【解】颈动脉(的).

car·o·tin [ˈkærətin] *n.* = carotene.

ca·rous·al [kəˈrauzəl] *n.* 欢乐喜闹的酒宴; 闹饮.

ca·rouse [kəˈrauz] *n., vi.* 聚饮; 痛饮, 大喝大闹. ~ *it* 大喝,畅饮.

car·ou·sel [ˌkærəˈzel] *n.* ①【史】马上比枪; 骑术比赛. ②(游艺场中的)旋转木马. ③旋转式传送带.

carp[1] [kɑːp] *n. (pl. ~, ~s)* 【动】鲤鱼; 鲤科〔属〕鱼. *the black ~* 青鱼. *the silver ~* 白鲢. *the golden [Prussian] ~* 鲫鱼.

carp[2] [kɑːp] *vi.* 挑剔,找错,吹毛求疵. *~ing criticism* 吹毛求疵的批评. *~ing tongue* 刻薄嘴. *make irresponsible and ~ing comments* 说风凉话.

carp. = carpenter; carpentry.

-carp *comb. f.* 表示"果实".

carpal [ˈkɑːpl] *n., a.* 【解】腕关节(的). ~ *bone* 腕骨.

car·pa·le [kɑːˈpeiliː] *n. (pl. -li·a* [-ə]*)* = carpal.

Car·pa·thi·an Mountains [kɑːˈpeiθjənz] (中欧)喀尔巴阡山山脉 ***(= the Carpathians)***.

car·pe di·em [ˈkɑːpi ˈdaiem] 〔L.〕 ①抓住时机(及时行乐). ②一种鼓吹及时行乐思想的抒情诗.

car·pel [ˈkɑːpel] *n.* 【植】心皮; 果爿.

Car·pen·ter [ˈkɑːpintə] *n.* 卡彭特〔姓氏〕.

car·pen·ter [ˈkɑːpintə] *n.* 木匠,木工(尤指粗木工);【海】船匠. ***the ~'s son*** 木匠之子〔耶稣〕. — *vt.* 以木工手艺造〔修〕(家具、器物、房屋等). ~ *lieutenant* 【海】海军船匠特务上尉. **~'s mate** 【海】海军船匠. **~'s rule** 折尺. **~'s scene** 幕间节目〔以便换布景道具〕. **~'s shop** 木匠店. **~'s square** 角尺,曲尺.

car·pen·try [ˈkɑːpintri] *n.* ①木匠业. ②〔总称〕木工; 木器.

carp·er [ˈkɑːpə] *n.* 吹毛求疵的人.

car·pet [ˈkɑːpit] *n.* ①地毯,桌毯; 毛毯,绒毯. ②【建】磨耗层. ③地毯状覆盖物. ④(装在飞机上的)雷达电子干扰仪. ~ *of flowers* 繁花似锦. ***on the ~*** ①在审议中, 在研究中. ②(仆役,下级等)被叫去, 被训斥 *(to have sb. on the ~* 责备某人. *be called on the ~ for sth.* 为某事被召去受责备). ***red ~*** 红地毯; 〔喻〕隆重的接待〔礼遇〕. ***roll out the red ~ for sb.*** 铺开红地毯接待某人. ***shove sth. under the ~*** 掩盖某事. —*vt.*①在…上铺绒毯〔地毯(等)〕; 把(花等)栽成地毯状. ②〔英〕把(仆役等)叫来责斥. **~-area** 〔英〕室内面积. **~bag** 毡制旅行提包. **~-bagger** 〔美〕(南北内战刚结束时,利用南部的未安定局面去谋利的)冒险家; 不受欢迎的外来者〔政客, 候选人等〕. ~ **bed** (绒毯一样的) 花坛. ~ **blanket** 厚毛毯. **~bomb** *vt.* 对…实行地毯式轰炸. ~ **bombing** (把全区炸平的)地毯轰炸. ~ **dance** (在地毯上跳的)即兴跳舞. ~ **fire** 地毯轰炸造成的大火灾. ~ **herb** 地皮草. ~ **knight** 地毯骑士〔生活优裕的非战斗军人〕; 吃喝玩乐的人. ~ **rod** (扣住梯毯的)金属条. ~ **snake** (澳州) 锦蛇, 斑蛇. ~ **sweeper** 扫毯器. **~weed** 【植】粟米草. **-ing** *n.* 地毯料子〔织品〕; 〔集合词〕地毯,桌毯. **-less** *a.* 没有铺地毯的.

car·pi [ˈkɑːpai] *n.* carpus 的复数.

carp·ing [ˈkɑːpiŋ] *a.* 吹毛求疵的; 苛刻的; 强词夺理的. **-ly** *ad.*

carpo- *comb. f.* 表示"果实": *carpology*.

car·po·go·ni·um [ˌkɑːpəˈgəuniəm] *n. (pl. -ni·a* [-ə]*)* 【植】果胞.

car·pol·o·gy [kɑːˈpɔlədʒi] *n.* 【植】果实(分类)学.

car·poph·a·gous [kɑːˈpɔfəgəs] *a.* 【动】食果实的,以果实为生的.

car·po·phore [ˈkɑːpəfɔː] *n.* 【植】①心皮柄; 果瓣柄. ②子实体.

car·po·phyl(l) [ˈkɑːpəfil] *n.* 【植】大孢子叶.

car·port [ˈkɑːpɔːt] *n.* 〔美〕简陋的汽车棚.

car·po·spore [ˈkɑːpəspɔː] *n.* 【植】果孢子.

car·pus [ˈkɑːpəs] *n. (pl. -pi* [-pai]*)* 【解】腕骨; 腕; (马的)膝头; 脉端; 翅痣.

car·rack [ˈkærək] *n.* 西班牙大帆船(= galleon).

carra·g(h)een ['kærəgiːn] *n.* 【植】鹿角菜〔一种海藻〕.

car·re·four [ˌkærə'fuə] *n.* ①十字路口. ②(位于道路交叉点上的)广场.

car·rel, car·rell ['kærəl] *n.* (图书馆在书库为个别读者提供的)特设小阅览室.

car·ri·age ['kæridʒ] *n.* ①车;(四轮)马车;〔英〕(铁路)客车车厢(=〔美〕car);【空】牵引车;(汽车的)座位. ②运输,输送. ③运费. ④体态,步态;姿态; 风度;〔古〕举止,行动. ⑤炮架;【机】车架,台架,支架;(打字机等的)滑架, 托架; (机床的)拖板, 溜板; 楼梯架. ⑥〔古〕经营;办理. ⑦(议案的)通过. *a close [an open]* ~ 有盖[无盖]马车. *a state* ~ 豪华的礼仪马车,花车. *a composite* ~ 混合客车. *a graceful* ~ 优美的姿势,优雅的态度. ~ **and pair [four]** 双马[四马]马车. ~ **by land [sea]** 陆路[水路]运输. **keep [drive] a** ~ 自备马车. **start [set up] a** ~ 开始备置自用马车. ~ **clock** 正歪放置都会走动的钟. ~ **drive** ①(名胜公园内的)车道. ②(大住宅院内的)马车道. ③汽车道. ~ **folk**〔俚〕有自备马车的人们. ~**-forward** *ad.*〔英〕运费由收货人支付. ~**-free** *ad.* 运费免付. ~**-paid** *ad.* 运费已付. ~ **porch** 停车廊. ~ **trade** (自备马车的)上等顾客. ~**-way** 车行道 (*a dual* ~*way* 复式车行道〔中央有分隔带〕. ①手提的. ②可通行马车的.

car·ri·age·ful ['kæridʒful] *n.* 整整一(马)车的量.

Car·rie ['kæri] *n.* ①卡里〔姓氏〕. ② 卡丽〔女子名, Caroline 的昵称〕.

car·rick ['kærik] *n.* ~ **bend** 【船】(接两根绳子时所用的一种)单花大绳接结. ~ **bitts** 【船】卷扬机柱, 系缆桩.

car·ried ['kærid] *a.* ①被携带的; 被载运的. ②〔英方〕失神落魄的,精神恍惚的.

car·ri·er ['kæriə] *n.* ①运送人,搬夫;负荷者;使役;〔美〕信差,邮递员;送报人;〔英〕运输行, 运输业者. ②传书鸽,信鸽. ③(车后的)货架;吊架; 托架. ④水管, 引水沟. ⑤运载工具;搬运机;移动滑车. ⑥【医】带菌者, 病媒. ⑦航空母舰. ⑧【电】载波; 载流子;【拓】承载子;【化】载体;填料; 导染剂. *a mail [letter]* ~ 邮递员. *a band* ~ 传送带. ~ **aircraft** ①舰载机. ②客机,货机,邮机. ③母机. ~ **bag**〔美〕(购物用)拎包,提包(=〔美〕shopping bag). ~**-based,** ~**-borne** 舰载的. ~**-gear** 过桥齿轮. ~**-nation** 海运业国家. ~ **pigeon** 信鸽. ~ **plane** 舰载飞机. ~**-rocket** *n.* 运载火箭. ~ **ship** 航空母舰. ~**'s note**【商】提货证,提单. ~ **wave** 【无】载波.

car·ri·ole ['kæriəul] *n.* ①小单人马车; 小篷车. ②(加拿大的)狗拉雪车.

car·ri·on ['kæriən] *n.* 腐尸;腐肉;腐臭之物. —*a.* ①腐尸的;腐肉的;腐臭的. ②吃腐肉的. ~ **crow**【鸟】吃腐肉的乌鸦,黑兀鹰.

Car·rol(l) ['kærəl] *n.* 卡罗尔〔姓氏,男子或女子名〕.

car·rom ['kærəm] *n.* 〔美〕①【台球】连中二球的一击(= cannon).②撞击后弹回. —*vi.* ①【台球】连中二球(=cannon). ②撞击后弹回.

car·ron·ade [ˌkærə'neid] *n.* (旧时)大口径短炮.

car·rot ['kærət] *n.* ①【植】胡萝卜. ②〔*pl.*〕〔口〕红头发(的人). ③〔喻〕空洞的政治许诺. *a policy of (the) stick and (the)* ~ 胡萝卜加大棒的政策,又打又拉的政策. ***the donkey's*** ~ 梦想. ~**-top**〔美〕红发人.

car·rot·y ['kærəti] *a.* ①胡萝卜色的. ②〔俚〕(头发)红的;红发的.

car·rou·sel [ˌkæru'zel] = carousel.

car·ry ['kæri] *vt.* ①搬运, 装运. ②携带; 佩带, 怀有. ③支持;掮,肩挑,担(重物);悬挂(旗、帆等). ④举动,处身,自处. ⑤移转;传达,传送,传导.⑥领去,带去. ⑦扩张, 伸到. ⑧使满意, 使服气, 使佩服. ⑨推行, 贯彻(自己主张);使 (议案等) 通过, 使 (候选人等) 当选. ⑩有,含有(意义);记得,不忘记;附带(权利、义务等);生(利息). ⑪占领, 夺取, 攻陷; 获胜. ⑫【会计】转记;结转(次页);【数】进位;(由…)移来, 移上一位. ⑬〔美〕登载,登出(消息等). ⑭(把货物)摆在店里, 卖; 赊卖. ~ *a box on one's shoulder* 把箱子掮在肩头上走. ~ *a gun* 带着枪走. *C- arms!* 举枪! *The timber carries the whole weight of the roof.* 栋梁支承屋顶全重. ~ *an election* 竞选获胜. ~ *conviction* (议论等)令人佩服. ~ *one's point* 贯彻主张. *The motion is carried.* 这一提议业已通过. *be carried [away; out of oneself; to idleness]* 入迷,被迷住;发狂;变懒惰. *The sense these words ~ is ….* 这几个字的含义是…. *We ~ a full line of canned goods.* 本店运销各种罐头. —*vi.* ①担任运送者. ②(声音等)能达到(多远),(枪等)能打到(多远). ③(泥)粘附(鞋子等). ④保持某种姿势. ⑤主张获得赞同, (议案等)获得通过. ⑥被携带. ⑦有感染力. *The trunks don't ~ easily.* 这些大箱子不便于携带. *This gun carries nearly a mile.* 这枪几乎能打一英里远. *These guns ~ true.* 打得准. ~ **a bone in the mouth [teeth]** 【海】开足马力破浪前进. ~ **a flag**〔美俚〕无业游民改姓易名旅行. ~ **a safe**【美棒球】慢慢跑. ~ **a torch for** 见 torch 条. ~ **a tune** 准确地唱,一板一拍地唱. ~ **all [everything] before one [it]** 获巨大成功, 势如破竹, 所向无敌. ~ *(sb.)* **along** 使人佩服 (*They were all carried along by his speech.* 他们都佩服他的话). ~ **away** ①带去,拿去,搬去;冲走; 获得(印象). ②使冲昏头脑,使入迷,使神魂颠倒 (*Music has carried him away.* 音乐使他陶醉). ~ **back** 拿回,带转来;使回想,使想起. ~ **down** 搬下;取下;结转, 滚入. ~ **forward** ①结转, 滚入,转入(下页,下期等). ②使进行;推进, 扩张(业务);发扬 (~ *the glorious tradition forward* 发扬光荣传统). ~ *(sb.)* **high and dry** 逗恼, 戏弄(某人). ~ **into effect [execution]** 实施,实行. ~ **it** 占优势;取胜. ~ **off** ①得(奖); 夺去; 诱拐;(病)夺去人命. ②坚持 (~ *it off well* 若无其事,装作无事. *He was carried off by cholera.* 他患霍乱死了). ~ **on** ①继续; 经营, 处理; 开展. ②不得体[狂乱,幼稚]地行动. ③与…有暧昧关系;与…调情*(with)*. ~ **one's life in one's hands** 冒生命危险. ~ **one's liquor like a gentleman** 慢慢地喝(酒). ~ **oneself well [gracefully]** 举止彬彬有礼[文雅]. ~ **out** ①完成,成就,了结. ②开展;贯彻,落实,实行,执行 (*He hasn't the funds to ~ out his design.* 他没有落实他的计划的资本). ~ **over** ①贮存(货物等)供下季供应. ②将(帐目等)结转(次页);〔英〕(在交易所中)将…转期交割. ③(从以前的阶段、领域等)继续下去, 遗留下来. ④延期至…. ~ **the baby**〔口〕担负麻烦工作;担任不愿担任的工作. ~ **the can**〔英口〕单独承担全部风险[责任]. ~ **the day** 取胜. ~ **the house** 博得满堂喝彩. ~ **the war into the enemy's country [camp]** 在辩论中进一步反攻, 反驳; (战争中)反攻. ~ **the world before one** 取得大成功. ~ **things (off) with a high hand** 用高压手段〔采取断然措施〕处理事情. ~ **through.** ①坚持到底,支持到底. ②贯彻,实行,完成(计划等). ~ *(sth.)* **too far [to extremes]** 过度[走极端]. ~ **true** 奏效,恰到好处. ~ **weight** (意见等)有力,有份量;(人物)有势力 [地位];【赛马】(使优势马匹)负担较多重量. ~ *(sth., sb.)* **with one** ①随身携带(某物,某人);在记忆中保留(某事,某人). ②说服(某人). —*n.* ①(枪的) 射程. ②〔英〕二轮车. ③〔Scot.〕云的去向, 云,空. ④运载,携带;运载[携带]方法;〔美〕运输,水陆联运;(两条水道间)陆上运送. ⑤【军】举枪 (或掮枪) 的姿势;持剑礼;旗手持旗前进的姿势. ⑥【高尔夫球】(球的)距离. ⑦【数】移位,进位; 进位数, 进位指令. ⑧〔美俚〕需用救护车[担架]运送的病人. ~ **all**〔美〕单马拉轻便篷车;万用旅行提包;大型载客汽车;【矿】轮式铲运机. ~**-cot**〔英〕= car bed. ~**on** ①*n.* (飞机乘客的)随身行李. ②*a.* (飞机乘客的行李)可随身携带的. ~**out** *a.* (饭馆等) 饭菜供携出店外的, 外卖的, 送饮食上门的.

～**-over** 余存部分；遗留物；余粮；【商】滞销品；【会计】滚存，结转（～*-over influence* 后效）。～ **topper**（可放在机车顶上载送的）车顶小艇。

car·ry·ing [ˈkæriiŋ] *a.* ①装载的。②运送的，运输的。— *n.* ①运送，运输。②【纺】垫纱，给线。～ **capacity** 装载量，负荷载，输送力；【电】含储电量，荷电量。～ **charge** ①拥有财产所带来的费用〔如纳税〕。②（分期付款购货的）附加价格。～ **over**【股】递延交易。～**s-on**〔俚〕轻薄行为，蠢举，丑态。～ **trade** 运输业。

car·sick [ˈkɑːsik] *a.* 晕车的。**-ness** *n.*

Car·son [ˈkɑːsn] *n.* 卡森〔姓氏，男子名〕。～ **City** 卡尔逊城〔美国内华达州首府〕。

cart [kɑːt] *n.* ①（二轮运货）马车，大车；手推车。②一车之量。*a rubber-tired* ～ 胶轮大车。*a bullock* ～ 牛车。***be in the*** ～〔俚〕为难，陷于困境，被打败。***put [set] the*** ～ ***before the horse*** 前后倒置，本末颠倒。— *vt.* 用车装运。— *vi.* ①赶运货马车。②〔俚〕装运到过远的地方。～ ***off***（强行）运走，拿走，带走（～*yourself off!* 去你的！）。

cart·age [ˈkɑːtidʒ] *n.* 马车运输；（马车）运费。

Car·ta·ge·na [ˌkɑːtəˈdʒiːnə; Sp. ˌkartaˈxena] *n.* ①卡塔赫纳〔哥伦比亚港市〕。②卡塔赫纳〔西班牙港市〕。

carte [kɑːt] *n.*（击剑手）手掌向上刺敌人右胸的姿势（= quart）。～ ***and tierce*** 剑术。

carte [kɑːt] *n.* ①〔F.〕菜单；价目表。②名片；〔罕〕纸牌。③〔*pl.*〕纸牌戏。④〔罕〕地图，海图。***à la*** ～ 点菜。～ ***blanche*** [ˈkɑːtˈblɑ̃ːnʃ] 白纸；署名空白纸；全权委任。～ ***de visite*** [ˈkɑːtdəvi(ː)ˈziːt] 名片；（旧时作名片用的）小相片。

car·tel [kɑːˈtel] *n.* ①俘虏交换协定。②决斗书，挑战书。③卡特尔，联合企业；政党间的联盟。**-ship** *n.* 俘虏交换船。

car·te·li·za·tion [ˌkɑːtəlaiˈzeiʃən] *n.* 卡特尔化。

car·tel·ize [kɑːˈtelaiz] *vt., vi.*（把…）组成卡特尔。

Car·ter [ˈkɑːtə] *n.* 卡特〔姓氏，男子名〕。

cart·er [ˈkɑːtə] *n.* 赶（运货）马车的人。

Car·te·sian [kɑːˈtiːzjən] *a.*（法国哲学家）笛卡尔(Descartes) 的；笛卡尔哲学的。— *n.* 笛卡尔哲学的信徒。～ **co-ordinates**【数】笛卡尔座标。～ **devil [diver]**【物】浮沉子。～ **geometry** 解析几何。**-ism** 笛卡尔哲学〔主义〕。

cart·ful [ˈkɑːtful] *n.*（运货马车）一车的量。

Car·thage [ˈkɑːθidʒ] *n.*【史】（北非）迦太基。

Car·tha·gin·i·an [ˈkɑːθədʒiniən] *a., n.* 迦太基(Carthage)的〔人〕。

Car·thu·sian [kɑːˈθjuːzjən] *n.* ①卡尔特教团〔1086年 St. Bruno 在法国 Chartreuse 山中成立的教团，提倡苦修冥想〕。②（英国）卡尔特公学的学生〔校友〕〔该公学即 Charterhouse School，校址即原来的卡尔特教团修道院〕。— *a.* ①卡特尔教团的。②卡特尔公学学生〔校友〕的。

car·ti·lage [ˈkɑːtilidʒ] *n.*【解】软骨（组织）。

car·ti·lag·i·nous [ˌkɑːtiˈlædʒinəs] *a.*【解】软骨（质）的。

cart·load [ˈkɑːtləud] *n.*（运货马车）一车的装载量；〔口〕大量。***come down (on sb.) like a*** ～ ***of bricks*** 大骂（某人），怒责。

car·to·gram [ˈkɑːtəgræm] *n.* 统计图。

car·to·graph [ˈkɑːtəgrɑːf] *n.* 地图，（特指）插画地图。

car·tog·ra·pher [kɑːˈtɔgrəfə] *n.* 制图员。

car·tog·raph·ic, -i·cal [ˌkɑːtəˈgræfik(əl)] *a.* 制图的。

car·tog·ra·phy [kɑːˈtɔgrəfi] *n.* 制图法，制图学。

car·to·man·cy [ˈkɑːtəuˌmænsi] *n.* 纸牌占卜。

car·ton [ˈkɑːtən] *n.* ①纸板，卡片纸；纸（板）匣；一纸匣的量〔东西〕。②靶心；正中靶心（的子弹）。

car·toon [kɑːˈtuːn] *n.* ①（壁画、织锦等的）草图，底图。②（报刊上的）漫画；连环画。③【影】动画（=animated ～s）。—*vt., vi.* ①（为…）画草图，（为…）画底样。②（使）漫画化；（把…）画成漫画〔动画〕。**-ist** *n.* 底图画家；漫画家；动画家。

car·touch(e) [kɑːˈtuːʃ] *n.* ①【建】（柱头、纪念碑等的）涡卷饰。②（古埃及碑上王和神的名字周围一种椭圆形的）象形文字花框。③装饰镜板。④〔废〕弹药筒。

car·tridge [ˈkɑːtridʒ] *n.* ①【军】弹药筒；子弹。②【物】释热元件；【无】拾音器心座；（电唱机上的）针头。③【机】夹头，卡盘；灯座；（圆珠笔上盛油墨的）笔芯。④【摄】软片，胶卷。*a ball* ～ 实弹。*a blank* ～ 空弹。～ **bag** 弹药包。～ **belt** 子弹带，弹链。～ **box**（串在皮带上的）子弹盒。～ **case** 药筒；子弹壳。～ **chamber** 药室；弹膛。～ **clip**（机关枪等的）弹夹。～ **igniter**【火箭】爆管，导火管。～ **paper** 弹壳纸，火药纸；图画纸。～ **pouch** 弹药盒。

car·tu·lar·y [ˈkɑːtjuləri] *n.* ①契据〔证书〕集，契据登记簿。②契据登记员；契据〔记录〕保存处。

cart-wheel, cart wheel [ˈkɑːthwiːl] *n.* ①大型车轮。②〔俚〕大银币；五先令银币，〔美俚〕一元银币。③〔俚〕（四肢张开，象轮子转动似的）打虎跳；侧身筋斗。***turn [throw]*** ～ 翻侧身筋斗。

Cart·wright [ˈkɑːt-rait] *n.* 卡特赖特〔姓氏〕。

cart·wright [ˈkɑːt-rait] *n.* 车匠。

car·un·cle [ˈkærəŋkl] *n.* ①（鸡的）肉冠，肉瘤。②【解、医】肉阜，息肉。③【植】脐阜，种阜。

car·va·crol [ˈkɑːvəkrɔl, -krəul] *n.*【化】香芹酚。

carve [kɑːv] *vt.* ①切割，切开（盘中的肉）。②雕刻，刻；〔喻〕开拓 *(out)*。～ *a figure out of stone* 用石头雕像。*an image* ～*d out of stone* 石像。— *vi.* ①做雕刻工。②切开熟肉。～ ***a niche*** ①挖出壁龛。②【美体】创记录。～ ***for oneself*** 自由行动。～ ***(stone) into*** 把（石头）雕成。～ ***out a career for oneself*** 独立谋生，自己开辟前途。～ ***out a victory***【美体】费九牛二虎之力获胜。～ ***(a head) out of*** 用…雕刻（头像）。～ ***out one's [a] way*** 开辟道路（～ *out a way through the enemy* 杀开一条血路）。～ ***up*** 切成几份，分切（肉等），瓜分，划分（遗产等）。～**-up**〔俚〕分得的一份（战利品等）。— *n.*〔美俚〕（作为食物、菜肴的）肉。

car·vel [ˈkɑːvəl] *n.* = caravel.

car·vel-built [ˈkɑːvəl-ˌbilt] *a.*【船】（船体木板）平镶的。

carv·en [ˈkɑːvən] *a.*〔古〕雕刻的。

Car·ver [ˈkɑːvə] *n.* 卡弗〔姓氏〕。

carv·er [ˈkɑːvə] *n.* ①雕刻师，雕工；切肉人。②切肉刀；〔*pl.*〕切肉用具。*a* ～ *in wood* = *a wood* ～木刻家，木雕者。

carv·ing [ˈkɑːviŋ] *n.* ①雕刻（术）；雕刻物，雕刻品。②切肉。～ **fork** 切肉叉。～ **knife** 切肉刀。

Car·y [ˈkeəri] *n.* 卡里〔姓氏，男子名〕。

car·y·at·id [ˌkæriˈætid] *n.* (*pl.* ～*s*, ～*es* [-iːz])【建】女像柱。

cary(o)- *comb. f.* 核：*caryopsis*.

car·y·op·sis [ˌkæriˈɔpsis] *n.* (*pl.* **-opses** [-siːz], ***-opsides*** [-sidiːz])【植】颖果。

car·zi·no·my·cin [ˈkɑːzinəuˈmaisin] *n.*【药】癌霉素。

ca·sa·ba [kəˈsɑːbə] *n.* ①【植】（产生小亚细亚卡萨巴的）香瓜，甜瓜。②〔美俚〕球。

Ca·sa·blan·ca [ˌkæsəˈblæŋkə] *n.* 卡萨布兰卡〔即 Dar el Beida 达尔贝达〕〔摩洛哥港市〕。

cas·al [ˈkeisəl] *a.*【语法】（关于）格的。

ca·sa·va [kəˈsɑːvə] *n.* = cassava.

cas·bah [ˈkɑːzbɑː, ˈkæs-] *n.* ①（北非）要塞，城堡。②北非城市；〔C-〕（阿尔及尔的）古旧闹市。

cas·ca·bel [ˈkæskəbel] *n.* ①（由炮口装弹的炮的）尾座，尾钮。②【动】响尾蛇；（响尾蛇的）响尾。③球形穿孔的铃。～ **plate**【军】尾座板。

cas·cade [kæsˈkeid] *n.* ①（陡岩落下的）瀑布；【园艺】人工瀑布。②瀑布状物；波状花边。③【物】级；级联，串联；【无】格，栅，格状物；【空】叶栅；【化】阶式蒸发器。— *vt.*, *vi.* ①〔罕〕(使)成瀑布落下. ②(使阶式地)串接,串联.

cas·car·a [kæsˈkɑːrə] *n.* 【植】药鼠李(= ~ buckthorn). ~ **sagrada** [sɑːˈgrɑːdə] 药鼠李皮〔可作缓泻剂〕.

cas·ca·ril·la [ˌkæskəˈrilə] *n.* ①【植】卡藜,苦香皮,加斯加利刺 *(Croton eluteria)*. ②加斯加利刺的树皮〔用作兴奋剂,健胃剂〕.

case[1] [keis] *n.* ①情况,状况;真相. ②(实)例,事例. ③诉讼(事件),案件,判例;问题. ④立场,主张;论据,论辩. ⑤病症;病例;病人,患者. ⑥〔美口〕怪人;迷恋(的对象). ⑦【语法】格. *a ~ of poverty* 穷苦的状况. *a ~ for conscience* 道义问题,良心问题. *a ~ for life and death* 生死问题. *a ~ in point* 恰当的实例,范例. *a ~ of small pox* 天花病人. *a civil [criminal] ~* 民事[刑事]诉讼. *a murder ~* 杀人事件[案件]. *a leading ~* 判(决)例. *That is not the ~.* 事实不是那样. *The plaintiff has no ~.* 原告无话可辩. *a gone ~* 不可救药的人. *a hard ~* 难症;难处的人,难缠的人;无赖,光棍. *a singular ~* 奇例;怪人. ***as is often the case*** 这是常有的事 (*He was absent, as is often the ~.* 他没有来,这是常有的事). ***as the ~ may be*** 看情形,根据具体情况. ***as the ~ stands*** 照现在的状况,事实上. ***be in good [evil] ~*** 幸福[不幸福],境况好[不好],身体好[不好]. ~ ***by*** ~ 逐一,一件一件地;相机行事地;具体问题具体处理. ***Circumstances alter ~s.*** 随机应变. ***drop a ~*** 撤回诉讼. ***give the ~ for [against] sb.*** 作出对某人有利[不利]的判决. ***in all ~s*** 一切,在一切情况下 (*to proceed in all ~s from the interests of the people* 一切从人民的利益出发). ***in any ~*** 无论如何,总之. ***in ~*** ①如果,若是,假如万一…,在…的时候〔用作连词〕(*In ~ it should rain, don't expect me.* 如果天下雨,我就不来了). ②以防,免得〔用作连词〕(*Take your umbrella, in ~ it rains.* 带伞去吧,以防下雨). ③作为准备;以防万一. 〔用作状语〕(*It may rain, you'd better take your umbrella (just) in ~.* 天可能下雨,你最好带上伞以防万一). ***in ~ of*** 要是,如果,万一 (*in ~ of war* 如果[万一]发生战争. *in ~ of need* 遇必要时,在紧急时). ***in nine ~s out of ten*** 十之八九,多半 (*He will not come in nine ~s out of ten.* 他十之八九[多半]不会来了). ***in no ~*** 决不. ***in some ~s*** 有时候. ***in the ~ of*** 就…说,至于…,论到,提到. ***in this [that] ~*** 既然是这[那]样,假若是这[那]. ***just in ~*** 以防万一;作为准备. ***lay the ~*** 陈述. ***make out [state] one's ~*** 摆明自己的理由. ***put (the) ~ that ...*** 〔古〕比如说,假定. ***such [that] being the ~*** 情况既然如此,因此. ***There are ~s where....*** 有时候…. ~ **book** 专题资料[案例]汇编. ~ **history** 病历;个人历史. ~ **law** 【法】判例法〔以判例为根据的法律〕. ~ **lawyer** 熟悉判例的律师. ~ **load** 办案量;病例数. ~ **note** 〔美〕一元钞票. ~**work** ①(对申请户状况进行调查等的)社会福利工作;(社会学家进行的)个别情况调研.

case[2] [keis] *n.* ①箱,盒. ②鞘,袋,套子,壳,罩,容器. ③外侧,外板;框架. ④(一)组,一对,两个. ⑤〔美俚〕旅行箱. ⑥【印】活字(分格)盘. ⑦〔美口〕元,块. *a jewel ~* 宝石盒. *a knife ~* 刀鞘. *upper [lower] ~* 【印】大写[小写]字盘;大写[小写]字母. *work at ~* 排字. *a 5-~ note* 一张五元钞票. — *vt.* ①把…装入箱内[袋内];把…插入鞘内;给…加框. ②包,围 *(with; up; over)*. ③〔美俚〕查看(地点),观察,窥探(尤指罪犯作案前的察看地点). ~ ***the joint*** 〔美俚〕(罪犯作案前的)现场窥探. ~ **bay** 【建】桁间. ~ **bottle** (装箱)方瓶;有套瓶. ~**harden** *vt.* ①【冶】使(铁合金)表面硬化,淬火. ②使厚颜无耻,使冷酷无情. ~**-hardened** ①【冶】表面硬化的. ②(思想等)已定型的;无情的. ~ **knife** 带鞘小刀;餐刀. ~ **shot** 霰弹. ~ **worm** *n.* 【虫】蛴螬.

ca·se·ase [ˈkeisieis] *n.* 【生化】酪蛋白酶.

ca·se·ate [ˈkeisieit] *vi.* 【医】干酪性坏死.

ca·se·a·tion [ˌkeisiˈeiʃən] *n.* ①变成干酪,干酪化. ②【医】干酪性坏死.

ca·se·fy [ˈkeisiˌfai] *vt., vi.* (使)变成酪状.

ca·se·in [ˈkeisiːin] *n.* 【化】酪朊,酪蛋白;酪素.

ca·se·in·o·gen [ˌkeisiˈinədʒən, keiˈsinə-] *n.* 【生化】酪素原,酪蛋白原.

case·mate [ˈkeismeit] *n.* 【军】①(堡墙上的)掩蔽部. ②隐蔽炮台,暗炮台. ③【海】(军舰上的)炮塔.

Case·ment [ˈkeismənt] *n.* 凯斯门特〔姓氏〕.

case·ment [ˈkeismənt] *n.* ①(可以开关的)窗框. ②〔诗〕窗;窗帘布. ③【建】窗扉,孔模. ~ **cloth** 细棉布. ~ **window** (普通的)玻璃窗.

ca·se·ose [ˈkeisiˌəus] *n.* 【生化】酪脲.

ca·se·ous [ˈkeisiəs] *a.* 干酪(状)的.

ca·sern(e) [kəˈzəːn] *n.* 〔常 *pl.*〕(设防城镇中的)兵营.

cash[1] [kæʃ] *n.* 现款,现金;〔口〕钱;小额支票. *a hard ~* 硬币. *idle ~* 〔口〕游资. ***be in [out of] ~*** 有[无]现款. ***be short of ~*** 现金不足,支付短少. ~ ***and carry*** 【商】现金出售运输自理. ~ ***down*** 【商】即期现款,即付 (*sell for ~ down* 现卖). ~ ***in hand*** 现有金额(=〔美〕~ ***on hand***). ~ ***on delivery*** 货到收款〔略 C.O.D.〕;售价. ***equal to ~*** 〔口〕真正有价值[功劳]的. ***keep the ~*** 做现金出纳. ***run out of ~*** 现金短缺. — *vt.* ①把…兑换现款;为…付[收]现款 *(for)*. ②【牌】先出(赢牌). ~ *a check* 把支票兑现. — *vi.* 赚钱. ~ ***in*** 〔美俚〕①赚到钱,抓到赚钱的机会. ②死. (*After her husband ~ in, she lived with her sons.* 丈夫死后,她和儿子住在一起). ③清算,决算,结束;断绝关系. ④兑换成现金;变卖财产. ⑤预先准备;乘机行事. ~ ***in on*** 〔美口〕用…赚钱;利用 (*~ in on one's ability to speak* 利用自己的口才). ~ ***in one's checks [chips]*** (赌毕)以筹码换现钱;〔俚〕死. ~ **account** 现金帐. ~ **articles** 现金证券. ~ **bar** 现卖饮料柜台〔与免费供应的 open bar 相对〕. ~**book** 现金帐(簿). ~**box** 钱箱[柜]. ~**boy** (往来营业柜台与现金帐台之间的)送款童子. ~ **carrier** 送款机. ~ **credit** 暂欠货款. ~ **crop** 【农】商品作物. ~ **customer** 〔美〕买票入场的人. ~ **payment** 付现. ~ **price** 现款售价. ~ **register** 现金收入记录机,现金出纳机. ~ **sale** 现卖.

cash[2] [kæʃ] *n.* 〔*sing., pl.*〕(印度和中国旧时的)铜钱,小铜币.

ca·shaw [kəˈʃɔː] *n.* 【植】南瓜,倭瓜(= cushaw).

cash·ew [kæˈʃuː] *n.* 【植】(美洲热带的)槚如树(属);腰果(槚如树坚果或其果仁,=cashew nut).

cash·ier[1] [kæˈʃiə] *n.* 出纳员;〔美〕(银行的)财务主任. ~**'s order [cheque, check]** 银行本票.

ca·shier[2] [kəˈʃiə] *vt.* ①把…撤职;驱逐,革除. ②废除,抛弃.

cash·mere [kæʃˈmiə] *n.* 开士米〔克什米尔产细羊毛;细羊毛绒线,织物,呢子〕;开士米围巾〔羊毛衫,呢大衣〕. ~ **hair** 开士米山羊毛. ~ **silk** 开士米毛葛.

cas·ing [ˈkeisiŋ] *n.* ①装箱,装袋,入鞘. ②〔集合词〕包装箱〔鞘、袋、筒、框等〕. ③(窗等的)框子;围子,围墙. ④(做香肠用的)肠衣. ⑤外(车)胎;套管;罩壳.

ca·si·no [kəˈsiːnəu] *n.* 〔It.〕①(可跳舞、赌博的)夜总会. ②(意大利的)小别墅,小住宅. ③(公园等处的)凉棚. ④一种纸牌戏.

cask [kɑːsk] *n.* 桶;一桶.

cas·ket [ˈkɑːskit] *n.* ①珠宝盒[信件盒等]. ②(知识等的)宝库. ③〔美〕棺材;骨灰盒.

Cas·lon [ˈkæzlən] *n.* 卡斯隆〔姓氏〕.

Cas·pi·an [ˈkæspiən] *a.* 里海(附近)的. ~ **Sea** 里海.

casque [kæsk] *n.* ①〔主诗〕盔. ②【植】盔瓣.

Cass [kæs] *n.* 卡斯〔姓氏〕.

cas·sa·ba [kəˈsɑːbə] *n.* 【植】香瓜,甜瓜 (= casaba).

Cas·san·dra [kəˈsændrə] *n.* ①卡姗德拉〔女子名,爱称 Cass〕. ②卡姗德拉〔荷马史诗中 Troy 王 Priam 之女,能预知祸事〕. ③不受人相信的凶事预言者.

cas·sa·tion [kæˈseiʃən] *n.* 【法】(原判决的)撤销,废除. *the Court of C-* (法国、比利时等国的)最高上诉法院.

cas·sa·va [kəˈsɑːvə] *n.* ①【植】木薯属 (Manihot) 植物. ②木薯属植物的根[淀粉]〔可做面包和食用淀粉〕.

cas·se·role [ˈkæsərəul] *n.* ①(有柄)砂锅,砂锅菜品. ②【化】勺皿;瓷勺,柄皿.

cas·sette [kɑːˈset] *n.* ①(放珠宝或文件的)匣子;摄影胶卷暗匣;弹夹. ②录音带盒. ③〔口〕盒式录音带. ~ **tape recorder** 盒式录音机. ~ **television [TV]** 盒式录象电视(机).

Cas·sia [ˈkæsiə] *n.* 【植】山扁豆属;〔c-〕低级肉桂. ~ *bark [lignea]* 桂皮,肉桂. ~ *oil* 肉桂油.

cas·si·mere [ˈkæsimiə] *n.* 开士米细毛呢 (= cashmere).

Cas·si·o·pe·ia [ˌkæsiəˈpi(ː)ə] *n.* 【天】仙后座 (= ~'s Chair).

cas·si·o·pe·ium [ˌkæsiəˈpiːəm] *n.* 【化】镥(= lutecium).

cas·sis [kæˈsiː] *n.* 黑醋栗酒〔常掺入苦艾酒〕.

cas·sit·er·ite [kəˈsitərait] *n.* 【矿】锡石.

cas·sock [ˈkæsək] *n.* ①(教士穿的)黑袍法衣;军人长大衣;女外套. ②〔喻〕牧师,教士.

cas·sou·let [ˌkæsuˈlei] *n.* 砂锅燉肉豆.

cas·so·war·y [ˈkæsəweəri] *n.* 【动】食火鸡.

cast [kɑːst] *vt.* ***(cast; cast)*** ①投,扔,掷,抛.★此义动词通常用 throw, cast 只用于若干特殊句子. ②丢弃,抛弃;脱掉(衣服);(蛇)脱(皮),(鸟)换(毛),(鹿)换(角);(树)落(叶);(马)脱落(掌铁). ③(兽)早产;(果树)落(果). ④【冶】浇铸,铸造;【印】把(纸型)浇成铅版. ⑤计算;合计. ⑥【剧】分配(角色),选派(角色). ⑦【法】使败诉. ⑧解雇,辞退,赶走,撵走;淘汰(不及格学生). ⑨投射(影子、光线) *(on)*;(眼光)钉住(某物). ⑩筑,挖造. ⑪算(卦),占卜. ⑫【海】使改变航向. ⑬使弯曲[翘起];扭弯. ~ *anchor* 抛锚. ~ *a net* 撒网. ~ *seed* 撒种,播种. ~ *a vote* 投票. ~ *a dice* 掷骰子. ~ *the lead* 【海】锤测(水深). ~ *the blame on sb.* 加罪[嫁祸]于人. ~ *a shoe* (马)掉了铁掌. ~ *a spell on sb.* 迷惑人. ~ *a stone at sb.* 拿石子打人;攻击[中伤]人. ~ *a glance at* 把(眼光)钉住,用(眼光)一扫. ~ *a (new) light on* 给与(新的)解决线索[解释]. ~ *accounts* 计算. *be* ~ *in a different mould* 性质[气质]不同. *be* ~ *in a suit* 败诉. *be* ~ *in [for] damages* 被判决赔偿损失. *be* ~ *in heroic mould* 有英雄的性格. ~ *a lot* 抽签. —*vi.* ①抛出钓丝,垂钓. ②〔英方〕呕吐. ③计算. ④占卜,算卦;〔古〕预测;筹划. ⑤〔Scot.〕褪色. ⑥【猎】分头追寻. ⑦【海】改变航向. ⑧浇铸成形. ⑨产. *Timber ~s.* 木料会起翘. *Overheated metals may ~ badly.* 加热过甚的金属可能难浇铸成型. *The wheat ~s well.* 小麦年景好. ~ ***about*** ①设法,计划. ②【海】掉转航向. ~ ***about for*** ①找,寻觅;搜集;物色. ②考虑,想(方法等). ③(船)向…掉头. ~ ***ashore*** (浪把船)抛到岸上. ~ ***aside*** 抛弃,排除,废除(习惯等),消除(疑虑等). ~ ***away*** 抛弃;浪费;排斥;使(船只)破坏 (*be ~ away* 漂流). ~ ***back*** 退回;恢复;追溯;回想. ~ *(sth. [sb.])* ***behind*** 把…抛在脑后;疏远. ~ *(past deeds)* ***behind one's back*** (把往事)忘掉,置之脑后. ~ *(sth.)* ***in sb.'s teeth*** 以(某事)当面责备某人. ~ ***beyond the moon*** 任意推测. ~ ***by*** 放弃;排除. ~ ***down*** 推倒,打掉;打倒;放低,压低;使胆寒 (*be ~ down* 丧胆,意气沮丧). ~ ***forth*** 抛出;逐出. ~ ***(in) one's lot with*** 与…共命运. ~ ***into the shade*** 使黯然失色;使向隅. ~ ***loose*** 解开,放开;(自行)放开. ~ ***off*** ①丢弃,脱掉(衣服);抛弃,放弃. ②【纺】织完,收针. ③【海】放(船),解(缆). ④【印】(据原稿)计划篇幅[版面]. ~ ***on*** 急忙穿上(衣服);起针编织. ~ ***oneself on [upon]*** 委身于,依赖,仰仗. ~ ***out*** ①扔出;逐出,赶出. ②吐出,呕吐. ③〔Scot.〕吵闹,争吵。~ ***over*** 【纺】绕针. ~ ***up*** ①合计,计算. ②责备. ③呕吐,吐出. ④打上,摔上;堆起(泥土). ⑤〔Scot.〕突然出现;(云)密集;责备 *(to)*. —*n.* ①投;掷骰子;抛石子;撒网;垂钓;一掷,一举,试. ②【冶】浇铸,铸造;铸型,模子;铸成品. ③(目光)投射;瞥见;轻微的斜视〔眼睛的一种缺陷〕. ④(容貌、性质等的)特征;外观;倾向,型式;色调;种类. ⑤计算. ⑥角色分配,演员;演员表. ⑦【海】锤测. ⑧【印】版;纸版,铅版. ⑨(木板等的)反翘;(弓的)弹力. ⑩脱落之物,(蛇的)蜕皮;(蚯蚓等翻到地面的)泥土(等). *a bow's* ~ 一箭的射程. *a* ~ *of the net* 撒一次网,一网. *a good* ~ (钓鱼或撒网的)好地方. *try another* ~ 再试一试. *a* ~ *in the eye* 轻微的斜视. *a woman of the old* ~ 旧式女人. *a man of noble* ~ 人品高尚的人. *an all star* ~ 名演员大会演. ~ *of features* 容貌. ~ *of mind* 脾气. ~ *of thought* 思想倾向. ***the last*** ~最后一着;最后机会. ~ **charge** (火箭发动机的)浇注火药柱. ~ **iron** 铸铁. ~ **steel** 铸钢.

Cas·ta·li·a [kæsˈteiliə] *n.* 【希神】帕纳苏斯 *(Parnassus)* 山的神泉;诗的灵感的源泉. **Cas·ta·li·an** [kæsˈteiliən] *a.* 诗的灵感源泉的.

cas·ta·nets [ˌkæstəˈnets] *n.* 〔*pl.*〕【乐】响板〔套在大中指上舞蹈时合击发音〕.

cast·a·way [ˈkɑːstəwei] *n.* ①遭难船;坐船遇难的人. ②漂泊无依的人,流浪者,光棍. —*a.* ①遭了难的. ②为世人所抛弃的;流浪的.

caste [kɑːst] *n.* ①(印度世袭的)种姓〔分婆罗门 (Brahman), 刹帝利 (Kshatriya), 吠舍 (Vaisya), 首陀罗 (Sudra) 四等〕;(世袭的)阶级,等级(制度). ②(昆虫的)职别〔如工蜂等〕. ~ *system* 种姓等级制度. *lose* ~ 失却社会地位,失去特权.

cas·tel·lan [ˈkæstələn] *n.* (古时的)城主,堡主,寨主.

cas·tel·la·ny [ˈkæstileini] *n.* ①城主职位. ②城堡领地.

cas·tel·lat·ed [ˈkæsteleitid] *a.* ①造成城形的,构造如城的. ②有城的,多城的.

cas·tel·la·tion [ˌkæsteˈleiʃən] *n.* ①城堡形建筑. ②【建】雉堞墙.

cast·er [ˈkɑːstə] *n.* ①投掷者. ②赌博者. ③铸工. ④〔印〕铸字机(=casting machine). ⑤计算者. ⑥占卜者,算命先生. ⑦分配角色的人. ⑧= castor[2].

cas·ti·gate [ˈkæstigeit] *vt.* ①惩戒,严厉批评. ②鞭责. ③修订(文章等). **-ga·tion** [ˌkæstiˈgeiʃən] *n.*

cas·ti·ga·tor [ˈkæstigeitə] *n.* ①惩戒者. ②鞭责者. ③修订者.

Cas·tile [kæsˈtiːl] *n.* 卡斯提尔〔古代西班牙中部北部地名〕. ~ **soap** 橄榄油香皂.

Cas·til·i·an [kæsˈtiliən] *a.* 卡斯提尔 (Castile) 的. —*n.* ①卡斯提尔人. ②卡斯提尔语. ③纯正的西班牙语.

cast·ing [ˈkɑːstiŋ] *n.* ①投,掷. ②【冶】铸造;铸件. ③【动】脱弃,脱落物〔如毛、皮等〕. ④计算. ⑤想法,手法. ⑥(木材等的)翘曲. ⑦【剧】配角. ~ **vote** (赞成与反对同数时,主席所作的)决定性投票.

cast-i·ron [ˈkɑːstˈaiən] *a.* ①铸铁制的. ②硬的,无伸缩性的. ③刚直的,不通融的. ④强健的. *a* ~ *law [regulation]* 严厉的法律[规章]. ~ ***will*** 坚强的意志. *a* ~ *stomach* 强健的胃.

cas·tle [ˈkɑːsl] *n.* ①城;(城堡形)建筑物. ②船楼. ③(国际象棋中的)车. ④〔the C-〕都伯林城. ⑤(不受侵扰的)避居地. *the Windsor C-* (英国的)(英国国王居住的)温莎宫. ~ ***in the air [in Spain]*** 空中楼阁,空想. —*vt.* ①把…置于城堡中;筑城堡防卫. ②(下国际象棋时)用车护(王). ~**-builder** 空想家. ~ **nut** 【机】开花螺帽.

cast·off [ˈkɑːstˈɔ(ː)f] *a.* 被丢弃的,无用的,废弃的. ~ *clothes* 不再穿的旧衣服.

Cas·tor [ˈkɑːstə] *n.* 【天】北河二〔双子座 α 星〕.

cas·tor[1] [ˈkɑːstə] *n.* ①【动】海狸. ②海狸皮;海狸皮帽.

③〔俚〕帽. ④【药】海狸香. ⑤一种大衣呢.

cas·tor² [ˈkɑːstə] *n.* ①(餐桌上的)调味瓶,调味瓶架子. ②(桌椅等的)脚轮. ~ **sugar** (餐桌上用的)细白砂糖.

cas·tor³ [ˈkɑːstə] *n.*【海】(暴风雨时的)桅头电光.

cas·tor⁴ [ˈkɑːstə] *n.* 蓖麻 (= ~-oil plant). ~**-bean**〔美〕蓖麻(子). ~**-oil** 蓖麻油. (*a* ~*-oil artist*[*merchant*]〔美俚〕医生,郎中).

cas·trate [kæsˈtreit] *vt.* ①割除(睾丸、卵巢),阉割;【植】去雄. ②〔喻〕删改,窜改(书籍).

cas·tra·tion [kæsˈtreiʃən] *n.* 阉割;【植】去雄;〔喻〕删改,窜改.

cas·tra·to [kɑːsˈtrɑːtəu] *n.* (*pl.* *-ti* [-iː]) 阉歌手〔过去为使男孩歌手保持女高音或女低音的声调而把他阉割〕.

cas·u·al [ˈkæʒjuəl] *a.* ①偶然的;碰巧的. ②临时的,不定期的;即席的. ③〔俚〕荒唐的,漫不经心的. ④随便的,非正式的. *a* ~ *visitor* 不速之客. *a* ~ *labourer* [*worker*] 临时工. *a* ~ *revenue* 临时收入. *the* ~ *poor* (需要临时救济的)无业游民. *a* ~ *remark* 临时想起的话,信口而出的话. *a* ~ *air* 满不在乎的态度. ~ *clothes* 便服. ~ *decisions* 草率的决定. *a very* ~ *sort of a man* 非常不尊重别人的人. —*n.* ①零工,散工 (= ~ labourer). ②〔英〕〔*pl.*〕(无业)游民;不定期接受救济金的人. ③【军】暂编人员〔暂时编在某一单位等候调配的军官士兵〕. ④偶然来访者. ~ **house** 〔英〕济贫院. ~ **ward** 〔英〕(济贫院的)临时收容所. **-ness** *n.*

cas·u·al·ly [ˈkæʒjuəli] *ad.* 偶然;不在意地;临时. *not to treat this* ~ 不要等闲视之.

cas·u·al·ty [ˈkæʒjuəlti] *n.* ①事故,横祸,灾难;损坏. ②死伤(者),受伤者. ③〔*pl.*〕【军】伤亡(人数). *heavy casualties* 巨大的伤亡[损失]. *the total casualties* 伤亡总数. ~ *clearing station* 野战医院〔略 C.C.S.〕. ~ **insurance** 灾害保险;火险. ~ **ward** 战地临时收容室.

cas·u·a·ri·na [ˌkæsjuəˈriːnə] *n.*【植】(大洋洲、西印度产)木麻黄.

cas·u·ist [ˈkæzjuist] *n.* 独断论者;决疑者;诡辩家.

cas·u·is·tic(al) [ˌkæzjuˈistik(əl)] *a.* 独断的;决疑的;诡辩的.

cas·u·ist·ry [ˈkæzjuistri] *n.* ①决疑法;诡辩术. ②用伦理学判断行为的是非.

ca·sus [ˈkɑːsus] *n.*〔L.〕事件;案例. ~ ***bel·li*** [ˈbeli:]〔L.〕开战的理由,宣战的原因[借口]. ~ ***foe·der·is*** [ˈfedəris] 条约中所涉及的事项.

CAT = clear air turbulence 晴空湍流(颠簸).

cat¹ [kæt] *n.* ①猫,(尤指)母猫〔公猫为 tomcat〕;猫科动物 (= the Cats, the great Cats)〔狮、虎、豹等〕;〔英〕山猫 (=lynx). ②脾气不好[爱骂人]的女人;爱抓人的孩子. ③(运煤等的)独桅艇. ④【海】起锚滑车. ⑤(无论如何摆放都用三脚站立的、有三对活动脚的)六脚器. ⑥(一种有九条皮带的)九尾鞭 (= cat-o'-nine-tails). ⑦〔英〕(一种击球游戏用的)橄榄状木球;(用棒击木球的)木球戏(= tipcat). ⑧〔美俚〕(任何)人,男人;娼妓;流动工人;爵士音乐演奏者[爱好者]. ⑨可惜,可怜;遗憾,抱歉. ***a barber's*** ~ 面有病容和饥色的人. ***A*** ~ ***has nine lives.*** 猫有九条命〔不易死亡〕. ***a*** ~ ***in the pan.*** 〔俚〕临阵脱逃者,叛徒. ***A*** ~ ***may look at a king.*** 猫也有权看看国王〔小人物也该有些权利〕. ***a queer*** ~ 怪人. ***a swell*** ~ 好家伙. ***as sick as a*** ~ 作恶心,不舒服;患重病. ***bell the*** ~ 为别人冒险,为公共的事冒险. ***Care killed the*** ~. 久虑伤身. ***cat-and-mouse act*** 〔美俚〕绝食囚犯假释令. ~***s and dogs*** ①〔口〕大量. ②〔美俚〕不值钱的股票,不确实的有价证券;杂品. ~***'s eye-brow [meow]*** 〔美俚〕了不得的,极美的,极好的. ~***'s pyjamas [pajamas]*** 〔美俚〕(自以为)了不起的东西,不平常的东西. ~***'s sleep*** 打盹. ***Dog my*** ~***s!*** 〔口〕畜牲!该死的! ***enough to make a*** ~ ***laugh [speak]*** 真可笑[漂亮],真蠢[好]. ***fight like Kilkenny*** ~***s*** 死斗,死拼. ***lead a cat-and-dog life*** 过猫狗生活〔特指夫妇经常吵架的生活〕. ***let the*** ~ ***out of the bag*** 使秘密泄漏,露马脚. ***Let the old*** ~ ***die.*** 〔儿〕静等秋千自身慢慢停下来. ***like a*** ~ ***on hot bricks [tiles]*** 焦躁不安,如热锅上的蚂蚁. ***make a*** ~***'s paw of sb.*** 利用他人作为利己的工具. ***no [not] room to swing a*** ~ ***in*** 地方窄狭. ***not a*** ~***'s chance*** 毫无机会. ***rain*** ~***s and dogs*** 大雨倾盆. ***see which way the*** ~ ***will jump*** 观望形势(然后行动). ***shoot [jerk] the*** ~ (因饮酒过多而)呕吐. ***tear a*** ~ 妄语,傲语. ***That*** ~ ***won't jump.*** 〔口〕那可不行,那一手行不通. ***turn the*** ~ ***in the pan*** 变节,见利思迁. ***wait [watch] for the*** ~ ***to jump*** 观望形势(然后行动). ***When the*** ~***'s away, the mice will play.*** 猫儿不在,老鼠翻天. —*vt.* ①【海】把(锚)吊放在锚架上. ②(用九尾鞭)鞭打. —*vi.* ①〔口〕呕吐. ②宿娼. ~**-and-dog** *a.* ①不和谐的,爱争吵的. ②〔俚〕投机性的. ~**-and-mouse** *a.* 折磨人的. ~**bird**〔美〕猫声鸟(鸫属)(~*bird seat* 有权力的职位). ~ **block** 吊锚滑车. ~**boat** 独桅艇. ~ **burglar** 〔俚〕(由屋顶潜入的)窃贼. ~**call** ① *n.* (会议或剧场内表示反对或喝倒彩的)嘘声. ② *vt.* 发嘘声反对,奚落. ③ *vi.* 发出嘘声. ~ **cracker** (石油)裂化催化器. ~ **davit**【船】有档锚吊杆. ~ **door** 猫门〔板壁等上供猫出入的小门〕. ~**-eyed** *a.* 能在黑暗中辨别东西的. ~**fall**【船】吊锚索. ~**fish**【动】鲇;(美洲)鲴. ~**gut** 肠线〔網球拍等用〕;弦乐器. ~**head** 锚架. ~ **hole**【船】锚链孔. ~ **hook**【船】吊锚钩. ~ **house**〔美俚〕妓院. ~**-ice** ① *n.* (水面下降后与水面隔开的)乳白色薄冰. ② *a.* 乳状的;发泡的;不规则的. ~**lap**〔美俚〕(茶等)非浓缩的饮料. ~**-let**〔美〕小猫;顽皮的姑娘. ~ **nap** 打盹. ~**nip**【美植】假荆芥. ~**-o'-nine'-tails** [ˈkætəˈnainteilz] ①九尾鞭. ②【植】香蒲. ~**'s cradle** 编花框,翻绞绞〔小儿用绳子玩的游戏〕. ~**'s-eye**【矿】猫眼石玻璃珠;(汽车等的)小型反光装置. ~**'s-foot**【植】积雪草,连钱草. ~**-shark** 鲨鱼. ~**-silver**〔古〕云母. ~ **skinner**〔美俚〕牵引车的司机. ~**-sleep** 打盹(= cat nap). ~**'s-paw** ①被人利用〔愚弄〕的人. ②【海】微风,猫掌风 (*make a* ~*'s-paw of sb.* 拿某人当工具〔傀儡〕). ~**'s stabber**〔美俚〕刺刀. ~**'s-tail** *n.*【植】问荆. ~ **suit** (连衫)喇叭裤. ~**-tackle**【海】起锚绞车. ~**tail**【植】香蒲属植物. ~**walk**〔美俚〕狭窄的人行道,桥上人行道;狭窄的过道. ~**'s-whisker**【无】触须,晶须;〔*pl.*〕〔美俚〕(自以为)了不起的东西,引以自夸的东西,不平常的东西 (=~**'s pyjamas**). ~**walk** 狭窄人行道[过道].

cat² [kæt] *n.*〔军俚〕履带式拖拉机,任何有履带的车辆.

cat. = catalog(ue); catechism.

cat(a)- *comb. f.* 表示"在下";"相反";"完全";"关于": *cata*comb, *cata*genesis.

cat·a·bol·ic [ˌkætəˈbɔlik] *a.*【生理】分解代谢的. **-ally** *ad.*

ca·tab·o·lism [kəˈtæbəlizəm] *n.*【生理】分解代谢 (*opp.* anabolism).

ca·tab·o·lite [kəˈtæbəlait] *n.*【生理】分解(代谢)产物.

ca·tab·o·lize [kəˈtæbəˌlaiz] *vi., vt.*【生理】(使)发生分解代谢.

cat·a·caus·tic [ˌkætəˈkɔːstik] *a.*【物】反射焦散曲线的. —*n.*【物】反射焦散曲线.

cat·a·chre·sis [ˌkætəˈkriːsis] *n.* (*pl.* *-ses* [-siːz])【修】①(在特定上下文中)语词的误用〔如 *the fruitful river in the eye*〕. ②(由于不了解语源、修辞手法生硬等导致的)比喻的乱用,引伸错误〔如 *blind mouth* 的比喻〕.

cat·a·clas·tic [ˌkætəˈklæstik] *a.*【地】碎裂的.

cat·a·cli·nal [ˌkætəˈklainl] *a.*【地】下倾型的.

cat·a·clysm [ˈkætəklizəm] *n.* ①特大洪水. ②【地】(地壳突然隆起而造成的)灾变;天翻地覆;(政治或社会的)大变动,大动乱. **-al, -mic** *a.*

cat·a·comb [ˈkætəkəum] *n.* ①〔常 *pl.*〕地下墓窟. ②酒窖.

cat·ad·ro·mous [kæ'tædrəməs] *a.*【动】(鱼等)下海繁殖的;(为产卵而顺流)入河的，降河性的 (*opp.* anadromous). ~ *fish* 降海[河]产卵鱼.
cat·a·falque ['kætəfælk] *n.* 灵柩台;灵柩车.
Cat·a·lan ['kætələn] *a.* (西班牙)加泰罗尼亚 (Catalonia) 地区的;加泰罗尼亚人[语]的. — *n.* 加泰罗尼亚人[语].
cat·a·lase ['kætəleis] *n.*【生化】过氧化氢酶,接触酶.
cat·a·lec·tic [kætə'lektik] *a.*【诗】最后缺少一音节的,韵脚不完全的.
cat·a·lep·sy ['kætəlepsi], **cat·a·lep·sis** [-'lepsis] *n.*【医】僵住(症状),强直性昏厥,倔强症.
cat·a·lep·tic [ˌkætə'leptik] *a., n.* 僵住症的(患者).
cat·a·lin ['kætəlin] *n.*【商标】铸塑酚醛塑料.
cat·a·lo ['kætələu] *n.* (*pl.* ~,~*s*〔美〕(家牛与野牛杂交生下的)杂种牛.
cat·a·log(ue) ['kætəlɔg] *n.* ①(图书或商品)目录，目录册. ②〔美〕(大学的)学校周年大事表,学校便览. ★ 美语中多用 catalog, 但②义则多用 catalogue. ~ *card* 目录卡. ~ *drawer* 目录抽屉. ~ *of articles for sale* 待售品目录. ~ ***raisonné*** [rezɔ'nei]〔F.〕附有说明的分类目录. — *vt., vi.* ①(为…)编目录,(把…)编目. ②(把…)按目录分类.
ca·ta·log(u)·er ['kætəlɔgə] *n.* 编目者.
ca·tal·pa [kə'tælpə] *n.*【植】梓;〔C-〕梓树属.
ca·tal·y·sis [kə'tælisis] *n.* (*pl.* **-ses** [-si:z])【化】接触反应,触媒作用,催化(作用). ~ **converter** 催化转化器〔汽车上的一种消除污染装置〕.
cat·a·lyst ['kætəlist] *n.*【化】触媒,催化剂,接触剂〔又作 catalytic agent〕;〔喻〕触发因素;〔口〕(善用热情、言语等打动他人的)有感染力的人.
cat·a·lyt·ic [ˌkætə'litik] *a.*【化】催化(的). **-i·cal·ly** *ad.*
cat·a·lyze ['kætəlaiz] *vt.*【化】催化. **-r** 催化剂.
cat·a·ma·ran [ˌkætəmə'ræn] *n.* ①长筏,捆扎筏. ②连筏船;双连小船. ③〔口〕泼妇,悍妇.
cat·a·me·nia [kætə'mi:niə] *n.*〔*pl.*〕【医】月经.
cat·a·mite ['kætəmait] *n.* 娈童.
cat·a·mount, cat·a·moun·tain ['kætəmaunt, ˌkætə'mauntin] *n.*【动】野猫,山猫;〔美〕美洲狮;猞猁狲;〔喻〕爱吵架的人.
Ca·ta·ni·a [kə'teinjə] *n.* 卡塔尼亚〔意大利港市〕.
cat·a·pho·re·sis [ˌkætəfə'ri:sis] *n.*【物、化】阳离子电泳;电(粒)泳.
cat·a·phyll ['kætəˌfil] *n.*【植】低出叶,芽苞叶.
cata·plane ['kætəplein] *n.*【空】弹射(起飞)飞机.
cat·a·pla·si·a [ˌkætə'pleiʒiə] *n.* (*pl.* **-si·ae** [-ʒii:,-zii:])【生】退变. **-plas·tic** [-'plæstik] *a.*
cat·a·plasm ['kætəplæzəm] *n.*【医】糊剂,泥罨[敷]剂.
cat·a·plex·y ['kætəˌpleksi] *n.*【医】猝倒.
cata·pult ['kætəpʌlt] *n.* ①【史】弩炮;石弩. ②〔英〕(儿童玩的)弹弓. ③【军】(导弹、飞机等的)弹射器;弹射座椅. — *vt.* ①用弩炮[弹弓、弹射机]发射;用发射机射出(飞机). ②〔美〕突然把…捧出名. — *vi.* (象被弹射似地)迅猛行动. ~ **passage** 飞机弹射道.
cat·a·ract ['kætərækt] *n.* ①急瀑布,大瀑布;暴雨;奔流. ②【医】(白)内障. ③【机】(矿山唧筒的)水力制动机,节动机. *vt., vi.* (使)象瀑布似地注流.
ca·tarrh [kə'tɑ:] *n.* ①【医】卡他,(鼻)黏膜炎. ②〔英口〕感冒. *bronchial* ~ 支气管炎. **-al, -ous** *a.*
cat·ar·rhine ['kætərain] *n., a.*【动】狭鼻猿(的).
ca·tas·ta·si [kə'tæstəsis] *n.* (*pl.* **-ses** [-ˌsi:z])①(古代戏剧中悲剧收场前或为全剧尾声作伏线的)高潮. ②(修辞中引出主旨的)开端叙述.
ca·tas·tro·phe [kə'tæstrəfi] *n.* ①大变动,突变,激变. ②灾祸,事故;(人生的)灾难,大祸. ③【地】灾变. ④【剧】(尤指悲剧的)结局.
cat·a·stroph·ic [ˌkætə'strɔfik] *a.* ①大突变(灾难)的. ②悲惨结局的.
ca·tas·tro·phism [kə'tæstrəfizəm] *n.* ①【地】灾变说. ②大难难免论,劫数难逃论. **-phist** *n., a.* (信奉)灾变说的(人);(信奉)大难难免论的(人).
cat·a·to·ni·a [ˌkætə'təuniə] *n.*【精】紧张症. **-ton·ic** [-'tɔnik] *a., n.* 紧张症的(患者).
Ca·taw·ba [kə'tɔ:bə] *n.* ①(北美印第安 Sioux 族的)卡托巴部族人;卡托巴语. ②(美国东部产的)卡托巴葡萄;卡托巴白葡萄酒.
catch [kætʃ] *vt.* (***caught*** [kɔ:t]; ***caught***) ①捕捉;逮着,捕获,拦截;用网捕(鸟等);迷惑住. ②看到,看穿,看出,发觉. ③听到,听清;领悟,了解,理会(意味). ④使进退两难,使害怕;(暴风雨等)袭击. ⑤赶(得上)(火车等);追着. ⑥钩住;挂住,绊住;(因说错话等而)突然中止(发言等);【机】挡住;(盆)承受(雨水),接住(球等);【棒球等】接住球(使击球员退出);打(中);碰着;(偶然)碰见. ⑦感染,传染上,患(传染病等). ⑧着(火),烧. ⑨惹得,引起(注意). ⑩遭受(处罚等). ⑪打(个盹),扫(一眼). ⑫〔美俚〕抽(烟). ~ *sb. by the arm* 抓住某人手臂. *be caught red-handed* 当场捉住. *A nail caught her dress.* 钉子挂住了她的衣服. ~ *one's finger in a door* 门夹住指头. *The stone caught me on the nose.* 石头打中我的鼻子. *She caught him one in the eye.* 她在他的眼睛上打了一下. *The wind ~es a sail.* 风顶着船帆. *I caught (a) cold.* 伤了风,招了寒. *The flames caught the adjoining house.* 火延烧到隔壁. ~ *one's breath* 忍住呼吸. *I did not ~ what you said.* 我没有听懂[清]你说什么. ~ *the tune* 听出是什么曲调. *The dog ~es the scent.* 狗闻出臭迹. ~ *a likeness* 画一个像. ~ *a nap* 打个盹. ~ *a glimpse of* 看一眼. — *vi.* ①(想)捉住,(想)抓住 (*at*);(想)领悟 (*at*). ②(门)被闩住,锁住;挂住,绊住,(手指)夹住,(脚)陷进 (*in*);〔英方〕(水)结冰;(声音等)闷住,塞住. ③着火,发火. ④传染;时兴,流行. ⑤【棒球】做接球员. ⑥〔美口〕(庄稼)发芽. ⑦〔英俚〕得人缘. *The match will not ~.* 火柴擦不着. *The kite caught in a tree.* 风筝被树挂住了. *The door lock ~es.* 这把门锁锁得牢. ~ *for the entire game* (打棒球时)整场比赛都当接球手. *Will the disease ~?* 这病有传染性吗? *The lake ~es.*〔英方〕湖面结薄冰了. ***be caught in*** (*the rain, a trap*) 遇(雨);落入(陷阱,圈套). ***be caught over*** (指水面)结满了冰. ~ ***a crab*** (划船时)一桨未划好〔划得过深或未入水〕. ~ ***as*** ~ ***can*** 用尽一切办法,能抓到什么就抓到什么. ~ ***at*** 抓住(东西);欢迎(意见等) (*He caught at the idea.* 他立即采纳了这个意见). ~ ***away*** 攫去,抢去. ~ ***hold of*** 抓住,捉住;乘机抓住(对方的失言). ~ ***it***〔口〕挨骂,受责备,受罚 (*You will ~ it (hot).* 你会受(严厉)责备[处罚]的). ***Catch me*** (*at it, doing that*)!〔口〕你看吧,我决不会干的!(*C- me ever telling him anything again.* 下次决不告诉他了). ~ ***off*** 睡着. ~ ***on***〔口〕①投合人心,受欢迎(*The play caught on well.* 这场戏大受欢迎). ②理解,明白 (*I don't ~ on.* 我不明白). ~ ***one's death*** (***of cold***) 因(重伤风)而死. ~ ***out***【棒球】①接住球使击球员退出. ②看破,看出,发觉 (*He was caught out.* 他的错误被发觉了). ~ ***sb. at*** [***doing***]... ~ ***sb. napping*** 乘某人不注意. ~ ***sb. red-handed*** 当场捉住某人. ~ ***the bird*** 睡午觉. ~ ***the Speaker's eye*** (议会)获准发言. ~ ***up*** ①追着,赶上,与…并驾齐驱 (*to; with*). ②扰乱(说话人). ③立即采纳(新意见、新词等). ④握住,吸住,把…卷入. ⑤把…迅速拿[拾]起来. ⑥指出差错 (*on*) (~ *sb. up on the details* 指出某人所说细节有出入). — *n.* ①捕捉,把握;【棒球】接球,接球员;捕获数,渔获量. ②利益;〔口〕希望得到的东西[人],动心的事物. ③(门的)拉手,把手,门扣,门钩. ④陷阱,圈套,诡计;料不到的困难. ⑤(声息等的)梗塞,噎. ⑥【机】凸轮;制动器,掣子,轮档;抓爪;捕捉器;【化】(接)受器. ⑦【乐】滑稽轮唱歌曲;(歌曲的)片断. ⑧(庄稼的)茁壮. *a good* ~ (*of fish*) 巨大的渔获量. *a great*

～ 红人. *There is a ～ in his question.* 他的问话中有圈套. ***by ～es*** 时而, 常常, 屡(停)屡(作), 时(断)时(续) (*a diary written by ～es* 时断时续地写日记). ***no ～ = not much of a ～*** 买了上当的物品, 不合算的东西. ***the ～ of the season*** 社交季节中男女互相追逐. —*a.* ①引人注意的, 有趣味的. ②设有圈套的. *a ～ phrase* 妙语, 警句. *a ～ question* 设有圈套的问题. **～all** 〔俚〕①*n.* 垃圾箱; 装零杂物品的东西, 手提包; 【化】截液器, 分沫器; 总受器. ②*a.* 包括诸色人等的, 品色复杂的, 包罗一切的. **～-as-～-can** ①*n.* (各种抓法都可使用的)兰开夏式摔跤. ②*a.* 不择手段的; 乱七八糟的; 无计划的, 胡搞的. **～ basin** ①(阴沟等洞口的)滤污器. ②贮水池. **～-colt** 〔美〕私生子. **～ crop** 【农】间作; 填闲作物. **～ cry** (旨在使人注意或争取支持的)呼号〔口号〕. **～ drain** 截水沟; 承水渠. **～fly** 【植】捕蝇麦, 捕蝇草. **～light** 反射光. **～line** 宣传性标语; 【剧】滑稽插话, 噱头. **～penny** *a., n.* 骗钱的(东西), 花哨而不值钱的(东西). **～phrase** 警句, 引人注意的话. **～ pit** = ～ basin. **～pole, ～poll** 法警. **～-stitch** (裁缝的) Z形针迹. **～-up** (生产等停滞后的)加紧弥补. **～up** 〔美〕= ketchup. **～weed** 【植】猪殃殃. **～weight** *a., ad.* (参加比赛者)无体重限制的〔地〕(*a ～weight wrestling match* 无体重限制的摔跤赛). **～word** ①时髦语, 流行语; 标语, 口号. ②(词典的)眉题〔页上标示起迄的词〕. ③【剧】(对话中引起对手接说的)提示语. ④【印】(印在上页右下角的下页首词)提示词.

Catch-22 [ˈkætʃ ˈtwentiˈtuː] *n.* 第二十二条军规, 不可逾越的障碍.

catch-'em-a·live-o [ˈkætʃəməˈlaivəu] *n.* 捕蝇纸.

catch·er [ˈkætʃə] *n.* ①捕捉者. ②捕机; 收集器; 【化】(接)受器. ③【棒球】接球员. *a dust ～* 吸尘器. *a devil ～* 〔美俚〕牧师, 教士.

catch·i·ly [ˈkætʃili] *ad.* ①有吸引力地, 打动人地. ②有欺骗性地, 费解地. ③时断时续地.

catch·i·ness [ˈkætʃinis] *n.* ①吸引性, 动人之处. ②迷惑性, 费解之处. ③断续性.

catch·ing [ˈkætʃiŋ] *a.* ①(疾病)传染性的. ②动人的, 迷人的, 受欢迎的, 有感染力的.

catch·ment [ˈkætʃmənt] *n.* ①排水; 集水. ②贮水池. ③流域. **～area, ～basin** 流域.

catch·y [ˈkætʃi] *a.* ①投合时好的; 动人的, 迷人的. ②(曲调)易记的. ③(问题)费解的; 易使人上当的, 有圈套的. ④断断续续的; 反复不定的.

cate [keit] *n.* 〔古〕美食; 珍馐, 美味; 可口之物.

cat·e·chet·ic, cat·e·chet·i·cal [ˌkætiˈketik(əl)] *a.* ①问答式(教学法)的. ②【宗】教义问答的.

cat·e·chin [ˈkætitʃin, -kin] *n.* 【药】儿茶酸.

cat·e·chism [ˈkætikizəm] *n.* ①问答教学法. ②【宗】教义问答集. ③(口试时的)盘问, 提问. ***put sb. through a ～*** 详细盘问.

cat·e·chist [ˈkætikist] *n.* ①问答式教学者. ②传道师.

cat·e·chize [ˈkætikaiz] *vt.* ①(常指宗教上)用问答法教授. ②盘问.

cat·e·chol [ˈkætitʃəul] *n.* 【药】焦儿茶酚; 邻苯二酚 (= pyrocatechol).

cat·e·chu [ˈkætitʃuː] *n.* 【药】儿茶. *Acacia ～* 【植】儿茶.

cat·e·chu·men [ˌkætiˈkjuːmen] *n.* ①【宗】新入教者; 新信徒. ②初学者, 新来者.

cate·gor·e·mat·ic [ˈkætigɔriˈmætik] *a.* 【逻】可单独使用的 (*opp.* syncategorematic 必须与另一词结合使用的).

cat·e·gor·i·cal [ˌkætiˈgɔrikəl] *a.* ①【哲】范畴的. ②绝对的, 无条件的. ③明确的; 直言的, 断言的. **～ imperative** 【伦】无上命令. **～ judg(e)ment [proposition]** 【逻】直言判断〔命题〕. **-ly** *ad.*

cat·e·go·rize [ˈkætigəraiz] *vt.* 把…分门别类, 把…分类. **-za·tion** [-ˈzeiʃən] *n.*

cat·e·go·ry [ˈkætigəri] *n.* ①类型, 部门, 种类, 类别; 类目. ②【哲、逻】范畴. ③〔*pl.*〕体重等级. *average ～ values* 【数】各处理平均值. *～ of ships* 【军】舰种. *～ of tax* 税目. **～ sales** (书籍)提类销售, 按类发售.

ca·te·na [kəˈtiːnə] *n.* (*pl.* **-nae** [-niː]) 〔L.〕连锁, 连续, 链条. *a ～ of events* 一连串事故.

cat·e·nane [ˈkætnein] *n.* 【化】双环化合物.

ca·te·na·r·i·an, cat·e·nar·y [ˌkætiˈnɛəriən, kəˈtiːnəri] *n., a.* ①链(状的). ②【数】悬链线(状的), 垂曲线(的). ③(电缆)吊线(的). *a ～ bridge* 垂曲线桥.

cat·e·nate [ˈkætineit] *vt.* ①链接; 使连成一串. ②〔喻〕(滚瓜烂熟地)记住.

cat·e·na·tion [ˌkætiˈneiʃən] *n.* ①链接; 耦合. ②熟记.

ca·ten·u·late [kəˈtenjulit, -leit] *a.* 链状的; 链状排列的.

ca·ter[1] [ˈkeitə] *vt.* 为(宴会等)供应酒菜. *～ a party* 为酒会包办酒菜. —*vi.* ①供应伙食, 给人包伙; 包办宴席; 筹办娱乐节目. ②迎合, 投合. *～ for [to] a banquet* 包办酒宴. *～ for [to] sb.'s enjoyments* 设法使某人高兴; 为某人安排娱乐.

cater[2] [ˈkeitə] *n.* (骰子, 纸牌的)四点.

cat·er·an [ˈkætərən] *n.* 〔Scot.〕苏格兰高地的强盗, 绿林好汉, 草莽英雄.

cat·er-cor·nered [ˈkætəˌkɔːnəd] *a.* 对角线的. —*ad.* 成对角线地 (= cater-corner).

ca·ter-cous·in [ˈkeitəˌkʌzn] *n.* 〔古〕密友, 好友.

ca·ter·er [ˈkeitərə] *n.* 包办伙食〔宴席〕的人; (娱乐节目等的)筹办者; 逗人乐的人.

cat·er·pil·lar [ˈkætəpilə] *n.* ①【动】鳞翅目幼虫, 蠋, 毛虫. ②【机】链轨, 履带; 履带拖拉机 (= ～ tractor). ③贪心汉. **～ track [tread]** (坦克车等的)履带. **～ grinder** 链式碎木机. **～ tractor** 〔美〕履带拖拉机.

cat·er·waul [ˈkætəwɔːl] *vi.* (猫)叫春; (象叫春的猫一样)尖叫; 〔蔑〕求爱, 追求. —*n.* 猫的叫春声.

cat·form·ing [ˈkætˌfɔːmiŋ] *n.* 【化】催化重整.

cath- *pref.* 〔用于送气音前〕= *cata-*, 如: *cathode.*

Cath. = Catholic.

cath. = cathedral.

Catha·rine-wheel *n.* = Catherine-wheel.

ca·thar·sis [kəˈθɑːsis] *n.* ①【医】导泻(法), 通便(法); 精神发泄. ②【哲】(通过对悲剧等艺术品的观赏而)感情净化. ③(精神分析学所说通过自觉或表达)忧惧消解.

ca·thar·tic [kəˈθɑːtik] *n.* 【医】泻药. —*a.* 【医】利泻的; 洗涤(胃肠)的 (= cathartical).

Ca·thay [kæˈθei] *n.* 〔古、诗〕中国. **-an** *a.* 中国(人)的.

ca·thect, ca·thec·ti·cize [kæˈθekt, -ˈθektəsaiz] *vt.* (精神分析学所说)精神专注于(某人, 某事或某种想法). **-thec·tic** *a.*

ca·the·dra [kəˈθiːdrə] *n.* ①主教座位. ②(教授的)讲坛, 讲座.

ca·the·dral [kəˈθiːdrəl] *n.* (英国教会等设有主教座位的)总教堂, 大教堂 (= ～ church); 大圣堂, 大会堂. —*a.* ①(象)大教堂的. ②庄严的, 权威的. **～ glass** 嵌花〔马赛克〕玻璃.

ca·thep·sin [kəˈθepsin] *n.* 【生化】组织蛋白酶.

Cath·er [ˈkæðə] *n.* 卡瑟〔姓氏〕.

Cath·er·ine [ˈkæθərin] *n.* 凯瑟琳(女子名). **～ politician** 看风转舵的政治家. **～ wheel** ①轮圈外缘装有倒钩的车轮. ②【建】轮形窗. ③轮形图案. ④轮转烟火. ⑤侧身筋斗 (*turn ～-wheels* 翻侧身筋斗).

cath·e·ter [ˈkæθitə] *n.* 【医】导(液)管. **-ize** *vt.* 在…插入导管.

ca·the·to·me·ter [ˌkæθiˈtɔmitə] *n.* 【物】测高计, 高差计.

ca·thex·is [kəˈθeksis] *n.* (精神分析学中所说的)精神专注〔指精神集中于某人, 某事, 某种想法或自己身上〕.

Cath·leen [ˈkæθliːn] *n.* 凯瑟琳〔女子名，Catherine 的异体〕.

cath·ode [ˈkæθəud] *n.* 【电】阴极，负极. ～ **leg** 阴极引线. ～ **ray** ①(阴极发射出的)高速电子. ②阴极射线. ～**-ray gun** 电子枪.

Cath·o·lic [ˈkæθəlik] *a.* ①天主教的. ②〔c-〕统括一切的,普遍的;宽宏大量的. *Holy ～ Church* 圣公会. *Science is truly c-.* 科学是真正具有普遍性的. *His tastes are very c-.* 他的嗜好很广泛. —*n.* 旧教徒;(尤指)天主教徒;旧教信奉者〔指信奉宗教改革前的教会信条的人〕. **-i·cal·ly** *ad.*

Ca·thol·i·cism [kəˈθɔlisizəm] *n.* ①天主教的信条〔主张〕. ②〔c-〕普遍性;宽宏大量.

cath·o·lic·i·ty [ˌkæθəˈlisiti] *n.* ①普遍性; 宽宏大量. ②〔C-〕= Catholicism.

ca·thol·i·cize [kəˈθɔlisaiz] *vt., vi.* ①(使)一般化,(使)普遍化. ②〔C-〕(使)变成天主教徒.

ca·thol·i·con [kəˈθɔlikən] *n.* ①万灵药. ②〔C-〕(希腊正教的)主教教堂.

cath·o·lyte [ˈkæθəlait] *n.* 【化】阴极电解液.

cath·o·my·cin [ˌkæθəˈmaisin] *n.* 【药】新生霉素.

Cath·ryn [ˈkæθrin] *n.* 凯瑟琳〔女子名, Catherine 的异体〕.

Cathy, Cathie [ˈkæθi] *n.* 凯茜〔女子名, Catherine 的昵称〕.

Cat·i·li·nar·i·an [ˌkætələˈnɛəriən] *a.* 从事阴谋〔叛逆〕活动的〔源出罗马进行阴谋活动的政治家 Catilina〕. —*n.* 参加阴谋活动的人;阴谋家.

cat·i·on [ˈkætaiən] *n.* 【化】阳离子, 正离子 (*opp.* anion).

cat·ish [ˈkætiʃ] *a.* 〔美俚〕美的;漂亮的.

cat·kin [ˈkætkin] *n.* 【植】葇荑花序;杨花;柳絮.

cat·like [ˈkætˌlaik] *a.* 如猫的;无声的,偷偷的.

cat·ling [ˈkætliŋ] *n.* ①小猫. ②(外科用)双刃小刀. ③肠线; 〔*pl.*〕弦乐器.

cat·mint [ˈkætmint] *n.* 【植】猫薄荷.

cat·nip [ˈkætnip] *n.* 〔美〕= catmint.

C.A.T.O. = catapult-assisted take-off【空】弹射起飞.

Ca·to [ˈkeitəu] *n.* ①加图〔人名〕. ②**Marcus Porcius** ～ 老加图〔234—149 B.C.,罗马政治家,将军〕. ③**Marcus Porcius** ～ 小加图〔95—46 B.C., 罗马斯多噶派哲学家,政治家,为老加图之曾孙〕.

cat-o'-moun·tain [ˌkætəˈmauntn] *n.* = catamountain.

cat-o'-nine-tails [ˌkætəˈnainˌteilz] *n.* (*pl.* **-tails**) 九尾鞭.

ca·top·tric [kəˈtɔptrik] *a.* 【物】反射(镜)的. ～ **system** 反射光组.

ca·top·trics [kəˈtɔptriks] *n.* 【物】反射光学.

Cats·kill Mountains [ˈkætskil] 卡茨基尔山〔美国纽约州东部山脉〕(= the Catskills).

cat·sup [ˈkætsəp] *n.* 番茄酱〔沙司〕(= ketchup).

cat·(t)a·lo [ˈkætələu] *n.* 〔美〕(野牛和家牛杂交生下的)杂种牛.

Cat·tell [kæˈtel] *n.* 卡特尔〔姓氏〕.

cat·tery [ˈkætəri] *n.* ①养猫场. ②〔美俚〕妇女团体〔公寓〕,女生宿舍.

cat·ti·ly [ˈkætili] *ad.* ①敏捷地. ②狡猾地, 恶毒地. **cat·ti·ness** *n.*

cat·tish [ˈkætiʃ] *a.* 猫一般的;狡猾而阴险的; 心怀不良的.

cat·tle [ˈkætl] *n.* 〔*sing., pl.*〕①牛;家畜; 〔俚〕马,牲口. ②〔骂〕畜生. ③〔美俚〕女学生. *beef [dairy]* ～ 肉〔奶〕牛. ～ *breeding* 畜牧(业). ～ *for dual-purpose* 乳肉兼用牛. *C- low.* 牛叫. *kittle* ～ 难以应付的人〔事〕. ～**-lifter** 偷牛贼, 偷家畜的贼. ～**-lifting** 偷牛. ～ **leader** 牛鼻环. ～**man** 〔英〕牧〔养〕牛人;〔美〕牧场主. ～ **pen** 牛栏,牛圈,畜槛. ～ **piece** (风景画家的)家畜画,牧牛图. ～ **plague** 牛疫. ～ **rustler** 〔美〕偷牛贼. ～ **show** 家畜〔畜牛〕展览会.

cat·tle·ya [ˈkætliə; kætˈliə, -ˈleiə] *n.* 【植】卡特来兰属植物.

cat·ty[1] [ˈkæti] *n.* 斤〔东方各国的重量单位,约 0.5—0.6 kg.〕,(中国的)斤.

cat·ty[2] [ˈkæti] *a.* = cattish.

CATV = Community antenna television 有线电视.

Cau·ca·sia [kɔːˈkeiziə] *n.* 高加索(高原)〔苏联〕.

Cau·ca·sian [kɔːˈkeiziən] *a.* ①高加索的;高加索人的,高加索语的. ②【人类】白种人的. —*n.* ①高加索人;高加索语. ②【人类】白种人.

Cau·ca·soid [ˈkɔːkəsɔid] *a.* 高加索人种群的. —*n.* 高加索种群的人.

Cau·ca·sus [ˈkɔːkəsəs] *n.* ①高加索山脉〔苏联〕(= the ～ Mountains). ②= Caucasia.

cau·cus [ˈkɔːkəs] *n.* 〔美〕(政党等的)干部会议; 秘密会议;核心小组; 〔英〕(有决策权的)地方议员会决策委员会. —*vi.* 〔美〕召开〔参加〕干部(秘密)会议; 〔英〕采用地方议员会议制度,由地方议员会议决定.

cau·dad [ˈkɔːdæd] *ad.* 【解、动】向尾,向后;在后部.

cau·dal [ˈkɔːdl] *a.* 【解、动】尾的;尾部〔侧〕的;尾状的. ～ *fin* 尾鳍. ～ *appendage* 尾.

cau·date, cau·dat·ed [ˈkɔːdeit(id)] *a.* 【动】有尾的.

cau·dil·lo [kɔːˈdiːljəu] *n.* 〔Sp.〕军事首脑;总指挥,(尤指游击队的)领导人.

cau·dle [ˈkɔːdl] *n.* (病人食用的)粥汤〔粥中加入葡萄酒、香料、鸡蛋等〕.

caught [kɔːt] catch 的过去式及过去分词.

caul [kɔːl] *n.* ①【解】胎膜; 大网膜. ②(旧时妇女的)发网,户内妇女头饰的后部.

caul- *comb. f.* = caulo- 〔用于元音前〕.

caul·dron [ˈkɔːldrən] *n.* = caldron.

cau·les·cent [kɔːˈlesnt] *a.* 【植】有茎的.

cau·li·flow·er [ˈkɔliflauə] *n.* ①【植】花椰菜, 菜花. ②〔Scot.〕啤酒泡. ③〔美俚〕(在拳击中打残废的)菜花耳(= ～ ear). ～ **code** 〔美俚〕拳赛规则. **C- Garden** 〔美〕= Madison Square Garden (纽约市的)麦迪逊广场花园. ～ **vernacular** 〔美〕拳击用语〔行话〕.

cau·line [ˈkɔːlain] *n.* 【植】茎(上)的;茎上部的.

cau·lis [ˈkɔːlis] *n.* (*pl.* **-les** [-liːz]) 【植】茎.

caulk [kɔːk] *vt.* ①用麻丝填塞(船缝). ②堵(缝). ③【机】敛(钢板的)铆缝〔锤打铆好的钢板, 使铆缝不致漏水、气〕. **-er** 填船缝工,敛铆缝工;堵缝的人; 堵缝工具. **-ing** *n.* 堵缝;敛缝;挤缝,冲缝;砸边.

caulo- *comb. f.* 表示植物的"柄,茎": *caulo*caline.

cau·lo·ca·line [ˌkɔːləuˈkeiliːn] *n.* 【植】成茎素.

caus. = causative.

caus·a·ble [ˈkɔːzəbl] *a.* 可被引起的. **-a·bil·i·ty** *n.*

caus·al [ˈkɔːzəl] *a.* ①(有)原因的; 构成原因的;因果律的;【逻】表示原因的. ②因果关系的. ～ *relation* 因果关系. *a* ～ *force* 构成原因的力量. —*n.* 【语法】表示原因的词〔结构〕. **-ly** *ad.*

cau·sal·gi·a [kɔːˈzældʒiə, -dʒi] *n.* 【医】灼痛.

cau·sal·i·ty [kɔːˈzæliti] *n.* ①因果关系, 因果性. ②诱发性;原因作用. *the law of* ～ 因果律.

cau·sa si·ne qua non [ˈkɔːzə ˈsaini kwei ˈnɔn] 〔L.〕不可缺少的原因〔条件〕,必要原因〔条件〕.

cau·sa·tion [kɔːˈzeiʃən] *n.* ①引起,惹起,导致. ②因果关系. ③原因作用,原因力. *the law of* ～ 因果律.

caus·a·tive [ˈkɔːzətiv] *a.* ①成为…的原因的,惹起…的. ②【语法】使役的. **be** ～ **of** 为…的原因, 引起…. ～ **agent** 【医】病原体. ～ **value** 发展价值. ～ **verb** 使役动词. —*n.* 【语法】使役词,使役形式.

cause [kɔːz] *n.* ①原因,起因;缘故,理由,根据,动机. ②【法】诉讼事由;诉讼案件;诉讼程序. ③事业,事项,事件;(奋斗的)目标;问题. ④主张,主义,目的,…运动. *the formal* ～ 形式原因. *the immanent [transient]* ～ 内

〔外〕因. *the immediate [remote]* ～ 近〔远〕因. *the occasional* ～ 偶因,机缘. *a* ～ *for (complaint)* (抱怨)的原因〔理由〕. ～ *and effect* 原因与结果, 因果. ～ *of (revolution)* (革命)事业. *the temperance* ～ 戒酒运动. ***have* ～ *for*** *(joy)* 有理由(高兴),当然(高兴),应当(高兴). ***in the* ～ *of*** 为…(而工作等). ***make common* ～ *with*** 与…协力,与…合作, 和…一致. ***plead one's* ～** 辩护,分辩. ***show* ～**【法】提出理由,说明所以然. ***the first* ～**【哲】第一推动力;【宗】造物主;上帝 ***without (due)* ～** 无缘无故. —*vt.* ①成为…的原因,惹起,引起,使发生. ②使遭受,给…带来,致使. ～ *sb.'s ruin* 致使某人身败名裂. ***be* ～*d by*** 起因于,因…而起. ～ *(sb.) to (do)* 促使(人)(作)…. ～ *(sth.) to be (done)* 叫人(做)(某事、物)(*He* ～*d a house to be built.* 他叫人盖了一所房子).

'cause [kɔːz] *conj.*〔口〕= because.

cause cé·lèb·re [kəuz seˈlebr] (*pl.* ***causes cé·lèb·res*** [kəuz seˈlebr])〔F.〕著名的〔轰动一时的〕讼案〔论战〕.

cause·less [ˈkɔːzlis] *a.* 无原因的;无理由的;偶然的.

caus·er [ˈkɔːzə] *n.* 引起者;根由.

cau·se·rie [ˈkəuzəri(ː)] *n.*〔F.〕(*pl.* ～*s* [-z]) ①漫谈,非正式讨论. ②(报章杂志上的)随笔,随感录.

cause·way, causey [ˈkɔːzwei, -zei] *n.* ①(低湿地中的)堤道. ②(比马路高的)人行道. ③公路. — *vt.* 在…上〔穿过…〕修建堤道〔人行道,公路〕.

caus·tic [ˈkɔːstik] *a.* ①【化】腐蚀性的; 苛性的. ②讽刺的,刻薄的, 挖苦的. ③【物】焦散的. ～ *comments* 尖刻的评论. — *n.* ①刻薄;讽刺. ②【医】腐蚀剂. ③【物】焦散面;〔*pl.*〕焦散线. ④【化】苛性碱. *common [lunar]* ～【化】硝酸银. ～ **curve**【物】焦散曲线. ～ **potash**【化】苛性钾, 氢氧化钾. ～ **silver** 硝酸银. ～ **soda**【化】苛性钠〔苏打〕,氢氧化钠,烧碱. ～ **surface**【物】焦散面. **-al·ly** *ad.*

caus·tic·i·ty [kɔːsˈtisiti] *n.* 腐蚀性; 苛性度; (言语等的)刻薄,辛辣.

caus·tic·i·za·tion [ˌkɔːstisaiˈzeiʃən] *n.*【化】苛化作用.

cau·ter·ant [ˈkɔːtərənt] *a.* (能)烧灼的. — *n.* 烙器,烙铁;有烧灼作用的物质.

cau·ter·i·za·tion [ˌkɔːtəraiˈzeiʃən] *n.* ①【医】烧灼,烙,腐蚀(作用). ②(良心等的)麻木.

cau·ter·ize [ˈkɔːtəraiz] *vt.* ①【医】烙,烧灼; 腐蚀. ②使(良心等)麻木.

cau·ter·y [ˈkɔːtəri] *n.* ①【医】烧灼(术),烙(术), 腐蚀. ②烧灼器,烙器. ③烧灼剂,腐蚀剂.

cau·tion [ˈkɔːʃən] *n.* ①小心,谨慎, 慎重. ②警惕;告诫,警告. ③〔Scot.〕【法】担保,保证. ④〔口〕须警惕的事〔人〕;怪物,怪人. *Well, you're a* ～*!* 你这个要提防的家伙! 我可要留心你! ***exercise [use]* ～** 小心, 谨慎. ***fling* ～ *to the winds*** 不顾一切,莽撞从事. ***for* ～*'s sake*** 为慎重起见. ***give* ～ *to*** 警告,训诫. ***take* ～ *against*** 防备, 提防, 留心. ***with* ～** 留心,慎重. — *vt.* 使小心, 警告 (*against, to do, not to do*); 告诫. — *vi.* 告诫 (*against*). ～ **money**〔英〕大学入学保证金;法学协会入会保证金.

cau·tion·a·ry [ˈkɔːʃənəri] *a.* ①警戒的,提醒注意的;告诫的. ②〔Scot.〕担保的, 保证的. ～ *advice* 忠告. ～ *tales* 警诫性的故事.

cau·tious [ˈkɔːʃəs] *a.* 谨慎的,小心的. ***be* ～ *of*** 留意,谨防. **-ly** *ad.* **-ness** *n.*

cav·al·cade [ˌkævəlˈkeid] *n.* ①骑兵队;车队;船队; 一队人马. ②游行队伍.

cav·a·lier [ˌkævəˈliə] *n.* ①骑士; (某种)勋章获得者. ②骑士风度的男子, 向妇女献殷勤的男子. ③〔美俚〕拳击选手. ④〔C-〕【英史】(查理一世时代的)保王党党员. — *a.* ①豪爽的,满不在乎的;勇敢的;傲慢的. ②骑士风度的,向女子献殷勤的. ③〔C-〕(查理一世时代)保王党的. *He treated us in a* ～ *fashion.* 他待我们很不客气. — *vt.* ①护送(女人),(对女子)有骑士风度. ②态度傲慢. **-ly** *ad.*

ca·val·la [kəˈvælə] *n.* (*pl.* ***-la, -las***)【动】①巨鲐,马鲛鱼(= cero). ②长面鲹(= crevalle). ★上列两种鱼,在英国亦称 horse mackerel.

cav·al·ry [ˈkævəlri] *n.* ①〔集合词〕(一队)骑兵;骑兵队. ②〔集合词〕骑者;马;〔废〕马术. ③【军】高度机动的地面部队. *heavy [light]* ～ 重〔轻〕骑兵. *a* ～ *orderly* 骑兵传令兵. ～**man** 骑兵. ～ **twill** 马裤呢.

ca·vate [ˈkeiveit] *a.* 挖空岩石而成的;形成〔象〕山洞的.

cav·a·ti·na [ˌkævəˈtiːnə] *n.* (*pl.* ***-ne*** [-nei])〔It.〕【乐】短抒情曲;(歌剧中的)独唱短曲.

cave[1] [keiv] *n.* ①洞,穴,岩洞;〔方〕地窖. ②【英史】(从自由党分离出来的)分离派; 脱党(者). ～ *period* 穴居时代. — *vt.* ①在…挖洞. ②使陷下;使倒坍;使崩溃. ③暗中破坏. — *vi.* ①陷下,倒坍. ②投降,停止抵抗. ～ ***(back) over*** 倒下,翻转. ～ ***in*** ①(地面)下陷,塌陷;(墙壁、帽子)凹进去,塌. ②〔口〕屈服,投降;〔美〕倒塌. ～ **dweller** (史前的)穴居人;〔口〕(都市高层住宅的)大楼居民. ～ **dwelling [house]** 窑洞. ～**-in** ①〔口〕陷落(处),塌方. ②投降;失败,堕落.

ca·ve[2] [ˈkeivi] *int.* 〔英学俚〕小心〔老师来了〕! ***keep* ～** (学生干坏事时)把风.

ca·ve·at [ˈkeiviæt] *n.* ①【法】中止诉讼的申请;〔美〕保护发明特许权的请求书;【商】停止支付的通知. ②防止误解的说明; ③要求停止某些行动的告诫, 警告. ***enter [put in] a* ～** 提出中止某事的申请.

ca·ve·at emp·tor [ˈkeiviæt ˈemptɔː]〔L.〕【商】购者留心〔货物出门概不退换〕.

ca·ve ca·nem [ˈkɑːvei ˈkɑːnəm]〔L.〕当心恶犬!

Cav·ell [ˈkævl, kəˈvel] *n.* 卡维尔〔姓氏〕.

cave-man [ˈkeivmæn] *n.* ①(史前)穴居人; 野蛮人. ②〔喻〕(感情,行为等)粗野的人(尤指对待妇女). ～ **stuff**〔美俚〕野蛮的求爱,强奸.

Cav·en·dish [ˈkævəndiʃ] *n.* 卡文迪什〔姓氏〕.

cav·en·dish [ˈkævəndiʃ] *n.* (压成块的)板烟.

cav·ern [ˈkævən] *n.* 大山洞, 大洞穴. — *vt.* ①置…于山洞中. ②挖空 (*out*). *The rock was* ～*ed out to make a tunnel.* 挖空岩石造隧道. **-ed** [-d] *a.* 有洞穴的;洞窟状的;在洞穴中的.

cav·ern·ous [ˈkævənəs] *a.* ①洞穴(状)的;(眼等)凹的;塌的. ②多洞穴的. ③瓮音的. ④多孔的, 海绵状的. ～ **body** 海绵体. ～ **roar** (狮子的)瓮音式吼声.

cave(s)son [ˈkævisən] *n.* (训练马时用的)鼻勒, 鼻带〔马具〕.

ca·vet·to [kəˈvetəu] *n.* (*pl.* ***-vetti*** [-veti], ***-vettos***)【建】截面为九十度弧的凹线脚.

ca·vi·ar(e) [ˈkæviɑː] *n.* ①(俄式)鱼子酱; 美味. ②〔俚〕被检查员涂掉的句子. ～ ***to the general*** 曲高和寡的事物.

cav·il [ˈkævil] *vi.* (**-ll-**) 挑剔, 吹毛求疵 (*at; about*). — *vt.* 对…挑剔,对…吹毛求疵. — *n.* 无端指摘, 吹毛求疵. **-(l)er** *n.* 吹毛求疵的人.

cav·i·ta·tion [ˌkæviˈteiʃən] *n.* ①【空】气穴现象;气涡现象. ②【物】成穴,空化;(超声波的)空穴作用;【医】成洞,成腔. ～ **tunnel**【船】空泡式验筒.

cav·i·ty [ˈkæviti] *n.* ①【解】穴,窝,盂,腔;空腔;【医】(空)洞. ②【物】模槽;气蚀区;空腔谐振器;【原】(反应堆中的)小室,暗盒. *the abdominal [mouth]* ～ 腹〔口〕腔. *the* ～ *in a tooth* 齿窝. ～ **magnetron** 发电力巨大的磁控管. **vortex** ～ 涡流区.

ca·vo-ri·lie·vo [ˈkævəuriliˈeivəu] *n.* (*pl.* ～*s*)〔It.〕【美】凹浮雕,沉雕.

ca·vort [kəˈvɔːt] *vi.* ①〔美口〕(马)跳跃, (骑者)骑马腾跃. ②放荡地玩乐.

ca·vort·ings [kəˈvɔːtiŋz] *n.* 下流放荡的行为.

CAVU = ceiling and visibility unlimited【空】云高及

可见度无限制.

ca·vy [ˈkeivi] *n.* 【动】天竺鼠,豚鼠.

caw [kɔː] *vi.* (乌鸦)哇哇地叫; (人)乌鸦似地叫 *(out)*. — *n.* 乌鸦的叫声.

Cax·ton [ˈkækstən] *n.* ①卡克斯顿〔姓氏〕. ②**William** ~ 威廉·卡克斯顿〔1422?—1491, 最初把印刷术传入英国的人〕. ③〔*pl.*〕卡克斯顿版本;卡克斯顿活字.

cay [kei] *n.* 珊瑚礁;沙洲,小岛.

Cay·enne [keiˈen] *n.* 卡宴〔圭亚那(法)首府〕.

cay·enne [keiˈen] *n.* 辣椒(粉) (=~ pepper).

cay·man [ˈkeimən] *n.* 【动】(中南美的)大鳄鱼.

Cay·man Is·lands [ˈkeimən ˈailəndz] *n.* 开曼群岛(英)〔拉丁美洲〕.

Ca·yu·ga [keiˈjuːɡə, kai-] *n.* *(pl. ~s, ~)* ①卡育加人〔易洛魁印第安人的一个部族,居住于纽约州卡育加湖一带〕. ②卡育加语. ~ **Lake** 卡育加湖.

cay·use [kaiˈjuːs] *n.* ①〔美西部〕印第安种小马,〔口〕马.②卡育斯人〔俄勒冈州东北部山区印第安人的一个部族〕.

cazic, ca·zique [kəˈziːk] *n.* = cacique.

CB = ① construction battalion 〔美军〕修建营. ②= chemical and biological 化学及生物的.

C.B. = ①Cape Breton 【地】布雷顿角. ②Chirurgiae Baccalaureus 外科学士. ③Companion of the Bath. 〔英〕(第三等的) 最低级巴斯勋位爵士. ④= citizens band 〔美〕私人波段〔政府拨给私人无线电通讯使用的波段〕.

C.B., c.b., CB = confinement to barracks 〔美军〕禁止外出.

c.b. = centre of buoyancy 【物】浮心.

Cb =①【化】(= columbium) 钶〔niobium 铌的旧名〕. ②【气】cumulonimbus 积雨云.

CBC = Canadian Broadcasting Corporation 加拿大广播公司.

CBD = cash before delivery 【商】交货前付款.

C.B.E. = Commander (of the Order) of the British Empire (第二等的)高级英帝国勋位爵士.

C.B.E.L., CBEL = Cambridge Bibliography of English Literature 〔英〕《剑桥(大学)英国文学书目》〔期刊名称〕.

C.B.er [ˈsiːbiːə] *n.* (政府拨给的) 私人无线电通讯波段使用者.

CBR = chemical, bacteriological, and radiological 化学的、细菌学的和放射学的.

CBS = Columbia Broadcasting System 〔美〕哥伦比亚广播公司.

CBU = cluster bomb unit 集束炸弹(装置).

CBW = chemical and biological warfare 化学生物战.

C.C. = ①compte courant (〔F.〕 = current account 往来帐户,存款帐户). ②cashier's check 〔美〕(银行)本票.③Circuit Court 巡回法庭. ④City Council(lor) 市议员. ⑤Civil Court 民事法庭. ⑥Common Councilman〔美〕市政会成员,地方议会议员. ⑦County Council 〔英〕郡议会. ⑧County Court 〔英〕郡法院. ⑨Cricket Club 板球俱乐部.

cc.=chapters.

cc.,c.c.= ①carbon copy 复写本. ②cubic centimeter 立方厘米. ③ centre to centre 中心间距,轴间距.

C.C.A. = ①carrier controlled approach (system) (航空母舰)舰控飞机进场指挥(系统). ②Circuit Court of Appeals 〔美〕巡回上诉法院.

C.C.C. = Corpus Christi College 【英宗】基督圣体节学院.

C.C.P. = Court of Common Pleas 〔英〕高等民事法庭; 〔美〕中级民事及刑事法庭.

C.Cr.P. = Code of Criminal Procedure 刑法典.

CCS = Combined Chiefs Staff 〔旧〕(英美)参谋长联席会议.

C.C.S. = Casualty Clearing Station 伤员后送站.

CCTV = closed-circuit television 闭路式电视, 工业电视.

CCUS = Chamber of Commerce of the U.S. 美国商会.

ccw = counterclockwise 反时针(方向).

Cd = cadmium 【化】镉.

cd. = cord ①绳,索. ②木材堆的体积单位.

CD =①coastal defense 海岸防御,海防. ②civil defense 民防.

C/D, c/d = certificate of deposit 存款单,存据.

c.d. = ①cash discount 【商】付现折扣. ②cum dividend 附有红利,附股息.

Cdr., CDR = Commander.

Ce = cerium 【化】元素铈的符号.

C.E. = ①Chemical Engineer 化学工程师. ② Chief Engineer 总工程师;【海】轮机长; 工兵主任. ③Church of England 【宗】英国国教, 圣公会. ④Civil Engineer 土木工程师. ⑤Council of Europe 欧洲理事会.

-ce *comb. f.* 构成抽象名词 (= 〔L.〕-tia): diligen*ce*, indigen*ce*.

CEA =①Commodity Exchange Authority 〔美〕(农业部)农产品交易管理局. ②council of Economic Advisers 〔美〕(总统) 经济顾问委员会.

ce·a·no·thus [ˌsiːəˈnəuθəs] *n.* 【植】(鼠李科的)美洲茶(属); 美洲茶〔所含生物碱可作泻剂〕.

cease [siːs] *vi.* ˈ停,终止,息. ~ *from quarrelling* 停止吵闹. *The rain has ~d.* 雨停了. *vt.* 停止,结束. ~ *payment* 停止支付. *Cease fire!* 【军】〔命令〕停火,停止射击. ~ ***out*** 绝迹. ~ ***to be*** *(sth.)* 不再是(某事物). ~ ***to exist*** 不再存在, 死亡; 灭亡. ★ cease *(to do; doing)*是书面语,现在普通说 stop *(doing)*. — *n.* 终止,停止 〔现在仅用于成语 without ~ 中〕. ***without*** ~ 不断地,不停地. ~**-fire** 停战 (*a ~-fire agreement* 停战协定).

cease·less [ˈsiːslis] *a.* 不停的,不绝的, 无限的. **-ly** *ad.* 不断地. **-ness** *n.*

ceas·ing [ˈsiːsiŋ] *n.* 终止,停止,间断.

Ce·bu [seˈbuː] *n.* ①宿务岛〔菲律宾〕. ②宿务〔菲律宾港市〕.

CECF = Chinese Export Commodities Fair 中国出口商品交易会.

ce·cidi·um [seˈsidiəm] *n.* 【动、植】瘿.

Ce·cil [ˈsesl, ˈsisl] *n.* 塞西尔〔姓氏,男子名〕.

Ce·cile [ˈsesil, ˈsesiːl] *n.* 塞西尔〔女子名, Cecilia 的异体〕.

Ce·cil·ia [siˈsiljə] *n.* 塞西莉亚〔女子名〕.

Cec·i·ly [ˈsisili] *n.* 塞西莉〔女子名〕.

ce·ci·ty [ˈsiːsiti] *n.* 〔古〕(精神上的)盲目.

ce·cro·pi·a moth [siˈkrəupiə mɔθ] *n.* 【动】天蚕蛾 *(Samia cecropia)*.

ce·cum [ˈsiːkəm] *n.* *(pl. -ca* [-kə]*)* ①【解】盲肠; 盲端. ②【动】单向腔孔 (= caecum). **ce·cal** [ˈsiːkəl] *a.*

CED = ①cohesive energy density 内聚能密度. ②Committee for Economic Development 〔美〕经济开发委员会.

ce·dar [ˈsiːdə] *n.* 【植】①雪松; 雪松木,杉木杆. ②香椿. ~ **wood** 雪松属木料,杉木.

ce·darn [ˈsiːdən] *a.* 〔诗〕雪松(制)的,杉木(制)的.

cede [siːd] *vt.* 让与,割让,放弃(权利、领土等). ~ *territory to ...* 向…割让领土. ~ *a point in debate* 在某一争论点上让步. **-er** *n.* 割让者,让步者.

ce·di [ˈsediː] *n.* *(pl. -dis)* 塞地〔加纳货币单位〕.

ce·dil·la [siˈdilə] *n.* 【语】(法语某些词中字母c下的)勾形符号(ˌ) 〔表示 a, o, u 前的c 为 [s] 音: *façade*〕.

ce·drol [ˈsiːdrɔːl] *n.* 【化】雪松醇, 雪松脑〔亦称柏木脑〕.

ced·u·la [ˈsedʒulə] *n.* (西班牙语国家所颁发的)证明书，证件，执照.

cee [siː] *n.* (英语字母) C, c. — *a.* C字形的. *a Cee-spring* 【机】(支持车身的) C形弹簧 (= C spring).

cei·ba [ˈseibə, saibə] *n.* ①【植】吉贝〔木棉科植物〕; 木棉树. ②木棉花; 木棉.

ceil [siːl] *vt.* ①在…装天花板; 在…装壁板. ②在(木船)上装船底隔板.

ceil·ing [ˈsiːliŋ] *n.* ①天花板，顶板，顶篷. ②(垫船底的)隔板，舱室垫板. ③(物价、工资等的)最高限度 *(opp.* floor*)*; 【空】升限，上升限度; 云幕高度，低层云与地面间的距离 (= ~ height). *hit the* ~〔美俚〕①发脾气; 生气. ②(大学里)考试不及格. ~ **capacity** 【空】上升能力. ~ **height** 【空】升限.

ceil·o·me·ter [siːˈlɔmitə] *n.* 【空】云高计; 【气】云幕计.

cel. = celebrated.

cel·a·don [ˈselədɔn] *n.* ①灰绿色. ②青瓷色. ③(中国产的)青瓷器. — *a.* 青瓷色的.

cel·an·dine [ˈseləndain] *n.* 【植】白屈菜.

cel·an·ese [ˌseləˈniːz] *n.* 【商标】纤烷丝〔一种人造丝〕.

-cele *comb. f.* 肿，曲张: varicocele.

celeb [siˈleb] *n.* 〔美口〕名人; 要人.

cel·e·brant [ˈselibrənt] *n.* ①司仪神父，主持弥撒的神父. ②参加庆祝典礼的人. ③(某一事物或人的)赞赏者.

cel·e·brate [ˈselibreit] *vt.* ①举行(仪式); 庆祝(胜利等). ②表扬，赞美，歌颂. ③公布，发表. ~ *a marriage* 举行婚礼. ~ *one's birthday* 庆祝生日，做生日. *a man* ~*d in the headlines* 被报纸大加表扬的人. — *vi.* ①举行宗教仪式〔庆典〕. ②〔口〕欢宴作乐. **-brat·er, -brat·or** *n.* 庆祝的人.

cel·e·brat·ed [ˈselibreitid] *a.* 驰名的，有名的，大名鼎鼎的.

cele·bra·tion [ˌseliˈbreiʃən] *n.* ①庆祝，庆祝会. ②(某些宗教性的)仪式; (尤指)圣餐礼(的举行). ③称赞，赞美. *in* ~ *of* 为庆祝…. *hold a* ~ 举行庆祝会.

ce·leb·ri·ty [siˈlebriti] *n.* ①名声，扬名. ②名人，知名之士. *of great* ~ 大名鼎鼎的.

ce·le·ri·ac [səˈleriæk] *n.* 【植】块根芹 *(Apium graveolens rapaceum)*.

ce·ler·i·ty [siˈleriti] *n.* 〔书〕(行动的)迅速，神速; 敏捷.

cel·er·y [ˈseləri] *n.* 【植】芹菜. ~ **cabbage** (中国)白菜. **wild** ~ 【药】独活.

ce·les·ta [siˈlestə] *n.* 【乐】钢片琴.

ce·leste [siˈlest] *n.* ①天蓝色. ②(风琴的)音节栓. — *a.* 天蓝色的.

ce·les·tial [siˈlestjəl, siˈlestʃəl] *a.* ①天的，天空的; 天上的; 天体的. ②天国的; 神圣的. ③〔C-〕中国的，天朝的〔指封建时代的中国〕. ④天体导航法的. *the C- City* 【宗】天国. *the C- Empire* 天朝〔指封建时代的中国〕. — *n.* ①天人，神仙. ②〔C-〕(指封建时代的)中国人，天朝之人. ~ **body** 天体. ~ **fire** 诗的灵感. ~ **globe** 天球仪. ~ **fix** 天体导航法测定船位. ~ **latitude** *[longitude]* 黄纬〔经〕. ~ **mechanics** 天体力学. **-ly** *ad.* **-ness** *n.*

cel·es·tine [ˈselistin, -tain; siˈlestin] *n.* 天青石(= celestite).

cel·es·tite [ˈselistait] *n.* 【矿】天青石.

Cel·ia [ˈsiːljə] *n.* 西莉亚〔女子名，Cecilia 的昵称〕.

ce·li·ac [ˈsiːliæk] *a.* 【解】腹的，腹腔的.

cel·i·ba·cy [ˈselibəsi] *n.* ①独身(生活). ②禁欲，贞洁.

cel·i·ba·tar·i·an [ˌselibəˈteəriən] *n., a.* 独身主义者(的).

cel·i·bate [ˈselibit] *n., a.* 独身者(的).

cell [sel] *n.* ①小室，单室; 隔间，舱; 〔诗〕茅舍; (单个的)蜂窝，蜂房. ②〔诗〕墓穴，墓. ③(大修道院附属的)小修道院. ④单人牢房. ⑤【生】细胞; 【电】电池; 元件; 【建】(天花板的)方格板; 隔板; 【空】机翼构架; 【原】晶格，晶胞; 【计】单元，元件; 【植】花粉囊; 药室; (气球等的)气囊. 【气】单体，环型. ⑥基层组织，小组. ⑦管，盒，槽. *a queen [royal]* ~ (养蜂)王台. *the phase* ~【统】相格. *a secondary* ~ 蓄电池. *a photosensitive* ~【无】光电管. *a rectifier* ~【无】整流片. *the narrow* ~ 墓. ~**block** (若干牢房组成的)监狱分区. ~ **division** 细胞分裂. ~ **lumina** 空胞. ~ **membrane [wall]** 细胞膜〔壁〕. ~ **nucleus** 细胞核; 窝，凹处.

cel·la [ˈselə] *n.* 【建】(希腊神庙的内殿)神坛.

cel·lar [ˈselə] *n.* ①地窖，地下室; 〔英〕(都市住宅的)地下煤窖. ②地下酒窖; 窖藏(葡萄)酒. ③【机】油盒. *a salt* ~ 盐瓶. ~ *smaller* 〔美〕酒徒. ~ *tenants* 【美体】比赛中成绩最坏的一队. *the* ~ 〔口〕(竞赛组别中的)最低级位. *from* ~ *to rafter* 楼上楼下. *keep a good [small]* ~ 藏有大量〔少量〕的酒. — *vt.* 把…藏入地窖〔酒窖〕.

cel·lar·age [ˈseləridʒ] *n.* ①〔总称〕地窖. ②窖藏费. ③地窖的容积.

cel·lar·er [ˈselərə] *n.* ①管窖人; 酒窖管理员; (寺院等的)食品管理员. ②酒商.

cel·lar·et(te) [ˌseləˈret] *n.* (餐馆的)酒柜; 酒橱.

cel·lar·way [ˈseləˌwei] *n.* 〔美〕地窖入口〔尤指梯口〕.

celled [seld] *a.* 含有(某种或若干)细胞〔小单位、小室等〕的〔一般用作构词成分〕. *a single-*~ *organism* 单细胞生物.

cel·list, 'cel·list [ˈtʃelist] *n.* 大提琴演奏者 (= violoncellist).

cel·lo, 'cel·lo [ˈtʃeləu] *n. (pl.* ~*s)* ①【乐】大提琴 (= violoncello). ②〔美俚〕嗄嗓子女演员.

cel·loi·din [siˈlɔidn] *n.* (制作显微镜切片用的)火棉.

cel·lo·phane [ˈseləfein] *n.* 玻璃纸; 胶膜，赛璐珞.

cel·lu·lar [ˈseljulə] *a.* ①【生】细胞的，细胞质〔状〕的. ②【建】区划〔分格〕式的; 小室的. ③多孔的; 有窝的. ~ **rubber** 泡沫橡胶. ~ **shirt** 网眼衬衫. ~ **system** ①【植】细胞组织. ②(犯人的)分隔监禁法. ~ **tissue** 【解】蜂窝状结缔组织.

cel·lu·lar·i·ty [ˌseljuˈlæriti] *n.* 【生】细胞性，细胞结构.

cel·lu·lase [ˈseljuleis] *n.* 【生化】纤维素酶.

cel·lu·late [ˈseljuleit] *a.* = cellular. — *vt.* 使有细胞状组织. **-d** *a.* 细胞状的，蜂窝状的.

cel·lu·la·tion [ˈseljuˈleiʃən] *n.* 细胞组织; 蜂窝状组织.

cel·lule [ˈseljuːl] *n.* ①【医】小细胞，小房. ②【空】翼组.

cel·lu·lif·er·ous [ˌseljuˈlifərəs] *a.* 【医】有小细胞的，产生小细胞的.

cel·lu·li·tis [ˌseljuˈlaitis] *n.* 【医】蜂窝织炎.

cel·lu·loid [ˈseljulɔid] *n.* ①【化】赛璐珞(明胶); 假象牙. ②〔美俚〕电影(胶片). — *a.* 细胞状的. ~ *fans* 〔美俚〕影迷.

cel·lu·lose [ˈseljuləus] *n.* 【植】细胞膜质，纤维质; 【化】纤维素. — *vt.* 用纤维素处理. ~ **acetate** 醋酸纤维素. ~ **plant** 纸浆厂.

cel·lu·los·ic [ˌseljuˈləusik] *a.* 纤维质的. — *n.* 纤维素质.

cel·lu·lous [ˈseljuləs] *a.* 〔罕〕有细胞的，充满细胞的.

ce·lom [ˈsiːləm] *n.* 体腔 (= coelom).

Cel·o·tex [ˈseləˌteks] 〔美〕赛璐特克斯〔隔音板的商标名称〕. —〔c-〕 *n.* 隔音板.

Cels. = Celsius.

Cel·si·us [ˈselsiəs] *a.* 摄氏的. ~ **thermometer** 摄氏温度计.

Celt [kelt, Am. selt] *n.* 【史】凯尔特人. *the* ~*s* 凯尔特族.

celt [selt] *n.* 【考古】石凿，凿斧〔史前石制或金属工具〕.

Celt. = Celtic.

Cel·tic [ˈkeltik; Am. ˈseltik] *a.* 凯尔特人的，凯尔特族的; 凯尔特语的. — *n.* 凯尔特语. *the* ~ *fringe* 凯尔

特系外缘人口〔指英国内的 Scots, Irish, Welsh 和 Cornish 人后裔〕.
cem. = cemetery.
cem·ba·lo [ˈtʃembələu] *n.* (*pl.* **-li** [-liː], **-los**)【乐】①= harpsichord. ② = dulcimer.
ce·ment [siˈment] *n.* ①水泥. ②胶泥; 胶合剂, 接合剂, 胶;【医】(牙科等用的)黏固粉. ③【解】(牙齿的)白垩质. ~ *gland* 黏腺. *glass* ~ 玻璃胶. —*vt.* ①用水泥粘合, 用水泥涂. ②胶合, 接合; 溶接. ③【冶】对…作渗碳处理. ④巩固, 加强(友谊等), 强化(关系等); 把…结合在一起. ~*ed steel* 渗碳钢. —*vi.* 粘紧, 粘牢. ~**ing process**【冶】渗碳法.
ce·men·ta·tion [ˌsiːmenˈteiʃən] *n.* ①【医】黏固(作用). ②接合; 胶合, 黏结. ③【化】胶结, 硬化. ④【冶】渗碳(法), 渗碳处理.
ce·ment·ite [siˈmentait] *n.*【冶】渗碳体, 碳化铁体; 西门体(结晶).
ce·men·tum [siˈmentəm] *n.* ①【解】牙骨质. ②黏固粉, 水泥.
cem·e·ter·y [ˈsemitri] *n.* 墓地, 公墓.
cen. = centre; central; century.
cen·acle [ˈsenəkl] *n.* ①晚餐室;〔C-〕耶稣与门徒进最后晚餐的房间. ②聚会室. ③(作家等的)结社, 小组.
Cen. Am. = Central America 中美洲.
-cene *comb. f.* 表示"新", "最近".
ce·nes·the·sia [ˌsiːnisˈθiːʒə, -ʒiə; ˌsenis-] *n.*【心】普通感觉 (= coenesthesia, cenesthesis).
ceno-[1] *comb. f.* 表示"新", "最近".
ceno-[2] *comb. f.* 表示"共同".
ce·no·bite [ˈsiːnəubait] *n.* = coenobite.
ce·no·gen·e·sis [ˌsiːnəˈdʒenisis, ˌsenəu-] *n.*【生】新性发生; 新生性变态. **-ge·net·ic** [-dʒiˈnetik] *a.*
ce·no·phyte [ˈsiːnəufait] *n.*【植】新生代植物.
ce·no·spe·cies [ˈsiːnəspiʃiːz, ˈsenə-] *n.*【生】群型种, 杂交种.
cen·o·taph [ˈsenətɑːf] *n.* 衣冠冢; (葬于别处的死者)纪念碑. *the C-* (伦敦)第一次世界大战阵亡将士纪念碑.
ce·no·te [siˈnəuti] *n.*【地】(石灰岩溶蚀形成的)天然水井.
Ce·no·zo·ic [ˌsiːnəˈzəuik] *n., a.*【地】新生代(的), 新生界(的).
cense [sens] *vt.* ①(向神)焚香. ②用香熏.
cen·ser [ˈsensə] *n.* 香炉.
cen·sor [ˈsensə] *n.* ①(古罗马调查户口、检查社会风纪等的)监察官; (书刊等的)审查员, (信件等的)检查员. ②(牛津大学等的)学监. ③有恶意的评论者. ④【心】抑制性潜意识. —*vt.* ①审查(书刊等); 检查(信件等). ②删改.
cen·so·ri·al [senˈsɔːriəl] *a.* ①监查官的; 检查员的. ②批判的, 谴责性的.
cen·so·ri·ous [senˈsɔːriəs] *a.* 检查员一样的; 爱挑剔的, 苛评的, 吹毛求疵的; 批判式的, 谴责性的. **-ly** *ad.* **-ness** *n.*
cen·sor·ship [ˈsensəʃip] *n.* ①审察员[检查员]的职权; 古罗马监察官的职权. ②检查(制度), 审查(制度). ③【心】潜意识中的抑制力.
cen·sur·a·ble [ˈsenʃərəbl] *a.* 可批评的, 该谴责的. **-bly** *ad.*
cen·sure [ˈsenʃə] *vt., n.* 指责, 批评; 谴责 (*opp.* praise). ~ *sb. for a fault* 谴责某人的错误. *a vote of* ~ 不信任决议[投票].
cen·sus [ˈsensəs] *n.* ①人口[户口, 国情]普查;【生】种群普查; 调查. ②(调查获得的)统计数字. *take a* ~ *(of the population)* 举行(人口)普查. —*vt.* 调查(某地区等的)人口数字; 统计…的数字. ~ **paper** 人口调查表. ~ **quadrat** 普查采样区〔一块划定的方形地区〕. ~ **taker** (人口)普查员.
cent [sent] *n.* ①〔美〕分〔货币单位〕; 分币, 零钱. ②(作单位的)百. *per* ~ 百分之…. ~ *per* ~ 百分之百; 毫无例外. *don't care a (red)* ~ 毫不在乎. *put in one's two* ~*s (worth)* 发表意见; 发言.
cent. = centigrade; centimetre; central; centum; century; centime.
CENTAG = Central Army Group (of NATO) (北约)中央军集团.
cent·age [ˈsentidʒ] *n.* 〔罕〕百分率.
cen·tal [ˈsentl] *n.* 百磅〔称谷物用的重量单位, 美国习惯说作 hundredweight〕.
cen·tare [ˈsentɑː] *n.* 平方米, 平方公尺 (= centiare).
cen·taur [ˈsentɔː] *n.* ①【希神】半人半马的怪物. ②(马术精妙的)名骑手. ③〔C-〕【天】半人马座.
cen·tau·re·a [senˈtɔːriə] *n.*【植】矢车菊属 (*Centaurea*) 植物.
Cen·tau·rus [senˈtɔːrəs] *n.*【天】半人马(星)座.
cen·tau·ry [ˈsentɔːri] *n.*【植】矢车菊.
cen·tavo [senˈtɑːvəu] *n.* 分, 仙〔墨西哥、南美等国的小辅币, = 1/100 peso〕.
cen·te·nar·i·an [ˌsentiˈnɛəriən] *n.* 百岁(以上)的老人. —*a.* 百岁(以上)的; 一百周年的.
cen·te·nar·y [senˈtiːnəri] *a.* ①一百年的, 一世纪的. ②一百周年纪念的. —*n.* ①百年间, 一世纪. ②一百周年纪念.
cen·ten·ni·al [senˈtenjəl, -niəl] *a.* ①(每)百年的; 一百周年纪念的. ②活了一百岁的, 继续了百年之久的. —*n.* 一百周年(纪念). *the C- State* 美国科罗拉多州的别称〔该州于 1876 年开国一百周年时加入合众国〕.
cen·ter [ˈsentə] *n., vt., vi.* 〔美〕= centre.
cen·ter·board [ˈsentəˌbɔːd] *n.*【船】滑动龙骨, 活动防浪板, 垂板龙骨.
cen·tered [ˈsentəd] *a.* ①位于中心的. ②以某一对象为(活动)中心的. *consumer-*~ 以消费者为中心的.
cen·ter·fire [ˈsentəˌfaiə] *a.* 中心点火的.
cen·ter·ing [ˈsentəriŋ, ˈsentriiŋ] *n.* ①定(中)心, 定圆心, 对中. ②【建】临时穹顶支架, 拱膺架(装置).
cen·tes·i·mal [senˈtesiməl] *a.* 百分之一的;【数】百分的, 百进位的.
cen·tes·i·mo [senˈtesiˌməu] *n.* (*pl.* **-mos** [-ˌməuz]; It. **-mi** [-ˈmiː]) ①分〔意大利货币单位, 为 1/100 里拉〕; 分〔乌拉圭货币单位, 为 1/100 比索〕; 分〔巴拿马货币单位, 为 1/100 巴波亚〕; 分〔智利货币单位, 为 1/100 埃斯库多〕. ②上述某些货币中的硬币.
centi- *comb. f.* 百; 百分之一: *centimeter*.
cen·ti·are [ˈsentiɛə] *n.* 百分之一公亩, 平方米.
cen·ti·bar [ˈsentibɑː] *n.*【物】厘巴 (=1/100 bar.).
centi·grade [ˈsentigreid] *a.* ①百分度的. ②摄氏温度计的. ~ **thermometer** 摄氏温度计.
cen·ti·gram(me) [ˈsentigræm] *n.* 厘克 (=1/100 gram, 略作 cg.).
cen·tile [ˈsentail, -til] *n.* 百分位点 (= percentile).
cen·ti·li·tre, -ter [ˈsentiˌliːtə] *n.* 厘升 (=1/100 litre, 略作 cl.).
cen·til·lion [senˈtiljən] *num.* ①〔英、德〕100 万的 100 次乘方. ②〔美、法〕1000 的 101 次乘方.
cen·time [ˈsɑ̃ːntiːm] *n.* 〔F.〕生丁 (法国货币单位 = 1/100 franc).
cen·ti·me·tre, -ter [ˈsentiˌmiːtə] *n.* 厘米, 公分 (=1/100 metre, 略作 cm.).
cen·ti·me·tre-gram-sec·ond [ˈsentiˌmiːtəˈgræmˈsekənd] *a.* 厘米克秒制的.
cen·ti·mil·li·me·tre, -ter [ˈsentiˈmiliˌmiːtə] *n.* 忽米 (= 1/1,000 厘米, 略作 cmm.).
cen·ti·mo [ˈsentiməu] *n.* (*pl.* ~*s*) ①分〔西班牙货币单位, 为 1/100 比塞塔〕; 分〔委内瑞拉货币单位, 为 1/100 波利瓦〕; 分〔哥斯达黎加货币单位, 为 1/100 科

郎]; 分〔巴拉圭货币单位，为 1/100 瓜拉尼〕. ②上述某些货币的硬币.

cen·ti·pede ['sentipi:d] *n.* 【动】蜈蚣.

cen·ti·poise ['sentipɔiz] *n.* 【物】厘泊〔黏度单位〕(= 1/100 poise).

cen·ti·stere ['sentistiə] *n.* 百分之一立方米.

cent·ner ['sentnə] *n.* 生奈尔〔德国、丹麦等 = 50 公斤; 英国 = 100 磅; 分析用微衡为 1 dram〕. *a metric [double]* ~ 一公担, 100 公斤.

CENTO=Central Treaty Organization 中央条约组织.

cen·to ['sentəu] *n. (pl. ~s)* ①(摘录别的作品拼成的)集锦诗; 集锦曲. ②拼接成的衣服, 百纳衣; 马鞍垫布. ③拼凑而成的东西, 大杂烩.

centr- *comb. f.* 中心: *centr*al.

cen·tra ['sentrə] *n.* centrum 的复数.

cen·trad ['sentræd] *ad.* 【解】中向. — *n.* 【数】百分之一弧度 (=1/100 radian).

cen·tral ['sentrəl] *a.* ①中心的, 中央的. ②重要的, 主要的. ③中枢的; 中枢神经系统的. ④(政治上)走中间道路的. ⑤【语】(中)央的. — *n.* 〔美〕电话总局; 接线员. *C- Executive Committee* 中央执行委员会. *C- Reserve Banks* 〔美〕中央准备银行. *C- Reserve Cities* 〔美〕中央准备市〔New York, Chicago, St. Louise 三市〕. ~ **city** 特别市的中心城市. ~ **figure** (绘画、戏剧等的)中心人物. ~ **force** 向心力, 辏力. ~ **heating** (大厦的)中央供暖法, 暖气. ~ **staging** 观众围坐舞台四周的剧场. ~ **station** 中央发电厂. ~ **tendency** 【统】集中趋势. ~ **time** 〔美〕中部标准时间. ~ **treasury** 中央金库. ~ **vowel** (中)央元音. **-ly** *ad.* **-ness** *n.*

cen·tral·ism ['sentrəlizəm] *n.* 中央集权制, 集中制. *democracy and* ~ 民主和集中. *democratic* ~ 民主集中制.

cen·tral·ist ['sentrəlist] *n.* 中央集权主义者. — *a.* 中央集权的; 拥护中央集权的.

cen·tral·i·ty [sen'træliti] *n.* ①中心性, 中央状态. ②中心地位. ③向心性, 归心性.

cen·tral·i·za·tion [ˌsentrəlai'zeiʃən] *n.* 中央集权; 集于中心, 集中(化).

cen·tral·ize ['sentrəlaiz] *vt.* ①把(权力)集中; 使(国家等)实行中央集权制. ②成为…的中心, 把…集中起来. — *vi.* 形成中心, 集中.

cen·tre, cen·ter ['sentə] *n.* ①中心; 中心点; 圆心; 中央; 中枢, 核心; 中心人物; 根源, 起源. ②〔常 C-〕(政治上的)中间派. ③(足球等的)中锋; (军队、舞台等的)中央部分. ④【建】假框, 拱架. ⑤【机】承轴; 顶尖, 顶针. ⑥〔*pl.*〕中心距. *recruiting ~s* 征兵站. *cultural ~s* 文化馆. ~ *field* 【棒球】中外垒. ~ *forward* 【曲棍球等】中锋中卫. ~ *of attraction* 引力中心; 惹眼的东西, 有名的东西; 注意力的中心, (一个场所的)中心人物. ~ *of gravity* 重心. ~ *of motion* 动心. — *vt.* ①把…集中, 使聚集于一点 *(in, at, on, round, about)*. ②把…置于中部. ③定…的中心; 矫正 (透镜等的)中心. ④(足球等)传(球)给中锋. — *vi.* ①居中. ②有中心; 做中锋. ~**bit** ①(木匠用的)绳钻, 转柄钻. ②【机】中心钻, 打眼钻. ~**board** 【船】①(船底中心的)垂直升降板. ②装有升降板的小船. ~**drill** = ~**bit**. ~**fielder** 【棒球】中锋. ~**fold** (报纸期刊的)中间折页〔常连成一大张多印彩色图片等〕. ~ **forward** 〔足球〕中锋. ~**piece** 【建】中心装饰; 放在(桌子等)中央的装饰. **-less** *a.* 无中心的. **-most** *a.* 在正中心的.

centri- *comb. f.* = centr-.

cen·tric, cen·tri·cal ['sentrik(əl)] *a.* ①中心的; 中央的; 围绕着中心的. ②神经中枢的. **-ly** *ad.*

cen·tric·i·ty [sen'trisiti] *n.* 中心, 归心性.

cen·trif·u·gal [sen'trifjugəl] *a.* ①离心的 *(opp.* centripetal*)*; 应用离心力的. ②【生】输出的, 排泄的. — *n.* 离心机. ~**-box** 【化纤】离心式纺丝罐. ~ **blower** 离心吹风机. ~ **effect** 离心作用. ~ **force** 离心力. ~ **inflorescence** 【植】远心花序, 上花先开. ~ **machine** 离心机. ~ **pump** 离心泵. ~ **sugar** 分蜜糖. **-ly** *ad.*

cen·trif·u·gal·ize [sen'trifjugəlaiz] *vt.* 使受离心作用, 离心分离.

cen·trif·u·ga·tion [senˌtrifju'geiʃən, -ə'gei-] *n.* 离心(分离).

cen·tri·fuge ['sentrifju:dʒ] *n.* 离心[分离]机; 离心式脱水机.

cen·tring ['sentriŋ] *n.* =centering.

cen·tri·ole ['sentriəul] *n.* 【生】中心粒.

cen·tripe·tal [sen'tripitl] *a.* ①向心的 *(opp.* centrifugal*)*; 应用向心力的. ②【生】输入的. ~ **force** 向心力. ~ **inflorescence** 【植】向心花序, 下花先开. ~ **pump** 向心泵. **-ly** *ad.*

cen·trist ['sentrist] *n.* 〔常 C-〕(议会中的)中间派〔中立〕议员; 稳健派, 温和派.

centro- *comb. f.* = centr-.

cen·tro·bar·ic [ˌsentrə'bærik] *a.* 与重心有关的.

cen·troid ['sentrɔid] *n.* 〔物〕矩心; 质心, 质量中心 (= centre of mass); 形心曲线; 心迹线.

cen·tro·mere ['sentrəˌmiə] *n.* 【生】着丝点[粒]. **-meric** [-'merik, -'miə-] *a.*

cen·tro·plasm ['sentrəplæzəm] *n.* 【生】中心质.

cen·tro·plast ['sentrəplæst] *n.* 【生】中心质体.

cen·tro·some ['sentrəsəum] *n.* 【生】中心小体.

cen·tro·sphere ['sentrəsfiə] *n.* ①【地】地心圈, 地核. ②【生】中心球; 星状球.

cen·trum ['sentrəm] *n. (pl. ~s, -tra* [-trə]*)* 中心; (地震的)震源; 【解】椎体, 中枢; 【生】中心体.

cen·tum ['sentəm] *n.* 〔L.〕百. *per* ~ = per cent.

cen·tu·ple ['sentjupl] *a.* 百倍的. — *n.* 百倍. — *vt.* 使增为百倍, 用百乘.

cen·tu·pli·cate [sen'tju:plikit] *n.* 百倍. *in* ~ (印)一百份. — *a.* 百倍的. — [-keit] *vt.* 使增为一百倍.

cen·tu·ri·al [sen'tjuriəl, -'tur-] *a.* 百年的, 一世纪的.

cen·tu·ri·on [sen'tjuəriən] *n.* (古罗马军团的)百人队队长.

cen·turi·um [sen'tjuriəm] *n.* 【化】钲〔现名 fermium 镄〕.

cen·tu·ry ['sentʃuri, -tʃəri] *n.* ①百年, 一世纪. ②(古罗马)(军队的)百人队, (选举的)百人团. ③百, 百个; 【板球】百分. ④百镑(钞票); 〔美俚〕百元(钞票); 百码赛跑. *the twentieth [20th]*~ 二十世纪 (1901—2000年). *a ~ note* 〔美俚〕百元钞. *a ~ title* 〔美〕百码赛跑锦标. **centuries-old** *a.* 历史悠久的. ~ **plant** 【植】龙舌兰.

ceorl ['tʃeiˌɔ:l] *n.* ①【英史】底层自由民. ②〔古〕= churl.

cephal- *comb. f.* 〔用于元音前〕= cephalo-.

ceph·a·lad ['sefəˌlæd] *ad.* 【解、动】头向 *(opp.* caudad*)*.

ceph·a·lal·gi·a [sefə'lældʒjə] *n.* 【医】头痛.

ce·phal·ic [se'fælik] *a.* ①头(部)的. ②向着头部的; 头附近的.

ceph·a·lin ['sefəlin] *n.* 【生化】脑磷脂.

ceph·a·li·zation [ˌsefəli'zeiʃən] *n.* ①头部形成. ②头向集中.

cephal(o)- *comb. f.* 〔用于辅音前〕头: *cephalo*pod.

ceph·a·lo·chor·date [ˌsefələ'kɔ:deit] *a.* 【动】无头纲的, 头索动物纲的. — *n.* 无头纲动物, 头索动物纲动物.

ceph·a·lom·e·ter [ˌsefə'lɔmitə] *n.* 头测量器. **-lom·e·try** 头测量. *n.*

cepha·lo·pod ['sefələupɔd] *n., a.* 【动】头足纲动物〔乌贼等〕(的).

ceph·a·lo·spo·rin [ˌsefələu'spɔ:rin] *n.* 【药】头孢霉菌素.

ceph·a·lo·tho·rax [ˌsefələu'θɔ:ræks] *n.* 【动】(甲壳类

的)头胸部.
ceph·a·lous ['sefələs] *a.* 有头的.
-ceph·a·lous *comb. f.* 有头的: bicephalous.
Ceph·e·id (variable) ['sefiid, 'si:fi-] 【天】造父变星.
Ce·pheus ['si:fju:s] *n.* 【天】仙王座.
-ceptor *comb. f.* 表示:"接受者,接受器".
cer- *comb. f.* 〔用于元音前〕 = cero-.
ce·ra·ceous [si'reiʃəs] *a.* 蜡状的;蜡质的.
ce·ram·al [si'ræməl] *n.* 金属陶瓷, 合金陶瓷 (= cermet).
ce·ram·ic [si'ræmik] *a.* 陶器的,陶瓷的,陶质的; 制陶的. *the ~ industry* 陶瓷业, 窑业. *~ manufactures* 陶器, 瓷器. *~ fibre* 硅酸盐纤维, 陶瓷纤维. — *n.* (一件)陶器.
ce·ram·ics [si'ræmiks] *n.* ①陶瓷学; 陶瓷工艺,制陶术, 窑业. ②〔总称〕陶器.
ce·ram·ist ['serəmist] *n.* 陶瓷工人[技师]; 窑业家.
ce·rar·gy·rite [si'rɑ:dʒirait] *n.* 【矿】角银矿.
ce·ras·tes [si'ræsti:z] *n.* 【动】角蛇属毒蛇 (尤指角蝰 *(Cerastes cornutus)*).
Ce·ras·ti·um [si'ræstiəm] *n.* 【植】寄奴花属; 卷耳属.
ce·rate ['siərit] *n.* 【药】蜡膏,蜡剂;【化】铈酸盐.
ce·rat·o·dus [si'rætədəs, ˌserə'təudəs] *n.* ①澳大利亚肺鱼属 *(Ceratodus)* 的鱼. ②澳大利亚肺鱼 (= barramunda).
cer·a·toid ['serətɔid] *a.* 角状的; 角质的; 有角的.
ce·rau·no·graph [sə'rɔ:nəgrɑ:f] *n.* 【气】雷电计.
Cer·ber·us ['sə:bərəs] *n.* 【希神、罗神】冥府守门狗〔蛇尾三头,长年不眠〕. ***a sop to ~*** (收买看守、官员、敌对者等的)贿赂.
cer·ca·ri·a [sə'keriə] *n.* *(pl.* ***-ri·ae*** [-rii:]*)* 【动】摇尾幼虫,尾蚴.
cer·cis ['sə:sis] *n.* 【植】紫荆.
cer·cus ['sə:kəs] *n.* *(pl.* ***cerci*** [-si]*)* 【动】尾须, 尾铗, 尾毛.
cere[1] [siə] *n.* 【动】(鹦鹉、猛禽类等鸟喙底部的) 蜡膜.
cere[2] [siə] *vt.* ①〔古〕用蜡布包裹(尸体). ②〔罕〕给…上蜡,涂蜡于.
ce·re·al ['siəriəl] *a.* 谷类的; 谷类植物的; 谷类制成的. — *n.* 〔常 *pl.*〕禾谷类,谷物;〔美〕(加过工的)谷类食物〔麦片粥等〕. *coarse ~s* 杂[粗]粮. ~ **crops** 谷(类作)物. ~**-leguminous crops** 豆类作物.
cer·e·bel·lum [ˌseri'beləm] *n.* *(pl.* *~s,* ***-la*** [-lə]*)* 【解】小脑.
cer·e·bral ['seribrəl] *a.* ①大脑的,脑的. ②(文艺等)触动理智的;理智方面的; 非感情方面的. ~ **anaemia** 脑贫血. ~ **haemorrhage** 脑溢血. ~ **hyperaemia** 脑充血. ~ **hemispheres** 大脑两半球.
cere·bral·ism ['serəbrəlizəm] *n.* ①唯大脑机能论. ②理智至上主义; 抽象主义.
cer·e·brate ['seriˌbreit] *vi.* 用脑; 思索.
cer·e·bra·tion [ˌseri'breiʃən] *n.* 大脑作用[机能]; 思想活动; 思考.
cer·e·bri·tis [ˌseri'braitis] *n.* 【医】大脑炎.
cerebro- *comb. f.* 〔用于辅音前〕脑〔元音前用 cerebr-〕.
cer·e·bro·ma·la·cia [ˌseribrəumə'leisiə] *n.* 【医】脑软化.
cer·e·bro·scle·ro·sis [ˌseribrəu-skliə'rəusis] *n.* 【医】脑硬化.
cer·e·bro·side ['seribrəusaid] *n.* 【生化】脑苷脂类.
ce·re·bro·spi·nal [ˌseribrəu'spainl] *a.* 【解】脑脊髓的. *epidemic ~ meningitis [fever]* 流行性脑脊膜炎.
cer·e·brum ['seribrəm] *n.* *(pl.* *~s,* ***-bra*** [-brə]*)* 【解】大脑; 脑.
cere·cloth ['siəklɔθ] *n.* (防水或包尸的)蜡布.
cer·e·ment ['siəmənt] *n.* ①包裹木乃伊的蜡布. ②〔常 *pl.*〕尸衣.

cer·e·mo·ni·al [ˌseri'məunjəl] *a.* 礼仪上的; 讲究仪式的; 正式的. ~ **drill** 军仪教练. ~ **usage** 礼仪上的惯例. — *n.* 仪式,礼仪; 仪式书. ~ **dress** 礼服. **-ism** *n.* 讲究仪式, 拘泥形式, 形式主义. **-ist** *n.* 墨守礼法的人, 拘泥形式的人. **-ly** *ad.* 仪式上,礼仪上.
cer·e·mo·ni·ous [ˌseri'məunjəs, -niəs] *a.* ①礼仪的. ②仪式郑重的, 隆重的. ③(过分)讲究礼节的, 客套的, 古板的. *a ~ reception* 隆重的欢迎. **-ly** *ad.* **-ness** *n.*
cer·e·mo·ny ['seriməni; Am. 'seriˌməuni] *n.* ①典礼, 仪式. ②礼仪,礼节. ③虚礼; 客气. *a wedding ~* 结婚仪式. *the Master of (the) Ceremonies* (英国皇室的) 掌礼官; (正式集会的) 司仪. ***stand on [upon] ~*** 墨守礼法,讲究仪式; 讲客套, 客气. ***with ~*** 正式,隆重. ***without ~*** 不拘礼节地,随便地.
Ce·res ['siəri:z] *n.* ①【罗神】谷(类女)神. ②【天】谷神星.
cer·e·sin(e) ['serisin] *n.* (纯)地蜡.
ce·re·us ['siəriəs] *n.* 【植】仙影拳;〔C-〕仙影拳属.
ce·ri·a ['siəriə] *n.* 【化】二氧化铈.
ce·ric ['siərik, 'ser-] *a.* 【化】高铈的,四价铈的.
cer·if, cer·iph ['serif] *n.* 〔罕〕 = serif.
ce·rif·er·ous [si'rifərəs] *a.* 产蜡的,生蜡的.
ce·rise [sə'ri:z] *n., a.* 〔F.〕淡红[鲜红]色(的), 樱桃色(的).
ce·rite ['siərait] *n.* 【矿】铈硅石.
ce·ri·um ['siəriəm] *n.* 【化】铈.
cer·met ['sə:met] *n.* = ceramal.
CERN = 〔F.〕 *Conseil Européen pour la Recherche Nucléaire* 欧洲原子核研究委员会 〔现称 *Organisation Européene pour la Recherche Nucléaire* 欧洲原子核研究组织〕.
cer·nu·ous ['sə:njuwəs] *a.* 【植】俯垂的.
cero- *comb. f.* 表示"蜡": *ceroplastic.*
ce·ro ['siərəu] *n.* *(pl.* *~, ~s)* 【动】巨鲐, 马鲛鱼 *(Scomberomorus cavalla).*
ce·ro·graph ['si:rəgrɑ:f] *n.* = cerotype.
ce·rog·ra·phy [si'rɔgrəfi] *n.* 蜡版雕刻术; 蜡版印刷术; 蜡画术[法].
ce·ro·plas·tic ['siərəu'plæstik] *a.* 蜡塑的. *~s* 蜡塑术.
ce·rot·ic [si'rɔtik] *a.* 蜜蜡的,蜡脂的; 出自蜜蜡的, 出自蜡脂的.
ce·ro·type ['siərəˌtaip] *n.* 蜡面雕钢版; 蜡版印制品.
ce·rous ['siərəs] *a.* 【化】三价铈的,(正)铈的.
cert. = certainly; certificate; certify.
cert [sə:t] *n.* 〔俚〕 = certainty. *a dead [an absolute] ~* 绝对确实的事物. ***for a ~*** 的确,确实.
cer·tain ['sə:tən] *a.* ①(数量、日期等)已确定的; (证据等)确凿的,无疑的; (知识、技术等)正确的, 可靠的. ②必然〔后接不定式〕; 有把握, 确信 *(of, that)* 〔只用作表语〕. ③某,某一; 某种, 某些; 相当的, 一定程度的; (某种)不好意思说出来的 〔只用作定语〕. *a ~ remedy for* 治…的一种特效药. *face ~ death* 面临无可避免的死亡. *a ~ Smith* 一个叫做史密斯的人. *a ~ unit* 某部队[单位]. *a lady of ~ age* 相当年龄的[四五十岁的]女人. *a woman in a ~ condition* 孕妇. *a woman of a ~ description* 行为不好的女人; 娼妇. *There is a ~ charm about him.* 他有某种说不出的可爱处. *feel a ~ reluctance* 觉得有些讨嫌. *to a ~ degree* 到某种程度, 多少. *I am ~ of success.* 我对成功有把握. *He is ~ to succeed.* 他一定成功. *be morally ~ that* 确有把握,决不致, 包管. *~ evidence* 确实的证据. *~ illness* 某种病〔指性病〕. ***for ~*** 的确,一定 *(I know for ~ ...* 我确实知道). ***make ~ [of, that]*** 把…弄明白, 弄确实, 保证. *(make ~ when the guests leave* 弄清楚客人何时动身. *make ~ of the date of his arrival* 搞清楚他来的日期). *pron.* 某几个,某些. *~ of his relatives* 他的某些亲戚.
cer·tain·ly ['sə:tənli] *ad.* ①的确,无疑,一定,必定. ②

〔口〕〔回答语〕当然,自然可以;不错,的确是那样,的确是的. *C-, you may take the keys.* 没问题,你当然可以把钥匙拿去. *It is ~ the case that ..., but ...,* (…)虽然很对,可是….

cer·tain·ty [ˈsəːtnti] *n.* 确实(性); 确定性; 确实[定]的事,必然的事; 确信,肯定. *the ~ of death* 死的必然性. *bet on a ~* 十拿九稳地赌. ***a dead ~*** (竞赛时)必胜的马; 十拿九稳,势所必然. ***for [to, of] a ~*** 的确, 显然; 毫无疑问. ***moral ~*** 靠得住,定准,一定. ***with ~*** 确信,的确.

cer·tes [ˈsəːtiz] *ad.* 〔古〕的确,诚然,必然.

certif. = certificate(d).

cer·ti·fi·a·ble [ˈsəːtifaiəbl] *a.* 可证明的. **-bly** [-bli] *ad.*

cer·tif·i·cate [səˈtifikit] *n.* ①证明书; 执照,凭照; (毕业)文凭. ②证券,单据. ③明证. *be married by ~* 不依据宗教仪式结婚. *a health ~* 健康证明书. *a leaving ~* 毕业[肄业,离职]证书. *a medical ~* 诊断书. *a gold ~* 〔美〕金库券. *a ~ of birth [death]* 出生[死亡]证. *a ~ of deposit* 存款凭单. *a ~ of efficiency* 工作能力(优良)鉴定书. *a ~ of measurement* 【美商】木材尺寸检查证. *a ~ of merit* 【美军】奖状. *a ~ of shares [stock]* 记名股票. *a ~ of shipment* 【英商】出口许可证. *a ~ of bravery* 勇敢品质的明证. — [səˈtifikeit] *vt.* 发证明给…,批准; 认可,鉴定. *a ~d teacher* 鉴定合格的教员,正式教员.

cer·ti·fi·ca·tion [ˌsəːtifiˈkeiʃən] *n.* ①证明, 鉴定, 保证. ②证明书的发给,执照的授与. ③证明书.

cer·ti·fied [ˈsəːtifaid] *a.* ①被证明了的, 有保证的; 鉴定的. ②持有证明书的. *a ~ cheque* 〔美〕保付支票. *a ~ public accountant* 〔美〕(执有证书的)合格会计师. ~ **mail** 只负责递送的邮件〔不保证赔偿〕. ~ **milk** 消毒牛乳.

cer·ti·fi·er [ˈsəːtifaiə] *n.* 证明者.

cer·ti·fy [ˈsəːtifai] *vt.* ①(以保证书或许可证)证明. ②〔英〕证明…有精神病. ③〔美〕(银行)担保(支票)可付款. *I hereby ~ that ....* 兹证明…无误. — *vi.* (以书面形式)证明 *(to)*; 保证 *(for)*. I can ~ to her honesty. 我可以证明她是诚实的.

cer·ti·o·ra·ri [ˌsəːtiɔːˈrɛərai] *n.* 〔L.〕〔常作 writ of ~〕(上级法院向下级法院等发出的)诉讼文件[案卷]调取令(书).

cer·ti·tude [ˈsəːtitjuːd] *n.* ①确信; 确定. ②确实(性), 必然性.

ce·ru·le·an [siˈruːljən] *n., a.* 天蓝色(的).

ce·ru·men [siˈruːmen] *n.* 【医】耳垢,耵聍.

ce·ruse [ˈsiəruːs] *n.* ①铅粉,铅白化妆品. ②【化】碳酸铅白.

ce·rus(s)·ite [ˈsiərəsait] *n.* 【矿】白铅矿.

Cer·van·tes [səːˈvæntiz], **Miguel de ~** 塞万提斯〔1547—1616, 西班牙作家,《唐·吉诃德》的作者〕.

cer·van·tite [səːˈvæntait] *n.* 【矿】锑赭石,黄锑矿.

cer·vi·cal [ˈsəːvikəl] *a.* 【解】①颈(部)的. ②子宫颈的.

cer·vi·ces [ˈsəːvisiːz, səˈvai-] *n.* cervix 的复数.

cer·vi·ci·tis [ˌsəːviˈsaitis] *n.* 【医】子宫颈炎.

cer·vid [ˈsəːvid] *a.* 【动】鹿科的.

cer·vine [ˈsəːvain] *a.* ①鹿的; 鹿一样的. ②鹿毛色的, 茶褐色的.

cer·vix [ˈsəːviks] *n.* *(pl. ~es, -vi·ces* [-visiːz]*)* 【解】①颈; 颈部. ②子宫颈.

Ce·sar·e·an, -ri·an [si(ː)ˈzɛəriən] *a.* = Caesarean.

ce·si·um [ˈsiːzjəm] *n.* 【化】铯 (= caesium). ~ **clock** 铯原子钟.

Ces·ko·slo·ven·sko [ˈtʃeskɔslɔˈvenskɔ] 捷克斯洛伐克〔捷文名称〕.

ces·pi·tose [ˈsespitəus] *a.* 簇生的,丛生的,密生的; (似)草皮的.

cess[1] [ses] *n.* 〔Scot.〕田赋; 〔Ir.〕地方税〔英国今用 rate〕.

cess[2] [ses] *n.* 〔Ir.〕运气〔只用于下一短语〕. ***Bad ~ to you!*** 你真该死!

ces·sa·tion [səˈseiʃən] *n.* 停止, 休止. *~ of arms [hostilities]* 停战 [停止敌对行动]. *~ of friendship* 绝交.

ces·ser [ˈsesə] *v.* 【法】(期限、责任等的)中止,结束.

ces·sion [ˈseʃən] *n.* (领土的)割让, (权利等的)让与, 转让.

ces·sion·ar·y [ˈseʃənəri] *a.* 割让的,让与的; 转让了财产的. — *n.* 【法】受让人.

cess·pit, cess·pool [ˈsespit, ˈsespuːl] *n.* 污水坑; 粪坑; 〔喻〕污秽场所. *the ~ of iniquity* 罪恶的渊薮.

ces·ta [ˈsestə] *n.* 回力球戏的手筐〔捆在腕上,用来接球和扔球〕.

c'est-à-dire [setəˈdiː] 〔F.〕就是说; 即是.

c'est la vie [seləˈviː] 〔F.〕这就是生活; 生活就是这样的.

ces·tode [ˈsestəud] *n.* 【动、医】多节绦虫亚纲的动物, 绦虫. — *a.* 绦虫的,多节绦虫亚纲的.

ces·toid [ˈsestɔid] *n., a.* = cestode.

ces·tus[1] [ˈsestəs] *n.* (古罗马拳击用的)皮带手套.

ces·tus[2] [ˈsestəs] *n.* ①带; 【罗神】(爱神的)饰带. ②【动】带水母,带海蜇.

ce·su·ra [si(ː)ˈzjuərə] *n.* = caesura.

ce·ta·cean [siˈteiʃjən] *n.* 鲸类的动物〔鲸、海豚等〕. — *a.* 鲸类动物的.

ce·ta·ceous [siˈteiʃjəs] *a.* 鲸类动物的.

ce·tane [ˈsiːtein] *n.* 【化】十六烷,鲸蜡烷. ~ **number** 【化】十六烷值.

cet·e·ris pa·ri·bus [ˈsitəris ˈpæribəs] 〔L.〕(如)其他条件[情况]均同[均保持不变].

ce·tol·o·gy [siˈtɔlədʒi] *n.* 鲸类学. **-lo·gist** *n.* 鲸类学家. **-log·i·cal** [-ˈlɔdʒikl] *a.* 鲸类学的.

Ce·tus [ˈsiːtəs] *n.* 【天】鲸鱼座.

Ce·u·ta [ˈsjuːtə] *n.* 休达〔摩洛哥境内一港口, 属西班牙〕.

ce·vi·tam·ic [ˌsiːvaiˈtæmik, -vi-] *a.* ~ **acid** 【药】抗坏血酸,维生素 C.

Cey·lon [siˈlɔn] *n.* 锡兰〔斯里兰卡 (Sri Lanka)的旧称〕〔亚洲〕. ~ **moss** 【植】锡兰藻〔一种红藻,可提取琼胶〕.

Cey·lo·nese [ˌsiːləˈniːz] *a.* 锡兰(人)的. — *n.* 〔*sing., pl.*〕锡兰人.

C.F., c.f., C.&F. (= cost and freight) 【商】离岸加运费价格,成本加运费价格.

C.F. = Chaplain to the Forces〔英〕随军牧师.

Cf = californium 【化】锎.

c/f = carried forward 【会计】转下页.

cf. = 〔L.〕*confer.*

c.f. = 【棒球】centre field.

C.F.C. = consolidated freight classification 【商】统一运费分类表.

C.F.I., c.f.i. = cost, freight, and insurance 【商】到岸价格,成本加运费、保险费价格.

c.f.m. = cubic feet per minute 立方英尺/分.

c.f.s. = cubic feet per second 立方英尺/秒.

CG = ①centre of gravity 【物】重心(有时用 cg). ②Coast Guard 海岸警卫队. ③commanding general 【军】(将军级)司令官. ④consul general 总领事.

cg. = centigram(me)(s).

C.G.H. = Cape of Good Hope 【地】好望角.

cgm. = centigram.

CGS, C.G.S. = ①centimetre-gramme-second (system) 厘米、克、秒(制)〔也可用 c.g.s. 或 cgs〕. ②Chief of the General Staff 总参谋长.

CGT = 〔F.〕*Confédération Générale du Travail* 法国总工会 (=General Confederation of Labo(u)r).

Ch. = Charles; China; Chinese; Church.
ch. = chapter; chief; 〔L.〕 *chirurgiae* (= of surgery); choice; church; chain.
C.H. = ①Captain of the Horse 〔英旧〕骑兵大尉. ② clearing house 票据交换所; (技术)情报交换所. ③ Court House 法院. ④Custom-House 海关.
c.h. = courthouse.
chab·a·zite [ˈtʃæbəzait] *n.*【矿】菱沸石.
Cha·blis [ˈʃæbliː] *n.* (原产于法国沙百里的一种)无甜味白葡萄酒.
cha·b(o)uk [ˈtʃɑːbuk] *n.* 东方某些国家施行(体刑用的)马鞭.
cha·cha [ˈtʃɑːtʃɑː] *n.* 恰恰舞〔源出拉美的一种三拍子的、节拍急速的交际舞〕. — *vi.* 跳恰恰舞 (= cha-cha-cha).
chac·ma [ˈtʃækmə] *n.*【动】南非大狒狒, 山都 (= *Papio comatus*).
cha·conne [ʃɑːˈkɔn] *n.* 恰空舞(曲).
cha·cun à son goût [ʃəˈken nə səun ˈguː] 〔F.〕各有所好.
Chad [tʃæd] *n.* 乍得〔非洲〕. **-i·an** [-iən] *n.* 乍得人.
Chad·band [ˈtʃædbænd] *n.* 巧言令色的伪君子〔原为英国作家Dickens 所著小说 *Bleak House* 中的人物〕.
chae·ta [ˈkiːtə] *n.* ***(pl. -tae*** **[-i])**【动】(尤指某些毛虫身上的)体毛,毫毛,刚毛.
chae·tog·nath [ˈkiːtəgnæθ] *n.*【动】毛颚动物门 *(Chaetognatha)*动物.
chae·to·pod [ˈkiːtəpɔd] *n.*【动】毛足纲 *(Chaetopoda)* 动物.
chafe [tʃeif] *vt.* ①把(手、皮肤)擦热. ②擦破; 擦伤; 擦痛. ③惹怒, 使急躁. ~ *one's cold hands* 搓手取暖. — *vi.* ①(动物在铁栏等上)擦身体 *(against)*; (河)冲洗(崖岸等) *(against)*. ②(皮肤等)擦伤, 擦痛. ③发怒; 着急,焦躁. ~ **at** 生…的气. ~ ***under*** *(teasing)* 因(受戏弄)而生气,发火. ~ ***at the bit*** (马)焦躁;(人)(因延误而)不耐烦,想加快速度. — *n.* ①摩擦;擦伤. ②急躁,恼怒. ③(防止擦伤马的)马鞍环套皮. ***in a ~*** 愤然,发火.
chaf·er[1] [ˈtʃeifə] *n.* 烧开水的器具; 火炉.
chaf·er[2] [ˈtʃeifə] *n.*【虫】金龟子.
chaff[1] [tʃɑːf] *n.* ①粗糠,禾壳. ②切细的稻草〔饲料〕,秣; 麻杆碎屑; 废物. ③不值钱的假货. ④(干扰雷达的)金属碎箔. ***be caught with ~*** 受骗,上当. ***~ and dust*** 废物. ***offer ~ for grain*** 挂羊头卖狗肉. ~ **cutter** 去糠机; 切草机.
chaff[2] [tʃɑːf] *n., vt., vi.* 戏弄,开玩笑〔多指无恶意的〕.
chaff·er[1] [ˈtʃɑːfə] *n.* 戏弄者,恶作剧者.
chaf·fer[2] [ˈtʃæfə] *n.* 讨价还价, 讲价. — *vi.* ①讨价还价. ②〔英〕闲谈, 聊天, 交谈. — *vt.* ①为…讨价还价. ②交换; 以…作为交换物.
chaf·fer·er [ˈtʃæfərə] *n.* 讲价者,讨价还价者.
chaf·finch [ˈtʃɑːfintʃ] *n.*【动】(欧洲)苍头燕雀.
chaff·y [ˈtʃɑːfi] *a.* ①禾壳状的, 多糠的. ②无用的, 无价值的.
chaf·ing dish [ˈtʃeifiŋdiʃ] *n.* (在食桌上做菜或保持菜肴温度的)酒精炉盆,热水盆,火锅.
Cha·gas [ˈtʃɑːgɑːs] *n.* 查格斯〔人名〕. **~'s disease**【医】南美锥虫病〔查格斯氏病〕.
cha·grin [ˈʃægrin; Am. ʃəˈgrin] *n.* 悔恨, 懊恼; 委屈. *to one's ~* 使人懊恼的是. — [ˈʃægrin, ʃəˈgriːn; Am. ʃəˈgrin] *vt.* 使懊恼, 使悔恨. ***be [feel] ~ed at [by]*** 因…而悔恨〔懊恼〕.
chain [tʃein] *n.* ①链子,链条; 项圈; 表链. ②连锁; 连续, 一系列,一连串; (山)脉. ③〔常 *pl.*〕镣铐; 羁绊,拘束. ④【化】链;【测】测链〔100 节全长 20 米或 66 英尺〕;【海】锚链;【纺】经线;【电】电路,回路,通路; 信道,波道. ⑤(同属一家业主的)联号. *an endless ~* 环链. *the home radar ~* 飞机归航地面雷达链. *The camera ~* 摄像系统. *a ~ of events* 一连串事件. *a ~ of mountains* 山系,山脉. *She owned a restaurant ~.* 她是几个饭馆的老板. ~ *of command* 指挥系统. *A [The] ~ is not stronger than its weakest link.* 〔谚〕一环薄弱, 全局不稳. ***be in ~s*** 被链条拴着; 被拴在牢房内. ~ ***and ball*** ①〔美〕带铁球的脚镣. ②束缚, 拘束. ③〔喻〕未婚妻, 爱人. ***in the ~s***【海】站在舷侧测海水深度的链台上. — *vt.* ①用链子拴住; 束缚; 连结. ②【测】用测链测量. ~ *up a dog* 把狗拴起来. *be ~ed to the desk* 拴在书桌上,被工作拴住(不能脱身). ~ **armo(u)r** = ~ **mail**. ~ **belt** 链带. ~ **brake** 链制闸,链刹车. ~ **bridge** 铁链吊桥. ~ **cable**【海】锚链; 链索. **~-cloth** (工业)滤布. ~ **coupling**【铁路】链接,【机】链形联接器. ~ **gang** 用链子拴成串的囚犯. ~ **locker**【海】锚链舱. ~ **mail [armour]** 锁子甲. **~man** [ˈtʃeinmən]【海】测链员. ~ **mo(u)lding**【建】链条花边. ~ **plate**【海】舷侧扣住支(桅)索的铁板. ~ **pump** 链斗式水车. **~-react** *vi.* 发生连锁反应. **~-reaction**【原】连锁反应, 链式反应. ~ **riveting** 排钉, 链式铆. **~-rule**【数】连锁法. ~ **shot** 链弹. **~-smoke** *vi., vt.* 一支接一支地吸(烟). ~ **smoker** (把将吸完烟头接在另一支烟上)连续抽烟的人. **~-stitch** *vt., vi.*【纺】锁缝, 用链状针脚缝. ~ **stitch**【纺】链状针迹; 链状线圈; 绞花组织. ~ **store** 〔美〕联号〔同一公司下属的商店,英国叫 multiple shop〕. ~ **timber** (石匠的)系木. ~ **wale**【海】拥桅索承扣板. ~ **wheel** (自行车的)锁链轮, 飞轮. **-less** *a.* 无链的; 无束缚的. **-let** 细链.
chair [tʃɛə] *n.* ①椅子; 〔古〕轿子 (=sedan). ②(大学的)讲座; 大学教授的职位. ③主席〔议长、会长〕的席位〔职位〕; 主席,议长,会长; 〔美〕总统〔州长〕的职位; 〔英〕市长职位. ④【铁路】(固定枕木的)轨座;【矿】罐座,垫板;【天】星座. ⑤〔美俚〕电椅. ⑥轻便单马车. ⑦〔美〕证人席. *an easy ~* 安乐椅. *a double ~* 鸳鸯椅, 双人椅. *a folding ~* 折椅. *a Morris ~* 大安乐椅. ~ **of state** 王位. *sit in [on] a ~* 坐在椅子上. ★有扶手的椅子用 *in*, 无扶手的椅子用 *on*. ***address the ~*** 向主席建议. ***appeal to the ~*** 请主席裁决. ***be above [below] the C-*** 〔英〕(伦敦市参议会议员)有〔无〕市长资历. ***Chair! Chair!*** 主席! 主席! 〔要求维持会场秩序〕. ***~(-)borne troops*** 〔美谑〕美国陆军航空队的地勤人员. ***escape the ~*** 〔美俚〕得免死刑〔免坐电椅〕. ***go to [be sent to, get] the ~*** 〔美俚〕被处死刑〔坐电椅〕. ***in the ~*** 担任会长〔主席〕; 处主席地位; 〔俚〕(请客时)做东道. ***leave the ~*** 离开主席座位; 散会. ***sit on two ~s*** 脚踏两头船. ***take a ~*** 入座,就座. ***take the ~*** 就任主席; 主持会议; 开会. — *vt.* ①使就座, 使入座. ②使就职, 使就位. ③将(得胜者)用椅子抬着游行. **~bed** 坐卧兼用床. **~-borne** *a.* 〔美俚〕坐办公室的〔尤指不上前线的军官〕. ~ **car** 〔美〕①没有活动坐椅的(铁路)客车. ②设有特别单人坐椅的豪华客车. ~ **lift** (山区游览用的)架空滑车. **~one, ~person** 主席,主任,主持人. ~ **rail**【建】护墙板. ~ **warmer** 〔美俚〕①长坐在旅馆门厅中休息的人〔不是付钱的住宿者〕. ②懒鬼.
chair·man [ˈtʃɛəmən] *n.* (*pl.* = ***men*** [-mən]) ①议长, 会长,主席,主任,委员长. ★可男女兼用,称呼时可说作 Mr. Chairman 和 Madame Chairman. ②〔古〕轿夫. —*vt.* 当(会议等)的主席〔议长等〕. **-ship** *n.* 议长〔会长、主席、委员长〕的地位〔身分〕.
chair·wom·an [ˈtʃɛəˌwumən] *n.* (*pl.* ***-wom·en*** [-ˌwimin]) 女主席,女议长,女会长,女主任,女委员长.
chaise [ʃeiz] *n.* 二轮轻便马车; 四轮游览马车.
cha·la·za [kəˈleizə] *n.* ***(pl. -zae*** [-ziː], ***-zas)*** ①【植】合点. ②【动】卵(黄系)带; (昆虫的)毛突. **-l** *a.*
chal·can·thite [kælˈkænθait] *n.*【化】胆矾, 五水(合)硫酸铜,蓝矾.
chal·ced·o·ny [kælˈsedəni] *n.*【矿】玉髓.

chal·cid [ˈkælsid] *n.*【动】寄生蜂 (= fly).

chalco- *comb. f.* 黄铜 〔元音前用 chalc-〕.

chal·co·cite [ˈkælkəsait] *n.*【矿】辉铜矿.

chal·cog·ra·phy [kælˈkɔgrəfi] *n.* 铜版雕刻(术).

chal·coph·a·nite [kælˈkɔfənait] *n.*【矿】黑锌锰矿.

chal·co·py·rite [ˌkælkəˈpaiərait] *n.*【矿】黄铜矿.

Chal·da·ic [kælˈdeiik] *n.* = Chaldean.

Chal·de·an, Chal·dae·an [kælˈdi(ː)ən] *n.* ①(古代巴比伦的)迦勒底人; 古代巴比仑人. ②占星者; 预言者. ③迦勒底人用的闪族语. — *a.* 迦勒底(人)的; 迦勒底语[文化]的.

Chal·dee [kælˈdiː] *a., n.* = Chaldean.

chal·dron [ˈtʃɔːldrən] *n.* 焦尔伦〔旧干量单位,英国为 32 至 36 蒲式耳,美国为 2,500 至 2,900 磅,用于称量煤、石灰等〕.

chal·et [ˈʃælei] *n.* ①(瑞士的)木造农舍, 牧人小屋. ②(农舍式)木造别墅. ③(街道)公厕.

chal·ice [ˈtʃælis] *n.* ①(高脚)酒杯;【宗】圣餐杯. ②〔诗〕杯. ③【植】杯状花.

chalk [tʃɔːk] *n.* ①白垩; 粉笔. ②用粉笔画的记号; 〔英〕(比赛)得分纪录; 记入借方的款项. ③〔美俚〕牛奶. *French* ~ = *tailor's* ~ (裁缝画线用的) 划粉. *coloured* ~*s* 彩色粉笔. ***(as) different as*** ~ ***from cheese*** = ***(as) like as*** ~ ***and [to] cheese*** 外貌相似实质不同, 似是而非. ***by a long*** ~ = ***by long*** ~***s*** = 〔英口〕***by*** ~***s*** 相差很多, 强得多, 好得多. ***come up to (the)*** ~ 〔美俚〕够标准, 好; 重行开始. ***make sb. walk a*** ~ 使人服从命令. ***not know*** ~ ***from cheese*** 不辨黑白, 不知好歹. ***not to make*** ~ ***of one and cheese of the other*** 公平待遇, 一视同仁, 毫无偏袒. ***stump one's*** ~ = ***walk one's*** ~ 〔俚〕走掉, 逃走. ***walk the*** ~ 〔俚〕笔直地走〔不醉的表现〕; 严格遵守公共秩序; 行为正派. — *vt.* ①用粉笔写[记下]. ②用白垩粉擦; 使苍白. ③打…的图样. ~ ***it up*** 公布, 公告. ~ ***on a barn door*** 〔美口〕大概算一算. ~ ***out*** ①标出. ②打样; 设计. ~ ***up*** ①用粉笔记下(分数、货帐等); 用粉笔写(在墙上等). ②把…归因于… ***(to)***. ③增多(利益等). ④〔美〕提高(价格); 赊出. ⑤达到, 得到. ~ **bed**【地】白垩层. ~**board** (浅色)黑板. ~ **line** 白粉笔线 (*walk the* ~ *line* 保持直线; 循规蹈矩). ~ **mixture** 幼孩用止痢药. ~**stone**【地】石灰岩;【医】痛风结石. ~**talk** (用粉笔边在黑板上边作图、边作说明的)图示演说[讲课].

chalk·y [ˈtʃɔːki] *a.* ①白垩(质)的; 富于白垩的; 白垩色的. ②无反响的;【摄】走了光的, 模糊不清的. **chalk·i·ness** *n.*

chal·lah [ˈhɑːlə] *n.* (犹太人安息日和节日吃的)白面包卷 (= hallah).

chal·lenge [ˈtʃælindʒ] *n.* ①挑战; 挑战书, 决斗书; (比赛等的)提议. ②要求, 需求, 鞭策. ③(哨兵对行人的)盘问, (对飞机等的)信号盘问; 口令. ④质问; 怀疑, 驳斥; 异议. ⑤艰巨任务, 难题. ⑥【法】(对陪审官等的) 要求回避, 表示反对, 拒绝. ⑦【医】(用接触致病性传染物进行的)免疫性试验. *give [write] a* ~ 挑战. *accept [take] a* ~ 应战. ***beyond*** ~ 无可非议; 无与伦比. ***rise to the*** ~ 应战; 迎着困难上. ***take a*** ~ ***lying down*** 在困难面前俯首贴耳. —*vt.* ①向…挑战. ②要求, 需要; 引起. ③【军】向…发出盘问口令[信号]. ④质问; 怀疑, 驳斥. ⑤【法】对(陪审官等)要求回避, 宣布反对, 拒绝. ⑥〔美〕不承认(投票人有投票资格). ~ *attention* 要求人们的注意. ~ *sb.'s interest* 使某人发生兴趣. ~ ***a result*** 质问表决结果, 对之表示异议. ~ ***(sb.) to (a duel; a game)*** 要求和(某人)(决斗; 比赛). —*vi.* ①提出挑战. ②【法】表示异议. ③(猎犬发现猎物时)吠叫. ~ **cup [flag]** 优胜杯[旗]. **-leng·ing** *a.* ①挑战的. ②引起争论[兴趣]的.

chal·leng·er [ˈtʃælindʒə] *n.* ①挑战人, 要求决斗者. ②提出异议者; 质问者; 驳斥者;【法】要求(陪审官等)回避者. ③提出盘问者.

chal·lis, chal·lie [ˈtʃælis, ˈtʃæli] *n.* 【纺】印花毛[棉]薄织物.

chal·one [ˈkæləun] *n.*【生化】抑素.

chal·u·meau [ˈʃæljuˌməu] *n.*【乐】①芦笛. ②竖笛的最低音区.

cha·lutz [hɑːˈluːts] *n.* *(pl.* **-lutz·im** [-luːˈtsiːm]*)* 哈鲁茨〔以色列农业居民点中最早移入的犹太拓荒者〕(= halutz).

cha·lyb·e·ate [kəˈlibiit] *a.* (矿泉)含铁质的. — *n.* 含铁矿泉, 铁剂.

cham [kæm] *n.* 〔废〕= khan[1]. *the Great C-* ①鞑靼王, 大可汗. ②文坛权威〔特指 Samuel Johnson〕.

cha·made [ʃəˈmɑːd] *n.* 〔F.〕〔古〕求和号 [鼓], 投降号 [鼓]; 退却信号.

Cha·mae·le·on [kəˈmiːljən, -ˈmiːliən] *n.*【天】蝘蜓(星)座 (= Chameleon).

cham·ae·phyte [ˈkæmiəfait] *n.*【植】地上芽植物.

cham·ber [ˈtʃeimbə] *n.* ①〔古、诗〕室, 房间; 寝室, 卧室; 〔*pl.*〕套房; 〔*pl.*〕律师[法官]办公室. ②会议室, 会场; 议会, 议院; 协会. ③箱, 暗箱; 蜂箱. ④(枪的)弹膛, 药室; (留声机内的); 螺管(动植物体的)窝, 穴, 腔; 心室. ⑤便壶, 尿罐(= ~ pot). ⑥【矿】矿车. *the upper [lower]* ~ 上[下]议院. *C- of Commerce* 商会. *C- of Deputies* (法、意、智利等的)下院. *C- of Peers* (旧时葡萄牙的)上院. *C- of Representative* (比利时的)众议院. — *vt.* ①把…关在室内, 禁闭. ②(枪上)装(子弹). ③使有房间. — *a.* ①秘密的. ②【乐】在小厅内表演的, 小乐队演奏的. ~ *concert* 室内音乐会. ~ **council** 秘密会议. ~ **counsel** 法律顾问; (律师的)私人意见, 鉴定. ~**maid** (旅馆的)女侍; 〔美〕(一般)女仆; 〔古〕侍女. ~ **music** 室内音乐. ~ **orchestra** 室内乐队. ~ **pot** 尿罐, 便壶.

cham·bered [ˈtʃeimbəd] *a.* 有 (…) 房间的; 处在房间[小室]里的. ~ **corridor** 两旁边侧有房间的走廊. ~ **rein**【矿】束状矿脉.

Cham·ber·lain [ˈtʃeimbəlin] *n.* 钱伯林, 张伯伦〔姓氏〕. **(Arthur) Neville** ~ 张伯伦〔1869—1940, 英国政治家, 1937—40 年任首相〕.

cham·ber·lain [ˈtʃeimbəlin] *n.* ①(国王的)侍从; (贵族的)管家. ②(村镇的)收款员, 财务管理人; 〔古〕(旅馆的)房间管理人. *the Grand C-* 侍从长. *the Lord C- (of the Household)* (英王的)宫内大臣; 侍从长. *the Lord Great C- (of England)* 掌礼大臣.

Cham·bers [ˈtʃeimbəz] *n.* 钱伯斯〔姓氏〕.

cham·bray [ˈʃæmbrei] *n.* 条格布.

cha·me·le·on [kəˈmiːljən] *n.* ①【动】石龙子, 变色龙〔蜥蜴类〕. ②反复无常的人. ③〔the C-〕【天】蝘蜓(星)座. ~ **solution** 【化】(过)锰酸钾溶液, 变色液.

cha·me·le·on·ic [kəˌmiːliˈɔnik] *a.* 变色龙一样的; 反复无常的.

cham·fer [ˈtʃæmfə] *n.* ①【建】削角. ②槽, 凹线; 〔美〕圆槽. ③斜面, 切角面, 棱角. ④【机】圆角, 倒角, 倒棱, 斜切. — *vt.* ①在…上雕槽[刻沟]. ②去…的角, 斜切. ③〔美〕(用圆凿)刳(木、石等), 在…上挖圆槽.

cham·fron, cham·frain [ˈtʃæmfrən] *n.* 马头甲, 马盔.

cham·ois [ˈʃæmwɑː] *n.* *(pl.*~ [ˈʃæmwɑːz]*)* ①【动】(南欧及西亚的)小羚羊. ②羚羊皮, 麂皮, 油鞣革.

cham·o·mile [ˈkæməmail] *n.* = camomile.

Cha·mor·ro [tʃɑːˈmɔːrəu] *n.* ①*(pl.* ~*)* 夏莫洛人〔关岛和马里亚纳群岛本土人的一个部族〕. ②夏莫洛人讲的印尼语.

cha·motte [ʃəˈmɔt] *n.*【建】火泥. ~ **brick** 耐火砖.

champ[1] [ˈtʃæmp] *vt.* ①(马)嚼(草料); 格格地咬 (马嚼子). ②捣烂. — *vi.* ①(马) 大声咀嚼. ②(人) (兴奋得) 牙齿颤响, (怒得) 咬牙切齿. ③不耐烦, 焦急. ~

the bit (马)咬马嚼子;(人)(因拖延等而)焦急,不耐烦. —*n.* 嚼;嚼声.

champ² [ˈtʃæmp] *n.* 〔美俚〕 = champion.

cham·pac, cham·pak [ˈʃæmpæk] *n.*【植】金香木.

cham·pagne [ʃæmˈpein] *n.* ①香槟酒. ②微黄色,极淡的黄绿色;香槟酒似的颜色. ③〔C-〕香槟省〔法国东北部一省〕. *still* ～ 无泡香槟酒. ～ **cider** 苹果香槟酒;苹果汽酒. ～ **cup** ①香槟汽水. ②大酒杯.

cham·paign [ˈtʃæmpein] *n.* 原野,平原. —*a.* (地势)平坦的.

cham·per·ty [ˈtʃæmpə(ː)ti] *n.*【法】(帮人诉讼胜诉后互分利益的)帮诉;帮诉罪.

cham·pi·gnon [tʃæmˈpinjən] *n.*【植】香蕈,食用伞菌.

cham·pi·on [ˈtʃæmpjən] *n.* ①战士;斗士;监督执行者;维护者,拥护者 *(for)*. ②锦标保持人,优胜者,冠军 (*cf.* runner-up);(博览会中的)特等奖得奖人〔动物〕. ③倡导人,提倡者. *a national* ～ 全国冠军. ～ *flag* 优胜旗. ～ *race* 锦标赛跑. *a* ～ *for [against] justice* 正义的维护者〔反对者〕. *King's [Queen's] C-, C- of England* (世袭的)英王加冕典礼护卫官. —*a.*〔口〕头等的,优秀的;非常的. *a* ～ *idiot* 大傻瓜. *a* ～ *blunder* 大错. —*vt.* ①维护,拥护,主张;为…而斗争. ②监督执行,主持. ～ *a cause* 维护一项事业. **-less** *a.* 无冠军的.

cham·pi·on·ship [ˈtʃæmpjənʃip] *n.* ①拥护,支持;提倡;拥护者〔支持者,提倡者〕的身分. ②锦标;优胜;冠军称号〔地位〕. ③锦标赛 (=～ series). ④保持冠军称号的时期.

champ·le·vé [ʃɑːnliˈvei] *a.* 〔F.〕雕刻铜版的. — *n.* 雕刻铜版搪瓷器皿.

Chanc. = Chancellor; Chancery.

chance [tʃɑːns] *n.* ①偶然;运气,命运;偶然事件,意外事件 (*opp.* necessity). ②机会,良机;幸运,侥幸;机缘. ③〔常 *pl.*〕概率,几率,或然率,可能性,或然性,把握,希望;形势. ④〔美〕危险,冒险;赌博;彩票. ⑤〔美俚〕大学校长. ⑥〔美俚〕时间;大量,许多. *a game of* ～ 碰运气的游戏;没有把握的行动;碰运气的(偶然的)事情. *If* ～ *will have me king.* 万一我做国王. *I will give you a* ～. 我姑且给你一个改过的机会〔下次不再宽恕了〕. *The* ～*s are against it.* 形势不利. *I stood there a pretty considerable* ～. 〔美〕我在那儿站了很久. *a smart [powerful]* ～ *of apples* 〔美〕许许多多苹果. ***a dog's*** ～ 极微小的一点儿机会. ***a fat*** ～ 机会"多得很"〔反语〕. ***an off*** ～ 万一的希望,很小的可能. ***by any*** ～ 万一,碰巧. ***by*** ～ 偶然,意外地 (*by the merest* ～ 完完全全是偶然的,极意外地). ***by some*** ～ 不知道为什么. ***even*** ～ 胜败各半,成败相等. ***fighting*** ～ 虽有可能性但很难得到的机会. ***have no*** ～ ***whatever*** 谈不上;没有任何希望. ***leave things to*** ～ 听天由命,听其自然. ***lose no*** ～ ***for*** 不放松,抓紧. ***on the*** ～ ***of*** 指望,期待 (*I came on the* ～ *of finding you.* 我来是想碰到你). ***on the off*** ～ 适值千载一时的机会,侥幸. ***run a*** ～ ***of failure*** 〔美〕有失败的危险. ***stand a good [fair]*** ～ ***of*** 有相当把握,大有希望. ***stand no*** ～ ***against*** 对…不操胜算〔无把握〕. ***stand one's*** ～ 听天由命. ***take a (long)*** ～ = ***take (long)*** ～ 冒险一试. ***take one's [the]*** ～ 好歹试试看. ***the main*** ～ 最有利的机会,绝好机会;赚钱机会 (*have an eye to the main* ～ 追求个人利益,唯利是图,竭力钻营). —*a.* 偶然的,意外的. *a* ～ *meeting* 邂逅. *a* ～ *child* 私生儿. —*vi.* 偶然发生,料不到会,偶然得到. *I* ～*d to meet him.* 偶然碰到了他. *He* ～*d to be present.* 他碰巧在场〔此义现在一般用 happen〕. —*vt.* 冒…的险;〔口〕〔常作 ～ it〕试试看,碰碰看;〔美俚〕抓住(机会). *I will* ～ *it.* 好歹试试看,碰碰运气看. ***and*** ～ ***it*** 〔俚〕无论怎样,好歹. ***as it may*** ～ 按当时形势. ～ ***on [upon]*** 偶然发现,碰巧看见. ～ ***one's arm*** 〔口〕冒险一试;抓牢机会. ～ ***the consequence*** 成败由天.

chance·ful [ˈtʃɑːnsful] *a.* ①多变的;多事的. ②〔古〕取决于机会的;冒险的,危险的.

chan·cel [ˈtʃɑːnsəl] *n.*【宗】(教堂中祭坛周围设有祭司及唱诗班席位的)高坛,圣坛.

chan·cel·ler·y [ˈtʃɑːnsələri] *n.* ①大臣〔大法官、总理等〕的职位. ②大臣官邸,总理公署、官邸,大法官法庭. ③(大使馆或领事馆的)办事处;大使〔领事〕馆全体人员. *news to disturb the chancelleries of Europe* 震惊欧洲外交界的消息.

chan·cel·lor [ˈtʃɑːnsələ] *n.* ①〔英〕(财政)大臣,司法官〔职位名〕. ②〔美〕平衡法院的首席法官;(大使馆等的)秘书长;〔英〕大学名誉校长,〔美〕大学校长. ③【史】(东罗马帝国的)掌玺官. ④【史】(旧时德、奥等国的)总理. *a* ～ *of a diocese* (英国教会)主教法律顾问. *the C- of the Exchequer* 〔英〕财政大臣. *the Lord (High) C-* = *the C- (of England)* 〔英〕大法官〔阁员之一,议会开会期间兼任上院议长〕. **-ship** 大臣〔大法官、总理〕的职位〔任期〕.

chan·cel·lor·y = chancellery.

chance-med·ley [ˈtʃɑːnsˈmedli] *n.* ①【法】偶然杀人,过失〔自卫〕杀伤. ②偶然(行动).

chan·cer·y [ˈtʃɑːnsəri] *n.* ①〔C-〕〔英〕大法院〔今为高等法院的一部〕. ②〔美〕平衡法院;平衡法院的法律〔诉讼事务〕. ③档案处,记录处. ④大臣〔总理、大法官〕的办事处. ***a ward in*** ～ 受大法官监护的未成年人. ***in*** ～ ①在平衡法院〔大法官法庭〕诉讼中的. ②【拳】〔喻〕头被挟在对手腋下;进退两难.

chan·ci·ness [ˈtʃɑːnsinis] *n.* 不确定性,危险性.

chan·cre [ˈʃæŋkə] *n.*【医】(硬性)下疳.

chan·croid [ˈʃæŋkrɔid] *n.*【医】软下疳(=soft chancre).

chanc·y [ˈtʃɑːnsi] *a.* ①〔口〕不确实的,危险的. ②〔Scot.〕幸运的〔常用于否定句〕.

chan·de·lier [ˌʃændiˈliə] *n.* 枝形吊灯;【军】撑墙.

chan·delle [ʃɑːnˈdel] *n.*【空】急跃升. —*vi.* 作急跃升.

chan·dler [ˈtʃɑːndlə] *n.* ①蜡烛制造人,蜡烛商. ②(杂货)零售商.

chan·dler·y [ˈtʃɑːndləri] *n.* ①蜡烛类;杂货类. ②蜡烛店;杂货店. ③蜡烛〔杂货〕仓库.

chanel [ʃəˈnel] *a.* 沙诺尔式的〔一种妇女的服装形式,尤指无领无腰身的上衣〕.

change [ˈtʃeindʒ] *vt.* ①改变,变更,变换,变革. ②交换;兑换;把(大票等)换成零钱;把(支票等)兑成现金. ③换(车、衣服),更换. ④〔口〕使(味)变酸〔坏〕. ～ *one's habits [way of thinking]* 改变习惯〔想法〕. ～ *a horse [cars]* 换马〔倒车〕. ～ *a fivepound note* 把一张五镑钞票兑换成零钱. ～ *a fivepound note into gold* 把一张五镑钞票兑换成金币. — *vi.* ①变,改变,起变化. ②换车,换衣服,改换办法〔策略等〕. *Where do we* ～? 我们在哪里换车? *It took me only five minutes to* ～. 我只用五分钟就换好了衣服. ～ ***about*** 转变方向;变节;首尾互异,反复无常. ～ ***arms***【军】换(掮枪的)肩. ～ ***at …*** 在(某处)换车. ～ ***breath*** 〔美俚〕换换口味〔换喝另一种酒〕. ～ ***colo(u)r*** 变脸色. ～ ***down [up]*** (汽车)改成慢档〔快档〕;开慢〔快〕. ～ ***foot [step]*** 变方向;变态度;变步骤. ～ ***for …*** 换车往(某处). ～ ***for the better [worse]*** 变好〔坏〕. ～ ***… for …*** 以…换… (～ *the old shoes for the new ones* 以旧鞋换新鞋). ～ ***front***【军】改变攻击方向;〔喻〕转变论调. ～ ***into*** ①改穿(～ *into flannels* 换上法兰绒裤). ②变成 (*Water* ～*s into steam.* 水变成汽). ～ ***one's note [tune]*** 〔口〕(言谈中)改变口气〔态度〕. ～ ***oneself*** 换衣裳. ～ ***oneself into*** 变成…,化为. ～ ***over*** (使)改变(目的,位置);改期. ～ ***side*** 改变立场;脱党,变节. ～ ***(seats) with (sb.)*** 与(人)换(座位). —*n.* ①变化;改变,变换,变更;变动,变迁;改革;更迭. ②交换,交替;换衣服;换车;换环境. ③找头,零钱. ④【乐】转调,换调;钟声的变调. ⑤〔C-〕交易所(= 'Change, Exchange). *a* ～ *of address* 住址的变更. *a* ～ *of cars* 换车. *a* ～ *of clothes* 换衣服. *a* ～

of heart 变心;改变主意. *the* ~ *of the moon* 月亮的(圆缺)变化;新月的出现. *a* ~ *of tide* 潮的交替;危机. *a changing bag* (换胶卷用的)暗袋. *I have no* ~ *about me.* 我没有零钱. *You need a* ~. 你应该改变改变环境. **be [go] on** ~ 在交易所(做事). ~ **of air** 迁地(疗养). ~ **of life** (妇女的)更年期,经绝期,停经. ~ **of pace** 换口味;变手法. ~ **of voice** (青春期的)变嗓音. **for a** ~ 为了改变一下,为了换换花样. **get no** ~ **out of (sb.)** 〔俚〕从(某人)处得不到什么便宜;从(某人)探听不出什么. **give (sb.)** ~ 给某人以报答;〔俚〕向某人报复,对某人予以还击. **give (sb.) no** ~ 〔口〕不让某人知道;对某人秘而不宣. **put the** ~ **on [upon] (sb.)** 瞒,欺骗(某人). **ring the** ~**s** 打钟打出(各种)调子;用种种言语〔方式〕说明;用种种方法试办. **small** ~ 零钱. **take the** ~ **out of (sb.)** 〔口〕报复,复仇. **Take your** ~ **out of that!** 〔还嘴、报复时语〕这就是回答! ~ **gear [wheel]** 【机】变速轮. ~**over** *n.* ①改变,转变;变更,转换. ②(电影换片时的)换机放映. ~**room** 更衣室. ~**-up** *n.* 【垒球】(投球手每次投球的)变换手法.

change·a·bil·i·ty [ˌtʃeindʒəˈbiliti] *n.* 易变,不安定;可变性.

change·a·ble [ˈtʃeindʒəbl] *a.* 可变的,易变的,会变的;不确定的;无恒心的. **-ness** *n.* 易变,三心二意.

change·a·bly [ˈtʃeindʒəbli] *ad.* 易变地;不安定地;会变似地.

change·ful [ˈtʃeindʒful] *a.* 变化多的,易变的,不确定的. ~ **gear** 【机】变速齿轮. **-ly** *ad.*

change·less [ˈtʃeindʒlis] *a.* 不变的,确定的;单调的. **-ness** *n.*

change·ling [ˈtʃeindʒliŋ] *n.* ①(迷信说法中被仙女)偷换后留下的丑孩子;矮小丑陋的人〔动物〕. ②〔古〕低能儿. ③〔古〕见异思迁的人;不忠实的人,变节者. ④(集邮)颜色起化学变化的邮票.

chang·er [ˈtʃeindʒə] *n.* 变更者;更换器;(电唱机)自动换片器.

chan·nel[1] [ˈtʃænl] *n.* ①水路,水道,渠,沟;海峡;河床,河底. ②(柱等的)槽,凹缝;【机】槽铁,凹形铁. ③〔喻〕路线,手段;媒介;脉络,系统,途径. ④【无、电】波道;电路;信道;磁道;频道. *a talk* ~ 通话线路. *a vision* ~ 电视信道,视频信道. *the (English) C-* 英伦海峡. *C-fever* 〔英〕怀乡病. ~ *of command [communication]* 指挥〔通讯〕系统. *through a reliable* ~ 通过可靠途径. **through the proper** ~ 经由正当途径〔手续〕. — *vt.* (〔英〕**-ll-**) ①在…开〔形成〕水道;在…上凿沟〔凹缝〕. ②开(路),开辟(途径). ③为…开辟途径,引导. ~ *one's interests* 对自己的兴趣加以引导. — *vi.* 形成水道〔凹槽〕. ~**groping** 英国近海巡航.

chan·nel[2] [ˈtʃænl] *n.* 〔常 *pl.*〕【海】突出舷侧承扣支索的铁板.

chan·nell·ed [ˈtʃænəld] *a.* 有沟(凹缝)的. ~ **iron** 【机】U 形铁.

chan·nel·ize [ˈtʃænəlaiz] *vt.* = channel *vt.* **-i·za·tion** *n.*

chan·son [ˈʃænsən] *n.* 〔F.〕歌. ***C- de Roland*** 《罗兰之歌》〔法国中世纪的民族史诗〕.

chant [tʃɑːnt] *n.* ①【宗】颂歌;圣歌,赞美诗. ②单调的歌;吟诵语调,单调的语调. — *vt., vi.* ①单调地唱,吟诵. ②歌颂;颂扬,赞扬. ~ ***horses*** 夸马(骗卖),登骗人广告. ~ **the praises of** 极口称赞,颂扬.

chan·tage [ˈtʃɑːntidʒ] *n.* 〔F.〕勒索,讹诈.

chan·te·cler 见 chanticleer.

chant·er [ˈtʃɑːntə] *n.* ①歌唱者;领唱人. ②(风笛的)指管. ③骗人的马贩子. ④【动】篱雀.

chan·te·relle [ˌtʃæntiˈrel, ˌtʃæn-] *n.* 【植】鸡油菌属 *(Cantharellus)* 植物〔尤指鸡油菌〕*(Cantharellus cibarius)*.

chan·teuse [F. ʃɑ̃tøːz] *n.* 女歌手〔尤指女民歌手〕.

chant·ey [ˈʃɑːnti] = chanty.

chan·ti·cleer, chan·te·cler [ˌtʃæntiˈkliə, -ˈklɛə] *n.* 雄鸡(先生)〔法国古代文学作品《列那狐的故事》中拟人化的雄鸡〕.

chan·tor [ˈtʃɑːntə] *n.* = chanter.

chantress [ˈtʃɑːntris] *n.* 〔诗〕女歌手.

chan·try [ˈtʃɑːntri] *n.* ①(施主捐款建造的)歌祷堂;歌祷堂的捐建. ②附属小礼拜堂.

chan·ty [ˈʃɑːnti] *n.* 水手起锚歌(= chantey)

Cha·nu·kah [ˈkɑːnuˌkɑː] *n.* 犹太圣节(= Hanuka).

cha·os [ˈkeiɔs] *n.* ①〔常 C-〕(天地未出现前的)浑沌世界. ②混乱. ③〔古〕无底深渊.

cha·ot·ic [keiˈɔtik] *a.* 浑沌的;混乱的. **-i·cal·ly** *ad.*

chap[1] [tʃæp] *n.* ①〔口〕家伙,小伙子. ②〔英方〕买者,顾客. *a funny little* ~ 有趣的小家伙. *my dear* ~ = *old* ~ 老兄.

chap[2] [tʃæp] *n.* ①〔*pl.*〕(动物的)颚;(人的)面颊. ②猪头肉的颚颊部分. **lick one's** ~**s** 淌着口水等待(好菜),馋涎欲滴;(吃东西时)咂舌头.

chap[3] [tʃæp] *n.* 〔常 *pl.*〕皲;皲裂(处),龟裂(处). — *vt., vi.* (使)(皮肤等)皲裂〔发皲,龟裂,变粗糙〕.

chap[4] [tʃæp] *n.* 〔Scot.〕(钟)报(时).

chap. = chapel; chaplain; chapter.

cha·pa·ra·jos, -rejos [ˌtʃæpəˈrɑːhəus, -ˈreihəus] *n.* 〔美西部〕牧人皮套裤.

chap·ar·ral [tʃæpəˈræl] *n.* 〔美西部〕小槲树(的丛林);(一般)树丛.

chap-book [ˈtʃæpbuk] *n.* ①(旧时小贩沿街叫卖的)民间文艺(廉价)小册子〔唱本〕. ②小书,小册子.

chape [tʃeip] *n.* ①(剑鞘的)铜包头. ②(皮带上的)小圈.

cha·peau [ʃæˈpəu] *n.* (*pl.* ~**s**, **-peaux** [-ˈpəuz]) 〔F.〕帽. *C- bas* [ˈbɑː]! 脱帽! ~ *de poil* 海獭帽. ~**-bras** 〔F.〕可折叠的三角帽.

chap·el [ˈtʃæpəl] *n.* ①小教堂,附属教堂;〔英〕(国教分离派的)教堂;(学校、营房等的)附属礼拜堂〔室〕;(在学校礼拜室中做的)礼拜. ②印刷(厂工人)工会. ③〔美俚〕殡仪馆. **a** ~ **of ease** 〔英〕(偏远教区的)小教堂. **father of the** ~ 印刷厂工人工会主席. **hold a** ~ 开印刷厂工会会议. **hold** ~ (教皇等)参加礼拜. **keep a** ~ 〔牛津、剑桥大学〕(按时)做礼拜. **keep one's** ~**s** 只按时做礼拜(此外不做). **lose [miss] a** ~ 没有去做礼拜.

cha·pelle ar·dente [ʃæˈpel ɑːˈdɑ̃ːnt] 〔F.〕(名人死后点着蜡烛供人瞻仰的)停尸室.

chap·er·on(e) [ˈʃæpərəun] *n.* (在交际场中监护少女的)年长女伴;保护人. — *vt.* 陪伴,伴随;护送(少女). **-age** *n.* 陪伴,伴随(少女).

chap·fall·en [ˈtʃæpˌfɔːlən] *a.* ①下颚下垂的. ②〔喻〕沮丧的,垂头丧气的.

chap·i·ter [ˈtʃæpitə] *n.* 【建】柱头.

chap·lain [ˈtʃæplin] *n.* 随军〔校内,院内〕教士〔军队、学校、医院、监狱等中的教士,有时亦由非教士担任〕. **-cy, -ship** *n.* (随军等的)教士职位.

chap·let [ˈtʃæplit] *n.* ①花冠;项圈. ②念珠;【建】串珠饰. ③(孔雀)冠毛;(昆虫)刺冠. **-ed** *a.* 戴着花冠的.

Chap·lin [ˈtʃæplin] *n.* 查普林,卓别麟〔姓氏〕.

Chap·man [ˈtʃæpmən] *n.* 查普曼〔姓氏〕.

chap·man [ˈtʃæpmən] *n.* 叫卖小贩;行商.

chap·pie, chap·py[1] [ˈtʃæpi] *n.* 〔口〕①花花公子. ②家伙,小伙子.

chap·py[2] [ˈtʃæpi] *a.* 皲裂的.

chaps [tʃæps] *n.* 〔*pl.*〕= chaparajos.

chap·ter [ˈtʃæptə] *n.* ①(书籍、文章的)章,部分;(历史或人生的)一段经过. ②(大教堂)教士会;教士会集会,骑士团〔修士团〕的集会(会场). ③〔美〕(俱乐部,协会,校友会等的)分会;〔美〕一次比赛. ④(钟表盘面上的)数字,符号. **a** ~ **of accidents** 一连串(不幸的)事故. **enough on that** ~ 这个问题就到此为止. **give** ~ **and verse**

for 注明引证出处；指明确切依据. *read (sb.) a ~* 教训(某人). *to [till] the end of the ~* 到最后；永远. ~ **house** 教士会礼堂；〔美大学〕校友会会所.

char[1] [tʃɑː] *n., vi., vt.* = 〔美〕chare. ~**lady,** ~**woman** 打杂女工. ~**man** 勤杂工.

char[2] [tʃɑː] *n.* 木炭，炭；烧焦之物. — *vt.* 把…烧成炭；烧焦(木材表面). — *vi.* 变焦黑.

char[3] [tʃɑː] *n.* *(pl. ~s)* 【鱼】红点鲑，白点鲑.

char[4] [tʃɑː] *n.* 〔英俚〕茶.

char-à-banc [ˈʃærəbæŋ] *n.* *(pl. ~s* [z]*)* 〔F.〕游览车. *a motor ~* 游览汽车.

char·a·cin [ˈkærəsin] *n.* 【动】特色鱼 *(Characinidae)* 〔产于南美，中美和非洲〕.

char·ac·ter [ˈkæriktə] *n.* ①性格，品格；特性，性状，特征；【生】形质. ②身分，地位，资格. ③名声，声望. ④(戏剧、小说中的)角色，人物. ⑤人，〔口〕怪人，奇人. ⑥字，字母；数字；(印刷)符号；电码组合；【计】字符. ⑦品德证明书，鉴定，推荐书. ⑧人物[性格]素描. *a man of ~* 有个性[骨气]的人. *the national ~ = the ~ of a people* 国民性. *a generic ~* 【生】属的特征，属性. *a leading ~* 主角. *a bad ~* 坏人，歹徒，恶棍. *He is quite a ~.* 他简直是一个怪人. *a Chinese ~* 汉字. *~ portrayal* 性格描写. *~ sketch* 人物简评[素描]. ***get a good [bad] ~*** 得好[坏]名. ***give (sb.) a good [bad] ~*** 推奖[攻击](某人). ***have an insight into ~*** 有知人之明. ***in ~*** (在)性格上；正合担任[扮演]；适当，相称. ***in the ~ of*** 以…的资格；扮演. ***out of ~*** 不适当[适合]，不称(*go out of ~* 越分妄为). ***take away sb.'s ~*** 夺人名誉. ***take on ~*** 有特征[特色]. — *vt.* ①〔诗、古〕写，画；刻. ②表现…的特性；使具有特性. ~ **actor** 性格演员. ~ **assassination** (对知名人士等的)人格毁损. ~ **book** 征信录，各界人士录. ~ **building** 性格陶冶. **-less** *a.* 无特征的，平凡的.

char·ac·ter·is·tic [ˌkæriktəˈristik] *a.* 有特性的；表示…特性的，…特有的. *Japan's ~ art* 日本特有的艺术. —*n.* 特性，特征，性能，特色. *be ~ of* …所独有的特征，有…的特色. *~ of logarithm* 对数的首数. ~ **curve** 特性曲线. ~ **function** 示性函数. ~ **radiation** 【物】标志辐射. ~ **species** 典型种. ~ **test** 【机】特性试验 **-cal·ly** *ad.*

char·ac·ter·i·za·tion [ˌkæriktəraiˈzeiʃən] *n.* 特性记述[表示、赋与]；性格描写；鉴定.

char·ac·ter·ize [ˈkæriktəraiz] *vt.* ①叙述[描写]…的特性；鉴定. ②表示…的特性；以…为特性；使带有…的特征. *a style ~d by brevity* 具有简洁特色的文体. — *vi.* (文学作品中)塑造人物，描写性格. ***be ~d by*** 有…的(显著)特点，突出地表现为….

char·ac·ter·y [ˈkæriktəri] *n.* 〔集合词〕符号，文字.

char·ac·to·nym [kəˈræktənim] *n.* 说明某人特征的词[名称].

char·ac·tron [ˈkærəktrɔn] *n.* 【无】显象管；显示管，字码管.

cha·rade [ʃəˈrɑːd; Am. ʃəˈreid] *n.* ①(用诗、画、动作等构成的)哑剧字谜；哑剧字谜的谜底〔一个词或一句话〕. ②〔喻〕荒谬的借口，几乎不加掩饰的伪装.

char·bon [ˈʃɑːbɔ̃ːŋ] *n.* 〔F.〕【医】炭疽(脾脱疽).

char·broil [ˈtʃɑːbrɔil] *vt.* 用木炭火烤(肉).

char·coal [ˈtʃɑːkəul] *n.* ①(木)炭；【医】生物炭. ②(画用)炭笔. ③木炭画. *activated ~* 活性炭. *animal ~* 骨炭，兽炭. ~ **biscuit** (胃肠病吃的)炭饼干. ~ **burner** 烧炭人；炭炉. ~ **crayon** 炭笔. ~ **drawing** 木炭画. ~ **lily** 黑皮肤的少年. ~ **rot** 【植】黑腐病.

chard [tʃɑːd] *n.* 【植】莙荙菜，牛皮菜 *(Beta vulgaris cicla).*

chare [tʃɛə] *n.* ①〔美〕〔常 *pl.*〕(家庭中的)零碎工作，杂活，家务. ②〔口〕打杂女用人，临时女帮工，计时女佣. — *vt., vi.* ①(给…)打杂，(为…)做零活. ②清扫，修理. *~ a leak* 检修屋漏.

charge [tʃɑːdʒ] *vt.* ①填；装(子弹)；充(电)；使饱和；使充满；堆积，装载. ②命令；促；谕示，指令. ③责备；告诫. ④使承担(责任). ⑤把…归咎于 *(to, on, upon)*；告发，在控告 *(with)*. ⑥要求收(费)；索(价)；课(税). ⑦为…支出；在(帐)上记入…，记入…帐内[名下]. ⑧【军】向…进击，袭击. *~ a pen* (钢笔)上墨水. *a charging machine* 装料机. *air ~d with moisture* 充满潮气的空气. *~ sb. with theft* 以窃盗罪控告某人，控告某人行窃. *I shall ~ you five dollars.* 我要你付五元. *~ a tax on …* 对…征税. *I ~d him to see that all was right.* 托他妥为照料. — *vi.* ①收费，要价. ②【军】冲锋，向前冲. *He ~s high for it.* 他对之要高价. ~ ***and cheer*** 一边冲锋一边呐喊. ***C- bayonet!*** 上刺刀！〔冲锋前的号令〕. ~ ***off*** 【会计】(在帐簿中)注销(损失等)，报损. ~ ***off … to*** 把…归于某一项[看作某事的一部分]. ~ ***oneself with*** 负起…的责任，承担. ~ ***to sb.'s account*** 记入某人帐下 (*C- these cigars to my account [against me].* 这些雪茄烟请算在我帐里). ~ ***(sb.) with*** 托付，使…负担；使负…的罪名，认为有…的嫌疑；使受…的责备. — *n.* ①负荷，装载物；(火器的)装填；充气；充电，电荷；(一定量的)炸药. ②保护，监督，管理. ③责任；义务，任务. ④委托，委托物. ⑤命令，指令. ⑥控诉；告发；指责；嫌疑；罪状，罪过. ⑦〔常 *pl.*〕费用；捐税；代价；记帐. ⑧【军】冲锋，进击；冲锋号；(足球)截住对方攻球，阻住对方前进；(猛兽的)袭击. ⑨〔美俚〕快感，刺激. ⑩【徽】(盾上)图形，图案. ⑪〔*pl.*〕〔美〕棒球队队员. ⑫〔口〕麻醉剂，毒品. *a bursting ~* 炸药. *a rocket ~* 火箭火药柱. *The books are under my ~.* 这些书归我保管. *a carrying ~* 维修费. *a false ~* 诬告. *a terminal ~* (给用户的)结算. *sound the ~* 吹冲锋号. *at moderate ~s* 以公道的代价. ***at one's own ~*** 自费. ~ ***for trouble*** 手续费. ~ ***of sheer bone and muscle*** 肉搏战. ~***s forward*** 运费等货到后由收货人自付. ~ ***of quarters*** 营舍值班(士官). ~***s paid*** 各费付讫. ***free of ~*** 免费. ***give in ~*** 寄存，委托(某物给某人)；交付(犯人给警察). ***have ~ of*** 承受，承担. ***in ~*** 主任[主管] (*the doctor in ~* 主任医师). ***in ~ of*** 主持，领导，管理[处理]…的，看管…的，受托…的 (*the nurse in ~ of the child* 照管孩子的保姆). ***in full ~*** 负全责；猛然，突然. ***in [under] the ~ of*** 在…看护下的，交…照看的 (*the child in the ~ of the nurse* 交保姆照看的孩子). ***lay to sb.'s ~*** 归罪于，指控(某人). ***make a ~ against*** 责备；袭击；控告. ***no ~ for admission*** 免费入场. ***on (a) ~ of*** 以…罪控告. ***on the ~ of*** 因…的嫌疑. ***put in ~ of*** 委托. ***return to the ~*** 再重新进攻；改变(意见等). ***take ~*** 掌管；〔俚〕(事物)控制不住，弄糟. ***take ~ of*** 担任，保管，看守，看管，监督，负责. ***take over ~ of*** 承受，接办. ***take personal ~*** 亲自处理[照管]. ~ **account** 【会计】赊销(户头). ~ **nurse** (某一个病房的)责任护士. ~**-a-plate,** ~ **plate** 赊货牌. ~ **sheet** (警察局的)事故[案件]记录.

charge·a·ble [ˈtʃɑːdʒəbl] *a.* ①(税)应征收的. ②(罪)应指控的. ③应由某人负担[应负责]的. ④可充电的. **charge·a·bil·i·ty** *n.*

char·gé d'af·faires [ˈʃɑːʒei dæˈfɛə] *(pl. chargés d'affaires* [ˈʃɑːʒeiz dæˈfɛə]*)* 〔F.〕①代理大使，临时代办(正式说作 ***chargé d'affaires ad interim***). ②代办.

charg·er [ˈtʃɑːdʒə] *n.* ①委托者；控诉者. ②插弹夹；充电器，装料机. ③突击者；【军】军官坐骑；战马. ④〔古〕大盘子.

char·i·ly [ˈtʃɛərili] *ad.* ①小心地，谨慎地. ②节俭地，吝啬地.

char·i·ness [ˈtʃɛərinis] *n.* ①小心，谨慎. ②节俭，吝啬.

char·i·ot [ˈtʃæriət] *n.* ①(古代双轮马拉)战车；(十八世纪的)四轮轻便马车；〔诗〕花车，凯旋车；长途马车. ②〔美俚〕汽车. ③【电】齿车；托架. — *vt.* 用马车[战车]

运送.

char·i·ot·eer [ˌtʃæriəˈtiə] *n.* ①马车[战车]驾驶者. ②〔the C-〕【天】驭夫座.

char·ism [ˈkærizəm] *n.* = charisma.

cha·ris·ma [kəˈrizmə] *n.* (*pl.* **-ma·ta** [-mətə]) ①【神】(迷信者所说的领袖人物的)超凡魅力, 神授能力. ②众望所归的作领导的特殊本领〔品质〕. **charis·mat·ic** [ˌkærizˈmætik] *a.*

char·i·ta·ble [ˈtʃæritəbl] *a.* 仁爱的; 慈善的; 厚道的. **-ness** *n.*

char·i·ta·bly [ˈtʃæritəbli] *ad.* 仁爱地; 慈善地.

char·i·tari·an [ˌtʃæriˈteiriən] *n.* 〔美〕慈善家.

char·i·ty [ˈtʃæriti] *n.* ①慈爱; 仁爱, 博爱,【宗】上帝之爱, (基督徒之间的)教友之爱. ②(对别人的)仁慈; 宽大, 宽容; 慈悲心. ③〔常 *pl.*〕慈善(行为), 施舍, 捐助; 抚恤金; 慈善事业; 慈善机关[团体]; 施诊所. ***as cold as*** ~ 极冷淡〔讽刺形式上的慈善〕. ***be in [out of]*** ~ ***with*** 爱[不爱]. ~ ***ball [concert]*** 慈善募捐舞会[音乐会]. ***C- begins at home.*** 〔谚〕仁慈先从亲属始〔常作拒绝捐款的借口〕. ~ ***hospital*** 慈善医院, 施诊所. ***for*** ~***'s sake*** = ***in*** ~ = ***out of*** ~ 为慈善故, 以仁爱精神. ~ **boy [child, girl]** 孤儿院[慈善学校]中的男孩[孩子, 女孩]. ~ **school** 慈善学校.

cha·ri·va·ri [ˈʃɑːriˈvɑːri] *n.* ①(在新婚者屋前敲铁锅、铜罐等的)逗闹音乐; 大嚷闹, 嘈杂. ②〔C-〕《逗闹》杂志〔法国一滑稽刊物〕. *The London C-* 〔英〕幽默刊物 *Punch* 杂志的别称.

char·la·tan [ˈʃɑːlətən] *n.* ①骗子; 假内行. ②庸医. — *a.* 假充内行的, 骗人的. **-ism, -ry** *n.* 吹牛; 蒙混, 欺骗. **-ish** *a.* 庸医般的, 骗人的.

Charle·magne [ˈʃɑːləˈmein] *n.* 查理曼大帝〔742—814, 世称 Charles the Great 或 Charles I, 于 768—814 为法兰克王, 并于 800—814 为西罗马帝国皇帝〕.

Charles [tʃɑːlz] 查尔斯〔姓氏, 男子名〕.

Charles's Wain [ˈtʃɑːlziz ˈwein] 〔英〕北斗七星.

Charles·ton [ˈtʃɑːlstən] *n.* ①查尔斯顿〔美国南卡罗来纳州港市〕. ②查尔斯顿〔美国西弗吉尼亚州城市〕. ③查尔斯顿舞〔本世纪二十年代开始流行〕. — *vi.* 跳查尔斯顿舞.

Char·ley, Charlie [ˈtʃɑːli] *n.* 查利〔男子名〕. ***c- horse*** 〔美口〕(因运动过度或受伤所致的)筋肉硬直.

Char·lie [ˈtʃɑːli] *n.* ① = Charley. ②通讯中代表字母 C 的词.

char·lock [ˈtʃɑːlɔk] *n.* 【植】田芥菜.

Char·lotte [ˈʃɑːlət] *n.* 夏洛特〔女子名〕.

char·lotte [ˈʃɑːlət] *n.* 〔F.〕水果奶油布丁.

Char·lotte A·ma·lie [ˈtʃɑːlə əˈmɑːljə] 夏洛特阿马利亚〔美属维尔京群岛首府〕.

charm [tʃɑːm] *n.* ①(迷人的)魔力, 诱惑力; 〔常 *pl.*〕妩媚; 妖媚, 风骚, 风韵, 色相. ②咒文; 护符, 符咒. ③(表链等的)小装饰品, 小玩意儿. ④〔*pl.*〕〔美俚〕钱. *feminine* ~*s* 女性(特有)的妩媚. ***act like a*** ~ = ***to a*** ~ (药物等)效验如神; 神妙地, 十二万分地. — *vt.* ①迷(人), 诱惑, 夺(人)魂魄; 使陶醉, 使喜爱. ②〔古〕对…行魔法, 用魔法保护[治疗]; 把(蛇等)养乖. *I shall be* ~*ed to see you tomorrow.* 我真希望明天能见到你. — *vi.* ①行魔法. ②有魅力, 令人陶醉. *Goodness* ~*s more than beauty.* 心地好胜过容貌好. ***be*** ~***ed with*** 心醉于, 给…迷住. ***bear [have, lead] a*** ~***ed life*** 有刀枪不入的能耐 (*She bore a* ~*ed life, and prospered amid dangers and alarms.* 她似乎是刀枪不入的, 经过种种危险还好好活了下来). ~ ***(sb.) asleep*** 用魔力催眠. ~ ***away*** *(the fiend)* 用符咒驱除(恶魔). ~ *(a secret)* ***out of*** *(sb.)* 哄出(某人)的(秘密)来. **-ed** *a.* 着迷的; 被施了魔法的; 陶醉的; (蛇)养乖了的.

charm·er [ˈtʃɑːmə] *n.* 弄蛇人; 魔术师; 使人着魔的人[物]; 〔古、讽〕美女.

char·meuse [ʃɑːˈməːz] *n.* 【纺】软缎. ~ **cotton** 棉缎.

charm·ing [ˈtʃɑːmiŋ] *a.* 迷人的, 娇媚的, 可爱的; 有趣的. **-ly** *ad.*

char·nel [ˈtʃɑːnl] *n.* 骨灰堂, 藏骸所(= ~ house). — *a.* 藏放尸骨场所的; 死一样的.

Cha·ron [ˈkeərən] *n.* 【希神】(将亡魂渡到阴界去的)冥府渡神; 〔讽〕摆渡的人. ***~'s boat [ferry]*** 临终.

char·poy [ˈtʃɑːpɔi] *n.* (印度等地的)轻便床 (= charpai).

char·qui [ˈtʃɑːki] *n.* (秘鲁)干牛肉.

char·rette [ʃəˈret] *n.* (一个团体请专家协助讨论的)问题研究会.

char·ring [ˈtʃɑːriŋ] *n.* 烧焦, 炭化(法), 焦化(法).

char·ry [ˈtʃɑːri] *a.* 炭状的.

chart[1] [tʃɑːt] *n.* ①海图, 航(线)图, 航海图; 地势图 (= physical ~), (军用)地形图 (= topographic ~). ②图, 略图; 图表; (物价、温度等的)曲线图, 线标图. ③(仪器中用的)刻度记录纸. *a bathygraphic* ~ 海洋水深图. *a hydrographic* ~ 水道图. *a duty* ~ 工作时间[进度]表. *a flow* ~ 工艺流程图. *a record* ~ 自动记录带. *a toll rate* ~ 长途电话价目表. — *vt.* ①绘制…的海图[地图], 把(航线等)绘入海图; 〔喻〕指引(航向). ②用图表示〔说明〕. ③制订…的计划. ~ **house [room]** (船上的)海图室. **-ist** *n.* 制图者. **-less** *a.* ①尚未绘入海图[地图]的. ②无图可凭的. **-let** 【海】小海图.

chart[2] [tʃɑːt] *n.* 乐曲的改编; 改编的乐曲.

char·ter [ˈtʃɑːtə] *n.* ①(准许成立自治都市、工会等的)特许状; 凭照, 执照, (社团对成立分会等的)许可证. ②特权, 豁免权, 专利权, (铁路等的)铺设权. ③宪章. ④契据, 证书; 【商】租船契约; 租船合同 (= ~ party). ⑤(船只、飞机、公共汽车等的)租赁. *the C- of the U.N.* 联合国宪章. ***a blank*** ~ 行动自由权, 空白委任状. ***the Great C-*** (= Magna Charta)【英史】大宪章. ***a time*** ~ 定期租船契约. — *vt.* ①给…发特许执照, 特许(成立公司等). ②(凭契约)租[包](船、车等); 〔口〕雇(车等). ~ **member** 〔美〕(公司等的)创立委员. ~ **party** 租船契约[合同].

char·tered [ˈtʃɑːtəd] *a.* ①(受)特许的. ②(船等)租的. *a* ~ *bank* 特许银行. *a* ~ *ship* 租用的船. ***a*** ~ ***libertine*** 世所公认的浪子. ~ **accountant** 〔英〕特许会计师〔略 C.A.〕. ~ **cities** 特别市.

char·ter·er [ˈtʃɑːtərə] *n.* (车、船等的)租用者.

Char·ter·house [ˈtʃɑːtəhaus] *n.* ①卡尔特修道院. ②〔the ~〕卡尔特养老院〔1611 年在伦敦卡尔特修道院旧址上设立, 故名〕. ③卡尔特豪斯公立学校 (= ~ School)〔曾设立在卡尔特修道院旧址〕.

Chart·ism [ˈtʃɑːtizəm] *n.* 【英史】(1837—1848 年的)宪章运动; 宪章主义.

Chart·ist [ˈtʃɑːtist] *n.* 宪章运动者; 宪章主义者, 宪章派.

char·tog·ra·pher [kɑːˈtɔgrəfə] *n.* 制图家.

char·tog·ra·phy [kɑːˈtɔgrəfi] *n.* 制图法; 制图术 (= cartography).

char·treuse [ʃɑːˈtrəːz] *n.* ①〔C-〕(法国)沙特勒兹修道院. ②(沙特勒兹修道院所制)荨麻酒. ③鲜嫩的黄绿色.

char·tu·lar·y [ˈkɑːtjuləri] *n.* = cartulary.

char·y [ˈtʃeəri] *a.* ①细心的, 谨慎的. ②谦恭的, 腼腆的. ③节俭的 (*of*). *be* ~ *of giving offense* 尽量避免伤人感情[得罪人]. *be* ~ *of strangers* 怯生, 腼腆. *be* ~ *of one's praise* 不轻易称赞.

Cha·ryb·dis [kəˈribdis] *n.* ①【希神】女妖. ②(Sicily 岛海面的)大旋涡.

Chase [tʃeis] *n.* 蔡斯〔姓氏〕.

chase[1] [tʃeis] *vt.* ①追赶, 追击; 追随, 追逐. ②追寻, 寻觅. ③驱逐, 驱除. ④〔俚〕(男女间)竭力追求. ⑤〔俚〕端递(食物), 上(菜). ~ *fear from the mind* 驱除恐怖心. ~ *a cat out of the garden* 把猫赶出花园去. *Please* ~ *the milk this way.* 请把牛奶递到这边来. — *vi.* ①追逐, 追赶; 跟踪

(after). ②东奔西跑,匆忙地走. ~ ***a wild goose*** 作徒劳的搜索[无益的举动]. ~ ***all over*** = ~ ***around*** 在…到处奔走. ~ ***around a stump*** 〔美〕讲废话浪费时间. ~ ***away*** 赶走. ~ ***off after*** 尾追. ~ ***oneself*** 〔美〕走开,逃走. ***C- yourself!*** 〔美俚〕别打搅我,走开; — *n.* ①追赶,追击; 追猎; 追求. ②〔the ~〕打猎. ③〔英〕(私人的)猎场; 狩猎地,(一定地区内的)狩猎权. ④追求物; 被追的野兽[人]; 被驱赶的船[车等]. ⑤〔美俚〕紧张忙乱的活动. ⑥(网球的)一种击球法. ***give ~ to*** 追踪; 追击. ***have [hold] in ~*** 在追求[追赶、追击]中. ***in ~ of*** 追赶,追踪; 追求. ***in full ~*** 拼命追赶. ***lead sb. a (merry) ~*** 使追者困恼不堪; 使追者追不着; (女性)对追求者设置种种困难. ***lovers of the ~*** 爱打猎的人. ~ **gun [piece]** (追击时用的)舰首[尾]炮. ~ **port** 船首[尾]炮门.

chase[2] [tʃeis] *vt.* 在(金属上)雕花(作装饰); 在(金属上)打出浮凸花样的装饰; 刻镶(宝石); 用螺纹梳刀刻(螺纹).

chase[3] [tʃeis] *n.* ①沟; 槽; (墙上的)水管槽,竖沟. ②(炮的)前身〔炮耳至炮口部分〕,炮身. ③【印】(已排好的)活字版的框架. — *vt.* 在…上开槽.

chas·er[1] [ˈtʃeisə] *n.* ①追赶者; 追求者; 追猎者,猎人. ②【海】追击舰; 追击炮; 反击炮; 【空】战斗机; 歼击机. ③(越野) 障碍赛跑参加者. ④〔美俚〕酒后喝的少量清水[汽水等]; 咖啡后喝的酒. ⑤〔英〕压台戏; 观众退场时奏的进行曲.

chas·er[2] [ˈtʃeisə] *n.* ①镂刻者,金属浮雕艺人. ②【机】螺纹梳刀,梳刀盘.

chasm [ˈkæzəm] *n.* ①【地】(地壳的)裂口; 陷坑; 裂罅,断层; 峡谷. ②(感情等的)分歧,隔阂. *a ~ in time* 空白时间. *bridge over a ~* 弥补隔阂.

chas·mal [ˈkæzəməl] *a.* ①【地】裂口的,断层的. ②(感情、意见等)分歧[隔阂]巨大的.

chas·mog·a·my [kæzˈmɔgəmi] *n.* 【植】开花受精.

chas·my [ˈkæzmi] *a.* 裂口多的,深壑多的; 深壑般的.

chasse [ʃɑːs] *n.* 〔F.〕(喝咖啡或抽雪茄烟后喝的)小杯芳香浓烈甜酒,加味酒.

chas·sé [ˈʃæsei; F. ʃase] *n.* 〔F.〕(舞蹈的) 快滑步,追步. — *vi.* 走[跳]快滑步. ~ ***croisé*** [ˈkrwɑːzei] 双重快滑步; 〔喻〕无意义的来回移动.

chasse·pot [ʃɔsˈpəu] *n.* 后膛快枪〔1866 年和 1874 年间法国军队使用〕.

Chas·sid·im [ˈhæsidim] *n. pl. (sing.* ***Chas·sid*** [ˈhæsid]*)* 虔敬派信徒(= Hasidim). **Chas·sid·ic** *a.* **Chas·sid·ism** *n.*

chas·sis [ˈʃæsi] *n. (pl.* ~ [ˈʃæsiz], *~es* [ˈʃæsisiz]*)* ①(马车、汽车车身的)底盘,底架,车台; 炮座,炮底架; (收音机等的)机壳; 【纺】轧液槽; 【空】机架,机脚; 机壳,机箱; (窗等的)框. ②〔美俚〕(尤指女性的)体态,身段. *a ~ mount* 装框炮架. *a colour ~* 彩色电视接收机机壳.

chaste [tʃeist] *a.* ①贞节的,忠于配偶的; 纯洁的,童贞的; 高雅的. ②(文体等)简洁的,朴素的. ③〔古〕未婚的. **-ly** *ad.* **-ness** *n.*

chas·ten [ˈtʃeisn] *vt.* ①惩戒,责罚. ②遏制,使…缓和. ③磨炼(思想等); 精练,推敲(文章等). **-ed** *a.* (文章等)精练的; (思想等)有磨练的; 变乖了的. **-er** *n.* 惩戒者; 遏制者; 推敲(文章)者.

chas·tis·a·ble [tʃæsˈtaizəbl] *a.* 该受责备的; 应责备的,应惩戒的.

chas·tise [tʃæsˈtaiz] *vt.* ①惩戒,惩罚,惩办. ②〔美〕(比赛时)打败(对方). ③〔古〕纯化,净化. **-r** *n.* 惩戒者.

chas·tise·ment [ˈtʃæstizmənt, Am. tʃæsˈtaizmənt] *n.* 惩罚,惩戒.

chas·ti·ty [ˈtʃæstiti] *n.* ①贞节,贞操; 童贞. ②(思想、感情的)纯洁; (文章的)简洁,朴素.

chas·u·ble [ˈtʃæzjubl] *n.* 【宗】(神父举行弥撒时穿的)无袖长袍.

chat[1] [tʃæt] *n.* ①闲谈,聊天. ②鸣禽. *have a ~ with* 与…闲谈,与…聊天 *(with)*. — ***(-tt-)*** *vi.* 闲谈,聊天. ~ **show** (电台或电视台的)现场采访节目.

chat[2] [tʃæt] *n.* = chit[1].

châ·teau [ˈʃɑːtəu] *n. (pl.* ***~s, -teaux*** [təuz]*)* 〔F.〕①城堡. ②邸宅,公馆; 大别墅. ③大葡萄园. ~ ***en Espagne*** 空中楼阁. **C- wine** 高级葡萄酒.

chat·e·lain [ˈʃætlein] *n.* 城堡的主人; 城主,城守.

chat·e·laine [ˈʃætəlein] *n.* ①女城堡主人; 大公馆的女主人. ②〔新闻用语〕女主人. ③女人腰带上的饰链.

Chat·ham [ˈtʃætəm] *n.* 查塔姆〔姓氏〕.

cha·toy·ant [ʃəˈtɔiənt] *a.* 变色的,闪光的. ~ *silk* 闪光丝. — *n.* 猫眼石,金绿宝石. **cha·toy·ance, cha·toy·an·cy** *n.* 闪光.

chat·tel [ˈtʃætl] *n.* ①【法】物,有体财产. ②〔古〕奴隶. ~ *personal* 动产. ~ *real* 准不动产〔借地权等〕. *goods and ~s* 有体动产,家具什物.

chat·ter [ˈtʃætə] *vi.* ①瞎谈,饶舌. ②(牙齿、机器等)振动,打颤; 卡嗒地响. ③(鸟等)鸣,啁啾; (猴等)吱吱叫. — *vt.* ①瞎谈,喋喋不休地说. ②使(牙齿)抖得卡嗒卡嗒地响. ③〔英方〕撕碎. — *n.* ①饶舌,瞎谈. ②卡嗒声. ③啁啾. *monkey ~* 〔口〕(电话) 串话,交叉失真.

chat·ter·box [ˈtʃætəbɔks] *n.* ①唠叨多言的人. ②〔军俚〕机关枪.

chat·ter·er [ˈtʃætərə] *n.* ①多言的人,嘴老是不停的人. ②燕雀类小鸟.

Chat·ter·ton [ˈtʃætətn] *n.* 查特顿〔姓氏〕.

chat·ty [ˈtʃæti] *a.* ①爱唠叨的,爱闲聊的. ②聊家常似的,亲切的. **-ti·ly** *ad.*

Chau·cer [ˈtʃɔːsə] *n.* ①乔瑟(乔叟)〔姓氏〕. ②**Geoffrey** ~ 乔叟〔1340—1400,英国诗人,《坎特伯雷故事集》*(Canterbury Tales)* 的作者〕.

Chau·ce·ri·an [tʃɔːˈsiəriən] *a.* 乔叟的; 有关乔叟著作的. — *n.* 乔叟著作[生平]研究者.

chaud·froid [ˈʃəuˈfrwɑː] *n.* 〔F.〕肉冻.

chauf·fer [ˈtʃɔːfə] *n.* 小火炉,小炭盆,手炉.

chauf·feur [ˈʃəufə] *n.* ①(私人雇用的)汽车司机. ②〔美俚〕飞机师. — *vi.* 做汽车司机. — *vt.* ①开(汽车等). ②开汽车运送.

chauf·feur·ette [ʃəufəˈret] *n.* 〔美〕女(汽车)司机.

chauf·feuse [ʃəuˈfəːz] *n.* 女(汽车)司机.

chaul·mau·gra, chaul·moo·gra, chaul·mu·gra [tʃɔːlˈmuːgrə] *n.* 【植】大风子. ~ *oil* 大风子油.

chaunt [tʃɔːnt] *n.* 〔古〕歌; 赞美诗. *vi., vt.* 单调地唱(赞美诗)(= chant).

chausses [ʃəus] *n. pl.* 马裤〔尤指中古骑士的腿铠〕.

chaus·sure [ʃəuˈsjuə] *n.* 〔F.〕鞋; 履; 靴; 拖鞋.

Chau·tau·qua [ʃəˈtɔːkwə] *n.* ①(美国纽约州的)肖陶扩湖; 肖陶扩村〔有名的夏令文娱活动中心〕. ②〔c-〕〔美〕野外文化讲习会.

chau·vin·ism [ˈʃəuvinizəm] *n.* ①沙文主义,大民族主义. ②本性别第一主义,男[女]性至上主义. *great-nation [-power]* ~ 大国沙文主义. *dominant-nation* ~ 民族沙文主义. *male [female]* ~ 男子[女子]至上主义,大男[女]子主义.

chau·vin·ist [ˈʃəuvinist] *n.* 沙文主义者; 男子[女子]至上主义者. — *a.* 沙文主义的; 男[女]子至上主义的.

chau·vin·is·tic [ˌʃəuviˈnistik] *a.* 沙文主义的.

chaw [tʃɔː] *vt., vi.* 〔方、卑〕嚼,咀嚼. ~ ***up*** 〔美〕(在比赛中)把…打得惨败,把…打成重伤. — *n.* 〔口〕所嚼物; 一满嘴; (嚼烟草的)一口; 〔美〕嚼烟草. **~-round** 〔美〕会话,谈话.

chay [tʃei, tʃai] *n.* 【植】①伞形花耳草 *(Oldenlandia umbellata)*. ②伞形花耳草植株.

cha·yo·te [tʃɑːˈjəuti] *n.* 【植】佛手瓜 *(Sechium edule)*.

chaz·an, chaz·zan [ˈhɑːzn] *n.* (犹太教堂的)合唱指挥; 领唱者(= hazan).

Ch. Clk. = Chief Clerk.
Ch. E. = Chemical Engineer 化学工程师.
cheap [tʃiːp] *a.* ①廉价的,便宜的,贱 *(opp.* dear*)*. ②(钱)贬了值的;有折扣的. ③粗劣的;恶俗的,低劣的,可鄙的;虚伪的. ④〔俚〕身体虚弱的; 垂头丧气的. ⑤(商店等)索价低的;〔英〕大减价的. *buy* ~ *and sell dear* 贱买贵卖. *dirt* ~ 〔俚〕极便宜的,便宜透顶的. ***A*** ~ *son of a bitch!* 吝啬鬼! ~ *and nasty* 价廉而质劣的. ***feel*** ~ 〔俚〕①觉得身体不舒服. ②扫兴,灰心,气馁;惭愧. ***get things on the*** ~ 贪便宜. ***hold*** *(sb.)* ~ 瞧不起,藐视,轻蔑. ***make oneself too*** ~ 过份自卑,过份自轻〔动辄迁就别人〕. ***on the*** ~ 便宜地,经济地. ~ **car (ticket)** 减价电车(票). ~**-Jack,** ~**-John** (走街串巷的)小贩,廉价商品兜销贩. ~ **mit** 〔美俚〕小气鬼,吝啬鬼. ~ **money** 利息低廉的借款. ~ **skate** 〔美俚〕吝啬鬼,小气鬼. ~ **trip [tripper]** 廉价旅行〔旅行者〕. **-ly** *ad.* 便宜,廉价. **-ness** *n.* 廉价.
cheap•en [ˈtʃiːpən] *vt., vi.* ①(使)减价, (使)跌价. ②(使)降低威信〔地位〕. ③(使)变低级〔粗俗〕.
Cheap•side [ˈtʃiːpˈsaid] *n.* 切普赛德街〔伦敦中部东西向大街名,中古时为闹市〕.
cheat [tʃiːt] *vi.* ① 哄骗,作弊. ②〔俚〕(男女关系上)不忠实 *(on)*. *He never* ~*s to pass exam.* 他考试从不作弊. — *vt.* ①哄骗,欺骗,诈取. ②消磨(时间),解(闷),消除(疲劳). ③逃脱(法网); 用计挫败(对方). *C- the devil!* 混蛋! 〔水手骂人话〕. ~ *the law by suiside* 以自杀逃避法律制裁. ~ ***at*** *(cards)* (玩纸牌)作弊(骗钱). ~ ***in*** *(business)* (做生意)行骗. ~*(sb.)* ***into*** 诱骗(人)使…. ~ *(sth.)* ***of [out of]*** *(sb.)* 骗(人)(东西). ~ ***the journey*** 消磨旅途的寂寞. — *n.* ①欺骗,欺诈. ②骗子. ③雀麦,稗草. ④〔美俚〕(汽车上的)反光镜. ⑤〔the ~〕〔卑〕绞刑架. *put a* ~ *upon* 使上当;欺骗.
cheat•ee [ˈtʃiːtiː] *n.* 〔美〕易受骗的人.
cheat•er [ˈtʃiːtə] *n.* ①骗子. ②〔*pl.*〕〔美俚〕眼镜;女衬裤;赌博作弊物〔如作了记号的纸牌,骰子等〕.
cheat•ing [ˈtʃiːtiŋ] *a.* 欺骗的. ~ **stick** 〔美俚〕计算尺.
che•cha•ko [tʃiːˈtʃɑːkəu] *n.* 〔Can.〕新来者,生手.
check [tʃek] *n.* ①(象棋)将军(!),被将军的局面. ②(突然的)妨碍〔制止,阻止〕;停顿,挫折;【猎】(猎狗闻不出臭迹时的)站住;【语音】默止音. ③制止,斥责;(军队等的)牵制,阻止,拦截;控制. ④制止物〔扣绳、制动机、塞子等〕;制止者. ⑤〔美〕支票〔英国作 cheque; 美国为表示郑重起见有时也用 cheque〕. ⑥号牌,号码单,联单;对号,查对标记;核对,校对,验算;已核对的记号(✓);〔美〕收据,发票,(餐馆)帐单;〔美军〕(赌钱用的)筹码. ⑦棋盘格,方格图案;方格花布;小方块,小方格. ⑧(木料的)裂缝,罅缝;【建】幅裂;槽口. ⑨〔美〕同意,允诺,答应. ~ ***to bearer*** 见票即付的支票,无记名支票. ~ ***to order*** 记名支票. ~ ***variety*** 【植】对照品种. ***draw a*** ~ 开发支票. ***discover*** ~ (象棋中)移动一子露出棋路向对方将军. ***hand [pass] in one's*** ~*s* ①交还筹码给赌场主. ②〔俚〕死;放弃. ***hold [keep] in*** ~ 防止,阻止;制止. — *vt.* ①【象棋】将(对方的王棋)一军. ②抑制,阻止,妨碍;击退. ③在…上附加号牌,给…系上标签;(凭号牌)寄存,托运. ④在…上记上查验记号,在…上打勾号〔✓号〕;在…上加上双联号码;检查,检验,校对,核对;对照,比较. ⑤使产生裂缝,在…上画〔印〕方格图案;【农】条插,方形栽植. ⑥【棒球】牵制. *Small parcels* ~*ed here.* 本处寄存手提包裹. — *vi.* ①【猎】(猎狗)因臭迹中断而站住. ②〔美〕开发支票. ③〔美〕(帐目)相符. ④(油漆面等)干裂成小方块. ⑤【象棋】将军. ~ ***at*** 对…发火,气愤. ~ ***in*** (在旅馆)登记,办理住宿手续;〔美俚〕死;〔美口〕签到;作笔记. ~ ***into*** 〔美口〕去…上班. ~ ***it*** 〔美〕吓唬;假装. ~ ***off*** 查讫;记上查讫记号. ~ ***(up) on*** 检查. ~ ***out*** 〔美〕开支票(提款); (旅客)付帐后离开;合格,及格;辞职;〔美俚〕死. ~ ***up*** 检查,核对,对照;〔美〕试验(工作的效率,精确程度等). ~ ***(up) with*** 与…相符合. — *int.* ①【象棋】将军! ②〔口〕行! 对! ~ **beam** 【空】验位电波. ~**book** 支票簿;存折. ~ **cross** 验证杂交. ~ **experiment** 对比〔核对〕试验. ~ **formula** 验算公式. ~**in** *vi.* 〔美〕报到; (旅馆)登记. ~**ing account** 〔美〕活期存款. ~**ing-room** 衣帽间,衣帽寄放处. ~**list** 〔美〕(核对用)清单; (特指选举人的)名单; 调查表. ~**mate** *vt., n.* (象棋)将军; 困死〔通常说 mate 即可〕;打败,击破; (使)失败, (使受)挫折 (*play* ~*mate with* 使进退两难). ~ **nut** 螺钉帽. ~**off** 〔美〕(工会)会费的催收. ~**out** ①最后检查; (对新机器等的)使用练习. ②(购货时的)结帐. ③(旅馆规定结帐后必须离去的)离馆时限. ~**-pawl** 【机】棘爪. ~ **plot** (试验地的)对照小区. ~**-point** 公路检查站,关卡;【军】试射点. ~**rein** 勒马缰绳. ~**room** 〔美〕物品寄放处,衣帽间. ~**row** ①*n.* 方格谷物列; 方格树列. ②*vt.* 把…种成方格形. ~**stand** (超级市场的)验货收款台. ~ **taker** (戏院、车站等的)收票人. ~**up** 〔美〕核对,对照;检验;(严格的)健康检查 (*a* ~*up committee* 查帐委员,查帐委员会. *general* ~*up* 全身检查). ~ **valve** 【机】止回阀,单向活门.
checked [tʃekt] *a.* ①格子花的,棋盘花的. ②【语音】受阻的,封闭的. ~ **syllable** 受阻音节,闭音节. ~ **vowel** 闭音节〔封闭〕元音.
check•er [tʃekə] *n., vt.* 〔美〕= chequer. ~**berry** 【植】平铺白珠树. ~**board** ①*n.* 〔美〕跳棋盘. ②*vt.* 在…上纵横交错地排列〔分布〕. ~**work** 棋盘形结构;【建】甃.
check•ered [ˈtʃekəd] *a.* = chequered; 〔美〕有波折的,有变化的;受挫折的.
Ched•dar [ˈtʃedə] *n.* (原产英国 Cheddar 地方的)切达干酪 (= ~ cheese).
chedd•ite [ˈtʃedait, ˈʃed-] *n.* 谢德炸药〔最初在法国 Chedde 地方制造〕.
che•der [ˈkeidə] *n.* 犹太儿童宗教学校 (=heder).
Che. E. = Chemical Engineer 化学工程师.
cheek [tʃiːk] *n.* ①脸,面颊. ②〔口〕冒失行为〔言语〕,无耻行为〔言语〕;厚颜无耻. ③〔*pl.*〕事物成对的两例;两侧成对的部件〔器物〕;【机】滑车的外壳;颊板. ④(炸药的)面皮. *None of your* ~! 莫说了,没皮没脸的! 别吹牛! ~ ***by jowl with*** (和…)亲密地,(和…)紧靠着. ***give*** ~ 说无耻话. ***have plenty of*** ~ 老脸厚皮. ***have the*** ~ ***to*** *(do)* 厚着脸皮(做). ***sour one's*** ~*s* 哭丧着脸. ***to one's own*** ~ 自己专用. ***tongue in*** ~ 不老实,口是心非. ***turn the other*** ~ 泰然容忍〔被人打一耳光后,再转过一面给人打〕. —*vt.* 厚着脸皮去,无耻地说. ~ ***it*** 厚着脸皮干下去. ~ ***up*** 无耻地回答. ~**bone** 颊骨,颧骨. ~**tooth** 臼齿.
cheek•y [ˈtʃiːki] *a.* 〔口〕厚脸皮的; 无耻的. **-i•ly** *ad.* **-i•ness** *n.*
cheep [tʃiːp] *vi.* (小鸟等)吱吱地叫. — *n.* 吱吱的叫声. *He didn't even* ~. 他一声不吭.
cheep•er [ˈtʃiːpə] *n.* 吱吱叫的小鸟;毛娃娃.
cheer [tʃiə] *n.* ①欢呼,喝采; 鼓励. ②心情. ③兴致勃勃,愉快. ④款待;丰盛的菜肴〔食品〕,好菜. ⑤〔古〕表情. *What* ~? 你好吧? *Be of good* ~! 加油! 鼓(起)劲儿(来)! *The fewer the better* ~. 人少些,吃得多些. *words of* ~ 鼓励话. ~ *leader* 〔美〕啦啦队队长. *enjoy good* ~ 享受盛宴. *give three* ~*s for* 欢呼三声〔三呼 Hip, hip, hurrah!〕. ***make good*** ~ 欢乐,笑笑闹闹;〔古〕欢宴. ***with good*** ~ 高高兴兴地,乐意地. — *vt.* ①使振奋,使喜欢,使快慰,安慰. ②对…欢呼;为…喝彩; (以欢呼声)鼓舞,奖励. ~ *them (on) to victory* 声援他们取得胜利. *the cups that* ~ *(but not inebriate)* 使人提神而不醉的饮料〔指茶〕. — *vi.* ①欢喜,高兴,快活. ②欢呼,喝彩. *C- up!* 鼓起劲儿来! 别灰心! ~ ***to the echo*** 欢声雷动. ~ ***up at*** *(the news)* 听见(消息)兴奋

起来.

cheer•ful [ˈtʃiəful] *a.* ①高兴的，兴致勃勃的，欢乐的，快活的；爽快的. ②使人愉快[振奋]的. ③心甘情愿的. ④〔反〕讨厌的，使人发愣的，可慨叹的. *a* ～ *room* 舒适的房屋. *a* ～ *worker* 兴致勃勃的工作者. *That's a* ～ *remark.* 〔反〕那真听不过去[听了使人发愣]. **-ly** *ad.* 高高兴兴地，兴致勃勃地. **-ness** *n.* 高兴，快活；愉快，爽快.

cheer•ing [ˈtʃiəriŋ] *n.* 欢呼，喝彩；鼓励，安慰.

cheer•i•o(h), cheer•o [ˈtʃiəriˈəu, ˈtʃiərəu] *int.* 〔英口〕珍重！再会！〔干杯贺语〕恭喜恭喜！— *n.* 告别话；祝酒词.

cheer•less [ˈtʃiəlis] *a.* 郁郁不乐的，沉闷的.

cheer•ly [ˈtʃiəli] *a.* 〔古〕欢乐的，快活的. — *ad.* 【海】欣然，高高兴兴地.

cheers [tʃiəz] *int.* 祝你健康！〔用于祝酒〕.

cheer•y [ˈtʃiəri] *a.* 高兴的，快活的；愉快的，爽快的. **-i•ly** *ad.* **-i•ness** *n.*

cheese¹ [tʃi:z] *n.* ①干酪，乳酪；干酪状的东西. ②〔美俚〕重要人物；上品，珍品. ③【纺】筒子纱；④〔学俚〕微笑. *green* ～未熟干酪；绿皮干酪；(低级)乳清干酪. ***bread and*** ～ 粗食；糊口之道. ***chalk and*** ～ 形似而实非. ***big [small]*** ～ 〔俚〕伟大[渺小]的人. ***get the*** ～ 碰钉子，失望. ***hard*** ～ 倒霉. ***make*** **～*s*** 飘裙游戏〔女学生在旋转中突然弯下身子使裙子张大的游戏〕；(女人)弯腰行礼招呼. ***Say '～'!*** (照相时叫对方)笑！ ***That is [quite] the*** ～〔俚〕十分对头[得当]. ～ **burger** 牛肉饼加乳酪. ～**cake** ①干酪蛋糕. ②〔美俚〕显示优美的女性体态〔特别是大腿〕的摄影. ～**cloth** 干酪包布〔一种粗棉布〕. ～ **cutter** 大切刀；〔美俚〕自行车. ～ **mite** 干酪虫. ～**monger** 乳品(干酪、奶油等)商. ～**paring** ① *n.* 干酪的碎皮屑；吝啬；〔*pl.*〕无用的琐碎东西；私财. ② *a.* 吝啬的，小气的. ～ **plate** 干酪盘子，中号盘子；大钮扣. ～ **rennet** 酪条. 【植】白花蓬子叶. ～ **straws** [美 **sticks**] 〔*pl.*〕酥皮干.

cheese² [tʃi:z] *vt.* 〔俚〕停止. ***Cheese it!*** ①停止吧！〔美〕别吵！静一点！注意！②逃呀！走吧！

chees•y [ˈtʃi:zi] *a.* ①干酪质[味]的. ②〔俚〕俊俏的，时髦的，潇洒的. ③〔美俚〕粗制滥造的，低级的；脸色苍白的，面黄肌瘦的；不愉快的.

chee•tah [ˈtʃi:tə] *n.* 【动】(驯养后用以行猎的)猎豹；猎豹皮.

chef [ʃef] *n.* 〔F.〕男厨师长；大师傅，厨师. ～**'s salad** 【烹】大师傅沙拉〔足够吃饱一顿饭的一大盆什锦冷菜〕.

chef d'œuvre [ʃeiˈdə:vr] *n.* ***(pl. chefs d'-)*** 〔F.〕杰作.

cheir(o)- *comb. f.* = chiro-.

Che•ka [ˈtʃekə] *n.* 【苏联史】契卡，肃反委员会.

Che•khov [ˈtʃekɔf], **Anton Pavlovich** 契诃夫〔1860—1904，俄国剧作家，短篇小说家〕.

che•la¹ [ˈki:lə] *n.* *(pl.* ***-lae*** *[-li:])* (蟹、虾等的)螯；钳爪；倒钩骨.

che•la² [ˈtʃeilə] *n.* 〔印度〕学徒，门徒，(学道的)徒弟.

che•late [ˈki:leit] *a.* 【化】螯合的，螯形的. — *n.* 【化】螯合物. — *vt.* 【化】螯合，与(金属)结合成螯合物. — *vi.* 【化】生成螯合物. **-la•tion** 【化】螯合作用.

che•lic•er•a [kəˈlisərə] *n.* *(pl.* ***-er•ae*** *[-əri])* 【动】螯角，螯肢，钩角. **-er•ate** [-əˌreit,-ərit] *a.* 有螯角[肢]的.

che•lif•er•ous [kiˈlifərəs] *a.* 【动】具螯的，具钳爪的.

che•li•form [ˈki:liˌfɔ:m] *a.* 【动】螯形的，钳爪状的.

Chel•le•an [ˈʃeliən, ʃeˈliən] *a.* 【考古】(旧石器时代初期)莎楞文化的.

che•loid [ˈki:lɔid] *n.* 【医】瘢痕瘤；瘢痕疙瘩(=keloid).

che•lo•ni•an [kiˈləuniən] *n., a.* 【动】龟鳖类(的)；蠵鱼科(的)；海龟(的).

Chel•sea [ˈtʃelsi] *n.* (伦敦市)彻西区〔伦敦的文化区，作家、艺术家多居于此〕. ～ *bun [pensioner]* 彻西残废军人休养院的残废军人. ～ *Hospital* 彻西残废军人休养院. *dead as* ～ 人虽没死但已残废. *the Sage of* ～ 彻西区的圣人〔英国十九世纪作家 Thomas Carlyle 的别号〕.

chem. = chemical, chemist, chemistry.

chem- *comb. f.* 〔用于元音前〕= chemo-.

chemi- *comb. f.* 表示"化学": *chemi*sorb.

chem•ic [ˈkemik] *a.* ①〔古〕炼金术的. ②化学的.

chem•i•cal [ˈkemikəl] *a.* 化学的，化学作用的；应用化学的，用化学方法获得的. ～ *combination* 化合(作用). ～ *compounds* 化合物. ～ *cotton* 漂白棉子绒. ～ *formula* 化学式. ～ *industry* 化学工业. ～ *reaction* 化学反应. ～ *warfare* 化学战. ～ *weapon* 化学武器. ～ *works* 制药厂. — *n.* 〔常 *pl.*〕化学制品；药品. *fine* ～*s* (用量微小的)精制化学品[药品]. *heavy* ～*s* (用量巨大的)农工业用化学品. **-ize** *vt.* 用化学药品处理. **-ly** *ad.*

chemico- *comb. f.* 〔用于辅音前〕= chemi-.

chem•i•co•bi•olo•gy [ˌkemikəubaiˈɔlədʒi] *n.* 生物化学.

chem•i•co•physics [ˌkemikəuˈfiziks] *n.* 物理化学，化学物理学.

chem•i•cul•ture [ˌkemiˈkʌltʃə] *n.* 【农、植】水栽法.

Chemigum [ˈkemigʌm] *n.* 【商标】丁腈橡胶.

chem•i•loon [ʃemiˈlu:n] *n.* 〔美〕(女用)连裤内衣.

chem•i•lu•mi•nes•cence [ˌkemiˌlu:miˈnesns] *n.* 【化】化学发光，化合光. **-cent** *a.* 化学发光的.

che•min de fer [ʃəˌmæn dəˈfεə] 〔F.〕十一点〔一种纸牌戏，法语原义为"铁路"〕.

che•mise [ʃiˈmi:z] *n.* ①(女人的)无袖衬衫. ②(堤的)护岸.

chem•i•sette [ˌʃemi(:)ˈzet] *n.* (女人的)胸衣，紧胸衬衣.

chem•ism [ˈkemizəm] *n.* 化学作用[过程，机理].

chem•i•sorb [ˈkemisɔ:b, -ˌzɔ:b] *vt.* 使用化学方法吸附. **-sorp•tion** *n.* 化学吸附.

chem•ist [ˈkemist] *n.* ①化学家；化学工作者. ②〔英〕化学药品商；〔英〕药剂师. *a* ～*'s shop* 〔英〕药房. *a technical* ～ 药学士.

chem•is•try [ˈkemistri] *n.* ①化学. ②物质的组成和化学性质；化学作用[现象]. ③〔喻〕神秘的变化(过程). *medical* ～ 药物学. *organic [inorganic]* ～ 有机[无机]化学. *the* ～ *of logic* 逻辑过程.

chem•i•type [ˈkemitaip] *n.* 化学蚀刻凸版.

chemo- *comb. f.* "化学" = *chemo*ceptor.

chem•o•au•to•troph•ic [ˌkeməuˌɔtəˈtrɔ:fik, ˌkiməu-] *a.* 化学自养的. **-i•cal•ly** *ad.* **-tot•ro•phy** [-ˈtɔ:trəfi] *n.* 化学自养.

chem•o•cep•tor [ˌkeməuˈseptə] *n.* = chemoreceptor.

chem•o•ki•ne•sis [ˌkeməukiˈni:sis, -kai-, ˌki:məu-] *n.* (生物的)化学运动性.

chem•o•mor•pho•sis [ˌkeməuˈmɔ:fəsis] *n.* 【生】化学诱变.

chem•o•pro•phy•lax•is [ˌkeməuˌprəufiˈlæksis] *n.* 【医】(传染病的)化学预防. **-lac•tic** [-ˈlæktic] *a.*

chem•o•re•cep•tor [ˌkeməuriˈseptə] *n.* 化学受体，化学感受器. **-tive** *a.*

chem•os•mo•sis [ˌkemɔsˈməusis] *n.* *(pl.* ***-ses*** *[-si:z])* 化学渗透作用. **-mot•ic** [-ˈmɔtik] *a.*

chem•o•sphere [ˈkeməsfiə] *n.* 【气】光化圈，臭氧层.

chem•o•ster•i•lant [ˌkeməuˈsterilənt, ˌki:məu-] *n.* (灭虫的)化学绝育剂.

chem•o•syn•the•sis [ˌkeməuˈsinθəsis] *n.* 【化】化学合成.

chem•o•tac•tic [ˌkeməuˈtæktik] *a.* 【生】趋化性的，趋药性的.

chem•o•tax•is [ˌkeməuˈtæksis] *n.* 【生】趋化性，趋药性.

chem•o•ther•a•peu•tant [ˈkeməuˌθerəˈpju:tənt] *n.* 化学治疗药.

chem•o•ther•a•py [ˌkeməuˈθerəpi] *n.* 【医】化学疗法(=chemotherapeutics). **chem•o•ther•a•pist** *n.* 化学疗

法专家.
chem·o·troph [ˌkeməuˈtrɔf] *n.* 【生】化能营养. **chem·o·troph·ic** *a.*
chem·o·troph·y [ˌkeməuˈtrɔfi] *n.* = chemotroph.
chem·ot·ro·pism [ˈkemɔtrəpizm] *n.* 【医】向药性. **-trop·ic** [-ˈtrɔpik] *a.*
chem·ur·gy [ˈkeməːdʒi] *n.* 农业化学.
che·nar [tʃiˈnɑː] *n.* = chinar.
che·nille [ʃəˈniːl] *n.* ①绳绒线, 雪尼尔花线. ②假绳绒线,毛虫状绒线(编织品).
che·no·pod [ˈkiːnəpɔd, ˈkenə-] *n.* 【植】藜科植物.
che·ong·sam, che·ong-sam [tʃeˈɔːŋˈsɑːm] *n.* 〔Chin.〕旗袍〔广东话"长衫"的音译〕.
Che·ops [ˈkiːɔps] *n.* 基奥普斯〔公元前 3—4 世纪埃及第四王朝的法老,金字塔的建造者〕.
cheque [tʃek] *n.* 【英商】支票. *a ~ for 100 dollars* 百元支票. *a blank ~* 空白支票;〔喻〕自由行动的权力. *a crossed ~* 画线支票. *a ~ drawer [holder]* 支票出票人[持票人]. *raise a ~* 增改支票上金额. **~book** 支票簿.
cheq·uer [ˈtʃekə] *n.* ①〔英〕棋子; 〔*pl.*〕西洋跳棋 (= draughts). ②〔*pl.*〕棋盘图案,格子花;棋盘格子;【建】方格式排列的石块. ③【植】花楸果. — *vt.* 使成格子花样; 使(象光和影一样)交错; 使变化多端〔常用被动语态〕. — *vi.* 盛衰不定;(情绪等)变化多端.
cheq·uered [ˈtʃekəd] *a.* 〔英〕①格子花样的;交错的. ②变化多端的, 盛衰无常的. *~ light and shade* 交错的光和影,光与影的交错. *a ~ fortune [career]* 波折重重的命运[一生].
Cheq·uers [ˈtʃekəz] *n.* (伦敦郊外)旧英国首相乡间别墅〔1917 年捐赠给国家〕.
cher·a·lite [ˈtʃerəlait] *n.* 【矿】富钍独居石.
Cher·bourg [ˈʃɛəbuəg] *n.* 瑟堡〔法国港市〕.
cher·ish [ˈtʃeriʃ] *vt.* ①抚育. ②爱护. ③怀有,抱有(希望等). *~ fond dreams of* 做…的美梦. *~ a grudge against* 对…怀恨. *~ justice* 坚持正义. *~ed desire* 夙愿.
cher·no·zem [ˈtʃɛənəzem] *n.* 【地】黑土,黑土地带.
Cher·o·kee [ˌtʃerəˈkiː] *n.* (*pl.* *~, ~s*) (北美印第安人的)柴罗基部族. **c- rose** 【植】金樱子.
che·root [ʃəˈruːt] *n.* 平头雪茄烟.
Cher·ry [ˈtʃeri] *n.* 彻丽〔女子名〕.
cher·ry [ˈtʃeri] *n.* ①樱桃;樱桃树. ②樱桃色; 樱桃酒. ③〔美俚〕处女膜,处女状态,童贞. — *a.* ①樱桃色的. ②鲜红的. ③有樱桃味的; 樱桃木制的. ④处女的. **~ bay** 月桂,桂树. **~ bomb** 球形红色烟火. **~ brandy** 樱桃白兰地. **~ coal** 软煤. **~ picker** 〔俚〕(修理电线等用的)车载升降台. **~ pie** ①樱桃酱馅饼. ②【植】香水草;柳叶菜(= heliotrope). **~ red** 〔英俚〕街斗靴 (= bovver boot). **~ stone** ①樱桃核. ②(北美)小蛤蜊. **~ tree** 樱桃树.
cher·so·nese [ˈkəːsəniːz, -niːs] *n.* 半岛.
chert [tʃəːt] *n.* 【矿】燧石,黑硅石.
cher·ub [ˈtʃerəb] *n.* ① (*pl.* ***cher·u·bim*** [ˈtʃerəbim], 【圣】***-bin*** [-bin]) (画上象征智慧与正义的)有翅的小天使. ②(*pl.* *~s*) 天真无邪的儿童;胖娃娃.
che·ru·bic [tʃeˈruːbik] *a.* 小天使似的; (面孔等)白胖可爱的.
cher·vil [ˈtʃəːvil] *n.* 【植】细叶芹属.
Chesh·ire [ˈtʃeʃə] *n.* 柴郡〔英国郡名〕. ***grin like a ~ cat*** 露着牙齿嘻嘻笑. **~ cat** 动不动露着牙齿嘻嘻笑的人. **~ cheese** 英国饼状干酪.
Ches·nut(t) [ˈtʃesnʌt] *n.* 切斯纳特〔姓氏〕.
chess[1] [tʃes] *n.* 国际象棋. *have a game of ~* 下一盘象棋. *play (at) ~* 下象棋. **~board** 棋盘. **~man** 棋子. **~tournament** 象棋比赛.
chess[2] [tʃes] *n.* (*pl.* *~es*) 架浮桥的木板.
chess[3] [tʃes] *n.* 【植】雀麦;稗草.
ches·sel [ˈtʃesəl] *n.* 制干酪的模型.
chess·y·lite [ˈtʃesilait] *n.* 【矿】蓝铜矿[石青].
chest [tʃest] *n.* ①箱,函,柜,匣. ②银箱;金库; 公款,资金. ③胸部,胸腔;(特指)肺. *an ice ~* 冰箱. *a medicine ~* 药箱. *~ of drawers* 五屉柜. *~ trouble* 肺病. *~ voice* 胸声. *cold in the ~* 咳伤风. ***get sth. off one's ~*** 〔口〕吐出心里的话. ***throw a ~*** 〔俚〕挺起胸部. **~note** 【乐】最低音调,胸音. **~ protector** (绒布)护胸. **~ voice** 最低的歌声[话声].
-chest·ed [ˈtʃestid] *comb. f.* 胸部…的,有…胸的: *pigeon-~* 【医】鸡胸的. *broad [flat, full]-~* 胸部宽阔[扁平,挺出]的.
Ches·ter[1] [ˈtʃɔstə] *n.* 切斯特〔男子名〕.
Ches·ter[2] [ˈtʃestə] *n.* 柴郡〔英国郡名〕(= Chestshire); 柴郡的首府. **~ White** 〔美〕切斯特种早熟白猪.
Ches·ter·field [ˈtʃestəfiːld] *n.* 切斯特菲尔德〔姓氏〕.
ches·ter·field [ˈtʃestəfiːld] *n.* ①睡椅,长靠椅. ②〔Can.〕沙发;(丝绒领的)单排扣大衣.
Ches·ter·ton [ˈtʃestətən] *n.* 切斯特顿〔姓氏〕.
chest·nut [ˈtʃesnʌt] *n.* ①栗子, 板栗〔Spanish ~ 或 sweet ~ 的果实〕. ②栗树. ③栗色, 褐色. ④栗毛马. ⑤马前腿内侧胼胝. ⑥〔美口〕陈腐话,滥调. — *a.* 栗色的;栗毛的. *water ~* 菱. *(Chinese) water ~* 荸荠. ***pull (sb.'s) ~s out of the fire*** 为(某人)火中取栗,为解决别人困难而自己承担后果.
chest-on-chest [ˈtʃestɔnˈtʃest] *n.* 叠式立柜〔连在一起的两个柜,下面的那个比上面的大一些〕.
chest·y [ˈtʃesti] *a.* ①〔口〕胸腔宽的; 〔英口〕有(肺病等)胸腔病症状的; 〔俚〕(女人)胸部(乳房)突出的. ②〔美〕自负的,自命不凡的,骄傲的.
che·tah [ˈtʃiːtə] *n.* = cheetah.
cheth [ket] *n.* 希伯来文第八个字母 (= het).
che·val [ʃəˈvæl] *n.* (*pl.* ***-vaux*** [-ˈvəu]) 〔F.〕马. ***~-de-frise*** [ʃəˈvældəˈfriːz] 〔F.〕 chevaux-de-frise 的单数形式.
che·va·let [ʃəvalɛ] *n.* 〔F.〕【乐】弦乐器.
che·val-glass [ʃəˈvælglɑːs] *n.* (活动)穿衣镜.
Chev·a·lier [ʃəˈvæljei] *n.* 谢瓦利埃〔姓氏〕.
che·val·ier [ˌʃevəˈliə] *n.* ①骑士. ②爵士,各级爵位〔勋位〕的成员. ③法国贵族的见习军官, 法国最下级贵族. ④勇士,义士,侠客. *~* ***d'industrie*** [dɛ̃ːdysˈtriː] = ***a ~ of industry*** 骗子.
che·vaux-de-frise [ʃəˈvəudəˈfriːz] *n. pl.* 〔F.〕【军】(阻止骑兵进攻的)拒马,防栅,刺栏;(墙上的)防贼钉.
cheve·lure [ʃəvˈljuːə] *n.* 〔F.〕头发〔尤指假发〕.
che·vet [ʃəˈvei] *n.* 〔F.〕(教堂的)圆室,多角室.
Chev·i·ot [ˈtʃeviət] *n.* ①(英国)舍维绵羊. ②〔c-〕舍维呢. *~ Hills* 舍维山〔英格兰与苏格兰之间的丘陵地带〕.
chev·ron [ˈʃevrən] *n.* ①【徽】山形符号;【军】(下级军官的)山形袖章. ②【建】波浪饰. ***in ~*** (盾状徽内的)虚线山形. ***per ~*** (盾状徽内的)黑山形.
chev·ro·tain [ˈʃevrəutein] 【动】麝鹿;鼷鹿.
chev·y [ˈtʃevi] *n.* 〔口〕追赶,追猎声;(游戏)捉俘虏. — *vt.* ①追赶, 追捉. ②使发窘, 使困惑. — *vi.* 快跑, 逃窜.
chew [tʃuː] *vt.* 咀嚼,嚼碎;嚼(烟). — *vi.* ①咀嚼. ②沉思,细想 (*over, upon*). ③〔口〕嚼烟. ④〔美俚〕吃;讲,谈话. ***bite off more than one can ~*** 〔美口〕自不量力;过份自信. ***~ out*** 〔俚〕严厉责备. ***~ the cud*** (牛等)反刍;熟思,玩味 (*of*). ***~ the fat [rag]*** 〔美俚〕闲谈,聊天;辩论,争吵. ***~ the scenery*** 〔美俚〕做得过分(象做戏一样);发牢骚. ***~ upon [over]*** 沉思,细想. — *n.* 咀嚼;一口.
chewing-gum [ˈtʃu(ː)iŋ-gʌm] *n.* 橡皮糖,口香糖.
chew·y [ˈtʃuːi] *a.* (***chew·i·er; chew·i·est***) 耐嚼的. **~ candy** 橡皮糖;口香糖. **chew·i·ness** *n.*

Chey·enne [ʃaiˈen,-ˈæn] *n.* *(pl. ~s, ~)* ①晒延人〔美国印第安人的一个部落的成员〕. ②晒延语.

chez [ʃei] *prep.* 〔F.〕在,在家.

chg. = change; charge.

C.H.H. (= chain home high) 〔英〕海岸高空远程警戒雷达网.

chi [kai, kiː] *n.* 希腊语字母表第 22 字母 (X, χ) 〔相当于英语的 ch〕. *a chi² (= χ²) square test* 【生】卡方测验.

Chi. = Chicago.

Chi·an [ˈkaiən] *a.* (希腊)凯奥斯岛(Chios)的. — *n.* 凯奥斯岛人.

Chi·an·ti [kiˈænti] *n.* (意大利)基安蒂红葡萄酒.

chi·a·ro·scu·ro [kiˌɑːrəsˈkuərəu] *n.* *(pl. ~s)* 〔It.〕【美】明暗对比法;浓淡的映衬;明暗对比画.

chi·as·ma [kaiˈæzmə] *n.* *(pl. ~s, -mata* [-mətə]*)* 【生】染色体交叉点;【解】(视神经)交叉. **-l** *a.*

chi·as·ma·typ·y [kaiˈæzməˌtaipi] *n.* 【生】染色体交叉.

chi·as·mus [kaiˈæzməs] *n.* *(pl. -mi* [-mai]*)* 【修】交错配列法〔例: *we live to die, but we die to live*〕. ***-as·tic*** [kaiˈæstik] *a.*

chiaus [tʃaus, tʃauʃ] *n.* 〔Turk.〕使者;军曹.

Chi·ba [ˈtʃiːbə] *n.* 千叶〔日本城市〕.

Chib·cha [ˈtʃibtʃə] *n.* *(pl. ~s, ~)* ①切布查人〔美洲印第安人一个部落的成员〕. ②已消亡的切布查语.

Chib·chan [ˈtʃibtʃən] *a.* 切布查语的.

chibol [ˈtʃibəl] *n.* 〔英方〕带茎洋葱.

chi·bouk, chi·bouque [tʃiˈbuːk] *n.* (土耳其的)(长杆)旱烟袋.

chic [ʃiːk, ʃik] *n.* 〔F.〕〔口〕(美术上的)独创风格;别致,潇洒,时髦. — *a.* 别致的,潇洒的,漂亮的.

Chi·ca·go [ʃiˈkɑːgəu] *n.* 芝加哥〔美国城市〕.

chi·ca·lo·te [ˌtʃikəˈləuti] *n.* 【植】阔果蓟罂粟(老鼠艻) *(Argemone platyceras)*.

chi·ca·na [ʃiˈkɑːnə] *n.* 〔Sp.〕住在美国的墨西哥女人.

chi·cane [ʃiˈkein] *n.* ①卑鄙手法,诈骗;狡辩,诡辩. ②【英牌】(一手没有王牌的)牌. — *vt., vi.* ①〔罕〕蒙骗,欺诈. ②狡辩. — *vt.* 诈骗.

chi·can·er·y [ʃiˈkeinəri] *n.* ①卑鄙手法,诈骗. ②狡辩,诡辩. *use* ~ 玩卑鄙手段.

Chi·ca·no [tʃiˈkɑːnəu] *n.* 〔Sp.〕*(pl. ~s)* 墨西哥裔美国人;在美国的墨西哥男人.

chic·co·ry [ˈtʃikəri] *n.* = chicory.

chi·chi [ˈʃiːˈʃiː] *a.* ①装饰精致的,华美的. ②装模作样的,小题大做的. ③赶时髦的.

chick¹ [tʃik] *n.* 小鸡,小鸟;小宝宝;〔美俚〕少妇,年轻女人. — *a.* 〔美〕雅致的,潇洒的,漂亮的;小的. ***the ~s*** (家庭中的)孩子们.

chick² [tʃik] *n.* 〔印〕竹帘子.

chick·a·bid·dy [ˈtʃikəbidi] *n.* 〔儿〕小鸡,鸡宝宝.

chick·a·ree [ˈtʃikəriː] *n.* 【动】(美洲)红松鼠.

chick·a·saw [ˈtʃikəˌsɔː] *n.* *(pl. ~, ~s)* ①契卡索人〔美国马斯科吉印第安人一个部落成员,过去住在密西西比州北部和田纳西州的部分地区,现在住在俄克拉何马州〕. ②契卡索语.

chick·en¹ [ˈtʃikin] *n.* *(pl. ~,~s)* ①鸡雏,小鸡;〔美口〕鸡. ②鸡肉,童子鸡. ③小海虾. ④小儿,娃娃. ⑤〔美俚〕漂亮姑娘,年轻女人. ⑥胆小鬼,懦夫. ⑦〔美俚〕军纪细节. *She is no ~.* 她不是小娃娃. *Don't be a ~.* 不要害怕. ***count one's ~s before they are hatched*** 蛋未孵出先数鸡,过早乐观. ***like a ~ with its head off*** 发疯一样地. ***play ~*** 〔美俚〕互相挑战和威胁(以吓倒对方). ***That's your ~.*** 那是你自己的事(与人无关). **~-and-egg** *a.* 难分先后的,难分因果关系的. **~ breast** 【医】鸡胸. **~-breasted** *a.* 鸡胸的. **~ broth** 鸡汤. **~ cholera** 鸡瘟,家禽霍乱. **~ colonel** 〔美军俚〕上校. **~ feed** 鸡食;〔美口〕小钱币〔五分铜币等〕;一笔小数目的钱. **~ fixings** 〔美〕炸童子鸡. **~ head** 〔美俚〕笨蛋,蠢货. **~hearted, ~livered** *a.* 胆怯的,软弱的. **~ money** 〔美俚〕海军军人退职金. **~ pox** 【医】鸡痘,水痘. **~ roost** 〔美俚〕戏院最上层座位. **~ yard** 鸡圈.

chick·en² [ˈtʃikin] *n.* 〔印〕刺绣.

chick·en·y [ˈtʃikini] *a.* 胆小的.

chick·let(te) [ˈtʃiklit] *n.* 〔美俚〕少女.

chick·ling [ˈtʃikliŋ] *n.* ①小鸡. ②【植】野豌豆〔亦作 ~ vetch〕.

chick·pea [ˈtʃikpiː] *n.* 【植】鹰嘴豆.

chick·weed [ˈtʃikwiːd] *n.* 【植】繁缕.

chic·le [ˈtʃikl] *n.* 〔美〕糖胶树胶〔做橡皮糖用〕.

chi·co [ˈtʃiːkəu] *n.* *(pl. ~s)* 【植】黑肉叶刺茎藜 (= greasewood).

chic·o·ry [ˈtʃikəri] *n.* 【植】菊苣〔根可充作咖啡〕.

chide [tʃaid] *vt.* *(~d, chid* [tʃid]; *chidden* [ˈtʃidn], *chid)* 呵叱,责骂;骂走,斥逐 *(from; away)*. —*vi.* ①责备,责骂. ②〔书〕(风、猎犬等)怒号,咆哮.

chief [tʃiːf] *n.* ①首领,领袖;酋长,族长. ②〔口〕主管人员,长官〔部长、局长、科长等〕. ③重要部分. *~ of a section* 科长,组长. *~ pilot* 正驾驶员. *~ itch and rub* 〔美俚〕头子. *C- of Administrative Services* 陆军后勤总部行政处处长. *~ of staff* 参谋长. *C- of the Royal Air Force* 英国空军大元帅. ***in ~*** 居领导地位的,最高的,长官的;主要,【法】直接 (*the commander in ~* 总司令. *for many reasons, and this one in ~* 理由很多,但主要是这个理由). — *a.* 首,长;主要的,第一的. *a ~ accountant* 会计主任,会计科科长. *~ attractions* 主要节目. *~ clerk* 〔美〕= a ~ secretary 书记长,秘书长. *~ editor* 总编辑. *the C- Executive* 〔美〕总统;州长;市长. *~ judge [justice]* 审判长. *the C- Justice of the Common Pleas* 〔英〕民事高等法院院长. *the C- Justice of the King's Bench* 英国高等法院院长. *the C- Justice of the United States* 美国高等法院院长. *a ~ justiciar* 审判长;首席法官. *a ~ officer [mate]* 【海】大副. *a ~ radio man* 【美军】一等电讯兵. ***~ [~est] of all*** 尤其是,最重要的是. **-dom, -ship** *n.* 首领的地位〔资格〕.

chief·ly [tʃiːfli] *ad.* 第一,首先;主要. — *a.*领袖(般)的.

chief·tain [ˈtʃiːftən] *n.* 首领;族长;酋长;(土匪等)头子,〔诗〕指挥官,队长. **-cy, -ship** chieftain 的身分,地位.

chiel [tʃiːl] *n.* 〔Scot.〕小伙子,青年(= chield).

chiff·chaff [ˈtʃiftʃæf] *n.* 【动】嚣鹪.

chif·fon [ˈʃifɔn] *n.* 〔F.〕①雪纺绸,薄绸. ②〔*pl.*〕女服花边. — *a.* 薄绸制成的;薄绸般透明〔柔软〕的.

chi·ffo·nier [ˌʃifəˈniə] *n.* 梳妆镜柜,小衣橱;碗碟柜.

chig·ger [ˈtʃigə] *n.* ① = chigoe. ②【动】恙螨.

chi·gnon [ˈʃinjɔ̃ːŋ] *n.* 假髻.

chig·oe, chig·re [ˈtʃigəu] *n.* 【动】沙蚤.

chik [tʃik] *n.* = chick².

chil·blain [ˈtʃilblein] *n.* 〔常 *pl.*〕【医】冻疮. *have ~s* 生冻疮. **-ed** *a.* 生冻疮的.

child [tʃaild] *n.* *(pl. children* [ˈtʃildrən]*)* ①孩子,儿童;胎儿,婴儿. ②孩子气的人,幼稚的人. ③子孙;后裔;(空想等的)产物. ④追随者,崇拜者,弟子. ⑤某个时代的产物. *a forward ~* 早熟[慧]儿. *a male [female] ~* 男[女]孩. *a natural ~* 私生子. *a spoilt ~* 宠子,娇儿. *The ~ is father of [to] the man.* 从小看大. *Don't be a ~!* 不要孩子气! *fancy's children* 想象的产物,空想. ***~ of fortune*** 幸运儿. ***~ of nature*** 自然的宠儿;天真的人. ***~ of the devil*** 魔鬼之子,恶人. ***~ of the people*** 人民的儿子〔在人民中成长起来的人〕. ***as a ~*** 在幼年时代. ***drag up a ~*** 〔口〕把孩子拉扯大. ***from a ~*** 自幼. ***own a ~*** 承认自己是孩子的父亲. ***this ~*** 〔美俚〕我,鄙人. ***with ~*** 怀孕. **~bearing**

生产,分娩. ~bed 产褥,分娩. ~birth 分娩,生产. ~ bride 年轻的新娘子;童养媳. ~ care [welfare] 保育事业. ~hood 幼年(时代) (*second ~hood* 第二幼年,老耄期). ~ labour 童工(劳动). ~-placement agency〔美〕有幼孩待人领养的机关. ~proof *a.* 使儿童无法开启的,保护儿童安全的(指家用电器等). ~ psychology 儿童心理学. ~'s play 儿戏;轻而易举的事情. -like *a.* 孩子似的;天真烂漫的,直率的,老实的.

Child(e) [tʃaild] *n.* 蔡尔德〔姓氏〕.

childe [tʃaild] *n.* 〔古〕贵胄,贵族青年〔尤指骑士的候补者〕.

child·ing [ˈtʃaildiŋ] *a.* ①〔古〕怀孕的. ②【植】花旁生花的.

child·ish [ˈtʃaildiʃ] *a.* ①孩子似的,孩子气的;孩子的,幼年的. ②幼稚的,傻里傻气的. -ly *ad.* -ness *n.*

child·less [ˈtʃaildlis] *a.* 无儿女的.

child·ly [ˈtʃaildli] *a.*, *ad.* 孩子似的[地].

chil·dren [ˈtʃildrən] child 的复数. ~ *of iniquity* 歹人. ~ *of Israel* 犹太人. ~ *of Izaak Walton* 爱钓鱼的人们. ~ court 少年法庭. C-'s Day 儿童节.

Chil·e [ˈtʃili] *n.* 智利〔拉丁美洲〕. ~ pepper 辣椒. ~ saltpetre 智利硝.

chile con car·ne [ˈtʃili kɔn ˈkɑːni] 〔Sp.〕 辣椒肉末〔墨西哥菜〕.

Chil·ean, Chil·ian [ˈtʃiliən] *n.* 智利讲的西班牙语;智利人. — *a.* 智利(人)的;智利文化的.

chil·i [tʃili] *n.* = chilli. ~-eater *n.* 〔美俚〕墨西哥人.

chil·i·ad [ˈkiliæd] *n.* 一千;一千年.

chil·i·arch [ˈkiliˌɑːk] *n.* (古希腊)千夫长.

chill [tʃil] *n.* ①冷,寒冷,发冷;冷却;冷冻;【冶】冷模,冷铸. ②冷淡;薄情. ③扫兴;沮丧,寒心. *a ~ in the air* 恶冷,透骨的冷. *cast a ~ over* 使扫兴,泼冷水. *catch a ~* 受寒,发冷. *~s and fever* 〔美方〕间歇热,疟疾,打摆子. *feel [have] a ~* 打冷颤,发冷. *take a ~* 受寒,发冷. *take the ~ off* 热一热,烫一烫(酒等). — *a.* ①〔书〕冷,寒. ②冷淡的,薄情的;隔膜的;冷酷的;扫兴的,使…寒心的. — *vt.* ①使变冷;使感觉冷;冰冻(食物);冷却,冷藏. ②使扫兴,使寒心. ③【冶】冷铸,冷淬. ④〔口〕把(酒等)温一下,热一下. — *vi.* 冷却,变冷;发冷. -ing·ly *ad.*

chilled [tʃild] *a.* 已冷的,冷却了的;冷淬过的;(肉等)冷冻了的,经过冷藏的. ~ *castings* 冷硬铸件. ~ *meat* 冷藏肉. *a ~ shell* 硬铁弹. *a ~ projectile* 破甲弹. ~ *to the bone* 冷彻骨髓.

chill·er [ˈtʃilə] *n.* ①惊险小说. ②(冰箱中的)冷冻格. ③冷却装置. ④冷冻工人.

chil·li [ˈtʃili] *n.* (*pl.* ~*es*) ①干辣椒. ② = chile con carne. ~ sauce 蕃茄辣酱.

chill·i·ness [ˈtʃilinis] *n.* 寒冷,严寒,恶冷;冷淡,疏远.

chill·y[1] [ˈtʃili] *a.* ①寒冷的;怕冷的. ②使心恐惧的. ③冷淡的,疏远的. *a ~ story* 令人打冷战的故事. — *ad.* 〔罕〕冷,冷淡地.

chil·ly[2] [ˈtʃilli] = chilli.

chilo- *comb. f.* = lip, labial.

chi·lo·pod [ˈkailəpɔd] *n.* 【动】唇脚类动物〔蜈蚣、蚰蜒等〕.

Chil·tern Hundreds [ˈtʃiltəːn ˈhʌndrədz] 〔英〕切尔吞皇室领地〔在 Chiltern Hills 附近〕. *accept [apply for] the Chiltern Hundreds* 解除[请求解除]下院议员职务〔受任这个皇室领地的挂名主管人,等于辞去下院议员职务〕.

chi·mae·ra [kaiˈmiərə] *n.* = chimera.

chim·ar [ˈtʃimə] *n.* = chimere.

chimb [tʃaim] *n.* = chime[2].

chime[1] [tʃaim] *n.* ①(音调谐和的)一套钟;铁琴. ②〔*pl.*〕合奏钟声,钟乐. ③谐音,韵律;调和,一致. ④单调. *fall into ~ with* 与…调和,与…一致. *in ~* 调和,一致. *keep ~ with* 和…步骤一致. — *vt.* ①打(一套钟),奏(钟乐);敲钟报(时),打钟召集(人). ②机械地重复,单调啰嗦地说. — *vi.* ①(乐器、钟等)奏出和谐的音调. ②合节奏;调和. ~ *in with* 赞成,同意,附和,为…帮腔,与…一致[协调].

chime[2] [tʃaim] *n.* ①(啤酒桶两端的)凸边. ②【海】(甲板上的)沟.

chi·me·ra [kaiˈmiərə] *n.* ①【希神】〔常 C-〕吐火女怪〔狮头、羊身、龙尾〕;怪物;【建】狮头羊身蛇尾装饰. ②妄想,奇想. ③【遗传】嵌合体,嫁接杂种.

chi·mere [tʃiˈmiə] *n.* (主教穿的)无袖罩袍.

chi·mer·i·cal [kaiˈmerikəl] *a.* 空想的,妄想的;幻想的,梦一般的. -ly *ad.*

chim·ney [ˈtʃimni] *n.* ①烟囱;(煤油灯的)灯罩;烟囱状东西. ②(火山的)喷烟口;【地】冰川井柱状矿体;冰川竖井;【登山】(岩面可容一人攀登的)直立裂口. ③〔美方〕壁炉. ④〔美俚〕老抽烟的人. ~ cap 烟囱帽. ~ corner 壁炉边〔通常设有的座位〕(*the ~-corner law* 〔美〕习惯法). ~ jack 旋转式烟囱帽. ~piece 壁炉架 (= mantelpiece). ~ pot 烟囱顶管;高顶礼帽. ~-pot hat 高顶礼帽. ~ rock 柱状石. ~ shaft (房顶上的)烟囱;(工厂等的)大烟囱. ~ stack 丛烟囱;(工厂等的)大烟囱. ~ stalk 〔英〕(工厂等的)大烟囱;屋顶烟囱. ~ swallow 〔英〕(在烟囱上作巢的)燕子. ~ sweep(er) 扫烟囱的人; ~ swift 〔美〕 = ~swallow.

chimp [tʃimp] *n.* 〔口〕黑猩猩.

chim·pan·zee [ˈtʃimpənˈziː] *n.* 【动】黑猩猩.

chin [tʃin] *n.* ①颏,下巴. ②〔美俚〕闲谈. ③【体】(单杠)引体向上动作. *have a ~* 〔美〕聊天. *keep one's ~ up* 〔口〕始终精神昂扬,不泄气,不灰心. *stick one's ~ out* 暴露自己;自惹麻烦;甘冒风险. *take it on the ~* 〔俚〕吃败战,彻底失败;忍痛. *up to the ~* = ~-deep. *wag one's ~* 唠叨. — *vt.* ①〔口〕用下巴夹住(提琴等). ②〔~ oneself〕(单杠)引体向上使下巴高过横杠; — *vi.* 〔美俚〕说,讲,谈话,唠叨,聊天. ~ armor 〔美俚〕连鬓胡子. ~bone 颏骨. ~ buster 〔美俚〕拳击选手. ~deep *a.* 到下巴的,深深陷入的. ~ music 〔美俚〕闲谈,空谈;口才;责骂. ~ turret 机头[舰首]炮塔. ~-wag *n.*, *vi.* 〔美讽〕闲聊,闲谈. ~-wagger 〔美〕碎嘴子.

Chin. = Chinese, China.

Chi·na [ˈtʃainə] *n.* 中国. *the People's Republic of ~* 中华人民共和国. *from ~ to Peru* 到处. ~ aster 【植】翠菊. ~ bark = quinine. ~ bean 豇豆. ~ blue 青瓷色. ~ cotton 鸡脚棉. ~ crape 广东绉纱. ~ cup 茶碗. ~ grass 【植】苧麻,线麻. ~-green 【植】亮丝草,广东万年青. ~ ink 墨. ~jute 苘麻,青麻. ~man 〔旧,蔑〕中国佬. ~ orange 橙. ~ rose 月季花. ~-teasel 【植】华川续断. ~town 唐人街,中国城. ~ tree 【植】楝树,苦楝. ~ wood oil 桐油.

chi·na [ˈtʃainə] *n.* 瓷器;瓷料,白瓷土,瓷质粘土. *a piece of ~* 一件瓷器. ~ clay 瓷土. ~ closet 瓷器橱. ~ mania 瓷器搜集热. ~ maniac 瓷器搜集迷[人]. ~ plate 〔英俚〕伙伴. ~ shop 瓷器店. ~ stone 做瓷器的石料. ~ware 瓷器. ~ wedding 瓷婚,结婚二十年纪念.

china·ber·ry [ˈtʃainəberi] *n.* 【植】楝树.

chi·na·crin(e) [ˈkinəkriːn] *n.* 【药】阿的平.

Chinar [tʃiˈnɑː] *n.* 【植】悬铃木,法国梧桐.

chinch [tʃintʃ] *n.* ①臭虫. ②〔美〕麦椿象 (= chinch bug).

chin·che·rin·chee [ˌtʃintʃəˈrintʃi] *n.* 【植】好望角虎眼万年青 (*Ornithogalum thyrsoides*).

chin·chil·la [tʃinˈtʃilə] *n.* ①【动】南美栗鼠(皮). ②栗鼠呢,珠皮呢. ③银灰色.

chin·cough [ˈtʃinkɔf] *n.* 百日咳.

chine[1] [tʃain] *n.* ①脊骨；脊肉。②山脊，山岭。③【船】舷线。~ *boat* 一种快艇。— *vt.* 切出(脊肉)，沿…脊梁切开。

chine[2] [tʃain] *n.* 〔英方〕狭而深的峡谷，幽谷。

chine[3] [tʃain] *n.* = chime[2].

Chi·nee [tʃaiˈniː] *n.* 〔俚〕中国人。

Chi·nese [ˈtʃaiˈniːz] *a.* 中国(人)的；中国(话)的。*the ~ Wall* 万里长城。— *n.* 〔*sing.*, *pl.*〕中国人；中国话，汉语。~ **copy** 惟妙惟肖的描摹[临写]。~ **indigo** 蓝靛。~ **ink** 墨。~ **lantern** 灯笼。~ **linen** 夏布。~ **puzzle** (九连环等)中国玩具；难解的问题。~ **red** 大红；朱红。~ **white** 白色颜料，氧化锌。~ **wood oil** 桐油。

chin·fest [ˈtʃinfest] *n.* 〔美俚〕茶话会；争论。

chi·ni·o·fon [kiˈniəfən] *n.* 【药】喹碘方，药特灵。

chink[1] [tʃiŋk] *n.* ①(金属)叮当声。②〔俚〕硬币；现款。— *vi.*, *vt.* (使)叮当响。

chink[2] [tʃiŋk] *n.* 裂缝，裂口；漏洞，弱点。— *vi.* 破裂，开裂。—*vt.* ①使开裂。②〔美〕塞…的裂缝。

chinky [ˈtʃiŋki] *a.* 有[多]裂缝的。

-chinned [tʃind] *comb. f.* 长着…下巴的〔构成复合词〕：*double*~双下巴的。

Chi·no- *comb. f.* = China. ~-*Japanese* 中日的。

chi·no [ˈtʃiːnəu, ˈʃiː-] *n.* ①丝光卡其布。②〔*pl.*〕丝光卡其布男衬裤。

chin·oise·rie [ˌʃiːnwɑːz(ə)ˈriː] *n.* (欧洲18世纪摹仿的)中国艺术风格；具有中国艺术风格的物品。

Chi·nook [tʃiˈnuːk] *n.* (*pl.* ~, ~*s*) ①〔美〕切奴克族印第安人；切奴克族及其他印第安人语言和英语及法语的混合语。②〔常 c-〕俄勒冈州的温暖西南湿风；落矶山东边的暖燥风(=c- wind)。

Chi·nook·an [tʃiˈnuːkən] *n.* (北美印第安人的)切奴克族。—*n.* 切奴克语。

chin·qua·pin [ˈtʃiŋkəpin] *n.* 【植】美国栗树，板栗。

chintz [tʃints] *n.*, *a.* (*pl.* ~*es* [-iz]) 擦光印花棉布(的)。

chintz·y [tʃintsi] *a.* ①印花布的。②〔口〕廉价的；低劣的；卑劣的；尖刻的；小气的；琐碎的。

chi·o·no·phil·ous [kiəˈnɔfiləs] *a.* 【植】适雪的，喜雪的。

chi·o·no·pho·bous [ˌkiənəuˈfəubəs] *a.* 【植】避雪的，嫌雪的。

chip[1] [tʃip] *n.* ①碎片，削片，薄片；碎屑；薄木片；无价值的东西。②(陶器等的)缺损(处)。③(赌博用)筹码；〔*pl.*〕〔英俚〕钱。④〔*pl.*〕〔口〕炸马铃薯片。⑤(作燃料的)干牛[马]粪。⑥集成电路唱片[块]。⑦〔口〕小粒金刚石[水晶]。***a ~ of [off] the old block*** (脾气等)完全象父亲的儿子；一家的典型人物。***(as) dry as a ~*** 枯燥无味的。***buy ~s*** 投资。***cash [pass] in one's ~s*** 把筹码兑现；〔俚〕死。~ ***in porridge [pottage, broth]*** 无关重要的东西，可有可无的东西。***do not care a ~ for*** 毫不介意。***have a ~ on one's shoulder*** 〔美俚〕盛气凌人；好打架；好争吵。***have one's ~s on*** 孤注一掷。***in the ~s*** 〔美俚〕有钱的。***let the ~s fall where they may*** 不管后果如何。***when the ~s are down [get on the line]*** 万不得已的时候，紧急时候。— *vt.* ①切，削，凿，刻。②把…削成薄片；弄缺(刀口，瓷器等)。③〔口〕戏弄；挖苦。④(鸡雏等)啄碎(蛋壳)。—*vi.* ①出现缺口。②碎裂，瓦解，破碎(*off*)。~ ***at*** 对准…打；谩骂。~ ***in*** 〔口〕插嘴，加入(打架等)；捐助；拿钱赌(*They all chipped in to buy it.* 大家都要买了)。~ ***off*** 切下来，削下来。~**board** 废纸制成的纸板；刨花板。~**bonnet** **[hat]** 刨花帽。**chip·pings** (削下或凿下的)屑片。

chip[2] [tʃip] *n.* (摔交时)用绊腿把对方摔倒的一种技巧。— *vt.* (用绊腿)摔倒(对方)。

Chip·e·wy·an [ˌtʃipiˈwaiən] *n.* ①契帕瓦人〔加拿大西北部阿撒巴斯卡印第安人的一个部族〕。②契帕瓦语。

chip·muck, chip·munk [ˈtʃipmʌk, ˈtʃipmʌŋk] *n.* 【动】花栗鼠〔北美产〕。

Chip·pen·dale [ˈtʃipəndeil] *n.* (英国家具师切宾代尔设计的)切宾代尔样式(的家具)。— *a.* (家具)切宾代尔式的。

chip·per[1] [ˈtʃipə] *a.* 〔美口〕活泼的；潇洒的，漂亮的；精力充沛的。— *vt.*, *vi.* (使)鼓起精神，(使)高兴起来(*up*)。

chip·per[2] [ˈtʃipə] *n.* ①削片者。②削片机；錾刀，凿刀。

chip·per[3] [ˈtʃipə] *vi.* (鸟)唧唧地叫；(人)喊喊喳喳地闲谈。

Chip·pe·wa, Chip·pe·way [ˈtʃipəwɑː, -wei] *n.* (北美印第安人)齐帕威部族〔又叫 Ojibway, Ojibwa〕。

chip·ping[1] [ˈtʃipiŋ] *n.* 〔*pl.*〕(削、凿下的)碎屑，破片，薄片；【机】切屑。

chip·ping[2] [ˈtʃipiŋ] *a.* (雀，栗鼠等)唧唧叫的。

chip·py[1] [ˈtʃipi] *a.* ①碎片的。②〔俚〕枯燥无味的。③(因饮酒过多而)心烧气躁的；易怒的。

chip·py[2] [ˈtʃipi] *n.* ①〔美俚〕行为不检的年轻荡妇；妓女。② = chipmunk.

chirk [tʃəːk] *a.* 〔美〕活泼的，高兴的。— *vi.* ①使快活[高兴]起来(*up*)。②(鸟、鼠等)唧唧地尖叫。—*vt.* 使快活[高兴]起来。

chirm [tʃəːm] *n.* 〔方、罕〕喃喃声；啾啾声；嗡嗡声；远处的喧噪声。— *vi.* 〔方、罕〕作啾啾声；作嗡嗡声等。

chir(o)- *comb. f.* = hand: *chiro*graphy.

chi·rog·no·my [ˈkaiəˈrɔgnəmi] *n.* 手相术。

chi·ro·graph [ˈkaiərəgrɑːf] *n.* 【法】亲笔字据；教皇的亲笔特许证书。

chi·rog·ra·phy [ˌkaiəˈrɔgrəfi] *n.* 笔迹；书法。

chirology [kaiˈrɔlədʒi] *n.* 手语法；手的研究。

chiro·man·cer [ˈkaiərəmænsə] *n.* 手相家。

chi·ro·man·cy [ˈkaiərəmænsi] *n.* 手相术。

chi·rop·o·dist [kiˈrɔpədist] *n.* 【医】手足病医生〔尤指足病医师〕。

chi·rop·o·dy [kiˈrɔpədi] *n.* 【医】手足病治疗。

chi·ro·prac·tic [ˌkaiərəˈpræktik] *n.* 【医】①(脊柱)按摩疗法。② = chiropractor.

chi·ro·prac·tor [ˈkaiərəˌpræktə] *n.* 【医】(脊柱)按摩疗法医生。

chi·rop·ter [kaiˈrɔptə] *n.* 【动】蝙蝠。**-an** *a.*

Chi·rop·te·ra [kaiəˈrɔptərə] *n. pl.* 【动】翼手目。**-n** *a.*

chirp [tʃəːp] *n.* (鸟的)啁啾声，(虫的)唧唧声；(无线电的)啁啾声信号。— *vi.* ①(鸟等)啁啾地叫，(蟋蟀等)唧唧地叫。②(人)喊喊喳喳地讲话。— *vt.* 喊喊喳喳地讲出。

chir·py [ˈtʃəːpi] *a.* 唧唧叫的；快活的，活泼的。

chirr [tʃəː] *vi.* (蟋蟀等)唧唧地叫。— *n.* 唧唧声。

chir·rup [ˈtʃirəp] *n.* (颤动舌头哄婴孩或催马的)啧啧声；(鸟、虫等)不断发出的唧唧声。—*vi.* 发出啧啧声〔哄婴孩或催马等〕；唧唧地叫；〔俚〕(在戏院中替自己人)喝采。— *vt.* 啧啧地说出。

chi·rur·geon [kaiəˈrəːdʒən] *n.* 〔古〕= surgeon.

chis·el [ˈtʃizl] *n.* ①凿子，凿刀；錾子。②〔俚〕诈骗。*a chipping* ~ 石錾子，平切錾。*a cold* ~ 錾子。*a cross-mouth* ~ (打眼的)圆凿。*a pneumatic* ~ 气凿。*the* ~ 雕刻刀具；雕刻术。— (*-ll-*) *vt.* ①凿，錾，镌，雕，刻。②凿成，錾成，镌成，雕琢(*into*)；加工，润饰(文章)。③〔美俚〕欺诈，骗取；不正当地处置。— *vi.* ①凿，錾，镌，雕，刻。②〔美俚〕骗，欺诈；弄手段，考试时作弊。③钻进(*in*)。~ ***in*** 干涉，钻空子。***full*** ~ 〔美俚〕飞快地；猛冲。**-(l)ed** *a.* 凿过的，凿光的；轮廓清晰的(*chiselled features* 〔口〕(象雕成一样的)轮廓清晰的脸盘)。

chis·el·er [ˈtʃizlə] ①凿工。②〔美俚〕骗子，行为不正的人。

chi-square [ˈkaiskwɛə] *n.* 【统】χ^2 检验法。

chit[1] [tʃit] *n.* 幼芽，嫩芽。— *vi.* 〔方〕发芽。— *vt.* 〔口〕摘去…的芽。

chit[2] [tʃit] *n.* 小孩;少女;黄毛丫头.
chit[3] [tʃit] *n.* ①短信,字条. ②收条,帐单. ③(受雇用者等的)保单,保证书. ~**-book** 送文簿,签收簿. ~ **system** 单据支付制度[对现金支付而言].
Chi·ta [tʃi'tɑː] *n.* 赤塔[苏联城市].
chi·tal ['tʃiːtəl] *n.* (印度等地产的)白斑鹿.
chit·chat ['tʃittʃæt] *vi.* (*-tt-*) 闲谈,聊天. — *n.* 闲聊.
chi·tin[1] ['kaitin] *n.* 【动】(甲)壳质,明角质.
chi·tin[2] ['kaitin] *n.* 【生化】几丁质,壳多糖.
chi·tin·ous ['kaitinəs] *a.* 【生化】几丁质的,壳多糖的.
chit·lins, chit·lings ['tʃitlinz] *n. pl.* = chitterlings.
chi·ton ['kaitɔn] *n.* [古希腊]长内衣.
chit·tack ['tʃitæk] *n.* 吉塔克[印度重量单位,相当于一盎斯].
Chit·ta·gong ['tʃitəgɔŋ] *n.* 吉大港[孟加拉国港市].
chit·ter ['tʃitə] *vi.* ①[美]嘁嘁喳喳地闲聊. ②[Scot.][方]冷得发抖.
chit·ter·lings ['tʃitəliŋz] *n. pl.* (猪等的)小肠 (= chitlings).
Chit·ty ['tʃiti] *n.* 奇蒂[姓氏].
chiv [ʃaiv] *n.* [美俚] = chive[2].
chiv·al·ric ['ʃivəlrik] *a.* [诗] = chivalrous.
chiv·al·rous ['ʃivəlrəs] *a.* ①(象)骑士的;勇武的,豪侠的. ②骑士时代的,骑士制度的. ③敬重女人的. **-ly** *ad.* **-ness** *n.*
chiv·al·ry ['ʃivəlri] *n.* ①骑士制度. ②骑士气概[精神(等)],豪侠. ③骑士团. ④妇女崇拜(者). *laws of* ~ 骑士制度的条例. *the flower of* ~ 骑士(制度)的典范.
chive[1] [tʃaiv] *n.* 【植】细香葱.
chive[2] [tʃaiv] *n.* [美俚]小刀.
chiv·(v)y ['tʃivi] *n., vt., vi.* = chevy.
Ch. J. = Chief Justice 审判长,首席法官;法院院长.
C.H.L. (= chain home low) [英]海岸低空飞机远程警戒雷达网.
chlam·y·date ['klæmideit] *a.* 【动】有覆盖的.
chla·myd·o·spore [klə'midəspɔː] *n.* 【生】厚垣[壁,膜]孢子.
chla·mys ['kleiməs, 'klæməs] *n.* (*pl.* ~*es, chlam·y·des* ['klæmidiz]) (古希腊人的)短外套.
chlor- *comb. f.* [用于元音前] = chloro.
chlo·ral ['klɔːrəl] *n.* 【化】氯醛,三氯乙醛;三氯乙二醇[麻醉剂,又名 ~ hydrate 水合氯醛]. **-ism** *n.* 三氯乙醛中毒症.
chlor·am·bu·cil [klɔ'ræmbjusil] *n.* 【药】苯丁酸氮芥,瘤可宁[抗肿瘤药].
chlo·ra·mine ['klɔːrəmiːn] *n.* 【药】氯胺,氯阿明.
chlor·am·phen·i·col [ˌklɔːræm'fenikɔːl, -kəul] *n.* 【药】氯霉素.
chlo·rate ['klɔːrit] *n.* 【化】氯酸盐.
chlor·dan(e) ['klɔːdein] *n.* 【化、农】氯丹,八氯化甲桥茚,1068[剧毒杀虫剂].
chlor·di·az·epox·ide [ˌklɔːdaiˌeizi'pɔksaid] *n.* 【药】利眠宁,甲氨二氮䓬[安定药].
chlo·rella [klɔː'relə] *n.* 【植】小球藻.
chlo·ren·chy·ma [klə'reŋkimə] *n.* 【植】(含叶绿素的)绿色组织.
chlo·ric ['klɔːrik] *a.* 【化】氯的,含五价氯的,从氯制得的.
chlo·ride ['klɔːraid] *n.* 【化】氯化物;[口]漂白粉 (= ~ of lime [soda, potash]). *sodium* ~ 氯化钠,食盐.
chlo·ri·dize ['klɔːridaiz] *vt.* 【摄】用氯化物处理;在…上涂氯化银;使氯化.
chlo·ri·nate ['klɔːrineit] *vt.* 使氯化,给…加氯,用氯气处理.
chlo·rin·a·tion [ˌklɔːri'neiʃən] *n.* 【化】氯化(作用),加氯(消毒)法.
chlo·rine ['klɔːriːn] *n.* 【化】氯(气). ~ *water* 氯水[漂白液].
chlo·rite ['klɔːrait] *n.* 【矿】绿泥石;【化】亚氯酸盐.
chlor·mad·i·none [klɔ'mɑːdinəun] *n.* 【药】氯地孕酮[避孕药] (= ~ acetate).
chloro-, *comb. f.* [用于辅音前] ①【动、植】绿. ②【化】氯: *chloro*plast.
chlo·ro·ben·zene [ˌklɔːrə'benziːn] *n.* 【化】氯苯.
chlo·ro·dyne ['klɔ(ː)rədain] *n.* 【医】哥罗颠[止痛麻醉药].
chlor·o·form ['klɔ(ː)rəfɔːm] *n.* 【化、医】三氯甲烷,氯仿. — *vt.* 用氯仿(麻醉);用氯仿杀死[处理]. **-ism** *n.* 氯仿中毒. **-ist** *n.* 管氯仿的人[外科医生助手];爱用氯仿的医师.
chlo·ro·hy·drin(e) [ˌklɔːrə'haidrin] *n.* 【化】氯(乙)醇.
chlor·o·my·cetin [ˌklɔ(ː)rəumai'siːtin] *n.* 【药】氯霉素.
chlo·ro·phyl(l) ['klɔ(ː)rəfil] *n.* 【植】叶绿素.
chlo·ro·phyl·lite ['klɔ(ː)rəfilait] *n.* 【矿】绿叶石.
chlo·ro·pic·rin [ˌklɔːrə'pikrin] *n.* 【化】氯化苦,三氯硝基甲烷 (= nitrochloroform).
chlo·ro·plast ['klɔ(ː)rəplæst] *n.* 【植】叶绿体.
chlo·ro·prene ['klɔ(ː)rəpriːn] *n.* 【化】氯丁二烯. ~ **rubber** 氯丁(二烯)橡胶.
chlo·ro·quine [ˌklɔ(ː)rə'kwiːn] *n.* 【药】氯奎.
chlo·ro·sis [klɔ'rəusis] *n.* 【医】萎黄病;【植】缺绿病,褪绿,失绿. **chlo·rot·ic** [klɔː'rɔtik] *a.*
chlo·rous ['klɔːrəs] *a.* 【化】与氯化合的;亚氯的;阴电性的. ~ **acid** 亚氯酸.
chlor·phe·nir·a·mine [ˌklɔːfeni'ræmin] *n.* 【药】氯苯吡胺,扑尔敏[商品名称].
chlor·pic·rin [klɔː'pikrin] *n.* = chloropicrin.
chlor·prom·a·zine [klɔː'prəuməzin] *n.* 【药】氯普鲁马嗪[商品名].
chlor·prop·a·mide [klɔː'prəupəmaid] *n.* 【药】氯磺丙脲[降血糖药,治轻度糖尿病].
chlor·tet·ra·cy·cline [ˌklɔːˌtetrə'saiklin] *n.* 【药】氯四环素,金霉素 (= aureomycin).
chm. = chairman; checkmate.
chmn. = chairman.
cho·a·na ['kəuənə] *n.* (*pl.* *-nae* [-niː]) 【解】鼻后孔,内鼻孔.
Choate [tʃəut] *n.* 乔特[姓氏].
choc·ice [tʃɔk'ais] *n.* 涂有巧克力的冰淇淋.
chock [tʃɔk] *n.* ①(防止滑动的)塞子,楔子;垫木;【机】垫块;(甲板、码头上的)角状柱;[*pl.*]【海】(大轮船上安置救生艇的)定盘,楔形木垫. ②导缆钩,导缆器. — *vt.* 用楔子垫阻;把(救生艇)收置定盘上. ~*up* ①用楔子垫稳. ②(用…)摆满,塞满(屋子) (*with*). —*ad.* 紧,牢,稳;完全. *stand* ~ *still* 呆呆地站着. ~**-a-block** *a.* 摆满,塞满 (*with*). ~**-full** *a.* 塞满了的.
choc·o·late ['tʃɔkəlit] *n.* ①巧克力(糖果). ②巧克力饮料. ③巧克力色. *a bar [box] of* ~ 一块[盒]巧克力. *a cup of* ~ 一杯巧克力茶. ~ *in cake [powder]* 块状[粉状]巧克力. — *a.* ①(含有)巧克力的. ②巧克力色的. ~ **cream** 奶油巧克力(糖). ~ **drop** [美][贬]黑种女孩. ~ **soldier** 非战斗部队的军人.
choc·taw ['tʃɔktɔː] *n.* (*pl.* ~, ~*s*) ①【溜冰】花式溜冰的一种. ②[C-] (印第安人的)巧克陶族;巧克陶语;难懂的语言[解释等].
choice [tʃɔis] *n.* ①选择;挑选;选择力,选择权,选择的自由. ②选择物,所爱好的物品;被选中的东西;入选者;精选品,精华. ③供选择的种类. ④审慎. ⑤[美]移民的选定地. *the girl of one's* ~ 自己选中的女子,所爱好的姑娘. *Every man to his* ~. 各取所好. *There is no* ~ *between the two.* 二者半斤八两. *Which is your* ~? 你要哪一个? *a great [large]* ~ *of* 备有大量…以供选购. *a poor* ~ 备货少(无从选择). *at one's own* ~ 随

意,任意;自由选择地. *by* ~ 出于自己的选择. *for* ~ ①出于自择. ②要选(的话)就选…; 特别, 宁愿(要). *have a [the]* ~ (可以)选择. *have a wide [large]* ~ *of* 有很多, …齐备. *have no (particular)* ~ ①哪个都好,并不特别喜欢哪一个. ②无法选择. *have no* ~ *but to (do)* 除…外别无他法,只好…. *have one's* ~ 选择听便,可以挑选 (*You have your* ~ *between the two.* 两者之中任拣一个). ***Hobson's*** ~ 就是这个要否听便[不许挑选]. *make* ~ *of* 选择. *make [take] one's* ~ 任意选取 (*You may take your* ~ *for one dollar.* 每样一元听凭选择). *of* ~ 精选的, 特别好的. *of one's* ~ 自己选择[喜欢]的. *offer a* ~ 听凭选择. *without* ~ 不分好歹地,无选择地. — *a.* ①精选的,上等的,优良的; 值得选用的. ②爱选择的,挑七拣八的. ③〔美〕宠爱的, 爱惜的. *be* ~ *of* 好挑剔 (*be* ~ *of one's cloth [food]* 讲究衣着[饮食]的); 〔美〕珍视 (*It's my mother's trunk, and she is very* ~ *of it.* 这是我母亲的箱子, 她很珍视它). *be* ~ *over* 珍爱, 溺爱. ~ *bit of calico* 〔美俚〕迷人的姑娘. ~ **goods** 尖儿货,精选货品. **-ly** *ad.* 精选地, 七挑八选地, 认真地, 严查地. **-ness** *n.* 精巧, 优良; 精选.

choir [ˈkwaiə] *n.* ①(教堂的)唱诗队, 唱诗班; 唱诗队席位. ②合唱团,舞蹈组,(天使、鸟、星等的)群, 组; 队. — *vt., vi.* 〔诗〕合唱,合奏. ~ **boy [girl]** 唱诗班男[女]童. ~ **organ** (教堂内)合唱伴奏风琴. ~ **screen** 内坛围栏.

choke [tʃəuk] *vt.* ①使闭气,使闷死; 使闷塞; 扼(喉), 绞死. ②堵塞,填塞;【机】(为获得浓缩的燃料混合物而)阻塞…的气门. ③阻止,妨止,扼止; 干死(植物); 灭(火); 压住,抑制(情感). ④【棒球】握(球棒)中段. *Let go, you* ~ *me!* 放开呀,闷死我啦. — *vi.* ①窒息, 噎, 哽. ②(管道等)塞住; 说不出话来. ③窘住; 举止失措,行动失当. *The pipe* ~*s.* 管子塞住了. ~ *back* 抑压住(感情),忍住(哭泣). ~ *down* 硬用力咽下; 硬忍着(气), 抑制住(感情、眼泪等). ~ *in* 〔美俚〕紧张得发呆[说不出话来]. ~ *off* 把…闷死, 绞死; 使中止,使放弃(计划). ~ *up* 使闷死; 枯死; 〔口〕激动得说不出话来, 紧张得发呆. ~ *up with* 阻塞,填塞, 塞满. — *n.* ①窒息; 哽,噎; 拥塞. ②(管的)闭塞部,节气门;【无】扼流圈[又作~ coil]. ~**berry**【植】唐棣属(植物). ~**bore** 越近枪口越窄的枪筒. ~**cherry** 〔美〕苦樱桃. ~**damp** (煤坑、深井中的)碳酸气. ~ **pear** 味涩的梨; 难忍受的责备[事实]. ~**-full** *a.* = chock-full.

chok·er [ˈtʃəukə] *n.* ①使窒息的人,扼住喉咙的人; 窒息物; 难咽下的东西; 〔俚〕使人哑口无言的事物, 使人点头佩服的事物. ②【电】扼流线圈. ③〔口〕很紧的项圈; 硬高领; 〔美俚〕阔领带; 〔美俚〕= cheese. *a white* ~ 〔俚〕(教士夜礼服上的)宽大白颈巾; 教士. *That's a* ~. 这倒使我没话可说了.

chok·ing [ˈtʃəukiŋ] *a.* ①窒息的, 闷人的. ②闭紧的; (声音)哽住的. ③【电】扼流(作用)的. *a* ~ *coil*【电】扼流线圈. — *n.* 闷气,闷住; 拥塞,堵塞,塞住.

chok·y[1] [ˈtʃəuki] *a.* 窒息的,闷人的.

chok·y[2] [ˈtʃəuki] *n.* ①〔英俚〕拘留所,监狱. ②〔印俚〕警察所; (征收过境税的)关卡.

chol(e)- *comb. f.* 胆汁: *chol*emia 胆血症.

cho·lane [ˈkəulein] *n.*【化】胆(甾)烷.

cho·late [ˈkəuleit] *n.* 胆酸盐(酯).

chol·e·cyst [ˈkɔlisist, ˈkəuli-] *n.* 胆囊.

chol·e·cys·tec·to·my [ˌkɔlisisˈtektəmi, ˌkəuli-] *n.* 胆囊切除术.

cho·le·cys·ti·tis [ˌkɔlisisˈtaitis] *n.*【医】胆囊炎.

chol·er [ˈkɔlə] *n.* 〔诗、古〕脾气,怒气; 胆汁(症).

chol·er·a [ˈkɔlərə] *n.*【医】霍乱. *Asiatic [epidemic, malignant]* ~ 亚洲[传染性、恶性]霍乱. ~ *morbus* 〔L.〕急性胃肠炎. *European [English, bilious, summer]* ~ 欧洲[非传染性,急性]霍乱. ~**-belt** *n.* 预防霍乱症的肚围.

chol·er·a·ic [ˌkɔləˈreiik] *a.* 霍乱症的, 霍乱性的; 类似霍乱的.

chol·er·ic [ˈkɔlərik] *a.* 易怒的,躁急的; 愤怒的; 〔古〕胆汁质的. ~ **temperament** 胆汁质.

chol·er·ine [ˈkɔlərain] *n.*【医】轻霍乱.

cho·le·sta·sis [ˌkɔliˈsteisis] *n.*【医】胆汁郁积[阻塞].

cho·les·ter·in(e) [kəˈlestərin] *n.* = cholesterol.

cho·les·ter·ol [kəˈlestərəul, -rɔl] *n.*【生化】胆固醇, 胆甾醇,异辛甾烯醇.

cho·lic [ˈkəulik] *a.* ~ **acid**【生化】胆酸.

cho·line [ˈkəuliːn] *n.*【生化】胆硷.

cho·lin·er·gic [ˌkəuliˈnəːdʒik, ˌkɔli-] *a.* ①类胆碱(功)能的. ②类胆碱(功)能药物的.

cho·lin·es·ter·ase [ˌkɔliˈnestəreis] *n.* 胆碱酯酶.

chol·la [ˈtʃəujə] *n.* 仙人掌属植物〔产于美国西南部及墨西哥〕.

cholo- *comb. f.* = 〔用于元音前〕chol-.

chol·o·lith [ˈkɔləliθ] *n.*【病】胆石.

chomp [tʃɔmp] *vt., vi.* 〔方〕①吧哒吧哒地使劲咀嚼; 格格地咬. ②不断地咬. — *n.* 嚼; 嚼声. **-er** *n.* 使劲咀嚼者.

Chomsk·i·an [ˈtʃɔmskiən] *a.* (美国语言学家) 乔姆斯基 (Chomsky) 语言理论的.

chon [tʃɔn] *n.* *(pl.* ~*)* 分〔朝鲜货币名称, 为一元的1/100〕.

chon·drin(e) [ˈkɔndrin] *n.*【化】软骨胶.

chondri·o·some [ˈkɔndriəsəum] *n.*【生】线粒体.

chon·drite [ˈkɔndrait] *n.*【地】球粒状陨石. **-drit·ic** [kɔnˈdritik] *a.*

chondro- *comb. f.*【生】粒子: *chondro*ma.

chon·dro·cra·ni·um [ˌkɔndrəuˈkreinjəm] *n.* *(pl.* **-nia** [-njə]*)* *n.*【解】软骨颅.

chon·dro·ma [kɔnˈdrəumə] *n.* *(pl.* **-mas, -ma·ta** [-mətə]*)* 软骨瘤.

chon·drule [ˈkɔndruːl] *n.* 陨石球粒.

choo-choo [ˈtʃuːtʃuː] *n.* 〔儿〕火车头; 火车头的噗噗声. — *vi.* 火车头发出噗噗声; 坐火车旅行.

choose [tʃuːz] *(chose* [tʃəuz]; *chosen* [tʃəuzn]*)* *vt.* ①选, 选择, 挑选, 拣, 选定. ②宁愿. ③〔口〕欲, 好, 想,愿〔后接不定式〕. *He was chosen deputy to the National People's Congress.* 他被选为全国人民代表大会代表. *There is nothing [little; not much] to* ~ *between them.* 全无[几乎没有; 无多大]差别. — *vi.* ①选择. ②喜欢,看中. *She is deaf when she* ~*s.* 不合适她就不听. *(How) can I* ~ *but weep?* 我哪能不哭? *if you* ~ *(to go)* 你若想(去). *as you* ~ 任便,听便. *cannot* ~ *but* 不得不, 只好. ~ *A before B* 宁选 A 不选 B, 宁愿要 A 不要 B. ~ *up (sides)* 〔口〕指定(运动)选手, 分组(比赛). *Let's* ~ *up to see* ... 看是选定…呢, 究竟是让…呢. *pick and* ~ 仔细挑选.

choos·er [ˈtʃuːzə] *n.* 选择者; 选举人; 投票者.

choos·(e)y [ˈtʃuːzi] *a.* 〔美口〕爱挑剔的,爱小题大作的.

chop[1] [tʃɔp] *vt.* *(-pp-)* ①切,砍(柴),伐,劈,断,剁(肉). ②切细,剁碎. ③辟(路), 开(路)前进. ④【网球】搓(球). —*vi.* ①切, 砍, 剁. ②插嘴 *(in)*. ③【网球】搓球. ~ *about* 乱砍(树木等); (风)突然转变方向,突变; 迷,变心. ~ *at* 打,砍. ~ *away* 切掉,割去. ~ *down* 斩掉,砍倒. ~ *fine* 切细. ~ *in* 多嘴,插嘴; 切成. ~ *into* 切成. ~ *off* 切开,切断,切去. ~ *out* (地层等)突然露出. ~ *up* 切细; (地层等)突然露出; 〔喻〕割断(历史等). — *n.* ①砍,劈,剁,切断; (砍伐成的)裂缝. ②排骨, (连骨的)一块肋肉. ③随风翻变的波浪.

chop[2] [tʃɔp] *n., pl.* ①牙床, 颚; 腮; 滑车的腭. ②(港湾、峡谷等的) 入口. *lick one's* ~*s* 切盼, 对…馋涎欲滴 (over). ~**-fallen** *a.* = chapfallen.

chop[3] [tʃɔp] *n.* ①公章,官印; 出港证; 登陆护照; 旅行护照. ②〔口〕牌号,商标; 品种,品质; 等级. *the* ~ *of tea*

[silk] 同一牌子的茶〔生丝〕. *the first [second]* ~〔口〕头〔二〕等. ***no [not much]*** ~〔澳,新俚〕质量不佳.
chop⁴ [tʃɔp] *vi.* ①(风、浪)骤变,突变; ②〔英方〕(思想)动摇,波动,踌躇. ~ ***back*** 急忙退回,急忙掉转方向. ~ ***round*** 风突变. ~ ***upon***〔俚〕突遇;袭来.— *vt.*〔古〕交换;辩论. ~ ***logic*** 强词夺理地诡辩. ~ ***words*** (相)骂. — *n.* 骤变,突变. ~ *and change (about)* 常常改变(方针、意见、职业),反复无常.
chop-chop [ˈtʃɔpˈtʃɔp] *ad., int.* 快快,赶快.
chop·fall·en [ˈtʃɔpˌfɔːlən] = chapfallen.
chophouse [ˈtʃɔphaus] ①小饭馆,烤肉馆. ②(旧中国的)海关.
cho·pin(e) [tʃəuˈpiːn] *n.* (十七世纪妇女穿的)厚底鞋.
chop·per [ˈtʃɔpə] *n.* ①切者,砍者,剁者;伐木人. ②〔美俚〕验票员. ③斧子;屠刀,大砍刀;切碎机. ④【电】斩波器;断路器;遮光器,限制器. ⑤〔美俚〕机关枪;充当机关枪手的匪徒. ⑥【原】中子选择器. ⑦〔美俚〕直升飞机. ⑧〔*pl.*〕〔俚〕牙齿. ⑨特别设计的摩托车.— *vi.*〔美俚〕搭直升飞机. — *vt.*〔美俚〕用直升飞机运送.
chop·ping¹ [ˈtʃɔpiŋ] *n.* ①砍,伐,剁. ②树已伐尽的林中空地. *green* ~ 收青〔庄稼未成熟时即收割〕. ~ **block [board]** 俎,砧板,肉砧. ~ **knife** 菜刀.
chop·ping² [ˈtʃɔpiŋ] *a.* 波涛汹涌的.
chop·ping³ [ˈtʃɔpiŋ] *n.*〔英口〕(儿童)身体强壮的.
chop·py¹ [ˈtʃɔpi] *a.* ①(风向、市场等)紊乱的,变动频繁的; 波浪滔滔的.
chop·py² [ˈtʃɔpi] *a.* ①裂缝多的; 断断续续的. ②不匀称的;结构拙劣的.
chop·stick [ˈtʃɔpstik] *n.*〔常 *pl.*〕(中国的)筷子.
chop-su·ey [ˈtʃɔpˈsuːi] *n.*〔美〕炒杂碎〔中国菜〕; 中国菜馆.
cho·ra·gus [kəuˈreigəs, kə-] *n.* *(pl. -gi [-dʒai])* ①古希腊戏剧中的歌队的队长. ②合唱队,乐队领队. **cho·rag·ic** [-ˈrædʒik] *a.*
cho·ral [ˈkɔrəl] *a.* 合唱队的,圣诗队的;合唱(曲)的. ~ **service** 合唱礼拜. **-ly** *ad.*
cho·ral(e) [kɔˈrɑːl] *n.* (合唱的)赞美诗〔歌〕;(唱赞美诗的)专业合唱团.
cho·ral·ist [ˈkɔːrəlist] *n.* 合唱队员; (教会)唱诗班成员,赞美诗歌手.
chord [kɔːd] *n.* ①〔诗〕(琴)弦; (心)弦; 【乐】和弦,和(谐)音. ②【空】翼弦; 【数】弦; 【解】腱,带; 【建】弦材,桁材. *the major [minor]* ~ 大〔小〕三和弦. *the spinal* ~ 脊髓. *the* ~ *organ* 和音(电子)风琴. *vocal* ~*s* 声带. ***strike a responsive*** ~ 打动对方心弦. ***touch the right*** ~ 触及心弦. — *vt.* 上…的弦; 调(弦). — *vi.* ①调和,和谐. ②弹奏.
chor·da [ˈkɔːdə] *(pl. -dae [-diː])* *n.*【解】索,带,腱. ~ *dorsalis* 脊索. ~ *tendinae* 腱索.
chor·dal [ˈkɔːdəl] *a.*【解】(脊)索的.
Chor·da·ta [kɔˈdeitə] *n.*【动】脊索动物类.
chor·date [ˈkɔːdeit] *n.*【动】脊索类动物.
chordless [ˈkɔːdlis] *a.* 使用干电池的. *a* ~ *shaver* 干电剃刀.
chore [tʃɔː] *n., vi.*〔美〕= chare. ~ ***around***〔美〕作短工.
cho·re·a [kɔˈriə] *n.*【医】舞蹈病.
cho·reg·ra·phy [kəˈregrəfi] *n.* 舞蹈(尤指芭蕾舞)编写法,舞蹈设计;(芭蕾)舞蹈艺术,舞蹈表演.
chore·ic [kɔ(ː)ˈriːik] *a.* 舞蹈病的.
cho·re·o·graph [ˈkɔ(ː)riəgrɑːf] *vt.* ①为(芭蕾舞等)设计舞蹈动作. ②设计,筹划. — *vi.* 从事舞蹈设计. **-er** (芭蕾)舞蹈动作设计者. **-ic** *a.* (有关)舞蹈艺术的.
cho·re·og·ra·phy [ˌkɔ(ː)riˈɔgrəfi] *n.*〔英〕= choregraphy.
chori- *comb. f.*〔用在元音前〕= chorio.
chor·i·amb, chor·i·am·bus [ˈkɔ(ː)riæmb, -bəs] *n.*【韵】扬抑抑扬格. **-bic** *a.*
chor·ic [ˈkɔːrik] *a.* (古希腊剧)合唱曲的; 合唱歌舞式的.
cho·rine [ˈkɔːriːn] *n.*〔美〕歌剧合唱队女歌唱〔舞蹈〕队员 (= chorus girl).
cho·ri·o·al·lan·to·is [kɔːriˌəuəˈlæntwis] *n.* 绒(毛)膜尿囊. **-lan·toic** [-ˌælənˈtəuik] *a.*
cho·ri·oid [ˈkɔːriˌɔid] *a.*【解】似脉络膜的;似胎囊的.— *n.*【解】脉络膜.
cho·ri·on [ˈkɔːriɔn] *n.* *(pl. -ria [-riə])*【解】绒(毛)膜,浆膜;【动】卵壳.
cho·ri·pet·al·ous [ˌkɔːriˈpetələs] *n.*【植】离瓣的.
cho·rist [ˈkɔːrist] *n.* 合唱者,合唱歌手.
chor·is·ter [ˈkɔristə] *n.*① (教堂的)合唱者;少年合唱队队员. ②唱诗班领唱者;〔美〕合唱队指挥员. *feathered* ~*s* 嘈杂啁啾的鸟群.
cho·ro·graph·ic [ˌkɔːrəˈgræfik] *a.* (地方性)地图绘制术的;地方地理学的.
cho·rog·ra·phy [kɔːˈrɔgrəfi] *n.* ①地方地理学;地方志,地方志编纂. ②地方地图(绘制术).
cho·roid [ˈkɔːrɔid] *a.*【解】似脉络膜的;似胎囊的. — *n.*【解】脉络膜;【生理】黑衣;【虫】黑基膜.
cho·rolo·gy [kɔːˈrɔlədʒi] *n.* 生物分布学,生物地理学,动植物分布论.
chortle [ˈtʃɔːtl] *n.* 哈哈大笑(声).— *vi.* ①哈哈大笑. ②高兴地唱歌. ~ ***about [over]***〔英俚〕对…表示高兴.
cho·rus [ˈkɔːrəs] *n.* ①【乐】合唱; 合唱队;合唱歌(曲). ②〔古希腊〕歌舞剧合唱的唱词;【英古剧】(宣读开场白和收场白的)剧情解说员. ③(歌的)迭句;合唱句,合唱. ④歌舞团(表演)的歌舞. *join in a* ~ 参加合唱; 唱合唱部分. *laugh [protest] in* ~ 齐声发笑〔反对〕. *meet with a* ~ *of protest* 遭到多数人的齐声反对. *in* ~ 合唱;异口同声地. — *vt.* 合唱; 齐诵;异口同声地说. ~ **girl** 歌剧合唱队女队员〔配唱演员〕. ~ **master** 合唱队指挥.
chose¹ [tʃəuz] choose 的过去式.
chose² [ʃəuz] *n.*【法】物,动产. ***a*** ~ ***in action*** 无形动产〔可依法获得但尚未实际占有〕. ***a*** ~ ***in possession*** 所有财产,所有物〔已实际占有〕.
chose jugée [ʃəuz ʒyˈʒei]〔F.〕无庸议论的事情,既定的事情.
cho·sen [ˈtʃəuzn] choose 的过去分词. — *a.* 拣过的;精选的,纯良的. *my* ~ *profession* 我所爱好的职业. ***the*** ~ ***people***【宗】上帝的选民〔指犹太人〕.
chott [ʃɔt] *n.* 北非小盐湖盆地.
chou [ʃuː] *n.*〔F.〕①(妇女衣帽上的)球结,花结,蝶结. ②〔爱称〕= darling.
chough [tʃʌf] *n.*【鸟】红嘴乌鸦.
chouse [tʃaus] *vt., n.*〔口〕骗,诈骗;欺骗.
chow [tʃau] *n.* ①中国(黑鼻)狗. ②(中国的)州. ③〔澳口〕中国人. ④〔美军俚〕食品,军粮;吃饭. ~ ***mein*** (中国)炒面.
chow-chow [ˈtʃauˈtʃau] *n.* ①中国咸菜,醃菜; 中国食品;杂碎,杂拌. ②中国种的狗. — *a.* 杂,什锦的. ~ **box** (日本的)漆制食盒. ~ **shop** (中国的)杂货店.
chow·der [ˈtʃaudə] *n.* (纽芬兰、美国和新英格兰地区以鱼或蛤加洋葱、猪肉等做的)杂脍. ~**head** 呆子,傻瓜.
CHQ = Corps Headquarters 军(司令)部.
Chr. = Christ; Christian; Christopher.
chre·ma·tis·tics [ˌkriːməˈtistiks] *n.* 理财学,货殖论;政治经济学.
chres·tom·a·thy [kresˈtɔməθi] *n.* ①有注解的文选;文章选读. ②(作家的)选集.
Chris¹ [kris] *n.* 克里斯〔男子名, Christopher 的爱称〕.
Chris² [kris] *n.* 克莉丝〔女子名, Christiana 或 Christine 的略称〕.
chrism [ˈkrizəm] *n.*【宗】圣油;圣油礼.

chrismal [ˈkrizməl] *a.*【宗】圣油的.
chris·ma·to·ry [ˈkrizmətəri] *n.*【宗】圣油瓶. — *a.* 圣油的.
chris·om [ˈkrizəm] *n.* ① = chrism. ②〔废〕婴孩的洗礼衣. ③不满月死亡的婴儿;〔古〕(天真无邪的)婴儿;幼儿(= ~ child).
Christ [kraist] *n.* ①【基督】〔the ~〕救世主. ②基督〔原为 Jesus 的称号,用作 Jesus the Christ, 后来才变成 Jesus Christ 这一固有名词〕. ***Before*** ~ 公元前〔略作 B. C.〕. ***in*** ~***'s name*** 究竟〔强调语气〕(*What in* ~*'s name are you doing out there?* 你究竟是在那里干什么). ***to*** ~ 真正,十分 (*I do hope to* ~ *he isn't going.* 他真的不去就好了). — *int.* 〔俚〕哎呀! 岂有此理!〔表惊愕、愤怒等〕. *Christ, it's cold.* 真冷呀! ~**-Church** *n.* (牛津大学的) 基督学院. ~**-cross** *n.* = crisscross.
Chris·ta·bel [ˈkristəbel] *n.* 克里斯塔贝尔〔女子名〕.
Christ·church [ˈkraist-tʃəːtʃ] *n.* 克赖斯特彻奇〔新西兰城市〕.
christ·cross [ˈkristkrɔs] *n.* 十字形的记号[签押]. ~**-row** 字母表,字母系统.
chris·ten [ˈkrisən] *vt.* ①【宗】为…施洗礼(使成基督教徒); 施洗礼时命名. ②(举行仪式)命名(轮船等); 给…取绰号. ③隆重地首次启用(汽车、轮船等);〔口〕开始使用. *be* ~*ed John after one's father* (施洗礼时)照父名命名为约翰. **-ing** *n.* 施洗礼仪式;命名仪式.
Chris·ten·dom [ˈkrisəndəm] *n.* 基督教界;〔集合词〕基督教徒. ***by my*** ~ 的确〔强调语势〕.
Christ·hood [ˈkraisthud] *n.* 基督的品格[身分].
Chris·tian[1] [ˈkristjən, -tʃən] *n.* ①基督教徒; 信徒. ②〔口〕人类; 文明人; 正派人. — *a.* ①基督(教)的; 信基督教的. ②〔口〕人(类)的; 文明的;〔口〕正派的,高尚的. *a good* ~ *dinner* 丰盛的酒席. ~ **era** 西历纪元. ~ **faith** 基督教(信仰). ~ **name** 教名,洗礼名.
Chris·tian[2] [ˈkristjən] *n.* 克里斯琴〔男子名〕.
Chris·ti·an·a [ˌkristiˈɑːnə] *n.* 克里斯蒂安娜〔女子名〕.
Chris·ti·an·i·a [ˌkristiˈɑːniə] *n.* ①克里斯蒂安尼亚〔挪威首都旧名,现名 Oslo〕. ②【滑雪】急转弯 (= ~ turn).
Chris·ti·an·ism [ˈkristjənizəm] *n.* = Christianity.
Chris·ti·an·i·ty [ˌkristiˈæniti] *n.* 基督教; 基督教信仰;〔集合词〕基督教徒; 基督徒精神.
Chris·tian·ise, -ize [ˈkristjənaiz] *vt., vi.* (使)成为基督教徒,(使)基督教化.
Chris·tie [ˈkristi] *n.* 克里斯蒂〔姓氏〕.
Chris·ti·na [krisˈtiːnə] *n.* 克里斯蒂娜〔女子名〕.
Chris·tine [ˈkristiːn, krisˈtiːn] *n.* 克里斯廷〔女子名〕.
Christ·less [ˈkraistlis] *a.* 违反基督精神的, 不信基督教的.
Christ·like, Christ·ly [ˈkraistlaik, -li] *a.* 具有基督精神[德性]的; 象基督一样的.
Christ·mas [ˈkrisməs] *n.* 圣诞节〔12 月 25 日, 略写作 Xmas〕. ~ **beetle**【动】食根虫. ~ **box** 圣诞节礼品;〔英口〕圣诞节给雇用人员的礼物或赏钱〔暗示明年继续雇用〕. ~ **card** 圣诞贺片. ~ **carol** 圣诞节颂歌. ~ **Day** 圣诞节. ~ **Eve** 圣诞节前夜[日]. ~ **flower**【植】一品红. ~ **holidays** 圣诞节假期; (学校等)寒假. **C-Island** 圣诞岛〔一在 Java 南,一在太平洋〕. ~ **log** = Yule log. ~ **rose**【植】黑儿波. ~ **stocking** 圣诞老人袜〔圣诞节前夕, 孩子们睡觉前挂在床边, 让圣诞老人把礼物塞在里面〕. ~ **tree** 圣诞树. ~ **waits** 圣诞节夜晚挨户唱歌的艺人. ~**tide** 圣诞节节期〔12 月 24 日至 1月 6 日〕. **-(s)y** *a.* 圣诞节似的,圣诞节情调的.
Chris·tol·o·gy [krisˈtɔlədʒi] *n.* (研究耶稣基督的)基督学.
Chris·toph·a·ny [krisˈtɔfəni] *n.*【宗】基督再现.
Chris·to·pher [ˈkristəfə] *n.* 克里斯托弗〔男子名〕.
Christ's-thorn [ˈkraistsθɔːn] *n.*【植】滨枣.

Christy minstrels [ˈkristi ˈminstrəlz] 黑面歌手〔指涂黑面孔沿街唱黑人歌曲的卖艺人〕.
-chroic *comb. f.* (皮肤、植物等的)色.
chrom- *comb. f.* 色,色素;【化】铬(= chromo-).
chro·ma [ˈkrəumə] *n.* 色彩纯度; 色品, 色度.
chromat- *comb. f.* 〔用于元音前〕= chromato-.
chro·mate [ˈkrəumit] *n.*【化】铬酸盐.
chro·mat·ic [krəˈmætik] *a.* ①色彩的; 着色的, 彩色的. ②【生】染色质的. ③【乐】半音(阶)的. ~ *aberration*【摄、电视】(镜头的)色(度象)差, 色散. ~ *printing* 套色版; 彩色印刷. *a* ~ *scale* 半音音阶. *a* ~ *semitone* 变化半音,花半音. ~ *signs* 变音号. **-i·cal·ly** *ad.* ①上色, 套色. ②成半音阶.
chro·ma·tic·i·ty [ˌkrəuməˈtisiti] *n.* 染色性.
chro·mat·ics [krəˈmætiks] *n. pl.* 颜色学.
chro·ma·tid [ˈkrəumətid] *n.*【生】染色单体.
chro·ma·tin [ˈkrəumətin] *n.*【生】染色质, 染色粒.
chro·ma·tism [ˈkrəumətizəm] *n.* ①【植】变色. ②色散, 色差.
chro·mat·ist [ˈkrəumətist] *n.* 颜色学家.
chromato- *comb. f.* 色; 染色质: *chromato*graphy.
chro·mat·o·gram [krəuˈmætəgræm] *n.*【化】色层(分离)谱, 色彩谱.
chro·ma·to·graph [ˈkrəumətəgrɑːf] *vt.* ①用套色印刷复制. ②用色层法分离(物质). — *n.*〔古〕套色版.
chro·ma·tog·ra·phy [ˌkrəuməˈtɔgrəfi] *n.*【化】层析, 色层(分离)法.
chro·ma·tol·y·sis [ˌkrəuməˈtɔlisis] *n.*【医】染色质消失[溶解]. **-mat·o·lyt·ic** [krəuˌmætəˈlitik] *a.*
chro·mat·o·phore [ˈkrəumətəfɔː] *n.*【生】色素细胞; (载)色体.
chro·mat·o·scope [ˈkrəumətəskəup] *n.*【天】闪烁反射望远镜;【医】彩光折射率计.
chro·ma·tron [ˈkrəumətrɔn] *n.* 彩色电视显象管.
chro·ma·trope [ˈkrəumətrəup] *n.* (成双的)旋转彩色幻灯片.
chro·ma·type [ˈkrəumətaip] *n.* 铬盐相片, 彩色相片; 铬盐片照相法.
chrome [krəum] *n.*【化】①铬(= chromium). ②铬黄(= ~ yellow); 黄色. ③镀铬物件. ~ **ocher** 铬华. ~ **red** 铬铅红. ~ **steel** 铬钢. — *vt.* 镀以铬; 用镀铬化合物印染.
chro·mic [ˈkrəumik] *a.*【化】铬的. ~ **acid** 铬酸.
chro·mide [ˈkrəumaid] *n.*【动】丽鱼科鱼(= cichlid).
chro·mi·nance [ˈkrəuminəns] *n.*【无】①色品, 色度. ②彩色信号.
chro·mite [ˈkrəumait] *n.*【矿】铬铁(矿).
chro·mi·um [ˈkrəumjəm] *n.*【化】铬.
chro·mize [ˈkrəumaiz] *vt.* 对(金属)作渗铬处理, 铬化(金属). **chro·miz·ing** *n.* 渗铬(处理), 铬化(处理).
chro·mo [ˈkrəuməu] *n.* 彩色石印版.
chromo- *comb. f.* 色: *chromo*graph.
chro·mo·gen [ˈkrəumədʒən] *n.*【化】发色团, 生色团; 色(素)原, 色母, 产色细菌;【纺】铬精.
chro·mo·graph [ˈkrəuməgrɑːf] *n.* 胶版复制品. — *vt.* 用胶版复制器复制.
chro·mo·lith·o·graph [ˈkrəuməˈliθəgrɑːf] *n.* 彩色石印图画. **-ic** *a.* 彩色石印术的. **-y** *n.* 彩色石印术.
chro·mo·mere [ˈkrəuməmiə] *n.*【生】染色粒. **-mer·ic** [-ˈmirik] *a.*
chro·mo·ne·ma [ˌkrəuməˈniːmə] *n.* (*pl.* **-ma·ta** [-tə])【生】染色线. **-mal** *a.*
chro·mo·phil [ˈkrəuməfil] *a.*【生】易染的. — *n.*【生】易染细胞; 易染细胞部分.
chro·mo·phore [ˈkrəuməfɔː] *n.*【生】载色体; 发色团, 生色团. **-phor·ic** [-ˈfɔːrik] *a.*
chro·mo·pho·to·graph [ˈkrəuməˈfəutəgrɑːf] *n.* 彩色

照相. **-tog·ra·phy** *n.* 彩色照相术.
chro·mo·plast [ˈkrəuməplæst] *n.* 【生】有色体.
chro·mo·pro·tein [ˌkrəuməˈprəutiːn] *n.* 【生】色蛋白.
chro·mo·scope [ˈkrəuməskəup] *n.* (电视)显色管.
chro·mo·some [ˈkrəuməsəum] *n.* 【生】染色体. ~ **complex**【生】染色体群.
chro·mo·sphere [ˈkrəuməsfiə] *n.* 【天】(太阳的)色球层.
chro·mo·type [ˈkrəumətaip] *n.* 彩色印刷术;彩色摄影.
chro·mo·xy·lo·graph [ˈkrəuməˈzailəgræf] *n.* 套色[彩色]木版画.
chro·mous [ˈkrəuməs] *a.* 【化】①亚铬的, 二价铬的. ②铬的.
chro·myl [ˈkrəumil] *n.* 【化】①铬酰. ②氧铬基.
Chron. = Chronicle.
chron., chronol. = chronology; chronological.
chron-, *comb. f.* 表示"时间". *chronology.*
chro·nax·ie, chro·nax·y [ˈkrəunæksi] *n.* 【医】时值.
chro·n·ic, -i·cal [ˈkrɔnik(l)] *a.* ①慢性的; 长期的; 积习成癖的. ②〔英俚〕剧烈的, (天气等)恶劣的. *a* ~ *disease* 慢性病,痼疾. *a* ~ *grumbler* 一年到头牢骚不停的人. *a* ~ *liar* 说谎成癖的人. — *n.* 慢性病人. **-i·cal·ly** *ad.* 慢性地,不断地.
chro·nic·ity [krəˈnisiti] *n.* 慢性,长期性.
chron·i·cle [ˈkrɔnikl] *n.* ①年代记, 编年史; 记录. ②〔C-〕«…新闻»〔报刊名〕. ~*history [play]* 年代史剧,纯史剧. *the Chronicles*【圣】«历王纪». *The San Francisco* ~ «旧金山新闻»〔报纸名〕. — *vt.* 把…载于编年史中,记录.
chron·i·cler [ˈkrɔniklə] *n.* ①年代记作者, 编年史家. ②记录者.
chro·nique scan·da·leuse [krɔːˈniːk skaːŋdaˈləːz] 〔F.〕丑闻录.
chrono- *comb. f.* 〔用于辅音字母前〕= chron-.
chron·o·gram [ˈkrɔnəgræm] *n.* ①(用大写罗马数字之和表示的)纪年铭文: *LorD haVe MerCIe Vpon Vs* = 50+500+5+1,000+100+1+5+5 = 1666 〔铭文意为"求主怜悯我们", 其中嵌入 L. D. V. M. C. I. V. V 等表示数字的大写罗马数字〕. ②时间记录(图象).
chron·o·graph [ˈkrɔnəgrɑːf] *n.* 计时器,录时器.
chron·o·lo·ger, -gist [krəˈnɔlədʒə, -dʒist] *n.* 年代学者; 年表编制者.
chron·o·log·i·c(al) [ˌkrɔnəˈlɔdʒik(əl)] *a.* 年代学的,编年的,按照年月顺序的. **-ly** *ad.*
chro·nol·o·gize [krəˈnɔlədʒaiz] *vt.* 把…按年排列,把…编年,给…作年表.
chro·nol·o·gy [krəˈnɔlədʒi] *n.* ①年代学. ②年表. ③(资料等)按年代次序的排列.
chro·nom·e·ter [krəˈnɔmitə] *n.* 精密计时表; 航海时计,经线仪;天文钟;【乐】拍节机.
chron·o·met·ric, -ri·cal [ˌkrɔnəˈmetrik(əl)] *a.* (用)精密计时表[天文钟等](测定)的.
chro·nom·e·try [krəˈnɔmitri] *n.* 时刻测定;测时术,记时法.
chron·o·pher [ˈkrɔnəfə] *n.* 电气报时器.
chron·o·scope [ˈkrɔnəskəup] *n.* 瞬时计〔尤指炮弹等的速度测量器〕.
chrys- *comb. f.* 〔用于元音字母前〕【化、矿】黄色的; 金黄的,金的(= chryso).
chrys·a·lid [ˈkrisəlid] *a.* 【动】蝶蛹的;〔喻〕准备期的. — *n.* = chrysalis.
chrys·a·lis [ˈkrisəlis] *n.* (*pl.* ~*es, chrysalides* [kriˈsælidiːz]) ①蝶蛹; 蝶蛹茧. ②〔喻〕过渡期, 准备期; 过渡期中的事物.
chrys·an·the·mum [kriˈsænθəməm] *n.* 【植】菊(花); 〔C-〕菊属. ~ *flower* 菊花.
chrys·a·ro·bin [ˌkrisəˈrəubin] *n.* 【医】柯桠素.
chrys·el·e·phan·tine [ˌkriseliˈfæntain] *a.* 用金和象牙做成的.
chryso- *comb. f.* 〔用于辅音字母前〕= chrys-.
chrys·o·ber·yl [ˈkrisəberil] *n.* 【矿】金绿宝石.
chry·so·lite [ˈkrisəlait] *n.* 【矿】贵橄榄石.
chrys·o·prase [ˈkrisəpreiz] *n.* 【矿】绿玉髓.
chrys·o·tile [ˈkrisəˌtail] *n.* 【矿】温石绵,织蛇纹石.
chs. = chapters.
chtho·ni·an [ˈθəuniən] *a.* 【希神】冥府的; 冥府鬼神的.
chthon·ic [ˈθɔnik] *a.* ①= chthonian. ②阴暗的; 原始的,神秘的.
chub [tʃʌb] *n.* (*pl.* ~*s*, 〔集合词〕~)【鱼】雪鲦.
Chubb [tʃʌb] *n.* (英国伦敦产的)丘伯锁(=Chubb lock).
chub·by [ˈtʃʌbi] *a.* 圆胖的, 鼓鼓的, 丰满的. **-ness** *n.*
chuck¹ [tʃʌk] *vt.* ①〔口〕抛出,扔出; 逐出. ②〔美〕辞职,退职; 放弃; 丢弃. ③呕出,吐出. ④拍; 抚摸. ~ ***away*** 扔弃; 浪费(金钱); 失去(机会). ~ ***in*** 挑战. ***Chuck it!*** 〔俚〕停下来! 别吵[闹]了! ~ ***one's weight about*** 摆架子,倨傲. ~ ***out*** 赶出, 撵出; 〔口〕否决(议案). ~ ***over*** 驱逐. ~ ***up*** 缩手,放弃,厌弃. ~ ***up the sponge*** 认输. — *n.* ①抛出,扔弃;〔口〕放弃; 辞退. ②轻抚, 爱抚. ***give sb. the*** ~ 辞退[开除]某人. ***get the*** ~ 被辞退[开除].
chuck² [tʃʌk] *n.* 【机】(车床等的)卡盘, 轧头; (罐头)封罐机. *independent* ~ 分动[四爪]卡盘. *scroll* ~ 三爪卡盘. — *vt.* 【机】用卡盘夹紧.
chuck³ [tʃʌk] *int., n.* 咕咕〔呼鸡声〕, 喔喔〔呼马声〕; 咯咯〔母鸡叫声〕. — *vi.* 咕咕[咯咯,嘟嘟]地叫; 喔喔地赶马.
chuck⁴ [tʃʌk] *int., n.* 亲爱的,宝贝, 心肝〔对妻子、爱儿、小鸡等的爱称〕.
chuck⁵ [tʃʌk] *n.* ①(牛等的)颈肉. ②〔美西部〕食品, 粮食, 伙食. ~ **box** 食物匣. ~ **wagon** (牧场等的) 炊事车,伙食车.
chuck-a-luck [ˈtʃʌkəˌlʌk] *n.* 掷骰赌博 (= chuck-luck).
chuck·er(-out) [ˈtʃʌkəˈraut] *n.* 〔英〕(戏院、旅馆等雇来撵走捣乱者的)护场员,护馆员.
chuck-far·thing [ˈtʃʌk-ˈfɑːθiŋ] *n.* (比赛用钱币投进小洞穴内的)投钱戏. ***play (at)*** ~ ***with*** 孤注一掷, 冒险一试.
chuck-full [tʃʌk-ful] *a.* (塞) 满了的, 挤得满满的 (= chock-full).
chuck·hole [ˈtʃʌkhəul] *n.* 人行道上的坑洼.
chuck·le [ˈtʃʌkl] *n.* ①(母鸡的) 咯咯声. ②吃吃的笑, 嘻嘻轻笑声. — *vi.* ①(母鸡) 咯咯地叫. ②嗤的一笑, 轻声地笑,暗笑. ~ ***out*** 笑嘻嘻地说. ~ ***over [at]*** 开心得笑嘻嘻,暗自得意. ~ ***to oneself*** 独自发笑; 暗中好笑[高兴]. ~**head** 〔口〕傻瓜, 笨蛋. ~**headed** *a.* 〔口〕愚蠢的,呆笨的.
chuck·wal·la [ˈtʃʌkˌwɑːlə] *n.* 【动】叩壁蜥属蜥蜴〔产于墨西哥西北部和美国西南部〕.
chuck-will's-widow [ˌtʃʌkˌwilzˈwidəu] *n.* 【动】蚊母鸟.
chuck·y [ˈtʃʌki] *n.* 〔英方〕鸡.
chud·dar [ˈtʃʌdə] *n.* (印度毛料)披巾.
chuff¹ [tʃʌf] *n.* ①乡下佬. ②粗暴的人. ③吝啬鬼.
chuff² [tʃʌf] *a.* 〔英方〕①胖的,健壮的. ②得意的, 趾高气扬的.
chuff³ [tʃʌf] *n.* (火车头排气的) 噗噗声. — *vi.* (火车) 噗噗地前进; (蒸气机等) 噗噗地运转. *The train* ~*ed along.* 火车噗噗地前进.
chuff·y [ˈtʃʌfi] *a.* 〔方〕矮胖的; 肥胖的.
chug [tʃʌg] *n.* 〔美〕(发动机等短而钝的) 嚓嘎声. — *vi.* *(-gg-)* (发动机等)嚓嘎嚓嘎地响; 〔口〕(火车、汽船等) 嚓嘎嚓嘎地前进. ~-~ 〔口〕旧火车头,旧机车.
chug-a-lug [ˈtʃʌgəlʌg] *ad.* 〔美俚〕咕咚咕咚地喝完. — *vt., vi.* *(-gg-)* 〔美俚〕咕咚咕咚地喝完; 痛饮,牛饮; 狼吞

虎咽.

chu·kar [tʃəˈkɑː] *n.* 【动】石鸡 *(Alectoris graeca)*〔原产于亚洲和欧洲〕.

chuk·ker [ˈtʃʌkə] *n.* (马球戏)一局〔7 分 30 秒〕.

chum[1] [tʃʌm] *n.* 〔口〕(大学等的) 同室朋友，同房间的人；密友；同事. *a great* ～ 极要好的朋友. *a new* ～〔大洋〕新来的移民. ***get [make]*** **～*s with*** 和…成好朋友. ***split*** **～*s*** 绝交. — *vi.* 同室居住；成为好朋友. ～ ***up with*** 〔口〕与…成好朋友.

chum[2] [tʃʌm] *n.* 鱼饵〔尤指切成小块作饵的鱼〕.

chum·mage [ˈtʃʌmidʒ] *n.* ①同室居住，同室交谊；合住. ②〔俚〕(监狱新来囚犯的)入伙钱.

chum·mer·y [ˈtʃʌməri] *n.* 同住一个房间的人.

chum·my[1] [ˈtʃʌmi] *a.* 〔口〕亲密的，有交情的. ***be*** ～ ***with*** 与…交好〔关系亲密〕. —*n.* ①〔俚〕好友，密友. ②微型汽车. ～ **flyabout** 〔美〕私人用的小飞机. ～ **roadster** 〔美〕郊游用的小汽车.

chummy[2] [ˈtʃʌmi] *n.* 〔俚〕扫烟囱的小伙子.

chump [tʃʌmp] *n.* ①木片；木块. ②大块肉片 (= ～ chop). ③〔俚〕头；〔口〕笨人，呆头傻脑的人. ***(go) off one's*** ～ 〔英〕疯狂，发狂. ***make a*** ～ ***out of*** 使…丢脸，侮辱.

chunk [tʃʌŋk] *n.* ①大块. ②大量，相当大的部分. ③〔美〕矮胖结实的人；结实的马. *a* ～ *of bread [meat]* 一大块面包〔肉〕.

chunk·y [ˈtʃʌŋki] *a.* 〔美〕矮胖的，结实的.

chun·nel [ˈtʃʌnəl] *n.* 水底火车隧道.

Church [tʃəːtʃ] *n.* 丘奇〔姓氏〕.

church [tʃəːtʃ] *n.* ①教堂，礼拜堂；〔C-〕教会；教派. ②教徒团体；〔集合词〕基督教徒. ③〔the ～〕牧师〔神父〕职位，圣职. ④【宗】(教堂的)礼拜〔不用冠词 the〕. ⑤教会的组织；教权. *C- of Humanity* 人道主义者，孔德主义者. *the* ～ *invisible* 天上的基督教徒们；天上教会. *the visible* ～ 地上的基督教徒们；地上教会，现世教会. *the Eastern C-* 东正教 (会)，希腊正教. *the Western C-* 西正教(会)，罗马天主教会. *the established [state]* ～ 国教. *the C- of England [English C-, Anglican C-]* 英国国教，圣公会. *the High [Low] C-* (重礼仪的)高教〔(不重礼仪的) 低教〕教会. ***after*** ～ (在教堂)做礼拜之后，从教堂出来. ***as poor as a*** ～ ***mouse*** 非常贫穷. ***be at*** ～ = ***be in*** ～ 正(在教堂)做礼拜. ***between*** ～***es*** 上次做礼拜与下次做礼拜相隔期间. ***enter the C-*** = ***go into the*** ～ 做牧师，任圣职. ***go to [attend]*** ～ 上教堂去做礼拜；〔口〕结婚. ***talk*** ～ 讲有关宗教信仰的话〔枯燥无味的话〕；〔古〕讲行话. — *vt.* ①使(某人)去教堂接受宗教仪式. ②为(妇女) 做产后感恩礼拜. ③按教会规章申斥〔处罚〕. ～**goer** (经常)上教堂去做礼拜的信徒. ～**-going** ① *a.* 经常上教堂去的. ② *n.* 上教堂去. ～ **key** (开罐头用的)三角开刀. ～**man** 〔古〕教士，牧师；〔英〕国教教徒. ～ **rate** (教区内征收的)教堂维持费. **C- scot** 教区百姓供养教士的捐款. ～ **service** 礼拜；祈祷书；说教. **C- session** 长老会. ～ **text** 墓碑上的黑体字；【印】黑体字. ～**warden** ①教区委员，教会执事. ②〔英口〕陶制长烟斗. ～**woman** (英国国教的)女教徒. ～**yard** 教堂庭院；(教堂的)墓地 (*a* ～*yard cough* 〔英〕衰竭无力的干咳. *a fat* ～*yard* 坟多的公墓). **-ing** (妇女) 安产感恩礼拜. **-ism** 墨守教会仪式；英国国教主义. **-ly** *a.* ①教会的，符合教会规章. ②虔诚的.

Church·ill [ˈtʃəːtʃil] *n.* 丘吉尔〔姓氏〕. **Sir Winston Leonard Spencer** ～ 温斯顿·丘吉尔〔1874—1965，英国政治家，曾于 1940—45 年，1951—55 年两次任首相〕.

church·y [ˈtʃəːtʃi] *a.* 固守教会教条〔礼仪〕的，教会万能主义的.

churl [tʃəːl] *n.* ①粗鄙的人；乡下人；吝啬鬼，守财奴；脾气坏的人，执拗的人. ②【英史】下层自由民. ***put a*** ～ ***upon a gentleman*** 好酒喝后喝劣酒.

churl·ish [ˈtʃəːliʃ] *a.* ①乡下人的. ②粗鄙的；脾气坏的. ③吝啬的. ④(土地)难耕种的. **-ness** *n.*

churn [tʃəːn] *n.* (提制奶油用的)搅乳桶；〔英〕奶桶；【纺】黄化鼓；【机】摇转搅拌桶. — *vt.* ①(用搅乳桶) 搅拌(牛奶等)，制造(黄油等). ②用力搅拌(使起泡沫). — *vi.* ①用搅乳器搅拌. ②(浪等)猛烈冲洗海岸，(风)翻腾(波浪)，(牛乳等)发泡. ～***(out)*** 制造〔做出〕许多(粗制滥造的东西). ～**dasher,** ～**staff** 搅乳装置，搅乳棒. ～**ing** *n.* 搅乳；一次提制的奶油.

churr [tʃəː] *vi., n.* (鹧鸪等)颤鸣(声).

chut [tʃʌt] *int.* 啧！咄！〔焦急时的咂嘴声〕.

chute [ʃuːt] *n.* ①奔流，急流，瀑布；射水路. ②斜槽；流槽；筏路；险陡滑道. ③〔口〕降落伞〔parachute 的缩写〕. *an air* ～ 降落伞. *a flare* ～ 照明伞. — *vt., vi.* (使)顺斜道滑行. ～ *the* ～*s* 〔口〕滑斜坡游戏.

chute-the-chute [ˈʃuːtðəʃuːt] *n.* ①(儿童乐园的) 惊险滑梯. ②惊险情节.

chut·nee, chut·ney [ˈtʃʌtni] *n.* (印度式调味用)酸辣酱.

chutz·pah, chutz·pa [ˈ*k*hutspə] *n.* 〔美口〕厚颜无耻；胆大妄为.

chyle [kail] *n.* 【生】乳糜.

chyme [kaim] *n.* 【生】乳糜汁，食糜.

chym·ist [ˈkimist] *n.* 〔古〕= chemist.

chy·mo·tryp·sin [ˌkaiməˈtripsin] *n.* 【生化】胰凝乳蛋白酶，糜蛋白酶.

Ci = cirrus. 【动】触毛. 【植】卷须.

C.I. = ①cast iron 铸铁，生铁. ②Channel Islands 海峡群岛. ③Colour Index 【医】血色指数，比色指数.

CIA = Central Intelligence Agency 〔美〕中央情报局.

Cia = 〔Sp.〕Compania (= Company).

ciao [tʃəu] *int.* 〔It.〕〔见面问候语或告别语〕你好！再见！

ci·bo·ri·um [siˈbɔːriəm] *n.* (*pl.* ***-ria*** [-riə]) ①〔古〕祭坛天盖. ②【天主】圣体盒.

Cic. = Cicero 西塞罗.

C.I.C. = ①Counterintelligence Corps 〔美〕反情报队. ②Combat Information Center 战斗情报中心. ③Commander in Chief 总司令.

ci·cada [siˈkeidə, siˈkɑːdə] *n.* (*pl.* ～***s, -dae*** [-diː]) 【动】蝉.

ci·ca·la [siˈkɑːlə] *n.* (*pl.* ***-le*** [-le]) 〔It.〕= cicada.

cic·a·trice [ˈsikətris] *n.* (*pl.* ～***s*** [-siz]) ①痂，伤痕，疤痕. ②【植】叶痕，脱离痕.

cica·tri·cle [ˈsikətrikl] *n.* 【生】(卵黄的)胚点；【植】叶痕，脱离痕.

cic·a·trix [ˈsikətriks] *n.* (*pl.* ***cic·a·trices*** [sikəˈtraisiːz]) = cicatrice.

cic·a·tri·za·tion [ˌsikətraiˈzeiʃən] *n.* 长疤，生疤，愈合.

cic·a·trize [ˈsikətraiz] *vi., vt.* (使) 长疤，(使)形成疤痕；(使)愈合.

Cic·e·ly [ˈsisili] *n.* 西塞莉〔女子名〕.

cic·e·ly [ˈsisili] *n.* 【植】欧洲汤药属植物，野胡萝卜属植物〔可供食用〕.

Cice·ro [ˈsisərəu] *n.* ①西塞罗〔**Marcus Tullius** ～，公元前 106—43 年，古罗马政治家、雄辩家、著作家〕. ②西塞罗市〔美国都市〕.

cic·e·ro·ne [ˌtʃitʃəˈrəuni, sisə-] *n.* (*pl.* ～***s, -ni*** [-niː]) 〔It.〕(名胜古迹)讲解导游人. *do the* ～ 担任讲解导游.

Cic·e·ro·ni·an [ˌsisəˈrəunjən, -niən] *a.* 西塞罗式的，雄辩的；文字精炼优美的. — *n.* 西塞罗崇拜者〔研究家〕.

cich·lid [ˈsiklid] *n.* 【动】丽鱼科 *(Cichlidae)* 鱼. — *a.* 丽鱼科的.

ci·cis·be·o [ˌtʃitʃizˈbeiəu] *n.* (*pl.* ***-bei*** [-bii]) 〔It.〕(17—18 世纪时期) 已婚贵妇的公开爱慕者，贵妇人的骑士扈从.

C.I.D. = ①Committee of Imperial Defence〔英〕帝国国防委员会. ②Criminal Investigation Department〔英〕刑事调查局.
Cid [sid] *n.*〔Sp.〕首领. *The Cid* ①熙德〔十一世纪与摩尔人作战的西班牙英雄 Ruy Diaz 的称号〕. ②«熙德之歌»〔赞美熙德功绩的西班牙文学中最古老的史诗〕.
-cidal *suf.* 以 -cide 作后缀的形容词形式.
-cide *suf.* 杀…者;杀[灭]…药: sui*cide*, insecti*cide*.
ci·der ['saidə] *n.* 苹果汁, 苹果酒. *sweet [hard]* ~ 未发酵的苹果汁[发过酵的苹果酒]. ***All talk and no*** ~ 空谈不已,结论全无;空谈而无实惠. ***more*** ~ ***and less talk*** 内容丰富些,空话少些. ***Smith C-*** 柳玉(品种)苹果. ~ **brandy** 苹果白兰地酒. ~**cup** 汽水酒. ~**drunk**〔美〕喝苹果酒的人;喝苹果酒喝醉了的. ~**press** 苹果汁榨取器.
ci·de·vant [si:də'vɑ̃:ŋ] *a.*〔F.〕在前的, 以前的. *a* ~ *governor* 前任县长. —*n.* 过时的人[物]; 已失去权势的人.
cie = 〔F.〕Compagnie (= company).
Cien·fue·gos [sjen'fwegɔ:s] *n.* 西恩富戈斯〔古巴省名〕.
CIF, C.I.F., c.i.f. = cost, insurance, and freight 到岸价格,成本加保险费、运费价格.
C.I.F.& E. = cost, insurance, freight and exchange 到岸价格加汇费价格.
C.I.F. & I. = cost, insurance, freight and interest 到岸价格加利息价格.
cig〔美〕= cigarette.
ci·ga·la, ci·gale [si'gɑ:lə, -'gɑ:l] *n.*【虫】蝉 (= cicada).
ci·gar [si'gɑ:] *n.* 雪茄烟, 叶卷烟. *Have a* ~? 〔美俚〕你好. ~**-end** 雪茄烟的烟蒂. ~**fish**【动】圆鲹. ~**-holder** 雪茄烟烟嘴. ~**-shaped** *a.* 雪茄烟状的.
cig·a·ret(te) [,sigə'ret] *n.* 香烟,卷烟,纸烟;烟卷状的催眠剂或其他药品. *a pack [tin] of* ~*s* 一包[听]香烟. ~ **case** 香烟盒. ~ **end** 烟头. ~ **girl** (餐厅等地)卖香烟女子. ~ **holder** 烟嘴. ~ **paper** 卷烟纸. ~ **store** 香烟店.
cig·a·ril·lo [,sigə'riləu] *n.* *(pl.* ~*s)* 小雪茄;香烟.
C.I.G.S., CIGS = Chief of the Imperial General Staff〔英〕帝国参谋总长.
cil·i·a ['siliə] *n.* (*sing.* ***cili·um*** [-əm])〔*pl.*〕【解】睫毛;【生】纤毛;(叶、翅等的)细毛.
ci·l·i·ar·y ['siliəri] *a.* 眼睫毛的,睫状体的;纤毛的. ~ **movement** (低级动物的)睫毛运动.
cili·ate ['siliit] *n.*【动】纤毛虫. — *a.* 有睫的, 有纤毛的.
cil·i·at·ed ['silieitid] *a.* 有睫毛的;有纤毛的.
cil·i·a·tion [,sili'eiʃən] *n.* ①具有睫毛. 〔总称〕睫毛;纤毛.
cil·ice ['silis] *n.* 粗毛布;粗毛布衣服.
cil·i·o·late ['siliəlit, -leit] *a.*【植、动】具短纤毛的.
cil·i·um ['siliəm] *n.* cilia 的单数.
cim·ba·lom, cym·ba·lom ['simbələm] *n.*【乐】辛巴龙〔匈牙利民乐器〕.
ci·mex ['saimeks] *n.* (*pl.* ***cim·i·ces*** ['simisi:z])【动】臭虫*(Cimex)*.
Cim·me·ri·an[si'miəriən] *n.*【希神】西米里族人〔荷马史诗中描写的,生活在阴暗潮湿国土上的〕西米里 (Cimmerii) 族. — *a.* 西米里族人的; 黑暗的, 阴惨的. ~ *darkness* 一团漆黑.
C-in-C = commander in chief 总司令.
cinch [sintʃ] *n.*〔美〕①(马鞍等的)肚带. ②〔口〕紧握. ③〔俚〕必定会发生的事. ④〔口〕容易做的事, 轻松的工作. *be a* ~ …是确实的[有把握的,简单的]. — *vt.* ①系(马的)肚带. ②〔美俚〕确定, 弄清楚, 弄明白, 确实掌握,确保. ~ **notice**〔美〕对成绩不良的警告.
cin·cho·na [siŋ'kəunə] *n.* ①〔C-〕【植】金鸡纳树属. ②金鸡纳树,规那树;规那树皮;金鸡纳霜,奎宁.
cin·cho·nine ['siŋkəuni:n], **cin·choni·a** [siŋ'kəuniə] *n.*【药】去甲氧基奎宁碱,辛可宁,金鸡宁.
cin·cho·nism ['siŋkənizəm] *n.*【医】奎宁中毒.
cin·cho·nize ['siŋkənaiz] *vt.*【医】用奎宁处理, 用辛可宁治疗.
Cin·cin·nat·i [,sinsi'næti] *n.* 辛辛那提〔美国城市〕.
CINCLANT ['siŋklənt] = Commander in Chief of the Atlantic Fleet〔美〕大西洋舰队司令.
cinc·ture ['siŋktʃə] *n.* ①围绕;〔诗〕带. ②【建】环带,边轮. — *vt.* ①用带子缠绕. ②给(柱头)加饰轮.
CINCUS = Commander-in-chief, United States Navy 美国海军总司令.
cin·der ['sində] *n.* 煤渣;【冶】熔渣;煅渣;剥片;熔岩渣,火山渣;〔*pl.*〕灰烬. ***burn to a*** ~ 烧成灰烬. ~**-burner**〔美〕径赛运动员. ~ **carnival** =〔美〕~ **classics**〔美〕(径赛)运动会. ~ **path** 煤渣跑道. ~ **sifter** 煤灰筛子;〔美〕沿铁路流浪的游民. ~ **specialists**〔美〕田径选手. ~ **track** = ~ path. ~ **trials**〔美〕径赛.
Cin·der·el·la [,sində'relə] *n.* ①灰姑娘〔童话中一美丽姑娘,被后母虐待,终日与煤渣为伴,故称灰姑娘〕. ②美丽的贫苦姑娘, 无名美女; 前妻所生的姑娘. ③打杂女仆. ④价值被埋没的人[货品等]; 一举成名的人〔男人或女人〕. ⑤以夜半12时为止的小跳舞会〔又叫 ~ dance〕.
cin·der·y ['sindəri] *a.* 煤渣的,煤灰多的.
cine ['sini] *n.* 电影(院).
cine- *comb. f.* = cinema.
cin·e·an·gi·o·gra·phy ['sini,ændʒi'ɔgrəfi] *n.* 血管活动摄影术.
ci·n·é·aste ['siniæst] *n.*〔F.〕①电影制片业人士. ②影迷;电影鉴赏家.
cin·e·cam·er·a ['sini,kæmərə] *n.* 电影摄影机.
cin·e·cism ['sinisizəm]〔美〕电影批评,影评.
cin·e·col·o(u)r ['sini'kʌlə] *n.* 彩色电影.
cin·e·cult ['sinikʌlt] *n.* 电影热潮,电影崇拜.
cin·e·film ['sinifilm] *n.* 电影胶片.
cin·e·kodak ['sini'kəudæk] *n.* (柯达克) 小型电影摄影机.
cin·e·ma ['sinimə] *n.* ①电影院. ②电影, 影片. ③电影工业;电影制片术. ***go to*** ~ 看电影去.
cine·mact ['sinimækt] *vi.*〔美〕做电影演员.
cin·e·mac·tor [,sini'mæktə] *n.*〔美俚〕电影演员.
cin·e·mac·tress [,sini'mæktris] *n.*〔美俚〕电影女演员.
cin·e·mad·dict ['sinimædikt] *n.*〔美俚〕影迷.
cin·e·ma·go·er ['sinimə-gəuə] *n.* 常看电影的人; 影迷.
cin·e·ma·nu·fac·ture ['sini,mænju'fæktʃə] *n.*〔美〕影片摄制法. — *vt., vi.* 摄制(影片).
cin·e·ma·scope ['siniməskəup] *n.*〔有时作 C- S-〕【商标】立体声宽银幕电影.
cin·e·mas·ter ['sini'mɑ:stə] *n.*〔美〕电影明星.
cin·e·ma·theque [,sinimə'tek] *n.* ①影片贮藏库; 影片图书馆. ②(放映文献片、非正规影片的)实验电影院.
cin·e·mat·ic [,sini'mætik] *a.* 电影的. **-s** *n. pl.* 电影摄制(术).
cin·e·ma·tize ['sinimətaiz] *vt., vi.*〔英〕①把(小说、舞台剧等)拍摄成电影. ②拍摄 (= cinematograph).
cin·e·mat·o·graph [,sini'mætəgrɑ:f] *n.* ①电影摄影机;〔英〕电影放映机. ②电影制片术. ③电影(院). — *vt., vi.* ①(把…)拍摄成电影. ②摄制(影片). **-ic** *a.*
cin·e·ma·tog·ra·pher [,sinimə'tɔgrəfə] *n.* 电影摄影师.
cin·e·mat·o·graph·ic [,sini,mætə'græfik] *a.* 电影摄影术的. **-i·cal·ly** *ad.*

cin·e·ma·tog·ra·phy [ˌsinimə'tɔgrəfi] *n.*电影摄影术.
cin·é·ma vér·i·té ['siːneimə 'veiriː'tei] 〔F.〕实况纪录影片.
cin·e·mi·cros·cop·y ['sinimai'krɔskəpi] *n.* 电影显微术.
cin·e·ole ['siniəul] *n.* 桉树脑(= eucalyptol).
cin·e·pan·o·ram·ic ['siniˌpænə'ræmik] *n.* 全景宽银幕电影.
cin·e·phile ['sinifail] *n.* 电影迷.
cin·e·pro·jec·tor ['sinipre'dʒektə] *n.* 电影放映机.
cin·e·ram·a [ˌsinə'rɑːmə] *n.* 宽银幕立体电影.
cin·e·rar·i·a [ˌsinə'rɛəriə] *n.* ①【植】爪叶菊. ②cinerarium 的复数.
cin·e·rar·i·um [ˌsinə'rɛəriəm] *n.* (*pl.* ***cin·e·rar·i·a*** [-riə]) 骨灰存放所.
cin·e·rar·y ['sinərəri] *a.* (存放)骨灰的; 灰的.
cin·er·a·tor ['sinireitə] *n.* 火葬场; (垃圾)焚化炉.
cin·e·ra·tion [ˌsinə'reiʃən] *n.*【化】灰化; 煅灰法.
cin·e·re·cord [ˌsinəri'kɔːd] *vi.* 拍摄记录电影.
cine·re·ous [si'niəriəs] *a.* ①已成灰的; 灰一样的. ②(羽毛等)灰色的.
cin·er·in ['sinərin] *n.*【化、农】丁烯除虫菊酯.
cin·e·the·o·dol·ite [ˌsinəθi'ɔdəlait] *n.* 电影经纬仪.
Cin·ga·lese [ˌsiŋgə'liːz] *n., a.* (*pl.* ~) 锡兰岛人 [语] (的); (斯里兰卡) 僧加罗人 (的); 僧加罗语 (的) (= Sinhalese).
cin·gu·late, cin·gu·lated ['siŋgjəlit, -leit; -leitid] *a.*【动】(昆虫腹部)有色带环绕的(亦作 cingulated).
cin·gu·lum ['siŋgjuləm] *n.* (*pl.* ***-la*** [-lə]) 【动】色带; 系带.
cin·na·bar ['sinəbɑː] *n.*【矿】朱砂,辰砂,银朱;【化】一硫化汞. — *a.* 朱红色的. ~ **stick** 朱墨.
cin·nam·ic [si'næmik] *a.* ①肉桂的; 由肉桂提炼出来的. ②肉桂酸的.
cin·na·mon ['sinəmən] *n.* ①【植】樟属植物; 樟属中几种树的芳香内皮,肉桂,桂皮; 肉桂树. ②肉桂色,黄棕色. **Chinese** ~ 肉桂. — *a.* 肉桂色的,黄棕色的. ~**oil** 肉桂油. ~**stone**【矿】钙铝榴石.
cin·na·mon·ic [ˌsinə'mɔnik] *a.* 肉桂的; 由肉桂提炼出来的.
cinq(ue) [siŋk] *n.* (骰子等的)五点; 五. *Cinque Ports* 五港〔英国东南海岸的五个特别港 Dover, Sandwich, Hastings, Romney, Hythe〕.
cin·quain [siŋ'kein] *n.* 五行诗.
Cin·que·cen·tist [ˌtʃiŋkwi'tʃentist] *n.* ①十六世纪意大利的艺术家[诗人]. ②十六世纪意大利文艺的研究者.
cin·que·cen·to [ˌtʃiŋkwi'tʃentəu] *n.* 十六世纪意大利艺术.
cin·que·foil ['siŋkfɔil] *n.* ①【植】委陵菜属. ②【建】五叶形[梅花形]装饰.
C.I.O. = Congress of Industrial Organizations 〔美〕产联〔产业工会联合会〕.
ci·on ['saiən] *n.*【植】接穗(= scion).
-cion *comb. f.* (= -tion): suspi*cion*.
Ci·pango [si'pæŋgəu] *n.* 〔诗〕= Japan 日本国〔源出"马可波罗游记"〕.
ci·pher ['saifə] *n.* ①零〔即0〕. ②数码, 阿拉伯数字. ③暗号,暗码, 密码; 密码索引 (=~ key). ④(姓名首字母的)组合字, 花押字. ⑤【乐】(风琴出毛病时的)连响. ⑥无价值的人[物]. *a mere* ~ 一无所长[毫无价值]的人. *a number of 5* ~*s* 五位数. ~ ***in algorism*** 零; 傀儡. ***in*** ~ 用密码. — *vt., vi.* ①计算; 〔美口〕算出. ②用密码书写. ~ ***out*** ①〔美口〕想出,考虑出. ②算出,解出. ③(风琴出毛病时)发出(呜呜的连响). ~ **code [telegram]** 数字密码[电报]. ~ **device** 译码机. ~ **key** 暗号索引[密码释译本]. ~ **officer** 译电员.
cip·o·lin ['sipəlin] *n.* (意大利的)白底绿花大理石.
cir., circ. = circa; circular.
cir = circumference.
cir·ca ['səːkə] *prep., ad.* 〔L.〕大约, 前后〔用于年代前,通常略作 c., ca., cir., circ. 或 C.〕. *circ. 1800* 约 1800 年.
cir·ca·di·an [sə'keidiən] *a.*【生】24 小时周期的; 生理节奏的; 日常生理律动性的〔指地球 24 小时转动一圈而产生于人的生活和生理的规律性反应,如新陈代谢,睡眠等〕. ~ **rhythm** 生理节奏. **-ly** *ad.*
cir·can·ni·an [sə'kæniən] *a.* 一年周期的, 周年节奏的; 每年活动或循环一次的.
Cir·ce ['səːsi] *n.*【希神】女妖锡西〔荷马史诗《奥德赛》中把人变成猪的妖妇〕; 妖媚的女人.
Cir·ce·an [sə(ː)'si(ː)ən] *a.* 妖妇锡西的; 有魅惑力的.
cir·ci·nate ['səːsineit] *a.*【植】拳卷的.
Cir·ci·nus ['səːsinəs] *n.*【天】两脚规座.
Cir·cit·er ['səːsitə] *prep., ad.* 〔L.〕= circa.
cir·cle [səːkl] *n.* ①圆; 圆周; 圈; 环; 环状物. ②圆形场地,马戏场; (铁路的)环行交叉口; (体育场的)圆形看台; (剧场的)楼厅. ③周期,循环; (天体运行的)轨道; (体操的) 环转运动;【逻】循环论法〔= vicious ~〕; (科学等的)完整体系,整体. ④党派,圈子,集团,…界,(活动、势力、思想等的)范围. *the Arctic [Antarctic] C-* 北极[南极]圈. ~ *of acquaintance* 交际圈. *the dress* ~ (戏院的)花楼; 月楼. *the upper* ~ 楼厅后座. *the upper* ~*s* 上层社会. *business [military, political]* ~*s* 实业[军、政]界. (*have*) ***a large*** ~ ***of friends*** 交游广阔. ***a swing around [round] the*** ~ 发表政见的巡回旅行. ***a vicious*** ~ ①恶性循环. ②【逻】循环论证. ~ ***of illumination***【天】昼夜分界圈. ~ ***of latitude [longitude]***【天】黄纬 [黄经] 圈. ~ ***of vegetation***【生】群落环. ***come full*** ~ 绕了一圈,兜了一个圈子. ***full*** ~ (*thinking*) 充分的 (考虑). ***go all round the*** ~ (话)婉转,兜圈子. ***in a*** ~ 成圆形地, 围着(…坐) (*argue in a* ~ 用循环论法论证). ***run round in*** ~***s*** 〔口〕忙得团团转. ***square the*** ~ 求与圆面积相等的正方形; 试图做不可能的事,妄想. — *vt.* 围,环绕; 绕过. — *vi.* ①盘旋,环行,兜圈子; 旋转,回转. ②流传.
cir·clet ['səːklit] *n.* ①小圈, 小环. ②(手镯等)环形饰物.
cir·cle·wise ['səːklwaiz] *ad.* 成圈状,成圆形.
cir·cling ['səːkliŋ] *n.*【马术】环骑.
circs [səːks] *n.* 〔*pl.*〕〔口〕= circumstances.
cir·cuit ['səːkit] *n.* ①(某一范围的)周边一圈; 巡回,周游; 巡回路线[区域]; 迂路. ②巡回审判(区); 巡回律师会. ③【电】电路,线路; 回路,环道. ④同行业联合组织; (戏院等的)轮演系统; 轮回演出(节目)[上映(影片)]的戏院. ⑤事物变化的顺序. *a postman's* ~ 邮递员的送信路线. *closed [open]* ~【电】通[断]路. *return* ~【电】回路. *integrated* ~ 集成电路. ***be in*** ~ ***with*** 和…接成电路. ***go the*** ~ ***of*** 绕…环行. ***make a*** ~ 绕远路,迂回. ***make the*** ~ ***of*** 绕…一圈. ***ride the*** ~ (巡回法官)作巡回审判. — *vt., vi.* (绕…)环行. ~ **attorney** 〔美〕地方检查官. ~ **binding** 包边装订. ~ **breaker**【电】断路开关. ~ **camera** 环转照相机. ~ **closer**【电】通路器. ~ **court** 巡回法庭. ~ **drive [clout]**【棒球】本垒打. ~ **judge** 巡回法官. ~ **rider** 〔美〕(美以美教派的)巡回牧师.
cir·cu·i·tous [sə(ː)'kju(ː)itəs] *n.* ①绕行的, 迂回的. ②间接的,迂远的. **-ly** *ad.* **-ness** *n.*
cir·cuit·ry ['səːkitri] *n.* 电路学; 电路图; 电路系统; 电路.
cir·cu·i·ty [sə'kjuːiti] *n.* 迂回; (说话等的)转弯抹角; 间接手法.
cir·cu·lar ['səːkjulə] *a.* ①圆的, 圆[环]形的. ②循环的; 巡回的. ③通告的,环游的; 供传阅的. ④伙伴的,团体的. ⑤【逻】循环论证的. ***a*** ~ *arc [cone]* 圆弧[锥].

a ~ *argument* 循环论证. ~ *numbers* 循环数. *a* ~ *tour* 环游,周游. *a* ~ *letter* 传阅文件,通知. — *n.* ①传阅文件; 通报, 通知; 传单, 报单. ②无袖女外衣. ~ **measure** 弧度法. ~ **note** 旅行支票; (特指外交方面的) 传阅文件. ~ **saw** 圆锯. ~ **stair** 环状楼梯. ~ **ticket** 环程(车、船)票. **-ly** *ad.* 成圈状; 循环地.

cir·cu·lar·i·ty [ˌsəːkjuˈlæriti] *n.* ①圆, 圆形, 圈状, 环状. ②【化纤】充实度.

cir·cu·lar·ize [ˈsəːkjuləraiz] *vt.* ①对…发送通知; 送…请传阅; 传递; 分发; 向(多方面)征询意见[吁请支援]. ②(用通知等)公布. ③把…弄成圆形.

cir·cu·late [ˈsəːkjuleit] *vt.* ①使(血液等) 循环,使运行; 使传观. ②使流传; 散播(谣言等). ③使(货币等)流通,使周转. *a* ~*d cheque* 流通支票. — *vi.* ①循环,运行. ②流传; 流行; 传播. ③流通, 周转. ④〔美〕巡回,各处访问.

cir·cu·lat·ing [ˈsəːkjuleitiŋ] *a.* 流通的, 循环的, 运行的. ~ **capital** 流动资本. ~ **decimal** 循环小数. ~ **door** 旋转门. ~ **library** 流通图书馆. ~ **medium** 通用货币; 流通票据. ~ **real capital** 动产,流动资产.

cir·cu·la·tion [ˌsəːkjuˈleiʃən] *n.* ①循环; 运行. ②传播; 环流(量),流通(量). ③(杂志等的)发行(额),销数,销路. ④通货,货币; 流通证券. ⑤【空】环量,环流. *the* ~ *of the blood* 血液的循环. *have a good [bad]* ~ 血液循环良好 [不好]. *the active* ~ 纸币的实际流通额. *the passive* ~ 纸币的准备额. *the* ~ *of a bank* 银行的纸币发行额. ***be in*** ~ 传播中; 流通中,通行着. ***put in [into]*** ~ 传播; 使(纸币等)流通,通用,使用. ***withdraw ... from*** ~ 收回; 停止发行.

cir·cu·la·tive [ˈsəːkjuleitiv] *a.* ①循环性的; 促进循环的. ②(货币、报刊等)有流通性的.

cir·cu·la·tor [ˈsəːkjuleitə] *n.* ①(谣言等的)传播者. ②循环器. ③【数】循环小数.

cir·cu·la·to·ry [ˈsəːkjuleitəri] *a.* (血液)循环的; 循环上的.

CIRCUM = circumference.

cir·cum- *pref.* 周,围,环,诸方: *circum*aviation 环球飞行.

cir·cum·am·bi·ent [ˌsəːkəmˈæmbiənt] *a.* 周围的,环绕的。**-ence, -ency** *n.* 环绕,围绕.

cir·cum·am·bu·late [ˌsəːkəmˈæmbjuleit] *vt., vi.* ①(绕…)运行,巡行,巡逻. ②转弯抹角打探; 绕着圈子说. **-tion** *n.* **-to·ry** *a.*

cir·cum·a·vi·ate [ˌsəːkəmˈeivieit] *vt.* 环绕 (地球) 飞行. **-tion** *n.* **-tor** *n.* 环球飞行员.

cir·cum·bend·i·bus [ˌsəːkəmˈbendibəs] *n.* (说话,写文章等的)绕圈子; 兜圈子的说法.

cir·cum·cen·tre, -ter [ˌsəːkəmˈsentə] *n.*【数】外心〔外接圆的中心〕.

cir·cum·cir·cle [ˌsəːkəmˈsəːkl] *n.*【数】外接圆.

cir·cum·cise [ˈsəːkəmsaiz] *vt.* ①【宗】为…行割礼〔割除包皮,小阴唇,阴蒂〕. ②【医】环切. ③〔古〕使(心)净化,清除(罪孽).

cir·cum·ci·sion [ˌsəːkəmˈsiʒən] *n.* ①【宗】割礼;【医】包皮环切 (术); (精神) 净化. ②〔C-〕【宗】割礼节〔一月一日〕. ③〔the ~〕〔总称〕犹太人; (心地)纯洁的人.

circ·um·fer·ence [səˈkʌmfərəns] *n.* 四周,周围; 圆周; 圈线; 周线. *ten miles in* ~ 周长十英里.

cir·cum·fer·en·tial [səˌkʌmfəˈrenʃəl] *a.* ①周围的,四周的. ②委婉的.

cir·cum·flect [ˌsəːkəmˈflekt] *vt.* ①把…弯成圆形; 卷缠. ②附加音调[长音]符号于.

cir·cum·flex [ˈsəːkəmfleks] *n.*【语】音调 [长音] 符号〔如 ˆ ˜ ~〕. — *a.* 有音调[长音]符的; 发长音的; 曲折的. — *vt.* 附加音调[长音]符号于.

cir·cum·flu·ence [sə(ː)ˈkʌmfluəns] *n.* 环流, 回流.

cir·cum·flu·ent, cir·cum·flu·ous [sə(ː)ˈkʌmfluənt, -fluəs] *a.* 环[回]流的; 缠绕的,围绕的.

cir·cum·fuse [ˌsəːkəmˈfjuːz] *vt.* ①使(光)向周围照射,在周围浇(水等); 在周围散布. ②缠绕,围绕.

cir·cum·fu·sion [ˌsəːkəmˈfjuːʒən] *n.* 周围灌注; 散布; 围绕.

cir·cum·gy·rate [ˌsəːkəmdʒaiəˈreit] *vi.* 回转, 旋转; 周游. — *vt.* 使回转.

cir·cum·gy·ra·tion [ˌsəːkəmdʒaiəˈreiʃən] *n.* ①旋转. ②〔谑〕翻筋斗. ③周转,东挪西移.

cir·cum·ja·cent [ˌsəːkəmˈdʒeisnt] *a.* 周围的,邻接的,围绕着的.

cir·cum·lit·tor·al [ˌsəːkəmˈlitərəl] *a.* 沿海的,临海岸的.

cir·cum·lo·cu·tion [ˌsəːkəmləˈkjuːʃən] *n.* ①语言冗长,罗唆. ②躲闪, 遁辞; 婉转曲折(的说法). *C- Office* 拖拉衙门〔Dickens 小说 *Little Dorrit* 中办事拖拉的官僚机关〕.

cir·cum·loc·u·to·ry [ˌsəːkəmˈlɔkjutəri] *a.* ①迂回的,委婉曲折的. ②冗长的,罗唆的.

cir·cum·lu·nar [ˌsəːkəmˈluːnə] *a.* 环月的,绕月的.

cir·cum·nav·i·gate [ˌsəːkəmˈnævigeit] *vt.* 环航(世界).

cir·cum·nav·i·ga·tion [ˈsəːkəmˌnæviˈgeiʃən] *n.* 环球航行.

cir·cum·nav·i·ga·tor [ˌsəːkəmˈnævigeitə] *n.* 环球航行者.

cir·cum·nu·tate [ˌsəːkəmˈnjuːteit] *vi.*【植】(茎、卷须等)回旋转头.

cir·cum·nu·ta·tion [ˌsəːkəmnjuˈteiʃən] *n.*【植】回旋转头运动.

cir·cum·po·lar [ˌsəːkəmˈpəulə] *a.* ①【地】极圈的, 极地周围的. ②【天】拱极的,围绕天极的. ~ **stars** 周极星〔永远高于地平线〕.

cir·cum·ro·tate [ˌsəːkəmˈrəuteit] *vi.* 旋转,循环. **-tation** *n.*

cir·cum·scis·sile [ˌsəːkəmˈsisəl] *a.* 【植】周裂的〔指果实〕.

cir·cum·scribe [ˈsəːkəmskraib, ˌsəːkəmˈskraib] *vt.* ①在…周围画线; 为…立限界. ②限定, 限制. ③【数】使外接, 使外切. ④为…下定义. ~*d circle* 外接圆. ~*d figure* 外接形.

cir·cum·scrip·tion [ˌsəːkəmˈskripʃən] *n.* ①限界,限制. ②【数】外接. ③界线; 范围, 区域. ④〔古〕定义. ⑤(硬币周围的)齿刻,花边.

cir·cum·so·lar [ˌsəːkəmˈsəulə] *a.* 围绕着太阳的,太阳周围的,绕日的.

cir·cum·spect [ˈsəːkəmspekt] *a.* 慎重的,细心的,谨慎小心的,周到的,精密的. **-ly** *ad.* **-ness** *n.*

cir·cum·spec·tion [ˌsəːkəmˈspekʃən] *n.* 慎重,周到.

cir·cum·stance [ˈsəːkəmstəns] *n.* ①〔常 *pl.*〕(周围的)情况,情形,环境. ②〔*pl.*〕(人的)境遇,境况. ③(事情的)详情,细节,本末,原委; (一桩)事故,事情,事实. ④〔古〕形式,仪式; (仪式的)隆重. ⑤命运, 机会. *adverse [favourable]* ~*s* 逆〔顺〕境. *act according to* ~*s* 临机应变,因时制宜. *private* ~*s* 内幕,内情. *the whole* ~*s* 前后原委,始末根由. ***a mere [remote, poor]*** ~〔美口〕无用的东西; 不足道的人. ***at no*** ~***s*** 在任何情况下都不…. ***in bad [needy, reduced]*** ~***s*** 穷困. ***in easy*** ~***s*** 生活安乐. ***in good*** ~***s*** 顺遂. ***in no*** ~***s*** = under no ~s. ***in straitened*** ~***s*** 困苦, 穷困. ***in the*** ~***s*** = under the ~s. ***not a*** ~ ***to*** 〔美口〕远不及, 不能与…相比. ***pomp and*** ~ 排场; 装腔作势. ***under all*** ~***s*** 无论如何. ***under certain*** ~***s*** 在某种情况下, 看情形, 有时. ***under no*** ~***s*** 无论如何不, 决不. ***under the*** ~***s*** 在这种情形下, 因为这种情形. ***with*** ~ 详细. ***without*** ~ 不讲虚套(仪式)地,直截地. ***without omitting a single*** ~ 毫无遗漏地. — *vt.* 把…置于某种情况下.

cir·cum·stanced [ˈsəːkəmstənst] *a.* 在(某种)情形[情况]下. ～ *as I am* 情形如此，所以我…. *differently* ～ 情形不同. *so* ～ *that* 事已如此(故). *well* ～ 处境顺遂.

cir·cum·stan·tial [ˌsəːkəmˈstænʃəl] *a.* ①按照情况(推测)的; 看(当时)情形的. ②(故事等)详细的. ③偶然的,不测的;不重要的. ④礼节隆重的，仪节完备的. ～ *report* 详尽报导. ～ ***evidence***【法】间接证据，旁证. ***of*** ～ ***importance*** 次要的. **-ly** *ad.*

cir·cum·stan·ti·al·i·ty [ˈsəːkəmˌstænʃiˈæliti] *n.* ①情况详尽,富有细节. ②〔*pl.*〕详情;具体细节. ③偶然性.

cir·cum·stan·ti·ate [ˌsəːkəmˈstænʃieit] *vt.* 证实(每一细节);(提供事实)详细说明,(提供证据)证明.

cir·cum·ter·res·tri·al [ˌsəːkəmtəˈrestriəl] *a.* 围绕地球的.

cir·cum·val·late [ˌsəːkəmˈvæleit] *vt.* 用城墙[壕沟,壁垒等]围住.

cir·cum·val·la·tion [ˌsəːkəmvəˈleiʃən] *n.* ①被壁垒[城墙、壕沟等]围绕. ②壁垒,城墙.

cir·cum·vent [ˌsəːkəmˈvent] *vt.* ①围绕，包围，围困. ②用计超过[胜过、包围];(用欺骗手段)陷害. ③用计防止;避免.

cir·cum·ven·tion [ˌsəːkəmˈvenʃən] *n.* ①包围，围困. ②欺骗;计谋. ③胜过;防止.

cir·cum·vo·lute [səːˈkʌmvəljuːt] *vt.* 围绕…旋转;卷绕,缠绕.

cir·cum·vo·lu·tion [ˌsəːkəmvəˈljuːʃən] *n.* ①卷缠,(围绕某物的)旋转,周转;涡线. ②迂回运行.

cir·cum·volve [ˌsəːkəmˈvɔlv] *vt., vi.* (绕…)旋转;缠绕.

cir·cus [ˈsəːkəs] *n.* ①(圆形的)马戏场;杂技场(古罗马的)圆形竞技场. ②杂技团,马戏团;杂技[马戏]表演. ②〔英〕圆形十字路口,圆形广场. ③〔口〕乱哄哄的热闹场面;在作某种表演的一群人. ④【地】外轮山. ⑤〔军俚〕游击队;飞行队;飞行表演. *pitch* [*put up*] *a* ～ 搭临时卖艺[马戏]场. *run a* ～ 演马戏,演出杂技. *travelling* ～ 流动杂技[马戏]团. **C- Maximus** 罗马的大竞技场. **Bread and ～es** 面包和竞技 〔古罗马统治者有时为民众免费提供用以欺骗和麻醉他们的一种手段;〔泛指〕统治者的小恩小惠〕.

ci·ré [səˈrei] *a.* 涂蜡的. —*n.* 蜡光丝,蜡光草.

cirque [səːk] *n.* ①圆形场地;〔诗〕(天然)半圆形剧场. ②【地】冰斗,冰雪坑. ③圆圈,环行物.

cir·rate [ˈsireit] *a.*【生】①有触毛的，有触须的. ②有棘毛的. ③(腕足类)有腕丝的. ④(棘皮)有卷肢的. ⑤(甲壳类)有蔓足的. ⑥(昆虫)有细干卷的. ⑦(昆虫)有阳茎的.

cir·rho·sis [siˈrəusis] *n.*【医】肝硬化;(任何器官的)慢性间质炎.

cir·ri [ˈsirai] *n.* cirrus 的复数.

cirri- *comb. f.* = cirro.

cir·ri·ped, cir·ri·pede [ˈsiriped, -piːd] *n.*【动】蔓脚类动物.

cirro- *comb. f.* 触毛;卷须;卷云: *cirrose.*

cir·ro·cu·mu·lus [ˈsirəuˈkjuːmjuləs] *n.*【气】卷积云，絮云.

cir·rose, cir·rous [siˈrəus, ˈsirəs] *a.* ①(象)卷云的. ②有[似]卷须的;有[似]触毛的.

cir·ro·stra·tus [ˈsirəuˈstrɑːtəs] *n.*【气】卷层云.

cir·rus [ˈsirəs] *n.* (*pl.* ***cir·ri*** [ˈsirai]) ①【植】卷须;孢子角. ②【动】粗纤毛,触毛;触须;(腕足类的)腕丝;(甲壳类的)蔓足;(虫类的)阳茎. ③【气】卷云.

cir·soid [ˈsəːsɔid] *a.*【医】静脉怒张的，静脉肿胀的,静脉肿的.

cis- *comb. f.* ①这一边 (*opp.* trans-, ultra-). ②以后 (*opp.* pre-). ③【化】顺(式),顺向: *cis*atlantic.

cis·al·pine [sisˈælpain] *a.* 阿尔卑斯山这边〔南侧〕的，意大利方面的〔有时指从欧洲北部等地说,也指阿尔卑斯山北侧〕.

cis·at·lan·tic [ˌsisətˈlæntik] *a.* 大西洋这边的.

cis·co [ˈsiskəu] *n.* (*pl.* ～*es*, ～*s*)【美动】加拿大雪鲦.

cis·lu·nar [sisˈluːnə] *a.*【天】位于地球与月球(轨道)之间的.

cis·mon·tane [sisˈmɔntein] *a.* ①(阿尔卑斯)山这边[北侧]的，非意大利方面的. ②=cisalpine. ③在山这一边的.

cis·pa·dane [ˈsispədein] *a.* 在波河 (Po) 这边〔南侧〕的;在罗马这一方面的.

cis·soid [ˈsisɔid] *n.*【数】(尖点)蔓叶(曲)线. —*a.* 蔓叶线内的,凹边的〔指两条相交蔓叶线的夹角〕.

Cis·sy [ˈsisi] *n.* 锡西〔女子名，Cecilia 的昵称〕.

cis·sy [ˈsisi] *n.* 〔美俚〕没骨气的人;胆小鬼.

cist [sist] *n.*【考古】石柜,石棺.

Cis·ter·ci·an [sisˈtəːʃjən] *n.,a.* (法国 Robert de Molesme 于 1098 年在 Cistercium 地方创建的) 西斯特教团修士(的).

cis·tern [ˈsistən] *n.* ①(贮水用的)水缸[桶,箱,槽]. ②(天然的)水塘〔池〕. ③(餐桌上的) 水瓶，洗手钵. ④【解】(贮分泌液的)池囊,淋巴间隙.

cis·ter·na [sisˈtəːnə] *n.* (*pl.* ***-nae*** [-niː])【解】池. **-l** *a.*

cis·tron [ˈsistrɔn] *n.*【生】顺反子,作用子.

cis·tus [ˈsistəs] *n.*【植】岩蔷薇属植物.

cit [sit] *n.* ①〔古〕市民〔蔑称〕. ②〔美〕都市人，城里人;老百姓. ③〔*pl.*〕〔美〕便服.

CIT = California Institute of Technology 〔美〕加利福尼亚理工学院.

cit. = citation; cited; citizen.

cit·a·ble [ˈsaitəbl] *a.* ①可引用[引证]的. ②可叫来(作证)的,可传呼来[传讯]的.

cit·a·del [ˈsitədəl] *n.* ①(居高临下的)城寨,城堡,要塞. ②(军舰上的)炮廓. ③〔喻〕根据地,大本营;避难所.

ci·ta·tion [saiˈteiʃən] *n.* ①引证,引用,引文;例证;说到,列举. ②【法】传讯;传票;(对于法律先例等的)援引. ③〔美〕(对杰出人物等的)表扬(证书)，荣誉状，奖品;【军】嘉奖令. **-to·ry** *a.*

cite[1] [sait] *vt.* ①引用,引证;举(例),列举;说到. ②【法】传讯. ③召集,发动. ④〔美〕表扬;【军】传令嘉奖.

cite[2] [sait] *n.* 〔口〕例证,引文 (= citation).

cith·a·ra [ˈsiθərə] *n.* 古希腊的三角竖琴;筝.

cith·er(n) [ˈsiθə(n)] *n.*【乐】(十六、七世纪流行的吉他状)七弦琴.

cit·ied [ˈsitid] *a.* ①有城市的. ②城市一样的.

cit·i·fied [ˈsitifaid] *a.* 〔美,主蔑〕有城市(人)风的,城市化的.

cit·i·fy [ˈsitifai] *vt.* 使城市化.

cit·i·zen [ˈsitizn] *n.* ①市民,城市居民. ②〔美〕(区别于军人而言的)平民,老百姓. ③人民，公民，国民. ④居民;栖息者. *an American* ～ 美国公民〔*cf.* a British subject〕. ～ *of the world* 世界公民(指对全世界情况有兴趣的人,四海为家的人). **～'s arrest** 公民扭送〔不成文法,公民发现罪犯,可扭送法院〕. **～s' band**【无】(专供私人无线电通信用的)民用波段. **～s' committee** 〔美〕自警团. **～s' rally** 市民大会. **-hood** *n.* ①公民[市民]身分;公民权. ②国籍. **-ry** 〔总称〕市民，公民;〔美〕(不同于军人的)平民. **-ship** *n.* ①公民〔市民〕身分，公民的权利和义务. ②国籍. ③个人品德表现.

cit·i·zen·ess [ˈsitizənis] *n.* 〔罕〕女市民[公民].

citr- 〔用于元音前〕*comb. f.* 柠檬,柑橘(= citro-).

citra- *comb. f.* = cis-.

cit·ral [ˈsitrəl] *n.*【化】柠檬醛.

cit·rate [ˈsitrit] *n.*【化】柠檬酸盐.

cit·re·ous [ˈsitriəs] *a.* 柠檬色的,柠檬的.

cit·ric [ˈsitrik] *a.*【化】柠檬性的. ～ **acid** 柠檬酸.

cit·ri·cul·ture [ˈsitriˌkʌltʃə] *n.* 柑桔栽培.

cit·rin [ˈsitrin] *n.* 【化】柠檬素,维生素 P.
cit·rine [ˈsitrin] *a.* 柠檬的, 柠檬色的. —*n.* ①柠檬色. ②【矿】黄水晶.
cit·rin·in [ˈsitrini] *n.* 【化】橘霉素.
citro- 〔用于辅音前〕. *comb. f.* = citr-.
cit·ron [ˈsitrən] *n.* 【植】①香橼,枸橼. ②香橼皮蜜饯. ③柠檬色. *the fingered* ~ 佛手柑.
cit·ron·el·la [ˌsitrəˈnelə] 【植】香茅; 香茅油. ~ *circuit* 〔常作 C- C-〕暑期剧团的巡回演出.
cit·ron·el·lal [ˌsitrəˈnelæl] *n.* 【化】香茅醛.
cit·rul·line [siˈtrʌliːn] *n.* 【化】瓜氨酸.
Cit·rus [ˈsitrəs] *n.* ①【植】柑桔属. ②〔c-〕柠檬, 柑桔. ~ *Metropolis* 〔美〕柑桔市〔洛杉矶 (Los Angeles) 市的别号〕.
cit·tern [ˈsitən] *n.* = cithern.
cit·y [ˈsiti] *n.* ①城市; 市〔英国指设有大教堂的特许市; 美国指大于 town 的重要城市〕; 都市. ②〔the ~〕全市, 全体市民. ③〔the C-〕伦敦商业中心区 (= the C- of London). ④【希史】城邦 (= ~ state). *be in the C-* 是实业家; 在商业中心做事. *C- of a Hundred Towers* 百塔城〔意大利 Pavia 的别号〕. *C- of Brotherly Love* 友爱城〔〔美〕Philadelphia 市的别号〕. *C- of God* 天国. ~ *of homes* 〔美〕家乡城〔Philadelphia 的别号〕. *C- of Light* 灯城〔巴黎的别号〕. *C- of Masts* 桅城〔伦敦的别号〕. *C- of Prophet* 先知城〔阿拉伯 Medina 的别号〕. *C- of the dead* 墓地,公墓. *C- of the Seven Hills* 七山城〔罗马的别称〕. *C- of Victory* 胜利城〔埃及 Cairo 的别号〕. *the eternal* ~ 永恒之城〔指罗马〕. **C- article** (伦敦报纸上的)商业经济新闻. ~ **assembly** 市议会. ~ **billy** 〔美〕在城市中长大的乡村音乐演唱者. ~ **chicken** 串烤(小)牛肉(等). **C- Company** 伦敦市商会. ~ **convention** 〔美〕(政党的)市代表会议. ~ **council** 市参议会. ~ **councillor** 市参议会议员. ~ **dads** 〔美俚〕市参议员. ~ **editor** 〔美〕(报馆的)本市栏编辑主任; 〔英〕〔C-〕(报馆的)经济栏编辑. ~ **employee** 市府公务员. ~ **fathers** 〔美俚〕市参议员(= ~ dads). ~ **hall** 市政厅. ~ **item** 【商】本市汇划汇票. **C- man** 〔英〕实业家,资本家. ~ **manager** 〔美〕(市行政委员会任命的) 市执政官. ~ **office** 市政厅. ~ **plan** 市街区划,都市计划. ~ **room** 本市新闻版编辑(室). ~**scape** ①城市风光画片. ②市容,市景. ~ **slicker** 〔口〕(农民眼中的)城市滑头. ~-**state** (古希腊的)城邦. ~**ward(s)** *ad.* 向都市.
Ciudad Tru·jil·lo [sjuːˈðɑːð truˈhijo] *n.* 特鲁希略城〔西印度多米尼加首都, 使用过的新名,现又恢复旧称 Santo Domingo〕.
civ. = civic; civil; civilian.
civ·et [ˈsivit] *n.* ①【动】香猫,麝猫. ②【化】麝猫香. ~ **cat** 香猫(皮).
civ·ic [ˈsivik] *a.* ①城市的. ②市民的,公民的. ~ **center** 市中心区. ~ **crown** 槲叶环〔古罗马赠与救护市民者的荣冠〕. ~ **life** 城市生活. ~ **rights [duties]** 市民权,公民权〔义务〕. ~-**minded** *a.* 关心社会福利的, 有公德心的; 有市〔公〕民意识的. ~ **ethics,** ~ **virtues** 文明礼貌,公民道德.
civ·i·cism [ˈsivisizəm] *n.* ①市政; 市政至上主义. ②公民道德,市民思想.
civ·ics [ˈsiviks] *n.* 市政学; 〔美〕公民学.
civ·ie [ˈsivi] *n.* = civvy.
civ·ies [ˈsiviz] *n. pl.* 〔军俚〕便装,便服; 〔美〕便衣警探.
civ·il [ˈsivl] *a.* ①市民的,公民的; 民用的; 【法】民事的; 根据民法的,法律规定的. ②国内的,国民间的. ③有礼貌的; 文明的. ④非军职的,文职的,文官的. ⑤非圣职的,非宗教的. ⑥历法规定的. *do the* ~ 行动郑重,为人诚恳. *keep a* ~ *tongue in one's head* 说话有礼貌. *say something* ~ 说恭维话, 说应酬话. ~ **action** 民事诉讼. ~ **administration** 市政. ~ **architecture** 民用建筑. ~ **aviation** 民用航空. ~ **bond** (地方)公债. ~ **case** 民事案件. ~ **clothes** 便装, 便服〔与军服等相对〕. ~ **code** 民法. ~ **contract** (不依据宗教仪式的)民间契约,世俗约定〔如结婚等的〕. ~ **day** 日历日; 【海】常用日. ~ **death** 褫夺公权; 放逐; 无期徒刑. **C- Defence** (主指防空的)民间防卫(组织)〔略 C.D.〕. ~ **engineering** 建筑工程. ~ **law** 民法; 罗马法. ~ **liberty** 公民自由; 法律范围内的个人自由. ~ **life** 社会生活, 公民生活 (*return to* ~ *life* 复员,退役). ~ **list** 〔美〕文官薪级表; 文官薪俸(总额); 〔英〕〔C-L-〕皇室费. **Civil Lord** (英海军部的) 文官委员. ~ **marriage** 不举行宗教仪式的婚姻. ~ **obligation** 公民义务. ~ **occasion** 犯罪; 过失; 诱惑. ~ **possession** 民法上的占有. ~ **power** 统治权, 政权. ~ **procedure [proceedings]** 民事诉讼(程序). ~ **right** 公民权. ~ **sanction** 民事上的制裁. ~ **servant** (〔英〕 **C- Servant**)公务员,文职人员,文官. ~ **service** 〔英〕**C- Service** 全体公务员〔文官〕; 行政机构〔与军事机构相对〕. ~ **state** (除军人、僧侣以外的)全体国民. ~ **time** 民用时. ~ **war** 内战 (*the Civil War* 〔英〕(1642—49 年的)查理一世与议会的战争; 〔美〕(1861—1865 年的) 南北战争). ~ **year** 日历年. **-ly** *ad.*
ci·vil·ian [siˈviljən] *n.* ①市民. ②平民; (军队中的)无军职人员. ③文官. ④民法学者, 民法家; 罗马法专家. ~ **airman [aviator]** 民航飞行员. ~ **clothes** 便装,便衣.
ci·vil·i·ty [siˈviliti] *n.* ①礼貌; 文明态度; 〔*pl.*〕礼仪. ②〔古〕文明,文化. *vapid civilities* (陈腐的)虚礼.
civ·i·liz·a·ble, -lis·a·ble [ˈsivilaizəbl] *a.* 可开化的, 可教化的.
civ·i·li·za·tion, -sa·tion [ˌsivilaiˈzeiʃən] *n.* ①文明, 文化. ②教育,教化,开化. ③文明世界; 文明利器; 文明事物.
civ·i·lize, -lise [ˈsivilaiz] *vt.* 使文明; 启发,教化,开化; 教育. — *vi.* 变成文明(社会). ~ ***away*** 用文化教育革除(野蛮习性等).
civ·i·lized, -lised [ˈsivilaizd] *a.* ①文明的; 有礼貌的; 有教养的. ②已变成文明(社会)的.
civ·ism [ˈsivizəm] *n.* 公民精神,公民〔国民〕道德.
Civ. Serv. = Civil Service. 文职人员; 行政机构.
civ·vy [ˈsivi] *n.* ①〔军俚〕平民; 非军人. ②〔*pl.*〕便衣, 便服. *C- Street* 〔俚〕平民生活.
CJ,C.J. = Chief Justice 审判长, 首席法官; 法院院长.
C.J.C.S. = Chairman of the Joint Chiefs of Staff 〔美〕参谋长联席会议主席.
ck. = cask; chalk; check; cook.
ckd = completely knocked down.
ckw = clockwise.
Cl = chlorine 【化】氯.
cl. = centilitre; claim; class; classification. clause; clergyman; cloth.
clab·ber [ˈklæbə] *n.* 凝结变酸的牛奶, 酸牛奶, 酸酪. — *vt., vi.* (使)(牛乳等)变酸而凝结.
clach·an [ˈklɑːkhən] *n.* 〔Scot.〕村庄; 乡村客店; 乡间教堂.
clack [klæk] *vi.* ①发毕剥声. ②〔方〕唠叨, 剌剌不休地讲. ③(家禽)咯咯地叫. — *vt.* ①使发毕剥声. ②唠叨地说. —*n.* ①毕剥声. ②喋喋不休, 饶舌, 唠叨. ③【机】瓣(阀); 【空】翼门止回阀. *Hold your* ~! 住嘴! 别作声! ~ **box** 【空】翼门止回阀箱. ~ **valve** 【机】瓣阀.
clad [klæd] 〔古〕 *clothe* 的过去式及过去分词. — *a.* ①穿衣的. ②被覆盖的. ③镀过(另一种)金属的; 用金属包被的. *an iron-~ vessel* 装甲舰. — *vt.* ***(clad; cladding)*** 在(金属)外面包上另一种金属. **cladding** *n.* 【物】镀; 包层.
clad- *comb. f.* 〔用于元音前〕=clado-.

cla·dis·tic [klə'distik] *a.* 基于遗传因素的.
clado- *comb. f.* 芽;枝: *clado*phyll.
cla·doc·er·an [klə'dɔsərən] *n.*【动】枝角目.
clad·ode ['klædəud] *n.* = cladophyll.
clad·o·phyll, clado·phyl·lon ['klædəfil,-filən] *n.*【植】叶状枝[茎].
claim [kleim] *n.* ①(根据权利而提出的)要求,请求;认领,索取. ②(应得的)权利;(…的)资格. ③主张,断言,声称,自称. ④要求权;要求物;(矿区等的)申请购买地. *He has no ~ to scholarship.* 他不配称做学者. *I have many ~s on my time.* 我很忙. *~s agent* 〔美〕专门代人向议会要求赔偿[救济]的代理人. *~ to order* 记名债权. ***hold down a ~*** 留住一地以便获得对土地的所有权. ***jump a ~*** 〔美〕强占别人申请的购买地. ***lay ~ to*** 声称,要求(…是自己的);以…自任[自居],自以为是. ***put in a ~ for*** = ***enter a ~ for*** 提出(某项)要求;认领(某物). ***set up a ~ to*** 声明对…的权利,提起对…的要求. ***stake out [off] a ~*** 〔美〕立界标表明(土地等的)所有权;坚持要求(得到某物). —*vt.* ①要求(应得权利). ②主张,断言;声称,自称;要求承认. ③理应获得,值得(重视等),需要(注意等),赢得. *~ a reward* 要求报酬. *~ a victory* 声称取得胜利. *This question ~s attention.* 这个问题需要注意。*His heroism ~s our admiration.* 他的勇敢行为应该得到我们的赞美. —*vi.* 〔罕〕要求赔偿损失 *(against)*. ~ **jumper** 〔美〕非法占取他人采矿权或土地所有权者.
claima·ble ['kleiməbl] *a.* 可要求的;可认领的;可索取的.
claim·ant, claim·er ['kleimənt, 'kleimə] *n.* 提出要求者,索取者,申请者 *(to, for)*;【法】原告,债权人.
claims·man ['keimzmən] *n.* (*pl.* **-men**) (灾害保险的)调查员.
clair·audi·ence [kleər'ɔːdjəns] *n.* 透听,透听力,超人的听力.
clair·au·di·ent [kleər'ɔːdjənt] *a.* 有超人听力的. —*n.* 听力超人者,顺风耳.
Claire [klεə] *n.* 克莱尔〔女子名, Clara 的异体〕.
clair·voy·ance [klεə'vɔiəns] *n.* ①超人的视力,透视力,千里眼. ②洞察力.
clair·voy·ant [klεə'vɔiənt] *a., n.* ①视力超人的(人). ②明察秋毫的(人),有洞察力的(人).
clam[1] [klæm] *n.* (*pl.* ~, ~s) ①【动】蛤;蛤肉. ②〔美口〕沉默寡言的人,嘴紧的人. ③〔美俚〕银币,一元. *razor ~* 蛏. ***as close as a ~*** 〔美〕一毛不拔的;守口如瓶的. ***happy as a ~ (at high tide)*** 〔美口〕极幸福的. —*vi.* ①捞蛤. ②〔美俚〕嘴紧,话少. ~ ***up*** 嘴紧,死不开口. ~ ***catchers*** 〔美〕新泽西州人的别号. ~**-face** 〔美〕胆小鬼. ~ **trap** 〔美俚〕嘴. **-like** *a.* 象蛤的;一言不发的.
clam[2] [klæm] *n.* 〔英〕钳,夹子.
clam[3] [klæm] *n.* 〔美俚〕(爵士音乐中)错误的音. —*vi.* 奏出[唱出]错音.
cla·mant ['kleimənt] *a.* 〔书〕①(孩子等)吵闹的,嚷的. ②紧急的,迫切的,迫在眉睫的.
clam·a·to·ri·al [ˌklæmə'tɔːriəl] *a.*【动】鹟科的.
clam·bake ['klæmbeik] *n.* ①〔美〕(海滨)吃蛤会;以吃蛤为主的海滨旅行. ②〔美俚〕即兴爵士音乐演奏会. ③〔美俚〕不精彩的广播[电视]节目.
clam·ber ['klæmbə] *vt., vi.* 爬,攀登. ~ *down the slope* 爬下陡坡. ~ *to one's feet* 爬了起来. ~ ***up*** 攀登,爬上. —*n.* 攀登.
clam·my ['klæmi] *a.* ①滑腻的,粘糊糊的. ②(蛙身等)冰冷粘湿的. ③(态度)冷淡的. **-mi·ly** *ad.*
clam·or·ous ['klæmərəs] *a.* 吵闹的;扰嚷的. **-ly** *ad.* **-ness** *n.*
clam·o(u)r ['klæmə] *n.* 吵闹,扰嚷;(表示抗议、支持等的)叫喊,(舆论的)鼎沸,哗然. —*vi.* 大嚷大叫,叫喊,吵闹,喧嚷. ~ ***for*** 叫嚣;吵吵闹闹地要求. ~ ***against*** 吵吵闹闹地反对. —*vt.* ①用吵吵嚷嚷的方法迫使. ②吵吵闹闹地发出[表示]. ~ ***down*** 吵得使(演讲者等)说不下去[把演讲者哄下台]. ~ ***(sb.) into [out of] doing sth.*** 吵吵闹闹迫使(某人)做[停止做]某事.
clamp[1] [klæmp] *n.* ①钳,夹子. ②【机】压板,压铁;【建】夹板;【船】支梁板. —*vt.* (用夹钳等)夹紧,夹住. *~ing bolt*【机】夹紧螺栓. ~ ***down*** ①箝制,压迫;取缔;勒紧. ②强制执行(宵禁等). ~**down** *n.* 压制,取缔. ~**-screw** 制动螺旋.
clamp[2] [klæmp] *n.* 〔英方〕(砖等的)堆. —*vt.* 把(砖等)堆高 *(up)*;堆存.
clamp[3] [klæmp] *vi.* 叭哒叭哒地行走,脚步很重地走. —*n.* 重踏的脚步声.
clamp·er ['klæmpə] *n.* ①〔*pl.*〕夹子. ②接线板. ③(防滑用)鞋底钉.
clam·shell ['klæmʃəl] *n.* 蛤壳;蛤壳状挖泥器.
clan [klæn] *n.* ①克兰〔苏格兰高地人的氏族,部族〕. ②氏族,部族;〔口〕家族,一门. ③【生】异种集团,系. ④党派,小集团. ⑤【美体】队. **-ship** *n.* ①氏族[部族]制度. ②氏族[部族]状态. ③小集团精神.
clan·des·tine [klæn'destin] *a.* 秘密的,暗中的,私下的. ~ *dealings* 秘密交易. *a ~ marriage* 秘密结婚. ~ *evolution* 不知不觉中的演化. **-ly** *ad.* **-ness** *n.*
clang [klæŋ] *vt.* 使发铿锵[丁当]声. —*vi.* ①发铿锵[丁当]声. ②(鹤等)鸣唳. —*n.* ①铿锵(声),丁当(声). ②【乐】音色,音质,音调. ③(鹤、雁等嘹亮而似乎有回声的)鸣唳.
clang·er ['klæŋə] *n.* 〔英口〕大错误;荒唐的错误.
clan·gor·ous ['klæŋgərəs] *a.* 丁丁当当响的,响亮的. **-ly** *ad.*
clan·go(u)r ['klæŋgə] *n.* 铿锵声,丁当声. —*vi.* 铿锵地[丁当地]响.
clank [klæŋk] *vt., vi.* (使)丁当地响. —*n.* 丁当(声);铿锵(声).
clan·nish ['klæniʃ] *a.* ①克兰的,部族的. ②宗派的;小集团的. **-ly** *ad.* **-ness** *n.*
clans·man ['klænzmən] *n.* 同氏族[部落]的人.
clap[1] [klæp] *vt.* ①拍,轻拍;拍打;轻敲. ②振(翼),拍(翅膀). ③拍地关上[碰上,装上]. ④急促地放;急忙处理. ~ *one's hands* 拍手(喝采). ~ *spurs to a horse* 急急忙忙踢马飞跑. —*vi.* ①拍手. ②发出噼拍声[碰撞声]. ~ ***by the heels*** 捉住;逮捕;投入监狱. ~ ***eyes on*** 瞥见,(偶然)看见〔常与 never 等否定词连用〕. ~ ***hold of*** 急忙捉住. ~ ***(sb.) in prison [gaol]*** 猛地(把某人)关进牢房. ~ ***on*** ①急忙张(帆). ②征(税). ~ ***(sb.) on the back*** 用手掌拍拍(某人的)脊背(以示打招呼、称赞). ~ ***up*** ①赶忙处理[办理];赶忙决定[订定、讲妥](交易、契约等). ②赶着做(椅子、箱子等). —*n.* ①噼拍声;破裂声. ②拍手(喝采),鼓掌;轻拍. *a ~ of thunder* 雷鸣,霹雳. *give him a ~* 给他鼓掌. ***in a ~*** 忽然,突然;迅速地. ***in two ~s of a lamb's tail*** 立即,赶快,急忙. ~**ped-out** 〔俚〕精疲力尽的;(器物因过分使用,长年无人照管等而)破烂不堪的.
clap[2] [klæp] *n.* 〔俚〕〔the ~〕淋病.
clap·board ['klæpbɔːd] *n.* 〔美〕护墙板,隔板;〔英〕桶板;【影】(开拍前在镜头前敲响的)音影对号板.
Clap·ham ['klæpəm] *n.* 克拉彭〔姓氏〕.
clap·net ['klæpnet] *n.* (捕鸟)网.
clap·per ['klæpə] *n.* ①拍手者. ②铃舌;钟舌,钟铎;拍板;(田间吓鸟雀的)鸣子;〔俚〕舌头. ③〔常 *pl.*〕响板. ***like the ~s*** 〔英俚〕迅速地,很快地.
clap·trap ['klæptræp] *n.* 哗众取宠的言语[诡计]. —*a.* 博人喝彩的,哗众取宠的.
claque [klæk] *n.* 〔F.〕〔集合词〕(戏院雇用的)鼓掌者,喝彩者,捧场者;随声附和的谄媚者.
claqueur [klæ'kəː] *n.* 〔F.〕(受雇用的)喝彩者;随声附和

者,谄媚者.
clar. = 【印】中长黑体铅字(= clarendon type).
Clar·a [ˈklɛərə] *n.* 克莱拉〔女子名〕.
clar·a·bel·la [klærəˈbelə] *n.* 【乐】风琴的强音笛音栓.
Clare [klɛə] *n.* 克莱尔〔女子名, Clara 的异体〕.
Clar·ence [ˈklærəns] *n.* 克拉伦斯〔男子名〕.
clar·ence [ˈklærəns] *n.* (旧时伦敦街上兜揽顾客的)四轮马车.
clar·en·don [ˈklærəndən] *n.* 【印】中长黑体铅字. **C- Press** 牛津大学出版部印刷所〔原为 Clarendon 伯爵所创办〕.
clar·et [ˈklærət] *n.* ①(法国波尔多产)红葡萄酒. ②〔美俚〕血. ③紫红色. ***tap sb.'s*** ~ 把人打得鼻孔出血. — *a.* 紫红色的. ~ **colo(u)r** 紫红色. ~**-colo(u)red** *a.* 紫红色的. ~ **cup** 客拉例冰汽酒〔红葡萄酒、白兰地、柠檬、苏打水、冰糖、香料等调成〕.
clar·i·fi·ca·tion [klærifiˈkeiʃən] *n.* ①澄清(作用); 澄清法; 净化. ②说明.
clar·i·fy [ˈklærifai] *vt.* ①澄清(液体等); 【生】透化. ②说明,讲清楚,阐明. ③使(头脑等)变清楚. — *vi.* ①(液体等)澄清,净化. ②变得清楚易懂.
clar·i·net [ˌklæriˈnet] *n.* 【乐】单簧管.
clar·i·net·(t)ist [ˌklæriˈnetist] *n.* 单簧管演奏者.
clar·i·on [ˈklæriən] *n.* (中世纪一种声音嘹亮的)号角〔喇叭〕. ②〔主诗〕号角声, 清脆嘹亮的音响. — *a.* 响亮清澈的.
clar·i·o·net [ˌklæriəˈnet] *n.* = clarinet.
Cla·ris·sa [kləˈrisə] *n.* 克拉丽莎〔女子名〕.
clar·i·ty [ˈklæriti] *n.* 清澈; 明晾; 明确.
clar·keite [ˈklɑːkait] *n.* 【矿】水标铀矿.
Clark(e) [klɑːk] *n.* 克拉克〔姓氏,男子名〕.
Clar·ki·a [ˈklɑːkjə] *n.* 【美植】山字草属.
cla·ro [ˈklɑːrəu] *n.* 〔Sp.〕 一种色淡味纯的雪茄烟. — *a.* (雪茄烟)色味俱淡的.
clar·y [ˈklɛəri] *n.* 【植】鼠尾草属; 南欧丹参.
clash [klæʃ] *n.* ①(金属撞击的)当当声,铿锵声,丁当声. ②(意见、利益等的)抵触,冲突; 龃龉; 不一致, 不调和. ③〔美〕比赛. *the border ~es* 国界冲突. *avoid a ~ with* 避免和…冲突. — *vt.* ①使当当〔丁丁〕地响. ②使猛撞. — *vi.* ①(金属)碰撞作声,当当地响. ②猛撞, 冲突, 抵触. ③〔美〕比赛; 〔口〕(色调等)不调和 *(with)* ~ *into (sb.)* 猛地撞上(某人).
clasp [klɑːsp] *vt.* ①扣住,钩住; 扣紧. ②紧紧抱住; 握紧; (藤等用卷须)紧紧缠住. ~ ***hands*** 紧紧握手; 互相结合; 结成联盟. ~ ***one's hands*** 两手十指交叉〔哀求、绝望等的表示〕. — *vi.* ①扣住, 钩住; 扣紧. ②紧紧握手. *The hook won't ~.* 这钩子钩不紧. — *n.* ①扣子, 钩子; (挂徽章的)银质棒状扣; 别针. ②紧握; 拥抱, 搂抱; 握手. ~ **hook** 抱合钩, 弯脚钩. ~ **knife** (比一般铅笔刀大些的)折叠式刀.
clasp·er [klɑːspə] *n.* ①扣, 钩, 扣紧物; (卷须等)缠绕物. ②【动】鳍脚; 交合突,交尾器官.
class [klɑːs] *n.* ①阶级; 社会等级. ②学级; 班级, 年级, 级,班; 组; (有组织的)讲习班; 〔美〕同年毕业班; 【军】同年入伍士兵. ③(高低、优劣的)等级; 类别. ④〔英大学〕(荣誉考试)优等; 〔俚〕高级,优秀; 漂亮, 优雅. ⑤【生】(分类学的)纲; 【矿】晶族. ⑥(一节)课. *the working ~es* 工人阶级. *No ~ today.* 今天没课. *C- is over.* 下课. *boycott ~es* 罢课. *the first [second] ~* 头〔二〕等. *high [low] ~* 高〔低〕级. *There's a good deal of ~ about him.* 他有很多优点. *He is not ~ enough.* 他没有什么了不起. ***at the top of one's*** ~ 出类拔萃; 居首要位置. ***be no*** ~ 〔俚〕不足道,无价值. ~ ***of the field*** 〔美〕比赛的优胜候补人. ***get a*** ~ = obtain a ~. ***in a ~ by itself*** 特好, 出众. ***in*** ~ 在上课中. ***in the same*** ~ 〔美〕同一类型的,同等的. ***no*** ~ 〔俚〕等外的,极坏的,蹩脚的〔用作表语〕. ***not in the same ~ with*** 不能同…相比,无法和…相提并论,比不上…. ***obtain a ~ = take a ~*** 毕业考试得优等. ***take a ~ at*** *(Oxford)* 在(牛津大学)进荣誉班. ***take a ~ of*** *(beginners)* 担任(初级)班(的教师). ***take ~es in*** *(history)* 听(历史)课; 选修(历史)课程. ***the ~es*** 上层社会; 知识阶级. ***the ~es and masses*** 各阶级和各阶层. — *vt.* 把…分类; 把…分等〔分级〕; 给…定等级; 把…分组. — *vi.* 属于…类〔等、级、组〕. ~ **action** 【法】集体诉讼. ~ **baby** 〔美俚〕同班生中最年轻者; 同班生结为夫妻所生的子女. ~**book** 教科书; 〔美〕毕业纪念册. ~ **champion** 优秀选手. ~**-conscious** *a.* (有)阶级意识〔觉悟〕的. ~ **consciousness** 阶级意识,阶级觉悟. ~ **day** 〔美〕毕业联欢会〔常作 C- D-〕. ~**fellow** 同班同学. ~**-for-itself** 自为的阶级. ~**-in-itself** 自在的阶级. ~**list** 班级名簿; 〔英大学〕考试成绩优等生名簿. ~**man** (英大学)优等考试及格生 (*opp.* passman). ~**mate** 同班生,同班同学, 级友. ~ **meeting** 班会, 级会. ~ **noun [name]** 【语法】类名词. ~**room** 教室. ~ **scrap** 〔美〕大学各级对抗比赛. ~ **strife [struggle, war]** 阶级斗争. ~ **work** 课堂作业. **-able** *a.* 可分类〔等级〕的. **-less** *a.* 无阶级的.
class. = classic; classical; classification; classified.
clas·sic [ˈklæsik] *a.* ①最优秀的, (艺术作品等)第一流的; 高尚的,优雅的; 模范的, 标准的. ②古典(派)的; 古希腊〔古罗马〕的; 有名的,有历史渊源的. ③传统的; 不朽的; 历史上值得纪念的; 与古典名著〔作家〕有关的. ④确实的,可靠的,典型的. *modern ~ writers* 第一流的当代作家. *a ~ example* 范例, 典范. *~ style* 古典派风格; 简练朴素的文体. *~ taste* 高尚的趣味. ***become*** ~ 被公认为杰作,被列入经典著作中. —*n.* ①文豪, 大艺术家; 古典〔经典〕作家; 古典主义者. ②〔*pl.*〕古典文学,古典语言〔特指希腊、拉丁语言〕. ③〔*pl.*〕名著,名作,杰作. ④〔美〕锦标赛大比赛. ⑤〔俚〕传统式样女服. ⑥典范,楷模; 典型事例; 可靠的出典. ***the ~s*** (古希腊、罗马的)古典文学. ~ **city** 〔美〕波士顿 (Boston) 市的别号〔旧时美国知识分子大都集中在该地〕. ~ **myth** 希腊〔罗马〕的神话. ~ **races** (英国传统的)五大赛马.
clas·si·cal [ˈklæsikəl] *a.* ①(文艺等)古典的, 传统的, 权威的; 古典文学的; 古典语文的; 古希腊〔古罗马〕的; 古典主义的,经典的. ②人文科学的,文科的. ③= classic ①. ~ **education** 古典文教育. ~ **music** 古典音乐. ~ **school** 古典(经济)学派. ~ **silk** 【纺】次优级生丝. **-ly** *ad.*
clas·si·cal·ism [ˈklæsikəlizəm] *n.* ①古典主义. ②古典文体〔成语、风格〕. ③古典崇拜; 拟古主义, 古典模仿,古希腊、罗马美术的模仿. ④古典文学研究; 古典文学〔知识〕.
clas·si·cal·i·ty [ˌklæsiˈkæliti] *n.* ①卓绝; 优美, 优雅. ②精通古典文学; 古典文学知识.
clas·si·cism [ˈklæsisizəm] *n.* = classicalism.
clas·si·cist [ˈklæsisist] *n.* 古典主义者; 古典学者; 拟古派.
clas·si·cize [ˈklæsisaiz] *vt.* 使古典化. — *vi.* 模仿古典.
clas·si·fi·a·ble [ˈklæsifaiəbl] *a.* 可分类的, 可分等级的.
clas·si·fi·ca·tion [ˌklæsifiˈkeiʃən] *n.* ①选别; 分等, 分级; 分选. ②【动、植】分类(法). 〔分类级别为: phylum 【动】及 division 【植】门, class 纲, order 目, family 科, genus 属, species 种, variety 品种〕. ③类别; 等级; (文件的)保密级. *a ~ yard* (车站的)调车场.
clas·si·fi·ca·to·ry [ˌklæsifiˈkeitəri] *a.* 分类上的,类别的.
clas·si·fied [ˈklæsifaid] *a.* ①分类〔分级〕的. ②机密的,保密的. ~ **ad(vertising)** (报刊上的)分类广告. ~ **documents** 保密文件.
clas·si·fi·er [ˈklæsifaiə] *n.* ①分类者. ②【矿】分级机.

③【化】分粒器. ④(汉语等中的)量词.
clas·si·fy [ˈklæsifai] *vt.* ①把…分类,〔分部; 分等, 分级〕. ②把…列为密件.
clas·sis [ˈklæsis] *n.* (*pl.* **-ses** [-siːz])【宗】地区教会委员会 〔由一地区的教会代表组成的管理教会事务的机构〕; 设有教会委员会的地区.
class·y [ˈklɑːsi] *a.* 〔俚〕上等的, 优等的; 〔美俚〕漂亮的, 时髦的, 美丽的. **-i·ly** *ad.* **-i·ness** *n.*
clas·tic [ˈklæstik] *a.*【地】碎屑状的;【生】分裂的, 分解的, 可分离的.
clath·rate [ˈklæθreit] *a.* ①【植】粗筛孔状的. ②【化】笼形的. — *n.*【化】笼形化合[包合]物.
clat·ter [ˈklætə] *n.* 〔只用 *sing.*〕①(马蹄的)得得声, (金属物品碰撞的)铿锵声, (机器等运转的)卡嗒声. ②喊喊喳喳的谈笑声. ③喧嚷, 骚动. — *vi.* ①得得[铿锵, 卡嗒]地响. ②喊喊喳喳地说笑. — *vt.* 使得得[铿锵、卡嗒]地响. ~ ***along*** 得得地跑; 骑马飞跑. ~ ***down*** 哗拉拉地落下. **-er** *n.* 得得作响的东西; 饶舌者.
clat·ter·ing·ly [ˈklætəriŋli] *ad.* ①得得[铿锵、卡嗒]响地. ②喋喋不休地, 咕咕呱呱地.
Claud(e) [klɔːd] *n.* 克劳德〔男子名〕.
Clau·di·a [ˈklɔːdjə] *n.* 克劳迪娅〔女子名〕.
clau·di·ca·tion [ˌklɔːdiˈkeiʃən] *n.*【医】跛, 跛行.
claus·al [ˈklɔːzl] *a.* ①【语法】子句的, 从句的, 分句的. ②条款的.
clause [klɔːz] *n.* ①(章程、条约等的)条, 项; 条款. ②【语法】子句, 分句, 主谓结构, 从句. *memorandum* ~*s* 附加条款. *penal* ~*s* 罚则. *saving* ~*s* 附则, 附言. *noun* ~ 名词从句. *principal* [*subordinate*] ~ 主要[从属]分句.
claus·tral [ˈklɔːstrəl] *a.* 修道院的; 隐遁的.
claus·tro·pho·bi·a [ˌklɔːstrəˈfəubjə] *n.*【心、医】幽闭[独居]恐怖症.
claus·tro·pho·bic [ˌklɔːstrəˈfəubik] *a.*【心、医】幽闭恐怖症的.
cla·vate, cla·vat·ed [ˈkleiveit, -veitid] *a.*【植】棒状的, 纺锤状的, 一端粗大的.
clave [kleiv] cleave² 的过去式.
claver [ˈkleivə] *n.* 〔Scot.〕闲谈; 闲话.
Clav·i·ceps [ˈklæviseps] *n.*【微】麦角菌属.
clav·i·chord [ˈklævikɔːd] *n.* 翼琴〔钢琴的前身〕.
clav·i·cle [ˈklævikl] *n.*【解】锁骨; 棍状体.
clav·i·corn [ˈklævikɔːn] *a.*【动】(昆虫)锤角组的. **-ate** [-ˈkɔːneit] *a.*
cla·vic·u·lar [kləˈvikjulə] *a.*【解】锁骨的.
clav·i·er [ˈklæviə] *n.* ①(钢琴等的)键盘; (练习用)无音键盘. ②[kləˈviə] 键盘乐器.
clav·i·form [ˈklævifɔːm] *a.* 棒形的.
claw [klɔː] *n.* ①(动物的)爪; (蟹等的)钳; 爪形器具, 钩. ②〔贬〕(瘦得象爪子一样的)手; 魔爪. ~ ***thumpers*** 〔美〕马里兰州人. ***cut*** [***clip, pare***] ***sb.'s*** ~***s*** 斩断魔爪; 解除…的武装. ***draw in one's*** ~***s*** 收敛气焰, 抑制怒气; 放弃强硬办法. ***escape from the*** ~***s of sb.*** 逃出某人的魔掌. ***get one's*** ~***s into*** (*sb.*) 狠狠地揍人一顿; 恶意中伤某人. ***in sb.'s*** ~***s*** 在某人魔掌下. — *vt.* ①用爪子抓[挖, 掘, 撕]. ②〔英方〕搔; 用爪捕捉, 用手探索. ③〔美俚〕逮捕; (入)贪婪地抓住; 搜刮(钱等). —*vi.* 用爪子抓[挖, 掘, 撕]. ~ ***back*** 〔英〕(政府用增税等办法)设法弥补. ~ ***favour*** 献媚, 拍马屁. ~ ***hold of*** 抓紧. ***C- me and I'll*** ~ ***thee.*** 善来好往, 一逗一诺, 互相迎合. ~ ***off*** [***away***] ①【海】把船头转朝上风. ②退避, 摆脱. ③责骂. ~**-back** 〔英〕①弥补. ②欠缺, 不利. ~ **bar** 撬杆. ~ **hammer** ①羊角榔头, 拔钉锤. ②〔俚〕燕尾服〔又叫 ~-hammer coat〕.
clax·on [ˈklæksn] *n.* 电气警笛;【机】电器喇叭 (= klaxon).
Clay [klei] *n.* 克莱〔男子名, Clayton 的昵称〕.
clay [klei] *n.* ①粘土; 泥土. ②(相对于灵魂而言的)人体, 肉体; 资质, 天性. ③陶制烟斗 (= ~-pipe). ④粘土状物. *potter's* ~ 陶土. *porcelain* ~ 瓷土. *a man of common* ~ 普通人, 常人. ***a yard of*** ~ 陶制长烟管. ***as*** ~ ***in the hands of the potter*** 要捏成什么样就是什么样; 听凭摆布. ***dead and turned to*** ~ 死. ***feet of*** ~ 泥足〔象征站不住脚的事物〕. ***moisten*** [***soak, wet***] ***one's*** ~ 饮酒. ~**-cold** *a.* 土一样冷的; 死的. ~ **court** 红布网球场. ~**-pigeon** (投掷空中练习射击的)鸽形土靶; 〔美俚〕易被捉弄的人; 容易的工作. ~**-pipe** 陶制烟管. ~**-slate**【地】粘板岩. ~**-stone**【地】变朽粘土岩. **-ish** *a.* 粘土(多)的; 粘土似的; 泥质的.
clay·bank [ˈkleiˌbæŋk] *a.* 棕黄色的. *a* ~ *horse* 棕黄马.
clay·ey [ˈkleii] *a.* 粘土(多)的, 粘土似的; 泥质的 (= clayish).
clay·more [ˈkleimɔː] *n.* 剑; (十六世纪苏格兰高地部落的)双刃大砍刀. ~ **mine** (爆炸时飞出金属颗粒的)霰粒爆炸装置.
Clay·ton [ˈkleitn] *n.* 克莱顿〔姓氏, 男子名〕.
clay·to·ni·a [kləˈtəuniə] *n.* ①【植】春美草. ②〔C-〕春美草属.
-cle *comb. f.* = -cule.
clead·ing [ˈkliːdiŋ] *n.* ①【机】(汽锅等的)保热套, 套板;【矿】(隧道的)护尘板, 衬板, 覆板. ②〔Scot.〕衣服.
clean [kliːn] *a.* ①清洁的, 干净的; 未染污的; (核武器等)无放射性尘埃的. ②(精神、品质等)纯洁的, (历史等)清白的; 不淫猥的. ③(心地)正直的, 光明正大的, 不作弊的. ④彻底的, 完全的, 十足的. ⑤巧妙的, 高明的; 干净利落的. ⑥有洁癖的, 爱干净的; 洗干净的. ⑦没有用过的, 新(鲜)的; 无杂质的; 无瑕疵的 ⑧没有疾病的; 〔俚〕没有麻醉毒瘾的. ⑨光洁的; 整齐的, (身材、四肢等)匀称的, 好看的, 端正的. ⑩〔美俚〕分文没有的, 两袖清风的; 〔美俚〕不暗藏枪枝[毒品等]的, (船舱等)已卸空的. ⑪(肉等)可供食用的; (鱼)非产期而宜食的. ⑫(田里)不生杂草的. *lose a* ~ *hundred dollars* 丢了整整一百元. *wine* ~ *to the taste* 爽口的葡萄酒. ***as*** ~ ***as a pigsty*** 〔反〕象猪圈一样干净. ***be*** ~ ***in one's person*** 爱干净, 服装整洁. ~ ***author*** 不作猥亵描写的作家. ~ ***ball*** 好球. ~ ***bill of health*** 健康证明书; 船内安全报告; 〔口〕人事保证. ~ ***bill of lading***【海】无故障船货提单. ***have*** ~ ***hands*** = ***keep the hands*** ~ 廉洁清正, 无可疵议. ***keep it*** ~ 〔俚〕不下流, 守规矩. ***keep oneself*** ~ 保持身体清洁干净. ***lead a*** ~ ***life*** 过清白日子. ***make a*** ~ ***breast of*** 完全吐露, 彻底坦白; 剖白. ***make a*** ~ ***sweep of*** 一扫, 廓清. ***show a*** ~ ***pair of heels*** 一溜烟逃走, 溜掉. — *ad.* ①完全, 十分, 彻底地. ②干净地, 清洁地. ③巧妙地, 干净利落地. ***be*** ~ ***bowled*** 〔俚〕被打得大败. ***be hit*** ~ ***in the eye*** 正打中眼睛. ~ ***full*** 使满帆; 扯满所有风帆. ~ ***gone*** 无影无踪. ~ ***wrong*** 完全错误. ***come*** ~ 〔俚〕吐露真情, 供认. ***cut*** ~ ***through*** 洞穿. — *vt.* ①把…弄清楚, 把…收拾干净, 扫除; 洗涤. ②把…擦干净, 擦亮, 刷. ③收清, 搬空. ④【化】纯化, 净化; 精炼, 提纯. ~ *field for sowing* 整地播种. ~ *sb.* 〔美〕骗取(某人)所有的钱〔财物〕. — *vi.* ①被弄干净. ②打扫, 扫除, 做清洁工作. ~ ***away*** [***off***] 擦去, 清除. ~ ***down*** 清扫(墙壁等); 喝干; 洗(马等). ~ ***house*** 整顿, 清洗(组织). ~ ***one's plate*** 吃得盘底精光. ~ ***out*** 扫除干净; 〔俚〕(把钱)花完, 输完. ~ ***up*** 收拾干净, 扫除清洗, 肃清, 扫荡;【机】改正, 加工, 园工; 〔俚〕赚厚利, 发财. ~ ***up on*** 〔美俚〕打垮. ***have one's clothes*** ~***ed*** 送衣服去干洗. ~ **anchorage** 安全抛锚处. ~ **bond** 无背书公债. ~**-bred** *a.* 纯血种的. ~ **copy** 清整的原稿; 誊清稿. ~ **credit**【商】无条件信用书. ~ **cultivation**【农】无覆盖播种. ~ **culture**【农】单播. ~**-cut** *a.* 样子好的, 好看的, 轮廓鲜明的; 品格优良的; 正确的, 明确的. ~ **fallow**【农】

绝对休闲. ~ **fielding** (棒球等) 无懈可击的防守. ~ **fingered** *a.* 廉洁的;(手)灵巧的. ~ **fish** (非产期的)食用鱼. ~**-handed** *a.* 正直的,清白的. ~**-limbed** *a.* 手足匀称的,姿势好的. ~**-living** *a.* 生活作风正派的. ~ **operation** 扫荡战. ~**out** 清除. ~ **page** 空白页. ~ **proof**【印】清样. ~ **record** 清白履历. ~ **room** 净室;绝对无尘室;无菌室. ~ **shave**〔美〕无可疵议的工作,美满完成的工作. ~**-shaved** 剃净胡须的;干净利落的. ~ **ship** 全无收获的捕鲸船. ~**-skin**〔Aus.〕不打烙印的放牧牲畜. ~ **slate** 白纸(主义)〔不受义务、口约等所拘束〕;无疵可寻的履历. ~ **shot** 高明的射手. ~ **stroke** (打球等)干净利落的一击. ~ **sweep**〔美〕决定性胜利,大胜. ~ **talk** 清谈. ~ **timber** 无节疤的木料. ~ **tongue** (不说脏话的)干净嘴 (*keep a ~ tongue* 不说下流话). ~**up** *n.* ①〔口〕扫除,清扫运动;【化】提纯,净化,精炼,澄清. ②〔美西部〕(金矿产地等定期的)清选. ③〔俚〕赚头.

clean·er [ˈkliːnə] *n.* ①清洁工人;(干洗)洗衣工人. ②洗衣店(老板). ③除垢器. *a lower* ~【纺】下绒辊. ***take sb. to the ~s***〔俚〕把(某人)钱财骗光,使输光.

clean·ing [ˈkliːniŋ] *n.* ①清洁法;扫除;清洗,洗涤;(种子的)清选. ②〔常 *pl.*〕(牛、羊等的)胞衣. ③【林】除伐. ④〔*pl.*〕垃圾. ⑤〔口〕(比赛等的)惨败,输光. ⑥〔口〕巨额利润. *a general [thorough]* ~ 大扫除. ***take a*** ~ (球队等)惨败. ~ **brush** 枪刷,除尘毛刷. ~ **doctor**【纺】刮浆刀. ~**rod** (枪口的)通条.

clean·li·ly [ˈklenlili] *ad.* 清洁,干净.

clean·li·ness [ˈklenlinis] *n.* 清洁.

clean·ly[1] [ˈklenli] *a.* ①爱清洁的;干净的,清洁的. ②〔古〕纯洁的.

clean·ly[2] [ˈkliːnli] *ad.* ①干净地,清洁地. ②清白地,纯洁地. ③【古】完全,统统.

cleanse [klenz] *vt.* ①把…弄清洁,把…洗干净;消毒;澄清. ②净化,使(思想等)变纯洁;【圣】治愈. ***~ one's bosom of perilous stuff*** 清心寡欲.

cleans·er [ˈklenzə] *n.* ①做清洁工作的人. ②清洁剂〔肥皂等〕,去污粉;擦亮粉. ③滤水器,清洁器.

cleans·ing [ˈklenziŋ] *n.* ①〔古〕清洁化,净化. ②〔*pl.*〕垃圾;(牛羊等的)胞衣. —*a.* 清洁用的,洗涤用的.

clear [kliə] *a.* ①(水等)清澈的,透明的;(天气等)晴朗的,明净的,爽朗的;明亮的,皎洁的. ②明白的,明了的,清楚的;显明的,容易分辨的. ③无遮拦的,无障碍的;畅通的;开阔的,豁然的. ④无疑的,的确的,确实的. ⑤(船)已卸净(货)的. ⑥纯粹的,十足的;整整的;净得的. ⑦无疵瑕的;(木材)无节疤的. ⑧脱离的,还清(债务)的;清除了(障碍等)的;摆脱了(束缚等)的 (*of*). *Do I make myself ~?* 你明白我的意思吗? *He made it ~ that* …他说明…. *The train is ~ of the station.* 火车已离开车站了. *a ~ head* 清晰的头脑. *~ intellect [sight]* 明智. *a ~ outline* 鲜明的轮廓. *a ~ sky* 晴空. *a ~ space* 空地. *a ~ water* 开阔无阻的水面. *roads ~ of traffic* 没有人来往的路. *a ~ width* (布的)净阔,纯幅. *a ~ profit* 纯(收)益. *a ~ month* 整整一个月. *the ~ contrary* 恰恰相反. *a ~ majority* 绝对多数,过半数. *a ~ timber* 无节疤的木料. ***All*** ~ 无敌机,解除警报. ***(as) ~ as a bell*** 很清楚;很健全. ***(as) ~ as day*** 极明白,显而易见. ***be ~ from** (suspicion)* 没有(嫌疑). ***be ~ of** (debt; worry)* 无(债、忧). ***~ as mud***〔美〕不明显,很模糊,一塌糊涂. ***get ~ away [off]*** 完全离开,逃掉. ***get ~ of*** 脱离,离开,避掉. ***get ~ out*** 完全脱离[离开]. ***keep ~ of*** 避开,离着. ***see one's way*** ~ 前途无阻[顺畅]. —*ad.* ①显然地,清楚地. ②离开,不接触. ③一直. *hang ~* 挂开点,挂远点. *speak loud and ~* 说话又响又清楚. *five miles ~* 整整五英里. *~ on to the end* 一直到底. — *vt.* ①使变清澈,使无污垢. ②把…弄明白,使清楚. ③澄清;消除(嫌疑),宣布开释,辩明(无罪). ④(议案等)通过(批准手续);批准,准许. ⑤付清;抵消,结清;清讫. ⑥扫除,除去;赶走,驱逐;打发掉. ⑦开垦,砍伐,开拓. ⑧穿过,超过;跳过,通过;突破(难关). ⑨为(船或船货等)结关〔办好出港手续〕,(船)结关后离开(港口). ⑩【商】抛卖,贱卖,脱售;交换清算(票据);兑现(支票). ⑪【商】净赚,净得. *~ a fishing line* 解开钓丝. *~ an examination paper* 答完所有试题. *~ the air* 祛除郁暑;扫清疑惑[疑团]. *~ (the decks) for action* (收拾甲板)准备战斗. *~ the hurdle*〔美〕克服障碍,走向成功. *~ a fence* 跳过栅栏. *~ a port* 出港. *~ the land* 驶离陆地. *My car only just ~ed the lorry.* 我的车险些儿没有避开卡车. — *vi.* ①变清澈,变澄清;(天气)开晴. ②(船只等)办清出港手续,出港 *(from)*;〔俚〕离去;走出;逃掉. ③【商】交换票据. ④(文件等)送审,报批. *great reduction in order to ~* 出清存货大贱卖. *The sky is ~ing.* 天正转晴. ~ ***away*** 扫除,收拾(餐具);排除,砍去;(雾等)消散. ~ ***expenses*** 抵消开支. ~ *(1,000 pounds)* ***from*** 因…赚得(一千镑). ~ … ***of*** 从…扫清… (*~ one's mind of doubt* 消除心中疑团. *~ the city of undesirables* 驱逐不良分子出市). ~ ***off*** 完成,做好,理清(工作等);清算,了清(债务等);卖掉;驱逐,撵走;(雨)停,(云)散;〔俚〕走掉,逃掉. ~ ***oneself of** (a charge)*, 洗清(嫌疑),表白. ~ ***out*** ①扫出;〔俚〕掏空腰包[钱袋];卖光,出清. ②出港;〔俚〕离去. ~ ***the land*** (船)离开陆地(以免触礁). ~ ***the way*** 作好准备. ~ ***up*** ①整顿,理清. ②解决,说明. ③(天气)转晴,变好. —*n.* ①【机】间隙,余隙. ②【建】中空体内部的尺寸. ③= clearance. ***in the*** ~ ①(两边之间的)内宽. ②自由,无罪. ③明码,不用暗号. ④〔美俚〕没有债务. ~ **cole** (打底子的)油灰. ~**-cut** *a.* 轮廓鲜明的,清晰的. ~**-eyed** *a.* 目光锐利的,能判明是非的. ~**-headed** *a.* 头脑清楚的,聪明的. ~**-sighted** *a.* 英明的,聪明的,精明的. ~**starch** *vt., vi.* 给(衣服等)上浆. ~**story**【建】开窗假楼;〔美〕(火车车顶下面的)气窗 (= clerestory). ~**way** (立体交叉,限制进入,保证畅通的)超高速公路. ~**wing**【动】透翅蛾 *(Aegeriidae)*. **-ly** *ad.* **-ness** *n.*

clear·age [ˈkliəridʒ] *n.* 清除,清理,出清.

clear·ance [ˈkliərəns] *n.* ①清除,扫除,除去;解除. ②【林】终伐;(伐去树木后的)林间空地. ③出[入]港证;放行证;(军事、飞行等方面的)许可(证);出入港手续. ④【机】(公差的)公隙;余隙,间隙;【建】净空〔如车辆通过隧道时两边所留空隙〕. ⑤【商】结算,清算;纯益;票据交换(额). ⑥辞职照准. ⑦(美国罗斯福实行"新政"时代呈递的)请示. *a ground ~* (飞机起落轮中心的)离地距离. ***for*** ~ (足球)踢球门球. ~ **fee** 出港手续费. ~ **permit** 出港许可;出港证. ~ **sale**〔英〕出清存货大贱卖.

clear·cole [ˈkliəkəul] *n.* (油漆墙壁等打底用的)细白垩胶,白铅胶. — *vt.* 为…上细白垩[白铅]胶.

clear·ing [ˈkliəriŋ] *n.* ①清除,扫除,除去;清洁,纯化. ②表白,雪冤,昭雪. ③【林】集材;(森林中的)开辟地,开垦地. ④【军】扫海. ⑤【商】清算;(银行间的)汇划结算;票据交换;〔*pl.*〕票据交换[汇划结算]额. ~ **bank** 参加票据交换的银行. ~ **hospital** 野战医院. ~**-house** ①票据交换所. ②(技术)情报交流所. ~ **items** 交换项目[物件]. ~ **label** 出港证. ~ **lamp** (电话)话终灯. ~ **line [mark]** (航海图上的)避险标记. ~ **sheet** 交换[结算]清单. ~ **station**【军】医疗后送站,师救护所.

cleat [kliːt] *n.* ①(木器、鞋后跟等上的金属或木料的)楔形加固角;【空】加强[固]角片;【电】磁夹板. ②【船】系缆角[耳];羊角. — *vt.* 用楔子加固;给…装楔子.

cleav·a·ble [ˈkliːvəbl] *a.* ①劈得开的;易劈的. ②【物,矿】可解理的. **-bil·i·ty** *n.*

cleav·age [ˈkliːvidʒ] *n.* ①劈开,劈裂;劈开处. ②【生】卵裂;分裂;【矿】解理,劈理.

cleave[1] [kliːv] *vt.* (***~d, clove*** [kləuv], ***cleft*** [kleft];

~d, cloven [kləuvn], *cleft)* ①劈,劈开. ②把…分成若干小部分[小派别等]. ③(船)破(浪)前进; 开(路). — *vi.* ①(木头等顺着纹路)被劈开,裂开. ②(船等)破浪前进; (鸟等)掠过空中. ~ *down* 劈倒. ~ *in two* 把…劈成两半. ~ *one's way through* 排开…前进.

cleave[2] [kliːv] *vi.* *(~d, clave* [kleiv]; *~d)* ①死守着,坚守; 坚持; 依恋 *(to)*; 紧密结合*(together)*. ②〔古〕粘着,粘住 *(to)*.

cleav·er [ˈkliːvə] *n.* ①劈东西的人[器具]; 切肉大菜刀. ②(冰河或雪原的)岩脊.

cleav·ers [ˈkliːvəz] *n.* 〔*sing., pl.*〕①【植】八重葎, 猪殃殃. ②〔英方〕杂草(丛).

cleek, cleik [kliːk] *n.* ①〔主 Scot.〕铁钩; 挂钩. ②高尔夫球铁头球棒.

clef [klef] *n.* 【乐】谱号. *F [G]* ~ 低[高]音谱号.

cleft[1] [kleft] *v. cleave*[1] 的过去式和过去分词. —*a.* 劈开的,裂开的;【植】尖裂的,半裂的. ***in a ~ stick*** 进退两难. **~-grafting**【园艺】劈接(法). ~ **lip** 兔唇. ~ **palate** 裂腭. ~ **sentence**【语法】分裂句.

cleft[2] [kleft] *n.* ①裂缝, 裂口, 裂痕, V字形凹刻. ②裂片.

cleg [kleg] *n.* 〔英〕虻,马蝇,牛蝇.

cleis·tog·a·mous [klaisˈtɔgəməs], **cleis·to·gam·ic** [-təˈgæmik] *a.* 【植】闭花受精的.

cleis·tog·a·my [klaisˈtɔgəmi] *n.* 【植】闭花受精.

clem [klem] *vt., vi.* 〔英方〕(使)挨饿,(使)受饥渴寒冷之苦.

Clem·a·tis [ˈklemətis] *n.* 【植】女萎属; 〔c-〕女萎,铁线莲.

clem·en·cy [ˈklemənsi] *n.* ①(气候等的)温和,温暖. ②仁慈,宽厚.

Clem·ens [ˈklemənz] *n.* 克莱门斯〔姓氏〕. **Samuel Langhorne** ~ 塞缪尔·克莱门斯〔美国小说家 Mark Twain的真实姓名〕.

clem·ent [ˈklemənt] *a.* ①仁慈的,宽厚的,宽大的. ②(气候)温和的,温暖的.

Clem·ent [ˈklemənt] *n.* 克莱门特〔男子名〕.

clench [klentʃ] *vt.* ①握紧(拳头); 咬紧(牙关). ②(为加固目的)敲弯(钉头); 敲紧, 敲牢. ③捏紧, 抓牢. ④解决, 确定(论据等), 决定(交易等). ~ *a bargain* 定契约. ~ *one's teeth [jaws]* 咬紧牙关; 下决心. — *vi.* 〔通常用 clinch〕(铆钉等)钉牢;【拳】揪扭,扭住; (手)握紧; 咬紧. — *n.* ①敲弯的钉头. ②钉牢; 咬紧牙关; 咬牙切齿. ③【拳】揪扭.

clench·er [ˈklentʃə] *n.* = clincher.

cle·o·me [kliˈəumi] *n.* 【植】醉蝶花,紫龙须; 〔C-〕醉蝶花属,紫龙须属.

Cle·o·pa·tra [kliəˈpɑːtrə] *n.* ①克娄巴特立〔女子名〕. ②(古埃及)克娄巴特拉女王〔公元前 69—30〕; 〔喻〕绝世美人. ③〔c-〕鲜蓝色. *~'s needle* 古埃及方尖碑〔指现已被移置伦敦泰晤士河畔及纽约中央公园的两块〕. *~'s nose*〔喻〕历史发展中的偶然性因素,克娄巴特拉之鼻〔意谓她的容貌假如不美, 就会使由此引起的一系列历史事件改观云云〕.

clepe [kliːp] *vt.* ①〔废〕呼唤(人),对(人)说话. ②〔古〕呼名; 命名. ★ 过去分词通常使用已废弃的 **yclept, ycleped.**

clep·sy·dra [ˈklepsidrə] *n.* *(pl. ~s, -drae* [-driː]*)* 漏壶,水漏,铜壶滴漏〔古代计时器〕.

clep·to·ma·ni·a [ˌkleptəˈmeinjə] *n.* 【心、医】盗癖,偷窃癖 (= kleptmania).

clere·sto·ry [ˈkliəstəri] *n.* ①天窗; 高侧窗; 长廊, 楼座. ②(火车车顶下面的)气窗 (= clearstory).

cler·gy [ˈkləːdʒi] *n.* ①教士[牧师]职务; 〔集合词〕教士, 牧师. ②〔废〕学问.

cler·gy·man [ˈkləːdʒimən] *n.* *(pl. cler·gy·men)* 教士, 牧师. *~'s sore throat*【医】(因说话过多所患的)慢性喉头炎. *~'s week [fortnight]* 包括两个[三个]星期日的假期.

cler·gy·wom·an [ˈkləːdʒiˌwumən] *n.* *(pl. cler·gy·wo·men* [-ˌwimin]*)* ①女牧师,女教士. ②〔谑〕牧师太太,牧师小姐; 牧师的女性家属.

cler·ic [ˈklerik] *n.* 教士,牧师; 教堂[宗教机构]中的工作人员. — *a.* 〔古〕= clerical ①.

cler·i·cal [ˈklerikəl] *a.* ①教士的,牧师的. ②职员[办事员,事务员]的, 办公室工作的. — *n.* ①牧师,教士. ②〔贬〕(议会中主张扩张教士势力的)教士派议员. ③〔*pl.*〕牧师服,教士服. ~ **error** 笔误. ~ **force** 职员们,事务员们. ~ **staff** (全体)职员,办事员. ~ **type** 书写体. ~ **work** 文书工作,事务,杂务. **-ism** *n.* 教权主义; 教士(不应有的)权力. **-ist** *n.* 教权主义者. **-ly** *ad.*

cler·i·sy [ˈklerisi] *n.* 〔旧〕知识阶层,(作为一个阶层的)受过相当教育的人们.

clerk [klɑːk; Am. kləːk] *n.* ①(银行、公司等的)事务员,办事员,职员,管理员; 〔美〕(商店的)店员. ②【宗】教会文书, 执事. ③(团体等的)秘书. ④〔古〕牧师, 教士; 识字的人, 学者. *a town* ~ 市政府的公务员. *a bank* ~ 银行职员. *a correspondence* ~ 处理信件的秘书. *a ~ of the works* 监工. ***~ in holy orders*** 牧师,教士〔英国教会的正式用语〕. ***~ of St. Nicholas = St. Nicholas's ~*** 盗贼, 路劫. ***C- of the Weather*** 风伯雨师; 〔美谑〕气象台长. — *vi.* 担任事务员[职员]; 〔美〕做店员.

clerk·dom [ˈklɑːkdəm] *n.* 职员的身分[职位].

clerk·ly [ˈklɑːkli] *a., ad.* ①〔古〕教士(似)的[地]. ②职员的[地]. ③〔古〕学者似的[地]; 善书写的[地]. ~ **hand** 学者一样的笔迹.

clerk·ship [klɑːkʃip] *n.* ①职员的职位[身分]; 牧师的职位. ②〔古〕博学. ③(医科学生的)住院实习.

cleve·ite [ˈkliːvait] *n.* 【矿】钇铀矿.

Cleve·land [ˈkliːvlənd] *n.* ①克利夫兰〔美国城市〕. ②克利夫兰〔姓氏〕.

clev·er [ˈklevə] *a.* ①灵巧的,能干的; 聪明的; 伶俐的,机敏的. ②〔美方〕性情温良的,和蔼可亲的. ③〔美方〕英俊的,神气的; 壮健的; 恣态美好的; 风采优雅的. *He is ~ at cricket.* 他擅长板球. ~ ***fingers*** 巧手, 妙手. ~ ***horse*** 善能跳越障碍物的马. ~ ***dog*** 〔美俚〕聪明乖觉的人. **-ish** *a.* 有小聪明的,灵巧的. **-ly** ① *ad.* 灵巧,能干; 聪明; 伶俐,机敏; 〔方〕完全,全然. ② *a.* 〔美俚〕壮健, 结实. **-ness** *n.*

clev·is [ˈklevis] *n.* (连接拖车等用的) U 字形铁扣, 两齿叉形接头.

clew [kluː] *n.* ①线团,线球; (希腊神话中带人出迷宫的)引路线; (解决问题等的)线索, 暗示. ②【海】帆耳〔横帆的下角及纵帆的后角〕; 帆下角的铁圈. ③〔*pl.*〕吊床两头的绳子. ***from ~ to earing*** 由(帆的)一角到另一角; 从头到尾; 完全地. ***spread a large [small] ~*** 多上[少上]风帆; 大张[收缩]气势. — *vt.* ①把…绕成线球. ②扯(帆)上桁. ~ ***down (a sail)*** (张帆时)拉下风篷. ~ ***up*** ①绕线球. ②把帆下角扯到桁上; 完成(工作).

cli·ché [ˈkliːʃei; Am. kliːˈʃei] *n.* 〔F.〕【印】电铸版,(由纸型翻铸的)铅版; 〔喻〕陈词滥调,老生常谈; (小说等)陈腐的题材[场面]. — *a.* 陈腐的.

click[1] [klik] *vi.* ①(开枪扣扳机,关门上锁时)卡嗒一声响. ②哇啦哇啦地说. *The pistol ~ed empty.* 手枪卡嗒一声射出子弹. *The door ~ed shut.* 门卡嗒一声关上. — *vt.* ①使卡嗒响. ②(马)碰响(前后蹄铁掌). ~ *one's heels (together)* (兵士等敬礼时) 卡地一声并拢双脚. ~ *the door* 卡嗒一声关上门. — *n.* ①卡嗒声,的答声; 啧啧声. ②门闩,插锁; 【机】棘爪, 挡爪. ③【语音】(非洲霍屯督语、布须曼语等的)倒吸气音. **~-beetle** 叩头虫.

click[2] [ˈklik] *vi.* ①正相吻合; 一见如故; 情投意合, (男女)一见倾心. ②〔美俚〕成功; 做得好,达到目的; (演技)博得喝彩,大受欢迎; 赌赢.

click·er [ˈklikə] *n.* ①【英印】排字工头. ②制鞋工头.

click·e·ty·clack [ˈklikətiˈklæk] *n.* 火车车轮的咔哒声. — *vi.* 发出车轮的咔哒声.

cli·ent [ˈklaiənt] *n.* ①诉讼〔辩护〕委托人；顾客，客人. ②〔古罗马〕(依附贵族的)门客；受保护者，依附他人者. ③附庸国 (= ~ state). **-less** *a.* (律师等)没有人委托的；(商店等)没有顾客的.

cli·ent·age [ˈklaiəntidʒ] *n.* ①委托关系；保护关系. ② = clientele.

cli·en·tele [ˌkliːɑ̃ːnˈteil]〔集合词〕*n.* ①诉讼委托人；顾客；(戏院的)常客. ②被保护者；追随者.

cliff [klif] *n.* (海岸等的)峭壁，断崖，绝壁，悬岩. *walls of a* ~ 断崖侧面. ~ **dweller**〔俚〕①住公寓大厦的人. ②美国西南史前印第安悬岩洞人. ~**-hanger** (连载的)惊险小说；惊险〔紧张〕的事件〔比赛〕. ~**-hanging** *a.* 扣人心弦的. ~ **swallow** 崖燕.

Clif·ford [ˈklifəd] *n.* 克利福德〔姓氏，男子名〕.

cliffsman [ˈklifsmən] *n.* 惯于攀登险崖的人.

cliff·y [ˈklifi] *a.* 有峭壁陡岩的，险峻的.

cli·mac·ter·ic [klaiˈmæktərik] *n.* (女性的)更年期，绝经期；(果实的)完熟期；(据信人的命运每七年一次的)关口，转折点. *the grand* ~ 大关〔据信为 63 岁〕. — *a.* = **climac·teri·cal** [klaimək'terikl] 更年期的；危机的；关口上的.

cli·mac·tic [klaiˈmæktik] *a.* 极点的，顶点的，高潮的. **-ally** *ad.*

cli·mate [ˈklaimit] *n.* ①气候；水土，风土；地带. ②(社会思想等的)趋势，倾向，风气，思潮. *continental [marine]* ~ 大陆性〔海洋性〕气候.

cli·mat·ic [klaiˈmætik] *a.* ①气候的，水土的，风土的. ②一般趋势的，风气的. ~ **year**〔美〕气候年〔10月1日——次年9月30日〕. **-ly** *ad.*

cli·ma·tol·o·gy [ˌklaiməˈtɔlədʒi] *n.* 气候学，风土学. **-log·ic** *a.*

cli·ma·tron [ˈklaimətrɔn] *n.* (大型不分隔的)人工气候室.

cli·max [ˈklaimæks] *n.* ①【修】渐强(而达顶点的)修辞法. ②顶点，最高峰，极点；(事件的)高潮. ③【生】顶极(群落)，演替顶极. *come to a* ~ 达到顶点，达到高潮. — *vi., vt.* (使)达到顶点〔高潮〕. ~ **forest stage**【林】最后森林阶段.

climb [klaim] *vi.* ①攀登，爬上；(太阳等)徐徐上升；(飞机)爬高；(植物)攀缘向上. ②向上爬，钻营. ③(物价)上涨；(数目)渐增. — *vt.* ①爬，攀登；爬上. ②(植物)依附…攀缘向上. ③使(飞机)爬高. ~ *(up) a mountain [tree]* 爬山〔树〕. *The sun has* ~*ed the sky.* 太阳已经高照. ~ ***aboard***〔美〕上车. ~ ***down*** 爬下来；(从高位)退下来；断念，放弃(要求)；让步，屈服. ~ ***into the square***〔美〕爬上拳击台开始比赛. ~ ***into [out of] one's overalls*** 匆忙穿上〔脱下〕工作服. ~ ***on the band wagon***〔美〕加入轰轰烈烈的运动；和群众共同行动. ~ ***over*** *(a wall)* 翻过(墙壁). ~ ***the rigging*** 发脾气. ~ ***through the ropes***〔美〕= ~ into the square. ~ ***to power*** 爬到掌权地位，掌权. ~ ***up*** 攀登，冒险爬. — *n.* ①攀登；【空】爬高. ②需要攀登的地方，山坡. ~**-down** *n.* ①向下爬. ②〔口〕(议论等的)让步；退让，屈服；(声明的)撤回. ~**out**【空】急速爬升.

climb·a·ble [ˈklaiməbl] *a.* 可攀登的，爬得上去的.

climb·er [ˈklaimə] *n.* ①爬山者. ②【植】攀缘植物；【动】〔*pl.*〕攀禽类〔啄木鸟等〕. ③〔喻〕野心家，向上爬的人. ④(登山靴上的)助爬钉.

climb·ing [ˈklaimiŋ] *a.* 攀缘而上的；上升的. — *n.* 攀登；【空】爬升. ~ **angle**【空】上升角. ~ **fern**【植】蟹草属. ~ **fish [perch]**【动】攀木鱼. ~**iron** *n.* 攀树器；〔*pl.*〕(登山鞋上的)助爬钉. ~ **plant**【植】攀缘植物. ~ **power**【空】上升力. ~ **turn**【空】上升盘旋.

clime [klaim] *n.*〔诗〕地区；气候，风土.

cli·mo·graph [ˈklaiməgræf] *n.* 气象图.

cli·nan·dri·um [kliˈnændriəm] *n.* *(pl.* ***-dri·a*** [-ə]*)*【植】某些兰科植物的药床.

clinch [klintʃ] *n., vt., vi.* ① = clench. ②〔美俚〕热烈拥抱.

clinch·er [ˈklintʃə] *n.* ①敲弯钉尖的用具；紧钳，夹子. ②〔口〕定论，无可置辩的议论. ③(汽车的)钳入〔紧钳〕式轮胎. ***That's a*** ~. 那就叫我没话可说了. ~**-built** *a.* = clinker-built.

cline [klain] *n.*【生】(物种演变曲线中的)倾斜. **-nal** *a.*

cling [kliŋ] *vi.* *(clung* [klʌŋ]*)* ①粘住；缠住，绕住，抱住 *(to)*. ②沿(岸)前进，贴着(墙)走 *(to)*. ③依恋(朋友等)；依靠，依附；赖住，守牢(家庭)；抱定(希望)；坚信，坚持，墨守 *(to)*. ~ ***like grim death to*** 死抱住…不放. ~ ***to the last hope*** 抱定最后希望，决不灰心. ~ ***to the peak***【美棒球】保持联赛中的最高地位. ~**ing garments** 紧身衣. ~**ing vine**〔美俚〕惯于依靠男人的妇女.

cling·fish [ˈkliŋˌfiʃ] *n.* *(pl.* ~*,* ~*es)*【动】腹印鱼目 *(Xenopterygii)* 的鱼.

cling·stone [ˈkliŋstəun] *n.* (果肉与核分离不开的)粘核桃.

cling·y [ˈkliŋi] *a.*〔罕〕粘住的，紧贴的.

clin·ic [ˈklinik] *n.* ①临床讲授；临床实习课. ②诊所；门诊部. ③特殊病例分析；会诊.

clin·i·cal [ˈklinikəl] *a.* ①临床(讲授)的；病房(用)的；诊所的. ②(态度等)冷静的，慎重的. ~ **lectures** 临床讲义. ~ **medicine** 临床医学. ~ **thermometer** 体温表. **-ly** *ad.*

cli·ni·cian [kliˈniʃən] *n.* 临诊医师，门诊医师〔心理学家〕.

cli·nique [kliˈniːk] *n.*〔F.〕临床讲义.

clink[1] [kliŋk] *vi., vt.* ①(使)丁当地响. ②〔诗〕(使)押韵. ③〔英方〕痛打. ~ *one's money in one's pocket* 使钱在口袋里丁当丁当地响. ~ *glasses* (干杯时)丁当碰杯. ~ ***down [off]***〔英方〕急忙走开. — *n.* ①丁当声. ②〔Scot.〕〔俚〕硬币，现金. ③〔方〕瞬间. ④〔俚〕猛击；搬弄是非. ⑤音韵. ⑥【冶】裂缝.

clink[2] [kliŋk] *n.*〔英口〕监狱. ***be in*** ~ 在坐牢.

clink·er[1] [ˈkliŋkə] *n.* ①炼砖，缸砖，硬砖. ②【冶】渣块，烧结块，铁渣；煤渣. ③〔美俚〕饼干. ④〔*pl.*〕〔美俚〕硬币；现金；系囚犯的铁链. ⑤〔俚〕大错；大失败. ⑥【拳】猛击. ~*-free cement* 无熟料水泥. — *vt., vi.* (使)矿石〔煤等〕(在燃烧中)结成硬块，炼渣.

clink·er[2] [ˈkliŋkə] *n.*〔英俚〕上等品，极好的东西. *a regular* ~ 上等品；妙人.

clink·er-built [ˈkliŋkəˌbilt] *a.*【船】重迭搭造的，鳞状搭造的〔指木船言，铁船用 lap-jointed〕.

clink·ing [ˈkliŋkiŋ] *a.* ①丁当丁当响的. ②〔英俚〕无比的，无上的，极好的. — *ad.*〔英俚〕很，极. *a* ~ *fine day* 天气极好的日子.

clink·stone [ˈkliŋkˌstəun] *n.*【矿】响岩.

cli·nom·e·ter [klaiˈnɔmitə] *n.*【机】倾斜仪；测角器；磁倾计. *a gyroscopic* ~【空】陀螺式倾斜仪.

clin·quant [ˈkliŋkənt] *a.*〔古〕金光闪闪的，银光闪闪的；闪亮的. — *n.*〔古〕镀金叶子；(金属)箔，仿金箔.

Clin·ton [ˈklintən] *n.* 克林顿〔姓氏，男子名〕.

clin·to·ni·a [klinˈtəuniə] *n.*【植】七筋菇；〔C-〕七筋姑属.

Cli·o [ˈklaiəu] *n.* ①克莱奥〔女子名〕(Gr. = famous). ②【希神】主管历史，史诗的女神.

clip[1] [klip] *v.* *(clipped* [-t]*; clipped, clipt* [klipt]*)* — *vt.* ①剪去，剪短，修剪；剪取；轧(车票等)；〔美〕剪辑(报纸等). ②删削；削减. ③(拼法、发音等) 省略，缩略；说漏(语音). ④〔美俚〕殴打，痛打. ⑤〔俚〕诈骗(钱财). ~ *sheep* 剪羊毛. ~ *one's hair close* 把头发剪短. — *vi.* ①剪下，剪短；剪辑. ②〔口〕急走，飞跑，快速动作. ~ ***and keep*** (剪下后保存起来)剪贴. ~ ***sb.'s wings*** 剪掉翅膀；使某人活跃不起来，使无能为力. ~ ***one's words***

发音不明，使语尾变浊．***clipped words*** 缩略词〔例如 bus (< omni*bus*), ad (<*ad*vertisement)〕．—*n.* ①剪短,修剪;〔*pl.*〕剪刀,指甲刀．②一剪,(一季或一次的)剪毛量．③〔美俚〕痛打;鞭子的一抽．④〔口〕快速动作,进度,速度．⑤〔美口〕一次，一度．***a ~ on the ear*** 一个耳光．*(a week)* ***at a ~*** 连续(一星期)．***at one ~*** 一次．***go at a good ~*** 飞快地去．**~ joint** 〔美俚〕索价高昂的咖啡馆〔夜总会等〕; 专敲顾客竹杠的场所．**~ sheet** (为剪贴方便而)单面排印的新闻〔通告等〕.

clip[2] [klip] *n.* ①夹子，钳子；纸夹，钢夹；曲别针；可别在衣服上的装饰物．②【军】(机关枪的)弹夹．③【无】接线柱．*a diamond ~* 一枚钻石别针．—*vt., vi.* ①握紧；夹牢；紧紧围住；〔古〕拥抱．②(美式足球中)在(对方球员)身后冲撞〔下绊〕．**~board** 有夹纸装置的书写板．**~-fed** *a.* (子弹)自动上膛的．**~-on** *a.* 用夹子夹上去的.

clip·per ['klipə] *n.* ①剪取人；削取人；〔*pl.*〕大剪刀，剪子．②快速大帆船；快速大飞艇；快马．③【无】削波器，限幅器．④〔俚〕上等品，上好的东西；第一流人物．*a nail-~s* 指甲剪〔刀〕．*the barber's ~s* 理发推子.

clippie ['klipi] *n.* 〔口〕(电车等的)女售票员.

clip·ping ['klipiŋ] *n.* 剪断，剪裁；剪取物；〔美〕(报纸等的)剪辑(=〔英〕cutting)；剪报；(报纸的)杂讯栏；〔*pl.*〕零头衣料．*the hair ~s* 剪下的头发．*~ bureau* 〔美〕报纸、杂志资料供应社；剪报服务社．—*a.* ①剪的．②〔口〕快速的．③〔俚〕头等的，极好的；恰好的．*Come in ~ time.* 来得恰好.

clipt [klipt] clip 的过去式和过去分词.

clique [kli:k] *n.* 派系，集团，帮会；〔美俚〕棒球队．*an academical ~* 学术小系派 —*vi.* 〔口〕结党.

cliquey ['kli:ki] *a.* = cliquy.

cli·quish ['kli:kiʃ] *a.* 有派系成见的，党同伐异的；小集团的．**-ly** *ad.* **-ness** *n.*

cli·quism ['kli:kizəm] *n.* 派系心，派系成见，宗派主义，小集团倾向.

cli·quy ['kli:ki] *a.* 有派系成见的；党同伐异的；小集团主义的.

clis·tog·a·my [klais'tɔgəmi] *n.* = cleistogamy.

cli·tel·lum [klai'teləm] *n. (pl.* ***-la*** [-lə]) 【动】(蚯蚓等的)环带〔生殖带〕.

cli·to·ris ['klaitəris] *n.* 【解】阴核，阴蒂.

Clive [klaiv] *n.* 克莱夫〔姓氏，男子名〕.

clk. = clerk; clock.

clo·a·ca [klou'eikə] *n. (pl.* ***-cae*** [-ki:]) 〔L.〕①下水道，阴沟，暗渠；厕所．②【鸟】泄殖腔.

cloak [klouk] *n.* ①斗篷；大氅〔有时也指有袖子的〕，外套．②覆盖物．③托辞，口实，借口；幌子，伪装．***under a ~ of*** *(snow)* 被(雪)盖着．***under the ~ of*** ①借口，借名，假装 (*under the ~ of charity* 假装慈善)．②在…的掩护下，趁着 (*under the ~ of night* 趁黑)．—*vt.* ①给…披斗篷；给…穿外套．②盖，覆，遮掩，包庇．**~-and-dagger** *a.* ①间谍的，特务的，阴谋活动的．②(作品、作家等描写间谍等)惊险性的．**~-and-suiter** ①服装店；(特指)现成服装店．②〔美〕犹太人.

cloak-room ['kloukru(:)m] *n.* ①(戏院等的)寄物处，衣帽间；〔美〕议员休息室；(车站的)随身物品寄存处．②〔英，婉〕厕所.

clob·ber ['klɔbə] *vt.* 〔美俚〕①连续打击；打破．②彻底打垮.

clo·chard [klɔ'ʃɑ:] *n.* 〔F.〕流浪者，流浪乞丐.

cloche [klouʃ] *n.* 〔F.〕①(圆顶狭边的)钟形女帽．②(防植物霜害的)玻璃罩.

clock[1] [klɔk] *n.* ①钟；挂钟，坐钟，上下班计时计．②〔俚〕记秒表，卡马表；〔美俚〕〔*pl.*〕驾驶仪表，速度表，里程计．③〔英俚〕(人的) 面孔．④〔C-〕【天】时钟座〔星座名〕．⑤【自】(电子计算机的) 时钟脉冲 (器)．*a Dutch ~* (报时发杜鹃鸣声的) 杜鹃钟 (=cuckoo-~)．*an eight-day ~* 八日上一次发条的钟．*a musical ~* 八音钟．*the face of a ~* 钟的字码盘．*What of the ~?* 〔古谑〕= *What o'clock is it?* 现在是几点钟？*wind up the ~* 上(钟的)发条．***around the ~*** = ***round the ~***．***~ calm*** 海面平静如镜．***fight the ~*** 抢时间．***like a ~*** 钟表似地，准确地，按部就班地．***put [set, turn] back the ~*** 把钟拨慢，倒拨；〔喻〕阻碍进步；复古；开倒车；隐瞒年龄；扭转历史车轮．***race the ~*** 争分夺秒．***regulate [set] a ~ by ...*** 根据…对钟．***round the ~*** = ***the ~ round*** 昼夜不停，连续一整天．***set ahead a ~*** 把钟拨快．***when one's ~ strikes*** 临终．***work against the ~*** 抢时间做完．—*vt.* ①为(比赛等)计时；(运动员等)用…时间跑〔游〕完．②(用机械)记录(速度、距离、次数等)．*~ a swimmer* (用跑表)记录游泳选手的成绩．*~ five minutes for the whole distance* 用 5 分钟跑〔游〕完全程．—*vi.* (在自动计时器上) 记下考勤．***~ in [out]*** = ***~ on [off]*** (用钟铃装置自动)鸣报开始〔终止〕时间；(职工用自动记录时钟)记录上班〔下班〕时间．***~ in*** *(an hour)* ***at*** *(the work)* 花(一小时)在(工作上)．**~-hour** 60 分钟一节课．**~maker** (制造、修理时钟的)钟匠．**~ radio** 定时(开动及停止)收音机．**~ watch** 报时表；自鸣钟．**~ watcher** 混工作的人〔老是看钟点盼望下班〕．**-er** *n.* (比赛等的)计时员；交通量计算员.

clock[2] [klɔk] *n.* 袜子跟部〔侧面下方〕的织绣花纹．—*vt.* 织〔绣〕上袜跟部〔侧下方〕花纹.

clock·ing ['klɔkiŋ] *a.* 〔英方〕(母鸡)伏窝孵卵的.

clock·like ['klɔk,laik] *a.* 准确如时钟的；时钟般有规律的.

clock·wise ['klɔkwaiz] *a., ad.* 顺时针方向转动的〔地〕，正转的〔地〕.

clock·work ['klɔkwə:k] *n.* 钟表机构，发条装置．***like ~*** 有规律地；精确地；准确无误地．***with ~ precision*** 简直象机械一样精确地．**~ feed** 发条．**~ toys** 有发条装置的玩具.

clod [klɔd] *n.* ①(土)块，泥块．②〔the ~〕泥土；〔喻〕(相对于灵魂而言的)肉体．③牛肩肉．④【矿】煤层顶底板页岩．⑤老粗，乡下人；呆子，傻瓜．⑥〔英俚〕〔*pl.*〕铜币．*a ~ of earth* 一块土．*break (up) the ~s* 耕地．*this corporeal ~* 肉体．—*vt., vi.* ***(-dd-)*** (向…) 掷土块.

clod·dish ['klɔdiʃ] *a.* ①土块一样的．②土头土脑的，粗鲁的；呆笨的，笨拙的.

clod·dy ['klɔdi] *a.* ①土块多的，土块一样的．②不值钱的．③矮而结实的.

clod·hop·per ['klɔd,hɔpə] *n.* ①〔贬〕乡下佬．②笨人，粗人．③〔*pl.*〕大土鞋〔一种笨重的大鞋子〕.

clod·hop·ping ['klɔd,hɔpiŋ] *a.* 粗鲁的，乡下佬似的.

clod·pate, clod·pole, clod·poll ['klɔdpeit, -pəul] *n.* 笨人，呆子.

clo·fi·brate [klou'faibreit] *n.* 【药】祛脂乙脂，安妥明.

clog [klɔg] *n.* ①阻碍，阻塞；制动器；(系在兽脚上限制其行动的)坠子；枷．②木底鞋；木屐；木屐舞．—*vt.* ①阻碍，妨碍．②塞满，填满(管子、道路等)．—*vi.* ①(油垢等)腻住，粘住；凝成一块．②(容易)阻塞；(心胸)闷塞．③跳木屐舞．**~-dance** 木屐舞〔用鞋底的木块踏出响亮的拍子〕.

clog·gy ['klɔgi] *a.* ①易粘牢的；黏糊糊的．②妨碍的，易阻塞的.

cloi·son·né [klwɑ:'zɔnei] *a.* 〔F.〕景泰蓝(制)的．—*n.* 景泰蓝 (= ~ enamel).

clois·ter ['klɔistə] *n.* ①修道院；修道院生活；隐居地．②(修道院、学校等地的)回廊，走廊．***the ~*** 修道院生活，隐居．—*vt.* ①把…关在修道院里；使出家，使与尘世隔绝．②在…设回廊．**-ed** *a.* ①住在修道院中的，隐居的．②有走廊的.

clois·tral ['klɔistrəl] *a.* ①(关入)修道院的；修道院式的．②隐居的，遁世的；静寂的.

cloke [kləuk] *n.* 〔古〕 = cloak.
clomb [kləum] climb 的过去式和过去分词的古体.
clom·i·phene [ˈkləməfi:n] *n.*【药】克罗密芬〔一种助孕剂〕(= ~ citrate).
clomp [kləmp] *vi.* 以刺耳的脚步声行走; 顿着脚走.
clon(e) [kləun] *n.*【生】纯种细胞,无性系. — *vt.* 把…培养为纯种细胞; 无性繁殖. **clon·al** *a.*【生】无性系的.
clon·ic [ˈklənik] *a.*【医】阵挛(性)的.
clonk [kləŋk] *n.* 〔口〕①沉闷的金属声; 沉重的一击. ②〔俚〕笨蛋. — *vt., vi.* 发出沉闷金属声移动[撞击](= clunk).
clo·nus [ˈkləunəs] *n.*【医】阵挛(性).
cloop [klu:p] *n.* 砰〔拔瓶塞声〕. — *vi.* 发出砰声.
clop [kləp] *n.* (兽蹄声似的)得得响. — *vi.* ***(-pp-)*** 作得得响,发出脚步声[蹄声].
clo·qué [kləuˈkei] *n.* 泡泡纱(状织物).
close[1] [kləuz] *vt.* ①关(窗等),闭(眼等); 盖(盖子等); 锁闭,封闭; 塞,隔绝. ★ 对 door, box, drawer 等,口语较常用 shut. ②完结; 结束; 停闭. ③讲好(价钱等),商定(交易等),结清(帐目等). ④【电】接通(电流); 使靠拢,使接近;【海】靠近,逼近(其他船只等);【军】使(队伍)靠紧. *His eyes are ~d.* 他死了. *My mouth is ~d.* 无话可说. *That chapter is ~d.* 话已完结,问题已有结果. *~ a hole* 填穴. *~ a speech* 结束演说. *~ a bargain* 订约,讲好买卖,成交. *~ a discussion* (主席)宣布讨论终结. — *vi.* ①(门等)关上; 闭合; (烟斗)塞住. ②完结, 结束, 散会. ③接近,挨近,靠近, (船)靠岸. ④接战, 格斗, 扭打. ⑤集合. ⑥同意, 与…一致 *(on, upon, with)*. ***~ about [around, round]*** 包围, 围住; 逼近…周围. ***~ sb.'s eye*** 打肿(某人的)眼睛. ***~ accounts*** 结算,清帐. ***~ an account*** (清帐后)停止信用交易,停止赊购. ***~ down*** 〔美〕关掉,封闭; 停止,(电台)停播. ***~ down on*** 限制,禁止; 抓牢,逼迫. ***~ in*** ①围拢,迫近. ②(白天)渐短. ***~ it up*** 靠拢 (*You people ~ it up now!* 大家靠拢一点!) ***~ off*** 结(帐); 隔离; 封锁; 阻塞. ***~ on [upon]*** 围拢,围上来; 隐没; 协议,同意. ***~ one's career [life, days]*** 死. ***~ one's parent's eyes*** 给父母送终. ***~ one's purse to*** 不出钱给…. ***~ out*** 〔美〕处理(物品),抛售; 〔美〕停闭(业务). ***~ over*** 封盖; 淹没. ***~ the door on*** 停止讨论…,对…关门. ***~ the door upon*** 堵塞…的门路,不给与…机会. ***~ the rank [files]*** ①使队伍排紧,使密集. ②(政党等)巩固阵营, 加强团结. ***~ together*** 密集. ***~ up*** ①密集,靠紧. ②(伤)愈合. ③密闭,阻塞; 〔美〕结束. ***~ upon*** (手、指)握紧(某物); (箱子)关着; (夜)渐深,(眼向着某物)渐闭; 死. ***~ upon (the world)*** 死. ***~ with*** ①突击,与…肉搏. ②谈妥; 与…达成协议; 同意,答应. ***have [with] one's eyes ~d*** 看不见; 不肯看; 不管,不理会. — *n.* ①完结,终结,终. ②【乐】终止(法); 结尾复纵线(‖). ③肉搏(战),白刃战. ④(私人的)围地,围场; 围墙内; 学校场院. ⑤〔英方〕(大街通到场院的) 小路. ***bring to a ~*** 结束,弄完. ***~ of the year*** 年底. ***come [draw] to a ~*** 将完,临终. **~-down** *n.* ①(工厂等的)关闭,停歇,封闭. ②(夜幕)降临. ③(电台)停止播音.
close[2] [kləus] *a.* ①关闭着的, 密闭的. ②窄狭的, 局促的; 严密的; 紧密的; 严丝合缝的,吻合的. ③闷气的, 闷热的. ④有限制的,限定的. ⑤不公开的,秘密的. ⑥吝啬的,小气的. ⑦近的,紧贴的,接近的; 亲密的. ⑧密集的,稠密的. ⑨绵密的,精密的,详细的. ⑩危急的,千钧一发的. ⑪差不多相等的; 〔美〕(选举上)势均力敌的. ⑫【语音】闭塞音的. ⑬禁猎的. ⑭沉默的, 嘴紧的. ⑮(钱等)难弄到的. *a ~ lid* 严密的盖子. *a hot ~ day* 闷热的日子. *Money is ~.* 钱紧. *a ~ corporation* (股票不对外公开的) 内股公司. *a ~ crop* 接近根部地割剪. *a ~ combat* 肉搏战. *a ~ district* 〔美〕 竞选激烈的选举区. *a ~ election* 〔美〕势均力敌的选举战. *a ~ game* 势均力敌的比赛. *a ~ friend* 亲密的朋友. *a ~ order [formation]*【军】密集队形. *a ~ copy* 准确的复写[复制品]. *a ~ investigation* 细查. *a ~ translation* 忠实的[准确的] 翻译. *a ~ port* 闸港. *a ~ season* [〔美〕*a closed season*] 禁猎期. —*ad.* ①精密地,细密地,紧密地. ②秘密地. ③接近,密接; 亲密地. ***a ~ call [thing]*** 千钧一发的情况; 侥幸的脱险. ***a ~ shave*** ①剃光头发. ②(差点打中的)危险的子弹; 侥幸的脱险 ***(=a ~ shot)***. ***~ about a matter*** 对一件事情严守秘密. ***be ~ to*** 接近; 不离. ***be ~ with one's money*** 用钱吝啬. ***~ at hand*** 就在眼前; 紧迫. ***~ by*** 近, 旁边. ***(a) ~ call [thing]*** 〔口〕千钧一发; 十分危险的情况. ***~ cut*** 〔美〕近路,间道,捷径. ***~ on (upon)*** 大概,差不多; 紧接着. ***~ quarters*** 狭窄拥挤处; 肉搏战 (*come to ~ quarters* 接战). ***~ to*** 接近于; 在附近. ***cut ... ~*** 接近根部割剪. ***fit ~*** 吻合. ***live ~*** 俭约地过日子. ***in ~ proximity to*** 逼近,贴近; 近似. ***keep ~*** 隐匿着. ***keep (sth.) ~*** 把(东西)收藏着. ***lie ~*** 隐藏着. ***press sb. ~*** 紧逼某人. ***run sb. ~*** (赛跑)几乎赶上,紧紧跟住. ***stand [sit] ~*** 站[坐]拢. **~ breeding** 近亲繁殖. **~ buyer** 专买便宜货的人. = **~-cropped, ~-cut** *a.* (头发等) 剪短的. **~-fisted** *a.* 吝啬的,小气的. **~-fitting** *a.* 紧身的,贴身的. **~-grained** *a.* 木理细密的; 有条不紊的. **~-hauled** *a.*【海】迎风开的, 抢风开的. **~-in** *a.* ①近战的, ②接近(市)中心的. **~-knit** *a.* ①紧紧结合在一起的. ②(论据等) 严谨的. **~-lipped, ~-mouthed** *a.* 嘴紧的. **~ planting** 密植. **~ shot** (电影等的) 近景. **~ stool** 马桶(箱). **~-up**【影】特写; 〔美俚〕精密观察; 详细检查; 详图; 用扩音器播送出来的声音. **-ly** *ad.*
closed [kləuzd] *a.* ①关闭着的,封闭着的; 密闭着的; 保密的. ②〔美〕准备好了的; 定了契约的. ③【语音】闭音节的. ***with ~ door*** 禁止旁听. **~ association**【植】郁闭群丛. **~ book** 未知之事,不可理解的事情. **~ bundle**【生】有限维管束. **~ circuit**【无】闭路式(电视). **~-circuit** *a.* 闭路式的. **~-door** *a.* 绝密的, 不公开的. **~ doorism** 关门主义. **~-end** *a.* 资本额固定的. **~ loop**【无】闭合回路. **~ pipe** 一端封闭的管子. **~ port** 不开放海港. **~ primary** 仅由一个政党的成员参加的预选. **~ rule** (议会禁止对某一议案再提修正案的) 议决规定. **~ sea** 领海 (*opp.* open sea 公海). **~ shop** 不雇用非工会会员的工厂 (*opp.* open shop).
close·ness [ˈkləusnis] *n.* ①密闭,紧密; 狭窄; 闭塞; 闷热. ②接近. ③严密; 精密. ④亲密. ⑤吝啬.
clos·er [ˈkləuzə] *n.* ①关闭者; 闭塞器. ②【建】镶墙边的砖石. *a king [queen] ~*【建】去角[纵剖]砖.
clos·et [ˈkləzit] *n.* ①内室,小间; 议事室,密室. ②〔美〕壁橱; 碗橱; 衣橱. ③盥洗室,厕所; 抽水马桶 (= water ~). *~ consultation* 秘密会议. ***of the ~*** 理论的, 不切实际的. — *vt.* 把…关进小室; 把…引入内室密谈. ***be ~ed with*** 与…密谈. — *a.* ①隐蔽的, 暗藏的, 不公开的. ②闭门造车的, 空谈的. *~ racist* 隐蔽的种族主义者. *~ homosexual [queen, queer]* 隐蔽的搞同性爱者. ***~ play [drama]*** 仅供阅读的剧本,不适宜上演的戏剧. ***~ strategist*** 纸上谈兵的战略家.
clos·ing [ˈkləuziŋ] *n.* ①封闭,停闭; 封闭口;【植】郁闭. ②终结,结尾; 完工. ③(交易等的)谈妥; 结帐; 地产成交会. — *a.* 结尾的,末了的; 闭会的. *a ~ account* 决算. *a ~ address* 闭会词. *a ~ hour* 停止营业的时间; 临终时刻. *the ~ date* 决算日. *the ~ day* 截止日期. *the ~ time* 截止时间; 停止时间. **~ costs** 地产成交价. **~ quotations** 收盘市价.
clos·trid·i·um [kləsˈtridiəm, kləs-] *n.* *(pl.* ***-trid·i·a***[-ə]*)*【生】梭菌(属). **-trid·i·al** *a.*
clo·sure [ˈkləuʒə] *n.* ①关闭,停业; 截止; 末尾,结束; 〔英议会〕终止辩论(=〔美〕cloture). ②闭塞物;【建】隔板; 围墙; 填塞砖;【空】节气门;【数】闭包;【机】锁合;【电】闭合;【地】闭合度. — *vt.* 使结束,使停止辩论.
clot [klət] *n.* ①泥团; (血等的)凝块. ②(人、动物等的)聚

集,群集. ③〔俚〕呆子,笨蛋. —*vi., vt.* (使)凝结;(使)群集,(使)拥塞. *clotted cream* 凝结成块的奶油. *clotted hair* 结成一团的头发. **clotted** *a.* ①凝结的;(头发等)结成一团的;拥塞的. ②〔英口〕纯粹的(*clotted nonsense* 纯粹一派胡言).

cloth [klɔ(:)θ] *n.* *(pl.* ~*s* [klɔ(:)θs] 〔用于 kinds of ~ 之意〕, [klɔ:ðz]〔用于 pieces of ~ 之意〕*)* ①织物,布类,毛织品,呢绒;(一块)布;衣料;(白)桌布;擦布,揩布. ②(职业)制服,(特指)黑色教士服;〔the ~〕牧师,教士. ③【海】帆. ④【剧】布景画布. *American* ~ 彩色防水布,人造革. *Italian* ~ 意大利棉毛呢;黑色直贡呢. *long* ~ 漂白细棉布. ~ *merchant* 呢绒布匹商. ***all*** ~ ***made*** 【海】满帆, 鼓着风. ***bound in*** ~ 布面装订的. ***carry much*** ~ 【海】张大风帆. ~ ***of gold [silver]*** 金[银]线锦. ~ ***of state [estate]*** 宝座背上的饰布. ***cut from the same*** ~ 一路货色,一丘之貉. ***cut one's coat according to one's*** ~ 量入为出,量布裁衣. ***draw the*** ~ (饭后)收拾餐桌. ***have [shake] a*** ~ ***in the wind*** 〔口〕有点醉意;〔转〕穿破烂衣服. ***lay the*** ~ 在餐桌上铺桌布放餐具预备开饭. ***made out of whole*** ~ 凭空捏造. ***out of the whole*** ~ 〔美〕彻头彻尾(瞎说,谎言等). ***remove the*** ~ (饭后)收拾餐桌. ***renounce the*** ~ (修士等)还俗. ~**back** 布面装订的书. ~-**binding** (书的)布面装订,布封面 ~**bound** *a.* 布面装订的. ~-**cap** *a.* 〔英〕布帽的〔指工人及劳动者〕. ~-**eared** *a.* 重听的,听觉不灵的. ~ **ears** 重听,听觉迟钝. ~ **measure** 布尺. ~ **yard** ①布码尺(3 英尺). ②长箭(3 英尺).

clothe [kləuð] *vt.* *(clothed,* 〔古〕 *clad* [klæd]; *clothed, clad)* ①给…穿衣,给…衣服,把衣服穿(在身上);使披上,覆盖上. ②(用语言)表现(思想等). ③使蒙受(耻辱) *(with; in)*. ④赋与…以(权力、特性等). ~ *one's family* 使全家人有衣服穿. *fields* ~*d with trees* 树木蔽野. *be* ~ *with shame* 受辱,蒙耻. *be* ~*d [clad] in rags* 穿着破烂衣裳. *trees* ~*d in fresh leaves [with verdure]* 长满了嫩叶的树木. — *vi.* 穿衣服.

clothes [kləuðz] *n.* ①衣服. ②〔集合词〕被褥. ③(送去洗的)衬衣被单等. *Fine* ~ *make the man.* 马靠鞍装人靠衣裳. ***in long*** ~ 在襁褓中的,幼稚的. ~**bag,** ~-**basket**盛放待洗〔已洗净〕衣物的袋〔篮〕. ~**brush** 衣刷. ~-**horse** 晒衣架; 爱穿时髦服装的人(特指女人). ~**line** 晒衣绳;〔美俚〕爱搬弄是非的人. ~**man** 〔俚〕旧衣商. ~ **moth** (蛀蚀衣服等的)蠹虫. ~**peg,**〔美〕~**pin** (晒衣用的)衣夹. ~ **pole [prop]** 晒衣绳支架. ~**press** 衣橱. ~ **tree** 柱式衣架,衣帽架. ~ **wringer** 衣服绞干器.

cloth·ier [ˈkləuðiə] *n.* ①呢绒布匹商;服装商;织布业者. ②织布工,裁缝.

cloth·ing [ˈkləuðiŋ] *n.* ①〔集合词〕衣服,衣类;被服. ②【海】帆装. ~ **hair** 【动】披毛〔披覆动物全身的毛〕.

Clo·tho [ˈkləuθəu] *n.* 【希神】(命运三女神中)纺生命之线的女神,命运之神.

clot·ty [ˈklɔti] *a.* 易凝固的;多团块的.

clo·ture [ˈkləutʃə] *n.* (美议会) 辩论终结;限期结束辩论. — *vt.* 结束对(问题等的)辩论.

clou [klu:] *n.* 〔F.〕 最令人感兴趣之点;最吸引人的东西[节目,部分];中心思想.

cloud [klaud] *n.* ①云. ②云状尘埃、烟(等);(鸟、虫、飞机等的)大群,大队. ③(水晶等的)雾斑,(镜子等上的)云斑. ④(显出疑惑、不满、悲哀等的)阴郁脸色;遮暗物,阴影. ⑤(编结的质地轻柔的)女围巾. ⑥(名誉等的)污点. *a* ~ *of steam* 雾气. *a* ~ *of dust* 一团尘雾. *a* ~ *of birds* (象云一样的) 一大群鸟. *a* ~ *of arrows* 一阵稠密的乱箭. ***a*** ~ ***of words*** 暧昧话. ***be lost in a*** ~ 烟消云散. ***be lost in the*** ~ 隐入云中. ***blow a*** ~ 〔俚〕抽烟,吞云吐雾. ***cast a*** ~ ***(up)on*** 在…上投下一层暗影. ***Every*** ~ ***has a silver lining.*** 乌云朵朵衬白底,黑夜漫漫有尽头; 任何困难情况都有可盼的希望. ***drop from the*** ~ 从天而降. ***(lose oneself) in the*** ~***s*** ①在云层中; 〔喻〕虚无缥渺. ②(人)空想,呆想,茫然;(事情)不落实,不现实. ***kick the*** ~***s*** 〔俚〕被绞死. ***on a*** ~ 〔俚〕满心欢喜,兴高采烈. ***under a*** ~ ①不得意,失宠,受嫌疑,遭白眼,处困境. ***under*** ~ ***of night*** 趁黑. ***wait till the*** ~***s roll by*** 等乌云散开,等时机到来. —*vt.* ①使乌云密布,使变黑暗. ②在(心)上投下苦恼的[忧愁的]暗影,使心情黯然. ③破坏(名誉),损伤(友谊). *face* ~*ed with anger* 因为生气而面色阴沉. —*vi.* ①云层密布,变黑暗;(镜面等)布满云斑. ②(心)变忧郁,变黯然 *(over, up)*;(脸色)阴沉下来. ~**berry** 【植】野生黄莓. ~-**built** *a.* 云一样的,空想的. ~**burst** 倾盆大雨,暴雨. ~-**capped** *a.* 白云笼罩着的,高耸云霄的. ~ **castle** 空中楼阁,空想,幻梦. ~-**compeller** 云神;〔谑〕吞云吐雾的人,抽烟人. ~ **drift** 浮云,飞云. ~ **chamber** 【物】云室. ~ **hopping** 【空】云中飞行,穿云飞行. ~-**kissing** *a.* 高耸云霄的. ~**land** 云界,云景;幻境,仙境 (= ~-cuckoo). ~ **line** 幸福感,兴高采烈. ~ **nine** 〔俚〕狂喜,幸福状态 (*to be on* ~ *nine* 感到无比幸福). ~ **point** 浊点. ~ **rack** 断云层,浮云. ~**scape** 云景,云的景致;云的图画. ~ **seeding** (人工降雨的)云的催化. ~ **stone** 陨石. ~**world** = ~land. -**less** *a.* 无云的,晴朗的. -**let** *n.* 微云,朵云,片云.

cloud·ed [ˈklaudid] *a.* ①阴云密布的,阴暗的;有暗影的. ②(人) 糊涂的. ③愁容满面的. ④有云状花纹的. *a* ~ *tiger* 云纹老虎.

cloudi·ly [ˈklaudili] *ad.* 云雾迷漫;黯然;朦胧.

cloud·ing [ˈklaudiŋ] ①(染色面的)云状花纹,闷光,无光泽. ②【无】(图象)模糊,云斑.

cloudi·ness [ˈklaudinis] *n.* 朦胧;阴暗;【化】混浊性,(混)浊度.

cloud·y [ˈklaudi] *a.* ①阴天的,阴云密布的. ②云(状)的. ③朦胧的. ④愁容满面的. ⑤受人怀疑[蔑视]的. ⑥(水晶等)带云雾纹的;(酒等)混浊的. — *n.* 多云天.

clough [klʌf] *n.* 〔英方〕深谷;峡谷.

clout [klaut] *n.* ①〔古、方〕补丁;破布,碎布;布片;抹布,揩布. ②婴儿的衣服. ③(射箭的)靶心;(箭的)命中. ④(鞋底的)角铁[铁片];鞋底大头钉(= ~-nail);(防止磨损的)铁掌. ⑤〔口〕(用指关节往头上的)一击,一敲;【美拳】打击;【棒球】击球. ⑥〔美口〕势力,影响力;权势. *a* ~ *king* 击球大王. ***In the*** ~***!*** 命中!着! — *vt.* ①〔古、方〕(用布片等)补;用破布盖上; 用布擦. ②给(鞋跟等)加上铁掌;给(鞋底)钉大头钉. ③〔口〕(用手)猛击,击打,敲打. ~ **nail** 鞋底大头钉. ~-**shoe** 穿粗布鞋的人,农民. ~ **shooting** 远距离射击. -**ed** *a.* 打了补钉[铁掌]的.

clove[1] [kləuv] cleave[1] 的过去式.

clove[2] [kləuv] *n.* 【植】丁香. ~ **hitch** 【海】丁香结,酒瓶结.

clove[3] [kləuv] *n.* 【植】小鳞茎,珠芽.

clove[4] [kləuv] *n.* 〔美〕溪谷,壑,峡;山路.

clo·ven [ˈkləuvn] cleave[1] 的过去分词. — *a.* ①劈开的,裂开的. ②【动】分趾的,偶蹄的. ***show the*** ~ ***hoof [foot]*** 现原形,露马脚〔旧时以为魔鬼的脚象牛羊那样是偶蹄的〕. ~-**hoofed** *a.* ①偶蹄的. ②恶魔的.

clo·ver [ˈkləuvə] *n.* 【植】三叶草,车轴草. *bur* ~ 苜蓿. *Dutch* ~ 白三叶草. *sweet* ~ 草木樨. *white [yellow] sweet* ~ 白花[黄花]草木樨. ***in (the)*** ~ 养尊处优;富裕;飞黄腾达. ***pigs in (the)*** ~ 暴发户.

clo·ver·leaf [ˈkləuvəli:f] *n.* *(pl. -leaves)* 苜蓿叶形立交路口〔公路交叉点的一种天桥设计,便于四面车子畅通无阻〕. — *a.* (公路口等)苜蓿叶形的,立体交叉的.

Clow [kləu] *n.* 克洛〔姓氏〕.

clown [klaun] *n.* ①(马戏团、喜剧等中的) 小丑,丑角. ②乡下佬;笨拙粗鲁的人. ③经常闹笑话的人;好说笑话的人;逗人笑乐的人;可笑的人. ④〔美俚〕村镇警察;小气鬼,守财奴. — *vi.* 扮小丑;闹笑话;说笑话,逗趣.
clown·er·y [ˈklaunəri] *n.* 滑稽;可笑;粗鲁;笨拙.
clown·ish [ˈklauniʃ] *a.* 滑稽的;粗鲁的;笨拙的.
cloy [klɔi] *vt.* ①使过饱,使吃腻(美味等). ②(因享乐等过度而)使(人)腻烦 *(with)*. ~ *the appetite by eating too much food* 因吃油腻过多而倒了胃口. *be ~ed with pleasure* 享乐过度而玩腻了. —*vi.* 过饱,倒胃口,吃腻;玩腻.
cloze [kləuz] *a.*【教】补漏测验法的. ~ **procedure**【教】补漏测验法〔语文教学中,教师在选读一段文字时,有计划地缺漏一些单字,看学生能否补足,以测验学生的语文能力〕.
C.L.R. = Central London Railway〔英〕伦敦中央铁道.
C.L.S.C. = Chautauqua Literary and Scientific Circle.〔美〕肖托夸湖畔文学科学讲习会.
club [klʌb] *n.* ①棍棒;(马球等的)球棒;【生】锤节,(昆虫触角中的)棒,棒状构造〔器官〕. ②俱乐部,夜总会,会,社,(俱乐部等的)会所. ③(纸牌的)梅花;〔*pl.*〕一组梅花牌. *an Alpine* ~ 登山俱乐部. *a compaign* ~〔美〕竞选俱乐部. *Indian ~s* (体操用)健身棒. ***be on the*** ~ 得到互助会的金钱支援. ***Christmas*** ~ 圣诞礼品储金〔每月储蓄一个固定数目,到十二月份付还〕. —*vt.* ①用棍棒打;把(枪等)当棍棒用;使形成棒状物,把(头发等)束集成棍棒状. ②凑集(款项等),贡献(意见等). ③〔主英〕使乱成一团. ~ *a dog to death* 用棍子打死一只狗. ~ *a rifle* 倒拿着枪(当棍子用). — *vi.* ①组成俱乐部,联合 *(together, with)*. ②共摊费用. —*a.* ①俱乐部的. ②客饭性质的〔不自行点菜〕. ~**foot** 畸形足. ~**-footed** *a.* 畸形足的. ~ **hair** 杵状毛. ~**hand** 畸形手. ~**haul** *vt.*【海】弃锚抢风把(船)掉转方向〔避往下风海岸〕. ~**house** 俱乐部会所,运动员更衣室. ~**-land** (伦敦 St. James's 宫附近俱乐部集中的)俱乐部区. ~ **law** 暴力政治. ~**man** 俱乐部会员;〔美〕交际家;〔英〕拿棍棒的人. ~ **moss**【植】石松. ~**room** 俱乐部礼堂〔聚会厅〕. ~ **root**【植】根肿病. ~ **sandwich**〔美〕鸡肉夹心烤面包. ~ **steak** 小牛排. ~**woman** 俱乐部女会员;爱往俱乐部交际的女人.
club·(b)a·ble [ˈklʌbəbl] *a.* 合乎俱乐部会员资格的,爱交际的,善于交际的.
club·bed [klʌbd] *n.* 棒状的〔指畸形的手、植物、果实等〕.
club·by [ˈklʌbi] *a.*〔口〕①亲切近人的,热忱对人的. ②(某些俱乐部)会员资格限制很严的,排他的.
cluck[1] [klʌk] *vi.* ①(母鸡)咯咯地叫. ②(谈话中)发出吸气声. — *n.* ①咯咯的叫声. ②(言谈中的)吸气声,啧啧的赞叹声.
cluck[2] [klʌk] *n.*〔俚〕傻瓜,糊涂虫.
clue [klu:] *n.* (调查、研究等的)线索;迹象;(故事的)关键情节;〔罕〕= clew. *give a* ~提供线索. —*vt.* 为…提供线索;提示.
clum·ber [ˈklʌmbə] *n.*〔或 C-〕矮脚长耳猎犬.
clump [klʌmp] *n.* ①丛,薮; 树丛; 密集的大群人〔建筑物〕. ②沉重的脚步声; 加厚(皮)鞋底;根基. ③(土、细菌等的)凝集硬块;一团;一块. *~s of Frenchmen* 一大群法国人. — *vt.* ①把…栽成一丛;使成群;使结块〔结团〕. ②给(靴子)加厚鞋底. — *vi.* ①用沉重的脚步行走. ②丛生;【生】群生;成群;结块〔团〕. ~ **block**【海】强厚滑车. ~ **foot** 畸形足(= club foot). ~ **sole** 特厚鞋底.
clump·y [ˈklʌmpi] *a.* 凝块的;多树丛的;笨重的.
clum·si·ly [ˈklʌmzili] *ad.* 笨拙,粗陋;粗俗.
clum·sy [ˈklʌmzi] *a.* ①(手脚)笨拙的. ②愚笨的,不圆滑的. ③制作粗陋的;(文体等)臃肿的. **clum·si·ness** *n.*
clunch [klʌntʃ] *n.*【地】硬化粘土,耐火粘土;硬质白垩.
clung [klʌŋ] cling 的过去式及过去分词.
clunk [klʌŋk] *n.* = clonk.
clunk·er [ˈklʌŋkə] *n.*〔俚〕年久失修的机器〔尤指噪音很大的破旧汽车〕.
clu·pe·id [ˈklu:pi:id] *n.*【动】鲱科鱼. — *a.* 鲱科的.
clu·pe·oid [ˈklʌpiɔid] *a.*【动】青鱼科鱼的; 青鱼科状鱼的. — *n.* 青鱼科鱼.
clus·ter [ˈklʌstə] *n.* ①丛集,一丛;(葡萄等的)串,挂;(花)团;(秧)蔸;组. ②(蜂、人等的)丛,群,群集. ③【物】聚集,组件;【化】类族,基;(原子)团;【天】星团. ④【美军】(表示又一个同等勋章的)金属片. ⑤【语音】音丛,音群,义丛,词组. ⑥集中建筑群〔在一大片土地上集中兴建住宅,以提供较大的公共休息场所〕. ***in a*** ~ 成串的;成团〔群〕的. — *vi., vt.* (使)成群;(使)群集. *~ed column*【建】簇柱. ~ **bomb unit** 集束炸弹. ~ **college** (文科大学中模仿牛津、剑桥的)独立学院,专科学院. ~ **point**【数】聚点.
clutch[1] [klʌtʃ] *vt., vi.* 抓,抓住,攫住;握紧. ***at a straw*** (危急时)捞稻草;急不暇择;急来抱佛脚; ~ ***the gunny***〔美〕不及格. — *n.* ①(一把)抓住;〔常 *pl.*〕掌握;(抓牢不放的)手,魔掌,毒手. ②【海】有叉支柱;〔*pl.*〕(鹰等的)爪;【机】离合器(踏板). ③(女用)没有提梁的手提包〔由于需用手抓住〕. ④〔美口〕(体育比赛中的)紧要关头. *be in sb.'s ~es* 在某人掌握之下. *fall [get] into the ~es of* 遭…毒手,被…抓牢. *get out of the ~es of* 逃脱…魔掌. ***in the ~es*** 在紧急关头. ***within*** ~ 在抓得到的地方,在伸手可及之处. ~ **coupling**【机】离合联轴节. ~ **pedal**【汽车】离合器踏板.
clutch[2] [klʌtʃ] *n.* 一次孵的蛋; 一窝雏; 一捆(书等),一组(人等). *a whole ~ of chorus girls* 整整一队女子合唱团团员.
clut·ter [ˈklʌtə] *n.* ①〔方〕喧嚣. ②混乱,(房屋等)拥挤杂乱的一团. — *vt.* 〔英方,美〕弄乱,搅乱;乱七八糟地堆满*(up, with)*. — *vi.* 〔方〕喧闹,吵吵闹闹地跑 *(along)*.
Clyde [klaid] *n.* 克莱德〔姓氏,男子名〕.
Clydes·dale [ˈklaidzdeil] *n., a.* 强健的拖车马(的)〔源出苏格兰 Clyde 地方所产名马〕.
clyp·e·ate [ˈklipieit] *a.*【生】①盾形的. ②有唇基的,有盾状甲片的(= clypeated).
clyp·e·us [ˈklipiəs] *n.* *(pl.* ***clyp·e·i*** [ˈklipiai]*)* (古代的)圆盾;(昆虫的)盾部,额板,唇基.
clys·ter [ˈklistə] *n.* 〔罕〕【医】灌肠(剂),灌肠法. — *vt.* 给…灌肠.
Cm = 【化】curium 锔.
cm. = centimetre.
C.M., c.m. = ① common metre〔诗〕普通韵律. ② corresponding member (学会、协会的)通讯会员. ③ Church Missionary 教会传教士. ④ Court-Martial 军事法庭. ⑤ circular mil 圆密耳(直径为密耳数的金属丝面积单位). ⑥ centre of mass 质量中心.
CM = Command Module 指挥舱,指令舱.
C.M.A. = Circulation Managers' Association.〔美〕发行经理协会.
C.M.B. = coastal motorboat 沿海摩托艇.
CMEA,C.M.E.A. = Council for Mutual Economic Assistance [Aid] 经济互助委员会〔简称"经互会"〕.
cml. = chemical; commercial.
cmm. = centimillimetre(s).
C'mon [kmɔn] *int.* 来吧 (= Come on)!
CMP = cytidine monophosphate【化】一磷酸胞苷,胞苷酸.
cmpd = compound【化】化合物;化合.
C.M.S. = ① centre-of-mass system【物】质心系统. ② Church Missionary Society 教会传教士协会.
C.M.T.C. = Citizens' Military Training Camps〔美〕国民军事训练营.
CNO = Chief of Naval Operations〔美〕海军作战部部长.
C-note [ˈsi:nəut] *n.*〔美俚〕百元钞票.
C.O. = ① cash order 现金票据;现金订货单. ② Colonial Office;〔英旧〕殖民部. ③ Commanding Officer 指挥官.

Co = ① cobalt【化】钴. ② concentration 浓度;浓缩;【矿】富集,选矿.

Co., co. = ① company. ② county.

C.O., CO = ① Colonial Office〔英〕殖民部. ②commanding officer 指挥官. ③ conscientious objector (为了道德或宗教上的原因)拒服兵役者.

c/o, c.o. = ① care of 由…转交. ② carried over (簿记用语)转入.

co- *pref.* ①与,共同,共通,相互:*co*heir. ②辅,陪;【数、天】余,补(= complement):*co*sine. ③副:*co*-flyer.

co·ac·er·vate [kəuˈæsəveit] *n.*【化】凝聚层.

co·ac·er·va·tion [kəuˌæsəˈveiʃən] *n.* 凝聚.

coach [kəutʃ] *n.* ①轿式马车;(四马拉)公共马车,驿车. ②【铁路】客车(=〔美〕day ~);〔美〕卧车. ③(四门)轿式汽车,(长途)公共汽车. ④私人教师,家庭教师;辅导员;【体】教练. ⑤【海】(军舰顶层后甲板下面的) 舰长专舱. ⑥【美,棒球】= coacher. ⑦汽车拉的活动房屋. ⑧客机二等舱. ***a slow*** ~ 动作[头脑]迟钝的人,落后分子. ***drive a ~-and-four through a new law [an Act of Parliament]*** 明目张胆地钻新法案的空子,设法使新法案无效. — *vt.* ①用马车运送. ②教,指导,辅导;教练,训练(应考生、运动员等). — *vi.* ①坐马车旅行. ②准备应考. ③受训练[辅导]. ④作指导[辅导,教练]. **~-built** *a.* (汽车车身) 木制的. **~-and-four [-six]** 四[六]马拉大马车. ~ **box** (马车)驾驶人座位. ~ **dog** 看车狗. ~ **fellow** (同拉一车的)马伴儿;伴侣,伙伴. ~ **house** 马车房. **~man** ①马车夫. ②(钓鱼用的)假蝇钩. **~whip** ①马鞭. ②马鞭蛇. **~work** 汽车车身的设计、制造和装配.

coach·ee[1] [kəuˈtʃiː] *n.* (马车)车夫.

coach·ee[2] [kəuˈtʃiː] *n.* 受指导[训练]的人.

coach·er [ˈkəutʃə] *n.* ①辅导员;教练. ②〔美〕(公共)马车. ③【棒球】跑垒及击球指挥员.

co·act [kəuˈækt] *vi.* 协作,协力.

co·ac·tion[1] [kəuˈækʃən] *n.* 强制;强迫. **-ac·tive** *a.*

co·ac·tion[2] [kəuˈækʃən] *n.* ①协力. ②【生态】相互作用.

co·ac·ti·vat·ed [kəuˈæktiveitid] *a.*【化】共激活的.

co·ac·ti·va·tor [kəuˈæktiveitə] *n.*【化】共激活剂,共活化剂.

coad. = coadjutor.

co·ad·ja·cent [ˌkəuəˈdʒeisnt] *a.* 互相邻接的,毗邻的;(思想)接近的.

co·ad·ju·tant [kəuˈædʒutənt] *a.* 相助的;互补的,互助的. — *n.* 协力者,合作者,帮手.

co·ad·ju·tor [kəuˈædʒutə] *n.* 助手;【宗】副主教.

co·ad·u·nate [kəuˈædjunit] *a.* 连结的,接合的. ②【植】叶茎连生的.

co·a·gent [kəuˈeidʒənt] *n.* 帮手,伙伴;合作[协助]因素.

co·ag·u·la·ble [kəuˈægjuːləbl] *a.* 能凝结的. **-bil·i·ty** *n.* 可凝结性.

co·ag·u·lant [kəuˈægjulənt] *n.*【化】凝结剂.

co·ag·u·lase [kəuˈægjuːleis] *n.*【生化】凝固酶.

co·ag·u·late [kəuˈægjuleit] *vt., vi.* (使)凝结;(使)成一体. — *a.* 凝结的.

co·ag·u·la·tion [kəuˌægjuˈleiʃən] *n.* 凝固(作用);凝结物.

co·ag·u·la·tive [kəuˌægjuˈleitiv] *a.* (引起)凝结的.

co·ag·u·la·tor [kəuˌægjuˈleitə] *n.*【化】凝结器[剂].

co·ag·u·lum [kəuˈægjuləm] *n.* *(pl. -la* [-lə]*)* 凝结物;凝(结)块.

coal [kəul] *n.* ①煤; 煤块, 煤堆. ②〔*pl.*〕〔美〕(一堆)烧红的煤. ③〔常 *pl.*〕〔英〕(几块)供燃烧的煤. ④木炭. *broken* ~ 碎煤. *brown* ~ 褐煤. *craw [crow]* ~ 劣煤. *hard* ~〔美〕无烟煤,硬煤. *small* ~ 煤屑. *soft* ~〔美〕烟煤. *white* ~ (发电用的)水力. *a live* ~ 通红的火炭. ***a cold ~ to blow at*** 无成功希望的工作. ***blow hot ~s*** 暴怒. ***blow the ~s*** 嗾使,唆使,挑唆,煽动. ***call [haul] over the ~s*** 申斥,谴责. ***carry [bear] ~s*** 做低三下四的工作; 甘受屈辱 (*Gregory, on my word, we'll not carry ~s.* 格列高里,我们绝对不能忍辱受屈呀). ***carry [send] ~s to Newcastle*** 多余的举动,徒劳无益〔Newcastle 是产煤地〕. ***heap [cast, gather] ~s of fire on sb.'s head*** 使某人痛苦[惭愧]难当. ***stir ~s*** 挑拨(是非). ***take in*** ~ 上煤(到船内). ***take [rake, drag] over the ~s*** = call over the ~s. — *vt., vi.* ①(给…)上煤,(给…)加煤. ②(把…)烧成炭. ~ **bed** 煤层. **~-black** *a.* 漆黑. ~ **box** 煤箱;〔军俚〕发黑烟的炸弹. ~ **breaker** = ~ cracker. ~ **bunker** 煤舱. ~ **capacity** 载煤量. ~ **cellar** 地下煤库. ~ **cracker** 碎煤机. ~ **cutter** 采[截]煤机. ~ **cutting** 采[截]煤. ~ **drop** 卸煤机. ~ **dust** 煤粉. ~ **endurance** 续航力. ~ **face** 采煤工作面. ~ **factor** 煤商. **~field** 煤田,产煤区. **~fish**【鱼】黑鳕,军曹鱼. ~ **gas** 煤气. ~ **hatch** (船的)上煤口. **~heaver** 上[卸]煤工人;运煤工人. **~hole** (地下)煤库; 地下煤库通到街上的洞穴. **~ing station** 装煤港[站]. **~master** 煤矿主. ~ **measures**【地】煤系. ~ **mine** 煤矿. ~ **miner** 煤矿工人. **~mouse** = **~tit**. ~ **oil** 石油,原油;煤油. ~ **pit** 煤矿坑,竖井;〔美〕炭窑. **~sack** 装煤麻袋;【天】煤袋〔银河中靠近南十字座的黑斑〕. ~ **plant** 煤中所含的树木化石 ~ **screen** 煤筛. ~ **scuttle** 煤篓;(舷侧)上煤口. ~ **seam** 煤层. ~ **series**【地】煤系. **C- State**〔美〕煤州〔Pennsylvania 州的别名〕. ~ **tar** 煤焦油. **~tit**【鸟】四十雀. ~ **vase** = ~ **scuttle.** **~-whipper** 卸煤工人;卸煤机.

coal·er [ˈkəulə] *n.* ①煤船;煤车;运煤铁路. ②〔*pl.*〕〔美〕运煤铁路股票;煤炭搬运工人;煤商.

co·a·lesce [ˌkəuəˈles] *vi.* ①(断骨等)接合;(创口等)愈合,合口. ②结合;(政党等)合并,联合;合作.

co·a·les·cence [ˌkəuəˈlesns] *n.* 接合;结合;合并,联合;愈合;【化】聚结. **-les·cent** *a.*

coal·i·fi·ca·tion [ˌkəulifiˈkeiʃən] *n.*【矿】煤化(作用).

coal·ing [ˈkəuliŋ] *n.* 装煤,上煤. **~base, ~place, ~-station** 供煤港;(供)煤站.

Coal·ite [ˈkəulait] *n.*【商标】固来特煤〔一种无烟燃料〕.

co·a·li·tion [ˌkəuəˈliʃən] *n.* 结合,合并;(政党等的)联合,联盟. ~ **cabinet [ministry]** 联合内阁. ~ **government** 联合政府.

co·a·li·tion·ist [ˌkəuəˈliʃənist] *n.* ①(政治上主张)联合论者. ②参加联盟者.

coal·y [ˈkəuli] *a.* 多煤的;煤质的;煤(状)的;墨黑的.

coam·ing [ˈkəumiŋ] *n.*〔*pl.*〕档水围栏;井栏;【船】舱口栏板[围板].

co·apt [kəuˈæpt] *vt.* 使(骨头等)接合,接(骨),使接牢.

co·ap·ta·tion [ˌkəuæpˈteiʃən] *n.* 接合;【医】接骨术.

co·arc·tate [kəuˈɑːkteit] *a.*【生】①狭缩的,缩窄的. ②(某些虫蛹的)密闭于最后一层蛹皮内的. **-ta·tion** *n.*

coarse [kɔːs] *a.* ①粗糙的;粗劣的,粗制滥造的,下等的. ②粗鄙的,粗俗的,粗暴的,下流的;猥亵的,(言语等)鄙俗的. ~ *fare* 粗食. ~ *fish* 杂鱼. ~ **counts**【纺】(纱的)粗支(数),低支(数). **~-fibred** *a.* 粗纤维的;〔喻〕粗鲁的. **~-grained** *a.* ①粗粒的;木理粗糙的. ②粗鲁不文的. **-ly** *ad.* **-ness** *n.*

coars·en [ˈkɔːsn] *vt., vi.* (使)变粗糙.

coast [kəust] *n.* ①海岸;海滨. ②〔美〕(雪橇等的)滑下,下坡;【空】滑翔,惯性飞行. ③〔古〕边疆. ④(吸毒者等过瘾后的)飘然状态. ***Clear the ~!***〔俚〕躲开! 让开! ***off the*** ~ 在海面上. ***on the*** ~ 在岸上,沿岸. ***skirt the*** ~ 沿海岸航行;谨慎行事. ***the C-***〔美〕太平洋沿岸;太平洋沿岸各州. ***The ~ is clear.***〔走私黑话〕道路通畅,无问题,时机正好! — *vi.* ①沿岸航行[旅行]. ②(由坡上)滑(行)下(去),溜下. ③(人)一帆风顺. ④(吸毒者等)飘飘然. ~ **home**〔美〕轻易得胜. ~ **in**〔美〕

轻易夺得锦标. ~ **artillery** 海岸炮(兵). ~ **defence ship** 海防舰. ~ **guard** 水上警察;〔英〕海岸警备队;〔C- G-〕〔美〕海岸救难〔缉私〕警备队(队员). ~-**guard(s)man** 沿岸警备队队员. ~-**land** 沿海地带. ~**line** 海岸线. ~ **pilot** 〔美〕(政府出版的)沿岸航海指南. ~ **waiter** 海关沿岸检查员. ~**ward** *ad., a.* ~-**wards** *ad.* 朝着[向着]海岸. ~**wise** ① *a.* 近海(岸)的,沿岸的. ② *ad.* 顺着海岸,沿岸;靠近海岸.

coast·al [ˈkəustl] *a.* 沿海的,临海的;沿岸的. — *n.*〔英〕海防飞机. **C- Command** 空军海防总队. **C- Eastern** 〔美〕美国东部大西洋沿岸使用的美国英语. ~ **plain** 滨海平原. ~ **waiter** 〔英〕= coast waiter.

coast·er [ˈkəustə] *n.* ①沿岸贸易[航行]者;沿岸贸易船[航船];沿海居民. ②(餐桌上放酒瓶的带轮)银盆;(杯盘等的)垫子. ③(儿童的)滑板,橇;滑翔机;滑行者;【军】惯性滑翔导弹. ④(自行车的)前叉放脚处. ~**brake** (自行车的)倒轮闸,脚煞车.

coast·ing [ˈkəustiŋ] *n.* ①沿岸航行,沿岸贸易;(雪橇等的)滑降游戏;海岸线. ②【机】惰转;惰行. ~ **flight** 【空】惯性飞行;滑翔飞行. ~ **lead** 【海】(120—360 英尺水深的)滨海测锤.

coat [kəut] *n.* ①上衣;外衣,外套. ★ 厚大衣叫 over*coat*,〔英〕great*coat*. ②(女人、孩童的)短大衣. ③锁子甲. ④(动物的)毛皮,被覆;(植物的)表皮. ⑤(漆等的)涂层;【解】外膜,膜. ⑥〔*pl.*〕〔古〕裙子. *first (floating; setting)* ~ (漆等的)头(二、三)道. ~*s of the stomach* 胃膜. ~ *of mail* 锁子甲. ***black*** ~ 牧师,教士. ***change one's*** ~ 变节;改变立场. ~ ***and skirt*** 妇人外出服装. ~ ***of arms*** 战袍;(代表某一个人,家族,团体等的)盾形纹章. ***dust [smoke] sb.'s*** ~ ***(for him)*** 殴打某人. ***in*** ~ ***and skirt*** (妇女)穿着出门的衣服. ***lace sb.'s*** ~ 鞭打某人. ***pick a hole in sb.'s*** ~ 找人短处[错儿]. ***take off one's*** ~ 脱掉上衣(预备打架或使劲干). ***The*** ~ ***fits.*** 衣服合身;说[想]对了. ***trail one's*** ~ 故意地找碴子争吵,挑衅. ***turn one's*** ~ 变节;改变立场. ***wear the king's [queen's]*** ~ 〔英〕服兵役,当兵. — *vt.* ①给…穿上上衣[外套]. ②包上,涂上,盖上. *be* ~*ed with* 用…包上[涂上、蒙上]. ~*ed paper* 铜板纸,上浆纸. *a* ~*ed tape* 涂粉磁带. ***My tongue is*** ~***ed.*** 长舌苔了. ~-**armo(u)r** 铠甲上穿的外衣;纹章,家徽. ~**card** (纸牌中)有人像的牌,花牌. ~ **hanger** 衣架. ~ **holder** 给(争斗者、竞技人等)拿上衣的人,旁观者. ~**room** 衣帽间. ~**rack** 衣帽架.

coat·tail [ˈkəutteil] *n.* ①男上衣后摆;男子燕尾服的尾;〔*pl.*〕女子长外衣的下摆. ②〔*pl.*〕〔美口〕(可提携声望较差的候选人的)政治威信,政治影响. ***ride on sb.'s*** ~***s*** 依靠别人的声望荣升(指政治方面),附骥尾. ***trail sb.'s*** ~***s*** 向(某人)挑衅,招惹(某人).

coat·ee [ˈkəuti:, kəuˈti:] *n.* 紧身短上衣.

co·a·ti [kəuˈɑ:ti] *n.*【动】(美洲产)长吻浣熊(= ~-mundi, ~-mondi).

co·au·thor [kəuˈɔ:θə] *n.* 合著者,合作者,共同研究者.

coat·ing [ˈkəutiŋ] *n.* ①被覆,表皮,涂层;包覆物;(食品上的)面衣,糖衣;涂料. ②上衣料;细呢,花呢.

coax [kəuks] *vt.* ①用好话劝诱;哄. ②巧妙地[用心地]处理,轻轻地弄好. ~ *sb. to do [into doing]* 哄某人去做…. ~ *a fire to burn* 轻轻把火拨燃. — *vi.* 哄骗. ~ *and plead* 又哄又劝. ~ *round* (用好话)搪塞,哄骗. — *n.* 〔俚〕①油嘴滑舌的人. ②花言巧语. ③同轴电缆(= coaxial cable). -**ing** *n., a.* 哄骗(的).

co·ax·al, co·ax·i·al [kəuˈæksəl, -iəl] *a.*【数】同轴的,共轴的. ~ **cable** 同轴电缆.

cob[1] [kɔb] *n.* ①(面包等的)小圆块;〔常 *pl.*〕(煤、石头、矿石等的)圆块,一小堆. ②〔美〕玉米的穗轴(= corncob). ③雄天鹅(= ~-swan). ④结实的短脚马. ⑤〔英口〕蜘蛛. ⑥大榛子,欧洲榛(= cobnut). ⑦〔英方〕要人. ~ **coal** 圆煤块. ~ **house** 土墙房子. ~**loaf** 圆面包.

cob[2] [kɔb] *n.* (掺有干草的)抹墙泥.

cob[3] [kɔb] *vt.* *(-bb-)* ①打碎,捣碎. ②(用扁物)打(臀部).

co·bal·a·min [kəuˈbɔləmin] *n.*【生化】钴胺素,维生素 B_{12}.

co·balt [kəˈbɔ:lt, ˈkəubɔ:lt] *n.* ①【化】钴. ②钴类颜料. ③深蓝色. ~ **blue** 钴蓝,深蓝. ~ **bomb** 钴弹. ~ **green** 钴绿. ~ **yellow** 钴黄.

co·bal·tic [kəuˈbɔ:ltik] *a.*【化】(三价)钴的,含钴的.

co·balt·ite cobalt·ine [kəuˈbɔ:ltait, -in] *n.*【矿】辉砷钴矿.

co·bal·tous [kəuˈbɔ:ltəs] *a.*【化】(正)钴的;二价钴的. ~ **sulphate** 硫酸钴.

cob·ber [ˈkɔbə] *n.*〔澳俚〕(男)朋友,伙伴.

cob·bies [ˈkɔbiz] *n.*〔*pl.*〕一种镶有楔形后跟的女式平底鞋.〔又名 wedgies〕.

cob·ble[1] [ˈkɔbl] *n.* ①鹅卵石;【地】中砾. ②〔*pl.*〕卵石路;〔*pl.*〕圆煤块. — *vt.* 在…铺鹅卵石.

cob·ble[2] [ˈkɔbl] *vt.* ①修补(鞋). ②马虎地修补*(up)*. ③粗制滥造 *(up)*. — *n.*〔俚〕粗制滥造的物品.

cob·bler [ˈkɔblə] *n.* ①补鞋匠,皮匠. ★ 现通用 shoemaker. ②手艺笨拙的工匠. ③〔美〕果馅饼. ④冰杜松子酒柠檬水. ⑤〔*pl.*〕〔英〕愚蠢而不诚恳的话;胡说. ~**'s wax** 鞋线蜡.

cob·bler·y [ˈkɔbləri] *n.*〔美〕补鞋店.

cob·ble·stone [ˈkɔblstəun] *n.* 圆石,鹅卵石.

cob·bly [ˈkɔbli] *a.* 用大鹅卵石铺的;崎岖的.

cob·by [ˈkɔbi] *a.* ①象结实的矮脚马似的. ②〔英方〕活跃的;执拗的.

Cob·den [ˈkɔbden] *n.* ①科布登〔姓氏〕. ② **Richard** ~ 李查·科布登〔1804—65英国工业家,商人,经济学家,政治家〕. -**ism** *n.* 科布登主义,自由贸易主义. -**ite** *n.* 科布登主义[自由贸易主义]信徒.

co·bel·lig·er·ent [ˌkəubiˈlidʒərənt] *n.* 共同参战国[参战者];友邦.

Cob·ham [ˈkɔbəm] *n.* 科伯姆〔姓氏〕.

co·bi·a [ˈkəubiə] *n.* 【动】军曹鱼*(Rachycentron canadus)*.

co·ble, cob·ble [ˈkəubl] *n.* ①(英国东北部的)一种小渔船. ②(苏格兰的)一种平底渔船.

cob·nut [ˈkɔbnʌt] *n.* ①大榛子,欧洲榛. ②碰榛子游戏〔以线端所系榛子互相碰击的游戏〕.

COBOL [ˈkəubəul] *n.* 【计】通常事务语言〔*co*mmon *b*usiness *o*riented *l*anguage〕.

co·bra[1] [ˈkəubrə] *n.*【动】眼镜蛇,毒帽蛇.

co·bra[2] [ˈkəubrə] *n.*〔澳〕头;头盖骨.

cob·web [ˈkɔbweb] *n.* ①蜘蛛网,蛛丝. ②蛛网状的薄织物[纱帕等]. ③(蛛网一样)易破的东西. ④〔*pl.*〕薄弱的推论;混乱的思想;混乱,陈腐,暧昧. ~*s of the law* 陈腐的法律. ***blow [clear] away the*** ~***s from one's brain*** 使头脑清醒一下. ***have a*** ~ ***in the throat*** 口渴. — *vt.* *(-bb-)* 使布满蛛网. ~ **throat** 〔美〕没有喝酒;想喝酒.

cob·web·bed [ˈkɔbwebd] *a.* ①布满蛛网的;蛛网状的. ②〔美〕头脑混乱的.

cob·web·by [ˈkɔbwebbi] *a.* ①蛛网似的;布满蛛网的. ②长久不用的;粘满了灰尘的.

co·ca [ˈkəukə] *n.* 【植】古柯〔南美药用植物〕;古柯叶;古柯叶制剂.

co·ca-co·la, Co·ca-Co·la [ˈkəukəˈkəulə] *n.*〔美〕可口可乐〔一种饮料,商标名〕.

co·caine [kəˈkein] *n.*【药】可卡因,古柯碱.

co·cain·ism [kəˈkeinizəm] *n.*【医】古柯碱瘾;古柯碱中毒.

co·cain·ize [kəˈkeinaiz] *vt.* 用古柯碱麻醉. -**cain·i·za·tion** *n.*

co·car·boxy·lase [ˈkəukɑːˈbɔksileis] *n.*【生化】辅羧酶，羧化辅酶.
cocc-, cocci- *comb. f.* 小球状体，浆果：*cocci*diosis.
coc·ci [ˈkɔksai] *n.* coccus 的复数.
coc·cid [ˈkɔksid] *n.*【动】介壳虫.
coc·cid·i·oi·do·my·co·sis [kɔkˌsidiˌɔidəumaiˈkəusis] *n.*（牲畜的）球孢子虫病.
coc·cid·i·o·sis [kɔkˌsidiˈəusis] *n.*【医】（人体）球虫病.
coc·cif·er·ous [kɔkˈsifərəs] *a.*【植】结浆果的，有浆果的.
cocco- *comb. f.* = cocc-.
coc·co·lith [ˈkɔkəliθ] *n.*【植】颗石藻.
coc·cus [ˈkɔkəs] *n.* *(pl. cocci)* ①【微】球菌. ②【植】（果实的）分果爿.
coc·cyg·eal [kɔkˈsidʒiəl] *a.*【解】尾骨的.
coc·cyx [ˈkɔksiks] *n.* *(pl. coccyges* [kɔkˈsaidʒiːz], *~es)*【解】尾骨.
Co·cha·bam·ba [Sp. ˌkotʃaˈbambə] *n.* 科恰班巴〔玻利维亚城市〕.
Co·chair·man [kəuˈtʃeəmən] *n.* ①联合主席，两主席之一. ②副主席.
Co·chin, co·chin [ˈkəutʃin]【动】（越南的）交趾鸡.
Cochin-China [ˈkɔtʃinˈtʃainə] *n.* ①【史】交趾支那. ②〔cochin-china〕交趾支那鸡.
coch·i·neal [ˈkɔtʃiniːl] *n.* ①【动】胭脂虫. ②（由胭脂虫制成的）虫红，洋红（颜料）.
coch·le·a [ˈkɔkliə] *n.* *(pl. -ae* [-iː], *~s)*【解】（耳）蜗；【植】卷荚.
coch·le·ate, coch·le·ated [ˈkɔkliit, -eit; -eitid] *a.*【动】螺旋状.
cock[1] [kɔk] *n.* ①雄鸡，公鸡. ②雄禽. ★有时与其他动物名连用；表示雄性. ③ 雄螯蝦〔蟹、鲑〕. ④野鹬〔= wood ~〕. ⑤首领，领袖；架子十足的人. ⑥塞子；【机】（水管等的）龙头，开关，旋塞；（活）栓；节气门. ⑦（枪的）击铁，扳机，系机；击铁待发位置，准备击发（状态）. ⑧风标，风信鸡；（日晷、天平等的）指针. ⑨（帽的）卷边；（鼻子的）上翘；（眼梢的）翘起；（帽子等）歪戴，歪着. *a three way* ~ 三通旋塞. *turn the* ~ 开龙头. ***at [on] full [half]*** ~ 把击铁扳上[拨上一半]，处于全[半]击发状态；充分准备[准备未周]. ~ ***of the loft [dunghill]*** 小霸主，土皇帝，地头蛇，自命不凡的头子. ~ ***of the north***【鸟】花鸡. ~ ***of the school*** 学生领袖；（校中）最横行霸道的学生. ~ ***of the walk***〔美〕有威望的头领. ~ ***of the wood***【鸟】（北美产的）一种啄木鸟. ***go off at half-cock*** 操之过急. ***live like fighting ~s***（象斗鸡一样）吃得好，过阔气日子. ***Old ~!***〔昵称〕老兄！***red*** ~ 纵火引起的火灾. ***set (the) ~ on (the) hoop*** 纵饮，放纵. ***That ~ won't fight.*** 那一手行不通，那种话说不过去. — *vt.* ①扳上（枪的）扳机. ②使朝上，使翘起，耸起（耳朵）；（把帽檐翘起）歪戴（帽子）. — *vi.* ①（狗）翘尾巴，翘起，竖起. ②扳上扳机（准备击发）. ③趾高气扬（地走）. ~ ***a snoot (at)*** 不屑一顾，轻视. ***~ed and primed*** 装上弹药和扳起扳机；作好（战斗）准备. ***~ed hat*** 卷边帽；（海军军人等的）三角帽；三柱球戏. ~ ***one's eye at***〔俚〕向上一瞟；使眼色. ~ ***one's nose*** 抬起鼻子〔轻蔑的表情〕. ~ ***up*** 耸起，竖起，翘起；〔学俚〕打板子. **~-and-hen** *a.* 适用于两性的. **~boat**（附设于大船上的）小艇. ~ **chafer**【虫】金龟子. **~crow(ing)** 黎明，清晨. **~-eyed** *a.* 斗鸡眼的；〔俚〕歪在一边的；愚蠢的；可笑的；狂乱的，喝醉的. **~fighting** ① *n.* 斗鸡（戏）(*This beats ~-fighting.* 这有趣极了). ② *a.* 爱斗鸡的. **~horse** ① *n.*（骑在上面可前后摇动的）玩具木马. ② *ad.* 得意地；趾高气扬地. **~pit** 斗鸡场；战场；（戏院的）正厅；（军舰内的）伤兵室；【空】（飞机上的）座舱；船尾座位 (*the ~pit of Europe* 比利时的别号). **~roach**【虫】蟑螂，油虫. ~ **robin** 雄知更鸟；（知更鸟一样）灵巧的矮子. **~shy, ~shot** 掷棒打靶游戏；掷棒戏的靶子，投掷一次. ~ **sparrow** 公麻雀，矮小强悍的人. **~spur**（鸡的）距；【植】稗属植物；【虫】跳蝼蛄. ~ **strut**〔美〕骄傲自大的步态. **~sure** *a.* 确信 *(of; about)*；（事情）一定会发生；一定…*(to do)*；独断的，太自信的 *(of)*. **~swain**〔古〕= coxswain. **~tail** ①*n.* 鸡尾酒；（正菜前用蟹肉，牡蛎肉或水果等做成的）开胃小吃；尾巴切短的马；非纯种的赛马；出身低微的人. ②*a.* 鸡尾酒的 (*a ~ party* 鸡尾酒会. *the ~ hour*〔美〕喝鸡尾酒时间，指下午五时左右)；（女服）在半正式场合穿的. **~tail belt**（经常出席酒会的）上流人士住宅区. **~tailed** *a.* 切短了尾巴的. **~up** ① *a.* 尖儿向上翘起的. ② *n.*【印】（篇首的）特高大写字母；附在字母右肩上的字，〔大写字等〕上角字[码]；〔俚〕一团糟，混乱.
cock[2] [kɔk] *n.*（圆锥状）干草堆；粪堆. — *vt.* 把（干草等）堆成圆锥状小堆.
cock·ade [kɔˈkeid] *n.* ①帽章，帽上的花结. ②〔C-〕〔美〕马里兰 (Maryland) 州的别号.
cock-a-doo·dle-doo [ˈkɔkəduːdlˈduː] *n.* *(pl. ~s)* ①（雄鸡的）喔喔叫声，鸡鸣. ②〔儿〕大公鸡.
cock-a-hoop [ˈkɔkəˈhuːp] *a., ad.* 得意洋洋的[地]；骄傲的[地]. **-ness** *n.*
Cock·aigne, Cock·ayne [kɔˈkein] *n.* ①（幻想中的）安乐乡. ②伦敦的别号〔= the land of C-〕.
cock-a-leek·ie [ˈkɔkəˈliːki] *n.* 韭菜鸡肉汤（= cocky-leeky）.
cock·a·lo·rum [ˌkɔkəˈlɔːrəm] *n.* ①小公鸡；自负不凡的小人物. ②蛙跳游戏（= high ~）. ③大话，吹牛.
cock·a·ma·mie [ˈkɔkəˌmeimiː] *a.*〔美俚〕愚蠢的；荒唐可笑的；质量极差的，劣等的〔表示很不赞许的一般用语〕.
cock-and-bull [ˈkɔkənˈbul] *n.* 荒唐话，无稽之谈. — *a.* 荒唐无稽的.
cock·a·teel, cock·a·tiel [ˌkɔkəˈtiːl] *n.*【动】澳大利亚玄凤〔一种鹦鹉〕*(Nymphicus hollandicus)*.
cock·a·too [ˌkɔkəˈtuː] *n.* ①【动】白鹦. ②〔澳俚〕小农. ③〔俚〕（替盗贼）把风者. *a rose* ~【鸟】红鹦鹉.
cock·a·trice [ˈkɔkətrais] *n.* ①（传说中的）鸡身蛇尾怪；（传说人被它看上一眼即死的）毒蛇. ②妖妇；极恶毒的人.
Cocke [kəuk] *n.* 科克〔姓氏〕.
cocked [kɔkt] *a.* ①翘起的，竖起的. ②（枪）处于准备击发状态的. ~ *hat* 三角帽，两端尖的帽子. ***knock (the plan) into a ~ hat*** 使（计划等）完全失败. ***make a ~ hat of sb.*** 把某人打得一蹶不振.
Cock·er [ˈkɔkə] *n.* 科克尔〔姓氏〕. **Edward** ~ 爱德华·科克尔〔1631—1675，英国有名的数学教师. 著有《算术大全》*(The Complete Arithmetician)*〕. ***acccording to*** ~ 精确的；精确地说.
cock·er[1] [ˈkɔkə] *vt.* 娇养，溺爱，放纵 *(up)*.
cock·er[2] [ˈkɔkə] *n.* 一种矮脚长耳猎犬（= ~ spaniel）.
cock·er[3] [ˈkɔkə] *n.* 斗鸡迷.
cock·er·el [ˈkɔkərəl] *n.*（未满一岁的）小公鸡；血气方刚的青年.
cock·i·ly [ˈkɔkili] *ad.*〔俚〕趾高气扬地，自高自大地.
cock·i·ness [ˈkɔkinis] *n.* 自大；过于自信；趾高气扬.
cock·le[1] [ˈkɔkl] *n.* ①【贝】乌蛤；海扇壳. ②（浅底）小船. ***~s of the heart*** 内心深处，心底的感情 *(delight [warm] the ~s of the heart* 令人深深满意[深感温暖]. **~boat** 轻舟. ~ **hat**（朝香者）以海扇壳装饰的帽子. **~-stair** 螺旋楼梯.
cock·le[2] [ˈkɔkl] *n.*【植】麦仙翁.
cock·le[3] [ˈkɔkl] *n.*（纸张等的）皱折，褶. — *vt., vi.*（使）皱折.
cock·le[4] [ˈkɔkl] *n.* 火炉.
cock·le·bur [ˈkɔklbəː] *n.*【植】苍耳属 *(Xanthium)*.
cock·le·shell [ˈkɔklˌʃel] *n.* ①海扇[乌蛤]壳. ②这类贝壳的通称. ③小艇.

cock·loft [ˈkɔklɔft] *n.* (小)顶楼,阁楼,顶层.
cock·ney [ˈkɔkni] *n.* ①〔亦作 C-〕伦敦佬〔尤指伦敦东区的人〕;伦敦话,伦敦口音〔含轻蔑意〕. ②〔主美〕柔弱的都市人. ③装模作样的女人. ④〔罕〕被宠坏的孩子. — *a.* 〔贬〕①伦敦佬的,伦敦佬气派的. ②伦敦腔的. ~ **accent** 伦敦口音. **-dom** ①〔集合词〕伦敦佬;伦敦佬的脾性. ②伦敦佬居住区;伦敦人居民区的社会. **-fy** *vt.* 使有伦敦佬的派头〔腔调〕. **-ish** *a.* 伦敦佬派头的;带点伦敦腔的. **-ism** 伦敦佬派头,伦敦口音〔语调〕. **-ize** *vt., vi.* (使)有伦敦佬派头;用伦敦语调说话.
cocks·comb [ˈkɔkskəum] *n.* ①鸡冠. ②【植】鸡冠花. ③ 小丑的帽子 (= coxcomb).
cocks·foot [ˈkɔksfut] *n.* 【植】鸭茅.
cock·sy [ˈkɔksi] *a.* 骄傲自大的,趾高气扬的(= coxy).
cock·y [ˈkɔki] *a.* 〔口〕骄傲的,自大的;过分自信的;趾高气扬的. *be* ~ *(at success)* (因为成功而)翘尾巴.
cock·y-leek·y, cock·y-leek·ie [ˈkɔkiˈli:ki] *n.* 〔Scot.〕韭菜鸡肉汤.
cock·y·ol·(l)y bird [ˌkɔkiˈɔli bə:d] 〔儿〕鸟儿〔对小鸟的爱称〕.
co·co [ˈkəukəu] *n.* *(pl.* ~*s* [-z]*)* ①【植】椰子树 (= coconut tree [palm], ~-palm); 椰子. ②〔美俚〕(人的)脑袋. — *a.* 椰子壳纤维制的.
co·coa [ˈkəukəu] *n.* ①可可粉,可可(茶). ②可可树. ③深褐色. ~ **bean** 可可豆. ~ **butter** 可可脂〔药用,化妆用〕. ~**mat** 椰子树片编织物; (置于门口的)席垫. ~ **nibs** 可可豆的子叶. ~ **powder** 一种褐色火药.
co·co(a)·nut [ˈkəukənʌt] *n.* ①椰子(果). ②〔俚〕头,脑袋. ***That accounts for the milk in the*** ~. 〔谑〕啊,原来是这样. ~ **butter** =~ oil. ~ **matting** 椰毛编织的垫子,棕垫. ~ **milk [water]** 椰子汁. ~ **oil** 椰子油〔可食用或制肥皂用〕. ~ **palm [tree]** 椰子树.
co·con·scious [kəuˈkɔnʃəs] *a.* ①意识到同样事物的. ②并(存)意识的. **-ness** 【心】并(存)意识.
co·con·spir·a·tor [ˈkəukənˈspirətə] *n.* 共谋者.
co·coon [kəˈku:n] *n.* ①(蚕)茧;(昆虫的)卵袋,(蚯蚓等的)土房;(蜘蛛等的)子囊. ②茧状物; (军用物品等的)塑料披盖,防护喷层. — *vt.* ①作茧包藏,把…包在茧内. ②以茧状物〔喷层〕包(军用品等). ~ *the patient in blanket* 把病人裹在毯子里. — *vi.* 作茧,成茧状. ~ **shells** 出壳茧. ~ **strippings** 茧皮.
co·coon·e·ry [kəˈku:nəri] *n.* 养蚕场,蚕室.
co·cotte[1] [kəˈkɔt] *n.* 〔F.〕妓女〔尤指(巴黎的)高等娼妓〕;淫妇,作风不正派的女人.
co·cotte[2] [kəˈkɔt] *n.* 砂锅〔饭馆中用来蒸煮原汁菜肴之用〕.
co·co·zel·le [ˌkəukəˈzeli, -ˈzel] *n.* 可可绿皮南瓜〔西葫芦之类〕.
co·crys·tal·li·za·tion [ˈkəuˌkristəlaiˈzeiʃən] *n.* 【物】共结晶.
co·cur·ric·u·lum [ˌkəukəˈrikjuləm] *n.* *(pl.* ***-la*** [-lə]*)* 辅助课程.
cod[1] [kɔd] *n.* *(pl.* ~, ~*s)* 【鱼】鳕 (= ~fish) *the Bank* ~ 纽芬兰鳕. ~**-liver** 鳕肝. ~**-liver oil** 鱼肝油.
cod[2] [kɔd] *n.* ①〔方〕荚,壳,蒴 (= pod); 〔古〕袋,阴囊. ②〔Scot.〕枕头,靠垫.
cod[3] [kɔd] *vt., vi.* 〔俚〕哄骗,愚弄.
cod[4] [kɔd] *a.* 〔英方〕滑稽的,讽刺的.
COD, C.O.D. = ① cash on delivery 货到付款. ② collect on delivery 货到收款. ③ Concise Oxford Dictionary 〔英〕《简明牛津词典》.
co·da [ˈkəudə] *n.* 〔It.〕①【乐】结尾. ②(小说、戏剧等的)结局部分.
cod·ding [ˈkɔdiŋ] *n.* 捕鳕,捕鳕业.
cod·dle [ˈkɔdl] *vt.* ①娇养,溺爱;过分细心地照料. ②用文火煮,嫩煮(鸡蛋等). ~ ***oneself*** 对自己过分娇养. — *n.* 〔口〕娇生惯养的人,身体虚弱的人.
code [kəud] *n.* ①法典;法规. ②规则,准则;(社会、阶级等的)惯例,习俗,制度. ③(电)码,代码,密码,暗码;代号,略号,暗号. ④【生】遗传(密)码. *the civil [criminal]* ~ 民[刑]法典. *the moral* ~ 道德准则. ~ *of signals* 信号密码(本) ~ *of the school* 校规. ~ ***and conventions*** 规章制度. ***C- Napoléon*** [ˈkɔ:d-nəpəuleiˈɔ:ŋ] 拿破仑法典. ***C- of Hammurabi*** (古代巴比伦的)汉穆拉比法典. ~ ***of honour*** 社会礼法;决斗惯例. ~ ***of written law*** 成文法典. ***the International Code*** 国际电码. ***the Morse*** ~ 摩尔斯电码. — *vt.* ①把…编成法典〔法规〕. ②把…译成〔编成〕电码;编(码);译(码). ~ **address** 电报挂号. ~ **book** 电码本,密码本. ~**breaker** 密码译电员. ~ **flag** 信号旗. ~ **machine** 译码机. ~**-message** 密码电信. ~ **name** 代号. ~**switching** 【计】编码系统转换. ~ **translator** 译码机. **-r** *n.* 【自】编码装置;【讯】记发器.
co·dec·li·na·tion [ˌkəuˌdekliˈneiʃən] *n.* 【天】极距 (= polar distance), 赤纬的余角.
co·de·fend·ant [ˈkəudiˈfendent] *n.* 【法】共同被告,株连被告.
co·de·in(e) [ˈkəudi:in] *n.* 【药】可待因(碱).
co·dep·o·si·tion [ˈkəuˌdepəˈziʃən] *n.* 【化, 物】共淀积.
co·det·ta [kəuˈdetə] *n.* 〔It〕【乐】小结尾.
co·dex [ˈkəudeks] *n.* *(pl.* ***codi·ces*** [ˈkəudisi:z, ˈkɔdisi:z]*)* 〔L.〕(圣经等古籍的)抄本. ②〔古〕法典. ③【医】处方书,药典.
cod·fish [ˈkɔdfiʃ] *n.* 【动】鳕, 大头鱼. ~ *aristocracy* 〔美〕捕鳕致富的人,暴发户.
codg·er [ˈkɔdʒə] *n.* 〔口〕怪人,有怪癖的老头子;家伙;〔英方〕吝啬鬼.
cod·i·cil [ˈkɔdisil] *n.* ①【法】遗嘱的附录. ②附注;备考,附录.
cod·i·cil·la·ry [ˌkɔdiˈsiləri] *a.* 附注的;备考的.
cod·i·fi·ca·tion [ˌkɔdifiˈkeiʃən] *n.* 法规汇编.
cod·i·fy [ˈkɔdifai, ˈkəud-] *vt.* ①把…编成法典. ②编纂,整理.
cod·ing [ˈkəudiŋ] *n.* 编码;译成电码.
cod·lin, cod·ling[1] [ˈkɔdlin, -liŋ] *n.* (做菜用的)尖头苹果;未成熟的小苹果.
cod·ling[2] [ˈkɔdliŋ] *n.* 幼鳕.
co·don [ˈkəudən] *n.* 【生】(遗传)密码子.
cod·piece [ˈkɔdˌpi:s] *n.* 十五、十六世纪男子短裤前面所悬的袋状物.
cods·wal·lop [ˈkɔdzˌwɔləp] *n.* 〔英俚〕胡说八道,愚蠢而没有价值的话〔文章〕.
Co·dy [ˈkəudi] *n.* 科迪〔姓氏〕.
co·ed [ˈkəuˈed] *n.* 〔美口〕(男女同校的)女生〔co-education 的略语〕. — *a.* 男女同校的,(男女同校)女学生的. **co·ed·i·sm** *n.* 〔口〕男女同校制度.
co·ed·na [kəuˈednə] *n.* 〔美〕女大学生.
co·ed·u·cate [kəuˈedjukeit] *vt., vi.* ①(使…)实行〔受〕男女同校教育. ②〔美口〕(使)和异性交际.
co·ed·u·ca·tion [ˈkəuˌedju(:)ˈkeiʃən] *n.* 男女同校;〔美口〕与异性交际. **-al** *a.*, **-al·ly** *ad.*
coef., coeff. = coefficient.
co·ef·fi·cient [kəuiˈfiʃənt] *a.* 共同作用的. — *n.* ①共同作用,协同因素. ②【数,物】系数,率;程度. ~ *of absorption* 吸收率〔系数〕. ~ *of expansion* 膨胀系数. ~ *of displacement* 排水量〔系数〕.
coe·la·canth [ˈsi:ləˌkænθ] *n.* 【古生】空棘鱼(化石).
coe·len·ter·ate [siˈlentəreit] *n., a.* 【动】腔肠动物(的).
coe·len·ter·on [siˈlentərɔn] *n.* *(pl.* ***-ter·a*** [-rə]*)* 【动】体肠腔.
c(o)e·li·ac [ˈsi:liæk] *a.* 【生理】腹的,下腹的,腹腔的.
coe·lom, coe·lome [ˈsi:ləm,ˈsi:ləum] *n.* *(pl.* ***coe·lo·ma·ta*** [siˈləumətə], ~*s)* 【动】体腔.

coe·lo·stat [ˈsiːləˌstæt] *n.* 【天】定天镜.
co·emp·tion [kəuˈempʃən] *n.* ①囤积，搜购. ②【罗马法】买卖婚姻.
coen-, coeno- *comb.f.* 共同: *coeno*cyte.
coe·nen·chy·ma [siˈlenkimə] *n.* *(pl.* ***-ta*** [-tə]*)* 【动】共质轴；共骨骼.
coe·nes·the·sia [ˌsiːnisˈθiːzjə] *n.* 【心】一般感觉(= coenesthesis).
coe·no·bite [ˈsiːnəubait] *n.* 修道院住院修士.
coe·no·bit·ism [ˈsiːnəubaitizəm] *n.* 修道院制.
coeno·cyte [ˈsiːnəusait] *n.* 【生】多核细胞，多核体；合胞体.
coe·no·gen·e·sis [ˌsiːnəuˈdʒenisis] *n.* 【生】后生变态.
coe·no·sarc [ˈsiːnəuˌsɑːk] *n.* 【生】共体，共肉.
coe·no·zygote [ˌsiːnəuˈzaigəut] *n.* 【生】多核合子.
coe·nu·rus [siˈnjurəs] *n.* *(pl.* ***-ri*** [-ai]*)* 【动】共尾幼虫.
co·en·zyme [kəuˈenzaim] *n.* 【生化】辅酶.
co·e·qual [kəuˈiːkwəl] *a., n.* (地位、能力等)互相平等的(人)，同权的(人)，同身分的(人). **-ly** *ad.*
co·e·qual·i·ty [ˌkəui(ː)ˈkwɔliti] *n.* 互相平等，同等，同权.
co·erce [kəuˈəːs] *vt.* 强制，强迫，胁迫；压制. ~ ***sb. into (doing)*** 强迫某人(做).
co·er·ci·ble [kəuˈəːsibl] *a.* ①可强迫的. ②可压凝的；可压缩成液态的.
co·er·cion [kəuˈəːʃən] *n.* 强迫；胁迫；高压政治〔统治〕. ~ ***and bribery*** 威胁利诱. ***No ~!*** 反对强制〔高压统治〕.
co·er·cion·a·ry [kəuˈəːʃənəri] *a.* = coercive.
co·er·cion·ist [kəuˈəːʃənist] *n.* 高压统治论者，强制主义者.
co·er·cive [kəuˈəːsiv] *a.* 强制的，强迫的，胁迫的；高压的. ~ **force** 【物】矫顽〔磁〕力. **-ly** *ad.*
coes·ite [ˈkəusait] *n.* 【矿】柯石英.
co·es·sen·tial [ˌkəuiˈsenʃəl] *a.* 同素的，同体的，同质的.
co·e·ta·ne·ous [ˌkəuiˈteiniəs] *a.* = coeval.
co·e·ter·nal [ˌkəuiˈtəːnl] *a.* 同样永存的，永远共存的.
co·e·val [kəuˈiːvəl] *a.* 同时代〔年代、时期、年龄〕的 *(with)*. — *n.* 同时代的人，同年代的人〔东西〕.
co·e·val·i·ty [ˌkəuiːˈvæliti] *n.* 同时代，同时期；同年龄.
co·ex·ec·u·tor [ˌkəuigˈzekjutə] *n.* *(fem.* ***-trix*** [-triks]*)* 【法】(遗嘱的)共同执行人，共同受托人.
co·ex·is·tence [ˈkəuigˈzistəns] *n.* 共存，共处. *peaceful* ~ 和平共处.
co·ex·ist [kəuigˈzist] *vi.* (在同地)同时存在，同在，共存 *(with)*. ~ *with ... peacefully* 与…和平共处.
co·ex·ist·ent [ˌkəuigˈzistənt] *a.* 同在的，共存的，同时代的.
co·ex·tend [ˈkəuiksˈtend] *vi., vt.* (在时、空方面)(使)共同扩张.
co·ex·ten·sive [ˈkəuikstensiv] *a.* 同广阔的，同久远的，(时空)共同扩张的. **-sion** *n.*
co·fac·tor [kəuˈfæktə] *n.* ①【数】余因子. ②【生】辅助因素.
C. of C. = Chamber of Commerce.
C. of E. = Church of England.
cof·fee [ˈkɔfi] *n.* 咖啡(树、豆、粉或色). *a cup of* ~ 一杯咖啡. *black* ~ (不加牛奶的)清咖啡. *white* ~ 牛奶咖啡. ~***-and*** 〔美口〕一杯咖啡和少许糕点等. ~ **bar** 〔英〕咖啡馆. ~ **bean,** ~**berry** 咖啡豆. ~ **break** (上班时的)喝咖啡休息〔一般在上午十时和下午三时〕. ~ **cake** 早餐点心〔以面粉、奶油、蛋、糖等制成〕. ~ **cooler** 偷懒耍滑的人. ~ **cup** 咖啡杯. ~ **extract** 咖啡精. ~ **grinder** ①咖啡磨. ②〔美俚〕飞机引擎. ~ **grounds** 咖啡渣. ~ **hour** 正式会议后的自由聚谈〔多有咖啡招待〕. ~**house** 咖啡馆. ~ **maker** 煮咖啡的壶. ~ **lightener** 掺在咖啡里的人造牛奶. ~ **mill** 咖啡豆的磨具；〔美军俚〕机关枪. ~ **palace** = ~house. ~ **pot** 咖啡壶；〔美俚〕小餐馆. ~ **room** 咖啡室〔店〕. ~ **shop** 咖啡店，(一般的)小餐馆. ~ **stall,** ~ **stand** (街头)咖啡摊. ~ **table** 咖啡桌〔放在沙发前的小桌或茶几〕. ~**-table** *a.* ①陈设在咖啡小桌上的. ②(画报等)精装大本多插图的. ~ **tavern** (不卖酒的)小餐馆. ~ **tree** 咖啡树. ~ **whitener** = ~ lightener.
cof·fer [ˈkɔfə] *n.* ①贵重品箱；保险箱，银柜. ②〔*pl.*〕资产，财源；国库，金库. ③围堰；潜水箱，沉箱；浮船坞；【船】隔离舱；【建】天花板的镶板，藻井. *the ~s of the state* 国库. — *vt.* ①把…装入箱内，把…放存金库内，贮藏. ②【建】用镶板装饰. ~ **dam** *n.* 围堰；沉箱；隔离舱. **-ing** *n.* 格子天花板.
Cof·fey [ˈkɔfi] *n.* 科菲〔姓氏〕.
Cof·fin [ˈkɔfin] *n.* 科芬〔姓氏〕.
cof·fin [ˈkɔfin] *n.* ①棺材. ②(马的)蹄槽. ③【印】木框. ④(不适于航海的)破旧的船(=~-ship). ⑤(运送放射性物质的)重屏蔽容器. ***drive a nail into sb.'s ~*** 促人早死. ***in one's ~*** 已死，已葬. — *vt.* 把…入殓，收殓；收藏(书籍等). ~ **boat** 〔美〕猎野鸭的小船. ~ **bone** 蹄骨. ~ **joint** 蹄关节. ~ **nail** 〔美俚〕香烟，烟卷儿. ~ **plate** 棺盖上的金属名牌〔记生死年月日〕. ~ **varnish** 〔美〕烈酒.
cof·fin·ite [ˈkɔfinait] *n.* 【矿】水硅铀矿.
cof·fle [ˈkɔfl] *n.* (连锁着的)一长列奴隶〔兽类〕.
co·flyer [kəuˈflaiə] *n.* 副飞行员.
co·found·er [kəuˈfaundə] *n.* 共同创立者.
C of S = chief of staff 参谋长.
co·func·tion [kəuˈfʌnkʃən] *n.* 【数】余函数.
cog[1] [kɔg] *n.* 【机】(齿轮的)钝齿，嵌齿；【建】雄榫，凸榫. ***have a ~ loose*** (脑子等)有些不正常，有点毛病. ***hunting ~s*** 【机】追逐齿；〔口〕处于从属地位但不可缺少的人〔物〕. ***slip a ~*** (意外地)失算；失错，疏漏. — *vt., vi.* (在…上)装齿轮，(在…上)楔榫. ~**wheel** 嵌齿轮.
cog[2] [kɔg] *vt.* (用假骰子)欺骗；行贿. ~ *a die [the dice]* 用骗人手段掷骰子.
cog[3] [kɔg] *n.* 小船；附属于大船的供应船.
cog. = cognate; cognate with.
co·gen·cy [ˈkəudʒənsi] *n.* ①说服力；(理论等的)中肯；恳切. ②〔*pl.*〕有说服力的说法.
co·gent [ˈkəudʒənt] *a.* 有说服力的，使人信服的；无法反驳的. **-ly** *ad.*
cogged[1] [kɔgd] *a.* 有齿轮的.
cogged[2] [kɔgd] *a.* 有弊的，骗人的.
Cog·ge·shall [ˈkɔgzɔːl] *n.* 科格索尔〔姓氏〕.
cog·ging [ˈkɔgiŋ] *n.* 【建】接头；〔集合词〕榫.
cog·i·ta·ble [ˈkɔdʒitəbl] *a.* 可以思考的，可以想象的.
cog·i·tate [ˈkɔdʒiteit] *vi., vt.* 慎重思考，考虑；【哲】思维.
cog·i·ta·tion [ˌkɔdʒiˈteiʃən] *n.* 思考，考虑；思考力；〔常 *pl.*〕思想；计划，设计.
cog·i·ta·tive [ˈkɔdʒitətiv] *a.* 深思熟虑的，有思考力的.
cog·i·ta·tor [ˈkɔdʒiteitə] *n.* 深思熟虑的人.
co·gi·to er·go sum [ˈkɔdʒiˌtəuˈəːgəuˈsʌm] 〔L.〕 我思故我在〔笛卡儿语〕.
cogn. = cognate.
co·gnac [ˈkəunjæk, ˈkɔn-] *n.* (法国)柯纳克(Cognac)产的白兰地酒；〔口〕(品质优良的)白兰地酒.
cog·nate [ˈkɔgneit] *a.* ①同族的；【法】女系亲戚的，母族的. ②同类的，同性质的，同种的 *(with)*. ③【语言】同源的；同语根的；同语族的. — *n.* ①【法】亲族；外戚. ②同源物；同性物. ③【语言】同源〔根〕词. ~ **languages** 同语族语言. ~ **object [accusative]** 【语法】同义宾语〔例: tell a tale 中的 tale〕.
cog·na·tion [kɔgˈneiʃən] *n.* ①同族；亲戚；外戚，女系亲戚. ②【语言】同语族；同词源.
cog·ni·tion [kɔgˈniʃən] *n.* 认识；认识力；(在认识过程

中形成的)知识. **-al** *a.*

cog·ni·tive [ˈkɔgnitiv] *a.* 认识的; 有认识力的. ~ *powers* 认识力. ~ **dissonance**【心】内心冲突.

cog·ni·za·ble [ˈkɔgnizəbl, ˈkɔn-] *a.* ①可认识的. ②【法】可受理的,审判权限内的. **-bly** *ad.*

cog·ni·zance [ˈkɔgnizəns] *n.* ①认识; 承认; 认识范围. ②管辖(权),监督(权);【法】审理; 审判权. ③纹章图案; 标记,记号. ***beyond [out of] one's*** ~ 认识不到的; 不受…管辖的. ***come to one's*** ~ 知道. ***have*** ~ ***of*** 认识到; 注意到; 有审判权. ***lack of*** ~ 认识不足. ***take*** ~ ***of*** 认识; 受理审判. ***take no*** ~ ***of*** 对…置之不理. ***within one's*** ~ 可以认识到的; 在…管辖以内.

cog·ni·zant [ˈkɔgnizənt] *a.* ①认识,知道. ②有管辖权的,有审判权的. ***be*** ~ ***of*** 认识到,知道.

cog·nize [kɔgˈnaiz] *vt.* 知道,认识.

cog·no·men [kɔgˈnəumen] *n.* *(pl. ~s, cog·no·min·a* [kɔgˈnominə]*)* 姓; (古罗马人的) 家名, 第三名〔例: Caius Julius Caesar 的 Caesar〕; 别名; 绰号.

co·gno·scen·te [ˌkɔnjəuˈʃenti] *n.* *(pl.* ***-ti*** [-tiː]*)* 〔It.〕(美术品的)鉴定家.

cog·nos·ci·ble [kɔgˈnɔsibl] *a.* 可以认识到的; 可以打听明白的,可知的.

cog·no·vit [kɔgˈnəuvit] *n.*【法】(承认原告诉讼理由为正当的)被告承认书,具结.

Co·gon [kəˈgəun] *n.* 【植】白茅属〔尤指白茅, 茅针 *(Imperata cylindrica)*〕.

co·hab·it [kəuˈhæbit] *vi.* (男女) 同居 *(with)*; 〔旧〕共同生活.

co·hab·i·tant [kəuˈhæbitənt] *n.* 同居者.

co·hab·i·ta·tion [ˌkəuhæbiˈteiʃən] *n.* 同居,同住,同国.

Co·han [kəuˈhæn] *n.* 科汉〔姓氏〕.

co·heir [ˈkəuˈɛə] *n.* 共同继承人.

co·heir·ess [ˈkəuˈɛəris] *n.* 女性共同继承人.

Co·hen [ˈkəuin] *n.* 科恩〔姓氏〕.

co·here [kəuˈhiə] *vi.* ①(互相)挤紧, 粘合, 凝聚. ②一致 *(with)*, 团结. ③(理论等)前后一贯,有条理,紧密.

co·her·ence, co·her·en·cy [kəuˈhiərəns, -si] *n.* ①紧密的结合,凝聚. ②统一,首尾一贯; 一致性. ③【物】同调;【光】相干性,相参性;【化】内聚力; 内聚现象.

co·her·ent [kəuˈhiərənt] *a.* ①紧密地结合着的; 凝聚性的. ②(话等)有条理的,首尾一贯的; 一致的. ③【光】相干的,相参的.

co·her·er [kəuˈhiərə] *n.* ①密聚[凝聚]者. ②【电】金屑[粉末]检波器.

co·he·sion [kəuˈhiːʒən] *n.* ①(各部的)结合;【物】(分子的)凝聚,内聚,内聚力, 内聚性; 〔喻〕结合力, 团结. ②【植】连着. *It undermines* ~ *and creates dissension.* 这件事会破坏团结,制造纠纷.

co·he·sive [kəuˈhiːsiv] *a.* 有粘着力的, 有附着力的; 凝聚性的; 内聚性的,有结合力的. ~ **force** 凝聚力,内聚力,粘合力. **-ly** *ad.* **-ness** *n.*

co·ho [ˈkəuhəu] *n.* *(pl.~,~s)*【动】银大马哈鱼〔原产北太平洋, 现大量引进美国北部淡水湖(河)〕(= coho salmon).

co·ho·bate [ˈkəuhəubeit] *vt.* 再[多次]蒸馏.

co·hort [ˈkəuhɔːt] *n.* ①(古罗马的)步兵大队(300—600人). ②〔常 *pl.*〕军队; 一群,队 *(of)*. ③【生】区,股. ④助手; 同伴; 共犯,同谋者; 追随者.

co·hosh [ˈkəuhɔʃ, kəˈhɔʃ] *n.*【植】①毛茛科植物〔如升麻、类叶升麻〕. ②唐松草叶葳岩仙 *(Caulophyllum thalictroides)*.

C.O.I. = Central Office of Information 〔英〕中央新闻署.

coif [kɔif] *n.* ①一种紧包在头上的小帽; 【史】(盔下戴的)衬帽. ②(高级律师 sergeant-at-law 戴的)白帽; 高级律师的地位[身份]. ③ [kwɑːf] = *coiffure n.* — *vt.* 使戴布帽[白帽].

coif·feur [kwɑːˈfəː] *n.* 〔F.〕理发师.

coif·fure [kwɑːˈfjuə] *n.* 〔F.〕理发; 发型,发式; 头饰. — *vt.* 把(头发)做成某种发式.

coign(e) [kɔin] *n.*【建】外角; 隅; 隅石; 楔. ~ ***of vantage*** 有利地位.

coil[1] [kɔil] *vt., vi.* 卷, 盘绕, (把…)盘[卷]成一圈 *(up)*. — *n.* ①(一)卷,(一)盘,(一)圈. ②螺旋管, 蛇管. ③【电】线圈,绕组. ~ **paper** 筒纸,卷纸. ~ **spring** 螺形弹簧.

coil[2] [kɔil] *n.* 〔古〕混乱; 纠纷. ***(shuffle off) this mortal*** ~ (摆脱)人世的纷扰.

COIN = counterinsurgency.

coin [kɔin] *n.* ①硬币; 〔俚〕金钱. ②〔古〕= coign. *a base* ~ 劣币. *a false* ~ 伪币; 赝品. *a silver* ~ 银币. *a small* ~ 小钱. *a subsidiary* ~ 辅币. ***pay (sb.) (back) in his own*** ~ 以其人之道还治其人之身. ***ring a*** ~ 敲响硬币检查真假. — *vt., vi.* 铸造(货币); 制造, 新创(新语等); 靠…赚钱. ~ ***money*** 〔俚〕大发其财,发横财; 情况好. ~ ***one's brains*** 动脑筋挣钱. ~ **certificate** 〔美〕(政府发行的)兑换券. ~ **telephone** 投币式公用电话. ~**ing rate** (贵金属)铸造比率.

coin·age [ˈkɔinidʒ] *n.* ①造币; 铸币; (某国某时代的)货币(全部); 货币制度; 造币费. ②创制品; 新造语词. *the* ~ *of new words* 新词的创造. *the* ~ *of fancy [one's brain]* 空想[头脑]的产物.

co·in·cide [ˌkəuinˈsaid] *vi.* 与…一致, 相合, 符合, 相符,相巧合 *(with)*. *My opinion* ~*s with his.* 我的意见跟他巧合. *These two triangle* ~. 这两个三角形相互重合. *These two lines* ~ *with each other.* 这两条线彼此相合.

co·in·ci·dence [kəuˈinsidəns] *n.* 一致(性), 符合; 巧合, 暗合;【数】重合,迭合(素); 同时发生[存在]. ***a mere*** ~ 偶合,巧合.

co·in·ci·dent [kəuˈinsidənt] *a.* (与…)一致[符合]的, (与…)暗合[巧合]的; 同时发生的. ~ *indicator* 【经】(与经济状况直接相关的) 相关指数 [指示物]. — *n.* 【经】= ~ indicator. **-ly** *ad.*

co·in·ci·den·tal [kəuˌinsiˈdentl] *a.* 符合的,暗合的,巧合的. **-ly** *ad.*

coin·er [ˈkɔinə] *n.* 造币者; 伪币制造者; (新词等的)创造者.

co·in·stan·ta·ne·ous [ˈkəuˌinstænˈteinjəs] *a.* 同时(发生的).

co·in·sti·tion·al [kəuˌinstiˈtjuːʃənəl] *a.* (中学等)男女分班的.

co·in·sur·ance [kəuinˈʃuərəns] *n.* 共同担保[保险].

co·in·sure [kəuinˈʃuə] *vt., vi.* ①(保险业的)联保. ②(保险业的)分保.

coir [ˈkɔiə] *n.* 椰子皮壳纤维[制品]. ~ **rope** 棕绳.

cois·trel, cois·tril [ˈkɔistrəl] *n.* 〔古〕①(骑士的)马僮,跟班. ②恶棍,无赖,流氓.

co·i·tal [ˈkəuitl] *a.* 交媾的.

co·i·tion, coi·tus [kəuˈiʃən, ˈkəuitəs] *n.* (特指人类的)交媾,交合.

Coke [kəuk, kuk] *n.* 科克〔姓氏〕.

coke[1] [kəuk] *n.* 焦(炭). *mineral* ~ 天然焦. *a* ~ *oven* 炼焦炉. — *vt.* 把…炼制成焦炭. — *vi.* 炼焦; 成焦炭.

coke[2] [kəuk] *n.* ①〔俚〕= cocaine. ②〔美口〕可口可乐 (= coca cola). ***go and eat*** ~ 别作打扰别人的事 [少管闲事].

co·ker·nut [ˈkəukənʌt] *n.* = cocoanut.

col [kɔl] *n.* ①(峰与峰之间的)山口, 坳口. ②【气】鞍状等压线,气压谷.

col. = collector; college; colony; colour; column.

Col. = Colonel; Colorado; Colossian; Columbia.

col-[1] 〔用在 l 字母前〕= com-.

col-[2] = colo-.

co·la[1] [ˈkəulə] *n.* ①【植】(非洲)可乐树. ②可乐〔可乐树子制成的饮料〕.
co·la[2] [ˈkəulə] *n.* colon 的复数.
col·an·der [ˈkʌləndə] *n.* (洗菜等用的)滤器,漏勺.
co·lat·i·tude [kəuˈlætitjuːd] *n.*【天】余纬(度).
col·can·non [kəlˈkænən, kɔl-] *n.* (爱尔兰式)土豆燉白菜泥.
col·chi·cin(e), col·chi·ci·a [ˈkɔltʃisi(ː)n, kɔlˈkiʃiə] *n.*【生化】秋水仙硷.
col·chi·cum [ˈkɔltʃikəm] *n.*【植】秋水仙;秋水仙制剂.
Col·clough [ˈkəukli, ˈkɔlklʌf] *n.* 科尔克拉夫〔姓氏〕.
col·co·thar [ˈkɔlkəθə] *n.*【化】铁丹〔由硫酸亚铁烧成的褐红色铁氧化物〕.
cold [kəuld] *a.* ①冷,寒,冻;冰凉的. ②冷静的,冷淡的,无情的,冷酷的;无趣味的,沉闷的;令人打冷颤的;扫兴的;【美】有冷感的,冷色的. ③(谜语)难猜中的 (*opp.* hot). ④(猎物臭迹)已变淡的. ⑤(土壤)粘湿的;(肥料)腐熟缓慢的. ⑥〔俚〕已死亡的. *He has to quit* ~. 他不得不完全放弃. *be* ~ *in manner* 态度冷淡. ~ *as all get out* 〔美〕冷极. ***get [have] sb.*** ~ 〔口〕任意摆布(某人). ***give [show] the*** ~ ***shoulder to*** 冷待,对…冷淡. ***have*** ~ ***feet*** 〔军俚〕意气沮丧,吓破了胆子. ***in*** ~ ***blood*** 无动于衷地,冷酷地,若无其事地 (*kill in* ~ *blood* 杀人不眨眼). ***leave sb.*** ~ 对人冷酷无情;未说动某人. ***make sb.'s blood run*** ~ 使某人不寒而栗. ***pour [throw]*** ~ ***water on*** (对他人计划等)泼冷水,扫…的兴. ***turn the*** ~ ***shoulder on*** 冷待,对…冷淡. — *n.* ①寒冷;冰点下. ②感冒,着凉,伤风. *fifteen degrees of* ~ 冰点下15度. ***be left out in the*** ~ 被…冷遇〔摈弃〕. ***catch [take]*** ~ 着凉,伤风. ~ ***in the head*** 鼻炎,淌清鼻涕,鼻塞. ***come in from the*** ~ 不再被忽视;摆脱孤立. ~ ***on the lungs*** 伤风咳嗽. ***Feed a*** ~ ***and starve a fever.*** 伤风要吃,发热要饿. ***have a*** ~ 伤风. ~**-blooded** *a.* 冷血的;杂种的(马等);怕冷的;冷酷的,冷淡的. ~ **chisel** 冷錾. ~**coil** 冷却用蛇管. ~**colours** 冷色〔灰、蓝、绿等〕. ~ **comfort** 敷衍人的安慰. ~ **counsel [news]** 不愿听的忠告〔通知〕. ~ **cream** 冷霜〔化妆品〕. ~ **cuts** 什锦冷盘. ~ **deck** 〔美俚〕作弊用的牌. ~**-drawn** *a.* (金属丝等)冷抽的;(油等)冷提的. **C- Duck** 〔美〕冷鸭酒〔杂酒〕. ~ **feet** 冰冷的脚;〔美俚〕害怕,胆小. ~ **game** 〔美〕胜败分明的比赛. ~ **hardening** 加工硬化. ~ **hardiness** 耐〔抗〕寒力. ~**-hearted** *a.* 冷酷的. ~**-livered** *a.* 冷淡的. ~ **meat** 冷的熟肉;经济菜;〔美俚〕死尸. ~**-meat party** 〔美俚〕守夜;丧事. ~ **pig** 〔口〕(使人清醒的)冷水浇脸〔参看 ~-pig〕. ~**-pig** *vt.* 〔口〕使洗冷水澡(解乏);对…泼冷水(使清醒). ~**-proof** *a.* 御寒的. ~ **purse** 无钱;贫穷. ~**resistance** 抗〔耐〕寒性. ~ **room** 冷藏室. ~ **scent** 【猎】(已走远了的野兽留下的)轻微的气味. ~ **seeds** 瓜子. ~ **sheets** 贞操. ~**short** *a.* 一冷就脆的,(金属)冷脆的. ~ **shoulder** 冷冻烤羊排;藐视,冷眼对待. ~**shoulder** *vt.* 疏远. ~ **shudder** 〔美俚〕没钱的同伴,被人讨厌的人. ~ **snap** 乍冷,骤冷. ~ **sore** 嘴边〔脸上〕的疹子. ~ **steel** 利器〔刀剑等〕. ~ **storage** 冷藏;冷藏库;〔俚〕牢监. ~ **turkey** 无准备,即席;突然,莽撞;〔美俚〕定价出售. ~ **war** 冷战. **C-Warrior** 冷战政治家. ~**-water** *a.* 没有水暖系统的. ~ **wave** ①寒流. ②冷烫(头发). ~ **weld** 冷焊. ~**-work** 冷变形. **-ly** *ad.* **-ness** *n.*
coldish [ˈkəuldiʃ] *a.* 微冷的.
Cole [kəul] *n.* 科尔〔姓氏〕.
cole [kəul] *n.* 蔬菜〔芸苔等,特指油菜〕.
co·lec·to·my [kəˈlektəmi] *n.*【医】结肠切除术.
Cole·man [ˈkəulmən] *n.* 科尔曼〔姓氏〕.
cole·man·ite [ˈkəulmənait] *n.*【矿】硬硼钙石,硬硼酸钙石,硼炭石.
co·le·op·ter [ˌkɔliˈɔptə] *n.* ①【动】独角虫. ②环翼飞机,直升飞机.
Co·le·op·ter·a [ˌkɔliˈɔptərə] *n.* 〔*pl.*〕【动】甲虫类,鞘翅目.
co·le·op·ter·on [ˌkəuliˈɔptəˌrɔn, kɔli-] *n.* (*pl.* **-ter·a** [-ə])【动】鞘翅目昆虫 (= coleopteran).
col·e·op·ter·ous [ˌkɔliˈɔptərəs] *a.*【动】甲虫类的,鞘翅目的.
co·le·op·tile [ˌkəuliˈɔptl, -ˌkɔli-] *n.*【植】胚芽鞘.
co·le·o·rhi·za [ˌkəuliəˈraizə] *n.* (*pl.* **-zae** [-ziː])【植】胚根鞘.
Co·le·ridge [ˈkəulridʒ] *n.* ①科尔里奇〔姓氏〕. ②**Samuel Taylor** ~ 萨·柯勒律治〔1772—1834, 英国诗人〕.
cole·seed [ˈkəulsiːd] *n.*【植】油菜(籽).
cole·slaw [ˈkəulslɔː] *n.* 凉拌卷心菜 (= coldslaw).
cole·us [ˈkəuliəs] *n.*【植】锦紫苏.
cole·wort [ˈkəulwəːt] *n.*【植】海甘兰,油菜(等).
C.O.L.I. = cost of living index 生活费指数.
col·ic [ˈkɔlik] *n.*【医】(腹)绞痛;疝痛. — *a.*【医】(腹)绞痛的;疝痛的.
col·ic·in [ˈkɔlisin] *n.*【生化】大肠杆菌素.
col·ick·y [ˈkɔliki] *a.* (腹)绞痛的.
col·ic·root [ˈkɔlikˌruːt] *n.* ①【植】被粉肺筋草 (*Aletris farinosa*). ②任何可治腹痛等的植物〔如块根马利筋〕.
col·ic·weed [ˈkɔlikˌwiːd] *n.* 加拿大荷包牡丹 (=squirrel corn).
co·li·form [ˈkəuliˌfɔːm, ˈkɔli-] *a.* 筛状的;筛骨的.
Co·lin [ˈkɔlin] *n.* 科林〔男子名, Nicholas 的昵称〕.
col·in [ˈkɔlin] *n.*【动】鹑.
-coline = -colous.
col·i·seum [ˌkɔliˈsiəm] *n.* ①〔C-〕= Colosseum. ②戏院;音乐厅;体育场.
co·li·tis [kəuˈlaitis] *n.*【医】结肠炎. *acute* ~ 急性结肠炎.
col·khoz [kɔlˈkəuz] (苏联的)集体农庄 (= kolkhoz).
coll. = collateral; colleague; collection; collector; college; colloquial; 〔L.〕collyrium.【药】洗眼剂;栓剂.
col·lab·o·rate [kəˈlæbəreit] *vi.* ①合作,共同研究;(国家间的)协调,提携. ②与敌合作,通敌;勾结 (*with*).
col·lab·o·ra·tion [kəˌlæbəˈreiʃən] *n.* ①合作,合著,共同研究. ②与敌合作,通敌,勾结. ***in*** ~ ***with*** ①与…合作〔合著、合编〕. ②与…勾结. **-ism** 鼓吹与敌人合作;通敌. **-ist** *n.* 通敌分子,卖国贼.
col·lab·o·ra·tor [kəˈlæbəreitə] *n.* ①合作者,共同研究者. ②与敌合作分子,通敌分子,卖国贼.
col·lage [kɔˈlɑːʒ] *n.* ①(用火柴商标、车票、纸牌等拼贴而成的)拼贴(画). ②抽象派拼贴画. ③(互不相干物件的)大杂烩.
col·la·gen [ˈkɔləˌdʒən] *n.*【生化】(骨)胶原,成胶质. **-ic** *a.*
col·lap·sar [kəˈlæpsɑː] *n.*【天】崩塌(恒)星,黑洞 (= black hole).
col·lapse [kəˈlæps] *vi.* ①(屋顶等)倒塌,塌下;(政府等)崩溃,瓦解. ②(价格等)暴跌;(计划等)失败;(身体、健康等)衰退,消沉,颓丧. ③(用具等)折叠,压扁;压缩. — *vt.* 使倒坍;使崩溃;使衰弱. ②折叠. — *n.* ①倒塌,崩溃,衰弱. ②(价格等的)暴跌. ③【医】虚脱;萎陷.
col·lap·sar [kəˈlæpsɑː] *n.* 塌陷星,太空黑洞.
col·laps·i·ble, col·laps·a·ble [kəˈlæpsəbl] *a.* (椅子等)可折叠的,可压扁〔压缩〕的. *a* ~ *chair* 折椅. ~ **tube** 收缩管,软管.
col·lar [ˈkɔlə] *n.* ①衣领;硬领;项圈;护肩,(牲口的)轭. ②环状物;【机】端箍,轴环;【建】柱环;系梁,底梁;【植】根颈. ③(猪肉等的)肉卷. ④(一杯啤酒表面的)泡沫. ⑤【橄榄球】紧抱. ⑥〔美俚〕逮捕. ***against the*** ~ (马上坡时)轭具勒紧肩膀;冒着困难,下死力(干等),千辛万苦. ***be hot under the*** ~ 〔俚〕发怒;奋激. ***be in [out of]*** ~ (马套上[卸下]轭具)听候[解除]役使;〔俚〕有[无]工作,担任[失去]职务. ***in the*** ~ 受压制[束缚]. ~ ***of SS [esses]*** SS 连锁形颈章. ***fill one's*** ~ 〔口〕尽本分,尽职. ***keep sb. up to the*** ~ 把人当牛马使唤. ***seize [take] (sb.) by the*** ~ 抓住领口. ***slip the*** ~ 避开困难;挣脱,逃脱. ***wear sb.'s*** ~ 〔口〕听人差遣.— *vt.* ①扭住领口;上衣领;使戴项圈. ②〔口〕捕,捉;取,窃取;拉用,扯用;(不断谈话)留住不放. ③【橄榄球】抱住. ④做(肉)卷. *Who's ~ed my pen?* 谁拿走了我的钢笔? ~ **beam**【建】系梁. ~**-bone**【解】锁骨. ~ **button [stud]** (把硬[软]领扣在无领衬衫上用的)领扣. **C-day** 〔英〕颈饰日;〔谑〕绞刑日. ~ **gall** 马颈上的擦伤. ~ **harness** 颈部的马具. ~ **work** 吃力的工作;【冶】冷作.

col·lard [ˈkɔləd] *n.* 【植】(菜叶不包卷起来的)散叶甘兰.

col·lared [ˈkɔləd] *a.* 有领的,戴着领圈的;(肉)成卷的.

col·lar·et(te) [ˌkɔləˈret] *n.* 女用围巾,女用领巾.

col·lat. = collateral; collaterally.

col·late [kɔˈleit] *vt.* ①核对,对照,校对;(装钉)整理,检查. ②【宗】授与牧师职.

col·lat·er·al [kɔˈlætərəl] *a.* ①侧面的;旁边的;旁系的;间接的;副的;附属的,附带的;附加的,追加的. ②平行的,并列的. — *n.* ①旁系亲属. ②〔美〕附属担保物(*cf.* 〔英〕security);附带事项,附属部分. ③【解】侧突. ~ **evidence** 旁证,间接证据. ~ **issue** 附带诉讼. ~ **office** 兼职. ~ **relatives** 旁系亲属. ~ **security** 附属担保物. ~ **surety** 副保证人. **-ly** *ad.*

col·la·tion [kɔˈleiʃən] *n.* ①核对,校对,校勘;整理,(页码的)检查. ②牧师职的委任. ③小吃,零食,茶点;(斋日的)夜点.

col·la·tor [kɔˈleitə] *n.* 核对者,校对者;整理人;牧师职授任者.

col·league [ˈkɔliːg] *n.* 同事,同行.

col·lect[1] [kəˈlekt] *vt.* ①收集,收藏;召集;征收(税等),募(捐),领取(信件等). ②集中,整理(思想);镇定;鼓起(勇气);把牢(缰绳). ③〔古〕推测. ~ *a horse* 将马把牢. — *vi.* 聚集;堆积;募捐 *(for)*;〔美〕收帐,收款. ~ ***on delivery*** 〔美〕= cash on delivery. ~ ***oneself*** 平心静气,镇定一下. — *a., ad.* 由接收者付款的[地]. *to telephone* ~ 打一个由受话者付款的电话. ~**ing agent** 收款代理人.

col·lect[2] [ˈkɔlekt] *n.*【宗】短祷.

col·lect·a·ble, col·lect·i·ble [kəˈlektəbl] *a.* 可收集的,可收取的;可代收的.

col·lec·ta·ne·a [ˌkɔlekˈtɑːnjə] *n.* 〔L.〕〔*pl.*〕总集,文集;杂录,杂集.

col·lect·ed [kəˈlektid] *a.* ①收集成的. ②泰然自若的,镇定的. ~ *papers* 论文集. ~ *works* 全集. **-ly** *ad.* 泰然,冷静地. **-ness** *n.* 镇定.

col·lec·tion [kəˈlekʃən] *n.* ①收集,采集;集团;收集品,珍藏;(收藏丰富的)美术馆. ②征收,收款;征税;捐款;募捐. ③〔*pl.*〕(牛津大学等各学院的)学期考试. ***make [take up] a*** ~ ***for*** 为…募捐.

col·lec·tive [kəˈlektiv] *a.* 集合的;聚合性的;共同的,集体的,集团的. ~ *wishes of the people* 人民的共同愿望. — *n.*【语法】集合名词;【统】集体. ~ **action** 集体行动. ~ **agreement [bargaining]** (劳资间的)集体协定[合同]. ~ **behaviour** 集体行为. ~ **effort** 集体的力量,协力. ~ **farm** = kolkhoz. ~ **farming** 集体农业. ~ **fire** 集合射击. ~ **fruit**【植】聚合果〔桑子等〕. ~ **goods** 集体财产,公共设施[公园、道路等]. ~ **intervention** 共同干涉. ~ **note** 连名通知. ~ **noun**【语法】集合名词. ~ **ownership** 集体所有(制). ~ **species**【植】综合种. **-ly** *ad.*

col·lec·tiv·ism [kəˈlektivizəm] *n.* 集体主义.

col·lec·tiv·ist [kəˈlektivist] *n., a.* 集体主义者(的).

col·lec·tiv·i·ty [ˌkɔlekˈtivity] *n.* 全体,总体;集体,集团;集体主义,集体精神;集体状态.

col·lec·tiv·ize [kəˈlektivaiz] *vt.* 使成为共同的,使集体化.

col·lec·tor [kəˈlektə] *n.* ①收集家;采集者;收集器. ②收税员;收款员;募捐人;〔美〕(海关的)征收员;收票员. ③【电】集电器,集电极;集流器[环];整流子;换向器;【机】集合器;集尘器;【计】编辑机. **-ship** *n.* ①收税员[收款员等]的职权. ②(古董等的)收集,收藏.

col·leen [ˈkɔliːn] *n.* 〔Ir.〕少女,(金发碧眼的)姑娘;〔美〕爱尔兰姑娘. ~ *bawn* [bɔːn] 漂亮的姑娘.

col·lege [ˈkɔlidʒ] *n.* ①(综合大学中的)学院. ②〔美〕分科[单科]大学;高等(专科)学校;〔英〕大学预科专门学校. ③(以上各学校的)校舍;院;(牛津、剑桥等大学的自治组织)宿舍. ④(英国的)私立中等学校[亦称"公学"];(法国的)私立高等学院. ⑤团体,学会. ⑥【宗】长老会,红衣主教团. ⑦〔俚〕监牢,感化院;(老弱残废人的)收容所. *C- of Arms* = *Herald's C-* 徽章院. *C- of Cardinals* = *Sacred C-* (梵蒂冈教廷的)枢密院. *C- of Justice* 苏格兰高等法院. ~ *of the apostles* (十二)使徒团. *C- of Surgeons* 外科医学会. ~**-bred** *a.* 受过大学教育的. ~ **cap** 大学帽. ~ **forest** 实验林. ~ **ice** 〔美〕= sundae. ~ **living** 大学牧师的薪水. ~ **man** 高等学校毕业生. ~ **pudding** 一人一份的葡萄干布丁. ~ **woman** 女大学生,高等学校毕业女生.

col·leg·er [ˈkɔlidʒə] *n.* ①〔英〕伊顿(Eton)公学的公费生. ②〔美〕大学生.

col·le·gi·al [kəˈliːdʒiəl] *a.* = collegiate.

col·le·gi·al·i·ty [kəˌliːdʒiˈæliti] *n.* ①共同掌权. ②【天主】教皇与主教分权的原则.

col·le·gi·an [kəˈliːdʒiən] *n.* ①高等学校[专科学校等]的学生[毕业生]. ②某些团体[集体]的成员. ③〔古、俚〕监狱中同房间的人.

col·le·gi·ate [kəˈliːdʒiit] *a.* ①学院的,大学的,高等学校(学生)的;大学程度的. ②(某些)集体组织的. ③〔美俚〕愉快的,有趣的. — *n.* 学院[高等学校,大学]学生. ~ *church* 置有牧师会的大教堂;〔Scot.〕由几个牧师共同管理的教堂;〔美〕协同教会[教堂]. ~ *education* 大学教育.

col·legi·um [kəˈliːdʒiəm] ①学院. ②长老会. ③(尤指苏联政府各部中计议重要业务的)委员会.

col·lem·bo·lan [kəˈlembəulən] *n.*【动】弹尾目昆虫(= springtail).

col·len·chy·ma [kəˈleŋkimə] *n.*【植】厚角组织.

col·let [ˈkɔlit] *n.* ①(戒指上的)宝石座. ②【机】有缝夹头,套爪;(钟表中的)油丝固着环.

col·lide [kəˈlaid] *vi.* (车等)碰撞 *(with)*;(意志等)冲突,抵触 *(with)*.

col·lie [ˈkɔli] *n.* 柯利狗[苏格兰牧羊长毛狗].

Col·lier [ˈkɔliə] *n.* 科利尔[姓氏].

col·li·er [ˈkɔliə] *n.* ①〔英〕(煤矿的)矿工. ②煤船;煤船船员[水手]. ③〔废〕煤商.

col·lier·y [ˈkɔljəri] *n.* (包括建筑、设备在内的)煤矿.

col·lie·shang·ie [ˈkɔliʃæŋi] *n.* 〔Scot.〕争吵.

col·li·gate [ˈkɔligeit] *vt.* ①把…绑扎在一起. ②总括(事实),综合.

col·li·mate [ˈkɔlimeit] *vt.* ①瞄准,校准,使准直. ②使成平行. *a ~d light beam* 平行光束.

col·li·ma·tion [ˌkɔliˈmeiʃən] *n.* 校准,瞄准;【物】准直.

col·li·ma·tor [ˈkɔlimeitə] *n.*【物】准直仪,准直管,平行光管.

col·lin·e·ar [kɔˈlinjə] *a.*【数】共线的.

Col·lins[1] [ˈkɔlinz] *n.* 柯林斯[姓氏].

Col·lins[2] [ˈkɔlinz] *n.* 〔亦作 c-〕果汁水酒〔鸡尾酒的一种〕.

Col·lins[3] [ˈkɔlinz] *n.*〔英口〕(访客走后寄来的)感谢信.

col·lin·si·a [kəˈlinziə, -siə] *n.* 【植】寇林希草属的草.
col·li·sion [kəˈliʒən] *n.* 碰撞;冲突,抵触,(政党等的)倾轧. ***come into ~ with*** 和…相撞[冲突,抵触]. ***in ~ with*** 和…相撞[冲突]. **~-mat** 【海】防漏毯.
col·lo·cate [ˈkɔləkeit] *vt.* 把…并置,并列;排列,配置. *~ books on a shelf* 把书排列在书架上.
col·lo·ca·tion [ˌkɔləˈkeiʃən] *n.* ①并列,并置;排列,配置,安排,布置. ②【语法】连语(法),(习惯上的)搭配(关系).
col·loc·u·tor [ˈkɔləkjuːtə] *n.* 谈话的对手,对话者.
col·lo·di·on, colodium [kəˈləudjən, -diəm] *n.* 【化】珂珞酊,火棉胶,胶棉. **-ize** *vt.* 用胶棉处理. **~ silk** 胶丝.
col·logue [kəˈləug] *vi.* 密谈;〔方〕密谋 *(with)*.
colloid [ˈkɔlɔid] *a., n.* 胶质(的),胶体(的),胶态(的). **~ chemistry** 胶质化学.
col·loi·dal [kəˈlɔidl] *a.* 胶质的,胶态的.
col·lop [ˈkɔləp] *n.* ①〔英方〕薄肉片;小薄片. ②〔古〕(肥胖动物或人的)皮肤的皱折.
col·loq. = colloquial(ism); colloquially.
col·lo·qui·al [kəˈləukwiəl] *a.* 口语的;通俗语的,会话上的. **-ism** *n.* 口语(体). **-ly** *ad.* 用口语.
col·lo·quist [ˈkɔləukwist] *n.* (正式会谈的)会谈者;对谈者.
col·lo·qui·um [kəˈləukwiəm] *n. (pl. **-qui·a** [-ə], ~s)* 学术讨论会.
col·lo·quy [ˈkɔləkwi] *n.* ①(正式的)会谈;讨论;对谈,会话;(美议会)自由讨论. ②对话体著作.
col·lo·sol [ˈkɔləusɔl] *n.* 【化】溶胶.
col·lo·type [ˈkɔləutaip] *n.* 【印】珂罗版(印刷品,印刷术).
col·lude [kəˈljuːd] *vi.* 共谋. *~ with* 勾结.
collun. = collunarium.
col·lu·nar·i·um [ˌkɔljuˈnɛəriəm] *n. (pl. **-nar·i·a** [-ˈnɛəriə])* 【医】点鼻剂.
col·lu·sion [kəˈljuːʒən] *n.* 共谋,互相勾结. *the parties in ~* 参加共谋的几方面(人). ***in ~ with*** 与…串通[勾结].
col·lu·sive [kəˈljuːsiv] *a* 共谋的.
col·lu·to·ri·um [ˌkɔləˈtɔriəm] *(pl. **-to·ri·a** [-tɔriə])* = collutory.
col·lu·to·ry [ˈkɔlətəri] *n.* 漱口剂;漱口药.
col·lu·vi·al [kəˈluːviəl] *a.* 【地】崩积的.
col·lu·vi·um [kəˈluːviəm] *n. (pl. **-vi·a** [-ə], ~s)* 【地】崩积层.
col·ly[1] [ˈkɔli] *n.* = collie.
col·ly[2] [ˈkɔli] *n.* 煤灰;锅灰. — *vt.* 〔英方〕(被煤灰等)弄黑,弄脏.
col·lyr·i·um [kəˈliriəm] *n. (pl. **-ia** [-iə])* 【医】洗眼剂;眼药(水).
col·ly·wob·bles [ˈkɔliˌwɔblz] *n. pl.* 〔口、谑〕肚子痛,肚子响,肚子不舒服.
Col·man [ˈkəulmən] *n.* 科尔曼〔姓氏〕.
Col·ney Hatch [ˈkəuniˈhætʃ] (伦敦的)一所疯人院.
Colo. = Colorado.
col·o·bus [ˈkɔləbəs] *n.* 【动】疣猴.
co-lo·cate [ˈkəuləuˈkeit, Am. kəuˈləukeit] *vt., vi.* (两个以上部队等的)共同驻扎一地,共处在一地. **-ca·tion** *n.*
col·o·cynth [ˈkɔləsinθ] *n.* 【植】药西瓜〔干果可作导泄药〕.
Co·logne [kəˈləun] *n.* ①科隆〔德意志联邦共和国城市〕. ②〔c-〕科隆香水,花露水(= ~ water).
Co·lom·bi·a [kəˈlɔmbiə] *n.* 哥伦比亚〔拉丁美洲〕.
Co·lom·bi·an [kəˈlɔmbiən] *a.* 哥伦比亚(人)的. — *n.* 哥伦比亚人.
Co·lom·bo [kəˈlʌmbəu] *n.* ①科伦坡〔斯里兰卡首都〕. ②【天】月面第四象限的壁平原.
Co·lón [kəˈlɔn] *n.* 科隆〔巴拿马港市〕.
co·lon[1] [ˈkəulən] *n.* 冒号(:).
co·lon[2] [ˈkəulən] *n. (pl. ~s, **co·la** [-lə])* 【解】结肠,大肠.
co·lon[3] [kəuˈləun] *n.* 科朗〔哥斯达黎加和萨尔瓦多的货币单位〕.
co·lon[4] [kəˈləun] *n.* 〔F.〕殖民者〔尤指种植园主〕.
colo·nel [ˈkəːnl] *n.* 〔美〕陆军〔空军、海军陆战队〕上校,〔英〕陆军〔海军陆战队〕上校〔空军上校叫 group captain〕. *a lieutenant ~* 〔美〕陆军〔空军〕中校,〔英〕陆军中校〔空军中校叫 wing commander〕. *~ commandant* 〔英〕旅长. *~-in-chief* 〔英〕名誉团长(皇族). **-cy, -ship** *n.* 陆〔空〕军上校的职位,团长的职位.
co·lo·ni·al [kəˈləunjəl] *a.* ①殖民(地)的;殖民地化的. ②〔常 C-〕〔美〕英领殖民地时代的,美国初期的;从前的,旧时的. ③【生】群体的,集群的. — *n.* 殖民地居民;〔*pl.*〕〔英〕殖民地股票. *old ~ days* (独立前美国)英领殖民地时代. *the C- Bureau [Secretary]* 殖民局〔大臣〕. **~ architecture** (美国初期)殖民时代建筑式样. **~ militia** 屯田兵. **C- Office** 〔英〕殖民部.
co·lo·ni·al·ism [kəˈləunjəlizəm] *n.* ①殖民主义,殖民政策. ②殖民地特征. ③〔美〕守旧主义.
co·lon·ic [kəˈlɔnik] *a.* 结肠的.
col·o·nist [ˈkɔlənist] *n.* ①殖民者,移住民;殖民地居民. ②【生】外来动[植]物. *summer ~s* 避暑客.
co·lo·ni·tis [ˌkɔləˈnaitis] *n.* 【医】结肠炎.
col·o·ni·za·tion [ˌkɔlənaiˈzeiʃən] *n.* 殖民;殖民地化,拓殖;【生】移植.
col·o·nize [ˈkɔlənaiz] *vt.* ①在(某处)开拓殖民地. ②向(殖民地)移民. ③〔美〕把选民非法移入(某地区)〔以扩充政党势力〕. ④〔美〕(为政治目的)打入,混入(某部门等). ⑤【生】移植[植物]. — *vi.* ①开拓殖民地. ②移居于殖民地;移植植物.
col·o·ni·zer [ˈkɔlənaizə] *n.* 殖民地开拓者,殖民者.
col·on·nade [ˌkɔləˈneid] *n.* ①【建】柱廊,列柱. ②成列的街树,行道树. *the method of ~ foundation* 【建】(桥梁工程中的)管柱钻孔法.
col·o·ny [ˈkɔləni] *n.* ①殖民地;【希史】殖民城市;【罗史】征服区驻防地. ②殖民[移民]团. ③侨居地,侨民区;〔集合词〕侨民. ④(外交家等的)聚居地. ⑤【动】(鸟、蚁、蜜蜂等的)集团,群;【生】群体,集群;【地】(异系统内的)化石群. ⑥(有特殊作用的)居住区〔如失业救济,收容难民等〕. *a leper ~* 麻风病人隔离区. *~ formation* 群居生活. *morale of the ~* (蜂)群势. *size of ~s* 群势的大小. ***the Colonies*** (英国在美国最初设立的)东部十三州.
col·o·phon [ˈkɔləfən] *n.* ①(印有著者、发行者及出版日期等的书籍的)末页,底页,版权页. ②(书籍的)扉页. ③出版社的商标[徽章]. *from title page to ~* (全书)从头到尾.
col·o·pho·ny [kəˈlɔfəni] *n.* 松香,松脂,树脂(= resin).
col·o·quin·ti·da [ˌkɔləˈkwintidə] *n.* = colocynth.
col·or [ˈkʌlə] 〔美〕=〔英〕colour.
color- (= colour-).
col·or·a·ble [ˈkʌlərəbl] *a.* (= colourable).
Col·o·rad·o [ˌkɔləˈrɑːdəu] *n.* ①科罗拉多〔美国州名〕. ②〔the ~〕科罗拉多河〔北美洲〕. **~ beetle** 马铃薯岬虫.
col·o·ram·a [ˌkʌləˈrɑːmə] *n.* 【物】彩色光. **~lighting** 色光照明.
col·or·ant [ˈkʌlərənt] *n.* 色料,颜料,染料.
col·or·a·tion [kʌləˈreiʃən] *n* ①染色(法),着色(法). ②(天然)色,色彩. ③【乐】赋色. *protective ~* 保护色.
col·o·ra·tu·ra [ˌkɔlərəˈtuərə] *n.* 〔It.〕【乐】①花腔. ②花腔女高音(歌手)(= ~ soprano).
col·or·cast [ˈkʌləˌkɑːst, -ˌkæst] *n.* 彩色电视广播 — *vt., vi. (~, ~ed; ~, ~ed)* 用彩色电视广播.

col·or·i·fic [ˌkɔlə'rifik] *a.* ①能产生颜色的,能传色的. ②色彩的;着了色的. ③(文体等)华丽的.

col·or·im·e·ter [ˌkʌlə'rimitə] *n.* 色度计, 比色计. **-metry** [ˌkʌlə'rimitri] *n.* 比色法. **-met·ric** *a.*

co·los·sal [kə'lɔsl] *a.* ①巨像(似)的;巨大的,庞大的. ②〔口〕异常的,非常的. *a* ~ *scheme* 宏伟的计划. ***by a*** ~ ***accident*** 由于异常事故. ***in one's*** ~ ***ignorance*** 因为丝毫不知道.

Col·os·se·um [ˌkɔlə'siəm] *n.* ①罗马椭圆形竞技场. ②〔c-〕公共娱乐场.

Col·os·sian [kə'lɔʃən] *n.* (小亚细亚古城) 歌罗西 (Colossae) 人[基督教徒].

col·os·sus [kə'lɔsəs] *n.* ***(pl. -si*** [-sai]; ***~es*** [-iz]*)* ①巨像; 巨人, 巨物. ②〔C-〕(Rhodes 港入口处) 阿波罗 (Apollo) 神青铜巨像〔约 36 米〕. ③巨大的势力.

co·los·to·my [kə'lɔstəmi] *n.* 【医】结肠造口术.

co·los·trum [kə'lɔstrəm] *n.* (产妇的)初乳.

co·lot·o·my [kə'lɔtəmi] *n.* 【医】结肠切开术,人工肛门造成术.

col·our, col·or ['kʌlə] *n.* ①颜色,色彩;色调;着色;色素,颜料,染料;〔*pl.*〕图画颜料. ②脸色,血色;(有色人种的)肤色. ③(声音、文章等的)格调,情调,风格;【乐】音色. ④个性,特色;外观;口实;〔*pl.*〕立场,观点. ⑤〔常 *pl.*〕军旗,团旗,军舰旗;船旗;优胜旗;【美海军】对军舰旗的敬礼. ⑥〔*pl.*〕(作为某种标志的)彩色装饰[衣饰],徽记,绶带. ⑦〔美口〕精采,生动,有声有色. ⑧〔美〕(矿砂中)贵金属微粒[量]. ⑨【印】油墨用量. *fundamental [primary, simple]* ~*s* 原色〔一般指红、蓝、黄〕. *secondary* ~*s* (二原色混合成的)等和色. *oil [water]* ~*s* 油画[水彩画]颜料. *fading [fugitive]* ~*s* 易褪的颜色. *fast* ~*s* 经久不变的颜色. *contrast* ~*s* 反衬色. *He has very little* ~. 他脸色不好. *Her* ~ *came and went as she listened.* 她一面听一面脸色忽红忽白. *a high* ~ 良好的血色. *true [false]* ~*s* 真[假]面目. *The program lacks* ~. 〔美口〕节目欠精采. *local* ~ 地方色彩. *a person of* ~ 非白种人,(特指)黑人. *some* ~ *of truth* 若干真实味. *call to the* ~*s* 征兵,召服军役[入伍]. *change* ~*s* (激动得)变脸色. ***come off with flying ~s*** 旌旗飘扬地凯旋; 大告成功; 获得重大胜利. ***come out in their true ~s*** 暴露本来面目. ***desert one's ~s*** 变节;逃走. ***gain [gather]*** ~ 血色变好. ***get [win] one's ~s*** 〔英〕当选为(运动)选手. ***give sb. his*** ~ 选某人为选手. ***give a false*** ~ ***to*** 把…描画得[渲染得]象真的一样,歪曲. ***give*** ~ ***to*** 使(话说得)象真的一样,使…动听[生色],渲染; 润饰. ***haul down one's ~s*** 投降. ***hang out false ~s*** 带着假面具, 挂羊头卖狗肉; 假表态. ***have a high*** ~ 面色红润. ***in one's true ~s*** 露原形, 发挥本性. ***join the ~s*** 入伍. ***(the) King's [Queen's]*** ~ 英国军队的团旗. ***lay on the ~s (too thickly)*** 渲染太过;夸大. ***lose*** ~ 脸色变青,失色;退色. ***lower one's ~s*** 降低要求; 退让; 放弃权利[主张]; 投降. ***nail one's ~s to the mast*** 高竖旗帜, 坚决主张. ***off*** ~ (瓷器等)色泽不佳;音色不好;〔俚〕脸色不好,没有精神;〔美俚〕低级趣味的. ***paint in bright [dark] ~s*** 画得鲜艳[晦暗]; 赞扬 [贬损]. ***put false ~s upon*** 歪曲, 故意曲解. ***sail under false ~s*** (船)挂着别国的国旗航行;打着骗人招牌,凭伪善、欺骗过日子. ***salute the ~s*** 对军旗敬礼. ***see [not see] the*** ~ ***of sb.'s money*** 接受 [不接受] 某人款项. ***see things in their true ~s*** 看清事物真相. ***serve (with) the ~s*** 服兵役,当兵. ***show one's ~s*** 打出鲜明旗帜,说出自己意见[计划],现出本来面目. ***show one's true ~s*** 露出真面目, 露马脚. ***stick to one's ~s*** 严守原则; 坚持自己的立场. ***strike one's ~s*** 放下旗帜(投降). ***take one's*** ~ ***from*** 仿效,模仿. ***under*** ~ ***of*** 在某种幌子下. ***with ~s flying and band playing*** 大张旗鼓,得意扬扬. ***with the ~s*** 当着兵;现役. ***without*** ~ 不加渲染;无特色. — *vt.* ①给…着色,给…上色;染. ②渲染,粉饰,使带上色彩,歪曲. ③使具有特征. *an account* ~*ed by prejudice* 带有成见色彩的报道. — *vi.* ①获得颜色. ②(水果因熟)变黄[红等]; 脸红 *(up)*. ~ *up to the temples* (脸)红到发根. ~ **bar** 对有色人种的歧视[隔离]. ~ **bearer** 旗手. ~**-blind** *a.* ①不辨颜色的,色盲的. ②无种族歧视的. ~ **blindness** 色盲. ~ **box** 颜料盒. ~**-cast** *v., n.* 彩色电视广播. ~ **caster** 讲评精彩的广播员. ~ **chest** 信号旗箱. ~**-code,** ~**-key** *vt.* 对(电线、管道等)作上色彩标记. ~ **combination** 配色. ~**-distinction** 种族歧视. ~ **film** 彩色胶片[影片]. ~ **filter** 〔摄〕彩色滤光片. ~ **guard** 护旗队. ~ **line** = ~ bar. ~**man** 颜料商;染色师. ~ **painter** 突出着色的抽象派画家. ~ **photography** 彩色摄影. ~**plate**【印】彩色版;套色彩印图片. ~ **printing** 套色版,彩印. ~ **response** 色谱敏感性. ~ **question** 人种问题. ~ **sergeant** 护旗中士. ~ **stuff** 〔美口〕生动的记事文. ~ **television** 彩色电视. ~ **telly** 〔英俚〕彩色电视. ~ **transparency** 彩色幻灯片. ~ **wash** 彩色涂料;刷色. ~ **way**【纺】配色,色组.

col·our·a·ble ['kʌlərəbl] *a.* ①可着色的. ②经过渲染的. ③貌似有理的; 表面上的; 虚伪的. ~ *imitation* 外观好看的仿制品. ~ *sorrow* 假悲伤. **-bly** *ad.*

col·our·ant ['kʌlərənt] *n.* 颜料,染料.

col·our·a·tion [ˌkʌlə'reiʃən] *n.* = coloration.

col·oured ['kʌləd] *a.* ①有彩色的, 着了色的, 染过的. ②有色(人种)的, 皮肤黑的;〔美〕黑种人的. ③虚饰的, 花哨的,似是而非的. *a* ~ *person* 非白人;黑人. ~ **stone** (钻石之外各种色彩的)宝石. — *n.* 〔the ~〕有色人种的人〔尤指黑人〕;混血种人.

co·lour·ful ['kʌləful] *a.* 富于色彩的, 花哨的; 华美的; 精采的; 丰富多采的; 有趣的; 生动活泼的. **-ly** *ad.* **-ness** *n.*

col·our·ing ['kʌləriŋ] *n.* ①着色(法), 彩色颜料, 染料. ②(脸上的)血色. ③外观; 外貌, 伪装. ④渲染; 特色; (某种)倾向,色彩. ~ *matter* 色素,染料.

col·our·ist ['kʌlərist] *n.* ①着色者,善用彩色的人[配色师,画家]. ②笔墨生动的作家.

col·our·less ['kʌləlis] *a.* ①无色的; 苍白的; 退了色的. ②不精采的, 无特色的. ③中立的, 公平的, 无偏袒的; (新闻报道等)无倾向[色彩]的. **-ly** *ad.* **-ness** *n.*

col·our·y ['kʌləri] *a.* 多色的,多彩的;【商】(货物) 色泽优良的.

-colous *suf.* 住在[生在]…的.

col·pi·tis [kɔl'paitis] *n.* 【医】阴道炎.

col·por·tage ['kɔlˌpɔːtidʒ] *n.* 宗教书刊贩卖.

col·por·teur ['kɔlpɔːtə] *n.* 〔F.〕书贩; (尤指)贩卖圣经等宗教书籍的小贩.

Col.-Sergt, Col.-Sgt = Colour-Sergeant 掌旗军士; 〔英〕(海军陆战队)上士.

Colt [kəult] *n.* 柯尔特式自动手枪(= ~ revolver).

colt [kəult] *n.* ①幼小的公马[骆驼]; 顽皮小伙子; 不懂事的男孩子. ②没有经验的新手;【体】生手. ③【海】笞绳,绳鞭. — *vt.*【海】用绳鞭抽打. ~**'s tail**【气】凹凸云,卷云. ~**'s teeth** 轻薄,放荡.

col·ter ['kəultə] *n.* 前小犁,犁刀,犁头(=〔美〕coulter).

colt·ish ['kəultiʃ] *a.* 小马似的; 没有经验的; 轻浮的.

colts·foot ['kəultsfut] *n.*【植】款冬.

col·u·brid ['kɔlubrid] *n.* 黄颔蛇.

col·u·brine ['kɔljubrain] *a.* ①蛇(似)的. ②无毒蛇的. ~ *nature* 蛇似的性格.

co·lu·go [kə'luːgəu] *n.* 【动】猫猴 〔东南亚树居的一种哺乳动物〕(= flying lemur).

Col·um ['kɔləm] *n.* 科勒姆〔姓氏〕.

Co·lum·ba [kə'lʌmbə] *n.*【天】天鸽座.

col·um·ba·ri·um [ˌkɔləm'bɛəriəm] *n.* ***(pl. -ria*** [-riə]*)* ①(古罗马的)鸽棚[房]. ②(一格一格的) 骨灰匣壁龛; 骨灰安置所.

col·um·bar·y [ˈkɔləmbəri] *n.* 鸽棚,鸽房.

Co·lum·bi·a [kəˈlʌmbiə] *n.* ①哥伦比亚〔美国 Carolina 州的首府〕;(纽约的)哥伦比亚大学. ②〔诗〕美洲,美国〔意为 Columbus 发现之地〕. ③哥伦比亚杂交羊〔Lincoln 种和 Rambouillet 种的杂交,体格特大〕. ***the District of*** ～ 哥伦比亚特区〔美国首都华盛顿所在的行政区域,略作 D. C.〕 ～ **University** 哥伦比亚大学.

Co·lum·bi·an [kəˈlʌmbiən] *a.* ①哥伦比亚的. ②〔诗〕美国的. ③哥伦布 (Columbus) 的. — *n.*【印】一种活字.

col·um·bine[1] [ˈkɔləmbain] *a.* 鸽的,鸽似的;鸽色的. ～ *innocence* 鸽子一样纯洁无邪的.

col·um·bine[2] [ˈkɔləmbain] *n.*【植】美洲耧斗菜.

co·lum·bite [kəˈlʌmbait] *n.*【矿】铌铁矿.

co·lum·bi·um [kəˈlʌmbiəm] *n.* 〔废〕【化】钶〔现名 niobium〕.

Co·lum·bus [kəˈlʌmbəs] ①哥伦布〔地名,美国 Ohio 州首府〕. ②**Christopher** ～ 哥伦布〔1446?—1506,据传于 1492 年发现北美洲〕. ～ ***Day***〔美〕哥伦布节〔10 月 12 日,= Discovery Day〕.

co·lu·mel·la [ˌkɔljuˈmelə] *n.* ***(pl. -lae*** [-liː]***)*** ①【生】小柱;【动】(爬虫的)中耳小骨;(螺的)轴柱,壳轴. ②【植】蒴轴,果轴.

col·u·mel·li·form [ˌkɔljuˈmelifɔːm] *a.* 小柱形的.

col·umn [ˈkɔləm] *n.* ①【建】圆柱;圆柱状物〔如烟柱〕. ②【军】纵队 *(opp.* line*)*;队;(舰队的)纵阵,纵列,舰列. ③(报纸的)栏;【数】(纵)行;【印】栏,【化】塔. ④【植】雌雄合体的柱状花芯. ⑤〔美〕(党派、候选人的)全体支持者. ⑥(报纸上的)专栏(文章). *the* ～ *of the nose* 鼻梁. *spinal* ～ 脊柱,脊梁. *advertisement [literary]* ～ 广告〔文学〕栏. ～ *of fours* 四路纵队. ～ *of mercury [water]* 水银〔水〕柱. ～*s of smoke* 烟柱. *in* ～ *of sections [platoons, companies]*【军】按分队〔小队,中队〕编队. ***in our [these]*** ～***s***〔报纸编者用语〕在本栏内,在本报上. **-ed** *a.* 圆柱(状)的,有圆柱的.

co·lum·nar [kəˈlʌmnə] *a.* ①圆柱的,柱状的,圆筒形的. ②(报纸等)专栏的.

co·lum·ni·a·tion [kəˌlʌmniˈeiʃən] *n.* ①【建】列柱,列柱法. ②(页的)分栏.

co·lumni·form [kəˈlʌmnifɔːm] *a.* (圆)柱状的.

col·um·nist [ˈkɔləmnist] *n.* 〔美〕(报纸的)专栏作家.

co·lure [kəˈljuə] *n.*【天】分至圈,两至圈,分至经线,四季线. *the equinoctial* ～ 二分圈,昼夜平分圈. *the solstitial* ～ 二至圈.

Col·vin [ˈkɔlvin] *n.* 科尔文〔姓氏〕.

col·za [ˈkɔlzə] *n.* 菜籽(油). ～**-oil** 菜(籽)油.

COM = ①Computer-Output Microfilm 计算机输出缩微胶卷. ②Computer-Output Microfilmer 计算机输出缩微摄影机.

Com. = Commander; Commission(er); Committee; Commodore.

com. = comedy; comic; comma; commander; commentary; commerce; commercial; commission; committee; commodore; common(ly); communication.

com- *pref.* 与,共,总共,全,等〔在 b, p, m 前用 com-;在 l 前改用 col-;在 r 前改用 cor-;在元音及 h, gn 前改用co-;在其他场合下改用 con-〕.

co·ma[1] [ˈkəumə] *n.* ***(pl.*** ～***s)*** ①【医】昏迷(状态). ②怠惰;麻木.

co·ma[2] [ˈkəumə] *n.* ***(pl. -mae*** [-miː]***)*** ①【植】种毛,种缨;序缨;树冠. ②【天】(彗星的)彗发. ③【物】(透镜的)彗形像差.

co·make [ˈkəumeik] *vt.* ***(-made; -mak·ing)*** (担保)联署;共同签字 (= cosign). **-r** *n.* (担保)联署者;共同签字者.

Co·man·che [kəuˈmæntʃiː] *n.* (北美印第安人的)科曼奇族(语).

co·mate[1] [ˈkəumeit] *a.*【植】有种发的,有芒刺的;毛状的.

co·mate[2] [kəuˈmeit] *n.* 伙伴.

co·ma·tose [ˈkəumətəus] *a.* ①【医】昏迷的. ②怠惰的;麻木的.

co·mat·u·la, co·mat·u·lid [kəuˈmætʃuːlə, -lid] *n.* *(pl. -lae* [-liː]*)*【动】毛头星 (= feather star).

comb[1] [kəum] *n.* ①梳,篦,梳机;【纺】精梳机;【空】排管. ②鸡冠;鸡冠形物〔山顶、浪头等〕. ③蜂房;【动】栉. ④刻螺纹的某些器具. ***cut the*** ～ ***of*** 挫其锐气,杀傲慢气焰,使屈辱. ***go through [over] with a fine*** ～ 详细检查〔研究〕. — *vt.* 刷(毛),梳(发);(到处)搜寻,搜遍. — *vi.* (波浪)涌起浪花. ～ ***sb.'s hair the wrong way*** 使人发怒. ～ ***out***〔泛指〕彻底清除;搜罗;梳掉(脱落的毛发等);严密搜索. ～**-out** *n.* ①除掉不需要的人〔物〕. ②彻底搜查. ③搜罗. ④发型的梳理.

comb[2] [kuːm] *n.* = combe.

com·bat [ˈkɔmbət] *n.* ①格斗,搏斗;战斗. ②论战. ③〔美〕竞赛,比赛. *a single* ～(一对一的)格斗. *air* ～ 空战. — *vi.* 打,战斗;(和…)斗争 *(with; against)*;(为…)奋斗 *(for)*. — *vt.* 反对(不良现象等);防止. ～ *forest fires* 防止林火. ～ **car** 战车. ～ **crew** 战斗人员. ～ **fatigue** 战斗疲劳症. ～ **gains** 战绩. ～ **gasolines** 军用级汽油. ～ **orders** 战斗命令. ～**-plane**〔美〕战斗机. ～**-ready** *a.* 作好战斗准备的. ～**-unit** 战斗部队. ～**-worthy** *a.* 有战斗力的.

com·bat·ant [ˈkɔmbətənt] *a.* (参加)战斗的;好斗的. — *n.* ①斗士,战士;战斗部队,战斗员 *(opp.* noncombatant*)*. ②【美体】队员;【徽】二兽相斗式. ～ **branch** (陆军)战斗部队. ～ **nation** 交战国.

com·bat·ive [ˈkɔmbətiv] *a.* 好战的,斗志旺盛的. **-ly** *ad.* **-ness** *n.*

combe [kuːm] *n.*〔英〕(三面皆山或深入海中的)峡谷.

comb·er [ˈkəumə] *n.* ①梳者;精梳机,梳棉机. ②卷浪,碎浪.

com·bi·na·tion [ˌkɔmbiˈneiʃən] *n.* ①结合,合并;混合;联合,配合,组合. ②合作;共谋,同谋;同党. ③〔*pl.*〕〔英〕连裤衬衣. ④【化】化合(物);【矿】聚形;〔*pl.*〕【数】组合;【语法】组合词. ⑤附有旁坐的摩托车. ⑥暗码锁(的暗码). *a crystal* ～ 合晶. *a missile-cruiser* ～ 配备有导弹的巡洋舰. ***in*** ～ ***with*** 和…共同〔结合、协同、协力、共谋〕. ～ **car**〔美〕(头二三等的)混合客车. ～ **cracking**【化】(液相和汽相)联合裂化. ～ **gas** 富(含石油气的)天然气. ～ **lock** 暗码锁. ～ **room** (剑桥大学的)特别研究员餐后休息室. ～ **salad**〔美俚〕垃圾. ～ **vessel** 客货(混合)船.

com·bi·na·tive [ˈkɔmbinətiv] *a.* 结合(性)的,集成的.

com·bine[1] [kəmˈbain] *vt.* ①使结合,合并. ②兼备,兼有(各种性质等). ③使化合. *be* ～*d in* 化合成. *be* ～*d with* 与…结合着,与…分不开. ～ *A with B* 使甲乙相结合〔化合〕;兼备甲乙. ～*d accounts* 总帐. ～*d card* 联合梳麻机. ～*d efforts* 合作,协力. ～*d operations*【军】(海陆空军的)联合作战. ～*d parlour and sitting room* 客房. — *vi.* ①联合,合并,合作,配合,协力. ②化合. ～ *with* 与…联合;与…化合. **combining stress** 复应力. **combining form**【语法】构词成分. **combining power**【化】化合力.

com·bine[2] [ˈkɔmbain, kəmˈbain] *n.*〔美口〕①(政治上的)联合. ②联合企业〔工厂〕,综合工厂. ③联合收割机 (= ～ harvester). ④〔美口〕组合艺术. — *vt.* 用联合收割机收割(庄稼). ～ **harvester** 联合收割机.

comb·ing [ˈkəumiŋ] *n.*【纺】①精梳. ②〔*pl.*〕各级精梳毛;精梳落棉;短亚麻稭. ～ **machine** 精梳机.

com·bo [ˈkɔmbəu] *n.* ①=combination. ②〔口〕小爵士乐队. ③〔澳俚〕与土著女子结婚的白人.

com·bus·ti·bil·i·ty [kəmˌbʌstəˈbiliti] *n.* 燃烧力,可燃性.

com·bus·ti·ble [kəmˈbʌstəbl] *a.* ①易燃的，燃烧性的．②易怒的．— *n.*〔常 *pl.*〕燃料，可燃物．*a high-strung ~ nature* 一碰就发火的性格．

com·bus·tion [kəmˈbʌstʃən] *n.* ①燃烧，发火，点火．②(有机体内营养料的)氧化．③骚动．*spontaneous ~* 自燃．~ **bomb** 燃烧弹．~ **engine** 内燃机．

com·bus·tor [kəmˈbʌstə] *n.*【机】燃烧室．

comb·y [ˈkəumi] *a.* 蜂窝似的，蜂房状的．

comd. = command.

comdg. = commanding.

comdr. = commander.

comdt. = commandant.

come [kʌm] *vt.* (**came** [keim]; **come**) ①来，过来；去，上，赴．*He came (to my house) last night.* 他昨晚(到我家里)来过．*Come nearer (to me).* 再过来一点．*Come (and) see me = Come to see me.* 来(我家)玩呀．〔俚语尤其美国俚语中常略去and或to〕．*I will ~ (to see you) soon.* 我过几天去(看你)．*Let 'em all ~!*〔俚〕要来的都来！*Light ~, light go.* 来得容易去得快．*Will you ~ with me to Beijing?* 你愿意和我一道去北京吗？②(时间、季节等)到来．*Spring has ~.* 春天到了．*The time will ~ when....* …的时候快到了．*in the years to ~* 在今后的几年里．*in time(s) to ~* (在)将来．*the world to ~* 来世 *(It will be) two years ~ Christmas (= when Christmas ~s).* 到圣诞节就两年了〔例句中的 come 是虚拟语气现在时〕．③(事情)发生，落到…身上 *(to)*．*whatever ~s to me* 我无论发生什么事 (都…)．④来源于 *(of)*，得自 *(from)* *Dispute came of a trifling.* 争论是由一件小事引起的．*His money ~s from ....* 他的钱是从…那里得到的．⑤生自，出身于，是在…生长大的 *(of; from)*．*~ of a poor family* 出身贫苦．*I ~ from Shanghai.* 我是在上海生长大的，我是上海人．⑥想起，想出，想得；(东西)出来，出现于．*A good plan came to me.* 我想起一个好办法．*It ~s on page 10.* 那在第十页上．*A knock came to my door.* 有人敲门了．⑦日渐成熟．*The wheat began to ~.* 小麦发芽了．⑧达到，伸展到．*The road ~s to the station.* 大路一直通到车站．⑨做成．*The butter will not ~.* (怎样搅拌)奶油(始终)搅不出来．⑩有，装，存．*This shirt ~s to three sizes.* 这种衬衫有三个尺寸．*The lemonade ~s in a can.* 柠檬水是罐装的．⑪变…了，…起来，开始…；会，以至于，终于是〔接不定式或形容词型表语〕．*Things will ~ right.* 一切会顺利进行的．*I have ~ to like him.* 我对他喜欢起来了．*~ into sb.'s favour* 为某人所器重．*~ to grief* 失败．*~ to harm* 受伤，受害．*~ apart* 分开了．⑫〔与 how 连用〕(怎么)会的．*How ~ you to hear of it?* 你怎么知道的？⑬需要（某种）代价（才能买到、实现、得到等)．*Good service ~s high.* 服务好，收费高．⑭生活过得(如何)．*How is she ~ing these weeks?* 她这几个星期(过得)怎么样？⑮合计成；归结为．*Your bill ~s to 5 dollars.* 尊帐共计五元．*What you say ~s to this.* 你所说的总括来就是这样．⑯装作〔冒充〕…的样子．*~ the swell [great man]* 装阔，装做了不起的样子．⑰〔命令法〕喂！嘻！唉唉！*Come, tell me all about it.* 喂！全告诉我吧．*Come, don't flatter me.* 嘻！不要乱捧我．⑱〔口〕变得开始有同情心．⑲〔美俚〕达到肉体刺激的顶点．**Come!**〔美〕请进来 (= Come in!) ~ ***about*** ①发生 *(How did all this ~ about?* 这一切是如何发生的？)．②发生；(风等)变向；【海】抢风调向．~ ***across*** ①(穿过…)来到．②(偶然)遇见(某人)，无意中发现 *(~ across one's friend in [on] the street* 街上遇见朋友)．③〔美俚〕还(债)；尽(义务)．④难理解，不可信．⑤招认．~ ***after*** 相继；跟着…来，续来；探寻，找；来取．~ ***again*** 〔美俚〕请再说一遍．~ ***along*** ①一道来．②进步；同意，赞成．③〔祈使语气〕请过来，快一点儿！~ ***and get it*** 〔美口〕(饭预备好了)请过来吃．~ ***and go*** 来来去去，忽(来)忽(去)；变化无定 *(Her colour came and went.* 她的脸色一忽儿红一忽儿白)．~ ***around*** = ~ round．~ ***at*** ①袭击，向…打来．②赶上；得到；达到 (*~ at a true knowledge of* 得知…的真相．*Just let me ~ at you!* 让我跟你比一下；来，我跟你比！*First-class men are hard to ~ at.* 第一流人物难得)．~ ***away*** ①脱掉．②(一同)离开(某地) ★ Go away 则是叫人‘走开’．~ ***back*** ①回来；想起来；〔口〕复原，恢复，复苏．②〔美俚〕还嘴．~ ***before*** ①先来；优于．②被交付(审判等)，被提出．~ ***between*** 介入…之间；离间．~ ***by*** ①〔by 介词〕到手，获得．②〔by 副词〕通过附近；〔美俚〕拜访，看望．~ ***clean*** 〔美俚〕①坦白承认，说出实话，和盘托出．②修完课程．~ ***down*** ①降，落，下来；走向台口；(物价)下跌；(树)被砍倒，(屋)被毁．②(俚) 大学毕业．③传，传下来 *(from)*．④败落，没落；〔美口〕病了起来 *(with)*．⑤〔口〕(慷慨)解囊，拿出钱 (常加 *with*) *(He came down when I was hard up.* 我困难时他照顾过我)．~ ***down on [upon]*** ①袭击；反对；责备，骂；②向…索取(钱财) *(for)*．③严厉追究．~ ***down out of the tree*** 〔美〕拿出精神来；留神点；好好地干．~ ***down with*** ①害病；病倒．②〔口〕出(钱)，付．~ ***for*** 来取(物)；来迎接(人)．~ ***forth*** 出来；涌现；提出，公布．~ ***forward*** ①出来，出现；出头；(候选人)出来候选，应(众望)而起，自告奋勇，挺身而出．②增长．~ ***home*** ①回家．②【海】锚脱掉．③说得正对；刺中(…心病)，打动人心，影响深远 *(to sb., sb.'s heart, etc.)* ~ ***in*** ①进入，进来，入场 (*Come in* 请进来！请过来！)②当选，就任；上台，当权；(党派)组阁，取得政权．③到达．④流行起来；兴起．⑤到时候；到成熟期．⑥有用(起来)(*~ in useful* 有用，中用)．⑦(现款)收进，到手，(比赛中)获得…名．⑧起作用，有效；(幽默话的)有意义 (*Where do I ~ in?* 我的作用在哪儿呢？我的好处在哪儿呢？*Where does the joke ~ in?* 什么地方好笑〔意义在那里〕?)．⑨干涉，妨碍．⑩〔美俚〕(母牛)下仔．~ ***in for*** 来取；接受，领取(份儿)；受到(处分等)．~ ***in on [upon]*** 打动…，留在某人心里．~ ***in through the cabin window*** 〔美〕靠亲戚关系发迹，走后门．~ ***into*** ①归入，进入，开始 (*~ into notice* 使人注目，引起注意．*~ into sight* 被人看见，出现，靠近．*~ into use* 开始应用．*~ into the world* 生出，出世)．②缔结，订立，赞成，加入；支持．③得到，继承．~ ***into one's own*** ①收回自己的正当权利，恢复地位．②被人认识．~ ***it over*** 胜过；欺骗．~ ***it strong*** 〔口〕使劲〔坚决〕干；干得过分；夸大 (*He ~s it too strong.* 他干得过分了)．~ ***near*** ①不劣于，不亚于，及得上．②几乎，差一点就…．~ ***of*** ①由于，是…的结果 (*~ of drinking* 是喝酒所致)．②生自，出身，是在…生长大的．~ ***of age*** 成年．~ ***off*** ①(人)走了；(扣子、齿、发)脱落，(油漆)剥落．②成为 (胜利者等) (*~ off victorious* (战争)胜利．*~ off a gainer [loser]* (做生意等)赚钱〔蚀本〕)．③(计划等)实现，实行 (*When does the ceremony ~ off?* 仪式什么时候举行？)．④(预言)应验．⑤(事业)完成，结果 (*~ off well [badly]* 成功〔失败〕，顺利〔不顺利〕．*They came off with flying colours.* 他们凯旋而归．*Everything came off satisfactory.* 结果事事如意)．⑥离开，〔祈使语气〕停止！别那么说啦！(*~ off your high horse*〔美〕别那样骄傲，不要那样自大，不要那样固执．*~ off your perch*〔美〕不要那样神气，放下你的臭架子)．⑦〔美口〕孵出．~ ***off with*** 发表(言论)，讲出，宣布．~ ***on*** ①〔on 介词〕= ~ upon．②〔on 副词〕(演员)出台；进步，进行(得好)，发展 (*The crops are ~ing on nicely.* 庄稼长得很好)．③(冬、夜等)来临，接近；(敌人)袭来，攻来；(雨)下起来 (*It came on to rain.* 下起雨来了)．④(暴风雨等)起，发作；(病、苦痛等)加深，加重；(人物)给人突出印象，取得扎实的效果．⑤(问题)提交讨论；(事件)被提出来．⑥〔祈使语气〕跟我来！〔挑斗〕来吧！快点来！(*He is coming on.* 他(一天天)好起来了．*A trial ~s on.* 要开审了)．~ ***on in*** 〔美〕= ~ on．~ ***out*** ①出来；(花)开出．②(书等)出版，发行．③(秘密等)现出，露出．④(新玩

意儿)初次出现;初次登台，初进社交界；参加 *(for)*. ⑤【数】解答出来. ⑥罢工,罢业. ⑦〔美〕结果是;考取(第…名) (*The play ~s out well on the stage.* 这个剧本演出效果不错. *You ~ out well in that photo.* 你那张相片照得很好. *Nothing came out of all this talk.* 谈来谈去，结果全无. *The truth ~s out.* 真相大白，水落石出). ⑧消失. ~ **out against** 出头反对,反抗. ~ **out of** 出自,生自;(冲破…)出来. **Come out of that!** 走开!〔美俚〕去你的! 滚蛋! ~ **out with** ①发表,公布;讲出;泄露(秘密) (~ *out with an advertisement* 登出广告). ②展出,供应. ③跟…同行. ~ **over** ①〔over 介词〕(云) 密布(天空);(变化)发生在…;(感情)抓住(人). ②〔over 副词〕从远方来,渡过来,传来;(从敌方)过来,投奔过来;变卦,变节;〔口〕欺骗;顺便来访. ~ **right** 无事. ~ **pass** 通过. ~ **round** ①来，轮到. ②(生气的人)消除怒气;(病后)复原;苏醒. ③(风向等)改变;改变意见. ④让步,同意. ⑤笼络,诱骗 (*You can't ~ round me with such yarns.* 你别想用这套花言巧语来哄骗我). ~ **through** ①成功,胜利;脱险. ②(消息)传出;(电话)接通;通用,通行. ③〔美〕改变信仰,变节;欺骗. ④终结,完成. ⑤招认,坦白. ⑥支付;捐献. ~ **to** ①〔to 介词〕总计为,达到;结果是,终于 (*Has it ~ to this?* 弄到这个地步了吗? 弄成这个样子了吗?). ②〔to 副词〕苏醒,复原;把船朝着风头,逆风;停泊. ~ **to a point** 渐渐变尖. ~ **to think of it** 〔口〕这样一想，那么. ~ **to bat** 遇到难题,需要对付困难[考验等]. ~ **to no good** 弄不好,结果不好. ~ **to oneself [one's senses]** 苏醒;醒悟;复原. ~ **to pass** 发生,兴起,遭遇. ~ **to stay** 〔美〕木已成舟,(事)成定局,变成永久性的东西. ~ **to the point** 恰当,得要领. ~ **to the same thing** 殊途同归. ~ **to the scratch** 采取断然处置,采取行动. ~ **to time**〔美〕服从命令;满足要求. ~ **together** 会合. ~ **together again** 和好如初. ~ **under** ①编入,归入…类[项目]. ②受…的(影响),被…支配. ~ **unstuck** 碰到困难;垮台,失败. ~ **up** ①来，走近. ②上升;发芽;抬头. ③(暴风雨等)起,发作. ④上京,晋京. ⑤〔英〕搬进(学校)宿舍. ⑥流行起来. ⑦被提出. ~ **up against** 遇到(困难),遭到(反对);与…矛盾. ~ **upon** ①碰到，碰见;忽然想到;突袭. ②要求 (~ *upon sb. for sth.* 向某人要求某物). ③(人)成为…的累赘[负担];(工作)落到(…头上) (*The disabled men ~ upon the town.* 残废人得到地方照顾). ~ **up to** 到达;及得上,不亚于;不负(期待),适合(标准等). ~ **up with** ①赶上. ②补充;提供,提出. ③(向人)报仇. ~ **what may [will]** = ~ **weal or woe** 无论发生什么事情,怎样都,反正都. **for months to** ~ 此后数月. **How ~?** 〔口〕为什么? **How ~s it that …?** 怎么会…了呢? **the to-come** 〔俚〕未来,将来〔作名词用〕. ~**-and-go** ① *n.* 往来,来回,交通;收缩膨胀. ②*a.* 近似的,大致的;易变的. ~**-at-able** *a.*〔口〕易接近,易见面;不远;容易到手的. ~**back** 〔口〕①(声望等的)恢复;重整旗鼓，转好. ②〔俚〕巧妙的反驳[回答];〔美俚〕还嘴 (*have a ~back like a cork* 随即恢复[振作起来]. *stage a ~back* 卷土重来;复辟). ③〔美俚〕不满[抱怨]的理由 (*He was well treated and had no ~.* 他得到很好的待遇,没有什么可抱怨的了). ~ **down** 败落,落魄,没落;退步;(飞机的)下降. ~**-hither** ① *a.*〔美俚〕诱惑人的,迷人的. ② *n.* 诱惑,挑逗. ③〔对家畜呼叫声〕来来! ~**-on** ① *n.* 引诱;诱惑物;受骗者. ② *a.* 有诱惑力的. ~**-outer** 〔美〕脱党[退会]分子;急进分子.

COMECON, Comecon = *C*ouncil for *M*utual *Econ*omic Assistance[Aid] 经互会.

co·me·di·an [kəˈmiːdiən] *n.* ①喜剧演员;滑稽人物. ②〔罕〕喜剧作家.

co·me·dic [kəˈmiːdik, -ˈmedik] *a.* (关于)喜剧的.

co·me·di·enne [kəˌmediˈen] *n.* 〔F.〕喜剧女演员;滑稽妇女.

co·me·di·et·ta [kəˌmediˈetə] *n.* 小喜剧.

co·m·e·dist [ˈkɔmidist] *n.* 喜剧作家.

com·e·do [ˈkɔmidəu] *n.* (*pl.* ***com·e·do·nes*** [ˌkɔmiˈdəuniːz], **~s**)【医】(黑头)粉刺.

com·e·dy [ˈkɔmidi] *n.* 喜剧;喜剧场面,喜剧事件;喜剧性. *a light* ~ 轻松喜剧. *a low* ~ 滑稽戏. *a musical* ~ 音乐喜剧. ~ **of manners** (英国十七世纪末的) 风俗喜剧. **cut the** ~ 〔俚〕不再开玩笑. ~ **relief** 【影】穿插在紧张场面中的轻松镜头.

come·li·ness [ˈkʌmlinis] *n.* ①清秀，美丽. ②〔古〕合宜,适当.

come·ly [ˈkʌmli] *a.* ①好看的，清秀的，美丽的. ②〔古〕适当的,合宜的;满意的.

com·er [ˈkʌmə] *n.* ①来的人,前来(申请…)的人. ②〔美口〕有(成功)希望的人[事]. *a chance* ~ 偶然的来客,不速之客. *the first* ~ 先来者. **all ~s** 全体来人(申请人、应征者、中途加入者等) (*open to all ~s* 随意加入,欢迎加入).

co·mes·ti·ble [kəˈmestibl] *a.* 可以吃的. —*n.* 〔常 *pl.*〕食粮,食物.

com·et [ˈkɔmit] *n.*【天】彗星;【空】彗星机. ~ **finder [seeker]** 观测彗星用的一种望远镜，寻彗镜. ~ **wine** (彗星出现年酿造的)葡萄酒,醇美的葡萄酒.

com·et·ar·y, co·metic [ˈkɔmitəri, kɔˈmetik] *a.* 彗星(状)的.

co·meth·er [kəuˈmeðə] *n.* 〔英爱、方〕①事情，事件;情况. ②友谊,友好关系. **put the ~ on** 劝说,劝诱.

come·up·pance [kʌmˈʌpəns] *n.* 〔美口〕报应;应得的惩罚.

com·fit [ˈkʌmfit] *n.* (球状)糖果; 蜜饯，糖衣果仁. ~ **cocoons** 僵蚕茧.

com·fort [ˈkʌmfət] *n.* ①安慰. ②安慰的东西,慰劳品;安慰者. ③舒适，愉快. ④〔常 *pl.*〕(现代化)生活舒适用品[设备]. ⑤〔美〕鸭绒被. ⑥〔古〕【法】援助. *cold* ~ 聊胜于无的安慰. *creature [bodily]* ~*s* 物质上的舒适(指衣、食等). *What ~?* 〔古〕你好吗? **be cold** ~ 不很畅快. **be of (good)** ~ 畅快. **gifts of ~ and thanks** 慰问品. **give ~ to** 安慰. **live in** ~ 生活舒适. **take ~ in** 以…自慰. —*vt.* 安慰;使(痛苦等)缓和,使安乐;〔古〕援助，帮助. ~**bag** 慰问袋. ~**station [room]** 〔美〕公厕. ~ **stop** 〔美〕长途汽车中途的休息停车. **-less** *a.* 无安慰的,不舒服的;孤单的,孤寂的.

com·fort·a·ble [ˈkʌmfətəbl] *a.* 愉快的，安乐的，舒适的;令人感到安慰的. — *n.* 绒线围巾;〔美〕鸭绒被. **-ness** *n.*

com·fort·a·bly [ˈkʌmfətəbli] *ad.* 愉快，安乐，称心如意地.

com·for·ter [ˈkʌmfətə] *n.* ①慰问者. ②〔the C-〕【宗】圣灵. ③〔英〕毛围巾. ④〔美〕鸭绒被. ⑤〔英〕(哄小孩的)橡皮奶头.

com·fort·ing [ˈkʌmfətiŋ] *a.* 安慰的; 令人鼓舞的. **-ly** *ad.*

com·frey [ˈkʌmfri] *n.*【植】①紫草科植物. ②= daisy.

com·fy [ˈkʌmfi] *a.* (***-fi·er; -fi·est***)〔口〕= comfortable.

com·ic [ˈkɔmik] *a.* ①喜剧的. ②滑稽的,好笑的. ③连环图画的. — *n.*〔美〕①滑稽品;滑稽新闻. ②连环漫画. ③〔英俚〕(杂技团的)丑角,滑稽演员. **the** ~ 人间喜剧〔文学、人生等滑稽有趣的一面〕. ~ **book** 〔美〕连环漫画杂志. ~ **opera** 喜歌剧. ~ **paper** 报纸的连环图画版. ~ **relief** = comedy relief. ~ **strip** 连环漫画.

com·i·cal [ˈkɔmikəl] *a.* 滑稽的，好笑的，有趣的;喜剧性的;〔方、俚〕奇妙的. **-ly** *ad.*

com·i·cal·i·ty [ˌkɔmiˈkæliti] *n.* 诙谐,滑稽;滑稽的人[物].

Com-in-Ch = **Com-in-Chf** = Commander-in-chief.

Com·in·form [ˈkɔminfɔːm] *n.* (欧洲) 共产党(及工人

党)情报局〔1947—1956〕.

com·ing [ˈkʌmiŋ] *a.* ①就要来的,正在来到的,来(年),次(日),下(月、周). ②有前途的;正在崛起的,蒸蒸日上的,(人)新进的. —*n.* 进来;到达;〔美方〕发芽;〔*pl.*〕萌芽. *C-, Sir!* (本人)马上就来! *She is ~ nineteen.* 她快要满十九岁了. *the ~ week* 下星期. ***~ up*** 〔美口〕立正! 预备! ***~ out*** 【商】新发行的股票 (*bargain for the "C- Out"* 新股买卖). ***have it ~*** (奖、惩等)是应得的. ***have sb. ~ and going*** 使无路可逃,使进退维谷. ***the ~ thing*** 〔美口〕就要变得时髦[有重要性]的东西. **~-in** *n.* (*pl.* ~s-in) ①进入,开始. ②〔常 *pl.*〕收入. **~-of-age** *n.* 〔*pl.* ~s-of-age〕成年;成熟. **~-on** *a.* 顺从的.

Com·in·tern [ˈkɔmintəːn] *n.* 第三国际 (=Komintern) 〔1919—1943〕.

co·mique [kɔmik] *n.* 〔F.〕丑角;滑稽歌手;滑稽歌曲.

co·mi·ti·a [kəˈmiʃiə] *n.* 〔*sing., pl.*〕(古罗马的)公众议事集会,公民会议.

comitus gentium [ˈkɔmitəs ˈdʒentiəm] 〔L.〕国际礼让.

com·i·ty [ˈkɔmiti] *n.* 礼貌,礼让. ***the ~ of nations*** 国际礼让〔指互相尊重对方法律、风俗等〕.

coml. = commercial.

comm. = commentary; commander; commerce; commission; committee; commonwealth.

com·ma [ˈkɔmə] *n.* ①逗号(,). ②【乐】小音程,差音程. *inverted ~s* = quotation-marks. **~bacillus**【生】弧杆菌.

com·mand [kəˈmɑːnd] *vt.* ①命令,指令;指挥,统率(军队等). ②左右,支配,控制,管理,掌握. ③自由使用. ④博得,得到(同情等). ⑤(某一地点)远望,俯瞰,俯视. *You ought to ~ us.* 请随意指派我们吧. *~ the sea [air]* 掌握制海[空]权. *~ one's temper* 压制忿怒. *~ a good price* 能以高价卖出. *~ a ready sale* 获得畅销. *~ a view of* 眺望,俯瞰,展望. —*vi.* 指挥,命令. *Who ~s here?* 谁在这里指挥?这里的指挥人是谁? ***~ oneself*** 克己,自制. ***~ the services of*** 可自由使用. ***Yours to ~*** 敬请赐示〔信末的客套话〕. —*n.* ①命令,号令;指挥,统率;指挥权;支配权;【自】指令,信号. ②部属;管区. ③控制力,自由运用[操纵]力. ④司令部,指挥部;统帅地位. ⑤眺望,俯瞰,展望. ***at ~*** 得自由使用;支配自如. ***at [by] sb.'s ~*** 照某人嘱咐,听某人支配. ***~ of the air [sea]*** 制空[海]权. ***get ~ of*** 控制…(的要地). ***have a good ~ of (English)*** 能自由应用(英语). ***have at one's ~*** 得自由使用[能充分掌握]. ***in ~ of*** 指挥(着). ***lose ~ of oneself*** 失却自制力. ***take ~ of*** 担任指挥. ***under ~ of*** 在…指挥下,由…所统率. **~ car** 〔美〕指挥车. **~ code**【计】指令码,操作码. **~ module**【宇】(宇宙飞船上的)指挥[指令]舱. **~ night** 〔英〕举行御前演出的晚场. **~ performance** 〔英〕奉命进行的演出,御前演出. **~ post**【军】(战地)指挥部[所]. **-ism** 命令主义. **-ist** *a.* 命令主义的.

com·man·dant [ˌkɔmənˈdænt] *n.* ①司令官;指挥官;防区[要塞]司令官. ②〔美〕(陆军军官学校的)校长.

com·man·deer [ˌkɔmənˈdiə] *vt.* ①征用;强征(壮丁等),征发(粮食等). ②〔口〕强取,强占.

com·mand·er [kəˈmɑːndə] *n.* ①指挥者;【军】指挥官,司令官. ②【海军】中校,副舰长. ③木槌. *the supreme ~* 最高统帅. ***the C- of the Faithful*** 大教长〔Sultan 或 Caliph 的称号〕 ***the ~ of the point*** 侦察组组长.

com·mander in chief [kəˈmɑːndərinˈtʃiːf] *n.* (*pl.* *~s in chief*) 总司令;(海军的)舰队司令.

com·mand·er·y [kəˈmɑːndəri] *n.* ①〔古〕骑士团管领地. ②〔美〕社团〔秘密结社等〕的分团.

com·mand·ing [kəˈmɑːndiŋ] *a.* ①指挥的. ②威风凛凛的,外表庄严的. ③占有险要地位的,(高处等)居高临下的.

com·mand·ment [kəˈmɑːndmənt] *n.* 【宗】戒律;诫条,训条. ***the ten ~s***【圣】十诫;〔俚〕十指. ***taboos and ~*** 清规戒律.

com·man·do [kəˈmɑːndəu] *n.* (*pl.~s, ~es*) ①【史】(南非布尔战争时代的)义勇队. ②突击队(队员). ***~-Glider Corps*** 〔美〕滑翔登陆部队. **~ vessel** 登陆艇.

com·meas·ure [kəˈmeʒə] *vt.* 使等量,使成比例. **-ur·a·ble** *a.* 可成比例的.

comme il faut [F. kɔm il fo] 〔F.〕〔只作表语用〕得当;得体;合乎礼仪.

com·mem·o·ra·ble [kəˈmemərəbl] *a.* 可纪念的,值得纪念的.

com·mem·o·rate [kəˈmeməreit] *vt.* 纪念,庆祝;(某物)成为…的纪念.

com·mem·o·ra·tion [kəˌmeməˈreiʃən] *n.* ①纪念(物);纪念节日,庆祝会. ②〔C-〕牛津大学校庆. ***in ~ of*** 为纪念…,纪念…的.

com·mem·o·ra·tive, com·mem·o·ra·to·ry [kəˈmemərətiv,-təri] *a.* 纪念(性)的.

com·mence [kəˈmens] *vt., vi.* ①开始. ②〔英〕获得(*M.A.* 等的)学位. ***~ on*** 着手. ***~ with*** 从…开始.

com·mence·ment [kəˈmensmənt] *n.* ①开始,发端. ②〔the ~〕学位授予典礼,毕业典礼;〔美〕授奖典礼日 (=〔英〕speech-day).

com·mend [kəˈmend] *vt.* ①交托,委托,委任. ②褒奖,称赞. ③推荐,推举. *~ sth. to sb.'s care* 委托某人照管某物. *~ him to the directory* 向董事会推荐某人. ***~ itself [oneself] to (sb.)*** 给(某人)留下好印象,中(某人)的意. ***C- me to*** 〔古〕①请代我向…致意. ②〔口〕我还是比较喜欢[以为…比较好];〔常作反语用〕(*C- me to a decayed country parson for a dull dog.* 说到胡涂虫,那就要数老朽的乡下牧师了).

com·mend·a·ble [kəˈmendəbl] *a.* 值得赞美[推荐]的,很好的. **-ably** *ad.* **-ness** *n.*

com·men·dam [kəˈmendæm] *n.* ①(在正式牧师出缺时代理其职务时所享受的)薪俸代领权. ②代领的薪俸.

com·men·da·tion [ˌkɔmenˈdeiʃən] *n.* ①称赞,赞美. ②推荐. ③奖品. ④〔旧〕赞词,祝词;问候.

com·mend·a·to·ry [kɔˈmendətəri] *a.* ①称赞的,表扬的. ②推荐的.

com·men·sal [kɔˈmensəl] *a.* ①同桌共餐的. ②【生】共生的,共栖的. —*n.* ①共食者. ②【生】共生生物. **-ism, -ity** [ˌkɔmenˈsæliti] *n.*【生】共生.

com·men·su·ra·bil·i·ty [kəˌmenʃərəˈbiliti] *n.* ①【数】公度性,通约性. ②同单位;相应,相称.

com·men·su·ra·ble [kəˈmenʃərəbl] *a.* ①有公度的;有等数[等量]的,同单位的;能通约的 (*with*). ②相应的,匀称的;成比例的;相称的 (*to*). **~ number [quantity]**【数】可通约数[量].

com·men·su·rate [kəˈmenʃərit] *a.* ①同量的,同大的,同单位的 (*with*). ②相称的,相应的,相当的 (*to; with*);能通约的.

com·men·su·ra·tion [kəˌmenʃəˈreiʃən] *n.* ①公度,通约. ②相称,相应.

com·ment [ˈkɔment] *n.* ①注解,说明. ②评语;评论,批评;闲话,流言. *Her strange behavior caused a good deal of ~.* 她的反常行为引起了不少闲话. —*vi.* 注释;评论,提意见 (*upon, on*). *~ on [upon] a text [a current topic]* 对原文[一个当前问题]作评论. ***No ~.*** 无可奉告〔对新闻记者等提问时的惯用语〕. ***without ~*** 不必多说.

com·men·tar·y [ˈkɔməntəri] *n.* ①注释,评注. ②(编者的)按语;评论,批评. ③〔常 *pl.*〕纪事. *the Commentaries of Caesar* 恺撒的《高卢战记》. ***a running ~*** (书)逐句[逐段]的评注;(时事等的)系统评述;【无】(运动等的)实况广播[报道].

com·men·tate [ˈkɔmənˌteit] *vt.* ①给(文章等)作注解,释义,评注. ②连续地口头评述(比赛等). —*vi.* 作评论员[注释者].

com·men·ta·tor [ˈkɔmenteitə] *n.* ①注解者,注释者. ②(电台的)时事评论员，实况广播报道员. ③主持［解释］宗教仪式的非教士.

com·men·ter [ˈkɔmentə] *n.* 批评家;注解者.

com·merce [ˈkɔmə(:)s] *n.* ①商业,商务,贸易. ②社交;(思想的)交流;交际，应酬. ③〔古〕性交. *a chamber of* ～ 商会. *the world's* ～ 国际贸易. *have no* ～ *with* 跟…无来往［交往］. ～**-destroyer** *n.* 通商破坏舰.

com·mer·cial [kəˈmə:ʃəl] *a.* ①贸易的,商业上的;营业性的. ②〔美〕(能)大量生产的;营利(性质)的;面向市场的;〔美〕(广播)广告性质的. ③〔美〕中等的〔指商品肉的等级〕. — *n.* 〔英口〕跑生意的,旅行兜销员(= ～ traveller);〔美〕商业广告广播［节目］. ～ **agency** 商业征信所. ～ **agent** 贸易事务官;商务官;代理商. ～ **analysis**【化】商品分析. ～ **articles** 商品;(报上的)商业新闻. ～ **attaché** (大使馆)商务参赞. ～ **availability**【化】工业效用. ～ **chestnut** 〔美〕商业文件中的陈词滥调. ～ **company** 贸易公司. ～ **credit bureau** = ～ **inquiry office** 商业征信所. ～ **firm [concern]** 商店,贸易公司. ～ **museum** 商品陈列馆. ～ **operation** 商业行为,交易. ～ **paper** 商业票据. ～ **par** 商业平价. ～ **room** (旅馆中租给行商的)客商室. ～ **run**【化】工业过程,工业方法. ～ **size**【化】工业规模. ～ **sulphuric acid** 工业用硫酸. ～ **treaty** 通商条约. ～ **unit** 工业设备;工商业单位. ～ **usage** 商业习惯. ～ **value** 交换价值. ～ **weight** 正量,原量. **-ese** [-ʃəˈli:z] *n., a.* (函件上的)商业用语(的). **-ism** *n.* 商业主义,商业精神,商业习惯;商业文体［用语］. **-ist** *n.* 商业家,商业主义者,营利主义者. **-ize** *vt.* 使商业化,使商品化;使成营业性质;使供应市场 (**commercialized vice** 公娼制度). **-ly** *ad.*

com·mie [ˈkɔmi] *n., a.* 〔口,常 C-〕= Communist.

com·mi·nate [ˈkɔmineit] *vt.* (以上天的惩罚来)威吓.

com·mi·na·tion [ˌkɔmiˈneiʃən] *n.* 威吓;【宗】以蒙受神谴进行威吓. *the* ～ *service* (英国教)大斋忏悔. **-to·ry** *a.*

com·min·gle [kɔˈmiŋgl] *vt., vi.* 混合;掺合.

com·mi·nute [ˈkɔminju:t] *vt.* 把(矿物等)粉碎;研细;把(土地等)细分,分割.

com·mi·nu·tion [ˌkɔmiˈnju:ʃən] *n.* ①粉碎;研细. ②磨损. ③【医】粉碎性骨折 (=comminuted fracture).

com·mis·er·a·ble [kəˈmizərəbl] *a.* 可怜悯的.

com·mis·er·ate [kəˈmizəreit] *vt.* 怜悯;同情,哀悼.

com·mis·er·a·tion [kəˌmizəˈreiʃən] *n.* 怜悯，同情;〔*pl.*〕悼词.

com·mis·er·a·tive [kəˈmizəreitiv] *a.* 有怜悯［同情］心的;哀悼的. **-ly** *ad.*

com·mis·sar [ˌkɔmiˈsɑ:] *n.* ①政(治)委(员)=political ～). ②〔旧〕(苏联的)人民委员〔1946年前各部部长旧称〕. *a political* ～ 政治委员.

com·mis·sar·i·al [ˌkɔmiˈsɛəriəl] *a.* ①代表的,委员的. ②【宗】代理主教的. ③【军】兵站部的.

com·mis·sar·i·at [ˌkɔmiˈsɛəriət] *n.* ①【军】兵站部,军粮经理部;给养,军粮. ②〔旧〕(苏联的)人民委员部〔1946年前政府各部旧称〕.

com·mis·sar·y [ˈkɔmisəri] *n.* ①代表,委员;【宗】代理主教. ②【军】粮秣员,兵站负责人员;= commissar;〔美〕(军队、矿山等的)日用物资供销店;【影】(制片厂等的)内部食堂. ～ **general** 兵站总监. ～ **line** 补给线.

com·mis·sion [kəˈmiʃən] *n.* ①命令,训令;委任,委托;任务;职权. ②委员,委员会. ③(陆海军军官的)任命. ④【商】代办,经纪;手续费,佣金. ⑤【法】作为,犯(罪). *the C- of Overseas Chinese Affairs* 华侨事务委员会. ～ *agency* 代办业,经纪业. ～ *agent* 代办人,代办商. ～ *broker* 经纪人,掮客. ～ *of inquiry* 调查委员会. ～ *of the peace* 〔英〕治安裁判权;治安陪审团. ～ *sale* = *sale on* ～ 代售,寄售,经销. ～ *weaver* 代加工织造厂. *sin of* ～ 违法罪. ***get one's*** ～ 被任命为军官. ***go beyond one's*** ～越权. ***go out of*** ～ 退役;衰老死亡. ***in*** ～ ①现役的,服役中的. ②被委任的,带有任务的. ③委员代办的 (*put a ship in* ～ 征船;把军舰编入现役队). ***on*** ～ 受委托 (*sell on* ～ 托销);收取佣金. ***on the*** ～ 担任治安陪审员. ***out of*** ～ 退役,非现役;搁置不加使用中;(武器等)已损坏 (*put a ship out of* ～ 放回征用船;把军舰编入预备役). — *vt.* ①给与…以职权，委任;任命. ②委托. ③把(军舰)编入现役. ④(军官)被委任指挥(舰只). ～*ed officer* (少尉以上的)军官. ～*ed ship* 现役舰.

com·mis·sion·aire [kəˌmiʃəˈnɛə] *n.* 〔英〕①(穿制服的)门警. ②(伦敦退役军人转业的)雇工协会会员.

com·mis·sion·er [kəˈmiʃənə] *n.* ①(官厅委任的)专员委员;特派员. ②(税务等的)督察(官). ③(某些地方或机构的)长官. ～ *of banking* 〔美〕银行督察(官). ～ *of education* 〔美〕教育局长.

com·mis·su·ral [ˌkəmiˈsjuərəl] *a.* 接缝的,连合的.

com·mis·sure [ˈkɔmisjuə] *n.* ①接缝处,缝口. ②【植】(心皮的)接着面;【解】连合. ③(昆虫的)神经接索.

com·mit [kəˈmit] *vt.* ①犯(罪等);干(坏事等),做(某事). ②托,委;委任;(把议案等)交付委员会. ③【法】提(审);判处;收(监),下(牢). ④使承担义务,使作保证;【军】使投入战斗. ⑤损坏(名誉等),累及. ⑥说明自己立场［身分等］. ～ *an infringement* 违犯规则. ～ *a crime* 犯罪. ～ *sin* 犯(宗教、道德上的)罪过. ～ *robbery* 抢劫. ～ *suicide* 自杀. ～ *outrages* 蛮干,横行. ～ *sb. to prison* 监禁某人. *be in no way committed to* 决不偏袒. ～ ***one's soul to God [God's mercy]*** 逝世,寿终正寝. ～ ***oneself to*** 委身于,专心致志于. ～ ***to memory*** 记住. ～ ***to oblivion*** 置之脑后. ～ ***to sb.'s care*** 委托某人. ～ ***to paper [writing]*** 写上,记下. ～ ***to the earth*** 埋葬. ～ ***to the water [flame]*** 投入水中［烧掉］;水［火］葬. ***feel oneself committed*** 觉得有损自己名誉,觉得自己受到牵连［受义务束缚］.

com·mit·ment [kəˈmitmənt] *n.* ①(某种)作为;犯罪. ②委任,委托;(对委员的)托付. ③许诺,诺言;(受)约束;(承担)义务;债务. ④拘留,关押. ⑤信仰;赞助. ⑥投入(战斗). ⑦【股】买卖(契约).

com·mit·tal [kəˈmitl] *n.* = commitment.

com·mit·tee [kəˈmiti] *n.* ①委员会;〔集合词〕(全体)委员. ②[ˌkɔmiˈti:]【法】受托人,财产代管人,保护人,(白痴等的)监护人. *the Central C- of the Communist Party of China* 中国共产党中央委员会. *the (Communist) Party C-* 党委会. *The* ～ *meets at three today.* 委员会今天三点钟开. *The* ～ *get together with difficulty.* 委员会召集困难〔指人难到齐,通常用作 *sing.* 为宜〕. ***in*** ～ 由委员会审议中. ～ ***English*** 公文英语. ***C- of One*** 一人委员会〔被授与全权、行使一个委员会职权的个人〕. ***C- of Supply*** 〔英〕预算委员会. ***C- of the whole (House)*** 议院全体委员会. ***C- of Ways and Means*** 岁入调查委员会. ～**man** 委员. ～**woman** 女委员.

com·mix [kɔˈmiks] *vt., vi.* 〔古、诗〕混合. **-ture** *n.* 混合(物).

commn. = commission.

com·mode [kəˈməud] *n.* ①五斗柜. ②洗脸台. ③便桶 (=night-～).

com·mo·di·ous [kəˈməudiəs] *a.* ①宽敞的. ②方便的,便利的. **-ly** *ad.* **-ness** *n.*

com·mod·i·ty [kəˈmɔditi] *n.* ①〔常 *pl.*〕日用品;商品;农［矿］产品;有用物品. ②〔旧〕便利;利益. *prices of commodities* 物价. *staple commodities* 主要商品. ～ **money** 商品货币.

com·mo·dore [ˈkɔmədɔ:] *n.* ①海军准将. ②〔英〕分舰队司令官. ③〔用作客气的称呼〕前任舰长［船长］;游艇俱乐部会长;领港长. ④商船队的向导船. *an air* ～ 〔英〕空军准将.

com·mon [ˈkɔmən] *a.* ①共通的,共同的,共有的. ②公

众的;公共的. ③普通的,通常的,寻常的,平常的. ④平凡的,通俗的;粗俗的,低劣的. ⑤【数】共通的,公约的;【语法】通性的;通格的. *be ~ to* 共通. *by ~ consent* 全场一致,无异议,按公意. *~ as dirt* 最平凡的. *~ or garden* 普普通通的. *~ run of* 最普通的. — *n.* ①公(有)地. ②(牧场等的)共[公]用权 (=right of ~). ③〔*pl.* 作 *sing.* 用〕见 commons 词条. *above [beyond] the ~* = out of the ~. *in ~ (with)* 共通,共同,(与…)同样 (*charges borne in* ~共同负担的费用). *keep [be in] ~s* (在大学等)聚餐. *the (House of) C-*〔英〕下院,众议院. *out of (the) ~* 异常的,非凡的. ~ **beam** 标准天平;标准. ~ **cardinal vein** 总主静脉. ~ **carrier** 【法】运输业者,运输公司,转运行. ~ **cold** 感冒. ~ **council** 市会;村会. ~ **crier** 广告员,报告员. ~ **denominator** 公分母;共同特色. ~ **doings** 常食,粗食. ~ **factor**【数】公约数. ~ **gender**【语法】通性. ~ **good** 公益. ~ **honesty** 常有的诚实. ~ **jury** 小陪审团. ~ **knowledge** 常识. ~ **language** 共同语言. ~ **law** 习惯法,不成文法律. **~-law** *a.* 根据习惯法;按习惯法同居的;(子女等)由同居男女所生的. (*~-law marriage* 【法】非正式结婚,同居. *a ~-law wife* 同居的配偶). ~ **manners** 粗鲁. ~ **market**【经】共同市场(组织). **C-Market** 欧洲共同市场〔即"欧洲经济共同体"〕. ~ **measure**【数】公约数;【乐】= ~ time. ~ **nuisance** 妨害治安. **C- Pleas**〔英〕高等民事法院;〔美〕高等法院. ~ **right** 公民权. ~ **room** (牛津大学)特别研究员的餐后休息室;(学校的)教员公用室. ~ **salt** 食盐. ~ **saying** 俗话,谚语. ~ **school**〔美〕公立小学校. ~ **scold** 爱吵架的女人. ~ **sense** 通情达理,常情. **~-sense** *a.* 有常识的;明白的,一望而知的. ~ **stock**【经】普通股. ~ **talk** 传闻. ~ **time**【乐】普通拍子. ~ **touch** 平易近人的特征. ~ **welfare** 公共福利. ~ **trust fund** 托拉斯联合基金. ~ **woman**私娼. ~ **year**【天】平年〔相对于闰年而言〕. **-ly** *ad.*

com·mon·a·ble [ˈkɔmənəbl] *a.* ①可于村、镇公地放牧的. ②(土地)共有的,公用的,共同的.

com·mon·age [ˈkɔmənidʒ] *n.* ①(牧场的)共用权. ②共有地;公地. ③〔集合词〕平民,老百姓.

com·mon·al·i·ty [ˈkɔməˈnæliti] *n.* ①民众,老百姓. ②共同性;共通性.

com·mon·al·ty [ˈkɔmənəlti] *n.* ①平民,老百姓,民众. ②〔集合词〕法人,团体. ③〔罕〕平凡的事物. *the ~ of mankind* 人类社会.

com·mon·er [ˈkɔmənə] *n.* ①平民. ②(牛津大学等的)自费生;普通学生〔不是 fellow (特别研究员), scholar (官费生)或 exhibitioner (领助学金的学生)的学生〕. ③有共有权的人. ④〔罕〕英国下院议员. *the First C-*〔英〕(现指)枢密院议长;(原指)下院议长.

com·mon·place [ˈkɔmənpleis] *a.* 平凡的;陈腐的. — *n.* ①平常话;口头禅,常套话. ②常事,平常物品. ③备忘录 (=~ book). —*vt.* ①把…记入备忘录. ②由备忘录中摘出. ~ **book** 备忘录;笔[札]记本. **-er** *n.* 作笔记者.

com·mons [ˈkɔmənz] *n.* 〔*pl.* 常用作单数〕①平民,民众. ②众议院(议员). ③公共餐桌,公共食堂;〔牛津、剑桥大学〕份食;(一般)食物. ④公地. *a ~ of bread and butter* 一份黄油面包. *short ~* 质量不好的份食. *be (put) on short ~* 吃不饱,被减食.

Com·mons [ˈkɔmənz] *n.* 康芒斯〔姓氏〕.

com·mon·sen·si·ble, com·mon·sen·si·cal [ˌkɔmənˈsensibl, -sikəl] *a.* 通情达理的,符合常情的.

com·mon·weal [ˈkɔmənwiːl] *n.* ①公益. ②〔古〕国家;共和国;全体公民,公民社会.

com·mon·wealth [ˈkɔmənwelθ] *n.*① 公民(社会);团体. ②国家;(尤指)共和国;联邦. ③〔美〕州〔只用于 Massachusetts, Pennsylvania, Virginia 及 Kentucky 州〕. *the British C- of Nations* = the British Empire. *the C-*【英史】(1649—1956年的)共和政体.

com·mo·tion [kəˈməuʃən] *n.* 动荡,动摇;骚扰,骚动,暴动. *be in ~* 在动荡中.

com·move [kəˈmuːv] *vt.* 使动荡,搅乱.

commr.= commander; commissioner; commoner.

com·mu·nal [ˈkɔmjunl] *a.* ①自治体的,公社的,村社的;巴黎公社的;〔印〕部落的. ②群居的;社会的,公共的. ③对立宗教[种族]间的,社区[公社]间的. ~ **marriage** 共婚,杂婚,群婚. ~ **politics** 社会政治学. ~ **socialism** 地方自治社会主义. **-ism** *n.* ①地方自治主义. ②公社制(社会组织). **-ist** *n.* ①地方自治主义者. ②(1871年的)巴黎公社参加者.

com·mu·nal·ize [ˈkɔmjunəlaiz] *vt.* 把…收归地方团体所有. **com·mu·nal·i·za·tion** [-ˈlaiˈzeiʃən] *n.*

Com·mu·nard [ˈkɔmjunɑːd] *n.* 〔F.〕 巴黎公社社员;巴黎公社支持者. *the Wall of the ~s* 巴黎公社社员墙〔1871 年一批巴黎公社社员曾在此墙下英勇牺牲〕.

com·mune[1] [kəˈmjuːn] *vi.* ①(亲密地)商量,交谈,谈心 (*with*). ②〔美〕接受圣餐. *~ with oneself [one's own heart]* 沉思,内省. — [ˈkɔm-] *n.* 亲密的会谈;沉思.

com·mune[2] [ˈkɔmjuːn] *n.* ①公社. ②法、意、比利时等国最小行政区划的市区、村镇自治体. ③〔美〕(嬉皮士等的)群居组织. *the people's ~* 人民公社. *the Paris C-* 巴黎公社.

com·mu·ni·ca·ble [kəˈmjuːnikəbl] *a.* 可以传达[传授]的;(疾病)可传染的;〔古〕爱说话的. **-ness** *n.* **-bly** *ad.*

com·mu·ni·cant [kəˈmjuːnikənt] *n.* ①圣餐接受者. ②(消息等的)传达者. — *a.* ①通信息的;相通的,相交往的 (*with*). ②接受圣餐的.

com·mu·ni·cate [kəˈmjuːnikeit] *vt.* ①传达;传授. ②【宗】授与(圣餐). ③传染(疾病). —*vi.* ①通信,交通 (*with*). ②相通 (*with*). ③【宗】接受圣餐. ④传,移 (*to*). *~ by telegram* 用电报通信. *This room ~s with another room.* 这间屋子和另外一间屋子相通.

com·mu·ni·ca·tion [kəˌmjuːniˈkeiʃən] *n.* ①通讯,通知;交换;信息;书信,口信,通报. ②传达,传授;传播;传染. ③交通,交通机关;联系,连络(设备). ④【宗】接受圣餐. *a means of ~* 交通工具. *~ equipment* 通讯设备. *cut off ~* 切断连络[通讯]. *have no ~ with* 与…无联系[不通信息]. *in ~ with* 与…连络[通信息]. *privileged ~* 【法】①法律准许不外泄的内情. ②法律准许作为证词而提供的内情〔不构成诽谤罪等〕. ~ **cord** (火车中的)报警索. **~s carrier**〔美〕信息递送者. ~ **gap** 信息沟,通讯隔阂〔不同年龄、阶层等的人们因缺乏互通信息而产生的隔阂〕. ~ **[~s] theory** 信息论,传播理论. ~ **trench**【军】交通壕. ~ **zone**【军】后勤区.

com·mu·ni·ca·tive [kəˈmjuːnikətiv] *a.* ①爱传话的;爱说话的,藏不住话的. ②通讯联络的.

com·mu·ni·ca·tor [kəˈmjuːnikeitə] *n.* ①通信员,传达者. ②发信机;报知器;通话装置. *agitate the ~*〔口〕拨动某种传递信息设备铃〔如使用通话装置等〕.

com·mun·ion [kəˈmjuːnjən] *n.* ①共享,共有;共同参与. ②亲密交谈;(思想、感情的)交流. ③同信仰的人[团体,教派]. ④〔C-〕【宗】圣餐式;圣餐拜受. = (Holy C-). *be of the same ~* 是同派教友. *hold ~ with* 与…有(思想上)交往. *hold ~ with oneself* 沉思,内省. *in ~ with* 与…有连络,有共同利害关系. ~ **cup** 圣餐杯. **C- Service** 圣餐礼 **-ist** *n.* 领圣餐者.

com·muni·qué [kəˈmjuːnikei] *n.* 〔F.〕公报,官报.

com·mu·nism [ˈkɔmjunizəm] *n.* 共产主义.

com·mu·nist [ˈkɔmjunist] *n.* 共产主义者,共产党员. — *a.* 共产主义(者)的;共产党(员)的. *the international ~ movement* 国际共产主义运动. *C- Party* 共产党. *~ style* 共产主义风格. *C- Manifesto* 共产党宣言.

com·mu·nis·tic [ˌkɔmjuˈnistik] *a.* 共产主义(者)的. **-cal·ly** *ad.*

com·mu·ni·tar·i·an [kə͵mju:niˈtɛəriən] *a.,n.* 公有制社会的(成员)；鼓吹公有制社会的(人)．

com·mu·ni·ty [kəˈmju:niti] *n.* ①公社；村社；社会，集体；乡镇，村落；【生】群落，群社．②共有，共用；共同体，共同组织；联营(机构)．③共(通)性；一致(性)；类似性．*the European Atomic* ～ 欧洲原子能联营．*the European Coal and Steel* ～ 欧洲煤钢联营．～ *of interests* 利害相通．～ *of property* 财产的共有．*the Jewish* ～ 犹太人社会〔一个地区全部犹太人的〕．～ **antenna television** 共用天线电视．～ **centre** 〔美〕公共礼堂．～ **chest** 〔美〕共同(募捐来的)基金；公共资金．～ **singing** 团体合唱．～ **welfare department** 〔美〕社会福利部．

com·mut·a·ble [kəˈmju:təbl] *a.* 可以交[互]换的；可以折换[抵偿]的．*offences not* ～ *by fine* 不能用罚款折换刑罚的罪行．

com·mu·tate [ˈkɔmjuteit] *vt.*【电】使(电流)换向；变换(交流电)为直流电．

com·mu·ta·tion [͵kɔmju(:)ˈteiʃən] *n.* ①换算，交换，变换．②减刑；抵偿；抵偿金；划拨．③【电】整流，换向．④〔美〕使用长期票(在两地间)经常来往．～**-ticket** 〔美〕长期来往车[机]票，月(季)票〔英国作 season ticket〕．

com·mut·a·tive [kəˈmju:tətiv] *a.* 相互的，交互的，(可)交[互]换的．～ **law** 互换律．～ **field**【数】域(体)．

com·mu·ta·tor [ˈkɔmjuteitə] *n.* ①【电】换向器，整流器．②整流子．③交换机，交换台．④【数】换位子．～ **circuit**【计】环形计数器．～ **rectifier**【电】换向整流器．

com·mute [kəˈmju:t] *vt.* ①交换，变换；互换，兑换；划拨，换算．②减免(刑罚)．③抵偿，折算 *(into; for)*．④【电】变向，整流．～ *stone into gold* 点石成金．～ *foreign currency to domestic* 兑换外币为本国货币．～ *imprisonment into a fine* 以罚款代监禁．—*vi.* ①交换．②用钱折算 *(into; for)*．③划拨．④【数】对易．⑤〔美〕使用长期票经常旅行［来往］，通勤来往 *(between)*．—*n.* 通勤来往；通勤来往的途程[距离]．

com·mut·er [kəˈmju:tə] *n.* ①交换者．②〔美〕使用长期票经常来往者，使用月票上下班者，长期票通勤旅客．③【电】＝commutator．～ **belt [～land, ～dom, ～ville]** (在市内上班的)郊区通勤人员居住区．～ **time** 上下班时间．

Com·my [ˈkɔmi] *n.* ＝ commie.

COMNAVFE, Comnavfe [kɑmˈnævfi] ＝ Commander, United States Naval Forces, Far East 美国驻远东海军司令．

Com·o·ro [ˈkɔmərəu] **Islands** *n.* 科摩罗群岛〔非洲〕．

Com·o·ros [ˈkɔmərəus] *n.* 科摩罗〔非洲〕．

co·mose [ˈkəuməus] *a.*【植】具有丛毛的；多毛的．

comp[1] [kɔmp] *n.* 〔美〕恭维话；招待券．

comp[2] [kɔmp] *n.* 〔口〕排字(工人)．

comp[3] [kɔmp] *vi.* 进行(不规则的)爵士乐自由伴奏〔accompany 的缩略〕．

comp. ＝ comparative; compare; compiler; composer; composition; compositor; compound; comprising.

com·pact[1] [ˈkɔmpækt] *n.* 契约，协议，条约．*by* ～ 照契约．*enter into a* ～ 订契约，订合同．

com·pact[2] [kəmˈpækt] *a.* ①挤满的，密集的；紧密的；(物质)致密的；(体格)结实的．②简洁的，(文体等)紧凑的；【拓】紧列的．③〔诗〕由…组成的 *(of)*．—*vt.* ①把…弄紧密，把…弄结实，压实．②使(文体)简洁，简化．③使紧凑地组合成，由…组成．—*vi.* 变紧密，变结实．—[ˈkɔm-] *n.* 随身携带的粉盒；小型汽车．**-ly** *ad.* **-ness** *n.*

com·pac·tion [kəmˈpækʃən] *n.* 紧密；致密；压缩．

com·pa·dre [kəmˈpɑ:drei] *n.* 〔美〕知友，至交；伙伴．

com·pa·ges [kəmˈpeidʒi:z] *n. pl.* 骨架，结构．

com·pag·i·nate [kəmˈpædʒineit] *vt.* 使牢固结合．

com·pa·ñe·ro [͵kæmpəˈnjerəu] *n.* 〔*Sp.*〕同伙，伙伴．

com·pan·ion[1] [kəmˈpænjən] *n.* ①伙伴，侣伴；朋友．②(一对中的)一方．③最下级勋爵．④〔书籍杂志名〕指南，必读，必携，手册．⑤〔*pl.*〕伴生种，伴(细)胞；【天】伴星(＝～ star)．⑥雇来照料病人[老人]的人．*a boon* ～ 酒友．～ *for life* 终身侣伴[配偶]．*a Teachers' C- to...*, 教师用…(参考书)．～ *volume* 姐妹篇．***a ladie's*** ～ 女人手提包．～ ***at [in] arms*** 战友．*C- of the Bath* 第三级[最下级]巴斯勋爵．***make a*** ～ ***of*** 与…作伴，与…为友．—*vt.*(与…)同行，(跟…)搭伴儿去．～ **crops**【农】混间作物．～ **lode**【矿】副矿脉．**-ship** 伙伴关系；交往，友谊；〔英〕排字的伙伴．

companion[2] [kəmˈpænjən] *n.* ①【船】升降口．②＝～ hatch [head]．③＝～ ladder 或 ～way. ～**hatch [head]**【船】升降口盖[罩]．～ **ladder [～ way]** ①【船】升降口扶梯．②【空】坐舱走道．

com·pan·ion·a·ble [kəmˈpænjənəbl] *a.* ①可交往的．②爱与人作伴的；人缘好的．

com·pan·ion·ate [kəmˈpænjənit] *a.* 〔美〕伙伴的；友好的．～ **marriage** 试婚；同居．

com·pa·ny [ˈkʌmpəni] *n.* ①交际，交往；作伴；伴侣；朋友；来客．②(社交)集会，聚会．③一队，一行；(演员的)一班．④行会；公司，商号，商社；合伙者．⑤【军】连，中队；【海】全体船员．⑥消防队．*love one's own* ～ 爱独自一人(生活，行事等)．*Two's* ～, *three's none.* 二人成一对，三人不顺遂．*a theatrical* ～ 剧团．*a strolling* ～ 流动剧团．*a City C-* 伦敦的商业[同业]公会．*a limited liability* ～ 〔英〕有限公司〔略 Co., Ltd.〕．*... and Co.*… 公司；…之流，…一伙，…等．*Hitler and Co.* 希特勒之流．*bear [keep] sb.* ～陪伴某人．*be good [bad]* ～ 是个能[不能]相处得很好的伙伴．***fall into*** ～ ***with*** 和…交往［作伴］．***find (sb.) poor*** ～ 觉得(某人)不是个能相处的人．***for*** ～ 陪着．***get [receive] one's*** ～ 升为连长［上尉］．***give (him) one's*** ～ 陪他．***go into*** ～ 到大伙中．***have*** ～ 有客．***in sb.'s*** ～ 与某人一道［同席］．***in*** ～ 在大伙中，在人面前(假装做…)．***in*** ～ ***with*** 和…一道．***keep*** ～ ***with*** 和…常来往；同…结伴．***keep good [bad]*** ～ 与好人[坏人]来往．***keep to one's own*** ～ 独自一人．***know sb. by his*** ～ 观友见其人．***like sb.'s [one's own]*** ～ 爱和某人在一起［独自一人］．***part*** ～ ***with*** 与…告别［有分歧；绝交］．***present*** ～ ***excepted*** 在场者[在座者]除外．***see a great deal of*** ～ 交际广．～ **commander** 连长．～ **manners** 在客人面前的虚礼，客套．～ **officers**【军】尉级军官．～ **union** 〔美〕公司(的御用)工会．

compar. ＝ comparative; comparison.

com·pa·ra·ble [ˈkɔmpərəbl] *a.* ①可相比的 *(with)*；敌得上…的 *(to)*．②类似的．**-bly** *ad.*

com·par·a·tist [kəmˈpærətist] *n.* 比较语言学［文学］研究者．

com·par·a·tive [kəmˈpærətiv] *a.* ①比较(上)的．②相当的，还可以的．③【语法】比较级的．—*n.* ①可匹敌者；可比拟物．②〔the ～〕【语法】比较级．*in* ～ *comfort* 相当舒适地．*with* ～ *ease* 比较容易地．～ **adjective** 比较级形容词．～ **method** 比较(研究)法．**-ly** *ad.* (*-ly speaking* 比较地说来〔插入语〕)．**-tiv·ist** ＝ comparatist.

com·pa·ra·tor [ˈkɔmpəreitə] *n.*【机】比测器，比较仪，比长仪；【化】比色计；比…器；【无】比较器；比较电路．～ **block**【生】比色匣．

com·pare [kəmˈpɛə] *vt.* ①比较，对照 *(with)*；参照．②把…比作为 *(to)*．③【语法】把(形容词、副词)变成比较级［最高级］．—*vi.* 相比，匹敌 *(with)*．***(as)*** ～***d with*** 和…比起来．***be*** ～***d to*** 好比 (*Life is* ～*d to voyage.* 人生好比航海)．～ **notes** 对笔记；交换意见．—*n.* 比较．***beyond [past, without]*** ～ 无与伦比的，不可及的．

com·par·i·son [kəmˈpærisn] *n.* ①比较，对照；类似．②【语法】比较法；【修】比喻．*There is no* ～ *between the two.* 两者无法相比．***bear [stand]*** ～ ***with*** 不亚于，比得上．

beyond ～ 天壤之别; 不可相比. *by* ～ 比较起来. *Comparisons are odious [odorous].* 不怕不识货,只怕货比货;不和人家比,不显自己臭. *in* ～ *with* 和…比起来. *without* ～无与伦比.

com·part [kəmˈpɑːt] *vt.* 区划;隔开,分割.

com·part·ment [kəmˈpɑːtmənt] *n.* ①间隔, 区划;(小)室,隔室;舱,隔水舱;(火车的)分格车室;【林】林班. ②(英国议院在政府规定期限内讨论的)特殊协议事项. *a smoking* ～ (舟车中的)吸烟室. *a control* ～【火箭】操纵舱. ～ *under regeneration*【林】更新地. *be [live] in water-tight* ～ 和别人完全隔绝. ～ **ceiling** 格子天花板. ～ **roofing** 分区划的屋顶. **-al** *a.*

com·part·men·tal·ize [kəmˌpɑːtˈmentəlaiz] *vt.* 把…分成各自独立的几部分, 把…分成区; 把…分门别类. **-i·za·tion** *n.*

com·pass [ˈkʌmpəs] *n.* ①周围;界限,区域,范围;【乐】音域. ②罗盘,罗针仪,指南针. ③〔*pl.*〕两脚规,圆规. ④迂回的路径. *a radio* ～ *station* 无线电定向台. *beyond sb.'s* ～ 某人力所不及. *beyond the* ～ *of* 越出…范围以外. *fetch [go] a* ～迂回,绕道. *in small* ～紧凑,简洁,在小范围内. *keep (one's desires) within* ～ 克制着(欲望),不作妄想. *speak within* ～ 谨慎小心地说. *within sb.'s* ～ 某人力所能及. *within the* ～ *of a lifetime* 在人的一生中. —*vt.* 〔古〕围绕;沿着…划一圆圈,沿…绕行一圈. ②达成,完成(目的). ③图谋,计划. ④了解,领悟. ～ *the death of* … 图谋杀害…. ～ *one's object* 达到目的. ～ **card** 罗盘的盘面. ～ **plane** 凹刨,刳刨. ～ **plant** 指向植物. ～ **saw** 截圆锯. ～ **timber** 弯料. ～ **window**【建】半圆形凸窗.

com·pas·sion [kəmˈpæʃən] *n.* 怜悯,同情. *have [take]* ～ *on* 怜悯,同情. *fling oneself on [upon] sb.'s* ～ 乞求某人怜悯.

com·pas·sion·ate [kəmˈpæʃənit] *a.* ①富于同情心的. ②(津贴等)特赐的. ～ *allowance* 特别津贴. ～ *leave* 特准的休假. —[-ʃəneit] *vt.* 怜悯,体恤,同情. **-ly** *ad.*

com·pat·i·bil·i·ty [kəmˌpætiˈbiliti] *n.* 适合, 适应;兼容(性);一致(性),协调(性).

com·pat·i·ble [kəmˈpætəbl] *a.* ①协调的,相容的,可两立的,不矛盾的(*with*). ②【无】兼容的. ～ **colour** 黑白电视机亦可收看的彩色电视节目. ～ **colour TV system** 兼容制彩色电视,兼容彩色电视制式.

com·pat·ri·ot [kəmˈpætriət] *n.* 同国人,同胞. — *a.* 同国的. **-ic** *a.*

com·peer [kɔmˈpiə] *n.* (等级、能力等)同等的人,同辈;伙伴.

com·pel [kəmˈpel] *vt.* 强迫;胁迫;使不得不;迫使(服从、沉默等). ～ *sb. to one's will* 逼人服从自己. ～ *tears from one's audience* 使观众掉泪. *a compelling argument* 使对方无话可说的论据. *a compelling smile* 迷人的微笑. *a compelling gaze* 咄咄逼人的凝视. *be compelled to (do)* 不得不(做). **com·pel·la·ble** *a.* 可强迫的, **com·pel·la·bly** *ad.*

com·pel·la·tion [ˌkɔmpəˈleiʃən] *n.* ①称呼;呼唤(对方的名字或称谓). ②头衔;姓名.

com·pend [ˈkɔmpend] *n.* = compendium.

com·pen·di·ous [kəmˈpendiəs] *a.* 简明扼要的; 简略的. **-ly** *ad.* **-ness** *n.*

com·pen·di·um [kəmˈpendiəm] *n.* (*pl.* ～*s*, *-dia* [-diə]) 梗概,概论;摘要,概略;纲领;总目录.

com·pen·sa·ble [kəmˈpensəbl] *a.* 有权要求补偿[赔偿]的;应予以补偿[赔偿]的;可补偿[赔偿]的.

com·pen·sate [ˈkɔmpenseit] *vt.* ①赔偿,补偿. ②酬劳,〔美〕给…付工钱,给…报酬. ③【经】(调整金币成色以)稳定(货币的)购买力. ④【物】补偿…的变差;【机】补整. — *vi.* 补偿; 赔偿 (*for*). ～ *(sb.) for loss [services]* 赔偿某人损失[付予酬劳]. *compensating gear*【机】差动齿轮.

com·pen·sa·tion [ˌkɔmpenˈseiʃən] *n.* ①赔偿;补偿(金);报酬 (*for*);〔美〕薪水,工资 (*for*);【机】补整;【船】补强. ～ *for damage* 损害赔偿. ～ *for removal* 退职金,遣散费. ～ **balance** 补整平衡. ～ **method** 补偿法,对消法. ～ **pendulum**【物】补偿摆. *in* ～ *for* 以作…的赔偿[报酬].

com·pen·sa·tive, com·pen·sa·to·ry [kəmˈpensətiv, -təri] *a.* 赔偿的,补偿的;报酬的;补充的.

com·pen·sa·tor [ˈkɔmpenseitə] *n.* ①赔偿者. ②【机】补偿器;胀缩件;补偿棱镜;【电】调相机.

compère [ˈkɔmpɛə] *n.* 〔F.〕(演出等的)节目主持人, 报幕员. — *vt.* 主持(演出节目).

com·pete [kəmˈpiːt] *vi.* ①竞争 (*with; in*); 比得上,及得上;匹敌. ②比赛. *There is no book that can* ～ *with this.* 没有一本书抵得上这本的. ～ *in a race* 参加赛跑. ～ *with [against] (others) for (a prize)* 和(人们)争夺(奖赏). ～ *with (sb.) in* 和(某人)竞争.

com·pe·tence, com·pe·ten·cy [ˈkɔmpitəns, -si] *n.* ①资格,能力 (*for; to do*); 反应能力,胜任(性); 相当的资产[财力];(对于某种语言的)运用能力. ②【法】权能,权限. ③【生】(细菌的)遗传变化力,耐药力. *acquire a* ～ 得到相当的财产. *challenge the* ～ 对权限提出疑问. *exceed one's* ～ 越权. *have* ～ *over* 对…具有管辖权.

com·pe·tent [ˈkɔmpitənt] *a.* ①适任的,称职的,有能力的,有资格的. ②有职权的;正当的;合法的;有管辖权的. ③充足的,相当的. ④【生】(对抗生素等)有适应力的,有耐药性的;有抵抗力的. *It is perfectly* ～ *for me to refuse* 我拒绝是十分正当的. *It is* ～ *to Parliament to prohibit it* 议会有禁止它的权力. ～ *income* 相当的收入. *the* ～ *authorities* 主管当局. *the* ～ *minister* 主管部长. **-ly** *ad.*

com·pe·ti·tion [ˌkɔmpiˈtiʃən] *n.* ①竞争. ②竞赛, 比赛. ③【生】生存竞争. *a boxing* ～ 拳击比赛. ～ *in arms* 军备竞赛. *be [stand] in* ～ *with (sb.) for* 为…和(某人)竞争. *put (sb.) in [into]* ～ *with* … 使(某人)与(另一人)竞争.

com·pet·i·tive [kəmˈpetitiv] *a.* 竞争的, 竞赛的. ～ *bidding system* 招标制. ～ *examination* 竞争考试. ～ *exhibition* 竞赛(展览)会. ～ **shading**【植】(植株间的)互相荫蔽. **-ly** *ad.*

com·pet·i·tor [kəmˈpetitə] *n.* 竞争者;敌手.

com·pet·i·to·ry [kəmˈpetitəri] *a.* = competitive.

com·pet·i·tress, com·pet·i·trix [kəmˈpetitris, -triks] *n.* 女竞争者;女对手.

com·pil·a·tion [ˌkɔmpiˈleiʃən] *n.* 汇集, 编辑(物);汇编.

com·pil·a·to·ry [kəmˈpailətəri] *a.* 汇集的,编辑的.

com·pile [kəmˈpail] *vt.* 汇集,编辑,编制;搜集(资料). ～ *a dictionary* 编词典. ～ *a budget* 编预算.

com·pil·er [kəmˈpailə] *n.* ①汇集者,编辑(人). ②【计】自动编码器;自动编码[编译]程序.

compl. = complement.

com·pla·cence, com·pla·cen·cy [kəmˈpleisns, -si] *n.* 满足,(特指)骄傲自满,自得.

com·pla·cent [kəmˈpleisnt] *a.* 满足的,(特指)自满的,得意的,自得的. *We must not become* ～ *over any success.* 我们决不能一见成绩就自满. **-ly** *ad.*

com·plain [kəmˈplein] *vi.* ①(对某事)诉苦,抱怨,叫屈;发牢骚. ②(病人)自诉有…病痛(*of*). ③向某人(*to*)申诉,控诉 (*of, about*). ④〔诗〕呻吟,呜咽,哀号. *He* ～*ed to the manager about the service.* 他抱怨服务员态度不好. ～ *of a stomach-ache* (病人)自诉有胃痛病. ～ *to the city authorities of a public nuisance* 向市政当局控诉公害. — *vt.* 抱怨,控诉[与 that 从句连用]. *They* ～*ed that the price of books had increased.* 他们抱怨说书籍价格提高了.

com·plain·ant [kəmˈpleinənt] *n.* ①诉苦者, 抱怨者. ②控诉者;原告.

com·plaint [kəmˈpleint] *n.* ①不平,牢骚,委屈,意见,怨

言。②不平的来由，痛苦根源。③控诉；申诉；【美】(民事诉讼中原告一方的)指控。④疾病，病痛；【医】主诉。*a bowel* ~ 肠炎。***make [lodge, lay] a* ~ *against*** 控告。~ **department** 顾客意见接纳处。

com·plai·sance [kəmˈpleizəns] *n.* 殷勤，恳切，亲切(行为)；讨好(行为)。

com·plai·sant [kəmˈpleizənt] *a.* 殷勤的；恳切的；讨好的。**-ly** *ad.*

com·pla·nate [ˈkɔmplənit] *a.* 平坦的；平面的。

com·pla·na·tion [ˌkɔmpləˈneiʃən] *n.* ①平面化。②【数】曲面求积法。

com·plect [kəmˈplekt] *vt.* 〔古〕交缠，交织。

com·plect·ed [kəmˈplektid] *a.* 〔美方，口〕面色…的，肤色…的。〔常用以构成复合词〕*a light-*~ *boy* 肤色白的少年。

com·ple·ment [ˈkɔmplimənt] *n.* ①补足(物)；补全；互补(成分)，补充。②(必需的)定量，全量；整套，整组；【海】(船员的)定额；【军】编制人数，定额装备。③【语法】补(足)语；【数】余角，余弧，余数；余集；【计】补数，补码；反码；【乐】补足音程；【生】补体[免疫]；组[细胞]。*The regiment had its* ~ *of men.* 这个团的兵员已足额。~ *of nine's* 十进制反码。~ *of one's* 二进制反码。~ *of ten's* 十进制补码。~ *of two's* 二进制补码。~ *of an angle* 余角。— [ˈkɔmpliment, ˌkɔmpliˈment] *vt.* 补充，补足。~ *each other* 互为补充。

com·ple·men·tal, com·ple·men·ta·ry [ˌkɔmpliˈmentl,-təri] *a.* 补充的；补足的；互补的；【生】互配(力)的。~ **colour** 余色，补色。~ **event**【统】相补[互补]事件。~ **factor** 互补因子。~ **interval**【乐】补足音程。~ **minor**【数】余子式。

com·ple·men·tar·i·ty [ˌkɔmplimenˈtæriti] *n.* 互补(性)；互关性；【物】并协性；【生】(核苷酸的)互配能力。

com·plete [kəmˈpli:t] *a.* ①完全的，圆满的；全面的；全能的。②完成的，结束的。③〔古〕老练的。*a* ~ *ass* 大傻瓜。~ *works* (作品的)全集。*a* ~ *set* 全套。*a* ~ *success [failure]* 大成功[失败]。*This month is now* ~. 本月到此结束。*The task is* ~. 任务完成了。*a* ~ *divorce*【法】离婚。*a* ~ *angler* 钓鱼名手。— *vt.* 完成，使完满，使完工，完结；配齐，凑满。~ *a task* 完工。~ *sb.'s happiness* 使某人快乐到极点。~ *the whole course* 修毕全部课程。***To* ~ *(the sum of) one's misery.*** 不幸之上再加不幸，祸不单行。**-ly** *ad.* **-ness** *n.*

com·ple·tion [kəmˈpli:ʃən] *n.* ①成就，完成，实现；【数】求全法。②满期；毕业。*bring [be brought] to* ~ 使完成[完工]。~ *of a course* 修毕课程，毕业。~ *of a term* 满期，结束。

com·plex [ˈkɔmpleks] *a.* ①复杂的，错综的。②合成的，综合的；【化】络合的。③【语法】复合的；含有从属子句的。— *n.* ①复杂；合成物。②联合企业。③【化】络合物，复合物，综合体；【生】染色体组；【数】复数；线丛；【语法】复合句；【心】意结，情结，变态[复合]心理。*an iron and steel* ~ 钢铁联合企业。*the inferiority* ~ 自卑情结〔一种由自卑感引起的复杂心理状态〕。*the superiority* ~ 自高情结〔由自我优越感引起的一种复杂心理〕。~ *of circles*【数】圆丛。~ *of external conditions* 外界条件总体。~ **builder**【化】螯合剂。~ **ion**【化】络离子。~ **plane** 复数平面。~ **sentence**【语法】复合句。

com·plex·ion [kəmˈplekʃən] *n.* ①面色，气色，肤色。②(天)色，情况，形势，局面；【物】配容。③〔古〕(人的)天性，气质。*give a fair* ~ 装得美丽漂亮。*put a false* ~ *on a remark* (故意)歪曲某一句话。*put another* ~ *on* 改变…的局面。*the* ~ *of the war* 战局。**-al, -ed** *a.* 〔常用以构成复合词〕面[肤]色…的；天性…的 (*fair- [dark-]* ~*ed* 面[肤]色白[黑]的)。**-less** *a.* (面色等)苍白的。

com·plex·i·ty [kəmˈpleksiti] *n.* ①复杂性，复合状态。②复合物；复杂的事物[情况]。

com·pli·a·ble [kəmˈplaiəbl] *a.* = compliant.

com·pli·ance, com·pli·an·cy [kəmˈplaiəns,-si] *n.* ①应允，答应(要求等)。②和蔼，温和；顺从，服从；盲从；【物】柔量；【数】顺性。*feigning* ~ 阳奉阴违，假装同意。***in* ~ *with*** *(your wishes)* 遵照(您的愿望)。

com·pli·ant [kəmˈplaiənt] *a.* 应允的；服从的；温顺的。

com·pli·ca·cy [ˈkɔmplikəsi] *n.* ①复杂性，错综性；混乱状态。②错综复杂的事物[情况]。

com·pli·cate [ˈkɔmplikeit] *vt.* 把…弄复杂，使错综，使混乱。*That would* ~ *matters.* 那会使事情弄得更麻烦的。*be* ~*ed in* 卷入…(的麻烦中)。— *vi.* 变复杂。— *a.* ①复杂的，麻烦的。②(昆虫的翅)纵折的。

com·pli·cat·ed [ˈkɔmplikeitid] *a.* 复杂的，错杂的，混乱的，麻烦的。**-ly** *ad.* **-ness** *n.*

com·pli·ca·tion [ˌkɔmpliˈkeiʃən] *n.* ①错杂，混杂；纠纷。②【医】并发症。③【心】混化，复化；精神错乱。*to cause* ~ 节外生枝。

com·plice [ˈkɔmplis] *n.* 〔古〕同谋者，从犯。

com·plic·i·ty [kəmˈplisiti] *n.* 共谋，共犯；牵连(*in*)。

com·pli·er [kəmˈplaiə] *n.* 依从者，听从者。

com·pli·ment [ˈkɔmplimənt] *n.* ①恭维话，赞辞；敬意，礼仪。②〔*pl.*〕道贺，贺词，问候。③〔古，美〕礼物，慰劳品。*He did me the* ~ *of listening.* 他郑重其事地[很客气地]倾听了我的话。*Your presence is a great* ~. 承蒙光临，不胜荣幸。*a doubtful [left-handed]* ~ 挖苦[恶意]的恭维话。***Give [Present] my* ~*s to*** 请向…致意[问候]。***make [pay, present] one's* ~*s*** 问好，问候。***make [pay] a* ~ *to*** 恭维，夸奖，颂扬；问候，表示敬意。***return the* ~** 答礼，还礼；报复。***send one's* ~*s*** 致意，致候。***the* ~*s of the season*** 恭贺佳节〔贺年等〕。***with the* ~*s of*** *(the author)* = ***with*** *(the author's)* ~***s*** (著者)敬赠。— *vt.* ①向…问候[致敬]。②恭维，夸奖；祝贺。③赠呈。— *vi.* 说恭维话。~ ***away*** 说好话解决。~ *(sb.)* ***into*** *(compliance)* 用恭维话使(某人)应允。~ *(sb.)* ***on*** *(his courage)* 夸奖(某人勇敢)。~ *(sb.)* ***out of*** *(his money)* 恭维(某人)以骗取(钱财)。~ *(sb.)* ***with*** *(a book)* 赠(书)给(某人)。

com·pli·men·ta·ry [ˌkɔmpliˈmentəri] *a.* ①问候的，祝贺的，致敬的；称赞的。②会说恭维话的，善于辞令的。③免费赠送的。*He is too* ~. 他太客气[会说恭维话]。~ **address** 贺辞。~ **ticket** 招待券，优待券。

com·plin(e) [ˈkɔmplin] *n.*【宗】晚祷。

com·plot [ˈkɔmplɔt] *n.* 共谋；密谋。— [kəmˈplɔt] *vt., vi.* 〔古〕共谋。

complt. = complainant.

com·ply [kəmˈplai] *vi.* 应允，答应，依从，同意；遵照。*To* ~ *with sb.'s request* 答应某人要求；~ *with the rules* 遵守规则行事。~ ***with a formality*** 履行手续。

com·po[1] [ˈkɔmpəu] *n.* ①混合(物)；组合(物)；混合涂料，灰沙；人造象牙。②(船员的)部分工资，预付的部分工资。~ **rations** 大包综合配给口粮〔供若干天食用的〕。

com·po[2] [ˈkɔmpəu] *n.* 〔澳俚〕工伤赔偿金。

com·po·nent [kəmˈpəunənt] *a.* 构成的，组成的，合成的，成分的。~ *motion*【物】分运动。~ *part* 组成部分。— *n.* 部分，成分；【物】分力，分向量；【自】元件，组件，部件。~ *of force*【物】分力。~ *(star)*【天】子星。~*s of cost* (各种)生产费用。

com·port [kəmˈpɔ:t] *vt.* 〔书面语〕处身，持己，表现；举动，行为 (*oneself*)。~ *oneself with dignity* 举止庄重。*He* ~*ed himself as if he had already been elected.* 他表现出好象他已经当选了似的。— *vi.* 与…一致，相称，相适应。*His remark simply does not* ~ *with his known attitude.* 他的发言同他一贯的态度极不相称。

com·pose [kəmˈpəuz] *vt.* ①组成，构成。②创作(诗歌，乐曲等)；撰写；为(歌词等)谱曲；构(图)，设计。③【印】排(字)。④使安定[平静，镇定]。④正(容)；整顿；安顿(死尸)。⑤调停(纷争等)。~ *a poem* 作诗。~ *a novel*

写小说. ~ *a dispute* 调解纷争. ~ *one's features* 使面色[态度]平静下来. ~ *one's thoughts for action* 打定主意[考虑好办法]准备行动. ~ *one's mind* 平心静气,安心. — *vi.* ①创作,作曲. ②排字. ***be ~d of*** 由…组成. ~ ***oneself*** 使自己镇定[安心]下来 (*to sleep* 等).

com·posed [kəmˈpəuzd] *a.* 镇静的,沉着的,从容自若的. **-ly** [-zidli]*ad.* **-ness** *n.*

com·pos·er [kəmˈpəuzə] *n.* ①作曲家;作者. ②调停人,和解人. ③设计者,制图者.

com·pos·ing [kəmˈpəuziŋ] *a.* 起镇静作用的,镇静的. — *n.*【印】排字. ~ **frame** 排字架. ~ **medicine** 镇静剂. ~ **machine** 排字机. ~ **stick** 排字盘.

com·pos·ite [ˈkɔmpəzit, -zait] *a.* ①并合的,复合的,混成的,合成的,集成的. ②【建】混合式的;【船】铁骨木壳的. ③【植】菊科的. — *n.* ①合成物;混合蜡烛,混合客车,综合照片;混合式(建筑物). ②【植】菊科植物. ~ **candle** 混合蜡烛. ~ **carriage** 混合客车. ~ **forest** 中林. ~ **number**【数】合成数,非素数. ~ **photograph** (由几张底片合印成的)综合照片. ~ **ship** 铁骨木皮船. ~ **system** 金银本位并用制;【电】报话复合制.

com·po·si·tion [ˌkɔmpəˈziʃən] *n.* ①作文(法),作诗(法),作曲(法);作品,文章;乐曲;文体,措辞. ②编制;结构,构造,组成,组织;成分;合成物. ③素质,性格. ④构图,配合,布置. ⑤妥协,和解(条件);(私下了结的)和解费,(议定的)偿付额. ⑥【印】排字. ⑦【逻】综合法,合成推理;【语法】复合法;【社】结合体. *Latin prose ~s* 拉丁散文作品. *a stone ~* 石刻品. *He has not a spark of generosity in his ~.* 他(性格中)一点肚量也没有. *a ~ of 5 sh. in the pound* 每镑照赔五先令. ~ *for violin* 提琴曲. ~ *of a picture* 绘画构图. ~ *of air* 空气成分. ***make a ~ with*** *(sb.'s creditors)* 和(各债权人)议定偿还办法. ~ **billiard-ball**【台球】人造象牙球. ~ **book** 〔美〕作文簿. ~ **cloth** 防水帆布.

com·po·si·tion·a·lism [kɔmpəˈziʃənəlizəm] *n.*【文艺】构成派.

com·po·si·tive [kəmˈpɔzitiv] *a.* 合成的,综合的.

com·pos·i·tor [kəmˈpɔzitə] *n.*【印】排字工人.

compos mentis [ˈkɔmpɔs ˈmentis] 〔L.〕【法】精神健全[正常]的.

com·pos·sible [kɔmˈpɔsəbl] *a.* 可共存的;并行不悖的. *The two theories vary, but they are ~.* 这两种理论虽然各有千秋,但它们是并行不悖的.

com·post [ˈkɔmpɔst] *n.* ①混合物,合成物. ②【农】混合肥料,堆肥;混合涂料,灰泥. — *vt.*【农】使成混合肥料[堆肥];给…施堆肥.

com·po·sure [kəmˈpəuʒə] *n.* 镇静,沉着. ***keep [lose] one's*** ~ 沉住[沉不住]气. ***with great*** ~ 泰然自若,极镇静.

com·po·ta·tion [ˌkɔmpəˈteiʃən] *n.* 〔书〕共饮,会饮,聚饮.

com·po·ta·tor [ˈkɔmpəteitə] *n.* 酒伴,共饮者,会饮者.

com·pote [ˈkɔmpəut] *n.* 水果糖浆〔如糖水樱桃等〕;〔美〕(饭后的)一碟甜食. ②(高脚)果碟.

com·pound[1] [kəmˈpaund] *vt.* ①使混合,调合,配合;【语】复合,合成. ②(通过互相让步等)解决(纠纷);用钱了结(债务等);一次清算;部分偿还. ③【电】复绕[复激、复卷]. ~ *a medicine* 配药. ~ *a felony*【法】用钱抵赎罪罚. — *vi.* 和解,谈妥,和平了结. ~ ***with*** *(sb.)* 与(某人)和解[和平了结]. — [ˈkɔmpaund] *a.* 混合的,复合的;合成的,复式的. — *n.* 混合物,合成品;【化】化合物;【语】复合词. *cutting ~* 润削剂. *filling ~* 填料. *sealing ~* 封口胶. ~ **animal**【动】群栖动物. ~ **addition [subtraction]** 复名数加[减]算. ~ **discount**【商】复贴现. ~ **engine**【机】复合机. ~ **eye**【动】复眼. ~ **flower**【植】聚合花. ~ **fracture**【医】哆开[开放]骨折,有创骨折. ~ **glass** 多层玻璃. ~ **motor** 复激电动机. ~ **number**【数】复名数. ~ **sentence**【语法】并列句. ~ **statement**【计】复合语句. ~ **word** 复合词.

compound[2] [ˈkɔmpaund] *n.* ①(印度等地工厂、住宅的)圈占地区(南非等地用围墙等围起的)矿工居住区. ②圈有围墙[篱笆]等的场地〔临时战俘营收容所等〕;(同族聚居的)村寨.

com·pra·dor(e) [ˌkɔmprəˈdɔː] *n.* (旧时中国的)买办.

com·preg [ˈkɔmpreg] *n.* (渗)胶合(缩)木材.

com·pre·hend [ˌkɔmpriˈhend] *vt.* ①了解,领悟. ②包含,包括.

com·pre·hen·si·bil·i·ty [ˈkɔmpriˌhensəˈbiliti] *n.* 能理解,易了解.

com·pre·hen·si·ble [ˌkɔmpriˈhensəbl] *a.* 能理解的.

com·pre·hen·sion [ˌkɔmpriˈhenʃən] *n.* ①理解,理解力. ②包含,包括,含蓄;概括公理;【逻】内包;【修】推知法;【宗】包容政策. *a term of wide ~* 意义广泛的术语[名词]. ***be above [pass, be beyond]*** ~ 难理解,不可解.

com·pre·hen·sive [ˌkɔmpriˈhensiv] *a.* ①广泛的,全面的,完整的,包含多的,综合的. ②有理解力的,悟性好的. *a ~ knowledge* 渊博的知识. *a ~ mind* 宽大的心胸. *a ~ account [description]* 全面的说明[记载]. *a ~ survey* 全面调查. ~ *faculty* 理解力. *a ~ English-Chinese dictionary* 综合英汉词典. *be ~ of* 包含…. ~ *utilization* 综合利用. **-ly** *ad.* **-ness** *n.*

com·press [kəmˈpres] *vt.* 压缩,浓缩;使(文章等)变简练. — *vi.* 经受压缩. —[ˈkɔmpres] *n.* ①【医】压布,敷布;罨,敷. ②(棉花等的)打包机. *hot ~* 热敷布;热敷法. *ice ~* 冰罨.

com·pressed [kəmˈprest] *a.* ①压缩过的;(文字)简练的. ②【植】(左右)扁平的;【动】侧扁的,宽度大于长度的. ~ *air* 压缩空气. ~ *wallboard* 压扁壁板.

com·pres·si·bil·i·ty [kəmˌpresiˈbiliti] *n.* 欽缩性,压缩性;压缩系数.

com·pres·si·ble [kəmˈpresəbl] *a.* 可压紧的,可压缩的.

com·pres·sion [kəmˈpreʃən] *n.* ①压缩,压紧;浓缩;紧缩. ②加压;压抑. ③(表现的)简练. ④应压试验. ~ *of ideas* 思想的概括. ~ *of the earth* 地球椭[扁]率. ~ **joint** 压力接合;承压缝,挤压节理. ~ **member** 抗压构件. ~ **pump** 压气泵. ~ **test** 耐压试验.

com·pres·sive [kəmˈpresiv] *a.* 有压力的,压缩的,压榨的. ~ **strength** 抗压强度. **-ly** *ad.* **-ness** *n.*

com·pres·sor [kəmˈpresə] *n.* ①压缩物. ②压缩器,压气机,压榨器. ③【解】收缩肌,压肌.

com·pris·al, com·priz·al [kəmˈpraizəl] *n.* ①包含,包蓄. ②梗概,大要.

com·prise, com·prize [kəmˈpraiz] *vt.* 包含,包括;由…组成[合成]. *The house ~s nine bedrooms.* 这栋房子有九间卧室. *the chapters that ~ the first part of the book* 构成该书第一部的几章. — *vi.* 由…构成 *(of)*. *funds comprising of subscriptions* 由捐款构成的基金.

com·pro·mise [ˈkɔmprəmaiz] *n.* ①妥协,调和,和解,互让了结,私下了结 *(between)*. ②妥协方案,折衷方案,调和契约;中间物,折衷物. ③(名誉等的)损害;连累;危及. ~ ***between a fish and a snake*** 非鱼非蛇的中间生物. ~ ***of principles*** 原则上的让步. ***make ~ with*** 和…妥协. — *vt.* ①对…妥协,和解,互让了结,私下了结. ②连累,危及. ③损伤(名誉等),放弃(原则等);泄露(秘密等). *be ~d by* 被…所危害[连累]. ~ *oneself* 做出有失体面[有损自己名誉]的事情. ~ *(one's own) reputation* 损坏(自己)名誉. — *vi.* 妥协,和解,让步. ~ *with (sb.) on (a point)* (在某点上)和(某人)和解[妥协].

com·pro·vin·cial [ˌkɔmprəˈvinʃəl] *a.* 同一省区的;同一管区的.

comp·to·graph [ˈkɔmtəgrɑːf] *n.* 自动计算器.

comp·tom·e·ter [kɔmpˈtɔmitə] *n.* 【商标】业务用计算机.
Comp·ton [ˈkɔmptən] *n.* ①康普顿(姓氏). ②**A. H.** ~ 康普顿〔1892—1962, 美国物理学家〕.
comp·trol·ler [kənˈtrəulə] *n.* 审计员〔官〕,主计员.
com·pul·sion [kəmˈpʌlʃən] *n.* ①强迫,强制. ②打动人的力量. ③【心】难抗拒的冲动. ***by*** ~ 强迫地. ***on [upon, under]*** ~ 被迫,不得不. ***take part under*** ~ 胁从;被迫参与.
com·pul·sive [kəmˈpʌlsiv] *a.* 强迫的,有强迫力的;在强迫下发生〔造成〕的,不由自主的. **-ly** *ad.* **-ness** *n.*
com·pul·so·ri·ly [kəmˈpʌlsərili] *ad.* 强迫,强制.
com·pul·so·ry [kəmˈpʌlsəri] *a.* 强迫的,强制的;义务的;必修的. ~ **contribution** 勒捐,派捐. ~ **education** 强迫教育,义务教育. ~ **execution** 强迫执行. ~ **measures** 强迫手段. ~ **service** 征兵,义务兵役. ~ **subjects** 必修科目.
com·punc·tion [kəmˈpʌŋkʃən] *n.* 良心的责备,后悔,懊悔,悔恨. ***without (the slightest)*** ~ 毫不在乎,无动于衷.
com·punc·tious [kəmˈpʌŋkʃəs] *a.* (使)内疚的,惭愧的;(使)后悔的. **-ly** *ad.*
com·pur·ga·tion [ˌkɔmpəːˈgeiʃən] *n.* 〔古〕【法】根据证人宣誓证实宣布被告无罪.
com·pur·ga·tor [ˈkɔmpəːˌgeitə] *n.* 被告无罪证实人.
com·put·a·ble [kəmˈpjuːtəbl] *a.* 能计算的,能算出的.
com·pu·ta·tion [ˌkɔmpju(ː)ˈteiʃən] *n.* ①计算,估算. ②计算法. ③计算结果,得数.
com·pu·ta·tion·al [ˌkɔmpju(ː)ˈteiʃənəl] *a.* 计算的. ~ **linguistics** 【语言】(用)计算机(进行研究的)语言学.
com·pute [kəmˈpjuːt] *vt., vi.* 计算;估计;算定. ~ *tare* 估计皮重. *computing centre* 计算中心. ~ *(one's loss)* ***at*** …(损失)估计为…. ~ ***from*** 由…起算. —*n.* 计算,估计. ***beyond*** ~不可计量.
com·put·er [kəmˈpjuːtə] *n.* ①计算者. ②(电子)计算机;计量器. *an electronic* ~ 电子计算机. ~ **graphics** 电子计算机制图. ~ **language** 电子计算机语言. ~-**like** *a.* 计算机般的. ~-**on-a-chip** 微型电子计算机. **-ism** 电子计算机主义〔认为电子计算机万能等〕. **-er·ite, -nik** 计算机专家;计算机工作者.
com·put·er·ize [kəmˈpjuːtəˌraiz] *vt., vi.* ①(给…)装备电子计算机,(使)电子计算机化. ②用电子计算机计算〔操纵,操作,编排等〕. **-za·tion** *n.*
Comr. = Commissioner.
com·rade [ˈkɔmrid] *n.* 同志;伙伴,同事;战友. ***~ in arms*** 战友. **-ship** *n.* 伙伴关系,友谊(关系). (*~ship in arms* 战斗友谊).
COMSAT = 〔美〕Communication Satellite Corporation 通信卫星公司.
com·sat [ˈkɔmsæt] *n.* 通信卫星.
Com·so·mol [ˈkɔmsəmɔl] *n.* = Komsomol.
Com·stock [ˈkʌmstɔk, ˈkɔmstɔk] *n.* 康斯托克〔姓氏〕.
Com·stock·er·y [ˈkɔmstɔkəri] *n.* 对妨害风化的文化艺术的干涉.
COMSUBRON = Commander, Submarine Squadron 〔美〕潜艇分遣队司令.
Comte [kɔ̃ːnt, kɔːnt], **Auguste** 孔德(1798—1857), 法国实证主义哲学家.
Com·ti·an [ˈkɔ̃ːntiən] *a.* 【哲】(孔德的)实证主义(学派)的.
Comt·ism [ˈkɔ̃ːntizəm] *n.* 【哲】(孔德的)实证主义〔哲学〕.
Comt·ist [ˈkɔ̃ːntist] *n.* 【哲】实证主义者.
Com. Ver. = Common Version (Bible) (基督教《圣经》的)普通译本.
Co·mus [ˈkəuməs] *n.* 【希、罗神】宴会欢乐之神.
Com Z = Communication Zone 【美军】兵站区.

con [kɔn] *prep.* 〔It.〕【乐】以, 用. ~ ***amore*** [əˈmɔːri] 亲切地,热烈地,真诚地. ~ ***brio*** [ˈbriːəu] 活泼地,精神勃勃地. ~ ***espressione*** [ˈespresˈsjɔːnei] 有表现力地,富于表情地. ~ ***fuoco*** [ˈfwɔːko] 充满热情. ~ ***gracia*** [ˈgrɑːtʃiə] 愉快地.
con[1] [kɔn] *vt.* 精读,研读,研究;熟读;默记 *(over)*.
con[2] [kɔn] *vt., vi.* 【海】指挥(操舵), 指挥(船的)航路. *a conning tower* (军舰的)司令塔. — *n.* 指挥操舵;指挥操舵者的位置.
con[3] [kɔn] *n.* 反对(论点);反对票,反对者. ***the pro and ~s*** 赞成者和反对者;赞成票数与反对票数;正面理由和反面理由. —*ad.*反对. — *prep.* 反对. *forces pro and ~ the act* 赞成和反对法案的两支力量.
con[4] [kɔn] *vt.* 〔美俚〕欺骗, 欺诈. — *a.* 欺诈的, 骗取信任的. *a ~ game* 骗局. *a ~ man* 骗子.
con[5] [kɔn] *n.* 〔美俚〕囚犯 (= convict); 肺病 (= consumption); 电车售票员 (= conductor).
con- *pref.* = com-.
con. = concerto; conclusion; conics; connection; consigned; consignment; *contra* (〔L.〕 = against); consolidate(d); contra.
Con. = Consul.
CONAC = Continental Air Command 〔美〕本土空军司令部.
CONAD=Continental Air Defense Command 〔美〕本土防空司令部.
Co·na·kry [ˈkɔnəkri] *n.* 科纳克里〔几内亚首都〕.
Co·nan [ˈkəunən, ˈkɔnən] *n.* 科南〔男子名〕.
Co·nant [ˈkɔnənt] *n.* 科南特〔姓氏〕.
co·na·tion [kəuˈneiʃən] *n.* 【心】努力,企求,欲求.
con·a·tive [ˈkɔnətiv, ˈkəunə-] *a.* ①【心】努力企求的,欲求的. ②【语法】增强性的,(动词)表示努力企求的,意动的. ~ **verb** 【语法】意欲动词.
co·na·tus [kəuˈneitəs] *n.* *(pl.* ~*)* ①努力; 企图; 尽力. ②【生】(动植物的)自然企求力,自然倾向.
conc. = concentration; concerning.
con·cat·e·nate [kɔnˈkætineit] *vt.* 使(成串地)连结〔衔接〕起来. —*a.* 连锁状的.
con·cat·e·na·tion [kɔnˌkætiˈneiʃən] *n.* 连锁; 连结成串,连续.
con·cave [ˈkɔnˈkeiv, ˈkɔnkeiv] *a.* 凹的, 凹面的 *(opp.* convex*)*. —*n.* 凹,凹线,凹面(物). ***the (spherical)*** ~ 〔诗〕穹苍. — *vt.* 把…弄成凹(面). ~ **lens** 凹透镜. ~ **mirror** 凹面镜. ~ **tile** 牝瓦. **-ly** *ad.* **-ness** *n.*
con·cav·i·ty [kɔnˈkæviti] *n.* 凹状; 凹性;凹度; 凹处,凹面;成凹形.
con·ca·vo-con·cave [kɔnˈkeivəuˈkɔnkeiv] *a.* 两面凹进的,双凹的.
con·ca·vo-con·vex [kɔnˈkeivəuˈkɔnveks] *a.* 一面凹一面凸的,凹凸的.
con·ceal [kənˈsiːl] *vt.* 隐藏,隐蔽,隐匿. ~ ***from (sb.)*** 对(人)隐蔽 (*I ~ nothing from you.* 我对你一切公开). ~ ***oneself*** 躲起来,躲藏,潜伏,埋伏.
con·ceal·ment [kənˈsiːlmənt] *n.* ①隐匿,隐蔽;潜伏. ②埋伏处,躲避处. ***remain in*** ~ 隐藏着,躲着.
con·cede [kənˈsiːd] *vt.* ①(勉强)承认. ②让与, 放弃赢得…的希望. ③〔俚〕【体】失(局). ~ *a point in (argument)* 在(争论)中退让一步. ~ *a game* 输一局. ~ *that (the statement is true)* 勉强承认(陈述是真实的). — *vi.* 让步. ~ *to (sb.)* 对(某人)让步.
con·ced·ed·ly [kənˈsiːdidli] *ad.* 〔美〕明白地, 众所承认地.
con·ceit [kənˈsiːt] *n.* ①自负,自大,自满. ②奇想,幻想;(作品的)做作, (比喻的)牵强附会, (构思的)奇巧. ③意见, 想法; 私见, 独断. ④不切实用的花哨物品. ⑤〔古〕理解力. ⑥〔英方〕喜欢,中意. ***be full of*** ~ 十分自负. ***be out of*** ~ ***with*** 厌倦, 嫌弃, 厌弃. ***in one's***

own ~ 自以为；自夸（*He is wise in his own* ~. 他自以为聪明）. *lose* ~ *of oneself* 失去自信. *put (sb.) out of* ~ *with (sth.)* 使（某人）厌弃. *take the* ~ *out of (sb.)* 打消（某人的）傲气[自信]；挫折，折磨（某人）. — *vt.* ①〔方〕想象. ②〔英方〕喜欢，中意于. ③〔古〕理解.

con·ceit·ed [kən'siːtid] *a.* ①自负的，自夸的，逞能的. ②狂想的，奇想的. ③花哨的. ④〔旧〕聪明的，机智的. *He is* ~ *and short-sighted.* 他自高自大，目光短浅. *a well* ~ *play* 构想巧妙的戏剧. *be* ~ *about* 自负，自夸. **-ly** *ad.* **-ness** *n.*

con·ceiv·a·ble [kən'siːvəbl] *a.* 可以想到的，可以想象的，可能的. *by every* ~ *means* 千方百计，用一切手段. *It is* ~ *that ...?* 难道是…的吗？ **-bil·i·ty** [-'biliti] *n.* **-ness** *n.*

con·ceiv·a·bly [kən'siːvəbli] *ad.* 想得到地，想象上.

con·ceive [kən'siːv] *vt.* ①怀(胎). ②想到（计划等）；想象；以为；想出；怀(恨等)，蓄(意)，抱有(思想)；〔旧〕理解. ③〔常用被动语态〕表达，陈述. ~ *a child* 怀胎. ~ *a hatred* 怀恨. *a badly* ~*d petition* 词不达意的请愿书. *a badly* ~*d scheme* 拙劣的计划. ~ *prejudices* 抱偏见. ~ *an aversion to* 对…抱反感. — *vi.* ①怀孕. ②想像，设想 *(of)*. ~ *of (a plan)* 想出(计划).

con·cel·e·brate [kɔn'selibreit] *vt.* 共同做(弥撒)〔由两个或更多的司祭牧师一起进行祷告〕. **-bra·tion** *n.*

con·cent [kən'sent] *n.* 〔古〕①(音乐的)谐调，和谐. ②协调；一致.

con·cen·ter [kɔn'sentə] *vi., vt.* 〔美〕= concentre.

con·cen·trate ['kɔnsentreit] *vt.* ①集中；使…集中于一点. ②【化】提浓，浓缩，凝缩；【冶】汰选. ~ *fire* 集中火力(射击). —*vi.* 专心，凝(神)；倾全力. ~ *in class* 专心听讲. ~ **one's attention on [upon]** 把注意力集中在。~ **on [upon]** 集中在；专心于. —*n.* 浓缩物；【畜】精料；【矿】精砂.

con·cen·trat·ed ['kɔnsentreitid] *a.* ①集中了的；浓缩了的；汰选出来的. ②聚精会神的. ~ *fire* 集中射击，集中火力. ~ *food [feed]* 浓缩食品[饲料]. ~ *study* 悉心研究，专心学习.

con·cen·tra·tion [ˌkɔnsen'treiʃən] *n.* ①集中. ②【化】提浓，蒸浓，浓缩；浓度；稠密度；【矿】汰选，选矿，富化. ③集中注意，专心. *multi-stage ore* ~ 多段选矿法. *with deep* ~ 专心. ~ **camp** (俘虏等的) 集中营. ~ **cell** 浓差电池. ~ **ring**【军】集索圈.

con·cen·tra·tive ['kɔnsentreitiv] *a.* ①集中(性)的. ②一心一意的，专心的.

con·cen·tra·tor ['kɔnsentreitə] *n.* ①集中者；浓缩器；【冶】选矿厂，选矿机；【电】集线器. ②(特定课题的)钻研者.

con·cen·tre, con·cen·ter [kɔn'sentə] *vi., vt.* (使)聚集于同一中心；(使)集中；(使)会聚.

con·cen·tric [kɔn'sentrik] *a.* 同心的，同轴的 *(with)*；集中的，会聚的. **be** ~ **with** 与…同心. ~ **circles**【数】同心圆. ~ **fire** 集中火力. **-al·ly** *ad.* **-i·ty** *n.*

Con·cep·ción [kənˌsepsi'əun] *n.* 康塞普西翁〔智利城市〕.

con·cept ['kɔnsept] *n.* ①【哲】概念. ②观念，思想，意思，心意. *the* ~ *of operations* 作战方针，作战思想. ★ concept 指具体的概念，conception 则着重指概念的形成.

con·cep·ta·cle [kən'septəkl] *n.*【植】(某些藻类的)生殖窠.

con·cep·tion [kən'sepʃən] *n.* ①妊娠，受孕；胚胎，胎儿；起源，发端. ②概念作用；概念；印象. ③设想，构想；见解，看法. *a clear [vague]* ~ 清楚的[模糊的]概念. *a clever* ~ 聪明的想法. *a poetic* ~ 诗的构想. *his* ~ *of himself* 他对他自己的看法. *have too rigid a* ~ *of* 对…的看法太刻板. *the materialistic* ~ *of history* 唯物史观. *the idealist* ~ *of history* 唯心史观. *the* ~ *of the United Nations* 联合国的创立. **form a** ~ **of** 对…抱有一种想法. **have no** ~ **of** 完全不知[不懂].

con·cep·tion·al [kən'sepʃənəl] *a.* 概念的.

con·cep·tive [kən'septiv] *a.* ①概念(上)的；设想上的. ②〔罕〕会受孕的.

con·cep·tu·al [kən'septʃuəl] *a.* 概念的. ~ *knowledge* (抽象的)概念知识(比较：perceptual knowledge 感性知识). ~**art** (表达概念而不是形象的)概念艺术. **-ism** *n.*【哲】(介乎唯名论与实在论之间的) 概念论. **-ist** *n.* 概念论者.

con·cep·tu·al·ize [kən'septjuəlaiz] *vt.* 使形成概念，使产生想法；使概念化. **-za·tion** *n.*

con·cern [kən'səːn] *vt.* ①关系到；影响，涉及(某人的)利害. ②〔用被动语态〕干与，干涉，参加，从事 *(in)*. ③使关心 *(with)*，担心，挂念，忧虑 *(for, about, over)*〔参看 ~*ed*〕. *It doesn't* ~ *me.* = *I am not* ~*ed with it.* 那件事和我没关系[我不知情]. *I am* ~*ed to tell you of it.* 我打算把那件事告诉你. *I am much* ~*ed to hear that ...* 我听见…后十分着急. *be* ~*ed about* 关心；挂念，顾虑. *Don't* ~ *yourself about his opinion.* 不要管他的意见. *be* ~*ed in* 和…有关系，牵涉到. *be* ~*ed with* 干与，参与；关怀. ~ *oneself about* 关心，挂念. ~ *oneself with [in]* 从事，参与，干与，干涉. *My honour is* ~*ed.* 有关我的名誉. **as** ~**s** 关于. **so far as I am** ~**ed** 就我个人来说. —*n.* ①关系；利害关系. ②关心，挂念，担心. ③商行，公司；财团；康采恩；事业，业务；〔*pl.*〕事件，事情. ④〔口〕(泛指)事物，家伙〔指有缺点的人〕. *It is no* ~ *of mine.* 与我无关. *a flourishing* ~ 兴盛的事业[商号]. *a going* ~ 开着的商店. *a rickety old* ~ 年久失修的老建筑. *a petty* ~ 细事. *a selfish* ~ 自私的家伙. *everyday* ~*s* 日常事务. *worldly* ~*s* 世事. *I can manage my own* ~*s.* 自己的事总可以解决. *feel* ~ *about* 担心，挂念. *have a* ~ *in* 和…有利害关系. *have no* ~ *for* 毫不关心；完全不怕. *have no* ~ *with* 和…毫无关系. *matter of the utmost* ~ (关系)重大的事件. *of* ~ 关系重大的；有关系的. *with* ~ 忧虑着，惦记着. *He inquired with (grave)* ~. 他殷切询问. *without* ~ 不关心；不怕.

con·cerned [kən'səːnd] *a.* ① 担心的，挂虑的. ②关心政治的，关心社会的. ③〔常用于名词之后〕有关(方面)；被牵连的. *the authorities* ~ 有关当局. *the parties* ~ 关系人，当事人. *I'm not* ~. 于我无关. *Everyone* ~ *in the murder case has been identified.* 与凶杀案有牵连的人都已查明. **be much** ~ **about** 十分挂念. **with a** ~ **air** 用关心的态度. **-ly** [kən'səːnidli] *ad.*

con·cern·ing [kən'səːniŋ] *prep.* 关于，论及，就…说. ~ *the matter* 提到那件事.

con·cern·ment [kən'səːnmənt] *n.* ①关系；参与；重要. ②悬念，挂念. ③关系事项，事务. *(a matter) of* ~ 关系重大的(事情). **of general** ~ 一般的. **of vital** ~ 关系非常重大的.

con·cert ['kɔnsət] *n.* ①音乐会，演奏会；合奏(曲)；【乐】协奏曲. ②一致，协力，和谐. **in** ~ 异口同音地，同声；齐. **in** ~ **with** 和…相呼应 [合作] *(act in* ~ *with* 和…一致行动. *proceed in* ~ *with* 和…采取一致步骤). — [kən'səːt] *vt.* 协商；合订（计划）. —*vi.* 协同工作 *(with)*. ~ **grand** 演奏会用大钢琴. ~ **hall [room]** 音乐堂[厅]. ~**master,** ~**meister**【乐】音乐指挥；首席小提琴演奏者. ~ **needles** (留声机)唱针. ~ **pitch**【乐】合奏调，较高音调；较高效能.

con·cert·ed [kən'səːtid] *a.* 商定的，协商好的；预定的；协力一致的；【乐】合拍调的. *a* ~ *plan of operations* 协商好的作战计划. *take* ~ *action* 取一致行动.

con·cer·ti·na [ˌkɔnsə'tiːnə] *n.* ①六角手风琴. ②【军】(可移动) 蛇腹式铁丝网. ~ **movement** 折叠[蛇腹]式构造. ~ **table** 折叠桌.

con·cer·ti·no [ˌkɔntʃə'tiːnəu] *n.*【乐】①小协奏曲〔通

常只有一个乐章〕。②主奏组〔协奏曲中的一组独奏乐器〕。

con·cert·ize [ˈkɔnsətaiz] *vi.* 独唱〔独奏〕表演〔在音乐会上独唱或独奏，尤指巡回演出时〕。

con·cer·to [kənˈtʃə:təu] *n.* 〔It.〕【乐】协奏曲。

con·ces·sion [kənˈseʃən] *n.* ①让步；迁就；让与。②(政府的)核准，许可，特许；特许权。③租借地，租界。④〔美〕(商店等在公园、球场等公共场所的)场地特许使用(权)，特许使用的场地。*an oil* ～ 石油开采权。*make a* ～ *to* 对…让步。

con·ces·sion·aire [kənˌseʃəˈnεə] *n.* 受让人；特许权获得者 (= concessioner)。

con·ces·sion·ar·y [kənˈseʃənəri] *a.* 让与的；让步的；让渡特权的。—*n.* 受让人；特许权获得者。

con·ces·sive [kənˈsesiv] *a.* 让与的；让步的。～ **clause** 【语法】让步从句。

conch [kɔŋk, kɔntʃ] *n.* (*pl.* ～*s* [-ks], ～*es* [-tʃiz])【希神】海神特里顿 (Triton) 的响螺；【动】凤螺，海螺；海螺壳。②【建】半圆形穹顶。③【解】外耳；耳壳；(鼻)甲。④〔俚〕西印度巴哈马 (Bahama) 岛人。

con·cha [ˈkɔŋkə] *n.* (*pl.* -*chae* [-ki:]) ①【解】外耳，耳壳；(鼻)甲。②【建】半圆形穹顶。

con·chie [ˈkɔntʃi] *n.* = conchy.

con·chif·er·ous [kɔŋˈkifərəs] *a.* 有贝壳的；【地】生贝壳的。

con·choid [ˈkɔŋkɔid] *n.* 【数】蚌线，螺旋线；螺线管；【矿、地】贝壳状断面。

con·choi·dal [kɔŋˈkɔidl] *a.* 贝壳状的；【数】蚌线的。

con·chol·o·gist [kɔŋˈkɔlədʒist] *n.* 贝壳学者，贝类学者。

con·chol·o·gy [kɔŋˈkɔlədʒi] *n.* 贝壳学，贝类学。

con·chy [ˈkɔntʃi] *n.* 〔英俚〕由于信仰的驱使而抵制者〔拒绝服兵役者〕(= conscientious objector)。

con·ci·erge [kɔ̃:nsiˈεəʒ] *n.* 〔F.〕①门房，门警。②(公寓等的)管理员。③(大旅馆中能说几种外语的)接待员。

con·cil·i·ar [kənˈsiliə] *a.* 议(事)会的，来自〔通过〕议(事)会的。

con·cil·i·ate [kənˈsilieit] *vt.* ①安抚，抚慰，劝慰，说服(反对者)。②赢得(支持，好感)。③调停，调解。

con·cil·i·a·tion [kənˌsiliˈeiʃən] *n.* ①安抚，劝慰；说服。②调停，调解；妥协。③迎合；获得。*Court of* ～【法】调解法庭。*The C- Act* 〔英〕(工潮的)调停法。-**ism** *n.* 调和主义。-**ist** *n.* 调和主义者。

con·cil·i·a·tive, con·cil·i·a·to·ry [kənˈsiliətiv, -liətəri] *a.* 安抚的，说服的；和解的，调解的。

con·cil·i·a·tor [kənˈsilieitə] *n.* 安抚者，说服者；调停者，和解者。

con·cin·ni·ty [kənˈsiniti] *n.* (文章等的)妥贴，和谐，优雅，优美。

con·cise [kənˈsais] *a.* 简洁的，简明扼要的。*Talks and articles should all be* ～ *and to the point.* 讲话和写文章都应该简明扼要。-**ly** *ad.* -**ness** *n.*

con·ci·sion [kənˈsiʒən] *n.* ①简洁，简明。②〔废〕切断；切分；切除。

con·clave [ˈkɔnkleiv] *n.* ①秘密会议。②【天主】教皇选举密议室；教皇选举会议；(教廷内的)红衣〔枢机〕主教团。*be in* ～ *with* 和…密议中。*sit in* ～ *(with)* (与)密议。

con·clude [kənˈklu:d] *vt.* ①结束，终止，使完毕。②议定，缔结(条约等)。③推断，断定。④〔美〕(最后)决定。～ *a speech* 终止演说。～ *peace* 缔结和约。～ *a treaty* 订立条约。*From what you say I* ～ *that* …从你的话中我断定…。—*vi.* ①结束，终止。②断定，决定，达成协议。*to be* ～*d* (连载的文章)下期〔次〕登完。*to* ～ 最后(一句话)。

con·clu·sion [kənˈklu:ʒən] *n.* ①终结，结局，最后结果。②结论；决定，断定。③缔结；商定，议定。*at the* ～ *of* 当…完结时。*bring to a* ～ 使结束；谈定(买卖等)。*come to a* ～ 结束，告一段落；得到一个结论。*come to the* ～ *that*… 所得结论是…，断定。*draw the* ～ 得出结论，推断。*foregone* ～ 可预断的〔免不了的〕结果。*in* ～ 最后，总之。*leap [jump] to a* ～ 冒然断定，过早下结论。*try* ～*s with* 和…决最后胜负，争(最后)优劣。-**al** *a.* -**al·ly** *ad.*

con·clu·sive [kənˈklu:siv] *a.* 决定的，结论性的，确定性的；最后的，无争论余地的。*a* ～ *answer* 断然的回答。～ **evidence [proof]** 确证，真凭实据，结论性的证据。～ **presumption** 【法】(不容反驳的)决定性推断。-**ly** *ad.*

con·coct [kənˈkɔkt] *vt.* ①调制，炮制(汤、饮料、肥皂等)。②捏造，编造，虚构。③图谋，策划，计划。～ *a new dish* 配制新菜。～ *a story* 虚构事实。～ *a plot* 图谋不轨。

con·coc·tion [kənˈkɔkʃən] *n.* ①调制；调合〔混合〕品。②捏造。③策划，图谋。*meat* ～*s* 串荤〔荤素混合菜，杂烩〕。

con·coc·tive [kənˈkɔktiv] *a.* 调制的；捏造的；图谋的。

con·col·o(u)r·ous [kənˈkʌlərəs] *a.* 同色的，单色的。

con·com·i·tance, con·com·i·tan·cy [kənˈkɔmitəns, -tənsi] *n.* ①相伴，并在；共存。②【宗】(圣餐中)耶稣的血肉并在。

con·com·i·tant [kənˈkɔmitənt] *a.* 相伴的，并在的，伴生的，附随的。—*n.* 〔常 *pl.*〕相伴物，附随物。-**ly** *ad.*

con·cord [ˈkɔŋkɔ:d] *n.* ①协和，一致；(国际间的)和谐。②(国际间的)协定，协约。③【乐】谐音，协和音；【语法】(数、性、格、人称等的)一致。*Book of* ～【宗】信仰忏悔录。*in* ～协和，和谐；一致。

con·cord·ance [kənˈkɔ:dəns] *n.* ①(著作、作家的)词汇索引(*to*)。②协和，调和，一致；【统】和谐性。③【地】整合，整一。*be in* ～ 一致，协和。*in* ～ *with* 依照。

con·cord·ant [kənˈkɔ:dənt] *a.* 协和的，一致的 *(with)*；【乐】协和音的；【地】整合的。～ **twin** 相似孪生。-**ly** *ad.*

con·cor·dat [kɔnˈkɔ:dæt] *n.* ①协定。②【宗史】(罗马教皇与各君主〔政府〕间的)宗教事务协约。③(宗派间的)协议。-**da·to·ry** *a.*

Con·cor·di·a [ˈkɔŋkɔ:diə] *n.* 【罗神】协和女神。

con·course [ˈkɔŋkɔ:s] *n.* ①集合；辐辏；合流，总汇；群集。②〔美〕(公园中的)中央广场，(车站内的)中央大厅。③车道，马路，林荫路。

con·cres·cence [kənˈkresns] *n.* ①【生】接合，结合，会合；合生。②增生，增殖。

con·crete [ˈkɔnkri:t] *a.* ①具体的，有形的；实在的，实际的。②固结成的，混凝土制的。③图案诗歌的(参阅～poetry)。*a* ～ *fact* 具体事实。*a* ～ *vessel* 混凝土船。*in the* ～ 具体地，实际上。—*n.* 具体物；凝结物；混凝土，三合土；【逻】具体名词；【文学】具体诗歌。*a* ～*-mixer* 混凝土搅拌器〔机〕。*mushy [poured]* ～ 注入的混凝土。*reinforced [armoured]* ～ 钢筋混凝土。—*vt.*, *vi.* ①[kənˈkri:t](使)固结，(使)凝固；(使)结合。②[ˈkɔnkri:t]用混凝土修筑；(在…上)浇注混凝土。～ **noun**【语法】具体名词。～ **number**【数】名数。～ **poetry**【文学】(用形象的字母、单词、符号等而不是用传统的文句来表达的)图案诗歌。-**ly** *ad.*

con·cre·tion [kənˈkri:ʃən] *n.* ①凝结，固结；具体化。②固结物；连生体；【医】结石；凝结物；硬块；【地】结核，凝岩。-**ary** *a.* 凝固的，已凝结的；【地】结核性的(构造)，由凝岩形成的。

con·cret·ism [kɔnˈkri:tizəm] *n.* 【文艺】具体主义〔具体诗歌的理论和实践〕。

con·cre·tive [kənˈkri:tiv] *a.* 凝结性的，有凝固力的；【医】结石的；凝结(物)的。

con·cre·tize [ˈkɔnkri(:)taiz] *vt.*, *vi.* (使)具体化；(使)凝固。～ *abstractions* 使抽象概念具体化。

con·cu·bi·nage [kɔnˈkju:binidʒ] *n.* ①非法同居。②蓄妾，妾的地位。

con·cu·bi·nar·y [kɔnˈkju:biˌnəri] *a.* (作)妾的；妾生的。

con·cu·bine [ˈkɔŋkjubain] *n.* 妾；姘妇。

con·cu·pis·cence [kən'kju:pisəns] *n.* ①性欲. ②【宗】贪欲,世俗欲念.

con·cu·pis·cent [kən'kju:pisnt] *a.* ①好色的, 色欲旺盛的. ②多欲的,贪婪的.

con·cu·pis·ci·ble [kən'kju:pisəbl] *a.* 由性欲引起的.

con·cur [kən'kə:] *vi.* ①同时发生,并发; 合作, 共同作用*(with)*. ②同意,一致 *(with)*. *Everything concurred to make him happy.* 每一件事都凑在一起使他快活[幸福]. *They all concurred in giving him the prize.* 他们一致同意给他奖赏.

con·cur·rence [kən'kʌrəns] *n.* ①同时发生,并发. ②同意,一致;合作,联合. ③【数】(数线的)交点. ④【法】(权利的)共有,权利等同.

con·cur·rent [kən'kʌrənt] *a.* ①同时发生的,并发的;并存的, 共存的;合作的. ②(意见)一致的. ③【动】趋合的;【数】共点的;【机】并流的. ④(权力等)由两个负责当局共同行使的,有相等裁定权的. ~ *insurance (policy)* (对于一投保物的)共同保险(合同). ~ *post* 兼职. ~ *sentence* (适用于多个被告的)共同判决. —*n.* ①并发事件;共存[共有]物;并在原因. ②竞争者. ③【数】共点. **-ly** *ad.* (*hold a post concurrently* 兼任).

con·cuss [kən'kʌs] *vt.* ①猛烈撞击(使成脑震荡); 使震动,使震伤. ②〔Scot.〕胁迫,恐吓.

con·cus·sion [kən'kʌʃən] *n.* ①震动,冲击,撞击,冲激. ②【医】(脑)震荡. ③〔Scot.〕威胁,胁迫. *a ~ of the brain* 脑震荡. ~ **fuse** 触发信管. ~ **grenades** 触发手榴弹.

con·cus·sive [kən'kʌsiv] *a.* 震荡的,有激动[冲击]力的,震动性的.

cond. = condenser; conditional; conductivity; conductor.

con·demn [kən'dem] *vt.* ①定(某人)罪,判(某人)罪,宣告(死刑等). ②责备,谴责. ③宣告(患者)无法治疗. ④宣告…完全无用;决定废弃,报废. ⑤宣告没收(船舶、私货等). *His looks ~ him.* 他的模样显得是有罪的. *be ~ed to death* 被宣告(死刑). ~ *(sth.) as unfit for* 宣告(某物)不适于….

con·dem·na·ble [kən'demnəbl] *a.* ①该定罪的. ②该谴责的. ③该废弃的.

con·dem·na·tion [ˌkɔndem'neiʃən] *n.* ①定罪,宣告有罪. ②谴责,非难. ③定罪理由. ④报废. ⑤征用; (宣告)没收. *conditional ~* 缓刑. ~ **factor** 报废率.

con·dem·na·to·ry [kən'demnətəri] *a.* 处罚的,宣告有罪的;谴责的.

con·demned [kən'demd] *a.* ①已被定罪的; 已被定罪者使用的. ②被认为不当的; 受谴责的. ③被认为不适用的. ~ **cell [ward]** 死刑犯监房.

con·den·sa·bil·i·ty [kənˌdensə'biliti] *n.* 可凝结性,可冷凝性,可压缩性.

con·den·sa·ble [kən'densəbl] *a.* 可凝结的; 可压缩的;可缩短的.

con·den·sate ['kɔndinseit, kən'denseit] *n.* 浓缩物;【化】冷凝物[液]. —*a.* 浓缩的,冷凝的,凝结的.

con·den·sa·tion [kɔnden'seiʃən] *n.* ①浓缩; 【物】冷凝(作用),凝聚(作用);压缩;缩合;凝块. ②(著作等的)压缩;压缩后的形式,节本. ~ **point**【物】凝点. ~ **trail** 【空】凝结尾〔喷气式飞机经过后肉眼可见的白带状水气凝结物〕. ~ **wave**【物】凝聚波.

con·den·sa·tor [kən'denseitə] *n.* = condenser.

con·dense [kən'dens] *vt.* ①压缩;使浓缩;聚集(光线); 加强(电力). ②【物、化】冷凝,使凝结. ②(著作等的)缩短, 压缩. *~d film* 缩合膜. *~d milk* 炼乳. *~d spark* 高电炉火花. *condensing lens* 聚光透镜. ~ *vapour into rain* 使水气凝结成雨. ~ *an essay* 压缩一篇文章. —*vi.* ①浓缩;凝结. ②(气体)变成液体[固体].

con·dens·er [kən'densə] *n.* 冷凝器;凝汽器;电容器;聚光器;【纺】集棉器; 搓条机. ~ **leg (pipe)** 冷凝器气压管. ~ **paper** 绝缘纸. ~ **pipe** 冷凝管.

con·den·ser·y, con·den·sar·y [kən'densəri] *n.* 〔美口〕炼乳厂.

con·den·si·ble [kən'densəbl] *a.* = condensable.

con·de·scend [kɔndi'send] *vi.* ①谦虚地做,俯就,屈尊. ②堕落到做(下流事情). ③抱着优越感施惠于人, 以恩赐[高高在上]态度对待别人. ~ *to accept a bribe* 堕落[不要脸]到接受贿赂. *She does not ~ to such little things.* 她不屑理睬那种小事. ~ **upon** 〔Scot.〕不厌其烦地细说. **-ing** *a.* 屈尊的;抱恩赐态度的. **-ing·ly** *ad.*

con·de·scend·ence [ˌkɔndi'sendəns] *n.* ①= condescension. ②〔Scot.〕详细列举[细述].

con·de·scen·sion [ˌkɔndi'senʃən] *n.* 屈尊; 恩赐[高高在上]态度.

con·dign [kən'dain] *a.* 相当的, 应得的, 适当的. ~ *punishment [vengeance]* 应得的处罚[报复].

con·di·ment ['kɔndimənt] *n.* 佐料, 调味品. **-al** [-'mentəl] *a.*

con·di·tion [kən'diʃən] *n.* ①状态,状况,情形;品质. ②〔*pl.*〕外界状况,周围情形. ③地位, 身分. ④条件;【语法】条件从句. ⑤【纺】含潮量;(套毛)含脂含杂量. ⑥健康状态; 〔口〕病痛. ⑦〔美〕补考及格才能随班附读的规定条件;补考学科. *the ~ of affairs* 事态. *a man of ~ [humble ~]* 有身分的[身分低的]人. *the ~s of peace* 媾和条件. ***be in a certain [an interesting] ~*** 在怀孕. ***be in [out of] ~*** (人)健康[不健康], 身体好[不好]; (物)保存良好[不好]; 合用 [不合用]; 耐[不耐]…, 堪[不堪]…. ***change one's ~*** 〔口〕结婚. ***in [under] favourable [difficult] ~s*** 在顺利[困难]景况[条件]下. ***in good [bad, poor] ~*** 情况良好[不好];健康[不健康];(物件)无[有]破损; (食品)新鲜[不新鲜]. ***make ~s*** 规定条件. ***make it a ~ that*** 以…为条件. ***make no ~*** 毫无条件. ***on [upon] ~ that*** 在…的条件下; 若…则. ***on this ~*** 在这一条件下. ***on no ~*** 在任何条件下都不…. ***under existing ~s [the present ~]*** 就现况说. —*vt.* ①决定;规定,作为…的条件,限定;制约. ②改善;增进(牛、马等的)健康; 调节 (室内空气). ③使适应, 使习惯于 (环境). ④〔美〕(若要升级)必须补考…. ⑤【心、生】使发生条件反射. ⑥【商】检验(生丝,棉纱等). *to ~ public opinion* 煽动舆论. *She ~ed her leaving upon the weather.* 她动身与否,视天气而定. *Diligence ~s success.* 勤奋为成功的条件. *the things that ~ happiness* 决定幸福的事物. ***be ~ed by*** 以…为转移[条件],受…所制约. ***the ~ed*** 【哲】受制约物;【逻】(条件推论的)后项.

con·di·tion·al [kən'diʃənl] *a.* ①带有条件的,有限制的;视…而定的. ②【语法】条件的,假定的. ③引起条件反射的. —*n.* 【语法】条件从句, 条件词. ***be ~ on [upon]*** 在…条件下, 以…为条件, 取决于. **~condemnation** 缓刑. ~ **contract** 有条件契约,暂行契约. ~ **reflex**【心】条件反射. ~ **sale** 搭卖(法). **-ity** *n.* 受限制性,有条件性,制约性;条件限制. **-ly** *ad.*

con·di·tioned [kən'diʃənd] *a.* ①有条件的,有限制的. ②〔美〕暂准入学[升级]的. ③情形…的; 适合…的. ④有…调节的. ⑤习惯于…的*(to)*. *the ~ air (of a theater)* (戏院中的)有调节的空气. *a ~ reflex [response]*【心】条件反射[反应]. *become ~ to the rough weather* 已适应恶劣气候.

con·di·tion·er [kən'diʃənə] *n.* ①【机】调节器; (冷、暖)空气调节装置. ②(硬水)软化剂. ③【体】教练员. ④(商品)检查员. *soil ~* 土壤改良剂.

con·di·tion·ing [kən'diʃəniŋ] *n.* ①(商品的)检验. ②(空气、湿度等)调节. ③【冶】整修. ④【心】条件作用. *a silk ~ house* 生丝检验所. *air ~* 空气调节. ~ **oven** 烘箱.

con·do ['kɔndəu] *n.* (多层公寓中有独立所有权的)一套公寓房间,一个住宅单元〔condominium 的缩略词〕.

con·do·la·to·ry [kən'dəulətəri] *a.* 吊唁的,慰问的.

con·dole [kən'dəul] *vi.* 吊慰，表示悼念；慰问. *He ~d with me on [upon] the death of my father.* 我父亲死了，他向我表示吊唁. — *vt.* 〔古〕哀悼. **-ment** *n.* = condolence.

con·do·lence [kən'dəuləns] *n.* 吊唁，吊慰；悼词；追悼. *express one's ~ to* 向…表示吊唁. *a letter of ~* 吊唁信.

con do·lo·re [kɔːn dɔː'lɔːre] 〔It.〕【乐】悲哀地.

con·dom ['kɔndəm] *n.* 阴茎套，男用避孕套.

con·do·min·i·um [ˌkɔndə'miniəm] *n.* ①共管(地)，共同统治(地)；共同所有权. ②(多层公寓中有独立所有权的)一套公寓房间，一个住宅单元.

Con·don ['kɔndən] *n.* 康登〔姓氏〕.

con·do·na·tion [kɔndəu'neiʃən] *n.* 赦免，宽恕(特指对配偶有通奸行为的宽容).

con·done [kən'dəun] *vt.* ①宽恕，宽容(配偶的通奸行为). ②用(行动、事实)抵消(罪行)，赎罪.

con·dor ['kɔndɔː, 'kɔndə] *n.* ①【动】(南美)秃鹰，神鹰. ②[kɔn'dɔr] 〔Sp.〕(智利等国的)秃鹰金币.

con·dot·tie·re [It. ˌkondo'tjɛːrə] *n.* 〔It.〕 (*pl.* ***-ri*** [-riː]) (14—16世纪的)雇佣兵队长；(军事)冒险家，投机分子.

con·duce [kən'djuːs] *vi.* 导致；有助于，有益于. *Rest ~s to health.* 休息有助健康.

con·duc·i·ble [kən'djuːsəbl] *a.* = conducive.

con·du·cive [kən'djuːsiv] *a.* 导致…的；有助于…的，助长…的. *be ~ to (health)* 增进(健康).

con·duct ['kɔndəkt] *n.* ①行为，举动；操行，品格. ②指导；带领；护送. ③处理，管理，经营；指挥. ④(戏剧等的)处理法，进展，情节，趣向；方法，做法. ⑤〔英〕伊顿(Eton)公学礼拜堂的牧师. *a testimonial of good ~* 操行优良证明. *a safe ~* (战时)护照，通行证. *~ of the background* 背景处理法. ***under the ~ of*** 在…指导[管理]下. — [kən'dʌkt] *vt.* ①〔~ oneself〕行动，表现，为人. ②指导；带领；护送；陪伴(游客等). ③处理，管理，经营，办(事)；指挥. ④传导，传(热、电等). *~ a business* 经营生意. *~ an orchestra* 指挥管弦乐队. *~ a campaign* 指挥作战. *~ oneself nobly* 为人高尚. — *vi.* ①引导，带领；指导；指挥乐队演奏. ②传导. ③(道路)通向(*to*). *He ~ed well.* 他对乐队演奏指挥得法. *A metal ~s well.* 金属是良导体. *a ~ing-wire* 导线. *~ (sb.)* ***into [to]*** 引导(某人)…. *~ (sb.) over (a place)* 引导[陪伴](某人)参观(某处). ~ **sheet**【军】操行[奖惩]记录.

con·duct·ance [kən'dʌktəns] *n.* 【电】电导；电导系数；传导(性).

con·duct·i·bil·i·ty [kənˌdʌkti'biliti] *n.* 传导性[力].

con·duct·i·ble [kən'dʌktəbl, -ibl] *a.* 可传导的.

con·duc·tion [kən'dʌkʃən] *n.* (用管对流体的)引流；【物】传导，导电；【生理】神经脉冲的传导.

con·duc·tive [kən'dʌktiv] *a.* 传导(性)的，有传导力的.

con·duc·tiv·i·ty [ˌkɔndʌk'tiviti] *n.*【物】传导性[力]，传导率；导电率[性，系数]. ~ **water** 校准电导水.

con·duc·tom·e·ter [ˌkɔndʌk'tɔmitə] *n.* 【物】热导计，电导计.

con·duc·tor [kən'dʌktə] *n.* ①指导者，向导者；护送者；处理人，管理人；指挥人；【乐】指挥. ②(电车、公共汽车上的)售票员；【美铁路】(列车)乘务长(=〔英〕guard)；列车员；【英军】下士. ③【物】导体；导管，导线；【数】前导子；【建】竖承霤；避雷针 (= lightning-~). *a good [bad, poor, non-] ~* 良[不良、非]导体. **-to·ri·al** [-'tɔːriəl] *a.*

con·duc·tress [kən'dʌktris] *n.* conductor 的女性.

con·duit ['kɔndit] *n.* 导管(= ~ pipe)；水管，水道，沟渠，暗渠；【电】导线管，管道(电缆). ~ **system** (电车的)地下电线[管道]系统；(电灯的)暗线装置[系统].

con·du·pli·cate [kən'djuːplikit] *a.*【植】(叶)对摺的.

con·dy ['kɔndi] 过锰酸钾液【商标】(= Condy's fluid 一种消毒剂).

con·dyle ['kɔndil] *n.*【解】髁；(关节处)骨顶部，骨阜，髁状突起.

con·dy·loid ['kɔndilɔid] *a.* 髁(状)的.

con·dy·lo·ma [ˌkɔndi'ləumə] *n.* (*pl.* ***-ma·ta*** [-mətə])【医】湿疣.

cone [kəun] *n.* ①圆锥，锥形物；锥面；锥体. ②火山锥，圆锥形火山；锥状地区. ③【植】球果，球花. ④风暴信号. ⑤【动】芋螺 (= cone shell). *~ of rays*【光】光锥. *an ice cream ~* 蛋卷冰淇淋. *a parasitic ~* 寄生火山锥. — *vt.* ①使成锥形；把…卷于锥状体上. ②〔用被动语态〕(探照灯)集中探照(敌机). — *vi.* (松树等)结球果. **~-buoy** 锥形浮标. ~ **gear** 锥轮联动机. ~ **pulley** 锥形轮.

cone·flow·er ['kəunflauə] *n.*【植】金光菊(属).

Con·el·rad ['kɔnəlræd] *n.*【无】电磁波辐射控制(=control of electromagnetic radiation).

cone·nose ['kəunnəuz] *n.*【动】锥鼻虫 (*Conorhinus sanguisuga*)〔见于美国南部和美洲热带地区〕.

Con·es·to·ga (wagon) [ˌkɔnis'təugə] *n.* 〔美〕康内斯托加式宽轮大篷马车〔拓荒者在草原地带使用〕.

co·ney ['kəuni] *n.* = cony.

conf. = confer; confessor; conference.

con·fab ['kɔnfæb] *n.*, *vi.* 〔口〕= confabulation, confabulate.

con·fab·u·late [kən'fæbjuleit] *vi.* ①谈论，谈笑，闲谈，谈心 (*with*). ②【心】(在记忆的缺失处)插入虚构情节. **-la·tion** [-'leiʃən] *n.* **-fab·u·la·to·ry** [-'fæbjulətəri] *a.*

con·fab·u·la·tor [kən'fæbjuleitə] *n.* 谈笑者，闲谈者.

con·far·re·a·tion [kənˌfæri'eiʃən] *n.* 【史】献糕式婚礼〔古罗马最隆重的结婚仪式，由大司祭主持，向朱庇特献奉斯佩尔特小麦糕〕.

con·fect ['kɔnfekt] *n.* 糖果. — [kən'fekt] *vt.* 制造；调制；泡制.

con·fec·tion [kən'fekʃən] *n.* ①(糖果等的)制造，调制；糖果蜜饯[点心]；【医】糖果剂. ②精巧的制品；妇女时装用品. — *vt.* 〔古〕调制.

con·fec·tion·ar·y [kən'fekʃənəri] *a.* 糖果点心(业、商)的. — *n.* 〔总称〕糖果点心(店).

con·fec·tioner [kən'fekʃənə] *n.* 糖果(点心)制造人[商]，糖果点心店.

con·fec·tion·er·y [kən'fekʃənəri] *n.* ①糖果点心类〔糖果，蜜饯，糕点等总称〕. ②糖果点心铺. ③糖果点心制造(法、业).

Confed. = Confederate, Confederacy.

con·fed·er·a·cy [kən'fedərəsi] *n.* ①同盟，联盟，邦联. ②共谋；秘密结社；帮派. *the C-*【美史】(南北战争时的)南部邦联〔正式名称为 the Confederate States of America〕.

con·fed·er·al [kən'fedərəl, -'fedrəl] *a.* 同盟的，联盟的，邦联的.

con·fed·er·ate [kən'fedəreit] *vt.*, *vi.* (使)结成同盟，(使)联合；(使)成帮派[秘密结社] (*with*). ***~ oneself with*** 与…结盟、联盟，结成一帮. — *n.* ①同盟者；〔口〕联合者；联盟成员. ②共谋者，同伙. ③〔the C-〕【美史】(南北战争时)南部邦联的支持者. ***play ~ to*** 策应. — [kən'fedərit] *a.* 同盟的，联合的；〔C-〕【美史】(参加)南部邦联的.

con·fed·er·a·tion [kənˌfedə'reiʃən] *n.* ①同盟，联盟；(特指)邦联. ②〔the C-〕【美史】(1781—1789年)十三州邦联；【史】加拿大联盟〔指英属加拿大四省联盟，于1867年获得自治领地位〕.

con·fed·er·a·tive [kən'fedərətiv] *a.* 同盟[联盟，邦联]的.

con·fer [kən'fəː] *vt.* 授与，颁与(称号、学位等). *~ a medal [title] on [upon] sb.* 授与某人以勋章[称号].

— *vi.* 商议,协商,谈判. ～ *with sb. on [about] sth.* 与某人协商[商议]某事.

con·fer [kənˈfəː] 〔L.〕 *vt.* 〔祈使语气〕比较,对照,参看〔略作 cf.〕.

con·fer·ee [ˌkɔnfəˈriː] ①会议的参加者[出席者],参加商谈者. ②被授(学位、称号)者.

con·fer·ence [ˈkɔnfərəns] *n.* ①协商,谈判,商议;讨论会,协商会;会议. ②(学位等的)授与. ③〔美〕(宗教,学术,运动团体的)联合会. *a press [news]* ～ 记者招待会. *be in* ～ 会议中. *call [convene, convoke] a* ～ 召集会议. *call together (the members of a society) to a* ～ 召集(会员)开会. *have a* ～ *with* 和…协商〔谈判〕. *hold a* ～ 开会. ～ **call** 电话会议.

con·fer·ment [kənˈfəːmənt] *n.* (学位等的)授与.

con·fer·ree [ˌkɔnfəˈriː] = conferee.

con·fer·rer [kənˈfəːrə] 授与人.

con·fer·va [kənˈfəːvə] *n.* (*pl.* **-vae** [-viː], ～**s**) 【植】水绵属植物. **-l** *a.*

con·fer·void [kənˈfəːvɔid] 【植】 *a.* 水绵状的. — *n.* 水绵.

con·fess [kənˈfes] *vt.* ①自白,承认,供认. ②表白(信仰);忏悔. 向上帝[神父等]忏悔(罪恶). ③(教士)听取(教徒)忏悔. ④证明. ～ *oneself to be in the wrong* 承认错误. ～ *oneself (to be) guilty* 承认有罪. ～ *a crime* 坦白罪行. ～ *allegiance to ...* 表明忠诚于… *The priest* ～*ed the young man.* 神父听取那个青年的忏悔. — *vi.* ①供认,承认. ②忏悔. ③(神父)听取忏悔. ～ *before a priest* 在神父面前忏悔. ～ *to a weakness for smoking* 承认有爱吸烟的缺点. ～ **and avoid** 【法】承认所控事实但同时举出其他事实抗辩,主张所控罪名在法律上不能成立. ***I*** ～ ***(that)...*** 〔口〕得承认,这实在是. ***to*** ～ ***the truth*** 说实话.

con·fessed [kənˈfest] *a.* ①众所公认的,已有定论的,明白的. ②已认罪的,已自首的. ③【宗】已向神父忏悔(而得到赦免)的. ④被公开信仰的. *a* ～ *and unconquerable difficulty* 众所公认的无法克服的困难. *a* ～ *fact* 明白的事实. ***stand*** ～ ***as*** 被揭露为,被认为是.

con·fess·ed·ly [kənˈfesidli] *ad.* 已公开承认;明白无疑地,众所公认地.

con·fes·sion [kənˈfeʃən] *n.* ①自白;承认,坦白;(对神父所作的)忏悔. ②【法】自白书,口供. ③【宗】(基督教会具有某种特殊教规的)殉教者坟墓[祭坛]. ④信仰的宣告[声明];教规;教派. ～ ***of faith*** 信仰声明〔获准入教前所作〕. ***make an*** ～ 交代. **-sion·al, -sion·ary** ① *a.* 自白的;忏悔的. ② *n.* 听取忏悔室.

con·fes·sor [kənˈfesə] *n.* ①坦白者,自首者;忏悔者. ②(遭遇宗教迫害时)声明自己信仰的人. ③听忏悔的牧师[神父].

con·fet·ti [kənˈfeti(ː)] *n.* *pl.* (作单数用) ①糖果. ②(婚礼中投掷的)五彩碎纸.

con·fi·dant [ˌkɔnfiˈdænt] *n.* 〔F.〕(可以秘密托付的)心腹朋友.

con·fi·dante [ˌkɔnfiˈdænt] *n.* 〔F〕知心女友.

con·fide [kənˈfaid] *vt.* ①吐露(秘密). ②信托,交托,委托. ～ *a secret to (sb.)* 对(某人)吐露秘密. ～ *a task to (sb.)* 对(某人)托付任务. — *vi.* ①(对知己)吐露秘密 *(in).* ②信任,信赖 *(in).* ～ *in one's friend* 向朋友谈个人心事.

con·fi·dence [ˈkɔnfidəns] *n.* ①信任,信赖. ②自信,确信;自恃. ③(偷偷吐露的)秘密,心事. ④(多指怀恶意的)胆量;厚脸,无耻. *exchange* ～*s* 互谈心事. *forfeit* ～ 丧失信用. ～ *game* 〔美〕 = ～ trick 〔英〕骗局. ～ *in oneself* 自信 (= self-～). ～ *man* 〔美〕骗子. ***enjoy [have]*** *(sb.'s)* ～ 受到某人的信赖. ***give*** ～ ***to*** = ***have*** ～ ***in*** 信任,信赖. ***have the*** ～ ***to*** *(deny it)* 胆敢,无耻(否认). ***in*** ～ 秘密地,偷偷地,暗中. ***in the*** ～ ***of*** 受…信任;参与…的机密. ***make*** ～***s*** ***[a*** ～***] to (sb.)*** = ***take (sb.) into one's*** ～ 对(某人)吐露秘密,把(某人)当做心腹朋友. ***misplace one's*** ～ 误信(某人),信任不可靠的人. ***place [put, repose, show]*** ～ ***in*** 信任,信赖. ***want of*** ～ ***in the Cabinet [Ministry]*** 〔英〕对内阁不信任. ***with (great)*** ～ 很有把握地,满怀信心地. — *a.* 骗得信任的,欺诈的. *a* ～ *tricker* 骗子. ～ **belt** 【自】置信带. ～ **game** 〔美〕骗局. ～ **man** 〔美〕骗子. ～ **trick** 〔英〕 = ～ game.

con·fi·dent [ˈkɔnfidənt] *a.* ①确信,深信;自信 *(in; of; that).* ②有自信的;沉着的. ③大胆的,过分自信的;厚颜无耻的. *a* ～ *manner [smile]* 充满信心的态度[微笑]. *a* ～ *attack* 大胆的攻击. *a very* ～, *uppish young man* 极其冒失逞能的小伙子. *be* ～ *of (success)* 对(成功)满怀信心. *I am* ～ *that* 我深信. — *n.* 知己,心腹朋友. **-ly** *ad.*

con·fi·den·tial [kɔnfiˈdenʃəl] *a.* ①极信任的,心腹的. ②秘密的,机密的. ③(语气等)亲密的. *Confidential* (此系)密件[信封用语]. *Strictly* ～ 绝密. *a* ～ *clerk* 极受信任的职员. *a* ～ *creditor* 优先债权人. *a* ～ *inquiry* 秘密调查[打听]. *a* ～ *opinion* 心里话. *a* ～ *document* 密件,保密文献. ～ *papers* 机密文件. ～ *communication* 密告;(不对外公开的)秘密通知. ～ *price list* (内部的)秘密价目单. **-ly** *ad.* **-ness** *n.*

con·fid·ing [kənˈfaidiŋ] *a.* 信任的;轻信的,相信不疑的. *a* ～ *nature* 不疑人[轻信]的性格. *a* ～ *wife* 十分信任丈夫的妻子.

con·fig·u·ra·tion [kənˌfigjuˈreiʃən] *n.* ①结构;构造;图形,外形. ②组合,布置;配置. ③地形;【天】(行星等的)相对位置,方位;【化】(分子中原子的)构型,排列;【物】位形;组态.

con·fig·u·ra·tion·ism [kənˌfigəˈreiʃəˌnizm] *n.* 形态心理学;格式心理学 (= Gestalt psychology).

con·figure [kənˈfigə] *vt.* 使成形.

con·fine [kənˈfain] *vt.* ①限制 *(to; within);* 【物】约束,吸持. ②幽禁,监禁;使闭居,蛰居. — *vi.* 〔罕〕接界,邻接 *(with).* ***be*** ～***d*** 闭居;坐月子,分娩. ***expect to be*** ～***d (on a date)*** 预期在(某日)分娩. ***be*** ～***d to barracks*** (士兵)被禁止外出. ***be*** ～***d to one's bed*** 卧病床上 (*He is* ～*d to his bed with a cold.* 他因为伤风病倒了). ～ ***oneself to*** 在…闭门不出;以…为限. — [ˈkɔnfain] *n.* ①〔常 *pl.*〕境界,界限,国界,疆界;边界,边境. ②限度;范围. ***between the*** ～***s of ...*** 之间的界线. ***on the*** ～***s of*** 濒于,差一点儿就 (*on the* ～*s of the indecent* 再进一步就流于猥亵了). ***the*** ～***s of a town*** 城区,市区. ***within the*** ～***s of*** 在…范围内.

con·fined [kənˈfaind] *a.* ①有限的,狭窄的. ②被禁闭着的. ③产期内的. ④受约束的. ～ *water* 受压水,有压水.

con·fine·ment [kənˈfainmənt] *n.* ①限制,界限,拘束;(电磁)吸持. ②幽禁,监禁;拘留;【物】密封,密闭. ③闭居,退隐. ④产期,分娩期. *major [minor]* ～ 重[轻]监禁. *solitary* ～ 单独监禁. *a difficult* ～ 难产.

con·firm [kənˈfəːm] *vt.* ①使更坚固[坚定,坚强]. ②(进一步)证实[确定]. ③【法】使有效,确认,批准,认可. ④【宗】给…行按手礼[坚信礼]. ⑤坚持认为 *(that).* ～ *a treaty* 批准条约. ～ *sb. in his belief* 使某人信仰更坚定. *It wants yet to be* ～*ed* 还待确证. ～ *an order* (卖主)确证已收到订单. ～ *a plane reservation* (乘客)向航空公司确认所订机票不作变动. **-able** *a.* 可确定的;能证实的;可批准的.

con·fir·mand [ˌkɔnfəˈmænd, ˈkɔnfəˌmænd] *n.* 【宗】请受坚信礼[按手礼]者.

con·fir·ma·tion [ˌkɔnfəˈmeiʃən] *n.* ①(进一步)确定[确立、证实]. ②确认,认可,批准. ③【宗】按手礼;坚信礼. ***in*** ～ ***of*** 以(便)证实….

con·firm·a·tive [kənˈfəːmətiv], **con·firm·a·to·ry** [-təri] *a.* 确证的,确定的;批准的;【宗】坚信礼的.

con·firmed [kənˈfəːmd] *a.* ①坚定的；确定[证实]了的。②根深蒂固的；难治的，慢性的。*a* ~ *disease* 老毛病。*a* ~ *fool* 无可救药的傻瓜。*a* ~ *habit* 积习。*a* ~ *invalid* 痼疾病人。
con·fis·ca·ble [kənˈfiskəbl] *a.* 可没收[充公]的。
con·fis·cate [ˈkɔnfiskeit] *vt.* 没收，把…充公；征用。**-ca·tion** [-ˈkeiʃən] *n.*
con·fis·ca·tor [ˈkɔnfiskeitə] *n.* 没收者。
con·fis·ca·to·ry [kənˈfiskətəri] *a.* 没收的，充公的。
con·fit·e·or [kɔnˈfitiɔː] *n.* 【宗】忏悔祈祷(文)。
con·fi·ture [ˈkɔnfitʃuə] *n.* 糖果，蜜饯，糖渍。
con·fla·grant [kənˈfleigrənt] *a.* 燃烧的，炽燃的。
con·fla·gra·tion [ˌkɔnfləˈgreiʃən] *n.* 大火(灾)；战火。
con·fla·tion [kənˈfleiʃən] *n.* 熔合；合成；(两种不同版本、异文的)合刊本。
con·flict [ˈkɔnflikt] *n.* ①争斗；纠纷，倾轧。②冲突，矛盾，抵触。③〔美俚〕竞赛，比赛。*a* ~ *of opinions [views]* 意见的冲突。*a* ~ *of laws* 法律条文的相抵触。*undergo an inner* ~ 思想上产生矛盾。***come into*** ~ ***with*** 和…冲突。***in*** ~ ***with*** 和…冲突[矛盾]。— [kənˈflikt] *vi.* ①争斗，倾轧 *(with)*。②冲突，抵触，矛盾 *(with)*。
con·flict·ing [kənˈfliktiŋ] *a.* 互相斗争的，互不相容的；相冲突的，矛盾的。~ *emotions* 矛盾情绪。~ *purposes* 互相冲突的目的。
con·flu·ence [ˈkɔnfluəns] *n.* ①合流；汇流(处)；汇合而成的河流。②会合，群集；汇聚(的人群)。
con·flu·ent [ˈkɔnfluənt] *a.* 合流的，汇合的；【植】会合的。②【医】融合性的。— *n.* 汇流；支流。
con·flux [ˈkɔnflʌks] *n.* = confluence.
con·fo·cal [kɔnˈfəukl] *a.* 【数】共焦(点)的。
con·form [kənˈfɔːm] *vt.* 使一致[符合]；使顺应，依照(习惯)；使遵照 *(to)*。~ *one's habits to those of the local inhabitants* 使自己的习惯与当地居民相一致。— *vi.* ①一致；遵照；依据 *(to, with)*。②【宗】遵奉国教。~ *to customs [rules]* 遵守习惯[规则]。~ ***(oneself) to*** 遵照；顺应；遵守。**-a·bil·i·ty** *n.* 适合，一致，顺应，相似；顺从；【地】(地层的) 整合性。**-able** *a.* 相似；一致，适合，依照 *(to; with)*；遵从 *(to)*；【地】整合的。**-ably** *ad.*
con·for·mal [kɔnˈfɔːml] *a.* ①【数】共形的，保形的，保角的。②(地图等)形状完全如实[相似]的。
con·form·ance [kənˈfɔːməns] *n.* 相似，相符，一致。
con·for·ma·tion [ˌkɔnfɔːˈmeiʃən] *n.* ①适应，相应，符合，一致。②构造；形态；结构，组成。**-tion·al** *a.* **-al·ly** *ad.*
con·form·ist [kənˈfɔːmist] *n.* ①(法律、习惯等的)遵守者。②〔常 C-〕英国国教徒。
con·form·i·ty [kənˈfɔːmiti] *n.* ①相似，符合；适合，一致。②遵从，顺从；【英史】遵奉国教。③【地】整合。***in*** ~ ***to [with]*** 和…相适应，和…一致[符合]；遵照。
con·found [kənˈfaund] *vt.* ①混淆，使混同[混杂]，使混乱。②使惊慌失措，使狼狈；使羞愧。③反驳；挫败(计划、希望等)。④[ˈkɔnˈfaund]〔口〕〔比 damn 轻的骂语〕让…死掉，可恶，活该。*be ~ed at [by] the sight of* 看见…大惊失色。*be ~ed with ...* 和…混淆了。~ *right and wrong* 混淆是非。~ *the means with the end* 把手段与目的相混淆，颠倒本末。***C- you [him]!*** 这个[那个]家伙；混蛋，去你[他]的！***C- it!*** 讨厌，该死的！
con·found·ed [kənˈfaundid] *a.* ①混乱的，狼狈的。②[ˈkɔnˈfaundid]〔口〕讨厌的，无理的，非常的。*I've been kept waiting a* ~ *long time.* 叫我傻等多时。*a* ~ *idiot* 十足的大傻瓜。**-ly** *ad.*〔口〕非常，极度，特别。
con·fra·ter·ni·ty [ˌkɔnfrəˈtəːniti] *n.* (宗教、互助、慈善性质的)团体；协会，公会。
con frère [ˈkɔnfreə] *n.* 〔F.〕同事；同仁，同行；(同一结社的)会员，社员。
con·front [kənˈfrʌnt] *vt.* ①面对；在…的正对面；勇敢正视；对付(危险等)。②(困难等)横阻在…的面前。③使面临；使对质，使对证。④对照，使对比。*be ~ed with [by] (a difficulty)* 碰到(困难)。~ *(the accused) with (his accuser)* 使(被告)和(原告)对质。*the hardships ~-ing the miners* 矿工们面临的艰苦环境。
con·fron·ta·tion [ˌkɔnfrʌnˈteiʃən] *n.* 面对；遭遇；对峙；对抗；对质。**-ist** *n.* 主张在国际关系中持对抗态度的人，对抗[对峙]主义者。
con·fu·cian [kənˈfjuːʃjən] *a.* 孔子的；儒家的。— *n.* 孔门弟子[门徒]；儒家。**-ism** *n.* 孔子学说，儒教，儒家(学说)。
Con·fu·cius [kənˈfjuːʃiəs] *n.* 孔子。
con·fuse [kənˈfjuːz] *vt.* ①使混乱，弄乱；混淆；弄错。②使慌乱，使困窘，使狼狈；使胡涂〔常用被动语态〕。~ *accounts* 搞乱帐目。~ *dates* 弄错日期。~ *liberty with license* 混淆自由和放纵。*be [become, get]* ~*d with one's blunder* 因做错事而发慌[窘]，不知所措。
con·fus·ed [kənˈfjuːzd] *a.* 混乱的；慌乱的，狼狈的。**-ly** *ad.* ness *n.*
con·fu·sion [kənˈfjuːʒən] *n.* ①混乱，紊乱；混同，混淆。②慌乱，狼狈。③〔骂〕混帐，该死。④〔古〕毁灭。*be thrown into* ~ 陷入慌张失措[混乱]中。*chaotic* ~ 大混乱。*covered with* ~ 慌慌张张。*drink* ~ *to (the enemy)* 为(敌人)完蛋干杯。*in* ~ 狼狈；慌乱；胡乱。*in the* ~ *of the moment* 趁着混乱。***C-!*** 该死！***C- on [upon] ...!*** …该死！~ ***worse confounded*** 更加混乱，一团糟。
con·fu·ta·tion [ˌkɔnfjuːˈteiʃən] *n.* 驳倒；反证。
con·fute [kənˈfjuːt] *vt.* ①驳倒。②〔旧〕糟蹋。
cong. = congregation; congress(ional).
con·ga [ˈkɔŋgə] *n.* 〔美〕康茄舞(曲)。— *vi.* 跳康茄舞。
con·gé [ˈkɔ̃ːnʒei] *n.* 〔F.〕①(突然的)撤职。②辞行，告别，行告别礼 (= congee[1])。③离去的许可。④【建】四分之一弧凹形边饰，拇指圆饰。~ ***d'élire*** (国王颁发的)主教选举许可令。***get [receive] one's*** ~ 被免职。***give sb. his*** ~ 免某人职。***pour prendre*** ~ [F. pur prɑ̆dr kɔ̃ʒe] (= to take leave) 辞行〔略作 *P.P.C.*，辞行时写在名片下端〕。***take one's*** ~ 告别。
con·geal [kənˈdʒiːl] *vi., vt.* (使)冻结，(使)凝结。*Fear ~ed my blood.* 吓得我血液都凝结起来了。**-able** *a.* 可冻结的，可凝结的。**-er** *n.* 冷冻机，冷却器，冷藏箱。**-ment** *n.* 冻结，凝结。
con·gee[1] [ˈkɔndʒiː] *n., vi.* 〔古〕辞行，告别；行告别礼[鞠躬]。
con·gee[2] [ˈkɔndʒiː] *n.* 粥，稀饭。
con·ge·la·tion [ˌkɔndʒiˈleiʃən] *n.* ①冻结(物)，凝结(物)。②冻伤，冻疮。
con·ge·ner [ˈkɔndʒinə] *n.* ①同属的动植物。②同一种类的人[东西]。*Compare the Russian peasant with his English* ~. 比较一下俄国农民和英国农民。
con·ge·ner·ic [kɔndʒiˈnerik] *a.* 同源[种、属、类]的。
con·gen·ial [kənˈdʒiːnjəl] *a.* ①同性质的，性格相似的，意气相投的，思想感情相同的 *(with; to)*。②适意的，合适的 *(to)*。~ *spirits* 意气相投的人物。*a* ~ *work* 合意的工作。*be* ~ *to* 对…意趣相合的。*in* ~ *society* 与意气相投的人们在一起。
con·ge·ni·al·i·ty [kənˌdʒiːniˈæliti] *n.* 思想感情相同，趣味相同，意气相投；适意，合适。
con·gen·i·tal [kənˈdʒenitl] *a.* 生来的，天赋的，先天的。~ *deformity* 先天的残废人。**-ly** *ad.*
con·ger, con·ger·eel [ˈkɔŋgə, -gəˈriːl] *n.* 【动】海鳗。
con·ge·ries [kɔnˈdʒiəriːz] *n.* 〔*sing., pl.*〕团集，聚集(体)；堆积，堆。
con·gest [kənˈdʒest] *vt., vi.* ①(使)充血。②充满，拥塞。*a ~ed district* 人口稠密[拥挤]的地方。*The cold ~ed his sinuses.* 他因受凉堵了鼻子。
con·ges·tion [kənˈdʒestʃən] *n.* ①【医】充血。②(交通

的)拥挤;(货物的)充斥;(人口)过剩，稠密. *traffic* ～ 交通拥塞. ～ *of the brain* 脑充血.

con·ges·tive [kən'dʒestiv] *a.*【医】充血的,充血性的. ～ *symptoms* 充血性征候.

con·gi·us ['kɔndʒiəs] *n.* (*pl.* **-gi·i** [-ai]) ①【史】康吉斯〔古罗马液量单位，略小于七品脱〕. ②【药】一加仑.

con·glo·bate ['kɔngləubeit] *vt., vi.* (使)变成球,(使)形成球状. — *a.* 成球(状)的.

con·glo·ba·tion [ˌkɔngləu'beiʃən] *n.* 球形,球形体.

con·glom·er·ate [kən'glɔmərit] *a.* ①成球(状)的; 结成团块的. ②由不同种类的各部分组成的，混杂会聚在一处的. ③【地】砾岩(性)的. — *n.* ①团集物. ②集团;联合大企业,多种经营大公司,多业公司. ③【地】砾岩. — [kən'glɔməreit] *vt., vi.* (使)结聚成一团.

con·glom·er·a·tion [kənˌglɔmə'reiʃən] *n.* ①结聚作用;结聚. ②团块;堆集. ③集团.

con·glom·er·a·tor [kən'glɔməreitə] 联合大企业[多业公司]的组成者[主持人].

con·glu·ti·nant [kən'glu:tinənt] *a.* ①粘合的; 愈合的;收口的. ②【医】促使(伤口)愈合的,加速(伤口)收口的.

con·glu·ti·nate [kən'glu:tineit] *vt., vi.* (使)粘合,(使)粘在一块;【医】(使)愈合. — *a.* 粘合的;【医】愈合的.

con·glu·ti·na·tion [kənˌglu:ti'neiʃən] *n.* 粘合,粘着;【医】愈合.

Con·go ['kɔŋgəu] *n.* 〔the ～〕①刚果〔非洲〕. ②刚果河〔即扎伊尔河〕〔非洲〕. ～ **dye,** ～ **colour** 一种偶氮染料. ～ **eel [snake]**【动】蛇状两栖鲵. ～ **paper** 一种化学试纸〔遇酸变蓝色，遇碱变红色〕. ～ **red** 刚果红〔一种染料〕.

Con·go·lese [ˌkɔŋgə'li:z] *a.* 刚果(人)的; 刚果语的. — *n.* 刚果人;刚果语.

con·go(u) ['kɔngəu] *n.* (中国的)工夫红茶.

con·grat·u·lant [kən'grætjulənt] *a.* 祝贺的. — *n.* 祝贺者.

con·grat·u·late [kən'grætjuleit] *vt.* 祝贺,向…致祝词. *I* ～ *you on your success [birthday].* 我祝贺你的成功[生日]. *I* ～ *myself on [upon] my narrow escape.* 我庆幸自己死里逃生.

con·grat·u·la·tion [kənˌgrætju'leiʃən] *n.* 祝贺;〔*pl.*〕祝词，贺辞. *a matter for* ～ 值得庆贺的事情. *offer one's* ～*s* 致祝词,道贺. *Congratulations!* 恭喜恭喜!

con·grat·u·la·tor [kən'grætjuleitə] *n.* 祝贺者.

con·grat·u·la·to·ry [kən'grætjulətəri] *a.* 祝贺的. *a* ～ *address* 祝词. *a* ～ *telegram* 贺电.

con·gre·gant ['kɔŋgrigənt] *n.* (会众中的)召集人.

con·gre·gate ['kɔŋgrigeit] *vt., vi.* (使)聚集，集合. — *a.* 聚集的;集团的.

con·gre·ga·tion [ˌkɔŋgri'geiʃən] *n.* ①集合;(特指宗教的)集会;会众，听众. ②〔the C-〕【犹史】以色列人(全体);犹太民族(＝C- of the Lord.). ③(牛津大学的)教职员全体会议. ④〔美〕(殖民时代的)教区,行政区,农庄,农垦地.⑤(遵守共同教规的)天主教结社;(由几个修道院结合起来的)修士团分团;(教廷中协助教皇处理各种事务的)十一个常设委员会之一;(处理某种特殊问题的)主教会议.

Con·gre·ga·tion·al [ˌkɔngri'geiʃənəl] *a.* ①【宗】公理会的. ②〔c-〕集会的;(教堂、教会)会众的. **-ism** ①【宗】公理会. ②〔C-〕地方教会自治主义. **-ist** ①*n.* 公理会教友. ②*a.* 公理会的.

con·gress ['kɔŋgres] *n.* ①(代表)大会. ②国会;国会会期;〔C-〕美国国会. ③集会,交际;社交. ④协会. ⑤群. *a medical* ～ 医学会议. *the National People's C-* 全国人民代表大会. *in C-* 〔美〕在国会开会期间. — [kən'gres] *vi.* 开会,集合. ～ **boot [gaiter, shoe]** 〔美〕两侧有松紧布的半统靴. ～**man** 〔美〕(男性)国会议员,(特指)众议院议员. ～**person** 国会议员〔妇权运动者用语〕. ～**woman** 〔美〕国会女议员.

con·gres·sion·al [kən'greʃənəl] *a.* 会议的;委员会的;〔C-〕〔美〕国会的. **C- district** 〔美〕选举区. **C- Record** 〔美〕国会议事录.

Con·gress·ite ['kɔŋgresait] *n.* 印度国大党党员.

Con·greve ['kɔŋgri:v] *n.* 康格里夫〔姓氏〕.

con·gru·ence, con·gru·en·cy ['kɔŋgruəns(i)] *n.* ①适合,和谐,【语法】一致. ②【数】叠合,相合,全等;同余(式)(线)汇. ～ **field**【数】同余域. ～ **lines** 线汇.

con·gru·ent ['kɔŋgruənt] *a.* ①适合的,相合的,一致的. ②【数】全等的，叠合的，同余的. ～ **points** 叠合点.

con·gru·i·ty [kɔŋ'gru(:)iti] *n.* ①适合,一致，调和. ②【数】全等. *a* ～ *of ideas* 思想一致.

con·gru·ous ['kɔŋgruəs] *a* ①一致的，适合[协调]的,符合的 *(with; to)*. ②【数】全等的.

con·ic ['kɔnik] *n.* 圆锥(形);圆锥[二次]曲线;〔*pl.*〕锥线法[论]. — *a.* 圆锥(形)的. ～ **pendulum** 锥动摆. ～ **projection** 锥顶射影. ～ **section** 圆锥截面;圆锥[二次]曲线. ～ **spring** 锥形弹簧.

con·i·cal ['kɔnikəl] *a.* 圆锥(体、形)的. **-ly** *ad.*成圆锥形.

co·nic·i·ty [kəu'nisiti] *n.*【物】锥削度.

con·i·coid ['kɔnikɔid] *n.*【数】二次曲面，(特指)双曲面.

co·nid·i·al [kəu'nidiəl] *a.*【植】①无性芽胞(状)的. ②产生无性芽胞的(＝ conidian).

co·nid·i·o·phore [kəu'nidiəfɔ:] *n.*【植】分生孢子柄[梗].

co·nid·io·spore [kəu'nidiəspɔ:] *n.*【微】分生孢子.

co·nid·i·um [kəu'nidiəm] *n.* (*pl.* **-nidia** [-'nidiə])【植】分生孢子.

co·ni·fer ['kəunifə] *n.*【植】针叶树.

co·ni·f·er·ae [kəu'niferi:] *n.* 〔*pl.*〕【植】松柏科.

co·nif·er·ous [kəu'nifərəs] *a.* 结球果的,松柏科的.

co·ni·form ['kəunifɔ:m] *a.* 圆锥形的.

co·ni·ine ['kəunii:n, -in] *n.*【化】毒芹碱 (＝ conine).

co·ni·ol·o·gy [ˌkəuni'ɔlədʒi] *n.*【气】微尘学 (＝ koniology).

Co·ni·o·se·li·num [ˌkəuniəusi'lainəm] *n.*【植】川芎属.

co·ni·um ['kəuniəm] *n.* 毒芹属植物〔如芹叶钩吻*(Conium maculatum)*〕.

conj. ＝ ①conjugation. ②conjunction; conjunctive.

con·jec·tur·a·ble [kən'dʒektʃərəbl] *a.* 可推测[猜想]到的.

con·jec·tur·al [kən'dʒektʃərəl] *a.* 推测的,猜想的. **-ly** *ad.*

con·jec·ture [kən'dʒektʃə] *n.* 推测,猜想;辨读;设想. ～ *of the most vague and shadowy description* 瞎猜，捕风捉影的推测. ***form [make]*** ～***s upon*** 推想. ***found a*** ～ ***on*** 根据…推测. ***hazard [venture] a*** ～ 猜猜看,估估看. — *vt., vi.* 推测,猜想,估量;辨读,设想.

con·jee ['kɔndʒi:] *n.* ＝ congee².

con·join [kən'dʒɔin] *vt., vi.* (使)结合，(使)连接;(使)联合.

con·joined [kən'dʒɔind] *a.* 结合的;联在一起的;【徽】重叠的,相连的.

con·joint ['kɔndʒɔint] *a.* 相连的，粘合的,结合的;连带的,共同的. ～ *action* 共同动作. — *n.* 〔*pl.*〕夫妇. **-ly** *ad.*

con·ju·gal ['kɔndʒugəl] *a.* 婚姻上的，夫妇(间)的. ～ *affection* 夫妇爱. ～ *laws* 婚姻法. ～ *understanding* 婚约. **-i·ty** [-'gæliti] *n.* **-ly** *ad.*

con·ju·gant ['kɔndʒəgənt] *n.*【生】配合体[子].

con·ju·gate ['kɔndʒugit] *a.* 成对的; 结合的;【语法】

同源[根]的;【数、物、化】共轭的,缀合的;【生】配合的;【植】对生的. ~ *angles* 共轭角. *a* ~ *point* 共轭点. —[-geit] *vt.* ①使结合,使配合. ②【语法】列举(动词)变化,变位. — *vi.* ①结合;(动物)交尾;【生】配合. ②【语法】(动词)变化. ~*d protein*【化】缀朊.

con·ju·ga·tion [ˌkɔndʒuˈgeiʃən] *n.* ①结合(作用),配合. ②【语法】动词的变化[变位]. ③【化】共轭,缀合;【生】(雌雄配子等的)接合(作用),配合. *strong* [*weak*] ~【语法】强[弱]变化,不规则[规则]变化.

con·junct [kənˈdʒʌŋkt] *a.* 连接的,结合的;联合的. **-ly** *ad.*

con·junc·tion [kənˈdʒʌŋkʃən] *n.* ①连合,结合,连接;联合;联系. ②(事件的)同时发生. ③【语法】连(接)词. ④【天】(行星等的)会合,(月的)朔;【数】契合,合取;【计】逻辑乘法,逻辑乘积. *coordinate* [*subordinate*] ~*s* 并列[从属]连词. *in* ~ *with* 与…共同,与…协力,联络着;连带着. **-al** *a.*

con·junc·ti·va [ˌkɔndʒʌŋkˈtaivə] *n.* [L.] (*pl.* ~*s*, *-vae* [-viː])【解】(眼球的)结膜.

con·junc·tive [kənˈdʒʌŋktiv] *a.* ①连结(着)的;【数】契合的,合取的;【语法】(有)连接(作用)的. ②【计】逻辑乘法的. — *n.*【语法】连词. ~ **mood**【语法】连接语态. ~ **symbiosis**【生】合体共生. **-ly** *ad.*

con·junc·ti·vi·tis [kənˌdʒʌŋktiˈvaitis] *n.*【医】结膜炎.

con·junc·ture [kənˈdʒʌŋktʃə] *n.* ①局面,场合,地步;(某种)机缘;紧要关头,非常时候. ②结合;连接. *at* [*in*] *this* ~ 在这(危急)时候.

con·ju·ra·tion [ˌkɔndʒuəˈreiʃən] *n.* ①祈求;恳求. ②魔法;咒语. ③【法】犯罪图谋[合谋].

con·jure [ˈkʌndʒə] *vt.* ①使用魔术变出. ②[kənˈdʒuə] 祈求. ③想象出 (*up*). *I* ~ *you by all that is holy to desist.* 务祈作罢. ~ *an egg out of an empty cup* 从空杯里变出一枚鸡蛋. — *vi.* 施魔法;变戏法. ~ ***away*** 念咒驱逐[消除]. ~ ***down*** 召来(魔鬼). ~ ***out*** 念咒语使出现;变戏法变出. ~ ***up*** 念咒召来;(凭想象)作出,使现出,想象出.

con·jur·er, con·jur·or [ˈkʌndʒərə] *n.* ①咒法家,邪术家;魔术师. ②[口]极聪明厉害的人. *He is no* ~. 他不大行. ***without being a*** ~ 虽不怎样精明.

con·jur·y [ˈkʌndʒəri] *n.* 咒法,邪术;魔术.

conk[1] [kɔŋk] *n.* [俚]鼻子;[美俚]头,脑袋;头上的一击. — *vi.* [口](机械等)坏掉,出毛病;疲劳已极,累透(*out*);昏厥;死亡. — *vt.* [美俚] 打…的脑袋,敲…的头. ~ *out* [美口]突然停止,发生故障. ~**out** *n.* 发生故障.

conk[2] [kɔŋk] *vt.* 把(非洲人卷紧的头发)弄成波浪形或弄直. — *n.* 把卷紧的头发展平[成波浪形]的发式.

conk·er [ˈkɔŋkə] *n.* ①【植】七叶树. ②[*pl.*][动词用单数]打栗子[一种儿童游戏,双方各执一串七叶树栗,以打碎对方的一串为胜].

conk·y [ˈkɔŋki] *a.*, *n.* [俚]鼻子大的(人).

con mo·to [kɔn ˈmәutәu] *n.* [It.]【乐】速度加快.

conn [kɔn] *vt.* (驶)船,掌握(船的)驾驶. — *n.* 驶船(指挥).

Conn. = Connecticut.

con·nate [ˈkɔneit] *a.* ①生来的;先天的;【生】原生的;合生的. ②同源[族]的;同性质的. *a* ~ *deposit* 原生沉积. *a* ~ *disease* 先天性疾病.

con·nat·u·ral [kəˈnætʃərəl] *a.* ①生来的,固有的 (*to*). ②同性质的,同种[族]的.

con·nect [kəˈnekt] *vt.* ①连接,接合,连结. ②使有联系;为…接通电话. ③联想. *tow towns* ~*ed by a railway* 由铁路连接的两个市镇. *The telephone operator* ~*d us.* 话务员给我们接通了电话. — *vi.* 连通,连接,衔接,连续 (*with*). *This pipe* ~*s with a smaller one.* 这管子和一个较小的管子连通着. ***be*** ~***ed with*** 与…有关[联]系. ***be well-***~***ed*** 有有钱有势的亲戚[朋友][主要指亲戚,也可扩大到指某种后台]. ~ (***up***) ***with*** 和…有关系. ★~ up 是美语. ~ ***oneself with*** 和…联系. ***You are*** ~***ed.*** (电话)接通了[话务员用语].

con·nect·ed [kəˈnektid] *a.* 有联络的,联系着的;连续[贯]的. ~ *ideas* 连贯的思想. *a* ~ *plan* 通盘计划. **-ly** *ad.* **-ness** *n.*

Con·nect·i·cut [kəˈnetikət] *n.* 康涅狄格[美国州名].

con·nect·ing [kəˈnektiŋ] *a.* 连结着的;起连结作用的. ~ **trenches**【军】交通壕. ~ **tube** 导管.

con·nec·tion [kəˈnekʃən] *n.* [美] = connexion.

con·nec·tive [kəˈnektiv] *a.* 连接的. — *n.* ①连接物. ②【语法】连接语,连词. ③【植】药隔;【动】连索. ~ **fibre** [**tissue**]【解】结缔纤维[组织]. **-ly** *ad.*

con·nec·tor [kəˈnektə] *n.* ①连合者;连结者. ②连接物. ③【电】连接器,接头,插塞,插头,连接管.

con·nex·ion [kəˈnekʃən] *n.* ①连结;关系,联系;【电】合闸. ②联络;交情,交际;男女关系. ③团体;教派,宗派. ④[总称]主顾,顾客;有贸易关系的商号[人物]. ⑤(前后)关系;连贯(性);联想. ⑥亲戚;社会关系[多指有权有势的]. ⑦交通手段;联运船[车]. ⑧(电报、电话)通讯线. ⑨性交. ⑩[美俚]毒品贩子. *There is no* ~ *between them.* 他们无关系. *You are in* ~. (电话)接通了. *hot water* ~*s* 热水管. *outside* ~ (电话)外线. *criminal* ~ 通奸. *break off a* ~ 断绝关系. ***enter into a*** ~ ***with*** 与…发生关系[打交道]. ***form useful*** ~***s*** 构成有帮助的社会关系. ***have a*** ~ ***with*** 和…有关系,通着,勾搭着. ***have*** ~ ***with*** 和…发生关系,和…勾搭上. ***in*** ~ ***with*** 和(车、船等)联络着;与(人)共同,与…有关系[联络]. ***in this*** ~ 就此而论,关于这一点. ***make*** ~***s at*** (火车、轮船等)在…衔接[联络、转搭]. ***miss one's*** ~ (搭火车等)迟到而未搭上. ***sever*** ~ 脱离关系;分手. ***take up one's*** ~***s*** [美俚] 离开学校. ~ ***ticket*** (车、船)联运票. ~**-peg** 临时接通电流的插头.

Con·nie [ˈkɔni] *n.* 康妮[女子名,Constance 的昵称].

con·ning·tower [ˈkɔniŋtauə] *n.* (军舰的)司令塔;(潜艇的)指挥塔[亦用作出入口].

con·nip·tion [kəˈnipʃən] *n.* [美口]歇斯底里发作;大发脾气,激怒 (= ~ fit). ***throw a*** ~ 大发雷霆.

con·niv·ance, con·niv·an·cy [kəˈnaivəns(i)] *n.* 默许,放任,纵容;【法】(不当的对罪行的)默许 (*at*; *in*).

con·nive [kəˈnaiv] *vi.* ①假装不见;默许,纵容,放任 (*at*). ②共谋,成立默契,私通 (*with*). ③【生】逐渐集中一处,靠合.

con·niv·ent [kəˈnaivənt] *a.*【生】会接的,靠合的,逐渐集中的.

con·nois·seur [ˌkɔniˈsəː] *n.* (美术品的)鉴定家,行家,内行,权威 (*in*, *of*). ~ *in wine* 葡萄酒鉴定家. *play the* ~ 充内行. **-ship** 鉴赏能力;行家地位[资格].

Con·nor(s) [ˈkɔnə(z)] *n.* 康纳(斯)[姓氏].

con·no·ta·tion [ˌkɔnəuˈteiʃən] *n.* ①言外之意,含蓄;(词的)涵义. ②【逻】内涵,内包.

con·no·ta·tive [ˈkɔnəuteitiv, kəˈnəutətiv] *a.* ①含蓄的;有涵义的. ②【逻】内包的,包涵的. **-ly** *ad.*

con·note [kɔˈnəut] *vt.* ①暗示,指点. ②含蓄,包含;意味;【逻】内涵;包摄 (*opp.* denote). ③[俚]意思就是.

con·nu·bi·al [kəˈnjuːbjəl] *a.* 婚姻的,结婚的;夫妇的;配偶的. ~ *love* 夫妇爱. **-ly** *ad.* 婚姻上,作为夫妇来说(*not connubially inclined* 不想结婚).

con·nu·bi·al·i·ty [kəˌnjuːbiˈæliti] *n.* 夫妇关系;结婚(状态);结婚风俗.

co·no·dont [ˈkəunədɔnt, ˈkɔnə-] *n.*【古生】牙形虫.

co·noid [ˈkəunɔid] *n.* 圆锥体[形];【数】劈锥曲面. — *a.* 圆锥形[体]的. **-al** *a.*

co·no·scope [ˈkəunəskəup] *n.*【物】锥光偏振仪.

con·quer [ˈkɔŋkə] *vt.* ①征服;攻克;打败(敌人). ②克服(困难等),改正(恶习等);抑制(情欲等). ③[古、诗]赢得(名誉,某人的感情等). ~ *the enemy* 征服敌人.

~ *bad habits* 克服不良习惯. ~ *passions* 压制情欲. *the ~ed* 被征服者,败者. — *vi.* 得胜. ***stoop to ~*** 忍辱取胜;降低身分以达到目的. ***To ~ or to die.*** 非胜即死,不成功便成仁.

con·quer·a·ble [ˈkɔnkərəbl] *a.* 可征服的; 能赢得的; 能克服的.

con·quer·or [ˈkɔŋkərə] *n.* ①征服者, 胜利者. ②〔废〕决胜败的争斗. ***play the ~***〔口〕(游戏中同分数者)举行决赛. ***William the C-***【英史】征服者威廉第一〔1066 年征服英国的 Normandy 公爵 William〕.

con·quest [ˈkɔŋkwest] *n.* ①征服; 获得(物); 赢得(物); 征服地, 占领地. ②感情上被征服的人; 受笼络[诱惑]的人. ***for the ~ of*** 为要征服…. ***make a ~ of*** 征服; 赢得…的感情. ***the C-***【英史】1066 年威廉的征服英国.

con·qui·an [ˈkɔŋkiən] *n.* 碰对牌戏 (= cooncan).

con·quis·ta·dor [kɔnˈkwistədɔː] *n.* *(pl.* ~s, ~es) 〔Sp.〕征服者〔指 16 世纪征服秘鲁、墨西哥等地的西班牙人〕.

Con·rad [ˈkɔnræd] *n.* 康拉德〔姓氏, 男子名〕.

cons.=consecrated; 〔L.〕【处方】conserva (=conserve 请保存); consigned; consignment; consolidated; consonant; constable; constitution; construction; consul.

con·san·guin·e·ous [ˌkɔnsæŋˈgwiniəs] *a.* 血亲的, 近亲的,同血统的. *a ~ marriage* 血亲婚姻,近亲婚姻.

con·san·guin·i·ty [ˌkɔnsæŋˈgwiniti] *n.* ①血族,血缘, 血亲, 亲族. ②密切关系. *a collateral ~* 旁系亲族. *a lineal ~* 直系亲族.

con·science [ˈkɔnʃəns] *n.* 良心. *a bad [guilty] ~* 做贼心虚, 深感内疚. *a good [clear] ~* 问心无愧, 安然自得. *a matter of ~* 良心问题. *liberty of ~* 信仰自由. ***for ~(') sake*** 为了良心关系 [问心无愧], 请凭良心(做某事). ***have sth. on one's ~*** 觉得内疚, 感到心中难受. ***have the ~ to (do)*** 竟厚着面皮 (做某事). ***in (all) ~***〔口〕真的, 当然. ***My ~!*** 哎呀,哼, 嗯, 呸〔表示惊讶、反驳、疑心等〕. ***sleep on a calm ~*** 安心睡眠. ***upon my ~*** 凭良心说, 的确, 一定. **~ money** (为求良心安逸而拿出的) 悔罪金. **~-smitten** *a.* 受良心责备的. **~-strick·en** [ˈkɔnʃəns-ˌstrikən] *a.* 内疚的,悔恨的;良心不安的. **-less** *a.* 没良心的,没有道德心的.

con·sci·en·tious [ˌkɔnʃiˈenʃəs] *a.* ①认真(负责)的,真心实意的. ②有[凭]良心的,诚实的, 正大光明的, 耿直的. ③严正的; 谨慎的. ***be far from ~*** 很不认真. **~ *objector*** 真心实意拒绝参加罪恶战争(等)的人. **-ly** *ad.* **-ness** *n.*

con·scion·a·ble [ˈkɔnʃnəbl] *a.* 〔古〕凭良心办理的, 正直的,正当的.

con·scious [ˈkɔnʃəs] *a.* ①有意识的, 有知觉的; 神志清醒的. ②自觉的, 自己知道的, 明明知道的 *(of; that)*; 有意识的,故意的. ③(痛苦、感情、冷气等)感觉得到的; 意识到的. ④= self-conscious. ⑤有…意识的〔常用以构成复合词〕. *Man is a ~ being.* 人是有意识的生物. *He became ~.* 他清醒[苏醒]了. *a hardly ~ movement* 不自觉 [自然而然] 的动作. *a class-~ worker* 一个有阶级意识的工人. *be [become] ~ of* 意识到. *be ~ of one's own blame* 自知理亏. *be too ~* 极腼腆. *the ~ simper* 忸怩的强笑. *with a ~ air* 故作谦虚地. *with ~ superiority* 带着故作高人一等的神气. **-ly** *ad.*

con·scious·ness [ˈkɔnʃəsnis] *n.* 意识; 知觉; 觉悟(性); 自觉. *class ~* 阶级觉悟, 阶级意识. ***lose [recover] one's ~*** 失去[恢复]知觉, 不省人事 [苏醒过来]. **~-expanding** *a.* 迷幻的,使人感到飘飘然的.

con·scribe [kənˈskraib] *vt.* 征募,招募;征用.

con·script [ˈkɔnskript] *a.* 被征入伍的. — *n.* 应征新兵. — [kənˈskript] *vt.* = conscribe. **~ fathers** (古罗马,中世纪意大利的)元老院议员;〔谑〕立法议会议员.

con·scrip·tee [ˌkɔnskripˈtiː] *n.* 〔美口〕被征入伍者.

con·scrip·tion [kənˈskripʃən] *n.* 征兵; 征集, 征发, 征用. ~ *of wealth* (对不服兵役者所征)兵役税;【经】资本课税. **~ age** 适役年龄. **~ system** 征兵制度.

con. sec. = conic sections.

con·se·crate [ˈkɔnsikreit] *vt.* ①献奉, 献祭. ②把…奉为神圣,尊崇. ③(用宗教仪式)授予…以某种职位. *a ~d ground* 圣地. *a life ~d to science* 献身科学的一生.

con·se·cra·tion [ˌkɔnsiˈkreiʃən] *n.* ①献祭; 奉献. ②神圣化. ③授(圣)职. ④献身.

con·se·cra·to·ry [ˈkɔnsikreitəri] *a.* 使神圣化的, 授(圣)职的; 奉献的.

con·se·cu·tion [ˌkɔnsiˈkjuːʃən] *n.* ①连贯; (逻辑) 顺序,推理顺序[步骤]; 前后关连. ②【语法】(词序, 语法变化等的)连贯,一致.

con·sec·u·tive [kənˈsekjutiv] *a.* ①连续的, 串联的, 依次相续的; 连贯的. ②【语法】表示结果的. *It rained four ~ days.* 连续下了四天雨. *~ account of the accident* 事件的顺序叙述. *~ days* 连续几天. **~ clause**【语法】(表示结果的)连贯分句. **~ fifths**【乐】连续五度. **~ numbers**【数】相邻数. **-ly** *ad.* **-ness** *n.*

con·se·nes·cence, con·se·nes·cen·cy [ˌkɔnsiˈnesns, -si] *n.* 衰老.

con·sen·su·al [kənˈsenʃuəl] *a.* ①【法】在双方同意下成立的. ②【生理】交感反应的. ③【心】(指本能活动) 意识作用激发的,交感的.

con·sen·sus [kənˈsensəs] *n.* ①(意见等的)一致, 合意. ②【生理】交感. *The ~ of opinion is that ....* 一致的意见是…. ***~ gentium***〔L.〕民意,公论.

con·sent [kənˈsent] *vi.* 同意,赞成,应允,答应 *(to; to do; that)*. *~ to a proposal* 赞同提案. *~ to give a lecture* 答应演讲. — *n.* 同意, 赞同, 赞成, 答应. *Silence gives ~.* 不说话就是答应. ***age of ~***【法】承诺年龄〔尤指少女法律上达到可以自主的年龄〕. ***give [refuse] one's ~*** 答应 [拒绝]. ***with one ~ = by common ~*** 异口同声,全体一致. ***with the ~ of*** 得…的同意.

con·sen·ta·ne·ous [ˌkɔnsenˈteiniəs] *a.* ①同意的; 一致的. ②合意的; 适合的 *(to; with)*.

con·sent·er [kənˈsentə] *n.* 同意者,答应者,赞同者.

con·sen·tient [kənˈsenʃənt] *a.* 同意的, 赞同的; 一致的.

con·se·quence [ˈkɔnsikwəns] *n.* ①结果,成果,影响,后果;【数】后承;【逻】结论. ②重要(性); 重大意义. ***answer for the ~s*** 对后果负责. ***face the ~s of one's action*** 自食其果. ***in ~*** 因此,结果. ***in ~ of*** …的结果, 因为…的原故, 由于. ***of ~*** 有势力的; 重要的 *(a man of ~* 有势力的人物. *a matter of no ~* 没有什么重要性的事). ***take the ~s*** 自食其果, 承担责任 *(He must take the ~s of his own deeds.* 他得自食其果). ***take upon oneself the ~s*** 自己承担后果.

con·se·quent [ˈkɔnsikwənt] *a.* ①继起的,因…而起的 *(on; upon)*; (逻辑上)必然的,当然的. ②【地】顺向的. — *n.* (当然的) 结果;【逻】后件; 结论;【数】后项;【语法】(条件结构中的) 结果从句. **~ divide** 顺向分水岭. **~ drainage** 顺向水系. **~ pole**【物】庶极. **-ly** *ad.*

con·se·quen·tial [ˌkɔnsiˈkwenʃəl] *a.* ①随之而起的, 后果的; 继起的; 必然的. ②有重要性的. ③以重要人物自居的, 傲慢的. **~ damages**【法】间接损害. **-ly** *ad.* **-ness** *n.*

con·ser·van·cy [kənˈsəːvənsi] *n.* ①(天然资源的) 管理,保管,保护,保存; 水土保持; 资源保护区. ②(河、港等的) 管理局[委员会];〔集合词〕管理员. *build water ~ projects* 兴修水利. *a water ~ project* 水利工程. *the Thames C-* 泰晤士河管理委员会.

con·ser·va·tion [ˌkɔnsə(ː)ˈveiʃən] *n.* ①保存, 维持(健康),保守; 保护; 保护森林[河道](等). ②【物】守恒, 不灭. *~ of energy [mass]* 能量[质量]守恒. *~ of heredity*

遗传性的保守性. ～ *of water and soil* 水土保持. ～ *of wildlife* 野生动物保护. ～ **plant** 废料再生工厂; 废料利用工厂. **-al** *a.*

con·ser·va·tion·ist [ˌkɔnsəˈveiʃənist] *n.* 自然资源保护论者.

con·ser·va·tism [kənˈsəːvətizəm] *n.* ①保守主义,守旧(性). ②〔C-〕〔英〕保守党(的主张〔政策〕).

con·ser·va·tive [kənˈsəːvətiv] *a.* ①保守的,守旧的; 有保存力的. ②〔C-〕保守党的 (*opp.* Liberal, Radical). ③稳健的; (估计等)谨慎的. — *n.* ①保守主义者; 〔C-〕保守党员; 稳健派. ②防腐剂; 保护料. ～ *grazing* 适度放牧. *C- party* (英国的)保守党. **-ly** *ad.* **-ness** *n.*

con·ser·va·toire [kənˈsəːvətwɑː] *n.* 〔F.〕音乐〔艺术〕学校〔学院〕.

con·ser·va·tor [ˈkɔnsə(ː)veitə] *n.* ①保存者,保护者; 管理人; 〔英〕(河、港、森林等的)管理委员. ②[kənˈ-]〔美〕(疯子等的)监护人; (银行的)监督.

con·ser·va·to·ry [kənˈsəːvətri] *a.* ①(有)保存(力)的. ②保管人的. — *n.* ①(植物的)暖房,温室. ②音乐〔艺术、戏剧〕学院. ③防腐剂.

con·serve [kənˈsəːv] *vt.* ①保存. ②糖渍. ③【物,化】使守恒. — *n.* 〔常 *pl.*〕糖食,蜜饯; 果酱; 【医】糖剂.

con·sid·er [kənˈsidə] *vt.* ①考虑,细想; 估量,斟酌; 留意,研究. ②尊重; 体谅; 给(赏钱〔小费〕). ③以为,认为〔后接 that 引导的从句〕. ④把(某人、某事)看作…,认为(某人、某事)如何〔后接 as …, of …, (to be) … 等〕. ～ *a matter well before deciding.* 慎重考虑后再决定. ～ *her ill health* 照顾她体弱. ～ *the servants* 给仆役赏钱. ～ *reform as revolution* 认为改革是一场革命. ～ *sb. (to be) a fool* 拿人当傻瓜. — *vi.* 考虑,细想. *Let me ～ a moment.* 让我想一想.

con·sid·er·a·ble [kənˈsidərəbl] *a.* ①该注意的,应考虑的,不可忽视的,重要的. ②相当(大,多)的,不少的; 很多的,大量的,巨额的. ***by*** ～〔美口〕不少,大大. ～ ***of***〔美口〕大量. — *ad.*〔美口〕= **-a·bly** *ad.* **-ness** *n.*

con·sid·er·ate [kənˈsidərit] *a.* ①对…关心爱护的,体谅(人)的,照顾到…的 (*of*). ②〔古〕经过斟酌的,细心的,慎重的. **-ly** *ad.* **-ness** *n.*

con·sid·er·a·tion [kənˌsidəˈreiʃən] *n.* ①考虑,考察; 讨论,商量. ②照顾,关心; 体谅,体恤. ③报酬,补偿. ④尊敬,敬意. ⑤原因,理由; 须考虑到的事实〔问题〕; 理由. ⑥〔罕〕重要性. *a man of* ～ 要人. *That's a* ～. 那是一个值得考虑的问题. ***after due*** ～ 经相当考虑后. ***be of no*** ～ 并不紧要,没有什么问题. ***for a*** ～ 为求报酬,为求补偿 (*He sold it for a* ～. 为了换取一点补偿,他把它低价卖掉了). ***for the*** ～ ***of*** 作为…的参考. ***give adequate*** ～ ***to*** 适当照顾. ***in*** ～ ***of*** 考虑到,因,由于; 以作…的谢礼,酬劳. ***leave out of*** ～ 置之度外,不以…为意. ***not on any*** ～ 决不. ***(be) of*** ～ 值得考虑〔重要〕的. ***on no*** ～ 决不 (*On no* ～ *could I consent.* 我决不能同意). ***out of*** ～ ***for your feelings*** 看你面上,由于照顾你的情绪. ***take into*** ～ 估量到,斟酌. ***show [have]*** ～ ***for (sb.'s position)*** 考虑〔照顾〕到(某人处境). ***taking one*** ～ ***with another*** 对各方面进行考虑. ***the first*** ～ 第一要件,最重要的事. ***under*** ～ 考虑中,研究中. ***under no*** ～ 决不. ***without due*** ～ (不假思索)贸然,轻率.

con·sid·ered [kənˈsidəd] *a.* 考虑过的; 被尊重的.

con·sid·er·ing [kənˈsidəriŋ] *prep.* 就…而论,照…说来,与…比起来,以…看起来. *C- her age, she looks young.* 照年龄说来,她显得年轻. ～ *(that) she is a woman* 因为她是一个妇女,所以…. *That is not so bad,* ～ *(the circumstances).* 照(实情)说,那还算不错; 从多方面说来,还过得去. — *ad.*〔口〕细想起来,认真说,委实. *The boy does well,* ～. 认真说,那个小孩干得是不错的.

con·sign [kənˈsain] *vt.* ①委托,托付; 【商】托运. ②托卖,寄售; 寄存,存(款). ③用作,当作 (*to*). ～ *a task to s'.* 把一项任务交付给某人. *We beg to* ～ *the following per s.s. 'London'.* 请由'伦敦'号轮船运交下列各物. ～ *money in a bank* 把款子存在银行里. ～ *a letter to the post* 付邮. *be* ～*ed to misery* 陷入可悲境地. ～ *sth. to oblivion* 把某事置之脑后; 忘却.

con·sig·na·tion [ˌkɔnsaiˈneiʃən] *n.* 交付,委托; 寄存. ***to the*** ～ ***of*** 运交〔寄交、转交〕…处.

con·sign·ee [ˌkɔnsaiˈniː] *n.* 收存人,受托人; 收货人,承销人.

con·sign·er, con·sign·or [kənˈsainə; (和 consignee 相对应时作) ˌkɔnsaiˈnɔː] *n.* 交付者,委托者; 发货人,托运人,托销的货主.

con·sign·ment [kənˈsainmənt] *n.* ①交付,委托. ②寄售,托卖 (=～ sale); 托卖货. *a new* ～ *of summer suit* 新到夏服. ～ *goods* 托卖品. ～ *invoice* 发货单. ～ *note* 发货通知书. ～ *out* 寄销品. ～*-sheet* 收货清单. ***on*** ～ 寄售,以寄售方式处理.

con·sil·i·ence [kənˈsiliəns] *n.* 符合,一致.

con·sist [kənˈsist] *vi.* ①由…组成 (*of*). ②存在于 (*in*). ③(与…)一致,适合; 并存,并立 (*with*). ④〔古〕生存; 共存. *The book* ～*s of eight chapters.* 那书共有八章. *Happiness* ～*s in contentment.* 幸福在乎知足. *Health does not* ～ *with intemperance.* 健康与纵欲〔无节制〕不能相容.

con·sis·tence, con·sis·ten·cy [kənˈsistəns, -si] *n.* ①无矛盾,相容(性); 始终一贯; 稳定(性); (言行)一致,(色调)调和. ②坚强,坚定; 坚固,结实; 坚实度. ③浓度,稠度; 粘度.

con·sist·ent [kənˈsistənt] *a.* ①一致的,协调的,相容的,不矛盾的 (*with*); 首尾一贯的. ②言行一致的; 坚定的,有操守的. ③坚实的,密实的,稠的,浓厚的. *a policy* ～ *with public good* 符合公众利益的政策. *the firm and* ～ *policy* 坚定不移的方针. *He is not* ～ *in his statement.* 他的陈述前后不符. **-ly** *ad.*

con·sisto·meter [kənˈsistəmitə] *n.* 【物】稠度计.

con·sis·to·ri·al [ˌkɔnsisˈtɔːriəl] *a.* ①宗教法庭的. ②【天主】教廷议会上院的.

con·sis·to·ry [kənˈsistəri] *n.* ①宗教会议,宗教法庭; 【天主】(教廷的)参议院; 【英国教】主教法庭; (长老派的)长老法庭. ②集会,协议会,参议会.

con·so·ci·ate [kənˈsəuʃieit] *vt., vi.* (使)结合〔结成一伙〕, (使)联合 (*with*).

con·so·ci·a·tion [kənˌsəusiˈeiʃən] *n.* ①联合,组合. ②【宗】宗教法庭. ③【生】单优种社会,小社会群.

consol. = consolidated.

con·sol·a·ble [kənˈsəuləbl] *a.* 可安慰的.

con·so·la·tion [ˌkɔnsəˈleiʃən] *n.* ①安慰,慰藉,安抚,抚恤. ②安慰物,抚恤金. ～ **money** 抚恤金; (辞退被雇用者时给的)慰藉金. ～ **prize** (给落选人的)安慰奖,副奖. ～ **race [match, game]** (特为竞赛失败者举行的)安慰赛.

con·sol·a·to·ry [kənˈsɔlətəri] *a.* 安慰的. *a* ～ *letter* 慰问信. ～ *words* 安慰话.

con·sole¹ [kənˈsəul] *vt.* 安慰,慰问.

con·sole² [ˈkɔnsəul] *n.* 【建】①悬臂(梁),突梁,肘托, (涡卷形)托石; 角(撑)架. ②(用落地支架靠墙安设的)蜗形支腿桌案 (= ～-table). ③【机、空】(计算机等的)控制台,操纵台; 仪表板〔台〕; 键盘台; (管风琴的)演奏台. ④(收音机、电视机的)落地式支座.

con·sol·i·date [kənˈsɔlideit] *vt.* ①使坚固,巩固; 加固,强化. ②合并,统一; 整顿,整理(公债、土地、公司等). ③【医】变实,愈合. — *vi.* 结成一体,变巩固.

con·sol·i·dat·ed [kənˈsɔlideitid] *a.* 加固的; 整理过的,统一的. ～ **annuities**〔英〕统一公债〔简称 consols〕. ～ **school**〔美〕合并的公立小学〔常指农村小学〕. ～ **ticket office**〔美〕(各路火车)联合售票处.

con·sol·i·da·tion [kənˌsɔliˈdeiʃən] *n.* ①巩固,强化,

加强；凝固，固结，压实，渗压。②【经】统一，合并，调整（期）。③【医】变实，愈合；【植】着生。*Party* ～ 整党。*training and* ～ 整训。～ **line** 渗压曲线。

con·sols [kənˈsɔlz] *n.* 〔*pl.*〕（英国）统一公债。

con·so·lute [ˈkɔnsəljuːt] *a.* 【化】会溶质（会与另一液体完全混溶的液体）的，混溶质的。

con·som·mé [kənˈsɔmei] *n.* 〔F.〕【烹】清炖肉〔鸡〕汤。

con·so·nance [ˈkɔnsənəns] *n.* ①【乐】谐和音；【物】共鸣。②和谐，调和，一致。***in*** ～ ***with*** 和…一致〔调和、共鸣〕。

con·so·nan·cy [ˈkɔnsənənsi] *n.* ①协和，协调，一致。②【乐】谐和音。

con·so·nant [ˈkɔnsənənt] *a.* （和…）一致的，调和的 *(with; to)*；【乐】谐和（音）的；【语音】辅音的。— *n.* 【语音】辅音（字母）；谐和音。**-al** [-ˈnæntl] *a.*

con·sort [ˈkɔnsɔːt] *n.* ①配偶（特指在位君主的夫或妻）。②伙伴，会员。③僚舰，僚艇。④合作，协力，协同。⑤一组乐师；一组同类乐器。*a prince [king]* ～ 女王的丈夫。*a queen* ～ 王后。***in*** ～ ***with sb.*** 和某人共同〔协力〕。— [kənˈsɔːt] *vt.* 〔～ oneself〕使结合，使陪伴。— *vi.* 一致，调和，相称 *(with)*。*His practice does not* ～ *with his preaching.* 他言行不一。

con·sor·ti·um [kənˈsɔːtjəm] *n.* ①（国际）财团；（国际性）金融协议；组合，共同体。②【法】配偶的地位和权利。③〔美〕（小型大学集中人力、物力办学的）大学联盟协定。

con·spe·cif·ic [ˌkɔnspiˈsifik] *a.* 【动、植】同种的。

con·spec·tus [kənˈspektəs] *n.* 梗概，大要，大纲，纲要，一览（表）。

con·spic·u·ous [kənˈspikjuəs] *a.* ①显著的，显眼的。②（服装等）过分花哨的；令人注目的，触目的；明显的；著名的，特出的，出众的。*be* ～ *by its absence* 因为（某人）缺席反而引人注意。～ *error* 显著的错误。***cut a*** ～ ***figure*** 放异彩，令人注目。***make oneself*** ～ （标新立异）惹人注目。～ **consumption** 摆阔性消费〔出于炫耀财产而花钱购物等，并非出于需要〕。**-ly** *ad.* **-ness** *n.*

con·spir·a·cy [kənˈspirəsi] *n.* ①共谋。②阴谋，反叛 *(aganist)*。*form a* ～ *against* 秘密策划进行反对〔破坏、杀害等〕。*take part in a* ～ 参与阴谋。*get scent [wind] of a* ～ 发觉阴谋。～ ***of silence*** 保守秘密的约定。***in*** ～共谋，搞派系活动。

con·spir·a·tor [kənˈspirətə] *n.* 共谋者，阴谋家，谋反者。

con·spir·a·tress [kənˈspirətris] *n.* 女共谋者，女阴谋家。

con·spir·a·to·ri·al [kənˌspirəˈtɔːriəl] *a.* ①阴谋的，阴谋者的；阴险的。②（爱）搞阴谋的。③共谋的。**-ly** *ad.*

con·spire [kənˈspaiə] *vi.* ①（结党）密谋，同谋，搞阴谋。②协力；巧合；共同促成。～ *against the state* 图谋卖国。*All things* ～*d to make him happy.* 事事巧合使他心满意足。*All things* ～ *against me.* 事事凑合起来跟我作对。～ **with** 勾结。— *vt.* 〔罕〕共谋，图谋。

con spi·ri·to [kɔnˈspiritəu] *n.* 〔It.〕【乐】热烈地，精神饱满地。

con·spue [kənˈspjuː] *vt.* 叫嚷着表示憎恶；要求驱逐〔废除〕（人物，政策等）；唾弃。

Const. = Constantine; Constantinople.

const. = ①constable. ②constant. ③constitution. ④construction.

Con·sta·ble [ˈkʌnstəbl, ˈkɔnstəbl] *n.* 康斯特布尔〔姓氏〕。

con·sta·ble [ˈkʌnstəbl] *n.* ①〔英〕警察，警官。②【史】（中世纪的）王室〔贵族〕总管；王室〔贵族〕城堡的主管。*Chief C-* 〔英〕警察厅长。*a special* ～ （非常时期的）临时民警。***outrun [overrun] the*** ～ 负债。***the C- of France*** （法国王朝时代的）元帅。***the Lord High C- of England*** （英国中古的）保安长官，（现指举行仪式时临时任命的）侍从武官长。

con·stab·u·lar·y [kənˈstæbjuləri] *n.* ①警区。②（全体）警察。③（负责治安的）保安部队。— *a.* 警察的，治安的。

Con·stance [ˈkɔnstəns] *n.* 康斯坦斯〔女子名〕。

con·stan·cy [ˈkɔnstənsi] *n.* ①恒定不变，定型性，恒久（性）。②恒心；不屈不挠，坚忍不拔；坚贞；忠实。

con·stant [ˈkɔnstənt] *a.* ①恒定不变的，固定的，稳定的，恒久的；继续不断的。②不屈不挠的，坚韧的。③忠实的，有节操的。*be* ～ *in love* 忠贞不渝的爱情。*two days of* ～ *rain* 两天接连下雨。～ *to one's duty* 忠于职守。～ *wind* 恒风。— *n.* 【数、物】常数，恒量；恒定（值）；（常）系数，率；【语法】（转换语法用语）定项。*the circular* ～ 圆周率。～ **current** 直流电。～ **error** 常在误差。～**-level balloon** （搜集大气层资料的）定高气球。～ **temperature** 恒温。**-ly** *ad.*

Con·stan·ta, Con·stan·tsa [kənˈstɑːntə,-tsə] *n.* 康斯坦察〔罗马尼亚港市〕。

con·stant·an [ˈkɔnstəntæn] *n.* 【冶】（温度系数接近恒定不变的）康铜。

Con·stan·tine[1] [ˈkɔnstəntain] *n.* ①康斯坦丁〔男子名〕。②～ **the Great** 康斯坦丁大帝，罗马皇帝(288?—337)〔全名是 *Favius Valerius Aurelius Constantinus*〕。

Con·stan·tine[2] [ˈkɔnstəntain] *n.* 君士坦丁〔阿尔及利亚城市〕。

Con·stan·ti·no·ple [ˌkɔnstæntiˈnəupl] *n.* 君士坦丁堡〔Istanbul 伊斯坦布尔的旧称〕〔土耳其港市〕。

con·stel·late [ˈkɔnstəleit] *vt.* ①形成星座；使群集。②用星群样的饰物装饰。*the* ～*d sky* 群星灿烂的天空。— *vi.* ①形成星座。②群集。

con·stel·la·tion [ˌkɔnstəˈleiʃən] *n.* ①星座；星群；（占星术中认为与某人命运有关的）星宿；（杰出人物等的）灿如明星的集团。②型。③（组织上的）配合。④【心】（思想感情）丛。⑤【语法】并列关系。⑥〔C-〕美国 C-69 型星座式远程客机。

con·ster·nate [ˈkɔnstə(ː)neit] *vt.* 使惊愕〔常用被动语态〕。

con·ster·na·tion [ˌkɔnstə(ː)ˈneiʃən] *n.* 惊愕，恐怖，惊惶失措。***throw (sb.) into*** ～ 使（某人）大吃一惊，使愕然。***to one's*** ～ 极其可惊的是。***with*** ～ 愕然。

con·sti·pate [ˈkɔnstipeit] *vt.* ①使呆滞，使闭塞。②【医】使便秘。*be* ～*d* 便秘；〔俚〕吝啬。

con·sti·pa·tion [ˌkɔnstiˈpeiʃən] *n.* 【医】便秘。

con·stit·u·en·cy [kənˈstitjuənsi] *n.* ①（议员所代表的）选民（全体）；选（举）区。②〔集合词〕顾客；（期刊的）订户；赞助者。***nurse a*** ～ 笼络一批选民。

con·stit·u·ent [kənˈstitjuənt] *a.* ①构成的，组织的，成分的。②有选举权的，有提名权的，有宪法制定〔修改〕权的。～ **parts of water** 水的成分。～ **power** 宪法制定〔修改〕权。— *n.* ①要素，成分，组分。②构成者，制定者，设立者。③选民。④（指定代理者的）委托人，当事者本人。⑤【语言】（结构）成分，组成成分。**C- Assembly** 【法史】国民议会。～ **assembly** 宪法制定〔修改〕会议。～ **body** 选民团。～ **corporation** 【经】子公司。～ **republics** 构成联邦的各共和国。～ **structure** 【语法】（转换语法用语）成分结构。

con·sti·tute [ˈkɔnstitjuːt] *vt.* ①构成，组成，成为…的本质。②制定，设立。③委托…为（代表），指定，任命。④引起（某种状态等）；等于。*Seven days* ～ *a week.* 七天为〔构成〕一星期。*What* ～*s virtue?* 美德的本质是什么？*I am not so* ～*d that ...* 我不是…性格的人。*be* ～*d representative of ...* 当选为…的代表。～*d authorities* 当局。*He* ～*d himself as their judge.* 他自命为他们的裁定人。

con·sti·tu·tion [ˌkɔnstiˈtjuːʃən] *n.* ①构成，构造，结构；组织；成分。②体格，体质，素质。③制定，设立；任命。④【政】宪法；政体；法规，章程；【法】制度组织。*the C-*

of the Communist Party of China 中国共产党章程. *a republican* ～ 共和政体. *a written* ～ 成文宪法. *a draft* ～ 宪法草案. *a nervous* ～ 神经质. **by** ～ 天性, 体质上. ***have a good [poor]*** ～ 体格好[差]. ***suit [agree with] sb.'s*** ～ 适合某人体质[性格]. ***undermine sb.'s*** ～ *(by...)* (因…)伤害身体.

con·sti·tu·tion·al [ˌkɔnstiˈtjuːʃənl] *a.* ①生来的, 固有的; 体质上的. ②宪法(上规定)的; 立宪的, 拥护宪法的; 法制的. ③有益健康的, 保健的. ④组织的, 构成的. — *n.* 保健运动[散步]. *a* ～ *disease [disorder]* 体质病. *a* ～ *convention* [美]制宪[修宪]代表会议. *a* ～ *government* 立宪政体 [政治]. *a* ～ *formula* 【化】结构式. ～ *infirmity* 生来的虚弱. ～ *law* 宪法. ～ *walk* 保健散步. *take a* ～ 散步. *the C- assembly* 制宪会议. **-ism** *n.* 立宪制度, 立宪主义, 宪政; 宪法论, 拥护宪政, 护宪论. **-ist** *n.* 宪法学者; 立宪主义者, 护宪论者, 拥护宪政者.

con·sti·tu·tion·al·i·ty [ˌkɔnstiˌtjuːʃəˈnæliti] *n.* 立宪(性), 合法性.

con·sti·tu·tion·al·ly [ˌkɔnstiˈtjuːʃənəli] *ad.* ①本质地; 体质上. ②宪法上, 按照宪法.

con·sti·tu·tive [ˈkɔnstitjuːtiv] *a.* ①构成的, 组织的; 要素的, 本质的. ②有制定权的. ***be*** ～ ***of*** 由…构成.

con·sti·tu·tor [ˈkɔnstitjuːtə] *n.* 构成者, 组织者; 制定者.

con·strain [kənˈstrein] *vt.* ①强迫, 强制 *(to)*. ②束缚, 约束; 使紧张, 紧压, 使不舒服[不自由]. ③把…关进, 监禁. *be* ～*ed to (do)* 不得不; 被迫. ～ *oneself* 勉强, 自制. ～*ing force* 抑制力; 【物】约束力. *feel* ～*ed* 觉得不自如[受压迫, 不舒服].

con·strain·ed [kənˈstreind] *a.* 被强迫的; 受压制的; 不自然的, 勉强的. *a* ～ *manner* 不自然的[局促的]样子. *a* ～ *smile* (勉强做作的)苦笑. **-ly** [-ˈstreinidli] *ad.*

con·straint [kənˈstreint] *n.* ①强迫, 拘束. ②约束, 压抑, 拘泥. ③强制力. ④紧张感[状态]. *by* ～ 勉强, 强迫. *feel* ～ 觉得局促不安, 感受压迫. *show* ～ 显得局促. *under [in]* ～ 被迫, 不得不; 被束缚着.

con·strict [kənˈstrikt] *vt.* ①压缩, 使收缩. ②妨害, 阻碍. *a* ～*ed outlook* 狭窄的眼界. — *vi.* 收缩.

con·stric·tion [kənˈstrikʃən] *n.* ①压缩, 收缩; 狭窄, 缩窄. ②(胸部等的)压迫感, 憋闷感. ③压束物, 阻塞物. ④被压束部分; 缩颈.

con·stric·tive [kənˈstriktiv] *a.* 收缩(性)的, 压缩的, 紧缩的.

con·stric·tor [kənˈstriktə] *n.* ①压缩物, 收缩物; 压缩器; 收缩器; 【火箭】收敛[尾部收缩]式燃烧室. ②【解】括约肌 (= ～ muscle). ③【动】大蟒 (= boa-～).

con·stringe [kənˈstrindʒ] *vt.* 压缩, 使紧缩.

con·strin·gen·cy [kənˈstrindʒənsi] *n.* 收缩(性), 收敛, 压缩.

con·strin·gent [kənˈstrindʒənt] *a.* 使收缩的, 收敛性的.

con·stru·a·ble [kənˈstruːəbl] *a.* ①(句子等)能理解的, 能作语法分析的. ②可解释为…的 *(as)*.

con·struct [kənˈstrʌkt] *vt.* ①构成, 建造, 建筑, 铺设, 架设; 【数】作(图); 【语法】造(句), 作(文). ②构想, 创立. ③解释. ～ *a bridge* 造桥. ～ *a theory* 创立学说. — [ˈkɔnstrʌkt] *n.* ①结构(物). ②思维产物; 构想; 【心】构成概念. ③【语法】结构(体), 结构成分.

con·struc·tion [kənˈstrʌkʃən] *n.* ①建筑, 结构, 构造, 架设, 铺设; 建设; 设计; 工程; 建筑法, 构造法, 建筑物; 【剧】搭置, 布景, 结构, 编排. ②(法律等的)解释; 推定. ③【语法】结构(体); 句法结构; 构词法; 【数】作图. *capital* ～ 基本建设. *socialist* ～ 社会主义建设. *the order of* ～ 施工程序. *a sandwich* ～ 层状结构. ***bear a*** ～ 可作某一解释; 可解释为. ***put a false*** ～ ***on*** 故意曲解. ***put a good [bad]*** ～ ***upon*** 善[恶]意解释. ***under [in course of]*** ～ 建筑中, 建造中. ～**-way** 临时铁路, 毛路. ～ ***engine*** 工程机车. ～ ***gang*** [美] 铁路土方工人队. ～ ***gauge*** 【工】建筑界限. ～ ***labourer*** [美]铁路土方工人. ～ ***problem*** 【数】作图题. ～ ***train*** 建设材料运输列车. ～ ***work*** 建设工程. **-al** *a.*

con·struc·tion·ism [kənˈstrʌkʃənizəm] *n.* 【数】构造论; 【美学】构成主义, 构成派.

con·struc·tion·ist [kənˈstrʌkʃənist] *n.* ①(法律条文等的)解释者; ②【美】构成派画家. *a strict [liberal]* ～ (对法律条文等)作严格[自由]解释者.

con·struc·tive [kənˈstrʌktiv] *a.* ①构成的, 建设(性)的; 积极的. ②【法】推定的; 解释(性)的. ③【数】作图的; 【物】相长的. ～ *criticism* 建设性的批评. *a* ～ *faculty* 组织力, 建设力. ～ **crime** 【法】推定罪行. ～ **fraud** 【法】推定欺诈 [虽非恶意诈骗但已通过其不实之言行而使他人或公共利益受到侵害之行为]. ～ **total loss** (水险)准海损. **-ly** *ad.* **-ness** *n.*

con·struc·tiv·ism [kənˈstrʌktivizəm] *n.* 【美学】结构主义.

con·struc·tor [kənˈstrʌktə] *n.* ①建造者, 建设者. ②【海军】造船技师.

con·strue [kənˈstruː] *vt.* ①分析(语法); (逐字)翻译, (特指)口译. ②解释, 给…下注解; 推论. ③结合, 连用; 使与…联系 *(with)*. *"Depend" is* ～*d with "on". Depend* 与 *on* 连用. — *vi.* 解释; 能解释; 能分析. *The sentence does not* ～. 那一句不能分析. — [ˈkɔnstruː] *n.* ①【语法】语法分析; 分析练习句. ②解释. ③直译.

con·sub·stan·tial [ˌkɔnsəbˈstænʃəl] *a.* ①同质的, 同体的. ②【神】三位一体的. *The Son is* ～ *with the Father.* 圣子与圣父同体. **-ly** *ad.* **-ism** [-ʃəlizm] — *n.* 【神】圣体共在论. **-ist** [-ʃəlist] *n.* 圣体共在论者.

con·sub·stan·ti·al·i·ty [ˌkɔnsəbstænʃiˈæliti] *n.* 【神】同体, 同质, 同性. ～ *of the three Persons of the Trinity* (把上帝、耶稣、圣灵当作一身同体看的)三位一体.

con·sub·stan·ti·ate [ˌkɔnsəbˈstænʃieit] *vt.* 使同体[同质, 同性]. — *vi.* 变成同体; 【宗】鼓吹圣体共在论.

con·sub·stan·ti·a·tion [ˈkɔnsəbˌstænʃiˈeiʃən] *n.* 【宗】圣餐中面包和酒与耶稣的血肉同在(论).

con·sue·tude [ˈkɔnswitjuːd] *n.* (有法律效力的)习惯, 惯例.

con·sue·tu·di·nar·y [ˌkɔnswiˈtjuːdinəri] *a.* 习惯(上)的; 习惯法的. *a* ～ *law* 习惯法, 不成文法. — *n.* 习惯法, 不成文法; (教堂的)惯例书, 宗仪书.

con·sul [ˈkɔnsəl] *n.* ①领事. ②【罗马史】执政官. ③【法史】执政. *an acting* ～ 代理领事. *a* ～*-general* 总领事. *an honorary* ～ 名誉领事. *a vice* ～ 副领事. *the Chinese* ～ *at ...* 中国驻…领事. **-ship** *n.* 领事职位, 领事任期.

con·su·lage [ˈkɔnsjulidʒ] *n.* 领事签证手续费.

con·su·lar [ˈkɔnsjulə] *a.* ①领事的. ②【史】执政官的. *a* ～ *agent* 代理领事. *a* ～ *attaché* 领事随员. *a* ～ *invoice* 领事签证.

con·su·late [ˈkɔnsjulit] *n.* ①领事职位; 领事任期. ②领事馆. ③[C-]【法史】执政府时代. ④(古罗马)执政官职位. ～ *general* 总领事馆.

con·sult [kənˈsʌlt] *vi.* 商量, 协商, 商议 *(with)*; 【医】会诊. ～ *with a friend about [on] a matter* 和朋友商量一件事. — *vt.* ①请教, 咨询; 与…商量. ②查考, 查阅(参考书); 看(表). ③上(医生处去)就诊, 请…鉴定. ④考虑, 顾及, 谋(便利), 图(利益). ～ *a dictionary* 查词典. ～ *a doctor* 找医生诊治. ～ *a mirror [watch]* 照镜子[看表]. ～ *one's own interests* 考虑到自己的利益. ～ *sb.'s pleasure* 观察[考虑]某人高兴不高兴. ～ *the meeting* 征求与会者意见. ～ ***one's pillow*** 通夜思索.

con·sult·ant [kənˈsʌltənt] *n.* ①求教者, (与人)商议者, 征求意见者, 查阅者. ②(受人咨询的)顾问; 会诊医生, (顾问)医生.

con·sul·ta·tion [ˌkɔnsəlˈteiʃən] *n.* ①商量, 协商, 评议;

(专家的)会议,协商会,审议会. ②【医】会诊;(律师的)鉴定. ③参考,查阅.

con·sult·a·tive [kən'sʌltətiv] *a.* 商议的,协商的;咨询的,顾问的. *Chinese People's Political C- Conference (C. P. P. C. C.)* 中国人民政治协商会议. *a ~ body* 咨询机关. *a ~ committee* 顾问委员会.

con·sult·er [kən'sʌltə] *n.* 与人商量者;向人咨询者;查阅者.

con·sult·ing [kən'sʌltiŋ] *a.* 咨询的,顾问的. *a ~ engineer* 顾问工程师. *a ~ physician* 会诊医生. **~-room** 诊室.

con·sul·tor [kən'sʌltə] *n.* 顾问;(天主教会主教的)顾问神父.

con·sum·a·ble [kən'sju:məbl] *a.* 可消费的,可消耗的,能用尽的. *a ~ ledger* 消费[耗]品总帐. — *n.*〔*pl.*〕消费[耗]品.

con·sume [kən'sju:m] *vt.* ①消费,消耗,用掉;浪费. ②毁灭,消灭. ③吃光,喝光. ④烧光. *a half ~d cigar* 吸剩半根的雪茄烟. *be ~d by a fire* 烧掉. — *vi.* ①消费掉,用掉,用完. ②烧光;消尽,消灭. ③消磨. ④枯萎;衰萎,憔悴. *The flowers ~d away.* 花枯萎了. *be ~d with (envy, fever, ambition)* (因嫉妒,热病,野心)而憔悴[心疲力竭]. *~ away with (grief)* (因抑郁)而逐渐憔悴[死去].

con·sum·ed·ly [kən'sju:midli] *ad.* 过分地,极端地.

con·sum·er [kən'sju:mə] *n.* ①【经】消费者,用户. ②用电设备. ③【生】消费有机体. *a small ~*【电】普通用户. *~s' cooperative society* 消费合作社. **~-city** 消费城市. *~* **('s) credit** 分期付款销售(法);给予分期付款购买者的信贷. **~s' goods** 消费品. *~* **strike** (消费者的)罢购.

con·sum·er·ism [kən'sju:mərizəm] *n.* ①保护用户[消费者]利益主义. ②【经】消费主义〔认为社会消费力愈大对整个经济愈有利〕. ③(商品和劳务的)消费,销售. **con·sum·er·ist** [-rist] *n.* 用户第一主义者;主张消费主义经济理论的人.

con·sum·mate ['kɔnsʌmeit] *vt.* 使圆满;作成,完成;使(幸福等)达到顶点. *~ a marriage* 成婚,完婚. *His happiness was ~d when he heard the good news.* 他听到喜讯后快乐到极点. — [kən'sʌmit] *a.* 无上的,至上的,完全的,圆满的;无比的. *~ happiness* 无上的幸福. *a ~ ass* 大傻瓜. **-ly** *ad.*

con·sum·ma·tion [ˌkɔnsʌ'meiʃən] . ①圆满,完备;成就,完成;顶点,极端;终结,终极. ②成婚. *Death is the ~ of life.* 死是生命的终结.

con·sum·ma·tor ['kɔnsʌmeitə] *n.* 圆满完成者;(某方面的)专家,能手.

con·sump·tion [kən'sʌmpʃən] *n.* ①消费(量);消尽,消耗,灭绝. ②【医】结核病;痨病,肺痨 (= pulmonary *~*). *The speech was meant for foreign [home] ~.* 那篇讲话是让国外[本国人]听的. *~ goods* 消费品. *~ of the bowels* 肠结核. *~ tax [duty]* 消费税.

con·sump·tive [kən'sʌmptiv] *a.* ①消费的;消耗性的. ②痨[结核]病的. *~ warfare* 消耗战. — *n.* (肺)结核病患者.

cont. = ① containing. ② contents. ③ continent. ④ continue. ⑤ contract.

con·ta·bes·cence [ˌkɔntə'besns] *n.* 萎缩;衰萎;【植】雄蕊萎缩.

con·tact ['kɔntækt] *n.* ①接触;联系;交涉. ②〔美〕(有势力的)熟人;门路. ③【数】相切;【电】接触;触头;触点;【无】通讯;【军】(飞机和地上部队的)联络. ④曾与传染病接触者;【医】传染病带菌嫌疑人. *a man of many ~s* 交际广[门路多]的人. *an auxiliary ~* 联锁触头. *first ~*【天】初亏. *fourth [last] ~*【天】复圆. *a radar ~* 雷达搜获目标. ***be in ~ with*** 和…接触着,和(某人)接近. ***break ~*** 断开电路. ***brought … into ~ with …*** 使…和…接触. ***come in (to) ~ with*** 和…接触[冲突];碰见. ***make ~*** 接通电路. ***make useful ~s with …*** 和…进行有用[利]的来往. — [kən'tækt] *vt.* ①使接触. ②【无】与…通讯;与…通话. ③〔美口〕与…交际,接近(某人). *~ a station in America* 和美国一电台通话[接触]. —*vi.* 接触,联系. ★ contact 作动词,多用于商业上或极亲密的朋友之间. — *a.* ①保持接触的,有联系的;由接触引起的. ②【空】可看见地面景物的. — *ad.*【空】以目力观察(飞行). — [kən'tækt] *int.* 开动〔让飞机发动的信号〕. *~* **action** 接触作用. *~* **agent** ①【化】触媒. ②【军】卫生联络员. *~* **breaker**【电】接触断路器. *~* **flying [flight]** 目视飞行 (*opp.* blind flying). *~* **lens** (装在眼睑内的)隐形镜片. *~* **light** (机场)跑道灯. *~* **maker**【电】电流开关装置. *~* **man** (厂商雇用的)交际员,跑街. *~* **mine** 触发水雷. *~* **twin**【矿】接合双晶.

con·tac·tee [ˌkɔntæk'ti:] *n.* 被接触者(尤指被所谓不明飞行物上的外星球人接触过的人).

con·tac·tor ['kɔntæktə] *n.*【电】接触器,开关.

con·ta·di·na [It. ˌkonta'di:nə] *n.* 〔It.〕 *(pl.* ***-ne*** [-nei]*)* 农妇.

con·ta·di·no [It.ˌkonta'di:no] *n.* 〔It.〕 *(pl.* ***-ni*** [-ni:]*)* 农夫.

con·ta·gion [kən'teidʒən] *n.* ①(接触)传染;传染病;(传染性的)病原体,病毒,病菌. ②(思想,风气等)传播,蔓延,流行. ③(传播中的)不良影响,歪风邪气.

con·ta·gi·os·i·ty [kənˌtædʒi'ɔsiti] *n.* 接触传染率.

con·ta·gious [kən'teidʒəs] *a.* ①传染病的;传染性的;会蔓延的,有感染力的. ②为对付传染病用的. *a ~ disease* 传染病. *a ~ ward* 传染病病房. **-ly** *ad.* **-ness** *n.*

con·ta·gi·um [kən'teidʒiəm] *n.* *(pl.* ***-gi·a*** [-dʒi]*)*【医】接触传染病原体[病菌,病毒].

con·tain [kən'tein] *vt.* ①含有,包含;能容纳. ②相当于,等于. ③克制,忍耐. ④【数】除尽,整除;(边)夹(角),包围(图形). ⑤【军】牵制,箝制,拦截,包围;遏制. *This box ~s soap.* 这只箱子装着肥皂. *I cannot ~ my urine.* 小便急得憋不住了. *15 ~s 3 and 5.* 15 能用 3 和 5 除尽. *4 is ~ed in 12 three times.* 12 是 4 的 3 倍. *~ing force*【军】牵制部队. *be ~ed between [within]* 被包容[挟在]…之间[之中]. — *vi.* 自制. *She could ~ no longer.* 他再也克制不住自己. *~* ***oneself*** 克制自己,忍耐 (*I could not ~ myself for joy.* 我喜欢得忍耐不住). **-ment**【军】牵制 (*the policy of containment* 遏制政策).

con·tain·er [kən'teinə] *n.* ①容器,箱,匣. ②集装箱. **ship** 集装箱船. *~* **shipping** 集装箱运输. **-i·za·tion** *n.* (运输)集装箱化. **-ize** *vt.* 使用集装箱运输;使集装箱化.

con·tam·i·nant [kən'tæminænt] *n.* 沾染物(质),(使清洁空气等污染的)污染物.

con·tam·i·nate [kən'tæmineit] *vt.* ①沾染,弄污,弄脏,污染;使受放射性物质影响而无法使用. 损害,毒害. *a ~d area* 撒毒区,(放射性粒子等的)污染地区. *~d blood* 污血. *~ a laboratory* 使实验室受到放射性物质的影响而无法使用. — *a.*〔古〕污染的.

con·tam·i·na·tion [kənˌtæmi'neiʃən] *n.* ①污染;污秽,污物;(语言的)交感,感染错合;(文章,故事等的)混合,拼凑. *ideological ~* 精神污染.

con·tam·i·na·tive [kən'tæminətiv] *a.* (使)污染的;弄脏了的.

con·tan·go [kən'tæŋgəu] *n.* *(pl. ~es)* (伦敦股票交易所)交易延期费,延期日息. *a ~ day* 交割限期日.

contd. = *continued.*

conte [kɔ̃:nt] *n.* 〔F.〕(极短的、多为情节奇特的)短篇小说,小故事.

con·te ['kɔ:nte] *n.* 〔It.〕伯爵.

con·temn [kən'tem] *vt.* 轻蔑,藐视.

contemp. = contemporary.
con·tem·plate [ˈkɔntempleit] *vt.* ①熟视,注视,细心观察. ②熟思,细想,仔细考虑. ③期待,预期;企图,打算. *I'm ~ visiting France.* 我打算上法国去游览. — *vi.* 沉思,冥想.
con·tem·pla·tion [ˌkɔntemˈpleiʃən] *n.* ①注视,凝视;静观. ②仔细考虑;沉思,默想,冥想. ③打算,企图,计划;期待,预期. ④【宗】默祷;感知神之存在. ***under [in]*** ~计划中的 (*a new building under ~* 计划兴建的新楼). ***be lost in*** ~ 想得出神. ***have (sth.) in*** ~ 企图,筹划.
con·tem·pla·tive [ˈkɔntempleitiv] *a.* ①熟思的;爱默想的,冥想的. ②【宗】默祷的. ***be ~ of*** 注视,细想,仔细考虑.
con·tem·pla·tor [ˈkɔntempleitə] *n.* 冥想者,沉思者,深思熟虑的人.
con·tem·po·ra·ne·i·ty [kənˌtempərəˈni:iti] *n.* 同时代(性),同时期(性);同时发生性.
con·tem·po·ra·ne·ous [kənˌtempəˈreinjəs] *a.* 同时期的,同时代的;同时发生的. ***be ~ with*** 与…同时代[同时期,同时发生]. **-ly** *ad.* **-ness** *n.*
con·tem·po·ra·ry [kənˈtempərəri] *a.* ①当代的,现代的. ②同年龄的;同时代的. *be ~ with* 和…同时代. *~ literature* 当代文学. *~ opinion* 时论. — *n.* ①同时代的人,同代者;同年龄的人,同年者. ②同时代的报刊,报刊同业. *our contemporaries* 同时代的人们,当代人物. *our ~* 我们同代的报刊,报刊同业.
con·tem·po·rize [kənˈtempəˌraiz] *vt., vi.* ①(使)成同时代. ②(使)合乎时代. ③(使)同时发生. *This writer has a power of contemporizing himself with the bygone times.* 这位作家能把古代写得栩栩如生.
con·tempt [kənˈtem*p*t] *n.* ①轻蔑,藐视. ②耻辱,屈辱. ③不管,不顾. *bring into ~* 污辱. *bring upon oneself the ~ of* 自讨…屈辱. *~ of court* 藐视法庭[法官]罪. *feel ~ for* 对…发生轻蔑心理. *have a ~ for* 对…有轻蔑感. *live in ~* 在屈辱中生活. *show ~ for sth.* 对某事表示轻视. *have [hold] … in ~* 藐视,看不起,轻视. ***fall into*** ~受辱,丢脸. ***in ~ of*** 看不起,蔑视.
con·tempt·i·ble [kənˈtem*p*təbl] *a.* 可鄙的,可轻视的,下贱的;不值一谈的. **con·tempt·i·bil·i·ty** [-ˈbiliti] *n.* **-i·bly** *ad.* **-ness** *n.*
con·temp·tu·ous [kənˈtem*p*tjuəs] *a.* (表示)轻蔑的;傲慢不恭的. *be ~ of* 瞧不起. *~ air* 傲慢态度. **-ness** *n.*
con·tend [kənˈtend] *vi.* ①争夺,竞争;斗争,战斗. ②争论,争辩. *~ against one's fate* 和自己的命运斗争. *~ with difficulties [an opponent]* 和困难[对手]斗争. *~ with each other for hegemony* 互相争霸. *~ with sb. about a matter* 与某人争辩某事. —*vt.* (坚决)主张 (*that*). *It is ~ed that …* 人们坚持认为…. ~ ***for*** 争取. ***have much to ~ with*** 有不少困难待克服.
con·tent[1] [ˈkɔntent] *n.* ①容积,容量,含量,【数】容度;收容量. ②【哲】内容 (*opp.* form);要旨,真意. ③〔*pl.*〕内容,内含物;(一本书的)目次. *a table of ~s* 目录. *the unity of ~ and form* 内容和形式的统一. *linear ~(s)* 长,长度. *solid [cubical] ~(s)* 容积,体积. *superficial ~(s)* 面积. *a ~ word* 实义词.
con·tent[2] [kənˈtent] *vt.* 使满意,使满足. *~ oneself with* 自满于,甘于. *Nothing can ~s her.* 她永无厌足之时. — *n.* ①满足,自得. ②〔*pl.*〕(英国上院)(投)赞成票(者). ***to one's heart's*** ~ 尽情,尽量. — *a.*〔只作表语用〕①满足,甘心. ②喜欢,满意;赞成〔英国上院不说yes, no 而说 ~, not ~, 下院则说 ay, no〕. ***be ~ with*** 以…为满足. ***cry ~ with*** 满足于. ***live [die]*** ~ 心满意足地过日子[死去].
con·tent·ed [kənˈtentid] *a.* 满足的,满意的;甘心的. *He is ~ with his lot.* 感到满足. *a superior hard to be ~* 难于使之感到满意的上司. *a ~ look* 满意的表情. ***be ~ to do*** 乐意地[甘心情愿地]做…. **-ly** *ad.* **-ness** *n.*
con·ten·tion [kənˈtenʃən] *n.* ①斗争,竞争;争论. ②(争论中的)论点,主张.
con·ten·tious [kənˈtenʃəs] *a.*①好争吵的,爱议论的. ②引起争论的,有争论的. *be of a ~ disposition* 好争辩的性格. *~ case* 抗争事件,诉讼事件. ~ ***clause in a treaty***条约中有争议的条款. **-ly** *ad.*
con·tent·ment [kənˈtentmənt] *n.* ①满意,知足. ②〔古〕令人满意(的事物).
con·ter·mi·nal [kɔnˈtə:minl] *a.* = conterminous.
con·ter·mi·nous [kɔnˈtə:minəs] *a.*①具有共同边界的,邻接的. ②(时、空意义等)同广度的. ③处于同一范围以内的;美国本部内的〔指阿拉斯加和夏威夷以外的美国国土〕.
con·test [ˈkɔntest] *n.* ①竞争;争论. ②竞赛,比赛. *a musical ~* 音乐比赛会. *an oratorical ~* 辩论会. *the ~ of strength* 力量的较量. — [kənˈtest] *vt.* ①争夺(胜败,土地等). ②争议,辩驳,争论. *~ a prize* 争夺奖赏. *~ an election* 竞选. *~ed election* 竞选;〔美〕有异议的选举. *~ed passage* (文中)有争论的段落[文句]. — *vi.* 争夺;竞争;争论 (*against, with*). ~ ***with [against]*** (*an adversary*) 和(敌方)竞争.
con·test·ant [kənˈtestənt] *n.* ①〔主美〕竞争者;争论者;竞赛参加者,选手. ②(对选举结果)有异议者.
con·tes·ta·tion [ˌkɔntesˈteiʃən] *n.* 争论,论战;论点;争讼. ***in*** ~ 争执中的.
con·test·ee [ˌkɔntesˈti:] *n.* 竞争者;竞赛者;〔美〕有争议的候选人.
con·text [ˈkɔntekst] *n.* ①上下文;文章的前后关系[脉络]. ②(事情等的)关节,范围,场合,处境,条件;来龙去脉. *tell the meaning of a word from its ~* 从一个字的上文下推知其字义. ***in one*** ~ 在一定场合,在某一范围内. ***in the ~ of*** 在…情况下. ***in this*** ~ 关于这一点,在这种场合下. ***outside the ~ of*** 在…之外.
con·tex·tu·al [kɔnˈtekstjuəl] *a.* (按照)上下文的,由(文章)前后关系来看的. *a ~ quotation* 原文引用. **-ly** *ad.*
con·tex·ture [kɔnˈtekstʃə] *n.* 组织,构造,结构;交织(物);上下文.
con·ti·gu·i·ty [ˌkɔntiˈgju:iti] *n.* ①接触,接近,邻接. ②〔罕〕连续(物).
con·tig·u·ous [kənˈtigjuəs] *a.* 连接,接近,邻接 (*to*). *The bridge is ~ to the house.* 桥屋相邻. *a ~ angle* 【数】邻角,接角. **-ly** *ad.* **-ness** *n.*
con·ti·nence, con·ti·nen·cy [ˈkɔntinəns(i)] *n.* ①克己,自制;节欲,禁欲. ②克制力.
con·ti·nent[1] [ˈkɔntinənt] *a.* ①自制的. ②节欲的,贞洁的;禁欲的.
con·ti·nent[2][ˈkɔntinənt] *n.* ①大陆;陆地. ②〔the C-〕欧洲大陆;〔美〕北美洲大陆.
con·ti·nen·tal [ˌkɔntiˈnentl] *a.* ①大陆的,大陆性的. ②〔C-〕欧洲大陆的;〔C-〕〔美〕(独立战争时)美洲殖民地的. — *n.* ①欧洲大陆人. ②〔美〕(独立战争中的)美国兵[纸币]. ③〔C-〕〔美俚〕(起源于英国的)欧洲大陆发式. ***do not care a*** ~〔美俚〕毫无关系. ***not worth a*** ~〔美俚〕毫无价值. ~ **bill** 汇到欧洲大陆的票据〔汇到英国的叫做 a sterling bill〕. ~ **breakfast** 包括面包与热饮料的早餐. ~ **climate** 大陆性气候. ~ **code** 大陆电码〔即莫尔斯电码〕. ~ **currency** 欧陆的通货. **C- Divide** (北美) 洛矶山脉分水岭. ~ **drift** 大陆飘移. ~ **facies** 陆相. ~ **island** 陆边岛. ~ **seating** 不留中间过道的剧场座位. ~ **shelf**【地】陆棚,陆裙,大陆架. **con·ti·nen·tal·i·za·tion** [ˌkɔntiˌnentəlaiˈzeiʃən] *n.* ①欧洲大陆化. ②【地】大陆成形.
con·tin·gence [kənˈtindʒəns] *n.* ①接触. ② =contingency.
con·tin·gen·cy [kənˈtindʒənsi] *n.* ①偶然[可能](性). ②(意外)事故;意外事件,临时[可能]事件. ③临时费.

future contingencies 以后的偶然[可能]事件. ***in case of ~ = in the supposed ~*** 在万一[可能]的情况下. ***not by any possible ~*** 未必…可能. ***provide against contingencies*** 以备万一. ~ **fund** 应急费用. ~ **reserve** 应急费用储备金. ~ **table**【统】列联表.

con·tin·gent [kən'tindʒənt] *a.* ①可能的; 偶然的 *(to)*; 临时的; 附随的. ②因情况而异的, 视条件而定的 *(upon)*. ③应急(用)的. ~ *fund* 应急费. *Such risks are ~ to the trade.* 这种危险对于那种生意是可能有的. — *n.* ①偶然[可能]事件. ②部分,份额;【军】小分队,分遣队[舰队]; 代表团. *a crack ~* 精锐部队. *reduce ... down to token ~s* 把…裁减到象征性的限额. *~s of the people's militia* 民兵师. ***~ on [upon]*** 视…而定 *(fee [remuneration] ~ on success* 成功才给的报酬). **-ly** *ad.* 偶然,意外; 看情况,相应地.

con·tin·u·al [kən'tinjuəl] *a.* 不断的, 连续的; 频繁的. *~ bouts of toothache* 一阵接一阵的牙痛. **-ly** *ad.*

con·tin·u·ance [kən'tinjuəns] *n.* ①持续; 继续, 连续. ②继续期间; 继续部分,(小说等的)续篇;【法】诉讼延期. *a ~ of [in] prosperity* 长时期的繁荣. *of long ~* 长期不断的.

con·tin·u·ant [kən'tinjuənt] *a.*【语音】连续音的. — *n.* 连续音[可拖长发音的 f. v. s. r 等辅音];【数】鯨夹行列式.

con·tin·u·ate [kən'tinjueit] *a.* [废]①继续的. ②连续的; 持久的.

con·tin·u·a·tion [kən,tinju'eiʃən] *n.* ①继续,连续; 持续. ②延续,续篇;(线路等的)延长. ③【乐】延留音. ④[*pl.*] 连接短裤的帮腿; [俚] 裤子,袜子. *C- follows.* 待续. ~ **day** [英](交易所)交割限期日. ~ **school** (成人业余)补习学校;(加拿大边区的)简易中学.

con·tin·u·a·tive [kən'tinjuətiv] *a.* 连续的; 继续的;【语法】接续的.

con·tin·u·a·tor [kən'tinju,eitə] *n.* [L.] 继续者, 续作者.

con·tin·ue [kən'tinju(:)] *vi.* ①连续,继续; 延伸. ②仍旧,依旧,留. *The rain ~d all day.* 雨终日不停. *The door ~d to bang all night.* 这门砰当砰当地响了一晚上. *He ~d at his post.* 他留任原职. *~ at school* 留校. *~ in command.* 继续担任指挥. *~ on page 20.* 下接 20 页. — *vt.* 接续,继续; 使留任; 延续,延长;【法】使(诉讼) 延期. *To be ~d.* 待续. *~ a boy at school* 使孩子继续求学. **~d bond** 延期偿付公债. **~d fraction** 连分数. **~d story** (报刊上的)连载小说[故事].

con·tin·u·ing [kən'tinjuiŋ] *a.* 继续的,连续的,持续的. ~ **education** 进修教育. ~ **partner** 继续合伙人.

con·ti·nu·i·ty [,kɔnti'nju(:)iti] *n.* ①连续(性),继续; 连结,连合,连锁. ②【影】剪辑; 分镜头电影剧本;(详细分段的)广播[电视]剧本; 广播节目[电视]的情节说明; 连环画的故事梗概说明. ~ **girl** [口](影片的)剪辑员. ~ **writer** 分镜头电影剧本作者.

con·tin·u·o [kən'tinjuəu] *n.* *(pl. ~s)*【乐】(西欧室内音乐中)键盘乐器的低音部; 连续的低音伴奏,通奏低音.

con·tin·u·ous [kən'tinjuəs] *a.* ①连续的, 继续的,无间断的. ②【植】无节的. *a ~ current* 恒(向电)流. *~ fire* 连续射击. *~ rain* 连绵不断的雨. *a ~ train of thoughts* 一连串的思想. *a ~ wave (radar)* 等幅波(雷达). **-ly** *ad.*

con·tin·u·um [kən'tinjuəm] *n.* *(pl. -ua* [-uə]*)*【哲】连续(统一体);【数】连续统, 闭联[连续]集;【物】连续区. *space-time ~* 时空连续.

contl. = Continental.

cont·line ['kɔntlain] *n.* (绳子的股与股之间; 并排放的桶与桶之间的)空隙.

Cont O【美军】= Contact Officer.

con·to ['kɔntəu] *n.* *(pl. ~s)* 康多[货币计算名称, 在葡萄牙等于 1000 埃斯库多,在巴西等于 1000 克鲁赛罗].

con·tort [kən'tɔ:t] *vt.* 扭,扭歪,拧弯; 曲解(文义等). *~ one's features* 扭歪着脸[如由于疼痛、忧愁].

con·tor·tion [kən'tɔ:ʃən] *n.* 扭弯,扭歪; 曲解;【医】捩转,转位,脱节. **-ist** *n.* ①柔软杂技演员. ②(语义的)曲解者.

con·tour ['kɔntuə] *n.* ①外形,轮廓; 周线,轮廓线. ②等高线,恒值线;【电视】等场强线 (= ~-line). ③概略,大要; 形势. ④【电】回路. *the irregular ~ of the coast* 曲折的海岸线. *the ~s of things* 情势. — *a.* ①与轮廓相合的. ②(表示[循着])等高线的. — *vt.* ①描画…的轮廓; 画…的等高[等值]线. ②顺等高线(作业)[如开沟,筑路等]. ~ **chasing**【空】低空飞行. ~ **map** 等高线(地)图, 曲线地图. ~ **planting** 等高造林. ~ **plowing** 等高耕作.

contr. = ① contract(ed). ② contraction. ③ contractor. ④ contrary. ⑤ control.

con·tra ['kɔntrə] *n.* ①反对(意见), 反对票. ②【会计】对方[尤指贷方]. *pros and ~s* 赞成与反对. — *ad.* 反对地. — *prep.* 对于. *~ credit [debit]* 对于贷方[借方].

contra- *pref.* 反,逆,抗,对应.

con·tra·band ['kɔntrəbænd] *n.* ①非法买卖[运输]; 走私. ②(战时)禁运品 (= ~ of war); 走私品,私货. ③【美史】南北战争时私逃投奔[被秘密送往]北军的黑人. — *a.* 禁运的, 非法的. **-ist** *n.* 买卖走私品者; 走私者.

con·tra·bass ['kɔntrə'beis] *n.*【乐】,倍低音乐器[提琴等]. — *a.* 倍低音的,最低音的.

con·tra·bas·soon [,kɔntrəbə'su:n] *n.*【乐】低音大管[巴松管].

con·tra·cept ['kɔntrəsept] *vt.* 使避孕.

con·tra·cep·tion [,kɔntrə'sepʃən] *n.* 避孕(法).

con·tra·cep·tive [,kɔntrə'septiv] *a.* 避孕(用)的. — *n.* 避孕药物[用品].

con·tra·clock·wise [,kɔntrə'klɔkwaiz] *a., ad.* 反时针方向的[地].

con·tract[1] ['kɔntrækt] *n.* ①契约,合同. ②婚约. ③承包(合约). ④【法】契约法. ⑤【牌戏】定约; 合约桥牌. ⑥[主英方]月(季)票. ⑦[美]工作,事情. ⑧[美俚] 小恩小惠,贿赂. *It's a bit of a ~.* [美] 这是相当难的工作. *a bare ~* 无条件契约. *a simple [parole] ~* 誓约. *a verbal [oral] ~* 口头约定. *be built by ~* 包工建造. *draw up a ~* 拟订合同. *~ drawing* 承包施工图. *~ system* 承包制. *~ work* 包工. ***make [enter into] a ~ with*** 与…订约. ***put out to ~*** 包出去, 给人承包. — [kən'trækt] *vt.* ①订(约),立(合同); 约定. ②订婚[通例用被动语态],把…许配给 *(to)*. ③结交(朋友等). ④招,患(病),染(恶习). ⑤负债. *~ed a bad cold.* 得了重伤风. *be ~ed to* 是…的未婚夫[妻]. *~ an alliance (with)* 结盟. *~ a marriage with* 与…订婚. *~ friendship with* 与…交朋友. ***~ oneself out of*** 订立契约免除…, 照契约不必…. — *vi.* 订约; 订婚; 承包. *~ing parties* 订约双方当事人. *High Contracting Parties [powers]* 缔约国. *~ for labour and material* 包工包料. ~ **bridge** 合约桥牌. ~ **miner** 按工计酬的矿工.

con·tract[2] [kən'trækt] *vt., vi.* ①收缩,紧缩; (使)皱起. ②(使)缩短,(使)缩小. ③【语法】缩略, 缩约. *~ one's brows* 皱拢眉头. *~ing muscles* 收缩肌.

con·tract·ed [kən'træktid] *a.* ①收缩了的, 缩小的; 缩略的;(心胸,思想等)狭小的; 贫困的. ②订过(婚)约的. **-ly** *ad.* **-ness** *n.*

con·tract·i·ble [kən'træktəbl] *a.* 会缩的,可缩的.

con·trac·tile [kən'træktail] *a.* 会缩的,有收缩性的. *~ force* 收缩力.

con·trac·til·i·ty [,kɔntræk'tiliti] *n.* 收缩性; 收缩力.

con·trac·tion [kən'trækʃən] *n.* ①缩短, 收缩;【医】挛

缩．②(开支等)缩减；收敛，狭窄；缩度．③【语法】缩略〔如将 never 略成 ne'er, do not 略成 don't 等〕；略体，缩写〔如 department 缩为 dep't〕．④得病；习染；招致；(负债等的)陷入．

con·trac·tive [kən'træktiv] *a.* 收缩(性)的．

con·trac·tor[1] [kən'træktə] *n.* 立约人，承包人．

con·trac·tor[2] [kən'træktə] *n.*【解】收缩肌．

con·trac·tu·al [kən'træktjuəl] *a.* 契约上(规定)的．**-ly** *ad.*

con·trac·ture [kən'træktʃə] *n.*【医】挛缩．

con·tra·dance ['kɔntrədɑːns] *n.* = contredanse.

con·tra·dict [kɔntrə'dikt] *vt.* ①反驳，反对，抗辩；否认．②与…矛盾，与…抵触．～ *the rumour* 辟谣．～ *oneself* 自相矛盾．— *vi.* 反驳．**-able** *a.* 可反驳的．**-or** *n.* 反驳者；相矛盾的人；抵触者．

con·tra·dic·tion [ˌkɔntrə'dikʃən] *n.* ①反驳，抗辩；否定，否认．②矛盾，抵触，相反．*class* ～*s* 阶级矛盾．*a* ～ *in terms* 语词矛盾〔如 *a square circle* 一个正方的圆形〕．

con·tra·dic·tious [ˌkɔntrə'dikʃəs] *a.* ①相抵触[矛盾]的．②爱争辩的．**-ly** *ad.* **-ness** *n.*

con·tra·dic·to·ri·ly [ˌkɔntrə'diktərili] *ad.* 反驳；相反，矛盾．

con·tra·dic·to·ry [ˌkɔntrə'diktəri] *a.* ①反驳的，反对的，抗辩的．②矛盾的，相反的．— *n.* 对立的一方，矛盾的一方；【逻】正反对(命题)．

con·tra·dis·tinc·tion [ˌkɔntrədis'tiŋkʃən] *n.* 对照的区别，对比的区别，对比．***in*** ～ ***to[from]*** 与…对比；与…截然不同．

con·tra·dis·tin·guish [ˌkɔntrədis'tiŋgwiʃ] *vt.* 通过比较来区别，通过对照来区别，对比．

con·trail ['kɔntreil] *n.*【空】(飞机、导弹等航迹中云状的)凝结尾流[迹]，凝迹；逆增[转换]轨迹．

con·tra·in·di·cate [kɔntrə'indikeit] *vt.*【医】禁忌(某种疗法等)．

con·tra·in·di·ca·tion[ˌkɔntrəˌindi'keiʃən] *n.*【医】(表明不宜采用某种疗法的)禁忌征象．**-dic·a·tive** *a.*

con·tra·lat·er·al [ˌkɔntrə'lætərəl] *a.*【解】对侧的．

con·tral·to [kən'træltəu] *n.* (*pl.* ～*s*, *-ti* [-tiː])【乐】女低音；女低音歌手[角色]．— *a.* 女低音的．

con·tra·mis·sile ['kɔntrə'misail] *n.* 反导弹导弹．

con·tra·pose ['kɔntrəpəuz] *vt.* ①以…针对着；使对照 *(to)*．②【逻】换(命题)的质位．

con·tra·po·si·tion [ˌkɔntrəpə'ziʃən] *n.* ①对置；对照；对位．②【逻】换质换位法〔例：若"A 是 B"，则可推演为"非 B 就非 A"〕．***in*** ～ ***to [with]*** 跟…位置相反．

con·tra·po·si·tive [ˌkɔntrə'pɔzətiv] *a.* 对照的；针对的．

con·tra·prop ['kɔntrəprɔp] *n.*【空】同轴成相对方向旋转的推进器．

con·trap·tion [kən'træpʃən] *n.* 〔口〕新设计，新发明；〔蔑〕样子古怪的新发明(物品)．

con·tra·pun·tal [ˌkɔntrə'pʌntl] *a.*【乐】对位(法)的．

con·tra·pun·tist ['kɔntrəpʌntist] *n.*【乐】擅长对位法的作曲家．

con·trar·i·ant [kən'treəriənt] *a.* 反对的，对立的，敌对的．

con·tra·ri·e·ty [ˌkɔntrə'raiəti] *n.* ①反对，矛盾，矛盾性．②〔*pl.*〕相反物；矛盾物；对立面．

con·tra·ri·ly ['kɔntrərili] *ad.* ①反之，相反地，反对地，逆．② [kən'treərili] 〔口〕故意闹别扭．

con·tra·ri·ness ['kɔntrərinis] *n.* ①对立，相反，反对．②〔口〕乖张，别扭．

con·trar·i·ous [kən'treəriəs] *a.* 〔罕〕相反的〔尤指别扭的，乖张的〕．

con·tra·ri·wise ['kəntrəriwaiz] *ad.* 反之，相反地，反对地．

con·tra·ry ['kɔntrəri] *a.* ①反对的，相反的；格格不入的，矛盾的，对抗的．②〔口〕[kən'treəri] 乖张的，别扭的，执拗的．③【植】直角的．*He looked the* ～ *way.* 他把脸转了过去．*be* ～ *to expectations* 出乎意外．～ *child* 不听话的孩子．～ *wind* 逆风．— *ad.* 反对地，相反地．～ *to* 跟…相反[相违背]（～ *to his expectation* 跟他的预料相反．*act* ～ *to nature* 违反自然[常情]）．— *n.* ①反对；矛盾．②〔*pl.*〕对立物；【逻】反对命题[名词]．*Quite the* ～. 正相反．*He is neither tall nor the* ～. 他不高不矮．***by contraries*** 正反对地，相反地，出乎预料地 (*Dreams go by contraries.* 梦是相反的〔旧时一种圆梦的说法〕．*interpret by contraries* 相反地解释)．***on the*** ～ 反之，正相反．***to the*** ～ 反对地，和这相反的 (*a rumour to the* ～ 完全相反的谣言．*There is no evidence to the* ～. 没有反证．*Unless I hear to the* ～. 除非我听说不是那样．*I know nothing to the* ～. 我不知道有和这相反的情况)．

con·trast ['kɔntræst] *n.* ①对照，对比；(对照中的)差异．②对立面，对照物；【摄】反差．③【修】对照法．*What a* ～ *between them!* 他们之间真是大不相同！～ *colours* 反衬色．***for the sake of*** ～ 为了对比[反衬]．***gain by*** ～ 对比之下显出优点．***in*** ～ ***with*** 和…成对比；和…大不相同．***present [form] a striking*** ～ ***to*** 和…成显著的对比．— [kən'træst] *vt.* 使对照，使对比．*C- birds with fishes.* 拿鸟和鱼对比．— *vi.* (和…)形成对照；(和…)成很好的对照 (*with*)．～ ***finely with*** … 和…对比起来更加鲜明．

con·trast·y [kən'træsti] *a.* (尤指照相负片)调子硬的，明暗对比强的，反差强的．

con·trate ['kɔntreit] *a.*【机】横齿的．

con·tra·test ['kɔntrətest] *a.* 对比试验的．

con·tra·val·la·tion [ˌkɔntrəvæ'leiʃən] *n.*【军】(防止被围者突围的)对垒(工事)．

con·tra·vene [ˌkɔntrə'viːn] *vt.* ①违反，违背，犯(法等)．②否定，反驳，推翻(论据等)．③背叛(主义)，抵触，与…不相容．

con·tra·ven·tion [ˌkɔntrə'venʃən] *n.* ①违反，违背．②〔Scot.〕【法】违警罪．③否定，反驳．***in*** ～ ***of*** *(the law)* 违(法)．

con·tre·coup ['kɔntrəˌkuː, 'kəun-] *n.*【医】对侧反激伤〔如头部正面受冲击，后脑勺撞在墙上而伤在后脑部〕．

con·tre·danse ['kɔntrəˌdɑːns, 'kauntrəˌdæns] *n.* ①对列舞〔一种农村舞〕．②对列舞曲．

con·tre·temps ['kɔ̃ːntrətɑ̃ːŋ] *n.* 〔F.〕①令人窘困的(意外)事故；意料不到的困难[阻碍]．②【乐】节调，约调，切分法．

contrib. = contributor.

con·trib·ute [kən'tribju(ː)t] *vt.* ①捐赠(款项)．②投稿(给杂志等)．③贡献出．*Everybody* ～*s his ideas and his strength.* 人人想办法，个个出力量．～ *(money) to* 捐(款)给．～ *(an article) to (a magazine)* 投寄(一篇论文)给(某杂志)．— *vi.* ①出力，作出贡献．②捐款，捐献．③投稿．～ *to [towards]* 捐助，帮助，贡献，出力；给…投稿．*contributing factors* 促成因素．*contributing editor* 特约编辑[撰稿人]．

con·tri·bu·tion [ˌkɔntri'bjuːʃən] *n.* ①贡献，赠送；捐赠，捐助．②投稿，来稿．③捐款，献金；献品，补助品．④【军】(向占领地人民征收的)军税；【法】分担(额)．***lay under*** ～ 强制派捐，勒派军税．***make a*** ～ ***to [towards]*** 捐赠；贡献给．

con·trib·u·tive [kən'tribjutiv] *a.* ①捐赠的；贡献的，出资[分担]的．②有帮助的，增进…的．

con·trib·u·tor [kən'tribju(ː)tə] *n.* ①贡献者．②捐助者，赠送者．③投稿人．

con·trib·u·to·ry [kən'tribjutəri] *a.* ①捐助的；参加力量的；有贡献的．②有助于 *(to)*．*various* ～ *factors* 各种起配合[促进]作用的因素．～ *negligence*【法】(车祸等

中)受伤一方本身的粗心。
con·trite [ˈkɔntrait] *a.* ①悔罪的，悔悟的，悔恨的。②表示悔罪[忏悔]而作出的。**-ly** *ad.* **-ness** *n.*
con·tri·tion [kənˈtriʃən] *n.* 悔罪，悔悟，悔恨。
con·triv·able [kənˈtraivəbl] *a.* 可设计的；可发明的；可设法做到的。
con·triv·ance [kənˈtraivəns] *n.* ①发明，设计(方案)，计划。②发明[设计]的才能；机巧，巧思。③奇巧的制作物，新发明，装置，设备。④计策，奸计，诡计。⑤人为的修饰，巧饰。*an automatic* ~ 自动装置。
con·trive [kənˈtraiv] *vt.* ①发明，创制，设计。②图谋，企图。③设法做到。④挖空心思(而弄巧成拙)，周到反而弄得(不利等)。~ *a new kind of tape recorder* 设计出一种新型录音机。~ *a robber* 企图抢劫。~ *to do it well* 设法做好这件事。*He ~d to make a mess of the whole thing.* 他挖空心思反而把事情全盘弄糟了。*He ~d to persuade me.* 他千方百计想说服我。*He ~d to get himself disliked.* 他费了许多苦心反而弄得大家都讨厌他了。— *vi.* ①妥为料理；设法[巧妙]应付 *(to do)* 〔尤指治家，料理家务〕。②设计，图谋。*I can ~ without meat.* 我没有肉也能凑合(吃这顿饭)。***cut and ~*** 妥善地安排[应付]。
con·trived [kənˈtraivd] *a.* 使用机巧的；人为的；非天然的。
con·triv·er [kənˈtraivə] *n.* ①发明者，设计者，创制者；筹谋者。②善于安排[应付]的人；善于持家的人。
con·trol [kənˈtrəul] *n.* ①支配，管理，管制，统制，控制；监督。②抑制(力)；压制，节制，拘束；【农】防治。③检查；核对；(试验中的)对照(处理)。④(记录等的)留底；底本；存根。⑤【空】驾驶；〔*pl.*〕操纵装置。⑥(飞机的修理站；(车赛等的)慢行地区；(同上地区内车身等的)检查站。⑦【棒球】制球力。*remote [distance]* ~ 远距离操纵，遥控。*homing* ~【火箭】导引；自导。*traffic* ~交通管制。*public* ~ 普查。*biological* ~生物防除。*birth* ~ 生育控制，节(制生)育。*automatic* ~ 自动控制(装置)。~ *of light* 灯火管制。***beyond*** ~ 无法控制。***in*** ~ ***(of)*** 由…控制(住)，管理。***get out of*** ~ 失掉控制(能力)，控制不住。***get under*** ~ 抑制，治理(水患)，防制(火灾) *(The fire was got under ~.* 火已压下去了)。***have ~ of [over] oneself*** 控制[克制]自己。***have no ~ over*** 不能控制，无控制力。***keep under*** ~ 抑制，控制，统制。***lose ~ of*** 失却对…的控制力，控制不住。***out of ~*** 失去控制。***under the ~ of*** 受管制[管理、支配]，在…管辖下的。***without*** ~ 不受管制地，无拘束地。— *vt.* ①管理，统制；节制，抑制，控制；监督；防治。②核对，核实，对照；检查。~ *oneself* 自制。~ **board** 仪表板。~ **chart** (工厂中的产品质量)控制图。~ **company**【经】控股公司。~ **dam** 节流闸。~ **experiment** 受控[对照]实验。~ **figures** (计划中的)控制数字。~ **lever [stick]**【空】操纵杆。~ **line**【林】防火线。~ **room** (潜艇的)调度室，操纵室。~ **stick** (飞机的)操纵杆。~ **top**【军】桅楼指挥所。~ **tower**【空】机场中的起落指挥塔。
con·trol·la·ble [kənˈtrəuləbl] *a.* 可支配[管理]的；可抑制[控制]的，可操纵的。
con·trol·ler [kənˈtrəulə] *n.* ①管理人，主管人。②(会计的)主计人，检查员；〔英〕(特指宫廷、海军等的)出纳官〔常作 comptroller〕。③(电车的)驾驶器；【机】控制器；操纵杆，舵；【电】整流器；【船】(锚链的)制链器。~ **general** 主计长。
con·tro·ver·sial [ˌkɔntrəˈvəːʃəl] *a.* ①(有)争论的；被争论的。②好争论的。*a ~ issues* 有争论的问题。**-ism** *n.* 争论癖。**-ist** *n.* 争论者，有异议者。
con·tro·ver·sy [ˈkɔntrəvəːsi] *n.* (尤指纸上的)争论，辩论，论战 *(with; about; between)*. *a barren* ~ 无结果[无益]的争论。*be in a ~ with sb.* 和某人争论中。***beyond [without]*** ~ 无争论余地。***enter into a ~ with*** 和…论争。
con·tro·vert [ˈkɔntrəvəːt] *vt.* 争论；辩驳，反驳，攻击。— *vi.* 参加争论。**-er, -ist** *n.* 争论者；辩驳者。
con·tro·vert·i·ble [ˈkɔntrəvəːtəbl] *a.* 可争论的；可辩驳的。
con·tu·ma·cious [ˌkɔntju(ː)ˈmeiʃəs] *a.* ①抗拒的，拒不服从的，顽抗的。②【法】违抗法院命令的，蓄意藐视法庭的。
con·tu·ma·cy [ˈkɔntjuməsi] *n.* ①抗拒，顽抗，不服从。②【法】违抗法院命令，蓄意藐视法庭。
con·tu·me·li·ous [ˌkɔntju(ː)ˈmiːljəs] *a.* 傲慢无礼的，轻侮的。
con·tume·ly [ˈkɔntju(ː)mli] *n.* 傲慢无礼；轻侮，侮辱。
con·tuse [kənˈtjuːz] *vt.* 打伤，挫伤，撞伤，(尤指)使受暗伤，使受内伤。
con·tu·sion [kənˈtjuːʒən] *n.* 殴打；伤害；受(内)伤；【医】打伤，挫伤。
co·nun·drum [kəˈnʌndrəm] *n.* (字)谜，谜语；难解的问题。
con·ur·ba·tion [ˌkɔnəˈbeiʃən] *n.* (由中心大城市及卫星城镇构成的)集合城市。
CONUS= Continental United States 美国大陆。
con·va·lesce [ˌkɔnvəˈles] *vi.* (病后逐渐)复元，恢复，康复。
con·va·les·cence [ˌkɔnvəˈlesns] *n.* ①康复，恢复。②康复期的，恢复期的。
con·va·les·cent [ˌkɔnvəˈlesnt] *a.* ①病后渐愈的。②康复期的。*become ~* 逐渐复元。— *n.* 康复期病人。*a ~ hospital* 疗养院，休养所。
con·vect [kənˈvekt] *vi.* 对流传热。— *vt.* 使(热空气)对流循环；借对流传(热)。
con·vec·tion [kənˈvekʃən] *n.* ①传送。②【物】运流，环流；【气】对流，上升气流。~ **current** 对流；【电】运流。~ **light** 集中光束。
con·vec·tive [kənˈvektiv] *a.* ①有传送力[运输力]的，传送性的。②【物】对流的。
con·vec·tor [kənˈvektə] *n.* 对流式热空气循环加热器。
con·ven·a·ble [kənˈviːnəbl] *a.* 可召集的，可召唤的。
con·ve·nance [ˈkɔ̃ːŋvinɑ̃ːns] *n.* 〔F.〕习俗，惯例；〔*pl.*〕仪式，礼仪。
con·vene [kənˈviːn] *vt.* 召集。— *vi.* 聚集，集合。
con·ven·ience [kənˈviːnjəns] *n.* ①便利，方便(机会)。②〔*pl.*〕(生活上的)便利设备。③〔英〕厕所。④〔古〕公共马车。*a marriage of ~* 有某种谋利目的的婚姻。*await sb.'s ~* 等某人方便时。*a ~ outlet*【电】万能插头。***as a matter of ~*** 为了方便。***at one's (own) ~*** 顺便；得便时，方便的时候。***at your earliest ~*** 务请从速，有便即请。***for ~(') sake*** 为了便利起见。***for the ~ of*** 为…的方便起见。***make a ~ of (sb.)***〔口〕利用(某人) *(He is simply making a ~ of me.* 他不过是利用我罢了)。***suit sb.'s ~*** 对某人便利 *(if it suits your ~* 若对你方便)。***suit [consult] one's own ~*** 只图一己方便。~ **food** 方便食品〔指罐头食物，方便面条等〕。
con·ven·ient [kənˈviːnjənt] *a.* ①便利的，合宜的。②〔英方，美〕附近的，不远的。*if it is ~ to you* 若你方便。*place ~ for bathing* 适宜游泳的地方。**-ly** *ad.*
con·vent [ˈkɔnvənt] *n.* 修(道)女团；女修道院。***go into a ~*** 去做修女。
con·ven·ti·cle [kənˈventikl] *n.* ①集会；【宗】秘密集会。②【英史】集会(场所)；〔蔑〕独立教派的小教堂；(苏格兰长老派的)野祷(场所)。
con·ven·tion [kənˈvenʃən] *n.* ①集会，会议；【英史】(1660，1688 年的)(非由英王召集的)非常议会；〔美〕(政党等的)全国代表大会，〔集合词〕(出席的)代表们。②(国际间的)公约，协定。③(社会)习俗，惯例，常规；【牌】(玩牌者公认的)规定〔出牌或叫牌法〕。*stage ~s* 舞台惯例[程式]。*break away from ~* 打破常规[习俗]。***the***

National C- ①【法史】国民议会〔1792—1795〕. ②【英史】宪章党员大会. ③〔美〕(政党决定总统候选人的)全国代表大会. ～ **money** (两国以上协定发行的)同本位货币.

con·ven·tion·al [kən'venʃənl] *a.* ①因袭的,传统的. ②习用的; 平常的,常规的; 形式上的. ③约定的, 协定的; 会议的. *a ～ ceremonial* 常礼,惯例. *a ～ greeting* 常规的问候. ～ *morality* 相沿成习的道德. *the ～* 相沿成习的事物, 传统. ～ *neutrality* 约定中立, 义务中立. *the ～ wisdom* 公众的一般看法, 群众意见, 公众态度. *a ～ phrase* 常套语. ～ **duties** 协定关税. ～ **tariffs** 协定税率. ～ **war [weapon]** (不使用核武器的)常规战争[武器]. **-ism** *n.* 依从俗例; 因袭主义; 惯例,习惯做法, 常规旧套; 陈言套语;【数】约定论. **-ist** *n.* 拘泥习俗[遵守惯例]的人. **-ly** *ad.*

con·ven·tion·al·i·ty [kən,venʃə'næliti] *n.* ①因袭(性). ②传统; 常套; 惯例,习俗.

con·ven·tion·al·ize [kən'venʃənəlaiz] *vt.* 使照惯例, 使习俗化,使按传统形式. *～d flowers* (照传统形式画成的)定型的花.

con·ven·tion·eer [kən,venʃə'niə] *n.* 到会者; 〔美〕(代表大会的)出席代表.

con·ven·tu·al [kən'ventjuəl] *a.* ①女修道院(似)的. ②〔C-〕圣芳济会修士(团)的. — *n.* 修(道)女; 〔C-〕圣芳济会修士.

con·verge [kən'və:dʒ] *vi.* ①会聚,集中(于一点或一处); 辐辏. ②【物、数】收敛. *converging fire* 集中射击. — *vt.* 使聚合[集中]于一点,使辐辏 *(on; upon)*. **-r** *n.* 〔美口〕擅长精细推理的人.

con·ver·gence, con·ver·gen·cy [kən'və:dʒən, -dʒənsi] *n.* ①聚合, 会聚, 辐辏, 汇合. ②集合点; 【数、物】收敛;【生】趋同(现象).

con·ver·gent [kən'və:dʒənt] *a.* ①渐集一点的, 会聚性的; 包围集中的. ②【数】收敛的. — *n.* 【数】收敛子; 渐近分数. ～ **evolution** 趋同进化. ～ **lens** 会聚透镜. ～ **pencil** 【物】会聚光线锥. ～ **series**【数】收敛级数.

con·vers·a·ble [kən'və:səbl] *a.* 健谈的; 谈得来的; 适于闲聊的.

con·ver·sance, con·ver·san·cy [kən'və:səns, 'kɔnvə-; -si] *n.* ①亲近, 接近. ②熟悉, 通晓, 精通.

con·ver·sant [kən'və:sənt] *a.* ①亲近的,有交情的. ②精通…的, 熟悉…的. ③有关的 *(in; about; with)*. *be ～ with* 精通; 和…有交情.

con·ver·sa·tion [,kɔnvə'seiʃən] *n.* ①会话,谈话; 会谈 *(on; about)*; (人与计算机的)人机对话. ②接交, 交往, 交际. ③交媾, 性交. ～ *goes on [stagnates, languishes, stops, revives]* 会谈正在进行[不畅, 冷落, 停止, 重新活跃]. *drop [break off, interrupt, close, resume] ～* 停止[中止,打断,结束,又开始]谈话. *a topic of ～* 话题. *criminal ～* 通奸. *enter into ～ with* 和…谈起来. *hold [have] a ～ with* 和…交谈. ～ **piece** ①一种有情节的人物画. ②可作话题的东西, 题材. ～ **pit** 谈话间 (指客厅等内供谈话用的专设场所).

con·ver·sa·tion·al [,kɔnvə'seiʃənl] *a.* ①会话的, 谈话的. ②健谈的, 善应酬的.

con·ver·sa·tion(·al)·ist [,kɔnvə'seiʃən(əl)ist] *n.* ①谈话者. ②健谈者,会应酬的人.

con·ver·sa·zi·o·ne ['kɔnvə,sætsi'əuni] *n.* *(pl.* *～s,* 〔It.〕 *-ni* [-ni:]) 〔It.〕(学术性)座谈会.

con·verse[1] [kən'və:s] *vi., n.* ①〔书〕谈话 *(with; on; upon)*; (人与计算机)对话. ②〔古〕交际; 接交; 交往; 性交.

con·verse[2] ['kɔnvə:s] *n.* 【逻】倒转命题, 逆命题; 逆叙 (= ～ statement);【数】逆,反. — *a.* 倒转的,逆(转)的. ～ **proposition**【逻】逆命题. ～ **statement** 逆叙〔把 if I were you 说作 if you were I 等〕. **-ly** *ad.*

con·ver·sion [kən'və:ʃən] *n.* ①变换,转化,转换; 换算, 换位. ②(意见、信仰等的)改变〔特指改信基督教〕; (车身, 设备等的) 改装, 改造. ③【法】变更; 强占; 【数】换算法;【逻】换位(法); 【心】(心理冲突转化为生理病态的)变形表现, 变形发泄; 【军】改换装备, 改装; 【商】兑换; 更换(字据等). ④【橄榄球】触地得分, (篮球)罚球得分. ～ **parity** 兑换平价. ～ **pig** 炼钢生铁. ～ **table** 换算表. ～ **unit** 【化】反应设备.

con·vert [kən'və:t] *vt.* ①变换, 转换, 转化; 更改, 改造, 改装. ②使改变信仰[意见、立场],使弃恶从善; 使转变; 使回心转意. ③【法】强占. ④【逻】转换, 换位; 【商】兑换,更换. ⑤【橄榄球】使触地得分. ～ *sugar into alcohol* 把糖变为酒精. ～ *notes into gold* 把纸币兑换为黄金. *～ed goods* 加工织物. *be [get] ～ed* 悔改. ～ *(sb.) to* 使(某人)改信(某教, 尤指改信基督教). *～ed cruiser* 改装巡洋舰. *～ed timber* 锯制材. — ['kɔnvə:t] *n.* 改宗者, 皈依者, 改变信仰者. *make a ～ of sb.* 使某人转变[改变]信仰.

con·vert·er [kən'və:tə] *n.* ①使转变[改变信仰]的人. ②改装者,改装品. ③【冶】炼钢炉, 吹风转炉;【电,无】换流器,变压器; 变频器;【自】变换器; 密码翻译[编制]机. ～ **pig** 转炉(用)生铁.

con·vert·i·bil·i·ty [kən,və:tə'biliti] *n.* ①可改变,可变换; 可兑换; 可转化性,可转变性.

con·vert·i·ble [kən'və:təbl] *a.* ①可转换的; 可转变的; 可改装的; 可兑换的. ②(汽车) 车篷可折起 [取掉] 的. — *n.* ①可改变的事物. ②敞篷车〔有活动折篷的汽车〕. ～ **husbandry**【农】轮作. ～ **note [paper]** 可兑换纸币[证券]. ～ **terms** 同义语,可代换用语. **-bly** *ad.*

con·vert·i·plane [kən'və:tiplein] *n.* 【空】垂直起落换向式飞机,平直两用飞机.

con·vert·ite ['kɔnvə,tait] *n.* 〔古〕= convert.

con·vex ['kɔn'veks] *a.* 中凸的, 凸圆的, 凸面的. — *n.* 凸状, 凸面, 凸圆体. ～ *glasses* 远视眼镜,老光眼镜. ～ **lens** 凸透镜. ～ **mirror** 凸面镜. **-ly** *ad.*

con·vex·i·ty [kɔn'veksiti] *n.* 凸度; 凸状; 凸面(体).

con·vex·o-con·cave [kɔn'veksəu'kɔnkeiv] *a.* 一面凸一面凹的, 凸凹(形)的.

con·vex·o-con·vex [kɔn'veksəu'kɔnveks] *a.* 双凸面的.

con·vex·o-plane [kɔn'veksəu'plein] *a.* 一面凸一面平的, 凸平形的.

con·vey [kən'vei] *vt.* ①输送; 搬运, 转运, 运输. ②传达, 传递; 传导; 传播; 通知, 通报; 表达(意义). ③【法】让与, 转让(财产等). ④〔古〕偷. ⑤〔废〕秘密带走. ～ *goods in a lorry* 用卡车运货. *Words fail to ～ our grateful feelings.* 我们的感激之情非言语所能表达. *Please ～ to him my best wishes.* 请向他转达我最良好的祝愿. **-able** *a.*

con·vey·ance [kən'veiəns] *n.* ①运输; 输送. ②运输用具(车船等), 输送带, 搬运器. ③【法】(不动产的)让与; 让与证据, 卖据. ～ *by land [water]* 陆路[水路]运输. *means of ～* 交通[运输]工具. *a push-plate ～* 无限连锁式传送工具(运煤用).

con·vey·anc·er [kən'veiənsə] *n.* ①运输者; 传达者. ②【法】不动产让与(证书)经办人.

con·vey·anc·ing [kən'veiənsiŋ] *n.* (律师的)财产转让业务; 让与证书制作(业); 不动产让与手续.

con·vey·er, con·vey·or [kən'veiə] *n.* ①运送者, 传达者; 传送器, 运送机. ②让与人. *a ～ belt* 传送带. *a green ～* 轮饲牧场. *a coal ～* 送煤机.

con·vict [kən'vikt] *vt.* ①证明…有罪, 宣告…有罪, 定…的罪. ②使知罪, 使认罪. *be ～ed of arson* 被判决为放火犯. ～ *(sb.) of (murder)* 判决 (某人) 有 (杀人) 罪. *a person ～ed of sin* 自知有罪的人. *～ed prisoner* 已定罪人. — ['kɔnvikt] *n.* ①罪犯. ②(长期服刑的) 囚犯. ③〔美俚〕马戏团的斑马. *ex-～* 有前科的罪犯, 惯犯. ～ **goods** 服劳役囚犯生产的物品. ～ **prison** 徒刑监狱. ～ **system** 徒刑制度; 流刑制度.

con·vic·tion [kən'vikʃən] *n.* ①有罪判决，定罪。②确信，坚信。③服罪，【神】悔罪。 ***be open to*** ～ 能够[愿意] 接受正当理由，愿意服理。 ***carry*** ～ (话，论点等)令人信服。 ***in the full*** ～ ***that*** 充分信服…。 ***listen with*** ～ (虚心)倾听。 ***under*** ～【宗】悔悟中。

con·vic·tive [kən'viktiv] *a.* 有说服力的；定罪的。 **-ly** *ad.*

con·vince [kən'vins] *vt.* ①使确信，说服，使承认。②使悔悟；使认错[罪]。 ～ *people by sound arguments* 以理服人。 ***be*** ～***d of [that]*** 确信，深知。 ***be fully*** ～***d*** 充分相信。 ～ ***(sb.) of [that]*** 使 (人) 承认 [信服]。 ～ ***oneself of*** 充分弄明白。

con·vin·ci·ble [kən'vinsəbl] *a.* 可说服的，可使信服的。 *a* ～ *person* 知情达理的人。

con·vinc·ing [kən'vinsiŋ] *a.* 使人信服的，有说服力的，令人心悦诚服的。 *a* ～ *argument* 有说服力的论点。 **-ly** *ad.* **-ness** *n.*

con·viv·i·al [kən'viviəl] *a.* ①宴会的，欢宴的；欢乐的，快活的。②爱(和人)吃喝玩乐的。 *a* ～ *meeting [gathering]* 联欢会，欢乐的宴会。 **-ist** *n.* 爱吃喝玩乐的人。 **-ly** *ad.*

con·viv·i·al·i·ty [kənˌvivi'æliti] *n.* ①宴乐；欢宴。②爱(和人)吃喝玩乐的性格。

con·vo·ca·tion [ˌkɔnvə'keiʃən] *n.* ①(会议的)召集；集会。②[美] (圣公会)主教区会议[管区]；(牛津大学等的)评议会；(加拿大某些大学的)学位授与典礼。 *to address a* ～ 寄发开会通知。

con·voke [kən'vəuk] *vt.* 召集(会议等)，召集…开会。 ～ *Parliament* 召开国会。

con·vo·lute ['kɔnvəljuːt] *a.* ①【动、植】包卷形的，回旋状的。②【医】迂曲的，蟠曲的。③迂迴的，盘旋形的。— *n.* 包旋体。— *vt., vi.* 盘旋，包卷。 **-d** *a.* = ①convolute。②复杂的，难解的。 (～ *convoluted horns* 回旋状的(羊)角。 ～ *arguments* 绕弯子的论证，难解的论点。 ★ 作形容词用时，多用 convoluted 而不常用 convolute)。

con·vo·lu·tion [ˌkɔnvə'ljuːʃən] *n.* ①回旋，卷旋，盘旋；旋圈，卷褶；涡流。②【动、植】包卷，旋绕；【解】回转(部)；脑回；【数】褶[卷]积；褶合式；【统】结合式。

con·volve [kən'vɔlv] *vi., vt.* 卷绕，缠绕。

con·vol·vu·lus [kən'vɔlvjuləs] *n.* *(pl.* ***-li*** [-lai], ～***es)*** 【植】旋花属植物[如旋花，牵牛花等]。

con·voy ['kɔnvɔi] *n.* ①(战时的) 护航队。②被护送者。③护送。 *a* ～ *of transport ships* 有护航的运输船队。 *under* ～ 在护航[护送]下。 *under the* ～ *of troops* 在军队护送下。— [kɔn'vɔi] *vt.* 护航，护送；[古]引导(宾客等)；伴送。 *a merchant ship* ～*ed by a destroyer.* 由驱逐舰护航的一艘商船。

con·vulse [kən'vʌls] *vt.* ①使(地等)震动；震撼[震动](全国等)。②[常用被动语态]使痉挛；使大笑不止。 ***be*** ～***d*** 惊厥；(小儿)惊风。 ～ ***sb. with laughter*** 令人捧腹，使人绝倒。 ***be*** ～***d with laughter*** 捧腹大笑。

con·vul·sion [kən'vʌlʃən] *n.* ①震动，激动；动乱；【地】激变，灾变。②【医】[常 *pl.*] 惊厥；搐搦；惊风。③[*pl.*] 捧腹大笑。 ～ ***of the whole kingdom*** [英] 全国鼎沸。 ***have*** ～***s*** 惊厥。 ***throw into*** ～***s*** 使惊厥；使捧腹大笑。

con·vul·sion·a·ry [kən'vʌlʃənəri] *a.* ①剧烈震动的；灾变性的；激动(性)的。②惊厥的。— *n.* 惊厥者。

con·vul·sive [kən'vʌlsiv] *a.* 痉挛性的；惊厥的；骤发的；震动性的。 *a* ～ *effort* 拼死努力。 ～ *laughter* 捧腹大笑。 ～ *rage* 震怒。 **-ly** *ad.* **-ness** *n.*

co·ny, co·ney ['kəuni] *n.* ①兔；兔皮。②(在《圣经》中提到的)蹄兔。③【动】狗鱼。④笨伯；受骗者。 **～-catcher** 骗子。

coo¹ [kuː] *vi., vt.* (鸽等)咕咕地叫；低声软语地谈(情话)。温柔亲切地说。 ～ *one's words* 轻轻地说话。 ***bill and*** ～ 亲热地抚爱[亲吻]。— *n.* 鸽叫声。

coo² [kuː] *int.* (伦敦话)哦！呀！[表示惊异]。

cooch [kuːtʃ] [美俚](色情的)扭肚舞。 ～ *dancer* 扭肚舞舞女。

coo·coo ['kuːkuː] *a.* [俚]狂乱的；愚蠢的，傻的 (= cuckoo)。

coo·ee, coo·ey ['kuːi(ː)] *n., int.* 喂！[澳洲本地人的招呼声]。— *vi.* 叫一声喂！

coo·er ['ku(ː)ə] *n.* 鸽；语言柔和而可爱的人，甜言蜜语的人。

cook [kuk] *vt.* ①烹调，煮，烧(食物)。②[口]虚报，窜改(帐目等)，捏造(报告等)。③[美俚]损坏，破坏。④[英俚](热得)使发昏，使筋疲力竭。⑤[俚]给…上电刑。 ～ *food* 做饭。 *be* ～*ed alive in the tropics* 在热带地方热得象活活被火烤似的。 ～ *accounts* 伪造帐目。— *vi.* ①(食物)在煮[烧]着。②做饭，做菜；当厨师。③[美口]发生。 *What's* ～*ing at the station?* 车站上出了什么事？ *The dinner is* ～*ing.* 晚餐正在做。 ～ ***off*** (火药包、炮弹等因过热而)走火。 ～ ***sb.'s goose*** [俚]破坏某人的计划，使某人彻底失败[完蛋]。 ～ ***up*** 捏造，炮制；[美]计划，图谋 (～ *up a report* 捏造报告)。 ～ ***well*** 容易煮 (*Eggs* ～ *well.* 鸡蛋容易煮熟)。 ***sb.'s goose is*** ～***ed*** 某人的计划[前途，名誉等]已完蛋。— *n.* ①厨子；厨娘。②(工业、技术上的)煮制过程。 ***a cold*** ～ [俚]做殡仪馆生意的人。 ***Too many*** ～***s spoil the broth.*** 厨子多了煮坏汤。 **～book** [美]①烹调全书，食谱(大全)。②详细说明书。 **～house** 厨房；船内厨房；露天厨房。 **～house yarns** 忽然流传起来的谣言。 **～-in** 烹饪讲座。 **～ off** 烹饪比赛。 **～out** 野餐郊游。 **～room** (= ～house)。 **～shop** 菜馆；饭店。 **～stove** [美] 烹调用火[电]炉。 **～top** ①炉灶口。②(山等的)平顶。

Cook(e) [kuk] *n.* 库克[姓氏]。

cooked [kukt] *a.* ①煮得…的。②(报告等) 捏造的。③[俚](热得)要死的。④(跑得人)筋疲力尽的。⑤[俚]喝醉了的。⑥【影】(胶片)露光过久的。

cook·er ['kukə] *n.* ①炊具，蒸煮器。②[口]菜果(适于做菜的果类)。③虚报帐目的人；造谣者，说谎者。 *a gas* ～ 煤气灶。 *a pressure* ～ 高压锅。

cook·er·y ['kukəri] *n.* ①烹调术。②[美]厨房。 **～-book** [英] = cookbook。

cook·ie ['kuki] *n.* ① [Scot.] 甜面包；[美](家常)小甜饼；饼干。②[俚]厨娘；厨师助手。③[口](对心爱的人的称呼)亲爱的。④[俚]精明能干的家伙；吸引人的年轻妇女。⑤[*pl.*] [俚] 吃到肚里的食物。 *a tough* ～ 硬汉子。 *shoot one's cookies* [美俚]呕吐。

cook·ing ['kukiŋ] *a.* 烹调用的(水果、锅、炉等)。— *n* 烹调(法)。

Cook Islands *n.* 库克群岛[南太平洋]。

cook·y ['kuki] *n.* = cookie.

cool [kuːl] *a.* ①凉，凉爽。②沉着的，冷静的，慎重的。③冷淡的，薄情的；不动感情的，冷酷的。④[口](价格)不夸大的，实价的；(数额)不打折扣的，整整。⑤【猎】(动物臭迹)淡薄的，些微的，一点点的。⑥(颜色)素净的，冷色的[指以蓝、绿光谱段为基调的]。⑦[美俚]极好的，绝妙的。⑧轻描淡写的，不作充分说明的。⑨冷藏着的；有冷藏设施的。⑩厚脸皮的，无礼的。⑬(音乐、绘画等)超然冷漠的，强调理性的。⑭未被放射性污染的。 *a* ～ *customer [card, fish, hand]* (不动感情，不怕羞的)厚皮脸[指男人]。 *a* ～ *head* 头脑冷静(的人)。 *a* ～ *matting* 凉爽的席子。 *a* ～ *thousand pounds* 整整一千镑。 *a real* ～ *comic* 一个十分出色的喜剧演员。 ～ *chamber* 冷藏室。 ～ *cheek* 厚脸皮。 ～ *frock* 单薄的外衣。 ～ *tankard* 冷饮。 ～ ***as a cucumber*** 冷静沉着。 ***get*** ～ 冷了；凉了。 ***keep*** ～ 冷(藏)着；乘凉；沉住气。 ***keep*** ～***!*** 别慌。 ***leave sb.*** ～ 不能引起某人兴趣。 ***play it*** ～ [美俚] 压住感情，冷静处理[对待]。 ***remain*** ～ 保持冷静，很沉着。— *vt.* ①使冷却，冷一冷，冰一冰(酒)。②使消除放射性，使减少放射性。③使镇定，使冷静，止(怒)。— *vi.* ①凉了，冷了；变冷却。②(怒气)平息；变冷静，沉着。 ～ ***down*** 冷起来,凉了;冷却;冷静下来. ～ ***it*** 〔俚〕沉着;轻松冷静地〔从容不迫地〕做. ～ ***off*** 〔口〕沉着,变冷静,平静下来. ***～ one's coppers*** 喝解醉饮料. ～ ***one's heels*** 久等. — *n.* ①冷气;凉爽的空气;凉快的地方〔时间、东西等〕. ②平静,冷静,镇定. ③〔美〕一种较保守的爵士音乐. ***in the ～ (of the evening)*** (晚)凉时候. **-ly** *ad.* **-ness** *n.*

cool·ant [ˈkuːlənt] *n.* 【机】冷却剂;(减热的)润滑剂.

cool·er [ˈkuːlə] *n.* ①冷却器;冰箱. ②冷却剂;冷饮,清凉饮料. ③〔美俚〕监狱;单人监房;〔军俚〕兵营仓库. ***put in the ～*** 〔口〕搁置起来,搁到一边.

cool-head·ed [ˈkuːlˈhedid] *a.* 头脑冷静的,沉着的.

coo·li·bah [ˈkuːlibə] *n.* 澳洲橡胶树.

Coo·lidge [ˈkuːlidʒ] *n.* ①库利奇〔姓氏〕. ② **Calvin ～** 卡尔文·库利奇〔1872—1933, 美国第三十任总统,任期为1923—1929〕.

coo·lie, coo·ly[ˈkuːli]*n.* 苦力(特指东方的廉价劳动力).

cool·ing [ˈkuːliŋ] *n., a.* 冷却(的). ～ **cup** 冷却杯. ～ **down** 【体】准备活动. ～ **drink** 冷饮. ～ **fins** 【机】散热片. ～ **room** 冷却室. ～**-off** *a.* 可使头脑冷静的,缓和情绪的 ***(～-off period*** 发生劳资纠纷时的缓和期〔在此期间不罢工,先行协商〕).

cool·ish [ˈkuːliʃ] *a.* 微冷的;觉得冷的,有冷意的.

cool·ly[1] [ˈkuːlli] *ad.* 冷,沉着,冷静;冷淡;厚着脸皮.

cool·ly[2] [ˈkuːli] *n.* = coulee.

coolth [kuːlθ] *n.* 〔谑〕= coolness.

coom [kuːm] *n.* 煤灰,煤烟;〔Scot.〕煤;〔方〕锯屑.

coomb(e) [kuːm, kəum] *n.* 深谷,小山沟;(三面皆山的)无川狭谷;海边小溪崖.

coon [kuːn] *n.* ①【美动】浣熊(= racoon). ②〔口〕猾头,机灵鬼. ③〔美俚〕黑人〔对黑人的蔑称〕. ***an old ～*** 老奸巨猾的人. ***a ～'s age*** 很长一段时日,好多年. ～ ***skinners*** 〔美〕乡下佬. ***go the whole ～*** 〔美〕彻底干. ***(a) gone ～*** 没希望的人,不可救药的家伙. ***hunt [skin] the same old ～*** 〔美俚〕老是干同一工作. ***tree the ～*** 〔美口〕追究问题的原因;穷追. ～ **cat** 【动】蓬尾浣熊 (= cacomistle). ～**skin** *n., a.* 浣熊皮(制的). ～ **songs** (美国南部感伤的)黑人歌曲.

coon·can [ˈkuːnkæn] *n.* 碰对牌戏〔一种用两副纸牌玩的牌戏〕.

coon·tie [ˈkuːnti] *n.* 【植】全绿叶泽米.

coon·y [ˈkuːni] *a.* (浣熊一样)狡猾的,机灵的.

coop [kuːp] *n.* (养鸡兔等的)笼〔栏,小舍〕;〔英〕捕鱼笼;牢狱. ***fly the ～*** 〔美俚〕逃走. — *vt.* ①把(家禽)关进笼子〔棚〕. ②把…关起来 ***(in; up)***. — *vi.* 〔美俚〕(值夜班警察)在警车内打瞌睡.

co-op [ˈkəuɔp] 〔口〕= co-operative store [society].

co-op. = cooperative.

Coop·er [ˈkuːpə] *n.* 库珀〔姓氏〕.

coop·er [ˈkuːpə] *n.* ①桶匠. ②(装桶贩卖的)酒商. ③(由葡萄酒和烈啤酒合成的)混合黑啤酒. ④(北海上的)小贩船. ***dry [wet] ～*** 干品用〔液体用〕桶类制造者. ***white ～*** (普通)桶匠. — *vt.* ①修理(桶类). ②把…装入桶内. ③〔口〕修饰外表 ***(up)***. — *vi.* 做桶匠.

coop·er·age [ˈkuːpəridʒ] *n.* 木桶业;桶匠工作;桶匠工钱;桶铺.

co-op·er·ant [kəuˈɔpərənt] *a.* 合作的.

co-op·er·ate [kəuˈɔpəreit] *vi.* 合作;协作;互助. ～ ***with (sb.) for (a purpose)*** 为(某目的)和(某人)合作. ***～ with (sb.) in (a work)*** 和(某人)合作(某事).

co·op·er·a·tion [kəuˌɔpəˈreiʃən] *n.* 合作;协作;互助. *a consumers' [consumptive] ～* 消费合作. *a producers' [productive] ～* 生产合作. ***in ～ with*** 和…合作〔协作,共同〕.

co·op·er·a·tive [kəuˈɔpərətiv] *a.* ①合作的,协作的,共同的. ②合作社的. ③〔美〕(大学文科)有关〔包含〕各种实习活动的. *a ～ society* 合作社. *a ～ store* 合作商店. — *n.* 合作社. **-ly** *ad.* **-ness** *n.*

co·op·er·a·tor [kəuˈɔpəreitə] *n.* 合作〔协作〕者;合作社社员.

coop·er·y [ˈkuːpəri] *n.* 箍桶活;桶店;桶器.

co·opt [kəuˈɔpt] *vt.* ①(原有成员)增选(新成员). ②选用,任命. ③吸取,罗致. **-ion, -a·tion** *n.* **-a·tive** *a.*

co·or·di·nal [kəuˈɔːdinl] *a.* 【植、动】同目〔属〕的.

co·or·di·nate [kəuˈɔːdinit] *a.* ①同等的,同位的;协调的,配合的;【语法】并列的. ②【数】座标的. ③(图书、资料编目)交叉索引查阅法的. — *n.* ①同等者,同等物;同位. ②〔*pl.*〕【数】座标;(图书、资料编目的)交叉索引. — [kəuˈɔːdineit] *vt.* 使成同等;使成同位;使配合;使(各部分)动作协调,调整. ～ ***with each other*** 互相策应〔配合〕. ～ **bond [link]** 【化】配价键. ～ **clause** 【语法】并列分句. ～ **valence** 【化】配位价. ～ **paper** 座标纸. ～ **system** 座标系.

co·or·di·na·tion [kəuˌɔːdiˈneiʃən] *n.* 同等,同位,对等;同等关系;调整;配合;协作,协调;【生理】(器官等的)共同调济,协调(一致);【物,化】配位;【语法】并列(关系) *the close ～ between two partners* 两个合伙人之间的紧密配合.

co·or·di·na·tive [kəuˈɔːdinətiv] *a.* (使)同等的,同位的;协调的;配合的;整合的. 【语法】并列的.

co·or·di·na·tor [kəuˈɔːdineitə] *n.* ①同等的人;同等物;配合者〔物〕;整合物;【生理】共同调济器(官). ②协调人. ③【语法】并列连接词.

coot [kuːt] *n.* ①【鸟】水鸭,大鹬;〔美〕黑鸭. ②〔俚、方,美〕笨人,傻瓜. ***(as) bald as a ～*** 头发光秃. ***(as) stupid as a ～*** 笨拙.

coot·ie [ˈkuːti] *n.* 〔美军俚〕虱子.

co-own·er [kəuˈəunə] *n.* 【法】共有人.

Cop. = ① Copenhagen. ② Copernican. ③ Coptic.

cop[1] [kɔp] *n.* ①纺锤状线团,管纱;纡子. ②〔英方〕(山)顶;(鸟)冠毛.

cop[2] [kɔp] *n.* 〔俚〕警察. *a plain clothes ～* 便衣警察. ～ **shop** 〔口〕警察局;派出所.

cop[3] [kɔp] *vt.* 〔俚〕①捕捉,逮捕(犯人). ②取胜,赢得. ③偷. ～ ***a plea*** 自首,招认(希望减轻刑罚). ～ ***big*** 〔美俚〕胜利,赢得;巧中. ～ ***hours*** 〔美俚〕优胜,获胜. ～ ***it*** 〔学俚〕挨骂,遭罚;被杀死. ～ ***out*** 〔美俚〕①自首(并告发同犯). ②反悔,失信,躲赖;逃避(义务);放弃,妥协;退出;离开. ～ ***the curtain*** 【美剧】谢幕. — *n.* 〔俚〕抓获,捕捉. ***a fair ～*** 不小的胜利. ***no ～, not much ～*** 没有什么价值〔用处〕. ～**-out** *n.* ①逃路. ②躲避. ③逃跑者.

co·pa·cet·ic [ˌkəupəˈsetik] *a.* 〔美俚〕极好的;令人十分满意的;完全正确的.

co·pai·ba, co·pai·va [kəuˈpaibə, -və] *n.* 【医】苦配巴香脂;苦配巴香胶.

co·pal [ˈkəupəl] *n.* 硬树脂;柯巴脂.

co·palm [ˈkəuˌpɑːm] *n.* ①【植】香枫. ②香枫脂膏.

co·par·ce·nar·y [ˌkəuˈpɑːsinəri] *n.* 【法】共同继承(的土地);共同所有(的土地). — *a.* 共同所有〔继承〕的.

co·parce·ner [ˈkəuˈpɑːsinə] (土地的)共同继承人.

co·part·ner [ˈkəuˈpɑːtnə] *n.* 合作者;(有平等权利的)合伙人. **-ship** *n.* 合作;损益分担;合伙人(身份).

co·pa·set·ic [ˌkəupəˈsetik] *a.* = copacetic.

cope[1] [kəup] *vi.* ①竞争,抗衡,对抗 *(with)*. ②对付,应付;克服,善处(困难等) *(with)*. ③【古】接触 *(with)*. *He was scarcely able to ～ with the situation.* 他几乎不知道如何去应付这个局面. — *vt.* ①〔英口〕应付. ②〔废〕遇见,接触.

cope[2] [kəup] *n.* ①(教士等举行宗教仪式等时穿的)斗篷式长袍,罩袍;(剑桥大学神学博士举行仪式时穿的)肩衣. ②笼罩物;夜幕;苍穹. ③铸钟模型顶部;【建】顶盖,墙帽. *under the ～ of night* 在夜幕的遮盖下. ～ ***in steel beam*** 【建】削梁. ***under the ～ of heaven*** 普天之下. — *vt.* ①给…穿上教士罩袍. ②加盖于,覆盖,给…砌上顶盖[墙帽]. ③【铸】修型 *walls ~d with broken bits of china* 顶部覆盖有碎瓷片的墙. — *vi.* 突出如墙帽 *(over)*.

co·peck [ˈkəupek] *n.* 戈比〔旧俄及苏联货币,值1/100卢布〕;〔美俚〕一元银币.

Co·pen·hag·en [ˌkəupənˈheigən] *n.* 哥本哈根〔丹麦首都〕. **-i·an** *n.* 哥本哈根人.

co·pe·pod [ˈkəupiˌpɔd] *n.*【动】桡脚亚纲的动物.

Co·pep·o·da [kəuˈpepədə] *n.* 〔*pl.*〕【动】桡脚亚纲.

cop·er¹ [ˈkəupə] *n.* 〔英方〕马贩子.

cop·er² [ˈkəupə] *n.* (北海的)烟酒贩卖船.

Co·per·ni·can [kəuˈpəːnikən] *a.* 哥白尼(学说)的. ~ **theory** 太阳中心说,地动说.

Co·per·ni·cus [kəuˈpəːnikəs], **Nicolaus** 哥白尼〔1473—1543,波兰天文学家〕.

co·pe·set·ic [ˌkəupəˈsetik] *a.* = copacetic.

cope·stone [ˈkəupstəun] *n.* ①墙帽,盖顶石. ②盖面活;收尾工作,尾活. ***put the ~ on sb.'s embarrassment*** 使人在窘迫时更加窘迫.

cop·i·er [ˈkɔpiə] *n.* ①誊写[复写]员;抄录者. ②仿效者;剽窃者. ③誊写笔,复印机.

co·pi·lot [ˈkəupailət] *n.*【空】副驾驶员;自动驾驶仪.

cop·ing [ˈkəupiŋ] *n.* (墙等的)顶盖. ~ **saw** 钢丝锯. **~-stone** *n.* = copestone.

co·pi·ous [ˈkəupjəs] *a.* ①丰富的;大量的. ②冗长的. *a ~ harvest* 丰收. *~ material* 丰富的材料. *~ notes* 详注. *a ~ speaker* 多言者. *a ~ style* 冗长的文体. *~ tears* 大量的眼泪. *a ~ vocabulary* 丰富的词汇. *a ~ writer* 多产作家. **-ly** *ad.* **-ness** *n.*

co·pla·nar [kəuˈpleinə] *a.*【数】共面的.

Cop·land [ˈkɔplənd, ˈkəuplənd] *n.* 科普兰〔姓氏〕.

co·pol·y·mer [kəuˈpɔlimə] *n.*【化】共聚物.

co·pol·y·mer·ize [kəuˈpɔliməraiz] *vt., vi.*【化】(使)异分子聚合.

co·pol·y·mer·i·za·tion [kəuˌpɔliməraiˈzeiʃən] *n.*【化】共聚[聚合](作用).

cop·per¹ [ˈkɔpə] *n.* ①铜;紫铜. ②铜币,铜钱;〔*pl.*〕零钱. ③铜器;铜罐,铜壶,铜锅;铜管;铜制品. ④(紫)铜色. ⑤〔*pl.*〕〔俚〕喉咙. ~ *nitrate* 硝酸铜. *a few ~s* 几枚铜币. ***cool [clear] ones ~*** 喝点解酒饮料润润喉(见 cool 条). ***have hot ~s*** 〔俚〕喝大量酒后觉得喉咙干燥发烧. — *a.* ①铜(制)的. ②(紫)铜色的. ~ *pipe* 铜管. ~ *plate [sheet]* 铜板. —*vt.* 用铜板[铜皮]盖[包]. ~ **beech**【植】铜红山毛榉. ~ **bit** 铜焊夹. **~bottom** *vt.* 用铜板包(船底等). **~-bottomed** *a.* 铜板包底的(船);航海经久的,结实的. ~ **captain**〔英〕假船长,冒充的大人物. ~ **facing** 镀铜. **~-head**【动】铜斑蛇;〔C-〕【美史】南北战争时同情南方的北方人. ~ **hearted** *a.*〔美〕说谎的,靠不住的. ~ **Indian** (北美)印第安人. **~nose** (红鼻子)酒鬼. **~plate** ①*n.* 铜板;铜版(印刷) (*write like ~ plate* 写得非常工整). ②*a.* 用铜板雕刻的;用铜版印刷的;(印刷似地)美丽的(字体). **~skin** *n.* = redskin. **~smith** 铜匠;铜器制造人. **C- State**〔美〕威斯康星 (**Wisconsin**) 州的别号. **~sulphate [vitriol]** 胆矾,硫酸铜. ~ **sulphide** 硫化铜. **~top**〔俚〕红毛人. ~ **wire** 铜丝. **~-worm** 蛀船虫;衣裳蛀虫;癣虫. **-ish** [ˈkɔpəriʃ] *a.* 有点象[含]铜的. **-ize** [ˈkɔpəraiz] *vt.* 镀铜于…;用铜处理.

cop·per² [ˈkɔpə] *n.* 〔英俚〕警察.

cop·per·as [ˈkɔpərəs] *n.*【化】(水)绿矾;皂矾;呈天然结晶状态的硫酸亚铁.

Cop·per·belt [ˈkɔpəbelt] *n.* 铜带省〔赞比亚省名〕.

Cop·per·field [ˈkɔpəfiːld] *n.* 科波菲尔〔姓氏〕.

cop·per·y [ˈkɔpəri] *a.* 含铜的;铜一样的;铜制的,铜质的;(紫)铜色的.

cop·pice [ˈkɔpis] *n.* 〔英〕矮林,小树林,灌木林;萌生林,杂木林 (= ~-wood).

copr. = copyright.

cop·ra [ˈkɔprə] *n.* 椰肉干〔可榨油〕.

co·precipitate [ˌkəupriˈsipiteit] *vt., vi.* (使)一同沉淀.

copr(o)- *comb. f.* 粪: *coprolite*.

cop·ro·dae·um [ˌkɔprəˈdiːəm] *n.*【动】粪道.

cop·ro·lite [ˈkɔprəlait] *n.*【地】粪化石.

cop·rol·o·gy [kɔˈprɔlədʒi] *n.* ①【医】粪便学. ②污物;猥亵文字[图画]. **-log·i·cal** *a.*

co·p·roph·a·gous [kɔˈprɔfəgəs] *a.*【动】(甲虫等)吃粪的.

cop·ro·phil·i·a [ˌkɔprəˈfiliə] *n.*【心医】嗜粪癖.

copse [kɔps] *n.* = coppice.

copse·wood [ˈkɔpswud] *n.* ① = copse. ②(杂木林下的)矮树丛.

Copt [kɔpt] *n.* ①哥普特人〔古埃及原住民的后裔〕,埃及本地人. ②【宗】哥普特教会〔埃及的基督教派〕.

cop·ter [ˈkɔptə] *n.* 〔美〕helicopter (直升飞机)的缩略词.

Cop·tic [ˈkɔptik] *a.* ①哥普特人[语]的. ②【宗】哥普特教会的. — *n.* 哥普特语[人].

cop·tis [ˈkɔptis] *n.*【植】黄连;〔C-〕黄连属.

cop·u·la [ˈkɔpjulə] *n.* (*pl.* *~s, -lae* [-liː]) ①【逻,语法】系词〔be, seem, appear 等〕. ②【解】联桁,结合肌. ③【法】交媾;【生】交合. ④介体,介沟. **-r** *a.* 连系(动词)的.

cop·u·late [ˈkɔpjuleit] *vi.* ①性交,交配,交尾. ②结合;连接,连系. — *a.* 连接的,配合的.

cop·u·la·tion [ˌkɔpjuˈleiʃən] *n.* ①性交,交配,交尾. ②接合,结合,连系.

cop·u·la·tive [ˈkɔpjulətiv] *a.* ①结合的. ②交配的. ③【语法】系词的. — *n.*【语法】连词,系词〔*and* 等〕.

cop·u·la·to·ry [ˈkɔpjulətəri] *a.* 连接的;交配的.

cop·y [ˈkɔpi] *n.* ①抄本,缮本,誊本,摹本,复制品,【影】拷贝;【法】副本 (*opp.* script). ②(书的)一部,一册,(报纸的)一份. ③〔不用不定冠词及 *pl.*〕(印刷的)原稿;新闻材料. ④〔罕〕范本,习字帖 (= copybook);〔英口〕(学校的)作文(习题). *duplicate copies* 正副两本. *a clean [fair] ~* 誊清的稿子[文件];清样. *a foul [rough] ~* 底稿,草稿. *make a rough ~ of* 起草. *~ of verses* 短诗;习作诗. ***hold ~*** 做校对员的助手. ***keep a ~ of*** 留副本. ***make good ~*** 成为(报纸等的)好材料. ***paint [write] from a ~*** 临画[临帖]. ***take a ~*** 复写. — *vt., vi.* ①抄,誊,临(帖),模写,复写. ②模仿,仿效. ③〔英学俚〕抄袭(别人试卷). *~ a great man* 模仿伟人. *~ into a notebook* 做笔记. *~ fair* 誊清. *~ out a document* 全文抄下一份文件. *~ from (the) life* 写生. **~book** 习字帖;〔美〕复写簿 (*blot one's ~book* 做了损害自己名誉的事情. *~books maxims [morality]* 陈腐浅薄的格言[教训]). ~ **boy** 〔美〕(递送原稿、印样等的)送稿生. **~cat** ①*n.* 盲目模仿者. ②*vt.* 盲目模仿. ~ **chief** 〔美〕(报馆的)编辑主任,主编. **~cutter** (剪贴新闻稿的)报馆排版工人. ~ **desk** (报馆内马蹄形的)编辑桌;〔转义〕编辑部. ~ **editor** 〔美〕报馆编辑. **~graph** 油印机;油印图. **~hold** *n., a.*【英法】誊本保有权;登录不动产保有权. **~holder** ①【英法】誊本保有权者. ②校对助手. ③(打字机的)原稿压. **~money** 稿费;版税. **~reader** 〔美〕(报馆、出版社的)编辑. **~right** ①*n.* 版权,著作权 (*~right reserved* 版权所有). ②*a.* 版权的,著作权的. ③*vt.* 为(书等)取得版权 (*~righted* 版权所有. *~right a book* 为一本书取得版权). **~writer** 撰稿人〔尤指写广告文字者〕.

cop·y·ing [ˈkɔpiiŋ] *n., a.* 复写(的),誊写(的). ~ **ink** 复写墨(水). ~ **paper** 复写纸. ~ **pencil** 字迹很难擦去的铅笔. ~ **press** 拷贝机. ~ **ribbon** (打字机的)墨带,色带.

cop·y·ist [ˈkɔpiist] *n.* 誊写者,抄写员;模仿者;剽窃者.

coq au vin [kɔk əu ˈvæn] 〔F.〕酒烹嫩炸鸡.
coque [kɔk] *n.* 装饰女帽的小丝带圈[羽毛圈].
coque·li·cot [ˈkəuklikəu] *n.* ①【植】虞美人草. ②鲜艳的橙红色.
co·quet [kəuˈket] *vi.* ①(女子)卖弄风情,卖俏;闹着玩儿〔指轻佻无诚意的调情〕. ②玩弄;轻浮对待,玩忽. ~ *with (a man)* 玩弄(男子). ~ *with (an affair)* 玩忽(职务). — *n.* = coquette.
co·quet·ry [ˈkəukitri] *n.* ①(女子的)卖弄风情,卖俏,撒娇. ②娇态,媚态,妖娆. ③玩弄.
co·quette [kəuˈket] *n.* ①(轻佻的)卖弄风情的女子. ②蜂鸟. — *vi.* = coquet.
co·quet·tish [kəuˈketiʃ] *a.* 卖弄风情的,卖俏的;轻佻的;妖娆的. **-ly** *ad.* **-ness** *n.*
co·quille [kəuˈkiːl; F.kɔkij] *n.* 〔F.〕①用贝壳(状容器)盛的菜. ②贝壳状容器.
co·qui·na [kəˈkiːnə] *n.* 【矿】(可供筑路用的)(介)壳灰岩,贝壳岩.
co·qui·to (palm) [kəuˈkiːtəu] *n.* 【植】智利棕榈〔树液和壳果可供食用〕.
Cor. = ① Corinthians. ② Coroner.
cor. = corner; cornet; corrected; correction; correlative; correspondent; corresponding.
cor- *pref.* = com-.
Cor·a [ˈkɔːrə] *n.* 科拉〔女子名〕.
cor·a·ci·i·form [ˌkɔːriˈsaiəfɔːm] *a.* 【动】佛法僧目的〔鱼狗,犀鸟等鸟〕.
cor·a·cle [ˈkɔrəkl] *n.* (用柳条扎成骨架并覆以防水布的)柳条艇.
coraco- *comb. f.* 表示"喙突";"喙".
cor·a·coid [ˈkɔːrəkɔid, ˈkɔr-] *a.* 【解】喙骨的. — *n.* 【解】喙骨;喙突.
cor·al [ˈkɔrəl] *n.* ①珊瑚;珊瑚虫;珊瑚工艺品,珊瑚玩具. ②珊瑚色. ③龙虾卵. — *a.* 珊瑚的;珊瑚色的. ~ *island* 珊瑚岛. ~ **polyp** 珊瑚虫. ~ **rag** 珊瑚石灰岩. ~ **reef** 珊瑚礁. **C- Sea** (大洋洲东北的)珊瑚海.
cor·al·bells [ˈkɔːrəlˌbelz] *n.* *(pl.* ~ 【植】珊瑚钟 *(Heuchera sanguinea)*.
cor·al·ber·ry [ˈkɔːrəlˌberi] *n.* 【植】小花雪果 *(Symphoricarpos orbiculatus.)*
coralli- *comb. f.* 表示"珊瑚";"珊瑚形状".
cor·al·line [ˈkɔrəlain] *a.* 珊瑚的;珊瑚状的;珊瑚色的;生产珊瑚的. — *n.* 【动】珊瑚(虫);珊瑚状动物,蓟苔虫;珊瑚状构造;【植】珊瑚藻. ~ **crag** 山灰岩. ~ **ware** 珊瑚色陶器.
cor·al·lite [ˈkɔrəlait] *n.* ①【地】珊瑚单体;珊瑚石. ②珊瑚色大理石.
cor·al·loid [ˈkɔrəlɔid] *a.* 珊瑚状的.
Cor·al·root [ˈkɔːrəlruːt, -rut] *n.* 【植】珊瑚兰属 *(Corallorhiza)*.
co·ram [ˈkɔːrəm] *prep.* 〔L.〕在…的面前. ~ **judice** [-ˈdʒuːdisi] 在法官面前. ~**populo** [-ˈpɔpjuləu] 在民众面前,公然.
Co·ran [kɔ(ː)ˈraːn] *n.* = Koran.
cor an·glais [ˈkɔːr ˈɔŋˌglei] *n.* 〔F.〕= English horn.
co·ran·to [kəˈræntəu] *n.* 库兰特舞;库兰特舞曲 (= courante①).
cor·beil [ˈkɔːbel] *n.* 【建】花篮饰;【筑成】小堡篮.
cor·bel [ˈkɔːbəl] *n.* 【建】翅托. — *vt.* 用翅托支承,给…砌上翅托. — *vi.* 砌翅托. ~ **arch** 突拱. ~ **course** 突腰线. ~ **piece** 挑出块. ~*-steps* 挑出踏步,马头墙. ~ **table** 挑檐.
cor·bic·u·la [kɔːˈbikjulə] *n.* 【动】蚬.
cor·bie [ˈkɔːbi] *n.* 〔Scot.〕大鸦. ~ **steps** = corbel-steps.
cor·cho·rus [ˈkɔːkəurʌs] *n.* 【植】黄麻.
cord [kɔːd] *n.* ①绳子,索子;弦;【电】软线,塞绳. ②〔常 *pl.*〕束缚. ③【纺】灯芯绒;布上凸起的楞条;棱凸纹;〔*pl.*〕〔口〕灯芯绒裤. ④【解】索状组织,韧带,神经. ⑤层积〔柴薪体积单位,合 8×4×4 立方英尺〕. *the spinal* ~ 脊髓. *the vocal* ~*s* 声带. ~ *of discipline* 纪律的束缚. *the silver* ~ 生命. — *vt.* 用索子捆[绑、扎];堆积(柴薪). ~ **adjuster** 【电】磁葫芦.
cord·age [ˈkɔːdidʒ] *n.* ①绳索,(船的)索具. ②(柴薪的)层积数量.
cor·date [ˈkɔːdeit] *a.* 【植】心脏形的.
cord·ed [ˈkɔːdid] *a.* ①用绳索捆扎的; ②(柴草)按层积堆积的. ③绳制的. ④起棱纹的. ⑤(肌肉)紧张的.
cor·delle [kɔːˈdel] *n.* 〔美〕纤绳. — *vt.* 用纤拉(船).
cor·dial [ˈkɔːdjəl] *a.* ①真心诚意的,恳挚的,热诚的. ②提神的,强心的. *a* ~ *smile* 由心里发出的微笑. *a* ~ *welcome* 热诚的欢迎. *a* ~ *meeting* 一次亲切的会见. ~ *medicine* 强心剂,补药. — *n.* ①爽心之物. ②【医】补药,强心药,兴奋剂. ③甘露酒,浸果酒. **-ly** *ad.* 诚心诚意地;恳挚地 (~*ly yours* = yours ~ly 〔美〕谨上〔信尾语〕). **-ness** *n.*
cor·di·al·i·ty [ˌkɔːdiˈæliti] *n.* 诚实;恳挚,热诚. *hate [love] with great* ~ 痛恨[深爱].
cor·di·er·ite [ˈkɔːdiərait] *n.* 【矿】堇青石.
cord·i·form [ˈkɔːdifɔːm] *a.* 心脏形的.
cor·dil·le·ra [kɔːdiˈljeərə] *n.* 〔Sp.〕山脉. **-ran** *a.*
cord·ing [ˈkɔːdiŋ] *n.* ①绳索. ②棱纹[楞条]织物〔如灯芯绒〕;【纺】吊综工作.
cord·ite [ˈkɔːdait] *n.* 无烟线状火药,硝棉甘油石油脂火药.
cord·less [ˈkɔːdlis] *a.* ①无绳的. ②不用电线的;可用电池供电的. *a* ~ *electric shaver* 干电池剃刀.
Cór·do·ba [ˈkɔːdəuvə] *n.* ①科尔多瓦〔阿根廷城市〕. ②科尔多瓦〔西班牙城市〕.
cor·do·ba [ˈkɔːdəbə] *n.* 科多瓦〔尼加拉瓜货币单位〕.
cor·don [ˈkɔːdən] *n.* ①【筑城】(堡垒外濠的)壁顶冠石;【建】带饰. ②【军】哨兵线;警戒线,封锁线;防疫隔离线. ③饰带,绶章;衣带. ④【园艺】单干形. *a sanitary* ~ 防疫线. ~ *of police* (警察站成一线形成的)警戒线. *post [place, draw] a* ~ 佈设警戒线. ~ **bleu** [kɔːdõbləː] ①(法国 Bourbon 王朝时最高勋位的)蓝绶章. ②名流;〔谑〕第一流厨师. ~ ***sanitaire*** [kɔːdõsaniteːr] 〔F.〕①防疫钱. ②(国家之间的)封锁线. — *vt.* 佈设警戒线,封锁交通.
cor·do·va [ˈkɔːdəvə] = cordoba.
Cor·do·van [ˈkɔːdəvən] *a.* (西班牙)科尔多瓦城的. — *n.* ①科尔多瓦人. ②〔c-〕科尔多瓦皮革.
cor·du·roy [ˈkɔːdərɔi] *n.* ①灯芯绒;〔*pl.*〕灯芯绒的衣服[裤子]. ②〔美〕铺木路 (= ~ road). — *a.* ①用灯芯绒做的. ②(路)用木头铺成的. — *vt.*〔美〕铺筑木路于;用木排修(路).
cord·wain·er [ˈkɔːdweinə] *n.* ①〔古〕科尔多瓦皮制造工人. ②鞋匠.
cord·wood [kɔːdwud] *n.* (堆成 128 立方英尺出售的)层积柴堆.
CORE = Congress of Racial Equality〔美〕争取种族平等大会.
core [kɔː, kɔə] *n.* ①果心. ②(事物、问题等的)中心,核心;精髓. ③(地球的)地核;【地】岩心;【铸】型心;【建】衬心;【电】(线)心,芯线,(计算机的)磁心;(原子反应堆的)堆芯,活性区;(燃料元件)芯体. ④(羊内脏中的)肿瘤. ⑤〔美〕(各专业学生共修的)基础课. ***throw away the apple because of the*** ~ 因噎废食. ***to the*** ~ 到心,彻底 (*rotten to the* ~ 透心腐烂;坏入骨髓,糟糕透顶. *English to the* ~ 道地的英国人). — *vt.* 挖去…的果心. ~ **city** (大都市的)中心城市. ~ **loss** 【电】铁心损失. ~ **memory [storage]** (计算机的)磁心贮存器. ~ **tube** (插入大堆物质抽取样品的)取样器. ~ **wall** 隔水墙.
Co·re·a(n) [kɔːˈriən] *a., n.* = Korea(n.)
co·re·la·tion [ˌkəuriˈleiʃən] *n.* 〔英〕= correlation.

co·re·li·gion·ist [ˈkəuriˈlidʒənist] *n.* 同宗教[教派]的人.
cor·e·op·sis [ˌkɔriˈɔpsis] *n.* ①【植】金鸡菊属植物;〔C-〕金鸡菊属. ②波斯菊.
cor·er [ˈkɔːrə] *n.* (水果的)去心器;岩心钻取器.
co·re·spond·ent [ˈkəurisˌpɔndənt] *n.*【法】(离婚诉讼中的)共同被告〔指私通者双方〕.
corf [kɔːf] *n.* 〔英〕①运煤[矿]小车;煤炭箩. ②鱼笼.
cor·gi [ˈkɔːgi] *n.* ①(威尔斯产脚短身长的)狗. ②〔俚〕微型汽车.
cor·i·a·ceous [ˌkɔriˈeiʃəs] *a.* 皮革制的;皮革一样(牢)的.
cor·i·an·der [ˌkɔriˈændə] *n.* ①【植】芫荽,胡荽,香菜;芫荽[胡荽]子. ②〔卑〕钱.
Cor·inth [ˈkɔrinθ] *n.* 科[考]林斯〔希腊南部港口城市,《新约》中译本作哥林多〕.
Co·rin·thi·an [kəˈrinθiən] *a.* ①科林斯(人)的;【建】(古希腊)科林斯(式)的 〔尤指带有叶形饰钟状柱顶的建筑〕. ②古雅的. ③奢侈的;〔古〕放荡的. — *n.* ①科林斯人〔《新约》旧译作哥林多人〕. ②耽于奢华生活的人;富有的享乐者;富有的业余运动爱好者〔尤指游艇运动爱好者〕. ~ **order**【建】科林多柱型.
Cor·in·to [kəuˈrintəu] *n.* 科林托〔尼加拉瓜港市〕.
Cor·i·o·lis force [ˌkɔːriˈəulis] 地球自转偏向力〔得名于法国数学家科里奥利〕.
co·ri·um [ˈkɔːriəm] *n.* *(pl.* **-ria** [-riə]*)* ①【解】真皮. ②革片;(古罗马的)皮铠.
Cork [kɔːk] *n.* 科克〔爱尔兰共和国港市〕.
cork [kɔːk] *n.* ①软木;木栓;软木塞,塞子;(钓鱼用)软木浮子. ②【植】外皮. ③〔美俚〕落第. *burnt* ~ (演员化妆用的)软木炭. ~ *jacket* 软木救生衣. ~ *oak* 栓皮槠. **like a** ~ 精神活泼地;马上恢复元气. — *vt.* ①用软木塞塞紧. ②抑制,制止,压制(感情)〔常与 *up* 连用〕. ③(滑稽歌剧化妆中)用软木炭把脸涂(黑). — *a.* 用软木制的. ~ **cambium**【植】木栓形成层. ~ **oak**, ~ **tree**【植】栓皮槠. ~ **opera** 〔美俚〕演员把脸涂黑的滑稽歌剧.
cork·age [ˈkɔːkidʒ] *n.* 拔去塞子,塞上塞子;(在餐馆中喝自备的酒所付的)开塞费.
corked [kɔːkt] *a.* 塞着塞子的;软木底的,软木后跟的(鞋子等);有软木塞气味的(酒等);〔美俚〕喝醉了的.
cork·er [ˈkɔːkə] *n.* ①塞瓶工人;塞瓶机[器]. ②〔美俚〕定论,定局. ③大谎话. ④杰出的惊人的人[物]. *That show was a* ~*!* 那场演出真好[十分动人]; ***play the*** ~ 举动过火(叫人看不顺眼).
cork·ing [ˈkɔːkiŋ] *a.* 〔美俚〕极好的. — *ad.* 极,非常. ***have a*** ~ ***time*** 过[玩]得非常愉快.
cork·screw [ˈkɔːkskruː] *n.* (拔瓶塞的)螺丝锥;【空】螺旋飞行. — *a.* 螺旋形的. ~ *cloth* 螺旋斜纹呢. ~ *curl* 螺状卷发. ~ *dive*【空】螺旋降落. — *vt., vi.* 蜿蜒前进[移动];扭成螺旋;〔俚〕探听(消息). ~ ***a secret cut*** *(of sb.)* 把(某人的)秘密探听出来.
cork·wood [ˈkɔːkwud] *n.* 轻木.
cork·y [ˈkɔːki] *a.* ①软木塞一样的;干缩的. ②软木塞气味的. ②〔口〕没有分量的,轻佻的;活泼的. ③〔口〕喝醉了的.
corm [kɔːm] *n.*【植】球茎;群居体.
cor·mel [ˈkɔːməl] *n.*【植】新生小球茎.
cormo- *comb. f.* 表示"茎","根","干".
cor·mo·rant [ˈkɔːmərənt] *n.* ①【动】鸬鹚,鹈鹕,水老鸦. ②贪吃的(人),贪婪的人. — *a.* 水老鸦似的;食欲大的.
corn¹ [kɔːn] *n.* ①谷粒;(胡椒等的)子;谷类;谷物. ②一个地区的主要谷类;〔美〕玉米;〔Scot.〕〔爱〕燕麦;〔英〕小麦. ③〔美俚〕威士忌酒;零钱;平凡的音乐[戏剧];陈腐的艺术. *a sheaf of* ~ 一捆谷子. *Chinese* ~ 谷子,粟,小米. *gather* ~ 拾谷子. *grow [raise]* ~ 种谷物. *house* ~ 把谷类堆入谷仓里. *Indian* ~ = *Turkey* ~ 玉米. ~ *in the ear* 带总苞的玉米棒子. *waxy* ~ 糯玉米. *pop* ~ 〔美〕爆玉米;爆玉米花. ***acknowledge [admit, confess] the*** ~ 认罪,认输. ***be worth [earn]*** ~ 〔口〕仅够工本. ~ ***and horn go together*** 谷贱肉亦贱. ***eat one's*** ~ ***in the blade*** 钱未到手先花销,寅吃卯粮. ***measure another's*** ~ ***by one's own bushel*** 按自己尺度去衡量别人;以己律人. ***up*** ~, ***down horn*** 谷贵(牛)肉贱. — *vt.* ①制成细粒. ②播种玉米;用玉米喂(牛). ③用盐腌;用盐水泡. ④〔俚〕使醉. — *vi.* (谷穗)成熟,结子 ~ **ball** ① *n.* 爆玉米花糖;〔俚〕乡下人. ② *a.* 陈腔滥调的. ②多愁善感的. ~ **beef** 咸牛肉. **C- Belt** ①美国中部主要产玉米地带. ②~ **belt** 玉米主要产区. ~ **binder** 玉米收割机. ~ **borer** 玉米螟虫. ~ **brash** 粗钙质砂岩. ~ **bread** 玉米面包. ~ **chandler** 粮食零售商. ~ **cob** ①棒子芯,玉米穗轴. ②棒子芯烟斗. ~ **cockle**【植】麦仙翁;瞿麦. ~ **colour** 淡黄色. ~-**cracker** 〔美蔑〕美国南方的穷苦白人. ~ **crake** 秧鸡. ~ **dodger** 〔美〕玉米饼,玉米团子. ~ **earthwarm** 棉铃虫. ~-**exchange** 谷物交易所. ~-**factor** 谷物商(=〔美〕**grain broker**). ~-**fed** ①*a.* 〔英〕喂粮食的;〔美〕精神饱满的;健壮的;天真的(音乐家). ②*n.* 健康的人. ~**field** 稻田;麦田;玉米田. ~ **flag**【植】水仙菖蒲. ~**flakes** 玉米楂儿. ~ **flour** 玉米面. ~**flower**【植】矢车菊. ~**land** 适于种谷物的土地. **C- Law** 〔英史〕谷物法. ~**loft** 谷仓. ~**meal** 玉米粉. ~ **mill** ①〔英〕面粉机. ②〔美〕玉米面粉机. ~ **picker** 玉米收割机. ~ **pone** 玉米饼. ~ **salad**【植】野苣. ~ **silk**【植】玉米花丝. ~ **smut** 玉米黑粉病. ~ **snow** (早春的)粒雪. ~ **syrup** 玉米糖浆. ~**stalk** 麦秸,玉米杆(等);高个子(人);〔C-〕澳洲土生白人. ~**starch** 玉米淀粉. ~ **whisky** 玉米威士忌酒.
corn² [kɔːn] *n.* 【医】(脚趾上的)鸡眼,钉胼. ***tread [trample] on sb.'s*** ~***s*** 揭人疮疤,伤某人的感情.
Corn. = ① Cornish. ② Cornwall.
corn·cake [ˈkɔːnˌkeik] *n.* 〔美〕玉米饼(=Johnnycake).
corn·crib [ˈkɔːnˌkrib] *n.* 〔美〕玉米透风仓,玉米囤.
cor·ne·a [ˈkɔːniə] *n.* 【解】角膜. ~ *transplant*【医】角膜移植. **-l** *a.*
corned [kɔːnd] *a.* 弄成细粒的;盐腌的;〔英俚〕醉了的. ~ *beef* 罐头咸牛肉.
cor·nel [ˈkɔːnel] *n.*【植】山茱萸(的果实).
Cor·nel·ia [kɔːˈniːljə] *n.* 科妮莉亚〔女子名〕.
cor·nel·ian [kɔːˈniːljən] *n.*【矿】光[肉红]玉髓.
Cor·nel·ius [kɔːˈniːljəs] *n.* 科尼利厄斯〔男子名〕.
Cor·nell [kɔːˈnel] *n.* 科内尔〔姓氏〕.
cor·ne·ous [ˈkɔːniəs] *a.* 角(质)的;角状的.
cor·ner [ˈkɔːnə] *n.* ①(桌等的)角,棱,隅. ②天涯海角,僻远地方;偏僻处,角落. ③(街道)拐角,壁角;【数】隅角;边缘. ④困境,绝境. ⑤【商】囤积居奇;【棒球】(本垒的)棱角〔投球员方面〕;(足球)踢角球. *meet a friend at the corner of a street* 在马路拐角地放遇见一位朋友. ***a tight*** ~ 困境. ***from every*** ~ ***of the earth*** 由世界各地. ***around the*** ~ = 〔英〕***round the*** ~. ***cut*** ~***s*** 〔美〕抄近路;节约 *(cut* ~*s on production costs* 节约生产费用). ***cut off a*** ~ 抄近路. ***do in a*** ~ 秘密干. ***drive into a*** ~ 把…逼入死地,追究. ***establish [make] a*** ~ ***in (wheat)*** 垄断[囤积](小麦). ***four*** ~***s*** 四隅;十字路口 *(the four* ~*s of the earth* 世界各处. *within the four* ~*s of a document* 文件的范围). ***keep a*** ~ 保住一角,占据一角. ***on the*** ~ 〔口〕失业. ***put [stand] (a child) in the*** ~ (罚小儿)立壁角. ***out of the*** ~ ***of one's eyes*** 斜着眼睛偷(看). ***rough*** ~***s*** 粗鲁. ***round the*** ~ 〔英〕在拐角处;在附近. ***the C-*** 〔俚〕伦敦 Tattersall's 马市场和赛马场. ***turn the*** ~ 拐过街角;(疾病等)有转机;脱险. — *vt.* ①使有棱[角];收在[放在]角内;角相接;转角,拐弯. ②(把)逼入绝境,紧逼,

使无路可走。③垄断,囤积居奇。 ～ *the market* 垄断市场。— *vi.* ①位于(拐)角上 *(on)*。②形成一个角。③垄断,囤积 *(in)*。— *a.* ①在拐角处的;适于拐角地方的。②(美式足球)翼卫的。 ～**back** *n.* (美式足球)翼卫。 ～**boy** 〔英〕游民,光棍。 ～**man** 翼卫队员;囤积居奇的人。 ～**stone** 隅石;(奠基礼的)基石;基础,柱石。 ～**wise**, ～**ways** *ad.* 斜,斜交成角地. **-ed** *a.* 有…角的。

cor·ner·er [ˈkɔːnərə] *n.* 【商】垄断者,囤积居奇者。

cor·net [ˈkɔːnit] *n.* ①【乐】(有音栓的)短号〔又名～*-à-pistons*〕;(风琴的)音栓。②(修女团团员的)大白帽。③【英史】骑兵旗手;海军信号旗。④三角纸袋;〔英〕(圆锥形)蛋卷冰淇淋。

cor·net-à-pis·tons [kɔːˈnetəpistənz] *n.* *(pl.* ***cor·nets-à-pis·tons*** [-nˈetsə-]*)*【乐】短号 (= cornet)。

cor·net·(t)ist [ˈkɔːnitist] *n.* 短号吹奏者。

corn·ey [ˈkɔːni] *a.* 〔俚〕= corny ④。

corn·husk·er [ˈkɔːnkʌskə] *n.* 玉米穗剥皮人[机]。*C- State* 〔美〕内布拉斯加州的别号。

corn·husk·ing [ˈkɔːnˌhʌskiŋ] *n.* 〔美〕①剥玉米。②剥玉米会〔玉米收下后亲友邻里大家来帮着剥玉米,一般还有舞会等余兴〕。

cor·nice [ˈkɔːnis] *n.*【建】上楣(柱);【登山】雪檐。～ *boarding* 花檐板。

cor·niche [ˈkɔːniʃ] *n.* 悬崖盘旋道路。

Cor·nish [ˈkɔːniʃmən] *a.* 〔英〕康瓦尔 (Cornwall) 郡的。 ～**man** 康瓦尔郡人。

cor·no·pe·an [kəˈnəupjən] *n.*【乐】= cornet。

cor·nu [ˈkɔːnjuː, -nuː] *n.* *(pl.* ***-nu·a*** [-njuə]*)*【解】角状突起,角状物;【医】钉胼,鸡眼。**-al** [-əl] *a.*

cor·nu·co·pi·a [ˌkɔːnjuˈkəupjə] *n.* ①【神话】丰饶角。②丰产的象征;丰富,丰饶;圆锥形糖果容器,糖果角。

cor·nu·co·pi·an [ˌkɔːnjuˈkəupjən] *a.* 丰产的,丰饶的。

cor·nut·ed [kɔːˈnjuːtid] *a.* 有角的。

cor·nu·to [kɔːˈnuːtɔː] *n.* 〔It.〕 *(pl.* ***-ti*** [-tiː]*)* 奸妇的丈夫 (=cuckold)。

Corn·wal·lis [kɔːnˈwɔlis] *n.* 康沃利斯〔姓氏〕。

corn·y[1] [ˈkɔːni] *a.* ①谷类的;谷类丰富的。②〔英方〕酒醉的。③〔美俚〕(爵士音乐)伤感的 *(opp.* hot)。④〔美俚〕陈腐的,枯燥的;天真的,朴素的;粗野的。

corn·y[2] [ˈkɔːni] *a.* 有鸡眼的。

coroll. = corollary.

co·rol·la [kəˈrɔlə] *n.*【植】花冠。

cor·ol·la·ceous [ˌkɔrəˈleiʃəs] *a.* 花冠(状)的。

cor·ol·lar·y [kəˈrɔləri] *n.*【逻、数】系,系定理;推论;必然的结果。

Co·ro·na [ˈkɔrənə] *n.* 科罗娜〔女子名〕。

co·ro·na [kəˈrəunə] *n.* *(pl.* ***-nae*** [-niː]*)* ①(古罗马授与立功战士的)花冠。②【植】小冠,副冠;【解】(齿等的)冠;【动】(海胆的)壳;(轮虫的)轮盘;【建】花檐底板;(教堂的)圆形烛架。③【天】(全蚀时的)日冕;【电】电晕放电。④花冠牌雪茄烟。*C- Australis [Borealis]*【天】南[北]冕座。

cor·o·nach [ˈkɔrənək, -nəx] *n.* 〔Scot., In.〕葬歌,挽歌,哀乐。

co·ro·na·graph [kəˈrəunəˌgræf] *n.*【天】日冕仪。

co·ro·nal [ˈkɔrənl] *n.* 冠;花冠;冠状物;【解】冠状合缝。— [kəˈrəunl] *a.* 冠的;花冠的;【解】头颅的;冠状合缝的;【天】日冕的;【语音】舌尖的。

cor·o·nar·y [ˈkɔrənəri] *a.* 冠的,花冠的;冠状的。*the ～ arteries [veins]* (心脏的)冠状动脉[静脉]。～ *thrombosis*【医】冠状动脉血栓形成。

cor·o·nate [ˈkɔrəneit] *vt.* 给…加冕。— [ˈkɔrənit] *a.* ①【动】冠端的。②【植】有副花冠的。

cor·o·na·tion [ˌkɔrəˈneiʃən] *n.* 加冕礼,即位典礼。

cor·o·ner [ˈkɔrənə] *n.* ①验尸官。②(从前英国的)王室私产管理官。*Coroner's Court* 验尸法庭。～*'s inquest* 验尸。

cor·o·net [ˈkɔrənit] *n.* ①(贵族、王族的)宝冠;(女用)冠状头饰;【诗】花冠。②【建】华丽的三角墙;【兽医】蹄冠。**-ed** *a.* 戴冠的;贵族的,高贵的。

cor·o·noid [ˈkɔrənɔid] *a.*【解】鸟喙状的。

co·ro·zo [kəˈrəuzəu] *n.*【植】(南美)象牙棕榈。 ～**nut** 象牙棕榈果。

corp. = ① corporal. ② corporation.

cor·po·ra [ˈkɔːpərə] *n.* corpus 的复数。

cor·po·ral[1] [ˈkɔːpərəl] *a.* 肉体的,身体上的;〔罕〕个人的,人身的;【动】躯干的。— *n.* 圣餐布。～ *defects* 身体上的缺点。～ *oath* 〔古〕用手接触圣餐布、圣经(等)所行的宣誓。～ *punishment* 体罚,体刑〔主指笞刑〕。

cor·po·ral[2] [ˈkɔːpərəl] *n.* ①【军】下士,班长。②〔美〕牧牛头子。③〔C-〕〔美〕单段式地对地导弹。*a lance ～* 代班长。～*'s bull* 〔美〕香烟头,烟蒂。～*'s guard* (班长带领的)少数卫兵;少数随员;少数人的会集(等)。*the Little C-* 矮小的下士〔拿波仑第一的绰号〕。

cor·po·ral·i·ty [kɔːpəˈræliti] *n.* ①具体性;肉体;物质。②〔美〕体格;身体。③〔*pl.*〕肉欲。

cor·po·rate [ˈkɔːpərit] *a.* ①〔古〕团结的。②法人的,团体的。③共同的,全体的。④(大)公司的。⑤总体国家的。*a ～ body* = *a body ～* 法人团体。～ *responsibility* 共同责任。*a ～ town* 自治城市。***in one's ～ capacity*** 以法人身份。～ **image** 公司形象,公司给人的印象。～ **spying** 商业间谍活动。

cor·po·ra·tion [ˌkɔːpəˈreiʃən] *n.* ①团体;协会,公会;法人;(市)自治体。②〔美〕(股份有限)公司 (= joint-stock ～)。③〔口〕(凸出的)大肚子。*a closed ～* 股权不能外让的公司。*a trading ～* 贸易公司。*the municipal ～.* = *the C-* 市自治体,市政府。*develop a ～* 肚子肥大凸出。～ **aggregate** 集合法人,社团法人。～ **cork** (水管、煤气管的)总开关。～ **farm** 〔美〕规模巨大的农场。～ **law** 〔美〕公司法。～ **lawyer [attorney]** 〔美〕公司法律顾问。～ **police** 〔美〕(公司等的)自备警察。～ **sole** 单独法人,单一法人。

cor·po·rat·ist [ˈkɔːpərətist] *a.* 社团主义的,各阶级合作性质的。**-ism** *n.*

cor·po·ra·tive [ˈkɔːpəreitiv, -rə-] *a.* 法人(团体)的,团体的,全体的。～ **state** 总体国家〔指法西斯统治时期的意大利〕。

cor·po·ra·tor [ˈkɔːpəreitə] *n.* ①(一个团体的)成员,发起人。②公司的股东〔尤指最初的创办人〕。③市政机关职员。

cor·po·re·al [kɔːˈpɔːriəl] *a.* 肉体的;物质的 *(opp.* spiritual);【法】有形的。～ *property [movables]* 有形财产[动产]。**-ly** *ad.* 肉体上;物质上。

cor·po·re·al·i·ty [kɔːˌpɔːriˈæliti] *n.* 肉体的存在;有形[有体]状态;肉身;〔谑〕身体。

cor·po·re·i·ty [ˌkɔːpəˈriːiti] *n.* 形体的存在;物质性;〔谑〕身体;体格。

cor·po·sant [ˈkɔːpəzænt] *n.* 桅顶电光〔一种雷电发生时在高塔等尖顶上出现的放电现象〕(= St. Elmo's fire)。

corps [kɔː, 〔*pl.*〕 kɔːz] *n.* *(sing., pl.)* ①【军】军(团)。②【军】特殊兵种的部队[单位];特殊部队。③某种工作者的全体,团体。④(德国大学的)校友会。*a ～ commander* 军长,军团司令。*an army ～* 军团。*the Army Ordnance C-* 陆军军械部。*the Army Service C-* 辎重部队,陆军兵站部。*the marine ～* 海军陆战队。～ *area.* 军管区。～ *d'armée* [ˈdɑːmei] 〔F.〕军团。～ *de ballet* [də ˈbælei] 〔F.〕舞剧团。～ *d'élite* [dəˈlit] 〔F.〕精选出来的骨干[拔尖]人物。～ *diplomatique* [diplomæˈtiːk] 〔F.〕外交(使)团 (= diplomatic ～)。～ *dramatique* [drəmæˈtiːk] 剧团。～ *troops* 军直属部队。～ *volant* [vɔlɑːŋ] 游击队。

corpse [kɔːps] *n.* ①尸体。②行尸走肉;没有活动力的人[牲畜]。— *vt.* 〔俚〕杀死。～ **candle [light]** 预兆死亡

的鬼火.

corps·man [ˈkɔːzmən] *n.* (*pl.* **-men** [-mən]) 战斗部队医务员 (= aidman).

cor·pu·lence, cor·pu·len·cy [ˈkɔːpjuləns, -si] *n.* 肥胖.

cor·pu·lent [ˈkɔːpjulənt] *a.* 肥胖的. **-ly** *ad.*

cor·pus [ˈkɔːpəs] *n.* (*pl.* **-po·ra** [-pərə]) ①躯体,身体;〔主谑〕尸体. ②(法典等的)集成,全集. ③(事物的)主体;【法】主体(财产),基金;本钱,资本. ④【解】(脂肪)体;【植】原体. ⑤【语】资料. ~ *adiposum* 脂肪体. ~ *callosum* 胼胝体. ~ *delicti* [diˈliktai]【法】犯罪事实.(谋杀案中的)被杀尸体. ~ *juris* [ˈdʒuəris] 法令大全. ~ *luteum*【解】黄体;【医】黄体激素,妊娠激素. ~ *striatum*【解】纹状体.

cor·pus·cle, cor·pus·cule [ˈkɔːpʌsl, kɔːˈpʌskjuːl] *n.* 小体,细胞;【物】微粒,粒子. *blood* ~*s* 血细胞,血球. *bone* ~*s* 骨小体,骨细胞. *red [white]* ~*s* 赤[白]血球;红[白]细胞.

cor·pus·cu·lar [kɔːˈpʌskjulə] *a.*【物】微粒子的.

corr. = ① correction. ② correlative. ③ correspond (-ence; -ent; -ing). ④ corrupt(ion).

cor·rade [kəˈreid] *vt., vi.*【地】(流水、冰川等的)磨蚀,侵蚀. **-ra·sion** [-ˈreiʒən] *n.* **-ra·sive** [-siv] *a.*

cor·ral [kɔˈrɑːl] *n.*〔美〕畜栏,畜槛;(捕象等用的)栅栏;(用车辆等拦成的)应急防御车阵,车栅. —*vt.*〔美〕关在槛内,养在槛内;(把车辆)排成围栅;〔口〕围捕;〔美口〕捕获,获得,取得.

cor·rect [kəˈrekt] *a.* 正确的;恰当的,合式的;(品行等)端正的. *a* ~ *account* 正确的说明. *a* ~ *young man* 品行端正的青年. *the* ~ *card*〔俚〕(运动会等的)节目单,次序表;礼仪,规章. *the* ~ *thing*〔俚〕正事,应该的事. —*vt.* 改正,更正,修正,订正;调整,补正(机件等);校正(印件等);矫正,制止(恶劣倾向等);使中和,解(毒);惩罚,训斥. ~ *the proof sheets* 改正校样. ~ *a child for disobedience* 训斥不听话的孩子. *I stand* ~*ed.* 我承认错误,接受改正. **-ly** *ad.* **-ness** *n.*

cor·rec·tion [kəˈrekʃən] *n.* 修正,改正;校正;矫正;〔古〕惩罚;勘误表,补正. *a copy disfigured by numerous* ~*s* 修改得一塌糊涂的文稿. *first* ~ *of proofs* (校样的)初校,头校. *a free air* ~ 海平校正数. *Gregorian* ~*s*【天】格列高里改正历,阳历. *a steering* ~【火箭】控制信号,稳定信号. ***under [subject to]*** ~ 容有错误,尚待订正(*I speak under* ~. 我说的不一定都对). **-al** *a.*

cor·rect·i·tude [kəˈrektitjuːd] *n.* 正确(性);(品行的)端正.

cor·rec·tive [kəˈrektiv] *a.* 纠正的,改正的;矫正的,惩治的;【药】矫味[中和]的. —*n.* 改善办法[措施];矫正物;补救办法;矫味[中和]剂[药].

cor·rec·tor [kəˈrektə] *n.* 修正者,校正者,校对(员),矫正者,惩治者;【医】矫味剂,中和剂. *a* ~ *of the press*〔英〕校对员 (= proof-reader).

correl. = correlative(ly).

cor·re·late [ˈkɔrileit] *n.* 互相关联,相互关系;相关物. —*vi.* 和…相关 (*with; to*). —*vt.* 把…同某事结合起来;使互相关联 *Her research results* ~ *with his.* 她的研究成果和他的研究成功相关联. *The diameter and the circumference of a circle* ~. 圆的直径与圆周互相关联. ~ *facts* 使事实互相关联. ~ *geography with other studies* 把地理学同其他学科联系起来. —*a.* 关联的,相关的.

cor·re·la·tion [ˌkɔriˈleiʃən] *n.* 相互关系,相关(性);对比;交互作用;【数】对射,异射. ~ *index* 关联指数. ~ *mineral* 对比矿物.

cor·rel·a·tive [kɔˈrelətiv] *a.* 有相互关系的,相关的 (with; to). —*n.* 有相互关系的人[物],互相依赖的人[物],伙伴;【语法】关联词,相关连词〔例 both ... and; such ... as 等〕. ~**conjunction**【语法】关联连词. ~ **figures** 对射图形. ~ **terms**【心】相关名词. **-ly** *ad.* 相关地.

cor·rel·a·tiv·i·ty [kəˌreləˈtiviti] *n.* 相互关系,相关(关系).

cor·re·spond [ˌkɔrisˈpɔnd] *vi.* ①相当(于),【数】对应;与…一致,符合 (*to; with*). ②通信 (*with*). *The broad lines on the map* ~ *to roads.* 图上粗线表示[相当于]道路. *His words* ~ *with his action.* 他言行一致. *We* ~ *regularly.* 我们经常通信.

cor·re·spon·dence [ˌkɔrisˈpɔndəns] *n.* ①通信;信件. ②符合,一致;相当;对应. ③【文艺】通感. ~ *column* (报上的)读者来信栏. ~ *course*〔美〕函授课程. ~ *department* 文书科. ~ *school* 函授学校. ***bring ... into*** ~ ***with*** 使…与(…)一致起来;使某人与另一人通信. ***drop [let drop] one's*** ~ ***with*** 停止和…通信. ***enter into*** ~ ***with*** 开始与…通信. ***keep up*** ~ 保持通信.

cor·re·spon·den·cy [ˌkɔrisˈpɔndənsi] *n.* ①符合,一致. ②相当,类似.

cor·re·spond·ent [ˌkɔrisˈpɔndənt] *n.* 通信者;通讯员;【商】外地客户,外地代理店. *a bad* ~ 不爱写信的人. *a good* ~ 爱写信的人. *our London* ~ 本社伦敦通讯员. *a special* ~ (报馆的)特派记者. *a war* ~ 随军记者. **-ly** *ad.*

cor·re·spond·ing [ˌkɔrisˈpɔndiŋ] *a.* ①相当的,对应的,符合…的 (*to; with*). ②通信的. ~ *angles*【数】同位角. ~ *member*〔英〕通信会员;〔美〕(无表决权的)准会员. ~ *period of last year* 去年中的同一时期.

cor·re·spon·sive [ˌkɔriˈspɔnsiv] *a.*〔古〕= corresponding.

cor·ri·da [kɔːˈriːðɑː] *n.*〔Sp.〕斗牛.

cor·ri·dor [ˈkɔridɔː] *n.*【建】走廊;通路;【筑城】覆道. ~ *carriage*〔英〕有走廊的客车. ~ *train* 通廊列车.

cor·rie [ˈkɔri] *n.*〔Scot.〕(圆形)山凹;冰坑,冰斗.

cor·ri·gen·dum [ˌkɔriˈdʒendəm] *n.* (*pl.* **-da** [-də]) 应改正的错误;〔*pl.*〕勘误表.

cor·ri·gent [ˈkɔridʒənt] *n.*【药】矫味[中和]药.

cor·ri·gi·ble [ˈkɔridʒəbl] *a.* 可改正的;易矫正的.

cor·ri·val [kəˈraivəl] *n.*〔罕〕竞争者.

Corr. Mem. = corresponding member (学、协会的)通讯会员.

cor·rob·o·rant [kəˈrɔbərənt] *a., n.*【医】滋补(性)的;补药;确定的(事实).

cor·rob·o·rate [kəˈrɔbəreit] *vt.* ①使(信仰等)坚定,使巩固;使加强. ②确定,证实.

cor·rob·o·ra·tion [kəˌrɔbəˈreiʃən] *n.* 加强,坚固,坚定;确定,证实. *in* ~ *of sb.'s argument* 为了证实某人的论据.

cor·rob·o·ra·tive, cor·rob·o·ra·tory [kəˈrɔbərətiv, -rətəri] *a.* ①确定的,证实的. ②滋补的. —*n.* 强壮剂,滋补剂.

cor·rob·o·ra·tor [kəˈrɔbəreitə] *n.* 证实者.

cor·rob·o·ree [kəˈrɔbəri] *n.* (澳洲原住民的)庆祝跳舞会[舞歌];狂欢宴会[集会];大集会.

cor·rode [kəˈrəud] *vt.* 腐蚀,侵蚀;渐渐消灭. —*vi.* 腐蚀.

cor·ro·den·tia [kɔrəuˈdenʃiə] *n.*〔*pl.*〕【动】啮虫目.

cor·rod·i·ble [kəˈrəudəbl] *a.* 可腐蚀的;可侵蚀的.

cor·ro·sion [kəˈrəuʒən] *n.* 腐蚀,侵蚀;【植】溶蚀. ~ *preventive* 防腐剂.

cor·ro·sive [kəˈrəusiv] *a.* 腐蚀(性)的,侵蚀性的. —*n.* 腐蚀物,腐蚀剂. ~ *action* 腐蚀作用. ~ *sublimate*【化】氯化汞,升汞. **-ly** *ad.*

cor·ru·gate [ˈkɔrugeit] *vt., vi.* (使)成波状;〔古〕(使)起皱纹;皱缩成波状. — [-git] *a.* 起皱的,波状的,有沟纹的. ~*d bar* 竹节钢筋[条]. ~*d glass* 波纹玻璃.

cor·ru·ga·tion [ˌkɔruˈgeiʃən] *n.* 起皱;皱纹,皱折;波曲度,波纹度;(铁皮等的)波状;沟纹;沟畦.

cor·ru·ga·tor [ˈkɔrugeitə] *n.* 波纹[瓦楞]板轧制机; 波纹纸制造工[机];【解】皱眉肌.
cor·rupt [kəˈrʌpt] *a.* ①腐败的,腐烂的,污浊的; 道德败坏的,堕落的,品行坏的; 贪污的(官吏等). ②(文献等)错误百出的,不可靠的. ~ *air* 污浊的空气. ~ *morals* 坏风气. ~ *officials* 贪污的官吏. ~ *practices* 舞弊,行贿. ~ *language* 传讹语. — *vt., vi.* 使腐败,使颓废; 使堕落; 行贿收买; 败坏(风俗等), 抄错,印错, 转述错(文献,原词等); 腐败,恶化. **-ly** *ad.* **-ness** *n.*
cor·rupt·i·ble [kəˈrʌptəbl] *a.* 易腐败的; 易堕落的; 易贿赂[收买]的; 易传讹[讹误]的. **-bil·i·ty** *n.* **-bly** *ad.*
cor·rup·tion [kəˈrʌpʃən] *n.* ①腐败,堕落,败坏; 恶化; 贪污, 舞弊, 贿赂. ②(文献等的)讹误;【语】传讹. ③〔美〕脓. ~ *in language* 语言的传讹.
cor·rup·tion·ist [kəˈrʌpʃənist] *n.* 贪污腐化分子,行贿受贿分子.
cor·rup·tive [kəˈrʌptiv] *a.* 使腐败[堕落]的; 腐败性的; 败坏的.
cor·sage [kɔːˈsɑːʒ] *n.* (女服的)胸部,腰身; 胸衣;〔美〕女服腰部或肩部的装饰花束.
cor·sair [ˈkɔːsɛə] *n.* ①私掠船. ②海盗; 海盗船.
corse [kɔːs] *n.* 〔诗〕= corpse.
Corse [法 kɔrs] *n.* = Corsica.
Cor. Sec. = Corresponding Secretary (学会、协会的)干事,文书,公文秘书.
cor·se·let, cors·let [ˈkɔːslit] *n.* 胸甲,体甲; 胸衣; (昆虫的)前胸(部),(鱼的)胸甲.
cor·set [ˈkɔːsit] *n.* (常 *pl.*) 女服胸衣;【医】胸衣. *a* ~-*cover* 罩在胸衣外面的背心. **-ed** *a.* 带有胸衣的,穿着胸衣的.
cor·se·tiere [ˌkɔːsiˈtiə, -tjə] *n.* ①女服胸衣裁缝. ②女服胸衣商.
cor·set·ry [ˈkɔːsitri] *n.* 女服胸衣类缝制业,胸衣类销售(商店).
Cor·si·ca [ˈkɔːsikə] *n.* 科西嘉(岛)〔法国〕.
Cor·si·can [ˈkɔːsikən] *a., n.* 科西嘉岛的(居民). *the* ~ "科西嘉人"〔拿破仑第一的绰号〕.
cor·tège [kɔːˈteiʒ] *n.* 〔F.〕①(葬礼等)行列,仪仗. ②扈从人员.
Cor·tes [ˈkɔːtes, -tez] *n.* 〔*pl.*〕(西班牙、葡萄牙的)议会,国会.
cor·tex [ˈkɔːteks] *n.* (*pl.* **-ti·ces** [-tisiːz]) 外皮;【解】皮质,皮层;【药】(药用植物的)皮.
cor·ti·cal [ˈkɔːtikəl] *a.* 外皮的; 皮质的,皮层的.
cor·ti·cate, cor·ti·cat·ed [ˈkɔːtikeit, -kit, -keitid] *a.* 有外皮的,有皮层的.
cor·ti·coid [ˈkɔːtikɔid] *n.* =corticosteroid.
cor·ti·co·ste·roid [ˌkɔːtikəuˈstiərɔid] *n.*【生化】(肾上腺)皮质激素类,皮质甾(类).
cor·ti·cos·ter·one [ˌkɔːtiˈkɔstərəun] *n.*【生化】(肾上腺)皮质甾酮.
cor·ti·co·tro·phin [ˌkɔːtikəuˈtrəufin] *n.*【生化】促肾上腺皮质激素 (= corticotropin).
cor·tin [ˈkɔːtin] *n.*【生化】(肾上腺)皮质激素.
cor·ti·sol [ˈkɔːtiˌsəul] *n.*【生化】皮质醇;【药】氢可的松.
cor·ti·sone [ˈkɔːtiˌsəun, -zəun] *n.*【生化】(肾上腺)皮质酮[素];【药】可的松.
co·run·dum [kəˈrʌndəm] *n.*【矿】刚石,刚玉;【机】金钢砂(磨料); 金刚砂磨轮.
cor·us·cate [ˈkɔrəskeit] *vi.* 闪烁; (才气)焕发.
cor·us·ca·tion [ˌkɔrəsˈkeiʃən] *n.* 闪光; 焕发.
cor·vée [ˈkɔːvei] *n.* ①(封建社会的)徭役; ②(强派的)劳役.
corves [kɔːvz] *n.* corf 的复数.
cor·vet(te) [kɔːˈvet] *n.* (旧时木造帆装的)海防舰; 轻巡洋舰; (现代的)小型护卫舰.
cor·vi·na [kɔːˈviːnə] *n.*【动】①无鳔石首鱼. ②细须石首鱼和犬牙石首鱼属 (= corbina).
cor·vine [ˈkɔːvain] *a.* 乌鸦(似)的.
Cor·vus [ˈkɔːvəs] *n.*【天】乌鸦座.
Cor·y·bant [ˈkɔriˌbænt] *n.* (*pl.* ~*s*, ~*es* [-tiːz]). ①【希神】母神 (Cybele) 的狂欢乱舞的随从; 供奉母神的阉割过的祭司. ②〔c-〕喝酒狂欢的人.
Cor·y·ban·tic [ˌkɔriˈbæntik] *a.* (有关) Corybant 的; 疯狂的,狂欢乱舞的.
co·ryd·a·lis [kəˈridlis] *n.*【植】紫堇(属).
cor·ymb [ˈkɔrimb] *n.*【植】伞房花序.
cor·ym·bose [kəˈrimbəus, kɔrimˈbəus] *a.*【植】伞房状的.
cor·y·phae·us [ˌkɔriˈfiːəs] *n.* (*pl.* **-phaei** [-ˈfiːai]) ①(古希腊合唱队的)领唱歌手. ②(派系、运动等的)领导人,领袖.
cor·y·phée [ˈkɔrifei] *n.* 芭蕾舞(仅次于主要演员的)重要演员.
co·ry·za [kəˈraizə] *n.*【医】鼻炎,鼻感冒[伤风].
cos [kɔs] *n.*【植】科斯(岛产的)长叶莴苣.
C.O.S., COS = cash on shipment 装货付款.
Co·sa Nos·tra [ˈkausə ˈnəustrə] "科萨•诺斯特拉"〔美国黑手党犯罪集团的秘密代号,1962 年始被揭露,意为"我们自己的事"〕.
co·saque [kɔˈzaːk] *n.* = cracker (bonbon).
cose [kəuz] *vi., n.* = coze.
cosec. = cosecant.
co·se·cant [ˈkəuˈsiːkənt] *n.*【数】余割.
co·seis·mal, co·seis·mic [kəuˈsaizməl, -mik] *a.*【地】同震的[同时受地震影响的]. *a* ~ *area* 同震区.
co·sey [ˈkəuzi] *a., n.* = cosy, cozy.
cosh [kɔʃ] *n.* 〔英俚〕(金属心、外包橡皮的)棍子; 警棍. — *vt.* 用棍子打.
cosh·er[1] [ˈkɔʃə] *vt.* ①给吃好东西. ②溺爱,娇养. — *vi.* 享受盛宴款待.
cosh·er[2] [ˈkɔʃə] *n.* 〔口〕开怀畅谈.
cosh·er[3] [ˈkəuʃə] *v.* = kosher.
co·sign [ˈkəuˈsain] *vt., vi.* ①担保联署. ②联署,共同签字. **-er** *n.*
co·sig·na·to·ry [ˈkəuˈsignətəri] *a.* 联署的,连名的. — *n.* 联署人[国].
co·si·gner [ˈkəusainə] *n.* 联署人.
co·si·ly [ˈkəuzili] *ad.* 舒适地,适意地.
co·sine [ˈkəusain] *n.*【数】余弦.
co·si·ness [ˈkəuzinis] *n.* 舒适,安乐; 适意.
cosm- *comb. f.* 〔用于元音前〕= cosmo-.
cos·met·ic [kɔzˈmetik] *n.* 〔常 *pl.*〕化妆品; 美发油,发蜡; 美容术. — *a.* ①化妆用的; 美发用的. ②装点门面的; 表面的. *a* ~ *urge* 〔美〕化妆品广告. ~ **surgery** 美容手术. **-ti·cian** [-ˈtiʃən] 制造[出售,使用]化妆品者.
cos·met·i·cize [kɔzˈmetəsaiz] *vt.* 用化妆品打扮; 粉饰,为…涂脂抹粉.
cos·me·tol·o·gy [ˌkɔzməˈtɔlədʒi] *n.* 〔美〕美容术; 美容业.
cos·mic [ˈkɔzmik] *a.* ①宇宙的; 宇宙论的. ②有秩序的,有条不紊的. ③广大无边的. ~ **dust** 宇宙尘. ~ **fog [clouds]** 星云. ~ **inventory** 宇宙万物. ~ **philosophy** 宇宙(演化)哲学. ~ **rays** 宇宙(射)线. ~ **year**【天文】宇宙年. **-cal·ly** *ad.*
cos·mi·cal [ˈkɔzmikəl] *a.* = cosmic.
cos·mism [ˈkɔzmizəm] *n.*【哲】宇宙(演化)论.
cosmo- *comb. f.* 〔用于辅音前〕= cosmos: *cosmo*drome.
cos·mo·dom [ˈkɔzməudəm] *n.* 太空站.
cos·mo·drome [ˈkɔzməudrəum] *n.* (苏联的)人造卫星及宇宙飞船发射场; 太空站的降落部分.
cos·mog·o·ny [kɔzˈmɔgəni] *n.* ①宇宙的发生[起源,演化]. ②星原学,天体演化学,宇宙(演化)论.
cos·mo·grad [ˈkɔzməugrəd] *n.* 太空城.

cos·mog·ra·pher [kɔzˈmɔgrəfə] *n.* 宇宙志学者.
cos·mo·graph·ic [ˌkɔzməˈgræfik] *a.* 宇宙志的.
cos·mog·ra·phy [kɔzˈmɔgrəfi] *n.* 宇宙志.
Cos·mo·line [ˈkɔzməˌliːn] *n.* "柯斯莫林"重油〔商标名,尤指武器等的防锈润滑油〕; 〔c-〕(柯斯莫林)防腐润滑油. — *vt.* 〔c-〕涂以(柯斯莫林)防腐润滑油.
cos·mo·log·i·cal [ˌkɔzməˈlɔdʒikəl] *a.* 宇宙论的.
cos·mol·o·gist [kɔzˈmɔlədʒist] *n.* 宇宙论者.
cos·mol·o·gy [kɔzˈmɔlədʒi] *n.* 宇宙论.
cos·mo·naut [ˈkɔzmə*u*nɔːt] *n.* 宇(宙)航(行)员.
cos·mo·naut·ic [ˌkɔzmə*u*ˈnɔːtik] *a.* 宇(宙)航(行)的.
cos·mo·nau·tics [ˌkɔzməˈnɔːtiks] 宇宙航行学[术].
cos·mo·plas·tic [ˌkɔzməˈplæstik] *a.* 宇宙形成的.
cos·mop·o·lis [kɔzˈmɔpəlis] *n.* 国际[世界]都市〔指居民中有许多不同国籍的人〕.
cos·mo·pol·i·tan [ˌkɔzməˈpɔlitən] *n.* 世界主义者. — *a.* ①世界主义的. ②全世界的. ③世界性的; 全世界各地都有的. *a ~ population* 世界各地的人都有的居民. *a ~ city* 国际都市. **-ism** *n.* 世界主义. **-ize** *vt., vi.* (使)世界主义化.
cos·mop·o·lite [kɔzˈmɔpəlait] *n., a.* ① = cosmopolitan. ②【生】世界种,遍生种.
cos·mo·ra·ma [ˌkɔzməˈrɑːmə] *n.* 世界各地景色图片.
cos·mos [ˈkɔzmɔs] *n.* ①宇宙. ②完整的体系. ③秩序,和谐 *(opp.* chaos*).* ④【植】大波斯菊(属); 秋英(属). *~ fibre* 破麻布再生纤维.
cos·mo·tron [ˈkɔzməˌtrɔn] *n.* 【原】宇宙线级回旋加速器,(高能)同步稳相加速器,质子同步加速器.
COSPAR = Committee On Space Research (国际科学协会理事会)空间研究委员会.
co·spon·sor [ˌkə*u*ˈspɔnsə] *n.* 联合发起[主办]人之一. — *vt.* 作…的联合发起[主办]人. **-ship** *n.*
Cos·sack [ˈkɔsæk] *n.* 哥萨克人; 哥萨克骑兵; 哥萨克式服装; 〔美〕(用以镇压工人斗争的)骑警. — *a.* 哥萨克的,哥萨克人的.
cos·set [ˈkɔsit] *n.* 亲手饲养大的小羊; 亲手饲养的禽兽; 宠儿. — *vt.* 宠养; 宠爱.
cost [kɔst] *n.* ①费用; 代价,价格; 成本. ②牺牲; 损害,损失. ③〔*pl.*〕讼费. *living ~s* 生活费用,物价. *first [prime, initial] ~* 生产成本. ***at all ~s*** = ***at any ~*** 无论如何,不惜任何牺牲. ***at ~*** 照成本. ***at sb.'s ~*** 某人出钱; 损及某人. ***at the ~ of*** 以…为牺牲,舍…而. ***~ and freight*** 成本加运费〔略作 C. & F.〕. ***~ of living*** 生活费(用). ***~ of living index*** 物价指数. ***~ of operation*** 管理费用. ***count the ~*** 估计费用; 先盘算盘算. ***free of ~*** 免费,(奉)送. ***to sb.'s ~*** 归某人负担,算作某人损失; 叫某人受累; 某人吃亏后才 (*as I know to my ~* 我吃亏后才知道. *I knew it to my ~.* 这个我(因吃过苦头)是见而有戒了. *He found to his ~ that motoring is dangerous.* 他(吃过苦头后才)知道开汽车是危险的). — *vt.* ①值,要价(若干); 花费,需要. ②使花费,使损失,牺牲. ③估定(…的)成本. — *vi.* 花费,付代价. *It ~s five dollars.* 值五元,要价五元. *It ~ me much labour.* 费了我不少劳力[麻烦]. *His ambition ~ him his life.* 他的野心断送了自己一条命. ***~ (sb.) dear(ly)*** 代价极大,费用极高; 闯大祸,吃大亏 (*If you attempt it, it will ~ you dear.* 你试试看,一定要吃大亏的.) ***~ what it may*** 不惜任何代价,无论代价多少; 无论如何. ~ **accounts** 成本帐(户). ~ **accounting** 成本会计. ~**-effective** *a.* 节省成本的. ~**-free** 免费的,奉送的. ~ **keeper** 成本会计师. ~ **price** 成本(价格). ~**-push** 成本增加(趋势). ~ **taking** 成本计算. ~ **sheet** 成本单.
cos·ta [ˈkɔstə] *n. (pl.* ***-tae*** [-tiː]*)*【解】肋骨;【虫】前缘脉;【植】缘; 中脉,主脉.
cos·tal [ˈkɔstl] *a.* 【解】肋骨的; 前缘脉的. *~ fold* 膜垂; 前缘褶.
co-star [kə*u*ˈstɑː] *vt., vi.* 【影】(使)共同主演〔充任并立主角〕. — *n.* 合演主角,并立主角.
cos·tard [ˈkʌstəd] *n.* 英国大苹果(树); 〔古、谑〕头.
Cos·ta Ri·ca [ˈkɔstə ˈriːkə] *n.* 哥斯达黎加〔拉丁美洲〕.
cos·tate [ˈkɔsteit] *a.* 【解】有肋骨的; 有中脉的.
cost-book [ˈkɔstbuk] *n.* 成本帐.
cos·tean, cos·teen [ˈkɔstiːn] *vi.* 【矿】井探,掘井勘探,水力冲刷勘探.
Cos·tel·lo [kɔsˈtelə*u*] *n.* 科斯特洛〔姓氏〕.
cos·ter, cos·ter·mon·ger [ˈkɔstə, -mʌŋgə] *n.* 〔英〕(水果、鱼类的)叫卖小贩.
cos·tive [ˈkɔstiv] *a.* ①便秘的. ②吝啬的. ③〔美〕昂贵的.
cost·li·ness [ˈkɔstlinis] *n.* 高价,昂贵; 奢华.
cost·ly [ˈkɔstli] *a.* 昂贵的,费用大的; 奢华的,浪费的. *a ~ victory* 代价高的胜利.
cost·mar·y [ˈkɔstmɛəri] *n.* 【植】艾菊.
costo- *comb. f.* 肋骨: *costo*tomy.
cos·tot·o·my [kɔsˈtɔːtəmi] *n.* 肋骨切除术.
cost-plus [ˈkɔːstˈplʌs] *a.* (定货合同中)成本加利润(价格)的.
cos·trel [ˈkɔstrəl] *n.* 〔古,方〕背挎水瓶,腰挎水瓶.
cos·tume [ˈkɔstjuːm, -ˈtjuːm] *n.* ①服装,装束; 衣服. ②女服; 女装. ③服装式样; 化装用服装; 戏装. *a bathing-~* 游泳衣. — [kɔsˈtjuːm] *vt.* 为…提供服装. ~ **ball** 化装跳舞会. ~ **designer**【剧、影】服装设计员. ~ **piece [play]** 古装戏.
cos·tum·er, cos·tu·mi·er [kɔsˈtjuːmə, -miə] *n.*〔美〕①服装[戏装]供应〔缝制,出售或出租〕商. ②衣帽架.
co·sy [ˈkəuzi] *a.* ①舒适的,舒服的,安乐的; 容易的. ②畅快的; 投合的; 亲切友好的. ③自满的,自得的. *a ~ job* 容易的工作. — *n.* ①有宝盖的双人座位. ②保暖罩〔例: tea-~ 茶壶暖罩〕. — *vt.* 〔口〕使放心,保证; 哄骗 (along). — *vi.* 〔美口〕 ***~ up to*** 巴结,奉承,讨好,表示好感.
cot. = cotangent.
cot[1] [kɔt] *n.* ①〔诗〕= cottage; 小屋. ②(羊)槛,(鸽)舍. ③套子,罩子.
cot[2] [kɔt] *n.* ①帆布床; (船上的)吊床,吊铺. ②小儿卧床; 儿科病床. ~ **death**【医】(原因不明的)婴孩猝死(症).
co·tan·gent [ˈkəuˈtændʒənt] *n.* 【数】余切.
COTAR = correlation tracking and range 相关跟踪测距系统.
cote [kəut] *n.* (家畜、家禽的)槛,栏.
co·teau [kəuˈtəu] *n.* 〔F.〕*(pl.* ***-teaux*** [-z]*)*〔美、加拿大〕高地,高原.
co·tem·po·ra·neo·us, co·tem·po·rar·y [kəutempəˈreinjəs, -rəri] = contemporaneous, contemporary.
co·ten·ant [ˈkəuˈtenənt] *n.* 共同租户[租地人,租屋人]; 共同佃户.
co·te·rie [ˈkəutəri] *n.* 同人俱乐部; 小集团,小圈子.
co·ter·mi·nous [kəuˈtəːminəs] *a.* = conterminous.
co·thur·n(us) [kə*u*ˈθəːn(əs)] *n. (pl.* ***-ni*** [-nai]*).* (古希腊罗马)悲剧角色厚底高统靴; 〔诗〕〔the ~〕悲剧(风格).
co·tid·al [kəuˈtaidl] *a.* 等潮(时)的,同潮的. *~ lines on a map* 地图上的等潮(时)线.
co·til·l(i)on [kəˈtiljən, kəu-] *n.* ①一种不断更换舞伴、热闹的交际舞; 这种舞曲. ②(为初进社交界的少女开的)正式舞会.
co·to·ne·as·ter [kəˌtəuniˈæstə] *n.* 【植】栒子.
Co·to·nou [ˌkəutəˈnuː] *n.* 科托努〔达荷美港市〕.
cot·quean [ˈkɔtˌkwiːn] *n.* 〔古〕①泼妇. ②做家务的男子.
Cots·wold [ˈkɔtswəuld] *n.* (英国)柯茨窝尔山; 柯茨窝尔羊. *the ~ lion* 〔谑〕羊.
cot·ta [ˈkɔtə] *n.* ①短袖或无袖白色短法衣; 外衣,束腰外衣. ②极粗劣的毯子.

cot·tage [ˈkɔtidʒ] *n.* ①〔英〕乡下房子,农舍;小房子. ②〔美〕(农舍式的)别墅;(郊外的)新式住宅;(大院内的)单幢住宅;〔澳〕平房. ③竖式小钢琴 (= ~ piano). ~ **cheese** 〔美〕用酸牛奶做的软干酪. ~ **hospital** (无住院医生的诊疗所,(乡下)小医院;医院分院. ~ **industry** 家庭手工业. ~ **loaf** 大小两个叠合的面包. ~ **piano** 竖式小钢琴. ~ **pudding** 〔美〕乡下布丁.

cot·tag·er [ˈkɔtidʒə] *n.* 住乡下房子的人;〔英〕农场雇工;〔美〕(避暑地等的)别墅客,度假客.

cot·tar, cot·ter[1] [ˈkɔtə] *n.* 住屋狭小的人,贫农;〔Scot.〕农场雇工.

cot·ter[2], **cot·ter·el** [ˈkɔtə, -rəl] *n.* 【机】栓,销; 开尾销 (= ~ pin).

cot·ti·er [ˈkɔtiə] *n.* 〔英〕(住在农村小舍里的)小〔贫〕农;〔爱〕(投标定租的)佃农.

Cotton [ˈkɔtn] *n.* 科顿〔姓氏〕.

cot·ton [ˈkɔtn] *n.* 【植】草棉;棉,棉花;棉线;棉布,棉织品;〔美口〕脱脂棉. *upland [sea-island]* ~ 陆地〔海岛〕棉. *tree* ~ 木棉. *ginned* ~ 皮棉. *unginned* ~ 籽棉. *raw* ~ 原棉. *dead* ~ 废棉. — *vi.* 一致,赞同 *(with)*; 接近,亲近 *(to; with)*; (对提案等)抱好感,欢迎. **~ to [with]** 发生好感,喜欢起…来. **~ on to** 〔俚〕明白,了解. **~ up** 〔口〕接近,亲近 *(to)*. —*vt.* 娇养,娇宠. **C- Belt** 〔美〕(东南部)产棉地带〔区域〕. ~ **cake** 棉籽饼. ~ **gin** 轧花机. ~**grass** 【植】羊胡子草 (属). ~ **gum** 紫树(属). ~ **holiday** 〔美〕(因生产过剩)暂时停种棉花. ~ **lord** 棉花大王; 纱业大王. ~**manies** [-ˈmeini:] 〔美〕田纳西州人〔别号〕. ~ **meal** 棉籽饼. ~ **mill** 纱厂. ~ **oil** 棉子油. ~ **picker** 采棉机. ~ **piece goods** 棉布类(商品). ~**plant** 棉株,草棉. ~ **plantation** 〔美〕(盛栽棉花的) 亚拉巴马州的别号. ~ **print** 印花棉布. ~ **seed** 棉子. ~ **shirting** 细棉布. **C-State** 〔美〕亚拉巴马州的别号. ~ **stainer** 棉椿象. ~-**tail** 【动】美洲白尾灰兔. ~ **thread** 棉线. ~ **textile [tissue]** 棉织品. ~ **tree** 木棉 (树). ~ **waste** (揩擦机械用的) 纱头. ~ **weed** 【植】母子草, 鼠麴草. ~ **wood** 加拿大杨;三角叶杨. ~ **wool** 原棉; 棉絮; 脱脂棉. ~ **yarn** 棉纱.

cot·ton·oc·ra·cy [ˌkɔtənˈɔkrəsi] *n.* 〔口〕棉纱业暴发户〔集团〕;〔美〕(南北战争前南部的)棉花种植场主.

Cot·ton·op·o·lis [ˌkɔtənˈɔpəlis] *n.* 〔谑〕棉都〔英国 Manchester的别号〕.

cot·ton·pick·ing [ˈkɔtənpikən] *a.* 〔美俚〕糟透的,该死的,可恨的.

cot·ton·y [ˈkɔtni] *a.* ①棉花状的;柔软的. ②有绒毛的. ③棉质的,粗劣的.

cot·y·le·don [ˌkɔtiˈli:dən] *n.* 【植, 解】绒毛叶, 子叶. **-don·ous, -don·al** *a.*

cot·y·loid [ˈkɔtilɔid] *a.* 【解】髋臼状的,杯状的.

couch[1] [kautʃ] *n.* ①〔诗〕床,卧榻. ②躺椅,长沙发椅〔背部比沙发低〕. ③休息处; (兽)窝,窟, 巢穴. ④【绘】底子. ⑤【酿造】麦芽床. *a studio* ~ 坐卧两用沙发. —*vt.* ①横躺着(身体),使横卧〔常用被动〕. ②挺着(枪). ③表述,暗含(真意),暗示(要求等). ④【医】除去白内障. *be ~ed on a bed of flowers* 生活奢华. ~ *one's refusal in polite terms* 婉言拒绝. —*vi.* ①躺,睡. ②蹲着,弯着身子(作要跳的姿势); 埋伏. ③(树叶等)堆积〔发酵,沤肥〕.

couch[2] [kautʃ] *n.* 【植】= ~ *grass.* —*vt.* 铲除麦斛. ~ **grass** 麦斛,匍匐冰草,茅根.

couch·ant [ˈkautʃənt] *a.* 【徽】昂首蹲着的 (兽), 昂首伏卧状的.

cou·che [ˈku:ʃei] *a.* 〔F.〕【徽】微微前倾的.

cou·chee [ˈku:ʃei] *n.* ①重伤兵. ②晚上的接见.

cou·chette [ku:ˈʃet] 〔F.〕【铁道】(客车上的)卧铺分隔间; 卧铺铺位.

cou·gar [ˈku:gə] *n.* 【动】美洲豹.

cough [kɔf] *n.* ①咳,咳嗽. ②咳嗽声, 咳嗽病. ③(机关枪等的)连续发射声. — *vi.* ①咳嗽. ②(引擎等) 发噗噗声. — *vt.* 咳; 咳出 *(out; up)*; 咳哑 (声音). ~ ***down*** (听众)用咳嗽声轰演讲者. ~ ***oneself hoarse*** 咳嗽得嗓子嘶哑. ~ ***out [up]*** 咳出;〔美俚〕(被迫)说出; 付出,交出 (~ *up one's dough* 说出〔吐出〕藏金). ~ ***up one's cookies*** 〔美俚〕呕吐. ~ **drop** 咳嗽糖. ~ **lozenge** 咳嗽片. ~ **mixture** 止咳药水. ~ **syrup** 止咳糖浆.

could [强 kud; 弱 kəd] *auxil. v.* (can 的过去式). ①〔特殊用例〕打算,要,想. *I ~ laugh for joy.* 我喜欢得想笑. *Really I ~ not think of it.* 真的那是我不愿意考虑的. *I couldn't think of allowing it.* 我没有允许的意思. ★could 与感觉动词连用时,表示"要,想";与一般动词连用而表示"能够"时,为避免与"要,想"混淆起见,通例不说 could 而改说 was [were] able to, 若所指行动须经过努力或会遇到困难,则通例不说 could 而改说 managed to, succeeded in -ing. 例: I *could* do it = I *was able to* do it. He *could* reach the top of the mountain. = He *managed to* reach *[succeeded in reaching]* the top of the mountain. ②〔用于虚拟语气的条件句〕*if I ~* 〔现在〕如果可能的话(但事实上不可能). *if I ~ have done so* 〔过去〕如果做到了(但事实上没有做到). ③〔用于虚拟语气的结论句〕*I ~ if I would.* 〔现在〕我如果要做就可以做到〔但事实上不打算做〕. *I ~ have done.* 〔过去〕我本来是可以做到的〔但未做〕.

could·n't [ˈkudnt] = could not.

couldst [kudst] 〔古、诗〕could 的单数第二人称.

cou·lee [ˈku:li] *n.* ①〔美〕斜壁峡谷;低地;(时干时流的)深山沟(山溪). ②【地】熔岩流;(熔岩)岩席.

cou·leur de rose [ˈku:lə(:) də ˈrəuz] 〔F.〕玫瑰色;粉红色;乐观(情绪);美好的前景.

cou·lisse [ku:ˈli:s] *n.* ①【机】滑槽;滑板;滑动片;游标. ②【剧】侧面布景;〔*pl.*〕二片侧面布景之间的空间; 〔*pl.*〕后台. ③【建】穿堂门厅. *the gossip of the ~s* 后台传闻,剧坛消息. *experienced in the ~s of* 熟悉…的内幕.

cou·loir [ˈku:lwɑ:] *n.* 〔F.〕①峡谷. ②挖泥机,浚泥机. ③通道;管道.

cou·lomb [ˈku:lɔm] *n.* 【电】库仑.

cou·lom·e·ter [ku:ˈlɔmitə] *n.* 【电】电量计,库仑计.

coul·ter [ˈkəultə] *n.* = colter.

cou·ma·rin(e) [ˈku:mərin] 【化】香豆素, 氧杂萘邻酮.

cou·ma·rone [ˈku:məˌrəun] *n.* 【化】香豆酮,氧茚,苯并呋喃.

coun·cil [ˈkaunsil] *n.* ①议事〔行政,参议,立法〕机构;委员会;理事会;公会. ②【宗】宗教〔教法〕会议; 〔美〕地方工会代表会议. ③计议,协商,讨论;〔美〕忠告,劝告. *the China C- for the Promotion of International Trade* 中国国际贸易促进委员会. *a cabinet* ~ (内)阁(会)议. *a municipal [city]* ~ 市政参议会. *a common* ~ 〔美〕市〔镇〕参议会. *a county* ~ 〔英〕州(议)会. *the World Peace C-* 世界和平理事会. *the United Nations Security C-* 联合国安理会. *the C-* 〔英〕= *the Privy C-* 枢密院. *C- of Defence* 国防会议. *C- of State* (法国等的)参议院,国务会议. ~ *of war* (战地的)军事会议;〔喻〕行动方针的商讨;(英美以外的)军事参议院. *the State C-* (中国)国务院. ~ **board** 会议桌;(正在进行的)会议. ~ **chamber** 会议室. ~ **house** 会堂, 议场; 〔Scot.〕市政厅;州〔市〕营住宅. ~**man** 议事机构的成员;〔美〕市〔镇、村〕会议员〔英国通常用 councillor〕. ~ **manic** 〔美〕市〔镇、村〕议员的. ~ **school** 〔英〕(市政议会主办的)公立小学校.

coun·cil·(l)or [ˈkaunsilə] *n.* (市会、镇会等的)参议员;委员;顾问,参赞. *a county* ~ 〔英〕州议员. *a Privy C-* 枢密顾问官〔略 P. C., 用在名字之后〕. **-ship** 参议员〔顾问等〕的职位.

coun·sel [ˈkaunsəl] *n.* ①商议;劝导,忠告. ②〔古〕深思熟虑,审慎. ③意图,目的,计划. ④法律顾问,辩护人.

Deliberate in ~, prompt in action. 熟虑果断. *He takes ~ of his heart, but not of his head.* 他感情用事而不理智. *the King's [Queen's] C-* 王室法律顾问. ***adopt a ~ of despair*** 采取自暴自弃[不顾一切]的态度. ***~ for the Crown*** [英]检察官. ***follow sb.'s ~ close*** 牢记某人忠告. ***give ~*** 提出忠告[建议]. ***keep one's own ~*** 不暴露自己意图. ***take ~ (with)*** 与…商量. ***take [hold] ~ together*** 协商. ***take ~ with oneself*** 好好考虑考虑. ***take sb. into one's ~*** 和某人商量. —*vt.* 忠告, 劝告. —*vi.* 互相商议; 提出劝告[建议]; 接受劝告[建议].

coun·sel·(l)or [ˈkaunsələ] *n.* ①顾问, 参事; 参赞; 辅导员; [美, 爱]法律顾问, 律师 (= ~-at-law). ②(儿童夏令营等中的)领队[教导员].

count[1] [kaunt] *vt.* ①计数, 计算, 列举, 清点. ②算进, 计进; 包括. ③认为, 相信为; 算为. *~ heads [noses]* 数人数. *I ~ that he will come.* [美俚]我想他会来的. —*vi.* ①计数, 计算. ②【乐】打拍子. ③被算入…数内; 有价值, 重要, 值得考虑. ④指望, 期待, 依赖 (*on; upon*). *That does not ~.* 那不作数; 不算问题. *See that everything ~s.* 事事都不可疏忽; 要事事都办妥贴. *Every vote ~s.* (选举时) 每一张票都值得重视. ***be ~ed on one's fingers*** 屈指可数. ***~ sb. among*** *one's friend* 把某人看做朋友. ***~ against*** *sb.* 认为…对某人不利. ***~ ... as [for]*** 以为, 当作是 (*~ sb. as dead* 当他是死了). ***~ down*** (9, 8, 7, ... 0 地)倒数; (火箭发射时)倒数秒数. ***~ for little [nothing]*** 无足轻重, 不足取. ***~ for much*** 非常重要. ***~ in*** 算入, 归入…中计算. ***~ kin (with)*** (与…)是近亲; [Scot.](与)比血统[门第]. ***~ off*** (点算后)分出, 挑出; [口令]报数. ***~ on [upon]*** 指望; 依赖. ***~ on one's fingers*** 掐指计算. ***~ out*** ①一面数一面取出, 点数; 一面数一面分开; 除开, 忽视. ②[美](开票时)少算一部分票数 (使某候选人落选) [常用被动式]. ③【拳】(对被打倒者数完十下后)宣告失败. ***~ out the House*** [英下院](议长)(因不足法定人数)宣告延会. ***~ out a measure [a member]*** [英](议长因不足法定人数)宣布停止讨论某议案[某议员发言]. ***~ ... over*** 重算; 数完. ***~ the house*** 清点出席人数. ***~ (the) ties*** [美]沿着铁路徒步旅行. ***~ up to*** 数到, 数完, 总计. —*n.* ①计算; 数(目); [古]总数, 总计; 顾虑, 考虑. ②价值, 评价. ③【法】起诉理由, 罪状. ④【纺】支[每克纱的米数]; [美]论件出售的东西; (英下院)由于法定人数不足的延会; 【拳】(给被击倒者再起来比赛的宽延时间)数十秒. ***his ~ of years*** 他的年龄. ***keep [lose] ~ (of)*** 无错漏地数下去[因点错而数不下去]. (*There were so many that he couldn't keep ~ of them.* 太多了, 他无法数清他们). ***on all ~s*** 从所有方面说; 【法】就所有诉讼理由[罪状]说. ***out of ~*** 数不完的, 无数的. ***set no ~ on*** 看不起, 轻视, 眼中没有. ***take ~ of*** 清点; 重视. ***take [make] no ~ of*** 眼中没有, 轻视. ***take the ~*** 【拳】(裁判员对被击倒者) 数十下. **-able** ①*a.* 可数 [计算]的. ②【语法】*n.* 可数名词.

count[2] [kaunt] *n.* (英国以外的)伯爵[英国叫 earl].

count·down [ˈkauntˌdaun] *n.* ①(火箭、核弹等准备发射、爆炸时的)时间计算(阶段); (火箭、核弹发射、爆炸前)计时系统. ②(雷达的)回答脉冲比; (电视的)脉冲分频[脱漏]. ③读数, 示度; 计数损失[漏失].

coun·te·nance [ˈkauntinəns] *n.* ①容貌, 相貌; 脸色, 气色; 面目. ②奖励; 鼓励; 纵容; 支持, 赞助. ③镇定. *a sad [jovial] ~* 悲苦[欢快]的面容. *a man with an expressive ~* 脸上富于表情的人. *catch some familiar ~* 认出是相识. ***find no ~ in*** 不受欢迎, 得不到…的支持. ***for (a) ~*** 为了面子. ***get out of ~ = lose ~.*** ***give [lend] ~ to*** (暗暗)嘉奖, 支持, 默认. ***give ~ to*** 赞成. ***give oneself ~*** 沉住气. ***have the ~ of*** 得到…的援助. ***in the light of sb.'s ~*** 由于某人帮助. ***keep (sb.) in ~*** 留人面子, 不抓破某人面子; 不叫人为难. ***keep one's ~*** 泰然自若, 不露声色; 忍住不笑. ***lose ~*** 失色, 慌张起来. ***put (sb.) out of ~*** 使狼狈, 使丢脸. ***stare (sb.) out of ~*** 盯着看, 使人不好意思起来. ***with a good ~*** 十分沉着. —*vt.* 暗暗奖励, 嘉奖; 支持, 赞助, 鼓动; 纵容, 默认.

count·er[1] [ˈkauntə] *n.* ①计算者; 计算器; 计数器. ②筹码, 号码; 伪币; 劣币; [蔑]钱; 棋子; 凑数的人, 玩具似的人. ③柜台, 帐台; [英](旧时)债务人监狱. *~s for gambling* 赌博用筹码. *a girl behind the ~* 女店员. ***pay over the ~*** 在(进门处)帐柜上交款. ***sit [serve] behind a ~*** 当店员; 做商人. ***under the ~*** 私下(交易).

coun·ter[2] [ˈkauntə] *n.* ①反对物, 反面. ②(鞋底的)后跟. ③马的前胸部; 船尾突出部. ④【乐】反对次中音. ⑤【拳】回击, 迎击; 【溜冰】逆转. ⑥铅字笔划间的凹处. —*a.* 相反的, 反对的; 一对中之一, 副的. *a ~ list* 副名单. —*ad.* 相反地, 反对地; 逆向地. ***act [run, go] ~ to*** 违反, 与…相反. ***hunt [go, run] ~*** 向相反方向追猎. —*vt.* ①对抗; 反击, 反抗, 反对; 针对. ②(象棋)下针锋相对的一着. ③换鞋跟; 打后掌. —*vi.* 进行反击; 还击 (*against*).

coun·ter- *comb. f.* 反对, 反, 逆, 防; 对应, 补, 副: *counter-agent.*

coun·ter·ac·cu·sa·tion [ˌkauntəˌækjuˈzeiʃən] *n.* 反控.

coun·ter·act [ˌkauntəˈrækt] *vt.* 对…采取直接反对行动; 抵抗, 抵制, 阻碍, 打破(计划); 消减, 抵消, 解(毒), 中和. *~ a man's influence* 削弱某人的影响.

coun·ter·ac·tion [ˌkauntəˈrækʃən] *n.* 反对行动; 反作用, 反动, 对抗(作用); 中和, 抵消.

coun·ter·ac·tive [ˌkauntəˈræktiv] *a.* 反对的, 抵抗的, 反作用的; 中和性的, 起抵消作用的. —*n.* 中和剂; 中和力.

coun·ter·a·gent [ˌkauntəˈreidʒənt] *n.* 对抗力[者, 物]; 中和力, 反抗力, 反对动作; 反作用[中和]剂.

coun·ter·ap·proach [ˈkauntərəprəutʃ] *n.* [常 *pl.*] 筑城对壕(作业); (守军的)反抗行动.

coun·ter·at·tack [ˈkauntərəˌtæk] *vt., vi., n.* 反攻, 反击.

coun·ter·at·trac·tion [ˈkauntərəˌtrækʃən] *n.* 反[对抗]引力; 对抗物.

coun·ter·bal·ance [ˌkauntəˈbæləns] *vt.* 使平均, 使平衡; 补充, 弥补; 抵消(…的作用). — [ˈkauntəbæl-] *n.* 抗衡, 等衡, 平衡量; 平衡力; 【机】平衡锤.

coun·ter·blast [ˈkauntəblɑːst] *n.* ①对抗气流, 逆风. ②强硬的抗议, 猛烈的反驳.

coun·ter·blow [ˈkauntəˌbləu] *n.* 反击. *deliver a ~ against the aggressor* 对侵略者予以反击.

coun·ter·buff [ˈkauntəbʌf] *n., vt.* 反击; 击退; 挫败.

coun·ter-cei·ling [ˈkauntəˌsiːliŋ] *n.* 【建】(隔音, 隔热)吊平顶.

coun·ter·change [ˌkauntəˈtʃeindʒ] *n., vt., vi.* 交换, 交替, 掉换; (起)交互作用; (使)交错, (使成)棋盘花[杂色].

coun·ter·charge [ˈkauntətʃɑːdʒ] *n., vt.* 反攻; 【法】反诉, 反告.

coun·ter·check [ˈkauntətʃek] *n.* 阻挡, 对抗; 制止; 核对, 复查; [古]反驳, 回嘴. *the quarrelsome ~* 对骂. —*vt.* 制止, 防止; 核对, 复查.

coun·ter·claim [ˈkauntəkleim] *n., vi., vt.* (提出)反要求; 反诉.

coun·ter·clock·wise [ˌkauntəˈklɔkwaiz] *a., ad.* 反时针方向的(地).

coun·ter·cul·ture [ˈkauntəkʌltʃə] *n.* 反传统[主流]文化 [六十年代以来在美国青少年中盛行的一种思潮言行].

coun·ter·cur·rent [ˈkauntəˌkʌrənt] *n.* 逆流, 对流, 反流; 【电】逆[反向]电流.

coun·ter·deed [ˈkauntədiːd] *n.* 【法】反对证书[声明前一文件无效的文件, 大都为密件].

coun·ter·dem·on·stra·tion [ˈkauntəˌdemənsˈtreiʃən] *n.* 反示威〔指反对某一示威的反示威〕.
coun·ter·de·vice [ˈkauntəˌdivais] *n.* ①对抗装置. ②【军】反导弹装置.
coun·ter·drain [ˈkauntədrein] *n.* (堤底的)副渠, 漏水渠,副阴沟.
coun·ter·drive [ˈkauntədraiv] *n.* 【军】反攻, 反袭击.
coun·ter·es·pi·on·age [ˈkauntəˌrespiəˈnɑːʒ] *n.* 反间谍行动.
coun·ter·ev·i·dence [ˈkauntəˈrevidəns] *n.* 反证.
coun·ter·feit [ˈkauntəfit] *a.* 仿造的, 假冒的; 虚伪的, 假的. *a* ~ *note* 伪钞. ~ *sickness* 假病. — *n.* 伪物, 伪品,仿造品; 伪币; 伪作; 肖像,画像; 〔古〕骗子. — *vt., vi.* ①作伪; 伪造(货币、文件等). ②假冒, 伪; 仿造, 仿效,摹仿. ~ *death* 装死.
coun·ter-fire [ˈkauntəfaiə] *n.* 【林】迎火,逆火.
coun·te·flow [ˈkauntəfləu] *n.* 逆流.
coun·ter·foil [ˈkauntəfɔil] *n.* 存根,票根.
coun·ter·force [ˈkauntəˌfɔːs] *n.* 反击力〔尤指用战略空军和导弹核武器在战争一开始就摧毁敌方核攻击力量〕.
coun·ter·fort [ˈkauntəfɔːt] *n.* 【建】护墙, 扶壁; 后扶垛,拱柱;【地】山的支脉.
coun·ter-glow [ˈkauntəgləu] *n.* 【天】对日照.
coun·ter-guard [ˈkauntəgɑːd] *n.* 筑城堡障,垒障.
coun·ter·in·sur·gen·cy [ˌkauntərinˈsəːdʒənsi] *n.* 反暴动(行动),反骚动(行动),反叛乱(行动).
coun·ter·in·tel·li·gence [ˈkauntərinˌtelidʒəns] *n.*【军】对敌〔反〕情报活动; 反情报部队〔机构〕 (= C- Corps).
coun·ter-ir·ri·tant [ˌkauntəˈriritənt] *n.* 【医】对抗刺激剂,诱导剂.
coun·ter·irritate [ˈkauntəˈririteit] *vt.* 对抗刺激〔指施加刺激以抵消附近的炎症〕; 对…施用对抗刺激剂.
coun·ter·jum·per [ˈkauntədʒʌmpə] *n.*〔口、蔑〕商店售货员,站柜台的.
coun·ter·light [ˈkauntəlait] *n.* 面对面的窗子; 逆光.
count·er·man [ˈkauntəˌmæn, -mən] *n.* *(pl.* *-men* [-ˌmen,-mən]*)* (自助餐馆等)柜台服务员.
coun·ter·mand [ˌkauntəˈmɑːnd] *vt., n.* ①(下反对命令)取消(前一命令); 撤回, 召回,调回. ②改变定货,取消(定货).
coun·ter·march[ˈkauntəmɑːtʃ] *n.* 【军】反向行进; 后退,倒退. — *vi., vt.* (使)向反对方向行进.
coun·ter·mark [ˈkauntəmɑːk] *n.* ①(金首饰等上的)戳记,刻印. ②(货物等上的)副标记,附加记号. ③【兽医】(隐瞒马四年龄而作的)人造齿瘢. — *vt.* 刻印记; 加副号.
coun·ter·meas·ure [ˈkauntəmeʒə] *n.* 对案, 对策; 对抗〔报复〕手段;【无】干扰.
coun·ter·mine [ˈkauntəmain] *n.* 【军】(对敌军所挖地道的)对抗地道; (反炸敌人水雷的)反水雷; 对抗计划〔谋略〕. — *vt.* 用反地道防御; 用对抗计策挫败〔破坏〕.
coun·ter·move [ˈkauntəmuːv] *n.* 对抗行动; 对抗手段,报复手段〔行动〕.
coun·ter·mure [ˈkauntəmjuə] *n.* 筑城副壁.
coun·ter·of·fen·sive [ˈkauntərəˌfensiv, ˌkauntərəˈfensiv] *n.* 反攻,反击.
coun·ter·of·fer [ˈkauntəˌɔːfə] *n.* 还价,反建议.
coun·ter·pane [ˈkauntəpein] *n.* 床罩.
coun·ter·part [ˈkauntəpɑːt] *n.* ①【法】(正副两份中的)一份,(尤指)副本; 极相似的人〔物〕,一对中之一个, 骑缝图章的一半. ②相对物; 变体, 变型. ③【乐】对应部. *It has no* ~ *in the world.* 举世无双.
coun·ter·plea [ˈkauntəpliː] *n.* 【法】附带抗辩.
coun·ter·plot [ˈkaunˈtəplɔt] *n.* 对抗策略. — *vt., vi.* 用对抗策略对付.
coun·ter·point [ˈkauntəpɔint] *n.* ①【乐】对位法,对位音; 旋律配合法; 重复旋律法. ②对偶; 对比; 对照(法). — *vt.* 用对照法衬托.
coun·ter·poise [ˈkauntəpɔiz] *vt.* (使)均衡〔平衡〕; 补偿,抵补. — *n.* 平衡, 均衡; 平衡力, 衡重体; 秤锤,砝码;【无】平衡网络,地网. *be in* ~ 保持平衡〔均衡〕.
coun·ter·pro·duc·tive [ˈkauntəprəˌdʌktiv] *a.* 起反作用的.
coun·ter·pro·gram·ming [ˈkauntəˈprəugræmiŋ] *n.* 竞争〔对抗〕性节目编排.
coun·ter·pro·po·sal [ˈkauntəprəˌpəuzl] *n.* 反建议, 反提案.
coun·ter·ref·or·ma·tion [ˈkauntəˌrefəˈmeiʃən] *n.* 反改革.
coun·ter·rev·o·lu·tion [ˈkauntərevəˈljuːʃən] *n.* 反革命. **-ary** *n., a.* 反革命分子(的). **-ist** *n.* 反革命(分子).
coun·ter·scarp [ˈkauntəskɑːp] *n.* (堡垒濠沟的)外削壁.
coun·ter·sea [ˈkauntəsiː] *n.* 逆浪,逆行海流.
coun·ter·shaft [ˈkauntəʃɑːft] *n.* 【机】副轴,对轴,平行轴,逆转轴; 天轴.
coun·ter·sign [ˈkauntəsain] *n.* ①【军】(对哨兵盘问时)回答口令; 呼应暗号; 【海】应讯信号. ②副签, 副署; 【商】会签. — *vt.* 副署,连署; 同意,承认.
coun·ter·sig·na·ture [ˌkauntəˈsignitʃə] *n.* 副署, 连署.
coun·ter·sink [ˈkauntəsiŋk] *vt.* *(-sunk* [-sʌŋk]*)* 打孔装埋(螺钉头), 打埋头孔. — *n.* 埋头钻; 埋头孔, 暗钉眼.
coun·ter·spy [ˈkauntəspai] *n.* 反间谍.
coun·ter·stroke [ˈkauntəstrəuk] *n.* 反击; 还击, 回击; 【医】反击损伤.
coun·ter·ten·or [ˈkauntəˈtenə] *n.* 【乐】上次中音〔男声最高音部〕; 上次中音歌手.
coun·ter·type [ˈkauntəˌtaip] *n.* ①相反典型. ②对等型; 相似型.
coun·ter·vail [ˈkauntəveil] *vt., vi.* ①对抗; 抵敌; 与…势均力敌. ②补偿; 抵消.
coun·ter·view [ˈkauntəvjuː] *n.* ①反对意见. ②对质.
coun·ter·weigh [ˌkauntəˈwei] *vt.* 使平衡; 抵消.
coun·ter·weight [ˈkauntəweit] *n.* 平衡重量; 砝码; 抗衡. — *vt.* = counterweigh.
coun·ter·word [ˈkauntəwəːd] *n.* 转用词, 代用词〔例: swell 意为 first-rate 等〕.
coun·ter·work [ˈkauntəˈwəːk] *vt., vi.* 对抗行动; 阻碍; 破坏. — *n.* 对抗;【军】对垒.
count·ess [ˈkauntis] *n.* ①伯爵夫人〔英国指 earl 的妻子,欧洲大陆指 count 的妻子〕. ②女伯爵.
count·ing [ˈkauntiŋ] *n.* 计算. ~ *house* 〔英〕 = ~ *room* 〔美〕帐房; 会计室; 事务室. ~ *overseer [witness]* (投票的)唱票监察人.
count·less [ˈkauntlis] *a.* 无数的,数不尽的.
count·out [ˈkauntˈaut] *n.* (英下院) 不满法定人数 (40人) 的休会; 【拳】(对被击倒者宽限的) 十秒, 数十下; 〔美〕被故意少报票数而落选的候选人.
coun·tri·fied [ˈkʌntrifaid] *a.* 土里土气的; 粗鲁的.
coun·tri·fy [ˈkʌntrifai] *vt.* 使土头土脑,使成乡下派头; 使粗鲁.
coun·try [ˈkʌntri] *n.* ①国家; 国土; (全)国民, 民众. ②本国,祖国; 家乡,故乡. ③乡下,农村; 土地; 地方,地区; 领域,范围. ④(代表群众的)陪审(团). ⑤【矿】围岩(= ~ rock). ⑥【海】(船内的)室,间; 士官室 (= the officer ~). ⑦【板球】外野. *a developing* ~ 发展中的国家. *a beautiful* ~ 美丽的地区. *town and* ~ 城乡. *a flat* ~ 平原地区. *a hill* ~ 丘陵地带. — *a.* ①地方的,乡村的; 粗鲁的. ②祖国的; 故乡的,家乡的. ③〔美乐〕乡村音乐的. *across* ~ (不走正路)横断田野,越野的(赛跑等). ~ *cousin* 乡下亲戚, (衣着朴素态度悬直的)

乡下人. ~ *gentleman* 乡下地主. ~ *note* 地方(银行发行的)钞票. ~ *party* (代表农村利益的)农民党. ***go (out) into the*** ~ 下乡〔美国说 ***go up (the)*** ~〕. ***go [appeal] to the*** ~〔英〕解散议会(进行普选),吁请国民决定国是. ***in the*** ~ 在乡下;【板球】远离三柱门. ***live in the*** ~ 住在乡下〔美国说 ***live up*** ~〕. ***put [throw] oneself upon the*** ~ 要求陪审团审判. ~ **and western**〔缩 C&W〕*a.*【美乐】西部乡村音乐的. **~-born** *a.* 生在乡下的. **~-bred** *a.* 在乡下长大的. ~ **damage**【商】因风雨或处置失当所造成的损失. **~-dance** (英国的)土风舞,乡村舞. ~ **folk** 乡下人;同国人,同胞. ~ **house** (乡绅贵族等的)庄宅(*opp.* town house);庄园式地主住宅;〔美〕别墅. ~ **jake**〔美〕乡下人. **~man** 乡下人;某地[国]的人;同国人,同胞,同乡. (*fellow ~men* 同胞). ~ **mile** 很远的距离. **~people** 乡下佬. ~ **rocky**【美乐】西部乡村摇摆音乐. ~ **seat** = ~ house. **~side** 乡下,农村;地方;地方居民. **~wide** *a.* 全国(性)的. **~woman** 乡下妇女;女同胞,女同乡.

coun·ty [ˈkaunti] *n.* ①〔英〕郡〔与专有名词连用时用 shire. 例: Yorkshire = the ~ of York〕. ②〔英〕郡中世家,郡中社交频繁的阶层;全郡居民. ③〔美〕县. ***the home counties***〔英〕伦敦附近六州. ~ **alderman** 郡参议员. ~ **borough** 市. ~ **commissioner**〔英〕郡治安法官;〔美〕县长. ~ **corporate**〔英〕自治市,特别市. ~ **council** 郡议会. ~ **council school**〔英〕郡立小学校. ~ **court**〔英〕郡法院,〔美〕县法院;县监察委员会. **~-court** *vt.*〔英口〕向郡法院控告. ~ **family**〔英〕郡中世家. ~ **farm [house]**〔美〕县济贫农场,县贫民收容所. ~ **hall** 郡议事厅;〔the C- H-〕(特指)伦敦郡议事厅. ~ **seat**〔美〕县城. ~ **sessions** 郡治安法官执行的四季裁判. ~ **society** 郡中上层社会(集团). ~ **town**〔英〕郡城;〔美〕县城.

coup [kuː] *n.*〔F.〕①突然的一击. ②突然而敏捷的行动;大成功. ③(军事)政变. ***at one*** ~ 一举,一气. ***make [pull off] a great*** ~ 大大成功. ~ ***de foudre*** [ˈkuː də ˈfuːdrə]〔F.〕雷击;晴天霹雳;一见钟情. ~ ***de grâce*** [ˈkuːdəˈgrɑːs]〔F.〕(使其少受痛苦而)一下打死;一举消灭;致命一击. ~ ***de main*** [ˈkuːdəˈmɛ̃ːŋ]〔F.〕【军】奇袭. ~ ***de maître*** [kuːdəˈmetrə]〔F.〕巧妙的手段. ~ ***d'état*** [ˈkuːdeiˈtɑː]〔F.〕(武装)政变. ~ ***de théâtre*** [ˈkuːdəteiˈɑːtr]〔F.〕(富有效果的)戏剧(性)手法. ~ ***d'œil*** [ˈkuːˈdəːi]〔F.〕一瞥,概观;【军】能迅速看清局势的眼力.

cou·pé [ˈkuːpei] *n.*〔F.〕双座四轮轿式马车;轿式小汽车;〔英〕(客车末端的)分隔车厢.

coup·ist [ˈkuːist] *n.* 企图(军事)政变者;支持(军事)政变者.

cou·ple [ˈkʌpl] *n.* ①一对,一双. ②配偶,夫妇,未婚夫妻;一对舞伴. ③〔口〕交媾;【物】力偶;电偶;【天】联星. ④〔口〕(少数)几个,两三个. *an old* ~ 老两口儿. *a married* ~ 夫妇. *a pack of 20* ~ 二十对的一群猎犬. *a thermo-electric* ~ 温差电偶. *a* ~ *of days* 二三日,数日. ***go [hunt, run] in ~s*** 总是成双成对;协力. — *vt.* ①(两支)拴在一起,配合,连接. ②使结婚;(使)交配. ③由…联想到(…);把…同联系起来. ~ *two railroad coaches* 把两节铁路车厢连接起来. ~ *the name of Lenin with the idea of revolution* 把列宁的名字同革命的思想联系起来. — *vi.* 拥抱,搂抱;交尾;结婚;结合,配合.

cou·pler [ˈkʌplə] *n.* ①连结者,配合者. ②联结器;【无】耦合器;【铁路】车钩;【摄】发色剂;【乐】(风琴上连结两组键盘的)联奏器.

cou·plet [ˈkʌplit] *n.* 两行诗〔两行构成一节的诗体〕;对句;〔*pl.*〕对联. *the heroic* ~ 英雄史诗式两行诗.

cou·pling [ˈkʌpliŋ] *n.* 联结;交尾;【机】管箍;联结器;轴接;(火车的)车钩;【电】耦合.

cou·pon [ˈkuːpɔn, ˈkuːpɔ̃ːŋ] *n.* ①【商】(附在证券上的)息票;(火车等使用一次剪下一张的)票,通票. ②【商】赠券;(连在广告上的)预约券,优待券. ③配给票. ④〔英俚〕(政党领袖提出的)候选人名单. ⑤【技术】试样,试件,试棒,试片,切片. *a food [oil]* ~ 粮[油]票. ~ *system* 附送赠品的商品推销法. ~ *ticket* (使用一次剪下一张的)多次入场票. *cum* ~ =~ *on* 带有息票的(公债票等). *ex* ~ = ~ *off* 不带息票的.

cour·age [ˈkʌridʒ] *n.* 勇气,胆量;精神;〔美俚〕钱. *Dutch* ~〔俚〕酒后之勇,虚勇. *moral* ~ 精神之勇,坚信不移之勇. *physical* ~ 不怕身体危险的勇气,刚勇. *stoic* ~ 坚忍不拔的精神. ***have the*** ~ ***of one's convictions [opinions]*** 勇于坚持自己的主张[信仰]. ***lose*** ~ 丧气,丧胆. ***take [muster up, pluck up, screw up]*** ~ 鼓起勇气. ***take one's*** ~ ***in both hands*** 勇敢地干,敢作敢为.

cou·ra·geous [kəˈreidʒəs] *a.* 勇敢的,英勇的. **-ly** *ad.* **-ness** *n.*

cou·rant [kuˈrænt] *n.* 报(纸)〔现仅作报名用〕. — *a.*【徽】步行状的.

cou·rante, cou·rant [kuːˈrɑ̃ːnt] *n.* ①库兰特舞. ②库兰特舞曲. ③〔英方〕乱跑.

cou·reur de bois [kuːˈrəː dəˈbwɑː] (*pl.* ***cou·reurs de bois***) (早期在加拿大边界流窜的)法国非法毛皮贩子;非法猎取毛皮者.

cour·gette [kuːəˈʒet]〔F.〕绿皮南瓜汁〔一种冷饮〕.

cour·i·er [ˈkuriə] *n.* ①信使,急件递送人. ②(欧洲的)伴游服务员. ③〔C-〕(用作报名)信使报. *the Liverpool C-.* 利物浦信使报.

cour·lan [ˈkulən] *n.*【动】(美洲热带的)哭鸟,长嘴鸟.

course [kɔːs] *n.* ①进程,经过,过程,趋势;经过期间. ②进路;水路;路程;路线;航线;【火箭】导引. ③行进方向;航向;走向,(矿)脉;(行动的)方针,方法;程序;举动,行动;〔*pl.*〕〔古〕品行,行为. ④行列,层次. ⑤学科,课程,教程;【医】疗程. ⑥经历,生涯. ⑦赛跑场;跑道;跑马场. ⑧(用狗)追猎. ⑨(比赛的)一场,一回合;一道菜;【建】一层(砖等),一排;【船】下桁大横帆. ⑩〔*pl.*〕月经. ⑪〔又写作 'course〕〔俚,美〕= of ~. *a dog* ~ = *a pursuit* ~【空】追踪飞行. *a pre-computed* ~【火箭】程序控制导引;自动导航. *a collision* ~【空】迎面航向;拦截方向. *What* ~ *do you advise?* 你说怎么办好呢? *the science [literature]* ~ (大学的)理[文]科. *the preparatory* ~ 预科. *a dinner of five ~s* 五道菜的一餐饭. *a* ~ *of lectures* 连续讲演,讲座. *a degree in* ~〔美〕(经过)正式(课程而获得的)学位. ***(as) a matter of*** ~ (作为)当然的事情. ***adopt a middle*** ~ 采取稳健办法. ***be on her [its]*** ~ (船)航向不变. ***by*** ~ ***of*** 照…的常例. ~ **bond** = ~ ***of headers***【建】丁砖层. ~ ***crabbing***〔美俚〕讨好老师,取得老师的欢心. ~ ***of events*** 事件的经过. ~ ***of exchange*** (外汇)兑换率[行情表]. ~ ***of things*** 事态,趋势. ~ ***of treatments***【医】疗程. ***follow a middle*** ~ 采取稳健办法. ***follow [persue] her*** ~ 照一定航线航行. ***hold [keep on] one's*** ~ 不变方向;抱定宗旨. ***in*** ~ ①〔美〕按正规课程(得到的). ②〔俚〕= of ~. ③〔古〕= ***in due*** ~. ***in*** ~ ***of*** 在…中(*The house is in* ~ *of construction.* 房子正在建造中). ***in due*** ~ 及时;顺次,依次序. ***in full*** ~〔口〕快;用全速. ***in mid*** ~ 在半路,中途. ***in short*** ~〔口〕立即,马上. ***in the*** ~ ***of*** 在…之中(*in the* ~ *of today* 在今天以内. *in the* ~ *of things* 在事情顺利发展中,在正常情况下). ***in the ordinary*** ~ ***of events*** 按正常趋势. ***lay the*** ~ 砌砖. ***of*** ~ 当然. ***run its [their]*** ~ (疾病、岁月等自然而然地)经过,进展. ***shape one's*** ~ 决定路线;制定方针. ***stay the*** ~ 坚持到底,始终不渝. ***take a*** ~【海】採一定航路. ***take one's own*** ~ 按自己办法,走自己的道路. ***take to evil ~s*** 开始放荡. ***walk over the*** ~【赛马】(因无劲敌)从容

得胜。— *vt.* 追，赶，猎；跑马；越过，跑过，横断（原野）。— *vi.* （用猎狗）追猎；（马、孩子等的）快跑；（血液）循环；（眼泪）不住地淌；（云等）乱飞；决定航线［方针］。~-**dinner** （丰盛的）正式晚餐。

cours·er[1] [ˈkɔːsə] *n.* ①快跑者，行进者［人或物］。②追猎者。③猎狗。

cours·er[2] [ˈkɔːsə] *n.* 〔诗〕骏马；军马。

cours·er[3] [ˈkɔːsə] *n.* 【动】（亚洲和非洲产的）快跑走禽。

cours·ing [ˈkɔːsiŋ] *n.* ①（使用猎狗）追猎。②快跑，追赶；运行，奔驰。

court [kɔːt] *n.* ①法院，法庭；法官。②宫廷，朝廷；朝臣；朝见，谒见；御前会议；（公司等的）委员会，董事会；委员，董事。③院子，天井；场子，网球场；（展览会中的）馆。④奉承，讨好；（尤指男人向女人）求爱，求婚。⑤短巷，短街。*a law* ~ 法庭。*the People's C-* 人民法院。*a summary* ~ 即决法院。*the Crown C-* 〔英〕刑事法院。*the High C- of Parliament* 英国议会。*a grass [hard]* ~ 草地［硬地］网球场。***appear in*** ~ 出庭。***at*** ~ 在宫中，在朝廷上。***be presented at*** ~ 在宫中受接见。***C- of Admiralty***【英史】海军法庭。***C- of Appeal*** 上诉法院。***C- of Claims*** 〔美〕（华盛顿）行政法院。***C- of Conscience [Requests]*** （少额）债权法院；〔喻〕良心。~ ***of inquiry*** 咨询会议。~ ***of justice [judicature]*** = ~ *of law* 法院，法庭。***C- of St. James's*** 英国宫廷。***go to*** ~ 觐见。***hold a*** ~ ***(C-)*** 开庭，开审；举行（觐见礼）。***in*** ~ 在法庭上。***laugh out of*** ~ 置之一笑，一笑了之。***order the*** ~ ***to be cleared*** 命令旁听人退庭。***out of*** ~ 在法庭外；无审判价值的，无诉讼权利的；无足轻重的，不值一顾的（议论等）。***pay [make] one's*** ~ ***to*** 奉承，献殷勤，（向女人）求爱，求婚。***present at*** ~ 陪…入宫谒见，做谒见陪客。***put out of*** ~ 不顾，蔑视。***put oneself out of*** ~ 做出［讲出］让人瞧不起的事情［话］。***settle (a case) out of*** ~ （在法院外）私下和解。***take (a matter) into*** ~ 弄到上法庭，提出诉讼。— *vt., vi.* 献殷勤；（向女人）求爱，求婚；寻求；博（人喝采等），招惹（祸事等），诱（人）*(into; to; from)*；〔英俚〕向法院控诉。~ **card** 〔英〕有人头的纸牌〔King, Queen, Jack〕。~ **circular** 宫廷公报。~ **day** 开庭日，审判日；（朝廷中的）典礼日。~ **dress** 朝服，大礼服。~ **fool** 朝廷中的弄臣。~ **guide** 〔英〕名绅录。~ **house** 法院；〔美〕县政府。~ **lady** 朝廷中女官，宫女。~ **martial** 军事法庭；〔俚〕交军事法庭。~ **mourning** 宫丧，废朝。~ **plaster** （往时英国宫女贴在脸上增进美感的膏膏，转为）橡皮膏；〔俚〕死缠不休的求婚者。~ **roll** （租佃）地册，地籍登记簿。~**room** 审判室。~**ship** （男向女）求爱，求婚；求爱期间；【动】求偶（现象）。~**yard** 庭院，院子。

cour·te·ous [ˈkəːtjəs] *a.* 有礼貌的；殷勤的，周到的。*(opp.* rude*)*. **-ly** *ad.* **-ness** *n.*

cour·te·san, cour·te·zan [ˌkɔːtiˈzæn] *n.* 高等妓女；原指王公显贵的情妇。

cour·te·sy [ˈkəːtisi, ˈkɔːtisi] *n.* 礼貌，殷勤周到；亲切；好意；〔古〕行礼，请安。***be granted the*** ~ ***[courtesies] of the port*** 〔美〕准予在海关免除检查。***by*** ~ 按惯例，礼貌上；〔美〕情面上。***by [through]*** ~ ***of*** 〔美〕由于…好意，蒙…特许。~ ***of the port***【海】外国军舰入港时相互访问的礼节。~ **light** （汽车车门打开后即自动开灯的）车箱灯。~ **title** （非法律规定的）礼貌上的尊称。

court·i·er [ˈkɔːtjə] *n.* ①朝臣。②谄媚者；受宠遇者。

court·li·ness [ˈkɔːtlinis] *n.* 礼让，殷勤，周到。

court·ly [ˈkɔːtli] *a.* 朝廷的；有礼貌的，殷勤的；周到的。

cous·cous [ˈkuːskuːs, kuːsˈkuːs] *n.* 【烹】（北非的）粉蒸羊肉；粉蒸鸡。

cous·in [ˈkʌzn] *n.* ①堂［表］兄弟，堂［表］姊妹；亲戚，远亲。②卿〔国王对贵族或别国元首的敬称〕。③朋友，伙伴。④同族者，同类者，同辈。⑤〔美俚〕容易受骗的人；无意中使对方占便宜的人。*first [full, own]* ~*s* （第一代）嫡堂［表］兄［弟、姊、妹］。*first* ~*s once removed* =〔俚〕*second* ~*s* （第二代）隔房堂［表］兄［弟、姊、妹］。*call* ~*s (with)* 认（某人）是亲戚；称兄道弟，建立亲密关系。*C- Anne* 〔美俚〕威尔斯人矿工的妻子。*C- Jack* 〔美俚〕到美国来谋生的威尔斯人矿工。~ *Jacky [Jan]* 〔英俚〕康瓦尔 (Cornwall) 人的绰号。*C- Johnathan* 美国人的绰号。~**-german** = *first* ~. ~**hood,** ~**ship** 堂［表］兄弟［姊妹］关系；亲戚关系。**-ly** *a.* 堂［表］兄弟［姐妹］关系（一样）的；亲戚似的。

cous·in·ry [ˈkʌzənri] *n.* 〔集合词〕表兄弟姊妹们，堂兄弟姊妹们；亲戚们。

coûte que coûte [ˈkuːt kə ˈkuːt] 〔F.〕无论代价如何，不惜任何牺牲。

couth [kuːθ] *a.* ①〔谑〕文雅的；有教养的；文明的。②〔古〕人所共知的；熟悉的。

couth·ie [ˈkuːθi] *a.* 〔Scot.〕①友好的，和善的。②舒适的。

cou·ture [F. kuˈtyːr] *n.* 妇女时装业；妇女时装。

coutu·rier [F. kutyrˈje] *n.* *(fem.* ***-rière*** [-riˈɛə]*)* 〔F.〕妇女时装设计师；时装店主。

cou·vade [kuːˈvɑːd] *n.* 父代母育风俗〔某些原始部族的风俗，婴儿出生后，父亲代替母亲卧床〕。

co·va·lence [kəuˈveiləns] *n.* 【化】共［协］价；共价电子；共价键。**-va·lent** *a.*

co·var·i·ance [kəuˈvɛəriəns] *n.* 【统】协方差，协变性；共离散。

co·var·i·ant [kəuˈvɛəriənt] *a., n.* 【统】协变的［式］。

cove[1] [kəuv] *n.* ①（河）湾；小海湾，崄岨的海角［山凹］。②【建】穹窿，拱。③凹圆线。— *vi., vt.* （使）成拱形；（使）内凹。

cove[2] [kəuv] *n.* 〔英俚〕家伙；〔澳俚〕老板（特指牧场经理）。*a rum* ~ 可笑的家伙。

cov·en [ˈkʌvən, ˈkəuvən] *n.* （女巫）大聚会；集会。

cov·e·nant [ˈkʌvinənt] *n.* ①协议，协定；协议书，协定条款。②【宗】誓约；（上帝对信徒的）圣约。③〔the C-〕国联盟约；【史】（1638 年苏格兰长老会反对主教派教会的）国民契约（= the National C-）；（1643 年英格兰和苏格兰议会协议保护长老会的）严肃盟约（= the Solemn League and C-）。④【法】契约（条款）；违约诉讼。— *vi., vt.* （订）协定，缔结盟约 *(with; for; to do; that)*.

cov·e·nan·tee [ˌkʌvinænˈtiː] *n.* 契约受益方。

cov·e·nant·er [ˈkʌvinəntə] *n.* 协定者，结盟者；〔C-〕【史】国民契约及严肃同盟的结盟者。

Cov·ent Garden [ˈkɔvənt gɑːdn] 考文特花园〔指 ①伦敦中部一个蔬菜花卉市场。② = the Covent Garden Theatre 伦敦中心戏院〕。

cov·en·trate, cov·en·trize [ˈkɔvəntreit, -traiz] *vt.* 集中轰炸摧毁〔来自 Coventry，英国城市名，1940 年几乎全部被纳粹空军炸毁〕。

Cov·en·try [ˈkɔvəntri] *n.* 考文垂〔英国城市〕。***send sb. to*** ~ 逐出社交圈子，抵制，与…绝交。

cov·er [ˈkʌvə] *vt.* ①覆盖，遮蔽，包裹；戴帽子；包庇，隐蔽，掩盖；灭迹，（用纸）裱（墙）。②孵（小鸡）；（种马）交配。③（炮火等）控制；对准射击；【军】掩护。④涉及，包括，包含；网罗；适用。⑤通过，走过（若干里）；讲完（几课）；看完（几节）。⑥足敷，足以抵补［补偿］；（用保险办法）保护；出大牌压倒（对方）。⑦【商】补进（预先卖出的商品）。⑧【宗】恕宥。⑨〔美〕采访（新闻；报导会议情形等）。⑩掩没。⑪（与雌的）交配。~ *the table* 铺桌布和摆餐具（准备开饭）。*Pray be* ~*ed.* 请戴好帽子。*The troops* ~*ed the country.* 军队遍布国内。~ *the landing [retreat] of an army* 掩护军队登陆［退却］。*His studies* ~*ed a wide field.* 他的研究涉及广大范围。*The rules* ~ *all cases.* 那规则普遍适用。*He once* ~*ed a mile in three minutes.* 他有一次在三分钟内跑了一英里。*My fee barely* ~*s my expenses.* 我的薪水刚刚够用。***be*** ~***ed with*** 盖满，覆满

(灰尘等),落满(苍蝇等),充满(恐慌、羞耻等). ~ **in** 用屋顶遮盖;用土填洞等. ~ ***into the Treasury*** 〔美〕解交国库. ~ ***oneself with*** 蒙受,获得 (*He ~ed himself with glory.* 享受荣誉). ~ ***over*** 遮遍, 完全封蔽. ~ ***shorts [short sales]*** (交易所)补进空头股数. ~ **up** ①蒙盖;隐藏. ②包庇(某人); 为某人打掩护. —*vi.* ①展延. ②代替 (*for*). ③(拳击中)掩护脸部. — ***n.*** ①覆盖物,盖子,套子,罩子,(书的)封面,壳子; (车轮的)外胎. ②隐蔽,遮蔽;假托,借口,假装. ③掩护物〔森林、凹地等〕;(禽兽)隐藏处. ④(一份)餐具. ⑤【商】担保,保证金. ⑥【板球】后卫场所;【网球】防守范围;【乒乓】触球. *a dinner of 50 ~s* 供五十个人食用的一次正餐. *Covers were laid for five.* 预备了五份饭菜. ***be under ~*** 是秘密的,在隐蔽处. ***break ~*** 由隐藏处跳出〔飞出〕. ***draw a ~*** 把(猎物)由树丛中赶出. ***from ~ to ~*** 从头到尾〔指书籍〕. ***provide ~ for*** 给…打掩护. ***take ~*** 【军】利用〔凭〕掩护物;隐蔽. ***under separate ~*** 另函包寄. ***under (the) ~ of*** 躲在…之下; 在…掩护下; 趁着(夜色等);借…为口实. ***under ~ to*** 附在…信中. ***under the same ~*** 在同一包〔封〕中, 附在信中. ~ **charge** (饭店)附加费,服务费. ~ **crop** 护田〔肥田〕的农作物,覆盖作物. ~ **girl** 封面女郎. ~**lid** = ~let. ~ **note** 暂保单,保险证明. ~ **point** 【板球】后卫. ~**-up** [ˈkʌvərʌp] *n.* 掩盖手段〔手法〕.

cov·er·age [ˈkʌvəridʒ] *n.* 范围,规模,总额;〔美〕保险额;保证金,现金准备;〔美〕(新闻)报导(范围);【植】优势度. ~ *diagram* 【空】搜索范围.

cov·er·all [ˈkʌvəˌrɔːl] *n.* 〔通常为 *pl.*〕连衣裤工作服.

Cov·er·dale [ˈkʌvədeil] *n.* 科弗代尔〔姓氏〕.

cov·ered [ˈkʌvəd] *a.* 隐蔽着的,掩藏着的;有屋顶的,有盖的; 戴着帽子的; 〔复合词〕盖满…的〔如: moss-~〕. *a ~ position* 隐蔽阵地. *a ~ wagon* 〔美〕有篷马车;汽车拉着走的活动房子. ~ **smut** 【农】坚黑穗病. ~ **way** 【军】覆道,暗道;【建】廊道.

cov·er·ing [ˈkʌvəriŋ] *n.* 被覆,外被;外封;房顶;上覆物,掩护;【商】了结,补进. ~ *fire* 掩护射击. ~ *for (chair, hand ...)* (椅、手…) 套. ~ *letter* (寄送物件等作为说明的)附信. ~ *note* 【火灾保险】承保通知单. ~ *party* 【军】掩护队. ~ *price* (一切计算在内的)总价.

cov·er·let [ˈkʌvəlit] *n.* ①床单,桌布(等). ②盖子,罩子.

cov·ert [ˈkʌvət] *a.* 隐蔽的,偷偷摸摸的,隐密的;【法】有丈夫(保护)的. *a feme ~* 【法】有夫之妇. ~ *cloth* 细纹薄呢. — [ˈkʌvə, ˈkʌvət] *n.* 掩蔽物; 隐伏处〔树丛等〕; 〔*pl.*〕【动】复羽. ***break ~*** = break cover. ***draw a ~*** = draw a cover. **-ly** *ad.*

cov·er·ture [ˈkʌvətjuə] *n.* ①被覆;保护;掩护物,隐伏处. ②【法】有夫之妇的身份. ***under ~*** 有丈夫.

cov·et [ˈkʌvit] *vt., vi.* 妄想 (别人东西), 贪求. *All ~ all lose.* 贪多无所得. **-able** *a.* 可垂涎的,可羡慕的.

cov·et·ous [ˈkʌvitəs] *a.* 贪婪的. ***be ~ of*** 渴望,贪求. **-ly** *ad.* **-ness** *n.*

cov·ey [ˈkʌvi] *n.* (鹌鹑、鹧鸪等的)一群,一窝;〔谑〕(人的)一群,一伙;(东西的)一套,一批.

cov·in [ˈkʌvin] *n.* ①变节;背信;欺诈;阴谋集团,诈骗集团. ②【法】共谋暗算他人.

cov·ing [ˈkəuviŋ] *n.* (河等的)湾,弯处;【建】弧形饰;穹窿,拱;凹圆线.

cow[1] [kau] *n.* (*pl.* ~*s*, 〔古、方〕 *kine* [kain]) ①母牛,乳牛 (*opp.* bull); (象、犀、鲸等的)母兽. ②〔美、方〕〔*pl.*〕= cattle. ③〔美俚〕牛奶,奶油;牛肉;〔俚〕粗壮邋遢的女人;〔卑〕儿女多的妇女;老妓. ***give 'em Brown's ~*** 〔美〕(马戏团)缩短表演. ***salt the ~ to catch the calf*** 〔美口〕用间接手段达到目的. ***till the ~s come home*** 长久,永远. ~**age** 【植】发痒黧豆. (= ~hage). ~**bane** 【植】毒芹. ~**bell** (牛的) 颈铃; 【植】白玉草. ~**berry** 【植】牙疙疸,越桔. ~**bind** 【植】白泻根; 异株泻根. ~**bird** 【鸟】(北美产)燕八哥. ~**boy** 牧童;〔美、加拿大〕骑马牧童;〔美俚〕违章驾驶的汽车司机;〔美俚〕西部风味的夹心面包. ~**boy boot** 〔美〕牛崽靴. ~**boy hat** 〔美〕牛崽帽. ~**boy suit** (儿童)牛崽装. ~**catcher** 〔美〕(车头前面的)排障器;(电车的)救助网;〔美俚〕无线电广播要目前后的广告. ~ **chips** 〔美〕(燃料)粪干. ~**college** 〔美俚〕农业学院; 小而不出名的大学. ~**-fat**, ~**-herb** 【植】麦篮菜. ~**fish** 【动】海牛;角鱼;海豚. ~**grass** 【植】紫云英. ~**gun** 〔海俚〕海军重炮. ~**hage** = ~age. ~**hand** 〔美方〕 = ~boy. ~**heel** 牛蹄冻; 炖(牛)蹄筋. ~**herd** 牧牛者. ~**hide** ① *n.* 牛皮;〔美〕牛皮鞭. ② *vt.* 用牛皮鞭抽打. ~**house** 牛棚. ~**lick** 〔美〕(牛舐过似的)一绺梳不平的乱发. ~ **lily** 【植】萍蓬草属. ~**man** 〔英〕放牛者;〔美〕牧牛业者; 牧场主人. ~**parsnip** 【植】欧洲防风,欧洲防风根;白芷属植物. ~**pea** 〔美〕 豇豆〔饲料〕; 豇豆. ~**poke** 〔美俚〕 = ~boy. ~**-pony** 〔美〕(牧牛者骑的)矮种马. ~**pox** 牛痘. ~**puncher** 〔美口〕 = ~boy. ~***'s breakfast*** 〔美俚〕草帽. ~**shed** 牛舍, 牛棚. ~**shot** 【板球】弯身用力斜打. ~**skin** 牛皮;〔美〕牛皮鞭. ~**slip** 【植】黄花九轮草,立金花. ~**'s-tail**, ~ **tail** 散开的绳头. ~ **to cover** 〔美〕 = butter. ~**tree** (南美产)乳树. ~ **with the iron tail** 〔美俚〕牛奶掺水用唧筒. 【植】黄花九轮草,西洋樱草;〔美〕猿猴草的一种.

cow[2] [kau] *vt.* 吓(倒), 恐吓. ***be ~ed*** 被吓退〔吓倒〕.

Cow·ard [ˈkauəd] *n.* 考厄德〔姓氏〕.

cow·ard [ˈkauəd] *n.* 懦夫, 胆小鬼; 【赛马】胆小的马. — *a.* 〔诗〕怯懦的;【徽】夹着尾巴的. *a greyhound ~* 夹着尾巴的猎犬.

cow·ard·ice, cow·ard·li·ness [ˈkauədis, -linis] *n.* 怯懦,懦弱,胆小.

cow·ard·ly [ˈkauədli] *a., ad.* 怯懦的〔地〕.

cow·er [ˈkauə] *vi.* 畏缩,退缩.

Cowes [kauz] *n.* 考斯〔英格兰 Isle of Wight 的港口,著名海滨浴场及快艇竞赛场〕.

cow·ish [ˈkauiʃ] *a.* 牛一样的;笨拙的;怯懦的.

cowl [kaul] *n.* ①(修道士的)头罩,带头罩的僧衣;兜帽;苏格兰睡帽. ②烟囱罩;(风筒上的)通风帽. ***take the ~*** 出家当修士.

cowled [kauld] *a.* ①带有头罩的. ②【动、植】僧帽状的.

Cow·ley [ˈkauli] *n.* 考利〔姓氏〕.

cowl·ing [ˈkauliŋ] *n.* 【机】罩,外壳,盖,帽.

cowl·staff [ˈkaulˌstɑːf, -ˌstæf; ˈkəul-] *n.* 〔古〕扁担.

co-work·er [ˈkəuˈwəːkə] *n.* 共同工作者,合作者,帮手,同事.

Cow·per [ˈkaupə, ˈkuːpə] *n.* 考珀〔姓氏〕.

Cow·rie, cow·ry [ˈkauri] *n.* 【贝】玛瑙贝.

cox [kɔks] *n.* 〔口〕(赛艇的)舵手,艇长. — *vt., vi.* 做舵手〔艇长〕.

cox·a [ˈkɔksə] *n.* (*pl.* *coxae* [ˈkɔksiː]) ①【解】髋. ②【虫】基节.

cox·al [ˈkɔksəl] *a.* 基节的; 髋骨的. ~ *gland [joint]* 腰腺(节). ~ *process* 基节突.

cox·al·gi·a [kɔkˈsældʒiə, -dʒə] *n.* 【医】①髋痛. ②髋关节结核. **-al·gic** *a.*

cox·comb [ˈkɔkskəum] *n.* ①纨袴子. ②【史】(中世纪丑角的)鸡冠帽. ③【植】鸡冠花.

cox·comb·i·cal [kɔksˈkəumikəl] *a.* 纨袴气的,虚浮的,浮夸的.

cox·comb·ry [ˈkɔkskəumri] *n.* 虚浮,浮夸; 爱打扮; 纨袴子弟.

cox·swain [ˈkɔkswein, ˈkɔksn] *n.* (赛艇的)艇长,舵手〔略 cox〕; (舰船的)艇手. ~ ***of the plow*** 〔美〕新水兵. ~***'s box*** 舵手坐位. — *vt.* 充当(赛艇的)艇长.

cox·y [ˈkɔksi] *a.* 〔学俚〕 = cocky.

Coy [kɔi] *n.* 科伊〔姓氏,男子名〕.

Coy = company.

coy [kɔi] *a.* ①腼腆的,羞怯的;对…感到害羞*(of, about)*. ②献媚的,卖弄风情的. ③〔古〕隐蔽的,偏僻的(地方). *be ~ of speech* 怕羞说不出话来. *~ tricks* 卖弄风情. **-ly** *ad.* **-ness** *n.*

coy·ote [ˈkɔiəut, kɔiˈəuti] *n.* *(pl. ~s,* 〔集合词〕 *~)* 【动】(美国西部大草原中的)草原狼,郊狼.〔喻〕歹人,恶棍.

coy·pu [ˈkɔipuː] *n.* *(pl. ~s,* 〔集合词〕 *~)* 【动】(南美)海狸鼠〔毛皮称 nutria, 颇名贵〕.

coz [kʌz] *n.* 〔口〕 = cousin.

coze [kəuz] *vi.* 聊天,谈心. — *n.* 亲热的谈话〔茶话〕.

coz·en [ˈkʌzn] *vt.* ①骗走某人的某物 *(out of sth.)* ②诱哄某人做某事 *(into doing sth.)* — *vi.* 招摇撞骗. **-age** *n.* 欺骗,;招摇撞骗.

co·zi·ly [ˈkəuzili] *ad.* = cosily.

co·zi·ness [ˈkəuzinis] *n.* = cosiness.

co·zy [ˈkəuzi] *a.* = cosy.

CP = ①Communist Party 共产党. ②Command Post 【军】指挥所. ③Common Pleas 〔美〕中级法院.

C. P. = ① chemically pure 化学纯的. ②Common Pleas 〔美〕(某些州的)中级法院. ③Court of Probate 〔美〕遗嘱(检验). ④current paper 最新文献.

cp. = ①compare. ②centipoise.

c.p. = candlepower.

CPA, CPAL = Canadian Pacific Airlines 加拿大太平洋航空公司.

C. P. A. = Certified Public Accountant. 〔美〕(特许)会计师.

CPC = Communist Party of China 中国共产党.

CPI = Consumer Price Index 消费者价格指数.

Cpl, cpl. = Corporal 下士.

cpm = counts per minute 计数/分.

cpn. = coupon 【会计】息票,利息券;(食品、布匹等的)配给券.

CPPCC = Chinese People's Political Consultative Conference 中国人民政治协商会议.

C. P. R. = Canadian Pacific Railway 加拿大太平洋铁路.

cps = ①counts per second 计数/秒. ②cycles per second 周/秒.

CPSU = Communist Party of the Soviet Union 苏联共产党.

CPSU(B) = Communist Party of the Soviet Union (Bolsheviks) 联共(布).

CPU = Central Processing Unit 【自】中央处理机.

CQ = ①call to quarters 〔公告等的广播开始信号;业余无线电爱好者相互通讯前的信号〕. ②charge of quarters 【军】内务值班;内务值班军士.

CQD = Come quick, danger 〔遇难求救信号〕.

Cr = Chromium.

cr. = ①credit; creditor. ②crown(s).

C. R., CR = Costa Rica.

crab[1] [kræb] *n.* ①蟹;蟹肉;〔C-〕【天】巨蟹座, 巨蟹宫. ②【虫】阴虱. ③〔*pl.*〕(骰子)双么. ④〔口〕不利,失败;【机】起重绞车. ⑤〔空俚〕侧飞;偏差,偏出. *a case of ~s* 失败,不利的下场. ***catch a*** ~ (划船)插桨入水过深,〔俚〕一桨没划好,划坏. ~ ***fleet*** 〔美俚〕蟹舰队〔学生练习舰队〕. ***turn out [come off]*** ~***s*** 终于失败. — *vt.* ①用爪抓. ②使侧航;使斜行. — *vi.* 捕蟹;〔美口〕缩手,摆脱;侧航,偏飞. ~ ***out of*** 〔美口〕摆脱. ~ ***the wind*** 【美空】横飞. ~ **apple** 【植】山楂. ~ **louse** 【虫】阴虱. ~**sidle** *vi.* 侧航;横行. ~ **winch** 起重机.

crab[2] [kræb] *vt.* ①〔美口〕苛责,挑剔,贬损;〔美俚〕干涉,②使人扫兴;使变乖戾. —*vi.* 抱怨;发牢骚 *(about)*. ~ ***sb.'s act*** 〔美俚〕干涉人,扫人兴.

crab[3] [kræb] *n.* 【植】沙果;沙果树(= ~ apple, ~ tree).

Crabb(e) [kræb] *n.* 克拉布〔姓氏〕.

crab·bed [ˈkræbid] *a.* ①乖张的;刻薄的;执拗的. ②晦涩的(文章等);难辨认的(字迹等). ③又酸又涩的.

crab·ber[1] [ˈkræbə] *n.* 捕蟹人;捕蟹小船.

crab·ber[2] [ˈkræbə] *n.* 专爱挑剔〔吹毛求疵〕的人;爱发牢骚的人.

crab·bing [ˈkræbiŋ] *n.* 捕蟹;【纺】(染色)煮呢. *a ~ machine* 煮呢机.

crab·by[1] [ˈkræbi] *a.* 蟹似的;蟹多的.

crab·by[2] [ˈkræbi] *a.* 乖张的,别扭的,执拗的.

crab·fest [ˈkræbfest] *n.* 〔美〕牢骚(话),诉苦(话).

crab·like [ˈkræblaik] *a., ad.* 蟹似的(地).

crab·stick [ˈkræbˌstik] *n.* ①沙果树木棍棒. ②〔古〕脾气坏的人.

Crab·town [ˈkræbtaun] *n.* 〔美〕(美国海军学校所在地) Annapolis 的别号.

crack [kræk] *vt.* ①使破裂;敲破,敲碎,砸碎(陶器等);嗑(瓜子等);【化】裂化(石油等). ②把(枪打得、鞭子抽得)噼啪噼啪(等)地响. ③打开(酒瓶)喝. ④弄伤,损坏(信用等);弄哑(嗓子);使发狂. ⑤说(笑话). ⑥〔口〕解决;辨认(暗号);破(案). ⑦〔美俚〕兑开(钞票). ⑧〔口〕闯入. ⑨撬开(门). ⑩微启窗户. ⑪刻苦攻读. — *vi.* ①破裂;断掉;(地面等)拆裂;皲裂;缩裂;〔美〕破晓(= day ~s). ②发拆裂〔爆裂〕声,(手枪、鞭子等)噼啪噼啪地响. ③(嗓子)发哑;(发育期)变嗓子. ④损坏;(精神)受打击. ⑤〔Scot., 北英〕谈,谈话;〔俚〕说笑话;讥讽. *This is a hard nut to ~.* 这是一个难解决的问题. ~ *sunflower seeds* 嗑瓜子. ~ ***a book*** 〔美俚〕读书,用功. ~ ***a bottle with*** 和…开瓶酒喝. ~ ***a crib*** 〔口〕溜门撬锁(偷窃). ~ ***a mark [record]*** 【美军】打破纪录,创新纪录. ~ ***a prospect*** 〔美俚〕推销成功. ~ ***a smile*** 〔俚〕微笑. ~ ***back*** 〔美俚〕回嘴. ~ ***down*** 〔美俚〕敏捷地做;拼命做. ~ ***down on*** 〔美俚〕对…采取严厉措施,对…进行制裁. ~ ***on*** 满帆前进;〔俚〕开足马力前进,飞快前进;继续前进. ~ ***out laughing*** 发笑. ~ ***the lingo*** 〔美俚〕讲本行行话. ~ ***the party*** 〔美俚〕不请自来赴会. ~ ***up*** ①夸奖;吹捧某人(~ *oneself up* 自夸,自大). ②(人、身体等)疲惫不堪,有气无力;〔美俚〕(飞机)坠毁,撞毁;引起(哄堂)大笑;忍不住大笑;笑痛肚子. ~ ***wise*** 〔美〕讲俏皮话,打哈哈. ***get ~ing*** 〔俚〕开动,动工;动手,开始做. — *n.* ①裂缝,裂纹,皲裂,龟裂;【化】裂化. ②破裂声,爆裂声,(手枪、鞭子等的)噼啪声;打击声,打击. ③疵瑕,缺点;精神错乱. ④(发育期)换嗓,变声. ⑤〔口〕第一流人物;名马;(竞技的)名手;优良的船. ⑥〔古、俚〕自大,自夸;〔Scot., 北英〕闲谈;〔*pl.*〕奇闻. ⑦〔美俚〕警句;俏皮话,挖苦话. ⑧〔口〕一会儿,片刻. ⑨〔俚〕溜门撬锁. *Open the window a ~.* 把窗子开一条缝. *the ~ of a whip* 鞭声. *the ~ of thunder* 雷鸣. *a ~ on the head* 头上的一击. *There is a ~ in your head.* 你有点疯啦. ***(at) ~ of day*** 〔英方,美〕(在)黎明,天亮时. ~ ***of doom*** 世界末日的霹雳信号 *(till the ~ of doom* 到世界毁灭时,到最后). ***in a ~*** 即刻,立刻. —*a.* 〔口〕最好的,第一流的;出名的,响当当的. *a ~ hand* 妙手,能手. *a ~ performer* 名演员. *a ~ player* (竞赛等的)能手. *a ~ regiment* 精锐团. *~ troops* 精锐部队. *a ~ team* 名队. — *ad.* 噼啪地,啪的一声,尖锐地. *The pistol went off ~.* 手枪啪的一声打了出去. ~**brain** 精神错乱的人. ~**brained** *a.* 精神错乱的. ~**down** 〔美俚〕制裁;猛击. ~**jaw** *a.* 〔口〕难发音的;拗口的.

crack·a·jack [ˈkrækədʒæk] *n.* 〔美〕 = crackerjack.

cracked [krækt] *a.* ①弄破了的,弄裂了的. ②嗓子弄哑了的,声音起了变化的. ③〔口〕疯了的,精神失常的. ~ *ice* 碎冰;〔美俚〕钻石. *a ~ reputation* 坏名. *be ~* 声音发哑;发疯. ~ *wheat* (碎)麦片.

crack·er [ˈkrækə] *n.* ①爆竹;鞭炮. ②〔美〕脆饼;〔美〕饼干(=〔英〕biscuit). ③〔学俚〕谎话. ④〔*pl.*〕胡桃夹,

破碎器;〔谑〕牙齿. ⑤〔C-〕〔美南部〕贫穷的白种人. ⑥〔俚〕全速力. ⑦破门撬锁者. ⑧说大话的人. ⑨(石油)裂化设备. *the C- State* 〔美〕乔治亚州的别名. *go a* ～ 开足马力;压扁.

crack·er·jack ['krækədʒæk] *n.* ①〔美〕玉米花核桃饼. ②〔美俚〕专家,能手,杰出人物. — *a.* 〔美俚〕熟练的,第一流的.

crack·ers ['krækəz] *a.* 〔俚〕发疯,发狂〔常用作表语〕. *drive sb.* ～ 使某人发狂. *go* ～ *about sth.* 给…迷住;热中于.

crack·ing ['krækiŋ] *a.* 分裂的,分解的;〔美俚〕极快的,猛裂的. ～ *distillation* 【化】裂化蒸馏(法). ～ *salt* 响盐. *get* ～ *(on)* 〔俚〕忙起来;发奋,努力.

crack·le ['krækl] *n.* 噼啪声,爆裂声;(碎瓷上的)裂纹;【医】尖锐的肺泡音. — *vi.* 噼噼啪啪地响;生气勃勃,兴奋不安(等).

crack·le·ware ['krækl,wɛə] *n.* 碎纹陶瓷.

crack·ling ['krækliŋ] *n.* 噼噼啪啪的响声;(饼干等的)松脆;(烧猪的)脆皮;〔主美〕猪油渣.

crack·ly ['krækli] *a.* 劈劈拍拍响的;松脆的.

crack·nel ['kræknəl] *n.* 脆饼;〔*pl.*〕〔英方,美〕脆煎(猪)肉饼;〔*pl.*〕猪油渣.

crack·pot ['krækpɔt] *n., a.* 〔美俚〕疯子,怪人;想入非非的,不切实际的. *Joe's* ～ *scheme* 空想的计划.

cracks·man ['kræksmən] *n.* 〔俚〕强盗.

crack·up ['krækʌp] *n.* (车辆的)相撞;(飞机的)坠毁;〔口〕(体力或精神的)垮掉.

crack·y ['kræki] *a.* *(-i·er; -i·est)* 多裂缝的,易破的;〔口〕疯狂的.

Cra·cow ['krækəu] *n.* 克拉科夫〔波兰城市〕.

-cra·cy [krəsi] *suf.* 统治(权),统治阶级.

cra·dle ['kreidl] *n.* ①摇篮. ②婴儿时代;(文化等的)发源地. ③(雕铜版用的)凿刀. ④【农】(附在大镰刀上,使割下的谷物整齐排列的)配禾架;(船厂的)船架,活动滑台;(砌拱洞等的)支架;(电话的)听筒架;【医】(骨折)护架,接骨台;【矿】淘汰机;炮鞍;(支持有反座力的炮身的)摇架. ⑥〔美俚〕无盖货车. *the* ～ *of an art* 一种艺术的发祥地. *a launching* ～ 【火箭】发射台. *from the* ～ 自幼. *from the* ～ *to the grave* 从生到死,一生中. *in the* ～ 在初期,在幼年时代. *rob the* ～ 选比自己小得多的人做情人〔配偶〕. *stifle in the* ～ 把…掐死在摇篮里,防患于未然. *the* ～ *of the deep* 海. *watch over the* ～ 看着长大. — *vt.* ①放在摇篮内,摇摇篮催眠(小孩);抚养. ②刈割;用架支住;淘洗(矿沙). **～land** 发祥地. **～song** 摇篮曲.

cra·dling ['kreidliŋ] *n.* 选矿,淘汰;抚育,育成;【建】弧顶架.

craft [krɑːft] *n.* ①〔古〕技巧,手腕;鬼聪明,诡计. ②技术,技能,手艺;手工业;工艺;(需要特殊技能的)专业,行业;同业,同行;同业工会. ③〔单复同形〕船舶;飞机,飞船. ④〔美〕竞赛中的同组同志. *a hydrofoil* ～ 水翼船. *art(s) and* ～*(s)* 艺术和手工艺,美术工艺. *by* ～用诡计〔手腕〕. *with* ～ 有技巧地,巧妙地. ～ *brother* 同行. ～ *guild* 技艺〔手工艺〕行会. ～ *union* 职业工会. *the* ～ *of the wood* = *the woodcraft. the gentle* ～ 钓鱼术;钓鱼伙伴.

-craft *comb. f.* 术,法;行业.

craft·i·ly ['krɑːftili] *ad.* 狡猾地,诡计多端地.

craft·i·ness ['krɑːftinis] *n.* 狡猾,诡计多端.

crafts·man ['krɑːftsmən] *n.* 手艺人,工匠,名匠. **-ship** *n.* (工匠的)技术,技艺.

craft·y ['krɑːfti] *a.* 狡猾的,诡诈的;〔古〕巧妙的,灵巧的,能干的.

crag[1] [kræg] *n.* 岩崖,巉崖;岩石碎块. ～ *and tail* 一边有巉岩另一边有缓坡的地层,鼻尾丘.

crag[2] [kræg] *n.* 〔Scot.〕脖子;喉咙;(鸡等的)嗉子.

crag·ged ['krægid] *a.* = craggy. **-ness** *n.*

crag·gy ['krægi] *a.* 多岩石的,嵯峨的,崎岖的. **-gi·ness** *n.*

crags·man ['krægzmən] *n.* 爬岩崖名手.

Craig [kreig] *n.* 克雷格〔姓氏,男子名〕.

Craig·a·von [kreig'ævən] *n.* 克雷加文〔姓氏〕.

Crai·gie ['krægi] *n.* 克雷吉〔姓氏〕.

Craik [kreik] *n.* 克雷克〔姓氏〕.

crake [kreik] *n.* 【鸟】秧鸡;秧鸡的叫声. — *vi.* (秧鸡等的)叫.

Cram [kræm] *n.* 克拉姆〔姓氏〕.

cram [kræm] *vt.* *(crammed, cram·ming)* 塞入,填入;喂饱,填饱(鸭子等),塞满(屋子等);填鸭式地教,死记*(up)*. *a bus crammed with passengers* 挤满乘客的一辆公共汽车. ～ *papers into a drawer* 把文件塞入抽屉. — *vi.* 狼吞虎咽地吃;吃得太饱;填鸭式地死用功;考试前临时抱佛脚〔死背硬记〕. ～ *up on mathematics* 仓促准备应付数学考试. ～ *(sth.)* **down** *sb.'s* **throat** 填饱;反复地对人说(某事). *to sit up late* ～*ming* 开夜车准备功课. ～ *oneself* 塞满肚皮;吃饱. — *n.* 填塞;填鸭式用功;考试前临时硬记;超额拥挤;〔俚〕压碎;〔俚〕瞒骗.

cram·be ['kræm,biː] *n.* 【植】埃塞俄比亚海甘蓝〔一种地中海油料作物〕*(Crambe abyssinica)*.

cram·bo ['kræmbəu] *n.* ①对韵游戏. ②拙劣的诗词〔韵文〕.

cram·mer ['kræmə] *n.* 填塞者;赶教应考者的补习老师,填鸭式用功〔死背硬记〕的学生;〔俚〕谎话.

cram·ming ['kræmiŋ] *n.* 填鸭式〔死背硬记〕的学习〔教法〕.

cram·oi·sy, cram·oi·sie ['kræm,ɔizi] *a.* 〔古〕深红色的. — *n.* 〔古〕红布.

cramp[1] [kræmp] *n.* ①夹子;扣钉,爬钉(= ～ iron). ②(制靴)弓状木. ③束缚,约束. — *a.* ①难懂的,难读的;难认的. ②受拘束的;狭窄的. *a* ～ *word* 难认的字. *a* ～ *corner* 狭窄的角落. — *vt.* 用夹子夹紧;用扒钉接牢;拘束,束缚(自由等);禁闭(up). ～ *sb.'s style* 〔美俚〕拘束某人使不能充分发挥才能.

cramp[2] [kræmp] *n.* 【医】(痛性)痉挛;〔*pl.*〕〔美口〕(经期)腹痛. — *vt.* 使痉挛,使抽筋;〔美俚〕使扫兴. *writer's* ～ 书写痉挛.

cramp·fish ['kræmpfiʃ] *n.* 【动】电鳐.

cram·pon ['kræmpən] *n.* ①〔常 *pl.*〕(起重,搬冰块等用的)钩铗;(登山)鞋底尖钉. ②【植】攀缘根,气根.

cran [kræn] *n.* 〔Scot.〕鲱斗〔计量鲱鱼用单位,= $37\frac{1}{2}$ 加仑〕.

cran·age [kreinidʒ] *n.* 起重机的使用(费).

cran·ber·ry ['krænbəri] *n.* 【植】酸果蔓(属);大酸果蔓. ～ **bush [tree]** 【植】三裂叶荚蒾. ～ **glass** 带青紫色的透明红玻璃.

cran·dall ['krændəl] *n.* (石工)小锤.

Crane [krein] *n.* 克兰〔姓氏〕.

crane [krein] *n.* ①鹤;〔口〕苍鹭,鹭鸶,鹳;〔C-〕【天】天鹤座. ②起重机,吊车,摄影升降机;虹吸器;(机车的)上水管;(炉边挂铁壶的)吊钩. *a sacred* ～ 丹顶鹤. *a whiteheaded* ～ 锅鹤. *a white-naped* ～ 灰鹤. *a floating* ～ 水上起重机. *a gantry [gauntry]* ～ 龙门起重机. *a slewing* ～ 旋臂起重机. *a universal* ～ 万能起重〔装卸〕机. — *vt.* 伸(颈);用起重机搬移. — *vi.* 伸着脖子(看) *(out; over; down)*;踌躇 *(at)*. ～ **fly** 【动】大蚊,蚊姥;〔美〕盲蜘蛛. **～s'-bill** 【植】老鹳草(属),天竺葵;【医】钳子.

cra·ni·al ['kreinjəl] *a.* 头盖(骨)的;颅形的.

cra·ni·ate ['kreiniit] *a.* 有头盖(骨)的.

cra·ni·o- *comb. f.* 头盖,头: craniology.

cra·ni·ol·o·gist [,kreini'ɔlədʒist] *n.* 头盖骨学者,颅骨学者.

cra·ni·ol·o·gy [,kreini'ɔlədʒi] *n.* 头盖骨学,颅骨学.

cra·ni·om·e·ter [,kreini'ɔmitə] *n.* 颅〔头盖〕(骨)测

量器.

cra·ni·om·e·try [ˌkreiniˈɔmitri] *n.* 颅〔头盖〕骨测定学.

cra·ni·o·sa·cral [ˌkreiniəuˈsækrəl, -ˈseikrəl] *a.* ①颅骶骨的. ②副交感神经的 (=parasympathetic).

cra·ni·ot·o·my [ˌkreiniˈɔtəmi] *n.* ***(pl.* -mies)**【医】颅骨切开术;穿颅术.

cra·ni·um [ˈkreinjəm] *n.* ***(pl.* -nia** [-niə]*)*【解】头盖(骨),颅(骨);脑壳;脑袋,头.

crank[1] [kræŋk] *n.* ①【机】曲柄;(刑具)旋盘. ②(言语或思想的)奇特的转折;狂想,幻想;〔美俚〕想法古怪的人;〔口〕脾气乖戾的人. ③〔古〕弯曲,曲折. ～ *axle* 曲柄轴. — *vi.* 转动曲柄;弯曲而行;(转动电影摄影机的曲柄)拍摄. — *vt.* 弯成曲柄状;装上曲柄,用曲柄连结;转动曲柄开动(引擎) *(up)*;(转动电影摄影机的曲柄)摄影. ～ ***out*** 制作,制成. ～ ***up*** 开动;加快;作好准备. ～ **axle** 曲柄轴. ～ **case** 曲柄轴箱. ～**pin**【机】曲柄销,拐轴销. ～**shaft**【机】曲轴,机轴.

crank[2] [kræŋk] *a.* (建筑物等)松松垮垮的,摇晃不稳的;(船)易翻的,象要翻似的;〔英方〕不健康的,虚弱的.

crank[3] [kræŋk] *a.* 〔美、英方〕①活泼的,精神好的. ②骄傲的,逞能的.

cran·kle [ˈkræŋkl] *vt., vi., n.* 弯曲;扭弯;(弄成)曲曲弯弯.

crank·ous [ˈkræŋkəs] *a.* 〔Scot.〕胡思乱想的;急躁的,易怒的.

crank·y [ˈkræŋki] *a.* ***(-i·er; -i·est)*** ①胡思乱想的;疯狂的;古怪的,易发脾气的. ②(多)弯曲的. ③易翻倒的,动摇不稳的;虚弱的. ***be*** ～ ***on*** 〔俚〕全神贯注在…,热中于,被…迷住.

cran·nied [ˈkrænid] *a.* 有[多]裂缝的.

cran·ny [ˈkræni] 裂缝,隙缝. *search every* ～ 到处寻找.

Cran·ston [ˈkrænstən] *n.* 克兰斯敦〔美国城市〕.

crap[1] [kræp] *n.* 掷双骰子〔一种赌博〕;(掷输的)一掷. — *v.* 〔仅用于〕 ～ ***out*** ①〔俚〕放弃计划(等). ②〔俚〕休息;打盹. ③(赌博)掷输.

crap[2] [kræp] *n.* ①〔卑〕大便,粪便. ②费话,胡话. ③夸张,吹牛;谎话. ④垃圾,废料,破烂东西. — *vi.* ①〔卑〕拉屎. ②〔美俚〕胡搞. *He used to* ～ *around like that.* 他老做那样的傻事.

crape [kreip] *n.* ①(丧服用的)黑纱,(帽子等上面的)黑丧章. ②绉纱,绉绸 (= crêpe). —*vt.* ①使绉. ②用黑纱覆盖. ③使穿戴黑纱. ～ **hanger** 忧郁悲观的人;〔俚〕扫兴的人. ～ **myrtle**【植】百日红,紫薇属.

craped [kreipt] *a.* 戴黑纱[丧章]的;绉的.

crap·pie [ˈkræpi] *n.* 〔美〕【动】克勒皮鱼,日鲈.

craps [kræps] *n.* 〔用作 *sing.*〕〔美〕掷双骰子〔一种赌博〕. *shoot* ～ 掷双骰子.

crap·shoot·er [ˈkræpˌʃuːtə] *n.* 掷双骰子赌徒.

crap·u·lence [ˈkræpjuləns] *n.* 暴饮暴食(致病,酗酒);无节制;纵欲.

crap·u·lent, crap·u·lous [ˈkræpjulənt, -ləs] *a.* 无节制(而致病)的,吃得[喝得]过多的;大醉的,中酒毒的.

crap·y [ˈkreipi] *a.* ①绉纱状的. ②戴黑纱[丧章]的. ③弯弯曲曲的,波状的.

crash[1] [kræʃ] *vi.* ①砰的碎掉,粉碎,哗啦一声坏掉;哗啦啦地倒坍 *(down, through)*;(雷、炮)隆隆地响 *(out)*;(轰隆一声)碰到,撞在 *(into; against)*. ②(计划等)失败,破产;(飞机)坠毁;(飞机师)摔死;(汽车)碰撞,撞坏. ③〔美俚〕(从服用麻醉品迷幻状态中)恢复常态,醒过来. ④〔美俚〕躺下睡觉,住宿. — *vt.* ①撞击(使发大声). ②使粉碎,打碎;使(飞机)坠毁;击落(敌机);使(汽车)碰撞. ③〔美俚〕擅自闯入. ④〔美俚〕轰动一时地取得(…地位). ～ *the headlines* 成了轰动一时的头条新闻. ～ *in [on]* 〔俚〕闯入,擅自进入. ～ *the gate* 〔美俚〕擅自闯进(招待会等),无票进入(戏院等). — *n.* ①(坍塌等时的)猛烈声音,轰隆声;【剧】轰隆声发声装置. ②(碰得)粉碎,毁坏;撞击;(飞机的)坠毁. ③失败,破产;崩溃,瓦解. *a sweeping* ～ (经济等的)总崩溃. ～ *dive* (潜艇)急速潜入水中. *with a* ～ 轰隆[哗啦]一声. — *ad.* 〔口〕= *with a* ～. *A stone came* ～ *through the window.* 一块石头哗啦一声打破窗子飞了进来. ～ **barrier** 〔英〕(置于快速公路中线的)防撞栏. ～**-helmet** (摩托运动员等戴的)防护头盔. ～ **land** *vt., vi.* (使)强行着陆. ～ **pad** 〔美俚〕临时住宿处,栖身处. ～ **program** 应急计划. ～**worthy** *a.* 防[耐]碰撞的.

crash[2] [kræʃ] *n.* 粗(麻)布.

crash·ee [ˈkræʃiː] *n.* 〔美〕破产的资本家.

crash·er [ˈkræʃə] *n.* 发猛烈声音的东西;痛击,猛撞;〔美俚〕擅自闯入者 (= gate-crasher).

crash·ing [ˈkræʃiŋ] *a.* 〔口〕完全的;彻底的. *a* ～ *bore* 讨厌已极的人.

cra·sis [ˈkreisis] *n.* ***(pl.* -ses** [-siːz]*)* ①(体质成分的)配合;体质,气质. ②【语】(二元音的)融合,异词元音结合〔如拉丁语中 coopia 融合为 copia〕.

crass [kræs] *a.* ①〔书〕非常的,澈底的;〔古〕粗厚的(麻布等). ②愚钝的. **-ly** *ad.*

cras·si·tude [ˈkræsitjuːd] *n.* 粗糙,粗厚;愚钝.

-crat *suf.* (某种统治形式,统治集团的)支持者;参与者: aristo*crat*, auto*crat*, demo*crat*.

cratch [krætʃ] *n.* 〔英方〕饲料箱,饲料架.

crate [kreit] *n.* ①竹篾[柳条]篮[篓、筐];条板箱;一箱(60×30×30cm)的量. ②〔俚〕旧飞机;旧汽车;牢监. — *vt.* 〔美〕(用篮筐或板条箱)装起来,装箱.

cra·ter [ˈkreitə] *n.* ①火山口. ②〔C-〕【天】巨爵座;(月球上的)环形山. ③(炸成的)弹坑;陨石坑;陷口. — *vt., vi.* (使)成坑状. ～**-kin**, ～**-let** 小火山口. ～ **wall** 火山口壁. **-d** *a.* 形成火山口的.

cra·ter·i·form [ˈkreitərifɔːm] *a.* 火山口状的,漏斗状的.

craunch [ˈkrɔːntʃ, krɑːntʃ] *vt., vi., n.* 嘎扎嘎扎地咀嚼〔碾压,踏过〕(= crunch).

cra·vat [krəˈvæt] *n.* (旧式)领带;〔古〕(男用)围巾;三角绷带;(女用)领饰. *a hempen* ～ 〔古〕绞索.

crave [kreiv] *vt.* ①切望,热望,渴望. ②恳求,恳请,乞求. ③(情形)要求,需要. — *vi.* 热望,渴望,恳求〔同 for, after 连用〕.

cra·ven [ˈkreivən] *n.* 懦夫. — *a.* 怯懦的,畏缩的,胆小的. *cry* ～ 叫饶,投降. **-ly** *ad.*

crav·en·ette [kreivənˈet, kræv-] *n.* 【商标】(伦敦)克来文雨衣(料).

crav·ing [ˈkreiviŋ] *n.* 渴望,热望;恳请,恳求. ***have a*** ～ ***for*** 渴求.

craw [krɔː] *n.* ①【鸟】嗉子. ②【动】胃. ③〔美俚〕喉咙. ～*thumper* 〔美〕马里兰 (Mariland) 州人(的绰号).

craw·dad [ˈkrɔːdæd] *n.* 〔美俚〕= crawfish.

craw·fish [ˈkrɔːfiʃ] *n.* ①【动】淡水小龙虾,蝲蛄(= crayfish). ②〔美口〕后退者,变节者,叛徒. ～ *land* 〔美〕低湿的地方. — *vi.* 〔美口〕①捕小龙虾(作为消遣). ②(象蝲蛄一样)向后退,退缩;撒手;变节.

crawl[1] [krɔːl] *vi.* ①爬;爬行;(车辆、病人等)慢吞吞地行进;(时间)慢慢过去;偷偷地溜走;爬来爬去. ②巴结. ③(皮肤)发痒. ④(虫)成群地蠕动 *(with)*. ⑤用自由式游;〔美俚〕跳舞. ⑥(地毯等)移动皱缩(不平). ⑦〔英俚〕(出租汽车)往来兜生意. ⑧〔美俚〕食言;悔约. ～ *home on one's eyebrows* 〔口〕累得精疲力尽地慢慢走回家. — *n.* 爬行,徐行;〔美俚〕跳舞;自由式游泳. *a pub* ～ 〔俚〕一连走几家酒店喝串门酒. ***go at a*** ～ 慢吞吞地走;(出租汽车等)往来兜生意. ***go for a*** ～ 去散散步. ***the*** ～ 爬泳,自由式游泳 (=～-stroke). ～**way** (为运输火箭或宇宙飞船而修建的)慢速道.

crawl[2] [krɔːl] *n.* (圈养鱼类的)鱼围;〔罕〕= kraal.

crawl·er [ˈkrɔːlə] *n.* ①爬行者,爬行动物,爬虫. ②〔美口〕蛇蜻蜓的幼虫;虱子. ③拍马屁的人;懒汉. ④〔英口〕(沿街兜生意的) 出租汽车. ⑤〔主 *pl.*〕〔英〕(婴孩的)爬服,罩衣. ⑥自由式游泳者. ⑦履带式牵引车.

crawl·y [ˈkrɔːli] *a.* *(-i·er; -i·est)* 〔口〕痒痒的,麻辣辣的;毛骨悚然的.

cray·fish [ˈkrei-fiʃ] *n.* = crawfish①.

cray·on [ˈkreiən] *n.* 颜色(铅)笔, 色粉笔, 蜡笔; 色粉〔蜡笔〕画; (弧光灯的)碳精棒. ***in ~(s)*** 用色粉〔蜡笔〕画的. — *vt.* 用色粉〔蜡笔〕画; 勾轮廓; 拟计画.

craze [kreiz] *vt.* ①使发狂〔通常用被动语态〕. ②使(陶器)现裂纹. — *vi.* 发狂; (陶器)出现裂纹. ***be ~d about*** 热中于. — *n.* ①疯狂; 狂妄; 狂热, 热中, 大流行. ②(陶器的)裂纹; 裂痕. ***be the ~*** 大流行. ***~for (gold)*** (发财)狂.

crazed [kreizd] *a.* ①疯狂的; 狂热的. ②有裂纹的.

cra·zy [ˈkreizi] *a.* ①摇晃不稳的, 破烂的(船、房子等); 〔古〕(身体)孱弱的. ②疯狂的; 狂妄的; 怪诞的, 古怪的; 〔口〕对…极度热心〔迷恋〕*(about)*. ③〔美俚〕极好的, 极妙的; 令人惊异的. *Are you ~?* 你疯了吗? ***be ~ for*** 渴望, 痴想. ***be ~ with (pain)*** (痛苦)得发狂. ***~ as a bedbug*** 〔美〕发疯的; 荒唐的. ***like ~*** 发狂似地, 激昂地. **~ act** 〔美〕滑稽戏. **~ bone** 〔美〕= funny bone. **~ cat** 〔美〕笨蛋, 傻瓜. **~ (patch) work** 碎料拼活 (工艺). **~ quilt** 〔美〕碎料缝成的褥子. **~ pavement [walk]** 碎石铺道.

cra·zy·weed [ˈkreiziˌwiːd] *n.* 【植】疯草, 黄芪属植物和棘豆属植物(= locoweed).

creak [kriːk] *n.* 吱吱嘎嘎声, 辗轧声. ***with a ~*** 吱嘎一声(开门). — *vi.* 吱吱嘎嘎地响.

creak·y [ˈkriːki] *a.* *(-i·er; -i·est)* (容易)吱吱嘎嘎响的.

cream [kriːm] *n.* ①奶油, 乳皮; 奶油色, 淡黄色; 液面皮. ②〔the ~〕精华; 真髓; 妙处. ③奶油色的马. ④奶油糕点〔冰淇淋等〕; (化妆用)雪花膏, 香脂; 【化】乳剂. **~** *cake* 奶油蛋糕. **~** *de goo* [-dəˈguː] 〔美俚〕牛奶烤面包. **~** *ice* 〔英〕= ice ~. **~** *laid paper* 嫩黄色平行罗纹纸. **~** *of lime* 石灰乳. **~** *of tartar* 酒石酸氢钾. **~** *of the crop* 〔口〕精华, 精选物. **~** *of the society* 社会名流. **~** *puff* 奶油气鼓饼; 可爱的人; 〔美俚〕懦夫; 无骨气的男子; 〔美俚〕外观特好的旧汽车. **~** *separator* 奶油分离器. ***get the ~ of*** 取其精华. — *vt.* ①提取奶油, 取乳皮. ②抽取精华, 拔粹. ③【烹】搅成奶油状; 加奶油(在菜, 茶里). ④搽雪花膏. ⑤〔俚〕痛打, 打伤. — *vi.* ①结乳皮, 成奶油状. ②起泡沫. **~-colo(u)red** *a.* 奶油色的; 淡黄色的. **~ware** 奶油色陶器.

cream·cups [ˈkriːmkʌps] *n.* 【植】美国平蕊罂粟 *(platystemon californicus)*.

cream·er [ˈkriːmə] *n.* ①撇取乳皮的盆〔人〕. ②奶油分离器. ③〔美〕(餐桌上的)奶油瓶.

cream·er·y [ˈkriːməri] *n.* 奶油干酪厂; (兼卖茶的)奶品商店.

cream·y [ˈkriːmi] *a.* 奶油状的; 含奶油的; 奶油色的; 浓厚的, 浓艳的.

crease¹ [kriːs] *n.* ①(衣等的)折痕, 折缝; 皱折. ②【地】古冰川流迹. ③【板球】投手〔打手〕界线. — *vt., vi.* ①使有折缝, 变皱. ②〔美口〕(被流弹)擦伤.

crease² [kriːs] *n.* = creese.

creas·er [ˈkriːsə] *n.* 压折缝的器具.

cre·a·sote [ˈkriːəsəut] *n.* = creosote.

creas·y [ˈkriːsi] *a.* 折缝多的, 有折痕的, 变皱了的.

cre·ate [kri(ː)ˈeit] *vt.* ①创造; 创作; 产生, 引起. ②创设, 设立; 建设(国家等). ③封爵; 把…封为(贵族). **~** *peers* 册封贵族. *be ~d (a) baron* 被封为男爵. — *vi.* ①(进行)创作. ②〔俚〕大叫大喊; 发牢骚. *be quick to imitate but powerless to ~* 善于模仿拙于创作. *You need not ~ about it.* 你不必大惊小怪. ***~ about nothing*** 无事自扰.

cre·a·tin(e) [ˈkriːətin] *n.* 【生化】肌酸, 肌肉素.

cre·at·i·nine [kriːˈætiˌniːn, -nin] *n.* 【生化】肌酸酐.

cre·a·tion [kri(ː)ˈeiʃən] *n.* ①创造, 创作; 发生. ②创造物; 天地万物, 宇宙. ③创设; 建设. ④(爵位等的)封授. ⑤创造性演出, 新型服装. ⑥〔美口〕(作感叹词用)哎呀, 天哪. *since the ~* 从开天辟地以来. *the whole ~* 万物; 宇宙, 全世界. *That beats [licks, whips] (all) ~.* 〔美口〕那倒是惊人极了; 那打破一切纪录了. *C-! how he looked.* 嗳呀; 他那个面孔. *the latest Paris ~s* 最新巴黎式样(服装). ***~ of genius*** 天才作品. ***~ of new species*** 新种的发生. ***in all ~*** 〔美口〕究竟, 到底. ***like all ~*** 〔美口〕拼命, 猛烈, 严重.

cre·a·tion·ism [kri(ː)ˈeiʃənizəm] *n.* 【生】神造论, 特创说.

cre·a·tive [kri(ː)ˈeitiv] *a.* 有创造力的, 创造的; 造成的. *be ~ of* 能产生…的. *~ power* 创造力, 创作力. *~ talent* 创作的才能.

cre·a·tiv·i·ty [ˌkriːeiˈtiviti] *n.* 创造力; 艺术创新.

cre·a·tor [kri(ː)ˈeitə] *n.* ①创造者; 创作家; 创设者; 发生原因; 新衣设计人; 新演技创造人, 新型演员. ②【宗】〔the C-〕造物主, 上帝.

cre·a·tress [kri(ː)ˈeitris] *n.* 女创造者; 女创办人; 女创作家.

crea·ture [ˈkriːtʃə] *n.* ①创造物; 生物, (特指)动物; 〔美〕牛马, 家畜. ②(某人)一手提拔的人; (某人设置的)私人, 工具; 奴才, "走狗. ③〔怜爱、轻蔑〕人, 家伙, 东西. *good ~s* 衣服饮食. *dumb ~s* 牲畜. *fellow ~s* 和我们同样的人, 同胞. *a pretty ~* 美丽的女人. *Poor ~!* 可怜的家伙! *that ~ there* 那家伙. *What a ~!* 好家伙! ***~ of circumstances*** 环境的奴隶〔产物〕. ***~ of the age*** 时代的产物. ***~s of the dictators*** 独裁者的走狗. ***the ~*** [ˈkriːtə, ˈkreitə] 〔谑〕烈酒, (特指爱尔兰产的) 威士忌酒〔常照爱尔兰音拼作 crater, crat(h)ur 等〕. **~ comforts** = good ~s.

crèche [kreiʃ] *n.* ①(日托) 托儿所. ②育婴堂, 孤儿院. ③【宗】马槽中初生耶稣画像.

cre·dal [ˈkriːdl] *a.* 信条的, 教义的, 纲领的.

cre·dat Ju·dae·us (A·pel·la) [ˈkriːdæt djuˈdiːəs(əˈpelə)] 〔L.〕只有犹太的迷信者(阿佩拉)相信〔我可不信〕.

cre·dence [ˈkriːdəns] *n.* ①信用; 信任; 凭证. ②【宗】祭器台, 供桌; (中世纪欧洲的)餐具柜, 餐桌旁的伺服用桌. *a letter of ~* 介绍信, (大使等的)国书. *find ~* 受到信任. ***give [refuse] ~ to*** 相信〔不信〕.

cre·den·da [kriˈdendə] *n.* 〔*pl.*〕*(sing.* ***-den·dum*** [-dəm]*)* 信条; 教条.

cre·dent [ˈkriːdnt] *a.* ①〔罕〕相信的, 有信仰的. ②〔废〕可信的.

cre·den·tial [kriˈdenʃəl] *a.* 〔罕〕信任的. — *n.* 凭证, 证件; 〔*pl.*〕国书. *present one's ~s* 呈递国书. *~s committee* 资格审查委员会. **-ism** 文凭主义, 资格主义〔特指使用人员中过分重视学历〕.

cred·i·bil·i·ty [ˌkrediˈbiliti] *n.* 可靠性, 确实性. *It rests on the ~ of ....* 那要看…的是否可靠了. *an account lacking in ~* 靠不住的话. **~ gap** 信用差距〔指政府官员等言论与事实的不符〕; (两类人之间的)缺乏信任; (言行等的)不相符合; 可信性的不足.

cred·i·ble [ˈkredəbl, -ibl] *a.* 可信的, 可靠的. *It is hardly ~ that.* 想不到.

cred·i·bly [ˈkredəbli, -ibli] *ad.* 确实, 由可靠方面. *I am ~ informed that* 由可靠方面听说.

cred·it [ˈkredit] *n.* ①信用, 信任. ②名誉, 名望, 声望. ③赞扬, 称许; 光荣, 功劳, 勋绩, 荣誉. ④信贷; 赊销; 贷款; 存款; 债权. ⑤【会计】贷方(金额)〔略 Cr.〕*(opp.* debit). ⑥〔美〕(某科目)学分及格证; 〔俚〕优等. ⑦【商】活支汇信, 信用状 (= letter of ~). ⑧【美无】广告. *a man of ~* 德高望重的人. *an open ~* (无担保)信用贷款; 无条件活支汇信. ***be a ~ to*** 是…的光荣〔功劳〕. ***be bare of ~*** 名誉不好, 没有信用; 没有名气. ***be to sb.'s ~*** 是某人的光荣〔功劳〕. ***deserve no ~*** 不足信,

可疑. ***do ~ to sb.*** = do sb. ~ 使某人大为光荣,增加某人的身价; 证明某人具有某种才能或品质. ***gain [lose] ~*** 得[失]信任. ***get ~ for*** 因…出名. ***get the ~ of*** 得到…的名誉[光荣] (*The wrong man got the ~ of it.* 给别人抢了功). ***give (a person) ~ for*** 把…贷给(某人),把…记入(某人)付方; 把…归功于(某人),认为是…的功劳; 认为当然有(某种性质等) (*I gave you ~ for more sense.* 我以为你还要聪明一些 (那晓得这样笨). *I did not give you ~ for such skill.* 我没想到你有这个本事). ***give ~ to*** 相信. ***have ~ at*** 有存款在; 在…有势力[信誉]. ***have ~ for*** = *get ~ for*. ***have ~ with*** 对…有信用. ***have the ~ of*** = *get the ~ of*. ***lose ~ with sb.*** 失去某人的信任. ***on ~*** 赊 (*deal on ~* 信用交易,赊帐买卖). ***open ~ with*** 和…开始信用交易. ***place [put] ~ in*** 相信. ***reflect ~ on*** 使…光荣,成为…的光荣. ***take ~ for*** = *get ~ for*. ***take ~ to oneself*** 把功劳归自己. ***to sb.'s ~*** 在某人贷方,值得嘉奖[表扬],是…的光荣. — *vt.* 信用,信任; 【会计】记入贷方; 归(功于某人); 〔美〕发及格证给(学生). *He is ~ed with the invention.* 这个发明是他的功劳. ~ ***(sb.) with*** *(an amount; a quality)* 把(某数)记入(某人)帐户的贷方,记入为(某人)存款; 相信(某人)具有(某性质). ~ *(an amount; success)* ***to*** *(sb.)* 把(某数)记入(某人)帐户的贷方; 把(成功)归(某人). ~ **bureau** (商业)征信所. ~ **hour**【教育】学分. ~ **line** ①(出版物、展出物等上标注的)作者名,来件人姓名(等). ②(= ~ limit) 贷款限额,信用限额. ~ **man** 信用调查员. ~ **sales** 赊销. ~ **worthy** *a.* (资产殷实)可给予[扩大]信贷的.

cred·it·a·ble [ˈkreditəbl] *a.* 声誉好的,可钦佩的; 可信任的; 可称许[赞扬]的; 可信用[给予信贷]的. **-bil·i·ty** [-ˈbiliti] *n.*

cred·it·a·bly [ˈkreditəbli] *ad.* 美满地,有信誉地; 值得称许地; 不愧,有体面,很好地.

cred·i·tor [ˈkreditə] *n.* 债权人 (*opp.* debtor); 【会计】贷方〔略 Cr.〕. ~ *nation* 债权国. *~'s sale*〔美〕破产者所有股票的拍卖.

cre·do [ˈkriːdəu] *n.*【宗】教义; 信条.

cre·du·li·ty [kriˈdjuːliti] *n.* 轻信.

cred·u·lous [ˈkredjuləs] *a.* 轻信的,易受骗的. **-ly** *ad.* **-ness** *n.*

Cree [kriː] *n.* 北美印第安人的克里族; 克里语.

creed [kriːd] *n.* ①【宗】教义,信条. ②主义,纲领; 宗派.

Creek [kriːk] *n.* 克里克人〔以马斯科吉部族为主的美国一印第安大部族,原住美国佐治亚州和阿拉巴马州,现住俄克拉何马州〕; 克里克语.

creek [kriːk] *n.* ①(河、湖的)小湾; 小港. ②〔美〕小川,支流,溪河; 山间小平地. ③〔废〕弯曲狭窄的通路. ***up the ~***〔俚〕困难起来; 处于困难中.

creek·y [ˈkriːki] *a.* 多小湾的; 曲折的.

creel [kriːl] *n.* ①(捕)鱼篮; 捕虾篮. ②【纺】经轴架,筒子架. *coup the ~s*〔Scot.〕弄乱,变杂乱.

creep [kriːp] *vi.* (***crept*** [krept]; ***crept***) ①爬行; (蔓、根等)蔓延. ②偷偷前进,(病人,老者)衰弱迟缓地前进 (*in; into; up* 等); 蠕动; 【铁路】潜动; 【纺】蠕变,潜伸. ③〔喻〕讨好[巴结]. ④(文章等)单调,生涩. ⑤(身上)发痒; 毛骨悚然,发抖. ⑥【海】用探海钩探海底. *Age ~s upon us.* 我们不知不觉地就老了. ~ ***away*** 偷偷离开. ~ ***in*** 悄悄混进. ~ ***into sb.'s favour*** 逐步巴结而取得某人的好感. ~ ***on*** (时间)悄悄地过去. ~ ***out*** 偷偷出去. ~ ***over*** *(sth.)* (蔓等)爬上; 〔喻〕偷偷逼近(进行袭击). ***make sb.'s flesh ~*** = *make sb.* ~ *all over* 令人不寒而栗,令人毛骨悚然. — *n.* ①爬行,匍匐; 徐行; 蠕动, 【纺】蠕变,潜伸. ②〔*pl.*〕虫爬似的感觉,毛骨悚然的感觉. ③(动物)爬穿的洞. (铁路路基下的)拱洞. ④【地】潜动,蠕动. ***give (sb.) the ~s*** 使毛骨悚然. ~ **hole** (动物)躲藏的洞穴; 遁辞,借口. ~ **joint**〔美口〕流窜赌场; (盗骗顾主财物的)妓院; 下流暗娼. ~ **rate** 蠕变率. ~ **ratio** 蠕流比.

creep·age [ˈkriːpidʒ] *n.* 缓慢移动; 蠕动; 渗水; 【纺】蠕变; 【电】漏电.

creep·er [ˈkriːpə] *n.* ①爬行物; 蠕虫,爬虫; 卑躬屈节[巴结讨好]的人. ②攀缘植物; 匍匐枝; 啄木鸟. ③【机】螺旋[定速]输送器. ④打捞钩,探海钩. ⑤〔*pl.*〕〔美〕(绑在脚下防滑用的)铁钉板. ⑥〔*pl.*〕【建】藤蔓浮雕. ⑦滚球. ⑧【机】上螺丝器. ⑨(用于在汽车下面工作的)躺人小车. ⑩(大卡车的)爬坡排挡(= ~ gear). ⑪(婴儿的)爬行服. ⑫(斯里兰卡的)种茶学生.

creep·ie-peep·ie [ˈkriːpiˈpiːpi] *n.* 携带式电视摄像机.

creep·ing [ˈkriːpiŋ] *a.* ①爬行的; 蠕动的; 蠕变的; 遍地蔓延的. ②迟缓的,悄悄的. ③巴结奉承的. ④痒痒的; 毛骨悚然的. ~ *discharge*【电】蠕缓[潜流,沿面]放电. ~ *Jesus*〔英俚〕怕迫害而躲藏的人,胆小鬼. ~ *motion* 蠕动. ~ *things* 爬虫类.

creep·mouse [ˈkriːpmaus] *n.* 爬行的老鼠; 老鼠爬行般的刺痒.

creep·y [ˈkriːpi] *a.* 慢慢爬行的; 痒痒的; 毛骨悚然的; 〔英学〕讨好老师的. **~-crawly** *a.* (动物,虫类)爬行的; 毛骨悚然的.

creese [kriːs] *n.* (马来人的)波刃短剑(= cris, kris).

creesh [kriːʃ] *n.*, *vt.*〔Scot.〕油脂,润滑脂; 涂油,搽油.

cre·mains [krəˈmeinz] *n. pl.* (尸体火化后的)骨灰.

cre·mate [kriˈmeit] *vt.* 烧成灰; 火葬.

cre·ma·tion [kriˈmeiʃən] *n.* 烧化,火葬; (垃圾)焚化(法). **-ist** *n.* 火葬论者.

cre·ma·tor [kriˈmeitə] *n.* 火葬者,焚尸人; 焚尸炉; 垃圾焚化炉. **-to·ri·al** [-ˈtɔriəl] *a.*

cre·ma·to·ri·um [ˌkreməˈtɔːriəm] (*pl.* ~*s*, *-ria* [-riə]) *n.* 火葬场,垃圾焚化场.

cre·ma·to·ry [ˈkremətəri] *n.* = crematorium. — *a.* 火葬的.

crème [kreim] *n.*〔F.〕= cream; 奶油状溶液. ~ ***de cacao*** 可可酒. ~ ***de la*** ~ [dəlaː-] 尖子; 头等人物; 精华. ~ ***de menthe*** [-dəˈmɑ̃ːnt] 薄荷酒.

Cre·mer [ˈkriːmə] *n.* 克里默〔姓氏〕.

Cre·mo·na, c- [kriˈməunə] *n.* (意大利)克里莫纳提琴.

cre·nate(d) [ˈkriːneit(id)] *a.*【植】圆(形锯)齿状的,钝齿状的.

cre·na·tion [kriˈneiʃən] *n.* 圆齿状,钝齿状; (红细胞的)皱缩.

cren·a·ture [ˈkrenətʃə] *n.* (叶边的)圆齿,钝齿.

cren·el, cre·nelle [ˈkrenəl, kriˈnel] *n.* ①雉堞(上的枪眼); 〔*pl.*〕城垛. ②= crenature.

cren·el·ate,〔英〕**cren·el·late** [ˈkrenileit] *vt.* 造雉堞,开枪眼. *~d moulding*【建】圆齿状花边[线脚].

cren·el(l)a·tion [ˌkreniˈleiʃən] *n.* 筑雉堞; 开枪眼(工作); 圆齿状突出.

cren·el·et [ˈkrenilit] *n.* 小雉堞.

creno- *comb. f.* 泉水.

cren·u·late [ˈkrenjuːlit, -ˈleit] *a.* 具小扇的; 细圆齿状的; 具细圆齿的 (=crenulated).

cren·u·la·tion [krenjuːˈleiʃən] *n.* 小钝锯齿(状).

cre·o·dont [ˈkriəˌdɔnt] *n.*【古生】肉齿亚目,古肉食亚目.

Cre·ole [ˈkriːəul] *n.* ①克里奥尔人〔西印度及南美各地的西班牙、法国移民的后裔〕(= ~ white). ②〔c-〕黑白混血种; 西印度、南美等处生长的黑人 (= ~ negro). ③〔美〕路易斯安那州的法国移民的后裔; 路易斯安那州的法国土话. — *a.* 克利奥尔人(特有)的. ~ **State** 美国路易斯安那州〔别号〕.

cre·o·sol [ˈkriəˌsəul, -ˌsɔːl] *n.*【化】木焦油酚,甲氧甲酚.

cre·o·sote [ˈkriəsəut] *n.*【化】杂酚油,烟油,【商】石炭酸 (= carbolic acid). ~ *oil* 杂酚油.

cre·owls [ˈkriːəuls] *n.* 〔美〕路易斯安那州人〔别号〕.
crepe, crêpe [kreip] *n.* 〔F.〕 ①绉绸〔纱〕. ②黑纱丧章. ③油煎薄饼. ~ *de Chine* [ˈkreipdəˈʃiːn] 【纺】双绉. ~ *hanger* 忧郁悲观的人; 扫人兴的人. ~ *paper* 绉纸. ~ *rubber* 绉纹薄橡皮板.
crêpes su·zette [ˌkreipsuˈzet] *n.* 白兰地油煎饼.
crep·i·tant [ˈkrepitənt] *a.* ①劈拍响的. ②【医】咿轧音的,捻发音的.
crep·i·tate [ˈkrepiteit] *vi.* ①(火里的盐等)劈拍响,作碎裂声. ②(肺炎病人等的肺)发咿轧音.
crep·i·ta·tion [ˌkrepiˈteiʃən] *n.* 劈拍声,爆裂声; 裂声; 【医】咿轧音,捻发音.
cré·pon [ˈkrepɔ̃ːŋ] *n.* 〔F.〕 重绉纹织物.
crept [krept] creep 的过去式及过去分词.
cre·pus·cu·lar [kriˈpʌskjulə] *a.* ①朦胧的,微明的, 半明半暗的; 拂晓的; 黄昏的; 薄暮的. ②在黄昏时候活动的(动物). ③曙光时代的,半开化的,蒙昧的. ~ *ray* 曙光; 朦胧的微光.
cre·pus·cule [kriˈpʌskjuːl] *n.* 黄昏,薄暮; 曙光(= crepuscle).
cres., cresc. = crescendo.
cres·cen·do [kriˈʃendəu] *ad.* 〔It.〕【乐】渐强; (感情、动作)逐渐加强. — *n.* 渐强音〔音节〕; 声音渐强; (向高潮)进展.
cres·cent [ˈkreznt, ˈkresnt] *n.* ①新月,娥眉月. ②新月状物〔街巷等〕; (旧土耳其帝国的)新月旗, 土耳其帝国, 土耳其军; 伊斯兰教(新月形记号). ③〔美〕 月牙形面包(= ~ bun [roll]). ***the Cross and the C-*** 基督教和伊斯兰教. — *a.* 新月(形)的,月牙形的; 〔诗〕(新月一般)渐渐增大的, 逐渐变圆的. **C- citizen** 〔美〕新奥尔良市民. **C- City** 〔美〕新奥尔良市〔别号〕.
cres·cent·ade [kresnˈteid] *n.* 新月军,伊斯兰教军.
cres·cive [ˈkresiv] *a.* 〔罕〕增长的,增加的.
cre·sol [ˈkriːsɔl] *n.* 【化】甲酚〔防腐等用〕.
cress [kres] *n.* 【植】水芹.
cres·set [ˈkresit] *n.* 号灯,标灯,篝灯; 油盏.
crest [krest] *n.* ①鸡冠; 冠毛. ②羽毛饰,(盔上的)饰毛, 翎毛,顶饰; 〔诗〕盔. ③(山)脊,山顶; (浪)峰, 浪头. ④(动物的)颈脊; (马等的)鬣; 【徽】(楯形上部的)饰章; 【建】脊饰; 【解】头上隆起,骨栉,脊突. ~ *voltmeter* 【电】巅值伏特计. ~ *table* 【建】墙帽. ~ *tile* 屋脊瓦. ***erect [elevate] one's*** ~ 〔古〕 得意洋洋. ***on the ~ of the wave*** 在波浪顶上; 得意已极. ***one's ~ falls*** 垂头丧气. — *vt.* ①加上顶饰. ②用作顶饰. ③到达…的顶部. — *vi.* ①形成冠毛状顶部; (波浪)山涌. ②到达顶部. **~*ed note-paper*** 顶上印有标章的信纸. **~fallen** *a.* 垂头丧气的.
crest·ing [ˈkrestiŋ] *n.* 【建】屋〔墙〕脊饰.
cre·syl·ic [kriˈsilik] *a.* 【化】甲酚的; 杂酚油的; 从甲酚〔杂酚油〕中提取的.
cre·ta [ˈkriːtə] *n.* 【化】 ①白垩. ②漂白土.
cre·ta·ceous [kriˈteiʃəs] *a.* 白垩(质)的. ~ *period [system]* 【地】白垩纪〔系〕. — *n.* 〔C-〕【地】白垩纪〔系〕.
Cre·tan [ˈkriːtən] *a., n.* 克里特岛的(人).
Crete [kriːt] *n.* 克里特(岛)〔希腊〕.
cre·tic [ˈkriːtik] *n.* 【韵】扬抑扬音步.
cret·in [ˈkretin, ˈkriːtin] *n.* 【医】呆小病患者,愚侏病患者. **-ism** *n.* 【医】(阿尔卑斯山地常有的)呆小病, 愚侏病. **-ous** *a.*
cre·tonne [kreˈtɔn] *n.* 〔F.〕 大花帘布; 印花装饰布.
cre·val·le [kriˈvæli] *n.* 【动】长面鱼参 *(Caranx hippos)*.
cre·vasse [kriˈvæs] *n.* 〔F.〕 (冰河等的)裂隙; 裂口.
crev·ice [ˈkrevis] *n.* 罅隙,裂缝. ~ *plant* 石隙植物.
crew[1] [kruː] *n.* (全体)乘务员,(中下级)船员,水手; 【体】划艇队员; 〔蔑〕同伴; 组,班,队,群; 〔美〕同事们,工友们. *officers and* ~ 高级和低级全体船员. ***a train*** ~ 列车乘务员. ***air [ground] ~s*** 空勤〔地勤〕人员. ***the whole ~ of Jingoes*** 主战派全班人马. ~ **cut** (发式)平头. **~-man** 〔美〕(飞机、轮船等的)乘务员; (军队的)部队人员.
crew[2] [kruː] 【罕】crow 的过去式.
crew·el [ˈkru(ː)il] *n.* ①刺绣用的细绒线. ②= ~**work** 绒线刺绣.
crib [krib] *n.* ①秣槽; 牛栏, 牛舍. ②(有围栏的)儿童床; 〔俚〕摇篮. ③框; 【建】叠木框架, 脚手架. ④木头小屋; 小房间,狭小的地方. ⑤〔俚〕偷窃, 剽窃 *(from)*. ⑥(学生用的)本国文与外国文对照本,注解书. ⑦(盗贼隐语)人家,店家, 仓库, 保险柜(等行窃对象). ⑧〔俚〕= cribbage. ⑨〔美俚〕酒吧,赌场,妓院(等). ⑩〔英〕(工人带到工地吃的)盒饭. *crack a* ~ 闯入行窃地点. — *vt.* ①关进(狭小的地方); 拘束. ②〔俚〕偷; 剽窃,抄袭. ③搁秣槽(在牛栏等里). — *vi.* ①剽窃,抄袭. ②(学生考试时)作弊,作挟带; 用注释本. ③(马等)咬秣槽. ~ **death** 【医】婴儿猝死综合症.
crib·bage [ˈkribidʒ] *n.* 【牌】每人发牌6张,先凑足121分或61分者为赢牌的玩法.
crib·ber [ˈkribə] *n.* ①剽窃者, 作弊者. ②(缚住马颈以防马咬秣槽的) 皮带. ③有咬秣槽淌口水习癖的马. ④支撑物.
crib·bing [ˈkribiŋ] *n.* 剽窃〔抄袭〕行为; (学生的)作弊, 作挟带; = crib-biting.
crib-bit·ing [ˈkribiŋ] *n.* (马)咬住秣槽喘气的习癖.
crib·ble [ˈkribl] *n.* 粗筛; 粗粉. — *vt.* (用粗筛子)筛.
crib·el·lum [kriˈbeləm] *n.* *(pl. -la* [-lə]) 【动】(蜘蛛等的)纺绩突起.
crib·ri·form [ˈkribrifɔːm] *a.* 筛状的.
crib·work [ˈkribwəːk] *n.* 【建】叠木框架.
cri·ce·tid [kraiˈsiːtid, -ˈset-] *n.* 【动】啮齿科动物〔包括美洲鼠在内〕; 仓鼠.
Crich·ton [ˈkraitn] *n.* 克赖顿〔姓氏〕.
Crick [krik] *n.* 克里克〔姓氏〕.
crick [krik] *n.* 【医】(颈、脊、腰等的)肌肉〔关节〕痉挛. — *vt.* (颈等)引起痉挛.
crick·et[1] [ˈkrikit] *n.* 【虫】蟋蟀. ***as merry as a*** ~ 极快活的.
crick·et[2] [ˈkrikit] *n.* 【体】板球〔双方各11人玩的球戏,英国最为流行〕; 光明正大,公正的行为〔态度〕. — *a.* 〔口〕公正的. ***It's not*** ~. 【俚】这个不公正. ***play*** ~ 打板球; 光明正大地做.
crick·et[3] [ˈkrikit] *n.* 〔美〕矮木凳; 垫脚凳.
crick·et[4] [ˈkrikit] *n.* 斜沟小屋顶.
crick·et·er [ˈkrikitə] *n.* 板球运动员.
cri·coid [ˈkraikɔid] *a.* 【解】环状的.
cri de cœur [F. kri də kæːr] 衷心的呼喊; 强烈抗议; 满腹牢骚.
cri·er [ˈkrai-ə] *n.* ①喊叫者, 哭喊者, 哭娃娃. ②(乡下) 传布公告的 (= town ~). ③大声宣扬做广告的. ④(法院的)传唤者,法警. ⑤叫卖小贩.
cri·key [ˈkraiki] *int.* 〔俚〕嗳呀! 唷! 〔又作 By ~!〕.
crim. con. = criminal conversation.
crime [kraim] *n.* 犯罪; 罪恶; 〔俚〕坏事; 〔口〕蠢事. — *vt.* 指控犯罪; 判定犯罪; 处罚军事犯. *a capital* ~ 死刑罪. *commit a* ~ 犯罪. *collude with ... as partners in* ~ 与…狼狈为奸 〔进行犯罪活动〕. ~ *sheet* 【军】处罚记录. ~*s against the State* 国事犯. ***put [throw] a ~ upon sb.*** 把罪推在某人身上.
Cri·me·a [kraiˈmiə] *n.* 克里米亚(半岛), 克里木(半岛)〔苏联〕. *the ~ Conference* (1945年英美苏联的) 克里米亚会议 〔= Yalta Conference〕. **-an** *a.*
crim·i·nal [ˈkriminl] *a.* 犯罪的; 刑事上的; 〔口〕恶劣的, 蛮不讲理的. — *n.* 罪犯,犯人. *a habitual* ~ 惯犯. *a war* ~ 战犯. ~ **abortion** 坠胎罪. ~ **act** 犯罪行为. ~ **action** 刑事诉讼 (= ~ suit). ~ **assault** 强奸. ~ **attempt** 犯罪未遂. ~ **conversation [connexion]** 通奸. ~ **jurisprudence** 刑法学. ~ **law** 刑法. ~ **offence** 刑

事罪. ~ **operation** 坠胎罪. ~ **psychology** 犯罪心理学. ~ **suit** 刑事诉讼. **-ist** *n.* 刑事学家,罪犯学家.

crim·i·nal·is·tics [ˌkriminəˈlistiks] *n. pl.* 犯罪侦察学,刑事学.

crim·i·nal·i·ty [ˌkrimiˈnæliti] *n.* 犯罪(行为),罪行,罪恶.

crim·i·nal·ly [ˈkriminəli] *ad.* 刑法上; 犯罪. *proceed against sb.* ~ 对某人提起刑事诉讼.

crim·i·nate [ˈkrimineit] *vt.* ①控告…有罪. ②证明…有罪; 定罪. ③责备. ~ *oneself* 说出对自己不利的事情;泄露[证明]自己有罪.

crim·i·na·tion [ˌkrimiˈneiʃən] *n.* 控告; 定罪; 责备. *~s and recriminations* 互相告发〔指责对方犯罪〕.

crim·i·na·tive, crim·i·na·to·ry [ˈkriminətiv, ˈkrimineitəri] *a.* 控告的,举罪告发的; 责难的.

crim·i·ne, crim·i·ny [ˈkrimini] *int.* 〔俚〕嗳呀!〔惊叹声〕.

crim·i·no·log·i·cal [ˌkriminəˈlɔdʒikəl] *a.* 犯罪学(上)的.

crim·i·nol·o·gy [ˌkrimiˈnɔlədʒi] *n.* 犯罪学, 刑事学.

crim·i·nous [ˈkriminəs] *a.* 犯罪的. *a ~ clerk* 犯罪僧,破戒僧.

crim·mer [ˈkrimə] *n.* 克里默羔皮(= krimmer).

crimp[1] [krimp] *vt.* ①卷(头发). ②使有折缝, 使发皱. ③(在鱼肉等上)划裂痕(使挛缩). ④(把鞋革等)做成鞋形. ⑤轧在一起,叠在一起. ⑥妨碍, 阻碍. — *n.* 〔常 *pl.*〕〔美〕卷发; 卷缩机; 抑制物, 障碍. ***put a ~ in(to)*** 〔美俚〕妨[阻]碍.

crimp[2] [krimp] *n.* 兵贩子, 人贩子. — *vt.* 诱骗…(当兵等).

crimp·ing·iron *n.* [ˈkrimpiŋ aiən] 卷发器,烫发铁.

crim·ple [ˈkrimpl] *n.* 绉折, 折缝. — *vt., vi.* (使)绉, (使)缩, (使)卷缩.

crimp·y [ˈkrimpi] *a.* ***(-i·er; -i·est)*** ①绉缩[卷缩]的. ②〔美俚〕冷得要命的.

crim·son [ˈkrimzn] *n.* 深红, 鸡冠红, 绯红; 深红色颜料. — *a.* ①深红的. ②〔喻〕流血的,血腥的. — *vt., vi.* 染成[变成]深红色; (脸)变通红. **C- Beauty** 艳红品种苹果. ~ **lake** 洋红〔图画颜料〕. ~ **pool** 〔美俚〕亏空. ~ **satin** 牙兰缎.

cri·nal [ˈkrainl] *a.* 毛发的.

cringe [krindʒ] *n., vi.* 畏缩; 卑躬曲膝, 战战兢兢.

crin·gle [ˈkriŋgl] *n.*【船】索眼; 索圈.

cri·nite [ˈkrainait] *a.* 毛发状的;【动】有发状尾的;【植】有长毛的,长毛的.

crin·kle [ˈkriŋkl] *n.* ①绉纹,折痕; 条子泡泡纱. ②【植】绉叶病. ③沙拉沙拉声. — *vt.* 使绉. — *vi.* ①起绉,卷缩. ②沙拉沙拉地作声. *~d paper* 绉纸.

crin·kle·root [ˈkriŋklˌruːt,-ˈrut] *n.* 【植】二叶石芥花 *(Dentaria diphylla)*.

crin·kly [ˈkriŋkli] *a.* (衣料等)起绉的,绉折多的; 波状的; (毛发等)卷曲的; 沙拉沙拉响的. ~ *curve* 怪曲线.

crin·kum-cran·kum [ˈkriŋkəmˈkræŋkəm] *n.* 〔口〕弯曲; 弯弯曲曲的东西. — *a.* 弯弯曲曲的,错综复杂的.

cri·noid [ˈkrainɔid,ˈkrin-] *a.* 海百合类的. — *n.* 海百合.

Cri·noi·de·a [kraiˈnɔidiə] *n.* 〔*pl.*〕【动】海百合纲.

crin·o·line [ˈkrinəliːn] *n.* ①做裙衬的硬毛布[马鬃布]; 裙子的衬架; 有硬毛布衬(架)的裙子. ②(军舰的)水雷防御网.

cri·num [ˈkrainəm] *n.*【植】文殊兰属.

cri·o·llo [kriːˈəuləu] *n.* ***(fem. cri·o·lia)*** ①西班牙裔拉美人; 西班牙、拉美混血儿. ②拉美繁殖的家畜. — *a.* 西班牙裔拉美人的; 西班牙、拉美混血儿的.

cri·o·sphinx [ˈkraiəsfiŋks] *n.* 狮身羊头像.

crip·ple [ˈkripl] *n.* 跛子,瘸子, 瘫子, 残废(人). ②〔美方〕杂木满地的沼地. ③脚凳; 脚手架; 〔美俚〕破汽车. *be a ~ for life* 成终生残疾. — *vt.* 使成瘫子[跛子], 使残废; 削弱; 使失去战斗力. — *vi.* 〔Scot.〕一瘸一瘸地走 (along). *be financially ~d* 财政拮据. *~d soldier* 残废士兵. **-dom, -hood** *n.* 残废; 无能.

Cripps [krips] *n.* 克里普斯〔姓氏〕.

cris [kriːs] *n.* = creese.

cri·sis [ˈkraisis] ***(pl. -ses*** [-siːz]***)*** *n.* ①危急关头,紧要关头; (政治、经济上的)危机,危局; 恐慌; 激变. ②【医】转变期,骤退; 临界; 危象. ③【剧、影】危急情节,转折点. *a cabinet ~* 内阁危机. *a financial ~* 金融恐慌, 财政危机. *economic ~* 经济危机. *political ~* 政治危机. ~ **of confidence** 信任危机. ~ **of conscience** 精神危机, 信仰危机. ***bring to a ~*** 使紧迫[危急]. ***face a ~*** 面临危局. ~ **centre** 个人疑难咨询中心.

crisp [krisp] *a.* ①卷缩的; 起绉的; 有微波的. ②脆的, 易碎的. ③有脆声的(纸). ④新鲜的,爽快的; 有力的, 有劲儿的(文章等); 干脆的, 够味的(说法等). *the ~ air* 清新的空气. *a ~ manner [utterance]* 干脆的态度 [语调]. *eat ~* 吃着松脆. — *vt.* ①弄卷 (头发); 使起绉; 使生小波浪. ②烘脆(面包等); (寒冷使地面)冻硬. — *vi.* ①卷曲; 起绉; 起小浪. ②变脆; (地面等)冻硬. — *n.* 脆(性);【俚】钞票;〔*pl.*〕〔英〕油炸马铃薯片. *(burned) to a ~* (烧)脆[焦]. **-ly** *ad.* **-ness** *n.*

cris·pate [ˈkrispeit] *a.* 卷缩起皱的,卷曲的;【动、植】卷缩状的,皱成波状的,有皱缘的.

crisp·er [ˈkrispə] *n.* (电冰箱中的)新鲜蔬菜储藏格.

cris·pin [ˈkrispin] *n.* 鞋匠; 〔美〕鞋匠工会会员. **St.** ~ (罗马神话中的)鞋匠之神.

crisp·ing·iron [ˈkrispiŋaiən] *n.* 卷发器,卷发铁,烫发剪.

crisp·y [ˈkrispi] *a.* 卷曲的; 脆的, 松脆的,易碎的; 爽快的,干脆的.

criss·cross [ˈkriskrɔs] *n.* ①(文盲代替签名划的) 十字押,十字号[图案]; 十字交叉形式. ②龃龉,抵触; 混乱. ③〔古〕字母 (= christ-cross). ④〔美〕= *tick-tack-toe.* — *a., ad.* ①十字形的[地]; 交叉的[着]. ②龃龉; 脾气大,警扭. *a ~ pattern* 十字形花样. ~ *traffic* 纵横交叉的交通. ***go ~ with*** 跟…作对. — *vt.* 画十字押; 做成十字形; 使交叉. **~-row** *n.* 字母. **-ing** *n.* 交叉回交.

cris·sum [ˈkrisəm] *n.* ***(pl. -sa*** [-ə]***)***【解】①肛周. ②围肛羽. **cris·sal** *a.*

cris·ta [ˈkristə] *n.* ***(pl. -tae*** [-tiː]***)***【解、动】脊; 卵鞘脊.

cris·tate [ˈkristeit] *a.* 鸡冠状的; 有冠毛的.

crit. = critical; criticism; criticized.

cri·te·ria [kraiˈtiəriə] *n.* criterion 的复数.

cri·te·ri·on [kraiˈtiəriən] *n.* ***(pl. -ria)*** (评判等的)标准,准则.

crith [kriθ] *n.* 克瑞〔气体重量单位,摄氏0度、气压760毫米下1公升氢的重量, = 0.0896克〕.

crit·ic [ˈkritik] *n.* ①批评家,评论家; 鉴定家. ②吹毛求疵的人. ③〔废〕= critique. *a dramatic [literary] ~* 戏剧[文学]评论家.

crit·i·cal [ˈkritikəl] *a.* ①批判的,批评的; (在某方面)有鉴定力的 *(in)*. ②吹毛求疵的; 爱挑剔别人的 *(of, about)*. ③危机的, 危急的; 决定性的, 重大的; 急需的 (物资等);【医】危象的; 极期的. ④【数,物】临界的; 中肯的; 足够发生连锁反应的. *I am nothing, if not ~.* 只有这张刻薄的嘴,是俺的长处. *be ~ about* 爱挑剔. ~ **acumen** 明察秋毫的敏锐. ~ **age** (妇女的)绝经期. ~ **angle** 临界角. ~ **condition** (病的)危险状态; 临界状态. ~ **days** (病的)危险期. ~ **evidence** 决定性证据. ~ **length** (纤维的)致断长度. ~ **moment** 危机; 紧要关头,关键时刻. ~ **path (analysis)** 统筹方法,关键路线法, 主要矛盾线路法. ~ **point**【物】临界点,驻点. ~ **radius** 中肯半径. ~ **region**【统】判域. ~ **situation** 严重的局势[形势]. ~ **temperature** 临界温度. ~ **writer** 评论家. **-ly** *ad.*

crit·ic·as·ter [ˈkritikæstə] *n.* 低劣的批评家.

crit·i·cise [ˈkritisaiz] *vt., vi.* = criticize.

crit·i·cism [ˈkritisizəm] *n.* ①批评,批判,评论;非难. ②鉴定,审定;考证,校勘;鉴定法. ③【哲】批判主义[哲学]. ④评论文章;文艺批评理论. *the higher [lower, textual]* ~ 义理方面的[文字上的]校勘. *self-*~ 自我批评. ***be beyond [above]*** ~ 无可批评. ***be beneath*** ~ 无批评价值. ***open to*** ~ 待批评的.

crit·i·cize [ˈkritisaiz] *vt., vi.* 批评,批判;鉴定;校勘;非议,非难,挑剔.

crit·i·co- *comb. f.* 批评的.

cri·tique [kriˈtiːk] *n.* 批评,批判,评论;鉴定,审定;校勘;检阅;批评法;鉴定法.

crit·ter, crit·tur [ˈkritə] *n.* 〔方〕动物等(= creature).

CRM =① counter-radar measures 反雷达措施. ②counter-radar missile 反雷达导弹. ③counting rate metre 计数率测量计,计数表.

c. r. o. = cathode-ray oscilloscope.【无】阴极射线示波器.

croak [krəuk] *n.* ①(鸦、蛙等的)哇哇的鸣声;嘎声. ②怨言,牢骚. ③不吉利的话. *give a* ~ *of a laugh* 发出一声干笑;哑然失笑. — *vi.* ①哇哇地叫;发嘎声. ②喊冤,抱怨;发牢骚. ③预报不吉;哭丧着说. ④〔美俚〕死,断气. — *vt.* ①用阴抑的语声叙述(不吉的事情等). ②〔美俚〕杀死.

croak·er [ˈkrəukə] *n.* ①哇哇叫的东西. ②喊冤者,抱怨者. ③预报凶事者;悲观者. ④〔俚〕尸首. ⑤(北美产)叫鱼. ⑥〔美俚〕医生. *yellow* ~ 黄(花)鱼.

croak·y [ˈkrəuki] *a.* ①哇哇叫的. ②嘎声的. ③阴抑不吉的(声音等).

Cro·at [ˈkrəuət] *n.* 克罗地亚人[语].

Cro·a·tia [krəuˈeiʃjə] *n.* 克罗地亚〔南斯拉夫一地区〕.

Cro·a·tian [krəuˈeiʃən] *a.* 克罗地亚的.

croc [krɔk] *n.* 〔口〕= crocodile.

cro·ce·ate [ˈkrəusieit] *a.* 藏红花(色)的.

cro·ce·in [ˈkrəusiin] *n.*【化】藏(红)花精.

cro·chet [ˈkrəuʃei] *n.* ①钩针编织(品). ②【动】趾钩. *the fillet [single]* ~ 方格[简单]编织法. ~ *hook* 编花边等的钩针. — *vt., vi.* 用钩针织.

cro·cid·o·lite [krəˈsidəlait] *n.*【矿】青石棉.

crock¹ [krɔk] *n.* ①(瓦)罐,(瓦)缸;碎瓦片;〔英方〕三足铁釜. ②〔俚〕荒唐的话[行为];不老实的话;胡说;自相矛盾的话.

crock² [krɔk] *n.* 废马,老马;〔Scot.〕老母羊;无用的人,病弱残废人;(学校等中)不(能)运动的人;废物. — *vt.* 〔俚〕使无用,使成残废,弄成废物. — *vi.* 变衰竭;破损. ~ *sb. up* 使人无法工作. ~ *up* 〔美俚〕(飞机)坠毁,跌碎;(人体)变衰弱.

crock³ [krɔk] *n.* ①〔方〕(炊具等的)烟垢,煤臭. ②(色布上)掉下的有色物质. — *vt.* 用烟垢弄脏. — *vi.* (布)掉色. ~**-meter** 耐摩擦度测定器.

crock·er·y [ˈkrɔkəri] *n.* 〔集合词〕陶器,瓦器.

crock·et [ˈkrɔkit] *n.*【建】卷叶饰.

Crock·ett [ˈkrɔkit] *n.* 克罗基特〔姓氏〕.

croc·o·dile [ˈkrɔkədail] *n.* ①鳄鱼. ②假装慈悲的人,伪善者. ③〔英俚〕双列女学生队;(汽车等的)长蛇阵. ~ **bird** (非洲)鳄鸟. ~ **tears** 假慈悲〔据说鳄鱼一面吃一面哭它所吃的动物〕.

croc·o·dil·i·an [ˌkrɔkəˈdiliən] *a.* 鳄鱼(一样)的. — *n.* 鳄鱼(类动物).

cro·co·i·site [ˈkrəukəuzait] *n.* = crocoite.

cro·co·ite [ˈkrəukəuait] *n.*【地】铬铅矿.

cro·cus¹ [ˈkrəukəs] *n.* (*pl.* ~*es, cro·ci* [-sai]) ①【植】藏红花(属);英国报春花. ②藏红花色,桔黄色. ③紫红(氧化)铁粉〔一种研磨料〕.

cro·cus² [ˈkrəukəs] *n.* 〔美俚〕庸医.

Croe·sus [ˈkriːsəs] *n.* 克利萨斯〔公元前六世纪 Lydia 王,以富有著称〕;大富豪.

Croft [krɔft] *n.* 克罗夫特〔姓氏〕.

croft [krɔft] *n.* 〔英〕(住宅附近的)园地,小农场,小牧草地. **-er** *n.* (苏格兰西部)小农场佃农.

Crofts [krɔfts] *n.* 克罗夫茨〔姓氏〕.

crois·sant [krəˈsɑːnt] *n.* 新月形小面包.

Cro·ker [ˈkrəukə] *n.* 克罗克〔姓氏〕.

Cro-Mag·non [krəuˈmænjɔ̃ːŋ] *n., a.* 克罗马尼翁人(的)〔欧洲史前人种〕.

crom·lech [ˈkrɔmlek] *n.*【考古】①=dolmen. ②(史前)环列巨石柱群.

Cromp·ton [ˈkrʌmptən] *n.* ①克朗普顿〔姓氏〕. ②**Samuel** ~ 萨穆尔·克伦顿〔1753—1827,英国纺纱机发明人〕.

Crom·well [ˈkrɔmwəl] *n.* ①克伦威尔〔姓氏〕. ②**Oliver** ~ 奥利弗·克伦威尔〔1599—1658,英国将军,政治家〕.

crone [krəun] *n.* 皱皮老太婆;老母羊.

Cro·nin [ˈkrəunin] *n.* 克罗宁〔姓氏〕.

cro·ny [ˈkrəuni] *n.* 密友,好友,老友.

crook [kruk] *n.* ①(河道等的)弯曲(部). ②钩;壶钩;锅钩;曲把拐杖. ③诡计,狡计. ④〔俚〕骗子,盗贼,恶棍,坏蛋. ⑤【乐】弯曲管,调管. ***a*** ~ ***in one's lot*** 〔Scot.〕不幸,灾难,波折. ***by hook or by*** ~ 千方百计地,不择手段地. ***have a*** ~ ***in one's back [nose, character]*** 驼背[鹰钩鼻,性情别扭]. ***on the*** ~ 用不正当手段. — *a.* ①= crooked. ②不正当的,骗人的;歹徒的. — *vt.* ①弄曲,弄弯,弄成钩状. ②用钩钩,钩取;〔美俚〕偷. — *vi.* 弯曲. ~ ***the elbow [the little finger]*** 〔俚〕喝酒. ~**back** *n.* 驼背. ~**backed** *a.* 弓腰驼背的.

crooked [ˈkəukid] *a.* ①弯曲的;歪扭的. ②不正当的;诈欺的;〔俚〕用不正当手段得来的. ③[krukt] 有钩状柄的. ~ ***as dog's hind leg*** 〔美俚〕极不老实的. ~ **money** 不义之财. ~ **stick** (牧羊者的)曲把手棍;顽固分子,顽梗的人. **-ly** *ad.* **-ness** *n.*

Crookes [kruks] *n.* ①克鲁克斯〔姓氏〕. ②**Sir William** ~ 克鲁克斯〔1832—1919,英国化学、物理学家〕. ~ **rays** 克鲁克斯射线,阴极射线. ~ **tube** 克鲁克斯(真空)管. ~ **vacuum** 克鲁克斯真空.

crook·neck [ˈkruknek] *n.* 〔美〕长颈南瓜.

croon [kruːn] *vi.* 低声歌唱,低吟,哼(歌曲). — *vt.* ①低唱[哼]. ②低声哼着安慰(小儿等). ~ *a child to sleep* 低声哼着使小孩睡觉. — *n.* 低唱[哼],低吟;单调的哼歌曲声;低声哼的感伤性流行歌曲.

croon·er [ˈkruːnə] *n.* 〔美〕低声哼唱感伤性流行歌曲的歌手.

crop [krɔp] *n.* ①农作物,庄稼;收获;收成;〔**the** ~**s**〕一季的收获量,产量. ②(同一时期出现的人物等)一批,一群,大量. ③剪短;短发. ④猎鞭;鞭柄. ⑤〔鸟〕嗉囊. ⑥(家畜的)耳印. ⑦(树等的)顶,梢,尖儿;【建】叶尖;【矿】露头. *an abundant [a bumper]* ~ 丰收. *a bad [poor]* ~ 歉收. *a rice* ~ 水稻作物. *industrial* ~*s* 经济作物. *row* ~*s* 中耕作物. *standing [growing]* ~*s* 植株,青苗. *a catch* ~ 填闲作物. *the black* ~ 豆类作物. *the green* ~ 菜类作物;牧草类作物. *the white* ~ 谷类作物. *this year's* ~ *of students* 今年毕业的一批学生. *a* ~ *of troubles* 麻烦一大堆. *a close* ~ 剪短发. *a* ~ *of (disputes; questions)* 一大批(争论;问题). *a* ~ *of pimples* 一大批[一大片]粉刺[疙瘩]. ~ *and root* 全部. ~ *capacity* 谷物单位面积产量. ~ *rotation* 轮作(法),轮种. ~ *succession* 轮作顺序. ~ *tree* 林木. ~ *yield* 茬地作物的产量. ***in [under]*** ~ 种着作物,在耕种. ***out of*** ~ 未种作物,未耕种. ***the*** ~***-mowing season*** 收割季节. — ***[cropped, cropt]*** *vt.* ①修剪,剪(树枝、头发等);割去(动物耳朵的)一角(作标记),剪掉(书上的)多余白边;(马)啃去(草尖等). ②收割,收获. ③种植,栽培,播种. — *vi.* ①生产;发生,发芽. ②(性质等)突然出现,(问题等)突然发生,(矿床等)露出(*out; forth; up*). ③(羊、鸟等)吃去嫩芽. *All sorts of unexpect-*

ed difficulties ~ped up. 种种想象不到的困难都发生了. *cropping system* 耕作制度. **~-dust** *vi., vt.* 撒药飞行. **~-duster** 撒药飞机. **~-eared** *a.* 割耳的;【英史】剪短头发露出耳朵的, 短发的. **~-over**〔西印度群岛〕甘蔗收割后的狂欢庆祝.

crop·per [ˈkrɔpə] *n.* ①种植者; (以收成一部分作佃租的)佃农. ②刈割者; 修剪者; (布等的)剪头机, 刈毛机. ③作物, 庄稼. ④〔口〕倒转坠下, 栽跟斗; 大失败. ⑤【动】大膆〔球胸〕鸽. *a heavy [light]* ~ 丰〔歉〕收. ***come [fall, get] a ~***〔口〕(从马上等)摔下来; 垮台; 大失败.

crop·pie [ˈkrɔpi] *n.* *(pl.* ~*s*, ~*)*【动】北美日鲈 (= crappie).

crop·py [ˈkrɔpi] *n.* 头发剪成平头的人; (1798年爱尔兰同情法国革命的)光头派; 清教徒.

cropt [krɔpt]〔罕〕crop 的过去时和过去分词.

cro·quet [ˈkrəukei, -ki] *n.*【体】(户外)槌球.

cro·quette [krəuˈket] *n.*〔F.〕炸丸子, 炸肉饼.

cro·quis [ˈkrəuki:] *n.* *(pl.* ~[-ki, -ki:z]*)* 草图〔尤指妇女时装草图〕.

crore [krɔ:] *n.*〔印〕一千万(卢比).

cro·sier [ˈkrəuʒə] *n.* ①【宗】牧杖〔主教职标〕. ②【植】(蕨等嫩叶的)卷头.

cross[1] [krɔs] *n.* ①十字架; 〔the C-〕耶稣受刑的十字架. ②〔the C-〕基督教(教义, 国家). ③不幸, 苦难; 挫折, 折磨, 考验. ④十字〔+, ×, †, ✚, T 等〕; 十字形(物); 十字装饰; 十字形花押; 十字勋章; 十字杖; 十字路;【天】南〔北〕十字星座. ⑤(字母 T 等的)横线. ⑥杂种, 杂交; 混合物, 中间物. ⑦〔俚〕欺诈, 骗局; (拳斗等)骗人的比赛. ⑧〔俚〕钱. ⑨【机】十字管, 四通;【电】交扰;【测】直角器. *the Buddhist* ~ 卍字. *a double* ~ 双杂交. *an off-*~ 天然杂交. *a* ~ *between a horse and a donkey* 马与驴的杂交种. *a* ~ *between a breakfast and lunch* 早午餐合并的上午饭. *bear one's* ~*es* 忍受苦难. ~ *and pile*〔古〕钱的正反面; 事物的两方面; (卜卦的)运气. ~ *of St. Andrew* × 形十字, 斜十字. ~ *of St. Anthony* 丁字十字. ~ *of St. George* (英格兰的)白底红色正十字. ~ *of St. Patrick* (爱尔兰的)白底红色 T 形十字. ***in*** ~ = *per* ~. ***make one's*** ~ (文盲)画十字花押. ***on the*** ~ 斜着; 〔俚〕不老实地, 为非作歹地(生活等). ***go on the*** ~ 走坏路, 入邪道. ***per*** ~ 照十字形; 交叉地. ***take (up) one's*** ~ 忍受苦难. ***take (up) the*** ~【史】接受十字章, 加入十字军; (教徒)为信仰受难. ***the True C-*** 钉死耶稣的十字架. — *a.* ①横斜的, 交叉的. ②反对的, 相冲突的; 逆向的; 不吉的, 不幸的. ③〔口〕暴躁的, 易怒的, 脾气不好的. ④相互的, 交替的. ⑤杂种的. ⑥〔俚〕不正当的; 用非法手段(得来)的. *a result* ~ *to a purpose* 与目的相反的结果. ***be as ~ as two sticks [as a bear with a sore head]***〔俚〕非常不高兴, 非常恼火. ***run ~ to*** 与…相反, 逆着. — *vt.* ①使交叉; 使相交; 搭着放, 横放; 画横线, 画线. ②渡(河), 横越, 翻(山)越(岭), 穿过; 使穿过; 〔口〕跨上(马); 擦过, 错过; 妨碍. ③(用手)画十字. ④打叉叉〔画线〕勾消, 划掉. ⑤使杂交. — *vi.* ①交叉. ②越过, 横断, 穿过, 渡过. ③相交; 错过〔双方的信件〕. ④杂交, 成杂种. ***be ~ed in*** 对…失望. ***be ~ed in love*** 失恋. ~ ***a cheque*** 把支票画上平行线. ~ ***a horse*** 跨上马. ~ ***each other on the road*** 在路途上互相错过. ~ ***keys***【徽】交叉钥匙. ~ ***mallets***〔美〕打马球. ~ ***off accounts*** 销帐. ~ ***one's arms*** 抱着手臂. ~ ***oneself*** 在自己身上画十字. ~ ***one's fingers*** (把中指与食指交叉搭住)期待好运; 希望减轻罪过. ~ ***sb.'s hand with silver*** 悄悄给以贿赂. ~ ***one's legs*** 交叉着腿(坐). ~ ***one's mind*** 想起. ~ ***one's lips*** 说出来. ~ ***sb.'s path*** 碰见, 遇见; 遮拦, 阻碍. ~ ***one's t's*** 不遗忘画 t 字的一横; 一笔一划〔一举一动〕都不草率. ~ ***out [off]*** 划掉, 取消, 注销. ~ ***over*** 横越, 穿过; 〔美〕死;【生】(染色体的)交杂. ~ ***swords with*** 与…斗剑, 与…交战; 与…争论〔论战〕. ~ ***the cudgels*** 不参与(争斗等). ~ ***the dope***〔美〕(比赛结果)和预料相反. ~ ***the line*** (船等)越过赤道. ~ ***the path of*** 碰到, 遇着; 拦阻. ~ **action**〔法〕反诉. ~**arm** 电线杆上的横木. ~**bar** 闩, 横木; 横臂; 十字管, 四通;【橄榄球】决胜柱的横木. ~**beam** 大梁, 横桁. ~**-bearer** 十字杖捧持者; 为耶稣忍苦受难的人; 支持炉格的横杆. ~ **bedded** *a.*【地】交错层的. ~**belt** 斜挂在肩上的子弹带〔武装带〕. ~**-bench** ① *a.* 中立的; ② *n.* 中立议员席. ~**-bencher** 中立议员; 中立人士. ~**-bias** 一种倾向〔偏见〕掩盖着的另一种倾向〔偏见〕. ~**bill**【鸟】交喙鸟. ~**birth**【医】横产. ~**bones**〔*pl.*〕交叉的大腿骨〔通常画在骷髅下, 象征死亡〕. ~**bow** 石弓, 弩. ~**bred** *n., a.* 杂交的, 杂种(的). ~ **breed** ①*n.* 杂交; 杂种. ②*vt., vi.* *(p., p.p.* ~**-bred***)* (使)杂交. ~ **bun** (耶稣蒙难节用的)蒙难节圣糕〔也叫 hot cross bun〕. ~**-buttock** *n., vt.*【摔交】拦腰抱掷; 冷不防的投掷〔打〕. ~**-check** *n., vt.* 反复核对; 多方查证. ~**-counter**【拳】反击. ~**-cloth** (妇女)扎头带. ~**-country** *a.* 越野的; 横越(全国)的. ~ **cousins** 姑表或舅表兄弟姐妹. ~**-coupling** ① *n.* 相互作用; 交叉耦合(干扰). ②*a.*【空】交感的. ~**current** 逆流; 相反思潮〔意见, 倾向〕. ~**cut** ①*n.* 横切; 直路, 捷径;【矿】横巷, 石门;【建】横锯. ②*a.* 横切的, 斜切的; 横锯的; 纹路交叉的(锉子). ③ *vt.* 横断. ~ **debt** 互相抵消的债务; 冲帐. ~**-disciplinary** *a.* 两种以上学科的, 多学科的. ~**-dress** *vi.* 穿着异性服装〔女扮男装或男扮女装〕. ~**-examination**【法】反复讯问, 盘问. ~**-examine** *vt.*【法】反复讯问, 盘问. ~**eye** 内斜视〔眼〕. ~**-eyed** *a.* 内斜视(眼)的; 〔美俚〕喝醉了的. ~**-fertilization** 异花〔异体〕受精. ~ **-fertilize** *vt., vi.* (使)异花〔异体〕受精. ~**-file** *vi.*〔美〕在初选中申请备案作为两个以上政党的候选人. ~**-garnet** T 字蝶铰. ~**-grained** *a.* (木料)纹理不规则的, 扭丝的; (性子)拗的, 倔强的, 脾气大的. ~ **hairs** (光学仪器等上的)十字(丝)准线. ~**hatch** *vt.* (钢笔画等)画上横直交叉平行线的阴影. ~**head** *n.*【机】T 字头; (报纸等的)小标题(= cross-heading). ~**-index** *vt., vi.* 编制〔附有〕相互参照的索引〔注释〕. ~**jack** 后桅下桁上挂的大横帆. ~**-legged** *a.* 交叉着腿的. ~**let** (徽章的)小十字形. ~**light** 交叉光线; 不同的看法〔意见〕. ~**-link** 交叉〔横向〕耦合; (聚合物的)交联(键). ~**over**【铁路】岔道, 转线路;【生】(染色体的)交杂, 交换; 交换型; 〔英〕(交搭胸前的)女围巾. ~**patch** 脾气坏的人; 淘气的孩子. ~**-piece** 腕木, 横木; 横档儿; (剑的)小锷. ~**ply** (轮胎的)交叉帘布. ~**-pollination**【植】异花授〔受〕粉. ~**-purpose** 相反的目的〔意志, 计划〕; 〔*pl.*〕(一种滑稽游戏)答非所问 (*be at* ~*-purpose* 矛盾, 龃龉; 互相误解). ~**-question** *vt., n.* 盘问; 反复讯问 (~*-question and crooked answers* 答非所问, 答非所问游戏). ~ **rate** 第三国外汇牌价. ~**ratio** 交比, 非调和比, 重比. ~**-refer** *vi., vt.* 相互参照. ~**-reference** 相互参照(条目), 互见条目. ~**road** 横路; 交叉道路; 〔*pl.*〕(英国旧时埋葬自杀者的)十字路口; 〔美〕大路交会处所〔多成为居民点〕, 村镇中的闹市; 活动、聚会中心地点. ~**-section** (有代表性的)横截面, 剖面; 抽样, 样品;【原】有效截面. ~**-sterility** 杂交不育. ~**-stitch** 十字缝, 十字形针迹. ~ **talk** (电话)串话, 串线; 斗嘴, 争论, 口角; 对口相声. ~**tie**〔美〕【铁路】枕木. ~**-town** *a.* 横贯全城镇的, 穿城的. ~ **trade** 买空卖空. ~ **traffic** 设红绿灯的交叉路口. ~**trees**〔*pl.*〕【船】桅顶横桁; 撑持桅楼的横档. ~**-under**【物, 电】穿接; 交叉; 交迭. ~**-walk** 人行横道; 斑马线. ~**way** 十字路口; 活动、聚会的中心地点. ~**ways**, ~**wise** *ad.* 斜横; 成十字状, 交叉; 相反地; 别扭地, 恶意地. ~**word (puzzle)** 纵横字谜. ~**yard**【海】横桁.

Cross(e) [krɔs] *n.* 克罗斯〔姓氏〕.

crosse [krɔs] *n.* (加拿大 lacrosse 球戏用来抛球和捕球

的)有网曲棒.
crossed [krɔst] *a.* 十字的,装成十字的; 交叉的; 画线的(支票);注销的,划十字勾销掉的;受到阻碍的(爱情、野心等). ～ **cheque** 划线支票.
cros·sette [krɔˈset] *n.*【建】(钉于门窗下缘一角的)门耳,窗耳.
cross·ing [ˈkrɔsiŋ] *n.* ①交叉,相交;横切,横断;横越,横渡. ②交叉点;十字街口;人行横道;(河的)渡口,(铁路的)闸口. ③〔古〕阻碍,挫折. ④画十字; 画线. ⑤【生】杂交. ⑥(横加)阻挠. *have a good [rough]* ～ 风平浪静[风浪险恶]的渡航. *a grade* ～〔美〕= *a level* ～〔英〕平面交叉. *a street [footway]* ～ 人行横道. *zebra* ～ 斑马线.
cross·ing-o·ver [ˈkrɔːsiŋˈəuvə] *n.*【生】交换.
cross·ite [ˈkrɔːsait] *n.*【地】青铝闪石.
cross·ly [ˈkrɔsli] *ad.* 横,斜;发着脾气,别扭地,拗着.
cross·ness [ˈkrɔsnis] *n.* 情绪坏,别扭.
cros·sop·te·ryg·i·an [krəˌsɔptəˈridʒiən] *n.*【动】总鳍组鱼.
cross·ruff [ˈkrɔːsˌrʌf] *n.*【牌】惠斯特纸牌戏的一种玩法.
crotch [krɔtʃ] *n.* ①(人的)胯. ②叉状物;(树等的)丫叉;【海】叉柱;〔美〕(路等的)岔口.
crotch·et [ˈkrɔtʃit] *n.* ①小钩;叉架, 叉柱; 【筑城】钩形路;【解、植】枝叉,桠叉. ②怪想, 奇想;怪癖. ③【乐】四分音符.
crotch·et·eer [krɔtʃiˈtiə] *n.* 奇想家,奇癖家,怪人.
crotch·e·ty [ˈkrɔtʃiti] *a.* 有怪想的,有怪癖的.
cro·ton [ˈkrəutən] *n.*【植】巴豆(属). ～ **bug** 小蟑螂. ～ **oil** 巴豆油.
crouch [krautʃ] *vi., vt.* 蹲下;蜷着,缩着;弯腰低头 *(to).* — *n.* 蹲;【滑雪】屈膝姿势. ***be ～ing in a corner*** 缩在角落里. ***～ing start***【体】蹲下起跑法.
croup [kruːp] *n.*【医】假膜性喉炎,格鲁布,哮吼.
croup(e) [kruːp] *n.* (马等的)臀部;〔谑〕(人的)屁股.
croup·er [ˈkruːpə] *n.* = crupper.
crou·pi·er [ˈkruːpiə] *n.* ①(赌场上的)管钱人. ②(公共宴会的)副主持人.
croup·ous, croup·y [ˈkruːpəs, -pi] *a.* 【医】格鲁布性(的).
Crouse [kraus] *n.* 克劳斯〔姓氏〕.
crouse [kruːs] *a.* 〔英方〕活泼的;大胆的;生气勃勃的.
croû·ton [ˈkruːtɔn] *n.* 〔F.〕油炸面包丁.
crow[1] [krəu] *n.* ①鸦〔包含 raven, rook, jackdaw, chough, 英国特指 carrion crow〕. ②=～ bar. ③〔C-〕【天】乌鸦座. ***as the ～ flies = in a ～ line*** 笔直. ***eat (boiled)～***〔美口〕忍辱,屈服. ***have a ～ to pick [pluck, pull] with (sb.)*** 有一件非与(某人)争论不可的事,非得跟某人讲个明白不可. ***white ～*** 珍奇的东西,珍品;南非产秃鹰. **～bar** 铁挺,铁橇; 起货钩;【物】急剧短路,断裂. **～ber·ry**【植】岩高兰(属);〔美〕红莓苔子. **～-foot** ①*(pl.* -foots*)*【植】毛莨(属);玉柏;牛角花;臭荠状车前;老鹳草(属). ②*(pl.* -feet*)*【军】铁蒺藜, 拦路钩;【摄】防滑三角架. ③*(pl.* -feet*)*【海】吊索. ～ **-quill** 乌鸦的羽毛(管),鸦羽笔;(作图用)细笔尖. **～bill, ～'s-bill**【医】鸦嘴钳. **～'s-foot** *(pl. -feet)* ①(眼外角的)鱼尾(纹). ②【军】= caltrop. ③【空】(控制气球,飞船的)拉索钢缆. **～'s-nest** 桅楼守望台. **～step** 屋侧山形墙头的墙级. **～toe**【植】百脉根. ～ **vetch**【植】草藤,广布野豌豆.
crow[2] [krəu] *n.* 鸡叫声; 儿童欢闹声. — *vi.* ***(～ed, crew; ～ed)*** ①(雄鸡)叫,鸣,报晓. ②(儿童)欢叫. ③欢呼;欢笑,得意洋洋. ～ ***over one's enemy [victory]*** 向敌人呼喊示威[欢呼胜利].
crowd[1] [kraud] *n.* ①人群;拥挤. ②〔the ～〕民众,群众,大众,老百姓. ③(物的)大量,许多. ④〔美口〕一伙, 伙伴;〔美军〕家伙,东西;〔美〕一群;〔军俚〕部队. ***～s [a ～] of people*** 一大群人. *He belongs to a fast* ～. 他是一个放荡鬼. *He's a bad* ～. 他是一个坏东西. *a* ～ *of (books)* 许许多多的(书). ～ *psychology* 群众心理. ***far from the madding ～*** 远离扰攘的公众. ***follow [go with] the ～*** 随大流. ***in ～s*** 成群,大群地. ***might [would] pass in a ～***〔俚〕不会十分坏;可以过得去. — *vt.* ①挤;排挤. ②塞满,挤满. ③〔美俚〕逼迫;勒索. ～ *a child out of his way* 将小孩挤开. ～ *sb. for money* 催某人付款. — *vi.* 群聚,拥挤 *(about; round; in; to)*; (大群人)挤进 *(into)*. *a ～ing pen*〔美〕给牲畜烧烙印的小围场. ***be ～ed with*** 被…挤满; 满是…. ***come ～ing in*** 一拥而入. ～ ***about*** 围住, 包围. ～ ***on [in] upon*** 蜂拥而来,逼拢来. ～ ***out*** 挤出,推开,排挤,驱逐. ～ ***(on) sail***【海】扯满所有风帆. ～ ***the mourners***〔美俚〕急躁地行动; 操之过急. ～ ***up*** 推上, 挤上. ～ ***upon one's mind*** (百感)交集,涌上心头.
crowd[2] [kraud] *n.* = crwth.
crowd·ed [ˈkraudid] *a.* 拥挤的, 挤满人的,客满的;充满(东西)的; 多事的;【植】郁闭的. *a ～ career* 丰富的经历. *a ～ hour* 事情安排得紧紧的时间. *a ～ week* 忙忙碌碌的一周. ～ *solitude* 在人群中感到的孤独.
crown [kraun] *n.* ①(胜利的)花冠;荣誉;〔美俚〕锦标. ②王冠,冕;王位;君权;〔the C-〕国王, 君主. ③王冠印记[图案]. ④印有王冠的硬币;〔旧〕五先令英国硬币;克朗〔某些国家的货币单位名称〕. ⑤(一切东西的)顶部;头顶,(特指)圆形的顶部;帽顶;峰顶;绝顶,极致, 至上. ⑥【解】齿冠;【海】锚冠;【建】冠顶;【植】冠;根茎; 副花冠 (= corona);【动】冠状部. ⑦一种纸张尺寸〔15×20英寸;〔美〕15×19英寸〕. ⑧晕,光环,光轮,圆光. ⑨【机】隆起;凸面. ⑩冕牌玻璃. *an officer of the* ～ (国王任命的)官吏. ***pleas of the ～***【英法】公诉. ～ *and anchor* (在印有王冠、铁锚等的盘子上用骰子玩的)掷冕锚游戏. ～ *of one's labors* 工作中的最终成就. ～ *of the head* 头顶. ～ *of the year* 秋收季节. ～ *of thorns*【植】虎刺; 棘冕, 荆冠; 痛苦. — *vt.* ①为…加冕, 使戴王冠; 使登极,立…为君主;(跳棋)加冕使成为王棋. ②加在顶上;戴;装饰…的顶,作…的冠饰;【齿】装金帽,镶齿冠. ③授予荣誉,表扬,酬劳. ④作…的最后点缀,完成,成就. ⑤〔美俚〕打脑门顶. ⑥【农】打顶尖. ⑦镶上齿冠. *a high [low] ～ed hat* 高顶 [低顶] 帽子. *be ～ed with success* 最后得到成功, 以成功结束. ～ *a tooth* 镶齿罩[冠]. *～ed heads* 国王与王后. ***to ～ all*** 在一切之上更…的是. ～**bud** 根茎芽. ～ **cap** 铁皮瓶盖. **C- Colony** 英国直辖殖民地. ～ **density** 郁闭度. **C- Derby** 英国 Derby 制陶器〔印有王冠商标〕. ～ **forest**〔英〕王室林. ～ **gear** = ～ **wheel**. ～ **glass** 冕牌玻璃. ～ **imperial** 皇冠;【植】壮丽贝母. ～ **jewels**〔英〕加冕礼用珠宝类. ～ **land**〔英〕王室领地;(自治领的)公有土地. ～ **law**〔英〕刑法. ～ **lawyer**〔英〕王室律师;刑事律师. ～ **layer** 树冠层. ～ **lens** 冕牌玻璃透镜;消色差凸透镜. **C- Office** ①英国高等法院的习惯法事务处理部. ②大法官厅的国玺部. ～ **piece** (旧制) 旧五先令硬币. ～**piece** 顶部,冠饰;马笼头顶部. ～ **prince** 皇太子. ～ **princess** 皇太子妃. ～ **saw** 筒形锯. ～ **vetch**【植】多变小冠花. ～ **wheel**【机】冕状轮〔差动器侧面伞形齿轮〕. ～ **witness**【英法】(刑事案件的)原告证人. ～ **work**【筑城】冠状工事;【齿科】(镶装)假齿冠[罩].
crown·er [ˈkraunə] *n.* ①授冠者; 授予荣誉者. ②最后完成者. ③倒栽葱;(因而)跌伤头顶. ④〔英方〕验尸官(coroner).
crown·ing [ˈkrauniŋ] *a.* 无上的; 无比的; 登峰造极的;顶部的. ～ *glory* 无上光荣. — *n.* ①加冕. ②圆满完成;终结;登峰造极.
croy·don [ˈkrɔidn] *n.* 轻快二轮单马车.
croze [krəuz] *n.* ①(木桶的) 栓槽; 桶顶槽. ②凿槽具.
cro·zier [ˈkrəuʒə] *n.* = crosier.

c. r. s. = cold-rolled steel 冷轧钢.
CRT = cathode-ray tube 阴极射线管.
cru·ces [ˈkruːsiːz] *n.* crux 的复数.
cru·ci·al [ˈkruːʃjəl, ˈkəuːʃəl] *a.* ①严酷的;极为困难的. ②极紧要的;决定性的. ③【医】十字形的. *the ~ moment* 关键时刻,重要关头. *a ~ incision* 十字切开.
cru·cian [ˈkruːʃən] *n.*【动】鲫鱼. *~ carp* 欧洲鲫.
cru·ci·ate [ˈkruːʃiit] *a.*【植、动】十字形的;交叉的.
cru·ci·ble [ˈkruːsibl] *n.* ①坩埚;熔罐. ②很严酷的考验. ***in the ~ of*** 处于…的残酷考验中.
cru·ci·fer [ˈkruːsifə] *n.* ①十字花科的植物. ②【宗】捧持十字架者.
Cru·cif·e·rae [kruːˈsifəriː] *n.* 〔*pl.*〕【植】十字花科.
cru·cif·er·ous [kruːˈsifərəs] *a.* ①【植】十字花科的;有十字形花的. ②【宗】捧持十字架的.
cru·ci·fix [ˈkruːsifiks] *n.* (十字架状)耶稣受难像;(象征基督教信仰的)十字架.
cru·ci·fix·ion [ˈkrusifikʃən] *n.* ①被钉死在十字架. ②〔the C-〕耶稣被钉死在十字架上的画. ③苦痛的考验;受难;极大的痛苦.
cru·ci·form [ˈkruːsifɔːm] *a.* 十字形的,十字架状的.
cru·ci·fy [ˈkruːsifai] *vt.* ①钉[绑]在十字架上;处以钉在十字架的死刑. ②迫害,虐待,折磨. ③抑制,压灭〔情欲等〕.
crud [krʌd] *n.* ①〔俚〕沉渣. ②可鄙的人或物. ③〔美〕怪病. ④〔方〕= curd. — *vi., vt.* (使)凝结(成块).
crude [kruːd] *a.* ①天然的,未加工的. ②粗(制)的,低级的;未熟的,生的;生硬的;粗糙的,粗杂的,粗鲁的. ③赤裸裸的;未加修饰的(现实情况等). ④【统】未整理的. ⑤【语法】无词尾变化的. — *n.* 原[生]材料,天然物质;原油. *~ materials* 原料. *~ (mineral) oil* = *~ petroleum* 原油. *~ rubber* 生橡胶. *~ manners* 粗鲁的态度. *a ~ method* 粗暴的方法. *the ~ birth rate* 总出生率. *a ~ fact* 赤裸裸的事实,事实真相. **-ly** *ad.* **-ness** *n.*
cru·di·ty [ˈkruːditi] *n.* 生,未熟;生硬;芜杂,粗杂;未成熟物,未成品;粗鲁的行为[言语].
cru·el [ˈkruəl] *a.* ①残忍的,残酷的. ②令人痛苦的;无情的;严酷的,铁面无私的. — *ad.* 〔口〕极度,非常. *It hurt me something ~.* 痛极了. **-ly** *ad.* **-ness** *n.*
cru·el·ty [ˈkruəlti, -il-] *n.* ①残酷,冷酷,刻毒. ②〔*pl.*〕残酷行为,横蛮行为. ③【法】(残酷)虐待.
cru·et [ˈkru(ː)it] *n.* ①(餐桌上的)调味瓶(瓶架). ②【宗】祭坛用瓶. ~ **stand** 调味瓶架.
cruise [kruːz] *n.* ①(军舰等)巡逻,巡航. ②〔口〕游览,旅行,周游. *~ missile* 巡航导弹. — *vi.* ①巡逻,巡航,游弋. ②〔口〕游览,漫游. ③(营业汽车)在街上慢行兜揽生意. ④〔美〕森林勘查,估测. ⑤(在公共场所)勾搭异性(舞伴等). — *vt.* (在公共场所)勾搭(异性舞伴等). ~ **missile** 巡航导弹. **cruising radius**【海】续航距离. **cruising taxi** 在街上兜揽搭客的出租汽车.
cruis·er [ˈkruːzə] *n.* ①巡洋舰. ②游艇 (= cabin ~). ③巡航飞机;远程导弹. ④〔美〕漫游者;(警察)巡逻汽车;揽客汽车. ⑤〔拳口〕= ~weight. ⑥〔美〕森林勘查者(穿的长统靴). ⑦〔俚〕(在街上来回走动勾搭嫖客的)娼妓. *an armoured ~* 装甲巡洋舰. *an auxiliary ~* 补助巡洋舰[武装商船]. *a battle ~* 巡洋战舰. *a converted ~* 改装[伪装]巡洋舰. *a protected ~* (有装甲甲板的)装甲巡洋舰. **~weight** 〔拳口〕轻重量级拳击家〔161磅至176磅〕.
crul·ler [ˈkrʌlə] *n.* 〔美〕油炸麻花;〔方〕煎饼,油炸面包圈.
crumb [krʌm] *n.* ①〔常 *pl.*〕(面包的)碎屑;碎片;团粒. ②面包心(*opp.* crust). ③些少,少许. ④〔美俚〕可鄙的人物. *pick up a few ~s of information* 稍微打听一下. *~ brush* (餐桌用)面包屑刷子. *~ of comfort* 些许的安慰. *to a ~* 精细地;仔细周到地. — *vt.* 捏碎,弄碎;【烹】裹上面包屑(用油煎),加面包屑使(汤)变浓;〔美口〕扫去(餐桌上的)面包屑. ~**cloth** (铺在餐桌下地毯上的)面包屑承接布. ~ **structure** 团粒[屑粒状]结构.
crum·ble [ˈkrʌmbl] *vt.* 弄碎,粉碎. — *vi.* 破碎;崩溃,溃散;灭亡,消灭. *~ to [into] dust* 化为尘土.
crum·bly [ˈkrʌmbli] *a.* 易碎的,脆弱的.
crumb·y [ˈkrʌmi] *a.* ①尽是面包屑的;裹了面包屑的;柔软的(面包). ②〔美俚〕肮脏,可厌,劣等,低廉,可鄙的;虱子多的.
crum·mie, crum·my[1] [ˈkrʌmi] 〔英方〕曲角牛;牛.
crum·my[2] [ˈkrʌmi] *a.* ①〔英俚〕丰满的,健美的(女人);娇媚的,可爱的. ②有钱的. ③〔英俚〕尽是虱子的,肮脏的;低廉的,劣等的.
crump [krʌmp] *vi.* ①嘎扎嘎扎作声. ②(炸弹)猛然爆炸. — *vt.* ①嘎扎嘎扎地嚼. ②〔俚〕猛打(板球);③〔军俚〕用巨弹猛轰. — *n.* ①嘎扎嘎扎的咀嚼声. ②猛打. ③〔军俚〕猛轰;(炮弹)爆裂声;爆裂弹.
crum·pet [ˈkrʌmpit] *n.* ①〔英〕松脆热煎饼. ②〔俚〕娇媚(的女性). ③〔俚〕头. ***be barmy [balmy] on the ~ = be off one's ~*** 疯狂的;神经不正常的.
crum·ple [ˈkrʌmpl] *vt., vi.* 揉皱;击溃;变皱,折坏;崩溃. ***~... into a ball*** 揉成一团. ***~ up*** 揉皱;压倒;垮台,崩溃.
crum·pled [ˈkrʌmpld] *a.* 变皱了的;弯扭的(牛角等).
crum·ply [ˈkrʌmpli] *a.* 易皱的;易弄皱的. *~ paper* 皱纹纸.
crunch [krʌntʃ] *vi., vt.* 嘎扎嘎扎地咀嚼(饼干等);(车轮、皮靴等)嘎喳嘎喳地(在砂砾路上)碾过[踏过] (*through*). *The dog was ~ing a bone.* 狗正在啃骨头. — *n.* ①咬碎,咬,嚼;〔方〕碎屑;嘎扎嘎扎的响声. ②〔美俚〕摊牌(时刻),紧要[决定性]关头;困境;(经济等)紧缩状态.
crunch·y [ˈkrʌntʃi] *a.* (咀嚼时)嘎吱作响的. **-i·ness** *n.*
cru·or [ˈkruːɔː] *n.* 凝血,血块.
crup·per [ˈkrʌpə] *n.* (勒在马的臀部上的)后鞦;马屁股;〔俚、谑〕(人的)屁股. — *vt.* 上屁鞦.
cru·ral [ˈkruərəl] *a.*【解】股的,腿的;腕钩的.
crus [krʌs] (*pl.* ***crura*** [ˈkruərə]) *n.*【解】下腿(由膝至踝的部分);腕钩.
cru·sade [kruːˈseid] *n.*【史】十字军;(宗教性的)圣战;讨伐;改革运动;肃清运动,扑灭运动. ***~ against Fascism*** 肃清法西斯运动. ***~ in favour of birth control*** 节制生育运动. — *v.* 发动十字军,加入十字军;讨伐,从事改革[肃清]运动.
cru·sad·er [kruːˈseidə] *n.* 十字军从军骑士;十字军战士;参加讨伐者;改革运动参与者.
cruse [kruːz] *n.* 〔古〕瓦罐,坛子. *a widow's ~* 寡妇的坛子[喻取之不竭的资源].
crush [krʌʃ] *vt.* ①压碎;压扁,压坏(帽子等);捣碎,弄碎;挤榨. ②压倒,压服,扑灭(疫病等);打倒;击溃(敌人等);扼杀;(使受)挫折. ③喝(酒等). ④〔口〕压皱,揉皱(衣服等). — *vi.* ①(被)压扁,压坏,压烂. ②(人群)挤进,蜂拥而来,向前推进 (*into; through*). ③变皱. *~ a beetle with the foot* 用脚踩烂一只甲虫. ***be ~ed to pieces*** 压成碎片. ***~ down*** 镇压,压服;碾碎. ***~ out*** 扑灭,歼灭;榨取,榨出,挤出;〔美俚〕越狱. ***~ up*** 粉碎,碾碎;揉成一团;挤过来. — *n.* ①压烂,压碎,碾碎,粉碎. ②拥挤;〔口〕扰嚷的集会;〔军俚〕部队. ③〔澳〕(给牲畜打火印设置的)漏斗状围栏. ④(榨出的)鲜果汁. ⑤〔美俚〕(特指女子对男性的)迷恋. ***have [get] a ~ on*** 迷恋. ~ **barrier** (公共场所拦阻人群挤入的钢制)栏栅. ~ **hat** 可折摺而不致损坏的帽子(= opera hat.). **~-proof** *a.* 防碰撞的. ~ **room** (戏院等的)休息处.
crush·er [ˈkrʌʃə] *n.* ①压碎者,压碎器[机]. ②〔口〕猛烈的一击;压服人的议论,使人哑然失色的事实. ③〔俚〕警察.
crush·ing [ˈkrʌʃiŋ] *a.* 压倒的,决定性的. *a ~ defeat* 大溃败. *a ~ sorrow* 肝肠欲碎的忧愁. *a ~ retort* 使人闭口无言的反驳,斩钉截铁的回答.

Cru·soe [ˈkruːsəu] *n.* ①鲁宾逊·克鲁索〔英国作家笛福 (Defoe) 所作小说《鲁宾逊飘流记》的主人公〕. ②象鲁宾逊一样飘流到荒岛上的人,孤独的人.

crust [krʌst] *n.* ①面包皮 *(opp.* crumb*)*; 干面包片; 生活口粮,糊口之资. ②外皮,壳;〔美〕雪壳;【地】地壳;【动】甲壳;【医】痂; (酒等的)浮渣; 水垢. ③(事物的)皮相,外表,表面. ④〔美俚〕老面皮,厚颜无耻; 没礼貌; (人的)脑壳. ~ *movement* 地壳移动. ***earn one's*** ~ 挣钱糊口. ***have a*** ~〔美俚〕脸皮太厚; 太大胆,太卤莽,太冒失. ***the upper*** ~〔古、俚〕上层社会. — *vt., vi.* 用外皮覆盖; 结成硬皮; 生痂儿. *The snow has ~ed over.* 雪在地上结成冰壳. **~-hunt** *vi.*〔美〕在硬雪上猎麋鹿(等).

Crus·ta·ce·a [krʌsˈteiʃjə] *n.*〔*pl.*〕【动】甲壳纲.

crus·ta·ce·an [krʌsˈteiʃjən] *a., n.* 甲壳类的(动物).

crus·ta·ce·ous [krʌsˈteiʃjəs] *a.* 外皮的; 硬皮的; (甲)壳(质)的;【动】甲壳类的; 有甲壳[硬壳]的;【植】坚脆的; (地衣)覆生的.

crus·tal [ˈkrʌstl] *a.* 外壳的〔尤指地球外壳〕.

crust·ed [ˈkrʌstid] *a.* 外面结成硬皮的,有壳的; 长了酒垢的; 古色古香的; 陈腐的; 顽梗的. ~ *habit* 陋习. ~ *Tories* 顽固的守旧分子.

crust·i·ly [ˈkrʌstili] *ad.* 执拗地,顽固地,态度顽梗地.

crust·i·ness [ˈkrʌstinis] *n.* 执拗,顽固,倔强.

crust·y [ˈkrʌsti] *a.* 壳一样的; 有(硬)壳的,(面包)皮硬的 *(opp.* crumby*)*; 执拗的,顽固的; 态度恶劣的,脾气乖戾的.

crutch [krʌtʃ] *n.* ①拐杖,(跛子腋下的)T字杖. ②支柱,叉柱;〔喻〕支持; 依靠(物). ③【船】船尾肘木,叉木; 桨架. ④〔古〕(人的)胯部. *the ~ of one's declining years* 老来依靠. ***from cradle to*** ~ 从小到老. — *vt.* 用拐杖[支柱等]支住.

crutched [krʌtʃt] *a.* ①拄着T字杖[拐杖]的; 用支柱撑着的. ②[ˈkrʌtʃid] 带[挂]着十字架的.

crux [krʌks] *n.* *(pl.* ~*es* [-iz], ***cruces*** [ˈkruːsiːz]*)* ①【徽】十字(架)形. ②要点; 症结; 难题,难点; 难解的谜. ③〔C-〕【天】南十字座. ~ *ansata* T字形十字. ~ *play* 悬疑剧.

cru·zei·ro [kruːˈzeirəu] *n.* *(pl.* ~*s)* 克鲁塞罗〔巴西货币单位,等于一百 centavos〕.

crwth [kruːθ] *n.* ①克楼得〔凯尔特古乐器〕. ②〔英方〕小提琴(= crowd).

cry [krai] *vi.* ①叫,喊; (禽兽)啼,鸣,嗥,(犬)吠. ②哭泣; 号哭. — *vt.* ①叫,喊,大声叫喊,大声说. ②呼报,呼告; 叫卖. ③〔古〕乞求. ④〔美俚〕诉委曲,发牢骚,哭诉. ⑤哭出; 以哭泣促使. ~ *the news all over the town* 遍街大声报导消息. ~ *one's wares* 叫卖货物. ~ *against* 对…大声反对. ~ ***back***〔Scot.〕叫回来;【猎】(狗)跑回来,折回来; (动物等)重现祖先的性状,反祖遗传. ~ ***bitter tears*** 痛哭流涕. ~ ***down*** 轰下,轰走(演讲者等),贬损,侮蔑,责骂. ~ ***for*** 乞求,请求; 要求,哭着要; 迫切需要 (~ *for the moon* 空想,妄想). ~ ***for company*** 陪哭. ~ ***halves*** 要求平分. ~ ***from [on] the house-top(s)*** 公开宣称,扬言. ~ ***halt*** 命令停止. ~ ***hands off*** 叫(竞争者)放手,警告退避. ~ ***in company*** 陪哭. ~ ***on the God*** 求神. ~ ***off (from)*** 撤回,取消(前约等); (从交易等上)撒手; 宣布退出. ~ ***oneself to sleep*** (婴儿)哭到睡着. ~ ***one's eyes out*** 把眼都要哭瞎了,长时间大哭. ~ ***one's heart out*** 极伤心地痛哭. ~ ***out*** 大叫,对…大声反对 *(against)*; 喊着要求 *(for)*. ~ ***out before one is hurt***〔喻〕牢骚发得太早. ~ ***over*** 叹惜(不幸等). ~ ***over spilt milk*** 作无益的后悔[谴责]. ~ ***quarter*** 乞命,求免一死. ~***quits*** 见 quits 条. ~ ***shame upon*** 责备,非难,大骂. ~ ***stinking fish*** 叫卖臭鱼; 暴露自已的丑事. ~ ***to [unto]*** 向…求援,求…保护; 苦求. ~ ***up*** 夸奖,褒扬. ~ ***up wine and sell vinegar*** 挂羊头卖狗肉. ~ ***wolf*** 作虚假的警报; 谎报军情. — *n.* ①叫喊; 呼声; 叫声; 哭声; 吠声; 号哭. ②喝彩,呐喊; 大声宣扬; 呼吁; 叫卖声. ③哭诉,哀求. ④谣传,舆论; 运动,风尚. ⑤(政党的)口号,标语. ⑥一群猎狗(的呼叫声). ***a far*** ~ 远距离; 悬殊很大的东西. ***all ~ and no wool = more ~ than wool. all the ~*** 大流行; 最新式样. ***be within ~ of*** …声听得见的地方[距离]. ~ ***against*** 反对…的呼声,…的反对运动. ~ ***for*** 要求…的呼声,…的要求运动. ***follow in the ~*** 随声附和. ***give a ~*** 大喊一声. ***have a good ~*** 尽情痛哭. ***in full ~*** 猎狗一齐追赶着,在拼命追赶中; 一齐. ***more ~ than wool = much [a great] ~ and little wool*** 雷声大雨点小; 力气花得不少,结果甚微. ***out of all ~*** 过份,过度. ***out of ~*** 在叫声不能听到的地方;〔喻〕力量够不着的地方. ~ **baby** 爱哭[诉]的人.

cry·ing [ˈkraiiŋ] *a.* 叫喊的,嚎哭的; 突出的,显著的,厉害的; 紧急的. *a ~ evil* 突出的[急应矫正的]弊病. *a ~ need* 迫切需要. *a ~ shame* 奇耻大辱.

cryo- *comb. f.* 低温,冷,冰,霜.

cry·o·bi·ol·o·gy [ˈkraiəubaiˈɔlədʒi] *n.* 低温生物学〔尤指研究低温下热血动物的生命的科学〕. **-biol·o·gist** *n.*

cry·o·chem·is·try [ˈkraiəuˈkemistri] *n.* 低温[深冷]化学.

cry·o·e·lec·tron·ics [ˌkraiəuiˌlekˈtrɔniks] *n.* 低温电子学.

cry·o·gen [ˈkraiəudʒen] *n.*【化】制[致]冷剂,冷冻剂; 低温[冷却]粉碎.

cry·o·gen·ic [ˌkraiəuˈdʒenik] *a.* 低温学的; 低温实验法的.

cry·o·gen·ics [ˌkraiəuˈdʒeniks] *n.* 低温(物理)学; 低温实验法.

cry·og·e·ny [kraiˈɔdʒini] *n.* 低温物理学冷却法.

cry·o·hy·drate [ˌkraiəˈhaiˌdreit] *n.* 冰盐; 低(共)熔冰盐结晶; 饱凝分晶体.

cry·o·lite [ˈkraiəulait] *n.*【矿】冰晶石.

cry·om·e·ter [kraiˈɔmitə] *n.* 低温计,深冷[低温]温度计.

cry·on·ics [kraiˈɔniks] *n.*【医】人体冷冻学.

cry·o·phil·ic [ˌkraiəuˈfilik] *a.*【生】好冷性的,嗜寒的,喜低温的,低温下繁茂的.

cry·oph·o·rus [kraiˈɔfərəs] *n.*【物】凝冰器〔显示水因自身蒸发而结冰的仪器〕.

cry·o·phyte [ˈkraiəufait] *n.*【植】冰雪植物.

cry·o·probe [ˈkraiəuˌprəub] *n.*【医】冰冻探子,冷冻器,冷刀.

cry·o·pump [ˈkraiəupʌmp] *n.*【机】低温泵.

cry·o·scope [ˈkraiəuskəup] *n.*【物】冰点测定器.

cry·os·co·py [kraiˈɔskəpi] *n.* 冰点测定学; 冰点降低测定法.

cry·o·stat [ˈkraiəuˌstæt] *n.* 低温恒温器; 致冷器,低温箱.

cry·o·sur·ger·y [ˌkraiəuˈsəːdʒəri] *n.* 冷冻手术; 冷冻破坏法. **-sur·gi·cal** *a.*

cry·o·ther·a·py [ˌkraiəuˈθerəpi] *n.*【医】冷(冻)疗法.

cry·o·tron [ˈkraiəutrɔn] *n.* 冷子管,低温管; 冷持元件.

crypt [kript] *n.* ①地窖,地穴; (特指)教堂地下室〔常作墓穴用〕. ②【解】滤胞腺,腺窝,小囊,隐窝.

crypt- (接元音) = crypto- (接辅音).

crypt·a·nal·y·sis [ˌkriptəˈnælisis] *n.* 密码分析,密码分析学. **-lyst** [-ˈtænəlist] *n.* **-lyt·ic** [-tænəˌlitik] *a.*

cryp·tic, cryp·ti·cal [ˈkriptik, -kəl] *a.* ①隐藏的,秘密的; 神秘的; 难解的. ②【动】(适于)隐藏的. ~ *colouring*【动】保护色. *a ~ remark* 有言外之意的话. ~ *species*【生】同形种.

cryp·to [ˈkriptəu] *n.* (政党、社团等的)秘密成员,秘密支持者.

crypto- *comb. f.* 隐藏,隐蔽,潜藏; 秘密.

cryp·to·clas·tic [ˌkriptəuˈklæstik] *a.*【矿】隐屑质的.

cryp·to·com·mer·cial·ism [ˈkriptəukəˈməːʃəlizəm]

n. 勾心斗角的商业竞争.

cryp·to·crys·tal·line [ˈkriptəuˈkristlin] *a.* 【矿】潜晶(质)的,隐晶(质)的.

cryp·to·gam [ˈkriptəugæm] *n.* 【植】隐花植物 (*opp.* phanerogam).

cryp·to·ga·mi·an, cryp·to·gam·ic, cryp·tog·a·mous [ˌkriptəuˈgeimiən, -ˈgæmik, kripˈtɔgəməs] *a.* 隐花(植物)的.

cryp·to·gen·ic [ˌkriptəuˈdʒenik] *a.* 【医】隐原性的,隐发性的,病原不明的.

cryp·to·gram [ˈkriptəugræm] *n.* 密码(文件);暗号.

cryp·to·graph [ˈkriptəugrɑːf] *n.* 密码;密码打字机;暗码记录法. — *vt.* 译成密码.

cryp·tog·ra·pher [kripˈtɔgrəfə] *n.* 密码员 (包括译电员;编码员);暗号使用者.

cryp·tog·ra·phy [kripˈtɔgrəfi] *n.* 密码学;密码翻译术;密写术.

cryp·tol·o·gy [kripˈtɔlədʒi] *n.* ①隐语. ②密码学[术].

Cryp·to·me·ri·a [ˌkriptəuˈmiəriə] *n.* 【植】柳杉属 (植物).

cryp·to·nym [ˈkriptəunim] *n.* 匿名,假名.

cryp·to·pine [ˈkriptəupiːn] *n.* 隐品碱.

cryp·to·sex·u·al [ˈkriptəuˈseksjuəl] *a.* 难辨性别的.

cryp·to·xan·thin, cryp·to·xan·thol [kriptəuˈzænθin, -təˈzænθəul] *n.* 隐黄质.

cryst. = crystalline; crystallized.

crys·tal [ˈkristl] *n.* ①结晶,(结)晶体;晶粒;水晶(= rock ~);石英. ②【无】晶体. ③结晶玻璃;雕玻璃;〔美〕水晶玻璃. ④〔诗〕水晶一样的东西〔冰、水、泪、眼睛等〕. ⑤〔俚〕神秘的朕兆;预言,占卜. ⑥〔美俚〕厕所. *eyes as clear as ~s* 一双眼睛明如秋水. *a necklace of ~s* 水晶珠项练. *the ~s of sugar* 糖的结晶体. — *a.* ①水晶(制)的. ②水晶一般的;透明的,清澈的. ③【无】晶体的,运用晶体检波器的. ~ *water* 晶莹的水. ~ *ball* (占卜者用的)水晶球. ~**-ball** *vt., vi.* (用水晶球)占卜. ~**-clear** *a.* 象水晶一样透明的,清澈的,明白的. ~ **detector** 晶体检波器. ~ **diode [triode]** 晶体二极管[三极管]. ~ **receiver [set]** 矿石[晶体]收音机. ~ **gazer** (用水晶球)占卜的人,预言者. ~ **wedding** 晶婚〔结婚15周年〕.

crys·tal·lif·er·ous [ˌkristəˈlifərəs] *a.* 生结晶体的,含结晶体的.

crys·tal·line [ˈkristəlain] *a.* 水晶的,由水晶做成的;结晶的,【化、矿】结晶质的;透明的. — *n.* 结晶质,结晶体;晶态;(眼球)水晶体. ~ **lens [humour]** (眼球的)水晶体. ~ **nucleus** 雏晶.

crys·tal·lite [ˈkristəˌlait] *n.* 【矿】①雏晶,微晶;细晶体,晶粒(子). ②雏晶岩. **-lit·ic** [-ˈlitik] *a.*

crys·tal·liz·a·ble [ˈkristəlaizəbl] *a.* 可结晶的.

crys·tal·li·za·tion [ˌkristəlaiˈzeiʃən] *n.* 晶化,结晶(作用,过程);结晶体;具体化,明朗化.

crys·tal·lize [ˈkristəlaiz] *vt.* ①使结晶. ②使(计划、思想等)明确化,具体化. ③使沾糖,使包上一层糖. — *vi.* ①晶化,结晶. ②明确化,具体化. *~d sugar* 冰糖. *~d fruit* 沾糖水果. *~d ginger* 糖薑.

crys·tal·log·ra·phy [ˌkristəˈlɔgrəfi] *n.* 结晶学.

crys·tal·loid [ˈkristəlɔid] *a.* 似晶的;结晶状的;透明的. — *n.* 【化】(类)晶体,(似)晶质;【植】假结晶,假晶体.

crys·tal·lon [ˈkristəlɔn] *n.* 【化】籽晶.

CS = ① chief of staff 参谋长. ②civil service〔总称〕文职人员;(军队以外的全部)行政机构.

cs. = case(s).

C. S. = ①*capital stock*【商】股本. ②*Chemical Society*〔美〕化学学会. ③Court of Session〔英〕苏格兰最高民事法庭.

Cs = 【化】c(a)esium.

C/S, c/s = cases; cycles per second.

C×S = count × strength 品质指标.

C. S. A. = ①Confederate States Army【美史】南部联邦军队. ②Confederate States of America【美史】美国南部联邦.

C. S. B.〔美〕= Central Statistical Board.

C. S. C. = Conspicuous Service Cross〔英〕特等功勋十字章.

CSC = Civil Service Commission 文官委员会.

c/sec = cycles per second 周/秒.

C Sig O = Chief Signal Officer 通信主任.

CSM = *Christian Science Monitor*〔美〕《基督教科学箴言报》.

Csn =【军】caisson.

C.S.N. = Confederate States Navy【美史】南部联邦海军.

C. S. O. = Chief Signal Officer 通信主任.

C. S. T. = Central Standard Time〔美〕中部地区标准时间.

Ct =【化】celtium.

Ct. = Connecticut; Count; Court.

ct. = carat; cent; certificate; count; county; court.

c. t. =【电】current transformer.

C. T. C. = Cyclists' Touring Club〔英〕自行车旅行俱乐部.

ctr. = center.

cts. = certificates, cents.

ct/sec = counts per second 计数/秒.

cten- (接元音), **cteno-** (接辅音) *comb. f.* 有栉状部分的.

cte·noid [ˈtiːnɔid] *a.* 【动】栉状的;有栉齿状边缘的;栉齿鳞科的. — *n.* 栉鳞鱼.

cte·noph·o·ran [tiˈnɔfərən] *a.* 【动】栉水母的;栉水母纵带的. — *n.* 栉水母类动物,栉水母门(ctenophore).

cten·o·phore [ˈtenəˌfɔː, ˈtiːnə-] *n.* 【动】栉水母门动物.

CTP = 【化】Cytidine triphosphate 三磷酸胞苷.

cts. = centimes; cents.

CTU = centigrade thermal unit.

Cu =【化】cuprum

C.U. = Cambridge University.

cu. =【天】cumulus (clouds).

cu., cub. = cubic.

cub [kʌb] *n.* ①仔兽;幼狐;〔美〕小熊;(狼、虎等的)仔. ②〔谑、蔑〕小捣乱,野娃娃〔指男孩〕,不懂事的小伙子〔小姑娘〕〔常叫 an unlicked ~〕;〔美〕生手记者 (= ~ reporter);生手,没经验的人;幼年童子军(= wolf~). — *a.* 没经验的. — *vi.* ①(野兽)生仔. ②捉幼狐〔仔兽〕.

Cu·ba [ˈkjuːbə] *n.* 古巴〔拉丁美洲〕.

cu·bage, cu·ba·ture [ˈkjuːbidʒ, ˈkjuːbətʃə] *n.* 求容积〔体积〕法;容积,体积.

Cu·ban [ˈkjuːbən] *a., n.* 古巴的〔人〕.

cu·ba·ture [ˈkjuːbətʃə] *n.* ①求容积法,求体积法. ②容积,体积.

cub·bing [ˈkʌbiŋ] *n.* 【猎】捉仔兽〔幼狐等〕.

cub·bish [ˈkʌbiʃ] *a.* ①幼兽一样的;笨拙的. ②粗野的,没规矩的.

cub·by [ˈkʌbi] *n.* 整齐的场所〔小房间〕;狭窄的房间;小柜,(鸽舍式)小书架,分类架;〔军俚〕小壕沟(等). **~-hole** = cubby.

cube[1] [kjuːb] *n.* ①立方体[形],正六面体. ②立方,三次幂,三乘;〔*pl.*〕〔美俚〕骰子. ③立体闪光灯 (= flash-cube). *magic* ~ 魔方〔积木式玩具〕. — *vt.* ①三乘;求体积;使成立方体;铺方石. ②(把土豆等)切成(小)方块;切成丁. ~ **powder** 方形火药. ~ **root**【数】立方根. ~ **sugar** 方糖.

cu·be[2] [ˈkjuːbei, ˈkuː-] *n.* 【植】尼古矛果 (*Lonchocarpus nicou*).

cu·beb [ˈkjuːbeb] *n.* 【植】荜澄茄;〔美〕荜澄茄卷烟〔旧时

用来治伤风鼻炎]。

cub·hood [ˈkʌbhud] *n.* (兽类的)仔兽期，幼稚期；〔喻〕(事物的)初期。

cubi- *comb. f.* 表示"立方体","立方": *cubi*form.

cu·bic [ˈkju:bik] *a.* ①立方体[形]的，正六面体的。②【数】三次的，立方的。—*n.*【数】三次曲线；三次方程式；三次多项式；三次函数。~ **content** 体积，容积。~ **density** 假比重。~ **displacement**【船】排水量[吨位]。~ **measure** 容量。~ **saltpetre** 智利硝石。~ **sugar** 方糖。~ **system**【物】立方晶系。

cu·bi·cal [ˈkju:bikəl] *a.* ①立方(体)的。②【数】三次方的。③体积的，容积的。

cu·bi·cle [ˈkju:bikl] *n.* 寝室，(特指学校宿舍中分隔开的)小卧室；小室；(设在书架旁的)库内阅览席，单人阅览室；室；部分，段；(游泳池的)更衣室。

cu·bic·u·lum [kjuˈbikjuləm] *n.* (*pl.* **-u·la** [-lə]) ①(地下墓窟的)停柩室；殡葬室。②小卧室；小室。

cu·bi·form [ˈkju:bifɔ:m] *a.* 立方形的。

cub·ism [ˈkju:bizəm] *n.* 〔美〕(艺术上的)立体派。

cub·ist [ˈkju:bist] *n.* ①立体派艺术家。②玩魔方的人，魔方专家。

cu·bit [ˈkju:bit] *n.*【史】腕尺〔约 18 至 22 英寸〕。

cu·bi·tal [ˈkju:bitl] *a.*【解】肘的；前膊的；尺骨的。~ *vein* 肘脉。

cu·bi·tus [ˈkju:bitəs] *n.*【解】肘；肘骨，尺骨；前臂。

cu·boid [ˈkju:bɔid] *a.* ①立方形的；骰子形的。②【解】骰骨的。—*n.* ①【解】骰骨。②长方体，矩形体。~ *bone (of the foot)* (足的)骰骨。**-boi·dal** [kju(:)ˈbɔidəl] *a.*

cu·chi·fri·to [ˌku:tʃi:ˈfri:təu] *n.*【烹】油炸猪肉丁。

cuck·ing stool [ˈkʌkiŋ stu:l] *n.* (旧时把行为不端的妇女绑在上面示众的)惩椅。

cuck·old [ˈkʌkəld] *n.* 〔谑〕乌龟〔奸妇的本夫〕。—*vt.* 使戴绿头巾，使做乌龟；与…的妻子私通。

cuck·old·ry [ˈkʌkəldri] *n.* ①(与有夫之妇的)私通，通奸。②做乌龟，戴绿头巾。

cuck·oo [ˈkuku:] *n.* ①【鸟】郭公鸟，杜鹃，布谷鸟。②杜鹃的啼声。③傻子；〔俚〕人，家伙。—*a.* 〔美俚〕疯狂的，傻，笨。*the ~ in the nest* 夺取[破坏]他人骨肉之爱(父母对儿女之爱)的人，破坏他人家庭感情的人。~ **clock** (报时似杜鹃鸣声的)杜鹃钟。~**flower**【植】布谷鸟剪秋罗(=ragged robin)。~**pint**【植】斑叶阿若母。

cu.cm. = cubic centimeter(s).

cu·cu·li·form [kjuˈkju:ləˌfɔ:m, ˌkə-] *a.* (似)杜鹃的；杜鹃鸟目的。

cu·cul·late(d) [ˈkju:kəleit(id)] *a.* 戴僧(状)帽的；【植】兜[勺]状的。

cu·cum·ber [ˈkju:kəmbə] *n.*【植】黄瓜；〔美〕锐叶木兰。*(a) sea ~* 海参。*(as) cool as a ~* ①(令人感到爽快地)冰凉的。②极冷静地，沉着地。~ **tree**【植】(美洲)渐尖木兰。

cu·cur·bit [kju(:)ˈkə:bit] *n.*【植】葫芦；【化】(葫芦形)蒸馏瓶。

cu·cur·bi·ta·ceous [kju(:)ˌkə:biˈteiʃəs] *a.*【植】葫芦科的。

cud [kʌd] *n.* ①反刍的食物。②瘤胃〔反刍兽类的第一胃〕。③〔俚〕嚼烟；口香糖。*chew the ~* ①(牛等)反刍。②细想，反省。~**-chewer** 反刍动物〔牛、羊等〕。

cud·bear [ˈkʌdbɛə] *n* 石芯地衣；苔色素〔紫色染料〕。

cud·dle [ˈkʌdl] *vt.* 拥抱，搂抱，怀抱。—*vi.* 紧贴着身子睡，抱着睡 *(together)*；蜷着身子(睡) *(up)*。—*n.* 搂抱，拥抱。*have a bit of a ~* 紧紧拥抱。~**some** *a.* 引人拥抱(似)的；可爱的。

cud·dly [ˈkʌdli] *a.* ①引人拥抱的，可爱的。②喜欢拥抱的。

cud·dy[1] [ˈkʌdi] *n.* ①〔Scot.〕驴子 (= ~ ass)；傻瓜。②三脚铁梯，三脚杠杆。③【动】军曹鱼，绿鳕。

cud·dy[2] [ˈkʌdi] *n.* (从前船上兼做客厅的)餐厅；(小船的)厨房，餐具室；(船头、船尾的)小室；(渔船的)渔网台。

cudg·el [ˈkʌdʒəl] *n.* (粗短的)棍棒；〔美俚〕(棒球)棒。*take up the ~s for* 拿棍防卫；毅然为…辩护[辩论]。—*vt.* (〔英〕**-ll-**) 用棍棒打。~ *one's brains* 绞脑汁，伤脑筋。~ **play** 斗棍；棍术比赛。

cud·weed [ˈkʌdwi:d] *n.*【植】鼠麯草(属)。

Cud·worth [ˈkʌdw(:)θ] *n.* 卡德沃斯[姓氏]。

cue[1] [kju:] *n.* ①【剧】(暗示对方接言的)尾白，提示。②暗示，指示，线索，暗号。③情绪，心情。④(必需扮演的)角色；必需做的事。⑤刺激。—*vt.* ①给…暗示[出主意]。②把…插入演出。~ *sb. on his lines* 给某人提示台词。~ *in a violin section* 插进一段小提琴演奏的曲调。*be in ~ for* 想…，有意要…。*be in good ~* 心情好。*be not in the (right) ~ for* 不想，无意。*drop a ~* 〔俚〕进棺材，死亡。*give (sb.) the ~* 暗示给人，递点子。*miss a ~* 搞错；〔口〕抓不着要点，领会错误。*take one's ~ from* 得到某人的指点[暗示]。

cue[2] [kju:] *n.* ①【台球】球竿。②发辫 (=queue)；尾，尾状物。③(买票等的)排队。*stand in ~* 排队(站着)。~ **ace** 〔美〕台球选手。

Cuen·ca [ˈkweŋka:] *n.* ①昆卡〔厄瓜多尔城市〕。②昆卡〔西班牙城市〕。

cue·ist [ˈkju:ist] *n.* 〔口〕台球家，打弹子的名手。

cues·ta [ˈkwestə] *n.*【地】鬣丘，单面山。

cuff[1] [kʌf] *n.* ①袖口；(套袜的)罗口；〔美〕裤脚的卷折。②〔*pl.*〕手拷。~ *cover* 袖套。~ *links* [〔美〕buttons] 袖扣。*off the ~* 〔美俚〕马上，(未作预先准备)当场；即兴地；非正式地。*on the ~* 〔美俚〕①赊。②免费。*shoot one's ~s* (在上衣袖口下)露出一截衬衫袖口〔意味着服装整齐〕。

cuff[2] [kʌf] *n., vt., vi.* (用拳头或手掌)打，殴打。*be at ~s* 打架。*~s and kicks* 拳打脚踢。*fall [go] to ~* 打起架来。*give sb. a ~* 给某人一巴掌。

cu. ft. = cubic foot [feet] 立方英尺。

cui bo·no [ˈkwi:ˈbɔnəu] 〔L.〕什么人得益？〔转义〕有什么益处[目的]？为了谁？

cui·rass [kwiˈræs] *n.* ①妇女胸衣。②胸甲；【动】保护(骨)板，鳞甲；(军舰的)装甲。*vt.* 给…披上胸甲。**-ed** [-t] *a.* 穿着胸甲的；(军舰等)装甲的。

cui·ras·sier [kwirəˈsiə] *n.*【史】(法国的)胸甲骑兵。

cui·sine [kwi(:)ˈzi:n] *n.* ①厨房；烹调法，烹饪。②菜肴。

cuisse, cuish [kwis, kwiʃ] *n.* 腿甲。

culch [kʌltʃ] *n.* ①(铺垫牡蛎养殖场水底的)贝壳屑，砂砾。②牡蛎卵。③〔方〕垃圾，碎屑，废物。

cul-de-sac [ˌkuldəˈsæk] *n.* 〔F.〕①死巷，死胡同。②【军】(三面被围的)绝境；困境；绝路。③【解】盲管，盲肠。

-cule *comb. f.* 小：animal*cule*; poeti*cule*.

cu·let [ˈkju:lit] *n.* (打磨成首饰的)钻石的底面。

cu·lex [ˈkju:leks] *n.* (*pl.* **-li·ces** [-lisi:z])【动】(普通)家蚊。

cu·lic·id [kju:ˈlisid] *a.*【动】蚊科的。—*n.* 蚊子。

cu·li·nar·y [ˈkʌlinəri] *a.* 厨房的；烹任的，烹调用的。~ *arts* 烹饪术。

cull[1] [kʌl] *vt.* 〔书〕①采，摘(花)；拣，选拔。②拣出，剔出。—*n.* 拣出的东西；拣剩的东西；(不合格的)等外品；(社会中的)败类。

cull[2] [kʌl] *n.* 〔俚〕= cully.

cul·len·der [ˈkʌlində] *n.* = colander.

cul·let [ˈkʌlit] *n.* (供回炉的)碎玻璃。

cul·lion [ˈkʌljən] *n.* 〔废〕卑下可鄙的人。

cul·lis [ˈkʌlis] *n.*【建】承霤；沟。

cul·ly [ˈkʌli] *n.* ①〔英俚〕呆子，傻瓜。②〔俚〕伙伴；家伙。—*vt.* 欺骗。

culm[1] [kʌlm] *n.*【植】(竹、芦、草等空心的)茎，杆。—*vi.* 长成(空心)茎杆。

culm[2] [kʌlm] *n.* ①低级无烟煤。②碎煤，灰煤；③〔C-〕

【地】碳质页岩.

cul·mif·er·ous [kʌlˈmifərəs] *a.* ①【地】含有碳质页岩的. ②【植】生成空心茎杆的.

cul·mi·nant [ˈkʌlminənt] *a.* ①达到顶点的, 绝顶的. ②【天】子午线上的, 中天的.

cul·mi·nate [ˈkʌlmineit] *vi.* ①到绝顶, 达于极点, 达最高潮;【天】到中天[最高度]. ②告终 *(in)*. —*vt.* ①使达到顶点. ②使告终. ~ ***in*** ... (…到极点)终至成为, (结果)竟成 *(Animal life ~s in man.* 动物发达到顶点而成为人).

cul·mi·na·tion [ˌkʌlmiˈneiʃən] *n.* ①顶点, 极点, 极度. ②最高潮; 极盛期, 绝顶; 成就, 完成. ③【天】中天.

cu·lottes [kju(ː)ˈlɔts] *n.* (女用)裙裤.

cul·pa [ˈkulpə, ˈkʌl-] *n.* 〔L.〕 ①过失; 犯罪. ②【法】疏忽; 过失.

cul·pa·bil·i·ty [ˌkʌlpəˈbiliti] *n.* 该罚, 有罪.

cul·pa·ble [ˈkʌlpəbl] *a.* 该责备的, 应受罚的; 有罪的, 有过失的. ~ *negligence* 应受惩罚的疏忽[失职]. *hold (sb.)* ~ 认为(某人)有罪[应受惩罚, 谴责].

cul·pa·bly [ˈkʌlpəbli] *ad.* 该罚地, 该责备地; 有罪地.

cul·prit [ˈkʌlprit] *n.* ①犯人, 罪犯. ②【英法】刑事被告, 未决犯, 嫌疑犯.

Cul·ross [ˈkʌlrɔs] *n.* 卡尔罗斯〔姓氏〕.

cult [kʌlt] *n.* ①(宗教)崇拜; 祭礼, 祭仪, 礼拜; 信仰; 邪教, 异教, 会道门. ②狂热崇拜, 迷信(对象). ③巫术疗法, 祈祷疗法. ④〔集合词〕崇拜[歌颂]者; (狂热的)信徒. *the personality* ~ 个人崇拜. ***the* ~ *of*** ..., …崇拜, …的流行[风尚], …热 (*the ~ of the individual* 个人崇拜. *the ~ of nature [beauty]* 自然[美]的歌颂[崇拜]. *the ~ of the eye-glass* 单眼镜的大流行. *the ~ of the jumping cat* 观望主义). **~-figure** 崇拜对象.

cultch [kʌltʃ] *n.* = culch.

cul·ti·gen [ˈkʌltidʒen] *n.*【植】栽培种.

cul·ti·va·ble [ˈkʌltivəbl] *a.* ①可耕种的, 可栽培的. ②可培养的; 可教化的.

cul·ti·var [ˈkʌltiˌvɑː, -ˌvə] *n.*【植】栽培变种.

cul·ti·vate [ˈkʌltiveit] *vt.* ①耕作, 耕种; 开垦; 〔美〕中耕, 培土; 养(鱼等); 栽培. ②教化, 培养, 养成; 修习, 磨练. ③谋求; 追求; 发展, 培养(友谊、感情等); 细心照料. ~ *a moustache* 留胡子. ~ *the acquaintance of* 设法与…交往, 谋求与…结识.

cul·ti·vat·ed [ˈkʌltiveitid] *a.* ①在耕种[栽培]中的. ②有修养[教养]的, 文雅的. ~ *land* 耕地. ~ *plants* 栽培植物. ~ *silk* 桑[家]蚕丝. ~ *taste* 高雅的趣味.

cul·ti·va·tion [ˌkʌltiˈveiʃən] *n.* ①耕种, 耕作; 中耕; 开垦; 造林; 栽培; (细菌等的)培养; (鱼等的)养殖. ②教养, 研究, 修养; 优雅, 高尚. *intensive [extensive]* ~ 集约[粗放]耕作. ***bring*** *(waste land)* ***under*** ~ 开垦(荒地). ***land under*** ~ 耕地.

cul·ti·va·tor [ˈkʌltiveitə] *n.* ①耕种者; 栽培者. ②教养者; 修习者. ③中耕机. *a multi-purpose* ~ 多用途耕作机.

cul·trate, cul·trated [ˈkʌltreit, -id] *a.* 小刀状的, 锐利的.

cul·tur·al [ˈkʌltʃərəl] *a.* ①耕作的, 开垦的, 栽培[培养]的. ②教养的, 修习的. ③文化的. ~ *control* 耕作防除. ~ *exchange* 文化交流. **-ly** *ad.* (*a culturally advanced country* 高度文明的国家).

cul·tu·ra·ti [ˌkəltʃəˈrɑːti] *n.* 〔*pl.*〕 有文化的阶层; 有文化的人们; 文化人.

cul·ture [ˈkʌltʃə] *n.* ①教养; 修养, 磨练. ②文化, (精神)文明. ③人工培养, 养殖; 培养菌, 培养组织. ④耕作; 栽培; 造林. *a man of* ~. 有教养的人, 文化人. ~ *of mind and body* 身心修养. *intellectual [moral, physical]* ~ 智[德、体]育. ~ *of cotton* 棉花栽培. *silk* ~ 养蚕. —*vt.* ①使有教养. ~ **gap** 文化沟〔两种文化间的差异〕. ~ **fluid [tube]** 培养液[管]. ~ **medium** 培养基. ~ **pan** 种植钵, 营养钵. ~ **pearl** 人工培养的珍珠. ~ **shock** 文化休克〔在陌生的文化环境中不知所措等〕. **~-vulture** 〔美俚〕文化秃鹰〔对文化艺术有高度或过分兴趣的人〕.

cul·tured [ˈkʌltʃəd] *a.* ①有教养的, 有修养的, 高尚的. ②耕作了的; 所种植的. ③(人工)培养[栽培, 养殖]的. ***the*** ~ ***minds*** 有(文化)教养的人们.

cul·tur·ist [ˈkʌltʃərist] *n.* ①栽培者; 培养者; 养殖者. ②文化主义者.

Cul·tus [ˈkʌltəs] *n.* 〔L.〕 = cult.

cul·ver [ˈkʌlvə] *n.* 〔英方〕鸽; 野鸽.

cul·ver·in [ˈkʌlvərin] *n.* ①(中世纪)火枪. ②(15—16世纪的)长炮, 重炮.

cul·vert [ˈkʌlvət] *n.* 暗渠, 阴沟;【电】电缆管道; 涵洞.

cum [kʌm] *prep.* 〔L.〕 ①= with. ②附属, 联合〔用于固有名词间〕; 兼. *Stow-cum-Quy,* Stow 与 Quy 的联合教区. *a dwelling-cum-workshop* 兼作住宅的工厂, 住宅兼工厂. ~ ***call*** 附催缴款项通知单. ~ ***coupon*** 附有息单. ~ ***dividend*** 附有红利(*opp.* ex div.). ~ ***grano (salis)*** 〔L.〕 [ˈgreinəu (ˈseilis)] 有保留地, 打个折扣 (听等) (*Take things ~ grano salis.* 〔口〕事事应加斟酌. *Take what he says ~ grano salis.* 〔口〕他讲的话要打个折扣听). ~ ***laude*** 〔L.〕 [ˈlɔːdiː] 受到赞许, 优等〔以优等成绩毕业〕. ~ ***new*** 附有新股.

cum. = cumulative.

cum·ber [ˈkʌmbə] *vt.* 拖累, 妨害, 阻碍; 阻塞(地方). —*n.* 妨碍(物).

Cum·ber·land [ˈkʌmbələnd] *n.* ①〔英〕坎伯兰郡〔英格兰一郡名〕. ②坎伯兰〔姓氏〕.

cum·ber·some [ˈkʌmbəsəm] *a.* ①麻烦的; 讨厌的. ②繁重的; 笨重的, 累赘的. **-ly** *ad.* **-ness** *n.*

cum·brance [ˈkʌmbrəns] *n.* 麻烦[讨厌]的负担.

Cum·bri·an [ˈkʌmbriən] *a.* (英国古代)坎伯兰 (Cumbria) 王国的; (现代)坎伯兰(郡)的. —*n.* 坎伯兰人.

cum·brous [ˈkʌmbrəs] *a.* = cumbersome.

cum d. = cum dividend【会计】附有红利, 附股息.

cum·in [ˈkʌmin] *n.*【植】枯茗, 欧莳萝, 小茴香; 小茴香子.

cum·mer, kim·mer [ˈkʌmə, ˈkimə] *n.* 〔Scot.〕 ①教母. ②女伴, 女友. ③女人; 姑娘.

cum·mer·bund [ˈkʌməbʌnd] *n.* (印度人的)腰围, 腰带; 徽带, 绶带.

cum·min [ˈkʌmin] *n.* = cumin.

Cum·ming(s) [ˈkʌmiŋ(z)] *n.* 卡明(斯)〔姓氏〕.

cum·quat [ˈkʌmkwɔt] *n.* = kumquat.

cu·mu·late [ˈkjuːmjulit] *a.* 堆积的, 累积的. —[-leit] *vt.* 堆积, 积累, 蓄积.

cu·mu·la·tion [ˌkjuːmjuˈleiʃən] *n.* 堆积; 积累; 累积法; 蓄积; 重叠.

cu·mu·la·tive [ˈkjuːmjulətiv] *a.* ①累积的, 蓄积的; 渐增的; 累加的, 附加的. ②【法】(证据等与同一事实)相重的; (判刑等)加重的. ~ **dividend** 累加红利. ~ **evidence**【法】累积证据, 复证. ~ **medicine** 少量常服的缓效药. ~ **offence** 累犯. ~ **preference shares** 累积优先股, 累积红利先取股. ~ **time** 总[累积]时间. ~ **volume** 总[累积]体积.

cu·mu·li [ˈkjuːmjulai] *n.* cumulus 的复数.

cu·mu·li·form [ˈkjuːmjuliˌfɔːm] *a.*【气】有积云状的.

cumulo- *comb. f.* 表示"积云": *cumulo*cirrus.

cu·mu·lo·cir·rus [ˈkjuːmjuləuˈsirəs] *n.*【气】叠卷云, 积卷云.

cu·mu·lo·nim·bus [ˈkjuːmjuləuˈnimbəs] *n.*【气】积雨云.

cu·mu·lo·stra·tus [ˈkjuːmjuləuˈstreitəs] *n.*【气】层积云.

cu·mu·lous [ˈkjuːmjuləs] *a.*【气】积云状的, 由积云形

成的.

cu·mu·lus [ˈkjuːmjuləs] *n.* (*pl.* **-li** [-lai]) ①堆积;丘群. ②【气】积云.

cunc·ta·tion [kəŋkˈteiʃən] *n.* 〔罕〕耽搁,迟延. **-ta·tive** [ˈkʌŋkteitiv, -tətiv] *a.*

cu·ne·al, cu·ne·atic [ˈkjuːniəl, -niːætik] *a.* 楔的,楔形的.

cu·ne·ate [ˈkjuːniit, -eit] *a.* (叶等)楔形的.

cu·ne·i·form [ˈkjuːniifɔːm] *a.* 楔形的;楔形文字的;楔状骨的. —*n.* ①楔形文字〔文献〕. ②【解】楔状骨.

cu·nette [kjuˈnet] *n.* 壕底(排水)渠.

cun·ning [ˈkʌniŋ] *a.* ①狡猾的,诡诈的. ②巧妙的,灵巧的;老练的;精巧的. ③〔美口〕(孩子等)伶俐的,可爱的. *a* ~ *baby* 可爱的婴儿. —*n.* 狡猾;诡诈;机巧,巧妙. *have a great deal of* ~ 很狡猾. **-ly** *ad.* **-ness** *n.*

Cun·nin·gham [ˈkʌniŋəm] *n.* 坎宁安〔姓氏〕.

cunt [kʌnt] *n.* 〔俚〕①女性阴部. ②〔贬〕人,女人.

cup [kʌp] *n.* ①(有柄的)茶杯;(有脚)(酒)杯;奖杯,优胜杯;圣餐杯. ②一杯(约 1/2 pint). ③酒;(圣餐礼的)葡萄酒,饮酒. ④〔喻〕命运;人生经验. ⑤杯状物;【植】萼;【解】杯状窝,骨臼;【勺球】球洞;【火箭】罩帽,喷注室. ⑥【医】干吸杯,火罐. ⑦杯状凹地,盆地. ⑧(酒、糖、冰等配成的)冷饮. ⑨【数】求并运算. ***One's [The]*** ~ ***of happiness [misery] is full.*** 幸福〔不幸〕极了,快乐〔悲苦〕极了. ***One's*** ~ ***of happiness runs over [overflows].*** 太幸福了. *a* ~ *of wine* 一杯酒. *a queen* ~ 【养蜂】王台. ***a*** ~ ***of cold water*** 象征性的施舍. ***a*** ~ ***too low*** 无精打采,意气消沉. ***be*** ~ ***and can*** 好友. ***between the*** ~ ***and the lip*** 差不多要成功〔到手〕之时;眼看要成功但尚未最后定夺时. ***bitter*** ~ 艰苦的经历. ~ ***and ball*** 杯球〔一种玩具〕. ~***-and-ball joint*** 【解】球窝关节. ~ ***and saucer*** 一套茶杯和碟子. ***drain [drink up] the*** ~ ***of humiliation*** 忍受耻辱. ***drain the*** ~ ***of life to the bottom [dregs]*** 备尝辛酸;享尽快乐. ***have had (got) a*** ~ ***too much*** 〔俚〕喝醉了. ***in one's*** ~***s*** 在酒醉的时候,醉熏熏地. ***kiss the*** ~ 呷,饮;饮酒. ***sb.'s*** ~ ***of tea*** 〔口〕①(某人)喜爱之物;(对某人)适宜的事物. ②命运. ③颇堪怀疑的东西. ***the*** ~***s that cheer but not inebriate*** 茶. ***win the*** ~ 优胜. ***withhold the*** ~ 不喝圣餐葡萄酒尽吃面包. —*vt.* ①把…弄成杯形(凹形). ②把…置于杯内. ③【医】给…拔火罐,用吸杯吸. ④【高尔夫球】用打棒打(地面)作发球势. —*vi.* ①成杯形(凹形). ②【医】使用吸杯. ~**bearer** (宫廷筵席上的)上酒人;侍臣. ~ **event** 【体】锦标赛. ~ **final** 【体】决赛. ~ **holder** 奖杯保持者. ~ **product** 【拓】上积. ~ **seaming** 包缝缝合. ~ **tie** 优胜杯决赛. ~**-tied** *a.* 〔英〕参加优胜杯比赛的.

cup·board [ˈkʌbəd] *n.* 食橱,碗柜;〔英〕小厨. ***cry*** ~ 〔口〕喊饿,想吃东西. ~ ***love*** 有所意图的亲热表示. ***skeleton in the*** ~ 家丑.

cup·cake [ˈkʌpkeik] *n.* ①杯形蛋糕. ②〔美俚〕女人模样的家伙;讨厌的人.

cu·pel [ˈkjuːpəl] *n.* 【冶】(鉴定贵金属用的)烤钵,灰皿,灰吹盘. —*vt.* (〔英〕 **-ll-**) 用烤钵鉴定,用灰皿提炼. ~ **furnace** 灰吹炉.

cu·pel·la·tion [ˌkjuːpəˈleiʃən] *n.* 【冶】烤钵鉴定法;烤钵冶金法.

cup·fer·ron [ˈkʌpfəˌrɔn, ˈkuːp-] *n.* 【化、冶】铜铁灵,铜铁试剂.

cup·ful [ˈkʌpful] *n.* 一满杯,一杯之量〔约 1/2 pint〕.

Cu·pid [ˈkjuːpid] *n.* ①【罗神】丘比特〔爱神,其形象为一背生双翼、手持弓箭的美童〕. ②〔c-〕美童,美少年. ~***'s bow*** 爱神的弓;弓形嘴唇.

cu·pid·i·ty [kju(ː)ˈpiditi] *n.* 贪欲,贪婪.

cu·po·la [ˈkjuːpələ] *n.* ①圆顶;圆顶篷;圆顶阁. ②【冶】化铁〔冲天〕炉. ③【军】旋转炮塔. ④【解】钟形感器. ***a blast*** ~ 化铁炉.

cup·pa [ˈkʌpə] *n.* 〔英口〕一杯茶. *what about a* ~? 想喝杯茶吗?

cup·ping [ˈkʌpiŋ] *n.* ①【医】杯吸术. ②(木材的)翘曲. ~ **axe** 【林】采脂斧. ~ **glass** 【医】吸杯,火罐.

cup·py [ˈkʌpi] *a.* ①杯形的;凹的. ②(地面上)窟窿多的.

cu·pre·ous [ˈkjuːpriəs] *a.* 含铜的;似铜的,铜色的.

cu·pri- *comb. f.* 表示"铜";"二价铜": *cupri*ferous.

cu·pric [ˈkjuːprik] *a.* 【化】(正;二价)铜的;含铜的. ~ **chloride** 氯化铜. ~ **oxide** 氧化铜. ~ **sulphate** 硫酸铜.

cu·prif·er·ous [kju(ː)ˈprifərəs] *a.* 含铜的,产铜的.

cu·prite [ˈkjuːprait] *n.* 【矿】赤铜矿.

cu·pro- *comb. f.* 表示"铜";"一价铜": *cupro*nickel.

cu·pro·nick·el [ˈkjuːprəuˈnikl] *n.* 铜镍合金,白铜.

cu·prous [ˈkjuːprəs] *a.* 【化】亚〔一价〕铜的; = cupreous. ~ **oxide** 氧化亚铜.

cu·prum [ˈkjuːprəm] *n.* 【化】铜.

cu·pu·late [ˈkjuːpjuleit] *a.* ①杯状的,壳斗状的. ②有壳斗的.

cu·pule [ˈkjuːpjuːl] *n.* 杯形器,杯状凹,杯状托;【动】(杯状)吸盘;【植】杯状体,壳斗.

cur [kəː] *n.* ①野狗,杂种狗. ②卑劣可鄙的人.

cur. = currency; current.

cur·a·bil·i·ty [ˌkjuərəˈbiliti] *n.* ①(病的)治愈可能性. ②(水果等的)可保存性能.

cur·a·ble [ˈkjuərəbl] *a.* ①可医治的,医得好的. ②(水果等)能贮存的.

Cu·ra·çao, cu·ra·ço·a [kjuərəˈsəu, -ˈsəuə] *n.* ①(委内瑞拉西北的)库拉索岛. ②〔c-〕陈皮酒.

cu·ra·cy [ˈkjuərəsi] *n.* 副牧师的身份〔职位〕.

cu·ra·re, cu·ra·ri [kjuˈrɑːri] *n.* ①(南美印第安人用以涂箭头的)箭毒. ②【植】马钱子,番木鳖;可提取箭毒的植物.

cu·ra·rine [ˈkjuərərain] *n.* 【化】箭毒碱.

cu·ra·rize [kjuˈrɑːraiz, ˈkjuːrəˌraiz] *vt.* ①【医】对…施用箭毒. ②用箭毒使瘫痪. **-za·tion** [kjuˌrɑːriˈzeiʃən, ˈkjuːrəri-] *n.*

cu·ras·sow [ˈkjuərəsəu] *n.* 【动】(中、南美的)凤冠鸟.

cu·rate [ˈkjuərit] *n.* ①〔英〕副牧师;教区牧师. ②〔谑〕拨火棍. ***(good in parts, like) the*** ~***'s egg*** 〔英谑〕好坏混杂(之物).

cur·a·tive [ˈkjuərətiv] *a.* 治疗的;有疗效的. —*n.* 医药,药品;治疗物〔法〕.

cu·ra·tor [kjuəˈreitə] *n.* ①(博物馆、图书馆等的)馆长;保管员. ②(幼年继承人等的)监护人. ③〔英〕(大学)学监;校董会中的财务保管员. ~**ship** *n.* 馆长〔学监等〕的职位〔身份〕. **-to·ri·al** [-ˈtɔːriəl] *a.*

curb [kəːb] *n.* ①勒马绳,马衔索. ②限制,抑制,拘束;制止. ③(生于后足使马成瘸脚的)硬瘤. ④(街道的)镶边石;井栏;【建】缘饰. ⑤〔美〕(证券的)场外市场〔又作 ~ market (=〔英〕kerb market)〕;场外经纪人. ~ *for fire place* 壁炉槛. ***on the*** ~ 〔美〕(交易所开市前)在街头,在场外. ***put [place] a*** ~ ***on [upon]*** 限制,抑制. —*vt.* ①给(马)扣上马衔. ②制止,束缚. ③用石块镶…的边;在…处设井栏. ***one's desires*** 抑制欲望. ~ **bit** 马嚼子. ~ **exchange,** ~ **market** (股票的)场外交易. ~ **roof** 【建】复斜屋顶. ~ **service** (给来往乘客坐在车上吃的)饮食供应业务. ~**side** 街头. ~**stone** ①*n.* 边石,栏石(=〔英〕kerbstone);〔*pl.*〕〔美俚〕烟头,烟屁股. ②*a.* 场外(证券)交易的 (*a* ~*-stone broker [operator]* 〔美〕场外经纪人;非内行的 (*a* ~*-stone critic* 门外汉批评家).

curb·ing [ˈkəːbiŋ] *n.* ①做路边石的材料. ②= curb.

curch [kəːtʃ] *n.* 〔Scot.〕妇女头巾.

cur·cu·li·o [kəːˈkjuːliəu] *n.* 【动】象鼻虫.

cur·cu·ma [ˈkəːkjumə] *n.* 【植】姜黄;〔C-〕姜黄属. ~

paper 姜黄纸.

curd [kəːd] *n.* 凝乳; 凝乳状物〔食品〕. *bean* ~*(s)* 豆腐. ~*s and whey* 凝乳,奶酪. — *vt., vi.* (使)成凝乳状. ~ **soap** 乳白肥皂.

cur·dle [ˈkəːdl] *vt.* ①使凝结,使凝固. ②使(牛奶等)凝结变质,使变坏. — *vi.* ①凝结,凝固. ②(牛奶等)变质,变坏. ~ ***the [sb.'s] blood (with horror) = make sb.'s blood*** ~ 使极度恐怖.

curd·y [ˈkəːdi] *a.* 凝乳状的,凝结的.

cure[1] [kjuə] *n.* ①治愈,痊愈;医治,治疗 *(of)*;(对社会问题等的)处治,对策. ②药,治疗用剂 *(for)*; 疗法. ③疗养;疗程;矿泉疗养地. ④补救(办法),矫正法 *(for)*. ⑤牧师的职位[职责]. ⑥〔美俚〕离婚〔医治家庭病的良药之意〕. ⑦(橡胶的)硫化;干固,固化. ⑧(鱼等用腌、熏、晒、烤等的)加工保藏(法). *the best* ~ *for a cough* 止咳良药. *a good* ~ *for lying* 治谎良策. *a* ~ *for unemployment* 失业问题的对策. — *vt.* ①治愈,治疗,医治. ②救治,矫正,扫除(恶习等). ③(用腌、熏等法)保藏(鱼肉等),加工. ④硫化(橡胶). *be* ~*d of (a disease)* (病)治好了. ~ *drunkenness* 矫正[改掉]酒癖. ~ *mental worry* 消除精神烦恼. ~ *oneself of* 自行矫正,自己改正(恶习等). — *vi.* ①医病;治愈. ②(谷草等)晒干; (鱼等用腌熏等法)进行加工. ③(橡胶)受硫化. *The hay is curing in the sun.* 谷草正在太阳下晒干.

cure[2] [kjuə] *n.* 〔俚〕怪人,奇人.

cu·ré [kjuəˈrei] *n.* 〔F.〕教区牧师.

cure-all [ˈkjuərɔːl] *n.* 〔美〕万应良药.

cure·less [ˈkjuəlis] *a.* ①病入膏肓的,无法医治的. ②已难补救的,难以矫正的.

cur·er [ˈkjuərə] *n.* ①熏腊食品制造人. ②治疗者; 治疗器. ③(加工食品等的)烘焙机. *fish* ~ 腌鱼商.

cu·ret·tage [ˌkjurəˈtaːdʒ, kjuˈretidʒ] *n.*【医】刮除术〔尤指刮子宫〕.

cu·ret(te) [kjuˈret] *n.*【医】刮匙;刮器. — *vt.*【医】用刮器刮(宫).

cur·few [ˈkəːfjuː] *n.* ①(中世纪通知已到规定熄灯时间的)晚钟(声); 晚钟时刻. ②(戒严时期的)宵禁(时间); 熄灯令. *impose [lift] a* ~ 实行[撤消]宵禁.

cu·ri·a [ˈkjuəriə] *n.* *(pl. -ri·ae* [-riiː]*)* ①(古罗马行政区划的)族区; 族区礼拜堂; 元老院. ②〔the C-〕【史】罗马教廷 (=the C- Romana). ③〔英〕封建时代的法庭. **-l** *a.*

Cu·rie [ˈkjuəri] *n.* ①居里〔姓氏〕. ②**Marie** ~ 居里夫人〔1867—1934,著名女物理学家〕. ③**Pierre** ~ 皮埃尔·居里〔1859—1906,法国物理学家,与居里夫人共同发现镭〕.

cu·rie [ˈkjuəri] *n.*【物】居里〔放射性强度单位〕.

cu·ri·o [ˈkjuəriəu] *n.* 古董,骨董,(珍奇)古玩.

cu·ri·o·sa [ˌkjuəriˈəusə, -zə] *n.* 〔*pl.*〕①珍品. ②色情书籍.

cu·ri·os·i·ty [ˌkjuəriˈɔsiti] *n.* ①好奇心; 爱打听的癖好. ②引起好奇心的事物;珍品,古董;奇人. ③奇特性. ~ *shop* 古玩铺. ***from*** ~ = ***out of*** ~ 在好奇心驱使下. ***in open*** ~ 公然出头过问与己无干的事.

cu·ri·o·so [ˌkjuəriˈəusəu] *n.* 〔It.〕*(pl. -si* [-sai], ~*s)* 美术品爱好家,古董搜集家.

cu·ri·ous [ˈkjuəriəs] *a.* ①好奇心旺盛的; 好事的,爱看热闹的. ②稀奇的,古怪的, 奇妙的. ③(书等)猥亵的,趣味低级的. ④〔古〕非常细致的,精细的. *He is very* ~. 他是好管闲事的(人). *a* ~ *inquiry* 寻根问底. ***be*** ~ ***about (sth.)*** 对(某事物)感到好奇. ***be*** ~ ***to say*** 说来真稀奇. **-ly** *ad.* 好奇地;奇妙地;〔加强语气〕怪,很,非常 (*a curiously bad accent* 怪重的土腔). **-ness** *n.*

cu·rite [ˈkjuərait] *n.*【矿】板铅铀矿.

cu·ri·um [ˈkjuəriəm] *n.*【化】锔.

curl [kəːl] *vt.* ①使卷曲,使成螺旋状; 弄卷(毛、发), 捻(髭); (狗等)蜷着(身子); 使(水等)起波纹. ②用卷毛装饰. — *vi.* ①卷曲,卷缩; (烟等)缭绕,袅袅上升; (蔓等)绕缠; (球、路等)弯曲. ②〔Scot.〕冰上作溜石饼游戏. ③〔美口〕得到极好成绩. ~ ***one's lip*** (轻蔑地, 厌恶地)歪歪嘴,翘翘上唇. ~ ***up*** ①卷缩; 卷起. ②〔口〕衰弱,无精神; 蜷做一团. ③〔俚〕(使)崩溃,垮台;打倒,驳倒,说服 (~ *oneself up* 把身体蜷作一团,蜷着睡). ***make sb.'s hair*** ~ 〔口〕使战慄,吓坏. — *n.* ①卷发,卷毛;卷曲物. ②蜷缩, 盘曲; 涡流. ③(植物的)卷叶病. ④【机】旋度. ~ *of the lip* (轻蔑的) 歪嘴, 抿嘴. ~ *of wave* 波浪的翻滚. ***go out of*** ~ 〔口〕无精打采,精疲力尽. ***keep the hair in*** ~ 卷着头发. **-er** *n.* ①卷曲者;卷曲物. ②作冰上溜石饼游戏者.

cur·lew [ˈkəːluː] *n.* *(pl.* ~, ~*s)*【鸟】杓鹬(属);麻鹬.

curl·i·cue, curl·y·cue [ˈkəːlikjuː] *n.* ①卷曲装饰;(字的)花体. ②花式溜冰法. ***cut a*** ~ (在冰、雪等上)作花式滑行. — *vt.* 以花体装饰. — *vi.* 形成花体.

curl·i·ness [ˈkəːlinis] *n.* 卷缩,卷曲;旋涡.

curl·ing [ˈkəːliŋ] *n.* ①卷缩;卷曲. ②(苏格兰) 冰上溜石饼游戏. ~ **irons [tongs]** 卷发夹. ~ **stone** (玩冰上溜石饼游戏用的)石饼.

curl-pa·per [ˈkəːlpeipə] *n.* 卷发纸.

curl·y [ˈkəːli] *a.* ①卷缩的; 有卷毛的. ②蜷作一团的; 翘翘的. ③旋涡形的. ④(植物)有卷叶病的. ~ **dwarf**【植】卷叶病,萎缩病. ~ **grains** 绉状纹理. ~ **top**【植】曲顶病.

curl·y·cue [ˈkəːlikjuː] *n.* = curlicue.

curl·y·locks [ˈkəːlilɔks] *n.* 〔*pl.*〕〔美〕头发卷曲的人.

curl·y-pate [ˈkəːlipeit] *n.* 〔口〕头发卷曲的人.

Curme [kəːm] *n.* 柯姆〔姓氏〕.

cur·mudg·eon [kəˈmʌdʒən] *n.* ①脾气坏的人. ②〔古〕讨厌的吝啬鬼. **-ly** *a.*

curn [kəːn] *n.* 〔Scot.〕①谷物,谷类. ②少量.

curr [kəː] *vi.* (鸽子、猫等)发出低微的咕咕声;低语.

cur·rach, cur·ragh[1] [ˈkʌrə] *n.* 〔Scot., Ir.〕= coracle.

cur·ragh[2] [ˈkʌrə] *n.* 沼泽地.

cur·ra·jong, cur·re·jong, cur·ri·jong [ˈkəːrəˌdʒɔŋ, -ˌdʒɔːŋ] *n.*【植】异叶瓶木(=kurrajong).

cur·rant [ˈkʌrənt] *n.* ①无核小粒葡萄干. ②【植】茶藨子, 穗状醋栗〔= garden ~〕. *black* ~*s* 茶藨子. *red [white]* ~*s* 红[白]茶藨子.

cur·ren·cy [ˈkʌrənsi] *n.* ①通货. ②通用,流通;流传,传播. ③市价, 行情. ④流通时间. *fractional* ~ 辅币. *paper* ~ 纸币. *metallic* ~ 硬币. ***gain*** ~ ***with*** 流行开,流通开, 得到…信任. ***give*** ~ ***to*** 散播 (谣言等). ***in common*** ~ 一般通用. ***lose*** ~ ***with*** 停止流通[使用]; 失却…的信任. ~ **notes** 流通券. ~**system** 币制.

cur·rent [ˈkʌrənt] *a.* ①通用的, 流行的. ②现在的, 现时的; 当时的. ③流畅的; 草写的. *the* ~ *price* 市价. ~ *news* 时事. ~ *expenditure* 经常费. ~ *expenses* 日常费用. *the* ~ *issue [number]* (杂志的)本期. *the* ~ *week* 本星期. *the* ~ *year* 今年. *the 10th* ~ *[curt.]* 本月十日. ~ *account* 往来存款帐;【法】交互计算. ~ *English* 现代通行英语,日常英语. ~ *handwriting* 草书. ~ *money* 通行货币. ~ *rate* 现价, 成交价. ~ *thoughts* 现时代思潮. ***pass [run, go]*** ~ 通用, 流行. — *n.* ①水流; 气流; 电流. ②思潮,潮流;趋势, 倾向. ③进行,过程. *a cold* ~ 寒流. *the Japan* ~ 日本海流,黑潮. *the great* ~ *of events* 天下大势. *a density* ~ 密着(海)流. *an alternating [a direct]* ~【电】交[直]流电. ~ *of air* 气流. ~ ***of time [the times]*** 时势,时代潮流 (*go [swim] with [against] the* ~ *of the times* 顺应[违反]时势). ~ **breaker**【电】断流器. ~ **density** 电流密度. 扩散流密度. ~ **feed** 电流馈接. ~ **gauge [meter]** 电流表;流速计,流量计. ~ **transformer** 变流器.

cur·rent·ly [ˈkʌrəntli] *ad.* ①通常,一般;现在. ②容易;流畅.

Cur·rer [ˈkʌrə] *n.* 柯勒〔姓氏〕.
cur·ri·cle [ˈkʌrikl] *n.* 双马二轮小马车.
cur·ric·u·la [kəˈrikjulə] *n.* curriculum 的复数.
cur·ric·u·lar [kəˈrikjulə] *a.* 课程的,功课的.
cur·ric·u·lum [kəˈrikjuləm] *n.* ***(pl. ~s, -la*** [-lə]***)*** ①(一个学校,专业,或学科的)全部课程. ②(取得毕业资格等的)必修课程. ~ ***vitae*** [ˈvaitiː] 〔L.〕(简短的)履历. ~ **schedule** 课程表.
cur·rie [ˈkʌri] *n.* = curry¹.
cur·ried [ˈkʌrid] *a.* ①(菜)用咖喱烧的. ②(马等)梳刷过的. ③(皮革)鞣制过的. ~ *rice with beef* 咖喱牛肉饭.
cur·ri·er [ˈkʌriə] *n.* ①制革工,鞣皮匠. ②梳马工人.
cur·ri·er·y [ˈkʌriəri] *n.* ①鞣皮业; 制革业. ②鞣皮工场; 制革厂.
cur·rish [ˈkəːriʃ] *a.* ①恶狗似的; 爱吵闹的,脾气坏的. ②卑劣的,下贱的. **-ly** *ad.* **-ness** *n.*
Cur·ry [ˈkʌri] *n.* 柯里〔姓氏〕.
cur·ry¹ [ˈkʌri] *n.* 【烹】咖喱(粉); 咖喱饭菜. ~ *and rice* 咖喱炒饭. *a chicken* ~ 咖喱鸡. — *vt.* 在…中加咖喱粉调味. *curried rice* 咖喱饭. ~ **paste** 咖哩酱. ~ **powder** 咖喱粉.
cur·ry² [ˈkʌri] *vt.* ①制(革),鞣(皮). ②用马梳梳(马毛等). ③打(人),鞭笞. ~ ***below the knee*** 〔美〕过分讨好,巴结. ~ ***favour with*** *(sb.)* 巴结,讨好(某人),拍(某人)马屁. ~**comb** ① *n.* 马梳. ② *vt.* 用马梳梳.
curse [kəːs] *vt.* *(~d, curst* [kəːst]*;~d, curst)* ①咒,诅咒 (*opp.* bless); 咒骂; 恶骂. ②咒逐,把(某人)逐出教门. ③使遭天罚; 使受灾祸; 使苦恼,使困苦〔多用被动语态〕. *C- it!* 混帐! *C- you [your folly]!* 笨蛋! ***be ~d with*** 受到某种灾祸; 被…所苦; 生(疮等). — *vi.* 诅咒,咒骂. ***~ and swear*** 咒骂. — *n.* ①诅咒,恶骂; 咒语. ②咒逐,逐出教门. ③祟,天罚; 祸害,灾祸; 灾害的原因,祸因. ④〔俚〕〔the ~〕月经(期间). ***call down a ~ (up)on*** =***lay sb. under a ~*** 诅咒(某人遭受灾祸). ***Curses come home to roost.*** 诅咒他人,反而应验到自己身上[害人反害己]. ~ ***of drink*** 饮酒之害. ~ ***of Scotland*** 【牌】方块九点. ***C- upon it!*** 混帐! ***not care [give] a ~ (for)*** 丝毫不顾; 不以为意,怎么都好. ***not worth a ~*** 毫无价值. ***under a ~*** 被诅咒,受某种灾害.
curs·ed [ˈkəːsid] *a.* ①被诅咒的. ②该罚的; 该咒的,可恶的; 〔口〕讨厌的. ③[ˈkʌsid] 〔古〕性子拗的,脾气坏的. **-ly** *ad.* **-ness** *n.*
cur·sive [ˈkəːsiv] *a.* (字迹)草写的,手写体的. — *n.* 草书; 手写原稿. ~ *characters* 草字. *a ~ hand [handwriting]* 草书,行书. **-ly** *ad.* **-ness** *n.*
cur·sor [ˈkəːsə] *n.* (计算尺的)游标.
cur·so·ri·al [kəːˈsɔːriəl] *a.* 【动】走禽类的; 疾走的. ~ *insects* 只走不飞的昆虫. ~ *birds* 走禽兽.
cur·so·ry [ˈkəːsəri] *a.* 匆促的,仓卒的; 草率的; 粗率的,(知识等)浅薄的. **-ri·ly** *ad.* **-ri·ness** *n.*
curst [kəːst] curse 的过去式及过去分词.
curt [kəːt] *a.* 简短的; 简略的; 草率的,粗率的,敷衍了事的. *a ~ answer* 草率无礼的回答. *a ~ refusal* 不客气的拒绝. **-ly** *ad.* **-ness** *n.*
cur·tail [kəːˈteil] *vt.* ①缩短,省略(讲话、节目等). ②削减,节减(经费等). ③褫夺,剥夺(特权、官衔等). ~ *him of his title* 取消他的官衔. *~ed words* 缩略词〔例: bus, phone 等〕. *have one's pay ~ed* 被减薪. **-ment** *n.*
cur·tain [ˈkəːtən] *n.* ①帘幕; 窗帘,帘子. ②(舞台的)幕; 启[落]幕. ③幕状物; (两棱堡间的)中堤幕墙; 【建】隔壁,间壁. ④〔*pl.*〕〔美俚〕死; 终结. *The ~ rose on the war.* 战争揭幕[开始]了. ~ *of smoke* 烟幕. ***behind the ~*** 在幕后,秘密. ***call an actor before the ~*** 要求演员到幕前来(谢幕); 叫幕. ***C-!*** 听众注意! ***draw a ~ on [over]*** 拉(窗)帘遮住(窗子等); (把话头)截止,停讲(不谈下文). ***draw the ~*** 拉幕〔开幕或闭幕〕. ***draw the ~s*** 拉上所有窗帘. ***drop [raise] the ~*** 闭[开]幕,停[开]演. ***lift the ~ on*** 开始; 扯开幕布使看; 公布; 明说. ***ring down the ~*** 响铃闭幕; 使结束; 使终止(事件). ***take a ~*** (演员到幕前)谢幕. ***work up the ~*** (戏剧)在收场时作出兴奋激昂的表演. — *vt.* 在…挂帘子; 用幕[帘子]隔开[遮住] *(off)*; 遮蔽,隐藏. ~ **call** (要求演员到幕前来的)叫幕声. ~ **fall** 闭幕; (事件的)结尾,大团圆. ~ **fire** 【军】弹幕,掩护射击. ~ **lecture** (妻子对丈夫说的)帐中私话,对丈夫的训斥. ~ **line** 全剧[一幕]的最后一行台词. ~ **raiser** 开幕戏; (球赛等的)开幕战; (大事发生前的)小事. ~ **ring** 窗帘圈. ~ **rod** 窗帘棍. ~ **speech** (剧作者、演出人等)剧终在幕前的致词. ~ **time** 开幕时间. ~**-up** (表演开始时的)幕启.
cur·tal [ˈkəːtl] *a.* 〔废〕切短的; 削减的. — *n.* 〔废〕①剪短尾的马. ②切短物,截短物. ~ **ax** 短弯刀(= cutlass).
cur·ta·na [kəːˈteinə, kəːˈtɑːnə] *n.* 无尖刀,慈悲剑〔英王加冕式上表示仁慈的器物〕.
cur·tate [ˈkəːteit] *a.* 削短的,缩短的,缩减的.
cur·te·sy [ˈkəːtisi] *n.* 【法】鳏夫产权.
cur·ti·lage [ˈkəːtilidʒ] *n.* 【法】庭园,宅地.
Cur·tis(s) [ˈkəːtis] *n.* 柯蒂斯〔姓氏〕.
curt·sey, curt·sy [ˈkəːtsi] *n.* (女子的)屈膝礼. ***make [bob, drop] a ~*** 请个安,行屈膝礼. — *vi.* 行屈膝礼 *(to)*.
cu·rule [ˈkjuəru(ː)l] *a.* 〔古罗马〕有权坐公共集会显要席的; (官职)显要的. ~ *chair [set]* 显要席; 高位,显职. ~ *office* 显要官位.
cur·va·ceous [kəːˈveiʃəs] *a.* 〔口〕(女性)有曲线美的,(身段)苗条的.
cur·va·ture [ˈkəːvətʃə] *n.* ①弯曲(部分). ②【数】曲率,曲度.
curve [kəːv] *n.* ①曲线; 弯曲; 弯曲物. ②曲线规(= French ~); 【机】曲线板; 【棒球】曲线球; 【统】曲线图. ③诈欺; 〔美〕使对方难应付的策略. ④〔*pl.*〕(圆)括号. ~ *of beauty* 曲线美. — *vt.* 弄弯; 使弯曲. — *vi.* 成弯曲状; (依)曲线行进; 呈曲线美. ~ **ball** (乒乓球的)弧圈球; 〔喻〕狡滑手段. ~ **fitting** 【统】曲线求律法,曲线拟合.
cur·vet [kəːˈvet] *n.* *(-tt-)* *vi.* 【马术】腾跃; 〔古〕嬉戏,跳跃. ***cut [make] a ~*** 腾跃; 跳跃.
cur·vi·lin·e·al, cur·vi·lin·e·ar [ˌkəːviˈliniəl, ˌkəːviˈliniə] *a.* 曲线的. *a ~ tracery* 【建】曲线花样窗格.
curv·y [ˈkəːvi] *a.* ***(curv·i·er; curv·i·est)*** ①弯曲的. ②〔口〕体态丰满的,有曲线美的. *a ~ road* 弯曲的道路.
Cus·co [ˈkuːskəu] *n.* = Cuzco.
cus·cus [ˈkʌskʌs] *n.* 【动】袋貂属 *(Phalanger)*.
cu·sec [ˈkjuːsek] *n.* 秒立方英尺〔灌溉流量单位,每秒一立方英尺, cubic feet per second 之略〕.
cush [kʌʃ] *n.* 〔美俚〕钱; 薪水; 收入〔尤指利润、贿赂〕.
cush·at [ˈkʌʃət] *n.* 〔英方〕(欧洲)斑鸠.
cu·shaw [kəˈʃɔː] *n.* 【植】南瓜,倭瓜 *(Cucurbita moschata)*.
cush·i·ly [ˈkuʃili] *ad.* 轻松地,舒适地.
Cush·ing [ˈkuʃiŋ] *n.* 库欣〔姓氏〕.
cush·ion [ˈkuʃən] *n.* ①软垫,椅垫,靠垫. ②【机】缓冲垫层,汽垫,胶垫,缓冲器; 【植】叶枕. ③(台球台盘四边的)橡皮衬垫. ④(猪等的)后腿肉. ⑤(衬裙子的)腰垫. ⑥假发. ⑦针扎,针插(=pin-~). ⑧(马的)蹄叉. ⑨【棒球】〔俚〕= base. ⑩〔*pl.*〕〔美〕安慰,慰藉,安慰物; 安乐,奢侈. ⑪〔俚〕积贮,存款. — *vt.* ①把…摆在坐垫[桌垫]上; 给…安上垫子,用软垫垫上,给…装上汽垫. ②【台球】使(球)碰触台边衬垫〔先碰触后击中另一球或先击中一球后碰触衬垫后再击中另一球〕. ③使(反抗,冲击等)变缓和; 掩饰(丑闻等). *a ~ed voice* 柔软的声音. ~*ing effect* 缓冲作用. ~ **capital**【建】罗曼式〔带枕〕柱头. ~**craft** 气垫汽车；气垫船. ~ **tyre**（填满碎橡皮的）半实心轮胎.

cush·ion·y [ˈkuʃəni] *a.* ①垫子似的；柔软的. ②= cushy.

Cush·it·ic [kʌˈʃitik, kuʃ-] *a.*（东非的）库什特语族的. —*n.* 库什特语族.

cush·y [ˈkuʃi] *a.* ①〔俚〕容易的，（工作）轻松的，舒适的. ②〔军俚〕（伤等）轻的，不要紧的. *all very* ~〔口〕非常愉快.

cusk [kʌsk] *n.* (*pl.* ~*s*，〔集合词〕~)【动】卡斯克鳕，单鳍鳕.

cusp [kʌsp] *n.* ①（齿、叶等的）尖端，尖头. ②【天】月角；【建】尖角；【数】（二曲线的）尖点，歧点，会切点；（曲线等的）波峰. **-ed** [kʌspt] *a.* 有尖的（~*ed arch*【建】尖拱）.

cus·pate [ˈkʌspit, -ˌpeit] *a.* 尖的，（叶子等）有尖端的（= cuspated, cusped）.

cus·pid [ˈkʌspid] *n.*（人的）犬齿.

cus·pi·dal [ˈkʌspidl] *a.* 尖的，有尖端的.

cus·pi·date, cus·pi·dat·ed [ˈkʌspideit, -id] *a.* 尖的；（叶子等）有尖端的. *a* ~ *tooth* 犬齿.

cus·pi·da·tion [ˌkʌspiˈdeiʃən] *n.*【建】尖形饰，饰以尖头〔尖顶〕.

cus·pi·dor(e) [ˈkʌspidɔː] *n.*〔美〕痰盂.

cuss [kʌs] *n.* ①〔口〕粗话，诅咒. ②〔美口〕古怪可憎的东西〔指人或动物〕. *a queer* ~ 怪家伙. ***not care a*** ~ 毫不介意. ***not worth a tinker's*** ~ 一文不值. —*vt.*, *vi.*〔口〕= curse.

cuss·ed [ˈkʌsid] *a.*〔美口〕①= cursed. ②别扭的，性子拗的. **-ly** *ad.*〔口〕别扭地，拗着.

cuss·ed·ness [ˈkʌsidnis] *n.*〔美口〕乖戾；（事情）别扭；不如意.

cus·tard [ˈkʌstəd] *n.* 乳蛋糕，蛋羹. ~ **apple**【植】番荔枝，释迦果. ~ **glass** 乳黄色（不透明）玻璃. ~ **pudding** 乳蛋布丁.

Cus·ter [ˈkʌstə] *n.* 卡斯特〔姓氏〕.

cus·to·des [kʌsˈtəudiːz] custos 的复数.

cus·to·di·al [kʌsˈtəudjəl] *a.* 看管的，管理的，保管的；看守的. *a* ~ *engineer*〔美〕房屋看管人. *a* ~ *officer* 物资保管员；〔美〕狱吏. —*n.*【宗】圣物保藏器.

cus·to·di·an [kʌsˈtəudjən] *n.* 看管人，管理人；保管人. **-ship** *n.* 看守人〔保管人〕的职位〔责任〕.

cus·to·dy [ˈkʌstədi] *n.* ①保管，管理；保护，监护，看守. ②拘留，监禁，收容. ***be in the*** ~ ***of*** 托…保管，受…监视；受…保护. ***have the*** ~ ***of*** 保管；保护. ***in*** ~ 被监禁，被拘留着. ***in the*** ~ ***of*** 在……监护下. ***keep (sb.) in*** ~ 拘留（某人）. ***take sb. into*** ~ 逮捕，拘留（某人）.

cus·tom [ˈkʌstəm] *n.* ①习惯，风俗；惯例，常规；【法】习惯法. ②经常光顾；〔集合词〕顾客，主顾. ③〔the ~s〕海关；〔*pl.*〕关税. ④【史】经常赋役. *as his* ~ *then was* 照他当时的习惯. *social* ~*s* 社会风俗. ***have plenty of*** ~（商店等）经常主顾多. ***have sb.'s*** ~ 受某人照顾. ***present [give] one's*** ~ ***to*** … 经常光顾，成为 … 的经常主顾. —*a.*〔美〕（衣服等）定做的，定制的. ~**-built** *a.* 定制的. ~ **cloth [suit]**〔美〕定做的（讲究的）衣服. ~**s detention** 海关扣留. ~**(s)house [office]** 海关（*a* ~*(s) house broker* 代客报关服务行）. ~**-made** = ~**-built**. ~**tailor** ①*n.*〔美〕承接定做衣服的裁缝. ②*vt.* 定制，定做. ~**s clearance** 出口结关. ~**s duty[due]** 关税. ~**s entry** 进口报关. ~**s shed [warehouse]** 海关仓库，关栈. ~**s tariff** 关税率. ~**-tailor** *vt.* 分别对待，分别计划.

cus·tom·a·ble [ˈkʌstəməbl] *a.*〔主美〕可征收关税的.

cus·tom·a·ri·ly [ˈkʌstəmərili] *ad.* 照例，通常，素来，习惯上.

cus·tom·a·ry [ˈkʌstəməri] *a.* 通常的，向来的；照惯例的. *a* ~ *law* 习惯法. —*n.*〔*pl.*〕风俗志，习俗志.

cus·tom·er [ˈkʌstəmə] *n.* ①（经常的）顾客，主顾，客户，买主. ②〔口〕（打交道的）人，家伙；〔*pl.*〕〔美口〕观众，听众. *a queer* ~ 怪人，好笑的家伙. *a tough* ~ 粗暴的〔难对付的〕家伙.

cus·tom·ize [ˈkʌstəmaiz] *vt.* 定制，定做；按规格改制.

cus·tos [ˈkʌstɔs] *n.*〔L.〕(*pl.* ***cus·to·des*** [kʌsˈtəudiːz])〔L.〕保管人；看守人. ~ ***rotulorum*** [rɔtjuˈlɔːrəm]〔英〕（兼管文件的）郡法院首席法官.

cus·tu·mal [ˈkʌstjuməl] *n.*（某一城市的）习俗志.

cut [kʌt] *vt.* (***cut; cut·ting***) ①切，割，截，斩，砍（树），剪（发等）；切断，割下；采伐；剪下；修剪，刈，割. *I have* ~ *my finger.* 我切伤了指头. *I had my hair* ~ *at the barber's.* 我在理发店里理了发了. ②削减（物价等），节减（费用）；删节（文章等）. ~ *prices* 降价. ~ *an article* 删节一篇文章. ③开辟，开凿，挖掘；（船）破（浪）前进；（鸟）掠（空）而飞. *The ship* ~ *her way through the waves.* 船破浪前进. ④雕，刻；琢磨（宝石等）. ~ *a figure in stone* 雕刻石像. ⑤剪裁，裁（衣）. *The jacket was cut too long.* 这件短上衣裁剪得太长. ⑥〔口〕停止，断绝（关系）；〔口〕缺（课），怠（课），停（课）；〔口〕假装没看见，不睬，不理. ~ *school* 逃学. *He* ~ *me in the street.* 他在街上假装没看见我. ⑦【数】（线）切，交，相交. *One line* ~*s another at right angels.* 两线相交成直角. ⑧〔口〕显出. *He* ~*s a poor figure.* 他显得可怜，他显得寒酸. ⑨（用鞭子）抽打；使象刀切一样疼痛；使极为痛心；（风等）刺骨，透彻心肺. *The cold wind* ~*s me to the bone.* 寒风刺骨. ~ *to the heart* 使深深地感到痛心. ⑩溶解，搀，混合. ~ *resin with alcohol* 用酒精溶解树脂. ⑪生，长，出（牙齿）. ⑫阉割，骟（马）. ⑬（球）斜打，削（球）；【牌】切（牌）〔把另一人洗好的一叠牌从上面随便拿一部分换在下面〕；【影】停止拍摄；剪辑（胶片）. ⑭录音于（磁带等上）. —*vi.* ①切；（锐利）能切，（被）切，（被）割断，（被）剪裁. *This knife* ~*s well.* 这把小刀很快. ②切开，切进 (*through*). ③（牙齿）长出. ④横切，横穿过，直穿过，走近路 (*across*). ⑤〔口〕急忙走开，跑开；跑；〔命令〕去！滚！ *I* ~ *after him with all speed.* 我拼命赶他. *I must* ~. 我要跑了. *C-(it)!* 滚！ ⑥象刀割似地使人感到疼痛. *The wind* ~*s.* 风如刀割. ⑦（画色）过浓. ⑧〔俚〕缺课. ⑨〔美〕尽投一〔二〕人的票. ⑩【牌】切牌；削球. ~ ***a fat hog***〔美俚〕虚摆架子，虚张声势. ~ ***a joke*** 说笑，打诨. ~ ***a loss*** 趁损失不大而及早丢手，相机撒手，知难而退. ~ ***a melon***〔美俚〕分配〔分得〕巨大利益. ~ ***a swath***〔美俚〕成名，有名起来. ~ ***a ticket***〔美俚〕全给一个候选人投票. ~ ***a tooth*** 长牙齿；长见识. ~ ***about*** 乱跑. ~ ***across*** 抄近路穿过，对直穿过. ~ ***adrift*** 分别，永远走掉. ~ ***and carve*** 切开，分割. ***C- and come again***（请）尽量吃. ~ ***and run***〔口〕连忙逃走. ~ ***at*** 猛打，痛打；〔口〕使（精神上）受重大打击；打断（希望等）；砍，斩. ~ ***away*** ①匆匆跑掉，逃走. ②切开，剪去，切去；连砍，乱砍. ~ ***back*** ①回叙往事；（影片中为强调前面某一镜头而）再次映出；倒叙. ②中止（合同等）. ③【化】稀释. ④缩减. ⑤修剪（树枝等）. ⑥（足球）急退. ~ ***both ways*** 抱骑墙态度. ~ ***(sb.) dead*** 见到（某人）假装不认识，不理睬（某人）. ~ ***down*** 砍倒；削减，缩减；减价，减低；使失色，夺去…活动力，（疾病）使（人）躺倒. ~ ***fine*** 只能得到极少的利益. ~ ***in*** ①突然插入. ②（汽车）超车. ②抢去别人的舞伴. ③在电话里窃听. ④把…剁入. ⑤（电）接通. ~ ***into*** 插入话头；多嘴，干涉；打断（话头）；突然加入. ~ ***it***〔命令式〕停止！ 别响！ ~ ***it (too) fat***〔俚〕做得过分，做得过火. ~ ***it fine*** 尽量节约（时间、用费等）. ~ ***it out***〔俚〕停止！ 别响！ ~ ***it quick*** 快去，快逃！ ~ ***loose*** ①割断绳索〔铁链〕，放下，放开；断绝（关系），摆脱（束缚）. ②逃；随意去做，自由行动. ③开始攻击；开始活动. ④〔美俚〕痛痛快快讲，痛饮. ~ ***lots*** 抽签. ~ ***no ice***〔俚〕毫无效果，不起作用；无关紧要. ~

off ①切开,切断,割掉,削除,伐除;截止;截断(退路等),断绝(关系等). ②妨害;使(人)闭口无言. ③(病等)把(人)弄死 (*be ~ off in one's prime* 盛年夭折). *~ **off with a shilling*** (只给一先令)实际断绝继承关系. *~ **on*** 急速前进. *~ **on the right side*** 〔美俚〕赚到钱. *~ **one's coat according to one's cloth*** 量入为出,量体裁衣. *~ **one's stick*** 逃. *~ **out*** ①割掉;除去,删去;剪下;开辟. ②裁制(衣服). ③使适合 (*be ~ out for the job* 天性适合那个工作). ④筹划,设计,准备,预备. ⑤遮断 *(from)*. ⑥取而代之,抢先一着,胜过;夺取,捕获(敌船). ⑦〔美俚〕停止(*~ it [that] out* 停止! 别响!). *~ **over*** 【林】主伐. *~ **prices*** [〔美〕 ***rates***] (为竞争而)减价. *~ **round*** 〔美〕卖弄,夸示,故意做给人看. *~ **short*** ①打断(讲话);使停止. ②缩减;缩短,从简 (*to ~ the matter short* 简单地说,总之. *C- it short!* 〔口〕讲得简单点! 别说了! *I ~ him short.* 不让他讲下去). *~ **the buck*** 〔美俚〕满足要求. *~ **the comedy*** 〔美俚〕别开无聊的玩笑,别演戏吧! *~ **the gun*** 制止发动机〔马达〕. *~ **the (Gordian) knot*** 快刀斩乱麻似地处理(难事). *~ **the mustard*** 〔美俚〕满足要求. *~ **the record*** 【体】打破纪录. *~ **the rough stuff*** 〔美俚〕矫正粗鲁的行为. *~ **to pieces*** 切碎,粉碎(敌军);严厉批评(新书). *~ **to the bone*** (把价钱等)减到不能再减. *~ **under*** 〔美〕落价卖,亏本卖. *~ **up*** ①割裂;弄伤;歼灭(敌军). ②酷评,痛骂,使心痛. ③连根拔除,根绝;【林】带伐. ④〔美〕引起(骚动). ⑤卖弄,耍花招. ⑥杀,宰;可宰;可裁. ⑦留下遗产(*This ox will ~ up well.* 这条牛壮得可以宰杀了. *He ~ up fat [very well].* 他留下不少财产). *~ **up rough [savage, crusty, stiff, ugly, nasty]*** 忿怒,发脾气,横暴起来.

— *a.* ①切过的,切下的,修过的,剪过的,剪下的;【植】尖裂的. ②刻好的,雕好了的;磨过的;加过工的. ③削减了的,缩小了的. ④(牲畜等)阉过的;〔俚〕喝醉了的. *~ flowers* 瓶花. *~ gloss* 雕花玻璃. *~ horse* 骟过的马. *~ plane* 剖面. *~ alchy* [ˈælki] 〔美俚〕酒. ***at ~ rate*** 〔美〕打折扣(卖等). *~ **out for*** 〔口〕适于,合适. ***finely ~ features*** 端正秀丽的容貌.

— *n.* ①刀伤,切口,伤口;一切,一击,一刀〔剑、鞭等〕. ②隧道;坑;运河,沟渠;挖土,挖方. ③一片,一块,切片;〔美〕肉片;〔口〕分得的份儿;(一张唱片内的)一首歌曲;【影】剪辑;画面〔镜头〕的突然转变;〔美〕被排挤掉的候选人. ④(印刷用的)铜版,木版(等);版画,木刻画;插画,插图. ⑤【牌】(牌洗好后)切牌;切牌人;(球戏)斜打,削球. ⑥近路,捷径 *(= short ~)*. ⑦剪裁(法),做法;制作,加工;样式,类型. ⑧无情的攻击,尖锐的讽刺;不理睬,不打招呼. ⑨削减,削除;删节;减价;〔美〕折扣,减低(租金等). ⑩(学生的)旷课,缺课,逃学. ⑪黄麻支数长度单位(〔英〕 = 300 码). ***a ~ above [below]*** 〔口〕高〔低〕一等,胜〔次〕于. ***(This was) a ~ at (me).*** (这是)对(我)的攻击. ***a ~ off the nut*** 〔谑〕菜食,素食. *~ **of one's face*** 相貌. *~ **of one's jib*** 外表,仪表. *~ **of timber*** 木材的采伐量. *~ **of wool*** 剪毛量. ***draw ~s*** 抽签. ***give** (one) **the ~ direct*** (故意)不理睬(人). ***have [take] a ~*** 吃(一片肉的)简单的饭食. ***the most unkindest ~ of all*** 无情到极点的作风〔举动〕. **~-and-come-again** *n.* (肉等的)尽量吃;丰富,丰饶. **~-and-dry [-dried]** *a.* ①早已准备好的. ②呆板的. **~ and thrust** 劈刺;肉搏;激战;激烈争吵. **~-and-thrust** *a., n.* 劈刺两用的(剑). **~-and-try** *a.* 试验性的. **~ away** *a., n.*下摆裁成圆角的(上衣)(特指常礼服). **~back** (电影等)倒叙;【园艺】剪枝;修剪过的果树;〔美〕削减生产,减产. **~bank** 陡岸. **~-grass** 【植】李氏禾(属). **~-in** ①*n.* 【影】插入字幕;【印】(插图等的)插入,排入;【火箭】接通,开动. ②*a.* 插入的. **~ number** 【影】镜头号码. **~off** ①〔美〕近路,捷径. ②【机】停车(装置);【火箭】切断,停止工作. ③〔美〕运河. **~out** ①挖去,剪去;(幼儿书的)剪纸;(动画片中用的)剪纸画;嵌花;(著作等的)删去部分. ②【电】断流器,保险装置;(内燃机的)排气阀. **~over** ①〔美〕树木砍光了的原野 (*a ~over forest* 主伐林). ②【讯】接入. **~purse** 扒手. **~-rate** *a.* 减价的,便宜的;次等的. **~throat** ① *n.* 凶手;〔Scot.〕角灯;〔美〕(涩味)红葡萄. ② *a.* 杀人的,凶恶的,残忍的;剧烈的;【牌】三人玩的. **~up** ①打击,酷评,痛骂. ②〔美俚〕爱打诨的人,爱诙谐的人. **~water** ①【海】船头破浪处;桥墩的分水角. ②黑色撇水鸟. **~work** 挖花花边〔桌布等〕. **~worm** 【虫】夜盗虫,鳞翅目幼虫.

cut·a·bil·i·ty [ˌkʌtəˈbiliti] *n.* ①可割,可分割. ②净肉〔屠宰后牲畜躯体上可供出售的瘦肉的分量〕.

cu·ta·ne·ous [kju(ː)ˈteinjəs] *a.* ①皮肤(上)的,影响皮肤的. ②肤浅的,皮毛的.

cutch [kʌtʃ] *n.* 【植】儿茶 (= catechu).

cut·cher·ry, cut·chery [kʌˈtʃeri] *n.* 〔印度〕行政机关;法院;种植园事务所.

cute [kjuːt] *a.* 〔美口〕①聪明的,伶俐的;逗人爱的. ②做作的. *~ **as a bug's ear*** 〔美口〕非常可爱的〔美丽的〕. — *n.* 〔美俚〕25 分(硬币). **-ly** *ad.* **-ness** *n.*

cu·tey [ˈkjuːti] *n.* ①〔口〕灵巧的美人儿〔尤指少妇〕. ②〔俚〕(安插在敌方内部的)内线;巧妙的策略〔手腕〕.

Cuth·bert [ˈkʌθbət] *n.* ①卡斯伯特〔姓氏, 男子名〕. ②〔c-〕〔英俚〕(借口公务)逃避兵役的人.

cu·ti·cle [ˈkjuːtikl] *n.* 【解】表皮, 护膜;【植】角质层;角皮,小皮;(液面的)薄膜. **-u·lar** [-ˈtikjulə] *a.*

cut·ie [ˈkjuːti] *n.* ①= cutey. ②机智灵巧的运动员. ③欺骗行为. ***a ~ pie*** ①灵巧可爱的人;情人. ②携带式辐射能测定仪.

cu·tin [ˈkjuːtin] *n.* 【植】角质,腊状质.

cu·tin·i·za·tion [ˌkjuːtiniˈzeiʃən] *n.* 【植】角化(作用). **cu·tin·i·ze** [-aiz] *vt., vi.* (使)角化.

cu·tis [ˈkjuːtis] *n.* *(pl. ~es, cu·tes* [ˈkjuːtiz]*)* 〔L.〕【解】真皮,下皮肤;【植】表皮. *~ **plate*** 生皮层,皮节.

cut·las(s) [ˈkʌtləs] *n.* (从前水手用以肉搏的)短剑〔刀〕,弯刀.

cut·ler [ˈkʌtlə] *n.* 刀匠;卖刀人;磨刀人;刀具商,刀具制造人.

cut·ler·y [ˈkʌtləri] *n.* 刀具;餐刀;刀剑制造〔修理、贩卖〕业者.

cut·let [ˈkʌtlit] *n.* (炸)肉片,(炸)肉排.

cut·or [ˈkjuːtə] *n.* 〔美俚〕检察官.

cut·ter [ˈkʌtə] *n.* ①切者;裁衣人;【影】剪辑员. ②切刀,切断机;刻纹〔录音〕头;利齿,门牙,前牙. ③〔美〕(单马)小橇;〔美俚〕检察官. ④【海军】小汽艇;独桅前后帆快船. ⑤砌面砖. ⑥〔美〕老牛. ***a life ~*** 救生艇.

cut·ting [ˈkʌtiŋ] *n.* ①切断,切下;切片;【园艺】扦插,插条;〔英〕剪裁,(报纸等的)剪辑;(宝石等的)加工,琢磨;开凿. ②大贱卖;剧烈的竞争. ③【林】采伐;【畜】剪毛. ④(马的)互踢. ⑤【机】切削. *~ **into the womb*** 剖腹产术. — *a.* ①切得动的,锐利的. ②象刀割似的;刺骨的. ③讽刺的,尖酸刻薄的. ④(目光)炯炯的,敏锐的. ⑤〔俚〕卖得贱的. *~ wind* 刺骨的寒风. *~ retort* 尖锐的反驳. *~ trade* 薄利多销. **~continuity** 【影】剪辑用脚本. *~ **paper dolls*** 〔美口〕被打得头昏眼花,眩晕. *~ **tool*** 切削工具. **-ly** *ad.*

cut·tle·bone [ˈkʌtlbəun] *n.* 乌贼骨,墨鱼骨,海螵蛸.

cut·tle·fish [ˈkʌtlfiʃ] *n.* 【动】乌贼,墨鱼. *~ **tactics*** (驱逐舰等的)烟幕战术.

cut·ty [ˈkʌti] *a.* 〔Scot.〕①切短的. ②性急的. — *n.* ①短匙;(陶制的)短柄烟斗;矮胖的女人. ②〔口〕品行坏的女人;〔谑〕脾气大的女人. ③兔子;气枪. *~ stool* 矮凳;〔古〕〔Scot.〕(给奸妇坐的)忏悔椅.

cu·vette [kjuːˈvet] *n.* (度谱术和光度术使用的)小玻璃管;透明小容器;小池,电池.

Cu·vier [ˈkju:viei] *n.* ①居维叶(姓氏). ②George ~ 格·居维叶[1769—1832,法国自然科学家,比较解剖学的创始者].
Cuz·co [ˈku:skəu] *n.* 库斯科[秘鲁城市].
cv. = convertible.
c.v. = coefficient of variation【纺】变异系数,变差系数.
C. V. = Common Version (基督教《圣经》的)通行本.
CW, cw, c-w = ① continuous wave 等幅波; 连续波. ② cosine wave 余弦波. ③ clockwise 顺时针(方向).
CWA = Civil Works Administration〔美〕土木工程署.
CWAR = continuous wave acquisition radar 等幅波搜索雷达.
cwm [ku:m] *n.*【地】圆形峪 (= cirque).
c. w. o. = cash with order【商】定购即付,定货付款.
C. W. O. = Chief Warrant Officer〔美〕(陆军或空军)一级准尉.
CWS = Chemical Warfare Service〔美〕化学兵,化学勤务.
cwt. = hundredweight (= [L.] *centum* + *weight*).
cy. = copy; currency.
-cy *suf.* 表示"状态","性质","职权","地位": ①加于词尾为 -t 或 -n 的名词后: bankrupt*cy*, captain*cy*. ②使动词变成名词: occupan*cy* (< occupy), vacan*cy* (< vacate). ③使词尾为 -ant, -ent, -te, -tic 等的形容词变成名词: ascendan*cy* (<ascend*ant*), expedien*cy* (< expedi*ent*), adequa*cy* (< adequa*te*), luna*cy* (< luna*tic*).
cyan- *comb. f.* (接元音或 h-) = cyano-.
cy·an·am·ide [saiˈænəmaid] *n.*【化】①氰(化)胺,氨基氰. ②氨腈 (RNHCN).
cy·a·nate [ˈsaiəneit] *n.*【化】氰酸盐.
cy·an·ic [saiˈænik] *a.* ①【化】氰的,含氰的. 青蓝色的. ~ **acid** 氰酸.
cy·a·nide [ˈsaiənaid], **cy·a·nid** [-nid] *n.*【化】氰化物. ~ *process* 氰化(物)法[用氰化物从矿物中提取贵金属的方法]. — *vt.* 用氰化法处理.
cy·a·nine [ˈsaiənain] *n.* 花青(染料).
cy·a·nite [ˈsaiənait] *n.*【矿】蓝晶石.
cyano- *comb. f.* 表示①氰(基). ②氰化物. ③青色,深蓝.
cy·a·no·co·bal·a·min [ˌsaiənəukəˈbɔləmin] *n.*【生化】维生素 B_{12}.
cy·an·o·gen [saiˈænədʒin] *n.*【化】氰[即乙二腈 ethane dinitrile].
cy·a·no·ge·net·ic, cy·a·no·gen·ic [ˌsaiənəudʒiˈnetik, ˌsaiənəuˈdʒenik] *a.* 能产生氰化物的.
cy·a·no·hy·drin [ˌsaiənəuˈhaidrin] *n.*【化】偕醇腈,氰醇.
cy·a·nom·e·ter [ˌsaiəˈnɔmitə] *n.* (测量天空、海洋蓝度的)蓝度表.
Cy·a·no·phy·ce·ae [ˈsaiənəuˈfaisei:] *n.*【植】蓝藻纲. **-phy·cean** *n., a.* 蓝藻(的).
cy·a·no·sis [ˌsaiəˈnəusis] *n.*【医】青紫,发绀.
cy·a·not·ic [ˌsaiəˈnɔtik] *a.*【医】发绀的,青紫的.
cy·an·o·type [saiˈænətaip] *n.* 蓝晒[氰印]相片(法); 晒蓝图.
cy·a·nu·rate [ˌsaiəˈnju:reit, -it] *n.*【化】三聚氰酸酯,三聚氰酸盐.
cy·a·nu·ric [ˌsaiəˈnjuərik] *a.* ~ **acid**【化】氰尿酸,三聚氰酸.
Cyb·e·le [ˈsibili] *n.*【希神】母神[小亚细亚神话中女神,作为自然之母的象征].
cy·ber·cul·ture [ˈsaibəˌkʌltʃə] *n.* 电脑文化[指社会文化在电子计算机影响下的状态]. **-tural** *a.*
cy·ber·nate [ˈsaibəneit] *vt.* 以电子计算机和自动化控制,使电子计算机化和自动化.
cy·ber·na·tion [ˌsaibəˈneiʃən] *n.* 电子计算机和自动化控制.
cy·ber·net·ic [ˌsaibə:ˈnetik] *a.* 控制论的.
cy·ber·net·i·cist [ˌsaibə:ˈnetisist] *n.* 控制论学者,自动化专家.
cy·ber·net·ics [ˈsaibə:ˈnetiks] *n.* 控制论.
cy·borg [ˈsaibɔ:g] *n.* ①(在太空)靠机械装置维持生命的人. ②受控机体[部分机能被各种电子装置控制或代替了的人或其他生物体].
cyb·o·tac·tic [ˌsibəˈtæktik] *a.*【化】群聚的.
cyc., cyclo. = cyclopaedia; cyclopaedic.
cy·cad [ˈsaikæd] *n.*【植】苏铁(科).
cy·cas [ˈsaikəs] *n.*【植】苏铁(属).
cycl- *comb. f.* (循)环; 回旋[转]; 环(状,合,化); 圆[辅音前用 cyclo-].
cy·cla·mate [ˈsaikləmeit, ˈsiklə-] *n.*【化】环己(基)氨基磺酸盐.
cyc·la·men [ˈsikləmən] *n.*【植】仙客来(属).
cy·cle [ˈsaikl] *n.* ①循环,周期,一转. ②周时,周年,年纪. ③(诗、故事等的)始末. ④自行车,三轮车,摩托车. ⑤【电】周波;【数】环;【拓】闭链;【地】旋回;【植】(从枯凋到再生的)一轮廻; 天体运转的轨道. *the business* ~ 商业盛衰的周期性. *the life* ~【生】生活周期,生活史. *the Arthurian* ~ 《亚瑟王记》. *the Calippic* ~ 七十六年周期. *the Trojan* ~ 《特洛依战争史诗集》. — *vi.* ①轮转,循环. ②骑自行车[三轮车等]. — *vt.* 使循环,使轮转. ~**car** (机动)三轮车[四轮车]. **-ry** (出售或修理自行车的)自行车铺.
cy·cler [ˈsaiklə] *n.* ①【空】周期计. ②〔主美〕= cyclist.
cy·cler·y [ˈsaikləri] *n.* 自行车商店.
cy·clic, cy·cli·cal [ˈsaiklik(kəl)] *a.* ①周期的; 轮转的,循环的. ②【化】环状的;【植】轮列的,轮卷的. ④组诗的; 故事始末的. ~ **flower** 轮生花. ~ **number**【数】完全数. ~ **poets** (歌咏特洛依战争等故事的)史诗诗人.
cy·clist [ˈsaiklist] *n.*〔英〕骑自行车[摩托车]的人.
cy·cli·za·tion [ˌsaikliˈzeiʃən] *n.*【化】环合,环的形成.
cy·cli·zine [ˈsaikliˌzi:n] *n.*【药】环嗪,马内嗪[一种抗组胺药].
cy·clo [ˈsi:kləu, ˈsaikləu] *n.* (出租载客的)三轮摩托车 (= ~taxi). ~**-pousse** [ˌsi:kləuˈpu:s] (载客的)脚踏三轮车,摩托三轮车.
cyclo- *comb. f.* = cycl-.
cy·clo·bu·tane [ˈsaikləuˈbju:tein] *n.*【化】环丁烷.
cy·clo·cross [ˌsaikləuˈkrɔs] *n.*【体】摩托车越野赛.
cy·clo·graph [ˈsaikləugrɑ:f] *n.* ①圆弧规. ②【摄】轮转全景照相机. ③金属硬度测定仪.
cy·clo·hex·ane [ˌsaikləuˈheksein] *n.*【化】环己烷.
cy·clo·hex·i·mide [ˌsaikləuˈheksimaid] *n.*【微】放线(菌)酮,环已酰亚胺.
cy·cloid [ˈsaiklɔid] *n.* ①【数】摆线,旋轮[圆滚]线. ②【动】圆鳞鱼. ③循环精神病. — *a.* ①圈状的,圆形的. ②(有)圆鳞的. ③易患循环精神病的.
cy·cloi·dal [saiˈklɔidl] *a.* ①摆线的. ②(鱼鳞)圆形的.
cy·clom·e·ter [saiˈklɔmitə] *n.* ①回转计,转数表. ②里程表. ③圆弧测定器.
cy·clom·e·try [saiˈklɔmitri] *n.*【数】测圆法.
cy·clone [ˈsaikləun] *n.* ①【气】气旋; 旋风. ②旋风器,吸尘器. ③【化】环酮,四芳基茂酮. ~ *cellar [pit]*〔美〕(草原地带的)旋风避难穴; 逃避处. ~ *wind* 气旋风. **cy·clon·ic** *a.*
cy·clo·nite [ˈsaikləunait] *n.*【化】旋风[黑索今]炸药,六素精,三次甲基三硝基胺.
cy·clo·o·le·fin [ˌsaikləuˈəuləfin] *n.*【化】环烯.
cy·clo·p(a)e·di·a [ˌsaikləuˈpi:djə] *n.* 百科全书.
cy·clo·p(a)e·dic [ˌsaikləuˈpi:dik] *a.* 百科全书的; 渊博的,广泛的.
cy·clo·par·af·fin [ˌsaikləuˈpærəfin] *n.*【化】环烷(属)烃,环烷.

Cy·clo·pe·an, Cy·clo·pi·an, Cy·clop·ic [saiˈkləupjən, ˌsaiˈklɔpik] *a.* ①【希神】独眼巨人的. ②〔c-〕巨大的;【建】巨石堆积的.
cy·clo·pen·tane [ˌsaikləuˈpentein] *n.*【化】环戊烷.
cy·clo·ple·gi·a [ˌsaikləuˈpliːdʒiə] *n.*【医】睫状肌麻痹. **-ple·gic** [-dʒik] *a.*
cy·clo·pro·pane [ˌsaikləuˈprəupein] *n.*【药】环丙烷〔麻醉剂〕.
Cy·clops [ˈsaiklɔps] *n.* *(pl. Cy·clo·pes* [saiˈkləupiːz], *~es)*【希神】独眼巨人;〔喻〕独眼人.
cy·clo·ra·ma [ˌsaikləuˈrɑːmə] *n.* ①环形画景. ②【剧】半圆形透视背景. **-ram·ic** *a.*
cy·clo·sis [saiˈkləusis] *n.*【生】(细胞中的)胞质环流.
cy·clos·to·mate [saiˈklɔstəmeit] *a.*【动】①有圆口的. ②圆口动物的(= cyclostomatous).
cy·clo·stome [ˈsaikləustəum] *n.*【动】圆口类(亚纲).
cy·clo·style [ˈsaikləustail] *n.* ①滚齿轮铁笔复写器. ②围柱式建筑物.
cy·clo·thyme [ˈsaikləuθaim] *n.*【医】(躁郁)循环性精神病患者.
cy·clo·thy·mi·a [ˌsaikləuˈθaimiə] *n.*【医】(躁郁)循环性气质. **-thy·mic** *a., n.*
cy·clo·tron [ˈsaiklətrɔn] *n.*【物】回旋加速器. ~ **resonance** 迴旋共振.
cy·der [ˈsaidə] *n.*〔英〕= cider.
cyg·net [ˈsignit] *n.* 小天鹅.
Cyg·nus [ˈsignəs] *n.* ①【鸟】天鹅属. ②〔the ~〕【天】天鹅座.
cyl. = cylinder; cylindrical.
cyl·in·der [ˈsilində] *n.* ①圆筒;机筒;烘筒;量筒;(印刷机等的)滚筒. ②【数】柱(面),柱体. ③【机】汽缸;【化】(装氧气等的)钢筒,钢瓶. ④(左轮手枪的)旋转弹膛. ⑤【考古】(巴比伦和亚述的)圆筒形石印(= ~ seal);(雕有阿拉伯人楔形文字的)圆柱形陶器. ***(work) on all ~s*** 〔口〕尽全部力量(大干). ~ **ga(u)ge** 缸径规,圆筒内径测量器. ~ **head [cap]** 汽缸盖. ~ **mirror** 柱面镜. ~ **machine** 圆网(造纸)机. ~ **press**〔美〕= ~ **printing machine** 轮转[滚筒]印刷机.
cy·lin·dri·cal [siˈlindrikəl] *a.* 圆柱体的,圆柱形的,长圆形的. **-cal·i·ty** [-ˈkæliti] *n.*
cyl·in·droid [ˈsilindrɔid] *n., a.*【数】①圆柱性面(的),拟圆柱面(的). ②椭圆柱(的).
cy·lix [ˈsailiks, ˈsiliks] *n.* *(pl. cyl·i·ces* [ˈsilisiːz]*)* (古希腊)高脚双柄宽口浅酒杯(= kylix).
cy·ma [ˈsaimə] *n.* *(pl. ~s, -mae* [-miː]*)* ①【建】反曲线;波状花边[线脚]. ②【植】= cyme.
cy·mar [siˈmɑː] *n.* (宽大无袖的)女便袍,女衬袍.
cy·ma·ti·um [siˈmeiʃiəm] *n.* *(pl. -tia* [-ʃiə]*)*【建】反曲线状;波状(拱顶)花边.
cym·bal [ˈsimbəl] *n.*〔常*pl.*〕【乐】铙钹,钗(钹). **-ist** *n.* 击钹者.
cym·bid·i·um [simˈbidiəm] *n.*【植】兰属.
cym·bi·form [ˈsimbifɔːm] *a.*【解】【植】船形的,舟状的.
cyme [saim] *n.*【植】聚伞花序.
cy·mene [ˈsaimiːn] *n.*【化】伞花烃,百里香素;甲基[异丙基]苯.
cymo *comb. f.* 表示"波": *cymo*scope.
cy·mo·gene [ˈsaiməudʒiːn] *n.*【化】粗丁烷,近纯丁烷.
cy·mo·graph [ˈsaiməugrɑːf] *n.* = kymograph.
cy·moid [ˈsaimɔid] *a.*【植】聚伞状的,聚伞花序状的.
cy·mom·e·ter [saiˈmɔmitə] *n.*【电】波长计,自记波频计.
cy·mo·phane [ˈsaiməufein] *n.* 猫眼石,金绿宝石.
cy·mo·scope [ˈsaiməuskəup] *n.*【无】检波器,振荡指示器.
cy·mose, cy·mous [ˈsaiməus, ˈsaiməs] *a.*【植】有聚伞花的;聚伞状的.
Cym·ric [ˈkimrik, ˈsimrik] *a.* = Welsh.
Cym·ry [ˈkimri, ˈsimri] *n.* 威尔士族.
Cyn·ic [ˈsinik] *n.* ①(古希腊)犬儒学派的门徒. ②〔c-〕好挖苦人的人,好嘲笑的人;玩世不恭的人,愤世嫉俗的人. — *a.* ①犬儒学派的. ②〔c-〕= cynical.
cyn·i·cal [ˈsinikəl] *a.* 爱嘲笑人的,冷嘲热讽的,讥诮的;玩世不恭的,愤世嫉俗的. ***be ~ about (sincerity)*** 不相信(人的诚实). **-ly** *ad.* **-ness** *n.*
cyn·i·cism [ˈsinisizəm] *n.* ①〔C-〕(古希腊的)犬儒哲学,犬儒主义. ②讥诮(癖),冷笑(癖);玩世不恭,愤世嫉俗.
cyno- *comb. f.* 犬: *cyno*phobia.
cy·no·ceph·a·lus [ˌsainəuˈsefələs] *n.* ①【动】犬面狒狒. ②【神话】狗头人身的人(像).
cy·no·pho·bia [ˌsainəuˈfəubiə] *n.*【医】恐犬病.
cyn·o·sure [ˈsinəzjuə, ˈsain-] *n.* ①〔*C-*〕【天】小熊座(Little Bear 的别名),北极星. ②指针,目标;众目之的,众望所归,赞美的目标. *the ~ of all eyes [of the world]* 人人注意的目标.
Cyn·thi·a [ˈsinθiə] *n.* ①辛西娅〔女子名〕. ②〔诗〕月亮〔拟人化的说法〕. ③【罗神】女神狄安娜(Diana)的别名.
cy·pher [ˈsaifə] *n., v.* = cipher.
cy-pres [ˈsiːˈprei] *n.*【法】力求近似(原则)〔指对于遗嘱等文件的解释有困难时,力求使解释接近立遗嘱者的愿望,尤其适用于公益捐款等方面〕. — *a., ad.*【法】力求近似的[地].
cy·press [ˈsaipris, -prəs] *n.* ①【植】柏(属);扁柏,丝柏;丝柏木料. ②丝柏枝〔哀悼标记〕;志哀黑纱. ~ **vine**【植】茑萝.
Cyp·ri·an [ˈsipriən] *a.* ①塞浦路斯[人,语]的. ②关于爱神阿芙罗狄蒂(Aphrodite)的;色情的,淫荡的. — *n.* ①塞浦路斯人[语]. ②爱神阿芙罗狄蒂的崇拜者;淫荡的人,娼妓.
cy·prin·o·dont [siˈprinədɔːnt, siˈprainə-] *n.*【动】鳉科鱼.
cyp·ri·noid [ˈsiprinɔid] *a.*【动】鲤科的. — *n.* 鲤科鱼(= cyp·ri·nid [-nid]).
Cyp·ri·ot, Cyp·ri·ote [ˈsipriət, -əut] *a.* 塞浦路斯岛的;塞浦路斯人[语]的. — *n.* 塞浦路斯人[语].
cyp·ri·pe·di·um [ˌsipriˈpiːdiəm] *n.* *(pl. ~s, -dia* [-ə]*)*【植】①杓兰(属). ②兜兰(属)*(Paphiopedilum)*.
Cy·prus [ˈsaiprəs] *n.* 塞浦路斯〔亚洲〕.
cyp·se·la [ˈsipsələ] *n.* *(pl. -lae* [-ˌliː]*)*【植】连萼瘦果.
Cy·re·na·ic [ˌsaiəriˈneiik] *a.* ①(北非古城)昔勒尼的. ②昔勒尼学派的. — *n.* ①昔勒尼人. ②昔勒尼学派的信徒. **-i·cism** [-isizəm] *n.* 昔勒尼学派〔古希腊一种鼓吹享乐为人生唯一目的的学派〕.
Cy·ril [ˈsiril] *n.* 西里尔〔男子名〕.
cy·ril·lic [siˈrilik] *a.* 西里尔(Cyril)字母的. ~ **alphabet** 西里尔字母〔九世纪时传教士西里尔发明的字母,系现代俄语等字母的本源〕.
cyrto- *comb. f.* 弯曲,弓状: *cyrto*meter.
cyr·tom·e·ter [səːˈtɔmitə] *n.* ①圆量尺,测曲面器. ②测胸围器,测头颅器.
Cy·rus [ˈsaiərəs] *n.* 赛勒斯〔男子名〕.
cyst [sist] *n.* ①【生】胞,囊;包囊;膀胱. ②【医】囊肿. ③【植】孢囊,胚囊. *the urinary ~* 膀胱. **-ic** *a.*
cyst-〔接元音〕, **cysti-**〔接辅音〕 *comb. f.* = cysto-: *cyst*eine, *cysti*cercus.
cys·tec·to·my [sisˈtektəmi] *n.*【医】囊切;(胆囊,膀胱)切除(术).
cys·te·ine [ˈsistin] *n.*【生化】半胱氨酸.
cyst·ic [ˈsistik] *a.* ①膀胱的;胆囊的. ②胞的,囊的. ③胞状的,囊状的;有胞的,有囊的.

cys·ti·cer·coid [ˌsistiˈsəːkɔid] *n.* 【动】拟囊尾幼虫.
cys·ti·cer·co·sis [ˌsistisəˈkəusis] *n.* (*pl.* **-co·ses** [-ˈkəusiːz]) 【医】囊尾幼虫病.
cys·ti·cer·cus [sistiˈsəːkəs] *n.* (*pl.* **-ci** [-sai]) 【动】囊尾幼虫.
cys·ti·form [ˈsistifɔːm] *a.* 胞状的,囊状的.
cys·tin(e) [ˈsistiːn] *n.* 【生化】胱氨酸.
cys·ti·tis [sisˈtaitis] *n.* 【医】膀胱炎.
cysto- *comb. f.* 表示"胞","囊","膀胱": *cysto*cele.
cys·to·carp [ˈsistəkɑːp] *n.* 【植】囊果.
cys·to·cele [ˈsistəsiːl] *n.* 【医】膀胱突出(症).
Cy·sto·flag·el·la·ta [ˈsistəuˌflædʒəˈleitə] *n. pl.* 【动】胞状鞭毛虫类.
cys·toid [ˈsistɔid] *a.* 胞囊状的,囊肿一样的. — *n.* 【医】类囊肿,假囊肿.
cys·to·lith [ˈsistəliθ] *n.* ①【医】胆石; 膀胱结石. ②【植】钟乳体.
cys·to·scope [ˈsistəskəup] *n.* 【医】膀胱镜.
cys·tos·to·my [sisˈtɔstəmi] *n.* 【医】膀胱造口(导尿)术.
cys·tot·o·my [sisˈtɔtəmi] *n.* 【医】膀胱切开术, 膀胱结石[肿疡]截除术.
cyt- *comb. f.* = cyto-.
cy·tase [ˈsaiteis] *n.* 【生化】细胞溶(解)酶.
-cyte *suf.* 细胞,球: leuco*cyte*.
Cyth·er·e·a [ˌsiθəˈri(ː)ə] *n.* 【希神】爱神〔阿芙罗狄蒂(Aphrodite) 的别称〕.
Cyth·er·e·an [ˌsiθəˈri(ː)ən] *a.* 【希神】爱神的, 阿芙罗狄蒂的. — *n.* 爱神崇拜者.
cyto- *comb. f.* 细胞(质): *cyto*logy.
cy·to·chem·is·try [ˈsaitəuˌkemistri] *n.* 细胞化学.
cy·to·chrome [ˈsaitəuˌkrəum] *n.* 【生】细胞色素.
cy·to·gen·e·sis [ˌsaitəuˈdʒenisis] *n.* 【生】细胞发生, 细胞生成.
cy·to·ge·net·ics [ˌsaitəudʒiˈnetiks] *n.* 细胞遗传学. **-net·ic, -neti·cal** *a.* **-neti·cal·ly** *ad.* **-net·i·cist** *n.*
cy·tog·e·nous [saiˈtɔdʒinəs] *a.* 【生】细胞发生的,细胞生成的.
cy·to·ki·ne·sis [ˈsaitəukaiˈniːsis] *n.* 【生】胞质分裂, 减数分裂.
cy·to·kin·in [ˌsaitəuˈkinin] *n.* 【生】细胞激动素.
cy·tol·o·gist [saiˈtɔlədʒist] *n.* 细胞学者.
cy·tol·o·gy [saiˈtɔlədʒi] *n.* 细胞学.
cy·tol·y·sin [saiˈtɔlisin] *n.* 【生】溶细胞素.
cy·tol·y·sis [saiˈtɔlisis] *n.* 【生】细胞溶解. **cy·to·lyt·ic** [ˌsaitəˈlitik] *a.*
cy·to·mem·brane [ˌsaitəuˈmembrein] *n.* 【生】细胞膜.
cy·to·plasm [ˈsaitəuplæzəm] *n.* 【生】(细)胞质.
cy·to·plast [ˈsaitəuˌplæst] *n.* 【生】= cytoplasm. **-ic** *a.*
cy·to·sine [ˈsaitəsiːn] *n.* 【生化】胞(核)嘧啶,胞嗪.
cy·to·tax·on·o·my [ˌsaitəutækˈsɔnəmi] *n.* 细胞分类学.
cy·to·troph·o·blast [ˌsaitəuˈtrɔfəblæst] *n.* 【生】细胞滋养层. **-ic** *a.*
cy·to·sol [ˈsaitəusɔl] *n.* 【生】细胞溶质.
cyt·u·la [ˈsitjulə] *n.* 【生】合子;受精卵.
C. Z. = Canal Zone (Panama) (巴拿马)运河区.
czar [zɑː] *n.* = Tsar.
czar·das [ˈtʃɑːdæʃ, -dɔʃ] *n.* (匈牙利) 恰尔达什舞(曲).
cza·ri·na [zɑːˈriːnə] *n.* = tsarina.
czar·ism [ˈzɑːrizəm] *n.* = tsarism.
czar·ist [ˈzɑːrist] *n., a.* = tsarist.
Czar·i·tz·a [zɑːˈritsə] *n.* = tsarina.
Czech, Czekh [tʃek] *n.* 捷克人[语]. — *a.* 捷克的, 捷克人[语]的.
Czech·ic, Czech·ish [ˈtʃekik, ˈtʃekiʃ] *a.* 捷克的,捷克人[语]的.
Czech·o·slo·vak [ˈtʃekəuˈsləuvæk] *n.* 捷克斯洛伐克人. — *a.* 捷克斯洛伐克(人)的.
Czech·o·slo·vak·i·a [ˈtʃekəusləuˈvækiə] *n.* 捷克斯洛伐克〔欧洲〕.
Czech·o·slo·vak·i·an [ˈtʃekəusləuˈvækiən] = Czechoslovak.

D

D,d [diː] (*pl.* **D's, d's** [diːz]) ①英语字母表第四字母. ②【乐】D音, D调. ③【数】第四个已知数. ④第四. ⑤(学业成绩)劣或勉强及格. ⑥ D 字形物. *D flat* 【乐】降 D 调. *D major* [*minor*] 【乐】D 大调 [小调]. *D sharp* 【乐】升 D 调. *a D student* 劣等生. *a D slide valve* D 形滑阀.
D [diː] ①【化】= deuterium 元素氘的符号. ②(罗马数字) 500. *CD* = 400. *DC* = 600. $\bar{D}$ = 500,000 〔有时 = 5,000〕.
D. = ① December. ② Democrat; Democratic. ③ Doctor. ④ Don. ⑤ Duchess. ⑥ Duke. ⑦ Dutch.
d. = ① date. ② daughter. ③ day(s). ④ dead. ⑤ degree. ⑥ dele; delete. ⑦〔L.〕*denarius; denarii* (旧)便士 (= penny; pence). ⑧ deputy. ⑨ deserted; deserter. ⑩ diameter. ⑪ died. ⑫ dime. ⑬ director. ⑭ dividend. ⑮ dollar. ⑯ dorsal. ⑰ dose. ⑱ dyne.
'd [d] 〔口〕① = had: *I'd* ... = I had ... . ② =did: *Where'd* ... = Where did.... ③= should (或 would): *He'd* ... = He should (或 would). ④ =-ed: *foster'd*.
d' [d] 〔口〕① = do: *How d'you* ... = How do you .... ② = did.
da [dɑː] *n.* 〔口〕= dad.
D.A., DA = District Attorney 〔美〕地方检察官.
D.A. = delayed action (bomb) 定时(炸弹); direct action; documents against [for] acceptance.
D/A, d/a ① = days after acceptance. ② = deposit account.
d.a. = duck's ass 〔美俚〕鸭屁股男发型.
dab[1] [dæb] *vt.* ①轻敲,轻拍; 轻抚 (*sth.*). ②〔美俚〕在…上摁指纹印. *a plaster to be wetted and dabbed on* 润湿后轻轻敷上的膏药. ~ *one's forehead with a handkerchief* 用手帕轻拍脑门(揩汗). — *vi.* 轻拍轻敷; 涂擦 (*on, at*); (鸟)啄. — *n.* ①轻打,轻拍; 轻抚. ②涂擦. ③啄. ④指纹印. ⑤少量,些许; 一小块. *a* ~ *of butter* 一小块奶油. *a* ~ *of powder* 一刷子白粉.
dab[2] [dæb] *n.* 小鲽;比目鱼.
dab[3] [dæb] *n.* 〔口〕名手, 能手 (*at*). *a* ~ *at tennis* 网球能手.

DAB, D.A.B. = Dictionary of American Biography.
dab·ber ['dæbə] *n.* ①轻拍的人[物]. ②(木版印刷的)涂墨擦. ③(打纸型的)硬毛刷.
dab·ble ['dæbl] *vt.* ①弄湿,溅湿. ②蘸,浸,沾. *be ~d with mud* (被)溅满泥浆. —*vi.* ①玩水. ②浅尝,涉猎,涉足. *~ in literature* 涉猎文学. *~ in [with] stocks* 经营一部分股票. *~ with the text* 窜改原文.
dab·bler ['dæblə] *n.* ①玩水者. ②浅尝者,涉猎者;(业余)爱好者. *~ in [at] wood engraving* 业余木刻者.
dab·chick ['dæbtʃik] *n.* 【鸟】䴙䴘.
dab·ster ['dæbstə] *n.* ①〔英方〕能手,老手. ②〔口〕业余爱好者.
da ca·po [dɑː'kɑːpəu] 〔It.〕【乐】从头(重复一遍). 〔略作 D.C.〕
Dac·ca ['dækə] *n.* 达卡〔孟加拉国首都〕.
dace [deis] *n. (pl. ~s,* 〔集合词〕*~)* 【鱼】(鲤科)鲦鱼.
dach·a, datch·a ['dɑːtʃə] *n.* 〔Russ.〕别墅,乡间邸宅.
dachs·hund ['dækshund] *n.* 达克斯狗〔体长脚短,常用于猎獾、狐等〕.
da·coit [də'kɔit] *n.* (印度、缅甸的)土匪,强盗. **-coit·y** [-i] *n.* 土匪的抢劫.
Da·cron ['deikrɔn, 'dækrɔn] *n.* ①【商标】达可纶. ②〔d-〕聚酯纤维;达可纶;涤纶织物〔俗名的确良〕.
dacry(o)- *comb. f.* 泪: *dacryo*cyst 泪囊.
dac·tyl ['dæktil] *n.* ①【韵】扬抑抑格,长短短格〔如: take her up tenderly〕. ②【动】指,趾.
dac·tyl·ic [dæk'tilik] *a., n.* 扬抑抑〔长短短〕格的(句子).
dactyl(o)- *comb. f.* 指,趾: *dactylo*gram.
dac·tyl·o·gram [dæk'tiləgræm] *n.* 指纹.
dac·ty·log·ra·phy [ˌdækti'lɔgrəfi] *n.* 指纹学,指纹法;指纹术.
dac·tyl·ol·o·gy [ˌdækti'lɔlədʒi] *n.* (聋哑人的)指语术.
dac·ty·los·co·py [ˌdækti'lɔskəpi] *n.* 指纹鉴定法.
dad[1] [dæd] *n.* 〔口〕爹爹,爸爸.
dad[2] [dæd] *int.* 〔美口〕神. *~-blasted [-blamed]* 讨厌,可恶.
Da·da = Dadaism.
dad·a ['dædə] *n.* 〔儿〕= dad[1].
Da·da·ism ['dɑːdəizəm] *n.* 达达派〔1916—1922年间兴起的一种西方文艺流派,其特征为运用怪诞的象征手法以表达潜意识的东西,运用虚无主义的讽刺手法等〕.
Da·da·ist ['dɑːdəist] *n.* 达达派艺术家.
dad·dy ['dædi] *n.* ①〔口〕= dad[1]. ②〔俚〕爱在少女身上花钱的老色迷(= sugar ~).
dad·dy-long·legs ['dædi'lɔŋlegz] *n.* ①大蚊子. ②长脚蜘蛛.
da·do ['deidəu] *n. (pl. ~s, ~es)* ①【建】(柱墩的)墩身;护壁板,墙裙. ②(木工的)开榫槽.
DAE, D.A.E. = *Dictionary of American English* «美国英语词典».
dae·dal ['diːdl] 〔诗〕*a.* 巧妙的;错综复杂的;千变万化的. *the ~ hand of nature* 大自然的鬼斧神工.
Dae·da·le·an, Dae·da·li·an [di'deiljən] *a.* ①代达罗斯(Daedalus)的. ②〔d-〕错综复杂的;巧妙的.
Dae·da·lus ['diːdələs] *n.* 【希神】代达罗斯〔建造 Crete 迷宫的名匠〕.
dae·mon ['diːmən] *n. (pl. ~s, ~es [-iːz])* = demon.
daff[1] [dæf] *vi.* 〔Scot.〕演丑角;举止滑稽.
daff[2] [dæf] *vt.* 〔废〕①推开. ②丢开. *~ ... aside* 摆脱.
daf·fa·down·dil·ly [ˌdæfədaun'dili] *n.* 〔诗〕= daffodil.
daf·fo·dil, daf·fo·dil·ly ['dæfədil,-i] *n.* ①【植】水仙. ②鲜黄色.
daff·y ['dæfi] *a.* 〔美口〕①疯狂的,愚笨的. ②轻浮的.
daft [dɑːft] *a.* ①愚蠢的. ②疯狂的. ③〔Scot.〕玩闹的. *go ~* 发狂;发痴.
dag. = decagram(me).
dag·ga ['dægə] *n.* ①大麻. ②大麻干叶子(= marijuana).
dag·ger ['dægə] *n.* ①短剑,匕首. ②【印】剑号〔即 †〕. ③〔*pl.*〕敌意. *a double ~* 双剑号〔即‡〕. ***at ~s drawn*** 势不两立,互相仇视,剑拔弩张. ***look ~s at*** 瞪着眼看,怒视. ***speak ~s to*** *(sb.)* 说刻毒话,恶言伤人. —*vt.* ①用剑刺. ②用剑号标明.
dag·gle ['dægl] *vt., vi.* ①拖脏(衣服等). ②溅湿,弄脏. ③拖着(衣服)走. *clothes ~d by the splash of passing vehicles* 过路的车辆把衣服溅脏.
dag·lock ['dægˌlɔk] *n.* (羊犬等的)凝污卷毛.
da·go ['deigəu] *n. (pl. ~s, ~es)* 〔常 D-〕〔美蔑〕意大利或西班牙血统的人. *~* **red** 〔美〕(意大利人酿的和喝的)低级红葡萄酒.
da·go·ba ['dɑːgəbə] *n.* (印度的)舍利子塔.
Da·gon ['deigɔn] *n.* (古代腓力斯人和腓尼基人的)半人半鱼的神.
da·guerre·o·type [də'gerəutaip, -rətaip] *n.* (从前的)银板照相(法).
dah[1] [dɑː] *n.* 无线电或电报电码中的一长划.
dah[2] [dɑː] *n.* (缅甸人的)大刀.
da·ha·bee·yah, da·ha·bi·ah, da·ha·be·ah, da·ha·bi·yeh [dɑːhə'biːjə, -'biːə, -'biːə, -'biːje] *n.* 〔Ar.〕尼罗河中的舫式渡船.
dah·li·a ['deiljə] *n.* ①【植】大丽花. ②浓紫色. *a blue ~* 不会有的东西.
Da·ho·man [də'həumən] *n.* 达荷美人. —*a.* 达荷美人的;达荷美的.
Da·ho·mey [də'həumi] *n.* (西非)达荷美.
da·hoon [də'huːn] *n.* 达宏冬青.
Dail Eir·eann ['dail 'ɛərən] 爱尔兰的众议院.
dai·ly ['deili] *a.* 逐日的,每日的. —*n.* ①日报(= ~ (news)paper). ②〔英口〕日佣女用人(= ~ girl) *~ bread* 每日食粮,生计. *~ capacity* 每日产量. *~ interest* 日息. —*ad.* 每日,逐日,天天. *~* **double** 两场连赌法〔赛马或赛狗赌博中对连续两场比赛的结果统押一注的赌法〕;〔喻〕同时在两个不同的领域取得成功. *~* **dozen** 每天的体育健身活动.
dai·mon ['daimɔn] *n.* = demon.
dain·ti·ly ['deintili] *ad.* ①优雅,好看. ②好吃,爽口. ③讲究,考究. *be ~ dressed* 衣着雅致. *fare ~* 吃得好.
dain·ti·ness ['deintinis] *n.* ①优雅,美丽. ②美味. ③讲究,考究.
dain·ty ['deinti] *a.* ①优美的,好看的,雅致的. ②好吃的,爽口的. ③讲究的,有洁癖的. *a ~ lass* 美极了的姑娘. *~ bits* 美味. *a ~ feeder* 考究吃的人. *born with a ~ tooth* 生来嘴馋. —*n.* 美味,可口之物.
dai·qui·ri ['daikəri] *n.* 台克利酒,鸡尾酒.
dair·y ['dɛəri] *n.* ①(制)酪场,牛奶棚;牛奶场. ②牛奶店. ③奶品制造业. *~* **cattle** 〔集合词〕奶牛. *~* **farm** 奶场. *~* **farmer** 奶农. *~***maid** 奶场女工. *~***man** 奶场场主;挤奶工人;奶品商. *~* **products** 奶产品. *~* **stock** 奶牛. **-ing** 奶品制造业.
da·is ['deiis] *n.* ①(为贵宾或演说者设置的)上座;讲坛. ②(大厅一端的)台,高台〔用以放置高桌、宝座等〕. ③(露天的)平台. ④〔古〕(宝座上的)华盖.
Dai·sy ['deizi] *n.* 戴西〔女子名〕.
dai·sy ['deizi] *n.* ①〔英〕雏菊,延命菊. ②〔美〕牛眼菊(= oxeye ~). ③〔美俚〕上品,逸品;〔美〕卓越人物. ④去骨肩胛肉熏制的火腿(= ~ ham). ***turn (up) one's toes to the daisies*** 〔俚〕死. ***under the daisies*** 〔俚〕葬在地下. —*a.* 〔美俚〕极好的;可爱的. *~* **chain** ①(给女学生戴的)雏菊花环. ②〔俚〕搞同性恋爱的集团. *~* **cutter** 〔俚〕①跑时举足极低的马. ②【板球等】(贴近地面的)滚球. ③【军】榴霰弹. *~* **ham** 去骨熏腿.

Dak·ar [ˈdækə] *n.* 达喀尔〔塞内加尔首都〕.

da·koit [dəˈkɔit] *n.* = dacoit.

Da·ko·ta [dəˈkəutə] *n.* ①达科他人〔北美印第安人〕. ②达科他语. ③达科他〔美国过去一地区名,现分为南、北达科他州〕. — *a.* ①达科他人的. ②达科他语的. ③(南、北)达科他(州)的. **the ~s** 南、北达科他.

dal [ˈdɑːl] *n.* = dhal.

dal. = decalitre.

Da·la·dier [dɑlɑˈdjei] *n.* ***the ~ line*** 达拉第防线〔在法国、比利时、卢森堡之间,是马奇诺防线 (Maginot line) 的延长部分, 由当时法国总理 (1938—1940) 兼国防部长 Edouard Daladier (1884—1970) 负责筑成〕.

da·lai la·ma [ˈdælai ˈlɑːmə] *n.* 达赖喇嘛.

Dale [deil] *n.* 戴尔〔姓氏,男子名,女子名〕.

dale [deil] *n.* 〔诗、方〕谷, 山谷. ***o'er hill and ~*** 翻山越岭.

dales·man [ˈdeilzmən] *n.* (英国北部的)山谷居民.

da·leth, da·ledh [ˈdɑːlet, ˈdɑːləd] *n.* 希伯来字母表中的第四个字母.

Dal·las[1] [ˈdæləs] *n.* 达拉斯〔姓氏,男子名〕.

Dal·las[2] [ˈdæləs] *n.* 达拉斯〔美国城市〕.

dal·li·ance [ˈdæliəns] *n.* ①调戏; 调情, 调笑; 嬉戏. ②浪费时间,混日子.

dal·ly [ˈdæli] *vi.* ①调戏; 调情, 嬉戏; 戏弄 *(with)*. ②闲荡; 延误(时机等) *(over)*. — *vt.* 浪费(时间). ~ ***away*** 混日子; 延误. ~ ***with danger*** 瞎冒险.

Dal·ma·tia [dælˈmeiʃjə] *n.* 达尔马提亚〔南斯拉夫一地区〕.

Dal·ma·ti·an [dælˈmeiʃiən] *a.* 南斯拉夫达尔马提亚地方的. — *n.* ①达尔马提亚人. ②达尔马提亚狗〔白毛,有黑斑或褐斑〕.

dal·mat·ic [dælˈmætik] *n.* ①(主教等的)法衣. ②(英国国王的)加冕服.

dal se·gno [dæl ˈseinjəu] 〔It.〕【乐】反复记号〔从 $ 记号处开始重复一遍,略号 D.S.〕.

Dal·ton [ˈdɔːltən] *n.* ①多尔顿〔姓氏,男子名〕. ②**John** ~道尔顿〔1766—1844,英国化学、物理学家,原子学说首倡人,红绿色盲的发现者〕.

dal·ton·ism [ˈdɔːltənizəm] *n.* 【医】色盲; (特指)先天性红绿色盲.

Da·ly [ˈdeili] *n.* 戴利〔姓氏〕.

dam[1] [dæm] *n.* ①水闸, 坝, 堰. ②坝中的水. ③【矿】坑道堰. ④(牙科用的)橡皮障. ⑤〔喻〕障碍. *a regulating* ~ 拦洪坝. *a fascine* ~ 草坝. *a hydraulic* ~ 现代水闸. *a storage* ~ 蓄水坝. *weir* ~ 量水堰. — *vt.* ①筑水闸堵住. ②阻塞,遮断. ③抑制. ~ *up inflation* 抑制通货膨胀. ~ *back one's tears* 忍住眼泪.

dam[2] [dæm] *n.* ①母兽. ②〔古、蔑〕母亲.

dam·age [ˈdæmidʒ] *n.* ①损害, 损伤; 〔口〕伤害, 毁坏. ②〔口〕费用, 代价. ③ 〔*pl.*〕【法】赔偿损失; 赔偿金. *What's the ~?* 〔口〕要花多少钱? *a claim for ~s* 赔偿损失的要求. *costs and ~s* 讼费和损害费. *I will stand the ~* 我来掏腰包好啦. ***do [cause, inflict] ~ to*** 损害. ***sustain great ~*** 受到重大损害. — *vt.* 损坏 (房屋等), 损伤; 毁坏(名誉等). ~ *one's reputation* 毁坏名誉. — *vi.* 被损害. **-able** *a.* 易受损害的.

dam·an [ˈdæmən] *n.* 非洲蹄兔, 蹄兔 (= hyrax).

dam·ar [ˈdæmə] *n.* ①澳洲松脂. ②达马脂〔用以制油漆〕.

Dam·a·scene [ˈdæməsiːn] *a.* 大马士革的. — *n.* ①大马士革人. ② 〔d-〕 西洋李子. ③ 〔d-〕 (钢铁等烧后现出的)波状花纹. ④ 〔d-〕 镶嵌; 金银线镶嵌工艺. — *vt.* 〔d-〕 (在金属上)用金银线镶嵌; 使现波状花纹.

Da·mas·cus [dəˈmæskəs] *n.* 大马士革〔叙利亚首都〕. ~ *steel* = damask steel.

dam·ask [ˈdæməsk] *n.* ①缎子, 花缎, 锦缎; 花布. ②(呈现波状花纹的)大马士革钢 (= ~ steel). ③淡红色. — *a.* ①淡红色的. ②缎子的. ③大马士革钢的. ~ *rose* 淡红色玫瑰. — *vt.* 使织出花纹; 使呈淡红色.

dam·as·keen [ˌdæməsˈkiːn] *vt.* = damascene.

dame [deim] *n.* ①〔古、诗〕贵妇人; 〔古〕(私塾的)女先生; 〔古〕主妇. ②太太, 夫人; 〔美口〕妇女; 少女. ③〔英〕(knight 或 baronet 的)夫人. ④(英国 Eton 学院的)舍监〔现在是男人〕. *an old ~* 〔谑〕老太婆.

dam·mar, dam·mer [ˈdæmə] *n.* ①澳洲松脂. ②达马(树)脂.

damn [dæm] *vt.* ①指责, 攻击. ②毁坏, 糟踏. ③咒骂, 诅咒; 〔古〕使堕地狱. ④讨厌; 该死; 什么话; 〔常讳作 D— 或 d—n〕. *I'll be [I am] ~ed if it is so [if I do].* 我决不会有这样的事[我决不做这种事]. *D- me, but I'll do it.* 我一定要干,我死也要干. *God ~ you! = Be ~ed to you! = D- you!* 混帐! *Oh d—!* 讨厌! *D- [God~] (it)!* 该死! 糟了! *D- the rain!* 讨厌的雨! — *vi.* 咒骂. ~ ***all*** 完全没有. ***do [know] ~ all*** 简直什么都不干[知道]. ~ ***with faint praise*** 用冷淡的称赞反对[贬责]. — *n.* ①诅咒. ②些微. ***not care [give] a ~*** 毫不在乎. ***not worth a ~*** 毫无价值. ***Who gives a ~?*** 谁管呢? — *ad.* 〔俚〕= damned.

dam·na·ble [ˈdæmnəbl] *a.* ①该罚的,该死的. ②〔俚〕讨厌的. ~ *weather* 讨厌的天气.

dam·na·bly [ˈdæmnəbli] *ad.* ①该罚地, 该死地. ②讨厌地. *It is ~ hot.* 热得要命.

dam·na·tion [dæmˈneiʃən] *n.* ①指责. ②该死, 该下地狱. ③诅咒, 痛骂. ④毁坏, 破灭. — *int.* 糟了! 完了! 该死! *curse a person to ~* 咒骂某人不得好死.

dam·na·to·ry [ˈdæmnətəri] *a.* ①该咒的, 该罚的, 该死的. ②指责的. ~ *evidence* 不利的证据; 铁证.

damned [dæmd] *a.* ①该死的; 该咒的, 该罚的. ②讨厌的. ③〔俚〕要命的, 非常的. *a ~ lie* 弥天大谎. *You ~!* 该死! 混蛋! — *ad.* 非常, 极, 要命地. *It was so ~ hot.* 热死了. ***do [try] one's damnedest [damndest]*** 拼命干.

dam·ni·fi·ca·tion [ˌdæmnifiˈkeiʃən] *n.* 【法】损伤, 损害.

dam·ni·fy [ˈdæmnifai] *vt.* 【法】损害, 损伤.

damn·ing [ˈdæmiŋ] *n.* 咒诅. — *a.* ①该死的. ②身败名裂的; 逃避不了的. ~ *evidence* 逃避不了的罪证.

Dam·o·cles [ˈdæməkliːz] *n.* 达摩克里斯〔Syracuse 国王 Dionysius 的廷臣〕. ***the sword of ~*** 即将临头的危险〔Damocles 常说帝王多福, Dionysius 乃以一发悬剑,命他坐其下, 以示帝王多危〕. **-cle·an** [-ˈkliːən] *a.*

dam·oi·selle, dam·o·sel, dam·o·zel [ˌdæməˈzel] *n.* 〔古、诗〕小姐.

Da·mon and Pyth·i·as [ˈdeimən ənd ˈpiθiæs] 生死朋友,莫逆.

damp [dæmp] *n.* ①湿气, 潮湿. ②(矿井里的)有毒气体. ③消沉, 沮丧. ***cast [throw, strike] a ~ over [into]*** 给…泼冷水,使沮丧. — *a.* ①有湿气的, 潮湿的. ②消沉的,沮丧的. ~ ***squib*** 〔俚〕湿爆竹; 〔喻〕完全的失败; 无效的东西,没用的东西; 引不起注意[同情]的事情. — *vt.* ①弄湿, 濡湿, 打湿. ②给…泼冷水,使沮丧. ③抑止, 阻抑. ④【电】阻尼, 使减幅, 使衰减. ⑤(用灰等)封(火) *(down)*. ⑥【乐】制止弦的振动. — *vi.* ①变湿. ②(振幅)衰减. ~ *down* (用灰把火)封上. ~ ***off*** (植物因霉病而)枯萎. **~ing coil** 阻尼线圈. **damp·ing-off** 【植】枯萎病. **~proof** *a.* 防湿的, 耐湿性的. **-ly** *ad.*

damp·en [ˈdæmpən] *vt.* ①使潮湿. ②抑制; 减少; 减轻. ~ *a sponge* 把海绵弄湿. *~sb.'s spirits* 打击某人的情绪. — *vi.* 变潮湿.

damp·er [ˈdæmpə] *n.* ①使人扫兴的人[事]. ②【乐】(钢琴的) 制音器. ③【电】阻尼器; 减震器. ④(火炉等的)风门, 节气闸. ⑤〔美俚〕现金记录机. ⑥〔澳〕(在篝火上烤的)硬烧饼. *an air ~* 气压制动器. *an acous-*

tical ～ 消声器. ～ *pedal* 制音踏板. ***cast a ～ on*** 使…扫兴.
Dam·pier [ˈdæmpjə] *n.* 丹皮尔〔姓氏〕.
damp·ing [ˈdæmpiŋ] *n.* 【物】阻尼,减幅,衰减. ～ *resistance* 阻尼电阻.
damp·ish [ˈdæmpiʃ] *a.* 湿渍渍的,潮湿的.
damp·ness [ˈdæmpnis] *n.* 潮湿,润湿;湿度.
dam·sel [ˈdæmzəl] *n.* ①〔古、诗〕闺女,姑娘.
dam·son [ˈdæmzən] *n.* ①西洋李子. ②(暗)紫色. ～ *cheese* 蜜李〔一种甜食〕.
Dan[1] [dæn] *n.* 丹〔男子名 Daniel(l) 的昵称〕.
Dan[2] [dæn] *n.* 〔古诗〕= Master; Sir.
Dan[3] [dæn] 【圣】①雅各的第五子. ②在巴勒斯坦北部定居的一族,其后裔即为以色列族.
Dan [dɑːn] *n.* 〔Jap.〕段〔表示棋手等技术水平的级别〕.
Dan. = Daniel; Danish.
Da·na [ˈdeinə, ˈdænə] *n.* 戴纳〔姓氏,男子名,女子名〕.
Dan·a·ë [ˈdæneiiː] *n.* 【希神】达那厄〔Argos 王之女,天神宙斯化作金雨与她相会,后生子 Perseus〕.
Da Nang [ˈdɑːˈnɑːŋ] 岘港〔越南港市〕.
dance [dɑːns] *vi.* ①跳舞,舞蹈,舞. ②跳跃,(影子等)摇晃,(水波)荡漾.—*vt.* ①使跳舞,跳(狐步等)舞. ②舞弄(孩子). ～ ***after*** 仰…鼻息,听从…指挥,百依百顺地服从(某人). ～ ***attendance upon [on]*** *(sb.)* 侍奉(某人). ～ ***away [off]*** 继续不断地跳舞;错过,失去;跳掉(～ *one's chance away*(因跳舞)失去机会.～ *one's sense off* 跳得忘形). ～ ***on [upon] air [a rope]*** 被吊死. ～ ***oneself into*** *(a room; sb.'s favour)* 舞进(房间)里;舞得(某人宠爱). ～ ***to another tune*** 改变意见〔态度、行动等〕. ～ ***to sb.'s pipe [tune]*** 跟着某人笛子跳舞,唯某人马首是瞻. ～ ***upon nothing*** 被吊死. — *n.* ①跳舞,舞蹈. ②舞曲. ③舞会. *a social* ～ 交际舞. *a stage* ～ 舞台舞. ～*s and delight* 极愉快的跳舞 (= delightful ～). ～ *of joy* 〔美〕五月一日的野外土风舞. ***give a*** ～ 举行跳舞会. ***lead*** *(sb.)* ***a pretty [jolly]*** ～ 拖昏〔拖疲〕(某人). ***lead the*** ～ 领头跳;提倡.
danc·er [ˈdɑːnsə] *n.* 舞女; 舞蹈家. *a taxi* ～(舞厅里的)舞女. *merry* ～*s* 〔Scot.〕北极光.
danc·ery [ˈdɑːnsəri] *n.* 跳舞厅.
dan·cette [dɑːnˈset] *n.*【建】曲折饰(=chevron molding).
danc·ing [ˈdɑːnsiŋ] *n.* 跳舞,舞蹈(法). ～ *girl* 舞女. ～ *hall* 〔美〕舞厅. ～ *master [mistress]* 舞蹈教师〔女教师〕. ～ *party* 舞会. ～ *saloon* 〔英〕跳舞场. ～ *steps* 【建】(螺旋形)均衡梯级〔梯级的一端略窄于另一端,也称为 balanced steps〕.
dan·de·li·on [ˈdændilaiən] *n.* 【植】蒲公英.
D and D, D & D=〔美俚〕① drunk and disorderly (警察用语)醉酒后扰乱治安的. ② deaf and dumb 又聋又哑的;〔喻〕装聋作哑的(尤指因为怕报复而对坏事不加告发).
dan·der [ˈdændə] *n.* ①头垢,头皮屑. ②〔口〕怒气. *get one's* ～ *up* 发怒.
dan·di·a·cal [dænˈdaiəkəl] *a.* 纨袴子弟 (dandy)似的,打扮漂亮的. *a* ～ *pose* 吊儿郎当的样子.
Dan·die Din·mont (terrier) [ˈdændi ˈdinmɔnt] 矮鬃犬〔脚短身长的垂耳小犬, Dandie Dinmont 系 Scott 的小说中的人物,他养了两只这种小犬,故名〕.
dan·di·fy [ˈdændifai] *vt.* 使象花花公子;使打扮得花哨〔时髦〕. *dandified ways* 纨袴子弟的行为.
dan·dle [ˈdændl] *vt.* ①(上下颠动着) 舞弄 (孩子). ②宠爱,娇养.
dan·driff, dan·druff [ˈdændrif, -drəf] *n.* 头垢,头皮屑. **-y** *a.* 头垢多的.
dan·dy[1] [ˈdændi] *n.* ①纨袴子弟,花花公子,服装时髦的人. ②〔口〕最好的东西,上品. ③【英海】(船尾装有一桅的)快艇. *a* ～ *of a boy* 〔美口〕漂亮的少年. — *a.* ①时髦的,服装华丽的. ②花花公子的. ③〔美口〕最好的,第一流的. ～ **brush** 鲸须马刷. ～ **cart**〔英〕(送奶人用的)弹簧货车. ～ **fever** 【医】登草热 (=dengue). ～ **roll** 造币业中做水印的滚筒.
dan·dy[2] [ˈdændi] *n.* = ～ fever.
dan·dy·ish [ˈdændiʃ] *a.* 花花公子似的,时髦的.
dan·dy·ism [ˈdændiizəm] *n.* ①华丽,时髦. ②花花公子的派头〔行为〕.
Dane[1] [dein] *n.* 戴恩〔姓氏〕.
Dane[2] [dein] *n.* 丹麦人. *the* ～ 丹麦民族. *a Great* ～ 丹麦种大狗.
Dane·geld [ˈdeinˌgeld] *n.* 抗丹税〔盎格鲁-萨克逊时代为反丹麦入侵而征收的一种税,后作为土地税沿袭征收〕.
dang [dæŋ] *v., n.* 〔俚〕= damn.
dan·ger [ˈdeindʒə] *n.* ①危险. ②危险物,威胁. ③〔废〕权力,势力范围. *The signal is at* ～.【铁路】(前面)有危险信号. *a* ～ *to peace* 对和平的威胁. *You stand within his* ～*, do you not?* 你的生命捏在他手里呀. ***be in*** ～ ***of*** 有…危险. ***in*** ～ 在危险中,垂危. ***run the*** ～ ***of*** 冒…的危险. ***out of*** ～ 脱离危险. ～ **money** 从事危险工作的额外报酬,风险补贴. ～ **signal** 危险信号. ～ **space** (子弹)危险界;(高射炮的)爆炸圈. ～ **zone** 危险地带〔区域〕.
dan·ger·ous [ˈdeindʒrəs] *a.* 危险的. *a most* ～ *dog* 恶狗. *look* ～ 表现凶狠(不可接近). **-ly** *ad.* 危险. **-ness** *n.*
dan·gle [ˈdæŋgl] *vi.* ①(晃来晃去地)吊着;悬挂着. ②尾随,追逐(女人) *(about; after; round).* — *vt.* 使(晃来晃去地)吊着;吊着晃来晃去地引诱. *He* ～*d a bone in front of the dog.* 他晃动骨头逗狗. **dangling participle** 【语】垂悬分词〔如 After marrying him, her trouble began 中的 marrying〕.
dan·gler [ˈdæŋglə] *n.* ①吊着晃来晃去的东西. ②追逐女人的男人.
Dan·iel [ˈdænjəl] *n.* ①丹尼尔〔姓氏,男子名〕. ②(旧约圣经)《但以理书》. ③有名法官.
da·ni·o [ˈdæniˌəu] *n. (pl.* ～*s)* 鲤科鱼.
Dan·ish [ˈdeiniʃ] *a.* 丹麦的;丹麦人的;丹麦语的. — *n.* 丹麦语.
Dan·ite [ˈdænait] *a.* 达恩希伯来族的. — *n.* ①达恩希伯来族人. ②达恩分子〔摩门教的秘密组织的成员〕.
dank [dæŋk] *a.* ①潮湿的. ②(杂草等)繁茂的. — *n.* ①潮湿. ②沼泽地,低湿地.
danse du ventre [dɑːns djuː ˈvɑːntrə] 〔F.〕肚皮舞.
danse ma·ca·bre [dɑːns məˈkɑːbr] 〔F.〕死的舞蹈;死亡的象征(尤指中世纪绘画中出现的象征死亡的骷髅带领人们走向坟墓的舞蹈).
dan·seur [dɑːŋˈsəːr] *n.* 芭蕾舞男演员. ～ *noble* 芭蕾舞男演员.
dan·seuse [dɑːnˈsəːz] *n. (pl.* ～*s [-səːz])* 〔F.〕芭蕾舞女演员.
Dan·te [ˈdænti], **Alighieri** 但丁〔1265—1321,意大利诗人,《神曲》*(Divine Comedy)* 作者〕.
Dan·te·an [dænˈtiːən] *n.* 但丁研究者;以但丁作模范的人,崇拜但丁的人. — *a.* 但丁的;但丁式的.
Dan·tesque [dænˈtesk] *a.* 但丁式的.
Dan·ube [ˈdænjuːb] *n.* 多瑙河〔欧洲〕.
Danu·bi·an [dænˈjuːbiən] *a.* 多瑙河的.
Dan·zig [ˈdæntsig] *n.* 但泽〔波兰港口,波兰语叫 Gdansk〕.
dap [dæp] *vi.* ***(dapped; dap·ping)*** ①将钓饵轻轻放在水面上钓鱼;垂钓. ②(球)弹跳;(石片在水面上)漂掠. ③(鸟)轻捷地潜入(水中). ④(在木材上)切出槽口. — *n.* ①(球的)弹跳. ②(木材衔接处的)槽口.
Daph·ne [ˈdæfni] *n.* ①达夫妮〔女子名〕. ②【希神】为躲避 Apollo 的追逐而变作月桂树的女神. ③〔d-〕【植】瑞香.
dap·per [ˈdæpə] *a.* ①短小精悍的,小巧玲珑的. ②整

洁的．*be ~ in dress* 衣冠楚楚．*be ~ in appearance* 风度翩翩．
dap•per•ling [ˈdæpəliŋ] *n.* 短小精悍的人．
dap•ple [ˈdæpl] *n.* ①斑纹．②花斑马(等)．— *a.* 有斑纹的，花斑的．— *vt., vi.* (使)起斑纹．*a ~d deer* 梅花鹿．*a ~d shade* 斑斑点点的树荫．**~-gray** 〔英〕**~-grey** *a., n.* 有灰黑花斑的(马)．
D.A.R. = Daughters of the American Revolution 美国革命女儿会．
darb [dɑːb] *n.* 〔美俚〕出众的人；高级的东西．
dar•by [ˈdɑːbi] *n.* ①(瓦工用的)双耳抹子．②〔俚〕钱．③〔*pl.*〕〔俚〕手铐．
Dar•by and Joan [ˈdɑːbi ənd ˈdʒəun] 白头偕老的夫妇．
Dard [dɑːd] *n.* 达尔德语族〔阿富汗东北部、巴基斯坦西部和克什米尔居民讲的印欧语〕(=Dardle).
Dar•da•nelles [dɑːdəˈnelz] *n.* 达达尼尔海峡．
dare [dɛə] *vi.* **(~d** [dɛəd], 〔古〕 ***durst*** [dəːst]; **~d),** *v. aux.* 〔在陈述句中，用作主要动词，接带 to 的不定式；在疑问、否定、条件句中，用作助动词，其后接不带 to 的不定式．〕①敢，胆敢．*He ~ not fight.* 他不敢打．*D- he do it?* 他敢做那件事吗？*He won't ~ (to) deny it.* 他未必敢否认那件事．*He ~s to insult me.* 他竟敢侮辱我．*Don't you ~ to touch me.* 你敢碰我？！ — *vt.* ①冒险；敢于承担．②挑逗〔激〕(某人做某事) *~ all dangers* 冒种种危险．*I ~ damnation.* 我不怕刀山火海．*He ~d me to jump.* 他挑唆我跳．*I will do it if I am ~d to.* 如果有人激我，我一定做．***I ~ say*** ①我想，我看(大概) (*I ~ say you are mistaken.* 我认为你错了)．***I~ swear*** 我确信，一定．— *n.* 〔口〕①胆量，勇气．②挑逗．
dare•dev•il [ˈdɛəˌdevl] *a., n.* 胆大的(人)，冒失的；冒失鬼．**-il•try,** 〔英〕**-il•ry** *n.* 鲁莽，冒失．
Dar el Bei•da [ˈdɑːr el baiˈdɑː] 达尔贝达〔即 Casablanca 卡萨布兰卡〕〔摩洛哥港市〕．
daren't [dɛənt] = dare not.
dare•say [ˈdɛəsei] *v.* = dare say.
Dar es Sa•laam [ˈdɑːr es səˈlɑːm] 达累斯萨拉姆〔坦桑尼亚首都〕．
dar•ing [ˈdɛəriŋ] *a.* ①胆大的，勇敢的．②意气风发的．*Never before have they been so inspired, and so ~ as at present.* 从来也没有看见他们象现在这样精神振奋，意气风发．— *n.* 大胆，勇敢．**-ly** *ad.* **-ness** *n.*
Da•ri•us [dəˈraiəs] *n.* **Hystaspis** 大流士一世 (558？—486 B.C.)，古代波斯王，在位期间 521—486 B.C.，世称 ~ the Great.
Dar•jee•ling [dɑːˈdʒiːliŋ] *n.* (印度)大吉岭茶．
dark [dɑːk] *a.* ①暗，暗黑的；微暗的，阴沉的．②浅黑的，(皮肤)带黑色的；深，浓(色)．③秘密的，隐密的．④难解的，(句法等)含糊的．⑤阴郁的；希望暗淡的．⑥愚昧的，蒙昧无知的．⑦狠毒的，(计划等)阴险的．⑧郁郁不乐的．⑨(戏院等)已熄灯关门的．⑩【语音】浊．⑪(咖啡)搀了少量牛奶〔奶油〕的．*look on the ~ side of things* 看事物的黑暗面，悲观．*keep a thing ~* 保守某事的秘密．*in a ~ temper [humour]* 不高兴．***keep ~*** 隐瞒；隐藏．— *n.* ①暗黑；暗处；暗色．②愚昧，无知．③隐晦，隐秘．④夜，傍晚．⑤〔美〕阴影；浓(淡)．***at ~*** 黄昏时候．***in the ~*** ①在暗处．②秘密，暗中 (*plot in the ~* 暗中策划)．③不知 (*be in the ~ about it* 完全不知道那个．*leave one in the ~* 不给某人知道)．**~-adapt** *vt.* 使(瞳孔)适应黑暗．**~ ages** (中世纪的)黑暗时代．**~ blue** 深蓝色．**~ comey** 黑色幽默，黑色喜剧 (*cf.* black 条)．**~ day** ①密云〔浓雾〕笼罩下的日子；不吉利的日子，倒霉时候．②〔*pl.*〕失意时代，不得意的时候；(冬季)夜长昼短的日子．**~ deeds** 坏事．**~ horse**【赛马】实力未明的马；(竞赛等的)预想不到的劲敌；'黑马'．**~ lantern** 有遮光装置的提灯．**~ lantern caucus** 〔美〕秘密会议．**~ l** 浊音 l〔辅音前或语尾的 l: silk., tall. 元音前的 l 叫清音 l: look, clear〕．**~ light** 不可见光．**~ plan** 秘密计划．**~ room**【摄】暗室．**~ secret** 谁也不知道的秘密．
dark•en [ˈdɑːkən] *vt.* ①使暗，遮暗．②弄模糊．③使愁闷．④弄污．⑤弄瞎．— *vi.* ①变黑暗，阴．②变瞎．***~ counsel*** 使乱上加乱，使更加纠纷．***~ sb.'s door*** 访人 (*Don't ~ my door again.* 下次不要再到我家来了)．
dark•ey [ˈdɑːki] *n.* 〔蔑〕= darky.
dark•ish [ˈdɑːkiʃ] *a.* 微黑的；浅黑的；阴暗的．
dar•kle [ˈdɑːkl] *vi.* ①变黑；变暗；阴沉下来．②板起面孔．③躲进暗处．
dark•ling [ˈdɑːkliŋ] 〔古〕 *a.* ①在黑暗中的．②朦胧的．— *ad.* 在黑暗中．
dark•ly [ˈdɑːkli] *ad.* ①暗；黑．②朦胧，模糊．③秘密，暗中．④恶，毒．*seeing a ship but ~ against the horizon* 隐约看见天边一只船．*The storm clouds gathered ~.* 阴云密集．*glancing ~ at his opponent* 恶狠狠地看着敌人．
dark•ness [ˈdɑːknis] *n.* ①黑暗，阴暗．②秘密．③盲目．④蒙昧，无知．⑤黑心，阴险．⑥含糊．***the velvet ~*** 乌黑．*Egyptian ~* 漆黑．***cast sb. into the outer ~*** 赶走，解雇．***deeds of ~*** 坏事，罪恶．***the Prince of ~*** 魔王，恶魔．
dark•some [ˈdɑːksəm] *a.* ①〔诗〕微暗的；带黑色的，阴暗的，阴郁的．②〔古〕晦涩难解的．
dark•y, darkie [ˈdɑːki] *n.* 〔美蔑〕黑人．
dar•ling [ˈdɑːliŋ] *n.* ①爱人，情人．②宠儿；宠物．*My ~!* 亲爱的〔夫妻间的称呼〕；宝宝〔父母对儿女的称呼〕．***the ~ of fortune*** 幸运儿．— *a.* 心爱的；中意的；宝贵的．
darn[1] [dɑːn] *vt., n.* ①缝补，补缀．②补丁．
darn[2] [dɑːn] *vt., n.* 〔主美〕= damn. *D- it!* 讨厌！*He could not see a ~ without his glasses.* 他不戴眼镜就什么也看不清楚了．
darned [dɑːnd] *a.* 〔美〕= damned.
dar•nel [ˈdɑːnl] *n.* 【植】毒麦．
darn•ing [ˈdɑːniŋ] *n.* 缝补；缝补物 **~ ball [egg]** (衬着缝补衣物用的)缝补球．**~ last** 缝补台．**~ needle** 缝补针；〔美方〕蜻蜓．
Darn•ley [ˈdɑːnli] *n.* 达恩利〔姓氏〕．
Dar•row [ˈdærəu] *n.* 达罗〔姓氏〕．
Dar(r)yl [ˈdæril] *n.* 达里尔〔男子名〕．
dar•shan [ˈdəːʃən, ˈdɑː-] *n.* (能见伟人一面而)有德；沾光，增禄；得福〔印度教徒的迷信〕．
dart [dɑːt] *n.* ①标枪，短矛；镳．②〔*pl.*〕掷标枪．③突进．④(虫的)螯，刺．⑤(缝纫)暗针，暗线；捏褶．⑥飞快的一瞥；飞快的移动．⑦突然的刺痛．— *vt., vi.* ①投掷(标枪等)；发射，放射．②急冲；突进．
darter [ˈdɑːtə] *n.* ①掷标枪的人；突进者．②【鸟】鹈类．③【鱼】飞鱼．
dar•tle [ˈdɑːtl] *vt., vi.* 连续发射；不断突进；不断伸缩．*an adder's dartling tongue* 蝰蛇的不断伸缩的舌头．
Dart•moor [ˈdɑːtmuə] *n.* ①(英国 Devon 州的)达特姆尔高原．②达特姆尔监狱．③达特姆尔羊(毛粗而长)．
Dart•mouth [ˈdɑːtməθ] *n.* ①(英国 Devonshire 的)达特茅斯港口．②达特茅斯皇家海军学校．
Dar•von [ˈdɑːvɔːn] 达而丰〔一种止痛药的商标〕．
Dar•win[1] [ˈdɑːwin] *n.* ①达尔文〔澳大利亚港市〕．
Dar•win[2] [ˈdɑːwin] *n.* ①达尔文〔姓氏，男子名〕．**Charles ~** 达尔文〔1809—1882，英国博物学家，进化论创始人〕．②月面第三象限的壁平原．
Dar•win•i•an [dɑːˈwiniən] *a.* 达尔文的．— *n.* 达尔文派(的人)．**~ Theory** 达尔文的进化论．
Dar•win•i•sm [ˈdɑːwinizəm] *n.* 达尔文主义，进化论．**-win•ist** *n.* 进化论者．
DASH = drone antisubmarine helicopter 无线电遥控

反潜艇攻击机.

dash [dæʃ] *vt.* ①猛冲,猛撞;猛掷. ②撞破,碰碎,打碎,掼碎. ③浇,洒,泼(水等);溅. ④乱涂. ⑤匆忙完成 *(down; off)*. ⑥(少量)搀,混和. ⑦使(计划等)失败;使失望. ⑧使沮丧,使狼狈. ⑨〔英〕= damn. ~ *a mirror to pieces* 把镜子摔得粉碎. ~ *water in [over] a person's face* 泼水到脸上. *D- it!* 可恶! 讨厌! *I'll be ~ed if* = I'll be damned if. — *vi.* ①猛冲,猛进. ②猛击. ③炫耀衣着. ~ ***against [upon]*** 与…碰撞,撞在…上. ~ ***down*** 猛掷,猛掼. ~ ***forward*** 突进,猛冲. ~ ***in*** 跳进. ~ ***off*** ①飞出;急忙离开. ②一气写成[写完](文章等). ~ ***out*** ①删去,涂掉. ②跳出,跑开. ~ ***to pieces*** 粉碎. ~ ***up*** 冲上前;跑来. — *n.* ①猛冲,猛进;冲锋,突击. ②碰撞. ③(浪、雨等)打击声. ④(少量的)搀和;少量的搀和物. ⑤锐气,闯劲. ⑥笔触,笔势. ⑦炫耀,虚饰;外观,门面. ⑧挫折,打击. ⑨【印】长划,破折号. ⑩(莫尔斯电码的)长划〔与 dot 相对〕. ⑪【体】短跑. ⑫ = ~board. *a ~ of brandy* 少许白兰地. *red with a ~ of purple* 有点发紫的红色. *a hundred-meter ~* 百米赛跑. *a swung ~* 代字号〔即 ~, 又叫 tilde〕. ***a ~ to one's hopes*** 希望落空. ***at a ~*** 一气,一举. ***cut a ~*** 大出风头;铺张门面,打扮漂亮. ***have both skill and ~*** 既有技巧,又有干劲. ***make a ~ for*** 向…猛冲. **~board** ①(马车的)遮泥板. ②【海】防波板. ③(墙的)遮雨板. ④(汽车的)仪表盘. ~ **light** 仪表板灯. ~ **plate**【机】缓冲板. **~pot** 缓冲器,减震器,阻尼延迟器.

da·sheen [ˌdæˈʃiːn] *n.*【植】芋头(= taro).

dash·er [ˈdæʃə] *n.* ①猛冲者. ②(奶油)搅拌器. ③〔美〕遮泥板;遮水板. ④〔口〕有干劲的人.

dash·ing [ˈdæʃiŋ] *a.* ①勇敢的,有锐气[干劲]的. ②浮华的,打扮漂亮的. **-ly** *ad.*

dash·y [ˈdæʃi] *a.* 外表好看的,浮华的;漂亮的,时髦的.

das·sie [ˈdɑːsiː] *n.* 蹄兔科动物.

das·tard [ˈdæstəd] *n.* 懦夫〔尤指干了坏事而不承当责任的人〕. — *a.* 怯懦的,畏缩的. **-ly** *a.* (*a dastardly act* 卑劣的行为).

das·yure [ˈdæsijuːə] *n.*【动】袋猫.

da·ta [ˈdeitə] *n.* ① 资料,材料〔此词系 datum 的复数,但 datum 罕用,一般即以 data 作为集合词,在口语中往往用单数动词;如系指一件资料,则说作 this ~〕. ②〔美〕(观察所得的)事实,知识. *a ~ book* 参考资料书. *gather ~ on* …收集…的资料[数据]. *The ~ is not enough to be convincing.* 资料不足,尚难令人信服. ~ **bank** 资料库,数据库. ~ **logging**【自】数据记录. ~ **phone**【讯】数据送话机. ~ **processing**【自】数据处理.

dat·a·ble [ˈdeitəbl] *a.* 可推定[测定]日期[年代]的.

da·tal·ler [ˈdeitələ] *n.* = daytal(l)er.

da·ta·ry [ˈdeitəri] *n.*【天主】①(罗马教庭)教庭官员资格与圣俸审查官署. ②掌管此官署的红衣主教.

datch·a [ˈdɑːtʃɑː] *n.* = dacha.

date¹ [deit] *n.* ①日期. ②时期;时代,年代. ③〔美口〕(和异性的)约会;〔美俚〕约会的对象. ④〔口〕同日;本日. *make a ~* 定一个(会面的)日期. *She is his ~.* 她跟他有约会. ***at an early ~*** 日内. ***bear ~*** …载有(某某)年月日. ***break [cut] the ~*** 不遵守约会. ***down to ~*** = to ~. ***of early ~*** 初期的,古代的. ***out of ~*** 过时的,陈腐的,旧式的. ***to ~*** 到今天,至今,到现在. ***under ~ (of) (Jan. 5)*** 于(一月五号). ***up to ~*** ①直到现在(的),直到最近(的). ②最新式的,时兴的. ***without ~*** 〔美〕无期. — *vt.* ①给…注明日期. ②断定(事物的)年代. ③〔美口〕和…约会. *a bill ~d the 7th of May* 五月七日期的支票. — *vi.* ①记有日子. ②起,始 *(from)*. ③进行约会. ~ ***back to*** 回溯至,(年代)远在. ~ **bait** 〔美俚〕勾引男子与自己约会的女子. ~ **book** (记载约会日期等的)记事册. ~ **line** ①【天】日界线〔东经或西经 180 度的子午线〕. ②=~line. **~line** ① *n.* 日期;〔口〕电讯电头. ② *vt.* 注明电讯发稿日期和地点,写上电讯电头. **~mark** 日戳. **-less** *a.* ①无日期的,年代不明的. ②太古的. ③〔美俚〕没有异性伴侣的. ④经住时间考验的. ⑤无限期的. ~ **slip** (图书馆)借书卡. ~ **stamp** 邮戳.

date² [deit] *n.* ①海枣属. ②海枣. *a Chinese ~* 枣,中国枣. ~ **palm** 枣椰树.

dat·er [ˈdeitə] *n.* 日期戳子.

dat·ing [ˈdeitiŋ] *n.* ①记日期. ②【商】(支付的)延期日期;③〔美〕幽会. ~ **machine [perforator]** 日期戳子. ~ **nail**【铁路】(钉在枕木上的)日期钉.

da·tive [ˈdeitiv] *n.*【语法】与格. — *a.* ①【语法】与格的. ②【法】(物品等)可随意赠与他人的;(官员等)可免职的.

da·to, dat·to [ˈdɑːtəu] *n.* *(pl. ~s)* (菲律宾)摩洛部族首长.

da·tum [ˈdeitəm] *n.* *(pl. da·ta* [ˈdeitə]) 〔L.〕①〔常 *pl.*〕数据,资料. ②论据,作为论据的事实. ③【数】已知数. ④【测】基点,基线,基面. ~ **level** 基准水平面. ~ **line** 基准线. ~ **mark**【测】基(准)点. ~ **plane**【测】基(准)面.

da·tu·ra [dəˈtjuərə] *n.*【植】蔓陀罗.

daub [dɔːb] *n.* ①涂抹. ②涂料. ③拙劣的画. — *vt., vi.* ①涂,涂抹 *(with)*. ②弄脏;乱涂(颜料). ③胡画(拙劣的画). ~ *a wall with mud* 用泥巴抹墙. *a poor picture carelessly ~ed over* 草率画成的蹩脚画.

daub·er [dɔːbə] *n.* ①涂抹者;涂抹工具. ②拙劣的画匠. ③泥水匠. ④〔美俚〕精神,勇气. *Just keep your ~ up and your mouth shut.* 打起精神,闭住嘴.

daub·ster [ˈdɔːbstə] *n.* 拙劣的画家.

daub·y [ˈdɔːbi] *a.* ①粘性的. ②潦草的,乱画的.

daugh·ter [ˈdɔːtə] *n.* ①女儿 (*opp.* son). ②(某地的)妇女. ③【生】子体,子代;④【原】子核;产物. ~ *of revolution* 革命女儿. ~ ***of Eve*** 女人. ~ ***of Momus*** 受嘲弄的人,滑稽的人. — *a.* ①女儿(般)的. ②【生】第一代的. ~ **cell** (经细胞分裂而新形成的)子细胞. ~ **element**【化】子元素. **~hood** ①女儿的身分;女儿时代. ②〔集合词〕女儿们. **~-in-law** *(pl. ~s-in-law* [ˈdɔːtəzinlɔː]) 儿媳妇;继女. **-ly** *a.* 女儿(似)的.

daunt [dɔːnt] *vt.* ①吓,恐吓;②使畏缩,使胆怯,使气馁. *No difficulties in the world can ~ us.* 世界上任何困难都吓不倒我们. *He was ~ed by the amount of work still to be done.* 他被那百废待举的形势弄得灰心丧气. **-less** *a* 不屈不挠的,大胆的,大无畏的.

dau·phin [ˈdɔːfin] *n.* 法国皇太子〔1349 年至 1830 年的称呼〕. **-e** [ˈdɔːfi(ː)n], **-ess** [-nis] *n.* 法国皇太子妃.

daut [dɔːt, dɔt] *vt.* 〔Scot.〕爱抚;宠爱.

Dav·en·port [ˈdævnpɔːt] *n.* 达文波特〔姓氏〕.

dav·en·port [ˈdævənpɔːt] *n.* ①〔英〕(有盖)书桌. ②〔美〕(坐卧两用)长沙发.

Da·vid [ˈdeivid] *n.* ①大卫〔《圣经》古以色列国王〕. ②戴维〔姓氏,男子名〕. ~ ***and Jonathan*** 同生共死的朋友.

Da·vid·son [ˈdeividsn] *n.* 戴维森〔姓氏〕.

Da vin·ci [də ˈvintʃi], ***Leonar·do*** 达芬奇〔1452—1519, 意大利的画家、雕刻家、建筑家、工程师〕.

Da·vis [ˈdeivis] *n.* 戴维斯〔姓氏,男子名〕. ~ **cup** 戴维斯杯〔美国人 D. F. Davis 捐献给国际网球比赛的银杯〕. ~ **tournament** 戴维斯杯锦标赛.

Da·vis·son [ˈdeivisn] *n.* 戴维森〔姓氏〕.

dav·it [ˈdævit] *n.* ①(轮船上的)吊艇柱,吊艇架. ②(放锚和起锚用的)吊柱,吊杆.

Da·vy [ˈdeivi] *n.* 戴维〔男子名, David 的昵称〕. ~ **Jones** 〔海俚〕海魔 *(go [be sent] to ~ Jones's locker* 淹死,葬身海底). ~ **lamp** (初期的)矿灯.

da·vy [ˈdeivi] *n.* 〔俚〕= affidavit. ***take one's ~*** 宣誓,发誓.

daw¹ [dɔː] *n.*【鸟】= jackdaw.

daw² [dɔː] *vi.* 〔Scot.〕破晓,黎明.

daw•dle [ˈdɔːdl] *vt., vi.* 混日子,偷懒,磨蹭. ～ *away one's time* 混日子. **-r** 游手好闲的人,懒人.

dawk [dɔːk] *n.* (政治、外交主张)介乎鸽派 (dove) 和鹰派(hawk)之间的中间派,非鹰非鸽派.

dawn [dɔːn] *n.* ①黎明,拂晓;曙光. ②开端,发端,端绪,萌芽. ③醒悟. *before the ～ of history* 有史以前. ***at ～*** 拂晓,天一亮. ***from ～ till dusk*** 从早到晚. — *vi.* ①破晓,东方发白,露曙光. ②开始出现,渐露端倪. ③渐渐明白,渐悟 *(on, upon)*. *It [Day, Morning] ～s.* 天亮了,东方发白了. *This fact has just ～ed upon me.* 这件事我现在才明白了. *～ing consciousness* 开始醒悟.

dawn•ing [dɔːniŋ] *n.* ①黎明,拂晓. ②东方. ③开端,端绪. ④曙光. *the ～ of a new era* 新时代的曙光.

Daw•son [ˈdɔːsn] *n.* 道森〔姓氏〕.

dawt [dɔːt, dɔt] *vt.* 爱抚;宠爱 (= daut).

Day [dei] *n.* 戴〔姓氏〕.

day [dei] *n.* ①日,一日. ②节日;规定的日期,约定的日子. ③昼,白昼,白天;日光. ④〔常 *pl.*〕时代;全盛时代. ⑤寿命,生平. ⑥(某日的)战斗;胜负,胜利. *May 1st International Labour D-* 五一国际劳动节. *the National D-* 国庆节. *in a ～ or two* 过一二日,一两天内. *a creature of a ～* 短命的生物. *before ～* 天亮前. *His ～ is done.* 他的得意时代已经过去了. *Every dog has his ～.* 每人一生中总有得意的日子. *The ～ is doubtful.* 胜负难料. *The ～ is ours!* 胜利是我们的. *How goes the ～?* 战况如何? ***all ～ (long)*** 终日,一天到晚. ***at that ～*** 那时候. ***better ～s*** 黄金时代 (*have seen better ～s* 曾过过好日子). ***between two ～s*** 通夜,终夜. ***by ～*** 白天,在白天. ***by the ～*** 计日,论日(工作等). ***(We will) call it a ～.*** 〔俚〕今天就这样算了,结束了. ***carry the ～*** 得胜;胜利完成. ***～ about*** 隔日. ***～ after ～ = ～ by ～*** 成天,天天,每天. ***～ and night*** 日日夜夜,昼夜. ***～ in (and) ～ out*** 日日夜夜,一天到头. ***～ of grace*** 到期票据的宽限日〔通常为缓期三天〕. ***～ of obligation*** 须停止工作去做礼拜的日子. ***～ to money*** 暂时的借款. ***during the ～*** = by ～. ***end one's ～s*** 死. ***every other ～*** 每隔一天. ***for ～s on end*** 接连数日. ***from ～ to ～*** 日日,日复一日,一天一天. ***from this ～ forth*** 从今天以后. ***give the time of ～*** 问候,致意. ***have one's ～*** 转运,走运,有得意的时候. ***if a ～*** 至少 (*He is fifty, if a ～.* = *He is fifty, if he is a ～ old.* 他至少五十岁). ***in a ～*** 一日,一朝一夕. ***in broad ～*** 在大白天. ***in ～s gone by*** = ***in ～s of old [yore]*** 在从前,已往. ***in ～s to come*** 将来,后世. ***in one's ～*** 年青时候;在旺盛的时候. ***in our ～s*** 如今,目下. ***in the ～s of old*** 从前,已往. ***in these ～s*** 如今,目下. ***in those ～s*** 当时,那时候. ***keep one's ～*** 守约. ***man of other ～s*** 古人. ***man of the ～*** 当代名人. ***name the ～*** (女子)决定(结婚等的)日期. ***night and ～*** 不分昼夜,始终. ***of the ～*** 当时的;现在的(问题等). ***one ～*** (过去或将来的)某一天. ***one of these (fine) ～s*** 日内,不日. ***one ～ before [after] the fair*** 过早[迟],太早[迟]. ***one's ～ has gone*** 大势已去. ***pass the time of ～*** 问候,致意. ***some ～*** 有一天,哪天. ***the ～ after tomorrow*** 后天. ***the ～ before yesterday*** 前天. ★上两条美语常省去 the. ***the ～ of ～s*** 重大的日子. ***The ～ will come when....*** 终归有一天将会…. ***the other ～*** 前几天. ***these ～s*** 现在,今天. ***this ～ week [year]*** 上星期[去年]的今日;下星期[明年]的今日. ***till this ～*** 到今天. ***to a ～*** 恰恰,正巧 (*It is now five years to a ～.* 正好五年). ***to this ～*** 直到今天. ***up to this ～*** 到今天. ***win [lose] the ～*** 打胜[败]. ***without ～*** 无期,不定期. **～bill** (戏剧等的)海报,广告招贴. **～ bed** 兼作沙发用卧铺. **～ blindness** 昼盲症. **～ boarder** 走读生. **～book** ①【商】日记帐,流水簿. ②【海】航海日记. **～break** 黎明,拂晓. **～-by-～** *a.* 每日的(*a ～-by-～ account* 每日汇报) **～ clock** 每日上一次的钟. **～ coach** 普通客车. **～dream** 幻想,空想. **～dreamer** 空想家. **～flower** 鸭跖草属. **～fly**【虫】蜉蝣. **～ hospital** 只看门诊的医院. **～ labo(u)r** 日工,零工. **～labo(u)rer** 做零工的工人. **～ letter** 〔美〕(比一般电报缓慢的)日间电报. **～long** *a.* 终日的,整天整日的;*(ad.)* 终日,一日到头. **～man** ①按日计工的人. ②做日班的人. **～ nursery** 日间托儿所. **～-off** 休息日. **～room** (学校等的)休息室;(军营等的)娱乐室. **～ school** 日校;走读学校. **～spring** ①〔诗〕黎明,拂晓. ②开端. **～star** ①晨星. ②〔诗〕太阳. **～tal(l)er** 按日雇用的短工. **～time** 日间,白天. **～-to-～** *a.* 日常的. **～work** *n.* ①白天的工作. ②按日或按小时计酬的工作.

Day•ak, Dyak [ˈdaiæk] *n.* ①达雅克人〔婆罗洲内地的本土人〕. ②达雅克语.

Day-Glo [ˈdeiˈgləu] "狄格洛"加色剂〔一种颜料,染料的加色剂的商标名〕. — *a.* "狄格洛"加色剂的;"狄格洛"加色剂状的.

day•light [ˈdeilait] *n.* ①日光;白昼,白天;清早,黎明. ②公开,发表. ③(竞赛中船与船间等的)间隔. ④〔*pl.*〕〔俚〕眼睛;视力;智力;活动力. ***at ～*** 黎明,拂晓,天一亮. ***beat [frighten, scare] the (living) ～s out of sb.*** 痛打,威吓. ***burn ～*** 白费精力,做无益的事. ***～ lamp*** 日光灯. ***～ saving*** 日光节约. ***～-saving time*** 夏季时间. ***in broad ～*** 在大白天,在光天化日之下. ***let ～ into*** 〔俚〕开孔;刺死. ***No ～!*** (主人对客人)斟满〔指酒与酒杯边缘之间没有间隔〕. ***see ～*** 〔俚〕①了解. ②有(完成、解决的)希望.

daze [deiz] *vt.* ①使眼花,耀眼. ②使迷乱,使茫然. — *n.* 迷乱,茫然.

daz•zle [ˈdæzl] *vt.* ①使眼花,耀眼,使眼花缭乱. ②使茫然. — *vi.* 闪,耀;晃眼. — *n.* ①眩惑;炫耀. ②使人眼花缭乱的事物. **～ lamps [lights]** (汽车的)强光前灯. **～ paint** (涂在船身上的)掩护色.

daz•zling [ˈdæzliŋ] *a.* 晃眼睛的,灿烂的. *a ～ advertisement* 五光十色的广告.

db.【物】= decibel(s) 分贝(电平、音强单位).

D.B. = double bottom 双层底; daybook 日记帐;〔美〕=disciplinary barracks 军人监狱.

D.B.H. = diameter breast high【林】树干直径.

dbt. = debit 借方.

DC, D.C. = ① direct current 直流电: *a DC generator* 直流发电机. ② District of Columbia 哥伦比亚特区〔美国首都华盛顿所在的行政区域〕: Washington, *D.C.* 美国首都华盛顿. ③〔It.〕*da capo* (=repeat from the beginning). ④ Deputy Consul 副领事. ⑤ District Court 〔美〕地方初审法院.

D.C.L., DCL = Doctor of Civil Law 民法学博士.

D.C.M. = ① Distinguished Conduct Medal 〔英〕(陆军)特等军功章. ② District Court-Martial 地方军事法庭.

DC of S = Deputy Chief of Staff 副参谋长.

D.D. = ① Doctor of Divinity 神学博士. ② double deck 双层甲板的.

d.d. = *dono dedit* 〔L.〕 作为礼物赠送.

D/D = demand(ed) draft 即期汇票.

D/D, D/d, d.d. = days after date 期后日数 (票据).

d/d = delivered 已交付,已交货.

d—d [diːd, dæmd] = damned 〔口〕该死的.

D-Day [ˈdiː-dei] *n.* ①(第二次世界大战中盟军在西欧发起反攻的)反攻日. ②(一般的) 攻击发起日. ③十进日〔英国将货币与度量衡改为十进制的日子〕.

DDD = dichloro-diphenyl-dichloroethane【化】二氯二苯二氯乙烷;滴滴滴〔一种杀虫剂〕.

D.D.S. = Doctor of Dental Surgery 〔美〕牙外科博士.

DDT = dichloro-diphenyl-trichloroethane【化】二氯二苯三氯乙烷;滴滴涕〔一种杀虫剂〕.

D

DE = destroyer escort 护航驱逐舰.

de[1] [diː] *prep.* 〔L.〕 = down from, from, off. ***de fac•to*** [-ˈfæktəu] 事实上(的). ***de fide*** [-ˈfaidi] 该作信条遵守的. ***de in•te•gro*** [-ˈintigrəu] 重行,另行,再. ***de jure*** [ˈdʒuəri] 根据权利的,(王等)正当的,权利上的,法律上的. ***de no•vo*** [-ˈnəuvəu] 从头, 再. ***de pro•fun•dis*** [ˈdiːprəuˈfʌndis] 从深处, 从心底上; 从(悲哀、绝望等的)深渊中发出来的叫声.

de[2] [də] *prep.* 〔F.〕 = of; from. ***de haut en bas*** [dəoːtɑ̃ba] 傲慢地,侮蔑地,不客气地. ***de luxe***[-ˈluks] 豪华的,上等的,特制的,精装(版本等) (*train de luxe* 花车). ***de nou•veau*** [F. də nuvo] 从新,另,再. ***de règle*** [F. də rɛgl] 习惯的; 适当的. ***de ri•gueur*** [riˈgəː; F. rigœːr] 不可缺少的, 礼仪上必要的. ***de trop*** [ˈtrəu; F. tro] 多余的,不受欢迎的,碍事的. ★①元音前的 de 常作 d': *coup d'état*. ②贵族出身者的名前常加用 de: *Guy de Maupassant; d'Alembert*.

de- *pref.* ①表示"离开","除去": *de*pilate, *de*rail. ②表示"向下": *de*press, *de*cline. ③表示"完全": *de*funct. ④表示"相反","解除": *de*frost, *de*code.

Dea. = Deacon.

dea•con [ˈdiːkən] *n.* ①【宗】(新教,长老会等的)执事; (英国教会,罗马教会的)副主祭,(希腊教会的)助祭. ②〔Scot.〕 工会会长. ③〔美〕初生小牛(皮). — *vt.* ①把(水果等)包装成全象一级品. ②搀混, 蒙混. ③屠宰幼畜. **-ess** *n.* 女执事; 慈善妇女会会员. **~hood, -ry, -ship** *n.* 执事的职位.

de•ac•ti•vate [diːˈæktiveit] *vt.* ①解散(军队),使复员; 使(军队)处于非战斗状态. ②使失去活力[作用]. ③取下(炮弹等的)雷管使成死弹. ④【化】使不活化, 去除活化.

dead [ded] *a.* ①死的; 无生命的, 无生物的. ②无感觉的. ③(炭等)已熄灭的; 无生气的,呆滞的,停顿的; 冷落的,不景气的; (土地)贫瘠的; 不生产的,(货物等)积压着的; (饮料)走了味的. ④静寂的,死一样的; 无声响的,发音钝浊的; 无光泽的,(色调等)阴沉沉的. ⑤已废的,不通行的,已成空文的. ⑥无凸凹的, 平滑的. ⑦完全的, 全然; 必然的, 确实的. ⑧〔美〕被矫正过来的, 改邪归正的. ⑨〔美口〕精疲力竭的. *Aren't you ~?* 你是不是太疲劳了? *She is ~.* 她死了. *~ sleep* 酣睡. *~ law* 已废的法律. *a ~ certainty* 绝对确实. *a ~ failure* 完全失败. ***be ~ and done for*** 死定了. ***be ~ to...*** 对…无感觉. ***be shot ~*** 被枪打死. ***be stone ~*** 死定,全无气息. ***come to a ~ stop [stand]*** 完全停止[停顿]下来. ***~ above the ears*** 〔美俚〕笨的,蠢的,傻的. ***~ act*** 【美剧】不受欢迎的一幕. ***~ and alive*** 〔口〕郁郁不乐,烦闷; 无聊,无趣味. ***~ and gone*** 死去. ***~ as a dodo*** 〔美俚〕已废的,老朽的,消灭了的. ***~ as mutton [as a doornail, as a herring, as a salmon]*** 死透,死定; 完蛋; 不活泼. ***~ to shame*** 无廉耻,不知耻. ***~ to the world*** 〔美俚〕对世事不闻不问; 熟睡; 烂醉. ***fall ~*** 死; (风)平息. ***in a ~ line*** 一直线. ***in ~ earnest*** 十分认真, 真心实意. ***more than half ~*** 快死的. ***on a ~ level*** 真正的水平. ***over sb.'s ~ body*** 不顾别人的激烈反对, 硬要. — *ad.* 全然, 完全, 十足. ***~ asleep*** 熟睡. ***~ straight*** 一直,对直. ***~ ahead*** 直接向前. ***be ~ against** (a plan)* 坚决反对(某项计划). ***be ~ sure*** 确信,包管. ***cut** (a person)* ~ 假装不认识(某人)似地走过. — *n.* ①死者. ②(死一样的)寂静. ③极寒时候. *Let the ~ bury their ~.* 既往不咎. ***at [in the] ~ of night*** 在深夜. ***in the ~ of winter*** 在隆冬. ***rise [raise] from the ~*** (使)复活. ***the quick and the ~*** 生者和死者. **~-alive, ~-and-alive** *a.* 郁郁不乐的,无精神的; 烦闷的; 单调的. **~ angle**【军】死角. **~ beat** *n.* 〔美俚〕无经济收入的人; 赖债不还的人; 游手好闲者. **~-beat** *a.* 〔俚〕精疲力尽的. **~beat** ①*a.* 非周期的; 差拍的; 不摆的. ②*n.* 不摆; 无差拍; 〔美俚〕赖账的人. **~ beer** 走了气的啤酒. **~ block**(货车等的)缓冲板. **~ calm**全然无风,极平静. **~ center**【机】(冲程的)死点; (车床的)死顶尖. **~-colour**底色. **~ description**缺乏生气的描写. **~ duck**〔美俚〕无价值的人[物],注定要失败的人. **~ end** ①(铁路等)终点; 尽头; 死胡同. ②僵局,绝境(*The discussion reached a ~ end.* 讨论陷入僵局). **~-end** *a.* 行不通的; 没出路的. **~eye** ① *n.* 神枪手; 三眼滑轮. ② *a.* 精确的. **~fall** ①陷阱. ②堆倒下的树木. ③〔美〕下等酒店,博场. **~ fingers** (冻)僵了的手指. **~ fire** 桅顶电光. **~ floor** 无反响的地板. **~ forms** 形式,虚礼. **~ freight** (包船位装货不满时应付的)空舱运费. **~-from-the-neck-up** 〔俚〕笨的,愚钝的. **~ ground** ①【军】(火力不能达到的)死角. ②【电】完全接地. **~ hand** ①永远管业. ②过去对现今的影响. **~head** ①*n.* 木浮标; 免票的人; 光吃饭不干事的人; 跑空趟的车子. ② *vt.* 优待某人免票看戏 [搭车]; 使火车放空车. ③ *vi.* 免票看戏 [搭车]; 放空车. **~ heat** 不分胜负的赛跑. **~ horse** ①预付的工资. ②旧债. ③无益的话题, 徒劳的事物. **~ hours** 深更半夜. **~house** 停尸所, 太平间. **~ language** 死语 [拉丁语等]. **~ leaves** 枯叶. **~ letter** ① (无法投递的) 死信. ②(法律上)已废的规定,空文. **~ lift** ①(不用滑车) 凭气力往上拉. ②〔古〕需全力以赴的难事. **~light** 【海】舷窗盖. **~line** ①(囚犯逾越即格杀勿论的)死线. ②截止时间. ③(新闻)原稿截止时间. **~ load** ①静荷重,自重; 底载. ②【电】固定负载. **~ loan** 呆帐,倒帐. **~lock** ①停顿,停滞. ②僵局. ③没有弹簧的锁 (*break the ~lock* 打开僵局. *come to a ~lock* 陷于僵局). **~locked** 【美体】实力相等的,得分相同的,不分胜负的. **~ matter** 无机物. **~ melting** 静熔. **~ men [marines]** 〔俚〕空酒瓶. **~ men's shoes** 死后遗留下的财产[地位]. **~ office** 丧礼,葬礼. **~pan** ① *n.* 没有表情的脸, 一点也不笑的丑角,毫无表情的喜剧演员. ② *a., ad.* 没有表情的(地),不带感情色彩的(地). **~ pigeon** 〔美俚〕注定要完蛋的人. **~ point** = ~ center. **~ pull** = ~ lift. **~ reckoning** 【海】(根据仪器推算而不是根据天文观察的)船位推测法. **~ river** 平静得好象没有流动的河流. **~ room** 静室,消声室. **D- Sea** 死海. **~ season** 停滞季节, 淡季. **~ set** ①猎犬指示猎物所在的不动姿势. ②(为得到某物而做的)坚决的努力. ③坚决的攻击[反对](*make a ~ set at sb.* 断然反对某人). **~ shot** 百发百中的人, 神枪手; 命中弹. **~ soil** 不毛之地. **~ soldier** 〔美俚〕空酒瓶. **~ spot**〔美〕无线电收音困难的地区. **~ stand** 完全的静止. **~ stick landing** 【美空】停止发动机降落. **~ stock** ①呆滞商品[资金]. ②农具,农业机械 (*opp.* livestock). **~ sure** 〔美〕 绝对可靠[确实]的. **~ surface** 无光泽的表面. **~ time** 停滞期. **~ wall** 无窗户的墙壁. **~ water** ①死水,静水. ②船驶过所成的旋涡. ③炮火达不到的水面. **~ weight** ①重负,重担. ②净重. ③【船】总载重量. ④【铁路】(车身的)自重. ④按重量收费的货物. **~weight ton** 长吨, 载重吨(= 2,240 磅). **~weight tonnage** (商船的) 载重容量. **~ wind** 逆风. **~wood** ①枯枝; 沉木. ②卖不掉的货, 陈货. ③没用的东西, 没用的人. ④〔美俚〕 优势 (*have [get] the ~wood on sb.* 占某人上风).

dead•en [ˈdedn] *vt.* ①缓和,使弱, 使钝; 使消失, 使(酒等)走味. ②使无声音; 使不发光; 使失知觉. —*vi.*死灭; 减弱,变钝; 变哑; 走味.

dead•en•ing [ˈdedəniŋ] *n.* ①隔音材料. ②去光泽的涂料.

dead•li•ness [ˈdedlinis] *n.* 致命伤.

dead•ly [ˈdedli] *a.* ①要命的, 致命的, (伤等)致死的. ②(脸色等)死人似的. ③极其有害的. ④不共戴天的(仇敌等). ⑤〔口〕非常的,极. ***be perfectly ~*** 〔口〕太厉害,真受不了. ***be insidious and ~*** 阴险毒辣. ***in ~ haste*** 飞快. ***the seven ~ sins*** 七项可遭天罚的大罪〔指骄、贪、欲、怒、馋、妒、懒〕. — *ad.* ①死了一样地. ②

〔口〕极,非常. ~ **nightshade**【植】颠茄 (= belladonna). ~ **sins**【宗】(应受天罚的)大罪. ~ **weapon** 凶器.

dead·ness [ˈdednis] *n.* ①死;死的状态. ②无生气,无感觉. ③(酒等的)走味.

de·aer·ate [diˈeiəreit] *vt.* 使除去空气;使除去气体;使除去氧气.

deaf [def] *a.* ①聋. ②不听的;不理的,装聋的. *be ~ to advice* 不听劝告. *~-and-dumb alphabet* (聋哑人用的)指语字母 (= manual alphabet). ***~ as an adder [a post, a door, a door-post]*** 全聋. ***None so ~ as those that won't hear.*** 最聋者莫过于不听劝说的人. ***the ~*** 聋子. ***turn a ~ ear to*** 充耳不闻,不听,完全不理. **-ness** *n.* 聋;不听.

deaf·en [ˈdefn] *vt.* ①使聋;使听不见. ②震聋. ③(用更大的声音)淹没(声音). ④【建】使(墙等)不漏音.

deaf·en·ing [ˈdefniŋ] *a.* 震耳欲聋的,吵聋耳朵的. — *n.* 防音[隔音]装置[材料].

deal[1] [diːl] ***(dealt*** [delt]***)*** *vt.* ①分派,分配 ***(out; round)***. ②分,发(牌). ③分给;授,赐,给与,使受(打击). *~ determined counter-blows to the interventionists* 给干涉者以坚决的回击. *~ a blow at sb.* 打人. —*vi.* ①做买卖,交易. ②处理;应付,对付. ③从事,参与. ④(和…)来往,交际,打交道. ⑤发牌. *~ honourably* 光明正大地行事. ***~ (fairly) by [with] sb.*** (秉公)待人,(秉公)发落某人. ***~ in*** 买卖(货物);办理;经营,参与. ***~ with*** 办理,处理;对待;与…交涉,与…交往;与…交易 (*He is hard to ~ with.* 他很难对付). — *n.* ①发牌(者);所发的牌;一圈,一场. ②〔口〕交易,买卖;〔美〕密约,(秘密)协定. ③〔美〕(尤指经济上的)政策. ***a raw ~***〔口〕不公平的待遇[处理]. ***a square [fair] ~***〔口〕公平待遇[处理]. ***a big ~***〔美口〕要人;重要的事. ***Big ~!*** 妙极了!〔假装赞叹的讽刺语〕. ***do a ~ with*** 与…交易;与…妥协,与…说合. ***Good ~!***〔美俚〕好极了! ***It's a good ~.***〔口〕我同意你提的条件. ***make a big ~ out of*** 对…极为重视;就…小题大做. ***the New D-***〔美〕(1933年罗斯福实行的)新政(策).

deal[2] [diːl] *n.* 量,数额;〔口〕大量. *a vast ~* 非常(多). ***a ~ = a great [good] ~*** 很多. ***by a great ~*** 远远 (*He is cleverer than you by a great ~.* 他远比你聪明).

deal[3] [diːl] *n.* (松等的)木板;木材,木料. —*a.* 松木的.

de·a·late [diːˈeileit] *a.*【动】脱翅的. **-la·tion** [-ˈleiʃən] *n.*

deal·er [ˈdiːlə] *n.* ①商人,…商. ②发牌人,庄家. ③以某种方式待人的人. *a ~ in grocery* 杂货商. *a wholesale [retail] ~* 批发[零售]商. *~ aids [helps]* 推销员;广告(等). *a fair [plain] ~* 行为正直的人. *a double-~* 表里不一的人.

deal·er·ship [ˈdiːləʃip] *n.* 商品经销特许权;商品特许经销商.

deal·ing [ˈdiːliŋ] *n.* ①待遇;处置. ②(对人的)行为,举动. ③〔*pl.*〕生意,交易;交际. ④纸牌的分发. *have ~s with* 和…有关系;和…有交往.

dealt [delt] deal[1] 的过去式及过去分词.

de·am·bu·la·to·ry [diːˈæmbjulətəri] *a., n.* = ambulatory.

de·am·i·nase [diːˈæmineis] *n.*【生化】脱氨基酶.

de·am·i·nate [diːˈæmineit] *vt.* 脱去氨基;去掉氨基. **-na·tion** [-ˈneiʃən] *n.*

de·am·i·nize [diːˈæminaiz] *vt.* = deaminate. **-za·tion** [-ˈzeiʃən] *n.*

Dean [diːn] *n.* 迪安〔姓氏,男子名〕.

dean[1] [diːn] *n.* ①【宗】副主教;地方主教. ②(大学的)院长,系主任;(美大学)辅导主任;(牛津大学的)学监. ③(一个团体中的)老前辈 (= doyen). *the ~ of the diplomatic corps* 外交团团长.

dean[2] [diːn] *n.*〔英〕(树林繁茂的)深谷.

Deane [diːn] *n.* 迪恩〔姓氏,男子名〕.

dean·er·y [ˈdiːnəri] *n.* 地方主教[院长、系主任、学监等]的职位[宅邸].

dear[1] [diə] *a.* ①亲爱的,心爱的,可爱的,敬爱的. ②贵重的,宝贵的 *(to)*. ③昂贵的,高价的. ④热切的. *D- Sir = My ~ Sir* 先生,老兄〔亲切的招呼用语,有时含有奚落之意,在一般书信中作抬头称呼用语〕. ★ D- Mr.… 在英国是形式上的称呼,在美国是亲爱的称呼. My D- Mr.… 在英国是亲爱的称呼,在美国是形式上的称呼. *one's ~est wish* 真诚的愿望. *a ~ year* 物价昂贵的年份. ★ dear 与 high, cheap 与 low 的不同用法: The price of this book is high [low]. = This book is dear [cheap]. ***for ~ life*** 拼命 (*run for ~ life* 拼命跑). ***hold (sb.) ~*** 重视,宠爱,觉得可爱. — *n.* 爱人;可爱的人[东西],宠物. *There's a ~.* (做得好)真是好孩子; = *That's a ~.* 好孩子. *What ~s they are!* 多可爱! *My ~ [~est]* 亲爱的,您,老兄. — *ad.* 贵. *sell ~* 贵卖. *That will cost him ~.* 他那样做会吃苦头的[要付出很大代价的]. — *int.* (表示惊愕、怜悯等)哎呀!啃! *D-, ~! = D- me! = Oh, ~!* 啃!哎呀!嗳呀妈呀!天哪! *Oh, ~, no!* 呀,没有什么;呀,不行! **D- John letter** 女子给男子的断情书.

dear[2] [diə] *a.*〔古〕严厉的,厉害的.

dear·ie [ˈdiəri] *n.* = deary.

dear·ly [ˈdiəli] *ad.* 深深地(爱等);昂贵. *a ~ bought victory* 付出巨大牺牲得到的胜利.

dear·ness [ˈdiənis] *n.* ①高价. ②贵重. ③亲爱. *~ allowance* 物价津贴.

dearth [dəːθ] *n.* ①缺乏. ②饥荒. *a ~ of food* 粮食缺乏. ***in time of ~*** 饥荒时候.

dear·y [ˈdiəri] *n.*〔口〕亲爱的,宝贝儿〔用作表示亲爱的称呼,有时也含有讽刺或幽默的意思〕.

dea·sil [ˈdiːzəl] *ad.* 顺时针方向地.

death [deθ] *n.* ①死,死亡. ②死状,死法;惨死;死因. ③褫夺公权. ④死刑. ⑤绝灭,消灭. ⑥谋杀;惨案. ⑦〔古〕瘟疫;黑死病 (=black ~). ⑧〔D-〕死神;杀气. *as pale as ~* 死人一样苍白. *die a hero's ~* 壮烈牺牲. *black ~* 黑死病. *civil ~* 褫夺公权. *the ~ of one's hope* 希望的破灭. *D- was in the air.* 杀气冲天. ***as sure as ~*** 必定,的确. ***be at ~'s door*** 将死. ***be ~ on***〔俚〕①善于,是…的能手. ②极爱. ③极恨,极反对. (*He's ~ on curves.* 他善于投转弯的球. *He is ~ on brandy.* 他极爱喝白兰地. *The publisher is ~ on sloppily typed manuscripts.* 出版商极反对打字不清的原稿). ***be in at the ~*** ①(猎狗)看到猎获物已死. ②看到事情的结果. ***be the ~ of***〔口〕成为…致死的原因,要了…的命;逼得…苦死;把人笑死〔指笑话〕. ***be worse than ~*** 坏极了. ***D-!*** 要死啦!糟糕!不得了啦! ***hang [hold] on like grim ~*** 死不放手. ***put to ~*** 处死刑,杀死(=〔古〕do to ~). ***to ~*** 到极点,已极,…死了 (*tired to ~* 疲倦死了. ***to the ~*** 至死,到底 (*fight to the ~* 战斗到底). ~ **adder** (澳洲)一种毒蛇. ~ **agony** 临终时痛苦. ~**bed** ①*n.* 死亡时的卧床;临终(时). ②*a.* 临终时做的 (*~ bed will* 遗嘱. *~ bed sonfession* 临时的坦白). ~ **bell** 丧钟. ~ **blow** 致命打击. ~ **certificate** 死亡证书. ~ **chair** 电椅. ~ **chamber** ①死了人的房间. ②(罪犯)行刑室. ~ **cup** 鬼笔鹅膏〔一种有毒的蘑菇〕. ~ **dust** 放射室. ~ **duty**【英法】遗产税. ~ **feud** 不共戴天之仇. ~ **house** 死囚行刑前的监房. ~ **knell** 丧钟. ~**penalty** 死刑. ~ **point**【生】死点. ~ **rate** 死亡率. ~ **rattle** 临终时痰声. ~ **ray** 死光. ~ **roll** 死亡表册. ~ **row** 死囚室. ~ **sand**【军】(含有放射能的)摧命沙. ~ **toll** 死亡人数. **D- Valley** 死谷〔美国 California 州东部不长树木的干燥盆地〕. ~ **warrant**【法】死刑执行令;致命的打击. ~**'s-head** [ˈdeθshed] (象征死的)骷髅;骷髅画,骷髅像. ~**'s-head moth**【虫】骷髅蛾. ~**trap** ①不安全的建筑物.

②死的陷阱. ~**watch** ①临终病人的看护; 守夜. ②死囚看守人. ③【虫】蛀木器的小甲虫.
death·ful [ˈdeθfəl] *a.* ①死一样的. ②致命的; 杀人的.
death·less [ˈdeθlis] *a.* 不死的,不朽的,永恒的,不灭的.
death·ly [ˈdeθli] *ad.* ①死一样地. ②非常, 十分. — *a.* 死一样的; 致死的,致命的;〔诗〕死的.
deb [deb] *n.* = debenture;〔口〕débutante.
de·ba·cle, *dé·bâ·cle* [deiˈbɑːkl] *n.* 〔F.〕①(冰河的)溃裂,解冻;(河水的)奔溢,泛滥. ②【地】山崩. ③溃散; 瓦解,崩溃,毁灭. ④突然地大混乱;(政府等)大崩溃.
de·bag [diːˈbæg] *vt.* 〔英口〕剥下裤子(取闹、惩罚).
de·bar [diˈbɑː] *vt.* 阻止, 防止, 禁止; 排除. ~ *(sb.)* ***from*** 使…不,阻止 (~ *a person from a place* 禁止某人进某处. ~ *a person from doing something* 禁止某人做某事). **-ment** *n.*
de·bark [diˈbɑːk] *vt., vi.* = disembark.
de·bar·ka·tion [ˌdiːbɑːˈkeiʃən] *n.* 上岸,登陆.
de·bar·rass [diːˈbærəs] *vt.* 解除疑难,使摆脱(累赘等).
de·base [diˈbeis] *vt.* 贬损(品格等),降低(品质);(使货币)贬值. ~ *the value of the dollar* 使美元贬值. ~ *oneself for money* 为金钱而卑躬屈膝. ~**ment** (品质的)降低,贬质; 贬值; 变坏,堕落.
de·based [diˈbeist] *a.* ①下贱的; 品质恶劣的. ②【徽】反形的.
de·bat·a·ble [diˈbeitəbl] *a.* ①可争辩的. ②成问题的. ③(土地)有争执的. *a* ~ *ground [land]* 争执不决的边境.
de·bate [diˈbeit] *n.* 讨论,争论,辩论. ***the ~s*** (议会的)讨论报告. ***hold ~ with oneself*** 独自考虑〔盘算〕. — *vt., vi.* ①辩论; 讨论. ②细想, 盘算. ③〔古〕争(胜负等),争执. ~ ***upon [on]*** *(a question)* 讨论(问题). ~ ***with oneself*** 盘算. ~ ***the victory*** 争取胜利. **-bating society** 讨论会, 辩论会.
de·bat·er [diːˈbeitə] *n.* 讨论者; 辩论者.
de·bauch [diˈbɔːtʃ] *vt.* 使堕落; 诱奸(妇女); 败坏,伤害(风俗),使(趣味)低下. — *vi.* 放荡,淫逸. — *n.* 放荡,淫逸,沉湎酒色; 暴饮暴食.
deb·au·chee [debɔːˈtʃiː,-ˈʃiː] *n.* 荡子.
de·bauch·er·y [diˈbɔːtʃəri] *n.* ①放荡. ②诱惑,诱奸. ③〔*pl.*〕大吃大喝的宴会.
de·ben·ture [diˈbentʃə] *n.* ①(公司)债券. ②(海关)退税凭单. ~ ***stock*** 〔英〕公司债券.
de·bil·i·tate [diˈbiliteit] *vt.* 使虚弱,使衰弱.
de·bil·i·ty [diˈbiliti] *n.* 虚弱,衰弱.
deb·it [ˈdebit] *n.* ①(帐簿的)借方. ②增入(栏) *(opp.* credit). ~ ***side*** 【会计】增入栏,借方. — *vt.* 把…记入增入栏. ~ *one with $ 100* = ~ *$ 100 against [to] sb.* 记入某人增入栏内 100 元.
de·blai [ˈdeiblei] *n.* 〔F.〕(筑城)壕沟掘出土.
deb·o·rair [ˌdebəˈnɛə] *a.* 〔古〕殷勤的; 温雅的; 快活的.
de·boost [diːˈbuːst] *vi.* (导弹、宇宙飞船等)减速.
Deb·o·ra(h) [ˈdebərə] *n.* 黛博拉〔女子名〕.
de·bouch [diˈbautʃ] *vi.* (河水等)流出; (军队)进入(开阔地). — *n.* = débouché. **-ment** 河口; 【军】前进(地点).
dé·bou·ché [ˌdeibuːˈʃei] *n.* 〔F.〕 ①【军】(通向开阔地的)进路; 出口. ②(商品的)销路.
De·bre·cen [ˈdebretsen] *n.* 德布勒森〔匈牙利城市〕.
dé·bride·ment [F. debridmã] *n.* 【医】(外科)清创术.
de·brief [diˈbriːf] *vt.* ①听取(飞行员、使者等的)报告执行任务情况; (飞行员等) 报告 (执行任务情况). ②指令(离职人员等) 保守机密. ~ *one's mission* 述职. — *vi.* (飞行员等)汇报执行任务情况. **-ing** *n.*
deb·ris [ˈdebriː, ˈdeib-] *n.* 〔*sing., pl.*〕①(破坏物的)碎片, 破片. ②【地】岩屑. ③(登山中遇到的崩落的)冰块堆.
dé·brouil·lard [F. debrujɑːr, -ard] *n., a.* 〔F.〕 机灵的(人),有办法的(人),足智多谋的(人).
Debs [debz] *n.* 德布斯〔姓氏〕.
debt [det] *n.* ①借款,欠款,债务,债. ②情义,恩,恩义. ③【宗】罪孽. *a floating* ~ 暂借款,短期负债. *a national* ~ 国债. *contract [incur] a* ~ 借债. ***be deep in*** ~ 一身是债. ***be in ~ (to)*** 借着…的钱,受着…的恩惠. ***be in sb.'s*** ~ 欠某人的债; 受某人恩惠. ***be out of*** ~ 不欠债. ~ ***of gratitude*** 恩情. ~ ***of honour*** 因打赌或赌博而欠下的债务. ~ ***of [to] nature*** 死 (*pay one's ~ to nature* 死,归土). ***fall in ~= get into ~ = run into ~. get out of ~*** 还债. ***keep out of ~*** 不借债. ***out of ~, out of danger*** 〔俚〕无债一身轻. ***pay off a ~*** 清欠. ***run into ~*** 借债,负债.
debt·ee [deˈtiː] *n.* 债权人.
debt·or [ˈdetə] *n.* ①债务人. ②借方. ③受恩人. ~ ***and creditor*** 借方和贷方.
de·bug [diːˈbʌg] *vt.* ***(-bugged; -bug·ging)*** ①驱除(某处的)害虫. ②排除(飞机等的)故障; (自动化装置中)移去(程序等中的)错误. ③【无】调整, 调谐. ④寻出并拆除…内的窃听器. ⑤(用电子仪器) 使 (窃听器) 失效.
de·bug·ger 拆除窃听器专家.
de·bunk [diːˈbʌŋk] *vt.* 〔美口〕①暴露,揭穿真面目. ②说…的坏话.
de·bunk·er [diːˈbʌŋkə] *n.* 〔美俚〕暴露者, 揭穿真面目者.
de·bus [diːˈbʌs] *vt., vi.* 上下公共汽车.
dé·but [ˈdeibuː] *n.* 〔F.〕 ①初次登台. ②初次参加社交活动. *make one's* ~ ①初次登台. ②初次参加社交活动.
dé·bu·tant [debju(ː)ˈtɑ̃ːŋ] *n.* *(fem.* ***-tante*** [-ˈtɑ̃ːnt]) 〔F.〕①初次登台的演员. ②初次参加社交活动的人.
Dec. = December.
dec. = deceased; decimeter; declaration; declension; declination; decrease.
dec(a)- *comb. f.* 表示"十": *decagon, decameter.*
dec·ad·al [ˈdekədəl] *a.* 十的; 十年间的.
dec·ade [ˈdekeid] *n.* ①十, 十个一组. ②十年, 十年间. ***for ~s on end*** 数十年如一日.
dec·a·dence, dec·a·den·cy [ˈdekədəns(i)] *n.* 衰退, 退步,堕落; (文学等的)颓废.
dec·a·dent [ˈdekədənt] *a.* ①堕落的; 颓废的. ②文艺颓废期的,颓废派的. ~ *wave* 【物】减幅波. — *n.* 颓废派艺术家〔文人〕.
de·caf·fein·ate [diːˈkæfəneit], **de·caf·fein·ize** [diːˈkæfinaiz] *vt.* 除去…中的咖啡因.
dec·a·gon [ˈdekəgən] *n.* 【数】十角形,十边形.
de·cag·o·nal [diˈkægənl] *a.* 十角形的.
dec·a·gram, dec·a·gramme [ˈdekəgræm] *n.* 十克.
dec·a·he·dral [dekəˈhedrəl] *a.* 【数】有十面的, 十面体的.
dec·a·he·dron [dekəˈhedrən] *n.* *(pl.* ~***s*** [-z], ***-dra*** [-drə]) 十面体.
de·cal [diˈkæl], **de·cal·co·ma·ni·a** [diˌkælkəˈmeinjə] *n.* ①移画印花法〔把绘在特殊纸上的图案移印到瓷器、玻璃等上的方法〕. ②移画印花法所用的图画〔图案〕.
de·cal·ci·fy [diːˈkælsifai] *vt.* 使(骨头)脱钙.
de·ca·les·cence [ˌdikəˈlesns] *n.* 钢条吸热. **-lescent** *a.*
dec·a·li·ter, dec·a·li·tre [ˈdekəˌliːtə] *n.* 十升.
dec·a·log(ue) [ˈdekəlɔg] *n.* 【宗】十诫 (= ten commandments).
De·cam·er·on [diˈkæmərən, deˈkæm-] *n.* ①《十日谈》〔意大利14世纪作家 Boccaccio 的名著〕. ②〔d-〕《十日谈》式的故事,语涉色情的故事.
Dec·a·mer·on·ic [diˌkæmərˈɔnik] *a.* (文学作品等)《十日谈》式的.
dec·a·me·ter, dec·a·me·tre [ˈdekəmiːtə] *n.* 十公尺.

dec·a·me·tric [ˌdekəˈmiːtrik] *a.* ①十公尺的. ②【无】波长为十公尺的,高频无线电波的.

de·camp [diˈkæmp] *vi.* ①撤营. ②逃走,逃亡. **-ment** *n.*

de·ca·nal [diˈkeinl] *a.* 副主教[院长、学监等](管辖)的.

dec·ane [ˈdekein] *n.*【化】癸烷.

de·cant [diˈkænt] *vt.* ①轻轻倒出(液体);滗. ②(把液体从一容器)移注(另一容器). ③卸(货),下(客). *to ~ passengers at an ideal site for lunch* 让乘客在理想的地点下车用餐.

de·can·ta·tion [ˌdiːkænˈteiʃən] *n.* ①移注. ②滗. ③【化】倾析.

de·cant·er [diˈkæntə] *n.* ①有玻璃塞子的圆酒瓶. ②滗析器.

de·cap·i·tate [diˈkæpiteit] *vt.* ①把…斩首. ②〔美俚〕(因政治原因而)解雇,免…的职.

de·cap·i·ta·tion [diˌkæpiˈteiʃən] *n.* ①斩首. ②解雇.

de·cap·i·ta·tor [diˈkæpiteitə] *n.* ①刽子手. ②解雇者.

dec·a·pod [ˈdekəpɔd] *a.* 有十足的,有十臂的. — *n.* ①【动】十足类〔蟹、虾等〕. ②【动】十腕类〔乌贼等〕.

de·car·bon·ate [diˈkɑːbəneit] *vt.* *(-at·ed; -at·ing)* 除去碳素,除碳.

de·car·bon·ize [diːˈkɑːbənaiz] *vt.*【化】使脱碳.

de·car·box·y·la·tion [ˌdikɑːˌbɔksiˈleiʃən] *n.* ①【化】脱羧基. ②【医】脱羧(作用). **-box·y·late** *vt., vi.*

dec·are [ˈdekeə] *n.* 十公亩.

dec·a·stere [ˈdekəstə] *n.* 十立方米 (= 10 m³).

dec·a·style [ˈdekəstail] *a.*【建】十柱式的. — *n.* 十柱式柱廊.

de·ca·sua·lize [diːˈkæʒjuəlaiz] *vt.* 使无临时工人.

dec·a·syl·lab·ic [ˌdekəsiˈlæbik] *n., a.* 十音节(的).

dec·a·syl·la·ble [ˈdekəsiləbl] *n.* 十音节的一行诗.

de·cath·lon [diˈkæθlɔn] *n.* 十项运动〔指百米、四百米、跳远、铅球、跳高、一百一十米跳栏、铁饼、撑杆跳、标枪、一千五百米,总分最高者为优胜者〕.

de·cau·ville [dəˈkɔːvil] *a.* 轻便铁路的. *~ railway* 轻便铁路.

de·cay [diˈkei] *vi.* ①朽,腐烂. ②衰减,衰退. ③凋谢,枯. — *vt.* 使朽坏;使衰退. — *n.* ①衰微,衰退. ②朽,腐烂. ③【无】衰变. *tooth ~* 蛀牙. ***be far gone in ~*** 衰弱过甚,凋落不堪. ***go to ~ = fall into ~*** 腐朽,凋谢,衰微.

de·cay·ed [diˈkeid] *a.* 已朽的,腐烂了的;衰退了的. *a ~ tooth* 龋齿,蛀牙.

decd. = deceased.

de·cease [diˈsiːs] *n., vi.* 死,死亡.

de·ceased [diˈsiːst] *a.* 已死的. *the ~ father* 先父. *the ~ wife* 亡妻. *the ~* 死者,已故者.

de·ce·dent [diˈsiːdənt] *n.*【美法】死者.

de·ceit [diˈsiːt] *n.* 欺骗,欺诈;诡计. *a man of ~* 奸诈的人.

de·ceit·ful [diˈsiːtful] *a.* 欺诈的,虚假的,骗人的;不诚实的. **-ly** *ad.*

de·ceiv·a·ble [diˈsiːvəbl] *a.* 容易受骗的.

de·ceive [diˈsiːv] *vt.* ①欺,瞒. ②使弄错,使失望. *~ oneself* 骗自己;误解,想错. *~ sb.'s hopes* 辜负某人的希望. — *vi.* 欺诈,欺骗.

de·ceiv·er [diˈsiːvə] *n.* 欺骗者.

de·cel·er·ate [diːˈseləreit] *vt., vi.* 降低速度.

de·cel·er·on [diˈselərɔn] *n.* (飞机的)减速副翼〔副翼和减速板的组合〕.

De·cem·ber [diˈsembə] *n.* 十二月.

De·cem·brist [diˈsembrist] *n.* (俄国)十二月党人.

de·cem·vir [diˈsemvə(ː)] *n.* *(pl. ~s; -vi·ri* [-virai]*)* ①(古罗马)十大执政官之一. ②十人团的一人.

de·cem·vi·rate [diˈsemvirit] *n.* 十大执政官的职位〔任期〕;十头政治.

de·cen·cy [ˈdiːsnsi] *n.* ①正派,庄重,端庄. ②〔*pl.*〕礼仪,礼节;面子. ③〔古〕合宜,适当. ④〔*pl.*〕过体面的生活所需要的东西. *public ~* 风俗. ***D- forbids.*** 君子自重不可小便(等). ***for ~'s sake*** 为了面子.

de·cen·na·ry [diˈsenəri] *n., a.* 十年间(的).

de·cen·ni·ad [diˈseniæd] *n.* 十年间.

de·cen·ni·al [diˈsenjəl] *a.* ①十年间的. ②每十年发生一次的. — *n.* 〔美〕十周年,十周年纪念. **-ly** *ad.*

de·cen·ni·um [diˈseniəm] *n.* *(pl. ~s, -ni·a* [-niə]*)* 十年间.

de·cent [ˈdiːsnt] *a.* ①正派的,庄重的. ②(服装等)相称的,合宜的. ③〔口〕象样的,相当好的,过得去的. ④〔学俚〕宽宏的,不严格的. ⑤〔口〕穿好了衣服的. *a very ~ fellow* 老好人. *live in ~ conditions* 生活相当好. *quite a ~ house* 很不错的一所住宅. *a ~ fortune* 相当多的财产. ***Are you ~?*** 〔口〕您穿好衣服了吗? ***get ~ marks*** (学生)得分相当多. **-ly** *ad.*

de·cen·tral·ize [diːˈsentrəlaiz] *vt.* ①分散(行政权). ②疏散(工厂、人口等). *a ~d state* 实施地方分权的国家. **-li·za·tion** [-laiˈzeiʃən] *n.*

de·cep·tion [diˈsepʃən] *n.* ①瞒骗,欺诈. ②受骗. ③骗局;骗人的东西.

de·cep·tive [diˈseptiv] *a.* 骗人的,靠不住的,虚伪的. *Appearances are ~.* 不可貌相. **-ly** *ad.* **-ness** *n.*

de·cern [diˈsəːn] *vt.* ①辨别,分辨. ②辨认;弄清. ③【苏格兰法】判决.

de·chris·tian·ize [diːˈkristjənaiz] *vt.* 使非基督教化.

deci- *pref.* 十分之一: *deci*gram.

dec·i·are [ˈdesieə] *n.* 十分之一公亩 (= 10 m²).

dec·i·bel [ˈdesibel] *n.*【物】分贝〔音量单位〕.

de·cid·a·ble [diˈsaidəbl] *a.* 可决定的,可判定的.

de·cide [diˈsaid] *vt.* ①决定,决心. ②使下决心,使决断;使解决. ③裁决,判决. — *vi.* ①决定,决心,选定. ②判决. *That ~s me.* 那使我下了决心. ***~ against*** 决心不…,决定不采取;决定反对;判决(某人)败诉. ***~ between*** 于…中抉择其一,判断. ***~ for [in favour of]*** 决定;判定(某人)胜诉. ***~ on [upon]*** *(a course of action)* 决心,决定(采取某种行动).

de·cid·ed [diˈsaidid] *a.* ①明白的,明确的,无疑的. ②决定的;断然的,果断的. *a ~ success* 明显的成功. **-ly** *ad.* **-ness** *n.*

de·cid·er [diˈsaidə] *n.* ①决定者. ②【体】决赛.

de·cid·u·a [diˈsidʒuːwə] *n.*【胚胎】蜕膜. **-u·al** *a.*

de·cid·u·ous [diˈsidjuəs] *a.* ①【动、植】(在某个生长期或季节)脱落的. ②每年落叶的. ③非永久的,暂时的. *~ teeth* 乳齿. *a ~ tree* 落叶树.

dec·i·gram, dec·i·gramme [ˈdesigræm] *n.* 分克 (= 1/10 克).

dec·ile [ˈdesil] *n.* (10 分中的)一分,一成.

dec·i·li·ter, dec·i·li·tre [ˈdesiˌliːtə] *n.* 分升 (= 1/10 升).

de·cil·lion [diˈsiljən] *n.* ①〔美、法〕1000 的 10 乘方〔在 1 后加 33 个零所得的数〕. ②〔英、德〕100 万的10 乘方〔在 1 后加 60 个零所得的数〕.

dec·i·mal [ˈdesiməl] *a.* 十数的,以十作基础的,十进的;小数的. *~ carry* 十进制进位. *~ classification* (图书等的)十进制分类(法)〔用三位数字表示图书的主要分类,用小数点后的数字表示次要分类〕. *~ coinage* 十进币制. *~ currency* 十进制通货,小通货. *~ fraction* 小数. *~ notation* 十进记数法. *~ numeration* 十进法. *a ~ point* 小数点. *the ~ system* 十进制;十进法. — *n.* ①小数. ②〔*pl.*〕十进算术. *a circulating [recurring, repeating] ~* 循环小数. *to three places of ~s* 到小数第三位.

dec·i·mal·ism [ˈdesiməlizəm] *n.* 十进法〔制〕.

dec·i·mal·i·za·tion [ˌdesiməlaiˈzeiʃən] *n.* 十进法化,采用十进制.

D

dec·i·mal·ize [ˈdesiməlaiz] *vt.* ①使成为十进制. ②使变为小数. ~ *the currency* 使货币成为十进制.
dec·i·mal·ly [ˈdesiməli] *ad.* ①用十进法. ②用小数, 用小数形式.
dec·i·mate [ˈdesimeit] *vt.* ①从十个…中抽一. ②抽杀[罚]…的十分之一人.③(传染病等)使死去多人.④【史】向…征收(十一税). *Famine ~d the population.* 饥饿使人口大批死亡. **-ma·tion** [-meiʃən] *n.*
dec·i·me·tre, dec·i·me·ter [ˈdesiˌmiːtə] *n.* 分米(=1/10 米).
de·ci·pher [diˈsaifə] *vt.* ①译解(密码等). ②解释(古代文学). ③辨认, 辨读(潦草字迹). — *n.* 密电(或密信)的译文.**-able** *a.* 译得出的, 辨认得出的. **-ment** *n.* ①译解,解释,辨认. ②译文.
de·ci·sion [diˈsiʒən] *n.* ①决定. ②判决. ③决议. ④决心;决断. ⑤【美拳】(根据分数而不是根据击倒对方做出的)裁判. *a man of ~* 有决断力的人, 果断的人. ***come to a ~*** 做出决定. ***~ by majority*** 取决于多数. ***give a ~ for [against]*** 判决对…有利[不利]. ***with ~*** 断然. ~ **table** (列出对付某问题各项可选择办法的)决策表.
de·ci·sive [diˈsaisiv] *a.* ①决定性的. ②决然的, 断然的;果断的;明确的. *a ~ battle* 决战. *a ~ evidence* 确证. ~ *measures* 断然的措施. ***be ~ of*** 对…具有决定性. **-ly** *ad.* **-ness** *n.*
dec·i·stere [ˈdesiˌstiə] *n.* 十分之一立方米.
de·civ·i·lize [diˈsivilaiz] *vt.* 使陷入野蛮状态. *the decivilizing effect of the wars* 战争的使人陷入野蛮状态的作用.
deck [dek] *n.* ①甲板,舱板;覆盖物. ②【建】平屋顶;桥面;【铁路】客车车顶. ③〔俚〕地面, 地. ④〔主美〕(纸牌的)一组.⑤(报纸的)副标题. ⑥〔美口〕装海洛因等毒品的袋子. ⑦录音座. ⑧(打了孔的)卡片组. *fly close to the ~* 低空飞行. *clear the ~s (for action)* (战舰)准备战斗[动作]. ~ *passenger* (没有船舱铺位的)甲板船客. ***hit the ~*** 〔俚〕①起床. ②倒在地上. ③准备行动. ***on ~*** ①到舱面上,在甲板上. ②准备好. ③(打棒球)依次等着, 下一个轮到. ***sweep the ~s*** (海浪) 漫过甲板. — *vt.* ①给(船)铺甲板. ②装饰, 修饰 *(with)*. *a double ~ed bridge* 铁路公路两用桥. ~ **beam**【建】上承梁. ~ **bridge** 上承桥,跨线桥. ~ **chair** 帆布睡椅. ~ **hand** 甲板水手, 普通水手. ~**house** 舱面船室. ~ **load** 放在甲板上的露天货物. ~ **log** (船上的) 守望记事簿. ~ **passage** 甲板舱位〔最廉价的舱位〕,统舱. ~ **plate** 铁甲板. ~**-tube** 上甲板水雷发射管. ~ **watchman** 停泊值班水手.
Decker [ˈdekə] *n.* 德克〔姓氏〕.
deck·er [ˈdekə] *n.* ①装饰者. ②〔口〕甲板水手; 甲板船客. ③有(多少)层的东西,有(多少)层甲板的船. ④(造纸用的)脱水机. *a two-~* 两层军舰. *a double-~* 双层公共汽车[电车].
deck·le [ˈdekl] *n.* ①(造纸用的模子四边的)稳纸框. ②毛边. ~ *edge* 纸的毛边.
de·claim [diˈkleim] *vt., vi.* ①巧辩, 雄辩. ②(口若悬河地)演说. ③朗诵,朗读. ④(用激动的语气)攻击. ~ ***against*** 抗议,攻击. **-er** *n.*
dec·la·ma·tion [ˌdekləˈmeiʃən] *n.* ①雄辩, 雄辩法. ②(口若悬河的)演说. ③朗读, 背诵. **-clam·a·to·ry** [-ˈklæmətəri] *a.* ①适于朗诵的. ②慷慨激昂的, 口若悬河的.
de·clar·a·ble [diˈklærəbl, -ˈkler-] *a.*可申报(交税)的,须报关纳税的.
de·cla·ra·tion [ˌdekləˈreiʃən] *n.* ①宣言, 布告; 公告, 声明. ②【法】(原告的)申诉; (证人的)陈述, 口供. ③(纳税品在海关的)申报. ④【牌】摊牌; 叫牌. *~ of intention* 【法】(外国人归化某国的)意志的表示. *~ of the poll* 选举结果公告. *~ of war* 宣战公告. ***the D- of Independence*** (美国) 独立宣言〔1776 年 7 月 4 日〕. ***the D- of Rights*** (1689 年规定英国宪法基本原则的) 民权宣言.
de·clar·a·tive, de·clar·a·to·ry [diˈklærətiv, -təri] *a.* ①宣言的, 布告的. ②呈诉的; 陈述的, 叙述的. *a ~ sentence* 【语法】陈述句.
de·clare [diˈklɛə] *vt.* ①声称 *(that)*; 声称[宣布]某人是; 宣布. ②公布; 发表; 披露. ③声明; 断言 *(that)*. ④【法】招,供述,陈述. ⑤申报(纳税品). ⑥【牌】摊牌; 宣布(某种牌)是王牌. *~ a state of emergency [peace]* 宣布紧急状态[和平]. *~ sb. winner* 宣布某人获胜. *Anything to ~?* 有东西要报税吗? — *vi.* 表明态度 *(for, against)*. ~ ***against*** 声明反对. ~ ***for [in favour of]*** 声明赞成. ~ ***off*** 宣布…作废[作罢],宣布退出,毁约. ~ ***oneself*** 发表意见,表明态度,宣布自己身分 *(They openly ~ themselves as atheists.* 他们公开宣布自己是无神论者).~ ***war on [upon]*** 对…宣战. ***…, I ~!*** 的确是…的. ***Well, I ~!*** 怪了!
de·clared [diˈklɛəd] *a.* 公开宣称的. *a ~ atheist* 自命的无神论者. *a ~ value* (进口货在海关纳税的)申报价格.
de·clar·ed·ly [diˈklɛəridli] *ad.* 公然.
de·class [diːˈklɑːs] *vt.* 使某人失去社会地位, 使某人降低社会地位.
dé·clas·sé [deiˈklæsei; Am. ˌdeiklɑːˈsei] *a.* *(fem.* ***-sée*** [-sei]) 〔F.〕 丧失了(社会)地位的。— *n.* 落伍者, 落魄者.
de·clas·si·fy [diˈklæsifai] *vt.* (文件报告等)不再作机密论,降低机密等级并公开化. **-fi·ca·tion** [ˈdiˌklæsifiˈkeiʃən] *n.*
de·clen·sion [diˈklenʃən] *n.* ①【语法】(名词、代词、形容词的)变格,词形变化. ②倾斜, 偏差. ③堕落; 衰微, 衰退. ④婉言谢绝. *the ~ of virtue* 道德败坏. *his ~ of the nomination* 婉言谢绝被提名. **-al** [-əl] *a.*
de·clin·a·ble [diˈklainəbl] *a.* 【语法】可以变化词尾的, 可以变格的.
dec·li·na·tion [ˌdekliˈneiʃən] *n.* ①下倾, 倾斜. ②衰微. ③谢绝, 拒绝. ④【天】赤纬. ⑤【物】偏角, 偏差, 磁偏角. **-al** *a.* 下倾的,偏差的;赤纬的.
dec·li·na·tor [ˈdeklineitə] *n.* 偏差仪; 测斜仪; 赤纬计.
de·cline [diˈklain] *vi.* ①下倾,下降; 跌落; 歪斜; (树枝等)下垂,(头)低下. ②衰落,衰老. ③堕落,退步; 落魄. ④接近终了; 近尾声. ⑤进行词形变化.⑥谢绝,拒绝. *The birth rate in our country has been declining for several years.* 我国人口的出生率几年来一直在下降. *Prices begin to ~.* 物价开始下降. *the rotten and declining system* 腐朽没落的制度. *She invited me to dinne but I ~d on account of urgent business.* 她请我吃饭,但我因有急事谢绝了. — *vt.* ①谢绝,拒绝. ②使下倾,使下降,使歪斜,使(头)低垂. ③【语法】变化(名词、代名词、形容词的)词尾. *She ~d her head in despair.* 他垂头丧气. *He never ~s to do what his mother asks him to do.* 母亲叫他做什么,他从来不拒绝. *~ an invitation* 谢绝邀请. ~ ***… with thanks*** 婉言谢绝. — *n.* ①倾斜. ②衰退, 减退. ③(物价的)下落. ④衰弱(病),(特指)肺病. ⑤斜坡,下坡. *in the ~ of his life* 在他的晚年. ***fall [go] into a ~*** 衰弱; 患肺病. ***on the ~*** 没落; 在低落中,在下坡路上; 在衰退中.
dec·li·nom·e·ter [ˌdekliˈnɔmitə] *n.* 偏角计,测斜仪.
de·cliv·i·tous [diˈklivitəs] *a.* 向下倾斜的,下坡的.
de·cliv·i·ty [diˈkliviti] *n.* ①倾斜, 下斜. ②倾斜面, 斜坡.
de·cli·vous [diˈklaivəs] *a.* 向下的,倾斜的,下坡的.
de·clutch [ˌdiːˈklʌtʃ] *vi.* 脱开(汽车上的)离合器. — *vt.* (脱开离合器)使停止运转.
de·co [ˈdekəu] *n.* 〔口〕 = decoration.
de·co·coon [ˈdiːkəˈkuːn] *vt.* (装配或使用前)除去(设

备等的)外包皮.
de·coct [diˈkɔkt] *vt.* 煎,熬,煮.
de·coc·tion [diˈkɔkʃən] *n.* ①煎,煮. ②煎汁;煎好的药;煮成的东西.
de·code [ˌdiːˈkəud] *vt.* 译码;解码;译出指令.
de·cod·er [diːˈkəudə] *n.* 译电员;译码机;解码器;判读器.
de·col·late [diˈkɔleit] *vt.* ①斩(首),杀(头). ②拆散(电子计算机的多层复印副本).
de·col·la·tion [ˌdiːkəˈleiʃən] *n.* ①斩首. ②【医】(难产胎儿的) 头截断术. ③(电子计算机多层复印副本的)拆散.
dé·col·le·tage [deiˌkɔliˈtaːʒ] 〔F.〕 *n.* ①袒胸露肩衣服的低领. ②袒胸露肩衣服.
dé·colle·té [deiˈkɔltei] *a.* 〔F.〕 袒胸露肩的;穿袒胸露肩衣服的. *a robe* ~ 露胸女人夜礼服.
de·col·o·ni·za·tion [diːˌkɔlənaiˈzeiʃən], **de·co·lo·ni·al·i·za·tion** [diːkəˌləuniəliˈzeiʃən] *n.* 非殖民主义化.
de·col·o·nize [diːˈkɔlənaiz] *vt.* 使非殖民主义化.
de·col·o(u)r [diːˈkʌlə] *vt.* 使脱色,漂白.
de·col·o(u)r·ant [diːˈkʌlərənt] *a.* 脱色的;漂白的. — *n.* 漂白剂,脱色剂.
de·col·o(u)r·a·tion [diːkʌləˈreiʃən] *n.* 脱色,退色;漂白.
de·col·o(u)r·ize [diˈkʌləraiz] *vt.* 使脱色,漂白. **-za·tion** [-ˈzeiʃən] *n.*
de·com·pen·sa·tion [diːˌkɔmpənˈseiʃən] *n.* 【医】(心脏)代偿失调;心力衰竭.
de·com·pose [ˌdiː-kəmˈpəuz] *vt., vi.* ①(使)分解,分析,(使)还原. ②(使)腐烂;衰变. ~*d dung* 腐熟厩肥. **-pos·able** *n.* 可分解[分析]的. ~**r** 【微】分解体.
de·com·po·site [ˌdiːˈkɔmpəzit] *a.* ①再混合的,与混合物混合的. ②【植】重复状的,数回复生的. — *n.* ①再混合物. ②二重合成语〔 newspaperman 等〕.
de·com·po·si·tion [ˌdiːkɔmpəˈziʃən] *n.* ①分解,分析,溶解,还原(作用). ②腐朽,解体.
de·com·pound [ˌdiː-kəmˈpaund] *vt.* ①再混合,使与混合物混合. ②分解. ③使腐败. ④【生化】多回分裂. ⑤【植】多回复出. — [diˈkɔmpaund] *a., n.* = decomposite.
de·com·press [ˌdiː-kəmˈpres] *vt.* 使减压,降压. **-or** *n.* 减压装置. **-pres·sion** *n.*
de·con·cen·trate [diˈkɔnsəntreit] *vt.* 使[权力]分散. **-tra·tion** [-ˈtreiʃən] *n.*
de·con·gest·ant [ˌdikənˈdʒestənt] *n.* 减充血剂.
de·con·se·crate [diːˈkɔnsikreit] *vt.* 把(教堂等)改供俗用.
de·con·tam·i·nate [ˈdiː-kənˈtæmineit] *vt.* ①纯化,净化,去污,弄清洁. ②清除毒气;消除(放射性)污染. ③对(文件等)作删密处理,删除(将公开发表的文件的)保密部分. **-na·tion** [-ˈneiʃən] *n.*
de·con·trol [ˌdiː-kənˈtrəul] *vt., n.* 解除管理[管制].
dé·cor [ˈdeikɔː] *n.* 〔F.〕①舞台装置,电影布景. ②装饰(品);布置.
dec·o·rate [ˈdekəreit] *vt.* ①修饰,装饰,布置. ②把(勋章)授给(某人). ~ *a house for May Day* 装饰房子过五一节. ~ *sb. with a medal* 授与某人勋章. ~**d architecture [style]** 盛饰[尖拱式]建筑.
dec·o·ra·tion [ˌdekəˈreiʃən] *n.* ①装饰,装璜. ②〔*pl.*〕装饰品. ③勋章. **D- Day** 〔美〕先烈纪念日〔在美国大多数州,将 5 月最后一个星期一定为法定纪念日,纪念在所有战争中阵亡的将士〕.
dec·o·ra·tive [ˈdekərətiv] *a.* 装饰的. ~ **art** 装饰美术. ~ **procelain** 彩瓷. **-ly** *ad.* **-ness** *n.*
dec·o·ra·tor [ˈdekəreitə] *n.* 室内装饰师[油漆匠等];【剧】制景人员. — *a.* 适于室内装饰的.
dec·o·rous [ˈdekərəs] *a.* 有礼貌的,端庄的,正派的,谦恭的. **-ly** *ad.* **-ness** *n.*
de·cor·ti·cate [diˈkɔːtikeit] *vt.* 使脱皮 [脱壳等]. ~*d rice* 脱壳大米.
de·co·rum [diˈkɔːrəm] *n.* ①礼貌;端庄,正派. ②〔*pl.*〕礼节,礼仪. *behave with* ~ 行为得体. *lose one's* ~ 失礼.
de·cou·page, dé·cou·page [ˌdeikuːˈpaːʒ] *n.* ①剪贴工艺. ②剪画,剪影.
de·coy [diˈkɔi] *n.* ①引诱物,囮子. ②诱捕鸟兽的场所,圈套. ③诱骗者,诱人入圈套的东西. ~ *bird* 囮子. ~ *duck* 做囮子的野鸭;囮子. *a police* ~ 警察的密探. — *vt.* 引诱. ~ *enemy troops into a place* 把敌军诱到某地.
de·crease [ˈdiːkriːs] *n.* ①减少,减小,减退. ②减少额,减小量. *a* ~ *in production* 生产减少. *Cases of this nature are on the* ~. 这类案件正在减少. — [diːˈkriːs] *vt., vi.* 减,减少;减退;(温度表等)下降. ~ *the number to …* 把数目减少到…. ~ *in size* 尺寸减小.
de·creas·ing·ly [diːˈkriːsiŋli] *ad.* 渐减地.
de·cree [diˈkriː] *n.* ①法令,命令,公告. ②天命,天意. ③【法】判决. ④(教会的)教令. ~ ***nisi*** [ˈnaisai] 【英法】离婚判决书〔六星期内无异议即生效〕. — *vt.* 颁布(法令);判决;(命运)注定. — *vi.* 发布命令.
dec·re·ment [ˈdekrimənt] *n.* ①消耗,递减,减缩. ②减少率,减缩量;减幅. ③【数】减缩率.
de·crem·e·ter [diˈkremitə] *n.* 【无】减缩量计,衰减计,减幅计.
de·crep·it [diˈkrepit] *a.* 衰老的,老弱的;老朽的. *a* ~ *stove* 破旧的火炉. *be* ~ *with old age* 年老体衰.
de·crep·i·tate [diˈkrepiteit] *vt.* 毕里剥落地烧 (盐等),烧爆. — *vi.* 烧得毕里剥落响,爆裂. **-ta·tion** [-ˈteiʃən] *n.*
de·crep·i·tude [diˈkrepitjuːd] *n.* 衰老,老朽.
de·cre·scen·do [ˈdiːkriˈʃendəu, ˈdei-] *a., ad.* 〔It.〕【乐】渐弱. — *n.* 渐弱音,渐弱音演唱的片段.
de·cres·cent [diˈkresnt] *a.* ①渐小的, 渐少的. ②下弦的(月).
de·cre·tal [diˈkriːtl] *a.* 法令的. — *n.* ①法令. ②罗马教皇的教令;〔*pl.*〕教令集.
de·cre·tive [diˈkriːtiv] *a.* 命令的,法令的.
dec·re·to·ry [ˈdekritəri] *a.* ①根据命令解决的. ②有法令性质的,有法令效力的.
de·cri·al [diˈkraiəl] *n.* 诽谤,诋毁.
de·crus·ta·tion [ˌdiːkrʌsˈteiʃən] *n.* 脱皮,脱壳.
de·cry [diˈkrai] *vt.* ①谴责. ②诋毁. ③大声反对. ④(公告钱币等的)贬值.
de·crypt [diˈkriːpt] *vt.* 解…的密码[暗号].
de·cub·i·tus [diˈkjuːbitəs] *n.* ①【医】褥疮 (= bedsore). ②卧姿,卧床.
de·cum·bence, de·cum·ben·cy [diˈkʌmbəns(i)] *n.* 俯伏,匍匐.
de·cum·bent [diˈkʌmbənt] *a.* ①爬卧地上的,俯伏性的. ②(植物的茎)匍匐地上而枝端向上的.
dec·u·ple [ˈdekjupl] *a.* ①十倍的. ②以十计的. — *n.* 十倍. — *vt.* 使成十倍,将…乘以十.
de·cu·ri·on [diˈkjuriən] *n.* 【罗马史】①十人长,什长. ②市或殖民地元老院的元老.
de·cur·rent [diˈkʌrənt] *a.* 【植】(叶)向下生长的,下延的.
de·curved [diˈkəːvd] *a.* 【动】下曲的,向下弯的. ~ bill 向下弯的鸟嘴.
dec·u·ry [ˈdekjuri] *n.* 【罗马史】①十人团体. ②(审判官的)十人小组.
de·cus·sate [diˈkʌseit] *vt., vi.* 交叉成×形,交叉成十字形,交错. — [-sit] *a.* 交叉着的,×形的;【植】交互对生的.

de·cus·sa·tion [ˌdiːkʌˈseiʃən] *n.* 十字交叉,×形交叉.
de·dal [ˈdiːdəl] *a.* = daedal.
de·da·li·an [diːˈdeiljən] *n.* = daedalian.
de·dans [dəˈdɑ̃ːŋ] *n.* 〔F.〕 ①网球场发球线背后的看台. ②〔the ~〕网球赛观众.
ded·i·cate [ˈdedikeit] *vt.* ①献给,奉献,供奉,献上 *(sth. to)*. ②〔用反身代词〕献身,委身 ③(把精力、时间等)专门用于某事 *(to)*. ④(在自己著作前)题献(给某人). *The ancient Greeks ~d many shrines to Aphrodite*. 古代希腊人为女神阿芙罗狄蒂造了许多神庙. ~ *a memorial* 献纪念品. ~ *one's life to* ... 毕生致力于. ~ *oneself to* 献身于,致力于. *Mornings were ~d to reading and afternoons to writing*. 早上一心读书,下午专事写作. *Dedicated to* ... 谨以本书献给….
ded·i·ca·tee [ˌdedikəˈtiː] *n.* 被题献者.
ded·i·ca·tion [ˌdediˈkeiʃən] *n.* ①奉献. ②忘我精神,献身. ③题献;题辞,献辞.
ded·i·ca·tor [ˈdedikeitə] *n.* 奉献者;题献者;献身者.
ded·i·ca·to·ry [ˈdedikətəri] *a.* 奉献的;题献的.
de·duce [diˈdjuːs] *vt.* ①推论,推断,演绎 *(from)*. ②追溯根源.
de·duc·i·ble [diˈdjuːsəbl] *a.* 可推断的.
de·duct [diˈdʌkt] *vt.* ①扣除,除去. ②(演绎地)推论. ~ *10% from the cost* 由费用中扣去一成.
de·duc·tion [diˈdʌkʃən] *n.* ①扣除,折扣. ②扣除额,折扣额. ③推论,推定;【逻】演绎法 *(opp.* induction).
de·duc·tive [diˈdʌktiv] *a.* 推论的,推断的;演绎的. ~ *method* 演绎法. ~ *reasoning* 演绎推理. **-ly** *ad.*
dee¹ [diː] *n.* D 字;(兜住马鞍的) D 字形铁环;D 形物.
dee², **deed** [diː(d)] *a.* = damned.
deed¹ [diːd] *n.* ①行为,行动;实行;事实. ②事迹,功绩. ③【法】证书,契约. *a title* ~ 地契. *a trust* ~ 财产信托证书〔常用以进行抵押〕. ~ ***of arms*** 战功. ***in ~ and not in name*** 有实有名,不是名义上而是实际上. ***in ~ as well as in name*** 有名有实. ***in name, but not in ~*** 有名无实. ***in word and (in) ~*** 言行俱…. ***in (very) ~*** 实际上,真的. — *vt.* 〔美〕立契转让(财产).
deed² [diːd] *ad.* 〔口〕 = indeed.
dee·jay [ˈdiːdʒei] *n.* = DJ.
deem [diːm] *vt., vi.* 〔古〕想,以为,认为;相信. *I ~ it proper to refuse*. 我想以拒绝为好. ~ *highly [meanly] of* 尊重[轻视].
de·em·pha·sis [diːˈemfəsis] *n.* ①降低重要性. ②不强调;去加重,减加重.
de·em·pha·size [diːˈemfəsaiz] *vt.* 降低…重要性,不再加以强调. **-em·pha·sis** *n.*
deem·ster [ˈdiːmstə] *n.* (英属 Man 岛的)法官.
deep [diːp] *a.* ①深的;深处的;…深的,有深度的. ②深远的;深奥的,奥妙的;深谋远虑的. ③深陷…中;埋头…中,热中于*(in.)* ④重大的,深刻的. ⑤(同情等)强烈的,痛切的,深厚的. ⑥心计深的,奸滑的. ⑦(颜色)浓厚的. ⑧(声音等)深沉的. *The lot is 100 feet ~*. 地基进深 100 英尺. *soldiers four rows ~* 排成四排的军队. ~ *breathing* 深呼吸. ~ *disgrace* 奇耻大辱. ~ *drinker* 酒量大的人. ~ *fat* 炼得火辣的油. ~ *gaming* 滥赌. ~ *gratitude* 重谢,铭感. ~ *oil* 深成油,埋藏很深的石油. ~ *one* 〔俚〕心计深的家伙,阴险的家伙. ~ *red* 深红. ~ *road* 泥泞的道路. ~ *sigh* 长叹. ~ *sleep* 熟睡. ~ *thinker* 哲学家. ~ ***in*** 沉湎(冥想等)中,埋头(书本等)中,专心致力于;深陷(债务等)中;深入…中 (~ *in debt* 遍身是债. ~ *in a subject* 造诣深). ***go off [go off at, go in at] the ~ end*** 〔美俚〕①跳入深水. ②冒险从事一项事业. ③发脾气,变兴奋. ***in ~ waters*** (因债务等)愁困不堪;潦倒困顿. — *n.* ①〔诗〕〔*the ~*〕海,大洋. ②〔常 *pl.*〕(海、河的)深度,深处,深渊. ③正当中. *wonders of the ~* 海的奇迹. *in the ~ of winter* 在隆冬. — *ad.* 深;迟. *drink ~* 狂饮. *talk ~ into the night* 谈到深夜. ***Still [smooth] water runs ~***. 水静河深;大智若愚,深谋者寡言. ***the ~ six*** ①〔美海军俚〕海葬. ②〔美俚〕完全拒绝 *(give his plans the ~ six* 完全拒绝他的计划). **~-browed** *a.* 眉宇间智慧焕发的. **~-chested** ①胸膛厚的. ②发自肺腑的. **~-drawn** *a.* (叹息、呼吸等)深长的. **~-dyed** *a.* ①染得浓艳的. ②深染恶习的,坏透的 (*a ~-dyed villain* 大坏蛋). **~-felt** *a.* 深深感觉到的,深刻的. **~freeze** ①*n.* 冷藏箱,电冷箱(= ~freezer); 冷藏; 停止活动. ② *vt.* 冷藏,冷冻. **~freezer** 电冷箱. **~-going** *a.* 深入的,深刻的. **~laid** *a.* 秘密策划的,深谋远虑的. **~-mouth·ed** *a.* 声音沉重、洪大的 (猎犬). **~-read** *a.* 深通的,精通的. **~rooted** *a.* 根深蒂固的. **~-sea** *a.* 深海的(*~-sea fishing* 远洋渔业). **~-seated** *a.* 根深蒂固的,由来已久的,顽固的(*~-seated disease* 老毛病,慢性病). **~set** *a.* (眼睛等)深陷的. ~ **space** (太阳系以外的)深太空,远太空. ~ **structure** (转换生成语法所讲的)深层结构. **~water** *a.* 深水的,深海的;靠近海洋的.
deep·en [ˈdiːpən] *vt.* 加深;加重;加浓;使(音调等)深沉. — *vi.* 变深;变深沉;变浓.
dee·pie [ˈdiːpi] *n.* 〔口〕立体电影.
deep·ly [ˈdiːpli] *ad.* ①深深地. ②深刻地. ③(颜色)浓,深. ④(声音)低沉. ⑤巧妙. ***be ~ versed in*** 精通,深通. ~ ***committed*** 深陷(某事中)无法自拔. ***feel ~ for*** 痛感.
deer [diə] *n.* 〔*sing., pl.*〕鹿. *a river ~* 獐. *small ~* 〔集合词〕无足轻重的动物[东西]. ~ *forest* 猎鹿的旷地. ~ *lick* (鹿常去舐食的)含盐的泉水或湿地. ~ *mouse* 鼷鼠. ~ *neck* 鹿颈〔指瘦长的马颈说〕. ~ *park* 猎鹿场. ~ *shot* 猎鹿用的子弹. ***run like a ~*** 飞跑. ***stalk ~*** (偷偷逼近)猎鹿. **~hound** 猎鹿的狗. **~lick** 含盐的泉水[沼泽地](鹿常去舐食盐分,故名). ~ **neck** 鹿颈(指瘦长的马颈). **~skin** 鹿皮. **~stalker** 猎鹿的人;旧式猎帽.
de·es·ca·late [diːˈeskəleit] *vi., vt.* 逐步降(级);缩小(冲突范围),降低(战争等的)等级. **-la·tion** [-ˈleiʃən] *n.*
def. = defective; defendant; defense; deferred; defined; definite; definition.
de·face [diˈfeis] *vt.* ①损伤…的外观. ②涂销,盖销(邮票等). ③毁伤,磨灭(碑文等). ~ *a wall by writing on it* 墙上题字有损观瞻. **-ment** *n.* 毁损,磨灭;涂销.
de·fal·cate [ˈdiːfælkeit] *vi.* 挪用[盗用、侵吞]公款,亏空.
de·fal·ca·tion [ˌdiːfælˈkeiʃən] *n.* ①盗用公款. ②亏空额.
de·fal·ca·tor [ˈdiːfælkeitə] *n.* 盗用公款者.
def·a·ma·tion [ˌdefəˈmeiʃən] *n.* 毁谤. ~ *of character* 毁谤人格.
de·fam·a·to·ry [diˈfæmətəri] *a.* 毁谤的. ~ **writer** 以中伤别人为能事的作者.
de·fame [diˈfeim] *vt.* 毁谤,中伤,破坏…的名誉;丑化.
de·fat [ˈdiːˈfæt]***(de·fatted; de·fatt·ing)****vt.* 使脱去脂肪.
de·fault [diˈfɔːlt] *n.* ①不履行; 违约; 拖欠. ②【法】不履行债务;缺席. ③欠缺,缺乏. *judgment by ~* 缺席裁判. *make ~* 缺席. *suffer a ~* 受缺席裁判. ***be in ~*** 不履行(契约). ***in ~ of*** 因无…,若缺少…时,若没有…时*(He was silent in ~ of any excuse*. 他无可推委,哑口无言). — *vi., vt.* ①拖欠(欠款等),不履行. ②(使)不到案;(比赛)不出(场),不参加到底. ③缺席裁判(某人);因不出场而输掉(比赛). *~ing subscriber* (电话)欠费用户.
de·fault·er [diˈfɔːltə] *n.* ①不履行者; 拖欠者; 缺席者. ②亏空(公款)者. ③〔英〕违犯军规者. ~ **sheet**【军】违犯军规登记表〔*cf.* conduct sheet〕.
de·fea·sance [diˈfiːzəns] *n.* ①(契约的)作废,废止,废除. ②使契约作废的条款.
de·fea·si·ble [diˈfiːzəbl] *a.* 可作废的.

de·feat [di'fi:t] *vt.* ①打破，摧毁(计划等). ②打败(敌人)；使受挫折. ③【法】宣告无效，作废，废除. *be ~ed* 被打败. *be ~ed in one's design* 计划被打破. — *n.* ①战胜，击败. ②战败，失败；挫折. ③【法】废除. ***bring ~ upon oneself*** 招致失败. ***suffer a ~*** (战斗、比赛中)失败. **-ism** *n.* 失败主义(的态度、行为)，失败情绪. **-ist** *n.* 失败主义者.

de·fea·ture [di'fi:tʃə] *vt., n.* 损坏外貌.

def·e·cate ['defikeit] *vt.* 澄清，提净，滤净. — *vi.* ①澄清. ②通便. **-ca·tor** *n.* 澄清器，滤清器. **-ca·tion** [-'keiʃən] *n.*

de·fect[1] [di'fekt] *n.* ①缺陷，缺点，弱点；疵伤. ②不足，缺乏. *have some ~ in eyesight* 目力不佳. *have the ~s of one's qualities* 美中不足之处. ***in ~ of*** 若无…时；因无.

de·fect[2] [di'fekt] *vi.* 叛变；逃走. *He ~ed to the West.* 他叛逃到西方.

de·fec·tion [di'fekʃən] *n.* ①缺点. ②缺乏，丧失. ③叛党，脱党，叛教，变节. ④不履行义务；不尽职. *a sudden ~ of courage* 突然失去勇气. *~ from a party* 脱党.

de·fec·tive [di'fektiv] *a.* ①有缺陷[缺点]的，有瑕疵的，不完全的 *(in)*. ②【语法】变化不全的. ③智力低于正常的. — *n.* ①身心有缺陷的人. ②变化不全的词. ***~ verb***【语法】不完全变化动词 (*may, must, can* 等). **-ly** *ad.* **-ness** *n.*

de·fence [di'fens] *n.* ①防御，防备. ②保卫，保护；辩护. ③防卫物；〔*pl.*〕【军】防御工事，堡垒. ④护身术. ⑤【法】(被告的)抗辩，答辩；被告一方(包括被告及其辩护律师). ⑥【体】守方. *legal ~* 正当防卫. *line of ~* 【军】防线. *national ~* 国防. *The best ~ is offence.* 最好的防御是进攻，先下手为强. *counsel for the ~* (刑事被告的)辩护人. *a ~ against an attack* 防御(敌人的)进攻. ***~ in depth*** 纵深防御. ***in ~ of*** 以防卫，为保护…，为…辩护. ***put oneself in the state of ~*** 摆开防御姿势. ***the D- of the Realm Act***〔英〕国防条例〔略 DORA, 1914 年 8 月的法令，规定政府在战争期间有广泛的权力〕. ***the science [art] of ~*** 护身术〔拳术、剑术等〕.

de·fence·less [di'fenslis] *a.* 无防御的，无防备的；不设防的；无可辩护的. **-ly** *ad.* **-ness** *n.*

de·fend [di'fend] *vt.* ①保卫(国家等)；防御，防守，保护…使免于 *(from, against)*. ②为(某观点)辩护，作(某人)的辩护律师，为…进行辩护，抗辩. ③〔罕〕禁止. ***~ against [from]*** 保卫，抵抗；否认. ***~ oneself*** 自卫；自行辩护，答辩. ***God ~!*** 断断没有(这种事).

de·fend·ant [di'fendənt] *n., a.*【法】被告(人)(的) (*opp.* plaintiff). *the ~ company* 被告方面.

de·fend·er [di'fendə] *n.* ①防御者，保卫者；辩护人. ②【体】锦标保持者. ***D- of the Faith*** 护教者〔英国君主的称号，最初由教皇利奥十世授给亨利八世〕.

de·fen·es·tra·tion [di:fenis'treiʃən] *n.* 扔出窗外，掷出窗外.

de·fense [di'fens] *n.* 〔美〕= defence.

de·fen·si·ble [di'fensəbl] *a.* 能防御的；能辩护的. **-bly** *ad.* **-bil·i·ty** [-'biliti] *n.*

de·fen·sive [di'fensiv] *a.* ①防卫的，防御的；守势的. ②辩护的. *assume a ~ attitude* 采取守势. *a ~ alliance* 防守同盟. *a ~ warfare* 防御战. *~ works* 防御工事. — *n.* ①守势. ②辩护. ***assume the ~*** 采取守势. ***be [stand, act] on the ~*** 取防守姿态，在防御立场上. **-ly** *ad.* **-ness** *n.*

de·fen·so·ry [di'fensəri] *a.* = defensive.

de·fer[1] [di'fə:] *vt.* ①拖延，迁延，展缓；扣存. ②【军】使延期入伍. *His military service was deferred.* 他被允许缓期服役. *deferred annuity* 扣存退休费. *deferred pay* 〔英〕(兵士死亡或离队时发还的)扣存薪饷. *deferred shares* 〔英〕红利扣存股，红利后取股. *deferred telegram* (收费较廉的)慢(发)电(报). —*vi.* 迁延；因循.

de·fer[2] [di'fə:] *vi.* 服从，听从，遵从 *(to)*. *We all ~ to him in these matters.* 在这类事情上我们都听从他. — *vt.* 把(某事)交由(某人)决定 *(to)*. *We ~ questions of this kind to him.* 我们把这类问题交给他决定.

def·er·ence ['defərəns] *n.* ①服从；依从，敬服. ②敬意，尊敬. *blind ~* 盲从. ***in ~ to*** *(your wishes)* 遵从，听从(您的意愿). ***pay [show] ~ to*** 对…表示敬意. ***treat with ~*** 谦逊地对待. ***with all due ~ to you*** 尊意虽好，但是…〔表示不同意时的客气讲话〕.

def·er·ent[1] ['defərənt] *a.* 传送的，输送的. *a ~ duct* 【解】输送管，输精管.

def·er·ent[2] ['defərənt] *a.* = deferential.

def·er·en·tial [ˌdefə'renʃəl] *a.* 表示敬意的，谦让的，谦逊的，恭敬的.

de·fer·ment [di'fə:mənt] *n.* 拖迟，延期，展期.

de·fer·ra·ble, de·fer·a·ble [di'fə:rəbl] *a.* 能延期的；能缓役的. — *n.* 〔美〕有缓役资格者.

de·fer·ves·cence [ˌdi:fə'vesns, ˌdefə-] *n.* 【医】退烧，退热期.

de·fi·ance [di'faiəns] *n.* ①挑衅，挑战. ②反抗；蔑视. ***be at open ~ with*** 公然反抗. ***bid ~ to ... = set ... at ~*** 反抗；蔑视，藐视. ***in ~ of*** 无视，不顾，不管.

de·fi·ant [di'faiənt] *a.* ①挑战的；反抗的. ②大胆的. ③无礼的，目中无人的. ***be ~ of*** 蔑视. **-ly** *ad.* **-ness** *n.*

de·fib·ril·late [di'fibrileit, -'faibri-] *vt.* 用电流停止心脏纤维性颤动. **-ril·la·tion** *n.* **-ril·la·tor** *n.*

de·fi·cien·cy [di'fiʃənsi] *n.* ①缺乏，不足，短缺. ②缺陷. ③不足额；亏空. *a ~ of food* 食物不足. *~ disease* 亏损病，维生素(等)缺乏病. ***make good [up for] a ~*** 补足亏空.

de·fi·cient [di'fiʃənt] *a.* ①不足的，缺乏的. ②不完全的，有缺陷的. ③痴呆的. — *n.* 有缺陷的人[东西]. ***be ~ in*** 欠缺. ***be mentally ~*** 精神上有缺陷.

def·i·cit ['defisit] *n.* 不敷，亏空(额)，赤字；欠缺. *cover the ~* 弥补亏欠. *What? Another ~!* 咳！又亏了！ *~ financing* 赤字财政〔政府为刺激生产和消费而大量增加开支的做法〕. *~ spending* 赤字开支〔政府通过借债而不是通过税收来支付开支〕.

de·fi·er [di'faiə] *n.* 挑战者；反抗者；蔑视者.

def·i·lade [ˌdefi'leid] *vt.* 【军】根据地势部署军队. — *n.* 【军】遮蔽(物)，掩护(物).

de·file[1] [di'fail] *vt.* ①弄脏，污损. ②损坏(名誉等). ③亵渎，玷污. *They that touch pitch will be ~d.* 近墨者黑.

de·file[2] [di'fail] *vi.* 排成纵列[单列]前进. — ['di:fail] *n.* ①隘路，狭路，峡谷. ②纵列行进.

de·fin·a·ble [di'fainəbl] *a.* 可限定的，有界限的；能下定义的.

de·fine [di'fain] *vt.* ①为…立界限，限定，规定. ②(弄)明确. ③为…下定义，定界说. *be well ~d* 划分明白. *~ one's meaning [position]* 明确自己心意[立场]. *ill-~d duties* 权限不明的任务. *a well-~d word [figure]* 意义明确的文字[轮廓分明的图象].

de·fin·i·en·dum [ˌdifini'endəm] (*pl.* ***de·fin·i·en·da*** [-ə]) *n.* 被下了定义的词.

de·fin·i·ens [di'finiˌenz] (*pl.* ***de·fin·i·en·tia*** [diˌfini'enʃə]) *n.* 定义.

def·i·nite ['definit] *a.* ①明确的；确定的. ②一定的. ③【植】(雄蕊等)有一定数目的. *be more ~ in your statements* 请说得更明白点. *a ~ answer* 明确的答复. *a ~ article* 定冠词〔即 the〕. **-ness** *n.*

def·i·nite·ly ['definitli] *ad.* ①明确. ②〔口〕的确，一定. ③〔有否定词时〕决，绝对. *Will you go?* — *D-.* 你去吗？一定去. *I will not do it, ~.* 我绝对不干.

def·i·ni·tion [ˌdefi'niʃən] *n.* ①限定. ②定义，界说.

③明确. ④(透镜的)明晰度. ⑤(收音机的)清晰度. ⑥(印花)轮廓.

de·fin·i·tive [deˈfinitiv] *a.* ①限定的; 明确的. ②确定的,决定(性)的,最后的. ~ *host*【生】定局[最后]宿主. ~ *organs*【生】定形器官. ~ *sentence* 最后判决. **-ly** *ad.* **-ness** *n.*

de·fin·i·tude [deˈfinitjuːd] *n.* 明确,精确.

def·la·grate [ˈdefləgreit] *vt., vi.* (使)突然燃烧,(使)暴燃. **def·la·gra·tion** [ˌdefləˈgreiʃən] *n.* 暴燃(作用); 焚烧. **-gra·tor** *n.*【电】突燃器,爆燃器.

de·flate [diˈfleit] *vt.* ①抽去(空气等). ②降低…的重要性,使泄气. ③收缩,紧缩(通货). **de·fla·tion** *n.* ①抽气; (汽球的)放气. ②通货收缩. ③【地】风蚀, 吹蚀.

de·fla·tion·a·ry [diˈfleiʃənəri] *a.* 通货收缩的.

de·flect [diˈflekt] *vt.* 使偏斜,使转向,使弯曲. — *vi.* 偏移,偏转,偏离. ~ *a stream from its original course* 使河流改道. **de·flec·tion** *n.*〔美〕= deflexion. **-tor** [diˈflektə] *n.* 偏导装置,转向装置,折转板; 导流片,导风板;【海】偏针仪.

de·flex·ion [diˈflekʃən] *n.* ①歪斜, 偏斜. ②【物】偏转(度); 偏差. ③【工】挠曲; 挠度. ④【军】(枪弹的)偏差. ~ *shooting* (把飞机的移动计算在内而把炮火射到飞机前面的)修正瞄准射击.

de·flo·rate [diːˈflɔːrit] *a.*【植】过了开花期的.

de·flo·ra·tion [ˌdiːflɔːˈreiʃən, def-] *n.* ①摘花,采花. ②摘录书中精彩部分,拔萃. ③奸污处女,破坏贞操.

de·flow·er [diːˈflauə] *vt.* ①摘花, 采花. ②抽取…的精华. ③奸污(处女),破坏(处女贞操); 蹂躏.

De·foe [diˈfəu, dəˈfəu] *n.* ①迪福〔姓氏〕. ② **Daniel** ~ 笛福〔1659?—1731, 英国小说家,《鲁宾逊飘流记》(*Robinson Crusoe*) 的作者〕.

de·fog [diːˈfɔg] *vt.* 扫(雾). **de·fog·ger** [diːˈfɔgə] *n.* 扫雾器.

de·fo·li·ant [diːˈfəuliənt] *n.* 脱叶剂,落叶剂.

de·fo·li·ate [diːˈfəulieit] *vt., vi.*【植】(使)落叶. — *a.*〔罕〕落了叶的. **-li·a·tion** [diˌfəuliˈeiʃən] *n.* 落叶; 叶子的脱落.

de·force [diˈfɔːs] *vt.*【法】①霸占, 强占. ②不让人享有合法权益. **-ment** *n.*

de·for·ciant [diˈfɔːʃənt] *n.*【法】强占者,霸占者.

De For·est [dəˈfɔrist] *n.* ①德福雷斯特〔姓氏〕. ② **Lee** ~德福来斯特〔1873—1961, 改进收音机、有声电影及电视机的美国发明家〕.

de·for·est [diˈfɔrist] *vt.* 砍伐森林; 去掉树木. **-a·tion** [-ˈteiʃən] *n.*

de·form [diˈfɔːm] *vt.* ①使变丑,毁伤…的形体, 使成畸形. ②【物】使变形. — *vi.* 变形. **-a·tion** [-ˈmeiʃən] *n.* ①(形体的)损伤; 改丑 (*opp.* reformation). ②畸形. ③【物】变形. **-ed** *a.* 变了形的; 丑陋的; 畸形的.

de·form·i·ty [diˈfɔːmiti] *n.* ①畸形,残废,残疾; 丑陋. ②(制度等的) 缺陷. ③畸形的人〔东西〕.

de·fraud [diˈfrɔːd] *vt.* 骗取,诈取; 欺骗. ***be ~ed of (one's estate)*** 被骗去(财产). ***~ a person of something*** 骗去某人的东西. ***with intent to ~***【法】蓄意诈骗.

de·fraud·er [diˈfrɔːdə] *n.* 诈骗者.

de·fray [diˈfrei] *vt.* 支付,支给. *The expenses are ~ed by the company.* 费用由公司支付. **-al, -ment** *n.* 支付,支出.

de·frock [diˈfrɔk] *vt.* 剥夺…的牧师资格(或职务),免去…的圣职 (= unfrock).

de·frost [di(ː)ˈfrɔ(ː)st] *vt.* 使溶解,使解冻,去冰霜. — *vi.* 解冻.

de·frost·er [di(ː)ˈfrɔ(ː)stə] *n.* (飞机等的)熔冰机; 除霜器.

deft [deft] *a.* 灵巧的,巧妙的,熟练的 (*opp.* awkward). *She is a ~ hand with a needle.* 她针线做得好. **-ly** *ad.* **-ness** *n.*

de·funct [diˈfʌŋkt] *a.* ①死了的; (公司)倒闭了的,已不存在的. ②已废止的,已失效的. ***the ~*** 故人,死者.

de·fuse, de·fuze [diˈfjuːz] *vt.* ①拆除…的雷管; 使失去导火线. ②使变为无害. **~r** *n.* (危险局面的)调解人.

de·fy [diˈfai] *vt.* ①挑, 激. ②蔑视,藐视,不顾,公然反抗. ③使不能,使落空. *~ing laws human and divine* 无法无天. *~ death to defend ...* 誓死保卫. *I ~ you to do that.* 我看你敢不敢那么干. *They ~ all comparison.* 没有能和他们比较的. *~ description* 难以形容. *The door defies all attempts to open it.* 门怎么也弄不开.

deg. = degree.

dé·ga·gé [F. degaʒe] *a.* 〔F.〕潇洒的,不拘束的.

de·gas [diːˈgæs] *vt.* 排气; 排除煤气.

de·gauss [ˈdiːˈgaus] *vt.* 使消磁; 消除(船只的)磁场〔以防磁性水雷〕. *~ing cable* (防磁性水雷的) 消磁电缆.

de·gen·er·a·cy [diˈdʒenərəsi] *n.* ①退步,退化; 衰退. ②堕落,颓废.

de·gen·er·ate [diˈdʒenəreit] *vi.* ①腐化,堕落,颓废. ②衰败;【生】退化 (*to*);【生理】变质. *Liberty often ~s into lawlessness.* 自由常常变质为无法无天. — [diˈdʒenərit] *a., n.* ①腐化的,堕落的,颓废的(人); 退化的(动物). ②蜕化变质的(分子); 变了质的(东西); 变态性欲的(人).

de·gen·er·a·tion [diˌdʒenəˈreiʃən] *n.* ①退步; 恶化. ②颓废,堕落. ③【生理】变性, 变质. ④【生】简并,退化(病). ⑤【物】退化,简并化.

de·gen·er·a·tive [diˈdʒenərətiv] *a.* 变坏的; 退化的; 变性的; 堕落的.

de·glu·ti·nate [diˈgluːtineit] *vt.* 从…中提取麦麸. **-na·tion** [-ˈneiʃən] *n.*

de·glu·ti·tion [ˌdiːgluːˈtiʃən] *n.* 咽,吞,咽下,吞咽能力.

deg·ra·da·tion [ˌdegrəˈdeiʃən] *n.* ①降级; 免职. ②退化; 堕落. ③【地】(地表的)剥蚀. ④【化】降解,递降分解(作用). ⑤【物】(能的)退降. *advancement and ~* 升级和降级.

de·grade [diˈgreid] *vt.* ①降格,降级. ②撤职; 免职. ③降低品格[身价、价值(等)]; 使堕落; 使受屈辱. ④【化】降解. ⑤【生】使退化. ⑥【地】使剥蚀. — *vi.* ①降低; 堕落. ②【生】退化. ③(剑桥大学)把名誉学位考试延期一年. **de·grad·ed** *a.* 被降了级的; 被免了职的; 堕落了的; 贬低了的; 退化了的. **de·grad·ing** *a.* 堕落的,可耻的,卑鄙的.

de·grease [diːˈgriːz] *vt.* 去除…的油污;【化】使脱脂.

de·gree [diˈgriː] *n.* ①程度; 等级. ②阶层,地位. ③学位,学衔. ④度,度数. ⑤【数】次; 幂. ⑥【乐】阶,度, 音程. ⑦【语法】(形容词和副词的)级. ⑧【法】亲等. *He was tired to such a ~ that he fainted.* 他疲乏得昏了过去. *people of every ~* 各阶层的人们. *a man of high ~* 地位高的人们. *give [take] a ~* 授与[取得]学位. *the prohibited ~s (of marriage)* 禁止结婚的亲等〔一、二、三等亲〕. *third ~*〔美〕(警察的)严厉的拷问. ***by ~s*** 渐次,渐渐,逐渐. ***by slow ~s*** 慢慢,一点儿一点儿地. ***~ of frost*** 零下 (*10 ~s of frost* 零下 10 度). ***in a ~*** 有一点儿. ***in its ~*** 各有(所长等) (*Each is useful in its ~.* 各有不同程度的用处). ***in some ~*** 多少. ***to a certain ~*** 相当. ***to a ~*** 非常;〔美〕有点. ***to the last ~*** 极端,再…没有了. **~-day** 度-日〔气温较标准每降低 1°时, 一日内暖房所需燃料单位〕.

de·gres·sion [diˈgreʃən] *n.* ①下降. ②(税率的)递减. **-sive** *a.*

de·gust [diˈgʌst] *vt., vi.*〔罕〕尝味〔尤指品尝〕. **-gus·ta·tion** [ˌdiːgəsˈteiʃən] *n.*

de gus·ti·bus non dis·pu·tan·dum (est) [diˈgʌstibəs nɔn ˌdispjuːˈtændəm]〔L.〕各有所好,无可计较.

D.E.H. = diameter at height of the eye.【林】目高(树干)直径.

de·hisce [diˈhis] *vi.* ①张嘴,开口. ②【植】(种皮、豆荚

等的)裂开. **-his·cence** [diˈhisns] *n.* 【植】裂开,张开. **-cent** [-ˈhisnt] *a.* 【植】裂开性的.

de·horn [diˈhɔːn] *vt.* ①〔美〕除去(牛等的)角. ②〔军俚〕除去(炸弹的)雷管.

de·hor·ta·tion [ˌdiːhɔːˈteiʃən] *n.* 劝阻,劝戒. **-ta·tive** [diːˈhɔːtətiv] *a.* 劝戒的.

de·hu·man·ize [diːˈhjuːmənaiz] *vt.* 使失人性;把(人)看成(动)物;使(艺术作品等)失去个性.

de·hu·mid·i·fy [ˌdiːhjuːˈmidifai] *vt.* 使除去湿气〔水分〕. **-i·fi·ca·tion** [ˈdiːhju(ː)ˌmidifiˈkeiʃən] *n.* **-fi·er** [-hju(ː)ˈmidifaiə] *n.*

de·hy·drate [diːˈhaidreit] *vt., vi.* (使)脱水. *~d eggs* 蛋粉. *~d vegetables* 脱水蔬菜.

de·hy·dro·canned [diːˌhaidrəˈkænd] *a.* 脱水装罐头的.

de·hy·dro·freez·ing [diːˈhaidrəuˈfriːziŋ] *n.* 脱水冷冻.

de·hy·dro·gen·ase [diːˈhaidrədʒəˌneis, ˌdiːhaiˈdrɔdʒəˌneis] *n.* 脱氢酶.

de·hy·dro·gen·ate, de·hy·dro·gen·ize [diːˈhaidrəudʒəneit, -naiz] *vt.* 脱氢;去氢. **-gen·a·tion** [diːˌhaidrəudʒəˈneiʃən] *n.*

de·hyp·no·tize [ˈdiːˈhipnətaiz] *vt.* 使解除催眠状态,使解除催眠术.

de·ice [diːˈais] *vt.* 除去…上的冰;防止…结冰. **de·ic·er** [-ə] *n.* (机翼上的)除冰装置.

de·i·cide [ˈdiːisaid] *n.* 杀神(者).

deic·tic [ˈdaiktik] *a.* 直接指出的;直接证明的;【逻】直证的;【语法】指示的.

de·i·fi·ca·tion [ˌdiːifiˈkeiʃən] *n.* ①祀为神,奉作神圣. ②神化,神格化. ③神的化身.

de·i·form [ˈdiːifɔːm] *a.* 神一样的;神性的.

de·i·fy [ˈdiːifai] *vt.* 把…祀奉为神,奉…为神圣. *~ prudence* 慎重第一.

deign [dein] *vi.* ①俯准,垂顾. ②降低身分;屈尊. *~ to visit* 光临. *He doesn't ~ to acknowledge his old friends.* 他连老朋友也不理了. —*vt.* 惠准,赐予. *He ~ed no reply.* 他不予答复.

de·i gra·ti·a [ˌdiːai ˈgreiʃiei] 〔L.〕凭上帝的恩典.

deil [diːl] *n.* 〔Scot.〕①恶魔. ②歹徒.

de·i·on·ize [diːˈaiəˌnaiz] *vt.* 【物】除去…的离子.

de·ism [ˈdiːizəm] *n.* 自然神论〔17、18世纪的学说,说上帝创造世界及其自然规律,但此后不再参与其事〕.

de·ist [ˈdiːist] *n.* 自然神论者. **-tic** [diːˈistik] *a.*

de·i·ty [ˈdiːiti] *n.* ①神;神性;神的身分. ②〔the D-〕上帝,造物主. *a society in which money is the only ~* 金钱万能的社会.

dé·jà vu [ˌdeiʒɑː ˈvjuː] 〔F.〕【心】记忆幻觉;【医】似曾相识症.

de·ject [diˈdʒekt] *vt.* 使沮丧,使寒心,使气馁. *be ~ed* 垂头丧气.

de·jec·ta [diˈdʒektə] *n.* 〔*pl.*〕排泄物,粪便.

de·ject·ed [diˈdʒektid] *a.* 垂头丧气的,郁郁不乐的. **-ly** *ad.* **-ness** *n.*

de·jec·tion [diˈdʒekʃən] *n.* ①沮丧,气馁,灰心,失意. ②【医】排泄(物);粪便.

dé·jeu·ner [ˈdeiʒənei] *n.* 〔F.〕早餐;午餐.

deka- *pref.* = deca-.

Dek·ker [ˈdekə] *n.* 德克〔姓氏〕.

dek·ko [ˈdekəu] *n.* 〔俚〕看一眼,看一看. *Let's have a ~.* 给我们看一看.

Del. = Delaware. **del.** = delegate; delete; *delineavit* (〔L.〕 = he [she] drew it) 此画为某某所画;〔美〕deliver.

de·laine [dəˈlein] *n.* ①细毛料,棉毛混纺布料. ②一种羊毛〔用以作精纺毛纱〕.

de·la·foss·ite [ˌdeləˈfɔsait] *n.* 【地】铜铁矿.

de·lam·i·nate [diːˈlæmiˌneit] *vt., vi.* (使)分层.

de·lam·i·na·tion [diːˌlæmiˈneiʃən] *n.* 分层〔尤指胚胎的分层〕.

De·land [ˈdiːlənd] *n.* 迪兰〔姓氏〕.

de·late [diˈleit] *vt.* ①控告,告发. ②〔古〕宣扬,公布. **-la·tion** *n.* 告发,控告.

Del·a·ware [ˈdeləwεə] *n.* ①特拉华〔美国州名〕. ②〔美〕特拉华河. ③ *(pl. ~, ~s)* 居住在特拉华河流域的一种印第安人.

de·lay [diˈlei] *vt.* 延迟,拖延,耽搁. *We'll ~ the party for two week.* 我们要把会期延迟两周. *The train was ~ed by heavy snow.* 火车因大雪误点了. — *vi.* 耽搁,耽误,迟误. *It's getting late; don't ~.* 时间已晚,别再耽误了. — *n.* 延迟,拖延,耽搁,耽误. *No more ~s, comrades.* 同志们,再迟不行了. ***admit of no ~*** 不能耽搁. ***without ~*** 赶快,立刻,马上. **~-line** 延迟线. **-er** *n.* 延迟器;缓燃剂.

de·layed-action [diˈleidˈækʃən] *a.* (雷管、炸弹等)延期爆炸的,定时的. — *n.* 延迟动作〔作用〕.

del cred·e·re [delˈkredəri] 〔It.〕(掮客对)买主支付能力的保证.

de·le [ˈdiːli(ː)] *vt.* 〔L.〕【印】(校对用语)删去〔略 d.〕.— *n.* 删去号.

de·lec·ta·ble [diˈlektəbl] *a.* ①使人愉快的. ②美味的. **-ness** *n.* **-bly** *ad.*

de·lec·ta·tion [ˌdiːlekˈteiʃən] *n.* ①愉快. ②娱乐,享受.

de·lec·tus [diˈlektəs] *n.* (学习用)拉丁〔希腊〕文选.

del·e·ga·cy [ˈdeligəsi] *n.* ①选出代表,被选为代表. ②代表权. ③代表团.

del·e·gate [ˈdeligeit] *n.* ①委员,代表,特派员. ②〔美〕(Virginia, West Virginia, Maryland 等州的)众议院议员. ③(众议院中准州地区的)代表〔无投票权〕. *~s without power to vote* 列席代表. *a walking ~* (工会的)交涉代表. — *vt.* ①派…做代表. ②委任,委托. *~ authority to sb.* 授权某人.

del·e·ga·tion [ˌdeliˈgeiʃən] *n.* ①(代表的)委派,派遣. ②代表团. ③〔美〕(某)州议员团. *a ~ bringing gifts and thanks* 慰问团.

de·lete [diˈliːt] *vt.* 删去. *His name was ~d from the list.* 他的名字从名单上删去了.

del·e·te·ri·ous [ˌdeliˈtiəriəs] *a.* (对身心)有害的,有毒的. **-ly** *ad.* **-ness** *n.*

de·le·tion [diˈliːʃən] *n.* ①删除. ②删除部分. ③(遗传学上染色体的)缺失.

delf, delft [delf, delft] *n.* 荷兰德尔夫特出产的陶器. **~ware** 荷兰蓝白彩釉陶器.

Del·hi [ˈdeli] *n.* 德里〔印度城市〕.

del·i [ˈdeli] *n.* *(pl. del·is)* 〔美口〕熟食店 (= delicatessen).

Del·ia [ˈdiːljə] *n.* 迪莉娅〔女子名〕.

de·lib·er·ate [diˈlibəreit] *vt.* ①考虑. ②商议. *~ the question* 考虑那个问题. *They are deliberating what to do.* 他们正在商议该做什么 — *vi.* 思考 *(on, over)*;与某人 *(with)* 协商,讨论某事 *(over, upon, on)*. *I ~d with him on his future plans of study.* 我和他商讨关于他将来学习的计划. *~ on [over] a question* 思考问题. — [diˈlibərit] *a.* ①深思熟虑的,盘算周到的. ②故意的,蓄意的. ③审慎的,慎重的;沉着的,从容的. *a ~ aim* 从容不迫的瞄准. *a ~ decision* 慎重的决定. *a ~ murder* 蓄意谋杀. **-ly** *ad.* **-ness** *n.*

de·lib·er·a·tion [diˌlibəˈreiʃən] *n.* ①深思熟虑. ②协商,评议. ③故意. ④慎重,细心;沉着. ***after long ~*** 经过深思熟虑后. ***be taken into ~*** 被审议. ***under ~*** 在考虑中;在审议中. ***with ~*** 慎重.

de·lib·er·a·tive [diˈlibəreitiv] *a.* ①考虑过的,慎重的. ②协商的,评议的. *a ~ body [assembly]* 协商机关〔会议〕. *have a ~ voice* 有协商发言权. *a ~ speech* 提案审查报告.

del·i·ca·cy [ˈdelikəsi] *n.* ①优美;精巧,精致. ②柔弱,脆

D

弱．③敏感；审慎，周到，体贴．④微妙；棘手．⑤美味，好菜．⑥正派，一本正经．⑦【语言学】(语言范畴中各亚类的) 细微差别．*a ~ of constitution* 虚弱的体质．*the ~ of one's sense of right and wrong* 敏锐的正义感．*diplomatic negotiations of great ~* 极微妙的［极伤脑筋的］外交谈判．*the delicacies of the season* 应时好菜．***feel a ~ about*** 对…伤脑筋．*fake ~* 假正经，一本正经．

del·i·cate [ˈdelikit] *a.* ①巧妙的，优美的，优雅的．②柔弱的；脆弱的．③精巧的，精致的；(仪器)灵敏的．④美味的，鲜美的．⑤敏感的；周到的．⑥需要审慎的，微妙的，伤脑筋的．⑦有洁癖的，爱挑剔的．*a ~ touch* 巧妙的笔锋，精致的手艺．*~ colours* 淡色，柔和的颜色．*a ~ balance* 准确的天平．*~ food* 美味．*a ~ operation* 困难的手术．*a ~ hint* 微妙的暗示．***be in ~ health*** 身体虚弱．***be in the ~ condition*** 〔美俚〕有喜，怀孕．***have a ~ ear for music*** 对音乐有鉴赏力．**-ly** *ad.* **-ness** *n.*

del·i·ca·tes·sen [ˌdelikəˈtesn] *n.* 〔*pl.*〕〔美〕①现成食品，熟食．②〔用作单数〕熟食店，现成食品店．

de·li·cious [diˈliʃəs] *a.* ①美味的，好吃的，可口的．②美妙的，爽快的；极有趣的．—*n.* 〔D-〕〔美〕"美味"苹果〔一种冬季的红苹果〕．**-ly** *ad.* **-ness** *n.*

de·lict [ˈdiːlikt, diˈlikt] *n.* 不法行为，违警罪．***in flagrant ~*** 在作案时．

de·light [diˈlait] *n.* ①欢喜，高兴，愉快．②爱好的事物；嗜好．*The dance was a ~ to see.* 这个舞蹈看着愉快．*scorn ~s and live laborious days* 唾弃欢乐，刻苦度日．***take ~ in*** 喜欢；嗜好．***to one's ~*** 说来真使某人高兴．***with ~*** 欣然．— *vt.* 使欢喜，使高兴，使快乐．*I shall be ~ed to come.* 我一定来．—*vi.* 欢喜，快乐．*They ~ in travels.* 他们喜欢旅行．***be ~ed with*** 喜欢，中意，合意．***~ in music*** 喜欢音乐．***~ to hono(u)r*** 衷心尊敬［称赞］．

de·light·ed [diˈlaitid] *a.* 喜欢的，高兴的．*a ~ look* 喜气洋洋．**-ly** *ad.*

de·light·ful [diˈlaitful] *a.* ①极快乐的，极愉快的．②可爱的，讨人欢喜的．**-ly** *ad.* 大喜，欣然．**-ness** *n.*

de·light·some [diˈlaitsəm] *a.* 〔古、诗〕= delightful.

De·li·lah [diˈlailə] ①(《圣经》中)迪莱勒〔力士Samson的情妇，她把 Samson 出卖给腓力斯人〕．②妖妇．

de·lim·it [diːˈlimit], **de·lim·i·tate** [di(ː)ˈlimiteit] *vt.* 为…定界，划界．**de·lim·i·ta·tion** [diˌlimiˈteiʃən] *n.* 定界，划界；区划．**de·lim·it·er** *n.* 定义符，定界符〔表示一个数据单位开始或终结的字符，如磁带上的这类字母〕．

de·lin·e·ate [diˈlinieit] *vt.* ①描…的外形，画…的轮廓，勾画．②叙述，描写．

de·lin·e·a·tion [diˌliniˈeiʃən] *n.* ①描写，描画．②轮廓，图形，略图；线条写生画．③叙述．

de·lin·e·a·tor [diˈlinieitə] *n.* ①描写者，描画者，制图者．②叙述者．③图型．④描画器．⑤(夜间公路上标示拐弯处的)一排照明灯．

de·lin·quen·cy [diˈliŋkwənsi] *n.* ①懈怠，失职，怠工．②过失，失职罪；罪过；【法】(青少年的)不法行为，罪行．③拖欠的债务［税款］．*juvenile ~* 少年犯罪．

de·lin·quent [diˈliŋkwənt] *a.* ①不尽责的，怠工的．②〔美〕拖欠(税款)的．③有过失的，有罪的．—*n.* ①懈怠者．②过失者；违犯者．③少年罪犯．

del·i·quesce [ˌdeliˈkwes] *vi.* ①融解，溶化．②【化】潮解．③【植】(叶脉的)扩散；(蘑菇等因成熟、衰老)变软而液化．

del·i·ques·cence [ˌdeliˈkwesns] *n.* ①溶解．②【化】潮解(性)．③【植】(叶脉的)扩散；(蘑菇等的)液化．

del·i·ques·cent [ˌdeliˈkwesnt] *a.* ①溶解的，溶化的．②【化】潮解性的．③【植】扩散的，液化的．

del·i·ra·tion [ˌdeliˈreiʃən] *n.* 〔罕〕谵妄，精神错乱．

de·lir·i·ous [diˈliriəs] *a.* ①谵妄的，精神错乱的，语无伦次的．②极兴奋的，发狂的．*~ with joy* 狂喜．

de·lir·i·um [diˈliriəm] *n.* (*pl.* ***~s, ri·a*** [-riə]) ①精神错乱，谵妄．②极度兴奋，发狂．*lapse into ~* 陷入谵妄状态，说起胡话来．***~ tremens*** [ˈtriːmenz] 【医】(醉后的)酒狂，震颤性谵妄．

del·i·tes·cence [ˌdeliˈtesns] *n.* ①(传染病等的)潜伏期，潜伏状态．②(炎症等的)突然消退．**-cent** *a.*

de·liv·er [diˈlivə] *vt.* ①救，救出，解放出 *(from)*．②引渡，移交，交付 *(up; over; to; into)*．③递送，投递，送(信等)；传达，传(话等)．④发表(意见)．⑤加，给与(打击等)；抛，投球．⑥射出，喷出．⑦陈说，讲述，吐露．⑧使分娩，助产．*~ sb. from danger* 从危险中救出某人．*The oil well ~s 500 tons a day.* 这口油井每天喷油500吨．*a well ~ed sermon* 天花乱坠的说教．***be ~ed of*** 生(孩子)；作(诗)；说(俏皮话)．***~ a gaol [jail]*** 把囚犯提交法院．***~ battle*** 开始攻击．***~ oneself of*** *(an opinion)* 发表(意见)．***~ oneself to*** *(the police)* (向警察)自首．***~ oneself well*** 讲得不错．***~ the goods*** 交货；履行诺言；〔美〕不负所望．

de·liv·er·ance [diˈlivərəns] *n.* ①救援，救助；释放．②陈述；(意见的)发表．③(正式)意见；判决．

de·liv·ered [diˈlivəd] *a.*【商】在…交货的；包括运费在内的．*~ at station* 车站交货．*~ price* 包括运费在内的价格．

de·liv·er·er [diˈlivərə] *n.* ①救助者．②引渡人，交付者．③递送人．④〔罕〕陈述者．

de·liv·er·y [diˈlivəri] *n.* ①引渡，交付；【商】交货；【法】正式让渡．②运送；投递；传送．③分娩．④陈述，讲演；口才．⑤【棒球】投球．⑥救助；释放．*the means of ~* 发射工具．*an express ~* 快信，快件．*the two o'clock ~* 两点钟投递的邮件．*aerial ~* 空投．*easy [difficult] ~* 顺［难］产．*a good [poor] ~* 能说会道［笨嘴拙舌］．*~ book* 交货簿，送货簿．*~ of canal* 渠道输水量．*~ port* 输出港．***~ on arrival*** 货到交付．***~ on term*** 定期交付．***take ~ of*** 收到送货 (*The balance will be paid on taking ~ of the machine.* 收到机器就付还差额)．*~* **book** 交货簿．*~* **order** 出栈凭单．*~* **port** 输出港．*~* **receipt** 送货回条．*~* **room** ①医院的分娩室，产房．②出纳台，图书馆的借书处．

dell [del] *n.* (有树林环抱的)小山谷．

Del·lin·ger [ˈdelindʒə] *n.* 德林杰〔姓氏〕．

Del·mar·va [ˈdelmɑːvə] *n.* 美国 Delaware, Maryland, Virginia 三州的总称．

de·lo·cal·ize [diːˈləukəlaiz] *vt.* ①使离开原位．②使不受局部地方限制；消除地方性．③【物】使(电子)移位．*~ an industry* 使工业不偏重于一方．*~sb. accent* 使无地方口音．

de·louse [ˈdiːˈlaus] *vt.* 灭虱．

Del·phi [ˈdelfai] *n.* 特尔斐〔古希腊城市，因有阿波罗神殿而出名〕．

Del·phi·an, Del·phic [ˈdelfiən, ˈdelfik] *a.* ①(希腊)特尔斐的；阿波罗神殿的．②神示的；神秘的，玄妙的；模棱两可的．

del·phi·nine [ˈdelfiniːn, -nin] *n.*【化】翠雀宁．

del·phin·i·um [delˈfiniəm] *n.* 飞燕草；翠雀属植物．

Del·phi·nus [delˈfainəs] *n.* 海豚(星)座．

del·ta [ˈdeltə] *n.* ①希腊语字母表第四字母〔Δ, δ〕．②(河流的)三角洲；三角形物．③〔D-〕通讯中用以代替 d 的词．*~ metal* δ 齐，δ 合金．*the ~ of the Nile* 尼罗河三角洲．*~* **rays**【物】δ 射线．*~* **ware**【生】三角波〔显示熟睡状态的脑电波〕．

del·ta·ic [delˈteiik] *a.* (有)三角洲的；三角形的．

del·ti·ol·o·gist [ˌdeltiˈɔlədʒist] *n.* 图画明信片收藏家．

del·toid [ˈdeltɔid] *a.* 三角形的；三角肌的．—*n.*【解】三角肌 (= ~ muscle).

de·lude [diˈluːd] *vt.* 欺骗，哄骗．*~ oneself* 自欺；误解．

del·uge [ˈdeljuːdʒ] *n.* ①大洪水；泛滥．②倾盆大雨．③洪水般的涌来．*a ~ of rain* 大雨．*a ~ of tears* 泉涌似的泪．*a ~ of fire* 火海．***After me the D-!*** (身)后

(之)事于我何干! *the D-*【圣】诺亚(Noah)时的洪水. —*vt.* 泛滥;涌集. *be ~d with applications* 申请书雪片似地飞来.

de·lu·sion [di'lu:ʒən] *n.* ①欺骗,迷惑. ②幻想;【心】妄想. ③误解,谬见,误会. *have a ~ that* 幻想. ***labour under a ~*** 因妄想而苦恼;误解. ***be under no ~ as to*** 对…所见不差,对…没有误解.

de·lu·sion·al [di'lu:ʒənl] *a.* 幻想的,妄想性的.

de·lu·sive [di'lju:siv] *a.* 欺骗的,虚妄的,不可靠的. **-ly** *ad.* **-ness** *n.*

de·luxe [di'lʌks, di'luks] *a.* 豪华的,奢侈的,高级的. *a ~ edition* 精装本.

delve [delv] *vt., vi.* 〔古、方〕①掘,挖. ②探究,钻研. —*n.* 穴,凹,坑. *~ into books* 钻研书本. *~ into the past* 调查过去的情况.

dem [dem] *v.* 〔卑〕= damn.

Dem. = Democrat(ic).

de·mag·net·ize ['di:'mægnitaiz] *vt.* 除去…的磁性,给…退磁. **-mag·net·i·za·tion** [-ˌmægnitai'zeiʃən] *n.* 退磁.

dem·a·gog·ic, -i·cal [ˌdemə'gɔgik(əl)] *a.* 煽动(性)的,造谣生事的,蛊惑的. **-gog·ism,** 〔美〕**-gog·uer·y** *n.* 煽动主义,煽动行为;造谣生事.

dem·a·gogue, dem·a·gog ['deməgɔg] *n.* ①煽动者,蛊惑人心者,造谣生事的人. ②(古代的)民众领袖.

dem·a·gog·y ['deməgɔgi] *n.* 煽动的行为,蛊惑的性质.

de·mand [di'mɑ:nd] *vt.* ①要求,请求;需要. ②询问,盘问,追究. ③【法】召唤. *~ an interview* 要求会面. *The work ~s care.* 那项工作需要细心. *~ sb.'s name* 询问姓名. *~ (sth.) of [from] (sb.)* 向(某人)要求(某物). *She ~ed that we let her in.* 她要我们让她进来. —*vi.* 要求,查问. ★后面从句中的动词,美国人多用虚拟语气现在式,即第三人称单数现在时不加 -s, 如: She ~s that he *assume* the responsibility. (她要求他承担责任.)英国人则用 *should assume.* —*n.* ①要求,请求. ②需要;销路. *I have a ~ to make of him.* 我对他有一个要求. *supply and ~* 供给和需要. *~ for a commodity* 商品的需要[销路]. *There are many ~s on my purse.* 我有许多事情要花钱去办. ***be in ~*** 有需要,销路好. ***on ~*** 请求即 (*a bill payable on ~* 见票即付的票据). ***present one's ~s*** 提出要求. *~* **bill [draft, note]** 见票即付的票据,即期票据. *~* **deposit** 活期存款. *~* **inflation,** *~*-**pull**【经】需求膨胀. **-er** *n.* 要求者.

de·mand·a·ble [di'mɑ:ndəbl] *a.* 可要求的.

de·mand·ant [di'mɑ:ndənt] *n.* ①要求者. ②询问者. ③【法】原告.

de·mand·er [di'mɑ:ndə] *n.* 要求者,请求者.

de·man·toid [di'mæntɔid] *n.* 翠榴石,钙铁榴石.

de·mar·cate [di'mɑ:keit] *vt.* ①划界,定界线. ②区别,分开.

de·mar·ca·tion [ˌdi:mɑ:'keiʃən] *n.* ①边界,分界. ②划界,设界限. ③区分,划分. *a line of ~ between* …之间的界线. *draw a clear line of ~* 划清界线.

dé·marche ['deimɑ:ʃ] *n.* 〔F.〕①(外交用语)手段,步骤,措施,反措施. ②(口头的或书面的)表示. ③行动的方针.

de·mark [di'mɑ:k] *vt.* = demarcate.

de·ma·te·ri·al·ize ['di:mə'tiəriəlaiz] *vt., vi.* (使)非物质化,(使)失去物质的性质.

deme [di:m] *n.* ①【希腊史】(古 Attica 的)市区. ②【生】同类群.

de·mean[1] [di'mi:n] *vt.* 〔古〕〔~ oneself〕行动,表现,举动. *~ oneself well [ill]* 行为好[不好].

de·mean[2] [di'mi:n] *vt.* 〔通例 ~ oneself〕降低(身分),损坏(人品). *to ~ oneself by taking a bribe* 因受贿而贬低自己.

de·mean·or, de·mean·our [di'mi:nə] *n.* 态度,行为,举动;品格,品行. *assume a haughty ~* 采取高傲的态度.

de·ment [di'ment] *vt.* 〔罕〕使发狂.

de·ment·ed [di'mentid] *a.* 疯狂的,发狂的. *be [become] ~* 发狂. *drive (sb.) ~* 〔口〕(忧愁等)使(人)发狂.

dé·men·ti [dei'mɑ̃:nti:] *n.* 〔F.〕(外交上)正式否认,正式辟谣.

de·men·ti·a [di'menʃiə] *n.* 【医】痴呆. *epileptic ~* 癫痫性痴呆. *~ praecox* ['pri:kɔks]【医】早发性痴呆,精神分裂症.

de·mer·it [di:'merit] *n.* ①缺点,短处;过失. ②(学校的)记过. *the merits and ~s* 优点缺点;功过. *He already has three ~s on his record.* 他已记过三次.

dem·e·rol ['deməɔl] *n.* 【商标】德美罗〔止痛药〕.

de·mesne [di'mein] *n.* ①(土地的)占有;地主的不出租的地产. ②(领主的)领地,庄园周围的土地. ③范围,领域. *hold estates in ~* 有许多地产. *a Royal ~*〔英〕御地. *a State ~* 国有地.

De·me·ter [di'mi:tə] *n.* 【希神】德墨特尔〔主管生产、社会治安等的女神〕.

de·mi ['di:mai] *n.* demos 的复数.

demi- *pref.* 表示"半","部分","略小": *demigod, demitasse.*

dem·i·god ['demigɔd] *n.* 半神半人;神与人所生的后代;神一样的人.

dem·i·john ['demidʒɔn] *n.* (用柳条编壳保护着的)小颈大瓶.

de·mil·i·ta·rize ['di:'militəraiz] *vt.* 解除武装,废除军备,解除军事管制. **-rized** *a.* 非武装的. *~d zone* 非军事区.

dem·i·lune ['demilu:n] *n.* ①半月,新月. ②半月形堡垒.

dem·i·min·i ['demi'mini] *a.* 超超短的. —*n.* 超超短裙.

dem·i·mon·daine [ˌdemimɔn'dein] *n.* 〔F.〕妓女;交际花.

dem·i·monde ['demi'mɔ̃:nd] *n.* 〔F.〕①〔集合词〕名声不好的女人. ②妓女. ③娼妓界. ④形迹可疑的一群人.

dem·i·re·lief [ˌdemiri'li:f] *n.* 半浮雕.

dem·i·rep ['demirep] *n.* 名声不好的妇女,不正派的妇女.

de·mise [di'maiz] *n.* ①【法】(不动产的)转让;遗赠. ②让位. ③崩,薨;〔口〕逝世,死. *the ~ of the Crown* 王位的继承. —*vt.* ①转让,遗赠. ②逊(位),让(位). *~ the Crown* 让位. **de·mis·a·ble** *a.*

dem·i·sem·i·qua·ver ['demisemiˌkweivə] *n.* 【乐】三十二分音符.

de·mis·sion [di'miʃən] *n.* ①放弃(职务,权力);辞职. ②免职,撤职.

de·mit [di'mit] *vt.* ①辞(职),放弃. ②〔古〕罢免. —*vi.* 辞职.

dem·i·tasse ['demitɑ:s] *n.* 小咖啡杯;一小杯咖啡.

dem·i·tint ['demitint] *n.* (介乎浅色与深色之间的)晕色.

dem·i·urge ['demiə:dʒ] *n.* (*pl.* *-ur·gi* [-dʒai]) ①〔D-〕(柏拉图哲学里所说的)造物主. ②(古希腊城邦的)行政官.

dem·i·ur·gic, dem·i·ur·gi·cal [ˌdi:mi'ə:dʒik(əl)] *a.* 造物主的;创造世界的.

dem·i·volt ['demivəult] *n.* (骑马时马前足抬起的)半腾空.

Dem·o ['deməu] *n.* (*pl.* *-os*)〔美〕民主党员.

dem·o ['deməu] *n.* 〔美口〕①示威. ②示威者. ③(新歌手等用以试探听众反应的)示范唱片,试播唱片. ④(游行示威时播放示威内容的)示威唱片.

de·mob [di:'mɔb]〔英口〕*n.* ① = demobilization. ② 复员军人. —*vt.* = demobilize.

de·mo·bi·li·za·tion ['di:ˌməubilai'zeiʃən] *n.* 复员;遣散. *~ order* 复员令.

de·mo·bi·lize [di:'məubilaiz] *vt.* 【军】复员;遣散. *a*

D

~d soldier 复员军人.

de·moc·ra·cy [diˈmɔkrəsi] *n.* ①民主政治;民主政体,民主制度;民主主义;民主精神. ②民主国家. ③〔D-〕〔美〕民主党. ④〔the ~〕平民,老百姓.

dem·o·crat [ˈdeməkræt] *n.* ①民主主义者. ②〔D-〕〔美〕民主党党员. ~ **wagon** 〔美〕(农场用的)二马轻便马车.

dem·o·crat·ic [ˌdeməˈkrætik] *a.* ①民主政体的,民主主义的;民主作风的. ②民众的;平等的. ③〔D-〕〔美〕民主党的. ~ *centralism* 民主集中制. ~ *parties and groups* 民主党派. *the D- party* (美国的)民主党. ~ *personnel.* 民主人士.

de·moc·ra·tism [diˈmɔkrətizəm] *n.* 民主主义;民主制;民主原则.

de·moc·ra·tize [diˈmɔkrətaiz] *vt., vi.* 民主化,民主起来. **de·moc·ra·ti·za·tion** [diˌmɔkrətaiˈzeiʃən] *n.*

De·moc·ri·tus [diˈmɔkritəs] *n.* 德谟克利特 (460?—370? B.C.) 古希腊哲学家. **-te·an** [-tiːən] *a.*

dé·mo·dé [F. demɔde] *a.* 〔F.〕 过时的,已不时兴的,老式的.

de·mod·ed [diːˈməudid] *a.* 过时的,老式的.

de·mod·u·late [diːˈmɔdjuːˌleit] *vt.* 【无】解调;检波.

de·mod·u·la·tion [diːˌmɔdjuˈleiʃən] *n.* 【无】解调,反调制;检波.

De·mo·gor·gon [ˈdiːməuˈgɔːgən] *n.* (古代神话中的)魔王.

de·mo·graph·ic [diːməˈgræfik] *a.* 人口统计(学)的.

de·mog·ra·phy [diˈmɔgrəfi] *n.* 人口统计学.

de·moi·selle [demwɑːˈzel] *n.* 〔F.〕 ①(未婚)少妇,少女. ②【鸟】蓑羽鹤. ③【虫】豆娘〔一种蜻蜓〕. ④【地】菌状石. ⑤【动】一种在珊瑚礁里栖栖的热带鱼.

de·mol·ish [diˈmɔliʃ] *vt.* ①拆毁(建筑物等),毁坏,破坏(组织等),推翻(计划、制度等). ②〔俚〕吃光. *The automobile was ~ed in a collision the train.* 汽车与火车相撞而被毁坏. *They simply ~ed that turkey.* 他们把那只火鸡一下子吃光.

dem·o·li·tion [ˌdeməˈliʃən] *n.* ①爆破,破坏. ②〔*pl.*〕废墟. ③〔*pl.*〕爆破的炸药. ~ **bomb** 爆破炸弹. ~ **derby** 撞车比赛〔参加者驾车互撞,直至最后有一辆仍可驶行者获冠军〕.

de·mon [ˈdiːmən] *n.* ①鬼,恶魔. ②恶棍. ③精力过人的人. ④(古希腊的)守护神. *the little ~ (of a child)* 调皮娃娃. *a regular ~* 坏家伙. *He is a ~ for work.* 他做起工作来真是精力过人. *the ~ of a bulldog* 凶猛的斗犬.

de·mon·e·tize [diːˈmʌnitaiz] *vt.* ①使(货币)失去标准价值. ②停止用(金银)做货币本位. **-mon·e·tiza·tion** [-ˌmʌnitaiˈzeiʃən] *n.*

de·mo·ni·ac [diˈməuniæk] *a.* ①着魔的. ②恶魔的. ③恶魔似的,凶恶的,疯狂的. — *n.* 着魔的人.

de·mo·ni·a·cal [ˌdiːməˈnaiəkəl] *a.* = demoniac. ~ *possession* 着魔,凶神附体.

de·mon·ic [diːˈmɔnik] *a.* ①有魔力的,神通广大的,超人的. ② = demoniac.

de·mon·ism [ˈdiːmənizəm] *n.* 对魔鬼的信仰. **de·mon·ist** *n.* 魔鬼信仰者.

de·mon·ize [ˈdiːmənaiz] *vt.* 使成鬼;使着魔.

demono- *comb. f.* = demon.

de·mon·oc·ra·cy [diːməˈnɔkrəsi] *n.* 魔鬼的统治〔支配〕.

de·mon·ol·a·try [ˌdiːməˈnɔlətri] *n.* 崇拜魔鬼.

de·mon·ol·o·gy [ˌdiːməˈnɔlədʒi] *n.* ①对魔鬼的研究;对魔鬼的信仰. ②〔美俚〕仇敌名单.

de·mo·nop·o·lize [ˌdiːməˈnɔpəlaiz] *vt.* 解除专卖权.

dem·on·stra·ble [ˈdemənstrəbl] *a.* 可表明的;可论证的. **-bil·i·ty** [ˌdemənstrəˈbiliti] *n.* 论证可能性. **-bly** *ad.* 可证明地,确然,了然.

dem·on·strate [ˈdemənstreit] *vt.* ①表明,表示(感情). ②论证,证明. ③(用实例、实验)说明,示范,表演. ~ *one's anger by slamming a door* 把门砰地关上表示愤怒. ~ *a philosophical principle* 论证一次哲学原理. ~ *how to cook with a pressure cooker* 当众表演如何使用高压锅. —*vi.* ①举行示威运动. ②【军】示威,佯动.

dem·on·stra·tion [ˌdemənstˈreiʃən] *n.* ①表明,表示. ②论证,证明. ③实物示教,示范;实物说明. ④示威(运动);示威游行. ⑤【军】示威行动,佯动. *give a ~ of love* 表示爱情. *to ~* 决定地,断然,明确地. **-al** *a.* 示威(运动)的. **-ist** *n.* 参加示威运动者.

de·mon·stra·tive [diˈmɔnstrətiv] *a.* ①论证的,证明的. ②【语法】指示的. ③感情外露的,易动感情的. — *n.*【语法】指示词. *a ~ person* 易动感情的人. *a ~ pronoun* 指示代词. **-ly** *ad.* **-ness** *n.*

dem·on·stra·tor [ˈdemənstreitə] *n.* ①证明者;示范者;实验示教者;实物说明者. ②示威者. ③用来向顾客作示范表演的产品.

de·mor·al·ize [diˈmɔrəlaiz] *vt.* ①败坏风纪〔道德〕,伤风败俗. ②挫折锐气;【军】使士气沮丧. ③使陷入混乱. **-za·tion** [-ˈzeiʃən] *n.* 道德败坏,风纪败坏;士气沮丧.

de mor·tu·is nil ni·si bo·num [diːˈmɔːtʃuːis nil ˈnaisai ˈbəunəm] 〔L.〕 对于死者唯有称美.

de·mos [ˈdiːmɔs] *n.* (*pl.* ***de·mi*** [ˈdiːmai]) ①(古希腊的)平民. ②(一般的)人民,民众.

De·mos·the·nes [diˈmɔsθəniːz] *n.* 德摩斯梯尼,(公元前 384—322) 古希腊的政治家、雄辩家.

Dem·os·then·ic [ˌdemɔsˈθenik] *a.* 雄辩的.

de·mote [diˈməut] *vt.* 〔美〕使降级 (*opp.* promote).

de·moth·ball [diːˈmɔːθbɔl] *vt.* 重新使用(已转入后备役保存起来的船舶、飞机、大炮等).

de·mot·ic [di(ː)ˈmɔtik] *a.* ①民众的;通俗的. ②(古埃及经过简化的)通俗文字的. — *n.* ①(古埃及经过简化的)通俗文字. ②〔D-〕现代希腊日常用语 (*opp.* Katharevusa).

de·mo·tion [deˈməuʃən] *n.* 降级.

de·mount [diːˈmaunt] *vt.* 卸除. *to ~ a motor* 卸除马达. **-able** *a.*

de·mul·cent [diˈmʌlsnt] *a.* 【医】缓和的,止痛的. —*n.* 缓和药;润药.

de·mul·si·fy [diˈmʌlsifai] *vt.* 【化】反乳化. **-si·fi·ca·tion** [-sifiˈkeiʃən] *n.* 反乳化作用.

de·mur [diˈməː] *vi.* ①表示异议,反对 (*to; at*). ②(因怀疑或反对而)迟疑. ③【法】抗辩. — *n.* 异议,反对. *No ~.* 没有异议. *without ~* 无异议.

de·mure [diˈmjuə] *a.* ①娴静的,拘谨的,庄重的. ②假装正经的. *a quiet and ~ woman* 文雅端庄的妇女. **-ly** *ad.* **-ness** *n.*

de·mur·ra·ble [diˈməːrəbl] *a.* 可抗辩的,可提出异议的.

de·mur·rage [diˈmʌridʒ] *n.*【商】(轮船、货车因未能如期装卸、运行而)逾期;逾期费. ②(英格兰银行的)金银块兑换费.

de·mur·rer [diˈmʌrə] *n.* ①【法】异议,抗辩. ② [diˈməːrə] 抗辩者. *enter [put in] a ~* 提出异议,反对.

de·my [diˈmai] *n.* ①〔英〕$22\frac{1}{2} \times 17\frac{1}{2}$ 英寸开(的纸);〔美〕21 × 16 英寸开(的纸). ②(英国牛津大学 Magdalen College 的)半津贴生.

de·my·e·lin·ate [diːˈmaiəlineit] *vt.*【医】脱髓鞘. **-na·tion** [-ˌmaiəliˈneiʃən] *n.*

de·my·thol·o·gize [ˌdiːmiˈθɔlədʒaiz] *vt.* 去掉(《圣经》等中的)神话色彩(以便于理解和领受).

Den. = Denmark.

den [den] *n.* ①兽穴,窝. ②匪窟,贼窝. ③小而脏的屋子. ④小而舒适的书斋. ⑤〔Scot.〕溪谷. ⑥(幼年童子军的)小组,小队. — *vi.* ①穴居. ②入洞,进窝(冬眼)。— *vt.* 把…赶入洞中。
de·nar·i·us [di'nɛriəs] *n.* (*pl.* **-ri·i** [-riai])第纳里〔古罗马银币,英国旧便士 (penny, pence) 以该词首字母 d 为缩略号〕。
de·na·ry ['di:nəri] *a.* 十的,十进的,十倍的。~ *scale* 十进法。
de·na·tion·al·ize [di:'næʃənəlaiz] ①使(国家)失去国家地位[特点]。②使(人)失去国籍[公民权]。③使(企业)非国有化,变成私营。**-za·tion** ['di:,næʃənəlai'zeiʃən] *n.*
de·nat·u·ral·ize [di:'nætʃrəlaiz] *vt.* ①使不自然;使改变本性。②剥夺国民[市民]权利,开除…的国籍。**-za·tion** [-'zeiʃən] *n.*
de·na·tur·ant [di:'neitʃərənt] *n.* 变性剂。
de·na·ture [di:'neitʃə] *vt.* ①使变性。②使(酒精)不能饮用。③使(蛋白质)变质。④使(核燃料)中毒〔加入不裂变物质使裂变物质不适于制造原子弹〕。~*d alcohol* 变性酒精。~*d protein* 变性蛋白质。
de·na·zi·fy [di:'nɑ:tsifai] *vt.* 消除…的纳粹影响;清除…的纳粹分子,使非纳粹化。
dendr(i)- *comb. f.* 〔用于辅音前〕= dendro-.
den·dri·form ['dendrifɔ:m] *a.* 树木状的。
den·drite ['dendrait] *n.* ①【矿】松树石,树石。②【化】枝状晶体。③【解】(神经的)枝状突起;树突。
den·drit·ic, den·drit·i·cal [den'dritik(əl)] *a.* 枝状的。
dendr(o)- *comb. f.* 树木〔元音前用 dendr-〕。
dendroi·d(al) [den'drɔid(əl)] *a.* 树状的;分枝状的。
den·dro·lite ['dendrəulait] *n.* 树木化石,化石植物。
den·drol·o·gy [den'drɔlədʒi] *n.* 树木学。
den·drom·e·ter [den'drɔmitə] *n.* 测树器。
den·dron ['dendrɔn] *n.*【解】= dendrite.
dene[1] [di:n] *n.* (树木繁茂的)幽谷。
dene[2] [di:n] *n.* (海滨的)沙地;沙丘。
Den·eb ['deneb]【天】天津四〔天鹅座 α〕。
D. Eng. = Doctor of Engineering 工程学博士。
den·e·ga·tion [,deni'geiʃən] *n.* 否认;拒绝。
den·gue ['deŋgi] *n.*【医】登革热〔蚊子传染的热带病,症状为关节痛、发烧、出疹子〕。
de·ni·a·ble [di'naiəbl] *a.* 可否认的,可反对的;可拒绝的。
de·ni·al [di'naiəl] *n.* ①否认,否定。②拒绝承认,拒绝相信,拒绝接受。③克制 (= self-~)。*general* [*specific*] ~ 全部[部分]否认。*make a* ~ *of* 否定,否认。*take no* ~ 不许否认,不许说不,硬要。
de·nic·o·tin·ize [di:'nikətinaiz] *vt.* (从烟草中)除去尼古丁。**-za·tion** [-,nikətinai'zeiʃən] *n.*
de·ni·er[1] [di'naiə] *n.* 否认者;拒绝者。
de·nier[2] ['diniei] *n.* ①法国古银币名。②纤度,紫〔生丝纤度单位,长 450 米重 0.05 克时为 1 denier〕。~**meter** 纤度计。
den·i·grate ['denigreit] *vt.* ①涂黑。②污蔑,诽谤。**-gra·tion** [,deni'greiʃən] *n.* **-grat·or** *n.* 诽谤者。**-gra·to·ry** [-grətəri] *a.*
den·im ['denim] *n.* ①斜纹粗棉布。②〔*pl.*〕(蓝色斜纹粗棉布制成的)工作服,工装裤。
Den·ise [də'ni:z, de'ni:z] *n.* 丹妮斯〔女子名〕。
de·ni·trate [di:'naitreit] *vt.* 从…除去硝酸盐,使脱硝。
de·ni·tra·tion [di:nai'treiʃən] *n.* 脱硝。
de·ni·tri·fy [di:'naitrifai] *vt.* ①去掉…的氮气。②使脱去硝酸盐。~*ing bacteria* 反硝化细菌;脱氮细菌。
den·i·zen ['denizn] *n.* ①居民。②(享有某些或全部公民权的)外籍居民,归化者。③外来语;外来动植物。④暂住某处的人;常去某处的人。*winged* ~*s of the forest* 森林中的鸟类。— *vt.* 给与…以市民权;准许…归化;移植。
Den·mark ['denmɑ:k] *n.* 丹麦〔欧洲〕。
Den·(n)is ['denis] *n.* 丹尼斯〔姓氏,男子名〕。
de·nom·i·nate [di'nɔmineit] *vt.* 为…命名,给…取名,把…叫做,把…称做。
de·nom·i·na·tion [di,nɔmi'neiʃən] *n.* ①命名;名目,名称。②(度量衡等的)单位;票面金额。③种类;教派,宗派;派别。*plants falling under different* ~*s* 种种植物。*money of small* ~*s* 小钱,零钱。*What* ~? 什么票面的钱币? *all sects and* ~*s* 各党各派。**-al** [-nl] *a.* 名称上的;宗派的,教派的。
de·nom·i·na·tion·al·ism [di,nɔmi'neiʃənəlizəm] *n.* ①宗派原则。②宗派制度。③宗派主义。④分成宗派。
de·nom·i·na·tive [di'nɔminətiv] *a.* ①有名称的;可命名的。②【语法】出自名词[形容词]的。*"To eye" is a* ~ *verb.* To eye (目视)是来自名词的动词。
de·nom·i·na·tor [di'nɔmineitə] *n.* ①命名者。②【数】分母。③(爱好、见解等的)标准。④共同特性。*a* [*the least*] *common* ~ 公[最小公]分母。*manufacturers catering to a low* ~ *of public taste* 制造商致力于满足公众的低标准的爱好。*Only a single* ~ *do they share.* 他们只有一种共同的特点。
de·not·a·ble [di'nəutəbl] *a.* 可表示[指示]的。
de·no·ta·tion [,di:nəu'teiʃən] *n.* ①指示,表示。②名称;符号。③(字面)意义 (*cf.* connotation)。④【逻】外延。⑤命名。
de·no·ta·tive [di'nəutətiv] *a.* ①指示…的,表示的 (*of*)。②【逻】外延的 (*opp.* connotative)。**-ly** *ad.*
de·note [di'nəut] *vt.* ①指示,表示;意味着。②【逻】概述,概指 (*opp.* connote)。*Dark clouds* ~ *rain.* 黑云表示有雨。**-ment** 指示,表示,表示方法。
dé·noue·ment [dei'nu:mɑ̃:ŋ] *n.* 〔F.〕(小说等的)大团圆,收场;结局。
de·nounce [di'nauns] *vt.* ①指责,谴责;声讨,斥责。②〔古〕恐吓,扬言要(报仇等)。③告发,揭发。④通告废除(条约等)。~ *a man as a traitor* 指责某人是叛徒。~ *a person to the police* 向警察告发某人。~ *vengeance against* 扬言要向…报仇。**-ment** *n.* = denunciation.
dense [dens] *a.* ①密集的,(物质等)密度大的,(人口等)稠密的。②(烟、雾等)浓密的,浓厚的。③愚钝的。④(摄影底片)反差强的。*a* ~ *forest* 密林。*a* ~ *metal* 密度大的金属。*a* ~ *fog* 浓雾。*a man with a* ~ *brain* 头脑愚昧的人。*My* ~ *lady, can't you follow?* 哎呀,我的傻太太,你真的听不懂吗? **-ly** *ad.* **-ness** *n.*
den·si·fy ['densifai] *vt.* 使增加密度。**-fi·ca·tion** [-fi'keiʃən] *n.*
den·sim·e·ter [den'simitə] *n.* 比重计,密度计。
den·si·tom·e·ter [,densi'tɔmitə] *n.* ① = densimeter. ②(测量底片的)显影密度计。
den·si·tom·e·try [,densi'tɔmitri] *n.* 测密度术;测光密度术;显微测密术。
den·si·ty ['densiti] *n.* ①稠密;浓厚。②【物】浓度;密度;比重。③愚钝,昏庸。*traffic* ~ 交通量。*the* ~ *of population* 人口密度。~ **recorder** 自记比重计,比重记录器。
den·som·e·ter [den'sɔmitə] *n.* ①(纸张的)透气度测定计。②=densimeter.
Dent [dent] *n.* 登特〔姓氏〕。
dent[1] [dent] *n.* ①凹,凹痕,压痕。②〔英方〕打,击。③削减。④进展。**make a** ~ 使注意;开始有进步[有进展] (*The doctor told him to stop smoking, but it didn't make a dent.* 医生让他停止抽烟,但没有引起注意。*I haven't even made a* ~ *in this job.* 我这工作没有取得进展)。— *vt.* ①敲凹,使凹下。②削减。— *vi.* 凹进。
dent[2] [dent] *n.* (齿轮等的)齿;【纺】竹筘齿格。
dent- (接元音) = denti-.
dent. = dental; dentist; dentistry.
dent·al ['dentl] *a.* ①牙齿的;牙科(用)的。②【语音】齿音的。— *n.* ①【语音】齿音;齿音字 [d, t, n 等]。②〔谑〕牙齿。*a* ~ *parlor* 〔美〕牙医诊室。~ *paste* 牙膏。*a* ~ *surgeon* 牙医生。~ *surgery* 牙科,口腔外科。**-ize**

vt. 使齿音化. **-gi·a** [den'tældʒiə] *r.* 齿痛.

den·ta·li·um [den'teiliəm] *n.* *(pl.* **-li·a** [-lə]*)* 角贝属动物.

den·tate ['denteit] *a.* ①有牙齿的. ②【植】(叶子)锯齿状的.

den·ta·tion [den'teiʃən] *n.* 齿状(构造).

denti- (接辅音) *comb. f.* 齿,牙: *denti*form.

den·ti·care ['dentikɛə] *n.* (加拿大等国实行的)儿童牙齿免费保健计划.

den·ti·cle ['dentikl] *n.* ①小牙; 细齿状突起. ②【建】齿饰. **-tic·u·lar** [den'tikjulə] *a.* 细齿状的. **-tic·u·late** [den'tikjulit] *a.* 有细齿的, 锯齿状的. **-tic·u·la·tion** [den,tikju'leiʃən] *n.* 细齿状 (突起); 〔常 *pl.*〕一副细齿.

den·ti·form ['dentifɔ:m] *a.* 齿形的.

den·ti·frice ['dentifris] *n.* 牙粉; 牙膏.

den·tig·er·ous [den'tidʒərəs] *a.* 生齿的,有牙齿的.

den·til ['dentil] *n.*【建】(屋檐下的)齿饰.

den·ti·la·bi·al [,denti'leibiəl] *a., n.* = labiodental.

den·ti·lated ['dentileitid] *a.* 形成齿状的.

den·ti·lin·gual [,denti'liŋgwəl] *a.*【语音】齿舌音〔[θ], [ð] 等辅音〕的.

den·tin, den·tine ['dentin, -ti:n] *n.* (牙齿的牙釉下的)牙质.

den·tist ['dentist] *n.* 牙科医生.

den·tist·ry ['dentistri] *n.* 牙科医术; 牙医业.

den·ti·tion [den'tiʃən] *n.* ①出牙齿,长牙齿. ②牙列,齿列. ③〔集合词〕(一口)牙齿.

dento- *comb. f.* = denti-

den·toid ['dentɔid] *a.* 牙齿状的.

Den·ton ['dentən] *n.* 登顿〔男子名〕.

den·to·sur·gi·cal [,dentəu'sə:dʒikl] *a.* 牙外科的.

den·ture ['dentʃə] *n.* ①一副牙齿. ②一副假牙. *a full [partial]* ~ 全副[一部分]假牙.

de·nu·cle·ar·ize [di:'nju:kliəraiz, -'nju:-] *vt.* 使非核武器化. **-za·tion** [-,nju:kliərai'zeiʃən] *n.*

de·nu·cle·ate [di:'nju:klieit] *vt.* 除去 (原子、分子、动物细胞等的)核,使去核. **-cle·a·tion** [-,nju:kli'eiʃən] *n.* 去核(作用).

de·nu·da·tion [,di:nju:'deiʃən] *n.* ①剥裸; 除光,裸露. ②【地】剥蚀. ③【林】滥伐.

de·nude [di'nju:d] *vt.* ①除光,剥裸. ②剥去; 剥夺. ③【地】剥蚀. ④【化】溶蚀; 去垢. *Most trees are ~d of their leaves in winter.* 许多树木冬季都要落叶.

de·nu·mer·a·ble [di'nu:mərəbl, -'nju:-] *a.* 可数的.

de·nun·ci·ate [di'nʌnsieit, -ʃieit] *vt.* = denounce.

de·nun·ci·a·tion [di,nʌnsi'eiʃən] *n.* ①指责,弹劾. ②控诉,告发,揭发. ③警告, 恐吓. ④声讨檄文. ⑤废约通告.

de·nun·ci·a·tor [di'nʌnsieitə] *n.* 指责者; 告发者; 恐吓者.

de·nun·ci·a·to·ry [di'nʌnsiətəri] *a.* 指责的; 恐吓的.

Den·ver ['denvə] *n.* 丹佛〔美国城市〕. **-ite** [-vərait] *n.* 丹佛人.

de·ny [di'nai] *vt.* ①否定,否认; 不承认. ②拒绝(要求等),不给与. ③不接受,推卸; 摒弃. ④谢绝(宾客). *He denied the charges against him.* 他否认他有嫌疑. *There is no ~ing the fact.* 事实无可否认. *~ one's signature* 否认是自己的署名. *This night before the cock crows, you shall ~ me three times.* 今夜鸡叫以前,你要三次不认我. *I was denied this = This was denied (to) me.* 这个我未曾得到. *I was denied satisfaction.* 我未曾满足. *Peace was denied him.* 他心境不安. ~ ***oneself*** ①自制, 克己. ②放弃 (*He must ~ himself many of the comforts of life.* 他必须放弃自己生活上的许多享受). ~ ***oneself to*** 不会见客人等 (*She denied herself to all callers.* 她不会见任何来客). ~ ***sb. to*** *(callers)* 使某人不会见客人 (*I told the door-keeper to ~ me to all callers.* 我关照传达室不接见任何客人). — *vi.* 否定; 拒绝.

de·ob·stru·ent [di'ɔbstru:ənt] *n., a.*【药】便通剂(的).

de·oc·cu·py [di'ɔkjupai] *vt.* 解除对…的占领.

de·o·dar ['diəuda:] *n.*【植】喜马拉雅杉. ~ *ceder* 雪松.

de·o·dor·ant [di:'əudərənt] *a.* 除臭的. —*n.* 防臭剂,除臭药.

de·o·dor·ize [di:'əudəraiz] *vt.* 除去…的臭味, 防止…的臭味. **-ri·za·tion** [di,əudərai'zeiʃən] *n.* 防臭, 脱臭(作用). **-iz·er** [-zə] *n.* 除[防]臭剂; 防臭喷雾器.

de·on·tol·o·gy [di:ɔn'tɔlədʒi] *n.*【伦】义务论,道义学.

de·or·bit [di:-'ɔ:bit] *vt.* 使脱轨. — *n.*, 脱轨.

De·o vo·len·te ['di:əu vəu'lenti] 〔L.〕若承天意; 若无阻碍〔略 D.V.〕.

de·ox·i·di·za·tion, de·ox·i·da·tion [di:,ɔksidai'zeiʃən, -'deiʃən] *n.* 脱氧; 还原.

de·ox·i·dize, de·ox·i·date [di:'ɔksidaiz, -deit] *vt.*【化】使脱氧; 使还原.

de·ox·i·di·zer [di:'ɔksidaizə] *n.* 脱氧剂; 还原剂.

de·ox·y·gen·ate [di:'ɔksidʒineit] *vt.* = deoxidize.

de·ox·y·ri·bo·nu·cle·ic [di:'ɔksi,raibəunju:'kli:ik] *a.* ~ **acid**【生化】脱氧核糖核酸 (DNA).

de·ox·y·ri·bo·nu·cle·o·tide [di:'ɔksi,raibəunju:'kli:ətaid] *n.*【生化】脱氧核(糖核)苷酸〔DNA 的组成成分之一〕.

dep. = department; departs; departure; deponent; deposed;【银行】deposit; depot; deputy.

de·part [di'pa:t] *vi., vt.* ①〔古、诗〕离开. ②(火车等)开行 *(opp.* arrive*)*. ③不合(情理等) *(from)*. ④死亡,消失. ~ *at 5:30* 五点半开〔略作 dep. 5:30 a.m.〕. ~ *from (this) life* 去世,死. ~ ***this life*** 去世. ~ ***for*** *(London)* 去(伦敦). ~ ***from*** 不合(习惯等); 背离; 违反(*~ from one's word* 违约). ~ ***hence*** 由这儿去.

de·part·ed [di'pa:tid] *a.* ①已往的,过去的. ②已去世的. *the* ~ 死者,故人.

de·part·ment [di'pa:tmənt] *n.* ①部门; 〔美〕部 (=〔英〕ministry); 〔英〕局,课,科; 车间. ②(法国等的)省,县. ③【军】军(管)区. ④(学校、学术机构的)系; 学部. ⑤知识范围; 活动范围. ⑥(期刊或广播节目的) 专栏. *the physics [literature]* ~ 物理学[文学]部. *D- of the Interior* 〔美〕内政部. *the State D-* 〔美〕国务院. *the accountant's* ~会计科. *the Statistics D-* 〔英〕统计局. *the Hawaiian D-* 〔美〕夏威夷军区. ~ *store* 百货商店,百货公司. *D- of Trusteeship Council* (联合国)托管理事会.

de·part·men·tal [,di:pa:t'mentl] *a.* 部门[科、系、局等]的. **-ism** *n.* 分散主义; 本位主义. **-ize** [-aiz] *vt.* 把…分成部门. **-ly** *ad.*

de·par·ture [di'pa:tʃə] *n.* ①起程,出发; (火车的)开行. ②背离,违反 *(from)*; 偏差. ③【测】东西距离,横距. ④〔古〕逝世. ⑤【海】航迹推算起点. ~ ***and arrival*** 开出和到达. ~ ***from the truth*** 失真,伪. ***new*** ~ 新政策,新方案. ***take one's*** ~ 出发, 起身. ~ **hall** (飞机场的)候机室. ~ **platform** 发车月台.

de·pas·ture [di:'pa:stʃə] *vt., vi.* ①(使)吃草; 放牧. ②(把)(某地)作放牧[牧草]基地. **-pas·tur·age** [-'pa:stʃəridʒ] *n.* 放牧(权).

de·pau·per·ate [di:'pɔ:pəreit] *vt.* ①使贫穷. ②使衰落; 使萎缩. —*a.* ①贫穷的. ②发育不全的, 萎缩的. **-a·tion** [-,pɔ:pə'reiʃən] *n.* ①贫穷. ②衰落. ③【植】萎缩,变质.

de·pau·per·ize ['di:'pɔ:pəraiz] *vt.* ①〔美〕使贫穷. ②〔英〕使脱离贫穷.

de·pend [di'pend] *vi.* ①取决于,因…而定,靠,凭 *(on; upon)*. ②依赖,依靠; 信任 *(on; upon)*. ③(树枝等)下垂,悬挂 *(from)*. ④〔古〕(案件等)悬而不决. ⑤【语法】从属. *Success ~s on [upon] your own exertions.* 成功全靠自己努力. *You can ~ on him.* 你信任他好了. ~ *on*

depth to avoid breakthrough【军】以纵深配备防止突破. ***a man to be ~ed on*** 可靠的人. ***~ on [upon] ... for*** 要看…,靠…供给…,赖…做… (*He ~s on his pen for his living.* 他靠写作吃饭). ***D- upon it!*** 靠得住! 的确的! 你看好啦! 你相信好啦(*D- upon it, you will succeed.* 你准能成功). ***That ~s = It all ~s.*** 那要看情况了,不能一概而论,要看时间与地点而定 (*Sometimes I support him, and sometimes he supports me; that ~s.* 有时我支持他,有时他支持我,这要看情况而定).

de·pend·a·ble [diˈpendəbl] *a.* 可靠的,可信任的. **-bly** *ad.* **-bil·i·ty** [-ˌpendəˈbiliti] *n.* 可靠性, 可信任程度. **-ness** *n.* 可靠,可信任.

de·pend·ant [diˈpendənt] *n., a.* = dependent. *family ~s* 供养的直系亲属.

de·pend·ence [diˈpendəns] *n.* ①依赖, 依靠. ②依靠之物,靠山. ③信任,信赖. ④从属; 隶属. ⑤【物】依存(关系). ⑥【法】未决.

de·pend·en·cy [diˈpendənsi] *n.* ①依存; 从属. ②从属物. ③属国,属地,保护地.

de·pend·ent [diˈpendənt] *a.* ①依靠的, 依赖的. ②从属的,隶属的,【语法】从属的. ③由…决定的. ④下垂的,悬吊的. *be ~ on [upon]* 依靠; 取决于. —*n.* ①受赡养者,靠人生活的人. ②扈从,侍从. ③依存[从属]物. *~ clause*【语法】从属子句[从句,分句]. *~ nexus* 从属二元语核. *a ~ domain* 领地. *He listed four ~s on his income-tax form.* 他在所得税表格上填写了四个受赡养人.

de·perm [diːˈpəːm] *vt.* 减少[消除](船体周围)的磁性.

de·per·son·al·ize [diːˈpəːsənəˌlaiz] *vt.* ①使…失去个性; 对…作客观处理. ②使失去自我感. **-per·son·a·li·za·tion** [-ˌpəːsənəlaiˈzeiʃən] *n.*

De·pew [diˈpjuː] *n.* 迪皮尤〔姓氏〕.

de·phased [diːˈfeizd] *a.*【无】有相位差的; 相位移后的.

de·phleg·mate [diːˈflegmeit] *vt.*【化】除去…的过量水分; 使分馏,使分凝. **-ma·tion** [ˌdiːflegˈmeiʃən] *n.* 分馏; 分凝. **-tor** *n.* 分馏塔; 分凝器.

de·phos·phor·ize [diːˈfɔsfəraiz] *vt.* 使脱去磷酸.

de·pict [diˈpikt] *vt.* ①画,刻画. ②描写, 叙述. **de·pic·tion** [-ˈpikʃən] *n.* 描写; 叙述. **de·pic·tive** [-ˈpiktiv] *a.* 描写的. **-ture** [-ˈpiktʃə] *vt.* = depict.

dep·i·late [ˈdepileit] *vt.* 使脱毛,除去…的毛. **-la·tion** [ˌdepiˈleiʃən] *n.* 脱毛. **-to·ry** [diˈpilətəri] *a., n.* ①有除毛力的. ②【医】脱毛剂.

de·plane [diːˈplein] *vi.* 下飞机.

de·plen·ish [diˈpleniʃ] *vt.* 弄空 *(opp.* replenish*)*. *a ~ed house* (没有家具的)空荡荡的房子. *a ~ed purse* 囊空如洗.

de·plete [diˈpliːt] *vt.* ①减少,损耗. ②弄空,耗尽,用尽. ③【医】减液,放血. *~ one's strength* 竭尽全力. *a lake recklessly ~d* 乱捕鱼(使鱼源枯竭)的湖.

de·ple·tion [diˈpliːʃən] *n.* ①损耗. ②弄空; 耗尽. ③【医】减液; 放血; (缺液引起的)衰竭(状态).

de·ple·tive [diˈpliːtiv] *a.* ①引起枯竭的,有耗尽作用的. ②减液的; 放血的.

de·ple·to·ry [diˈpliːtəri] *a.* = depletive.

de·plor·a·ble [diˈplɔːrəbl] *a.* 可叹的,悲惨的. ***in ~ order*** 极杂乱. **-ness** *n.* **-bly** *ad.* **-bil·i·ty** [diˌplɔːrəˈbiliti] *n.*

de·plore [diˈplɔː] *vt.* ①悲悼,痛惜. ②悔恨. *~ the death of one's friend* 哀悼朋友的逝世. **-plor·ing·ly** *ad.*

de·ploy [diˈplɔi] *vt., vi.* ①【军】展开,散开,疏散开. ②部署. ③(使)张开. *~ a battalion* 使队伍散开. *The army ~ed to the right.* 部队向右方展开. **-ment** *n.* 部署 (*rational deployment of labour power* 合理安排劳动力).

de·plume [diːˈpluːm] *vt.* ①拔去…的羽毛. ②夺去,剥夺(荣誉、财产等).

de·po·lar·ize [diːˈpəuləraiz] *vt.* ①【物】减极,去极,退极化. ②消除(偏见等); 使丧失(信心等). **-zer** [-zə] *n.* 退极化剂. **-za·tion** [ˈdiːˌpəuləraiˈzeiʃən] *n.*

de·po·lit·i·cize [ˌdiːpəˈlitisaiz], **de·po·lit·i·cal·ize** [ˌdiːpəˈlitikəlaiz] *vt.* 使非政治化.

de·pone [diˈpəun] *vt., vi.* 〔古〕发誓证明.

de·po·nent [diˈpəunənt] *a.* 【拉丁语语法】异态的, 词形被动词义自动的. —*n.* ①异态(词形被动词义自动的)动词,异相动词. ②【法】宣誓作证者.

de·pop·u·late [diːˈpɔpjuleit] *vt.* (战争,疫病等)消灭[减少](某地的)人口. —*vi.* 〔罕〕人口减少. —*a.* 〔古〕人口减少的. **-la·tion** [-ˌpɔpjuˈleiʃən] *n.*

de·port [diˈpɔːt] *vt.* ①〔*~ oneself*〕行动,举动. ②运输,输送. ③把…驱逐出境. *~ oneself well [ill]* 行为好[坏]. *~ dangerous aliens* 把危险的外国人驱逐出境. **-ta·tion** [ˌdiːpɔːˈteiʃən] *n.* 驱逐出境. **-tee** [ˌdiːpɔːˈtiː] *n.* 被驱逐出境者.

de·port·ment [diˈpɔːtmənt] *n.* 行为,品行; 举止,态度.

de·pos·al [diˈpəuzəl] *n.* 罢免,免职; 废位.

de·pose [diˈpəuz] *vt.* ①把…免职, 废黜(国王等). ②【法】宣誓证明 *(that)*. ③放置. *~ sb. from office* 免去某人的职务. *~ sth. on the table* 把某物放在桌上. —*vi.* 宣誓作证. *~ to a fact* 宣誓证明某事. **-a·ble** *a.* 可废除的,可罢免的.

de·pos·it [diˈpɔzit] *vt.* ①放置,安置. ②使淤积,使沉淀. ③储蓄. ④付保证金. ⑤寄存,委托保管. ⑥(把硬币)放入(自动售货机). *~ money in the bank* 把钱存入银行. *~ sth. with sb.* 把某物委托某人保管. —*vi.* ①淤积,沉淀; 附着. ②存贮; 寄存. —*n.* ①淤积[沉积]物;【矿】矿藏, 矿床. ②储蓄; 存款. ③保证金, 押金. ④寄存,寄存品. ⑤寄存处,仓库. *oil ~s* 石油埋藏量. *current [fixed] ~* 活期[定期]存款. *money on ~* 存款. *have [place] money on ~* 有存款[攒、存钱]. ***~ at bank*** 银行存款. ***~ at call*** 活期存款. ***~ in security*** 保证金, 押金. ***~ in trust*** 信托存款. **~ account** 存款帐户.

de·pos·i·ta·ry [diˈpɔzitəri] *n.* ①受托人,保管人. ②保管所,贮藏所,仓库.

dep·o·si·tion [ˌdepəˈziʃən, diː-] *n.* ①免职,罢免; 废位. ②淤积[沉积](物, 作用). ③耶稣从十字架上放下(的画、雕刻). ④寄存,委托; 委托物. ⑤【法】口供,证言; 口供书.

de·pos·i·tor [diˈpɔzitə] *n.* ①存放人; 存款人. ②沉淀器.

de·pos·i·to·ry [diˈpɔzitəri] *n.* ①寄存处,存放处,贮藏所,仓库. ②受托人,保管人. *a ~ of learning* 知识的宝库. *~ library* 〔美〕指定免费接受政府出版物的图书馆.

dep·ot [ˈdepəu; Am.ˈdiː-] *n.* ①〔英〕贮藏所,仓库. ②〔美〕火车站; 航空站. ③【军】兵站,补给站. ④〔英〕团司令部; 新兵训练站; 俘虏收容所. *~ ship* 供应舰,修配舰.

de·prave [diˈpreiv] *vt.* ①使堕落,使腐化. ②弄坏,败坏. **-d** *a.* 堕落的,腐败的. **-va·tion** [ˌdeprəˈveiʃən] *n.* 颓废,堕落.

de·prav·i·ty [diˈpræviti] *n.* ①堕落; 腐败; 邪恶. ②〔*pl.*〕恶劣行为,腐化堕落的行为.

dep·re·cate [ˈdeprikeit] *vt.* ①不赞成,反对(战争等). ②祈免,求免(灾殃等). ③贬低. *~ sb.'s anger* 求某人息怒. **-ca·tion** [ˌdepriˈkeiʃən] *n.* ①不赞成,反对. ②求免,求情. **-ca·to·ry** [ˈdeprikətəri] *a.* ①反对的. ②求情的,道歉的. *a ~ letter.*

de·pre·ci·ate [diˈpriːʃieit] *vt.* ①使减值,使贬值; 使跌价. ②贬低,轻视. —*vi.* 减价,贬值. **-at·ing·ly** [-ˈpriːʃieitiŋli] *ad.* 轻视地, 贬低地(*speak depreciatingly of* 贬损,讥笑).

de·pre·ci·a·tion [diˌpriːʃiˈeiʃən] *n.* ①减价,贬值. ②折旧;【机】损耗. ③藐视,轻视. *~ in price* 减价. *a ~ of currency* 通货贬值. *~ funds* 折旧费.

de·pre·ci·a·tive, de·pre·ci·a·to·ry [diˈpriːʃjətiv,

-ətəri] *a.* ①价值低落的,减价的,贬值的. ②蔑视的,贬低的.

dep·re·date [ˈdeprideit] *vt., vi.* 掠夺,劫掠 *(sth., on sth.).* **-da·tion**[ˌdepriˈdeiʃən] *n.* 劫掠;〔*pl.*〕劫余残迹.

de·press [diˈpres] *vt.* ①压下, 压低(声调等), 放低 *(opp.* raise). ②使沮丧, 使消沉, 抑制. ③使萧条,使跌价. ④使衰弱.

de·press·ant [diˈpresənt] *a.* ①【医】有镇静作用的. ②使消沉的. ③引起萧条的. —*n.* 镇静剂.

de·pressed [diˈprest] *a.* ①被压下的,被压低了的. ②中间凹下的. ③抑郁的,消沉的. ④萧条的. ⑤【动、植】扁平的〔横向扁者叫 depressed, 纵向扁者叫 compressed〕. *feel* ~ 闷闷不乐. *The market is* ~. 市况萧条. ~ *area*〔英〕不景气地区. ~ *classes* 最下层人民. ~ *roadway* 低陷的道路.

de·press·i·ble [diˈpresibl] *a.* 可压低的.

de·press·ing [diˈpresiŋ] *a.* 抑压的;郁闷的. **-ly** *ad.*

de·pres·sion [diˈpreʃən] *n.* ①压低,降低,陷落. ②凹洼;洼地,沉降地. ②不景气,萧条,不振. ③沮丧,消沉. ④低气压. ⑤【天】地平线以下星体的角度距离;【测】俯角. ⑥【病】机能降低;抑郁症. *atmospheric* ~ 低(气)压. *nervous* ~ 神经衰弱. *suffer from [be affected with]* ~ 患神经衰弱症.

de·pres·sive [diˈpresiv] *a.* ①抑压的,压下的. ②郁闷的,消沉的.

de·pres·so·mo·tor [diˈpresəuˌməutə] *a.* 抑制运动功能的. —*n.* 运动抑制剂.

de·pres·sor [diˈpresə] *n.* ①抑压者. ②【化】抑制剂. ③(血压)降压剂. ④【解】下牵肌. ⑤【医】压舌板, 压低器. ~ *nerve* 减压神经. *a tongue* ~ 压舌板.

de·priv·a·ble [diˈpraivəbl] *a.* 可剥夺的.

de·priv·al [diˈpraivəl] *n.* 剥夺,褫夺.

dep·ri·va·tion [ˌdepriˈveiʃən] *n.* ①剥夺;(圣职等的)褫夺,免职;废止. ②丧失(氧气、维生素等).

de·prive [diˈpraiv] *vt.* ①剥夺,使 *(sb.)* 不能享受 *(of).* ②免职(特指圣职). ~ *(sb.) of* ... 使(人)失去 *(An accident* ~*d him of his sight.* 意外的事故使他失明). ***be*** ~***d of*** 失却 *(I was* ~*d of education at ten.* 我十岁时就失学了).

de pro·fun·dis [ˌdiː prəuˈfʌndis, ˌdei-] ①悲悯以极的. ②〔*D- P-*〕《圣经》第一百三十诗篇〔篇首语是此二词,故以之代篇名〕;哀悼经.

dep·side [ˈdepsaid, -sid] *n.* 【化】缩酚酸.

dept. = ① department. ② deponent. ③ deputy.

depth [depθ] *n.* ①深;深度. ②(色泽的)浓度;(声音的)低沉;(感情等的)深厚,深沉,深刻. ③进深. ④〔常 *pl.*〕深处;深渊,深海,海. ⑤正中,当中. ⑥深奥,奥妙. ***beyond [out of] one's*** ~ 在深不着底的地方;不能理解,力所不及. ~ ***bomb [charge]*** 深水炸弹. ~ ***of shade*** 色度. ***from the*** ~ ***of the mind*** 诚心,真心,从心底里. ***in*** ~ 广泛,彻底,详细. ***in the*** ~ ***of*** 在正中;在深处. ***keep within one's*** ~ 在(某人)可能限度内蹚水;做(某人)力所能及的事情. ***to the*** ~***s of one's heart*** 内心深处. ***with a great*** ~ ***of feeling*** 深深同情.

dep·u·rate [ˈdepjureit] *vt.* 除去…的杂质, 净化, 提纯. **-ra·tion**[ˌdepjuˈreiʃən] *n.* 净化(作用); **-ra·tive** [ˈdepjurətiv,diˈpjuər-] *a., n.* 净化的;净化剂. **-ra·tor** [ˈdepjureitə] *n.* 净化器;净化剂.

dep·u·ta·tion [ˌdepju(ː)ˈteiʃən] *n.* ①代理,代表;代表团. ②派代表,委派. *a* ~ *to the conference* 参加会议的代表团.

de·pute [diˈpjuːt] *vt.* 使…做代理,派为代理;委托代理.

dep·u·tize [ˈdepjutaiz] *vt.* 〔美〕委任…为代表. —*vi.* 〔口〕做代理人 *(for).*

dep·u·ty [ˈdepjuti] *n.* ①代理,代表. ②〔D-〕(法、意等的)下院议员. ③〔英〕(客栈的)管理员. —*a.* 代理的,副的. *a* ~ *to the National People's Congress* (中国)人民代表大会代表. ***by*** ~ 由别人代理〔代表〕. ***the Chamber of Deputies*** (法国等的)国民议会,下院. ~ **chairman** 副主席,代理主席. ~ **director** 副主任. ~ **mayor** 副市长. **D- Speaker** 副议长,代理议长.

De Quin·cey [də ˈkwinsi] *n.* 德昆西〔姓氏〕.

der. = derivation; derivative; derived.

de·rac·i·nate [diˈræsineit] *vt.* ①根除,灭绝. ②隔绝,隔离.

de·raign [diˈrein] *vt.* 【法】(当事人)以决斗来解决(争端).

de·rail [diˈreil] *vt.* 使(火车等)出轨. —*vi.* 出轨. ***be [get]*** ~***ed*** 出轨. **-ment** *n.* 出轨.

de·range [diˈreindʒ] *vt.* ①扰乱(秩序),打乱(计划). ②使精神错乱,使发狂. *be* ~*d* 发疯. **-ment** *n.* ①扰乱;混乱. ②(精神)狂乱,错乱〔较 insanity 轻〕.

de·rate [diːˈreit] *vt., vi.* 减税,免税.

de·ra·tion [ˈdiːˈræʃən] *vt.* 取消(粮食等的)定额分配.

de·ray [diˈrai] *n.* 〔废〕混乱〔尤指狂乱无度的饮闹〕.

Der·by[1] [ˈdɑːbi; Am. ˈdəːbi] *n.* ①(英国 Epsom Downs 的)德比赛马. ②大赛马;大竞赛. ③〔d-〕[ˈdəːbi]〔美〕常礼帽,圆顶礼帽(= ~ hat).

Der·by[2] [ˈdɑːbi; Am. ˈdəːbi] 德比(英国 Derbyshire 的首府). ~ **china** 德比瓷器〔一种精致的彩色瓷器〕.

der·by·lite [ˈdəːbilait] *n.* 【矿】锑钛铁矿.

de·reg·is·ter [diˈredʒistə] *vt.* 撤销…的登记.

de·re·ism [diːˈriːizm] *n.* 【心】内闭性〔对外部世界不感兴趣,背离正常的逻辑思维〕. **-is·tic** *a.*

De·rek [ˈderik] *n.* 德里克〔男子名〕.

der·e·lict [ˈderilikt] *a.* ①被抛弃了的,(船等)无主的. ②〔美〕玩忽职守的. —*n.* ①【法】遗弃物,无主物,(特指)漂流船. ②海水减退后露出的新陆地. ③被(社会所)唾弃的人,无家可归的人,无固定职业的人. ④〔美〕玩忽职守的人.

der·e·lic·tion [ˌderiˈlikʃən] *n.* ①遗弃,放弃. ②玩忽职守,懈怠 *(of).* ③海水退后露出的新陆地. ~ ***of duty*** 玩忽职守.

de·req·ui·si·tion [diːˌrekwiˈziʃən] *vt.* 取消对…的征用.

de·re·strict [ˈdiːrisˈtrikt] *vt.* 取消对…的限制.

de·ride [diˈraid] *vt.* 嘲弄,愚弄,嘲笑. ~ *a person's ignorance* 嘲笑某人无知.

de·rid·er [diˈraidə] *n.* 愚弄者,嘲笑者.

de·rid·ing·ly [diˈraidiŋli] *ad.* 嘲弄似地,愚弄地,嘲笑地.

de ri·gueur [də riːˈgəː]〔F.〕①礼节上所必需的;合乎礼数的. ②时髦的,追求新奇的.

de·ris·i·ble [diˈrizibl] *a.* 该当嘲笑的.

de·ri·sion [diˈriʒən] *n.* ①嘲笑. ②被嘲笑的人[事物];笑柄. ***be in*** ~ 被嘲笑. ***be the*** ~ ***of*** ... 是…的笑柄,被…嘲笑. ***bring*** ... ***into*** ~ 使成笑柄,使受嘲笑. ***hold [have] a person in*** ~ 嘲弄[愚弄]某人. ***in*** ~ ***of*** 嘲弄.

de·ri·sive de·ri·so·ry [diˈraisiv, -səri] *a.* ①嘲弄的,愚弄的. ②可笑的,值得嘲笑的. **-ly** *ad.*

de·riv·a·ble [diˈraivəbl] *a.* 可引伸出来的,可诱导出来的;可推论出来的.

der·i·va·tion [deriˈveiʃən] *n.* ①引出,导出. ②出处,由来,起源. ③【语】词源;派生. ④衍生;衍生物.

de·riv·a·tive [diˈrivətiv] *a.* 导出的;派生的. —*n.* ①派生物. ②【语】派生词. ③【化】衍生物. ④【医】诱导法〔剂〕. ⑤【数】导数,纪数,微商. **-ly** *ad.*

de·rive [diˈraiv] *vt.* ①得到,导出 *(from).* ②追寻起源. ③推论,推究 *(from).* —*vi.* 由来;派生出来. ***be*** ~***d from*** 由…而来[生出]. ~ ***itself from*** 由…而来. ~**d fossils** 转生化石. ~**d protein** 【生化】衍生朊.

derm [dəːm] *n.* = derma.

-derm *suf.* 皮.

der·ma[1] [ˈdəːmə] *n.*【解】真皮;皮肤.
der·ma[2] [ˈdəːmə] *n.* 面包馅烤肉.
der·mal [ˈdəːməl] *a.* 真皮的,皮肤的.
der·mat- *comb. f.* = dermato-.
der·ma·ti·tis [ˌdəːməˈtaitis] *n.* 皮肤炎,皮炎.
der·ma·to- *comb. f.* 皮(肤)的.
der·mat·o·gen [dəˈmætədʒən] *n.*【植】表皮原.
der·ma·tog·ra·phy [ˌdəːmæˈtɔgrəfi] *n.* 皮肤解剖记录.
der·ma·toid [ˈdəːmətɔid] *a.* 象皮肤的.
der·ma·tol·o·gist [ˌdəːməˈtɔlədʒist] *n.* 皮肤学者,皮肤科医生.
der·ma·tol·o·gy [ˌdəːməˈtɔlədʒi] *n.* 皮肤(病)学. **-log·i·cal** [-ˈlɔdʒikəl] *a.*
der·ma·tome [ˈdəːmətəum] *n.* ①【解】生皮节. ②皮刀,植皮刀.
der·ma·to·neu·ri·tis [ˌdəːmətənjuˈraitis] *n.* 神经性皮炎;皮肤神经炎.
der·ma·top·a·thy [ˌdəːməˈtɔpəθi] *n.* 皮肤病.
der·ma·to·phyte [ˈdəːmətəufait, dəˈmætə-] *n.* 皮肤真菌,皮癣霉菌.
der·ma·to·plas·ty [ˈdəːmətəuplæsti] *n.* 皮成形术,植皮术. **-tic** [-ˈplæstik] *a.*
der·ma·to·sis [ˌdəːməˈtəusis] *n.* 皮肤病.
der·mic [ˈdəːmik] *a.* = dermal.
der·mis [ˈdəːmis] *n.*【解】= derma.
der·mo- *comb. f.* = dermato-.
der·moid [ˈdəːmɔid] *a.* ①皮样囊肿的. ②皮状的.
der·mop·ter·an [dəˈmɔptərən] *n.* 皮翼目动物〔包括猫猴〕.
der·mo·trop·ic [ˌdəːməˈtrɔpik] *a.* 亲皮肤的;趋向皮肤的.
dern [dəːn] *v.*〔美卑〕= darn.
der·ni·er [ˈdəːniə; F. dɛrnje] *a.*〔F.〕最后的. ~ ***ressort*** [reˈsɔːr] 最后手段.
der·nier cri [dəːˈnjei kriː]〔F.〕(服装等)最新样式;极品.
der·o·gate [ˈderəgeit] *vi., vt.* ①毁损,减损. ②贬损,贬低. *He ~d from his ancestors.* 他毁坏了祖祖辈辈的声名. *~ from rights* 丧失权利. **-ga·tion** [ˌderəˈgeiʃən] *n.* ①毁损,减损(权力、地位等). ②(法律等的)部分废除. ③贬低自己,失去地位.
de·rog·a·to·ry [diˈrɔgətəri] *a.* 减损…的,毁损(名誉)的;有伤品格的. *~ from authority* 有损权威的. *~ to one's dignity* 降低品格的. *"Politician" is used in a ~ sense.* "政客"是贬义用法.
der·rick [ˈderik] *n.* ①【机】动臂起重机,塔式起重机;起货桅. ②油井架,钻(井高)塔;(飞机的)起飞塔. ③〔美俚〕小偷. **~-car** 起重机车.
der·ri·ère [ˌderiˈɛə] *n.* 臀部.
der·ring-do [ˈderiŋˈduː] *n.*〔古〕蛮勇;大胆行为.
der·rin·ger [ˈderindʒə] *n.* 大口径短筒手枪.
der·ris [ˈderis] *n.* 鱼藤属植物.
der·vish [ˈdəːviʃ] *n.* 伊斯兰教苦修教士.
de·sal·i·na·tion [diːˌsæliˈneiʃən], **de·sal·i·ni·za·tion** [diːˌseilinaiˈzeiʃən] *n.* 脱盐(作用),减少盐分. **-nate, -nize** *vt.* 脱盐化.
de·salt [diːˈsɔːlt] *vt.* 除去…的盐分. **-er** *n.* 脱盐设备.
de·scale[1] [ˈdiːˈskeil] *vt.* 除去…的锅垢.
des·cant [ˈdeskænt] *n.* ①〔诗〕歌曲,曲调. ②【乐】童高音. — *vi.* 唱歌.
des·cant[2] [disˈkænt] *n.* 详谈,评论. — *vi.* 详谈,评论(*on, upon*). *~ on the wonders of nature* 畅谈大自然的奇迹.
Des·cartes [deiˈkɑːt, dekart], **René** 笛卡儿〔1596—1650〕,法国哲学家,数学家〕.
de·scend [diˈsend] *vi.* ①下来,下降. ②下斜,下倾. ③(财产等)传给,传下,遗传. ④系出,是…的后裔(*from*). ⑤转而说到,涉及(细节等). ⑥降低身分去做. ⑦突然袭击,突然访问. ⑧【天】移向南方,移向地平线. *~ from a hill* 由山上下来. *~ to particulars [details]* 转而谈到细节. *He never ~s to such meanness.* 他决不干那种卑鄙事. — *vt.* 下,降. ***~ from* = *be ~ed from*** 是…的后裔. ***~ on [upon]*** 袭击;突然访问.
de·scend·a·ble [diˈsendəbl] *a.* = descendible.
de·scend·ant [diˈsendənt] *n.* ①子孙,后代(*opp.* ancestor). ②弟子,门生. ③从某一来源派生的东西;派生物. — *a.* = descendent.
de·scend·ent [diˈsendənt] *a.* ①祖传的,遗传的. ②下降的,下行的. ③派生的.
de·scend·i·ble [diˈsendibl] *a.* ①能遗传[遗赠]的. ②能走下[降下]的.
de·scend·ing [diˈsendiŋ] *a.* 下降的,下行的;递降的. *a ~ letter* 下垂字母〔g, p, y 等〕. *~ powers*【数】降幂. *a ~ scale*【乐】下行音阶.
de·scen·sion [diˈsenʃən] *n.* 降下,降落.
de·scent [diˈsent] *n.* ①下降,降下. ②下坡,倾斜. ③家世,门第,血统. ④【法】继承,世袭. ⑤一代;〔古〕子孙,后裔. ⑥突然袭击. ⑦屈尊,降格. *be of France ~* 祖籍是法国. ***be of good ~*** 出身好. ***~ of man*** 人类由来. ***make a ~ upon*** 袭击,侵入.
des·cloi·site, des·cloi·zite [deiˈklɔizait] *n.*【矿】钒铅锌矿.
de·scrib·a·ble [disˈkraibəbl] *a.* 能描写的.
de·scribe [disˈkraib] *vt.* ①记述,叙述,描写,形容;评述. ②制(图),画(图形),作图. ③(行星等)周转,运行. *the falling star describing a long curve in the sky* 流星在空中划下长长的一道曲线. *~ sb. as* 把某人评为,叫某人做.
de·scrib·er [disˈkraibə] *n.* 叙述者,描写者;制图人.
de·scri·er [disˈkraiə] *n.* 发现者.
de·scrip·tion [disˈkripʃən] *n.* ①记述,叙述,描写;记载. ②叙事文;(物品)说明书;相貌说明书. ③种类. ④作图;绘制. *a man answering (to) that ~* 和相貌说明书符合的人. *pencils of every ~* 各种铅笔. *persons of that ~* 那一类人. *a speech of the poorest ~* 内容平淡到极点的演说. *beyond ~* 难以形容. *give [make] a ~ of* 叙述…的样子;说明. *the ~ of a circle* 画圆圈.
de·scrip·tive [disˈkriptiv] *a.* 记述的,叙述的;说明的. *a ~ catalogue* 带有说明的目录. *a ~ writing* 叙事文. *the ~ geometry* 画法几何(学). ***~ of*** 描写…的,记述…的,说明…的. **-ly** *ad.*
de·scrip·tor [disˈkriptə] *n.*【自】(数据处理中表示某一项目的)主字码.
de·scry [disˈkrai] *vt.* ①远远地看出[看到]. ②(由调查等)发现.
des·e·crate [ˈdesikreit] *vt.* 把(神物)供俗用;亵渎,玷污. **-cra·tion** [ˌdesiˈkreiʃən] *n.* 亵渎神圣.
de·seg·re·gate [diːˈsegriˌgeit] *vt., vi.* 废除种族隔离. **-ga·tion** [diːsegriˈgeiʃən] *n.*
de·se·lect [ˌdiːsiˈlekt] *vt.* 中途淘汰(培训的选手).
de·sen·si·tize [ˌdiːˈsensitaiz] *vt.* ①【摄】使减少感光度. ②【医】使减少敏感性. ③使感觉迟钝. **-tiz·er** [ˈdiːˈsensitaizə] *n.* 减感剂,脱敏剂.
De·ser·et [ˈdezərit] *n.*〔美〕犹他州的别名.
des·ert[1] [ˈdezət] *a.* 荒芜的,不毛的;沙漠的;无人的. *a ~ island* 荒岛. — *n.* ①沙漠;荒漠. ②〔喻〕荒凉的境地;枯燥无味的学科;历史上的荒芜时代(等). *the Gobi D-* 戈壁滩.
de·sert[2] [diˈzəːt] *vt.* ①丢开,抛弃. ②擅离(职守). *~ one's colours* (兵)开小差;叛变. *His presence of mind ~ed him.* 他失去镇静. — *vi.* 逃亡,逃走(*from*);开小差. *He ~ed to the enemy.* 他投敌去了.
de·sert[3] [diˈzəːt] *n.* ①功过;该受奖赏[处罚]的品质[行动]. ②应得的报酬,应得的奖赏[处罚]. ③功劳,美德. *get [meet with] one's ~s* 受相当奖赏[处罚]. *The honour*

is above my ～. 荣誉过当.

de·sert·ed [di'zə:tid] *a.* 无人居住的,荒废了的;被抛弃了的. *a* ～ *village* 荒村.

de·sert·er [di'zə:tə] *n.* 遗弃者;脱党者;逃亡者;逃兵.

de·ser·tion [di'zə:ʃən] *n.* ①遗弃,抛弃. ②脱党;逃走. ③荒废.

de·serve [di'zə:v] *vt.* 应受,该得,值得,当. ～ *attention [sympathy]* 值得注意[同情]. *He* ～*s his fate.* 他命该如此. —*vi.* 应受赏[罚]. ～ *to be rewarded [punished]* 该奖[罚]. ～ **ill [well] of** 有罪[功]于 (*He has* ～*d well of his country.* 他有功于国家).

de·serv·ed [di'zə:vd] *a.* 该奖[罚]的,理所当然的. **-ly** *ad.*

de·serv·ing [di'zə:viŋ] *a.* ①该奖[罚]的. ②有功劳的. ③值得…的 (*of*). ④值得帮助的. *be* ～ *of death* 该死. *(a crime)* ～ *of death* 该处死刑的(罪). *the* ～ *poor* 值得帮助的穷人. —*n.* 赏罚,功过. **-ly** *ad.*

de·sex [di:'seks] *vt.* ①使无性欲. ②使失去性特征. ③使失去性能力.

de·sex·u·al·ize [di:'seksjuəlaiz] *vt.* (= desex). **-za·tion** [di:ˌseksjuəlai'zeiʃən] *n.*

des·ha·bille [ˌdeizæ'bi:ei] *n.* 〔F.〕 = dishabille.

des·ic·cant ['desikənt] *a.* 干燥用的,去水分的,去湿气的. —*n.* 干燥剂.

des·ic·cate ['desikeit] *vt.* ①干燥,弄干,晒干(等);使脱水. ②用干燥法保存(食物). ③使(生命力等)枯竭. ～*d milk* 奶粉. *desiccating agent* 干燥剂. *a* ～*d woman* 干瘦的妇女. —*vi.* 变干. **-ca·tion** [ˌdesi'keiʃən] *n.* 干燥,干化. **-ca·tive** [de'sikətiv] *a., n.* = desiccant. **-ca·tor** [-tə] *n.* ①(鱼等的)干货制造者. ②干燥器,吸湿器.

de·sid·er·a·ta [diˌzidə'reitə] *n.* desideratum 的复数.

de·sid·er·ate [di'zidəreit] *vt.* 迫切需要,渴望得到. ～ *an impossibility* 希求不可能的事情. **-a·tion** [diˌzidə'reiʃən] *n.*

de·sid·er·a·tive [di'zidərətiv] *a.* 【语法】希求的. —*n.* (动词的)希求[愿望]语气;愿望动词.

de·sid·er·a·tum [diˌzidə'reitəm] *n.* (*pl.* **-ta** [-tə])〔L.〕急需品,需要物.

de·sign [di'zain] *vt.* ①计划,企图,立意要…. ②指定,预定;留给,留着. ③设计,草拟,拟定,筹划;起草,画草图,打(图)样. ～ *an attack* 计划进攻. ～ *one's son for [to be] a soldier* 立意要儿子做军人. ～ *a room for one's library* 指定一间屋子做某人书房. —*vi.* 计划;打样,打图样 (*for*). —*n.* ①计划,企图;目的,意图;野心,阴谋. ②(小说等的)提纲,结构,构想,情节. ③设计,图案,图样. **by** ～ **and not by accident** 是故意不是偶然. **have a** ～ **on** 对…有野心,企图. **have** ～**s upon [against] sb. life** 拟加害某人. ～ **paper** 制图纸.

de·sign·a·ble[1] [di'zainəbl] *a.* 能设计[计划]的,可企图的.

des·ig·na·ble[2] ['dezignəbl] *a.* 能指定的.

des·ig·nate ['dezigneit] *vt.* ①指出,指明. ②指出…的名字;把…叫做 (*as*). ③指定,选定,任命某人任某职. (*to; for*). —[-nit] *a.* 指定而尚未上任的;选出而尚未上任的〔用在名词后〕. *a captain* ～ 指定而尚未上任的船长. **-tive, -tory** *a.*

des·ig·nat·ed ['dezigneitid] *a.* 指定的,派定的.

des·ig·na·tion [ˌdezig'neiʃən] *n.* ①指出,指明. ②任命,选派. ③名称,称呼;【军】番号.

des·ig·na·tor ['dezigneitə] *n.* ①指定者. ②〔古罗马〕定席次的官.

de·signed [di'zaind] *a.* 设计好的;故意的,有计划的. **-ly** *ad.* 特意,故意,有计划地.

des·ig·nee [ˌdezig'ni:, des-] *n.* 被指名人.

de·sign·er [di'zainə] *n.* ①设计师,打样师,制图员. ②阴谋者.

de·sign·ing [di'zainiŋ] *a.* ①狡猾的,有野心[阴谋]的. ②计划性的,有远见的. —*n.* 设计(工作).

de·sir·a·ble [di'zaiərəbl] *a.* ①理想的,希望到手的. ②称心的,令人满意的. —*n.* 称心如意的人[东西]. **-ness** *n.* **-bil·i·ty** [diˌzaiərə'biliti] *n.* **-a·bly** *ad.*

de·sire [di'zaiə] *vt.* ①想要,欲望,希望(做某事). ②要求某事 (*sth.*); 要求做到 (*that*); 要求[请求]某人做某事. *He* ～*s to see you.* 他想要见见你. *We* ～ *to have a good result.* 我们但愿有个好结果. *I* ～ *an immediate answer of yours.* 我请您立即回信. *They* ～ *that you will come at once.* 他们要求你马上来. *He* ～*d me to wait.* 他要我等着. *Please* ～ *him to come in.* 去请他进来. —*vi.* 愿望,期望. **leave much [nothing] to be** ～**d** 缺点不少[一点也没有]. —*n.* ①愿望,欲望. ②要求. ③食欲,情欲. ④想望的东西. **at one's** ～ 照某人希望. ～ **for fame** 虚荣心. **get one's** ～ 得到所希望的东西.

de·sir·ous [di'zaiərəs] *a.* 〔用作表语〕要,想,欲 (*to do; that*). **be** ～ **of** 想得到,想 (*Everybody is* ～ *of success [to succeed].* 每人都想获得成功).

de·sist [di'zist] *vi.* 停止,休想,断念. *You had better* ～. 你最好打消念头吧. ～ *from talking [a scheme]* 停止谈话[一项计划].

de·size [di:'saiz] *vt.* 【纺】除去…的浆液.

desk [desk] *n.* ①书桌,办公桌. ②值勤台. ③[美]讲道坛. ④〔the ～〕文书工作. ⑤(报馆的)编辑部. ⑥乐谱架. ⑦(一机构中专门负责某方面事务的)部,司,组. ⑧(乐队里演奏者的)席位,席次. *He is at his* ～. 他在用功[办公]呢. *a roll-top* ～ 有活动盖板的办公桌. *an inquiry* ～ 问事处. *the city* ～ (报馆的)社会部. ～ *lamp* 台灯. ～ *work [job]* 文书工作,办公室工作. *a first-*～ *violinist* 第一提琴手. *sit at the* ～ 写着字;办着公. —*a.* 书桌上用的. —*vt.* 派某人做办公室工作. ～ **bound** *a.* 埋头事务的,书呆子气的;内勤的;后勤的 (*chair-borne commandos and* ～ *bound doughboys* 支前民兵和后勤步兵). ～**man** (*pl.* ～**men**) ①新闻助理编辑. ②坐办公桌的人. ～ **room** *[space]* (在别人办公室内租借的)办公地位. ～ **pad** ①(附有吸水纸的)书桌垫. ②便条,便笺. ～ **set** 一套文具. ～ **study** 纸上谈兵,桌上研究〔指未经过实地的或实验室的试验〕.

D. ès L. 〔F.〕 = *Docteur ès Lettres* (= Doctor of Letters) 文学博士.

des·man ['desmən] *n.* (*pl.* ～*s*) 食虫水栖鼹鼠.

des·mid ['desmid] *n.* 绿藻门植物 (亦作 desmidian).

desm(o) *comb. f.* 表示"结合的";"带状的";"丝状的": *desmo*bacteria.

des·mo·bac·ter·i·a [desməbæk'tiəriə] *n.* 【医】丝状细菌属.

des·mo·en·zyme [ˌdezmə'enzaim] *n.* 【生化】不溶性酶;固定酶.

des·moid ['desmɔid] *a.* ①似韧带的. ②(肿瘤)纤维样的,纤维性的.

Des Moines [di'mɔinz] *n.* 得梅因〔美国衣阿华 Iowa 州的首府〕.

des·mo·lase ['desməleis] *n.* 【生化】碳链酶.

des·mol·y·sis [dez'mɔlisis] *n.* (*pl.* **-ses** [-si:z])【化】碳链分解作用;解链作用.

Des·mond ['dezmənd] *n.* 德斯蒙德〔男子名〕.

des·o·late ['desəlit] *a.* ①荒无人烟的,荒凉的;荒废的. ②孤独的;凄凉的. —['desəleit] *vt.* ①使荒无人烟,使荒芜. ②使凄凉,使孤单. **-ly** *ad.* **-ness** *n.*

des·o·la·tion [ˌdesə'leiʃən] *n.* ①荒芜,荒凉. ②寂寥,孤独;凄凉. ③荒地,废墟.

de·sorb [di'sɔ:b] *vt.* 【化】使解除吸附,使放出. **-sorp·tion** [-'sɔ:pʃən] *n.* 解吸(作用).

de·soxy- *comb. f.* 脱氧 (= deoxy-).

des·ox·y·date [di'sɔksideit] *vt.* 【化】使脱氧.

de·spair [dis'pɛə] *n.* ①绝望,失望. ②令人绝望的原因

〔指人或事〕. ③望尘莫及的人〔事物〕. *Defeat after defeat filled us with* ~. 接二连三的失败,使我们感到绝望. *She gave up the attempt in* ~. 她失望地放弃尝试. *He is my* ~. 他是无可救药的了〔他是我万万赶不上的〕. *He is his mother's* ~. 他使他妈绝望了. ***abandon oneself [give oneself up] to*** ~ 只会悲观失望. ***be driven to*** ~ 遭到失望. ***in*** ~ 绝望地. ***out of*** ~ 出于绝望而…. ***the*** ~ ***of*** 使某人失望;使某人感到望尘莫及. ***yield [give way] to*** ~ 打断念头,深自绝望. —*vi.* 绝望,失望. ~ *of success* 失却成功希望. *His life is* ~*ed of.* 他的一生完了.

de·spair·ing [dis'pɛəriŋ] *a.* 感到绝望的,表示失望的. *a* ~ *look* 绝望的样子. **-ly** *ad.*

des·patch [dis'pætʃ] *n., v.* = dispatch.

des·per·a·do [ˌdespə'rɑːdəu, -'rei-] *n.* *(pl.* ~*s,* ~*es)* 无赖;〔美〕暴徒〔尤指美国西部的土匪〕;亡命徒.

des·per·ate ['despərit] *a.* ①不顾死活的,拼命的. ②悲观失望的,穷途末路的,无可救药的. ③猛烈的,厉害的. ④极想得到的. *D- diseases require* ~ *remedies.* 绝症需猛药. *a* ~ *remedy* 非常手段,最后手段. ~ *weather* 恶劣的天气. *a* ~ *fool* 大傻瓜. ***be*** ~ ***for*** *(a cup of tea)* 极想(喝一杯茶). **-ly** *ad.* 绝望地;拼命;〔口〕非常,极. **-ness** *n.* 拼命;绝望.

des·per·a·tion [ˌdespə'reiʃən] *n.* 拼命,不顾死活;绝望. ***be driven to*** ~ 不得不拼命. ***drive (a person) to*** ~ 使拼命;〔口〕使大发脾气. ***in*** ~ 拼死,无可奈何地.

des·pi·ca·ble ['despikəbl] *a.* 恶劣的,卑鄙的,可鄙的. **-bly** *ad.*

de·spise [dis'paiz] *vt.* 轻视,藐视,看不起. *Strategically we should* ~ *all our enemies.* 在战略上我们要藐视一切敌人. **-spis·ing·ly** *ad.*

de·spite [dis'pait] *n.* 〔古〕①恨,怨恨,憎恨. ②恶意. ③轻蔑;侮辱. —*prep.* 不管,不顾,任凭. ***(in)*** ~ ***of*** … 不管,任凭,不把…当事儿. ***die of*** ~ 抱恨而死,冤死. ***in one's own*** ~〔古〕无可奈何地.

de·spite·ful [dis'paitfəl] *a.* 〔古〕= spiteful.

de·spit·e·ous [dis'pitiəs] *a.* 〔古〕怀恨的;恶意的.

de·spoil [dis'pɔil] *vt.* 剥夺;掠夺. ~ *sb. of his right.* 剥夺某人权利. **-ment** *n.*

de·spo·li·a·tion [disˌpəuli'eiʃən] *n.* 掠夺,强夺;遭受掠夺.

de·spond [dis'pɔnd] *vi.* 灰心,消沉. —*n.* 〔古〕沮丧,失望. **-ence, -cy** *n.* 灰心,消沉.

de·spond·ent [dis'pɔndənt] *a.* 垂头丧气的,心灰意懒的.

de·spond·ing·ly [dis'pɔndiŋli] *ad.* 垂头丧气地,心灰意懒地.

des·pot ['despɔt] *n.* 专制君主;暴君. *a local* ~ = *a* ~ *landlord* 恶霸(地主). **-pot·ic** [des'pɔtik] *a.* 专制的,专横的,暴虐的. **-pot·i·cal·ly** *ad.*

des·pot·ism ['despətizəm] *n.* ①专制;专制政治. ②暴政,苛政. ③专制国家,专制政府.

de·spu·mate ['despjumeit] *vt.* ①除去浮沫. ②当做浮沫扔掉. [ˌdespju'meiʃən] **-tion** *n.*

des·qua·mate ['deskwəmeit] *vi.* 【病】脱屑,脱皮. **-ma·tion** [ˌdeskwə'meiʃən] *n.*

des·sert [di'zəːt] *n.* ①餐后食品〔点心、水果等〕. ②〔英〕甜食后的新鲜水果. *a* ~ *service* 一套餐后食品用具. ~**spoon** 点心匙. *a* ~ **wine** 强烈的葡萄酒.

de·sta·bi·lize ['diː'steibilaiz] *vt.* 使打破平衡;使不稳定.

de·stain [diː'stein] *vt.* 使标本脱色(以便用显微镜观察).

de·ster·i·lize [diː'sterilaiz] *vt.* 〔美〕①解封(黄金)〔解封库存黄金,存入中央银行,以扩大信贷和货币发行〕. ②恢复使用(长期闲置的物资).

de Stijl [də stail] *n.* (荷兰)德斯太尔抽象画派.

des·ti·na·tion [ˌdesti'neiʃən] *n.* ①〔罕〕指定,预定,注定. ②目的地,指定地. ③目的,目标. *We are at last at our* ~. 我们终于到达目的地. *the port of* ~ 目的港.

des·tine ['destin] *vt.* 〔常用被动语态〕①命定,注定. ②派定,指定,预定. *My letter was* ~*d never to reach him.* 我的信注定是交不到他手里了. *a building* ~*d for that purpose* 指定作那一目的用的建筑物.

des·ti·ny ['destini] *n.* ①命运,天数,定数. ②〔the Destinies〕命运的三女神〔the three Fates〕. *a master of one's own* ~ 掌握自己命运的人.

des·ti·tute ['destitjuːt] *a.* ①缺乏…的,无…的 *(of)*. ②贫穷的. *The people are* ~. 民不聊生. ***be*** ~ ***of*** *(morality)* 无(道德)的. ***be left*** ~ 贫穷下去. ~ ***and homeless*** 流离失所. ***the*** ~ 穷人.

des·ti·tu·tion [ˌdesti'tjuːʃən] *n.* ①缺乏. ②贫穷,穷困.

des·tri·er ['destriə, des'triə] *n.* 〔古〕军马,战马.

de·stroy [dis'trɔi] *vt.* ①毁坏,破坏;摧残. ②肃清,消灭,歼灭(敌人),扑灭(害虫等),驱除. ③打破〔希望,计划〕,使失败. *be* ~*ed by fire* 被火烧毁. ~ ***itself*** 自灭. ~ ***oneself*** 自杀.

de·stroy·er [dis'trɔiə] *n.* ①破坏者;扑灭者,驱除者. ②驱逐舰. ~ *escort* 护航驱逐舰.

de·struct [dis'trʌkt] *vi.* (中途失灵的导弹、火箭等)自毁(以防落入敌方手中). —*n.* 自毁〔此词系从 destruction 逆生而成〕.

de·struct·i·ble [dis'trʌktəbl] *a.* 能毁坏的,易破坏的. **-bil·i·ty** [diˌstrʌkti'biliti] *n.* 破坏性,破坏力.

de·struc·tion [dis'trʌkʃən] *n.* ①破坏;灭亡;消灭,扑灭,驱除. ②毁灭的原因;破坏手段. *Over confidence was his* ~. 自负是他垮台的原因. **-ist** *n.* 破坏分子;破坏主义者.

de·struc·tive [dis'trʌktiv] *a.* 破坏性的;有害的. ***be*** ~ ***of*** 对…有破坏作用. ***be*** ~ ***to*** 有害…的. ~ **bird** 害鸟. ~ **distillation** 干馏. ~ **interference** 【物】相消干涉. ~ **range** (炸弹等的)破坏半径. **-ly** *ad.* **-ness** *n.*

de·struc·tor [dis'trʌktə] *n.* ①〔英〕垃圾焚毁炉. ②破坏器;爆破装置.

de·suda·tion [desju'deiʃən] *n.* 【医】大量出汗.

des·ue·tude [di'sjuːitjuːd] *n.* 废止,废除. ***fall [pass] into*** ~ (习惯、风俗等)不时兴,衰废.

de·sul·phur·ize [diː'sʌlfəraiz] *vt.* 使脱硫. **-za·tion** [-ˌsʌlfərai'zeiʃən] *n.* 脱硫.

des·ul·to·ry ['desəltəri] *a.* ①散漫的,杂乱的. ②不连贯的,无条理的. ③离奇的,古怪的. *a* ~ *conversation* 漫谈. *a* ~ *remark* 唐突话. *a* ~ *research* 漫无边际的研究. *a* ~ *walk* 漫步. *a* ~ *project [thought]* 离奇的设想. **-i·ly** *ad.* **-i·ness** *n.*

de·su·per·heat·er [diˌsjupə'hiːtə] *n.* 过热蒸气降温器.

det. = ①detach. ②detachment. ③detail. ④detector.

Det. = detective.

DET = diethyltryptamine 二乙色胺〔一种迷幻药〕.

de·tach [di'tætʃ] *vt.* ①分开,分离,拆开 *(opp.* attach*)*. ②派遣(军队等). ***be*** ~***ed from*** 脱离. **-a·ble** *a.* 可分离的;可派遣的. **-ly** *ad.* **-ness** *n.*

de·tached [di'tætʃt] *a.* ①分离的,孤立的. ②分遣的;派遣的. ③公平的;超然的. *a* ~ *house* 独立式住宅. *a* ~ *palace* 离宫. *a* ~ *force* 分遣队,别动队. ~ *duty* 【军】临时任务. *a* ~ *mind* 超然的见解. ***in a*** ~ ***way*** 客观地. ***take a*** ~ ***view*** 抱客观〔公平〕态度.

de·tach·ment [di'tætʃmənt] *n.* ①脱离,分离. ②超然,超脱,不偏不倚. ③派遣;分遣队,支队.

de·tail ['diːteil, di'teil] *n.* ①〔*pl.*〕详细;详情. ②细目;琐事,小事. ③【军】支队;〔英〕行动指令. ④详图,明细图. ⑤零件,元件. *a matter of* ~ 琐事. ***beat [defeat] in*** ~【军】各个击破. ~ ***by*** ~ 逐一. ***go [enter] into*** ~***(s)*** 详述,逐一细说. ***in*** ~ 详细. —*vt.* ①详述,详记. ②【军】特派,选派 *(for; to do)*. ~ *particulars of* *an event* 详述某事的细节. ～ *a man for sentry duty* 派人站岗. —*vi.* 画详图. ～ **man** 制药厂的推销员.

de·tailed [ˈdiːteild] *a.* ①详细的,明细的. ②错综复杂的,千头万绪的. *a* ～ *account* 详细的叙述. *a* ～ *problem* 一个错综复杂的问题.

de·tain [diˈtein] *vt.* ①留住,阻住. ②扣留;拘留. *He was* ～*ed by business.* 他因有事而留下了. ～ *sb. as a suspect* 把某人当做嫌疑犯而加以拘留. **-er** *n.* ①阻留者. ②【法】(财产的)非法占有;拘留,扣押;继续拘留指令.

de·tain·ee [ˌdiːteiˈniː] *n.* 被拘留者(多指政治犯等).

de·tas·sel [diːˈtæsl] *vt.* **(～(l)ed, ～(l)ing)** 去掉(玉蜀黍的)穗状雄花(以杂交).

de·tect [diˈtekt] *vt.* ①发觉,发见,看破. ②【化】检定;【无】检波. *be* ～*ed in(doing)…* 做(坏事等)被发觉. ～ *a flaw in an argument* 发现论点中有破绽. **-a·ble, -i·ble** *a.* 能发觉的;能检查出来的.

de·tec·ta·phone [diˈtektəfəun] *n.* (窃听电话的)窃听器,偵听器.

de·tec·tion [diˈtekʃən] *n.* ①探知;发见,发觉;败露. ②【化】检定,检查;【讯】检波.

de·tec·tive [diˈtektiv] *a.* 侦查(用)的. *a* ～ *agency* 秘密侦探所. *a* ～ *police* 侦探,密探. *a* ～ *story* 侦探小说. —*n.* 侦探,密探.

de·tec·tor [diˈtektə] *n.* ①发觉者. ②侦查器. ③【化】检定器. ④【电】检电器. ⑤【讯】检波器,指示器. *a crystal [tube]* ～ 晶体[真空管]检波器.

de·tent [diˈtent] *n.* ①【机】(棘)爪,掣子;扳手. ②(钟表机件的)擒纵装置.

dé·tente [deiˈtɑ̃ːnt] *n.* 〔F.〕(国际关系等的)缓和.

de·ten·tion [diˈtenʃən] *n.* ①阻止;阻留. ②扣留,拘留,监禁. ③(罚学生的)课后留校. ④(非法)占有. ～ *barracks [camp]* (俘虏等的)临时收容所. ～ *home* 青少年罪犯的拘留所. ～ *hospital* (传染病的)隔离病院. *under* ～ 拘留中,扣留中.

dé·te·nu [deitəˈnuː] *n.* 〔F.〕*(fem.* ***détenue)*** 被扣留者.

de·ter [diˈtəː] *vt.* 防止,阻止,制止,使不敢,使踌躇. *paint sth. to* ～ *rust* 涂漆防锈. ～*(sb.)* ***from*** 制止(人)….

de·terge [diˈtəːdʒ] *vt.* 洗净(伤口等).

de·ter·gen·cy, de·ter·gence [diˈtəːdʒənsi, -dʒəns] *n.* 脱垢力,去垢性.

de·ter·gent [diˈtəːdʒənt] *a.* 有洗净力的. —*n.* 洗净剂;除垢剂,去污剂. *synthetic* ～ 合成洗涤剂.

de·te·ri·o·rate [diˈtiəriəreit] *vt., vi.* ①弄坏,使恶化. ②败坏(风俗);降低(品质等). ③堕落. ～ *one's health* 弄坏身体. ～ *relations with other countries* 恶化同其他国家的关系.

de·te·ri·o·ra·tion [diˌtiəriəˈreiʃən] *n.* ①恶化;变质;退化. ②堕落,颓废. ③凋萎;衰败. **-tive** *a.*

de·ter·ment [diˈtəːmənt] *n.* ①制止,威慑. ②制止物,威慑物.

de·ter·mi·na·ble [diˈtəːminəbl] *a.* ①可决定[确定]的. ②可终止的.

de·ter·mi·na·cy [diˈtəːminəsi] *n.* ①确定性. ②坚定性.

de·ter·mi·nant [diˈtəːminənt] *a.* 决定性的,限定性的. —*n.* ①决定因素. ②【逻】限定词. ③【数】行列式. ④【生】决定体,遗传因素.

de·ter·mi·nate [diˈtəːminit] *a.* ①确定的,一定的,决定的. ②毅然决然的. ③【植】(花序)有限的. ④【数】有定值的,有定数的. *a* ～ *variation* 定向变异. *a* ～ *reply* 毅然决然的回答. — [diˈtəːmineite] *vt.* 〔罕〕①确定,确保. ②认明. **-ly** *ad.* 明确地;断然. **-ness** *n.*

de·ter·mi·na·tion [diˌtəːmiˈneiʃən] *n.* ①决心,决意. ②决定,确定. ③倾向. ④【法】判决;(权利的)消失,终止. ⑤【物】测定,鉴定. ⑥【逻】规定,限定. ⑦【医】(血的)涌集.

de·ter·mi·na·tive [diˈtəːminətiv] *a.* 决定的;指定的;限定的. — *n.* ①决定因素. ②【语法】限定词.

de·ter·mi·na·tor [diˈtəːmiˌneitə] *n.* ①决定因素. ②【语】限定词.

de·ter·mine [diˈtəːmin] *vt.* ①决心,决意. ②使下决心〔多用被动结构〕. ③决定;断定,推定,确定;限定,规定. ④【法】了结,使终结. ⑤限制. ⑥【物】测定. *They* ～*d to do this at any cost.* 他们不惜任何牺牲来作此事. *I'm* ～*d to learn French.* 我决心学习法语. *The news* ～*d her against further delay.* 这消息使她下决心不再拖延. *to* ～ *what metals are present in the ore* 测定矿石中有什么金属存在. *A hill* ～*d my view.* 一座山挡住我的视线. —*vi.* ①决心;决定. ②【法】终结,终止.

de·ter·mined [diˈtəːmind] *a.* 坚决的;毅然的;确定的. *a* ～ *character* 果断的性格. *in a* ～ *manner* 决然. **-ly** *ad.* **-ness** *n.*

de·ter·min·er [diˈtəːminə] *n.* ①决定因素. ②【语法】限定词〔如 the, a, an 等〕.

de·ter·min·ism [diˈtəːminizəm] *n.*【哲】宿命论. **-min·ist** [-minist] *n.* 宿命论者. **-min·is·tic** [diˌtəːmiˈnistik] *a.* 宿命论的.

de·ter·rence [diˈterəns] *n.* ①制止,威慑. ②制止物,威慑力量;制止因素,威慑因素 (指保持庞大军力以遏制敌方不敢发动战争).

de·ter·rent [diˈterənt] *a.* 制止的,威慑的. —*n.* 阻碍物,制止物;威慑物. ～ *policy* 威慑政策. ～ *power* 威慑力量.

de·ter·sive [diˈtəːsiv] *a.* 有清洁效力的. —*n.* 洗净剂,清洁剂.

de·test [diˈtest] *vt.* 嫌恶,憎恶,嫌. ～ *evil* 嫉恶如仇. **-a·ble** *a.* 极可恶[讨嫌]的. **-a·bly** *ad.*

de·tes·ta·tion [diːtesˈteiʃən] *n.* ①憎恶,嫌恶,讨厌. ②极讨厌的东西. ***be in*** ～ 被厌恶. ***hold [have] in*** ～ 嫌恶,讨厌. ***regard with great*** ～ 非常讨厌.

de·throne [diˈθrəun] *vt.* ①废黜,废立. ②撵走,推翻. **-ment** *n.* 废立,废位.

det·i·nue [ˈdetinjuː] *n.*【法】对他人动产的非法扣留;收回被非法占有动产的诉讼.

det·o·nate [ˈdetəuneit] *vt., vi.* ①(使)爆炸,(使)爆发. ②触发(一连串事件). *detonating agent* 起爆剂. *detonating cap* 雷管. *detonating fuse* 导爆索;起爆信管. *detonating powder* 起爆(火)药.

det·o·na·tion [ˌdetəuˈneiʃən] ①爆炸,爆发. ②爆炸声. **-na·tor** *n.* ①发爆剂;雷管;发爆管,起爆剂. ②【铁路】(浓雾时作信号用的)爆鸣器.

de·tour, dé·tour [ˈdeituə] *n.* ①弯路,迂路. ②迂回,曲折. *make a* ～ 迂回. —*vt., vi.* 迂回,(使)绕道.

de·tox·i·cate [diːˈtɔksikeit] *vt.* = detoxify.

de·tox·i·fy [diːˈtɔksiˌfai] *vt.* 除去…的毒物,使解毒. **-fi·ca·tion** [-ˌtɔksifiˈkeiʃən] *n.*

de·tract [diˈtrækt] *vt., vi.* ①降低,减损(价值、名誉等). ②诬蔑,损坏,伤害. ③转移(注意). ～ ***from*** 损伤,损坏 (*That does not* ～ *from his merit.* 那无损于他的功绩). **-tion** *n.* **-tive** *a.* **-tor** *n.* 诬蔑者.

de·train [diːˈtrein] *vi.* 〔英〕下火车. —*vt.* 使(军队等)下车. **-ment** *n.*

de·trib·a·lize [diːˈtraibəlaiz] *vi., vt.* (使)脱离部落,使消除部落习惯. **-za·tion** [diːˌtraibəlaiˈzeiʃən] *n.*

det·ri·ment [ˈdetrimənt] *n.* ①损害,伤害. ②有害物. ***to the*** ～ ***of*** 有损于,不利于. ***without*** ～ ***to*** 不损害[损伤],无损于.

det·ri·ment·tal [ˌdetriˈmentl] *a.* 有害的,不利的 *(to)*. —*n.* ①〔俚〕不受欢迎的求婚者. ②有害的人[物]. **-ly** *ad.*

de·tri·tion [diˈtriʃən] *n.* 耗损,磨损.

de·tri·tus [diˈtraitəs] *n.* ①【地】碎岩;碎屑. ②碎石堆.

de trop [də 'trəu] 〔F.〕多余的;无用的. *A topcoat was ~ with the thermometer standing at 72 degrees.* 温度72度时,大衣是多余的.

de·trude [di'truːd] *vt.* ①推下,推落. ②推走,推出. **-tru·sion** *n.*

de·trun·cate [diː'trʌŋkeit] *vt.* 削去,切去(…的一部分).

de·tu·mes·cence [ˌdiːtu(ː)'mesns, -tjuː-] *n.*【医】消肿. **-cent** *a.*

deuce[1] [djuːs] *n.* ①(纸牌的)两点. ②【网球】(终局前的)平分. ③〔美〕二元券[纸币]. —*vt.*【网球】扯平.

deuce[2] [djuːs] *n.* 〔口〕①不幸,遭殃,倒霉. ②魔鬼. ③〔美〕胆小鬼. ④〔用作感叹词〕讨厌! 哼! ★相当于 devil, 表示厌恶、忿怒、惊奇、强意否定等. *The ~ is in it if I cannot.* 我要不能那就见鬼了. *The ~ he isn't.* 他不是那才见鬼啦. *The (very) ~ is in them!* 他们真的见了鬼啦! *The ~ it is!* 奇怪,见鬼! *The ~ you are!* 你这样还了得(岂有此理)! ***a ~ of a ...*** 非常(讨厌的,愉快的) (*a ~ of a lovely day* 愉快的一天). ***(the) ~ a bit*** 完全不,一点儿不,毫不 (*(The) ~ a bit I care.* 毫不在乎). ***(the) ~ a man*** 一个人也没有. ***(the) ~ a one*** 没有一个[一种等]. ***D- knows!*** 天晓得! ***D- take it!*** 他妈的! 糟了! ***go to the ~*** 灭亡 (*Go to the ~!* 滚! 去见你的鬼去!). ***like the ~*** 猛然. ***play the ~ with*** 把…弄得一团槽. ***The ~!*** 见鬼! 糟了! ***the ~*** 究竟 (*Who [What] the ~ is that?* 那究竟是谁[什么东西]? *Why [Where] the ~ ...?* …究竟为了什么[在哪儿]?). ***the ~ and all*** 好好歹歹全都;全没一个好的. ***the ~ of a*** = a ~ of a. ***the ~ to pay*** 此后困难,后患 (*There will be the ~ to pay.* 后果可怕;后患堪虞). **~-ace** ①(骰子的)丁丁[两点和一点]. ②倒霉.

deuced [djuːst, 'djuːsid] *a., ad.* 〔口〕过度,非常;很,极,异常. ~ *bad* 极坏. *a ~ fine girl* 非常美丽的姑娘. *in a ~ hurry* 急急忙忙. **-ly** *ad.*

De·us ['deius, 'diəs] 〔L.〕上帝.

de·us ex ma·chi·na ['diːəs eks 'meikinei] 〔L.〕①(古希腊、罗马戏剧中)用舞台机关送出来参与剧情进展的神仙. ②(小说等中)突然出现以解围的人物. ③在紧要关头突然出现而扭转局面的人.

Deut. = Deuteronomy.

deu·ter·ag·o·nist [ˌduːtə'rægənist, 'djuːt-] *n.* ①(古希腊戏剧中)演二流角色的演员. ②给别人当配角的人.

deu·ter·an·ope ['djuːtərəˌnəup, 'duːt-] *n.* 绿色盲患者.

deu·ter·an·o·pi·a [ˌdjuːtərə'nəupiə, duːt-] *n.* 绿色盲,第二型色盲.

deu·ter·at·ed ['djuːtəreitid, 'duːt-] *a.* 氘化了的,氘水合物的,重水合物的.

deu·ter·ide ['djuːtəraid, 'duːt-] *n.* 重氢化合物.

deu·te·ri·um [djuː'tiəriəm] *n.*【化】氘,重氢. ~ **oxide** 重水.

deu·ter·o- *comb. f.* 表示"第二","再": *deutero*plasm.

deu·ter·o·ca·non·i·cal [ˌdjuːtəˌrəukə'nɔnikl, ˌduːt-] *a.*【圣】圣典别集的.

deu·ter·og·a·my [ˌdjuːtə'rɔgəmi] *n.* 再婚. **-mist** 再婚者.

deu·ter·o·gen·e·sis [ˌdjuːtərəu'dʒenisis] *n.* 〔L.〕【生】后期发生.

deu·ter·on ['djuːtərɔn] *n.*【化】氘核.

Deu·ter·on·o·mist [ˌdjuːtə'rɔnəmist] *n.* 圣经旧约申命记的作者[编者].

Deu·ter·on·o·my [ˌdjuːtə'rɔnəmi] *n.* 《申命记》〔旧约圣经中的一卷〕.

deu·ter·op·a·thy [ˌdjuːtə'rɔpəθi] *n.*【医】继发病.

deu·to- *comb. f.* = deutero-.

deu·ton ['djuːtɔn] *n.* 〔美〕= deuteron.

deu·to·plasm ['djuːtəplæzəm] *n.*【生】滋养质,副浆,卵黄质.

deutsch ['dɔitʃ] *a.* 〔G.〕德国的.

deut·sche mark ['dɔitʃəˌmaːk] 〔G.〕马克〔西德货币名称,缩写为 DM〕.

Deut·sches Reich ['dɔitʃəs 'raiç] *n.* 〔G.〕德意志帝国〔第二次世界大战前德国的正式国名〕.

Deutsch·land ['dɔitʃlənd] *n.* 〔G.〕德国,德意志.

deut·zi·a ['djuːtsjə] *n.*【植】溲疏属植物.

Dev. = Devonshire.

de·va ['deivə] *n.* (印度神话的)神,善灵.

de·val·u·ate, de·val·ue [diː'væljueit, -ljuː] *vt.* 使降低价值;【经】使减低币值.

de·val·u·a·tion [ˌdiːvælju'eiʃən] *n.*【经】(货币)贬值. **-ist** *n.*【经】主张货币贬值者.

De·va·na·ga·ri [ˌdeivə'nɑːgəri] *n.* 天城文书〔梵文等所由派生的文字〕.

dev·as·tate ['devəsteit] *vt.* 蹂躏,破坏;使荒废. *a devastating blow* 毁灭性的打击. **-ta·tion** [ˌdevəs'teiʃən] *n.* 蹂躏;荒废;〔*pl.*〕劫后余迹. **-ta·tor** ['devəsteitə] *n.* 蹂躏者,劫掠者.

dev·el ['devl] *n.*〔Scot.〕沉重打击;令人发晕的一击. —*vt.*〔Scot.〕给…以沉重的一击.

de·vel·op(e) [di'veləp] *vt.* ①使发达,使发展;使发生;使进化. ②开发,开展,扩大. ③【摄】使显影. ④【军、数】展开. ⑤使显出,产生,研制;发现(新事实). ⑥〔美〕揭露,暴露. ~ *industry and agriculture simultaneously* 工业与农业同时并举. ~ *a mine* 开矿. *a motor that ~s 100 horse-power* 一百匹马力的发动机. —*vi.* ①发育;发生,进化. ②发展,发达 (*from*); 发达成 (*into*). ③(剧情等)展开;(局面)进展;(像)显现出来. ④〔美〕(新事实等)发现,出现. *a developing country* 发展中的国家. **~ing paper**【摄】显像纸.

de·vel·op·er [di'veləpə] *n.* ①开发者. ②【摄】显影剂,显像剂.

de·vel·op·ment [di'veləpmənt] *n.* ①发展,发达;进化. ②展开;扩充;开发. ③发达物,新事物,发展阶段. ④【生】发育(史);【军、数】展开;【摄】显影,显像;【乐】展开(部);研制,研制成果. ~ *area* 〔英〕新开发地区. ~ *of heat* 放热,生热.

de·vel·op·men·tal [diˌveləp'mentəl] *a.* ①发展的,开发的. ②促使成长的,发育上的;进化的. ~ *diseases* 发育病. *a long-range ~ program* 长期发展规划.

de·verb·a·tive [di'vəːbətiv] *a.* 从动词派生的. —*n.* 动词派生词.

de·vest [di'vest] *vt.* = divest.

de·vi·ant ['diːviənt] *a.* 离经叛道的,偏离正道的. —*n.* 行为不轨的人. **-vi·an·cy, -vi·ance** *n.*

de·vi·ate ['diːvieit] *vi.* 越(轨),脱离(常轨);违背;误入歧途 (*from*). —*vt.* 使脱离常轨. —*a.* 脱离常轨的. —*n.* 脱离常轨的人.

de·vi·a·tion [ˌdiːvi'eiʃən] *n.* ①脱离,越轨,背离 (*from*). ②偏向,偏差. ③(统计上的)误差. ④【海】(故意)偏航. ⑤【数】偏差数. *the ~ of the magnetic needle* 磁针的偏差. **-ism** *n.* (政治上的)脱离正道. **-ist** *n.* 脱离正道者,异端分子.

de·vice [di'vais] *n.* ①设计,计划;方法,手段. ②〔*pl.*〕意志,欲望. ③谋略,策略,诡计. ④器具,器械,设备,装置. ⑤图案,图样,花样;纹章;标记,商标;(纹章上的)题铭. *a safety ~* 安全设备. *a pressure ~* 压力计. *a homing ~* 自动寻的[导引]装置. ***leave sb. to his own ~s*** 让某人自行其是.

dev·il ['devl] *n.* ①魔鬼,恶魔;〔the D-〕魔王. ②人面兽心的人,恶棍. ③冒失鬼. ④精力绝伦的人. ⑤可怜的家伙. ⑥猛兽. ⑦…鬼,…狂者. ⑧斗志,好胜心. ⑨难事;难操纵的东西. ⑩(律师等的)代笔者;(印刷厂等的)学徒;见习护士;助手. ⑪【烹】辣子肉. ⑫【机】切碎机. ⑬〔口〕飞沙走石的风暴,尘卷风. ⑭〔口〕〔the ~〕表示"究竟","决不"等惊叹语气〔与 who, how, why, where, what 等连用〕. *a poor* ～ 可怜的家伙. *a printer's* ～ 印刷所学徒. *He has lost his job, poor* ～. 他失业了,这个可怜的家伙. *Who the* ～ *is he?* 他究竟是谁? *The* ～ *I will.* 我决不干. *work like the* ～ 拼命工作. ***a*** ～ ***of a*** … 异常的, 吓人的; 麻烦的, 讨厌的, 愉快的(等). ***and the*** ～ ***knows what*** 其他种种. ***be a*** ～ ***for*** … 是…狂 (*He is a* ～ *for gambling* 他是赌棍). ***between the*** ～ ***and the deep sea*** 进退两难. ***blue*** ～***s*** 意气消沉. ～ ***a bit*** 毫不. ～ ***a one*** 无一个. ***D- take it!*** 糟了! 该死! ***give the*** ～ ***his due*** 平心而论,公平对待. ***go to the*** ～ ①败落,落魄. ②〔生气时用语〕滚开 (*Go to the* ～*!* 去见你的鬼去! 滚!). ③惨败,落空. ***have the*** ～***'s (own) luck*** (坏人) 得意一时. ***like the*** ～ 猛烈,拼命. ***Needs must when the*** ～ ***drives.*** 情势所迫,只好如此. ***paint the*** ～ ***blacker than he is*** 诽过其实. ***play the*** ～ ***with*** 损害,糟踏;使为难. ***raise the*** ～ ①起哄,作乱. ②引起麻烦. ③弄得非常热闹. ***say the*** ～***'s paternoster*** 嘟哝不满,发牢骚. ***Talk of the*** ～ ***and he will appear.*** 谈鬼鬼到, 说起某人某人就到. ***the*** ～ ***among the tailors*** 〔英〕吵闹; 一种烟火. ***the*** ～ ***and all*** 一切坏事. ***the*** ～ ***(of it)*** 难点. ***the*** ～***'s own luck*** 〔俚〕极好 [坏] 的运气. ***the*** ～***'s own time*** 非常痛苦的经验. ***The*** ～ ***take the hindmost.*** 让逃得最慢的人被魔鬼抓去吧〔意为不管别人,只顾自己逃命等〕. ***the*** ～ ***to pay*** 此后困难, 后患. ***whip the*** ～ ***round the stump [post]*** 推卸责任. — *vt.* (〔英〕*-ll-*) ①用辣子烤(肉等). ②(用切碎机)切碎. ③〔美口〕虐待,折磨,纠缠. — *vi.* (替作家、律师等) 做助手 *(for)*. ～**-box** 〔口〕电子计算机. ～ **dog** 〔美俚〕水兵,海军陆战队队员. ～**dodger** 牧师,教士. ～**dom** ①魔鬼的统治. ②魔鬼所在地区. ③〔集合词〕魔鬼. ～**fish** 【动】鸢魟; 灰色鲸; 鮟鱇, 琵琶鱼; 章鱼, 乌贼. ～ **horse** 螳螂. ～**-may-care** 不顾一切的; 嬉闹的,满不在乎的,随遇而安的. ～**'s advocate** 吹毛求疵的人, 故意唱反调的人. ～**'s bedpost** 【牌】梅花四点. ～**'s bones** 骰子. ～**'s books** 纸牌. ～**'s darning needle** 〔美俚〕蜻蜓. ～**'s dozen** 十三. ～**'s food cake** 巧克力蛋糕. ～**'s tattoo** 用手指或脚在桌上或床上得得得的敲击.

dev·il·ish [ˈdevliʃ] *a.* ①魔鬼似的; 可怕的,穷凶极恶的. ②〔口〕异常的,非常的. — *ad.* 〔口〕非常,极. **-ly** *ad.*

dev·il·ism [ˈdevlizəm] *n.* ①魔鬼似的品性,魔鬼似的行为. ②魔鬼崇拜.

dev·il·kin [ˈdevəlkin] *n.* 小魔鬼; 小精灵.

dev·il·ment [ˈdevlmənt] *n.* ①鬼脾气; 鬼举动. ②怪事,怪现象. ③恶作剧.

dev·il·ry [ˈdevlri] *n.* ①恶劣行为. ②魔法, 妖术. ③恶作剧; 胡作非为. ④妖怪学. ⑤魔界.

dev·il·try [ˈdevltri] *n.* = devilry.

de·vi·ous [ˈdiːvjəs] *a.* ①远离大路的, 偏僻的. ②误入歧途的; 无一定路线的. ③不正当的; 狡猾的,诡计多端的. ④迂回的,曲折的. *Let's take the* ～ *route home to avoid the crowds in the main roads.* 为了避免大街上的拥挤,我们还是绕道回家去吧. **-ly** *ad.* **-ness** *n.*

de·vis·a·ble [diˈvaizəbl] *a.* ①能想出[发明、设计]的. ②【法】能遗让的.

de·vis·al [diˈvaizl] *n.* 设计, 计划; 图谋.

de·vise [diˈvaiz] *vt.* ①设计,制定,创造, 发明. ②图谋; 策划. ③【法】遗让(财产). *They* ～*d a plan to escape from prison.* 他们设计越狱. — *n.* ①遗让,遗赠(财产). ②遗赠财产的遗嘱(或其中的条款). ③遗赠的财产.

de·vi·see [diˈvaiˈziː] *n.* 【法】被遗赠者, 受遗让者.

-vis·er *n.* ①设计者, 发明者. ②图谋者. ③【法】= devisor.

dev·i·sor [ˌdeviˈzɔː, divaiˈzɔː] *n.* 【法】遗赠者.

de·vi·tal·ize [diːˈvaitəlaiz] *vt.* ①使失去生命,使失去生命力. ②使伤元气,使衰弱. **-za·tion** [diːˌvaitəlaiˈzeiʃən] *n.*

de·vi·ta·min·ize [diːˈvitəminaiz] *vt.* (烹调或去皮壳时)使(食物)失去维生素.

de·vit·ri·fy [diːˈvitrifai] *vt.* 使失去玻璃光泽; 使玻璃不透明.

de·vo·cal·ize [diːˈvəukəlaiz, ˈdiːˈvəu-] *vt.* 【语音】使(浊音)变成清音.

de·voice [diˈvɔis] *vt.* = devocalize.

de·void [diˈvɔid] *a.* 无…的, 缺…的 *(of)*. *a book* ～ *of content* 一本毫无内容的书. *be* ～ *of common sense* 缺乏常识. ～ *of vegetation* 草木不生的.

de·voir [dəˈvwaː ˈdevwaː] *n.* ①本分,义务. ②〔*pl.*〕敬意; 问候. ***do one's*** ～ 尽本分. ***pay [tender] one's*** ～***s to*** 表示敬意,问候…,对…致敬.

de·vo·lute [ˈdiːvəljuːt] *vt.* 〔罕〕= devolve.

de·vo·lu·tion [ˌdiːvəˈljuːʃən] *n.* ①(责任、权利、财产等的)转移. ②(议会对所属委员会的)授权代理. ③(中央对地方的)权力下放. ④【生】退化.

de·volve [diˈvɔlv] *vt.* 转移,移交. ～ *a work on somebody else* 将工作交代给别人. — *vi.* ①移归,授与. ②流[滚]向下[向前]. *the work that* ～*s upon sb.* 移归某人负责的工作. *streams devolving from the mountains* 从山上流下的河流.

Dev·on [ˈdevn] *n.* 德文郡〔英国郡名〕(= ～shire).

De·vo·ni·an [deˈvəuniən] *a.* ①(英国) 德文郡的. ②【地】泥盆纪的. — *n.* ①德文郡人. ②【地】泥盆纪.

Dev·on·shire [ˈdevnʃiə] *n.* (英国)德文郡.

de·vote [diˈvəut] *vt.* ①献(身),专心致力于,贡献. ②把…专用于 *(to)*. ③听任. *He* ～*d his life to art.* 他终生献身艺术. *I don't think we should* ～ *any more time to this question.* 我认为我们在这个问题上不应当花费更多的时间了. ～ *one's country to evil fate* 听任国家遭受噩运的摆布. ～ ***one's energy to*** 用全力. ～ ***oneself to (study; amusement)*** 致力于,专心从事(研究); 一味贪玩.

de·vot·ed [diˈvəutid] *a.* ①献身…的,埋头…的, 热中…的 *(to)*. ②深爱 *(to)*; 忠实的. ③注定要遭殃的. *a* ～ *wife* 忠实的妻子. **-ly** *ad.* 一心; 忠实. **-ness** *n.*

dev·o·tee [ˌdevəuˈtiː] *n.* ①热爱者. ②皈依者 *(of)*. *a* ～ *of the ballet* 芭蕾舞爱好者.

de·vo·tion [diˈvəuʃən] *n.* ①信仰,信心; 〔*pl.*〕祈祷. ②献身; 热诚,忠诚; 专心,热心 *(to)*. ③充作, 派用, 利用. *He works with greater* ～. 他工作更安心了. *be at one's* ～*s* 正在祈祷. *the* ～ *of a mother for her child* 母亲对儿女的热爱. *the* ～ *of one's time to scientific advancement* 把个人的时间用于科学的发展. **-al** *a.* 虔诚的; 祈祷的. — *n.* 简短的礼拜.

de·vour [diˈvauə] *vt.* ①狼吞虎咽地吃,拼命吃; 吞没, 吃光; 舐光. ②吞灭,毁灭. ③赶(路); 贪读; 盯,盯着看,凝视; 倾听. ④使 (好奇心、忧虑等) 被吸引住, …到极点. *He is* ～*ing novel after novel.* 他一味贪看小说. ～ *the way* 〔诗〕(马等)兼程急进. *I am* ～*ed with anxiety.* 我忧愁极了. *He* ～*ed every word.* 他一字不漏地倾听着.

de·vour·ing·ly [diˈvauəriŋli] *ad.* 贪婪地,贪; 吞灭似地.

de·vout [diˈvaut] *a.* 热诚的; 虔诚的. **-ly** *ad.* **-ness** *n.*

dew [djuː] *n.* ①露; 露水一样的东西(泪等). ②爽快,清新, 轻快. ～**-lit** *eyes* 〔诗〕挂着泪珠的双眼. *the* ～ *of youth* 青春的朝气. *the timely* ～ *of sleep* 甜睡. — *vt.* 喷湿, (露水等) 弄湿. — *vi.* 结露水. *It* ～*s.* 结露水. ～**berry** 【植】悬钩子. ～ **cell** 露管〔测定露点的仪器〕. ～**claw** (狗等脚上不与地面接触的) 无机能趾; 悬蹄. ～**drop** 露, 露珠. ～**fall** 结露, 起露; 黄昏(起露的)时刻. ～**lap** (牛等颈部) 垂皮, 垂肉. ～ **point** 【物】露点. ～ **pond** 露池〔山区高地用以蓄水的浅池〕. ～**ret** *vt.* 把(麻等)放在雨露下浸湿. ～ **worm** (作鱼饵用的) 蚯蚓.

de·wan [diˈwaːn] *n.* 〔印〕财政部长; 邦政府的首席部长.

Dew·ar [ˈdju(ː)ə] *n.* 迪尤尔〔姓氏〕.
Dew·ar ves·sel [ˈdjuːə ˈvesəl] *n.* 保温真空瓶〔又作 **Dewar, Dewar flask.** 苏格兰物理学家 Sir James Dewar 发明〕.
de·wa·ter [diːˈwɔːtə] *vt.* 使脱水,使浓缩.
de·wax [diːˈwæks] *vt.*【化】使脱蜡.
Dew·ey [ˈdju(ː)i] *n.* 杜威〔姓氏〕.
dew·i·ly [ˈdjuːili] *ad.* ①带露水地; 露水般地. ②纯洁地,清新地.
de·windt·ite [dəˈwintait] *n.*【矿】磷铅铀矿.
dew·i·ness [ˈdjuːinis] *n.* 露水大; 湿润.
DEW line = Distant Early Warning line【军】远程早发警报线.
DEW radar = Distant Early Warning radar【军】远程早发警报雷达.
DEWS = Distant Early Warning System【军】远程早发警报系统.
dew·y [ˈdjuːi] *a.* ①露大的, 带露水的; 似露的. ②(眼睛)泪汪汪的. 舒服的(睡眠等). ③纯洁的,清新的. ~ *tears* 晶莹的泪滴. *a* ~ *maiden* 纯洁直率的姑娘.
dex·i·o·trop·ic [ˌdeksiəˈtrɔpik] *a.* (如软体动物的螺形外壳等)向右的,右旋的.
Dex·e·drine [ˈdeksidriːn, -drin] *n.*【药】右旋苯异丙胺〔dextroamphetamine 的商标名,用作中枢神经兴奋剂〕.
Dex·ter [ˈdekstə] *n.* 德克斯特〔男子名〕.
dex·ter [ˈdekstə] *a.* ①右边的, 右手的. ②(因面向右边或出现在右边而) 预兆吉利的. ③【纹】(盾徽) 右边的 (*opp.* sinister).
dex·ter·i·ty [deksˈteriti] *n.* ①(手)灵巧, 熟练, 巧妙. ②(头脑)敏捷; 机敏. ③用惯右手.
dex·ter·ous [ˈdekstərəs] *a.* ①灵巧的,巧妙的,手快的,手巧的. ②敏捷的, 机敏的. ③右手灵便的. **-ly** *ad.* **-ness** *n.*
dex·tral [ˈdekstrəl] *a.* ①在右(边)的, 向右(边)的. ②用右手的. ③(软体动物的螺形外壳等)右旋的, 右卷的 (*opp.* sinistral). **-i·ty** [deksˈtræliti] *n.* **-ly** *ad.*
dex·tran [ˈdekstrən] *n.*【化】葡聚糖.
dex·trin [ˈdekstrin] *n.*【化】糊精.
dex·tro [ˈdekstrəu] *a.*【化】①右旋的, 顺时针向的. ②(某些水晶)使光的偏振右旋的.
dextro- *comb. f.* 表示"向右的","右旋的": *dextro*rotatory.
dex·tro·am·phet·a·mine [ˌdekstrəuæmˈfetəˌmiːn] *n.* 右旋苯异丙胺,右旋安非他明〔中枢神经兴奋药〕.
dex·tro·glu·cose [ˌdekstrəuˈgluːkəus] *n.* 葡萄糖; 右旋糖.
dex·tro·gy·rate [ˈdekstrəuˈdʒairit] *a.* ①右旋的, 顺时针向的. ②(某些水晶)使光的偏振右旋的.
dex·trone [ˈdekstrən] *n.* = dextran(e).
dex·tro·ro·ta·tion [ˌdekstrəurəuˈteiʃən] *n.* 右旋, 顺时针方向旋转.
dex·tro·ro·ta·to·ry [ˌdekstrəuˈrəutəˌtəri] *a.* ①右旋的,顺时针方向的. ②(某些水晶)使光的偏振右旋的.
dex·trorse [ˈdekstrɔːs] *a.*【植】右旋的, 右旋向上的. ~ *vine* 右旋葡萄藤.
dex·trose [ˈdekstrəus] *n.*【化】右旋糖,葡萄糖.
dex·trous [ˈdekstrəs] *a.* = dexterous.
dey [dei] *n.* 总督; 帕夏〔土耳其人建立的奥斯曼帝国在北非的官员〕.
D.F. = ①Dean of the Faculty (大学的)系主任. ②direction finding 测向. ③Doctor of Forestry. 林学博士. **D/F** = direction finding. **d/f** = day of fire (每)日弹药基数.
D.F.C. = Distinguished Flying Cross〔英〕优异飞行十字勋章.
D.F.E. = directional frictional effect 方向性摩擦效应.
D.F.M. = Distinguished Flying Medal〔美〕优异飞行勋章.
dft. = defendant; draft.
D.G. = ①*Dei gratia* (= by the grace of God)【宗】蒙上帝保佑. ②*Deo gratias* (= thanks to God) 感谢上帝. ③Director-general 总裁. ④Dragoon Guards〔英〕龙骑兵近卫团.
dg. = decigram(me)(s).
d.h. ① *das heisst*〔G. = that is to say〕. ②deadhead.
DH = designated hitter〔棒球〕指定击球手.
dhal [dɑːl] *n.* (印度的)木豆.
dhar·ma [ˈdɑːmə] *n.* ①〔印〕【佛】宇宙法规(包括自然法规和道德法规). ②遵守法规. ③〔D-〕达摩.
dhar·na [ˈdɑːnə] *n.* 〔印〕绝食伸冤〔印度曾流行过的一种消极斗争方式,受冤毒的人坐在当事人家门口,长坐绝食而至于死〕.
dho·bi(e) [ˈdəubi] *n.* 〔印〕洗衣工人. ~ **itch** 腹股沟癣〔据说是送到外面洗的衣服传染的〕.
dho·ti, dhoo·ti [ˈdəuti, ˈduːti] *n.* 〔印〕(男子的)围腰布.
dhow [dau] *n.* (阿拉伯沿海的)独桅帆船.
D.H.Q. = 〔美〕Division Headquarters 师部.
dhur·na [ˈdəːnə] *n.* = dharna.
dhur·rie [ˈdʌri] *n.* 〔印〕厚棉布; 厚棉布地毯.
di-¹ *pref.* = dis-¹.
di-² *pref.* 二,双,二重,二倍: *di*archy.
di-³, dia- *pref.* 〔后接辅音时用 dia-, 接元音时用 di-〕. ①表示"通过","横过": *dia*phragm, *dia*gonal. ②表示"分离": *dia*gnose, *dia*critical.
di(a). = diameter.
di·a·base [ˈdaiəbeis] *n.*【矿】辉绿岩.
di·a·be·tes [ˌdaiəˈbiːtiːz, -tiːs] *n.*【医】①糖尿病〔又作 ~ mellitus〕. ②尿崩症〔又作 ~ insipidus〕.
di·a·bet·ic [ˌdaiəˈbetik, -ˈbiːtik] *a.* (害)糖尿病的; —*n.* 糖尿病病人.
di·a·ble·rie, di·ab·le·ry [diˈɑːbləri, diˈæbləri] *n.* ①魔法, 妖术. ②妖怪传说. ③妖魔世界.
di·a·bol·ic, -i·cal [daiəˈbɔlik(əl)] *a.* ①〔通例 diabolic〕恶魔(一样)的. ②〔通例 diabolical〕凶暴的, 穷凶极恶的. *diabolic arts* 魔术.
di·ab·o·lism [daiˈæbəlizəm] *n.* ①魔术, 妖术. ②相信魔鬼,崇拜魔鬼. ③魔鬼行径,恶行.
di·ab·o·lize, di·ab·o·lise [daiˈæbəlaiz] *vt.* ①使成恶魔. ②把…描绘成恶魔.
di·ab·o·lo [diˈɑːbələu] *n.* 空竹 (*cf.* the devil on two sticks).
di·a·chron·ic [ˌdaiəˈkrɔnik] *a.*【语】历时的语言学的〔指语言系统在历史过程中的变化而言〕. ~ **linguistics**【语】历时语言学. **-cal·ly** *ad.*
di·ach·ron·y [daiˈækrəni] *n.*【语】历时语言学.
di·ach·y·lon, di·ach·y·lum [daiˈækilɔn, -əm] *n.*【医】铅硬膏.
di·ac·id [daiˈæsid] *a.*【化】①二酸的. ②二价酸的. —*n.* 二酸.
di·ac·o·nal [daiˈækənl] *a.* deacon 的.
di·ac·o·nate [daiˈækənit] *n.* ①副主祭〔执事〕的职位〔任期〕. ②副主祭团; 执事团.
di·a·cous·tic [ˌdaiəˈkuːstik] *a.* 折声的. **-tics** *n.* 折声学.
di·a·crit·ic [ˌdaiəˈkritik] *a.* ① = diacritical. ②【医】= diagnostic. —*n.* = diacritical mark.
di·a·crit·i·cal [daiəˈkritikəl] *a.* 区分的, 区别的. ~ **marks [points, signs]** 区别音符〔如 ā, ă, ä 所标的 -, ˘, ¨ 等〕.
di·ac·tin·ic [ˌdaiækˈtinik] *a.*【物】有化学线透射性能的,能透光化线的.
di·ac·tin·ism [daiˈæktinizəm] *n.* 透光化线性能.
di·ad¹ [ˈdaiæd] *n.* ①二; 一双. ②【数】并矢(量). ③

【化】二价元素；二价基。④【生】二分体；二分细胞。

diad² [ˈdaiæd] *a.* 【物】二重(对称)的。～ *axis* 二重轴。

di·a·del·phous [ˌdaiəˈdelfəs] *a.* 【植】①(雄蕊的)二体排列的。②二体雄蕊的。

di·a·dem [ˈdaiədem] *n.* ①王冠，冕〔尤指东方君主的头带〕。②王权，王位。— *vt.* 用王冠装饰；授以王冠。

di·ad·ro·mous [daiˈædrəməs] *a.* ①【植】(叶子)扇形脉序的。②【动】(鱼等的)洄游于海水和淡水中的。

di·aer·e·sis [daiˈiərisis] *n.* *(pl. -ses* [-siːz]*)* ①二连续元音的音节区分。②(表示二连续元音须分别发音的)区分音符〔如 coöperate 中的 ..；cooperate, zoology 等常用词常有省去 .. 的倾向；naïve 等外来语则仍沿用〕。

diag. = diagonal; diagram.

di·a·gen·e·sis [ˌdaiəˈdʒenisis] *n.* 【地】成岩作用，岩化作用。

di·a·ge·o·tro·pism [ˌdaiədʒiˈɔtrəpizm] *n.* (植物枝、茎的)横向地性。**-trop·ic** [-ˌdʒiəˈtrɔpik] *a.*

di·a·glyph [ˈdaiəglif] *n.* 凹雕 (= intaglio).

di·ag·nose [ˈdaiəgnəuz] *vt.* ①【医】诊断(疾病)。②判断(问题)。*The doctor ～d her illness as diabetes mellitus.* 医生诊断她患糖尿病。*The teacher ～d the boy's reading difficulties.* 老师找出那孩子阅读上困难的原因。

di·ag·no·sis [ˌdaiəgˈnəusis] *n.* *(pl. -ses* [-siːz]*)* ①诊断。②【生】(分类学上的)特征简述。③调查分析，判断。*mistake in ～* 误诊。*form a correct ～ on [upon] a disease* 确诊。

di·ag·nos·tic [ˌdaiəgˈnɔstik] *a.* ①诊断的。②特征的。— *n.* ①征候，特征。②〔*pl.*〕诊断法，诊断学。**-ti·cal·ly** *ad.* 诊断上，按照诊断。

di·ag·nos·ti·cian [ˌdaiəgnɔsˈtiʃən] *n.* 诊断者，诊断专家。

di·ag·o·nal [daiˈægənl] *a.* ①对角线的。②斜的；斜纹的。— *n.* ①【数】对角线，对顶线。②斜纹布。～ **matrix** 【数】对角(矩)阵。**-ly** *ad.* 斜，斜对。

di·a·gram [ˈdaiəgræm] *n.* 图，图形，图解；【数】作图。*a ～ of an engine* 发动机设计图。— *vt.* *(-gram(m)ed; -gram·ming)* 用图表示，图解。

di·a·gram·mat·ic, -i·cal [ˌdaiəgrəˈmætik(əl)] *a.* 图解的，图式的；概略的。**-i·cal·ly** *ad.*

di·a·gram·matize [ˌdaiəˈgræmətaiz] *vt.* 把…作成表，用图表示。

di·a·graph [ˈdaiəgrɑːf] *n.* 分度画线仪；分度尺；绘图器；放大绘图器。

di·a·ki·ne·sis [ˈdaiəkaiˈniːsis] 【生】(生殖细胞分裂的)丝球期〔指母染色体和父染色体在核中配对的时期〕。

di·al [ˈdaiəl] *n.* ①日晷(= sun-～)。②(钟表等的)针盘；(仪表等的)标度盘；(电话的)拨号盘。③矿用罗盘；航海罗盘。④〔俚〕脸(盘)。*a radio ～* 收音机刻度盘。— *vt., vi.* *(～(l)ed; ～(l)ing)* 拨(电话号码)，打(自动电话)；用矿用罗盘测量。～ *a radio* 转动收音机的旋钮选收。～**-a-bus** 〔亦作～**-a-ride**〕*n.* 〔美口〕电话传呼出租汽车业务。～ **indicator** 千分表。～ **plate** (针盘的)标度板。～ **telephone** 自动电话机。

dial. = ①dialect. ②dialectic.

di·a·lect [ˈdaiəlekt] *n.* ①方言，地方话。②【语】语支。③(某人的)谈风，语调。④(某职业的)专业用语。*the Lancashire ～* 兰开夏的方言。*English is an Indo-European ～.* 英语是印欧语的一支。*the lawyer's ～* 律师用语。～ **atlas** 方言分布图。**di·a·lec·tal** *a.*

di·a·lec·tic [ˌdaiəˈlektik] *a.* ①辩证(法)的。②方言的。— *n.* ①【哲】辩证法。②〔常 *pl.*〕(以问答方式进行的)论证；雄辩术。*Dialectics studies how opposites can become identical.* 辩证法研究对立物是怎样变统一的。*materialistic ～* 唯物辩证法。

di·a·lec·ti·cal [ˌdaiəˈlektikəl] *a.* ①辩证(法)的。②方言的。～ *materialism* 辩证唯物论。*the ～-materialist theory of knowledge* 辩证唯物论的认识论。**-ly** *ad.*

di·a·lec·ti·cian [ˌdaiəlekˈtiʃən] *n.* ①辩证家；逻辑学家。②方言学家。

di·a·lec·tics [ˌdaiəˈlektiks] *n.* 辩证法。*materialist ～* 唯物辩证法。

di·a·lec·tol·o·gy [ˌdaiəlekˈtɔlədʒi] *n.* 方言学。**-logist** 方言学家。

di·al·lage [ˈdaiəlidʒ] *n.* 异剥石。

di·al·ling [ˈdaiəliŋ] *n.* ①日晷制作；以日晷测时。②(自动电话)拨号。～ *system* (电话机的)自动式。～ *tone* (自动电话的)拨号音。

di·a·log(ue) [ˈdaiəlɔg] *n.* ①问答，对话。②问答体，对话体。③(小说中的)对白。*in ～* 用对话体，照问答体。— *vi.* 对话。— *vt.* 用对话表达。**-log·ic** *a.* 对话(体)的，问答体的。**-al·o·gism** [-ˈælədʒizəm] *n.* 对话式讨论法。**dial·o·gist** [daiˈælədʒist] *n.* 问答者，对话者；对话体作者。

di·a·lyse [ˈdaiəlaiz] *vt.* 【化】渗析，透析。

di·a·lys·er [ˈdaiəlaizə] *n.* 透析器，渗析器；渗析膜。

di·al·y·sis [daiˈælisis] *n.* *(pl. -ses* [-siːz]*)* ①分离，分解。②【化】渗析，透析。

di·a·lyt·ic [ˌdaiəˈlitik] *a.* 【化】有分离力的，透析的，渗析的。

di·a·lyze [ˈdaiəlaiz] *vt.* 〔美〕 = dialyse.

diam. = diameter.

di·a·mag·net·ic [ˌdaiəmægˈnetik] *a.* 【物】抗磁性的。— *n.* 抗磁性体。**-ally** *ad.*

di·a·mag·net·ism [ˌdaiəˈmægnitizəm] *n.* 【物】①抗磁性。②抗磁力；抗磁现象。③抗磁学。

di·a·man·té [ˌdiəˈmɑːnˈtei, -ˈmɑːntei] *a.* 嵌以钻石的；饰以闪光珠宝的。～ *sandals* 嵌着钻石的拖鞋。— *n.* 珠光宝气的装饰品。

di·a·man·tif·er·ous [ˌdaiəmænˈtifərəs] *a.* = diamondiferous.

di·am·e·ter [daiˈæmitə] *n.* ①直径。②(显微镜等的)放大倍数。*a lens magnifying 2,000 ～s* 能放大二千倍的透镜。

di·am·e·tral [daiˈæmitrəl] *a.* 直径的。

di·a·met·ric, di·a·met·ri·cal [ˌdaiəˈmetrik(əl)] *a.* ①直径的。②正好相反的。*They are in diametrical opposition to each other.* 他们彼此针锋相对。**-cal·ly** *ad.*

di·am·ine [daiˈæmiːn, ˈdaiəˌmiːn] *n.* ①二胺化合物；②肼，联氨。③二(元)胺；双胺染料。

di·a·mond [ˈdaiəmənd] *n.* ①金刚钻，金刚石，钻石。②菱形；菱饰；(纸牌的)方块。③【棒球】内场；棒球场。④【印】钻石体活字〔$4\frac{1}{2}$点〕。⑤(切玻璃用的)钻刀。⑥〔D-〕〔美〕Delaware 州的别名。⑦〔*pl.*〕〔美俚〕煤。— *a.* ①钻石(一样)的；钻石制成的，镶有钻石的。②菱形的。～ *in the rough* = *rough ～* ①天然金刚石。②言行粗鲁而心地善良的人。③〔美俚〕初露光芒的设想。*black ～s* 黑金刚石；煤。*a small ～* 一副方块同花牌中最小的牌。～ *cut ～* 以强制强，硬碰硬，棋逢对手。～ *of the first water* 最好的钻石；第一流人物。～**back** *a.* 菱纹背的。～ **drill** 金刚锥。～ **field** 钻石产地。～ **jubilee [aniversary]** 60(或 75)周年纪念。～**-point** *a.* 有钻石尖的；用有钻石尖的工具制作的。～ **point** ①钻石刻刀。②【交】铁轨菱形交叉处。～ **snake** 菱纹蛇。～ **spar** 刚石，钢玉。**D- State** 美国 Delaware 州的别名。～ **wedding** 钻石婚，结婚 60(或 75)周年纪念。～**-wise** *ad.* 成菱形。

di·a·mon·dif·er·ous [ˌdaiəmənˈdifərəs] *a.* 产钻石的。

Di·an·(n)a [daiˈænə] *n.* 黛安娜〔女子名〕。

Di·an·a [daiˈænə] *n.* ①【罗神】狄安娜(月亮和狩猎的女神)。②〔诗〕月。③女猎人；善骑的女人；女独身主义者。

di·an·drous [daiˈændrəs] *a.* 【植】具有两雄蕊的。

di·a·no·et·ic [ˌdaiənəuˈetik] *a.* 逻辑推理的；从逻辑推理出发的；非直觉的。

di·an·thus [daiˈænθəs] *n.* 石竹属植物〔如麝香石竹(康耐馨),美国石竹等〕.

di·a·pa·son [ˌdaiəˈpeisn, -ˈpeizn] *n.* ①和声;旋律. ②全声域;全音域. ③有管风琴的主要音栓. ④音叉. ⑤领域;范围.

di·a·pause [ˈdaiəˌpɔːz] *n.*【生】滞育〔指某些昆虫的发育停滞〕.

di·a·pe·de·sis [ˌdaiəpiˈdiːsis] *n.*【医】血细胞渗出.

di·a·per [ˈdaiəpə] *n.* ①菱形花样;织成的菱形花纹. ②【建】菱形格子. ③菱纹麻布;手巾. ④(婴儿)尿布. —*vt.* ①用尿布衬上. ②用菱形花纹装饰. ～ *cover* 衬尿布的橡皮布.

di·aph·a·nous [daiˈæfənəs] *a.* ①半透明的. ②朦胧的,缥渺的;模糊不清的. ～ *cloth* 半透明的布料.

di·a·phone [ˈdaiəfəun] *n.*【语音】类音〔如 half, 读 [hæf] 或 [hɑːf]〕.

di·a·pho·re·sis [ˌdaiəfəˈriːsis] *n.* (大量)发汗,出汗.

di·a·pho·ret·ic [ˌdaiəfəˈretik] *a., n.* 发汗的;发汗剂.

di·a·phragm [ˈdaiəfræm] *n.* ①隔膜, 膜. ②【物】光圈, 光阑. ③【机】隔板. ④【解】横隔膜, 膈. ⑤(电话机等的)振动膜. ⑥(避孕用)子宫帽. **-mat·ic** [ˌdaiəfrægˈmætik] *a.* 膈的,隔膜的.

di·aph·y·sis [daiˈæfisis] *n.* (*pl.* **-ses** [-siːz])【解】骨干〔指长骨的中间部分〕.

dia·pos·i·tive [ˌdaiəˈpɔzitiv] *n.* 透明的照相正片(如幻灯片).

di·ar·chi·al [daiˈɑːkiəl] *a.* 二人执政的,两头政治的.

di·arch·y [ˈdaiɑːki] *n.* 两头政治.

di·ar·i·al [daiˈɛəriəl] *a.* 日记的;日记体的.

di·a·rist [ˈdaiərist] *n.* 记日记的人.

di·a·ris·tic [ˌdaiəˈristik] *a.* 日记体的.

di·a·rize, di·a·rise [ˈdaiəraiz] *vi.* 记日记. —*vt.* 把…记入日记.

di·ar·rh(o)e·a [ˌdaiəˈriə] *n.*【医】腹泻. *have* ～ 下痢,泻肚子. **-rh(o)e·al** [-əl], **-rh(o)e·ic** [ˌdaiəˈriːik], **-rh(o)et·ic** [ˌdaiəˈretik] *a.*

di·ar·thro·sis [ˌdaiɑːˈθrəusis] *n.* (*pl.* **-ses** [-siːz])【解】动关节.

di·a·ry [ˈdaiəri] *n.* 日记,日志;日记簿. *a pocket* ～ 袖珍日记. *keep a* ～ 记日记.

Di·as·po·ra [daiˈæspərə] *n.* ①犹太人的分散;分散各地的犹太人;犹太人散居的地方. ②〔d-〕(同一起源的人民的)分散,散居.

di·a·spore [ˈdaiəˌspɔː] *n.*【矿】水铝石.

di·a·stase [ˈdaiəsteis] *n.*【生化】淀粉(糖化)酶. **-stat·ic** [ˌdaiəˈstætik] *a.*

di·as·ta·sis [daiˈæstəsis] *n.*【医】①(骨骼等的)脱离,分离. ②心舒张后期.

di·a·stem [ˈdaiəˌstem] *n.*【地】(沉积物沉积的)小间断.

di·a·ste·ma [ˌdaiəˈstiːmə] *n.* (*pl.* **-ste·ma·ta** [-tə])【齿】间隙,齿隙. **-mat·ic** [-stiˈmætik] *a.*

di·as·ter [daiˈæstə] *n.*【生】(有丝分裂的)双星体,双星期. **-tral** *a.*

di·as·to·le [daiˈæstəli] *n.* ①【生理】(心)舒张;心舒张期. ②【诗】音节延长. **-tolic** [ˌdaiəˈstɔlik] *a.*

di·as·tro·phism [daiˈæstrəfizəm] *n.* 地壳的变动;(一般的)变形,变动.

di·a·tes·sa·ron [ˌdaiəˈtesərən] *n.* (由四福音书改编成的)一览福音书.

di·a·ther·mal [ˌdaiəˈθəːməl] *a.*【物】透热(辐射)的.

di·a·ther·man·cy [ˌdaiəˈθəːmənsi] *n.*【物】透热性.

di·a·ther·ma·nous [ˌdaiəˈθəːmənəs] *a.*【物】透热的.

di·a·ther·mia [ˌdaiəˈθəːmiə] *n.*【医】透热疗法.

di·a·ther·mic [ˌdaiəˈθəːmik] *a.* ①有关透热(疗)法的. ②透热的.

di·a·ther·mize [ˌdaiəˈθəːmaiz] *vt.* 施透热法.

di·a·therm·y, di·a·ther·mi·a [ˈdaiəθəːmi, ˈdaiəˈθəːmiə] *n.* 透热(疗)法.

di·ath·e·sis [daiˈæθisis] *n.*【医】(易患某种疾病的)素质,体质. *tuberculous* ～ 易患结核病的体质. **-a·thet·ic** [ˌdaiəˈθetik] *a.*

di·a·tom [ˈdaiətəm] *n.*【植】硅藻.

di·a·to·ma·ceous [ˌdaiətəˈmeiʃəs] *a.* (含)硅藻的. ～ *earth* 硅藻土.

di·a·tom·ic [ˌdaiəˈtɔmik] *a.*【化】双原子的. ～ *acid* 二价酸.

di·at·om·ite [daiˈætəmait] *n.* 硅藻土,矽藻土.

di·a·ton·ic [ˌdaiəˈtɔnik] *a.*【乐】全音阶的. *the* ～ *scale* 全音阶,自然音阶.

di·a·tribe [ˈdaiətraib] *n.* 恶骂;酷评.

di·at·ro·pism [daiˈætrəpizəm] *n.*【植】斜屈性. **-pic** [ˌdaiəˈtrɔpik] *a.*

di·a·ze·pam [ˌdaiəˈzepem] *n.*【药】苯甲二氮䓬〔一种镇静安眠药〕.

di·a·zin(e) [ˈdaiəziːn, daiˈæzin] *n.*【化】二嗪,二氮(杂)苯. ～ *colours* 二嗪染料.

di·az·i·non [daiˈæzinɔn] *n.* 二嗪农(农药).

di·a·zo [daiˈæzəu] *a.*【化】重氮基的. ～ **colours** 重氮染料.

di·az·o·am·i·no [daiˌæzəuəˈmiːnəu, daiˌeizəu-] *a.*【化】重氮氨基的,重氮胺撑的.

di·a·zo·ni·um [ˌdaiəˈzəuniəm] *a.* 重氮(化)的.

di·az·o·tize [daiˈæzətaiz] *vt.*【化】使形成重氮化合物,使重氮化. **-zation** [-ˌæzətaiˈzeiʃən] *n.* 重氮化(作用).

dib[1] [dib] *n.* ①(羊等的)关节骨,羊拐子;〔*pl.*〕把关节骨当球玩的儿戏. ②(打牌用的)骨制筹码. ③〔*pl.*〕〔美〕要求,权利,保留权. ④〔俚〕(小额的)钱. *have* ～*s on* 对…有权利,对…有要求(*I have* ～*s on that piece of cake.* 我要吃那块蛋糕).

dib[2] [dib] *vi.* (**dib·bed, dib·bing**) = dap.

Di·bai [diˈbai] *n.* = Dubai.

di·bas·ic [daiˈbeisik] *a.*【化】二碱价的,二元的;二代的. ～ *acid* 二元酸. ～ *ester* 二价酸酯. ～ *salt* 二代盐.

dib·ber [ˈdibə] *n.* = dibble.

dib·ble[1] [ˈdibl] *vt.* ①用小锹在(地)上掘穴. ②穴植,点播. —*vi.* 使用点播器;点播. —*n.* 掘穴具,点播器. ～ *in potatoes* 穴播马铃薯.

dib·ble[2] [ˈdibl] *vi.* ①= dib. ②= dable.

dib·buk, dyb·buk [ˈdibək] *n.* (犹太民间传说)阴魂附体.

di·bran·chi·ate [daiˈbræŋkiːit] *a.*【动】二鳃目的,属于二鳃目的.

di·car·box·yl·ic [daiˌkɑːbɔkˈsilik] *a.*【化】二羧基的; ～ *acid* 二羧酸.

di·cast [ˈdikæst, ˈdaikæst] *n.* (古雅典法庭的)审理官.

DICBM = detection (of) intercontinental ballistic missile (system) 洲际弹道导弹的探测(系统).

dice[1] [dais] *n.* 〔本为 die[2] 的复数;但在口语中亦可作单数用,其复数形为 ～(s)〕①骰子;掷骰子. ②小方块. *cut potatoes into* ～ 把马铃薯切成丁. *play at* ～ 掷骰子. *no* ～ 〔俚〕反对,拒绝;失败(*As for the rest, no* ～. 其余各人全都失败[落空]了). —*vt.* ①把…切成骰子形[小方块],把…切成丁. ②掷骰子赌…. —*vi.* 掷骰子. ～ *away* 赌输.

dice[2] [dais] *n.* 〔美俚〕(赛车名次的)激烈争夺. —*vi.* (赛车)争夺名次.

di·cen·tra [daiˈsentrə] *n.* 荷包牡丹属植物〔如:荷包牡丹和兜状荷包牡丹〕.

di·ceph·a·lous [daiˈsefələs] *a.* (某些怪胎的)有双头的.

dic·er [ˈdaisə] *n.* ①掷骰子的人,赌钱人,赌徒. ②(食物)切丁机. ③〔俚〕帽子(尤指圆顶礼帽).

dic·ey [ˈdaisi] *a.* 〔主英口〕危险的,冒险的;不确实的.

dich- = dicho-.

di·cha·si·um [daiˈkeiziəm, -ʒiː-] *n.* *(pl.* **-si·a** [-ə]*)* 【植】二歧聚伞花序,二歧式.
di·chlo·ride, di·chlo·rid [daiˈklɔːraid, -rid] *n.* 【化】二氯化物.
di·chlo·ro·di·phen·yl·tri·chlor·o·eth·ane [dai-ˈklɔːrəu daiˌfenil traiˌklɔːrəuˈeθein]【化】滴滴涕,二氯二苯三氯乙烷, DDT.
dicho- *comb.f.* 二分,分为二: *dicho*tomy.
di·chog·a·my [daiˈkɔgəmi] *n.* 【植】(为防止自花授粉而)雌雄〔蕊〕异熟. **-a·mous, -cho·gam·ic** [ˌdaikəˈgæmik] *a.*
di·chon·dra [daiˈkɔndrə] *n.* 旋花科葵苔属植物.
di·chot·o·mic [ˌdikəˈtɔmik] *a.* = dichotomous.
di·chot·o·mize [diˈkɔtəmaiz] *vt., vi.* 二分,对分,叉分;(把…)分成两叉. ~ *the animal world into vertebrate and invertebrate* 把动物界分为脊椎动物和无脊椎动物.
di·chot·o·mous [diˈkɔtəməs] *a.* ①两分的. ②对生的;二歧的;二叉的. ~ *branching* 叉状分枝. **-ly** *ad.*
di·chot·o·my [diˈkɔtəmi] *n.* ①二等分. ②【天】弦月,半月. ③【植】对生;二歧式;二叉分枝式. ④【逻】二分法. *a* ~ *into the good and the evil* 善与恶的一分为二.
di·chro·ic, di·chro·it·ic [daiˈkrəuik, -itik] *a.* 有二色的. ~ *crystal* 有二色的水晶.
di·chro·ism [ˈdaikrəuizəm] *n.* ①【物】二向色性. ②【物】二色性.
di·chro·mate [daiˈkrəumeit] *a.* 【化】重铬酸盐.
di·chro·mat·ic [ˌdaikrəˈmætik] *a.* ①现二色的,二色性的. ②【生】二色变异的. ③【医】二色性色盲的.
di·chro·ma·tism [daiˈkrəumətizəm] *n.* ①【物】二色(性). ②【生】二色变异. ③【医】(红、蓝、绿三色中只能辨别二色的)二色性色盲.
di·chro·mic [daiˈkrəumik] *a.* 重铬的. ~ *acid* 重铬酸.
di·chro·scope, di·chro·o·scope [ˈdaikrəˌskəup, dai-ˈkrəuəˌskəup] 二(向)色镜.
dic·ing [ˈdaisiŋ] *n.* ①掷骰子. ②(皮面的)菱形花纹. *a* ~ *house* 赌场.
dick [dik] *n.* ①〔口〕家伙. ②〔俚〕皮围裙. ③〔俚〕誓言,声明. ④〔美俚〕侦探. ⑤标准. *take one's* ~ 发誓. *up to* ~ 合乎标准.
Dick·ens [ˈdikinz] *n.* ①迪肯斯〔姓氏〕. ②**Charles** ~ 狄更斯〔1812—1870,英国小说家〕.
dick·ens [ˈdikinz] *n.* ① = devil, deuce. ②困难. *What the* ~ *is it?* 究竟是什么? *The* ~*!* 哎呀! 糟了! 混帐. *as the* ~ 真是,实在是 (*He is noble as the* ~ 他真高尚).
Dick·en·son [ˈdikinsn] *n.* 迪肯森〔姓氏〕.
dick·er¹ [ˈdikə] *n.* 【商】十;〔特指〕十张皮革.
dick·er² [ˈdikə] *n.* 〔美〕①小生意; 物物交换; 讨价还价. ②【美政】谈判,交涉. — *vi.* 做小生意,用物换物;讨价还价.
dick·ey, dick·y¹ [ˈdiki] *n.* 〔俚〕①(公)驴. ②小鸟 (= ~-bird). ③衬衫假前胸,小孩围嘴. ④(马车的)车夫坐位;(随员坐的)马车后坐.
dick·y² [ˈdiki] *a.* 〔俚〕(脚)站不稳的,软弱的;靠不住的;可怜的. *It's all* ~ *with him.* 他完全靠不住了〔无希望了〕. *The table was in a* ~ *state.* 桌子不行了.
dick·y-bird [ˈdikibəːd] *n.* 〔儿〕小鸟.
di·cli·nous [daiˈklainəs] *a.* 【植】雌雄异花的, 单性的. **-nism** [ˈdaiklainizəm], **-ny** [-ni] *n.*
di·cot [ˈdaikɔt] *n.* 双子叶植物 (= dicotyledon).
di·cot·y·le·don [ˈdaiˌkɔtiˈliːdən] *n.* 双子叶植物. **-ous** *a.*
di·cou·ma·rin, di·cou·ma·rol [daiˈkuːmərin, dai-ˈkuːmərɔl] *n.* 双香豆素〔用作抗凝血药〕.
di·crot·ic [daiˈkrɔtik] *a.* 【医】重脉的, 二重脉搏的. **-ism** *n.* 重脉.
dict. = dictation; dictator; dictionary.
dic·ta [ˈdiktə] *n.* dictum 的复数.
dic·ta·phone [ˈdiktəfəun] *n.* 【商标】录音机.
dic·tate [dikˈteit] *vt.* ①(将信稿等内容向某人)口授,(口述文句等叫人)听写 (*sth. to*). ②命令,支配. ~ *some letters to a secretary.* 口述几封信叫秘书笔录下来. *The teacher* ~*d the phrase to the class.* 老师让全班同学听写这个短语. ~ *peace terms to a conquered enemy* 向被征服的敌人提出和谈条件 — *vi.* ①口述,听写. ②命令,支配,摆布. *I will not be* ~*d to.* 我不愿受人指挥. — [ˈdikteit] *n.* 〔常 *pl.*〕命令,指挥,指令,意旨. *the* ~*s of fancy* 时兴的趋向. *the* ~*s of conscience* 良心的驱使.
dic·ta·tion [dikˈteiʃən] *n.* ①默写,听写;口授. ②命令,指令,指挥.
dic·ta·tor [dikˈteitə] *n.* ①发号施令者,(特指)独裁者;专政者. ②口授者. ③〔古罗马〕执政官.
dic·ta·to·ri·al [ˌdiktəˈtɔːriəl] *a.* 执政者的;专政的,独裁的;傲然的,唯我独尊的. **-ly** *ad.* **-ness** *n.*
dic·ta·tor·ship [dikˈteitəʃip] *n.* ①执政者的职位〔任期〕. ②专政,独裁. ③独裁权. *the* ~ *of the proletariat* 无产阶级专政.
dic·ta·to·ry [ˈdiktətəri] *a.* = dictatorial.
dic·ta·tress [dikˈteitris] *n.* 女独裁者.
dic·tion [ˈdikʃən] *n.* ①用语的选择;措辞,用字. ②〔美〕(讲话、唱歌的)发音法, 朗诵法. *good* [*faulty*] ~ 确切的〔错误的〕说法. *bad* [*poor*] ~ 不妥当的措辞. *a Latin* ~ 拉丁用语.
dic·tion·a·ry [ˈdikʃənəri] *n.* 字典,词典;【自】代码字典. *consult a* ~ 查阅词典. *a walking* [*living*] ~ 活字典,知识渊博的人. *a* ~ *of English* 英语词典. ~ **catalog-gue** (图书馆按字母顺序编排的) 词书体书目. ~ **English** [*style*] 古板的英语〔体裁〕.
Dic·to·graph [ˈdiktəgrɑːf] *n.* 【商标】窃听器;电话录音器;室内传话器.
dic·tum [ˈdiktəm] *n.* *(pl.* ~*s,* **-ta** [-tə]*)* ①断言, 断定. ②名言,格言. ③【法】法官的意见.
dic·ty [ˈdikti] *a.* 〔美俚〕①高级的, 上等的. ②傲慢的;势利的.
di·cu·ma·rol [daiˈkuːmərəl] *n.* 【化】血液凝固防止剂.
di·cy·an [daiˈsaiən] *n.* 【化】①氰. ②二氰(基).
did [did] do 的过去式.
di·dact [ˈdaidækt] *n.* 说教者.
di·dac·tic [diˈdæktik, daiˈd-] *a.* 教导的;启发人的;说教的. *a* ~ *manner* 启发人的态度. **-ti·cal·ly** *ad.* 在教导上;启发式地. **-tic·ism** *n.* 教导法;教师的品质;启发.
di·dac·tics [diˈdæktiks, dai-] *n.* 教授法,教学法.
di·dap·per [ˈdaidæpə] *n.* = dabchick.
did·dle [ˈdidl] *vt.* 〔口〕①骗 (钱等). ②浪费(时间). ③快速摇动. — *vi.* 前后移动,前后摇摆.
Di·de·rot [ˈdiːdərəu] *n.* ① 狄特罗〔姓氏〕. ②**Denis** ~ 〔1713—1784,法国哲学家,百科全书编者〕.
did·n't [ˈdidnt] = did not.
di·do [ˈdaidəu] *n.* *(pl.* ~*es,* ~*s)* 〔美口〕〔常 *pl.*〕胡闹,开玩笑. *cut* (*up*) ~*s* 乱开玩笑.
Di·do [ˈdaidəu] *n.* 传说中迦太基 (Carthage) 的建国者和女王.
didst [didst] 〔古、诗〕(thou 后用的) did.
di·dy [ˈdaidi] *n.* 〔口〕尿布.
di·dym·i·um [daiˈdimiəm] *n.* 镨钕混合物.
did·y·mous [ˈdidiməs] *a.* 【植、动】双生的,孪生的.
di·dyn·a·mous [daiˈdinæməs] *a.* 【植】二强雄蕊的.
die¹ [dai] *vi.* ①死. ②灭亡,消灭;熄灭;枯死,凋落. ③漠然不受影响,感觉不到 (*to*). ④泄气. ⑤〔口〕渴望,盼望〔参看 dying〕. ⑥【棒球】出局. *I thought I should have* ~*d.* 要命要命〔大笑后口吻〕. *The secret* ~*d with him.* 秘密跟他同时埋葬了〔至死未曾吐露秘密〕. *My heart died within me.* 我疲倦死了. ~ **a beggar** 穷困潦倒而死. ~ **a dog's death** 死得可鄙. ~ **a glorious death**

死得光荣,壮烈牺牲. ~ ***a martyr*** 杀身成仁,殉道,殉教. ~ ***an unnatural [untimely] death*** 死于非命;暴卒. ~ ***at one's post*** 殉职. ~ ***away*** (风、声音等)渐息,渐弱;渐渐凋落,枯萎. ~ ***back***【植】顶枯;枯萎(根未死). ~ ***by violence*** 凶死. ~ ***daily*** 虽生犹死;遭受精神的痛苦. ~ ***down*** = ~ away. ~ ***for one's country*** 殉国,为国牺牲. ~ ***from*** *(a wound)* 因伤致死. ~ ***game*** 奋战而死,至死不屈. ~ ***hard*** 壮烈牺牲;难断气;难绝灭. ~ ***in harness*** 至死不倦,积劳而死,殉职. ~ ***in one's bed*** = ~ ***a natural death*** 寿终正寝,老死,好死. ~ ***in one's shoes [boots]*** ①横死;被绞死. ②至死犹劳累不倦. ~ ***in the last ditch*** 奋斗到死. ~ ***of*** 因…而死. ~ ***of age*** 老死. ~ ***of hunger*** 饿死. ~ ***off*** 一个一个死去;顺次枯死. ~ ***old [young]*** 寿终[(夭)折]. ~ ***on the air*** (钟声等)渐渐消失. ~ ***on the vine*** (计划等)失败,中途夭折. ~ ***out*** 消灭,死绝. ~ ***standing by***【美剧】演出无人喝采. ~ ***the death*** 毙命;受死刑. ~ ***to self*** 舍己,无我. ~ ***to shame*** 死不要脸,恬不知耻. ~ ***unto sin*** 不受罪恶的摆布. ***Never say ~!*** 不要气馁;不要悲观; **~-in** *n.* (以死亡相威胁的)死亡抗议,死亡示威. **~-up** *n.* ①(因天灾等而造成的)牲畜的大批死亡. ②大批死亡的牲畜.

die² [dai] *n. (pl. dice [dais])* ①骰子;骰子状物;一粒骰子. ②*(pl. dies [daiz])* 钢型,硬模;冲模;螺丝模;拉丝模. ③【建】(柱墩的)墩身. ~ ***casting*** 模铸. ***straight [level, true] as a*** ~ 笔直的,平坦的;决无错误的. ***The ~ is cast.*** 事已决定,事已至此,无可翻悔. ***upon a [the]*** ~ 在危急存亡关头,有关…的存亡. **~-cast** *a.* 以印模铸造的. ~ **maker** 雕刻印模者.

die-away [ˈdaiəwei] *a.* 没精神的,颓丧的,忧郁的. *a ~ look* 无精打采的样子.

die•back [ˈdaiˌbæk] *n.*【植】顶枯病,顶死.

di•e•cious [daiˈiːʃəs] *a.* = dioecious.

dief•fen•bach•i•a [ˌdiːfnˈbækiə] *n.* 花叶万年青属植物.

die-hard [ˈdaihɑːd] *n.* ①拼死抵抗的人,顽强的人. ②【政】顽固[保守]分子,死顽固. — *a.* 极右派的,死硬派的.

diel•drin [ˈdiːldrin] *n.*【化】狄氏剂,氧桥氯甲桥萘[一种长效杀虫剂].

di•e•lec•tric, di•e•lec•tri•cal [ˌdaiiˈlektrik(əl)] *a.* 非传导性的,绝缘的,介电的. — *n.* 电介质,电介体,绝缘体. ~ **constant** 介电常数;介电恒量,电容率.

Dien Bien Phu [ˈdjen ˈbjen ˈfuː] 奠边府[越南城镇].

di•en•ceph•a•lon [ˌdaienˈsefələn] *n.*【解】间脑. **-ce•phal•ic** [-siˈfælik] *a.*

di•er•e•sis [daiˈiərəsis] *n. (pl. -ses [-siːz])* = diaeresis.

Di•es [ˈdaiiːz] *n. (sing., pl.)* [L.] 日. ~ ***Irae*** [ˈaiəriː] ①最后审判日. ②由 ~ Irae 开头的拉丁文赞美诗. ***dies non*** [ˈnɔn] ①停审日,休庭日. ②(须扣除不算的)假日.

Die•sel [ˈdiːzəl] *n.* ①[d-] = ~ engine [motor] 柴油机,内燃机. ~ *oil* 柴油. ②**R.** ~ 狄赛尔 (1858—1913),德国柴油机发明者.

die•sel•ize [ˈdiːzəlaiz] *vt.* 用柴油发动机装备(轮船).

die•sink•er [ˈdaisiŋkə] *n.* 制模工.

di•e•sis [ˈdaiəsis] *n. (pl. -ses [-ˌsiːz])* 双剑号 (‡) (= double dagger).

die•stock [ˈdaiˌstɔk] *n.* (切削螺纹用的)板牙扳手,扳牙架,螺丝绞板.

di•es•trum, di•es•trus [daiˈestrəm, -trəs] *n.*【生】间(动)情期. **-trous** [-trəs] *a.*

di•et¹ [ˈdaiət] *n.* ①饮食,食物;规定的饮食. ②日常看[听]的东西,日常做的事情. *a subsistence ~* 维持健康所必需的最少食量. *a vegetable [meat] ~* 素[肉]食. — *vt.* 给与(病人)规定的饮食. ~ *oneself on vegetables* 吃素. — *vi.* 吃规定的饮食,忌嘴,忌口. ~ **pill** [美口]减肥丸. **-er** (旨在减肥的)节食者.

di•et² [ˈdaiət] *n.* [常 D-] (丹麦、日本等的)议会,国会.

di•et•a•ry [ˈdaiətəri] *a.* 饮食的;规定食物的. — *n.* 规定的食物;规定的食量;食谱. *a ~ cure* 食物疗法.

di•e•tet•ic, die•tet•i•cal [ˌdaiəˈtetik(əl)] *a.* 饮食的,营养的;(特指限制糖分的)特定饮食的. **-ly** *ad.* **-tet•ics** *n.* 饮食学,营养学. **-ti•tian, -ti•cian** [ˌdaiəˈtiʃən] *n.* 饮食学家,营养学家.

di•eth•yl [daiˈeθil] *n.*【化】二乙基的. ~ **ether**【化】二乙醚. ~ **ketone**【化】二乙酮,戊酮.

di•eth•yl•stil•b(o)es•trol [daiˌeθilstilˈbestrəul] *n.*【药】已烯雌酚[雌性激素的代用品].

Dieu et mon droit [ˈdjɔ ei məun ˈdrɔit] [F.] 上有天帝,我有权利[英王的座右铭].

dif- *pref.* = dis-¹.

diff. = difference; different; differential.

dif•fer [ˈdifə] *vi.* ①不同,不一样,不一致,有差别. ②意见不同[不合]. ~ *in opinion* 意见不同. ***I beg to ~.*** 很抱歉,我不赞成. ***agree to ~*** 求同存异;彼此保留不同意见. ~ ***from*** ①和…不同,和…不一致. ②和…意见不同 (*~ from each other* 互异). ~ ***with*** 和…意见不同.

dif•fer•ence [ˈdifrəns] *n.* ①差异,差别. ②不和,争论. ③【数】差,差额. ④【逻】特殊性. *There is no ~ between them.* 两者毫无差别. *the ~ of jetsam from flotsam* 弃货不同于浮货. *What ~ can it make?* 不是一样吗? *He is an artist with a ~.* 他是别具风格的艺术家. ***distinction without ~*** 无聊的区别. ***make a ~*** 发生差别;使…有差别;(结果等)是重要的,有关系[影响] (*One false step will make a great ~.* 失之毫厘谬以千里. *Don't let it make any ~.* 没关系. *make a ~ between A and B* 使甲乙有别,对甲乙不一样). ***pay [meet] the ~*** 付差额金. ***seek common ground while reserving ~s*** 求同存异. ***settle ~s*** 调停. ***split the ~*** ①折中,妥协. ②均分剩下的东西. — *vt.* [罕]区别,使有差别.

dif•fer•ent [ˈdifrənt] *a.* ①不同的,不一致的,有差别的. ②各种的,各色各样的. ③[美]异常的. *That is a ~ pair of shoes.* 那是另外一件事. ***be ~ from*** 和…不同,和…有别. **-ly** *a.*

dif•fer•en•ti•a [ˌdifəˈrenʃiə] *n. (pl. -ti•ae [-ʃiiː])* ①差异. ②【逻】(同类的东西中使这一种有别于另一种的)特殊性.

dif•fer•en•ti•a•ble [ˌdifəˈrenʃiəbl, -ʃə-] *a.* ①可鉴别的. ②【数】可微分的. **-bil•i•ty** [difəˌrenʃiəˈbiliti] *n.*

dif•fer•en•ti•al [ˌdifəˈrenʃəl] *a.* ①差别的,区别的;特定的. ②【数】微分的. ③【物、机】差动的,差速的,差示的. — *n.* ①(铁路不同路线之间为保持运输平衡而规定的)运费差. ②(同一行业中熟练工和非熟练工的)工资差别. ③【数】微分. ④【机】差动器. ~ **blood count** 白血球分类计数. ~ **calculus**【数】微分. ~ **diagnosis**【医】鉴别诊断. ~ **equation** 微分方程式. ~ **duties** 特定[差别]关税. ~ **gear** 差动齿轮. ~ **medium** 鉴别性培养基. ~ **pressure** 分压,不均匀压力. ~ **rate** (铁路的)特定运费率. ~ **thermometer** 差示温度计. **-ly** *ad.*

dif•fer•en•ti•ate [ˌdifəˈrenʃieit] *vt.* ①使有差别,区别,划分,区分. ②使分化,使变异. ③【数】求…的微分. ~ *one thing from another* 使甲乙互异. — *vi.* ①产生差别. ②区分,区别. ③【生】分化,变异.

dif•fer•en•ti•a•tion [ˌdifəˌrenʃiˈeiʃən] *n.* ①差别,区别;区分,划分. ②【生】分化,变异. ③【地】(从共同的岩浆产生出不同的岩石的)分异作用. ④【数】微分法. *class ~* 阶级分化.

dif•fi•cile [ˈdifisiːl] *a.* [F.] 困难的;难对付的.

dif•fi•cult [ˈdifikəlt] *a.* ①困难的,(工作等)艰难的. ②执拗的,顽固的. *a ~ disposition* 执拗的性情. ~ *of access* 难接近. ~ *to answer* 难答.

dif•fi•cul•ty [ˈdifikəlti] *n.* ①困难;难事,难局,逆境;障碍. ②异议;争论,纠葛. ③[常 *pl.*] 财政困难,(经济)

拮据. ***be in difficulties*** 财政困难,经济拮据. ***make a*** ~ 不同意,反对. ***make [raise] difficulties*** 刁难. ***make no*** ~ ***in*** *(granting the request)* 立即同意[应允]. ***tide over difficulties*** 渡过难关. ***with*** ~ 好容易才,千辛万苦才. ***without*** ~ 容容易易就,轻易.

dif·fi·dence [ˈdifidəns] *n.* ①缺乏自信. ②羞怯,腼腆;谦虚. ③〔古〕疑惑,猜疑. *with nervous* ~ 提心吊胆地. *with seeming* ~ 假装着害羞.

dif·fi·dent [ˈdifidənt] *a.* ①缺乏自信的. ②羞怯的,胆怯的. *He is* ~ *of his success.* 他对成功缺乏信心. **-ly** *ad.*

dif·flu·ent [ˈdifluənt] *a.* ①流出性的,分流性的 *(opp.* confluent*)*. ②溶解的;溶化的. ~ *rivers* 分流河. **-ence** [-əns] *n.* ①流出;分流. ②溶解,潮解.

dif·fract [diˈfrækt] *vt.* 分解;【物】(光等)折射,衍射. **-tion** *n.* 折射,衍射 (*diffraction grating [fringe]* 衍射光栅[条纹]). **-tive** *a.* 折射的,衍射的.

dif·fuse [diˈfjuːz] *vt.* ①使(水分)渗出;(使气体等)扩散,发散. ②散布(谣言等);普及(教育);传播(知识). ③【物】使(光)漫射. — *vi.* ①扩散;渗出. ②传播;散布. ③【物】漫射. — [-s] *a.* ①四散的;散乱的. ②(文章等)冗长的,啰嗦的,铺张的. ~ *nebula* 弥漫星云. ~ *sound* 漫射声. **-ly** *ad.* **-ness** *n.*

dif·fus·er, dif·fu·sor [diˈfjuːzə] *n.* ①散布者,传播者. ②【物】(使光线均匀分布的)漫射体. ③【机】扩散器.

dif·fus·i·ble [diˈfjuːzəbl] *a.* 会扩散的,会散开的;弥漫性的. **-bil·i·ty** [diˌfjuːzəˈbiliti] *n.* 散播力,散布性,弥漫性;【物】扩散率.

dif·fu·sion [diˈfjuːʒən] *n.* ①散布,发散. ②传播,普及. ③冗长. ④【化】渗滤. ⑤【物】扩散,漫射. *the* ~ *of knowledge* 知识的传播. ~ *of speech* 演说的冗长. ~ *of light* 光线的漫射.

dif·fu·sive [diˈfjuːsiv] *a.* ①散布性的;扩散的. ②(奉承话等)啰啰嗦嗦的,冗长的.

dig [dig] *vt.* **(dug** [dʌg], 〔古〕 ***digged; dug,*** 〔古〕 ***digged)*** ①挖,掘(土),凿(井等),采掘(山芋、矿物等). ②探究 *(up; out)*. ③〔口〕(把指尖等)戳进,插进,刺入 *(into; in)*. ④〔美俚〕理解. ⑤〔美俚〕赞成;喜欢. ⑥〔美俚〕看,看到. — *vi.* ①挖土;开凿,掘进,挖穿 *(in; through; under)*. ②探究,发掘 *(for; into)*. ③〔美俚〕苦学,苦干,钻研 *(at)*. ④〔俚〕住. ~ ***a pit for*** 挖陷阱(陷人). ~ ***deep*** 〔美俚〕挖深;掏出来. ~ ***down*** ①挖倒,挖下,挖去. ②掏腰包. ~ ***down into sb.'s mind*** 探察某人心理. ~ ***in*** ①挖进,埋进(肥料等). ②戳进. ③苦学,苦干. ④坚持主张. ⑤开始吃. ⑥= ~ oneself in. ~ ***[poke]*** *(a person)* ***in the ribs*** 用指头戳(某人)胸脯. ~ ***into*** ①掘进. ②钻研. ③用掉,用去. ④吃. ~ ***oneself in*** 挖战壕防守. ~ ***out*** ①挖出;查出(事实). ②〔美口〕慌慌忙忙走开[逃走]. ~ ***one's way*** 挖进 *(in; into)*, 挖出 *(out)*, 挖穿 *(through)*. ~ ***over*** 探掘. ~ ***up*** ①开垦(荒地等);采掘(山芋等). ②查出;(偶然)发现,找到,得到. ③〔美俚〕出钱,捐助,支付. ④挑起(~ *up the hatchet* 挑起战端). — *n.* 〔口〕①一挖;一戳;一撞. ②挖苦,讽刺 *(at)*. ③〔美口〕刻苦钻研的学生. ④(考古的)挖掘,挖掘地点. ⑤〔*pl.*〕〔英口〕学生宿舍,单身宿舍;住处.

dig. = digest.

dig·a·mist [ˈdigəmist] *n.* 再婚者.

dig·a·my [ˈdigəmi] *n.* 再婚. **-mous** [-məs] *a.* 再婚的.

di·gas·tric [daiˈgæstrik] *a.* 【解】二腹的;二腹肌的. — *n.* (下颚的)二腹肌.

di·gen·e·sis [daiˈdʒenisis] *n.* 【生】(有性生殖和无性生殖的)世代交替.

di·gest [diˈdʒest, dai-] *vt.* ①消化,助消化. ②玩味,领会,体会(文意). ③容忍,忍受,甘受(侮辱等). ④(系统地)整理;汇编(法律);摘要. ⑤【化】浸煮,煮解. — *vi.* ①消化. ②【化】浸煮. *This food* ~*s well [ill].* 这食品易[难]消化. *This conduct is more than I can* ~. 这种行为我忍受不了. — [ˈdaidʒest] *n.* ①文摘;摘要. ②法律汇编;〔the D-〕罗马法典〔公元六世纪罗马皇帝查士丁尼命令汇编的罗马法典,共五十卷〕.

di·gest·er [diˈdʒestə, dai-] *n.* ①消化者. ②助消化的药[食品]. ③汇编者. ④【化】浸煮器;蒸煮锅.

di·gest·i·ble [diˈdʒestəbl, dai-] *a.* ①易消化的. ②可摘要的. **-bil·i·ty** [diˌdʒestiˈbiliti] *n.* 消化性[率].

di·ges·tion [diˈdʒestʃən, dai-] *n.* ①消化;消化力,消化作用. ②(精神上的)同化吸收,融会贯通. ③【化】浸煮(作用),浸提. ④菌致分解〔用细菌分解法处理污水〕. ***be easy [hard] of*** ~ 易[难]消化. *I have a weak [good]* ~. 我的消化力弱[强].

di·ges·tive [diˈdʒestiv, dai-] *a.* ①有消化力的;助消化的;易消化的. ②【化】浸煮的. *He suffers from* ~ *trouble.* 他消化不好. ~ *juice [fluid]* 消化液. ~ *organs* 消化器官. — *n.* 消化剂. **-ly** *ad.* 在消化上,用消化作用.

dig·ga·ble [ˈdigəbl] *a.* 可采掘的.

dig·ger [ˈdigə] *n.* ①挖掘者;采金矿工. ②地蜂,穴蜂 (= ~ wasp). ③挖掘器. ④〔口〕澳洲人,澳洲兵;新西兰人. ⑤〔澳〕老兄,朋友. ⑥〔美俚〕扒手;为金钱而与男人交朋友或结婚的女人. ⑦〔the D-〕〔美〕专挖草木根吃的印第安人. ⑧〔英史〕掘地派成员〔十七世纪英国的平均地权者开挖耕种某些公有土地,以抗议私有财产制度〕. ⑧〔美俚〕为黄牛代购戏票的人. ⑨〔美俚〕〔D-〕乐于帮助同伙的嬉皮士.

dig·ging [ˈdigiŋ] *n.* ①挖掘,采掘. ②〔*pl.*〕开采物. ③矿区,金矿. ④〔*pl.*〕〔美俚〕住处,〔英俚〕公寓.

dight [dait] *vt.* 〔古、诗〕整顿;装饰;装备.

dig·it [ˈdidʒit] *n.* ①手指,足趾. ②一指之宽〔约 3/4 英寸〕. ③【天】太阳(或月亮)直径的 1/12〔用作测定日食、月食的单位〕. ④阿拉伯数字〔0,1,2,… 9. 有时将 0 除外,仅指 1 至 9〕. ★古人以指、趾计数,故称数字为 digit. *The number 301 contains three* ~*s.* 数字 301 是三位数. *binary* ~ 二进制数字[数位].

dig·it·al [ˈdidʒitl] *a.* ①手指的;指状的. ②数字的. — *n.* ①(钢琴等的)琴键. ②手指. **a** ~ **computer** 数字型电子计算机. 〔相对于 analogue computer 即模拟型电子计算机而言〕.

dig·i·tal·in [didʒiˈtælin, -ˈteilin] *n.* 地芰他灵,洋地黄苷,毛地黄苷.

dig·i·ta·lis [ˌdidʒiˈteilis] *n.* ①【植】毛地黄属. ②毛地黄干叶;毛地黄制剂〔强心剂〕.

dig·i·tal·ize [diˈdʒitəlaiz] *vt.* 用毛地黄治疗(心脏病). **-zation** [-ˌdʒitəlaiˈzeiʃən] *n.*

dig·i·tate, dig·i·tat·ed [ˈdidʒiteit, -id] *a.* ①有指的,有趾的. ②指状的,掌状的. ~ *leaves* 掌状叶.

dig·i·ta·tion [didʒiˈteiʃən] *n.* 指状分裂;指状突起.

digiti- *comb. f.* 表示"指";"趾": *digiti*grade.

dig·i·ti·form [diˈdʒitifɔːm] *a.* 指状的.

dig·i·ti·grade [ˈdidʒitigreid] *a.* 【动】(脚跟不落地而)用足趾行走的,趾行的. — *n.* 趾行动物〔狗、猫、马等〕.

dig·i·tize [ˈdidʒiˌtaiz] *vt.* 使计数化,使数字化,使成为数字.

dig·i·tox·in [ˈdidʒiˈtɔksn] *n.* 毛[洋]地黄毒苷〔用以制强心剂〕.

di·glot [ˈdaiglɔt] *a.* 两种语言的,使用两种语言的. — *n.* 两种语言对照版本.

dig·ni·fied [ˈdignifaid] *a.* 有威风的,有威严的;显贵的,高贵的.

dig·ni·fy [ˈdignifai] *vt.* ①使有威严,使高贵;授以荣誉. ②把…夸大为. *to* ~ *cowardice by calling it prudence* 把怯懦美化为谨慎.

dig·ni·ta·ry [ˈdignitəri] *n.* ①高贵的人,高官显贵. ②〔特指〕高僧. — *a.* 高官的,权贵的.

dig·ni·ty [ˈdigniti] *n.* ①威严,威风;端庄;尊严,高贵;体面. ②高位,显职. ③高官显贵. ***impair one's*** ~ 有伤

体面. *a little on one's* ~ 有点摆架子. ***be upon [stand upon] one's*** ~ 摆架子,闹气派. ***beneath one's*** ~ 损害尊严,不合身分. ***with*** ~ 庄严地; 端着架子, 神气十足地.

di·gox·in [daiˈgɔksin] *n.* 【药】异羟基洋地黄毒苷〔作用较快的强心药〕,(商品名)地高辛,狄戈辛.

di·graph [ˈdaigrɑːf] *n.* (读作一音的) 复合字母〔如 ch, ea〕.

di·gress [daiˈgres] *vi.* 脱轨,离题. ~ *from the point* 离开要点.

di·gres·sion [daiˈgreʃən] *n.* ①离题; 枝节话. ②【天】偏离特定路线. *to return from the* ~ 言归正传, 闲话休讲.

di·gres·sive [daiˈgresiv] *a.* 离题的,枝节的. **-ly** *ad.*

di·he·dral [daiˈhedrəl, daiˈhiːdrəl] *a.* 由两个平面构成的, 二面的. — *n.* 【数】二面角 (= ~ angle); 【空】上反角 (= positive ~); 下反角 (= negative ~).

di·hy·brid [daiˈhaibrid] *n.* 【遗传】二对因子杂种〔杂合子〕.

di·hydrate [daiˈhaidreit] *n.* 【化】二水合物.

di·hy·dro·chlo·ride [daiˌhaidrəˈklɔːraid] *n.* 二氢氯化物; 二盐酸化物.

di·hy·dro·strep·to·my·cin [daiˌhaidrəuˌstreptəuˈmaisin] *n.* 【药】双氢链霉素.

Di·jon [ˈdiːʒɔːŋ] *n.* 第戎〔或译迪戎,法国城市〕.

dik-dik [ˈdik-dik] *n.* (非洲)小羚羊.

dike[1] [daik] *n.* ①堤,堤防,堰堤. ②沟, 濠, 渠. ③【矿】岩脉. ④障碍物. — *vt.* ①用堤[濠沟]围绕. ②开沟排水.

dike[2] [daik] *n.* 搞同性恋的女人. **dik·ey** *a.*

dike[3] [daik] *vt.* 〔美俚〕使穿得漂亮,打扮 (*out, up*). *They were all* ~*d out for the party.* 他们都为赴晚会打扮得漂漂亮亮.

dike-grave [ˈdaikgreiv] *n.* ①(荷兰的) 堤防监督. ②〔英方〕(沼泽地区的)沟渠[堤防]监视官.

dik·tat [dikˈtɑːt] *n.* (强加于战败国等的) 单方面的苛刻解决条件.

dil. =【化】dilute.

di·lac·er·ate [diˈlæsəˌreit] *vt.* 撕裂,裂碎.

di·lan·tin [daiˈlæntin] *n.*【化、药】地仑丁,二苯乙内酰脲〔抗癫痫药〕.

di·lap·i·date [diˈlæpiˌdeit] *vi., vt.* ①使(局部)毁坏,(部分)损坏. ②〔古〕浪费,乱花(钱财等).

di·lap·i·dat·ed [diˈlæpideitid] *a.* 破烂的(衣服等),要坍的(房子等); 破落的, 衰败的. *a* ~ *fortune* 衰败的家道.

di·lap·i·da·tion [diˌlæpiˈdeiʃən] *n.* ①破烂,破败. ②浪费, (家产的)荡尽. ③(崖岸等的)崩塌; 崩塌物. ④(向居住教会房屋的圣职者索取的)房屋维修费.

di·lap·i·da·tor [diˈlæpideitə] *n.* 损坏者; 浪费者.

di·lat·a·ble [daiˈleitəbl] *a.* 会膨胀的,可扩张的. **-bil·i·ty** [daiˌleitəˈbiliti] *n.* 膨胀性 [率].

di·lat·ant [daiˈleitnt, di-] *a.* ①膨胀的,有膨胀之势的. ②(颗粒物质)因变形而膨胀的. ③(胶状溶液)受压而凝固的. — *n.* 膨胀物. **-an·cy** *n.*

dil·a·ta·tion [ˌdaileiˈteiʃən], **-la·tion** [ˌdaiˈleiʃən] *n.* ①扩张, 膨胀. ②【医】扩张(症); 扩张术. ③(说话、写文章的)铺叙,详述.

di·late [daiˈleit] *vt.* 使膨胀. *with* ~*d eyes* 瞪着眼睛. — *vi.* ①扩张,膨胀. ②详述. ~ *on [upon] a subject* 对问题详加叙述.

di·la·tion [daiˈleiʃən] *n.* ①膨胀, 扩大. ②【医】扩张(症).

dil·a·tom·e·ter [ˌdiləˈtɔmitə, dailə-] *n.*【物】膨胀计.

di·la·tor [daiˈleitə] *n.* ①使膨胀[扩张]的人. ②【医】扩张器. ③【解】扩张肌,开大肌.

dil·a·to·ry [ˈdilətəri] *a.* 缓慢的,拖拉的. *a* ~ *measure* 拖延办法. **-to·ri·ly** *ad.* 迟迟,拖拖拉拉地. **-to·ri·ness** *n.*

di·lem·ma [diˈlemə, dai-] *n.*【逻】(使对手在两个或多个对他不利的事物中进行选择的)双关论法, 双刀论法; 二难推论. ②窘境,困境,进退两难. ***be in a*** ~ = ***be on the horns of a*** ~ 进退维谷,左右为难.

dil·em·mat·ic [ˌdiləˈmætik] *a.* ①双关论法的. ②左右为难的.

dil·et·tan·te [ˌdiliˈtænti] *n.* (*pl.* ~*s*, **-ti** [-tiː]) ①文学、艺术的爱好者. ②(艺术或科学的)业余爱好者,浅薄的涉猎者. — *a.* 爱好文艺的; 业余的. **-tan·tish** [-ˈtæntiʃ] *a.* 业余(性质)的.

dil·et·tant·ism [diliˈtæntizəm] *n.* 业余艺术; 业余嗜好; 业余知识.

dil·i·gence[1] [ˈdilidʒəns] *n.* 勤勉,努力. *study with* ~ 勤奋学习.

dil·i·gence[2] [ˈdilidʒəns; F. diliʒɑ̃ːns] *n.* 四轮公共马车,驿站马车.

dil·i·gent [ˈdilidʒənt] *a.* 勤勤恳恳的 (*in*); 刻苦的, 勤奋的. *He is* ~ *in his studies* 他学习勤奋. **-ly** *ad.*

Dill [dil] *n.* 迪尔〔姓氏〕.

dill[1] [dil] *n.* ①【植】莳萝. ②莳萝子, 莳罗叶〔可作香辣佐料〕. ③莳萝泡菜 (= ~ pickle).

dill[2] [dil] *vt.* 〔英方〕安慰,使镇静.

Dil·lon [ˈdilən] *n.* 狄龙〔姓氏〕.

Dil·ly, Dil·i [ˈdili] *n.* 帝力〔东帝汶首都〕.

dil·ly [ˈdili] *n.* 突出人物,优秀人物; 突出事物. *a* ~ *of a movie* 优秀的电影.

dil·ly·dal·ly [ˈdilidæli] *vi.* 吊儿郎当,闲混,闲逛.

dil·u·ent [ˈdiljuənt] *a.* 稀释用的. — *n.*【医】稀释剂.

di·lute [daiˈljuːt, diˈl-] *vt., vi.* ①冲淡,搀淡,稀释. ②(掺杂) 使变薄弱. ~ *wine with water* 用水把酒冲淡. *The quality of the novel is* ~*d by the bad writing.* 因写得不好而使小说质量有所减色. — *a.* 稀释的; 淡的. ~ *nitric acid* 稀硝酸.

di·lu·tion [daiˈljuːʃən, diˈl-] *n.* ①冲淡; 稀释. ②稀度,淡度. ③稀释物. ④削弱, 削减. ⑤(把技术性操作分成若干加工过程而用生手替换熟手的) 劳动力的削减 (= ~ of labour).

di·lu·vi·al [daiˈljuːvjəl], **delu·vi·an** [-vjən] *a.* ①(Noah 的)大洪水的. ②【地】洪积(层)的. ~ **deposits [formations]** 洪积层. ~ **epoch**【地】洪积世.

di·lu·vi·um [daiˈljuːvjəm, diˈl-] *n.* ①冰河冲积物. ②【地】洪积层.

Dilys [ˈdilis] *n.* 迪莉斯〔女子名〕.

dim [dim] *a.* ①微暗的, 朦胧的; 暗淡的, 混沌的. ②模糊不清的. ③无光泽的,消光的. ④迟钝的. *a* ~ *light* 微亮. *a* ~ *memory* 模糊的记忆. ~ *prospects* 暗淡的前景. *take a* ~ *view of* 抱悲观[怀疑]的看法. ***be*** ~ ***and remote*** 渺茫. — *vt., vi.* (使)暗淡, (使)朦胧, (使)模糊; (使)变朦胧. *Her eyes became* ~*ed with tears.* 她泪眼朦胧. ~ *out* 〔美〕熄灯,实行灯火管制. — *n.* ①〔古、诗〕暗淡. ②(汽车的)弱光前灯. ~**out** 灯火管制. ~**wit** 〔美俚〕笨蛋,傻子. ~**-witted** *a.* 〔美俚〕愚蠢的.

dim. = dimension; diminuendo; diminutive.

dime [daim] *n.* ①(美、加拿大)一角银币. ②少数的钱. *a* ~ *a dozen* 便宜的, 按堆卖的; 容易获得的. ***do not care a*** ~ 毫不在乎. ***on a*** ~ ①在极小的地方 (*This car can turn on a* ~. 这车能在极小的地方转弯). ②立刻(*stopped on a* ~ 立刻停止). ~ **museum** 简陋的博物馆,收费极少的展览. ~ **novel** 廉价小说〔多为黄色小说〕. ~ **store** 一角商店〔出售五分、一角等廉价商品的商店〕.

di·men·hy·dri·nate [ˌdaimenˈhaidrəˌneit] *n.*【药】乘晕宁,海晕宁; 氯茶硷苯海拉明.

di·men·sion [diˈmenʃən] *n.* ①尺寸. ②【数】次元, 度(数),维(数). ③【物】因次,量纲. ④〔*pl.*〕容积; 面积;

大小,规模,范围. ⑤〔*pl.*〕〔口〕女性的胸腰臀尺寸. *of great [vast] ~s* 非常大的; 极重大的. *of one ~* 线(长度)的. *of three ~s* 立体的. *of two ~s* 平面的. *scheme [calamity] of vast ~s* 宏大的计划〔范围广阔的灾害〕. *The girl's ~s were 38-24-36.* 女孩的标准胸腰臀尺寸是38-24-36英寸. — *a.* (石料、木材)切成特定尺寸的. *~ lumber [stone]* 切成特定尺寸的木材[石料]. — *vt.* ①使形成所需的尺寸. ②在…上标出尺寸.

di·men·sion·al [diˈmenʃənəl] *a.* ①尺寸的. ②空间的. ③【数】因次的; …次(元)的. *a two ~ object* 平面. *a three-~ picture* 立体影片. *two [three] ~* 二[三]度空间的. *~* **sound** 立体音响.

di·mer [ˈdaimə] *n.*【化】二聚物. **-mer·ic** [-ˈmerik] *a.*

dim·er·ous [ˈdimərəs] *a.* ①分成两部分的. ②(花的轮生体)有二基数的. ③(昆虫)有二跗节的.

dim·e·ter [ˈdimitə] *n.* 二韵脚诗句〔如: He is gone on the mountain, / He is lost to the forest〕.

di·mid·i·ate [diˈmidiit] *a.* ①两分的,对开的, 折半的. ②【生】只一半发达的. — *vt.* 〔古〕将…对分, 将…折半.

di·min·ish [diˈminiʃ] *vt.* 减少, 减低 (*opp.* increase); 【建】使成尖顶;【乐】减半音. — *vi.* 减少, 缩小;【建】成尖顶. *~ed arch* 平圆拱〔指高度不及宽度的一半的圆拱〕. *~ed fifth*【乐】减五度. *hide one's ~ed head* 失势退隐. *~ing* **returns** 报酬递减〔指资本和劳动力增加到一定程度后, 生产率不能与资本和劳动力成比例地增加上去〕. **-ing** *a.* 渐减的,递减的.

di·min·u·en·do [diˌminjuˈendəu] *ad.* 〔It.〕【乐】渐弱 (= decrescendo).

dim·i·nu·tion [ˌdimiˈnjuːʃən] *n.* ①减少, 减缩, 缩小. ②【建】(柱子等的)逐渐变尖.

di·min·u·tive [diˈminjutiv] *a.* ①小的,小型的. ②【语法】指小的 (*opp.* augmentative). *a ~ suffix* 指小后缀〔如: cigar*ette*〕. — *n.* ①极小的人[物]. ②【语法】指小词缀〔如: bird*ie* stream*let*〕. ③爱称, 昵称〔如: Jack*ie*〕. ④小的人[东西].

dim·is·so·ry [ˈdimisəri, daiˈmisəri] *a.* ①免职的; 允许离开的. ②【宗】准许迁往[调往]其他教区的.

dim·i·ty [ˈdimiti] *n.* 凸纹条格细棉布.

dim·ly [ˈdimli] *ad.* 暗淡,朦胧,模糊.

dim·mer [ˈdimə] *n.* ①使变暗淡的人[物]. ②(舞台电灯的)减光器,调光器. ③〔*pl.*〕减光车头灯; (汽车上的)停车信号灯.

dim·mish [ˈdimiʃ] *a.* 暗淡的,朦胧的.

dim·ness [ˈdimnis] *n.* ①暗淡, 朦胧, 模糊. ②蒙昧, 愚钝. *the ~ of the room [one's memory]* 屋子阴暗 [记忆淡薄].

di·mor·phic, di·mor·phous [daiˈmɔːfik, -fəs] *a.* ①【生】二态的,二形的. ②【矿】双晶的. *a ~ flower* 二形花. **-phism** [-ˈmɔːfizəm] *n.* ①【生】二态性, 二态现象. ②【矿】双晶现象.

dim·ple [ˈdimpl] *n.* ①靥, 酒窝; 凹. ②波纹,涟漪. — *vi., vt.* ①(使)现酒窝, (使)生酒窝. ②(使)起波纹. **-pled** *a.* ①有酒窝的. ②起波纹的.

dim·ply [ˈdimpli] *a.* ①有酒窝的. ②起波纹的.

DIN [din] = 〔G.〕 *Deutsche Industrie Normen* (= German Industry Standard) 德国工业标准.

din [din] *n.* 噪音,喧嚣,鼓噪. — *vi.* ***(dinned, din·ning)*** 喧嚣,聒耳,嘈杂. *The noise ~ned in his ears.* 他听到聒耳声. *A hundred horn ~ned in protest as traffic ground to a stop.* 在车辆的流动受阻时,成百的喇叭齐鸣以示抗议. — *vt.* 以喧声聒人; 喋喋不休地说. ***~ something into sb.'s ears [head]*** 喋喋不休地说给某人听.

Di·na(h) [ˈdainə] *n.* 黛娜〔女子名〕.

di·nar [diˈnɑː] *n.* ①第纳尔〔阿尔及利亚、伊拉克和南斯拉夫的货币单位〕.

din·dle [ˈdindl, ˈdinl] *vi.* 〔苏格兰、英方〕(由于巨响、惊吓等而)发颤,发抖. — *n.* 〔苏格兰、英方〕抖动, 震颤.

dine [dain] *vt.* ①供吃; 招待膳食; 宴请. ②可容…人用餐. *~ a famous scholar* 宴请一位出名的学者. *This table ~s twelve.* 这张餐桌能坐12人. *I request her to ~ with me this night.* 今晚我请她吃饭. ***~ and wine*** *(a person)* 宴请(某人). ***~ forth*** 出外吃晚饭. —*vi.* 吃饭, 进餐. ***~ on [off, upon]*** *(a chicken)* 吃(鸡). ***~ out [in]*** 在外[在家]吃饭. ***~ with Duke Humphrey*** 饿着.

din·er [ˈdainə] *n.* ①吃饭的(客)人. ②〔美〕餐车. ③餐车式的饭馆. **~-out** 常被宴请的人[应酬多的人].

di·ner·ic [daiˈnerik] *a.*【物】(在同一容器中二液体间的)临界面的.

di·ner·o [diˈnɛərəu] *n.* 〔美口〕钱.

di·nette [daiˈnet] *n.* ①(厨房旁边的)小吃饭间. ②小吃饭间里的桌椅.

ding[1] [diŋ] *vi.* ①(钟等)叮当地响. ②啰嗦, 唠叨. ③〔美俚〕打; 扔; 占上风; 咒骂; 冲撞. — *vt.* 唠叨地讲. *~ into sb.'s ears* 唠唠叨叨地讲.

ding[2] [diŋ] *vi.* (**dang** [dæŋ]) 〔Scot.〕 (雨)猛下.

ding-a-ling [ˈdiŋəˈliŋ] *n.* 〔俚〕笨蛋; 怪人.

ding·bat [ˈdiŋbæt] *n.* ①东西, 玩意儿 (= dingus). ②〔美口〕(石子、木棍等)投掷物. ③【印】(用于段落开始处的)装饰标志.

ding·dong [ˈdiŋˈdɔŋ] *n.* 丁当,丁冬.— *a.* 丁当作响的; (比赛等)激烈的. *a ~ race [fight]* (各方相继领先的)势均力敌的赛跑 [激烈的战斗]. — *ad.* 丁当作响地, 使劲儿, 拼命. *go [be] at it ~ = hammer away at it ~* 〔俚〕拼命工作. *fall to work ~* 拼命[认真]工作起来. — *vi.* 丁当作响. — *vt.* 一再重复(以加深印象).

dinge [dindʒ] *n.* 〔美俚〕黑人.

din·ger [diŋə] *n.* 〔美俚〕①非常奇特的事物. ②铁路车站站长.

din·gey, din·ghy [ˈdiŋgi] *n.* (印度的)小船; 舰载小艇; (附属大船的)供应小船; 无甲板单桅比赛用小船; 救生橡皮筏.

din·gi·ly [ˈdindʒili] *ad.* 暗淡地; 肮脏地; 褴褛地.

din·gi·ness [ˈdiŋdʒinis] *n.* 暗淡; 肮脏; 褴褛.

din·gle [ˈdiŋgl] *n.* 〔诗〕有树木的幽谷.

din·go [ˈdiŋgəu] *n.* (澳洲)野狗.

ding·us [ˈdiŋgəs] *n.* 〔美俚〕东西, 玩意儿.

din·gy[1] [ˈdindʒi] *a.* ①暗黑的. ②肮脏的. ③褴褛的.

din·gy[2] [ˈdiŋdʒi] *n.* = dingey.

dining [ˈdainiŋ] *n.* 吃饭, 进餐. *~* **alcove** 小餐厅. *~* **car** 餐车. *~* **hall** 大餐厅. *~* **room** 饭厅. *~* **table** 餐桌.

dinitro- *comb. f.*【化】二硝基: *dinitro*benzene.

di·ni·tro·ben·zene [daiˌnaitrəuˈbenziːn] *n.* 二硝基苯〔用于染料,有机合成物〕.

dink [diŋk] *a.* 〔Scot.〕 (衣着) 整洁的. — *vt.* ①打扮, 装饰. ②(网球)打靠近网边的吊球. — *n.* 〔美〕(猎野鸭的)小船.

Din·ka [ˈdiŋkɑː] *n.* ①丁卡人〔居住在苏丹南部的苏丹黑种部族人〕. ②丁卡语.

dinkey [ˈdiŋki] *n.* 〔美〕①(铁道停车场作运输、调车等用的)小型机车. ②小型电车.

dink·um [ˈdiŋkəm] *n.* 〔澳俚〕工作, 劳动. — *a.* 纯粹的, 真正的, 可靠的, 公正的. *~* **oil** 〔澳俚〕真情实况, 真相.

dink·y [ˈdiŋki] *a.* ①〔英口〕整洁的; 可爱的; 漂亮的. ②〔口〕小的; 微不足道的. — *n.* = dinkey.

din·ner [ˈdinə] *n.* 正餐, (现通例指)晚餐; 午[晚]宴, 宴会. ★英美中级以下人家通例叫午餐为 dinner, 中级以上人家则叫晚餐为 dinner. *ask sb. to ~* 请某人吃饭. *give a ~* 举办午[晚]宴. *at ~* 吃着饭. *early ~* 中饭. *late ~* 晚饭. ***after ~, mustard*** 饭后上芥末; 雨后送伞. ***give a ~ for [in honour of]*** *(sb.)*

宴请(某人),特为(某人)请客. ***make a good [poor]*** ~ 吃盛餐[便饭]. ***sit down to*** ~ 入席. ~ **bell** 开饭铃[钟]. ~ **bucket** =~ pail. ~ **cloth** 正餐桌巾. ~ **clothes** 餐服. ~ **coat [jacket]** 〔英〕男子无尾晚礼服〔美国叫 tuxedo〕. ~ **dress** 一种半正式的妇女餐服〔通常有袖或短外衣〕. ~ **fork** (通常有四个叉齿的)大桌叉. ~ **hour** 正餐时间. ~ **knife** 餐刀. ~ **party** 宴会. ~ **pail** 饭盒. ~ **ring** 正式场合带的大戒指. ~ **service [set]** 成套餐具. ~ **table** 餐桌. ~ **wagon** 脚轮送菜车.

dino- *comb. f.* 恐怖: *dino*saur.

di·noc·er·as [daiˈnɔsərəs] *n.*【古生】恐角兽.

di·no·flag·el·late [ˌdainəˈflædʒilit, -ˌleit] *n.* 腰皮鞭毛目动物.

di·nor·nis [daiˈnɔːnis] *n.*【古生】恐鸟.

di·no·saur [ˈdainəsɔː] *n.*【古生】恐龙. **-saur·i·an** [ˈdainəsɔːriən] *n., a.* 恐龙(的).

di·no·there [ˈdainəθiə] *n.*【古生】恐兽.

dint [dint] *n.* ①打痕,凹痕. ②打击. ③暴力; 力量. ***by ~ of*** 凭…的力量,靠,凭借. — *vt.* 打凹,压凹.

di·oc·e·san [daiˈɔsisən] *a.* 主教管区的. — *n.* 主教.

di·o·cese [ˈdaiəsis] *n.* 主教管区.

di·ode [ˈdaiəud] *n.*【无】二极管.

di·o·done [ˈdaiədəun] *n.*【药】碘造影剂.

di·oe·cian, di·oe·cious [daiˈiːʃən, daiˈiːʃəs] *a.*【生】雌雄异株[体]的.

di·oe·cism [daiˈiːsizəm] *n.*【生】雌雄异株[体].

di·oes·trum, di·es·trum [daiˈestrəm, -ˈiːs-] *n.*【生】间(动)情期.

Di·og·e·nes [daiˈɔdʒiniːz] *n.* 提奥奇尼斯〔住在桶中白昼点灯寻找正人君子的古希腊哲学家, 纪元前 412—323〕.

Di·o·nys·i·a [ˌdaiəˈniziə] *n.* 〔*pl.*〕酒神节. **-c** [daiəˈniziæk], **-n** [-iən] *a.* 酒神狄俄尼索斯的; 酒神节的; 狂欢的.

Di·o·ny·sus, Di·o·ny·sos [ˌdaiəˈnaisəs] *n.*【希神】狄俄尼索斯〔酒神〕.

di·op·side [daiˈɔpsaid] *n.*【矿】透辉石.

di·op·tase [daiˈɔpteis] *n.*【矿】透视石,绿铜矿,翠铜矿.

di·op·ter, di·op·tre [daiˈɔptə] *n.* (透镜的)屈光度.

di·op·tom·e·ter [ˌdaiɔpˈtɔmitə] *n.* 屈光计. **-try** *n.* 屈光测量.

di·op·tric [daiˈɔptrik] *a.* 屈光的, 折光的. ~ *glass [lens]* 屈光镜[透镜]. ~ *strength* 焦度. ~ *system* 屈光组.

di·op·trics [daiˈɔptriks] *n.* 屈光学.

di·o·ra·ma [ˌdaiəˈrɑːmə] *n.* ①(从小孔窥视的)透明幕上的画面, 西洋景, 洋片. ②有人物塑象的缩型立体布景. ③模拟动物野生状况的博物馆展览. **dio·ram·ic** [ˌdaiəˈræmik] *a.*

di·o·rite [ˈdaiərait] *n.*【矿】闪长岩.

di·ox·ane [daiˈɔksein] *n.*【化】二氧杂环已烷, 二噁烷〔用做油脂溶剂〕.

di·ox·ide [daiˈɔksaid] *n.*【化】二氧化物.

dip [dip] *vt.* ***(dipped,*** 〔古〕 ***dipt; dip·ping)*** ①浸,泡,蘸; (微微)弄湿, 濡湿; 浸染. ②把(旗等)稍稍放下又急速升起〔做信号或敬礼〕. ③汲出, 汲取, 舀 ***(out; up)***. ④(把烛芯反复置于融蜡中以)浸制(蜡烛). ⑤为…施浸礼. ⑥(把猪羊等放在杀虫液里)浸洗. ⑦〔口〕使欠债〔常用被动语态〕. ~ *out soup with a ladle* 用勺子舀[打]汤. ~ *a curtsy* 屈膝行礼. *I am slightly dipped.* 我有一点儿债. — *vi.* ①浸; (微微)一浸. ②【空】(升前)急降. ③沉, 沉落; (地层)沉陷. ④(路)向下倾斜. ⑤(手)伸入(袋内), 掏取, 汲取. ⑥浏览; 稍加探究. ⑦〔俚〕扒窃. *The sun dipped below the horizon.* 太阳落到地平线下了. ~ ***into*** ①舀出; 取出, 掏出 (~ *into one's purse* 挥霍, 乱花). ②看一看, 查一查. ③探究, 细想 (~ *deep into the future* 细想将来). ④潜入. ~ ***one's finger in*** 染指. — *n.* ①泡, 浸渍, 沾湿; 洗浴. ②(汤等的)一勺; 浸液, 洗羊的消毒水; (布丁的)浇汁. ③(地、路等的)倾斜, 凹下, 窪, 坑. ④【空】(升前的)急降. ⑤(磁针的)倾角, 俯角. ⑥(电线等下垂的)弛度. ⑦(双杠上的)双臂屈伸, 拔双扛. ⑧蜡烛. ⑨〔美俚〕扒手. *a ~ in price* 跌价. ~ *of the needles* 磁针的俯角. ***at the*** ~【海】(旗)微降〔表示敬意〕. ***have a ~ in the sea.*** 洗海水澡. ~ **circle** 磁倾仪. ~**-dye** *vt.* 浸染(针织物). ~ **grain** (木材的)曲走纹理. ~ **needle** = dipping needle. ~ **net** 长柄的捞鱼网. **dipping needle**【物】磁倾针.

di·par·tite [daiˈpɑːtait] *a.* 分成几部分的.

di·pet·al·ous [daiˈpetələs] *a.*【植】有两瓣的.

di·phase, di·pha·sic [ˈdaiˌfeiz, -ˈfeizik] *a.* 二相的.

di·phas·er [daiˈfeizə] *n.* 二相发电机.

di·phen·yl [daiˈfenl, -ˈfiːn-] *n.*【化】①联(二)苯. ②二苯基.

di·phen·yl·a·mine [daiˌfeniləˈmiːn] *n.* 二苯胺〔用以制造炸药稳定剂和染料〕.

di·phos·gene [daiˈfɔsdʒiːn, -ˈfɔz-] *n.* 双光气〔在化学战中用作毒气〕.

diph·the·ri·a [difˈθiəriə, dip-] *n.*【医】白喉. **-ri·al** [-riəl], **-ric** [difˈθerik], **-rit·ic** [ˌdifθiˈritik, dip-] *a.* (患)白喉的.

diph·the·roid [ˈdifθərɔid] *a.* 白喉状的, 白喉样的. — *n.* 假白喉.

diph·thong [ˈdifθɔŋ, ˈdip-] *n.* ①复合元音〔oil 之 ɔi 等〕. ②〔口〕复合元音词〔oil 之 oi 等〕; 元音连字〔æ, œ 等〕. ③复合辅音〔ch ([t] + [ʃ]), j([d] + [ʒ]) 等〕. **-al** *a.*

diph·thong·ize [ˈdifθɔŋgaiz] *vt.* 使复合元音化; 使照复合元音一样发音. — *vi.* 变成复合元音.

diph·y·cer·cal [ˈdifiˌsəːkl] *a.* (鱼)双尾的, 圆尾的.

di·phy·let·ic [ˌdaifaiˈletik] *a.* 二源的〔在血统的继承上有两个来源的〕.

di·phyl·lous [daiˈfiləs] *a.* 有两叶的.

di·phy·o·dont [daiˈfaiəˌdɔnt, diˈfiə-] *a.* 有两期牙齿的. — *n.* 有乳齿和永久齿两期牙齿的哺乳类动物.

dipl. = diplomat; diplomatic.

dipl(o)- *comb. f.* 双, 复, 重: *diplo*coccus.

di·ple·gi·a [daiˈpliːdʒiə] *n.* 两侧瘫痪, 两侧麻痹, 双瘫.

di·plex [ˈdaipleks] *a.*【电】同向双工的, 收发信号同时同向传送的. ~ *telegraph* 单向双路电报.

dip·lo·blas·tic [ˌdipləˈblæstik] *a.*【动】双胚层的.

dip·lo·coc·cus [dipləuˈkɔkəs] *n.* ***(pl. -coc·ci*** [-ˈkɔksai]***)*** 双球菌.

di·plod·o·cus [diˈplɔdəkəs] *n.* 梁龙〔古生物恐龙的一种〕.

dip·lo·ë [ˈdipləˌiː] *n.* (头颅骨里的)板障(骨). **di·plo·ic** [diˈpləuik] *a.*

dip·loid [ˈdiplɔid] *a.* ①二重的; 两数的, 二倍的. ②二倍体的. — *n.* ①【生】二倍体, 二倍染色体. ②(结晶)偏方 24 面体.

di·plo·ma [diˈpləumə] *n.* ***(pl. ~s,*** 〔罕〕 ***-ma·ta*** [-mətə]***)*** ①特许证, 执照. ②毕业文凭, 学位证书. ③奖状. ④公文; 〔*pl.*〕古文书. — *vt.* 发给执照[学位证书等]. ~ **mill** 〔美俚〕滥发文凭的大学. ~ **piece** 为文凭[证书]而写的论文.

di·plo·ma·cy [diˈpləuməsi] *n.* ①外交; 外交手腕. ②交际手段; 权谋. ③外交使团. *shuttle* ~ 穿梭外交. *use* ~ 应用外交手腕.

dip·lo·mat [ˈdipləmæt] *n.* ①外交官; 外交家. ②善于交际的人.

dip·lo·mate [ˈdipləmeit] *n.* 领有文凭的专科医生, 学位证书持有者.

dip·lo·mat·ese [ˌdipləməˈtiːz] *n.* 外交语言.

dip·lo·mat·ic [ˌdipləˈmætik] *a.* ①外交(上)的; 有外交

手腕的；外交使团的．②古抄本的；不改真本原样的．*the* ~ *body [corps]* 外交使团．*a* ~ *copy* 一字未改的抄稿［誊本］．~ *agent* 外交工作人员．~ *evidence* 文献上的证据．*resume [sever]* ~ *relations* 恢复［断绝］外交关系．~ **immunity** 外交豁免权．~ **pouch** 外交文件袋．~ **service** 外交官勤务．

dip·lo·mat·i·cal·ly [ˌdipləˈmætikəli] *ad.* 外交上；用外交手腕．

dip·lo·mat·ics [ˌdipləˈmætiks] *n.* ①古文书学．②外交手腕 (= diplomacy).

dip·lo·ma·tism [dipˈləuməˌtizəm] *n.* ①外交，外交活动．②外交手腕．

dip·lo·ma·tist [diˈpləumətist] *n.* 〔主英〕= diplomat.

dip·lo·ma·tize, di·plo·ma·tise [diˈpləumətaiz] *vi.* 运用外交方法，施展外交手腕；折冲樽俎．— *vt.* ①用外交方法处理．②〔古〕给…颁发证书．

dip·lon [ˈdiplɔn] *n.* 【化】氘核．

dip·lont [ˈdiplɔnt] *n.* 【动、植】二倍体．

di·plo·pi·a, dip·lo·py [diˈpləupiə, ˈdipləpi] *n.* (病)复视 (*opp.* haplopia).

dip·lo·pod [ˈdipləˌpɔd] *n.* 千足虫 (= millipede).

di·plo·sis [diˈpləusis] *n.* (染色体的)倍加作用．

dip·no·an [ˈdipnəuən] *a., n.* 肺鱼类的；肺鱼．

Dip·noi [ˈdipnɔi] *n.* 【动】肺鱼亚纲．

dip·o·dy [ˈdipədi] *n.* *(pl. -dies)* 【韵】二重韵脚．**di·pod·ic** [daiˈpɔdik] *a.*

di·po·lar [daiˈpəulə] *a.* 双极的(磁石)．

di·pole [ˈdaipəul] *n.* 【物、化】①偶极．②偶极天线．

dip·per [ˈdipə] *n.* ①(有柄的)勺．②【摄】显影液槽．③浸渍工人，浸制工人〔如浸制蜡烛、火柴头等〕．④【鸟】川乌类的鸟，善于潜水的鸟．⑤浸礼会会友．⑥〔D-〕北斗七星．⑦读书很快的人．⑧〔俚〕扒手．*the Big [Great] D-* 北斗七星．*the Little D-* 小北斗〔小熊星座的七颗主星〕．

dip·py [ˈdipi] *a.* *(-i·er; -i·est)* 〔俚〕①疯狂的．②愚蠢的，古怪的．*be* ~ *about peanuts* 嗜爱花生．*be* ~ *with love for her* 对她大为倾倒．

di·pre·pel·lant [ˌdaiprəˈpelənt] *n.* (火箭的)二元推进剂 (= bipropellant).

dip·se·ma·ni·a [ˌdipsəuˈmeiniə] *n.* 嗜酒狂，酒癖；【医】间发性酒狂．**-ni·ac** [-niæk] ① *a.* 有间发性酒狂的．② *n.* 嗜酒狂人．

dip·stick [ˈdipˌstik] *n.* ①(测量容器内液体深度的)量杆，量尺．②鼻烟棍 (= snuff stick).

dipt [dipt] 〔古〕dip 的过去式及过去分词．

Dip·ter·a [ˈdiptərə] *n.* 〔*pl.*〕【虫】双翅目〔包括苍蝇、蚊子等〕．

dip·ter·al [ˈdiptərəl] *a.* ①【虫】双翅类的．②【植】(种子)有双翅的．③【建】四周有两排柱子的．

dip·ter·an [ˈdiptərən] *a.* 【虫、植】= dipteral. — *n.* 双翅目的虫子〔包括苍蝇，蚊子〕．

dip·ter·os [ˈdiptərɔs] *n.* 四周有两排柱子的建筑物．

dip·ter·ous [ˈdiptərəs] *a.* 【虫、植】= dipteral.

dip·tych [ˈdiptik] *n.* ①〔古罗马〕可折合的双连记事板．②(祭坛后的)可折合的双连画［雕刻］．③由两个平行的或相对的部分组成的东西．

dir. = director.

Di·rac [diˈræk] *n.* 迪拉克〔姓氏〕．

dir·dum [ˈdiədəm, ˈdəːdəm] *n.* 〔苏格兰、英方〕①吵闹，喧嚣．②斥责．③噩运．

dire [ˈdaiə] *a.* ①可怕的；悲惨的；不吉利的．②迫切的，极端的．*a* ~ *need* 迫切的需要．**the** ~ **sisters** 专管复仇的女神 (= the Furies).

direc.prop. = 〔L.〕*directione propria* 【处方】依照适当指导．

di·rect [diˈrekt, dai-] *a.* ①笔直的，一直线的；正面的．②直接的．③直截了当的，直率的，明白的．④直系的，正统的．⑤【语法】直接法的．⑥【天】由西向东运行的．⑦(不用媒染剂)直接染色的．*a* ~ *road* 直路．~ *rays* 直射光．~ *vision* 直视．~ *pressure* 正面追击；【物】定向压力．~ *proportion* 正比例．~ *tax* 直接税．~ *action* 直接作用；直接行动〔如罢工、商品抵制等行动〕．~ *relatives* 直系亲属．*a* ~ *address* 称呼．~ *motion* 顺行．— *ad.* 笔直，一直，直接．— *vt.* ①(把…)针对(某人)，把…指向某人 *(at; to; towards)*；暗指着说．②指挥，指导；【美剧、影】导演；命令；管理，掌管；支配．③指点某人，为某人，指示方向．④寄(信等)给，写寄发地址．*I* ~*ed my remarks to you.* 我的话是暗指你说的．~ *a business [campaign]* 指挥业务［战斗］．*a film* ~*ed by* … 某人导演的影片．*Will you* ~ *me to the station?* 请问车站往哪里走？*D- the letter to my business address.* 请把这封信寄交我的办公地址．— *vi.* 指挥，指导；管理．**as** ~**ed** 照说明，按处方．~ **current**【电】直流电〔略作 D.C. 或 d.c.〕．~ **current dynamo [generator]** 直流发电机．~ **current motor** 直流电动机．~ **dye** 直接染料 ~ **mail** (向广大群众投寄的)直接邮件．~ **method**【语】直接教学法．~ **primary (election)** 由选民直接投票的预选．~ **proportion**【数】正比例．~ **speech**【语法】直接引语．

di·rect·ed [diˈrektid, ˈdai-] *a.* ①有指导的；定向的．②【数】标出(数、角、线段的)正负的．~ **number**【数】(有加减号的)有向数．~ **variants** 定向变异．

di·rec·tion [diˈrekʃən, daiˈ-] *n.* ①方位，方向；范围，方面．②〔*pl.*〕指挥，指导；管理．③〔常 *pl.*〕指示，命令，吩咐；用法说明．④导演；(乐队)指挥．⑤寄发地址．⑥趋向，倾向．*Full* ~*s inside.* 内有详细说明．~ *finder [detector]* 【无】测向仪．~ *finding* 定向．~ *finding station* 无线电测向站．~ *for use* 用法说明．***in all*** ~***s*** 四方八面，各方面．*(reforms)* ***in many*** ~***s*** 各方面的(改革)．***in the*** ~ ***of*** 向…方面．***take a new*** ~ 有新倾向．***under the*** ~ ***of*** 在…指导下．~ **angle**【数】方向角．

di·rec·tion·al [diˈrekʃənəl,dai-] *a.* ①方向的．②【无】指向的，定向的．~ **antenna** 定向天线．~ **derivative**【数】方向导数．~ **gyro**【空】陀螺方向仪．~ **radio** 无线电定向．

di·rec·tive [diˈrektiv, dai-] *n.* 〔美〕命令，训令，指令；方针．— *a.* ①指导的，指挥的；管理的．②【无】指向［定向］式的．*a* ~ *antenna* 定向天线．*rules* ~ *of our actions* 支配我们行动的法则．

di·rect·ly [diˈrektli, dai-] *ad.* ①径直地；直接地．②直截了当地，直率地．③正好地，恰好地．④不久；〔英〕立刻，立即．— *conj.* [常 ˈdrekli]〔口〕一…(就)．***I will come*** ~ ***I have finished.*** 我一完就来．

di·rect·ness [diˈrektnis, dai-] *n.* 直接；率直，坦白．*the* ~ *of manner [speech]* 态度［谈吐］坦率．

Di·rec·toire [diˈrektwɑː]〔F.〕*n.* (1795—1799年法国革命政府的)五人执政内阁．— *a.* 法国五人执政内阁时期的〔尤指家具、衣服等的式样〕．

di·rec·tor [diˈrektə, dai-] *n.* ①指导员，指挥者；长官；理事，董事；校长，社长；(工厂的)厂长，(车间)主任．②【剧】导演；【乐】指挥．③(1795—1799 年法国革命政府的)执政官，行政委员．④【医】有沟探针．⑤【机】司动部分．⑥【军】炮兵射击指挥仪．⑦【无】引向器；导向器．*a board of* ~*s* 理事会，董事会．*an assistant* ~【影】助理导演．~ **circle** 准圆．~ **firing**【军】指挥仪射击．**D- General** 总裁，总监．~**'s chair** 导演椅〔一种可折叠的轻便椅〕．

di·rec·to·rate [diˈrektərit, dai-] *n.* ①指导者(董事、导演等)的职位．②理事会，董事会．

di·rec·to·ri·al [diˌrekˈtɔːriəl] *a.* ①指挥［指导］的，管理的．②指挥者的，管理者的．③〔D-〕(1795—1799 年法国革命政府的)执政内阁的．

di•rec•tor•ship [diˈrektəʃip] *n.* 董事[理事、主任、社长等]的职务[任期].

di•rec•to•ry [diˈrektəri] *n.* ①姓名地址录,工商人名录. ②(教堂的)礼拜规则书;(记载规则、指令等的)指南. ③理事会,董事会;〔集合词〕一群董事[理事]. ④〔D-〕= Directoire. *a telephone* ~ 电话号码簿. — *a.* 指导的,指挥的,管理的.

di•rec•tress [diˈrektris, dai-] *n.* ①女指导者;女董事. ②女导演;女指挥.

di•rec•trix [diˈrektriks, dai-] *n.* (*pl.* ~*es* [-iz], *-trices* [-trisiːz]) ①〔古〕= directress. ②【数】准线.

dire•ful [ˈdaiəful] *a.* 可怕的;悲惨的;预兆不祥的. **-ly** *ad.*

dirge [ˈdəːdʒ] *n.* ①挽歌,悼歌. ②凄凉的歌[诗、乐曲].

dir•ham [diəˈhæm] *n.* ①迪拉姆〔摩洛哥货币单位〕. ②里亚尔的 1/100〔卡塔尔的货币名〕.

dir•i•gi•ble [ˈdiridʒəbl] *a.*【空】可操纵的. *a* ~ *torpedo* 可操纵的鱼雷. — *n.* 飞船,飞艇(=~ balloon).

dir•i•ment [ˈdirimənt] *a.* 使无效的. ~ ***impediments***【法】(使结婚无效的)绝对障碍.

Dirk [dəːk] *n.* 德克〔男子名, Derek 的异体〕.

dirk [dəːk] *n.* 短剑,匕首. — *vt.* 用短剑刺.

Dirk•sen [ˈdəːksn] *n.* 德克森〔姓氏〕.

dirl [diəl, dəːl] *vt., vi.* 〔苏格兰、北英方〕发颤,发抖.

dirn•dl [ˈdəːndl] *n., a.* 紧身连衣裙.

dirt [dəːt] *n.* ①污物;烂泥;油垢;灰尘. ②泥土;土地;【矿】含金土. ③毫无价值的东西. ④肮脏,下贱,卑鄙. ⑤骂人话,恶言. ⑥下流话,下流作品. ⑦〔美俚〕闲谈,聊天;钱;糖;秘密情报;〔美乐俚〕= blues. *treat a person like* ~ 视某人如草芥. *common as* ~ 草芥一样到处皆是的,平凡的. *yellow* ~〔蔑〕黄金. ***(as) cheap as*** ~ 极其便宜的. ***cut*** ~〔美俚〕逃走. ***do sb.*** ~〔美〕用卑鄙手段[恶言恶语]陷害某人. ***eat*** ~ 忍辱. ***fling [throw]*** ~ ***at*** 臭骂. ***hit the*** ~ 落在地上. ***talk*** ~ 说下流话[猥亵话]. ~**-cheap** *a., ad.* 极便宜的[地]. ~ **bed**【地】泥土层. ~ **eating** 食土癖. ~ **farmer**〔美口〕自耕农 (*opp.* gentleman farmer). ~ **floor** (屋内未铺地板的)泥土地面. ~ **money**〔英俚〕装卸污臭货物时额外付给码头工人的补贴. ~ **pie** (小孩游戏做的)泥饼. ~**-poor** *a.* 很穷的. ~ **road**〔美〕(未铺路面的)砂土路. ~ **track** 砂土[煤渣]跑道. ~ **wagon**〔美〕垃圾车.

dirt•i•ly [ˈdəːtili] *ad.* 龌龊;卑鄙,下贱.

dirt•i•ness [ˈdəːtinis] *n.* 龌龊;卑鄙,下贱.

dirt•y [ˈdəːti] *a.* ①龌龊的,肮脏的,污秽的,不干净的;(原子核)污染的. ②(手段等)卑鄙的. ③下流的,猥亵的. ④(钱财等)不正当的. ⑤恶意的(话). ⑥(脸色)难看的. ⑦(天气)恶劣的. ⑧(颜色等)浑浊的. ⑨(喇叭)声调邪乎的. ⑩有毒瘾的,吸毒的 (*opp.* clean). *That's a* ~ *shame!* 真丢脸! *a* ~ *fighter* 无耻的拳斗选手. *a* ~ *crack* 〔美俚〕尖酸刻薄的话,挖苦话. *a* ~ *dig*〔美俚〕刻薄嘴,骂人话. *a* ~ *trumpet* 声调邪乎的喇叭. ***do one's*** ~ ***work for another*** 为某人效劳,做某人部下. ***do the*** ~ ***on*** … 对…干卑鄙的勾当. — *vt.* 弄脏;沾污. ~ *one's hands* 弄脏自己的手脚;有损于自己的人格. — *vi.* 变脏. ~ **linen** 家丑. ~ **money [gains]** 不义之财. ~ **pool**〔美俚〕不诚实的行为,不公正的竞技. ~ **work**〔美俚〕诈骗;不法行为. ~ **wound** 已化脓的伤口.

Dis [dis] *n.*【罗神】阎王;冥府,地狱.

dis. =〔美〕discharged; discipline; disconnect; discontinued; discount; distance; distribute.

dis-[1] *pref.* 〔动词前缀〕①表示"离开","分离": *dis*miss, *dis*perse. ②表示"剥夺","除去": *dis*frock, *dis*bar. ③表示"相反": *dis*able. ④表示"未能","停止","拒绝": *dis*satisfy, *dis*appear, *dis*allow. ⑤〔形容词前缀〕表示"不","非","相反": *dis*honest, *dis*satisfied, *dis*pleasing. ⑥〔名词前缀〕表示"相反","缺少": *dis*ease, *dis*union.

dis[2]**-** *pref.* = di-[2]: *dis*sylable.

dis•a•bil•i•ty [ˌdisəˈbiliti] *n.* ①无力,无能;残疾. ②【法】无能力,无资格.

dis•a•ble [disˈeibl] *vt.* ①使不中用,使无能 (*from doing; for*);使残废. ②【法】使无能力,使无资格. *Old age* ~*d him for hard labour.* 年迈使他不能胜任繁重工作了. *I was* ~*d from walking by a fall.* 我摔跤后连路也走不动了. *be* ~*d* 成残废;(军舰)失去战斗力. *a* ~*d soldier* 残废军人. *a* ~*d ship* 废船. **-ment** *n.* 无能;残废.

dis•a•buse [ˌdisəˈbjuːz] *vt.* 去除…的错误想法,使省悟,纠正. ~ *sb. of superstition* 破除某人迷信.

di•sac•cha•ride [daiˈsækəraid] *n.* 二糖类〔如蔗糖、麦芽糖、乳糖〕.

dis•ac•cord [ˌdisəˈkɔːd] *vi., n.* 不一致,不和谐,不和;不同意. *Your theory* ~*s with my experience.* 你的理论和我的经验不一致. ~*s among nations* 国家间的不和.

dis•ac•cred•it [ˌdisəˈkredit] *vt.* 对(某人)不再信任;撤销对(某人)的授权,撤销对…的委托. ~ *a diplomat* 对某外交官不再信任.

dis•ac•cus•tom [disəˈkʌstəm] *vt.* 使(对某事物)失去习惯,摆脱…的习惯. *In the country I was* ~*ed of rising late.* 我在农村去掉了晚起的习惯.

dis•ad•van•tage [ˌdisədˈvɑːntidʒ] *n.* ①不利,不便;不利的处境[地位]. ②(名誉、信用等的)损害,损失. ***be at a*** ~ 处不利地位,吃亏. ***sell goods to*** ~ 吃亏卖出货物. ***take sb. at a*** ~ 突然[乘隙]打击某人. ***to sb.'s*** ~ = ***to the*** ~ ***of*** …对(某人)不利地. — *vt.* 使不利,使吃亏. *I was* ~*d by illness.* 我因病而处于不利地位.

dis•ad•van•taged [ˌdisədˈvɑːntidʒd] *a.* 社会地位低下的;被剥夺了基本权利的;生活条件差的. ~ *children* 没有得到适当照顾的儿童.

dis•ad•van•ta•geous [ˌdisædvɑːnˈteidʒəs] *a.* 不利的,吃亏的,有害的,不便的. *What is* ~ *to John may be advantageous to Henry.* 对约翰不利的事情也许对亨利有利. **-ly** *ad.* **-ness** *n.*

dis•af•fect [ˌdisəˈfekt] *vt.* 使疏远;使不满;使不忠. *The dictator's policies had soon* ~*ed the people.* 独裁者的政策很快就使人民大为不满.

dis•af•fect•ed [ˌdisəˈfektid] *a.* (对政府等)生厌的;不满的,不平的;不义的,不忠的.

dis•af•fec•tion [ˌdisəˈfekʃən] *n.* (尤指政治上的)不满,不平;厌恶;不服. *D- often leads to outright treason.* 政治上的不满常常导致断然的背叛.

dis•af•fil•i•ate [disəˈfilieit] *vt.* 分离,拆散,使脱离关系. *He* ~*d himself from the church.* 他与教会脱离关系. — *vi.* 与…结束往来;与…脱离关系. **-a•tion** *n.*

dis•af•firm [ˌdisəˈfəːm] *vt.* ①反驳,反对,拒绝. ②【法】否认;取消,废弃(以前的判决). ~ *a judicial decision* 取消判决.

dis•af•firm•ance, dis•af•fir•ma•tion [disəˈfəːməns, disæfəːˈmeiʃən] *n.* 反驳;【法】否认;废弃.

dis•af•for•est [ˌdisæˈfɔrist, disəˈfɔrist] *vt.* ①【英法】把(森林地)开辟成不受森林法约束的普通地. ②伐除…上的森林. **-a•tion** [ˌdisæˌfɔrisˈteiʃən] *n.*

dis•a•gree [ˌdisəˈgriː] *vi.* ①不合,不对,不符合,不一致 (*with; in*). ②争持,不同意 (*with*). ③不适宜,有害 (*with*). *His conduct* ~*s with his words.* 他言行不一. *The food* ~*d with me.* 这食物对我不适合.

dis•a•gree•a•ble [ˌdisəˈgriəbl] *a.* ①不愉快的,讨厌的. ②难对付的,难打交道的. *a thoroughly* ~ *person* 十分讨厌的家伙. — *n.* 〔常 *pl.*〕讨厌的事,不愉快的事.

dis•a•gree•a•bly [ˌdisəˈgriəbli] *ad.* 讨厌,无聊.

dis•a•gree•ment [ˌdisəˈgriːmənt] *n.* ①不一致,不调和;差异. ②异议;不和,争论. ③不适合,有害. *a* ~ *between accounts* 帐目不一致.

dis·al·low [ˈdisəˈlau, dis-] *vt.* 不许,不准;不承认,驳回. ~ *the veracity of a report* 不承认报告的真实性. **-ance** *n.*

dis·an·nul [ˌdisəˈnʌl] *vt.* 取消,废弃. ~ *a contract* 废除契约.

dis·a·noint [ˌdisəˈnɔint] *vt.* 不再把…奉若神明. ~ *a king* 不把国王奉为神明.

dis·ap·pear [ˌdisəˈpiə] *vi.* ①消失, 消散. ②失踪,绝迹. ~ *from sight* 消失不见. ~**ing bed** 立体多用床. **-ance** *n.*

dis·ap·point [ˌdisəˈpɔint] *vt.* ①使失望,使沮丧. ②使(计划等)落空,打破…的念头,使受挫折. ③对…失信. *be greatly ~ed to hear that ...* 听见…而大失所望. ***be agreeably ~ed*** 庆幸未如所想. ***be ~ed in a person [thing]*** 对某人[某事]失望. ***be ~ed of one's purpose [hopes]*** 目的[希望]落了空.

dis·ap·point·ed [ˌdisəˈpɔintid] *a.* 失望了的,受了挫折的;失恋的. *a ~ hope* 落空的希望. **-ly** *ad.*

dis·ap·point·ing [ˌdisəˈpɔintiŋ] *a.* 使人失望的, 沮丧的,令人扫兴的,使人不痛快的. **-ly** *ad.*

dis·ap·point·ment *n.* ①失望,失意,沮丧; 挫折. ②使失望的人[事情]. ~ ***in love*** 失恋. ***to one's ~*** 失望的是.

dis·ap·pro·ba·tion [ˌdisæprəuˈbeiʃən] *n.* 不认可,不答应,不赞成;指责,非难.

dis·ap·pro·ba·tive [disˈæprəubeitiv], **dis·ap·pro·ba·to·ry** [-bətəri] *a.* 不赞成的,不答应的;对…表示不满的. *cast a ~ glance at the boy* 对小孩投以不赞成的眼光.

dis·ap·prov·al [ˈdisəˈpruːvəl] *n.* 不准, 不赞成;非难. *express ~ of the plan* 对计划表示不赞成. *shake one's head in ~* 摇头表示不赞成. *All watched him with ~.* 大家都用非难的目光看着他.

dis·ap·prove [ˌdisəˈpruːv, dis-] *vt.* 不答应,不准,不赞成;不满,指责. *The court ~d the verdict.* 法庭不赞成陪审团的裁决. — *vi.* 不赞成, 反对 *(of)*. *I ~ of ladies' smoking.* 我反对妇女抽烟. **-prov·ing·ly** *ad.* 不以为然地,以为不可地.

dis·arm [disˈɑːm, diz-] *vt.* ①缴械,解除…的武装; (劈剑)打落对方武器. ②缓和(敌意);冰释(疑虑);消除(怒气). ③取出…的信管. *~ed criticism by frank avowal of his errors* 坦率承认错误,避免了批评. — *vi.* 解除武装;裁减[废除]军备.

dis·ar·ma·ment [disˈɑːməmənt] *n.* 缴械; 解除武装; 裁军. *general and complete ~* 全面彻底的裁减军备. *~ conference* 裁军会议.

dis·arm·ing [disˈɑːmiŋ] *a.* 使人消除敌意(或怀疑、怒气等)的. **-ly** *ad.*

dis·ar·range [ˈdisəˈreindʒ] *vt.* 扰乱,搅乱,弄乱. **-ment** *n.* 混乱,紊乱.

dis·ar·ray [ˈdisəˈrei] *vt.* ①弄乱,搅乱. ②〔古〕脱去[剥去]衣服 *(of)*. — *n.* ①混乱. ②衣冠不整.

dis·ar·tic·u·late [ˈdisɑːˈtikjuleit] *vt., vi.* (使)关节脱离. **-la·tion** [ˌdisɑːˌtikjuˈleiʃən] *n.*

dis·as·sem·ble [ˌdisəˈsembl] *vt.* 拆卸, 拆除, 拆散; 分解.

dis·as·sem·bly [ˌdisəˈsembli] *n.* 拆卸,分解.

dis·as·sim·i·la·tion [ˌdisəˌsimiˈleiʃən] *n.* 分解代谢, 异化作用.

dis·as·sim·i·late [ˌdisəˈsimileit] *vt.* 【生】使进行分解代谢.

dis·as·so·ci·ate [ˌdisəˈsəuʃieit] *vt.* = dissociate. **-ation** [ˌdisəˌsəusiˈeiʃən] *n.* = dissociation.

dis·as·ter [diˈzɑːstə] *n.* 天灾,灾害;不幸,事故.

dis·as·trous [diˈzɑːstrəs] *a.* 引起灾难的;悲惨的; 损害重大的;不幸的. *with consequences ~ beyond imagination* 后果不堪设想. **-ly** *ad.*

dis·a·vow [ˈdisəˈvau] *vt.* 不承认,否认,推翻(前言),推卸(责任). **-al** *n.*

dis·band [disˈbænd] *vt., vi.* 解散, 遣散 (军队等). **-ment** *n.*

dis·bar [disˈbɑː] *vt.* 【法】取消律师资格.

dis·be·lief [ˈdisbiˈliːf] *n.* 不信. ~ *in superstition* 不迷信.

dis·be·lieve [ˌdisbiˈliːv, dis-] *vt., vi.* 不信, 怀疑 *(in)*.

dis·bench [disˈbentʃ] *vt.* 【英法】取消法律协会会员资格.

dis·branch [disˈbrɑːntʃ] *vt.* ①从…剪掉树枝. ②分开,切断.

dis·bud [disˈbʌd] *vt.* ①疏芽, 疏蕾〔以改进花的质量〕. ②除去(牛等的)幼角.

dis·bur·den [disˈbəːdn] *vt.* ①卸下(重担);摆脱,解除(烦闷等). ②说明,剖白(心地等). ~ *one's mind to* 向…吐露心怀. ~ *a donkey* 卸下驴子的重担. ~ *a person of grief* 解除某人的忧虑. — *vi.* 卸货.

dis·burse [disˈbəːs] *vt.* ①支付,支出. ②分配,分散. *~d $50,000 for roads* 支付5万美元来筑路. *Our troops were ~d over a wide area.* 我们的军队分布在广大地区. *She ~d the flowers to the children.* 她把花分给孩子们. **-ment** *n.* ①支付,支出. ②付出款;开销.

disc[1] [disk] *n.* = disk. ~ **brake** 碟形制动器,圆盘式刹车.

disc[2] = discothèque〔此词不如 disco 常用〕.

disc. = discount; discover(ed).

disc·al [ˈdiskəl] *a.* 盘状的.

dis·cal·ce·ate, dis·calced [disˈkælsi(e)it, disˈkælst] *a.* (僧侣等)赤脚的;穿草鞋的.

dis·card [disˈkɑːd] *vt.* ①放弃,抛弃. ②解雇. ③(纸牌戏中)垫(牌). ~ *one for another* 舍甲取乙. — *vi.* 垫牌. — [ˈdiskɑːd] *n.* ①垫牌;垫出的牌. ②抛弃;被抛弃的人[物]. ***go into the ~*** 被抛弃 (*Sword and spear and battle-ax have gone into the ~ of time.* 刀枪剑戟已被时间所淘汰). ***throw into the ~*** 〔美〕放弃.

dis·cern [diˈsəːn] *vt.* ①辨别,分清. ②看出,认出. ~ *good and evil* = ~ *good from evil* = ~ *between good and evil* 辨别善恶. ~ *a distant object* 看出远处目标. ~ *no difference* 看不出差别. — *vi.* 辨别. **-i·ble** *a.* 可辨别[看出]的. **-i·bly** *ad.* **-ing** *a.* 眼力好的,眼光敏锐的. **-ing·ly** *ad.* **-ment** *n.* 辨别(力);眼力;精明.

dis·cerp·ti·ble [diˈsəːptibl] *a.* 可分解的,可剖析的. **-bility** [-ˌsəːptiˈbiliti] *n.*

dis·cerp·tion [diˈsəːpʃən] *n.* 分离,割断;断片.

dis·charge[1] [disˈtʃɑːdʒ] *vt.* ①发射(炮等),打(枪),射(箭). ②起,卸(货). ③排泄,排出,放出(水等). ④释放;解除,免除(义务等);遣散(军人),使退役;放走,放行,罢免,解雇. ⑤尽(义务等),履行,践(约等);清偿(债务). ⑥【电】放(电). ⑦(印染中)除去染料〔颜色〕,漂白,拔染. ⑧【法】撤销(命令). ~ *a bow* 开弓. ~ *an arrow from a bow* 射箭. ~ *a gun* 开炮. ~ *a ship* 卸货. ~ *one's duties* 尽责. *A chimney ~s smoke.* 烟囱冒烟. — *vi.* ①卸货, 起货. ②(疮等)出脓,出水. ③(染料、墨水等)洇, 沁, 渗. ④放电. ⑤(枪炮等)发射. ~ ***(sb.) from*** *(service; office; hospital; prison)* 解(雇); 免(职); 使出(医院);使出(狱). ***(The river) ~ (itself) into*** *(the sea)* (河)流注(海中). ~ ***oneself of one's duty*** 尽(义务). — *n.* ①发射,射出. ②起货,卸货. ③流出,排泄,流量;排泄物. ④免除,释放;退伍,退役;解雇,免职. ⑤退伍[解职、释放]证明书. ⑥履行;清帐,清偿欠款;(担保的)解除. ⑦【电】放电. ⑧【纺】(印染中的) 漂白(剂). *be ready for the ~ from the hospital* 随时皆可出院. ~ *from the ears [eyes, nose]* 耳屎 [眼屎,鼻涕]. *the ~ of contract* 契约的勾销. ~ **gas** 废气. ~ **jetties** 卸货码头. ~ **liquid** 废液.

dis·charg·er [disˈtʃɑːdʒə] *n.* ①发射者;发射装置;启动装置. ②卸货人;开释人;履行者. ③【电】放电器; 避电

器；火花间隙；【染】拔染剂. **static** ～ 静电放射器.

dis·ci·form [ˈdis(k)ifɔːm] *a.* 圆形的；椭圆形的.

dis·ci·ple [diˈsaipl] *n.* ①徒弟，门徒，信徒，弟子，追随者. ②【宗】耶稣十二门徒之一. *a* ～ *of Freud* 弗洛伊德学说的信徒. *a* ～ *of the Hindus* 印度教徒. *the (twelve)* ～*s* 耶稣十二门徒. **-ship** *n.* 徒弟的身份；做徒弟的时期.

dis·ci·pli·nal [ˈdisiplinəl] *a.* ①训练上的. ②纪律上的，惩戒的.

dis·ci·plin·ant [ˈdisiplinənt] *n.* ①苦行者，苦行僧. ②〔D-〕(西班牙古时基督教)鞭身教派教徒.

dis·ci·pli·nar·i·an [ˌdisipliˈnɛəriən] *a.* ①训练上的. ②训育的，惩戒性的，有关纪律的. — *n.* ①训练者. ②严格执行纪律的人；严格的教员. *The teacher is a formidable* ～. 这位老师对纪律抓得很严.

dis·ci·pli·na·ry [ˈdisiplinəri] *a.* ①训练上的. ②纪律的；惩戒性的. ～ *barracks* 【美军】惩戒所. *a* ～ *committee* 惩戒委员. ～ *punishment* 纪律处分. *take* ～ *action* 采取纪律措施，实行处分. **-ri·ly** *ad.*

dis·ci·pline [ˈdisiplin] *n.* ①训练，锻炼；(逆境等的)磨炼；修养；教养. ②纪律，风纪；【宗】宗规，戒律. ③训戒，惩戒；惩罚. ④〔古〕学科. *courage without* ～ 匹夫之勇，蛮勇. *good* ～*s in an army* 一支军队的良好军纪. *school* ～ 校规，校训. *strict* ～ 严格的训练. *be under perfect* ～ 训练严格. *enforce [maintain]* ～ 坚持[维持]纪律. *a commission for* ～ *inspection* 纪律检查委员会. *keep one's passions under* ～ 节制情欲. — *vt.* ①训练，锻炼，操练. ②训导，强使守纪律. ③惩戒，惩罚. ～ *oneself for an end* 为某一目的训练[锻炼]自己. ～ *an outlaw* 强使一个亡命徒守纪律. *be* ～*d for one's failure* 因失败受罚. **-plin·a·ble** *a.* 可训练的；应惩罚的.

dis·cip·u·lar [diˈsipjulə] *a.* 门徒的，信徒的，追随者的.

dis·claim [disˈkleim] *vt.* ①放弃，【法】对…弃权，不认领，不索取. ②否认，不承认. ～ *all participation* 否认参与其事. — *vi.* ①【法】表示弃权. ②〔废〕否认有关系. **-a·tion** *n.* **-er** *n.* ①弃权；否认. ②弃权者，否认者.

dis·cli·max [ˈdisˈklaimæks] *n.* (由于耕种等而)破坏或改变生态平衡.

dis·close [disˈkləuz] *vt.* ①露出；泄露(秘密等). ②揭发，揭开；表明. ～ *a secret* 泄露一个秘密. *The violets* ～ *their petals.* 紫罗兰绽开花瓣. *a* ～*d ballot* 无封投票. ～ *one's intentions* 表明心意.

dis·clo·sure [disˈkləuʒə] *n.* ①泄露，暴露；(发明等的)公开. ②揭发；显示；开诚布公的话. *make a* ～ *of* 暴露.

dis·co [ˈdiskəu] *n.* 迪斯科(=disthèque). ～**-beat** 强劲急促的迪斯科音乐节拍. ～**-girl** 迪斯科女郎. ～**-pub** 迪斯科酒吧. ～**-set** 迪斯科乐队.

dis·cob·o·lus [disˈkɔbələs] *n.* (*pl.* **-boli** [-bəlai]) ①(古代的)铁饼掷手；掷铁饼者. ②〔D-〕铁饼掷手像〔公元前五世纪雕刻家 Myron 所作青铜像〕.

dis·cog·ra·phy [disˈkɔgrəfi] *n.* ①唱片分类学. ②唱片分类目录. **-ra·pher** *n.* 唱片分类目录编制者.

dis·coid [ˈdiskɔid] *a.* ①圆饼状的，盘状的. ②【植】花盘上的；只有管状小花的. — *n.* 圆饼状物.

dis·col·our, dis·col·or [disˈkʌlə] *vt.* 使变色；使褪色；污染，弄脏. *wallpaper* ～*ed by age* 褪色的陈年糊壁纸. — *vi.* ①变色；褪色，脱色. ②污染，变脏. **-a·tion** [ˌdiskʌləˈreiʃən] *n.* **-ment** *n.* 变色，褪色.

dis·com·bob·u·late [ˌdiskʌmˈbɔbjuleit] *vt.* 〔美口〕破坏，搞乱，扰乱，打乱(计划等). *plans* ～*d by the turn of events* 因事态演变而遭打乱的计划.

dis·com·fit [disˈkʌmfit] *vt.* ①破坏，搞乱，打乱(计划、目的等). ②使狼狈，使为难. ③〔古〕击溃，打败. *be* ～*ed by a question* 被质问得很狼狈. **-fi·ture** [-ˈkʌmfitʃə] *n.* ①为难，狼狈. ②失望；挫折. ③失败；溃败.

dis·com·fort [disˈkʌmfət] *n.* ①不舒适，不方便；困难. ②不安；不愉快，烦闷. *neglect minor* ～*s* 对小小的不愉快不放在心上. — *vt.* ①使不安，使不愉快，使苦恼. ②使不舒适，使不便. **-able** *a.* 〔古〕使人不舒适的；使人失望的.

dis·com·mend [ˌdiskəˈmend] *vt.* ①〔罕〕不赞许. ②〔废〕劝说；非议，贬.

dis·com·mode [ˌdiskəˈməud] *vt.* ①使不方便. ②使为难，使烦恼.

dis·com·mod·i·ty [diskəˈmɔditi] *n.* 〔古〕①不便；不利. ②无使用价值的东西.

dis·com·mon [disˈkɔmən] *vt.* ①把(公地)占为私有；剥夺…的公地使用权. ②(英牛津大学等)禁止(商人、市民等)和学生做买卖.

dis·com·pose [ˌdiskəmˈpəuz] *vt.* ①使不安，使烦恼，使失常. ②扰乱(秩序等). *be* ～*d by bad news* 听到坏消息深感不安. **-pos·ed·ly** [-ˈpəuzidli] *ad.* 不安地，心绪不宁地. **-po·sure** [-ˈpəuʒə] *n.* 不安，烦乱，失常.

dis·con·cert [ˌdiskənˈsəːt] *vt.* ①使为难，使困窘，使仓皇失措，使失常. ②挫败，打乱(计划等). *be* ～*ed by the unexpected question* 因遇到意想不到的问题而为难. **-ed** *a.* 心烦意乱的，不安的. **-ing·ly** *a.* **-ment** *n.* 失措；挫折.

dis·con·form·i·ty [diskənˈfɔːmiti] *n.* ①〔古〕不一致，不调合. ②【地】假整合.

dis·con·nect [ˌdiskəˈnekt] *vt.* ①分开，隔开，使(一物)与(另一物)分离 *(from; with).* ②割断，切断(联络)，挂断(电话)，折断. ～ *the telephone* 挂断电话. *We were* ～*ed.* 我们失去了联络. ～ *the fuse from [with] a bomb* 从炸弹上卸下导火线. — *vi.* ①结束联系. ②退隐，离群索居. ～ *into silence* 隐居，销声匿迹.

dis·con·nect·ed [ˈdiskəˈnektid] *a.* ①断了联络的，分离的. ②支离破碎的，无系统的，(演说等)乱七八糟的. ～ *argument* 首尾不一贯的论点. *His letters have lately been* ～. 他的来信近来时断时续. **-ly** *ad.* 无联络地，断断续续地.

dis·con·nex·ion, dis·con·nec·tion [ˌdiskəˈnekʃən] *n.* 分离；分开；断开，切断. *partial* ～【电】半断接(线).

dis·con·so·late [disˈkɔnsəlit] *a.* ①郁闷的，愁闷的；忧伤的. ②(前景等)阴暗的. ～ *prospects* 暗淡的前景. *The team returned* ～ *from three losses.* 连输三场的球队归来时闷闷不乐. **-ly** *ad.* **-ness** *n.*

dis·con·tent [ˈdiskənˈtent] *n.* ①不满；不平；不愉快. ②不满的人. ～ *among unemployed workers* 失业工人的不满. — *a.* 不满的，不安分的；不平的 *(with).* ～ *with one's work [lot]* 对自己的工作[处境]不满意. — *vt.* 〔通例用被动语态〕使不满意，使不平. *be* ～*ed with sb.* 对某人不满. **-ment** *n.*

dis·con·tent·ed [ˈdiskənˈtentid] *a.* 不平的；不满的. *For all their wealth, they were* ～. 他们尽管有钱，还是感到不满. **-ly** *ad.* **-ness** *n.*

dis·con·tin·u·ance [ˌdiskənˈtinjuəns] ①停止，废止，中止，断绝. ②【法】(诉讼等的)撤销，(诉讼手续等的)中止. *the* ～ *of a business* 企业歇业.

dis·con·tin·u·a·tion [ˈdiskənˌtinjuˈeiʃən] *n.* =discontinuance ①. *repeated* ～ *of work* 工程的多次停顿.

dis·con·tin·ue [ˈdiskənˈtinju(ː)] *vt.* ①搁下，中止，停止；中断；暂停. ②【法】撤销(诉讼等)；放弃(权利等). ～ *a newspaper* 停止订阅报纸. ～ *a correspondence* 停止通信. — *vi.* ①中止，中断，停止，暂停. ②(报纸等)停刊. *This magazine will* ～. 这家杂志将停刊.

dis·con·ti·nu·i·ty [ˈdisˌkɔntiˈnju(ː)iti] *n.* ①断绝，中断；间断. ②【物】不连续性，突变性，突变点；【数】不连续点；断续函数.

dis·con·tin·u·ous [ˈdiskənˈtinjuəs] *a.* ①不连续的，断断续续的；中断的. ②突变的. ～ *function*【数】不连续函数. **-ly** *ad.*

dis·co·phile [ˈdiskəfail] *n.* 唱片收藏[鉴别]家.

dis·cord [ˈdiskɔːd] *n.* ①不和，倾轧. ②不一致，不调和；【乐】不谐和(音). ③嘈杂声，喧闹. *marital* ～ 夫妇不

和. *sow* ~ 挑拨. ***be in*** ~ ***with*** 和…闹别扭，与…不和. ***the apple of*** ~ 见 apple 条. — [dis'kɔːd] *vi.* ①不调和，不一致；倾轧，冲突 *(with; from)*. ②【乐】不谐和，发乱音.

dis·cord·ance, dis·cor·dan·cy [dis'kɔːdəns, dis'kɔːdənsi] *n.* ①不一致，不和，倾轧. ②【乐】(音的)不谐和；【地】不整一，不整合.

dis·cord·ant [dis'kɔːdənt] *a.* ①不一致的，不和的，倾轧的. ②【乐】不谐和的；【地】不整合的. ~ *opinions* 众说纷纭，互不一致的意见. **-ly** *ad.*

dis·co·thèque ['diskətek] *n.* 夜总会；(播放流行歌曲唱片的)"迪斯科"舞厅. — *vi.* 在迪斯科舞厅内跳舞. ~ **dress** 迪斯科装(尤指一种底领、黑底色、底边有褶的短女装).

dis·count ['diskaunt] *n.* ①折扣，让头. ②【商】贴现，贴现率，折息，扣息. ③不考虑，不重视，不全信. *5 percent* ~ *for cash* 现金付款，九五折优待. *an arithmetical [true]* ~ 真折扣. *a bank* ~ 银行贴现. *10 percent* ~ *on tickets* 票价打九折. *accept his story with some* ~ 打折扣听他的故事. *at 25%* ~ 打七五折. ~ *of 10%* 九折. ***at a*** ~ ①(股票等的处理)低于票面价格〔参看 at a premium〕，打折扣. ②(货物等的)跌价；无销路. ③不受重视，不受欢迎 (*Superstitions are at a* ~ *today.* 迷信的习俗今天已不受欢迎). ***give [allow, make] a*** ~ 打折扣 *(on)*. — ['diskaunt, dis'kaunt] *vt.* ①打去(若干)折扣；打折扣买〔卖〕；【商】把(票据等)贴现，(借款时)先扣(若干)利息. ②打着折扣听，不全信；低估；忽视，藐视. ③(通过事先采取行动)减弱(事件等的效果). ④【台球】向(对方)让分. *be* ~*ed at 10% percent* 打九折. *The store* ~*ed all clothing for the sale.* 该店的服装全部减价出售. ~ *a politician* 对政客持怀疑态度. *They had* ~*ed the effect of a decline in the stock market.* 他们已经考虑到股票市场跌风的影响而事先作出估算. ~ **bank** 贴现银行. ~ **broke** 贴现掮客. ~ **house** 廉价商店. ~ **rate** 贴现率. **-er** *n.* = ~ **house**.

dis·count·a·ble ['diskauntəbl] *a.* ①可打折扣的；【商】可贴现的. ②该打折扣听的，不可全信的.

dis·coun·te·nance [dis'kauntinəns] *vt.* ①使…丢脸，冷淡对待，使尴尬，使羞愧. ②不赞成，不支持，使泄气. *Teachers* ~*ed smoking by the students.* 教师们反对学生吸烟. *He survived every attempt to* ~ *him.* 他经受住了种种冷遇. — *n.* 不赞成，不支持.

dis·cour·age [dis'kʌridʒ] *vt.* (*opp.* encourage) ①使受挫折；使沮丧，使泄气. ②劝阻，使打断念头；阻止，阻碍. *be* ~*d with life* 对生活失去信心. *Low prices* ~ *industry.* 低物价妨碍工业发展. ~ *sb. from smoking* 劝止某人吸烟. **-ment** *n.* ①挫折，气馁，沮丧，失意. ②阻碍，拦阻 *(give up (sth.) in complete* ~ 完全气馁而放弃不干(某事). *Poor health is grave* ~. 身体不好是一个严重的障碍).

dis·cour·ag·ing [dis'kʌridʒiŋ] *a.* ①使人沮丧〔气馁〕的. ②阻止的. **-ly** *ad.*

dis·course [dis'kɔːs] *n.* ①演说；【宗】讲道，说教. ②讲稿；论说，论文. ③〔古〕会话，谈话. ④【语法】叙述法. ⑤〔古〕推理能力. *make a stirring* ~ 作了一次激动人心的演讲. — *vi.* ①讲演，论说 *(on; upon; of)*；说教，讲道. ②写论文，写讲稿. ③谈，讲，谈论. *D- on Method*《方法论》〔法国哲学家笛卡尔的著作〕.

dis·cour·te·ous [dis'kəːtjəs] *a.* ①不懂礼的，无礼的. ②粗鲁的. **-ly** *ad.* **-ness** *n.*

dis·cour·te·sy [dis'kəːtisi] *n.* ①无礼貌，失礼 (*opp.* courtesy). ②粗鲁，鲁莽行为.

dis·cov·er [dis'kʌvə] *vt.* ①看出，发现，看到. ②〔古〕现出，露出；显示，泄露；【象棋】(移开己方挡道棋子)将(对方)一军. ~ *America* 发现美洲. *Try to* ~ *what is best to do.* 想办法找出最好的对策. *His poems* ~*ed vast realms of the spirit.* 他的诗显示出广阔的精神天地. ***be*** ~***ed*** 【剧】幕一开就在舞台上. ~***ed check***【象棋】(移开己方的一子露出另一有攻击力的棋子)将(对方)一军. ~ ***oneself*** 显露自己的身份，通名，自我介绍. — *vi.* 有所发现. **-able** *a.*

dis·cov·er·er [dis'kʌvərə] *n.* ①发见者，发现者. ②〔D-〕(美国的)"发现者"号卫星. ~ *of electricity* 发现电的人.

dis·cov·ert [dis'kʌvət] *a.* 【法】无夫的，(女子)未婚的，寡居的.

dis·cov·er·y [dis'kʌvəri] *n.* ①发见，发现，发觉. ②〔古〕显示，暴露，显露. ③(剧情的)发展. ④被发现的事物. ⑤【法】(审判前当事一方必须作出的)显示证据. ~ *ship* 探险船. *make many discoveries about the heavenly bodies* 在天体方面有许多新发现. **D- Day**〔美〕美洲发现纪念日〔十月十二日〕. ~ **well** 油田的第一口油井.

dis·cred·it [dis'kredit] *n.* ①丧失信用，丧失信任. ②丧失名誉，丢脸，耻辱. ③不信，疑惑. *It is no* ~ *to him.* 那是无损于他的名誉的. *His theories met with general discredits.* 他的理论遭到普遍怀疑. ***bring*** ~ ***on sb.'s name*** 玷污某人名誉. ***bring*** ~ ***on oneself*** 使自己失信〔丢脸〕. ***fall into*** ~ 声名狼藉. ***throw [cast]*** ~ ***on [upon]*** 使人疑心…. — *vt.* ①不信，怀疑；使成为不可信. ②损害…的信誉，丢…的丑. *an effort to* ~ *certain politicians* 设法使某些政界人士丧失信誉. *His behaviour* ~*s him.* 他的行为使他名誉扫地. *There was good reason to* ~ *the witness.* 有充足的理由怀疑证人. **-a·ble** *a.* 损害信用的，不名誉的；丢脸的，耻辱的. **-a·bly** *ad.*

dis·creet [dis'kriːt] *a.* ①考虑周到的，用心深远的. ②慎重的，谨慎的，小心的. *He is very* ~ *in giving his opinions.* 他发表意见时十分慎重. *a* ~ *silence* 用心深远的沉默. **-ly** *ad.* **-ness** *n.*

dis·crep·an·cy [dis'krepənsi] *n.* 差异，矛盾；不符合，不一致. *a* ~ *between two versions of a story* 一篇故事两个不同讲法之间的差别. *There are obvious discrepancies between what you practice and what you preach.* 你言行不一. **-crep·ant** *a.* 互有差别的 (*discrepant accounts* 互有差异的报道).

dis·crete [dis'kriːt] *a.* ①分离的，分立的；显然有别的. ②不连续的；【数】离散的；【哲】抽象的 (*opp.* concrete). *A nebula is really a* ~ *mass of innumerous stars.* 一团星云实际上是无数星体不连续的集合体. ~ **quantity**【数】分离量. ~ **smallpox**【医】稀疏性天花. ~ **space**【物】离散空间. **-ly** *ad.*

dis·cre·tion [dis'kreʃən] *n.* ①判断(力)，辨别(力). ②慎重，谨慎，考虑周到. ③(行动、判断或选择的)自由，自行裁决，斟酌；【法】任意决定权. ④〔古〕离散，间断，不连续. *D- is the better part of valour.* 考虑周到胜过勇敢. ***act at [on] one's own*** ~ 相机处理，自行决断. ***age [years] of*** ~【法】解事年龄，责任年龄，成年〔英国法律规定为 14 岁〕. ***at*** ~ ①随意，任意. ②无条件 (*be allowed to work overtime at* ~ 被允许自由加班. *surrender at* ~ 无条件投降). ***at the*** ~ ***of*** 随…的意思，凭…自行处理. ***be in [within] one's*** ~ ***to*** *(do)* (做…)是某人的自由〔权限〕. ***leave to sb.'s*** ~ 交某人酌(办)，任某人自由决定. ***use one's own*** ~ 相机处理. ***with*** ~ 慎重，审慎.

dis·cre·tion·al [dis'kreʃənl], **dis·cre·tion·a·ry** [dis'kreʃnəri] *a.* 任意的，自由决定的. *a* ~ *power to act* 可自由采取行动的权力，可便宜行事权. ~ **account [order]**【商】由经纪人〔中间人〕全权处理的资本帐户〔自由裁决的定货〕. ~ **income** 可以自由处理的收入(指扣除纳税和衣食住等必需开支后的收入部分). ~ **principle** 独断主义. ~ **wiring method**【电】选择布线法.

dis·crim·i·na·ble [dis'kriminəbl] *a.* 可区别的，可辨别的.

dis·crim·i·nant [dis'kriminənt] *n.*【数】判别式.

dis·crim·i·nate [dis'krimineit] *vt.* ①区别，鉴别，识别.

②区分出,辨出. *a mark that ~s the original from the copy* 使原本与抄本有所区别的特征. *He can ~ minute variations in tone.* 他能辨别出音调的细微变化. — *vi.* ①识别,区别. ②分别对待,歧视,排斥. ~ **against** 歧视,排斥 (~ *against foreigners* 排外). ~ **between (one thing) and (another)** 区别开(一物)和(另一物)(~ *between right and wrong* 辨明是非). ~ **in favour** 优待 (*He ~s in favour of his relatives.* 他优待自己的亲戚). —[dis'kriminit] *a.* ①能识别的,有分辨能力的. ②〔古〕明确的;显著的. *D- people choose carefully.* 有眼光的人作选择时总很细心. **-ly** *ad.*

dis·crim·i·nat·ing [dis'krimineitiŋ] *a.* ①有辨别力的,有鉴别力的. ②有差别的,区别对待的. ③形成区别的,特征显著的. ④辨别的,分析的. *a ~ tariff* (关税等的)差别税率. *a ~ test* 分析试验. *a ~ eye* 有鉴别力,有眼力. ~ *audiences* 有鉴赏力的观众. *a ~ mark* 形成差别的标志. **-ly** *ad.*

dis·crim·i·na·tion [dis,krimi'neiʃən] *n.* ①辨别,区别,鉴别. ②辨别力,识别力,鉴赏力,眼力. ③不公平的待遇,差别对待,歧视,排斥. *racial and religious ~* 种族和宗教歧视. *a man of ~* 有眼光[见识]的人. *a policy of ~ against foreigners* 排外政策. ~ *between right and wrong* 辨明是非. *bombing without ~* 狂轰滥炸. **-na·tor** [dis'krimineitə] *n.* ①辨别者. ②歧视者. ③【无】鉴频器.

dis·crim·i·na·tive [dis'kriminətiv] *a.* ①有辨别力的. ②有区别的,差别分明的. ③区别对待的,歧视的 (*the ~ features of man* 人的独有特征. ~ *organs* 识别器官. ~ *tariff* 差别关税).

dis·crim·i·na·tor [dis'krimineitə] *n.* 辨别者.

dis·crim·i·na·to·ry [dis'kriminətəri] *a.* = discriminative.

dis·crown [dis'kraun] *vt.* 使退位,废黜…的王位.

dis·cul·pate [dis'kʌlpeit] *vt.* 开脱…的罪责.

dis·cur·sion [dis'kəːʃən] *n.* ①东拉西扯的谈话[文章]等. ②(文章、谈话等的)散漫,东拉西扯,支离破碎. ③【哲】推论.

dis·cur·sive [dis'kəːsiv] *a.* ①(谈话、文章等)散漫的,东拉西扯的,不着边际的,离题的. ②【哲】推论的 (*opp.* intuitive). *a ~ talk* 漫无边际的谈话. **-ly** *ad.* **-ness** *n.*

dis·cus ['diskəs] *n.* (*pl.* ~*es* [-iz], *dis·ci* ['diskai]) ①【体】铁饼;掷铁饼. ②【动】盘;盘域;【植】花盘. *the ~ ~ throw(ing)* 掷铁饼.

dis·cuss [dis'kʌs] *vt.* ①议论;讨论,辩论. ②论述,详述. ③〔口〕津津有味地吃[喝]完;欣赏…的味道. ④【法】对(主要债务人)起诉. ~ *what should be done* 讨论应该做什么. *They ~ed a bottle of wine.* 他们津津有味地喝完酒. *demand to ~ the principal debtor* 要求对主要债务人提起诉讼. — *vi.* 讨论;谈话. ~ **with** *sb.* 和某人谈话.

dis·cuss·ant [dis'kʌsənt] *n.* 应邀参加讨论的人,讨论会列席者.

dis·cus·sion [dis'kʌʃən] *n.* ①议论,讨论;辩论,审议. ②详述,论述. 〔口〕(对食品的)品尝,尝味 (*of*). *a question under ~* 审议中的问题. *a bill down for ~* 一项被提出讨论的议案.

dis·dain [dis'dein] *vt.* ①轻蔑,鄙视,藐视,瞧不起. ②不屑做. ~ *a coward* 鄙弃懦夫. ~ *a man for his snobbishness* 鄙视势利小人. ~ *to reply an insult* 不屑于理睬别人的侮辱. — *vi.* 〔主美〕被轻蔑,遭鄙视. — *n.* 轻蔑,鄙视. ~ *of riches* 鄙视财富. *be treated with ~.* 他遭人轻视. **-ful** *a.* 轻蔑的,藐视的,倨傲的 (*a ~ look* 蔑视的目光. *be ~ of danger* 藐视困难). **-ful·ly** *ad.*

dis·ease [di'ziːz] *n.* ①病,疾病;【植】病害. ②(精神等的)病态,弊病. ③(酒等的)变质;(食物等的)腐败. ④〔废〕不安. *an acute [chronic] ~* 急性[慢性]病. *a family ~* 遗传病. *foot-and-mouth ~*【兽医】口蹄疫. *tin ~* 铁皮的锈蚀. *the various ~s of civilization* 文明带来的弊害. **be cured of a ~** 治好病. **catch [suffer from, take] a ~** 患病.

dis·eased [di'ziːzd] *a.* ①有病的;【植】有病害的. ②有弊病的;(精神等)病态的. *the ~ part* 患部. *a ~ society* 病态的社会. *a ~ mind* 病态心理.

dis·economy ['disi(ː)'kɔnəmi] *n.* ①不经济,成本(或费用)的增加. ②使成本(或费用)增加的因素.

dis·em·bark ['disim'bɑːk] *vt.* 使离船上岸;(从船上)卸下. — *vi.* 离船登岸. **-a·tion** [,disembɑː'keiʃən] *n.*

dis·em·bar·rass ['disim'bærəs] *vt.* 解脱,使摆脱(忧虑等),使脱离(困窘等);使安心. *He ~ed himself of his heavy coat.* 他脱下了沉重的外衣. ~ *oneself from troublesome trivialities* 摆脱令人烦恼的琐事. **-ment** *n.*

dis·em·bod·y ['disim'bɔdi] *vt.* ①使…脱离肉体,使不具形体〔主要以过去分词形式作定语用〕. ②〔罕〕解散,遣散(军队). *a disembodied soul* 脱离肉体的灵魂. **-bod·i·ment** *n.*

dis·em·bogue [,disim'bəug] *vi.* ①(河水等)流出;流注 (*into*). ②(内容等)倾吐出. ③〔罕〕(船)驶出港湾. *a river that ~s into the ocean* 一条流入大洋的江河. —*vt.* (河流等)将(河水)倾吐出. *a river that ~s itself [its waters] into the ocean* 一条注入大洋的江河.

dis·em·bos·om [,disim'buzəm] *vt.* 说出,透露,公开(秘密等). ~ *oneself of a secret* 说出心中的秘密. ~ *oneself* 说出心里话. ~ *a secret* 透露秘密.

dis·em·bow·el [,disim'bauəl] *vt.* (〔英〕*-ll-*) ①除去…的内脏,取出…的肠子. ②取出…的内容. ③(蜘蛛)吐(丝). ~ *oneself* 剖腹自杀. **-ment** *n.*

dis·em·broil [,disim'brɔil] *vt.* 排解…的纠纷,把…从纷扰中解脱.

dis·em·ployed [,disim'plɔid] *a.* 失业的〔尤指由于技术、学识等方面不称职而失业的〕.

dis·en·chant [,disin'tʃɑːnt] *vt.* ①使清醒,使摆脱幻想,使不再着迷. ②使…从邪祟中解脱. *The harshness of everyday reality ~ed him of his idealistic hopes.* 冷酷的日常现实使他从理想主义的幻梦中清醒过来. *He will be ~ed with her.* 他对她将不再着迷. **-ment** *n.*

dis·en·cum·ber ['disin'kʌmbə] *vt.* 消除(成见等),摆脱(烦恼、负担等). ~ *the mind from prejudice* 消除成见. ~ *one's mind from [of] cares* 消除烦恼.

dis·en·dow ['disin'dau] *vt.* 剥夺(教会、学校等的)捐款[基金]. **-ment** *n.*

dis·en·fran·chise [,disin'fræntʃaiz] *vt.* = disfranchise.

dis·en·gage ['disin'geidʒ] *vt.* ①放开,解开(束缚等),解除(契约等),使脱开(约束等). ②【机】使(离合器等)分开;【军】使脱离(接触),使中止(战斗);【化】使分离,使游离,使离析. ~ *a clutch*【机】使离合器分开. ~ *oneself from the promise of marriage* 解除婚约. *She ~d quickly from his hold.* 她很快挣脱开他. *He accepted the invitation, but was later forced to ~ himself.* 他接受了邀请,但后来被迫失约. *Our army ~d the enemy.* 我军和敌军脱离了接触. **disengaging zone**【化】分离层.

dis·en·gaged ['disin'geidʒd] *a.* ①被解开的,已脱离的;已断绝关系的;已解除婚约的. ②自由的,闲着的,空着的. ③【军】脱离接触的,【化】离析的,分离的;【机】脱开的. *I'll be ~ on Friday* 我星期五就有空了. *Is this room ~?* 这房子空不空?

dis·en·gage·ment [,disin'geidʒmənt] *n.* ①解开,脱离. ②解约;解雇. ③闲暇,自由. ④【化】分离,离析;【军】脱离接触. *a ~ zone* 脱离接触区. *hours of ~* 空闲时间.

dis·en·tail ['disin'teil] *vt.*【法】解除(地产等的)限定继承权.

dis·en·tan·gle ['disin'tæŋgl] *vt.* 解脱,解开(结扣等);解决(纠纷等);清理(破产的公司等). ~ *a complicated knot* 解开复杂的结扣. ~ *oneself from the intrigues* 从勾心斗角中解脱出来. — *vi.* ①(结扣等)解开. ②(纠纷等)解决.

dis·en·thral(l) [ˌdisinˈθrɔːl] *vt.* 使摆脱(奴役状态); 使解除(束缚). *be ~ed from morbid fantacies* 从病态的幻想中解放出来. **-ment** *n.*

dis·en·throne [ˌdisinˈθrəun] *vt.* 废黜, 使退位. **-ment** *n.*

dis·en·ti·tle [disinˈtaitl] *vt.*【法】剥夺…的权利; 剥夺…的官衔. *~ sb. to the right of inheritance* 剥夺某人的继承权.

dis·en·tomb [ˌdisinˈtuːm] *vt.* 从坟墓中挖出; 发掘.

dis·en·twine [ˌdisinˈtwain] *vt., vi.* 解开; 解决(纠纷), 摆脱(瓜葛).

di·sep·al·ous [daiˈsepləs] *a.*【植】有两萼片的.

dis·e·quil·i·brate [ˈdisˌiːkwiˈlaibreit] *vt.* 使失去平衡, 打破…的平衡. **-bra·tion** *n.*

dis·e·qui·lib·ri·um [disˌiːkwiˈlibriəm] *n.* *(pl. ~s, -ri·a* [-ə]) 不平衡; 失去平衡〔尤指经济发展不平衡〕.

dis·es·tab·lish [ˈdisisˈtæbliʃ] *vt.* ①使(教会)与政府分离. ②废除(成规), 打破…的现状; 解除…的官职. *~ the authority of an outdated code* 废除过时的法典. **-ment** *n.*

dis·es·teem [ˌdisisˈtiːm] *vt., n.* 厌恶, 轻视.

dis·fa·vour, dis·fa·vor [ˈdisˈfeivə] *n.* ①不赞成; 厌弃; 疏远, 冷淡. ②失众望, 失宠. ③不利. *He regarded my suggestions with ~.* 他不赞成我的建议. *The minister incurred the king's ~.* 这位大臣招致国王的冷遇. ***be [live] in ~*** 过受气日子, 失宠, 不受欢迎, 受冷遇. ***fall [come] into ~*** 失宠, 失众望, 不受欢迎. — *vt.* 疏远, 冷待; 嫌弃.

dis·fea·ture [disˈfiːtʃə] *vt.* 毁损…的容貌.

dis·fig·ure [disˈfigə] *vt.* ①毁损…的外形〔外貌〕, 使破相, 使变丑. ②毁损…的优点〔价值〕. *Old towns ~d by tasteless new buildings.* 古老的城镇被平庸的新建筑弄得很难看. **-ment** *n.* 破相, 外貌变丑; 疵瑕; 毁形.

dis·for·est [disˈfɔrist] *vt.* 采伐…的森林 (= disafforest).

dis·fran·chise [disˈfræntʃaiz] *vt.* ①褫夺…的公权〔选举权〕. ②〔英〕剥夺(某地)选派议会议员的权利. **-ment** *n.*

dis·frock [disˈfrɔk] *vt.*【宗】解除…的圣职.

dis·gorge [disˈgɔːdʒ] *vt.* ①吐, 呕吐出; 吐出(赃物等). ②(江河等)流出. *The soldiers had to ~ the jewels which they had plundered.* 士兵被迫交出抢劫的珠宝. *trains disgorging thousands of passengers* 吐出成千上万旅客的火车. — *vi.* ①呕吐. ②(河流等)流注. *where the river ~s into the sea* 河流入海的地方.

dis·grace [disˈgreis] *n.* ①失宠, 受气; 耻辱, 出丑, 丢脸. ②丢脸的事, 出丑的人. *the ~ of criminals* 罪犯身份的耻辱. *a humiliating ~* 奇耻大辱. *Choose death before ~.* 宁死不屈. ***be a ~ to*** 是…的耻辱 (*He is a ~ to his school.* 他给学校丢脸). ***bring ~ on [upon] (oneself)*** 玷辱(自己), (自)失体面. ***fall into ~ (with sb.)*** (在某人面前)失宠. ***in ~*** 失宠, 受气; 丢脸. — *vt.* ①玷污(名誉); 使丢脸. ②使失宠; 贬黜. *~ oneself* 丢脸. *~ one's name* 玷污自己的名誉. *be ~d at court* 在宫廷中失宠.

dis·grace·ful [disˈgreisful] *a.* 可耻的, 丢脸的, 不光采的, 不名誉的. *~ behavior* 不光采的行为. **-ly** *ad.* **-ness** *n.*

dis·grun·tle [disˈgrʌntl] *vt.* 使不满, 使不平; 使不高兴. *He was ~d at their absence.* 他对他们的缺席不满. *members ~d with their president* 对会长不满的会员们. **-d** *a.* 不平的, 不满的; 不高兴的. **-ment** *n.*

dis·guise [disˈgaiz] *n.* ①假装, 伪装, 幌子; 化装服, 伪装衣. ②托辞, 口实, 借口. *throw off all ~* 抛开一切假面具. *No words can be the ~ of base intentions.* 没有任何说法可以作为卑鄙用心的托辞. ***in ~*** 假装的; 伪装的 (*a policeman in ~* 便衣警察. *Misfortune might be a blessing in ~.* 因祸可能得福, 塞翁失马安知非福). ***in [under] the ~ of*** ①以…为口实, 托辞…. ②装做, 假扮做. ***make no ~ of one's feelings*** 真情毕露. ***(speak) without ~*** 摆明(说). — *vt.* ①假装, 假扮, 佯装, 扮作. ②隐藏(真意等), 隐瞒, 掩饰. *The king was ~d as a peasant.* 国王假扮做农民. *~ oneself with a false mustache* 用假胡须化装. *a door ~d as a book-case* 做成书橱一样的门. *be ~d in [with] drink* 装醉. *~ one's age* 瞒岁数. *~ one's voice* 改变说话腔调. **-guis·ed·ly** *ad.*

dis·gust [disˈgʌst] *vt.* ①使作呕. ②令人嫌恶, 招人唾弃〔反感〕. *Your vacillations ~ me.* 你的优柔寡断使人讨厌. ***be ~ed at [by, with]...*** 嫌, 讨厌, 唾弃; 对…作呕. — *n.* ①作呕. ②厌恶, 憎恶, 反感 *(at; for; towards; against)*. ***take a ~ at*** 嫌, 讨厌…. ***to one's ~*** 可厌的是; 令人作呕的是. **-ed·ly** *ad.* **-ful** *a.* ①令人作呕的. ②使人讨厌的. **-ing, -ful** *a.*

dish [diʃ] *n.* ①碟子, 盘子. ②盘菜; 盘装食品; 菜. ③盘形, 盘状(物). ④一盘的容量, 满满一盘. ⑤〔美俚〕漂亮的女人. ⑥〔美俚〕心爱物; 爱好. ⑦下陷, 凹处;【物】抛物面;【无】抛物面天线反射镜. *a meat ~* 盛肉盘. *a wooden ~* 木盘. *a ~ of beans* 一盘豆子. *a cold ~* 冷盘(菜). *Chinese ~es* 中国菜, 中国口味. *a plain [dainty] ~* 清淡的〔好吃的〕菜. *Rice is an inexpensive ~.* 大米是一种廉价食品. *an evaporating ~* 蒸发皿. *one's favourite ~* 爱吃的菜. *a standing ~* 每日例菜; 老生常谈, 老调. *Mathematics is not my ~.* 我不喜欢数学. ***~ of gossip*** 闲谈. ***eat off a ~*** 由盘中取食. ***made ~es*** 拼盘. — *vt.* ①把(食物)盛在碟〔盘〕子里. ②使成盘形; 把…挖空. ③〔俚〕瞒, 骗; 打败, 破坏, 挫败(计划等). *~ food onto plates* 把食物装进盘子里. *She ~ed him some breakfast.* 她用盘子给他装上早餐. — *vi.* ①成盘状, 成中凹形. ②闲谈. ***be ~ed*** 输了, 完了. ***~ it out*** 〔口〕吃责; 嚷叫; 〔美俚〕处罚 (*the woman dishing it out to her children* 大声责骂孩子的妇女). ***~ sb. out of sth.*** 骗去某人的某物. ***~ out*** ①上(菜), 把(菜等)装盘端上; 分配(饭菜等). ②〔喻〕托出, 抛出; 提供, 发布(消息等). ③把…挖成空盘状. ④滔滔不绝地讲. ***~ up*** ①把(食物)盛在盘里端出. ②(把故事等)说得动听 (*~ up the story in a humorous way* 以幽默的语调把故事讲得娓娓动听). **~cloth** (洗盘碟用的)抹布. **~cloth gourd** 丝瓜. **~clout** ① = **~cloth**. ②〔美俚〕软弱而愚蠢的人. **~ cross** 十字形盘碟架. **~pan** 洗碗碟等物的浅桶 (*~pan hands* 家庭主妇因经常洗碗碟等而变粗糙的手). **~rag** = ~cloth. **~ ring** 环形盘垫. **~towel** 〔美〕(擦干碗碟的)抹布. **~washer** ①洗盘子的人; 洗碟机. ②【鸟】鹡鸰. **~water** ①洗过盘子的脏水. ②〔喻〕味道差的汤〔茶〕等; 〔美俚〕没有力量的话, 滥调 (*dull as ~* 十分枯燥乏味, 令人厌烦). **-ful** *n.* 满盘, 一碟.

dis·ha·bille [ˌdisæˈbiːl] *n.* ①衣着随便, 穿着便服〔睡衣等〕. ②便服. ③邋遢, 散漫; 混乱, 杂乱; (心理)失常. ***in ~*** 穿着便服, 穿得很随便.

dis·ha·bit·u·ate [ˌdishəˈbitjueit] *vt.* 使丢弃习惯.

dis·har·mo·ni·ous [ˌdishɑːˈməunjəs] *a.* 不调和的, 不谐和的. **-ly** *ad.*

dis·har·mo·nize, dis·har·mo·nise [disˈhɑːməˌnaiz] *vt.* 使不和谐. — *vi.* 失去和谐.

dis·har·mo·ny [ˈdisˈhɑːməni] *n.* 不调和, 不一致; 不协调.

dis·heart·en [disˈhɑːtn] *vt.* 使沮丧, 使泄气, 使垂头丧气. *He was ~ed at the result.* 这个结果使他垂头丧气. *be ~ed by the unlucky event* 因运气不佳而泄气. **-ing** *a.* 使人沮丧的. **-ing·ly** *ad.* **-ment** *n.* 沮丧.

dished [diʃt] *a.* ①凹, 瘪, 盘形凹陷的; (房间)有圆屋顶的, 穹窿形的. ②〔俚〕筋疲力尽的. *a ~ face* 凹陷的脸. ③〔美俚〕完蛋了的, 受挫折的. *~ bottom* 碟形底.

dis·her·i·son [disˈherizn] *n.* 剥夺继承权.

di·shev·el [diˈʃevəl] *vt.* (〔英〕 **-ll-**) 弄乱, 搅乱 (头发等). *The wind ~ed the papers on the desk.* 风把桌上的纸吹乱了. **-ed** *a.* 散乱的; (头发等)乱蓬蓬的; 服装不整

洁的 (*dishevel appearance* 衣容不整洁).

dis·hon·est [disˈɔnist] *a.* 不诚实的;不正直的;狡猾的,阴险的;不可靠的. ~ *gains* 不正当收入,不义之财. **-ly** *ad.*

dis·hon·es·ty [disˈɔnisti] *n.* ①不正直,不诚实;狡猾;阴险. ②不诚实的行为. *a piece of* ~ 一桩不老实的行为. *many dishonesties* 许多不诚实的行为. *a man of* ~ 不诚实的人.

dis·hon·our, dis·hon·or [disˈɔnə] *n.* ①不名誉,丢脸;耻辱,侮辱. ②【商】(票据的)拒付,拒收. *I offered him no* ~. 我未曾侮辱他. *do sb. a* ~ 侮辱人. *a notice of* ~ 【商】拒付通知. ***be a ~ to*** 是…的耻辱. ***bring sb. to ~*** 使蒙受耻辱. ***To the ~ of …*** 对…说来丢脸的是. — *vt.* ①使蒙受耻辱,侮辱,败坏(名誉). ②使(契约等)作废;【商】拒付,拒收(票据). ③奸污(妇女). *a ~ed bill* 被拒收的票据. *a ~ed cheque* 空头支票. **-a·ble** *a.* 不名誉的,耻辱的;卑鄙的,无耻的. **-a·bly** *ad.*

dis·horn [disˈhɔːn] *vt.* 除去(动物的)角.

dish·y [ˈdiʃi] *a.* 〔美俚〕称心的,合意的;有吸引力的.

dis·il·lu·sion [ˌdisiˈluːʒən] *n.* 觉醒;幻灭. — *vt.* 使觉醒,使幻灭,给…泼冷水. *Hamlet was ~ed in his mother.* 汉姆雷特对他母亲的幻想破灭了. ***be ~ed with*** 对…大失所望. **-ize** *vt.* **-ment** *n.*

dis·in·cen·tive [ˌdisinˈsentiv] *n.* (生产等方面的)障碍因素. — *a.* (对生产等)起阻碍作用的.

dis·in·cli·na·tion [ˌdisinkliˈneiʃən] *n.* 不喜欢,不愿,厌恶. *his ~ to the fair sex* 他对女性的厌恶. *have a ~ for work* 怕工作. ***with ~*** 很勉强地 (*read a book with ~* 勉强地读书).

dis·in·cline [ˈdisinˈklain] *vt.* 使不愿,使无意于. *be ~ed to* 无意于…. *feel ~d for any more sleep* 不想再睡了. *Your rudeness ~s me to grant your request.* 你的粗鲁态度使我不想答应你的要求.

dis·in·cor·po·rate [ˌdisinˈkɔːpəreit] *vt.* 解散(团体、公司、组织等).

dis·in·fect [ˌdisinˈfekt] *vt.* 给…消毒,给…灭菌;使洗净. ~ *drinking water* 给饮用水消毒. **dis·in·fect·ant** ① *a.* 消毒的. ② *n.* 消毒剂. **-fec·tion** *n.* 消毒(作用),灭菌(法). **-or** *n.* 消毒器;消毒剂;消毒者.

dis·in·fest [ˌdisinˈfest] *vt.* 消灭(某处的)老鼠[跳蚤等];除去(庄稼等)的害虫. **-ant** *n.* 除虫剂,杀虫剂.

dis·in·fla·tion [ˌdisinˈfleiʃən] *n.* 通货收缩. **-ary** *a.*

dis·in·for·ma·tion [disˌinfəˈmeiʃən] *n.* 假情报〔为迷惑敌方情报机关而故意泄露的虚假情报〕.

dis·in·gen·u·ous [ˌdisinˈdʒenjuəs] *a.* 不真诚的,无诚意的,虚伪的;奸诈的,阴险的. **-ly** *ad.* **-ness** *n.*

dis·in·her·it [ˈdisinˈherit] *vt.* 【法】与…断绝父子关系,废(嫡);取消…的继承权. *~ed people* 被取消继承权的人们. **-ance** *n.*

dis·in·te·grate [disˈintigreit] *vt.* ①使崩溃,使瓦解. ②使分裂,使分解,分化. *an empire ~d* 瓦解的帝国. *rocks ~d by frost and rain* 被风霜雨露剥蚀瓦解的岩石. ~ *the enemy troops* 瓦解敌军. — *vi.* ①崩,碎,分裂,分解. ②崩溃,溃散,瓦解 (*into*). ③【原】蜕变,衰变. *house gradually disintegrating with age* 房屋因年久失修而逐渐倾颓. *The national economy ~d.* 国民经济崩溃了. **-gra·tor** *n.* ①造成分裂者,分裂因素. ②粉碎机,解磨机;(造纸用)打浆机.

dis·in·te·gra·tion [disˌintiˈgreiʃən] *n.* ①分裂,分解,崩解. ②瓦解,崩溃,溃散. ③【地】剥蚀;【原】裂变,衰变,蜕变. *the atmospheric ~ of rocks* 岩石的风化. *the ~ of a society* 社会的瓦解. *the ~ of personality* 人格分裂. *radioactive ~* 【物】放射性蜕变.

dis·in·ter [ˈdisinˈtəː] *vt.* ①(从坟墓中或地下)掘出. ②发掘出,揭露出. **-ment** *n.*

dis·in·ter·est [disˈintrist] *n.* ①无利害关系. ②无兴趣,不关心,冷淡. — *vt.* 使无利害关系;使不关心. ~ *oneself* 置身事外,采取不干涉态度.

dis·in·ter·est·ed [disˈintristid] *a.* ①无私心的,廉洁的,公平的. ②〔美口〕不关心的,不感兴趣的 (~ *aid* 无私的援助. *a ~ decision* 公平的决定). **-ly** *ad.* **-ness** *n.*

dis·in·ter·me·di·a·tion [disˌintəmiːdiˈeiʃən] *n.* 〔美〕大量提款(指从储蓄银行中大量提款投入证券投资市场).

dis·in·vest·ment [ˌdisinˈvestmənt] *n.* 减少资本投资;变卖资本投资;抽回投资资本.

dis·jec·ta mem·bra [disˈdʒektə ˈmembrə] *n.* 〔L.〕〔*pl.*〕断片,残片;不连贯的引文.

dis·join [disˈdʒɔin] *vt.* 把…分开,拆散. — *vi.* 分开.

dis·joint [disˈdʒɔint] *vt.* ①使关节脱位,使脱臼. ②拆散(机械等). ③打乱(次序等). — *vi.* ①(关节等)脱位,脱臼. ②分离,脱开. **-ed** *a.* ①关节脱臼的. ②拆散了的,支离破碎的. ③无条理的,无系统的. **-ed·ly** *ad.* **-ed·ness** *n.*

dis·junct [disˈdʒʌŋkt] *a.* ①脱节的;不相连的. ②【乐】跳跃的. ③【动】(昆虫)头、胸和腹部由缢缩分开的. — [ˈdisdʒʌŋkt] *n.* 【逻】选言肢.

dis·junc·tion [disˈdʒʌŋkʃən] *n.* ①分离,折断. ②【数】(计算机的)析取;逻辑加法;逻辑和;【逻】选言,选言判断;选言推理.

dis·junc·tive [disˈdʒʌŋktiv] *a.* ①分离的,分离性的. ②【逻】选言的. ③【语】转折的;反意的. *a ~ proposition* 【逻】选言命题. ~ *conjunctions* 转折连词. — *n.* ①【语法】转折连词 (*but; yet* 等). ②【逻】选言判断.

disk [disk] *n.* ①圆盘;盘状,盘状物. ②【体】铁饼;〔美〕唱片. ③【植】花盘;【动】盘;【农】(圆盘)耙片. ④【自】(电子计算机的)数据存储盘;(照相排版机的)机盘. *the ~ of the sun* 太阳表面. ~ *recording* 灌唱片. — *vt.* ①使成圆盘状. ②用圆盘耙耕(地). ③灌(唱片),把…录制成唱片. ~ **harrow** 圆盘耙. ~ **jockey** 〔美俚〕唱片节目播音员. ~ **pack** 【自】可换式磁盘组〔电子计算机的存储设备〕.

dis·like [disˈlaik] *n.* 不喜欢,讨厌,反感. *likes and ~s* 喜欢与反感. *She has a ~ to [for, of] him.* 她不喜欢他. *I took an instant ~ to [for, of] him.* 我对他立刻产生了反感.

dis·limn [disˈlim] *vt.* 〔古〕使(画等的)轮廓模糊;使变模糊.

dis·lo·cate [ˈdisləkeit] *vt.* ①使脱离原来位置;使(骨关节)脱位,使脱臼. ②打乱…的正常秩序,弄乱…的位置;使混乱. *The glacier ~d the great stones.* 冰河搬动了巨石. *have [get] one's leg ~d* 腿关节脱臼. ~ *one's shoulder* 肩关节脱臼. *Traffic was ~d by the accident.* 车祸使交通陷入混乱. ~ *one's mind* 使心烦意乱. *strikes dislocating the economy* 打乱经济秩序的罢工.

dis·lo·ca·tion [ˌdisləˈkeiʃən] *n.* ①【医】脱位,脱臼;离位,转位,位移. ②【地】断层,断错;【物】位错. ③混乱,打乱. *a disastrous economic ~* 灾难性的经济混乱.

dis·lodge [disˈlɔdʒ] *vt.* ①把…从住地[窝巢等处]逐出;【军】击退;赶走. ②移去;取出. ~ *a stone with one's foot* 用脚把石子踢开. ~ *a beast* 把野兽从窝巢中逐出. ~ *the enemy from their fortifications* 把敌人从碉堡中逐出. — *vi.* 从住处退出. **-ment** *n.*

dis·loy·al [disˈlɔiəl] *a.* 不忠的;无信义的;不贞的 (*to*). *a ~ friend* 不忠诚的朋友. *be ~ to one's country* 叛国. *be ~ to the marriage bed* 不贞洁. **-ist** *n.* 不忠的人. **-ly** *ad.* **-ty** *n.* 不忠诚,不忠,无信义,不贞洁.

dis·mal [ˈdizməl] *a.* ①阴郁的,惨淡的,凄凉的;忧郁的,(叫声等)凄惨的. ②沉闷的,无趣的. ③〔废〕可怕的. *a ~ face* 忧郁的面孔. *a ~ room* 阴暗的房间. *the ~ days of winter* 萧瑟的冬天. *the ~ science* 沉闷的科学〔英美等国指政治经济学而言〕. *a ~ incidents* 不如意的事. — *n.* ①〔美南部〕沼地. ②〔the ~s〕〔口〕忧郁. **-ly** *ad.*

dis·man·tle [disˈmæntl] *vt.* ①拆除…的设备〔装备、家具、防御工事〕等. ②拆掉…的覆盖物; 剥掉…的衣服. ③拆卸,拆散(机器等). ④摧毁,夷平. ～ *a ship* 拆掉船上的装备. ～ *a fortress* 拆除要塞的防御设备. *They* ～*d the machine and shipped it in pieces.* 他们把机器拆开,分成零碎部件运出. *The wind* ～*d the trees of their leaves.* 风把树上的叶子吹个精光.

dis·mask [disˈmɑːsk] *vt.* = unmask.

dis·mast [disˈmɑːst] *vt.*【海】(暴风、大炮等) 打落〔打断、吹断〕桅杆.

dis·may [disˈmei] *n.* ①灰心; 沮丧, 丧失勇气. ②惊愕. *The enemy retreated in perfect* ～. 敌人沮丧地退去. *exclaim in* ～ 惊愕得叫喊起来. *To my* ～*, this university was closed.* 使我沮丧的是, 这所大学停办了. — *vt.* ①使沮丧. ②使惊愕. *The surprise attack* ～*ed the enemy.* 这次奇袭大灭了敌人的威风. *He was* ～*ed at the size of his adversary.* 对手的魁伟身材使他丧失了勇气.

dis·mem·ber [disˈmembə] *vt.* ①肢解, 割断…的肢体. ②割裂; 把…撕碎; 瓜分(国土等). *The revolts* ～*ed the country.* 叛乱使国家四分五裂. *a* ～*ed country* 一个被瓜分的国家. **-ment** *n.*

dis·miss [disˈmis] *vt.* ①使退去,让…走开, 打发走. ②遣散,解散(队伍等). ③解雇,把…免职; 开除(学生等). ④放弃(企图等); 断(念), 消除(顾虑等), 忘掉; 草草了结(讨论中的问题等). ⑤【法】驳回,拒绝受理. ⑥搁置; 不予考虑. *after school was* ～*ed* 放学以后. ～ *a suitor* 拒绝求婚者. *She* ～*ed the class early.* 她早早下课. ～ *an employee* 解雇雇员. *He was* ～*ed from the service for his careless behaviors.* 他因玩忽职守而被解除职务. ～ *one's fear* 打消恐惧. ～ *a suit* 对诉讼不予受理. — *vi.* (队伍等)解散. ***D-!*** 〔口令〕散队; 解散; ***the*** ～【军】解散口令.

dis·miss·al [disˈmisəl] *n.* ①解雇; 免职; 开除. ②退去, 打发走; 遣散; 解散. ③【法】驳回, 拒绝受理. ④免职令; 解雇通知; 开除通告.

dis·miss·i·ble [disˈmisəbl] *a.* ①可解雇的; 可免职的. ②可打发走的; 可拒绝的; 可不予考虑的.

dis·mis·sion [disˈmiʃən] *n.*〔罕〕= dismissal.

dis·mis·sive [disˈmisiv] *a.* ①拒绝的; 打发走的. ②轻蔑的, 瞧不起人的. *a curt* ～ *gesture* 挥一挥手把人打发走. *a* ～ *question* 盛气凌人的发问.

dis·mount [ˈdisˈmaunt] *vt.* ①使下马, 使下车; 使(敌人、骑者等)摔下马来. ②(从支架, 托座, 台子等上)取下, 卸下, 拿下. ③拆卸(机器等). *The horse twisted, kicked and finally* ～*ed its rider.* 那匹马又蹦又跳, 终于把骑手摔了下来. ～ *a picture* 从画框里取下画. ～ *a gun from its carriage* 从炮架上卸下大炮. — *vi.* (从车、马等上) 下来 *(from)*. ～ *from a horse* 下马. — *n.* 下马,下车;【体】跳下动作. ***the*** ～【军】下马令.

dis·na·ture [disˈneitʃə] *vt.* 使失去自然属性 (或形态); 使不自然.

Dis·ney[1] [ˈdizni] *n.* ①迪斯尼〔姓氏〕. ②**Walt** ～ 瓦尔特·迪斯尼〔1901—1966,美国电影动画片设计家〕.

Dis·ney[2] [ˈdizni] *n.* 迪斯尼动画片〔美国瓦·迪斯尼设计的电影动画片〕.

Dis·ney·land [ˈdizniˌlænd] *n.* 迪斯尼游乐园〔美国动画片制片人瓦·迪斯尼在洛杉矶附近设计的游乐场〕;〔喻〕奇妙的幻境.

dis·o·be·di·ence [ˌdisəˈbiːdjəns] *n.* 不服从, 不顺从, 违抗 *(to)*; 不孝. ～ *to the law* 违抗法律.

dis·o·be·di·ent [ˌdisəˈbiːdjənt] *a.* 不顺从的,不服从的 *(to)*; 违法的, 不孝的. *a* ～ *son* 不孝顺的儿子, 逆子. **-ly** *ad.*

dis·o·bey [ˈdisəˈbei] *vt.* 不服从, 违抗. ～ *one's parents* 对双亲不孝. ～ *a law* 违抗法律. — *vi.* 不听话; 不顺从. *The son* ～*s.* 儿子不听话.

dis·o·blige [ˈdisəˈblaidʒ] *vt.* ①使…失望,不满足…的愿望; 对…不通融. ②〔口〕使不便. ③得罪, 使生气. *We are sorry to* ～ *you, but the rooms you desire are already reserved.* 我们使您失望感到很抱歉, 不过您要的房间已经订出去了. *be* ～*d by a tactless remark* 因一句不得体的话而生气. *be* ～*d by an uninvited guest* 因为来了一位不速之客而被弄得很不方便. **-o·blig·ing** *a.* ①不亲切的,不通融的. ②(作为邻居等)不考虑别人的.

dis·or·der [disˈɔːdə] *n.* ①无秩序,混乱, 杂乱; 不合手续. ②骚乱, 纷扰. ③小病,(身心机能的)失调. ④【化】无序. *a* ～ *in legal proceedings* 法律诉讼的不合手续. *the* ～*s in universities* 大学里的骚乱. *a mild stomach* ～ 轻微的胃病. ***in*** ～ 混乱, 紊乱 (*papers in* ～ 胡乱堆放着的文件. *long hair in* ～ 乱蓬蓬的长发). ***fall into*** ～ 陷入混乱. ***throw into*** ～ 使混乱, 把…卷入动乱. — *vt.* ①扰乱,使混乱. ②使(身心等)失调, 使(神经等)错乱. **-ed** *a.* ①(秩序等)混乱的. ②(身心)失调的, 有病的. *a* ～*ed stomach [liver]* 胃〔肝〕病.

dis·or·der·ly [disˈɔːdəli] *a.* ①无秩序的,不规则的, 紊乱的. ②骚乱的,无法无天的;【法】妨害治安的; 伤风败俗的. *a* ～ *pile of clothes* 乱七八糟的一堆衣服. *charged with being drunk and* ～ 被控告犯酗酒和妨害治安罪. — *ad.* 无秩序地, 杂乱地. ～ **conduct**【法】妨害治安行为. ～ **house** 妓院, 赌场. ～ **person**【法】妨害治安者, 伤风败俗者. **-li·ness** *n.*

dis·or·gan·i·za·tion [disˌɔːgənaiˈzeiʃən] *n.* 分裂, 瓦解; 混乱, 紊乱.

dis·or·gan·ize [disˈɔːgənaiz] *vt.* 瓦解; 打乱, 使混乱. ～ *a political party* 使一个政党瓦解. ～ *a plan* 打乱一项计划.

dis·o·ri·ent [disˈɔːrient], **dis·o·ri·en·tate** [disˈɔːrienteit] *vt.* ①使不辨方向,使迷失方位. ②使精神混乱〔尤指不辨时间、地点和人物等〕. *The strange streets* ～*ed him.* 生疏的街道使他迷路了. *a society* ～*ed by changing values* 由于价值观点不断改变而迷失方向的社会. *They became deeply intoxicated and totally* ～*ed.* 他们酩酊大醉, 已经完全分不清东南西北了. **-a·tion** *n.*

dis·own [disˈəun] *vt.* ①不承认…和自己有关系; 否认…是自己的; 声明与(子女等)脱离关系. ②不承认…的权威性〔正确性、有效性〕等. ～ *one's heirs* 宣布和自己的继承人断绝关系. ～ *a letter* 否认是自己写的信. ～ *the doctrine* 不承认那个学说是正确的.

dis·par·age [disˈpæridʒ] *vt.* ①轻蔑, 轻视. ②污蔑; 贬损, 指责. *Your behaviour will* ～ *the whole family.* 你的行为将使全家丢脸. *Don't* ～ *good manners.* 不要把礼貌不放在心上. **-ment** *n.* 轻蔑; 贬损.

dis·par·ag·ing·ly [disˈpæridʒiŋli] *ad.* 轻蔑地; 毁谤地. *speak* ～ *of a man* 说人坏话.

dis·pa·rate [ˈdispərit] *a.* 根本不相同的; (种类)全异的; 不能互相比拟的;【逻】异类的. ～ *ideas* 根本不相同的看法. — *n.*〔常 *pl.*〕无法比较的东西. **-ly** *ad.* **-ness** *n.*

dis·par·i·ty [disˈpæriti] *n.* 不同,不等,不一致,不相称; 悬殊. ～ *in rank* 身份悬殊. *disparities between men and women* 男女差别.

dis·park [disˈpɑːk] *vt.* 开放(私人园地、猎苑等)改作别用.

dis·part[1] [disˈpɑːt] *vt.*〔古〕使分离,使分裂. — *vi.*〔古〕分裂,分离.

dis·part[2] [disˈpɑːt] *n.* 炮口与炮尾的中径差; 炮口准星.

dis·pas·sion [disˈpæʃən] *n.* ①不动感情,冷静. ②公平, 无偏见.

dis·pas·sion·ate [disˈpæʃənit] *a.* ①不动感情的, 冷静的. ②公平的, 无偏见的. *a* ～ *critic* 一位不偏不倚的批评家. **-ly** *ad.* **-ness** *n.*

dis·patch [disˈpætʃ] *n.* ①(迅速)发送, (火速)派遣. ②急报,快信,急件; (新闻)电讯. ③(敏速)处理,速办; 敏捷,急速. ④调度,调遣. ⑤(即刻)处死, (就地)正法. ⑥特电, 特别公报. ⑦运输行. *the date of the* ～ *of the* *parcel* 包裹发出的日期. *a Xinhua News Agency* ~ *from Beijing (on) Nov. 13* 新华社北京11月13日电. *quick* ~ *of business* 快速处理事务. *Proceed with all possible* ~. 火速进行. *a* ~ *carrier* 急件递送员. *the* ~ *of two companies to the front* 派遣两个连上前线. ***be mentioned in* ~*es***【英军】因建立殊勋而在特别通报上受表彰. ***send (sth.) by*** ~ (某物)作快件寄发. ***with*** ~ 火速,从速.—*vt.* ①(火速)发出(信件,电讯等),(急速)送出(公文等),(快速)派出(军队等). ②快办,快速处理,迅速了结;〔口语〕匆匆吃完(饭等). ③调度,调遣. ④(迅速)处决(罪犯等). ~ *troops to the border* 火速向边界派出部队. *spy promptly* ~*ed* 被立即处决的间谍. ~ *business* 赶快办完事情. ~ *a meal* 三口并作两口地把饭吃完. ~ *sb. on an errand* 差遣某人. —*vi.* 〔古〕赶快,匆忙做;就地处决人犯. ~ **boat** (传送公文的)通讯快艇. ~ **box [case]** 公文传送箱. ~ **rider** 骑兵[摩托]通讯员. **-er** *n.* ①(急件等的)发送人. ②(火车,飞机等的)调度员.

dis·pel [dis'pel] *vt.* *(-ll-)* ①驱散(云、雾等). ②消除(疑虑等). ~ *vapors* 驱散雾气. ~ *fears* 打消疑惧. *All doubts are now* ~*ed.* 所有的怀疑这时都一扫而空.

dis·pen·sa·ble [dis'pensəbl] *a.* ①可有可无的,可省的,不重要的. ②(金钱等)可分与的. ③(罪恶等)可恕免的. **-sa·bil·i·ty, -ness** *n.* 可省去,非必需.

dis·pen·sa·ry [dis'pensəri] *n.* ①配药处,药房. ②(免费或降价收费的)施药所. ③诊疗所,门诊部. ④〔美〕(酒类等的)配给处. ~ **system** 〔美〕中央配给制度.

dis·pen·sa·tion [ˌdispen'seiʃən] *n.* ①分配;分与;分配物. ②【医】处方,配方. ③【宗】天道,天命;天启. ④施行,管理,处理;制度,体制. ⑤【天主】(教会当局特许的对法律、誓言等的)豁免. ⑥省却,免除,不用 *(with)*. *under the new* ~ 按照新制度. *the* ~ *of Providence* 天意. *Total* ~ *of cigarettes can be difficult for a habitual smoker.* 吸惯烟的人要做到完全不吸烟不是一件容易的事. **-al·ism** *n.* 天命史观.

dis·pen·sa·to·ry [dis'pensətəri] *n.* ①药谱,药品说明书,药方解说. ②〔古〕药房.

dis·pense [dis'pens] *vt.* ①分配,分给;发放(施舍物等). ②配(药),配(方);发(药). ③施与(恩惠等). ④实施,施行(法律等). ⑤免除,豁免(义务等). ~ *wisdom* 传播智慧. ~ *a prize* 发奖. ~ *the law without bias* 施政公允;执法如山. ~ *a prescription* 配方. —*vi.* 〔古〕免除,特免. ~ ***with*** ①废,罢;省,免除 (*Let us* ~ *with formalities.* 我们别讲客套[免除礼节,节省手续]). ②不需要,没有也行 (*I can* ~ *with an overcoat.* 我没有外套也行). ③豁免 (~ *with a penal statute* 免于按刑法规定追究责任).

dis·pens·er [dis'pensə] *n.* ①药剂师,配药者. ②执行者,管理者. ③分与者;分配器;自动售货机.

dis·peo·ple ['dis'pi:pl] *vt.* = depopulate.

di·sper·mous [dai'spə:məs] *a.*【植】双种子的.

dis·pers·al [dis'pə:səl] *n.* = dispersion.

dis·perse [dis'pə:s] *vt.* ①使疏散,使散开;冲散(敌军等);解散(集会等);驱散(云、雾等). ②传播(知识、病菌等);散布(谣言等);【物】使(光线)色散,使弥散. ~ *the crowd* 驱散人群. *a book* ~*d throughout the world* 传布全世界的一本书. ~ *knowledge* 传播知识. *the fog* ~*d by the wind* 被风驱散的雾气. *Her sweet words* ~*d his melancholy.* 她的温柔话语驱散了他的忧愁. —*vi.* ①散开,分散,散去. ②(云、雾等)消散. *The smoke* ~*d into the sky.* 黑烟在天空中消散. *The crowd* ~*d.* 人群散去了. —*a.* 分散的;【物】弥散的. ~ **system**【化】分散体系. **-r** *n.* ①分散剂. ②(蒸馏塔中的)泡罩. ③扩散器,扩散装置.

dis·pers·ed [dis'pə:st] *a.* 分散的,散开的. ~ *element* (岩石、矿物中包含的)微量元素. ~ *dye* 弥散性染料. **-ly** *ad.* 四散地,散乱地.

dis·per·sion [dis'pə:ʃən] *n.* ①分散,散开;散布,传播;离散. ②【物】弥散,色散;【化】分散作用;被分散物;分散相,分散体系;【医】(炎症等的)消散;【统】离中趋势. ③〔the D-〕(犹太人的)离散异邦. *the* ~ *of heat* 热的扩散. *the* ~ *of an assembly* 集会的解散. ~ ***on the ground*** 炮弹在地面上的散布. ~ **error** (炮弹的)散布偏差. ~ **zone** (炮弹的)散布区,弹着区.

dis·per·sive [dis'pə:siv] *a.* ①散,分散的,散乱的,弥散的,消散性的. ②【物】色散的. *the* ~ *power of a lens* 透镜的色散率. *a* ~ *medium* 扩散媒介. **-ly** *ad.* **-ness** *n.*

dis·per·soid [dis'pə:sɔid] *n.*【化】弥散体,分散体.

dis·pir·it [dis'pirit] *vt.* 使气馁,使沮丧. *be* ~*ed from further exertions by an unexpected blow* 由于在意外的打击下意气沮丧,不想再作进一步的努力. **-ed** *a.* 意气消沉的,垂头丧气的. **-ed·ly** *ad.*

dis·pit·e·ous [dis'pitiəs] *a.* 〔古〕冷酷的,无情的,残忍的.

dis·place [dis'pleis] *vt.* ①换置,移置;顶替,取代. ②取代…的职位;迫使…离家[出国]. ③【化】置换,取代;【海】排(水). ④撤换,把…免职. *The ship* ~*s 500 tons.* 这条船排水量为500吨. *be* ~*d by the invaders* 被侵略者赶出家园. *huge rocks* ~*d by the earthquake* 因地震而移位的巨石. *Fiction* ~*s fact.* 虚构代替了事实. *Jet planes have* ~*d propeller ones.* 喷气式飞机取代了螺旋桨飞机. ~ *an officer from a regiment* 撤换团里的一名军官. ~**d mass**【地】移位岩体. ~**d person**【国际法】(由于战争、政治迫害等被迫离开原居住地或本国的)难民〔略作DP〕. **-r** *n.* ①【化】取代剂,置换剂. ②取代者,取代物. ③【药】过滤器.

dis·place·ment [dis'pleismənt] *n.* ①转位,移动;取代,置换;(人的)流离失所. ②撤换,免职. ③【机】(活塞)排气量;【海】排水量〔一般指军舰的排水量;商船的排水量一般用 gross [net] ton(nage)〕. ④【化】置换(作用),取代(作用);【物】位移;【医】移位;【生】替位;【药】滤过;【地】(断层)移动. ~ *nitration process*【化】取代硝化. ~ **stress**【物】位移应力. ~ **tonnage** 排水吨数.

dis·plant [dis'plɑ:nt] *vt.* 〔废〕移植;移去;移置.

dis·play [dis'plei] *vt.* ①显示;展示,表现出. ②展览,展出,陈列(商品等);展开(旗帜等),摊开(地图等). ③夸示,夸耀. ④【印】(用大号字)醒目地排印. ~ *bravery* 表现出勇气. ~ *fear* 流露出恐惧. ~ *a new automobile* 展出新汽车. ~ *one's learning* 卖弄学问. ~ *a map* 摊开地图. ~ *a sail* 张开风帆. ~ ***one's wares***〔美体俚〕显本领,露一手. —*n.* ①显示;展示. ②展览,陈列. ③显示物;展览品,陈列品. ④夸耀,夸示,虚饰. ⑤【印】醒目排印. ⑥【动】(雄性动物在繁殖期的)求偶夸耀行为. ⑦(用于电视电话、无线电传真等设备上的)显示器. *a great* ~ *of fireworks* 烟火大会. *a notable* ~ *of loyalty* 忠诚的明显表现. *be too fond of* ~ 太好卖弄. *a vulgar* ~ *of wealth* 庸俗地夸耀财富. ~ *flight* 表演飞行. ~ *sensitivity* 指示灵敏度. *make a* ~ *of* 夸耀;显示. *the* ~ *of national flag* 展开国旗. *foreign cars on* ~ 展出的外国汽车. ~ **ad** 〔口〕(有别于分类广告、用醒目大字排印的)普通广告. ~ **type**【印】(排广告等的)醒目大号铅字. ~ **window** 展览橱窗. **-ed** *a.*【纹】(鸟的翼爪等)张开的.

dis·please [dis'pli:z] *vt.* 使不愉快,使不高兴;触怒,使发火. *be* ~*d with the work* 嫌工作不合心意. *be* ~*d at his conduct* 对他的行为感到不愉快. *His reply* ~*d the king.* 他的答复触怒了国王. —*vi.* 令人不快,使人生气. *Bad weather* ~*s.* 恶劣的天气令人不快.

dis·pleas·ing [dis'pli:ziŋ] *a.* 使人不愉快的;令人发火的. *The noise was very* ~ *to him.* 噪音使他非常恼火. **-ly** *ad.*

dis·pleas·ure [dis'pleʒə] *n.* ①不愉快,不满意,不高兴. ②发怒,生气. *incur [arouse] the* ~ *of* 触犯…,得罪…,伤…的感情. *take a* ~ *in...* 对…觉得不高兴[生气].

dis·plode [dis'pləud] *vt., vi.* 〔废〕 = explode.
dis·plume [dis'plu:m] *vt.* 〔诗〕 = deplume.
dis·port [dis'pɔ:t] *vt.* 〔~ oneself〕嬉戏,玩,耍;娱乐. *~ oneself to one's heart's content* 玩个痛快. — *vi.* 玩,游戏,娱乐. *He ~ed among books, radio and tape recorder.* 他以读书、听收音机和录音机自娱.
dis·pos·a·ble [dis'pəuzəbl] *a.* ①可(任意)处理的. ②可自由使用的;可供使用的. *a ~ paper plate* 用一次就扔掉的纸碟. *Every ~ vehicle was sent.* 所有能够用得上的车子都派出去了. — *n.* 〔美口〕使用后随即抛掉的东西(尤指容器等). *Use returnables. Not ~s.* 请使用可回收容器,勿用需要抛掉的容器(以免污染环境). **~ income** 可用收入〔指个人所得纳税以后的部分〕. **~ weight** 飞机上遇紧急情况时可以丢弃的物件重量.
dis·pos·al¹ [dis'pəuzəl] *n.* ①配置,布置,安排. ②处置,处理. ③(财产等的)出售,让与. ④支配权;(自由)处置权,(自由)使用权. *the ~ of troops* 部队的配置. *the ~ of waste material* 废料的处理. *land ~* (放射性废料的)埋入地下. *the king's capricious ~ of offices* 国王授与官职,全凭一时之兴. *~ sth. by sale* 卖掉某物. ***at one's ~*** 随某人自由,由某人随意支配(*My books are at your ~.* 我的书请你随意看好了). ***put [leave] sth. at one's ~*** 把某物交某人自由处理.
dis·pos·al² [dis'pəuzəl] *n.* (厨房)垃圾粉碎机.
dis·pose [dis'pəuz] *vt.* ①安排,配置,布置. ②处置,处理. ③使倾向于,使有意于(*to sth.;to do*). ④〔古〕赋与. *outposts carefully ~d* 小心布置的岗哨. *The lamp was ~d on a table nearby.* 灯配置在附近的桌上. *Your words of cheer ~ me for the task.* 你的打气使我愿意接这项任务了. *He is well [ill] ~d to [towards] me.* 他对我有[没有]好感. — *vi.* 处置,处理;安排(*of*). **~ of** ①处理,处置,安排;解决,办妥(*~ of a business affair* 处理一件事务. *~ of oneself* 安排好自己,设法过日子. *~ of old clothes* 把旧衣服处理掉). ②卖掉,让与(*~ of one's possessions* 卖掉个人的财产). ③除掉,干掉,杀掉(*~ of the mice in the attic* 消灭阁楼上的老鼠). ④吃光,喝光(*~ of some food* 吃一些食品). ***Man proposes, God ~s.*** 谋事在人,成事在天.
dis·posed [dis'pəuzd] *a.* ①已处理了的. ②性情…的. ③有意于…;有…倾向,喜欢…. *ill [well] ~* 脾气坏[好]的. *I am ~ to think so.* 我倾向于这样想,也许是这样. *I'm not ~ to argue with him.* 我不想和他争论. *He is ~ to take offence at trifles.* 他容易为一点小事发脾气. *a man ~ to meditate* 喜欢沉思默想的人.
dis·po·si·tion [ˌdispə'ziʃən] *n.* ①配置,安排;【军】部署,布置;〔*pl.*〕战略[战术]计划. ②处理,处置;处置权,支配权. ③【法】(财产等的)让与. ④性情,素质,气质;性质. ⑤倾向,意向. ⑥〔古〕神意,天命. *a girl with a pleasant ~* 性格开朗的姑娘. *a ~ to gamble* 喜欢赌博. *the ~ of ice to melt when heated* 冰受热即溶解. *the ~ of furniture in the room* 房间里家具的布置. *a fair ~* 处置公平. *the ~ of one's estate* 卖掉不动产. *funds at one's ~* 可自行支配的资金. *the ~ of God* 神意,天命. **-al** *a.*
dis·pos·sess [ˌdispə'zes] *vt.* ①剥夺,使不再占有,霸占(*of*). ②撵走. *~ sb. of land* 夺去某人土地. *~ed refugees living in camps* 被逐出家园、住在帐棚里的难民. *men spiritually ~ed* 精神贫困的人. **-or** *n.* 霸占(他人财产、土地)的人. **-ion** *n.* ①抢夺,霸占,强占. ②驱逐.
dis·po·sure [dis'pəuʒə] *n.*〔古〕①布置;安排;部署. ②管理,处置. ③(财产的)出让. ④免除. ⑤支配权;安置权;管理权;控制. ⑥倾向,意向. ⑦心境;性情;脾气.
dis·praise [dis'preiz] *n., vt.* ①贬损,骂. ②指责. *speak in ~ of…* 指责,非难.
dis·prize [dis'praiz] *vt.* 〔古〕贬价;贱视.
dis·prod·uct [dis'prɔdəkt] *n.* 有害产品(尤指由于生产者的疏忽而造成者).
dis·proof ['dis'pru:f] *n.* ①反证,反驳. ②反证物,反驳的证据.
dis·pro·por·tion ['disprə'pɔ:ʃən] *n.* 不均衡,不相称,不相当,失调. *architectual ~* 建筑上的不均衡. *a supply in ~ with the demand* 供求失调. — *vt.* 使失平衡,使不相称. **-able** *a.* **-al** *a.* = disproportionate. **-a·tion** *n.* 【化】不均衡反应.
dis·pro·por·tion·ate [ˌdisprə'pɔ:ʃənit] *a.* 不均衡的,不匀称的,不相称的. **-ly** *ad.*
dis·prove [dis'pru:v] *vt.* ①证明…不成立,给与…反证. ②驳斥,反驳. *I ~ his claim.* 我证明他提出的索赔要求不能成立.
dis·put·a·ble [dis'pju:təbl] *a.* 有争论余地的,可质疑的(*opp.* indisputable). *~ statements* 可争论的说法.
dis·pu·tant [dis'pju:tənt] *n.* 争论者. — *a.* 争论的.
dis·pu·ta·tion [ˌdispju(:)'teiʃən] *n.* 争论,议论;(大学中的)辩论.
dis·pu·ta·tious [ˌdispju(:)'teiʃəs] *a.* 爱议论的;爱争论的;争论的. *~ litigants* 爱争论的诉讼当事人. **-ly** *ad.* **-ness** *n.*
dis·pu·ta·tive [dis'pju:tətiv] *a.* ①爱争论的,爱争辩的. ②有关争论的.
dis·pute [dis'pju:t] *vt.* ①驳斥,抗辩,对…提出质疑;争论,辩论. ②反对,反抗,阻止. ③争夺(土地、奖品、胜利等). *~ a proposal* 辩论一项建议. *~ a will* 对遗嘱提出质疑. *~ every inch of ground* 寸土必争. *~ the enemy's advance* 阻止敌人推进. *~ a victory [prize] with sb.* 和某人争夺胜利[奖品]. — *vi.* ①辩论,争论. ②争吵. *~ with [against] sb. over [on, about] sth.* 与某人争论某事. *~ as to who is the greatest English poet* 争论谁是最伟大的英国诗人. — *n.* 议论,争论;辩驳,抗辩;争吵;争端. *a bitter [hot] ~* 激烈的争论. *boundary ~* 边界纠纷. *a labour ~* 劳资纠纷,工潮. ***beyond [past, without, out of] ~*** 无争论余地;的确,无疑. ***in [under] ~*** (在)争论中的,未决的(*a point in ~*争端). **dis·put·a·tive** *a.* = disputatious. **-r** *n.* 争论者,争辩者.
dis·qual·i·fi·ca·tion [disˌkwɔlifi'keiʃən] *n.* ①无资格,不合格;取消资格. ②使不合格的事物[原因]. *His ~ for the team was a bad knee.* 他没有资格参加运动队是因为膝关节有毛病. *~ from office* 没有资格担任公职.
dis·qual·i·fy [dis'kwɔlifai] *vt.* 使无资格,使不合格;使不能;【体】取消…的比赛资格. *Age disqualified him for the job.* 年岁过大使他失去做这项工作的资格[能力等]. *disqualified sb. from being a witness* 使某人失去充当证人的资格. *~ him from further participation in the game* 取消某人继续参加比赛的资格.
dis·qui·et [dis'kwaiət] *vt.* 使不安,使忧虑,使烦恼. *~ing rumours* 扰乱人心的谣言. *My heart is ~ed.* 我心中不安. — *n.* 不安,不平静,忧虑,烦恼. *be filled with ~* 满心不安,满腹烦恼. *An uncertain but unceasing ~ is upon me.* 不知道什么缘故,我始终觉得心里七上八下的. **-ly** *ad.*
dis·qui·e·tude [dis'kwaiitju:d] *n.* 不安;忧虑.
dis·qui·si·tion [ˌdiskwi'ziʃən] *n.* ①专题论文;学术讲演. ②〔古〕(有系统的)研究. *~ on [about] a question* 关于某一问题的专题论文.
Dis·rae·li [diz'reili] *n.* ①迪斯雷利〔姓氏〕. ②**Benjamin ~** 本杰明·迪斯雷利〔1804—1888,英国著名政治家,小说家〕.
dis·rate [dis'reit] *vt.* 降价;降等;降级. *~ an officer* 把一个军官降职.
dis·re·gard ['disri'gɑ:d] *vt.* ①不理,不顾,不管. ②蔑视,轻视. *D- the footnotes.* 别去管那些脚注. *Disregarding both hunger and fatigue, I traveled forward.* 我不顾饥饿和疲劳,继续向前走. *~ an invitation* 不把邀请放在心上. — *n.* 不理,不顾;蔑视,轻视. *have a total ~ for rank* 不计较地位. *This order was in ~ of the Constitution.* 这项

命令置宪法于不顾. **-ful** *a.* 轻视,忽视;不顾.

dis·rel·ish [dis'reliʃ] *n.* 嫌恶,不喜欢,讨厌 *(for)*. *have a ~ for raw fish* 不喜欢吃生鱼. — *vt.* 嫌,讨厌.

dis·re·mem·ber [ˌdisri'membə] *vt.* 〔口〕〔美方〕忘记,忘掉.

dis·re·pair ['disri'pɛə] *n.* 失修,破损. *be in (a state of) ~* (房屋等)年久失修,破损. *These houses have been allowed to fall into ~.* 听凭这些房屋破损.

dis·rep·u·ta·ble [dis'repjutəbl] *a.* ①名誉不好的,声名狼藉的. ②不体面的,丢脸的. ③破烂不堪的,难看的. *He looked ~ in his gray three days beard.* 他的灰白胡子三天没有刮,看起来不象样子. **-ta·bil·i·ty** *n.* 声名狼藉 (*a man of disreputability* 声明狼藉的人). **-ness** *n.*

dis·re·pute ['disri'pju:t] *n.* 坏名声,声名狼藉;不体面,丢脸. ***be in ~*** 名声不好. ***bring a man into ~*** 使人声誉扫地. ***incur ~*** 招来坏名声,招来恶名. ***fall into ~*** 名誉变坏.

dis·re·spect ['disris'pekt] *n.* 失礼,失敬,无礼. *show ~ for one's seniors* 对长辈[上级]不尊重. — *vt.* 不尊敬,不尊重. *~ the law* 不尊重法律. **-able** *a.* 不值得尊敬的. **-ful** *a.* 不敬的,失礼的,无礼的 (*a disrespectful remark about teachers* 对老师不尊重地乱加议论). **-ful·ly** *ad.* 失礼地;无礼地.

dis·robe ['dis'rəub] *v.* = undress.

dis·root [dis'ru:t] *vt.* 连根拔除,消除. *replace a ~ed tree* 移植一棵连根拔起的树.

dis·rupt [dis'rʌpt] *vt.* ①使分裂,使瓦解;破坏,使混乱. ②打断,使中断. *The war ~ed the society.* 战争使社会陷入混乱. *Telephone service was ~ed for hours.* 电话中断了好几个小时. — *a.* 混乱的;瓦解的;中断的. **-er, -or** *n.* 造成混乱[破坏、分裂]者.

dis·rup·tion [dis'rʌpʃən] *n.* 分裂,破裂,瓦解;中断. *the ~ of rock* 岩石的破裂. *family ~* 家庭破裂. *The state was in ~.* 国家处于分崩离析之中. **the D-** (1843年苏格兰教会的)大分裂.

dis·rup·tive [dis'rʌptiv] *a.* 分裂(性)的;破裂的;破坏性的. *~ activities* 破坏活动. *~* **discharge**【物】破裂放电,火花放电. **-ly** *ad.*

dis·rup·ture [dis'rʌptʃə] *n.* = disruption.

dis·sat·is·fac·tion ['disˌsætis'fækʃən] *n.* ①不满,不平 *(with, at)*. ②令人不满的事物. *~ with the present world* 对世道的不满.

dis·sat·is·fac·to·ry ['disˌsætis'fæktəri] *a.* 令人不满的,使人不平的. *~ service* 令人不满的服务.

dis·sat·is·fy ['dis'sætisfai] *vt.* 使不满,使失望,使不平,使不服〔通常多用被动语气〕. *a ~ing book* 一部不能令人满意的书. ***be dissatisfied with [at]*** 不满于,对…不满. **-fied** *a.* 不满意的,不愉快的.

dis·seat [dis'si:t] *vt.* 〔古〕= unseat.

dis/sec = disintegrations per second【物】衰变/秒.

dis·sect [di'sekt] *vt.* ①解剖;剖开,切开;【地】分割. ②仔细分析. *~ed map* 明细地图. *~ed plateau*【地】切割台地. *~ an idea* 仔细分析一种思想. — *vi.* ①进行解剖. ②进行仔细分析. *~ed leaf*【植】深裂[多裂]叶. *~***ing knife [room]**【医】解剖刀[室]. **-ible** *a.* 可解剖的,可仔细分析的.

dis·sec·tion [di'sekʃən] *n.* ①解剖;【地】切割作用. ②详细分析. ③解剖标本;【商英】分类. *~ of a human body* 人体解剖. *image ~*【物】析象,图象分析.

dis·sec·tor [di'sektə] *n.* ①解剖者;解剖学家. ②解剖用具. ③分析者. *~* **tube**【物】析象管 (= image ~).

dis·seise, dis·seize ['dis'si:z] *vt.*【法】霸占,强夺 *(of)*. *~ sb. of his estate* 强占某人不动产.

dis·sei·see, dis·sei·zee [ˌdissi:'zi:] *n.*【法】被强夺者,被侵占者.

dis·sei·sin, dis·sei·zin [dis'si:zin] *n.*【法】霸占,侵占.

dis·sei·sor, dis·sei·zor [dis'si:zə] *n.*【法】强夺者,侵占者.

dis·sem·ble [di'sembl] *vt.* ①掩饰(感情、动机等). ②假装. ③假装不见. *~ one's incompetence* 掩饰自己的无能. *~ innocence* 装出清白无辜的样子. — *vi.* ①掩饰;作伪,作假. ②假装不知,装聋作哑. **-r** *n.* 作伪者,伪君子.

dis·sem·i·nate [di'semineit] *vt.* ①撒,播(种). ②传播,散布,普及. *the idea ~d by the newspaper* 报纸宣扬的观点. *~ Christianity* 传播基督教. — *vi.* 广为传播. **dis·sem·i·na·tion** [diˌsemi'neiʃən] *n.* 播种;传播,散布. **-na·tor** *n.* 播种者,撒种者;传播者,散布者.

dis·sen·sion [di'senʃən] *n.* ①(意见等的)不一致,分歧. ②不合;冲突,倾轧,纠纷. *sow ~s among...* 在…当中挑拨离间. *~ between the two nations* 两国之间的纷争.

dis·sent [di'sent] *vi.* ①持异议,有不同意见 *(from)*. ②〔英〕不信奉国教 *(from)*. *~ from sb. [sb.'s views]* 不同意某人的观点. *pass without a ~ing voice* 一致通过. *~ from the Church of England* 不信奉英国国教. — *n.* ①不同意,异议 *(from)*. ②〔英〕反对国教;〔集合词〕不信奉国教者. *None of them dares even mutter ~.* 没有人敢说半个不字. **-er** *n.* 反对者;持异议者,持不同政见者;〔英〕〔通例 Dissenter〕不信奉国教者.

dis·sen·ti·ent [di'senʃiənt] *a.* 不同意的. *The bill passed with one ~ vote.* 议案以一票反对被通过. — *n.* 不同意,异议;持不同意见者.

dis·sen·tious [di'senʃəs] *a.* 不和的,好争吵的;闹倾轧的.

dis·sep·i·ment [di'sepimənt] *n.*【植、动】隔膜,隔壁;(植物的)子房中隔.

dis·sert [di'sə:t], **dis·ser·tate** ['disəteit] *vi.* 论述,论说;写论文,讲演.

dis·ser·ta·tion [ˌdisə(:)'teiʃən] *n.* (专题)论述;论文,学位论文;学术讲演. *a doctoral ~* 博士学位论文.

dis·serve ['dis'sə:v] *vt.* 损害,伤害,危害. *~ the society* 危害社会.

dis·serv·ice ['dis'sə:vis] *n.* 损害,伤害,危害. *They do a great ~ to our society.* 他们给我们的社会带来很大危害.

dis·sev·er [dis'sevə] *vt.* 分裂,分离;分割. *~ a chicken* 把鸡斩成小块. *A quarrel ~ed the two friends.* 一场争吵使两个朋友绝交了. — *vi.* 分离,分手. **-ance** [-'sevərəns], **-ment** *n.*

dis·si·dence ['disidəns] *n.* (意见等的)不同,不一致,异议. *political ~* 政治意见的不同. **dis·si·dent** ['disidənt] ① *a.* 持不同意见的(人) (*opinions dissident from ours* 和我们不同的意见). ②*n.* 持不同意见者.

dis·sight [dis'sait] *n.* 〔罕〕难看的东西.

dis·sim·i·lar [di'similə] *a.* 不同的,不一样的 *(to, from, with)*. *The end would be ~ to the beginning.* 结局将不同于开始. **-ly** *ad.*

dis·sim·i·lar·i·ty [ˌdisimi'læriti] *n.* 不同,不相似;异点. *There are dissimilarities in our outlooks.* 我们的相貌有许多不同点.

dis·sim·i·late [di'simileit] *vt.* ①使不同,使有异点. ②【语】使异化. — *vi.* ①不同,有异点. ②【语】异化.

dis·sim·i·la·tion ['disimi'leiʃən] *n.* ①相异,异化(过程、作用、现象). ②【生】异化作用 (= catabolism);【语】(音的)异化 *(opp.* assimilation*)*.

dis·si·mil·i·tude [ˌdisi'militju:d] *n.* 相异,不同,异点;【修】对比.

dis·sim·u·late [di'simjuleit] *vt.* 假装(镇静),掩饰(感情等). *~ fear* 掩饰恐惧,强作镇静. — *vi.* 作伪,作假. **-la·tion** *n.* **-la·tor** *n.* = dissembler.

dis·si·pate ['disipeit] *vt.* ①使(云雾等)消散,驱散(忧虑等). ②浪费(时间等),挥霍(金钱等). *~ the mist* 驱散雾气. *~ the enemy force* 驱散敌军. *~ sorrows* 消除忧愁. *~ one's energy* 浪掷精力. — *vi.* ①消散;【化】散逸.

②放荡；浪费. *They ~ all night and sleep all day.* 他们白天睡觉，通夜鬼混. *Her anger was dissipating.* 她渐渐息怒. **-ed** *a.* ①被驱散的，【化】散失的. ②浪费掉的. ③放荡的. **-r, -tor** *n.* 浪子，败家子.

dis·si·pa·tion [ˌdisiˈpeiʃən] *n.* ①消散，分散；【化】散逸. ②浪费；消耗，损耗. ③放荡，闲游浪荡. ④消遣，娱乐. *the ~ of a fortune* 挥霍. *the ~ of one's time* 浪费时间，虚度光阴. *My only ~ is angling.* 钓鱼是我唯一的消遣. ~ **trail** 【空】(喷气式飞机飞过后留下的) 消散痕迹.

dis·si·pa·tive [ˌdisiˈpeitive] *a.* ①消散的. ②消耗(性)的，浪费的. ③放荡的. ~ *element* 【无】耗能元件.

dis·so·cia·ble [diˈsəuʃiəbl] *a.* ①可分离的；易分离的. ②不调和的. ③[diˈsəuʃəbl] 不爱交际的. *Worthy and unworthy motives are often not ~.* 高尚和不高尚的动机不是时常能够区别开来的.

dis·so·cial [diˈsəuʃəl] *a.* ①反社会的；自私的. ②不爱交际的，孤僻的. *solitary ~ habits* 与世寡合的孤僻性格.

dis·so·cial·ize [diˈsəuʃiəlaiz] *vt.* 使不爱交际，使孤僻.

dis·so·ci·ate [diˈsəuʃieit] *vt.* ①使分离，使脱离 *(from)*. ②【化】使离解；【心】分裂(意识等). ~ *the two ideas* 分开两种观念. ~ *oneself from the evil in one's past* 改邪归正. *It's difficult to ~ the man from his position.* 一想到这个人，就很难不同时想起他的职位. *~d personality* 【心】分裂人格. — *vi.* ①分离，游离. ②【化】离解.

dis·so·ci·a·tion [diˌsəusiˈeiʃən] *n.* ①分解，分裂；分离. ②【生】离异，分化变异(体)；【化】离解(作用)；【心】分裂；【统】不相联. *the ~ of church and state* 政教分离. ~ *of ideas* 观念的不相联. *electrolytic ~* 【物】电离(作用).

dis·so·ci·a·tive [diˈsəuʃiətiv] *a.* ①使分离的，分裂性的. ②【化】离解的；【心】分裂的；【生】离异的. ~ *capture* 【化】离解俘获.

dis·sol·uble [diˈsɔljubl] *a.* ①可分解的，可分离的；(机构等)可解散的. ②(婚约、职务等)可解除的；(财产等)可清算的，(法律等)可取消的. ③可溶解的，可液化的，可融解的. *Sugar is ~ in water.* 糖溶于水.

dis·sol·u·bil·i·ty [diˌsɔljuˈbiliti] *n.* 可溶性；溶(解)度.

dis·so·lute [ˈdisəlјu:t] *a.* 放荡的；自甘堕落的. *a ~ crew [set of people]* 一群荒淫放荡的男女. *a brilliant and ~ writer* 才气焕发而放荡不羁的[有才无德的]作家. **-ly** *ad.* **-ness** *n.*

dis·so·lu·tion [ˌdisəˈlјu:ʃən] *n.* ①分解，分离. ②溶解(作用)，融化，液化. ③(婚约等的)取消，(职务等的)解除，(法律等的)废除；(公司等的)解散. ④(财产等的)清算；(债务等的)结清. ⑤(机能等的)消失，消亡，死亡. ⑥腐朽，崩溃，解体. ⑦〔废〕放荡. *the ~ of the partnership* 合伙关系的取消. *the ~ of Parliament* 解散议会. *the ~ of the Republic* 共和国的崩溃. *the ~ of the body* 尸体的腐烂.

dis·solv·a·ble [diˈzɔlvəbl] *a.* ①可分解的. ②可溶(解)的. ③可解散的. **-ness, -a·bil·i·ty** [diˌzɔlvəˈbiliti] *n.* 可溶性.

dis·solve [diˈzɔlv] *vt.* ①溶，使溶解，使融化，使液化. ②使分解，使分离. ③解散(议会等)；【法】废除，撤消(法令等)，取消(契约等)，解除(婚约等). ④摧毁(希望等)，打破(魔法等)，揭开(秘密等)，解开(谜语等). ⑤使感动，软化. ⑥使(电影，电视画面)渐隐，使溶暗. ~ *salt in water* 使盐溶于水. ~ *sugar into syrup* 使糖融化为糖浆. ~ *a bond* 解除契约. ~ *Parliament* 解散议会. ~ *sb.'s hopes* 使某人的希望破灭. ~ *a spell* 破除魔法，解除符咒的魔力. ~ *a marriage* 解除婚约. ~ *the injunction* 取消禁令. ~ *partnership* 散伙，拆伙. *Time ~s all things.* 时光使一切事物都难以永存. *be ~d in tears* 因感动而流泪. ~ *one scene into another* 使(电影、电视等的)一个画面逐渐化入另一画面. — *vi.* ①分解；崩溃. ②溶解；融化. ③(议会等)解散；(婚约等)失效；(幻影等)消失. ④动感情，软化. ⑤(电影、电视等画面)渐隐，溶暗. *Sugar ~in liquid.* 糖溶于液体. *Ice ~s in the sun.* 冰在阳光下融化. *The assembly ~d.* 集会解散了. *Society must disintegrate once the family ~s.* 一旦家庭解体，社会也就必定崩溃. *She ~d in tears.* 她感动得泪流满面. ~ *into water* 溶化成水. ~ *into air* 在空气中消失. ~ ***out [in]*** (电影、电视等画面) 溶出［入］，化出［入］. — *n.*【影】(电影、电视等画面的)渐隐，溶暗. **dissolving views**【影】渐隐画面.

dis·solv·ent [diˈzɔlvənt] *a., n.* = solvent.

dis·so·nance [ˈdisənəns], **dis·so·nan·cy** [-si] *n.* ①不一致，不和谐. ②【乐】不协和音. ③倾轧，不和 *(opp.* consonance*)*. *cognitive ~* 认识上的分歧.

dis·so·nant [ˈdisənənt] *a.* ①不调和的；不一致的. ②【乐】不协和的；刺耳的. ③倾轧的，不和的. ~ *and loud voices* 又响又刺耳的声音. **-ly** *ad.*

dis·suade [diˈsweid] *vt.* 劝阻，劝止，劝戒 *(from)*. ~ *a friend from joining a society* 劝阻朋友不参加某团体. *She was ~d from leaving home.* 她受到劝阻，没有离家出走.

dis·sua·sion [diˈsweiʒən] *n.* 劝诫，告诫，制止.

dis·sua·sive [diˈsweisiv] *a.* 劝诫的，劝阻的，告戒的. *be ~ of* 劝止. *make ~ gestures* 用手势劝阻. **-ly** *ad.* **-ness** *n.*

dis·syl·lab·ic [ˈdisiˈlæbik] *a.*【语】双音节的.

dis·syl·la·ble [diˈsiləbl] *n.*【语】双音节词，双音节式.

dis·sym·met·ri·c(al) [ˈdissiˈmetrik(əl)] *a.* ①非对称的，不匀称的. ②(镜面内外、左右手等)相反对称的. ③【化】对映形态的.

dis·sym·me·try [ˈdisˈsimitri] *n.* ①非对称(现象). ②(镜面内外、左右手等的)相反对称. ③【化】对映形态.

dist. = distance; distant; distinguish(ed); distributed; distribution.

dis·taff [ˈdistɑ:f] *n.* ①(手工纺织用的)卷线杆. ②针线活，女活，妇女工作，妇道. ③〔集合词〕女性. ④女人. ~ *side* 母方，母系 *(opp.* spear side*)*. — *a.* 〔书〕女子的，女性的，妇道的. *cooking, sewing and such ~ matters* 做饭缝衣这类女活. **-er** *n.* 家庭中的女性.

dis·tal [ˈdistəl] *a.*【解】远端的，远侧的；末端的，末梢(部)的；【植】远基的，远轴的. *the ~ end of a bone* 骨头的末端部位. ~ **bite**【牙科】远心咬合.

dis·tance [ˈdistəns] *n.* ①距离，路程. ②远隔，远离；远处，远方. ③(时间的)间隔，长远，长久. ④悬殊. ⑤隔阂，疏远. ⑥【音】(二音间的)音程；【绘】远景；【拳击】规定的比赛时间. *The ~ between the two houses was exactly one mile.* 两座房屋正好相隔一英里. *What's the ~ from here to the station?* 从这里到车站有多远? *It's quite a ~ from here.* 离这里远得很. *A vast ~ of water surrounded the ship.* 船的四周都是辽阔的水面. *Every sound carries a great ~.* 每一种声音都传到远处. *the ~ between birth and death* 从生到死的这段时间. *a ~ of a century* 一世纪的间隔，经过一世纪. *Our philosophies are a long ~ apart.* 我们的哲学观点相去悬殊. *stare into the ~* 向远方凝视. *the extreme [middle] ~* (绘画的)远[中]景. *treat sb. with a little ~* 有点冷淡地对待某人. ***a good ~ off*** 很远，远隔着. ***at a ~*** 隔开一段距离，留有间隔，不挨近(*look to advantage at a ~*远看为好). ***at a respectful ~*** 敬而远之. ***at this ~ of time*** 经过这样长一段时间 (*It's impossible to judge at this ~ of time.* 经过这样长一段时间以后，再想作出判断是不可能的了.) ***be a great ~ away*** 离得很远. ***be out of (striking) ~ (from...)*** 太远，难(打)到. ***be within striking [hailing, hearing] ~*** (在)能打到［听到］(的地方). ***from a ~*** 从远方 (*It's a very beautiful house, especially from a ~.* 这是一所漂亮的房子，从远处看尤其如此). ***go [last] the ~*** 做完，坚持干到最后一次. ***in the ~*** 在远处，在很远的那边. ***Keep at a ~!*** 别靠近！ ***keep ~*** 留间隔. ***keep***

sb. at a ~ 与某人保持相当距离，敬而远之，疏远. ***keep one's*** ~ 避开,不接近 (*Keep your ~ from him.* 你不要接近他). ***know one's*** ~ 知分寸,守本分. ***to a*** ~ 到远方 (*spread to a ~* 伸展到远方). ***within*** ... ~ 在…距离内 (*within jumping ~* 在跳得到的地方). — *vt.* ①隔开，把…放在一定距离之外；使显得遥远. ②超过，赶过；胜过；(比赛中)把…甩在后面. *~ one's competitors* (竞赛中)把对手远远地甩在后面. *I feel I'm ~ed by him in every respect.* 我感到自己在各方面都赶不上他了. ~ **made good**【海】直航距离〔从船经过的某一点至其现在位置之间的距离，以海里表示〕. ~ **post** (赛马时用的)距离标杆. ~ **recorder**【无】遥测记录器.

dis·tant [ˈdistənt] *a.* ①远,远方的,远离的,远隔的；相距(若干路程)的. ②冷淡的,疏远的,有隔阂的. ③(亲戚)远族的,远房的；(朋友等)泛泛之交的，交情不深的. ④隐约的,不清晰的. *a ~ place* 远方. *a ~ view* 远景. *a ~ letter* 来自远方的信. *a ~ sound* 远处传来的声音. *~ ages* 往昔. *~ centuries past* 经过多少世纪. *10 miles ~ from here* 离这里十英里. *a ~ voyage* 远航. *a ~ politeness* 敬而远之. *a ~ air [manner]* 冷淡的态度. *a ~ connection [relative]* 远亲. *a ~ acquaintance* 点头之交. *one's ~ youth* 早已逝去的青年时期. *a ~ likeness [resemblance]* 约略相似. ***at no ~ date*** 不日,日内. ~ ***crossing [hybridization]***【植】远缘杂交. ***have not the most ~ idea (of a matter)*** 很不明白(某事). ***make a ~ allusion*** 迂回曲折地暗示. ~ **signal**【铁道】预告信号. **-ly** *ad.* 远地,遥远地(*be distantly related to* 和…是远亲).

dis·taste [ˈdisˈteist] *n.* 厌恶；不爱吃〔喝〕*(for)*. *He had hearty ~ for songs of pathos.* 他极不爱听感伤歌曲. *have a ~ for fish* 不爱吃鱼.

dis·taste·ful [disˈteistful] *a.* ①味道不好的，不合口味的. ②令人不愉快的,令人讨厌的 *(to)*. *a ~ medicine* 苦口的药. *I find him ~.* 我发现他很讨厌. *Drinking is ~ to me.* 我不喜欢喝酒. **-ly** *ad.* **-ness** *n.*

Dist. Atty. = District Attorney 〔美〕地方检察官.

Dist. Ct. = District Court 地方法院.

dis·tem·per[1] [disˈtempə] *n.* ①【兽医】犬瘟热；马腺疫；兽类传染性卡他. ②疾病〔尤指兽类疾病〕；不健康；(精神状态)不正常. ③(社会的)不安，骚动. *political ~* 政治骚乱. — *vt.* ①使(精神等)失常，使(机能等)失调〔常用被动语态〕. ②在…中造成动乱. *a ~ed fancy [illusion]* 由疾病引起的幻觉.

dis·tem·per[2] [disˈtempə] *n.* ①(壁画等用的)色粉颜料，胶画颜料. ②【化】水浆涂料. ③胶画. — *vt.* ①用胶画颜料画；用胶画颜料涂(壁等). ②用胶状物调制(颜料)，把(蛋黄、胶水、颜料等)调制成胶画颜料.

dis·tend [disˈtend] *vi.* 扩张；膨胀. *The sea ~ed about them.* 海水在他们周围上涨. *Habitual overeating has ~ed his stomach.* 经常大吃大喝把他的胃口撑大了.

dis·ten·si·ble [disˈtensəbl] *a.* 会膨胀的. **-bil·i·ty** *n.* 膨胀性,可张性.

dis·ten·sion, dis·ten·tion [disˈtenʃən] *n.* 膨胀(作用)，胀大. *~ of the abdomen* 腹部的胀大.

dis·thene [ˈdisθiːn] *n.*【矿】蓝晶石.

dis·tich [ˈdistik] *n.*【韵】(诗中押韵的)对联,对句.

dis·tich·ous [ˈdistikəs] *a.*【植】对生的，双列的.【动】(触角等) 双节的. *~ leaves*【植】双列叶. *~ antennae*【动】双节触角.

dis·til(l) [disˈtil] *vt.* ①蒸馏；用蒸馏法制造，用蒸馏法提取；蒸馏出 *(off; out)*. ②提取…的精华. ③使滴下. *~ whiskey from mash* 用麦芽汁蒸馏威士忌酒. *~ gasoline from crude oil* 从原油中蒸馏汽油. *~ out impurities* 蒸馏出杂质. *The cool of the night ~ the dew.* 深夜的寒气凝成露珠. *~ed liquors* 烧酒. *~ed water* 蒸馏水. *~ one's style* 使文体简洁. *A proverb ~s the wisdom of ages.* 谚语是许多世纪智慧的精华. — *vi.* ①蒸馏. ②滴下,渗出；凝成水滴. *Some water ~ed over the rocks from the moist undergrowth.* 岩石下潮湿的草丛使石上渗出水滴.

dis·til·land [ˈdistilænd] *n.*【化】被蒸馏物.

dis·till·ate [ˈdistilit, ˈdistileit] *n.* ①蒸馏液,馏出物. ②浓缩物；精华. *the ~ of their wisdom* 他们的智慧的精华，他们的心血结晶.

dis·til·la·tion [ˌdistiˈleiʃən] *n.* ①蒸馏(作用)；蒸馏法. ②蒸馏液；蒸馏物. ③精华，精萃. *dry [destructive] ~*【化】干馏(法). *fractional ~*【化】分馏,分解蒸馏(法). ~ **column [tower]** 蒸馏塔. ~ **plant** 蒸馏设备. ~ **yield** 馏出体积.

dis·til·la·to·ry [disˈtilətəri] *a.* 蒸馏(用)的. *a ~ vessel* 蒸馏器皿. — *n.* 蒸馏器；蒸馏场所.

dis·till·er [disˈtilə] *n.* ①蒸馏者. ②制酒者. ③蒸馏器. *a whiskey ~* 威士忌酒制造者. *~'s grain [solubles]* 酒糟.

dis·till·er·y [disˈtiləri] *n.* ①蒸馏室. ②酒厂.

dis·til(l)·ment [disˈtilmənt] *n.* 〔古〕蒸馏,蒸馏物,蒸馏液.

dis·tinct [disˈtiŋkt] *a.* ①独特的，性质，不同的 *(from)*. ②清楚的,明显的；明确的；显著的. ③难得的,不同寻常的. ④〔诗、古〕修饰过的；富于变化的. *things similar in effect but wholly ~ in motive* 效果相似而动机不同的东西. *Gold is ~ from iron.* 金子和铁不同. *a neat ~ handwriting* 字迹清楚. *a ~ pronunciation* 发音清晰. *a ~ improvement of living conditions* 生活条件的显著改善. *His praise is a ~ honour* 得到他的夸奖是一项难得的荣誉. ~ **roots**【数】相异根,不等根. **-ly** *ad.* 清楚地,显然(*be -ly audible* 声音清晰). **-ness** *n.*

dis·tinc·tion [disˈtiŋkʃən] *n.* ①差别，区别；区分. ②特征,特性,个性. ③优越,卓越；盛名. ④殊勋，大功，荣誉；勋章，荣誉称号. ⑤【电视】清晰度. ⑥〔废〕分割，分离. *His ~ of sounds is excellent.* 他辨别声音的能力很强. *a ~ between what he says and what he does* 他的言行不一. *There is no ~ in his appearance.* 他的面貌没有什么特殊的地方. *Death comes to all without ~.* 人皆有一死. *draw [make] a clear ~ between right and wrong* 辨别是非〔忠奸，正邪〕. *gain [win] ~* 出名，立功. *graduate from college with ~* 以优异成绩毕业. *serve with ~ in the war* 立下战功. *rise to ~* 出名. *a poet of ~* 名诗人.

dis·tinc·tive [disˈtiŋktiv] *a.* ①区别的，鉴别性的. ②独特的,有特色的. *the ~ stripes of the zebra* 斑马身上独特的条纹. ~ **feature**【语】示差特征. **-ly** *ad.* **-ness** *n.* 独特性.

dis·tin·gué [disˈtæŋgei] *a.* 〔F.〕(风度、服饰、容貌等) 高贵的,高雅的,雍容华贵的. *a rather ~ foreign diplomat* 一位风度高雅的异国外交官.

dis·tin·guish [disˈtiŋgwiʃ] *vt.* ①区别；辨别，识别，判别. ②(通过耳、目等)辨认出. ③把…分类. ④使具有特色；使显著,使触目〔通常用 ~ oneself〕. *~ the sound of piano in an orchestra* 在乐队合奏中分辨出钢琴的声音. *~ good from evil* 分别善恶. *~ her from her sister* 辨别出她和她的妹妹. *I can't ~ things so far.* 那么远的东西我可分不清. *the geniality that ~ed him* 他那特有的亲切风度. *be ~ed for one's vices* 恶名昭著. *~ oneself in battle* 作战勇敢，战功卓著. *~ oneself by scholarship* 学问超群. *Let us ~ the various types of metaphor.* 我们把各种譬喻加以分类. — *vi.* 区别,辨别；识别. *His mind could no longer ~ between illusion and reality.* 他的头脑已经不再能分清幻觉和现实. **-able** *a.* 可区别的,可辨别的；(通过耳、目等)可以辨认出的.

dis·tin·guish·ed [disˈtiŋgwiʃt] *a.* ①卓越的，卓著的. ②以…出名的. ③高贵的；(服饰、气度等) 高雅的. *a ~ scholar* 知名学者. *a ~ old gentleman* 一位气度不凡的老先生. ~ **marksman** 特等射手. ~ **services** 特殊的功劳〔贡献〕. **D- Conduct Medal** 〔英军〕殊功勋章. **D-Service Order**【美陆军】殊勋〔金十字〕勋章.

dis·tome [ˈdistəum] *n.*【动】双盘吸虫〔肝蛭,肺蛭等〕.
dis·to·mi·a·sis [ˌdistəˈmaiəsis] *n.*【医】双盘吸虫病.
dis·tort [disˈtɔːt] *vt.* ①使歪扭,弄歪(嘴脸、手足等). ②曲解,歪曲(事实等). ③使不正常. ④【电】使失真. *a mirror which ~s the features* 使人变相的镜,哈哈镜. *face ~ed with rage* 脸气得变了样. *~ the facts* 歪曲事实. *Arthritis ~ed his wrists.* 关节炎使他的手腕扭曲了. **-ed** *a.* 歪曲的;扭歪的;偏颇的. **-ed·ly** [-ˈtɔːtidli] *ad.* 被歪曲地.
dis·tor·tion [disˈtɔːʃən] *n.* ①歪扭,扭曲. ②【电】(信号、波形等的)失真;【物】(透镜成像产生的)畸变;【医】扭转,变形. ③窜改,歪曲,曲解. *a gross ~ of the news* 大肆歪曲的报道. *frequency ~*【无】频率失真. *undergo a sudden ~* (脸等)突然变形. **-al** *a.*
dis·tor·tion·ist [disˈtɔːʃənist] *n.* ①漫画家. ②擅长柔软体操〔武艺、杂技〕的人.
dis·tract [disˈtrækt] *vt.* ①分散(注意力等), 岔开(念头等) (*opp.* attract). ②〔多用被动语态〕弄昏;使发狂,使精神错乱. ③娱乐, 消遣. *Reading ~s the mind from grief.* 读书解忧. *The music ~ed him from his work.* 乐声使他不能专心工作. *I'm ~ed with [by] anxiety.* 我焦急得发狂. *Grief drived him ~ed.* 悲伤使他发狂. *~ oneself by talking* 闲谈消遣. *I'm bored with bridge, but golf still ~s me.* 我已经玩厌了桥牌,但是还喜欢玩高尔夫球.
dis·tract·ed [disˈtræktid] *a.* ①分神的,分散注意力的. ②心烦意乱的,精神失常的,发狂的. *lend a very ~ attention.* 根本心不在焉. *the ~ mother whose child had fallen ill* 因孩子生病而急得发狂的母亲. **-ly** *ad.*
dis·tract·ing·ly [disˈtræktiŋli] *a.* ①使人精神涣散的,使人分心的. ②使人心烦意乱的,使人发狂的.
dis·trac·tion [disˈtrækʃən] *n.* ①精神涣散,分心;使人分心的事情. ②心乱,心烦; 发狂, 精神错乱. ③消遣; 娱乐. *a good place to study, free from ~* 一个不使人分心的良好的学习场所. *be driven to ~ by love* 爱得发狂. *The child will drive me to ~.* 这孩子闹得简直要使我发狂. *He listened with ~.* 他心不在焉地听着. *Fishing is his major ~.* 钓鱼是他的主要娱乐. *without ~* ①全神贯注地,不分心地. ②心不乱地.
dis·train [disˈtrein] *vt.*【法】(为赔偿损失、担保债务等)扣押(财物). *~ goods for an amercement* 为罚款而扣押财物. — *vi.*【法】扣押 *(on; upon)*. **-ment** *n.*
dis·train·ee [ˌdistreiˈniː] *n.*【法】财物被扣押者.
dis·train·er, dis·train·or [disˈtreinə, ˌdistreiˈnɔː] *n.*【法】扣押他人财物者.
dis·traint [disˈtreint] *n.*【法】扣押财物(行动, 处分).
dis·trait [disˈtrei] *a.* 〔F.〕(因烦恼、忧惧等而)心不在焉的〔形容女性时用 distraite〕.
dis·traught [disˈtrɔːt] *a.* 心神错乱的;发狂的. *~ with terror* 恐怖得发狂.
dis·tress [disˈtres] *n.* ①苦恼,烦恼;悲痛,悲叹; 使人悲痛〔苦恼〕的事情;(肉体的)苦痛. ②贫苦,穷困. ③灾殃,危难,不幸;【海】海难. ④【英法】扣押财物; 被扣押的财物. *feel acute ~ at...* 对…深感苦恼〔悲痛〕. *relieve ~ among the poor* 减轻穷人的痛苦. *an old story of a damel in ~.* 少女落难之类老一套的故事. *a ship in ~* 失事的船只. *a signal of ~* 遇难信号. *levy a ~ upon* 对…实行扣押财物的处分. — *vt.* ①使苦恼, 使为难, 使悲痛. ②使贫困; 使困苦. ③【法】扣押(财物). *~ oneself* 焦虑,悲痛. *~ sb. into committing suicide* 因…的痛苦而自杀. ~ **call [signal]** 遇险信号,求救信号〔即 SOS〕. ~ **frequency**【无】遇险求救频率. ~ **gun [flag]** 遇险〔求救〕号炮〔信号旗〕. ~ **merchandize** 亏本出售的货物. ~ **rocket** 遇难求救火箭. ~ **warrant**【法】扣押令. ~**ed area** 灾区;经济萧条区.
dis·tress·ful [disˈtresful] *a.* ①苦难重重的,不幸的,悲惨的. ②使人苦恼的,使人痛苦的. *the ~ circumstances of poverty and sickness* 贫病交加的不幸境遇. *a ~ cry* 惨叫. **-ly** *ad.*
dis·tress·ing [disˈtresiŋ] *a.* 令人苦恼的; 使人痛苦的. *the ~ news* 使人痛苦的消息.
dis·trib·u·ta·ry [disˈtribjutəri] *n.* (分出后不再流入本河的)分流. *(opp.* tributary*)*.
dis·trib·ute [disˈtribju(ː)t] *vt.* ①分配,分给, 分发, 配给;〔古〕实施,颁布. ②区分, 把…分类. ③分布, 散布 *(over)*. ④【逻】周延;【电】配(电);【印】调(墨); 拆(版). *~ circulars* 散发传单. *a distributing centre* 集散地. *a distributing station* 配电站; 图书配给站. *~ foodstuffs among the underfed people* 在饥民当中分发食物. *~ money to the poor* 向贫民发放救济金. *~ seed over a field* 在田间播种. *The guest ~ed themselves in the garden.* 客人们在花园里散开. *The process is ~ed into three stages.* 工作进程分为三个阶段. *These plants were ~ed into 22 classes.* 这些植物分为22类. *~ justice to the criminals* 对犯罪分子施行法律. — *vi.* 分配;散布;【数】分布. **dis·trib·u·tee** [disˌtribjuˈtiː]【法】分配遗产受益人. **-r** *n.* = distributor.
dis·tri·bu·tion [ˌdistriˈbjuːʃən] *n.* ①分配,分发,配给;分配装置〔系统〕;配给品;配给量;【经】配给方法,配给过程;分红;【法】(无遗嘱死亡者的)财产分配. ②分布,配置, 分布状态;【生】(生物的)分布范围;【无】频率分布. ③分类,整理,区分. ④【电】配电;【机】配汽;【印】拆版;【逻】周延(性). ⑤销售. *the ~ of wealth* 财富的分配. *the accurate ~ of zoological specimens* 动物品种的精确分类. *live on charitable ~s alone* 完全依靠配给救济品生活. *the ~ of coniferous forests* 针叶林的分布范围. *the ~ of troops* 部队配置. *The ~ of our school paper is now 3000.* 我们校刊的发行量现在是3000份. *We have a good harvest but our ~ is bad.* 我们丰收了,但是产品卖不出去. ~ **cost**【商】推销费用. ~ **curve [function]**【统】分布曲线〔函数〕.
dis·trib·u·tism [disˈtribjutizəm] *n.* 分产主义〔主张把私人财产,尤其是土地,重新进行分配〕. **-tist** *n.* 分产主义者.
dis·trib·u·tive [disˈtribjutiv] ①(关于)分配的;分布的. ②【逻】周延的;【语法】个体的, 个别的. *a ~ agency for foodstuffs* 食品分配处. — *n.*【语法】个体词〔each, either, every 等〕. ~ **education**〔常作 D- Education〕分配性教育〔学校与企业合办,把课堂教学与职业训练结合起来〕. ~ **law**【数】分配律,分布律. **-ly** *ad.*
dis·trib·u·tor [disˈtribjutə] *n.* ①分发者, 分配者,配给者;散布者,分布者. ②【印】调墨胶辊; 自动拆版机; 拆版工人;【电】配电盘. ③销售者; 批发商. *oil ~*【机】分油器. ~ **bar**【印】自动拆版装置.
dis·trict [ˈdistrikt] *n.* ①区; 管区; 行政区, 市区. ②地区,区域. ③〔美〕(各州众议员)选举区;〔英〕教区,分区. *a military ~* 军区. *a police ~* 警察管区. *a shopping ~* 商业学区. *a Congressional ~* 美国各州众议员选区. *an agricultural [wooded] ~* 农业〔山林〕区. ***the D- of Columbia*** 哥伦比亚特区〔美国首都华盛顿所在的行政区〕. — *vt.* 把…分区. *the new ~ing of the city* 城市重新分区. ~ **attorney**〔美〕地方检察官. ~ **council**〔英〕地方议会. ~ **court**〔美〕地方法院. ~ **heating** 分区供暖系统〔可供应同一地区内暖气或热水需求的中央系统〕. ~ **man** 负责采访某一地区新闻的记者. ~ **office**〔美〕县公署;地方分店. **D- Railway** (伦敦)郊区铁路. ~ **school**〔美〕村立小学校. ~ **tug** 港用拖船. ~ **visitor** 教区牧师助理.
dis·trust [disˈtrʌst] *n.* 疑惑,不相信;不信任,猜疑. *have a ~ of sb.* 不信任某人. *His policy earned him the ~ of the Athenians.* 他的政策受到了雅典人的猜疑. — *vt.* 不信任,怀疑. *~ one's friend* 对朋友起疑心. **-ful** *a.* 不信任的, 疑心重的*(of)*; 可疑的 *(A distrustful dog is the best watch dog.* 疑心重的狗是最好的看门狗*)*. **-ful·ly** *ad.*

dis·turb [dis'tə:b] *vt.* ①搅乱，扰乱；打扰．②使不安，使烦恼．③妨害，妨碍；侵犯（权利）．*Please don't* ～ *me while I am sleeping.* 我睡觉时请不要打扰我．～ *the peace*【法】扰乱治安．～ *the smooth surface of a lake* 搅乱平静的湖面．— *vi.* 妨碍睡眠[休息等]．**Do not** ～．请勿打扰，现在恕不会客〔挂在会议室、旅馆房间门上用的字牌〕．～**ing force**【天】摄动力，扰力．**-er** *n.* 打扰者．

dis·turb·ance [dis'tə:bəns] *n.* ①动乱，变乱，骚乱．②烦闷；（心情）纷乱；（身心）失调．③【无】干扰；【气】扰动；【地】（地壳的）局部运动．④【法】侵犯（权利），妨害（治安）．*cause [make, raise] a* ～ 作乱，闹事，闹乱子．*quiet [suppress] a* ～ 平息骚乱．*magnetic* ～ 磁场干扰．*political* ～ 政治骚乱．～ ***of apprehension [attention, intelligence]***【医】领悟[注意，心理]障碍．

dis·turbed [dis'tə:bd] *a.* ①被打扰的；【天】受摄的．②不安的；心理失常的．③为心理失常者服务的．*the* ～ *children* 心理不正常的儿童．～ **body**【天】受摄体．～ **day**（地磁）受扰日．

dis·tyle ['distail] *n.*【建】双柱式门廊．— *a.*【建】双柱式的．

di·sul·fate, di·sul·phate [dai'sʌlfeit] *n.*【化】焦硫酸盐；硫酸氢盐，酸式硫酸盐．

di·sul·fide, di·sul·phide [dai'sʌlfaid] *n.*【化】二硫化物．～ *oil* 含二硫化物的油．

dis·un·ion ['dis'ju:njən] *n.* ①分离，分裂．②不一致，不统一；不和，倾轧．*the* ～ *of the body and soul* 肉体和灵魂的分离．*internal* ～ 内部倾轧．**-ism** *n.*【美史】（美国南北战争时主张南北分离的）分离主义．**-ist** *n.*【美史】分离主义者．

dis·u·nite ['disju:'nait] *vt.* ①使分离．②使分裂；使起纷争，（使）不和．*The issue* ～*d the party members.* 该问题在党员中造成分裂．— *vi.* ①分离．②分裂，不和．

dis·use ['dis'ju:s] *n.* 不用，废止，废弃．*The machine has become rusty from* ～．机器已经因不用而生锈．*Traditional customs are coming [falling] into* ～．老习惯正在破除．— ['dis'ju:z] *vt.* 不用，废止；废弃．*a* ～*d car* 废车．*a* ～*d meaning of the word* 一个词的废义．**-d** *a.* 已不用的，已废止的，已废弃的．

dis·val·ue [dis'vælju:] *vt.* ①〔古〕轻视．②使减价．— *n.* ①轻视．②贬值．

di·syl·lab·ic ['disi'læbik] *a.* 双音节的．

di·syl·la·ble [di'siləbl] *n.*〔英〕= dissyllable.

ditch [ditʃ] *n.* ①水沟，渠．②壕沟．*fall into a* ～ 跌进沟里．***be driven to the last*** ～ 陷入绝境．***die in the last*** ～ 奋战而死．***the Big D-***〔美俚〕①大西洋．②巴拿马运河．***the D-***〔美空军俚〕英吉利海峡；北海．***the last*** ～ ***struggle*** 垂死挣扎，负隅顽抗．— *vt.* ①在…开沟，在…挖壕沟；用壕沟围绕．②〔美〕使（火车）出轨，使（汽车）冲落沟内．③〔美俚〕摆脱，抛弃，甩开，避开（同伴等）；逃避（责任）等．④使（飞机）迫降海上．*a pasture hedged and* ～*ed* 用树篱和沟渠围起来的牧场．*be [get]* ～*ed*〔美俚〕（飞机）迫降海上．*I* ～*ed that old hat of yours.* 我把你那顶旧帽子扔掉了．*He* ～*ed the cops by turning off his lights and driving down an alley.* 他关掉车灯，朝胡同深处驶去，想用这样办法逃开警察．— *vi.* ①开沟，挖沟；修沟．②〔美〕（火车）出轨，（汽车）冲落沟内；（陆上飞机）迫降海上．～*ing device*（无人驾驶飞机的）迫降装置．*hedging and* ～*ing* 沟道和树篱的整修．～**-digger** ①挖沟者．②做小工的人．③开沟机．～**rider**〔美俚〕照管水渠的工人．～ **riding**〔美俚〕照管水渠的工作．～**water** *n.* 沟中死水（*as dull as* ～*water* 完全停滞的；单调乏味的）．

ditch·er ['ditʃə] *n.* ①挖沟者，掘壕者．②开沟机．③被迫使飞机降落水上的人．

di·the·ism ['daiθi(:)izəm] *n.*【宗】善恶二神说，二神教．

dith·er ['diðə] *n.* ①发抖，颤抖．②〔口〕（因兴奋、恐怖等而引起的）慌乱．③【物】高频振[脉]动．*have the* ～*s* 发抖．*throw sb. into a* ～ 使某人心慌意乱．*all of a* ～ 浑身发着抖．— *vi.* ①〔方〕（因兴奋、恐怖等而）发抖，颤抖．②优柔寡断；游移不决，三心二意．*He sat there* ～*ing over his decision.* 他坐在那里拿不定主意．～ **motor** 高频振动用电机．～ **pump** 高频振动泵．

dithi(o)- *comb. f.*【化】联硫基；二硫代：*dithio*nate.

di·thi·o·nate [dai'θaiəneit] *n.*【化】连二硫酸盐．

dith·y·ramb ['diθiræm*b*] *n.* ①〔古希腊〕酒神赞歌．②〔书〕狂热的诗歌[演说、文章等]．

dit·ta·ny ['ditəni] *n.*【植】白鲜属．

dit·to ['ditəu] *n.* (*pl.* ～*s*) ①同上，同前〔略号作 d° 或 do 或″或"，仅用于单据或表格中〕．②〔口〕同样的事物；一模一样的人；复制品．③〔*pl.*〕（衣裤）用同一种料子做的一套服装．*He is the* ～ *of his mother.* 他的长相和他母亲一模一样．*a suit of* ～*s* = *a* ～ *suit* 用同一料子做的一套服装．***be in*** ～***s*** 穿着（衣裤）用同一种料子做的一套服装；对…表示完全同意．***say*** ～ ***to*** 对…表示同意．— *ad.* 如前所述，和以上所说一样地；同样地．*act* ～ 采取同样的行动，同样办理．— *vt.* ①重复（别人的言论、行动等）．②（在复印机上）复印．～ **machine** 复印机．～ **mark**"同上"符号．

dit·to·graph ['ditəgrɑ:f] *n.*（书写、印刷中由疏忽而造成）重复的词，重复的字母．**-y** [di'tɔgrəfi] *n.*（词或字母的）印重，写重，重复．

dit·ty ['diti] *n.* 小曲，小调．*a plaintive* ～ 一首伤感的小曲．～ **bag**（水手等的）针线包，针线盒．～ **box** ①摄影道具箱．②= ～ bag.

di·u·re·sis [ˌdaijuə'ri:sis] *n.* (*pl.* ***-re·ses*** [-'ri:si:z])【医】利尿；多尿．

di·u·ret·ic [ˌdaijuə'retik] *a.*【医】利尿的．— *n.* 利尿剂．

di·ur·nal [dai'ə:nl] *a.* ①每日的；【天】周日的．②昼间的，白天的 (*opp.* nocturnal)．③【植】（花、叶等）昼开夜闭的；【动】（鸟等）昼出夜息的 (*opp.* nocturnal)；（昆虫）只活一天的；【医】（病等）夜轻日重的．*the* ～ *round of the mailman* 邮递员每日的巡行．～ *task* 每日任务，日常工作．～ *noises* 白昼的喧闹．～ *flowers* 白天开的花．— *n.* ①【宗】每日祈祷书．②〔古〕日报，日记．**-ly** *ad.* ①每日，天天．②只在白天．～ **cycle** 昼夜循环．～ **motion** 周日运动；（因地球自转而产生的星球每日似乎由东向西的）视移动．～ **tides** 潮汐．

div. = divide; dividend; divine; division; divisor; divorced.

di·va ['di:və] *n.*〔It.〕(*pl.* ～*s, di·ve* ['di:vei]) 歌剧女主角；主要女歌手；著名女歌唱家．

di·va·gate ['daivəgeit] *vi.* ①〔书〕流浪，漂泊．②（说话）离题．**-ga·tion** [ˌdaivə'geiʃən] *n.*

di·va·lent ['daiˌveilənt] *a.* ①【化】（化合价）二价的．②【生】（染色体）二价的．

di·van [di'væn] *n.* ①（土耳其等国的）国务会议；（政府的）局．②（土耳其等国的）国务会议室；接见厅；法庭；（海关等的）大楼．③（一般的）会议；委员会．④['daivæn]（靠墙放的）长沙发椅；沙发床．⑤烟茶室，咖啡室，…烟店．⑥波斯语诗集，阿拉伯语诗集．

di·var·i·cate [dai'værikeit] *vi.* ①（道路等）分为两叉．②【动、植】（树枝、翅膀、羽毛等）分叉．— *a.*【生】（树枝、翅、羽等）分歧的，分叉宽阔的，展开的．**-ca·tion** [daiˌværi'keiʃən] *n.* 分叉，分歧；交叉点；意义暧昧；意见分歧．

dive [daiv] *n.* ①潜水；【泳】跳水；【空】俯冲，（潜艇）下潜，急降．②猛冲，突然隐去；【拳】假装被击倒．③专心研究，探究．④（气温，股票价格等的）暴落．⑤〔英〕（常指地下室中的）小饭馆；〔美口〕低级酒馆；赌窟；匪窝．*a fancy* ～【泳】花式跳水．*a nose* ～【空】俯冲．*Rail stocks took a* ～ *on the stock market.* 铁路股票在股票市场上暴跌．***make a*** ～ ***for sth.*** 冲过去拿（某物）．

take a ~ into** (the subject)* 埋头(该问题)中. — *vi.* **(~d, *dove [dəuv]; **~d)** ①(头朝下)跳入水中. ②(潜艇等)下潜, (飞机等)俯冲. ③(飞机)俯冲, (气温, 物价等)突然下降. ④突然潜匿; (手等)插入口袋; 〔俚〕扒窃. ⑤埋头研究. ⑥〔美俚〕【拳】假装被打倒. *~ for pearls* 潜水取珍珠. *~ into a purse* 手伸进钱袋. *~ into the bushes* 潜入树丛中. *~ into (one's secret)* 探察(某人秘密). — *vt.* 使(潜艇等)下潜. *~ the submarine* 使潜艇下潜. **~-bomb** *vt., vi.* 俯冲轰炸. **~ bomber** 俯冲轰炸机. **~keeper** 低级酒馆、赌窟等的老板.

div•er [ˈdaivə] *n.* ①跳水者; 潜水员; 潜水采珠者. ②潜水鸟; 〔俚〕潜水艇; 俯冲轰炸机. *a pearl ~* 采珠人. **~'s connection** 潜水员的救难通知管.

di•verge [daiˈvəːdʒ] *vi.* ①(道路等)分岔, 分开; (意见等)分歧. ②【生】趋异 *(opp.* converge*)*; 【数】(级数等)无极限, 无限大. ③(点等)分出. ④离(题), 逸出(正轨) *(from)*. — *vt.* 使岔开, 使转向. **di•ver•ger** [daiˈvəːdʒə] *n.* 〔美口〕富有幻想力的人. *(cf.* converger*)*.

di•ver•gence [daiˈvəːdʒəns] *n.* ①分歧, 分岔, 分出 *(opp.* convergence*)*. ②【生】趋异 *(opp.* convergence*)*; 【心】离散; 【数、物】散度, 开度; 发散. ③离题. *a ~ in opinion* 意见分歧.

di•ver•gent [daiˈvəːdʒənt] *a.* ①叉开的, 分歧的; 背道而驰的. ②【物、数】发散的; 【生】趋异的. **~ adaptation** 【生】趋异适应. **~ pencil** 【物】发散光线锥. **~ series** 【数】发散级数. **~ squint** 【医】外斜视.

di•verg•ing [daiˈvəːdʒiŋ] *a.* = divergent. *~ star cluster* 【天】散开星团. **~ lens** 【物】发散透镜.

di•vers [ˈdaivə(ː)z] *a.* ①若干, 好几个. ②〔古〕= diverse. *~ articles* 若干物品. — *pro.* 若干人. *He chose ~ of them, who were asked to accompany him.* 他选择他们当中的几个人, 要他们和他作伴. — *n.* 〔美俚〕指头.

di•verse [daiˈvəːs] *a.* ①不同的, 别的. ②形形色色的, 多种多样的. *He is of a ~ nature from the rest of his family.* 他和他家里别的人气质不同. *~ interpretations of these ideas* 对这些思想所作的多种多样的解释. **-ly** *ad.*

di•ver•si•fi•ca•tion [daiˌvəːsifiˈkeiʃən] *n.* ①形形色色, 多样化. ②【商】(投资的)分散经营〔以避免押打一的经营有失败的风险〕.

di•ver•si•fied [daiˈvəːsifaid] *a.* ①形形色色的, 多样化的. ②(投资等)分散经营的. *~ investments* 分散经营的投资. *~ activity* 多种多样的活动. *~ economy* 多样化经济. *~ scenery* 绚丽多姿的风景.

di•ver•si•form [daiˈvəːsifɔːm] *a.* 各式各样的.

di•ver•si•fy [daiˈvəːsifai] *vt.* ①使多样化, 使不同. ②把(资金)分散投资. *~ a course of study* 使课程多样化. *~ investments* 把资金分散投放.

di•ver•sion [daiˈvəːʃən] *n.* ①转换, 转移, 转向; (河流、航线等的)改道; (资金等的)挪用; 〔英〕(因修路等车辆)绕行, 绕路. ②消遣, 娱乐. ③【军】箝制, 佯攻. *a flood ~ area* 分洪区. *a ~ of industry into the war effort* 工业转入作战生产. *Movies can be a worthwhile ~.* 电影可以成为一种有益的娱乐.

di•ver•sion•ar•y [daiˈvəːʃənəri, diˈvəːʒənəri] *a.* ①转移注意力的. ②【军】牵制性的, 声东击西的. **~ tactics** 牵制战术, 声东击西战术.

di•ver•sion•ist [daiˈvəːʃənist] *n.* ①(政治上的)异端分子. ②进行牵制活动者; 在敌后活动者.

di•ver•si•ty [daiˈvəːsiti] *n.* ①不同, 异样, 差异. ②繁多, 多种, 多样, 驳杂, 参差. *a ~ of methods* 方法的多种多样. *a ~ of interests* 多种多样的趣味.

di•vert [daiˈvəːt] *vt.* ①使转向, 使转换, 使转移 *(from; to)*; 挪用(资金等); 使(工作等)改行. ②使消遣, 使解闷, 使娱乐. ③【军】箝制, 佯攻. *~ the course of a stream = ~ a stream from its course* 改变河道流向. *~ one's attention* 转移注意力. *~ children by telling stories* 讲故事逗乐孩子. *They were greatly ~ed by the play.* 这场戏使他们很开心. *She was trained as a doctor but ~ed to diplomacy.* 她是学医的, 但是改行做外交工作了.

di•ver•tic•u•li•tis [ˌdaivəˈtikjuˈlaitəs] *n.* 【医】憩室炎.

di•ver•tic•u•lo•sis [daiˌvətikjuˈləusis] *n.* 【医】憩室形成.

di•ver•tic•u•lum [ˌdaivəˈtikjuləm] *n.* *(pl.* ***-u•la*** [-lə]*)* 【解】憩室; 支囊.

di•ver•ti•men•to [diˌvɛətiˈmentəu] *n.* *(pl.* ***-men•ti*** [-tiː], *~s)* 【乐】套曲; 嬉游曲, 赋格曲中的间插段; 由多个乐章组成的旋律优美的轻音乐曲.

di•vert•ing [daiˈvəːtiŋ] *a.* 有趣的, 消愁解闷的. *a ~ caricature* 有趣的漫画.

di•ver•tisse•ment [daiˈvəːtismənt, *F.* divɛrtisˈmɑ̃ŋ] *n.* ①娱乐; 余兴[舞蹈等]. ②【乐】= divertimento.

Di•ves[1] [ˈdaivz] *n.* 戴夫斯〔姓氏〕.

Di•ves[2] [ˈdaiviːz] *n.* 豪富, 财主〔源出《圣经》《路加福音》〕.

di•vest [daiˈvest] *vt.* ①剥去…的衣服. ②剥夺. ③摆脱. *The wind ~ed the trees of their leaves.* 风吹光了树的叶子. *be ~ed of one's coat* 被剥掉上衣. *~ sb. of his office* 撤销某人的职务. *He attempted to ~ himself of all responsibilities for the decision.* 他力图摆脱掉作出该项决定的一切责任. **-ment** *n.*

di•vest•i•ture [daiˈvestitʃə] *n.* ①剥夺. ②脱衣.

div•i [ˈdivi] *n.* 〔英俚〕(消费合作社等的)红利.

di•vide [diˈvaid] *vt.* ①分, 区分, 划分 *(into)*. ②分配, 分派, 分给; 分享, 分担, 分摊 *(with; between; among)*. ③分开, 隔开, 隔离 *(from)*. ④分裂, 使对立; 使(意见)分歧, 离间(朋友); 【化】分离. ⑤【数】除; 除尽; 【机】在…上刻[分]度. *~ words between syllables* 给单词分音节. *Administratively, the country is ~d into counties.* 这个国家在行政区划分上分为许多郡. *The river ~s the city into two parts.* 那条河把市区分成两部分. *Opinions are ~d on that point.* 意见就在那一点上对立起来了. *~ ten dollars among five persons* 十块美元五个人分. *~ profits with the stock-holders* 和股东共分利润. *D- 6 by 3 and you get 2.* 以3除6得2. *9 ~s 36.* 9能除尽36. *~ a sextant* 给六分仪分度. ***be ~d against itself*** 发生内讧 *(If a house be ~d against itself, that house cannot stand.* 家不和, 必自败*)*. — *vi.* ①分, 分开. ②分裂, (意见等)分歧. ③【数】除, 被除尽. ④(议会等)表决. *~ in one's mind* 内心徬徨, 犹豫不决. *We all ~ equally.* 我们平等分配, 各取一份. *The road ~s six miles from here.* 这条路在六英里之外有分岔. *He could add and subtract, but hadn't learned to divide.* 他会做加减法, 但还没有学会除法. *Eight ~s by four.* 8能被4除尽. *Five will not ~ into nine.* 5除不尽9. *D-! D-!* (议会等中提出)表决! 表决! — *n.* ①分, 分配. ②〔口〕分裂. ③分界; 〔美〕分水岭. ***~ and rule*** 分而治之. ***the Great D-*** ①〔美〕落矶山脉分水岭; 主要分水岭. ②大限, 死; 生死关头 *(cross the Great D-* 死*)*.

di•vid•ed [diˈvaidid] *a.* ①被分割的; 分离的; 对立的, 意见分歧的. ②【植】(叶)分裂的; 全裂的. *~ circle* 【机】刻度盘. *~ consonant* 【语】分裂辅音. *~ current* 【物】分歧电流. *~ highway* (对行道分开的)分行公路.

div•i•dend [ˈdividend] *n.* ①【数】被除数 *(opp.* divisor*)*. ②红利, 股息; 利息; (破产时清算的)分配金. ③(一般的)份儿; 报酬. *cum [ex] ~* 〔英〕= *~ on [off]* 〔美〕有[无]股息. *stock ~* 股息. *non-~ payer* 无红股户. *Swimming is a fun, and gives you the ~ of better health.* 游泳既是娱乐, 又有增进健康的好处. ***declare a ~*** 通告分红. **~-account** 股息帐户. **~-cheque** 股息支票, 股利券. **~-coupon** 股利券. **~ warrant** 股息单, 领取股息通知单.

di·vid·er [diˈvaidə] *n.* ①划者；分割者；分裂者，离间者．②间隔物；分裂的原因．③(割禾机等的)分切器；【数】除数；除法器；【电】分压器；【空】减速器．④〔*pl.*〕划规，两脚规，分线规．*a pair of ~s* 一副两脚规．

di·vid·ing [diˈvaidiŋ] *a.* 起划分［区分、分割］作用的．*a ~ line* 分界线．~ **machine [engine]**【机】分度机，刻度机．~ **ridge** 分水岭．

div·i-div·i [ˈdiviˈdivi] *n.*【植】(南美热带产)鞣科芸实；鞣科芸实的豆荚〔含大量单宁酸，可供染色、鞣革用〕．

di·vid·u·al [diˈvidjuəl] *a.*〔古〕①分开的；可分离的；可分割的．②各别的．③分配的，分享的．

Di·vi·na Com·me·dia [It. diˈviːnaː kɔːmˈmeːdjaː]〔It.〕《神曲》〔意大利诗人但丁 (Dante, 1265—1321) 的名著〕．

div·i·na·tion [ˌdiviˈneiʃən] *n.* ①占卜，卜卦．②先见；预言；预测．③直观的感知，本能的预知．*the ~ of the high priest* 大祭司的预言．

di·vine [diˈvain] *a.* ①神的；神性的．②神授的，天赐的．③敬神的，奉为神的；神圣的．④神学的．⑤神妙的；绝世的，天才的，非凡的；〔俚〕好透了的．~ *song* 圣歌．~ *judgements* 神意．*a ~ call* 天命．*the ~ kingdom* 天国．*What ~ weather!* 多好的天气！~ *beauty* 国色天香，绝代佳人．— *n.* ①神学家，宗教学者．②圣职人员；牧师，教士，神父，祭司．③〔the D-〕神，上帝，造物主．④〔the ~〕(人性中)崇高的一面．*He hated the lust but admired the ~ in men.* 他憎恶人的贪欲，欣赏人性中崇高的一面．— *vt., vi.* ①预测；占卜．②看穿，察觉；(凭直觉)推测，猜测．~ *sb.'s intention* 识破(看穿)某人企图．*He ~d from her look that something was in her mind.* 他从她的神色上看出她心上有事．***divining rod***"魔杖"〔古代以迷信法探矿的一种木叉，据说寻得矿脉、水源等即自动弯曲云云〕．***the ~ Being [Father]*** 神，上帝．***the D-Comedy*** = Divina Commedia. ***the ~ right of kings*** 帝王神权，王权神授说．~ **nature** 神性．~ **service** 礼拜式．**-r** *n.* 占卜者；预言者；推测者．**-ly** *ad.*

div·ing [ˈdaiviŋ] *a.* ①潜［跳］水的．②潜［跳］水用的．— *n.* 潜水；【泳】跳水．~ **bell** 潜水钟；〔美俚〕地下室酒馆．~ **board** 跳水板．~ **helmet** 潜水帽．~ **plane** (潜艇的)浮沉控制舵．~ **suit [dress]** 潜水服．

di·vin·i·ty [diˈviniti] *n.* ①神性；神力，神威；神德．②〔the D-〕神，上帝；〔a ~〕(异教的)神；天使，神人．③神学；(大学的)神学院．④神奇，尽善尽美．*Doctor of D-* 神学博士〔略作 D. D.〕．*the ~ of Beethoven's music* 贝多芬乐曲的神奇力量．~ **calf** (作书籍封面用的)暗褐色小牛皮．~ **fudge** 奶油馅蛋糕．~ **school** 神学校．

di·vis·i·bil·i·ty [diˌviziˈbiliti] *n.* ①可分割性，可分性．②【数】可除尽，整约性，整除性．③【物】(晶体的)解理性，可劈性．

di·vis·i·ble [diˈvizəbl] *a.* ①可分的，可分割的．②【数】除得尽的 *(by). 12 is ~ by 4.* 12 可用4除尽．

di·vi·sion [diˈviʒən] *n.* ①分，分开，分割；分划，区分．②分配；分派．③分裂，(意见)不一致，倾轧．④区域；〔英〕选区；部分，部门；(大学的)部；(政府机构等的)司，科．⑤间隔，隔墙，分界；标度．⑥〔英〕(议会的)表决．⑦【数】除法 *(opp.* multiplication*)*．⑧【陆军】师；【海军】分舰队；海军航空兵分队．⑨【园艺】分株；【生】门，类［科，属等］．⑩【体】(按体重，年龄，技术等划分的)级，组．*the present ~ in our society* 当代社会的分裂．*take a ~* 表决．~ *of business* 营业部．*cell ~* 细胞分裂．*the sales ~ of the Ford Motor Co.* 福特汽车公司的销售部．*the D- of Humanities of the University of Chicago* 芝加哥大学人文科学部．~ *of officer*【美海军】分队长．~ *of function* 机能分工．~ *of labour*【经】分工．*the heavy weight ~*【拳】重量级．~ *of powers* (中央和地方或立法、司法、行政的)分权．~ **bell** 通知会场外议员即将表决的铃声．~ **sign [mark]**【数】除号．~ **wall** 界墙．

di·vi·sion·al [diˈviʒənl] *a.* ①分开的，分割的；分区的，分部的．②【数】除法的；【陆军】师的；【海军】分(舰)队的．*a ~ commander* 师长．

Di·vi·sion·ism [diˈviʒənizəm] *n.*【美术】点画派 (= Pointillism).

di·vi·sive [diˈvaisiv] *a.* 引起分裂的，造成不和的．**-ly** *ad.* **-ness** *n.*

di·vi·sor [diˈvaizə] *n.*【数】除数，约数 *(opp.* dividend*)*．*common ~*【数】公约数．~ *of zero*【数】零因子．

di·vorce [diˈvɔːs] *n.* ①【法】离婚．②分离，脱离，(关系的)断绝 *(between; of; from)*．*the ~ rate* 离婚率．*get [obtain] a ~* 获准离婚．~ *by consent* 协议离婚．*a ~ between thought and action* 思想与行动脱节．— *vt.* ①与…离婚，使…离婚．②脱离，与…断绝关系；使分离，使脱节．*The judge ~d the couple.* 法官判决这对夫妇离婚．*She ~d her husband.* 她和丈夫离了婚．*He was ~d by his wife.* 他的妻子和他离婚了．*science ~d from religion* 和宗教脱离了关系的科学．~ *church from state* 使政教分离．*He is ~d from society.* 他脱离了社会．*Life and art cannot be ~d.* 生活与艺术不能脱离．~ *oneself [be ~d] from one's spouse* 和自己的配偶离婚．~ **court** 离婚裁决法庭．~ **mill**〔口〕= ~ court. **-ment** *n.*

di·vor·cé [diˈvɔːsei] *n.*〔F.〕离了婚的男子．

di·vor·cée [diˈvɔːsei] *n.*〔F.〕离了婚的女子．

di·vor·cee [diˈvɔːsiː] *n.* 被离婚者；离了婚的人．

div·ot [ˈdivət] *n.* ①〔Scot.〕(一块)草皮．②【高尔夫】(击球时球棒削起的)一块草根土．~ *digger*〔美〕= golfer.

di·vul·gate [diˈvʌlgeit] *vt.*〔古〕公布，宣布．**-r** *n.* 公布者．**-ga·tion** [ˈdaivʌlˈgeiʃən] *n.*

di·vulge [daiˈvʌldʒ] *vt.* ①泄漏(秘密等)；揭发，暴露(隐私等)．②〔古〕公布，宣布．~ *the source of one's information* 泄露情报来源．**-nce, -ment** *n.*

di·vulse [daiˈvʌls] *vt.*【医】撕开，扯裂．**-vul·sion** [-ˈvʌlʃən] *n.*【医】扯裂(术)．

div·vy [ˈdivi] *n.*〔美俚〕(分得的)份儿．— *vi.* 拿一份，分享．— *vt.* 分配，分摊 *(up)*．*They divvied up the profits among themselves.* 他们一伙瓜分利润．

di·wan [diˈwɑːn] *n.* = dewan.

Dix·i·can [ˈdiksikən] *n.* 美国南部各州的共和党人．

Dix·ie[1] [ˈdiksi] *n.* 迪克西〔女子名〕．

Dix·ie[2] [ˈdiksi] *n.* ①〔美〕美国南部各州的别名；【美史】(美国南北战争期间参加南部同盟的)南部同盟诸州．②【美史】南部同盟军军歌．**~crats**〔*pl.*〕〔美〕南部各州的民主党党员．~ **Land** = ~ ①．**~land**〔美〕(源出美国新奥尔良地方的)半即兴式爵士音乐．

dix·ie [ˈdiksi] *n.*〔英陆军俚〕(行军、露营等用的)大铁锅．~ **cup** (盛冰淇淋或其他饮料的)纸杯．

dix·it [ˈdiksit] *n.* 武断的讲话；独断的主张．

Dix·on [ˈdiksn] *n.* 狄克逊〔姓氏〕．

dix·y [ˈdiksi] *n.* = dixie.

D.I.Y.〔英俚〕= do it yourself 自己动手．

diz·en [ˈdaizn] *vt.*〔古〕= bedizen.

diz·zy [ˈdizi] *a.* ①头晕眼花的．②(高度、速度等)使人眼花缭乱的．③〔美俚〕被弄胡涂的；昏头昏脑的，愚蠢的．*a ~ speed [height]* 使人头晕目眩的速度［高空］．*get [feel] ~* 感到头晕．*The wet heat made him ~.* 蒸人的暑热使他头晕目眩．*He was ~ with shame.* 他羞愧得变胡涂了．*that ~ blonde* 那个愚蠢的金发女人．— *vt.* ①使头晕眼花，使发昏．②使变胡涂．*prospects so brilliant as to ~ the mind* 如此美好的前途使头脑变得发晕了．**diz·zi·ly** *ad.* **diz·zi·ness** *n.*

DJ = ①disc jockey〔美俚〕无线电唱片音乐节目广播员．②Dow Jones & Co.〔美〕道·琼斯公司．

D.J. = ①District Judge〔美〕地方初审法院法官．②

Doctor Juris (= Doctor of Law) 法学博士.

Dja·kar·ta [dʒəˈkɑːtə] *n.* 雅加达〔印度尼西亚首都〕. **-n** [-tən] *n.* 雅加达人.

djeb·el [ˈdʒebəl] *n.* 山, 高山〔阿拉伯语里常用于地名中〕(= jebel).

djel·la·ba, djel·la·bah [dʒiˈlɑːbə] *n.* 结拉巴长袍〔伊斯兰教国家男女均穿着的宽敞长袍〕.

DJI = Dow-Jones Index〔美〕道·琼斯指数〔以选取的若干工业、铁路、公用事业股票的每日平均价格为依据, 据此计算出的证券的相对价格指数〕.

Dji·bou·ti [dʒiˈbuːti] *n.* ①吉布提〔非洲〕. ②吉布提〔吉布提首都〕.

dk. = deka; deck; dock.

dkg. = decagram(me)(s).

dkl. = decalitre.

dkm. = decametre.

D.L., DL = Deputy Lieutenant〔英〕副郡长.

dl. = decilitre(s). **D/L** =〔美〕day letter; demand loan 活期贷款.

DL_{50} = 50% Lethal dose 致死中量, 半致死量.

dld. =〔美〕delivered.

D.Lit(t)., D Lit(t) = Doctor of Literature 文学博士.

D.L.O. = Dead-Letter Office (无法投递的) 死信招领处.

D.M. = Deputy Master (学院的)副院长.

D.M., DM = ①Doctor of Medicine 医学博士. ②Doctor of Mathematics 数学博士. ③〔DM〕deutsche mark 德意志联邦共和国马克.

dm. = decimetre(s); delta metal; dram.

d/m = disintegrations per minute 衰变/分.

D.M.D. = Doctor of Dental Medicine.

D.M.E. =【空】distance measuring equipment 测距装置.

D.M.I. = Director of Military Intelligence.〔英〕(帝国总参谋部)军事情报局局长.

dml. = demolition.

dmm. = decimillimetre(s).

D.M.S. = Doctor of Medical Science(s) 医学博士.

D.Mus., D Mus = Doctor of Music 音乐博士.

DMZ = demilitarized zone 非军事区.

D.N. = Daily News〔美〕《每日新闻》.

d-n. = damn〔委婉语〕.

DNA = ①deoxyribonucleic acid【生化】脱氧核糖核酸. ②deoxypentose-nucleic acid 脱氧戊糖核酸.

D.N.B. =〔英〕Dictionary of National Biography《英国人名词典》.

DNF = did not finish 未完成.

Dnie·per [dˈniːpə] *n.* (苏联)第聂伯河.

D Notice〔英〕D 号通告, 国防保密通告〔政府的一项备忘录, 要求报纸不要刊登某些涉密消息, 以确保国防安全〕.

do. [ˈditəu] = ditto.

do[1] [强 duː, 弱 du, də] (***did*** [did]; ***done*** [dʌn]; 陈述语气第三人称单数现在式 ***does*** [强 dʌz, 弱 dəz]) *vt.* ①行, 为, 作, 做, 办, 干; 尽(义务等), 竭(力), 担任, 从事. ~ *one's work* 干工作. ~ *odd jobs* 干杂活, 打零工. ~ *business* 做买卖. ~ *washing* 洗东西. *Who has done it?* 这是谁干的? ~ *the host* 做主人, 当东. ~ *one's duty* 尽义务. *crimes done deliberately* 蓄意犯罪. ~ *a good deed* 行善, 做好事. ~ *penance* 忏悔. ~ *one's best [utmost]* = ~ *the best one can* 竭尽所能. ~ *one's worst* 捣乱. *What can I* ~ *for you?* 有什么事吗? 我能帮你干什么吗? (店员招呼顾客)要买什么吗? *I have much to* ~ *to pay my monthly bills.* 我应付每月的开支不是容易的. ②完成, 做完. *I have done reading.* 我已经看完书了. *You have done it very well.* 你做得很好. *Now you've done it.*〔俚〕这可糟了! 可被你搞坏了! *But it was done now, and it could not be helped.* 生米已成熟饭, 没有办法了. ③给与; 带来, 产生; 加以, 使蒙受. *Too much exercise will* ~ *you harm.* 运动过度可能有害. *Such a book* ~*es credit to the writer.* 这样的书给作者带来声誉. *Will you* ~ *me a favor?* 能帮个忙吗? *It doesn't* ~ *any good.* 这不会有什么好处. ~ *homage to* 对…表敬意. ~ *sb. justice* 为某人说公平话; 不亏待某人. ④处理; 修理; 收拾(房间等); 洗; 整(容); 预备(功课); 解答(问题). ~ *the dishes* 洗碗碟. ~ *one's face* 整容, 化妆. ~ *the flowers* 把花摆设好. ~ *one's hair* 梳头发, 做头发. ~ *the room [kitchen]* 收拾房间[厨房]. ~ *one's homework* 做作业, 做功课. ~ *English* 学英语, 做英语作业. ⑤翻译; 改写; 创作; 抄, 誊写. ~ *a Latin passage into Chinese* 把一段拉丁文译成中文. ~ *a poem into prose* 把诗改写成散文. *She* ~*es oil portraits.* 她创作油画肖像. *I have to* ~ *ten copies* 我得抄十份. ⑥访问, 游览, 参观, 逛. *They did London in five days.* 他们花五天时间游览伦敦. ~ *the sights* 游览名胜. ⑦适合, 对…合宜, 对…够用. *That would* ~ *me very well.* 那对我很适合, 那好极啦. *Ten dollars will* ~ *me.* 十美元就够我用了. *Will this chair* ~ *you?* 这椅子行吗? ⑧走过, 跑过, 跋涉. *He did 20 miles a day on foot.* 他一天走了二十英里. ⑨扮演; 上演;〔口〕装出〔一般接 the + 形容词〕. ~ *Hamlet* 扮演哈姆莱特. *We did Othello* 我们演出《奥赛罗》. ~ *the amiable* 装得和蔼可亲的样子. ~ *the big* 充好汉. ⑩煮, 煎, 烧. ~ *the meat thoroughly* 把肉煮透. *steak done to a turn* 牛排煎得很好. ⑪〔俚〕欺骗; 打败. *I'm afraid (that) you've been done.* 我恐怕你已经受骗了. *be done for $500 at poker* 赌牌时被骗去 500 元. *That does me.* 那要叫我认输了. ⑫〔俚〕待, 对待; 招待, 款待. ~ *sb. well* 优待某人; 款待某人. *"I will* ~ *you next, please wait a minute."* "请稍等一下, 接着就轮到你了."〔理发师对顾客说的话〕. ~ *oneself well [proud]* 生活阔绰, 养尊处优. ⑬〔口〕使疲劳. *The long journey has done him.* 长途旅行使他疲劳不堪. ⑭〔古〕处置;〔口〕杀死. *If you stir, I will* ~ *you.*〔俚〕你要是动, 我就干[杀]掉你. ⑮〔口〕服(刑); 做满(任期). ~ *five years for forgery* 因犯伪造罪服刑 5 年. ~ *a year as chairman of the club* 任俱乐部主席一年. ⑯为(小说等)写评论. ~ *the fiction for a newspaper* 专门为一家报纸写小说评论.

— *vi.* ①做, 行动, 工作; 进行; 行事, 表现. *Let us be up and doing.* 打起精神来工作吧! ~ *like a gentleman* 做事正派. *When at [in] Rome,* ~ *as the Romans* ~. 入乡随俗. *He is* ~*ing very well at the Bar.* 他在律师界干得不错. *How shall we* ~ *for the great cost?* 我们怎么应付庞大的开支呢? ~ *without an automobile* 在没有汽车的情况下凑合着干. ②〔口〕发生. *There is nothing doing!* 没有发生什么事. *What's* ~*ing at the office?* 办公室里出什么事了? ③行, 可以, 适合, 合用(*for*); 够了. *This will never* ~. 这不中用, 这个不行. *Any time will* ~. 什么时候都行. *This sum will* ~ *for the present.* 这笔钱暂时够用了. *It would never* ~ *to neglect official obligations.* 玩忽职守是绝对不行的. *That will* ~. 那就好了, 够了. *These shoes won't* ~ *for mountaineering.* 这些鞋子不适合爬山. ④(植物等)生长, (健康等)进展. *Mother and child are* ~*ing fine.* 母亲和孩子的身体都很好. *Flax* ~*es well after wheat.* 收过小麦以后, 亚麻长得不错. ④办完, 结束. *After she had done in the kitchen, she went out.* 她在厨房干完活以后就出去了. *His work is never done.* 他总是不把事情做完. *It is done.* 做完了. ***be done with*** 与…分手, 结束 (*I'm quite done with the girl.* 我和那个姑娘的关系彻底结束了). ***can*** ~ ***with*** 将就, 勉强能对付 (*Can you* ~ *with cold mutton for lunch?* 你能凑合着吃点冷羊肉当午饭吗? *I can* ~ *with two meals a day.* 我一天只吃两顿饭也可以). ***could*** ~ ***with*** 需要, 希望得到 (*I could* ~ *with a good rest.* 我希望好好休息一下. *You could* ~ *with a shave.* 你需要刮

刮脸了). ~ ***away with*** ①除去，废除. ②干掉，杀死 (*Trivial formalities have to be done away with.* 繁文缛节必须废除. ~ *away with oneself* 自杀. *suspected of having done away with sb.* 有杀死某人的嫌疑). ~ ***by*** 对待，待 (*He ~es well by a friend.* 他对朋友很好. *Do as you would be done by.* 你愿意别人怎样待你，你就怎样待别人). ~ ***for*** ①〔口〕杀死，除掉；毁掉，坏掉；累垮 (*Once you are unemployed, you are done for.* 一旦失业，你就完了. *It was the shot that did for him.* 那颗子弹要了他的命). ②适合做 (*You won't ~ for a lawyer.* 你不适合当律师). ③〔英〕照料(家务)，照顾，帮助 (*She ~es for her brother.* 她给弟弟管家). ~ ***in*** 〔俚〕①杀死，害死. ②损坏，累垮. ③欺骗 (~ *oneself in* 自杀. ~ *one's car in* 车子坏了. *be done in by the heat* 热坏了. *You'd better watch out, or you'll be getting done in.* 你得当心点，不然会受骗). ~ ***it all*** 〔美俚〕服无期徒刑. ~ ***one's thing*** 做自己喜欢做的事. ~ ***one's bit*** 见 bit 条. ~ ***one's demnedest*** 〔俚〕苦干，拼命干. ~ ***off*** 〔古〕脱 (~ *off one's clothes* 脱衣). ~ ***or die*** 干到底，决一死战，死而后已. ~ ***out*** 打扫，收拾 (~ *out a room* 收拾屋子). ~ ***sb. out of*** ①驱逐某人. ②欺骗某人 (*He did me out of the job.* 他把我解雇了. *She did me out of several hundred dollars.* 她骗去了我几百元). ~ ***over*** ①重做，改做. ②重新装饰(房屋等) (~ *a room over* 重新装饰房间). ~ ***sb. proud*** 使某人感到荣幸. ~ ***time*** 服徒刑 (*It's hard to get a decent job once you've done time.* 一旦坐过牢，想再找个好工作就不那么容易了). ~ ***to*** 对待，处置 (~ *to death* 〔古〕处死). ~ ***unto*** 〔古〕= ~ to. ~ ***up*** ①包；捆 (~ *up a parcel* 包包裹). ②扣，结扎 (~ *up one's hair* 扎好头发. ~ *up one's dress* 扣上衣服). ③整顿，修理；修饰；洗 (~ *up one's shirts* 洗衬衫. *have one's house done up* 收拾屋子). ④〔口〕使累垮，使极疲劳 (*be done up with teaching all day* 教一天书下来累得要命). ⑤穿，打扮 (*The waitresses are all done up in costumes.* 女服务员都穿着制服). ~ ***well*** ①处置得当. ②(病人等)情况好；成功，发达；顺遂，成绩好. ③(植物)长得好 (*He did well to refuse.* 他拒绝得好). ~ ***with*** ①满足于，忍耐 (*You must ~ with what you've got.* 你必须知足. *I can't ~ with his insolence.* 我忍受不了他的侮辱). ②与…相处 (*It's difficult to ~ with her.* 和她不易相处). ③处置，对付 (*What shall I ~ with a man like that?* 怎样对付这样一种人呢?). ~ ***without*** 省去，无需 (*The store hasn't any, so you'll have to ~ without.* 店里没有，所以你就得将就一些了). ***Have done!*** 停止！结束！ ***have done with*** ①办完，用完 (*Have you done with the pen?* 你用好那支笔了吗？) ②已和…无关，和…断绝关系 (*I have done with her.* 我已和她断绝关系了). ***have to ~ with*** 和…有关系〔来往〕 (*Smoking has a great deal to ~ with lung cancer.* 吸烟和肺癌有很大关系. *have nothing to ~ with* 和…无关系). ***How ~ you ~?*** 您好〔被介绍时及打招呼时用语〕. ***make ~ with*** 将就，凑合着用 (*She can't afford a new coat and so will have to make ~ with the old one.* 她买不起新外衣，只能凑合着用旧的了.

— *v. substitute* (代动词)〔用来避免动词的重复〕. *Use a book as a bee does* (= uses) *flowers.* 象蜜蜂利用花一样地利用书吧. *Did you see him? Yes, I did* (= saw him). 你看见他了吗？嗯，看见了. ***So ~ I.*** 我也是，我也如此 (*You smoke sometimes, so ~ I.* 你有时吸烟，我也如此). ***So I ~.*** 是的，不错 (*You smoke sometimes.* — *So I ~.* 你有时吸烟吧. —是的). — *aux.v.* [强du:, 弱 du, də, d] ①〔构成疑问句〕*Do you go?* 你去吗？ *Did you go?* 你去了吗？ ②〔与 not 连用构成否定句〕. *I did not [didn't] go.* 我没有去. *I ~ not [don't] know.* 我不知道. ③〔用于加强语气和倒装语序的句中〕. *I ~* [ˈdu:] *think so.* 我的确是这样想的. *He did* [ˈdid] *come.* 他的确来过了. *Well ~ I remember it.* 那我是记得很清楚的. *Never did I see such a thing.* 我从来没有见过那样一种东西. ④〔命令和劝告〕. *Do not [don't] tell a lie.* 莫撒谎. *Do* [ˈdu:] *come.* 请一定来. *Do* [ˈdu:] *be quiet.* 务请肃静！

— [du:] *n.* (*pl.* ~***s***, ~***'s*** [du:z]) ①要求做到的事. ②〔俚〕骗局，欺骗. ③〔英口〕宴会；庆祝会. ④〔英军俚〕交战. ⑤〔罕〕〔*pl.*〕处置；行动；〔英方〕骚动. ⑥成功. ⑦〔*pl.*〕分配. *It's all a ~.* 这全是欺骗. *It was a tricky ~.* 这是一个狡猾的骗局. *We've got a ~ to-night.* 家里今晚请客. *make a ~ of it* 获得成功. *Fair do's!* 公平分配！ ~ ***one's ~*** 做能做的事. ***dos and don'ts*** 善恶好歹；注意事项；习惯；规章制度 (*Observe the following dos and don'ts.* 请遵守下列注意事项).

do² [dəu] *n.* 【乐】(全音阶的)第一音，do 音.

do. [ˈditəu] = ditto.

D/O, d. o. = delivery order.

D.O.A., DOA = dead on arrival 送达医院当即死去〔警察或验尸报告用语〕.

do·a·ble [ˈdu:əbl] *a.* 可做的，做得到的，可行的.

doat [dəut] *vi.* = dote.

do-all [ˈdu:ˈɔ:l] *n.* 杂役，勤杂工.

dob·ber [ˈdɔbə] *n.* 〔美〕(钓丝上的)浮标，浮子.

dob·bin [ˈdɔbin] *n.* 农用马；老驽马.

Do·ber·man pin·scher [ˈdəubəmən ˈpinʃə] (一种德国品种的)多伯曼短毛猎犬.

do·bie [ˈdəubi] *n.* 〔美口〕= adobe.

do·bla [ˈdəublɑ:] *n.* 多布拉〔西班牙古金币名〕.

do·bra [ˈdəubrə] *n.* 多布腊〔葡萄牙几种古金币之一〕.

Dob·son [ˈdɔbsn] *n.* 多布森〔姓氏〕.

do·by [ˈdəubi] *n.* 〔美口〕住处.

doc [dɔk] *n.* 〔美口〕①= doctor. ②〔常 D-〕先生〔对医生、兽医的称呼〕.

do·cent [ˈdəusənt] *n.* ①(美国某些大学的)代课教师. ②(大学)讲师.

do·ce·tic [dəuˈsi:tik] *a.* 基督幻影说的；基督幻影说者的.

Do·ce·tism [dəuˈsi:tizəm] *n.* 【宗史】基督幻影说〔早期基督教的一种非正统学说，认为基督系幻影，无肉身〕. **Do·ce·tist** *n.* 基督幻影说者.

doch-an-dor·rach [ˈdɔkənˈdɔrək] *n.* 〔英方〕(临行时喝的)告别酒.

doc·ile [ˈdəusail] *a.* ①(学生等)容易教的，听话的，俯首贴耳的. ②(马等)驯良的，容易驾御的. ③易处理的. *a ~ horse* 驯顺的马. *be ~ at school but unruly at home* 在学校里听话，在家里调皮. **-ly** *ad.*

do·cil·i·ty [dəuˈsiliti] *n.* 温顺；听话. *follow with docility* 俯首听命.

dock¹ [ˈdɔk] *n.* ①船坞，修船所；〔常 *pl.*〕(附设码头，仓库等的)造船厂；〔美口〕码头，停泊处. ②【铁路】终点站. ③〔空〕飞机检修架，飞机库，飞机修配厂. ④(舞台下部的)布景存放处. *a wet [dry, floating] ~* 泊船坞〔干坞，浮坞〕. *naval ~* 海军船坞. ***in dry ~*** 〔俚〕失业. — *vt.* ①把(船)引入船坞〔码头〕. ②在…设置船坞. ③【宇航】使(宇宙飞行器)在外层空间相接. — *vi.* ①(船)进入船坞〔码头〕. ②【宇航】(与另一飞船等)在外层空间相接，会合. **D- Board** 【海】港务局. ~ **charge [dues]** 入坞费，码头费. ~**hand** 码头工人. ~**man** *n.* (*pl.* **-men**) =~hand. ~**master** 船坞长，造船厂厂长. ~**side** *n.* 码头边，码头侧邻区. ~**-wallope** 码头上的短工，搬运工. ~ **warrant** 船坞仓库存货凭单. ~**yard** ①造船厂，船舶修造厂. ②海军船坞；〔英〕军舰修造所. **-ing** ① *n.* 入坞. ② *a.* 入坞的 (~ *accommodation* 入坞设备. ~ *facilities* 泊船设备). **-ize** *vt.* 为(港口)设码头；在(河道等处)设船坞.

dock² [dɔk] *n.* 【植】①酸模属草类；酸模. ②草本植物.

dock³ [dɔk] *n.* ①尾巴的骨肉部分. ②剪短的尾，去毛的尾. ③(套在短尾上的)套尾皮袋. — *vt.* ①截去, 剪短(尾巴等); 把…的尾巴[头发]剪短. ②削减, 缩减(供应、工资等). ③剥夺, 扣去…的应得工资[津贴等]. ~ *a tail* 剪短尾巴. ~ *the ears of cattle* 剪短牛耳. ~ *a horse* 剪短马尾. ~ *sb.'s wages* 削减某人的工资, 使某人减薪. ~ *an allowance* 削减津贴. ~ *sb. a day's pay* 扣某人一天工资. ~ *him of the pleasures of childhood* 剥夺他童年时代的欢乐. ~**-tailed** *a.* 尾巴剪短的.

dock[4] [dɔk] *n.* (刑事法庭的)被告席. ***be in the*** ~ 受审, 处于被告席. ~ **brief**【法】(英国律师为贫苦被告进行的)免费辩护.

dock·age[1] [ˈdɔkidʒ] *n.* ①入坞费, 码头费. ②船坞设备. ③入坞.

dock·age[2] [ˈdɔkidʒ] *n.* ①(经费、工资等的)削减, 缩减; 扣除. ②(谷物中的)杂质.

dock·er[1] [ˈdɔkə] *n.* 〔英〕码头工人; 船坞工人.

dock·er[2] [ˈdɔkə] *n.* ①剪尾工. ②剪尾器.

dock·et [ˈdɔkit] *n.* ①(公文的)概略, 摘要. ②【法】判决摘要书; 备审案件目录. ②(贴在货物等包装外皮上的)标签, 签条. ③应办事项(表); 议事日程, 记事条. ④〔英〕(准购管制或稀缺物资的)购货证; 关税完税证. — *vt.* ①(在公文等上)附加提要. ②在…上附加签条. ③【法】把…记入[列入]应办案件表; 给(判决等)作摘要. *judgments regularly* ~*ed* 按规定作出摘要的判词. *His papers were always neatly* ~*ed.* 他的论文总是附有眉目清楚的摘要. ***clear the*** ~ 结束所有案件的审理; 〔喻〕结束, 扫清(工作). ***on [off] the*** ~ ①【法】在[不在]审理中. ②〔喻〕在[不在]审办[考虑]中. ***trial*** ~ 〔美〕备审案件目录.

doc·tor [ˈdɔktə] *n.* ①博士〔略作D. 或 Dr.〕. ②医生, 医师, 大夫; 牙医; 兽医; 巫医. ③〔古〕学者, 教师; 【天主】权威神学家. ④【机】校正器, 调节器; 临时应急工具[装置]; 〔口〕修理师; 修理场, 修理室. ⑤〔海口〕大师傅〔船上或营地等对厨师的尊称〕. ⑥(钓鱼用的)人造彩色蝇. ⑦【印】刮片, 刮刀. ⑧【化】(精炼石油用的)试硫液. ⑨〔口〕凉爽的(海)风. *D- of Divinity [Laws, Literature, Medicine, Philosophy]* 神[法, 文, 医, 哲]学博士. *a good-for-nothing* ~ 庸医. *a chair* ~ 修椅子的人, 修椅工. *a car* ~ 修车师傅. ~ *knife* 刮刀. ~ *solution*【化】试硫液. *D- of the Church* (天主教的) 权威神学家. ~ *test*【化】(汽油)含硫试验. *Doctors' Commons* (伦敦从前处理遗嘱、结婚、离婚等的) 民法博士会馆. ~***'s stuff*** 药剂. ***practice as a*** ~ 开业行医. ***put the*** ~ ***on sb.*** 欺骗某人. ***see [consult] a*** ~ 去就医, 就诊. ***sent for a*** ~ 请医生(来), 延医治疗. ***When*** ~***s differs*** 〔谑〕当大学者们产生意见分歧的时候. — *vt.* ①诊治, 医治; 为…充当医师. ②修理, 修复. ③修正, 改写(文稿等). ④〔口〕窜改(文件、帐目等); 搀混(酒等); 阉割(家畜). ⑤授与…博士学位. *He* ~*ed his cold at home.* 他在家治感冒. ~ *oneself for a cold* 给自己治感冒. ~ *an old clock* 修理旧钟. ~ *the play to suit the audience* 修改剧本以迎合观众. ~ *the election returns* 窜改选举结果. ~ *the fact on his passport* 窜改护照上的记录. ~ *the drink with a stupefying dose* 在酒里掺麻醉剂. — *vi.* ①行医, 做医生. ②〔方〕服药. *He* ~*ed in Europe before coming to the U.S.* 他来美国以前在欧洲当医生. ~ **blade**【印】(改版用的)刮刀. ~ **book** 《家医》, 家用医书. ~**ship** 博士学位.

doc·tor·al [ˈdɔktərəl] *a.* 博士的; 学者的; 权威的. *a* ~ *dissertation [thesis]* 博士论文.

doc·tor·ate [ˈdɔktərit] *n.* 博士头衔[学位、资格].

docto·ri·al [dɔkˈtɔːriəl] *a.* = doctoral.

doc·tress [ˈdɔktris] *n.* 〔罕〕女医生; 女博士; 博士夫人.

doc·tri·naire [ˌdɔktriˈnɛə] *n.* 空谈理论的人, 教条主义者. — *a.* 教条的, 空谈理论的. *a* ~ *preacher* 一个空谈理论的说教者. **-nair·ism** [-ˈnɛərizəm] *n.* 教条主义, 空谈理论.

doc·tri·nal [dɔkˈtrainl] *a.* 教条的, 教义的; 学说上的. *a* ~ *dispute* 学说上的论争. ~ **theology**【宗】教义学.

doc·tri·nar·i·an [dɔktriˈnɛəriən] *a., n.* = doctrinaire. **-ism** *n.* = doctrinairism.

doc·trine [ˈdɔktrin] *n.* ①(宗教、政治方面的)教旨, 教条; 原则; 主义. ②学说; 〔口〕教训, 训导. *Catholic* ~*s* 天主教教义. *the* ~*s of Freud* 弗洛伊德的学说. *religious* ~*s* 宗教训导.

doc·trin·ism [ˈdɔktrinizəm] *n.* 教义至上主义; 对主义的信奉. **-trin·ist** *n.* 教义至上主义者; 主义的信奉者.

doc·u·ment [ˈdɔkjumənt] *n.* ①文献, 文件; 公文. ②证件, 证书, 凭证. ③记录影片, 记实小说. ③【海】船舶执照. *a diplomatic* ~ 外交文件. *public* ~*s* 公文. *a* ~ *of searching* 搜查证. *a* ~ *of shipping* 装货单据. *a human* ~ 人世间的记录. — [ˈdɔkjument] *vt.* ①用文件[证书等]证明, 为…提供文件[证书等]. ②根据事实材料制作(影片等). ③【海】为(船舶)提供执照〔表明船的国籍、容量、所有权等〕. *a* ~*ed vessel* 〔美〕有执照的船. *a carefully* ~*ed biography* 有详细文献根据的传记. ~ *a case* 为案件提供文件资料.

doc·u·men·tal [ˌdɔkjuˈmentəl], **doc·u·men·ta·ry** [ˌdɔkjuˈmentəri] *a.* ①文件的; 公文的; 证书的. ②记录的, 记实的. *a* ~ *bill [draft]*【商】跟单汇票. *a* ~ *committee* 起草委员会. *a* ~ *film* 记录影片. *a* ~ *evidence [proof]* 文件证明. *a* ~ *history* 历史资料. — *n.* 【影】纪录片 (= ~ film); 记实小说; 【无】实况录音. **-men·ta·ri·ly** *ad.*

doc·u·men·ta·tion [ˌdɔkjumenˈteiʃən] *n.* ①文件[证书等]的提供; 参考文件[证件等]的利用. ②提供的文件[证书等]. ③与历史事实的相符. ④(利用微型照片复制等技术进行的)文献的编集; 文件分类.

DOD = Department of Defense 〔美〕国防部.

do·dad [ˈduːdæd] *n.* 〔美俚〕= doodad.

Dodd [dɔd] *n.* 多德〔姓氏〕.

dod·der[1] [ˈdɔdə] *vi.* ①(因年老、中风等而)摇晃, 蹒跚; 抖颤. ②蹒跚而行. *an old man* ~*ing down the walk* 一个在人行道上摇摇晃晃行走的老人. **-y** [ˈdɔdəri] *a.* 衰老的, 老迈的; 蹒跚的.

dod·der[2] [ˈdɔdə] *n.*【植】菟丝子, 菟丝子属植物.

dod·dered [ˈdɔdəd] *a.* ①(树木等)枯朽脱枝的. ②衰弱的.

dodec(a)- *comb. f.* 十二. *dodecagon.*

do·dec·a·gon [dəuˈdekəgən] *n.*【数】十二角形, 十二边形. **-al** [ˌdəudiˈkægənəl] *a.*

do·dec·a·he·dron [ˌdəudikəˈhedrən] *n.* (*pl.* ~***s, -dra*** [-drə])【数】十二面体.

do·dec·a·phon·ic [dəuˌdekəˈfɔnik] *a.* 【乐】十二音体系的. **-phonist** [-ˌfəunist] *n.* 运用十二音体系作曲者. **-pho·ny** [-ˈfəuni], **-pho·nism** *n.* 十二音体系作曲法.

do·dec·a·style [dəuˈdekəstail] *n.*【建】十二柱式.

Dodge [dɔdʒ] *n.* 道奇〔姓氏〕.

dodge [dɔdʒ] *vi.* ①躲开, 闪开, 避开. ②掩饰, 托词逃避, 搪塞. *To avoid my friend, I* ~*d into the nearest café.* 为了避免和一个朋友见面, 我躲进了最近的一家咖啡馆. *When asked a direct question, he* ~*s.* 当被问到一个明确的问题时, 他就搪塞过去. — *vt.* 闪开, 躲开, 避开, 摆脱. ~ *a blow* 躲闪开打击. ~ *a question* 回避问题. ~ *a direct question* 把一个明确的问题搪塞过去. ~ ***about*** 东躲西避. ***dodging and dissembling*** 遮遮掩掩地. — *n.* ①躲避; 〔口〕推托, 搪塞. ②〔俚〕妙计, 窍门, 诡计; 新设计的装置[器具]. *by a swift* ~ *to the left* 很快向左一躲. *a* ~ *to win your confidence* 想赢得你的信任的一个诡计. ~ *times* 〔美〕闲暇, 空闲时间. ***be up to all*** ~***s*** 诡计多端. ***on the*** ~ 〔英口〕搞鬼, 蒙混; 躲避; 无固定住处(以逃避拘捕). **dodg·er·y** *n.* ①躲避. ②推托. ③用诡计, 欺诈.

dodg•em [ˈdɔdʒim] *n.* （游乐园中的）电动躲闪车〔乘者相互躲让着行驶，躲闪不及常互相碰撞，源出 dodge them 一语，亦作 ～ car〕.

dodg•er [ˈdɔdʒə] *n.* ①躲闪者；推托者，蒙骗者. ②〔美〕传单，广告单. ③〔美南部〕玉米饼. ④〔澳〕一大块（面包等）. ⑤【海】船桥上的防浪屏. *a draft* ～ 逃避服兵役者. *a tax* ～ 逃税者.

Dodg•son [dɔdʒsən] 道奇森〔姓氏〕.

dodg•y [ˈdɔdʒi] *a.* ①躲避的；推托的；会掩饰的. ②〔俚〕机警的，巧妙的.

do•do [ˈdəudəu] *n.* (*pl.* **～s, ～es**) ①【鸟】渡渡鸟〔原产于毛里求斯岛等地、已于十七世纪末绝种的一种鸽属巨鸟，性迟钝，不会飞〕；愚钝的人；落后者；〔俚〕不能单独飞行的飞行员. *The society is as dead as the* ～. 社交界一片死气沉沉.

dod•unk [ˈdɔdʌnk] *n.* 〔美俚〕笨人.

Doe [dəu] 无名氏〔法院用语，用以指姓氏不明者，如 John Doe, Jane Doe（某约翰，某珍妮）〕.

doe [dəu] *n.* (*pl.* **～s,** 〔集合词〕 ～) ①母鹿，母山羊，母羚羊，雌兔 (*opp.* buck). ②〔美俚〕社交场合无男伴的女子.

do•er [ˈdu:ə] *n.* ①行为者. ②做（某事）的人，生长（好、坏）的动植物〔常用以构成复合词〕. ③实干家. *He is a* ～, *not a talker.* 他是一个不说空话的实干家. *a good [poor]* **～**发育良好[不良]的动[植]物. *an evil* ～ 作恶者. *a* ～ *of good* 行善者，做好事者.

does [强 dʌz; 弱 dəz, dz] do 的第三人称、单数、现在式.

doe•skin [ˈdəuskin] *n.* ①母鹿〔兔、羚羊、山羊〕皮. ②【纺】仿鹿皮（织物）；驼丝棉；〔*pl.*〕羊皮手套.

does•n't [ˈdʌznt] = does not.

do•est [ˈdu(:)ist] 〔古、诗〕 do[1] 的第二人称、单数、现在式〔用于主语为 thou 时的场合〕.

do•eth [ˈdu(:)iθ] 〔古、诗〕 do[1] 的第三人称、单数、现在式.

doff [dɔf] *vt.* ①脱（帽、衣等）(*opp.* don). ②废除（习惯等）. ③【纺】落（纱）；落（卷）；落（筒）. ～ *one's hat* 脱帽（敬意）. *D- your stupid habits and live.* 抛弃你的坏习惯好好生活吧. — *n.* 【纺】落下的纱〔卷等〕. **-er** *n.* 【纺】①小滚筒，"道夫". ②落纱工. ③落纱机.

do•fun•ny [ˈdu:fʌni] *n.* 〔美俚〕那个，那东西〔叫不出或想不起名称的东西，尤指小装饰品或一些新设计品〕.

dog [dɔg] *n.* ①犬，狗；猎犬；犬科动物. ②（狼、狐等）雄兽，雄狗；类似犬的动物. ③卑鄙的人，无赖；废物，没用的人. ④〔口〕（…样的）家伙〔常加形容词修饰〕；〔美〕装阔气；妄自尊大. ⑤【机】轧头，挡块，止动器；卡爪，棘爪；拔钉钳；搭钩；挂钩环，钩；【船】（水密门）夹扣. ⑥【天】〔the D-〕大犬座，小犬座. ⑦（炉中的）铁架. ⑧〔*pl.*〕〔美口〕小红肠；红肠夹心面包. ⑨〔*pl.*〕（人的）双脚. ⑩【气】假日，幻日；雾虹；（预示有雨的）小雨云. ⑪〔美俚〕（戏剧、音乐等的）失败之作；劣质品；滞销商品；亏本投资，贬值股票；丑妇；〔*pl.*〕破产，毁灭. ⑫〔美俚〕妓女. ⑬〔英俚〕〔the ～s〕跑狗比赛. *treat sb. like a* ～ 把某人当狗一样对待. *a hunting* ～ 猎犬. *a* ～ *fox* 雄狐. *a lazy* ～ 懒家伙，懒骨头. *a lucky* ～ 幸运儿. *a dead* ～ 废料，没用的东西. *a dirty* ～ 下流坯. *a gay* ～ 快活人儿. *Don't be a* ～. 不要这样卑鄙. *My* ～*s are burned up.* 我的两只脚都烧伤了. *She's been standing on her* ～*s all day.* 她已经站了一整天. *That used car you bought is a* ～. 你买的那辆旧车是件废物. ***a dead*** ～ 无用的东西. ***a*** ～ ***in a blanket*** 葡萄卷饼，卷布丁. ***a*** ～ ***in the manger*** 狗占马槽，占着毛坑不拉屎的人，自己干不了又不肯让位的人，占住自己不能享用的东西又不肯给别人享用的人. ***a*** ～***'s age*** 〔口〕好久好久. ***Barking*** ～***s do not [seldom] bite.*** 叫狗不咬人，嘴狠手软，干叫唤不动手干. ***be top*** ～ 居于高位，居于支配地位. ***be under*** ～ 永远听人支配. ***call off the*** ～ ①停止追逐〔查询〕. ②岔开不愉快的谈话. ***die like a*** ～ = ***die a*** ～***'s death*** 死得惨；死得可耻. ～ ***and maggot*** 〔英军俚〕饼干和干酪. ～ ***before its master*** 〔英俚〕大风前的巨浪. ～***s of law*** 酷刑，苛法. ～***s of war*** 战争惨祸，兵燹. ***eat*** ～ 〔美〕忍辱. ***Every*** ～ ***has his day.*** 凡人皆有得意时. ***Give a*** ～ ***a bad [ill] name and hang him.*** 谗言可畏，欲加之罪何患无辞. ***get the*** ～ 〔美〕胜，赢. ***give [throw] sth. to the*** ～***s*** ①放弃，扔掉某物. ②牺牲某物保护自己. ***go to the*** ～***s*** 〔口〕没落，堕落；灭亡；〔美〕努力全成泡影，失败. ***help a lame*** ～ ***over a stile*** 助人渡过危难. ***lead (sb.) a*** ～***'s life*** （使某人）过苦日子. ***Let sleeping*** ～***s lie.*** 莫惹睡狗，不要惹事生非. ***Love me, love my*** ～. 爱屋及乌. ***not even a*** ～***'s chance*** 毫无机会. ***put on (the)*** ～ 〔美俚〕要威风，摆架子. ***try it on the [a]*** ～ ①牺牲别人进行试验. ②电影试演检验效果. ***wake a sleeping*** ～ 惹事生非. — *vt.* ①追猎；追随，尾随，跟踪，钉梢；（灾难等）紧紧缠住. ②【机】用钩抓住；用轧头夹住. *He kept dogging my tracks all the way to London.* 他一直跟踪我到伦敦. ～ ***down***【海】用钩扣牢. ～ ***it*** 〔俚〕打扮起来. ②摆阔. ③偷懒. — *ad.* 〔用作复合词〕极，非常: *I'm* ～*-tired.* 我累死了. **～berry**【植】山茱萸，山茱萸的籽实；梾木属植物. **～-biscuit** 喂狗的饼干；硬饼干. **～-box** 铁路上运狗的车箱. **～cart** ①狗拖的车. ②（二人背靠背坐的）单马拉双轮马车. **～-cheap** *a., ad.* 极便宜（地）. ～ **clutch**【机】爪形夹盘，爪卡盘. ～ **collar** ①狗项圈. ②〔俚〕（牧师等用的）项圈形胶领. ③〔口〕（用宝石等装饰的）项链. ～ **days** ①三伏天，大热天〔一般为 7 月 3 日—8 月 11 日〕. ②无精打彩的日子；无所作为的时期. **～-ear** *n., vt.* = ～'s-ear. **～-eat-～** *n., a.* 狗咬狗（的），损人利己（的）(*a* ～*-eat-*～ *war* 狗咬狗的战争. *The only rule of the market place was* ～*-eat-*～. 市场上的唯一准则是损人利己). **～face** 〔俚〕士兵，步兵. **～fall** （摔跤时）双方同时倒地，平局. ～ **fancier** 爱狗的人；狗商. **～fight** *n., vi.* ①【空】缠斗，混战. ②狗打架，狗咬狗. **～fish**【动】角鲨，星鲨. **～hole** ①狗洞. ②龌龊的房间. ③〔俚〕不安全的小煤矿. **～house** ①狗窝；小窝棚. ②监狱的监视塔 (*in the* ～*house* 〔美俚〕丢脸，挨骂；受耻辱). ～ **Latin** 不规范的拉丁语. ～ **lead** 狗绳，狗链. **～leg, ～-legged** *a.* （象狗的后腿一样）折曲的，罗圈腿（的）. ～ **napper** 〔美〕偷狗的人，狗贼. ～ **paddle** 狗爬式游泳. **～-paddle** *vi.* 进行狗爬式游泳. **～robber** 〔美〕军官的传令兵. ～ **salmon**【动】鲑，大马哈鱼. **～'s age** 〔俚〕很久. **～'s-body** ①豆粉布丁. ②〔英海俚〕打杂；低级船员. **～'s chance** 极有限的一点机会. **～'s-ear** ① *n.* （书页的）折角. ② *vt.* 把（书页）折角. **～'s-eared** *a.* （书页）折角的；（书）翻旧了的. **～'s letter** 犬音字母〔指 r，尤指其发卷舌音时〕. **～'s nose** 啤酒与杜松子酒的混合饮料. **～shore**【船】（船下水前用的）支船木. **～-sick** 恶心的. **～-skin** 狗皮. **～sleep** 假寐，打盹，时常惊醒的睡眠. ～ **spike** （铁路上的）狗头钉，钩头道钉. **～'s-tail**【植】洋狗尾草属植物. **D- Star** ①天狼星〔大犬座主星〕. ②南河三〔小犬座主星〕. **～'s-tongue**【植】倒提壶属植物. **～'s tooth** （作男子衣料的）格子花呢. **～'s tooth violet**【植】山茨菇. ～ **tag** ①狗牌，狗执照. ②〔军俚〕（战时士兵挂在颈上的）身份证明牌. ～ **tent** 〔军俚〕掩蔽帐篷. **～-tired** *a.* 极疲倦的. **～tooth** ①犬齿. ②【建】犬牙饰，四叶饰. ～ **trick** 恶作剧. **～trot** *n., vi.* 小跑 (*He* ～*-trotted home.* 他小步跑回家). ～ **tune** 〔俚〕二流歌曲. **～vane**【船】（桅上的）风向指示器. **～watch** ①【海】（二小时换班的）折半轮值〔午后 4—6 时，6—8 时〕. 夜班〔尤指最后一班〕. ②〔俚〕（报社记者等的）额外值班〔正班以外等待特殊重要消息的轮值〕. **～wood**【植】山茱萸，梾木属植物. **-dom** ①犬类. ②犬性. ③〔集合词〕爱犬的人，爱玩狗的人. **-hood** *n.* 狗性. **-let** 〔美〕小狗. **-like** *a.* ①狗一样的. ②忠于主人的.

dog·ged [ˈdɔgid] *a.* ①顽固的,固执的. ②顽强的. *a ~ scholar* 坚持自己主张的学者. *resume one's ~ effort* 重新开始顽强的努力. ***It's ~ (that* 或 *as) does it.*** 有志者事竟成;坚持就是胜利.

dog·ger [ˈdɔgə] *n.* 荷兰双桅渔船. ***the D- Bank*** (英国与丹麦之间的)陶格尔沙〔世界著名渔场之一〕.

dog·ger·el [ˈdɔgərəl] *n.* 歪诗,打油诗. — *a.* (诗)拙劣的. ②滑稽的. *~ lines of verse* 拙劣的诗句.

dog·ger·y [ˈdɔgəri] *n.* ①狗性;(狗一样)卑劣的行为. ②〔集合词〕狗. ③乌合之众;暴徒. ④〔美俚〕小酒馆,下等酒吧间.

dog·gie [ˈdɔgi] *n.* ①小狗;〔儿〕狗. ②〔美俚〕红肠. — *a.* 爱狗的. **~bag** 狗食袋〔餐馆给顾客把残羹剩菜带回喂狗的袋子〕.

dog·gi·ness [ˈdɔginis] *n.* 象狗;爱狗;狗臭.

dog·gish [ˈdɔgiʃ] *a.* ①狗的;狗一样的;卑鄙的. ②脾气大的,泼辣的,爱吵闹的. ③〔口〕爱花哨的,浮华的. *a ~ temper* 坏脾气. **-ly** *ad.* **-ness** *n.*

dog·go [ˈdɔgəu] *ad.* 〔俚〕一动不动地;隐蔽地. ***lie ~*** 〔英俚〕隐蔽,埋伏,一动不动地等候.

dog·gone [ˈdɔgɔn] *a.* 〔美俚〕①可恶的,讨厌的. ②非常的,无比的. *That was a ~ insult.* 那是一个可恶的侮辱. — *int.* 〔美俚〕讨厌! 可恶! 他妈的! 该死的! — *vt.* 〔常用被动语态〕〔口〕咒骂. *I'll be ~d if I'll go.* 我要去就是混蛋,我决不去. *D- Your silly ideas.* 去你的那套馊主意吧. — *n.* 诅咒. — *ad.* 非常,极. *I've worked ~ hard in my life.* 我这辈子干的苦活儿可真够呛.

dog·gy [ˈdɔgi] *a.* ①狗的,狗一样的. ②爱玩狗的. ③〔美俚〕时髦的;摆阔的. *a ~ smell* 狗臭. *the tweedy, ~ people* 衣着时髦的阔佬. — *n.* = doggie.

do·gie [ˈdəugi] *n.* 〔美方〕(牧场中)失去母牛的牛犊;孤犊儿.

dog·ma [ˈdɔgmə] *n.* (*pl.* ***~s, ~ta*** [-tə])〔罕〕①教义,教理,教条;信条. ②定论;独断论,武断的意见. *the ~ of the Assumption* 【宗】关于圣母升天的教义. *a political ~* 政治信条.

dog·mat·ic, dog·mat·i·cal [dɔgˈmætik(əl)] *a.* ①教条的,教义的. ②教条主义的,独断论的. ③固执己见的,武断的. *a ~ statement* 武断的说法. **dog·mat·i·cal·ly** *ad.* 独断地,专断地;教条式地.

dog·mat·i·cs [dɔgˈmætiks] *n.* 〔*pl.*〕【宗】教义学.

dog·ma·tism [ˈdɔgmətizəm] *n.* ①教条主义. ②武断,独断论. **dog·ma·tist** *n.* ①教条主义者,独断论者. ②【宗】教义学者.

dog·ma·tize, dog·ma·tise [ˈdɔgmətaiz] *vi.* ①教条式地说〔写,阐释〕,教条化. ②武断,独断 *(on, about)*. — *vt.* 把…说成教条,使教条化.

do·good [ˈduːgud] *a.* 〔贬〕(空想)改良社会的. *~ schemes* 改良社会的空想方案. **-er** *n.* 〔俚,蔑〕(空想的)社会改良家. **-ism** *n.* 空想的社会改良主义.

do·gy [ˈdəugi] *n.* = dogie.

Doha [ˈdəuhə] *n.* 多哈〔卡塔尔首都〕.

Do·her·ty [ˈdəuəti, dəuˈhəːti] *n.* 多尔蒂〔姓氏〕.

doi·ly [ˈdɔili] *n.* (垫碗碟或小摆设等的)小布巾;花边桌垫.

do·ing [ˈdu(ː)iŋ] *n.* ①做,干,实行. ②〔*pl.*〕行为,行动,举动,活动,所作所为. ③〔俚〕所需要的东西. ④〔*pl.*〕〔方〕做菜的材料. *Your misfortune is not of my ~.* 你的不幸不是我造成的. *daily ~s* 日常活动. *his ~s in England* 他在英国的活动.

doit [dɔit] *n.* ①古荷兰小铜币. ②小额,几文钱;小东西,琐事. *I don't care a ~ what he does.* 我对他干的事毫不放在心上. *not worth a ~* 毫无价值.

doit·ed [ˈdɔitid] *a.* 〔Scot.〕(老年人)昏愦的.

do-it-your·self [duːitjɔːˈself] *a.* (业余爱好者等)自制的,为业余爱好者设计成的. *a ~ kit for building a radio* 供业余爱好者装配收音机用的一套工具. **-er** *n.* 自己动手的人(指在家中自己制造和修理生活用具的人),自己动手的业余爱好者.

dol. = dollar(s).

do·lan·tin [dəˈlæntin] *n.* 【药】盐酸地美罗,度冷丁.

dol·ce [ˈdɔltʃi] *a., ad.* 〔It.〕【乐】非常温柔的〔地〕.

dol·ce far ni·en·te [ˈdɔltʃi fɑː niˈenti] 〔It.〕安逸,闲适.

dolce vi·ta [ˈdəultʃei ˈviːtə, ˈdɔltʃə ˈviːtɑː] *n.* 〔It.〕放荡,淫乱.

dol·drums [ˈdɔldrəmz] *n.* 〔*pl.*〕①郁闷,忧郁;沉闷;萎靡不振,无生气. ②【气】〔the ~〕赤道无风带. *be in the ~* 意气消沉;(船)在无风带内. *August is a time of ~ for many enterprises.* 许多企业在八月份营业清淡. *in a state of mental ~* 精神萎靡.

Dole [dəul] *n.* 多尔〔姓氏〕.

dole[1] [dəul] *n.* ①施舍物,赈济品;(微少的)施舍. ②〔the ~〕〔英口〕失业救济. ③〔古〕命运. *Happy man may be his ~!* 〔古、诗〕愿他幸福快乐. *the unemployment ~* 失业救济. *on the ~* 处于被救济状态. ***draw the ~*** 领失业津贴. — *vt.* 施舍,少量分发 *(out)*. *The last of the water was ~d out to their thirsty crew.* 最后一点水被少量地分给干渴的船员. **doles·man** [ˈdəulzmən] *n.* 接受施舍的人,领取失业救济的人.

dole[2] [dəul] *n.* 〔古、诗〕悲哀,悲叹. *make one's ~* 哀叹. **-ful** [-ful], **-some** [-səm] *a.* 悲哀的;凄凉的 (*a doleful look* 悲哀的神色. *one's doleful voice* 声音凄苦).

dol·er·ite [ˈdɔlərait] *n.*【矿】① 粗玄武岩. ②〔英〕辉绿岩(= diabase). ③〔美〕(玄武岩一样的)深色火成岩.

dol·i·cho·ce·phal·ic [ˈdɔlikəuseˈfælik] *a.* 【解】长头的〔头指数在 75 以下, *opp.* brachycephalic〕.

dol·i·cho·cra·ni·al [ˌdɔlikəuˈkreiniəl] *a.* 【解】长颅的〔颅指数在 75 以下者〕. **-cra·nic** [-nik], **-cra·ny** [-ni] *n.*

do·li·ne, do·li·na [dəˈliːnə] *n.* 【地】落水洞,石灰坑,斗淋.

do·little [ˈduːlitl] *n.* 〔口〕游手好闲的人,懒汉.

Doll [dɔl] *n.* 多尔〔女子名, Dorothy 的昵称〕.

doll [dɔl] *n.* ①玩偶,玩具娃娃. ②貌美心拙的妇女. ③〔美俚〕姑娘,少女;美女. ④(对女子)有吸引力的男子. *in my ~ days* 在我当姑娘的时候,在我的少女时代. *in a world where woman are only ~s* 在一个妇女只是玩偶的世界里. ***~'s face*** 美貌而呆板的面孔. ***~'s house*** 玩偶之家;小住宅. ***guys and ~s*** 青年男女. — *vt., vi.* 〔美俚〕着意打扮,浓装艳抹 *(up)*. *be ~ed up in furs and diamonds* 用珠宝和皮大衣打扮得很漂亮. *This old woman ~s herself up like a young lady.* 这个老妇人总是漂漂亮亮地把自己打扮得象个少妇. ~ **baby** ①洋娃娃. ②情人,爱人. ③漂亮可爱的少妇. ~ **carriage [buggy]** 娃娃车. **~face** 娃娃脸(的成年人). **~faced** *a.* 娃娃脸的. **-ish, -like** *a.* 玩偶似的,好看而没有头脑的. **-ishly** *ad.*

dollar [ˈdɔlə] *n.* ①美元〔符号为 $ 或 $〕. ②元〔加拿大等国的货币单位,如加元,澳元等〕. ③一元金币〔银币,纸币〕;〔英俚〕五先令银币 (= crown). ④〔the ~s〕金钱,财富. ⑤【物】元〔原子堆的反应性单位, 指缓发中子产生的反应性〕. *Hong Kong ~* 港币. ***bet one's bottom ~s*** 〔美口〕确信,必然 (*I'll bet my bottom ~s that he will succeed.* 我确信他必然成功). ***~-a-year man*** 〔美〕拿法定最低薪俸的现任官员. ***~s to buttons [doughnuts]*** 〔美俚〕确信,有把握 (*It is ~s to doughnuts.* 的的确确. *I'll bet you ~s to doughnuts.* 我敢肯定). ***fell [look] like a million ~s*** 〔美俚〕感觉〔看上去〕十分健康;(妇女)看上去特别吸引人. **~-a-year** *a.* 只领象征性的菲薄薪金的. ~ **area** 美元地区. ~ **bloc** 美元集团. ~ **diplomacy** 金元外交. **~fish** 【动】翻车鱼. ~ **gap [shortage]** 美元亏空〔国际贸易中与美元地区相互贸易而入超〕. ~ **mark** 美元符号 (即 $ 或 $). **~(s)-**

and-cent(s) *a.* 纯经济的. **-wise** *ad.* ①以美元计算的(*How much does a million francs amount to* ~? 一百万法郎合多少美元). ②在财政方面.

doll·ish [ˈdɔliʃ] *a.* 玩偶似的; 好看而没有头脑的. **-ly** *ad.* **-ness** *n.*

dol·lop [ˈdɔləp] *n.* 〔口〕①(粘土、奶油等的)一块, 一团. ②少量, 一点儿. ~*s of mud* 泥团. *a* ~ *of soda water* 少量苏打水.

Dol·ly [ˈdɔli] *n.* = Doll. ~ **Varden** (1870年前后流行的)花布女服; 饰花阔边女帽.

dol·ly [ˈdɔli] *n.* ①〔儿〕(玩具)娃娃. ②【矿】(矿石的)捣碎棒; 〔英方〕(洗衣用的)搅拌棒, 捣衣杵. ③(车间运料用的)小轮手推车; (采石场的)窄轨小机车; 移动式摄影车. ④(打桩用的)垫盘; 【机】铆顶; 抵座; (铁匠做钉头用的)型铁; (使用搅拌棒的)洗衣桶. — *vt.* ①用独轮车运(物). ②用搅拌棒洗(衣); 用捣棒捣碎(矿石). — *vi.* ①【影】推动移动式摄影车. ②用捣棒捣碎矿石; 用搅拌棒洗衣. ~ ***in [out, back]*** 向前[向后]推动移动式摄影车. ~**man** 使用小轮手推车的搬运工. ~**'s bird** 〔美俚〕打扮入时的漂亮姑娘. ~ **shop** ①〔美俚〕废品店, 低级当铺. ②〔英口〕船具店(= marine store). ~ **shot** 【影】移动式拍摄. ~ **tub** (使用搅拌棒的)洗衣桶.

dol·man [ˈdɔlmən] *n.* ①土耳其长外套. ②披肩式衣袖的女外衣. ③骠骑兵的斗篷式短外衣.

dol·men [ˈdɔlmen] *n.* 【考古】石桌状墓标.

dol·o·mite [ˈdɔləmait] *n.* 【矿】白云石, 白云岩. ***the Dolomites*** (意大利东北部的)白云石山脉. **D- Alps** = the Dolomites. ~ **marble** 【矿】粗粒白云石. **-mit·ic** [-ˈmitik] *a.* 含白云石的.

do·lour, do·lor [ˈdəulə] *n.* 〔诗〕悲哀, 忧伤. ***the*** ~***s of Mary*** 【宗】圣母玛利亚的悲哀. **dol·or·ous** [ˈdɔlərəs] *a.* 〔诗〕(令人)忧伤的, (令人)悲哀的 (*a dolorous melody* 感伤的曲调. *dolorous news* 令人悲哀的消息).

dol·phin [ˈdɔlfin] *n.* ①【动】海豚; 海豚科动物. ②(码头的)系船柱; 系船浮标. ③〔the D-〕【天】海豚座〔又作 Delphinus〕; 〔俚〕= the Dorado.

dol·phin·ar·i·um [ˌdɔlfiˈnɛəriəm] *n.* 海豚馆.

dolt [dəult] *n.* 呆子, 笨蛋, 傻瓜.

dolt·ish [ˈdəultiʃ] *a.* 愚钝的, 呆笨的. **-ly** *ad.* **-ness** *n.*

do·lus [ˈdəuləs] *n.* 【法】恶意欺诈〔大陆法用语〕. *One is liable for* ~ *resulting in damages.* 一个人要对恶意欺诈造成的损害负法律责任.

DOM 〔美〕DOM 幻觉剂 (= STP).

Dom [dɔm] *n.* ①阁下〔天主教高级修道士和圣职人员的尊称〕. ②= Don〔巴西、葡萄牙贵人名前的尊称〕.

dom. = ①domain. ②domestic. ③dominion.

-dom *suf.* ①地位, 职位; 领域: earl*dom*, duke*dom*, king*dom*. ②状态, 性质: wis*dom*, free*dom*. ③集团, 界, 派: official*dom*, christen*dom*.

do·main [dəuˈmein] *n.* ①领土, 版图; 领地. ②管区, 势力圈; (特定动物等的)生长圈; (学问、活动等的)领域, 范围; 【物】磁区, 畴; 【数】域; 整环. ③产业, 房地产; 【法】土地〔产业〕所有权. *the* ~ *of Great Britain* 英国的版图. *the* ~ *of science* 科学领域. *Geography is not within my* ~. 地理不是我的专长. *We enter the* ~ *of the pine trees.* 我们进入了松树生长带. ***be out of one's*** ~ 非所长. ~ ***of use*** 【法】地上权. ***eminent*** ~【法】(国家对一切产业的)支配权, 征用权. ~ **theory** 【物】磁畴说. **-al, -ni·al** [dəˈmeiniəl] *a.* ①属于某一领地[领域]的. ②拥有领地的.

do·mal [ˈdəuml] *a.* 【语】卷舌的.

dome [dəum] *n.* ①圆屋顶, 圆盖, 穹窿; 丘; 【机】钟形汽室; 【化】(蒸馏釜的)拱顶. ②〔诗〕高楼, 大厦, 大教堂, 殿宇. ③〔美俚〕脑袋, 头; 狗的额头; 油库. ④【地】穹地, 穹丘; 【化】(结晶的)坡面. *the great* ~ *of the sky* 广阔无垠的苍穹. *the* ~ *formed by the tree's branches* 树枝构成的圆顶. *that big* ~ *of yours* 〔俚〕你那个大脑袋. — *vt.* ①在…上加圆顶. ②使成钟形; 使呈穹状凸起. — *vi.* 成圆顶状, 成穹状凸起. *His forehead* ~*ed out in a curve.* 他的前额呈弯曲的半球形. ~ **car** (装有玻璃圆顶供旅客观看沿途风景用的)圆顶游览车箱. **-d** *a.* 圆顶的, 圆盖形的, 半球形的 (*a domed roof* 圆形屋顶). **-like** *a.* 穹顶的.

Do·mes·day Book [ˈduːmzdei buk] 【英史】(1086年英王威廉一世颁布的)土地调查清册.

do·mes·tic [dəˈmestik] *a.* ①家的, 家里的, 家庭的. ②国内的, 本国的, 对内的. ③热心家务的, 不喜外出的; 会持家的. ④家养的, 养驯了的 (*opp.* wild). ⑤自己制造的; 国产的. ~ *affairs* 家事; 内政. ~ *animals* 家畜. ~ *economy* 家庭经济. ~ *life* 家庭生活. ~ *expenses* 家用. *a* ~ *fowl* 家禽, 鸡. *a* ~ *woman* 只关心家务事的女人, 家庭妇女. ~ *science* 家政学. ~ *soap* 家用肥皂, 洗衣皂. ~ *loan* 内债. ~ *mail* 国内邮件. ~ *products [goods]* 国货, 国产. ~ *trade* 国内贸易. — *n.* ①家仆, 佣人. ②〔美〕〔*pl.*〕国货, 本国产品. ③家用织物. **-ti·ca·ble** *a.* ①易[可]养驯的; (植物)可移植的. ②习于家居的. **-ti·cal·ly** *ad.* 家庭式地, 在家事上, 适合家庭[国内]地.

do·mes·ti·cate [dəˈmestikeit] *vt.* ①养乖, 养驯(动物等); 培养(野生植物). ②使喜爱家庭; 使爱做家务. ③使归化; 使(移民等)服水土. ④引入(国外习俗等). ⑤使受教化. ~*d plants* 栽培植物. *Cats were* ~*d by the Egyptians.* 猫是由埃及人养驯的. ~ *foreign customs* 引入外国习俗. — *vi.* ①(动物等)驯化. ②喜爱家庭, 喜爱做家务. **-ca·tion** [-ˈkeiʃən] *n.* **-ca·tor** *n.* ①驯养者, 驯化者. ②使归化者.

do·mes·tic·i·ty [ˌdəumesˈtisiti] *n.* ①对家庭生活的爱好, 爱操持家务; 深居简出. ②家庭乐趣, 家庭生活. ③〔*pl.*〕家事, 家务. *the domesticities* 家事, 家务; 家风.

Domett [ˈdɔmit] *n.* 多米特〔姓氏〕.

dom·ic, dom·i·cal [ˈdəumik(əl)] *a.* 圆顶式; 有圆顶的. **-al·ly** *ad.*

dom·i·cile [ˈdɔmisail] *n.* ①住处, 住所. ②【法】本籍, 原籍. ③【商】期票支付场所. *a regular* ~ 固定住处. ~ *by birth* 原籍, 出生地. ~ *of choice* 【法】选择居留地. ~ *of origin* 原籍. — *vt.* ①决定(某人)住处, 使定居. ②指定(期票的)支付场所. *be* ~*d in [at]* 在(某处)住下来. ~ *oneself* 定居下来. — *vi.* 定居, 安家. *I temporarily* ~*d with my aunt.* 我暂时和婶母住在一起. **-d** *a.* ①(期票)指定支付地点的. ②定居的.

dom·i·cil·i·ar·y [ˌdɔmiˈsiljəri] *a.* ①住处的, 住所的. ②户籍的. *a* ~ *register* 户籍. *a* ~ *visit [search]* 【法】搜查住宅.

dom·i·cil·i·ate [ˌdɔmiˈsilieit] *vt., vi.* = domicile. **-a·tion** *n.*

dom·i·nance, dom·i·nan·cy [ˈdɔminəns, -si] *n.* ①权势; 统治, 控制, 支配. ②优势, 优越. ③【生】显性, 优势度. *come under the* ~ *of* 沦于…的统治之下.

dom·i·nant [ˈdɔminənt] *a.* ①支配的, 统治的; 有权威的. ②最有力的, 占优势的; 主要的; 突出的, 超群出众的. ③居高临下的, 高耸的. ④【生】显性的, 优势的 (*opp.* recessive); 【乐】第五音的, 属音的. *be in the* ~ *position* 居于支配地位. *the* ~ *party* 第一大党, 多数党. *Writing has become his* ~ *interest.* 写作已成为他的主要兴趣. *a* ~ *mountain peak* 主峰. *the* ~ *chord* 【乐】属和音. *the* ~ *chord of the ninth* 【乐】第九属和音. — *n.* ①主因, 要素, 主要的人[物]. ②【生】显性性状; 显性基因; 优势种; 【乐】全阶第五音, 属音. ~ **character** 【生】显性性状. ~ **mutant** 【生】显性突变型[体]. ~ **sex** 〔美俚〕女性. ~ **tenement [estate]** *n.* 【法】承役地.

dom·i·nate [ˈdɔmineit] *vt.* ①把持, 操纵, 支配, 统治; 左右, 控制. ②优于, 超出. ③高出, 俯视. ~ *a country commercially* 控制一国的商业. *Dahlias* ~ *the garden.* 园

子里开的大都是大丽花. ~ *one's passions* 抑制欲望. ~*d by greedy egotism* 为贪婪的私欲所左右. ~ *the conversation* 滔滔不绝地谈，不容他人插嘴. *The city is ~d by the castle.* 古堡俯视着城市. *a dominating position*【军】制高点. — *vi.* ①有统治权力，居于支配地位；占优势 *(over)*. ②巍然在上；高耸 *(over)*. *the castle dominating over the river* 高耸于河边的古堡.

dom·i·na·tion [ˌdɔmiˈneiʃən] *n.* ①把持，操纵，支配，统治；优势. ②【生】显性化. ③〔*pl.*〕【宗】主天使〔天使分九阶三级三队，中级三队为主天使〕. *world* ~ 世界霸权. *fall under the ~ of* 沦于…的支配〔统治〕之下. *the maternal* ~ 母权统治. *the French ~ of the cinema* 法国在电影业中的优势地位.

dom·i·na·tive [ˈdɔmineitiv] *a.* 支配的，占优势的.

dom·i·na·tor [ˈdɔmineitə] *n.* ①支配者，统治者；占优势者. ②支配力，统治力.

dom·i·neer [ˌdɔmiˈniə] *vi.* ①擅权，跋扈，作威作福 *(over)*. ②高耸 *(over)*. ~ *over one's inferiors* 对下级盛气凌人. — *vt.* ①对…飞扬跋扈；对…盛气凌人. ②高耸于…之上. *~ed by one's wife* 怕老婆，惧内. *The castle ~s the town.* 古堡高耸于城市之上. **-ing** *a.* 盛气凌人的，飞扬跋扈的.

Dom·i·ni·ca [ˌdɔmiˈniːkə] *n.* 多米尼加(岛)〔西印度群岛〕.

do·min·i·cal [dəˈminikəl] *a.*【宗】①主的，基督的. ②主日的，星期日的. *the ~ prayer* 主祷文. *the ~ day* 星期日，主日. *the ~ year* 公元，公历. ***the ~ letter*** 主日文字〔教会历上表示一月第一个星期日用的 A, B, C, D, E, F, G 七个字母，如某年一月一日是星期日，该年的主日字母即为 A；一月二日为星期日，该年主日字母即为 B；余类推〕.

Do·min·i·can[1] [dəˈminikən] *a.*【天主】多明我会的. *the ~ Order*【宗】多明我会. — *n.* 多明我会修道士.

Do·min·i·can[2] [dəˈminikən] *a.* 多米尼加共和国的. — *n.* 多米尼加共和国人. ***the ~ Republic*** 多米尼加共和国〔拉丁美洲〕.

Dom·i·nic(k) [ˈdɔminik] *n.* 多米尼克〔男子名〕.

Dom·i·nick [ˈdɔminik] *n.*【动】= dominique.

dom·i·nie [ˈdɔmini] *n.* ①〔Scot.〕教员，老师. ②[ˈdəumini]〔美〕(荷兰改革派教会的)牧师；教士.

do·min·ion [dəˈminjən] *n.* ①统治权，主权；支配，管辖 *(over)*；【法】所有权. ②〔常 *pl.*〕疆土，领土，版图；领地. ③〔D-〕(英帝国的)自治领；加拿大. *have [hold, exercise] ~ over* 具有对…的支配权，对…行使统治权. *the overseas ~s* 海外领地. ***D- Day*** 加拿大自治纪念日〔七月一日〕. ***D- of Canada*** 加拿大自治领〔俗简称 the D-〕. ***D- Parliament*** 加拿大议会. ***the Old D-***〔美〕Virginia 州的通称.

Dom·i·nique[1] [ˈdɔminiːk] *n.* 多米尼克(女子名)〔又作 Dominica〕.

Dom·i·nique[2] [ˈdɔminiːk] *n.*【动】美国多米尼克肉卵兼用鸡.

dom·i·no[1] [ˈdɔminəu] *n.* *(pl. ~es, ~s)* ①带有假面具的化装舞衣；(蒙住眼睛和部分面孔的)黑色假面具. ②穿戴假面具化装舞衣的人.

dom·i·no[2] [ˈdɔminəu] *n.*〔*pl.*〕①多米诺骨牌；多米诺牌戏. ②〔*pl.*〕〔美俚〕牙齿. ③〔俚〕打倒人的一击. *play ~s* 玩多米诺骨牌. ***It's all ~ with (sb.).***〔俚〕(某人)完蛋了. — *int.* 不行！~ **effect** 多米诺效应，一倒百倒，连锁效应. ~ **theory** 多米诺(骨牌)理论〔指一国崩溃，其他邻国就会相继垮台的政治局面〕.

Do·mi·nus [ˈdəumiːnus, ˈdɔminəs] *n.*〔L.〕上帝，主.

Dominus vo·bis·cum [vəuˈbiskum]〔L.〕上帝与你同在，上帝保佑你.

Don[1] [dɔn] *n.* 唐〔人名，Donald 的昵称〕.

Don[2] [dɔn] *n.*〔the ~〕顿河〔苏联〕.

don[1] [dɔn] *vt.*〔书〕穿(衣)，披(衣)戴(帽) (*opp.* doff). ~ *one's clothes* 穿上衣服. *Rioters donned handkerchiefs as gas masks.* 暴乱者扎上手帕捂住口鼻作为防毒面具. ~ ***the spikes***〔美俚〕参加棒球比赛.

don[2] [dɔn] *n.*〔Sp.〕①〔D-〕唐〔意为"先生","阁下"，西班牙人用在人名前的尊称〕. ②西班牙贵族，绅士；(一般)西班牙人. ③〔古〕大人物；〔俚〕名人，名家；专家 *(at)*. ④(英大学尤指剑桥、牛津大学的)导师；特别研究员；*a ~ at cricket* 板球名手. **D- Juan** [dɔn ˈdʒuːən, Sp. don ˈhwɑːn] ①唐璜〔西班牙传说中的风流贵族〕；风流荡子. ②英国诗人拜伦一部长诗的题目.

do·ña [ˈdəunjə] *n.*〔Sp.〕①〔D-〕夫人，太太〔加在人名前的尊称〕. ② 西班牙女人.

do·na(h) [ˈdəunə] *n.*〔Pg.〕①〔D-〕太太，夫人〔加在人名前的尊称〕. ②葡萄牙女人；〔英俚〕女人；情妇.

Don·ald [ˈdɔnəld] *n.* 唐纳德〔男子名〕.

Do·nar [ˈdəunə] *n.* (日尔曼神话中的)雷神〔相当于北欧神话中的 Thor〕.

do·nate [dəuˈneit] *vt.*〔美〕捐赠，捐献；赠给，送. ~ *blood to a blood bank* 向血库献血. ~ *1,000 dollars to an orphanage* 向孤儿院捐赠 1,000 美元. — *vi.* 捐赠，捐献 *(to, towards)*. *They used to ~ to the Red Cross every year.* 他们每年捐钱给红十字会.

do·na·tion [dəuˈneiʃən] *n.* ①捐赠，赠送，捐献. ②捐赠物，赠品；捐款. *a blood ~* 献血. *make [give] a ~* 捐赠. *make ~s to the calamity fund* 为救灾基金捐款.

Don·a·tist [ˈdɔnətist] *n.* 多纳特斯教派〔四世纪北非的一个基督教派〕教友. **Don·a·tism** *n.* 多纳特斯派教义.

don·a·tive [ˈdəunətiv] *a.* ①赠与的，捐赠的. ②【教会史】(圣职)直接授与的. *a ~ trust* 捐款托管. —*n.* 捐赠物；捐款.

do·na·tor [dəuˈneitə] *n.* ①捐赠者，捐款人. ②【化】= donor.

Don·bas(s) [dɔnˈbɑːs, ˈdɔnˌbɑːs] *n.* 顿巴斯〔苏联一地区〕.

done [dʌn] do[1] 的过去分词. — *a.* ①已完成的，完毕了的. ②疲倦极了的，精疲力尽的. ③烧熟了的〔通例用作复合词〕. ④受了骗的；吃了亏的，负了伤的. ④注定要完蛋的. ⑤符合礼仪的，(趣味等)时行的，合时的. *Our work is ~.* 我们的工作做完了. *What ~ is ~.* 木已成舟. *half-~* 半熟的. *over-~* 煮得〔烧得〕过火的. *under ~* 煮得〔烧得〕夹生的. *The fish is ~.* 鱼烧好了. *too ~ to go any further* 累得不能再走了. *It isn't ~.* 这样做是失礼的，那已经不时行了. — *ad.*〔美俚〕已经. ***be ~ brown*** ①烧成焦色. ②上大当，受骗. ***be ~ for*** ①筋疲力竭. ②身败名裂. ③不行了，完了 (*Three days without water and a man is ~ for.* 三天不喝水，人就完了). ***be ~ to the wide, be ~ up [in]*** 筋疲力尽，累透了. ***Easier said than ~.*** 做比说难，说起来容易做起来难. ***No sooner said than ~.*** 一说就做，说到做到. ***D-!*** 好！赞成！ ***Well ~!*** 干得好！ ***What's ~ cannot be undone.*** 事已定局，无可挽回；覆水难收. **-ness** *n.* 煮熟的程度.

do·nee [dəuˈniː] *n.*【法】受赠人 (*opp.* donor).

dong[1] [dɔːŋ, dɔŋ] *n.* (钟等的)咚咚声 — *vi.* (钟等)咚咚响.

dong[2] [dɔ(ː)ŋ] *n.* 盾〔越南货币单位〕.

don·ga [ˈdɔŋgə] *n.* (非洲南部等的)小峡谷，山峡.

don·jon [ˈdɔndʒən] *n.* (城堡)主楼，主塔〔dungeon 的古拼法〕.

don·key [ˈdɔŋki] *n.* ①驴子. ②傻瓜；蠢驴；顽固的人. ③〔美俚〕拖拉机. ④〔美〕(1874 年以后) 民主党的象征. *(as) stubborn [stupid] as a ~* 驴子般顽梗〔愚蠢〕的. — *a.*【机】辅助的. *a ~ boiler [pump]* 辅助锅炉〔泵〕. *a ~ engine* 辅助机车；辅助发动机. ***~'s years***〔口〕很长时期 (*I haven't seen him for ~'s years.* 我好久没有看到他了). ***talk the hind leg off a ~*** 讲个不停. ~ **act**〔美俚〕蠢举，失策. ~ **boiler** 辅助锅炉. ~ **boy** ①驴

车夫. ②轻便发动机操作者. ~ **engine** 辅助发动机; 轻便机车. ~ **jacket** 女式防风厚上衣. ~**man** 辅助发动机管理工. ~ **pump** 辅助泵. ~**'s breakfast**〔美俚〕草垫. ~**work** 苦活; 单调的日常工作.

Don·na [ˈdɔnə] *n.* 唐娜〔女子名〕.

don·na [ˈdɔnə] *n.* (*pl.* *donne* [ˈdɔni])〔It.〕①〔D-〕夫人, 女士〔加在已婚妇女名前的尊称〕. ②意大利女子.

Donne [dʌn, dɔn] *n.* 多恩〔姓氏〕.

don·née [dɔːˈnei] *n.*〔F.〕(小说、戏剧等的)基本思想; (形成行动的)基本环境.

don·nered, don·nard [ˈdɔnəd] *a.*〔Scot.〕①眼花的, 耀眼的. ②迷乱的, 茫然的.

don·nish [ˈdɔniʃ] *a.* ①(英国)大学学监的, 大学教师的. ②卖弄学问的, 学究式的. **-ly** *ad.* **-ness** *n.*

don·ny·brook [ˈdɔnibruk] *n.* 乱哄哄的争论, 瞎吵, 胡吵乱闹. *He was a center of a political ~.* 他是政治论战的中心人物. **D- Fair** 往时爱尔兰都柏林 (Dublin) 地区顿妮溪每年一次以酒色、赌斗著名的集市; 扰嚷吵闹的地方.

do·nor [ˈdəunə] *n.* ①赠送人, 捐款人. ②【生】移植体; 【电】施主; 【化】给予体, 供体; 【医】供血者, 输血者, (移植术中)皮肤[组织]供给者. ③【法】(财产归属的)指定权. *a universal ~* 全适型供血者. *a skin ~* 捐皮者, 供给皮肤者. *the ~ area* 【医】移植区.

do·noth·ing [ˈduːˌnʌθiŋ] *a.* ①游手好闲的, 什么也不做的, 懒惰的. ②无所作为的, 无为主义的. — *n.* 懒鬼, 饭桶. **-ism** *n.* ①懒惰习性. ②(不愿打破现状的)无为主义.

Do·no·van [ˈdɔnəvən] *n.* 多诺万〔姓氏, 男子名〕.

Don Quix·ote [dɔn ˈkwiksət] *n.* ①唐吉诃德〔西班牙作家塞万提斯 (Cervantes) 所著同名小说及其主人公〕. ②唐吉诃德式的人物, 充满幻想的理想主义者.

don't [dəunt] = do not; 〔卑, 美方〕= does not. *Oh, ~!* 哎, 不可以! 不行! *You know that, ~ you?* 你是知道的(是不是). — *n.*〔谑〕禁止; 〔*pl.*〕禁止事项. *a long list of ~s* 一长串禁止事项. ~**-know** *n.* 动摇分子(特指犹豫不决的投票人).

do·nut [ˈdəuˌnʌt] *n.* = doughnut.

doo·dad, do·dad [ˈduːdæd]〔美俚〕装饰品; 小玩意; 花哨而不值钱的东西. *a kitchen full of the latest ~s* 满是新玩意[新装置]的厨房.

doo·dah [ˈduːdə] *n.*〔俚〕激动, 惊慌. *all of a ~* 非常激动.

doo·dle[1] [ˈduːdl] *n.*〔英口〕"V"型飞弹(= buzz bomb).

doo·dle[2] [ˈduːdl] *vi.* ①心不在焉地乱写乱画. ②〔美口〕漫不经心地弹奏. *He ~d during the whole lecture.* 他一整节课都在胡写乱画. — *vt.*〔方〕欺骗. — *n.* ①乱写乱画. ②〔美口〕傻瓜; 吊儿郎当的人.

doo·dle[3] [ˈduːdl] *n.* = doodlebug.

doo·dle·bug [ˈduːdlbʌg] *n.* ①〔美方〕蚁狮〔一种蚁蛉科昆虫蛟蜻蛉的幼虫〕. ②(古时用迷信方式探测地下矿产、水源等的)风水卜杖. ③〔英口〕"V"型飞弹 = buzz bomb. ④〔军俚〕侦察车, 战车.

doo·fun·ny, doo·hick·ey, doo·hi·ckus [ˈduːfʌni, ˈduːˌhiki, ˈduːˌhikəs] *n.* = dofunny.

doo·lie[1], **doo·ly** [ˈduːli] *n.*〔印〕轿子; 轿式担架.

doo·lie[2] [ˈduːli] *n.*〔口〕(美国)空军学院一年级生.

doom [duːm] *n.* ①命运; 厄运; 劫数; 毁灭, 死亡. ②【史】法令. ③〔古〕(不利的)判决, 宣判. ④【宗】末日审判. *His ~ is sealed.* 他注定要遭厄运了, 他已经在劫难逃. *a sign of ~ and decay* 衰亡的征兆. *pass [pronounce] ~ of death on [upon] an offender* 判处罪犯死刑. ***fall to [go to, meet] one's ~*** 死, 灭亡. ***the day of ~*** = doomsday. ***till the crack of ~*** 直到世界末日. — *vt.* ①注定, 命定. ②判决, 决定(命运等). *be ~ed to failure* 注定要失败. *a ~ed vessel* 失事船, 正在沉没中的船. *~ sb. to life imprisonment* 判处某人无期徒刑. *~ sb.'s penal servitude* 判某人服劳役. ~ **palm**【植】埃及姜果棕.

dooms·day [ˈduːmzdei] *n.*【宗】最后的审判日, 世界末日; 〔古〕判决日. ***till ~*** 永远, 直到世界末日. **D- Book** = Domesday Book. **D- Machine** 末日机器〔幻想中的一种能触发核武器毁灭世界而无人能加以阻止的机器〕.

door [dɔː, dɔə] *n.* ①门, 户. ②入口, 门口; 通道, 门径, 门路, 关口. ③一户, 一家. ④【船、机】盖, 口. *the front [back] ~* 正[后]门. *a street ~* 临街大门. *shut the ~ behind [after] him* 把他身后的门关上. *Mind the ~!* 注意门户! *Is the ~ to?* 是从这道门走吗? *three ~s off* 前面第三家. *next ~* 隔壁. *live next ~ but one* 住在隔壁第二家. *a ~ to success* 成功之道. *the ~ to learning* 治学之道, 学习的门径. *a manhole ~*【船】入孔盖, 检修孔. ***answer [go to] the ~*** 应门, 去开门(迎客). ***at death's ~*** 命在旦夕, 处在死亡边缘 (*She remained at death's ~ for weeks.* 她的生命好几个星期处在危险状态). ***at the ~*** ①在门口, 在入口处. ②快, 即将 (*stand at the ~* 站在门口. *It's at our ~s.* 问题迫在眉睫, 时间很紧迫). ***behind closed ~s*** 秘密, 私下, 暗中 (*Family quarrels must be settled behind closed ~s.* 家丑不可外扬, 家庭争端必须私下解决). ***close the ~ to*** 关上…的大门, 使…成为不可能 (*His selfishness closes the ~ to our reconciliation.* 他的自私关上了我们和解的大门). ***close [shut] the ~ upon [on]*** ①把…拒于门外. ②把…的门堵死 (*close the ~ upon all peddlers* 堵上门禁止通行. *The incident closed the ~ upon his promotion.* 这次事故使他不可能晋升了). ***darken the ~*** 闯入. ***from ~ to ~*** 挨户, 家家. ***in ~s*** 在家内, 在屋内. ***keep open ~s*** 好客, 款待客人. ***lay (blame) at sb.'s ~ = lay (blame) at the ~ of sb.*** 把(责任等)归咎于 (*The blame of delinquency may be laid at the ~ of careless parents.* 少年犯罪可能要归咎于父母的放纵). ***lie at sb.'s ~ = lie at the ~ of*** (过失等)是某人造成的 (*One's mistakes generally lies at one's own ~.* 一个人犯错误多半是自己造成的). ***next ~ to*** ①邻接, 在…的隔壁. ②很象, 几乎 (*Who lives next ~ to you?* 你的邻居是谁? *It costs you next ~ to nothing.* 这几乎不要你花钱). ***open a [the] ~ to [for]*** 欢迎, 使…成为可能, 向…开门, 给…方便. ***out of ~s*** 在户外; 在外, 不在(家). ***point to the ~*** 下逐客令. ***put [set] sb. to the ~*** 解聘, 赶走. ***see sb. to the ~*** 送(客). ***show sb. the ~*** 驱逐, 撵走某人. ***throw open the ~ to*** 对…敞开门户. ***turn sb. out of ~s*** 把某人撵出门外. ***with closed ~s*** 不公开地, 秘密; 独自. ***with open ~s*** 公开. ***within ~s*** 在屋内, 在家里. ***without ~s*** 在户外. ~ **alarm [bell]** 门铃. ~ **case [frame]** 门框. ~ **chain** 门链〔使门只开一定宽度的防盗装置〕. ~ **check [closer]** 自动闭门装置. ~**-hinge** 门铰链. ~ **holder** 门开后固定门扉的装置. ~**keeper** 门警, 门房. ~**-key child** (父母整天都不在家的)带钥匙的孩子. ~ **knob** 球形门把手. ~**man** 看门人. ~**mat** ①(门口的)擦鞋棕垫. ②〔喻〕逆来顺受的人, 被人欺侮的人 (*He's no ~.* 他可不是那种逆来顺受的人). ~ **money** 入场费. ~**nail** 门上饰钉 (*as dead as a ~nail* 死定了). ~ **opener** ①(消防队员用的)开门器. ②推销员赠送的廉价礼物. ~**opening** 入口. ~**plate** 门牌. ~**post**【建】门柱. ~**sill**【建】门槛. ~**step** 门阶. ~**stone** 门口铺石. ~**stop** ①门垫〔防止门猛然撞上的垫片〕. ②制门器〔使门只开一定宽度的装置〕. ~**-to-~** *a.* ①挨门逐户的. ②(货物由发货场)直送用户的. ~**way** 门口, 出入口, 〔喻〕入门 (*a doorway to success* 成功之道). ~**yard**〔美〕门前庭院. **-ed** *a.* 有门的. **-less** *a.* 没有门的. **-wards** *ad.* 向着房门.

doo·zer, doo·zy [ˈduːzə, ˈduːzi] *n.*〔美俚〕非常出色的人[东西].

DOP = developing-out paper【摄】显象纸.
do·pa·mine [ˈdəupəˌmiːn] *n.*【药】多巴宁〔一种治脑神经病的药物〕.
dop·ant [ˈdəupənt] *n.*【物】掺杂剂,掺杂物.
dope [dəup] *n.* ①浓液,粘稠物,胶状物;【空】(涂机翼的)明胶,涂布油;浆料;〔美俚〕显象液.②〔俚〕麻醉品,安眠药〔鸦片等〕;〔俚〕(赛马前给马服用的)兴奋剂;常服麻醉品的人,吸毒者.③(制造炸药等用的)吸收剂,添加剂,填料〔锯屑等〕;(掺入汽油等的)防爆剂.④〔美俚〕(加在冰淇淋上的)香汁〔浇头〕,(任何)食品;〔美南部〕(没有酒精成份的)饮料〔尤指可口可乐〕.⑤〔美俚〕(赛马成绩等的)预测,情报,内部消息,(给新闻记者的)特别情报〔消息〕.⑥〔美俚〕傻子,笨蛋.⑦汽油.*a ~-peddler* 毒品贩子.*He could not sleep without ~.* 他不吃安眠药就睡不着觉.*Slip me the inside ~.* 给我透露一点内部消息.*have a ~ habit* 吸毒上瘾.*upset the ~* 预测完全不对.*fire-proof ~* 耐火涂料.— *vt.* ①在…上涂浓液;在…上涂明胶.②给(人等)吃麻醉品;偷偷给(马等)服兴奋剂;〔俚〕欺骗,麻痹.③〔美俚〕(在饮料内)加酒精;(给发动机)上汽油;给(炸药等)加填料;【物】给(半导体)掺杂质.④〔美俚〕预测(赛马等的结果).⑤解(题).*~d chemical*【物】掺杂元素.*~d fabric* 涂漆蒙布.*~d fuel* 加防爆剂的汽油.*~d glass* 掺杂玻璃.~ ***off***〔俚〕睡熟;昏昏沉沉.~ ***out*** ①解出(谜等).②〔美俚〕预测;想出(方法等);拟出(计划等).~**fiend**〔俚〕瘾君子,吸毒者.~ **room** 喷漆间.~**sheet**〔美俚〕比赛结果预测,(赛马的)内情简报.~ **shop**【空】上胶场.~ **story**(说明某一事实的背景、意义等的)辅助性报告.~ **transistor**【物】掺杂(质)晶体管.
dope·ster [ˈdəupstə] *n.*〔美俚〕(选举、赛马结果等的)预测家,内部消息供给人.*a political ~* 政治行情预测家.
dope·y, dopy [ˈdəupi] *a.*〔美俚〕①傻,笨,呆;迟钝的.②(因经常服用麻醉品等而)昏昏沉沉的.
dop·pel·gäng·er [ˈdɔpəlˌgæŋə] *n.*〔G.〕(迷信者认为存在的)活人的魂魄.
dopp·ler·ite [ˈdɔplərait] *n.* 弹性沥青,橡皮沥青.
dor [dɔː] *n.* ①【昆】欧洲粪金龟子(= ~beetle).②飞时发嗡嗡声的昆虫.~**hawk**〔英方〕【动】欧洲夜鹰,蚊母鸟.
Do·ra[1] [ˈdɔːrə] *n.* 多拉〔女子名,Dorothea 和 Theodora 的昵称〕.
Do·ra[2] [ˈdɔːrə], **D.O.R.A.**〔英〕(1914年的)领土防御法(=the Defence of the Realm Act).
do·ra·do [dəˈrɑːdəu] *n.* ①【动】鲯鳅.②〔the D-〕【天】剑鱼座.
Do·reen, Do·rene [dɔ(ː)ˈriːn, ˈdɔːriːn] *n.* 多琳〔女子名〕.
do·re·mi [ˌdəureiˈmiː] *n.*〔美俚〕钱.
Do·ri·an [ˈdɔːriən] *n.* 多利安人〔古希腊人的一支,居住在伯罗奔尼撒半岛、克里特岛等地〕.— *a.* 多利安人的;淳朴的.
Dor·ic [ˈdɔrik] *a.* ①多利安人的.②(口音)土音重的.③【建】陶立克式的〔纯朴、古老的希腊建筑风格〕.*the ~ order*【建】陶立克式.— *n.* ①(古希腊的)多利克方言.②(英语)方言土腔〔尤指苏格兰方言〕.③【建】陶立克式.*speak in broad ~* 满口乡下土腔.
Dor·is[1] [ˈdɔris] *n.* 多丽丝〔女子名〕.
Dor·is[2] *n.* 多利士〔古希腊中部地区〕.
Dor·king [ˈdɔːkiŋ] *n.*(英国多津地方出产的)肉用种五趾鸡.
dorm [dɔːm] *n.*〔美口〕宿舍(= dormitory).
dor·man·cy [ˈdɔːmənsi] *n.* ①睡眠(状态);冬眠,休眠.②潜伏,蛰伏,静止,休止.
dor·mant [ˈdɔːmənt] *a.* ①睡着的,处于睡眠状态的;冬眠的,蛰伏的,休眠的.②静止的,休止的;潜伏的;(才能等)潜在的;(资金等)没有利用的;(权利等)尚待争取的.*the ~ economy* 停滞的经济.*A long ~ memory stirred.* 长期潜藏着的记忆复活了.*~ rights* 有待争取的权利.*a ~ project* 有待实现的计划.*the girl's ~ talent* 这个女孩子潜在的才能.***lie ~*** 潜伏着;休眠着;冬眠着,蛰伏着.~ **capital** 游资.~ **buds**【植】休眠芽,潜伏芽.~ **seeds**【植】休眠种子.~ **partner**【商】匿名合伙人.~ **tree**【建】梁,楣.~ **volcano** 休眠火山.~ **window** 屋顶窗.
dor·mer [ˈdɔːmə] *n.*【建】屋顶窗,老虎窗(= ~ window).
dor·mice [ˈdɔːmais] *n.* dormouse 的复数.
dor·mi·tive [ˈdɔːmitiv] *a.* 安眠的.— *n.* 安眠药,麻醉药.
dor·mi·to·ry [ˈdɔːmitri] *n.* ①(学校等的)宿舍;集体寝室.②(在市内工作的人的)郊外住宅区.*a ~ town* 市郊住宅区.*~ suburb*(市内工作的人的)郊外住宅区.*a prosperous ~ community* 繁荣的市郊住宅区.
dor·mouse [ˈdɔːmaus] *n.*(*pl.* ***dor·mice*** [ˈdɔːmais])【动】睡鼠;〔喻〕爱睡的人.
dor·nick[1] [ˈdɔːnik] *n.* ①花缎、锦缎和其它装饰织物的统称.②(比利时制)多尼克地毯.
dor·nick[2] [ˈdɔːnik] *n.*(适于投掷的)小石块.
Dor·o·the·a [ˌdɔrəˈθiə] *n.* 多萝西娅〔女子名〕.
Dor·o·thy [ˈdɔrəθi] *n.* 多萝西〔女子名〕.~ **bag**〔英〕女用开口手提包.
dorp [dɔːp] *n.*〔废〕村子,小村庄.
Dorr [dɔː] *n.* 多尔〔姓氏〕.
dors- *comb. f.* 背,脊:*dorsad.*
dor·sad [ˈdɔːˌsæd] *ad.*【解、动】(身体)背部地,向后部.
dor·sal[1] [ˈdɔːsəl] *a.* ①【解、动】背的,脊的.②【植】远轴的.③【语】舌背音的.*~fin* 脊鳍.*~ muscles* 背肌.— *n.*【语】舌背音.
dor·sal[2] [ˈdɔːsəl] *n.* = dossal.
Dor·set(shire) [ˈdɔːsit(ʃiə)] *n.* 多塞特(郡)〔英格兰南部一郡〕.~ **Horn** 多塞特细毛羊.
dorsi-, dorso- *comb. f.* = dors-.
dor·si·ven·tral [ˌdɔːsiˈventrəl] *a.* = dorsoventral.
dor·so·ven·tral [ˌdɔːsəuˈventrəl] *a.* ①【植】有背腹性的.②【动】背腹的,背腹可区辨的(= dorsiventral).
dor·sum [ˈdɔːsəm] *n.*(*pl.* ***-sa*** [-sə])〔L.〕①【解】背(部).②背面:*the ~ of the hand* 手背.③【动】后缘〔鳞翅目的翅〕.
Dort·mund [ˈdɔːtmənd] *n.* 多特蒙德〔德意志联邦共和国城市〕.
dort·y [ˈdɔːti] *a.*〔Scot.〕坏脾气的;不高兴的.
do·ry[1] [ˈdɔːri] *n.*(北美东海岸渔船上配备的)平底小船.
do·ry[2] [ˈdɔːri] *n.*【动】①海鲂(= John D-).②黄麻鲈.
D.O.S.〔美〕= doctor of osteopathetic science 整骨医学博士.
dos-à-dos [dəuzəˈdəu] *ad.*〔F.〕背对背地.— *n.*(*pl.* ~ [-dəuz]) ①背对背长椅〔马车〕.②〔美〕背对背双人舞.
dos·age [ˈdəusidʒ] *n.* ①下药,配药.②剂,剂量,服用量.③(酒的)增味剂;增味;配料.
dose [dəus] *n.* ①(药的)一服,一剂;药量,剂量,用量.②苦药,讨厌的东西.③(酒中的)配料,增味剂.④(处罚等)一回,一次,一番.⑤〔美俚〕花柳病,梅毒.⑥【物】放射〔辐射〕剂量.*a ~ of medicine* 一服药.*take medicine in small ~s* 按小剂量服药.*administer a ~* 投药.*a ~ of flattery* 一番奉承.*administer ~s of punishment* 施行惩罚.*a hard ~ to swallow* 一服难咽的苦药.*a ~ of hard work* 一项苦差事.*the maximum [minimum] ~* 最大〔最小〕用量.*a lethal [fatal] ~* 致死剂量.*lethal ~ 50* 受照射者50%死亡剂量.*lethal ~ 50/30* 受照射者经过30天50%死亡剂量.— *vt.* ①给…服药,给(药).②把(药等)配分剂量.③在(酒)中加料.*~ a patient with quinine* 给病人服奎宁.*I ~d myself with hot milk.* 我拿热牛奶当药喝.*He ~d me with advice.* 他

给我以劝告. ~ *out powders* 把药剂配成(一定份量). — *vi.* 服药. ***like a ~ of salts*** 〔俚〕非常迅速地. ~ *rate*【物】剂量率. **dosing tank** 量斗, 投配器.

do·si·me·ter [dəu'simitə] *n.* ①【物】放射性剂量仪; 原子能辐射计. ②【化】量筒, 剂量计, 剂量仪器.

do·sim·e·try [dəu'simitri] *n.* ①(放射)剂量测定(法). ②药量测定.

doss [dɔs] *n.* 〔英俚〕①简陋睡铺, (尤指小客栈的)床位. ②睡眠. — *vi.* ①睡简陋床铺, 住小客栈. ②〔美〕睡. ~ *down in a car* 倒在车子里睡一觉. ~ *out* 露宿. ~ **house** 〔俚〕小客栈; 集体宿舍.

dos·sal, dos·sel ['dɔsəl] *n.* ①(祭坛后方或圣坛周围的)吊帐, 垂帘, 挂布, 幔布. ②(椅子的)靠背饰布〔尤指国王座椅的靠背〕.

dos·ser ['dɔsə] *n.* ①驼筐, 背筐. ②= dossal.

dos·si·er ['dɔsiei] *n.* 〔F.〕(有关一事、一人的)全套档案. *a complete ~ on an individual* 关于某人情况的全套档案. *a criminal's ~* 罪犯档案.

dos·sil ['dɔsl] *n.* ①(桶等的)栓, 塞子. ②【医】填入伤口的纱布. ③【印】(揩去铜板上余墨的)揩墨布卷.

dos·sy ['dɔsi] *a.* 〔俚〕漂亮的, 好看的.

dost [dʌst] *v.* 〔诗, 古〕(主语为 thou 时的) do 的第二人称、单数、现在式.

Dos·to·ev·sky [dɔstə'jefski], **Fedor Mikhaylovitch** 费·米·陀斯妥也夫斯基〔1821—1881, 俄国小说家〕.

Dot [dɔt] *n.* 多特〔Dorothea 的昵称〕.

dot[1] [dɔt] *n.* ①点; 圆点; 句点; 【乐】附点〔音符后的一点, 表示延长 1/2 拍〕. ②一点点大的东西, 小片, 少量, 小个子. ③【数】小数点; 相乘的符号. *There are ~s of soot on the window sill.* 窗台上有一点烟灰. *Put a ~ on [over] the i.* 给字母 i 加上一点. *a ~ of butter* 一点儿奶油. *a mere ~ of a child* 小小的孩子. ***in the year ~*** 〔口〕老早以前. ***off one's ~*** 〔俚〕傻头傻脑的; 发疯. ***on the ~*** 〔口〕按时; 准时. ***put ~s on*** 〔口〕使倦怠〔烦闷〕. ***to a ~*** 〔美〕完全, 全部 (*be correct to a ~* 完全正确). ***to the ~ of an i*** 一丝不苟地. — *vt.* ①打点于; 星罗棋布于, 点缀; 用点线表示. ②〔俚〕敲, 打. *D- your i's and j's.* 写字时不要忘记在 i 和 j 字上打一点. *the sea dotted with ships* 点缀着船只的海洋. *Trees ~ the landscape.* 树木点缀着景色. *Stars ~ the sky.* 星星缀满天空. *a dotted note* 【乐】附点音符. ~ *a line across the page* 横贯书页划一条虚线. ~ *sb. in the eye* 一拳打到某人眼上. *a dotted line* 虚线. ***~ and carry one*** 〔做加法时〕逢十进位〔儿童用语〕. ***~ and go one*** ①= ~ and carry one. ②*n.* (拄着丁字杖走的)瘸子; 一瘸一拐的步行声. ③*a., ad.* 一瘸一拐的〔地〕. ~ ***down*** 暂且记下来. ***~ one's i's and cross one's t's*** 打 i 的点画 t 的横线; 一笔不苟, 详述. ***sign on the dotted line*** 〔美〕在(信封、文件等留出供署名的)虚线上签名; 〔喻〕全盘接受. **~-and-dash** *a.* ①莫尔斯电码的. ②一点一划相间的 (*~-and-dash technique* 电报技术). ~ **mark** 刻印标记. ~ **pattern** 【无】光点图形. **~-sequential** *a.* 【无】(彩色电视)点顺序制的. ~ **weld** 【机】点焊.

dot[2] [dɔt] *n.* 【法】嫁妆, 嫁资, 妆奁. **-al** ['dəutəl] *a.*

dot·age ['dəutidʒ] *n.* ①老耄, 老胡涂. ②溺爱, 过分的偏爱. ***be in one's ~*** 年老昏愦.

do·tard ['dəutəd] *n.* ①年老昏愦的人, 老胡涂. ②溺爱者.

do·ta·tion [dəu'teiʃən] *n.* ①捐助. ②基金. ③天分, 天资.

dote [dəut] *vi.* ①衰老, 年老昏愦. ②溺爱, 过分偏爱 (*on, upon*). *She ~s on her youngest son.* 她溺爱最小的儿子. **dot·ing** *a.* 老胡涂的; 溺爱的. **dot·ing·ly** *ad.* **dot·ing·ness** *n.*

doth [dʌθ] 〔古、诗〕do 的第三人称、单数、现在式.

dot·tel ['dɔtl] *n.* = dottle.

dot·ter ['dɔtə] *n.* ①加点的人. ②描点器; 【军】(练习火炮瞄准的)点标器.

dot·tle ['dɔtl] *n.* (烟斗中吸剩的)焦烟丝.

dot·ty ['dɔti] *a.* ①有点子的; 点子多的. ②有弱点的. ③〔口、方〕脚步不稳的. ④〔俚〕疯疯癫癫的, 半痴的. *be ~ on one's legs* 脚步踉跄. *That's my ~ points.* 那是我的弱点. *be ~ about a lass* 迷恋一个姑娘. **dot·ti·ly** *ad.*

Dou·a·la [du(:)'ɑ:lə] *n.* 杜阿拉〔喀麦隆港市〕.

dou·ane [du(:)'ɑ:n] *n.* 〔F.〕海关.

Dou·ay, Dou·ai [du:'ei] *n.* 杜埃〔法国地名〕. ***the ~ Bible*** 杜埃版《圣经》〔罗马天主教会核定的英译本圣经, 于 1582 及 1609—1610 年由罗马天主教学者将新旧约分别从拉丁文译成英语, 在法国 Douai 出版, 又称 ~ *Version*〕.

doub·le ['dʌbl] *a.* ①两倍的, 加倍的. ②双的, 二重的, 双重的; 对, 双, 两, 复. ③双人用的; 折摺式的. ④(意义)双关的; 模棱两可的; 表里不一的, 两面派的, 阴险的; 一人演二角的. ⑤【植】重瓣的; 【乐】低八度的; 二拍子的. ~ *pay [portion]* 双薪〔份〕. *a ~ axe* 双刃斧. *a ~ bed* 双人床. *a ~ blanket* 双连毯. *an egg with a ~ yolk* 双黄蛋. *a ~ bottom* (箱等的)夹底. *a ~ coating* 两道漆〔粉刷〕. *a ~ door* 双扇门. *a ~ eagle* 【徽】双头鹰; 〔美〕20 元金币. *serve a ~ purpose* 一举两得. *a ~ use* 双重用途. *a ~ flower* 【植】重瓣花. ~ *petunias* 重瓣矮牵牛花. *a ~ letter* (表示名词复数的)复写字母〔如 *ll.* = lines, *pp.* = pages, *LLD* = Doctor of Laws〕. *a ~ personality* 双重人格. ~ *conduct* 两面派行为. *He wore a ~ face.* 他是一个两面派. ~ *summer time* 〔英〕(比标准时间快两个小时的)二重夏令时间. *a ~ suicide* 双双自杀, 情死. *work ~ tides [shifts]* 昼夜不停地工作. *a ~ meaning* 语义双关. *a ~ interpretation* 双重解释. *a ~ rôle* 【影】一人演二角. — *n.* ①双倍. ②相似者, 相似的人〔物〕; 幽灵; 副本; 【影】译制演员, 配音演员, 后备演员, 替身; 【剧】一人演二角的演员. ③急转弯, 突然转向; 折回. ④(辩论等用的)诡计, 谋略; 回避. ⑤褶子, 褶儿; 摺迭, 重迭. ⑥【印】排重, 复印; 【军】快步; 〔*pl.*〕(网球等的)双打; 【棒球】二垒打. ⑦【天】双星; 【乐】变奏曲. ⑧〔美〕带厢房的房子. *pay ~* 付双薪, 加倍付酬. *Four is the ~ of two.* 4 是 2 的双倍. *Send me this sample in ~.* 把样品送两份给我. *This dress is the ~ of that.* 这件服装和那件一模一样. *He is the ~ of his cousin.* 他和他的表兄弟长得极相象. *make a ~* 突然折回. *play a ~ game* 玩弄两面手法. *act as sb.'s ~* 作为某人的后备演员. *a mixed ~s* 【网球】男女混合双打. ***at [on] the ~*** 迅速地; 【军】快步走. ***come the ~*** 摆弄, 欺骗. ***~ or nothing [quits]*** (打赌等)要么债务加倍要么前帐勾销, 孤注一掷. ***put a ~ on sb.*** 用计骗人. —*ad.* ①双倍地. ②双重地. ③双双地. *at ~ the speed* 用加倍速度. *pay ~ the price* 加倍付钱. *be ~ as many [much] as ...* 比…多一倍. *ride ~* (二人)共骑一马. *see ~* (酒醉眼花)看见重像. *He bent ~ with explosive laughter.* 他大笑得直不起腰来. ***sleep ~*** (二人)共睡一床. — *vt.* ①是…的两倍, 使加倍. ②重复; 折叠, 把…对折; 握(拳). ③替代(演员); 兼演(两角); (在译制片中)为…配音. ④【海】绕过(岬角等). ⑤【乐】使…高〔低〕八度. ⑥(辩论时)回避(要害问题等). ⑦【牌】(以输赢加倍计算)叫(牌). ⑧使成伙伴, 使合住〔合骑等〕. ~ *a sum* 把数目加一倍. ~ *one's efforts* 加倍努力. *The baby ~d its weight in a year.* 婴儿的体重一年增加了一倍. *Their fortune ~s ours.* 他们的财产比我们的多一倍. ~ *the blanket* 把毯子对折起来. *He ~d his fists.* 他握紧双拳. ~ *Cape Horn* 绕过合恩角. ~ *a passenger with another* 使一旅客与另一旅客合住一室. ~ *the parts of* (一人)兼演两个角色. — *vi.* ①成两倍, 增加一倍; 【牌】加倍. ②快步走〔小跑〕. ③折叠起来; 弯腰 (*over*). ④急退, 急转, 突然迂回. ⑤加倍使力, 加倍努力. ⑥替代演出 (*for*), 兼演两角 (*as*); 兼作 (*as*). ⑦【乐】兼奏 (*on*). ⑧(辩论等场合)用计. ⑨

【牌】(将输赢加倍)叫牌. *His money ~d in three years.* 他的钱三年增加了一倍. ~ *over with pain* 疼得弯下腰. *He ~d back by another road and surprised us.* 他从另一条路绕回来，突然出现在我们面前. *D-!*【军】快步走! *We ~d up the hill.* 我们一路小跑上了山. *The girl ~d as secretary and receptionist.* 那姑娘兼做秘书和招待员. *The saxophonist ~s on drums.* 萨克斯管吹奏演员兼做鼓手. ~ ***back*** ①向后折叠. ②扭头往回跑. ~ ***in*** 向内折叠. ~ ***in brass***〔美俚〕同时做两种工作,兼差; 从两处拿钱. ~ ***over*** 折起(书页等) (~ *over the edge before sewing* 衣服折起来缝边). ~ ***up*** ①(旅客等)同住一室. ②弯着身子 (*He ~d up in agony.* 他痛得弯下了身子. ~ *up with laughter* 笑弯了腰). ③折,摺;捏起(拳头). ~ ***upon*** 迂回;突然袭击(~ *upon one's steps* 折回原路行走,走回头路. ~ *upon the enemy* 突然反击敌人). **~-acting** *a.* ①【机】双动的,往复式的. ②双重作用的. **~-action** ①【机】双向,双动. ②双重作用. **~-banked** *a.* (艇等)双座的; (船舰等)双层的. **~-barrel** ①*a.* = double-barrelled. ② *n.* 双筒枪. **~-barrelled,**〔美〕**-reled** *a.* ①(枪、望远镜等)双筒的. ②双重的;有两重目的的; 模棱两可的, 暧昧的. ③复姓的〔如 Forbes-Robertson〕. **~-bedded** *a.* 备有两张床的;备有双人卧铺的;双层床的. ~ **beer** 双料啤酒. ~ **bond**【化】双键. **~-breasted** *a.* (外衣等)双排扣的,对襟的. **~-chinned** *a.* 有双下巴的. **~-clock** *vt.*〔美俚〕欺骗. ~ **cover** 二盯一〔赛球时以两名队员盯住对方一名进攻手〕. ~ **cross** ①出卖,欺骗,(有奖拳赛等约定要输而又打赢的)违约. ②【生】双杂交. **~-cross**〔美俚〕*vt.* 出卖,欺骗(朋友等). ~ **dagger**【印】双箭号. **~-dealer** 两面派,口是心非的人. **~-dealing** ①*a.* 口是心非的,奸诈的,不诚实的. ②*n.* 两面派手法,奸诈. **~-decked** *a.* 双层结构的. **~-decker** 双层床; 两层甲板的船; (铁路公路两用的)双层桥; 双层电车[公共汽车]; 双层火室的汽机. **~dome**〔美俚〕智力甚高而格调高雅的人. ~ **Dutch** 难以理解的东西,(尤指)莫名其妙的话. **~-dye** *vt.*【纺】染两次. **~-dyed** *a.* ①两次染色的,重染的. ②罪恶昭彰的,坏透的. ③(信仰等)根深蒂固的. ~ **eagle** 双鹰币〔美国金币〕, 值 20 美元. **~-edged** *a.* ①双刃的. ②模棱两可的. ③双重目的的. ④同时有好坏两方面影响的. **~ender** 两头构造相同之物[头尾同形船、两头机车、两头可开的电车等]. ~ **entry** 复式簿记. ~ **exposure**【摄】两次曝光的. **~-faced** *a.* ①有两面的; (布料等)两面可用的,两面一样好的. ②口是心非的,伪善的. ~ **feature** (一部)上下两集电影. ~ **first**〔英大学〕①两门课考优等. ②两门课优等生. **~-header**〔美〕①双车头火车. ②【棒球】连赛〔同一对球队一日连赛两次〕. **~-jointed** *a.* ①双重关节的. ②(关节等)前后左右可以自由活动的. **~-leaded** *a.*【印】放宽行距的. **~-lock** *vt.* 上双锁于. ~ **march**【军】跑步. **~-minded** *a.* 三心二意的; 反复无常的. ~ **negative**【语法】双重否定〔口语中用 I didn't hear nothing 之类, 仍为否定意〕. **~-O** *n.*〔俚〕详细追究[检查] **-park.** ~ *vt., vi.* (把汽车)挨着其他汽车并排停放〔否则违章〕. ~ **possessive**【语法】双重所有格〔如 He is a friend of father's. 他是我父亲的一位朋友〕. **~-quick** ①*n.*【军】快步. ②*a.* 快步的;急速的. ③*ad.* (用)快步;迅速. ④*vi.* 快步前进. ~ **ratio**【数】交比. **~-refine** *n., vt.* 再精炼, 再精制. **~-ripper [runner]**〔美〕双联雪橇. ~ **room** 套间. **~-space** *vt., vi.* (在打字机上)隔行打印. ~ **star**【天】双星. ~ **take** ①〔口〕先是一怔后来才恍然大悟(*do a ~ take* 先大吃一惊, 后来才明白了). ②回头再看一看. **~-talk** ①不知所云的话. ②含糊其词. **~-team** ①*vt.*【体】双拦〔球赛时用两名队员拦阻对方一名进攻者〕. ②*vi.* 用两组牲口拉一部车; 使用两倍兵力 (*on, upon*). **~think** 矛盾想法. ~ **time** ①【军】快步走. ②(加班等的)双工资. **~-time** ①*vt.* 使快步走. ②*vi.* 快步行进. **~-tongued** *a.* 撒谎的, 欺骗的. **~-track** *vt.* (使铁路)成双轨. **~-tree** (马车的)双马轼. **-r** *n.* ①【无】倍压器,倍频器. ②【纺】并线机. ③【自】倍增器,乘 2 装置. **-ness** *n.* ①加倍,二倍;双重, 二重. ②诡诈, 欺骗. **-bly** *ad.* ①加倍. ②二重, 双重. ③〔古〕欺骗地 (*be doubly cautious* 加倍小心).

dou·ble en·ten·dre [ˈduːbl ɑ̃ːnˈtɑ̃ːndr]〔F.〕①(暗含下流、猥亵含义的) 双关语. ②含糊其词. *headlines containing double entendres* 含有暧昧词句的标题.

dou·blet [ˈdʌblit] *n.* ①〔古〕(十四至十六世纪欧洲的一种)男紧身上衣,马甲. ②成对物;对偶物;〔*pl.*〕孪生子;【语】(同源异形或异义的) 同源词〔如 cloak 和 clock, fashion 和 faction〕; 〔*pl.*〕(骰子的)一对〔如一对么,一对五等〕. ③一对中的一个, 一对孪生子[同源词、骰子等]的一个. ④【印】排重的字句;【猎】(用双筒枪) 同时打下的两只鸟. ⑤【物】(光谱)双(重)线; 电子偶; 偶极天线,偶极子,对称振子; 双合透镜. ~ ***and hose*** 男装; 便装;工装.

dou·bling [ˈdʌbliŋ] *n.* ①加倍,成双. ②重叠;对折. ③(逃避追赶时等的)折回,往回跑; 迂回, 绕行, 绕航. ④【化】再蒸馏;(橡胶的)重合, 夹胶. ⑤【船】防护板, 加强板. ⑥= doublure.

dou·bloon [dʌbˈluːn] *n.* ①旧时西班牙及中南美金币名. ②〔*pl.*〕〔美俚〕钱.

dou·blure [duːˈbljuə] *n.*〔F.〕(衣服的)里子; (书籍的)封面衬里.

doubt [daut] *n.* ①怀疑; 疑惑, 疑问. ②〔常 *pl.*〕疑惧. *a shadow of ~* 有一点怀疑. *have grave ~s about* 对…有严重怀疑. ***beyond [past] (all) ~*** 毫无疑问〔常用作插入语〕. ***give sb. the benefit of the ~*** 对某人可疑处给与善意的解释,在证据不足时先假定某人是无辜的. ***hang in ~*** 悬而未决 (*His life hangs in ~.* 他的死活难以逆料). ***in ~*** ①感到疑心,拿不准. ②被怀疑, 悬而未决 (*His appointment to the position is still in ~.* 任命他担任那项职务还没有决定). ***make no ~ of*** 毫不怀疑, 确信. ***no ~*** ①无疑地. ②〔口〕很可能. ***throw [cast] ~ upon*** 对…产生怀疑. ***without (a)~*** 无疑,的的确确. — *vt.* ①疑,怀疑;不信,拿不准〔后接名词从句时, 肯定句用 whether, if, when, what 等, 否定句及疑问句用 that, but, but that, 肯定句用 that 往往表示非常怀疑〕. *I ~ whether [if] he was there.* 我拿不准他在不在那里. *I do not ~ (but) that he was there.* 我相信他在那里. *I ~ that he will be there.* 我不相信他会到那里去[我看他多半不会去了]. *~ the truth of the story* 对那番话的真实性有怀疑. ②〔古、方〕怕, 恐怕. *I ~ they will be too strong for us.* 我怕敌不过他们. — *vi.* 怀疑, 不信 (*about; of*). *He ~ed of the importance of honesty.* 他不相信诚实有多么重要. **-able** *a.* 可疑的, 令人怀疑的. **-ably** *ad.* 可疑地. **-er** *n.* 怀疑者. **-ing** *a.* 怀疑心重的,惴惴不安的(*doubting Thomas* 疑心重的人, 多疑的人). **-ing·ly** *ad.* 起怀疑心地, 有怀疑地. **-ingness** *n.* 多疑.

doubt·ful [ˈdautful] *a.* ①怀疑的, 拿不准的, 不太相信的 (*of; about*). ②可疑的, 有疑问的; 未必好的. ③含糊的, 暧昧的. ④难以预料的, 未定局的. *He is ~ of [about] the news.* 他怀疑那个消息不尽可靠. *I'm ~ (as to) what I ought to say.* 我拿不准该说些什么. *a ~ proposition* 可疑的命题. *a ~ character* 可疑的人物. *magazine of ~ taste* 内容不太好的[低级趣味的]杂志. *a ~ reply* 含糊的回答. *a ~ future* 难以预料的未来. **-ly** *ad.* **-ness** *n.*

doubt·less [ˈdautlis] *ad.* ①无疑地, 必定. ②〔口〕很可能, 多半. *D- he was the strongest.* 他无疑是最强有力的. *You have ~ seen it.* 你很可能已经看见过它了. — *a.*〔罕〕无疑的. **-ly** *ad.* = ~. **-ness** *n.*

douce [duːs] *a.*〔Scot.〕安详的; 文静的; 清醒的. **-ly** *ad.* **-ness** *n.*

dou·ceur [duːˈsəː] *n.*〔F.〕①酒钱, 赏钱; 贿赂. ②〔古〕

和蔼可亲.

douche [duːʃ] *n.* 【医】灌洗(疗)法;冲洗,灌洗. ②灌洗器,注水器. — *vt.* 灌洗;对…施行灌洗(疗法). — *vi* 施行灌洗疗法.

dough [dəu] *n.* ①(揉好的)生面团. ②生面团似的一团〔如揉好的陶土、油灰等〕. ③〔美俚〕钱,现钞. ④〔美口〕步兵〔~boy 的缩略形式〕. *a ~-brake [-kneader, -mixer]* 和面器,碾面机. *a ~ head*〔美〕面包厂. ***in the ~***〔美俚〕①兴旺;有钱,富有. ②得胜,赢. ***My cake is ~.*** 我的蛋糕还是生面团, 我的计划失败了. ***throw one's ~ around***〔美俚〕浪费金钱. **-boy** ①油炸面团;汤团. ②〔美口〕(第一次世界大战时出征的)美国步兵. **~foot**〔美口〕步兵. **~head**〔美俚〕傻瓜.

Dough·er·ty ['dəuəti] *n.* 多尔蒂〔姓氏〕.

dough·face ['dəufeis] *n.* 〔美俚〕①假面具. ②【美史】(南北战争时不反对南方蓄奴制的)亲南方的北方人〔议员〕. ③优柔寡断的人,易受人左右的人. ④生面团似的面孔. **-d** *a.*

dough·nut ['dəunʌt] *n.* ①炸面饼圈. ②环状物. ③〔美俚〕汽车轮胎;电子回旋加速室,环形室. **~ foundry [factory]**〔美俚〕小吃店. **-er·y** *n.*〔美俚〕= ~ foundry.

Dough·ty ['dauti] *n.* 道蒂〔姓氏〕.

dough·ty ['dauti] *a.* 〔古、谑〕刚强的,勇猛的. **~ knights** 勇敢的骑士. **-ti·ly** *ad.* **-ti·ness** *n.*

dough·y ['dəui] *a.* ①面团似的;粘成团的. ②夹有生面的,半熟的. ③苍白的;软弱的. *a ~ complexion* 苍白的面容. *a ~ consistency* 面团般的粘性. **dough·i·ness** *n.*

Doug·las(s) ['dʌgləs] *n.* 道格拉斯〔姓氏,男子名〕. **~ fir [pine, spruce]**【植】黄杉属;花旗松,洋松.

doup·pi·o·ni, dou·pi·o·ni [ˌduːpiː'əuniː] *n.* 【纺】双宫丝;双宫绸.

doum [duːm, daum] *n.* 【植】埃及棕榈〔通常作 ~-palm〕.

dour [duə] *a.* 〔Scot.〕①阴郁的;严厉的. ②倔强的,执拗的. ③(土地)荒瘠不毛的,(岩石)嶙峋的. *a ~ warning* 严厉的警告. **-ly** *ad.* **-ness** *n.*

dou·rine [du'riːn] *n.* 〔F.〕【兽医】马交媾病,马花柳病.

douse [daus] *vt.* ①把…浸入(水中);在…上泼水,浇水. ②【海】急速收(帆等);放松(绳子等);关闭(舱窗等). ③〔俚〕熄灭(灯、火等). ④〔口〕脱(衣、鞋等). *~ the clothes in soapy water* 把衣服浸入肥皂水. *~ the thirsty plant with water* 给干旱的植物浇水. *~ the lights* 熄灯. *~ a sail* 急速收帆. *~ a rope* 放松绳子. *~ my cap on entering the porch* 进入门廊时脱帽. — *vi.* 浸,泡;浇,洒,泼. — *n.* ①〔英方〕一击. ②浸,泡;浇,洒,泼,倾注.

douze·pers ['duːzˌpeəz] *n. pl.* ①【法史】十二名可入上院的贵族. ②(中古传奇)查理曼大帝的十二名骑士.

dove[1] [dʌv] *n.* ①鸽;小野鸽〔亦作 *mourning dove, ring dove, rock dove, turtledove*〕. ②【宗】圣灵. ③纯洁的人,天真无邪的人,温柔和蔼的人;〔昵称〕宝贝. ④和平〔纯洁、温柔、天真无邪〕的象征. ⑤〔美〕(政界的)鸽派,主和派. ⑥【天】〔the D-〕天鸽座(= Columba). *my ~* 我的宝贝儿. *a soiled ~* 娼妓. **~ colour** 暖灰色,淡红灰色. **~cot, ~cote** 鸽棚,鸽房 (*flutter [cause a flutter in] the ~cots* 扰乱鸽棚,〔喻〕使平地起风波,无事生非). **~-eyed** *a.* 目光柔和的. **~ gray** 一种紫灰色. **-let** 幼鸽,乳鸽. **-like** *a.* 鸽子般的.

dove[2] [dəuv] *v.* 〔美口,英方〕dive 的过去式.

dove·kie, dove·key ['dʌvkiː] *n.* 【动】①扁脚海雀. ②海鸠.

Do·ver ['dəuvə] *n.* 多佛〔英、美港市〕. ***Strait of ~*** 多佛海峡. ***when ~ and Calais meet*** 永不,决不〔~和加来(Calais)为英法两国隔海相望的二港市〕. **~'s powder**【药】阿片吐根散〔一种镇痛发汗剂〕.

dove·tail ['dʌvteil] *n.* 【木工】①鸠尾榫,楔形榫. ②鸠尾接合(= ~ point). — *vt.* ①用楔形榫接合;把…制成楔形榫. ②使(事实、知识、计划等)相互吻合,使相呼应;和…吻合. *~ the end of a board* 把一块木板的末端做成鸠形榫. *~ one's investigation into these sociological works* 把自己的研究纳进这些社会学著作的框框. — *vi.* 吻合,严丝合缝地嵌进. **~ joint**【木工】**~ groove [slot]**【机】燕尾槽. **~ machine** 制榫机.

dow [dau] *vi.* (*~ed, dought* [daut]; *~ed, dought*)〔主 Scot.〕得以,能够(= be able to).

Dow., dow. = dowager.

dow·a·ger ['dauədʒə] *n.* ①王〔公等〕的未亡人;继承亡夫遗产〔称号〕的寡妇. ②〔口〕老年贵妇人. *a duchess [princess] ~* 公爵〔亲王〕未亡人. *a queen ~* (王国的)皇太后. *an empress ~* (帝国的)皇太后. *a wealthy ~* 一个有钱的年老贵妇人. — *a.* 王〔公等〕的未亡人的;年高贵妇的〔只作限定语用〕. *the ~ duchess* 公爵未亡人. *a ~ style of dress* 老年贵妇型服装.

dow·dy ['daudi] *a.* ①(妇女)服装不整洁的,邋遢的. ②(服装等)式样俗气的;不美观的;过时的. — *n.* 邋遢女人. **dow·di·ly** *ad.* **dow·di·ness** *n.* **-ish** *a.* 有点邋遢的;有点俗气的.

dow·el ['dauəl] *n.* ①【木工】榫钉;夹缝钉;暗销. ②【建】传力杆,合缝钢条. *a plug ~* (为装架子等而打入墙中的)木钉. — *vt.* (*~(l)ed; ~(l)ing*) ①用合板钉钉合;用(暗)销接合. ②在…设置传力杆.

dow·er ['dauə] *n.* ①遗孀产〔寡妇应享受的一分亡夫遗产〕. ②嫁妆,陪嫁. ③天赋,天禀. — *vt.* ①给(寡妇)以亡夫遗产. ②给…以嫁妆. ③赋与(才能).

dow·er·y ['dauəri] *n.* = dowry.

dow·las ['dauləs] *n.* ①(十六、十七世纪英国产的)粗亚麻布. ②粗棉布.

down[1] [daun] *ad.* (*~most*) ①向下(面);下,降;在下(面). *come ~* 下来;下(楼)来;(雨等)落下. *The ship went ~ with all on board.* 这条船连船带人都沉没了. *He is not ~ yet.* 他还没有下来呢. *Our lawn slopes ~ to the river.* 我们的草地向下倾斜到河边. *He is up, and ~.* 他起床下楼来了. *go ~ on one's knees* 跪下. *Sit ~, please.* 请坐下. *The sun is ~.* 太阳落山了. ②倒下,病倒;放下. *The temple was thrown ~ by the earthquake.* 神庙被地震震坍了. *fall ~* 跌倒. *Many are ~ with cold.* 很多人患感冒病倒了. *leave the blinds ~* 放下百叶窗. *Put ~ your load and rest.* 放下扛着的东西歇一会儿. *They shouted ~ the opposition.* 他们以大喊大叫把反对派的声音压了下去. *The speaker was hissed ~ by the crowd.* 人群把演讲者嘘下台. ③(势头,程度等)减退,低落;(潮)退;(煮)干;(磨)碎;(价格)下降,(声音)由响到弱;(体积)由大到小;(数量)由多到少. *The wind went ~.* 风逐渐停了. *His passion has gone ~.* 他的情绪平静了下来. *boil ~* 熬干,煮干. *grind ~* 磨碎. *The tyres are ~.* 轮胎没气了. *get ~ sb.'s report to three pages.* 把某人的报告压缩到三张纸. *Bread is ~.* 面包落价了. *The price of commodities have gone ~.* 商品降价了. *Out patients are ~ a lot.* 外来的病人数量大减. *Turn ~ the phonograph.* 把唱机开小一些. ④〔口〕潦倒;衰弱;(意气)消沉. *come ~ in the world* 没落,潦倒. *She is ~ in health.* 她身体衰弱. *The news put him ~.* 那个消息使他消沉下来了. ⑤(查究,追问)到底;(时间,顺序,地位等的)直到. *run ~ a thief* 穷追小偷. *The repair crew traced ~ the leak.* 修缮队查明漏水的地方. *We try to run ~ the rumour.* 我们竭力想查明谣言的出处. *every metal from gold ~ to lead* 从金到铅的每一种金属. *The art has passed ~ for centuries.* 这门手艺已经传下来好几百年了. *from 100 ~ to 10* 从一百到十. *~ to page nine* 直到第九页. *~ to date* 直到今天. ⑥用现金,现付. *pay ~* 付现. *He paid $40 ~ and $20 a month.* 他现付 40 元,另外 20 元一个月内付清. *ten dollars ~ and five dollars a week* 现付 10 元,5 元一周付清. ⑦记〔抄〕到纸〔帐,文件等〕上;约定,列入(计

划). *copy* ~ 抄，誊. *Write* ~ *the address.* 记下地址. *take [get]* ~ *sb.'s words* 记下某人讲的话. *Meeting is* ~ *for next week.* 约定下周会晤. *He is* ~ *to speak.* 预定他要发表讲演. ⑧出(城)，下(乡)；(从首都)往内地；(从上游)至下游；(由北)往南；离开(大学)；(从内陆)到海边；(列车等)下行，〔美〕(从西部)向东. *go* ~ *from town* 离城下乡. *go* ~ *to the store* (从住宅区等)去商店. *go* ~ *to Scotland* (由首都伦敦)去苏格兰. *live* ~ *in Florida* 住在南方的弗罗里达州. *We drove* ~ *from San Francisco to Los Angels.* 我们驱车从旧金山南下洛杉矶. *go* ~ *East [South]* 〔美〕(从西部)到东部；(从北方)到南方去. *a train going* ~ 下行列车. *go* ~ *from Oxford* (因毕业或退学)离开牛津(大学). *Some twenty students have been sent* ~. 大约二十名学生停学[退学]. ⑨【印】付印；〔棒球俚〕出场. *The paper was* ~. 报纸已付印. *The edition has already gone* ~. 这一版已付印. ⑩〔加强语气〕完全，彻底；认真地；(办，料理，安顿)妥当. *get* ~ *to work* 认真工作. *wash* ~ *a car* 把车子彻底洗干净. *Let's settle* ~ *to studies.* 让我们安下心来读书. ⑪【海】往下风. *Put the helm* ~. = *Down with the helm.* 转舵向下风. ***be* ~ *and out*** 〔口〕①〔拳〕被击倒不能再战. ②落魄，潦倒. ***be* ~ *for*** 被列入计划[名单等]；(议案)被发下(重新讨论)(*He was* ~ *for the competition.* 他被列入参加竞赛的名单). ***be* ~ *on [upon]*** 怒责；憎恶，轻视，痛恨；虐待，欺负(*We are* ~ *on him.* 我们很讨厌他). ~ ***below*** ①在下面[楼下，甲板下，地面下等]. ②【宗】在地狱中. ~ ***East*** 〔美〕在 New England 东部沿海地区. ~ ***in the bushes [mouth]*** 〔美口〕意气消沉；心灰意懒(*Why do you look so* ~ *in the mouth?* 你为什么显得这样消沉)？~ ***to the ground*** 全然，完全(*That suits me* ~ *to the ground.* 那对我完全合适). ~ ***under*** 对跖地，地球底下的那一面〔从英国看指大洋洲说〕(*from* ~ *under* 从大洋洲方面；从地球底下的那一面). ***D- with*** ①打倒. ②拿下，放下，取下(*D- with your rifles!* 放下枪，缴枪！*D- with oars!* 放下桨！*D- with tyranny!* 打倒暴政！*D- with your money!* 交出钱来)！***go*** ~ 下；(日)落；(船)下沉；(物价)下跌；(饮食等)能吃下，能吸收；(解释等)讲得通(*Such explanation will not go* ~. 那样的解释讲不通).

— *prep.* ①下；往下方；沿着…往下. ②顺(流)而下；在(河的)下游. ③(由郊区)进市区，(由住宅区)到商业区；在市区，在商业区. ④(时间上)自…以上. *ski* ~ *the slope* 沿着斜坡下滑. *run* ~ *the stairs* 下楼梯. *sail* ~ *the river* 沿河下航，顺流而下. *be situated* ~ *the river* 位于河的下游. *walk* ~ *the road* 沿着路走. *The custom remained the same* ~ *the ages.* 这个风俗自古以来一直没有变. ~ *(the) wind* 顺着风向；在下风头. *live* ~ *town* 住在商业区. *drive* ~ *a street* 开汽车上街去.

—*a.* ***(~most)*** ①向下(方)的. ②沿海的，河口地方的. ③下行的；向南开的. ④沮丧的，心灰意懒的. ⑤现付的. ⑥赌输的. ⑦做完的，考虑好的. 【赛马】下了赌注的；【体】(比对方)得分低. *a* ~ *elevator* 往下开的电梯. *a* ~ *look* 向下看. *the* ~ *trend of business* 商业的萧条趋势. *a* ~ *country* 〔美〕滨海地方，河口附近地方. *a* ~ *grade [slope]* 下坡. *a* ~ *platform* 下行车出发处. *a* ~ *[bus] train* 下行列车[公共汽车]. *a* ~ *expression* 沮丧的表情. ~ *payment* 现付. *be* ~ *three games* 负三局. *After an hour of poker, he was* ~ *$10.* 他玩一个小时牌输了10元. *with five* ~ *and one to go* 五件已做完，还剩下一件.

— *vt.* ①〔口〕打倒，击落，打下(鸟、飞机等)；使屈服. ②放下，扔下，丢下. ③〔英口〕咽下，吞下，忘掉(伤心事等). ~ *one's opponent* 把对手打翻在地. ~ *a signal* 降下信号旗. *The anti-aircraft* ~*ed ten bombers.* 高射炮部队击落十架轰炸机. ~ *a tankard of ale* 喝一大杯淡啤酒. ~ ***tools*** 丢下工具，开始罢工. — *vi.* ①下降. ②(感情等)平息. ③(食物等)吃下；好吃. *Life will up and* ~. 人生总有沉浮.

— *n.* ①下位，下行；〔常 *pl.*〕倒霉，潦倒，落魄，失意；下降，衰落. ②〔口〕嫌恶，怨恨，憎恶. ③(广播剧等叙事而非对话时用的)低声调. ④〔美俚〕抑制剂，镇静剂. ***have a* ~ *on*** 憎恶，怨恨. ***ups and* ~*s*** 浮沉，荣枯，盛衰. **~-and-out** ① *ad.* = ~ and out. ② *n.* 穷愁潦倒的人；被击垮的人. **~-and-outer** *n.* = ~-and-out. ②**~at-heel** *a.* 潦倒的，衣衫褴褛的. **~beat** ① *n.* 【乐】(指挥棒的)一挥；强拍；下降，衰落. ②〔口〕*a.* 阴郁的；悲观的. **~cast** ①*a.* (眼睛)向下看的；哀声叹气的，垂头丧气的，萎靡不振的，衰颓的. ②*n.* 没落，灭亡；俯视；【地】下落，陷落；【矿】通风井，下风井. **~come** *n.* ①下降；衰落. ②= ~comer. **~comer** 下水管；落水管；下导管. **~draft** (烟囱的)倒灌风；向下通风；向下气流. **~-Easter** ①〔美〕新英格兰人，东部沿海地区的人〔特指缅因州人〕. ②美国东部沿海地区造的船；从缅因州开出的船. **~fall** 坠落，滚落，陷落，落下；(雨等的)大下特下；(家、国等的)没落，灭亡，瓦解. **~fallen** *a.* 坠落[陷落、没落、灭亡]的，已垮台的. **~grade** ①*a.* 下坡的；衰落的. ②*n.* 下坡. ③*vt.* 降低(地位、级别、阶级等)，贬低(他人)；(美国政府文件)降低(保密级). **~hearted** *a.* 〔俚〕垂头丧气的，郁郁不乐的，无精打采的(*Are we* ~*-hearted?* 〔俚〕决不灰心！). **~hill** ①*n.* 下坡路(*the* ~ *of life* 晚年). ②*a.* 倾斜的，下坡的；【滑雪】向下的. ③*ad.* 下坡；降下，向下(*go* ~ 下坡；衰颓，衰败). **~hold** *n.* 限制. *vt.* 减少. ~ **home** 美国南部；南部气质. **~-home** *a.* 乡土的，淳朴的. **~lead** 【无】(天线的)下天线. **~line** *ad.* 沿(铁路)线. ~ **payment** 分期付款的首次交款. **~pipe** 水落管. **~-point** *vt.* 减少(配给品的份数). **~pour** *n.* ①(日光的)照射. ②倾盆大雨. **~-price** *vt.* 降低…的价格. **~range** *a.*, *ad.* 【宇】离开发射中心和沿着试验航向的(地). **~right** ①*a.* 明白的，露骨的；直率的，爽直的，坦白的；〔古〕真正的，纯粹的(*a* ~*right falsehood* 公然作伪. *a* ~*right no* 明确的否定. *a* ~*right sort of person* 脾气直率的人). ②*ad.* 彻底，完全，干脆，真正(*He is* ~*-right angry.* 他愤怒已极). **~-river** ① *a.* 下游的. ②*ad.* 向下游. **~side** *n.* ①底侧. ②下降趋势. **~scale** *vt.* 缩减…的规模. **~stage** *n.*, *a.*, *ad.* 舞台前方(的，地). **~stair** *a.* 楼下的(*a* ~*stair room* 地下室). **~stairs** ①*ad.* 在楼下，往楼下(*come* ~*stairs* 下楼. *Downstairs the radio was singing.* 楼下的收音机正在播放歌曲. *kick* ~*stairs* 逐出家门). ②*a.* = downstair. ③*n.* 楼下；〔美〕(戏院的)正厅. **~state** *n.*, *a.*, *ad.* 〔美〕南部各州(的，地). **~stater** 〔美〕南部各州的人. **~-stream** *ad.*, *a.* 顺流(的)；在下游(的). **~swing** 下降趋势. **~-the-line** *a.* 完全的，充分的；无保留的，真心诚意地. **~throw** *n.* ①【地】陷落；下落地块(*opp.* upthrow). ②投下；垮台；(声誉等的)低落. **~time** (工厂由于检修、待料等而暂时停工的)停工期[时间]. **~-to-earth** *a.* 切切实实的，脚踏实地的(*a* ~*-to-earth appraisal of the situation* 对形势作切实的估计). **~trodden** *a.* 被蹂躏的，被压制的. **~turn** *n.* ①向下；下转，向下折曲. ②下降趋势. **~wash** *n.* ①从高处冲刷下来的物质. ②【空】下冲[洗]气流；下冲，下洗. **~wind** ①*n.* 顺风；下降气流. ②*ad.*, *a.* 顺风(的).

down[2] [daun] *n.* ①冈，丘，开阔的高地；〔美〕砂丘. ②〔*pl.*〕丘陵地，丘原，(适于牧羊的)丘陵地草原. ③〔D-〕(英国南部丘陵草原产的)塘种绵羊. ***the D-s*** ①英国东南部的丘陵草原. ②多佛海峡的一部分〔为船舶停泊处〕. **~land** *n.* ①山地牧场. ②澳大利亚温带草原. ③【地】丘陵地.

down[3] [daun] *n.* ①(装被、褥等用的)鸭绒，绒毛；(鸟的)绒羽；柔毛. ②汗毛，软毛，毳毛；(男孩脸上初生的)细软短须. ③【植】茸毛，(蒲公英等的)冠毛.

down·er [ˈdaunə] *n.* 〔俚〕抑制剂，镇静剂〔如巴比妥盐、酒精饮料等〕.

Down·ing Street [ˈdauniŋ striːt] ①唐宁街〔伦敦的一条街，英国首相官邸及一些主要政府机关所在地〕. ②〔口〕(英国的)首相,现内阁,现政府.

down·town ① [ˈdauntaun] *n., a.* (市中)商业区(的),闹区(的). ②[ˈdaunˈtaun] *ad.* 到[在]商业区. *go [live]* ～去[住在]商业区. *a ～ store* 闹市区的一家商店. *live in ～ New York* 住在纽约闹市区.

down·ward [ˈdaunwəd] *a.* ①下方的,向下的,低下的. ②下降的; 下坡的; (市价)下跌的. *a ～ tendency* (物价的)跌势. *a ～ slope* 下坡. *He is on the ～ path.* 他正在走下坡路. — *ad.* = downwards. **-ly** *ad.* **-ness** *n.*

down·wards [ˈdaunwədz] *ad.* ①向下; 以下, 往下. ②趋向衰落,日趋没落,日益堕落. ③(年代等)以来,以后. *He lay face ～ on his bed.* 他脸向下伏在床上. *look ～* 向下看. *As the river flows ～, it widens.* 这条河愈到下游愈宽. *be handed ～ from generation to generation* 世代相传，一代代地传下来. *boys of ten and ～* 十岁以下的男孩.

down·y[1] [ˈdauni] *a.* ①长绒毛[茸毛]的; 汗毛遍身的. ②汗毛状的,茸毛似的; 柔软的. ③用绒羽制成的. ④〔俚〕狡猾的, 机警的. *a ～ cloud* 绒毛状的云. *a ～ fellow* 狡猾的人. *a ～ pillow* 鸭绒枕头. ***do the ～*** 躺在床上睡觉. ～ **mildew**【植】霜霉病. **down·i·ly** *ad.* **down·i·ness** *n.*

down·y[2] [ˈdauni] *n.* ①丘陵草原性的. ②丘陵起伏的. *a rolling ～ landscape* 丘陵连绵起伏的景色.

dow·ry [ˈdauəri] *n.* ①嫁妆,嫁资. ②天赋,天禀, 才能. ③〔古〕寡妇(继承亡夫的一份) 产业. ④〔古〕(丈夫给新娘的)财礼.

dowse[1] [daus] *vt.* = douse.

dowse[2] [dauz] *vi.* (古时用迷信的)卜棒探寻水脉[矿脉]. — *vt.* 用卜棒找到(水脉等). — *n.* (找寻矿脉等的) 卜棒.

Dow·son [ˈdausn] *n.* 道森〔姓氏〕.

dox·ol·o·gy [dɔkˈsɔlədʒi] *n.*【宗】(礼拜式上唱的) 荣光赞歌,荣耀颂.

dox·y[1], **dox·ie** [ˈdɔksi] *n.* 〔口〕①学说, 见解. ②宗教见解,宗教主张,教旨.

dox·y[2] [ˈdɔksi] 〔俚〕①情妇. ②淫妇; 娼妓.

dox·y·cyc·line [dɔksiˈsaiklin] *n.*【药】强力霉素.

doy·en [ˈdɔiən] *n.* 〔F.〕 (*fem.* ***doy·enne*** [dɔiˈjen]) ①(一个团体中的)老前辈, 资格最老者, 地位最高者. ②历史最悠久者. *the D- of the Diplomatic Corps* 外交使团团长. *the ～ of the country's newspaper* 全国报纸当中最老的一家.

doy·enne [dɔiˈjen] *n.* (一个团体中的)女性老前辈, 女性资格最老者.

Doyle [dɔil] *n.* 多伊尔〔姓氏,男子名〕.

doz. = dozen(s).

doze[1] [dəuz] *vi.* ①打瞌睡, 打盹. ②迷迷胡胡, 昏昏沉沉. *～ over a stupid book* 看着一本枯燥无味的书打瞌睡. *He ～ed off during the sermon.* 他在听说教的时候直打盹. — *vt.* 在瞌睡中度过(时间) *(away, out). He ～d away the afternoon.* 他在瞌睡中度过一下午. —*n.* 打瞌睡, 打盹,假寐. *fall [go off, drop off] into a ～*打起瞌睡来. *drop back into a comfortable ～* 舒舒服服地打个盹儿.

doze[2] [dəuz] *vt.* 用推土机清除[挖出、推平].

doz·en [ˈdʌzn] *n. (pl. ～, ～s)* ①一打,十二个〔作为实数及用作定语时,复数不加 -s〕. ②〔*～s*〕 若干, 许许多多. *two [three] ～ eggs* 两[三]打鸡蛋. *four ～ of these eggs* 四打这种鸡蛋. *some ～s of eggs* 好几打鸡蛋. *～s of eggs* 几十个鸡蛋. *some ～ (of) eggs* 一打左右鸡蛋. *a ～ of eggs* 一打鸡蛋. *sell eggs by the ～* 论打售蛋. *pack oranges in ～s* 按打包装橘子. *a round ～* 整整一打. *a baker's [devil's, long, printer's] ～* 十三个. ***～s of times*** 屡次. ***(talk) thirteen [nineteen] to the ～*** 〔英俚〕①(说个)不停. ②(说得)过分地,迅速地.

doz·enth [ˈdʌznθ] *num.* 〔俚〕 = twelfth.

do·zer[1] [ˈdəuzə] *n.* 打瞌睡的人.

do·zer[2] [ˈdəuzə] *n.* 推土机.

doz·y [ˈdəuzi] *a.* ①想睡的, 困倦的. ②(木材等)腐烂的.

DP = ①displaced person (由于战争或政治迫害等而逃离原居住地或本国的)难民. ②degree of polymerization【化】聚合度. ③Distributing Point【军】交付所,配给点[站]. ④data processing 数据处理.

d. p. = difference of potential【电】电位差,势差.

DPH, DPh(il),D. Ph(il). = Doctor of Philosophy 哲学博士.

D.P.H. = Doctor of Public Health 公共卫生博士.

D.P.I. = Director of Public Instruction 〔美〕(海岸警卫队)公共教练处处长.

D.P.L. = Delta pine land cotton【纺】岱字棉.

dpm = disintegrations per minute 衰变/分.

DPN = diphosphopyridine nucleotide 二磷酸吡啶核苷酸.

DPRK = Democratic People's Republic of Korea 朝鲜民主主义人民共和国.

dpt. = ①department. ②deponent.

Dr., Dr = Doctor.

dr. = ①debit. ②debtor. ③drachma(s). ④dram(s). ⑤drum.

drab[1] [dræb] *n.* ①灰黄色,淡褐色. ②【纺】淡褐色厚呢. ③单调, 乏味, 死气沉沉. *the ～ of country life* 蛰居乡间的单调生活. — *a.* ①淡褐色的. ②单调的. *a ～ life* 单调的生活. **-ly** *ad.* **-ness** *n.*

drab[2] [dræb] *n.*①邋遢女人. ②淫妇; 妓女. — *vi.* 嫖妓.

drab·bet [ˈdræbit] *n.* 家用本色斜纹亚麻布.

drab·ble [ˈdræbl] *vt.* 拖脏(衣服等),把(衣服等)弄得满是泥污. — *vi.* 拖泥溅水地走*(through)*; 在浑水里钓鱼.

dra·cae·na [drəˈsiːnə] *n.*【植】龙血树属植物.

drachm [dræm] *n.* ①= drachma. ②= dram.

drach·ma [ˈdrækmə] *n. (pl. ～s, **drach·mae*** [ˈdrækmiː] ①古希腊银币名. ②德拉克马〔现代希腊货币单位〕. ③古希腊衡量单位; 现代衡量单位〔尤指 dram〕.

Dra·co [ˈdreikəu] *n.* ①〔the ～〕【天】天龙座. ②〔d-〕【动】飞龙.

Dra·co·ni·an [dreiˈkəunjən], **Dra·co·nic** [dreiˈkɔnik] *a.* ①古代雅典执政官德拉科的. ②〔常 d-〕(法律等)严酷的,残酷的. *adopt ～ measures* 采取严厉措施. *face with the ～ law of …* 面临着…的严酷法律. **-ism** *n.* 严刑峻法,严法重典主义.

dra·co·ni·an [dreiˈkəuniən], **dra·con·ic** [dreiˈkɔnik] *a.* 龙一样的.

drae·ger·man [ˈdreigəmæn] *n.* 矿工救护队队员.

draff [dræf] *n.* ①渣滓, 糟粕. ②(喂猪的)残羹剩饭, 猪食. *D- is good enough for swine.* 喂猪只需用猪食〔意为不作不必要的浪费〕. **-y** *a.* 渣滓[糟粕]很多的; 无价值的.

draft [drɑːft] *n.* ①选拔队,别动队, 分遣队; (分遣队的)选拔; 〔美〕征兵; (不经某人同意而要他出来竞选的)敦请. ②汇票; 付款通知单; (款项的)支取; 〔喻〕强要,索取; 耗完. ③草稿,草案; 图案,草图, 轮廓. ④牵引, 拖,曳; 牵伸,拉伸. ⑤吸饮; 一饮,一吸; 汲出; (药水等的)一服; (捕鱼等的)一网, 一网打获量. ⑥【海】(船的) 吃水(深度). ⑦罅缝风,穿堂风, 贼风; 通风, 气流; 通风装置. ★ 英国除①②③用 draft 外, 通例用 draught; 美国除⑤用 draught 外, 通例用 draft. *a ～ system* 征兵制. *～ evasion* 逃避服兵役. *a telegraphic ～* 电(报)汇(款). *a ～ for $ 100 on [upon] the bank* 一张向银行支取100元的汇票. *a rough ～ for [of] a speech* 讲话草稿. *the first ～* 初稿. *the ～ of a future building* 未来大厦的草图. *a beast of ～* 役畜, 拉车的牲畜. *a ～ of air* 一

阵风. *sit in a* ～ 坐在通风处. *a* ～ *on sb.'s resources* 某人财力枯竭. *a vessel of 20 feet* ～ *[with a* ～ *of 20 feet]* 吃水 20 英尺的船. **at a** ～ 一口,一气. ～ **at B.O.** (=booking office) 【美剧】从卖座上看的演出成败情况. ～ **on demand** 见票即付的汇票. **feel the** ～〔俚〕(手头) 拮据. **make a** ～ **of money** 提款. **make a** ～ **on a bank** 向银行提款. **make a great** ～ **upon sb.'s confidence** 死赖着要某人信任. **make out a** ～ **of** *(the treaty)* 起草(条约). **on** ～ 随时可从容器中汲出的 (*beer on* ～ 桶装啤酒). — *vt.* ①选拔;选派;〔美〕征(兵). ②起草,拟(方案);画(草图,轮廓),为…打样,设计. ③汲出. ④在(石)上凿槽[琢边]. ～ *a professional athlete* 选拔一个职业运动员. *He was* ～*ed into the army.* 他被征召入伍. *water* ～*ed by pumps* 用水泵汲出的水. ～ *an act* 起草一项法案. — *a.* ①(马等)拉车用的,供役使的. ②(啤酒等)桶装的 (*opp.* bottled). ③正在起草中的. ～ *beer* 桶装啤酒. ～ *bill* 草案. *a* ～ *horse* 拉车的马,役马. ～**-age** *a.* 〔美〕应征年龄的. ～**animals** 耕畜,役畜. ～ **board** 〔美〕征兵局. ～**calls** 征兵人数. ～ **dodger** 逃避服兵役者. ～ **gauge** 风力计,风压表. ～ **mark**【海】(船的)吃水线. ～ **mill** = smoke-jack. ～**nik** 〔美俚〕反征兵者. ～ **tube** 汲管. **-ee**[drɑːfˈtiː] *n.* 〔美口〕壮丁,应征入伍者. **-er** ①起草者. ②役马,拖车的马.

draft·ing [ˈdrɑːftiŋ] *n.* ①起草. ②制图. ～ *committee* 起草委员会. ～ *board* 绘图板. ～ *paper* 绘图纸. ～ *room* 绘图室.

drafts·man [ˈdrɑːftsmən] *n.* *(pl. -men)* 起草人;制图员. **-ship** *n.* 制图技术[才能].

draft·y [ˈdrɑːfti] *a.* 〔美〕通风的;通风良好的;有罅缝风吹入的. *a* ～ *room* 通风良好的屋子. **draft·i·ly** *ad.* **draft·i·ness** *n.*

drag [dræg] *vt.* ①拖,曳;拖动,拖着 (脚、尾巴等);硬拖(某人)做(某事)[至(某地)]. ②打捞,(用捞锚等)探寻(水底等);用拖网捕捉. ③耙(地),耙平. ④(在车轮上)装煞车. ⑤〔美俚〕(去社交场合时)陪伴(女子);(讲话时)引入,带出. ⑥〔美俚〕深深地吸(香烟). ⑦把(讨论等)拖长. ⑧〔美俚〕厌烦[无聊]地度(时光). ⑨〔美俚〕背景;势力. ⑩〔俚〕街;路. ⑪男扮女装用的服饰. *The ship* ～*s her anchor.* 船拖动了锚[意为锚系不住船,已失去作用]. ～ *one's feet in the water* 在水中拖着脚步走. ～ *sb. out of the room* 把某人拖出房间. ～ *oneself through the day's work* 好不容易干完一天的活儿. ～ *the lake for the body of the missing man* 打捞湖底搜寻失踪者的尸体. *He always* ～*s his Ph. D. into every discussion.* 他讨论发言的时候总是要生拉硬扯到他的哲学博士头衔. ～ *the discussion out for three hours* 把讨论拖长到三个小时. — *vi.* ①拖曳;(原来下的锚)被拖动. ②慢吞吞地走,拖沓,拖着脚步走 *(along)*. ③拖宕,拖长. ④用拖网[捞锚]探寻 *(for)*. ⑤【乐】拖长声音. ⑥〔口〕(猛)吸(烟) *(on)*. *The minutes* ～ *like hours.* 一分钟长得象几小时,度日如年. *The negotiation dragged on until July.* 谈判一直拖到七月份. ～ *behind the party* 落在一行人后面. *a dragging pain* 长时间的痛苦. *a dragging market* 呆滞的市场. ～ *on one's cigar* 吸上一支雪茄. *The book* ～*s.* 这本书冗长无味. *The door* ～*s.* 门呆得很[不容易开关]. ～ **a date** 〔美俚〕带舞伴去参加舞会. ～ **a hoof** 〔美俚〕跳舞. ～ **by** (时间)一点一点地挨过去. ～ **down** 〔俚〕挣工资;赚(钱). ～ **in** ①把…拉进去. ②硬把(某人)拉扯进(某事). ～ **in (by the head and shoulders) a joke** 牵强附会地插进一句(不恰当的)俏皮话. ～ **it** 〔美俚〕走掉,跑掉;停止谈话;断绝关系;离职. ～ **on [out]** 迁延,拖延;使拖延;拉长(声调等),拖长(字眼等);挨过. ～ **one's feet [heels]** 〔美俚〕故意拖延. ～ **oneself along** (慢吞吞地)拖着脚步走. ～ **through** 好容易才完毕. ～ **up** ①拉上;拖上;拔出 (～ *up the roots of a tree* 把一棵树连根拔起). ②〔俚〕粗心大意地抚养(小孩) (*These children seem to have been dragged up.* 这些小孩似乎是被胡乱带大的). ～ **your freight** 〔美俚〕出去! — *n.* ①拖曳物;拖网;捞锚;(四匹马拉的)双层马车;沉重的大耙;粗笨的橇;运货慢车;刮路机. ②拖累物,阻碍物,累赘;极讨厌的人[物]. ③齿扣,煞车,制动器;海锚;【空】阻力. ③牵引;拖沓,拖延. ④【海】舳舻吃水差. ⑤【猎】(训练猎犬用的)人工臭迹;应用人工臭迹的行猎;野兽的臭迹. ⑥〔美俚〕(对人、机构等具有的)影响,势力. ⑦〔俚〕(男穿)女装,(女穿)男装. ⑧猛喝一口茶[酒],深吸一口烟. ⑨〔美俚〕茶会,舞会;跳舞;有男子陪伴去参加舞会的女子. ⑩〔美俚〕马路,街道. *the* ～ *of population growth on living standards* 人口增长对提高生活水平的阻碍. *His brother is a* ～ *to him.* 他的兄弟是他的一个累赘. *School is a* ～ *for some youngsters.* 学校是一些儿童很讨厌的地方. *Don't invite him — he's a* ～. 不要邀请他——他这个人讨厌极了. *walk with a* ～ 慢吞吞地走. *take a long* ～ *on his cigar* 深深地吸一口雪茄烟. *the boys [girls] in* ～ 穿女装的男孩[穿男装的女孩]. *He has* ～ *with the school authorities.* 他和学校当局很有些交情,他在学校当局那里说话挺管用. — *ad.* 〔美俚〕带着女伴. *Are you going stag or* ～*?* 参加舞会你是单身去呢还是带着女伴去? — *a.* 〔美俚〕男穿女服的;女穿男服的. ～ **anchor** ①【海】海锚,浮锚. ②阻力;障碍. ～ **chain**【机】牵引链;刹车链. ②〔喻〕障碍. ～**line** ①牵引绳索. ②【矿】索斗铲. ～**net** ①拖网,捕捞网. ②法网,〔美〕大举搜捕. ～ **parachute** 阻力伞〔飞机降落于跑道后减速的尾伞〕. ～ **queen** 〔美俚〕男扮女装的男性同性恋者. ～ **race** 〔美俚〕(汽车拆卸减重后举行的)短程加速比赛. ～**rope** (炮身等的)拖绳. ～ **sail** 拖锚,浮锚. ～**saw**【机】(锯长金属棒材用的)下料电锯. **dragging** *a.*

dra·gée [ˈdrɑːʒei] *n.* 〔F.〕①糖果[多指装饰蛋糕的银衣糖果]. ②【药】糖衣药丸.

drag·gle [ˈdrægl] *vt.* 拖脏,拖湿. — *vi.* ①(裙子等)拖曳;拖脏,拖湿. ②慢吞吞前进,落后. ～**tail** ①(拖着又长又脏的裙子的)邋遢[不正派]女人. ②长裙拖地的女服. ～**tailed** *a.* ①拖着长裙子的. ②(妇女等)邋遢的,堕落的. **drag·gly** *a.* ①拖脏的. ②不整洁的.

drag·gy [ˈdrægi] *a.* ①拖拉的;拖沓的. ②死气沉沉的;沉闷的;无聊的. *a* ～ *market* 呆滞的市面.

drag·o·man [ˈdrægəumən] *n.* *(pl.* ～*s, -men)* (土耳其等近东诸国的)翻译,译员;向导.

drag·on [ˈdrægən] *n.* ①龙. ②飞龙旗. ③凶暴的人;(年轻女子的)严格凶狠的监护人[多指老太婆]. ④〔the D-〕【天】天龙座. ⑤(十七世纪前后口径大而枪身短的)龙骑枪;佩带龙骑枪的士兵. ⑥【动】飞龙〔蜥蜴的一种,有翼膜,能滑翔〕. ⑦【动】(一种善飞的)信鸽. ⑧【圣】海怪[指鲸鱼,鲨鱼,鳄鱼;海蟒等]. ⑨【军】装甲牵引车. *the old D-* 魔王. *a regular [perfect]*～ (年轻女子的)凶狠的伴婆. ～*'s blood* 龙血树树脂. ～*'s teeth* 〔英俚〕①(多层排列的三角锥形)反坦克混凝土路障. ②相互争斗的根源〔出自日尔曼神话: Cadmus 种下龙齿,化为武士相互砍杀〕. ～**fly**【虫】蜻蜓. ～**head**【植】青兰属植物. ～**'s head**【天】升交点. ～**'s tail**【天】降交点. ～ **tree**【植】龙血树.

drag·on·et [ˈdrægənit] *n.* ①小龙,龙子. ②【动】鰤鱼,欧洲鰤鱼.

drag·on·nade [ˌdrægəˈneid] *n.* ①〔*pl.*〕【法史】龙骑兵迫害〔法国国王路易十四使龙骑兵对新教徒进行迫害〕. ②武力迫害,武力镇压. — *vt.* 用武力迫害.

dra·goon [drəˈguːn] *n.* ①重骑兵;(持龙骑枪的)龙骑兵. ②龙骑兵团〔英国一骑兵团名称〕. ③凶汉,暴徒. ④(一种善飞的)信鸽. — *vt.* ①用龙骑兵镇压. ②武力迫害,暴力镇压. *The authorities* ～*ed the peasants into leaving their farms.* 当局用武力把农民驱离田庄.

drag·ster [ˈdrægstə] *n.* 经改装[拆卸减重]而成的高速赛车.

drain [drein] *vt.* ①排去(水等液体),排泄,放干 (*away; off*). ②喝干,倒空. ③用完,花光. ④使…某物枯竭;使…耗尽某物 (*of*). ~ *off the rain* 排掉雨水. ~ *the flooded mine* 排干矿上的积水. ~ *a glass of beer* 喝干一杯啤酒. ~ *the cup of sorrow [pleasure] to the bottom* 备尝艰苦[享尽欢乐]. *He ~ed the last of the whiskey into our glasses.* 他把最后一点威士忌酒都倒进我们的杯子里. *be ~ed of all strength* 筋疲力竭. ~ *a country of its resources* 使国家资源枯竭. — *vi.* ①(水等液体)流掉,渐渐淌完 (*away, off*). ②(土地)排水;(衣服、碗碟等)滴干. ③(资源等)逐渐枯竭. *The water will soon ~ away.* 水很快就会流掉. *His anger ~ed from him.* 他的怒气逐渐消失. *This land won't ~.* 这块田排不出水去. *This land ~s into the river.* 这块地的水排到河里. *Put the dishes on the board to ~.* 把碗碟放到板上滴掉水. *Hope and energy ~ away over the years.* 岁月逐渐使精力和希望枯竭了. — *n.* ①排水渠;下水道,阴沟;〔*pl.*〕(建筑物的)排水系统. ②【医】引流,导液(管),排脓管. ③排水,放干;(财富等的)外流,枯竭;耗费,负担. ④〔口〕(酒的)一杯,一口. *the economic ~ of war* 战争的经济耗费. *Working too hard is a ~ on his strength.* 过分辛劳使他精力衰竭. **go down the ~**〔俚〕①(情况)愈来愈坏,(人)每况愈下. ②(资金等)被浪费;(计划等)失败,破产. **laugh like a ~**〔口〕狂笑. **~board** (倾斜着放置洗过的碗碟以便把水滴尽的)滴水板. **~pipe** 排水管. **~pipe trousers** 瘦裤腿裤子. **~trap** (下水道等的)防臭阀. **~way** 泄水道. **-less** *a.*〔书〕取之不竭的.

drain·age ['dreinidʒ] *n.* ①排水,放水;排水法;逐渐流出. ②下水道;排水设备,排水系统. ③水系,排水区域,流域. ④阴沟水,(排出的)污水. ⑤【医】引流,导液(法). ~ *work* 排水工程. ~ *and irrigation equipments* 排灌设备. ~ **area** 排水面积[区域];流域. ~ **basin** (河流的)流域. ~ **system** 排水系统;【地】水系. ~ **tube**【医】导液管,引流管. **~way** 排水设施.

drain·er ['dreinə] *n.* ①排水工,放水的人;下水道修建工. ②排水器,滤干器;滴水板 (= drainboard).

Drake [dreik] *n.* ①德雷克〔姓氏〕. ②**Sir Francis** ~ 杜雷克〔1540?—1596,英国航海家,最初环绕地球航行一周的人〕.

drake[1] [dreik] *n.* ①公鸭. ②(打水漂用的)石片. **play ducks and ~s** 玩打水漂游戏. **~stone** (打水漂用的)浮石片.

drake[2] [dreik] *n.* ①(钓鱼用的)蜉蝣. ②【史】(十七、十八世纪用的)小型火炮.

dram [dræm] *n.* ①打兰〔常衡 = 1/16 ounce (= 1.771g.),药衡 = 1/8 ounce (= 3.8879g.);液量 = 1/8 ounce (= 0.0037 lit.)〕. ②(威士忌酒等的)少许,一口,微量. *a ~ drinker* 爱浅斟慢饮的人. *be fond of a ~* 喜欢喝两口(酒). *have not one ~ of learning* 一点学问也没有. — *vi.*〔古〕少量饮酒. **~shop**〔古〕小酒店.

dra·ma ['drɑːmə] *n.* ①剧本;一出戏;戏剧;戏曲. ②〔the ~〕戏剧事业;戏剧艺术. ③(因有很多巧合和冲突而激动人心的)戏剧性事件,戏剧性场面. ④戏剧效果,戏剧性. *the musical ~* 音乐剧. *the poster ~* 活报剧. *a poetic ~* 诗剧. *the historical ~* 历史剧. *the ~ of a murder trial* 审判一件凶杀案的戏剧性场面. *For God's sake, don't make a ~ about it.* 看在老天分上,不要大事宣扬这件事吧!

Dram·a·mine ['dræməmin] *n.*【药】达姆明〔晕船药商标名〕.

dra·mat·ic [drə'mætik] *a.* ①戏剧的,剧本的;演剧的. ②戏剧一样的,戏剧性的,激动人心的,引人注目的. *a ~ piece* 一个剧本. ~ *art* 戏剧艺术. *(a) ~ performance* 演出. *a ~ critic* 剧评家. ~ *poetry* 戏曲. ~ *presentation [production]* 上演. ~ *right* 上演权. *a ~ scene [event]* 戏剧性场面[事件]. *a ~ speech* 激动人心的演说. ~ *colors* 引人注目的色彩. ~ **present**【语法】戏剧手法的现在式〔描写过去事件为增强效果而用现在式〕. **-al·ly** *ad.*

dra·mat·ics [drə'mætiks] *n.*〔单复同〕①(特指业余的或学生的)演出;演剧活动. ②演剧技术,舞台技术. ③戏剧性的行为,作假. *amateur ~* 业余演出活动. *His friends are tired of all his phony ~.* 他的朋友们对他那一套假做作都腻透了.

dram·a·tis per·so·næ (可略作 ***dram. pers.***) ['drɑːmətis pəː'səuniː]〔L.〕〔*pl.*〕【剧】①登场人物,剧中人. ②人物表.

dram·a·tist ['dræmətist] *n.* 剧作家,剧本作者.

dram·a·ti·za·tion, dram·a·ti·sa·tion [ˌdræmətai'zeiʃən] *n.* ①戏剧创作;戏剧化;戏剧性描写. ②(小说等的)改编为剧本. ③(由小说等)改编成的剧本.

dram·a·tize, dram·a·tise ['dræmətaiz] *vt.* ①(把小说等)改编为剧本. ②演戏似地表现;把…戏剧化;使引人注目. *He ~s his woes with sobs and sighs.* 他象演戏似地又哭泣又叹气,来表现他的痛苦. — *vi.* ①具有戏剧性;适于改编为剧本. ②(演戏似地)作假. *That incident would ~ well.* 那个事件很具有戏剧性. **-tiz·a·ble** *a.* **-tiz·er** *n.*

dram·a·turge ['dræmətəːdʒ], **dram·a·tur·gist** ['dræmətəːdʒist] *n.* 剧作家 (= dramatist).

dram·a·tur·gy ['dræmətəːdʒi] *n.* ①剧作理论,剧本作法. ②演出艺术. **-tur·gic, -gi·cal** [-'tuːdʒik(əl)] *a.*

drank [dræŋk] drink 的过去式.

drape [dreip] *vt.* ①(用布等)覆盖,披盖;(随便地)披上(衣服等). ②悬挂;装饰. ③把(衣服等)制成褶皱状. ④【医】在(手术室等处)挂上消毒帷帘. *buildings ~d with flags* 用旗帜装饰起来的建筑物. *Don't ~ your feet over the chair.* 坐得端正些,不要把腿悬空架在椅子边上. *a cleverly ~d suit* 一件有漂亮褶皱的服装. — *vi.* ①(窗帘、饰帷等)优美地挂着. ②(衣服等)成褶皱状. *This silk ~s beautifully.* 这块丝绸有美丽的褶皱. — *n.* ①〔*pl.*〕窗帘,布帘. ②褶皱,裥. ③服装式样. *the ~ of a skirt* 裙子的式样.

Dra·per ['dreipə] *n.* 德雷珀〔姓氏〕.

drap·er ['dreipə] *n.* 布店;绸布商. *a woollen ~* 呢绒商. *a ~'s* 布店. *go to the ~'s* 去布店(购买衣服).

dra·per·y ['dreipəri] *n.* ①绸缎,呢绒,布匹;织物,服装. ②绸缎业,布业;服装业;绸布店. ③〔*pl.*〕帐帘,帷幔. ④(画像、雕像等上的)衣饰. ~ *establishment [stores]* 绸布店. **-per·ied** *a.* 悬有(褶形)布帘的.

dras·tic ['dræstik] *a.* ①激烈的,猛烈的;果断的. ②(法律等)严厉的. *apply ~ remedies* 下烈性药. *take ~ measures* 采取果断措施[激烈手段]. ~ *purgatives* 猛泻药. *a ~ debate* 激烈的辩论. **-cal·ly** *ad.*

drat [dræt] *vt.*〔口〕咒骂〔语气比 damn, confound 较为温和〕. *D- it!* 讨厌! *D- the child!* 小鬼〔妇女骂小孩的用语〕! *D- you!* 讨厌! *D-, there goes another button!* 讨厌,又有一颗钮扣脱落了!

draught [drɑːft] *n., v., a.* = draft.

draught·board ['drɑːftbɔːd] *n.*〔英〕跳棋盘 (=〔美〕checkerboard).

draught·i·ness ['drɑːftinis] *n.* 通风.

draught·i·ly ['drɑːftili] *ad.* 通风地.

draughts [drɑːfts] *n.*〔*pl.*〕〔英〕跳棋(=〔美〕checkers).

draughts·man ['drɑːftsmən] *n.* (*pl.* ***-men***) ①起草人;打样人;制图员. ②〔英〕跳棋棋子.

draught·y ['drɑːfti] *a.* = drafty.

Dra·vid·i·an [drə'vidiən] *a.* (印度南部的)德拉维人[语]的. — *n.* 德拉维人[语]. ~ **language** 德拉维语〔流行于印度南部和斯里兰卡北部的一个语族〕.

draw [drɔː] *vt.* (***drew*** [druː]; ***drawn*** [drɔːn]) ①拉,牵,曳,张(弓等). ②拔(牙、钉等),抽出(刀),从(容器等中)倒出(物品);取出(鸡等的)内脏. ③惹,引,招,引起,招

致,吸引(注意等).④打(水),排干,汲出(水等液体);受,靠(人供给);领取,提取(钱款),获得(资源等),生(利),汲取(教训).⑤描写;草拟,制订,拟(稿);描(图),绘制,画(线等),勾(轮廓).⑥开给(汇票等),开立(票据等).⑦抽(签),拈(阄).⑧下(判断),引出(结论等),推断(结果等).⑨吸进(空气);(船)吃水(深、浅).⑩把…拉成丝,抽制(铁线等);缩;扭歪(脸)〔此义多用被动语态〕.⑪使打成平局.⑫〔口〕钓出,诱出(回话等),逗引…说话.⑬拖出;【猎】搜出(狐等);【医】抽(血),放(血);(用药)拔(脓);泡出(茶)味.⑭【机】退(火).⑮【牌】吊(牌);补(牌).~ *a wagon* 拉车.~ *a curtain* 拉幕.~ *a bow* 张弓.~ *a rope tight* 把绳子拉紧.*Music drew the shy girl out of her shell.* 音乐吸引那个害羞的姑娘走出了深闺.~ *a tooth* 拔牙.~ *water from a well* 从井里汲水.~ *a pond* 排干池塘里的水.~ *a cork from a bottle* 拔开瓶塞.~ *one's sword at [against] sb.* 拔剑指向某人.~ *sb.'s attention* 吸引某人注意.~ *sb. into conversation* 把某人引进谈话中来.~ *sb. on* 引某人谈(某事).~ *a large audience* 吸引大量听众.~ *a vase* 画花瓶.~ *a character in a novel* 在小说中描绘一个人物.~ *a will* 立遗嘱.~ *a picture of* 描绘.~ *perpendicular lines* 划垂直线.~ *a comparison [parallel, distinction] between A and B* 比较[对比,区别]甲乙.~ *a deep breath* 深深地吸一口气.~ *a sigh* 叹气.~ *one's first breath* 出生.~ *one's last (breath)* 咽气,死.~ *information from* 从…取得情报.~ *inspiration from Shakespeare* 从莎士比亚著作中汲取灵感.~ *a conclusion* 引出结论.~ *interest on a saving account* 储蓄生利.~ *a salary of $100 a week* 领取每周100美元的薪金.~ *trouble* 惹事.~ *a turkey* 掏出火鸡的内脏.~ *wire* 拉制金属丝.~ *filaments of molten glass* 把热熔玻璃拉成丝.~ *lots* 拈阄.~ *a prize* 抽彩票.*a face drawn with pain* 痛得扭歪了的脸.*The ship ~s six feet.* 这条船吃水六英尺.*The game was drawn.* 比赛打得不分胜负.— *vi.* ①拉,牵,曳,拖;拉开,张满;汲取.②向(某处)移动,挨近,靠近,走近,靠拢 (*to; towards*);(时间等)接近,逼近.③画,描;制图.④【医】(膏药等)吸脓,拔出牙齿.⑤拔刀,拔枪.⑥开立票据;支取;请求,征集,勒索.⑦缩,皱.⑧(船)吃水(深、浅);(茶)泡开.⑨(比赛)打成平局,不分胜负.⑩拈阄,抽签.⑪吸引人.⑫(烟囱等)通风.⑬(猎狗)追踪[接近]猎物.*all sails ~ing* 所有的帆都张开.*The carts ~ easily* 这些车辆拉起来很轻便.*Night ~s nearer.* 夜色临近.*~ing at the well* 从井里汲水.~ *into the shore* 靠岸.*drew, aimed and fired* 拔出枪瞄准射击.*Like ~s to like.* 同声相应,同气相求.~ *for prize* 抽签得奖,抽彩票.*The draftsman ~s well.* 这个绘图员描图的技术好.*His face drew up.* 他的脸皱缩起来.*This cigar does not ~ well.* 这根雪茄不好抽.*The chimney ~s well.* 烟囱通风良好.*give the tea time to ~* 让茶慢慢泡开.*The play ~s well.* 这戏叫座.~ *on sb. for help* 要求某人给予帮助.~ *on one's imagination* 要求发挥想象力.*My shoes drew.* 我的鞋子缩小了.*They drew as many as four times that year.* 他们那一年四次打成平局.*This ship ~s deep.* 这船吃水深.~ ***a bead on*** 向…瞄准.~ ***a blank*** ①抽空签.②〔口〕失败,无所得.~ ***a full house*** 客满,剧场满座.~ ***ahead***【海】变成逆风.~ ***a longbow*** = ~ the longbow.~ ***a term***〔美〕被判徒刑.~ ***away*** *(from)* ①拉走,引开;离开,退出.②拔出;(赛马、赛跑等)跑到前头,和(别人)拉开距离(*They started even but he soon drew away from the rest.* 他们起跑时不分先后,但他很快便跑到前面去了).~ ***back*** ①收回.②退回(转出口等的进口商品的关税).③犹豫;退却,缩手不办.④拉开(幕布等).~ ***bit [bridle, rein]*** ①勒住(马).②减低速度;遏制.~ ***down*** ①扯下,放下(~ *down the curtain* 闭幕).②招来,惹,引起.③煮稠,熬干.~ ***first blood*** ①发动初次攻击.②【美体】得第一名.~ ***forth*** 引出;博得(赞赏等).~ ***in*** ①拉入;引入,吸入,流入;收(网等);收回(借款等).②引诱;诱致;使加入.③退缩;缩小;(天)黑了;(日)渐短.④紧缩(开支等),节减(~ *in a breath of fresh air* 吸一口新鲜空气.~ *in one's expenditure* 紧缩开支.*be drew in to buy* 被骗去买某物).~ ***iron***〔美俚〕(从口袋里)掏出枪来.~ ***it fine*** ①(经费等)精打细算.②精确地区别;〔口〕吹毛求疵.~ ***it mild***〔口〕①心平气和地说;放谦虚一点.②不要吹;不要做得过火〔均为祈使语气〕.~ ***it strong*** 小题大做,夸张其词.~ ***level (with)*** 追上,赶上;扯平.~ ***lots [cuts]*** 抽签[抽签牌].~ ***lots of water***〔美〕重要而有势力.~ ***near [nigh]*** 挨近,靠近.~ ***off*** ①放干,排掉(水等);脱去(手套等).②消除(痛苦等).③转移(他人注意力等).④退走,撤退(军队等).⑤从…中取出.~ ***on*** ①穿,戴(~ *on a pair of boots* 穿靴.~ *on a pair of gloves* 戴手套).②引起(战争等).③引诱,勾引;招来.④依赖;靠;吸收,利用(~ *on one's imagination [memory]* 凭想象力[记忆力]讲述).⑤向…支取(*He ~ $50 on his checking account.* 他从支票帐上支付50美元).⑥接近,挨近,靠近 (*He felt death ~ing on.* 他感到自己快死了).~ ***oneself up*** *(to one's full height)* 立直,挺着胸脯;高视阔步.~ ***out*** ①拉长,拖长.②抽出;拔出;掏出;提出;【海】离(港等) *(from)*.引出,诱出,诱使…说出.③使(队伍等)排列整齐.④(日)渐长;(战争等)延长下去.⑤画,描;拟订,起草(计画).~ ***over*** 拉下遮盖.~ ***round*** 围拢(~ *round the fire* 围拢火炉).~ ***ruin upon oneself*** 使自己身败名裂.~ ***short and long*** 抽签.~ ***the longbow*** ①吹牛,夸口.②〔美〕(球等)玩得好,打得好.~ ***the pen [quill] against*** 写文章攻击….~ ***to*** 近,快(~ *to a close* 快完;收尾).~ ***to a head*** (疮等)化脓;(阴谋等)成熟.~ ***together*** 聚拢,一齐挨近.~ ***up*** ①曳上,拉起(鱼网等);(把水)抽上.②正容;整(队).③起草,写出,拟订.④(车、马等)停住,使(车、马等)停住.⑤逼近 *(to)*,追上 *(with)*.~ ***upon*** = ~ *on*.— *n.* ①牵引;抽出,拉,拖;服,吸.②拔出;拔牙,拔刀,拔枪;开弓;【医】(膏药等的)吸脓;支取,提(款).③平局,和局,无胜负.④有吸引力的人[物];精采节目.⑤抽签,拈阄;【牌】补进的牌.⑥〔美〕吊桥的可吊起部分;〔口〕侦探;【地】冲沟,干涸的河谷.*take a ~ on his pipe* 吸一口烟.*end in a ~* 终成平局,不分胜负.*The new play is a great ~.* 新戏非常叫座.***a sure*** ~ 肯定可搜出狐狸的地方;可引起议论之处.***be quick on the*** ~〔美俚〕反应敏捷.***beat to the*** ~ 先拔剑[枪];先下手.~ ***and quarter***〔古时刑罚〕四马分肢,肢解尸体.***play off a*** ~ 见 play 条.~**back** *n.* ①妨碍,障碍 *(to)*.②不利,失误;欠缺,缺点;弊端,疵瑕 *(in)*.③退款,退税.④【机】回火.~**bar**【机】拉杆,导杆;挂钩.~**bench**【机】拉丝机.~**boys**【纺】手工提花织物.~**bridge** 吊桥.~**down** (水位)下降,消耗.~**knife**, ~**shave** (两端有柄的)木工括刀(= drawing-knife).~ **well** 吊桶井,深井.-**a·ble** *a.*

draw·ee [drɔːˈiː] *n.*【商】(汇票等的)付款人,受票人 (*opp.* drawer).

draw·er [ˈdrɔːə drɔː] *n.* ①[ˈdrɔːə] 拖曳者;【商】(汇票等的)出票人,开票人;制图人;【机】拉丝工;〔古〕酒馆侍者.②[drɔː] 抽屉;〔*pl.*〕橱柜.③〔*pl.*〕[drɔːz] 汗裤,衬裤.*a chest of ~s* 有抽屉的橱柜.*a pair of ~s* 一条衬裤.*bathing ~s* 游泳裤.***out of the bottom*** ~ 最低级的.

draw·ing [ˈdrɔːiŋ] *n.* ①延引,牵引;引诱.②抽签;拈阄.③【机】拔丝;冲压成形.④描画,制图;图,图形;素描;图画.④【纺】练条;【机】回火,退火.⑤(支票等的)开发,付给;〔*pl.*〕〔英〕售得金额.*make a rough ~ of* 给…画草图.*a lineal [line] ~* 素描.*a watercolour ~* 水彩画.*a working ~* 施工图.***in [out]*** ~ (不)合画法,画得(不)准确;和环境(不)相称.***make a*** ~ 打

图样．～ **block [pad]** 图画纸本．～ **board** 制图板，画板．～ **card** (叫坐的)节目[场面,演员等]．～ **compasses** 制图圆规．～ **knife** (两端有柄的)木工刮刀．～ **machine**【机】拔丝机．～ **mill** 拉丝厂．～ **paper** 图画纸，制图纸．～ **pen** 画图笔，鸭嘴笔．～ **pin** 图钉．～ **pump** 吸入[抽出]泵．～ **room** ①客厅；〔*pl.*〕聚集在客厅中的宾客；上流社会(人士)．②〔美〕(火车的)特级专用车室．③〔英〕(王宫中的)接见(室)．④〔英〕制图室[美国叫 drafting room]〔*hold a ～ room* 接见〕．**～-room** *a.* 客厅的；上流社会的．～ **table** 绘图桌．

drawl [drɔːl] *vi., vt.* 慢声慢气地说[唱](出),拉长腔调地说[唱](出),拖拖沓沓地说[唱](出)．*affected ～ing speech* 装腔作势的演说．— *n.* 慢慢吞吞地说[唱]；慢慢说出的话[唱出的调子]．*say in one's slow ～* 拖长腔调说话．**-er** *n.* **-ing·ly** *ad.* **-y** *a.*

drawn [drɔːn] draw 的过去分词．— *a.* ①(刀、剑等)拔出鞘的．②互无胜负的．③(禽等)取出内脏的．④(线等)画好的．⑤被吸引的．⑥(钢丝等)被拔长的，延伸的,冷拉的．⑦(脸等)扭歪的．*a ～ sword* 出鞘的剑．*a ～ fowl* 掏出内脏的鸡．*face ～ with pain* 痛得扭歪了的脸．～ **butter**(用面粉调成的)奶油酱．～ **game** 平局,和局．～ **steel** 拉制钢，冷拉钢．～ **work**【纺】抽花手工．

dray [drei] *n.* ①(没有边帮的)大车，载重(马)车．②粗陋的雪橇．— *vt.* 用大车拖运．— *vi.* 赶大车；用大车运货．～ **horse** 重型挽马．**～man** (赶运货马车的)车夫．

dray·age [ˈdreiidʒ] *n.* ①用马车拖运．②马车运货费．

Dray·ton [ˈdreitn] *n.* ①德雷顿〔姓氏〕．②**Michael** ～ 米·德雷顿〔1563—1631,英国诗人〕．

dread [dred] *vt., vi.* ①恐怕,害怕,怕；担心,愁．②〔古〕敬畏．～ *death [dying, to die]* 怕死．～ *meeting sb.* 怕见到某人．— *n.* ①恐怖；担心,害怕．②〔古〕敬畏．③畏惧的事物．*be in ～ of* 怕,担心．*have ～ of speaking in public* 害怕在大庭广众讲话．*Fire is a ～.* 水火无情,火是一件可怕的东西．— *a.* ①令人恐惧的，非常可怕的．②可敬畏的．

dread·ful [ˈdredful] *a.* ①可怕的．②令人敬畏的．③〔口〕讨厌的,糟透了的,丑陋的．*a ～ storm* 可怕的暴风雨．*a ～ hat* 难看的帽子．～ *cooking* 饭菜做得坏透了．— *n.*〔英〕(趣味低级、售价便宜的)惊险小说[杂志]．*a penny ～* 廉价惊险小说．**-ly** *ad.* 可怕地；战战兢兢地；〔口〕特别,非常,极,极坏 (*be dreadfully tired* 累极了)．

dread·naught, dread·nought [ˈdrednɔːt] *n.* ①耐用厚呢；厚呢大衣．②无所畏惧的人,勇士．③〔D-〕(装备着旋转炮塔和大口径火炮的)无畏战舰,弩级战舰．

dream [driːm] *n.* ①梦．②幻想，梦想；空想．③理想，愿望．④梦一样美好的人[物等]，美景．*a hideous ～* 恶梦．*It is beyond my ～.* 那是我梦想不到的．*a fond ～* 一厢情愿的梦想．*(I wish you) sweet ～.* 晚安．*the land of ～s* 梦乡．*She is a perfect ～.* 她真是天仙一样的美女．***be [live, go about] in a*** ～ 梦一样地过日子．***go to one's ～s***〔诗〕入梦乡．***read a*** ～ 圆梦．***waking*** ～ 梦想,白日梦,幻想,空想．— *vi.* (*～ed* [dremt,〔罕〕driːmd], *～t* [dremt]; *～ed, ～t*) ①做梦；梦见,梦到 *(of; about)*．②幻想，梦想；想象．③向往，渴望 *(of)*．④〔与 little, not, never 等连用〕(很少,没有,决没有)想到．～ *of three mice* 梦见三只老鼠．*I never ～ed of it.* 我从没有想到过它．*Little did I ～ of succeeding so well.* 我很少想到会这样顺利．— *vt.* ①做(梦)；梦见．②想象，幻想；臆想．③(在空想中)虚度(光阴)．④〔与 little, not, never 等连用〕(很少，没有，决没有)想到．～ *a happy dream* 做了一个快乐的梦．*Last night I ～ed you.* 我昨晚梦见你．～ *away one's time* 在空想中虚度光阴．*I never [little] ～t that ...* 我决没有[很少]想到…．～ ***up***〔口〕凭空想出；凭空捏造出．***～away [out]*** *(one's time)* 象梦一样地度过,虚度．**～boat**〔美俚〕①理想的人[物]；理想的情人．②同类事物中最好的．**～hole** (仓库等的)风窗,气窗．**～land** ①梦境,梦乡．②幻想世界．**～ reader** 圆梦者，详梦者．**～scape** 梦幻一般的景色．**～world**＝～land．**-er** ①做梦的人．②空想家，梦想家．**-ful** *a.* 梦多的；常易梦见的．**-less** *a.* 无梦的，梦不见的 **-like** *a.* 梦一般的；梦幻的,朦胧的．

dreamt [dremt] *v.* dream 的过去式及过去分词．

dream·y [ˈdriːmi] *a.* ①(人)喜欢幻想的．②梦幻般的，朦胧的，模糊的；(精神等)恍惚的．③(乐曲等)悦耳的，轻柔的．④〔口〕漂亮的，顶呱呱的．⑤〔诗〕多梦的．*a ～ night's sleep* 多梦的一夜．*a ～ child* 喜欢幻想的孩子．*a ～ recollection of the event* 对那件事的模糊记忆．～ *music* 轻柔悦耳的音乐．*a ～ scheme* 充满幻想的计划．*He has a ～ new car.* 他有一辆顶漂亮的新车．**-i·ly** *ad.* **-i·ness** *n.*

drear [driə] *a.*〔诗〕＝ dreary.

drear·y [ˈdriəri] *a.* ①沉寂的,冷冷清清的；惨淡的,凄凉的；阴郁的．②沉闷的；枯燥的，无趣味的．③〔古〕悲哀的．*cheer a ～ mind* 使忧郁寡欢的心情振作起来．— *n.* 可怕的人物,可憎的人物〔多指历史名人〕．*a ～ tract of country* 荒凉的地方．*His speech was ～.* 他的讲演枯燥乏味．**-i·ly** *ad.* **-i·ness** *n.* **-i·some** *a.*

dredge[1] [dredʒ] *n.* ①疏浚机，挖泥机；挖泥船；捕捞船．②(采牡蛎、捕鱼等用的)拖网，捞网．③悬浮矿石．～ *ore* 贫矿石．～ *pump* 疏浚泵；污水泵．— *vt.* ①清淤,疏浚(河道等)；挖掘(泥土等)．②用拖网捞取．— *vi.* 疏浚；挖泥；挖掘；捕捞．

dredge[2] [dredʒ] *vt.* (烹调时)把面粉撒(在食物上)；撒(面粉)在食物上．～ *flour over meat* 把面粉撒在肉上．～ *meat with flour* 在肉上撒面粉．

dredg·er[1] [ˈdredʒə] *n.* ①疏浚机,挖泥机；挖泥船；(捕牡蛎等用的)采捞船．②疏浚工,挖泥工；使用拖网的渔夫．

dredg·er[2] [ˈdredʒə] *n.* (烹调时用的)撒粉器〔内装面粉、砂糖或其他调味品等,盖上有小孔〕．

dree [dri] *vt.*〔主 Scot.〕忍受，忍耐．～ ***one's weird***〔Scot.〕满足于自己的命运,安分守己．

dreg [dreg] *n.* ①〔常 *pl.*〕残滓,脚子；糟粕，渣滓；废物．②微量,少量的残剩物．*the ～s of society* 社会渣滓．*He left not a ～ in the glass.* 他把一杯水喝得点滴不剩．***drain [drink] to the ～s*** 喝干；享尽(快乐等)，受尽(痛苦等)．

dreg·gy [ˈdregi] *a.* 有渣滓的,脚子多的；浑浊的；污浊的．

Drei·bund [ˈdraibunt] *n.*〔G.〕三国同盟〔1882 年德、奥、意三国缔结的防守同盟〕．

D region [ˈdiː ˈriːdʒən]【气】D 区〔离地球表面 25 到 40 英里的电离层的最低部分〕．

Drei·ser [ˈdraisə] *n.* ①德赖瑟〔姓氏〕．②**Theodore** ～ 西奥多·德莱塞〔1871—1945,美国小说家〕．

drench [drentʃ] *vt.* ①使湿透,使浸透；浸泡．②使充满，使洋溢；包着，沐浴在…之下．③浸润；给(牲畜)灌药；〔古〕使饮．*be [get] ～ed with [by] rain.* 被雨淋透．*be ～ed to the skin [through and through]* 全身湿透．*garment ～ed in blood* 鲜血染透的罩衣．*trees ～ed with sunlight* 沐浴在阳光下的树木．*a woman ～ed in black* 裹着黑衣的妇女．*a letter ～ed with a great longing for home* 充满思乡之情的一封信．— *n.* ①弄湿，淋透；雨淋．②浸渍液；(制革时浸泡熟皮的)脱灰水．③(喝)一大口；一服药水〔尤指给牲畜吃的药水〕．*a ～ of rain* 大雨倾盆．**drench·ing·ly** *ad.* 湿透地；大雨倾盆地．

drench·er [drentʃə] *n.* ①〔口〕倾盆大雨．②(给牲畜治病用的)灌药器．③(制革行业用药液除去皮革石灰质的)脱灰工．

Dres·den [ˈdrezdən] *n.* 德累斯顿〔东德城市〕．

dress [dres] *vt.* (*～ed,*〔古〕***drest*** [drest]; *～ed, drest*) ①使穿衣,给…穿衣；打扮．②装饰，修饰；布置(橱窗等)．③加工(皮革等)；梳理(头发)，梳刷(马等)；敷裹，包扎(伤处)；烹调(饮食)，做(菜)．④整顿(队伍)．⑤【矿】选(矿)，洗(矿)．⑥修剪(树木等)；给(土地)除草；

为(庄稼)施肥;耕作(土地). ⑦使(石头、木材、织物等)表面平滑光洁. *a lady ~ed in black* 穿着丧服的妇女. *~ a baby* 给婴儿穿衣服. *be well [finely] ~ed* 衣着漂亮[讲究]. *get ~ed for a dinner party* 为出席宴会穿礼服. *~ a store window* 布置商店橱窗. *~ three chickens for dinner* 为晚餐做三只鸡. *~ meat* 做肉菜. *~ one's hair with taste* 头发的式样梳得秀气. *~ a horse* 给马梳刷. *~ one's wound* 给伤口包扎. *~ the ranks* 列队. *~ a field* 耕地. *~ a crop* 给作物除草施肥. — *vi.* ①穿衣服; 穿礼服; 打扮, 整装. ②整队;【军】看齐. ③(鸡等) 煺毛后净重. *to ~ for the opera* 穿上看戏的服装. *We don't ~ (for dinner).* 我们(在家里晚餐)不穿礼服. *~ well [badly]* 衣着漂亮[难看]. *Wake up and ~ now!* 醒醒穿衣服吧; *~ by [to] the right* 向右看齐. *~ (sb.)* **down** 〔口〕①梳刷(马). ②责骂; 鞭打;【美体】打败(对方). ③把(鸡等)煺毛. *~* **oneself** (外出时)换衣,打扮. *~* **out** ①打扮. ②装饰(船等). ③包扎(伤口). *~* **ship** ①【海】给船上挂彩旗. ②【美海军】全舰挂国旗. *~* **up** ①(把…)打扮得漂漂亮亮,着盛装; 化装. ②整队. *~* ***up like a plush hòrse [Mrs. Astor's plush horse]*** 〔美俚〕穿得过份考究. ***Right —~!*** 向右看——齐〔口令〕; — *n.* ①衣服,服装; 〔a ~〕女服,童装. ②礼服,盛装. ③(鸟等的)羽毛; 覆盖物; 外表, 形式. *try on a ~* 试穿衣服. *the ~ of the 18th century* 十八世纪的服装. *an evening ~* 晚礼服,燕尾服. *a morning ~* 普通礼服. *a full ~* 大礼服; 正装. *no ~* 服装请便〔请帖中用语〕. *a bird in its summer ~* 夏季羽毛丰满的鸟. *an old idea in a new ~* 新瓶装旧酒; 旧思想,新形式. — *a.* ①女服的; 童装的. ②礼服的, 盛装的. ③需要穿礼服的. *girls in their ~ kimono* 穿着和服式女晨衣的姑娘. *a ~ dinner* 要求穿礼服的晚宴. *~* **affair** 〔俚〕需要穿礼服的集会[场合]. *~* **ball** 盛装舞会. *~* **circle** 〔古〕二楼正座〔此处观众需穿晚礼服〕. *~* **coat** 燕尾服. *~* **form** (服装店橱窗中的)服装模特儿. *~* **goods** (妇女、儿童用的)衣料. *~* **guard** (女式自行车上的)护衣装置. *~* **improver** 妇女托裙腰垫. *~***make** *vi.* 做女服[童装]. *~***maker** 女服[童装]裁缝. *~***making** 女服[童装]制作业. *~* **parade** 【军】正装阅兵式. *~* **rehearsal** 【剧】彩排. *~* **shield** (女人腋下的)汗垫. *~* **shirt** ①礼服用衬衫. ②〔美〕时髦男子. *~* **suit** (一套)大礼服, (男子)晚礼服. *~* **tie** 礼服用领带. *~* **uniform** 〔美〕空军制服; 陆军青色制服; 海军青灰色冬制服. *~***-up** *a.* 要求穿礼服的.

dres·sage [dreˈsɑːʒ, ˈdresɑːʒ] *n.* 〔F.〕①驯马表演. ②驯马技术,对马的调教.

dress·er[1] [ˈdresə] *n.* ①(剧团的)服装员; 装饰师; 梳头师;〔口〕服装考究的人; 穿…服装的人. ②【纺】整经机; 浆纱机; 梳麻机. ③(树木)整枝剪; (石料、木材等的)打磨机; 整形器; 选矿机. ④外科手术助手,敷裹员. ⑤加工者; 加工用具. *a fancy ~* 服装迷. *a smart ~* 服装漂亮的人.

dress·er[2] [ˈdresə] *n.* ①食具柜;〔古〕案板,厨桌. ②〔美〕梳妆台,镜台; 化妆箱. *~* **set** 全套梳妆用具.

dress·ing [ˈdresiŋ] *n.* ①穿衣; 衣服, 服装; 打扮,装束; 装饰,修饰. ②(铸件等的)修整; (石料等的)修琢; (木材等的)打磨. ③(伤口的)包扎,敷裹; 包扎用品,敷料,绷带. ④烹调,做菜; (鸡鸭等的) 煺毛. ⑤调味品,加味品,填料. ⑥追肥; (旱地用的)肥料. ⑦【矿】选矿. ⑧【军】整队;【纺】整理; 上浆; 梳棉. ⑨〔口〕申斥, 责骂. *~* **bag [case]** 化妆用品袋[盒]. *~* **bell** 【剧】整装铃. *~***-down** *n.* 〔口〕责骂; 鞭打 (*get (receive) a dressing-down* 受到申斥). *~* **gown [robe]** 〔主英〕晨衣,浴衣〔美国通例叫 bathrobe〕. *~* **room** 化妆室; (舞台的)后台. *~* **station** 【军】(战地的)敷裹处,包扎处. *~* **table** 化妆台,镜架台. *~***-works** 选矿厂.

dress·y [ˈdresi] *a.* ①讲究穿戴的,爱装饰的. ②(衣着)漂亮的,时髦的. **dress·i·ness** *n.*

drest [drest] *v.* 〔古、诗〕= dressed.

drew [druː] draw 的过去式. — *vi.* ①滴,滴下 *(from)*; 湿透 *(with)*. ②漏下,撒下.

Drey·fus [ˈdreifəs, F. dreiˈfjus] *n.* ①德雷福斯〔法国人名〕. ②**Alfred ~** 阿尔弗列·德雷福斯〔1859—1935,法国炮兵军官, 法国历史上著名大冤案"德雷福斯案件"的受害者〕. *~* **affair** 德雷福斯事件〔法国近代史上的大事件之一, 1894 年德雷福斯被诬通敌下狱, 举国愤怒, 经过十余年反复斗争, 终于 1906 年获申雪〕.

drib [drib] *n.* 〔方〕点,滴; 少量, 微量〔主要用于短语 ~s and drabs 中〕. *~***s and drabs** 点点滴滴; 少量.

drib·ble [ˈdribl] *vi.* ①滴下, 点点滴滴地流. ②淌口水, 流涎. ③慢慢流动; 逐渐消散. ④(篮、足球等)带球,运球,短传. *uncontrollable dribbling of liquid* 难以控制的漏水. *~ at the mouth* 口角流涎. — *vt.* ①使滴, 使淌(口水). ②(篮、足球等)盘(球), 带(球), 运(球). ③逐渐发出 *(out)*; 逐渐消磨 *(away)*. *~ water on a plant* 给植物洒水. *~ away one's time [energy]* 逐渐消磨掉时间[精力]. *~ out money to one's children* 一点一点地把钱花在子女身上. — *n.* ①滴; 涓滴,少量. ②【体】盘球; 带球,运球. ③流涎. ④微雨, 毛毛雨. *call a plumber for ~s* 请管道工来修一下漏水的管子. *a ~ of revenue* 少量收入. *send money in ~s* 一点一点地送钱去. **-r** *n.* ①流口涎的人. ②带球前进的运动员.

drib·(b)let [ˈdriblit] *n.* ①少量; 少额. ②(液体的)涓滴. *by [in] ~s* 一点一点地,渐渐. *He felt a ~ of fear.* 他有点儿害怕. *~s coming through the ceiling* 渗过天花板滴下的水珠. *~* **cone** 【地】熔岩滴锥.

dried [draid] dry 的过去式及过去分词. — *a.* 干燥的, 干缩的. *~ alum* 【化】焦矾. *~ bêche-de-mer* 干海参. *~ beef* 牛肉干;〔美俚〕陈词滥调. *~ blood* 血粉(肥料). *~ goods* 干货,干制品,干制海味. *~ milk* 奶粉. *~***-up** *a.* 干缩的; 干燥的 (*a dried-up water hole* 干了的水坑).

dri·er [ˈdraiə] *n.* ①干燥工. ②干燥机. ③干燥物; 干料;【化】催干剂,干燥剂.

drift [drift] *n.* ①漂流; (潮流的)推进力. ②漂流物; 吹积物; 堆积物;【地】冰碛,漂砾. ③倾向,趋势; 动向. ④大意,要点,要旨. ⑤(政策等的)坐观, 放任自流. ⑥流速; (船等的)流程,漂流距离; (滑车的)伸展距离. ⑦(仪表的)漂移; 偏移;【海、空】偏航,偏流; (导弹的)航差;【无】偏移; 偏差. ⑧【矿】水平巷道; 小平道. ⑨〔南非〕浅滩,滩. ⑩【机】冲头,冲孔器; 打桩器. ⑪〔方〕(鸟等)群. *against the ~ of a current* 顶着潮流的压力. *be in a state of ~* 心不自主,放任自流. *D- is as bad as unthrift.* 放任自流和浪费一样坏. *a policy of ~* 放任主义[政策]. *a ~ of snow [leaves]* 吹积成的雪[树叶]堆. *the amount of ~* (船的)漂流距离. *a ~ toward nationalism* 民族主义的倾向. *the ~ of an argument* 争论的要点. *catch the ~ of a talk* 抓住谈话的要点. *a ~ of ice* 流冰. *a ~ of sheep* 羊群. *the ~ of Nature* 造化的威力. *electronic ~* 电子(仪器)的漂移. — *vt.* ①使漂流; 使漂积[冲积]; 把…吹积; (吹积物等)覆盖. ②【机】(用冲头)冲孔. *The current ~ed the boat to sea.* 水流把船冲到海里去了. *a trail ~ed with leaves* 小道上满是落叶. *The wind ~ed the snow.* 风把雪吹成小堆. — *vi.* ①漂,漂流; 漂移; 游荡. ②被吹积成堆. ③心不由主地走; 不知不觉地陷入 *(into)*; 渐渐趋向 *(toward)*. *perfume ~ing into the room* 漂进屋里的香气. *~ toward ruin [bankruptcy]* 逐渐走向毁灭[破产]. *He ~d from town to town.* 他在各个城市流浪. *~ing sand* 吹积成的沙堆. *~ apart from sb.* 逐渐疏远某人. *~ off to sleep* 慢慢地睡着了. *~ down the river* 顺流而下. *~ (along) (through life)* 随波逐流地过一辈子. *~* ***into*** *(errors)* 不自觉地犯了错误. ***let things*** *~* 听天由命. *~* **anchor** 【海】浮锚. *~* **angle** 【海、空】偏航角,漂移角. *~***bolt** 【机】

系栓. ~ **bottle** 海流瓶〔投入海中以测量海流〕. ~ **ice** 流冰, 漂冰. ~ **net**【海】漂网. ~ **sand**【地】流沙. ~ **sight**【航】偏流指示计. ~ **space**【无】漂移空间. ~ **tube**【无】漂移管. ~**weed** 漂浮海草[藻]. ~**wood** ①*n.* 浮木; 被扔弃的零星物品; 寄生虫. ②*a.* 浮木的.
drift·y *a.* ①漂移的; 漂流的; 流荡的. ②吹积的.
drift·age [ˈdriftidʒ] *n.* ①漂流(作用). ②漂流物; 吹积物. ③【海】偏航, 偏流, 漂流偏差; (船的)流程; (子弹等受风影响的)偏差.
drift·er [ˈdriftə] *n.* ①漂流者, 流浪者; 漂流物;【军】漂流水雷. ②(带有漂网的)扫海船; 漂网渔船, 使用漂网的渔夫. ③【矿】架式钻机.
drill[1] [dril] *n.* ①【军】操练, 演习; (严格而有系统的)盘练, 训练. 〔英口〕教官. ②【机】钢钻, 钻头; 钻床, 钻孔机;【矿】凿岩机. ③【动】(一种钻进牡蛎壳破坏牡蛎繁殖的)海蜗牛, 荔枝螺. ④〔英口〕正确的步骤, 惯常的程序[手续]. *soldiers at* ~ 训练中的士兵. *gun* ~ 练炮. *a fire* ~ 消防训练. *a* ~ *in spelling* 拼写练习. *a* ~ *on pronunciation* 发音练习. *a twist* ~【机】麻花钻. *a three-fluted* ~【机】三槽钻头. *a heavy duty* ~ 重型钻床. *a rock* ~ 钎子. *know the* ~ *perfectly* 完全懂得规定的步骤. — *vt.* ①教练; (严格)训练; 操练; 练习; (通过反复教导)使牢记 *(into)*. ②(用钢钻)钻(孔); 在…上(用钢钻)钻孔. ③〔美俚〕(用子弹)打穿, 枪杀. ④〔美俚〕走, 步行. ~ *soldiers* 练兵. ~ *schoolboys in grammar* 严格教学生练习语法. ~ *an idea into sb.* 通过反复教导向某人灌输一种思想. ~ *a board* 在板上钻孔. ~ *holes an inch apart* 每隔一英寸钻一个孔. ~ *sb. right between the eyes* 子弹正好穿过某人的两眼之间. *We had to* ~ *20 miles.* 我们得靠两条腿走二十英里了. — *vi.* ①操练; 训练; 做体操. ②钻孔; 钻通 *(through)*. ③(子弹等)穿过. ④(钻机、电话等)发出连续的嗡嗡声. ~ *for oil* 钻探石油. *daylight* ~*ing into the room* 射入房间的日光. *The telephone started* ~*ing all of a sudden.* 电话突然嗡嗡响起来. ~ **ammunition** 练习弹. ~ **bit**【机】钻; 钻头. ~ **book** [**regulations**]【军】操典. ~ **call** 出操号. ~ **chulk**【机】钻夹头. ~ **ground** 练兵场, 操练场. ~**log** 钻探剖面; 岩心记录. ~**master** 教练,【军】教官. ~**ship** 钻探船, 石油钻探平台. ~ **team** (专为接受检阅等训练的)操典队. ~ **tower** 消防训练塔. **-able** *a.*
drill[2] [dril] *n.* ①条播机. ②条播沟. ③条播种子, 条播作物. — *vt.* ①条播(作物); 在(土地)上条播. ②用播种机播(种), 用播种机撒(肥料). ~ *barley in rows* 条播大麦. ~ *a hill with seedlings* 在小山上条植树苗. — *vi.* 条播, 条植.
drill[3] [dril] *n.*【纺】斜纹棉布[麻布]; 厚斜纹布.
drill[4] [dril] *n.*【动】(西非的)鬼狒.
drill·ing[1] [ˈdriliŋ] *n.* ①钻孔;【矿】钻井; 〔*pl.*〕钻屑, 钻粉. ②操练, 训练. ~ *machine* 钻床. ~ *fluid* [*mud*] 钻探泥浆.
drill·ing[2] [ˈdriliŋ] *n.*【农】条播. *ridge* [*furrow*] ~ 垄[沟]播.
drill·ing[3] [ˈdriliŋ] *n.*【纺】斜纹布, 卡其.
drill·ing[4] [ˈdriliŋ] *a.* 尖锐的, 辛辣的. ~ *eyes* 敏锐的目光. ~ *taunt about politics* 辛辣的政治抨击.
drill·i·on [ˈdriliən] *n.* 〔美俚〕天文数字.
dri·ly [ˈdraili] *ad.* ①干燥地. ②冷冰冰地, 冷淡地. ③干巴巴地, 枯燥无味地; 不加渲染地 (= dryly).
dri·me·ter [ˈdrimitə] *n.* 含水量测定计; 湿度计.
drink [driŋk] *vt.* (**drank** [dræŋk]; **drunk** [drʌŋk], 〔诗〕 ***drunk·en*** [ˈdrʌŋkən]) ①饮, 喝; 喝干, 喝完; 〔~ oneself〕喝酒喝得…. ②举杯祝贺, 为…干杯. ③吸入, (植物等)吸收(水分). ④把(金钱等)花在喝酒上; 用喝酒打发掉(时间等). ⑤尽情欣赏, 领略, 陶醉 *(in)*. ~ *a glass of milk* 喝一杯牛奶. *I could* ~ *the sea dry.* 我渴死了. *Let us* ~ *success to him.* 举杯祝他成功. ~ *sb.'s health* 为某人的健康干杯. ~ *(the toast of) the Queen* 为女王干杯. *The sunburnt sands drank water like a sponge.* 被太阳晒烫的沙子象海绵一样吸收水份. ~*ing air into his lungs* 吸一口气. ~ *himself into oblivion* 喝得忘却一切. ~ *one's troubles away* 以酒解忧. ~ *one's income to the last penny* 喝光自己的收入. ~ *the hours away* 喝酒消磨时间. ~ *oneself drunk* 喝得大醉. ~ *oneself into illness* 喝出病来. — *vi.* ①饮, 喝. ②喝酒; 喝醉, 酗酒. ③吸, 吸收 *(of)*. ④干杯 *(to)*. ⑤〔废〕喝起来有…味. ~ *from a well* 喝井水. *eat and* ~ 饮食. *He never* ~*s.* 他从不喝酒. ~ *deep of the Chinese culture* 深受中国文化的熏陶. *This whisky* ~*s well.* 这种威士忌酒味道不错. ~ ***down*** ①(一口气)喝下. ②以酒消(愁). ③喝到灌醉对方(~ *down one's heartache* 以酒浇愁. ~ *sb. down* 喝到使某人酒醉). ~ ***hard*** [***deep, heavily***] 痛饮, 大喝; 酗酒. ~ ***in*** 吸收; 陶醉于 (*We drank in the beauty of the landscape.* 我们陶醉在美景中). ~ ***it*** 〔俚〕大喝. ~ ***like a fish*** 牛饮, 大口大口地喝. ~ ***of*** 喝一口; 分享一部分 (*He shall* ~ *of the cup.* 给他喝一口). ~ ***off*** 一气喝干. ~ ***oneself out of a position*** 因为喝酒丢掉了差事. ~ ***the cup of joy*** [***sorrow***] 享尽欢乐[尝尽酸辛]. ~ ***to*** 举杯祝贺; 为…干杯 (*I'll* ~ *to you.* 我要为你干杯). ~ ***(sb.) under the table*** = drink down ③. ~ ***up*** ①喝干, 喝完. ②吸入, 吸上来. — *n.* ①饮料; 酒. ②(酒等的)一口, 一杯. ③喝酒, 酗酒. ④〔the ~〕〔口〕(河、湖、海等的)一大片水〔尤指海洋〕. *soft* ~*s* (无酒精成分的)饮料. *strong* ~ 酒. ~ *and tobacco* 烟酒. *D- was his downfall.* 酗酒是他垮掉的原因. *stand him a* ~ 请他喝一口酒. *Give me a* ~ *of milk.* 给我喝一口牛奶. *I will duck him in the* ~. 我要把他按进水里. *fall in the* ~ 落进水里. ***a big*** ~ 〔美谑〕大河. ***be fond of*** ~ 爱喝酒. ***be given*** [***addicted***] ***to*** ~ 纵酒. ***do a drink*** 〔美〕喝酒. ~ ***offering*** 敬神酒, 奠酒. ***have*** [***take***] ***a*** ~ 喝一杯. ***in*** ~ 醉. ***on the*** ~ 常常喝酒, 有酒瘾. ***take to*** ~ 喝(酒)上瘾. ***the big*** ~ 〔美俚〕①大西洋或太平洋. ②密西西比河. ~ **money** [**penny**] 〔古〕赏钱, 酒钱, 小帐. ~ **offering** 祭献的酒.
drink·a·ble [ˈdriŋkəbl] *a.* 可以饮的, 饮用的. — *n.* 〔常 *pl.*〕饮料. *eatables and* ~*s* 食品和饮料.
drink·er [ˈdriŋkə] *n.* ①饮者. ②酒徒, 醉翁. ③(给家禽等喂水的)饮水器. *a great* [*hard, heavy*] ~ 酒豪, 酒量大的人, 酗酒者. *a little* [*small*] ~ 不爱喝酒的人, 酒量小的人. *the* ~ *of the toast* 干杯者, 举杯祝酒的人.
drink·er·y [ˈdriŋkəri] *n.* 〔美〕酒店, 酒吧间.
drink·ing [ˈdriŋkiŋ] *n.* ①喝, 饮. ②(经常或过度的)喝酒. ③〔美〕狂欢酒会. *give up* ~ 戒酒. — *a.* ①适于饮用的. ②喝酒用的. ③有酒瘾的, 喝酒的. *Is he a* ~ *man?* 他喜欢喝酒吗? *a* ~ *companion* 酒友. ~ **bout** 宴会. ~ **cup** 酒杯. ~ **fountain** (公园、路旁公用的)喷嘴式饮水龙头. ~ **paper** 吸水纸. ~ **song** 祝酒歌. ~ **water** 饮用水.
Drink·water [ˈdriŋkˌwɔːtə] *n.* 德林克沃特〔姓氏〕.
drip [drip] *n.* ①滴, 点滴, 水滴; 滴下, 滴滴答答〔水滴声〕; 〔*pl.*〕滴下的液体[油汁等]. ②【建】滴水, (屋)檐, 滴水槽. ③【机】滴水器; 滴口; 引管; 采酸管. ④【医】滴注(法); 滴注器. ⑤〔俚〕伤感, 爱哭. ⑥〔美俚〕平庸的人; 使人厌烦的人; 无聊的闲谈[劝告]; 恭维话. *in a* ~ 一滴一滴地. *fog* ~*s* 雾珠. *the irritating* ~ *of a faucet* 水龙头令人厌烦的滴水声. *intravenous* ~ 静脉滴注. —*vi.* ①滴, 滴下 *(from)*; 湿透 *(with)*. ②漏下, 撒下. *sweat dripping off one's brow* 额头滴下汗珠. *The rain water* ~*s from the eaves.* 雨水滴下屋檐. *the cheeks dripping with tears* 颊上满是泪珠. *sunlight dripping over the house* 阳光从房上漏下. *a story dripping with love* 一个渗透着爱情的故事. — *vt.* 使滴下. *a dress dripping moisture* 往下滴水珠的衣服. *her fingers*

dripping blood 她的手指滴血. ~ **chamber** 排水室，沉淀池. ~ **coffee**(用渗漏咖啡壶煮的)渗漏咖啡. ~-~, ~-**drop** *n.* 不断的滴水. ~-**dry** ① ['drip-drai] *a.* (衣服)用快速晾干料子做的〔洗后不用绞干，可快速晾干〕. ②['drip-'drai] *vi.* (衣服)易快速晾干；晾干自挺. ~-**feed** *vt.* 以静脉滴注法给(病人)输液；~ **mo(u)ld**【建】滴水槽. ~ **painting** 滴色画〔把颜料洒或滴在画布上而不用画笔的一种作画法〕；滴色画派. ~ **pan**【机】(车床等的)盛油[屑]盘. ~ **stone** *n.* ①【建】滴水石. ②【地】钟乳石，石笋.

drip·o·la·tor ['dripəleitə] *n.* 渗漏咖啡壶.

drip·ping ['dripiŋ] *n.* ①滴，滴下；滴水声. ②〔常 *pl.*〕滴下物，水滴，液滴；(烧肉上的)油滴. — *a.* 水滴滴的，湿淋淋的. *a ~ day* 下雨天. ***be ~ wet*** 淋透，湿透. ~ *eaves*【建】滴水檐. ~ **pan** (烤肉等接油滴用的)油盘.

drip·py ['dripi] *a.* ①滴水的. ②多小雨的. ③〔口〕容易伤感的. ~ *weather* 经常下毛毛雨的天气. *a ~ love story* 感伤的爱情故事.

drive [draiv] *vt.* (***drove*** [drəuv], 〔古〕***drave*** [dreiv]; ***driven*** ['drivn]) ①驱逐，赶，撵 *(along; away; back; down; in; off; out; forward* 等). ②赶(马车等)；驾驶，开(汽车等)；用车运，用车送. ③逼迫，强迫，驱使，迫使，使不得不. ④推动；推进；发动(机器等)；运(笔)；【无】激励. ⑤努力经营，促使(成交). ⑥把(钉、桩等)打进 *(into)*；挖(隧道)；钻(油井等)；(在多山地区)开(路等). ⑦推迟，拖延. ⑧【棒球】用力击(球)，猛力掷(球)；【网球】抽(球)；发(急球)；【高尔夫球】从球座打出. ⑨从…中轰出猎物. ~ *away the flies* 赶走苍蝇. ~ *off the pirates* 击退海盗. ~ *a carriage* 赶马车. ~ *a motorcar* 开汽车. ~ *sb. home* 用车子送人回家. ~ *a mule* 赶骡子. *a submarine driven by nuclear power* 核动力驱动的潜艇. *Wind ~s the mill.* 风推动磨盘. ~ *a nail into the wall* 把钉子敲进墙里. ~ *a stone at the dog* 拿石头掷狗. ~ *a quill* 挥毫书写，拿鹅毛笔写字. ~ *sb. mad with jealousy [to desperation]* 使某人嫉妒得发狂[绝望]. *The heat drove him to rest.* 酷热迫使他休息. *She was driven to admit it.* 她被迫承认那件事. ~ *a roaring trade* 生意兴隆. ~ *a good bargain* 努力做成了一笔好生意. ~ *a tunnel through a hill* 挖一条穿山隧道. ~ *a railroad through a mountainous district* 横贯山区铺设一条铁路. ~ *a wood* (打猎时)把林中的猎物哄赶出来. ~ *one's departure to the last moment* 拖延行期直到最后一刻才动身. — *vi.* ①赶马车；开车；〔美口〕领到驾驶执照. ②乘车，乘车旅行. ③急驶，猛冲；(在外力推动下)急行. ④努力争取. ⑤【棒球】用力击球；猛力掷球；【网球】抽球；发急球. *learn how to ~* 学开车. *In this state, you can't ~ until you are 18 years old.* 本州规定，年满十八岁方可领驾驶执照. *Do you ride or ~?* 骑马去还是开车去？*D- ahead!* 往前开！~ *across the wilderness* 在荒原上急驶. *Rain drove into our faces.* 雨猛打到我们脸上. *The ship drove before the wind.* 船顺风急驶. ~ *in a carriage* 坐马车. ~ *hard to make it a success.* 努力争取成功. ~ **at** 指望，打算，想 (*I can't make out what he is driving at.* 我不明白他是什么打算). ~ ***away at*** 〔口〕一心做，拼命做. ~ ***down*** 压低. ~ ***(sb.) hard*** 强迫(某人)拼命工作. ~ ***home*** ①(把钉)敲进去. ②(摆清事实)使领会，使明白，使痛感. ③用车把…送到家. ~ ***into*** ①把…赶进去；(风等把…)吹积成. ②把(功课等)灌输给…. ~ ***on the horn*** 〔俚〕乱揿(汽车)喇叭. ***let ~ (at)*** 对准…打，照准…发射 (*let ~ at the ball* 对准球一击). — *n.* ①驱逐，赶，撵；(猎物的)哄赶. ②开车，驾驶马车[汽车]旅行；旅程. ③【机】传动，驱动；传动装置；【无】激励. ④马车道，汽车路；(私宅内的)环形车路. ⑤驱使；(被驱赶着走的)畜群. ⑥(木材的)流放，流运；(流运中的)木材. ⑦冲力，动力；干劲；努力；魄力；精力. ⑧倾向；趋势. ⑨〔美〕(政治宣传、募捐等的)运动，热潮；竞争，廉价推销. ⑩【棒球】猛掷球，猛击球；【网球】抽球，发急球. ⑪【军】猛攻. ⑫【心】冲动，本能要求. *take [have, go for] a ~ in a motor-car* 乘汽车出游. *It's only a few minutes' ~ to the airport.* 坐车去机场几分钟就到了. *a ~ of cattle* 赶牲畜. *a ~ of logs* 流放木材. *the hunger ~* 吃饱肚子的需求. *a sexual ~* 性冲动. *a man with great ~* 进取心强的人，干劲大的人. *a propaganda ~* 宣传运动. *start a ~ to raise funds* 开展一项征募基金的运动. *His paintings has a ~.* 他的画有一种活力. *a ~ against Berlin* 猛攻柏林. *gear ~* 齿轮传动. *chain [screw] ~* 链[螺杆]传动. *front [rear] ~* (汽车的)前[后]驱动. ~ **gear**【机】传[主]动齿轮，传动机构. ~ **line** (汽车的)动力传动系统. ~ **pipe** 自流井(竖管). ~ **pulse**【无】驱动脉冲. ~ **shaft**【机】主动轴. ~**way** ①(由私人住房通到大路的)私人车道. ②马路，汽车道. ③〔美〕畜群道；马车道. ~ **wheel** =【机】主动轮，传动轮.

driv·a·ble, drive·a·ble *a.* ①可驾驭的. ②(道路等)可供汽车行驶的.

drive-in ['draiv-'in] *n.* 〔美〕(让顾客不下汽车即可吃饭、办事、看戏等的)路边饭店，路边银行；露天电影院. — *a.* (饭店、电影院等)路边服务式的；露天营业式的. *Drive-in business far exceeded walk-in business.* 露天营业式的企业远远压倒了室内服务式的企业.

driv·el ['drivl] *vi.* ①淌口水. ②说蠢话，说胡涂话. ③〔古〕喋喋不休地说. *a drivelling idiot* 说胡话的笨蛋. — *vt.* ①愚蠢地说. ②浪费(时间、精力等). ~ *one's time [energy]* 浪费时间[精力]. — *n.* ①口水. ②胡涂话. ~ ***away*** 白费(时间等). **-(l)er** *n.* 说胡话的人；呆子，胡涂虫. **-lin·ly** *ad.*

driv·en ['drivn] drive的过去分词. — *a.* ①被逼迫的，不得已的，被驱使的. ②打入的. ③吹积起来的. ④【机】从动的. ~ **snow** 吹积的雪. *a ~ sense of obligation* 紧迫的责任感. *a ~ pile* 入土[打入]桩. ~ **gear**【机】从动齿轮. ~ **shaft**【机】从动轮. ~ **wheel**【机】从动轮.

drive-on ['draiv-'ɔn] *a.* (船等)可让汽车直接开上去的.

driv·er ['draivə] *n.* ①驱逐者，驱赶者；(火车的)司机；(汽车等的)驾驶员；赶马车者. ②【机】传动轮，主动轮；推进器. ③锤，夯，打桩机. ④赶牲口的人；(监督奴隶等劳动的)监工. ⑤激励器. ⑥【船】后桅斜桁帆，尾纵帆；【高尔夫球】长打棒. *a pile ~* 打桩机. *a spike ~* 钉锤. *a screw ~* (螺丝)起子，改锥，旋凿. ***the ~'s seat*** ①驾驶座. ②发号施令的地位，控制地位. **~'s license** (汽车)驾驶执照. **-less** *a.* 无人驾驶的. **-ship** (汽车)驾驶、保养和维修技术.

drive-up ['draiv-'ʌp] *a.* 专为驾车者设计的(指驾车者毋需下车即可接受服务). ~ **window** (餐厅的)驾车者服务台.

driv·ing ['draiviŋ] *a.* ①推动的，起推动作用的. ②【机】传动的；主动的. ③猛冲的. ④精力充沛的，有上进心的；(监工等对工人)苛刻的. ⑤驾驶的，操纵的. *a ~ shaft* 驱动轴. ~ *force* 推动力. *the ~ seat* 驾驶台，操纵台. *a ~ storm* 狂风暴雨. *a ~ young salesman* 精力充沛的年轻推销员. ~ **axle** 主动轮. ~ **band [belt]** 传动带. ~ **box** ①司机台. ②主动轴箱. ~ **gear** 主动齿轮. ~ **iron** 一种铁头高尔夫球棒. ~ **licence** 驾驶执照. ~ **shaft** 主动轮，传动轴. ~ **wheel** (机械的)主动轮；(汽车的)驱动轮.

driz·zle ['drizl] *n.* ①细雨，毛毛雨，蒙蒙细雨. ②细水珠. — *vi.* 下毛毛雨. *a drizzling rain* 蒙蒙细雨. *It ~s.* 下毛毛雨. — *vt.* ①细雨般地撒下. ②用细水珠弄湿. **driz·zling·ly** *ad.*

driz·zly ['drizli] *a.* ①下着蒙蒙细雨的. ②毛毛雨似的.

dro·ger, dro·gher ['drəugə] *n.* (西印度沿岸的)笨重的帆船，货船.

drogue [drəug] *n.* ①(捕鲸标枪末端的)浮标. ②【海】浮

锚，海锚. ③【空】(飞机场上的)锥形风标. ④【空】(由飞机或降落伞牵引用于空战演习的)拖靶. ⑤【空】(空中加油飞机用的)漏斗形软管接头. ⑥【空】(减低飞行速度用的)减速小(降落)伞.

droit [drɔit] *n.* ①权利；【法】法定所得. ②〔*pl.*〕税，关税. ③法律，法. *the ~s of Admiralty*〔英〕捕获敌船(或从遇难船、弃船中所得的)财物收益享有权.

droit des gens [drwa dei 'ʒɑːn]〔F.〕国际法.

droit du sei•gneur ['drɔitdjuːsein'jəː] ①(封建领主对领地内新婚妇女蛮横索取的)初夜权. ②任何蛮横索取的类似权利.

droll [drəul] *vi.*〔古〕说笑话，开玩笑. *~ on [upon, at] sb.* 拿某人开玩笑. — *a.* 好笑的，滑稽的. — *n.* 逗人发笑的人；滑稽演员；小丑. **-ness** *n.* **-y** *ad.*

droll•er•y ['drəuləri] *n.* ①滑稽(举动)，诙谐. ②笑话，滑稽话；滑稽戏；〔古〕漫画.

drome [drəum] *n.*〔口〕飞机场，航空港 (= airdrome).

-drome *comb. f.* 场: air*drome*, hippo*drome*, picture*drome*.

drom•e•da•ry ['drʌmədəri] *n.*【动】单峰骆驼；(善跑的)乘骑骆驼.

drom•on(d) ['drɔmən(d)] *n.* (中世纪地中海的)快速大帆船.

drom•om•e•ter [drəu'mɔmitə] *n.* 速度计.

drone [drəun] *n.* ①雄蜂；〔喻〕懒人，寄生虫. ②(蜂等的)嗡嗡声；单调的低音；【乐】风笛的低音管；低音调；低音风笛. ③言语单调的人；单调沉闷的话. ④靶机，飞行靶标；(无线电遥控的)无人驾驶飞机. *a target ~* 靶机. — *vi.* ①(蜂、机械等)嗡嗡地响；用单调低沉的声音说话[唱歌]，懒洋洋地说[唱]. ②偷懒，混日子. *an aircraft droning through the stillness* 一架飞机打破寂静的嗡嗡声. *The old clergyman ~d on.* 那个老牧师懒洋洋地布道. — *vt.* ①用单调低沉的声音说出[唱出]. ②懒洋洋地打发(日子) *(away)*. *~ (out) the sutras* 懒洋洋地讲经. **dron•ing•ly** *ad.* 嗡嗡地，单调低沉地；懒洋洋地；吊儿郎当地.

drool [druːl] *vi.* ①〔英方，美〕= drivel. ②过分表示高兴. — *n.* = drivel. 胡涂话.

droop [druːp] *vi.* ①(头、树枝等)低垂，下垂；(眼睛)朝下. ②(草木)枯萎；(人)衰弱，(精神)颓丧，(意气)消沉；〔诗〕(太阳等)落山，西沉. *with one's head ~ing* 低垂着头. *His spirits ~ed.* 他意气消沉. — *vt.* ①使下垂；使(眼睛)朝下. ②使颓丧. — *n.* ①下垂，低垂. ②颓丧. ③(声调的)低沉. *a ~ of the eyes* 眼睛俯视着. *~* **nose [snout]** (飞机的)下垂式机头〔降落时飞机机头可下垂，使驾驶员获得更佳视野〕.

drop [drɔp] *n.* ①滴；液滴，水滴. ②〔*pl.*〕【药】滴剂；滴眼药. ③微量，点滴；一口[杯]酒. ④滴状物；耳坠；水果糖. ⑤急降，降落；(物价)下跌，(生产)减低；败落，没落；落下距离，高低平面间的相差距离；(地面的)陷落深度；陡坡；【水】落差；【军】弹道降落距离. ⑥(绞刑台的)踏板；(绞刑犯的)吊起高度. ⑦(邮箱的)投信口；门上的锁孔盖；【建】吊饰；【机】落锤；(戏院的)垂幕；吊装布景. ⑧中央保管所[仓库]. ⑨降落伞部队；空投(物资). ⑩【橄榄球】投踢 (= drop-kick)；【棒球】下曲球. ⑪【机】轴吊距；【海】横帆的纵幅. ⑫绞刑台. ⑬刚出生的小动物；落果. ⑭〔美俚〕(间谍等藏匿、传递情报的)情报点，秘密传递点. *a ~ of rain [water]* 雨[水]滴. *two ~s of quinine* 两滴奎宁. *a ~ of whisky* 一口威士忌酒. *a ~ of fever.* 有一点发烧. *the ~ of tears* 落泪. *a ~ in prices* 跌价. *a ten feet ~* 十英尺的落下距离[落差]. *a sharp ~ to the lake* 斜向湖边的陡坡. *lemon ~s* 柠檬水果糖. *a persimmon ~* 树上落下的柿子. ***a ~ in the bucket [ocean]*** 沧海之一粟. ***at the ~ of a [the] hat*** 〔美俚〕一发信号就；随即，立刻；欣然 (*He used to fight at the ~ of a hat.* 他总是一看到信号就大打出手). *~* ***by*** *~* 一滴滴，一点点. ***get [have] the ~ on (sb.)*** 〔美俚〕①先拔枪对准(某人)，先发制(人). ②胜过(某人). ***have a ~ in one's eye*** 〔俚〕微醉，带醉. ***take a ~*** 喝一杯 (*take a ~ too much* 喝醉了). — *vt.* ***(dropped, dropt*** [drɔpt]; ***drop•ping)*** ①使滴下，淌(汗等). ②垂下，放下；使落下，投下；空投；放低(声音等)；降低(速度等). ③(失手)落下，丢下；失落(钱包等). ④省略；遗漏. ⑤丢开(话题等)；改掉(习惯等)；断绝(来往等). ⑥随便地说出，无意中漏出. ⑦(把信)投入(邮筒)；(随便地)写、寄(信等). ⑧射落，打下(鸟等)；击倒；〔俚〕杀掉. ⑨降级；〔美〕解雇；开除(学生等). ⑩下(乘客)，下(车)；辞别(同行人). ⑪(动物)下(崽)，产(仔). ⑫【海】赶过，超越；使(岛等)从视线中消失. ⑬【橄榄球】把落地球踢进(球门)；【篮球】投球进(篮)；【牌】吊出(王牌等). ⑭〔俚〕(赌博等)输(钱)；(比赛)失(局等). ⑮把(鸡蛋)打入沸水中煮. ⑯〔美俚〕吞服(丸药). ⑰退修(课程). ⑱将(衣服的滚边)放长. *~ lemon juice into tea* 给茶加柠檬汁. *~ sweat [blood]* 流汗[血]. *~ a bottle* 失手打破一个瓶子. *I must have dropped my wallet in the taxi.* 我必定是把皮夹子遗失在出租汽车里了. *~ a line* 垂钓. *~ a curtain* 落幕. *~ one's eyes* 垂下眼睛. *let us ~ the subject.* 把这个问题放下吧. *~ one's speed by ten kilometers* 把每小时车速降低十公里. *~ smoking* 戒烟. *~ a hint* 暗示. *~ a sigh* (无意中)叹一口气. *~ sb. a line* 略写数语寄给[简告]某人. *~ sb. with a blow* 一拳把某人打倒在地. *~ one's voice to a whisper* 放低声音切切私语. *~ one's friend* 和友人断交. *be dropped from the club* 被俱乐部除名. *I'll ~ you at your door.* 我送你到家下车吧. *~ the ball through the basket* 投篮命中. *~ two games* 输掉两局. *~ a litter of six kittens* 下了一窝六只小猫. *~ 300 combat troops* 空投下300名战斗部队. *~ the island* 船驶过的岛屿已从视线中消失. — *vi.* ①滴，滴落；降落，落下，落；(慢慢地)顺流而下 *(down)*；(话等)无意中漏出；〔美俚〕(罪犯等)落网. ②(价格)跌落；(声音等)变弱，变低. ③倒下；倒毙；消失；完结，终止；(习惯等)停止，(交往等)断绝；(从窗口等)跳下. ④下垂；下山，下车；降；访问 *(in, by, over)*. ⑤落伍，落后. ⑥(猎犬找到猎物时)蹲下. ⑦(动物)下仔. ⑧〔口〕(从比赛等中)退出. ⑨【牌】被迫打出王牌. *Rain ~s from the cloud.* 云层中落下雨滴. *~ off a cliff* 从悬崖上坠下. *A pin could be heard to ~.* 一根针落在地上也听得见，寂静之极. *~ to the ground* 倒地. *There the matter dropped.* 事情到那一步就了结了. *Our correspondence has dropped.* 我们的通信中止了. *I will work till I ~.* 工作到死，鞠躬尽瘁. *~ from a race.* 退出赛跑. *~ out of college* 退学. *~ from [out of] sight* 消失不见. *Her voice dropped.* 她的声音低下去了. *~ into reminiscence* 陷入回忆. *~ down a river* 慢慢地顺流而下. ***be ready [fit] to ~*** 疲倦得要死. *~* ***a brick*** 〔口〕失言，出错，出丑. *~* ***across*** ①偶然碰见. ②谴责. *~* ***asleep*** 睡着. *~* ***astern*** 落在(他船)后面. *~* ***a stitch*** (编织时)漏掉一针. *~* ***away*** 一滴一滴落下；(一个个)走掉；(不知不觉间)跑掉 (*The guests ~ away one by one.* 客人一个个散了). *~* ***back*** ①退后，后撤. ②恢复旧习，故态复萌 *(into)*. *~* ***behind [back in line, to the rear]*** 落伍，落在后头. *~* ***by*** 〔美〕顺便到(某处)去一下，随便访问一下. *~* ***by*** *~* 一滴一滴地，一点一点地. *~* ***dead*** 倒毙，暴死. *~* ***down*** ①倒下. ②(风等)突然停止. ③沿(河)而下. *~* ***in*** 〔口〕①顺便到(某处)访问 (*Please ~ in to tea.* 请随便来我家喝茶. *~ in on sb.* 偶然访问某人). ②偶然遇见 *(with)*. *~* ***into*** ①跌入，落入. ②偶然进入 (*~ into a house* 偶然走进一所房屋). ③不知不觉地进入(某种状态)，不知不觉地养成(习惯等) (*~ into sleep* 不知不觉地睡着了. *~ into a habit* 养成某种习惯. *~ into discussion* 不知不觉地谈论起来). *~* ***off*** ①(客)(一一)散去，走掉. ②睡着. ③衰落. ④流出. ⑤〔口〕死. ***D- it!*** 停止！别闹了！别那样了！ *~* ***on [upon]*** 〔口〕严厉谴责. *~* ***on one's knees*** 跪下. *~* ***out*** ①退出，脱离；(因不满传统制度

而)退出正常社会,放浪形骸. ②失落,落出. ③消失,隐退 *(of)*. ~ ***short*** ①不足 *(of)*. ②〔口〕暴死. ~ ***the leather*** 〔美〕(篮球)投中得分. ~ ***through*** 彻底失败. ***let*** ~ ①忽略,遗漏. ②放弃,撒手. ~ **arch**【建】垂拱. ~**-bottom** 活底,底卸式. ~ **cloth** (家具等的)罩布. ~ **curtain** 吊幕,垂幕. ~**-front** *a.* 正面用铰链相接可放至水平位置的. ~**-forge** *vt.*【冶】用落锤锻造,锤锻,冲锻. ~ **hammer**【机】落锤. ~**head** ①活动头〔使打字机或缝纫机头藏在台板下的活动装置〕. ②(汽车的)活动帆布车顶. ~**-in** ①*n.* 偶然来访的客人;偶然到访的地方;〔美俚〕吸毒者的巢穴. ② *a.* 插入式的. ~**kick** *n.*【橄榄球】踢落地球. ~**leaf** *a.* (桌等)有折叠板的. ~ **letter**〔美〕由同一邮局收递的信件. ~**light** 活动吊灯. ~**-off** *n.* ①陡坡. ②衰减. ~**-out** *n.*〔美〕①中途退出;退学;落后. ②中途退出者;退学者;落后者;因不满意传统制度而退出正常社会者,放浪形骸者. ③(磁带上的)信息漏失点. ~ **press**【机】模锻压力机,落锤. ~**scene** ①垂幕吊装布景. ②压台戏. ③结局,最后下场. ~ **shot**【网球】扣球. ~ **shutter** (旧式照相机上下滑动的)快门,开关. ~**side** *a.* 侧卸的. ~ **table** (一边连在墙上、使用时可放下的)连墙桌. ~ **valve** (蒸汽机中上下活动的)活门,活阀. ~ **window** (窗门可滑进窗框下面去的)伸缩窗. ~ **wort**【植】六瓣合叶子. **-like** *a.* 水滴似的,滴状的. **-let** *n.* 微滴.

drop·page [ˈdrɔpidʒ] *n.* ①(使用或操作时的)额外损耗量. ②(成熟前的)落果量. ③〔总称〕落下的东西.

drop·per [ˈdrɔpə] *n.* ①落下者,落下物. ②滴管;(有滴管的)点药瓶. ③【矿】分脉,支脉. ~**-in** 〔美〕(习惯于)随便到人家串门子的人.

drop·ping [ˈdrɔpiŋ] *n.* ①滴下;落下,降下;【军】空降,空投,伞降. ②点滴;〔*pl.*〕滴下物;落下物. ③〔*pl.*〕(鸟等的)粪;【纺】落棉,落毛. *animal ~s* 畜粪. ~ **bottle**【医】点药瓶. ~ **fire**【军】(步枪的)疏射. ~ **funnel** 滴液漏斗. ~ **gear** 空投装置. ~ **ground**【军】空投场. ~ **satellite** (由运载器抛落的)抛射式人造卫星.

drop·si·cal [ˈdrɔpsikəl] *a.*【医】水肿的,浮肿的;似水肿的;患水肿病的. **-ly** *ad.* **-ness** *n.*

drop·sied [ˈdrɔpsid] *a.* 患水肿病的.

drop·sonde [ˈdrɔpsɔnd] *n.*【气】(由降落伞投下的)下投式探空仪.

drop·sy [ˈdrɔpsi] *n.*【医】水肿,浮肿,积水.

dropt [drɔpt] *v.* drop 的过去式及过去分词.

dros·er·a [ˈdrɔsərə] *n.* 茅膏菜属植物.

drosh·ky [ˈdrɔʃki] *n.* (帝俄时代的)轻便马车,敞篷四轮马车.

dros·ky [ˈdrɔski] *n.* = droshky.

dro·som·e·ter [drɔˈsɔmitə] *n.*【气】露量计.

dro·soph·i·la [drəuˈsɔfilə] *n.* *(pl. ~s, -lae* [-liː]*)* ①【动】果蝇 (= fruit fly). ②〔D-〕【动】果蝇属.

dross [drɔs] *n.* ①【冶】浮渣;铁屑,铁渣. ②渣滓;碎屑;杂质. ③【矿】劣质细煤. *transmute the ~ of reality into the gold of art* 把现实的渣滓熔炼为艺术的纯金. ~ **coal** 渣煤,不粘(结性)煤. **-y** *a.* ①渣状的. ②不纯的. ③无价值的 (*the drossiest work* 最低劣的作品).

drought [draut],〔诗, Scot., Ir., 美〕 **drouth** [drauθ] *n.* ①旱灾,干旱. ②〔喻〕(长期的)缺乏. ③〔古〕干渴;干燥. *a prolonged ~* 天久不雨,长期干旱. *a ~ of good writing* 长期缺乏好作品. ~**-enduring** *a.* 耐旱的. ~**-resistant** *a.* 抗旱的.

drought·y [ˈdrauti],〔诗,美〕 **drouth·y** [ˈdrauθi] *a.* 干旱的;旱灾的;干燥的;〔古〕口渴的. **drought·i·ness, drouth·i·ness** *n.*

drove[1] [drəuv] *v.* drive 的过去式.

drove[2] [drəuv] *n.* ①(被赶着走的)畜群. ②(一道走或行动的)人群. ③(石匠的)平凿;(用平凿)凿平的石面. ***in ~s*** 成群结队. — *vt.* ①赶(牲畜);(牲畜贩子)买卖(牲畜). ②用平凿凿(石料). — *vi.* ①赶牲畜. ②用平凿凿石. ~ **chisel** (石匠用的)平凿. ~ **work** (经过粗凿的)凿平的石面.

dro·ver [ˈdrəuvə] *n.* ①赶家畜上市场的人. ②牲畜商.

drown [draun] *vt.* ①使溺死,淹死. ②使浸湿;淹没. ③使沉溺于,使迷恋 *(in)*. ④消(愁),解(闷). ⑤(噪音等)盖掉(低声). ⑥搀淡,冲淡(饮料). ⑦(加水)化开(生石灰). *get [be] ~ed* 淹死. *~ oneself in a river* 淹死在河里. *eyes ~ed in tears* 泪汪汪的眼睛. *be ~ed in wine* 恋酒贪杯. *be ~ed in sleep* 在酣睡中. *His voice was ~ed by the coughing of the audience.* 他的声音被听众的咳嗽声淹没了. *~ one's whisky* 冲淡威士忌酒. *~ one's sorrows [cares] in wine* 以酒消愁[解忧]. — *vi.* 淹死;沉没. *fall in the water and ~* 落水淹死. *The boat ~ed but we were saved.* 船沉了,但我们幸而获救. *a ~ing man* 快要淹死的人. ~ ***out*** ①(洪水)把(人)赶跑. ②把(另一声音)压倒[淹没,盖住]. ***like a ~ed rat*** (湿得)象落汤鸡. ~**ed valley** 被海水淹没而成为出海口或海弯的山谷. ~**proofing** 浮水法〔利用人体浮力长时间浮在水面上的技巧〕. **-er** *n.* 溺死者.

drowse [drauz] *n.* 瞌睡. — *vt.* 使昏昏欲睡;胡里胡涂地度过*(away)*. *a lecture that ~s the students* 使学生打瞌睡的讲演. *He ~d away the morning* 他一上午都是昏昏沉沉的. — *vi.* ①打盹儿,打瞌睡. ②发呆;呆滞不动. *a village drowsing in the sun* 沉寂地躺在太阳光下的村庄.

drow·sy [ˈdrauzi] *a.* ①昏昏欲睡的,困倦的;打着瞌睡的. ②催眠的;使人懒洋洋的. ③(街市等)沉寂的. ④呆滞的. *feel ~* 昏昏欲睡. *~ spring weather* 使人懒洋洋的春天. *~ hills* 寂静的群山. ~**-head** 瞌睡虫,爱瞌睡的人. **-si·ly** *ad.* **-si·ness** *n.*

drub [drʌb] *vt.* ①用棒连续敲打. ②打败(敌方);(愤慨时)踏响(地板等). *~ a silly notion out of sb.'s head* 把一个糊涂念头从某人头脑中强行打消. *a book ~ed by every critic* 一本受到所有批评家抨击的书. — *vi.* ①敲击,连打. ②(用脚在地板等上)咚咚地踏. **drub·ber** *n.* 敲打者;跺脚者.

drudge [drʌdʒ] *vi.* 做苦工 *(at, over)*. *~ at a tedious work* 干单调无味的苦活. — *vt.* 强使(某人)做苦工. — *n.* ①苦工,单调乏味的工作. ②做苦工的人. ③【海】将官室[舰长室]的侍者;〔美俚〕生威士忌酒. *a daily ~* 枯燥无味的每日例行公事. **-r** *n.* **drug·ing·ly** *ad.* 辛劳地,苦役般地;单调乏味地.

drudg·er·y [ˈdrʌdʒəri] *n.* 苦工,单调辛苦的工作. *farm ~* 农场上的苦活. *household ~* 繁琐的家务劳动.

drug [drʌg] *n.* ①药,药品,药物,药剂. ②〔俚〕麻醉药品,麻醉剂,使人上瘾的毒品 (= narcotic ~s). ③〔*pl.*〕〔美〕卫生用品[牙刷、牙膏等]. ④滞销货. *poisonous ~* 毒药. *This ~ will do you good.* 这种药能治你的病. *the ~ habit* 常用麻醉剂的习惯,吸毒瘾. *go on ~s* 吸毒. *a ~ in [*〔美〕*on] the market* 滞销货. — *vt.* ①在(酒、食物等中)渗(麻醉)药,下(麻)药于. ②使服(麻醉)药,使麻醉. ③使沉醉;毒化. *a cup of drugged coffee* 一杯下了麻药的咖啡. *drugged sleep* 服下麻醉药后的熟睡. *She was drugged against the pain.* 她服麻醉药止痛. *be drugged with sleep* 睡觉太多而昏昏沉沉. — *vi.* 常用麻药;吸毒上瘾. ~ **addict** 吸毒者,瘾君子. ~**-fast** *a.* 【医】抗药性的,耐药性的. ~**store** ①药房. ②〔美〕(出售药物而兼卖化妆品、纸烟、杂志的)杂货店. ~**store cowboy**〔美俚〕①爱吹牛的年轻人. ②在杂货店里混日子的年轻人. ③讨女人欢喜的男人;女模女样的男子. ~**store whisky** 用医师单方从药房里配来的威士忌酒.

drug·get [ˈdrʌgit] *n.* ①粗毛地毯[台毯],棉毛混纺地毯. ②(铺地板等用的)粗织物. ③(旧时作衣料用的)羊毛织物,棉毛混纺织物.

drug·gist [ˈdrʌgist] *n.*〔美〕〔Scot.〕①药商. ②药剂师. ③〔美〕(卖药又兼卖糖果纸烟等的)杂货房老板. ~

rubber sundries 〔*pl.*〕医用橡胶制品.

drug·gy [ˈdrʌgi] *n.* 〔美俚〕吸毒者. — *a.* 吸毒后引起的.

dru·id, Dru·id [ˈdru(:)id] *n.* ①(古代高卢、不列颠和爱尔兰等地凯尔特人中的)祭司,巫师、占卜者. ②(威尔士等地的)诗人[音乐家]联谊会的主持人. **-ess** *n.* (古代凯尔特人中的)女祭司, 女巫师, 女占卜者. **-ic, -dical** *a.* **-ism** *n.* (古代高卢、不列颠和爱尔兰等地凯尔特人中)由祭司[巫师、占卜者]举行的仪式.

drum[1] [ˈdrʌm] *n.* ①鼓. ②鼓声,击鼓般的声音; 麻鸦的叫声;〔古〕鼓手. ③鼓状物; 圆桶,汽油桶;【机】滚筒,鼓轮; 卷线轴; 绕线架;【建】(作石柱用的)鼓形石块; (支持圆屋顶的)鼓形墙壁;【解】鼓室; 鼓膜; 中耳;【动】鼓形共鸣器; (自动步枪的)转盘弹匣. ④〔古〕夜会; (午后)茶会. ⑤【动】(发击鼓声的)石首鱼. *play [beat] the* ~ 击鼓. *a double* ~ 双面鼓. *a* ~ *of running feet* 奔跑的脚步声. *the* ~ *of a cicada* 蝉的共鸣器官. *a dozen* ~*s of lubricating oils* 十二桶润滑油. ***beat [rattle] the [a] big*** ~ *(for, about)* 为…鼓吹, 为…做广告. ***beat the*** ~ 宣传. ***with*** ~***s beating and colours flying*** 军容威武. — *vt.* ①咚咚地敲打, 连打, 打响. ②敲鼓奏(曲). 敲出(曲调). ③生硬地教给(学问). ④〔美俚〕敲鼓招揽; 鼓励,奖励. ~ *a march* 击鼓奏进行曲. ~ *a rhythm for dancers* 为跳舞的人击出鼓点. ~ *one's fingers on the desk* 用手指敲桌子. ~ *sb. from his work* 敲鼓把某人从工作岗位上召来. ~ *sb. into action* 鼓动某人行动. ~ *Latin into a boy* 硬叫孩子学拉丁文. — *vi.* ①敲鼓, 咚咚地敲. ②(鸟、昆虫振动翅膀等)发出嗡嗡声. ③奔走招募; 鼓吹 *(for)*. ~ *at the door* 咚咚咚地敲门. ~ *on the floor* 咚咚咚地踏响地板. *The rain drummed.* 雨声滴答. ~ *for a new film* 为新影片做广告. ***a drumming in the ears*** 耳鸣. ~ ***down*** (击鼓)使静默. ~ ***out*** 轰走; 开除 *(be drummed out of the university* 被开除出大学). ~ ***up*** ①招揽(顾客等); 招募(新兵等). ②鼓励; 激起 (~ *up recruits* 招募新兵. ~ *up customers* 招揽顾客. ~ *up enthusiasm for the new policies* 激起支持新政策的热情). ~**beat** 鼓声. ~**beater** ①鼓手,打鼓佬. ②鼓吹者, 支持者. ~ **brake** 制动圆筒. ~ **corps** 军乐队. ~**-fed gun** 转盘式机枪. ~**fire** (步兵进攻前的) 猛烈炮火 (*a* ~*fire of announcements* 连续发表强烈声明). ~**-fish**【动】石首鱼科的鱼. ~**head** ①*n.* 鼓面皮;【解】鼓膜;【机】绞盘头. ② *a.* (裁判等)即决的 (*a* ~*head execution* 就地处决. *a* ~*head court-martial* 临时军事法庭). ~ **major** ①【军】鼓手长. ②行进军乐队指挥. ~ **majorette** 军乐队女指挥. ~ **printer** 滚桶印刷机. ~ **stick** ①鼓槌. ②【烹】(煮熟的)家禽腿下部. ~ **table** (三足)可旋转鼓形立橱.

drum[2] [drʌm] *n.* = drumlin.

drum·lin [ˈdrʌmlin] *n.*【地】(冰河漂积成的)鼓丘.

drum·mer [ˈdrʌmə] *n.* ①鼓手. ②〔美口〕旅行推销员.

Drum·mond [ˈdrʌmənd] *n.* 德拉蒙德〔姓氏〕.

drunk [drʌŋk] drink 的过去分词. — *a.* 〔多用作表语〕①酒醉的. ②陶醉于*(with)*. *be* ~ *with [on] wine* 喝醉酒. *as* ~ *as a fiddler [lord, fish]* 大醉. *get beastly [blind, dead]* ~ 泥醉,烂醉. *be* ~ *with joy* 沉醉于欢乐之中. — *n.* ①醉汉. ②〔美口〕酒宴. ③喝醉,酒醉状态. *be on a* ~ 喝醉. *sleep off* ~*s* 睡觉解酒. ~ **tank** 〔谑〕醉汉拘留所.

drunk·ard [ˈdrʌŋkəd] *n.* 酒鬼,醉汉. *play the* ~ 发酒疯. *a chronic* ~ 老酒鬼. ~**'s chair** (英国18世纪时的一种)矮脚围椅.

drunk·en [ˈdrʌŋkən] *a.* ①〔多作定语〕酒醉的; 常醉的; 爱喝酒的. ②酒醉引起的. ③象喝醉酒似的, 摇摇晃晃的. *a* ~ *bum [sot]* 酒鬼. *a* ~ *brawl* 酒醉后的吵闹. *a* ~ *frolic* 酒醉后的胡闹. ~ **saw**【机】切[开]槽锯. **-ly** *ad.* 醉. **-ness** *n.* ①酩酊; 醉态. ②放荡,放纵.

drunk·o·meter [drʌŋˈkɔmitə] *n.* (用呼出的气体测定司机等体内酒精含量的)测醉器.

dru·pa·ceous [dru:ˈpeiʃəs] *a.* ①【植】核果(性)的. ②结核果的. ~ *fruit* 核果. ~ *trees* 核果树.

drup·el, drupe·let [ˈdru:pəl, ˈdru:plit] *n.*【植】小核果.

Druse [dru:z] *n.* 德鲁斯〔姓氏〕.

druse [dru:z] *n.*【矿】晶簇,晶洞.

Drus(z)e [dru:z] *n.* 朱斯教人〔叙利亚、黎巴嫩的一个秘密穆斯林教派〕. **Dru·s(z)i·an, Dru·s(z)e·an** [ˈdru:ziən] *a.*

druth·ers [ˈdrʌðəz] *n.* 〔美方〕(自由的)选择; 偏爱. *If I had my* ~*, I'd go fishing.* 如果我能选择的话, 我就去钓鱼.

DRV, D.R.V. = Democratic Republic of Vietnam 越南民主共和国.

DRVN, D.R.V.N. = Democratic Republic of Viet Nam 越南民主共和国.

dry [drai] *a.* ①干的, 干燥的; 无水分的, 干透了的. ②(井、河等)干涸的, 枯竭的; (气候)干旱的; 无奶的; 无泪的; 无痰的, 干咳的. ③〔俚〕口干的;〔美口〕禁酒的, 赞成禁酒的*(opp. wet)*. ④不新鲜的, 陈的. ⑤不用水操作的; 不用润滑油的. ⑥简慢的, 冷淡的. ⑦赤裸裸的, 露骨的; 不加渲染的; 不带个人偏见的. ⑧干巴巴的, 枯燥无味的; (嗓音等)干涩的. ⑨(酒等)无甜味的, 味淡的; (面包等)不涂黄油的. ⑩〔军俚〕空弹的, 演习的. ⑪无预期结果的, 没有收获的. ~ *air* 干燥的空气. ~ *fish* 干鱼. *a* ~ *winter* 无雨的冬天. *a* ~ *bucket* 空桶, 没有盛水的桶. *a* ~ *well* 枯井. *a* ~ *cow* 枯奶期的乳牛. ~ *sobs* 没有眼泪的啜泣. ~ *toast* 不涂黄油的烤面包. *with* ~ *eyes* 不流泪, 冷然. ~ *work* 使人累得口干舌燥的工作. *a* ~ *clutch* 不加润滑油的离合器. ~ *wall construction* 不用灰浆的(预制件)筑墙法. *a* ~ *book* 枯燥无味的书. ~ *thanks* 冷淡的感谢, 客套. ~ *facts* 毫无虚饰的事实. ~ *humour* 一本正经地讲的笑话. *the* ~ *years of the great artists* 伟大艺术家作品贫瘠的时期. ~ *lodging* 不供伙食的宿舍. *a* ~ *state* 禁酒的州. ~ *firing* 射击演习. ***a*** ~ ***eye*** 不流泪的眼睛, 有泪不轻弹. ***die a*** ~ ***death*** 老死. ~ ***as a bone*** 干透. ***go*** ~ 〔美〕颁布禁酒令. ***not*** ~ ***behind the ears*** 〔美俚〕未成熟的, 乳臭未干的, 不懂事的. ***row*** ~ 划桨时不使水花溅起. ***run*** ~ ①(乳牛)不产奶. ②(河等)水干枯 (*Most cows run* ~ *in about ten months.* 大部分乳牛有十个月不产奶. *This stream will never run* ~. 这条溪流永不会枯干). — *vt.* ①把…弄干, 使干燥; 晒干; 揩干; 排干(池塘等). ②使(乳牛)停止产奶. ~ *the dishes* 揩干碗碟. ~ *one's tears [eyes]* 擦干眼泪. ~ *one's hand on a napkin* 用餐巾揩干手. — *vi.* 变干; 干涸; 干枯. ~ ***out*** ①变干. ②戒酒. ~ ***up*** ①把…弄干, 使干. ②干涸; 逐渐枯萎. ③〔俚〕停止讲话; (演员)忘记台词 (*The spring dried up long ago.* 这泉水早就干涸了. *D- up!* 住嘴! *I wish the conversation would* ~ *up.* 我希望谈话不要再继续下去). — *n.* ①***(pl. dries)*** 干燥(状态); 干燥场; 干裂, (石头的)裂缝;〔常 *pl.*〕干季. ②***(pl. drys*** [draiz]) 〔美口〕禁酒主义者, 赞成禁酒的人. ***do a*** ~ (演员)记不起台词. ***in the*** ~ 没有碰到雨, 没有弄湿. ~**ball** *n.*〔美学俚〕死用功的学生. ~ **battery [cell]** 干电池. ~**-boned** *a.* 皮包骨头的, 骨瘦如柴的. ~**-bones** 骨瘦如柴的人. ~ **bread** ①没有涂黄油的面包. ②陈面包. ~**-bulb** *a.* (寒暑表)干球式的 (*a* ~*-bulb thermometer* 干球温度计). ~**-clean,** ~**-cleanse** *vt.* 干洗(衣服). ~ **cleaner** ①干洗剂. ②干洗商. ~ **cup**【医】吸杯. ~**-cure** *vt.* 腌(鱼肉等). ~ **distillation** 干馏. ~**-dock** *vi., vt.* (使)入干船坞. ~ **dock** 干船坞. ~**-farm** ① *vt.* 用旱作法栽培. ②*vi.* 实行旱作法. ~ **farming** 旱地耕作(法). ~ **fly** (钓鱼)假饵. ~**foot** *ad.* 不湿脚地. ~ **goods** 〔美〕绸缎呢绒类货品;〔英〕杂粮(等). ~ **hole** 〔美〕笨人, 蠢货. ~ **ice** 〔美〕干冰〔固体二氧化碳〕. ~

land ①干旱地区. ②陆地. ~ law〔美俚〕禁酒法. ~ light ①无阴影的光线. ②公平的见解, 公正无私. ~ measure (度量衡) 干量 (*opp.* liquid measure). ~ milk 奶粉. ~ money (小戏院等的) 收入, 售票所得. D-Navy〔美〕酒类缉私舰[艇]. ~ nurse 保姆,保育人员 (*opp.* wet nurse). ~-nurse *vt.* 保育, 抚育, 当…的保姆[保育人]. ~ plate【摄】干片. ~point ①*n.* (不用酸的) 铜版雕刻 (术); 铜版雕刻针; 铜版画. ②*vi.* 作铜版雕刻. ~ provisions [wares] 食用干品[干货]. ~ resistance 抗旱性. ~ rot ①【植】干腐病. ②腐化 (*Nepotism and lack of discipline often cause ~ rot in an organization.* 任人唯亲和缺乏纪律, 往往造成一个组织的腐化). ~ run【军】空弹演习; 假俯冲, 假投弹. ~-salt *vt.* = ~-cure. ~salter 干货商. ~saltery 干货业; 干货店; 干货类. ~ shampoo ①(头发) 干洗. ②(酒精性)洗发水[粉]. ~-shod *a., ad.* 不湿脚的[地], 不湿鞋的[地]. ~ skim milk 脱脂奶粉. ~ town〔美〕禁酒市. ~ wall 不涂泥灰的墙壁. ~ walling【建】无浆砌墙, 干砌. ~ weight ①(脱水) 干重. ②【空】(不包括汽油等在内的飞机的)自重. -able *a.* -ness *n.*

dry·ad, Dry·ad [ˈdraiəd] *n.* (*pl.* ~s, ~es [-ədiːz]) 【希神】林中女仙,树精. -ic [draiˈædik] *a.*

dry·as·dust [ˈdraiəzdʌst] *a.* 枯燥无味的, 兴味索然的; 学究式的. — *n.*〔常 D-〕令人乏味的学究 [考古学家、统计学家等].

Dry·den [ˈdraidn] *n.* ①德赖登〔姓氏〕. ②John ~ 约翰·德赖登〔1631—1700,英国诗人、剧作家、批评家〕.

dry·er [draiə] *n.* = drier.

dry·ly [ˈdraili] *ad.* = drily.

dry·o·pith·e·cine [ˌdraiəuˈpiθəˌsiːn, -ˌsain] *a.*【考古】类人猿属的. — *n.*【考古】森林古猿.

Ds =【化】dysprosium〔一般作 Dy〕.

DS, D.S. =〔It.〕*dal segno* (= repeat from the sign) 【乐】从记号 $ 处开始重复一遍. degree of substitution; Dental Surgeon; Distinguished Service; dry spinning.

d.s. = day's sight; days after sight.

D S(c), D.S(c). = Doctor of Science 理学博士.

D.S.C. = Distinguished Service Cross〔英〕优异服务十字勋章.

DSIF = deep space instrumentation facility 深空探测设备.

DSIR =〔英〕Department of Scientific and Industrial Research〔英〕科学与工业研究总署.

D.S.M. =〔美〕Distinguished Service Medal〔美〕优异服务勋章.

d/s =【美军】day of supply;【化】disintegrations per second.

D.S.O. =〔英〕(Companion of the) Distinguished Service Order; District Staff Officer.

d.s.p. = *decessit sine prole* (= died without issue).

DSRV = Deep Submergence Rascue Vehicle 深潜救助艇.

DST,D.S.T. = daylight saving time 经济时〔即夏令时〕.

'dst = wouldst; hadst.

D T(h), D.T.(h). = Doctor of Theology 神学博士.

D.T. = ①Daily Telegraph〔英〕《每日电讯报》. ②delirium tremens 震颤性谵妄.

d.t. = doubling time 加倍时间.

D.T.'s [ˈdiːˈtiːz]〔美俚〕= d.t.

Du. = Dutch; duke.

du·ad [ˈdjuːæd] *n.* (一)对,一双.

du·al [ˈdju(ː)əl] *a.* 二的; 二重的; 二体的; 二元的. ~ *personality* 双重人格. — *n.*【语法】双数;【数】对偶. *the D- Monarchy* 双重君主国〔指第一次世界大战前的奥匈帝国〕. ~ control ①双重管辖. ②【空】复式驾驶装置. ~-control machine 复式驾驶(飞)机. ~ firing (煤与石油)混合加热. ~ flying 复式驾驶飞行; 同乘飞行. ~-purpose *a.* ①双重目的的, 两用的. ②【农】(卵肉或乳肉)兼用的.

Du·a·la [duːˈɑːlɑː] *n.* = Douala.

du·al·in [ˈdjuːəlin] *n.* 双硝炸药.

du·al·ism [ˈdju(ː)əlizəm] *n.* ①二重,二体; 两重性; 二元性. ②【哲】二元论;【宗】(善与恶相斗争的) 二神论.

du·al·ist *n.* ①二元论者. ②身兼二职的人. -is·tic [ˌdju(ː)əˈlistik] *a.* 二重的; 两重性的,二元性的; 二元论的. -is·ti·cal·ly *ad.*

du·al·i·ty [dju(ː)ˈæliti] *n.* ①两重性, 二元性. ②【物】二象性;【无】对偶(性).

du·al·ize [ˈduːəˌlaiz] *vt.* 使二元化,使具有二重性.

dub[1] [dʌb] *vt.* ①授与…以称号, 把…叫做; 给…起诨名[绰号]叫…. ②用剑拍肩授与…以骑士爵位. ③涂油加工(皮革). ④把(木板)刮光, 把(铁片等)锤平. ⑤【钓】装(假饵)于钓钩. ⑥割去 (小公鸡的) 鸡冠. ~ *bright* 【船】刨光(木船)壁面. ~ *out* 弄平(木板等). ~ *up* 〔俚〕付清.

dub[2] [dʌb] *vt., vi.* 刺,戳; 撞,敲(*at*). — *n.* ①刺,戳; 撞,敲. ②敲打声.

dub[3] [dʌb] *vt.* ①为(影片、广播节目等)配音; 译制(影片). ②复制(录音、唱片等); 把(音乐、对话等)灌进录音带. *Chinese-dubbed foreign films* 汉语配音译制的外国影片. — *n.* 配入影片声带中的对话[音乐等].

dub[4] [dʌb] *n.*〔美俚〕庸才,技艺拙劣的人[演奏者、运动选手] (*at*).

dub[5] [dʌb] *n.*〔Scot.〕水池,水塘.

Dub. = Dublin.

dub. = dubious.

dub-a-dub [ˈdʌb-ə-dʌb] *n.* ①(鼓的)咚咚声 (= rub-a-dub). ②鼓手.

Dubai [ˈdjuːbai] *n.* ①迪拜〔组成阿拉伯联合酋长国的酋长国之一〕. ②迪拜港〔阿拉伯联合酋长国港市〕.

dub·bing[1] [ˈdʌbiŋ] *n.* 骑士爵位的授与.

dub·bing[2] [ˈdʌbiŋ] *n.* (皮革用)防水油脂.

dub·bing[3] [ˈdʌbiŋ] *n.* ①译制,配音. ②复制的唱片.

du·bi·e·ty, du·bi·os·i·ty [dju(ː)ˈbaiəti, djuːbiˈɔsəti] *n.* ①疑心,怀疑. ②疑点,疑难.

du·bi·ous [ˈdjuːbjəs] *a.* ①(对事情等)半信半疑的(*of, about*); 犹豫不决的. ②可疑的, 令人怀疑的. ③暧昧的,含糊的. ④(命运等)未定的; (工作等)无把握的. *a ~ reply* 含糊的回答. *a ~ battle* 胜负难卜的战争. -ly *ad.* -ness *n.*

du·bi·ta·ble [ˈdjuːbitəbl] *a.* 可疑的; 不定的. -ta·bly *ad.*

du·bi·ta·tion [djuːbiˈteiʃən] *n.*〔古〕怀疑, 半信半疑. -ta·tive *a.* 怀疑的,半信半疑的,踌躇不决的.

Dub·lin [ˈdʌblin] *n.* 都柏林〔爱尔兰首都〕.

Du Bois [dju(ː)ˈbɔiz] *n.* ①杜波依斯〔姓氏〕. ②William Edward ~ 威廉·爱·杜波依斯〔1868—1963, 美国黑人学者,作家〕.

du·cal [ˈdjuːkəl] *a.* 公爵的;公爵似的;公爵领地的.

duc·at [ˈdʌkət] *n.* (中世纪流通欧洲各国的)达卡银币[金币]. ②货币;〔*pl.*〕金钱,现款. ③〔美俚〕门票,入场券.

Du·ce [ˈduːtʃi, It. ˈduːtʃe] *n.* (*pl.* ~s, It. *du·cei* [ˈduːtʃi]) 〔It.〕领袖; 首领, 独裁者. ***Il*** [il] ~ "领袖"〔法西斯统治期间对墨索里尼的称呼〕.

duch·ess [ˈdʌtʃis] *n.* ①公爵夫人; 公爵未亡人; 女公爵; (公国的)女大公. ②气度威严的妇女. ③〔英俚〕叫卖小贩的妻子.

duch·y [ˈdʌtʃi] *n.* ①公国, 公爵领地. ②英国王室直辖领地.

duck[1] [dʌk] *n.* (*pl.* ~, ~s) ①鸭; 家鸭; 母鸭 (*opp.* drake); 鸭肉. ②〔口〕亲爱的,宝贝. ③有吸引力的人[物]. ④【体】鸭蛋,零分 (=~-egg). ⑤跛子,瘸子 (=

lame ~). ⑥〔美俚〕家伙. *the domestic [wild]* ~ 家[野]鸭. *She's a perfect* ~. 她可爱极了. *a lame* ~ 瘸子;不能运行的船只. *a sitting* ~ 容易捕获的猎物;〔喻〕容易击中的目标. ***be out for a*** ~ 吃鸭蛋[得零分]退场. ***chance the*** ~ 好歹试一试. ***dead*** ~ 注定已完蛋的人,无价值的东西. ***(play)*** ~***(s) and drake(s)*** 打水漂〔投石片滑行水面的游戏〕. ~ ***[~'s] egg*** 〔俚〕【体】零分. ***~'s quack*** 〔美俚〕极好的, 很好的. ***fine day for young ~s*** 雨天. ***fuck a*** ~ 〔美俚〕他妈的, 去你的. ***in two shakes of (a) ~'s tail*** 立刻,马上. ***knee-high to a*** ~ 很小的,微不足道的. ***like (a)*** ~ ***in (a) thunder-storm*** 惊慌失措. ***like (a)*** ~ ***to water***(象鸭子入水)很自然地. ***like water off (a) ~'s back*** 毫无作用,毫无影响, 漠不关心. ***play ~s and drakes of*** ①鲁莽地处理. ②浪费,挥霍. ③使混乱,给…造成困难. ***take to (sth.) like a*** ~ ***to water*** 极爱,最喜欢. ***Will a*** ~ ***swim?*** 那还用问吗? **~bill**①【动】鸭嘴兽; 多齿白鲟. ②【矿】鸭嘴装载机. **~billed** *a.* (嘴巴)象鸭嘴的. **~boards** 〔*pl.*〕〔军俚〕(战壕或泥地上的) 垫路木板. ~ **hawk**〔美〕隼;〔英〕泽鹰. **~-legged** *a.* 短腿的. **~-legs** (鸭子似的)矮脚人. **~pin** ①滚球戏. ②(滚球戏用的) 小柱子. ~ **soup**〔美俚〕轻而易举的事; 好欺侮的人. **~'s disease**〔谑〕短腿. **~weed**【植】(鸭爱吃的)浮萍属.

duck² [dʌk] *vi.* ①突然潜入水中; 把头忽然插入水中; 忽潜忽露. ②急忙低头,急忙弯腰; 躲避, 回避;〔美口〕跑掉,逃走. ~ *away from the ball* 避开球. ~ ***out***〔美口〕跑掉,逃走 (Let us ~ out of here. 我们离开这儿吧). — *vt.* ①把(人等) 猛然按入水中; 突然潜入(水中). ②突然低下(头),突然弯下(腰). ③〔美口〕躲避, 逃避; 回避. ~ *an embarrassing question* 回避令人难堪的问题.

duck³ [dʌk] *n.* ①(作衣料的)帆布; 粗布. ②〔*pl.*〕〔口〕帆布裤子,帆布衣服.

duck⁴ [dʌk] *n.*【美海军】水陆两用车;〔美空俚〕水陆两用飞机.

duck·er¹ [ˈdʌkə] *n.* 潜水人;潜水鸟.

duck·er² [ˈdʌkə] *n.* 养鸭人;猎野鸭人.

duck·ing [ˈdʌkiŋ] *n.* ①钻入水中; 全身湿透. ②急低头,急弯腰. ③猎野鸭;【拳】闪避;〔美俚〕帆布. ~ ***pond*** ①猎鸭池. ②(古时一种惩罚人的) 浸刑池. ~ ***stool*** (古时惩罚泼妇用的)浸刑椅.

duck·ling [ˈdʌkliŋ] *n.* 小鸭,子鸭.

duck·y [ˈdʌki] *n.* 〔口〕亲爱的 (=darling). — *a.* 〔美俚〕①漂亮的,迷人的,玲珑的,可爱的. ②令人满意的.

duct [dʌkt] *n.* ①管,导管,输送管; 漕, 沟, 渠道. ②【无】波道;【电】(电线,电缆等的)管道. *an ejaculatory* ~ 输精管. *a lachrymal* ~ 泪管.

-duct *comp. f.* 表示"管道","管": aque*duct*, via*duct*.

duc·tile [ˈdʌktail] *a.* ①(金属等)易拉长的,延性的,可延展的; 可锻的. ②(粘土等)可塑的, 易变形的; 柔软的. ③易教的,驯良的. **-til·i·ty** [dʌkˈtiliti] *n.* ①延性, 延度. ②可塑性; 韧性; 柔软. ③柔顺,驯良.

duc·ti·lim·e·ter [dʌktiˈlimitə] *n.* 塑性计.

duct·less [ˈdʌktlis] *a.* 无导管的. ~ *gland* 【解】无管腺,内分泌腺.

duct·ule [ˈdʌktjul] *n.* 小导管,小管道.

dud [dʌd] *n.* ①〔俚〕〔*pl.*〕衣服; 个人的衣服什物;〔罕〕破衣烂裳. ②〔军俚〕(没有爆发的)哑弹, 瞎弹. ③〔俚〕假货,伪品; 不中用的东西. ④〔俚〕失败,失望; 无用的人,没有进取心的人. — *a.* 假的,不中用的. ~ *coins [dollars]*〔美〕伪币.

dud·dy, dud·die [ˈdʌdi] *a.* 〔Scot.〕褴褛的,破烂的.

dude [djuːd] *n.* 〔美俚〕①纨袴子弟,花花公子,讲究穿戴的人. ②〔美方〕东部人, (休假时到西部牧场来的) 东部旅行者. ~ **hat** 〔美俚〕高帽. ~ **ranch** 〔美西部〕(供东部人休假时游息的) 休养农场; 仿西部农场造的休养处. ~ **wrangler** 带东部游客参观的牧童.

du·deen [duˈdiːn] *n.* = dudheen.

dudg·eon¹ [ˈdʌdʒən] *n.* 愤怒, 愤恨. ***in great [high deep]*** ~ 非常忿怒.

dudg·eon² [ˈdʌdʒən] *n.* 〔废〕①匕首柄木. ②黄杨木剑柄; 黄杨木柄匕首.

du·dheen [duˈdiːn] *n.* 〔Ir.〕磁烟嘴,磁烟管.

dud·ish [ˈdjuːdiʃ] *a.* 〔美俚〕纨袴子弟的, 花花公子般的,讲究穿戴的.

Dud·ley [ˈdʌdli] *n.* 达德利〔姓氏,男子名〕.

due [djuː] *a.* ①(债款等)当付的, 应该付给的; (票据等)到期(的), 满期(的). ②(车、船等按时间)应到达的; 预期的,约定的〔只用作表语〕. ③应有的; 应做的; 正当的; 当然的; 适当的,充分的; 正式; 照例. ④应给与的,应归与的; 起因于…,由于 *(to)*. *the* ~ *date* (票据等的)付款日, 满期日. *The bill is* ~ *on the 1st inst.* 这张支票本月一号到期. *We're* ~ *out!* 我们该走了! *He's about* ~. 他快来了. *When is the train* ~? 火车什么时候到? *a* ~ *margin for delay* 给意外延误留下足够的时间. *after [upon]* ~ *consideration* 经过充分考虑后. *protection due to their children* 应该给与孩子们的保护. ~ *process (of law),* ~ *course of law* 正当法律手续. ***be*** ~ ***to*** ①由于 (*The delay is* ~ *to the shortage of hands.* 事情耽搁下来是由于人手不足). ②应给,应归 (*The credit is* ~ *to you.* 荣誉[功劳]应该归你). ③预定 (*He is* ~ *to speak tonight.* 他预定今晚演说). ④应做的 (*It is* ~ *to him to say so.* 他这样说是应该的). ⑤应付给的, 欠的 (*Ten dollars is* ~ *to you.* 欠你十元). ***become*** ~ = fall ~. ~ ***bill*** 〔美〕借据, 借约. ~ ***from*** 应收. ***fall*** ~ (票据)到期,满期. ***in*** ~ ***course*** 及时地; 到一定时候, 到适当时候. ***in*** ~ ***form*** 正式,照例. ***in*** ~ ***time*** 到时候就, 在适当时候. ***with*** ~ ***ceremony*** 照正式仪式. ***with*** ~ ***regard [respect] to [for]*** 在给予…以应有尊重的情况下. — *ad.* (罗盘指针、方向等)正(南、北等). *a* ~ *north wind* 正北风. *The wind is* ~ *east.* 风是正东风. — *n.* ①应得物,正当报酬,当然权利,应得权益. ②〔常 *pl.*〕应付款; 税; 费用; 手续费; 租费; 会费. *give him more than his* ~ 给与他的过份多了, 给与他的超过了他应得的. *harbour ~s* 入港费. *light ~s* 灯塔费. *club ~s* 俱乐部会费. ***by [of]*** ~ 〔古、诗〕当然. ***for a full*** ~【海】十分,完全; 永久. ***give sb. his*** ~ 公平看待某人. ***give the devil his*** ~ 公平对待自己不喜欢的人. ~ ***date*** (借据等的)到期日,应付款日期.

du·el [ˈdju(ː)əl] *n.* ①决斗. ②竞争,斗争; 抗争;〔美〕运动比赛. *fight a* ~ *with sb.* 与某人决斗. *challenge sb. to a* ~ 向某人提出决斗. *the* ~ 决斗法, 决斗规则. *a* ~ *of wits* 斗智. *a verbal* ~ 舌战, 论战. — *vi.* (〔英〕***duelled)*** 决斗. **du·el·(l)ing** *n.* ①决斗(术), 斗争, 抗争.

du·el·(l)er [ˈdju(ː)ələ] *n.* 〔罕〕= duel(l)ist.

du·el·(l)ist [ˈdju(ː)əlist] *n.* ①决斗者. ②斗争者, 抗争者,角逐者.

du·el·lo [djuːˈeləu] *n.* (*pl.* ~*s,* 〔It.〕 ***du·el·li*** [djuˈeli]) 〔It.〕①决斗(术). ②决斗规则.

du·en·na [dju(ː)ˈenə] *n.* ①(西班牙家庭中的)保姆; (闺女的)陪媪. ②女家庭教师.

du·et(t), ***du·et·to*** [dju(ː)ˈet, dju(ː)ˈetəu] *n.* ①【乐】二重奏(曲), 二重唱(曲); 二重奏[唱]演出组. ②双簧; 对话; 对骂. ③一对,一双. ***play a*** ~ 演双簧,互相唱和.

duet·tist *n.* 二重奏[唱]者.

Duff [dʌf] *n.* 达夫〔姓氏〕.

duff¹ [dʌf] *n.* ①〔英方〕生面团,揉面. ②(通常嵌有葡萄干等蒸制的)布丁.

duff² [dʌf] *n.* 〔美俚〕臀部, 屁股. *get off one's* ~ 抬起屁股,(久坐后)站起来.

duff³ [dʌf] *n.* ①(森林中的)枯枝落叶堆积层, 地面腐殖质. ②煤屑,炭粉.

duff[4] [dʌf] *a.* 〔英俚〕(质量)低劣的；假的；不中用的．～ ***gen*** 〔军俚〕不可靠的情报．— *n.* 无价值的东西，伪品，假货．

duff[5] [dʌf] *vt.* 〔俚〕①伪造；欺骗；把(旧货)装扮成新的．②〔澳〕在(偷来的家畜身上)重打烙印；偷(家畜)．

duf·fel, duf·fle [ˈdʌfəl,ˈdʌfl] *n.* ①起绒粗呢．②(运动员、野营者等的)一套轻便用具，一套衣物；〔美口〕露营用品．～ **bag** (装杂物的)军用帆布袋．

duff·er [ˈdʌfə] *n.* ①废物，骗人货；伪币．②笨蛋，不中用的人．③〔俚〕兜售骗人货的小贩；〔*pl.*〕〔美俚〕参加走私的妇女；〔古〕行商．

Duf·fer·in [ˈdʌfərin] *n.* 达弗林〔姓氏〕．

dug[1] [dʌg] dig 的过去式及过去分词．

dug[2] [dʌg] *n.* (哺乳动物的)乳房，奶头．

du·gong [ˈdjuːgɔŋ] *n.* 【动】儒艮，人鱼〔一种海生哺乳动物〕．

dug·out [ˈdʌgaut] *n.* ①独木舟．②(太古人类居住的)岩洞；(挖在山坡或地下的)洞穴；【军】地下掩蔽部．③〔口〕(退役后的)复职军官；(超龄后)重新服役的军官．④【棒球】运动员休息室．

du·i [ˈdjuːiː] *n.* duo 的复数．

duke [djuːk] *n.* ①公，(公国的)君主；〔英〕公爵．②〔古〕司令官，首领，(古罗马的)省督．③(公爵种)樱桃．④〔*pl.*〕〔口〕手，拳头．*the D- of Wellington* 威林顿公爵．*Put up your ～s* 举起手来！*the Grand D-* 大公．***a ～'s mixture*** 〔美〕①集成物．②杂录，杂记．③混乱状态．***Royal D-*** 亲王兼公爵．

duke·dom [ˈdjuːkdəm] *n.* ①公爵领土，公国．②〔英〕公爵的地位〔身分〕．

Du·kho·bors [ˈduːkəbɔːz] *n.* 〔*pl.*〕【宗】杜霍波尔教派〔意为"灵魂力士派"，俄国的一种否认正教仪式的教派信徒，1875 年从希腊教会分化出来〕．**Du·kho·bor·tsy** [ˌduːkəˈbɔːtsi].

D.U.K.W.S., Dukws [dʌks] *n.* 水陆两用车〔美海军电报暗码代用语〕．

dul·cet [ˈdʌlsit] *a.* ①(音乐等)美妙的，优美动听的．②赏心悦目的，好看的．③〔古〕美味的，可口的，有香味的．

dul·ci·an·a [ˌdʌlsiˈænə] *n.* 【乐】(音调柔美似弦乐器的)风琴音栓．

dul·ci·fy [ˈdʌlsifai] *vt.* ①把…弄甜，加甜味于．②使愉快；使变温和．**-fi·ca·tion** [ˌdʌlsifiˈkeiʃən] *n.*

dul·ci·mer [ˈdʌlsimə] *n.* 洋琴．

Dul·cin·e·a [dʌlsiˈniə] *n.* ①达西妮亚〔小说《唐·吉诃德》中吉诃德先生心目中的情人〕．②〔d-〕 理想中的情人．

du·li·a [duːˈlaiə] *n.* 【天主】二等崇敬〔对于天使圣徒等的尊崇〕．

dull [dʌl] *a.* ①愚钝的，感觉迟钝的，呆笨的．②钝的，不快的，不锋利的 *(opp.* sharp*)*．③(天气等)阴郁的，阴暗的；(颜色等)暗淡的．④(市场等)呆滞的，萧条的；(谈话等)单调的，枯燥的，无聊的，沉闷的．⑤(光等)模糊的．*a ～ child* 头脑迟钝的孩子．*a ～ edge* 钝刃．*be ～ of hearing* 耳朵不灵．*a ～ fire* 文火．*a ～ pain* 钝痛，隐痛．*a ～ day* 阴天．*a ～ town* 萧条的市镇．*Trade is ～.* 生意清淡．*a ～ book* 枯燥无味的书．*a ～ landscape* 单调的景色．— *vt.* ①把…弄钝．②使阴暗，使阴郁．③缓和，减轻(痛苦等)．④使迟钝；使呆滞．*～ a razor's edge* 把刀片弄钝了．*one's sense ～ed by his emotion* 因激动而造成的感觉迟钝．*～ sorrow* 减轻哀愁．— *vi.* ①变钝；变迟钝．②(痛苦等)减少．③【纺】消光．*～ the edge of* ①弄钝刃口．②减弱(兴趣等)．*～***-brained** *a.* 头脑迟钝的．*～***-browed** *a.* 愁眉苦脸的，闷闷不乐的．*～***-head** 傻瓜，笨蛋．*～***-witted** *a.* 愚蠢的．**dul(l)·ness** *n.* **dul·ly** *ad.*

dull·ard [ˈdʌləd] *n.* 笨蛋，蠢汉．

Dul·les [ˈdʌlis, ˈdʌləs] *n.* ①达勒斯 (杜勒斯) 〔姓氏〕．②**John Foster ～** 约翰·福斯特·杜勒斯〔1888—1959，曾任美国国务卿〕．

dull·ish [ˈdʌliʃ] *n.* ①有点钝的；迟钝的．②有点沉闷的．

dulse [dʌls] *n.* 【植】掌状红皮藻．

du·ly [ˈdjuːli] *ad.* ①正当地，适当地；充分地．②及时，按时，准时．*Your letter is ～ to hand.* 来信已及时收到．*Eggs were ～ delivered.* 鸡蛋已按时运出．

Du·ma [ˈduːmə] *n.* 杜马〔帝俄国会〕．

Du·mas [djuˈmɑː] *n.* ①仲马〔法国姓氏〕．②**Alexandre ～** 大仲马〔1802—1870，世称 *Dumas père,* 法国剧作家，小说家，著有《三剑客》、《基督山伯爵》等．③**Alexandre ～** 小仲马〔1824—1895，世称 *Dumas fils,* 法国小说家及剧作家，为大仲马之子，其名著为《茶花女》〕．

Du Mau·ri·er [dju(ː) ˈmɔriei] *n.* 杜莫里埃〔姓氏〕．

dumb [dʌm] *a.* ①哑的，不能说话的．②沉默的，无言的．③无音的，无声的，不响的；打手势的，打哑语的．④口齿不清的，(在政府中)无代言人的，政治上无发言权的．⑤〔美口〕愚笨的．⑥没有自推力的．*a ～ animal* 不会说话的畜牲．*be ～ from birth* 一生下来就是哑巴．*the deaf and ～* 聋哑人．*be (remain) ～ on (sth.)* 对(某事)缄口不言．*be struck ～* 吓呆，吓得目瞪口呆．～ **barge [craft]** 无帆驳船，拖船．～**bell** ①【体】哑铃．②〔美俚〕笨蛋．～ **bid** (拍卖时物主所定而不宣布的)内定底价．～ **bunny [head, ox, sock]** 〔美口〕笨蛋，蠢东西．～ **card** 方位盘．～ **chamber** 无出口的房间，闷室．～ **cluck [Dora]** 〔美口〕笨女人．～ **creatures** 动物，牲畜．～**found(er)** *vt.* = dumfound．～ **piano** (练指用的)无声钢琴．～ **show** 默片，哑剧；手势．～**struck [～stricken]** *a.* 吓得目瞪口呆的．～ **waiter** 〔英〕回转式食品架；〔美〕送菜升降机．

Dum·bar·ton Oaks [dʌmˈbɑːtn əuks] *n.* 敦巴顿橡树园〔在华盛顿郊区，1944 年 8—10 月间，中美英苏四国代表为筹备建立联合国举行会议的地方〕．

Dum·bo [ˈdʌmbəu] *n.* 〔美海军口〕救护(搜索)飞机．

dum·dum [ˈdʌmdʌm] *n.* 【军】(旧时一种杀伤力很强的软头)达姆弹 (= ～ bullet)．

dum(b)·found [ˈdʌmˈfaund] *vt.* 吓哑，吓呆，使发愣．**-ment** *n.*

dum(b)·found·er [ˌdʌmˈfaundə] *vt.* = dum(b)-found．

dum·my [ˈdʌmi] *n.* ①〔口〕哑巴，经常沉默的人．②挂名代表；傀儡．③(橱窗中的)模型人；(拍电影用的)假人；人形靶；模型发式；模型货样，样品；(书的)样本；【军】模拟弹；虚设物；模仿物．④〔主英〕橡皮奶头．⑤〔口〕笨蛋．⑥(有凝汽器的)无声排汽机车．⑦【牌】(桥牌叫定后摊牌于桌上的)明家．*a wax ～* 蜡人．*a tailor's ～* 服装模型人．***sell the ～***【橄榄球】做递球假动作骗对方；〔喻〕声东击西．— *a.* ①摆样子的，做样品的，假的．②挂名的，傀儡的．*a ～ cartridge* 空弹．*a ～ bomb* (演习用的)模拟炸弹．*a ～ horse*【体】木马．*a ～ director* 名义董事．*a ～ state* 傀儡国．— *vt.* 把(书、报等)做成大样 *(up)*；把(书、报等)以大样印出 *(in)*．— *vi.* ①〔美俚〕装聋作哑，保守秘密 *(up)*．②〔澳方〕替别人占领土地．～**-head torpedo** (除去炸药的)演习用鱼雷．～ **run** 演习；排练．～ **variable**【数】虚变量．

dump[1] [dʌmp] *n.* ①铅制筹码．②(已作废的)澳洲旧银币；〔口〕小钱；〔*pl.*〕金钱．③(船上投环戏用的)绳圈；(造船用) 短粗螺钉；球形糖果；〔古〕矮胖子．*not worth a ～* 不值一文．*not care a ～* 毫不介意．

dump[2] [dʌmp] *n.* ①〔*pl.*〕〔口〕郁闷．②〔古〕忧郁的曲调．***in the ～s*** 不高兴，心情沮丧．

dump[3] [dʌmp] *vt.* ①〔主美〕倾倒(垃圾)，倾卸 *(out)*；解雇；解除(合同等)；使砰地落下，砰地放下 *(down)*；抛弃(废物，候选人等)；〔口〕故意输掉(比赛等)．②【商】(向海外)倾销；把(过剩移民)转送外国．③解雇，解(约)．④转嫁(责任等)．⑤(电子计算机) 转录，转储．— *vi.*

①砰地落下来. ②卸货. ③倾销. — *n.* ①砰的一声. ②卸货场所, 垃圾场; (矿山的)渣坑. ③(射流)放空孔, 排空孔; 【自】(计算机的)转储, 消除打印. ④(刚卸下的)货垛, 煤堆, 垃圾堆. 【军】(弹药等的)临时堆积处. ⑤〔美俚〕破陋的房子〔场所, 街道〕. ~ **car** (铁道上的)倾斜车, 自动卸货车. ~ **cart [truck]** 倒垃圾车.

dump·age [ˈdʌmpidʒ] *n.* ①〔美〕倾倒 (垃圾等). ②垃圾. ③垃圾倾倒权〔费〕.

dump·er [ˈdʌmpə] *n.* 〔美〕①垃圾倾倒车; (倾卸车上的)倾卸装置; 垃圾倾倒员. ②倾销者.

dump·ing [ˈdʌmpiŋ] *n.* ①倾倒(垃圾等), 抛弃. ②倾卸物, 垃圾. ③倾销. ~ **device** 卸料装置. ~ **field** 海外倾销市场. ~ **ground** 垃圾倾倒场.

dump·ish [ˈdʌmpiʃ] *a.* 忧愁的, 忧郁的.

dump·ling [ˈdʌmpliŋ] *n.* ①(有肉馅等的)汤团, 团子; 苹果布丁. ②〔口〕矮胖子; 矮胖的动物.

dump·y[1] [ˈdʌmpi] *a.* 矮胖的, 粗短的. *a ~ woman* 一个矮胖的女人. — *n.* 矮脚鸡. ~ **level** (测量用的)定镜水准仪. **-i·ly** *ad.* **-i·ness** *n.*

dump·y[2] [ˈdʌmpi] *a.* 忧郁的, 不高兴的.

dun[1] [dʌn] *n.* ①催促者, 纠缠不休者; 讨债人. ②催付, 追收. — *vt.* ①向…催讨. ②向…纠缠不休, 使烦恼. *a dunning letter* 讨债信. ~ *sb. for payment* 催某人还债. — *vi.* 催债, 讨债. **dun·ner** *n.* 讨债人.

dun[2] [dʌn] *a.* ①焦茶色的, 暗褐色的. ②〔诗〕微暗的, 阴暗的. ~ *clouds* 阴沉沉的云朵. — *n.* ①焦茶色, 暗褐色. ②暗褐色马. ③【动】蜉蝣的亚成虫; 毛翅目昆虫. ④暗褐色钓鱼假饵. — *vt.* 使成暗褐色; 腌(鳕等)成暗褐色.

Dun·bar [ˈdʌnbɑː] *n.* 邓巴〔姓氏〕.

Dun·can [ˈdʌŋkən] *n.* ①邓肯〔姓氏, 男子名〕. ②**Isadora** ~ 伊萨多拉·邓肯〔1878—1927, 美国女舞蹈家〕. ③ ~ **I** 邓肯一世 〔1034—1040 年在位, 被麦克佩斯暗害的苏格兰国王〕.

dunce [dʌns] *n.* 笨人; 低能儿; 劣等生. *an utter* ~ 十足的低能儿.

Dun·das [dʌnˈdæs, ˈdʌndæs] *n.* 邓达斯〔姓氏〕.

dun·der·head, dun·der·pate [ˈdʌndəhed, -peit] *n.* 傻瓜, 蠢才. **-ed** *a.* 笨的, 蠢的.

dune [djuːn] *n.* (海边被风吹积成的)沙丘. ~ **buggy** 沙滩车〔特别设计的轻型汽车, 专供在沙丘或海滩上行驶〕.

Dun·e·din [dʌˈniːdin] *n.* 达尼丁〔新西兰港市〕.

dung [dʌŋ] *n.* ①(牛马等的)粪; 肥料. ②〔喻〕丑恶的东西. — *vt.* 给(地)施肥〔上粪〕. ~ **beetle** 【动】粪金龟子, 蜣螂. ~ **cart** 粪车. ~ **deport** 粪库. ~ **fly** 粪蝇. ~ **fork** 粪耙.

dun·ga·ree [ˌdʌŋgəˈriː] *n.* ①(印度的)粗棉布, 粗蓝斜纹布. ②〔*pl.*〕粗蓝布工装, 粗布工作服.

dun·geon [ˈdʌndʒən] *n.* ①土牢, 地牢. ②(欧洲中世纪的)城堡主楼, 城堡主塔.

dung·hill [ˈdʌŋhil] *n.* ①粪堆, 堆肥. ②脏屋; 脏物. ③卑贱的状态〔地位〕. ***a cock on his own ~, a cock of the ~*** 地头蛇, 土霸王. ~ **cock [fowl]** (相对于"斗鸡"而言的)普通的农家公鸡.

dung·y [ˈdʌŋi] *a.* 到处是粪的; 沾上粪的; 粪一般的; 肮脏的.

du·nite [ˈduːnait] *n.* 【地】纯橄榄岩.

dun·i·was·sal [ˈduːniˈwɔsəl] *n.* 〔Scot.〕 二流绅士; (名门中)次子以下的子嗣.

dunk [dʌŋk] *vt.* ①〔主美方〕(吃前)把(面包等)在汤〔饮料〕中浸一浸. ②浸泡. ~ *the curtains in the dye* 把窗帘布浸在染色液里. — *vi.* 把自己浸入水中. *Let's ~ in the pool before dinner.* 我们饭前到池塘里泡一会儿. **-er** *n.*

Dun·kirk [dʌnˈkəːk], **Dun·kerque** [F. dœ̃kɛrk] *n.* ①敦刻尔克〔法国港市, 一九四〇年英军被德军击败后从此处撤回本国〕. ②类似敦刻尔克的大溃退.

dun·lin [ˈdʌnlin] *n.* (*pl.* ~, ~*s*) 【鸟】滨鹬.

Dun·lop[1] [dʌnˈlɔp, ˈdʌnlɔp] *n.* ①邓洛普, 邓禄普〔姓氏〕. ②**John Boyd** ~ 约翰·波义德·邓禄普〔1840—1921, 英国发明家〕.

Dun·lop[2] [ˈdʌnlɔp] *n.* ①邓禄普车胎 (= ~ tyre). ②〔Scot.〕邓禄普干酪 (= ~ cheese).

Dun·more [dʌnˈmɔː] *n.* 邓莫尔〔姓氏〕.

dun·nage [ˈdʌnidʒ] *n.* ①手提行李. ②【海】(防止所装货物动摇损伤的)衬板, 衬料〔木屑等〕.

Dunne [dʌn] *n.* 邓恩〔姓氏〕.

dun·nite [ˈdʌnait] *n.* D型炸药, 苦味酸铵〔一种能打穿装甲的高性能炸药, 为美国军官 B.W.Dunn 所发明〕.

dun·nock [ˈdʌnək] *n.* 【英, 动】篱雀, 岩鹨.

Duns·tan [ˈdʌnstən] *n.* 邓斯坦〔姓氏〕.

dunt [dʌnt] *n.* ①(陶器骤冷时的)爆裂. ②【空】与急降气流的碰击.

du·o [ˈdju(ː)əu] *n.* (*pl.* ~*s*, ***du·i*** [ˈdju(ː)iː]) ①【乐】二重唱, 二重奏. ②(演员的)一对. *a comedy* ~ 一对滑稽演员.

duo- *comb. f.* 表示"二, 双": *duo*logue.

du·o·cone [ˈdju(ː)əukəun] *n.* 【无】高低音扬声器.

du·o·dec·i·mal [ˌdju(ː)əuˈdesiməl] *a.* 【数】十二的; 十二分之几的; 十二进位制的. *the ~ system* 十二进位制. — *n.* ①十二分之一. ②〔*pl.*〕【数】十二进位制. **-ly** *ad.*

du·o·dec·i·mo [ˈdju(ː)əuˈdesiməu] *n.* (*pl.* ~*s*) ①(纸张的) 十二开〔约 4.5×7.5—5.25×8.125 英寸〕. ②(书的)十二开本〔略作 12mo 或 12°, 口语读作 twelve mo〕. ③微小的东西; 矮人. — *a.* (纸张)十二开的.

du·o·de·nal [ˌdju(ː)əuˈdiːnl] *a.* 【解】十二指肠的.

du·o·den·a·ry [ˌdju(ː)əuˈdiːnəri] *a.* = duodecimal.

du·o·de·ni·tis [ˌdju(ː)ədiˈnaitis] *n.* 【医】十二指肠炎.

du·o·de·num [ˌdju(ː)əuˈdiːnəm] *n.* (*pl.* ~*s*, ***du·o·de·na*** [ˌdju(ː)əuˈdiːnə]) 【解】十二指肠.

du·o·di·ode [ˌdju(ː)əuˈdaiəud] *n.* 【无】双〔孪〕二极管.

du·o·graph [ˈdju(ː)əugrɑːf] *n.* (照相制版)复影版.

du·o·logue [ˈdju(ː)əlɔg] *n.* ①对话. ②(戏剧等的)对白; 对话剧.

duo·mo [ˈdwɔːmɔː] *n.* (*pl.* ***-mi*** [-mi]) 〔It.〕(意大利的)大教堂, 中央教堂.

du·op·o·ly [djuˈɔpəli] *n.* 两家卖主垄断市场的局面.

du·op·so·ny [djuˈɔpsəni] *n.* 由两家买主独揽市场的局面.

du·o·rail [ˈdju(ː)əureil] *n.* 双轨铁路.

du·o·ser·vo [ˌdju(ː)əuˈsəːvəu] *a.* 双力作用的.

du·o·tone [ˈdju(ː)əutəun] *a.* 同色浓淡双色调的; 双色的. — *n.* 【印】同色浓淡双色调套印法, 双色网线版; 双色套印画.

dup., dupl. = duplicate.

dup·a·ble [ˈdjuːpəbl] *a.* 易受骗的. **dup·a·bil·i·ty** [ˌdjuːpəˈbiliti] *n.*

dupe[1] [djuːp] *n.* ①被愚弄的人; 容易受骗的人. ②盲从者. — *vt.* 欺骗, 愚弄, 蒙蔽. ~ *sb. into doing sth.* 骗某人去做某事.

dupe[2] [djuːp] *n., vt.* = duplicate (*n., vt.*).

dup·er·y [ˈdjuːpəri] *n.* ①诈欺; 欺骗. ②被愚弄, 上当, 受蒙蔽.

du·ple [ˈdjuːpl] *a.* ①二倍的, 二重的, 双的. ②【乐】二拍子的. ~ **time [measure, metre]** 【乐】二拍子〔2/2、2/4、2/8 拍等〕.

du·plet [ˈdjuːplit] *n.* 【原】粒子对, 粒子偶; 【化】电子对, 电子偶.

du·plex [ˈdjuːpleks] *a.* ①二倍的, 双的, 二重的. ②【机】双联式的, 复式. ③【讯】双向(通讯)的, (电报)双工的. — *n.* ①套楼公寓 (= ~ apartment). ②两户合住的房子 (= ~ house). ~ **apartment** (每套房间占有上下二层楼的) 套楼公寓. ~ **house** 〔美〕两户合

住的房子. ~ **pump** 联式泵. ~ *paper* 双层纸. ~ **telegraphy** 双工电报.
du·pli·cate [ˈdju:plikeit] *vt.* ①使加倍，使成双. ②使成双联式；使有正副两份，复制，复写，打印. ③重叠，双折. ④重演，重复. ~*d agencies* 骈枝机关. ~ *the document* 复制文件. *duplicating paper* 复写纸，打字纸. *He ~d his father's failure.* 他重蹈父亲的覆辙. — [ˈdju:plikit] *a.* ①双的，二倍的，二重的. ②双联的，双份的，复式的，成对的. ③重复的；副的，做底子的，抄存的. *a ~ copy* 副本，复本. ~ *copies* 正副两份. *a ~ ratio* 复比. *a ~ key* (另一把)备用钥匙. *a ~ letter* 信件留底. — [ˈdju:plikit] *n.* ①(绘画、相片等的)复制品；完全相似的对应物. ②誊本，复本，抄件，副本，副件 *(opp.* original*)*. ③对号牌子；当票. ④同义语. ⑤【牌】(桥牌比赛中的)换手重打. ⑥一式两份. *made [done] in ~* 制成一式两份. *type the letter in ~* 把这封信打成一式两份.
du·pli·ca·tion [ˌdju:pliˈkeiʃən] *n.* ①加倍，二重，重复. ②重叠，双折. ③复制，打印；复制品. ④【生】(由染色体迷乱造成的)部分遗传物质的复制，两岐. *save time by avoiding ~ of effort* 工作中避免重复以节约时间.
du·pli·ca·tor [ˈdju:plikeitə] *n.* ①复印机. ②复制者.
du·plic·i·ty [dju(:)ˈplisiti] *n.* ①口是心非，不诚实，欺骗性. ②二重性，重复.
Du Pont, Dupont [ˈdju:pɔnt] *n.* 杜邦[姓氏].
du·ra [ˈdjuərə] *n.*【解】硬脑[脊]膜 (=~ mater).
du·ra·ble [ˈdjuərəbl] *a.* ①经久的，持久的. ②坚牢的；耐用的. ~ *goods* 耐用品. ~ *cloths* 结实的衣料. *a ~ colour* 不易褪色的颜色. ~ *peace* 持久的和平. — *n.* 〔*pl.*〕耐久物品. ~ **goods** 耐久货物，耐久品 (=~s). ~ **press** 耐久性压制，风压〔用化学品在织物纤维上造成永久性的褶绉，略作 DP〕. **du·ra·bil·i·ty** [ˌdjuərəˈbiliti], **-ness** *n.* ①经久，坚牢. ②持久性[力]，耐久性[力]. **-bly** *ad.* 经久，坚牢；持久.
du·ral [ˈdjuərəl] *a.*【解】硬脑(脊)膜的.
du·ral·(u·min) [djuəˈræl(jumin)] *n.* (制飞机用的)硬铝，都拉铝. *a ~ bird* 铁鸟[飞机].
du·ra ma·ter [ˌdjuərə ˈmeitə] 〔L.〕【解】硬脑(脊)膜.
du·ra·men [djuəˈreimen] *n.*【植】心材.
dur·ance [ˈdjuərəns] *n.* ①〔古〕(长期)监禁. ②〔古〕持续. ***in ~ (vile)*** 遭(非法)拘禁.
Du·rant(e) [djuˈrɑ:nt, djuˈrænt] *n.* 杜兰特[姓氏].
du·ra·tion [djuəˈreiʃən] *n.* ①持久，持续. ②持续时间，存在时间；期间. *a disease of long ~* 长时间的疾病. *holidays of three weeks' ~* 三周的假期. *the ~ of flight* 【空】续航时间. *a ~ record* 【空】续航纪录. *the ~ of insurance [prescription]* 保险[有效]期间. *the ~ of day* 日照长度. *the ~ of life* 生存期间. *of long [short] ~* 长[短]期的. ***for the D-*** 〔俚〕战争未结束期间〔尤指第二次世界大战〕(*No vacations for the ~.* 战时一切假期取消). **-al** *a.*
dur·a·tive [ˈdjurətiv] *a.*【语法】持续的，连续的. *the ~ aspect* 【语法】持续体，连续体.
Dur·ban [ˈdə:bən] *n.* 德班〔南非(阿扎尼亚)港市〕.
dur·bar [ˈdə:bɑ:] *n.* ①(印度土邦君主等宫廷的)正式接见. ②(印度土邦君主等宫廷的)正式接见室.
dure [duə, djuə] *a.* 〔古〕冷酷的，苛刻的.
du·ress(e) [djuəˈres] *n.* ①【法】强迫，胁迫；强制. ②(非法)监禁. ***a plea of ~*** 【法】向法庭提出申请，宣告以前的契约[声明等]系在被胁迫情况下签订[发表]而现在要求宣告无效. ***be held in ~*** 在监禁中. ***~ of imprisonment*** 非法监禁. ***under ~*** 被迫，被劫持 (*a contract made under ~* 被胁迫签订的契约).
Dur·ham [ˈdʌrəm] *n.* ①达累姆〔英格兰一郡及其首府名〕. ②达累姆(产的)短角肉用牛.
du·ri·an [ˈdu:riən] *n.*【植】(马来群岛产的)榴莲果；榴莲树.
du·ri·crust [ˈdjuərikrʌst] *n.*【地】硬壳，钙质壳.
dur·ing [ˈdjuəriŋ] *prep.* 在…的期间；在…的时候. ~ *the day [morning, evening]* (在)白天[早上，晚上]. ~ *and after the crisis* 在危机期间和危机结束以后. ~ *sb.'s absence* 某人不在的时候.
du·ri·on [ˈdu:riən] = durian.
dur·mast [ˈdə:mɑ:st, -mæst] *n.*【植】栎属植物〔尤指柔毛栎〕.
durn [də:n] *vt., vi.* = darn.
du·ro [ˈduərəu] *n. (pl. ~s)* 元〔西班牙和拉丁美洲一些国家的银元〕.
Du·roc(·jer·sey) [ˈdjuərɔk(ˈdʒə:zi)] *n.*【动】(美国种体壮早熟的)短头红猪.
du·rom·e·ter [djuəˈrɔmitə] *n.* 硬度计.
dur·ra [ˈdurə] *n.*【植】(非洲原产、叶窄、株型中等的)食用高粱.
Dur·rell [ˈdə:rel] *n.* 德雷尔〔姓氏〕.
Dur·res [ˈdurəs] *n.* 都拉斯〔阿尔巴尼亚港市〕.
durst [də:st] 〔古〕dare 的过去式.
du·rum [ˈdjuərəm] *n.* 硬粒小麦 (=~ wheat).
Dur·ward [ˈdə:wəd] *n.* 德沃德〔男子名〕.
Du·sham·be [du:ˈʃɑ:mbə] *n.* 杜尚别〔苏联城市〕.
dusk [dʌsk] *a.* 〔诗〕= dusky. — *n.* ①薄暮，黄昏. ②幽暗；荫. *from dawn to ~* 从黎明到黄昏. *at ~* 在黄昏时刻. *in the ~ of the room* 在室内阴暗的光线中. — *vt.* 使变微黑[暗]. — *vi.* 变微暗[黑]；接近黄昏. ~ **action station**【军】薄暮(对空)战斗配置.
dusk·y [ˈdʌski] *a.* ①微暗的，暗淡的；微黑的. ②暗黑的；黑黝黝的；阴暗的. ③忧郁的. *a ~ brown* 深褐色. *a ~ frown* 愁眉不展. **-i·ly** *ad.* **-i·ness** *n.*
Dus·sel·dorf [ˈdusldɔ:f] *n.* 杜塞尔多夫〔西德城市〕.
dust [dʌst] *n.* ①尘，灰尘，尘土，尘埃. ②〔英〕垃圾，废品；灰烬. ③〔口〕金粉；粉末，粉剂；花粉. ④〔诗〕遗骸，尸体；人体，人. ⑤土，地面；葬地；废墟. ⑥混乱，骚乱. ⑦〔俚〕现金，钱. ⑧〔古〕肉体. *sweep up ~* 打扫灰尘. *insecticidal ~* 杀虫粉. *gold ~* 金粉. *the honoured ~* 荣誉显赫的遗骸. *Down with the [your] ~!* 〔口〕拿出钱来! ***as dry as ~*** 枯燥无味的. ***be humbled in [to] the ~*** 遭到奇耻大辱. ***be out for ~*** 努力挣钱. ***bite the ~*** 一败涂地；倒；倒毙；阵亡. ***crumble to ~*** 倒；垮；化为乌有. ***eat ~*** 含垢忍辱. ***have a little ~*** 交手，打一个回合. ***in the ~*** 死；屈辱. ***lay the ~*** (雨)压落尘埃. ***lick the ~*** ①卑躬屈膝. ②= bite the ~. ***lie in the ~*** ①成为废墟. ②战死. ***make [kick up, raise] a ~*** ①扬起灰尘. ②引起骚动. ***make the ~ fly*** 兴冲冲地干，蛮干. ***out of the ~*** 由灰尘中；由屈辱境遇中. ***raise sb. from the ~*** 提拔某人于微贱之中. ***shake the ~ off one's feet*** = ***shake off the ~ of one's feet*** 愤然[轻蔑地]离去. ***take the ~ of*** 落后，慢于，赶不上. ***the ~ and heat of the day*** 鏖战；竞争激烈. ***throw ~ in sb.'s eyes*** 〔口〕蒙蔽，欺骗. — *vt.* ①撣(灰)，打扫(灰尘). ②把…弄得满是灰尘，在…上撒粉；撒(粉等). ③使成为灰尘. ④〔古〕使蒙满灰. ~ *a table* 撣掉桌上的灰尘. ~ *the snow from one's knees* 把膝上的雪花撣掉. ~ *a cake with sugar* 在蛋糕上撒糖. ~ *DDT over the floor* 在地板上撒滴滴涕. *hairs ~ed with grey* 斑白的头发. ~ *oneself* 〔古〕弄得满身尘土. — *vi.* ①扫除灰尘. ②扬起灰尘. ③(鸟)沙浴. ④〔美口〕急忙跑掉. ***~'em off*** 〔美口〕用功. ***~ off*** 〔美口〕痛打，痛殴. ***~ sb.'s jacket [coat] for him*** 〔口〕打某人. ***~ the eyes of*** = ***~ a person's eye*** 瞒，骗. ~ **band** (表的)防尘圈. ~ **bin** 垃圾箱. ~ **bowl** (大草原中)久旱多尘暴的地区，"灰盆"地区. ~ **bowler** 住在干旱多尘土地区的人. ~ **brand** 〔英〕(麦子的)黑穗病. ~ **cart** 垃圾车. ~ **cloak [coat]** (防尘)罩衫. ~ **coal** 粉煤. **~-coat** 风衣，轻便的防尘外衣. **~-colo(u)r** *n.* 灰暗色. ~ **counter**【气象】计尘

器. ~ **cover** ①(家具等的) 布罩. ②(书的)护封. ~ **devil**【气】小尘暴,尘旋风. ~ **disease**〔口〕矽肺病. ~ **explosion** 煤屑爆炸. ~ **guard** (机器的) 防尘板[罩]. ~ **gun** 手提喷尘器. ~**heap** ①垃圾堆. ②闲置,默默无闻 (*be consigned to ~heap* 受到冷落). ~ **jacket** ①(书的)护封. ②(家具等的)防尘布套. ~**man** ①清洁工. ②(童话中的) 睡神, 瞌睡虫. ③【海】火夫. ~**off**〔美军俚〕救护用直升飞机. ~**pan** 畚箕. ~**proof** *a.* 防尘的. ~ **shot** 微型子弹. ~ **storm**【气】尘暴. ~**up**〔口〕争论,吵闹;打架;骚乱. ~ **well** 冰川表面由沙土等形成的洞. ~ **wrapper** = ~ jacket.

dust·er [ˈdʌstə] *n.* ①打扫灰尘的人, 打扫工. ②掸子,掸帚; 除尘器; 畚箕, 擦布, 揩布. ③撒粉器; 撒(胡椒等的)粉瓶. ④〔美〕防尘外衣, 风衣. *a DDT ~* 滴滴涕撒粉器.

dust·ing [ˈdʌstiŋ] *n.* ①打扫, 掸灰. ②【海】(暴风雨中船的) 颠簸. ③拌药; 撒粉; (火药等的) 筛分; 撒布; 防腐粉 (=~ powder). ④〔俚〕殴打, 鞭打. *a ~ of powder* 撒粉. ***give sb. a good ~*** 痛打某人一顿.

dust·y [ˈdʌsti] *a.* ①满是灰尘的, 灰蒙蒙的. ②土灰色的; (酒)浊的. ③灰尘似的, 粉状的. ④枯燥无味的. ⑤暧昧的; 含糊的. ⑥无价值的. *What a ~ answer!* 多含混的回答啊! *a ~ speech* 枯燥无味的演说. ***not [none] so ~*** 〔英俚〕还好. ~ **miller** ①【植】耳状报春花 (= auricula). ②(钓鲑等的) 假饵钩. ③〔美〕蠹蛾.

Dutch [dʌtʃ] *a.* ①荷兰(人)的;〔美方、口〕德国人的. ②荷兰语的. ③荷兰制的; 荷兰式的. — *n.* ①〔the ~〕荷兰人. ②荷兰语; 〔古〕(语言史上的) 德国语. ③〔the ~〕〔美方、口〕德国人. ④〔美俚〕怒气, 怒火. *double ~* 胡涂话, 莫名其妙的话. ***beat the ~*** 〔口〕做使人惊叹的事; 干的事叫人莫名其妙 (*Well, you women do beat the ~.* 好了, 好了, 你们女人真叫人伤脑筋). ***go ~*** 〔美口〕(聚餐等) 各人自己付钱. ***in ~*** 〔美俚〕①丢脸, 受气; 为难, 受窘. ②得罪 (上司等) (*get in ~ with sb.* 得罪了某人). ***talk to sb. like a ~ uncle*** 板着面孔唠唠叨叨地 [严厉地] 教训 [责备]. ~ **act** 〔美俚〕自杀. ~ **auction** 喊价逐步减低的拍卖. ~ **bargain** 酒席上讲成的买卖. ~ **barn** 〔英〕干草棚. ~ **butter** 人造黄油. ~ **cheese** 荷兰(球状)干酪. ~ **comfort [consolation]** 不幸时退一步着想而得到的安慰. ~ **concert** 〔口〕乱七八糟的合唱. ~ **courage** 酒后之勇, 虚勇. ~ **cousins** 老朋友. ~ **door** ①(上下两部分可各自分别开关的) 两截门. ②(夹在杂志中可抽出的) 散页广告. ~ **foil [gold leaf]** 人造金箔. ~ **lunch [supper]** 〔美〕聚餐式午餐[晚餐]. ~ **metal** 荷兰合金, 荷兰黄铜. ~ **oven** (盖上加炭的) 荷兰烤锅; (吊在火前烤的) 铁皮烤肉匣; 荷兰灶〔撤火后用余热烧东西的灶〕. ~ **pink** ①一种黄色颜料. ②〔俚〕血. ~ **rush**【植】木贼. ~ **school**〔美〕(以日常生活为题材的)荷兰画派. ~ **telescope** 荷兰式望远镜〔把凸镜作物镜, 凹镜作目镜〕. ~ **tile** 饰瓦. ~ **treat [party]** 〔美口〕(各人自己付钱的) 聚餐. ~ **uncle** 絮絮不休地教训人的人. ~ **wife** 竹夫人〔睡觉时减轻暑热用的藤具或竹具〕.

Dutch·man [ˈdʌtʃmən] *n.* ①(*pl.* **-men**) 荷兰人 (= 〔美〕 Hollander). ②〔美俚〕德国人. ③【海】荷兰船; 〔美俚〕德国船. ④(生于南非的) 荷兰血统人. ⑤(芬兰以外的) 北欧各国的海员. ⑥〔d-〕塞孔堵洞物; 遮盖物. ***I'm a ~ (if [or] …)*** 〔发誓语〕如果… 我就不是人! 决不会… (*It is true, or I'm a ~.* 我若说谎我就不是人. *You've passed the examination? Well, I'm a ~!* 你已经考试及格了! 我可不相信!).

Dutch·man's-breech·es [ˈdʌtʃmənsbritʃiz] *n.* 〔*sing., pl.*〕【植】兜状荷包牡丹.

Dutch·man's-pipe [ˈdʌtʃmənsˈpaip] *n.* 【植】美洲马兜铃.

du·te·ous [ˈdjuːtjəs] *a.* 忠实的, 顺从的, 守本分的, 尽职的. **-ly** *ad.* **-ness** *n.*

du·ti·a·ble [ˈdjuːtjəbl] *a.* (货物) 应缴税的; (输入品) 应课关税的. ~ *articles [goods]* 课税品.

du·ti·ful [ˈdjuːtiful] *a.* 孝顺的; 忠于职守的, 守本分的; (对长上)必恭必敬的. *a ~ child* 听话的孩子. *~ attention* 恭敬地谛听, 洗耳恭听. **-ly** *ad.* **-ness** *n.*

Dutt [dʌt] *n.* 达特〔姓氏〕.

du·ty [ˈdjuːti] *n.* ①义务, 本分; 责任; 职责, 职务, 职能. ②忠节, 孝顺; 恭敬, 尊敬, 敬意; 义, 谊. ③税, 关税; 【机】功; 能率; 灌溉率; 负荷, 生产量; 工作状态. ④【军】任务, 勤务; 兵役; 【宗】礼拜, (修行的) 功课. ⑤〔口〕(原指小孩的) 拉屎. *one's maternal ~* 做母亲的本分. *postmen's duties* 邮递员的职责. *filial ~* 做儿女的义务. *That's no part of my ~.* 那不是我管的事. *on radar ~ for two years* 当两年雷达兵. *~ call* 礼节性拜访. *customs duties* 关税. *export [import] duties* 出口 [进口] 税. *After graduation, he began his ~.* 他毕业后开始服兵役. ***be in ~ bound to (do sth.)*** 有义务(做某事). ***do ~ as [for]*** 代…用, 当…用 (*bookcases that do ~ as room dividers* 拿书柜当作分隔房间的墙壁). ***do [perform] one's ~*** ①尽义务, 尽职; 尽(友)谊. ②服兵役. ~ ***of water*** 一定区域内某种作物所需灌溉的水量. ***fail in one's ~*** 失职. ***off ~*** 在工作时间外, 不值班, 不值勤; 下班 (*go [come] off ~* 下班). ***on ~*** 在工作时间内, 值班, 值勤; 上班 (*go on ~* 上班). ***pay [send] one's ~ to*** 对…表示敬意. ***take sb.'s ~*** 替代某人的工作. ~-**bound** *a.* 义不容辞的. ~-**free** *a.* 无税的, 免税的. ~-**paid** *a.* 已完税的.

du·um·vir [dju(ː)ˈʌmvə] *n.* (*pl.* **~s** [-vəz], ***du·um·vi·ri*** [dju(ː)ˈʌmvirai]) (古罗马) 二头政治中的一个统治者; 两人掌权统治者中的一个.

du·um·vi·rate [dju(ː)ˈʌmvirit] *n.* ①二人共同负责的职务; 二头政治. ②共同统治的两个人.

du·vet [ˈdjuːvei] *n.* 〔F.〕鸭绒垫子.

du·ve·tyn, du·ve·tine, du·ve·tyne [ˈduːvətiːn] *n.* 【纺】起绒织物[丝毛混纺品].

dux [dʌks] *n.* (*pl.* ***~es, du·ces*** [ˈdʌksiz]) 〔Scot., N.Z., S.Afr.〕级长, 班长.

D.V. = *Deo Volente* (〔L.〕 = God willing; if God permits 如果上帝允许的话).

D.V.M. = Doctor of Veterinary Medicine. 兽医学博士.

d.w., dw = deadweight.

dwarf [dwɔːf] *n.* ①矮子. ②矮小的动物[植物]; 矮生植物. ③【北欧神话】(善做金属小工艺品的) 矮神. ④【天】矮星 (= ~ star). — *a.* 矮小的. *a ~ car* 小型汽车. — *vt.* 使矮小, 使(发育、知能等)受阻碍; 使相形见绌. *~ all one's rivals* 使所有的对手都相形见绌. *a ~(ed) tree* 盆栽树, 盆景. — *vi.* 变矮小. ~ **door** (活动门的下半截)小门. ~ **star**【天】矮星. **-ism** *n.* ①矮小. ②【植】矮态; 【医】侏儒症.

dwarf·ish [ˈdwɔːfiʃ] *a.* 比较矮小的.

DWC = deadweight capacity 【船】(总)载重吨位.

dwell [dwel] *vi.* (***dwelt*** [dwelt], ***~ed; dwelt, ~ed***) ①〔书〕住, 居住, 居留; 寓于 (***at; in, on***). ②(马跳障碍物时) 踌躇. *~ at a place* 住在一个地方. *~ for years in the same town* 在一个城市住了多年. *~ on the earth* 住在地球上. ***~ on [upon]*** ①细想; 详述; 仔细研究; 强调. ②拖长(发音); 仔细打量, 盯着看. ③减慢 (*~ on the pleasures of the past* 细想过去的欢乐. *~ on a stroke* 缓慢地荡桨. *Her eyes ~ on him.* 她盯着看他. *~ on a particular point in an argument* 详细阐述一个特殊论点. *~ on a syllabe* 拖长一个音节). **-er** *n.* ①居住者, 居民. ②(在障碍物前) 踌躇不跳的马 (*city and town dwellers* 城镇居民).

dwell·ing [ˈdweliŋ] *n.* ①居住. ②住宅, 寓所; 住处. *change one's ~* 搬家. *a portable ~* 活动房屋. *a modern ~* 现代化住宅. ~ **house** 住宅. ~ **place** 住处.

dwelt [dwelt] dwell 的过去式及过去分词.

Dwight [dwait] *n.* 德怀特[姓氏].

dwin·dle ['dwindl] *vi.* ①减少,变小,缩小;变瘦. ②衰落;变坏,退化. ~ *in size* 体积缩小. ~ *in numbers* 数量减少. ~ *away into [to] nothing* 减少到零,缩小到化为乌有. ~ *down to* 缩减到…. ~ *into* 缩小成. ~ *out* 逐渐消失. *His fame* ~*d.* 他的名声低落了.— *vt.* 使缩小,使减少. *Failing health* ~*d ambition.* 体弱雄心减.

DWT,D.W.T.,dwt = deadweight ton(s)【船】(总)载重吨位.

dwt., dwt = pennyweight(s).

DX = distance【无】远距离(常用以表示远距离播送).

DX., dx. =【讯】duplex.

Dy =【化】dysprosium.

dy = penny.

dy·ad ['daiæd] *n.* ①二个,一对;一双. ②【数】并矢(量);【化】二价元素;【生】二分体,二分细胞. ③〔美口〕双边对话,双边会谈;双边关系. *a chromosome* ~ 二分染色体. —*a.* 二数的,二价的. **dy·ad·ic** [dai'ædik] ①*a.*【数】二数的,二进的;【化】二价的;二重(对称)的,双值的. ②*n.*【数】并矢式,并向量,双积.

Dy·a(c)k ['daiæk] *n.* (婆罗洲的)达雅克人,达雅克语(=Dayak).

dy·ar·chy ['daiɑːki] *n.* = diarchy.

dyb·buk ['daibək] *n.* (犹太民间传说)阴魂附体.

Dyce [dais] *n.* 戴斯[姓氏].

dye [dai] *vt.* 染,染上,把…染色,给…着色. ~ *a dress green* 把衣服染成绿色. *A deep flush* ~*d her cheeks.* 她的双颊染上一层绯红. — *vi.* 着色,上色,染上颜色. *This cloth* ~*s easily.* 这种布容易上色. **be ~d in (the) grain [in the wool]** ①生染;被染透. ②〔喻〕造成不可改变的结果. ~ **well [badly]** 好[不好]染. — *n.* ①染料,染液. ②染色;色调. *acid [alkaline, basic]* ~*s* 酸性[碱性,盐基性]染料. *mordant [synthetic]* ~*s* 媒染[合成]染料. *take* ~ *well* 容易染色. ***(scoundrel) of the blackest [deepest]*** ~ 穷凶极恶的(无赖). ~**house** 染厂,染坊,染色间. ~**jigger**【纺】染缸,卷染机. ~**marker** 海水染色剂〔投在海中使水变色作为标志的染料〕. ~ **printing** 印染,印花. ~**stuff** 染料;颜料;(橡胶的)染色剂. ~ **vat** 染缸,染锅,染槽. ~**wood** 染料木. ~**-works**〔*sing., pl.*〕染厂. **-a·bil·i·ty** [-'biliti] *n.* 可染色性,可着色性.

dyed-in-the-wool ['daidinðə'wul] *a.* ①生染的,未纺织以前即染色的. ②纯粹的,十足的,彻头彻尾的,难以改变的.

dye·ing ['daiiŋ] *n.* 染色;染色法;染业. — *a.* 染色的.

dy·er ['daiə] *n.* 染色员,染工,染色师傅.

dy·er's-broom ['daiəzbruːm] *n.*【植】染料木.

dy·er's-weed ['daiəzwiːd] *n.* ①染料目(含染料的植物). ②【植】一枝黄花属植物;一枝黄花.

dy·ing ['daiiŋ] die 的现在分词. — *a.* ①垂死的,快死的;临终的. ②会死的,会灭亡的. ③(火)快熄灭的;快消灭的,行将完结的. ④〔口〕渴望,切盼,极想. *a* ~ *man* 快死的人. *one's* ~ *wish* 临终的心愿,遗嘱. *the* ~ *year* 年终岁尾. *a* ~ *fire* 行将熄灭的火. *the* ~ *moon* 下沉的月亮. *He is* ~ *to go.* 他很想去. ***be* ~ *for*** 对…想得要死. ***to [till] one's* ~ *day*** 直到老死.

dyke[1] [daik] *n.*〔英〕= dike.

dyke[2] [daik] *n.*〔俚〕爱搞同性爱的女性(尤指扮演男性角色者).

dyn., dynam. = dynamics.

dyna-, dynam- *comb. f.* 力,动力: *dyna*mics.

dy·nam·e·ter [dai'næmitə] *n.*【物】(望远镜的)倍率计.

dy·nam·ic, dy·nam·i·cal [dai'næmik, -kəl] *a.* ①动力的,动力学的;力学(上)的;动(态)的;起动的. ②有力的,有生气的;能动的;(工作)效率高的. ③【乐】力度强弱法的. ④【医】机能(上)的. ⑤【哲】动力论的,力本论的. *a* ~ *personality* 活跃的性格. *a* ~ *atmosphere* 生气勃勃的景象. *a* ~ *population* 动态人口. — *n.*〔限指 dynamic〕(原)动力;动态. ~ **agent** 起动原因. ~ **astronomy** 天体力学. ~ **behavior** 能动行为. ~ **characteristics**【讯】动态特性曲线. ~ **electricity** 动电. ~ **elevation** 动力势差[位差]. **dynamic geology** 地质力学. ~ **equilibrium** 动态平衡. ~ **meteorology** 气象力学. ~ **number** 重力势差[位差]数. **-al·ly** *ad.*

dy·nam·ics [dai'næmiks] *n. pl.* ①〔用作 *sing.*〕力学;动力学. ②动力,原动力. ③动态. ④【乐】力度强弱法.

dy·na·mism ['dainəmizəm] *n.* ①【哲】物力论,力本学. ②精力,活力;魄力,劲头. **-na·mist** *n.* 物力论者. **-na·mis·tic** [ˌdaiə'mistik] *a.*

dy·na·mi·tard ['dainəmitɑːd] *n.* (为某一政治目的采取行刺等暴力行动而)使用炸药的人;〔美〕使用炸药的盗匪.

dy·na·mite ['dainəmait] *n.* ①(一种爆炸力猛烈的)达那炸药,甘油炸药. ②具有爆炸性的事[物];有潜在危险的人. ③精力充沛的人. ④〔俚〕毒品〔指海洛英等〕. — *vt.* ①(用炸药)炸破. ②使完全失败. *Saboteurs* ~*d the dam.* 破坏者炸毁了堤坝. ~**-laden** *a.* (局势等)充满爆炸性的.

dy·na·mi·ter ['dainəmaitə] *n.* ①= dynamitard. ②〔美俚〕野心勃勃的人.

dy·na·mo ['dainəməu] *n.* ①【电】发电机〔尤指直流发电机〕. ②〔口〕勤奋肯干的人,精力充沛的人. *an alternating [direct] current* ~ 交[直]流发电机. *a compound (wound)* ~ 复绕[复激发]电机. *shunt (wound)* ~ 分绕[并励发]电机. ~**-electric** *a.* 电动的,机电的,机械能变为电能的,电能变为机械能的.

dy·na·mom·e·ter [ˌdainə'mɔmitə] *n.* ①测力计,拉力表. ②功率计;动力计;电力测工仪. **-y** 动力测定法.

dy·na·mo·tor ['dainəməutə] *n.*【电】电动发电机.

dy·na·po·lis [dai'næpəlis] *n.* (交通干线附近的)新兴城市.

dy·nast ['dinəst] *n.* (世袭王朝的)君主;统治者.

dy·nas·tic(al) [di'næstik(əl)] *a.* 朝代的;王朝的,皇朝的.

dy·nas·ty ['dinəsti, 'dainəsti] *n.* ①王朝,朝代. ②王朝统治;世袭统治. ③统治集团;统治家族. *the Ming* ~ 明王朝.

dy·nat·ron ['dainətrɔn] *n.*【无】(打拿)负阻管.

dyne [dain] *n.*【物】达因[力的单位].

Dy·nel [dai'nel]【纺】迪尼尔[美国制的一种合成纤维的商标名]. — *n.*〔d-〕【纺】迪尼尔线;迪尼尔皮毛.

dy·no ['dainəu] *a.*〔美口〕绝妙的.

dy·node ['dainəud] *n.*【无】①倍增器电极. ②打拿极,中间极.

dys- *comb. f.* 恶化,不良;困难: *dys*function.

dys·cra·sia [dis'kreizjə] *n.*【医】体液不调,恶液质. **-cra·si·al, -cras·ic** *a.*

dys·en·ter·y ['disntri] *n.* 痢疾. **-ter·ic** *a.* 痢疾(性)的.

dys·func·tion [dis'fʌŋkʃən] *n.*【医】机能障碍,机能不良. **-al** *a.*

dys·gen·ic [dis'dʒenik] *a.*【生】劣生的,遗传形质不良的. **-s** *n.*【生】劣生学.

dys·lex·i·a [dis'leksiə] *n.*【医】诵读困难. **-lex·ic** *a.*

dys·lo·gis·tic [dislə'dʒistik] *a.* 指责的,责难的;骂人的. ~ *terms* 骂人的话,出口伤人.

dys·men·or·rhe·a [ˌdismenə'riːə] *n.*【医】痛经,月经困难.

dys·pa·thy ['dispəθi] *n.*〔古〕无情;反感.

dys·pep·sia [dis'pepsiə] *n.* 消化不良,胃弱 (*opp.* eupepsia).

dys·pep·sy [dis'pepsi] *n.*〔方〕= dyspepsia.

dys·pep·tic [dis'peptik] *a.* ①消化不良的，胃弱的；由消化不良引起的. ②阴郁的,消沉的；易怒的. — *n.* 消化不良的人. **-cal·ly** *ad.*

dys·pha·gia [dis'feidʒiə] *n.*【医】咽下困难. **dis·phag·ic** *a.*

dys·pha·si·a [dis'feiʒiə] *n.*【医】语言困难.

dys·pho·ni·a [dis'fəuniə] *n.*【医】发音困难. **dis·phon·ic** *a.*

dys·pho·ri·a [dis'fɔːriə] *n.*【医】烦躁不安.

dys·pla·si·a [dis'pleiziə, -'pleiʒə] *n.*【医】发育异常. **-plas·tic** [-'plæstik] *a.*

dysp·n(o)e·a [dis'pniːə] *n.*【医】呼吸困难 (*opp.* eupnea). **-n(o)e·ic** [-'niːik] *a.*

dys·pro·si·um [dis'prəusiəm] *n.*【化】镝.

dys·to·cia [dis'təuʃiə] *n.*【医】难产.

dys·to·pi·a [dis'təupiə] *n.* 非理想化的地方，糟透的社会；地狱般的处境 (*opp.* utopia).

dys·tro·phic [dis'trɔfik] *a.* ①营养不良的，营养障碍的. ②发育不全的，畸形的；退化的.

dys·tro·phy ['distrəfi] *n.*【医】营养障碍，营养不良.

dys·u·ri·a [dis'juəriə] *n.*【医】排尿困难，尿痛. **dys·u·ric** *a.*

Dyu·sham·be [dju(ː)'ʃaːmbə] *n.* = Dushambe.

DZ = drop zone 空投(或伞降)地域.

dz. = dozen(s).

dzig·ge·tai [zi'getai] *n.* (蒙古的)野驴.

E

E, e [iː] (*pl.* *E's, e's* [iːz]) ①英语字母表第五字母. ②【乐】E 调，E 音. ③ E 字形. ④〔美〕(顺序)第五等，(成绩)'劣等'〔注意，有时 E 也作成绩优等 (excellent) 的符号〕.

E., e. = ① earth. ② east; eastern. ③ engineer(ing).

e- *pref.* [i; ə] 表示"出"，"出自"，"外面"，"缺"等意：*e*ject, *e*radiate, *e*scribe, *e*dentate.

EA = enemy aircraft 敌机.

ea. = each.

E.A.A. = Engineer in Aeronautics and Astronautics 航空学与航天学工程师.

each [iːtʃ] *a.* 各，各自的，每. ～ *man* 各人. ～ *side of the river* 河的两边. — *pro.* 每，各，各自. *E- (of us) has his likes and dislikes.* 各有各的好恶. *We* ～ *know what the other wants.* 我们彼此都知道各自的要求. *From* ～ *according to his ability and to* ～ *according to his work [needs].* 各尽所能，按劳[需]分配. — *ad.* 各个地. *These books cost one dollar* ～. 这些书每本的价钱一美元. ***bet*** ～ ***way***【赛马】赌两门. ～ ***and all*** 大家都，统统. ～ ***and every*** 每个都，人人都. ～***other*** 互相，彼此 (*They help* ～ *other.* 他们互相帮助). ***on*** ～ ***occasion.*** 每次.

Eads [iːdz] *n.* 伊兹〔姓氏〕.

ea·ger ['iːgə] *a.* ①〔多用作表语〕渴望，极想，热中于 (*after; about; for*). ②热切的，热情洋溢的. ③〔古〕(寒气等)凛烈的，酷烈的；(气味等)浓烈的. *be* ～ *to do sth.* 极想做某事. *I am* ～ *for [after] news about them.* 我渴望得到有关他们的消息. *She is* ～ *in her studies.* 她热中于学习. *one's* ～ *pursuit of pleasure* 一心追求享乐. *an* ～ *look* 热情洋溢的面孔. ～ **beaver** (为讨好上司)干活特别卖力的人. ～**-beaver** *a.* 巴结上司的，讨好卖乖的. **-ly** *ad.*

ea·ger·ness ['iːgənis] *n.* 渴望；殷切；热忱；热情. *He had a great* ～ *to join the army.* 他(当时)满腔热忱想要参军. *The recruit was all* ～ *to go to the front.* 新入伍的战士迫切盼望上前线.

ea·gle ['iːgl] *n.* ①鹰. ②鹰徽；鹰旗. ③〔美〕十元金币. ④〔E-〕【天】鹰座. ⑤〔E-〕〔美〕密西西比州别名，～ **boat**〔美〕小型反潜艇战舰. ～**-eyed** *a.* 眼力锐利的，目光炯炯的. ～ **owl**【动】鹏鸮.

ea·glet ['iːglit] *n.* 小鹰.

ea·gre ['eigə, 'iːgə] *n.*〔方〕(河口的)海潮，潮.

EAL = ① Ethiopian Airlines 埃塞俄比亚航空公司. ② Eastern Air Lines〔美〕东方航空公司.

-ean *suf.* 作名词和形容词的词尾，表示"…的"，"属于…"：Europ*ean*, Aeg*ean*, trach*ean*.

E and OE, E. & O.E. = errors and omissions excepted 如有错漏，可予更改〔常印在帐单上〕.

ear[1] [iə] *n.* ①耳朵. ②听觉；听力；倾听；注意. ③耳状物〔指水罐、茶杯等的把儿〕. ④报头两端刊登小广告、天气预报的地方. ***a flea in sb.'s*** ～ 刺耳的话. ***A word in your*** ～. 我跟你私下讲句话. ***about one's*** ～***s*** (某人)陷于尴尬[麻烦等]处境 (*bring the house about one's* ～*s* 遭全家反对). ***be all*** ～〔口〕专心倾听. ***be [go out] on one's*** ～***s***〔美俚〕发怒；无礼. ***bend sb.'s*** ～***s*** 讲得使某人厌烦；和某人谈要事. ***by the*** ～***s*** (动物)相斗；(人)扭打，倾轧；不和 (*set the whole neighbourhood by the* ～*s.* 挑拨离间，使四邻不和. *fall together by the* ～*s* 打起来). ***close [stop] one's*** ～***s to*** 完全不听. ***fall on deaf*** ～***s*** 不被理睬，不受注意. ***feel one's*** ～***s burning*** 感觉耳朵发烧(有人背地议论). ***get sb. on his*** ～〔美俚〕使某人发火. ***give sb. a thick*** ～ 把(某人)打得鼻青脸肿. ***give*** ～ ***to*** 听，倾听. ***give one's*** ～***s*** 不惜任何代价(要). ***have a good [poor]*** ～ 听力好[不好]. ***have an [no]*** ～ ***for music*** 懂[不懂]音乐. ***have [hold, keep] an*** ～ ***to the ground*** 注意舆论等的动向，留心可能发生的事情. ***have itching*** ～***s*** 爱听新奇消息、闲话. ***have [gain, win] sb.'s*** ～***s*** 得到某人注意. ***(go [through]) in at one*** ～ ***and out at the other*** 左耳进右耳出，听了就忘. ***kick [throw] sb. out on his ears*** 突然解雇某人. ***lend one's*** ～***s to*** = ***give*** ～ ***to.*** ***over head and*** ～***s*** = ***up to the*** ～***s.*** ***play [sing] by*** ～ ①不看乐谱演奏[歌唱]. ②〔口〕临时应付事态[事先没有计划]. ***prick up one's*** ～***s*** 竖起耳朵听. ***sleep upon both*** ～***s*** 酣睡. ***tickle sb.'s*** ～ 巴结，奉承某人. ***turn a deaf*** ～ ***to*** 装听不见[置若罔闻]. ***up to the*** ～***s*** 深陷(债务等). ***Walls have*** ～***s***〔谚〕隔墙有耳. ***(still) behind the*** ～***s*** 没有经验，缺乏训练. ～**ache** ['iəreik] 耳痛. ～**cap** 耳套. ～**drop** 耳饰，耳坠. ～**drops** 耳药水. ～**drum**【解】耳鼓. ～**-flap** (帽子的)护耳. ～**lap** ① = ～flap. ② = ～lobe. ③外耳. ～**lobe** 耳垂. ～**mark** ① *n.* (家畜耳朵上的)耳记；标记，特征；= dog-ear. ② *vt.* (给家畜)打耳记；指定(资金等的)用途. ～ **muffs**〔*pl.*〕〔美〕(防寒用的)耳套. ～**phone** 耳机，译意风. ～ **pick** 耳挖勺. ～**piece** ① = ～**phone.** ②眼镜腿. ～**-piecing** *a.* 刺耳的. ～**-plug** (防水或防噪声的)耳塞. ～ **reach** = ～**shot.** ～ **ring** 耳环. ～ **shell** ① = abalone. ②鲍鱼壳. ～**shot**

听力所及的范围 (*within [out of] the ~shot of the alarm* 在听得见[听不见]警报器的地方). **~ trumpet** (从前半聋人用的号筒形)助听器. **~wax** 耳垢. **~wig** ① *n.* 【动】蠼螋; 偷听者; 奉承者. ② *vt.* 在耳边说闲话(来打扰或企图影响某人).

ear² [iə] *n.* ①(稻麦等的)穗. ②〔*pl.*〕灯花. ***be in the ~*** 正在抽穗. ***come into ~s*** 抽穗. —*vi.* 抽穗. **~ developing stage** 孕穗期.

ear·bob [ˈiəbɔb] *n.* 〔方〕耳环.

eared [iəd] *a.* ①有耳朵的; …耳的. ②有把儿的; …把的. ③有穗的; …穗的.

ear·ful [ˈiəful] *n.* 〔口〕①听够了的话. ②大量的新闻[闲话]. ③耸人听闻的消息. ④训斥.

Ear·hart [ˈɛəhɑːt] *n.* 埃尔哈特〔姓氏〕.

ear·ing [ˈiəriŋ] *n.* 【海】(横帆角上的)耳索.

earl [əːl] *n.* (*fem.* **countess**) 〔英〕伯爵〔相当于欧洲大陆的 count〕. **E- Marshal** 英国纹章院院长.

earl·dom [ˈəːldəm] *n.* ①伯爵爵位[身份]. ②伯爵领地.

ear·less¹ [ˈiəlis] *a.* ①无耳的. ②听觉不佳的. **~ seal** 【动】海豹科 (*phocidae*) 动物.

ear·less² [ˈiəlis] *a.* 无穗的.

ear·li·ness [ˈəːlinis] *n.* 早, 早期.

Ear·ly [ˈəːli] *n.* 厄利〔姓氏〕.

ear·ly [ˈəːli] (*opp.* late) *a.* ①早; (果实等)早熟的. ②早日的, 及早的. ③早期的, 很久以前的, 古代的; 近日的. *at an ~ date* 早日, 在最近期间. *Please reply at your earliest convenience* 务请早日赐复. *~ death* 早死, 夭折. *~ maturity (of mind)* 思想早熟. *~ train* 早班车. ~ riser 早起的人; ~ rising 早起. ***~ bird*** 早起的人 (*The ~ bird catches [gets] the worm.* 〔谚〕捷足先登). ***~ habits*** 早起早睡的习惯. ***E- Modern English*** 早期现代英语(十五世纪中叶至十八世纪中叶). ***It is ~ days yet*** (*to make up one's mind*). ***one's ~ days*** 年轻时. (要下决心)现在还为时过早. ***keep ~ hours*** 早睡早起. —*ad.* 早, 先, 初; 幼小时候. *as ~ as May* 早在五月里. *Don't come too ~.* 不要来得太早. *~ in May* 五月初. ***earlier on*** 以前, 在更早的时候. ***~ and late*** 从早到晚. ***~ on*** 在早期. ***~ or late*** 迟早, 早晚. ***E- sow, ~ mow.*** 〔谚〕早种早收. ***rise [get up] ~*** 早起. **~ ag(e)ing** 【医】早衰. **~ ambulation** 【医】(外科手术后)早期下床活动. **~ door** (剧院的)提早入座门. **~ rice** 早稻. **~-Victorian** *a.* 维多利亚王朝初期的; (英国)(作家等)旧式的. **~-warning radar** 预先[远程]警报雷达.

earn [əːn] *vt.* ①赚得, 挣得. ②获得, 赢得, 博得(名声). *a well-~ed reward* 应得的报酬. *~ed income* 劳动收入. ***~ one's bread [living]*** 谋生, 挣钱. ***~ one's own living*** 自食其力.

ear·nest¹ [ˈəːnist] *a.* ①热心的; 诚挚的, 真挚的, 认真的. ②重要的. —*n.* 热心; 认真. ***in ~*** 诚挚, 认真 (*Are you in ~ (in what you say)?* 你(讲的话)当真吗? *It began raining in ~.* 雨真的下大了). ***in good [real, sober, sad, dead] ~*** 一本正经地, 非常认真地. **-ly** *ad.* **-ness** *n.*

ear·nest² [ˈəːnist] *n.* ①定钱, 保证金. ②预兆. **~ money** 定钱, 保证金.

earn·ings [ˈəːniŋz] *n. pl.* 所得, 收入, 工资, 报酬, 利润.

Earp [əːp] *n.* 厄普〔姓氏〕.

earth [əːθ] *n.* ①〔常 E-〕地球. ②大地, 陆地, 地面, 地上. ③土壤, 土. ④【化】土类; 泥. ⑤世界人类; 人的躯体. ⑥尘世, 人间, 世间; 世俗的事. ⑦〔英〕(狐、獾等的)洞, 穴. ⑧【电】接地. ⑨【化】难以还原的金属氧化物类〔如氧化铝、氧化钴等〕. *the whole ~* 全人类. *be brought to ~* 被击落地上. *alkaline ~* 【化】碱土. ***be of the ~*** 有点俗气. ***break ~*** 破土动工. ***come back [down] to ~*** 回到现实中来, 不再幻想. ***go the way of all the ~*** 死. ***go to ~*** (狐等)躲入洞内. ***move heaven and ~*** (*to do sth.*) 竭力, 用尽办法. ***on ~*** ①在地球上, 在人世间. ②到底, 究竟〔连用于 what, where; why, how 等词之后〕(*What on ~ are you?* 你究竟是什么人?). ③全然, 一点也〔用于否定语后〕(*No use on ~!* 一点也没有用!). ***on God's ~*** 普天之下. ***put to ~*** 【无】接地. ***run to ~*** = ***go to ~***. ***run ... to ~*** 穷追(狐等)直至其洞内; 查明, 查出. ***stop an ~*** 堵塞狐(等)的洞穴. ***take ~*** 逃入洞内; 隐匿. —*vt.* ①把…埋入土中, 用土掩盖, 给…培土; 把(萝卜等)保藏在土中 (*up*). ②追(狐等)到洞内. ③使(导体)接地〔美国用 ground〕. —*vi.* (狐等)躲进洞内. **~-bag** 【军】砂袋, 沙包. **~-based** *a.* 地面的. **~-bath** 泥浴. **~born** *a.* 地中生出的, 生在地上的; 人类的; 世俗的. **~bound** *a.* ①局限于地上的; 世俗的; 平凡的. ②朝地球走的. ③【电】接地的. **~-bred** *a.* 土生土长的; 卑贱的; 粗俗的. **~ closet** 撒土厕所 (*opp.* water closet). **~fall** 塌方. **~flow** 【地】泥流. **~ inductor** 【电】地磁感应器. **~light** 【天】= *~shine*. **~man** (*pl.* -men) (科学幻想小说中登上其他天体的)地球人, 地球上的来客. **~ metals** 碱(土)金属. **~mover** 挖土机. **~nut** 落花生. **~ oil** 〔古语〕石油. **~ plate** 【电】接地金属板. **~ satellite** 人造地球卫星; **~ science** 地球科学. **~ scraper** 刮土机. **~shaking** *a.* 翻天覆地的, 震撼世界的, 意义极其重大的. **~shine** *n.* 【天】大地光, 地(球反)照〔指新月暗部所呈现的微光, 系由地球反射的日光造成〕. **~ station** (接收及转播外层空间传来的讯号的)地面通讯站. **~ wave** 地震波. **~ wire** 【电】地线. **~work** ①土方(工程). ②土木工事; 土垒; 土炮台; 土堤. ③土石艺术〔利用泥土、石块等天然形态加工的艺术品〕. **~ worm** 蚯蚓, 蛐蟮; 鄙夫, 小人. **-ward(s)** *ad.* 向地面.

earthed [əːθt] *a.* 接地的, 通地的.

earth·en [ˈəːθən] *a.* ①土制的, 土的, 陶制的. ②大地的, 现世的. **~ware** *n.* 〔集合词〕陶器.

earth·i·ness [ˈəːθinis] *n.* ①土质, 土性. ② = earthliness.

earthing [ˈəːθiŋ] *n.* 【电】接地.

earth·li·ness [ˈəːθlinis] *n.* 世俗, 尘缘.

earth·ling [ˈəːθliŋ] *n.* 人类; 俗人.

earth·ly [ˈəːθli] *a.* ①地球的, 地上的. ②现世的, 世俗的. ③〔否定〕完全, 一点也 (= at all); 〔疑问〕究竟 (= on earth). ④〔古〕= earthy. *What ~ purpose can it serve?* 这究竟有什么好处呢? *~ passions* 情欲. ***have no ~ (chance)*** = ***not an ~ (chance)*** 〔英俚〕完全没有希望. ***of no ~ use [reason]*** 完全没有用处[道理].

earth·quake [ˈəːθkweik] *n.* ①地震. ②大变动, 动乱. **~ bomb** 地震炸弹. **~ centre** 震源. **~ country** 震区. **~ weather** 地震前的异常天气. **~-proof** *a.* 防震的.

earth·rise [ˈəːθraiz] *n.* 地出〔从月球或宇宙飞船上所见地球仿佛从月球地平线上升起的现象〕.

earth·y [ˈəːθi] *a.* ①土(状)的, 土质的. ②泥土气的; 粗俗的; 世俗的; 现世的. ③【化】土类的. **~ elements** 土族元素. **~iron ore** 泥状铁矿.

ease [iːz] *n.* ①快活; 安心; 悠闲; 自在. ②容易, 不费事. ③(衣服等)宽松. ***at ~*** ① = ***stand at ~***. ②快活, 自由自在, 心情舒畅, 安心. ***be [feel] ill at ~*** 不安心, 偏促不安, 心神不宁. ***ease of mind*** 心情舒畅. ***march at ~*** 【军】常步走. ***set sb.'s heart at ~*** 使安心. ***stand at ~*** 【口令】稍息. ***take one's ~*** 休息, 安心. ***well at ~*** 安心, 畅快. ***with ~*** 容易. —*vt.* ①使安逸, 使畅快; 使安心; 减轻(痛苦等). ②放松(绳索等), 使松动. ③小心地搬. ④〔谑〕抢, 偷. *~ sb. of his purse* 抢人钱包. *~ sb.'s mind* 使安心. —*vi.* ①减轻, 减缓 (*off, up*). ②小心搬动. ***E- all!*** 【赛艇】停划! ***~ down the speed*** 【海】减低速度. ***E- her!*** 【海】慢开! ***~ nature*** 解手. ***~ off [away]*** ① *vi.* (痛苦)渐减; 【海】(索等)松弛. ②

vt. 【海】放松；放开(小船)。③【商】(物价)松动[下跌]。~ *one's mind* 安心，宽心。~ *oneself* ①泄愤，出气。②= ~ *nature*. ~ *out* ①(以不伤和气的方式)解雇，使离任。②[美运]轻易得胜。*E- the helm [rudder]!* 【海】回舵；~**-up** *a.* 缓和的。

ease·ful [ˈiːzful] *a.* 安闲的，舒适的，轻松的，懒散的。**-ly** *ad.* **-ness** *n.*

ea·sel [ˈiːzl] *n.* 画架；黑板架。~ **picture [piece]** 画架画。

ease·ment [ˈiːzmənt] *n.* ①(苦痛等)减轻，(局势)缓和(的手段)。②便利；舒适。③【法】使用权，通行权。④附属建筑物。④使人舒适[便利]的东西。

eas·i·ly [ˈiːzili] *ad.* ①容易，不难。②顺利，流畅。③安逸。④远远；大大地。⑤多半，很可能。*It is ~ the best hotel.* 这无疑是最好的旅馆。*more easily said than done* [谚]说说容易实行难。*The train may ~ be late.* 火车多半要晚点。

eas·i·ness [ˈiːzinis] *n.* ①容易。②安乐，安逸。③轻松；从容。④温和。

east [iːst] *n.* ①东，东方。②东边，东面。③[the E-] 东方[美语作 the Orient]；[美]东部[密西西比河以东]。④[诗]东风。*the Far [Middle, Near] E-* 远[中、近]东。*go down E-* [美]去东部。~ ***by north [south]*** 【海，测】东偏北[南]。***E- or west, home is best.*** [谚]东好西好不如家好。***in the ~ (of)*** 在…的东部。***[on, to] the ~ of*** 在…的东方。—*a.* 东方的；从东方来的；东部的，东边的。**E- Central** (伦敦市)中央东部邮政区。**E- End** 伦敦东部(贫民区)。**E- Ender** 伦敦东部贫民。**E- India = E-Indies** 东印度群岛[印度、印度支那及马来群岛的总称]。**E- Indian** 东印度群岛的；东印度人。**E- Side** 纽约市东部(贫民区)。— *ad.* 向东，往东；在东方；从东方。

east·bound [ˈiːstˌbaund] *a.* 东去的，向东行的。

East·er [ˈiːstə] *n.* 【宗】复活节。~ **Day [Sunday]** 复活节日[春分满月后的第一个星期日]。~ **dues [offering(s)]** [英] 复活节献金。~ **egg** 复活节彩蛋。~ **Monday** 复活节次日。~ **term** ①(英法院)4月15日后约三个星期的开庭期。②(英大学)复活节后约六个星期的时期，春季学期。~**tide** 【宗】复活节季节[可分别指从复活节至升天节之间的四十天，或从复活节至圣灵降临节之间的五十天，或从复活节至三一节之间的五十七天]。~ **time** ①复活节季节[由复活节到圣灵降临节，共50日]。②= ~ week. ~ **week** 复活节一周间。

east·er·ly [ˈiːstəli] *a.* 东，向东方的；从东方来的。—*ad.* 向东方，从东方。— *n.* 东风；[*pl.*] 东风带。

east·ern [ˈiːstən] *a.* ①东(方的)；[E-] 东方的，东部(地方)的。②(风)从东吹来的。③朝东的。— *n.* ①东方人。②东正教信徒。*the E- Church* 【宗】东正教会。*the E- Empire* 【史】东罗马帝国。*the E- Hemisphere* 东半球。*the E- States* [美]东部各州。~ **larch** 【植】美洲落叶松。~ **red-bud** 【植】加拿大紫荆。~ **white pine** 【植】美洲五针松。~**most** *a.* 极东的，最东的。

east·ern·er [ˈiːstənə] *n.* ①东方人。②[E-][美]东部人，东部各州出身的人。

East·ern Sa·mo·a [ˈiːstən səˈmouə] *n.* 东萨摩亚[南太平洋]。

east·ing [ˈiːstiŋ] *n.* ①【海】东航[偏东航行]。②(天体的)东进；(风向的)偏东。③东行航程。④朝东方向。

East·man [ˈiːstmən] *n.* 伊斯曼[姓氏]。

east-north·east [ˈiːstˌnɔːθˈiːst] *n.* 【海、测】东东北。— *a., ad.* ①在东东北(的)，向东东北(的)。②自东东北(的)。

east-south·east [ˈiːstˌsauθˈiːst] *n.* 【海、测】东东南。— *a., ad.* ①在东东南(的)，向东东南(的)。②自东东南(的)。

East Ti·mor [iːstˈtimɔːr] *n.* 东帝汶[亚洲]。

east·ward [ˈiːstwəd] *a.* (向)东方的；朝东的。—*ad.* 朝东方，向东。— *n.* 东方，东部。**east·wards** *adv.* 向东。

east·ward·ly [ˈiːstwədli] *ad., a.* ①向东。②自东。

eas·y [ˈiːzi] *a.* ①容易的。②舒服的，安乐的，大方的；宽裕的；(衣服等)宽松的；懒散的，散漫的。③平缓的，从容的，缓慢的。④【商】(物资)丰富的；(物价)便宜的；(银根)松动的 *(opp.* tight*)*。⑤平易的，(笔墨等)流畅的。⑥慈善的；温厚的。⑦【牌】(无主桥牌局中的A牌)双方平等分配的。⑧随随便便的；易顺从的。*feel ~* 舒服；安心。*Make your mind ~.* 请放心。*free and ~* 悠然自得，毫不拘束。*E-!* 慢慢的，别急。~ *servicing* 小修。*Be ~!* 放心好了！~ *chair* 安乐椅，圈椅。~ *dress* 便衣。~ *grace* 优雅。~ *labour* 【医】顺产。~ ***on the ears*** [美俚]好听的。~ ***on the eye(s)*** [美俚] 好看的。~ ***on the trigger*** [美俚]易兴奋的，易怒的。~ ***to look at*** [美俚] = ~ ***on the eyes. in ~ circumstances = on ~ street*** (又作 ***E- Street***) [美口]生活优裕，小康。***a woman of ~ virtue*** 水性杨花的女人)。— *ad.* [口] 容易，轻易；慢慢，安然，悠然。*E- come, ~ go.* [谚]来得容易花得快。~ ***ahead!*** [口令] 轻步前进！【海】低速前进！***E- all!*** 【海】停桨！~ ***does it!*** 别急！***go ~*** 别急。***Stand at ~!*** 【军】稍息！***take things ~ = take it ~*** 从容不迫，别急。— *n.* ①[口语]暂时的休息，(桨手的)歇气。②[美口]易受欺骗的人，老好人。*without an ~* 不停地。***take an ~*** 歇一口气。~**-going** *a.* ①逍遥自在的，悠闲的。②懒散的；不严肃的。③(马)步子慢的。~ **meat** [英俚] 容易办的事。~ **mark** [美口] (容易受骗的)老好人，傻瓜，糊涂虫。②容易达到的目标。~ **money [dollars]** [美]①来得容易的钱。②松动的银根；低利资金。~**-payment system,** ~**-purchase system** 分期付款购货法。

eat [iːt] *vt.* *(**ate** [et, eit]; **eat·en** [ˈiːtn])* ①吃；喝(汤)。②蛀；腐蚀；消磨。~ *one's supper* 吃晚饭。~ *the soup first* 先喝汤。*posts ~en by termites* 被白蚁蛀蚀的柱子。—*vi.* ①吃，吃饭。②吃起来有…的味道；③蛀坏，腐蚀 *(into)*。④[美口]发怒，生气。*be good to ~* 可吃。~ *well* 好吃。*This cake ~s crisp [short].* 这点心吃起来酥脆。*It ~s like fish.* 吃起来味道象鱼。~ ***away*** 侵蚀，蚕食；继续吃下去。~ ***in [into]*** 蛀坏；腐蚀；消耗(钱财)。~ ***its head off*** [指牛马等]吃得多而又干不了活。~ ***of*** [古]吃。~ ***off*** 咬掉；腐蚀掉。~ ***one's fill*** 吃饱。~ ***one's heart out*** 烦恼，忧虑[常含不必要的意思]；默默伤心。~ ***one's terms [dinners]*** 学法律[在英国学法律的学生必须每学期参加律师公会的聚餐三次以上，才取得律师资格]。~ ***one's words*** 收回前言，俯首认错。~ ***out*** ①出去吃饭。②吃光；侵蚀。~ ***sb. out of house and home*** 把人吃穷。~ ***the wind out of*** 【海】占他船的上风。~ ***out of another's hand*** 听命于某人。~ ***up*** ①吃完；消耗 (~ *up one's savings* 耗尽积蓄)。②[常用被动语态]沉迷于，纠缠于 *(with)* *(be eaten up with pride [debt]* 自满极了[债务缠身])。③很快走完(距离) (*The road seems to be eaten up by him in half an hour.* 他好象半小时就走完了这段路)。***I'll ~ my hat [boots, hands, head] if*** 决不，决无，决非[发誓语]。***Well, don't ~ me!*** [谑] 唷，别那么凶啊！***What's ~ing you?*** [美口]你生什么气？你怎么啦？

eat·a·ble [ˈiːtəbl] *a.* 可食用的，可吃的。—*n.* [*pl.*] 食物，食品。*~s and drinkables* 吃的和喝的。

eat·en [ˈiːtn] eat 的过去分词。

eat·er [ˈiːtə] *n.* ①吃的人(或动物)；②腐蚀物，腐蚀剂。

eat·er·y [ˈiːtəri] *n.* [口] 小餐馆。

eat·ing [ˈiːtiŋ] *n.* ①吃。②食物。*good ~* 好吃的东西。— *a.* ①食用的。②可生吃的。③腐蚀的。~ *cares* 折磨人的心事。~ *apples* 供生吃的苹果 *(opp.* cooking apples*)*。~ **house** 饮食店，小餐馆，食堂。~**-out** 经常上馆子吃饭的习惯

Ea·ton [ˈiːtn] *n.* 伊顿[姓氏]。

eats [iːts] *n.* [*pl.*] [口]食物，饭食。

eau [ou] *n.* *(pl.* ***-x*** [ou]*)* [F.] 水。~ ***de Cologne*** [ˈou

de keˈləun] 科隆香水,花露水. ~ *de Nil* [niː] (象尼罗河水一样的)深绿色. ~ *de vie* [ˈəudvi] 白兰地酒. ~ *douce* [əu dus] 清水;软水. ~ *dure* [əu dyr] 硬水. ~ *sucrée* [əu syˈkre] 糖水.
eaves [iːvz] *n. pl.* 屋檐. ~**drop** ① *vi.* 偷听. ② *n.* 檐水. ~**dropper** 偷听的人.
EB = eastbound 向东航行的.
E.B. = Encyclopaedia Britannica《大英百科全书》.
ebb [eb] *n.* ①退潮, 落潮 (*opp.* flood; flow). ②衰退, 衰落. ***Every tide has its ebb.*** 〔谚〕凡事有盛必有衰. ***at a low*** ~ 衰败,不振. ***be at [on] the*** ~ (潮)正在退落;减少. ~ ***and flow*** 潮涨退;盛衰;消长. ***go out on the*** ~ (船)趁退潮出海. —*vi.* 退落;衰退,减退. ~ ***away*** 逐渐衰退. ~**tide** 落[低]潮.
Eb·en·e·zer [ˌebiˈniːzə] *n.* 埃比尼泽〔姓氏〕.
EbN, E by N = east by north 东偏北.
E-boat [ˈiːbəut] *n.* 〔英〕(第二次世界大战期间的) 敌方鱼雷快艇(= enemy ¦boat).
eb·on [ˈebən] *a.* 〔诗〕= ebony.
eb·on·ite [ˈebənait] *n.* 硬橡胶,胶木.
eb·on·ize [ˈebənaiz] *vt.* 使成黑檀色;使象乌木(色).
eb·on·y [ˈebəni] *n.* ①【植】乌木,黑檀. ②〔E-〕柿属. —*a.* 乌木制的;黑檀色的,乌黑的.
EbS, E by S = east by south 东偏南.
e·bul·lience, e·bul·liency [iˈbʌljəns, -si] *n.* ①沸腾;起泡. ②(感情等的)奔放. **-lient** [-ljənt] *a.* ①沸腾的. ②热情奔放的.
e·bul·li·om·e·ter [iˌbʌliˈɔmitə] *n.* 沸点测定计.
e·bul·li·o·scope [ˈibʌliəskəup] *n.* 沸点升高测定仪.
e·bul·li·os·co·py [iˌbʌliˈɔskəpi] *n.* 沸点升高测定法.
eb·ul·lism [ˌebəˈlizəm] *n.* 【医】体液起泡症〔由于气压突然减低,导致体内各种液体起泡〕.
eb·ul·li·tion [ˌebəˈliʃən] *n.* 沸腾;鼓泡;(感情等)迸发.
e·bur·na·ted [ˈebəːneitid] *a.* 象象牙一样坚硬结实的.
e·bur·na·tion [ˌebəˈneiʃən, ˌiːbəˈneiʃən] *n.* 【医】象牙质性变.
e·bur·ne·an, e·bur·ne·ous [iˈbəːnjən, iˈbəːnjəs] *a.* ①(颜色)象象牙的. ②用象牙制成的.
E.C. = ① Eastern Central 〔英〕(伦敦)东部中央邮(政)区. ②Established Church【英宗】国教.
ec [ek] *n.* 〔俚〕经济学 (= economics).
ec- *pref.* = ex-.
ECA = Economic Commission for Africa (of UN) (联合国)非洲经济委员会.
ECAFE = Economic Commission for Asia and the Far East (of UN) (联合国)亚洲及远东经济委员会.
é·car·té [eiˈkɑːtei] *n.* 〔F.〕一种两人玩的牌戏.
e·cau·date [iˈkɔːdeit] *a.* 【动】无尾的.
ec·bol·ic [ekˈbɔlik] *n.* 【医】催产药;流产剂.—*a.* 催产的.
ec·ce [ˈekei, ˈeksi] *int.* 〔L.〕看! 看呀! 瞧!
ecce homo [ˈetʃeiˈhəuməu, ˈeksiˈhəuməu] 〔L.〕①瞧! 就是这个人! 〔拉丁文《圣经》上彼拉多把荆冠戴在耶稣头上示众时说的话〕. ②头戴荆冠的耶稣画像.
ec·cen·tric [ikˈsentrik, ek-] *a.* ①【数】不同圆心的 (*opp.* concentric);【天】(轨道)不正圆的;【机】偏心的, 离心的;偏心器的,偏心轮的. ②目的[意思]不同的;(行为)异常的,反常的,偏执的. *an* ~ *person* 怪人. ~ *conduct* 古怪行为. —*n.* ①怪人. ②偏心圆;【机】偏心器,偏心轮;【天】离心圈. ~ **angle**【数】离心角,偏心角. ~ **anamoly**【天】偏近点角. ~**-cal·ly** [-kəli] *ad.*
ec·cen·tric·i·ty [ˌeksenˈtrisiti] *n.* ①反常, 怪癖. ②偏心,不同心,不对中;【数】偏心率;【机】偏心性. ③偏心半径,偏心距,偏心度.
ec·chy·mo·sis [ˌekiˈməusis] *n.* 【医】瘀斑,皮下溢血.
Eccl., Eccles. = Ecclesiastes.
eccl., eccles. = ecclesiastical.
ec·cle·si·a [iˈkliːʒiə] *n.* (*pl.* ***-si·ae*** [-ʒiiː, -ziiː]) ①古代雅典的人民会议. ②【宗】教会会友,会众.
Ec·cle·si·as·tes [iˌkliːziˈæstiːz] *n.* 【圣】《旧约·传道书》.
ec·cle·si·as·tic [iˌkliːziˈæstik] *n.* (基督教的)牧师. —*a.* = ecclesiastical.
ec·cle·si·as·ti·cal [iˌkliːziˈæstikəl] *a.* 基督教会的 (*opp.* secular, lay). ~ **calendar** 教会历. ~ **court** 宗教法庭. **-ly** *ad.* 依照教会法式,教规上.
ec·cle·si·as·ti·cism [iˌkliːziˈæstisizəm] *n.* 教会中心主义;教(会统治)权.
Ec·cle·si·as·ti·cus [iˌkliːziˈæstikəs]【宗】*n.* 《圣经外传》〔或称《外经》,伪经中的一卷,亦作Wisdom of Jesus〕.
ec·cle·si·ol·o·gy [iˌkliːziˈɔlədʒi] *n.* ①教会学. ②教堂建筑学.
ECCM = electronic counter-countermeasures 电子反干扰.
ec·crine [ˈekrin, ˈekrain] *a.* (人体)汗腺分泌的.
ec·cri·nol·o·gy [ˌekriˈnɔlədʒi] *n.* 分泌学.
ec·dem·ic [ekˈdemik] *a.* 【医】外来的.
ec·dys·i·ast [ekˈdiziæst] *n.* 〔谑〕脱衣舞女〔普通叫 striptease r〕.
ec·dy·sis [ˈekdisis] *n.* (*pl.* ***-dy·ses*** [-disiːz]) 【动】(蛇等的)蜕皮,(甲壳类的)脱壳;换羽.
ECE = Economic Commission for Europe (of UN) (联合国)欧洲经济委员会.
e·ce·sis [iˈsiːsis] *n.* 【动,植】定居.
ECG = electrocardiogram 心电图.
ech. = echelon.
ech·e·lette [ˌeʃəˈlet] *n.* 【物】红外光栅.
ech·e·lon [ˈeʃəlɔn] *n.* ①【军】梯队,梯阵;梯列. ②组织系统中的等级,指挥阶层;(负有特殊责任而占据同一等级的) 集团. ③特勤部队. ④【物】阶层光栅. *fly in* ~ 梯队飞行. *a rear* ~ 后方梯队. *in a higher* ~ 在高级指挥阶层. *a maintain* ~ 后勤保养队.— *vt.* 使成梯队. *an army* ~*ed along the road* 沿公路排成梯队的大军. — *vi.* 排成梯队. ~ **fire**【军】梯形炮火. ~ **grating**【物】阶梯光栅. ~ **lens**【光】阶梯透镜.
ech·e·ve·ri·a [ˌetʃiˈveriə, ˌek-] *n.* 【植】拟石莲花属 (*Echeveria*) 植物.
e·chid·na [eˈkidnə] *n.* (*pl.* ***-s, -nae*** [-niː]) 【动】针鼹.
ech·i·nate [ˈekiˌneit, əˈkainit] *a.* 布满刺针的;有刺的;棘皮的〔如豪猪〕(= ~d).
e·chi·no·coc·cus [iˌkainəˈkɔkəs] *n.* 【医】包虫,共尾虫. ~ **cyst** 包虫囊.
e·chi·no·derm [iˈkainəˌdəːm] *n.* (*pl.* ***-ma·ta*** [-mətə]) 【动】棘皮动物.
E·chi·no·der·ma·ta [iˌkainəˈdəːmətə] 〔*pl.*〕*n.* 【动】棘皮动物门.
e·chi·noid [iˈkainɔid, ˈeki-] *a.* 【动】海胆类的,海胆状的. — *n.* 【动】海胆类 (*Echinoidea*) 动物〔如海胆、饼海胆等〕.
Ech·i·noi·de·a [ˌekiˈnɔidiə] *n. pl.* 【动】海胆纲.
echi·nu·late [iˈkinjulit] *a.* 【生】刺毛状的,小棘状的;有刺毛的.
e·chi·nus [iˈkainəs] *n.* (*pl.* ***-ni*** [-nai]) ①【动】刺海胆. ②【建】拇指圆饰.
ech·o [ˈekəu] *n.* (*pl.* ***-es***) ①回声,反响;共鸣,反映. ②重复,摹仿;摹仿者;应声虫. ③【韵】与上句末音押韵的诗句. ④〔E-〕【希神】山林的女神. ⑤(雷达的)回波,反射波. ***find an*** ~ ***in sb.'s heart*** 得人共鸣. ***to the*** ~ 大声, 高声 (*applaud [cheer] to the* ~ 大声喝采). —*vt.* ①使反响. ②模仿, 重复. ③反射 (声音等)响. ~ *sb.'s words* 随声附和. — *vi.* ①发出回声, 共鸣 (*with*). ②重复. ③(桥牌戏中)打出报信牌. ~ **chamber** 回音室〔为制造回音及音响效果而特别设计的房间〕. ~ **sounder** 回音测深器.
e·cho·ic [eˈkəuik] *a.* ①回声的. ②【语】象声的, 拟声的.

ech·o·ism [eˈkəuizəm] *n.* 形声,象声,拟声.

ech·o·la·li·a [ˌekəˈleiliə] *n.* 模仿言语〔尤指精神不正常的一种症候〕. **-la·lic** [-ˈleilik] *a.*

ech·o·lo·cate [ˈekələkeit] *vi., vt.* 【物】用回音测定(方向或距离),回波定(位).

ech·o·lo·ca·tion [ˌekələˈkeiʃən] *n.* 【物】回波定位(法).

echt [ext] *a.* 〔G.〕 纯正的; 实在的; 可靠的.

ecks 〔美〕 = economics.

ECLA = Economic Commission for Latin America (of UN) (联合国)拉丁美洲经济委员会.

é·clair [F. eiklɛə] *n.* 〔F.〕 长圆形夹奶油的糖皮小点心.

é·clair·cisse·ment [F. eiklɛəsismɑ̃] *n.* 〔F.〕 ①说明,解释,澄清,明朗化. ② 〔E-〕 启蒙运动. *come to an ~ with* 得人谅解.

ec·lamp·si·a [iˈklæmpsiə] *n.* 【医】惊厥,子痫.

é·clat [ˈeiklɑː] *n.* 〔F.〕 光彩; 喝彩; 巨大成功; 名誉,光荣. *a diplomatist of great ~* 大名鼎鼎的外交家. *with great ~* 在大声喝彩中; 盛大地.

ec·lec·tic [ekˈlektik] *a.* 【哲】折衷(主义)的. —*n.* 折衷主义者. *the E- School* 折衷(学)派. **-cal·ly** *ad.*

ec·lec·ti·cism [ekˈlektisizəm] *n.* 折衷主义.

e·clipse [iˈklips] *n.* ①【天】食; (天体受到)遮蔽. ②亮光的丧失,漆黑,晦暗; (名声等的)丧失,黯然无光. *an annular ~* 环食. *a lunar ~* 月食. *a partial ~* 偏食. *a solar ~* 日食. *a total ~* 全食. ***in ~*** ①变暗; 失去光彩. ②(鸟)失脱求爱美毛. ***suffer an ~*** 黯然失色. —*vt.* ①(天体)食; 遮蔽(天体)的光. ②使失色; 超越,盖过.

e·clip·tic [iˈkliptik] *n., a.* 【天】黄道(的); 日[月]食(的). *obliquity of the ~* 【天】黄赤交角.

ec·lo·gite [ˈeklədʒait] *n.* 【地】榴辉岩.

ec·logue [ˈeklɔg] *n.* (两牧童对话形式的)牧歌,田园诗.

e·clo·sion [iˈkləuʒən] *n.* 【动】羽化; 孵化.

ECM = ①European Common Market 欧洲共同市场. ②electronic countermeasures 电子干扰.

eco- *pref.* 表示"生态(学)的": *eco*cide.

e·co·cide [ˈekəusaid,ˈiː-] *n.* 生态灭绝.

e·co·cline [ˈekəuklain,ˈiː-] *n.* 【生】生态差型.

ec·o·log·ic [ˌekəuˈlɔdʒik,ˌiː-], **ec·o·log·i·cal** [ˌekəuˈlɔdʒikl,ˌiː-] *a.* 生态学的. **-ly** *ad.*

e·col·o·gy [i(ː)ˈkɔlədʒi] *n.* ①生态学; 个体生态学. ②【社会学】环境适应学, 社会生态学. ③任何均衡的系统[制度等]. **-o·gist** *n.* 生态学家.

econ. = economical; economics; economist; economy.

e·con·o·met·rics [iˌkɔnəˈmetriks] *n. pl.* 〔动词用单数〕计量经济学. **-met·ric** *a.* **-me·tri·cian** [-miˈtriʃən] *n.* 计量经济学家.

e·co·nom·ic [ˌiːkəˈnɔmik,ek-] *a.* ①经济学的; 经济(上)的; 实用的. ②〔罕〕经济的,节俭的. *~ agreement* 经济协定. *~ base* 经济基础. *an ~ blockade* 经济封锁. *~ botany* 实用植物学. *~ circles* 经济界. *~ crisis* 经济危机. *~ geography* 经济地理学. *~ lifelines* 经济命脉. *an ~ policy* 经济政策. *~ principles* 经济原理. *~ sanction* 经济制裁. *~ structure* 经济结构.

e·co·nom·i·cal [ˌiːkəˈnɔmikəl] *a.* ①节俭的,俭约的; 经济的,合算的. ②经济学上的. *an ~ stove* 经济火炉. *be ~ of energy [time]* 节省精力[时间]. **-ly** *ad.*

e·co·nom·ics [ˌiːkəˈnɔmiks, ˌekəˈnɔmiks] *n.* ①经济学. ②(国家的)经济(状况); 经济.

e·con·o·mism [i(ː)ˈkɔnəmizəm] *n.* 经济主义.

e·con·o·mist [i(ː)ˈkɔnəmist] *n.* ①经济学家. ②〔古〕节俭的人.

e·con·o·mis·tic [ˌi(ː)kɔnəˈmistik] *a.* 经济主义的.

e·con·o·mi·za·tion [i(ː)ˌkɔnəmaiˈzeiʃən] *n.* 节约; 节省.

e·con·o·mize [i(ː)ˈkɔnəmaiz] *vt., vi.* 更经济地使用[处理]; 节约,节省.

e·con·o·miz·er [i(ː)ˈkɔnəmaizə] *n.* ①节俭者. ②节约装置. ③【机】废气预热器; 节油器; 省煤器,节热器; 废热锅炉.

e·con·o·my [i(ː)ˈkɔnəmi] *n.* ①经济. ②节约. ③(自然界的)法理,秩序,过程; 组织; 有机体. *domestic ~* 家政(学); 国内经济. *national [rural] ~* 国民[农村]经济. *state-owned ~* 国营经济. *political ~* 政治经济学. *diversified ~* 多种经营. *a man of ~* 节俭的人. *practice [use] ~* 节约,节省. *the ~ of nature* 自然界的秩序. *the ~ of a plant* 植物的机体. *~* **class** 二等舱〔尤指客机舱位〕.

ECOSOC = Economic and Social Council (United Nations) (联合国)经济及社会理事会.

e·co·spe·cies [ˈiːkəuˌspiːʃi(ː)z, ˈekəu-] *n.* 【生】生态种. **-spe·cif·ic** [-spiˈsifik] *a.*

e·co·sphere [ˈiːkəusfiə] *n.* 生态层〔海拔 12,000 英尺以下的空间,在此空间内,人类可不借助于氧气面罩等而自由呼吸〕.

e·co·sys·tem [ˌiːkəuˈsistəm] *n.* 【生】生态系(统).

e·co·tone [ˈiːkəutəun] *n.* 【生】交错群落(区).

e·co·type [ˈiːkəutaip] *n.* 【生】生态型. **-typ·ic** [-ˈtipik] *a.* **-typ·i·cal·ly** *ad.*

é·cra·seur [eikrəˈzəː] *n.* 〔F.〕【医】绞勒器.

ec·ru [ˈeikruː] *n.* 〔F.〕 (生丝等的)淡褐色. —*a.* 未漂白的; 本色的.

ECSC = European Coal and Steel Community 欧洲煤钢联营.

ec·sta·size [ˈekstəsaiz] *vt.* 使狂喜; 使入迷. —*vi.* 狂喜; 入迷.

ec·sta·sy [ˈekstəsi] *n.* 狂喜; 入迷; 销魂; 精神恍惚; (诗人的)忘我的境界. ***be in ecstasies over*** 对…心醉神迷. ***get [go, be thrown] into ecstasies*** 兴奋到极点,狂喜. ***in an ~ of joy [grief]*** 高兴[悲伤]到极点.

ec·stat·ic [eksˈtætik] *a.* 欣喜若狂的; 入迷的,出神的. **-cal·ly** *ad.*

ec·thy·ma [ˈekθimə] *n.* 【医】深脓疱,臁疮.

ecto- *pref.* 表示"外面","外部"等意 (*opp.* endo-; ento-): *ecto*blast, *ecto*derm.

ec·to·blast [ˈektəublæst] *n.* 【生】外胚层.

ec·to·chon·dral [ˌektəuˈkɔndrəl] *a.* 在软骨表面上的.

ec·to·com·men·sal [ˌektəkəuˈmensl] *n.* 【生】外共栖.

ec·to·crine [ˈektəukriːn] *n.* 【生】外分泌.

ec·to·derm [ˈektəudəːm] *n.* ①外胚层. ②外层. **-al, -ic** *a.*

ec·to·gen·e·sis [ˌektəuˈdʒenisis] *n.* 【生】体外发生. **-ge·net·ic** *a.*

ec·tog·e·nous, ec·to·gen·ic [ekˈtɔdʒinəs, ˌektəˈdʒenik] *a.* 【生】外生的.

ec·to·mere [ˈektəumiə] *n.* 外胚层裂球. **-mer·ic** [-ˈmerik, -ˈmiərik] *a.*

-ec·to·my *comb. f.* 表示"割除术","截除术": append*ectomy*, tonsill*ectomy*.

ec·to·par·a·site [ˌektəuˈpærəsait] *n.* 【生】外寄生物. **-a·sitic** [-ˈsitik] *a.*

ec·to·pi·a [ekˈtəupiə] *n.* 【医】出位,异位.

ec·top·ic [ekˈtɔpik] *a.* 【医】异位的. *~* **pregnancy** 子宫外妊.

ec·to·plasm [ˈektəuplæzəm] *n.* 【生】外胚层质,外质 (*opp.* endoplasm).

ec·to·proct [ˈektəuprɔkt] *n.* 【动】外肛亚纲 (*Ectoprocta*) 动物. **-an** *a.*

ec·to·sarc [ˈektəusɑːk] *n.* 【生】外质.

ec·to·therm [ˈektəuθəːm] *n.* 【动】冷血动物,变温动物.

ec·to·troph·ic [ˌektəuˈtrɔfik] *a.* 【植】外生的. *~ mycorrhiza* 外(生)菌根.

ec·to·zo·ic [ˈektəuzəuik] *a.* 体外寄生的.

ec·to·zo·on [ˌektəuˈzəuɔn] *n.* (*pl.* ***-zo·a*** [-ˈzəuə]) 【医】体外寄生虫.

ec·type [ˈektaip] *n.* 复制品; 副本.

é·cu [eiˈkjuː] *n.* *(pl.* **-cus** [-ˈkjuː]*)*〔F.〕法国古金币；法国古银币〔尤指 17—18 世纪时流通者〕.

Ec·ua·dor [ˌekwəˈdɔː, ˈekwədɔː] *n.* 厄瓜多尔〔拉丁美洲〕.

Ec·ua·do·ran [ˌekwəˈdɔːrən], **Ec·ua·do·re·an, Ec·ua·do·ri·an** [-riən] *n.* 厄瓜多尔人. —*a.* 厄瓜多尔的；厄瓜多尔人的.

e·cu·men·i·cal [ˌiːkju(ː)ˈmenikəl] *a.* ①普遍的，世界范围的. ②全基督教的.

ec·u·men·i·cism [ˌiːkjuˈmenisizəm] *n.* ＝ecumenism.

ec·u·me·nic·i·ty [ˌiːkju(ː)məˈnisiti] *n.* ＝ ecumenism.

ec·u·men·ism [ˈekjuminizəm] *n.* ①泛基督教主义. ②泛宗教主义〔促进各种宗教信仰的人们的合作和谅解〕(＝ ecumenicity). **-men·ist** *n.* 泛基督教〔宗教〕主义者.

E.C.W. ＝ Emergency Conservation Work〔美旧〕自然资源紧急保护事业局.

ec·ze·ma [ˈeksimə, ˈegzi-] *n.*【医】湿疹.

ED, E.D. ＝ electron device 电子器件〔装置〕.

ed. ＝ edited; edition; editor, education, educated.

-ed *suf.* ①用以形成规则动词的过去式及过去分词: call＞call*ed*, coll*ed* [kɔːld], talk ＞ talk*ed* [tɔːkt], mend ＞ mend*ed* [ˈmendid, -əd]. ②附于名词后面形成'…的','有…的'等意义的形容词: wing*ed* 有翼的.

e·da·cious [iˈdeiʃəs] *a.* 贪吃的，食量大的.

e·dac·i·ty [iˈdæsiti] *n.* 贪食；狼吞虎咽.

E·dam [ˈiːdəm] *n.* 伊顿干酪〔荷兰制球形干酪，外涂红腊，又叫 ～ cheese〕.

e·daph·ic [iˈdæfik] *a.*【生态】土壤的. ～ **formation** 土壤群系.

ed·a·phol·o·gy [edəˈfɔlədʒi] *n.* 土壤学.

e·da·phon [ˈedəfɔn] *n.* 土壤微生物(群).

E-day 英国加入欧洲共同市场日.

Ed.B. ＝ Bachelor of Education 教育学士.

Ed.D ＝ Doctor of Education 教育学博士.

E.D.D. ＝ English Dialect Dictionary《英语方言词典》.

Ed·da [ˈedə] *n.* 冰岛古代二文集之一. ***the Elder [Poetic]*** ～ 冰岛古代诗集. ***the Younger [Prose]*** 冰岛古代文集.

Ed·die [ˈedi] *n.* 埃迪〔男子名，Edward 的昵称〕.

Ed·ding·ton [ˈediŋtən] *n.* 埃丁顿〔姓氏〕.

ed·do [ˈedəu] *n.* *(pl.* *～es)*【植】芋.

Ed·dy [ˈedi] *n.* 埃迪〔姓氏〕.

ed·dy [ˈedi] *n.* (水、风尘等的)漩涡，涡流. — *vt., vi.* (使)起旋涡；(使)旋转.

e·del·weiss [ˈeidlvais] *n.*【植】火绒草.

e·de·ma [i(ː)ˈdiːmə] *n.* *(pl.* **-ta** [-tə]*)*【医】水肿，浮肿.

E·den[1] [ˈiːdn] *n.* ①【圣】*(Adam* 及 *Eve* 初住的*)*伊甸园. ②乐园.

E·den[2] [ˈiːdn] *n.* 伊登(艾登)〔姓氏〕. **Antony** ～ 艾登〔1897— ，曾任英国首相〕.

e·den·tate [iːˈdenteit] *a.*【动】无齿的；贫齿类的. —*n.* 贫齿目动物.

e·den·tu·lous [iːˈdentjuləs] *a.*【动】无齿的，无牙的.

Ed·gar [ˈedgə] *n.* 埃德加〔男子名〕.

edge [edʒ] *n.* ①刀口，(刀)刃；锋；端；锐利. ②边，棱，边缘，边界，界线，界限. ③优势，优越条件. ④(声调、议论、欲望的)尖锐，强烈. ⑤〔喻〕〔美俚〕微醉状态. *cutting* ～ 切削刀. *chisel* ～ 凿锋. *the water's* ～ 水边. *gilt* ～*s* (书的)烫金边. ～ *angle* 棱角. ～ *ball*【体】边插球. *a decisive* ～ *in military strength* 军事力量的决定性优势. *His remark has a fine* ～ *of cynicism.* 他的话带着强烈的讽刺. ***at hard*** ～ (练击剑时)用真剑；真刀真枪的〔地〕. ***be on a razor's*** ～ 在锋口上；处境危急. ***do the inside [outside]*** ～【溜冰】用冰刀里〔外〕刃滑. ***give an*** ～ ***to*** ①开(刀等的)刃. ②加强，刺激. ***give the*** ～ ***of one's tongue to*** 痛骂. ***have an*** ～ ***on*** 有点醉 *(He had an* ～ *on from beer.* 他喝了啤酒后微有醉意*)*. ***have an*** ～ ***on [over] sb.*** 〔美〕①怀恨某人. ②胜过某人. ***not to put too fine an*** ～ ***upon it*** 率直地说. ***on*** ～ ①竖着，直放着. ②易怒，紧张不安. ③急切，热望，忍不住 *(to do)*. ***on the*** ～ ***of*** 快要，眼看. ***put to the*** ～ ***of the sword*** 杀死. ***set on*** ～ ①把(书，箱子等)竖起来. ②把…弄锐利. ③使急躁，惹人生气 *(set sb.'s nerves on* ～ 使人心烦意乱. *set sb.'s teeth on* ～ 使人倒牙；使人厌恶*)*. ***take the*** ～ ***off*** ①使钝，挫伤锐气. ②使受挫折；减弱(胃口). ***turn the*** ～ ***of*** 弄钝…的锋芒，减弱…的锐气. —*vt.* ①使(刀、剑)锋利，给(刀等)开刃. ②给…镶边，滚边. ③渐渐移近，挤进 *(in; into)*；挤掉 *(out, off)*；挤过 *(through)*. ④鼓励；催促，促 *(on)*. — *vi.* ①沿边移动，向边缘移动. ②斜进，侧着身子进；渐进. ～ ***along*** 侧着身子移动. ～ ***away [off]*** 偷偷地离开；轻轻走开. ～ ***down upon [in, with]*** 徐徐斜行接近. ～ ***in*** ①插(话等). ②渐渐逼近. ～ ***oneself into*** 挤进，插进. ～ ***out*** ①(小心地)一步一步走出. ②排挤；〔美〕微微胜过. ～ ***out of*** 渐渐由…退出. ～ ***up*** 由边上慢慢靠拢. ～**bone** *n.* (牛的)臀骨. ～ **runner**【机】轮转机；碾子. ～**stone** ①(道路的)边缘石. ②(磨机的)立碾轮. **-less** *a.* 没刀刃的，钝的.

edg·ed [edʒd, ˈedʒəd] *a.* ①有刃的，有边的；锋利的. ②〔美俚〕微醉的. ～ *tool* 有刃之物，利器. *play with* ～ *tool* 玩弄利刃；〔喻〕干危险的事.

edg·er [ˈedʒə] *n.* ①轧边机. ②磨边器. ③【机】弯曲模膛. ④(园林)旋转剪修器.

edge·ways, edge·wise [ˈedʒweiz, -waiz] *ad.* ①刀刃(边缘)朝外(朝前). ②沿边；从旁边. ③边对边地. *put [get] a word in* ～ 插嘴.

Edge·worth [ˈedʒwəːθ] *n.* 埃奇沃斯〔姓氏〕.

edg·i·ly [ˈedʒili] *ad.* ①锋利地，锐利地. ②急躁地，易怒地. ③(绘画等的)轮廓过于分明地.

edg·ing [ˈedʒiŋ] *n.* ①(衣服的)边饰. ②镶边，磨边；修剪(草坪的)边缘. ～ **shears** (园林工人用)修边剪刀.

edg·y [ˈedʒi] *a.* ①锋利的；泼辣的，尖锐的. ②(画)轮廓过于分明的. ③神经紧张的，易激动的，急躁的.

edh [ˈeð] *n.* 古英语和冰岛语中所用的一个记号的名称〔表示 th 所发的舌齿摩擦音 [ð] 和 [θ]. 现代英语以 th 代之〕(＝eth).

ed·i·bil·ity [ˌediˈbiliti] *n.* 可食用性.

ed·i·ble [ˈedibl] *a.* 适合食用的，可以吃的. ～ *oil and fat* 食用油脂. — *n.* 〔*pl.*〕食品. **-ness** *n.*

e·dict [ˈiːdikt] *n.* 布告；命令. *an Imperial (a Royal)* ～ 敕令，诏书. **-al** [iːˈdiktəl] *a.* 布告的；法令的.

Edie [ˈiːdi] *n.* 伊迪〔男子名〕.

ed·i·fi·ca·tion [ˌedifiˈkeiʃən] *n.* 教诲，启发，开导.

ed·i·f·i·ca·to·ry [ˈedifikətəri] *a.* 教导的，教诲的，启发的.

ed·i·fice [ˈedifis] *n.* ①大建筑物，大厦. ②(知识的)体系，结构.

ed·i·fier [ˈedifaiə] *n.* 教导者，启发者.

ed·i·fy [ˈedifai] *vt.* ①训导，教导，启发，使受熏陶〔常作反语用〕. ②〔古〕建筑.

e·dile [ˈiːdail] *n.* 营造官〔古罗马掌管公共建筑物、保安警察等的官吏〕(＝ aedile).

Ed·in·burgh [ˈedinbərə] *n.* 爱丁堡〔英国城市〕.

Ed·i·son [ˈedisn] *n.* ①爱迪生〔姓氏〕. ② **Thomas** ～ 托马斯·爱迪生〔1847—1931，美国发明家〕.

ed·it [ˈedit] *vt.* ①编辑；编排；校订，订正. ②剪辑(影片，录音). ～ *out* (在编辑〔剪辑〕过程中)删除. —*n.* 编辑〔校订〕工作.

edit. ＝ edited; edition; editor.

E·dith [ˈiːdiθ] *n.* 伊迪丝〔女子名〕.

e·di·tion [iˈdiʃən] *n.* 版；版本；〔喻〕翻版. *the first* ～ 初版. *a cheap* ～ 廉价版. *a pocket* ～ 袖珍版. *rare* ～*s* 善本. *a popular* ～ 普及版. *a revised (and enlarged)* ～

修订(增补)版. ～ ***de luxe*** [də luks] 精装版,豪华版. ～ **time** 报纸截稿时间(即印刷开始的时间,亦作 press time).

e·di·tio prin·ceps [iˈdiʃiəu ˈprinseps] 〔L.〕初版,第一版.

ed·i·tor [ˈeditə] *n.* ①编者,编辑;校刊者;校订者. ②影片剪辑装置. ③社论撰写人(=〔美〕editorial writer,〔英〕leader writer). *chief* ～ = ～ *in chief* (*pl. editors in chief*) 总编辑,主编,主笔. *a city* ～ 商业金融栏编辑. *a contributing editor* 特约编辑. *a financial* ～〔美〕经济版编辑. *a managing* ～ 编辑主任,主编.

ed·i·to·ri·al [ˌediˈtɔːriəl] *a.* ①编辑的;编辑上的;主笔的,总编辑的. ②〔美〕社论的. — *n.*〔美〕(期刊的)社论. *an* ～ *article* 社论. *an* ～ *assistant* 编辑助理. *an* ～ *chair* 主笔职位. *an* ～ *office* 编辑室. *the* ～ *staff* 编辑部. *an* ～ *paragraph* [*note*] 短评. *an* ～ *writer*〔美〕社论作者,主笔. ～ **"we"** 编辑及作家用以代替"我"的"我们"(以避免"我"字用得太多或表示代表集体). **-ly** *ad.* ①在编辑上;以主笔身分. ②以社论形式.

ed·i·to·ri·al·ist [ˌediˈtɔːriəlist] *n.* 社论作者.

ed·i·to·ri·al·ize [ˌediˈtɔːriəlaiz] *vt., vi.* (*-iz·ed; -iz·ing*) ①(就某事)发表社论. ②(在报纸等的文章中)加编者按语. **-ali·za·tion** *n.* **-al·iz·er** *n.* 社论[编者按语]撰写者.

ed·i·tor·ship [ˈeditəʃip] *n.* 编辑[主笔]的职位;编辑[校订]工作.

ed·i·tress [ˈeditris] *n.* 女编辑,女校订.

Ed·mund [ˈedmənd] *n.* 埃德蒙〔男子名〕.

Ed·na [ˈednə] *n.* 埃德娜〔女子名〕.

E·do [ˈiːdəu] *n.* ①伊多人〔尼日利亚南部贝宁省人〕. ②伊多语.

E·dom [ˈiːdəm] ①【圣】伊多姆〔即雅各之兄伊索〕. ②伊多姆王国〔西南亚古王国名,在死海与亚喀巴湾之间〕.

E·dom·ite [ˈiːdəˌmait, -it] *n.* 【圣】伊多姆的后裔;伊多姆人. **-it·ish** *a.*

EDP = electronic data processing 电子数据处理.

E.D.S. = English Dialect Society 英语方言学会.

EDT = Eastern Daylight Time〔美〕东部夏季时间.

educ. = educated; education(al).

ed·u·ca·ble [ˈedjukəbl] *a.* 可教育的. **-bil·i·ty** [-ˈbiliti] *n.* 可教育性.

ed·u·cate [ˈedju(ː)keit, -dʒu(ː)-] *vt.* ①教育;教导. ②培养,训练. ③送…上学,为…负担学费. ～ *oneself* 自修. ～ *one's taste in literature* 培养文学兴趣. ～ *one's ear for music* 训练音乐欣赏能力. ***be ～d at [in]*** 在…受教育,在…读书 (*be ～d at a college* 受大学教育). **-ca·tor** *n.* 教师;教育(学)家. **-cat·ed** [ˈedju(ː)keitid] *a.* 受过教育的,有教育的,有训练的 (*opp.* uneducated; illiterate). **-cat·ee** [-ˈkeitiː] *n.* 受教育者,学生.

ed·u·ca·tion [ˌedju(ː)ˈkeiʃən] *n.* ①教育;训导;培养. ②教育学,教授法. ③(蜜蜂、蚕等的)饲养;(动物等的)训练. *elementary* [*secondary, higher*] *education* 初等[中等、高等]教育. *general* ～ 普通教育. *get* [*receive*] *a medical education* 受医学教育. *moral* [*intellectual, physical*] *education* 德[智、体]育. *professional* ～ 专[职]业教育.

ed·u·ca·tion·al [ˌedju(ː)ˈkeiʃənəl] *a.* 教育(上)的,有关教育的. *the* ～ *course* 学历. *an* ～ *worker* 教育工作者. *an* ～ *film* 教育影片. ～ *expenses* 教育费. *an* ～ *undertaking* 教育事业. ～ **park** 教育园〔大城市中为幼儿院至高等学校的学生开设的、公园式布局的教育设施〕. ～ **television** 教育电视. **-ly** *ad.* 教育上,用教育方式. **-(al)ist** [-ʃən(əl)ist] *n.*〔英〕①教师. ②教育学家.

ed·u·ca·tive [ˈedju(ː)kətiv] *a.* 有教育意义的,起教育作用的.

e·duce [i(ː)ˈdjuːs] *vt.* ①引出,唤起. ②推断;演绎. ③【化】离析.

e·du·ci·ble [i(ː)ˈdjuːsibl] *a.* 可引出的;可推断的.

e·duct [ˈiːdʌkt] *n.* ①【化】离析物,提出物,析出物. ②推断.

e·duc·tion [iˈdʌkʃən] *n.* 引出,抽出;推断;【化】离析,析出.

e·duc·tor [iˈdʌktə] *n.* ①喷射器. ②析出物.

e·dul·co·rate [iˈdʌlkəreit] *vt.* 从…中除去酸类等杂质;【化】纯化.

EDVAC = electronic discrete variable automatic computer 电子数据计算机.

Edward (略 **Edw.**) [ˈedwəd] *n.* 爱德华〔男子名;爱称 Ed, Eddie, Eddy, Ned, Neddie, Neddy, Ted, Teddie, Teddy〕.

Edwardian [edˈwɔːdjən] *a.* (英王)爱德华时代的〔在建筑方面,特指爱德华一世、二世、三世;在文学、艺术方面,特指爱德华七世〕. —*n.* 爱德华七世时代(1901—1910)的人.

Ed·wards [ˈedwədz] *n.* 爱德华兹〔姓氏〕.

Ed·win [ˈedwin] *n.* 埃德温〔男子名〕.

Ed·win·a [ˈedwinə] *n.* 埃德温娜〔女子名〕.

EE, E.E. = ① Electrical Engineer 电机工程师. ② Electrical Engineering 电机工程. ③ Early English 早期英语. ④ Envoy Extraordinary 特命公使.

e.e. = errors excepted. 如有错误,可予更正.

'ee [iː] *pro.*〔口〕*ye* (= you) 的简写: *Thank'ee.* 谢谢你.

-ee *suf.*〔作名词的词尾〕①表示"受动者": less*ee* 租户, pay*ee* 收款人. ②表示"动作者": absent*ee* 缺席者, refug*ee* 避难者. ③表示"与人(或物)有关或相似": barg*ee* 驳船船员, goat*ee* 山羊胡子.

EE & MP, E.E. & M.P. = Envoy Extraordinary and Minister Plenipotentiary 特命全权公使.

EEC = European Economic Community 欧洲经济共同体.

EEG = electroencephalography.

eel [iːl] *n.* ①鳝鱼;鳗类;(醋中所生的)小线虫. ②〔美俚〕精明油滑的人. ～ **buck** [**pot**] 捕鳝笼. ～ **grass** *n.* 【植】大叶藻. ～ **spear** *n.* 捕鳝叉. ～ **worm** *n.* 【动】小线虫,鳗蛔虫;线虫类 (Nematode) 动物〔一种植物寄生虫〕.

eel·pout [ˈiːlpaut] *n.* (*pl.* ～, ～*s*) ①锦鳚科 (*Zoarcidae*) 鱼. ②江鳕,淡水鳕 (= burbot).

eel·y [ˈiːli] *a.* 鳝鱼一样的;易滑脱的;油滑的.

e'en [iːn] *n., ad.*〔诗〕= even(ing).

e'er [ɛə] *ad.*〔诗〕= ever.

-eer *suf.* 表示"从事…的人": auction*eer*, election*eer*, mountain*eer*.

ee·rie, ee·ry [ˈiəri] *a.*〔Scot.〕①胆小的,害怕的. ②阴森可怕的,怪诞的. **-r·i·ly** *ad.* **-ri·ness** *n.*

E.E.T.S. = Early English Text Society 早期英语文本研究会.

ef- *pref.* 用于第一字母为 *f-* 的词前, = ex-¹.

eff. = efficiency.

ef·fa·ble [ˈefəbl] *a.*〔古〕可说明[表述]的.

ef·face [iˈfeis] *vt.* ①消去,抹去;抹煞;使消灭. ②忘却;漠视;使失色[相形见绌]. ～ *oneself.* 埋没自己,自卑;隐退. **-able** *a.* **-ment** *n.* **-r** *n.*

ef·fect [iˈfekt] *n.* ①结果. ②效能,效果,效力,效应,作用,功效;影响. ③感触,印象;外观,现象. ④旨趣,意义. ⑤实行,实施. ⑥(布的)花纹. ⑦〔*pl.*〕物品,动产,家财. ⑧〔*pl.*〕〔英〕仿制品. *cause and* ～ 因果. *curative* ～*s* 疗效. *general* ～ 大意,纲领. *household* ～*s* 家产,家具什物. *love of* ～ 爱面子,爱(修饰)外表. *no* ～*s* 无存款. *personal* ～*s* 私人财物;手提行李. *sound* ～*s* 音响效果. *three-dimensional* ～ 立体感. ***be in (full)*** ～ 正在实行[厉行]. ***bring [carry] into [to]*** ～ 实行,实现,贯彻. ***come [go] into*** ～ 开始实施[生效]. ***feel the ～s of*** 痛感…. ***for*** ～ 装门面. ***give ～ to*** 实行,实施. ***have an ～ on [upon]*** 对…有影响[效果]. ***in*** ～ 实际上;

总之;有效,生效. ***of no*** ~ 无效;无益,不中用. ***put into*** ~ 实行. ***take*** ~ 奏效,见效,有效验,应验;生效. ***to no*** ~ = ***without*** ~ 无效.不灵验. ***to the*** ~ ***that*** ... 大意是说…,内容是…(*A telegram to the* ~ *that* ..., 电报大意是说…). ***to this [that, the same]*** ~ 按这种[那种,同样]意思. ***with*** ~ 有效地. —*vt.* ①产生,招致,导致,引起. ②完成,达到,实现(目的等). ~ *a cure* 发挥治疗效果. ~ *an insurance* 参加保险. **-or** *n.* 〔生〕效应器,效应基因.

ef·fec·tive [iˈfektiv] *a.* ①有效(力)的,灵验的;显眼的;〔美〕生效的,被实施的;【军】有战斗力的. ②【经】实质上的,有实价的 (*opp.* potential, nominal). ③【军】精锐的. ~ *horsepower* 【物】有效马力. ~ *range* 有效射程. *an* ~ *shot* 命中(弹). *an* ~ *landing area*【空】安全降落区. *the* ~ *wind* 平均风速. ~ *segregation* 【生】正分离. ~ *coin [money]* 硬币. *the* ~ *strength of an army* 军队的战斗实力 [有生力量]. ***be far from*** ~ 很不得力. ***become*** ~ 〔美〕(法令等)生效. ***take*** ~ ***measures*** 采取有效措施. — *n.* 【军】〔*pl.*〕现役兵额,有生力量;精兵. **-ly** *ad.* ①有效地,有力地. ②实际上. **-ness** *n.* 有效;有力.

ef·fec·tu·al [iˈfektjuəl] *a.* 有效的; 有力的; 灵验的, **-ly** *ad.* **-i·ty** [-ˈæliti] *n.* **-ness** *n.*

ef·fec·tu·ate [iˈfektjueit] *vt.* 使有效,使实现;完成,贯彻. **-a·tion** *n.*

ef·fem·i·na·cy [iˈfeminəsi] *n.* 女人气,柔弱,娇气.

ef·fem·i·nate [iˈfeminit] *a.* 女人似的,女人气的,柔弱的;娇气的. —[-neit] *vt., vi.* (使)带女人气,(使)柔弱. **-ly** *ad.* **-ness** *n.*

ef·fen·di [eˈfendi] *n.* 〔Turk.〕①阁下,先生,老爷〔政府官员的尊称,1935年废止〕. ②(地中海东部各国的)权贵,有产者,学者.

ef·fer·ent [ˈefərənt] *a.* 【生理】输出的,传出的;远心的 (*opp.* afferent). — *n.* 【解】输出管,传出神经. ~ **duct** 输出管. ~ **nerve** 传出神经.

ef·fer·vesce [ˌefəˈves] *vi.* ①冒气泡,起泡沫;泡腾. ②兴奋 (*with*). **-ves·cence, -ves·cen·cy** [-sns, -snsi] *n.*

ef·fer·ves·cent [ˌefəˈvesnt] *a.* ①起泡的,泡沫翻滚的. ②奋发的. ~ **granules**【药】泡腾颗粒剂.

ef·fete [eˈfiːt] *a.* 精力枯竭的;已衰老的;疲惫的,衰弱的;无能的. *an* ~ *system of education* 衰败的教育制度.

ef·fi·ca·cious [ˌefiˈkeiʃəs] *a.* 有效的; (药等)灵验的. **-ly** *ad.* **-ness** *n.*

ef·fi·ca·cy [ˈefikəsi] *n.* 效力,功效.

ef·fi·cien·cy [iˈfiʃənsi] *n.* 功效. ②效率;效能;实力,能力. ③【物】性能. ~ **apartment** 简易公寓〔带小厨房和卫生设备的小套间〕. ~ **curve** 效率曲线. ~ **engineer [expert]** (研究降低成本、提高功效的) 效率技师〔专家〕. ~ **test** 效率试验.

ef·fi·cient [iˈfiʃənt] *a.* ①有效的,有力的;效率高的. ②有实力的;有能力的;有本领的;能胜任的. ~ *cause*【哲】动因. **-ly** *ad.*

Ef·fie [ˈefi] *n.* 埃菲〔女子名, Euphemia 的昵称〕.

ef·fi·gy [ˈefidʒi] *n.* 像,肖像,画像,雕像;模拟像. ***burn [hang] sb. in*** 焚烧〔绞死〕某人的模拟像(以泄愤).

ef·flo·resce [ˌeflɔ(ː)ˈres] *vi.* ①开花. ②【化】风化;粉化;(盐)起霜.

ef·flo·res·cence, ef·flo·res·cen·cy [ˌeflɔ(ː)ˈresns, -si] *n.* ①开花; 开花期; 花穗; (事业等)全盛(期). ②【化】风化;粉化;盐霜. ③【医】疹,皮疹.

ef·flo·res·cent [ˌeflɔːˈresnt] *a.* ①开花的. ②(易)风化的;起霜的. ③【医】发疹的;易发疹的.

ef·flu·ence [ˈefluəns] *n.* ①(液体、光、电、等的)流出;发出,放出. ②流出物,发射物.

ef·flu·ent [ˈefluənt] *a.*流出的,发出的. — *n.* ①流出物,发出物. ②排水渠,侧流. ③〔*pl.*〕废水,污水.

ef·flu·vi·al [eˈfluːviəl] *a.* 恶臭的.

ef·flu·vi·um [eˈfluːviəm] *n.* (*pl.* **-vi·a** [-viə], ~*s*) ①臭气,恶臭;臭液. ②【物】磁素,电素〔想象中磁、电微粒子〕. ③【无】无声放电;(臭气、液体等)散[放]出.

ef·flux [ˈeflʌks] *n.* ①流出,涌出. ②射流;流出量;流出物,【火箭】喷射气流,排出废气. ③时间经过;满期,终了.

ef·fort [ˈefət] *n.* ①努力,尝试,尽力. ②成就,努力的成果;杰作. ③〔英〕(募捐等的)运动. ④【机】作用力. ⑤工作;工作研究计划. *a great oratorical* ~ 动人的演说,雄辩. *literary* ~*s* 文学作品. *mutual co-operation* ~ 共同合作的努力. *That's a pretty good* ~. 那是很大的成绩. *one's maiden* ~ 处女作. *propelling* ~ 推进力. *space* ~ 空间研究计划. *tractive* ~ 牵引力. ***beyond human*** ~ 人力所不及. ***by human*** ~ 用人力. ~***s and resources*** 人力物力. ***make additional*** ~***s*** 再接再励. ***make an*** ~ = ***[make*** ~***s]*** 努力作出 (*to*). ***make every*** ~ 力求,尽一切努力 (*to*);费尽心血. ***redouble one's*** ~***s*** 加倍努力. ***spare no*** ~***s*** 不遗余力. ***with little*** ~ = ***without (any [an])*** ~ 不费力,不难,容易地.

ef·fort·less [ˈefətlis] *a.* ①不努力的,不出力的. ②不费力的,容易的. **-ly** *ad.* **-ness** *n.*

ef·front·er·y [iˈfrʌntəri,ˈef-] *n.* 厚颜无耻. ***have the*** ~ (*to do sth.*) 厚着脸皮,居然.

ef·fulge [eˈfʌldʒ, i-] *vt., vi.* (**-fulg·ed; -fulg·ing**)照耀,(使)发闪光.

ef·ful·gence [eˈfʌldʒəns, i-] *n.* 光辉,灿烂.

ef·ful·gent [eˈfʌldʒənt] *a.* 辉煌的,灿烂的. **-ly** *ad.*

ef·fuse [eˈfjuːz, i-] *vt.* 泻出;喷出;发散出;吐露. — *vi.* 泻出,流出;发出. — *a.* ①【植】疏展的. ②【动】豁开的〔指贝壳的唇边〕.

ef·fu·sion [iˈfjuːʒən, eˈf-] *n.* ①喷发,溢出,流出;渗出物;【医】渗出;【机】泻流. ②显露,流露,吐露(心情等). *an* ~ *of blood* 出血,流血,杀害. ~ *of blood in the brain* 脑溢血. *poetic* ~*s* 诗情奔放. *talk with an* ~ *of heart* 倾吐衷曲. *wild* ~*s of an angry man* 愤怒者的粗暴语言.

ef·fu·sive [iˈfjuːsiv] *a.* ①充溢的,流出的,喷出的,涌出的,射流的. ②吐露心情的,热情洋溢的. *be* ~ *in one's gratitude* 感谢不尽. *an* ~ *man* 热情洋溢的人. ~ **rocks** 【地】喷发岩. **-ly** *ad.* **-ness** *n.*

eft [eft] *n.* 【动】①〔美〕蝾螈. ②〔古〕蜥蜴,水蜥.

EFTA = European Free Trade Association 欧洲自由贸易联盟.

eft·soon [eftˈsuːn] *ad.* ①〔古〕一会儿之后; 立刻. ②〔废〕经常;常常. ③〔废〕又,再 (= eftsoons).

Eg. = ① Egypt; Egyptian. ② Egyptology.

e.g. = 〔L.〕*exempli gratia* 例如 (= for example).

e·gad [iˈgæd] *int.* 〔oh God 的委婉语〕天哪,哎呀!什么!

e·gal·i·tar·i·an [iˌgæliˈtɛəriən] *a.* 平等主义的;平均主义的 (= equalitarian). **-an·ism** *n.* 平等〔平均〕主义 (= equalitarianism).

é·ga·li·té [eigɑːliˈtei] *n.* 〔F.〕平等.

e·gest [iːˈdʒest] *vt.* 【医】排出, 排泄 (*opp.* ingest). **-ive** *a.*

e·ges·ta [iˈdʒestə] *n.* 〔*pl.*〕排泄物;粪便;汗.

e·ges·tion [iːˈdʒestʃən] *n.* 排出,排泄.

egg[1] [eg] *n.* ①蛋,鸡蛋;〔生〕卵,卵细胞;卵形物. ②〔俚〕炸弹,手榴弹;鱼雷. ③〔俚〕人,家伙. ④〔俚〕没有意思的玩笑;拙劣的表演. *fertilized* ~【生】受精卵,孕卵. *raw* ~ 生蛋. *soft-boiled* ~ 半熟蛋. ***a bad*** ~ 〔口〕①坏家伙. ②失败的计划. ***a good*** ~ 好人. ***as full as an*** ~ ***is of meat*** = ***as full of meat as an*** ~ 塞满的;满满的. ***as sure as*** ~***s is*** ~***s*** 确实,无疑. ***break the*** ~***s in sb.'s pocket*** 破坏别人计划. ***bring one's*** ~***s to a bad [wrong] market*** 失算, 失败. ~ ***and anchor [dart, tongue]*** 【建】卵锚相间图案的花饰. ***from the*** ~ ***to the apple*** 自始至终. ***go lay an*** ~

〔美〕别管闲事，滚开. *golden* ~ 厚利. *good* ~*!* 真好; *have [put] all one's* ~*s in one basket* 孤注一掷. *have* ~*s on the spit* 正忙得不可开交. *in the* ~ 未成熟的，尚在初期 (*kill a plot in the* ~ 防患于未然). *lay an* ~ ①生蛋，下蛋. ②(飞机) 扔炸弹. ③〔俚〕(演出等) 失败. *like as two* ~*s* 完全一样. *sit on* ~*s* 抱蛋，孵卵. *teach one's grandmother (how) to suck* ~*s* 班门弄斧. *tread [walk] upon* ~*s* 如履薄冰. *with* ~*s on one's face* 〔美〕受羞辱，处于窘困状态. ~ **apple** = ~**plant.** ~**beater [whisk]** *n.* ①打蛋器. ②〔美俚〕直升飞机. ~ **capsule [case]** 蛋壳. ~ **cell**【生】卵细胞. ~ **coal** 小块煤. ~**cup** *n.* (吃带壳蛋用的) 蛋杯. ~ **dance** 鸡蛋舞〔蒙上眼睛在放有鸡蛋的地上跳舞或头上顶蛋跳舞〕; 非常吃力的事. ~ **flip** = ~**head**〔讽俚〕知识分子. ~**nog(g)** *n.* 蛋酒. ~**plant** 茄子. ~ **roll** 蛋卷. ~**-shaped** *a.* 蛋形的; 易碎的. ~**shell** *n.* 蛋壳; 淡黄色. ~**shell china** 薄瓷器. ~ **tooth** *n.* 〔动〕破卵齿. ~ **tube**【解】卵巢管. ~ **white** 蛋白.

egg² [eg] *vt.* ①鼓动，煽动，怂恿 (on). ②用蛋制作(食物). ③向人扔鸡蛋. ~ ***sb. on to do sth.*** 怂恿某人干某事.

egg·er, egg·ar [ˈegə] *n.* 枯叶蛾科 (*Lasiccampidae*) 动物.

e·gis [ˈiːdʒis] *n.* = aegis.

eg·lan·tine [ˈegləntain] *n.*【植】①多花蔷薇. ②忍冬属的一种.

EGO = eccentrie geophysical observatory 偏心轨道地球物理观测卫星.

eg·o [ˈegəu, ˈiːgəu] *n.* (*pl.* ~*s*) ①【哲】自我. ②〔口〕自负; 自私. *emancipation of* ~ 自我解放. ~ **ideal**【心】自我理想. ~ **psychology** 自我心理学. ~ **trip** 追求个人成就. ~**-trip** *vi.* 表现自我,追求个人成就. ~**-tripper** 追求个人成就者.

eg·o·cen·tric [ˌegəuˈsentrik, ˈiːg-] *a.* 自我中心的; 利己的. — *n.* 自我主义者,以我为中心的人. **-i·ty** [-ˈtrisiti] *n.* 自我中心,利已.

e·go·cen·tri·cal·ly [ˌegəuˈsentrikəli,ˌiːg-] *ad.* 以自我为中心,利己地.

e·go·cen·trism [ˌegəuˈsentrizm,ˌiːg-] *n.* 自我中心; 自私自利.

eg·o·ism [ˈegəuizəm, ˈiːg-] *n.*【哲】自我主义; 利己主义 (*opp.* altruism); 自私,利已心. *departmental* ~ 本位主义. *national* ~民族利已主义.

eg·o·ist [ˈegəuist,ˈiːg-] *n.* 自我本位者; 利己主义者; 自私自利的人. **-tic, -ti·cal** *a.*

eg·o·ma·ni·a [ˌegəuˈmeiniə, ˈiːg-] *n.* 自负[大]狂，自我中心狂. **-ni·ac** [-niæk] *a.*

eg·o·tism [ˈegəutizəm,ˈiːg-] *n.* ①自我主义; 自我中心癖〔满口不离 I 或 me 的习惯〕; 自高自大. ②利己主义,自私自利. **-tist** *n.*

eg·o·tis·tic, -ti·cal [ˈegəˈtistik, -tikəl, ˈiːg-] *a.* ①自我中心的; 自高自大的. ②利己主义的; 自私的. **-ti·cal·ly** *ad.*

eg·o·tize [ˈegəutaiz,ˈiːg-] *vi.* 〔罕〕老是谈论自己; 自负，自私.

e·gre·gious [iˈgriːdʒəs] *a.* ①〔蔑〕无比的; 厉害的; 惊人的. ②〔古〕卓越的,显著的. *an* ~ *ass [fool]* 大傻瓜. **-ly** *ad.* **-ness** *n.* ①非常,极坏. ②〔古〕卓越,显著.

e·gress [ˈiːgres] *n.* ①外出〔退出〕的行为〔权利〕. ②出口，出路. ③【天】终切. — *vi.* 外出. ~ ***and ingress*** 出入.

e·gres·sion [i(ː)ˈgreʃən] *n.* 外出,退出.

e·gret [ˈiːgret, ˈeg-] *n.* ①【鸟】白鹭，鹭鸶. ②白鹭羽毛; 羽毛装饰. ③【植】冠毛.

E·gypt [ˈiːdʒipt] *n.* 埃及〔非洲〕.

E·gyp·tian [iˈdʒipʃən] *a.* ①埃及(人)的. ②〔古〕吉普赛(人) 的. — *n.* ①埃及人; 埃及语. ②〔古〕吉普赛. ***spoil the*** ~***s***【圣】夺取敌人财物.

E·gyp·tol·o·gy [ˌiːdʒipˈtɔlədʒi] *n.* 埃及学.

eh [ei] *int.* 啊? 嗯!〔表示疑问、惊奇、询商等〕: *Wasn't it splendid,* ~*?* 难道不好，嗯?

EHF, ehf = extremely high frequency【无】极高频.

EHP = effective horsepower 有效马力.

Ehr·lich [Germ. ˈeiəlix], **Paul** 爱尔利希〔1854—1915, 德国细菌学家，606 的发明者〕.

e.h.t. = extra-high tension 超高压.

EHV = extra high voltage【电】极高压.

E.I. = East India, East Indies. ①东印度群岛. ②东印度.

-eian *suf.* = -ean.

EIB(W) = Export-Import Bank (Of Washington)〔美〕(华盛顿)进出口银行.

ei·der [ˈaidə] *n.*【鸟】绒鸭,绒鸭的绒毛. ~ **down** 鸭的绒毛; 鸭绒垫. ~ **duck** 绒鸭.

ei·det·ic [aiˈdetik] *a.* (印象)非常鲜明的,(印象)极为逼真的. **-i·cal·ly** *ad.*

ei·do·graph [ˈaidəugrɑːf] *n.* 伸缩画图器,图画缩放仪.

ei·do·lon [aiˈdəulɔn] *n.* (*pl.* ~*s, -la* [-lə]) ①幻象. ②鬼怪.

Eif·fel [ˈaifəl] **Tower** (巴黎)爱斐尔铁塔〔高984 英尺〕.

ei·gen·func·tion [ˈaigənˌfʌŋkʃən] *n.*【数】特征函数，本征函数.

ei·gen·val·ue [ˈaigənvæljuː] *n.*【数】特征值,本征值.

eight [eit] *num.* 八，第八 (页等); 八人，八个 (东西). *E- minus four equals four.* 八减四等于四. *We are* ~. 我们是八个人. ~ *of them* 他们当中的八个人. *the* ~ *of them* 他们八个人. ★注意二者的不同. *Book E-* 第八册. *section* ~ 第八节. — *n.* ①八的记号. ②八人〔物〕一组; (八人的) 赛艇选手. ②8 字形(物);【溜冰】8 字形花样. ③八汽缸发动机,八汽缸汽车. ④八点钟; 八岁; 八号衣服〔鞋袜〕; (纸牌中的)8. ~*-fifteen* 8 点 15 分. *a piece of* ~ (西班牙从前的) 8R (= 8 reals) 银币. ***at*** ~ 在八点钟. ~ ***ball*** ①【美台球】标有 8 字的黑球〔把这球最先打进袋里,就全盘算输〕. ②【无】无定向话筒. ***be behind the*** ~ ***ball***〔美俚〕处境危险〔非常不利〕. ~ ***bells***【海】八击钟〔分别在四时半、八时半及十二时半各击钟一下，其后每半小时递增一击，逢四时、八时及十二时刚好八击〕. ***in*** ~***s*** 用八个音节的诗行. ***have one over the*** ~〔英俚〕醉得七颠八倒. ***the Eights*** 牛津及剑桥两大学的划船比赛. ~**-hour** *a.* 八小时制 (~*-hour(s') day* 一日八小时劳动制. ~*-hour labour* 八小时工作). ~ **pence** 八便士. ~**-penny** *a.* 八便士的.

eight·ball [ˈeitbɔːl] *n.* ①(美撞球戏中)有8 字记号的球〔此球落入袋中即输〕. ②〔美俚〕一种圆形扩音器. ***behind the*** ~〔美俚〕处于不利地位.

eight·een [ˈeiˈtiːn, eiˈt-, ˈeit-] *num.* 十八，十八个. — *n.* 十八岁; 十八的记号; 十九世纪; 十八点钟. ~ *months* 一年半. *in the* ~*-fifties* 在十九世纪的五十年代〔略作 in the 1850's〕.

eight·een·mo [eiˈtiːnməu] *n.*【印】十八开本 (= octodecimo).

eight·eenth [ˈeiˈtiːnθ] *num.* ①第十八，十八号. ②十八分之一的. — *n.* ①第十八. ②十八分之一. ③(每月的)第十八日.

eight·fold [ˈeitfəuld] *a., ad.* 八倍,八重.

eighth [eitθ] *num.* ①第八,八号. ②八分之一的. *five* ~*s* 八分之五. — *n.* 第八个; 八分之一; (每月的)第八日. ~ **note**【乐】八分音符. ~ **rest**【乐】八分休止符. **-ly** *ad.*

eight·i·eth [ˈeitiiθ] *num.* ①第八十. ②八十分之一的. — *n.* ① 第八十个. ②八十分之一.

eight·score [ˈeitˈskɔː] *n.* 一百六十.

eight·some [ˈeitsəm] *n.* 八人跳的苏格兰舞 (= ~ reel).

eight·y [ˈeiti] *num.* 八十,八十个. — *n.* 第八十; 八十的符

号. *the eighties* 八十多岁; 八十年代; 八十到九十的数目. ～-**niner** [-ˈnainə] 〔美〕1889 年开始移入俄克拉何马州的自耕农.
ei·kon [ˈaikɔn] *n.* = icon.
Ei·leen [ˈailiːn] *n.* 艾琳〔女子名〕.
Ein·stein [ˈainstain] *n.* ①爱因斯坦〔姓氏〕. ②**Albert** ～ 爱因斯坦〔1879—1955, 物理学家, 相对论的创立者. 获 1921 年诺贝尔物理奖〕. ～ **theory**【物】相对论. **-i·an** [ainsˈtainiən] *a.* 爱因斯坦(式)的; 相对论的.
ein·stein·i·um [ainˈstainiəm] *n.*【化】锿.
Eir·e [ˈɛərə] *n.* 爱尔兰共和国的旧名称.
ei·re·ni·con [aiˈriːnikɔn] *n.* (宗教斗争中的)和解提议.
Ei·sen·how·er [ˈaizənhauə] *n.* ①艾森豪威尔〔姓氏〕. ②**Dwight** ～ 德怀特·艾森豪威尔〔1890—1969, 美国第 34 任总统〕. ～ **jacket** 男用短茄克〔原系军用茄克衫〕.
eis·tedd·fod [aiˈsteðvɔd] *n.* *(pl. **-fods, -fod·au** [-dai])* 〔威尔斯〕(诗人、音乐家等的)艺术家年会.
ei·ther [ˈaiðə, ˈiːðə] *a.* 两者之一的; (两者之中)随便哪一个的; 两者中任何一方的. *sit on ～ side* 随便坐哪一边. *of ～ sex* 两性双方的. *curtains hanging on ～ side of the window* 挂在窗子两边的帘子. *E- view is correct.* 两种见解都对. ～ **way** 总之; 反正都; 两边都 (*abstain from voting ～ way* 两边的票都不投). **in ～ case** 两种情形都; 反正. — *pron.* 两者中的任何一个. *E- (of them) will do.* (他们)随便那个都行. — *conj.* 〔～ … or …〕或…或…, 不是…就是…, …呢还是…. *E- come in or go out.* 要末进来, 要末出去. *E- you or I must go.* 你跟我总要有一个人去. — *ad.* 〔与否定语连用〕①也(不…). *If you do not go, I shall not ～.* 你不去, 我也不去. *There is no time to lose, ～.* 再说, 这又是刻不容缓的事. ②而且还. *There was once a time, and not so long ago ～.* 有一次, 而且还是不久以前.
ei·ther-or [ˈaiðərˈɔː, ˈiː-] *a.* 非此即彼的, 二者择一的. — *n.* ①(自动控制)"异"; 按位加. ②二者择一.
e·jac·u·late [iˈdʒækjuleit] *vt., vi.* ①突然叫喊, 短促地喊叫着说. ②射出(精液等). **-la·tion** *n.* **-la·tor** *n.* ①突然叫喊者. ②【解】射出肌.
e·jac·u·la·to·ry [iˈdʒækjulətəri] *a.* ①喊叫的, 用喊话方式说的. ②【生理】射精的. ～ **duct** 射精管.
e·ject [iːˈdʒekt] *vt.* ①逐出, 撵出, 驱逐; 革(职), 排斥. ②喷出, 吐出(烟等); 发射, 喷射. ～ **sb. from** 把(某人)赶出…. — *n.*【心】投射; 推断的事物.
e·jec·ta [i(ː)ˈdʒektə] *n.* 〔*pl.*〕喷出物, 废物, 渣.
e·jec·tion [i(ː)ˈdʒekʃən] *n.* ①逐出, 赶出. ②排出, 推出; 喷出, 吐出; 发射, 喷射. ③排出物, 喷出物; 射出物. ～ **seat**【空】弹射座椅.
e·jec·tive [i(ː)ˈdʒektiv] *a.* 排出的, 喷出的; 逐出的.
e·ject·ment [i(ː)ˈdʒektmənt] *n.* ①驱逐; 排出, 喷出. ②【法】收回不动产的诉讼.
e·jec·tor [i(ː)ˈdʒektə] *n.* ①驱逐者. ②排出器[管]; 【机】弹射器, 喷射器; 喷射泵; 【医】射出器; (塑料)推顶器. ～ **pin** 顶杆, 顶销, 退件销. ～ **seat** = ejection seat.
e·ji·do [eˈhiːdəu] *n.* *(pl. **-dos**)* 〔Sp.〕(墨西哥农村的)公社, 村社.
EK = Eastman Kodak Company 〔美〕柯达公司.
eka- *pref.* 表示【化】"准"〔周期表中推定的某元素下一元素的暂用名〕. 例: *eka*-aluminium 准铝〔即现在的 gallium〕. *eka*-element 待寻元素.
eke[1] [iːk] *vt.* 〔古, 方〕①放宽, 放长. ②增补, 补充. ～ **out** 弥补不足; 辛辛苦苦维持(生活); 节省地消费 (*～ out one's salary with odd jobs* 做临时工弥补薪水的不足. *～ out a scanty livelihood* 勉勉强强过日子).
eke[2] [iːk] *ad.* 〔古〕又, 也; 加之.
EKG = electrocardiogram.
e·kis·tic·al [iˈkistikəl] *a.* 城市住区规划学的.
e·kis·ti·cian [iˈkistiʃən] *n.* 城市住区规划学家.
e·kis·tics [iˈkistiks] *n. pl.* 〔动词用单数〕城市住区规划学; 人类环境生态学.
ek·ka [ˈekɑː] *n.* 〔印英〕单坐马车.
el [el] *n.* ①英语字母 L, l. ②〔美口〕高架铁路(= elevated railroad).
e·lab·o·rate [iˈlæbəreit] *vt.* ①认真做; 用心作; 推敲(文章). ②详尽阐述. ～ *a plan for* 为…精心拟订计划. ～ *one's proposals* 阐述自己的建议. — *vi.* 增加细节, 详细说明: ～ *on [upon] a plan* 对计划作详细说明. — [iˈlæbərit] *a.* ①认真的, 精心的, 辛勤的. ②精巧的, 精细的, 精益求精的; 详尽的. **-ly** *ad.* **-ness** *n.* ①苦心经营, 费神. ②认真作出, 详尽发挥. ③精致; 缜密; 精巧.
e·lab·o·ra·tion [iˌlæbəˈreiʃən] *n.* ①认真做; 精练, 推敲. ②精巧; 细致的工作[作品]. ③【生】同化作用〔食物进入体内后, 由简单的物质变为复杂有机化合物的作用〕.
e·lab·o·ra·tive [iˈlæbərətiv] *a.* 认真做的, 精练的, 细致的. ～ **faculty**【心】思考力. **-ly** *ad.*
e·lab·o·ra·tor [iˈlæbəreitə] *n.* ①热心做事的人, 苦心经营的人. ②作详尽说明的人.
elaeo- *comb·f·* 表示"油": *elaeo*meter.
e·lae·om·e·ter [ˌeliˈɔmitə] *n.*【化】油比重计.
el·ae·op·tene [ˌeliˈɔptiːn] *n.*【化】油萜 (= eleoptene).
elaio- *comb. f.* = elaeo-.
e·lai·o·my·cin [iˈleiəmaiːsin] *n.*【药】油霉素, 伊霉素.
elai·o·plast [iˈlaiəplæst] *n.*【植】造油体.
E·lam [ˈiːləm] *n.* 伊拉姆古国〔古代巴比伦以东的一个古王国〕.
E·lam·ite [ˈiːləmait] *n.* ①伊拉姆古国人. ②伊拉姆语. — *a.* 伊拉姆的; 伊拉姆人的; 伊拉姆语的.
E·lam·it·ic [ˌiːləˈmitik] = Elamite.
é·lan [eiˈlɑ̃] *n.* 〔F.〕跃进; 冲动, 奔放. ～ ***vi·tal*** [viˈtɑl]【哲】生命的活力论.
e·land [ˈiːlənd] *n.*【动】(南非)大羚羊.
el·a·pid [ˈeləpid] *n.* 眼镜蛇科的蛇.
el·a·pine [ˈeləpain] *a.* 眼镜蛇科的〔包括眼镜蛇; 小尾眼镜蛇等〕.
e·lapse [iˈlæps] *vi.* (时间)经过, 消失. *Three years have ～d.* 已经过去三年了. — *n.* (时间的)消逝.
e·las·mo·branch [iˈlæzməˌbræŋk, -ˈlæs-] *a.*【动】软骨鱼类(纲)的. — *n.* 软骨鱼类动物〔如鲨鱼、鳐鱼、鹞鱼等〕.
e·las·tic [iˈlæstik] *a.* ①有弹力[弹性]的. ②伸缩自如的, 灵活的. ③机变的, 轻快的. *an ～ body* 弹性体. *～ braces* 松紧吊裤带. *～ force* 弹力. *an ～ principle* 灵活性的原则. *～ ribbon* 松紧带. *an ～ temperament* 开朗的性格. — *n.* 橡皮线, 松紧带, 橡皮圈. ～ **deformation**【物】弹性变形. ～ **sides** (紧口靴) 两边的松紧布; (两边有松紧布的)紧口靴. ～ **side(d)** *a.* 两边有松紧布的 (*～ side(d) boots* 紧口靴). ～ **tissue**【解】弹性(纤维)组织. **-al·ly** *ad.*
e·las·tic·i·ty [ˌelæsˈtisiti] *n.* ①弹力, 弹性; 伸缩力, 伸缩性, 灵活性. ②开朗的性情.
e·las·ti·cize [iˈlæstisaiz] *vt.* *(**-ciz·ed; -ciz·ing**)* 使弹性化.
e·las·ti·cized [iˈlæstisaizd] *a.* 用弹性线制成的.
e·las·tin [iˈlæstin] *n.*【生化】弹性硬蛋白.
e·las·ti·vi·ty [ˌelæsˈtiviti] *n.*【物】倒电容系数, 倒介电常数. **electric** ～ 介电常数的倒数.
e·las·to·mer [iˈlæstəmə] *n.* ①弹性体; 弹料. ②合成[人造]橡胶.
e·las·to·plast [iːˈlæstəplæst] *n.* ①【化】弹性塑料. ②弹性粘膏. **-ic** *n., a.* 弹性塑料(的).
e·late [iˈleit] *a.* 〔古〕= elated. — *vt.* 使得意, 鼓舞. ***be ～d at [by, with]*** 因…而得意洋洋.
e·lat·ed [iˈleitid] *a.* 欢欣鼓舞的, 兴高采烈的, 得意洋洋

的. *an* ~ *look* 得意的样子. **-ly** *ad.* **-ness** *n.*
el·a·ter [ˈelətə] *n.* ①【植】弹丝. ②【动】叩头虫(= elaterid).
e·lat·er·id [iˈlætərid] *n.* 叩头虫(= click beetle). — *a.* 叩头虫科的.
e·lat·er·in [iˈlætərin] *n.* 【化】喷瓜素.
e·lat·er·ite [iˈlætərait] *n.* 弹性沥青.
el·a·te·ri·um [ˌeləˈtiəriəm] *n.* 西洋苦瓜素, 喷瓜汁〔泻药或利尿药〕.
e·la·tion [iˈleiʃən] *n.* 兴高采烈, 振奋; 得意洋洋. ***with great*** ~ 怀着非常振奋的心情.
El·ba·san [ˌelbɑːˈsɑːn] *n.* 爱尔巴桑〔阿尔巴尼亚城市〕.
El·be [elb] *n.* 〔the ~〕易北河〔欧洲〕.
El·bert [ˈelbət] *n.* 埃尔伯特〔男子名, Albert 的异体〕.
el·bow [ˈelbəu] *n.* ①肘; 肘状物. ②(海岸线的)急弯, 曲折. ③(椅子的)扶手; 弯头; 【建】肘形管, 弯管, 弯头. ***at one's [the]*** ~ 在附近, 在左右. ***bend [crook, lift] one's*** ~ 喝酒太多. ***More [All] power to your*** ~! 祝你健康〔成功〕! ***out at (the)*** ~***s*** (上衣)露出肘部, 衣衫褴褛; 捉襟见肘, 穷困. ***rub [touch]*** ~***s with*** 与(人)交往. ***shake the*** ~***s*** 掷骰子, 赌博. ***up to the*** ~***s in*** 忙着, 埋头, 专心 (*We are up to the* ~*s in work.* 我们正埋头工作). — *vt., vi.* 用肘推; 挤进. ~ ***off [out]*** 推开〔推出〕. ~ ***one's way through (a crowd)*** 从人丛中挤过去. ~**-bending** *a.* 〔美俚〕酗酒的. ~ **board** 窗台(板). ~**chair** 扶手椅 (= armchair). ~ **grease** 〔口〕使劲擦拭; 苦干, 重活, 艰苦的工作. ~ **joint** 弯管接头. ~**room** 活动余地, 行动自由, 自由行动的机会. ~ **pipe** 【机】弯头. ~ **union** 【机】弯头套管. **-y** *a.* 用肘推的.
el·chee, el·chi [ˈeltʃi] *n.* (波斯与土耳其的)大使, 使节.
el·co·sis [elˈkəusis] *n.* 【医】溃疡.
eld [eld] *n.* 〔古、诗〕①从前, 古代. ②老年, 高龄.
eld. = eldest.
eld·er[1] [ˈeldə] *a.* 〔old 的比较级, 但不能与 than 并用〕①年长的; 资格老的. ②从前的. ③优先的. *one's* ~ *brother [sister]* 哥哥〔姊姊〕. — *n.* ①年长者; 长辈; 族长; 前人, 祖先; (教会的)长老. ~ *statesman* ①政界元老, 社会上有影响的人物. ②(日本史上天皇的)元老参事团参事. ~ *times* 古时侯. ~ *title* 优先权. ~ **care** *n.* 对穷苦老人的医疗照顾.
eld·er[2] [ˈeldə] *n.* 【植】接骨木.
el·der·ber·ry [ˈeldəˌberi] *n.* (*pl.* ***-ries***) ①接骨木属植物, 接骨木 (= elder). ②接骨木属植物之果.
eld·er·ly [ˈeldəli] *a.* 较老的, 年长的.
eld·er·ship [ˈeldəʃip] *n.* 长辈; 【宗】长老的职位.
eld·est [ˈeldist] *a.* 〔old 的最高级〕最年长的, 最老的, 领头的. ~ *daughter [son]* 长女〔子〕.
ELDO = European Launcher Development Organization 欧洲发射工具发展组织.
El·don [ˈeldən] *n.* 埃尔登〔姓氏, 男子名〕.
El Do·ra·do, El·do·ra·do [ˌel dəˈrɑːdəu] 〔Sp.〕(旧时西班牙征服者想象中的南美洲)黄金国; 〔喻〕宝山, 富庶之乡.
el·dritch [ˈeldritʃ] *a.* 〔Scot.〕怪异的; 可怕的; 有鬼怪出没的.
El·ea·nor [ˈelinə] *n.* 埃莉诺〔女子名〕.
El·e·at·ic [ˌeliˈætik] *a.* 伊利亚学派的〔公元前五、六世纪伊利亚的古希腊哲学流派〕. **-at·i·cism** *n.*
el·e·cam·pane [ˌelikæmˈpein] *n.* 【植】土木香; 用土木香根做香料作成的糖果.
elect. = electric; electrical; electrician; electricity.
e·lect [iˈlekt] *vt.* ①推选; 选(举)某人任某职. ②作出(…的)选择; 决定. ~ *sb. to the presidency [to be president]* 选某人当总统. ~ *to be a doctor* 决定当医生. — *vi.* ①进行(投票)选举. ②作出选择. ***be*** ~***ed*** 当选. ***the*** ~***ed*** 被选人; 当选人. ***the right to*** ~ ***and stand for election*** 选举权和被选举权. — *a.* 被选定的; 当选的; 当选而尚未就任的〔一般用于所修饰的名词之后〕. *the Mayor*-~ 当选市长. *the bride* ~ 被选中的未婚妻. — *n.* 〔the ~〕①当选人, 被选定的人. ②特权集团; 〔宗〕上帝的选民.
e·lec·tion [iˈlekʃən] *n.* ①选择. ②选举, 选出, 当选. ③选举权(利). ④【神】神的选择. *carry an* ~ 当选. *an* ~ *address* 竞选演说. *an* ~ *campaign* 竞选运动. *a general* ~ 普选, 大选. *a special* ~ 〔美〕补选〔在英国作 by-~〕. ***stand for*** ~ 做候选人. **E-Day** 美国总统及国会议员选举日. **E-Year** (美国总统)选举年.
e·lec·tion·eer [iˌlekʃəˈniə] *vi.* 为选举奔走, 进行竞选活动. — *n.* 〔英〕= **-er** 竞选的人. **-ing** *n.* 竞选活动.
e·lec·tive [iˈlektiv] *a.* ①选举的, 由选举产生的; 有选举权的. ②〔美〕随意选择的 (*opp.* required); 【化】有选择的. — *n.* 〔美〕选修课程. ~ **affinity** 【化】有择亲和势. ~ **course** 选修课程. ~ **culture** 选择培养. ~ **franchise** 选举权. ~ **system** (学校的)选课制度. **-ly** *ad.* **-ness** *n.*
e·lec·tor [iˈlektə] *n.* 选举人; 〔美〕总统选举团成员; 〔E-〕【史】选帝侯.
e·lec·to·ral [iˈlektərəl] *a.* ①选举的; 选举人的. ②【史】〔E-〕选帝侯的. ~ **college** 〔美〕(由各州所选出的)总统选举团. ~ **district** 选区.
e·lec·tor·ate [iˈlektərit] *n.* ①选民(全体). ②选举区. ③【史】选帝侯的爵位〔领土〕.
electr. = electric(al); electricity.
E·lec·tra [iˈlektrə] *n.* ①【希神】厄勒克特拉〔阿加麦农 (Agamemnon) 的女儿, 曾在 Troy 战争中率领希腊军队〕. ②女子名. ~ **complex** *n.* 【心】恋父(厌母)情结.
e·lec·tress [iˈlektris] *n.* ①女选举人. ②【史】选帝侯的夫人.
e·lec·tric [iˈlektrik] *a.* ①电的; 带电的; 起电的, 导电的, 发电的, 电动的. ②令人激动的, 紧张的, 惊人的. ③〔美口〕(乐曲等)用电吉他演奏的. ~ *eloquence* 惊人的口才. ~ *performance* 惊人的表演. *an* ~ *atmosphere* 紧张的气氛. — *n.* 〔口〕①带电物体. ②电动车辆. ~ **accumulator** 蓄电池. ~ **appliances** 电气设备. ~ **arc** 电弧. ~ **beacon** 灯光信标. ~ **bell** 电铃. ~ **blanket** 电(热床)毯. ~ **blue** 电光蓝色, 铁蓝色. ~ **bulb** 电灯泡. ~ **capacity** = electrical capacity. ~ **car** 电车. ~ **cell** 电池. ~ **chair** 死刑电椅. ~ **charge** 电荷. ~ **circuit** 电路. ~ **clock** 电钟. ~ **current** 电流. ~ **eel** 【动】电鳗. ~ **energy** 电能. ~ **engineering** 电机工程. ~ **eye** 光电池; 电眼. ~ **fan** 电风扇. ~ **field** 电场. ~ **furnace** 电炉. ~ **generator** 发电机. ~ **guitar** 【乐】电吉他. ~ **heater** 电热器; 电炉. ~ **iron** 电熨斗; 电烙铁. ~ **lamp** 电灯(泡). ~ **light** 电光〔注意, an ~ light 为"电灯"〕. ~ **locomotive** 电力机车. ~ **mains** 输电干线. ~ **motor** 电动机. ~ **organ** 电琴. ~ **outlet** 电源插座. ~ **potential** 电位(势). ~ **power** 电力. ~ **power house [station]** 发电厂. ~ **railway** 电气铁路. ~ **shock** 电震. ~ **torch** 电筒. ~ **tramway** 有轨电车. ~ **wave** 电波. ~ **welding** 电焊. ~ **wire** 电线.
e·lec·tri·cal [iˈlektrikəl] *a.* ①电力的, 电动的, 发电的; 电气科学的. ②令人激动的, 紧张的, 惊人的. ~ **artifice** 〔英军〕电气工匠兵. ~ **capacity** 电容. ~ **condenser** 电容器. ~ **engineer** 电机工程师. ~ **engineering** 电机工程. ~ **transcription** 广播用唱片; 录音广播. ~ **image transmission** 传真(照片). **-ly** *ad.* **-ness** *n.*
e·lec·tri·cian [ilekˈtriʃən] *n.* 电工; 电气技师; 电学家.
e·lec·tric·i·ty [ilekˈtrisiti] *n.* ①电, 电学; ②电流, 静电, 电荷. ③热心, 强烈, 紧张, 高涨的情绪. *negative* ~ 负〔阴〕电. *positive* ~ 正〔阳〕电. *a machine run by* ~ 电动机器.

e·lec·tri·fi·ca·tion [iˌlektrifiˈkeiʃən] *n.* ①起电；充电．②带电．③电气化．

e·lec·tri·fi·er [iˈlektrifaiə] *n.*【电】起电器．

e·lec·tri·fy [iˈlektrifai] *vt.* ①使起电，使通电；使充电；使电气化．②使触电．③使震惊，使兴奋，使激动．*an electrified body* 带电体．～ *an audience* 使观众震动．

e·lec·trize [iˈlektraiz] *vt.* = electrify. **e·lec·tri·za·tion** [-ˈzeiʃən] *n.*

e·lec·tro [iˈlektrəu] *n.* *(pl.* *～s)*〔口〕= electroplate, electrotype.

e·lec·tro- [iˈlektrəu] *comb. f.* 表示"电"，"电的"，"用电的"：*electro*analysis, *electro*form.

e·lec·tro·a·cous·tic, e·lectro·a·cous·ti·cal [iˈlektrəuəˈkuːstik, -əl] *a.*【电】电声的；电声学的．*an* ～ *system* 电声系统． **-cal·ly** *ad.*

e·lec·tro·a·cous·tics [iˈlektrəuəˈkuːstiks] *n.* *pl.*〔用作单数〕电声学．

e·lec·tro·af·fin·i·ty [iˌlektrəuəˈfiniti]【化】电亲和势．

e·lec·tro·a·nal·y·sis [iˌlektrəuəˈnælisis]【化】电解分析． **-lyt·i·cal** [-litikəl] *a.*

e·lectro·bal·li·s·tic [iˈlektrəubəlistik] *a.* 电弹道学的． **-cal·ly** *ad.*

e·lec·tro·bal·lis·tics [iˈlektrəubəlistiks] *n.* *pl.*〔用作单数〕电弹道学．

e·lec·tro·bath [iˈlektrəubaːθ] *n.*【化】电镀浴．

e·lec·tro·bi·ol·o·gy [iˌlektrəubaiˈɔlədʒi] *n.* 生物电学．

e·lec·tro·car·di·o·gram [iˌlektrəuˈkaːdaːdiəgræm] *n.*【医】心电图．〔常略作 EKG, E.K.G., ECG〕．

e·lec·tro·car·di·o·graph [iˌlektrəuˈkaːdiəgræf] *n.*【医】心电图描记器．

e·lec·tro·cau·ter·y [iˌlektrəuˈkɔːtəri] *n.*【医】电烙术；电烙器．

e·lec·tro·chem·is·try [iˌlektrəuˈkemistri] *n.* 电化学． **-i·cal** *a.* **-i·cal·ly** *ad.*

e·lec·tro·con·vul·sive [iˈlektrəukənˈvʌlsiv] *a.* 导电痉挛的．～ **therapy** 导电痉挛疗法．

e·lec·tro·cul·ture [iˈlektrəuˌkʌltʃə] *n.* 用电刺激植物的生长．

e·lec·tro·cute [iˈlektrəukjuːt] *vt.* ①把…处电刑．②使触电致死． **e·lec·tro·cu·tion** *n.*

e·lec·trode [iˈlektrəud] *n.* ①电极．②电焊条．*deflecting* ～【无】致偏电极．*focus(s)ing* ～【无】聚焦(电)极．*perforated* ～ 多孔电极． **-less** *a.* 无电极的．

e·lec·tro·de·pos·t [iˌlektrəudiˈpɔzit] *n.* 电解淀解物—*vt.* 电解淀解．

e·lec·tro·di·ag·no·sis [iˌlektrəuˌdaiəgˈnoːsis] *n.* 电诊断(术)．

e·lec·tro·di·al·y·sis [iˌlektrəudaiˈælisis] *n.*【化】电渗析． **-a·lit·ic** [-əlitik] *a.*

e·lec·tro·dy·nam·ic [iˌlektrəudaiˈnæmik] *a.* 电动力学的． **-s** [-ks] *n.* 电动力学．

e·lec·tro·dy·na·mom·e·ter [iˌlektrəuˌdainəˈnɔmitə] *n.* 电动测功计，电功率计；力测电流计．

e·lec·tro·en·ceph·a·lo·gram [iˌlektrəuenˈsefələgræm] *n.*【医】脑电图．

e·lec·tro·en·ceph·a·lo·graph [iˌlektrəuenˈsefələgræf] *n.* 脑电图描记器． **-ic** [-ik] *a.* **-y** [-i] *n.* 脑电图记录．

e·lec·tro·fax [iˌlektrəuˈfæks] *n.* 电子摄影．

e·lec·tro·form [iˈlektrəufɔːm] *vt.* 电铸．

e·lec·tro·gal·van·ize [iˌlektrəuˈgælvənaiz] *vt.* 用锌电镀．

e·lec·tro·graph [iˈlektrəugraːf] *n.* ①【讯】传真电报．②电刻器；电版机．③电图；X 光图象． **-ic** [-ik] *a.* 电图的，传真电报的． **-y** [-i] *n.* ①电版术．②电版法传真．

e·lec·tro·ki·net·ics [iˌlektrəukiˈnetiks] *n.* 电动学．

e·lec·tro·li·er [iˌlektrəuˈliə] *n.* 枝形(吊式)电灯架．

e·lectro·lu·mi·nes·cence [iˌlektrəuˌluːməˈnesəns] *n.*【物】电致发光，场致发光．

e·lec·tro·lyse, e·lec·tro·lyze [iˈlektrəulaiz] *vt.* 电解． **-r** *n.* 电解池，电解槽；电解装置．

e·lec·trol·y·sis [ilekˈtrɔlisis] *n.* ①电解(作用)，电蚀．②【医】用电针除去肿瘤、痣、毛发．

e·lec·tro·lyte [iˈlektrəulait] *n.* 电解质，电离质，电解(溶)液．

e·lec·tro·lyt·ic [iˌlektrəuˈlitik] *a.* 电解的；电解质的．～ **cell** 电解(电)池．～ **dissociation** 电离(作用)．～ **meter** 电解库仑计，电解库仑表．～ **rectifier** 电解(质)整流器．～ **refining** 电解法提纯，电解精炼．

e·lec·tro·mag·net [iˈlektrəuˈmægnit] *n.*【物】电磁体，电磁铁．

e·lec·tro·mag·net·ic [iˈlektrəumægˈnetik] *a.* 电磁的．～ **spectrum** 电磁波频谱．～ **unit** 电磁单位．～ **wave** 电磁波．

e·lec·tro·mag·net·ics [iˈlektrəumægˈnetiks] *n.* *pl.*〔动词用单数．〕电磁学．

e·lec·tro·mag·net·ism [iˈlektrəuˈmægnitizəm] *n.* 电磁；电磁学．

e·l ec·tro·mas·sage [iˌlektrəuˈmæsaːdʒ] *n.*【医】电推拿法，电按摩法．

e·lec·tro·me·chan·i·cal [iˌlektrəumiˈkænikəl] *a.* 电机的；电机学的．

e·lec·tro·me·chan·ics [iˌlektrəumiˈkæniks] *n.* *pl.*〔动词用单数〕*n.* 电机学．

e·lec·tro·mer [iˈlektrəumə] *n.*【物】电子异构体．

e·lec·trom·e·ter [ilekˈtrɔmitə] *n.* 量电表，静电计．*a differential [quadrant]* ～ 差动[象限]静电计．

e·lec·tro·met·ric [iˈlektrəuˈmetrik] *a.* 电测(量)的．～ **titration**【化】电势滴定． **-al** *a.* **-al·ly** *ad.*

e·lec·trom·e·try [ilekˈtrɔmitri] *n.* 电测，量电法，测电术．

e·lec·tro·mo·tive [iˈlektrəuməutive] *a.* 电动的．～ **force** 电动势．～ **series** 电动序．

e·lec·tro·mo·tor [iˌlektrəuˈməutə] *n.* 电动机．

e·lec·tron [iˈlektrɔn] *n.*【物】电子．*the* ～ *beam* 电子束．*the* ～ *theory* 电子(学)说．～ **accelerator** 电子加速器．～ **bomb** 镁壳燃烧弹．～ **camera** 电子摄像机．～ **gun** 电子枪．～ **lens** 电子透镜．～ **metal** (比铝轻的)镁合金．～ **microscope** 电子显微镜．～ **multiplier** 电子倍增器．～ **optics** 电子光学．～ **telescope** 电子望远镜．～ **tube** 电子管．～**-volt** *n.*【物】电子伏(特)．

e·lec·tron·a·tion [iˌlektrəuˈneiʃən] *n.*【化】增电子(作用)．

e·lec·tro·neg·a·tive [iˌlektrəuˈnegətiv] *a.*【物】负电性的，阴电性的．

e·lec·tron·ic [ilekˈtrɔnik] *n.* 电子的，电子操纵的；用电子设备生产的；用电子设备完成的．～ **analog(ue) computer** 电子模拟计算机．～ **brain [calculator, computer]** 电脑电子计算机．～ **charge** 电子荷．～ **control** 电子控制．～**-controlled** *a.* 电子控制的．～ **data processing** 电子数据处理．～ **digital computer** 电子数字计算机．～ **discrete variable automatic computer** 电子数据计算机．～ **engineering** 电子工程学．～ **image storage device** 电子录象设备．～ **intelligence**〔美〕电子情报．～ **media** 电子舆论工具〔指广播、电视〕．～ **music** 电子音乐．～ **numerical integrator and computer**【美军】电子数字积分计算机．～ **organ** 电子琴．～ **video recorder** 电子录象器． **-cal·ly** *ad.*

e·lec·tron·ics [ilekˈtrɔniks] *n.* *pl.*〔用作单数〕电子学．*molecular* ～ 分子电子学．

e·lec·tro·os·mo·sis [ilektrəuɔzˈməusis] *n.*【物】电渗透．

e·lec·trop·a·thy [ilek'trɔpəθi] *n.*【医】电疗学，电疗法．
e·lec·tro·phone [i'lektrəufəun] *n.* 送话器．**-nic** [-nik] *a.* 电响的．
e·lec·tro·pho·re·sis [iˌlektrəufə'risis] *n.* 电泳现象．
e·lec·troph·o·rus [ilek'trɔfərəs] *n.* (*pl.* **-ri** [-rai])【物】起电盘．
e·lec·tro·phys·i·ol·o·gy [iˌlektrəufizi'ɔlədʒi] *n.* 电生理学．
e·lec·tro·plate [iˌlektrəu'pleit] *vt.* 电镀．— *n.* ①电镀物品；镀银餐具．②【印】电铸版．**-ting** [-tiŋ] *n.* 电镀术．
e·lec·tro·po·lar [iˌlektrəu'pəulə] *a.* 电极性的；电极化的．
e·lec·tro·pol·ish [iˌlektrəu'pɔliʃ] *vt.* 电气抛光．
e·lec·tro·pos·i·tive [iˌlektrəu'pɔzitiv] *a.* (*opp.* electronegative) ①【物】正电性的，阳电性的．②【物】盐基性的，金属的．
e·lec·tro·re·fin·ing [iˌlektrəuri'fainiŋ] *n.* 电解提纯；电精炼．
e·lec·tro·psy·chrom·e·ter [iˌlektrəusai'krɔmitə] *n.* 电测湿度计．
e·lec·tro·scope [i'lektrəuskəup] *n.*【物】验电器．
e·lec·tro·sen·si·tive [iˌlektrəu'sensitiv] *a.* 电敏感的．
e·lec·tro·shock [i'lektrəuʃɔk] *n.* ①电休克．②【医】电震疗法，电休克疗法〔治疗精神病〕(= electrotherapy).
e·lec·tro·sol [i'lektrəusɔl] *n.*【化】电溶胶．
e·lec·tro·spin·o·gram [iˌlektrəu'spainəgræm] *n.*【医】脊髓电(流)图．
e·lec·tro·stat·ic(al) [i'lektrəu'stætik(əl)] *a.* 静电的，静电学的．～ **generator** 感应起电机，静电发电机．～ **printing** 静电印刷，静电复印．～ **unit** 静电单位．**-cal·ly** *ad.*
e·lec·tro·stat·ics [i'lektrəu'stætiks] *n. pl.* 〔用作单数〕静电学．
e·lec·tro·stric·tion [iˌlektrəu'strikʃən] *n.*【物】电致收缩．
e·lec·tro·sur·ger·y [iˌlektrəu'sə:dʒəri] *n.*【医】外科透热法．
e·lec·tro·tech·nics [iˌlektrəu'tekniks] *n. pl.* 〔用作单数〕电工技术；电工学．
e·lec·tro·ther·a·py [iˌlektrəu'θerəpi] *n.*【医】电疗法．
e·lec·tro·ther·mal, e·lec·tro·ther·mic [iˌlektrəu'θə:məl, -mik] *a.* 电热的．
e·lec·tro·ther··mics [iˌlektrəu'θə:miks] *n.* 电热学．
e·lec·tro·tim·er [i'lektrəu'taimə] *n.* 定时继电器．
e·lec·trot·o·nus [ilek'trɔtənəs] *n.*【医】电紧张．
e·lec·tro·type [iˌlektrəu'taip] *n.*【印】①电版；电铸版．②电铸术．③电版印刷物．— *vt.* 把…制成电版．— *vi.* 制电版．**-r** *n.* 电版技工．
e·lec·tro·va·lence [iˌlektrəu'veiləns] *n.* 电价．
e·lec·tro·win·ning [iˌlektrəu'winiŋ]【冶】电解冶金法．
e·lec·trum [i'lektrəm] *n.* ①金银合金；镍银．②【矿】银金矿．
e·lec·tu·a·ry [i'lektjuəri] *n.*【药】干药糖剂．
el·ee·mos·y·nar·y [ˌelii:'mɔsinəri] *a.* ①慈善的，施舍的．②受救济的；免费的．*an* ～ *corporation* 慈善团体．— *n.* 受救济的人．
el·e·gance ['eligəns] **-gan·cy** [-si] *n.* ①雅致，风雅，优美，高尚．②〔主 **-cies**〕雅事，优雅的言谈[举动]．
el·e·gant ['eligənt] *a.* 优雅的，雅致的；优美的，高尚的；讲究的．〔口〕极好的，漂亮的，一流的．～ *arts* 高尚的艺术．*an* ～ *vase* 别致的花瓶．*an* ～ *writer* 格调高的作家．**-ly** *ad.*
el·e·gi·ac [ˌeli'dʒaiək], **el·e·gi·a·cal** [i'li:dʒi:æk, -əl] *a.* ①〔希、罗诗〕挽歌的，哀歌的；挽(哀)歌体的．②挽(哀)歌式的．③悲哀的；哀怨的，忧伤的．— *n.* ①挽歌对句．②〔*pl.*〕一连串的对句；排律诗．
el·e·gise ['elidʒaiz] *v.* = elegize.
el·e·gist ['elidʒist] *n.* 挽歌作者．
e·le·git [i'li:dʒit] *n.*【法】(授权原告占有被告的财产直至债务还清的)扣押令．
el·e·gize ['elidʒaiz] *vt.* 作挽歌哀悼．—*vi.* 写哀歌 (*upon*).
el·e·gy ['elidʒi] *n.* 哀歌，挽歌．
e·lek·tron [i'lektrɔn] *n.* = electron.
elem. = element; elementary; elements.
el·e·ment ['elimənt] *n.* ①要素；成分；(构成)部分；分子．②【化】元素；【数】元，素；【机】单元；单体；【无】元件；【植】原种．③【电】电池；电极；电阻丝．④生存环境，活动范围；本行，本领．⑤〔*pl.*〕原理；初步；大纲．⑥〔*pl.*〕自然力；暴风雨．⑦【军】小队，分队．⑧〔*pl.*〕【宗】(圣餐用)面包和葡萄酒．*the four* ～*s* (古希腊哲学家认为组成世界的地、水、火、风)四元素．*discontented* ～*s* 不平分子．*daughter* ～【物】子元素．*control* ～ 控制元件．*the* ～*s of grammer* 语法基础．***in one's*** ～ 在自己活动范围内，如鱼得水．***out of one's*** ～ 在自己活动范围外，不得其所，格格不入．***strife [war] of the*** ～***s*** 暴风雨．
el·e·men·tal [ˌeli'mentl] *a.* ①基本的，本质的；原理的；初步的．②【化】元素的．③自然力的．④强大的，可怕的．～ *forces* 〔古〕自然力．～ *studies* 初步研究．～ *strength* 威力．— *n.* ①(古希腊)四元素的精灵．②〔*pl.*〕基本原理．**-ism** *n.* 自然力崇拜．**-ly** *ad.*
el·e·men·ta·ry [ˌeli'mentəri] *a.* ①初步的，初等的；基本的，根本的，本质的．②自然力的．③单元的，单体的．④【化】元素的．～ *arithmetic* 初等算术．～ *education* 初等教育．～ *knowledge* 基本知识．*an* ～ *school* 小学校．～ **particle**【物】基本粒子，元粒子．～ **species**【生】原种．～ **substances** 元素．**-ri·ly** [-rily; am. ˌelimen'terily] *ad.* **-ri·ness** *n.*
el·e·mi ['elimi] *n.*【化】橄榄树脂，榄香(脂)．
e·len·chus [i'leŋkəs] (*pl.* **-chi** [-kai]) *n.*【逻】反驳论证．*the Socratic* ～ 苏格拉底的问答法．
e·lenc·tic [i'leŋktik] *a.* 反驳论证的．
el·e·op·tene [ˌeli'ɔpti:n] *n.*【化】油萜．
el·e·phant ['elifənt] *n.* ①象．②象牌图画纸〔28×23英寸〕．***a white*** ～ ①(泰国、印度视作神物的)白象．②累赘的珍品，沉重的包袱．***double*** ～ 倍大画图纸〔40×26½ 英寸〕．～ ***dugout***【军】大壕沟，大防空洞．***see the*** ～〔美俚〕开眼界，见世面．～**'s-ear**【植】①秋海棠．②天南星科芋属 (*colocasia*) 植物〔尤指野芋 (*colocasia antiquorum*)〕．～**'s-foot** *n.*【植】蒟蒻．
el·e·phan·ti·a·sis [ˌelifən'taiəsis] *n.*【医】象皮病．
el·e·phan·tine [ˌeli'fæntain] *a.* 象(一样)的；巨大的；笨重的，粗笨的，累赘的．～ *humour* 笨拙的幽默．～ *movements* 迟钝的行动．～ *task* 累赘的任务．
el·eu·ther·o·ma·nia [eˌlju:θərəu'meiniə] *n.* 自由狂．
elev. = elevation.
el·e·vate ['eliveit] *vt.* ①举起，抬高(声音、炮口等)．②提升，提拔．③鼓舞，振起；使(意气)激昂；使(思想等)向上[高尚]．*an elevating gear* (炮)俯仰装置．*an elevating plane [rudder]* 升降翼[舵]．*elevating thoughts* 高尚思想．
el·e·vat·ed ['eliveitid] *a.* ①高的，升高的，提高的．②高尚的，严肃的．③欢欣的，振奋的．④〔口〕有点醉的．— *n.* 〔美口〕= ～ railroad. ～ **railroad**〔美〕高架铁路．～ **train**〔美〕高架(铁路)列车．
el·e·va·tion [ˌeli'veiʃən] *n.* ①高举，高升；【医】挺起，隆肿．②升级；上进，向上．③高尚．④高处，高地；高度，海拔；(枪炮的)仰角，射角；【测】标高．⑤【建】正视图；立视图．
el·e·va·tor ['eliveitə] *n.* ①起重工人．②〔美〕电梯，升降机 (=〔英〕lift)；(飞机的)升降舵；(建筑施工的)起卸机；【医】起子，牙挺．③〔美〕(备有起卸机的)谷仓．

④【解】提肌. *a belt* ~ 【讯】升降带. *a pneumatic* ~ 气压升降机. ~ **operator [man, boy, girl]** 开电梯的人. ~ **shaft** 电梯井.

el·e·va·to·ry [ˈeliveitəri] *a.* 举起的.

e·lev·en [iˈlevən] *num.* ①十一,十一个. ②第十一. —*n.* ①十一;十一个(人、东西). ②十一的记号. ③(足球、板球或曲棍球)球队. ***be in the*** ~ 是球队的队员. ***the E-*** ~【宗】耶稣的十一使徒〔犹大除外〕. **~-plus** *n.* 初中入学前预试〔英国私立学校对11—12岁学生升入初中前的预试,以决定其未来教育是否应为文科或理科〕. ~**fold** *a., ad.* 十一倍的〔地〕.

e·lev·ens(es) [iˈlevnz(iz)] *n.* 〔英口〕(午餐前吃的)茶点.

e·lev·enth [iˈlevənθ] *num.* ①第十一. ②十一分之一的. —*n.* ①第十一. ②十一分之一. ③(每月的)第十一日. ***at the*** ~ ***hour*** 在最后五分钟,刚好来得及,在危急的时候. **-ly** *ad.*

el·e·von [ˈelivɔn] *n.*【空】升降副翼.

ELF, elf = extremely low frequency【无】极低频.

elf [elf] *n.* (*pl. elves*) ①小精灵,小妖精. ②矮子,小东西. ③淘气鬼,小顽皮. ④小兽,小虫. ⑤小人,恶人. ~**bolt** 石镞. **~-fire** 鬼火. ~ **land** 妖窟,魔境. ~ **lock** 乱草蓬式的头发. **~-struck** *a.* 着迷的. **-like** *a.* 顽皮的,淘气的.

elf·in [ˈelfin] *a.* 小精灵的;小精灵一样的. —*n.* = elf.

elf·ish [ˈelfiʃ] *a.* 小精灵一样的;顽皮的,淘气的,恶作剧的. **-ly** *ad.* **-ness** *n.*

El·gar [ˈelgə] *n.* 埃尔加〔姓氏〕.

el·hi [ˈelhai] *a.* 〔美口〕中小学的,从一年级到十二年级的.

E·li·as [iˈlaiəs] *n.* 埃利阿斯〔男子名,爱称 Eliot〕.

e·lic·it [iˈlisit] *vt.* 引出,探出(事实等);诱出(回答等). ~ *information by inquiring* 打听出,问出. ~ *a laugh from somebody* 逗人发笑. ~ *a reply* 诱使别人回答.

e·lic·it·a·tion [iˌlisiˈteiʃən] *n.* 引出,导出,启发. *method of* ~ 启发式.

e·lide [iˈlaid] *vt.* ①削减,删节;不考虑. ②【语音】省略(元音等). ③【法】取消.

el·i·gi·ble [ˈelidʒəbl] *a.* ①有被选举资格的. ②适任的,合格的,适当的. ③〔俚〕适龄的,年龄适当的. ~ *for [to] membership* 可以作会员. —*n.* 合适的人. **el·i·gi·bil·i·ty** [ˌelidʒəˈbiliti] *n.* **-bly** *ad.*

e·lim·i·na·ble [iˈliminəbl] *a.* ①可消除的,可排除的. ②【数】可消去的.

e·lim·i·nant [iˈliminənt] *n.*【数】消元式,(消)结式.

e·lim·i·nate [iˈlimineit] *vt.* ①除去,消灭,逐出,淘汰,排出 (*from*). ②【数】消去. ~ *errors of misprint* 消灭印刷错误. *wastes* ~*d from the body* 体内排出的废物. **e·lim·i·na·tion** *n.* 除去,消除,淘汰,排除(作用);【化】弃置;【数】消去,消元法(~ *matches*【体】预赛,淘汰赛. *waste* ~ 消灭浪费). **e·lim·i·na·tor** 排除者;【电】消除器;【无】电源整流器 (*a battery* ~ 代电池).

e·lim·i·na·tive [iˈlimineitiv] *a.* ①抽出的,排除的,消除的. ②不加考虑的;不受理的;略去的. ③(比赛)淘汰的. ④【数】消去的,相消的. ⑤【生理】排泄的 (= eliminatory).

El·i·nor [ˈelinə] *n.* 埃莉诺〔女子名〕.

ELINT, elint [ˈelint] = electronic intelligence 〔美〕电子情报. *an* ~ *ship.* 电子情报舰.

el·in·var [ˈelinvɑː] *n.*【冶】镍铬恒弹性钢.

Eli·o·t [ˈeljət] *n.* ①埃利奥特〔姓氏〕. ②George ~ 乔治·埃利奥特〔1819—1880,英国女作家〕.

E·lis·a·beth [iˈlizəbəθ] 伊丽莎白〔女子名 = Elizabeth〕.

E·lise [eˈliːz] 埃莉斯〔女子名, Elizabeth 的异体, = Elyse〕.

e·li·sion [iˈliʒən] *n.*【语音】(元音、音节的)省略.

é·lite [eiˈliːt] *n.* 〔F.〕①〔集合词,作复数用〕精华;杰出人物,优秀分子,高贵者. ②精锐部队. ③一种打字机字母尺寸. *the* ~ *of society* 社会名流. ***corp d'*** ~ [ˈkɔːdeiˈliːt] 精锐部队.

e·lit·ism [eiˈliːtizm, iˈliːtizm] *n.* ①杰出人物统治论;对杰出人物统治论的鼓吹. ②高人一等的优越感. **e·lit·ist** *n.* ①杰出人物中的一个. ②杰出人物统治论的鼓吹者. —*a.* 具有高人一等优越感的.

e·lix·ir [iˈliksə] *n.* ①【药】酏剂,甘香酒剂. ②炼金药,长生不老药,灵丹妙药. ~ ***vitae*** [ˈvaitiː] 长生不老药,仙丹 (= ~ *of life*).

Eliz. = Elizabeth; Elizabethan.

E·liz·a·beth [iˈlizəbəθ] *n.* 〔女子名〕伊利莎白.

E·liz·a·be·than [iˌlizəˈbiːθən] *a.* 英国伊丽莎白女王的;伊丽莎白女王时代的. ~ *sonnet* = Shakespearan sonnet. —*n.* 伊丽莎白一世时代的人〔尤指诗人,剧作家,政治家等〕.

elk [elk] *n.* (*pl.* ~*s*, 〔集合词〕~) ①【动】麋,大角鹿 (=〔美〕moose;〔加拿大、北美〕wapiti). ②软鞣粗皮. ~**hound** = Norwegian elkhound.

ell, el [el] *n.* ①L 字母; L 状物;〔美〕(与正房成 L 形的)侧房. ②古尺名〔英 = 45 英寸; Scot. = 37 英寸〕. ***Give him an inch and he'll take an*** ~. 〔谚〕得寸进尺.

El·la [ˈelə] *n.* 埃拉〔女子名, Eleanor 的爱称〕.

El·len [ˈelin] *n.* 埃伦〔女子名, Helen 的异体〕.

El·lick [ˈelik] *n.* 男子名〔Alexander 的爱称〕.

el·lipse [iˈlips] *n.* ①【数】椭圆,椭圆形. ② = ellipsis.

el·lip·sis [iˈlipsis] *n.* (*pl.* **-ses** [-siːz]) ①【语法】省略法. ②【印】省略符号〔—,…,*** 等〕.

el·lip·so·graph [iˈlipsəgrɑːf] *n.*【数】椭圆规.

el·lip·soid [iˈlipsɔid] *n.*【数】椭圆;椭(圆)球. ~ *of stress* 应力椭(圆)面.

el·lip·tic [iˈliptik] *a.* ①椭圆(形)的. ②省略法的;有省略处的. **-ti·cal·ly** *ad.*

el·lip·tic·i·ty [ˌelipˈtisiti] *n.*【数】椭圆状;椭圆率.

El·lis [ˈelis] *n.* 埃利斯〔姓氏,男子名〕.

El·li·son [ˈelisn] *n.* 埃利森〔姓氏〕.

Ells·worth [ˈelzwəːθ] *n.* 埃尔斯沃斯〔姓氏,男子名〕.

elm [elm] *n.*【植】榆,榆木. **-y** *a.* 多榆树的 (~ *bark beetle*【动】荷兰榆皮蝍 (*Scolytus multistriatus*)).

El·mer [ˈelmə] *n.* 埃尔默〔男子名〕.

el·o·cu·te [ˈeləkjuːt] *v., n.* 〔美〕演说.

el·o·cu·tion [ˌeləˈkjuːʃən] *n.* ①雄辩术,演说术. ②朗诵法;发声法. *theatrical* ~ 舞台发声法. **-ar·y** *a.* 演说上的;朗诵上的;发声上的. **-ist** *n.* 雄辩家,演说家,朗诵者;演说术〔发声法〕教师.

e·lo·de·a [iˈləudiə] *n.* 伊乐藻属 (*Elodea*) 植物.

é·loge [F. elɔːʒ] *n.* 〔F.〕悼词(尤指新任法兰西科学院院士对已逝世的前任院士的悼念演说).

E·lo·him [eˈləuhim] *n.* (希伯来圣经中所说的)神,上帝.

E·lo·hist [eˈləuhist] *n.* 称"上帝"为"艾洛辛"的经典作者〔希伯来圣经某些篇章的作者,不称"上帝"为"耶和华",而称"艾洛辛"〕. **El·o·his·tic** [-tik] *a.*

e·loign, e·loin [iˈlɔin] *vt.* ①〔古〕〔~ oneself〕使走掉;退隐. ②带走(财产). ③【法】将(私有财产)转移至管辖区域之外. —*n.*【法】发还抵债物品. **-ment, -in·ment** *n.*

E. long. = east longitude 东经.

e·lon·gate [ˈiːlɔŋgeit] *vt., vi.* 拉长,(使)伸长;(使)延长. —*a.* 延长的;细长的. *an* ~ *leaf* 细长的树叶. **e·lon·ga·tion** [ˌiːlɔŋˈgeiʃən] *n.* ①延长,伸长;延长线;伸张度. ②【天】距角.

e·lope [iˈləup] *vi.* ①(女人)私奔 (*with*). ②逃亡;出走. **-ment** *n.*

el·o·quence [ˈeləkwəns] *n.* ①雄辩;口才,辩才. ②雄辩术;修辞法. *fiery* ~ 激烈的辩论. *a flow of* ~ 滔滔不绝的雄辩. ***Facts speak louder than*** ~. 事实胜于雄辩.

el·o·quent [ˈeləkwənt] *a.* ①雄辩的，善辩的，有口才的，有说服力的。②动人的，富于表情的，眉飞色舞的，意味深长的。**-ly** *ad.*

El·phin·stone [ˈelfinstən] *n.* 埃尔芬斯通〔姓氏〕。

El Sal·va·dor [el ˈsælvədɔː] *n.* 萨尔瓦多〔拉丁美洲〕。

else [els] *a.* 〔常用于疑问代词和不定代词后，起形容词作用，意为 other〕另外的，别的，此外的，其他的。*What* ~? 还有呢？*sb.* ~ 另外一个人。*sb.* ~'*s hat* 另外一个人的帽子。*Who* ~'*s?* = *Whose* ~? 另外什么人的呢？*What* ~ *do you want?* 你还要什么别的吗？*Who* ~ *is coming?* 还有谁来？*Nobody* ~ *knew.* 另外没有人知道。*What* ~ *shall I say?* 我还有什么可说呢？*What* ~ *can it be?* 不然是什么呢？***nothing*** ~ ***than*** 仅有，只是 (*It is nothing* ~ *than a hat.* 这不过是一顶帽子罢了)。★ 不可说 any book else, any city else 等。— *ad.* 〔常用在疑问副词后〕另外，其他(时间、地方、方式)。*When* ~ *will you come again?* 你们什么时候还会来呢？*Where* ~ *might I find this book?* 别的什么地方我能找到这本书呢？*I went to the library and nowhere* ~. 我到图书馆去了，其他什么地方也没去。*How* ~ *can you hope to win?* 用其他方法〔不这样〕你怎么能够希望胜利呢？***or*** ~〔前面加连词 or，构成复合连词，但 or 有时常被略去〕①否则，要不然 (*Make haste, (or)* ~ *you will be late.* 赶快，要不然就晚了)。②〔威胁一定照办，否则…〕不然的话，哼！否则给你个厉害看看！(*Do what I say, or* ~. 一定照我说的办，否则给你个颜色看看！)

else·where [ˈelsˈhweə] *ad.* 在别处，往别处；在另外一处。*You will have to look* ~ *for an answer.* 你一定要到别处去寻求答案。

El·sie [ˈelsi] *n.* 埃尔西〔女子名，Elizabeth 的爱称〕。

ELSS = extravehicular life support system (宇航员的)舱外生命维持系统。

El·ton [ˈeltən] *n.* 埃尔顿〔男子名〕。

el·u·ate [ˈeljuit, ˈeljuwit, -ˌweit] *n.* 【化】洗出液。

e·lu·ci·date [iˈlj uːsideit] *vt.* 阐明，说明，解释。**-a·tion** [-deiʃən] *n.* **-tive, -to·ry** *a.* **-tor** *n.* 阐明者，解释者。

e·lu·cu·bra·tion [iˌluːkəˈbreiʃən] *n.* ①刻苦钻研；苦思冥想。②苦心孤诣之作，苦心的著作。③〔常作 *pl.*〕〔谑〕学究气的作品。

e·lude [iˈlj uːd] *vt.* ①闪避，躲避(危险等)；逃避(追捕等)；避免。②难倒，使不懂。~ *sb.'s grasp* 逃脱，没有被人逮住。~ *the law* 规避法律。*The meaning* ~*s me.* 那个意义我摸不透。

El·ul [ˈelul] *n.* (犹太历)十二月。

e·lu·sion [iˈlj uːʒən] *n.* ①逃避，回避。②搪塞，遁辞。

e·lu·sive[iˈlj uːsiv] *a.* ①闪避的，逃避的。②无从捉摸的，油滑的；容易忘记的。**-ly** *ad.* **-ness** *n.*

e·lu·so·ry [iˈlj uːsəri] *a.* 难以捉摸的，容易逃逸的。

e·lute [iˈlj uːt] *vt.* 【化】洗提。**e·lu·tion** *n.*

e·lu·tri·a·te [iˈlj uːtrieit] *vt.* 【矿】淘洗，淘析，淘选。**e·lu·tri·a·tion** [iˌlj uːtriˈeiʃən] *n.*

e·lu·vi·al [iˈlj uːviəl] *a.* 【地】残积的，淋滤的。

e·lu·vi·ate [iˈlj uːvieit] *vi.* 【地】淋滤。

e·lu·vi·a·tion [iˌlj uːviˈeiʃən] *n.* 淋滤(作用)。

e·lu·vi·um [iˈlj uːviəm] *n.* 【地】残积层。

el·van [ˈelvən] *n.* 【矿】淡英斑岩。

el·ver [ˈelvə] *n.* 小鳗鱼。

elves [elvz] elf 的复数。

elv·ish [ˈelviʃ] *a.* = elfish.

El·y·ot [ˈeljət] *n.* 埃利奥特〔男子名〕。

É·ly·sée [ˌeliˈzei] *n.* 〔F.〕爱丽舍宫〔法国总统府〕。

E·ly·si·an [iˈliziən] *a.* 【希神】福地的；极乐的，天堂的，幸福的。~ ***Fields*** = Elysium. ~ ***joy*** 无上的快乐。

E·ly·si·um [iˈliziəm] *n.* 【希神】福地；理想的乐土。

el·y·troid [ˈelitrɔid] *a.* 【生】似翅鞘的。

el·y·tron [ˈelitrɔn], **el·y·trum** [ˈelitrəm] *n.* (*pl.* **-tra** [-trə]) 【动】鞘翅；膜质鳞，背鳞。

El·ze·vir [ˈelziviə] *n.* ①埃利居维〔荷兰古籍印刷出版家，1592—1680〕。②埃利居维版本〔铅字〕。— *a.* 埃利居维版的。

em[1] [em] *n.* ①字母 M, m. ②【印】全身〔12 点的字母 m〕。③欧美文字排版的字行长度单位。

em[2], **'em** [əm] *pro. pl.* 〔口〕 = them.

EM = enlisted man [men] 〔美〕士兵。

Em. = 【化】emanation; Emily; Emma; Emmanuel.

em- *pref.* ①〔用于 b, m, p 前〕 = en-[1]. ②〔用于 b, m, p, ph 前〕 = en-[2].

EMA = Electronic Missile Acquisition 导弹电子搜索系统。

e·ma·ci·ate [iˈmeiʃieit] *vt.* ①使憔悴，使衰弱，使消瘦。②减少，减弱(内容，效果，魅力等)。— *vi.* 消瘦，衰弱。**-d** *a.* 憔悴的，衰弱的，消瘦的。**-a·tion** [imeisiˈeiʃən] *n.* (因病或营养不良引起的)憔悴，消瘦。

em·a·nant [ˈemənənt] *a.* (气体、光等)发出的，发散的，放射的，流出的 (*from*)。*water* ~ *from the earth* 从地里流出的水。— *n.* 【数】放射式。

em·a·nate [ˈeməneit] *vi.* ①(光，气体等)发出，发散，放射 (*from*)。②起源 (*from*)。*Fragrance* ~*ed from flowers.* 香气从花中发散出来。

em·a·na·tion [ˌeməˈneiʃən] *n.* ①发散，放射。②由…发出的东西〔尤指人的美德、品质、精神力量〕。③【物】放射性元素。

em·a·na·tive [ˈeməneitiv] *a.* 发(散)出的，放射性的，流出的。

e·man·ci·pate [iˈmænsipeit] *vt.* ①解放 (*from*) 〔尤指从法律、政治、道德等的约束中解放〕。②解脱(疑虑、迷信、偏见等)。③【法】使(孩子)脱离父母的管束(获得行动自主权)。

e·man·ci·pat·ed [iˈmænsipeitid] *a.* 被解放的；不为习俗所拘束的，自由的，自主的。

e·man·ci·pa·tion [iˌmænsiˈpeiʃən] *n.* 解放；解脱。*the* ~ *of all mankind.* 全人类的解放。***E- Proclamation*** 【美史】奴隶解放宣言〔1863〕。**-ist** *n.*

e·man·ci·pa·tor [iˈmænsipeitə] *n.* 解放者。

e·man·ci·pa·to·ry [iˈmænsipeitəri] *a.* 解放的。

e·man·ci·pist [iˈmænsipist] *n.* 【澳史】刑满释放犯。

e·mar·gi·nate [iˈmɑːdʒinit, -neit] *a.* (叶子、翅膀等)微缺的，凹缘的。

e·mas·cu·late [iˈmæskjuleit] *vt.* ①给…去势，阉割，使柔弱。②减弱(文章语气等)。— [-lit] *a.* 阉割过的；无男子气的；删削了的。**e·mas·cu·la·tion** [iˌmæskjuˈleiʃən] *n.* **e·mas·cu·la·tive** [iˈmæskjulətiv], **-to·ry** [iˈmæskjuleitəri] *a.*

Emb. = Embassy.

emb. = embarkation.

em·balm [imˈbɑːm] *vt.* ①用防腐药物〔香料等〕保存(尸体)。②使不朽，使不被遗忘。③使充满香气。*fine sentiments* ~*ed in poetry* 保存在诗歌中的美好感情。**-ed** *a.* ①(尸体)被用防腐药物保存的。②充满香气的。③〔美俚〕喝得大醉的。**-ment** *n.*

em·bank [imˈbæŋk] *vt.* 筑堤(围绕，防护)。~ *a river* 筑河堤。**-ment** *n.* ①筑堤。②堤；(铁路等的)路基 (*the (Thames) Embankment* 伦敦泰晤士河河堤)。

em·bar·ca·der·o [emˌbɑːkəˈderəu] *n.* (*pl.* **-der·os**) 〔Sp.〕码头。

em·bar·ca·tion [ˌembɑːˈkeiʃən] *n.* = embarkation.

em·bar·go [emˈbɑːgəu] *vt.* ①封(港)，禁止(船只)出入港口；禁运，停止(通商)。②扣留征用(船只、货物)。— *n.* (*pl.* **-es**) ①禁止出〔入〕港；战时封港令。②禁运(令)，停止通商(令)。③禁止；限制；阻碍。~ *on (the export of) gold* = *gold* ~ 禁止黄金出口。***lay [put, place] an*** ~ ***on*** *(a ship)* 禁止(船只)出入；实行禁运。***lay an*** ~ ***on [upon] free speech*** 限制言论自由。***lift [take off, remove] the*** ~ ***on*** 解禁。***under an*** ~ 在禁运

中。

em·bark [imˈbɑːk] *vi.* ①上飞机，上船 *(on)*. ②从事，开始 *(in; on; upon)*. — *vt.* 载客，装货，搭载；使从事，使着手，投资。～ *in [on] a steamer* 上轮船。～ *for Shanghai* 乘船去上海。～ *in [on] matrimony* 开始过结婚生活。— *vt.* ①载(客)，装(货)；使上船，使上飞机；搭载。②使从事，使着手。③邀(某人)入股，投资于(某企业)。*a ship* ～*ing passengers and cargo* 载客兼装货的船。～ *money in an enterprise* 投资于某企业。**-ka·tion** [-ˈkeiʃən] *n.* ①乘飞机；乘船；装载(物)。②(事业等的)开始，从事。③启程。

em·bark·ment [imˈbɑːkmənt] *n.* = embarkation.

em·bar·ras [ɑ̃ːŋbæˈrɑː] *n.* 〔F.〕障碍；混乱；窘迫。～ ***de choix*** [də ˈʃwɑː]（因太多）难以选择。～ ***de richesse*** [də riˈʃes] 财富[东西]多得成了累赘。

em·bar·rass [imˈbærəs] *vt.* ①使窘迫，使困惑，使为难。②使穷困，使财政困难。③使(事件)发生纠纷，使(问题)复杂化。④使(行动)不便，妨碍，阻碍。*be [feel]* ～*ed in the presence of strangers* 在生人面前局促不安。*The decline of sales* ～*ed the company.* 销路下降使公司陷于财政困难。～**ment** *n.* 窘迫，困惑，为难。

em·bar·rass·ing [imˈbærəsiŋ] *a.* 令人为难的。～ *questions* 窘人的发问。**-ly** *ad.*

em·bas·sa·dor [imˈbæsədə] *n.* 〔古〕= ambassador.

em·bas·sage [ˈembəsidʒ] *n.* embassy（大使馆）的古变体。

em·bas·sy [ˈembəsi] *n.* ①大使馆。②大使的职务[地位]。③重任，差使。④使节；大使及其随员；大使馆全体人员。***go on an*** ～ 去当大使。***send sb. on an*** ～ 派某人出任大使。

em·bat·tle[1] [imˈbætl] *vt.* 〔一般用被动式〕①布阵，列阵，整军备战。②在…筑垒，设防于。

em·bat·tle[2] [imˈbætl] *vt.* 在…造城垛。

em·bat·tled [imˈbætld] *a.* ①摆好阵势的。②有城垛的，有雉堞墙的。

em·bat·tle·ment [imˈbætlmənt] *n.* = battlement.

em·bay [imˈbei] *vt.* ①使(船)入湾；(风)把(船)吹进湾内。②(象海湾那样)环抱，围住。③使成港湾。**-ment** *n.* ①湾，湾形物。②【地】形成港湾。

em·bed [imˈbed] *vt.* 〔一般用被动式〕①栽种。②埋置，嵌进；【医】植入。③深留(记忆中)。*slug embedded in the bone* 嵌进骨中的子弹。*These facts lie embedded in his mind.* 这些事实牢牢印在他的心中。**-ment** *n.*

em·bel·lish [imˈbeliʃ] *vt.* ①装饰，修饰，美化。②添加(故事的)细节；润色(文章)。**-ment** *n.*

em·ber [ˈembə] *n.* 〔*pl.*〕余火，余烬。— *a.*【宗】四季大斋日的。～ *days [week]*【宗】四季大斋日[周]。

em·be·zz·zle [imˈbezl] *vt.* 侵吞；盗用；挪用(代保管的财物等)。～ *public funds* 挪用公款。**-ment** *n.* **-er** *n.* 盗用[侵吞，挪用]者。

em·bit·ter [imˈbitə] *vt.* ①使变苦。②激怒，使怨恨。③加重(痛苦)。*Life is* ～*ed by disappointment.* 失望使得生活更难受。*Hops serve to* ～ *beer.* 酒花的作用是使啤酒发苦。**-ment** *n.*

em·blaze[1] [imˈbleiz] *vt.* 〔古〕①照亮。②点燃。

em·blaze[2] [imˈbleiz] *vt.* 〔废〕= emblazon.

em·bla·zon [imˈbleizən] *vt.* ①以纹章装饰(盾等)；用鲜艳颜色装饰。②颂扬，赞颂。**-ment** *n.* 描画纹章；装饰；颂扬。**-ry** *n.* 纹章描画(法)；纹章〔华美〕装饰。

em·blem [ˈembləm] *n.* ①标志，象征。②纹章，徽章。③标记，典型。〔古〕寓意画。*The olive branch is an* ～ *of peace.* 橄榄枝象征和平。*a state [national]* ～ 国徽。～ *book* 寓意画集。— *vt.* 用图案〔符号〕表示，用象征表示。

em·blem·at·ic [ˌembliˈmætik] *a.* 作为象征的，作为标记的 *(of)*. *Whiteness is* ～ *of purity.* 白色是纯洁的象征。**-cal·ly** *ad.*

em·blem·a·tise *vt.* = emblematize.

em·blem·a·tist [emˈblemətist] *n.* ①徽章制作者[设计者]。②寓言作者。

em·blem·a·tize [emˈblemətaiz] *vt.* 标志，象征。

em·ble·ments [ˈemblmənts] *n.* 〔*pl.*〕【法】庄稼；庄稼收益。

em·bod·i·ment [imˈbɔdimənt] *n.* 具体化，体现；化身，统一体。*an* ～ *of courage [health]* 勇敢[健康]的化身。

em·bod·y [imˈbɔdi] *vt.* ①使具体化，体现；使形象化。②使(精神等)肉体化。③归并。④包含，收录；【军】组编。～ *the feeling of the northland in his music* 在音乐中表现了北国情调。～ *troops in army corps* 把军队编成兵团。*This book embodies the works of many young writer.* 这本书收录了许多青年作家的作品。

em·bog [emˈbɔg] *vt.* 使陷在泥沼中；〔喻〕使陷入困境。

em·bold·en [imˈbəuldən] *vt.* 给…壮胆，使更大胆，鼓励。*His kind manner* ～*ed her to ask for help.* 他的和蔼态度使她大起胆子开口求助。

em·bo·lec·to·my [ˌembəˈlektəmi] *n.*【医】栓子切除术。

em·bol·ic [emˈbɔlik] *a.* ①栓塞的，血栓病的。②内陷的，内褶的；内陷[褶]中的。

em·bol·ism [ˈembəlizəm] *n.* ①(古代历法中的）闰月。②【医】栓塞。**-ic** *a.* (*an* ～ *month [year]* 闰月[年]).

em·bo·lus [ˈembələs] *n.* ***(pl. -li*** (-lai)**)**【医】栓子。

em·bo·ly [ˈembəli] *n.*【胚】内陷，内褶。

em·bon·point [F. ɑ̃bɔ̃ˈpwɛ̃] *n.* 〔F.〕（通常指妇女肥胖的客气话）发福。

em·bos·om [imˈbuzəm] *vt.* ①把…藏于怀内；拥抱；怀抱。②珍爱。③包围；遮掩，环绕。～ *hopes of success* 怀着成功的希望。*a house* ～*ed in trees* 树木围着的房子。*a village* ～*ed with hills* 群山环抱的村庄。

em·boss [imˈbɔs] *vt.* ①用浮雕装饰；在(图案，花样等)作浮雕。②使凸出；(用模子)压花，压纹。～ *the paper with a design* 把图案压在纸上。～ *a pattern on metal* 在金属材料上作出凸花。～*ed cloth* 拷花布，压花布。～ *work* 浮雕细工。**-er** *n.* ①压花技工。②压花机。**-ing** *n.*【工】凸花制法；【纺】浮雕印花，拷花，压花；【建】雕刻突饰。**-ment** *n.* 凸花装饰；浮雕工艺；浮雕花样 (*an embossment map* 立体地图)。

em·bou·chure [ˌɔmbuˈʃuə, ˈɔmbuˌʃuə] *n.* 〔F.〕①河口。②【乐】管乐器的吹口；管乐器吹奏法。

em·bow [emˈbəu] *vt.* 〔古〕把…成弓形，把…弄成弧形。**-ed** *a.* 弯曲的；弧形的。**-ment** *n.*

em·bow·el [imˈbauəl, em-] *vt.* (〔英〕***-ll-***) 从(体内)取出肠子(=disembowel)。

em·bow·er [imˈbauə,em-] *vt.* 用树叶遮蔽；把…隐藏在树林中，(有树)围绕。— *vi.* 〔古〕栖息在亭子[树荫]中。

em·brace[1] [imˈbreis] *vt.* ①拥抱，抱。②包括，包含；包围，环绕。③皈依，信奉。④抓紧(机会)，趁。⑤采用，接受。⑥参加，着手。⑦看出，领悟。*He* ～*ed his son in his arms.* 他把儿子抱在怀里。～ *an opportunity* 利用机会。～ *a good chance* 抓住好机会。～ *soldier's life* 从军。— *vi.* 相抱。— *n.* 拥抱；包围；接受；领会；【动】交尾。

em·brace[2] [imˈbreis] *vt.* 笼络[收买]陪审员。

em·brac·er[1] [imˈbreisə] *n.* 拥抱者。

em·brac·er[2], **em·brace·or** [imˈbreisə] *n.*【法】笼络[收买]陪审员的人。

em·brac·er·y [imˈbreisəri] *n.*【法】笼络[收买]陪审员的行为。

em·branch·ment [imˈbrɑːntʃmənt, -ˈbræntʃ-] *n.* ①分支，支脉；支流。②分支机构。

em·bran·gle [imˈbræŋgl] *vt.* 使纠缠；搞乱；使困惑。**-ment** *n.*

em·bra·sure [imˈbreiʒə] *n.* ①【军】枪眼，炮眼，射击孔。②【建】漏斗状斜面墙。③【医】楔状隙。

em·bro·cate [ˈembrəukeit] *vt.*【医】(以油膏、洗液等)

涂擦.

em•bro•ca•tion [ˌembrəuˈkeiʃən] *n.* ①【医】涂擦. ②涂擦剂.

em•broi•der [imˈbrɔidə] *vt.* ①刺绣,在…上绣花. ②修饰,润色,渲染. — *vi.* 刺绣,绣花. *an ~ing needle* 绣花针. **-er** *n.* 刺绣工. **-ess** *n.* 女刺绣工.

em•broi•dery [imˈbrɔidəri] *n.* ①刺绣,绣花. ②粉饰;修饰,润色. ~ **frame** 绣花架.

em•broil [imˈbrɔil] *vt.* ①使混乱,使纠缠,搅乱. ②牵连,卷入. *be ~ed in a quarrel* 卷入争吵中. **-ment** *n.*

em•brown [imˈbraun, em-] *vt.* 使成褐色,使成棕色;使变深色.

em•bry•ec•to•my [ˌembriˈektəmi] *n.* 【医】胎切除术〔尤指子宫外孕的胎切除术〕.

em•bry•o [ˈembriəu] *n.* *(pl. ~s)* ①【植】胚;【动】胚胎(对人来说,一般指三个月以内的胚胎). ②胚芽(时期),萌芽时期. ***in*** ~ 未发达的,初期的; 萌芽时期的; 在计划中的. — *a.* ①胚胎的,胚的. ②胚芽(时期)的,未发达的, 原始的, 初期的. ~ **grafting** 胚种嫁接. ~ **sac** 【植】胚囊.

em•bry•og•e•ny [ˌembriˈɔdʒini] *n.* 【生】胚形成 (=embryogenesis) **em•bry•o•gen•ic** [-ˈdʒenik], **em•bry•o•ge•net•ic** [-dʒəˈnetik] *a.*

em•bry•oid [ˈembriɔid] *a.* 胚胎(状)的.

em•bry•o•logic [ˌembriəˈlɔdʒik] *a.* 胚胎学的 (= bryological) **-cal•ly** *ad.* **-gist** *n.* 胚胎学家.

em•bry•ol•o•gy [ˌembriˈɔlədʒi] *n.* 胚胎学,发生学.

em•bry•o•nal [ˌembriˈəunəl] *a.* = embryonic.

em•bry•on•ic [ˌembriˈɔnik] *a.* ①胚胞的. ②开始的,初期的,未发达的. ~**layer** 【生】胚层. ~ **membrane** 【解】胚膜. **-al•ly** *ad.*

em•bry•ot•o•my [ˌembriˈɔtəmi] *n.* 【医】(难产时的)胎儿截割术,碎胎术.

em•bus [imˈbʌs] *vt., vi.* 【军】(使)人员[物资等]被载上机动车辆.

em•bus•qué [F. ɑ̃byske] *n.* 〔法〕逃避兵役的人.

em•cee [ˈemˈsiː] *n.* 〔美口〕司仪〔master of ceremonies的首字母 m c 的读音〕,电台节目主持人. — *vt.* 主持(电台节目等). — *vi.* 当司仪.

e•meer [əˈmiə] *n.* = emir. **-ate** [-it] *n.* = emirate.

e•mend [i(ː)ˈmend] *vt.* 校订,订正,改正,校勘,校正. ~ *the text of a book* 校勘某书. ~ *an author* 订正某作者著作. **-able** *a.*

e•men•date [ˈiːmənˌdeit] *vt.* ①校订,改正. ②校勘,校正. **e•men•da•tor** *n.* 校订者,校勘者. **e•mend•a•to•ry** [iˈmendəˌtəri] *a.*

e•men•tionda• [ˌiːmenˈdeiʃən] *n.* ①校订,订正. ②被校订的地方.

EMER = emergency.

em•er•ald [ˈemərəld] *n.* ①【矿】祖母绿,纯绿柱石. ②绿宝石,绿刚玉. ③鲜绿色. ④【印】一种活字〔相当于 $6\frac{1}{2}$ 点〕. — *a.* 祖母绿(制)的;鲜绿(色)的;纯绿宝石制的. ***the Emerald Isle*** 绿宝石岛〔爱尔兰别名〕. ~ **green** 翠绿,巴黎绿.〔图画颜料〕. ~ **nickel** 翠镍矿.

em•er•ald•ine [ˈemərəldain] *a.* 祖母绿一样的, 鲜绿的.

e•merge [iˈməːdʒ] *vi.* ①出现,显露,现出. ②(自困境等中)摆脱;脱颖而出. ③发生,暴露. ~ *from [out of] water* 从水中现出. *The sun ~s from behind the clouds.* 太阳从云里露出. ~ *from difficulties* 摆脱困难. ~ *into a street.* 在街上出现.

e•mer•gence [iˈməːdʒəns] *n.* ①出现,发生. ②【植】突出体;(柑果的)瓤胞. ③【虫】羽化. ④【哲】突创论.

e•mer•gen•cy [iˈməːdʒənsi] *n.* 突然事件;紧急情况,非常时期. *take ~ measures* 采取紧急措施. *be prepared [ready] for all emergencies* 以备万一. *in this ~* 在这个危急时刻. *meet emergencies* 采取应急措施. ***in [on] an ~ = in case of ~*** 在危急时刻,万一发生事变. ***rise to the ~*** 有应变之才,能够应付紧急事变. ~ **act** 紧急法令. ~ **airport** 应急机场. ~ **brake** 紧急刹车. ~ **bridge** 便桥. ~ **call** 紧急召集. ~ **case** 急诊病人. ~ **crops** 救荒作物,短期作物. ~ **door [exit]** 太平门. ~ **fund** 应急基金. ~ **man** 临时雇员;(球队等的)预备员,生力军. ~ **staircase** 安全楼梯. ~ **treatment** 紧急治疗,急诊.

e•mer•gent [iˈməːdʒənt] *a.* ①发出的,现出的. ②突现的,意外的;紧急的. ③自然发生的. *the recently ~ countries* 新兴国家. ~ **evolution** 【生】突生进化. ~ **year** (民族、国家等)计时开始的年代.

e•mer•i•tus [i(ː)ˈmeritəs] *a.* 保留头衔而退休的, 名誉的. *a professor ~ = an ~ professor* 名誉教授. — *n.* *(pl.* ***-ti*** [-tai, -tiː]*)* (教授、教士等的)荣誉退休者.

e•mersed [iˈməːst] *a.* (水生植物)伸出水面的.

e•mer•sion [i(ː)ˈməːʃən] *n.* ①现出;浮出 (*opp.* immersion). ②【天】复现.

Em•er•son [ˈeməsn] *n.* ①埃默森〔姓氏,男子名〕. ② **Ralph Waldo** ~ 埃默森〔1803—1882,美国评论家、哲学家、诗人〕.

em•er•y [ˈeməri] *n.* 粗金刚砂. ~ **bag** (磨针用的)砂袋. ~ **board** 砂板. ~ **cloth** 砂布. ~ **paper** 砂纸. ~ **wheel** 砂轮.

em•e•sis [ˈeməsis] *n.* 【医】呕吐.

e•met•ic [iˈmetik] *a.* 【医】催吐的. — *n.* 【药】催吐药. **-al•ly** *ad.*

em•e•tin(e) [ˈemətiːn] *n.* 【药】吐根碱,吐根素,依米丁.

é•meute [eiˈməːt] *n.* 〔F.〕起义;暴动.

E.M.F., EMF, e.m.f., emf = electromotive force 电动势. *back [counter] ~* 反电势.

-emia *n. suf.* = -aemia.

e•mic•tion [iˈmikʃən] *n.* ①排尿. ②尿.

em•i•grant [ˈemigrənt] *a.* (向外国)移居的;移民的,侨居的. — *n.* 移民,侨民;迁徙的动物;移植的植物. *Japanese ~s for Brazil* 日本移居巴西的侨民. *~s from China* 来自中国的移民.

em•i•grate [ˈemigreit] *vi.* ①移居(外国). ②〔口〕搬出,迁出(*opp.* immigrate). — *vt.* 使移居,使迁出.

em•i•gra•tion [ˌemiˈgreiʃən] *n.* 移居外国;〔集合词〕移民,侨民. ~ *policy* 移民政策.

em•i•gra•to•ry [ˈemigrətəri] *a.* = migratory.

é•mi•gré [ˈemigrei] *n.* 〔F.〕 移民; (因政治等原因而移居国外的)逃亡者,流亡者.

E•mile [eiˈmiːl] *n.* 埃米尔〔男子名〕.

Emily, Emilie [ˈemili] *n.* 埃米莉〔女子名〕.

em•i•nence [ˈeminəns] *n.* ①高处,高地. ②【解】(骨的)隆起,隆凸. ③高位,要职. ④高超,卓越;著名,杰出,显赫. ⑤〔E-〕【天主】阁下〔对主教的尊称,前面加 Your, His〕. *a man of ~* 名人. *have a position of ~ in the political world* 在政界居有显要地位. *attain ~ in literature* 在文学上享有盛名.

ém•i•nence grise [eimiːnɔnsˈgriːz], 〔F.〕 (政界、政党的)幕后操纵者.

em•i•nen•cy [ˈeminənsi] *n.* = eminence.

em•i•nent [ˈeminənt] *a.* ①杰出的,卓越的. ②著名的;显著的, 突出的. ~ *services* 功勋卓著. ~ *statesman* 杰出的政治家. *a man of ~ impartiality* 大公无私的人. *be ~ as a speaker* 以演说家著称. ~ **domain**【法】国家最高支配权;〔美〕土地征用权. ~ **souls** 社会名流. **-ly** *ad.*

e•mir [eˈmiə] *n.* ①埃米尔〔某些穆斯林国家的首长(或王子、长官)〕. ②穆罕默德后裔的尊称. **-ate** [eˈmiərit] *n.* 埃米尔的统治,首长国 (*the United Arab Emirates* 阿拉伯联合酋长国).

em•is•sa•ry [ˈemiseri] *n.* ①使者, 密使. ②间谍. — *a.* 密使的;间谍的.

e·mis·sion [iˈmiʃən] *n.* ①(光、热、气体等的)发出，发射，射出，放射；传播. ②(纸币等的)发行；发行额. ③发出物，放射物. ④【医】排出；遗精. ～ **spectrum**【物】发射光谱. ～ **theory**【物】微粒说.

em·is·sive [iˈmisiv] *a.* 发出的，发射的，放射(性)的. ～ *power*【物】发射力.

em·is·siv·i·ty [ˌemiˈsiviti] *n.* 发射率，辐射系数.

e·mit [iˈmit] *vt.* ①出(声)，发，放(光等)，发射，放射(热等). ②吐露(意见等). ③颁布(命令等)；发行(纸币等). *The sun ～s light.* 太阳放出光.

e·mit·ron [ˈemitrɔn] *n.* 光电摄像管.

e·mit·ter [iˈmitə] *n.* ①辐射体，辐射源. ②发射体，发射极. *beta* ～ β辐射体.

Em·ma [ˈemə] *n.* 埃玛〔女子名〕.

Em·(m)anuel [iˈmænjuəl] *n.* 伊曼纽尔〔男子名〕.

em·men·a·gogue [əˈmenəgɔg] *n.*【药】通经药，调经药.

em·mer [ˈemə] *n.* 粒小麦.

Em·met(t) [ˈemit] *n.* 埃米特〔姓氏，男子名〕.

em·met [ˈemit] *n.*【动】〔方、古〕蚁.

em·me·tro·pi·a [ˌeməˈtrəupiə] *n.*【医】正常眼，折光正常.

Em·my [ˈemi] *n.* (*pl.* **-mies, -mys**)(美国电视艺术与科学学院对在电视节目安排、演技等方面有卓越成就者所颁发的)埃美金像奖.

e·mol·li·ent [iˈmɔliənt] *a.* 使(皮肤等)柔软的，有缓和作用的. — *n.*【药】润肤剂，(皮肤的)缓和剂.

e·mol·u·ment [iˈmɔljumənt] *n.* 薪水，报酬.

Em·or·y [ˈeməri] *n.* 埃默里〔男子名〕.

e·mote [iˈməut] *vi.* 〔美口〕表现感情(尤指演戏或象在演戏).

e·mo·tion [iˈməuʃən] *n.* ①情感，情绪，感情. ②感动，激动. *a man of strong ～s* 感情强烈的人. *with* ～ 感动地，激动地. **-less** *a.* 没有感情的，冷漠的.

e·mo·tion·al [iˈməuʃənl] *a.* ①情绪的，感情的. ②容易激动的，易动感情的，感情脆弱的. ③感动人的，激起感情的. *an* ～ *actor* 善于表情的演员. *an* ～ *state* 兴奋状态. **-ism** [-izm] *n.* 感情主义，唯情论，情绪表露. **-ist** [-ist] *n.* 容易动感情的人；感情主义者，唯情论者. **-i·ty** [iˌməuʃəˈnæliti] *n.* 激动；富于感情. **-ise, -ize** *vt.* 使带感情色彩；使动感情. **-ly** *ad.*

e·mo·tive [iˈməutiv] *a.* 感情的，情绪的；表现感情的. **-ly** *ad.*

e·mo·tiv·i·ty [iˈməutiviti] *n.* 感触性，易感性.

Emp. = Emperor; Empress.

e.m.p.【医】照方处理 (= as directed).

em·pale [imˈpeil] *vt.* = impale.

em·pan·el [imˈpænl] *vt.* (〔英〕**-ll-**) 把(某人)记入陪审员名单；选任(陪审员等).

em·path·ic [emˈpæθik], **em·pa·thet·ic** [ˌempəˈθetik] *a.* ①(美学上)移情作用的. ②【心】神入的.

em·pa·thize [ˈempəθaiz] *vi.* 经历移情作用，感受移情作用.

em·pa·thy [ˈempəθi] *n.* ①移情作用. ②神入.

em·pen·nage [ˈempənidʒ] *n.*【空】尾翼(面)，尾部.

em·per·or [ˈempərə] *n.* (*fem.* **em·press**) 皇帝. *the Purple E-* 深紫蝶. **-ship** *n.* 皇帝的身分〔地位，统治〕.

em·per·y [ˈempəri] *n.* 〔诗〕①帝国，帝权. ②绝对统治权，权威.

emph. = emphasis, emphatic.

em·pha·sis [ˈemfəsis] *n.* (*pl.* **-ses** [-siːz]) ①【修】强调语势，强语气. ②强调，着重，重点，重要性. ③(形、色等的)显著，鲜明. ***lay [place, put]*** ～ ***on [upon]*** 着重在；强调，加强(语气). ***speak with*** ～ 着重说. ***underline words for*** ～ 在字下画线表示强调〔重要〕.

em·pha·size [ˈemfəsaiz] *vt.* ①强调，着重. ②使加强语气. ③使(事实等)突出(或显得重要).

em·phat·ic [imˈfætik] *a.* ①加强语气的，表现有力的，强调的. ②显著的，显眼的. *an* ～ *denial* 断然的否认. *an* ～ *honour* 特殊的光荣. *an* ～ *victory* 大胜. **-cal·ly** *ad.*

em·phy·se·ma [ˌemfiˈsiːmə] *n.*【医】气肿. *pulmonary* ～ 肺气肿. **-tous** [ˌemfiˈsemətəs] *a.*

em·phy·teu·sis [ˌemfiˈtjuːsis] *n.*【法】永佃权；永借权.

em·phy·teu·ta [ˌemfiˈtjuːtə] *n.*【法】永久佃户；永借人.

em·pire [ˈempaiə] *n.* ①帝国. ②帝王统治(权)；帝政；绝对统治权 *(over)*. (由某个人或集团控制的)大企业. *E- City [State]* 〔美〕纽约市〔州〕. *E- Day* 〔英〕帝国节〔5月24日，1958年改称 Commonwealth Day〕. *E- State Building* 纽约的帝国摩天大厦. *E- State of the South* 〔美〕佐治亚州. *the E-* 神圣罗马帝国；英帝国；(拿破仑统治下的)法兰西第一帝国. — *a.* ①〔E-〕法兰西第一帝国时期(1804—1815)的. ②〔E-〕(服装、傢具等)法国十九世纪头三十年款式的.

em·pir·ic [emˈpirik] *n.* ①凭经验办事的人，经验主义者. ②〔古〕庸医. — *a.* = empical.

em·pir·i·cal [emˈpirikəl] *a.* ①以经验为根据的，经验主义的. ②庸医的. ～ **formula**【化】实验式，经验式. **-ly** *ad.*

em·pir·i·cism [emˈpirisizəm] *n.* ①【哲】经验论 (*opp.* rationalism)；经验主义. ②庸医的医法.

em·pir·i·cist [emˈpirisist] *n.* ①经验主义者，经验论者. ②庸医.

em·pir·i·o-crit·i·cism, em·pir·i·o·crit·i·cism [emˌpiriəuˈkritisizəm] *n.*【哲】经验批判主义.

em·pir·i·o-mo·nism [emˌpiriəuˈmɔnizəm] *n.*【哲】经验一元论.

em·pir·i·o-sym·bo·lism [emˌpiriəuˈsimbəlizəm] *n.*【哲】经验符号论.

em·place [imˈpleis, em-] *vt.* ①放，置. ②【军】放列，使(火炮)进入阵地. ～**ment** *n.* ①定位置；【军】放列动作. ②炮兵掩体，炮台，炮位.

em·plane [imˈplein] *vi.* 乘飞机. — *vi.* 使乘飞机；把…装入飞机.

em·ploy [imˈplɔi] *vt.* ①用，使用. ②雇用. ③使专心于，使忙于，使从事于. ～ *one's time* 使用时间. *the ～ed* 雇工，雇员. *be ～ed* 被雇，受雇；从事. *be ～ed in drinking* 喝着酒. ～ *everything in one's power* 尽一切方法. ***～ oneself in [on]*** … 做(工作)，从事，时间花(在…). — *n.* ①使用. ②雇用. ③服务；工作；职业. *have many persons in one's* ～ 雇用着不少人. *in the* ～ *of sb.* = *in sb.'s* ～ 受某人雇用. ***out of*** ～ 失业.

em·ploy·a·ble [imˈplɔiəbl] *a.* ①能使用的. ②可雇用的〔尤指适于雇用的或满足起码雇用要求的〕. **em·ploy·a·bil·i·ty** [imˌplɔiəˈbiliti] *n.*

employé [ɔmˈplɔiei] *n.* (*fem.* **-ée** [-ei]) 〔F.〕= employee.

em·ploy·ee [ˌemplɔiˈiː, imˈplɔiiː] *n.* 雇员，雇工，受雇者. *office ～s* 职员.

em·ploy·er [imˈplɔiə] *n.* 雇主；雇用者.

em·ploy·ment [imˈplɔimənt] *n.* ①使用，利用. ②雇用. ③工作，职业. ④消遣. *the* ～ *of capital* 资金的运用. *the* ～ *of skilled labour* 熟练工人的雇用. *get [obtain]* ～ 就业. *lose* ～ 失业. ***a blind alley*** ～ ***[occupation]*** 没有前途的职业〔工作〕. ***in the*** ～ ***of*** 在…处工作，受雇于 …. ***out of*** ～ 失业，赋闲. ***seek for*** ～ 找工作. ***take (sb.) into*** ～ 雇用(某人). ***throw (sb.) out of*** ～ 解雇，取消(某人)差事. ～ **agency [bureau, office]** 职业介绍所. ～ **certificate** (学校发给适龄儿童可参加有酬工作的)从业证明书. ～ **exchange** 〔英〕(劳工部等设立的)职业介绍所.

em·poi·son [imˈpɔizn] *vt.* ①〔古〕使有毒；使污染. ②使怀恨，使狠毒.

em·po·ri·um [emˈpɔːriəm] *n.* (*pl.* ～**s, -ria** [-riə]) ①商场，商业中心. ②【商】商品陈列所，大百货店.

em•pow•er [im'pauə] *vt.* ①授权,准许. ②使能. ~ *sb. to do sth.* 授权某人可做某事. *Science* ~*s man to conquer natural forces.* 科学使人类能征服自然.

em•press ['empris] *n.* 女皇;皇后. ***an* ~ *dowager*** 皇太后.

em•presse•ment [F. ɑ̃:prɛsmɑ̃] *n.* 〔F.〕热诚,真挚.

em•prise, em•prize [im'praiz] *n.* 〔古,诗〕壮举;冒险;勇武.

emp•ti•ness ['em*p*tinis] *n.* ①空虚;空腹;空处. ②无智,无能.

emp•ty ['em*p*ti] *a.* ①空的,空着的. ②空虚的,空洞的. ③无聊的,愚蠢的. ④空闲的;无效的,徒劳的. ⑤杳无人烟的,空寂的. ⑥(母畜)未怀孕的. ⑦〔口〕空腹的,饿着肚子的. ⑧【逻】无元的,无分子的. *An* ~ *bag will not stand up right.* 〔谚〕空袋子,站不直;衣食足然后知礼义. *an* ~ *box* 空箱. ~ *hours* 空闲时间. *an* ~ *house* 空屋. ~ *lip service* 说得好听的空话. *an* ~ *talk* 空谈;废话. ~ *promises* 空洞许诺. *feel* ~ 觉得饿了. *drink on an* ~ *stomach* 空着肚子喝酒. *an* ~ *idea* 愚蠢的想法. ***be* ~ *of*** 无,缺,缺少 (*a life* ~ *of happiness* 缺乏幸福的生活). ***come away*** ~ 空手而回. — *n.* 〔*pl.*〕空箱,空桶;空瓶;空车. — *vt.* 弄空;用空;搬空,腾空,倒空 *(out)*. ~ *one's glass* 干杯. ~ *a drawer* 把抽屉腾空. ~ *a purse upon the table* 把钱袋里的钱统统倒在桌上. — *vi.* ①变空. ②流注,注入. ~ *(itself)* ***into***(河)流入(大海). **~-handed** *a.* 空手的,徒手的;空手,空着手. **~-headed** *a.* 没有头脑的,愚笨的. ~ **word**【语法】虚词. **emp•ti•ly** *ad.* **emp•ty•ing** *n.* ①倒空,空出. ②倒出的东西. ③〔*pl.*〕〔美俚〕用啤酒糟做的酵素.

em•pur•ple [im'pə:pl] *vt.* 把…弄成[染成]紫色.

em•py•e•ma [ˌempai'i:mə] *n.*【医】积浓;脓胸.

em•py•re•al [ˌempai'ri:əl, em'piriəl] *a.* 由净火形成的;最高天的,苍天的.

em•py•re•an [ˌempai'ri(:)ən, em'piriən] *n.*【宗】①最高天,上帝的住处. ②苍天,太空. — *a.* = empyreal.

e•mu ['i:mju:] *n.*【动】鸸鹋;高大而不飞的鸟.

E.M.U., EMU, e.m.u., emu = electromagnetic unit(s) 电磁单位.

em•u•late ['emjuleit] *vt.* ①与…竞赛[竞争]. ②努力赶上[超过]. ③仿效. ④【自】仿真,使用仿真器仿效(另一计算机系统).

em•u•la•tion [ˌemju'leiʃən] *n.* ①竞赛,竞争. ②仿效. ③【自】仿真(技术). *in a spirit of* ~ 以竞争的精神. *an* ~ *drive* 竞赛运动.

em•u•la•tive ['emjulətiv] *a.* 竞争的,好胜的,不服输的. **-ly** *ad.*

em•u•la•tor ['emjuleitə] *n.* ①竞赛者,竞争者. ②热心模仿的人. ③【自】仿真器,仿效器.

em•u•la•to•ry ['emjulətəri] *a.* 〔罕〕竞争的.

em•u•lous ['emjuləs] *a.* ①好胜的,竞争心强的. ②好仿效的. ③渴望的. ~ ***of*** ①热心模仿. ②渴望. **-ly** *ad.* **-ness** *n.*

e•mul•si•fi•a•ble [i'mʌlsifaiəbl] *a.* 可乳化的 (emulsible).

e•mul•si•fi•ca•tion [iˌmʌlsifi'keiʃən] *n.*【化】乳化(作用).

e•mul•si•fi•er [i'mʌlsifaiə] *n.*【化】乳化剂;乳化器.

e•mul•si•fy [i'mʌlsifai] *vt.* 使乳化. *a* ~*ing agent* 乳化剂.

e•mul•sion [i'mʌlʃən] *n.* 乳状液,乳胶;【医】乳剂. *sensitive* ~【摄】感光乳剂.

e•mul•sive [i'mʌlsiv] *a.* ①乳剂质的,乳化性的,生乳质物的. ②能乳化的.

e•mul•soid [i'mʌlsɔid] *n.*【化】乳胶(体).

e•munc•to•ry [i'mʌŋ*k*təri] *a.* 排泄用的. — *n.* 排泄器官.

en [en] *n.* ① 字母 N 或 n. ②【印】对开〔em 全身的一半〕.

en [ɑ̃] *prep.* 〔F.〕①在,在…中. ②用. ③象,如同. ***en bloc*** [-'blɔk] 总,全体 (*resign en bloc* 总辞职). ***en clair*** [-'klɛə] 用普通文字,明码. ***en famille*** [-fa'mi:jə] 在家,随意地,不拘礼地;一家人似地; ***en fête*** [-'fɛ:t] 在过节,如节日般地. ***en garçon*** [-'gɑrsɔ̃] (男子)独身. ***en masse*** [-'mas]〔法〕一同,一块儿;全部,整个地; ***en passant*** [-'pɑsɑ̃] ①顺便. ②【棋】吃掉一次进两格的敌卒〔敌卒已处于进一格便可吃掉的位置〕. ~ ***prise*** [ɑ̃ pri:z] 下棋处在容易被吃掉的地位. ***en rapport*** [-rɑ'pɔ:r] 同情;和谐,一致. ***en règle*** [-'rɛgl] 按部就班,照规则,正式. ***en route*** [-'ru:t] 在途中 *(to; for)*.

en- *pref.* (在 *p, b, m* 前作 *em-*) ①加在名词前,表示"放进","放在…上面","走上","赋予": *en*case, *en*throne, *em*bus, *em*power. ②加在名词或形容词前,表示"使成…": *en*slave, *em*bolden. ③加在动词前,表示"在里面","包住": *en*fold, *en*wrap. ★ en- 与 in- 常可通用,但在美国日常用语中多用 in-,英国一般多用 en-: *in*quire, *en*quire; *in*close, *en*close.

-en *suf.* ①加在形容词或名词后面构成动词,表示"弄","变","使","使有","变得","变得有": moist*en*,strength*en*, deep*en*, length*en*. ②加在物质名词后构成形容词,表示"由…构成的","由…制成的": earth*en*, wood*en*. 在非重音音节的 r 后面作 -n: silver*n*. ③加在不规则动词之后构成过去分词或形容词: spok*en*, fall*en*, beat*en*, drunk*en* ★ 在这一类词中,有的 -en 可改为 -ed〔如 shap*en* > shap*ed*〕,有的是古语〔如 *graven*〕,有的已略去 e〔如 *sworn*〕. ④加在名词之后构成复数名词: ash*en*. ox*en*. ⑤加在名词之后构成阴性名词: vix*en*. ⑥加在名词之后构成指小词: chick*en*, kitt*en*, maid*en*.

en•a•ble [i'neibl] *vt.* ①使能够,使得,使成为可能. ②授予…权力. ~ *sb. to (do)* 使人能(做)…. *an enabling act [statue]* 授予权力的条令.

en•act [i'nækt] *vt.* ①制定(法律);颁布;规定. ②扮演;演出. *as by law* ~*ed* 如法律所规定. ~*ing clauses*【法】说明法案制定经过的条文. **en•ac•tive** *a.* 有制定权的;制定法律的. **-ment** *n.* ①制定(法律),颁布. ②法令,条例,法规. ③(戏剧的)上演.

e•na•lite ['enəlait], *n.*【矿】水硅钍铀矿.

en•am•el [i'næməl] *n.* ①搪瓷,珐琅,瓷漆. ②搪瓷制品. ③指甲油. ④(牙齿的)珐琅质,釉质. — *vt.* (〔英〕**-ll-**) ①给…上珐琅,在…涂瓷漆. ②使光滑. ③给…上彩色,彩饰. ~ **paint** 瓷漆. ~ **ware** 搪瓷器皿. ~ **wire** 漆包(电)线.

en•am•el•er, en•am•el•ler [i'næmlə] *n.* 上釉工匠[技师](= enamelist 或 enamellist).

en•am•o(u)r [i'næmə] *vt.* 使迷恋,使倾心. ***be* ~*ed of [with]*** 恋慕;迷恋;醉心于.

en•an•ti•o•morph [i'næntiəumɔ:f] *n.*【化】对映(结构)体. **-phic** *a.* **-phism** *n.*【化】对映性.

en•an•ti•op•a•thy [enænti'ɔpəθi] *n.* = allopathy.

en•an•ti•ot•ro•py [iˌnænti'ɔtrəpi] *n.*【化】互变(现象),对映(异构)现象.

en•ar•gite [i'nɑ:dʒait] *n.*【矿】硫砷铜矿.

en ar•rière [F. ɑ̃ narjɛ:r] 〔F.〕①在后面;在…之后. ②拖欠,拖延.

en•ar•thro•sis [ˌenɑ:'θrəusis] *n.* (*pl.* ***-ses*** [-si:z])【解】杵臼关节,球窝关节.

en bro•chette [F. ɑ̃ brɔ'ʃɛt] 〔F.〕在烤肉的铁扦子上烤.

en brosse [F. ɑ̃ 'brɔs] 〔F.〕(毛发)刷状的.

enc. = enclosure(s).

en•cae•ni•a [en'si:niə] *n.* 〔*sing.*, *pl.*〕①创立纪念;教堂奠基纪念. ②〔E-〕牛津(或其他)大学校庆.

en•cage [in'keidʒ, en-] *vt.* 把…关进笼里,监禁.

en•camp [in'kæmp] *vi.* 扎营,露营. — *vt.* 使扎营,使宿营. **-ment** *n.* ①扎营,露营,野营. ②扎营地,露营地.

en•cap•su•late [in'kæpsjuleit, -sə-] *vt.* ①把…包于胶囊

等中. ②压缩，节略 (= encapsule). **-lant** *n.* 密封用的材料 **-la·tion** *n.*
en·car·nal·ize [inˈkɑːnəlaiz] *vt.* ①使具肉体，使成化身. ②具体化,体现,实现(理想等). ③使具肉感.
en·car·pus [enˈkɑːpəs] *n.*【建】垂花装饰.
en·case [inˈkeis] *vt.* ①把…装箱〔镶框子等〕. ②把…包在…内. **-ment** *n.* ①装箱;包装. ②箱子,鞘,套子,袋子.
en·cash [inˈkæʃ] *vt.*〔英〕兑现;付现. **-a·ble** *a.* **-ment** *n.* 兑现;付现;现金收纳.
en cas·se·role [enˈkæsirəul; F. ɑ̃ˈkasrɔl]〔F.〕用锅炖的;用锅盛出的(食物).
en·caus·tic [enˈkɔːstik] *a.* 带色陶土烧制的;蜡画法的. ~ *brick [tile]* 彩砖〔瓦〕. ~ *painting* 蜡画，瓷画. — *n.* 色腊〔涂后用熨斗加热固定〕;腊画.
-ence *suf.* 与形容词后缀 -ent 相对应的名词后缀，表示“动作”、“性质”、“状态”等: abs*ence*, dilig*ence*, indulg*ence*.
en·ceinte [enˈseint, F. ɑ̃ˈsɛ̃ːt] *n.*〔F.〕墙;城廓;城内的地方;围. — *a.*〔F.〕妊娠的,怀孕的.
En·cel·a·dus [enˈselədəs]【希神】恩塞拉都斯〔反对宙斯的百手巨人之一〕.
en·ce·ni·a [enˈsiːniə] *n.* = encaenia.
en·ce·phal·ic [ˌensiˈfælik] *a.* 脑的;头骨内的.
en·ceph·a·li·tic [enˌsefəˈlitik] *a.*【医】脑炎的.
en·ceph·a·li·tis [enˌsefəˈlaitis] *n.*【医】脑炎. *Jpaanese Type-B* ~ 流行性乙型脑炎. ~ *lethargica* 昏睡性脑炎.
encephal(o)- *comb. f.* 表示“脑的”: *encephali*tis, *encephalo*graphy.
en·ceph·a·lo·gram [enˈsefələugræm] *n.*【医】①脑电图 (electroencephalogram 的缩写). ②脑蛛网膜下腔充气图相 (pneumoencephalogram 的缩写).
en·ceph·a·log·ra·phy [enˌsefəˈlɔgrəfi] *n.*【医】脑照相术,气脑造影术.
en·ceph·a·lo·my·e·li·tis [enˌsefələuˌmaiəˈlaitis] *n.*【医】脑脊髓炎.
en·ceph·a·lon [enˈsefəlɔn] *n.* (*pl.* **-la** [-lə])【解】脑.
en·chain [inˈtʃein, en-] *vt.* ①用链锁住,束缚. ②抓牢,吸引住(注意力等). **-ment** *n.*
en·chant [inˈtʃɑːnt] *vt.* ①对…施行魔法，用妖术迷惑. ②使心醉，使销魂，使迷住. *an ~ed palace* (神话中的)魔宫. *be ~ed with [by]* 被迷住. **-er** *n.* 妖人,巫士. **-ing** *a.* 迷惑的，迷人的;艳丽的，标致的. **-ing·ly** *ad.* **-ment** *n.* 使妖术;妖术;迷惑;着迷;魅力. **-ress** *n.* 女巫;妖妇.
en·chase [inˈtʃeis, en-] *vt.* 嵌，镶;浮雕，镂刻.
en·ch(e)i·rid·i·on [ˌenkaiəˈridiən] *n.* (*pl.* ~*s*, **-rid·i·a** [-ˈridiə]) 手册,便览.
en·chi·la·da [ˌentʃiˈlɑːdə] *n.* 墨西哥的一种卷肉玉米面饼.
en·chon·dro·ma [ˌenkɔnˈdrəumə] *n.* (*pl.* **-ma·ta** [-mətə], **-mas**)【医】内生软骨瘤. **en·chon·drom·a·tous** [-ˈdrɔmətəs, -ˈdrəumətəs] *a.*
en·cho·ri·al [enˈkɔːriəl] *a.* ①某国特有的. ②古埃及通俗文字的.
en·ci·na [enˈsiːnə], *n.* = live oak.
en·ci·pher [inˈsaifə] *vt.* 把(电文)译成密码.
en·cir·cle [inˈsəːkl] *vt.* ①环绕，围绕;包围. ②围…绕行一周. *a lake ~d with [by] woods* 树林环绕的湖. ~ *the globe* 环绕地球〔特指外交,战略〕. **-ment** *n.*
encl. = enclosure.
en·clasp [inˈklɑːsp, en-] *vt.* 抱住,抱紧;握紧.
en·clave [ˈenkleiv; F. ɑ̃klɑːv] *n.* 插在别国领域中的领土,飞地.
en·clit·ic [inˈklitik, en-] *a.*【语法】与前一词结合的 (*opp.* proclitic)〔例: cannot 的 not〕. —*n.*【语法】前接成分.
en·close inˈkləuz] *vt.* ①(用篱、墙等)围起,圈起,包围,围绕. ②包,装. ~ *the land with walls* 筑墙围地. *I ~ herewith a cheque for 10 pounds* 随信附上十镑支票一张. *the ~d* 附件.
en·clo·sure [inˈkləuʒə] *n.* ①包围,围绕;封入. ②包入物,封入物;附件. ③圈占地,圈用地. ④围墙，围栏. *prisoners-of-war* ~ 临时战俘营.
en·clothe [inˈkləuð] *vt.*〔书〕= clothe.
en·cloud [inˈklaud] *vt.*〔书〕阴云遮蔽,使天阴;使阴郁.
en·code [inˈkəud] *vt.* 把(电文)译成电码〔密码〕. **-r** *n.* 译电员;〔自动控制〕编码器. **-ment** *n.*
en·co·mi·ast [enˈkəumiæst] *n.* 赞辞作者;赞美者;阿谀者. **-tic** *a.* **-ti·cal·ly** *ad.*
en·co·mi·um [enˈkəumjəm] *n.* (*pl.* ~*s*, **-mi·a** [-miə]). 赞辞,颂词;称赞,赞美,推崇.
en·com·pass [inˈkʌmpəs] *vt.* ①围绕,包围. ②包含. ③完成，贯彻. *be ~ed with perils* 被危险包围着. **-ment** *n.*
en·core [ɔŋˈkɔː] *n.* 要求再演;重唱,重演. *get an ~* 被要求重演 — *int.* 再来一个! — *vt.* 要求再演〔唱〕.
en·coun·ter [inˈkauntə] *n.* 遭遇;遭遇战，冲突. *an ~ action* 遭遇战. *an ~ of wits* 斗智. — *vt.* ①遇见，碰见;邂逅相逢(友人等). — *vi.* 偶然遇见;遭遇;冲突 (*with*). ~ **group** 病友谈心治疗小组〔美国现代的精神治疗方法,由患者互相畅谈内心感情〕.
en·cour·age [inˈkʌridʒ] *vt.* 鼓励,怂恿,促进，支持，赞助. ~ *sb. in his idleness* 助长某人的懒惰. ~ *sb. to (do)* 鼓励某人(做)…. **be ~d by** 受…鼓励〔鼓舞〕. **-ment** *n.* 奖励,鼓励;助长. **-ing** *a.* 鼓励的,赞助的,振奋人心的,令人欢欣鼓舞的. **-ing·ly** *ad.*
en·crim·son [inˈkrimzn] *vt.* 使成深红色.
en·cri·nite [ˈenkrinait] *n.*【古生】石莲.
en·croach [inˈkrəutʃ] *vi.* (逐渐)侵入,侵犯;侵略,侵占;侵害;侵蚀(*on, upon*). ~ *on [upon] another nation's territory* 侵略别国领土. ~ *on [upon] sb.'s right* 侵占他人权利. ~ *upon sb.'s time* 占用别人时间. ~ *upon the interests of sb. for one's own good* 损人利己. **-ment** *n.* ①侵入,侵犯,侵害;侵蚀,蚕食. ②侵占物,(海水的)侵蚀地.
en·crust [inˈkrʌst] *vt.* ①把…包上外壳. ②(用宝石等)镶饰(表面).— *vi.* 长壳〔皮〕. **-ment** *n.*
en·cul·tu·rate [inˈkʌltʃəreit] *vt.* 使适应时尚，使合时宜. — *n.* **-ra·tive** *a.*
en·cum·ber [inˈkʌmbə] *vt.* ①妨碍，阻碍;拖累，打扰. ②使负(债等). ③堆满(场所) (*with*). *be ~ed with debts* 负债,为债务所累. *be ~ed with a big family* 为大家庭所累. *an estate ~ed with mortgages* 已抵押出去的地产.
en·cum·brance [inˈkʌmbrəns] *n.* ①妨碍，阻碍，阻碍物;累赘;家累. ②【法】(不动产方面的)债权. ***without ~s*** 没有儿女的拖累.
ency(c)., encycl. = encyclop(a)edia.
-en·cy *suf.* 表示“性质”、“状态”的名词后缀: ag*ency*, depend*ency*.
en·cyc·lic, en·cyc·li·cal [enˈsiklik(əl), -ˈsaik-] *a.* 传阅的,通谕的. — *n.* (教皇的)通告,通谕.
en·cy·clo·p(a)e·di·a [enˌsaikləuˈpiːdiə] *n.* ①百科全书;专科全书. ②〔E-〕(十八世纪)法国狄德罗 (Diderot) 与达朗贝 (D'Alembert) 合编的《百科全书》〔包含启蒙主义思想〕.
en·cy·clo·p(a)e·dic(al) [enˌsaikləuˈpiːdik(əl)] *a.* 百科全书的;包含各种学科的;广博的,渊博的. ~ *knowledge* 渊博的知识. *an ~ mind* 博学的人.
en·cy·clo·pe·dism, en·cy·clo·pae·dism [enˌsaikləuˈpiːdizəm] *n.* ①百科全书的知识，知识渊博. ②〔E-〕(法国十八世纪)《百科全书》派的观点.
en·cy·clo·p(a)e·dist [enˌsaikləuˈpiːdist] *n.* ①百科全书编纂者. ②〔E-〕(法国十八世纪)《百科全书》派成员.
en·cyst [enˈsist] *vt.*【生】把…包在囊内. — *vi.*【生】被包

在囊内. **-ment, -ation** [ˌensisˈteiʃən] *n.* 被囊作用.

end [end] *n.* ①端,尖,末端,终点. ②边缘;极点,极限. ③结局,结果. ④目的. ⑤最后,死. ⑥【纺】经纱零头布,(丝的)头绪;〔*pl.*〕残片,残屑. ⑦〔美足球〕进攻、防守最前线两端位置上的球员. *As the year draws to its ~ ...* 在这一年将要结束的时候… *the ~ of the town* 市郊. *~s of a cigarette ~* 香烟头. *one's journey's ~* 旅行目的地. *achieve [gain, win] one's ~* 达到目的. *the East E- (of London)* 伦敦东区(劳动人民聚居区). *the West E- (of London)* 伦敦西区(富人聚居区). *The ~ crowns the work.* 〔谚〕工作贵在有始有终. *the supreme ~* 最高目的. ***a rope's end*** ①(两端以线相连的)打人用的短绳. ②绞索. ***a shoemaker's ~*** (带猪鬃的)绱鞋引线. ***at a loose ~*** 无固定职业,闲着. ***at loose ~s*** ①不安定. ②混乱. ***at the ~*** 最后,终于. ***at the ~ of*** 在…末端;在…的结尾. ***at the ~ of one's forbearance [patience]*** 忍无可忍. ***at the ~ of one's rescurces [rope, wits]*** 山穷水尽[束手无策,智穷计尽]. ***at the latter ~*** 在末期. ***be at an ~*** 尽;完结,终了(*Our intercourse is at an ~.* 我们的交往至此为止). ***be on the receiving ~*** 〔口〕①接收别人的礼物[善意]. ②成为攻击目标. ③【体】处于接球的一方. ***be the ~ of sb.*** 成为致死的原因(*You'll be the ~ of me.* 你真是要我的命). ***begin [start] at the wrong ~*** 一开头就错. ***bring to an ~*** 使结束. ***the business ~*** 起作用的一头(如针的尖,刀剑的锋). ***carry sth. through to the end*** 把某事进行到底. ***come out at [of] the little ~ of the horn*** 说过的话没做到. ***come to an ~*** 完结,终了,告终. ***come to a dead ~*** 走投无路. ***come to an untimely ~*** 短命,夭折. ***come to a sticky ~*** 落得痛苦的下场. ***~ and aim*** 目的. ***~ for ~*** 掉头,颠倒过来. ***the ~s of the earth*** 天涯海角. ***~ on*** 一端向前;正对着. ***~ to ~*** 头尾连接,衔接. ***~ up*** 直立着. ***for this ~*** 因这目的,因此. ***from ~ to ~*** 从头到尾. ***get [have] hold of the wrong ~ of the stick*** 完全误解. ***get the better ~ of sb.*** 机智胜人,占人上风. ***go (in) off the deep ~*** ①游泳时投入深水;冒险. ②控制不住自己;发脾气. ***have [take] an ~*** 告终,终了. ***have an ~ in veiw*** 有所企图. ***have sth. at one's fingers' [tongue's] ends*** 熟练,精通. ***have no ~ of a time*** 乐得忘记了时间. ***in the ~*** 终于,最后. ***In the ~ things will mend.*** 〔谚〕船到桥头自然直. ***keep one's ~ up*** 乐观地战斗,坚持到底. ***land in a dead ~*** 陷入困境. ***make an ~ of [to]*** 了结,结束,终止. ***make both ~s [~s] meet*** 使收支相抵,量入为出. ***a means to an ~*** 达到目的的手段. ***meet one's ~*** 死. ***(be) near one's ~*** 快要死了. ***no ~ (ad.)*** 〔口〕无限,非常(*I'm no end glad.* 我非常快乐). ***no ~ of*** 〔口〕很多,非常(*have no ~ of money* 钱多得不得了. *think no ~ of oneself* 自命不凡. *no ~ of a fool* 大傻瓜. *no ~ of a fellow* 极好的人). ***on ~*** ①竖着,笔直地. ②继续,不停地. (*work 10 hours on ~*连续工作十小时). ***play both ~s against the middle*** ①为私利而脚踏两只船. ②使人争吵而坐收渔人之利. ***put an ~ to*** 结束,了结,停止. ***right [straight] on ~*** 继续,接连;立刻. ***set one's hair on ~*** 使人毛骨悚然. ***to no ~*** 无益,徒劳. ***to that ~*** 因为那个原故,为要达到那个目的(所以). ***to the ~*** 到最后,始终. ***to the (bitter, very) ~*** 到最后,到底,直到死. ***to the ~ of time*** 永远. ***to the ~ of the chapter*** 到最后,到底,直到死. ***to the ~ that ...*** 为要,以便. ***To what ~?*** 为什么? ***without ~*** 无尽的;无穷的. ***with this ~ in view*** 抱着这一目的. ***world without ~*** 永久,无穷. — ***vt.*** ①使完结,了结,终止. ②使致死,杀. ③竖立,使直立着. ④成为…的结尾. *We ~ed the discussion on a note of optimism.* 我们以乐观的调子结束了这场讨论. *A bullet through the heart ~ed him.* 一颗子弹穿过心脏结束了他的生命. — ***vi.*** ①终止,完毕,结尾;收场. ②死. *The road ~s here.* 这条路到此地就到头了. *All is well that ~s well.* 〔谚〕有好结果,就算好事. ***~ by doing*** 以…结束(*He ~ed by thanking the audience* 最后他向听众道谢,结束演出). ***~ in*** 结果为…,终成,终归,终于. ***~ in bubble [smoke]*** 终归失败,终成泡影. ***~ off (up)*** 结束(*~ off one's talk with a joke* 用笑话结束讲话). ***~ up*** 结束;完事;〔俚〕死. ***~ up with*** 以…而告终. ***~ with*** 以…完结、终止. **~-all** 结尾,终结,收场;最终目的. **~-around** 循环. **~-consumer [user]** 目的用户(指最终应用产品的人). **~ game** (棋赛等的)残局. **~ ga(u)ge**【机】端面规块. **~ leaf = ~ paper.** **~ man** ①在一排末端的人. ②〔美〕(在化装演出黑人歌曲的剧团表演中)站在一排末端、同站正中扮领班者作滑稽对话的演员. **~ paper** (书的)补页. **~ point** 终点. **~ product** 最后产物,最终结果. **~-result** 最终结果,归宿. **~ run**〔美〕①【体】打橄榄球时在自己一端抱球左右兜圈前冲的动作. ②规避的伎俩. **~ table** (沙发旁的)茶几. **~ use** 最终用途. **~ zone**【足球】端区〔端线和球门线延长线至两边边线相交的区域〕.

end. = endorsed; endorsement.

en·dam·age [inˈdæmidʒ] *vt.* 使损坏,伤害.

en·da·moe·ba, en·da·me·ba [ˌendəˈmiːbə] *n.*【动】内变形虫属,内阿米巴属(*Endamoeda*). **en·da·moe·bic** *a.* [-ik].

en·dan·ger [inˈdeindʒə] *vt.* 危及,危害,使遭到危险. *~ one's life* 危及性命. **-ment** *n.*

en·darch [ˈendɑːk] *a.*【植】内始式的.

end·brain [ˈendˌbrein] *n.*【解】端脑(= telencephalon).

en·dear [inˈdiə] *vt.* 使受喜爱,使被爱恋. *~ oneself to one's friends* 受朋友们喜爱. **-ment** *n.* 亲爱;亲爱的行为[表示].

en·dear·ing [inˈdiəriŋ] *a.* 可爱的,惹人喜爱的. **-ly** *ad.*

en·deav·o(u)r [inˈdevə] *n.* 努力,尽力. ***do one's (best) ~(s)*** 尽全力. ***make every ~*** 尽一切努力,不遗余力. — *vi.* 尽力,竭力,努力,力图(*to do*). ***~ after [for]*** 竭力想,争取.

en·dem·i·c(al) [enˈdemik(əl)] *a.* ①(动、植物)某地特产的;(风土人情的)某地[某民族]特有的. ②地方病的. —*n.* ①某地特产的植物[动物]. ②地方病. **-ly** *ad.* **en·de·mic·i·ty** [ˌendiˈmisiti], **en·dem·ism** *n.* 地方性;风土性.

en·der·mic [enˈdəːmik] *a.*【医】经皮的,皮下的,经皮下吸收而作用的. ***the ~ method***【医】皮下疗法. **-cal·ly** *ad.*

En·ders [ˈendəz] *n.* 恩德斯[姓氏].

En·di·cott [ˈendikət] *n.* 恩迪科特[姓氏].

end·ing [ˈendiŋ] *n.* ①终止,完了,收场,结局,结尾. ②末期,最后. ③死. ④【语法】词尾. *nerve ~s*【解】神经末梢.

en·dive [ˈendiv] *n.* ①〔美〕苣荬菜. ②〔英〕= chicory.

end·less [ˈendlis] *a.* ①无尽的,无限的,无边的,无穷的;永远的;不断的. ②【机】环状的. *an ~ argument* 没完没了的议论. **~ band** 环带. **~ chain** 循环链. **~ saw** 环锯. **~ screw** 蜗杆. **-ly** *ad.* **-ness** *n.*

end·long [ˈendlɔːŋ] *ad.* 〔古〕①纵长地. ②竖立地,笔直地.

end·most [ˈendməust] *a.* 最末端的,极远的.

end(o)- *comb.f.* 表示"内","内部"(*opp.* ecto): *endo*crine.

en·do·bi·ot·ic [ˌendəubaiˈɔtik] *a.*【生】寄生于宿主组织内的.

en·do·blast [ˈendəuˌblæst] *n.* = endoderm.

en·do·car·di·al [ˌendəuˈkɑːdiəl] *a.*【解】①心脏内的. ②心内膜的.

en·do·car·di·tis [ˌendəukɑːˈdaitis] *n.*【医】心内膜炎.

en·do·car·di·um [ˌendəuˈkɑːdiəm] *n.*【解】心内膜.

en·do·carp [ˈendəukɑːp] *n.*【植】内果皮.

en·do·cen·tric [ˌendəuˈsentrik] *a.* 【语】向心结构的.
en·do·com·men·sal [ˌendəukəˈmensl] *n.* 【生】内共栖〔于宿主体内〕.
en·do·cra·ni·um [ˌendəuˈkreiniəm] *n.* (*pl.* **-ni·a** [-ə], **-ni·ums**) ①【解】硬脑(脊)膜(=duramater). ②(昆虫头盖里的)幕骨.
en·do·crine [ˈendəukrain] *a.* 内分泌的, 内分泌腺的,激素的. —*n.* 内分泌;内分泌腺,激素. ~ **disorders** 内分泌失调. ~ **glands** 内分泌腺.
en·do·cri·nol·o·gy [ˌendəukraiˈnɔlədʒi] *n.* 内分泌学.
en·do·derm [ˈendəudəːm] *n.* 【生】内胚层.
en·do·der·mis [ˌendəuˈdəːmis] *n.* 【植】内皮层.
en·do·don·tics [ˌendəuˈdɔntiks] *n.* *pl.* 〔用作单数〕【医】(牙)根管治疗术 (=endontia). **-don·tic** *a.* **-dontist** *n.* (牙)根管治疗医师.
en·do·en·zyme [ˌendəuˈenzaim] *n.* 【生】(胞)内酶.
en·do·gam·ic [ˌendəuˈgæmik] *a.* ①同族结婚的. ②【植】同系配合的;同花传粉的.
en·dog·a·mous [enˈdɔgəməs] *a.* 同族通婚的.
en·dog·a·my [enˈdɔgəmi] *n.* ①同族通婚. ②【植】同系配合 (*opp.* exogamy).
en·do·gen [ˈendədʒən] *n.* 【植】内生植物.
en·do·gen·ic [ˌendəuˈdʒenik] *a.* 【地】内成的.
en·dog·e·nous [enˈdɔdʒənəs] *a.* ①【生】内生的, 内长的;内原的. ②【地】内成的. ~ **metabolism** 内原代谢. ~ **plant** 单子叶植物.
en·dog·e·ny [enˈdɔdʒini] *n.* 【生】内生,内发,内长,内原;内生的细胞形成.
en·do·lymph [ˈendəulimf] *n.* 【解】内耳膜迷路内的液体,内淋巴.
en·do·me·tri·o·sis [ˌendəuˌmiːtriˈəusis] *n.* 【医】子宫内膜异位.
en·do·me·tri·tis [ˌendəumiˈtraitis] *n.* 【医】子宫内膜炎.
en·do·me·tri·um [ˌendəuˈmiːtriəm] *n.* 【解】子宫内膜.
en·do·mix·is [ˌendəuˈmiksis] *n.* 【生】内融合,内合. **-mic·tic** [-ˈmiktik] *a.*
en·do·morph [ˈendəumɔːf] *n.* ①【矿】内容矿物 (*opp.* perimorph) 〔指矿物内包含的另一矿体〕. ②【物】内容体. **-ism** 【矿】内容现象,内变质作用.
en·do·mor·phic [ˌendəuˈmɔːfik] *a.* ①【矿】内容矿物的;内变质的. ②【生】(胚胎的内胚层结构占优势的)腹体型的. **-phy** *n.*
en·do·mor·phism [ˌendəuˈmɔːfizm] *n.* 【矿】内变质(作用).
en·do·my·si·um [ˌendəuˈmiziəm] *n.* 【解】肌内膜,肌纤维衣.
en·do·neu·ri·um [ˌendəuˈnjuːriəm] *n.* 【解】神经内膜.
en·do·par·a·site [ˌendəuˈpærəsait] *n.* 【动】内寄生虫,内寄生物.
en·do·pep·ti·dase [ˌendəuˈpeptideis] *n.* 【化】肽链内切酶.
en·doph·a·gous [enˈdɔfəgəs] *a.* 【动】内食的.
en·do·phyte [ˈendəufait] *n.* 内生植物. **-phyt·ic** [-fitik] *a.*
en·do·plasm [ˈendəuplæzəm] *n.* 【生】内质 (*opp.* ectoplasm).
en·do·pleu·ra [ˌendəuˈplurə] *n.* 【植】内种皮.
en·dop·o·dite [enˈdɔpədait] *n.* 内肢;(昆虫的)内肢节.
en·do·proct [ˈendəuˌprɔkt] *n.* 【动】内肛亚纲 (*Endoprocta*)动物 (= entoproct).
en·dors·a·ble [inˈdɔːsəbl] *a.* 可背书的,可背署的;可担保的;可承认的;可赞成的,可批准的.
en·dorse [inˈdɔːs] *vt.* ①【商】在(支票等)背面签名,背书,背署. ②签署,签注,签收;批转,批注(公文等). ③保证,担保;承认,赞成. ④〔英〕在(驾驶员执照)上注明违章记录. ④〔南非〕把(进入城市的黑人)强制送回农村 (*out*). *have one's licence ~d* 〔英〕驾驶执照上被注明违章事件. ~ ***off*** 背书证明支取一部分票面金额. ~ ***over*** 背书(票据等)将所有权让与. **endorser, endorsor** *n.* 背书(让与)人. **endorsee** [ˌendɔːˈsiː] *n.* 被背书人,受让人.
en·dorse·ment [inˈdɔːsmənt] *n.* 背书;保证,承认. ~ *in blank* 无记名式背书. ~ *in full* 记名背书. ~ *to order* 指定背书. ~ *without recourse* 无偿还背书. *qualified ~* 有条件背书.
en·do·sarc [ˈendəusɑːk] *n.* 【生】= endoplasm.
en·do·scope [ˈendəuskəup] *n.* 【医】内窥镜.
en·dos·co·py [enˈdɔskəpi] *n.* 【医】内窥镜检查.
en·do·skel·e·tal [ˌendəuˈskelitl] *a.* 【解】内骨骼的.
en·do·skel·e·ton [ˌendəuˈskelitən] *n.* 【解】 内骨骼 (*opp.* exoskeleton).
en·dos·mo·sis [ˌendɔsˈməusis, -dɔz-] 【生】内渗. **endos·mot·ic** [-ˈmɔtik] *a.*
en·do·sperm [ˈendəuspəːm] *n.* 【植】胚乳.
en·do·sper·mous [ˌendəuˈspəːməs] *a.* 【植】胚乳的.
en·do·spore [ˈendəuspɔː] *n.* 【生】①内生孢子. ②(孢子)内壁. ③(花粉粒)内壁. **-spor·ic** *a.*
en·dos·te·al [enˈdɔstiəl] *a.* 【解】骨内(膜)的.
en·dos·te·um [enˈdɔstiəm] *n.* (*pl.* **-te·a** [-ə]) 【解】骨内膜.
en·do·ster·nite [ˌendəuˈstəːnait] *n.* 【动】腹内骨.
end·os·to·sis [ˌendɔsˈtəusis] *n.* 【医】软骨骨化.
end·os·tra·cum [enˈdɔstrəkəm] (*pl.* **tra·ca** [enˈdɔstrəkə]) *n.* 【动】壳内层.
en·do·style [ˈendəstail] *n.* 【动】内柱.
en·do·the·ci·um [ˌendəuˈθiːsiəm] *n.* (*pl.* **-ci·a** [-e]) 【植】(蒴)内层;药室内壁.
en·do·the·li·um [ˌendəuˈθiːliəm] (*pl.* **-a** [-ə]) *n.* 【解】内皮;【植】内种皮.
en·do·therm [ˈendəθəːm] *n.* 热血动物. **-al** [ˌendəuˈθəːməl] *a.*
en·do·ther·mic [ˌendəuˈθəːmik] *a.* 【化】吸热的 (= endothermal).
en·do·tox·in [ˌendəuˈtɔksin] *n.* 【医】内毒素.
en·do·tra·che·al [ˌendəuˈtreikiəl] *a.* 【解】气管内的.
en·dow [inˈdau] *vt.* ①捐赠基金 [财产等] 给(学校、医院等);留给(寡妇)一部分遗产. ②授与,赋与 (特权等). ~ *a school* 给学校捐赠基金. *an ~ed school* 拥有基金的学校. *He is ~ed with genius.* 他有天才. *She is richly ~ed by nature.* 她有极高天分,得天独厚.
en·dow·ment [inˈdaumənt] *n.* ①捐赠;捐款;基金;养老金. ②天赋, 天资. ~ **assurance [insurance]** 人寿定期保险. ~ **policy** 养老保险单.
en·drin [ˈendrin] *n.* 【化】艾氏剂,氯甲桥萘〔杀虫剂〕.
en·due [inˈdjuː] *vt.* ①授与, 赋与 (*with*). ②〔罕〕穿(衣);使穿上 (*with*).
en·dur·able [inˈdjuərəbl] *a.* ①可忍受的. ②能持久的. **-bly** *ad.* **-ness, en·dur·a·bil·i·ty** *n.*
en·dur·ance [inˈdjurəns] *n.* ①忍耐(力). ②耐久,持久(力),持久性, 耐久性. ***beyond [past]*** ~ 忍无可忍. ***cold*** ~ 耐寒性. ~ **flight** 【空】持久飞行. ~ **limit** 【机】疲劳极限. ~ **test** 耐力试验.
en·dure [inˈdjuə] *vt.* 忍耐,忍受;容忍. *I can not ~ her.* 我讨厌她. ~ *pain* 忍受痛苦. ~ *heat* 耐热. —*vi.* ①忍受,忍耐. ②支持,持久,持续. *as long as life ~s* 只要还有一口气. ~ *to the end* 忍耐到底,坚持到最后.
en·dur·ing [inˈdjuəriŋ] *a.* 持久的,永久的. ~ *fame* 不朽的声名. **-ly** *ad.* **-ness** *n.*
end·ways, end·wise [ˈendweiz, ˈendwaiz] *ad.* ①竖着;末端朝前[上]. ②(两端)连接着;向着两端. ③在末端.
En·dym·i·on [enˈdimiən] *n.* 【希神】安狄米恩〔月神狄安娜所爱的美貌牧童〕.

E.N.E., ENE, e.n.e. = east-northeast.
-ene *suf.*【化】〔构成烯属烃和苯系烃的名词〕: benz*ene*.
E·ne·as, E·ne·id = Aeneas, Aeneid.
en·e·ma ['enimə, i'ni:mə] *n.*【医】灌肠(法); 灌肠器; 灌肠剂. *barium* ~ 钡灌肠. *saline* ~ 盐水灌肠. *soapsuds* ~ 肥皂水灌肠.
en·e·my ['enimi] *n.* ①敌人,仇敌;〔集合词〕敌军,敌舰; 敌机; 敌国. ②危害物; 大害. *an* ~ *worthy of one's steel* 劲敌,强敌. *the public [King's, Queen's]* ~ 公敌. *a lifelong [mortal, sworn]* ~ 不共戴天之敌,死敌. *an* ~ *alien* 敌国侨民. *Better an open* ~ *than a false friend.* 〔谚〕宁要公开敌人,不要虚伪朋友. — *a.* 敌人的,敌方的. ***be an*** ~ ***to*** 危害; 仇视. ***be one's own*** ~ 自已害自已. ***go over to the*** ~ 投敌,附敌. ***the*** ~ ①敌(军). ②〔the E-〕恶魔. ③〔口〕时间 (*How goes the* ~? 现在几点钟?). ***the great [last]*** ~ 死神. ***the (old) E-*** = our ghostly ~ 恶魔.
en·er·get·ic [ˌenə'dʒetik] *a.* ①(措施等)积极的,有力的. ②精力旺盛的,精神饱满的. *an* ~ *effort* 积极努力. **-al** *a.* = energetic. **-al·ly** *ad.*
en·er·get·ics [ˌenə'dʒetiks] *n. pl.* 〔用作单数〕力能学; 动能学.
en·er·gid ['enədʒid] *n.*【生】活质体.
en·er·gism ['enədʒizəm] *n.* 活动主义,奋斗主义〔认为人生之至上幸福在于人的能力得到充分发挥的一种伦理学说〕.
en·er·gize ['enədʒaiz] *vt.* ①加强; 给与…以活力. ②【物】给与…能量; 给与…电压. —*vi.* 活动,用力,打起精神干. *To worry is often to* ~ *needlessly.* 忧虑往往是浪费精力.
en·er·gu·men [ˌenə:'gju:mən] *n.*【宗】①恶魔附身的人. ②狂热的信徒,狂热的人.
en·er·gy ['enədʒi] *n.* ①干劲,活力. ②(语言、行为等的)生动. ③*(pl.)* (个人的)精力; 能力. ④【物】能,能量. *What* ~ *you have!* 你真有精力呀! *be full of* ~ 精力旺盛. *act [speak] with* ~ 生气勃勃地干[说]. *conservation of* ~ 能量守恒,能量不灭. *kinetic [motive]* ~ 动能. *potential [latent]* ~ 势能. ***apply [devote, direct] one's energies to*** 致力于. ***brace one's energies*** 鼓起干劲,振作精神. ~ **budget** 能源预算〔对一个生态系统中能源的收入、利用与损耗的计算〕. ~ **level**【物】能(量)级(位). ~ **paper** 纸片电池.
en·er·vate ['enə:veit] *vt.* 使衰弱, 削弱. *an enervating climate* 使人困倦的气候. — *a.* = enervated.
en·er·vat·ed ['enə:veitid] *a.* 无力的,衰弱的. *an* ~ *style* 软弱无力的笔调. **-va·tion** *n.*
en·face [in'feis, en-] *vt.* 把(金额、日期、姓名等)填[印]在(票据等)上面,把(文字格式、备忘录等)写[印]在文件面上. *an* ~*d paper*【商】具名支票.
en·fants per·dus [F. ɑ̃fɑ̃ 'perdy] 〔F.〕敢死队.
en·fant ter·ri·ble [F. ɑ̃fɑ̃ teribl] 〔F.〕①早熟的儿童〔说话或提问常使大人为难〕. ②肆无忌惮的人.
en·fee·ble [in'fi:bl] *vt.* 使衰弱,弄弱. **-ment** *n.*
en·feoff [in'fef, -'fi:f, en-] *vt.*【史】①封与…领地,授与…封地[采邑]. ②转让,让渡. **-ment** *n.* ①领地的授与; 授与领地的证书. ②封地,采邑.
en·fet·ter [in'fetə, en-] *vt.* 给…上脚镣; 束缚; 使做奴隶.
en·fi·lade [ˌenfi'leid] *n.* ①【军】纵射炮火,纵向射击. ②易受纵射的地位. *an* ~ *barrage* 纵射弹幕. — *vt.* 对…进行纵射.
en·fin [F. ɑ̃fɛ̃] *ad.* 〔F.〕终于,最后.
en·fleu·rage [ɑ:nflæ'rɑ:ʒ] *n.* 〔F.〕花香吸取法.
en·fold [in'fəuld] *vt.* 〔主美〕①包,包进 *(in; with)*. ②抱; 拥抱. ③折叠.
en·force [in'fɔ:s] *vt.* ①推行,厉行,实施(法律等). ②强迫,强制,强派. ③坚持(要求、主张等). ~ *obedience to an order* 强迫服从命令. ~ *obedience on [from, upon] sb.* 强迫某人服从. ~*d education* 强迫教育,义务教育.
en·forc·ed·ly [in'fɔ:sidli] *ad.* 强迫地. **-ment** *n.* 实施;〔古〕强制. **-r** *n.* ①实施[强制]者. ②(流氓集团内为维护黑规矩而设的)执法人.
en·force·a·ble [in'fɔ:səbl] *a.* ①可实施的. ②可强行的, 可压服的. ③(法律的) 可强制服从的. **en·for·ci·bil·i·ty** *n.*
en·frame [in'freim] *vt.* 装(画)在框内,给…配上框子.
en·fran·chise [in'fræntʃaiz, en-] *vt.* ① 释放(奴隶). ②给与…公民权[选举权、参政权]; 给与…自治权. **-ment** [-tʃizmənt] *n.*
eng. = ①engine; engineer; engineering. ②engraved; engraver; engraving.
Eng. = England; English.
en·gage [in'geidʒ] *vt.* ①〔多用被动语态〕使从事,使忙于 *(in)*. ②(用誓约、义务等)束缚,约束,保证 *(oneself to do)*; 订婚 *(~d to)*. ③保证. ④雇,聘. ⑤预约,定(戏座等). ⑥使(军队)交战,与…交战; 使参加. ⑦【机】使(齿轮等)咬合,衔接 *(with)*. ⑧【建】使(柱)附墙. *Are you ~d?* 你有事吗? *Line [Number] is ~d.* (电话)占线了. ~ *sb.'s attention* 惹人注意. *This seat is ~d.* 座已定出. ~ *the enemy* 和敌人交战. — *vi.* ①约定,答应,允诺,保证 *(to do; for)*. ②从事,参加 *(in)*. ③交战 *(with)*. ④【机】(齿轮等)咬合. ***be ~d [~ oneself] in*** 正做着,正忙[在做,在忙]. ***be ~d [~ oneself] to*** 同…订婚. ***be ~d with*** 正与…接洽. ~ ***for*** 应承,保证; 约定 (*That's all I can* ~ *for.* 我能担保的只有这些). ~ ***in*** 从事,在忙; 参加(~ *in teaching* 当教员). ~ *in a game of tennis* 参加网球赛.
en·ga·gé [ɑ̃gaʒei] *a.* 〔F.〕(在政治等事件中)完全卷入的.
en·gage·ment [in'geidʒmənt] *n.* ①约会,约定; 约束,契约; 预约. ②婚约. ③雇用, 聘用期; 职业. ④义务; 〔*pl.*〕债务. ⑤【军】战斗. ⑥【机】接合,咬合. *break one's* ~ 毁约,违约. *fight several ~s* 打几仗. *fulfil one's* ~ 践约. *meet one's ~s* 偿清债务. *a meeting* ~ 遭遇战. *a minor* ~ 小规模交火. *a naval* ~ 海战. ***be under an ~ (to)*** 有约. ***enter into [make] an ~ (with)*** 同人定约. ~ **ring** 订婚戒指.
en·gag·ing [in'geidʒiŋ] *a.* 吸引人的,迷人的,可爱的. **-ly** *ad.*
en·gar·land [en'gɑ:lənd] *vt.* 〔诗〕给…戴上花环.
Eng. D. = Doctor of Engineering 工程学博士.
En·gels ['engəls, G.'eŋəls], **Friedrich** 弗里德里希·恩格斯〔1820—1895, 无产阶级革命导师〕.
en·gen·der [in'dʒendə] *vt.* 使发生,使产生; 惹起,酿成. —*vi.* 产生; 形成.
engin. = engineer(ing).
en·gine ['endʒin] *n.* ①机械,机器. ②引擎,蒸汽机,发动机. ③机车,车头. ④工具;〔古〕方法,手段. *a Diesel [steam]* ~ 柴油[蒸汽](发动)机. *an internal combustion* ~ 内燃机. *an auxiliary* ~ 辅助发动机. *a dental* ~ 钻牙机. *an* ~ *of torture* 刑具. *an* ~ *of warfare* 兵器,武器. *a fire* ~ 救火车,灭火机. *a gasoline* ~ 汽油机. *a pile* ~ 打桩机. *a race* ~ 比赛用汽车,赛车. *an empty* ~ (未挂列车的)空车头. — *vt.* 给…安装发动机. ~ **bearer** 发动机台. ~ **driver** 〔英〕火车司机. ~ **house** 救火车库、机车库. ~ **lathe** 普通车床. ~**man** *n.* = ~ driver. ~ **room** 发动机房,轮机舱. ~ **shed** 机车库. ~ **turning** (纸币等上面的)机绘花纹.
en·gi·neer [ˌendʒi'niə] *n.* ①技师; 工程师. ②机械设计者, 机车制造人. ③(轮船的)机师;〔美〕(火车的)司机; 驾驶员. ④(海军的)轮机军官; (陆军的)工兵. *a civil* ~ 土木工程师. *a naval [marine]* ~ 造船工程师. *a chief* ~ ①总工程师. ②轮机长. *a first* ~ 一级机工. *a student* ~ 见习技术员. *the Corps of Engineers* 工兵部队. *the Royal Engineers* 〔英〕皇家工兵. ~ ***in charge*** 主管工程师. ~ ***in chief*** 总工程师. —*vt.* ①设计,监督(工

程等). ②操纵. ③图谋,策划,策动. — *vi.* 做工程师. ~**ship** *n.* 工程师职务[地位].

en·gi·neer·ing [ˌendʒiˈniəriŋ] *n.* ①工程(技术),工程学. ②开车技术. ③土木工程,工事. ④操纵,管理. *civil [electrical, mechanical, mining]* ~ 土木[电机,机械,采矿]工程(学). *aeronautical [marine]* ~ 航空[轮机]工程. *the E-Corps* 工兵部队. ~ *geology* 工程地质. ~ *science* 技术科学. *a key* ~ *project* 关键工程. *military* ~ 工兵学. *an* ~ *worker* 技工. *field* ~ 安装技术. *rocket* ~ 火箭技术. *Nature* ~ 天工.

en·gine·ry [ˈendʒinəri] *n.* ①机械类. ②武器. ③谋略.

en·gird, en·gir·dle [inˈgəːd, -l] *vt.* 用带缠绕;围绕.

en·gla·cial [enˈgleiʃəl] *a.* 冰川内的,冰河内的.

Eng·land [ˈiŋglənd] *n.* ①英格兰〔英国的主要部分〕. ②(泛指)英格兰和威尔士. ③(泛指)英国.

Eng·lish [ˈiŋgliʃ] *a.* ①英格兰(人)的;英国(人)的. ②英语的. — *n.* ①英语. ②〔the ~〕英国人〔总称〕,英国人民;英军. ③〔e-〕【印】十四点活字. ④〔美〕(打网球、弹子时球的)旋转运动. *He is* ~. 他是英国人. *American* ~ 美国英语. *Basic* ~ 基本英语〔此处 Basic 系由 British American Scientific International Commercial 各词的第一字母组成〕. *current [present-day]* ~ 当代英语. *the king's [queen's]* ~ 纯正英语. *Middle* ~ (约 1150—1475 年的)中世纪英语. *Modern* ~ (约 1475 年以后的)近代英语. *Old* ~ (约 450—1150 年的)古代英语. *spoken* ~ 英语口语. *standard* ~ 标准英语. ~ *as she is spoke* 英语口语〔语音〕. *in plain* ~ 直率地说,说得通俗些. — *vt.* ①把…译成英语. ②使成英国式,使英国化. ③〔e-〕使(球)旋转前进. ~ **Channel** 英吉利海峡. ~ **daisy**【植】雏菊 *(Bellis perennis)*. ~ **disease** 〔主英〕支气管炎. ~ **horn** 英国管(中音双簧管). ~ **ivy** = ivy. ~ **muffin** 英式松饼. ~ **setter** 塞特狗,英国谍犬. ~ **sonnet** 英国十四行诗. ~ **sparrow** 家麻雀 *(Passer domesticus)* 〔产于欧洲,现今在北美极常见〕. ~ **springer spaniel**【动】英国长耳跳犬. ~ **toy spaniel**【动】英国长毛小犬. ~ **walnut** ①胡桃树 *(Juglans regia)*. ②胡桃. **-er** *n.* 英国人;翻译英语的人. **-ism** *n.* ①英语习惯用法. ②英国方式,英国人的特点. **-ry** *n.* (特指住在爱尔兰的英格兰籍)英国人.

Eng·lish·man [ˈiŋgliʃmən] *n.* (*pl.* **-men** [-mən, -men]) ①英吉利人,英国人;英国男子. ②英国船只. ~**'s tie** 锚结〔绳结的一种,又叫 anchor knot, fisherman's knot, true lover's knot, waterman's knot〕.

Eng·lish·ment [ˈiŋgliʃmənt] *n.* (外国著作的)英文版,英译本.

Eng·lish·wom·an [ˈiŋgliʃwumən] *n.* 〔*pl.* **-wom·en** [-wimin]〕英国女人.

en·glut [inˈglʌt] *vt.* 〔古、诗〕①吞下,咽下. ②使充满,使吃饱.

en·gobe [ɔnˈgəub] *n.*【化】釉底料.

en·gorge [inˈgɔːdʒ] *vt.* ①喂饱;狼吞虎咽地吃. ②使充血. *His eyes were* ~*d with blood.* 他双目充血. — *vi.* ①大吃,贪吃. ②吮足血. **-ment** *n.* 饱食;【医】充血.

engr. = engineer; engraving.

en·graft [inˈgrɑːft, en-] *vt.* ①嫁接(树木). ②灌输(思想等),使记牢. ③附加. **-a·tion, -ment** *n.*

en·grail [inˈgreil] *vt.* 使成锯齿状花边;使成波纹. **-ment** *n.*

en·grain [inˈgrein] *vt.* ①把(木料、纤维、纱、线等加工前)染色. ②〔喻〕深染〔尤指性格、思想、习惯〕. — *a.* = engrained 生来的;沾染的,根深蒂固的. *an* ~ *[~ed] habit* 积习,积癖. ~*ed scoundrel* 不可救药的恶棍. ~ *vices* 积弊.

en·grave [inˈgreiv] *vt.* ①雕上,刻上. ②镌刻(铜版);(用雕刻铜版)印刷. ②牢记,铭记(心上). ~ *a name on a stone* =~ *a stone with a name* 把名字刻在石头上. *be* ~*d on sb.'s memory* 给人留下深刻印象.

en·grav·er [inˈgreivə] *n.* 雕刻师,雕刻工,镌版工.

en·grav·ing [inˈgreiviŋ] *n.* ①雕刻,雕刻术. ②雕板. ③雕版印刷品;版画.

en·gross [inˈgrəus] *vt.* ①用大字体写,正式誊清. ②吸引(注意),占用(时间),使全神贯注. ③(以垄断方式)大量收购. ~ *the conversation* 只顾一个人说[不让别人开口]. *be* ~*ed in* 热中于,埋头,一心. **-ment** *n.*

en·gross·ing [inˈgrəusiŋ] *a.* 使人全神贯注的;极有趣味的;非常吸引人的. *an* ~ *task* 迷人的工作.

en·gulf [inˈgʌlf] *vt.* 把…卷入旋涡;吞没. **-ment** *n.*

en·hance [inˈhɑːns] *vt.* ①增加(价值、价格、力量、吸引力等),提高;增强. ②夸张;宣扬. **-ment** *n.*

en·har·mon·ic [ˌenhɑːˈmɔnik] *a.*【乐】等音的.

ENIAC, eniac = electronic numerical integrator and computer 电子数字积分计算机.

E·nid [ˈiːnid] *n.* 伊妮德〔女子名〕.

e·nig·ma [iˈnigmə] *n.* 谜;难解的话〔文章〕;不可解的事物〔人物〕.

e·nig·mat·ic(·al) [ˌenigˈmætik(əl), ˌiːnig-] *a.* 似谜的;令人迷惑的;神秘的. **-i·cal·ly** *ad.*

e·nig·ma·tize [iˈnigmətaiz] *vt.* 使成谜;使不可解.

en·isle [enˈail] *vt.* 使成(孤)岛;使孤立.

en·jamb·ment, en·jambe·ment [inˈdʒæmmənt; F. ɑ̃ʒɑ̃bmɑ̃] *n.*〔诗〕(诗句的)跨行进行.

en·join [inˈdʒɔin] *vt.* ①命令,吩咐;告诫;责成. ②〔美〕禁止. ~ *diligence on [upon] pupils* = ~ *pupils to be diligent* 叮嘱学生用功.

en·joy [inˈdʒɔi] *vt.* ①享受…之乐,欣赏,喜爱. ②享受,享有,取得. ~ *swimming* 喜欢游泳. *How did you* ~ *your trip?* 旅行如何? ~ *cherry-blossom(s)* 欣赏樱花. ~ *one's dinner* 饭吃得津津有味. ~ *good health* 健康. ~ *life* 享人生之乐. ~ *the esteem of one's friends* 受到朋友们的敬重. ~ *oneself* 过得快乐. **-a·ble** *a.* 愉快的,快乐的,有趣的. **-a·bly** *ad.* **-able** *a.* **-ness** *n.*

en·joy·ment [inˈdʒɔimənt] *n.* ①享乐,欣赏;愉快,乐事. ②享受,享有. *take* ~ *in* 喜欢,享受,欣赏. *be in the* ~ *of good health* 享有健康.

en·kin·dle [inˈkindl, en-] *vt.* 点着(火);使燃烧起来,激起(热情);挑起(战争等).

enl. = enlarged; enlisted.

en·lace [inˈleis] *vt.* ①卷上,把…卷起来. ②用带子捆扎. ③围绕,缠绕. **-ment** *n.*

en·large [inˈlɑːdʒ] *vt.* ①扩大,扩展,扩充;增大;【摄】放大. ②〔美〕〔古〕释放. ~ *one's views by reading* 以读书来开扩眼界. ~ *one's house* 扩建房屋. *an* ~*d edition* 增订版. *an* ~*d photograph* 放大照片. — *vi.* ①扩展,扩大. ②拉长说,详述 *(on; upon)*. **-ment** *n.* 扩大,扩张;增补;【摄】放大;【医】增大,肥大,肿大. **-r** [-ə] *n.* ①【摄】放大机. ②扩大者,增补者;详述者.

en·light·en [inˈlaitn] *vt.* ①启发,开导;教导;〔口〕使明白,使领悟. ②使摆脱偏见. ③〔古〕照耀. ~ *sb. on a subject* 使某人明白某问题. **-ed** *a.* 开通的,开明的,进步的,文明的;有知识的 *(an* ~ *age* 文明时代). **-ing** *a.* ①有启发作用的,使人领悟的. ②〔古〕照耀的,照明的. **-ment** *n.*

en·light·en·ment [inˈlaitnmənt] *n.* ①启迪,启蒙,启发;教化,开导. ②开明的状态. *the Enlightenment* (十八世纪欧洲的)启蒙运动. *the Age of Enlightenment* 启蒙时代.

en·link [inˈliŋk] *vt.* 把…连接起来,使紧密联系 *(with; to)*.

en·list [inˈlist] *vt.* ①使入伍;征募,招(兵). ②争取,谋取获得(赞助等). ~ *sb. in an enterprise* 在事业上得到某人赞助. ~ *the support of* 拉拢. *an* ~*ed man* 〔美〕士兵. — *vi.* ①应募;参加 *(in)*. ②协助,赞助,支持,偏袒. ~ *as a volunteer* 当志愿兵. ~ *in the army* 从军. ~ *under the banner of revolution* 加入革命队伍. **-ment** *n.* 募兵;征募,入伍;服兵役期.

en·li·ven [in'laivən] *vt.* 使快活,使有生气,给与生气;使生动;使活跃.

en·mesh [in'meʃ, en-] *vt.* ①把…绊在网上;使绊住.②使陷入. *be ~ed in difficulties* 陷入困难中. **-ment** *n.*

en·mi·ty ['enmiti] *n.* 敌意,仇恨,憎恨;反目,不和. ***at ~ with*** 与…不和. ***have [harbour] no ~ against sb.*** 对某人无冤无仇.

en·ne·ad ['eniæd] *n.* ①九个一组. ②〔E-〕(埃及的)九柱神.

en·ne·a·gon ['eniəgɔn] *n.*【数】九角形,九边形.

en·ne·a·hed·ron [ˌeniə'hedrən] *n.*【数】九面体.

en·ne·a·syl·la·ble [ˌeniə'siləbl] *n.* 九音节.

en·no·ble [i'nəubl] *vt.* ①使高贵;抬高. ②把…列入贵族,给…授爵. **-ment** *n.*

en·nui [F. ɑ̃nɥi; 'ɔnwiː] *n.* 〔F.〕厌倦,倦怠,无聊.

E·noch ['iːnɔk] *n.* 伊诺克〔男子名〕.

e·nol ['iːnɔl, -nəul] *n.*【化】烯醇. **e·no·lic** [iː'nɔlik] *a.* **e·nol·i·za·tion** [ˌenəlai'zeiʃən] *n.* 烯醇化(作用).

e·nol·o·gy [iː'nɔlədʒi] *n.* 葡萄酒酿制学. **e·nol·o·gist** *n.* 葡萄酒酿制术研究者〔专家〕.

e·nor·mi·ty [i'nɔːmiti] *n.* ①极恶,凶恶;暴行,大罪. ②巨大,庞大. *the ~ of the crime* 罪恶深重.

e·nor·mous [i'nɔːməs] *a.* ①巨大的,庞大的. ②无法无天的,罪大恶极的. *an ~ difference* 很大的分歧. *~ profits* 巨大的利益. *a man of ~ strength* 力气很大的人. **-ly** *ad.* **-ness** *n.*

e·nough [i'nʌf] *a.* 充足的,足够的. *~ eggs, eggs ~* 鸡蛋十分充足〔后者语气较弱〕. *~ noise to wake the dead* 吵得死人都不安. ***~ and to spare*** 绰绰有余. ***more than ~*** 太多. — *n.* 充足,满足,足够. *have ~ to eat* 有足够的东西吃. *E- of that!* 够了,别说了! *E- of this folly!* 不要再干这种傻事了! ***Cry '~'!*** 快认输吧! ***E. is as good as a feast.***【谚】饱食便是珍馐;知足常乐. ***have ~ to do*** 很吃力(*I had ~ to do to catch the tram.* 我好容易才赶上电车). ***have had quite [about] ~ of*** 感到厌烦. — *ad.* 〔用于被修饰语之后〕十分,充分,足,够. *I am warm ~.* 我够暖和的. *He was fool (= foolish) ~ to agree.* 他同意了,真够傻的. *She was clever ~ to take the management of her own house.* 她很能干,一定会管家. *The meat is roasted just ~.* 这肉烤得恰到好处. ***Be good [kind] ~ to reply early.*** 请早日赐复. ***be old ~ to*** 已经是可以…的年龄了. ***can not ... ~*** 无论怎样…都不够(*I cannot thank you ~.* 感谢不尽). ***curiously [oddly, strangely] ~*** 〔用作插入语〕说也奇怪,最奇怪的是. ***sure ~*** 确实,果然. ***well ~*** ①还不错,还可以. ②相当;很,极. — *int.* 够了! 别再说了!

e·nounce [i(ː)'nauns] *vt.* ①宣告,发表;声明,说明. ②发声读出. **-ment** *n.*

En·o·vid ['iːnəvid] *n.* 女用口服避孕药〔商标名〕.

e·now [i'nau] *a., n., ad.* 〔古〕= enough.

en·phy·tot·ic [ˌenfai'tɔtik] *a.*【植】恒定流行的.

en·plane [en'plein] *vi.* 乘飞机 (*cf.* deplane). *~ for Europe* 乘飞机去欧洲.

en·quire [in'kwaiə] *vi., vt.* = inquire.

en·quir·y [in'kwaiəri] *n.* = inquiry.

en·rage [in'reidʒ] *vt.* 触怒,激怒,使人愤怒. ***be ~d at [by] sth.*** 对某事愤慨,为某事激怒. ***be ~d with sb.*** 对某人发怒. **-d·ly** *ad.* **-ment** *n.*

en·rapt [in'ræpt] *a.* 狂喜的.

en·rap·ture [in'ræptʃə] *vt.* 使狂喜,使兴高采烈. **-d·ly** *ad.*

en·reg·i·ment [in'redʒimənt] *vt.* ①把…编成联队. ②把…严格地组织起来 (*cf.* regiment).

en·reg·is·ter [in'redʒistə] *vt.* 记录,登记.

en règle [F. ɑ̃'rɛgl] 〔F.〕照规则,按规定.

en·rich [in'ritʃ] *vt.* ①使富裕,使丰富. ②【矿】富集. ③(使)充实. ④使肥沃. ⑤加浓. ⑥浓缩. ⑥装饰. *~ oneself at sb.'s expense* 损人肥己. *~ed bread* 营养面包. *~ed uranium*【原】浓缩铀. **-ment** *n.* **-er** *n.* **-ing·ly** *ad.*

en·robe [in'rəub] *vt.* 使穿长袍. **-ment** *n.*

en·rol(l) [in'rəul] *vt.* ①把…记入名簿〔清单,目录〕;登记,编入;使入会,使入学. ②使入伍,使服兵役. *~ sb. a member of a club* 吸收某人为俱乐部会员. *~ oneself in the army* 应征入伍,参军. **-ment** *n.* ①登记,注册. ②入伍,参军. ③入会. ④注册人数.

en·roll·ee [inˌrəu'liː] *n.* 被录用的人;入会者;被征入伍者;入学者.

en·root [in'ruːt, -'rut] *vt.* 使根深蒂固,深植〔主要用作被动语态〕.

ens [enz] *n.* (*pl.* ***entia*** ['enʃiə]) = entity.

Ens. = Ensign 〔美〕海军少尉.

en·sam·ple [en'sɑːmpl] *n.* 〔古〕= example.

en·san·guine [in'sæŋgwin] *vt.* 血染,血污,血溅;使成血红色.

en·san·guined [in'sæŋgwind, en-] *a.* 血红色的.

en·sate ['enseit] *a.* = ensiform.

en·sconce [in'skɔns] *vt.* ①使安坐;安置. ②隐藏. *~ oneself in [on]* 安坐于…;把自己安置于….

en·sem·ble [F. ɑ̃sɑ̃ːbl] *n.* 〔F.〕①全体,总体;总(体)效果. ②全体演出,全体演出者. ③【乐】合唱,大合奏. ④整套(衣服). ⑤剧团,歌舞团,文工团. ⑥【自】集合,系集,信号群. ***~ playing*** 集体演出.

en·sep·ul·cher, en·sep·ul·chre [in'seplkə] *vt.* (***-chered, -chred; -cher·ing, -chring***) 把…葬入坟墓;埋葬.

en·sheathe [in'ʃiːð] *vt.* 把…插入鞘;用鞘套住.

en·shrine [in'ʃrain] *vt.* ①把…置于殿内祀奉;把…安置在龛内. ②秘藏. *memories ~d in one's heart* 珍藏在内心中的回忆. **-ment** *n.*

en·shroud [in'ʃraud, en-] *vt.* ①用寿衣包上. ②隐蔽,包藏. *be ~ed in mist* 笼罩在雾中.

en·si·form ['ensifɔːm] *a.*【植】剑形的.

en·sign ['ensain] *n.* ①徽章(表示职别等的). ②旗,国旗;团旗. ③['ensn] 军舰旗. ④〔美〕海军少尉;【英军】(从前做旗手的)步兵少尉〔现名 second lieutenant〕. *the national ~* 国旗. ***the blue ~*** 英国海军预备舰舰旗. ***the red ~*** 英国商船旗. ***the St. George's [white] ~*** 英国军舰旗. ***the white ~*** 英国海军与皇家快艇中队旗. **-cy** ['ensainsi] = **-ship** *n.* 少尉的职位〔任务〕.

en·si·lage ['ensilidʒ] *n.* 饲料青贮法;青贮饲料. — *vt.* 青贮(饲料).

en·sile [en'sail] *vt.* 青贮(饲料).

en·sky [in'skai] *vt.* ①使耸入天际. ②把…捧上天. — *vi.* 耸入天际.

en·slave [in'sleiv] *vt.* ①使做奴隶;征服. ②强制,使盲从. *be ~d to a habit* 成为习惯的奴隶. **-ment** *n.*

en·slav·er [in'sleivə] *n.* 奴役者,征服者.

en·snare [in'sneə] *vt.* ①用绊子捕捉,绊住. ②诱…入圈套;诱捕,诱惑,陷害. **-ment** *n.*

en·snarl [in'snɑːl] *vt.* 使缠结,使纠缠.

en·sor·cell, en·sor·cel [in'sɔːsl] *vt.* (***-celled; -cell·ing, -cel·ing***)〔古〕①迷,迷惑;(妖言)惑(众). ②令人心醉,使人心荡神移,恼(人).

en·soul [in'səul] *vt.* ①使深入灵魂. ②赋予…灵魂.

en·sphere [in'sfiə] *vt.* ①把…放置球中. ②包围;使成球形.

en·sta·tite ['enstətait] *n.*【地】顽辉石.

en·sue [in'sjuː, en-] *vi.* 跟着发生;(…的)结果是…(*from; on*). *the ensuing months* 随后数月. *the ensuing year = the year ensuing* 第二年. *Silence ~d.* 随即静默. *What will ~ from [on] this?* 这会产生什么结果呢? — *vt.*【圣】追求.

en·sure [in'ʃuə] *vt.* ①保护,使安全 (*against; from*). ②保证,担保;保险. *~ an income to sb.* 确保某人有一笔收

入. *It will ~ you success.* 这将保证你成功. **-r** *n.* 保证者;保护者.

en·swathe [in'sweið, -'swɑːð] *vt.* 绑;卷,缠. **-ment** *n.*

E. N. T. = ear, nose and throat 耳鼻喉.

-ent *suf.* ①加在动词后构成形容词,表示"动作"、"性质": insist*ent*. ②加在动词后构成名词,表示"动作者"、"生效物": presid*ent*, solv*ent*.

en·tab·la·ture [en'tæblətʃə] *n.* ①【建】柱上楣构,柱顶盘. ②(机器部件等的)支柱.

en·ta·ble·ment [in'teiblmənt] *n.* ① = entablature. ②承放雕像的平台.

en·tail [in'teil] *vt.* ①【法】限定(继承人). ②遗留给,传给(弊害等) *(on, upon)*. ③使蒙受,使产生,带来,引起;需要. *~ labour upon* 在…上要花费劳力. *~ great expense on sb.* 使某人承担大笔费用. — *n.*【法】①限定继承权. ②预定继承人的顺序. **-ment** *n.*

en·ta·moe·ba [ˌentə'miːbə] *n.* *(pl.* **-bae** [-biː], **-bas** [bəz]) = endamoeba.

en·tan·gle [in'tæŋgl] *vt.* ①使纠缠,缠住;使混乱. ②使卷入,使陷入;连累. ③困恼,迷惑. *be easily ~d by flattery* 易被甜言蜜语所迷惑. ***be [get] ~d in*** 给…缠住;被牵连,被卷入(*be ~d with sb.* 同某人有牵连).

en·tan·gle·ment [in'tæŋglmənt] *n.* ①缠结;纠纷,混乱. ②牵连. ③为难. *barbed wire ~s* 带刺的铁丝网.

en·ta·sis ['entəsis] *n.*【建】凸肚状.

en·tel·e·chy [en'teləki] *n.*【哲】①圆满实现. ②生命原理.

en·tel·lus [en'teləs] *n.*【动】(印度的)瘤猿.

en·ten·te [F. ɑ̃tɑ̃ːt] *n.* 〔F.〕①(国家间的)协定,协商. ②协约国;有协约关系的党派. *~* ***cordiale*** [kɔr'djal] 友好谅解. ***E- cordiale***(1904年的)英法协约. ***the (Triple) E-*** (1907 年的英、法、俄)三国协约.

en·ter ['entə] *vt.* ①入,进. ②把…放进. ③加入,参加;使加入,使入会,使入学. ④编入;记入,登记;申报. ⑤训练(狗、马等). ⑥【法】提出. ⑦开始. *~ the army* 参军. *~ a profession* 就业. *~ battle* 开始战斗. *~ details in a book* 把细目记入帐簿. *~ a protest* 提出抗议;把抗议列入记录. *~ an action against sb.* 控告某人. *~ a ship* 申报船只入港. *~ an appearance* 到案,出庭;到场,出席. — *vi.* ①入;挤进. ②【剧】上〔出〕场. ③参加,加入;入会,入学. *~ at the door* 从正门进来. *~ by a secret entrance* 偷进. *~ for (a race)* 参加(赛跑). *~ for an examination* 投考. *~* ***into*** ①入,挤入;动手,开始(谈话等). ②成为…的一部分. ③缔结(协约等). ④参加,参与(计划等). ⑤讨论(细节);着手处理. ⑥考虑;体会;体谅,同情. (*~ into sb.'s feelings* 体会某人心情. *~ into sb.'s troubles* 体谅别人困难. *~ into an agreement* 缔约). *~* ***on [upon]*** ①动手,开始. ②入,投身于. ③占有(土地、财产等)(*~ upon one's thirtieth year* 满29岁. *~ upon one's task* 动手工作. *~ upon a political career* 投身政界. *~ upon one's new duties* 开始担任新职). ***~ one's head*** 想起,想到. *~* ***up*** ①把…正式记入帐簿. ②【法】把…记入案件记录中. **-a·ble** *a.*

enter- *comb. f.* = entero- 表示"肠的": *enter*itis, *entero*cele.

en·ter·ic [en'terik] *a.* 肠的. *~* **fever** 伤寒,肠热病.

en·ter·i·tis [ˌentə'raitis] *n.*【医】肠炎.

en·ter·o- *comb. f.* "肠": *entero*cele.

en·ter·o·bi·a·sis [ˌentərəu'baiəsis] *n.*【医】蛲虫病.

en·ter·o·cele ['entərəusiːl] *n.*【医】肠疝,阴道后疝.

en·ter·o·co·li·tis ['entəˌrəukə'laitis] *n.*【医】小肠结肠炎.

en·ter·o·gas·trone [ˌentərəu'gæstrəun] *n.*【医】肠抑胃素.

en·ter·o·ki·nase [ˌentərəu'kaineis, -'kineis] *n.*【生化】肠致活酶.

en·ter·on ['entəˌrɔn] *n.* 肠,消化道.

en·ter·os·to·my [ˌentə'rɔstəmi] *n.*【医】肠造口术.

en·ter·o·to·my [ˌentə'rɔtəmi] *n.*【医】肠切开术.

en·ter·prise ['entəpraiz] *n.* ①(艰巨或带有冒险性的)事业,计划. ②企[事]业单位. ③企业心,事业心,进取心;冒险心;胆识. ④兴办(企业),开创(事业). *embark in [upon] an ~* 举办企业. *free ~* 自由企业. *a man of ~* 有进取心的人. *a rash ~* 轻率的计划. *a spirit of ~* 事业精神. ***undertake [take on] an ~*** 创办事业. **-pris·er** *n.* = entrepreneur.

en·ter·pris·ing ['entəpraiziŋ] *a.* 有事业心的,有创业精神的,有积极性的,大胆的. *an ~ young man* 富有事业精神的青年人. *~ spirit* 事业心,冒险精神,积极性. **-ly** *ad.*

en·ter·tain [ˌentə'tein] *vt.* ①招待,款待;使快乐;使感兴趣. ②怀抱(希望等),含有(感情等). ③容纳,接受,答应(请求等),愿意考虑. *The play ~ed us very much.* 那个戏很有趣. *~ the proposal* 愿意考虑建议. *be ~ed at [to] dinner* 受款待,被宴请. *~ doubts* 怀疑. *~ hopes* 怀抱希望. *~ friends with music [refreshments]* 用音乐〔茶点〕招待朋友. —*vi.* 进行招待〔款待〕的活动. *~* ***angels unawares*** 招待某人而不知其为贵宾〔出自《圣经·希伯来书》〕.

en·ter·tain·er [ˌentə'teinə] *n.* ①款待者. ②演艺者〔尤指民歌手,舞蹈、喜剧演员等〕.

en·ter·tain·ing [ˌentə'teiniŋ] *a.* ①有趣的,使人愉快的;招待好的. ②会应酬的. — *n.* 招待,款待. *~ expenses* 招待费,交际费. **-ly** *ad.*

en·ter·tain·ment [ˌentə'teinmənt] *n.* ①招待,款待;应酬;宴会;娱乐;游艺,余兴. ②怀抱. ③受理,采纳. ④招待会,表演会,文娱节目. *a house of ~* 娱乐场;旅馆;酒馆(等). *a farewell ~* 欢送会. *a musical ~* 音乐演奏,音乐余兴. ***give an ~ to sb.*** 招待(某人),宴请(某人). ***much to my ~*** 最有趣的是. *~* **tax** 娱乐捐.

en·thal·py ['enθælpi, en'θælpi] *n.*【化】热函;焓.

en·thral(l) [in'θrɔːl] *vt.* ①迷惑,吸引住. ②使役,使做奴隶. *be ~ed by a novel* 被小说迷住. **-ing** *a.* **-ment** *n.*

en·throne [in'θrəun] *vt.* ①使登基,立…为王;【宗】使就任主教;给予…最高地位. ②崇拜;尊崇. **-ment** *n.*

en·thro·ni·za·tion [inˌθrəunai'zeiʃən] *n.* = enthronement.

en·thuse [in'θjuːz] *vi., vt.* 〔口〕(使)表示热心;(使)变得热心.

en·thu·si·asm [in'θjuːziæzəm] *n.* ①热心,热情,热诚 *(for)*. ②爱好的事物;〔古〕宗教狂,笃信. *Music is his great ~.* 音乐是他最爱好的东西. ***be full of ~ about*** 热衷于. ***an outburst of ~*** 热情奔放. *~* ***for*** *(sport)* (运动)热. ***on momentary ~*** 凭一时热情. ***overflow with ~*** 热情洋溢. ***with ~*** 热衷,热心.

en·thu·si·ast [in'θjuːziæst] *n.* ①热心家,热情者,热衷者. ②〔古〕宗教狂.

en·thu·si·as·tic [inˌθjuːzi'æstik] *a.* 热心的,热情的;热烈的. **-cal·ly** *ad.*

en·thy·meme ['enθimiːm] *n.*【逻】省略推理法,省略三段论法. **en·thy·me·mat·ic** [ˌenθəmi'mætik], **en·thy·mem·ic** [ˌenθi'miːmik] *a.*

en·tice [in'tais] *vt.* 引诱,怂恿. *~* ***away from ...*** 从…诱出. *~ sb.* ***into*** *doing [to do]* 怂恿某人做…. **-ment** *n.*

en·tic·ing [in'taisiŋ] *a.* 迷人的,诱人的,动人心目的. **-ly** *ad.*

en·tire [in'taiə] *a.* ①整个的,完全的;全部的,完整的;全体的. ②纯粹的. ③【植】全缘的. ④(雄兽)没有阉过的. — *n.* 〔罕〕①整体;全部. ②〔英〕一种黑啤酒. ③种马. *~ affection* 纯真的爱情. *an ~ horse* 没有阉过的马. **-ly** *ad.* 彻底地,完全地. **-ness** *n.*

en·tire·ty [in'taiəti] *n.* 完全;全部,全体,总体. ***in its ~*** 整体,全部,全盘. ***possession by entireties***【法】共同占有,(不可分的)所有权.

en·ti·ta·tive ['entitətiv] *a.* 实体的,本质的.

en·ti·tle [in'taitl] *vt.* ①使…有资格(做某事);给与…权利[资格]. ②给…定名,把…叫做. *His talent ~s him to command.* 他的才能使他有资格指挥. *be ~d to say that* 有资格说. *be ~d to praise* 值得表扬. *be ~ed "Your Highness"* 被尊称为"殿下". **-ment** *n.* 权利.

en·ti·ty ['entiti] *n.* ①实体;统一体. ②存在(物). ③(有别于属性等的)本质.

en·to- *comb. f.* 表示"内": *ento*derm.

en·to·blast ['entəublæst] *n.* = endoblast.

en·to·derm ['entəudə:m] *n.* = endoderm.

en·to·gas·tric [ˌentəu'gæstrik] *a.* 胃内的.

en·toil [in'tɔil] *vt.* 〔古,诗〕使入圈套;诱惑;陷害.

en·tomb [in'tu:m] *vt.* 埋葬;成为…的坟墓. **-ment** *n.*

en·tom·ic(al) [in'tɔmik(əl)] *a.* 昆虫的.

en·to·mo·log·ic [ˌentəuməˈlɔdʒik] *a.* 昆虫学的.

en·to·mol·o·gist [ˌentəu'mɔlədʒist] *n.* 昆虫学家,昆虫学者.

en·to·mol·o·gize [ˌentəu'mɔlədʒaiz] *vi.* ①研究昆虫学. ②采集昆虫.

en·to·mol·o·gy [ˌentəu'mɔlədʒi] *n.* 昆虫学. *economic ~* 实用昆虫学,经济昆虫学.

en·to·moph·a·gous [ˌentəu'mɔfəgəs] *a.*【动】食虫的.

en·to·moph·i·lous [ˌentəu'mɔfiləs] *a.*【植】虫媒的. *an ~ flower* 虫媒花.

en·to·moph·i·ly [ˌentəu'mɔfili] *n.* 昆虫传花粉作用.

en·to·mos·tra·can [ˌentəu'mɔstrəkən] *n.* 切甲类(*Entomostraca*)动物.

en·to·phyte ['entəufait] *n.* 内寄生植物.

en·to·plas·tron [ˌentəu'plæstrən] *n.* (*pl.* **en·to·plastra** [ˌentəu'plæstrə])【动】内腹甲.

en·tou·rage [ˌɔntu'rɑ:ʒ] *n.* 〔F.〕①(建筑物的)周围,环境. ②随行人员,伴随者,近侍.

en·to·zo·a [ˌentəu'zəuə] *n.* entozoon 的复数.

en·to·zo·on [ˌentəu'zəuɔn] *n.* (*pl.* **-zoa** [-ə]) 内寄生动物. **en·to·zo·al** [-əl], **en·to·zo·ic** [-ik] *a.*

en·tr'acte ['ɔntrækt, ɔn'trækt] *n.* 〔F.〕①(多幕剧的)幕间休息. ②幕间休息时的插演节目(如音乐、舞蹈等).

en·trails ['entreilz] *n.* ①〔*pl.*〕内脏;肠. ②(物体的)内部.

en·train[1] [in'trein] *vt.* (用火车)输送(军队等). —*vi.* 上火车.

en·train[2] [in'trein] *vt.* ①〔罕〕拖. ②产生,导致. ③【化】带走;使(空气)在混凝土中成气泡. *~ed oil* 带走的油. **-er** *n.*【化】夹带剂.

en·train·ment [in'treinmənt] *n.*【化】雾沫. *dust ~* 带走粉尘量. *~ phenomena* 卷吸现象.

en·tram·mel [in'træml] *vt.* (〔英〕 *-ll-*) 纠缠;拘束,束缚;妨碍.

en·trance[1] ['entrəns] *n.* ①进入;入场;加入,入会;入学. ②开始,着手. ③就业,就职. ④(演员的)出场. ⑤入场权;入场费;会费;学费. ⑥入口,大门(口),楼梯口;【电】引入线. ⑦(海关)入港手续. ⑧【乐】起奏,起唱. ⑨【海】船头水线以下的部分. *~ examinations* 入学考试. *~ fee [money]* 入场费;会费;学费. *~ free* 免费入场. *~ requirements* 入学标准. ***force an ~ into*** 闯进. ***gain an ~*** 挤进去. ***have free ~ to*** 可以自由进入…. ***make [effect] one's ~*** 入场. ***No ~.*** 不准入内.

en·trance[2] [in'trɑ:ns] *vt.* 使出神,使神魂颠倒,使发迷;使狂喜. *be ~d with joy* 欢喜得发狂. *be ~d in thought* 想得出神. *be ~d with fear* 吓得魂不附体. **-ment** *n.*

en·tranc·ing [in'trɑ:nsiŋ] *a.* 迷人的,使人神魂颠倒的. **-ly** *ad.*

en·trant ['entrənt] *n.* ①进入者. ②新加入的人;新会员;(刚入大学的)新生;新就业者. ③参加竞赛者.

en·trap [in'træp] *vt.* ①俘获,使陷罗网. ②用计引诱,使堕术中.

en·treat [in'tri:t] *vt.* ①恳求,请求. ②〔古〕对待. *~ a favour of sb.* 请某人帮忙. *~ sb. for [to show] mercy* 求情. *~ sb.'s pardon* 请人原谅. *evil(ly) ~ sb.* 〔古〕虐待某人. —*vi.* 恳求,请求. **-ing·ly** *ad.* **-ment** *n.*

en·treat·y [in'tri:ti] *n.* 恳求,哀求.

en·tre·chat [ˌɑ:ntrə'ʃɑ:] *n.* 〔F.〕(芭蕾舞的)击足跳〔跃起两足腾空交叉数次〕.

en·tre·côte [F. ɑ̃trəko:t] *n.* 〔F.〕肋骨间的肉,去肋骨的肉片.

en·trée, en·tree ['ɔntrei] *n.* 〔F.〕①入场;入场许可,入场权. ②〔英〕鱼肉两正菜间的菜,〔美〕正菜. ③【乐】(舞剧的)开场舞,(歌剧的)开始乐章.

en·tre·mets ['ɔntrəmei, 〔*pl.*〕'ɔntrəmeiz] *n.* 〔F.〕*sing., pl.* 正菜之外的菜;甜食.

en·trench [in'trentʃ] *vt.* ①在…围以壕沟,用壕沟防护. ②盘踞,固守,牢固树立. ③深挖. —*vi.* ①侵犯,侵占. ②〔古〕接近(*on, upon*). ***be ~ed in ...*** 盘踞在…. ***~ oneself*** 挖壕沟自卫. ***~ed within tradition*** 墨守惯例. **-ment** *n.* ①掘壕沟,筑垒. ②壕沟,堡垒,阵地. ③保护. ④〔古〕侵犯.

en·tre nous [ɔ:ntrə 'nu:] 〔F.〕 ***(= between ourselves)*** 不要对外人说[只限你我知道].

en·tre·pôt ['ɔntrəpəu] *n.* 〔F.〕①仓库;关栈;保税仓库. ②货物集散地. **~ trade** 转口贸易.

en·tre·pre·neur [ˌɔntrəprə'nə:] *n.* 〔F.〕①企业家;创业人. ②承包人;主办人;促进者. **-ship** *n.* 企业家〔主办人等〕的身分[地位、职权、能力].

en·tre·sol ['ɔntrəsɔl] *n.* 〔F.〕【建】夹层,阁楼.

en·tro·py ['entrəpi] *n.* ①【物】熵. ②【无】平均信息量.

en·trust [in'trʌst] *vt.* 委托,付托;托. *~ sth. to sb.* = *~ sb. with sth.* 把某物交给某人. **-ment** *n.*

en·try ['entri] *n.* ①进入,入场;入城;(演员)出场. ②入口;门口. ③通道,路口;河口. ④登记;记载;申报;记录;记载事项,项目,条目. ⑤参加;(比赛的)参加人名单. ⑥(海关)报关手续,报单. ⑦【法】对土地的侵占;对家宅的侵入. *a triumphal ~* 凯旋入城. *a port of ~* 报关海港[口岸]. *double [single] ~* 复[单]式簿记. *word~* (词典的)词条. ***~ for consumption*** 进口货物报单. ***~ for free goods*** 免税货物报单. ***make an ~ (in)*** 记入,登记. ***make one's ~*** 出场. **~way** *n.* 入口通道.

en·twine [in'twain] *vt.* 缠住,盘绕;纠缠. *a tree ~d with ivy* 爬满常春藤的树. —*vi.* 缠绕. **-ment** *n.*

en·twist [in'twist, en-] *vt.* 缠结;捻,搓.

e·nu·cle·ate [i'nju:klieit] *vt.* ①〔古〕阐明. ②【医】摘出,剜出. ③【生】去核. **e·nu·cle·a·tion** *n.*

e·nu·mer·ate [i'nju:məreit] *vt.* ①数,点. ②枚举,列举. **e·nu·mer·a·ble** *a.* 可点数的,可列举的. **e·nu·mer·a·tion** [iˌnju:mə'reiʃən] *n.* ①计算;列举. ②详叙;细目. ③【统】点查(*defy ~* 不胜枚举. *the ~ method* 查点法). **-a·tive** *a.* 计算的,计数的;列举的.

e·nun·ci·a·ble [i'nʌnsiəbl, -ʃi:-] *a.* ①可断言的,可阐明的,可系统表达的. ②可宣布的;可发表的. ③可清晰发音的.

e·nun·ci·ate [i'nʌnsieit, -ʃi-] *vt.* 宣布,发表(学说等);阐明(宗旨等). —*vi.* (清晰)发音. **e·nun·ci·a·tion** [iˌnʌnsi'eiʃən] *n.* ①阐明;宣告;发表. ②清晰发音. **e·nun·ci·a·tive** [i'nʌnʃiətiv] *a.* ①阐明的;宣告的. ②发音(清晰)的. **e·nun·ci·a·tor** *n.* ①阐明者;宣告者,陈述者. ②发音清晰的人.

e·nure [i'njuə] *vt., vi.* = inure.

en·u·re·sis [ˌenju'ri:sis] *n.*【医】遗尿(症).

en·u·ret·ic [ˌenju'retik] *a.* 遗尿的. — *n.* 遗尿剂.

env. = envelope.

en·vei·gle [en'vi:gl] *vt.* = inveigle.

en·vel·op [in'veləp] *vt.* ①包,封;蔽. ②【军】包围. *an ~ing attack* 包围攻击. *be ~ed in* 被包围在. *~ oneself in a blanket* 包在毛毯中. —*n.* = envelope. *~* **table**

四边附有摺叶可以放大的桌子．～ **top** 桌子四边作放大桌面用的摺叶．**-ment** *n.* ①封,包;包围．②封皮,封套．

en·ve·lope ['envələup, 'ɔn-] *n.* ①信封;纸袋;包封,封皮．②壳层,外壳．③【数】包(络)线;包迹．④【空】气囊;【天】包层;【生】包膜,包被．*floral* ～【植】花被．

en·ven·om [in'venəm, en-] *vt.* ①置毒于,在…下毒．②使恶化;毒害．*an ～ed mind* 狠心．*～ed words* 恶毒的话． **en·ven·om·a·tion** [in,venə'meiʃən] *n.* 毒化;投毒．

en·vi·a·ble ['enviəbl] *a.* 引起妒忌的,值得羡慕的．**-ness** *n.* **en·vi·a·bly** *ad.*

en·vied ['envid] *a.* 被人妒忌的,被人羡慕的．

en·vi·er ['enviə] *n.* 嫉妒者,羡慕者．

en·vi·ous ['enviəs] *a.* 忌妒的,猜忌的,艳羡的．*be ～ of sb. for his success = be ～ of sb.'s success* 忌妒[羡慕]某人的成功．～ *looks* 嫉妒的神情,羡慕的眼光．**-ly** *ad.* **-ness** *n.*

en·vi·ron [in'vaiərən] *vt.* 包围,围绕．*be ～ed with [by] enemies* 被敌人包围．

en·vi·ron·ment [in'vaiərənmənt] *n.* ①周围,围绕．②围绕物;环境,四周,外界．③环境艺术作品;环境戏剧(*cf.* environmental art). *natural* ～ 自然环境． *social* ～ 社会环境．

en·vi·ron·men·tal [in,vaiərən'mentl] *a.* ①环境的,环境产生的．②环境艺术的．*an ～ factor* 环境的因素．～ **art** 环境艺术〔一种以作品包围观众,而不是把作品固定在观众面前的艺术形式〕．～ **engineering** 模拟运转条件的技术;环境工程． ～ **pollution** 环境污染．～ **radiation** 环境放射．～ **vresistance** (限制人口增长的)环境阻力．～ **science** (研究环境污染等问题的)环境科学．**-ly** *ad.*

en·vi·ron·men·tal·ism [in,vaiərən'mentlizm] *n.*【生】(同遗传论相对的)环境论〔认为环境系决定个体和群体发展的主要因素〕．

en·vi·ron·men·tal·ist [in,vaiərən'mentlist] *n.* ①环境论者．②环境保护论者,研究环境问题的专家．—*a.* 环境论的,环境论者的．

en·vi·rons ['envirənz, in'vaiərənz] *n. pl.* 附近,近郊,郊区．*the ～ of Paris* 巴黎郊区．

en·vis·age [in'vizidʒ, en-] *vt.* ①正视,面对(事实等)．②想象;设想．③观察,展望．～ *realities* 正视现实．*programs ～d by the municipal authority* 市政当局拟议中的计划．**-ment** *n.*

en·vi·sion [in'viʒən, en-] *vt.* 想象,预见,展望．

en·voi ['envɔi] *n.* = envoy.

en·voy[1] ['envɔi] *n.* 使节;代表,使者;全权公使;外交官．*an Imperial ～* 钦差(大臣)．*a peace ～* 媾和使节．*a special ～* 特使．*～ extraordinary and minister plenipotentiary* 特命全权公使．**-ship** *n.* 使节身份．

en·voy[2] ['envɔi] *n.* (诗等的)跋,书后;(作为高潮的概括或献词的)结尾诗节．

en·vy ['envi] *vt.* 羡慕;忌妒,猜忌．*How I ～ you!* 我真羡慕您! —*n.* ①羡慕;忌妒,猜忌．③忌妒的根由,羡慕的对象．*be in ～ of sb.'s success* 羡慕某人的成功．*out of ～* 出于忌妒[羡慕]．

en·wind [in'waind, en-] *vt.* 缠绕,包,卷．

en·womb [in'wu:m] *vt.* ①深包,隐藏．②使包藏于子宫内．

en·wrap [in'ræp] *vt.* ①包裹,包围,围绕．②吸引住,使专心,使迷于．

en·wreathe [in'ri:ð, en-] *vt.* 用花圈围住[装饰];缠,绕(= inwreathe).

en·wrought [in'rɔ:t] *a.* = inwrought.

en·zo·ot·ic [,enzəu'ɔtik] *n.* 地方性动物病．— *a.* 地方性动物病的．

en·zy·got·ic [,enzai'gɔtik] *a.*【生】同胚的,同一受胎卵发生的．

en·zy·mat·ic [,enzai'mætik] *a.*【生化】酶的,酶促的．**-al·ly** *ad.*

en·zyme ['enzaim], **en·zym** [-zim] *n.*【化】酶．*digestive ～* 消化酶．*induced ～* 诱导酶．

en·zy·mic [en'zaimik] *a.* = enzymatic. **-al·ly** *ad.*

en·zy·mol·o·gy [,enzi'mɔlədʒi] *n.* 酶(化)学．

eo- *comb. f.*【地、考古】表示"始新","原始": *Eocene, eohippus.*

e·o·bi·ont [,i(:)əu'baiənt] *n.*【生】生物前驱〔英国物理学家伯纳尔 (J. D. Bernal) 用语,假定生命起源于化学演变过程．生物前驱是生物具有生命前的一个发展期〕．

E·o·cene ['i(:)əusi:n] *a.*【地】始新世的,始新统的．— *n.*〔the ～〕【地】始新世;始新统;始新世岩石．～ **epoch**【地】始新世．～ **series** 始新统．

e·o·hip·pus [,i(:)əu'hipəs] *n.*【古生】始祖马 *(Eohippus).*

E·o·li·an [i(:)'əuliən] *a.* = Aeolian.

E·ol·ic [i(:)'ɔlik] *n., a.* = Aeolic.

e·o·lith ['i(:)əuliθ] *n.*【考古】原始石器．

e·o·lith·ic [,i(:)əu'liθik] *a.*【地、考古】始石器时代的．

E.O.M. = end of month 月底．

e·on ['i:ən, 'i:ɔn] *n.* 无限长的时代, 永世(= aeon).

e·o·ni·an [i:'əuniən] *a.* 永远的,永世的(= aeonian).

E·os ['i:ɔs] *n.*【希神】曙光女神,黎明女神〔相当于罗马神话的 Aurora〕．

e·o·sin(e) ['i:əsin] *n.*【化】曙红,四溴萤光素;类似曙红的染料．

e·o·sin·o·phil [,i:əu'sinəfil], **e·o·sin·o·phile** [-fail] *n.*【生】嗜曙红． **e·o·sin·o·phil·ic** [-'filik] *a.*

e·o·sin·o·phile [,i:əu'sinəfail] *a.*【化】易染曙红的．

e·os·phor·ite [i:'ɔsfərait] *n.*【矿】磷铝锰矿．

-eous〔形容词后缀〕= -ous. ①〔加在拉丁名词之后构成形容词〕: aque*ous*, ligne*ous*. ②〔加在末尾为 -ty 的法语名词之后构成形容词〕: bount*eous*, dut*eous*. ★ right*eous*, court*eous* 等是在类推之下形成的; beaut*eous*, plent*eous* 等是诗歌用语．

E·o·zo·ic [,i(:)əu'zəuik] *a.*【地】始生代的,前寒武纪的．— *n.*〔the〕始生代,前寒武纪．

ep- *pref.*〔用于元音前 = epi-〕: *ep*enthesis.

E.P. = electroplate.

e·pact ['i:pækt] *n.* ①闰余〔阳历一年间超过阴历的日数,通常为 11 日〕. ②元旦月龄,岁首月龄〔阳历元旦回溯至阴历当月初一的日数〕．

ep·arch ['epɑ:k] *n.* ①(古希腊的)州长;(近代希腊的)县长．②(东正教的)主教．

ep·arch·y ['epɑ:ki] *n.* ①(古希腊的)州;(近代希腊的)县．②(东正教的)主教管区．

é·pa·ter [F. epɑ'te] *vt.*〔F.〕使吃惊,使震惊．

ep·aul(e)·ment [e'pɔ:lmənt] *n.*【建】肩墙．

ep·au·let(te) ['epəulet] *n.*【军】肩章;肩章形的饰物．*win one's ～s* 升为军官．

E.P.B. = Economic Planning Board〔英〕经济计划局．

E.P.D. = excess profits duty 超额利润税．

é·pée [ei'pei] *n.*〔F.〕①(击剑用的)剑．②尖剑术．

ep·ei·rog·e·ny [,epai'rɔdʒini] *n.*【地】造陆作用． **e·pei·ro·gen·ic** [e,pairə'dʒenik], **e·pei·ro·ge·net·ic** [-dʒi'netik] *a.*

ep·en·ceph·a·lon [,epen'sefəlɔn] *n.*【解】①胎生体的后脑要素．②〔罕〕小脑．**-l·ic** *a.*

ep·en·dy·ma [e'pendimə] *n.*【动】室管膜．**-al, -ry** *a.*

e·pen·the·sis [e'penθisis] *n.* *(pl. -ses* [-si:z]*)* 插入字母,增音． **e·pen·thet·ic** [,epən'θetik] *a.*

e·pergne [i'pə:n; F. e'perɲ] *n.*〔F.〕(餐桌中央的)饰架．

ep·ex·e·ge·sis [e,peksi'dʒi:sis] *n.* 增词;附加说明．

ep·ex·e·get·ic(al) [e,peksi'dʒetik(əl)] *a.* 增词的,附加

说明的.
Eph. = Ephesians.
eph- *pref.* 〔用于 h 前〕(= epi-): *eph*emeral.
e·phah, e·pha [ˈiːfə] *n.* 以砝〔古希伯来干量具名,约合 1/3 到一个蒲式耳〕.
e·phebe [iˈfiːb, ˈefiːb] *n.* 男青年〔尤指古希腊刚成公民的男青年〕.
e·phe·bus [eˈfiːbəs], **e·phebe** [ˈefib,eˈfiːb] *n.* *(pl.* ***-bi*** [-bai]*)* 青年公民〔古雅典 18—20 岁接受体育和军事训练的男子〕. **e·phe·bic** *a.*
e·phed·rine, -drin [eˈfedrin, ˈefedriːn] *n.* 【药】麻黄素,麻黄硷.
e·phem·er·a [iˈfemərə] *n.* *(pl.* ***-s, -rae*** [-riː]*)* 【虫】蜉蝣;短命的东西.
e·phem·er·al [iˈfemərəl] *a.* 朝生暮死的;短命的,暂时的. —*n.* ①生命短暂的事物. ②短生植物. *an ~ fever* 一日热. *an ~ flower* 一天就凋谢的花. *~ joys* 短暂的欢乐. **-ly** *ad.*
e·phem·er·al·i·ty [iˌfeməˈræliti] *n.* ①短命,朝生暮死.②*(pl.* ***-ties*** [-tis]*)* 生命短暂的事物.
e·phem·er·id [iˈfemərid] *n.* 【动】蜉蝣,蜉蝣目昆虫.
e·phem·er·is [iˈfeməris] *n.* *(pl.* ***ephe·mer·i·des*** [ˌefəˈmerədiːz]*)* 【天】天体位置表;星历表.
e·phem·er·on [iˈfemərɔn] *n.* = ephemera.
E·phe·si·an [iˈfiːʒiən] *a.* 以弗所的. — *n.* ①以弗所人. ②〔*pl.*〕【圣】《以弗所书》〔见《新约》〕.
Eph·e·sus [ˈefisəs] *n.* 以弗所〔小亚细亚古都〕.
eph·od [ˈefɔd, -əd] *n.* 古时犹太教大祭司穿的法衣.
eph·or [ˈefɔ, -ə] *n.* *(pl.* ***-ors, -or·i*** [-ərai]*)* 古斯巴达五长官团长官.
E·phra·im [ˈiːfriim] ①【圣】伊弗列姆〔约瑟的次子〕. ②以色列伊弗列姆部族人. ③以色列王国.
ep·i- *pref.* 表示"在上";"在外";"在前";"在后";"在旁";"在其间";"除外"等〔元音前用 ep-, h 前用 eph-〕: *epi*blast, *epi*zoon.
ep·i·ben·thos [ˌepiˈbenθəs] *n.* 浅海生物.
ep·i·bi·ot·ic [ˌepibaiˈɔtik] *a.* ①【生】外生的,体外生的. ②残遗的. *~ species* 残遗种. —*n.* 残遗物;【生】残遗种.
ep·i·blast [ˈepiblæst] *n.* 【生】上胚层;外胚层.
e·pib·o·ly [iˈpibəli] *n.* 【胚】外包. **ep·i·bol·ic** [epiˈbɔlik] *a.*
ep·ic [ˈepik] *n.* ①叙事诗,史诗;写传说或历史中英雄事迹的诗. ②史诗般的文艺作品.—*a.* ①叙事诗的,史诗的. ②英雄的,壮丽的;宏大的. *~* **poem** 叙事诗 (= epic).
ep·i·cal [ˈepikəl] *a.* = epic. **-ly** *ad.*
ep·i·ca·lyx [ˌepiˈkeiliks, -ˈkæliks] *n.* *(pl.* ***-lyx·es, -ly·ces*** [-ləsiːz]*)*. 【植】副萼.
ep·i·can·thus [ˌepiˈkænθəs] *n.* 【医】内眦赘皮. **ep·i·can·thic** *a.*
ep·i·car·di·um [ˌepiˈkɑːdiəm] *n.* *(pl.* ***-di·a*** [-diə]*)* 【解】心外膜,心包脏层.
ep·i·carp [ˈepikɑːp] *n.* 【植】外果皮 *(opp.* endocarp*)*.
ep·i·ce·di·um [ˌepiˈsiːdiəm] *n.* 悼歌,挽歌.
ep·i·cene [ˈepisiːn] *a.* ①【语法】两性通用的,通性的.②【生】兼有两性的;无男女区别的;有女人气的. — *n.* ①通性词. ②兼有两性特征的人.
ep·i·cen·ter, 〔英〕 **ep·i·cen·tre** [ˈepisentə] *n.* 【地】震中;中心,集中点. **-tral** *a.*
ep·i·cen·trum [ˌepiˈsentrəm] *n.* *(pl.* ***-tra*** [-tra]*)* = epicenter.
ep·i·cist [ˈepisist] *n.* 史诗作者,叙事诗人.
ep·i·cor·a·coid [ˌepiˈkɔrəkɔid] *a.* 【解】喙突上的. — *n.* 上喙骨.
ep·i·cot·yl [ˌepiˈkɔtil] *n.* 【植】上胚轴.
ep·i·cot·yl·e·don·ar·y [ˌepikɔtiˈliːdnəri] *a.* 上胚轴的.
ep·i·cra·ni·um [ˌepiˈkreiniəm] *n.* *(pl.* ***-ni·a*** [-ə]*)* 【解、昆】头盖. **ep·i·cra·ni·al** *a.*
ep·i·crit·ic [ˌepiˈkritik] *a.* 【解】细觉的.
Ep·ic·te·tus [ˌepikˈtiːtəs] *n.* 埃皮克提图〔公元前一世纪时的希腊斯多噶派哲学家、教师〕.
ep·i·cure [ˈepikjuə] *n.* ①讲究饮食的人,美食家. ②享乐主义者.
ep·i·cu·re·an [ˌepikjuəˈri(ː)ən] *a.* ① 享乐主义的. ②讲究饮食的. *an ~ feast* 丰盛的筵席. — *n.* ①享乐主义者. ②美食家.
Ep·i·cu·re·an·ism [ˌepikjuəˈriənizəm] *n.* ①伊壁鸠鲁哲学;伊壁鸠鲁学派. ②信奉伊壁鸠鲁哲学. ③〔e-〕享乐主义,美食主义 (epicurism).
ep·i·cur·ism [ˈepikjuərizəm] *n.* 享乐主义,美食主义.
Ep·i·cu·rus [ˌepiˈkjuərəs] *n.* 伊壁鸠鲁〔公元前342?—270,古希腊杰出的唯物主义和无神论者〕.
ep·i·cy·cle [ˈepisaikl] *n.* ①【天】本轮. ②【数】周转圆.
ep·i·cy·clic [ˌepiˈsaiklik] *a.* ①【天】本轮的. ②【数】周转圆的. *~* **train** 【机】周转轮系.
ep·i·cy·cloid(al) [ˌepiˈsaiklɔid(əl)] *n.* 【数】圆外旋轮线,外摆线. **-al** [ˌepisaiˈklɔidəl] *a.*
ep·i·deic·tic [ˌepiˈdaiktik] *a.* (文体、演讲等)富于词藻的;夸耀的.
ep·i·dem·ic [ˌepiˈdemik] *n.* ①流行病,传染病,时疫.②(风尚等的)流行;(流行病的)蔓延. — *a.* ①传染的. ②流行性的. *~ encephalitis* 流行性脑炎.
ep·i·dem·i·cal [ˌepiˈdemikəl] *a.* = epidemic. **-ly** *ad.*
ep·i·de·mi·ol·o·gy [ˌepiˌdiːmiˈɔlədʒi, -ˌdemi-] *n.* 流行病学. **ep·i·de·mi·o·log·ic** [-əˈlɔdʒik], **ep·i·de·mi·o·log·i·cal** *a.* 流行病学的. **ep·i·de·mi·ol·o·gist** *n.* 流行病学家.
ep·i·den·drum [ˌepiˈdendrəm] *n.* 【植】兰属 *(Epidendrum* 即 *Cymbidium)* 植物〔小花朵,主指美洲热带寄生兰〕.
ep·i·der·mal, ep·i·der·mic [ˌepiˈdəːməl, -mik] *a.* 【生】表皮的,外皮的.
ep·i·der·mis [ˌepiˈdəːmis] *n.* 【解】表皮,外皮;【生】表皮层;(贝类的)壳.
ep·i·der·moid [ˌepiˈdəːmɔid] *a.* 表皮状的,表皮性的 (= epidermoidal).
ep·i·di·a·scope [ˌepiˈdaiəskəup] *n.* 实物幻灯机,透反射两用幻灯机.
ep·i·did·y·mis [ˌepiˈdidimis] *n.* *(pl.* ***ep·i·di·dym·i·des*** [-diˈdimidiːz]*)*. 【解】附睾. **ep·i·did·y·mal** *a.*
ep·i·dote [ˈepidəut] *n.* 【矿】绿簾石.
ep·i·fo·cal [ˌepiˈfəukəl] *a.* 【地】震中的.
ep·i·fo·cus [ˌepiˈfəukəs] *n.* 【地】震中.
ep·i·gam·ic [epiˈgæmik] *a.* 【动】吸引异性的,诱惑性的.
ep·i·gas·tric [ˌepiˈgæstrik] *a.* 【解】上腹部的.
ep·i·gas·tri·um [ˌepiˈgæstriəm] *n.* *(pl.* ***ep·i·gas·tri·a*** [ˌepiˈgæstriə]*)* 【解】上腹部;【动】第一腹片.
ep·i·ge·al, ep·i·ge·an [ˌepiˈdʒiəl, -ən] *a.* ①【植】生于地上的,贴地生长的;(子叶)出土的. ②【动】栖息于地上[浅水中]的. 亦 **ep·i·ge·an.**
ep·i·gene [ˈepiˌdʒiːn] *a.* 【地】外成的.*~* **rocks** 外成岩.
ep·i·gen·e·sis [ˌepiˈdʒenisis] *n.* ①【生】后成说,渐成说 *(opp.* preformation*)*. ②【矿】外成,外力变质.
ep·i·ge·net·ic [ˌepidʒiˈnetik] *a.* ①外成的;具有外成性质的. ②【地】生于地表的; 近地表生成的. ②【矿】后成的.
e·pig·e·nous [eˈpidʒinəs] *a.* 【植】附叶面生长的〔尤指某些真菌附在叶面上部生长的〕.
ep·i·ge·ous [ˌepiˈdʒiəs] *a.* = epigeal.
ep·i·glot·tic [ˌepiˈglɔtik] *a.* 【解】会厌软骨的.
ep·i·glot·tis [ˌepiˈglɔtis] *n.* 【解】会厌,会厌软骨.
ep·i·gone [ˈepigəun] *n.* *(pl.* *~s)* (哲学、文艺等方面的)后继者,追随者;蹩脚的模仿者.
ep·i·gon·ic [ˌepiˈgɔnik] *a.* (哲学、文艺等方面)后继

者的，追随者的；模仿者的。

ep·i·gram [ˈepigræm] *n.* 警句；讽刺短诗。

ep·i·gram·mat·ic [ˌepigrəˈmætik] *a.* 警句的；讽刺诗的。**-al·ly** *ad.*

ep·i·gram·ma·tism [ˌepiˈgræmətizəm] *n.* 警句的使用；警句文体。**-tist** *n.*

ep·i·gram·ma·tist [ˌepiˈgræmətist] *n.* 警句作者；讽刺诗作者。

ep·i·gram·ma·tize [ˌepiˈgræmətaiz] *vt.* ①以警句形式表达。②把…写成讽刺短诗。— *vi.* ①作讽刺短诗。②写[说]警句。

ep·i·graph [ˈepigrɑːf] *n.* ①(墓碑、肖像等的)题字，碑文。②(书前或章节前的)引语。

e·pig·ra·pher [eˈpigrəfə] *n.* 碑铭研究家，金石学家。

ep·i·graph·ic [ˌepiˈgræfik] *a.* 铭文的；碑文的；与铭[碑]文有关的(= exigraphical)。**-i·cal·ly** *ad.*

e·pig·ra·phist [eˈpigrəfist] *n.* = epigrapher.

e·pig·ra·phy [eˈpigrəfi] *n.* ①碑文，铭文。②碑铭学，金石学。

e·pig·y·nous [iˈpidʒinəs] *a.*【植】(花被，雄蕊等)上位的。**e·pig·y·ny** *n.*

ep·i·la·tion [ˌepiˈleiʃən] *n.*【医】脱毛(法)；拔毛(术)。

ep·i·lep·sy [ˈepilepsi] *n.*【医】癫痫，羊痫疯。*masked [minor]* ～ 轻微的羊痫疯。

ep·i·lep·tic [ˌepiˈleptik] *a.* 癫痫的；患癫痫的。— *n.* 癫痫病人。

ep·i·lep·toid [ˌepiˈleptɔid] *a.*【医】类癫痫的 (= epileptiform)。

ep·i·lim·ni·on [ˌepiˈlimniən] *n.* (湖水的)上温层。

e·pil·o·gist [eˈpilədʒist] *n.* ①跋的作者，写结束语的人。②念收场白的演员。

ep·i·log(ue) [ˈepilɔg] *n.* ①(文艺作品的)跋，后记，尾声，结尾部分。②(戏剧、广播和电视节目的)收场白。

ep·i·mer, e·pi·mer·ide [ˈepimə, iˈpiməraid] *n.*【化】差向[立体]异构体；差位[立体]异构体。

ep·i·mere [ˈepimiə] *n.*【解】(中胚层的)上段。

ep·i·my·si·um [ˌepiˈmisiəm,-ˈmiz-] *n.* (*pl.* *-sia* [-ziə])【解】肌外膜。

ep·i·nas·ty [ˈepinæsti] *n.*【植】偏上性。**-tic** *a.*

ep·i·neph·rin(e) [ˌepiˈnefrin, -riːn] *n.*【生化】肾上腺素。

ep·i·neu·ri·um [ˌepiˈnjuriəm, -ˈnur-] *n.*【解】神经外膜。

ep·i·no·sic [ˌepiˈnɔsik] *a.* 不卫生的，有害健康的。

E·piph·a·ny [iˈpifəni] *n.* ①【宗】(每年一月六日纪念耶稣显灵的)显现节。②〔e-〕(神的)显现；(对事物真意的)领悟。

ep·i·phe·nom·e·non [ˌepifiˈnɔminən] (*pl.* *-na* [-nə]) *n.* 副现象，附带现象；【医】偶发症状。

e·piph·y·sis [iˈpifisis] *n.* (*pl.* *-ses* [-siːz])【解】①骺。②脑上体〔全称 epiphysis cerebri [ˈserəˌbrai]〕。**ep·i·phys·e·al, ep·i·phys·i·al** [ˌepiˈfiziəl] *a.*

ep·i·phyte [ˈepifait] *n.* ①【植】附生植物。②(寄生于动物的)真菌。

ep·i·phy·tol·o·gy [ˌepifaiˈtɔlədʒi] *n.* 植物流行病学。

ep·i·phy·tot·ic [ˌepifaiˈtɔtik] *a.* 植物流行病的。— *n.* 植物流行病。

ep·i·plas·tron [ˌepiˈplæstrən] (*pl.* ～*s*, *-tra* [-trə]) *n.*【动】上腹甲。

ep·i·rog·e·ny [ˌepaiˈrɔdʒəni] *n.* = epeirogeny. **e·pi·ro·gen·ic** [iˌpairəˈdʒenik] *a.*

Epis(c) = Episcopal. **Epis(t)** = Epistle(s).

e·pis·co·pa·cy [iˈpiskəpəsi] *n.*【宗】①主教制度；主教职位[任期]。②〔the ～〕主教团。

e·pis·co·pal [iˈpiskəpəl] *a.* 主教的；主教管辖的；〔E-〕主教派的。*the E- Church* 英国圣公会。*the Protestant E-Church* 美国圣公会。**-ly** *ad.*

e·pis·co·pa·li·an [iˌpiskəˈpeiliən] *a.* 主教派的；圣公会的；〔E-〕新教徒主教教会的。— *n.* 主教派教友；圣公会教徒；主教制主义者。**-ism** *n.* 主教制主义。

e·pis·co·pate [iˈpiskəpit] *n.* 主教职务[权限，任期]；主教团；主教管区。

e·pis·cope [ˈepiskəup] *n.* 不透明物投影放大器。

e·pi·si·ot·o·my [iˌpiːziˈɔtəmi] *n.*【医】外阴切开术。

ep·i·sode [ˈepisəud] *n.* ①插话，(小说中的)一段情节。②(一系列事件中的)一个事件。③(古希腊悲剧中)两段合唱间的部分。④【乐】插部，间插段。⑤【影】(回想式的)插话。⑥【地】幕。

ep·i·sod·ic(al) [ˌepiˈsɔdik(əl)] *a.* 插曲的；插话(式)的；偶发的。**-al·ly** *ad.*

ep·i·some [ˈepəsəum] *n.*【动】因子副体。

ep·i·spas·tic [ˌepiˈspæstik] *a.*【医】发泡的。— *n.* 发泡药。

ep·i·sperm [ˈepispəːm] *n.*【植】外种皮。

e·pis·ta·sis [iˈpistəsis] *n.*【遗】上位，(遗传要素的)抑他性。

ep·i·stax·is [ˌepiˈstæksis] *n.*【医】鼻出血。

ep·i·ste·mic [ˌepiˈstiːmik] *a.* 认识的；与认识有关的。**ep·i·ste·mi·cal·ly** *ad.*

e·pis·te·mo·log·i·cal [iˌpisti(ː)məˈlɔdʒikəl] *a.* 认识论的。**-ly** *ad.*

e·pis·te·mol·o·gy [iˌpistiˈmɔlədʒi] *n.*【哲】认识论。

ep·i·ster·num [ˌepisˈtəːnəm] *n.* (*pl.* *-na* [-nə]) ①上胸骨。②(海胆)上腹板。③(昆虫)前侧片。**ep·i·ster·nal** *a.*

e·pis·tle [iˈpisl] *n.* 书信；书信体诗文；*the E-*【圣】使徒书。*the E- side*【宗】祭坛右侧。

e·pis·tler [iˈpislə] *n.* ①书信作家。②〔通常用 E-〕举行圣餐礼时朗读《使徒书信》的人(= epistoler [-tələ])。

e·pis·to·lar·y [iˈpistələri] *a.* 书信的，尺牍的；尺牍体的，书信体的；用书信进行的。

e·pis·tome [ˈepistəum] *n.*【动】(腕足类)口上突；(甲壳类)口上板；(甲壳类)口上区；(昆虫)口上片。

e·pis·tro·phe [iˈpistrəfi] *n.*【修】结句反复；(诗歌各句末的)叠句。

ep·i·style [ˈepistail] *n.* = architrave.

ep·i·taph [ˈepitɑːf] *n.* 墓志铭；墓志铭式的诗文。**-ial, -ic** *a.* **-less** *a.*

e·pit·a·sis [iˈpitəsis] *n.* (古典戏剧中)导致灾祸来临的高潮部分。

ep·i·tax·y [ˈepitæksi] *n.*【物】(晶体)取向附生，外延。**ep·i·tax·i·al, ep·i·tax·ic** *a.*

ep·i·tha·la·mi·um, -mi·on [ˌepiθəˈleimiəm] *n.* (*pl* ～*s*, *-mi·a* [-miə]) (祝贺新婚的)喜诗；颂歌。

ep·i·the·li·al [ˌepiˈθiːljəl] *a.*【生】上皮的；【植】皮膜的。**-i·za·tion** *n.*【生】上皮新生，上皮形成。

ep·i·the·li·oid [ˌepiˈθiːliɔid] *a.*【生】上皮状的。

ep·i·the·li·o·ma [ˌepiθiːliˈəumə] *n.* (*pl.* *-ma·ta* [-mətə], ～*s*)【医】上皮癌，上皮瘤。**-tous** *a.*

ep·i·the·li·um [ˌepiˈθiːljəm] (*pl.* ～*s*, *-lia* [ˌepiˈθiːljə]) *n.*【生】上皮；【植】皮膜。

ep·i·the·lize [ˌepiˈθiːlaiz] *vt.* (治溃疡时)以上皮覆盖(= epithelialize)。

ep·i·ther·mal [ˌepiˈθəːməl] *a.*【原】超热的；【地】浅成热液的。～ **neutron** 超热中子。

ep·i·thet [ˈepiθet] *n.* ①表示性质[属性]的定语。②称号，绰号。③【动、植】(一属中的)亚类名词。**-ic** *a.* 用性质形容词的。

e·pit·o·me [iˈpitəmi] *n.* ①梗概，摘要，节录。②缩影。

e·pit·o·mize [iˈpitəmaiz] *vt.* ①作…的摘要。②使成…的缩影；集中体现。

e·p·i·zo·ic [ˌepiˈzəuik] *a.*【生】体外寄生的。**ep·i·zo·ite** [-ait] *n.*

ep·i·zo·on [ˌepiˈzəuɔn] *n.* (*pl.* *-zo·a* [-ˈzəuə])【生】体

外寄生动物,皮上寄生虫.

ep·i·zo·ot·ic [ˌepizəuˈɔtik] *n., a.* 动物流行病(的). **-al·ly** *ad.*

ep·i·zo·ot·i·ol·o·gy [ˌepizəuˌɔtiˈɔlədʒi] *n.* 兽疫学;动物流行病学.

e·plu·ri·bus u·num [ˌiːˌpluːrəbəsˈjuːnəm] 〔L.〕合众为一〔美国的铭语〕(=one out of many).

ep·och [ˈiːpɔk, ˈepɔk] *n.* ①纪元,时代;时期. ②值得纪念的事件[日期]. ③【地】世,纪,期. ④【物】初相;【天】历元;【电】(信号)出现时间,恒定相位延迟. ***mark [form] an ~ (in)*** …(在…上)开辟新纪元. **~-making, ~-marking** *a.* 开新纪元的,划时代的,破天荒的.

ep·och·al [ˈepɔkəl] *a.* (新)时代的,划时代的,开新纪元的. **-ly** *ad.*

ep·ode [ˈepəud] *n.* ①一种长短句相间的抒情诗. ②古希腊抒情诗的第三部分.

ep·o·nym [ˈepəunim] *n.* ①名字被用来命名国家[地方等]的真人(或神话中的人). ②与某时期[运动,学说等]有关的人〔如构成 Elizabethan 一词的 Elizabeth〕. **-ic** *a.*

e·pon·y·mous [iˈpɔniməs] *a.* = eponymic.

e·pon·y·my [iˈpɔnimi] *n.* 名祖命名法〔用本民族中一个真实的或神话中的祖先名字作为本民族的名称的作法〕.

ep·oo·pho·ron [ˌepəˈɔfərɔn] *n.* 【动】卵巢冠.

ep·o·pee [ˈepəupiː], **ep·o·poe·a** [ˈepəupiːə] *n.* 史诗,叙事诗.

ep·os [ˈepɔs] *n.* 史诗,叙事诗,(口头传诵的)原始叙事诗;史诗事迹.

ep·ox·ide [eˈpɔksaid] *n.* 【化】环氧化物.

ep·ox·i·dize [eˈpɔksidaiz] *vt.* 【化】使环氧化.

ep·ox·y [eˈpɔksi] *a.* 环氧的. — *n.* 【化】环氧树脂.

eps. = envelopes.

ep·si·lon [epˈsailən] *n.* ①希腊语字母表第五字母〔E, ε =〔英〕短音 e〕. ②【数】小的正数.

Ep·som [ˈepsəm] *n.* ①埃普索姆〔英国伦敦南面的城市〕. ②埃普索姆的赛马场.

Ep·stein [ˈepstain] *n.* ①爱泼斯坦〔姓氏〕. ②**Jacob ~** 雅各·爱泼斯坦〔1880—1959,美国雕刻家〕.

E.P.T. = excess profits tax 超额利润税.

EPU = European Payments Union 欧洲支付同盟.

ep·u·rate [ˈepjuəreit] *vt.* 提纯,精炼.

ep·u·ra·tion [ˌepjuəˈreiʃən] *n.* ①提纯. ②清洗〔特指第二次世界大战后,法、意两国对官吏中法西斯党徒的刑事诉讼〕.

E.Q., EQ = educational quotient 教育商数.

eq. = equal; equalize; equation; equipment; equivalent.

eq·ua·bil·i·ty [ˌekwəˈbiliti, ˌiːk-] *n.* ①平稳,稳定;均等. ②平静.

eq·ua·ble [ˈekwəbl, ˈiːk-] *a.* ①平均的,均等的,一样的. ②均匀的. ③稳定的;(性情)恬静的. ④(法律等)公平的. *a man of ~ temper* 性情平静的人. **-bly** *ad.* **-ness** *n.*

e·qual [ˈiːkwəl] *a.* ①相等的;平等的,均等的 *(to; with)*;同等的;公平的;一样的. ②平静的;平稳的. ③势均力敌的;相当的. ④适合的;胜任的,经得起的. *the principle of ~ opportunity* 机会均等主义. *~ opportunity employer* 〔美〕标榜招工一视同仁的雇主. *an ~ plain* 平原. ***be ~ to*** ①等于(*The supply is ~ to the demand.* 供求相等. *Twice two is ~ to four.*二的二倍等于四). ②赶得上,敌得过. ③胜任,能干 (*He is ~ to anything.* 他事事能干). ④忍耐得住 (*be ~ to any trial* 经得起任何磨练). ***~ to the occasion*** 能应付局势 (*make a quick decision ~ to the occasion* 当机立断). ***~ to the task*** 胜任. ***~ pay for ~ work*** 同工同酬. ***in a firm, ~ tone*** 用坚定平稳的音调. ***on an ~ footing*** 以平等地位对待,在同一立场上. ***on ~ terms (with)*** (与…)平等相处. — *n.* ①地位相等的人,同辈. ②对等的事物. *mix with one's ~s and betters* 跟同辈和长辈交往. *be the ~ of one's word* 守约. *have no ~ in music* 在音乐方面没有人比得上. ***without (an) ~*** 无敌. — *vt.* (〔英〕*-ll-*) ①抵得上,比得上. ②等于. ③〔古〕使相等,使平等;同等看待;照样报答. *No man ~s him in strength.* 没有人比他气力大. **~-sign [mark]** *n.* 【数】等号〔=〕. **~ time** 〔美〕平等时间〔电台或电视天在另一天给予反对党同样长的发表政见的时间〕;〔喻〕均等的机会.

e·qual-ar·e·a [ˈiːkwəlˈeəriə] *a.* 等区的〔绘制地图投影上,子午线与纬线间地区按比例等于地球表面相应地区〕.

e·qual·i·tar·i·an [i(ː)kˌwɔliˈteəriən] *a.* 平均主义的,平等主义的. — *n.* 平均主义者,平等主义者. **-ism** *n.* 平均主义,平等主义.

e·qual·i·ty [i(ː)ˈkwɔliti] *n.* ①同等,平等,均一,均等;一样. ②【数】相等;等式. *~ between the sexes* 男女平等. *racial ~* 种族平等. *the sign of ~* 等号〔=〕. ***be on an ~ with*** 和…同等. ***the E- State***〔美〕(妇女在该处最先取得参政权的)怀俄明州.

e·qual·i·za·tion [ˌiːkwəlaiˈzeiʃən, -li-] *n.* 相等;均等;平均. *~ of landownership* 平均地权.

e·qual·ize [ˈiːkwəlaiz] *vt.* ①使相等,使平等. ②补偿. ③【电】使均衡;调整. — *vi.* ①相等,得到平衡. ②〔主英〕(与对方)打成平手,得分相等.

e·qual·iz·er [ˈiːkwəlaizə] *n.* ①使相等者,使平均者. ②【电】均压线;【自】补偿器;均衡器;平衡杆;平衡装置.

e·qual·ly [ˈiːkwəli] *ad.* 相等地;平等地;公正地.

e·qua·nim·i·ty [ˌiːkwəˈnimiti, ekwə-] *n.* 平静,沉着,镇定. ***with ~*** 沉着,泰然;安之若素.

e·quate [iˈkweit] *vt.* ①使相等. ②使平均;同等看待. ③【数】把…作成等式. *Politics cannot be ~d with art.* 政治并不等于艺术. — *vi.* 等同.

e·qua·tion [iˈkweiʃən] *n.* ①平衡,均衡;平均,相等. ②【数】方程式,等式. ③【天】(时)差;均分,等分. ④【化】反应式. *algebraic [linear, simple, quadratic, cubic, simultaneous] ~* 代数(一次,一元一次,二次,三次,联立)方程式. *differential ~* 微分方程. *an identical ~* 恒等式. ***~ of light*** 【天】光行时差. ***~ of payments*** 平均分期付款. ***~ of state*** 【物】物态方程式. ***~ of time*** 【天】时差. ***personal ~*** 【天】观测上的个人误差.

e·qua·tion·al [iˈkweiʃənl] *a.* ①方程式的. ②平均的. ③【语法】省略谓语动词的. **-ly** *ad.*

e·qua·tor [iˈkweitə] *n.* ①(地球或天球的)赤道. ②(平分球形物体的面的)圆;(任何)大圆. *the celestial ~* 天球赤道. *the earth's [terrestrial] ~* 地球赤道. *the magnetic ~* 地磁赤道. **-ward** *ad.* 朝赤道方向.

eq·ua·to·ri·al [ˌekwəˈtɔːriəl, iːk-] *a.* 赤道的;赤道附近的. *~ heat* 酷热. — *n.* 赤道仪. **E- Africa** 赤道非洲. **~ bulge** 赤道隆起带. **~ low** 赤道低压. **~ trough** 赤道槽. **~ telescope** 赤道仪. **-ly** *ad.*

E·qua·to·ri·al Guin·ea [ˌekwəˈtɔːriəl ˈgini] *n.* 赤道几内亚〔非洲〕.

eq·uer·ry [ˈekwəri, iˈkweri] *n.* ①马厩总管. ②〔英〕王室侍从.

e·ques·tri·an [iˈkwestriən] *a.* 马的;骑马的;骑术的,骑士(团)的. *~ feats* 马戏. *~ skill* 马术. *an ~ statue* 骑马塑像. — *n.* 骑马的人;骑手;马戏演员. **-ism** *n.* 马术.

e·ques·tri·enne [iˌkwestriˈen] *n.* 骑马女人;女骑手;马戏女演员.

e·qui- *comb. f.* 表示"同等": *equi*distant.

e·qui·an·gu·lar [ˌiːkwiˈæŋgjulə] *a.* 等角的. **-i·ty** *n.*

e·qui·axed [ˈiːkwiækst] *a.* 各方等大的〔特指金属晶粒〕.

e·qui·ca·lor·ic [ˌiːkwikəˈlɔrik] *a.* (能产生)同等热量

的. ～ *diets* 同等热量的饮食.
e·qui·cen·ter, e·qui·cen·tre [ˈiːkwiˈsentə] *n.* 【数】等心.
e·qui·dis·tance [ˌiːkwiˈdistəns] *n.* 等距离.
e·qui·dis·tant [ˌiːkwiˈdistənt] *a.* ①等距离的. ②(地图上所有方向的距离)同比例的. **-ly** *ad.*
e·qui·lat·er·al [ˌiːkwiˈlætərəl] *a.* 【数】①等边的, 等面的. ②两侧对称的. *an* ～ *figure* 等边形. —*n.* 等边形;(相应的)等边. ～ **hyperbola** 直角双曲线, 等轴双曲线. ～ **triangle** 等边三角形.
e·quil·i·brant [iˈkwilibrənt] *n.* 【物】平衡力,均衡力.
e·qui·li·brate [ˌiːkwiˈlaibreit] *vt.* 使平衡,使相称. —*vi.* 平衡,平均,相称.
e·quil·i·bra·tion [iˌkwilaiˈbreiʃən] *n.* 平衡, 平均, 均势,相称.
e·qui·li·bra·tor [ˌiːkwiˈlaibreitə] *n.* 保持平衡的物;平衡装置.
e·quil·i·brist [i(ː)ˈkwilibrist] *n.* 使自己保持平衡者(如走钢丝的人). **-ic** *a.*
e·qui·lib·ri·um [ˌiːkwiˈlibriəm] (*pl.* ～*s*, *-ri·a* [-riə]) *n.* ①平衡,均衡, 均势, 相称. ②(心情的)平静. ③(判断的)不偏不倚. ～ *constant* 【化】平衡常数. *the* ～ *of demand and supply* 供求均衡. *indifferent* ～ 【物】随遇平衡. *the theory of* ～ 【哲】均衡论.
e·qui·mo·lal [ˌiːkwiˈməuləl] *a.* 【化】克分子数相等的,重量克分子浓度相等的.
e·qui·mo·lar [ˌiːkwiˈməulə] *a.* 【化】克分子数相等的,体积克分子浓度相等的.
e·qui·mo·lec·u·lar [ˌiːkwiməuˈlekjulə] *a.* 【化】等分子的,克分子数相等的.
e·qui·mul·ti·ple [ˌiːkwiˈmʌltipl] *n.* 〔常 *pl.*〕 等倍数,等倍量.
e·quine [ˈiːkwain, ˈekwain] *a.* 【动】马的; 似马的; 马科的. — *n.* 马; 马科动物.
e·quin·ia [iˈkwiniə] *n.* (马)鼻疽.
e·qui·noc·tial [ˌiːkwiˈnɔkʃəl] *a.* ①【天】二分点的; 昼夜平分线的; 昼夜平分时的. ②春分的, 秋分的. ③(天球) 赤道的. — *n.* ①昼夜平分线,赤道. ②〔*pl.*〕 春分[秋分]周内的暴风雨. *the autumnal [vernal]* ～ *point* 秋分[春分]点. ～ **circle [line]** 【天】天球赤道, 昼夜平分线. ～ **gales** (春分或秋分时的)暴风雨. *the* ～ **point** (春分或秋分的)二分点. ～ **year** 分至年.
e·qui·nox [ˈiːkwinɔks] *n.* ①昼夜平分时,春[秋]分. ②【天】二分点. *the autumnal* ～ 秋分,秋分点. *the spring [vernal]* ～ 春分,春分点.
e·quip [iˈkwip] *vt.* ①配备,装备. ②使作好(智力等方面的)准备,训练. ～ *sb. for a trip*给人准备行装. ～ *a ship for a voyage* 装备船只出航. ～ *sb. with learning* 教人学习. ***be equipped with*** 安置着,装备着;身上穿着 (*be* ～*ped with modern machinery* 配备着现代化机械). ～ ***oneself*** 整装,预备行装,收拾.
eq·ui·page [ˈekwipidʒ] *n.* ①马车及仆从. ②(船、军队、士兵等的)装备,设备,用具. ③〔古〕成套用品. ④(贵族的)随员,扈从. *a dressing* ～ 一套化妆用品. *a tea* ～ 一套茶具.
e·qui·par·ti·tion [ˌiːkwipɑːˈtiʃən] *n.* 【物,化】均分,均隔,匀布,匀配. ～ *of energy* 【物】能量的平均分配.
e·quip·ment [iˈkwipmənt] *n.* ①〔常 *pl.*〕设备,装备,配件,配备物品. ②(一个企业除房地产以外的)固定资产. ③(工作必需的)知识,技能,修养. ④(火车)车辆;(汽车等)运输配备. *laboratory* ～ 实验室设备. *a machinery* ～ *plant* 机械装配厂. *military* ～*s* 军事装备. *the necessary* ～*s for a voyage* 航海必需的装备. *soldier's* ～ 士兵的装备. ～ *and parts* 器材.
e·qui·poise [ˈekwipɔiz] *n.* ①相称,平衡. ②平衡物;平衡力;平衡锤. — *vt.* ①使相称;使平衡. ②使相持不下.
e·qui·pol·lence, e·qui·pol·len·cy [ˌiːkwiˈpɔləns(i)] *n.* ①均等, 均势. ②【逻】(概念、判断的)等值,同义.
e·qui·pol·lent [ˌiːkwiˈpɔlənt] *a.* ①(大致)相等的,均等的. ②【逻】等值的,同义的. — *n.* = equivalent.
e·qui·pon·der·ance, e·qui·pon·der·an·cy [ˌiːkwiˈpɔndərəns, -si] *n.* 等重;均衡,平衡.
e·qui·pon·der·ant [ˌiːkwiˈpɔndərənt] *a.* 等重的, 均衡的. — *n.* 等重物,均衡物.
e·qui·pon·der·ate [ˌiːkwiˈpɔndəreit] *vi., vt.* (使)均重;(使)均力;(使)平衡.
e·qui·po·ten·tial [ˌiːkwipəuˈtenʃəl] *a.* ①潜力均等的,均势的. ②【物】等电位的,等能的,等势的,恒势的. **-i·ty** [-ˈæliti] *n.*
Eq·ui·se·tum [ˌekwiˈsiːtəm] *n.* 【植】①木贼属. ②〔e-〕(*pl.* ～*s*, *-ta* [-tə]) 木贼;问荆.
eq·ui·ta·ble [ˈekwitəbl] *a.* ①公平的,公正的,合理的. ②【法】衡平法上(有效)的. ～ **right** 在衡平法上的权利. **-ness** *n.* **-bly** *ad.*
eq·ui·tant [ˈekwitənt] *a.* 【植】跨状的,套折的.
eq·ui·ta·tion [ˌekwiˈteiʃən] *n.* 骑马;骑马术.
eq·ui·tes [ˈekwitiːz] *n.* 〔*pl.*〕【罗马史】特权市民阶层成员;骑士阶层.
eq·ui·ty [ˈekwiti] *n.* ①公平,公正. ②【法】衡平法(指补充成文法或普通法的公平原则, 必要时以纠正用法不公);衡平法上的权利. ③〔口〕(应付款额之外的)财产净价. ④〔英〕〔*pl.*〕(无固定利息的)股票,证券. ⑤〔E-〕〔英〕演员工会. ～ ***of redemption*** 衡平法上关于赎回担保物的权利. ～ ***of a statute*** 【法】法律条文的解释. ～ **capital** ①投资于新企业的资本. ②(资本)净值. ～ **stock** 股东手上持有的股票.
equiv. = equivalent.
e·quiv·a·lence, e·quiv·a·len·cy [iˈkwivələns, -si] *n.* ①均等,相等,相当. ②【化】等价, 化合价相当; 当量. ③等值;等量. ④(语词的)同义;同类. ⑤【数】等势;等效. ⑥【地】等时代.
e·quiv·a·lent [iˈkwivələnt] *a.* ①相当的,相同的,同等的. ②【化】等价的,当量的;【数】等价的;等量的;等势的;【物】等效的;【数】等面积的,等体积的. ③同意义的*(to)*. —*n.* ①同等物;【数】等价,等值,等价物,等值物,等量物;相当物. ②同义词,对应词句 *(of)*. ③【化】当量;克当量;等量. ④【地】同期地层. *a square* ～ *to a triangle* 同三角形等积的正方形. *five pounds or its* ～ *in books* 五镑或相当于五镑价值的书籍. *chemical* ～ 化学当量. *electrochemical* ～ 电化当量. *transmission* ～ 【电】传输衰耗等效值. *be* ～ *to* 等于;相当于. ～ **circuit** 等效电路. ～ **electrons** 同科电子. ～ **focal length** 【物】等值焦距. ～ **lens** 等焦透镜. ～ **mass** 等效质量. ～ **weight** 当量. **-ly** *ad.*
e·quiv·o·cal [iˈkwivəkəl] *a.* ①歧义的,语义双关的,多义的. ②暧昧的,含糊的,可疑的. ③不肯定的,不明确的. ～ **term** 多义名词. **-ly** *ad.* **-ness** *n.*
e·quiv·o·cal·i·ty [iˌkwivəˈkæliti] *n.* ①多义;暧昧;含糊,模棱两可. ②可疑性. ③不肯定性.
e·quiv·o·cate [iˈkwivəkeit] *vi.* 躲闪; 推诿; 含糊其词;说话支吾,态度暧昧.
e·quiv·o·ca·tion [iˌkwivəˈkeiʃən] *n.* 推诿;躲闪;说话支吾;含糊其词;暧昧. ***fallacy of*** ～ 【逻】一语多义的谬误;名词多义的谬误.
e·quiv·o·ca·tor [iˈkwivəkeitə] *n.* 说话支吾的人.
eq·ui·voque, eq·ui·voke [ˈekwivəuk] *n.* 两义语, 双关话;模棱两可;文字游戏.
E·quu·le·us [iˈkwjuːliəs] *n.* 〔the ～〕【天】小马(星)座.
E·quus [ˈiːkwəs] *n.* 〔L.〕【动】马属.
ER = emergency room 急救室.
er [ʌː,əː,ə] *int.* (表示踌躇不决的)呃,啊,这.
Er 【化】元素铒的符号 (= erbium).
E.R. = ①East Riding (of Yorkshire) 东赖丁(英国约克郡的一个行政区). ②East River 东河〔纽约市〕.

-er *suf.* ①加在名词、形容词、动词和动词词组构成的复合词后,构成名词. ⓐ表示"…的人[动物、植物]": hunter, singer, woodpecker. ⓑ表示"…的东西[器具、机械]", "…的事情": gasburner, eyeopener. ⓒ表示"…的物质","…剂": deodorizer. ⓓ表示"…(地方)的人","…居民": Londoner, westerner; cottager, villager. ⓔ表示"参与…的人","制造…的人","…商","…研究者","…学者": farmer gardener, hatter, geographer. ⓕ〔在近代口语中〕1. 构成该动作的名词: backhander (= back-handed blow), diner (= dining car). 2. 构成来自数词的名词: fiver (= 5 pound [dollar] note), tenner. 3. 使其他词尾的名词带有口语意味: Rugger (= Rug*by football*), Soccer (= *association football*). ②加在古法语名词或形容词的后面: carpenter, potter. sampler. ③加在形容词[副词]的后面构成比较级. ⓐ使单音节形容词,或末尾为 -y, -ly, -le, -er, -ow 的双音节形容词,或其他少数形容词〔尤其是重音在最末音节上的形容词〕成为比较级 (*cf.* -est): richer, lazier, likelier, tenderer, serener, narrower. 但在诗中及古体散文中,也有自由用其他形容词构成比较级的. ⓑ使末节不是-ly的(主要是与形容词同形的)副词构成比较级: harder,faster, sooner. ④构成有动作意义的名词: rejoinder, supper. ⑤表示动作发生多次或反复发生, ⓐ原为动词: wander (< wend), waver (< wave). ⓑ原为拟声语: chatter, twitter, flicker, glitter.

e·ra [ˈiərə] *n.* ①纪元;年代,时代. ②【地】代. *inaugurate [mark] a new* ~ 开[划]新纪元. *before [in] the Christian* ~ 公元前[后].

ERA, E.R.A. = ① Emergency Relief Administration 〔美旧〕紧急救济署. ② engine-room artificer【海】机舱机电军士.

e·ra·di·ate [i(:)ˈreidieit] *vt.* 发射,放射,辐射. **e·ra·di·a·tion** [i(:)ˌreidiˈeiʃən] *n.*

e·rad·i·ca·ble [iˈrædikəbl] *a.* 可以根除的,可以消灭的.

e·rad·i·cate [iˈrædikeit] *vt.* 连根拔除;根除,扑灭,使…断根.

e·rad·i·ca·tion [iˌrædiˈkeiʃən] *n.* 根除,扑灭,消灭.

e·rad·i·ca·tive [iˈrædikətiv] *a.* 根除的,消灭的. *an ~ medicine* 根治药.

e·rad·i·ca·tor [iˌrædiˈkeitə] *n.* ①根除者. ②除草器. ③去墨水液,褪色灵.

e·ras·a·ble [iˈreizəbl] *a.* 擦得掉的,可消除的,可删去的.

e·rase [iˈreiz] *vt.* ①擦掉,揩掉;消除(电子计算机中的记忆);涂掉,删掉(字句等). ②清除;除去. ③忘掉*(from)*;〔美俚〕杀死,暗杀掉. *The pencil marks were ~d.* 铅笔痕迹被擦去. *~ the recording* 抹去录音,洗掉录音. —*vi.* ①容易被擦掉[抹掉]. ②擦,抹. **erasing head** (录音机的)抹音磁头.

e·ras·er [iˈreizə] *n.* ①涂消者;【无】消磁器;抹音头. ②消除用具;挖字刀,消字灵,橡皮擦,黑板擦. ③〔美〕(在拳击中)打倒对手的猛击.

e·ra·sion [iˈreiʒən] *n.* ①擦抹,删去. ②【医】刮除术.

E·ras·mian [iˈræzmiən] *a., n.* 〔荷兰〕伊拉斯姆斯学派(的);伊拉斯姆斯的弟子(的);伊拉斯姆斯风(的).

E·ras·tian [iˈræstʃən] *a.* 伊拉斯图(Thomas Erastus)的. — *n.* 伊拉斯图派,国家全能论者. **-ism** *n.* 国家全能论.

e·ra·sure [iˈreiʒə] *n.* 擦掉;删去,删去部分[语句];涂擦痕迹.

er·bi·um [ˈəːbiəm] *n.*【化】铒.

ere [εə] *prep.* 〔诗、古〕在…以前. ~ ***long*** 不久,一会儿. — *conj.* 〔诗〕①在…之前. ②与其. ~ *it is too late* 趁着还不太晚. *He will die, ~ he will yield.* 他宁死不屈.

Er·e·bus [ˈeribəs] *n.*【希神】(人世与地狱之间的)黑暗区域. *as dark as ~* 漆黑.

e·rect [iˈrekt] *a.* ①直立的;【徽】垂直的; (头、手等)朝上举的; 直竖的. ②〔古〕不屈的,坚毅的; 谨慎的. ③【医】勃起的. *A flagpole stands ~.* 旗竿笔直地竖着. *an ~ figure* (直)立像. *an ~ image* 正像. *with (every) hair ~* 毛发直竖. *with tail ~* 竖着尾巴. — *vt.* ①使直立,树立,竖. ②建立,设立;创立(理论等);安装(机械等). ③【生】把(种)升为(属),提升. ④【数】作(垂直线). ⑤【医】使勃起. *an ~ing shop* 装配车间. *~ a house* 建造房子. *~ a monument* 立纪念碑. *~ oneself* 站起来. — *vi.*【医】勃起. **-ly** *ad.* **-ness** *n.*

e·rec·tile [iˈrektail] *a.* 直立的; 竖得起来的, 立得起来的;【医】有勃起能力的. *~ tissue* 勃起组织.

e·rec·tion [iˈrekʃən] *n.* ①直立;树立,建设,设立;架设;【机】安装,装配. ②建设物,建筑物. ③【医】勃起.

e·rec·tive [iˈrektiv] *a.* 直立的,竖起的;建立的.

e·rec·tor [iˈrektə] *n.* ①建立者,设立者. ②【机】安装工人, 装配工人; 安装器. ③【解】竖立肌. **~-muscle** *n.*【解】竖立肌.

ere·long [εəˈlɔŋ] *ad.* 〔古〕不久,即刻.

er·e·ma·cau·sis [ˌeriməˈkɔːsis] *n.*【化】慢性氧化.

er·e·mite [ˈerimait] *n.* 隐士.

er·e·mit·ic [ˌeriˈmitik] *a.* 隐士式的.

er·em·u·rus [ˌeriˈmjurəs] *(pl.* ***-u·ri*** [-ai]*)*【植】独尾属 *(Eremurus)* 植物.

ere·now [ˌεəˈnau] *ad.* 〔古、诗〕从前;至此,至今.

e·rep·sin [iˈrepsin] *n.*【生化】肠肽酶.

er·e·thism [ˈeriθizəm] *n.*【医】兴奋增盛,过敏.

ere·while [εəˈhwail] *ad.* 〔古〕片刻前,不久前.

Er·furt [ˈεəfuət] *n.* 埃尔富特〔德意志民主共和国城市〕.

erg [əːg] *n.*【物】尔格〔功的单位〕.

erg(o)-[1] *comb. f.* = work.

erg(o)-[2] *comb. f.* = ergot.

er·go [ˈəːgəu] *ad.* 〔L.〕所以,因此.

er·go·graph [ˈəːgəgrɑːf] *n.* 测力器,示功器.

er·gom·e·ter [əːˈgɔmitə] *n.* 测力计,测功计.

er·gom·e·try [əːˈgɔmitri] *n.*【物】测力学,测功学.

er·gon [ˈəːgɔn] *n.* ①【物】尔冈〔用热表示的功的单位〕. ② = erg.

er·go·nom·ic·al [ˌəːgəuˈnɔmikəl] *a.* 人体功率学的;工作环境改造学的.

er·go·nom·ics [ˌəːgəuˈnɔmiks] *n. pl.* 〔用作单数〕生物工艺学; 人类环境改造学;〔尤指〕工作环境改造学.

er·go·nom·ist [ˌəːgəuˈnɔmist] *n.* 工作环境改造学家, 生物工艺学家.

er·go·no·vine [ˌəːgəuˈnəuviːn] *n.*【化】麦角新硷.

er·go·pho·bia [ˌəːgəuˈfəubiə] *n.*【医】厌恶工作的病态.

er·gos·ter·ol [əːˈgɔstərɔl] *n.*【生化】麦角甾醇.

er·got [ˈəːgət] *n.* ①麦角,麦角碱,麦角菌. ②【农】(植物的)麦角病. **-ism** *n.*【医】麦角中毒.

er·got·a·mine [əˈgɔtəmiːn] *n.* 【药】(治周期性偏头痛的)麦角胺.

Er·ic, Erik [ˈerik] *n.* 埃里克〔男子名〕.

E·rid·a·nus [iˈridənəs]【天】〔the ~〕波江(星)座.

Er·ie [ˈiəri] *n.* 〔美〕①伊利市. ②伊利湖〔北美洲〕. ③伊利运河. ④伊利人(北美印第安人中的一支). ***on the*** ~〔美俚〕①竖起耳朵听,偷听. ②躲藏着.

e·rig·er·on [iˈridʒərɔn] *n.*【植】加拿大蓬 (=Erigeron canadense).

Er·in [ˈiərin] *n.* 〔诗〕爱尔兰. *Sons of ~* 爱尔兰人.

E·rin·ys [iˈrinis, iˈrainis] *n. (pl.* ***E·rin·yes*** [iˈriniiːz]*)*【希神】(复仇的女神)伊里逆丝.

e·ri·om·e·ter [ˌeriˈɔmetə] *n.* 纤维细度测定器.

E·ris [ˈeris] *n.*【希神】厄里斯〔司争吵、不和的女神〕.

er·is·tic [eˈristik] *a.* 争论的. — *n.* ①争论者. ②争论;辩论术. **-al·ly** *ad.*

Er·i·tre·a [ˌeriˈtri(ː)ə] *n.* 厄立特里亚〔埃塞俄比亚北部一省,濒临红海〕. **-n** ① *a.* 厄立特里亚的. ② *n.* 厄立特里亚人.

erk [əːk] *n.* 〔英〕①(英国空军中军阶最低的)空军兵,地勤人员. ②〔口〕无用的蠢人.
Er·lan·ger [ˈəːlæŋə] *n.* 厄兰格〔姓氏〕.
Er·len·mey·er [ˈəːlənmaiə] **flask** 【化】锥瓶,锥形烧瓶;爱伦美氏(烧)瓶.
erl·king [ˈəːlkiŋ] *n.* 【北欧神话】妖王.
er·mine [ˈəːmin] *n.* *(pl.* **-s,** 〔集合词〕 *~)* 【动】①貂;扫雪鼬;貂皮. ②标志法官地位和贵族身分的貂皮袍;【徽】白底黑斑的毛皮. ***wear the ~*** 就任法官职务. — *a.* 〔诗〕纯白的;纯洁的.
er·mined [ˈəːmind] *a.* 穿貂皮袍的;以貂皮装饰的.
-ern *suf.* 表示"方位": east*ern*, west*ern*.
ern(e) [əːn] *n.* 海鹰.
Er·nest [ˈəːnist] *n.* 欧内斯特〔男子名〕.
Er·nes·tine [ˈəːnəstiːn] *n.* 欧内斯廷〔女子名〕.
e·rode [iˈrəud] *vt.* ①侵蚀,腐蚀. ②腐蚀出,侵蚀成. *metals ~d by acids* 被酸腐蚀的金属. — *vi.* 受侵蚀,遭腐蚀.
e·rod·ent [iˈrəudənt] *a.* 侵蚀的,腐蚀的. — *n.*【医】腐蚀药.
e·rod·i·ble [iˈrəudəbl] *a.* 会被腐蚀的;受到腐蚀的.
e·rog·e·nous [iˈrɔdʒinəs] *a.* = erotogenic.
E·ros [ˈirɔs, ˈerɔs] *n.* ①【希神】爱神厄洛斯. ②性欲,性爱. ③精力,生命力.
e·rose [iˈrəus] *a.* ①不整齐的. ②【植、虫】啮蚀状的.
e·ro·sion [iˈrəuʒən] *n.* ①腐蚀,侵蚀(作用). ②【医】糜烂,齿质腐损.
e·ro·sive [iˈrəusiv] *a.* 腐蚀性的,侵蚀性的.
e·rot·ic [iˈrɔtik] *a.* 性爱的,色情的; 性欲的,情欲上的. — *n.* ①情诗. ②好色之徒. **-cal·ly** *ad.*
e·rot·i·ca [iˈrɔtikə] *n.* *pl.* 〔用作单数或复数〕色情书籍,色情画.
e·rot·i·cism [eˈrɔtisizəm] *n.* = erotism.
er·o·tism [ˈerətizəm] *n.* ①色情性,好色. ②性欲;性冲动;性行为. ③【医】性欲亢进.
e·ro·to·gen·ic [iˌrɔtəuˈdʒenik] *a.* 性感应区的.
e·ro·to·ma·ni·a [iˌrəutəuˈmeiniə] *n.* 【医】色情狂.
err [əː] *vi.* ①犯错误,错. ②做坏事. ③〔古〕入歧途,漫游. *To err is human.* 〔谚〕人孰无过. *~* ***from the truth*** 违背真理. *~* ***from the right path*** 误入歧途. *~* ***in believing*** 误信. *~* ***on the safe side*** 错也保险. *~* ***on the side of lenity [severity]*** 失之过宽〔过严〕.
er·ran·cy [ˈerənsi] *n.* 错误状态;犯错误的倾向;违背常规的事.
er·rand [ˈerənd] *n.* ①差使;差事;〔古〕使命. ②〔古〕口信. *a fool's ~* 徒劳的事. ***go on a fool's [gawk's]*** *~* 白白受累,无谓奔走. ***go on an ~ for sb.*** 为某人办事. ***run (on) ~s*** 跑腿. ***send sb. on an ~*** 差使某人. *~* **boy** 使童.
er·rant [ˈerənt] *a.* ①(冒险)周游的,漂泊的,漫游的. ②走错了的;错误的,迷路的. ③无定的,移动的. *~ conceptions* 谬见. — *n.* 游侠. **-ly** *ad.*
er·rant·ry [ˈerəntri] *n.* ①(中世纪骑士的)冒险周游;游侠行为. ②〔总称〕游侠.
er·ra·ta [eˈrɑːtə] *n.* erratum 的复数.
er·rat·ic [iˈrætik, eˈr-] *a.* ①飘忽不定的;(行为等)古怪的,反常的;(心意、爱情等)乖僻的,反复无常的. ②【天】轨道无定的;【地】漂移性的;【医】间断无定的,不规律的;游走的. — *n.* ①奇人,怪人;反复无常的人. ②【地】漂砾. *~* **blocks [boulders]**【地】漂砾;漂块. **an** *~* **star** 游星. **-cal·ly** *ad.* **-ism** *n.*
er·ra·tum [eˈrɑːtəm] *n.* *(pl.* **-ta** [-tə]*)* (书写或印刷中的)错误; 〔*pl.*〕勘误表.
er·rhine [ˈerain] *n.*【医】催嚏剂,引涕剂. — *a.* 催嚏的,引涕的.
err·ing [ˈəːriŋ] *a.* 做错了事的;有罪过的;走入歧途的. **-ly** *ad.*
er·ro·ne·ous [iˈrəunjəs, eˈr-] *a.* 错误的,不正确的. *~ opinions* 错误意见. **-ly** *ad.* **-ness** *n.*
er·ror [ˈerə] *n.* ①错误;失错. ②谬见,误想;误信;误解. ③罪过. ④【数】误差;【法】误审,违法;(棒球中的)错打. *commit [make] an ~* 犯[出]错. *correct ~s* 改正错误. *a clerk's [clerical] ~* 笔误. *mean ~s* 标准误差. ***a writ of*** *~* 【法】(推翻错误原判的)再审命令. *nature's ~* 天生畸形. ***in*** *~* 弄错了的;错误地. *~****s of commission [omission]*** 违犯〔疏忽〕罪. ***fall into*** *~* 误入歧途. ***nature's*** *~* 天生畸形. **-less** *a.* 无错误的,正确的.
er·satz [G. ɛəˈzɑːtz] *n.* 〔G.〕代用品. — *a.* 代用的,人造的,合成的.
Erse [əːs] *n.* (苏格兰高地或爱尔兰的)盖耳语. — *a.* 盖耳语的.
Er·skin(e) [ˈəːskin] *n.* 厄斯金〔姓氏〕.
ERTS = Earth Resources Technology Satellites 地球资源技术卫星(计划).
erst [əːst] *ad.* 〔古〕以前,从前,往昔.
erst·while [ˈəːst*h*wail] *ad.* 从前,往昔. — *a.* 以前的,从前的,原来的.
er·u·bes·cence [ˌeru(ː)ˈbesns] *n.* 变红,发红;脸红.
er·u·bes·cent [ˌeru(ː)ˈbesnt] *a.* 发红的,略带红色的;变红的;脸红的.
e·ruct, e·ruc·tate [iˈrʌkt, -teit] *vt.* 使打嗝;嗝出;喷出. — *vi.* 打嗝,嗳气.
e·ruc·ta·tion [ˌiːrʌkˈteiʃən] *n.* ①嗳气,打嗝儿. ②(火山等的)喷出;喷出物. **-tive** *a.*
er·u·dite [ˈeruːdait] *a.* 博学的,有学问的. *an ~ commentary* 学者的评论. — *n.* 饱学之士,有学问的人. **-ly** *ad.* **-ness** *n.*
er·u·di·tion [ˌeruːˈdiʃən] *n.* 博学;学识;学问. **-al** *a.*
e·rum·pent [iˈrʌmpənt] *a.* 突然现出的;【植】裂出的,迸出的.
e·rupt [iˈrʌpt] *vi.* ①(火山等)迸发,喷出,爆发. ②(人从房子里)涌出;(牙齿)冒出;(皮肤)发疹子. — *vt.* 喷发;喷射出. **-ble** *a.*
e·rup·tion [iˈrʌpʃən] *n.* ①【地】喷发;(战争、感情等)爆发,迸发. ②【医】疹,发疹;(牙齿)冒出. ③喷出物. **-al** *a.*
e·rup·tive [iˈrʌptiv] *a.* ①喷出的,爆发的,喷发的. ②【地】火山喷出的. ③【医】疹的,发疹性的. *~ fountain* 喷泉. — *n.* 火成岩,喷发岩 (= *~* rock). **-ly** *ad.* **-ness** *n.*
E.R.V. = English Revised Version 〔*cf.* Revised Version of the Bible〕.
Er·vin [ˈəːvin] *n.* 欧文〔姓氏,男子名〕.
Er·vine [ˈəːvin] *n.* 欧文〔姓氏〕.
Er·win [ˈəːwin] *n.* 欧文〔姓氏〕.
-er·y *suf.* ①〔加于名词或形容词之后〕表示"性质","行为","习性"等: brav*ery*, snobb*ery*. ②〔加于动词之后〕表示"职业","技术"等: arch*ery*, fish*ery*, surg*ery*. ③〔加于动词之后〕表示"厂","店","场所"等: bak*ery*, groc*ery*. ④〔加于名词之后〕表示"…类的产品": machin*ery*, pott*ery*. ⑤〔加于名词之后〕表示"集体": soldi*ery*. ⑥〔加于动词之后〕表示"境遇","身分","状况": drudg*ery*, slav*ery*.
e·ryn·go [iˈriŋgəu] *n.* *(pl.* **-goes***)* 【植】①刺芹属 *(Eryngium)* 植物. ②〔废〕海滨刺芹的糖煮根〔原用作春药〕.
er·y·sip·e·las [ˌeriˈsipiləs] *n.* 【医】丹毒.
er·y·sip·e·loid [ˌeriˈsipilɔid] *n.* 【医】类丹毒.
er·y·the·ma [ˌeriˈθiːmə] *n.* *(pl.* **-ma·ta** [-tə]*)* 【医】红斑,红皮病.
e·ryth·rism [ˈeriθrizəm, iˈriθrizəm] *n.* 异常红〔尤指哺乳动物的毛发和鸟羽〕. **-al, er·y·thris·tic** [-ˈθristik] *a.*
e·ryth·rite [iˈriθrait] *n.* 【化】①钴华. ②赤丁四醇,赤藓醇.
e·ryth·ri·tol [iˈriθrəˌtəul] *n.* 【化】赤藓醇;丁四醇.
e·ryth·ro- *comb. f.* 表示"红","赤": *erythro*mycin.
e·ryth·ro·blast [iˈriθrəublæst] *n.* 【生】成红血(球)细胞,有核红血球. **-ic** *a.*

e·ryth·ro·blas·to·sis [iˌriθrəublæsˈtəusis] *n.*【医】①骨髓成红血细胞增多症. ②胎儿、婴儿成红血细胞增多症.

e·ryth·ro·cyte [iˈriθrəusait] *n.*【医】红血细胞,红血球. **e·ryth·ro·cyt·ic** [-ˈsitik] *n.*

e·ryth·ro·cy·tom·e·ter [iˌriθrə*u*saiˈtɔmitə] *n.*【医】红血球计数器.

er·y·throid [ˈeriərɔid] *a.* ①色调微红的. ②属于红血球的,属于成红血球的原生细胞的.

e·ryth·ro·my·cin [iˌriθrə*u*ˈmaisin] *n.*【医】红霉素.

er·y·thron [ˈeriθrɔn] *n.*【解】红血球系统.

e·ryth·ro·phyll [iˈriθrəfil] *n.*【生化】叶红素.

e·ryth·ro·poi·e·sis [iˌriθrə*u*pɔiˈi:sis] *n.*【医】红血球生成. **e·ryth·ro·poi·et·ic** [-pɔiˈetik] *a.*

er·y·throp·(s)i·a [ˌeriˈθrɔp(s)iə] *n.*【医】红视症.

e·ryth·ro·sin [iˈriθrəsin] *n.* ①【化】赤鲜红;四碘萤光素. ②【纺】新品酸性红 (= erythrosine).

Es =【化】einsteinium.

es- *pref.* *ex-* 的异体: escape, *es*cheat.

-es *suf.* ①〔加于词尾为 s, z, sh, ch, o, y 的大多数名词之后,构成复数〕: glass*es*, fuzz*es*, bush*es*, peach*es*, hero*es*, lodi*es*, loav*es*. ②〔加于词尾为 s, z, sh, ch 等动词之后, 构成现在时陈述语气第三人称单数〕: buzz*es*, reach*es*.

ESC = Economic and Social Council (United Nations) (联合国)经济及社会理事会.

es·ca·drille [ˌeskəˈdril] *n.* 〔F.〕①(六机编成的)飞行小队. ②(八艘舰艇组成的)海军分队.

es·ca·lade [ˌeskəˈleid] *vt.* (用梯子)攀登;【军】(用云梯)爬(城). — *n.* ①爬云梯, 用云梯爬墙. ②活动人行道.

es·ca·late [ˈeskəleit] *vi.* ①乘自动梯上升;象乘自动梯上升. ②(战争) 逐步升级. ③迅速上涨,飞快增加〔如物价、工资等〕. — *vt.* 使逐步上升. **es·ca·la·tion** [ˌeskəˈleiʃən] *n.*

es·ca·la·tor [ˈeskəleitə] *n.* ①【建】自动楼梯. ②(规定工资定期按生活费用) 上下调整的条款. — *a.* (规定工资、价格定期按比例)上下调整的. ~ *clauses* 伸缩条款.

es·cal·lo·ni·a [ˌeskəˈləuniə] *n.*【植】鼠刺属植物;〔E-〕鼠刺属.

es·cal·(l)op [isˈkɔləp] *n.* = scallop.

es·cap·a·ble [isˈkeipəbl] *a.* 可以避免的;可以逃脱的.

es·ca·pade [ˌeskəˈpeid] *n.* ①越轨行为,恶作剧. ②逃走,逃避.

es·cape [isˈkeip] *vi.* ①逃走,逃亡;逃脱,逃逸;逃避,避免. ②(液体等)漏出, 漏气. ③(栽培植物)长成野生植物. *The gas is escaping somewhere.* 煤气有个地方漏气了. ~ *from prison* 越狱. —*vt.* ①避开,避免. ②漏掉;疏忽, 忘记. ③逸出; 从…发出. *narrowly [barely]* ~ *death [being killed]* 死里逃生. *Nothing* ~*s you!* 你真细心! *A groan* ~*d his lips.* 他不禁哼了一声. *an* ~*d convict* 越狱逃犯. ~ *one's lips* 脱口而出. *His name* ~*s me.*=*His name* ~*s my memory.* 他的名字我记不起来了. ~ *sb.'s notice* 未被别人注意. — *n.* ①逃避;逃亡;漏出,逸出. ②逃亡手段;避难装置;逃路. ③【机】排气管. ④野化植物,退化植物. ⑤【建】出口. *an air* ~ 放气管. *a narrow [hairbreadth]* ~ 九死一生. ***have an*** ~ 逃走. ***have one's*** ~ ***cut off*** 被切断逃路. ***make good one's*** ~ = ***effect one's*** ~ 逃脱. ***make one's*** ~ 逃走. ~ **artist** ①(魔术师或杂技演员等)有脱身术的人. ②善于越狱的人. ~ **canal** 排水渠. ~ **clause** (契约等的)例外条款. ~ **hatch** (危急时的)逃生出口;出路,办法. ~ **literature** 逃避现实的文学. ~ **mechanism**【心】逃避不愉快的现实的方法. ~ **pipe** 放出管. ~**-proof** *a.* 防逃脱的. ~ **shaft**【矿】太平竖井,安全竖井. ~ **stair** 太平梯. ~ **valve** 安全阀,放出阀,保险阀. ~ **velocity**【物】(火箭)第二宇宙速度,逃逸速度,脱离速度,克服地心吸力的速度. ~**way** 逃路;太平门,太平梯. ~ **wheel**【机】擒纵轮 (= scape wheel).

es·cap·ee [iˌskeiˈpi:, e-] *n.* 逃脱者〔尤指越狱犯人〕.

es·cape·ment [isˈkeipmənt] *n.* ①擒纵机;(钟、表等的)司行轮,摆轮;(打字机等上面的)棘轮装置. ②〔罕〕逃跑;〔古〕逃路,出口.

es·cap·ism [isˈkeipizəm] *n.* ①逃避现实, 空想, 幻想. ②逃避现实的文学[艺术].

es·cap·ist [isˈkeipist] *n.* 逃避现实的人. — *a.* 逃避现实的. ~ *literature* 逃避现实的文学.

es·ca·pol·o·gy [ˌeskəˈpɔlədʒi] *n.* 逃脱法,逃脱术.

es·car·got [F. ɛskargo] *n.* 〔F.〕蜗牛〔尤指食用蜗牛〕.

es·ca·role [ˈeskərəul] *n.*【植】菊苣,茅菜.

es·carp [isˈkɑ:p] *vt.* 使成急斜面. — *n.*【建】内壕, 壕沟内岸. **-ment** *n.* 急斜面;悬崖.

-esce *suf.* 〔用在拉丁语系动词之后〕表示"开始…","…起来","渐渐…","…化"(等): convale*sce*, efferv*esce*.

-escence *suf.* 构成与 -escent 结尾的形容词相对应的名词,表示"作用","变化","过程","状态"等: convales*cence*, lumin*escence*.

-escent *suf.* 构成形容词,表示"…期的","…性的": adol*escent*, recrud*escent*.

esch·a·lot [ˈeʃəlɔt] *n.* = shallot.

es·char [ˈeskɑ:] *n.*【医】焦痂.

es·cha·rot·ic [ˌeskəˈrɔtik]【医】生焦痂性的, 腐蚀性的. — *n.* 苛性剂,腐蚀剂.

es·cha·to·log·i·cal [ˌeskətəˈlɔdʒikəl] *a.*【宗】末世学的.

es·cha·tol·o·gy [ˌeskəˈtɔlədʒi] *n.*【宗】末世学〔研究人类和世界终局的神学〕.

es·cheat [isˈtʃi:t] *vi.*, *vt.*【法】(把)(无继承人的土地或财产)归属国家[领主或国王]; 充公. — *n.* ①(土地或财产的)归还国家,充公. ②归还的财产;没收地.

Esch·e·rich·i·a [ˌeʃəˈrikiə] *n.*【微】埃希氏菌属. ~ **coli** 大肠埃希氏菌,大肠杆菌.

es·chew [isˈtʃu:] *vt.*【修】避开;戒绝. ~ *wine [evil]* 戒酒[避开罪恶].

esch·scholt·zia [eˈʃɔltsiə] *n.*【植】花菱草,花菱草属植物.

es·clan·dre [esˈklɑ:ndr] *n.* 〔F.〕丑闻;纷扰.

es·co·lar [ˈeskəˌlɑ:] *n.* 玉梭鱼 *(Ruvettus pretiosus)* 〔产于大西洋热带地区〕.

es·cort [isˈkɔ:t] *vt.* 护卫,护送,伴随. — [ˈeskɔ:t] *n.* ①警卫,护送. ②护卫队,仪仗兵;护送者,护卫者;伴随者;护航舰[机]. *a convoy* ~ 车运警卫部队. ~ *carrier* 护航用小型航空母舰. *an* ~ *of jet fighters* 喷气战斗机护航队. *conduct* ~ *operations* 护航. *under the* ~ *of* 在…护送下.

e·scribe [esˈkraib] *vt.*【数】旁切. *an* ~*d circle* 旁切圆.

es·cri·toire [ˌeskriˈtwɑ:] *n.* 〔F.〕写字台.

es·crow [esˈkrəu] *n.*【法】(由第三者保存、待条件完成后即交受让人的)证书[契据]. ~ **agreement [bonds]** 有条件转让契约[债券].

es·cu·do [esˈku:du] *n.* *(pl.* ~*s)* 埃斯库多〔葡萄牙及智利等国的货币单位〕.

es·cu·lent [ˈeskjulənt] *a.* 适于食用的. — *n.* 食用品(尤指蔬菜).

es·cutch·eon [isˈkʌtʃən] *n.* ①用纹章装饰的盾. ②盾形物,盾纹面;昆虫小盾片. ③(船尾标志船名的)楣部. ④锁眼盖孔罩. ***a (dark) blot on [in] one's*** ~ 名誉上的污点.

E.S.E., ESE, e.s.e. = east-southeast.

-ese *suf.* ①〔接在地名之后〕表示"…语","…人": Chin*ese*, Japan*ese*. ②〔接在作家人名之后〕 表示 "…风格的","…体的","…笔调的": Carlyl*ese*, Johnson*ese*.

es·er·ine [ˈesəri:n] *n.* = physostigmine.

es·kar, es·ker [ˈeskə] *n.*【地】蛇形丘.

Es·ki·mo [ˈeskiməu] *n.* *(pl.* ~, ~*s*, ~*es* [-z]) 爱斯基摩人[语,狗]. — *a.* 爱斯基摩的. ~ **dog** 北极狼犬. ~

pie 〔美〕紫雪糕. **-an** [ˌeskiˈməuən] *a.*
ESL = as a second language 英语作为第二语言.
Es·mond(e) [ˈezmənd] *n.* 埃斯蒙德〔男子名〕.
e·soph·a·ge·al [i(ː)ˌsɔfəˈdʒi(ː)əl] *a.*【解】食管的.
e·soph·a·gus [i(ː)ˈsɔfəgəs] *n. (pl.* **-gi** [-gai])【解】食管.
es·o·ter·ic [ˌesəuˈterik] *a.* ①深奥的; 难解的. ②秘密的; 机密的. ③秘教的 *(opp.* exoteric); (弟子)受秘传的; 限于少数人的. — *n.* 受秘传的人. **E- Buddhism** 密教.
es·o·ter·i·ca [ˌesəuˈterikə] *n. pl.* 秘(密)事; 秘书; 秘教; 秘传.
es·o·tro·pi·a [ˌesəuˈtrəupiə] *n.*【医】辐辏性斜视, 内斜视.
ESP = extrasensory perception 超感官知觉, 超感觉力.
esp. = especially.
es·pa·drille [ˈespədril] *n.* 登山帆布鞋, 帆布便鞋.
es·pal·ier [isˈpæljə] *n.* 树墙, 树棚; 墙式果树, 棚式果树. ~ **growth form** 匍匐生长型. — *vt.* ①给(果树等)支棚架. ②使(果树等)成匍匐状.
es·pa·ña [esˈpɑːnjɑː] 〔Sp.〕 = spain.
es·par·to [esˈpɑːtəu] *n.* 〔Sp.〕【植】(可制纸、席的)茅草 (= ~ grass).
es·pe·cial [isˈpeʃəl] *a.* 特别的; 特殊的. *a matter of ~ importance* 特别重大的事件. *in ~* 特别, 格外, 尤其.
es·pe·cial·ly [isˈpeʃəli] *ad.* 特别, 格外, 尤其. ★口语中常把 especial(ly) 说成 special(ly).
Es·pe·ran·tist [ˌespəˈræntist] *n.* 世界语学者[提倡者]. — *a.* 世界语的, 世界语学者的.
Es·pe·ran·to [ˌespəˈræntəu] *n.* 世界语〔1887 年波兰人 Zamenhof 用 Dr. Esperanto 为笔名发表〕.
es·pi·al [isˈpaiəl] *n.* 侦察; 监视; 发觉.
es·piè·gle·rie [F. ɛspjɛgləri] *n.* 〔F.〕恶作剧; 顽皮, 淘气.
es·pi·o·nage [F. ɛspiəˈnɑːʒ, ˈespiənidʒ] *n.* 〔F.〕侦察, 监视; 谍报; 间谍活动. *electronic ~ equipment* 电子侦察设备.
es·pla·nade [ˌespləˈneid] *n.* ①(一般指为散步、驱车游玩的)平地, 广场; (尤指海滨、湖边供游人散步的)大道. ②【军】(要塞与市镇间的)空地.
es·pous·al [isˈpəuzəl] *n.* ①(对主义、事业等的)拥护, 支持. ②〔常 *pl.*〕订婚或订婚仪式; 结婚, 婚礼.
es·pouse [isˈpəuz] *vt.* ①信仰, 拥护, 采纳(主义、学说等). ②嫁娶(尤指娶妻).
es·pres·si·vo [ˌespreˈsiːvəu] *a., ad.* 〔It.〕【乐】富于表情的[地].
es·pres·so [eˈspresəu] *n. (pl. ~s)* 蒸馏咖啡〔用蒸汽加压煮出的咖啡〕.
es·*prit* [ˈespriː; 〔F.〕ɛspri] *n.* 〔F.〕精神; 活气; 才智. ~ ***de corps*** [dəˈkɔː] 集体精神, 团结精神. ~ ***de lois*** [dəˈlwɑː], 法律的精神. ~ ***fort*** [fɔːr] 意志坚强的人; 自由思想家.
es·py [isˈpai] *vt.* ①(偶然)看出; 发现(缺点等). ②窥探.
Esq. = Esquire.
-esque *suf.* 表示"…式的", "…风格的", "…似的": arab*esque*, pictur*esque*.
Es·qui·mau [ˈeskiməu] *n. (pl.* **-x** [-məuz]) *a.* = Eskimo.
es·quire [isˈkwaiə] *n.* ①〔英〕先生. ★信中或正式文件中用于男子姓名以后的尊称; 略作 Esq. 或 Esqre (写作 John Smith, Esq.; 头衔写作 John Smith, Esq.M.A.); 美国有时仅用 esquire 称呼律师. ②〔英〕(地位在骑士之下的)乡绅. ③(中世纪骑士的)扈从. ④〔古〕地主, 绅士. — *vt.* ①在(收件人姓名)后用先生的称号; 称…为先生. ②护送.
ESRO = European Space Research Organization 欧洲空间研究组织.
ess [es] *n. (pl. ~es* [ˈesiz]) ①字母 S, s. ②S 形物件.
ESS = Economic and Scientific Section 经济与科学部.
-ess *suf.* ①〔加在名词之后〕表示"阴性": poet*ess*, actr*ess*. ②〔加在形容词之后, 构成抽象名词〕: dur*ess*, larg*ess*.
es·say [ˈesei, ˈesi] *n.* ①(文艺上的)随笔, 漫笔; 小品文, 短论〔理论性强的学术论文叫 treatise, dissertation〕. ②尝试, 企图 *(at)*; 试验. ③(未被接受的)邮票[纸币]的图案印刷样张. — [eˈsei, ˈesei] *vt.* 试; 企图. ~ **question** (同填充题、是非题相对而言的)问答题. **-ist** *n.* 随笔[小品文等]作者.
es·se [ˈesi] *n.* 〔L.〕【哲】存在. ***in ~*** 存在着.
Es·sen [ˈesn] *n.* 埃森〔德意志联邦共和国城市〕.
es·sence [ˈesns] *n.* ①【哲】本质 *(opp.* phenomenon); 真髓, 精髓, 精华, 要素. ②香气; 香油, 香精, 香料. *~ of mint* 薄荷精, 薄荷油. ***in ~*** 本质上; 大体上. ***of the essence*** 绝对不可缺的. **-d** *a.* 香料的, 香气的.
es·sen·tial [iˈsenʃəl] *n.* ①本质的; 实质上的, 实在的. ②根本的, 必需的; 主要的, 紧要的 *(to)*. ③理想中的, 完美的. ④提炼的, 精华的;【乐】基本的;【医】特发的, 自发的. *~ elements* 要素. *~ ingredients* 主要成分. — *n.* 〔常 *pl.*〕本质; 要点, 要素, 要件. *~s of English Grammar* 英语语法要点. *~s of life* 生活必需品. ~ **anemia** 原发性贫血. ~ **character**【生】种特征. ~ **disease**【医】特发病. ~ **harmony**【乐】基本和声. ~ **oil**【化】(香)精油, 香料油. ~ **proposition**【逻】本质的命题. **-ly** *ad.* 本质上; 本来; 根本.
es·sen·tial·ism [iˈsenʃəlizəm] *n.*【哲】本质先于存在论. **-tial·ist** *n.* 本质先于存在论者.
es·sen·ti·al·i·ty [iˌsenʃiˈæliti] *n.* ①本性, 本质. ②重要性; 要点.
es·sen·tial·ize [iˈsenʃəlaiz] *vt.* ①提炼出, 使精炼. ②扼要地表达, 讲明…的本质, 用基本形式阐述.
es·ses [ˈesiz] *n.* 连写的 ss 〔ess 的复数〕.
es·so·nite [ˈesənait] *n.*【地】钙铝榴石.
EST = eastern standard time 〔美〕东部时间.
est. = ① established. ② estimate; estimated.
-est *suf.* ①〔接在大多数单音节的、某些双音节的和少数多音节的形容词和副词之后, 构成最高级〕表示"最": hard*est*, nobl*est*, polit*est*, lazi*est*. ★用法大体上如 -er; 比较级不用 -er 的 barren, fragile 等词, 最高级也常有采用 -est 的(末节为 -id 的词, 如 limpid, 也一样); 另外, 如 beautiful 这种三音节以上的词, 在诗里差不多全可自由应用 -est. ②〔在诗歌与古语中, 接在与 Thou 连用的动词之后, 构成陈述语气第二人称单数〕: Thou sing*est*.
estab. = established.
es·tab·lish [isˈtæbliʃ] *vt.* ①建立, 树立, 设立, 创立; 建设, 开设; 制定, 规定. ②安顿, 安排, 安置; 使开业; 使定居; 使固定. ③确定, 证实; 使承认, 使认定, 分辨. ④使(教会)成国教. *~ sb. in business* 使人立足商界. *~ a claim to* 确定有权…. *~ a law* 制定法律. *~ oneself as physician* 开业行医. — *vi.* (植物等)移植生长. **-able** *a.*
es·tab·lished [isˈtæbliʃt] *a.* ①被设立的; 确定的; 被制定的; 被认定了的; 既定的. ②固定的. ③【植】移植生长的. *an ~ clerk* 常设办事员. *an old ~ shop* 老铺, 老店. *an ~ customs* 成例, 常规. *an ~ fact* 既成事实. *an ~ variety* 移植的品种. *an ~ invalid* 慢性病人. *~ reputation* 定评. ***the E- Church*** 英国国教.
es·tab·lish·er [isˈtæbliʃə] *n.* 创办者, 建立者.
es·tab·lish·ment [isˈtæbliʃmənt] *n.* ①确定; 设置, 制定; 设立, 建立, 开设, 创设. ②建立的机构; 家庭; 产业; 机关, 商店, 学校(等); 〔英〕研究所. ③制度, 编制. ④定薪, (固定的)收入; 定职; 定员; 定居. ⑤【植】移植生长. ⑥〔the E-〕权力机构[体制]; 当局; 习俗社会. *keep a large ~* 拥有巨大家业. *an ammunition ~* 弹药库. *industrial and mining ~s* 工矿企业. *a manufacturing ~* 工业公司. *business ~s* 商店. *the E- newspaper* 官方报纸. *an atomic energy ~* 原子能科学研究所. *peace [war] ~*

【军】平时[战时]编制. ***the Civil Service E-*** 〔英〕文职定额. ***the (Church) E-*** (英国)国教. ***the ~ of the port*** 标准潮讯,潮候时差. ~ **period**【生】成林期.

es·tab·lish·men·tar·i·an [isˌtæbliʃmənˈtɛəriən] *n.* ①国教信徒,国教主义者. ②拥护既成权力体制的人. — *a.* ①国教的,国教信徒的. ②拥护既成权力体制的.

es·ta·mi·net [F. ɛstaminɛ] *n.* 〔F.〕小咖啡馆,小酒吧,小餐馆.

es·tan·cia [esˈtɑːnsjə] *n.* 〔Sp.〕(拉美的)大庄园〔尤指大牧场〕.

es·tate [isˈteit] *n.* ①财产;遗产;房地产. ②〔古〕身分,地位;家产. ③生活状况;等级;集团;情况,状态. ④财产权,所有权. ⑤庄园,种植园. ⑥人生阶段. *a housing* ~ 居民区. *an industrial* ~ 工业区. *landed* ~ 地产. *personal* ~动产. *real* ~ 不动产. *a tea* ~ 茶树种植园. *the third* ~ 第三等级(指平民);(法国革命前的)中产阶级. *the fourth* ~ 〔谑〕第四等级(指新闻界记者). *the fifth* ~ 第五等级(指科学界). ~ ***for life [years]*** 终身[定期]财产. ~ ***in fee*** 世袭领地. ~ ***upon condition*** 有条件的遗产. ***reach [come to] man's [woman's]*** ~ 成年. ***suffer in one's*** ~ 家道艰难. ***the Three Estates (of the Realm)*** (封建时代欧洲的)贵族、僧侣和庶民;〔英〕僧侣上院议员、贵族上院议员与下院议员. ***wind up an*** ~ 清算死者[破产人]的财产. ~ **agent**〔英〕①土地管理人. ②地产掮客. ~ **car**〔英〕客货两用轿车. ~ **duty [tax]** 财产税,遗产税. **-d** [-id] *a.* 有财产的,有产业的,有地产的.

Es·tates-Gen·er·al [iˈsteitsˈdʒenərəl] 三级会议〔法国1789年革命前的立法机构〕.

es·teem [isˈtiːm] *n.* ①尊重,尊敬. ②〔古〕评价. ***as a mark [token] of*** ~ 以表敬意. ***gain [get] the*** ~ ***of*** 受人尊敬. ***have a great*** ~ ***for*** 对…大为敬佩. ***hold sb. in*** ~ 尊重;尊敬. ***in my*** ~ 照我想[看]. — *vt.* ①尊重. ②认为;〔古〕评价. *I shall ~ it (as) a favour if ....* 若蒙…,不胜感谢. *an ~ed favor*【美商】订购信. *your ~ed letter* 尊函.

Es·telle [esˈtel] *n.* 埃斯特尔〔女子名〕.

es·ter [ˈestə] *n.*【化】酯. ~ **value** 酯化值.

es·ter·ase [ˈestəreis] *n.*【化】酯酶.

es·ter·i·fy [esˈterifai] *vt., vi.*【化】(使)酯化. **-fi·ca·tion** [-fiˈkeiʃən] *n.*【化】酯化.

Esth. = Esther, Esthonia.

Esth. = Esther.

Es·ther [ˈestə] *n.* ①埃丝特〔女子名〕. ②以斯帖〔《圣经》犹太女王名〕. ③〔the E-〕【圣】《以斯帖书》.

es·the·si·a [esˈθiːʒə, -ʒiə, -ziə] *n.* 感觉,感知;感觉力,知觉性.

es·the·si·om·e·ter [esˌθiːziːˈɔmitə] *n.*【医】触觉测量器.

es·thete [ˈiːsθiːt, ˈes-] *n.* ①唯美主义者. ②审美家;美学家 (= aesthete).

es·thet·ic(al) [iːsˈθetik(əl)] *a.* 美的;美学的,审美的;艺术的 (= aesthetic(al)). ~ **forest** 风景林. **-al·ly** *ad.*

es·the·ti·cian [ˌesθiˈtiʃən] *n.* 审美学者,审美学家 (= aesthetician).

es·thet·i·cism [iːsˈθetisizəm] *n.* 唯美主义;审美眼光;美的嗜好 (= aetheticism).

es·thet·ics [iːsˈθetiks] *n.* 〔用作单数〕美学 (= aesthetics).

Es·tho·ni·a [esˈtəuniə], **Es·tho·ni·an** [-niən] *n.* = Estonia. **-n** *a., n.* = Estonian.

es·ti·ma·ble [ˈestiməbl] *a.* ①值得尊重的;可估计的. ②〔古〕有价值的,可贵的. **-ness** *n.* **-bly** *ad.*

es·ti·mate [ˈestimeit] *vt.* ①估计,估算;估价;估量. ②评价,判断. ③〔古〕尊重. *an ~d sum* 估计总数. ~ *the loss at 1,000 yuan* 估计损失为一千元. — *vi.* 估计,估价. — [ˈestimit] *n.* ①估计;预测;〔英〕〔*pl.*〕预算,预算额;预算书;估价单;(从典型统计得出的)数值. ②评价,判断. *an intelligence* ~ 情报[敌情]判断. *a rough* ~ 据粗略的估计. ***at a moderate*** ~ 照适中的估计. ***by*** ~ 照估计. ***form an*** ~ ***of*** 给…作一估计;评价. ***the Estimates*** 〔英〕财政收支概算. **-d** *a.*

es·ti·ma·tion [ˌestiˈmeiʃən] *n.* ①估计,评价. ②预算,预算额;概算. ③尊重,尊敬. ④意见,判断. ⑤【化】估定;测定. *in my* ~ 据我估计,我认为. *in the* ~ *of the law* 从法律上来看. ***full [rise] in the*** ~ ***of the public*** 在公众心目中的评价下降[上升]. ***held in high*** ~ 极受尊重.

es·ti·ma·tive [ˈestimətiv] *a.* ①有估计能力的. ②可用以估计的;能作出判断的. ~ *figure.* 估计的数字.

es·ti·ma·tor [ˈestimeitə] *n.* 估计者;估计量.

es·ti·val [iːsˈtaivəl] *a.* = aestival.

es·ti·vate [ˈestiveit] *vi.* ①消夏. ②【动】夏眠,夏蛰.

es·ti·va·tion [ˌestiˈveiʃən] *n.* ①【动】夏眠,夏蛰. ②【植】花被卷叠式;夏眠〔指生态〕(=aestivation).

Es·to·ni·a [esˈtəunjə] *n.* 爱沙尼亚〔苏联加盟共和国国名〕.

Es·to·ni·an [esˈtəunjən] *a.* ①爱沙尼亚(人)的. ②爱沙尼亚语[文化]的. — *n.* ①爱沙尼亚人. ②爱沙尼亚语.

es·top [isˈtɔp] *vt.* ①【法】禁止翻供. ②〔古〕堵塞,遮拦. ③防止,禁止 *(from)*.

es·top·page [isˈtɔpidʒ] *n.*【法】禁止翻供. ②堵塞,阻止.

es·top·pel [isˈtɔpəl] *n.*【法】禁止翻供.

es·to·vers [esˈtəuvəz] *n.* 〔*pl.*〕【法】(法律上准许的)必需供给品〔如给租户作燃料或修理用的木材、给离婚妻子的赡养费等〕.

es·trade [esˈtrɑːd] *n.* 台,坛.

es·tra·di·ol [ˌestrəˈdaiəul, -ɔːl] *n.*【化】雌二醇.

es·trange [isˈtreindʒ] *vt.* ①使疏远;离间. ②隔离;使离开(习惯了的环境等). ③转用,移用. ***be [become]*** ~***d from each other*** 互相疏远. ~ ***oneself from*** 同…疏远起来. **-d** *a.* **-ment** *n.*

es·tray [eˈstrei] *n.* ①他去的人;不见了的东西. ②【法】无人认领的走失家畜;无主的走失家畜. — *vi.* 〔古〕迷路,走失.

es·treat [isˈtriːt] *n.*【法】(关于罚款等判决记录的)副本,抄本. — *vt.* 抄(判决记录);(按副本)追收(罚款等).

es·tri·ol [ˈestraiəul, ˈiːstriəl] *n.*【生化】雌三醇.

es·tro·gen [ˈestrədʒən] *n.*【生化】雌(性)激素.

es·tro·gen·ic [ˌestrəˈdʒenik] *a.*【生化】雌激素的,促进发情的.

Es·tron [ˈiːstrɔn] *n.* 醋酸纤维.

es·trone [ˈestrəun] *n.*【生化】雌素酮.

es·trous [ˈiːstrəs, ˈes-] *a.*【动】发情期的,有发情期特征的. ~ **cycle**【动】发情周期.

es·trum [ˈiːstrəm] *n.* = oestrum 或 estrus.

es·trus [ˈiːstrəs, ˈes-] *n.*【动】发情期.

es·tu·ar·i·al [ˌestjuˈɛəriəl] *a.* 三角港的,三角湾的,河口湾的,港湾的.

es·tu·ar·ine [ˈestjuːərin, -ain] *a.* ①江河口的;江河湾的;港湾的. ②(江河口、江河湾、港湾等)沉积的.

es·tu·ar·y [ˈestjuəri] *n.* 三角湾,河口湾,港湾. ~ **deposit** 港湾沉积.

E.S.U., ESU, e.s.u. = electrostatic unit 静电单位.

e·su·ri·ence, e·su·ri·en·cy [iˈsjuəriəns, -si] *n.* ①饥饿,贪吃,暴食. ②贪心,贪婪.

e·su·ri·ent [iˈsjuəriənt] *a.* ①饥饿的;暴食的,贪吃的. ②贪心的.

ESV = earth satellite vehicle 人造地球卫星.

ET = eastern time 〔美〕东部时间.

E.T. = ① English Translation. ② electric telegraph ③〔美〕electric transcription.

E·T [ˈiːtiː] *n.* 《外星人》〔美国的一部科学幻想影片〕.

-et[1] *suf.* ①〔主要加在法语的名词之后〕表示"小": bull*et*, fill*et*, isl*et*, sonn*et* (但 hatch*et*, pock*et*, pack*et* 等已失去"小"的意义). ②表示"组","组合": oct*et*, quart*et*.
-et[2], **ete** *suf.* 表示"…者","做…的人": aesth*ete*, athl*ete*, po*et*.
et [et] *conj.* 〔L.〕和, 以及 (=and). ***et al.*** [et'ɔl] ①= *et alibi*. ②= *et alii*. ***et seq(q)***. = ***et sq(q)***. = ***et sequentes [sequentia]*** [et'sikwenti:z, -ʃiə] 以及下列等等, 参看以下某句[某页] (= and those that follow).
ETA = estimated time of arrival 估计的到达时间.
e·ta ['i:tə] *n.* 希腊语字母表第七字母〔H, η., 相当英语的长音 e〕.
et alibi [et'ælibai] 〔L.〕以及其他地方 (= and elsewhere).
et alii [et'æliai] 〔L.〕以及其他人等 (= and others). ★ et alii 一般指人, 指物时用 etc.
et·a·mine ['etəmi:n] *n.* 【纺】纱罗; 筛绢.
é·tape [ei'tæp] *n.* 〔F.〕①兵站; 宿营地. ②一日的行程.
é·tat ['etɑ] *n.* 〔F.〕①国家. ②= estate.
é·ta·tisme, e·ta·tism [ei'tɑ:tizəm] *n.* 〔F.〕国家社会主义, 国家主义.
e·ta·tist, é·ta·tiste [ei'tɑ:tist] *a.* (拥护)国家社会主义的, (拥护)国家主义的. — *n.* 国家社会主义者, 国家主义者.
état-major ['eitɑ:mɑ:'ʒɔ:] *n.* 〔F.〕【军】参谋; 参谋部.
etc., &c. = 〔L.〕*et cetera*.
et cet·er·a [it'setrə] 〔L.〕等等, 以及其他〔指人时用 et al.〕.
et·cet·e·ras [it'setrəz] *n. pl.* 其他种种东西, 等等东西. *these* ~ 这种种东西. *100 dollars without* ~ 一百美元整.
etch [etʃ] *vt.* ①蚀刻, 浸蚀. ②刻划, 描述. ③铭刻. — *vi.* 进行蚀刻. — *n.* 腐蚀剂, 蚀刻剂. *mass* ~ (晶体的)粗蚀.
etch·ant ['etʃənt] *n.* 蚀刻剂.
etch·er ['etʃə] *n.* 蚀刻技工; 蚀刻器.
etch·ing ['etʃiŋ] *n.* ①蚀刻法; 蚀刻(铜)版画; 蚀镂术. ②蚀刻画, 蚀刻版, 蚀刻版印刷品. *close [rough]* ~ (晶体的)精[粗]蚀. *electrochemical* ~ 电化浸蚀, 电抛光. ~ **figure** 蚀像. ~ **ground** 蚀刻底子. ~ **needle** 蚀刻用钢针.
ETD = estimated time of departure 估计的离开时间.
e·ter·nal [i(:)'tə:nl] *a.* ①永远的, 永久的; 不变的, 不朽的. ②〔口〕不停的, 没完没了的. ~ *death* 死灭. ~ *life* 永生. ~ *truth* 永恒的真理. *the* ~ *triangle* 三角恋爱. ***the E-*** 【宗】上帝. ***the E- City*** 不朽的都市(指罗马). **-ly** *ad.* **-ity, -ness** *n.*
e·ter·na·lize [i(:)'tə:nəlaiz] *vt.* 使永恒, 使无穷, 使不朽.
e·ter·ni·ty [i(:)'tə:niti] *n.* ①无始无终, 无穷无尽. ②【宗】来世; 永生; 永劫. ***an*** ~ ***box*** 〔俚〕棺材. ***send sb. to*** ~ 送某人上西天. ***through all*** ~ 永远, 万古千秋.
e·ter·nize [i(:)'tə:naiz] *vt.* 使永恒, 使无穷, 使不朽. **e·ter·ni·za·tion** [i(:)ˌtə:nai'zeiʃən] *n.*
E·te·sian [i'ti:ʒiən] *a.* 一年一次的. — *n.* 〔常 *pl.*〕(定期发生的)地中海季风.
eth. = ethical; ethics.
-eth *suf.* ①〔加于以元音结尾的基数词以后, 构成序数词〕: forti*eth*. ②〔古〕〔加于动词之后, 构成第三人称单数现在时〕: ask*eth*, go*eth*.
eth·ane ['eθein] *n.* 【化】乙烷.
eth·a·no·ic [ˌeθə'nəuik] *a.* ~ **acid** 【化】醋酸, 乙酸.
eth·a·nol ['eθənɔ:l, -nəul] *n.* 【化】①醇. ②乙醇; 酒精 (= alcohol).
eth·a·nol·a·mine ['eθənəu'læmi:n] *n.* 【化】乙醇胺; 氨基乙醇.
Eth·el ['eθəl] *n.* 埃塞尔〔女子名〕.
eth·ene ['eθi:n] *n.* 【化】乙烯 (= ethylene).
e·the·o·gen·e·sis [ˌi:θiəu'dʒenisis] *n.* 【生】雄体单性生殖.
e·ther ['i:θə] *n.* ①【物】以太, 能媒. ②【化】醚; 乙醚. ③〔诗〕上空, 苍天. ④【哲】灵气; 气氛. ~ **wave** 以太波. **-ish, -like** *a.*
e·the·re·al, e·the·ri·al [i'θiəriəl] *a.* ①空气一样的; 轻飘的, 稀薄的. ②天上的, 太空的; 灵气的; 微妙的. ③【物】以太的. ④【化】用醚制的, 醚(性)的. ~ *oil* 香精油. **-ity** *n.* **-ly** *ad.*
e·the·re·al·i·za·tion [i(:)ˌθiəriəlai'zeiʃən] *n.* ①轻飘化, 稀薄化. ②微妙化. ③醚化, 气化.
e·the·re·al·ize [i(:)'θiəriəlaiz] *vt.* ①使轻飘, 使稀薄. ②使微妙. ③使成醚; 气化.
Eth·er·ege ['eθəridʒ] *n.* 埃瑟里奇〔姓氏〕.
e·the·ri·al [i'θiəriəl] *a.* = ethereal.
e·ther·i·fy [i'θerifai] *vt.* 【化】醚化.
e·ther·i·za·tion [ˌi:θərai'zeiʃən] *n.* 【医】麻醉.
e·ther·ize ['i:θəraiz] *vt.* 【医】用醚麻醉. **-r** *n.* 麻醉剂.
eth·ic ['eθik] *a.* = ethical. — *n.* = ethics.
eth·i·cal ['eθikəl] *a.* ①伦理的, 道德的; 伦理学(上)的; 合乎道德的. ②(药品)合乎规格的, 凭处方出售的. *an* ~ *principle* 道德原则. ~ *culture* 伦理教育. ~ **dative** 【语法】泛指的人称的与格. ~ **drug [pharmaceutical]** 凭处方出售的药品. ~ **genitive** 【语】泛指的第二人称的所有格. **-ly** *ad.* **-ness** *n.*
eth·i·cal·i·ty [ˌeθi'kæliti] *n.* 伦理性.
eth·i·cian [e'θiʃən] *n.* = ethicist.
eth·i·cist ['eθisist] *n.* 伦理学家 (= ethician).
eth·i·cize ['eθisaiz] *vt.* 使伦理化; 使变得道德的, 认为…合乎伦理.
eth·ics ['eθiks] *n.* ①伦理学. ②伦理, 道德. ③伦理学书籍[论文]; 伦理观, 道德标准. *practical* ~ 实用伦理学. *medical* ~ 行医道德. *press* ~ 新闻道德.
eth·i·nyl [e'θainl] *n.* 【化】乙炔基.
E·thi·op(e) ['i:θiɔp] *n.*, *a.* 〔古〕= Ethiopian.
E·thi·o·pi·a [ˌi:θi'əupjə] *n.* 埃塞俄比亚〔非洲〕.
E·thi·o·pi·an [ˌi:θi'əupjən, -piən] *a.* 埃塞俄比亚的, 埃塞俄比亚人的; 埃塞俄比亚语的. — *n.* ①埃塞俄比亚人; 埃塞俄比亚语. ②(泛指)黑人.
E·thi·op·ic [ˌi:θi'ɔpik, -'əupik] *a.* 埃塞俄比亚语的; 埃塞俄比亚人的; 埃塞俄比亚的. — *n.* 埃塞俄比亚语.
eth·moid ['eθmɔid], **eth·moi·dal** [-dəl] *a.* 【解】筛状的; 筛骨的. — *n.* 筛骨.
eth·narch ['eθnɑ:k] *n.* (拜占庭帝国等的)总督. **-y** *n.* 总督的职位[身分、统治权、管辖区].
eth·nic ['eθnik] *a.* = ethnical. — *n.* 少数民族的成员种族集团的成员.
eth·ni·cal ['eθnikəl] *a.* ①种族的, 种族上的, 人种学的. ②异教徒的. ~ *nation* 部落民族. ~ *psychology* 种族心理学. **-ly** *ad.*
eth·nic·i·ty [eθ'nisiti] *n.* 种族划分; 种族关系.
eth·no- *comb. f.* 表示"人种","种族","民族": *ethnography*.
eth·no·cen·tric [ˌeθnəu'sentrik] *a.* 种族[民族]中心主义的, 种族[民族, 集团]优越感的. **-al·ly** *ad.*
eth·no·cen·trism [ˌeθnəu'sentrizəm] *n.* 种族[民族]中心主义, 种族[民族, 集团]优越感.
eth·nog·e·ny [eθ'nɔdʒini] *n.* 人种起源学.
eth·nog·ra·pher [eθ'nɔgrəfə] *n.* 人种史[人种论]研究者, 人种史[人种论]学家.
eth·no·gra·phic(al) [ˌeθnəu'græfik(əl)] *a.* 人种学的.
eth·nog·ra·phy [eθ'nɔgrəfi] *n.* 人种史, 人种论.
ethnol. = ethnologic; ethnology.
eth·no·log·ic(al) [ˌeθnəu'lɔdʒik(əl)] *a.* 人种学的, 民族学的; 人类文化学的. **-al·ly** *ad.*
eth·nol·o·gist [eθ'nɔlədʒist] *n.* 人种学家, 民族学家; 人类文化学家.

eth·nol·o·gy [eθˈnɔlədʒi] *n.* 人种学，民族学；人类文化学.
eth·no·psy·chol·o·gy [ˌeθnəusaiˈkɔlədʒi] *n.* 人种心理学，民族心理学.
et hoc genus omne [et ˈhɔk ˈdʒiːnəs ˈɔmniː] 〔L.〕诸如此类 (= and all that kind of thing).
e·thol·o·gy [i(ː)ˈθɔlədʒi] *n.*【生】(个体)生态学. **-gi·c·(al)** *a.* **-gi·cal·ly** *ad.* **-gist** *n.* (个体)生态学研究者.
e·thos [ˈiːθɔs] *n.* ①性格，气质. ②民族精神，时代思潮；社会风气. ③文学作品中的客观因素〔指比决定人的行为的思想、感情更有普遍性的理性特征〕.
eth·yl [ˈeθil, ˈiːθail] *n.* ①【化】乙基，乙烷基. ②四乙铅〔加在汽油中的防爆剂〕. ③含四乙铅的汽车燃料. ～ **acetate** 醋酸乙酯，乙酸乙酯. ～ **alcohol** 乙醇. ～ **cellulose**【化】乙基纤维素. ～ **ether** = ether.
eth·yl·ate [ˈeθileit; 名词读作 -lit] *vt.*【化】使引入乙烷基类，使成乙醇. — *n.* 乙醇盐. **-tion** *n.*
eth·yl·ene [ˈeθiliːn] *n.*【化】乙烯；乙撑，次乙基. ～ **chloride** 氯化乙烯. ～ **dichloride** 二氯化乙烯.
e·thy·nyl [eˈθainl] *n.*【化】乙炔基.
-etic *suf.* 〔构成形容词或名词〕: em*etic*, gen*etic*.
e·ti·o·late [ˈiːtiəuleit] *vt.* ①使(叶子等)变白. ②使变苍白；使衰弱；使(工业等)萎靡. ③使褪色. — *vi.* 变白；变苍白；褪色.
e·ti·o·la·tion [ˌiːtiəuˈleiʃən] *n.* ①遮断日光使植物变白的方法；叶子等因不受日光而变白. ②褪色；萎靡.
e·ti·ol·o·gy [ˌiːtiˈɔlədʒi] *n.* = aetiology.
et·i·quette [ˌetiˈket, ˈetiket] *n.* ①礼仪，礼节；仪式，典礼. ②格式；成规. *a breach of* ～ 失礼. *be against the* ～ *of the game* 违反比赛规则. *It is against* ～ *to do so.* 这样做是违反礼仪的. *diplomatic* ～ 外交礼节. *legal [medical]* ～ 法律[医务]界成规.
et·na [ˈetnə] *n.* 酒精煮水器〔来自西西里岛 Etna 火山之名〕.
ETO = European Theatre of Operation (第二次世界大战时的)欧洲战区.
E·ton [ˈiːtn] *n.* ①〔英〕伊顿〔伦敦西面一市镇〕. ②伊顿公学〔培养英国上层政界人物的一所中学〕(= ～ college). ③〔*pl.*〕伊顿公学男生制服 (= ～ clothes). *go into* ～*s* 开始穿伊顿公学的制服，进伊顿公学. ～ **collar** 白色硬宽领. ～ **crop** (女子头发的) 男孩发型. ～ **jacket [coat]** 伊顿公学式短上衣.
E·to·ni·an [i(ː)ˈtəunjən, -niən] *a.* 伊顿公学的. — *n.* 伊顿公学学生.
E·tru·ri·a [iˈtruəriə] *n.* 伊特鲁里亚〔意大利中部的古国〕.
E·trur·i·an [iˈtruəriən], **E·trus·can** [iˈtrʌskən] *a.* 伊特鲁里亚人[语]的. — *n.* 伊特鲁里亚人；伊特鲁里亚语.
-ette *suf.* 〔加在名词以及少数形容词之后〕①表示"微小": cigar*ette*, statu*ette*. ②表示"女性": suffrag*ette*. ③表示"仿制品", "代用品": leather*ette*. ④表示"组", "组合": quart*ette*.
E.T.U. = Electrical Trades Union 〔英〕电气工会.
é·tude [eˈtjuːd] *n.* 〔F.〕练习；(绘画等的)习作；【乐】练习曲.
é·tui, e·twee [eˈtwiː] *n.* (*pl.* ～*s*) (放化妆品、针线等的)小盒子.
ETV = educational television 教育电视.
-ety *suf.* = 构成表示"状态"、"性质"的抽象名词: vari*ety*, sobri*ety*.
etym. = etymology.
et·y·mo·log·i·cal [ˌetiməˈlɔdʒikəl] *a.* ①词源学的，语源学的. ②词源的，语源的. *an* ～ *dictionary* 语源词典. **-ly** *ad.*
et·y·mol·o·gist [ˌetiˈmɔlədʒist] *n.* 词源[语源]学家，词源[语源]研究者.
et·y·mol·o·gize [ˌetiˈmɔlədʒaiz] *vt.* 发现(某词)的词源[语源]. — *vi.* 研究词源[语源]；探溯词源[语源].
et·y·mol·o·gy [ˌetiˈmɔlədʒi] *n.* ①词源，语源. ②词源[语源]学.
et·y·mon [ˈetimɔn] *n.* (*pl.* **-ma** [-mə]) ①词的原形，词源，词根. ②词的原义.
Eu =【化】europium.
eu- *pref.* 表示"善良", "美好", "优美"(*opp.* dys-); "真正": *eu*pepsia, *eu*phony; *eu*bacteria; *eu*ploid.
Eu·bac·te·ri·a [ˌjuːbækˈtiəriə], **Eu·bac·te·ri·ales** [juːˌbæktiəriˈeiliːz] *n. pl.*【微】真细菌类.
Eu·bac·te·ri·um [ˌjuːbækˈtiəriəm] *n.* Eubacteria 的单数.
Eu·boe·a [juːˈbi(ː)ə] *n.* (希腊东部的)优比亚岛〔埃维厄岛〕.
eu·caine [juːˈkein, ˈjuːkein] 优卡因〔成药名〕.
eu·ca·lypt [ˈjuːkəlipt] *n.* = eucalyptus.
eu·ca·lyp·tol, eu·ca·lyp·tole [ˈjuːkəˈliptəul, -tɔːl] *n.*【化】桉树脑.
eu·ca·lyp·tus [ˌjuːkəˈliptəs] *n.* (*pl.* ～*es*, *-ti* [-tai]) 桉树；〔E-〕桉树属. ～ **oil**【化】桉树油.
eu·cha·ris [ˈjuːkəris] *n.*【植】桉树属 (*Eucharis*) 植物.
Eu·cha·rist [ˈjuːkərist] *n.* ①【宗】圣餐；圣餐中用的面包和葡萄酒；圣体. ②〔e-〕感恩祈祷. **-ic(al)** *a.*
eu·chre [ˈjuːkə] *n.* 〔美〕尤卡牌戏〔二至四人打三十二张牌的纸牌戏〕. —*vt.* (玩尤卡牌戏时趁对方疏忽时)打赢；〔口〕智胜，打败；欺骗，耍弄. **-d** *a.*
eu·chro·ma·tin [juːˈkrəumətin] *n.*【生】常染色质.
eu·chro·mo·some [ju(ː)ˈkrəuməsəum] *n.*【生】常染色体.
eu·cil·i·ate [juːˈsiliːit] *n.*【动】真纤毛亚纲 (*Euciliata*) 动物.
Euck·en [ˈɔikən], **R.** 欧肯〔1846—1926，德国哲学家〕.
eu·clase [ˈjuːkleis] *n.*【地】蓝柱石.
Eu·clid [ˈjuːklid] *n.* ①欧几里得〔古希腊数学家〕. ②欧几里得几何学.
Eu·clid·e·an, Eu·clid·i·an [juːˈklidiən] *a.*【数】欧几里得的. ～ **geometry** 欧几里德几何，欧氏几何. ～ **space** 欧几里德空间，欧氏空间.
eu·col·loid [ˈjuːkəlɔid] *n.*【化】真胶体.
eu·d(a)e·mon·ism [juːˈdiːmənizəm] *n.*【哲】幸福论.
eu·d(a)e·mon·ist [juːˈdiːmənist] *n.* 幸福论者，幸福主义者.
eu·di·om·e·ter [ˌjuːdiˈɔmitə] *n.*【化】空气纯度测定管.
eu·di·o·met·ric(al) [ˌjuːdiəˈmetrik(əl)] *a.* 气体测定法的，量气管的. **-al·ly** *ad.*
eu·di·om·e·try [ˌjuːdiˈɔmitri] *n.*【化】气体测定(法)，空气纯度测定法.
Eu·gene [juːˈʒein, ˈjuːdʒiːn] *n.* 尤金〔男子名〕.
Eu·ge·ni·a [juːˈdʒiːnjə] *n.* 尤金妮亚〔女子名〕.
eu·gen·ic [juːˈdʒenik] *a.* 优生学的. **-i·cal·ly** *ad.*
eu·gen·i·cist [juːˈgenisist] *n.* 优生学家.
eu·gen·ics [juːˈdʒeniks] *n.* 优生学，人种改良学.
eu·gen·ist [ˈjuːdʒinist] *n.* = eugenicist.
eu·ge·nol [ˈjuːdʒinɔl, -nəul] *n.*【化】丁子香酚.
eu·gle·na [juˈgliːnə] *n.* 眼虫属 (*Euglena*) 动物.
eu·he·dral [juːˈhiːdrəl] *a.*【物】全形的，自形的.
eu·he·mer·ism [juːˈhiːmərizəm] *n.* 神话即历史论〔纪元前300年希腊哲学家 Euhemerus 的学说，认为神话来源于人间英雄的史实〕.
eu·he·mer·ist [juːˈhiːmərist] *n.* 神话即历史论者.
eu·he·mer·is·tic [juːˌhiːməˈristik] *a.* (基于)神话即历史论的. **-al·ly** *ad.*
eu·he·mer·ize [juːˈhiːməraiz] *vt.* 以神话即历史的观点解释(神话等).
eu·la·chon [ˈjuːləˈkɔn] *n.* = candlefish.
eu·la·mel·li·branch [ˌjuːləˈmelibræŋk] *n.* 真瓣鳃类

(Eulamellibranchia) 动物. **-bran·chi·ate** [-ˈbræŋkiːit] *n., a.*

eu·lo·gist [ˈjuːlədʒist] *n.* 颂扬者,作颂诗的人.

eu·lo·gis·tic(al) [ˌjuːləˈdʒistik(əl)] *a.* 颂扬的, 歌功颂德的. **-cal·ly** *ad.*

eu·lo·gi·um [juˈləudʒiəm] *n.* *(pl.* **~s, -gi·a** [-dʒiə]*)* 〔拉〕 = eulogy.

eu·lo·gize [ˈjuːlədʒaiz] *vt.* 称赞,颂扬.

eu·lo·gy [ˈjuːlədʒi] *n.* ①颂词; 颂文〔尤指对一位刚去世的人歌功颂德的演说、文章〕. ②称赞, 颂扬. ***chant the ~ of sb.*** 赞颂某人. ***pronounce sb.'s ~ = pronounce a ~ (up) on sb.*** 对某人致颂词.

Eu·men·i·des [juːˈmenidiːz] *n. pl.*【希神】复仇三女神 (= Furies).

eu·my·cete [juˈmaisiːt] *n.* 真菌.

Eu·nice [ˈjuːnis] *n.* 尤妮斯〔女子名〕.

eu·nuch [ˈjuːnək] *n.* 阉人; 太监,宦官.

eu·on·y·mus [juːˈɔniməs] *n.*【植】卫矛属 *(Euonymus)* 植物.

eu·pa·to·ri·um [ˌjuːpəˈtɔːriəm] *n.*【植】泽兰属 *(Eupatorium)* 植物〔包括雾花泽兰、贯叶泽兰等〕.

eu·pat·rid [juˈpætrid, ˈjuːpətrid] *n.* *(pl.* ***-rid·ae*** [-ridiː], ***-rids****)* 〔E-〕(古雅典)世袭贵族.

eu·pep·si·a [juːˈpepsiə] *n.*【医】消化 (力) 良好 *(opp.* dyspepsia*)*.

eupep·tic [juːˈpeptik] *a.* ①【医】消化良好的; 助消化的. ②乐观的,愉快的.

eu·phau·si·id [juˈfɔːziːid] *n.*【动】磷虾目 *(Euphausiacea)* 动物 (= euphausid).

euphem. = euphemism; euphemistic(ally).

Eu·phe·mia [juːˈfiːmjə] *n.* 尤菲米娅〔女子名〕.

eu·phe·mism [ˈjuːfimizəm] *n.*【修】委婉说法; 委婉话,婉言.

eu·phe·mis·tic [ˌjuːfəˈmistik] *a.* 婉言的; 委婉的. **-cal·ly** *ad.*

eu·phe·mize [ˈjuːfimaiz] *vi., vt.* 委婉地说,用委婉的话说.

eu·phen·ics [juˈfeniks] *n. pl.* 〔用作单数〕(用化学药物操纵父母的遗传基因来进行的)人种改良运动.

eu·phon·ic(al) [juːˈfɔnik(əl)] *a.* 声音和谐的, 悦耳的; 语音好的. **-al·ly** *ad.*

eu·pho·ni·ous [juːˈfəuniəs] *a.* 好听的,悦耳的,声音和谐的. **-ly** *ad.*

eu·pho·ni·um [juːˈfəuniəm] *n.*【乐】次中音号.

eu·pho·nize [ˈjuːfənaiz] *vt.* 使(声音)和谐,使(语音)悦耳.

eu·pho·ny [ˈjuːfəni] *n.* ①(声音、语音的)和谐,悦耳. ②和谐的声音; 悦耳的语音.

eu·phor·bi·a [juˈfɔːbiə] *n.* 大戟属植物,大戟(=spurge).

eu·pho·ri·a [juːˈfɔːriə] *n.* ①【心】幸福感. ②【医】欣快,精神愉快.

eu·pho·ri·ant [juˈfɔːriənt] *n.*【医】安乐药,欣快剂.

eu·phor·ic [juːˈfɔrik] *a.* 欣快症的; 欣快的.

eu·pho·tic [juˈfəutik] *a.*【生态】(水域的)光亮带的, 透光层的.

eu·phra·sy [ˈjuːfrəsi] *n.*【植】小米草.

Eu·phra·tes [juːˈfreitiːz] *n.* 幼发拉底河〔亚洲〕.

eu·phroe [ˈjuːfrəu, -vrəu] *n.* (船帆、帐篷等的) 绳索收紧器.

Eu·phros·y·ne [ju(ː)ˈfrɔsiniː] *n.*【希神】赐人欢乐与美丽的三女神之一〔另两女神为 Aglaia 和 Thalia〕.

eu·phu·ism [ˈjuːfjuːizəm] *n.* 绮丽体; 浮华的词句.

eu·phu·ist [ˈjuːfju(ː)ist] *n.* 用浮华词句的人.

eu·phu·is·tic [ˌjuːfju(ː)ˈistik] *a.* 夸饰的,浮华的; 绮丽体的. **-cal·ly** *ad.*

eu·plas·tic [juˈplæstik] *a.*【生理】易形成组织的; 易变成组织的. — *n.* 能成组织的物质.

eu·ploid [ˈjuːplɔid] *a.* 整倍体的. **-y** *n.*

eup·ne·a, eup·noe·a [jupˈniːə, ˈjuːpniə] *n.* 〔废〕【医】平静呼吸.

Eur. = Europe; European.

Eur·af·ri·ca [juəˈræfrikə] *n.* 欧非共同体.

Eur·ail·pass [juəˈreilpɑːs] *n.* 全欧火车特价证〔一种向旅欧游客提供的全欧铁路通用的廉价车票〕.

Eur·a·sia [juəˈreiʒə, -ʃə] *n.* 欧亚(大陆).

Eur·a·sian [juəˈreiʒiən, -ʃən] *a.* 欧亚(大陆)的; 欧亚混血的. — *n.* 欧亚混血人. ***the ~ Continent*** 欧亚大陆.

EURATOM, Euratom [ˈjuərətəm] = European Atomic Energy Community 欧洲原子能联营.

eu·re·ka [juəˈriːkə] *int.* 〔希〕我知道了! 有了! 〔阿基米德发现王冠所含纯金量时的欢呼〕.

eu·rhyth·mic [juəˈriθmik] *a.* ①(建筑式样) 匀称的,协调的. ②韵律体操的; 艺术体操的.

eu·rhyth·mics [ju(ː)ˈriθmiks] *n. pl.* 〔动词用单数〕韵律体操,艺术体操〔用即兴音乐伴奏〕.

eu·rhyth·my [juˈriðmi] *n.* ①韵律运动. ②匀称,和谐,协调.

Eu·rip·i·des [juəˈripidiːz] 欧里庇得斯〔480—406B. C., 古希腊悲剧作家〕.

Eu·rip·i·de·an [juəˌripiˈdiən] *a.* 欧里庇得斯的, 欧里庇得斯悲剧的.

eu·ri·pus [juˈraipəs] *n.* *(pl.* ***-pi*** [-pai]*)* 潮急水险的海峡,险流海峡.

Eu·ro·bond [ˈjuərəubɔnd] *n.* (美国公司以美元在国外买卖并计息的)欧洲债券.

Eu·roc·ly·don [juˈrɔklidɔn] *n.* ①【圣】地中海的东北暴风. ②暴风.

Eu·ro·crat [ˈjuərəukræt] *n.* 欧洲经济共同体的官员〔雇员〕.

Eu·ro-cur·ren·cy [ˈjuərəuˈkʌrənsi] *n.* 欧洲货币.

Eu·ro·dol·lar [ˈjuərəudɔlə] *n.* 欧洲美元〔美国在欧洲银行和借贷机关流通的美元〕.

eu·ro·ky [juˈrəuki], **eu·ry·o·ky** [ˌjuriːˈəuki] *n.*【生】广适性. **eu·rokous** [-kəs], **eu·ry·o·kous** [-ˈəukəs] *a.*

Euromart [ˈjuərəmɑːt] = European Common Market 欧洲共同市场.

Eu·ro·pa [juəˈrəupə] *n.*【希神】欧罗巴〔被宙斯化作白牛劫走的腓尼基公主〕.

Eu·rope [ˈjuərəp] *n.* 欧洲.

Eu·ro·pe·an [ˌjuərəˈpi(ː)ən, jɔːr-] *a.* 欧洲的; 全欧的; 欧洲人的. — *n.* 欧洲人. ~ *Atomic Energy Community* 欧洲原子能联营. ~ *Common Market* 欧洲共同市场. ~ *Economic and Monetary Union* 欧洲经济货币同盟. ~ *Economic Community* 欧洲经济共同体. ~ *plan* 欧洲旅馆收费制〔以日计旅馆费中包括房间和服务费, 膳食费另算〕 *(opp.* American plan). ~ *Recovery Plan* 欧洲复兴计划. *E- Theatre of War* 欧洲战区.

Eu·ro·pe·an·ism [ˌjuərəˈpi(ː)ənizəm] *n.* ①欧洲主义. 欧洲人的特征(指传统、习惯、思想、特性等).

Eu·ro·pe·an·i·za·tion [ˌjuərəˌpiənaiˈzeiʃən] *n.* 欧化.

Eu·ro·pe·an·ize [ˌjuərəˈpi(ː)ənaiz] *vt.* 使欧化,使具有欧洲风味.

eu·ro·pi·um [juəˈrəupiəm] *n.*【化】铕.

Eu·ro·po- *comb. f.* 表示"欧洲": *Europo*-centric.

Eu·ro·po·cen·tric [juəˌrəupəˈsentric] *a.* 欧洲中心主义的.

Eu·ro·po·cen·trism [juəˌrəupəˈsentrizəm] *n.* 欧洲中心主义.

Eu·ro·sis [ju(ː)ˈrəusis] *n.* 欧洲危机.

Eu·ro·vi·sion [ˈjuərəviʒən] *n.* 欧洲电视节目交换制.

eu·ry·bath [ˈjuəribɑːθ] *n.* 【生】(海洋的) 广深水性生物. **-ic** [-ˈbæθik] *a.*

Eu·ryd·i·ce [juəˈridisi(ː)] *n.*【希神】(歌手俄耳甫斯之

妻)欧律狄斯.

eu·ry·ha·line [ˌjuəriˈheilain, -ˈhælain] *a.*【生】广盐性的.

eu·ry·hy·gric [ˌjuəriˈhaigrik] *a.*【生】耐广湿性的.

eu·ryph·a·gous [juːˈrifəgəs] *a.*【生】广食性的.

eu·ryp·ter·id [juːˈriptərid] *n.*【古生】广翅鲎.

eu·ry·therm [ˈjuəriθəːm] *n.* 广温性生物. **-al, -ic, -ous** *a.*

eu·ryth·mic, eu·ryth·mi·cal [ju(ː)ˈriðmik, -kəl] *a.* = eurhythmic.

eu·ryth·mics [ju(ː)ˈriðmiks] *n.* = eurhythmics.

eu·ryth·my [ju(ː)ˈriðmi] *n.* = eurhythmy.

eu·ry·top·ic [ˌjuəriˈtɔpik] *a.*【生】广适性的. **-i·ty** [ˈjuəritəuˈpisiti] *n.*

eu·sol [ˈjuːsɔl] *n.*【药】优苏消毒水.

Eus·tace [ˈjuːstəs] *n.* 尤斯塔斯〔男子名〕.

Eu·sta·chi·an [juːsˈteiʃiən] *a.* (十六世纪意大利解剖学家)欧斯塔奇 (Eustachi) 的,欧氏的. ~ **tube**【解】耳咽管,欧氏管.

eu·sta·cy [ˈjuːstəsi] *n.*【地】海面升降,海面变化.

eu·stat·ic [juːˈstætik] *a.* 海面升降的,海面变化的. **-cal·ly** *ad.*

eu·stele [ˈjuːstil, juˈstiːli] *n.*【植】真中柱.

eu·tec·rod [juːˈtekrɔd] *n.*【机】共晶焊焊条.

eu·tec·tic [juːˈtektik] *a.*【化】低共熔的; 易熔的; 共晶的. — *n.* 低共熔混合物,共晶体. ~ **alloy** 低共熔合金. ~ **point**【化】低共熔点.

eu·tec·toid [juːˈtektɔid] *n.*【化、冶】类低共熔体,共析. — *a.* 类低共熔体的,共析的.

Eu·ter·pe [juːˈtəːpi] *n.*【希神】司音乐及抒情诗的女神. **-an** [-ən] *a.*

eu·tha·na·si·a [ˌjuːθəˈneiziə] *n.* ①安然去世, 无苦痛的死亡. ②(为结束不治之症患者的痛苦施行的)无痛苦致死术.

eu·then·ics [juːˈθeniks] *n. pl.* 〔用作单数〕优境学〔通过改善生活状况以改良人种的研究〕.

eu·the·ri·an [juːˈθiriən] *n.* 真兽亚纲动物. — *a.*【动】真兽亚纲的.

eu·troph·ic [juˈtrɔfik, -ˈtrəufik] *a.* ①(湖泊等)有充足养料可供动植物生长的. ②发育营养正常的. — *n.* 发育营养正常促进剂.

eu·troph·i·cate [juˈtrɔfikeit] *vi.* (河流、湖泊等)海藻污染. **eu·troph·i·ca·tion** [juˌtrɔfiˈkeiʃən] *n.*

eux·e·nite [ˈjuːksinait] *n.*【矿】黑稀金矿.

Eux·ine [ˈjuːksin, -sain] **Sea** 黑海的古称 (=the Black Sea).

E.V. = English Version (of the Bible) (《圣经》的) 英译本.

EVA = extravehicular activity【宇】太空人在飞船外的活动,出舱活动.

E·va [ˈiːvə] *n.* 伊娃〔女子名 Eve 的异体〕.

evac. = evacuation.

e·vac·u·ant [iˈvækjuənt] *a.*【医】促进排泄的,通便的. — *n.* 泻药,利尿剂.

e·vac·u·ate [iˈvækjueit] *vt.* ①抽空, 除清; 排泄, 泻出(粪便等). ②撤空,腾出(房子等); (有组织地)撤退; 疏散. ~ *water from a pond* 抽干池水. ~ *a city* 从城市中疏散人口. — *vi.* ①撤走,撤离,疏散. ②大小便.

e·vac·u·a·tion [iˌvækjuˈeiʃən] *n.* ①腾出; 撤退; (空袭时的)疏散. ②抽空; 排泄,排泄物. ~ *hospital* 后送医院. ~ *of bowels* 大便.

e·vac·u·ee [iˌvækju(ː)ˈiː] *n.* 撤退者,被疏散者.

e·vad·a·ble [iˈveidəbl] *a.* 可逃避的,可规避的.

e·vade [iˈveid] *vt.* 逃避, 躲避 (攻击等), 避免 (困难等); 回避,忌避; 避开(质问等); 漏(税). ~ *a question* 避免答复问题. ~ *paying one's debts* 逃债. ~ *(paying) taxes* 漏税,偷税. ~ *(military) service* 逃避兵役. *a term that ~s definition* 难下定义的词. ~ *discovery* 难发现. — *vi.* 躲避; 逃避; 规避. **-r** *n.* 躲避者,规避者. **e·vad·ing·ly** *ad.*

e·vag·i·nate [iˈvædʒineit] *vt.*【生】使(管状器官)外翻, 翻转. **e·vag·i·na·tion** *n.*【生】外翻; 外翻部分.

e·val·u·ate [iˈvæljueit] *vt.* ①对…估价,对…作评价. ②【数】求…的值.

e·val·u·a·tion [iˌvæljuˈeiʃən] *n.* ①估价,评价. ②【数】赋值,值的计算.

ev·a·nesce [ˌiːvəˈnes] *vi.* 渐渐消失,消散.

ev·a·nes·cence [ˌiːvəˈnesns] *n.* ①消失,消散; 幻灭. ②消失性,消散性,瞬息.

ev·a·nes·cent [ˌiːvəˈnesnt] *a.* ①(印象等)渐渐消失的. ②快消灭的; 短暂的,瞬息的. ③纤细的,轻盈的. ④【植】(叶脉)隐失的. ⑤【数】无限小的.

e·van·gel [iˈvændʒel] *n.* ①〔古〕基督救世的福音. ②〔E-〕【圣】四福音书之一. ③喜信,佳音. ④=evengelist.

e·van·gel·ic(al) [ˌiːvænˈdʒelik(əl)] *a.* ①福音(传道)的. ②〔常 -ical〕福音派的新教会的. ③E- 英国低教会的. ④衷于传道的. — *n.* 〔-ical〕福音派信徒. **-cal·ly** *ad.*

e·van·gel·i·cal·ism [ˌiːvænˈdʒelikəlizəm] *n.* 福音主义,福音派教义的信仰.

E·van·ge·line [iˈvændʒiliːn] *n.* 伊万杰琳〔女子名〕.

e·van·gel·ism [iˈvændʒelizəm] *n.* ①福音传道,传播福音. ②传道狂似的热情. ③=evangelicalism.

e·van·gel·ist [iˈvændʒilist] *n.* ①福音传教士. ②〔E-〕【圣】《福音书》的著者.

e·van·gel·ize [iˈvændʒilaiz] *vi.* 宣讲福音,传教. — *vt.* ①对…宣讲福音. ②使信奉基督教.

e·van·ish [iˈvæniʃ] *vi.* 〔诗〕消失; 消灭. **-ment** *n.*

Ev·ans [ˈevənz] *n.* 埃文斯〔姓氏〕.

e·vap·o·ra·ble [iˈvæpərəbl] *a.* 易蒸发的; 挥发的.

e·vap·o·rate [iˈvæpəreit] *vt.* ①使蒸发; 通过升华使(金属等)沉淀. ②使除去水分,使脱水. ③发射(电子). ④使消失,消灭. *water ~d by heat* 被热蒸发的水. — *vi.* 蒸发,挥发; 发散蒸气;〔口〕消失;〔谑〕(人)失踪,死亡;〔美俚〕跑掉,逃掉.

e·vap·o·rat·ed [iˈvæpəreitid] *a.* 浓缩的,脱水的,蒸发干燥的. ~ **milk** 淡炼乳. ~ **vegetable** 脱水蔬菜.

e·vap·o·ra·ting [iˌvæpəˈreitiŋ] *a.* 蒸发用的. ~ **column**【化】浓缩柱,蒸浓柱. ~ **dish**【化】蒸发皿.

e·vap·o·ra·tion [iˌvæpəˈreiʃən] *n.* ①蒸发(作用), 发散,升华沉淀作用. ②脱水(法). ③蒸气. ④(电子的)发射. ⑤蒸发量. ⑥消散. ~ **cooling** 蒸发冷却. ~ **gum test** (石油)蒸发胶质试验. ~ **nucleon**【原】蒸发核子.

e·vap·o·ra·tive [iˈvæpəreitiv] *a.* 蒸发的,使蒸发的,蒸发产生的. ~ *power* 蒸发力.

e·vap·o·ra·tor [iˈvæpəreitə] *n.* 蒸发器.

e·vap·o·rim·e·ter [iˌvæpəˈrimitə] *n.* 蒸发计.

e·vap·o·ro·graph [iˈvæpərəgrɑːf] *n.*【物】蒸发成像仪.

e·vap·o·trans·pi·ra·tion [iˌvæpəuˌtrænspiˈreiʃən] *n.* 土壤水分蒸发蒸腾损失总量.

e·vap·o·trans·pire [iˌvæpəuˈtrænspaiə] *vt.* 使 (土壤中的水分)蒸发,蒸腾.

E·varts [ˈevəts] *n.* 埃瓦茨〔姓氏〕.

e·va·sion [iˈveiʒən] *n.* ①逃避,规避,回避; (税的)偷漏. ②遁辞,借口推诿. ~ *tactics*【军】规避战术. ~ *of responsibility* 逃避责任. ~ *of taxes*=*tax* ~ 偷税. *take shelter in ~s* 找借口规避.

e·va·sive [iˈveisiv] *a.* ①逃避的,偷漏的; 托辞的, 推诿的,躲躲闪闪的. ②不可捉摸的. *an ~ action*【军】规避动作. *an ~ answer* 含糊的回答. *an ~ talk* 躲躲闪闪的谈话. **-ly** *ad.* **-ness** *n.*

Eve [iːv] *n.* ①伊夫〔女子名〕. ②夏娃〔基督教《圣经》中人类的女始祖,亚当之妻,见《创世纪》〕. ***daughters of ~*** 女人.

eve [iːv] *n.* ①节日的前日夜. ②(重大事件的)关头[前夕]. ③〔诗〕傍晚. *on the ~ of the battle* 战役前夕. *Christmas E-* 圣诞节前夜,圣诞之夜〔1月24日〕. *New Year's E-* 除夕. *on St. Tib's E-* 永远不,决不会〔St. Tib 为虚构的圣徒名,日历中无此节日〕.

e•vec•tion [iˈvekʃən] *n.* 【天】出差. *~ in latitude* 黄纬出差. *~ of the moon* 月球出差.

Ev•e•line [ˈiːvlin] *n.* 伊夫琳〔女子名〕.

Ev•e•lyn [ˈiːvlin, ˈevlin] *n.* 伊夫林〔姓氏〕.

e•ven[1] [ˈiːvən] *a.* ①平的,平坦的,平滑的. ②一样的,一致的;均匀的;同一的;同一水准的,高低相同的 *(with)*. ③不曲折的,无凹陷的,连贯的. ④单调的;平凡的. ⑤(心气)平静的,平稳的. ⑥公平的;平等的,对等的. ⑦【数】偶数的,双数的 *(opp. odd)*. ⑧整的,无零头的,恰好的. *~ country* 平坦的原野. *~ money* 同额赌注. *an ~ surface* 平滑的表面. *This will make all ~.* 这样就扯平了. *The snow is ~ with the window.* 雪同窗子一般齐. *an ~ color* 匀净的颜色. *an ~ tenor of life* 单调的生活. *an ~ bargain [exchange]* 公平交易. *an ~ money* 相等的赌注. *~ grain* 【植】均匀纹理. *an ~ temper* 温和的性情. *an ~ number* 偶数. *an ~ mile* 整整一英里. ***be [get] ~ with** (sb.)* ①和(某人)扯平,不亏欠(某人). ②向(某人)报复. ***break ~*** 〔口〕不赔不赚,不输不赢. ***evenly ~*** 能再分的偶数〔4除得尽〕. ***odd and ~*** 猜单双. ***make ~*** 排字时把最后一行排足. ***of ~ date*** 【法、商】同一日期的,即日. ***unevenly ~*** 不能再分的偶数〔2除得尽而4除不尽〕. ***with the ~ hand*** 公平. — *vt.* ①把…弄平坦. ②使平均;使相等. *~ the edges by trimming them* 修剪边缘. — *vi.* ①变平坦. ②变相等. *~* ***up*** 使平均;使平衡;使整齐. *~* ***up on*** 〔美〕报复. **-handed** *a.* 公平的,大公无私的. **-minded** *a.* 沉着的,泰然自若的. **-tempered** 性情平和的. **-ly** *ad.* **-ness** *n.*

e•ven[2] [ˈiːvən] *ad.* ①〔加强语气〕即使…也,连…还,甚至,也,都,还. ②〔与比较级连用〕更加,愈加. ③〔古〕正,恰恰,刚刚;即,就是. *E- children can understand it.* 连小孩子都知道的. *E- Homer sometimes nods.* 〔谚〕智者千虑,必有一失. *E- woods have ears* 〔谚〕隔墙有耳. *I ~ lent him my own books.* 我甚至把自已的书也借给他了. *He went away ~ as you came.* 你一来他就走了. *He did ~ better.* 他甚至做得更好. *~* ***as*** ①正在…时 *(Even as she spoke, it began to snow.* 恰恰在她说话的时候,天下雪了). ②正如 *(It happened ~ as I expect.* 情况正如我预料的那样). *~* ***if*** *= ~* ***though*** 即使…也. ***never ~*** 连…也不. *~* ***now*** ①甚至现在还. ②〔诗〕恰恰现在. *~* ***so*** ①即使如此. ②〔古〕正是那样. *~* ***then*** 甚至那时候都,连…都. ***or ~*** 乃至,以至.

e•ven[3] [ˈiːvən] *n.* 〔诗〕傍晚,黄昏 (= evening). *~***fall** *n.* 〔诗〕黄昏.

eve•ning [ˈiːvniŋ] *n.* ①傍晚,黄昏,晚. ②〔方〕午后〔从中午到黄昏〕. ③晚年;衰退期;末期. ④晚会. *an ~ edition* 夕刊. *~ gown* 女夜礼服. *an ~ paper* 晚报. *an ~ school* 夜校. *the ~ star* 晚星,金星. *~ student* 夜校学生. *the ~ of life* 晚年. *Good ~!* 晚安! *~ by ~* 天天晚上. *~ coat* 燕尾服. *~ glow* 夕阳. ***go out ~s*** 〔美〕 = ***go out in the ~*** 晚上出去,在黄昏时候出去. ***make an ~ of it*** 玩个通宵. ***of an ~*** 往往在晚上. ***on [in] the ~ of*** 在…日的傍晚. ***towards ~*** 快黑的时候. **-s** *ad.* 每晚,在绝大多数晚间. *~* **dress [clothes]** 夜礼服. *~* **gown** 女夜礼服. *~* **Prayer** 【宗】 = evensong. *~* **primrose** 【植】月见草,待宵草. *~* **wear** 晚礼服.

e•ven•song [ˈiːvənˌsɔːŋ] *n.* ①【天主】晚祷,晚课 (= vespers). ②【英国教】晚祷. ③黄昏时唱的歌. ④〔古〕黄昏.

e•ven-ste•ven, e•ven-ste•phen [ˈiːvnˈstiːvn] *a.* 〔口〕比分相等的,半斤八两的;各半的.

e•vent [iˈvent] *n.* ①事件;事情;事变;大事. ②偶然事件,可能发生的事. ③活动,经历. ④〔古〕结局. ⑤【体】项目(尤指重要比赛). ⑥【法】诉讼〔判决〕的结果. *It was quite an ~* 那确实是件大事. *current ~s* 时事. *a double ~* 双打比赛. *prophesy [wise] after the ~* 事后诸葛亮. *field and track ~* 田径赛. *a target ~* 射靶比赛. *a team ~* 团体赛. ***at all ~s*** *=* ***in any ~*** 无论怎样. ***in either ~*** 无论是这样还是那样. ***in no ~*** 决不能. ***in that ~*** 在那时候,在那种场合;如果那样. ***in the ~*** ①结果,终于. ②〔美〕如果. ***in the ~ of*** 万一在…的时候,若……. ***in the (natural) course of ~s*** 按自然趋势. ***pull off the ~*** 比赛得奖. *~* **counter** 信号计数器.

e•vent•ful [iˈventful, -fəl] *a.* 事故多的;重大的. *an ~ year* 多事之秋,多事的一年. **-ly** *ad.* **-ness** *n.*

e•ven•tide [ˈiːvəntaid] *n.* 〔诗〕黄昏.

e•vent•less [iˈventlis] *a.* 无大事的,平静无事的.

e•ven•tra•tion [ˌiːvenˈtreiʃən] *n.* 【医】腹脏突出.

e•ven•tu•al [iˈventjuəl] *a.* ①最后的. ②可能发生的,万一的. **-ly** *ad.* 最后,终于.

e•ven•tu•al•i•ty [iˌventjuˈæliti] *n.* 偶然性;不测事件. *provide against eventualities* 以备万一.

e•ven•tu•ate [iˈventjueit] *vi.* ①结果,终归 *(in)*. ②〔美〕发生,起. *~ well [ill]* 结果好〔不好〕.

ev•er [ˈevə] *ad.* ①〔表示否定、疑问和比较〕曾经,这以前. *Nothing ~ happens in this village.* 这个村里从来没有发生事情. *Have you ~ seen [Did you ~ see] a tiger?* 你以前见过老虎没有? *Have you ~ been there?* 以前你到过那里么? *Did you ~? = Did you ~ see [hear] the like?* 这种事你听[看]过么! *the nicest thing ~ = that ~ was on record* 迄今最好的东西. ②〔表示不耐烦等语气〕可能,总会. *Is he ~ at home?* 他也有在家的时候吗? ③〔表示条件、威胁等语气〕假如,要是. *If the band ~ plays again, we will dance.* 要是乐队再演奏的话,我们就跳个舞. *If I ~ catch him.* 我要是抓到他的话,哼〔就决不饶他〕! ④〔表示肯定,现在一般用 always〕常是,老是,始终,不断;永远是. *work hard as ~* 一向勤奋. *do better than ~* 做得比一向更好了. *He is ~ repeating the same words.* 他总是重复同样的话. *Yours ~ = E- yours* 〔信末语〕你永久的朋友. ⑤〔加强 as... as〕尽量. *Be as quick as ~ you can!* 尽量赶快. ⑥〔加强疑问词或最高级形容词,表示惊奇〕究竟,到底. *Which ~ way did he go?* 他究竟上哪一边去了? *What ~ can it be?* 那到底是什么? *Why ~ didn't you say so?* 你究竟为什么不那样讲? ⑦〔加强 so, such 等〕非常. *~ such a nice man* 非常好的人. ***as ~*** 仍旧;照常. *~* ***after [afterwards]*** 打那以后,以后老是. *~* ***and again*** *= ~* ***and anon*** 〔古〕时时,常常. *~* ***since*** 从…以来 *(I have known him ~ since he was a boy.* 从他是孩子的时候起,我就认识他了). *~* ***so*** 〔口〕大大,非常 *(The patient is ~ so much better.* 病人好得多了. *Thank you ~ so much.* 非常感激你. *I like it ~ so much.* 我非常喜欢它). *~* ***such*** 〔口〕很…的 *(It is ~ such a tool.* 这工具很有用). ***for ~*** 永远;〔俚〕一直 *(He would go on talking for ~.* 他一直不停地讲下去). ***for ~ and ~*** *=* ***for ~ and a day*** 永远. ***hardly [scarcely] ~*** 难得,几乎从不. ***seldom, if ~*** 就是有也极少见.

ever- *comb. f.* 〔放在形容词或动词、现在分词之前,构成复合形容词〕表示"常": *ever*-active; *ever*-present; *ever*-changeful, *ever*-increasing.

ev•er•bloom•ing [ˌevəˈbluːmiŋ] *a.* 四季开花的.

Ev•er•est [ˈevərist] *n.* 埃佛勒斯峰〔即珠穆朗玛峰〕.

Ev•er•ett [ˈevərit] *n.* 埃弗雷特〔姓氏,男子名〕.

ev•er•glade [ˈevəgleid] *n.* 〔美〕湿地,沼泽地. *the Everglade* 美国佛罗里达州南部大沼泽地.

ev•er•green [ˈevəgriːn] *a.* 常绿的 *(opp.* deciduous*)* — *n.* 常绿植物,常绿树;〔*pl.*〕(装饰用的)常绿树树枝. *E- State* 〔美〕华盛顿州的别名.

ev·er·last·ing [ˌevəˈlɑːstiŋ] *a.* ①永久的，耐久的，不朽的，无穷的. ②不断的；冗长的，使人厌烦的. ③【植】干后花的形状颜色不变的. — *n.* ①永久，无穷. ②〔英〕牢固耐久的毛呢. ③【植】蜡菊，蝶须，鼠曲草. ***from ~ to ~*** 永远无穷地. ***the E-*** 上帝，神. **~ cloth**【纺】永固缎纹织物. **~ cotton homespun**【纺】耐用的手工棉织品. **~ flower**【植】干后花的形状颜色不变的植物〔尤指季生菊科植物如蜡菊、灰毛菊等〕. **~ peas** 阔叶山黧豆. **-ly** *ad.* **-ness** *n.*

ev·er·more [ˌevəˈmɔː] *ad.* 始终；永远；将来，今后. ***for ~*** 永远.

e·ver·si·ble [iˈvəːsibl] *a.*【生】可外翻的，可翻转的.

e·ver·sion [iˈvəːʃən] *n.*【生】外翻，翻转. *~ of the eyelids* 眼睑外翻.

e·vert [i(ː)ˈvəːt] *vt.* ①使(眼睑等)外翻，使翻转. ②〔古〕颠复，推翻.

e·ver·tor [iˈvəːtə] *n.*【解】外转肌，外翻肌.

ev·er·y [ˈevri] *a.* ①所有的，一切的. ②无论哪个…都，凡…无不. ③充分的，一切可能的. ④〔与数词连用时，可用复数〕每. *~ one of them* 他们全都. *E- one thinks in his way.* 〔谚〕仁者见仁，智者见智. *I wish you ~ success.* 祝你事事如意. *~ day* 每日，天天. *~ four days = ~ fourth day* 每隔三日，每逢第四日. *have ~ reason* 有充分理由. *~ third man* 每三个人中有一个人. ***~ bit*** 从每一点，全部，完全. ***~ man Jack = ~ mother's son*** 人人，无例外地. ***~ now and again [then] = ~ once in a while [way]*** 时时，偶尔，间或. ***~ other [second]*** ①每隔(*~ other day* 每隔一天). ②所有其他. ***~ so often*** 〔口〕时时. ***~ time*** 每次，总是；每逢，每当. ***~ way = in ~ way.*** ***~ which way*** 〔美〕①四面八方. ②散乱 (*Railroads cross the country in ~ which way.* 铁路四通八达纵横全国). ***in ~ way*** 在每一方面，从各方面来看. ***not ~ ...*** 不见得 (*E- couple is not a pair. = Not ~ couple is a pair.* 〔谚〕成双未必能配对. ★①all 是对复数普通名词的总括性修饰语；every 是个别性的同时又是总括性的修饰语；each 则纯粹是个别性的. ②~ 和 each 的意思都是"每一"或"每个"，但 ~ 更强调全体或全部，而 each 更强调个人或各别. 此外，~ 只作形容词，而 each 除了作形容词外，还可用作代词和副词. ③all 和 every 虽有共同意义，但今日如说"All are happy." 仍不如说"Everybody is happy." 普通. ④~ 本应作单数处理，但在口语中因接用复数代名词而可作复数处理: Every one of them took off their hats.

eve·ry·bod·y [ˈevribɔdi, ˈevribədi] *pron.* 每人，人人. *~ else* 所有别人 (= all the others). ★ ~ 跟 everyone 同义，但在口语中 ~ 用得较广.

eve·ry·day [ˈevridei] *a.* ①每日的. ②日常的，平常的，普通的. *~ affairs* 日常琐事. *~ clothes* 便服. *~ English* 日常用英语. *an ~ occurrence* 日常的事. *~ people* 普通人. *the ~ world* 人世间.

Eve·ry·man [ˈevrimæn] *n.* ①15世纪道德剧中的主人公. ②〔e-〕平常人，普通人.

eve·ry·one [ˈevriwʌn] *pron.* = everybody.

eve·ry·place [ˈevripleis] *ad.* = everywhere.

eve·ry·thing [ˈevriθiŋ] *pron.* ①凡事，事事，万事；万物. ②(有关的)一切；最重要的东西. *be ~ to sb.* 某人认为是最重要的. *before ~* 在一切之上，比什么都重要. *E- has its time.* 〔谚〕物各有时. *E- is good for something.* 〔谚〕天生一物必有用. *Use is ~.* 实用最重要. *The book did ~ but sell.* 这本书就是卖不出去. *To know ~ is to know nothing.* 〔谚〕样样都通，样样稀松. ***and ~*** 等等. ***like ~*** 猛烈地，拼命地.

eve·ry·way [ˈevriwei] *ad.* ①不管从那方面来看；全然. ②各式各样的方法. *This candidate is ~ better than that one.* 这个候选人比那个更好. *They tried ~ to find the solution.* 他们想尽办法来解决问题.

eve·ry·where [ˈevriʰweə] *ad.* 处处，到处；无论什么地方.

e·vict [i(ː)ˈvikt] *vt.* ①(依法)收回(租屋、租地等). ②驱逐，赶出(房客等). *~ tenant from a house* 把房客赶出屋外.

e·vic·tion [i(ː)ˈvikʃən] *n.* ①(租地、租房等的)收回. ②(租户等的)驱逐，赶出. *an ~ man* 赶房客搬家的人.

e·vic·tor [i(ː)ˈviktə] *n.* 驱逐者；收回者.

ev·i·dence [ˈevidəns] *n.* ①根据，证据. ②形迹，迹象，痕迹. ③【法】证据，证人；证词. ④明白，明显，显著. *circumstantial ~* 间接(根据情况的)证据. *collateral ~* 旁证. *conclusive ~* 确定证据. *documentary ~* 书面证据. *external ~* 外来的证据. *historical ~* 历史上的证据. *internal ~* 内在的证据. *material ~* 物证. *oral [parol] ~* 口头证据. *verbal ~* 证言. ***bear ~*** 作证. ***bear [give, show] ~ of*** 有…的迹象. ***call sb. in ~*** 叫某人作证. ***~s of debt*** 借据. ***give ~*** 作证，提供证据. ***in ~*** 明显的，显而易见的 (*The child was nowhere in ~.* 到处都看不到那个小孩). ***turn King's [Queen's,*** 〔美〕***State's] ~*** 作检举同犯的证人；供出对同犯不利的证据. — *vt.* ①证明. ②显示.

ev·i·dent [ˈevidənt] *a.* 明白的，明显的. *with ~ pride* 得意扬扬地. **-ly** *ad.*

ev·i·den·tial [ˌeviˈdenʃəl] *a.* 证据上的；作为证据的，证明的. **-ly** *ad.*

ev·i·den·tia·ry [ˌeviˈdenʃəri] *a.* = evidential.

e·vil [ˈiːvl] *a.* ①邪恶的；有害的. ②不幸的，不吉利的. ③可厌的，不愉快的. ④〔古〕低劣的. ⑤〔美俚〕失望的，发怒的. ⑥〔美俚〕(表演等)有刺激性的. *~ days* 厄运. *~ devices* 奸计. *an ~ life* 不幸的生活. *~ news [tidings]* 噩耗，凶讯. *~ thoughts* 邪念. *~ tongue* 谗言；谗言者. ***in an ~ hour*** 在不幸的时刻. ***an ~ eye*** 恶毒[凶狠]的目光. ***the E- One***【宗】魔鬼. — *n.* ①邪恶；弊病；不幸. ②诽谤，恶言. ③【医】瘰疬 (= king's ~). *good and ~* 善恶. *Of two ~s choose the less.* 〔谚〕两害相权取其轻. *the social ~* 社会的罪恶；卖淫. *The ~s we bring on ourselves are the hardest to bear.* 〔谚〕自作孽不可活. ***do ~*** 干坏事. ***return good for ~*** 以德报怨. ***with ~ in one's heart*** 不怀好意. — *ad.* 恶毒地. *E- to him that ~ thinks.* 邪念伤身. ***speak ~ of*** 诽谤. **~-disposed** *a.* 性恶的. **~-doer** 作恶的人，坏人. **~-doing** 坏事，恶劣行为. **~-eyed** *a.* 目光恶毒的，目光凶狠的. **~-mind·ed** *a.* ①狠毒的，恶毒的；(带有)恶意的. ②好色的. **~-starred** *a.* 不幸的. **-ly** *ad.* **-ness** *n.*

e·vince [iˈvins] *vt.* 表示；表明；显示.

evin·ci·ble [iˈvinsəbl] *a.* 可表明的，可证明的.

e·vin·cive [iˈvinsiv] *a.* 证明性的，表明性的，显示的.

e·vi·rate [ˈiːvireit, ˈev-] *vt.* ①〔罕〕阉割. ②〔喻〕使软弱.

e·vis·cer·ate [iˈvisəreit] *vt.* ①取出…的内脏. ②抽去…的精华，挫伤…元气. ③切除(病人)器官. **e·vis·cer·a·tion** [iˌvisəˈreiʃən] *n.* 内脏切除术.

ev·i·table [ˈevitəbl] *a.* 可避免的.

ev·o·ca·tion [ˌevəuˈkeiʃən] *n.* ①引起，唤起. ②【法】案件的移送，调案. ③〔古〕召唤；招魂. ④【动】(胚胎中的)唤起.

e·voc·a·tive [iˈvɔkətiv, iˈvəu-] *a.* 唤起…的，引起…的 *(of)*. *~ words* 引起回忆或感情的言语. *The perfume was ~ of spring.* 那种香味令人想起了春天. **-ly** *ad.* **-ness** *n.*

ev·o·ca·tor [ˈevəkeitə] *n.* ①招魂者. ②(印象或记忆的)唤起人.

e·voc·a·to·ry [iˈvɔkətəri] *a.* =evocative.

e·voke [iˈvəuk] *vt.* ①召唤(死者灵魂等). ②唤起；引起，招致. ③【法】移送(案件到上级法院). *~ admiration [surprise, a smile, protests, memories of the past]* 引起羡慕[惊奇、微笑、抗议、对过去的回忆].

e·vo·lute [ˈiːvəluːt, ˈev-] *n.* ①【数】渐屈线,法包线,缩闭线. ②【机】展开线. — *a.* 【植】展开的, 反卷的. (*opp.* involute).

e·vo·lu·tion [ˌiːvəˈljuːʃən, ˌevəˈljuːʃən] *n.* ①发展,发育;开展. ②(气体等的)放出,散出;放出物,散出物. ③发生;演变;【生】演化,进化;进化论 (*opp.* creationism). ④【生】种族发生,系统发育; 个体发生; 个体发育. ⑤【天】(天体) 形成. ⑥【数】开方. ⑦【军】按计划行动,位置变换. ⑧(跳舞等的)规定动作. *an* ~ *unit*【军】机动单位. *the theory [doctrine] of* ~ 进化论. **-al, -ary** *a.* 发展的;进化(论)的; 展开的. **-ism** *n.* 进化论, 进化主义 (*opp.* creationism).

e·vo·lu·tion·ist [ˌiːvəˈljuːʃənist] *n.* 进化论者. — *a.* 进化的,进化论的,进化论者的 (= evolutionistic [ˌiːvəˌljuːʃəˈnistik]).

e·vo·lu·tive [ˌiːvəˈluːtiv, ˈev-] *a.* (促进)发展的,(促进)进化的.

e·volve [iˈvɔlv] *vt.* ①发展,展开,使逐渐形成. ②使进化. ③引伸出. ④放出,发出(热等). ⑤【化】离析. — *vi.* (情节等)进展;发展;进化. **-ment** *n.* 展开,发达;进化;发生.

EVR = electronic video recorder [recording] 电子录像机[录像].

e·vul·sion [iˈvʌlʃən] *n.* 拔出,拔去,强拔.

ev·zone [ˈevzəun] *n.* 希腊精锐部队中的步兵士兵.

E·we [ˈeiˌwei] *n.* ①埃维人〔居住于加纳、多哥境内和达荷美边境的黑人种族〕. ②埃维人讲的克瓦(Kwa) 语.

ewe [juː] *n.* 母羊. ~ *lamb* 小母羊. ***one's ~ lamb*** 自己最珍视的东西.

Ew·ell [ˈju(ː)əl] *n.* 尤厄尔〔姓氏〕.

ewe-neck [ˈjuːnek] *n.* (马和狗的) 母羊式脖颈. **-ed** [-nekt] *a.*

ew·er [ˈju(ː)ə] (盛洗脸水用的)大口水罐.

e·wig·keit [ˈeivigkait] *n.* 〔G.〕 永远, 永久. ***in [into] the*** ~ 〔谑〕在[进入]未知的领域[虚无缥渺]中.

EWR = early-warning radar 预先警报雷达, 远程警戒雷达.

ex[1] [eks] *n.* (*pl.* **-es**) ①英语 x 字母. ②X 形状的东西.

ex[2] [eks] *n.* 〔口〕离了婚的配偶.

ex[3] [eks] *n.* 〔口〕考试. — *vt.* 考试.

ex [eks] *prep.* 〔L.〕 ①由,从;为,因. ②【商】无,不,未 (*opp.* cum); 在(船上、码头)交货. ③〔美〕大学某班级中途退学的. ~ ***animo*** [ˈænimәu]衷心的(地). ~ ***bond*** 完税后关栈交货. ~ ***cathedra*** [ˈeks kəˈθiːdrə] 权威性地,用职权. ~ ***dividend*** 无红利〔略作 ~ div. 或 x-d.〕. ~ ***interest*** 无股息〔略 ~ int. 或 x-i.〕. ~ ***libris*** [ˈlaibris] (某某) 藏书. ~ ***new*** 〔英〕无权要求新股. ~ ***officio*** [ˈeks əˈfiʃiəu] 依据职权,当然(成员等). ~ ***parte*** [ˈeks pɑːti] 片面的,一方面的. ~ ***pede Herculem*** [eks ˈpiːdi ˈhəːkjuləm] 由部分可知全体. ~ ***pier [quay, wharf]*** 码头交货. ~ ***post facto*** [ˈeks pəust ˈfæktəu]【法】在事后; 溯及既往地. ~ ***rail*** 铁路旁交货. ~ ***rights*** 无新股特权〔略 Ex R.〕. ~ ***ship*** 船上交货. ~ ***store*** 仓库交货;〔美〕店铺交货. ~ ***voto*** [ˈvəutəu] 由于许愿; (许愿用的)供品. ~ ***warehouse*** 仓库交货. ***Yale*** ~ ***'47.*** 耶鲁大学一九四七班肄业.

Ex. = Exodus.

ex. =①examined. ②example. ③exception. ④exchange. ⑤excluding. ⑥excursion. ⑦executed; executive. ⑧exempt. ⑨exercise. ⑩exhibit. ⑪export. ⑫express. ⑬extra. ⑭extract. ⑮extremely.

ex- *pref.* ①= forth, without, thoroughly 等. ★ **ex-** 仅可接用于元音字母和 h, c, p, q, s, t 之前; f 之前用 *ef-*, 其他辅音字母前用 e- (略去 x): *ex*asperate, *ex*clude; *ef*ferent, *e*ducate. ②加在名词以前, 表示"以前的","前任的": *ex*-premier, *ex*-pow. ③=out, away, off. ★ 元音字母前用 **ex-**; 辅音字母前用 **ec-**: *ex*odus, *ex*orcize; *ec*centric,*ec*stasy. ④=exo.

ex·ac·er·bate [eksˈæsə(ː)beit] *vt.* ①使(病等)更重 [恶化],加深(痛苦等). ②激怒;使烦恼.

ex·ac·er·ba·tion [eksˌæsə(ː)ˈbeiʃən] *n.* ①增剧,加重. ②激怒,愤激. ③【医】病势加重,剧变,恶化.

ex·act[1] [igˈzækt] *a.* ①精密的,准确的. ②严格的,严正的;严厉的. ③严密的. ~ *discipline* 严格的纪律. *the* ~ *sciences* 精密科学. *the* ~ *sum* 准确的金额. *an* ~ *translation* 确切的翻译. ***be ~ to a cent*** 算得一分不差. ~ ***to the letter*** 原本原样,极正确. ~ ***to the life*** 和实物丝毫不差. ***to be*** ~ 精确地说〔插入语〕. ~ **differential** 【数】恰当微分.

ex·act[2] [igˈzækt] *vt.* ①勒索 (钱财等),强要. ②强制,逼使(服从等). ③急需;需要. *The task* ~*s the closest attention.* 这个工作需要周密注意. ~ *payments* 强要报酬.

ex·act·a·ble [igˈzæktəbl] *a.* 可以强取的,可以强求的.

ex·act·ing [igˈzæktiŋ] *a.* ①严格的;难以取悦的. ②强索的, 横征暴敛的. ③吃力的. *an* ~ *microbe* 对生存条件要求极高的微生物. ~ *work* 费力的工作. ~ *terms* 苛刻的条件. **-ly** *ad.* **-ness** *n.*

ex·ac·tion [igˈzækʃən] *n.* ①强求,勒索. ②苛刻的要求. ③苛捐杂税.

ex·ac·ti·tude [igˈzæktitjuːd] *n.* ①正确,精确. ②精密. 严正,严格.

ex·act·ly [igˈzæktli] *ad.* ①确切地,精确地; 恰好. ②十分. ③= yes. ***not*** ~ 不全是, 未必就 (*Those are not* ~ *the same* 那些并不完全一样). ~ ***true*** 千真万确.

ex·act·ness [igˈzæktnis] *n.* = exactitude.

ex·ac·tor [igˈzæktə] *n.* 勒索者;强征捐税的人.

ex·ag·ger·ate [igˈzædʒəreit] *vt.* ①夸张,夸大. ②使过大,使增大. ~ *an illness* 夸大病情. *shoes exaggerating the size of his feet* 使他的脚显得特别大的鞋子. — *vi.* 夸张,夸大,言过其实.

ex·ag·ger·at·ed [igˈzædʒəreitid] *a.* ①夸张的, 言过其实的. ②过大的,逾常的. *an* ~ *sense of one's importance* 自视过高. **-ly** *ad.*

ex·ag·ger·a·tion [igˌzædʒəˈreiʃən] *n.* 浮夸, 夸张; (艺术等的)夸张手法.

ex·ag·ger·a·tive [igˈzædʒəreitiv] *a.* 夸张的, 夸大的,小题大做的,言过其实的. **-ly** *ad.*

ex·ag·ger·a·tor [igˈzædʒəˌreitə] *n.* 夸张者.

ex·al·bu·mi·nous [ˌeksælˈbjuːminəs] *a.* 【植】无胚乳的. ~ **seed** 无胚乳种子.

ex·alt [igˈzɔːlt, eg-] *vt.* ①高举,升起. ②抬高(地位等) 提高(权力等). ③褒奖,捧. ④加强(想象力等),激发,发扬; 加浓(色彩等). ⑤使高兴,使得意. *He was* ~*ed to the skies* 他被捧上天了. *We were* ~*ed by his poems.* 他的诗激发了我们的想象力.

ex·al·ta·tion [ˌegzɔːlˈteiʃən] *n.* ①高举; 升高. ②提拔; 晋升. ③兴奋,得意. ④【冶】纯化;【化】炼浓. ~**-register** 缴款通知书.

ex·alt·ed [igˈzɔːltid] *a.* ①高贵的;高尚的,(目的等)崇高的. ②得意扬扬的,兴奋的. ~ *personages* 高贵人士.

ex·am [igˈzæm,eg-] *n.* 〔口〕考试 (= examination).

exam. = examination; examined.

ex·a·men [egˈzeimen] *n.* 批判性研究;详细探索.

ex·am·i·na·ble [igˈzæminəbl] *a.* ①可考查的,可检查的. ②在审查范围内的.

ex·am·i·nant [igˈzæminənt] *n.* 主考人, 审问者;检察人;审查人.

ex·am·i·na·tion [igˌzæmiˈneiʃən] *n.* ①考试 (*in*). ②(问题等的)检讨,考察;检查;审查,调查; 检定,检验;观察. ③审问. ④检察; 诊察. *an* ~ *in geography* 地理考试. *a civil service* ~ 文官考试. *an entrance* ~ 入学考试. *a medical* ~ 诊察. *a physical* ~ 体格检查. ~ *papers* 试卷. *an oral [verbal]* ~ 口试. *a written* ~ 笔

试. ~ ***in chief*** 【法】 己方律师对证人所作的直接讯问 (*cf.* cross-examination). ~ ***of party*** 【法】对方的讯问. ~ ***of the voir dire*** [vwar dir] 【法】对方对被传讯证人预先所作的讯问. ***an*** ~ ***of the witness*** 【法】律师对证人的质询. ***go in [up] for one's*** ~ 受考, 应试. ***make an*** ~ ***of*** 检查. ***on*** ~ 一检验, 一察看. ***pass [fail in] an*** ~ 考试及格[不及格]. ***sit for an*** ~ 应试. ***take an*** ~ 参加考试. ***under*** ~ 在调查[检查]中. ***undergo an*** ~ 受检查[诊察]. **-al** *a.*

ex·am·i·na·to·ri·al [igˌzæminəˈtɔːriəl] *a.* ①检查的, 审查的; 考试的. ②主考人的.

ex·am·ine [igˈzæmin] *vt.* ①调查, 检查, 审查; 检验, 检定; 观察, 研究. ②考试. ③审问 (*on*). ④诊察. *E- yourself.* 你反省反省吧. ~ *one's own heart [conscience]* 扪心自问, 反省. — *vi.* 调查 (*into*); 审问. ~ ***into a matter*** 调查事实. **examining judge** 预审法官.

ex·am·i·nee [igˌzæmiˈniː] *n.* 参加考试的人; 受审查的人.

ex·am·in·er [igˈzæminə, eg-] *n.* ①检查员, 审查人. ②主考人. ③检察官. *customs* ~ 海关检查员. *satisfy the* ~*s* 考试[审查]及格.

ex·am·ple [igˈzɑːmpl] *n.* ①例证, 实例; 标本, 样本. ②范例; 典型, 模范, 榜样; 例题. ③先例; 儆戒. *E- is better than precept.* 〔谚〕身教胜于言教. ***as an*** ~ = ***by way of*** ~ 例如, 举例来说. ***be an*** ~ ***to*** 是…的教训. ***beyond [without]*** ~ 无先例的, 空前的, 未曾有的. ~***s of the great masters*** 名家作品. ***follow the*** ~ ***of*** 照…的榜样, 以…作模范. ***for*** ~ 例如. ★ 日常用语中常说作 for instance. ***give [take] an*** ~ 举例; 示范. ***give [set] a good*** ~ ***to*** 以身作则. ***make an*** ~ ***of sb.*** 惩一儆百. ***take*** ~ ***by*** 临摹. — *vt.* 〔废〕作为…的示范〔常用被动语态〕.

ex·an·i·mate [igˈzænimit] *a.* ①已死的, 无生命的. ②没精神的, 没生气的; 意气消沉的.

ex·an·i·ma·tion [igˌzæniˈmeiʃən] *n.* ①【医】死; 假死, 昏厥. ②沮丧, 意气消沉.

ex·an·them [egˈzænθim] *n.* 【医】①皮疹; 皮肤溃烂. ②疹.

ex·an·the·ma [ˌeksænˈθiːmə] *n.* (*pl.* **-mas, -them·at·as** [-ˈθemətəz]) *n.* 【医】①皮疹. ②疹.

ex·arch[1] [ˈeksɑːk] *n.* ①(东罗马帝国的)总督. ②(东正教的)大主教; 主教特派使节.

ex·arch[2] [ˈeksɑːk] *a.* 【植】外始式的.

ex·arch·ate [ˈeksɑːkeit] *n.* 东罗马帝国总督[东正教主教等]的权限[职位、管区].

ex·as·per·ate [igˈzɑːspəreit] *vt.* ①激怒, 使恼怒. ②加剧, 加重, 使恶化. — *a.* [igˈzɑːspərit] ①被激怒的, 恼怒的. ②【生】具硬突起的, (表面) 粗糙的. **ex·as·per·at·ed·ly** *ad.*

ex·as·per·at·er [igˈzɑːspəreitə] *n.* 激怒他人者.

ex·as·per·at·ing [igˈzɑːspəreitiŋ] *a.* 使人恼怒的, 激怒人的. **-ly** *ad.*

ex·as·per·a·tion [igˌzɑːspəˈreiʃən] *n.* ①愤激, 激昂, 愤怒. ②激化, 恶化, 加剧.

exc. = ①excellent. ②except; excepted; exception. ③exchange.

Ex·cal·i·bur [eksˈkælibə] *n.* (传说中)英国国王亚瑟王的神剑.

ex ca·the·dra [ˌekskəˈθiːdrə] 〔L.〕有权威的, 有权力的 (尤指教皇的诏书).

ex·ca·vate [ˈekskəveit] *vt.* ①开凿, 挖掘. ②掘出, 发掘. — *vi.* ①凿, 掘开. ②变成空洞.

ex·ca·va·tion [ˌekskəˈveiʃən] *n.* ①开凿; 发掘; 挖掘; 挖土, 剜通. ②穴, 洞; 坑道, 开凿成的山路. ③【考古】出土文物, 发掘物.

ex·ca·va·tor [ˈekskəveitə] *n.* ①开凿者; 发掘者. ③挖掘器; 挖土机; 电铲. ③(牙科用的)钻孔器.

ex·ceed [ikˈsiːd] *vt.* ①超过(限度, 范围). ②越出. ③胜过, 优于, 凌驾. *a task that* ~*s one's ability* 不能胜任的工作. ~ *by five dollars* 超出五美元. ~ *one's authority [instructions]* 越权. ~ *sb. in courage* 勇气过人. ~ *the speed limit* 超出驾驶速率限制. — *vi.* (数量, 程度)超过其他, 领先, 突出. ~ *in size* 规模突出. **-a·ble** *a.* **-er** *n.*

ex·ceed·ing [ikˈsiːdiŋ] *a.* ①超越的, 胜过的. ②非常的; 极度的. — *ad.* 〔古〕 = -ly. **-ly.** *ad.*

ex·cel [ikˈsel] *vt.* 优于, 超过. ~ *sb. in knowledge* 学识过人. — *vi.* 胜过其他, 突出; 擅长. ~ *in (at) swimming* 擅长游泳. *She* ~*s as a dancer.* 她擅长跳舞.

ex·cel·lence [ˈeksələns] *n.* ①优越, 优秀, 杰出, 卓越; 〔*pl.*〕优点, 长处. ②〔E-〕阁下 = excellency. ~ *in English* 擅长英语, 英语优良.

ex·cel·len·cy [ˈeksələnsi] *n.* ①〔E-〕阁下; 被尊称为'阁下'的人. ②〔常 *pl.*〕优点; 美德 (= excellence). *Your E-* 阁下〔直接称呼时指 *you*〕. *His E-* 阁下〔间接提到时指 *he, him*〕. *Their Excellencies* 阁下〔间接提到时指 *they, them*〕. ★原用于王族的尊称, 目前限用于大臣、大使、全权公使、使节、总督等, 美国亦用于总统、州长以及外国大使; 其夫人称作 Your E-, Her E-.

ex·cel·lent [ˈeksələnt] *a.* 优秀的, 卓越的, 杰出的; 优良的, 精良的, 极好的. **-ly** *ad.*

ex·cel·si·or [ekˈselsiɔː] *n.* ①〔美〕(填塞用的) 木丝, 细刨花. ②【印】[3] 点活字. — *int.* 精益求精〔商标用语、箴言等〕. *the E- State* 美国纽约州(的别名). ***as dry as*** ~ 干透了的.

ex·cept [ikˈsept] *prep.* 除…之外. *We all failed* ~ *him.* 我们都失败了, 只有他除外. ~ ***for*** 只有, 除了…以外 (*The carpet is good* ~ *for its price.* 地毯很好, 只是价钱太高). ~ ***that*** 除了, 只是〔后接名词从句〕. ★ ~ 跟 besides 意义不同. 例如 "We all agreed ~ him." 是说"我们都同意, 只有他不同意". "We all agreed besides him." 是说"我们都同意, 他也同意". — *conj.* ①〔古〕除非, 如果不是 (= unless). ②只是, 要不是, 除…以外. *I would go* ~ *it's too far.* 要不是路太远, 我就去了. — *vt.* 把…除去, 把…除外 (*from*). *The minors are* ~*-ed from the regulation.* 未成年者不在此限. *nobody* ~*ed* 无人例外. *present company* ~*ed* 目前在场者除外. — *vi.* 反对 (*to, against*). ~ *to a statement* 反对某项声明. ~ *against a witness* 对证人提出异议. **-a·ble** *a.* 可例外的, 可除外的.

ex·cept·ing [ikˈseptiŋ] *prep.* 〔用于句首或 not, without, always 后面〕. 除…外. *E- his son, they are all right.* 除了他的儿子以外, 他们大家都好. *Everyone helped, not* ~ *John.* 每个人都帮了一把手, 连约翰也不例外. — *conj.* 〔古〕 = except. *conj.*

ex·cep·tion [ikˈsepʃən] *n.* ①例外; 除外, 除去. ②【法】抗告; 异议, 不服, 反对. *Every rule has its* ~*s.* 任何规则均有例外. ***by way of*** ~ 作为例外. ***liable [subject] to*** ~ 容易遭到反对的, 会引起异议的. ***make an*** ~ ***of*** 把…作为例外. ***make no*** ~***s*** 一视同仁, 一样看待. ***take*** ~ ①反对, 表示异议. ②有反感. ***take*** ~ ***at*** 发怒, 生气. ***take*** ~ ***to [against]*** 对…提出异议. ***without*** ~ 一概, 全都; 无例外地. ***with the*** ~ ***of*** 除…外. **-al·ly** *ad.* **-less** *a.* 无例外的.

ex·cep·tion·a·ble [ikˈsepʃənəbl] *a.* 可以反对 [抗议] 的, 会引起反对的. **-ness** *n.*

ex·cep·tion·al [ikˈsepʃənl] *a.* ①例外的, 特别的. ②格外的, 异常的, 稀有的, 较优的. *a man of* ~ *talent* 具有特殊才能的人. ~ *promotion* 破格提升. **-ly** *ad.* **-ness** *n.*

ex·cep·tion·al·ism [ikˈsepʃənəlizəm] *n.* 例外论.

ex·cep·tion·ali·ty [ikˌsepʃənˈæliti] *n.* ①例外, 除外. ②异常, 特别, 优越.

ex·cep·tive [ikˈseptiv] *a.* ①形成例外的, 特殊的, 有除

外含意的(如前置词 but, except, save 等). ②〔古〕好反对的,吹毛求疵的. *an ~ clause* 除外条款.

ex·cerpt [ˈeksəːpt] *n.* *(pl. ~s, -ta* [-ə]*)* 摘录,摘要;节录;抽印. — [ekˈsəːpt] *vt.* 摘录,摘要;引用,删节. **-er, -or** *n.* 摘录者,引用者. **-i·ble** *a.* 可摘录的.

ex·cerp·tion [ekˈsəːpʃən, ik-] *n.* 摘录,摘要;节录.

ex·cess [ikˈses] *n.* ①过量;过剩. ②超过,超越. ③超过数量. ④过度,(饮食等)无节制. ⑤〔*pl.*〕过分行为,暴行. *an ~ of enthusiasm* 过分热心. *an ~ of exports [imports]* 出[入]超. *an ~ of supply over demand* 供过于求. *an ~ of $100 over the estimate* 比预算超额100美元. *~ of authority* 越权. ***go [run] to ~*** 走极端. ***in ~*** 过度. ***in ~ of*** 超过. *(smoke)* ***to ~*** (吸烟)过度. ***with ~ of joy*** 因过度高兴. — [ˈekses] *a.* 过量的,超过限额的;过量的. *an ~ fare* 补票费. ~ **insurance** 超过损失保险. ~ **issue** (纸币的)额外发行. ~ **luggage** 超重行李. ~**-profits tax** 超额利润税. ~ **reserve** (现金的)超额储备.

ex·ces·sive [ikˈsesiv] *a.* ①过多的,过度的,极端的. ②份外的,额外的. **-ly** *ad.* **-ness** *n.*

Exch. = exchange; exchequer.

ex·change [iksˈtʃeindʒ] *vt.* ①(以某物与另一物)交换,调换*(for)*. ②互换,交流,交易. ③兑换. *~ one's labour for money* 以劳动换取报酬. *~ blows* 互殴. *~ civilities* 互相行礼. — *vi.* ①兑换*(for)*. ②交换;调换(职位,任务)*(from; into)*. *~ from [out of] one ship into another* 从甲船换乘乙船. — *n.* ①交换,互换. ②交流,交易. ③兑换;汇兑;汇划. ④汇兑行情,兑换率,汇水,贴水. ⑤〔*pl.*〕(票据)交换总额. ⑥交换品〔特指〕交换书刊. ⑦交易所. ⑧〔英〕职业介绍所. ⑨电话局,电话交换台. *an ~ of goods* 物资交流. *an ~ of prisoners* 交换俘虏. *~ of views* 交换意见. *foreign ~* 外汇. *domestic [internal] ~* 内汇. *a post ~* 〔美〕陆军消费合作社(PX). *a bill of ~* 汇票. *the rate [course] of ~ (= ~ rate)* 外汇率[行情,比价]. *a set of ~* 联单汇票[双联或三联]. *the first [second, third] of ~* 第一[第二、第三]联汇票. *the cotton ~* 棉花交易所. *a labour ~* 〔英〕职业[劳工]介绍所. *short ~* 短期汇票. *a stock ~* 证券交易所. *a [central] telephone ~* 中央电话局. *E- is no robbery.* 〔谑〕交换不是掠夺(为不公平交换辩解的话). ***in ~ for*** 换,调. ***make an ~*** 交换. ***value in [of] ~*** 交换价值(=~ value). ~ **area** (电话)通话区. ~ **broker** 证券交易所经纪人;汇兑掮客. ~ **control** 外汇管理. ~ **girl** 女接线员. ~ **professor** 交流讲学教授. ~ **quotations** 外汇行情. ~ **student** (两国间)交换的留学生. ~ **table** 汇兑换算表.

ex·change·a·bil·i·ty [iksˌtʃeindʒəˈbiliti] *n.* 可交换性,可交易性.

ex·change·a·ble [iksˈtʃeindʒəbl] *a.* 可交换的;可兑换的;可转换的*(for)*. ~ **value** 交换价值.

ex·chang·ee [iksˈtʃeindʒiː] *n.* 被交换者,交换的学生[教授、俘虏等].

ex·chang·er [iksˈtʃeindʒə] *n.* 交换器.

ex·cheq·uer [iksˈtʃekə] *n.* ①国库;资金;财源;〔口〕(个人的)财力. ②〔E-〕【英史】税务法庭(专管王室岁入并审理有关案件,1873年归并高等法院 = Court of E-). ③〔E-〕〔英〕财政部. *His ~ is low.* 他的经济状况不好. *Chancellor of the E-* 〔英〕财政大臣. **E- Bill** 〔英〕财政部证券. **E- Bond** 〔英〕国库债券.

ex·cide [ikˈsaid] *vt.* 割掉,切开.

ex·cip·i·ent [ikˈsipiənt] *n.* 【药】赋形剂.

ex·cis·a·ble [ikˈsaizəbl] *a.* 应纳国产货物税[执照税]税的.

ex·cise[1] [ekˈsaiz] *n.* ①(国产)货物税;消费税;(生产、贩卖)执照税. ②〔the E-〕(英国的)国产税务局〔现名 Commissioners of Customs and E-〕. *~ duties* 消费税. *the ~ law* 〔英〕酿酒法;〔美〕执照法. — *vt.* ①向…征收国产税[消费税]. ②〔英方〕向…索取高价. **-man** *n.* *(pl. -men)* 〔英古〕消费税征收官员(= E- officer).

ex·cise[2] [ekˈsaiz] *vt.* ①删去(文章等);切除. ②【动、植】在…上开槽,切开.

ex·ci·sion [ekˈsiʒən] *n.* ①删除. ②【医】切除(术). ③【宗】逐出教会.

ex·cit·a·bil·i·ty [ikˌsaitəˈbiliti] *n.* ①【物】可激发性. ②【医】兴奋性,敏感性;【生理】(感官的)刺激反应性.

ex·cit·a·ble [ikˈsaitəbl] *a.* 易激动的;敏感的. **-bly** *ad.*

ex·cit·ant [ˈeksitənt] *a.* 有刺激性的,使兴奋的. — *n.* 刺激物;兴奋剂.

ex·ci·ta·tion [ˌeksiˈteiʃən] *n.* ①刺激,兴奋,激发,鼓舞. ②【物】激发;【电】激励,励磁. ③【植】激感(现象).

ex·cit·a·tive [ekˈsaitətiv] *a.* ①刺激性的,兴奋性的,有刺激作用的;激发的. ②【电】励磁的.

ex·cit·a·to·ry [ekˈsaitətəri] *a.* ① = excitative. ②显示兴奋的,有激动迹象的.

ex·cite [ikˈsait] *vt.* ①刺激;使兴奋;使激动. ②激励;鼓励,激发,唤起(注意等),引起(兴趣);煽动. ③【电】激起(电流). ④【摄】使感光. *The good news ~d everybody.* 好消息使每一个人都很兴奋. *~ admiration* 引起羡慕. *~ jealousy in sb.* 引起某人嫉妒. *~ a nerve* 刺激神经. *~ heat by friction* 摩擦生热. — *vi.* 〔口〕兴奋,激动. *Don't ~.* 冷静点! *(= Don't ~ yourself).* ***get ~d at [by, about, over]*** 因…而激动[兴奋]起来.

ex·cit·ed [ikˈsaitid] *a.* ①激昂的,激动的,兴奋的. ②【物】激发的,励磁的. ~ **state** 【物】受激态. **-ly** *ad.* 激昂,兴奋.

ex·cite·ment [ikˈsaitmənt] *n.* ①刺激,兴奋,振奋;激昂,奋激;骚动. ②刺激的事物. *at a high pitch of ~* 极度激动[兴奋]. *great ~ caused by the fire* 由火灾引起的骚动. *be flushed with ~* 兴奋得脸色发红. ***in ~*** 兴奋地,激动地.

ex·cit·er [ikˈsaitə] *n.* ①刺激者;刺激物. ②【电】励磁机. 【无】激励器;主控振荡器;辐射器;主控振荡槽路.

ex·cit·ing [ikˈsaitiŋ] *a.* ①令人兴奋的,使人激动的. ②【电】励磁的. *~ news* 令人兴奋的消息. **-ly** *ad.*

ex·cit·on [ˈiksitɔn] *n.* 【物】激子. **-ic** [ˌiksiˈtɔnik] *a.* **-ics** *n. pl.* 〔用作单数〕【物】激子学.

ex·ci·tor [ikˈsaitə] *n.* ① = exciter. ②【解】兴奋反射神经.

excl. = exclusive.

ex·claim [iksˈkleim] *vt., vi.* 惊叫,呼喊,大声说. ~ ***against*** 指责. ~ ***at [on, upon]*** 抗议. ~ ***in [with] delight*** 欢呼. ~ ***over*** 感叹. **-er** *n.*

ex·cla·ma·tion [ˌekskləˈmeiʃən] *n.* ①惊叫,呼喊. ②感叹;【语法】感叹词;【修】咏叹法. ***the note [point] of ~ = the ~ mark [point]*** 感叹号[!].

ex·clam·a·to·ry [eksˈklæmətəri] *a.* 叫喊的;感叹的;咏叹式的.

ex·clave [ˈekskleiv] *n.* 飞地〔在别国境内的某国领土〕.

ex·clo·sure [iksˈkləuʒə, iks-] *n.* 围地〔尤指为防止家畜或野兽侵入而栅起来的地方〕.

ex·clude [iksˈkluːd] *vt.* ①拒绝;排除,排斥;把…除外. ②驱除,赶出. *~ sb. from membership in a society* 拒绝接纳,某人入会. *~ immigrants from a country* 不许移居入境. *There were fifteen present excluding myself.* 除我以外,有十五人出席. *None of these three can be ~d.* 这三者缺一不可. *the law of ~d middle* 【逻】排中律. ~ ***sb. from*** 不准进;把…赶出;剥夺(某人…的权利);拒绝(某人入会等). ~ ***the possibility of*** 排除…的可能性.

ex·clu·sion [iksˈkluːʒən] *n.* ①拒绝,杜绝;除去,排除,排斥;赶出. ②被排除在外的事物. ***the ~ policy*** 闭关政策. ***to the ~ of*** 把…除外;排斥. ~ **principle** 【物】(泡利)不相容原理(=Pauli ~ principle). **-ar·y** *a.*

ex·clu·sion·ism [iksˈkluːʒənizəm] *n.* 排外主义,闭关

主义；排他主义．

ex·clu·sion·ist [iks'klu:ʒəˌnist] *n.* 排他主义者．— *a.* 排他主义的．～ *attitude* 闭关自守的态度．

ex·clu·sive [iks'klu:siv] *a.* ①除外的；排外的，排他的，(俱乐部等)不公开的，势利的，非大众化的．②孤高的．③独占的；独有的，唯一的；专有的，专属的．④全部的．⑤〔美〕时髦的．⑥(商店、商品等) 高级的，价格高的，别处没有的．⑦不计及，不算入 *(of)* *(opp.* inclusive*)*. *an* ～ *aggressive bloc* 排他性的侵略集团．*an* ～ *agency policy* 独家代理政策．～ *jurisdiction* 专辖权．～ *of expenses* 除去费用不算．～ *privileges* 独有的特权．～ *rights for the sale of* 专售权．*an* ～ *selling agency* 独家经销店．*an* ～ *school* (限上层阶级子弟入学的)专设学校．～ *species*【植】确限种，专见种．～ *voice*【法】否认权，否决权．*an* ～ *hotel* 高级旅馆．*be* ～ *in manner* 态度傲慢．～ ***of*** 除；不算，不计 *(opp.* inclusive of*)* *(from 10 to 21* ～ 从 11 到 20〔10 和21除外〕*)*. —*n.* ①独家新闻．②专有权．③孤傲者．④【数】不可兼．**-ly** *ad.* **-ness** *n.*

ex·clu·siv·ism [iks'klu:sivizəm] *n.* = exclusionism.

ex·clu·siv·ist [iks'klu:sivist] *n.* 排他主义者．

ex·clu·siv·is·tic [iksˌklu:si'vistik] *a.* 排他主义的．

ex·clu·siv·i·ty [ˌeksklu:'siviti] *n.* 排外，排外主义；排他性，排他主义〔尤指搞宗派，拉山头，或闭关自守〕．

ex·cog·i·tate [eks'kɔdʒiteit] *vt.* 想出，设计，发明．

ex·cog·i·ta·tion [eksˌkɔdʒi'teiʃən] *n.* ①想出，设计，设法．②计划，计策，方案．

ex·cog·i·ta·tive [eks'kɔdʒiteitiv] *a.* 想出的，计划的，发明的．

ex·com·mu·ni·cate [ˌekskə'mju:nikeit] *vt.* ①把…革出教门，剥夺(教友)特权(如在教堂结婚、埋葬、领受圣餐等)．②开除 (会籍等)．— *a.* 被革出教门的 (= excommunicated)．— *n.* 被革出教门的人．

ex·com·mu·ni·ca·tion ['ekskəˌmju:ni'keiʃən] *n.* 革出教会；革出教会的公告．*major [greater]* ～ 大革出〔开除教籍〕．*minor [lesser]* ～ 小革出〔只停止领圣餐〕．

ex·com·mu·ni·ca·tive [ˌekskə'mju:nikətiv] *a.* 革出教会的；开除的．

ex·com·mu·ni·ca·tor [ˌekskə'mju:nikeitə] *n.* 革出教会者；开除者．

ex·co·ri·ate [eks'kɔ:rieit] *vt.* ①剥(皮)，磨掉，擦伤(皮肤等)．②严厉指责．

ex·co·ri·a·tion [eksˌkɔ:ri'eiʃən] *n.* ①剥皮，擦伤皮肤．②严厉指责．③【医】表皮脱落．

ex·cre·ment ['ekskrimənt] *n.* 排泄物；粪便．**-tious** *a.*

ex·cres·cence [iks'kresns] *n.* 赘疣，瘤；多余的东西．

ex·cres·cen·cy [iks'kresnsi] *n.* = excrescence.

ex·cres·cent [iks'kresənt] *a.* ①赘生的；无用的，多余的．②【语】赘音的．

ex·cre·ta [eks'kri:tə] *n. pl.*【生理】排泄物〔特指汗、尿、粪便等〕．

ex·crete [eks'kri:t] *vt.*【生理】排泄；分泌 (*cf.* secrete)．

ex·cre·tion [eks'kri:ʃən] *n.* ①排泄；分泌 (*cf.* secretion)．②排泄物；分泌物．

ex·cre·tive [eks'kri:tiv] *a.* 排泄的；分泌的，促进排泄〔分泌〕的；有排泄力的．

ex·cre·to·ry [eks'kri:təri] *a.* 有排泄功能的，排泄的．～ **cells** 排泄细胞．～ **ducts** 排泄管．～ **organ** 排泄器官．

ex·cru·ci·ate [iks'kru:ʃieit] *vt.* ①使苦恼〔痛苦〕．②〔古〕拷打；折磨．

ex·cru·ci·at·ing [iks'kru:ʃieitiŋ] *a.* ①使苦恼的；极痛苦的；难忍受的．②极度的，剧烈的．**-ly** *ad.*

ex·cru·ci·a·tion [iksˌkru:ʃi'eiʃən] *n.* ①苦恼，剧痛；折磨．②〔古〕酷刑，拷问．

ex·cul·pate ['ekskʌlpeit] *vt.* 开脱，申明…无罪，辩白．～ *oneself from a charge of theft* 辩白自己无盗窃嫌疑．

ex·cul·pa·tion [ˌekskʌl'peiʃən] *n.* 开脱，申明无罪；辩白；辩明无罪，昭雪．

ex·cul·pa·to·ry [iks'kʌlpətəri] *a.* 开脱罪责的；辩明无罪的．

ex·cur·rent [iks'kʌrənt] *a.* ①流出的．②【植】(茎)贯顶的，(树形)尖塔状的，(叶脉)延伸的．

ex·curse [iks'kə:s] *vi.* ①旅行，游览．②说话〔作文〕离题．③〔罕〕徘徊．

ex·cur·sion [iks'kə:ʃən] *n.* ①短途旅行，游览．②旅行团，游览团．③离题．④【机】冲程；【物】漂移，偏移．⑤【医】肺的一个完全呼吸动作．*amplitude* ～【物】振幅偏移．*an* ～ *bus [train]* 游览汽车〔列车〕．*go on [for] an* ～ *to* = *make [take] an* ～ *to.* 到…去旅行．～ *rates* 游览收费率．**-al, -ary** *a.* **-ist** *n.* 短途旅行者，游览者．

ex·cur·sive [iks'kə:siv] *a.* ①好旅行的．②容易离题的．③散漫的．*an* ～ *conversation* 漫谈．～ *reading* 涉猎性的阅读．**-ly** *ad.* **-ness** *n.*

ex·cur·sus [eks'kə:səs] *n.* *(pl.* ～, ～*es)* ①余论，补论；附注；补注；追记．②枝节的话，离题的话．

ex·cus·a·ble [iks'kju:zəbl] *a.* 情有可原的，可以饶恕的，可申辩的，不无理由的．**-bly** *ad.* **-ness** *n.*

ex·cus·a·to·ry [iks'kju:zətəri] *a.* 辩解的，表示歉意的．

ex·cuse [iks'kju:z] *vt.* ①原谅，宽恕．②免除，宽免．③为…辩解，表白；成为…的理由．***E-* me.** 对不起〔离开、打断别人说话、表示不同意或举止失礼时的道歉话〕．*E- me for interrupting you.* =*E- my interrupting you.* 原谅我打扰你了．*If you'll kindly* ～ *me* 请原谅…．～ *sb. for being late* 原谅某人迟到．*Sickness* ～*s his absense.* 他是因病才缺席的．～ ***oneself*** ①为自己辩解．②说声"对不起"就(要)走开 *(She* ～*d herself to us.* 她说声"对不起"就离开我们了*)*．～ ***oneself for*** 替自己辩解．～ ***oneself from*** 谢绝，托故推辞，申明不能．～ ***sb. from*** *(attendence)* 允许某人不(出席)．— [-'kju:s] *n.* ①原谅，饶恕．②辩解；解释；理由．③托辞，藉口．④〔*pl.*〕道歉，歉意．⑤请假条．*That is no* ～ *for your being late.* 那不能成为你迟到的理由．***an*** ～ ***for being [existence]*** 存在的理由．***be ill at making*** ～***s*** 不善辩解．***in*** ～ ***of*** 为…辩明．***make one's*** ～***s*** 辩解，推托．***make some*** ～ ***(for)*** 找借口．***without*** ～ 无故．

ex-di·rec·to·ry [ˌeksdi'rektəri] *a.* 〔英口〕电话簿上找不到的，未登记的．

ex·e·at ['eksiæt] *n.* 〔英〕①短期离校的许可．②牧师调换教区的许可．

ex·ec [ig'zek] *n.* ①〔美口〕行政长官．②〔美口〕主任参谋，副舰长．

exec. = executive; executor.

ex·e·cra·ble ['eksikrəbl] *a.* ①该诅咒的，讨厌的，可恶的．②(天气、食物等)恶劣的．**-bly** *ad.* **-ness** *n.*

ex·e·crate ['eksikreit] *vt.* ①诅咒，咒骂．②憎恶，嫌恶．—*vi.* 咒骂．**-cra·tion** *n.* ①诅咒，咒骂．②憎恶，嫌恶．③被诅咒的事物，嫌恶物；咒语．**-cra·tive, -cra·to·ry** *a.*

ex·e·cut·a·ble ['eksikju:təbl] *a.* 可执行的，可实行的，可以作成的．

ex·ec·u·tant [ig'zekjutənt] *n.* ①实行者，执行者．②【乐】演奏者．

ex·e·cute ['eksikju:t] *vt.* ①实行，实施，执行；履行；贯彻，完成．②作成，制成(美术品等)；奏(乐曲)，演(剧)．③〔英〕让渡(财产)；经过签名盖章等手续使 (法律文件等) 生效．④对…执行死刑，处决．～ *the captain's command* 执行船长命令．～ *a deed* 签名使契据生效．～ *fire*【军】开火．～ *one's [duties] office* 尽职．～ *the part of Hamlet* 扮演哈姆雷特．～ *a painting [statue]* 创作一幅画〔一件雕像〕．～ *one's promises* 践约，履行契约．～ *an estate* 让渡财产．～ *a will* 使遗嘱生效．***be summarily*** ～***d*** 就地正法，当场处决，立即处死．

ex·e·cu·tion [ˌeksi'kju:ʃən] *n.* ①实行，履行，执行；贯彻．②执行死刑；强制执行；执行命令．③作成，完成；签名盖印使法律文件生效；执行法律. ④扮演，演奏，(演奏)技巧，手法. ⑤成功，奏效；效果；(武器的)杀伤力. *forcible* ~ 强制执行. *The* ~ *leaves much to be desired, though the idea is good.* 设想虽好，执行起来很难如愿. ~ *by hanging* 绞刑. **carry [put] into** ~ 实行，实施. **do** ~ 奏效，见效；(武器有)摧毁作用 (*He did great* ~ *among the cakes.* 他吃掉很多饼.) ***Every shot did*** ~. 百发百中. ***E- Dock*** 【英史】(泰晤士 (*Thames*) 河畔处决海盗等的)死刑码头. ***make good*** ~【军】摧毁；使敌方受重大损失. ***put to*** ~ 处死刑，执行死刑. ~ **sale** 【法】强制拍卖.

ex·e·cu·tion·er [ˌeksiˈkjuːʃənə] *n.* ①死刑执行人；刽子手. ②(遗嘱、判决等的)执行人.

ex·ec·u·tive [igˈzekjutiv] *a.* ①执行的，实行的，实施的，有执行权力[手腕]的；行政(上)的. ②行政官的；总经理的. ~ *authorities* 行政当局. *an* ~ *branch [department]* ①行政部门. ②【海】作战部. ~ *committee* 执行委员会. ~ *board* 理事会. ~ *council* 谘询会议，行政会议，最高行政会议. *an* ~ *officer* = exec. — *n.* ①行政部门；行政官；执行委员会. ②【美商】总经理，董事. ***the (Chief) E-*** 〔美〕总统；州长；〔英〕国王. ~ **agreement** 〔美〕(政府行政部门就例行事务同外国政府签订的)行政协定. **E- Mansion** 〔美〕总统官邸；州长官邸. **E- Order** 〔美〕总统命令(=〔英〕*Order in Council*). ~ **part** 〔美〕(远离市中心的)商业机构办公区. ~ **session** 〔美〕(参议院的)秘密会议.

ex·ec·u·tor [igˈzekjutə] *n.* ①【法】指定遗嘱执行人. ②[ˈeksikjuːtə] 执行者. *a literary* ~ (遗嘱上指定的)遗著保管人. **-ship** [igˈzekjutəʃip] (遗嘱)执行人的职务.

ex·ec·u·to·ri·al [igˌzekjuˈtɔːriəl] *a.* 执行者的；执行上的.

ex·ec·u·to·ry [egˈzekjutəri] *a.* ①执行上的，行政上的；实施中的. ②【法】(契约等)将来有效的.

ex·ec·u·trix [igˈzekjutriks] *n.* ***(pl.*** ~***es, -tri·ces*** [-traisiːz]***)*** 【法】女遗嘱执行人.

ex·e·dra [ikˈsiːdrə, ˈeksi-] *n.* ***(pl. -drae*** [-driː]***)*** (古希腊的)对话间；座谈馆大楼；室外讨论会场.

ex·e·ge·sis [ˌeksiˈdʒiːsis] *n.* ***(pl. -ses*** [-siːz]***)*** *n.* (对《圣经》等宗教经典的)注释；注解.

ex·e·gete [ˈeksidʒiːt] *n.* (《圣经》等宗教经典的) 注释学者，评注家.

ex·e·get·ic [ˌeksiˈdʒetik] *a.* (关于《圣经》等宗教经典的)注释的. **-cal·ly** *ad.*

ex·e·get·ics [ˌeksiˈdʒetiks] *n.* (《圣经》等宗教经典的)注释学，训诂学.

ex·em·pla [igˈzemplə] *n.* exemplum 的复数.

ex·em·plar [igˈzemplə] *n.* 模范；典型；标本，样本.

ex·em·pla·ry [igˈzempləri] *a.* ①值得模仿的；典型的，示范的. ②惩戒性的. ~ *conducts* 模范行为. ~ *punishments* 作为惩戒的处罚. ~ **damages**【法】惩罚性赔偿〔超过实际损失的赔偿〕. **-ri·ly** *ad.* **-ri·ness** *n.*

ex·em·pli·fi·ca·tion [igˌzemplifiˈkeiʃən] *n.* ①举例，例证，例示；模范，适例. ②【法】核正誊本，正本.

ex·em·pli·fy [igˈzemplifai] *vt.* ①举例证明[解释]；示范；作…的范例. ②【法】复印；制成核正誊本.

ex·em·pli gra·ti·a [igˈzemplai ˈgreiʃiə] 〔L.〕例如(= for example，略作 e.g.).

ex·em·plum [igˈzempləm] *n.* ***(pl. -pla*** [-plə]***)*** ①(中世纪布道时讲的)劝喻性故事. ②例证，范例.

ex·empt [igˈzempt] *vt.* 免除，豁免 (*from*). ~ *sb. from an examination* 免考. — *a.* 被免除的，被豁免的 (*from*). *commodities* ~ *from taxes* 免税商品. — *n.* 被免除(义务、责任)的人；免税人.

ex·empt·i·ble [igˈzemptibl] *a.* 可享豁免权的.

ex·emp·tion [igˈzempʃən] *n.* ①免除；豁免，免税〔尤指部分所得税〕. ③取得豁免的原因. ~ *from taxation* 免税.

ex·en·ter·ate [ekˈsentəreit] *vt.* ①〔罕〕除去[取出]…的肠子；(蜘蛛)吐(丝). ②【医】摘除(某器官). **-ter·a·tion** [ekˌsentəˈreiʃən] *n.*

ex·e·qua·tur [ˌeksiˈkweitə] *n.* 〔L.〕= Let him perform. (驻在国政府发给他国领事或商务代表的) 许可证书.

ex·e·quies [ˈeksikwiz] *n.* exequy 的复数.

ex·e·quy [ˈeksikwi] *n.* 〔*pl.*〕葬礼，殡仪，出殡行列.

ex·er·cis·a·ble [ˈeksəsaizəbl] *a.* 可行使的，可实行的，可运用的；可操作的，可履行的.

ex·er·cise [ˈeksəsaiz] *n.* ①(精力等的)运用，使用；实行；执行. ②演习，操练；训练；〔常 *pl.*〕运动，体操. ③习题，练习，课程；(声乐、器乐的)练习曲. ④〔古〕礼拜；修行. ⑤〔*pl.*〕〔美〕典礼，仪式；传统[习惯]做法. ⑥学术辩论；(授学位前的)口试. *an* ~ *book* 练习簿. ~ *in mathematics* 数学习题. ~ *of the memory* 记忆力的锻练. *graduating* ~*s* 毕业典礼. *gymnastic* ~*s* 体操，健身操. *military* ~*s* 军事演习，军事操练. *opening* ~*s* 开会仪式. *public* ~*s* (音乐等的)公演，大会. *a religious* ~ 礼拜. ***do one's*** ~ 做功课. ***take*** ~ 运动. — *vt.* ①实行；行使(职权等)；使活动；运用；发挥(力量). ②练习，训练，操练. ③使受(影响等). ④使烦恼，使操心，使忧虑. ~ *a power* 行使权力. ~ *pressure* 施加压力. ~ *judgement* 运用判断力. — *vi.* 练习；运动. ***be*** ~***d about sth.*** 为某事担忧[操心]. ~ ***oneself in*** 练习….

ex·er·cis·er [ˈeksəsaizə] *n.* ①行使职权的人. ②受训练者. ③体育器械. ④训练马的马夫.

ex·er·ci·ta·tion [egˌzəːsiˈteiʃən] *n.* ①〔古〕练习；训练；实习. ②(能力、权力等的)运用，行使. ③演说练习；论文习作.

ex·ergue [ekˈsəːg] *n.* 钱币等反面底线下刻记年月日或铸造局名的地方.

ex·ert [igˈzəːt] *vt.* ①用(力)，尽(努力等)，行使(职权等). ②发挥(威力等)，使受(影响等) (*on; upon*). ~ *an influence* 施加影响. ~ *all one's powers* 尽全力. ~ ***oneself*** 努力，尽力，出力 (~ *oneself to the utmost* 尽全力).

ex·er·tion [igˈzəːʃən] *n.* ①努力，尽力. ②行使，运用. ***be no*** ~ ***to*** 不费力 (*It's no* ~ *to him to lift the stone.* 他不用费力就能把那块石头举起来). ***use [make, put forth]*** ~***s*** 尽力.

ex·er·tive [igˈzəːtiv] *a.* 努力的，费劲的，尽力的.

ex·es [ˈeksiz] *n.* 〔*pl.*〕〔口〕费用 (= expenses).

ex·e·unt [ˈeksiʌnt, -ənt] *vi.* 〔L.〕【剧】(某些演员)退场〔*cf.* exit〕. ~ *omnes* [ˈɔmniːz]全体退场，全体下.

ex·fil·trate [eksˈfiltreit] *vi., vt.* 〔美军俚〕偷偷溜出(敌占区)，偷越过(敌方封锁线).

ex·fil·tra·tion [ˌeksfilˈtreiʃən] *n.* 偷偷越过(封锁线等).

ex·fo·li·ate [eksˈfəulieit] *vt.* 象鳞片般剥下；使成片状. — *vi.* (岩面、皮肤等)剥落；【植】片状剥落；【动】鳞片样脱皮；【地】页状剥落；【医】表皮脱落.

ex·fo·li·a·tion [eksˌfəuliˈeiʃən] *n.* ①剥落；【医】表皮剥落；剥落物. ②分层(丝织品的)茸毛.

ex-GI [ˈeksdʒiːˈai] *n.* 〔美俚〕复员军人.

ex gra·tia [eksˈgreiʃiə] *a., adv.* 〔L.〕作为优惠的[地]；【商】通融的[地].

ex·hal·ant, ex·hal·ent [eksˈheilənt, egˈzei-] *a.* 呼气的；发散(性)的，蒸发(性)的. — *n.* 呼吸气管；发散管，蒸发管.

ex·ha·la·tion [ˌekshəˈleiʃən, egzə-] *n.* ①呼气；蒸发，(气味等的)发散；(怒气等的)发泄. ②(气体等)发散物；薄雾.

ex·hale [eksˈheil, egˈzeil] *vt.* ①呼(气) (*opp.* inhale). ②放出(蒸汽)；发散出(香味)；发泄(怒气). ③使蒸发. ④【医】渗出. — *vi.* ①呼气. ②散发，蒸发.

ex·haust [igˈzɔːst] *vt.* ①用尽，耗尽(资源等). ②排出

(空气),抽空,空出(容器等);汲干. ③提尽(可溶解的物质). ④使筋疲力尽,使疲备不堪〔多用 ~ *oneself* 或被动语态〕. ⑤彻底研究,详论. ~ *the water of a well* 把井水抽干. ~ *oneself walking* 走累. *feel quite* ~*ed* 感到累极了. *be* ~*ed by disease* 病得毫无力气. *be* ~*ed with toil* 劳累不堪. — *vi.* ①排出. ②排气. — *n.* ①排出;抽空. ②排气装置. ③(排出的)废气. *an* ~ *pipe [valve]* 排气管[阀]. ~ *steam [gas]* 废气.

ex·haust·ed [ig'zɔ:stid] *a.* ①耗尽的,枯竭的. ②筋疲力尽的. ~ *tea* 泡得无味的茶. *an* ~ *well* 枯井.

ex·haust·er [ig'zɔ:stə] *n.* 【机】排气机,抽风机.

ex·haust·i·bil·i·ty [igˌzɔ:stə'biliti] *n.* 可空竭;可用尽.

ex·haust·i·ble [ig'zɔ:stəbl] *a.* 可空竭的;可耗尽的,用得尽的.

ex·haust·ing [ig'zɔ:stiŋ] *a.* ①使耗尽的. ②使筋疲力尽的. **-ly** *ad.*

ex·haus·tion [ig'zɔ:stʃən] *n.* ①枯竭,用尽. ②排空,抽空. ③疲惫,衰竭. ④彻底的研究,详尽的论述.

ex·haus·tive [ig'zɔ:stiv] *a.* ①(论述等)详尽的;无遗漏的,彻底的. ②消耗的,使枯竭的. **-ly** *ad.* **-ness** *n.*

ex·haust·less [ig'zɔ:stlis] *a.* 用不完的,不会枯竭的. **-ly** *ad.* **-ness** *n.*

ex·her·e·date [eks'herideit] *vt.* 剥夺…的继承权.

ex·hib·it [ig'zibit] *vt.* ①表明,显示,显出. ②陈列,展览;〔罕〕公演. ③【法】提出(证据等). ④【医】〔废〕用(药). ~ *great bravery* 表现英勇. ~ *a charge* 提出控诉. ~ *a prize* 提供奖金. — *vi.* 开展览会;(产品、作品)展出. ~ ***wares*** 〔美俚〕参加比赛,露一手. — *n.* ①展出;展览会. ②陈列品,展览品. ③【法】证件,证物. **-ant, -er** *n.* = exhibitor.

ex·hi·bi·tion [ˌeksi'biʃən] *n.* ①表明,显示. ②陈列,展览. ③【法】(证据等的)提出. ④展览会;展览品,陈列品. ⑤(英国大学)奖学金. ⑥〔美〕(毕业典礼的)游艺会. *a competitive* ~ 评比会. *an art* ~ 美术展览会. ~ *flight* 【空】表演飞行. ~ *game [match]* 表演赛. ***make an* ~ *of oneself*** 丢脸,出丑. ***place [put] sth. on* ~** 展出某物.

ex·hi·bi·tion·er [ˌeksi'biʃənə] *n.* ①展出者. ②〔英〕得到奖学金的大学生.

ex·hi·bi·tion·ism [ˌeksi'biʃənizəm] *n.* ①【医】下体裸露癖. ②表现癖.

ex·hi·bi·tion·ist [ˌeksi'biʃənist] *n.* ①【医】下体裸露癖患者. ②好表现的人.

ex·hib·i·tive [ig'zibitiv] *a.* 供展览的,起显示作用的;能表示…的 *(of)*.

ex·hib·i·tor [ig'zibitə] *n.* ①展出者,展出厂商;展览会参加者. ②电影院老板[经理]. ③奖学金捐赠人. ③提供者,提出者〔= exhibiter〕.

ex·hib·i·to·ry [ig'zibitəri] *a.* ①展览的. ②显示的,表示的.

ex·hil·a·rant [ig'zilərənt] *a.* 令人高兴[兴奋]的. — *n.* 令人兴奋的东西,兴奋剂.

ex·hil·a·rate [ig'zilәreit] *vt.* 使高兴;使兴奋. **-d** *a.*

ex·hil·a·rat·ing [ig'zilәreitiŋ] *a.* 使人高兴的,令人兴奋的. *an* ~ *drink* 提神的饮料(指酒). **-ly** *ad.*

ex·hil·a·ra·tion [igˌzilə'reiʃən] *n.* 高兴,兴奋. **-ra·tive, -ra·to·ry** [ig'zilәreitiv, -rətəri] *a.* 令人高兴的,令人兴奋的.

ex·hort [ig'zɔ:t] *vt.* ①力劝;告诫;勉励. ②倡导. — *vi.* 劝告. **-hor·ta·tion** *n.* 劝勉;告诫. **-hor·ta·tive, -hor·ta·to·ry** *a.* 劝勉的;告诫的. **-er** *n.* 劝勉者,告诫者,倡导者.

ex·hume [eks'hju:m, igs'hju:m] *vt.* ①(从坟墓内)掘出(尸体等). ②〔喻〕发掘(被遗忘的东西). **-hu·ma·tion** [ˌekshju:'meiʃən] *n.* 发掘;掘墓.

ex·i·gence, -cy ['eksidʒəns, -si] *n.* ①危急,紧急,迫切. ②〔常 *pl.*〕迫切的需要,严酷的要求. ③危机,危急关头,非常时期;急变;急事;困境. ***in this extreme* ~** 在这危急关头. ***meet the exigencies of the times*** 应付当前的危局. ***suit the* ~** 应急.

ex·i·gent ['eksidʒənt] *a.* ①紧急的,危急的. ②(生活)艰苦的;苛求的. *be* ~ *of money* 急需金钱.

ex·i·gi·ble ['eksidʒibl] *a.* 可要求的,可强索的 *(from, against)*.

ex·i·gu·i·ty [ˌeksi'gju(:)iti] *n.* 微小;不足;贫乏. *an* ~ *of budget* 过少的预算.

ex·ig·u·ous [eg'zigjuəs] *a.* 细小的,微小的. *a merely* ~ *income* 微薄的收入. **-ly** *ad.* **-ness** *n.*

ex·ile ['eksail, 'egz-] *n.* ①流放,放逐,充军;流亡,亡命. ②充军者,流犯;流亡者;亡命者. ***go into* ~** 逃亡. ***live in* ~** 流亡(异乡). — *vt.* 放逐,处…以流刑,使充军,发配. ~ ***oneself*** 亡命(国外).

ex·il·i·an [eg'ziliən, ek'siliən], **ex·il·ic** [eg'zilik, ek'siliən] *a.* 放逐的,亡命的.

ex·il·i·ty [eg'ziliti, ek'sil-] *n.* 〔废〕微薄;微小;细微.

EXIM = Export-Import Bank 〔美〕进出口银行.

ex int. = ex interest 无利息.

ex·ist [ig'zist] *vi.* ①存在,有. ②生存;活着. ~ ***actually*** 实际存在. ~ ***as*** 作为…而存在,以…形态存在. ~ ***in*** 存在于…中. ~ ***on*** 靠…生活[生存].

ex·ist·ence [ig'zistəns] *n.* ①存在,实在,继续存在. ②生存,生活,生活方式. ③实体,存在物,生物. *a precarious [hollow]* ~ 朝不保夕的[空虚的]生活. *a struggle for* ~ 生存竞争. *be taxed out of* ~ 因税重而绝迹. ***bring [call] into* ~** 使发生,使产生,使成立. ***come into* ~** 产生;成立. ***in* ~** 现存的;存在的 (*the most miserable being in* ~ 世上最不幸的人. *the only copy to be known in* ~ 海内孤本). ***put out of* ~** 绝灭,使绝迹.

ex·ist·ent [ig'zistənt] *a.* = existing. — *n.* 生存者,存在的事物.

ex·is·ten·tial [ˌegzis'tenʃəl] *a.* ①关于存在的,依据存在经验的. ②【哲】存在主义的. ③【逻】存在判断的. *an* ~ *proposition* 存在判断的命题. **-ism** *n.* 【哲】存在主义. **-ist** *n.* 【哲】存在主义者.

ex·ist·ing [ig'zistiŋ] *a.* 存在的,现存的,实在的 (*opp.* extinct); 现行的,目前的. *the* ~ *circumstances [condition]* 现状,现况. ~ *equipments* 原[现]有设备. *the* ~ *situation* 当前形势.

ex·it ['eksit, 'egzit] *n.* ①出口,出路,太平门. ②【电】引出端;排气管. ③外出;离去;死亡;【剧】退场 (*opp.* entrance). ***make one's* ~** 退出;退场;去世. — *vi.* ①退出,离去. ②死,去世.

ex·it ['eksit] *vi.* 〔L.〕【剧】退场〔*cf.* exeunt; *opp.* enter〕.

ex li·bris [eks'laibris] *n.* 〔*sing., pl.*〕藏书签.

ex li·brist [eks'laibrist] *n.* 藏书签搜集者.

exo- *comb. f.* 表示"外","外部": *exo*ergic, *exo*skeleton.

ex·o·at·mos·phere [ˌeksəu'ætməsfiə] *n.* 外大气圈,外逸层〔地气大气圈的最高层〕.

ex·o·bi·ol·o·gy [ˌeksəubai'ɔlədʒi] *n.* 外(层)空(间)生物学〔探索地球之外存在生物的可能性的科学〕;宇宙生物学. **-o·log·i·cal** *a.* **-o·log·ist** *n.* 外空生物学家.

ex·o·carp ['eksəukɑ:p] *n.* 【植】外果皮(= epicarp).

ex·o·cen·tric [ˌeksəu'sentrik] *a.* 【语】离心结构的.

ex·o·coe·lom [ˌeksəu'si:ləm] *n.* 【生】胚外体腔.

ex·o·crine ['eksəkrain] *a.* 【医】外分泌的. — *n.* 外分泌腺.

ex·o·der·mis [ˌeksəu'də:mis] *n.* 【植】外皮层.

ex·o·don·tics [ˌeksəu'dɔntiks] *n.* 〔*pl.*〕【医】拔牙学(= exodontia). **-don·tist** *n.* 拔牙专家.

ex·o·dus ['eksədəs] *n.* ①离去,退出;(移民等大批)出国. ②〔E-〕古代以色列人出埃及. ③〔E-〕【圣】《出埃及记》.

ex·o·er·gic [ˌeksəu'ə:dʒik] *a.* 【物】放能的.

ex of·fi·ci·o [ˌeks əˈfiʃiəu] *ad.* 依据职权地. — *adj.* 职权上的.

ex·og·a·my [eksˈɔgəmi] *n.* ①异族结婚; 外婚 (*opp.* endogamy). ②【生】异系交配. **-o·gam·ic, -a·mous** [ˈeksəuˈgæmik, ekˈsɔgəməs] *a.*

ex·o·ge·nic [ˌeksəuˈdʒenik] *a.* = exogenous.

ex·og·e·nous [ekˈsɔdʒinəs] *a.* ①外部发生的, 外源的. ②【生】外因的. **-ly** *ad.*

ex·on·er·ate [igˈzɔnəreit] *vt.* ①证明…无罪; 开释; 昭雪. ②免除(义务等),解除(责任等). ~ *sb. from blame* 宽免某人的罪责.

ex·on·er·a·tion [igˈzɔnəreiʃən] *n.* 免罪, 昭雪; 免除, 解除.

ex·on·er·a·tive [igˈzɔnəreitiv] *a.* ①免罪的,免咎的. ②免除(义务)的,解除(责任)的.

ex·oph·thal·mos [ˌeksɔfˈθælməs] *n.* 【医】眼球突出症 (= exophthalmus, exophthalmia). **-thal·mic** *a.*

ex·o·plasm [ˈeksəuplæzəm] *n.* 【生】外质.

ex·op·o·dite [ikˈsɔpədait] *n.* 【动】外肢,外肢节.

exor. = executor.

ex·o·ra·ble [ˈeksərəbl] *a.* 心软的,容易说服的.

ex·or·bi·tance [igˈzɔːbitəns] *n.* ①(价格、收费、要求等的)过高, 过度. ②(倾向、性情的)过分. ③〔古〕无法无天; 混乱.

ex·or·bi·tant [igˈzɔːbitənt] *a.* 过高的,过度的,过分的. **-ly** *ad.*

ex·or·cise, ex·or·cize [ˈeksɔːsaiz] *vt.* 驱除(妖魔等); 从…驱魔 (*out of, from*). **-ment** *n.* **-r** *n.* =exorcist.

ex·or·cism [ˈeksɔːsizəm] *n.* 驱邪,祓魔.

ex·or·cist [ˈeksɔːsist] *n.* 祓魔师.

ex·or·di·al [ekˈsɔːdiəl] *a.* 绪言的,绪论的; 开端的.

ex·or·di·um [ekˈsɔːdiəm] *n.* (*pl.* *~s, -di·a* [-diə]) ①(事物的)发端; 开端. ②(论文的)绪言.

ex·o·skel·e·ton [ˌeksəuˈskelitn] *n.* 【解】外骨骼, 皮骨骼. **-e·tal** [-tl] *a.*

ex·os·mo·sis [ˌeksɔsˈməusis] *n.* 外渗. **-mot·ic** [-ˈmɔtik] *a.*

ex·o·sphere [ˈeksəsfiə] *n.* 【气】外逸层.

ex·o·spore [ˌeksəuˈspɔː] *n.* 【植】①外生孢子; (孢子)外壁. ②分生孢子 (= conidium).

ex·os·to·sis [ˌeksɔsˈtəusis] *n.* (*pl.* *-ses* [-siːz]) 【医】外生骨疣.

ex·o·ter·ic [ˌeksəuˈterik] *a.* ①外面的, 外界的. ②对外行开放的; 公开的. ③易懂的, 通俗的; 大众化的. ~ *doctrine* 公开的教义[主义]. **-cal·ly** *ad.*

ex·o·ther·mic [ˌeksəuˈθəːmik] *a.* 放热的 (= exothermal).

ex·ot·ic [igˈzɔtik] *a.* ①外来的, 外国产的 (*opp.* indigenous). ②异国情调的; 异乎寻常的; 〔口〕奇异的; 吸引人的. ③脱衣舞的. ④【物】极不稳定的,极难俘获的. — *n.* ①舶来品; 外来物; 外来品种; 外来语. ②脱衣舞演员(~ dancer). **-cal·ly** *ad.*

ex·ot·i·ca [igˈzɔtikə] *n.* 〔*pl.*〕 舶来品; 古董, 珍品; 奇风异俗.

ex·ot·i·cism, ex·ot·ism [igˈzɔtisizəm, -tizəm] *n.* ①异国趣味,异国情调. ②外来物; 外来语. ③外国化倾向; 对外国事物的兴趣.

ex·o·tox·in [ˌeksəuˈtɔksin] *n.* 【生化】(菌体)外毒素,外泌毒.

ex·o·tro·pi·a [ˌeksəuˈtrəupiə] *n.* 【医】外斜视.

EXP = experimental.

exp. = expense; expiration; export; exportation; express.

ex·pand [iksˈpænd] *vt.* ①扩大(范围等); 使增加; 扩张; 使膨胀. ②展开,张开. ③扩充, 使发展; 【军】扩编. ④【数】展开. ⑤详述,引伸,写出(缩体). ~ *one's knowledge* 增长知识. ~ *the business* 扩展企业. *birds ~ing its wings* 展开双翼的飞鸟. — *vi.* ①扩大,扩张. ②伸展,张开,延伸; 膨胀 (*opp.* contract). ③扩充; 发展 (into). ④详述,引伸 (*on; upon*). ⑤变得和蔼,感到舒畅. *The saplings have ~ed into trees.* 苗木已长成树. **-er, -or** *n.* 扩张器; 扩管器; 扩口器.

ex·pand·ed [iksˈpændid] *a.* ①膨胀的; 被扩大的; 被延伸的; (花瓣)展开的. ②【印】宽体的 (= extended). ~ *wings* 展开的翅膀. *an ~ program* 一项扩大了的计划. ~ **cinema** 舞台电影, 综合演出〔电影与舞台剧混合的演出〕. ~ **metal** 网形铁. ~ **plastics** 泡沫塑料 (亦称 foamed plastics). ~ **rubber** 多孔橡胶.

ex·panse [iksˈpæns] *n.* ①辽阔,广袤,太空,穹苍. ②膨胀; 扩张,展开. *the boundless ~ of the Pacific* 浩瀚无垠的太平洋. *the blue ~* 碧空.

ex·pan·si·bil·i·ty [iksˌpænsəˈbiliti] *n.* 扩张性; 膨胀性,延伸性.

ex·pan·si·ble [iksˈpænsəbl] *a.* 易扩张的; 能延伸的; 能膨胀的. *the ~ force of ice* 冰的膨胀力.

ex·pan·sile [iksˈpænsail] *a.* 易膨胀的; 膨胀性的. ~ *movement* 膨胀运动.

ex·pan·sion [iksˈpænʃən] *n.* ①张开,伸展. ②扩大; 扩建; 展开; 发展. ③广袤,辽阔. ④扩张物,扩大部分. ⑤(讲题等的)详述, 阐述. ⑥扩张. ⑦【物】膨胀;【数】展开(式). *the ~ of currency* 通货膨胀. *territorial ~* (= ~ of territory) 领土扩张. *arms [armaments, military] ~* 扩张军备. *the rate of ~* 膨胀率. *volume ~* 体积膨胀; 响度扩大. ~ **joint** 【建】伸缩(接)缝. **-ism** *n.* ①(通货的)膨胀论. ②(领土等的)扩张主义. **-ist** ①*n.* 通货膨胀论者,扩张主义者. ②*a.* 扩张主义的.

ex·pan·sion·ar·y [iksˈpænʃənəri] *a.* 引向膨胀的; 扩大性的; 扩张性的.

ex·pan·sive [iksˈpænsiv] *a.* ①易扩张的,膨胀性的. ②辽阔的, 浩瀚的. ③胸襟开阔的, 豁达的; 滔滔不绝的. ④豪华的. ⑤【心】自大狂的; 趾高气扬的. *an ~ forehead* 宽阔的前额. ~ *delusion* 自大狂. **-ly** *ad.* **-ness** *n.*

ex par·te [ˈeks ˈpɑːti] 〔L.〕偏袒的, 单方面的; 片面的.

ex·pa·ti·ate [eksˈpeiʃieit] *vi.* ①细说, 详述 (*on; upon*). ②漫游. **-a·tion** *n.* [eksˌpeiʃiˈeiʃən] **-a·to·ry** *a.*

ex·pa·tri·ate [eksˈpætrieit] *vt.* ①把…逐出国外. ②〔~ oneself〕移居国外, 放弃国籍. — *vi.* 放弃国籍; 移居国外. —[eksˈpætriit] *a.* 被逐出国外的, 移居国外的. — [eksˈpætriit] *n.* 被逐出国外的人,移居国外的人.

ex·pa·tri·a·tion [eksˌpætriˈeiʃən] *n.* ①放逐国外. ②移居国外;【法】脱离原国籍.

ex·pect [iksˈpekt] *vt.* ①期待, 预期, 预料 (*sth.; that*). ②指望[要求]某人做某事 (*to do*), 期望某人如何; 预期某事(发生、出现等). ③(对某人)有…期望[要求] (*sth. of sb.*). ④〔口〕想,料想,以为. *I ~ed you yesterday.* 我当你昨天会来的. *Don't ~ me.* 别指望我 (来) 吧. *I will do what is ~ed of me.* 我当尽我的本分. *I ~ (that) he will come.* 我想他会来的. *I shall not ~ you till I see you.* 便中随时请来好了. ~ *sb. home at six o'clock* 期望某人六点钟回家. *That must be ~ed.* 那是当然的. *I ~ to go there.* 我想到那里去. *Will he come today? — I ~ [don't ~] so.* 他今天会来吗? 我想会来〔不会来〕. — *vi.* ①〔废〕等待, 逗留; ②〔口〕怀孕. ***as one might ~*** 人们预料得到. ***as was ~ed (= as might have been ~ed)*** 果不其然,不出所料,如预期的那样. ***be ~ing*** 〔口〕(不久)要生孩子了 〔*cf.* expectant〕. ***~ an act of God*** 〔美俚〕希望生个孩子.

ex·pect·ance, ex·pect·an·cy [iksˈpectəns, -ənsi] *n.* ①预期,期望,期待. ②期望的东西. *life ~* 估计寿命. ***be on the very tiptoe of ~*** 焦急地等待.

ex·pect·ant [iksˈpectənt] *a.* ①预期的, 期望的; 期待的. ②【法】推定的,有继承权而期待占有的;【医】期待自然复原的. *an ~ attitude* 观望态度. *an ~ mother* 孕妇.

an ～ *method* [*treatment*]【医】自然疗法，期待疗法．— *n.* ①期待者．②预定任用者．③【数】期望值．**-ly** *ad.*

ex·pec·ta·tion [ˌekspekˈteiʃən] *n.* ①期待，期望；所希望的东西．②〔*pl.*〕前程，(发迹、继承遗产的)希望．③估计．④期待疗法．⑤【数】期望值．***against [contrary to]*** ～出乎预料．***answer [meet] sb.'s*** ～ ***(= come up to sb.'s*** ～***)*** 不负所望．***beyond*** ～ 料想不到地．～ ***of life*** 平均寿命 (=life expectancy)．***fall short of [do not come up to] sb.'s*** ～ 辜负期望；使人失望．***have [entertain, cherish] great*** ～***s*** 抱有极大的希望．***in*** ～ 指望中的．***in*** ～ ***of*** 预料着，指望着．***a man of (great)*** ～***s*** 有承受巨大遗产或取得高位希望的人．

ex·pec·ta·tive [iksˈpektətiv] *a.* 期待中的；等待的．

ex·pec·to·rant [iksˈpektərənt] *a.*【医】祛痰的．— *n.* 祛痰剂．

ex·pec·to·rate [eksˈpektəreit] *vt.* 咳出，吐(痰、血、唾液等)．— *vi.* 吐痰，咳痰．～ *phlegm* [*blood*] 吐痰[血]．

ex·pec·to·ra·tion [eksˌpektəˈreiʃən] *n.* ①吐痰，咳出痰．②咳出物；唾液．

ex·pe·di·ence, ex·pe·di·en·cy [iksˈpiːdiəns, -ənsi] *n.* ①便利，方便；得策，上策．②权宜手段[办法]；权宜之计．

ex·pe·di·ent [iksˈpiːdiənt] *a.* ①方便的，便利的，有利的；得当的，适当的．②权宜的，临时的．*Do whatever is* ～．权宜处置，怎么方便就怎么办．*measures* ～ *for public welfare* 有利公共福利的办法．*It is* ～ *that he should go.* 他最好还是走．— *n.* 应急办法，权宜手段．*He is full of [fruitful in]* ～*s.* 他办法多．*a temporary* ～ 临时办法．*resort to an* ～ 使手段．

ex·pe·di·en·tial [iksˌpiːdiˈenʃəl] *a.* 权宜之计的，为了便利的．*an* ～ *policy* 权宜之策．

ex·pe·dite [ˈekspidait] *vt.* ①加快，促进；迅速做好(工作等)．②派遣；发送，急送．— *a.* ①没有阻碍的．②迅速的．③便当的．**-ly** *ad.*

ex·pe·dit·er [ˈekspidaitə] *n.* 快干者，促进派，(企业和国家急要工程的)督办员，计划期成专员．

ex·pe·di·tion [ˌekspiˈdiʃən] *n.* ①远征，征伐；探险．②远征队，探险队．③迅速．*the Northern E-* (中国) 北伐战争．*an arctic* ～ 北极探险．*go [start] on an* ～ 去远征[探险]．*join an* ～参加远征队[探险队]．***go on a fishing*** ～〔美〕摸底，试探一下．***use*** ～ 从速，赶快．***with*** ～ 赶紧．

ex·pe·di·tion·ar·y [ˌekspiˈdiʃənəri] *a.* 远征的；探险的．*an* ～ *force* 远征军．— *n.* 远征队员，探险队员．

ex·pe·di·tious [ˌekspiˈdiʃəs] *a.* 迅速的，急速的，敏捷的，效率高的．*an* ～ *messenger* 急使．～ *measures* 应急手段．**-ly** *ad.* **-ness** *n.*

ex·pel [iksˈpel, eks-] *vt.* ***(-ll-)*** ①赶出；驱逐；开除．②射出(子弹等)，排出(气体等)．*He was expelled from the school.* 他被学校开除了．*bullets expelled from the gun* 从枪中射出的子弹．**-la·ble** *a.* 可驱逐的，应开除的．可击退的．**-ler** *n.* 驱逐者，开除者．**-lee** *n.* 被驱逐出国者．

ex·pel·lant, ex·pel·lent [iksˈpelənt] *a.* 驱逐的，有驱除力的．— *n.* 驱除剂，排毒剂．*mosquito* ～驱蚊药水．

ex·pend [iksˈpend] *vt.* ①使用，花费(金钱、劳力、时间等)；用光，耗尽．②【海】把(暂时不用的绳)绕在桅杆上．— *vi.*〔罕〕花钱．～ ***time [money] in [on]*** 把时间[金钱]花费在…上．★ ～ 与 spend 是同义词，"花钱"普通用 spend money.

ex·pend·a·ble [iksˈpendəbl] *a.* ①可消费的，可消耗的．②【军】消耗性的．～ *equipment* 使用一次的设备．～ *pattern material* 可熔化模型材料．— *n.* 〔常 *pl.*〕(战争中的)消耗品，牺牲者．

ex·pend·i·ture [iksˈpenditʃə] *n.* ①(时间、劳力、金钱等的)支出，花费．②消费；开销；费用，经费．③支出额，消费额．*a useless* ～ *of time* 时间的浪费．*annual* ～岁出．*current* ～ 经常费．*extraordinary* ～ 临时支出．*ordinary* ～ 经常支出．*revenue and* ～ 收支．

ex·pense [iksˈpens] *n.* ①(时间、精力、金钱等的) 消耗，花消，消费．②(无形的) 损失；牺牲．③〔常 *pl.*〕费用；(额外) 开支．④费钱的东西．*household [domestic]* ～*s* 家用．*sundry [miscellaneous]* ～*s* 杂费．*running [current]* ～*s* 经常费．*incidental* ～*s* 临时费．*school* ～*s* 学费．*travelling* ～*s* 旅费．***at a great*** ～ 以巨大费用．***at any*** ～ 无论花费多少．***at his [her, my*** 等***]*** ～ 嘲弄他[她，我等] (*They have a good laugh at his* ～．他们嘲笑他)．***at one's own [public]*** ～ 自[公]费 (*He went abroad at his own* ～．他自费出国)．***at the*** ～ ***of*** 以…为代价；由…出钱；牺牲… (*He attained his goal at the* ～ *of others.* 他牺牲别人来达到自己的目的)．***cut down [curtail] one's*** ～***s*** 节省开支．***free of*** ～ 免费．***go to*** ～ 花钱，用钱，出钱．***meet one's*** ～***s*** 足够开支．***put sb. to*** ～ 使人花钱，使某人负担用费，使破财．***regardless of*** ～ 不计钱财，不惜花费．***spare no*** ～ 不惜花费．～ **account** 支出帐目；报销帐单．～ **allowance** 交际费，额外开支．

ex·pen·sive [iksˈpensiv] *a.* 费钱的；昂贵的，高价的；浪费的，奢侈的(*opp.* inexpensive)．*an* ～ *mode of living* 奢侈的生活方式．*That will come very* ～．那是很费钱的．**-ly** *ad.* **-ness** *n.*

ex·pe·ri·ence [iksˈpiəriəns] *n.* ①经验，体验．②见识，经历，阅历．③〔*pl.*〕【宗】灵性的感受．*E- is the mother of science [wisdom].*〔谚〕经验为学问之母．*an unpleasant* ～一次不愉快的经历．*a man of vast worldly* ～ 富有处世经验的人．*have* ～ *with (persons)* 和 (某些人) 打交道有经验．～ *in teaching* 教学经验．***E- keeps a clear school.*** 经验学校学费高；苦头吃得多，学问也增多．***E- teaches.*** = ***E· does it.*** 经验使人聪明．— *vt.* ①经验，体验．②感受，经历．③(从经验中) 知道，发现．*be thoroughly [poorly]* ～*d in* 在…方面十分有[缺乏]经验．～ *great pleasure* 觉得很快活．**religion**〔美俚〕获得信仰．～ **meeting**【宗】宗教座谈会，灵性交流会；祈祷会．～ **table** (根据人寿保险公司资料拟出的) 寿命估计表，死亡率统计表．～**-a·ble** *a.* **-less** *a.* **-r** *n.*

ex·pe·ri·enced [iksˈpiəriənst] *a.* 有经验的，经验丰富的；老练的，熟练的．*have an* ～ *eye* 有眼光，看得准．

ex·pe·ri·en·tial [iksˌpiəriˈenʃəl] *a.* 经验(上)的，由经验得到的，来自经验的，从经验出发的．～ *philosophy* 经验哲学．**-ism** *n.* 经验主义．**-ist** *n.* 经验主义者．**-ly** *ad.*

ex·per·i·ment [iksˈperimənt] *n.* 实验，试验；尝试 (*of*)．*a scientific* ～ 科学试验，科学仪器设备．*a new* ～ *in education* 教育上的新尝试．～ *farm* 试验农场．～ *station* 试验站．***make [try] an*** ～ ***on [in, with]*** 做…实验．***prove by*** ～ 实验证明．— [-ment] *vi.* 做实验，进行试验；尝试 (*on; with; in*)．**-a·tive** *a.* **-a·tor,-er, -or** *n.* 实验者．

ex·per·i·men·tal [eksˌperiˈmentl] *a.* 实验(上)的；试验性的；经验上的．～ *parthenogenesis* 人工单性生殖，人工孤雌生殖．*an* ～ *farm* 试验农场．～ *psychology* 实验心理学．～ *science* 实验科学．— *n.*〔*pl.*〕实验性的东西．**-ism** *n.* 实验主义，经验主义．**-ist** *n.* 实验者，试验者；实验主义者，经验主义者．**-ize** *vi.* 实验．**-ly** *ad.*

ex·per·i·men·ta·tion [eksˌperimenˈteiʃən] *n.* ①实验，试验．②实验法．

ex·pert [ˈekspəːt] *n.* ①老手，熟手，内行，专家(*in; at*)；技师．②【法】鉴定人．③【军】特等射手．*a language [linguistic]* ～ 语言学专家．*a mining* ～ = *an* ～ *on mining* 矿山技师．— *a.* ①熟练的，老练的．②精巧的，巧妙的 (*in; at; with*)．③专家的，内行的，专门的．*an* ～ *accountant* 会计师．*an* ～ *botanist* 植物学专家．～ *evidence*【法】鉴定人的证明，鉴定．*an* ～ *witness*【法】鉴定者．***be*** ～ ***in [at]*** …在…方面是专家．**-ly** *ad.* **-ness** *n.*

ex·pert·ise [ˌekspəˈtiːz] *n.* ①专门技能；专门知识．②专家评价，鉴定．

ex·pert·ize [ˈekspətaiz] *vt., vi.* (对…)提出专业性意见[鉴定].

ex·per·to cre·di·te [eksˈpəːtəu ˈkrediti:] 〔L.〕相信有经验者的话 (=believe in the expert).

ex·pi·a·ble [ˈekspiəbl] *a.* 可赎的,可抵偿的.

ex·pi·ate [ˈekspieit] *vt.* 赎, 抵偿, 补偿. ～ *oneself* 赎罪,偿罪 ～ *sin (a crime)* 赎罪,赎前愆. **-a·tion** *n.* 赎罪, 消孽, 灭罪 (～ *of the sins of the dead* 超度死者. *in* ～ *of one's sin* 赎罪). **-a·tor** *n.* 赎罪者. **-a·to·ry** *a.* 赎罪的.

ex·pi·ra·tion [ˌekspaiəˈreiʃən] *n.* ①呼出空气, 呼气〔*cf.* inspiration〕; 呼出物, 嘘出的声音. ②〔古〕断气, 死亡. ③终止, 届满, 截止, 满期 (*of*). *at the* ～ *of three years* 三年期满后. *at the* ～ *of a contract* 合同到期后.

ex·pir·a·to·ry [iksˈpaiərətəri] *a.* 吐气的, 呼气的. ～ *movement* 深呼吸运动.

ex·pire [iksˈpaiə, eks-] *vi.* ①吐气, 呼气. ②断气, 死; 消灭. ③满期,届满. *The lease* ～*s in a month.* 租约再过一个月就到期了. — *vt.* 〔罕〕吐出; 排出.

ex·pir·ee [ˌikspaiəˈri:] *n.* = emancipist.

ex·pi·ry [iksˈpaiəri] *n.* ①终止,完满; 满期. ②呼气. ③〔古〕死亡,断气. ***at the* ～ *of the term*** 期满.

ex·pis·cate [eksˈpiskeit] *vt.* 〔Scot.〕查出, 探出; 搜出. **-ca·tion** *n.* **-ca·to·ry** *a.*

ex·plain [iksˈplein] *vt.* ①说明, 阐明; 解释. ②说明…的理由,替…辩解. ～ *one's behaviour* 为自己的行为作辩解. *Please* ～ *yourself.* ①请你把意思说清楚. ②请你讲讲你为什么要那样做. — *vi.* ①说明, 阐明. ②辩解. ～ ***away*** 巧辩过去,把…解释清楚,把…解释过去. ～ ***oneself*** 为自己的行为作解释; 说明自己心意[立场]. ～ **… *as*** … 把…解释为. **-a·ble** *a.* **-er** *n.*

ex·pla·na·tion [ˌekspləˈneiʃən] *n.* ①解释,注释; 说明. ②辩解,剖白. ③(消除误会后)和解. *notes in* ～ 注解. ***by way of*** ～ 作说明. ***come to an*** ～ ***with sb.*** 与人交谈后消除了误会. ***in*** ～ ***of*** 来解释,来说明.

ex·plan·a·tory [iksˈplænətəri] *a.* 解释的,说明的; 辩明的 (*of*). ～ *notes* 注释. ～ **title** 【影】字幕. **-a·to·ri·ly** *ad.* **-a·to·ri·ness** *n.*

ex·plant [eksˈplɑ:nt] *vt.* 【医】外植, 移植. — *n.* 外植体. **-plan·ta·tion** [-plɑ:nˈteiʃən] *n.*

ex·ple·tive [eksˈpli:tiv] *a.* 补足的,附加的; 多余的. — *n.* ①虚词,语助词; (无意义的)惊叹语; 赌咒发誓语. ②填补物,附加物.

ex·ple·to·ry [ˈeksplətəri] *a.* 补充的,附加的,多余的.

ex·pli·ca·ble [ˈeksplikəbl] *a.* 可解释的,可说明的, 可辩明的 (*opp.* inexplicable).

ex·pli·cate [ˈeksplikeit] *vt.* ①(详尽地) 解释, 说明,阐明. ②引伸,发展(概念等).

ex·pli·ca·tion [ˌekspliˈkeiʃən] *n.* ①解释, 说明; (观点的)阐明. ②(花等的)张开.

ex·pli·ca·tion de texte [ˌeksplikɑ:ˈsjɔn də ˈtekst] 〔F.〕对文艺作品各部分的精细分析.

ex·pli·ca·tive, -to·ry [eksˈplikətiv, eksˈplikətəri] *a.* 阐明意义的; 说明的,解释的.

ex·plic·it [iksˈplisit] *a.* ①明白的,明确的 (*opp.* implicit). ②直爽的,不隐讳的. ③显然可见的. ④(租金等)须直接付款的. ～ *definition* 【数】显定义. ～ *cost* 直接以货币支付的成本. ～ *function* 【数】显函数. *an* ～ *statement* 明确的声明. ～ *faith [belief]* 彻底了解教义后的明确的信仰. *be* ～ *in one's statement* 率直陈述. **-ly** *ad.* **-ness** *n.*

ex·plode [iksˈplud] *vt.* ①使爆炸, 爆破; 使爆发. ②破除(迷信等),打破,推翻(学说等). ③发 (p,b,t 等)爆裂音. — *vi.* 爆炸, 爆破, 爆发; 激发, 迅猛地发展. *an exploding population* 激增的人口. *exploding atom* 爆裂原子. ～ *with laughter* 哄笑.

ex·plod·ed [iksˈplәudid] *a.* 爆炸[爆破]了的; (理论、学说等)被推翻的, (迷信等) 被打破的. ～ **view** (机器的)部件分解图.

ex·plod·er [iksˈplәudә] *n.* ①爆炸者, 爆破手. ②爆炸物. ③信管,雷管; 爆炸,爆炸装置; 放炮器; 清除器.

ex·ploit[1] [ˈeksplɔit] *n.* 功绩, 功劳, 勋绩. *the* ～ *of the famous heroes* 著名英雄们的丰功伟绩.

ex·ploit[2] [iksˈplɔit] *vt.* ①利用; 利用…谋私利. ②剥削. ③开发, 开拓. *the* ～*ed class* 被剥削阶级. *the* ～*ing class* 剥削阶级. ～ *an office [a business]* 利用职权(以营私舞弊). ～ *the coal fields* 开采煤田. **-a·ble** *a.* 能利用的, 能开发的; 可剥削的. **-age** *n.* 利用,开发; 剥削. **-er** *n.* 剥削者; 开发者.

ex·ploi·ta·tion [ˌeksplɔiˈteiʃən] *n.* ①利用,非法利用. ②剥削. ③开发,开拓. ④宣传,广告. ～ *of man by man* 人剥削人.

ex·ploi(t·a·)tive [iksˈplɔi(tə)tiv] *a.* ①开发的. ②剥削的; 利用的[特指天然资源的滥用].

ex·plo·ra·tion [ˌeksplɔ:ˈreiʃən] *n.* ①勘探,探测,测定. ②探险; 调查. ③【医】(伤处等的)探查; (伤情)探查术. *pressure* ～ 压力分布测定. *space* ～ 星际探索,宇宙空间探索.

ex·plor·a·tive [eksˈplɔ:rətiv], **ex·plor·a·to·ry** [eksˈplɔ:rətəri] *a.* ①勘探的; 探测的. ②爱探究的, 爱调查的. ～ *operation on stomach* 开腹检查.

ex·plore [iksˈplɔ:] *vt.* ①勘探, 探测; 测定. 在…探险. ②调查. ③【医】探查 (伤处等); 探索, 研究. ～ *the Antarctic regions* 南极地区考察[探险]. — *vi.* 探测; 考察; 探险;【医】探查. *an exploring party [team]* 探测队, 考察队. *an exploring tube* 【医】探测管.

ex·plor·er [iksˈplɔ:rə] ①探测员,探险者. ②探矿机, 探测线圈;【医】探针;【空】搜索机. *an Arctic* ～ 北极探险家.

ex·plo·sim·e·ter [ˌiksplәuˈsimitә] *n.* 爆炸测定计.

ex·plo·sion [iksˈplәuʒən] *n.* ①爆炸,炸裂; 爆炸声. ②扩张,激增; (感情等的)爆发. ③【语】爆破. *air [subsurface]* ～ 空中[地下]爆炸. *nuclear* ～ 核爆炸. *a population* ～ 人口爆炸. ～ **chamber** (发动机的)燃烧室. ～ **gas turbine** 爆燃式燃气轮机.

ex·plo·sive [iksˈplәusiv] *a.* ①爆炸(性)的,爆发(性)的. ②暴躁的. ③【语】爆破音的. ④极易引起争论的. ～ *Gunpowder is* ～. 火药容易爆炸. *an* ～ *sustance* 易爆炸物. *an* ～ *temper* 暴躁易怒的性格. — *n.* ①易爆炸物,炸药; 爆破器材. ②【语】爆破音 (p, b, t, d, k, g 等音). *packages of* ～*s* 炸药包. ～ **bullet** 炸裂弹. ～ **compartment** 炸药室. ～ **engine** 爆发内燃机. ～ **forming** 爆炸成型. ～ **rivet** 炸药铆钉. ～ **train** 导火药, 分段装药,传爆系统. **-ly** *ad.* **-ness** *n.*

ex·po [ˈekspə] *n.* 〔美口〕博览会,展览会.

ex·po·nent [eksˈpәunənt] *n.* ①(学说、理论等的) 代表者,倡导者, 拥护者. ②典型, 样品. ③说明者, 解说员; 演奏者. ④【数】指数; 幂. *an* ～ *of Darwin's theory* 达尔文理论的倡导者. *an* ～ *of self-education* 自学成材的代表. *fractional* ～ 【数】分数指数. — *a.* 阐述的, 说明的,讲解的.

ex·po·nen·tial [ˌekspәuˈnenʃəl] *a.* 指数的, 幂的. ～ *curve* 指数曲线. ～ *function* 指数函数. ～ *sum* 指数和, 三角和. — *n.* 指数. *complex* ～ 复指数. **-ly** *ad.*

ex·po·nen·ti·a·tion [ˌekspәunənʃiˈeiʃən] *n.* 【数】取幂.

ex·port [ˈekspɔ:t] *n.* ①输出,出口. ②出口货; 〔*pl.*〕输出额. ③【无】呼叫, 振铃. *an* ～ *bill* 出口单. ～ *business* 出口事业. ～ *duty [tax]* 出口税. *an excess of* ～*s* 出超. ～ *trade* 出口贸易. ～ *trader* 出口商人. ～ *surplus* 出超. *invisible* ～*s* 无形输出[指船舶、保险、国外投资等的收入]. ***be engaged in*** ～ 做出口贸易. — *a.* 输出的,出口的. — [iksˈpɔ:t] *vt.* ①输出,出口 (*opp.*

import). ②带走,运走,排出. ~ *industrial goods* 输出工业品. *waste products* ~*ed by blood from the tissues* 由血液从身体内排出的废物. — *vi.* 输出物资.

ex·port·a·ble [iksˈpɔːtəbl] *a.* 可出口的.

ex·por·ta·tion [ˌekspɔːˈteiʃən] *n.* ①输出,出口.②出口商品. ③【无】呼叫,振铃.

ex·port·er [iksˈpɔːtə] *n.* 出口商;输出者,输出国.

ex·pos·al [iksˈpəuzəl] *n.* = exposure.

ex·pose [iksˈpəuz] *vt.* ①使暴露, 使曝露 (在日光、风雨等之中). ②【摄】使曝光,使感光. ③陈列(货物),露出. ④揭露, 揭发, 揭穿 (秘密等). ⑤使遭受, 招惹, 招致 (攻击、危险等). ⑥【史】扔弃(婴儿)〔如古代斯巴达人将弱婴弃置户外〕. ~ *one's skin to the sun* 使皮肤晒到太阳. *a situation* ~*d to every wind* 四面受风的地位. *a house* ~*d to the west* 西晒[正西]的房子. ~ *a plot* 揭穿阴谋. ~ *a card* 亮牌. *be* ~*d to danger* 可能遭受危险. ~ *oneself to ridicule* 使自己受嘲弄. ~ **... to** 使…受到;使…朝向….

ex·po·sé [eksˈpəuzei] *n.* 〔F.〕(事实的)陈述;(丑事、真相等的)暴露,揭露.

ex·posed [iksˈpəuzd] *a.* 无掩蔽的;暴露的,显露的. *an* ~ *position* 位置显露. ~ *wiring* 明线. **-ness** *n.*

ex·po·si·tion [ˌekspəˈziʃən] *n.* ①解释, 注释; 解说,说明. ②展览, 陈列; 展览会, 博览会. ③暴露,曝光. ④【剧】展示部分〔阐明情节、人物等〕. ⑤【乐】呈示部.

ex·pos·i·tive [iksˈpɔzitiv] *a.* 讲解的, 评注的, 说明的, 叙述的.

ex·pos·i·tor [iksˈpɔzitə] *n.* 解释者,解说员;说明者,评注者.

ex·pos·i·to·ry [iksˈpɔzitəri] *a.* = expositive.

ex post fac·to[ˈeks pəust ˈfæktəu] 〔L.〕 ①事后的,有追溯效力的,在事后. *an* ~ *law* 有追溯效力的法律.

ex·pos·tu·late [iksˈpɔstjuleit] *vi.* 劝导, 忠告 (*about; for; on*). ~ **with** *sb.* **on [about]** 告戒某人….

ex·pos·tu·la·tion [iksˌpɔstjuˈleiʃən] *n.* 劝导, 忠告.

ex·pos·tu·la·tor [iksˈpɔstjuleitə] *n.* 劝导者, 忠告者.

ex·pos·tu·la·to·ry [iksˈpɔstjulətəri] *a.* 告戒的.

ex·po·sure [iksˈpəuʒə] *n.* ①曝露; 曝晒; 揭发. ②【摄】曝光;胶卷(软片)张数;曝光时间. ③(房屋的)朝向, 方位. ④商品的陈列. ⑤【史】(婴儿的) 曝弃. ~ *meter* 曝光表. *correct* ~ 适度曝光. *There are three* ~*s left on this film.* 这个胶卷剩下三张没拍.

ex·pound [iksˈpaund] *vt.* ①详细说明(理论), 陈述; 为…辩护[解释]. ②解释(圣典). — *vi.* 阐述;解释,说明. **-er** *n.* 陈述者,说明者.

ex·press [iksˈpres] *vt.* ①表示,表现,表达〔*cf.* suppress; impress〕. ②【数】用符号表示. ③榨出, 压出. ④用快邮寄出;〔美〕快运; 快汇. ~ *regret* 表示遗憾. ~ *oneself* 表达自己的意思.~ *oneself (as) satisfied* 表示满意. ~ *oneself in English* 用英语说. ~ *the joice from grapes* 榨葡萄汁. ~ *the letter* 寄快信. — *a.* ①明白表示的;明确的. ②一模一样的. ③专门的,特殊的. ④快速的; 快递的. *an* ~ *provision* (法律)明文条款. *an* ~ *ticket* 快车票. *an* ~ *letter* 〔英〕快信. ~ *post [mail]* 快递邮件. *an* ~ *telegram* 急电. *You are the* ~ *image of your father.* 你跟你父亲一模一样. ***at*** ~ ***speed*** 火急. ***by his*** ~ ***consent*** 经他特别许可. ***for the*** ~ ***purpose of*** 特为, 特意. — *ad.* 乘快车; 用快递方式. — *n.* ①〔英〕专差; 专差急送的文件. ②快运; 快汇;快递(业务). ③快运货物,快汇款. ④快车. ⑤〔美〕快运公司. ***by*** ~ 乘快车;用快递方式. ~**bullet** 猎枪子弹. ~ **company** 〔美〕快运公司. ~ **delivery** 〔英〕快件〔美国叫 special delivery〕. ~ **highway** 高速公路. ~ **rifle** 高速猎枪. ~ **train** 特别快车. ~ **way** = ~ highway. **-a·ble** *a.* = **-i·ble.** **-less** *a.* **-ly** *ad.*

ex·press·age [iksˈpresidʒ] *n.* 〔美〕(小件包裹的) 快递业务;(小额款项的)快汇业务;快递费.

ex·press·i·ble [iksˈpresəbl] *a.* ①可表示的,可表达的. ②可榨出的.

ex·pres·sion [iksˈpreʃən] *n.* ①表现,表示,表达. ②词句;语句,措辞,说法. ③表情,脸色,态度; 腔调,声调. ④【数】式,符号. ⑤(油的)榨出,压榨. ⑥【生】表现度. *emotional* ~ 表情. *a happy* ~妙言. *an odd* ~ 怪话. *the* ~ *of the eye* 眼睛表情, 眼色. *a smiling* ~ 笑脸. ***beyond [past]*** ~ 形容不出,无法表达. ***find*** ~ ***(in)***(在…中)表现出来…,表现在…. ***give*** ~ ***to*** 表达,反映 (*give the fullest* ~ *to their initiative* 充分表现他们的积极性). ~ **mark** 【乐】表示感情色彩的符号. **-al** *a.* 表现的;表情的. **-ism** *n.* 【美】表现主义; 表现派. **-ist** ①*n.* 【美】表现主义者,表现派. ② *a.* 表现派的〔亦作 expressionistic〕. **-less** *a.* 缺乏表情的,呆板的.

ex·pres·sive [iksˈpresiv] *a.* 表现…的, 表示…的, 富于表情的; 意味深长的 (*of*). ~ *eyes* 富于表情的眼睛. *be* ~ *of feeling* 表现感情. *words* ~ *of gratitude* 表示感谢的话. **-ly** *ad.* **-ness** *n.*

ex·pres·siv·i·ty [ˌekspreˈsiviti] *n.* ①善于表达, 表达性. ②【生】基因的表现度.

ex·press·ly [iksˈpresli] *ad.* ①明白地,清楚地. ②特别地,特意地,专门地.

ex·press·man [iksˈpresmæn] *n.* *(pl.* ***-men)*** 运送员,递送员.

ex·pres·so [ekˈspresəu] *n.* = espresso.

ex·pro·pri·ate [eksˈprəuprieit] *vt.* ①没收(财产等); 征用(土地). ②让渡(所有权). ③把(他人财产)转到自己名下, 把…据为已有. ④剥夺…的所有权. *The state* ~*d the king.* 国家没收了国王的财产. **-a·tion** *n.* (土地的)征用. **-a·tor** *n.* 剥夺者,没收者,征用者.

ex·pul·sion [iksˈpʌlʃən] *n.* ①逐出,驱逐,开除.②排气. *the* ~ *of sb. from school* 某人被开除学籍. *the* ~ *of air from the lungs* 从肺中排出空气.

ex·pul·sive [iksˈpʌlsiv] *a.* 驱逐的;开除的.

ex·punc·tion [ikˈspʌŋkʃən] *n.* ①涂抹,拭去;删除,勾销,擦去. ②取消;抹煞. *make some* ~*s* 略加删节.

ex·punge [eksˈpʌndʒ] *vt.* ①涂掉;删去;抹掉. ②消灭,除去 (*from*). ~ *certain passages from the record* 从记录中删去几段.

ex·pur·gate [ˈekspəːgeit] *vt.* 使纯洁,删去(书籍的不妥处). *an* ~*d edition* 删改本;洁本.

ex·pur·ga·tion [ˌekspəːˈgeiʃən] *n.* 删改.

ex·pur·ga·tor [ˈekspəːgeitə] *n.* (书籍的)删改者.

ex·pur·ga·to·ri·al, ex·pur·ga·to·ry [eksˌpəːgəˈtɔːriəl, eksˈpəːgətəri] *a.* 删改的. ***Expurgatory Index*** 禁书目录.

ex·qui·site [ˈekskwizit] *a.* ①精致的,精巧的, 优美的, 优雅的. ②微妙的;细腻的;敏锐的.③(痛苦等)剧烈的, (快乐等)非常的. ~ *works of art* 绝妙的艺术品. *an article of* ~ *workmanship* 精致的工艺品. *a man of* ~ *taste* 趣味优雅的人. ~ *pain* 剧痛. — *n.* 过分讲究穿戴的人. *the young* ~*s* 过于讲究打扮的年轻人. **-ly** *ad.* **-ness** *n.*

exr. = executor.

exrx. = executrix.

ex·san·gui·nate [eksˈsæŋgwineit] *vt.* 【医】给…除血〔驱血〕;使无血. **-na·tion** [eksˌsæŋgwiˈneiʃən] *n.*

ex·san·guine [eksˈsæŋgwin] *a.* 无血的,贫血的.

ex·scind [ekˈsind] *vt.* 切开,割去;除去.

ex·sect [ekˈsekt] *vt.* 切去,割去;根除. **-sec·tion** *n.*

ex·sert [ekˈsəːt] *vt.* 【生】使突出,使伸出.

ex·sert·ed [ekˈsəːtid] *a.* 【生】伸出的.

ex·serv·ice [ˈeksˈsəːvis] *a.* 退役的;退伍的.

ex·serv·ice·man [ˈeksˈsəːvismæn] *n.* *(pl.* ***-men*** [-men]*)* 退役军人,复员军人 〔*cf.* veteran〕.

ex·sic·cate [ˈeksikeit] *vt.* 使干燥, 使干涸. — *vi.* 变干燥,变干涸.

ex·sic·ca·tion [ˌeksiˈkeiʃən] *n.* 干燥(法);除湿作用,干燥作用.
ex·sic·ca·tive [eksˈsikətiv] *a.* 使干燥的,除湿的. —*n.* 干燥剂.
ex·sol·dier [ˈeksˈsəuldʒə] *n.* 退伍[退役]军人.
ex·stip·u·late [eksˈstipjulit] *a.* 【植】无托叶的.
ex·stro·phy [ˈekstrəfi] *n.* 【医】(器官的)外翻〔尤指膀胱外翻〕.
ext. = extension; exterior; external; extinct; extra; extract.
ex·tant [eksˈtænt] *a.* ①现存的,尚存的. ②〔古〕突出的,显著的.
ex·ta·sy [ˈekstəsi] *n.* = ecstasy.
ext. dia. = external diametre 外径.
ex·tem·po·ra·ne·ous [eksˌtempəˈreinjəs] *a.* ①临时作成的,脱口而出的,即席的. ②不用讲稿的,善于即席讲话的. ③临时的,权宜之计的. *an ~ speech* 即席演说. *an ~ shelter* 临时遮蔽所. **-ly** *ad.*
ex·tem·po·ra·ry [iksˈtempərəri] *a.* = extemporaneous. **-rar·i·ly** *ad.* 即席,当场.
ex·tem·po·re [eksˈtempəri] *a.* 临时作成的,无准备的;当场的,即席的. —*ad.* 无准备地,临时地;即席地,当场地. —*n.* 即席之作,即兴诗文.
ex·tem·po·ri·za·tion [eksˌtempəraiˈzeiʃən] *n.* 即席作成;即席之作;即兴诗〔文〕.
ex·tem·po·rize [eksˈtempəraiz] *vt., vi.* 临时制作,当场作成;即席发(言);即兴演奏;即兴创作.
ex·tend [iksˈtend] *vt.* ①伸出(手等);伸展. ②延(期),延长(铁路). ③扩充,扩大,扩展;发挥(力量);延续. ④拉长,拉开(绳子等). ⑤寄与,给予(同情等). ⑥把(速记等)译出;详细写出. ⑦致(祝辞). ⑧提供,赠送(招待券). ⑨〔英〕【法】估价;扣押,没收(土地、房产等). ⑩【军】疏开,散开,展开. ⑪【数】开拓. ⑫使(竞赛者)拼命〔常用被动语态〕. ⑬搀杂(…以增加数量). ⑭会计把(数字)转入另一栏,算出…的总额,写出…的总额. *~ one's visit for a few days longer* 把访问期延长几天. *~ a building* 增建. *~ liquor* 用水掺酒. *~ an invitation [one's congratulations]* 向…发出邀请[致贺]. *Both man and horse ~ed themselves [were ~ed].* 人马竭尽全力. —*vi.* ①伸展;扩充;延长;延伸,绵亘,连续. ②【军】疏开,散开,展开. *The strike ~ed over ten weeks.* 罢工继续了十个星期.
ex·tend·ed [iksˈtendid] *a.* ①伸开的,展开的. ②延长的,继续的. ③(势力)扩大的;扩张的;(意思)引伸的. ④【印】(铅字)宽体的. *an ~ battle line* 拉长了的战线. ~ **bonds** 延期偿付的债券. ~ **formation [order]** 【军】疏开队形. ~ **play** 慢速唱片,密纹唱片. ~ **type** 宽体铅字.
ex·tend·er [iksˈtendə] *n.* ①补充剂,增量剂. ②补充部分,伸延部分.
ex·tend·i·ble, ex·ten·si·ble [iksˈtendəbl, -səbl] *a.* 可伸长的,可延长的,可扩张的. **-ness** *n.*
ex·ten·si·bil·i·ty [iksˌtensəˈbiliti] *n.* 延伸性,伸展性,伸长率,延伸度,可扩张性.
ex·ten·sile [eksˈtensail] *a.* ①【动】可伸展的,(爪子)伸长出来的. ②= extensible.
ex·ten·sion [iksˈtenʃən] *n.* ①伸长,伸展,延长,延伸,扩展,扩大;广度,范围. ②延期;〔美〕(房屋的)增建部分;(铁路等的)延长线;(电话的)分机;增设部分;附加物. ③(语句等的)铺张. ④【物】广延性. ⑤【军】延伸. ⑥【医】牵伸术;伸直;(病变)蔓延、扩展. ⑦【商】延期还债认可书. ⑧【逻】外延 (*opp.* intension); 【数】开拓; 广延性. ⑨会计从另一栏转来或算出的金额. *an ~ of a loan* 借款的延期偿还. *a university ~* 大学的附设部分(如函授班、夜校等). ~ **course** 大学函授班[夜校等]开设的课程. ~ **instrument** 附加仪表,外接仪器. ~ **ladder** (消防用)伸缩梯. ~ **line** 分机线. ~ **set** (电话)分机. ~ **spring** 牵簧. ~ **student** 在大学的附设部分(如函授班、夜校等)接受教育的学生. ~ **table** (可以加装活动板的)伸缩桌. ~ **work** 【军】疏开工事.
ex·ten·sion·al [iksˈtenʃənəl] *a.* ①【逻】外延的. ②延伸的,客观现实的;具体的,事实的.
ex·ten·si·ty [iksˈtensiti] *n.* ①扩张;扩大. ②【心】(空间知觉的)延长性.
ex·ten·sive [iksˈtensiv] *a.* ①广阔的,广大的,广博的;(交易等)大量的;范围广泛的. ②【物】广延的;【逻】外延的. ③【农】粗放的(*opp.* intensive). *~ knowledge* 广博的知识. *an ~ order* 大批定货. *~ reading* 泛读,粗读. *~ cultivation* 粗放的耕作. **-ly** *ad.* **-ness** *n.*
ex·ten·som·e·ter [ˌekstenˈsɔmitə] *n.* 【机】伸长计.
ex·ten·sor [iksˈtensə] *n.* 【解】伸(张)肌 (*opp.* flexor).
ex·tent [iksˈtent] *n.* ①广度,宽度,长度,一大片(土地). ②分量,程度;区域,范围,界限,限度. ③【逻】外延. ④【法】扣押,扣押令;〔美〕临时所有权令;〔英古〕土地估价. *interior ~* 【数】内延. *unlimited ~* 无限空间. *a vast ~ of land* 广大的土地. *the full ~ of the park* 公园的全景. *~ of the error* 误差量. *the ~ of one's patience* 忍耐限度. ***to a certain ~*** 在一定程度上,有点儿,多少,稍稍. ***to a great [large] ~*** 大部分,大大,在很大程度上. ***to some ~*** 在某种程度上,多少,有点儿,有些. ***to such an ~ that*** 达到这样的程度以至. ***to that ~*** 达到那种程度. ***to the ~ of [that]*** 达到…的程度. ***to the utmost [full] ~*** 到极点,极端;尽可能,尽力.
ex·ten·u·ate [iksˈtenjueit] *vt.* ①掩饰(坏事);(用借口来)减轻(罪过). ②〔废〕低估,藐视. ③〔古〕使细弱. *Nothing can ~ his base conduct.* 他的卑鄙行为无可掩饰. *try to ~ one's guilt* 试图减轻罪责.
ex·ten·u·at·ing [eksˈtenjueitiŋ] *a.* 使减轻的,情有可原的. *~ circumstances* 【法】可使罪行减轻的情况. **-ly** *ad.*
ex·ten·u·a·tion [iksˌtenjuˈeiʃən] *n.* ①减轻;酌量. ②【电】降低;衰减. *plead circumstances in ~ of one's guilt* 请求酌情减轻罪行.
ex·ten·u·a·tive [eksˈtenjueitiv] *a.* = extenuating.
ex·ten·u·a·to·ry [iksˈtenjuətəri] *a.* 减轻的;可酌量的. *an ~ defense* 有助于减罪的辩护.
ex·te·ri·or [eksˈtiəriə] *a.* ①外面的,外部的;外表上的,表面的 (*opp.* inward). ②外界的,外在的 (*opp.* internal, intrinsic). ③对外的,外交上的;外国的,外来的,外用的. *an ~ angle* 【数】外角. *~ lines* 【军】外线. *an ~ policy* 对外政策. —*n.* ①外部,外面,表面;外形,外观. ②【影、剧】户外布景;【影】外景(*opp.* interior). *a good man with a rough ~* 外貌粗鲁而内心善良的人. **-ly** *ad.*
ex·te·ri·or·i·ty [eksˌtiəriˈɔriti] *n.* = externality.
ex·te·ri·or·ize [eksˈtiəriəraiz] *vt.* ①= externalize. ②【医】用手术从腹中取出…. **-i·za·tion** *n.*
ex·ter·mi·nate [iksˈtəːmineit] *vt.* 消灭,扑灭,根绝.
ex·ter·mi·na·tion [iksˌtəːmiˈneiʃən] *n.* 根除,灭绝,消灭,扑灭.
ex·ter·mi·na·tor [iksˌtəːmiˈneitə] *n.* ①扑灭者,根绝者. ②根绝物(指杀虫剂等).
ex·ter·mi·na·to·ry [iksˈtəːminətəri] *a.* 扑灭的,绝灭的,根绝的.
ex·tern [ˈekstəːn] *a.* = external. —*n.* ①走读生. ②住院外的医生 (*opp.* intern);住院外的医科实习生.
ex·ter·nal [eksˈtəːnl] *a.* ①外部的,外面的;【哲】外界的,客观的,物质的. ②表面上的 (*opp.* intrinsic);肤浅的,浅薄的;形式上的. ③对外的;外国的;偶然的. ④【医】外用的. *~ diametre* 外径. *~ evidence* 外证. *~ grinding machine* 外圆磨床. *the ~ world* 外界,客观世界. *an ~ loan [debt]* 外债. *~ parameter* 外界参数. *~ temperature* 外界温度,室外温度,周围温度. *~ trade* 对外贸易. *~ remedies* 外用药. —*n.* ①外部,外面. ②〔*pl.*〕外形,外貌,外观;形式;外部情况. *judge by ~s* 从外观上判断. **~-combustion engine** 外燃(发动)机.

~ **examination** 由校外人士主持的考试. ~ **galaxy**【天】河外星系. ~ **respiration**【医】外呼吸. ~ **student** (获准入学并可参加学位考试的) 校外学生. **-ly** *ad.*

ex·ter·nal·ism [eks'tə:nəlizəm] *n.* ①形式主义; 讲究外表,拘泥形式. ②【哲】现象论,外在性,客观性,外在化.

ex·ter·nal·i·ty [ˌekstə:'næliti] *n.* ①外表,外貌,外部事物. ②【哲】客观存在性,外在性,客观性. ③形式主义,讲究外表.

ex·ter·nal·i·za·tion [eksˌtə:nəlai'zeiʃən] *n.* ①客观化,客观性; 外表化,外表性. ②仅具外表形式. ③客观[外表]化的事物.

ex·ter·nal·ize [eks'tə:nəˌlaiz] *vt.* ①赋与…以形体; 使客观化,使形象化,使具体化. ②以外因说明. *Language ~s thought.* 语言使思想具体化. ~ *sb.'s failure* 把某人的失败归咎于外因.

ex·terne [eks'tə:n] *n., a.* = extern.

ex·ter·o·cep·tor [ˌekstərəu'septə] *n.* 外感受器.

ex·ter·ri·to·ri·al [ˌeksteri'tɔ:riəl] *a.* = extraterritorial. **-ly** *ad.*

ex·ter·ri·to·ri·al·i·ty [eksˌteriˌtɔəri'æliti] *n.* = extraterritoriality.

ex·tinct [iks'tiŋkt] *a.* ①已消灭的,(火等)已熄灭的. ②(生物)已绝种的, 已灭绝的. ③(官职等)已废除的. ④【法】已过时效的,失效的. *an ~ family* 已绝嗣的家族. *an ~ species*已灭绝的物种. *an ~ volcano* 死火山. —*vt.* 〔古〕使熄灭; 使灭绝,消灭.

ex·tinc·tion [iks'tiŋkʃən] *n.* ①(权利等的)消灭,(生物等的)灭绝; (火等的)熄灭; (法律等的)废除. ②【物】消光; 自屏; 衰减. ~ *coefficent*【物】消光系数.

ex·tinc·tive [iks'tiŋktiv] *a.* 使熄灭的,使消灭的,使灭绝的.

ex·tin·guish [iks'tiŋgwiʃ] *vt.* ①熄(灯), 灭(火), 熄灭(希望等). ②消灭,扑灭. ③废除; 压制; 使沉默. ④使消声匿迹; 使暗淡; 使失色. ⑤【法】偿清. ⑥使失效, 废除,取消. ~ *one's hope* 使希望破灭. *She was ~ed by her sisters.* 她的姐妹使她相形见绌. ~ *one's opponents with a single word* 一句话把对方说得哑口无言. **-a·ble** *a.* 可熄的; 会绝灭的; 可扑灭的. **-er** *n.* ①消灭者. ②消除器; 熄灯器; 灭火器. **-ment** *n.* 消灭; 熄灭; 绝灭; 偿清.

ex·tir·pate ['ekstə:peit] *vt.* ①根除,根绝,绝灭,扑灭. ②【医】摘出,切除. ~ *weeds [evils]* 根除杂草[弊端]. ~ *superstition* 破除迷信. **-pa·tion** *n.*

ex·tir·pa·tor ['ekstə:ˌpeitə] *n.* 根绝者; 扑灭者.

extn. = extraction.

ex·tol(l) [iks'tɔl] *vt.* 赞美,称赞,颂扬; 吹捧. ~ *sb. to the skies* 把某人捧上天. **-ment** *n.*

ex·tol·ler [iks'tɔlə] *n.* 赞美者; 吹捧者.

ex·tort [iks'tɔ:t] *vt.* ①强夺; 敲诈,勒索 *(from)*; 强求,逼迫. ②曲解,牵强附会. *He ~ed a promise from me.* 他硬要我答应. ~ *a bizzare sense from the few words* 对片言只字作牵强附会的曲解. **-ive** *a.*

ex·tor·tion [iks'tɔ:ʃən] *n.* 强夺; 敲诈,勒索;【法】恐吓取财. **-ar·y, -ate** *a.* 强夺的; 敲诈的,横征暴敛的. **-er, -ist** *n.* 强求者; 敲诈勒索者.

ex·tra ['ekstrə] *a.* ①额外的,附加的,补充的. ②另外收费的. ③特大的; 特优的, 特级的. *an ~ loss* 额外损失. *an ~ train* 加车. *an ~ allowance* 特别津贴. *an ~ edition* 特号, 临时增刊. ~ *news* 号外. ~ *girls [ladies]* 临时女演员. *an ~ hand* 临时工. *Dinner 5 s., wine ~.* 晚餐五先令,酒资在外. *without ~ charge* 不另收费. *It is nothing ~.* 没有什么了不起的. —*n.* ①外加物; 赠品,附加物; 额外人手[津贴]; (报纸的)号外. ②特号; 特级品. ③【影】临时演员〔*cf.* supernumerary〕. ④【板球】额外得分. *a real ~* 上等产品〔广告用语〕. —*ad.* ①额外地,另外地. ② 格外地,非常地. ~ *good wine* 特好葡萄酒. *an ~ special (edition)* 最后版晚报特刊. *be charged ~* 额外收费. *try ~ hard* 特别尽力地试试看. ~**-base hit**【棒球】本垒打. ~ **bold** *n.*【印】超黑体字,特黑体字. ~**-fine** *a.* 超级的,极好的. ~**-hard** *a.* 异常硬的,超硬的. ~**-heavy** *a.* 特重的,超重的,超功率的.

extra- *pref.* 一般加在形容词之前表示"外","额外","格外","临时","超出": *extra*-fine, *extra*territorial.

ex·tra·ca·non·i·cal [ˌekstrəkə'nɔ:nikl] *a.*【宗】未入圣典的; 非钦定著作之列的.

ex·tra·cel·lu·lar [ˌekstrə'seljulə] *a.*【生】细胞外的 (*opp.* intra-cellular).

ex·tract [iks'trækt] *vt.* ①(用力)拔出,抽出. ②分离出,提取,蒸馏出,榨出. ③摘出(要点), 引用. ④推断出. ⑤【数】开(方),求(根). ⑥【军】退(弹). ~ *a tooth* 拔牙. *I could ~ no information from him.* 我从他那里一点儿消息也打听不出来. ~ *the root* 开方,求根. —['eks-] *n.* ①抽出物; 提出物,蒸馏品,精华,汁;【药】浸膏. ②拔萃; 摘录,摘记,抄. ~ *of beef.* = *beef ~* 牛肉汁. ~ *of roses* 玫瑰精. *make ~s* 精选,摘要. **-able, -ible** *a.*

ex·tract·ant [iks'træktənt] *n.* 提取剂,分馏物.

ex·trac·tion [iks'trækʃən] *n.* ①抽出,拔出. ②【化】提取(法); 回收物,提出物,精炼. ③精选,摘要. ④血统,家世,出身. ⑤【数】开方,求根. *spirit of the first ~* 原汁酒. *a man of foreign ~* 外国(血统的)人. *~s from a book* 一本书的内容摘录. *an ~ of 81 percent* 百分之八十一的出粉率,八一粉. *the ~ of root*【数】开方法,求根法. ~ **column** 提取塔. ~ **rates** 提取率.

ex·trac·tive [iks'træktiv] *a.* ①可提出的; 可抽出的. ②消耗资源的. —*n.* = extract. ~ *industries* 天然生产业[矿业、农业、渔业等]. *an ~ process* 抽提[提炼]过程.

ex·trac·tor [iks'træktə] *n.* ①提取者. ②抽出器; 分离器; 精选者;【医】提出器,拔出器;【军】退子钩; 退弹簧,退壳器;【林】推子钩; 脱模工具. *an air ~* 抽气机. *an electrostatic stalk ~* (茶叶) 静电拣梗机. *an ~ groove* 弹底槽.

ex·tra·cur·ric·u·lar, ex·tra·cur·ric·u·lum['ekstrəkə'rikjulə, -ləm] *a.* ①正课以外的. ②(娱乐等)业余的. ③(活动等)逾矩的,本分以外的. ~ *activities* 课外活动. ~ *athletics* 课外体育运动.

ex·tra·dit·a·ble ['ekstrədaitəbl] *a.* 可引渡的.

ex·tra·dite ['ekstrədait] *vt.* 引渡(外国的罪犯); 送还(逃犯). **-tra·di·tion** *n.*

ex·tra·dos [eks'treidɔs] *n.*【建】(拱的)拱背线,外弧面,外曲线 *(opp.* intrados*)*.

ex·tra·es·sen·tial [ˌekstrəi'senʃəl] *a.* 非主要的,本质以外的,非必要的.

ex·tra·ga·lac·tic [ˌekstrəgə'læktik] *a.* 银河系外的,(银)河外的. ~ *nebula [system]* 河外星系,河外星云. ~ *light* 银河以外传来的光.

ex·tra·ju·di·cial [ˌekstrədʒu(:)'diʃəl] *a.* 法院职权以外的,法律外的; 非正式的. **-ly** *ad.*

ex·tra·le·gal [ˌekstrə'li:gəl] *a.* 越出法律范围的; 法外的; 未经法律规定的. **-ly** *ad.*

ex·tra·li·mit·al [ˌekstrə'limitəl] *a.* (有机体、物种等)在某区域内不存在的.

ex·tra·mar·i·tal [ˌekstrə'mæritl] *a.* 婚姻外的,私通的,通奸的.

ex·tra·mun·dane [ˌekstrə'mʌndein] *a.* 超现实世界的,地球以外的; 宇宙外的.

ex·tra·mu·ral [ˌekstrə'mjuərəl] *a.* ①墙外的; 城外的. ②大学外的. ③(非校队参加的)校际比赛的. ~ *activities* 校外活动. ~ *classes* 校外班. ~ *hospital treatment* (医)院外治疗. *an ~ lecture* 为校外编写的讲义; (对校外人作的)公开讲授. ~ *teaching [courses]* 大学对外课程.

ex·tra·ne·ous [eksˈtreinjəs] *a.* ①体外的，外部的；外来的。②范围外的，局外的，无关的，不重要的，枝节的。～ *help [interference]* 外来援助[干涉]。**～ to the subject** 无关本题的。～ **reflex**【心】新异反射。～ **stimul**【心】新异刺激。～ **substance**【医】异物。**-ly** *ad.* **-ness** *n.*

ex·tra·nu·cle·ar [ˌekstrəˈnjuːkliə] *a.*【生、物】核外的。

ex·tra·of·fi·cial [ˌekstrəəˈfiʃəl] *a.* 职务外的，职权外的。

ex·traor·di·na·ry [iksˈtrɔːdnri, -dinəri] *a.* ①非常的，异常的，非凡的，卓绝的。②意外的，离奇的，可惊的；特别的。③[ekstrəˈɔːdinəri] 特命的，特派的；临时的。*a woman of ～ beauty* 非常美丽的女人。*an ～ event* 异常事件。*do ～ things* 干怪事。*～ rays*【物】非常光线。*an ～ session* 临时议会。*an ambassador [envoy] ～* 特使。**-r·i·ly** *ad.* **-ri·ness** *n.*

ex·trap·o·late [eksˈtræpəleit] *vt., vi.* ①【数】外推。②推断；判定。③推测，推论。**-o·la·tion** *n.* 推断，推知；【数】外推法。**-o·la·tive** *a.*

ex·tra·sen·so·ry [ˈekstrəˈsensəri] *a.*【心】超感觉的。*～ perception*【心】超感官知觉，超感觉力。

ex·tra·so·lar [ˌekstrəˈsəulə] *a.* 太阳系以外的。

ex·tra-spe·cial [ˌekstrəˈspeʃəl] *a.*〔口〕异常优秀的，特别优良的。

ex·tra·sys·to·le [ˌekstrəˈsistəliː] *n.*【医】(心脏)额外收缩。**-sys·tol·ic** [-sisˈtɔlik] *a.*

ex·tra·ter·res·tri·al [ˌekstrətəˈrestriəl] *a.* 地球外的，行星际的，大气圈外的，宇宙的。— *n.* 外星人，外星球的生物。

ex·tra·ter·ri·to·ri·al [ˈekstrəˌteriˈtɔːriəl] *a.* 治外法权的。**-ly** *ad.*

ex·tra·ter·ri·to·ri·al·i·ty [ˌekstrəˌteriˌtɔːriˈæliti] *n.* 治外法权。

ex·tra·u·ter·ine [ˌekstrəˈjuːtərain] *a.* 子宫外的。～ *pregnancy* 子宫外孕。

ex·trav·a·gance [iksˈtrævigəns], **ex·trav·a·gan·cy** [-si] *n.* ①奢侈，挥霍，铺张，浪费。②过分(的事情)。③放纵的言行。*check [avoid] ～* 制止[防止]浪费。*with ～* 过度地，过分地。

ex·trav·a·gant [iksˈtrævəgənt] *a.* ①过度的，过分的。②放肆的。③奢侈的，浪费的。④〔古〕游荡的。*an ～ price* 过高的价格。*load sb. with ～ praise* 过分赞扬某人。*～ in conduct* 行为放肆。*～ in dress* 穿着奢华。*～ habit* 奢侈的习惯。

ex·trav·a·gan·za [eksˌtrævəˈgænzə] *n.* ①狂文，狂诗，狂曲，幻想曲，滑稽剧。②狂妄的言行。③(电影、体育比赛等)铺张华丽的表演。

ex·trav·a·gate [iksˈtrævəgeit] *vi.*〔罕〕漂泊，放浪；越轨。

ex·trav·a·sate [eksˈtrævəseit] *vt.* 使(血液等由脉管中)渗出；使(熔岩等)溢出。*～d blood* 淤血。— *vi.* 外渗，外沉，溢出。— *n.* 渗出液。

ex·trav·a·sa·tion [eksˌtrævəˈseiʃən] *n.* ①【医】外渗，外沉；外渗液；溢血。②【地】熔岩外喷；(熔岩等的)溢出。

ex·tra·vas·cu·lar [ˌekstrəˈvæskjulə] *a.* 脉管外的；血管外的；导管外的。

ex·tra·ve·hic·u·lar [ˌekstrəviˈhikjulə] *a.* (宇航员)在宇宙飞船外部活动(使用)的；宇宙飞船外的。

ex·tra·ver·sion [ˌekstrəˈvəːʒən] *n.* = extroversion.

ex·tra·vert [ˈekstrəvəːt] *n.* = extrovert.

ex·tre·ma [iksˈtriːmə] extremum 的复数。

ex·tre·mal [iksˈtriːməl] *n.*【数】极值曲线，致极函数。

ex·treme [iksˈtriːm] *a.* ①极端的；过激的 (*opp.* moderate)。②极限的，非常的。③尽头的，末端的。④〔古〕最后的，临终的。*the ～ end of a rope* 绳索的末端。*～ measures* 极端手段。*～ old age* 极高龄。*an ～ case* 极端的例子。*～ unction*【天主】临终涂油礼。*～ value*【数】极值。*in one's ～ moments* 临终时刻。*the ～ hour of life* 临终。*the ～ lefts* 极左派。*the ～ penalty (of law)* 极刑。—*n.* ①极端；末端。②〔*pl.*〕两极端。③〔*pl.*〕困境。④【数】极限值，外项；【逻】(三段论法结论中的)小词或大词〔*cf.* middle〕。*the ～s of fortune* 盛衰荣枯。**be in ～s** 处困境。*Extremes meet.* 两极相通，物极必反。**go from one ～ to the other** 从一个极端转到另一个极端。**go to ～s = run to an ～** 走极端。**go to the ～ of** 采用…的极端手段。**in (the) ～** 极端，非常，很。**-ness** *n.*

ex·treme·ly [iksˈtriːmli] *ad.* 极端地，非常地。～ *high frequency*【无】甚高频。

ex·trem·ism [iksˈtriːmizəm] *n.* 极端主义。

ex·trem·ist [iksˈtriːmist] *n.* 过激主义者，极端分子。— *a.* 极端主义的，过激论的。

ex·trem·i·ty [iksˈtremiti] *n.* ①末端，尽头；极端，极度。②〔常 *pl.*〕困迫，绝境。③〔常 *pl.*〕最后手段，非常手段。④最后；〔常 *pl.*〕临终。⑤肢，手，足。*at the ～ of* 在…的尖端[末端]。*be in dire ～* 极端困迫。*be reduced [driven] to (the last) ～ [extremities]* 陷入困境。*resist to the last ～* 反抗到底，抵抗到最后。*the extremities* (人的)四肢，手足。**expect the ～** 作赴死准备，作万一准备。**proceed [go] to extremities** 采取最后手段。

ex·tre·mum [ikˈstriːməm] *n.* (*pl.* **-tre·ma** [-mə])【数】极值。

ex·tri·ca·ble [ˈekstrikəbl] *a.* 摆脱得了的；能救出的；能脱险的 (*opp.* inextricable)。

ex·tri·cate [ˈekstrikeit] *vt.* ①救出，使脱离 *(from)*。②【化】放出，游离。③分辨出。～ **oneself [itself] from [out of]** 从…中脱离，摆脱。

ex·tri·ca·tion [ˌekstriˈkeiʃən] *n.* ①救出，脱出。②【化】游离，放出。

ex·tri·ca·tor [ˈekstriˌkeitə] *n.* ①救出者，解脱者。②【化】游离器。

ex·trin·sic [eksˈtrinsik] *a.* ①外在的，非本质的 (*opp.* intrinsic, essential)。②附带的，外来的，外赋的；体外的。*That's something ～ to the subject.* 那是对本题无关宏旨的东西。**-cal·ly** *ad.*

extro- *pref.* = extra.

ex·trorse [eksˈtrɔːs] *a.*【植】(花药)向外的，外向的，外倾的 (*opp.* introrse)。**-ly** *ad.*

ex·tro·ver·sion [ˌekstrəuˈvəːʃən] *n.* (*opp.* introversion)【医】外翻；【心】外向性。**-versive** *a.* (*opp.* introversive)。

ex·tro·vert [ˈekstrəuvəːt] *n.* (*opp.* introvert)【心】外向性格的人。— *a.* 外向性的。— *vt.* 使成外向性格。— *vi.* 变成外向性格。**-ish** *a.* 有点外向性。

ex·trude [eksˈtruːd] *vt.* ①挤压，模压。②使(熔浆等)流出。③逐出 *(from)*。～ *tubing* 自模型内挤压出管子。— *vi.* 突出，伸出；挤压成形。**-r** *n.* 挤压机。

ex·tru·sion [eksˈtruːʒən] *n.* ①挤压，挤压成形；挤出。②逐出。③【地】(熔岩的)喷出；突出，伸出。～ **moulding** 挤压模塑法。～ **press** 挤压机。～ **stress** (塑性变形的)挤压应力。

ex·tru·sive [eksˈtruːsiv] *a.* ①挤出的；冲出的；迸出的；势在冲出的。②【地】喷出的；火山的。～ *rock* 火山岩。— *n.* 喷出岩体。

ex·tu·bate [eksˈtjuːbeit] *vt.* 从(身体某部)除管〔如气管〕。**-ba·tion** *n.*【医】除管法。

ex·u·ber·ance [igˈzjuːbərəns], **ex·u·ber·an·cy** [-si] *n.* ①繁茂，丰富。②充沛，充溢。～ *of foliage* 枝叶繁茂。

ex·u·ber·ant [igˈzjuːbərənt] *a.* ①茂盛的，繁茂的，丰富的。②(感情等)充溢的；(活力)充沛的，(精神)旺盛的；(词藻)过于华丽的，极度的。～ *growth* 繁茂生长。～ *spirits* 兴高采烈。*an ～ imagination* 丰富的想象。**-ly** *ad.*

ex·u·ber·ate [igˈzjuːbəreit] *vi.* ①充溢，富于，充满；显得茂盛。②沉溺 (in)。

ex•u•date [ˈeksjudeit] *n.* 渗出物,渗出液,流出物. *cellular* ~ 细胞渗出液.

ex•u•da•tion [ˌeksjuːˈdeiʃən] ①渗出(液),分泌(物),流出(物),溢泌(物). ②【冶】(跑铁水)胀箱;(打箱过早)跑火. *tin* ~ 锡汗.

ex•u•da•tive [igˈzjuːdətiv] *a.* 渗出的,流出的,溢泌的.

ex•ude [igˈzjuːd] *vt.* ①使渗出; 使流出. ②使发散. ~ *sweat* 流汗. — *vi.* ①渗出;流出. ②发散.

ex•ult [igˈzʌlt] *vi.* 欢跃;狂喜. ~ *at [in] a triumph* 为胜利而狂喜. *She* ~*ed to find that she had succeeded.* 她为自己的大功告成而狂喜. *an* ~*ing heart* 欢跃[得意]的心情.

ex•ult•ance, ex•ult•an•cy [igˈzʌltəns, -ənsi] *n.* = exultation.

ex•ult•ant [igˈzʌltənt] *a.* 兴高采烈的,欢欣鼓舞的;耀武扬威的. **-ly** *ad.*

ex•ul•ta•tion [ˌegzʌlˈteiʃən] *n.* 大喜,狂喜,欢跃;得意.

ex•um•brel•la [ˈeksʌmˈbrelə] *n.* 【动】上伞(水母伞顶部).

ex•urb [ˈegzəːb, ˈeksəːb] *n.* 城市远郊富裕阶层住宅区. **-an** *a.* 城市远郊的.

ex•ur•ban•ite [egˈzəːbənait] *n.* 城市远郊富裕居民〔尤指办公在市内,住在市郊的商人等〕. — *a.* 城市远郊的;城市远郊居民的;有城市远郊特点的.

ex•ur•bi•a [egˈzəːbiə] *n.* (总称)城市远郊.

ex•u•vi•ae [igˈzjuːviiː] *n.* 〔*pl.*〕蜕(蛇、蝉等的脱下的皮壳);〔喻〕空壳,残骸.

ex•u•vi•al [igˈzjuːvjəl] *a.* 蜕皮性的. ~ **glands**【动】蜕皮腺.

ex•u•vi•ate [igˈzjuːvieit] *vi., vt.* 脱(壳),蜕(皮).

ex•u•vi•a•tion [igˌzjuːviˈeiʃən] *n.* ①脱壳,蜕皮,脱皮.蝉蜕;蜕下的皮[壳等].

ex•vo•to [eksˈvəutəu] 〔L.〕 *n.* 还愿的奉献物. — *a.* 许愿的,还愿的.

ex•works [eksˈwəːks] *ad.* 〔口〕出厂(指出厂价格或价值等). *put down the price* ~ 压低出厂价格.

exx. = examples.

-ey *suf.* (用于末字母为 -y 的词后) = -y[1]: clay*ey*.

ey•as [ˈaiəs] *n.* (巢中的)雏鸟;雏鹰.

eye [ai] *n.* (*pl.* ~s 〔古〕 ***ey•en*** [ˈaiən]). ①眼睛,目. *blind in one* ~ = *lose an* ~ 一目失明. *compound* ~*s* (昆虫的)复眼. *the naked* ~ 肉眼. *Where are your* ~*s?* 难道你看不见? *His* ~*s are bigger than his belly.* 他眼馋肚饱. *What the* ~ *does not see, the heart does not grieve over.* 眼不见,心不烦. *Eyes, front!*【军】向前看! *Eyes left [right]!*【军】向左[右]看齐! ②〔常 *pl.*〕眼神,眼睛的表情. ③视觉,视力;眼力,鉴别力,眼光,观察力. *have a straight* ~ 能看出某物是否直或正的眼力. *have an* ~ *for the beautiful* 有审美眼光. *have an* ~ *in one's head* 颇有眼光. ④见解,观点;判断. *in sb.'s* ~ 照某人看来,按某人的看法. *in the* ~*(s) of (the) law* 从法律观点上看. ⑤注视,注意,注目. *keep one's* ~ *on the picture* 盯着图画看. *keep one's [both]* ~*s open* 提防,当心. ⑥眼状物;洞;孔;环;圈;(鱼卵、虫卵的)小黑点;色斑;(孔雀的)翎眼;眼状斑点;针眼;锚眼;钩眼;靶心;(索端的)索眼;圆窗. ⑦【气】风眼,风吹来的方向. *the* ~ *of a hurricane* 飓风眼,飓风中心部的平静区域. ⑧〔美俚〕侦探;私人侦探. ⑨【植】(马铃薯等的)芽眼,花心;(菊科的)花盘;【微】眼点;【物】光电池,光电管. *a magic* ~ 电眼,电子射线管. ***All my* ~ *(and Betty Martin) = all the eye*** 或 ***all in the eye*** 〔英〕瞎说,胡扯,无聊. ***an evil*** ~ 狠毒的眼光. ***an* ~ *for an* ~ = ~ *for* ~** 以眼还眼;报复. ***an* ~ *in the sky*** 〔美俚〕侦察卫星. ***apply the blind*** ~ 假装没看见. ***be all* ~*s*** 非常留意,注视. ***be bright in the*** ~〔口〕喝醉. ***before [under] sb.'s very* ~*s*** 当某人面前. ***black sb.'s* ~ = *give sb. a black*** ~ 把某人的眼眶打青. ***by the*** ~ 用眼睛估计,凭眼力. ***cast an* ~ *at [over] sth.*** 对某物随便看一眼. ***cast sheep's eyes on sb.*** 对某人飞媚眼. ***catch sb.'s* ~*(s)*** 引某人注意. ***catch [strike] the*** ~ 显眼. ***clap [set, lay]* ~*s on*** 看到. ***close one's eyes*** 死,逝世. ***close [shut] one's* ~*s to*** 拒绝注意. ***cry one's* ~*s out*** 哭得很伤心. ***do sb. in the*** ~ 〔俚〕骗人,愚弄人. ***dust the* ~*s of*** 欺骗,蒙蔽. ***easy as my*** ~ 易如反掌. ***easy on the* ~*s*** 〔俚〕悦目的,诱人的. ***feast one's* ~*s on*** 饱眼福. ***fix one's* ~ *on*** 盯,凝视. ***get [have] one's* ~ *well in*** (射击等)看得很准,(运动员)能用眼跟上球的方向. ***give an* ~ *to*** 照看,注意. ***give sb. the (glad)*** ~ 〔美〕对人做媚眼. ***half an*** ~ 随便一看 *(if you had half an* ~ 假若你稍加注意) ***have all one's* ~*s about*** 谨防,当心. ***have an* ~ *to*** ①照看,注意. ②以…为目的. ***have an* ~ *on [upon]*** 照看,注意. ***have* ~*s at the back of one's head*** 能看到一切. ***have* ~*s for*** 〔口〕对…极感兴趣;注意. ***have in one's*** ~ 心目中有…;考虑. ***hold the public*** ~ 吸引世人眼目. ***in a pig's*** ~ 〔美俚〕永不,决不. ***in sb.'s mind's*** ~ 在想象中,在心目中. ***in the* ~ *of the wind = in the wind's*** ~ 【海】逆风. ***in the* ~*s of = in one's* ~*s*** 在…的心目中,在…的眼里. ***in the public*** ~ 常公开露面〔在电视或报纸上〕;人人皆知. ***keep an [one's]* ~ *on [upon] = have one's* ~*s on*** ①照看. ②密切注意. ***keep an* ~ *[one's* ~*s] out for*** 注意,记住. ***keep one's* ~*s peeled [open, skinned]*** 时刻提防. ***look sb. in the*** ~ 无畏惧[无愧]地正视某人. ***make* ~*s at sb.*** 向某人送秋波;对…使眼色. ***make sb. open his* ~*s*** 使人吃惊. ***meet sb.'s* ~*s*** (偶尔)引起某人注意. ***Mind your* ~!** 〔口〕注意!当心! ***My* ~*(s)!*** 〔俚〕天啦!嗳唷!〔表示赞叹,反对,惊讶〕. ***never take one's* ~*s off*** 目不转睛. ***one's* ~*s draw [gather, pick] straw*** 〔废〕昏昏欲睡. ***open sb's* ~*s (to)*** 使某人认清. ***put a finger in one's*** ~ 哭. ***put one's* ~ *together*** 入睡. ***run one's* ~*s through [over]*** 浏览. ***see* ~ *to* ~ *with*** 跟…意见一致. ***see with one's own* ~*s*** 亲眼看见. ***set an* ~ *by*** 对…非常喜爱;极尊重. ***spit in the* ~ *of*** 藐视,蔑视. ***the blind man's* ~*s*** 瞎子用的拐杖. ***the* ~ *of day [the morning, heaven]*** 〔诗〕太阳. ***the* ~*s of night [heaven]*** 〔诗〕星. ***the* ~*s of a ship*** 船头;锚索眼. ***to one's mind's*** ~ 在心眼儿上,在心目中,在想象中. ***to the*** ~ ①从表面上看来. ②当面,公然. ***turn a [one's] blind* ~ *to*** 对…熟视无睹. ***up to one's [the]* ~*s in*** ①极忙,埋头(工作). ②深陷(债务中). ***wipe one's* ~*s*** ①抢在某人前面打别人瞄准的猎物. ②使人看到自己的狂妄. ***with all one's* ~*s*** 拼命,仔细. ***with an* ~ *on [to]*** 指望着,着眼于,为了要…. ***with dark [cold, dry]* ~*s*** 冷眼. ***with half an*** ~ 一看就…(不用细看) (*That can be seen with half an* ~. 那是显而易见的事). ***with one's* ~*s open*** ①明明知道. ②注意. ***with one's* ~*s shut*** 不注意,胡乱地. ***with open* ~*s*** 明知故犯. ***worth a Jew's*** ~ 〔古〕极为贵重. — *vt.* **(~d; ey(e)•ing)** ①看,观看;偷看;盯着看,注视,凝视. ②在…打眼. ~ *sb. askance* 用眼睛瞟人,斜着眼睛看人. ~ *narrowly* 细看. ~ *sb. jealously [with jealousy]* 嫉视某人. ~ *a needle* 打针眼. ~**ball** ① *n.* 眼球;瞳子 (~*ball to* ~*ball* 面对面的[地]). ② *vt.* 〔美俚〕打量. ~ **bank**【医】眼库. ~ **bath** 洗眼杯. ~**beam** 〔古〕目光. ~**bolt**【机】有眼螺栓,吊环螺栓. ~**bright**【植】小米草〔过去认为对眼疾具有疗效〕. ~**brow** ① *n.* 眉毛;【建】滴水;窗眉;【纺】飞花 (*knit the* ~*brows* 皱眉头. *raise the* ~*-brow* 扬起眉毛〔怀疑、吃惊的表情〕. ② *vt.* (皱起眉头)瞪 (~*brow sb. out of the room* 把(某人)瞪出房间). ~**-catcher** *n.* 特别引人注目的事物,醒目广告. ~**-catching** *a.* 〔美口〕引人注目的. ~ **chart** 视力检验表. ~ **cup** =~ bath. ~**dropper** *n.*【医】滴管. ~**end** *n.* 有眼端. ~**fidelity** 映象保真性,保真度. ~**glass**

①镜片；〔pl.〕眼镜，夹鼻眼镜．②(望远镜等装置中的)目镜．③洗眼杯．~-grabber 引人注目的事物．~ graffing 芽眼嫁接法．~hole 眼窝；窥视孔；(针等的)眼．~joint n. 眼榫接合．~lash 睫毛．~let, ~lethole 孔眼；小孔；(皮鞋等的)带眼；金属套圈；窥视孔；枪眼，炮眼，(孔眼)锁缝．— vt. 打小孔．~letting 用空心铆钉接合板材．~lid 眼睑；可调节喷口的半圆形调节片；可调节喷口 (*hang (on) by the ~lids* 一发千钧．*in the batting of an ~lid* 转瞬间．*lower ~lid* 下眼睑．*upper ~lid* 上眼睑)．~ liner 描眼膏．~ measurement 目测．~-mo 携带式(电视)摄像机．~-opener n. ①使人惊奇的事物，有启发的事物，迷人的人[物]．②〔美俚〕起床喝的醒眼酒．~-opening a. 使人惊奇的，有启发性的．~-piece 目镜．~-popping〔美〕使人吃惊的．~reach = ~shot. ~ rhyme 不完全韵〔拼写相近，但发音各异的词，如 lone, none〕．~-servant, ~-server〔古〕当面勤快而背地懒惰的佣人．~-service〔古〕①当面勤快而背地偷懒的帮佣．②敬仰的目光．~shade 眼罩．~ shadow 眼睑膏．~shot 眼界，视野；视力，眼力；一瞥，见解 (*beyond ~shot = out of ~shot* 在视界之外，不可见的地方．*in [within] ~shot* 在视界之内)．~-sight 视觉，视力，眼力；眼界，视野；见解，观察．~ socket n. 眼窝．~some a. 〔美〕媚人的，可爱的．~sore 刺眼的东西．~spot【动】①眼点．②眼状色斑．~-stalk【动】眼柄．~strain 眼疲劳．~strings 眼筋肉，眼神经．~tooth *(pl. ~teeth)* 上颚犬牙 (*cut one's ~teeth* 懂事，长大．*draw sb.'s ~teeth* 挫人的傲气)．~wall【气】眼壁〔飓风风眼外围的漏斗状云层 (= wall cloud)．~wash ①眼药水．②〔俚〕奉承；欺诈．~water 眼药，洗眼药水；泪．~wink 眨眼；一瞬；瞥见．~winker 睫毛，落入眼中的微粒．~witness 目击者，见证人．-less a. ①无眼的，瞎的．②盲目的，卤莽的．

eyed [aid] a. ①…眼的．②有孔眼的．③有眼状花纹的．④有(某种特点的)眼睛的；有眼状斑纹的．*blue-~* 蓝眼睛的．

eye·ful [ˈaiful] n. ①满眼．②被完全看到的东西．③〔俚〕值得一看的人[物]．*get [have] an ~*〔口〕好好看一下，看个够．*The bottle cap popped off and he got an ~ of beer* 瓶盖噗地一声掉了，他看见一满瓶啤酒．

ey·en [ˈaiən] n. eye 的古体和方言体的复数．

Eye·tie [ˈaiti] n. 〔英俚〕意大利人 — a. 意大利的〔带贬义，源于 Italian 的头两个字母〕．

eyot [eit, ˈeiət] n. 〔英方〕= ait.

eyre [ɛə] n.【史】巡回；巡回法院．*judices in ~* 巡回法官．

ey·rie, ey·ry [ˈɛəri] n. = aerie.

ey·rir [ˈeiriə] n. (pl. **au·rar** [ˈaurɑː]) 奥拉〔冰岛货币名，等于 1/100 克朗〕．

EZ = ①eastern zone 东区．②electrical zero【电】电零点．

E·ze·ki·el [iˈziːkjəl] n. ①伊齐基尔〔姓氏〕．②【圣】以西结〔希伯来预言家〕．③【圣】《以西结书》(旧约)．

Ez·ra [ˈezrə] n. ①【圣】以斯拉〔纪元前六世纪希伯来预言家〕．②【圣】《以斯拉书》(旧约)．③男子名．

F

F, f [ef] *(pl. F's, f's* [efs]*)* ①英语字母表第六字母．②第六．③〔F〕【乐】F 音，F 调．④〔F〕F 字形．⑤〔F.〕〔美〕(学业成绩)劣，不及格 (failure) 的符号．⑥【摄】光圈数 (f-number) 的符号．**F holes** (提琴上的) F 形孔眼．**F sharp** (F#) 升 F 调．

F = ①【化】fluorine. ②【生】(generation of) filial offspring;【植】子代〔F_1 杂种子 1 代．F_2 杂种子 2 代〕;【动】世代〔*cf.* f = force〕．

F. = ① Fahrenheit. ② Father. ③ Fellow. ④ Final (dividend). ⑤France. ⑥ French; Friday.

F,F/, f, f:, f/, f., *etc.* 见 *f-number* 条．

f. = and the following (page) *(pl. ff.)*.

f. = ①farad. ②farthing. ③【美军】fast. ④ fathom. ⑤ feet. ⑥feminine. ⑦field. ⑧ florin. ⑨folio. ⑩following. ⑪foot. ⑫*forte*.【棒球】⑬foul(s). ⑭franc(s). ⑮ from.

FA, F.A. = ①field artillery 野战炮；野战炮兵．②fine arts 美术．③Football Association (英国) 足球协会．④field ambulance 战地救护车；野战救护队．⑤first aid【医】(对病人的)急救．

fa [fɑː] n.【乐】全音阶的长音阶第四音．

f.a.a., FAA = free of all average 一切海损均不赔偿．

F.A.A. = Fleet Air Arm〔英〕海军航空兵．

FAA = Federal Aviation Administration〔美〕联邦航空局．

F.A.A.A.S. = Fellow of the American Association for the Advancement of Science 美国科学促进会会员．

F.A.A.S/C = Free from All Average Seizure and Capture 因船只被扣留与被掳掠而造成的损失及一切海损均不赔偿．

F.A.A.S/C *including* **R.D.C.** = Free from All Average Seizure and Capture including Running Down Clause 因船只被扣留与被掳掠而造成的损失及一切海损 (包括碰撞损失)均不赔偿．

FAB = Foreign Affairs Bureau 外事局．

fab [fæb] a. 〔口〕惊人的，极好的，难以置信的〔fabulous 的缩略〕．

fa·ba·ceous [fəˈbeiʃəs] a. ①【植】豆科植物的．②(蚕)豆状的．

Fa·bi·an [ˈfeibjən] a. ①古罗马大将费边 (Fabius) 式的，使敌人疲于奔命的，以逸待劳的，持久的．(*cf.* Fabius)．②费边社(社员)的．~ **society** (1884 在伦敦成立，主张以缓进的方法实现社会主义的) 费边社．— n. 费边社社员；费边主义者．**-ism** n. 费边主义；持久战术．**-ist** ① n. 费边主义者．② a. 费边主义的．

Fa·bi·us [ˈfeibjəs] n. 费比乌斯 (费边)〔?—公元前203年，罗马大将，以避免与敌作战和采取拖延政策的战略使敌师老无功，终于战胜迦太基军队〕．

fa·ble [ˈfeibl] n. ①寓言，童话〔*cf.* allegory, parable〕．②〔集合词〕神话，传说．③荒唐故事，无稽之谈．④〔古〕(史诗、剧本等的) 情节．⑤人人谈论的话题．*celebrated in ~* 传闻中大名鼎鼎的．**Aesop's ~s** 伊索寓言．**old wive's ~s** 闲话，奶奶经．— vi. 讲故事，编寓言．— vt. 虚构(故事)，杜撰，煞有介事地讲．**-r** n. = fabulist.

fa·bled [ˈfeibld] a. ①寓言中的，故事中有名的．②虚构的，荒唐无稽的；神话般的，传说式的．*a ~ chest of gold* 虚构的所谓金箱．*a ~ goddess* 传说中的女神．

fab·li·au [ˈfæbliəu] n. (pl. **-aux** [-ˌəuz]) (中世纪法国文学体裁) 诗体短篇小说，韵文故事．

Fa·bre [ˈfɑːbə], **J. H.** 法布尔〔1823—1915，法国昆

虫学家〕.

fab·ric [ˈfæbrik] *n.* ①构造物,建筑物;工厂;结构;(社会等的)组织;【地】组构. ②编织品,织物;纤维品;织法;质地. *aeroplane* ~【空】飞机蒙布. *the* ~ *of society* =*the social* ~ 社会组织. *a cloth of exquisite* ~ 织法精美的布. *soil* ~ 土壤结构. *synthetic* ~*s* 合成纤维织物. *woolen [silk]* ~*s* 毛[丝]织品. ~ **glove** 毛线手套. ~**proofing** 布上涂胶. **-a·ble** *a.* 可成型的,可塑造的.

fab·ri·cant [ˈfæbrikənt] *n.* 〔罕〕厂商,制造商,工厂主.

fab·ri·cate [ˈfæbrikeit] *vt.* ①构成;组成;〔美〕制作,建造. ②捏造,伪造,杜撰. ③创立(理论等). ~ *a document* 伪造文书. ~ *new theories* 创立新理论. ~ *automobiles* 制造汽车. *a* ~*d building* 装配式房屋. *a* ~*d ship* 组合船. **-ca·tion** [ˌfæbriˈkeiʃən] *n.* **-ca·tor** *n.* ①捏造者. ②装配工;修整工. ③金属加工厂.

Fab·ri·coid, Fab·ri·koid [ˈfæbrikɔid] *n.* 〔商标名〕(做书面等用的)漆布,人造革,防雨布.

fab·roil [ˈfæbrɔil] *n.* 纤维胶木.

Fab. Soc. = Fabian Society〔英〕费边社.

fab·u·list [ˈfæbjulist] *n.* ①寓言作家. ②虚构情节的人.

fab·u·los·i·ty [ˌfæbjuˈlɔsiti] *n.* ①神话;寓言性质;虚构性,无稽. ②〔古〕耸人听闻之言.

fab·u·lous [ˈfæbjuləs] *a.* ①寓言般的. ②传说上的,神话中的. ③荒唐无稽的;难以相信的;无比的,非常的. ④编写寓言的. ⑤〔口〕极好的. *a* ~ *price* (近乎荒唐的)非常昂贵的价格. ~ *wealth* 巨富. *a* ~ *writer* 寓言作家. *a* ~ *bird* 一种传说中的鸟. ~ **age** (一个国家开国初期的)神话时代. **-ly** *ad.* **-ness** *n.*

fac. = ①facsimile. ②factor. ③factory. ④faculty.

fa·cade, fa·çade [fəˈsɑːd] *n.* ①【建】正面. ②外表,外观;虚伪,浮面,(掩饰真相的)门面. *maintain a* ~ *of wealth* 保持富有的门面.

face [feis] *n.* ①脸,面孔;面貌,样子;面子,威信. ②愁容,苦脸;〔口〕老面皮,厚脸皮. ③外观,形势,局面. ④面前,眼前. ⑤面(部),表面;前面,正面;【物】荧光面;(钟表等的)字盘;(器具的)使用面. ⑥【军】方阵的一面. ⑦【商】票面,额面;(文件的)字面. ⑧【印】版面;【矿】(煤矿等的)采掘面;(矿石等的)晶面;【机】(刀具的)切削面. ⑨面部化妆. ⑩面具. *a sad* ~ 愁容. *a smiling* ~ 笑脸. *save one's* ~ 保全面子. *lose one's* ~ 丢脸. *the right [wrong]* ~ 表[反]面. *with a smile on one's* ~ 面带笑容. *the* ~ *of the note* 票面额. *a* ~ *of placid contentment* 一片宁静而自得其乐的外表. *the funny* ~*s* 假面具〔儿童玩具〕. *get one's* ~ *on* 作好面部化妆. ***a smooth face*** ①没有胡子的脸. ②讨好的面孔. ***accept the*** ~ ***of*** 保全[维护]…的面子;偏袒,偏爱. ***at [in, on] the first*** ~初初一看,乍看之下. ***before sb.'s*** ~ 当着某人的面. ~ ***to*** ~ 面对面. ***fall on one's*** ~ 脸朝下倒下. ***feed one's*** ~〔美俚〕吃饭. ***fly from the*** ~ ***of men*** 无面目见人. ***fly in the*** ~ ***of*** 悍然不顾;公然抗拒. ***grind the*** ~***s of the poor*** 压榨穷人. ***have*** *(the wind)* ***in one's*** ~ 朝着,逆着(风). ***have two*** ~***s*** 怀二心,口是心非;耍两面派;(语言)暧昧. ***hide one's*** ~ ***from*** 不理睬. ***in sb.'s*** ~ 正对着;当面. ***in the*** ~ ***of*** ①〔英〕在…前面;面临. ②不避,不惧;不管,不顾,尽管 (*in (the)* ~ *of the world* 公然,在众目睽睽下). ③反对. (*fly in the* ~ *of* 公开反抗). ***in the (very)*** ~ ***of day [the sun]*** 公然,在光天化日之下. ***keep a straight*** ~ 不露笑容,板着面孔. ***laugh in sb.'s*** ~ 当面嘲笑某人. ***lie [fall] on one's*** ~ 脸朝下趴[倒]下来. ***lift sb.'s*** ~ 为人整容〔尤指消除面部皱纹的整容外科〕. ***look sb. in the*** ~ = ***look in sb.'s face*** 瞧着某人的脸,正视. ***make a long*** ~ 拉下脸来,板着脸. ***make*** ~***s [a*** ~***]*** 做苦脸;做鬼脸. ***on [upon] the*** ~ ***of*** *(a document, etc.)* ①(文件等的)字面上,由句法上看. ②明明,可见 (*The story is false on the* ~ *of it.* 这个故事明明是假的). ***on the (mere)*** ~ ***of it*** (单)由外表判断,一看就…. ***open one's*** ~〔美俚〕开口,说. ***pull [put] a long*** ~ = make a long ~. ***pull*** ~***s [a*** ~***]*** = make ~s. ***put a bold*** ~ ***on*** 对…装做满不在乎. ***put a good*** ~ ***on*** ①给…装面子,粉饰,对…抱乐观态度,对…装作无事. ***put a new*** ~ ***on*** 使局面一新,使面目一新. ***run one's*** ~〔美俚〕硬要赊欠. ***set [put] one's*** ~ ***against*** 抵制,坚决反对. ***set one's*** ~ ***to [towards]*** ①向…方面. ②着手;决心. ***show one's*** ~ 露面,出面. ***slap sb. in the*** ~ 打人耳光;侮辱人. ***stare sb. in the*** ~ ①盯着人的脸看. ②就在眼前,迫在眉睫. ***straighten one's*** ~ 板起面孔. ***to sb.'s*** ~ 对着某人,向某人,在某人前面,当面. ***turn*** ~ ***about*** 背转过去,调转方向. ***turn one's*** ~ ***away*** 背过脸去. ***wear a long*** ~ = make a long ~. — *vt.* ①面向,面对,对着. ②对抗,抵抗;毅然承受,勇敢承当(难局等). ③给…包面;用…抹盖,涂上;把…的表面弄平,削平(石等). ④使转向;命令(队伍)转变方向;翻开(牌面). ⑤染(茶等的)色;镶(衣)边. ~ *the wall* 向着墙壁. *be* ~*d with danger* 面临危险. *The picture* ~*s page 8.* 插图在第8页对面. *a house facing the street* 临街的房屋. *a wall* ~*d with concrete* 水泥覆面的墙壁. — *vi.* ①面对着 (*on; to*). ②【军】…向…转;〔口令〕. ③朝某一方向. *About* ~*!* (口令) 向后转! *Left [Right]* ~*!* 向左[右]转! ~ ***about [round]*** (使)转过身来,改变主意 (*He* ~*d his men about.* 他命令他的队伍向后转). ~ ***sb. down*** 用目光压倒,降伏,挫败. ~ ***it [a matter] out*** 坚持到底,不让步. ***F- off!*** (冰上曲棍球)比赛开始! ~ ***off*** (在一场力量、耐力等的考验中与对手)对抗. ~ ***sth. out*** 把某事坚持到底. ~ ***the music*** 毅然面对难局;经受遣责,临危不惧. ~ ***the world*** 见世面. ~ ***up*** 着色,把表面弄得好看些. ~ ***up to*** 大胆面向;正面对付. ***let's*** ~ ***it.***〔美口〕面对现实(不要躲避退缩)吧;尽力对付吧. ~**-ache**【医】面部神经痛. ~**-around** *n.* 转变方向[态度]. ~ **bone** 颧骨. ~ **brick**【建】面砖. ~ **card** (纸牌中 K, Q, J. 三种)人头牌. ~**-centred** *a.*【物】(原子)面心的 (~*-centred crystal* 面心晶体). ~ **cloth** 面巾 (= washcloth). ~**-cream** 润肤香脂. ~**down** ① *ad.* 面朝下地. ② *n.* 〔美口〕= ~ off. ③摊牌. ~ **fly** 牛蝇. ~ **goods** 光洁毛织物. ~ **guard** (厂矿、击剑等用的)护面具,面罩. ~**-harden** *vt.*【冶】使(铁合金)表面硬化. ~**-lifting** ①(除去面部皱纹的)整容外科手术;整容. ②(建筑物、汽车等的)改建、翻新(门面). ~ **mask** ①面罩. ②面模. ~**-off** *n.* ①(冰上曲棍球)开球. ②对峙,敌对;摊牌;面对面的会议[争论,谈判]. ~ **par** 票面价格. ~**plate** ①【机】面板,花盘. ②(电灯开关等上的)护板,盖板. ~ **powder** 搽脸香粉. ~**-saver**〔美俚〕保全面子的事. ~**-saving** *a.* 保全面子的. ~**-to-**~ *a., ad.* 面对面的[地]. ~**-up** *ad.* 面朝上的. ~ **value** ①(钞票、债券等的)票面价值. ②表面价值 (*take a promise at* ~ *value* 把一项诺言信以为真.)

faced [feist] *a.* 具有…脸型的,有…表面的,有…贴边的〔多用以组成复合词〕. *a marble-*~ *brick building* 大理石面的砖房. *a neatly-*~ *terrice* 表面整齐的地坛. *round-*~ 圆脸蛋的. *satin-*~ *lapels* 缎子面的翻领. *straight-*~ 板面孔的.

face·less [ˈfeislis] *a.* ①没脸面的. ②面目不明的;缺乏鲜明个性的;没有个性的;匿名的.

fac·er [ˈfeisə] *n.* ①化妆师,美容师;对物品表面进行加工的人,用来覆盖或加工物品表面的材料. ②〔口〕(拳击的)面部打击. ③〔英口〕意外事故;意外障碍,大打击. ④【机】铣刀盘;平面铣刀.

fac·et [ˈfæsit] *n.* ①(宝石等的)小平面,刻面;平圆面. ②(事物的)方面. ③(昆虫的)小眼面. ④【建】柱槽筋,凸线. — *vt.* 在(钻石上)刻面. **facet(t)ed eyes** 复眼. **facet(t)ed pebbles** 棱石.

fa·ce·ti·ae [fəˈsiːʃiˌiː] *n.* 〔*pl.*〕①滑稽言语,诙谐. ②

〔书〕(黄色下流的)滑稽书,淫书.

fa·ce·tious [fəˈsiːʃəs] *a.* ①滑稽的,好笑的. ②爱开玩笑的. **-ly** *ad.* **-ness** *n.*

fa·ci·a [ˈfeiʃiə] *n.* = fascia.

fa·cial [ˈfeiʃəl] *a.* 面部的,颜面的. — *n.* 〔美俚〕面部按摩;美容. *a* ~ *layer* 表面的一层. ~ *expression* 面部表情. ~ **angle** 颜面角;(结晶的)面角. ~ **cream** 雪花膏,香脂. ~ *expression* 面部表情. ~ **index** (测定骨头)面部长宽比率. ~ **neuralgia**【医】面神经痛. ~ **nerve** 面神经. ~ **tissue** 纸巾,擦面用的薄纸.

fa·ci·es [ˈfeiʃiiːz, ˈfeiʃiːz] *n. pl.* 〔单复同〕①颜面,外观;外表. ②【生态】演替系列混优种社会,演替系列变群丛. ③【地】相. ④【医】面色;表面.

fac·ile [ˈfæsail, ˈfæsil] *a.* ①容易的;轻快的;轻便的. ②机敏的;流畅的. ③易亲近的;温和的;易打交道的. *a* ~ *task* 容易的工作. *a* ~ *liar* 随口撒谎的人. *a* ~ *style* 流畅的文体. *She has a* ~ *tongue* 她口齿流利,能说会道. *He is* ~ *tool.* 他容易被人利用. **-ly** *ad.*

fa·c'i·le prin·ceps [ˈfæsili ˈprinseps] 〔L.〕稳得第一的,独点鳌头. *In that special field of science he is* ~, *and has left all competitor behind.* 在这一专门的科学领域,他是出类拔萃的,使其他的竞争者望尘莫及.

fa·cil·i·tate [fəˈsiliteit] *vt.* ①使容易,使顺当. ②助长,促进. *The broken lock* ~*d my entrance into the empty house.* 门锁坏了,使我进入这个空房很容易. ★此词不以人作主语. **-ta·tion** [-ˈteiʃən] *n.*

fa·cil·i·ty [fəˈsiliti] *n.* ①容易,简易,轻便. ②机敏,灵巧,流畅. ③〔常 *pl.*〕方便,便利,设备,器材,工具,装置;机构. ④和善,柔和. *facilities of travelling* 旅游设施[机构]. *servicing facilities* 辅助设备;维护设备. *homing* ~ 归航设备. *monetary facilities* 金融机关. ~ ***and difficulty*** 顺利和困难. ***give [accord, afford] facilities for*** 给与…方便. ***with*** ~ ①容易. ②流利.

fac·ing [ˈfeisiŋ] *n.* ①【建】饰面,面层,覆盖面;敷面物,面料;面饰;墙面. ②(衣服等的)镶边,贴边,滚条. ③【机】衬片;刮面;刮面法. ④【军】〔*pl.*〕(军服的)领章,袖章. ⑤(茶等的)着色,色料. ⑥【军】转变队列方向,看齐. *a cement* ~ 水泥墙面. ***go through one's*** ~***s*** 被考试;受训练. ***put sb. through his*** ~***s*** 训练,教练(某人);考验某人的本领. ~ **slip** 邮包上注明目的地、日期等的标签. ~ **tool**【机】车面刀.

facs = facilities.

fac·sim·i·le [fækˈsimili] *n.* ①(通讯)传真. ②复制,摹写;摹本. *documents reproduced in* ~ 和原件维妙维肖的文件复制本. ***in*** ~ 逼真,毫不走样,唯妙唯肖. — *vt.* 复制,摹写. ~ **paper** 传真感光纸. ~ **telegraph** 传真电报. ~ **transmission [broadcasting]** 电传真迹.

fact [fækt] *n.* ①事实,实际,实情. ②犯罪行为. ③论据;证据. *an established* ~ 既定事实. *The* ~ *(of the matter) is that ...* 事实上是. *Facts are stubborn (things).* 〔谚〕事实是改变不了的. *Facts speak louder than words.* 事实胜于雄辩. *the hard* ~*s* 现实. *His* ~*s are open to question.* 他的论据有问题. ***after [before] the*** ~ 犯罪后[前],作案后[前] (*an accessary after the* ~ 事后从犯). ***as a matter of*** ~ 事实是,事实上. ***bring out the*** ~***s and reasons*** 摆事实,讲道理. ~***s of life*** ①性知识. ②严酷的现实. ~***s on file*** 小资料. ***from the*** ~ ***that*** … 从…的事实上来看. ***in*** ~ 其实,事实上,实际上;总之. ***be caught in the*** ~ 当场被捕. ***in point of*** ~ 实际上. ***turn the*** ~***s upside down*** 颠倒是非. ~**-finder** *n.* 事实调查者. ~**-finding** *n., a.* 进行实际调查(的) (*a* ~ *finding committee* 调查委员会).

fac·ta [ˈfæktə] factum 的复数.

fac·tion [ˈfækʃən] *n.* ①宗派,派别,小集团. ②派系纠纷,内讧. *sb.'s own* ~ 某人的嫡系. **-al, -ary,** *a.* **-al-ism** *n.* 派别活动;小团体主义,宗派主义. **-ist** *n.* 宗派[小团体]主义者.

-fac·tion *suf.* 加在词尾为 -fy 的动词后,形成表示其作用的名词: satis*faction.*

fac·tious [ˈfækʃəs] *a.* ①闹派别的;好捣乱的. ②起于派别的;由于搞宗派而产生的. **-ly** *ad.* **-ness** *n.*

fac·ti·tious [fækˈtiʃəs] *a.* ①人为的,人工的. ②装成的,不自然的;虚构的;假的. **-ly** *ad.* **-ness** *n.*

fac·ti·tive [ˈfæktitiv] *a.*【语法】作为的,使役的. *a* ~ *verb.* (直接宾语后须加补语的)使役动词. — *n.* 使役格.

fac·tor [ˈfæktə] *n.* ①〔英〕经销人;(代客买卖收取佣金的)经纪人;代理商;代办人;〔Scot.〕土地经管人. ②要素,因素;原动力. ③【物】系数,率;【数】因子,因数;【化】当量换算因数;【生】遗传因子,基因;【摄】曝光系数. ④倍;乘数;商. *amplification* ~ (电子管的)放大系数. *common* ~ 公因子,公因素. *the copper* ~ 含铜率. *engagement* ~【机】接触比,重叠系数. ~ *of safety* 安全系数. *the* ~ *of shape*【林】形数. *increase by a* ~ *of five* 增加四倍. *the key* ~ 关键. *the plant [utility]* ~ 设备使用率. *resolution into* ~*s* 因数分解. *the visibility* ~ 视度. *3 and 5 are* ~*s of 15.* 三和五是十五的因子. — *vt.* ①【数】把…化为因子[因数]. ②为…充当代理商;代理经营;代管(产业). ~ ***out*** 析出因数. ~ **group**【数】商群. ~ **ring**【数】商环.

fac·tor·age [ˈfæktəridʒ] *n.* ①代理[经纪]行业. ②佣金.

fac·to·ri·al [fækˈtɔːriəl] *a.* ①代理商的;工厂的. ②【数】因数的;阶乘的. — *n.*【数】阶乘;【统】阶乘积. *the* ~ *of 4* 四的阶乘. ~ **experiment** 析因实验. ~ **function** 阶乘函数.

fac·tor·ize [ˈfæktəraiz] *vt.*【数】把…化为因子[数]. **-tor·i·za·tion** [ˌfæktəraiˈzeiʃən] *n.*

fac·to·ry [ˈfæktəri] *n.* ①工厂,制造厂. ②〔古〕代理店. *an atomic-energy* ~ 原子能发电站. ~ *costs* 制造成本. *a* ~ *girl* 女工. *a* ~ *hand* 职工,工人. *The F- law [Acts]* 工厂法. ~ **ship** (设有鱼类加工设备的)加工渔船. ~ **town** 工业区,工厂区.

fac·to·tum [fækˈtəutəm] *n.* ①什么都得干的雇员[仆人];勤杂人员;打杂的(人). ②【印】特大型花体大写字母.

fac·tu·al [ˈfæktjuəl] *a.* 事实上的,实在的. ~ *writing* (某人的)手笔,真迹. **-i·ty** [ˌfæktjuˈæliti] *n.* 实在性. **-ly** *ad.* **-ness** *n.*

fac·tu·al·ism [ˈfæktjuəlizəm] *n.* 尊重事实,求实精神.

fac·tum [ˈfæktəm] *n.* 〔L.〕(*pl.* **-ta** [-tə])【法】①事实;行为. ②呈文,事实陈述书,辩驳书. ③(遗嘱的)正式订立.

fac·ture [ˈfæktʃə] *n.* ①〔古〕制造;(制)成品. ②制法〔尤指艺术品表面的加工〕.

fac·u·la [ˈfækjulə] *n.* (*pl.* **-lae** [-liː])【天】(太阳的)光斑〔*cf.* macula〕. **-lar, -lous** *a.*

fac·u·lae [ˈfækjuˌli] *n.* facula 的复数.

fac·ul·ta·tive [ˈfækəltətiv] *a.* ①特许的,特准的. ②任意的,随意的. ③能力上的,机能上的. ④【生】兼性的. ~ *money* 特准发行的货币. *a* ~ *course* 选修课程. ~ **parasite**【生】兼性寄生物,兼性寄生菌. ~ **plant**【植】不定型植物. **-ly** *ad.*

fac·ul·ty [ˈfækəlti] *n.* ①能力,才能;官能,机能;〔美〕技能,手腕. ②特权;特许;权能. ③〔英〕(大学的)专科,系;院;全院[系]教授;〔美〕教授会,教职员. ④任何一种专业的全体从业人员,公会. *the* ~ *of memory* 记忆力. *the imaginative* ~ 想象力. *a housekeeper of notable* ~ 极能干的女管家. *the students and* ~ 全院师生. *the F- of Engineering* 工学院. *the medical* ~ 医界同人. ***collect one's faculties*** 镇定下来.

fad [fæd] *n.* ①一时流行的风尚;一时的爱好. ②一时的怪念头. **-dish, -dy** *a.* 爱新奇的,一时流行的. **-di·ly** *ad.* ~**dism** *n.* 一时的狂热性;追随时尚. **-dist** *n.* 爱新奇的人,好事的人.

FAD = flavin adenine dinucleotide.【生化】黄素腺嘌呤

二核苷酸.

fade[1] [feid] *vi.* ①褪色;失去光泽. ②凋落,枯谢;衰老,憔悴. ③渐淡,渐渐消失. ④〔美俚〕离开,跑掉,逃掉. *The flowers have ~d.* 花已凋零. *All memory of his boyhood had ~d from his mind.* 他已经记不清自己童年时代的情景. — *vt.* 使褪色;使凋谢;使衰老. *a carpet ~d by the sun* 被晒得褪了色的地毯. *~ **in [out]***【影】(使)渐现[隐];【无】(使)(声音)渐高[消]. **~away** *n.* 逐渐消失. **~-in**【影】渐现,淡入;【无】(声音)渐高. **~-out**【影】渐隐,淡出;【无】(声音)渐消. **~-over**【影】淡入淡出. *~proof a.* 不褪色的. **-r** 音量[光量]调节器;混频电位器.

fade[2] [fɑːd] *a.* ①乏味的,平淡的. ②〔废〕萎谢褪色的;憔悴的.

fade·less [ˈfeidlis] *a.* 不凋谢的;不褪色的;不衰落的. **-ly** *ad.*

fa·do [ˈfɑːduː] *n.* 思乡曲〔葡萄牙民歌,带有忧郁、怀乡情调〕.

fae·cal [ˈfiːkəl] *a.* = fecal.

fae·ces [ˈfiːsiːz] *n.* 〔*pl.*〕= feces.

fa·e·na [fəˈeina] *n.* 〔Sp.〕(斗牛的)连续劈刺〔斗牛士在击杀牛前炫示技能的劈刺动作〕.

fa·er·ie, fa·er·y [ˈfeiəri, ˈfɛəri] *n.* (*pl.* ***fa·er·ies***) ①妖精之国,仙境. ②〔古〕妖精. — *a.* 妖精(一样)的;梦幻的.

Faer·oes [ˈfɛərəuz] *n.* 法罗群岛〔大西洋北部〕.

Faer·o·ese [ˌfɛərəˈiːz] *n.* ①法罗群岛的居民. ②法罗语. — *a.* ①法罗群岛居民的. ②法罗语的.

fag [fæg] *vt.* ①使疲劳. ②磨损,拆散(绳索的末端). ③(英国公学中旧生)强迫(新生)跑腿. — *vi.* ①拼命劳动 *(at)*,做苦工. ②替旧生跑腿. ***be fagged out*** 疲倦极了. ~ ***away*** 辛辛苦苦地做工. ~ ***out*** ①使筋疲力尽. ②【板球】使做外野手. — *n.* 〔英〕苦工;做苦工的人;疲劳. ②(英国学校中受旧生使唤的)当值新生. ③烟头,布头. ④〔美俚〕搞同性关系的男子. *It is too much (of a) ~.* 那是(一件)受不了的苦活. ~ **end** ①绳索的散端,末端,零头;烟头,布头(等). ②残渣,废渣. ③〔美俚〕上当,吃亏 (*get the ~ end* 上了当). **-gy** *a.* 〔美俚〕男性同性爱的;女性化的.

fag·got [ˈfægət] *n.* ①柴把,柴捆;束枝条. ②【冶】成束熟铁块,束铁. ③〔英〕(加调味品的)烤肝片. ④长条抽线,束芯装饰针迹. — *vt., vi.* ①捆,束. ②用花式针迹接(缝). ~ **vote**〔英〕(把一人财产暂时分与数人使享有选举权而进行的)结伙选举. ~ **voter** 结伙投票人. **-ry**〔美俚〕男性同性爱. **-y**〔美俚〕男性同性爱的;(男子)女性化的.

fa·gin [ˈfeigin] *n.* 小偷把头;教唆犯(原为狄更斯小说 *Oliver Twist* 中的人物).

fag·ot [ˈfægət] 〔美〕= faggot.

fag·ot·ing, fag·got·ing [ˈfægətiŋ] *n.* ①宽格花边抽花手工. ②花式针迹接缝.

Fahr. = Fahrenheit.

Fahr·en·heit [ˈfærənhait, ˈfɑːr-] *n., a.* 华氏温度计(的). *the ~ scale* 华氏温标. *a ~ thermometer* 华氏温度计.

fa·ience [faiˈɑːns] *n.* 〔F.〕彩釉陶器.

fail [feil] *vi.* ①失败,不及格 (*opp.* succeed);(判断)错误,不中目标. ②〔与 of 或不定式连用〕不能,不(做),忘记. ③(分量)不足,缺乏 *(in)*;(作物)歉收. ④(健康等)衰退,衰弱,停止作用;(水)断,风(停). ⑤倒闭,破产. ⑥(后嗣)全无,绝. *He ~s in truthfulness.* 他不够老实. *She never ~s to write me every week.* 她永不忘记每周给我写信. *I ~ to see.* 我弄不懂. *The wind ~ed.* 风停了. *Water supply has ~ed.* 供水中断. — *vt.* ①使失望;辜负;无助于;丢弃;不履行,玩忽. ②(考试)失败,不及格;〔口〕(考试人)不录取(考生),把(考生)评为不及格. *Words ~ed me at the last minute.* 到最后的时候我说不出话来了. *Time would ~ me to tell of it.* 没有那么多的时间去谈. *I ~ed exam in geography.* 我地理考试不及格. *The teacher ~ed me in physics.* 老师评我物理考试不及格. ***Don't ~ to*** 务必,一定 (*Don't ~ to write me.* 不要忘了给我写信). ~ ***of*** 不能达到,缺乏…能力 (*The debater's argument ~ed of logical connection.* 辩论者的论点缺乏逻辑的连贯性). ***never ~ to (do)*** 必定 (*He never ~s to come on Sunday.* 他星期天准来). — *n.* ①失败,失误;不及格;不及格者. ②【商】(期货交割)失期. ***without ~*** 必定,务必. **~-out** *n.* 故障后果. **~safe** ① *a.* (核弹运载机等)具有安全装置的;故障(自动)保险的. ② *vt., vi.* (使)具有自动保险装置. **F- Safe** (核弹运载机等的)自动保险装置. **~test** *n.* (零件故障)可靠性试验.

fail·ing [ˈfeiliŋ] *n.* 缺点,弱点,短处;失败. — *prep.* ①如果没有…. ②如果在…中失败. *F- good weather, the lecture will be held indoors.* 如果天气坏,讲演会改在室内举行. *F- election, she will return to her law practice.* 如果竞选失败,她将重操旧业去当律师. — *a.* 失败的,减弱中的,衰退中的.

faille [feil; F. faj] *n.*【纺】罗缎.

fail·ure [ˈfeiljə] *n.* ①失败 (*opp.* success);不及格. ②不足,缺乏;衰退;【医】衰竭. ③不履行,玩忽. ④破产,倒闭;(银行等的)无力支付. ⑤失败的事;失败者. ⑥【物】失效;【机】断裂,破坏,变钝. *F- is the mother of success.* = *F- teaches success.* 〔谚〕失败是成功之母. *a ~ of rain* 雨量缺乏. *~ in duty* 不尽职. *a crop ~ = (a) ~ of crops* 收成不好,歉收. *~ of electricity* 停电. *a ~ of issue* 无后(嗣). *~ of eyesight* 视力减退. *He is a ~ as a teacher.* 他教书不行. *heart ~*【医】心力衰竭. *a social ~* (社会上的)失败者. ***end in ~ = meet with ~*** 终归失败. ***invite ~*** 引起失败.

fain [fein] *a.* ①〔古、诗〕乐意的,愿意的. ②〔古〕不得不的,勉强的〔仅用作表语〕. *He was ~ to submit.* 他只好服从. — *ad.* 〔诗、古〕欣然,乐意〔与 *would* 连用〕. *I would ~ help you.* 我乐意帮助你.

fain(s) [fein(z)] *int.* 〔英学俚〕免除. *Fain(s) I keeping goal!* 可别叫我守球门.

fai·né·ant [ˈfeniənt; F. feneɑ̃] *a.* 〔F.〕懒惰的. — *n.* 懒人.

faint [feint] *a.* ①软弱的,无力的;无勇气的,怯懦的. ②轻微的,稀薄的,暗淡的,模糊的. ③〔只用作表语〕将昏倒似的. ④闷人的. *~ resistance* 微弱的抵抗. *a ~ heart* 懦夫,胆小鬼. *a ~ smell* 闷人的气味. *~ lines [rulings]* (练习本等上的)淡色横格. ***be ~ with hunger*** 饿得头晕眼花. ***feel ~*** 感到头昏眼花. — *vi.* ①昏晕,昏过去 *(away)*. ②渐渐不明,消失;〔古〕衰弱;颓丧. — *n.* 昏厥;眼花. ***go off in a ~*** 昏过去. ***fall (down) in a dead ~*** 昏倒,不省人事. **-ly** *ad.* **-ness** *n.* (*be attacked with faintness* 昏过去). **~-ruled** *a.* (纸张)印有淡色横格的.

faint·heart [ˈfeinthɑːt] *n.* 懦夫,优柔寡断的人,窝囊废. — *a.* 懦怯的;没有决断的;胆小的;羞怯的.

faint·heart·ed [ˈfeintˈhɑːtid] *a.* 懦怯的,缺乏决断的;胆小的;羞怯的. **-ly** *ad.* **-ness** *n.*

faint·ing [ˈfeintiŋ] *n.* 昏倒,昏厥. — *a.* 昏倒的. ~ **fit [spell]** 昏厥. **-ly** *ad.*

faint·ish [ˈfeintiʃ] *a.* ①发呆的;象要昏过去似的. ②(记号等)略为模糊的,(光线等)微弱的. **-ness** *n.*

faints [feints] *n.* 〔*pl.*〕(蒸馏威士忌时最初和最后滴出的)劣质酒精.

fair[1] [fɛə] *n.* ①〔英〕定期集市,庙会. ②义卖市场. ③商品展览会,展销会,商品交易会. *a World's F-* 世界博览会. *China's Export Commodities F-* 中国出口商品交易会. *a country ~* 本乡物资交易会. *village ~* 农村集市. *hold a ~ to raise money* 举办义卖筹款. *vanity ~* 浮华市集,名利场. ***a day after the ~ = a day too***

late for the ～ 过迟,太晚. ～ **ground**〔常 *pl.*〕集市场地;赛马场.

fair[2] [fɛə] *a.* ①〔古诗〕美丽的;女性的. ②(水等)清澈的,清洁的;(笔迹等)鲜明的;洁白的,干净的. ③(头发)金色的 (*opp.* dark);(皮肤)白嫩的. ④(风等)畅快的;爽朗的,(天气等)好的;顺畅的,(前途等)有希望的. ⑤正当的;公平的,合理的,正派的 (*opp.* foul). ⑥平坦的,平滑的. ⑦还可以的,相当的. ⑧充足的,不少的. ⑨嘴甜的,说着好听的. ⑩按法律可以捕猎的;可以据理攻击的. *a* ～ *lady* 美妇人. ～ *weather* 好天气. ～ *income* 相当高的收入. *a* ～ *crop* 还不错的收成. ～ *average quality*【商】中等品. *one's* ～ *name [fame]* 清白的名声. *a* ～ *month* 整整一个月. *a* ～ *one* 美人. *a* ～ *way* 坦途 .～ *words* 花言巧语. ***a*** ～ ***field and no favour*** 公平无私,对双方都不偏袒. ***be*** ～ ***game for ridicule*** 活该成为嘲笑的对象. ***be*** ～ ***in one's dealing*** 处置公平. ***be in a*** ～ ***way to*** 有希望,很可能. ***by*** ～ ***means*** 秉公. ***by*** ～ ***means or foul*** 千方百计,不择手段. ～ ***and softly*** 态度好些,稳重一些. ～ ***and square*** 光明正大的,磊落坦率的;公正地,公道地. ～ ***to middling***〔口〕中常的;过得去,还算好. ***see*** ～ ***play*** 公平裁判;公平对待,公平处理. ***to be*** ～ 说良心话. ***write a*** ～ ***hand*** 写一笔好字. — *ad.* ①好,清楚,明白. ②谦和,恳切. ③正直;光明正大,公平;漂亮. ④幸亏,好在;顺利,有望. ⑤直,挺直地,朝正面,正. ⑥十分. *deal* ～ *with sb.* 公平待人. *fall* ～ 直挺挺地倒下去. *play* ～ 光明正大地比赛,公平合理地处理(等). *speak sb.* ～ 彬彬有礼地对人讲话. *strike sb.* ～ *on the chin* 不偏不歪地打在某人下巴上. *write out* ～ 誊清. ***bid*** ～ ***to (do)*** 很有希望. — *n.* ①〔古、诗〕佳人;爱人;美好的事物. ②〔the ～〕女性. ③〔古〕幸运. ***for*** ～〔美口〕完全地,肯定的. ***see*** ～〔俚〕= see ～ play. ***through*** ～ ***and foul (weather)*** 在任何情况下.—*vt.* ①誊清. ②使表面平顺;【船、空】把…作成流线型,减阻,整流. — *vi.*〔英方〕(天气)好转. ～ **ball**【棒球】正打球,线内球. ～ **catch** (足球) 侵人犯规. ～ **copy** 誊正本,校正本;【印】清样. ～**-faced** *a.* 白嫩的;美貌的;好看的. ～ **game** ①准予捕猎的鸟兽. ②有正当理由可追击〔攻击、研究〕的对象. ～**-haired** *a.* 金发的;〔口〕被宠爱的. ～**-haired boy**〔美俚〕宠儿,红人. ～**lead** 引线孔,引出管. ～**light** *n.*〔英〕门顶窗,气窗 (= transom window). ～**minded** *a.* 公正的,没有偏见的. ～ **play** 正派的比赛;公平合理〔正大光明〕的处理〔态度〕,公平;漂亮. ～ **sex** 妇女,女性〔与定冠词连用〕. ～ **shake**〔美〕公平待遇. ～**-spoken** *a.* 谈吐文雅的,彬彬有礼的,和蔼的;亲切的;嘴甜的. ～**-trade** *vt.* 规定(商品)的最低零售价,按公平交易约定(买卖). ～**-trade agreement**〔美〕互惠贸易协定,(厂商与零售商所订)不擅自降低零售价格的协定. ～**way** 航路,水路;【空】水上飞机用水面跑道;【高尔夫球】(球的)正规通路;球座与终点间的草地. (*a* ～*way topnotcher* 高尔夫球名手). ～**-weather** *a.* 只适宜于好天气的;只适宜于顺利时候的 (*a* ～*-weather sailor* 仅能在风平浪静时值勤的水手. ～*-weather friends* 可共安乐而不可共患难的朋友).

Fair·bank(s) [ˈfɛəbæŋk(s)] *n.* 费尔班克(斯)〔姓氏〕.

fair·i·ly [ˈfɛərili] *ad.* 仙女似地;优雅地,身姿绰约地.

fair·ing[1] [ˈfɛəriŋ] *n.* 市场上买的礼物,酬谢物. ***get one's*** ～***s*** 获得应得的报酬. ***give sb. his*** ～ 给人以应得的报酬.

fair·ing[2] [ˈfɛəriŋ] *n.*【空】整流片;整流罩;【机】减阻装置.

fair·ish [ˈfɛəriʃ] *a.* 相当的;还算大〔好〕的.

fair·ly [ˈfɛəli] *ad.* ①公正地,正当地. ②明白地,清楚地. ③适当,相当. ④完全,简直. *write* ～ 写清楚. ～ *good* 还好. *I* ～ *cried with joy.* 我简直高兴得叫了起来. ***act*** ～ ***by all men***〔谚〕一视同仁. ***be*** ～ ***beside oneself*** 简直疯了. ***be*** ～ ***under way*** 在顺利航行中;完全就绪. ～ ***and squarely*** 光明正大.

fair·ness [ˈfɛənis] *n.* ①晴朗. ②公平. ③〔诗、古〕美丽;洁白. ④(头发)的金黄色. ⑤顺畅,适当. ***in*** ～ ***to*** 为了对…做到公平合理. ～ **doctrine**〔美〕(电台、电视台为辩论双方提供同等机会的)公平经营原则.

fair·y [ˈfɛəri] *n.* ①妖精;仙女. ②〔美俚〕漂亮姑娘. ③〔美俚〕妖里妖气的男子;搞同性恋爱的男子. — *a.* ①妖精(一样)的;仙女似的. ②幻想中的. ③美丽的,小巧玲珑的,可爱的;优雅的. *a* ～ *lamp [light]* 彩色小灯. *a* ～ *shape* 优美的姿态. ～ **circle** 仙女环蘑菇〔迷信传说中认为由于仙女跳舞而在茂草中丛生如环的蘑菇,故名〕. ～**dom** *n.* = fairyland. ～ **godmother** (危难时提供及时帮助的) 慷慨朋友,救星. ～**hood** ①妖精气质,魔性. ②〔集合词〕妖精们. ～**land** *n.* 仙境,奇境;胜地. ～**like** *a.* 妖精一样的,仙女般的. ～ **ring** = ～ circle. ～ **shrimp**【动】无甲目 (Anostraca) 动物;丰年虫. ～ **tale** ①神话故事,童话. ②谎言.

fait ac·com·pli [feta kɔːŋpˈliː]〔F.〕既成事实.

Faith [feiθ] *n.* 费丝〔女子名〕.

faith [feiθ] *n.* ①信用,信任. ②信仰,信心;信条,教义,教(派). ③约,誓约. ④信义,忠实,诚实,诚意. ⑤〔the F-〕宗教信仰〔指基督教信仰〕. *in bad* ～ 不诚实地. *in good* ～ 真诚地. ***break*** ～ 背弃信仰,不守信义. ***break one's*** ～ 背信食言. ***by my*** ～ = ***by the*** ～ ***of my fathers [body, love]*** = *upon my* ～. ***engage [pledge, plight] one's*** ～ 担保,发誓,答应. ***give one's*** ～ 担保,断定说. ***have*** ～ ***in*** 相信. ***have no*** ～ ***in*** 不相信. ***i' faith*** = ***in*** ～***!*** 实在,真,真正. ***keep*** ～ 忠于信仰,遵守信义. ***lose*** ～ ***in*** 对…失去信念. ***my*** ～ = in ～. ***on the*** ～ ***of*** 靠着…的信用,由…的保证. ***pin one's*** ～ ***on [to]*** 绝对信任,深信不疑. ***put*** ～ ***in*** 相信,信任. ***upon my*** ～ 我担保,一定. — *int.* 真正,真. ～ ***cure [healing]*** (用宗教,祷告等迷信方法的)信仰医疗. ～ **healer** 实行信仰疗法的人.

faith·ful [ˈfeiθful] *a.* ①忠实的,忠诚的;贞节的;信仰坚定的. ②可靠的;正确的. — *n.*〔the ～〕〔集合词〕信徒. **-ness** *n.* 诚实;正确.

faith·ful·ly [ˈfeiθfuli] *ad.* ①忠实地;诚心诚意地. ②(对契约等)切实遵守地. *deal* ～ *with* 诚恳地对待. *promise* ～〔口〕坚决保证,明确约定. ***Yours*** ～ = ***F- yours*** 你的忠实的〔信尾用语〕.

faith·less [ˈfeiθlis] *a.* ①无信义的,不忠实的;不贞的. ②靠不住的. ③没有信仰的. **-ly** *ad.* **-ness** *n.*

fai·tour [ˈfeitə] *n.*〔古〕骗子;流氓.

fake[1] [feik]〔口〕*n.* ①冒充,诈骗;冒牌货,骗人货. ②魔术用具;假动作,假消息. ③捏造者;〔美〕骗子. — *a.* 假的,冒充的,骗人的. ～ *diamonds* 假钻石. *a medical* ～ 冒牌医生. — *vt.* ①伪造;捏造 (*up*). ②假装,装做. ③即席演奏. ～ *an accompaniment* 即席伴奏. ～ *(up) a report* 捏造报告. ～ *illness* 装病. — *vi.* 作伪,造假货. *She's not sick, she's just faking.* 她没有病,是在装假呢. ～ ***a curtain***【美剧】(特雇观众所作的)假捧场. ～ ***it up*** 涂抹,装饰. ～ ***sb. out***〔口〕以欺骗、讹诈手法胜过某人. ～ **book** (盗印的只印有简单乐谱的) 流行歌曲集.

fake[2] [feik] *n.*【海】盘索;【电】线圈;软焊料. — *vt.* 卷(绳索).

fake·ment [ˈfeikmənt] *n.*〔口〕蒙骗;骗人货.

fa·keer [fəˈkiə] *n.* = fakir[1].

fak·er [ˈfeikə] *n.*〔口〕①骗子;卖假货的小贩. ②骗人货,伪造物.

fak·er·y [ˈfeikəri] *n.* ①伪造,捏造;伪装. ②假货,赝品.

fa·kir[1] [fəˈkiə, ˈfeikiə] *n.* (伊斯兰教或印度教的) 游方修士,托钵僧.

fak·ir[2] [ˈfeikə] *n.* = faker.

Fa·lange [Sp. feˈlæŋhei, ˈfeilændʒ] *n.* (西班牙)长枪党.

Fa·lan·gist [fəˈlændʒist] *n.* 长枪党党员.

fa-la, fal-la [fəˈlɑː, ˈfɑːlɑː] ①(古歌谣结尾音节)叠用词. ②(古代歌谣的)叠用曲.

Fa·la·sha [fɑːˈlɑːʃə] *n.* 法拉沙人〔住在埃塞俄比亚,信奉犹太教的含族人〕.

fal·ba·la [ˈfælbələ], **fal·be·lo** [ˈfælbeləu] *n.* (女子衣、裙等上的)荷叶边.

fal·cate(d) [ˈfælkeit(id)] *a.* 【植、动】镰刀状的. *a* ~ *leaf* 镰刀状叶片. — *n.* 镰刀形.

fal·chion [ˈfɔːltʃən] *n.* ①(中世纪的)弯形大刀,偃月刀. ②〔诗〕刀,剑.

fal·ci·form [ˈfælsifɔːm] *a.* 镰刀形的.

fal·con [ˈfælkən, ˈfɔːlkən, ˈfɔːk-] *n.* ①【动】隼,(猎鹰的)母鹰. ②(15—17世纪用的)轻炮. **-er** *n.* 养猎鹰的人;鹰猎者. **-et** *n.* ①小隼,小鹰. ②轻炮.

fal·con-gen·tle [ˈfɔːlkənˈdʒentl, ˈfɔːkən-] *n.* 【动】雌苍鹰,雌隼.

fal·con·ry [ˈfɔːlkənri] *n.* ①猎鹰驯练术. ②鹰猎.

fal·cu·la [ˈfælkjulə] *n.* (*pl.* **-lae** [-liː]) (猫等的)钩爪.

fal·de·ral [ˈfældəˈræl], **fal·de·rol** [ˈfældəˈrɔl] *n.* = folderol.

fald·stool [ˈfɔːldstuːl] *n.* ①(主教等坐的)折椅. ②(英国国教的)跪拜台;读经台.

Fa·ler·ni·an [fəˈləːniən] *n.* (意大利 Campania 地方的)费勒年(山)葡萄酒.

Falk·land Is·lands [ˈfɔːklənd ˈailəndz]〔与 the 连用〕福克兰群岛(即马尔维纳斯 (Malvinas) 群岛)〔大西洋〕.

Falk·ner [ˈfɔːknə] *n.* 福克纳〔姓氏〕.

fall [fɔːl] *vi.* (***fell*** [fel]; ***fall·en*** [ˈfɔːlən]) ①落下;散落,(毛发等)脱落;降落;(水银柱等)下降;(物价)下落,跌落;(帘、幕等)放下,垂下;(眼睛、脸色)下沉;(河流)流下,灌注;(地面等)倾斜. ②倒下,摔倒;趴下;坍倒;崩解;瓦解,垮台. ③陷落;失足. ④堕落;(女人)失身. ⑤死,战死. ⑥(精神等)衰退;(洪水等)减退,(风力)减弱;(潮水)退落. ⑦(瞌睡)沉沉,(恐怖)逼人;(光线等)当头. ⑧(小羊等)生下. ⑨(言语)漏出. ⑩忽然…起来,…出来,…下来(*to*). ⑪陷于(某种状态),变化,成为. ⑫(事故)发生;(时候)到来,正当,适逢;轮(到). ⑬属于;分为(…类). ⑬落入,留传给;(重音等)落在…上. ⑭(谈话等)停止. ⑮〔美俚〕被捕,落网. *The barometer is ~ing.* 气压正在下降. *The rain ~s.* 下雨了. *The curtain ~s.* 幕落. *Night ~s.* 夜色降临. *The fortress fell.* 要塞失守了. ~ *in battle* 战死. ~ *to sb.'s gun* 被人击毙. ~ *to the river* 向河边倾斜. ~ *within the jurisdiction of* 属于…管辖范围. *It ~s to our lot to do this.* 该我们来做这件事了. *His countenance [face] ~s.* 他脸色一沉. *His spirits fell at the news.* 他听到那个消息时垂头丧气. ~ *asleep* 睡着,入睡. ~ *ill* 病倒. ~ *into step* 进入同步. ~ *out of step* 失去同步. *He suddenly fell grave.* 他突然板起了面孔. *Not a word ~s from her lip.* 她一言不发. *The bill ~s due next week.* 支票在下周到期. *The shot ~s wide of (its) mark.* 那一枪没有打中. *She was tempted and fell.* 她被引诱而堕落. *The light fell on my book.* 灯光正照到我的书上. *The conversation fell suddenly.* 谈话声突然停止. *The novel ~s into six parts.* 小说分为六部分. *He fell thrice for theft.* 他因盗窃被捕过三次. ~ ***a sacrifice [victim] to*** 成为…的牺牲品. ~ ***aboard***【海】(与他船)相撞. ~ ***across*** 碰见. ~ ***among*** 遇见(盗匪等),偶然陷入…之中. ~ ***apart*** 崩溃,土崩瓦解. ~ ***at sb.'s feet*** 拜倒在某人脚下. ~ ***away*** ①疏远;背叛,变节;背离;(客人等)减少. ②渐退,隐退,消失. ③消瘦;变弱;死. ④分裂,(各级)分开,散开,排出. ⑤变懒,变懈怠. ⑥(地势)倾斜. ~ ***back*** 撤退,后退;退让,退缩;违约,不履行. ~ ***back on [upon]*** 退守,撤退到…线;投靠,求助于. ~ ***behind*** ①落后,跟不上. ②拖欠. ~ ***beyond*** 属于…外,在…外. ~ ***down*** (向下游)流下;〔美俚〕失败(~ *down on a job* 工作失败). ~ ***flat*** 失败,达不到预期结果. ~ ***for***〔美俚〕①被迷住,爱上. ②受骗上当. ~ ***from*** ①由…滚落下来;(由…口里)露出. ②〔古〕背叛(~ *from favour* 失宠). ~ ***home*** (木材或船侧上部)向里弯. ~ ***in*** ①(屋顶等)塌陷,往里坍塌;(眼等)洼下,凹进去. ②【军】排队,站队;集合. ③一致,符合. ④终止;(土地等)租借期满;(土地等)可以利用. ~ ***in for*** 参与,享受(~ *in for a share* 可分一份). ~ ***in [to] pieces*** 粉碎,破碎不堪. ~ ***into*** ①陷入(网等)中;陷入(坏习惯等)中,变成(~ *into line* 同人站成一排;跟人步调一致). ②渐渐(~ *into decay* 渐渐荒废). ③开始(~ *into conversation with* 和…谈起话来). ④流入. ⑤分成,分解(成几部分)(~ *into four divisions* 分成四个部分). ~ ***in with*** ①偶然碰见. ②同意;赞成. ③符合;适合. ~ ***off*** ①下降,跌落. ②离开;疏远;叛离. ③减退,销路减少;衰退;堕落. ④【海】偏向下风,(船只)不易驾驶,(飞机)侧降. ~ ***on [upon]*** ①开始(行动);进攻,袭击. ②(节日)正当,适逢. ③忽然看出来,想起来. ④(灾难等)临头,落在…上(~ *on the ball*〔美〕开始用功. ~ *on one's feet [legs]* 侥幸避免危难. ~ *on one's sword* 自刎. ~ *upon one's knees* 跪下). ~ ***on stony ground*** (计划等)落空. ~ ***out*** ①起纠纷,争吵(*They often ~ out over some trifling matter.* 他们常常因小事争吵). ②落下,脱落;【军】离队,原地解散. ③发生(…事),结果(是)(*It fell out that ...* 结果…). ④离队;【军】原地解散. ~ ***out of*** 放弃(习惯等). ~ ***over*** ①落在…上;落在…外. ②向前摔倒. ③(头发)披在(肩)上. ~ ***over one another***〔美〕争夺,竞争,争先恐后. ~ ***over oneself*** ①跌跤. ②拼命赶. ~ ***short (of)*** (…)缺乏;(…)不足;(子弹等)达不到(目标). ~ ***through*** 落空,失败. ~ ***to*** ①着手. ②开始用餐. ③争吵起来. ④开始攻击. ⑤(门等自动)关起来(*Let us ~ to!* 大家吃吧!; ~ *to work* 动手工作. ~ *to reading* 读起书来). ~ ***to the ground*** 落在地上;(计划等)落空. ~ ***under*** ①受(影响、检查等). ②归入(…部、类等);属于(~ *under sb.'s notice* 受某人注意,被某人看见). ~ ***within*** 属于,该当,适合. — *vt.* 〔美,英方〕击倒,斫倒(树木). — *n.* ①落下,坠落;(温度等的)下落,降落;(物价的)跌落;落差;降雨(量),降雪(量);(河水)流入,流下,倾泻;〔常 *pl.*〕瀑布. ②(树的)采伐,采伐量. ③跌倒,摔倒;陷落;坍倒;瓦解,崩溃;灭亡;战死. ④(对诱惑等的)屈服;堕落. ⑤减退,衰退;(潮的)退落;(太阳的)没落. ⑥【地】倾斜,斜度;【矿】冒落. ⑦(兽的)下仔;(羊等的)一胎. ⑧〔美〕秋天〔落叶期之意〕. ⑨下垂物;向下飘荡的服装,领子的翻下部分,(女帽上的)罩纱,(外衣的)宽下摆,大裤脚;(钢琴的)盖子. ⑩【摔交】把对手摔倒;一局摔角. ⑪【机】(滑车上的)拉绳,起重机绳;〔*pl.*〕【海】(放救生艇的)吊绳,辘绳. ⑫【猎】陷阱;〔美口〕被捕. ⑬【语】降调;【乐】乐曲终止. *Pride will have a ~.* 骄者必败. *A ~ into the pit, a gain in your wit.* 吃一堑,长一智. *the F- (of man)*【宗】人的堕落. *a heavy ~ of rain [snow]* 大雨[雪]. *a sharp ~ of temperature* 温度的剧降. *a waterfall with a ~ of 100 metres.* 落差一百公尺的瀑布. *in the ~ of 1980*〔美〕一九八〇年秋天. *the ~ of leaves* 落叶;秋天. ~ *of the hammer* (拍卖时)击槌成交. ~ *and spring yoke*〔美〕老少悬殊的婚姻. ***have a*** ~〔美俚〕被捕. ***nod to its*** ~ 摇摇欲坠. ***ride for a*** ~ ①乱骑马. ②闯乱子,准会失败. ***take a*** ~ 被打倒. ***try a ~ with*** 同某人较量一番. — *a.* 〔美〕秋天的,秋季的,秋天播种的;秋天成熟的;(衣服等)秋天用的. ~ *fashions* 秋季畅销货. ~ *goods* 秋季货品. ~ *wheat* 冬小麦. **~age** ①伐木. ②〔集合词〕伐下的树枝. **~away** *n.* 【宇】(火箭各级的)分开,散开,排出. **~back** ①后备物. ②撤退;退路. **~fish** 【动】风鱼 (*semotilus corporalis*)〔产于美国东北部清澈的江河湖海中〕. ~ **guy**〔美俚〕(无法脱身的)替罪羊,替死鬼,背黑锅者. ~ **line** ①【地】瀑布线. ②(滑雪的)直接下滑线. **~-off** *n.* ①下降,减少.

F

②【宇】(火线各级的)分开，散开，排出．~**out** *n.* ①【原】微粒回降；回降物，放射性尘埃．②意外的副产品，附带成果．③剩余物，残渣．(*radio active ~out* 放射性微粒回降．*a ~out shelter* 微粒掩蔽所)．~**-pipe** 水落管．~**-trap** 陷阱．~**up** 放射性尘埃对海洋地区的污染．【气】~ **wind**【气】下降风，下吹风．

fal·la·cious [fəˈleiʃəs] *a.* ①谬误的．②虚妄的；靠不住的，令人失望的．~ *hopes* 渺茫的希望．**-ly** *ad.* **-ness** *n.*

fal·la·cy [ˈfæləsi] *n.* 谬误，谬见，谬论，错误．*a pathetic ~* (诗人认为万物都有感情的)感伤的谬妄．

fal-lal [ˈfælˈlæl] *n.* (服装上的)妆饰品．

fal·lal·er·y [fælˈlæləri] *n.* 俗气的装饰品；虚饰．

fall·en [ˈfɔːlən] fall 的过去分词．— *a.* ①落下来的；倒了的．②陷落了的；已垮台的．③堕落了的；灭亡了的；破落了的；已死的．④憔悴的．~ *angel* 沦落的天使；恶魔．*a ~ woman* 堕落的女人．*persons ~ in battle* 阵亡者．*the ~* 阵亡者．~ *cheeks* 憔悴的双颊．

fall·er [ˈfɔːlə] *n.* ①伐木者．②【纺】(走锭纺纱机的)坠杆．

fal·li·bil·i·ty [ˌfæliˈbiliti] *n.* 易错；易受骗；虚妄．

fal·li·ble [ˈfæləbl] *a.* 易犯错误的；易受骗的；难免有错误的．*All men are ~.* 人皆有过．**-ness** *n.* **-li·bly** *ad.*

fall·ing [ˈfɔːliŋ] *n.* ①落下，坠落，下降．②洼进，凹陷；崩塌；垮台；陷落．③堕落．*the ~ of the leaf* 落叶时节，秋天．— *a.* ①落下的；垂下的；跌落的．②衰退的；变衰弱的．③〔美方〕(天气)象要下雨[下雪]似的．*a ~ intonation [tone]* 降调．~ *leaf*【空】落叶式降落．~ *market*【商】疲落的行市．~ **away** 反叛，叛教，叛党，脱党，变节．~ **in** 垮下，陷下〔*cf.* fall in〕．~ **leaf**【空】落叶式降落〔一种特技表演〕．~ **off** 衰落，衰败；(销路等的)减少 (*a ~ off place*〔美〕穷乡僻壤)．~ **out** 争执，冲突，不和．~ **sickness**〔罕〕癫痫．~ **sluice** 自动水闸．~ **star** 流星．~ **stone** 陨石．

Fal·lo·pi·an [fəˈləupiən] **tube** *n.*【解】输卵管，喇叭管．

fal·low[1] [ˈfæləu] *a.* (田地)休闲中的；荒芜的；(精神，智力等)松弛的，不活跃的；不熟练的．*lie ~* (田地)在休闲中．*lay land ~* 休闲田地．— *n.* 休闲地；休闲．— *vt.* 使(翻耕后的土地)休闲．*land in ~* 休闲地．*green ~* 绿肥作物休闲地．*black ~* 秋耕休闲地．*occupied ~* 半休闲．**-ness** *n.*

fal·low[2] [ˈfæləu] *a.* 淡棕色的．~ **deer**【动】黇鹿 (*Dama dama*)〔产于欧洲，夏天皮毛发黄，起白斑〕．

false [fɔːls] *a.* (*opp.* true) ①虚伪的，虚假的，捏造的；撒谎的，不诚实的；错误的．②不正的，非法的．③假造的，摹造的，人造的．④临时的，补助的．⑤【乐】不合调的．***be ~ of heart*** 不老实．***be ~ to*** = prove ~ to. ***bear [give] ~ witness*** 作假见证．***prove ~ to*** (背信)出卖，违背；辜负，欺骗．***sail [take] under ~ colours*** 挂别国国旗航行；冒充．— *adv.* 欺诈地；叛卖地．***play sb. ~*** 欺骗，出卖．~ **acacia**【植】刺槐 ~ **accusation [charge]** 诬告．~ **alarm** ①假警报，一场虚惊．②昙花一现的人物．~ **arrest**【法】(个人之间的)非法拘留．~ **attack**【军】佯攻．~ **attic**【建】假(屋)顶层．~ **bottom** ①(盒子等的)活底．②(威士忌酒杯的)假底．~ **card** 为迷惑对方而出的牌．~ **eggplant**【植】假茄子．~ **face** 假面具．~ **front** 骗人的外表．~ **fruit**【植】假果．~ **hair** 假发．~ **imprisonment** 非法监禁．~ **jaw**【机】虎钳口．~**-hearted** *a.* 奸诈的，不诚实的，虚伪的．~**hood** (*opp.* truth) 错误；虚伪，虚妄；撒谎；谎 (*tell a ~hood* 撒谎)．~ **keel**【船】副龙骨，保护龙骨．~ **position** 与心意[原则]相反的地位[立场]；尴尬的地位[处境]．~ **pretenses**【法】欺诈，诈骗(财物)．~ **pride** 妄自尊大．~ **ribs**【解】假肋．~ **roof** 屋顶状天花板．~ **smut**【农】稻麴病．~ **start**【体】错误的起步；慌张失措的开始．~ **statement** 伪证．~ **step** ①失足；绊倒．②社交性错误，不正当行为．~ **tooth** 假牙，义齿．~ **window**【建】假窗，配景窗．~**work**【建】脚手架，建筑架，工作架，临时支撑．**-ly** *ad.* 不正，误；不诚实；虚妄 (*be falsely accused* 被诬告)．**-ness** *n.* 虚伪；欺骗．

fal·set·tist [fɔːlˈsetist] *n.* 假嗓子歌手．

fal·set·to [fɔːlˈsetəu] (*pl.* ~*s*) *n.*〔It.〕假声，假嗓子〔*cf.* head voice〕；假嗓子歌手．*in ~* 用假声．— *a.* 用假声的．— *ad.* 用假声地．~ **tone** 假声[嗓子]．

fals·ies [ˈfɔːlsiːz] *n. pl.*〔美口〕妇女衬胸〔为使胸部丰满而衬在乳罩内的乳房形衬垫物〕．

fal·si·fi·ca·tion [ˌfɔːlsifiˈkeiʃən] *n.* ①弄虚作假；伪造；窜改；歪曲．②证明为虚伪，证明为无根据．~ *of accounts* 造假帐．~ *of wine* 酒里掺水作假．

fal·si·fier [ˈfɔːlsiˌfaiə] *n.* 伪造者；窜改者；弄虚作假的人，撒谎的人．

fal·si·fy [ˈfɔːlsiˌfai] *vt.* ①窜改，伪造(文件等)；歪曲．②证明…是假的[错的]．④搞错，误用．~ *certificates* 伪造执照．~ *records* 窜改记录．~ *a statement* 证明论述有误．*Her hopes have be falsified.* 她的希望已落空．— *vi.* 作假，撒谎．

fal·si·ty [ˈfɔːlsiti] *n.* 虚伪，不真实；欺诈；谎言．

Fal·staff [ˈfɔːlstɑːf], **Sir John** 约翰·福斯泰夫〔莎士比亚戏剧中一个肥胖、机智、乐观、爱吹牛的武士〕；爱吹牛的人．**-i·an** [-iən] *a.* 象福斯泰夫(一样)的．

falt·boat [ˈfɑːltbəut] *n.* 可以折叠的小艇．

fal·ter [ˈfɔːltə] *vi.* ①蹒跚，踉跄，摇晃．②颤抖，支吾，结巴．③逡巡，踌躇，迟疑；畏缩；(记忆力等)不确定，不稳定．— *vt.* 结结巴巴地说 (*out*)．— *n.* ①摇晃．②支吾，结巴．③踌躇，逡巡；不稳．

fal·ter·ing [ˈfɔːltəriŋ] *a.* ①踉跄的，摇晃的；不稳的．②颤抖的，支吾的．③踌躇的．*speak in a ~ voice* 用颤抖[吞吞吐吐]的声音说．**-ly** *ad.*

F.A.M., F. and A. M. = Free and Accepted Masons〔英〕共济会．

fam. = familiar; family.

fame [feim] *n.* ①名声，声望．②〔古〕传闻，风声．*a house of ill ~* 妓院．*ill ~* 污名，恶评，丑闻．*undying ~* 不朽之名．— *vt.* ①使出名，扬…的名．②〔古〕盛传．***come to ~ = win ~*** 成名．

famed [feimd] *a.* 闻名的，有名的，出名的．***be ~ for*** 以…出名．

Fa·meuse [fəˈmuːz] *n.* 晚熟的美国红苹果〔又名 snow apple〕．

fa·mil·ial [fəˈmiljəl] *a.* ①家庭的；涉及家庭的．②某家特有的．

fa·mil·iar [fəˈmiljə] *a.* ①亲密的，交情好的．②常见的，流行的．③熟悉…的，精通…的 (*with*)．④世所周知的，人人知道的 (*to*)．⑤平常的，普通的，通俗的；非正式的．⑥(男女间)亲昵；过分亲密，放肆．⑦家族[庭]的．~ *friends* 亲密的朋友．*a ~ song* 流行歌曲．*a ~ phrase* 惯用词句．*things ~ to us* 我们所熟悉的事物．*be ~ with English* 通晓英语．*a ~ essay* 小品文，随笔．*He made himself much too ~ with the girl.* 他对这位姑娘太放肆了．***be ~ with*** ①同…相好．②精通，熟习．***be on ~ terms with*** 同…交情好，同…熟识．~ ***spirit*** = familiar *n.* ⑤ ***make oneself ~ with*** 同…好[熟悉]起来，同…亲近起来．— *n.* ①亲友．②常客．③高级官吏的家属．④【天主】教皇[主教]的仆人．⑤传说中供女巫差遣的妖精．**-ly** *ad.*

fa·mil·i·ar·i·ty [fəˌmiliˈæriti] *n.* ①亲密，亲近；融洽．②熟悉，精通．③深交，不客气．④〔*pl.*〕爱抚；放肆的言行．*show thorough ~ with a language* 十分熟悉某种语言．***F- breeds contempt***.〔谚〕亲昵引起轻视，近之则不逊．

fa·mil·iar·i·za·tion [fəˌmiljəraiˈzeiʃən] *n.* ①亲密；熟识．②(思想等的)通俗化．

fa·mil·iar·ize [fəˈmiljəraiz] *vt.* ①使亲密，使熟习，使

熟知；使精通．②使尽人皆知，使通俗化*(to)*．～ ***oneself with*** 精通，熟习．

fam·i·lism [ˈfæmilizəm] *n.* 家庭主义〔强调家庭感情，以家庭为基本单位的社会结构〕．**-lis·tic** [ˌfæmiˈlistik] *a.*

fam·i·ly [ˈfæmili, ˈfæməli] *n.* ①家，家庭；〔集合词〕家庭成员，家属，子女；亲属．②氏族，家族，亲族．③〔美〕阁员，(特指国务部的)同僚；派别．④门第，家系；〔英〕门阀，名门．⑤人种，种族，民族．⑥系；族；科；【语】语族．⑦〔美俚〕(黑手党等犯罪集团的)行动小组．*His ～ is an old one*．他的家庭是一个旧式家庭．*My ～ are all well*．我全家都好．*the President's official ～*〔美〕总统的全体阁僚．*the Indo-European ～* 印欧语族．*the Teutonic ～* 条顿民族．*the chromium ～*【化】铬族．*the kantian ～* 康德学派．*the cat ～*【动】猫科．***a happy ～*** ①幸福家庭．②相安无事处于同一牢笼的不同类动物．***in a ～ way*** ①象家人一样随便，不拘形式地．②怀孕．***in the ～ way***〔美〕怀孕．***of (good) ～*** 出身门第很高的．***run in the ～*** (性格特征等)为一家所共有，世代相传 *(A gift for music runs in that family*．那一家人人有音乐天才)．— *a.* 家庭的，家族的．*a ～ likeness* 亲属之间的相似，隐约的相似．～ **allowance** (工资外的)家庭津贴．～ **Bible** 家用大型《圣经》．～ **butcher** 供应家庭的肉商〔区别于供应军队等〕．～ **circle** 家庭中常来的亲友们；【剧】家庭包厢．～ **coach**〔英〕①有顶大马车．②一种罚金游戏．～ **dissensions** 家庭纠纷．**F- Division**〔英〕(处理离婚、收养等方面诉讼的)高级民事法庭．～ *doctor* 家庭特约医师．～ **farm** 家庭农场．～ **friend** 世交；与全家人都来往的朋友．～ **hotel** (特别优待一家人住宿的)家庭旅馆．～ **man** ①爱管家务〔关心家庭〕的人．②有老婆孩子的人．～ **name** 姓．～ **planning** 计划生育．～ **room** 供一家人公用的起居室．～ **selection** 谱系选择．～ **skeleton** 不愿外扬的家丑．～ **style** 家庭式用餐法〔把大盘菜依次传递，自己拨取食物的进餐法〕．～ **ties** 家累．～ **tree** 家系图．～ **way** 怀孕 *She is in the ～ way again*．她又怀孕了．*She got herself in a ～ way*．她有喜了．

fam·ine [ˈfæmin] *n.* ①饥荒．②〔古〕饥饿．③极度缺乏．*a coal ～* 煤荒．*a water ～* 水荒．*die of ～* 饿死．～ **prices** 缺货时的高价．

fam·ish [ˈfæmiʃ] *vt.* 使饿，使饥饿；〔古〕使饿死．〔多用被动语态〕．*be ～ed for food* 缺粮挨饿，断炊．*be ～ed to death* 饿死．*I'm ～ing*．〔俚〕我饿坏了．*a ～ing wind* 冷得要命的风．— *vi.* 饿，挨饿；〔古〕饿死．

fa·mous [ˈfeiməs] *a.* ①有名的，出名的，驰名的 *(for)*．②〔口〕极好的．*a ～ scenic spot* 有名的风景区．*a ～ appetite* 胃口极好．*a ～ performance* 精彩的演出．***be a ～ hand at = be ～ at*** 是…的名手，善于．**-ly** *ad.* ①著名地．②非常，很．③〔口〕挺好．**-ness** *n.*

fam·u·lus [ˈfæmjuləs] *n.* *(pl.* ***-li*** [-lai]) (中世纪巫师或学者的)助手；侍从．

fan[1] [fæn] *n.* ①扇子；风扇，鼓风机．②簸箕；扬谷机；(风车的)定风翼；【空】螺旋桨，螺旋桨叶片．③扇状物(如孔雀尾，棕榈树叶等)．*a draft ～* 吸风机，通风扇．*an electric ～* 电风扇．*an exhaust ～*．抽风机，排气风扇．*a folding ～* 折扇．— *vt.* ①扇，扇动；激起．②(用扇子)驱走；簸(谷)；扬去(糠等)．③扇燃．④把(翅膀等)张开成扇形．⑤〔美俚〕拍打，鞭打；搜查；〔美俚〕连续急速扫射．⑥〔美俚〕搜查．～ *a fire* 扇火使旺．～ *the flies from the food* 从食物上扇走苍蝇．— *vi.* 飘动，拍翅；成扇形．～ ***away*** 扇去．～ ***in*** 扇进．～ ***oneself*** 扇扇子．～ ***out***【军】成扇形散开；【讯】分开(电缆心)．～ ***the flame*** 煽动情绪．**～-in** 【计】输出，输出端数．**～light** *n.*【建】楣窗，扇形气窗 (=〔美〕transom)．**～like** *a.* ①象扇的，象风扇般转动的．②折叠的．**～-out**【计】输出，输出端数．～ **palm**【植】扇叶棕榈．**～-shaped** *a.* 扇形的．～ **tracery**【建】扇形(花)格架．～ **truss**【建】扇形桁架．

fan[2] [fæn] *n.* 〔美俚〕(运动、影迷，球迷)狂热爱好者；狂慕者．*a film [movie] ～* 影迷．～ **mail** (影迷、球迷等写来的)表示敬慕的信．

fa·nat·ic(al) [fəˈnætik(əl)] *n.* 狂热宗教徒，狂信者；入迷的人．— *a.* 狂信的，狂热的，入迷的．**-i·cal·ly** *ad.*

fa·nat·i·cism [fəˈnætisizəm] *n.* 狂信，狂热．

fa·nat·i·cize [fəˈnætisaiz] *vt., vi.* (使)狂信；(使)变成狂信者；(使)变狂热．

fan·cied [ˈfænsid] *a.* 幻想的，空想出来的．

fan·ci·er [ˈfænsiə] *n.* ①空想家．②懂得一些窍门的行家；巧妙的设计师．③…迷．④(鸟兽的)饲养行家．*a bird ～* 养鸟迷；养鸟行家．

fan·ci·ful [ˈfænsiful] *a.* ①爱空想的；富于想象力的．②幻想中的．③奇异的．**-ly** *ad.* **-ness** *n.*

fan·cy [ˈfænsi] *n.* ①想象(力)．②幻想．③嗜好，爱好；嗜好品．④〔集合词〕〔the ～〕嗜好者，玩赏者；〔特指〕拳击爱好者；鸟兽(饲养)爱好者．⑤(玩赏动物)珍奇品种培育(法)．⑥花式；花式织物，花式货品．⑦〔古〕爱．*a passing ～* 一时的爱好．*a wild ～* 不着边际的空想．***after one's ～*** 合自己心意．***be full of fancies*** 幻想多；异想天开．***catch [please, strike, suit, take] the ～ of*** 投合…的心意，吸引．***go off into wild flights of ～*** 胡思乱想；异想天开．***have a ～ for*** 爱好，爱上；入迷．***have a ～ that*** 总觉得要[想]．***see in ～*** 想象．***strike sb.'s ～*** 投合某人心意．***take a ～ to [for]*** 爱好，爱上．***to one's ～*** 合自己心意．— *a.* ①煞费心机的，别出心裁的 *(opp.* plain)．②装璜用的；花式的，杂色的；变种的，品种珍奇的．③空想的，幻想的；异想天开的；异常的，特别的．④〔美口〕(水果等)特选的，特制的，高档的．⑤(价格)高昂的；供应高价品的．*a ～ ball* 化装跳舞会．*～ birds* 珍种奇鸟．*a ～ box* 装璜特别好看的商品盒子．*～ buttons* 饰钮．*～ cakes* 花式糕点．*～ coal* 上等煤，精选煤．*～ diving* 花式跳水．*～ dress* (化装舞会等的)化装服装．*a ～ fair*〔英〕小商品市场．*～ fishes* 观赏鱼．*～ fresh fruits* 特级鲜果．*～ goods* 花哨的小工艺品．*a ～ price* 十分昂贵的价格．— *vt.* ①想象，设想，幻想，妄想．②想…；爱好，欢喜．③认为，相信；〔俚〕自命为，自以为．⑤(为玩赏而)饲养，培养(变种动植物等)．*He fancies himself (to be) ill*．他以为自己病了．*I ～ he will come*．我想他会来的．*He fancies himself (to be) an authority*．他自以为是个权威．*I rather ～ he won't come*．我总以为他不会来．*She fancies herself still young*．她以为自己还年轻哩．*I don't ～ this place at all*．我一点也不喜欢这个地方．*Don't you ～ anything?* (问病人等)你想吃点什么吗？***F- (that)!*** 真想不到！奇怪！***F- his believing it!*** 谁想得到他竟会相信！— *vi.* 想象，幻想．***Just ～! = Only ～!*** 想想看！奇怪！**～-bred** *a.* ①由幻想而产生的．②(动物)品种优良的．～ **dan**〔美俚〕华而不实的人，喜欢耍花架子的运动员．**～-free** *a.* ①任凭想象随意驰骋的．②未婚的，情窦未开的，天真无邪的．～ **house** 妓院．～ **man** ①情夫．②靠女人倒贴而生活的男子．**～sick** *a.* 害相思病的．～ **woman [girl, lady]** ①情妇．②妓女．**～work** 钩编织品，刺绣品．

F. and A.M. = Free and Accepted Masons〔英〕共济会．

fan·dan·gle [fænˈdæŋgl] *n.* ①〔美俚〕(华丽但不值钱的)小装饰品．②〔俚〕胡闹，荒唐事．

fan·dan·go [fænˈdæŋgəu] *n.* *(pl.* *～s)* ①(一种轻快的)西班牙舞(曲)，方登戈舞(曲)．②胡闹，荒唐事．

fan·dom [ˈfændəm] *n.* 全体运动迷，全体球迷，全体影迷．

fane [fein] *n.* ①〔古，诗〕神庙．②〔古〕教堂．

fan·fare [ˈfænfɛə] *n.* ①(喇叭、铜鼓的)嘹亮吹奏声．②鼓吹，夸耀．— *vt.* 热闹地介绍〔宣布〕．*make [raise] a big ～* 大吹大擂．

F

fan·fa·ron·ade [ˌfænfærəˈnɑːd] *n.* ①浮夸,吹牛. ②= fanfare.

Fang [fæŋ] *n.* ①(分布在非洲几内亚湾东部海岸的)芳族,芳人. ②芳人讲的班图语.

fang [fæŋ] *n.* ①(犬、狼等的)尖牙;狼牙,犬齿;(蛇的)毒牙. ②牙根. ③(牙状的)尖端;(工具等的)齿,爪. — *vt.* ①以尖牙咬;在…上长有尖牙状物. ②灌水引动(水泵). *rocks ~ed with icicles* 上有尖牙状冰柱的岩石.

fanged [ˈfæŋd] *a.* 有尖牙的,有毒牙的.

fan·gle [ˈfæŋgəl] *n.* 新型. *new ~s of dress* 新款式的服装.

fan·ion [ˈfænjən] *n.* (士兵或测量员作为标志用的)小旗,测量旗.

fan·jet [ˈfænˌdʒet] *n.* ①【机】涡轮通风器. ②【空】鼓风式喷气飞机.

fan·ner [ˈfænə] *n.* ①扇风者. ②鼓风机,扬谷机.

Fan·nie [ˈfæni] *n.* = Fanny.

fan·nings [ˈfæniŋz] *n.* 〔*pl.*〕①簸出物;筛出的粗茶叶. ②(交换机电缆的)扇形编组.

Fan·ny [ˈfæni] *n.* 范妮〔女子名,Frances 的昵称〕.

fan·ny [ˈfæni] *n.* ***(pl. -nies)*** 〔俚〕臀部;屁股.

fan·on [ˈfænən] *n.* ①(祭师做弥撒时带的)臂巾. ②(教皇做弥撒时穿的)披肩.

fan·tab·u·lous [fænˈtæbjuləs] *a.* 〔美俚〕极好的,极妙的.

fan·tad [ˈfæntæd] *n.* = fantod.

fan·tail [ˈfænteil] *n.* ①扇状尾部. ②【动】扇尾金鱼. 扇尾鸽. ③【建】鸠尾榫. ④【船】鸭尾艄. ⑤(运煤工戴的)扇形帽. ~ *deck* 船尾甲板. **-ed** *a.* 扇形尾的.

fan·ta·si·a [fænˈteizjə, -ˈtɑː-] *n.* ①【乐】幻想曲. ②幻想作品.

fan·ta·size [ˈfæntəsaiz] *vt., vi.* 幻想,梦想. **-ta·sist** [-sist] *n.* 幻想家,梦想家.

fan·tasm [ˈfæntæzm] *n.* ①幻影;鬼. ②幻想,幻觉;空想(= phantasm).

fan·tas·ma·go·ri·a [fænˌtæzməˈgɔːriə] *n.* = phantasmagoria.

fan·tast [ˈfæntæst] *n.* 幻想家,空想家;神经不正常的人.

fan·tas·tic, fan·tas·ti·cal [fænˈtæstik, -tikəl] *a.* ①空想的,异想天开的. ②奇异的,古怪的. ③极大的,大得难以相信的. ~ *reasons* 奇怪的理由. — *n.* 〔古〕古怪的人. ***trip the light*** ~〔美〕跳舞. **-ti·cal·ly** *ad.* **-ism** *n.*

fan·tas·ti·cal·i·ty [fænˌtæstiˈkæliti] *n.* ①怪异;奇异. ②奇谈;怪事.

fan·tas·ti·cate [fænˈtæstikeit] *vt.* 使成为荒谬(的梦想). **-ca·tion** [fænˌtæstiˈkeiʃən] *n.*

fan·tas·ti·co [fænˈtæstikəu] *n.* 可笑的怪人.

fan·ta·sy [ˈfæntəsi, -zi] *n.* ①空想,幻想. ②怪念头,想入非非. ③想象力的产物,离奇的图案,奇妙的设计. ④【乐】幻想曲;幻想作品. ⑤观赏硬币〔专供收藏,并无流通使用价值〕. — *vt.* 想象;幻想;对…进行幻想. — *vi.* ①空想,幻想,梦想. ②奏幻想曲. ~**land** 梦境,幻想世界,幻境.

Fan·te(e), Fan·ti [ˈfæntiː] *n.* 〔*sing., pl.*〕(西非洲、加纳的)芬提族;芬提语. ***go*** ~ (欧洲人)芬提化,遵从西非当地的风俗习惯.

an·toc·ci·ni [ˌfæntəˈtʃiːniː] *n.* 〔*pl.*〕〔It.〕木偶,傀儡;木偶戏,傀儡戏.

fan·tod [ˈfæntəd] *n.* 焦躁不安;神经紧张. *the ~s* 焦急不安状态.

fan·tom *n.* = phantom.

fan·wise [ˈfænˌwaiz] *ad., a.* (展开)成扇形(的).

fan·wort [ˈfænˌwəːt] *n.* 【植】水盾草属 (= cabomba).

Fany, F.A.N.Y. = First Aid Nursing Yeomanry〔英〕急救护士队.

FAO, F.A.O. = Food and Agriculture Organization (联合国)粮食及农业组织.

F.A.P. = First Aid Post 急救所[站].

FAQ = ① fair average quality【商】中等品. ② free at quay 码头交货(价格).

fa·quir [ˈfɑːkiə, fəˈkiə] *n.* = fakir[1].

far [fɑː] *a.* ***(far·ther*** [ˈfɑːðə], ***fur·ther*** [ˈfəːðə]; ***farthest*** [ˈfɑːðist], ***fur·thest*** [ˈfəːðist]***)*** ①远隔的;离得远的;上远路的,长途的. ②较远的,远处的. ③久远的,上了年纪的. *a ~ country* 遥远的国家. *a ~ traveller* 远行者. *the ~ side of the room* 屋子的那一边. *the ~ side of a horse* 马的右边,下马的那边〔上马由左边〕. *a statesman of ~ sight* 目光远大的政治家. *the F- East* 远东. *the ~ past* 太古时候,很久以前. *the ~ West* (尤指美国)西部地方. — *ad.* 〔比较形同上〕①(地点)远,远隔,远在. ★口语中表示地点时 far 主要用于疑问句和否定句;肯定句中的表现方式是: We went a long way〔书面语… went far〕. The house is a long way off〔书面语… is far〕. ②(时间)遥远,久远. ③(程度)很,极,大,…得多. ~ *ahead* 远在前面. ~ *away [off]* 远隔,在老远处. *the ~ distant past* 久远以前. ~ *back in the past* 远古,在很久以前. *as ~ back as the 18th century* 远在十八世纪. *go so ~ as to* 竟然到…的地步,甚至…. ~ *into the night* 到深夜. ~ *better* 好得多. *I cannot say how ~ his story is true.* 我不能说他的话可靠到什么程度. ***a ~ cry*** 距离很远;不大相同(*It is a ~ cry to London.* 到伦敦很远. *It is a ~ cry from a magic lantern to television.* 电视与幻灯大不相同). ***as ~ as*** ①远到,直到(*go as ~ as Africa* 远至非洲). ②就;尽;至于(*as ~ as possible* 尽可能,尽量). ***as ~ as in me lies*** 尽我的力量. ***as [so] ~ as it goes*** 就现状来说,就其本身而言. ***as ~ as I know*** 就我所知 (= so ~ as I know). ***by ~*** (修饰比较级,最高级,表示数量、程度等)…得多;尤其;更(*This is by ~ the best.* 这个尤其好). ***~ and apart*** 远离着,远隔着. ***~ and away*** 非常;大大,…得多;肯定地,无疑地(*He is ~ and away the greatest poet living.* 他是目前最最伟大的诗人). ***~ and near [nigh]*** 远近,到处,四面八方. ***~ and wide*** 遍,广泛地,到处. ***~ be it from me*** 我决不会. ***(few and) ~ between*** 极少,偶尔. ***~ from*** ①远离. ②决不,决没有,完全不 (*~ from Paris* 远离巴黎的地方. *It's ~ from perfect.* 那还远远算不上完善). ***~ from it!*** 差得远呢! ***(be) ~ gone*** (病等)更加厉害;大醉;(欠债)更多. ***~ out*** 〔美俚〕①不寻常的. ②(政见等)极端的. ③奥秘的,秘传的. ***from ~*** 从远处. ***from ~ and near*** 从各处;远近都…. ***go ~*** ①成功,成名. ②长时间保持,大有帮助. ***go ~ towards*** 大有助于,大有贡献于. ***go ~ with*** 很能感动…,对…有巨大力量[影响]. ***how ~*** ①(离…)多远(*How ~ is it to the office?* 离办公室多远?). ②到什么程度[范围](*I don't know how ~ to trust them.* 我不知道应该相信他们到什么程度). ***in so ~ as*** (表示程度、范围)就…;尽…;至于. ***so [thus] ~*** 到目前(此地)为止;就此范围[程度]来说. ***So ~, so good.*** 到现在为止,一直都还不错. ***so ~ as*** 尽…说,就…说;只就…说(*So ~ as I know.* 就我知道的说). ***so ~ as … concerns*** 就…说. ~**away** [ˈfɑːrəˈwei] *a.* ①远方的;老早老早以前的. ②(眼色、神情等)走神的,恍惚的. ~**-back** *a.* ①古时的. ②遥远的. ~**-between** *a.* ①隔离的,远隔的. ②稀有的. ~**-end** (线路或电路的)远端. ~**-famed** *a.* 驰名的,闻名的. ~**-fetched** *a.* 强词夺理的,牵强附会的. ~**-flung** *a.* 〔书〕广泛的,漫长的,辽阔的. ~**-going** *a.* 范围广泛的. ~**-gone** *a.* ①(病等)日益加重的. ②遥远的. ③疲乏不堪的. ④已耗损的. ~**most** *a.* 遥远的. ~**-off** [ˈfɑːrɔːf] *a.* 远方的,远隔的;遥远的. ~**-out** *a.* ①在太空远处的. ②〔喻〕远离常规[传统方式]的;非常新颖的;先锋派(艺术)的. ~**-outer** 远离常规的人,反传统的人. ~**-point** 视远点〔眼睛看物的极限点〕. ~**-rang·ing** *a.* 远程的. ~**-reach-**

ing *a.* 深远的，效果［影响］大的；广泛的（~-*reaching designs* 远大的计划）．~-**red** *a.*【物】远红外的．~ **right** 极右分子［主义］．~-**right** *a.* 极右的．~-**seeing** *a.* 看得远的，目光远的；想得周到的，有先见之明的．~-**sighted** *a.* 远视的，有先见之明的；【医】远视的．~-**sightedness** 远视，远见．**-ness** *n.*

far. = ①farad. ②farthing.

far·ad [ˈfærəd] *n.* 法拉〔电容单位〕．**-a·ic** [-ˈdeiik], **-ic** [fəˈrædik] *a.* 感应电流的．**-ism** [ˈfærədizəm] *n.* 感应电应用，感应电疗法．

Far·a·day [ˈfærədi, -dei] *n.* ①法拉第〔姓氏〕．② **Michael** ~ 法拉第〔1791—1867，英国物理学家、化学家〕．③〔f-〕【电】法拉第〔电量单位〕．~ **dark space**【物】法拉第暗区．~ **disk**【物】法拉第圆盘．~ **effect**【物】法拉第效应．

far·a·dize [ˈfærədaiz] *vt.*【医】用感应电治疗〔刺激〕．**-za·tion** [ˌfærədaiˈzeiʃən] *n.* 感应电疗法．

farce [fɑːs] *n.* ①滑稽戏，笑剧．②滑稽，可笑的事物，冒充的东西．③馅儿．— *vt.* ①使带滑稽趣味，使（演说，作品等）有趣味．②〔古〕填塞；（用香料等）增进…的口味．

far·ceur [fɑːˈsəː] *n.* 〔F.〕 ①丑角，滑稽角色；笑剧作家．②爱说笑话的人．

far·ci·cal [ˈfɑːsikəl] *a.* 笑剧的，滑稽戏的；滑稽的．**-ly** *ad.* **-ness** *n.*

far·ci·cal·i·ty [ˌfɑːsiˈkæliti] *n.* 滑稽剧性质；滑稽性，滑稽味．

far·ci(e) [fɑːˈsiː] *a.* 有馅的．

far·cy [ˈfɑːsi] *n.* ①（马的）鼻疽；马皮疽．②家畜慢性致命性放线菌病．

far·del [ˈfɑːdl] *n.* 〔古〕①捆，包；包袱；重担．②不幸，灾祸．

fare [fɛə] *n.* ①运费，车费，船费．②乘客．③伙食．④（渔船的）捕获量．⑤精神食粮．*a single [double]* ~ 单程［来回］票价．*a bill of* ~ 菜单．*coarse* ~ 粗食．*simple [homely]* ~ 家常便饭．— *vi.* ①过日子，生活；受招待．②〔主语为 it〕（事）进行得（好、坏），处境（好，坏），结果（如何）．③吃，进食．④〔古〕去，前进，旅行．*How did you ~ in Paris?* 您在巴黎生活如何？*How ~s it with you?* 你近来怎样？你好吗？~ ***forth*** 〔古〕动身，去．~ ***ill*** 倒霉，过无聊日子；（事业等）吃亏，失败．~ ***well*** 走运；过得好；（事业）顺遂，成功．***F- you well!*** 〔古〕= farewell. ***You may go farther and ~ worse.*** 〔谚〕越走得远可能越倒楣〔劝人知足常乐，安于现状语〕．

fare-thee-well [ˌfɛəðiːˈwel], **fare-you-well** [ˌfɛəjəˈwel] *n.* 极度；完善．*to a* ~ 尽善尽美；登峰造极．

fare·well [ˈfɛəˈwel] *int.* 再见，再会，一路平安．— *a.* 告别的，送行的．*a ~ address* 告别辞．*a ~ dinner* 饯行宴会．*a ~ meeting* 欢送会．*a ~ present* 告别礼物．— *n.* ①告别．②欢送会．③告别辞．***bid*** ~ 辞行．***make one's ~s*** 道别，告辞．~ ***to life*** 辞世，死．***take a ~ of*** 向…辞行．***take one's*** ~ 辞行，告别．

fare·well-to-spring [ˈfɛəˈweltəˈspriŋ] *n.*【植】可爱高代花 (*Godetia amoena*)〔产于美国西部〕．

fa·ri·na [fəˈrainə, fəˈriːnə] *n.* ①谷粉．②淀粉．③粉状物质．④【植】花粉．

far·i·na·ceous [ˌfæriˈneiʃəs] *a.* ①谷粉制的．②含淀粉的．③粉状的．

far·i·nose [ˈfærinəus] *a.* ①产粉的，含粉的，粉质的．②【动、植】具粉的，被粉的．

far·kle·ber·ry [ˈfɑːklberi] *n.*【植】臼莓 (*Vaccinium arboreum*)〔美国南部的一种灌木〕．

farl(e) [fɑːl] *n.* 〔Scot.〕燕麦粉［面粉］薄饼．

Far·ley [ˈfɑːli] *n.* 法利〔姓氏〕．

farm [fɑːm] *n.* ①农场，农庄；农田；农场住宅，农家．②饲养场，畜牧场．③〔美〕别墅．④【英史】地租；出租田地；包租区．⑤〔美〕（棒球联合总会所属主要任务为训练新队员的）棒球分会．⑥育儿所，托儿所．*a state* ~ 国营农场．*F- Credit Administration* 〔美〕农场贷款署．*a fruit* ~ 果园．*a wheat* ~ 小麦地．*a chicken [poultry]* ~ 养鸡场．— *vt.* ①耕作，耕种，在…上经营农场；饲养（家畜等）．②佃出，出租；招人承包，包出（工件，活计、收租税等）(*out*)．③寄养（幼儿等）(*out*)．④把（囚犯等）作为劳动力出租 (*out*)．⑤使（地力）耗尽．~ *out the right to collect taxes* 包出收税权．*She ~ed out the baby with her mother.* 她把婴儿放在母亲家寄养．— *vi.* 耕作，经营农场［畜牧场］，务农．~ *for a living* 以农为生．~ *upon one's own land* 自耕．~ **bloc**【美政】（国会中由各农业州议员组成的）农业集团．~ **crops** 农作物．~**hand** 农业工人，农场工人；雇农．~**house** *n.* 农场住宅；农家．~ **implements [tools]** 农具．~ **labourer** = ~hand, ~**land** 农田．~ **machinery** 农业机械．~ **produce** 农产品．~**stead** 〔主英〕（包括住宅在内的）农场．~ **work** 农业劳动，农活．~**yard** 农家庭院．

farm·er [ˈfɑːmə] *n.* ①经营农业者，农场主〔*cf.* peasant〕；农夫．②（租税等的）包收人．③幼儿代养人．*a landed [tenant]* ~ 自耕［佃］农．*Farmer's Association* 农会．***an afternoon*** ~ 拖拖拉拉的人．***a dirt*** ~〔美口〕自耕农，小农．***gentleman*** ~ 乡绅，从事农业的贵族．~**like** *a.* 农夫般的．

farm·er·ette [ˌfɑːməˈret] *n.* 〔美口〕农场女工，农妇．

farm·ing [ˈfɑːmiŋ] *n.* ①农业，农作，耕作；饲养（畜禽）．②（租税等的）包收．③寄养幼孩．*mechanized* ~ 机耕．*small peasant* ~ 小农经济．*tank* ~ （用溶液培养植物的）无土栽培法．— *a.* 农业的；农场的．*the busy [slack]* ~ *season* 农忙［闲］季节．~ *implements* 农具．~ *land* 耕地．*a ~ region* 农业区．~ *system* 农作制度，农场管理制度〔*cf.* cropping system〕．

far·o [ˈfɛərəu] *n.*【牌】菲罗〔一种类似牌九的简单赌博〕．~ **bank** 玩菲罗牌戏的赌场．

fa·rouche [fəˈruːʃ] *a.* ①桀骜不驯的，凶猛的．②缺乏社交风度的；粗野失礼的；缺乏教养的．

far·ra·gi·nous [fəˈreidʒinəs] *a.* 杂凑成的，混杂的，乱七八糟的．

far·ra·go [fəˈrɑːgəu] *n.* (*pl.* ~*es*) 拼凑，大杂烩，混杂物．

Far·rar [fəˈrɑː] *n.* 法勒〔姓氏〕．

Far·rell [ˈfærəl] *n.* 法雷尔〔姓氏〕．

far·ri·er [ˈfæriə] *n.* 〔英〕①钉马掌［马蹄铁］的铁匠．②马医；兽医．③【军】管理军马的骑兵下士．

far·ri·er·y [ˈfæriəri] *n.* 〔英〕马掌钉法；兽医术．②马掌铺，马掌厂．

far·row [ˈfærəu] *n.* 一胎猪；猪下仔．*10 at one* ~ 一胎下十只猪崽．— *vt.* （猪）产一胎猪崽．— *vi.* 猪产崽 (*down*)．

fart [fɑːt] *n.* 〔卑〕①屁．②傻老头．— *vt., vi.* 放（屁）．

far·ther [ˈfɑːðə]〔far 的两种比较级形式之一，另一形式为 further〕*a.* ①再过去点的，再远点的；再进一步的，更往前一点儿的．②进一步的，另外的〔通常也用 further〕．*the ~ side of the hill* 山那边．*make no objection* 不再刁难［反对］．— *ad.* ①再过去点，再远点，再往前一点儿．②加之，更，还，并且〔通常也用 further〕．*I can go no ~.* 我不能再走了．***I'll see you ~ first.*** 我才不干呢！~ ***on*** ①（说明等）在下面；在后面．②更远些，再往前些 (*The village is about three miles ~ on.* 村子还在前面三英里左右的地方)．***No ~!*** 够了！到此为止！***until ~ notice*** 等到另行通知时．***wish sb.*** ~ 但愿某人［物］不在那里就好了．**F- India** 印度支那．

far·ther·most [ˈfɑːðəməust] *a.* 最远的．

far·thest [ˈfɑːðist]〔far 的两种最高级形式之一，另一种形式为 furthest〕*a.* 最远的，顶远的．*the ~ corner of the country* 最遥远的角落，最偏远的地方．— *ad.* 最远；最大程度地，最大限度地．*the seat ~ from the door* 离门最远的坐位．*the ~ thing from the ordinary*

最不寻常的事. *at (the)* ~ 最远也不过; 顶多也不过, 至迟也不过.

far·thing [ˈfɑːðiŋ] *n.* ①法新〔1961年以前的英国铜币, 等于四分之一便士〕. ②〔主要用于否定句〕一点儿, 极少量. *the uttermost* ~ 最后一个铜板. ***doesn't matter a*** ~ 无关紧要, 不足轻重. ***have not a*** ~ 一文不名. ***not care a*** ~ 毫不在乎. ***not worth a*** ~ 毫无价值, 一文不值.

far·thin·gale [ˈfɑˌðiŋgeil] *n.* (十六、七世纪妇女撑开裙子用的)鲸骨衬箍; 用鲸骨箍等撑大的裙子.

FAS = Federation of American Scientists 美国科学家联合会.

FAS, f. a. s. = free alongside ship 【商】船边交货(价格).

fas·ces [ˈfæsiːz] *n. pl.* 〔用作单或复, 其原来的单数形 fascis 较罕用〕〔L.〕束棒, 权标〔古罗马高级执法官吏的权标, 形状为一束棍棒, 中有一柄露出的斧头; 为"法西斯"一词的来源〕; 权威的标记. ②意大利法西斯党的标志.

fas·ci·a [ˈfæʃiə] *n.* *(pl.* ***fas·ci·ae*** [ˈfæʃiiː]*)* 〔常 *pl.*〕①带, 饰带. ②【医】绷带. ③【建】挑口饰, (柱顶)盘座面. ④(店门上的)招牌. ⑤〔英〕汽车仪表板. ⑥【解】筋膜; 【动】(昆虫的)横带. ~ **board** ①【建】挑口板. ②〔英〕汽车仪表板.

fas·ci·ate [ˈfæʃiˌeit] *a.* ①用带子捆束的. ②【植】扁化的; 生长于束簇内的; 簇生的. ③【动】具横带的 (= fasciated).

fas·ci·cle [ˈfæsikl] *n.* ①小束, 一簇. ②【植】(花、叶等的)束, 球, 簇; 密伞花序; 簇生叶, 丛生花. 【解】(神经、肌肉的)束. ③(书刊的)一卷, 一分册. **-d** *a.* 成束的, 簇生的.

fas·cic·u·lar [fəˈsikjulə] *a.* ①【解】(成)束的. ②【植】簇生的; 维管束的. ~ *fibres* 束状纤维. **-ly** *ad.*

fas·cic·u·late(d) [fəˈsikjulit(id)] *a.* = fascicular **-lat·ed·ly** *ad.*

fas·cic·u·la·tion [fæˌsikjuˈleiʃən] *n.* (成)束状; 【植】簇生.

fas·ci·cule [ˈfæsikjuːl] *n.*①(书籍的)分册. ②【解】(神经、肌肉的)束.

fas·cic·u·lus [fəˈsikjuləs] *n.* *(pl.* ***fas·cic·u·li*** [fəˈsikjulai]*)* ①【解】(神经、肌肉的)束. ②(书籍的)分册.

fas·ci·nate [ˈfæsineit] *vt.* ①迷住, 使神魂颠倒, 强烈地吸引住(蛇睨视青蛙等), 蛊惑; 使吓呆. *The boy was ~d by the toys.* 小孩被玩具迷住了. *The snake ~d its prey.* 蛇(用目光)吓住它要捕食的动物. — *vi.* 迷人, 极度吸引人.

fas·ci·nat·ing [ˈfæsineitiŋ] *a.* 魅惑的, 使人神魂颠倒的, 妖媚的. **-ly** *ad.*

fas·ci·na·tion [ˌfæsiˈneiʃən] *n.* ①迷惑力, 魅力. ②迷恋, 神魂颠倒; 强烈爱好.

fas·ci·na·tor [ˈfæsineitə] *n.* ①魅惑者, 迷人者; 妖艳迷人的妇女; 魔术师. ②网眼毛线披巾.

fas·cine [fæˈsiːn] *n.* ①(护堤岸用的)柴笼; (垫沟, 加固战壕等用的)柴捆, 木把, 捆. ②【林】粗杂材.

fas·cis [ˈfæsis] *n.* fasces 的单数〔罕用〕.

fas·cism [ˈfæʃizəm] *n.* 〔常作 F-〕法西斯主义.

Fa·scis·mo [It. faˈʃisməu] *n.* 〔It.〕= Fascism.

fas·cist [ˈfæʃist] *n.* 法西斯主义者, 法西斯分子. — *a.* 法西斯主义的, 法西斯主义者的. **-ic** [fəˈʃistik] *a.* **-i·cal·ly** *ad.*

Fa·scis·ta [fæˈʃistə] *n.* 〔It.〕【史】①意大利法西斯党党员. ②意大利法西斯党, 法西斯蒂.

Fa·scis·ti [fæˈʃistiː] *n.* Fascista 的复数.

fas·cist·i·za·tion [fəˌʃistaiˈzeiʃən] *n.* 法西斯化.

fash [fæʃ] *vt.* 〔Scot.〕使困恼, 使困窘; 使烦恼. **~oneself** 焦虑; 气恼. ~ ***one's beard [head, thumb*** 等***]*** 烦恼. — *n.* 烦恼, 焦虑; 使人厌烦的人〔物〕.

fash·ion [ˈfæʃən] *n.* ①时髦, 时兴; 风气, 潮流; 时新式样; 时兴货品; 〔集合词〕(资本主义社会中的)上流社会, 社交界; 时髦人物, 红人. ②制法, 方法, 风格, 方式; 式样; 型式; 〔古〕种类. *It is not the ~ to (do).*…现在通常不时兴了. *set [lead] the* ~ 开风气, 创先例. *the world of* ~ 社交界. *people of* ~ 社会名流. *a man of* ~ 有名人物; 时下名流. *He did it after (in) his own* ~. 他照自己的办法做了. *behave in a strange* ~ 举动奇怪. *the modern* ~ 摩登式样. *the present* ~ 时式. ***after [in] a [some]*** ~ 多少, 勉强, 好歹还…一点 (*He knows English after a* ~. 他多少懂一点英语). ***after the*** ~ ***of*** 照着, 模仿. ***be all the*** ~ 极时髦, 风行一时. ***be in (the)*** ~ 时新, 合乎时尚. ***be (all) the*** ~ 完全迎合时好, 极时新. ***be out of (the)*** ~ (人或物)不合时尚. ***bring into*** ~ 使流行(起来). ***come into*** ~ 流行起来, 正流行. ***follow the*** ~ 赶时髦. ***go out of*** ~ (渐渐)过时. ***in (the)*** ~ 时新的, 投合时好的. ***in the old*** ~ 照旧, 照老样. ***in this*** ~ 照这样. ***the latest*** ~ ***in*** *(shoes)* 最新流行式样的(鞋子). ***make*** ~ 作样子. ***set [lead] the*** ~ 开风气之先, 率先兴起新花样, 创先例. — *vt.* ①形成, 铸成, 造, 作 *(into; to)*. ②使适合, 使适应 (to); 改变, 改革. ~ *a vase from clay* = ~ *clay into a vase* 用粘土做一个花瓶. ~ *a whistle out of a piece of wood* 用木头做一个哨子. *doctrines ~ed to the varying hour* 因时而变的理论. ~ *sb. into a good teacher* 把某人培养成一名优秀教师. ~ **book** 时装录. ~ **designer** 时装设计商. ~ **monger** 赶时髦的人. ~ **plate** ①时装样片. ②衣着时髦的人. ~ **plate stem** 【船】(钢板)组成船首柱. ~ **show** 时装表演. **-less** *a.*

-fash·ion *comb. f.* 加在名词之后, 表示"…式的": *crab-~, Japanese-~.*

fash·ion·a·ble [ˈfæʃənəbl] *a.* ①时髦的; 流行的, 时新的. ②社交界的; 合乎上流社会口味的. ③(价格昂贵)高级的. *a ~ dressmaker* 时装裁缝. *a ~ restaurant* 高级饭馆. ***become ~ for a time*** 风靡一时. — *n.* 时髦人物, 场面人物. **-bly** *ad.* **-ness** *n.*

-fash·ioned [ˈfæʃənd] *comb. f.* 〔加在形容词或副词之后, 作为形容词〕表示"…式的"; "…作成的", "…形的": *old-~*, 老式的. *carefully-~* 精心作成的.

fast[1] [fɑːst] *a.* ①紧 *(opp.* loose), 牢实的, 坚牢的, 粘得紧的, 坚固的; 固定的. ②忠实的, 可靠的. ③耐久的; 不褪色的; 抗(酸等)的. ④(运动)激烈的, (睡眠)香甜的. ⑤*(opp.* slow*)* 迅速的; (钟表)走得快的; 敏捷的. ⑥贪快乐的, 放荡的. ⑦(球拍等)弹力好的; 【摄】感光快的, 曝光时间短的. *The door is ~.* 门关着. *a ~ colour* 经久不变的颜色. *a ~ fight* 【美体】激烈的比赛. *~ friends* 可靠的朋友. *~ friendship* 忠实的友情. *a ~ grip* 紧紧一握. *a ~ highway* 快速公路. *a ~ life* 〔美〕放荡的生活. *a ~ liver* 生活放荡的人. *a ~ track* 快行道. *a ~ train* 快车. *a ~ trip* 短期旅行. *a ~ woman* 放荡的女人. ***a ~ one*** ①(棒球中的)急球. ②〔俚〕骗局, 诡计. ③黄色笑话. ***as ~ as one's legs could carry (one)*** 拼命跑. ***be ~ in growth*** 成长迅速. ***be ~ with*** *(gout)* 因(痛风)而动不得. ***~ and hard*** 牢固稳定的, 一成不变的. ***lay ~ hold on*** = take ~ hold of. ***make ~*** 把…拴紧〔关紧〕; 把…打上结扣, 系, 拴 (*make a door ~* 把门关紧). ***pull a ~ one*** 欺骗. ***take ~ hold of*** 紧紧握住, 抓牢. — *ad.* ①紧紧地, 牢固地. ②酣畅地; (睡)熟. ③〔古、诗〕紧迫地, 逼近地 *(by; beside; upon)*; 接连不断地, 紧接着. ④快, 速. ⑤放荡. *F- bind, ~ find.* 〔谚〕藏得好, 丢不了. *speak ~* 说得快. *It is raining ~.* 阴雨连绵. ***live ~*** 生活放荡; 滥费精力. ***play ~ and loose (with)*** 反复无常, 靠不住. ***stand ~*** 不后退, 屹立不动; 不让步. ~ **ball** 【棒球】快速直球. ~ **break** ①(篮球的)快攻, 快速突破. ②(比赛的)迅速开始. **~-breeder (reactor)** 【物】快中子增殖反应堆. ~ **buck** 〔美俚〕轻易得来的钱; 来路不明的钱. **~coun-**

ter〔美〕伪报选举票数者；诡计多端的人；骗子．**~-fingered** *a.* ①非法的，不合法的．②聪明的，巧妙的．③狡猾的．**~-food** *a.* 供应汉堡包之类现成或快速食物的．**~-moving** *a.* ①快速移动的．②(小说等)情节紧凑的．**~-stepping** *a.* ①(马等)快速的．②积极的．**~-talk** *vt.* 花言巧语地企图说服［影响］．**~ time** 夏季时间 (= daylight-saving time).

fast² [fɑːst] *vi.* ①斋戒，禁食，绝食．②节制饮食；忌食某些食物．— *n.* (宗教上的)禁食，斋戒；绝食；斋期，禁食期，绝食期．***break one's ~*** ①开斋．②吃早餐．***~ on bread and water*** 过清水面包的斋戒生活．***keep [observe] a ~*** 守斋，断食．**~ day** 斋戒日，禁食日．

fast·back [ˈfɑːstbæk] *n.* (向尾部倾斜的)长坡度的汽车顶；有长坡度车顶的汽车．

fas·ten [ˈfɑːsn] *vt.* ①把…结牢[拴住]；锁，闩(门)；(用钉等)钉牢，使固定；加固；上紧，扣紧(钮子等)．②把(眼睛等)盯住 (*on*)．③把…归于，把…加在 (*on; upon*)．④使(颜色)不褪．*~ the documents ~ together* 把文件扎成一捆．*~ one's eyes on sb.* 把眼睛盯住某人．*~ one's shoes* 结上鞋带．*a rope ~ed to the post* 扣在柱子上的绳索．*~ the dyes into the cloth* 使布深染而不褪色．*She ~ed herself on him.* 她缠住他不放．*~ a crime on sb.* 归罪于某人．— *vi.* ①握牢，抓牢；坚持，集中注意力于．②(门等)关紧．*The door will not ~.* 门关不上．***~ a quarrel upon sb.*** 跟某人吵闹．***~ down*** (把箱盖等)钉上，盖紧；确定．***~ in*** 关进，装进．***~ off*** (打结、用针把线)扣牢．***~ on [upon]*** 握住，抓住，捉牢；盯住[纠缠]不放；一口咬定；牢牢注意．***~ up*** 使固着，使拴紧；捆，扎；钉牢．

fas·ten·er [ˈfɑːsnə] *n.* ①扣件，钮扣，揿钮，钩扣，扣钉，卡子，夹子，持着器，钉书机．②结扎者，结扎工．*belt ~* 皮带扣，引带扣．*slide [zip] ~* 拉链．*snap ~* 按扣，子母扣．*paper ~* 书钉．

fas·ten·ing [ˈfɑːsniŋ] *n.* ①扣紧，扎牢．②扣件，拴扣物(如锁、闩、钩、扣、钉等)．

fas·ti [ˈfæstai] *n.*〔*pl.*〕〔L.〕(古罗马的)行事日历；岁时纪；年代纪．

fas·tid·i·ous [fæsˈtidiəs] *a.* ①爱挑剔的，难讨好的，过分讲究的．②(微生物等)需要复杂营养的．*be ~ about one's food* 挑食．**-ly** *ad.* **-ness** *n.*

fas·tig·i·ate, -i·at·ed [fæsˈtidʒiit(id), -eit(id)] *a.* 锥状的，倾斜的；【植】帚状的；【动】圆束状的．**-ate·ly** *ad.*

fas·tig·i·um [fæsˈtidʒiəm] *n.* ①(疾病的)危急时刻，高峰期．②【解】(第四脑室的)尖顶．③【建】屋脊．

fast·ing [ˈfɑːstiŋ] *n.* 禁食．*F- comes after feasting.*〔谚〕开头大吃大喝，最后忍饥挨饿．— *a.* 禁食的．**~ blood-sugar level**【医】(空腹时的)血糖水平．**~ cure** 禁食疗法．

fas·tish [ˈfɑːstiʃ] *a.* ①相当迅速的，还快的．②有些放荡的．

fast·ness [ˈfɑːstnis] *n.* ①坚固，坚牢；固定，固着．②【纺】坚牢度；不褪色性；抗(毒)性．③迅速，急速．④放荡．⑤要塞，堡垒．*acid ~* 耐酸性．*~ to light* 耐光性，不褪色．*~ to washing* 耐洗度．

fas·tu·ous [ˈfæstjuəs] *a.* ①高傲的，傲慢的．②浮夸的，虚饰的．

fat [fæt] *a.* ①肥胖的，丰满的 (*opp.* lean, thin)〔*cf.* stout〕；多脂肪的，(肉等) 肥的；(猪等) 养肥了的．②(煤)含沥青的；〔美〕(松等)树脂多的等；粘性好的．③(土地等)肥沃的；(工作等)优厚的；收益多的，有利的；富裕的，兴旺的；(嗓音)圆润的；(香味)浓郁的．④【印】粗笔画的，黑体的．⑤迟钝的，愚钝的．*a ~ dividend* 优厚的红利．*~ [poor] lime* 纯[劣]质石灰．*a ~ salary* 高薪．*Laugh and grow [be] ~.* 心广体胖．*~ soil* 沃土．*a ~ page* (空白部分多、对印刷所)有利的版面．*a ~ year* 丰年．***a ~ lot*** 〔口〕〔反〕不多，少，一点也不 (*You know a ~ lot about it.* 你一点儿也不懂)．***cut it (too) ~***〔俚〕做得太过分；夸示．***cut up ~***〔俚〕留下大笔遗产．***get [grow] ~*** 发胖．***have a ~ chance of***〔俚〕〔反〕机会不多，希望不大．— *n.* ①肥肉 (*opp.* lean)．脂肪(质)；油脂．②最好部分；优厚的工作．③【剧】要角．④肥胖．⑤养肥可供销售的食用动物；树脂多的树．⑥多余额，积余，储备．⑦〔俚〕钱．*be somewhat inclined to ~* 略微显得肥胖．***(All) the ~ is in the fire.*** ①生米已成熟饭，事情已无可挽回．②危机迫在眉睫．***chew the ~***〔俚〕闲聊，嚼舌头．***fry the ~ out of***〔美俚〕摊派勒索．***live on one's own ~*** 吃老本．***live on [eat] the ~ of the land*** 极奢侈．— *vt.* ①养肥 (*out, up*)．②用油脂处理(皮革)．③在…加入脂肪．— *vi.* 长肥．***kill the fatted calf for sb.*** 宰肥牛欢迎某人，热诚欢迎某人．**~back** ①腌用猪板油．②(炼油或作肥料用)步鱼 (= menhaden)．**~-brained** *a.* 愚笨的．**~ cat**〔美俚〕①政治运动中出资多的人，对政治家(或政党)给予财政支援的大亨．②有钱有势的人．③洋洋自得的懒汉．**~ city**〔美俚〕极舒适的生活环境，富裕．**~ deposit** 脂肪沉积体．**~ farm**〔美俚〕减肥中心．**~head** 呆子，傻瓜．**~headed** *a.* 傻头傻脑的．**~ part**〔美剧俚〕重要角色．**~ stock** 供食用的家畜．**~ type**【印】黑体．**~-witted** *a.* 愚笨的；傻的，鲁钝的．**-less** *a.* **-ly** *ad.* **-ness** *n.*

fa·tal [ˈfeitl] *a.* ①命中注定的；避免不了的；必然的．②生死[成败]攸关的；致命的 (*to*)．③毁灭性的；铸成不可挽回的错误的；悲惨的，不祥的；严重的，意外的．*a ~ blow* 致命的打击．*a ~ disease* 不治之症．*a ~ wound* 致命伤．*a blow ~ to one's prospects* 危害前途的巨大打击．***~ and neglected*** 造成严重后果的疏忽(= fatally neglected)．***~ shears*** 死．***the ~ sisters*** 命运三女神〔*cf.* the Fates〕．***the ~ thread*** 生命线，生命，命脉．**-ly** *ad.* **-ness** *n.*

fa·tal·ism [ˈfeitəlizəm] *n.*【哲】宿命论．

fa·tal·ist [ˈfeitəlist] *n.* 宿命论者．

fa·tal·is·tic [ˌfeitəˈlistik] *a.* 宿命的，宿命论的．*~ attitude* 听天由命的态度．**-ti·cal·ly** *ad.*

fa·tal·i·ty [fəˈtæliti, fei-] *n.* ①宿命，天数，命运；命数．②灾难，惨事；惨死；死亡(事故)．***by a strange ~*** 由于不可捉摸的命运．**~ rate** 致死率．

fa·tal·ize, fa·tal·ise [ˈfeitəlaiz] *vt.* ①使倾向宿命论．②使受命运支配．— *vi.* 倾向宿命论．

Fa·ta Mor·ga·na [ˈfɑːtə mɔːˈgɑːnə]〔It.〕①(英国神话传说中) 阿瑟王 (King Arthur) 的妹妹变成的妖精．②〔f- m-〕空中楼阁 (特指西西里海岸上的海市蜃楼)．

fate [feit] *n.* ①命运，宿命．②灾难，死亡，灭亡．③结局；(正常发展的)可预期演变．④〔the (three) Fates〕【希、罗神】命运三女神．*There is no escape [flying] from ~.*〔谚〕在劫难逃．***(as) sure as ~*** 一定，千真万确地．***decide [fix, seal] one's ~*** 决定将来命运．***go to one's ~*** 自趋灭亡．***meet one's ~*** 死；送命．***the irony of ~*** 命运的播弄．

fat·ed [ˈfeitid] *a.* 宿命的，命运决定了的．*be ~ to be hanged* 注定要被绞死．*one's ~ lot* 宿命．

fate·ful [ˈfeitful] *a.* ①决定命运的；重大的，决定性的．②致命的，带来灾难的．③预言性的．**-ly** *ad.* **-ness** *n.*

fa·ther [ˈfɑːðə] *n.* ①父亲；〔口〕爸爸〔妻子对公公，女婿对岳丈通常也这样称呼〕，义父，继父．②族长；祖先；前辈，长辈．③〔F-〕圣父，上帝．④神父；教父；师傅；修道院长；早期基督教作家．⑤〔英〕(议会等的) 元老；前辈，长者；创造人，开山祖师，鼻祖；根源．⑥父亲的身分［情分］，父 (性) 爱．⑦〔*pl.*〕(古罗马的) 元老院议员．*Is your ~ a glazier?*〔谑〕你父亲是装玻璃的么?〔指责别人挡了光线〕．*The child is ~ of [to] the man.*〔谚〕从小看大，三岁看老．*Like ~, like son.*〔谚〕有其父必有其子．*The wish is ~ to the thought.* 希望是思想之父；有什么希望就有什么想法．***~s of a***

city 城市的耆老. *the F- of English poetry* 英国诗歌之父(指乔叟). *Fathers of the City* 市参议员. ***be a ~ to*** 象爹一样对待…. ***be gathered to one's ~s*** 去见祖宗,死. ***F- Christmas*** 〔英〕圣诞老人. ***~ of the Bar*** 年长律师. ***sleep [lie] with one's ~s*** 埋葬在故乡. ***the F- of lies*** 魔鬼. ***the F- of lights*** 上帝. ***the ~ of his country*** 国父. ***the F- Thames*** 泰晤士河. ***the F- of waters*** 江河之父(指伊洛瓦底江,尼罗河或密西西比河). ***the Holy F-*** 教皇. ***the Pilgrim Fathers*** 【英史】最初移居美国的清教徒. — *vt.* ①做…的父亲,生(孩子);创作,产生(新著作等);创立(计划等). ②自认是…的父亲;自认是…的作者[创立人](等). ③象父亲一样对待,保护;治理. ④确定(作品等)的作者;确定(儿童的)生父;确定(罪行的)责任. *He ~ed two sons.* 他生了两个儿子. *~ an orphan* 收养孤儿. *Investigations ~ed the baby on him.* 调查结果证明他就是那孩子的生父. *~ a crime upon the suspect* 确定该嫌疑犯即是作案者. ~ **confessor** 【天主】听忏悔的神父(= ghostly ~). ~**hood** 父亲的身分[资格];父性;父权;父道. ~ **image [figure]** 父亲般的人物,长者;(精神分析学中所指)被人当做父亲看待的人. ~**-in-law** *(pl. fathers-in-law)* 岳父;公公;舅父;〔俚〕干爹;〔古、罕〕继父. ~ **land** 祖国. ~ **right** ①父权. ②父系继承权. **F-'s Day** 〔美〕父亲节(每年六月的第三个星期日). ~**ship**= ~-hood. **F- Time** 时光老人〔拟人化说法〕. **-less** *a.* 没有父亲的,生父不明的. **-like** *a., ad.* 父亲般的[地].

fa·ther·ly [ˈfɑːðəli] *a.* ①父亲的. ②父亲般的;爱护的;慈祥的. —*ad.* 父亲般地. **-li·ness** *n.*

fath·om [ˈfæðəm] *n. (pl. ~s,* 〔集合词〕 *~)* ①英寻(测量水深用的长度单位,合6英尺,或1.829米). ②〔英〕剖面为一平方英寻的(木材)量. *piled ~* 劈柴层积(〔英〕= 6×6×6 英尺). — *vt.* ①测(水)深. ②推测,领会,看穿. *I can not ~ his meaning.* 我领会不透他的意思. *~ the universe* 探索宇宙. — *vi.* 测深;进行探索. **-a·ble** *a.* 深度可测的;可以了解的.

fa·thom·e·ter [fæˈðɔmitə] *n.* 【海】回音测深仪.

fath·om·less [ˈfæðəmlis] *a.* ①深不可测的;无法估量的. ②无法了解的. *the ~ depths of the ocean* 无法测量的海洋深处. *~ motives* 无法理解的动机. **-ly** *ad.* **-ness** *n.*

fa·tid·ic [fəˈtidik, fei-] *a.* 预言的;先见的 (= fatidical).

fat·i·ga·ble [ˈfætigəbl] *a.* 可使之疲劳的;易疲劳的. **-bil·i·ty** [ˌfætigəˈbiliti] *n.*

fa·tigue [fəˈtiːg] *n.* ①疲乏,劳累;劳苦;累活. ②【机】(金属屡经打击等后的)疲劳. ③【医】(组织、器官等对刺激失去反应能力的)疲劳. ④【军】(军务以外的)杂役劳动. ⑤〔*pl.*〕【军】(士兵服杂役等时穿的)工作服. *auditory ~* 【医】听觉疲劳. *photoelectric ~* 【物】光电疲劳. *~ strength* 疲劳强度. *~ tester* 疲劳试验机. — *vt.* 把(金属材料)弄疲劳,使疲乏. *feel ~d* 感到疲劳. — *vi.* ①疲劳. ②(士兵)担任杂役. ~ **clothes [dress]** 【军】工作服,劳动服装. ~ **duty** 【军】勤务. ~ **party** 【军】劳动队,杂役班. **-less** *a.* 不知疲劳的.

Fa·ti·ma [ˈfætimə] *n.* ①法蒂玛〔606?—632,穆罕默德的女儿〕. ②法国神话故事中专杀妻子的"蓝胡子"(bluebeard)的第七个妻子;好奇心重的女人.

Fat·i·mid [ˈfætimid], **Fat·i·mite** [-ˌmait] *a.* ①(穆罕默德女儿)法蒂玛后裔的. ②法蒂玛王朝(公元909—1171)的. — *n.* 法蒂玛王朝君主;法蒂玛的后裔.

fat·ling [ˈfætliŋ] *n.* 肥畜,养肥备宰的幼畜.

fat·so [ˈfætsəu] *n.* 〔口〕胖家伙〔作称呼用,含贬义〕.

fat-sol·u·ble [ˈfætˈsɔljəbl] *a.* 脂溶的,可溶于油脂的.

fat·ten [ˈfætn] *vt.* ①催肥,养肥*(up)*. ②使(变)肥沃. ③使充实,使增多. *~ one's child up with milk* 给孩子吃牛奶让他发胖. — *vi.* ①长肥;变肥沃. ②发财致富. ③增大,增多,变充实. **-a·ble** *a.*

fat·ten·er [ˈfætnə] *n.* ①养肥禽畜的人. ②养肥后供宰杀的禽畜.

fat·tish [ˈfætiʃ] *a.* 较肥的,稍肥的.

fat·ty [ˈfæti] *a. (-ti·er; -ti·est)* ①脂肪(质)的,油脂的,油腻的. ②肥胖的. ③【医】脂肪过多的. — *n.* 〔口〕胖子〔称呼用〕. ~ **acid** 【化】脂肪酸. ~ **compound** 【化】脂肪族化合物. ~ **degeneration** 【医】脂肪变性. ~ **liver** 【医】脂肪肝. **fat·ti·ness** *n.*

fa·tu·i·ty [fəˈtju(ː)iti] *n.* ①(自以为是的)愚蠢. ②蠢事.

fat·u·ous [ˈfætjuəs] *a.* ①愚蠢的,荒唐的. ②虚幻的,空虚的. *a ~ attempt* 妄举. *~ fires* 鬼火. *a ~ smile* 傻笑. **-ly** *ad.* **-ness** *n.*

fau·bourg [ˈfəubuəg, -bɔːg] *n.* 〔F.〕(特指巴黎的)郊区,近郊.

fau·cal [ˈfɔːkl] *a.* 咽喉的;喉音的. — *n.* 咽喉软颚音.

fau·ces [ˈfɔːsiːz] *n.* 〔*pl.*〕【解】咽门,喉头.

fau·cet [ˈfɔːsit] *n.* 〔美〕①(放水)旋塞,龙头. ②(连接管子的)承口,插口. *~ joint* 套筒接合.

fau·cial [ˈfɔːʃəl] *a.* 咽门的.

faugh [fɔː] *int.* 哼,呸〔表示轻蔑、厌恶〕.

Faulk·ner [ˈfɔːknə] *n.* ①福克纳〔姓氏〕. ②**William ~** 威廉·福克纳〔1897—1962,美国小说家,1949年诺贝尔文学奖金获奖者〕. **-i·an**, **~ian** (有关美国现代著名作家)福克纳的;福克纳风格的.

fault [fɔːlt] *n.* ①过失,过错;罪过,责任. ②缺点,缺陷,瑕疵. ③(猎狗的)失去嗅迹. ④【电】故障,误差;漏电;【地】断层. ⑤【网球】发球出界;犯规. *Faults are thick where love is thin.* 〔谚〕一朝情义淡,样样不顺眼. *~ detection* 【机】探伤. *The ~ is his own.* 这是他自己的错. *a grave ~ in a theory* 理论上的重大缺陷. *a ~ in the machine* 机械故障. *image ~* 【物】象差,影象失真. *numerical ~s* 数值误差. ***a ~ on the right side*** 因祸得福. ***be at ~*** ①(猎犬追捕猎物等时)失去嗅迹,踌躇不前;不知所措,正在为难. ②出毛病,有故障. ③ = in fault (*My memory is at ~.* 我想不起来了). ***find ~ in*** 看出…的缺点. ***find ~ with*** 找…的岔子. ***have no ~ to find with*** 无错可寻. ***hit off a ~*** (猎狗)闻出(曾一度错失的)嗅迹. ***in ~*** 有过错,有责任 (*Who is in ~?* 是谁的不是?). ***to a ~*** 过度,极端 (*He is kind to a ~.* 他过分老实). ***whip a ~ out of sb.*** 鞭打某人使之改过. ***with all ~s*** 不保证商品没有缺点. ***without ~*** 〔古〕无误,确实. — *vi.* ①【地】产生断层;有断层余迹. ②发球出界;犯规. ③〔方〕责备,挑剔. ④〔古〕犯错误,做错. — *vt.* ①找…的岔子,挑剔;〔方〕责备. ②【地】使产生断层. ③把…做错. *He ~ed my speech in two ways.* 他认为我的讲话有两点不妥. *~ one's performance* 表演发生失误. ~**age** 〔集合词〕【地】断层. ~ **block** 【地】(两个断层间的)零乱岩石. ~**finder** ①吹毛求疵者,喜欢挑剔的人. ②【机】故障探测器. ~**finding** ① *n.* 挑剔,找岔子. ② *a.* 吹毛求疵(的),喜欢挑剔的.

fault·i·ly [ˈfɔːltili] *ad.* 有过失地;不完善地;该指责地.

fault·i·ness [ˈfɔːltinis] *n.* 有过失,有瑕疵[缺陷];不完善;可指责.

fault·less [ˈfɔːltlis] *a.* 无过失的;无缺点的;完美无缺的. **-ly** *ad.* **-ness** *n.*

fault·y [ˈfɔːlti] *a. (fault·i·er; -i·est)* 有过失的,有缺点的;有毛病的;有错误的,该指责的;不完善的. *a ~ argument* 有漏洞的论点. *a ~ memory* 记忆力失常. *a ~ sentence* 病句. ~ **coal** 劣质煤. ~ **insulator** 故障绝缘子.

faun [fɔːn] *n.* 【罗神】半人半兽状的神.

fau·na [ˈfɔːnə] *n. (pl. ~s, -nae* [ˈfɔːniː]*)* ①(一个地区或时代的)全部动物;动物区系;动物群. ②动物志〔*cf.* flora〕. *marine ~* 水产动物. *the ~ of the Ice Age* 冰河时代的动物.

fau·nal [ˈfɔːnəl] *a.* ①动物区系的;动物群的. ②动物志的. **-ly** *ad.*

fau·nist [ˈfɔːnist] *n.* 动物区系研究者.

fau•nis•tic(al) [fɔːˈnistik(əl)] *a.* 动物区系(研究)的,动物区系研究者的.

Faust [faust] *n.* 浮士德〔欧洲中世纪传说中的人物,为获得知识和权力,向魔鬼出卖自己的灵魂,德国作家歌德曾创作同名诗剧〕. **-i•an** *a.*

faute de mieux [fəut də ˈmjəː]〔F.〕因别无更好的东西(= for want of sth. better).

fau•teuil [ˈfəutəːi] *n.*〔F.〕①扶手椅. ②戏院正厅前座.

fau•vism [ˈfəuvizm] *n.*〔常用 F-〕野兽派画风〔思潮;艺术家〕〔二十世纪初一个西方资产阶级画派〕. **fau•vist** *n.* 野兽派画家.

faux [fəu] *a.*〔F.〕虚假的;人为的;人造的.

faux pas [ˈfəu ˈpɑː] (*pl.* ***faux pas*** [fəuˈpɑːz])〔F.〕①过失;失着. ②违反习俗〔礼节〕的举动〔言语〕. ③(特指妇女的)失足.

fa•vel•a [fɑːˈvelɑː] *n.*〔Pg.〕(巴西城市近郊的)贫民窟〔区〕.

fa•ve•o•late [fəˈviəˌleit] *a.* 蜂窝状的;有蜂窝状小孔的;有气泡的.

fa•vo•ni•an [fəˈvəuniən] *a.*〔诗〕①西风的. ②温和的.

fa•vo(u)r [ˈfeivə] *n.* ①厚爱,恩惠;照顾;亲切;〔*pl.*〕(女人对男人的)委身. ②偏袒,偏爱. ③利益;赞成,支持;提倡;许可,宽恕. ④(表示好意或爱情的)礼物,纪念章,徽章,花结. ⑤〔古〕信函. ⑥〔古〕容貌. *I shall esteem it a ~ if....* 若蒙…不胜荣幸. *your ~ of yesterday* 昨日尊函. *a wedding ~* 婚礼用的花束、彩球(等). *under the ~ of night* 趁黑夜. ***ask a ~ of*** 请帮忙,请照顾. ***ask the ~ of an early reply*** 请早赐复. ***be [with] ~ of***……敬烦…转交〔信封上用语〕. ***be incapable of appreciating sb.'s ~*** 不识抬举. ***by [with] your ~*** 对不起;冒昧地说. ***curry ~ (with sb.)*** 拍人马屁,求宠于人. ***do sb. a ~*** 帮某人的忙,答应某人的请求,接济某人. ***find ~ with [in the eyes of] sb.*** 得某人的宠爱〔欢心〕. ***heap ~s upon*** 给予许多帮忙〔好处〕. ***in ~*** 时兴,流行(*What is now in ~?* 现在流行的是什么?) ***in ~ of*** ①赞成,支持(*I am in ~ of woman's suffrage.* 我赞成妇女参政). ②有利于(*The score was 80 to 78 in ~ of the guest team.* 比分为八十比七十八,客队获胜). ③付与(*cheque to be drawn in ~ of sb.* 开一张支票付给某人). ***in (high) ~ with*** 得人欢心,受人宠爱. ***in sb.'s ~*** 得某人好感〔欢心〕. ***in popular ~*** 得舆论拥护. ***out of ~ with*** 失宠,被嫌弃;不流行. ***show undue ~ to*** 偏爱,偏袒. ***stand high in sb.'s ~*** = in sb.'s ~. ***the last [ultimate] ~*** 女人以身相许. ***win sb.'s ~*** 得某人欢心〔好感〕. — *vt.* ①赞成,赞助,帮忙. ②便于,有利于;促进. ③惠赐,惠赠(*with*). ④偏袒,偏爱;善为照顾. ⑤证实(理论等). ⑥〔口〕容貌象. *~ a proposal* 赞成提案. *Fortune ~s the brave.*〔谚〕幸运找勇士. *The market ~s the buyers* 行市对买方有利. *Will you ~ us with a song?* 给我们唱一个歌,好吗? *Trusting to be ~d with your further orders.* 今后尚希源源定购. *The weather ~ed us.* 天公作美. *The boy ~s his father.* 这男孩长得象他父亲. *The man ~ed his sprained foot when he walked.* 那人走路时对他那只扭伤的脚很小心. ***Favoured by ...*** 敬烦…转交〔信封上用语〕.

fa•vo(u)r•a•ble [ˈfeivərəbl] *a.* ①顺利的;良好的;有利的,有望的. ②好意的,赞成的. ③起促进作用的. ④讨人喜欢的,赢得赞同的. *a ~ answer* 满意的答复. *a ~ balance of trade* 贸易顺差. *a ~ opportunity* 好机会. *a ~ wind* 顺风. *be ~ to a scheme* 赞成计划. ***be (not) ~ for*** (不)利于(*be ~ for a start* 利于起程). ***take a ~ turn*** (形势等)好转. **-a•bly** *ad.* **-ness** *n.*

fa•vo(u)red [ˈfeivəd] *a.* ①怀有好意〔好感〕的. ②(受)优惠的;有利的;有才能的;有某种特权的. ③〔作复合词用〕有…容貌的. *the most-~-nation clause* 最惠国条款. *ill ~* 丑陋的. *well-~* 标致的. **-ly** *ad.* **-ness** *n.*

fa•vo(u)r•er [ˈfeivərə] *n.* 宠爱者;照顾者;支持者;赞成者.

fa•vo(u)r•ing [ˈfeivəriŋ] *a.* = favo(u)rable. *~ winds* 顺风.

fa•vo(u)r•ite [ˈfeivərit] *n.* ①亲信,受宠信者. ②受人特别喜爱的人〔物〕;〔美〕党内有声望的政治家. ③有希望的获胜者(尤指马). *She is a general ~.* 人人都喜欢她. *The ~ came in third.* 被认为最有获胜希望的是跑在第三个位置上的人〔马〕. — *a.* 中意的;心爱的. *one's ~ author* 自己喜欢的作家. *one's ~ book(s)* 自己爱读的书. *a ~ child* 特别受宠爱的孩子. ***be a ~ with*** 是…的宠儿,在…面前走红运〔吃香〕. ***fortune's ~*** 幸运儿. ***~ son*** ①(由于有成就而受到乡里尊敬的)名人. ②州〔市〕政界领袖拥护的候选人〔如总统候选人〕. ***the ~*** (比赛中的)红马;红选手.

fa•vo(u)r•it•ism [ˈfeivəritizəm] *n.* 偏袒,偏爱,徇私. *It was thought that most promotions were based on ~.* 人们认为,这次提职大部分都不公平. *~ towards one's townsmen* 同乡观念.

fa•vus [ˈfeivəs] *n.*〔L.〕【医】黄癣,毛囊癣.

Fawkes [ˈfɔːks] *n.* 福克斯〔姓氏〕.

fawn[1] [fɔːn] *n.* ①小鹿;小山羊,小动物. ②鹿毛色,淡黄褐色. ***in ~*** (鹿)怀着小鹿. — *vi.* 生小鹿〔小山羊,小动物〕. — *vt.* 生(小鹿、小山羊或小动物). — *a.* 淡黄褐色的. **~ lily**【植】赤莲属植物;〔尤指〕美洲赤莲.

fawn[2] [fɔːn] *vi.* (狗等)摇尾乞怜;讨好,奉承(*on; upon*). **-er** *n.* 摇尾乞怜者;奉承者. **-ing** *a.* 摇尾乞怜的,奉承的. **-ing•ly** *ad.* **-ing•ness** *n.*

fax [fæks] *n.* ①传真(照片,文件)〔facsimile 的缩略词〕. ②电视(传真)画面;复印本. **~-mail** (无线电)传真邮件.

fay[1] [fei] *n.*〔诗〕仙女;小妖精.

fay[2] [fei] *n.*〔古〕信仰〔发誓语〕: ***by my ~*** 我保证,一定.

fay[3] [fei] *vt., vi.*【船】接合;合榫. **~ *in [with]*** (与)…恰相吻合.

Fay(e) [fei] *n.* 费伊〔女子名, Faith 的昵称〕.

faze [feiz] *vi.*〔美俚〕打扰,惊扰,使为难;使担忧.〔多用于否定句中〕. *The news did not ~ him.* 这个消息不会使他担心. — *n.* 混乱,狼狈;优虑.

FB = ①fire brigade 消防队. ②flying boat 水上飞机,飞船. ③freight bill 运货单. ④ fullback (足球)后卫;后卫的位置.

F.B.A. = Fellow of the British Academy 不列颠学会会员.

FBI = ①Federal Bureau of Investigation〔美〕联邦调查局. ②Federation of British Industries 英国工业联合会.

FBM = ①foot board measure (量木材用的)板尺. ②fleet ballistic missile 舰队弹道导弹.

FBR = fast breeder reactor 快中子增殖反应堆.

FC = ①fire control 消防;【军】实施射击;射击指挥;火力控制;(用电子仪器等进行的)射击控制. ②football club 足球俱乐部. ③footcandle【物】英尺烛光〔照度单位〕. ④free church 独立教会. ⑤Fighter Command【美军】战斗机指挥部.

fc = franc.

f.c. = ①fire control 火灾控制. ②follow copy【印】见原稿.

FCA = Farm Credit Administration〔美〕农业信贷署.

F.C.A. = Fellow of Chartered Accountants〔英〕特许会计师学会会员.

fcap, fcp = foolscap.

F.C.C. = ①Federal Communications Commission〔美〕联邦电信委员会. ②First Class Certificate 一级证件. ③Food Control Committee〔英〕粮食统制委员会.

F.C.S. = Fellow of the Chemical Society〔美〕化学学会会员. **f.c.s.** = free of capture and seizure【保险】

拘捕和扣留除外.

F.D. = 〔L.〕*fidei defensor* (= Defender of the Faith).

F/D = ①Free Docks 船坞交货. ②Forward Delivery【商】定期交货;来日交货.

FDC = fleur de coin (钱币)新铸的.

FE = Far East.

Fe = 【化】〔L.〕*ferrum* (= iron).

feal [fiːl] *a.* 〔古〕忠实的,诚实的.

fe·al·ty [ˈfiːəlti] *n.* ①【英史】(臣仆对封建主的)忠诚. ②〔诗〕信义,诚实.

fear [fiə] *n.* ①恐怖,畏惧. ②忧虑,担心,顾虑,不安. ③(对神的)敬畏. ④可能,机遇. ⑤令人害怕的事物. *He was overcome by* ~. 他吓坏了. *She could not speak for* ~. 她吓得说不出话来. *full of hopes and* ~*s* 充满希望和顾虑. *No* ~! 〔口〕没事儿! 当然不会那样! 不会(那样)的! *The is no* ~ *of their losing the battle.* 他们不会打败仗的. *There is not much* ~ *of that.* 那件事不大有可能发生. ***for*** ~ ***of*** 因为怕, 以免. ***for fear that [lest]*** 生怕,以免. ***from*** ~ 由于恐惧. ***go about in*** ~ ***of one's life*** 害怕会送命. ***have a*** ~ ***that***… 担心,怕(发生某事). ***in*** ~ ***and trembling*** 胆颤心惊,提心吊胆. ***out of*** ~ = from ~. ***with*** ~ 吓得,怕得. ***strike*** ~ ***into*** 使…感到害怕. ***without*** ~ ***or favour*** 公平,秉公. — *vt.* ①恐怕,害怕. ②畏敬. ③担忧. — *vi.* ①害怕. ②忧虑. *I* ~ *(that) he will get ill.* 我担心他要生病了. *I* ~ *it's too late.* 我怕太迟了. *Never* ~! 不怕! 放心好了! ★口语中一般不说 fear 而说 be afraid (of).

fear·ful [ˈfiəful] *a.* ①吓人的;可怕的. ②〔口〕非常的,厉害的. ③害怕的,担心的,胆怯的. *be* ~ *to look upon* 看起来可怕. *be* ~ *of falling* 怕摔倒. *be* ~ *to speak* 不敢讲话. ***be*** ~ ***that [lest]*** …担心,害怕…. **-ness** *n.*

fear·ful·ly [ˈfiəfuli] *ad.* ①可怕地. ②胆怯地. ③〔口〕非常地,十分. ~ *busy* 忙极了.

fear·less [ˈfiəlis] *a.* 无畏的,大胆的. *be* ~ *of* 不怕…. **-ly** *ad.* **-ness** *n.*

fear·nought, -naught [ˈfiənɔːt] *n.* ①粗绒大衣呢,粗绒大衣呢外套. ②【纺】开毛机,和毛机.

fear·some [ˈfiəsəm] *a.* ①可怕的,吓人的. ②胆小的,羞怯的. **-ly** *ad.* **-ness** *n.*

fea·sance [ˈfiːzns] *n.* 【法】实现条件;履行义务.

fea·si·bil·i·ty [ˌfiːzəˈbiliti] *n.* 现实性;可行性.

fea·si·ble [fiːzəbl] *a.* ①可实行的,行得通的. ②可能(有)的,有理的. ③可用的,适宜的. *a* ~ *plan* 可以实行的计划. *a road* ~ *for travel* 适于旅行[可通行]的道路. **-si·bly** *ad.* **-ness** *n.*

feast [fiːst] *n.* ①(宗教上的)节日; 节期,祝典. ②筵席;宴会,酒席. ③欢乐,娱乐;赏心乐事. *a death's head [a skeleton] at the* ~ 扫兴的人[事]. *a* ~ *for the eyes* 赏心悦目的事. *immovable* ~*s* 固定节日 [如圣诞节]. *movable* ~*s* 活动节日 [如复活节]. *a* ~ *for the gods* 精美的饮食; 使人愉快的事物. *a* ~ *of fat things* 山珍海味的酒席. *A cheerful look makes a dish a* ~. 〔谚〕脸上笑嘻嘻,便饭成筵席. ***a Dutch*** ~ 主人先醉的酒宴. ***a*** ~ ***of eyes*** 眼福. ***a*** ~ ***of reason and a flow of soul*** 富有教益的谈话;非常美妙的谈话. ***Enough is as good as a*** ~. 饱食即美餐;知足常乐. ***give [make] a*** ~ 请客. ***make a*** ~ ***of [upon]*** 大吃,饱吃. ***make*** ~ 〔古〕吃酒席, 作乐. ***the*** ~ ***of trumpets*** 犹太人的新年. — *vi.* ①摆节筵;参加宴会;赴宴. ②享受. ~ *on rare books* 愉快地读到大量珍本书籍. *F- today and fast tomorrow.* 〔谚〕今朝大吃大喝,明日忍饥挨饿. — *vt.* ①宴请. ②使享受,使精神愉快. ~ *one's friends* 宴请朋友. ~ *one's eyes on the beautiful scenes* 饱览美景. ~ ***a night away*** 通宵宴饮. ~ ***at the public crib*** 尸位素餐,(尤指)拿干薪. ~ ***one's eyes (up)on*** 以…大饱眼福. **-less** *a.*

feast·er [ˈfiːstə] *n.* 欢宴者.

feat[1] [fiːt] *n.* ①卓绝的手艺,技艺,本领;武艺. ②功绩,功劳,〔特指〕武功. *laudable* ~*s* 可称颂的事迹. ~*s in [of] arms* 武功. ~*s of horsemanship* 马术.

feat[2] [fiːt] *a.* 〔古〕①灵巧的. ②漂亮的, 整洁的. ③合适的. **-ly** *ad.*

feath·er [ˈfeðə] *n.* ①羽毛,翎毛; 羽饰; 箭羽. ②(同样)毛色;种类. ③鸟;〔集合词〕禽类〔*cf.* fur〕. ④(宝石等的)羽状瑕疵;【无】羽状回波; 轻如羽毛的东西; 零杂废物. ⑤(划船)桨叶的水平运动;(潜艇上潜望镜引起的)微波. ⑥【建】榫牙. ⑦【机】滑键;(铸件的)周缘翅片. ⑧服装,服饰. ⑨状态,心情. *Fine* ~*s make fine birds.* 〔谚〕佛靠金装,人靠衣装. *I am not of that* ~. 我不是那种人. *Birds of a* ~ *flock together.* 〔谚〕物以类聚. *fur, fin and* ~ 兽类、鱼类和鸟类. ***a*** ~ ***in one's cap [hat]*** 值得夸耀的事;荣誉. ***be spitting*** ~***s*** 大怒. ***birds of a*** ~ 同一类人,一丘之貉. ***crop sb.'s*** ~***s*** 杀某人的威风. ***cut a*** ~ 船头破浪前进. ***in*** ~ 有羽毛[羽饰]的. ***in full*** ~ (雏等)长满了毛的;盛装;精神抖擞. ***in good [high, fine, full]*** ~ 身强力壮,兴高采烈. ***knock sb. down with a*** ~ 使人十分惊奇. ***make the*** ~***s fly*** 〔美口〕①工作得很起劲. ②用激烈的语言或使用武力对付;引起争斗[争吵]. ***not a*** ~ ***to fly with*** 一文不名,一筹莫展. ***not care a*** ~ 毫不介意. ***rise at a*** ~ 〔美口〕一碰就冒火. ***ruffle one's*** ~***s*** 发怒. ***ruffle sb.'s*** ~***s*** 激怒某人. ***show the white*** ~ 示弱. ***singe one's*** ~***s*** 损害自己的名誉;使自己受损失. ***smooth sb.'s rumpled*** ~***s*** 稳住情绪,使平息怒气. ***wag the*** ~ 炫耀自己的身分. — *vt.* ①给…装上羽毛,用羽毛装饰,用羽毛覆盖;在…上装箭羽. ②使(桨)与水面平行;【空】使(螺桨)顺流交距,使(旋翼)周期变距. ③射掉(飞禽的)羽毛. ④(用楔形部件)使连接. ~ *an arrow* 上箭翎. ~ ***one's nest*** 贮备;肥私囊. — *vi.* ①长羽毛;成羽毛状;象羽毛似的动摇. ②使桨与水面平行;【空】(螺桨)顺流交距;(旋翼)周期变距. ~ ***out*** ①长出羽毛. ②(边缘、末端)稀疏开来;飘散开来. ③减弱;逐渐消失. ~ ***up to*** 〔美俚〕追求(女友). ~ **bed** ①羽毛褥垫,安有羽毛褥垫的床. ②安适的处境, 闲职. ③因轮藻丛生而形成的羽毛状池底[湖底]. ~**bed** ①*vi.* 要求资方限产超雇;担任闲职. ②*vt* 同意限产超雇,使成闲职;以政府津贴资助. ③*a.* 要求限产超雇的; 因限产超雇而闲散的 (*a* ~*bed soldier* 职务闲散的士兵; 放荡的人;嫖客). ~**bedding** 限产超雇(法)〔指工会为减少失业,在劳资合同中责成资方限制产量,或超额雇用工人〕. ~**bone** (用家禽羽茎制成的)鲸须代用品. ~**brain [~head, ~pate]** 愚蠢的人, 轻浮的人. ~**brained [~headed, ~pated]** *a.* 轻率的,愚忘的. ~ **duster** (羽毛)掸帚. ~**edge** ①*n.* (木板、剃刀等的)薄边. ②*vt.* 把(木板的边)削薄. ~**-footed, ~-heeled** *a.* 脚步很轻的,飞毛腿的,轻捷如飞的. ~**-light** *a.* 轻如羽毛的. ~ **palm** 羽叶棕榈, ~ **star**【动】毛头星〔海百合纲动物〕. ~**stitch** ① *n.* (毛线衣的) 羽状针织法. ② *vi., vt.* 把(毛衣等)织成羽状. ~**weight** ① *n.* 较轻的人[物];不重要的人[物];【拳】次轻级选手. ④*a.* 轻的;次轻级的;轻微的,琐细的. ~ **wit** 愚人,笨蛋,低能者. ~**like** *a.* ①轻如羽毛的. ②羽毛状的.

feath·ered [ˈfeðəd] *a.* ①有羽毛的. ②附装羽毛的; 用羽毛装饰的. ③羽毛状的;鸟一样飞得快的. ④边沿刨薄的. *the* ~ *tribe* 鸟类. *a* ~ *board* 边沿刨薄的木板.

feath·er·i·ness [ˈfeðərinis] *n.* ①长着羽毛(或羽状物). ②羽毛状. ③轻软.

feath·er·ing [ˈfeðəriŋ] *n.* ①羽毛. ②羽饰. ③羽状物;(狗脚等的)丛毛. ④【建】叶瓣饰. ⑤【乐】(提琴) 轻柔运弓法.

feath·er·less [ˈfeðəlis] *a.* 没有羽毛的. **-ness** *n.*

feath·er·y [ˈfeðəri] *a.* ①生羽毛[羽状物]的. ②羽毛似的(雪片等). ③轻软的.

fea·ture [ˈfiːtʃə] *n.* ①形状,外形;特色;(特指)好看的外

表；〔*pl.*〕脸形，五官；面目，容貌，面貌，相貌．②脸面的一部〔口、鼻、耳等〕．③部件，零件．④一条，一项．⑤特点，要点，性能．⑥地势，地形．⑦(电影)正片；故事片．⑧【剧】特别演出；(期刊的)特写，特辑．*the geographical ～s of a district* 一个地区的地理特征．*a ～ of the Sunday supplement* 星期日增刊上的一节特写．*a ～ film* 故事片，艺术片．*a man of handsome [poor] ～s* 面貌美好[丑陋]的男子．*Her eyes are her best ～.* 她的眼睛是她最好看的部分．***make a ～ of*** 以…为特色[号召]．— *vt.* ①使有特色，使成为…的特征；描写…的特征．②〔美〕以…作为号召物；使成为特色；以…作为报纸杂志等的特写；以…作为重要文章；给予(某事件、某文章等)以显要地位；【影】使(演员)主演．③〔俚〕想象．④〔口〕面貌象…．*a film featuring famous actresses* 以著名女演员作为号召的影片．*The mother was ～ed in the son.* 母亲长得很象儿子．*Can you ～ smoking here?* 在这种场合吸烟，你能想象吗？— *vi.* 起重要作用，作重要角色．**～-length** *a.* (电影) 达到正片(应有)长度的；(投稿文字)达到专题文章应有长度的．**-less** *a.* 没有特色的，平淡无奇的．

fea·tured [ˈfiːtʃəd] *a.* ①面貌秀丽的．②作为特色[号召物]的．③有…面貌特征的．*a ～ actor* 主要演员．*sharp-～* 面部轮廓分明的．**～ cast**【影】主要演员阵容．**～ story** (报刊)特载；特别详细的报导．

fea·tu·rette [ˌfiːtʃəˈret] *n.*【影】短故事片，短艺术片．

feaze[1] [fiːz, feiz] *vt.* = faze.

feaze[2] [fiːz] *vt., vi.*【海】解开．

Feb. = February.

feb·ri- *comb.f.* = fever.

fe·brif·ic [fiˈbrifik] *a.*〔古〕发烧的，发热的．

fe·brif·u·gal [fiˈbrifjugəl, ˌfebriˈfjuːgəl] *a.*【医】退热的，解热的．

feb·ri·fuge [ˈfebrifjuːdʒ] *n.*【医】退热药，解热剂．— *a.* 退热的．

fe·brile [ˈfiːbrail, ˈfeb-] *a.*【医】热病的；发热的．

Feb·ru·ar·y [ˈfebruəri] *n.* 二月．*～ fills dyke.*〔谚〕二月雨雪多，沟渠流成河．*All the months in the year curse a fair ～.*〔谚〕二月天气好，全年气候糟．

FEC = ①Far East Commission〔旧〕远东委员会．②Federal Exchange Commission〔美〕联邦交易委员会．

fee. = fecit.

fe·cal [ˈfiːkəl] *a.* 粪便的；排泄物的；糟粕的，渣滓的．

fe·ces [ˈfiːsiːz] *n. pl.* 粪便，排泄物；渣滓．

fe·cit [ˈfiːsit]〔L.〕(某某)画，(某某)作(=he [she] made [did] it)，〔略作 fec.〕*John Jones ～ = fec. John Jones* 约翰·琼斯画[作]．

feck·less [ˈfeklis] *a.*〔Scot.〕①没有气力的，没有精神的．②不中用的，无益的．③不负责任的．*two years of ～ negotiations* 拖了两年的毫无结果的谈判．**-ly** *ad.* **-ness** *n.*

fec·u·la [ˈfekjulə] *n.* (*pl.* ***-lae*** [-li]) ①淀粉．②沉渣．③虫粪．

fec·u·lence [ˈfekjuləns] *n.* ①污秽，混浊．②污物；渣滓．

fec·u·len·cy [ˈfekjulənsi] *n.* = feculence.

fec·u·lent [ˈfekjulənt] *a.* ①污秽的，混浊的．②粪便的；排泄物的．

fe·cund [ˈfiːkənd, ˈfe-] *a.* ①生殖力旺盛的．②多产的；丰饶的，肥沃的；创造力旺盛的．*a ～ mind* 创造力旺盛的头脑．

fe·cun·date [ˈfiːkəndeit, ˈfe-] *vt.* ①【动】使受孕，使受胎．②使多产，使丰饶，使肥沃．③【植】使结实．**-da·tion** [ˌfiːkəˈdeiʃən] *n.*

fe·cun·di·ty [fiˈkʌnditi] *n.* ①多产，富饶，肥沃．②【动】生育力，产卵力．③【植】结实性；结实力．*～ of imagination* 想象力丰富．

fed[1] [fed] *feed* 的过去式及过去分词．**-upness** ①过饱；吃饱．②极度厌倦．

fed[2] [fed] *n.*〔美俚，常作 F-〕联邦调查局人员；联邦政府(工作人员)．***the F-***〔美〕联邦储备制 (= the Federal Reserve System).

Fed.〔美〕= Federal; Federation.

fe·da·yee [feˈdɑːjiː] *n.* (*pl.* ***-yeen*** [-ˈiːn])〔Ar.〕(尤指反对以色列的)阿拉伯突击队队员．

Fed·er·a·cy [ˈfedərəsi] *n.* (*pl.* ***-cies*** [-siz]) 联盟；联邦．

fed·er·al [ˈfedərəl] *a.* ①同盟的，联合的．②联邦的，联邦制的；〔美〕联邦政府的，中央政府的；〔F-〕【美史】南北战争时北部联邦同盟的．***make a F- case out of sth.***〔美俚〕过分夸大[强调]某事重要．— *n.* ①联邦主义者．②〔F-〕【美史】北部联邦同盟盟员；联邦政府战士；联邦政府拥护者．**F- agent**〔美〕联邦调查局人员．**F- Aviation Commission**〔美〕联邦航空委员会．**F- Bureau of Investigation**〔美〕联邦调查局．**F- city** 联邦城(美国首都华盛顿市的别名)．**F- Constitution** 美国宪法．**F- Reserve Bank**〔美〕联邦储备银行．**F- Reserve Board**〔美〕联邦储备委员会，联邦储备银行董事会．**F- Government** (of the U.S.) 美国(中央)政府 (*opp.* State Government). **F- Trade Commission**〔美〕联邦贸易委员会．**-ism** *n.* 联邦制；〔F-〕【美史】联邦主义．**-ist** ① *n.* 联邦主义者；〔F-〕【美史】北部联邦同盟盟员．②*a.* (拥护)联邦制的；北部联邦同盟盟员的．**-ly** *ad.* 在全联邦范围内；在联邦政府一级．

fed·er·al·i·za·tion [ˌfedərəlaiˈzeiʃən] *n.* 联邦化，同盟化；置于联邦政府权力之下．

fed·er·al·ize [ˈfedərəlaiz] *vt.* ①使成联邦，使成联邦制．②把…置于联邦政府权力之下．③使结成同盟．

fed·er·ate [ˈfedərit] *a.* 同盟的，联合的；联邦制度(下)的．— [ˈfedəreit] *vt., vi.* (使)联合；(使)结成同盟[联邦]．

fed·er·a·tion [ˌfedəˈreiʃən] *n.* ①同盟，联盟．②联邦；联邦政府．**-ist** 联合主义者；联邦论者．

fed·er·a·tive [ˈfedərətiv] *a.* ①联合的，联盟的．②〔美〕有关整个国家的；有关外交和国家安全的．**-ly** *ad.*

FEDOM =〔F.〕Fonds Européen de Développement pour les Pays et Territoires d'Outre-Mer 欧洲海外开发基金组织 (= European Development Fund for Overseas Countries and Territories).

fe·do·ra [fiˈdɔːrə] *n.*〔美〕折顶弯帽檐软呢帽．

fee [fiː] *n.* ①报酬；薪水；公费；手续费；税；会费，学费，报名费，入场费．②赏金，小帐．③【史】(封建时代的)采邑，封地．④永租地；永业田，世袭地．⑤所有权；继承财产．*a doctor's ～ for a visit* 医生的出诊费．*a monthly ～* 月薪．*a license ～* 牌照费．*a membership ～* 会费．*a school [tuition] ～* 学费．*～ of permit* 执照税，牌照税．***hold in ～ (simple)*** 拥有无条件继承的权利．— *vt.* ①给…发薪水，给…小费，向…交手续费，缴(会费)[学费](等)．②〔英〕雇用，聘请．**～ absolute**【法】无条件继承权．**～ simple** (处置权不受限制的)土地绝对所有权；无条件继承的不动产(权)〔继承人身份不受限制〕，继承者身分不受限制的不动产权．**～-splitting** 病人介绍费(向医生介绍病人的佣金)．**～ tail** (限定继承人的) 土地所有权；具有一定身分的人才能继承的土地．**～-TV** 收费电视，投币电视．

Fee·bie [ˈfiːbiː] *n.*〔美俚〕联邦调查局人员．

fee·ble [ˈfiːbl] *a.* (***-bler; -blest***) ①无力的，虚弱的．②软弱的；微弱的；(声、光等)轻微的．*a ～ reason* 薄弱的理由．*a ～ joke* 不高明的俏皮话．*a ～ brain* 低能．**～-minded** *a.* 意志薄弱的，无决断的；低能的．**-ness** *n.*

fee·blish [ˈfiːbliʃ] *a.* 有点弱的．

fee·bly [ˈfiːbli] *ad.* 柔弱地，无力地；微弱地．

feed[1] [fiːd] fee 的过去式及过去分词．

feed[2] [fiːd] *vt.* ①给…饮食，给…东西吃；给(婴儿)喂奶．②喂养，饲养；使吃草，放牧(家畜)；用…作牧场 *(down)*．③(机器、煤炉等)加上(油、煤等) *(with)*；【物】馈给(信号)；通过线路向电台传送(节目)以供广播．④悦(目)，娱(耳)；满足(欲望等)；(用希望)安慰，使高兴 *(with)*. ⑤〔口〕给(演员)提台词. ⑥(足球)传(球). ⑦培养，增长，煽动(某种情绪). *F- a cold and starve a fever.* 〔谚〕受寒要吃，发烧要饿. ~ *wheat to cattle* = ~ *cattle with wheat* 用小麦喂牛. ~ *down the grassy land* 把(牛)放进草地吃草. ~ *the fire with fuel* 给火加燃料. *be well [poorly] fed* 吃得好[差]. *better fed than taught* 养而不教. *Well fed, well bred.* 吃得饱，懂礼貌[衣食足而后礼义兴]. ***be fed up with*** 〔美俚〕吃…吃得过饱；厌倦 *(I'm fed up with your grumbling.* 我对你的牢骚已经听厌了). ~ ***oneself*** 自己吃. ~ ***one's face*** 〔美俚〕吃饭. ~ ***out*** 催肥. ~ ***the flame of jealousy [anger]*** 使更加嫉妒[愤怒]. ~ ***to market*** 养肥出售. ~ ***up*** 供给食物〔营养〕；养肥；使吃饱. ~ ***with the money*** 贿赂. — *vi.* ①吃饭，进餐；吃东西，靠…生活，用…做食料；流入，进入. ②【物】馈入. *What time do we* ~? 我们什么时候开饭？*He* ~*s on hope.* 他靠希望支撑着生活. ~ ***at the high table*** = ~ high. ~ ***at the public trough*** 〔美〕吃公家饭，尸位素餐. ~ ***high [well]*** 吃得好. ~ ***on*** 吃…过日子；用…喂养(鸟兽等) (~ *on grass* 靠吃草生活. ~ *on hope* 寄托于希望). — *n.* ①喂养，饲养. ②饲料，饲草，草料；〔口〕饭食，吃饭. ③【机】进刀；传送，送料，上料；加水；馈电，供电；【机】送料管，运料槽. ④〔英口〕【剧】提台词〔特指提供给喜剧演员的笑料〕. ⑤〔口〕一餐，丰盛的一餐. ~ *for horses* 马料. *a* ~ *of oats* 燕麦的一次喂用量. *have a* ~ 吃饲料. *have a good* ~ 吃一顿丰盛的宴席. *automatic* ~【机】自动进刀，自动进给. *clockwork* ~ 钟表的发条. *cylinder* ~ 气缸进气. *hydraulic* ~【机】水力进给，水力进刀，液压输送. *jump* ~【机】(仿形切削的)快速越程，中间越程. *shunt* ~【电】并联馈电. *tape* ~ 磁带卷盘. *work* ~【机】工件进程. ***at one*** ~ 一顿. ***be off one's*** ~ 胃口不好. ***be on the*** ~ (鱼)在找吃，正吃着. ***be out at*** ~ (牛等)在牧场上吃着草. **~-back** ①【电】反馈，回授. ②回复，反应，反作用. ③成果，资料 (*negative* ~*-back* 负反馈. *positive* ~*-back* 正反馈). **~-back** *a.*【电】反馈的. ~ **bag** (系在马口下的)饲料袋 (*put on* ~ *bag* 〔俚〕吃饭). ~ **belt**【机】进料皮带. ~ **bin** 供应仓库. **~-box** 料箱；【纺】喂毛盒. ~ **cable**【电】馈电电缆，电源电缆. **~-in** ①*n.*【电】馈入. ②*n.* 施食(集会). ③*a.*【机】进给的，进料的. ~ **pipe** 供水管；送料管. ~ **pump** 给水泵，进水泵，进料泵. ~ **stock** (送入机器或加工厂的)原料. **~stuff** 饲料，饲料中的营养成分. ~ **system** 送料系统. **~-tank** 给水箱. **~through** 引线；馈入装置；连接线. ~ **trump** 中注管. **~water** (供给锅炉烧成水蒸气的)给水. ~ **well** 给水井.

feed·er [ˈfiːdə] *n.* ①给食者；喂食者；供应者，饲养员；煽动者，怂恿者，填鸭式教人的人. ②寄食者，使唤人；食客. ③奶瓶；〔英〕围涎；秣槽，料箱. ④支流；【矿】支脉；【铁路、空】支线；【电】馈(电)线. ⑤进料器；进刀装置；给水器；加煤器；加油器. ⑥配角；(主要剧情中的)陪衬情节. *a large [gross, prodigious]* ~ 大肚汉. ~ **line [road]** (铁路的)支线.

feed·ing [ˈfiːdiŋ] *n.* ①喂食，饲养，给食. ②送料，进料. ③牧场. *Is there good* ~ *here?* 这里的伙食好吗？— *a.* ①喂食的，饲养的，给食的. ②【机】进给的，进料的. ~ **adaptation** 摄食适应. ~ **bottle** (喂孩子的)奶瓶. ~ **migration** (鱼类的)就食回游. ~ **storm** 越来越厉害的暴风雨. ~ ***stuffs*** 〔美〕饲料.

fee-faw-fum [ˈfiː ˈfɔː ˈfʌm], **fee-fo-fum** [fiː fɔː fʌm] *int.* 唬唬唬！〔童话中表示要吃人的喊声，用以恐吓儿童〕. —*n.* ①吓人的话，(只能吓唬儿童的)胡言乱语. ②嗜杀成性的人；食人魔鬼.

feel [fiːl] *vt.* *(felt* [felt]; *felt)* ①触，摸；试探. ②感觉，觉得；感知. ③【军】侦探(敌情等). ④想，认为，以为 *(that)*. ⑤(无生物)受到…的作用，受影响于. ⑥〔~ oneself〕有…的感觉. ~ *sb.'s pulse* 按脉；试探某人的意图. ~ *a friend's death* 痛惜友人的死亡. ~ *music* 为音乐所感动. *I* ~ *that you are right.* 我以为你说得对. *The ship* ~*s the helm.* 船随舵转动. *She felt herself slighted.* 她感到自己受轻视. — *vi.* ①有感觉；有感情作用. ②摸上去有…感觉；象要. ③体谅，同情. ④摸索着寻找. *Ice and snow* ~ *cold.* 冰雪摸上去是冷的. *This room* ~*s hot.* (人在)这间屋子里觉得热. ~ *bad* 有病；心情不好. ~ *sad* 觉得心酸. ~ *sure* 有把握. ~ *one's pocket for a dime* 在衣袋里摸找角币. *Can animal* ~? 动物有感情吗？~ ***about [after]*** 摸索，探寻，探查. ~ ***as if [though]*** 觉得仿佛. ~ ***at home*** 畅快，舒松. ~ ***cheap*** 觉得丢脸. ~ ***empty*** 觉得饿. ~ ***for*** ①侦探(敌情)；探摸. ②同情，体谅 (~ *for the poor* 同情穷人). ~ ***free to*** 可以随便. ~ ***funny*** 感到不舒服，总觉得不对劲儿. ~ ***... in one's bones*** 深切感到. ~ ***like*** ①象要…似的 (*It* ~*s like rain.* 象要下雨似的). ②摸上去象是… (*It* ~*s like glass.* 那摸上去象玻璃). ~ ***like a boiled rag*** 觉得很不舒服，觉得虚弱无力. ~ ***like a fighting cock*** 精神健旺. ~ ***like a fish out of water*** 如鱼出水，感到不得其所. ~ ***like a million dollars*** 〔美口〕感觉身体〔精神〕很好. ~ ***like ...ing*** 觉得想… (*I don't* ~ *like taking a walk.* 我不想散步. ~ *like putting one on* 〔美〕很想上前帮助一下. ~ ***like [quite] oneself*** 觉得自在舒畅；沉着，镇定. ~ ***low*** 意气消沉. ~ ***mean*** 〔美〕感觉难为情. ~ ***of*** 〔美〕摸摸看. ~ ***one's legs [feet, wings]*** 相信自己的能力，自信. ~ ***one's way*** 摸索着走；行动谨慎. ~ ***out*** 探明，摸清. ~ ***seedy*** 觉得不舒服. ~ ***shaky*** 感到没有把握；感到不舒服. ~ ***slack*** 没精打采. ~ ***strongly about*** 对…抱有明确的态度. ~ ***the need of [for]*** 对…感到需要. ~ ***up [equal] to*** 〔口〕以为能承担，觉得能够胜任 (*I don't* ~ *up to a long hike today.* 我今天不能走远路). ~ ***with*** 同情. — *n.* 触，摸；触觉，感觉；感受. *Let me have a* ~. 让我摸一摸. ***get the*** ~ ***of sth.*** 掌握[学会，熟悉]某事. ***to the*** ~ 在触觉上 (*rough to the* ~ 摸起来很粗糙).

feel·er [ˈfiːlə] *n.* ①试探手段；探试者；试探器；探针. ②触角，触毛，触须. ③【机】测隙规，厚薄规. ④【军】侦察兵，探子. ⑤【无】灵敏元件. ⑥〔美俚〕手指. *a gauge* ~ 千分垫尺. ***put forth [send out*** 或 ***throw out] a*** ~ (用言语或动作)探听别人的反应；伸出触角(进行试探). ~ **gauge**【机】测隙规，厚薄规. ~ **pin**【医】探针. ~ **plug**【机】探孔规.

fee·lie [ˈfiːliː] *n.* 多感觉艺术品[物品]；多感觉宣传媒介〔指同时可以看见形象，闻到气味，有时并能听见音响的艺术品〕. — *a.* (艺术品)多感觉的.

feel·ing [ˈfiːliŋ] *n.* ①感触，感觉；知觉. ②〔常 *pl.*〕感情，心情，情绪. ③同情，怜悯，体谅. ④(对艺术等的)感受，敏感，鉴赏力. ⑤恶感，反感. ⑥看法，感想，(对市场行情的)预感. ⑦气氛，(艺术品的)情调. *speak with* ~*s* 带着感情说. *hurt sb.'s* ~*s* 伤人感情. ⑧事物给人的感觉. *good [ill]* ~ 好感[恶感]. *a man of fine* ~ 会体谅人的人. *a man of* ~ 易于伤感[富有同情心]的人. *a man without any* ~*s* 毫无感情的人. *monday* ~ 不爱工作的情绪. *public* ~ 人心. *No hard* ~*s.* 没有恶意. ***appeal to sb.'s better*** ~***s*** 诉诸某人的良心. ***be dead [lost] to all*** ~ 麻木不仁. ***enter into sb.'s*** ~***s*** 表同情，体谅. ***entertain a*** ~ ***against sb.*** 对某人怀恨在心. ***have a*** ~ ***for*** 对于…有一种体会 (*She has a deep* ~ *for beauty in nature.* 她对大自然的美有很深的感受力). ***have a*** ~ ***of [that]*** 觉得. ***have mixed*** ~***s*** 悲喜交集. ***have no*** ~ ***for*** 对…不同情. ***one's better*** ~***s*** 良心，天良. ***relieve one's feelings*** 发泄感情，泄愤. ***show much*** ~ ***for*** 对…大表同情. — *a.* ①富于感情的；富于同情心的. ②衷心的. *a* ~ *story* 动人的故事. ③动人的. ④表达感情的. *a* ~ *heart* 多情善感. *a* ~ *glance* 含情脉脉的一瞥. ***in a*** ~ ***way*** 富有感情

[同情]地,谆谆地,恳切地. **-ful** *a.* 充满感情的. **-less** *a.* ①没有感情的. ②没有知觉的. **-ly** *ad.* **-ness** *n.*

feet [fi:t] foot 的复数. ***die on one's*** ~ 垮台;倒塌. ~ ***of clay*** ①伟人或受崇拜者不为人所知的弱点. ②意料之外的严重缺点[错误] (*give the appearance of having* ~ *of clay* 显示出出人意外的弱点). ***vote with one's*** ~ 离去[避开]以表示不赞同. ~**-first** *ad.* ①脚先入水地. ②〔美俚〕死 (*be carried out* ~*-first* 死掉被抬走). **-less** *a.*

feeze [fi:z, feiz] *vt.* ①〔废、方〕驱,驱逐;吓唬;打;惩罚. ②打扰;妨碍,为难 (=faze). — *n.* ①〔英方〕冲击,猛冲,磨擦. ②〔口〕惊慌,激动.

feign [fein] *vt.* ①装作,假装. ②伪造(文件等),捏造(故事等). ~ *oneself sick* = ~ *that one is sick* 装病. ~ *ignorance* 假装不知. — *vi.* 做假,佯装. **-ed** *a.* ①假装的,做作的. ②虚构的.

feigned·ly [ˈfeindli] *ad.* 假装地,装聋作哑地.

feint [feint] *n.* ①(骗诱敌方的)佯攻;牵制运动. ②假托,伪装. ***by way of*** ~ 用声东击西的策略. ***make a*** ~ ***of ...ing*** 装作 (*make a* ~ *of studying hard* 装作用功读书). — *vi.* ①装作,假装. ②佯攻;虚击 (*at; on; upon; against*). — *a., ad.* 虚假的(地);不鲜明的(地),淡淡的(地). ~ *lines* 淡格子线. *an exercise book ruled* ~ 画有淡格线的练习簿.

feis [ˈfeʃ] *n.* (爱尔兰或其它地方的爱尔兰裔人一年一度的)文化艺术节.

feist [faist] *n.* 〔美方〕小狗;无用的人,脾气坏的人.

feist·y [ˈfaisti] *a.* 〔美口,方〕①精力充沛的;活跃的,坐立不安的. ②爱争吵的,好斗的.

feld·spar [ˈfeldspɑː] *n.* 【矿】长石.

feld·spath·ic [feldˈspæθik] *a.* 【矿】长石(质)的;含长石的;象长石的.

feld·spath·oid [feld*ˈ*spæθɔid] *n.* 【矿】似长石.

fe·li·cif·ic [ˌfiːliˈsifik] *a.* 造福的;带来幸福的.

fe·lic·i·tate [fiˈlisiteit] *vt.* 庆祝;庆幸;庆贺,祝贺. ~ *a friend on [upon] his success* 祝贺友人成功. *He* ~*ed himself that he had passed the entry examination.* 他庆幸自己通过了入学考试.

fe·lic·i·ta·tion [fiˌlisiˈteiʃən] *n.* 祝贺,庆祝;〔常 *pl.*〕祝词. *offer one's* ~*s* 道贺;致祝词.

fe·lic·i·ta·tor [fiˈlisiteitə] *n.* 祝贺者.

fe·lic·i·tous [fiˈlisitəs] *a.* ①巧妙的,适当的(措词等);善于措词的. ②〔罕〕可喜的,幸运的. **-ly** *ad.* **-ness** *n.*

fe·lic·i·ty [fiˈlisiti] *n.* ①幸福,幸运. ②(言词等的)巧妙,适切. ③巧妙[得当]的语言. ***rare*** ~ ***of phrase*** 稀有的佳句. ***with*** ~ 巧妙;得体.

fe·lid [ˈfiːlid] *n.* 【动】猫科动物.

Fe·lidae [ˈfiːlidiː] *n.* 〔*pl.*〕【动】猫科.

fe·line [ˈfiːlain] *a.* ①猫的,猫科的. ②猫一样的;狡诈的;阴险的. — *n.* 猫科动物. ~ *amenities* 笑里藏刀.

fe·lin·i·ty [fiˈliniti] *n.* 猫的特性,猫一样的残忍[阴险]性.

Fe·lix [ˈfiːliks] *n.* 费利克斯〔男子名〕.

fell[1] [fel] fall 的过去式.

fell[2] [fel] *vt.* ①砍倒(树等);弄倒;打倒. ②把(破缝边缘)缝平. — *n.* ①(树等)一季的采伐量. ②折进(边缘)缝平,(衣服等的)平缝.

fell[3] [fel] *a.* 〔古、诗〕残忍的,凶恶的,残暴的,致命的;尖锐的,剧烈的. *a* ~ *and barbarous enemy* 凶恶野蛮的敌人. *a* ~ *disease* 致命的病. **-ness** *n.*

fell[4] [fel] *n.* ①兽皮,毛皮,生皮. ②(人的)皮肤. ③羊毛,毛丛,发丛. *a* ~ *of hair* 乱蓬蓬的头发,发绺. ~**monger** *n.* 皮货商,生皮商,毛皮商.

fell[5] [fel] *n.* ①〔北英〕高沼;丘原. ②〔用作地名〕荒山,…岗,…丘陵.

Fell [fel] *n.* ***feel Dr.*** ~ ***towards sb.*** 不知为什么总觉得讨厌某人〔来自 Thomas Brown 的诗句: I do not love thee, Dr. Fell, / The reason why I cannot tell〕.

fel·lah [ˈfelə] *n.* (*pl.* ~*s*, 〔古〕~***in***, ~***een*** [ˈfeləˈhiːn]) (埃及等地的)农夫〔贫苦雇农〕.

fel·ler[1] [ˈfelə] *n.* ①伐木者,采伐者,樵夫;伐木机. ②平缝工,接缝工;(缝纫机的)平缝装置.

fel·ler[2] [ˈfelə] *n.* 〔俚〕= fellow.

fel·loe [ˈfeləu] *n.* 车轮外围,车辋辘,轮缘,轮辋.

fel·low [ˈfeləu] *n.* ①同伴,伴侣;帮手;同事,同辈;同类;酒友. ②同等者,匹敌者,对手;同代人;一员;类似的人[物];一对中的一个. ③〔常 ˈfelə〕〔口〕小伙子,家伙;某个人;男朋友. ⑤(英大学的)特别研究生;〔英〕(由毕业生中选出的管理学校的)大学评议员;(得奖学金的)特等校友,特别研究生. ⑥〔F-〕(学会中地位较高的)特别会员. ~*s at school* 同学. ~*s in arms* 战友. ~*feeling* 同情,相互了解. *pass all one's* ~*s* 超过同辈. ~*s of Shakespeare* 莎士比亚同时代的人们. *His shoes are not* ~*s.* 他的鞋不是一对. *a good [jolly]* ~ 有趣味的人,酒友. *that* ~ 那家伙. *my dear [good]* ~ 亲爱的朋友,老兄. *poor* ~ 可怜的家伙. — *a.* 同伴的,同事的;同在一处的;同道的. *a* ~ *countryman* 同国人,同胞. *a* ~ *passenger* 同车[船]旅客. *a* ~ *soldier* 战友. *a* ~ *student* 同学. ~ *sufferers* 难友. *a* ~ *townsman* 同乡. ~ *traders* 同行. ~ **commoner** ①〔英〕得与特别研究生共食的大学生. ②同桌吃饭的人;同一权利的享有者. ~ **creature** ①(动物的)同类. ②人类,同胞. ~**-man** 人,同胞. ~ **traveller** ①旅伴. ②(政治上的)同路人,同情者. ~**-travelling** *a.* (政治上)同路的.

fel·low·ship [ˈfeləuʃip] *n.* ①伙伴关系,交情,友谊. ②共处,共同,协力,提携 (*in; of*). ③会,团体;(基督徒的)团契. ④(英大学)特别研究生的地位[补助费];大学评议员的地位[报酬];(学会)特别会员的地位. — *vt., vi.* (〔美〕-pp-)〔美〕参加(教会团体). ***be admitted to*** ~ 获准入会. ***bear sb.*** ~ 与某人有交谊. ***give[offer]the right hand of*** ~ 同人结交;准许入伙.

fel·ly[1] [ˈfeli] *n.* = felloe.

fel·ly[2] [ˈfeli] *ad.* 〔古〕剧烈地;残酷地.

fe·lo-de-se [ˈfiːləudiˈsiː, ˈfeləu-] *n.* (*pl.* ***fe·lo-nes-de-se*** [fiˈləuniːzdiˈsiː], ***fe·los-de-se*** [ˈfiːləuzdiˈsiː]) 〔L.〕【法】①自杀者. ②〔仅用 *sing.*〕自杀.

fel·on[1] [ˈfelən] *n.* 重罪人,重罪犯. — *a.* 〔诗〕残忍的,凶恶的.

fel·on[2] [ˈfelən] *n.* 【医】瘭疽;甲沟炎;指头脓炎.

fe·lo·ni·ous [fiˈləunjəs, -niəs] *a.* 有重罪的;【法】重罪(犯)的;〔主诗〕凶恶的. ~ **homicide**【法】谋杀. **-ly** *ad.* **-ness** *n.*

fel·on·ry [ˈfelənri] *n.* 〔集合词〕重罪犯;犯人们.

fel·o·ny [ˈfeləni] *n.*【法】重罪 (*opp.* misdemeanor). ***compound a*** ~【法】受到赔偿而不起诉,私了案件. ~ **murder** 犯另一重罪时的凶杀(如强奸后杀死被害者).

fel·site [ˈfelsait] *n.*【矿】霏细岩,致密长石. **fel·sit·ic** *a.*

fel·spar [ˈfelspɑː] *n.* 〔英〕= feldspar.

fel·stone [ˈfelstəun] *n.* = felsite.

felt[1] [felt] feel 的过去式及过去分词. — *a.* 可以[显然]感觉到的. *a* ~ *earthquake* 感觉得到的地震. *a* ~ *want* 迫切的需要.

felt[2] [felt] *n.* 毛毡;毛布;毡制品;油毛毡. — *a.* 毡制的. *a* ~ *hat* 毡帽. — *vt.* ①把…制成毡. ②用毡遮盖,使粘结. — *vi.* 成毡,粘结起来.

felt·ed [feltid] *a.* ①毡制的. ②用毡覆盖的. ③粘结起来的. ~ *cloth* 薄毡料.

felt·ing [ˈfeltiŋ] *n.* ①制毡法. ②制毡材料. ③毡. ~ *products* 毡制品.

Fel·ton [ˈfeltən] *n.* 费尔顿〔姓氏〕.

felt·y [ˈfelti] *a.* ①毡状的. ②= felted.

fe·luc·ca [feˈlʌkə] *n.* (地中海沿岸的)二桅[三桅]小帆船.

fem [fem] *n.* 〔美俚〕女子. — *a.* 〔美俚〕女性化的,女人

似的. **F- Lib, Femlib**〔美〕妇解,妇女解放运动.

fem. = female, feminine.

fe·male [ˈfiːmeil] *a.* (*opp.* male) ①女性的. ②雌的; 【植】雌性的,雌蕊的. ③【机】阴的,内的. ④女人似的, 柔弱的. *the* ~ *sex* 女性, 女人. *a* ~ *operative* 女工. *a* ~ *flower* 雌花. *a* ~ *joint* 套筒接合. *a* ~ *screw* 阴螺丝,内螺丝. —*n.* ①女子. ②牝兽,雌禽,雌性动物. ③雌性植物,雌株. ~ **fern**【植】蹄盖厥,欧洲厥. ~ **impersonator** 男扮女的演员. ~ **sapphire** 淡色蓝宝石. ~ **suffrage** 妇女参政权〔选举权〕. ~ **voice**【乐】女声.

feme [fiːm; fem] *n.*【法】女子; 妻子. ~ **covert** 有夫之妇,已婚妇女. ~ **sole**【法】①未婚女子, 独身女子. ②寡妇,财产权独立的妻子.

fem·i·na·cy [ˈfeminəsi] *n.* (*pl.* **-cies** [-siz]) 女性, 女人的气质,女人的特性.

fem·i·nal·i·ty [ˌfeimiˈnæliti] *n.* ①女性; 妇女的特性. ②女用小型物品.

fem·i·ne·i·ty [ˌfemiˈniːiti] *n.* = femininity.

fem·i·nie [ˈfemini] *n.*〔集合词〕女性.

fem·i·nine [ˈfeminin] *a.* ①女性的, 女人的. ②妇女似的; 娇柔的; 柔弱的. ③【语法】阴性的〔*cf.* masculine〕. ④【诗】句尾有一多余轻音节的,弱韵的. ~ *beauty* 女性美. *the* ~ *gender* 阴性. — *n.* ①女性,温柔的女性. ②【语法】阴性; 阴性词. ~ **caesura** 不是紧接重音的诗行中断. ~ **rhyme** 弱韵〔押韵的双音节字的第二音节为非重音,如 motion; 或三音节字的第二、三音节为非重音, 如 happily〕. **-ly** *ad.* **-ness** *n.*

fem·i·nin·i·ty [ˌfemiˈniniti] *n.* ①女性,女人的特性; 温柔,柔弱. ②〔集合词〕妇女.

fem·i·nism [ˈfeminizəm] *n.* ①男女平等主义; 争取女权运动. ②女性. ③女人用的语言.

fem·i·nist *n.* 男女平等主义者,争取女权运动的人.

fe·min·i·ty [fiˈminiti] *n.* = femininity.

fem·i·nize, feminise [ˈfeminaiz] *vt., vi.* ①(使) 女性化; 【生】(使)雌性化 (*opp.* masculinize). ②(在某一地区或职业等方面) (使) 妇女占多数. **fem·i·ni·za·tion** [ˌfeminaiˈzeiʃən] *n.*

femme [fem, F. fam] *n.* ①【法】妻子. ②〔美俚〕女子; 在女子同性恋中充当女性角色者.

femme de cham·bre [F. fam də ʃɑ̃ːbr] (*pl.* ***femmes de chambre***)〔F.〕女仆, 侍女, 女服务员〔*cf.* chambermaid〕.

femme fa·tale [F. fam fatal] *n.* (*pl.* ***femmes fa·tales*** [F. fam fatal]) 荡妇〔尤指引诱男人堕落的女人〕.

fem·o·ral [ˈfemərəl] *a.* 大腿的,股骨的. ~ **artery**【解】股动脉.

fem·to- *comb.f.* 表示"毫微微"(=10^{-15}),"尘".

fe·mur [ˈfiːmə] *n.* (*pl.* **~s,** ***fem·o·ra*** [ˈfemərə])【解】股骨; 腿; (昆虫的)腿节.

fen[1] [fen] *n.* 沼泽; 沼泽群落. ***the Fens*** 英国剑桥郡附近的低地. — *vt., vi.*〔方〕= fend. ~ **fire** 沼地磷火. ~**land** *n.* 沼泽地. ~**man** *n.* 沼泽居民. ~ **pole**〔英方〕(沼地居民用的)跳沟撑竿.

fen[2] [fen] = fain[2].

fen[3] [fən] *n.*〔Chin.〕分.

fe·na·gle [fəˈneigl] *vi., vt.* = finagle.

fence [fens] *n.* ①栅栏,篱笆; 围墙. ②自卫术; 剑术. ③(机械的)防护物;〔古〕防壁, 防护. ④巧辩, 词令. ⑤〔俚〕买卖贼赃的人; 赃品买卖处, 贼市, 黑货市场. ⑥〔*pl.*〕〔美〕政党组织, 政治利益. *a thorn* ~ 刺篱. *a stone* ~ 石头围垣. *a sunk* ~ (不遮住视线的)矮篱,矮墙. ~ *riders*〔美〕修理牧场围墙的工人; 骑墙派. *a master of* ~ 剑术家; 雄辩家. *No* ~ *against a flail [an ill fortune]*.〔谚〕恶运难逃. ***be on both sides of the*** ~ 两面讨好. ***be on sb.'s*** ~ 帮助〔维护〕某人. ***be [sit, stand] on the*** ~ 观望形势,抱骑墙态度. ***be on the other side of the*** ~. 加入反对方面. ***be on the same side of the*** ~ 站在同一立场上, 和某方一致. ***descend [come down] on the right side of*** ~ 附和胜方. ***make [walk like] a Virginia*** ~〔美俚〕东倒西歪地走. ***mend [look after] one's*** ~***s*** 修补篱笆;〔美〕(国会议员) 改善自己政治地位. — *vi.* ①击剑. ②搪塞, 闪开. ③筑围墙, 用栅栏防护. ④(马) 跳过栅栏. ⑤〔俚〕买卖赃物. — *vt.* ①用墙围住,用栅栏防御〔护〕. ②防御,防护;〔古〕防止. ③(用栅栏)隔开,拦开,使成禁猎区. ④买卖(赃物). ~ ***about [up]*** 用栅栏围起来. ~ ***in*** 围进. ~ ***off [out]*** 挡开, 架开,用栅 (墙、篱笆等) 隔开. ~ ***round*** 搪塞开, 用围墙围住. ~ ***with*** 搪塞 (~ *with a question [questioner]* 避免正面答复). ~**-hanger** 未打定主意的人, 犹豫不决者. ~**-mending**〔美〕改善恶化的政治关系. ~**-off** *n.* (击剑比赛中)和局后的加赛. ~ **rider**〔美〕①修理牧场围墙的工人. ②骑墙派. ~ **shop** 黑货〔赃品〕商店. ~**-sitter** 骑墙派. ~**-straddler**〔美俚〕两面讨好者. ~ **time [month, season]** 禁猎〔渔〕期. **-less** *a.* 没有围墙的;〔诗〕不设防的.

fenc·er [ˈfensə] *n.* ①剑术师, 击剑家. ②篱笆匠. ③能跳过篱笆的马. *a good* ~ 善于越过篱笆的良马.

fenc·ible [ˈfensəbl] *a.* ①可以防卫的. ②〔Scot.〕能保卫国家的, 具有服兵役资格的. ③国防军的. — *n.*【史】〔主 Scot.〕国防军士兵.

fenc·ing [ˈfensiŋ] *n.* ①击剑, 剑术. ②辩论, 巧妙的搪塞. ③栅栏, 围栏, 篱笆. ④筑栅栏的材料. ⑤买卖赃物. ~ **cully**〔英俚〕窝藏赃物者. ~ **den [ken]**〔俚〕窝藏赃物的场所. ~ **foil** 练习剑. ~ **master** 击剑教练(员).

fend [fend] *vt.* ①闪避, 挡开(武器等). ②〔古〕防御,保护. ③〔英方〕供养. — *vi.*〔口〕①努力, 力争. ②供养, 照料. ~ ***for*** 筹措; 扶养 (~ *for oneself* 自己谋生; 照料自己). ~ ***off*** 挡开,架开; 避开(灾祸等).

fend·er [ˈfendə] *n.* ①防御者, 防护板, 防御物. ②火炉围栏. ③(车辆的)挡泥板. ④〔英〕(电车、机车等的) 缓冲装置,救护装置〔*cf.*〔美〕bumper〕. ~ **beam** (船舷上的)护舷物; (铁路终点的)止车障. ~ **board** 挡泥板. ~ **pile** 护舷棒. ~ **stool**〔英〕炉围前的脚凳. **-less** *a.* 无防撞物〔防护板〕的,无挡牌的.

fen·es·tel·la [ˌfenisˈtelə] *n.* (*pl.* ***-lae*** [-liː])【建】小窗; 窗状壁龛.

fe·nes·tra [fiˈnestrə] *n.* (*pl.* ***-trae*** [-triː])【解、动】窗〔如中耳内壁上的窗状小孔〕; 膜孔; (某些昆虫羽翼上的)透明斑点.

fe·nes·trate [fiˈnestrit] *a.* ①【动】具透明点的. ②【植】具窗孔的, 网状的.

fe·nes·trat·ed [fiˈnestreitid, ˈfenistreitid] *a.* ①有窗孔的; 有口的; 有孔的. ②【生】穿孔的; 具透明点的 (= fenestrate).

fen·es·tra·tion [ˌfenisˈtreiʃən] *n.* ①【建】窗户配列. ②【医】(耳科手术中的)开窗术.

Fe·ni·an [ˈfiːnjən] *n.* ①芬尼亚〔传说中的爱尔兰古代勇士〕. ②芬尼亚运动(指十九世纪爱尔兰争取民族独立的反英运动)成员. ~ ***Brotherhood*** 芬尼亚运动. — *a.* 芬尼亚运动(成员)的. **-ism** *n.* 芬尼亚共和主义.

fenks [feŋks] *n. pl.* (作肥料以及制作普鲁士蓝用的)鲸油渣.

fen·nec, fen·nek [ˈfenik] *n.*【动】耶狐 (*Fennecus zerda*)〔产于北非和阿拉伯的一种大耳大眼淡黄色小狐〕.

fen·nel [ˈfenl] *n.*【植】茴香(属). ~ **oil** 茴香油. ~ **water** 茴香水〔用作兴奋剂和驱风剂〕. ~**flower**【植】黑种草属.

fen·ny [ˈfeni] *a.* ①沼泽性的, 沼泽多的. ②生长在沼泽地带的.

fen·u·greek [ˈfenjugriːk] *n.*【植】胡芦巴〔一种豆科植物〕.

Fen·wick [ˈfenik, ˈfenwik] *n.* 芬威克〔姓氏〕.

feod [fjuːd] *n.* 采邑,领地.

feoff [fef, fiːf] *n.* 采邑, 领地. — *vt.* 把采邑[领地]授与[出售给](某人).

feoff·ee [feˈfiː, fiːˈfiː] *n.* ①领受采邑者, 不动产承受人. ②公共不动产管理人.

feof·fer [ˈfefə, ˈfiːfə] *n.* = feoffor.

feoff·ment [ˈfefmənt, ˈfiːf-] *n.* ①采邑授与. ②【法】土地及其他不动产的交付[让与]. ③不动产交付证.

feof·for [feˈfɔː; fiːˈfɔː] *n.* ①采邑授与者. ②不动产赠与[让与]人.

FERA = Federal Emergency Relief Administration 〔美旧〕联邦紧急救济署.

fe·ra·cious [fəˈreiʃəs] *a.* 〔罕〕多产的; 丰富的. **fe·rac·i·ty** [-ˈræsiti] *n.*

fer·ae na·tur·ae [ˈfiəri nəˈtjuəriː] 〔L.〕①野生的. ②【法】不属于私产的(野生动物).

fe·ral [ˈfiərəl] *a.* 野生的; 野蛮的, 凶悍的.

fer·bam [ˈfəːbæm] *n.* 【化】二甲胺基荒酸铁〔用作果树杀菌剂〕.

fer·ber·ite [ˈfəːbərait] *n.* 【矿】钨铁矿.

fer-de-lance [ˌfɛədəˈlɑːns] *n.* 【动】枪头蛇〔南美产大毒蛇〕.

Fer·di·nand [ˈfəːdinənd] *n.* 费迪南〔男子名〕.

fere [fiə] *n.* 〔古〕①同伴, 伙伴. ②配偶〔夫或妻〕.

fer·e·to·ry [ˈferitəri] *n.* ①【宗】放圣骨的神龛, (教堂内)安设神龛的地方. ②棺架, 尸架.

Fer·gus [ˈfəːgəs] *n.* 费格斯〔姓氏〕.

Fer·gu·s(s)on [ˈfəːgəsn] *n.* 费格森〔姓氏〕.

fe·ri·a [ˈfiəriə] *n.* (*pl.* ~***s***, ***-ri·ae*** [-iː]) ①〔*pl.*〕(古罗马)假日; 节日. ②【宗】(星期六或星期日以外, 尤指宗教节日或节日前夕以外的)平日. **-al** *a.*

fe·rine [ˈfiərain] *a.* = feral.

Fe·rin·ghee, Fe·rin·gi [fəˈriŋgi] *n.* 〔印蔑〕欧洲人; 欧亚混血儿; (尤指)在印度出生的葡萄牙人.

fer·i·ty [ˈferiti] *n.* 凶残; 野性; 未驯化.

fer·ma·ta [fəˈmɑːtə] *n.* 【乐】①延音. ②延长号(⌒)或(◡).

fer·ment [ˈfəːment] *n.* ①酶酵素. ②发酵. ③扰动, 骚动. *Yeast is a* ~. 酵母是一种发酵剂. *cause national* ~ 引起举国骚动. ***be in a*** ~在动乱中. — [fəːˈment] *vt., vi.* (使)发酵; (使)激动, (使)骚动. **-ta·ble** *a.* 发酵性的, 可发酵的. **-ta·tion** [ˌfəːmenˈteiʃən] *n.* 发酵; 激动, 激昂, 纷扰, 人心骚动. **-ta·tive, -tive** *a.* 发酵性的, 有发酵力的.

fer·mi [ˈfɛəmi, ˈfəː-] *n.* 【物】费密〔长度单位, 等于10^{-13}厘米〕.

fer·mi·on [ˈfɛəmiːˌɔn] *n.* 【原】费米子〔属费米系统的粒子〕.

fer·mi·um [ˈfɛəmiəm] *n.* 【化】镄.

fern [fəːn] *n.* 【植】蕨(纲), 蕨类植物. *royal* ~ (蕨类植物)王紫萁. ~**bracken,** ~**brake** 蕨; 羊齿丛. ~ **owl** 【动】欧夜鹰. ~ **seed** 蕨孢子.

fern·er·y [ˈfəːnəri] *n.* ①蕨类种植处, 蕨类种植盆. ②簇生的蕨.

fer·ni·co [ˈfəːnikəu] *n.* 【冶】费镍钴〔铁镍钴合金〕.

fern·y [ˈfəːni] *a.* 蕨的, 象蕨的, 多蕨的.

fe·ro·cious [fəˈrəuʃəs] *a.* ①凶猛的, 野蛮的, 残暴的. ②〔口〕非常的, 十分强烈的. *a* ~ *appetite* 特大的胃口. *a* ~ *look [feature]* 凶恶的相貌. *a* ~ *bore* 一个十分令人讨厌的家伙. **-ly** *ad.* **-ness** *n.*

fe·roc·i·ty [fəˈrɔsiti] *n.* ①凶猛, 野蛮, 残暴. ②暴行.

-fer·ous *suf.* 通常接在i以后, 构成形容词, 表示"含…的", "生…的", "产…的": pesti*ferous*, coni*ferous*, auri*ferous*.

fer·ox [ˈferɔks] *n.* 〔英〕大湖鳟, 猛鲑.

fer·rate [ˈfereit] *n.* 【化】高铁酸盐.

fer·rel [ˈferəl] *n.* =ferrule.

fer·re·ous [ˈferiəs] *a.* ①铁(制)的, 铁色的, 铁质的, 含铁的. ②硬如铁的. ~ **metals** 黑色金属 〔*cf.* non-~ metals〕.

fer·ret[1] [ˈferit] *n.* ①【动】(猎兔用的)白鼬, 雪貂. ②【动】(美西部)黑脚黄鼬. ③搜索者, 侦探. — *vt., vi.* 用雪貂(把兔等由隐藏处)驱出, 搜出; 搜寻. ~ ***about*** 四处搜寻. ~ ***for*** 探索. ~ ***out*** 探索出, 搜出; 肃清. ***go ferreting*** 带着雪貂去打猎.

fer·ret[2], **fer·ret·ing** [ˈferit, -iŋ] *n.* 细布[丝]带.

fer·ret·y [ˈferiti] *a.* 白鼬似的; 搜索者似的; 喜观窥视的.

fer·ri- *comb. f.* 【化】表示"含(正)铁的": *ferric, ferri*ferous.

fer·ri·age [ˈferiidʒ] *n.* ①摆渡; 渡船业. ②摆渡费.

fer·ric [ˈferik] *a.* ①铁的, 含铁的. ②【化】(正)铁的, 三价铁的. ~ **oxide** 三氧化二铁, 氧化铁. ~ **sulphate** 硫酸铁.

fer·ri·cy·a·nide [ˌferiˈsaiənaid] *n.* 【化】氰铁酸盐, 氰铁化物.

fer·rif·er·ous [feˈrifərəs] *a.* 含铁的, 含有三价铁的.

Fer·ris wheel [ˈferis] 阜氏转轮〔游艺场中供人乘坐可以飞快转动的玩具〕.

fer·rite [ˈferait] *n.* 【化】①铁素体, 纯粒铁, 纯铁体. ②铁酸盐. ③铁氧体, 铁淦氧.

fer·ro- *comb.f.* ①表示"铁": *ferro*concrete. ②表示"铁和…": *ferro*chrome. ③表示"亚铁": *ferro*cyanide.

fer·ro·al·loy [ˌferəuˈælɔi] *n.* 【化】铁合金.

fer·ro·chro·mi·um [ˌferəuˈkrəumiəm] *n.* 铬铁(合金)(= ferrochrome).

fer·ro·con·crete [ˌferəuˈkɔŋkriːt] *n.* 【建】钢[铁]筋混凝土, 钢骨水泥.

fer·ro·cy·a·nide [ˌferəuˈsaiənaid, -nid] *n.* 【化】氰亚铁酸盐, 亚铁氰化物.

fer·ro·e·lec·tric [ˌferəuiˈlektrik] *n., a.* 【物】铁电体(的); 强介质.

fer·ro·mag·ne·sian [ˌferəumægˈniːʃən] *a.* 【矿】含铁和镁的. *a* ~ *mineral* 铁镁矿物. — *n.* 铁镁矿物.

fer·ro·mag·net·ic [ˌferəumægˈnetik] *a.* 强铁磁(性)的, 铁磁的. **-mag·net·ism** [-ˈmægnitizm] *n.*

fer·ro·man·ga·nese [ˌferəuˈmæŋgəˌniːz, -ˌniːs] *n.* 铁锰合金, 锰铁.

fer·ro·mo·lyb·de·num [ˌferəuməˈlibdinəm] *n.* 【冶】钼铁, 钼钢.

fer·ro·nick·el [ˌferəuˈnikl] *n.* 【冶】镍铁, 铁镍齐.

fer·ro·phos·phor·ous [ˌferəuˈfɔsfərəs] *n.* 【冶】磷铁.

fer·ro·pseu·do·brook·ite [ˌferəuˌsuːdəuˈbrukait] *n.* 月铁板钛矿〔由阿波罗11号宇宙飞船带回地球的月球矿物〕.

fer·ro·sil·i·con [ˌferəuˈsilikən] *n.* 硅铁, 矽铁.

fer·ro·type [ˈferəutaip] *n.* 【摄】铁板照相(法). — *vt.* 用铁板给(照片)上光.

fer·rous [ˈferəs] *a.* ①铁的, 从铁得来的. ②【化】亚铁的, 二价铁的. ~ ***and non-*** ~ ***metals*** 黑色及有色金属. ~ **nitrate** 硝酸亚铁. ~ **oxide** 氧化亚铁. ~ **sulphate** 硫酸亚铁.

fer·ru·gin·o·si·ty [feˌruːdʒiˈnɔsiti] *n.* 含铁性.

fer·ru·gi·nous [feˈruːdʒinəs] *a.* ①铁(质)的, 含铁的. ②铁锈色的, 赤褐色的. *a* ~ *spring* 含铁矿泉.

fer·rule [ˈferuːl] *n.* ①(装于手杖、木柄、伞柄等顶端起加牢作用的)金属箍, 金属包头. ②【机】套圈, 箍. — *vt.* 用箍镶.

fer·rum [ˈferəm] *n.* 〔L.〕【化】铁.

fer·ry [ˈferi] *n.* ①渡口; 渡船; 摆渡权. ②〔美〕(出厂飞机的)现场输送〔指把飞机从接收地飞送至使用地等〕. *row the travelers over the* ~ 用摆渡船把旅客送过渡口. ***take the [charon's]*** ~ 死. — *vt.* 用船过渡, (用船等)运送, 运输. — *vi.* ①乘渡船; 摆渡; (小船)来往于渡口

(*upon*). ②乘飞机飞渡. ~ *across the river* 乘船渡河. — *vt.* ①用船渡(客、货等). ②用飞机运送. ~ *the traveler across a river* 用船把旅客摆渡过河. ~**boat** *n.* 渡船. ~ **bridge** (上下渡船用的)浮桥; 列车轮渡. ~**house** ①候船室. ②渡船船夫室. ~**man** *n.* 渡船工人. ~ **pilot** (把出厂飞机开到使用现场的) 飞机驾驶员. ~ **steamer** 渡轮.

fer·tile [ˈfəːtail] *a.* (*opp.* sterile) ①肥沃的, 丰饶的; 多产的,丰富的 (*of, in*). ②【生】能生育的,有繁殖力的; 已受孕[受精]的. ③【原】可变成裂变物质的. ~*egg* 受精卵. *a* ~ *land [soil]* 肥地. *a* ~ *plain* 沃野. ~ *pollen* 能育花粉. ~ *shower* 及时雨. *a* ~ *mind* 想象力丰富的头脑. *be* ~ *in expedients* 会临机应变的. *be* ~ *of imagination* 想象力丰富. ~ **material** 【原】(通过中子诱发核反应可变成裂变性燃料的)可转换物质[如铀238]; 燃料源物质; 变成核燃料的中子吸收剂. **-ly** *ad.* **-ness** *n.*

fer·til·i·ty [fəːˈtiliti] *n.* (*opp.* sterility) ①肥沃, 丰饶; 肥力,肥(沃)度; (土地的)生产力. ②【生】能育性, 繁殖力. ③(思想等的)丰富. *the soil* ~ 土壤肥力. ~ **agent** 致育因素. ~ **drug** (催女性排卵以医治不孕症的)受胎药.

fer·ti·li·za·ble *a.* 可施肥的,可受精的.

fer·ti·li·za·tion [ˌfəːtilaiˈzeiʃən] *n.* ①肥沃化, 使施肥; 丰饶化. ②【生】受孕[受精](作用,现象).

fer·til·ize, fer·ti·lise [ˈfəːtilaiz] *vt.* ①使肥沃,使丰饶, 使多产. ②【生】使受孕 [受精]. ~*d eggs* 受精卵. — *vi.* 施肥.

fer·til·iz·er [ˈfəːtiˌlaizə] *n.* ①肥料(特指化学肥料). ②受精媒介物(如蜂、虫、鸟、风、水等). *additional* ~ 追肥. *ground* ~ 基肥.

fer·til·i·zin [fəːˈtilizin] *n.* 【生】受精素.

fe·ru·la [ˈferulə] *n.* (*pl.* **-lae** [-liː]) ①【植】阿魏. ② = ferule[1].

fer·ule[1] [ˈferuːl] *n.* (责打学生用的)戒尺; 〔喻〕责罚; 纪律. *be under the* ~ 在教师鞭策之下; 受人支配. — *vt.* 用教鞭责打(手心).

fer·ule[2] [ˈferuːl] *n., vt.* = ferrule.

fer·ven·cy [ˈfəːvənsi] *n.* ①炽热. ②热情,热心,热烈.

fer·vent [ˈfəːvənt] *a.* ①炽热的. ②热情的,热心的,热烈的, 强烈的. ~ *heat* 白热. ~ *hatred* 痛恨. ~ *love* 热爱. *a* ~ *soul* 热情的人. **-ly** *ad.*

fer·vid [ˈfəːvid] *a.* ①〔诗〕炽热的. ②热烈的,热情的; 激烈的. ~ *loyalty* 赤胆忠心. **-ly** *ad.* **-ness** *n.*

fer·vid·i·ty [fəːˈviditi] *n.* ①炽热. ②热心,热烈.

fer·vo(u)r [ˈfəːvə] *n.* ①高温. ②强烈的感情, 激情, 热情.

F.E.S. = Fellow of the Entomological Society 昆虫学会会员.

Fes·cen·nine [ˈfesiˌnain, -nin] *a.* 〔常用 f-〕粗俗的; 猥亵的; 下流的.

fes·cue [ˈfeskjuː] *n.* ①教鞭, 指示棒. ②【植】羊茅, 酥油草.

fess(e) [fes] *n.* 【纹】(徽章中横跨盾形中央的)中线, 中横带.

fes·ta [ˈfestə] *n.* 〔It.〕喜庆日,节日.

fes·tal [ˈfestl] *a.* 节日的; 喜庆的, 欢乐的. *a* ~ *day* 节日. *a* ~ *mood* 节日气氛[情绪]. **-ly** *ad.*

fes·ter [festə] *n.* ①脓疮,溃烂. ②(怨恨等)郁积, 恶化. — *vt., vi.* ①(使)溃烂,(使)化脓. ②(使)烦恼, (使)恶化. *Jealousy* ~*ed his mind.* 嫉妒使他苦恼.

fes·ti·nate [ˈfestineit, -nit] *vt., vi.* 〔罕〕赶紧, 使赶快. — *a.* [ˈfestəneit, -nit] 〔罕〕急急忙忙的,匆忙的. *a* ~ *gait* 匆忙的步伐.

fes·ti·na·tion [ˌfestiˈneiʃən] *n.* 行走急促〔尤指某些神经疾病症状〕.

fes·ti·val [ˈfestəvəl] *a.* 节日的,喜庆的. — *n.* ①节日, 喜庆日; 庆祝典礼. ②贺宴; 会演; (定期)音乐节. *a* ~ *atmosphere* 节日的气氛.

fes·tive [ˈfestiv] *a.* 节日的,过节似的; 喜庆的; 欢乐的. *the* ~ *board* 筵席. *a* ~ *mood* 节日气象. *a* ~ *season* 节期. **-ly** *ad.*

fes·tiv·i·ty [fesˈtiviti] *n.* ①节日, 喜庆日; 喜庆, 欢乐. ②〔*pl.*〕祝宴,庆祝典礼.

fes·toon [fesˈtuːn] *n.* ①花彩; 穗边窗帘[门帘]. ②【建】垂花饰. ③花彩装饰物; 彩旗. — *vt.* ①给…结彩,在…饰以花彩. ②使成花彩形. **-e·ry** *n.* 〔集合词〕(一团)花丝; 彩饰.

Fest·schrift [ˈfestˌʃrift] *n.* (*pl.* **-schrift·en** [-ˌʃriftn], **-schrifts**) 〔亦 f-〕纪念册; (专为纪念某著名学者由其同事、学生等写成的)纪念文集.

fet·a (cheese) [ˈfetə] (用羊奶做的)希腊白软干酪.

fe·tal [ˈfiːtl] *a.* 胎儿的; 胎的. ~ **hemoglobin** 胎儿血红蛋白. ~ **membrane** 胎膜. ~ **position** 胎儿(状)姿势, (调气养身的)打坐.

fe·ta·tion [fiːˈteiʃən] *n.* 怀孕,受胎; 胚胎发育.

fetch[1] [fetʃ] *vt.* ①拿来,拿去; 请来, 接去. ②【海】到达; 赶上(别的船). ③使发生; 使出(血), 使流(泪), 使吐(气); 使发出(喊声等). ④卖得(好价钱). ⑤〔口〕给以打击,杀死. ⑥〔俚〕吸引, 使发生兴趣. ⑦激恼. ⑧推导出,演绎出. ⑨使信服 (*round*). ⑩〔方〕使苏醒. ~ *a doctor* 请医生来. *Please* ~ *me the pen.* 请把笔给我拿来. ~ *the harbour* (船)到港. ~ *way* 【海】开始航行. *The call* ~*ed him at once.* 一喊他就来了. ~ *a sigh* 发叹息声. ~ *a good price* 卖好价钱. *This old watch won't* ~ *you much.* 你这块旧表卖不出多少钱. *The beauty of the lake* ~*ed her completely.* 湖光美景完全吸引了她. *The film* ~*ed the public.* 影片博得好评, 受人欢迎. *A little flattery will* ~ *him.* 〔美俚〕稍一奉承他就软化了. — *vi.* ①取,拿来,带来. ②【海】航行,前进; 绕道走 (*about, round*). ③(猎犬)叼回猎物. ④〔方〕到达,抵达. *They* ~*ed home after a long ride.* 他们坐了很久的车之后,终于到家了. *To* ~! 〔命令猎犬〕去(把猎物叼回来)! ~ *headway [sternway]* 前进 [后退]. ~ ***about*** 迂回. ~ ***again*** 〔古〕使复活, 使苏生. ~ ***and carry*** ①(猎犬)把打死的猎物叼回. ②传播小道消息. ③当听差[仆役],打杂 (*for*). ~ ***around*** ①使确信, 说服. ②使复活. ~ ***away*** (桌上的物品因船只颠簸等而)滑离原处. ~ ***down*** 打下(射击物); 减轻(刑罚等); 落(价). ~ ***in*** 拉进; 招徕. ~ ***off*** ①使摆脱窘境. ②杀死. ③一口气喝光. ~ ***out*** 使显出(光彩等); 拿出; 引出. ~ ***to*** 使苏醒. ~ ***up*** ①拿出,想起; 引起, 产生. ②收回,取回(失品). ③呕吐; 扶养,养育. ④〔方〕苏醒. ⑤【海】到达,停止, 忽然停止 (~ *up all standing* 船驶上暗礁时, 风帆未下而忽然停止). ~ ***up with*** 追到, 赶上. ~ ***way*** = ~ away. — *n.* ①拿取,拿来. ②行程,(对岸)两点间的距离; 风浪区. ③诡计,谋略. ⑤〔古〕(想象力等的) 作用, 范围. *a far [long]* ~ 一段远距离. *the* ~ *of a bay* 海湾的全长度. ~**-up** *n.* 突然的停止. **-er** *n.* 取物的人,请人的人.

fetch[2] [fetʃ] *n.* ①(迷信者所说的)生魂,活人的魂, 人将死时的离魂. ②相同物. *be the exact* ~ *of* 和…一模一样. ~ **candle [light]** (迷信者所说的)人将死时从其家中飘向墓地的鬼火.

fetch·ing [ˈfetʃiŋ] *a.* 〔口〕动人的, 吸引人的, 迷人的. **-ly** *ad.*

fête, fete [feit] *n.* ①节日,喜庆日; 盛大招待会,盛宴; 游园会. ②生日. *a national* ~ 国庆节日. *a garden [lawn]* ~ 〔美〕游园会. — *vt.* 款待,盛宴招待; 给以巨大荣誉. ~ **champêtre** 〔F.〕游园大会. ~ **day** 节日; 庆祝日〔生日等〕.

fet·e·ri·ta [ˌfetəˈriːtə] *n.* 【植】非洲芦粟〔原产非洲,美国西南部种植为饲料,粒大,色白〕.

fe·tial [ˈfiːʃəl] *n.* (古罗马主持外交谈判, 宣布战争等职务的)外事祭司团成员. — *a.* ①古罗马祭司团的; 古罗马祭司团职务的. ②外交的,处理国家关系事务的.

fe·ti·a·lis [ˌfiːʃiˈeilis] *n.* (*pl.* **-a·les** [-liːz]) = fetial.

fe·tich(e) [ˈfiːtiʃ, ˈfet-] *n.* = fetish.

fet·ich·ism [ˈfetiʃizəm] *n.* = fetishism.

fet·ich·ist [ˈfetiʃist] *n.* = fetishist.

fet·i·cide [ˈfiːtisaid] *n.* 杀胎,堕胎(= foeticide).

fet·id [ˈfetid,ˈfiː-] *a.* 发臭的, 腐臭的. **-ly** *ad.* **-ness** *n.*

fe·tip·a·rous [fiːˈtipərəs] *a.* (有袋动物等)胎儿发育完全前生产的.

fet·ish [ˈfiːtiʃ, ˈfetiʃ] *n.* ①物神, 崇拜物. ②偶像, 迷信. ③【心】物恋的对象. ④物神崇拜的仪式. ***break with*** ~ 破除盲目崇拜. ***make a perfect ~ of*** 盲目崇拜.

fet·ish·ism [ˈfiːtiʃizəm,ˈfe-] *n.* ①物神崇拜, 拜物教. ②迷信,盲目崇拜. ③【心】(由异性的局部肢体或所用物件得到变态性欲满足的)物恋.

fet·ish·ist [ˈfiːtiʃist,ˈfe-] *n.* ①物神崇拜者; 拜物教徒. ②【心】恋物欲者.

fet·ish·is·tic [ˌfetiˈʃistik] *a.* ①拜物教(徒)的; 盲目崇拜的. ②【心】物恋的.

fet·lock [ˈfetlɔk] *n.* ①距毛,(马蹄上部的) 丛毛. ②(生距毛处的) 球节. ③(生距毛的) 肢关节. ***hairy about [at, in] the ~s*** 〔俚〕没教养的,没礼貌的.

fe·tol·o·gy [fiːˈtɔlədʒi] *n.*【医】胎儿学. **-o·gist** 胎儿学者.

fe·tor [ˈfiːtə, ˈfiːtɔː] *n.* 奇臭, 恶臭.

fet·ter [ˈfetə] *n.* 〔*pl.*〕脚镣; 囚禁; 束缚, 羁绊. *No man loves his ~s, be they made of gold.* 〔谚〕金铸的脚镣, 也没人喜好. ***be in ~s*** 上着脚镣, 被囚禁着. — *vt.* 给…上脚镣; 束缚. *be ~ed by tradition* 受传统的束缚. **~bush** *n.*【植】①(美国) 亮叶南烛 *(Lyonia lucida)*. ②美国马醉木 *(Pieris floribunda)*. **~lock** ①= fetlock. ②(马的) D 字形脚镣; D 字形徽章.

Fet·tes [ˈfetis] *n.* 费蒂斯〔姓氏〕.

fet·tle [ˈfetl] *n.* ①状态, 情绪. ②涂炉床材料. ***in good [fine]*** ~ 神采奕奕,兴高采烈. — *vt.* ①〔英方〕修补, 整顿. ②殴打. ③【冶】用矿渣等涂(炉床). — *vi.* 〔英方〕①准备好. ②纷扰,小题大做. **-r** *n.* 修理工,保养工.

fet·tling [ˈfetliŋ] *n.*【冶】涂炉床材料〔如硅石〕.

fet·tuc·ci·ne, fet·tu·ci·ne, fet·tu·ci·ni [ˌfetuːˈtʃiːniː] *n.* 〔It.〕*pl.* 〔动词常用单数〕黄油酱汁面条.

fe·tus [ˈfiːtəs] *n.* = foetus.

fet·wa [ˈfetwə] *n.* (根据伊斯兰教法规所作的)判决.

feu [fjuː] *n.* 〔Scot.〕【法】永久租借(权); 永久租借地; 封地. — *vt.* 准许永久租借.

feud[1] [fjuːd] *n.* (部落或家族之间的) 世仇; 仇恨, 不和; 争执, 纠纷. ***be at ~ with*** 与人不和. ***deadly*** ~ 不共戴天之仇, 世仇. ***sink a*** ~ 捐弃旧怨, 言归于好. — *vi.* 长期不和; 经常争吵. *spend one's time ~ing with the neighbours* 经常和街坊争吵.

feud[2] [fjuːd] *n.* (封建制度下的)封地, 采邑.

feu·dal[1] [ˈfjuːdl] *a.* ①封建的; 封建制度 [时代] 的. ②封地的, 采邑的. *the ~ age [days, times]* 封建时代. *the ~ system* 封建制度. *a ~ lord* 封建主, 诸侯. *~ estates* 封地, 采邑. **-ist** *n.* ①封建主义者. ②研究封建制度的学者. **-ly** *ad.*

feu·dal[2] [ˈfjuːdl] *a.* 世仇的; 不和的, 争吵的. **-ist** *n.* 结下世仇的人.

feu·dal·ism [ˈfjuːdəlizəm] *n.* ①封建主义, 封建制度. ②寡头制度. *industrial* ~ 工业上的寡头制度.

feu·dal·is·tic [ˌfjuːdəˈlistik] *a.* 封建制度的, 封建主义(者)的.

feu·dal·i·ty [fjuːˈdæliti] *n.* ①封建制度, 封建性. ②封地, 采邑.

feu·dal·ize [ˈfjuːdəlaiz] *vt.* 对(土地)实行封建制度, 使为领地. **-za·tion**[ˌfjuːdəlaiˈzeiʃən] *n.* 封建化.

feu·da·to·ry [ˈfjuːdətəri] *a.* ①封建的, 臣属的, 受有封地的. ②(邦上)隶属于外国的. — *n.* ①封建领主, 诸侯, 家臣. ②封邑.

feu de joie [ˌfəː də ˈʒwɑː] 〔F.〕①大篝火 (= bonfire). ②礼炮 (=fire of joy).

feud·ist [ˈfjuːdist] *n.* ①研究封建法的专家. ②〔美〕结下世仇的人; 仇敌.

Feu·er·bach [G. ˈfɔyərbax], **L. A.** 费尔巴哈〔1804—1872, 德国哲学家〕.

feu·il·le·ton [ˈfɔiitəːn] *n.* 〔F.〕①(报纸的) 副刊, 小品栏, 文艺栏; 小品文. ②连载小说, 通俗小说.

feuil·le·ton·ist [ˈfɔijətənist] *n.* (报刊的) 小品栏作家, 文艺栏作家, 连载小说作家, 法国报刊副刊[专栏]作家.

fe·ver [ˈfiːvə] *n.* ①发热, 发烧; 热度. ②热病. ③狂热; 兴奋. *~ and ague* 疟疾. *hectic ~* 消耗热, 痨病热, 潮热. *intermittent ~* 间歇热. *quartan ~* 间三日疟, 四日疟. *scarlet ~* 猩红热. *typhoid ~* 伤寒. *yellow ~* 黄热病. ***be in a ~ of impatience*** 焦虑不安. ***run a ~*** 发烧. ***send sb. into a ~ of excitement*** 使人非常激动. — *vt.* ①使发烧; 使患热病. ②使兴奋[发狂]. **~ blister [sore]**【医】唇疱疹, 口角疱疹 (= cold sore). **~few**【植】小白菊. **~ heat** 发烧时的体温; 高度兴奋, 狂热. **~ pitch** 高度兴奋, 狂热. **~ therapy**【医】高烧疗法〔提高患者体温以消灭病菌的一种旧疗法〕. **~ trap** 使人容易发热病的地方, 瘴疠之地. **~ tree**【植】蓝桉. **~ ward** 隔离病房. **~weed**【植】刺芹属植物. **~wort**【植】抱茎莛子藨. **-ed** *a.* 发烧的; 高度兴奋的.

fe·ver·ish [ˈfiːvəriʃ] *a.* ①发烧的, 有热病症状的; 热病的. ②容易引起热病的, 热病蔓延的. ③兴奋的, 狂热的, 焦躁的. *~ activities* 疯狂的活动. *with ~ excitement* 极端兴奋地. **-ly** *ad.* **-ness** *n.*

fe·ver·ous [ˈfiːvərəs] *a.* = feverish. **-ly** *ad.*

few [fjuː] *a.* (**~er; ~est**) ①〔无冠词 a (否定用法)〕少数的, 很少, 几乎没有 (*opp.* many) 〔*cf.* little〕. ②〔a ~ (肯定用法)〕有些, 几个 (*opp.* none) 〔*cf.* a little〕. *I have ~ friends.* 我朋友很少, 我几乎没有朋友. *a man of ~ words* 沉默寡言的人. *I have a ~ friends.* 我有少数几个朋友. *in a few days* 过几天, 在两三天内. — *n.* ①〔无冠词(否定用法)〕很少数, 几乎没有. ②〔*a ~* (肯定用法)〕少数, 几个. ③〔the ~〕(对'多数'说的) 少数. ***a ~*** ①几个, 两三个 (*A ~ of them come.* 他们来了几个人. *A faithful ~ remain.* 只剩下不多几个忠诚的友人[同道]). ②〔俚〕一点点; 〔反语〕很多, 的确. ***a good ~ =quite a ~, not a ~, some ~*** 〔美语〕不少, 相当多. ***at the ~est*** 至少. ***a very ~*** 极少数. ***every ~ days [minutes, weeks]*** 每隔几天[分钟、星期]. ***~ and far between*** 稀少, 隔很久才发生的. ***~ or no [none]*** 几乎没有. ***no ~er than*** 不下于, 多达. ***only a ~*** 仅仅少数, 一点点. ***to name (only) a ~*** 〔插入语〕(仅)举几个为例.

few·ness [ˈfjuːnis] *n.* 少, 少数.

few·trils [ˈfjuːtrilz] *n. pl.* 〔英方〕(琐碎的) 小事; 小物件; 少量.

fey [fei] *a.* 〔Scot.〕①该死的; 垂死的. ②象垂死的人一样心乱的. ③发狂似的. ④奇异的, 古怪的. ⑤能看见神仙的. ⑥非现世的.

fez [fez] *n.* (*pl.* **fez·zes** [ˈfeziz]) 土耳其帽.

ff. = ①〔It.〕【乐】*fortissimo*. ②folios 面数, 页数. ③following (pages) 以下(各页).

F/F = full(ly) fashioned【纺】全成形的.

FFA, f.f.a. = ①foreign freight agent 国外货运代理人. ②free from alongside 船边交货(价格).

F.F.A. = fellow of the Faculty of Actuaries 〔英〕保险统计师公会会员.

F.F.P.S. = Fellow of the Faculty of Physicians and Surgeons 〔英〕内外科医师公会会员.

F.F.V. 〔美俚〕= (a member of one of the) First Fam-

ilies of Virginia 贵族,俗不可耐的绅士;贵族派头的,俗不可耐的.
F.G. = ①Fire Guards〔英〕义勇消防队. ②foot-guards〔英〕近卫步兵.
FGA, f.g.a. = ①foreign general agent 国外一般代理人. ②foreign general average 国外共同海损险. ③free of general average 共同海损不保在内.
FGCM = field general court-martial 战地高等军事法庭.
F.G.S. = fellow of the geological society *(of London)*〔英〕(伦敦)地质学会会员.
F.G.S.A. = Fellow of the Geological Society of America 美国地质学会会员.
FH, F.H. = fire hydrant 消防栓,消防龙头,灭火龙头.
F.H.S. = Fellow of the Horticultural Society〔美〕园艺学会会员.
F.I. = Falkland Islands 福克兰群岛(即马尔维纳斯群岛)〔大西洋〕.
f.i. = for instance 例如.
F.I.A. = Fellow of the Institute of Actuaries〔英〕保险统计学会会员.
fi·a·cre [fiːˈɑːkə] *n.* 法国出租小马车.
fi·an·cé [fiˈɑ̃nsei; 美 ˌfiənˈsei] *n.*〔F.〕未婚夫.
fi·an·cée [fiˈɑ̃nsei; 美 ˌfiənˈsei] *n.*〔F.〕未婚妻.
fi·as·co [fiˈæskəu] *n.* (*pl.* ~*s*, ~*es*) (演奏等的)大失败;(特指)大为丢脸[出丑]的失败. ***end in a*** ~ 以完全失败告终.
FIAT [fiət, ˈfiːæt] = *Fabbrica Italiana Automobile Torine*〔It.〕菲亚特汽车公司.
fi·at [ˈfaiæt, -ət] *n.* ①命令, 法令. ②许可, 认可. — *vt.* ①认可. ②以命令宣布. ~ **money**〔美〕不兑换纸币,流通券.
fib¹ [fib] *n.* 小谎, 不伤大雅的谎话. — *vi.* 撒小谎. **fib·ber** *n.* 惯撒小谎的人.
fib² [fib] *n.*〔英〕一拳,一击. — *vt.* 击.
fi·ber [ˈfaibə] *n.*〔美〕= fibre. ~**ed** *a.* = fibred. ~**fill** = fibrefill. ~**-op·tic** = fibre-optic. ~ **op·tics** = fibre optics.
fi·ber·ize [ˈfaibəraiz] *vt., vi.* (使)成纤维,(使)纤维化.
fibr- *comb. f.* 表示"纤维": *fibrin.*
fi·bre [ˈfaibə] *n.* ①纤维,纤维质; 纤维制品,纤维板,硬纸板. ②【植】须根,木纹;〔口〕筋. ③性格,素质,骨气. *bast* ~【植】韧皮纤维. *nerve* ~【解】神经纤维. *synthetic* ~ 合成纤维. *a fabric of coarse [fine]* ~ 质地粗[细]的织物. *a man of real* ~ 有骨气的男子. ~**board** *n.* 硬纸板;纤维板. ~**fill** *n.* (被褥等的)纤维填塞物;合成纤维棉絮. ~**glass** 玻璃纤维, 玻璃丝. ~**-optic** *a.* 纤维光学的. ~ **optics** ①纤维光学. ②用于纤维光学的纤维. ~**scope** (利用光学纤维对胃等进行检查的)纤维镜. **-d** *a.* 含纤维的,纤维质的. **-less** *a.* 无纤维的,无骨气的.
fi·bri·form [ˈfaibrifɔːm] *a.* 纤维状的,象纤维的.
fi·bril [ˈfaibril] *n.* ①小纤维. ②【动】纤丝,原纤维. ③根毛. **-lar, -lar·y** *a.*
fi·bril·late [ˈfaibrileit] *a.* 有原纤维的,有纤维组织的. — *vt., vi.* ①(使)形成原纤维. ②(使)(心脏)作纤维性颤动.
fi·bril·la·tion [ˌfaibriˈleiʃən] *n.*【医】纤维性颤动.
fi·bril·li·form [faiˈbrilifɔːm] *a.* 小纤维状的.
fi·bril·lose [ˈfaibriləus] *a.* 小纤维的, 发丝的, 根毛的;似小纤维的,似发丝的,似根毛的.
fi·brin [ˈfaibrin] *n.* ①【生化】(血)纤维蛋白, (血)纤维朊. ②【植】麸植.
fi·brin·o·gen [faiˈbrinədʒən] *n.*【医】(血)纤维蛋白原.
fi·brin·o·gen·ic [ˌfaibrinəuˈdʒenik] *a.* ①纤维蛋白原的, 纤维蛋白原状的. ②可形成纤维蛋白原的 (= fibrinogenous).
fi·bri·nol·y·sin [ˌfaibrinəuˈlaisin] *n.*【生】纤维蛋白溶酶.
fi·bri·nol·y·sis [ˌfaibrinəuˈlaisis] *n.*【生】纤维蛋白溶解. **-lyt·ic** [-ˈlitik] *a.*
fi·brin·ous [ˈfaibrinəs] *a.* 纤维蛋白的; 纤维蛋白状的; 含纤维蛋白的.
fi·bro·blast [ˈfaibrəublɑːst] *n.*【生】成纤维细胞. **-blas·tic** [ˌfaibrəuˈblɑːstik] *a.*
fi·bro·cyte [ˈfaibrəusait] *n.*【生】纤维细胞.
fi·broid [ˈfaibrɔid] *a.* 纤维状的; 纤维性的; 由纤维组织的. — *n.*【医】纤维瘤.
fi·bro·in [ˈfaibrəuin] *n.*【生化】丝纤朊,丝(心)蛋白.
fi·bro·ma [faiˈbrəumə] *n.* (*pl.* ~*ta* [-tə], ~*s*)【医】纤维瘤. **-tous** *a.*
fi·bro·sis [faiˈbrəusis] *n.*【医】纤维变性,纤维化.
fi·bro·si·tis [ˌfaibrəuˈsaitis] *n.*【医】纤维织炎.
fi·brous [ˈfaibrəs] *a.* ①含纤维的, 纤维状的. ②能分成纤维的. ③坚韧的,有筋骨的. *the* ~ *husk of coconut* 椰子的纤维质外壳. ~ **glass** 纤维玻璃, 玻璃丝. ~ **roots**【植】纤维根,须根. ~ **tumour**【医】纤维肿(瘤). **-ly** *ad.* **-ness** *n.*
fi·bro·vas·cu·lar [ˌfaibrəuˈvæskjulə] *a.*【植】维管(组织)的.
fib·ster [ˈfibstə] *n.* 惯撒小谎的人.
fib·u·la [ˈfibjulə] *n.* (*pl.* ~*s*, *-lae* [-liː]) ①【解】腓骨 ②(古希腊、罗马的)饰针,别针. **-r** *a.*
F.I.C. = Fellow of the Institute of Chemistry〔英〕化学学会会员.
-fic *suf.* 构成形容词, 表示"…化的","引起…的","做成…的": speci*fic*, terri*fic*.
-fi·ca·tion *suf.*〔使末尾为 -fy 的动词变成名词〕表示"形成","…化": magini*fication*.
fi·celle [fiˈsel] *a.* 灰褐色的.
fiche [fiːʃ] *n.* ①卡片. ②微缩胶片 (=microfiche).
Fich·te [G. fixtə], **J.G.** 费希特〔1762—1814, 德国哲学家〕.
fich·u [ˈfiːʃuː] *n.* 三角形女用薄围巾.
fick·le [ˈfikl] *a.* 轻浮的,反复无常的,易变的. **-ness** *n.*
fi·co [ˈfiːkəu] *n.* (*pl.* ~*es*) ①〔古〕无价值的东西; 不足道的事. ②〔废〕= fig〔表轻蔑的手势〕.
fic·tile [ˈfiktail] *a.* ①可塑造的,塑造的. ②陶器的, 黏土制的. ③顺从的. *a* ~ *deity* 泥菩萨. ~ *ware* 陶器. — *n.* 陶制器.
fic·tion [ˈfikʃən] *n.* ①编造,想象,虚构; 捏造. ②编造的谎话. ③小说; 虚构的文学作品〔包括小说,剧本等〕. ④【法】假定,拟制. *Fact [Truth] is stranger than* ~.〔谚〕事实比小说还奇怪. **-eer** *n.* (特指粗制滥造的)小说作家. **-er, -ist** *n.* 小说家〔特指长篇小说作家〕.
fic·tion·al [ˈfikʃənəl] *a.* 虚构的; 小说的. **-ly** *ad.*
fic·tion·al·ize [ˈfikʃənəlaiz] *vt.* 把…编成小说, 使小说化 (=fictionize). **-i·za·tion** [ˌfikʃənəlaiˈzeiʃən] *n.*
fic·ti·tious [fikˈtiʃəs] *a.* ①虚构的, 编造的, 想象的; 虚伪的. ②假定的,虚设的. ③小说式的. *a* ~ *bill [paper]* 空头支票. *a* ~ *character* 虚构人物. *a* ~ *name* 假名. *a* ~ *price* 虚价. ~ *transactions*【商】买空卖空. ~ **person**【法】法人. ~ **year [star]**【天】假想年[天体]. **-ly** *ad.* **-ness** *n.*
fic·tive [ˈfiktiv] *a.* ①虚构的; 想象上的,假定的. ②用想象力进行创作的. ~ *tears* 虚情假义的眼泪. **-ly** *ad.*
fid [fid] *n.* ①支撑材, 固定材; 楔状铁栓. ②【船】桅栓. ③(解绳用的)硬木钉.
-fid *suf.* 表示"…分的","…叉的";【植】"…裂的": bi*fid*, tri*fid*.
fid. = fiduciary.
fid·dle [ˈfidl] *n.* ①〔口〕提琴,提琴类乐器. ②【海】防食器滚落的餐具框、栏. ③欺骗行为. ***as fit as a*** ~ ***[flea]*** 神采奕奕. ***hang up the*** ~ 隐退; 住手不干. ***hang up***

one's ~ when one comes home 在外谈笑兴致高，回家闷头睡懒觉。***have a face as long as a ~*** 板着面孔。***play first ~*** 做领头人，当第一把手，带头。***play second ~*** 做第二把手，充当副手。***play third ~*** 当第三把手，当配角。— *int.* = ~ sticks. — *vt.* ①用提琴演奏。②虚度（时光）。③〔俚〕欺骗，伪造（帐目等）。— *vi.* ①〔口〕拉提琴。②虚度光阴，鬼混。③（胡乱地，神经质地）摸弄；玩弄，瞎摆弄。*F- while Rome is burning.* 尽管大难临头，依然歌舞升平。*Stop fiddling around and get to work.* 别再鬼混，去干活吧！ ***~ about [around]*** 闲逛，混日子。***~ with*** （胡乱）玩弄，抚摸 *(He keeps fiddling with the dials on the radio, he is sure to put it out of order.* 他老是玩弄收音机上的度盘，一定会把它弄坏的）。**~back** *n.* 小提琴形状的东西。**~ bow** 提琴弓。**~ case** 提琴匣。**~deedee** *n. int.* 胡说，无聊话。**~-faddle**〔口〕①*n.* 无聊话，琐碎小事；懒人。②*a.* 无聊的，为琐事操心的。③*int.* 胡说！ ④*vi.* 无事忙；胡扯。**~head** ①（提琴头状的）船首饰。②（羊齿植物幼苗的）卷牙（= crosier）。**~ pattern**（刀、叉等柄部的）提琴形。**~stick** ①提琴弓。②无聊事（*not care a ~stick* 毫不在乎）。**~sticks** *int.* 胡说！ **~wood**【植】①美洲热带地区马鞭草科 *(Verbenaceae)* 植物或其硬木材。②同科的其他种树。

fid·dler [ˈfidlə] *n.* ①拉小提琴的人。②爱玩乐的人；游手好闲的人；（帐目等的）弄虚作假者。③= ~ crab. ***pay the ~*** 承担后果；负担玩乐的费用。**~ crab**【动】招潮属 *(Uca)* 蟹〔雄蟹的螯一大一小〕，招潮（蟹）。**~'s green**【海】水手的天堂〔指海员上岸饮酒作乐〕。

fid·dley [ˈfidli] *n.* = fidley.

fid·dling [ˈfidliŋ] *a.* 无用的，无足轻重的。

fi·de·ism [ˈfi:deiˌizm, ˈfaidi:ˌizm] *n.*【哲】唯信仰论，信仰主义。**fi·de·is·tic** [ˌfi:deiˈistik] *a.* **fi·de·ist** *n.* 信仰主义者。

fi·del·i·ty [fiˈdeliti, fai-] *n.* ①忠诚，忠实 *(to)*。②真实，翔实；（画等的）逼真度。③（收音，录音设备等的）保真度，重现精度。*a high ~ amplifier* 高保真度放大器。*~ to a principle* 忠于原则。*report with ~* 如实报告。*reproduce (the Ms.) with complete ~* （照原稿）原样复制。***high ~*** （收、录音设备等的）高保真度〔略作 hi-fi〕。

fidg·et [ˈfidʒit] *vi.* 坐立不安，烦躁。— *vt.* ①使烦躁，使坐立不安。②（心不在焉地或心烦意乱地）摆弄。— *n.*〔常 *pl.*〕坐立不安，烦躁；烦躁不安的人。***be in a ~*** 忐忑不安。***give sb. the ~s*** 使人烦躁不安。***have the ~s*** 心神不安，担心。

fidg·et·y [ˈfidʒiti] *a.* 坐立不安的，烦躁的；为小事操心的。**-i·ness** *n.*

fid·i·bus [ˈfidibəs] *n.*（点火用的）纸捻。

fid·ley [ˈfidli] *n.*【船】锅炉舱顶棚；锅炉（舱）栅。

FI·DO, Fi·do [ˈfaiˌdəu] *n.*（飞机跑道使用的）火焰驱雾法（= Fog Investigation Dispersal Operations）。

fi·do [ˈfaidəu] *n.* 有铸造缺陷的硬币〔系 freaks, irregulars, defects 和 oddities 四词的首字母缩合词〕。

fi·du·cial [fiˈdju:ʃəl] *a.* ①【测】基准的。②有信仰的。③可靠的，信用的。*a ~ line [point]* 基准线［准点］。*a ~ mark* 准标。

fi·du·ci·ar·y [fiˈdju:ʃəri] *a.* ①信用的，信托的。②受信托的。③信用发行的。*~ capacity [character]* 受托人身份。*a ~ guardian* 受托监护人。*a ~ institution* 信用机关。*~ issue* （纸币的）信用发行。*a ~ loan* 信用贷款。*~ notes* 无现金储备而发行的纸币。*~ property* 受托保管的财产。*a ~ relation* 信托关系。— *n.* 被信托者，受托人。**-ar·i·ly** *ad.*

fi·dus A·cha·tes [ˈfaidəs əˈkeiti:z]〔L.〕忠实的朋友；忠实的追随者；忠仆。

fie [fai] *int.* 呸！ ***Fie upon you!*** 去你的！ ***Fie, for shame!*** 呸，不要脸！

fief [fi:f] *n.* 采邑，封地。

fie-fie [ˈfaifai] *a.* 不象样子的，出丑的。

Field [ˈfi:ld] *n.* 菲尔德〔姓氏〕。

field [fi:ld] *n.* ①原野，旷野；（海、空、冰雪等的）茫茫一片。②田地，牧场；割草场；〔*pl.*〕〔集合词〕土地，田野；（地上的）庄稼。③广场，工作场。④（矿物的）产地，煤田，油田。⑤战斗，战役；战场，战地，作战训练［演习］区域。⑥【体】（跑道以内的）运动场；田赛场 *(opp.* track*)*，赛球场，【棒球】外场；（全体）外场守场员；（全体）运动员；（全体）游猎者；【赛马】（热门马以外的）马。⑦活动地，舞台；范围，方面；界（如学术界）。⑧【物】场；力场；区；【数】域；（望远镜等的）视界，视域。⑨（画等的）底子；【影，电视】画面，镜头。⑩影响人们行为的各种因素的综合；环境。⑪扫描场〔尤指隔行扫描制的半帧〕；【计】信息［符号］组，字段。*beast of the ~* 野兽。*a ~ of sea [sky]* 海域［天空］。*a snow ~* 雪原。*a wheat ~* 小麦地。*a coal ~* 煤田。*a bleaching ~* 漂白场。*a flying ~* 飞机场。*a good ~* 坚强的选手阵容。*gravitational ~* 重力场，引力场。*a hard-fought ~* 激战（地）。*magnet ~* 磁场。*a maiden ~* 未采的油田［矿区］。*real number ~*【数】实数域。*root ~*【数】根域。*a single ~* 一个对一个地打，单打。*terraced ~s* 梯田。*the ~ of battle* 战场。*~ of force*【物】力场。*a ~ of research* 研究范围。*a new ~ of inquiry* 研究的新领域。*a ~ of observation [view, vision]* 视界，视野。*the visual ~* 视界；雷达可见区。***be in the ~*** ①从军，参战，参加竞赛。②【物】在某种物理能的作用范围内。***be out in left ~***〔美俚〕发疯。***conquer the ~*** 获胜，占优势。***enter the ~*** 上场，上阵。***fair ~ and no favour*** 均等的比赛条件，公平无私。***~ of fire***【军】射界。***~ of honour*** 决斗场，战场。***hold [keep, maintain] the ~*** 守住阵地。***in one's own ~*** 在自己本行内。***in the ~*** ①实地，在现场。②在某一行中。***lead the ~*** 带头追猎。***leave sb. a clear ~*** 给人行动自由。***leave sb. the ~*** 输给某人。***leave the ~ open*** 不加干涉。***lose the ~*** 败退。***play the ~***〔美俚〕交好几个异性朋友；避免对专一的对象承担义务。***take the ~*** 出阵，开战。***take to the ~*** 接防，接守。***win the ~***〔古〕取得胜利，获胜。— *vt.* ①（棒球、板球运动中）接［截］（球），守（球）。②使（球队或球员）入场，把…投入战场。③把（谷物等）曝露场上。④当场圆满答复。— *vi.*（棒球赛等）担任外场员或守队队员；【赛马】冷门马。— *a.* ①田间的，野生的；野外的。②实地的。*~ care* 田间管理。*~ crops* 大田作物。*~ flowers* 野花。*~ operations* 野外作业。*a ~ worker* 实地工作者。**~ allowance**（军官）战地津贴。**~ ambulance** 战地救护车，野战救护队。**~ army** 野战军。**~ artillery**〔总称〕野战炮，野战炮兵。**~ball**【棒球】外野球。**~ book** 野外工作记录本。**~ capacity** 土壤容水量。**~ corn** 饲料玉米。**~ day** ①野外演习日。②户外集会。③体育比赛日。④野外科学活动日。⑤特别愉快的时刻，获得意外成功的时刻。⑥有重要活动的日子。**~ dressing**（战场上的）应急治疗。**~ driver**〔美〕兜捕无主家畜的警察。**~ editor**〔美〕（报馆的）地方通讯员；外埠通讯员。**~ effect transistor**【无】场效果晶体管。**~ event**【体】田赛。**~ exercise** 野外演习。**~ glasses** 双筒望远镜。**~ grade**【军】校级。**~ gun** 野战炮。**~ hand** ①（农场的）农工。②〔美〕干农活的黑人。**~ hockey** 曲棍球（= hockey）。**~ hospital** 野战医院。**~ house**（运动场周围的）更衣室［贮藏室］等房屋。**~ice**【地】冰原冰。**~ lens** ①【物】向场（透）镜。②（显微镜等的）物镜。**~ mail** 军邮。**~man** *n. (pl. -men)* 外务员〔推销员或其他不在公司内从事业务活动的人员〕。**~ magnet**【物】场磁体，场磁铁。**~ marshal**（英）陆军元帅，最高级陆军将官。**~ mouse** 野鼠，田鼠。**~ music** ①军乐队员［号手、鼓手等］。②军乐。**~ night** 有重要活动的夜晚。**~ pea**【植】紫花豌豆。**~ piece** 野战炮。**~ secretary** 地方联络员。**~-sequential** *a.*【无】（彩色电视）场序制的，帧序制的。**~ service** 野战勤务。**~s-man**

n. = ～er. ～ **sparrow**【动】原野春雀 *(Spizella pusilla)*〔北美的一种褐色白肚麻雀〕. ～ **sports** ①野外运动. ②田赛. ～ **strip** 拆卸检修(枪炮). ～ **telegraph** 军用电报，野战电报机. ～ **telegraphy** 军用电报学. ～**-test** *vt.* 对…作现场试验[工地试验，野外试验]. ～ **theory**【物】场论. ～ **trial** 猎狗的现场追猎试验. ～ **trip** (学生)校外旅行考查，(科研人员)社会调查. ～ **umpire**【棒球】垒裁判员. ～**ward(s)** *ad.* 向原野，向田野. ～ **winding**【物】(磁)场绕组. ～**work [survey, study]** ①野战工事. ②野外测量〔考察〕，实地调查，现场工作. **-er** *n.* (棒球、板球的)外场员，守队队员.

field·er [fiːldə] *n.*【棒球、板球】外场员，外野手；守队队员. ～*'s choice* 外场员的自由选择〔不扔球给一垒而扔给其他的垒〕.

field·fare [ˈfiːldˌfɛə] *n.* (冬季迁飞英国的)北欧鸫.

Field·ing [ˈfiːldiŋ] *n.* ①菲尔丁〔姓氏〕. ② **Henry** ～ 亨利·菲尔丁〔1707—1754，英国小说家〕.

field·ing [fiːldiŋ] *n.*【棒球】守备.

fiend [fiːnd] *n.* ①魔鬼；〔the F-〕魔王. ②恶毒的人，刻毒鬼. ③〔俚〕…迷，…狂. ④能手，神手. *a dance* ～ 跳舞迷. *an opium* ～ 鸦片鬼. *a theatre* ～ 戏迷. *a* ～ *at mathematics* 数学能手. **-like** *a.* 恶魔似的.

fiend·ish [fiːndiʃ] *a.* 恶魔(似)的；恶毒的，残忍的. **-ly** *ad.* **-ness** *n.*

fierce [fiəs] *a.* ①残忍的，凶猛的. ②猛烈的. ③〔英方〕精力旺盛的. ④狂热的，强烈的. ⑤〔美〕令人难受的，讨厌的. ～ *anger* 愤怒. ～ *look* 可怕的样子. ～ *heat* 酷暑. *a* ～ *offensive* 猛攻. *a* ～ *tempest* 狂风暴雨. ～ *pain* 剧痛. **-ly** *ad.* **-ness** *n.*

fi·e·ri fa·ci·as [ˈfaiərai ˈfeiʃiæs]〔L.〕【法】强制执行命令，扣押债务人动产令〔略 *fi. fa.*〕.

fi·er·y [ˈfaiəri] *a.* ***(fier·i·er; -i·est)*** ①火的，火焰的；燃烧的；火似的；如火如荼的. ②(眼光)炯炯有神的. ③热烈的，激烈的；急躁的，(马等)暴躁的. ④易燃烧的，易爆炸的. ⑤红肿的，火热的，火红的. ～ *eyes* 闪闪发光的眼睛. ～ *winds* 热风. ～ *heat* 炎热. ～ *red* 火红色. ～ *revolutionary struggles* 轰轰烈烈的革命斗争. *a* ～ *speech* 激昂的演说. *a* ～ *steed [courser]* 悍马. *a* ～ *taste* 刺激性的味道. ～ *temper* 暴躁的脾气. *a* ～ *sore* 红肿. ***go through a*** ～ ***trial*** 经过千锤百炼. ～ **cross** ①焦十字，血十字〔四端烧焦或染血的木十字架，古苏格兰高地人氏族出战的信号〕. ②火十字〔四端燃烧的木十字架，美国迫害黑人的三K党持之以制造恐怖〕. **fi·er·i·ly** *ad.* **fi·er·i·ness** *n.*

fi·es·ta [ˈfiːestaː, fiˈestə] *n.* ①宗教节日. ②喜庆日子；假日.

fi·fa. [ˈfaifei] =〔L.〕*fieri facias.*【法】扣押债务人动产令.

fife [faif] *n.* (主指军乐队的)笛子. — *vi., vt.* 吹(笛子)，用笛子吹奏(歌曲). ～ **rail**【海】桅脚栅栏，桅边系索杆.

fif·er [ˈfaifə] *n.* 吹笛人，笛手.

FIFO [ˈfaifəu] = first in first out 先进先出.

fif·teen [ˈfifˈtiːn] *num.* 十五. — *n.* ①十五；十五个(人、物)；十五岁；十五点钟(即下午三点)；十五的记号. ②十六世纪. ③(网球赢得第一球的得分叫法)15点，一分. ④〔英〕橄榄球队〔由15人组成〕. *in the* ～ *fifties* 在十六世纪五十年代. ～ **all** (在一盘网球中)双方各得一分. ～ **forty** (在一盘网球中)发球人得15点，接球人得40点，即1比3. ～ **love** (在一盘网球中)发球人得15点，接球人得0点，即1比0. ～**fold** *a., ad.* 十五倍.

fif·teenth [ˈfifˈtiːnθ] *num.* ①第十五. ②十五分之一. — *n.* ①每月的第十五日. ②【乐】(第)十五度音程.

fifth [fifθ] *num.* ①第五. ②五分之一. — *n.* ①〔美〕五分之一加仑(瓶). ②每月的第五日. ③【乐】五度音程，五度和音，第五音，属音. ④〔*pl.*〕五级品. ⑤〔F-〕= Fifth Amendment. *the* ～ *act* 第五幕，终幕；(人生的)晚境. *one* ～ 五分之一. *three* ～*s* 五分之三. *augmented [diminished]* ～【乐】增[减]五度. *smite (under) the* ～ *rib* 刺死，给以致命打击. **F- Amendment** 《美国宪法修正案》第五条〔规定不得强迫刑事犯罪者自证其罪〕. **F-Avenue** (美国纽约市最繁华的)第五号街. ～ **column** 第五纵队. ～ **columnism** 第五纵队战术，利用内奸. ～ **columnist** 第五纵队队员. **F- Monarchy**【宗】基督的王国. **F- monarchy men**【英史】十七世纪热烈盼望基督再次降临的基督教徒. **F- Republic** (法兰西)第五共和国〔成立于1958年〕. ～ **wheel** ①半拖车接轮；转向轮；试验(汽车行车距离的)专用轮. ②备用轮. ③多余的人[物]. **-ly** *ad.*

fif·ti·eth [ˈfiftiiθ] *num., n.* 第五十；五十分之一.

fif·ty [ˈfifti] *num.* 五十，五十个. — *n.* ①五十个人[物]；五十岁；五十的记号. ②〔*pl.*〕五十年代；〔*pl.*〕五十到五十九岁的时期. *in nineteen* ～ 在1950年. *the fifties* 五十几(岁)；(一世纪中的)五十年代. *in the nineteen fifties* (略1950's) 在二十世纪五十年代. — *a.* 许多的. *I have* ～ *things to tell you.* 我有许多话要和你说.

fif·ty-fif·ty [ˈfiftiˈfifti] *a., ad.*〔口〕扯平，各半. *go* ～ *with sb.* 与人平分(损失均摊). *on a* ～ *basis* 平分，对等.

fif·ty-fold [ˈfiftifəuld] *a., ad.* 五十倍.

fig[1] [fig] *n.* ①【植】无花果，无花果树，无花果属植物. ②少许，一点儿；无价值的东西，琐事. ③〔美〕(烟草等的)小片. ④表轻蔑的手势〔把拇指夹在两指之间或塞入口中〕. ***A*** ～ ***for this!*** 有什么了不起! ***Adam*** ～ 香蕉. ***Chinese*** ～ 柿子. ～***'s end*** 无价值的东西. ***not care a*** ～ 毫不在乎. ***not worth a*** ～ 毫不足取，一文不值. ～**eater**【动】无花果虫〔成虫靠食成熟水果为生，也称green June kettle〕. ～ **leaf** ①无花果叶. ②(雕塑)裸体像的遮羞叶，遮羞布. ～ **marigold**【植】日中花属(松叶菊属)植物. ～ **tree** 无花果树. ～ **wasp**【动】无花果小蜂，榕小蜂.

fig[2] [fig]〔口〕*n.* ①服装. ②健康状况. ***be in full*** ～ 盛装. ***be in good*** ～ 情况好，精神好. — *vt.* 使盛装，打扮. ～ *out [up] a horse* 把马装饰起来.

fig. = figurative(ly)；figure(s).

fight [fait] *vi.* ***(fought*** [ˈfɔːt]; ***fought)*** ①打仗，搏斗，打架. ②战斗，奋斗，斗争. ③当职业拳击手. — *vt.* ①与…作战，打(仗). ②争取，争夺. ③使斗，斗. ④指挥，操纵. ～ *a battle* 打一仗. ～ *the enemy head on* 正面进攻敌人，打硬仗. ～ *the fire [gale]* 与火灾[烈风]战斗. ～ *gun* 指挥开炮. ～ *a prize* 夺奖. *The captain fought his ship well.* 舰长出色地指挥军舰作战. ～ ***back*** 抵抗，还击. ～ ***down*** 打败，压服. ～ ***for a cause*** 为主义战斗. ～ ***for existence*** 为生存而斗争. ～ ***(for) one's own hand*** 争夺私利. ～ ***hand to hand*** 短兵相接. ～ ***it out*** 打个青红皂白，一决雌雄. ～ ***like kilkenny cats*** 死拼，斗得两败俱伤. ～ ***off*** 打退；竭力摆脱，克服. ～ ***on*** 继续战斗，继续斗争. ～ ***out*** 打出结果. ～ ***shy (of)*** ①回避，躲避. ②避开正面搏斗 *(The boy* ～*s shy of girls.* 这个男孩子怕和女孩子接触. ～ *shy of an invitation* 谢绝邀请). ～ ***to a finish*** 打到底. ～ ***together*** 打成一团. ～ ***tooth and nail*** 狠狠地打；拼命干. ～ ***under way*** (军舰)边走边打. ～ ***up against*** 与…力战[苦斗]. — *n.* ①战斗；搏斗；争吵，打架；斗争，竞争. ②战斗力，斗争性，斗志. ③拳击赛. *a free* ～ 乱斗. *a hand to hand* ～ 格斗，肉搏战. *a prize* ～ 职业拳击赛. *a running* ～ 追击战. *a sham* ～ 假打；〔英〕模拟战. *a stand up* ～ 光明正大的战斗. *a straight* ～ 一对一的二人竞选. *a* ～ *for higher wages* 为增加工资而斗争. *They have plenty of* ～ *in them.* 他们斗志旺盛. *take the* ～ *out of the enemy troops* 瓦解敌军斗志. ***give [make] a*** ～ 打一仗. ***put up a good*** ～ 善战，善斗. ***show*** ～ 显示斗志，不示弱. ～**-back** *n.* 回击，反击. ～**-off** *n.*

(拳击等的)决赛.

fight·er [ˈfaitə] *n.* ①战士,兵士;斗争者,奋斗者. ②【空】战斗机,歼击机. ③好斗的人. ④(职业)拳击手. *an escort* ~ 护航战斗机. *a jet* ~ 喷气式战斗机. ~-**bomber** 战斗轰炸机. ~ **escort** (护送轰炸机的)护航战斗机. ~-**interceptor** 战斗截击机. ~ **plane** 战斗机,歼击机.

fight·ing [ˈfaitiŋ] *a.* ①战斗的,斗争的,搏斗的. ②适于战斗的. ③好战的,好斗的. ④容易引起争斗的,挑战性的. *in* ~ *condition* 处在适于战斗的状态,斗志旺盛. ~ *words* 挑战性的话,招引是非的话. — *n.* 战争,战斗,作战. *a* ~ *field* 战场. *hand-to-hand* ~ 短兵相接,肉搏战. *house-to-house* ~ = *street* ~ 巷战. ~ *formation* 战斗队形. ~ *men* 战斗员,战士. ~ *spirit* 战斗意志. ~ **chance** 经过努力获得成功的机会. ~ **chair** 搏斗椅,钓鱼椅[牢固钉在船上供钓鱼者与上钩的鱼搏斗的坐椅]. ~ **cock** 斗鸡,好斗的人 (*feel like a* ~ *cock* 觉得斗志昂扬. *live like* ~ *cocks* 过奢侈生活). **F-French** (在第二次世界大战中,巴黎沦陷后继续抗战的)战斗的法国人. ~ **top** 军舰桅顶上的轻武器发射台[观测台].

fig·ment [ˈfigmənt] *n.* 虚构;虚构的事物.

fig·u·line [ˈfigjulin, -ˈlain] *ad.* 〔罕〕陶土的;陶土状的;陶制的. — *n.* 陶[瓷]器,陶瓷像.

fig·ur·a·bi·li·ty [ˌfigjurəˈbiliti] *n.* 能成形性,能定形性.

fig·ur·a·ble [ˈfigjurəbl] *a.* 能成形的,能定形的.

fig·u·ral [ˈfigjurəl] *a.* ①人物[动物]形象的. ②(绘画等)以人物[动物]形象构成的;以人物[动物]形象来表现的. ③比喻的. *the* ~ *representation* 人物画像.

fig·u·rant [ˈfigjurənt] *n.* 〔F.〕(芭蕾舞的)一般(男)演员;配角.

fig·u·rante [ˌfigjuˈrɑːnt] *n.* 〔F.〕(芭蕾舞的)一般女演员;女配角.

fig·u·ra·tion [ˌfigjuˈreiʃən] *n.* ①定形,成形(作用,过程). ②外形,轮廓. ③比喻表达法. ④图案装饰法,图案[符号]表现法;图象,形象. ⑤【乐】(音、旋律的)修饰.

fig·u·ra·tive [ˈfigjurətiv] *a.* ①比喻的,形容的 (*opp* literal);修饰多的,比喻多的,词藻华丽的;象征性的. ②用图形[形象]表现的. *the* ~ *art* 造形美术[绘画与雕刻]. *a* ~ *design* 象征的设计. *in a* ~ *sense* 在比喻的意义上. *a* ~ *style* 华丽的文体. **-ly** *ad.* **-ness** *n.*

fig·ure [ˈfigə, Am. figjər] *n.* ①外形,形状,外观;姿态. ②画像,塑像. ③图形,图案;插图;图表. ④人影,人形;人物. ⑤风度,态度,样子. ⑥数字,位数,符号;数值;价格;〔*pl.*〕计算,算术;【几何】图形. ⑦修辞手段,修辞格;【逻】(三段论法的)格;【乐】音型;(舞蹈中的)舞步形式,(溜冰、飞行的)花样,花式;动作所形成的轨迹. *a woman of good* ~ 身材好看的女人. *a slender* ~ 苗条的身段. *a fine* ~ *of a man* 优美的体态. *a half-length* ~ 半身像. *a rectangular* ~ 矩形. *the great* ~*s of history* 历史上的大人物. *a* ~ *of fun* 滑稽有趣的人物. *a person of* ~ 地位高的人. *significant* ~*s* 有效数字. *double [three]* ~*s* 两[三]位数. *an income of five* ~*s* 五位数字[数以万计]的收入. *cite [give]* ~*s* 列举数字. ***be good at*** ~ 会计算. ***cut [make] a*** ~ 露头角. ***cut [make] a brilliant [conspicuous, fine, good, great, splendid]*** ~ 露头角,出风头. ***cut [make] a poor [little, ridiculous, sorry]*** ~ 出丑. ***cut no*** ~ 〔美〕没有什么突出表现,默默无闻. ***do things on the big*** ~ 〔美〕大干特干. ~ ***of merit*** 【物】灵敏值,优值. ~ ***of speech*** 形象化说法,形象化比喻. ***get (sth.) at a low [high]*** ~ 低价[高价]买得(某物). ***go [come] the big [whole]*** ~ 〔美〕干到底,彻底地干. ***in round*** ~***s*** 用整数表示;大概,总而言之. ***keep one's*** ~ 保持体态苗条. ***lay*** ~ (画家用的)人体模型;虚构人物;傀儡. ***make an imposing*** ~ 仪表堂堂. ***miss a [one's]*** ~ 〔美〕失算,铸成大错. — *vt.* ①用图表示;用塑像等形象表现;描写. ②加图案于,画图案于,加花样于. ③想象. ④表示,象征,用比喻表现. ⑤用数字表示;计算;估计. ⑥〔口〕推测,判断,认为. ⑦懂,领会. ~ *the loss* 计算亏损. *Saints* ~*d on the wall.* 画在壁上的圣徒像. *the* ~ *cloth* 印花布. *I* ~ *he got angry.* 我想他是生气了. *He* ~*d himself a good scholar.* 他自以为很有学问. *She* ~*d the whole scheme at once.* 她立刻就懂得了整个计划. — *vi.* ①(作为…而)出现;扮演;突出,显露头角. ②计算. ③考虑,估计. ④跳某种(花式)舞步. ⑤〔美俚〕有道理,合乎情理. *He* ~*d in the war.* 他在战争中出了名. ~ *largely in a narrative* 在故事中极突出. ~ *for an election* 筹划选举. *Sure, that* ~*s.* 没错,那是合情合理的. ~ ***as*** 扮演…角色. ~ ***for*** 谋取,企图获得. ~ ***in*** ①算进. ②参加. ~ ***on*** ①依赖,指望. ②仔细考虑;计划;估计. ~ ***out*** ①算出,作出. ②估计,推测;解决;了解. ③〔口〕确定;发见;想出. ~ ***out at*** 总共…,合计…. ~ ***up*** 〔美〕总计. ~ **eight** 8 字形(如绳结、溜冰花式、飞行花式等). ~-**of-eight knot** 八字结〔绳结的一种〕. ~ **skating** 花式溜冰. ~**some** *a.* 有些显著的.

fig·ured [ˈfigəd] *a.* ①有形状的,用图形表示的. ②有花纹的,带图案的;富有文采的;【乐】华丽的,加了花的. ~ **fabrics** 有花纹的织品. ~ **iron** 型钢. ~ **satin** 花缎.

fig·ure·head [ˈfigəhed] *n.* ①船头雕饰;破浪神的雕像. ②(有名无实的)傀儡领袖. ③〔谑〕嘴脸.

fig·u·rine [ˈfigjuriːn] *n.* 小人像.

fig·wort [ˈfigwəːt] *n.* 【植】玄参,玄参属植物.

Fi·ji [fiːˈdʒiː, ˈfiːdʒiː] *n.* ①斐济〔西太平洋〕. ②斐济人,斐济语.

Fi·ji·an [fiːˈdʒiːən] *a., n.* ①(西太平洋)斐济群岛(的);斐济群岛人(的). ②斐济语(的).

fi·la [ˈfailə] *n.* filum 的复数.

fil·a·gree [ˈfiləgriː] *n.* = filigree.

fil·a·ment [ˈfiləmənt] *n.* ①细丝,丝状体. ②【纺】长丝;单纤维. ③【植】(雄蕊的)花丝. ④【电】灯丝;丝极;游丝. ~ **breakdown** 【电】丝状击穿. ~ **current** 丝状电流. **-ed** *a.* 有细丝的.

fi·lar [ˈfailə] *a.* ①线的,丝的;丝状或多线物的. ②(测微计的)视界里划有细线的.

fi·lar·i·a [ˈfiləəriə] *n.* 【动】(寄生人体内的)丝虫.

fi·lar·i·al [fiˈlɛəriəl] *a.* 丝虫的,带丝虫的,丝虫引起的. ~ *disease* 【医】丝虫病.

fil·a·ri·a·sis [ˌfiləˈraiəsis] *n.* 【医】丝虫病.

fil·a·ture [ˈfilətʃə] *n.* ①缫丝. ②缫丝机. ③缫丝厂,制丝厂. ~ **silk** 机缫生丝,厂丝.

fil·bert [ˈfilbət] *n.* ①【植】欧洲榛,欧洲榛果实,榛果实. ②〔美俚〕狂热者. *a football* ~ 足球迷.

filch [filtʃ] *vt.* 偷窃(小物品). — *vi.* 小摸小偷. **-er** *n.* 小偷.

file[1] [fail] *n.* ①纸夹,文件夹. ②钉成册的文件,档案,卷宗,案卷,合订本. ③【计】外存贮器,存贮带. ④行列;【军】纵列 (*opp.* rank). ⑤(象棋盘上的)纵线. ~ *computer* 编目计算机. *a column of* ~*s* 若干纵列组成的队伍〔如三路或四路纵队〕. *a* ~ *of men* 执行任务的二人小分队. *a blank* ~ 【军】(无后列时的)单列. *main* ~ 主文件;主存贮器. ~ ***by*** ~ 一列一列;陆续. ***half a*** ~ 二人小分队中的一人. ***in*** ~ 排成二列纵队;挨次,鱼贯地. ***in single [Indian]*** ~ 成一路纵队,成单行. ***keep on [in] a*** ~ 合订保存;归档. ***on*** ~ 合订成册,存档. — *vt.* ①按次序订存,编档保存,汇存. ②〔美〕提起,提出. ③命令(军队等)排成纵队行进. ④用电报[话]发稿. ~ *an information* 起诉,告发. ~ *a complaint with the authorities* 向当局申诉. — *vi.* 排成纵队前进;申请 (*for*);备案作候选人. *F- left [right]* (口令)各队向左(右)(走); ~ ***away [off]*** 排成纵队出发. ~ ***in*** 鱼贯而入,陆续编入. ~ ***out*** 鱼贯而出. ~ **clerk** 档案[卷宗]管理员.

~ **closer** (负值保持队形整齐的)队列官. ~ **memory** 外存贮器. ~ **signal** 档案分类标签.

file² [fail] *n.* ①锉刀. ②〔英俚〕滑头. *block* ~ 大方锉. *a close* ~ 吝啬鬼. *an old (a deep)* ~ 老滑头. ***bite [gnaw, lick] a*** ~ 自找苦吃; 徒劳. — *vt.* 锉; 磨炼(品性等); 推敲(文章等). ~ *one's fingernails* 锉指甲. — *vi.* 用锉刀锉工作. ~ ***away [off]*** 锉去(锈等). ~ ***down*** (用锉)锉开,锉坏. ~ ***one's teeth*** 锉牙齿; 咬牙切齿. ~ ***out*** 锉出.

file·fish [ˈfailˌfiʃ] *n.* 【动】①鲀. ②= triggerfish.

fil·e·mot [ˈfilimɔt] *n., a.* 枯叶色(的); 黄褐色(的).

fi·let [fiˈlei, ˈfiːlei] *n.* 〔F.〕①肉片, 鱼片. ②方网眼花边(= ~lace). ~ *net* 方网眼的网. ~ **de sole** 鲽鱼片. ~ **mignon** 烤里肌肉.

fil·i·al [ˈfiljəl] *a.* ①子女的,孝顺的. ②【生】子代的,后代的. ~ *affection* 子爱. ~ *duty* 做儿子的义务. ~ *obedience* 孝顺. ~ *piety* 孝道. *a* ~ *generation* 【生】杂交后代,子代. ***first*** ~ 杂交第一代,子一代〔略 作 F_1〕. ***second*** ~ 子二代〔略: F_2〕. **-ly** *ad.* **-ness** *n.*

fil·i·ate [ˈfilieit] *vt.* ①= affiliate. ②【法】确定(私生子的)父亲.

fil·i·a·tion [ˌfiliˈeiʃən] *n.* ①父子关系;【法】私生子父亲的鉴定; 私生子的确认. ②起源,由来; 血统,出身; (语言等的) 分支. ③关系的确定. *determine the* ~ *of a language* 确定一种语言的来源. ~ *of manuscripts* 对手稿的鉴定.

fil·i·beg [ˈfilibeg] *n.* 〔Scot.〕= kilt.

fil·i·bus·ter [ˈfilibʌstə] *n.* ①【史】掠夺兵,暴兵; 海盗. ②〔美〕(用冗长的发言)妨碍会议的议员; 会议妨碍行为. — *vt., vi.* ①掠夺,侵夺. ②〔美〕(因发言冗长) 妨碍(会议的进程).

fil·i·cide [ˈfiliˌsaid] *n.* ①杀子女者. ②杀子女的行为. **fil·i·cid·al** *a.*

fil·i·cite [ˈfilisait] *n.* 羊齿类化石.

fil·i·form [ˈfilifɔːm] *a.* 丝状的,线状的, 纤维状的.

fil·i·gree [ˈfiləgriː] *n.* ①金银细丝工艺. ②华而不实的东西. — *a.* 金银细丝工艺的. ~ *work* 金银细丝工艺(制品). — *vt.* ①用金银细丝饰品装饰. ②用华而不实的饰品装饰.

fil·ing [ˈfailiŋ] *n.* ①锉; 锉磨; 锉法. ②〔常 *pl.*〕锉屑. *iron* ~*s* 铁锉屑.

Fil·i·pine [ˈfiliˌpiːn] *a.* = Philippine.

Fil·i·pi·no [ˌfiliˈpiːnəu] *n.* (*pl.* ~*s*) (尤指信基督教的)菲律宾人. — *a.* = Philippine.

fill [fil] *vt.* ①注满,装满,装填,填充. ②(风)张满(帆),使(帆背)受风. ③充满,充实(知识等),普及. ④使满足; 使吃饱. ⑤占(地位); 补(缺), 填(空), 任(职). ⑥〔美〕满足(要求等); 供应(定货); 执行(命令等). ⑦配(药方). ⑧把…搀成杂质品. ~ *the heart with hope* 使心里充满希望. *a meal that* ~*s sb.* 一顿饱餐. ~ *an office satisfactorily* 尽职. ~ *an order* 供应定货. ~ *a prescription* 照方配药. — *vi.* ①充满. ②张满帆. ③堵塞. *The well* ~*s with water.* 井里充满了水. *The sails* ~*ed* 船张满帆. *My heart* ~*ed at the words.* 听到那话,我心中感到难过. ~ ***away*** 【海】转帆向风,顺风前进. ~ ***in*** 填充,装满; 填写(~ *in an application* 填申请书). ~ ***(sb.) in about [on]***… 〔美口〕对(某人)提供关于…的情况. ~ ***one's mind*** 充实知识,学习. ~ ***sb.'s place*** 代替. ~ ***out*** ① *vt.* 使充分,使完全; 使充实; 使扩张,使膨胀; 倾注(酒等); 〔美〕填满(空白). ② *vi.* 满杯; 长大; 变圆; 长胖. ~ ***the bill*** 如约完成; 满足需要,最为适合. ~ ***up*** ① *vt.* 装满, 填满; 补足; 填写. ② *vi.* 充满; (戏院等)客满; 填塞, 淤塞. ~ ***up time*** 消磨时光. — *n.* ①充满, 饱满. ②填塞物; 填土,填方,路堤. *a* ~ *of tobacco* 一袋烟,一烟斗烟草. ***drink [eat] one's*** ~ ***of*** 喝 [吃] 饱. ***have one's*** ~ ***of sorrow*** 饱经忧患. ***take one's*** ~ ***of rest*** 充分休息. ***grumble one's*** ~ 发够牢骚. ***weep one's*** ~ 尽情地哭.

fil·la·gree [ˈfiləgriː] *n., a., vi.* = filigree.

fill-dike [ˈfildaik] *n.* 春汛, 桃花汛〔又称 *February* ~〕. — *a.* 春汛到来的,沟渠满溢的.

fille [ˈfiːjə] *n.* 〔F.〕少女,姑娘.

filled [fild] *a.* 满的,填满的; 充气的; 加载的. ~ **gold** 镀金的金属〔铜、铁、铅等〕. ~ **milk** 加有植物油脂的牛乳. ~ **soap** 杂质肥皂.

fill·er [ˈfilə] *n.* ①装填者,斟酒人; 注入器,漏斗; 填充物. ②(杂志的)补白; 电影补白短片. ③雪茄烟烟心; (自来水笔的) 吸墨管. ④〔*pl.*〕【化】填料. ⑤(计算机的)进位填充数,填充位. *a tank* ~ (油箱的)注油孔.

fil·lér [ˈfiːlɛə] *n.* (*pl.* ~*(s)*) 〔Hung.〕菲勒〔匈牙利货币名,等于 1/100 福林〕.

fil·let [ˈfilit] *n.* ①带子, 带状物. ②头带, 束发带. ③肉片,鱼片. ④【建】平缘, 木摺; 突出横饰线. ⑤(书面等上的)饰线, 轮廓线. ⑥【机】嵌条, 内圆角. ⑦【解】襻, 丘系; 〔*pl.*〕(马、牛等的)腰部. *a* ~ *of veal [mutton]* 小牛[羊]肉片, 里脊片. *light* ~ 浅角焊缝. — *vt.* ①用带束(发), 给…加边线. ②把(鱼肉) 切片. ③修(图). ~*ed angle [corner]* 圆角[内圆角].

fil·li·beg [ˈfiliˌbeg] *n.* = filibeg (= kilt).

fil·li·bus·ter [ˈfilibʌstə] *n., v.* = filibuster.

fill-in [ˈfilˌin] *n.* ①(暂时)补缺者; 替工; 临时填补物. ②〔美口〕(有关事实的) 摘要. ③在等待时间所作的消遣. — *a.* 临时补缺的.

fill·ing [ˈfiliŋ] *n.* ①装满,填装; 填补. ②填料; 填土. ③(糕点内的)馅. ④(织品的)纬纱, 浆料. *gap* ~ 填缝. *gas* ~ 充气. *shell* ~ 外壳安装. ~ **pressure** 充填压力,充气压力,填料压力. ~ **station**〔美〕(汽车)加油站; 〔美俚〕小城市.

fil·lip [ˈfilip] *n.* ①弹指, 轻拍. ②刺激 (*to*). ③琐碎东西,小事,琐事. *make a* ~ 弹一弹,拍一拍. *a* ~ *to the memory* 唤起记忆的东西. ***not worth a*** ~ 毫不足取. — *vt.* ①用指头弹 (*away; down; forth; off*). ②激励,刺激. ~ *sb.'s memory* 唤起记忆. ~ *sb.'s spirits* 使某人振作精神. — *vi.* 弹指.

fil·li·peen [ˌfiliˈpiːn] *n.* = philopena.

fil·lis·ter [ˈfilistə] *n.* ①(刨凹槽用的) 凹刨. ②【建】凹槽; 刨槽, 开槽. ~ **plane**【木工】槽口刨.

Fill·more [ˈfilmɔː] *n.* 菲尔莫尔〔姓氏〕.

fil·ly [ˈfili] *n.* ①小母马 (*opp.* colt). ②〔口〕精神十足的小姑娘.

film [film] *n.* ①薄层, 薄膜; 薄雾, 轻烟, 细丝状的东西. ②【摄】感光乳剂,照相软片,电影胶片; 影片. ③〔*pl.*〕(集合词) 电影. ④(眼中的) 薄翳. *carbon resistance* ~ 【电】炭膜电阻. *a* ~ *of gossamer* 蜘蛛丝. *a roll [spool] of* ~ 一卷胶片. *a magnetic* ~ (录音)磁带. *a silent* ~ 无声影片,默片. *a sound* ~ 有声影片. *a talkie* ~ 有声对白影片. *a documentary [feature]* ~ 纪录[故事]片. *a three-dimensional* ~ 立体电影. ~ *actor [actress]* 电影男[女]演员. ~ *cutter* 电影剪辑员. ~ *play* 电影剧本. *have a* ~ *over the eyes* 看不清楚. — *vt., vi.* ①(在…上)蒙上薄膜; (使)生薄膜; (使)变朦胧. ②(把…)摄成影片; (使小说)电影化. ~**card** = fiche. ~**dom** 电影业,电影界 (= ~ land) ~**-fan** 电影迷. ~**goer** 看电影者,电影观众, ~**graph** 电影胶片,录音设备. ~**let** 短小的影片. ~ **maker** ①电影制作人,制片家,电影导演. ②(照片的)软片制作者. ~ **pack** 盒装胶卷. ~**set** ① *n.* 电影布景. ② *vt.* 【印】(照相版印刷术中)对(书稿等)作照相排版. ~ **star** 电影明星. ~**strip** 幻灯胶片; (教学用)电影胶片; 连续幻灯片. ~ **studio** 电影制片厂.

film·ic [ˈfilmik] *a.* 电影的, 有关电影的; 有关电影摄制术的.

film·ize [ˈfilmaiz] *vt.* 〔美〕把…改编成电影; 使电影化.

film·o·graph·y [filˈmɔgrəfi] *n.* ①(某一导演摄制或名

演员导演的)全部影片目录。②关于电影的著述。
fil·m·y [ˈfilmi] *a.* ***(film·i·er; -i·est)*** ①薄膜[细丝](状)的,薄膜[细丝]形成的。②蒙薄雾的,朦胧的。~ *ice* 薄冰。~ *clouds* 淡淡的云彩。**-i·ness** *n.*
fi·lo·po·di·um [ˌfiləˈpəudiəm, ˌfailə-] *n.* (*pl.* ***-di·a*** [-ə])【生】丝状假足。
fi·lose [ˈfailəus] *a.* 丝状的,线状的;有线状突出的。
fil·o·selle [ˌfiləˈsel] *n.* 〔F.〕绣花绒[丝]线。
fils [fiːs] *n.* 〔F.〕 儿子〔区别同名父子时附加于儿子名字以后的用语, = Jr.〕〔*cf.* père〕。***Dumas*** ~ 小仲马。
fil·ter [ˈfiltə] *n.* ①滤器,滤纸;过滤用料[砂、炭等]。②【无】滤波器;【物】滤光镜,滤色器。*acoustic* ~ 消声器。*bacterial* ~ 细菌滤器。*infrared* ~ 红外线滤光器。— *vt.* 过滤,用过滤法除去。— *vi.* ①过滤 *(through)*。②渗入,(消息)走漏 *(out; through; into)* 〔*cf.* infiltrate〕。③〔英〕(车辆在十字路口)开入另一车道。~ **bed** 滤垫,滤水池。~ **centre** 资料处理中心,情报整理处。~ **cigarette** 过滤嘴香烟。~ **paper** 滤纸(尤指定量滤纸)。~ **press**【化】压滤器,鱼油压榨机。~ **tip** ①香烟过滤嘴。②带过滤嘴的香烟。**~-tipped** *a.* 有过滤嘴的。
fil·ter·a·ble [ˈfiltərəbl] *a.* 可过滤的。~ **virus** 滤过性病毒。**-a·bil·i·ty** [ˌfiltərəˈbiliti] *n.*
filth [filθ] *n.* ①污物,污秽。②淫猥,猥亵语。③道德败坏。~ *disease* (由于不洁而引起的)肮脏病。
filth·y [ˈfilθi] *a.* ***(filth·i·er; -i·est)*** ①不洁的,污秽的。②丑恶的;猥亵的;道德败坏的。*a* ~ *lane* 肮脏的陋巷。***be*** ~ ***with dough*** 〔美俚〕有钱的。***be*** ~ ***with money*** 有钱的。~ **lucre** ①不义之财。②〔蔑〕臭钱。~ **pelf** 〔废〕= ~ lucre。**-i·ly** *ad.* **-i·ness** *n.*
fil·tra·ble [ˈfiltrəbl] *a.* = filterable. **-bil·i·ty** *n.*
fil·trate [ˈfiltreit] *vt., vi.* 过滤。— *n.* 滤液,滤过的水。
fil·tra·tion [filˈtreiʃən] *n.* 过滤;渗入。*automatic (centrifugal)* ~ 自动(离心)过滤。
fi·lum [ˈfailəm] *n.* (*pl.* ***-la*** [-lə])【解】丝状部分;丝。
fim·bri·ate [ˈfimbrieit] *a.* ①【生】有毛缘的。②用花带镶边的。— [ˈfimbrieit] *vt.* ①使有毛缘。②【纹】在…上镶以窄边。
Fin. = Finland; Finnish.
fin. = ①finance; financial. ②finish; finished. ③finis.
fin[1] [fin] *n.* ①鳍,鱼翅;鳍状物。②手,臂。③【海】潜水艇的)鳍板,水平舵;【火箭】舵;【空】稳定器,安定翼;【军】弹尾;【机】翅,尾翼,周缘翅片;散热片。④〔美口〕(人的)头。⑤汽车尾部的突起装饰物。⑥= flipper. *the anal [caudal, dorsal, pectoral, ventral]* ~ 臀[尾、脊、胸、腹]鳍。***~, fur and feather*** 鱼类,兽类与鸟类。*a cooling* ~ 冷却片。*damping* ~ 阻尼片。*rear* ~ 尾翼。*Shark's* ~ 鲨鱼翅。***Tip [give] us your*** ~.〔俚〕让我们握手。— *vt., vi.* ①把(鳍)切下。②(猛烈地)拍动(鳍)。③给…装上翅片[鳍板]。~ **keel** (游艇等的)鳍状龙骨。~ **ray** 鳍棘〔鱼鳍的软骨组织〕。
fin·a·ble [fainəbl] *a.* ①可罚款的,该罚款的。②可精制的,可提炼的。**-ness** *n.*
fi·na·gle [fiˈneigl] *vt.* 〔口〕用计取得[办妥];骗取,诈取,诱取。**-r** *n.*
fi·nal [ˈfainl] *a.* 最终的,最后的,终极的;结局的,结果的;决定性的。*the* ~ *ballot* 决选投票。*the* ~ *cause*【哲】终极原因;目的。*a* ~ *clause*【语法】目的从句。~ *game [contest]* 决赛。*a* ~ *issue* 最后结果。*the* ~ *round* 决赛。***in the*** ~ ***analysis*** 归根到底。— *n.* 结局,〔口〕(报纸的)末版;〔常 *pl.*〕〔美俚〕【体】决赛;最后[期终]考试。*the tennis* ~*s* 网球决赛。***prepare for the*** ~***s*** 准备参加期终考试。***run [play] in the*** ~***s*** 参加决赛。**F-Solution** 最后解决〔指纳粹对犹太人的大规模屠杀或任何一种种族灭绝运动〕。~ **thrill** 〔美俚〕死亡。
fi·na·le [fiˈnɑːli] *n.* ①结局,收尾。②【乐】终曲。③最后一幕;大团圆。
fi·nal·ist [ˈfainəlist] *n.*【体】决赛选手。
fi·nal·i·ty [faiˈnæliti] *n.* ①最后,定局,结尾。②最后的事物,最后的言行回答。③【哲】目的性;终极性。*an air of* ~ 最后的态度,摊牌的神气。*speak with* ~ 断言,咬定说。
fi·nal·ize [ˈfainəlaiz] *vt.* 使落实;使完成;把…最后定下来。**-zation** [ˌfainəlaiˈzeiʃən] *n.*
fi·nal·ly [ˈfainəli] *ad.* ①最后,最终。②决定性地;不可更改地。
fi·nance [faiˈnæns, fi-] *n.* ①财政,金融,财政学。②〔*pl.*〕岁入,财源,资金。*public* ~ 国家财政。*the Minister of F-* 财政部部长。*the Ministry of F-* 财政部。~ *bill* 财政法案。~ *company* 信贷公司。— *vt.* ①为…供给资金,给…通融资金。②赊货给…。~ *an enterprise* 供给企业资金。— *vi.* 掌握财政,处理财务。**fi·nancing** *n.* 资金的筹措,理财。
fi·nan·cial [faiˈnænʃəl, fi-] *a.* ①财政(上)的,财务(上)的,金融(上)的。②(会员)缴费的〔*cf.* honorary〕。~ *ability* 财力。~ *adjustment* 财政整理。~ *affairs* 财务。~ *capital* 金融资本。~ *circles* = *the* ~ *world* 金融界。*the* ~ *condition [situation]* 财政状况。~ *crisis* 财政危机,金融恐慌。*a* ~ *magnate* 金融巨头。*a* ~ *man* 财政家。*a* ~ *member* 普通会员。~ *reports* 会计报告。~ **statement** 资产负债表;借贷对照表;财政报告。~ **year** 〔英〕会计年度(=〔美〕fiscal year). **-ly** *ad.*
fin·an·cier [faiˈnænsiə, fi-] *n.* 财务官,财政家;金融家,资本家。— [ˌfainənˈsiə] *vt.* 对…提供资金,通融资金给;〔美〕骗取。— *vi.* 〔罕〕筹划财政,管理财务;从事(不正当的)金融活动。
fin·back [ˈfinˌbæk] *n.*【动】鳁鲸属动物〔尤指长须鲸〕。
fin·ca [ˈfiːŋkɑː] *n.* 〔Sp.〕(西班牙或拉美的)种植园,庄园;地产。
finch [fintʃ] *n.*【动】雀科鸣禽(如燕雀、金翅雀等)。
find [faind] *vt.* ***(found*** [faund]; ***found)*** ①找到;获得;发现;(偶然)看见;拾得,遇见。②想出,(炮弹等)打中;(锚)到达(海底)。③觉得,发觉;找出,查明。④供给;供应;筹措(资金等)。⑤【法】断定,裁决;宣判。⑥(江、河等)自然地形成,流向。⑦学会使用;恢复使用。~ *sb. dead* 发现某人死了。~ *sb. dying* 发现某人奄奄一息。~ *a good friend in sb.* 发现某人是个好朋友。*Water* ~*s its own level.* 水往低处流。*A bomb found him.* 炸弹打中了他。~ *time to do sth.* 有时间做某事。~ *food for friend* 供给朋友食物。~ *money for a plan* 为一项计划筹措经费。*Experience helped the young birds to* ~ *its wings.* 经验使小鸟学会用翅膀飞起。*The judge found the thief guilty.* 法官判决小偷有罪。~ *expression in* 在…表现出来。~ *it difficult to explain* 觉得难以说明。~ *tea for workmen* 给工人弄茶喝。*It will be found that* …下面将指出…。~ *sb. guilty* 断定某人有罪。~ *the cubic root of* 求…的立方根。— *vi.* ①作出判断。②找到猎物。***all [everything] found*** (工资以外)供给全部膳宿 (*wages $ 20 a month and all* ~ 工资每月二十元,另供膳宿)。***be found in [at]*** 在某地,到某地。***be well found in*** 在…方面设备齐全[修养很高]。***cannot*** ~ ***it in one's heart to …*** 不忍心…。~ ***fault with*** 吹毛求疵。~ ***favour in the eyes of*** 得到(某人的)看重。~ ***favour with*** 得宠。~ ***for [against] the defendant*** 下有利[不利]于被告的判决。~ ***it in one's hearts to …*** 有意,想。~ ***it (to) pay*** = ~ ***(that) it pays*** 看来合算(有利)。~ ***one's account in*** 认为…有利,由…得利。~ ***one's place in a book*** 在书中找到要找的一处。~ ***one's tongue [voice]*** 讲得出话,恢复说话能力。~ ***one's way*** 到达 (*How did it* ~ *its way into print?* 怎么会付印的?)。~ ***one's way out of*** 由…(脱离)出来。~ ***oneself*** ①发觉自己的处境。②(对于健康等的)自我感觉。③发现自己的特长并加以发挥。④自备衣食 (*three shillings a day and* ~ *yourself* 一天的报酬三先令,衣食自理)。~ ***one's feet [legs]*** 在

社会上站稳；对自己的能力有把握．～ ***out*** 发现，找出；猜着；想出；揭发(坏人等)．～ ***sb. in*** 供给某人(衣、食、费用等)．～ ***up*** 〔英方〕找出．～ ***what o'clock it is*** 查明事实真相．— *n.* 发现，发现物，拾得物，掘获物，被发觉的人材．*have [make] a great* ～ 有大发现，找出贵重宝物．***a sure*** ～ 一定能发现狐狸等的地方；〔俚〕必能找到的人〔物〕．

find·er [ˈfaində] *n.* ①发现者．②探测器；瞄准装置；寻象器；选择器，寻线机，测距器．*a fault* ～ 障碍寻找器，障碍位置测定仪．*a height* ～ 测高仪．*a range* ～ 测距仪，测远仪．*a view* ～ 寻象器，取景器．

fin de siè·cle [F. fɛ̃ də sjɛkl] *n.* 〔F.〕世纪末〔特指风气颓废的19世纪末〕．— *a.* 世纪末的，颓废的．

find·ing [ˈfaindiŋ] *n.* ①发现；发现的东西．②〔*pl.*〕结论；研究结果；【法】判决，(陪审员的)评定；(委员会等的)审查结果．③〔*pl.*〕〔美〕(服装，鞋，首饰制造用的)零件材料及工具．*a* ～ *store* 零件材料商店．

fine^1 [fain] *a.* ***(fin·er; -est)*** ①美好的，美丽的，优良的．②(天气)晴朗的，令人愉快的．③精制的；华美的；纯洁的；优雅的．④稀薄的，细致的，细微的，纤细的．⑤(刀)锐利的；(感觉)敏锐的，(区别)微妙的．⑥纯粹的；成色好的．*a* ～ *character* 品格高尚的人．～ *chemicals* 精制化学药品．*a* ～ *day* 晴天．*a* ～ *distinction* 细微的差别．～ *dust [powder]* 细粉．*a* ～*ear* 听觉灵敏．*a* ～ *edge* 利刃．～ *fibrous cotton* 细绒棉．*A* ～ *friend you have been.*〔谑〕你真够朋友．～ *gold 18 carats* ～ 十八开金．～ *grain* 细密的纹理．～ *linen [thread, china]*细麻布〔纱线，瓷器〕．～ *measuring instrument* 精密量具．*a* ～ *mind* 聪明的头脑．～ *ore*【矿】细矿粉．*a* ～ *pen* 笔头细的钢笔．*a* ～ *pencil* 画细线用的铅笔．～ *rain* 细雨．*a* ～ *sense of humour* 能体会幽默的微妙感．～ *skin* 细嫩的皮肤．～ *sugar [salt]* 精制糖〔盐〕．～ *tea* 高级茶叶．*have a* ～ *time* 〔俚〕过得高兴．*a* ～ *view* 壮观，壮丽的景色．～ *weather* 好天气．～ *words* 漂亮话．～ *workmanship* 精巧的制作．*as* ～ *[fit] as a fiddle* 很健康，精神好．*as* ～ *as silk* 柔软如丝；身体好．*F- feathers make* ～ *birds.* 〔谚〕人要衣装，佛要金装．*F- words dress ill deeds.* 〔谚〕口里仁义道德，心中男盗女娼．***F- excuse!*** 〔反〕好个辩护！～ ***feathered friend*** 〔美俚〕好朋友〔略带讽刺意味〕．～ ***paper [bill]*** 有信用的支票．～ ***thing*** 〔美俚〕好个东西〔表示厌恶的反语〕．***the New York finest*** 〔美俚〕纽约的警察．***not to put too*** ～ ***a point upon it*** 直截了当地说．***one*** ～ ***day [morning]*** 有一天，有一次〔讲故事时常用的开场白，有时也说明将来要发生不吉利的事〕．***one of these*** ～ ***days*** 改天，总有一天．***say*** ～ ***things about*** 恭维．— *n.* 晴天，好天气．***get home in the*** ～ 天晴时到家，顺利．***(in) rain or*** ～ 不拘晴雨〔*cf.* rain or shine〕．— *ad.* 〔口〕巧妙，很好；精巧地，细微地．*talk* ～ 说得好．***cut [run] it [things] (right)*** ～ 精打细算，(时间等)扣得紧，几乎不留余地．— *vt.* ①把…提纯，澄清；精制；使精细．②使稀薄，使细小．— *vi.* ①变好，变纯；变精致．②变稀薄．③(天气)转晴．～ ***away [down, off]*** 渐好；渐纯；缩小；渐渐消失．～ **arts** 美术(指绘画、雕刻、建筑、诗歌、音乐等)．～**-comb** *vt.* 仔细搜查．～**-cut** ① *a.* (烟草)细切的．② *n.* 烟丝．～**-draw** (-drew, -drawn) *vt.* ①细缝，密缝．②拉细(铁丝等)．③仔细讨论．～**-drawn** *a.* ①细(密)缝的，拉细了的；过于精致的．②(推理等)微妙的；(运动员)体重减轻了的．～**-grained** *a.* (木材、皮革等)纹理细密的．～ **print** (契约等)有限制性质的附属细则〔因其印刷字体较正文为小，故名〕．～**spun** *a.* 细纺的，拉细的，脆弱的；过分琐细的 (*a* ～*spun theory* 空洞的理论)．～ **structure** 微观〔显微〕结构．～**-tooth comb** = ～**-toothed comb** 细齿梳子 (*go over with a* ～*-tooth comb* 仔细检查；搜查)．～**-tune** *vt.* 精密〔仔细〕调校；仔细〔妥贴〕安排．～**-tooth-comb** *vt.* =仔细搜查 (=～-comb)．

fine^2 [fain] *n.* ①罚款．②【法】(获得或更新租契时交纳的)地租．③终结〔现限用于 in ～ 这一习语中〕．***in*** ～ 最后；总而言之．— *vt., vi.* (对…)处以罚款．

fi·ne^3 [ˈfiːne] *n.* 〔It.〕【乐】终止，完．*Al F-* 到末尾．

fine·a·ble [ˈfainəbl] *a.* = finable.

fine·ly [ˈfainli] *ad.* 精细地，美好地．

fine·ness [ˈfainnis] *n.* ①优良，精致．②细微，细度．③敏锐．④纯度；成色．⑤光洁度．～ **ratio**【航】细度比，径长比〔指流线型飞机机身长度同宽度的比例〕．

fin·er·y^1 [ˈfainəri] *n.* ①漂亮服装；美观的装饰品．②〔罕〕华丽，时髦．

fin·er·y^2 [ˈfainəri] *n.*【冶】精炼炉．

fines [ˈfainz] *n.* 〔*pl.*〕【矿】细粒〔尤指经过筛选的碎石〕．

fi·nesse [fiˈnes] *n.* ①手腕，手段，技巧；策略．②在桥牌中先出小牌，保留好牌以赢牌的手法，偷牌．*the* ～ *of love* 恋爱手腕．— *vt.* ①用手段实现，用巧计战胜．②保留大牌而先出(小牌)．～ *sb.'s rights away* 骗取他人权利．— *vi.* ①施巧计．②【牌】偷牌．～ *for the Jack* 把J牌偷打出去，偷跑J牌．

fin·ger [ˈfiŋgə] *n.* ①指头，手指〔一般指拇指以外的手指〕．②指状物；(手套的)指部；(钟表的)指针．③一指之阔〔约 $\frac{3}{4}$ 英寸〕；一中指之长〔约 $4\frac{1}{2}$ 英寸〕．④【乐】运指法．⑤〔美俚〕警察，告密的人．⑥〔美俚〕伸出中指表示侮辱的手势．*(a)* ～ *on the wall* 灾难的预兆．*Better a* ～ *off than aye wagging.*〔谚〕长痛不如短痛．*the first [index]* ～ 食指．*the little [small]* ～ 小指．*the middle [long]* ～ 中指．*the ring* ～ 无名指．*spring* ～ 弹簧夹．*His* ～*s are all thumbs.* 他笨手笨脚．***(a)*** ～ ***on the wall*** 灾难的预兆．***burn one's*** ～***s*** (管闲事)吃亏．***by a*** ～***'s breadth*** 差一点，险些．***by the*** ～ ***of God*** 靠神力．***count on the*** ～ 屈指计算．***crook one's little*** ～ 〔俚〕喝酒．***cross one's*** ～***s*** 把一个手指交叉放在同一只手的另一手指上〔迷信者认为这样可以逢凶化吉〕．***dig one's*** ～ ***in*** 染指．***give sb. the*** ～〔美俚〕使某人失败；让某人倒霉；亏待某人；侮辱某人．***have a*** ～ ***in the pie*** 参与，染指．***have at one's*** ～***s' ends [***～ ***ends,*** ～ ***tips]*** 熟识，精通．***in sb.'s*** ～ 在某人掌握中，听某人支配．***lay [put] a [one's]*** ～ ***on sb.*** 触犯，干涉．***lay [put] a [one's]*** ～ ***on sth.*** ①明白指出，记得．②发现，找到．***let sth. slip through one's*** ～***s*** 放走，放过，漏掉．***look through one's*** ～***s at*** 假装没有看见．***My little*** ～ ***told me*** 我当然知道．***not lift [stir] a*** ～ ***to help*** 一点不肯帮忙．*one's* ～*s itch to do sth.* 手痒，急于想干某事．***put one's*** ～ ***in*** 染指．***put one's*** ～ ***in one's eyes*** 哭泣．***put one's*** ～ ***[***～***s] in the fire*** 自讨苦吃．***put the*** ～ ***on*** 〔美俚〕向当局指明犯罪罪犯〔场所〕；指名告发．***rap sb.'s*** ～***s*** 处分某人，申斥某人．***slip between [through] sb.'s*** ～ 从某人的指缝中溜掉；(机会)被某人错过．***snap one's*** ～ ***at*** 打榧子〔向人捻拇指作响，表示轻蔑，不在乎等〕．***stick in [to] sb.'s*** ～ 被人中饱〔侵吞〕．***to the*** ～ ***nail*** 完全．***turn [twist, wind, wrap] sb. round [around] one's (little)*** ～ 把某人玩弄于股掌之上，任意摆布〔支配〕某人．***with a wet*** ～ 不费力地．***with one's*** ～ ***in one's mouth*** ①一事无成．②傻里傻气．***work one's*** ～ ***to the bone*** 不住手地工作．— *vt.* ①用指头摸弄〔触碰，捻摸〕．②接受(贿赂等)；偷．③用指头做；【乐】用手指弹〔奏〕；在乐谱上标明(指法符号)．④〔美俚〕尾随，监视；指责，告发．⑤指出，指认．⑥象手指般伸进．— *vi.* ①用手指触碰．②用手指弹奏．③象手指般伸出．～ **alphabet [language]** 手势语〔*cf.* dactylology〕．～ **board** ①(提琴等的)指板；(钢琴等的)键盘．②= ～ post．～ **bowl [glass]** (饭后用)洗指钵．～**-breadth** 指宽，指幅〔约为 $\frac{3}{4}$ 英寸到 1 英寸宽〕．～**fish**【动】海盘车．～ **food** (在正式宴会上可用手指拿取送入口中的)手拿食物．～**hold** *n.* ①以指支持．②微弱的支持．～ **hole** (管乐器、电话机等上的)指孔．～**man** 〔美俚〕(盗贼等的)眼线．～ **mark** 指迹．～**nail**

指甲. ~ **paint** 作手指画用的颜料. ~**-paint** *vi., vt.* 用手指画(画). ~ **painting** ①指画法〔用手指、手、胳臂代替笔刷来涂抹颜料〕. ②指画. ~**-parted** *a.* 如手指状辐射的. ~ **plate** (门等表面上)防止被手指染污的防护板〔层〕. ~ **post** ①指路牌,指向柱. ②指南. ~**print** ①*n.* 指纹,手印;〔喻〕特征. ② *vt.* 打下〔取下〕…的指纹印;(依据独特的标记)辨识出. ~ **reading** 盲人摸读法〔*cf.* braille〕. ~**stall** *n.* 护指套. ~ **wave** 手指卷发(指仅用手指、梳子等使头发呈波浪形,与电烫相区别). **-less** *a.*

fin·gered [ˈfiŋgəd] *a.* ①有指的;【植】指状的;掌状的. ②用手指弹奏的;被手指污染的. ③〔用以构成复合词〕表示"有…指的","手指…的. *a* ~ *citron* 佛手柑. *five-*~ 有五指的. *He was light-*~. 他手指纤巧;他手脚不干净(好偷东西). ~ *roots* 指状根.

fin·ger·ing[1] [ˈfiŋgəriŋ] *n.* ①用手指抚摸;用手指弹奏. ②【乐】指法;指法符号.

fin·ger·ing[2] [ˈfiŋgəriŋ] *n.* (织袜用)细绒线.

fin·ger·ling [ˈfiŋgəliŋ] *n.* ①小东西, 微不足道的东西,小事. ②长不及一指的小鱼;仔鱼.

fin·ger·tip [ˈfiŋgətip] *n.* ①指尖. ②(射箭等用的) 指尖套. ***have sth. at one's*** ~***s*** ①手头掌握了某物. ②精通某事. ***to one's [the]*** ~***s*** 完全地,彻底地 (*He was a gentleman to his* ~*s.* 他是十足的绅士).

fin·i·al [ˈfainiəl] *n.* ①【建】叶尖饰, 尖顶饰. ②物件顶端的装饰品.

fin·i·cal [ˈfinikəl] *a.* = finicky. **-ly** *ad.* **-ity -ness** *n.*

fin·ick·ing [ˈfinikiŋ] *a.* = finicky.

fin·ick·y [ˈfiniki] *a.* 苛求的,过于挑剔的;过于讲究的. **fin·ick·i·ness** *n.*

fin·i·kin [ˈfinikin] *a.* = finicky.

fin·ing [ˈfainiŋ] *n.* ①(酒等的)澄清;(金属的)精制. ②〔*pl.*〕(酒等的)澄清剂.

fi·nis [ˈfainis, ˈfiːnis] *n.*〔L.〕(书、电影等的)终止,终结;(生命的)结束〔时常印在书的结尾,表示"本书完"〕.

fin·ish [finiʃ] *vt.* ①完毕,完成,结束;使…毕业,使…卒业. ②磨光,【机】给…抛光;给…最后加工;润饰,修整,整理. ③用完,吃光. ④〔口〕杀掉,结果掉;累死;彻底征服,压服. ~ *doing sth.* 做完某事. *Where were you* ~*ed?* 你是哪里毕业的? ~ *sb. with a single blow* 一拳打死某人. *I am* ~*ed.* 我准备完毕了; 我累坏了. *The house will soon be* ~*ed.* 房子快要完工了. *be* ~*ed to gavge* 按尺寸精确加工. *surface* ~ 表面光洁度;表面抛光. *My arguments* ~*ed him.* 我的一番道理说得他哑口无言. — *vi.* 终了,完结;死;【体】到终点 *(up).* ~ ***off*** ①完成,结束;用完;吃完. ②〔口〕致…于死地,杀死. ~ ***up*** ①完成. ②吃光; 用尽. ~ ***up with*** 以…结束. ~ ***with*** ①完成,结束.②和…断绝关系.— *n.* ①结束,最后阶段;终点;完蛋的原因;〔美俚〕死,毁灭. ②完结,完成;完美;最后一道工序;抛光;【建】终饰;(态度等的)文雅. ***be in at the*** ~ 猎获猎物时亲自在场;〔喻〕目睹(比赛,战斗等的)最后情形. ***fight to a [the]*** ~ 打到底. ~ **allowance**【机】加工余量. ~ **line**〔美〕决胜线,(赛跑或赛马等的)终点线.

fin·ished [ˈfiniʃt] *a.* ①完成了的,完结了的. ②精巧的,制作完美的. ③〔美俚〕死了的;完蛋了的. ~ *goods* 完美的成品,精制品. ~ *products* 成品. *a* ~ *gentleman* 标准绅士. ~ *manners* 彬彬有礼.

fin·ish·er [ˈfiniʃə] *n.* ①修整工, 完工者;精加工工具. ②精作机,精轧机,末道清棉机. ③决定性的打击,决定性的事件. *the* ~ *of the law* 〔谑〕死刑执行人,刽子手.

fin·ish·ing [ˈfiniʃiŋ] *a.* 最后的. — *n.* 完成修整,精加工;结尾,结束. ~ **block** 拉细丝机. ~ **coat** (墙壁)最后一道涂工. ~ **material**【建】装饰材料. ~ **metal** 精炼金属. ~ **school** (青年妇女的) 进修学校,家事学校. ~ **touch [stroke]** (绘画等)最后修饰的笔触.

fi·nite [ˈfainait] *a.* 有限的;【语法】限定的;【数】 有穷的,有尽的. — *n.*〔the ~〕有限(性);〔集合词〕有限物. ~ **decimal** 有尽小数. ~ **induction** 数学归纳法. ~ **progression [series]** 有限极数. ~ **verb** 限定动词. **-ly** *ad.* **-ness** *n.*

fin·i·tude [ˈfainitjuːd] *n.* 有限,限定.

fink [fiŋk] *n.* 〔美俚〕①工贼. ②告密者. ③可鄙的家伙,讨厌的家伙,乞丐. —*vi.* ①告发同党. ②破坏罢工. — *vi.* 〔美俚〕退缩,撤退; 惨败. ~**-out** *n.* 〔美俚〕①大失败,大出丑. ②退出(不干);退缩.

Fin·land [ˈfinlənd] *n.* 芬兰〔欧洲〕. **Fin·land·i·za·tion** 芬兰化.

Fin(n) [fin] *n.* 芬兰人.

Finn [fin] *n.* 芬兰人.

fin·nan had·die [ˌfinən ˈhædi], **fin·nan·had·dock** [-ˈhædək] *n.*【动】熏鳕鱼.

finned [find] *a.* ①有鳍的; 有鳍状物的. ②〔用以构成复合词〕(有)…鳍的. *long-*~, *short-*~.

fin·ner [ˈfinə] *n.* = finback.

Finn·ic [ˈfinik] *a.* ①芬兰人的. ②芬兰语(族)的.

fin·nick·y [ˈfiniki] *a.* = finicky.

Finn·ish [ˈfiniʃ] *a.* ①芬兰的, 芬兰人的. ②芬兰语的. — *n.* 芬兰语.

Fin·no-U·gric [ˈfinəuˈjuːgrik, -ˈuː-] *a.* 芬兰-乌戈尔语系的. — *n.* 芬兰-乌戈尔语系 (=Finno-Ugrian).

fin·ny [ˈfini] *a.* ***(-ni·er; -ni·est)*** ①有鳍的; 鳍状的. ②〔诗、谑〕鱼类的; 多鱼的. *the* ~ *deep* 多鱼的深海. *the* ~ *tribe* 鱼族〔类〕.

fi·noc·chi·o [fiˈnəukiːəu] *n.*【植】茴香.

Fin·sen [ˈfinsən] *n.* **F- light [lamp]** 水银弧光灯.

fiord [fjɔːd] *n.* (尤指挪威海岸的断岩峭壁间的) 峡湾; 峡江 (= fjord).

fi·o·rin [ˈfaiərin] *n.*【植】小糠草.

fio·ri·tu·ra [ˌfjɔriːˈtuːrɑː] *n.* (*pl.* ***-tu·re*** [-re]) 【乐】装饰音.

fip·pence [ˈfipəns] *n.*〔英口〕= fivepence.

fip·pen·ny [ˈfipini, ˈfipni] **bit** *n.* 五便士币〔1857 年前在美国流通的西班牙银币,约合六美分〕.

fip·ple [ˈfipl] **flute**【乐】直笛.

fir [fəː] *n.* ①【植】冷杉属 (Abies); 枞; 松科常绿树(如黄杉等). ②冷杉木,枞木. ~**-apple,** ~**-ball,** ~**-cone** *n.* 冷杉球果. ~ **needle** 冷杉针叶, 枞叶. ~ **tree** 冷杉, 枞树.

FIR=food-irradiation reactor 食物辐射(杀菌)用反应堆.

fire [ˈfaiə] *n.* ①火,火焰;火灾;燃烧;炉火,烽火. ②射击;火力. ③火花;闪光;光辉. ④热情,热烈,热心;生气;(诗等的)灵感. ⑤发烧,发热,炎症. ⑥火刑;磨难,迫害. ⑦〔诗〕星. *A burnt child dreads the* ~.〔谚〕儿童被火烧,见火就逃跑;惊弓之鸟〔吃过亏的人〕格外胆小. *He who plays with* ~ *gets burned.* 玩火者必自焚. *It is too warm for* ~. 天气暖和不必生火. *F-!* 起火了! *council* ~ 印地安人在会议时点的篝火. *F- and water are good servants, but bad masters.*〔谚〕水火是忠仆,也能成灾主. *F- that's closest kept burns most of all.*〔谚〕火闷得越紧,烧起来越凶. *The* ~ *which lights [warms] us at a distance will burn us when near.*〔谚〕火在远处是明灯,到了近处烧死人. *ground* ~ 地面火力. *heavenly* ~*s,* ~*s of heaven*〔诗〕星星. *liquid* ~〔口〕烈性酒. *open [cease]* ~ 开〔停〕火. *rapid* ~ (轻武器或自动武器的)速射. *the* ~ *of a diamond* 钻石的光辉. *the* ~ *of lightning* 闪电光. *the* ~ *of love* 爱火,热烈的爱. *a speech lacking* ~ 缺乏热情的演说. *full of* ~ 充满热情〔愤恨〕. *Keep away from* ~*!* 切勿近火. *the* ~*s of persecution* 残酷的迫害. *Soft* ~ *makes sweet malt.*〔谚〕慢工出细活. ***amid*** ~ ***and thunder*** 轰轰烈烈. ***a running*** ~ ①连发,连射. ②一连串的批评指责. ***between two*** ~***s*** 腹背受敌,在两面夹攻中. ***blow the*** ~ 挑唆,煽动. ***build a*** ~ ***under oneself*** 作法自毙. ***by*** ~ ***and sword*** 杀人放火,

使用残暴方法. ***carry ~ in one hand and water in the other*** 两面三刀. ***catch ~*** 着火. ***~ and fag(g)ot*** 火刑. ***fight ~ with*** 以火攻火,以毒攻毒. ***~ and brimstone*** ①地狱里的磨难. ②见鬼! ***~ and fury*** 炽烈奔放的感情. ***flash [shoot] ~*** 眼中冒火, 怒目相对. ***go through ~ and water*** 赴汤蹈火. ***hang ~*** (火器) 发射不出, 迟缓发射; (作事)犹豫不决; 延迟. ***Hermes's ~*** = St. Elmo's ~. ***hold ~*** 忍着不表态. ***Kentish ~*** ①长时间的鼓掌. ②一片反对声. ***lay a ~*** 预备生火. ***lift ~***【军】①延伸射击. ②中止射击. ***make a ~*** 生火. ***miss ~*** (枪炮)打不响; 失败. ***nurse a ~*** ①看管火. ②烤火. ***on ~*** 燃烧着; 兴奋着, 热中. ***on the ~*** 〔美俚〕在考虑[审议]中. ***open ~*** ①开火. ②开始. ***play with ~*** 玩火, 轻举妄动. ***pour oil on ~*** 火上加油. ***pull (a game etc.) out of the ~*** 转败为胜. ***pull [snatch] sb. out of the ~*** 把某人救出火坑. ***put to ~ and sword*** 又烧又杀. ***save sth. out of the ~*** 把东西(从火中)抢救出来. ***set ~ to*** = ***set on ~*** 放火烧, 使燃烧; 使兴奋, 使激动. ***set the Thames [river] on ~*** 作惊人之举. ***show sth. the ~*** 把某物稍稍热一下. ***St. Anthony's ~***【医】丹毒. ***St. Elmo's ~*** 桅顶(飞机翼尖、塔尖等的)电辉火. ***stand ~*** 冒着炮火; 忍受批评. ***stir the ~*** 拨火. ***strike ~*** (用火石)打火, (用火柴) 擦火. ***take ~*** 着火燃烧; 激动起来. ***the sacred ~*** ①真挚的爱, 神圣的爱. ②天才. ***under ~*** 在炮火下; 受到攻击. — *vt.* ①烧, 点(火), 生(炉子). ②烧(瓦等); 烤(茶等). ③〔口〕扔, 投(石头等). ④射击, 打(枪), 开(炮); 炸破; 使爆发. ⑤激发(感情等). ⑥使发光辉. ⑦【兽医】(用烙铁) 烧灼. ⑧〔美俚〕解雇, 撵走 *(out)*. ~ *a house* 烧房子. ~ *a salute* 放礼炮. ~ *questions at sb.* 向某人提出(许多)质问. ~ *sb. with anger* 激怒某人. ~ *the blood of* 使热血沸腾. ~ *the imagination* 激发想象力. — *vi.* ①着火, 燃烧. ②激动. ③〔口〕扔石头(等). ④发射, 开火, 开炮 *(at; into; on; upon)*. *F-!* 开火! ~ *back in self-defence* 自卫还击. ***be ~d (out)*** 〔俚〕被解雇. ~ ***at*** 对…开枪, 向…射击. ~ ***away*** ①继续射击. ②〔口〕开始象连珠炮似地谈话或提问. ~ ***off*** ①发炮, 开炮. ②使爆炸, 炸掉. ③熄灭(火). ④开口. ⑤发射(火箭等). (~ *off questions* 提问题). ~ ***on*** = ~ at. ~ ***out*** 〔美〕撵走, 解雇. ~ ***up*** ①发动(机器); 生火. ②突然发怒. ~ **action**【军】火力交锋, 火战. ~ **alarm** 火警警钟, 火警; 报火机. ~ **ant**【动】火蚁, 火伤蚁〔美国南部的一种有害昆虫; 人被咬后, 有火辣的感觉〕. ~**-arm** 〔常 *pl.*〕 火器, 手枪, 步枪, 轻武器. ~ **apparatus** 消防设备. ~**back** ①(反射炉火的) 背壁. ②【动】(背部火红的) 南豆雉. ~**ball** ①火球; 流星; 〔诗〕太阳; 【军】(从前的) 燃烧弹. ②〔美口〕干劲十足的人. ~ **balloon** (下部置火使球内空气因热而上升的) 火气球; (升至高空后才爆炸燃烧的) 流星火花. ~ **bar** 炉条. ~**base**【军】火力基地, 重火力点. ~**bird**【动】①火红鸟. ②无线电信管. ~ **blast [blight]**【植病】火疫. ~**boat** 消防艇, 救火船. ~ **bomb**【军】燃烧弹. ~**bomb** *vt.* 用燃烧弹轰击. ~**box** ①【机】机车锅炉炉膛, 燃烧室. ②盛放火警报警器的箱子. ~**brand** ①火把. ②放火者; 煽动叛乱者, 挑动争执者. ~**break** 森林的防火线〔森林或草原上清除掉树木或草皮, 以防野火蔓延的空旷地带〕. ~**brick** (耐)火砖. ~ **brigade** 〔英〕 消防队; 〔美军俚〕特速紧急分遣队. ~**bug** 〔美〕萤火虫; 〔美口〕放火者, 纵火狂. ~ **call** = ~ alarm. ~ **chief** 消防署署长. ~ **clay** (耐)火泥, 耐火(黏)土. ~ **coat** 氧化膜. ~ **company** ①消防队. ②〔英〕火险公司. ~ **control** ①【军】实施射击, 射击指挥, 火力控制, 射击控制. ②消防. ~ **control system** 射击指挥系统, 射击指挥仪. ~**cracker** 爆竹, 鞭炮. ~**-cure** *vt.* 用烟熏(烟草等). ~**damp**【化】(煤矿内的)碳化氢, 沼气. ~ **department** 消防署. ~**dog** (炉中的)柴架, 炭架. ~ **door** 防火门, 炉门. ~**drake**, ~**dragon** (北欧神话中的) 喷火龙. ~ **drill** 消防演习; (工厂、学校等的) 防火训练. ~**-eater** ①吞火魔术师. ②爱打架的人, 暴性子. ~**-eating** *a.* 强暴的, 咄咄逼人的, 好战的. ~ **engine** ①救火车. ②〔泛指〕消防车〔运送消防队员和消防设备到火警现场的卡车等〕. ~ **escape** (防火) 太平门[梯], 安全出口. ~ **extinguisher** 灭火器. ~ **fight** 交火. ~ **fighter** 〔美〕消防人员; 〔英〕(空袭时的)临时消防员. ~ **fighting** 消防活动. ~**flood** 注火法〔一种石油开采程序〕. ~**fly** 萤火虫. ~ **grate** 炉篦, 炉条, 火床. ~**guard** ①火炉栏. ②= ~ break. ~ **hose** 救火蛇管, 水龙带. ~**house** = ~ station. ~ **hydrant** 消防栓, 消防龙头, 灭火龙头. ~ **insurance** 火(灾保)险. ~ **irons** 火炉用具(如火钳、通条、火铲等). ~ **ladder** 太平梯, 消防梯. ~ **lane** = ~ break. ~**light** (炉) 火光. ~**-lighter** 引火物. ~ **line** ①= ~ break. ②〔常 *pl.*〕(火灾现场的)消防警戒线, 交通封锁线. ③(草原、森林等的)火灾最前线. ~**lock** 火炮. ~**man** *(pl. men)* ①司炉工, 烧火工人. ②消防队员. ③【矿】救火员, 爆破工, 煤矿煤气检查员, 通风员. ~ **marshal** 〔美〕消防队长. ~**-new** *a.* 崭新的 (= brand-new). ~ **office** 〔英〕火灾保险公司. ~ **pan** 〔英〕火铲, 火斗, 火盆. ~**place** 壁炉; 炉床. ~**plug** 灭火塞, 消火栓. ~ **policy** 火(灾保)险单. ~ **position** 发射阵地; 战斗姿态. ~ **power**【军】①火力. ②火量〔单位时间发射炮弹数与重量〕. ~**proof** ①*a.* 耐火的, 防火的. ②*vt.* 使耐火, 使防火. ~**proofing** 使防火, 耐火, 耐火装置[材料]. ~**raising** 〔英〕放火. ~ **resistance** 耐火度. ~ **room** 锅炉间, 火室. ~ **sale** 火灾中受损物品的减价销售. ~ **screen** 火障, 炉围. ~ **ship** (火攻敌舰用的) 火攻船. ~**side** ①*n.* 炉边; 家; 家庭; 〔古〕家属. ② *a.* 炉边的, 亲切的, 毫无拘束的 (*the president's ~side chat* (美国) 总统的炉边谈话). ~ **station** 消防站. ~ **step** (战壕里射击时用的) 踏垛. ~**stone** 燧石, 耐火岩石, 耐火黏土, 黄铁矿. ~**storm** (原子弹爆炸等引起的) 风暴性大火. ~**teazer** 〔英俚〕烧炉员. ~ **thorn** 火棘属植物. ~ **tower** 森林火警了望塔. ~**trap** 无太平门的建筑物, 易遭火灾的建筑物. ~ **trench**【军】散兵壕. ~ **truck**【美】救火车. ~ **wall** 防火墙, 隔火墙. ~ **warden** 〔美〕防火监查员; 【林】防火了望员. ~**-watcher** 火灾警戒员. ~ **water** 〔口〕烈酒. ~**weed** (火烧过后长出的杂草) 火草. ~**wood** 木柴; 〔英〕柴火. ~**work** ①〔*pl.*〕焰火, 花火; 烽火. ②【军】烟火信号弹. ③〔常 *pl.*〕激情的表现. ④才气的焕发. ~ **worship** 拜火, 拜火教. **-less** *a.*

Fi·ren·ze [It. fi'rendze] *n.* 〔It.〕 = Florence.

fir·er ['faiərə] *n.* ①点火者, 放火者, 烧火工人. ②开炮者, 点火物. ③火器, 枪炮. *a quick ~* 速射炮. *a single ~* 单发枪.

fir·ing ['faiəriŋ] *n.* ①点火; (茶的)烘烤; (陶器等的)烧成. ②射击. ③燃料. ④添煤, 司炉. ⑤〔口〕解雇. ⑥【无】触发. ~ *practice* 开炮演习. ~ **iron** (兽医用的) 烙针. ~ **line** 第一线; 【军】火线; 前线部队. ~ **order** (发动机的) 发火次序. ~ **party** ①葬礼时的鸣枪队. ②行刑队. ~ **pin** (枪炮的) 撞针. ~ **point** 油的发火点; (打靶时的) 发射位置. ~ **range** ①靶场, 火箭试射场. ②射程. ~ **squad** = ~ party. ~ **step** = (战壕内射击时登上的) 踏垛 (= fire step).

fir·kin ['fəːkin] *n.* ①费尔金〔英国容量单位 合九加仑〕. ②(装油脂用, 容量为 8—9 磅的) 小木桶.

firm[1] [fəːm] *a.* ①坚固的, 坚牢的; 稳固的. ②坚定的, 坚决的. ③【商】固定的 (*opp.* optional); (货币) 坚挺的 (*opp.* easy, weak 疲软), 稳定的; (金融等) 紧缩的. ~ *belief* 确信. ~ *friendship* 牢不可破的友谊. ~ *ground* 陆地. ~ *step* 坚定的步伐. ***as ~ as a rock*** 安如磐石. ***be ~ on one's legs*** 站稳. ***be on ~ ground*** 脚踏实地; 在稳固的基础上. — *ad.* 稳固地, 坚定地. *hold ~* 固守. *stand ~* 站稳. — *vt., vi.* 使(变)坚固, 使(变)坚实, 使(变)稳定. ~**ware**【计】固件; 稳固设备(的微程

序控制)；(用器件实现的)操作系统；微程序语言.

firm² [fəːm] *n.* ①商号，商行；公司. ②工作集体〔如一组医生〕. *trading ~s* 商行. *a printing ~* 印刷公司. *a long ~*〔英〕(骗取货物而不付钱的)滑头商号.

fir·ma·ment [ˈfəːməmənt] *n.* 苍穹，天空. **-al** *a.*

fir·man [fəːˈmɑːn, ˈfəːmən] *n.* ①(土耳其皇帝等颁发的)诏书. ②许可证；执照；护照.

firm·er [ˈfəːmə] *n.* (木工所用的) 凿子〔圆凿〕.

firm·ly [ˈfəːmli] *ad.* 断然地，坚定地，坚固地.

firm·ness [ˈfəːmnis] *n.* 坚固，坚定，稳固.

firn [fəːn] *n.*【地】冰原，永久积雪〔俗名万年雪〕.

fir·ry [ˈfəːri] *a.* (*-ri·er; -ri·est*) ①冷杉木制的；枞木制的. ②多冷杉的，多枞的.

first [fəːst] *num.* 第一. — *a.* ①最初的，最早的. ②最上等的，第一流的. ③基本的，概要的. ④高音(调)的. *Judge not of men and things at ~ sight.*〔谚〕对人对事慢评论，初次印象未必真. *the ~ coat* (油漆等的)底涂，底层. *the ~ floor*〔美〕一楼；〔英、欧〕二楼. *the ~ impression* 最初印象. *the ~ instance*【法】初审. *the ~ snow of the season* 初雪. *the ~ train* 头班车. *the ~ two days* ＝〔古〕*the two ~ days* 头两天. ***at ~ hand*** 直接. ***at ~ sight [blush]*** 乍看；一见就. ***at the ~ opportunity*** 一有机会就. ***for the ~ time*** 第一次. ***in the ~ place [instance]*** 首先. ***on the ~ fine day*** 天一晴就. ***take the ~ opportunity*** 一有机会就. **the F- Commoner**〔英〕下议院议员. ***the ~ form***〔英〕(中等学校的)一年级. ***the ~ thing***〔俚〕首先. — *n.* ①最初，第一；第一位. ②每月的第一日，一号. ③【乐】高音部. ④第一等，头等，优等，甲等；〔*pl.*〕一级品. ⑤(棒球的) 第一垒. ⑥【汽车】起码〔最慢〕速度. *get [take] a ~* 考第一. *come in ~* 跑第一 *May (the) ~* ＝ *the ~ of May* 五月一日. ***at (the) ~*** 首先. ***be the ~ to (do)*** 最先…的. ***from ~ to last*** 自始至终. ***from the ~*** 从头，自始. ***the F-***〔英〕九月一号〔鹧鸪开猎日〕. —*ad.* ①第一，最初，首先. ②宁可. *safety ~* 安全第一. *F- come, ~ served.*〔谚〕先到先招待. *stand ~* 站在最前面. *He said he would die ~.* 他说他宁愿死掉 (也不作那样的事). *~ **and foremost*** 首先，第一. *~ **and last*** 总的说来. ***~, midst and last*** 彻头彻尾，始终，一贯. ***~, last and all the time***〔美〕始终一贯，绝对. *~ **of all*** 第一，首先. *~ **off*** 首先. *~ **or last***〔古、罕〕早晚，迟早. ~ **aid** 急救处理. **~-aid** *a.* 急救的 (*a ~-aid kit* 急救药箱). ~ **base**【棒球】一垒. *get to ~ base*〔俚〕获得初步成功，完成了第一步). **~-begotten** *a.* 最初生产的. ~ **blood** (在拳击等搏斗中)最初出血；〔喻〕从对手方面取得的最初胜利. **~born** ①*a.* 初生的；最年长的. ②*n.* 长子〔女〕；最初的结果. ~ **cause** ①首要原因；根源. ②【神】〔F- C-〕上帝，造物主. **~-chop** *a.*〔Ind.〕＝ **~-class** ①*a.* 头等的；第一类的；〔口〕最好的 (*a ~-class carriage* 头等车. *a ~-class paper* 信用优良的支票). ② *ad.* 乘头等舱〔车〕；作为第一类邮件；〔口〕极好 (*He plays ~* 他演得顶好. *travel ~-class* 乘头等车旅行). **~comer** 第一个来客，先到的人. ~ **cousin** 堂兄弟姐妹，表兄弟姐妹. ~ **day** 星期日〔一周的第一天，基督教公谊会用语〕. **~-degree** *a.* ①最低级的，最轻度的；【医】第一度的 (*~-degree burn* 第一度灼伤). ②最高级的，一级的，最严重的 (*~-degree combat readiness* 一级战斗状态). **F- Empire** (法兰西) 第一帝国〔1804—1815〕. ~ **estate** 第一等级(僧侣)〔欧洲封建时代的三个等级之一，其他两个等级是贵族和庶民〕. ~ **family** ①美国最早移民的黑裔. ②总统的家族. ~ **finger** 食指. **~-foot**〔Scot.〕元旦日第一个来客. ~ **floor** ①〔美〕一楼. ②〔英、欧〕二楼. ~ **fruits** 最初的结果，初次收获. **~-generation** *a.* 第一代的〔①指出生在外国的入籍公民. ②有时指父母入籍后出生的公民〕. **~hand**① *a.* 第一手的，直接的，亲自得到的. ② *ad.* 直接地. **F- International** 第一国际(1864—1876). ~ **lady**〔常作 F- L-〕第一夫人，总统夫人，元首夫人. ~ **lieutenant** ①(美陆军)中尉. ②(美海军) 中尉〔负责舰只或海军站的维修和保养〕. **~-line** *a.* ①【军】第一线的. ②头等的，最重要的. ~ **mate [officer]**【海】大副. ~ **name**〔美〕一个人姓名中的名字，教名(＝ given name). **~name** *vt* 不以姓而以名相称. ~ **night** (戏剧或歌剧等的)首夜演出. **~-nighter** 经常观看首夜演出者. ~ **offender**【法】初犯. ~ **papers**〔美国〕要求加入某国国籍的初步申请书. ~ **person** ①【语法】第一人称. ②用第一人称叙述的文体. ~ **quarter** ①上弦日子〔指阴历每月初八前后〕. ②上弦月. **~-rate** ①*a.* 第一等，最上等的. ②*ad.*〔口〕非常(好)地 (*feel ~-rate* 觉得精神极好). ③*n.* 一级战舰；一流人物. **~-rater** 一流人物；一级品. ~ **reading** (议会审议议案时的)正式初读. **F- Republic** (法兰西) 第一共和国〔1792—1804〕. **~-run** *a.*〔美〕头轮的〔指电影院〕. **~-runner**〔美〕头轮电影院. **F- Sea Lord**〔英〕海军部军事委员会第一军事委员. ~ **sergeant** (美陆、海军)军士长. **~-strike** *a.* (核战争中的) 第一次核打击的. **~-strike capability** 第一次核打击能力. **~-string** *a.* ①【体】正式(队员)的〔区别于候补(队员)的〕. ②第一流的，优秀的. **~-time** *a.* 初次的. **F- Triumvirate** (古代罗马的)前三雄执政〔指恺撒、庞培和克拉苏的三头执政团〕. ~ **water** (特指钻石、珍珠等) 最好品质，最纯洁的光泽，优等.

first·ling [ˈfəːstliŋ] *n.*〔常 *pl.*〕初生产物，初次收获；初产的幼畜；最初结果.

first·ly [ˈfəːstli] *ad.* 第一，首先. ★列举条目时常作: ~, secondly, thirdly, … lastly.

firth [fəːθ] *n.*〔Scot.〕＝ frith.

fisc [fisk] *n.* ①古罗马的皇室财库. ②国库，王室的财库.

fis·cal [ˈfiskəl] *a.* ①国库的. ②〔美〕财政上的；会计的. *a ~ policy* 财政政策. *~ resources* 财源. — *n.* ①财政部长；(苏格兰等的) 检察官；(西班牙及葡萄牙的)检察长. ②印花税票. ~ **agent** 财务代理人〔银行，商行〕. ~ **law** 会计法. ~ **stamp** 印花税票. ~ **year** 会计年度，财政年度.

Fish [fiʃ] *n.* 菲什〔姓氏〕.

fish [fiʃ] *n.* (*pl.* ~*es*,〔集合词〕~)①鱼；〔集合词〕鱼类；鱼肉. ★说鱼的若干种类时用 fishes，说几条鱼不用复数；鱼肉是不可数名词，无复数. ②〔口〕(特殊的)人物，家伙，东西. ③【海】钓锚器；撑夹桅杆的加固夹箍；【建】接合板，夹片，鱼尾板；悬鱼饰；【天】〔the Fish(es)〕双鱼宫. ④【军口】鱼雷. ⑤〔美口〕新囚犯；生手，笨蛋；容易受骗的人. ⑥〔美俚〕〔谑〕天主教徒. ⑦〔美俚〕美元. *eat three ~* 吃三条鱼. *lots of ~* 许多鱼. *F- begins to stink at the head.*〔谚〕上梁不正下梁歪，鱼要腐烂头先坏. *Gut no ~ till you get them.* ＝ *Never fry a ~ till it is caught.*〔谚〕鱼未捉到，别忙煎鱼. *He who would catch ~ must not mind getting wet.*〔谚〕捉鱼不要怕湿脚. *If you swear you will catch no ~.*〔谚〕咒骂不解决问题. *It is a silly ~, that is caught twice with the same bait.*〔谚〕智者不上两回当. *Never offer to teach ~ to swim.*〔谚〕别班门弄斧. *a big ~* 大亨，大人物. *a cool ~* 无耻之徒. *a dull ~* 钝汉. *a loose ~* 放荡鬼. *a queer ~* 怪人，莫名其妙的家伙. ***a ~ out of water*** 离水的鱼，不得其所的人. ***All is ~ that comes to his net.*** 到手的都要，便宜事来者不拒. ***as dumb [mute] as a ~*** 默不作声. ***big ~ in a little pond*** 矮子里头的长子. ***catch ~ with a silver hook*** 钓不到鱼之后花钱买鱼(冒充是自己钓的). ***cry stinking ~*** 拆自己的台. ***drink like a ~*** 牛饮. ***drunk as a ~*** 大醉. ***eat ~ on Fridays*** 斋戒日吃鱼〔有些基督教信徒在星期五不食肉，作为守斋〕. ***feed the ~es*** 晕船；葬身鱼腹. ***~ and chips***〔主英〕炸鱼加土豆片. ***have other ~ to fry***〔口〕别有要事. ***hook [land] one's ~*** 如愿以偿. ***make ~ of one and flesh [fowl] of another*** 厚此薄彼. ***neither ~, flesh, nor***

fowl [nor good red herring] 非驴非马，不伦不类．***(a) pretty [nice] kettle of ~*** 混乱；乱七八糟．***The best ~ smell when they are three days old.*** 〔谚〕鱼过三天就要臭；久居别家招人嫌．***The best ~ swim [are] near the bottom.*** 〔谚〕好鱼居水底，要得宝物不容易．***There's as good ~ in the sea as ever came out of it.*** 〔谚〕有水何患无鱼．***Venture a small ~ to catch a great one.*** 〔谚〕虾子钓鲤鱼，吃小亏占大便宜．— *vt.* ①在(…中)捕鱼，钓(鱼)，捉(鱼)，捕(鱼)．②捞出，搜出，查出，摸出．③【海】加夹箍夹牢；【工】用接合板连接〔加固〕；将(锚)吊起．④〔美俚〕奉承，巴结．~ *a pond* 在池塘里捕鱼．~ *trout* 钓鳟鱼．—*vi.* ①捕鱼．②搜查 *(after)*，探查，采(珊瑚等)．~ *for a living* 捕鱼谋生．~ ***in the air*** 缘木求鱼．~ ***in troubled waters*** 混水摸鱼，趁火打劫．~ ***or cut bait*** 要就大干要就不干．~ ***out [up]*** (从水中)吊起；捞出，搜出；把鱼捕尽．~ **ball [cake]** 鱼丸子．~**bone** *n.* 鱼骨．~ **bowl** ①玻璃鱼缸．②"玻璃鱼缸"场所〔喻一举一动易为人所知的地方〕．~ **crow**【动】渔鸦．~ **culture [breeding]** 养鱼法．~ **culturist** 养鱼家．~**-eye**【摄】(指镜头)超广角的〔视角特别广阔的〕；用超广角镜头拍摄的．~ **farm** 养鱼场．~ **farming** 养鱼(法)．~ **flake** 〔Can.〕晒鱼台．~ **flour** 鱼粉．~ **fork** 鱼叉；鱼钩．~ **fry** ①炸鱼．②吃炸鱼的野餐．③鱼秧．~ **globe** 金鱼缸．~ **glue** 鱼胶．~ **hawk**【动】鱼鹰，鹗．~**hook** 鱼钩，钓钩；【船】钓锚钩子．~**-in** 集体进入禁区钓〔捕〕鱼示威〔表示反对将该地列为钓〔捕〕鱼禁区〕．~ **joint** 夹板接合．~ **kettle** 有柄的椭圆形煮鱼锅．~ **knife** 鱼刀，食鱼用刀．~ **ladder** 鱼梯〔使鱼逐级向上游过水闸或瀑布的一系列台阶式水道〕．~**like** *a.* 鱼似的；冷淡的．~**-line** *n.* 钓丝．~ **meal** 鱼粉肥料，鱼粉饲料．~**monger** 〔主英〕鱼贩子．~**net** ①鱼网．②【军】伪装网．~ **paper** 青壳纸，鱼膏纸．~ **plate** 接合板；(铁轨接头处用的)鱼尾(夹)板．~**pond** 养鱼塘；〔谑〕海．~**pot** 捕鱼笼．~**pound** *n.* 〔方〕(捕鱼)潜网；鱼梁．~ **protein concentrate** (作食品用)精制鱼蛋白粉．~**skin** 鱼皮，(尤指)鲨鱼皮．~**skin disease**【医】鱼鳞癣 (= ichthyosis)．~ **slice** 〔英〕(侍者用)分鱼刀；煎鱼锅铲．~ **sound** *n.* 鱼鳔．~ **stick** 〔美〕炸鱼排〔一种长方形裹着面包粉的油炸鱼排或鱼饼〕．~ **story** 〔口〕牛皮，大话，靠不住的故事．~ **strainer** (从锅里捞鱼的) 笊篱．~ **tackle** 收锚复滑车．~**tail** ①*a.* 鱼尾状的．②*v.* 摆尾飞行 (~*tail burner* 鱼尾状煤气喷火口．~*tail wind* 扰乱弹道的不定风)．~ **torpedo** 鱼雷．~**way** = ~ ladder．~**weir** 鱼梁．~**wife,** ~**woman** 卖鱼妇；骂街的泼妇．~**works** 〔*sing., pl.*〕鱼场设备；水产制品厂．~**worm** 蚯蚓 (= angle worm)．

Fish·er [ˈfiʃə] *n.* 菲舍〔姓氏〕．

fish·er[1] [ˈfiʃə] *n.* ①渔夫；渔船．②【动】食鱼貂；以鱼为食的兽．*a ~ of men* 〔谑〕传教师．***the great ~ of souls*** 撒旦，魔鬼．

fish·er[2] [ˈfiʃə] *n.* 〔英俚、古〕一镑纸币．

fish·er·man [ˈfiʃəmən] *n.* ①捕鱼人．②渔船．*~'s bend* 渔人结．

fish·er·y [ˈfiʃəri] *n.* ①渔业，水产业．②渔场．③打鱼执照，捕鱼权．④渔业公司；养鱼术．*the pearl ~* 采珠场．

fish·i·fy [ˈfiʃifai] *vt.* 〔美俚〕为…供应鱼，使有鱼．

fish·ing [ˈfiʃiŋ] *n.* ①钓鱼，捕鱼；捕鱼权．②鱼尾接口．~ **banks [ground]** 渔场．~ **boat** 渔船．~ **expedition** ①审前盘问．②非法调查．~ **line** 钓丝．~ **net** 渔网．~ **pole** 钓竿〔只有竿、钩和钓丝的简单钓竿〕．~ **population** 渔民．~ **rod** 分节活动钓竿．~ **season** 渔汛期．~ **tackle** 钓具．

fish·y [ˈfiʃi] *a.* ***(-i·er; -i·est)*** ①鱼的，多鱼的；鱼肉做的，鱼似的．②腥臭的．③(眼光)模糊的；〔俚〕可疑的，靠不住的．*a ~ translation* 不忠实的翻译．*There's something ~ about it.* 这里面有鬼．**fish·i·ly** *ad.* **fish·i·ness** *n.*

fisk [fisk] *n.* = fisc.

fissi- *comb. f.* 表示"分裂"，"裂变"：*fissi*le, *fissi*parous.

fis·sile [ˈfisail] *a.* ①易分裂的，可分裂的．②【原】裂变的．~ *material* 可裂变物质，核燃料．

fis·sil·i·ty [fiˈsiliti] *n.*【原】可裂变性．

fis·sion [ˈfiʃən] *n.* ①裂开，分裂．②【生】分裂生殖．③【原】(核)裂变．*a ~ bomb* (裂变式)原子弹．~ *product* 裂变产物．*reproduction by ~* 分裂繁殖．*atomic ~* 原子分裂．*uranium ~* 铀核裂变．— *vt., vi.*【原】(使)裂变．~**-track dating**【地】铀裂变年代确定法．

fis·sion·a·ble [ˈfiʃənəbl] *a.* 可分裂的，可裂变的．— *n.* 〔常 *pl.*〕可裂变物质．**-bility** *n.*

fis·sip·a·rous [fiˈsipərəs] *a.*【生】分裂生殖的．**-ly** *ad.* **-ness** *n.*

fis·si·ped [ˈfisiped] *a.*【动】裂足的，叉指的 (= fissipedal)．— *n.* 裂脚亚目动物〔包括猫、狗等〕．

fis·si·ros·tral [ˌfisiˈrɔstrəl] *a.*【动】①宽阔而深裂的(指某些鸟类的喙)．②有裂喙的〔如褐雨燕、欧夜鹰〕．

fis·sure [ˈfiʃə] *n.* ①裂缝；裂隙．②(思想、观点等的)分歧．③【解】裂纹，沟．④【医】裂伤．*anal ~* 肛裂．— *vt., vi.* (使)裂开．

fist [fist] *n.* ①拳头；〔口〕手．②〔口〕笔迹．③【印】指标参见号．*clench [double] one's ~* 握拳．*Give us your ~.* 让我们握握手．*write a good [an ugly] ~* 字写得好〔丑〕．***grease sb.'s ~*** 向某人行贿．***make a good [poor] ~ at [of]*** 做得成功〔不成功〕．***the mailed ~*** 暴力，武力威胁．— *vt.* ①用拳打．②紧握；掌管(风帆等)，把(手)握成拳头．~ **fight** 打架．~ **law** 暴力主义．**-ed** *a.* ①有拳头的；握成拳头的．②〔组成复合词〕：*close [tight]-fisted* 吝啬的，手紧的．

fist·ful [ˈfistful] *n.* = handful.

fist·i·a·na [ˌfistiˈænə] *n.* 拳击界．

fist·ic(al) [ˈfistik(əl)] *a.* 〔口〕拳击的，拳术的．*a ~ arena* 拳赛场．*a ~ populace* 拳赛迷．

fist·i·cuff [ˈfistikʌf] *n.* ①拳的一击．②〔*pl.*〕互殴，乱斗．***come to ~s*** 打起架来．

fis·tu·la [ˈfistjulə] *n.* (*pl.* **~s, -lae** [-liː]) ①【动】细管，喙管．②【医】瘘(管)．**-r** *a.*

fis·tu·lous [ˈfistjuləs] *a.* ①烟斗状的，管状的；管子做的，有管的．②【医】瘘管(状)的 (= fistular).

fist·y [ˈfisti] *a.* = fistic(al).

fit[1] [fit] *vt.* ①适合．②使适合，使适应；使(服装等)合身；使合格，使胜任；〔美〕使准备(投考)．③为…提供设备，供给 *(with)*．④耕(地)．*This coat does not ~ me.* 这件上衣我穿着不合身．~ *a coat on sb.* 给某人试上衣样子．~ *the dress to the figure* 量体裁衣．~ *students for college* 训练学生使能升入大学．— *vi.* ①适合；调和，配合；(服装等)合身，合式；适应．②〔美〕准备(投考)．*Her clothes ~ well.* 她的衣服很合身．*The window ~s badly.* 这窗户关不上．~ ***in*** ①使适合，使顺应．②适合；调和 (~ *in with its surroundings* 适应环境)．~ ***into*** 顺应，调和．~ ***like a glove*** 完全合适．~ ***on*** ①装上；把…置于原处 (~ *the lid on* 把盖子盖上)．②试穿 (*have one's new coat fitted on* 试穿新上衣．~ ***oneself for*** 作好…的准备．~ ***out*** ①使装备齐全，准备好．②办妥(~ *out a ship for a voyage* 把船装备好以便远航)．~ ***the cap on*** 认为所指的是自己．~ ***up*** 准备，装备，设备 (*fit up the house with electric light* 给房子安装电灯)．— *a.* ①适当的，相称的，合适的，适宜的 *(for; to)*．②胜任的，合格的；有准备的．③〔口〕几乎要…的．④〔俚〕健康的，结实的．*be not ~ to be seen* 样子见不得人．*the survival of the fittest* 适者生存．*I walked till I was ~ to drop.* 我走到快累倒才停．*laugh ~ to burst oneself* 捧腹大笑．*Is he ~ for work [to travel] yet?* 他还能工作〔旅行〕吗？***as ~ as a fiddle [flea]*** 很健

康,精神好.*be ~ for* 适于,适合.*feel ~* 精神极好.*~ to be tied* 大发脾气 (*She looked ~ to be tied.* 她看上去气得要命). *~ to kill* 极度地,大大地 (*The girl was dressed up ~ to kill.* 这姑娘浓装艳抹). *keep ~* 保持健康. — *ad.* 适合地,恰当地;适时地〔仅用于下列成语〕: *see [think] ~ to (do)* … 认为应当(做…). — *n.* ①适当,妥当;合身. ②〔俚〕(投考)准备(*for*). ③【机】配合;密接部. *force ~* 压入配合. *shrink ~* 冷缩配合. *This coat is an easy [a bad, a poor] ~.* 这件衣服合身[不合身].

fit[2] [fit] *n.* ①(病的)发作,惊厥,(婴儿的)惊风. ②(感情的)激发;一时高兴. *a ~ of epilepsy* 癫痫发作. *have ~s of coughing* 一阵阵咳嗽. *fall down in a ~* 昏倒. *a ~ of fury* 勃然大怒. *a ~ of industry* 一时的勤勉. *beat [knock] sb. into ~s* 彻底打败某人. *by ~s (and starts)* 凭一时高兴,忽冷忽热地,一阵阵地. *give sb. ~s [a ~]*〔口〕使某人大吃一惊;使某人大发脾气. *go into ~s* (因癫痫等)昏过去. *have [throw] a ~*〔口〕大发脾气,大为不安. *in a ~ of rage [anger]* 一时气愤. *scream oneself into ~s* 狂叫,拼命叫. *when the ~ is on sb.* 当某人一时高兴时.

fit[3] [fit] *n.* 〔古〕①诗歌;故事. ②(诗歌的)一节.

Fitch [fitʃ] *n.* ①菲奇〔姓氏〕. ② **John ~** 约翰·菲奇〔1743—1798,美国汽船发明者〕.

fitch [fitʃ] *n.*【动】鸡鼬,鸡貂;鸡鼬毛.

fitch·et [fitʃit], **fitch·ew** [fitʃu] *n.* = fitch.

fit·ful [fitful] *a.* 发作的;间歇的;不定的. *a ~ breeze* 一阵阵微风. *a ~ gleam* 忽明忽灭的光. *a ~ wind* 方向不定的风. *a ~ worker* 忽作忽息的工人. **-ly** *ad.* **-ness** *n.*

fit·i·fied [ˈfitifaid] *a.*〔美〕①癫痫的. ②行为古怪的,反复无常的.

fit·ly [ˈfitli] *ad.* 适合地,合宜地,适时的.

fit·ment [ˈfitmənt] *n.* ①家具,设备. ②〔*pl.*〕附件,配件(=fittings).

fit·ness [ˈfitnis] *n.* ①适当,恰当,合理. ②健康. *the ~ of things* 事物的合情合理. **~ test** 健康检查.

fit-out [ˈfitaut] *n.* (旅行等的)准备;装备.

fit·ted [ˈfitid] *a.* 按实物尺寸做的. *~ bed sheets* 与床身宽长一致的床单. *a ~ coat* 定做的上衣.

fit·ter [ˈfitə] *n.* ①装配钳工. ②裁剪和试样的服装工人. ③〔*pl.*〕破片,碎片. *~'s shop* 装配车间.

fit·ting [ˈfitiŋ] *n.* ①配合,装配,装修. ②(衣样的)试穿. ③〔*pl.*〕【机】用具;零件,附件,(接头)配件. ④家具,装置,设备,器材. *a ~ shop* 装配车间;装配厂. *be ready for a ~* 准备试衣. *gas and electric-light ~s* 煤气和电灯设备. **~ school**〔美〕补习学校. — *a.* 适当的. **-ly** *ad.* **-ness** *n.*

fit-up [ˈfitʌp] *n.*〔英〕(可以带着走的)临时舞台装置[道具]. *a ~ company* 流动剧团.

Fitz- [fits-] *pref.* 表示"…的儿子"〔*cf.* Mac-, Mc-, O'-〕,旧时用来表示王族的庶子: *Fitz*roy (国王的庶子),*Fitz*clarence (Clarence 公爵的庶子).

Fitz·ger·ald [fitsˈdʒerəld] *n.* 菲茨杰拉德〔姓氏〕.

Fitz·john [fitsˈdʒɔn] *n.* 菲茨章〔姓氏〕.

Fitz·roy [fitsˈrɔi] *n.* 菲茨罗伊〔姓氏〕.

five [faiv] *num.* 五,五个;第五. — *n.* ①五岁;五点钟;(牌的)五点;【板球】得五分;5 镑钞票;〔*pl.*〕5 号大小的手套[鞋袜、衣服等]. ②〔俚〕〔*pl.*〕五厘公债(等);〔美〕五人篮球队;五个一组的东西. *~ and twenty* = *twenty-five* 二十五. *a bunch of ~s* 手,拳头. *~ senses* 五官. **~-by-~** *a.*〔美俚〕矮胖的. **~-case note**〔美俚〕五元钞. **F- Civilized Nations**【史】北美易洛魁(Cherokee)族五个印第安部落联盟. **~-fold** *a., ad.* 五倍,五重. **~ hundred** 五百;五百分〔纸牌游戏〕. **~-o'clock shadow** (清晨刮脸的人)傍晚已经长出的微微一层髭须. **~ o'clock tea** 午后茶点. **~-ouncers** 〔*pl.*〕〔美俚〕拳,一拳. **~pence**〔英〕五便士〔口 fppence〕;〔美〕5 分(铜币). **~ penny** *a.*〔英〕五便士的. **~ percents** 〔*pl.*〕五厘利债券;股息五厘的股票. **~-spot** ①五点的纸牌. ②〔美俚〕五元钞票. **~-star** *a.* 五个星的;五星级的;第一流的 (*a ~-star general* 美国的五星上将. *a ~-star film* 第一流影片). **F- Towns** 英国五大陶瓷名城. **F- Year Plan** 五年计划.

five-and-ten-cent (store) [ˈfaivnˈtenˈsent]〔美俚〕廉价品商店;五分一角钱商店.〔亦作 five-and-ten, five-and-dime.〕

five-fin·ger [ˈfaiv-ˌfiŋgə] *n.*【植】①(委陵菜;牛角花)(= cinquefoil). ②五叶地锦(= Virginia creeper). ③任何掌状裂叶或花冠的植物.

fiv·er [ˈfaivə] *n.*〔英俚〕五镑钞;〔美〕五元钞.

fives[1] [faivz] *n. pl.*〔用作单〕〔英〕(2 人或 4 人对墙投击的)手球.

fives[2] [ˈfaivz] *n.* (马等的)腺疫,传染性卡他.

fix [fiks] *vt.* ①使固定;安装. ②集中注意于,盯住,凝视. ③打定(主意),抱定(宗旨);牢记. ④决定;确定;规定. ⑤阉割. ⑥使固定;【化】使凝固,使不挥发;【摄】定(影). ⑦安排;准备. ⑧〔美口〕调整,整理;修理. ⑨〔口〕拉拢,收买,操纵,贿赂. ⑩〔口〕打败;偿清. ⑪烧(火);封(火). ⑫【生】(为显微镜检查等目的而)固定(机体,组织等). *bacteria that ~ nitrogen* 固氮菌. *~ all the blame on sb.* 把过失都推给某人. *~ bayonets* 上刺刀. *~ one's attention on [upon]* 集中注意力于…. *~ one's gaze [eyes] on [upon]* 注视. *~ sb. with one's eyes* 用眼睛盯牢某人. *~ a machine* 修理机器. *~ a jury* 买通陪审团. *~ one's account* 清帐. — *vi.* ①固着;固定. ②【化】凝固,不挥发. ③注目. ④决定,选定;〔美口〕准备,打算. *She is ~ing to go skating.* 她正准备去滑冰. *~ it*〔美口〕处理. *~ on [upon]* 决定 (*~ on a date for the meeting* 决定开会日期). *~ out* 把船具备齐,准备出航. *~ up* ①安顿住处. ②〔美口〕修理,修补;解决,商妥;组织,编成. ③打扮停当. (*~ up a dispute* 排解争端. *~ up sb. for the night* 安顿某人过夜. *~ sb. up with a job* 安排某人工作). — *n.* ①(船只、飞机等的)方位,定位. ②〔美口〕困境. ③〔美俚〕(比赛等)通过作弊预先安排好的结果[定局]. ④〔俚〕(吸毒者的)自我毒品注射. *navigator ~* 领航坐标. *radar [radio] ~* 雷达[无线电]定位. *be in a (pretty) ~* 束手无策,进退两难. *get oneself into a bad ~* 陷入困境. *in a fine ~* 情况好. *out of ~*〔美俚〕(钟表等)不准;(身体)不舒服.

fix·a·ble [ˈfiksəbl] *a.* 可固定的.

fix·ate [ˈfikseit] *vt., vi.* ①(使)凝视;(使)注意. ②(使)固定下来.

fix·a·tion [fikˈseiʃən] *n.* ①固定;凝固. ②凝视. ③【心】(青春早期的)固恋. ④【摄】定相;定影. *~ of tissues*【生】组织固定法.

fix·a·tive [ˈfiksətiv] *a.* ①固着的,固定的. ②定色的,防挥发的,防止褪色的. — *n.*【生、化】固定剂,固着剂;【摄】定影液.

fix·a·ture [ˈfiksətʃə] *n.* 发蜡.

fixed [fikst] *a.* ①固定的;确定的,不变的,固执的. ②【化】凝固的,不易挥发的. ③〔美口〕(在经济上)处境…的. ④〔美俚〕(比赛等)通过作弊预先安排好结果的. *a ~ deposit* 定期存款. *a ~ fact*〔美〕确定事实. *a ~ gun*【军】固定机枪. *a ~ income* 固定收入. *a ~ point* 警察常驻的地方. *~ par of exchange* 汇兑的法定平价. *a ~ oil* 不挥发性油,固定油. *well ~*〔美〕生活宽裕. **~ assets** 固定资产 (*opp.* current assets). **~ capital** 固定资本〔*cf.* circulating capital〕. **~ charge** 固定支出. **~ idea**【心】固执的思想;固定妄想. **~ price** 定价,标价. **~ property** 不动产. **~ rate** 固定汇率. **~ satellite** 固定人造卫星(如通讯卫星). **~ star** 恒星.

fix·ed·ly [ˈfiksidli] *ad.* 固定地;不变地;决心地;集中地.

fix·ed·ness [ˈfiksidnis] *n.* ①固定性,稳定性,耐挥发性. ②固定的东西.
fix·er [ˈfiksə] *n.* ①固定器. ②【摄】定影剂. ③维修工,保全工. ④〔美口〕向警察行贿[说项]者,在政党中奔走调停者. ⑤〔美俚〕贩毒的人.
fix·ing [ˈfiksiŋ] *n.* ①固着,固定;【摄】定影,定相. ②修理,整理. ③〔*pl.*〕〔美〕设备;装饰;〔美口〕(菜肴的)配料;调味品,花色配菜. *a* ~ *salt* (盐基性的)定色剂. *roast turkey and all the* ~*s* 烤火鸡以及配菜. ~ **solution** 【摄】定影液.
fix·i·ty [ˈfiksiti] *n.* = fixedness.
fixt [fikst] *v.* 〔诗〕fix 的过去式及过去分词.
fix·ture [ˈfikstʃə] *n.* ①固定,固定状态;固定物;【机】装置器,工件夹具. ②〔*pl.*〕【法】(不动产的)固定附着物〔房屋、树木等〕. ③【商】定期放款,定期存款. ④运动会举行日;比赛项目. ⑤固定在某地[某项工作]的人. *an A-*~ A 形电杆, A 形支柱. *gas* ~*s* 煤气设备. *racing* ~*s* 赛马日期.
fiz [fiz] *n., v.* = fizz.
fiz·gig [ˈfizgig] *n.* ①〔古〕轻浮的女子. ②发嘶嘶声的烟火. ③旋转的儿童玩具. ④鱼叉.
fizz [fiz] *n.* ①嘶嘶声. ②活跃. ③〔美〕发泡性饮料(特指香槟酒等). — *vi.* ①嘶嘶地响[发泡]. ②兴奋,高兴. ~ **water** 〔美〕苏打水〔*cf.* soda water, soda pop〕.
fiz·zle [ˈfizl] *n.* ①嘶嘶声. ②〔美口〕失败. — *vi.* ①发嘶嘶声. ②〔口〕失败. ~ *out* (燃烧物着水时)'嘶'的一声熄掉;〔口〕(计划等)失败.
fiz·zy [ˈfizi] *a.* **(-zi·er; -zi·est)** 发嘶嘶声的,起泡的. *a* ~ *drink* 汽水(或汽酒等).
fjeld [fjeld] *n.* (北欧诸国的)荒瘠高原.
fjord [fjɔːd] *n.* = fiord.
fl. = ①florin. ②floruit. ③flourished. ④flower. ⑤fluid.
Fl. = Flanders; Flemish.
Fla. = Florida.
flab [flæb] *n.* 〔口〕松弛的肌肉.
flab·ber·gast [ˈflæbəgɑːst] *vt.* 〔口〕使发愣,使大吃一惊.
flab·by [ˈflæbi] *a.* ①不结实的;松软的;松弛的. ②无力的;软弱的. ~ *muscles* 松弛的肌肉. **flab·bi·ly** *ad.* **flab·bi·ness** *n.*
fla·bel·late [fləˈbeleit], **fla·bel·li·form** [fləˈbeləfɔːm] *a.* 扇形的.
fla·bel·lum [fləˈbeləm] *n.* **(*pl.* -bel·la** [-ə]**)** ①教皇仪仗扇. ②【解】扇状器官[结构].
flac·cid [ˈflæksid] *a.* ①(肌肉等)不结实的,松弛的. ②软弱的. **-ly** *ad.* **-cid·i·ty** [ˌflækˈsiditi], **-ness** *n.*
flack[1] [flæk] *n.* 〔美俚〕 ①(剧团等的)新闻宣传员;广告代理人;(演员等的)宣传员 (= press agent). ②广告,宣传. — *vi.* 作(剧团等的)新闻宣传员等 (*for*). **-er·y** 广告宣传;大肆宣传.
flack[2] [flæk] *n.* = flak[2].
fla·con [flækn] *n.* 香水瓶;小玻璃瓶.
flag[1] [flæg] *n.* ①旗〔*cf.* banner, ensign, pennant, standard, colours〕;【海】司令旗,旗舰旗;旗舰. ②(狗,鹿等的)茸尾. ③〔*pl.*〕(鹰等)脚部长羽,(鸟的)次级飞羽. ④报头〔印刷报名处〕. *a black* ~ 黑旗〔海盗旗或升在监狱外宣布执行死刑的旗〕. *a yellow* ~ 黄旗,检疫旗. *a white* ~ (表示投降、休战、求和的)白旗. ***a*** ~ ***of convenience*** 【海】方便旗(指在外国登记船只而悬挂该国国旗). ***dip the*** ~ 将旗降下又立即升起以表示敬意. ***drob the*** ~ 落旗〔赛跑出发与决胜时的信号〕. ~ ***of truce*** 休战旗〔向敌人表示希望谈判的白旗〕. ***hang [show] the white*** ~ 竖白旗,投降. ***haul down one's*** ~ 投降. ***hoist a*** ~ ***half-mast high*** 下半旗致哀. ***hoist one's*** ~ (舰队司令等)升旗开始就职. ***keep the*** ~ ***flying*** 坚持战斗. ***strike [lower] the [one's]*** ~ 降旗表示敬礼〔投降〕;【海】舰队司令等降旗离职. ***under the*** ~ ***of*** 在…旗帜下. — *vt.* ①在…上升旗,悬旗于. ②用旗发出(信号),用旗通报[指挥等];打旗号[手势]使(车等)停下 (*down*). ③〔美军〕加旗形标识于(档案、卡片等)上(以防止改动). ~ *a train* 打旗号指挥火车. ~ *down a train* 打旗号使火车停下. ~ *down a taxi* 打手势让出租汽车停止. ~ *sb. a taxi* 为某人叫来一辆出租汽车. ~ *the streets* 街上到处悬挂出旗帜. ~**-boat** (做赛船目标的)旗艇;司令艇. ~ **captain** 【军】旗舰舰长. ~ **camer** 国家航空公司. ~ **commander** 【军】海军中校参谋. ~ **day** ①〔英〕(卖旗募捐的)旗日. ②〔F- D-〕〔美〕国旗制定纪念日(六月十四日). ~**-fall** 旗下挥(表示比赛开始). ~ **lady** 〔美〕女信号旗手. ~ **lieutenant** 【军】海军上尉参谋,海军将官的副官. ~ **list** 海军将官名册. ~**man** 信号兵,信号旗手,(铁道等的)旗工. ~ **officer** 海军将官. ~**pole** = ~**staff**. ~ **rank** 海军将官级军衔. ~**ship** 旗舰;〔喻〕(同类事物中)最优良或最重要的一个. ~**staff** 旗竿. ~ **station** (铁道上的)旗站,信号停车站. ~ **stop** 信号停车站〔公共汽车、火车等见停车信号方停车的地方〕. ~**-wagger** *n.* 〔主澳〕= ~*-waver.* ~**wagging** 〔军俚〕摇旗信号;(挑战性质的)豪言壮语. ~**-waver** 摇旗者;沙文主义者;摇旗呐喊的人,宣传鼓动者;激起沙文主义情绪的东西(如歌曲等). ~**-waving** 沙文主义情绪[宗派意识]的强烈表现[煽动].
flag[2] [flæg] *n.* ①(铺路用的)石板,扁石. ②〔*pl.*〕石板路. — *vt.* 用石板铺. ~**stone** (铺路用的)石板,扁石.
flag[3] [flæg] *n.* ①【植】菖蒲;鸢尾;香蒲. ②菖蒲叶[花].
flag[4] [flæg] *vi.* ①(帆等)无力地垂下,(草木等)萎垂. ②(力气、兴趣、热情等)松弛,减弱,衰退;失去吸引力.
fla·gel·la [fləˈdʒelə] *n.* flagellum 的复数.
flag·el·lant [ˈflædʒilənt] *n.* 【宗】鞭打自己以求赎罪的宗教教徒. — *a.* ①自行鞭打的. ②严厉抨击的.
flag·el·late [ˈflædʒeleit] *vt.* 鞭打. — *a.* ①【动】有鞭毛的,鞭毛形的. ②【植】有鞭状匍匐枝的. — *n.* 鞭毛藻,鞭毛虫. *a.* **-lator** *n.*
flag·el·la·tion [ˌflædʒeˈleiʃən] *n.* ①鞭身,鞭打〔尤指宗教悔过和变态性欲等行为〕. ②【动】鞭毛的发生.
flag·el·la·tor [ˈflædʒeˌleitə] *n.* 鞭打者. **-y** *a.* 鞭打的.
fla·gel·li·form [fləˈdʒelifɔːm] *a.* 鞭状的;细长的.
fla·gel·lum [fləˈdʒeləm] *n.* **(*pl.* ~*s*, -*gel·la*** [-lə]**)** ①【动】鞭毛,鞭状体;(昆虫触角的)鞭节. ②【植】鞭状匍匐枝. ③〔谑〕鞭子.
flag·eo·let [ˌflædʒəˈlet] *n.* ①六孔竖笛,哨笛. ②(风琴的)音栓.
Flagg [flæg] *n.* 弗拉格〔姓氏〕.
flag·ging[1] [ˈflægiŋ] *n.* ①石板路. ②〔集合词〕(铺路用的)石板.
flag·ging[2] [ˈflægiŋ] *a.* ①下垂的. ②萎靡不振的,松弛的,逐渐衰退的. — *n.* 下垂,松弛. **-ly** *ad.*
flag·gy[1] [ˈflægi] *a.* (岩石)会裂成扁石的;(土地)多扁石的.
flag·gy[2] [ˈflægi] *a.* 多菖蒲的;菖蒲状的.
fla·gi·tious [fləˈdʒiʃəs] *a.* 明目张胆为非作歹的,罪大恶极的,邪恶无耻的,狂暴残虐的. **-ly** *ad.* **-ness** *n.*
flag·on [ˈflægən] *n.* (有把的)酒壶[瓶],大肚酒瓶.
fla·granc [ˈfleigrəns] *n.* 臭名远扬,罪恶昭彰,明目张胆.
fla·grant [ˈfleigrənt] *a.* 罪恶昭彰的,臭名远扬的;公然的,明目张胆的. *a* ~ *offence* 明目张胆的罪行. *a* ~ *sinner* 明目张胆的为非作歹者. **-ly** *ad.*
fla·gran·te de·lic·to [fləˈgrænti dəˈliktəu] 〔L.〕当场. *be caught* ~ 被当场抓住.
flag-smut [flægsmʌt] 【植】杆黑粉病.
flail [fleil] *n.* ①连枷;古代一种类似连枷的武器. ②扫雷装置. — *vt., vi.* 用连枷打(谷类);鞭打,抽打. ~ **joint** 【解】连枷关节. ~ **tank** 扫雷坦克.
flair [flɛə] *n.* ①嗅觉. ②(某种)天资,(天生的)才能. ③

〔口〕鉴别力,眼力. *have a ~ for* 对…有鉴别力,有…的天资.

flak[1] [flæk] *n.* = flack[1].

flak[2] [flæk] *n.* ①高射炮火力;高射炮. ②恶评,谴责,漫骂;激烈的争论;反对. *a ~ area* 防空火力区. *~ installation* 高射炮掩体. *a ~ ship [train]* 防空军舰[火车]. **~ jacket [suit]** ①(飞行员的)护身衣. ②(警察的衬有钢片的)防弹背心.

flake[1] [fleik] *n.* ①薄片. ②火星,火花. ③【动】肌隔;【植】花瓣带条纹的石竹. ④〔美俚〕怪人. ⑤〔美俚〕(警察为了完成工作任务,用以充数的)"涉嫌"逮捕. *~ of snow* 雪片. *soap ~s* 肥皂片. *corn ~s* 玉米片. *huge ~s of flames* 火舌. ***fall in ~s*** 一片片地降落. — *vt.* ①使成薄片. ②象雪花般覆盖. — *vi.* ①剥落 *(away; off)*. ②雪片似地降下. **~board** 用碎木片胶压成的木板;刨花板. **~ white** 【化】碳酸铅白.

flake[2] [fleik] *n.* ①晒鱼架;食品搁架. ②(修船时用的)舷侧踏板.

flake[3] [fleik] *n., vt.* = fake[2]. **~ out** 〔俚〕①因疲劳而入睡. ②昏过去,不省人事. ③离去;消失.

fla·ko [ˈfleikəu] *a.* 〔美俚〕喝醉了的.

flak·y [ˈfleiki] *a.* *(flak·i·er; -i·est)* ①薄片状的. ②易成薄片的,易剥落的. ③〔美俚〕极古怪的,与常人不同的. **flak·i·ly** *ad.*, **flaki·ness** *n.*

flam [flæm] *n.* 〔口〕谎话;诈欺;诡计. —*vt.* 欺骗. *~ sb. off with lies* 用谎话骗人. *Stop your ~ing!* 别胡说.

flam·bé [flɑːnˈbei] *a.* (食物)燃烧着的〔指端上桌的食物是浸在燃烧着的白兰地、兰姆酒内的〕. — *n.* 浸在燃烧着的酒内的食物.

flam·beau [ˈflæmbəu] *n.* *(pl. ~s, ~x[-z])* ①火炬. ②华丽的大烛台.

flam·boy·ance [flæmˈbɔiəns, -si] *n.* ①火红. ②艳丽. ③过分华丽,装饰得过火.

flam·boy·ant [flæmˈbɔiənt] *a.* ①过分华丽的. ②艳丽的. ③火焰似的. ④火红色的. ⑤【建】火焰式的. ⑥夸张的,虚饰的. — *n.* 火焰色红花. **~-architecture** 火焰式建筑〔15—16世纪流行于法国,多采用火焰形或波状曲线〕. **-ly** *ad.*

flam·doo·dle [ˈflæmˌduːdl] *n.* 〔美俚〕①小物件,小玩意. ②(愚蠢的)胡说. ③吹牛;欺骗.

flame [fleim] *n.* ①火焰;光辉,光芒;【火箭】火舌. ②热情,激情. ③〔俚〕爱人,情人. *the ~ of sunset* 火红的晚霞. *~s of anger* 怒火. *an old ~ of mine* 我从前的情人. ***burst into ~(s)*** 烧起来. ***commit sth. to the ~s*** 把某物丢在火中,烧掉,付之一炬. ***fan the ~*** 激起热情;煽动. ***in ~s*** 燃烧着. — *vi.* 发火焰,燃烧;闪耀,发光;(激动地)爆发. *Her face ~d with shame.* 她的脸儿羞得通红. — *vt.* ①烧,加热,点燃,激起. ②发出(烽火,火焰等)信号. **~ *up [out, forth]*** 烧起来;极度兴奋,激怒;面孔发红. **~ bomb** 火焰炸弹. **~-colo(u)red** *a.* 火红的. **~ furnace** 反射炉. **~-out** (喷气发动机)熄火;燃烧中断. **~ projector, ~ thrower** 火焰喷射器. **~proof** *a.* ①耐火的. ②防火的. **~ tracer** 曳光弹. **~ tree** 凤凰木.

fla·men [ˈfleimen] *n.* *(pl. ~s, fla·mi·nes* [ˈflæminiːz]*)* (古罗马的)祭司.

fla·men·co [fləˈmeŋkəu] *n.* *(pl. ~s)* (西班牙安达鲁西亚地区吉普赛人的一种顿足拍手的)弗拉曼柯舞〔歌曲,乐曲〕.

flam·ing [ˈfleimiŋ] *a.* ①火焰熊熊的,燃烧灼热的. ②火红的,火焰般的,烂漫的. ③热情的,激情的. ④夸张的. *a ~ August* 赤日炎炎的八月. *~ eyes* 热情的眼光. *a ~ speech* 热烈的演说. **~ onions** 〔军俚〕火球形的高射炮火. **-ly** *ad.*

fla·min·go [fləˈmiŋgəu] *n.* *(pl. ~s, ~es)* 【动】火烈鸟.

Fla·min·i·an [fləˈminiən] **Way** 弗拉米尼乌斯大道〔罗马监察官弗拉米尼乌斯 (Flaminius) 于公元前220年修成的大道,从罗马通到阿里米尼乌姆〕.

flam·ma·ble [ˈflæməbl] *a.* 易燃的〔现今工商业界文件中多用之代 inflammable, 因后者虽同义,但其前缀 in-易引起误解〕. **-bil·i·ty** [ˌflæməˈbiliti] *n.* 易燃性.

flam·men·wer·fer [ˈflæmənvɛəfə] *n.* 〔G.〕火焰喷射器 (= flame projector).

flam·y [ˈfleimi] *a.* 〔罕〕火焰(似)的.

flan [flæn, flɑːn] *n.* ①(硬币)坯子;【机】毛坯. ②〔主英〕果馅饼.

Flan·a·gan [ˈflænəgən] *n.* 弗拉纳根〔姓氏〕.

Flan·ders [ˈflɑːndəz] *n.* 佛兰德〔中世纪欧洲一伯爵领地,包括现比、法、荷等地区,为第一次世界大战激战地〕.

flâ·ne·rie [ˈflɑːnəriː] *n.* 〔F.〕无目的闲步;游手好闲,无所事事.

flâ·neur [flɑːˈnəː] *n.* 〔F.〕无目的闲步者,懒人,游手好闲的人.

flange [flændʒ] *n.* ①【机】法兰(盘);凸缘;边凸缘制造机. ②(铁路)轨底. ③【建】(梁)翼缘. *a ~ coupling* 凸缘联轴节. *a mounting ~* 安装盘. *~ of bush* 衬套凸缘. *~ wheel* 轮缘. — *vt.* 在…上安装凸缘. *a ~d wheel* 凸缘轮.

flang·er [ˈflændʒə] *n.* ①【机】凸缘制造机. ②凸缘工人. ③(铁道)排雪板.

flank [flæŋk] *n.* ①胁腹;侧面. ②【建】厢房,侧翼建筑物. ③【军】侧翼,翼侧. ④【机】齿腹,面,齿侧;【激光】脉冲波前. *cover a ~* 掩护侧面. *a ~ attack [fire]* 翼侧攻击[侧射]. *the left [right] ~* 左[右]翼. ***in ~*** 从侧面,在侧面. ***take in ~*** 侧击. ***turn the ~ of the enemy*** 由侧面包抄敌人. — *vt.* ①在…的侧面. ②守[攻击、绕过]…的侧面. *a road ~ed with trees* 一边有树的道路. — *vi.* ①(堡垒等)和…的侧面相接 *(on, upon)*. ②占领两翼阵地. **~ speed** (船的)全速.

flank·er [ˈflæŋkə] *n.* ①【军】侧堡,侧面堡垒;〔*pl.*〕侧卫. ②【足球】侧翼后卫运动员(= ~ back).

flan·nel [ˈflænl] *n.* ①法兰绒;绒布;〔*pl.*〕法兰绒衣服〔如衬衫、运动衣、裤等〕. ②〔俚〕(骗人的)花言巧语;花招. *cotton ~* 绒布. — *a.* 法兰绒制的. — *vt.* *(*〔英〕*-ll-)* ①用法兰绒擦[包]. ②使穿法兰绒衣服. — *vi.* 〔俚〕耍花招. **~board** (作教学用具的)法兰绒板,绒布面揭示板〔可把用法兰绒包着的字母、阿拉伯数字等按压于其上〕. **~ cake** 〔美〕烤软饼. **~-mouthed** *a.* ①口齿不利落的,乡土音很重的. ②油嘴滑舌的,花言巧语的;耍花招的;爱吹牛的(人). **-ly** *a.* 法兰绒制的;象法兰绒一样的.

flan·nel·et(te) [ˌflænəˈlet] 绒布,棉法兰绒.

flan·nel·graph [ˈflænlgrɑːf] *n.* 可按压在绒布板上的示教图.

flap [flæp] *vt.* ①拍打,拍击;拍动(翅膀),扑动. ②拍打(蚊、蝇等);使(帆、帘子等)拍动. ③把(帽边等)拉下. ④合上,叠起,扔弃. —*vi.* ①拍动,摆动,飘动. ②拍翅飞行. ③垂下. ④乱吹,讲空话. ⑤〔俚〕激动起来,被搞糊涂. **~ *about*** 〔俚〕闲聊,讲空话. **~ *away [off]*** 拍走,拍去;拍着翅膀飞去. **~ *down*** 垂下. **~ *out*** 扑灭(灯火). — *n.* ①拍动. ②拍击;鼓翼. ③垂下物;前襟的翻褶;袋口盖;(帽)边;信封口盖. ④【机】(整流罩,散热器等的)风门片,鱼鳞片,瓣. ⑤(折叠式桌子的)折板,铰链板;(活板门的)活板;【造纸】挡水板;【空】襟翼,阻力板. ⑥(鱼鳃)盖;(狗等)下垂的长耳;(菌类)张开的伞. ⑦【医】(手术后遗下或移植用的)瓣. ⑧〔口〕兴奋,恐慌. ⑨〔口〕空袭(警报). *a ~ in the face* 打在脸上的一巴掌. *a ~ pocket* 有盖衣袋. *air ~* 风门片,鱼鳞片. ***be in a ~*** 在激动中,慌作一团. ***get into a ~*** 激动[慌乱]起来. **~ door** 吊门,活板门. **~dragon** 抢葡萄干游戏 (snap dragon 的原名). **~-eared** *a.* 大耳朵的,耳朵下垂的. **~ gasket** 平垫圈. **~jack** 〔英方,美〕①薄煎饼. ②(随身携带的)粉盒. **~-mouthed** *a.* (狗等)

嘴唇下垂的. ~**-seat** 折椅.

flap·doo·dle [ˈflæpˌduːdl] *n.*〔俚〕蠢话,胡说,瞎扯.

flap·pable [ˈflæpəbl] *a.* 缺乏自信的,性格软弱的;容易心慌的.

flap·per [ˈflæpə] *n.* ①拍击者;拍击物;〔俚〕手. ②苍蝇拍;(吓鸟的)叫子. ③片状悬垂物. ④阔鳍,鳍状肢,鸭脚板,橡皮脚掌. ⑤〔俚〕还不能飞的雏鸟;(不懂世故的)小姑娘;〔美俚〕摩登女郎,轻佻女郎. ⑥唤起记忆的人〔物〕. ~ **bracket** **[seat]** 机器脚踏车后面的座位. ~ **vote**〔英口〕妇女选举权. **-ish** *a.*〔美俚〕①小姑娘的. ②(女子)轻佻的.

flare [flɛə] *n.* ①摇曳的火焰,闪烁的火光,闪光(信号);曳光管;照明弹;(太阳的)耀斑,色球爆发. ②(突然)烧起;(怒气等的)爆发;(衣裙的)张开;炫耀,夸示. ③【摄】翳雾斑;【物】物镜反射光斑. ④(船只水线以上)船侧外倾. ⑤(足球的)短横传. ⑥〔*pl.*〕喇叭裤. *landing ~s* 着陆照明弹;机场着陆照明灯火. — *vi.* ①(火焰)摇曳,闪闪地燃烧 *(about; away; out)*,闪烁. ②(裙子等)张开. ③(船侧)外倾. — *vt.* ①使闪亮,使闪闪燃烧. ②用闪光作信号;夸示. ③使(裙子)张开. ④使(船侧)外倾. ~ ***out*** 突然闪亮;突然发怒. ~ ***up*** 突然烧起来;突然发怒;忽然喧噪起来. ~**back** ①火舌回闪,炮尾焰. ②短暂而意外的重新出现. ~ **bomb** 照明弹. ~ **path**【空】照明跑道. ~ **pistol** 闪光信号枪. ~ **point**【化】燃烧点,着火点. ~**-up** ①(突然)焚烧;(信号的)闪光. ②激怒. ③(一时的)盛况;狂欢. ④已平静后的突然爆发.

flar·ing [ˈflɛəriŋ] *a.* ①闪耀的;发光的,闪烁的. ②花哨的. ③外倾的;曲线形的,喇叭状张开的. **-ly** *ad.*

flash [flæʃ] *vt.* ①使闪光,使闪烁;反照,反射 *(back)*. ②晃;迅速传达出去,拍出,发出(电报等). ③使闪现;把(发亮的东西)晃一下,亮出一下;使掠过(心头) *(into; upon)*. ④灌水使(船)浮过障碍物,用水突然灌注. ⑤〔口〕炫耀,卖弄. ⑥将(玻璃)展成薄片;给(玻璃)镶盖. ⑦给(房顶)加覆盖物. ~ *a glance [a look, one's eyes] at* 用眼瞟一下,看一眼. *The news was ~ed across [over] the country*. 消息闪电般传遍全国. *His eyes ~ed defiance*. 他眼中显现出反抗的神色. — *vi.* ①(电光等)一闪;(火药等)忽然烧起来 *(off; out; up)*;(刀等)晃一晃. ②忽然显现,突然出现 *(forth; in; out)*. ③忽然想起;(机智、才能等)突然显现. ④飞驰,掠过. ⑤(河水等)冲泻,泛滥,暴涨. ⑥〔美俚〕(服迷幻药后)感到恍恍忽忽. ~ ***by [past]*** 一闪而过. ~ ***it away*** 〔俚〕炫耀,招摇. ~ ***on*** ①立刻心领神会. ②〔美俚〕(服迷幻药后)感觉飘飘然. ~ ***one's stuff*** 【美体】显出本领. ~ ***out [up]*** 勃然发怒. ~ ***upon*** 闪现心头,掠过心头,忽然想起. — *n.* ①闪光,闪发,焕发. ②刹那,一瞬间. ③浮华,浮夸,华而不实;衣饰漂亮的人. ④灌注的水,堰闸. ⑤【摄】闪光,闪光灯下摄成的照片. ⑥速报,急报,简短电讯. ⑦惹人注目的东西〔人物〕〔尤指优秀运动员〕. ⑧【军】徽章,肩章. ⑨(混合酒的)色料. ⑩(盗贼等的)隐语,黑话. *a ~ of hope* 一线希望. *~ of lightning* 闪电. *~ of merriment* 刹那的欢乐. *~ of wit* 灵机一动,突然出现的机智. ***a ~ in the pan*** 空枪;昙花一现(的人). ***in a ~*** 即刻,一刹那间. — *a.* ①闪光的,闪耀的,一闪而过的. ②浮华的,浮夸的,华而不实,假的. ③盗贼的,流氓的. ④〔俚〕(旅馆等)高级的. ⑤火速的;暴涨的. ⑥(相机)带有闪光设备的. ~ *language* 隐语. ~ *money [note]* 假钱〔钞票〕. ~**back** (电影的)闪回;(小说等的)倒叙;火舌回闪;(服迷幻药后)幻觉重现. ~**board** (调节水位的)闸板. ~ **bomb**闪光炸弹. ~ **bulb** (照相用)闪光灯(泡). ~ **burn** (原子弹等的)闪光灼伤. ~ **card** 单词、数目抽认卡〔上面写有单词、数目等的卡片. 教师逐一抽示,要求学生立即回答〕. ~**-cook** *vt.* 快速煮食. ~**cube** 立体闪光灯. ~**-dry** *vt.* 使快干. ~ **flood** 暴洪〔暴雨造成的急发性大洪水〕. ~**-forward** (小说、电影等)提前叙述未来事件. ~ **gun**【摄】(闪光灯的)闪光操纵器,闪光粉点燃器. ~ **house** (歹徒出入的)巢穴;魔窟. ~ **lamp**【摄】闪光灯. ~**light** ①(灯塔、机场等的)闪光信号灯;手电筒. ②【摄】闪光,闪光电. ③闪光灯下摄成的照片. ~**man** ①(通匪)劣绅. ②(拳赛的)赞助者. ~**over**【电】飞弧,闪络,跳火. ~ **photolysis**【化】闪光分解. ~ **picture** 用闪光灯拍的照片. ~ **point** (油的)燃烧点;(战争等的)爆发点. ~**tube** 闪光管.

flash·er [ˈflæʃə] *n.* ①闪光物;〔古〕华而不实的人物;【电】闪烁装置. ②自动断续装置.

flash·ing [ˈflæʃiŋ] *n.* ①闪光,炫耀. ②(坝水的)决放,(河水的)暴涨;【化】急骤蒸发. ③玻璃镶色. ④(房屋的)金属盖片,防雨板. — *a.* 闪烁的. *a ~ lantern* 闪光灯. *a ~ light* 闪光. ~ **point** = flash point.

flash·y [ˈflæʃi] *a.* ***(flash·i·er; -i·est)*** ①闪光的;瞬间的,昙花一现的. ②浮华的,只是外表好看的,华而不实的. ③(脾气等)暴烈的. **-i·ty** *ad.* **-i·ness** *n.*

flask [flɑːsk] *n.* ①瓶,长颈瓶. ②【化】烧瓶. ③(携带用)扁瓶. ④(打猎用的)火药筒. ⑤【机】沙箱,砂型.

flask·et [ˈflɑːskit] *n.* ①小瓶. ②〔古〕浅篮. ③(洗衣服用的)衣篮.

flat[1] [flæt] *n.* ①〔英罕〕地板;(房屋的)一层. ②一套房间;〔*pl.*〕分宅公寓〔美国高级公寓叫 apartment house〕. ③(轮船的)平台,甲板. **-let**〔英〕小套间.

flat[2] [flæt] *a.* ***(~ter; ~test)*** ①平的,平坦的,扁平的. ②浅的. ③伸平的,平展的. ④(图画等)平板的;(颜色等)单调的,不鲜明的;【摄】无深浅反差的. ⑤意气消沉的,无精打采的;单调的,无聊的;〔美俚〕没有钱的,不名一文的. ⑥(啤酒等)走了气的. ⑦(市面)呆滞的,萧条的,不景气的;(价钱)无涨落的. ⑧淡然的;直率的,直截了当的. ⑨【乐】降音的,降音号的. ⑩【语】平舌的;浊音的,带声的 *(opp.* sharp*)*;【语法】无语尾变化的. ⑪(风帆)绷紧的. ⑫【军】(弹道等)低平的. *crops ~ after a storm* 暴风雨后庄稼倒伏. *knock ~* 把人打倒在地. *a ~ price* (各种商品)一样的价格. *a ~ rate of 3%* 一律百分之三. *feel ~* 感觉无聊. *a ~ lie* 弥天大谎. *The market is ~*. 市面萧条. *Prices are ~*. 物价平平. *a ~ denial [refusal]* 断然否认〔拒绝〕. ***become ~*** 泄气. ***lay a city ~*** 把城市夷为平地. ***That's ~***. 当然;绝对这样. — *ad.* ①匍匐地,平直地. ②完全地;断然地,干脆地,直截了当地. ③恰恰,正好. ④【金融】无(利)息地; *tell sb. ~* 明白地告诉某人. *~ and plain* 简单明了,直截了当. *ten dollars ~* 拾元正. *~ aback* 吓了一跳. *the bond are sold ~* 公债无息出售. ***be ~ broke*** 完全破产. ***fall ~*** 跌倒;完全失败;全无效果,全无好评 (*fall ~ on the audience* 毫不动人). — *n.* ①平面;平面图;坪,平地;浅滩,低湿平地. ②平坦部分;扁平的东西;平底船;平底篮. ③〔俚〕(容易受骗的)傻子,蠢汉;泄气轮胎. ④【乐】降半音,降音号 [♭];【建】平顶;【机】台面;【剧】背景屏. ***(draw) from the ~*** 按照图样(描摹) (*opp. from the round* 按照实物). ***in the ~*** 在纸上;平面图的 *(opp.* in the round, in relief*)*. ***join the ~s*** 使(故事等)首尾呼应;装出始终如一的样子. ***on the ~*** = in the ~. — *vt.* ①使平;使降音. ②使(图画等)平淡. ③〔美〕丢弃(恋人). — *vi.* ①变平,变平淡. ②【乐】降音. ~ ***out***〔美〕渐薄;打错主意,终无结果,虎头蛇尾. ~**bed**, ~**-bed** ①*a.* 平板卡车(拖车等)的;【印】平面印刷机的. ② *n.* 平板卡车(拖车等);平面印刷机. ~**boat** (浅水)平底船. ~**-bottomed** *a.* 平底的. ~**car**〔美〕(无盖平板)货车. ~ **file** 扁锉. ~**fish** 比目鱼,平鱼,鲽鱼. ~**foot** ① *(pl. ~feet)* 平底脚. ② *(pl. ~foots)* 警察. ~**-footed** ① *a.* 平底脚的;拖着脚步走的;站稳脚跟的;果断的,无准备的. ② *ad.* 直截了当地,决意地 (*come out ~-footed*〔美俚〕打开窗子说亮话). ~**-hat** *vi.*【航】贴地飞行,不顾死活地低飞. ~**head** ①〔美俚〕傻子,无知识的人. ②(铆钉等的)扁平头. **F-head** 北美印第安人. ~**iron** 熨斗. ~ **knot** 旋圆两角结,缩帆结,平结 (= reef knot). ~**ling(s)** *ad.*

〔废、英方〕①直挺挺地．②以(刀剑等的)扁平面打击．~**long** *a.*〔废〕用(刀剑的)扁平面打击．(*a ~long blow* 用刀剑的扁平面给予的一击．) ~**-out** *a.* ①以最快速度的，以最大努力的．②十足的，不折不扣的．~ **pad**〔美口〕固定的导弹发射平台．~ **race** (无障碍物的)平地赛跑．~**-riser** 垂直起飞飞机．~**-roofed** *a.* (建筑物等)平顶的．~ **silver**〔美〕银质餐具．~ **spin** ①(飞机的)水平螺旋．②〔美俚〕精神错乱．~ **tire** 已爆破的车胎；〔美〕不中用的人，不善交际的人．~**top** ①平顶建筑物．②〔美俚〕航空母舰．~**ware** 盘碟类，银质餐具．~**ways** *ad.* 平面向下，平面与另一物接触着．~**woods** 地势平坦低洼处的树木．~**work** 通常用机械方法熨烫的毛巾、床单、衣服等．~**worm** 扁虫，扁平无环节的寄生虫．~**wise** *ad.* = ~ways.

flat·ly [ˈflætli] *ad.* ①水平地；平伏地，匍匐地．②平淡地，单调地．③断然地，直截了当地．*refuse* ~ 断然拒绝．

flat·ness [ˈflætnis] *n.* ①平坦，平滑．②直率，果断．③无变化，单调．④(音的)低沉；(市况的)萧条．

flat·ten [ˈflætn] *vt.* ①使平，弄平．②使倒伏．③【乐】使低半音．④使无光泽．⑤【拳】打倒．~ *one's opponent* 打倒对手．— *vi.* ①变平．②倒伏．③变单调；变呆板．④【乐】低半音．~ *out* ①打平，辗平．②变平；【空】取水平姿式．

flat·ten·er [ˈflætnə] *n.*【冶】压延工，压延机．

flat·ten·ing [ˈflætəniŋ] *n.* 整平，扁率．~ *oven*【化】平板(玻璃)炉．

flat·ter[1] [ˈflætə] *vt.* ①奉承，谄媚，阿谀．②使满意，使高兴．③(画像等的形象)美于(真人[实物])．*Oh, you ~ me.* 啊！你恭维我了．*His portrait ~s him.* 他的像画得比他本人漂亮．*The music ~ed his ears.* 音乐使他听得满意．***feel oneself's highly ~ed*** 得意洋洋．***~ oneself that*** 自以为，对自己(某方面)估价过高 (*She ~-ed herself (that) she might win the prize.* 她自以为会获奖)．

flat·ter[2] [ˈflætə] *n.* ①【机】平面锤；压平机，拉扁钢丝模，扁条拉模，扁平槽．②敲平的人．

flat·ter·er [ˈflætərə] *n.* 奉承[拍马]的人．*When ~s meet, the devil goes to dinner.*〔谚〕马屁精聚会的时候，魔鬼就无事可做了〔指吹牛拍马，使人丧失理智，必然产生恶果，就连魔鬼也不能干出更坏的事情来，因而赴宴去了〕．

flat·ter·ing [ˈflætəriŋ] *a.* ①谄媚的，讨好的，奉承的．②讨人欢喜的．③(画像等)比本人[实物]好看的．~ *prospects* 有希望的前途．*a ~ review* 捧场性的书评．*a ~ tongue* 甜嘴蜜舌．**-ly** *ad.*

flat·ter·y [ˈflætəri] *n.* ①谄媚，恭维，巴结．②恭维话，谄媚的举动．***be proof against*** ~ 不为阿谀所动．***be hood-winked by*** ~ 被捧得昏头昏脑．

flat·tie, flatty [ˈflæti] *n.* ①平的东西．②平跟[无跟](拖)鞋．③美国东部的平底船．④〔美俚〕警察．⑤〔美俚〕无立体感的老式电影．

flat·tish [ˈflætiʃ] *a.* ①稍平的．②有点单调[呆板]的．

flat·u·lence [ˈflætjuləns], **flat·u·len·cy** [-si] *n.* ①【医】肠胃气胀．②浮夸；空谈，吹嘘；自负．

flat·u·lent [ˈflætjulənt], **flat·u·ous** [ˈflætjuləs] *a.* ①肠胃气胀的．②(食物)能使肠胃气胀的．③浮夸的，空谈的，吹嘘的；自负的．**-ly** *ad.*

fla·tus [ˈfleitəs] *n.* ①气息；一阵风．②肠胃气．

Flau·bert [flouˈbɛr], **Gustave** 福楼拜〔1821—1880，法国小说家〕．

flaunt [flɔːnt] *vt.* ①(耀武扬威地)挥舞(旗帜等)．②宣扬，夸示，标榜．③〔美〕藐视．— *vi.* ①(旗等)飘扬，招展．②招摇，夸耀．— *n.* ①飘扬，招展．②夸示，夸耀；招摇．

flaunt·ing [ˈflɔːntiŋ] *a.* 招摇的，夸耀的，扬扬得意的．**-ly** *ad.*

flaunt·y [ˈflɔːnti] *a.* = flaunting.

flau·tist [ˈflɔːtist] *n.* = flutist.

fla·va·none [ˈfleivənəun, ˈflævə-] *n.*【化】黄烷酮(衍生物)．

fla·ves·cent [fləˈvesnt] *a.* 变成黄色的，带黄色的．

fla·vin(e) [ˈfleivin, ˈflæ-] *n.* ①【生化】(核)黄素．②【化】栎(黄)素染料；吖啶黄素．

fla·vone [ˈfleivəun, ˈflævəun] *n.*【化】黄酮(衍生物)．

fla·vo·nol [ˈfleivənɔl] *n.*【化】黄酮醇(衍生物)．

fla·vo·pro·tein [ˌfleivəuˈprəutiːn] *n.*【化】黄素蛋白，黄色酵素．

fla·vo·pur·pu·rin [ˌfleivəuˈpəːpərin] *n.*【化】黄红紫，煤染三号茜素红．

fla·vo(u)r [ˈfleivə] *n.* ①味，滋味．②风味，情趣，风趣．③〔古〕香味，气味．*give a ~ to* 加风味，使有风味．— *vt.* ①给…添风味[添情趣，添风趣]．②给…增加香气，给…调味．~ *the cake with chocolate* 在蛋糕里加巧克力提味．**-ed** *a.* ①提味的．②风味…的 (*chocolate-~ed cake* 有巧克力味道的蛋糕)．**-ing** *n.* 调味；佐料，调味料，香料．**-less** *a.* 无味的；无风趣的．**-ous** *a.* 味浓的；有香味的；有风趣的．

flaw[1] [flɔː] *n.* ①裂缝．②瑕疵，缺点．③(使证件等因而失效的)缺陷．*a ~ in an otherwise perfect character* 白璧之瑕，美德中仅有的缺点．— *vt., vi.* ①(使)生裂缝，(使)有裂纹．②(使)(证件等)因有缺陷而失效．~ **detector** 探伤仪．**-ed** *a.* 有裂纹的；有瑕疵的；有缺陷的．

flaw[2] [flɔː] *n.* 一阵狂风；短暂的风暴．

flaw·less [flɔːlis] *a.* 无裂隙的，无瑕疵的，完美无缺的．**-ly** *ad.* **-ness** *n.*

flax [flæks] *n.* ①【植】亚麻；亚麻皮，亚麻纤维．②亚麻布．③象亚麻的植物．***quench smoking*** ~ 使有希望的事夭折〔flax 的原意是烛芯，这个短语的意思是使火光熄灭了〕．~ **brake,** ~ **breaker** 剥麻机，亚麻碎茎机．~**seed** 亚麻籽[仁]．

flax·en [ˈflæksən] *a.* 亚麻的，亚麻制的；亚麻[淡黄]色的．~ *hair* 浅黄色的头发．

Flax·man [ˈflæksmən] *n.* 弗拉克斯曼〔姓氏〕．

flax·y [ˈflæksi] *a.* 亚麻的，似亚麻的；淡黄色的．

flay [flei] *vt.* ①剥…的皮．②抢夺，掠夺．③严厉批评．~ ***a flint*** 极吝啬，一钱如命．~**flint**〔古〕吝啬鬼，敲诈者．**-er** *n.* 剥皮者；抢劫者；痛责者．

flea [fliː] *n.* 跳蚤．①蚤目的昆虫．②(伤害植物叶、芽的)叶甲科的昆虫(= flea-beetle)．*a sand ~* 沙蚤．*a water ~* 水蚤．***a ~ in one's [the] ear*** 刺耳话，讥讽．***send sb. away with a ~ in his ear*** 用讥讽话气走某人．***skin a ~ for its hide*** 贪得无厌，爱财如命．~**bag**〔美俚〕①睡袋(= sleeping bag)；床铺．②〔美俚〕跳蚤窝〔条件很差的低廉旅馆〕．③生蚤的动物．④邋遢的老妇人．~**bane**【植】飞蓬(属)．~ **beetle** 叶甲科甲虫．~**-borne** *a.* 蚤传播的．~ **circus** (受过训练的)跳蚤杂技表演〔西方狂欢节的助兴节目之一〕．~ **collar** (围在家畜颈上而内藏灭蚤药的)杀蚤圈．~**hopper**【动】跳盲蝽〔棉作物害虫〕．~ **market** 欧洲街道上的廉价品和旧货市场．~**-pit**〔俚〕被认为有跳蚤或臭虫等的场所(如小旅店、电影院等)．~**wort**【植】①欧洲桂根旋复花．②欧洲亚麻子车前．

flea·bite [ˈfliːbait] *n.* ①蚤咬，蚤咬的疱痕．②小痛痒；小麻烦；少量的花费．③(白马的)小褐斑．*The cost is a mere ~.* 这点费用算不了什么．*Your misfortune is but a ~ to mine.* 和我比起来，你的不幸不值一提．

flea-bit·ten [ˈfliːbitn] *a.* ①被蚤咬的；生蚤的．②(马等)有红棕色斑点的．

fleam [fliːm] *n.* ①(兽医用的)放血针，刺血针；【医】静脉切开刀．②锯齿口和锯条面所成的角．

flèche [fleiʃ] *n.*〔F.〕①【筑城】凸角堡．②【建】(哥特式教堂的)尖顶塔．

fleck [flek] *n.* ①(皮肤上的)斑，雀斑．②(色、光的)斑纹，斑点．③微粒，小片．— *vt.* 使起斑点．*a sky ~ed with* *clouds* 白云朵朵的天空. **-less** *a.* 无斑点的,无缺点的. **-y** *a.* 斑纹点点的.

fleck·er [ˈflekə] *vt.* = fleck.

flec·tion [ˈflekʃən] *n.* 〔美〕= flexion. **-al** *a.* **-less** *a.*

fled [fled] flee 的过去式及过去分词.

fledge [fledʒ] *vt.* ①把(小鸟)喂养到长羽毛. ②用羽毛盖上;在…上装上羽毛. ~ *an arrow* 在箭上装羽毛. — *vi.* (小鸟)长羽,(幼虫)长翅. — *a.* 羽毛丰满的,能飞的. **-d** *a.* 羽毛丰满的;快会飞的. **-less** *a.* 还没有生羽毛的.

fledg(e)·ling [ˈfledʒliŋ] *n.* 羽毛未丰的小鸟;乳臭小儿. ~ *poets* 初出茅庐的诗人.

flee [fliː] *vi.* *(fled* [fled]; *fled)* ①逃走 *(from; before)*; 逃避,逃出 *(from)*. ②消失,消散. ~ *from temptation* 避免诱惑. *Life had [was] fled.* 死亡,断气. — *vt.* 避开,逃避. ~ *the dangerous place* 逃离险地. ~ *the presence of one's teacher* 避开老师. *F- temptation!* 避开诱惑!

fleece [fliːs] *n.* ①羊毛. ②一只羊一次所剪的毛. ③羊毛状物〔如白云、白雪、蓬发等〕. ④【纺】绒头织物,长毛大衣呢,粗梳回丝. ~ *fabric* 起绒织物. ***the Golden F-*** 【希神】金羊毛〔cf. Argo 条〕. ***(the Order of) the Golden F-*** 金羊毛勋章〔旧时奥地利、西班牙的最高勋章〕. — *vt.* ①剪(羊)毛. ②诈取. ③(羊毛般)盖满,装饰. ~ *sb. of all he possesses* 骗取某人全部所有. *a sky ~d with white clouds* 白云如絮的天空. **-able** *a.* ①可以剪取的. ②易受欺骗的. **-d** *a.* 【纺】(针织物)布面起绒的.

fleec·y [ˈfliːsi] *a.* *(fleec·i·er; -i·est)* 羊毛质的;羊毛似的;披盖有羊毛的. ~ *clouds* 如絮的白云. **-i·ly** *ad.* **-i·ness** *n.*

fleer[1] [fliə] *vi.* 〔方〕露牙微笑,作鬼脸表示轻蔑 *(at)*. — *vt.* 嘲笑. — *n.* 嘲笑,挖苦的言语[表情].

fle·er[2] [ˈfliːə] *n.* 逃走者.

fleet[1] [fliːt] *n.* ①舰队. ②船队;(飞机的)机队;(汽车、战车等的)车队. ③〔the ~〕海军兵力;海军. ④〔英〕连成一排的捕鱼网(具);有一百只钩子的钓索. *a combined ~* 联合舰队. *a ~ in being* 现有舰队. *a ~ of airplanes = an air [aerial] ~* 【军】大机群. *a ~ of trucks [taxis]* 卡车队〔出租汽车队〕〔指某一单位的全部车辆〕. ***Admiral of the F-*** 〔英〕海军元帅. **F- Admiral** 〔美〕海军五星上将;〔英〕海军总司令. ~ **air arm** 海军航空兵部队. ~ **base** 舰队基地. ~ **captain** 〔英〕舰队参谋长. ~ **engagement** 舰队战斗. ~ **fighter** 海军战斗机. ~**-owned** *a.* (出租汽车等)由公司拥有和经营的.

fleet[2] [fliːt] *vi.* ①疾飞,掠过. ②【海】(船员)变换位置. ③〔古〕(时间)飞逝. — *vt.* ①消磨(时间). ②【海】变换(位置). ③放下(绞盘的索、缆等). ~ *aft the crew* 把船员调到船尾.

fleet[3] [fliːt] *a.* ①〔诗、书〕快速的,敏捷的. ②短暂的,转瞬即逝的. *be ~ of foot* 腿快. ~**-foot(ed)** *a.* 走路快的,快腿的. **-ly** *ad.* **-ness** *n.*

fleet[4] [fliːt] *a.* 浅的. *a ~ soil* 浅土, 薄土. — *ad.* 浅,不深地. *plow ~* 浅耕. *sow ~* 浅种.

fleet[5] [fliːt] *n.* 〔英方〕①小湾;小河. ②〔the F-〕(伦敦)弗利特河. **F- marriage** 在弗利特河一带由名誉极坏的教士主持的秘密结婚. **F- Street** (伦敦报馆集中的)伦敦弗利特街;(英国)伦敦新闻界;新闻记者〔这条街因河而得名,一般误译为"舰队街"〕. **F- Streeter** 伦敦新闻界人士.

fleet·ing [ˈfliːtiŋ] *a.* 飞逝的,短暂的,飞跑的. ~ **target** 【军】瞬间目标. **-ly** *ad.* **-ness** *n.*

Fleet·wood [ˈfliːt-wud] *n.* 弗利特伍德〔姓氏〕.

Flem. = Flemish.

Flem·ing [ˈflemiŋ] *n.* 佛兰德人.

Flem·ish [ˈflemiʃ] *n., a.* 佛兰德(的);佛兰德人(的);佛兰德语(的). ~ **bond** 【建】荷兰式砌合. ~ **brick** 镶路硬砖. ~ **coil** 【海】平放在甲板上类似蒲团的绳圈. ~ **knot** 水手常用的"8"字形绳结.

flench [flentʃ], **flense** [flens] *vt.* 剥鲸鱼或海豹的皮,取鲸鱼或海豹的油.

flesh [fleʃ] *n.* ①肉; 肉食〔现多说 meat〕;(和鱼肉 fish、鸟肉 fowl 区别说的)兽肉. ②肉体; 肌肤. ③肉欲, 情欲;人性;人情. ④血肉之躯,肉身. ⑤果肉;菜蔬的鲜嫩部分. ⑥肉色,⑦亲属;亲骨肉〔主要用于短语中〕;众生,一切生物. *the pleasures of the ~* 肉体的快乐. ***after the ~*** 照凡人地,世俗地,粗鄙地. ***all ~*** 众生;人类. ***be made one ~ = become one ~*** 成为一体,结为夫妇. ~ ***and blood*** ①血肉;肉体;人性;人类. ②〔作定语用〕现世的,现实的. ~ ***and fell*** 全身; 完全地. ***gain ~ =*** make ~. ***go the way of all ~*** 逝世,死亡. ***grow in ~*** 发胖. ***in ~*** 肥胖的. ***in the ~*** ①以肉体形式;活着的. ②亲身,本人. ***live on ~*** 以肉食为主. ***lose ~*** 变瘦,消瘦. ***make ~*** 长肉,发胖. ***make sb.'s ~ creep*** 使人战慄,令人毛骨悚然. ***one's (own) ~ and blood*** 亲骨肉,亲属. ***pick up ~*** 病愈后长胖. ***proud ~*** 【医】浮肉,赘肉. ***put on ~ =*** make ~. ***the arm of ~*** 人力,人的努力. — *vt.* ①用肉喂养(猎狗等); 使尽量吃肉. ②使(猎狗等)闻到肉味. ③使 (兵士等) 惯于血战. ④使长肉,使发胖 *(up)*. 〔喻〕赋予…以血肉,使形象生动. ⑤(制革)刮去(皮上)的肉. ⑥〔古〕使满足. — *vi.* 〔口〕长肉,发胖. ~**-and-blood** *a.* 血肉般的;确有其人的,真实的. ~**-colo(u)red** *a.* 肉色的. ~**-eater** 食肉者,食肉动物. ~**-eating,** ~**-feeding** *a.* 食肉的. ~ **fly** 麻蝇. ~ **peddler** 〔美俚〕戏院的代理人. ~**pot** 肉锅;〔*pl.*〕丰盛的饮食[物质生活],奢侈的生活,寻欢作乐的场所 *(= the ~ pots of Egypt)*. ~**-printing** 鱼肉印象法〔电子追踪或记录鱼肉的蛋白质模式,用以进行辨别或研究〕. ~ **side** 兽皮贴肉的一面. ~ **tights** (演员穿的) 肉色紧身衣. ~**tint** 【绘】人体的肤色, 肉色. ~ **wound** 轻伤.

flesh·er [ˈfleʃə] *n.* ①皮革的刮肉人; 去肉工具. ②〔主 Scot.〕肉店,屠户.

flesh·i·ness [ˈfleʃinis] *n.* 多肉,肥胖.

flesh·ing [ˈfleʃiŋ] *n.* ①〔*pl.*〕(制革时) 刮肉. ②〔*pl.*〕(演员穿的)肉色紧身衣. ③(牲畜身上)肥肉和瘦肉的分布;长膘能力.

flesh·less [ˈfleʃlis] ①瘦弱的. ②无肉体的,非物质的.

flesh·ly [ˈfleʃli] *a.* *(-li·er; -li·est)* ①肉体的. ②肉欲的,肉感的, 刺激感官的. ③多肉的. ④尘世的. *the ~ envelope* 肉体,躯壳. **fresh·li·ness** *n.*

flesh·y [ˈfleʃi] *a.* *(flesh·i·er; -i·est)* ①肉的, 似肉的. ②多肉的,肥胖的. ③【植】肉质的. ~ *fruit* 肉果.

fletch [fletʃ] *vt.* 装上羽毛〔如装箭羽〕.

Fletch·er [ˈfletʃə] *n.* ①弗莱彻〔姓氏,男子名〕. ② **John ~** 约翰·弗莱彻〔1579—1625,英国剧作家〕. ③**John Gould ~** 约翰·古尔德·弗莱彻〔1886—1950 美国诗人〕.

Fletch·er·ism [ˈfletʃərizəm] *n.* 〔美〕细嚼进食健康论[法].

fleur-de-lis [ˌfləːdəˈliː, -ˈliːs] *n.* *(pl.* ***fleurs-de-lis*** [-lis, -liːz], ***-li'ses*** [-ˈliːsiz]*)* ①【植】鸢尾. ②艺术上的鸢尾花形,鸢尾〔百合〕花形纹章. ③法国王室纹章 (= fleur-de-lys).

fleur·et [ˈfluərit] *n.* ①小花形装饰. ②小剑;(击剑比赛用尖端为一小球的)钝头剑.

fleu·ry [ˈfluəri] *a.* 饰以鸢尾花徽记的.

flew [fluː] fly[1] 的过去式.

flews [fluːz] *n. pl.* (猎犬等的)上唇两旁的下垂部分.

flex [fleks] *vt., vi.* ①弯曲 (关节). ②折曲 (地层). ~ ***one's muscles*** 〔美俚〕显示力量. — *n.* ①弯曲,折曲. ②〔主英〕【电】花线,皮线.

flex. = flexible.

flex·i·bil·ity [ˌfleksəˈbiliti] *n.* ①揉屈性, 挠性,柔(韧)性. ②机动性,灵活性. ③弹形,塑性;(光的)折射性.

flex·i·ble [ˈfleksəbl] *a.* ①易弯的,挠性的. ②柔韧的;柔

顺的. ③灵活的. ～ **(lamp) cord**【电】花线,皮线. ～ **coupling**【机】弹性联轴节,活动耦合. ～ **pressure** 流体压力. ～ **rule** 软尺, 卷尺. ～ **tube** 挠性管. **flexibly** *ad.*

flex·ile [ˈfleksail] *a.* = flexible.

flex·ion [ˈflekʃən] *n.* ①弯曲; 弯曲部; 弯曲度. ②【语法】曲折, 词尾变化. **-al** *a.* 可弯曲的;【语法】屈折的, 词尾可变化的. **-less** *a.*

flex·o·me·ter [flekˈsɔmitə] *n.* 挠度计, 曲率计.

flex·or [ˈfleksə] *n.*【解】屈肌 *(opp.* extensor).

flex·time [ˈflekstaim] *n.* (职工)自定时间上班制.

flex·u·ose [ˈflekjuəus], **flex·u·ous** [ˈflekjuəs] *a.* ①弯曲的. ②动摇不定的. ③【植】锯齿状的, 波状的.

flex·u·os·i·ty [ˌflekjuˈɔsiti] *n.* 屈曲, 弯曲.

flex·ure [ˈflekʃə] *n.* ①屈曲, 挠曲, 弯曲(部). ②折褶. ③【数】歪度. ④【物】弯曲, 曲率. ⑤【地】单斜挠曲. ～ **coast**【地】单褶海岸.

flib·ber·ti·gib·bet [ˈflibətiˈdʒibit] *n.* ①轻浮、不负责任的人. ②爱散布流言蜚语的人.

flick[1] [flik] *n.* ①(用鞭子)轻打; (用手指)轻弹; (用手帕等)轻拂. ②(击球时手腕等)抽动. ③轻弹声. ④(溅着的)污点. *a ～ of the whip* 鞭子的轻轻一挥. —*vt.* ①轻轻鞭打. ②弹掉 *(away)*. ③轻轻拂去(尘灰) *(off)*. ～ *the dust from one's shoes* 从鞋子上轻轻拂去灰尘. —*vi.* ①轻击, 轻拂, 轻弹. ②(翅)拍动; (旗)飘扬. ～ **knife** 弹簧折刀 (= switch-blade knife).

flick[2] [flik] *n.* 〔英俚〕〔常 *pl.*〕①电影〔*cf.* flicker[1]〕. ②【军】照见(指探照灯照见空中飞机); 照见瞬间; (口令)集中照射.

flick·er[1] [ˈflikə] *n.* ①闪烁, 摇; 忽隐忽现; 扑动. ②〔美俚〕假装昏倒的乞丐. ③〔*pl.*〕〔美俚〕电影. ④〔～s〕〔美俚〕电影制片业. —*vi.* ①明灭不定, 闪烁; 闪变. ②(旗等)飘扬, (树叶等)摆动. ③〔美俚〕昏倒, 假装昏倒. *The fire ～s low.* 炉火颤动欲灭. —*vt.* 使闪烁; 使颤动.

flick·er[2] [ˈflikə] *n.* 〔美〕金翼啄木鸟.

flick·er·ing [ˈflikəriŋ] *a.* 扑动的; 闪烁的, 摇曳的, 忽隐忽现的. **-ly** *ad.*

Flick·er·tail State [ˈflikəˌteil] 〔美〕北达科他州〔别号〕.

flick·er·y [ˈflikəri] *a.* 忽明忽灭的, 不稳定的.

flied [flaid] 〔美〕fly 的过去式及过去分词.

fli·er [ˈflaiə] *n.* = flyer.

flight[1] [flait] *n.* ①飞行, 飞翔; (鹰对猎获物的)追赶. ②(候鸟等的)迁徙; 飞行的一群. ③(光阴)飞逝. ④(思想等的)飞跃, 奔放, (才智等的)焕发. ⑤航程, 飞行距离; 飞翔力; 定期客机, 班机; 搭机航行. ⑥(阶梯的)一段, 楼梯;【体】(跳栏的)一组跨栏; (箭等的)连发, 齐发. ⑦射远竞赛. ⑧飞行小队. *air patrol* ～ 空中巡逻飞行. *circular [circuitous]* ～ 回旋飞行, 圆圈飞行. *cosmic [space]* ～ 宇宙飞行. *dipping* ～ 俯冲飞行. *horizontal [level]* ～ 水平飞行. *interplanetary [interstellar]* ～ 星际航行. *inverted* ～倒飞. *long-distance* ～ 长距离飞行. *manned space* ～ 载人宇宙飞行。*night [nocturnal]* ～ 夜间飞行. *nonstop* ～ 不着陆飞行. *round-the-world* ～ 环球飞行. *soaring* ～ 滑翔飞行. *trick* ～ 特技飞行. *a ～ of swallows* 一群飞燕. ***a ～ of ambition*** 野心勃勃. ***a ～ of fancy*** 奇想, 想入非非. ***in the first*** ～〔口〕占首位; 领先. ***make [take] a*** ～ 飞行; 飞翔. ***a ～ of stairs*** 一段楼梯. ***the ～ of time*** 光阴流逝, 时光荏苒. ***wing a [one's]*** ～ 飞行. —*vt.* ①射击(飞鸟); 使(鸟)惊起. —*vi.* (鸟) 成群飞翔; (候鸟)迁徙. ～ **arrow** 远箭. ～ **bag** 航空手提包; 印有航空公司名字的帆布旅行袋. ～ **chart** 航空地图. ～ **commander** 〔英〕空军中校. ～ **control** ①(地面对飞机的) 飞行指挥, 飞行控制. ②地面飞行指挥站. ～ **course** 航线. ～ **crew** 〔集合词〕飞行人员. ～ **deck** (航空母舰上的)飞行甲板; 若干飞机内的仪器舱. ～**deliver** *vt.* 把(飞机) 直接从飞机从制造厂驾驶送往战地机场. ～ **engineer**【航】机上机械员. ～ **feather** (鸟翼的) 拨风羽. ～ **formation** ①飞行编队. ②空军小队. ～ **indicator** 陀螺地平仪. ～**leader**【航】飞行队队长; 编队长; 分队长. ～ **lieutenant** 〔英〕空军上尉. ～ **line** ①(机场的) 飞机保养场. ②飞行路线. ～ **log** 飞行记录簿. ～ **map** 航空照像用地图. ～ **nurse** 机上护士. ～ **officer** 〔美〕空军军官. ～ **path** (飞机、导弹等的)飞行经路, 航迹. ～ **pay [skins]** 飞行津贴. ～ **personnel** 〔集合词〕飞行人员. ～ **recorder** 飞行自动记录仪. ～ **refuel(l)ing** 空中加油. ～ **route** 飞行路线. ～ **sergeant** 〔英〕空军上士. ～ **shooting** (射箭的)射远比赛. ～ **simulator** (地面上训练飞行人员的)飞行摹拟装置. ～ **status** 飞行资格. ～ **strip** 着陆场, 简便机场. ～ **surgeon** 航空军医, 空军医生. ～**-test** *vt.* 对(飞机) 进行飞行试验, 试飞. ～ **time** 飞行时间, 开始飞行的时间. ～ **worthy** *a.* 能够飞行的; 可在航空飞行中使用的. **-less** *a.* 不能飞行的.

flight[2] [flait] *n.* ①溃逃, 逃走. ②(资金等的) 外逃. ～ *of capital* 资金外流. ***put [turn] to*** ～ 迫使溃逃. ***seek safety in*** ～ 溜之大吉. ***take (to)*** ～ = ***betake oneself to*** ～ 逃之夭夭. ～**ism** 逃跑主义.

flight·y [ˈflaiti] *a.* ①好作奇想的; 反复无常的; 轻浮的; 不负责任的; 不认真的. ②有些疯癫的; 愚蠢的; 发痴的. **-i·ly** *ad.* **-i·ness** *n.*

flim·flam [ˈflimflæm] *n.* 〔口〕①诡计, 欺诈, 欺骗. ②呓语, 梦话, 胡言乱语. —*vt.* 〔口〕欺骗, 欺诈. —*a.* ①欺诈的. ②胡言乱语的.

flim·flam·mer [ˈflimflæmə] *n.* 〔口〕骗子.

flim·sy [ˈflimzi] *a.* ***(-si·er; -si·est)*** ①薄的, 薄弱的. ②浮夸的. ③没有价值的, 不足取的. *a ～ excuse* 站不住脚的辩解. —*n.* ①薄纸. ②(新闻记者用的) 薄纸原稿. ③〔俚〕钞票. ④电报. **-si·ly** *ad.* **-si·ness** *n.*

flinch[1] [flintʃ] *vi.* 退缩, 畏缩 *(from)*. —*n.* 退缩, 畏缩.

flinch[2] [flintʃ] *v.* = flense.

flin·ders [ˈflindəz] *n.* 〔*pl.*〕破片, 碎片. *break [fly] into ～s* 破碎.

fling [fliŋ] *vt.* ***(flung*** [flʌŋ]; ***flung)*** ①扔, 抛, 掷, 丢; 摔倒; 摔下 *(off)*. ②关进 *(into)*. ③急伸, 挥动. ④急派(军队等); 急送(武器). ⑤乱花(钱财等); 〔书〕发出. ⑥〔美俚〕尝试. —*vi.* ①猛冲, 突进; 突然走开 *(away; forth; off; out)*. ②骂, 嘲笑. ③(马)暴跳 *(about; out)*. ～ ***about*** 跳来跳去; 抛散. ～ ***aside*** 丢弃. ～ ***away*** 抛弃; 愤然离开; 跳出; 浪费; 放过(机会等). ～ ***caution to the wind*** 鲁莽, 轻率. ～ ***down*** 摔倒, 打倒. ～ ***sth. in sb.'s teeth*** 当面斥责. ～ ***off*** 甩掉; 逃脱; 冲出; 挫败. ～ ***one's arms about*** 左右上下挥动双臂. ～ ***one's clothes on*** = ～ ***oneself into one's clothes*** 匆匆披上衣服. ～ ***oneself about in one's anger*** 气得暴跳如雷. ～ ***oneself into*** 跳进; 一屁股坐进; 投身. ～ ***oneself on [upon] sb.'s mercy*** 完全听任别人处置. ～ ***out*** 投出; 冲出; 粗声大气地骂; (马) 又踢又跳. ～ ***over*** 〔俚〕离弃. ～ ***the door open*** 猛然把门推开. ～ ***to the four winds*** 抛到九霄云外, 不再考虑. ～ ***up*** 抛弃, 放弃. —*n.* ①扔, 掷, 抛; (马的) 跳, 踢. ②谩骂, 讽刺, 攻击. ③跳舞. ④〔美俚〕尝试. ⑤放肆, 放纵. *the Highland ～* 苏格兰舞. ***at one*** ～ 一下子, 一气, 一举. ***have a ～ at sb.*** 挖苦某人. ***have a ～ at sth.*** 试图做某事. ***have one's*** ～ 花天酒地, 尽情放荡. ***in full*** ～ 莽撞地, 猛然地; 猛(跑).

Flint [flint] *n.* 弗林特〔姓氏〕.

flint [flint] *n.* ①燧石, 打火石. ②坚硬的东西. *a ～ and steel* 打火用具. *a heart of ～* 冷酷的心, 铁石心肠. ***fix sb.'s ～ for him*** 惩罚某人. ***get one's ～s fixed*** 〔美〕受处分. ***get [wring] water from a*** ～ 缘木求鱼. ***old*** ～ 老吝啬鬼. ***set one's face like a*** ～ 打定主意, 坚决不变. ***skin [flay] a*** ～ 贪鄙, 一钱如命. ～ **corn**【植】硬粒玉米〔一种印第安种玉米, 粒极硬, 粒端不凹进

去〕. ～ **glass** 火石玻璃，氧化铅玻璃. ～**-hearted** *a.* 冷酷无情的. ～ **knapper** 燧石匠. ～**lock** 燧发机；燧发枪. ～**stone** 燧石，打火石. ～ **ware** 〔美〕石器.

flint·y [ˈflinti] *a.* ***(flint·i·er; -i·est)*** 燧石的；燧石似的；强硬的，坚硬的. *a ～ heart* 冷酷的心. **-i·ly** *ad.* **-i·ness** *n.*

flip[1] [flip] *vi.* ①用指头弹；轻轻打. ②(用鞭子等)抽. ③叭嗒叭嗒地动；翻动纸张. ④跳上车. ⑤起强烈反应. ⑥〔美俚〕失去自制力；入迷；精神失常，发疯. ～ *at an ass with a whip* 用鞭子抽驴子. — *vt.* ①用指轻弹，轻击. ②(用鞭)抽打；急速挥动(扇子等)；急拉(鱼饵). ③翻动(纸牌等). ④跳上(驶行中的车辆). ～ *the ash from one's cigarette* 弹去烟头上的灰. ～ ***the pigskin*** 〔美〕(足球)递球. ～ ***up*** 掷钱币(按正反面决定事). — *n.* ①抛，弹；轻打. ②〔口〕(短距离)飞行〔传球〕. ③筋斗. ～ **chip**【计】叩焊，(反装)晶片，倒装片(法). ～ **side** 〔美口〕(唱片的)背面〔尤指所录乐曲不大有名的一面〕；〔喻〕对等的人物.

flip[2] [flip] *n.* (加有香料的)饮料酒〔如啤酒、葡萄酒、苹果酒等〕.

flip[3] [flip] *a.* ***(flipper, flippest)*** 〔美俚〕 = flippant.

flip-flap [ˈflipfˌlæp] *n.* ①啪嗒啪嗒的响声. ②爆竹，烟火. ③触发器，触发电路. ④〔俚〕(向后翻而手足轮流触地的)后空筋斗. ⑤(游乐场内装有座椅的)旋转器〔电子飞船等〕.

flip-flop [ˈflipˌflɔp] *n.* ①(杂技的) 后空筋斗. ②(观点的) 突然大转变. ③啪嗒啪嗒的响声. ④【电】触发器；触发电路，双稳态多谐振荡器. — *vi.* ①翻后空筋斗. ②观点突然改变. ③啪嗒啪嗒作声. — *ad.* 发出啪嗒声地.

flip·pan·cy [ˈflipənsi] *n.* ①轻率，无礼. ②轻率无理的言语〔行动〕.

flip·pant [ˈflipənt] *a.* ①轻率的，无礼的. ②〔古〕能说会道的. **-ly** *ad.*

flip·per [ˈflipə] *n.* ①阔鳍，(海豹、海象等的)鳍状肢. ②〔俚〕手. ③(潜水时缚在脚上的)鸭脚板，橡皮脚掌.

flip·per·ty-flop·per·ty [ˈflipətiˈflɔpəti] *a.* 松弛下垂的，(帽子等)耷拉着的.

flirt [flɜːt] *vt.* ①用指弹起；忽然扔掉. ②摆动，挥动. — *vi.* ①摆动，飘动. ②调情 *(with)*；玩弄. ③不认真考虑，不严肃对待. — *n.* ①急投；摆动. ②调情的人，卖弄风情者.

flir·ta·tion [flɜːˈteiʃən] *n.* (男女之间的)挑逗，调情.

flir·ta·tious [flɜːˈteiʃəs] *a.* 爱调情的，轻佻的.

flit [flit] *vi.* ①迅速飞过，掠过，飞来飞去 *(about; by; to and fro)*；轻轻走过. ②死亡. ③迁移，离开；(悄悄)搬走. *make [take] moonlight flitting* (为躲债)乘夜搬走. ～ ***about*** 翱翔. ～ ***by [past]*** 迅速飞过. ～ ***to and fro*** 飞来飞去. — *n.* ①飞去；夜逃；偷偷搬家. ②〔美俚〕男子同性恋者. ～ **gun** 喷雾器.

flitch [flitʃ] *n.* ①腌猪肋肉. ②(熏制或供熏制用的)(大比目鱼)鱼块；鲸油脂块. ③【建】贴板，桁板. ④(木材的)背板，料板. ～ ***of Dunmow*** = ***Dunmow*** ～ 英国 Dunmow 地方赠给终年和睦的夫妇的腌猪肉. — *vt.* 把(鱼)切成块；把(木材)截成板. ～**ed beam**【建】合板梁.

flite [flait] *vi.* 〔Scot.〕争吵，相骂. — *n.* 争吵，相骂.

flit·ter [ˈflitə] *vi.* 飞来飞去，匆忙来往. — *n.* 一掠而过的人〔物〕；避债夜逃者 (= moonlight ～). ～**mouse** *(pl.* ～***mice)***【动】蝙蝠.

fliv·ver [ˈflivə] *n.* ①〔美俚〕廉价小汽车；〔谑〕一般汽车；小吨位驱逐舰，小飞机，海军小艇；不值钱的东西. ②失败，挫折. ③欺骗. — *vi.* ①失败，挫折. ②乘坐廉价小汽车〔飞机〕.

flix [fliks] *n.* 毛皮；海狸绒.

flk. = 〔美军〕flank.

float [fləut] *vi.* ①漂浮，浮起 *(opp.* sink)；飘动，漂流. ②(谣言等)散布. ③(公司)成立；(计划)实行. ④(票据)流通. ⑤(货币)浮动. ⑥在数处投票；漂荡；旅行. ⑦犹豫不决 *(between)*. ⑧悠者游哉地生活，对世事不关心，消遥度日. ～ *before one's eyes [mind]* 浮现眼前〔心中〕. ～ *through life* 优游岁月. — *vt.* ①使漂浮；使浮动；使漂流. ②淹没，以水注满. ③创立(公司)；实行(计划)；筹(款)；使(计划等)获得支持. ④发行(公债等). ⑤(泥水工)把(灰泥等)用镘刀摊平. ⑥散布(谣言). ⑦使(货币)浮动. ⑧使平滑. *a ship ～ed by the tide* 因长潮而浮起的船. ～ *a loan* 发行公债，筹集贷款. ～ *an issue of stock* 发行一批股票. ～ ***off*** (搁浅的船)浮起. — *n.* ①漂浮. ②浮游物；浮萍，浮冰；木筏，浮码头；浮船坞；浮筒；浮标；水箱浮球，救生圈；【机】浮体；(钓鱼用的)浮子；(鱼的)浮囊. ③(水车的)蹼板，承水板；(轮船的)轮翼. ④【空】(水上飞机的) 浮舟. ⑤(泥水工的) 镘刀，单纹锉刀. ⑥(装运展览物的)平台卡车；彩车；花车；活动模型. ⑦【经】(货币等的)浮动. ⑧〔常 *pl.*〕(舞台的)脚灯. ⑨(织物上的)浮丝，织疵，跳花. ⑩土地许可证. ⑪运煤车. ⑫〔英〕(店铺每晨开始营业时备用作找付等用的)周转零款. *a joint currency* ～ 货币共同浮动. ***on the*** ～ 漂浮着. ～**board** (水车的)蹼板，承水板；(轮船等的)轮翼. ～ **bridge** 浮桥；(铁路轮渡的)固定浮坞. ～ **finish**【建】镘修整，浮镘出面. ～ **grass** 水草. ～ **period** 〔美〕课间休息. ～**plane** 水上飞机，浮筒飞机. ～**stone** (磨砖用的)磨石；轻石，浮石. ～ **valve** 浮阀.

float·a·ble [ˈfləutəbl] *a.* ①能浮起的. ②(水道)可航行的，可飘送木排的. ③【矿】可浮选的.

float·age [ˈfləutidʒ] *n.* ①漂浮；浮力. ②漂浮物〔尤指从失事船只中漂出的破烂物〕. ③(船体的)浮出水面部分. ④对漂浮物的占有权. ⑤火车轮渡费.

float·a·tion [fləuˈteiʃən] *n.* ①漂浮；(船的) 下水. ②【矿】浮选(法). ③(公债等的) 发行；(公司等的)设立；创业；(计划的)实行. *the ～ of a loan* 筹资. *the centre of* ～ 浮体的重心. *oil* ～ 浮油选矿. ～ **balance** 浮力秤. ～ **oil** 浮选油.

float·er [ˈfləutə] *n.* ①漂浮者；漂浮物；〔美〕浮尸；浮子；浮标. ②〔口〕游民；〔美〕流动选民；流动工，临时工. ③(公司的)发起人；(债券等的)发行人. ④(公认为有可靠担保物的)流通证券. ⑤(运输货物的) 保险. ⑥镘工. ⑦(未决定投任何一方票的)浮动选民〔投票人〕(= floating voter). ⑨〔美俚〕(受雇)于同一次选举中在多处作非法投票的人. ⑩警察限令某人离开城镇的命令.

float·ing [ˈfləutiŋ] *a.* ①漂浮的，浮动的，流动性的. ②【医】游离的. ③移动的；不定的. ④(涂工的)第二道(漆等). ⑤(船货) 未到埠的，在海上的，在运输中的. ～ *address* 浮动地址，可变通信处. ～ *exchange rate* 浮动汇率. ～ *capital* 游资，流动资本. *a ～ debt* 流动债务，短期债务. ～ *money* 游资. *a ～ pier [stage]* 浮码头. *the ～ population* 流动人口. ～ *tool*【机】浮动工具. ～ *trade* 海上贸易. ～ **aerodrome** 水上飞机. ～ **algae**【植】浮游藻类. ～ **anchor** 浮锚，海锚. ～ **axle** 浮轴. ～ **barge** (海洋)钻井浮船. ～ **battery** ①浮动蓄电池；浮置〔浮充〕电池组. ②(设于船上或筏上的)流动炮台. ～ **body**【物】浮体. ～ **bridge** 浮桥；缆索渡船. ～ **cargo** 未到埠船货. ～ **crane** 水上起重机. ～ **decimal**【计】浮动小数点. ～ **(dry) dock** 浮(船)坞. ～ **island** ①浮岛；浮动花园；浮在水面上的大片植物. ②奶油和蛋白盖面的蛋糕. ～ **kidney**【医】浮游肾. ～ **light** 浮标灯；灯船；桅顶灯；夜间用救命浮标. ～**-point** *a.*【数】浮点的. ～ **policy** 总保险单，船名未详保险(证书)，预定保险(证书). ～ **rate** 浮动汇率. ～ **rib** 浮动肋骨. ～ **voter** = floater⑦.

floc [flɔk] *n.* ①(浮悬的)絮状物. ②棉丛；丛毛；棉屑；毛屑；棉绒；毛绒 (= flock).

floc·ci [ˈflɔksai] floccus 的复数.

floc·ci-nau·ci-ni·hi·li·pi·li·fi·ca·tion [ˌflɔksiˌnɔːsiˌnaihiliˌpailifiˈkeiʃən] *n.* 〔英谑〕(把什么都看得毫无

价值的)藐视一切的心理[行为、脾气].

floc·cose [ˈflɔkəus] *a.* 羊毛状的;【植】被丛卷毛的.

floc·cu·late [ˈflɔkjuleit] *vt., vi.* 絮凝, 絮结. — *n.* 絮凝物; 絮结体. **-la·tion** [ˌflɔkjuˈleiʃən] *n.* **-lator** *n.*

floc·cule [ˈflɔkjuːl] *n.* 絮状物; 絮凝粒, 絮状沉淀.

floc·cu·lence [ˈflɔkjuləns] *n.* ①丛毛状. ②羊毛状. ③絮凝性,絮结性.

floc·cu·lent [ˈflɔkjulənt] *a.* ①丛毛状的. ②羊毛状的. ③【动】丛毛的; 絮凝的,絮结的.

floc·cu·lus [ˈflɔkjuləs] *n.* 〔L.〕 *(pl.* ***-li*** *[-lai])* ①【解】(小脑的)绒球. ②绒毛,絮状物. ③【天】(太阳表面的)谱斑.

floc·cus [ˈflɔkəs] *n. (pl.* ***floc·ci*** *[ˈflɔksai])* 绒毛丛; 绒毛团;【气】絮状云;【植】丛卷毛.

flock[1] [flɔk] *n.* ①(禽、畜等的)群,羊群. ②人群; (对牧师而言的)教徒; (对父母而言的)子女; (对老师而言的)学生. ③大量, 众多. ~*s and herds* 牛群和羊群, 牛羊家畜. *a whole* ~ *of visitors* 一大群访问者. *a* ~ *of pamphlets* 一大堆小册子. ***come in*** ~***s*** 成群涌来, 纷至沓来. ~***s and herds*** 羊和牛,家畜. ***flower of the*** ~ 鹤立鸡群, 某一集体中出类拔萃的人物. ***fire into the wrong*** ~ 打错目标. ***It is a small*** ~ ***that has not a black sheep.*** = ***There is a black sheep in every*** ~. 〔谚〕人多必有败类. — *vi.* 聚集, 成群 *(together)*; 成群地去[来] *(about; after; into; to; in; out)*. *People* ~*ed to see her.* 人们成群结队地去看她. *Sheep usually* ~ *together.* 羊通常总是成群的. ~**master** 羊群牧主,牧群管理人.

flock[2] [flɔk] *n.* ①棉丛; 丛毛. ②棉屑; 毛屑. ③棉绒; 毛绒. — *vt.* 用毛[棉]屑装填; 在…处植绒. ~ **bed** 有毛[棉]屑垫子的床. ~**paper** (糊墙用的)毛面纸. ~**ing** *n.* 植绒花纹.

flock·y [ˈflɔki] *a.* 羊毛状的; 绒毛丛生的,毛茸茸的.

floe [fləu] *n.* 大片浮冰,浮冰块. ~ **berg** 冰山.

flog [flɔg] *vt.* ①鞭打; 鞭挞. ②(抽打似地)扔放(钓丝). ③驱使, 迫使. ④〔英俚〕非法出售. ⑤〔俚〕打败, 胜过. ⑥严厉批评. ~ *a horse along* 策马前进. ~ *laziness out of sb.* 驱策某人使不再懒惰. ~ *Latin into sb.* 使人强记拉丁文. ~ ***a dead horse*** 徒劳无益. ~ ***a willing horse*** (不必要地)强迫勤奋的人, 滥加驱使.

flog·ging [ˈflɔgiŋ] *n.* 鞭打,笞打.

flong [flɔŋ] *n.* 【印】作纸型用的纸版.

flood [flʌd] *n.* ①洪水,水灾. ②溢流, 涨水,潮水最高点; 泛滥, 汹涌. ③〔诗〕河,湖; 海. ④充溢, 丰富; 大量,一大阵,滔滔不绝. ⑤〔口〕泛光灯,探照灯(=~ light). *ebb and* ~ 低潮与高潮. *golden* ~ 一股阳光. ~*s of ink* 连篇累牍. ~*s of rain* 倾盆大雨. *a* ~ *of anger* 怒气的爆发, 大发雷霆. *a* ~ *of light* 一大片明亮的光线. *a* ~ *of tears* 泪如泉涌. *a* ~ *of words* 滔滔不绝; 洋洋数千言. ***the F-*** = ***Noah's*** ~【圣】(旧约创世纪中所载)诺亚 *(Noah)* 遭逢的大洪水. ***at the*** ~ 正当高潮; 在恰好时机. ~ ***and field*** 海陆. ***go through fire and*** ~ 赴汤蹈火. ***in*** ~ 洋溢,滔滔, 大量; 泛滥. ***take at the*** ~ 利用有利时机. ***throw a*** ~ ***of light on sth***. 充分阐明. — *vt.* ①淹没,使泛滥; 涨满(河床). ②用水浇灌,灌溉. ③涌到; 冲进. *Applicants* ~ *the office.* 申请者挤满办事处. ~*ed districts* 水灾区域. *be* ~*ed with letters* 信件象潮水般涌来. — *vi.* ①发大水,泛滥; (潮)涨. ②涌到 *(in)*. ③【医】患子宫出血,血崩. *Applicants* ~*ed in.* 申请者如潮水般涌来. ~ **control** 治洪, 防洪, 洪水调节〔如修理水闸、水库,河堤等〕. ~**gate** ①水门, 水闸门; 防洪闸门. ②(怒气等的) 制约. ③大量. ~ **level** 最高洪水位,洪水警戒线. ~**light** ① *n.* 泛光灯, 泛光照明,探照灯. ② *vt.* 泛光照明,用泛光[探照]灯照亮. ~-**lighting** 泛光照明. ~**lit** *a.* 泛光灯照耀的. ~**mark** 满潮线. ~ **plain** 泛滥平原; 涝原,漫滩. ~ **tide** 涨潮 *(opp.* ebb tide); 高峰. ~**water** 洪水. ~**way** 分洪河道. ~**wood** 〔美〕漂流木,浮木.

flood·ing [ˈflʌdiŋ] *n.* ①泛滥; 灌溉. ②充溢. ③【化】溢流; (分馏时的)液阻现象; (油漆干燥或加热时的)变色. ④【医】血崩; 产后出血. ~ **irrigation** 漫灌.

flood·om·e·ter [flʌˈdɔmitə] *n.* 潮洪水位测量仪.

floo·ey, floo·ie [ˈfluːi] *ad.* 〔常用 go 连用〕糟,不行(= blooey).

floor [flɔː, flɔə] *n.* ①地板,地面. ②(楼房的)层. ③(船底的)肋板. ④(海洋、山洞等的)底. ⑤议员席; 经纪人席. ⑥发言权,发言机会. ⑦表演场地. ⑧最低数值[限度] *(opp.* ceiling). *dirt* ~ (没有铺装的) 泥地面. *a dressing* ~ 整理车间. *a moulding* ~ 翻砂车间. *a naked* ~ 未铺地毯的地板. *the* ~ *of bridge* 桥面. *a competition* ~ 室内比赛场. *founding* ~ 造型工地. *a threshing* ~ 打谷场. *the basement* ~ 地下室. *the top* ~ 顶楼. *the first [second]* ~ 〔英〕二[三]楼; 〔美〕一[二]楼. *The Senate from New York has the* ~. 该纽约州参议员发言了. *a price* ~ 底价, 最低价格. ***get [be let] in on the ground*** ~ 〔美口〕在有利条件下参加某种事业; 站在同等地位获得同等权利. ***be on the*** ~ ①正在发言[讨论]中. ②【影】正在拍摄中. ***cross the*** ~ ***of the House*** 议员从一党派转变到另一党派. ***get [obtain] the*** ~ 获得发言权. ***give the*** ~ ***to*** 给予发言权. ***go on the*** ~【影】开始拍摄. ***have the*** ~ 有发言权. ***mop [wipe] the*** ~ ***with sb.*** 把某人打得大败. ***take the*** ~ 〔美〕起立发言; 参加讨论; 参加跳舞. — *vt.* ① 在…上铺地板[基面]. ②〔英〕罚…坐地板. ③打倒; 〔口〕打败, 难倒,使认输. ④〔英俚〕做完(考卷等). ⑤〔美口〕把…减到最低限度, 把 (汽车加速器等) 压到最低一档. ~ ***sb. with one blow*** 一拳把人打翻在地. ~ ***an examination paper*** = ~ ***the paper*** 圆满答完考卷. ***get*** ~***ed*** 被打败,被压服. ~**board** ①适合做地板用的木材. ②一块地板(常指可以掀起的活动地板). ③汽车底部板. ~ **broker** 交易所场内经纪人. ~**cloth** 铺地板的漆布; (揩地板的) 拖布. ~ **exercise** 自由体操,地面体操〔不用器械, 在地毯上表演各种芭蕾舞式动作以及翻筋斗, 用手倒立等〕. ~ **frame**【机】地轴承架. ~ **knob** (装在地板上的) 门碰头. ~ **lamp** 落地灯. ~ **leader** (议会的)政党头目. ~ **manager** ①〔美〕政党提名大会中候选人的助选员. ②百货大楼中分管一层楼面业务的经理. ~ **partner** (经纪行派驻在交易所中的)驻所经纪人. ~ **plan**【建】楼面布置图. ~ **price** 最低价,廉价. ~ **push** 闸刀开关. ~ **sheet** 踏板. ~ **show** (舞厅里的) 余兴表演. ~ **slab** (铺设水泥楼面、地面的)水泥板. ~ **space** 地板[楼面]面积; 设备占用面积. ~-**through** (占有大楼整个一层楼面的) 公寓住所. ~ **time** 空闲时间. ~ **trader** 交易所场内商人. ~**walker** 〔美〕(百货商店中的) 巡视员〔其职务为引导顾客,防备窃贼和监督店员等〕. (=〔英〕shop walker). ~ **wax** 地板蜡. -**less** 无地板的.

floor·age [ˈflɔːridʒ] *n.* ①地板 [楼面] 面积; 设备占用面积(= floor space). ②做地板的材料.

floor·er [ˈflɔːrə] *n.* ①铺地板者. ②把人打倒的一击; 使人沮丧的消息; 难以置辩的论据. ③难以解答的试卷,难题.

floor·ing [ˈflɔːriŋ] *n.* ①室内地面; 铺地板. ②铺地板的材料. ~ **block** 嵌木地板. ~ **saw** 企口锯〔锯条两边都有锯齿的手锯〕.

floo·sie, floo·sy, floo·zie, floo·zy [ˈfluːzi] *n.* 〔美俚〕行为不检点[名声不好]的妇女; 妓女.

flop [flɔp] *vi.* ①鼓翼; 扑拍,跳动. ②啪嗒躺下 [放下,坐下]; 〔美俚〕上床. ③突然转变. ④彻底失败. ~ *down on one's knees* 扑通一声跪下. ~ *into an armchair* 蓦地坐到扶手椅子里. — *vt.* 啪啪地翻动; 噗地一声放下. ~ *the pages of a book* 啪啪作响地翻书页. — *ad.* 噗地一声, 恰巧. *fall* ~ *into the water* 噗通一声落到水里. *fall* ~ *on one's face* 噗地一声向前扑倒. — *n.* ① 扑通

(声)；啪嗒(声)；落下．②大失败；失败者．③〔美俚〕床；躲避处；过夜．~**-eared** *a.* (猎犬等)耳朵下垂的．~**house**〔美口〕①(按床位收费的)小客栈．②监狱．~**-nik**〔美俚〕失败了的卫星．~**-valve** 瓣．

flop·o·ver [ˈflɔpˌəuvə] *n.*【电视】场频不稳〔电视图象因受干扰而上下跳动〕．

flop·per [ˈflɔpə] *n.* ①(拍动翅膀学飞的)幼禽．②〔美俚〕变节者．③伪造事故骗钱的人．

flop·py [ˈflɔpi] *a.* *(-pi·er; -pi·est)*〔口〕①松软的．②松懈的；懒散的．~ **disc** (分者存电子计算机数据的)柔性塑料磁盘．**-pi·ly** *ad.* **-pi·ness** *n.*

flor. = floruit.

Flo·ra [ˈflɔːrə] *n.* ①弗洛拉〔女子名〕．②【罗神】花神．

flo·ra [ˈflɔːrə] *n.* *(pl.* ~*s,* ~*e* [-riː]*)* ①植物群；(某一地域的)全部植物．②植物区系；植物志．

flo·ral [ˈflɔːrəl] *a.* ①花(一样)的．②植物(群)的；植物区系的．③〔F-〕花神的．~ *designs* 花卉图案．*a* ~ *emblem* (代表一国、一州等的)象征之花．~ *envelope* 花被，花盖．*a* ~ *offering* 花制赠品．~ **clock** 花钟．~ **leaf** 花叶，苞片．~ **zone** 植物带．**-ly** *ad.*

Flor·ence [ˈflɔrəns] *n.* ①弗洛伦斯〔女子名〕．②佛罗伦萨〔意大利城市〕．

Flor·en·tine [ˈflɔrəntain] *a.* ①佛罗伦萨的．②佛罗伦萨画派的．— *n.* ①佛罗伦萨人．②〔f-〕佛罗伦萨厚绸，精纺背心呢，(夏季)斜纹裤料．

flo·res·cence [flɔːˈresns] *n.* ①开花，开花期．②兴盛〔全盛〕时期．

flo·res·cent [flɔːˈresnt] *a.* ①开花的，开花期的．②全盛时期的．

flo·ret [ˈflɔːrit] *n.* ①【植】(菊科植物的)小花．②【纺】绢丝．~ **silk** 优级绢丝．~ **yarn** 绢棉混纺纱．

Flo·rey [ˈflɔːri, ˈflɔuri] *n.* 弗洛里〔姓氏〕．

flori- *comb. f.* 表示"花"，"象花"：*flori*ated, *flori*culture.

flo·ri·at·ed [ˈflɔːrieitid] *a.* 有花卉装饰的．**-ation** *n.*

flo·ri·bun·da [ˌflɔːriˈbʌndə] *n.*【植】花束玫瑰〔人工培植的一种具有一簇簇花束的玫瑰〕．

flo·ri·cul·tur·al [ˌflɔːriˈkʌltʃərəl] *a.* 花卉栽培的．

flo·ri·cul·ture [ˈflɔːriˌkʌltʃə] *n.* 花卉栽培，园艺．

flo·ri·cul·tur·ist [ˌflɔːriˈkʌltʃərist] *n.* 花卉栽培家．

flor·id [ˈflɔrid] *a.* ①华丽的，丰富多采的；(绘画等)富丽的，(文章等)词藻华丽的．②红润的，血色好的．③花俏的，浮华俗气的．④〔古〕象花一样的，用花装饰的．*a* ~ *prose style* 华丽体(文章)．*a* ~ *writer* 词藻华丽的作家．**-ly** *ad.* **-ness** *n.*

Flor·i·da [ˈflɔridə] *n.* 佛罗里达〔美国州名〕．~ **Keys** 佛罗里达州南部一狭长的珊瑚岛群．~ **Strait** 佛罗里达海峡．**f- water** 花露水．

Flori·dan [ˈflɔridən], **Flo·rid·i·an** [ˈflɔridiən] *a.* 佛罗里达州的，佛罗里达人的．— *n.* 佛罗里达州人．

flo·rid·i·ty [flɔˈriditi] *n.* ①华丽，绚丽．②鲜艳．③花哨．

flo·rif·er·ous [flɔːˈrifərəs] *a.*【植】有花的，开花的，多花的．**-ly** *ad.* **-ness** *n.*

flor·i·gen [ˈflɔːridʒən, ˈflɔ-] *n.*【植】成花素．**-ic** *a.*

flo·ri·le·gi·um [ˌflɔːriˈliːdʒiəm] *n.* *(pl.* ***-gia*** [-dʒiə]*)* ①花谱，群芳谱．②名诗选，作品集锦；佳作选集．

flor·in [ˈflɔrin] *n.* ①〔1252 年发行于佛罗伦萨的〕一种金币．②英国的一种银币(值二先令)．③欧洲国家不同时代所用的金币或银币．

flo·rist [ˈflɔrist] *n.* ①种花者，花匠．②花商；花店．③花卉研究者．

flo·ris·tic [flɔːˈristic] *a.* ①花的．②(关于)植物种类地理学的．**-ti·cal·ly** *ad.*

flo·ris·tics [flɔːˈristiks] *n. pl.* 〔用作单数〕植物种类地理学．

-florous *suf.* 表示"…花的"：uni*florous.*

flo·ru·it [ˈflɔːrjuit] *n.*〔L.〕在世期，活跃时期〔用于生死年月不能确定的场合；略作 fl(or)，如：fl. A. D. 63—110〕；全盛时期．

flo·ry [ˈflɔːri] *a.* = fleury.

flos·cu·lar [ˈflɔskjulə] *a.* 花的，有小花的．

flos·cule [ˈflɔskjuːl] *n.* 小花．

flos·cu·lous [ˈflɔskjuləs] *a.* = floscular.

flos fer·ri [ˈflɔs ˈferai] *n.*【地】文石华，铁华，霰石华．

floss [flɔs] *n.* ①(蚕茧外的)乱丝，绪丝．②绣花丝线．③细绒线．④絮状物，木棉．⑤【植】绒毛．(玉米等的)黍须．⑥【冶】(浮于熔化金属表面的)浮滓．⑦(清除牙缝中食物碎屑的)牙缝拉线(= dental ~)．*candy* ~ 棉花糖．— *vi.* 使用牙缝拉线清除牙垢．~ **silk** *n.* 乱丝，绪丝；丝绵；丝线．

floss·y [ˈflɔsi] *a.* *(floss·i·er; -i·est)* ①乱丝的，绪丝的．②丝绵似的；轻软的，毛茸茸的．③〔美俚〕迷人的，装饰华丽的，穿得漂亮的．— *n.*〔美俚〕①浓装艳抹的轻浮女子．②任何女子(= flossie)．

flo·tage [ˈflɔutidʒ] *n.* = floatage.

flo·ta·tion [fləuˈteiʃən] *n.* = floatation.

flo·til·la [fləuˈtilə] *n.* ①小舰队．②海军纵队．③船队．*a destroyer* ~ 驱逐舰队．*a torpedo-boat* ~ 鱼雷艇队．

flot·sam [ˈflɔtsəm] *n.* ①(失事船只的)残骸和漂出物．②〔集合词〕流浪者．③零碎东西；废物，废料．~ ***and jetsam*** ①(失事船只的)残骸和漂出物．②流浪者．③零碎东西；废物．

flot·san [ˈflɔtsən] *n.* = flotsam.

flounce[1] [flauns] *n.* (裙子的)荷叶边．— *vt.* 给(裙子等)镶荷叶边．

flounce[2] [flauns] *vi.* ①肢体乱动，挣扎．②跳动，暴跳．③猝然离开 *(away; out; about)*．~ ***away [off]*** 挣脱．— *n.* 肢体乱动，急动，急转；暴跳．

flounc·ing [ˈflaunsiŋ] *n.* 荷叶边；做荷叶边的料子．

floun·der[1] [ˈflaundə] *vi.* ①挣扎 *(in)*，肢体乱动，踉跄．②着慌，勉强应付，行为〔言语〕错乱．~ ***through*** 胡乱地做完 (*The frightened girl* ~*ed through her song.* 那着慌的女孩疑三倒四地唱完了她的歌)．— *n.* 挣扎，踉跄前进．

floun·der[2] [ˈflaundə] *n.* *(pl.* ~*s,*〔集合词〕~*)*【动】比目鱼，鲽形目鱼．

flour [flauə] *n.* ①面粉；谷粉；粉，粉末．②粉状物质．*emery* ~ 金钢砂粉．*wood* ~ 木屑．— *vt.* ①在…撒粉．②〔美〕把…研成粉．— *vi.* 碎成粉．~ **bag** 面粉袋．~ **mill,**〔美〕~**ing mill** 面粉厂．

flour·ish [ˈflʌriʃ] *n.* ①挥动，挥舞．②华丽的辞藻，丰富多采．③花字；花边；花饰；雕花．④丰富多采〔热闹〕的演奏〔歌唱〕；【乐】有震颤音的花腔．⑤繁荣，茂盛；兴旺．⑥戏剧性动作．*She went away with a* ~ *of bonnet.* 她挥挥帽子走掉了．***a*** ~ ***of trumpets*** 响亮喧闹的喇叭声；〔喻〕大事件开场前的大肆宣扬．***in full*** ~ 全盛，极盛；盛行．***with a*** ~ ***of trumpets*** 自吹自擂地、耀武扬威地．— *vt.* ①挥舞；摇动(旗等)．②夸示．③以颜色〔花纹等〕装饰；以花体字作…的装饰．~ *one's wealth* 夸耀豪富．— *vi.* ①茂盛，繁荣，繁盛．②活跃，盛行，享有盛名．③手舞足蹈．④写花体字；使用华丽词句；花言巧语．⑤【乐】奏〔唱〕得精采响亮．*It's one thing to* ~ *and another to fight.* 舞剑是一回事，战斗是另一回事．

flour·ish·ing [ˈflʌriʃiŋ] *a.* ①繁茂的，繁生的．②繁荣的，兴盛的；茂盛的，蒸蒸日上的，欣欣向荣的．**-ly** *ad.*

flour·y [ˈflauəri] *a.* 面粉的；粉状的；多粉的．

flout [flaut] *vt.* 藐视，轻视，嘲笑．— *vi.* 表示轻蔑．— *n.* 嘲笑；侮慢，表示轻蔑的言行．**-ing·ly** *ad.*

flow [fləu] *vi.* ①流，流动．②(血液等)流通，循环．③流过；川流不息；(时间)飞逝；(言语等)流畅．④(衣服、头发等)飘动，飘拂，(旗等)飘扬．⑤流出，涌出．⑥(潮)涨 *(opp.* ebb*)*．⑦出血，行经．⑧充满，斟满，富有．⑨〔古〕泛滥．⑩来自．*Blood will* ~．一定会流血生事．

— *vt.* 溢过，淹没；使泛滥，使充溢．～ ***away*** 流走；流逝．～ ***down*** 流下．～ ***in*** 流入．～ ***like water*** (酒)源源不绝．～ ***out*** 流出．～ ***over*** 横流，溢出，泛滥．～ ***over into*** 涌入．— *n.* ①流，流水，逕流；气流．②流出，流入，流动；川流不息．③流量；消耗量；流速，流率；生产量．④涨潮．⑤〔常 *pl.*〕(特指尼罗河的)泛滥．⑥洋溢，饱满，丰满．⑦滔滔，流畅．⑧(衣服、头发等的)飘动，飘拂；(旗等的)飘扬．⑨【医】月经(＝ menstrual ～)．*soil* ～【地】流砂．*a* ～ *of eloquence* 谈吐流利．*a* ～ *of ten gallons a second* 每秒十加仑的流率〔量〕．*a good* ～ *of milk* 丰富的挤奶量．*ebb and* ～ 涨落，盛衰，消长．*The tide is on the* ～．正在涨潮．*a* ～ *of spirits* 精神饱满，兴致勃勃．*a* ～ *of soul* 推心置腹，融洽的交谈．～ *of talk [conversation, words]* 健谈，善于词令，滔滔不绝．*the* ～ *of time* 时光流逝．*a* ～ *of traffic* 车水马龙．～ **chart [sheet]** 生产流程图，作业图，生产过程图解．～**-line**【地】流理〔火成岩的纹理〕．～**meter** 流量表，流量计，流速计．～**rate** 流速；流量．

flow·age [ˈflәuidʒ] *n.* ①流动，流出，泛滥．②泛滥的河水，积水；溢出的液体，流出物．③【地】(岩石形状的)渐变．

Flow·er [ˈflauә] *n.* 弗劳尔〔姓氏〕．

flow·er [ˈflauә] *n.* ①花；花卉；花状装饰物．②精华 *(of)*．③开花，盛开．④少壮，青春，盛年，盛时．⑤〔*pl.*〕词藻．⑥〔*pl.*〕【化】华；(发酵时的)泡沫；〔古〕月经．*printer's* ～【印】(用于章末卷尾作为补白的)尾花图饰．*the language of* ～*s* 用花表达的话，以花作象征的意义．*the national* ～ 国花．*The* ～*s are out.* 花开了．*the* ～ *of the youth of the country* 国家的优秀青年．*the* ～ *of scholarship* 学界精华．～*s of sulphur* 硫华．*No* ～*s*. 花圈敬辞〔讣文上谢绝赠送花圈的用语〕．～*s of speech* 华丽的词藻(常含讽刺意味)．***in (full)*** ～ 开着花；盛开，怒放．***in the*** ～ ***of life (one's age)*** 在青春时代．— *vt.* 用花装饰；使开花．— *vi.* 开花；成长，兴旺．～ **arrangement** 插花术．～ **bed** 花坛．～ **child** 〔美俚〕花孩〔嬉皮士的一种，常戴花象征爱〕．～**-de-luce**【植】鸢尾．～ **girl** 卖花女；在新娘前撒花的女孩．～ **head**【植】头状花序(＝head)．～**like** *a.* 象花一样的．～**-of-an hour**【植】野西爪苗 *(Hipiscus trionum)*．～ **people** ＝～ children (～child 的复数)．～ **piece** 花卉画；花卉装饰．～**pot** 花盆，花钵．～ **power** 花的力量〔意即爱的力量，是～children 的口号〕．～ **show** 花卉展览．～ **stalk** 花柄，花梗．**F- state** 花州〔美国佛罗里达州的别号〕．～ **thinning**【园艺】疏花．**-less** *a.* 无花的，隐花的．**-like** *a.* 象花一样的．

flow·er·age [ˈflauәridʒ] *n.* ①花〔总称〕．②开花．

flow·ered [ˈflauәd] *a.* ①有花的．②以花形图案装饰的．

flow·er·er [ˈflauәrә] *n.* ①开花的植物．②(陶瓷、刺绣等的)描花人．*an abundant* ～ 花多的树．*an early [a late]* ～开花期早〔晚〕的花．

flow·er·et [ˈflauәrit] *n.* 小花；【建】小花饰．

flow·er·ing [ˈflauәriŋ] *a.* 开花的．*a* ～ *plant* 显花植物．～ **crab**【植】多花海棠．～ **peach**【植】碧桃．～ **quince** ①【植】贴梗海棠．②贴梗海棠果．

flow·er·y [ˈflauәri] *a.* ***(-er·i·er; -i·est)*** ①花的，花似的．②花多的；用花装饰的．③词藻华丽的．～ *language* 词藻丰富的语言．***the F- Kingdom [Land]*** 中华〔即中国〕．**-er·i·ly** *ad.* **-er·i·ness** *n.*

flow·ing [ˈflәuiŋ] *a.* ①流动的；如流的；(轮廓等)圆滑的，流畅的；连续不断的．②飘垂的．③上涨的．～ *lock's* 垂发．～ *tide* 涨潮．***a land*** ～ ***with milk and honey***【圣】流乳与蜜的地方，鱼米之乡．***sail with a*** ～ ***sheet [sail]***【海】放松帆脚减少风力，慢开．～ **well** 自喷井，自流井．**-ly** *ad.* **-ness** *n.*

flown[1] [flәun] fly[1] 的过去分词．

flown[2] [flәun] *a.* ①(陶瓷)涂有晕色的．②〔古〕满溢的．

fl. oz. ＝ fluidounce.

F.L.S. ＝ Fellow of the Linnean Society〔英〕林奈学会会员．

flt.【美军】＝ ①fleet．②flight．③float．

flu [flu:] *n.* 〔口〕【医】流行性感冒 (＝ influenza)．

flub [flʌb] *vt., vi.* ***(-bb-)*** (把工作等)搞坏；弄糟，做错．— *n.* 〔口〕错误，过失．

flub·dub [ˈflʌbdʌb] *n.* ①糊涂话；空话，哗众取宠的话．②(俗气的)艳丽服装．③〔美俚〕笨拙，蠢少年．～ ***and gulf*** 〔美〕夸大的空话，胡说八道．

fluc·tu·ate [ˈflʌktjueit] *vi.* ①波动，起伏，涨落；【物】脉动；(市价等)变动．②(意见等) 动摇不定．— *vt.* 使波动，使起伏．*a fluctuating market* 变动的行市．～ ***between hopes and fears*** 忽喜忽忧．

fluc·tu·a·tion [ˌflʌktjuˈeiʃәn] *n.* ①波动，起伏，涨落；【物】脉动．②动摇不定，踌躇．③【生】彷徨变异．

flue[1] [flu:] *n.* ①烟道，暖气管．②(管风琴的)唇管，唇管口．③〔俚〕(当铺中传送抵押品至收藏处的)滑槽，斜槽．***in [up;upon] the*** ～ 进了当铺；死了．～ **pipe** (管风琴的)唇管．

flue[2] [flu:] *n.* 绒毛；毛屑，棉屑．

flue[3] [flu:] *n.* 拖网；挂网；(任何)渔网．

flue[4] [flu:] *vt., vi.* (使)成喇叭形．

flue[5] [flu:] *n.* ＝ flu.

flue-cured [ˈflu:kjuәd] *a.* (烟草)烤干的．

flue·gel·horn, flu·gel·horn [ˈflu:glˌhɔ:n] *n.*【乐】夫吕号〔一种铜管乐器，结构和音调与短号差不多〕．

flu·en·cy [ˈflu(:)әnsi] *n.* 流畅，流利．～ ***of speech*** 口齿流利．***with*** ～ 流畅地，滔滔不绝．

flu·ent [ˈflu(:)әnt] *a.* ①流畅的，流利的．②畅流的，液态的．*speak* ～ *English* 说流利的英语．*a* ～*speaker* 口若悬河的演说家．*a* ～ *writer* 文笔流畅的作家．— **n.**【数】变数，变量．**-ly** *ad.*

flu·er·ic [ˈflu:әrik] *a.* ＝ fluidic.

flu·er·ics [ˈflu:әriks] *n.* ＝ fluidics.

flue·y [ˈflu:i] *a.* 绒毛似的，蓬松的．

fluff [flʌf] *n.* ①织物上的绒毛，柔毛；汗毛．②蓬松物．③说错；错误；〔美俚〕(戏剧、广播中)念错台词．④〔俚〕青年女子．⑤没有价值的东西〔言语〕．— *vi.* ①起毛，变松．②说错；念错台词，忘记台词；出错；搞糟．— *vt.* ①使起毛；抖开．②〔美俚〕说错；念错(台词)，忘记(台词)；搞糟．

fluff·y [ˈflʌfi] *a.* ①绒毛状的，有绒毛的；柔软的；蓬松的．②错乱的；糊涂的．**fluff·i·ness** *n.*

flu·id [ˈflu(:)id] *n.* 流体，液．*body* ～ 体液．*cooling* ～ 冷却液．— *a.* ①流动的；流体的；液体的．②容易〔可〕变动的；不固定的．③容易变成现金的；可以另派用处的．④流畅的．*a* ～ *analogue computer* 射流模拟计算机．～ *battle lines* 非固定作战线．～ *assets* 流动资产．～ *capital* 流动资本．*a* ～ *style* 流畅的文体．～ **drachm [dram]** 流量打兰(药衡名)．～ **drive**【机】液压传动．～**extract**【药】流浸膏剂．～ **mechanics** 水力学，流体力学．～ **ounce** 液量英两，液量盎司〔美国合 29.4 毫升，英国合 28.4 毫升〕．～ **pressure** 流体压力，流体静力学压力．**-ly** *ad.*

flu·id·ic [fluˈidik] *a.* 流体性的；射流的．

flu·id·ics [fluˈidiks] *n. pl.* 〔用作单数〕射流〔流体〕学；射流技术．

flu·id·i·fy [flu(:)ˈidifai] *vt.* 液化；使成流体．— *vi.* ①流体化．②积满液体．

flu·id·i·ty [flu(:)ˈiditi] *n.* 流动性，流度；流质；液流度，液性．

flu·id·ize [ˈflu:idaiz] *vt.* ***(-ized; -iz·ing)*** ①使液化，流化，使流质化．②用高速气流输送，使悬浮在气流中加以运送．**-zation** *n.*

flu·id·on·ics [ˌflu:iˈdɔniks] *n. pl.* ＝ fluidics.

fluke[1] [flu:k] *n.* ①锚爪，锚钩；(鱼叉等的)倒钩．②鲸尾叶突．

fluke[2] [flu:k] *n.* ①(台球)侥幸的击中. ②幸运,侥幸成功. ③偶然事件;倒霉,意外挫折. *win by a* ～ 侥幸得胜. — *vt.* 侥幸击中,侥幸做成. — *vi.* 侥幸成功,意外受挫.

fluke[3] [flu:k] *n.* ①【动】比目鱼, 鲽形目的鱼. ②肝蛭,吸虫. *blood* ～*s* 血吸虫.

fluk·ic·ide [ˈflu:kisaid] *n.*【药】杀吸虫剂.

fluk·y [ˈflu:ki] *a.* ***(fluk·i·er; -i·est)*** ①〔口〕侥幸的,靠运气的. ②偶然的,变化不定的. **-i·ly** *ad.* **-i·ness** *n.*

flume [flu:m] *n.*〔美〕①斜槽,渡槽,流水槽,滑运沟. ②峡流. ***go [be] up the*** ～〔美俚〕倒霉,垮台. — *vi.* 利用水槽,建造水槽. — *vt.* 用水槽运送(木材等).

flum·mer·y [ˈflʌməri] *n.* ①面粉糊; 冻状食品; 柔软易食的食物(尤指燕麦粥; 乳蛋黏糊; 乳蛋甜点心. ②假恭维,废话.

flum·mox [ˈflʌməks] *vt.*〔俚〕使狼狈, 使失措, 使慌乱. ～ *sb. by the lip* 说得(人)狼狈而退. — *n.* 失败.

flump [flʌmp]〔口〕*n.* 砰的一声,砰然落下. *fall with a* ～ 砰的一声倒落. — *vt.* 砰地放下. —*vi.* 砰地落下[移动].

flung [flʌŋ] fling 的过去式及过去分词.

flunk [flʌŋk] *n.*〔美俚〕(考试等)失败,不及格. ～ *in an examination* 考试不及格. —*vi., vt.* (使)失败; 放弃. *She* ～*ed English.* 她英语没有考及格. ～ ***out*** 考试不及格而退学. **-ee** [flʌŋˈki:] *n.* 因考试不及格而退学者,因工作不力而被解职者.

flun·k(e)y [ˈflʌŋki] *n.* ①(穿制服的) 仆从, 奴才, 走狗. ②马屁精, 势利小人. **-ism** *n.* 奴才相, 奴才气, 奴才作风.

flu·or [ˈflu(:)ɔ:, ˈflu(:)ə] *n.* = fluorite.

fluor- *comb. f.* ①表示"氟": *fluor*ide. ②表示"荧光": *fluor*escent.

flu·o·resce [fluəˈres] *vi.* 发萤光.

flu·o·res·ce·in [ˌfluəˈresi:in] *n.*【化】萤光素; 萤光黄.

flu·o·res·cence [fluəˈresns] *n.* 荧光(性).

flu·o·res·cent [fluəˈresnt] *a.* ①荧光的, 发荧光的. ②外表华丽的;光辉四射的. ③〔美口〕容光焕发的. — *n.*〔美口〕荧光灯. ～ **lamp [light, tube]** 荧光灯,日光灯. ～ **screen** 荧光屏.

flu·o·res·cer [fluəˈresə] *n.* 荧光增白剂.

fluori- *comb. f.* 表示"荧光": *fluori*meter.

fluor·i·date [ˈflu(:)ərideit,ˈflɔ:-] *vt.* 向(饮水等) 中加氟化物(以防儿童蛀齿). [-ˈdeiʃən]

flu·or·ide [ˈflu(:)əraid] *n.*【化】氟化物.

flu·o·ri·dize [ˈflu(:)əridaiz] *vt.* 用氟化物处理. **-di·za·tion** [-daiˈzeiʃən] *n.* **-r** ①氟化剂. ②(纺织品上可防水防油的)氟化面层.

flu·o·rim·e·ter [flu(:)əˈrimitə] *n.* = fluorometer.

fluor·i·nate [ˈflu(:)ərineit] *vt.* ①氟化. ②= fluoridate. **-na·tion** *n.*

flu·o·rine [ˈflu(:)əri:n] *n.*【化】氟.

flu·o·rite [ˈflu(:)ərait] *n.*【矿】荧石,氟石.

fluoro- *comb. f.* = fluor-.

flu·o·ro·car·bon [ˌflu(:)ərəˈkɑ:bən] *n.*【化】碳氟化合物.

flu·o·rog·ra·phy [flu(:)əˈrɔgrəfi] *n.* 荧光屏图象摄影术(= photofluorography).

flu·o·rom·e·ter [flu(:)əˈrɔmitə] *n.* 荧光(测定)计; 氟量计. **-metric** [ˌflu(:)ərəˈmetrik] *a.* **-metry** [-tri] *n.*

flu·o·ro·plas·tic [ˌflu(:)ərəˈplæstik] *n.*【化】氟塑料.

flu·o·ro·poly·mer [fluə(:)əˈpɔlimə] *n.*【化】含氟聚合物.

fluor·o·scope [ˈflu(:)ərəskəup] *n.* 荧光镜[屏]; 荧光检查器. — *vt.* 用荧光镜检查.

fluor·o·scop·ic [ˌflu(:)ərəˈskɔpik] *a.* 荧光镜的,荧光检查法的. **-i·cal·ly** *ad.*

flu·o·ros·co·py [flu(:)əˈrɔskəpi] *n.* ①荧光学. ②荧光屏检查; X 线透视(法),透视检查. **-co·pist** *n.* 透视科医师.

flu·o·ro·sis [flu(:)əˈrəusis] *n.*【医】(慢性)氟中毒.

flu·or·spar [ˈflu(:)əspɑ:] *n.*【矿】= fluorite.

flur·ried [ˈflʌrid] *a.* 混乱的, 慌张的. ***in a ～ manner*** 慌慌张张地.

flur·ry [ˈflʌri] *n.* ①阵风,急风. ②暴雨,风雪. ③慌张; (时间的)混乱. ④(股票市场行情等) 短时间波动. ***in a*** ～ 慌慌张张. — *vt.* 使激动[慌张], 搅乱; 使混乱. — *vi.* 慌张,匆忙.

flush[1] [flʌʃ] *vi.* ①奔流,涌进; 泛滥,充溢. ②(脸色等)骤然发红; 发亮; 辉耀. ③(植物) 冒新芽. *No tide* ～*es through this narrow inlet.* 这小湾潮水涌不过来. *Her face* ～*ed with anger.* 她气得满脸通红. — *vt.* ①淹没; 用水冲洗. ②使脸红; 使骤然发红. ③激励,使得意. ④使植物冒芽. *Shame* ～*ed his cheeks.* 他羞得两颊通红. *be* ～*ed with victory* 因胜利而洋洋得意. — *n.* ①奔流; 冲洗; 水车排出的水; 涨水. ②(草木的)冒芽,新芽; 新鲜; 旺盛; 激增. ③(脸的)晕红;〔诗〕(云的)霞光,(夕阳等的) 辉耀. ④【医】(热病等的) 发烧; 升火. ⑤(感情的)激发, 兴奋. *the* ～ *of grass* 嫩草. *the first* ～ *of spring* 春天萌发的嫩草. *the* ～ *of dawn* 朝霞. *the* ～ *of hope* 希望的曙光. ***young shoots in full*** ～ 嫩芽盛发. ***in the very ～ of youth*** 风华正茂. ***in the full ～ of triumph*** 在胜利的欢欣鼓舞中. ～ **gate** (水库等的)溢洪道[水门等]排水装置. ～ **tank** (抽水马桶上的) 水箱[水柜]. ～ **toilet** 抽水马桶.

flush[2] [flʌʃ] *a.* ①洋溢的, 注满的, 泛滥的. ②精力充沛的,有生气的. ③丰富的;富裕的,有钱的. ④挥霍的, 浪费的. ⑤齐平的,同平面的, 同高的 *(with)*;【印】左面每行排齐的, 没有缩排 (indention) 的. ⑥直接的. *a blow* ～ *in the face* 正中脸部的一击. *be* ～ *of [with] money* 钱多. *be* ～ *with one's money* 挥霍钱财. *The door is* ～ *with the casing.* 门跟门框严丝合缝. *The river is* ～ *with its banks.* 河水齐岸. — *ad.* ①齐平地,严丝合缝地. ②直接地. *a book cut* ～ 切齐的书. *a line set* ～【印】(边部与其他行)排齐的一行. — *vt.* ①弄平,嵌平,使齐平. ②【印】把(左面) 排齐. ～ **deck** (船的) 平甲板. ～**-decker** 平甲板船.

flush[3] [flʌʃ] *vi.* (鸟等)惊起,惊飞; 赶鸟. — *vt.* 使(鸟等)惊飞. —*n.* 飞起,一阵子飞起的鸟群; 赶鸟.

flush[4] [flʌʃ]*n.* (纸牌戏中的)一手同花的五张牌. *a royal* ～ 最强的一手牌〔以 A 打头的同花顺次五张牌〕. *a straight* ～ 次强的一手牌〔同花顺次的五张牌〕. ***a ～ sequence*** 同花顺.

flush·er [ˈflʌʃə] *n.* ①(阴沟、马路等的) 冲扫者. ②冲洗装置.

flush·ing [ˈflʌʃiŋ] *n., a.* 抽水冲洗(的). ～ **box [cistern, tank]** = flush tank.

flus·ter [ˈflʌstə] — *vt.* 扰乱, 使惊惶失措; 使酩酊. — *vi.* 混乱,慌张, 惊惶失措; 喝醉. — *n.* 混乱,慌张;醉. *all in a* ～ 惊慌失措.

flus·ter·a·tion [ˌflʌstəˈreiʃən], **flus·tra·tion** [flʌsˈtreiʃən] *n.* 慌乱,惊慌失措;酩酊大醉.

flute [flu:t] *n.* ①【乐】长笛; 长笛吹奏者; (风琴的)长笛音. ②(女服的)管状裙褶. ③(柱上的)凹槽. ④笛状物(如细长酒杯, 细长面包等). ⑤【机】(刀具) 出屑槽;【纺】沟槽. — *vi.* 吹长笛; 发笛声. — *vt.* ①用长笛吹(歌曲); 用长笛般的声音歌唱[说话, 吹口哨]. ②在…上刻凹槽. **-like** *a.* 象长笛(音)的.

flut·ed [ˈflu:tid] *a.* ①(似) 笛声的. ②有凹槽的. ～ *twist drill*【机】麻花钻. ～ *columns* 刻有凹槽的柱子. *the* ～ *notes of the birds* 小鸟清脆的啭鸣.

flut·er [ˈflu:tə] *n.* ①刻凹槽的人; 刻凹槽的器具. ②〔古〕长笛吹奏者.

flut·ey [ˈflu:ti] *a.* ***(flut·i·er, flut·i·est)*** 象长笛声的, 柔和而清亮的.

flut·ing [ˈfluːtiŋ] *n.* ①发长笛声，吹长笛. ②(刻)凹槽[沟槽]. ③凹槽装饰.

flut·ist [ˈfluːtist] *n.* 长笛吹奏者.

flut·ter [ˈflʌtə] *vi.* ①拍翅振翼；(旗帜)飘扬. ②颤动，(心)急跳，(脉搏)浮动. ③(心绪)不宁，坐立不安. *He ~ed about the room nervously.* 他心绪不宁地在房间里转来转去. — *vt.* ①振(翼)；拍(翅). ②扰乱；使不安. — *n.* ①振翼；飘扬. ②不安，焦急，波动. ③(身体部分的)病态阵跳. ④〔英俚〕投机，小赌. ⑤颤振. ⑥图象跳动，脉冲干扰，放音失真. *the ~ of wings* 翅膀的拍动. ***all in a ~*** 心慌意乱. ***cause [make] a great ~*** 轰动一时. ***fall into a ~*** 心慌意乱. ***in a ~*** 心里卜卜跳. ***put sb. in [into] a ~ = throw sb. into a ~*** 使忐忑不安. ~ **computer** 颤动(摸拟)计算机. ~ **kick** (爬泳或仰泳时小腿部的)浅打水. ~ **wheel** (置于水槽底部的)水轮. **-er** *n.* **-ing·ly** *ad.*

flut·y [ˈfluːti] *a.* *(flut·i·er; -i·est)* 笛声一样的；嘹亮的(= flutey).

flu·vi·al [ˈfluːviəl] *a.* ①河的，河流的. ②生在河中的. ③河流冲刷作用形成的. ~ *navigation* 河道航行. ~ *plants* 河生植物. ~ *soil [deposits]* 冲积土(物).

flu·vi·a·tile [ˈfluːviətail] *a.* = fluvial.

flux [flʌks] *n.* ①流，流出；流动. ②涨潮. ③不断的变动，波动. ④【物】流量，通量，电通量，磁通量. ⑤熔解，熔融；助熔剂；焊剂. ⑥【医】异常溢出；腹泻. *luminous ~*【物】光通量. *radiant ~*【物】辐射通量. *soldering ~* 焊剂. ***be [remain] in (a state of) ~*** 动荡不定，不断变动. ***~ and reflux*** (潮水的)涨落；(势力的)不断消长. — *vt.* ①熔化，使熔解. ②用助熔剂处理. — *vi.* ①(潮)涨；流出. ②熔化. ~ **density**【物】通量密度. ~ **gate** 地球磁力磁向测量仪，磁门. ~**meter** 磁通(量)计.

flux·ion [ˈflʌkʃən] *n.* ①流动. ②不断变化，转变. ③【数】微分，流数. *the method of ~s* (牛顿的)流数法.

flux·ion·al [ˈflʌkʃənəl], **-ar·y** [-nəri] *a.* ①流动的，变动的，不定的. ②【数】微分的，流数的. ~ **analysis [calculus]**【数】流数术，微积分.

fly[1] [flai] *vi.* *(flew* [fluː]; *flown* [fləun]*)* ①飞 *(about; away; forth; off; out)*，飞行；驾驶飞机，坐飞机旅行. ②飞跑；(时间等)飞逝；飞散，碎，(门)突然打开；突然…起来；〔古〕突击，扑向 *(at; on, upon)*. ③奔逃，逃走〔过去式和过去分词要用 *fled*〕；消失；褪色. ④(旗帜、衣服等)飘动，飞舞. ⑤(在棒球中)打飞球〔过去式和过去分词要用 flied〕. ⑥放鹰打猎. *The delegation flew from London to New York.* 代表团由伦敦飞往纽约. *She simply flew down the street.* 她沿着大街飞奔而去. *Fly for a doctor!* 快去请医生！*Time flies like an arrow.* 光阴似箭. *The dog flew at me.* 狗向我扑来. — *vt.* ①飞，驾驶，空运. ②放(风筝，鸟等). ③(坐飞机)飞过. ④使(旗帜)飘扬. ⑤逃避，逃出，从…逃开〔过去式和过去分词一般用 fled〕. ~ *the approach of danger* 逃避危险. ~ *the country* 亡命国外. ***~ a kite*** ①放风筝. ②试探舆论. ③开空头支票. ***~ about*** 翱翔；飞散. ***~ apart*** 飞散，粉碎. ***~ around [round]***〔美口〕飞绕，飞来飞去. ***~ at*** 扑向；责骂. ***~ at high game*** 胸怀大志；情绪高涨. ***~ blind*** 盲目飞行，完全靠仪表飞行. ***~ high*** = ~ at high game. ***~ in pieces, ~ into fragments*** = ~ apart. ***~ in the face of*** 勇敢反抗，违反. ***~ into*** 突然发作(~ *into a passion [rage]* 勃然大怒. ~ *into raptures* 欣喜若狂). ***~ low*** 谦卑；销声匿迹. ***~ off*** 飞速跑掉；飞出；挥发. ***~ [go] off at a tangent*** 说话离题，突然改变行径. ***~ [go, slip] off the handle***〔俚〕死去；发脾气. ***~ on [upon]*** = ~ at. ***~ one's flag*** (海军司令官)升司令旗，就司令职. ***~ open*** (门)突然打开. ***~ out*** ①冲出，激怒. ②升(旗). ***~ right***〔美俚〕为人正派. ***~ round*** (轮子)急转. ***~ short of*** 未达到应有水平. ***~ the iron beam*** 沿铁路飞行. ***~ to arms*** 急忙去拿武器，急忙作战斗准备. ***~ to sb.'s arms*** 投入某人怀抱. ***~ up*** 突然大怒. ***Go ~ a kite!***〔美俚〕走开！去你的！***let ~*** 放，射，投射 (*let ~ an arrow* 射出一箭). ***let ~ at*** 向…发射，向…射击；骂. ***make the dust [feathers, fur] ~*** 引起动乱. ***make the money ~*** 浪费金钱，挥霍. ***send sb. ~ing*** 逐出；驱散；解雇. ***send sth. flying*** 乱抛. ***with flags ~ing*** = with flying colours. — *n.* ①飞，飞行；飞行距离，飞程. ②〔*pl.* flys〕〔英〕轻便旅行马车. ③(服装的)钮扣遮布；(帐篷的)门帘；(旗帜的)外端[布幅]. ④〔*pl.*〕(舞台上部)布景控制处. ⑤【机】飞轮，整速轮；【印】(印刷机上的)拨纸器；(织机的)飞梭，锭翼，锭壳. 【纺】飞花，落棉，飞毛；(棒球中的)飞球. *have a ~* 作一次飞行. ***on the ~*** ①在飞行中. ②〔美俚〕匆忙地；③无所事事，在街头游荡，作乐. ④狡猾地，诡诈地. ~ **ash** 飞灰，煤灰〔尤指污染空气者〕. ~**away** ① *a.* 过于宽大的；(衣服)不合身的；轻浮的，轻率的；尖形的，翅状的；(造好的飞机)随时可以出厂的，包装好准备空运的. ② *n.* 轻浮的人；过于宽大；不合身的衣服；直接飞离飞机制造厂的新飞机；海市蜃楼；(单杠运动中的)翻筋斗跳下. ~ **ball** (棒球中的)飞球. ~**-bar** (造纸用的)飞刀. ~**boat** ①航行荷兰沿岸的平底船. ②快艇. ~ **bomb** 飞弹. ~**-boy**〔美俚〕空军人员，飞机驾驶员. ~**by**, ~**-by** *n.* *(pl. -bies)* 飞机或宇宙飞船的越过定点〔指定地点〕；飞越. ~**-by-night** ① *n.* (夜间在外不归的)夜游神；〔俚〕夜间潜逃的逃债者. ② *a.* 钱款上靠不住的，骗人的，无信用的. ~**-cruise** *n.* 空海联航站. ~ **front** 掩襟. ~ **ladder** 云梯顶部. ~**leaf** *n.* *(pl. -leaves)* (书籍前后的)空白页，衬页. ~**-man** *(pl. -men)* ①出租马车车夫. ②(舞台上的)道具管理员. ~**over** ①〔英〕立体交叉路跨线桥. ②(飞机)飞越，(举行庆典时的)低空编队飞行. ~**past**〔美〕①立交桥. ②(阅兵时的)空中分列式. ~ **post** *vt.* 仓卒地张贴(传单等). ~ **sheet** 广告，传单，小册子. ~**-tipping**〔英〕在街上乱倒垃圾废物. ~**way** 候鸟飞行路线. ~**wheel**【机】飞轮，整速轮.

fly[2] [flai] *n.* *(pl. flies* [flaiz]*)*，①蝇，苍蝇. ②(有透明翼的)飞虫. ③植物的蝇害，虫害. ④(钓鱼用的)假蚊钩. ***a ~ in amber*** 琥珀中的化石蝇；〔喻〕保存得很好的珍贵遗物. ***a ~ in the ointment*** 美中不足，杀风景的(小)事情. ***a ~ on the wheel*** 过分自恃的人. ***break [crush] a ~ on the wheel*** 小题大作；杀鸡用牛刀. ***Don't let flies stick to your heels.***〔口〕别磨蹭，快点. ***Let that ~ stick in [to] the wall.***〔Scot.〕对这件事[问题]不要再谈了. ***rise to the ~*** (鱼)上钩；(人)上当. ***There are no flies on sb. [sth.].***〔俚〕①(某人)很灵活[机灵]. ②(某人)可信赖. ③(某物，某事)没有弊病，不必生疑. ~ **agaric [amanita]**【植】蛤蟆菌. ~**bane** 灭蝇草；灭蝇药. ~**blow** ① *n.* 卵，麻蝇的幼蛆. ② *vt.* *(-blew; -blown)* 产蝇卵在…，使生蛆；玷污(声誉等). ~**blown** *a.* 被蝇卵弄脏了的，生了蛆的；(声誉)被玷污了的. ~**book** 假蚊钩盒. ~**-cast** *vi.* 用假蚊钩钓鱼. ~**catcher** ①【动】鹟科食虫鸟. ②【植】捕蝇草. ~**fish** *vi.* 用假蚊钓鱼. ~**-fisher** 用假蚊钓鱼的人. ~**flap** 蝇拍. ~ **net** 防虫网. ~**paper** 粘蝇纸，毒蝇纸. ~ **rod** 假蚊钩钓鱼竿. ~**speck** ① *n.* 蝇屎污点，小污斑，小点，小团. ② *vt.* 使玷上小污点. ~ **swatter** 蝇拍. ~**trap** ①捕蝇器. ②捕蝇草属植物. ~**weight** *n.* ①最轻级(拳击选手). ②小东西，无足轻重的东西.

fly[3] [flai] *a.*〔俚〕伶俐的；敏捷的，敏锐的. ~ *cop* 便衣侦探.

fly·a·ble [ˈflaiəbl] *a.* (天气等)适于飞行的，适航的；(飞机等)可以在空中飞行的.

fly·er [ˈflaiə] *n.* ①飞鸟；航空器，飞行物. ②飞行者，飞行员. ③能飞跑的动物；快马. ④快艇；快车. ⑤【纺】锭翼，锭壳. ⑥【建】梯级. ⑦跳，跃起. ⑧〔美口〕投机，孤注一掷. ⑨〔美〕(广告)传单. ⑩〔口〕野心勃勃的人. ***take a ~*** (滑雪赛中)从跳板上飞跳；〔喻〕冒险行事.

fly·ing [ˈflaiiŋ] *a.* ①飞的，飞行的，飞行员的. ②飘扬的，

飞舞的．③飞似的,飞速的．④临时的,短暂的．⑤到处流传的．⑥逃亡的．*a～ formation* 飞行队形．*a ～ suit* 飞行服．～ *time* 飞行时间．～ *corps* 飞行队，航空队．～ *man* 飞行员,航空员．～ *ship* 飞船．～ *visit* 走马观花的访问〔参观〕．***with colours ～ = with ～ colours*** 完全胜利,大获成功．— *n.* ①飞行,飞跑．②飞散物．③〔*pl.*〕【纺】飞毛，飞花． ～ **blowtorch**〔美俚〕喷气式战斗机．～ **boat** 飞船;水上飞机．～ **bomb**【军】飞弹．～ **bridge**【海】浮桥,舰桥,船上驾驶台．～ **buttress**【建】拱扶垛,飞拱．～ **colours** ①迎风飘扬的旗．②显著的胜利,巨大成功．～ **column**【军】快速突击部队,别动队．～ **crane** (用直升飞机作成的)飞行起重机．～ **dog** 吸血蝙蝠．**F- Dutchman** ①(传说中)注定要永远在海上飘流直至最后审判日的荷兰水手．②鬼船．～ **ferry** 滑钢渡,系留渡(指由钢索控制、借水流推动往返于两岸的渡船)．～ **field** 小型机场〔供小型飞机起落和小检修的机场〕,飞行场．～ **fish**【动】文鳐鱼,飞鱼．**F- Fortress** 飞行堡垒〔第二次世界大战中美国使用的B-17远距离重轰炸机．～ **fox**【动】狐蝠〔产于非洲、澳洲和南亚,头象狐,食果类〕, 大蝙蝠亚目动物．～ **frog**【动】大蹼树蛙〔产于东印度〕．～ **gurnard**【动】豹鲂鮄．～ **jib** 船首斜桅帆，三角帆．～ **jump,** ～ **leap** 助跑跳高．～ **lemur**【动】猫猴〔东南亚树居的一种哺乳动物〕．～ **machine** 航空机〔指飞机、飞船等〕．～ **mare**【摔交】后背包．～ **off** 起飞;离舰．～ **officer**〔英〕空军中尉．～ **phalanger**【动】大洋洲袋鼯．～ **rings** 吊环．～ **saucer** "飞碟"，真相未明的空中飞行物 (= UFO)．～ **school** 飞行学校,航空学校．～ **spot scanning**【电视】高速点扫描法．～ **squad** (警察等的) 摩托化紧急行动小组．～ **squadron** ①机动舰队．②(由受过专门训练的工人组成的)机动工组．～ **squirrel**【动】①北美鼯鼠．②= ～ phalanger. ～ **start** ①【体】疾足起步法〔先开始起跑，到起步线时全力飞跑〕．②任何迅速的开始．～ **windmill**〔美俚〕直升飞机．

Flynn [flin] *n.* 弗林〔姓氏〕．

flyte [flait] *vi.* = flite.

FM = ①Field Marshal〔英〕陆军元帅．②frequency modulation【物】调频，频率调制．③foreign mission 外交使团．

Fm = fermium【化】元素镄的符号．

fm. = ①fathom. ②from.

f.m.〔处方〕作成混合剂．

FMI =〔F.〕*Fonds Monetaire International* 国际货币基金组织 (= International Monetary Fund).

f-num·ber [ˈefˌnʌmbə] *n.*【摄】光圈数．

FO, F. O. = ①field officer.【军】校官．②Foreign Office (英国等的)外交部．③field order 野战命令．④Flying Officer〔英〕空军中尉．⑤forward observer【军】前进观察员．

fo. = folio.

FOA = Foreign Operations Administration〔美〕援外事务管理署．

foal [fəul] *n.* 驹(尤指一岁以下的马、驴、骡)．— *vt., vi.* 生(驹)．***be in [with]*** ～ (马)怀驹．～**foot** = coltsfoot.

foam [fəum] *n.* ①〔只用单数〕泡沫;(马等的)涎沫〔大汗〕．②泡沫材料，泡沫状物，泡沫橡皮;泡沫塑料．③〔诗〕海．***in a*** ～ (马等)浑身是汗．***sail the*** ～ 航海．— *vi.* ①起泡沫;(马等)出汗珠．②冒口水．③(浪)汹涌．— *vt.* 使起泡沫,使成泡沫状物．～*ing ale* 起泡的啤酒．～ ***at the mouth*** (狗等)口吐泡沫(发怒)．～ ***away [off]*** 成泡沫消失．～ ***over*** 起泡溢出．～**ed concrete**【建】泡沫混凝土．～**ed plastics** 泡沫塑料，多孔塑料．～ **rubber** 泡沫橡皮，海绵橡皮．**-less** *a.* 无泡沫的．**-like** *a.* 象泡沫的．

foam·y [ˈfəumi] *a.* ***(foam·i·er; -i·est)*** 起泡沫的,布满泡沫的,泡沫一样的．**-i·ly** *ad.* **-i·ness** *n.*

FOB, f.o.b. = free on board【商】船上交货,离岸价格．

fob[1] [fɔb] *n.* ①(男裤上的)表袋．②(怀表上的)表链及饰物．— *vt.* 把…装在表袋中．～**-chain** 表链及饰物．

fob[2] [fɔb] *vt.*〔古〕欺骗．～ ***off*** ①搪塞．②把冒充品当真品推销．③摈弃．～ *sth. inferior [spurious] off upon sb.* = ～ *sb. off with sth. worthless* 用劣货骗人．～ *sb. off with empty promises* 用空洞的诺言搪塞人．

FOBS = fractional orbit(al) bombardment system 部分轨道袭击系统〔一种核武器袭击系统，核弹头由绕地球运行的空间航空器发射,以避免被雷达发现〕．

fo·cal [ˈfəukəl] *a.* ①【物】焦点的,(集中在)焦点上的,有焦点的．②【医】病灶的,病灶性的．～ **distance [length]**【物】焦距．～ **infection**【医】病灶性感染．～ **plane**【物】焦平面．～ **point** 焦点．**-ly** *ad.*

fo·cal·ize, fo·cal·ise [ˈfəukəlaiz] *vt.* ①使聚焦,使集中在焦点上．②调节(焦距),使(注意等)集中．— *vi.* 聚焦,调焦距;集中注意．**-i·za·tion** [ˌfəukəlaiˈzeiʃən] *n.* **-r**【无】聚焦设备,聚焦装置．

Foch [fəuʃ], **Ferdinand** 福煦〔1851—1929,法国元帅,第一次世界大战联军总司令〕．

fo·ci [ˈfəusai] *n.* focus 的复数．

Focke [fɔk] *n.* 福克〔姓氏〕．

fo·co [ˈfəukəu] *n.*〔Span.〕"中心",游击活动中心．

fo·com·e·ter [fəuˈkɔmitə] *n.* 焦距计〔仪〕．

fo'c's'le [ˈfəuksl] *n.* = forecastle.

fo·cus [ˈfəukəs] *n.* *(pl.* ***fo·cus·es, fo·ci*** [ˈfəusai]*)* ①【物】焦点．②【物】焦距;聚焦,对焦点,配光,对光．③(活动兴趣等的)中心．④【医】病灶．⑤(地震的)震源．*the ～ of the world's attention* 世界注意的中心．*principal* ～【物】主焦点．*real [true]* ～【物】实焦点．*virtual* ～【物】虚焦点．*the ～ of a disease* 病的主要患部．*the ～ of an earthquake* 震源．***bring into ～ = bring to a ～.*** 使集中在焦点上配光,对光．***in ～*** 焦点对准,清晰．***out of ～*** 焦点没有对准,模糊．— *vt.* *(*〔英〕***-ss-)*** ①使聚焦,对焦．②调节镜头、焦距等．③集中注意力于．④使限制于小区域．— *vi.* 聚焦,注视,调焦距;限制于小区域．～**ing cloth**【摄】遮光黑布．～ **electrode**【无】聚焦电极．～**ing glass [screen]**【摄】调焦距用的毛玻璃．

fod·der [ˈfɔdə] *n.* ①饲料．②创作素材．③〔美俚〕弹药．④无价值的人．～ *crops* 饲料作物．***cannon ～*** 炮灰．***cut one's own ～***〔美〕管自己的事,自己谋生．— *vt.* 用饲料喂(家畜)．**-less** *a.* 没有饲料的．

foe [fəu] *n.* ①敌人;仇敌 *(opp.* friend*)*; 敌军,敌兵;(比赛的)敌手,对手．②危害物．*a ～ worthy of sb.'s steel* 劲敌,强敌．***our [the arch]*** ～【宗】魔鬼．

foehn [fein; G. fø:n] *n.* = föhn.

foe·man [ˈfəumən] *n.* *(pl.* ***-men)***〔古,诗〕敌兵,敌人．

foe·tal [ˈfi:tl] *a.* = fetal.

foe·ta·tion [fi:ˈteiʃən] *n.* = fetation.

foe·ti·cide [ˈfi:tisaid] *n.* = feticide.

foe·tid [ˈfetid,ˈfi:t-] *a.* = fetid.

foe·tor [ˈfi:tə] *n.* = fetor.

foe·tus [ˈfi:təs] *n.* = fetus.

fog[1] [fɔg] *n.* ①雾．②烟雾,尘雾．③【摄】(底片的) 雾翳;(影象的)模糊．④(灭火机喷出的)泡沫,喷雾．⑤困惑,迷惑不解,迷惘．*a dense ～* 大雾，浓雾．*the ～ of war* 战云．***be lost in a ～*** 如堕五里雾中,困惑不解．— *vt.* ①以雾笼罩．②使困惑,使迷惘．③【摄】使模糊,使起雾翳．— *vi.* ①被雾笼罩．②(在铁路沿线) 设立浓雾信号．③(植物因湿度过大而)烂死 *(off)*．④【摄】(影片) 模糊，有雾翳．～ **alarm** 浓雾警报．～ **bank** (海上)雾堤．～ **bell**【海】雾钟〔海岸等处所设，起雾时用以报警〕．～**bound** *a.* (船只)因浓雾而进退不得的．～**-bow** 雾虹．～ **broom** 除雾机．～ **buoy**【海】雾标〔装有铃或自动汽笛，起雾时用以使船拉开距离〕．～ **circle** = ～bow. ～**dog** 雾层 (～ bank) 中的明亮处．～**drip** 有雾时树上滴下的水滴．～**eater** ①= ～-

bow. ②雾中升起的满月. ～**horn** 雾角(雾中警号); 粗而响的嗓音. ～ **light** 汽车在雾中行驶时的灯光. ～ **signal** 浓雾信号,雾中信号. ～ **siren,** ～ **whistle** 浓雾警笛; 雾中警笛. **-less** *a.* 无雾的.

fog² [fɔg] *n.* ①割后再生的草. ②(地上未割的)过冬草,冬季原野上的枯草. ③〔方〕苔藓.

fo·gey [ˈfəugi] *n.* = fogy.

fog·gy [ˈfɔgi] *a.* ***(-gi·er; -gi·est)*** ①有雾的,多雾的. ②(玻璃等)不明净的. ③朦胧的. ④【摄】模糊的,有雾翳的. *a* ～ *night* 浓雾弥漫之夜. *a* ～ *idea* 模糊不清的思想. *have not the foggiest idea of* ... 丝毫不懂…的意义. **F- Bottom** 雾谷〔指美国国务院,常用以讽刺其发言人发布的话或其政策之含混不清〕. **fog·gi·ly** *ad.* **fog·gi·ness** *n.*

fo·gram [ˈfəugræm], **fo·grum** [-grʌm] *n.* 守旧的人,过时的人.

fo·gy [ˈfəugi] *n.* 〔俚〕守旧者,老古板〔通常说 *old* ～〕. **-ish** *a.* 守旧的,古板的. **-ism** *n.* 守旧(思想,作风),古板(性格).

foh [fɔː] *int.* = faugh.

Föhn [fein; G. fəːn] *n.* 〔G.〕【气】(阿尔卑斯山北部盆地的)暑热南风.

foi·ble [ˈfɔibl] *n.* ①(性格上的)弱点,小缺点. ②刀剑的前段〔指中段到刀尖,杀伤力不强部分〕 *(opp.* forte*)*.

foil¹ [fɔil] *n.* ①箔,金属薄片. ②(镜底的)银箔,(宝石等的)衬底. ③衬托物,陪衬的角色; 烘托,衬托. ④【建】叶形饰. ⑤水翼 (=hydrofoil); 气垫船. *gold* ～ 金箔. *tin* ～ 锡箔. ***serve as a*** ～ ***to*** 做陪衬. —*vt.* ①铺箔于,垫箔于. ②用…陪衬,衬托. ③【建】给…加上叶形饰.

foil² [fɔil] *n.* ①钝头剑,练习剑. ②〔*pl.*〕(使用钝头剑的)击剑比赛; 击剑术.

foil³ [fɔil] *vt.* ①挫败; 打破(对方策略). ②(打猎时)搞乱(臭迹〔足迹〕). ***be*** ～***ed in*** ... 失败. —*n.* ①猎兽的足迹. ②〔古〕击退. ***break her*** ～ (猎物)奔回原路逃跑. ***put to the*** ～ 挫败,击退. ***run (upon) the*** ～ (猎物)再在原路上奔跑使猎犬迷惑.

foiled [fɔild] *a.*【建】有叶形饰的.

foil·ing¹ [ˈfɔiliŋ] *n.*【建】叶形饰.

foil·ing² [ˈfɔiliŋ] *n.* (猎物的)臭迹.

foils·man [ˈfɔilzmən] *n. (pl.* ***-men*** [-mən]*)* 击剑运动员; 击剑手.

foin [fɔin] *vi., n.* 〔古〕【击剑】刺.

Fo·ism [ˈfəuizəm] *n.* (中国的)佛教.

foi·son [ˈfɔizn] *n.* ①〔古〕丰收,丰饶,大量. ②〔Scot.〕营养; 精力; 力气; 智力.

Fo·ist [ˈfəuist] *n.* 中国佛教徒.

foist [fɔist] *vt.* ①偷偷塞进,私自增加 *(into; in)*. ②偷偷安插(人); 骗卖(假货等); 冒称(作品)是某人所作 *(on, upon)*. ～ *sth. (off) on sb.* 把某物骗售给某人.

fol. = ①folio. ②following.

fo·late [ˈfəuleit] *a.*【生化】叶酸的.

fold¹ [fəuld] *n.* ①折,折叠. ②褶痕,褶层,褶页. ③(蛇、绳等的)一卷,一团. ④(起伏地的)凹处,洼; 〔*pl.*〕(地形的)重叠起伏; 【地】褶皱. ⑤【动】(腕足类的)中隆. ⑥【解】褶. *Another* ～ *gives a 32mo.* 再一折就是32开. —*vt.* ①折叠; 对折 *(back; in; over; together; up)*. ②合拢; 交叠; 叉手,盘(脚). ③抱住. ④和入,掺入,在(食物)中拌进(作料). ⑤包,笼罩. ⑥关掉,结束掉. ～ *a letter* 将信折起来. *The bird* ～*s its wings.* 鸟收拢翅膀. ～ *one's arms* 两臂抱拢〔多指袖手旁观〕. ～ *one's hands* 两手抱住(无所作为). ～ *sb. in one's arms* 抱住某人. *hills* ～*ed in the mist* 雾气笼罩的群山. —*vi.* ①折叠起来,对折起来. ②彻底失败; (戏剧等)因生意清淡而停演. ～ ***down [back]*** (将书页)折过来,折进去. ～ ***up*** ①折起. ②放弃. ③倒塌; 〔俚〕倒闭,破产. ***with*** ～***ed arms*** 两臂交叉抱着〔多指袖手旁观〕. ***with*** ～***ed hands*** 两手抱在一起(一无作为). ～**out** *n.* (书中的)折页.

fold² [fəuld] *n.* ①羊栏. ②羊群. ③〔集合词〕(具有共同信仰的)信徒. ***return to the*** ～ 浪子回头. —*vt.* 把…关进栏内.

-fold *suf.* 加在数词之后,表示"倍","重": three*fold*, mani*fold*, ★ 现在表示倍数意义的词一般多用 -ple, -ble 等拉丁后缀: tri*ple*, tre*ble*, quadru*ple* 等; 后缀为 -fold 的词多用作比喻或副词.

fold·a·way [ˈfəuldəwei] *a.* 可折叠存放的. *a* ～ *cot* 折叠小床. *a* ～ *ladder* 折梯.

fold·boat [ˈfəuldˌbəut] *n.* 折艇.

fold·er [ˈfəuldə] *n.* ①折叠者,折叠机. ②文件夹. ③〔美〕折叠式印刷品. ④〔*pl.*〕折叠式眼镜.

fold·e·rol [ˈfɔldərɔl] *n.* = falderal.

fold·ing [ˈfəuldiŋ] *a.* 可折叠的,折叠式的; (丝绸)起绉的. ～ **bed** 折叠床. ～ **bridge** 开合桥. ～ **chair** 折叠椅. ～ **doors** 〔*pl.*〕双扇门,折门. ～ **fan** 折扇. ～ **money** 〔美〕纸币; 巨款. ～ **rule** 折尺. ～ **screen** 折叠屏风. ～ **stair** 折梯. ～ **stool** 折凳. ～ **top** (汽车的)折叠式车顶.

Fo·ley [ˈfəuli] *n.* 富利〔姓氏〕.

Fol·ger [ˈfəuldʒə] *n.* 福尔杰〔姓氏〕.

fo·li·a [ˈfəuliə] *n.* folium 的另一复数形式.

fo·li·a·ceous [ˌfəuliˈeiʃəs] *a.* ①叶的; 叶状的; 有叶状器官的. ②层状的,(岩石等)分成薄层的.

fo·li·age [ˈfəuliidʒ] *n.* ①〔集合词〕(树的)叶子. ②【建】叶饰. ～ **leaf** 营养叶. ～ **plant** 观叶植物.

fo·li·aged [ˈfəuliidʒd] *a.* 有叶的. *dark-*～ 树叶浓密的.

fo·li·ar [ˈfəuliə] *a.* 叶的,叶状的,叶质的.

fo·li·ate [ˈfəulieit] *vt.* ①把…打成箔; 涂箔(在镜背等). ②【建】使加叶饰. ③把(书籍的)页数〔非面数〕编号. —*vi.* ①分裂成薄片. ②生叶. — [ˈfəuliit] *a.* ①【植】有叶的; 如叶的; 【动】叶状的. ②打成薄片的; 层状的.

fo·li·a·tion [ˌfəuliˈeiʃən] *n.* ①生叶. ②【植】叶卷叠式,幼叶卷叠式. ③打成箔,涂箔. ④【建】叶状饰. ⑤(书籍)标记页数.

fo·li·a·ture [ˈfəuliətʃə] *n.* 〔罕〕= foliage.

fo·lic acid [ˈfəulik ˈæsid]【生化】叶酸.

fo·lie à deux [fəuˌliː ɑː ˈdəː]【精】(两个接近的人的)病态感应,感应性神经病.

fo·lie de gran·deur [fəuˌliːdəgrɑːnˈdəː] 〔F.〕权势狂; 自大狂.

fo·li·ic·o·lous [ˌfəuliːˈikələs] *a.*【生】叶上生的, 寄生在叶上的〔如地衣、菌类、藻类等〕.

fo·lin·ic [fəuˈlinik] **acid** *n.*【化】柠胶(因)素〔= citrovorum factor〕.

fo·li·o [ˈfəuliəu] *n. (pl.* ～***s****)* ①(纸张的)对折,对开〔*cf.* quarto, sexto, octavo, duodecimo, sextodecimo, octodecimo〕; 对开本的书. ②【印】只有一个编码的正反两面,一张. ③张数号,页码. ④(写本的)一页. ⑤单位字数〔计算文件字数的单位,英国通常为 72 字或 90 字,美国为 100 字〕. ～ *volumes* = *volumes (in)*～ 对开本. *in* ～ 对开. —*a.* 对褶的,对开的. —*vt.* 编…的页码(张数号).

fo·li·o·late [ˈfəuliəleit] *a.* 具小叶的.

fo·li·ole [ˈfəuliəul] *n.* 小叶; 【动】叶状突.

fo·li·ose [ˈfəuliəus] *a.* 叶子覆盖的; 多叶的.

fo·li·um [ˈfəuliəm] *n. (pl.* ～***s,*** ***-li·a*** [-ə]*)* ①【地】薄层. ②【数】叶形线.

folk [fəuk] *n. (pl.* ～***s,*** ～*)* ①(常 ～***s,*** 〔古、方〕～) 人们. ②〔口〕家属,亲戚; 正派的人们. ③〔古〕民族,种族. —*a.* 民间的. *fine* ～*s* 名流. *town* ～*(s)* 城市人. *country* ～*(s)* 乡下人. *our* ～*s* 乡亲们. *my* ～*s* (全家)亲属们. *one's* ～*s* 家属. *the old* ～*(s)* 老人们. *the young* ～*s* 儿女. *your young* ～*s* 你家孩子们. ***just*** ～***s*** 〔口〕厚道热肠的人,淳朴的人. —*a.* 民间的. ～ **custom** 民间习俗. ～ **dance** 民间舞蹈. ～ **etymology** 民俗语源,

通俗词源;文字的通俗变化〔如 bridegome 变化 bridegroom, asparagus 变为 sparrow-grass 等〕. ~**lore** 民间创作;民间传说;民俗学. ~**lorist** 民间传说研究者,民俗学者. ~ **medicine** 土法治疗,民间疗法. ~**moot,** ~**mote** 〔废〕【史】(市、郡等的)群众大会. ~ **music** 民间音乐. ~**nik**〔俚〕民间歌手,民歌爱好者. ~**-rock** 民歌风摇摆舞音乐. ~**say**〔美〕俗话. ~ **song** 民歌. ~ **state** 由一个民族组成的国家. ~ **story,** ~ **tale** 民间故事,传说. ~**ways** 社会习俗,民间风俗习惯.

Folke·stone [ˈfəukstən] *n.* 福克斯通〔英肯特州一港口〕.

Fol·ke·ting, Fol·ke·thing [ˈfəulkətiŋ, Dan. ˈfɔlgəteŋ] *n.* 〔Dan.〕①(1953年以前的)丹麦议会的下院. ②(现在)丹麦一院制议会.

folk·sy [ˈfəuksiː] *a.* ***(-si·er,-si·est)***〔美口〕①爱交际的,友好的. ②随便的,无拘束的. ③有民间风味的. ~ **musical compositions** 有民间风味的音乐作品. **-i·ness** ***n.***

foll. = following (words, pages 等).

fol·li·cle [ˈfɔlikl] *n.* ①【解】(小)囊,滤泡,卵泡. ②【植】蓇葖. *a hair* ~ 毛囊. ~ **mite**【动】蠕形螨〔一种毛孔寄生虫〕. ~**-stimulating hormone** 促卵(成熟)激素,促卵泡激素.

fol·lic·u·lar [fəˈlikjulə] *a.* 【解】小囊的,滤泡的,卵泡的;【植】蓇葖的.

fol·lic·u·late(d) [fəˈlikjuleit(id)] *a.* = follicular.

fol·lic·u·lin [fəˈlikjulin] *n.*【生化】卵巢滤胞激素,经酮(= estrone).

fol·lies [ˈfɔliz] *n. pl.* 〔用作单数〕活报剧; 时事讽刺剧.

fol·low [ˈfɔləu] *vt.* ①跟着,跟随;接着,跟着发生,继…之后;(地位)在…之后. ②追赶,追求. ③顺…前进. ④因…而起,是必然结果. ⑤信奉,追随,遵循;听从(忠告等). ⑥仿效,照. ⑦从事. ⑧注视;倾听;注意(事态的发展等). ⑨(在理解上)跟得上;听得懂;领悟,了解. *Spring ~s winter.* 冬去春来. *F- this road to the corner.* 顺着这条路到转角处. *I do not quite ~ you.* 我听不大懂你的话. *Are you ~ing (me)?* 你听清楚没有? *~ the argument easily* 那个议论容易理解. *~ the world's affairs* 注意世界局势. —*vi.* 跟着,跟随,随后,继;结果发生;因而当然,那么…就. *Go on ahead and I'll ~.* 前面走着吧,我跟着你. *It ~s (from this) that ....* 由此得出,可见. ***as ~s*** 如下,如次. (*She wrote as ~s.* 她写的内容如下. *It reads as ~s.* 全文如下). ★ 主句的主语不论是单数还是复数,通常都不用 as ~. ***~ a course of action*** 采取一定行动. ***~ sb. about*** 跟踪,尾随. ***~ in [out]*** 跟着某人进去[出来]. ***~ after*** 紧跟,追求,力求达到. ***~ a lead***【牌】跟牌;跟着. ***~ in sb.'s steps*** 照某人成例,继某人衣钵. ***~ in the wake of*** 踏着…的足迹,继承着…的意愿;仿效. ***~ knowledge*** 求学. ***~ my leader*** = ~-my-leader. ***~ on*** 紧接着;继续下去. ***~ out*** 贯彻,进行到底;查明. ***~ the band***〔美〕追随群众;赶时髦. ***~ the drum*** 从军. ***~ the lead of sb.*** 效法某人. ***~ the stage*** 做演员. ***~ through***〔体〕(完成球棒或球拍击球后的)弧形动作;完成;坚持到底. ***~ up*** ①趁(机). ②穷追;贯彻到底. ③(足球队员)靠近盘球人作后援;【医】(在诊断或治疗后)随访(*~ up a victory* 乘胜穷追. *~ up a blow* 连打. *~ up work* 贯彻工作). ***in what ~s*** 在下文中. —*n.* ①跟随,追随. ②(台球)跟球. ③〔口〕添菜. ~**-my-leader** (游戏) (跟领头人一样动作,错则受罚的) 猴子学样. ~**-on** ① *n.* 随后发生的事;继任者. ② *a.* 后继的,随后发生的. ~**-scene [shot]**【影】跟镜头场面. ~**-the-leader** = ~-my-leader. ~**-through**【网球等】(球打出后的) 后续打姿;(一个举动的)最末部分;继续完成最后的行动.

fol·low·er [ˈfɔləuə] *n.* ①跟随者;追随者;跟踪者. ②随员;部下;信从者,信徒. ③〔英〕(特指女仆人的)情人. ④【火箭】跟踪装置. ⑤【机】从动件,从动轮,随动件. ⑥(契据的)附页. *unwilling ~s* 胁从分子.

fol·low·ing [ˈfɔləuiŋ] *a.* ①接着的,其次的. ②后面的;以下的,下述的. ③【海】(风)后面吹来的;(潮水)后面涌来的. *in the ~ year* = *in the year ~* 第二年. *on the ~ day* = *on the day ~* 在第二天. —*n.* ①随员,部属;追随者. ②〔the ~〕以下所说. *a political leader with a large ~* 拥有大批追随者的政治领袖. —*prep.* 在…以后. *F- the meeting, a dinner was given.* 会见后举行宴会. ~ **in range**【火箭】远距离跟踪.

fol·low-up [ˈfɔləuʌp] *n.* ①跟踪. ②【医】(诊断或治疗后对病人进行的)定期复查,随访. ③(报纸或广播的)补充[继续]报导. ④【机】随动装置. ⑤【商】经常发出的广告信. —*a.* 重复的;补充的;继续的,接着的. *~ pressure* 自动加压(法). *a ~ instruction* 补充指示. *a ~ letter* 补充寄来的信. *the ~ survey* 继续观察. ~ **system** 连续通信劝购法. ~**-up units**【军】后续部队.

fol·ly [ˈfɔli] *n.* ①愚笨,愚蠢. ②愚行,傻念头. ③〔古〕罪恶,放荡. ④花费巨大而无益的事,华而不实的大建筑〔常冠以设计者名字,例 *Allen's F-*〕. ⑤〔*pl.*〕时事讽刺剧. *commit a ~* 作蠢事. *The follies of youth are food for repentence in old age.*〔谚〕年轻时胡闹,年老时烦恼.

Fol·som man [ˈfɔlsəm, ˈfəul-] 佛索姆人〔冰河时代晚期居住在北美的一种人〕.

Fo·mal·haut [ˈfəumlˌhɔːt] 【天】北落师门〔南鱼座 α〕.

fo·ment [fəuˈment] *vt.* ①【医】热敷,热罨. ②酝酿,煽动,挑起. *~ dissension* 挑拨离间,散布不和. *~ a mutiny* 煽动哗变. **fo·men·ta·tion** [ˌfəumenˈteiʃən] *n.* **-er** *n.* 挑唆者.

fond [fɔnd] *a.* 〔常用作表语〕①喜欢,爱好 *(of)*. ②宠爱的,溺爱的. ③不大可能实现的. *be ~ of fishing* 爱钓鱼. *a ~ mother* 慈母. *a ~ dream* 黄粱美梦.

fon·dant [ˈfɔndənt] *n.* 奶油软糖;奶油软糖馅.

fon·dle [ˈfɔndl] *vt.* 爱抚;〔古〕溺爱… —*vi.* 爱抚 *(with; together)*.

fon·dling [ˈfɔndliŋ] *n.* ①爱抚. ②被宠爱的人[动物].

fond·ly [ˈfɔndli] *ad.* ①亲爱地. ②愚蠢地,毫无头脑地. *as I ~ imagined* 象我以前傻想的那样. *~ hope* 妄想;一厢情愿的希望.

fond·ness [ˈfɔndnis] *n.* ①喜欢,嗜好 *(for)*. ②宠爱;溺爱. ③傻想法,轻信. ***have a ~ for*** 爱好.

fon·du(e) [fɔnˈduː] *n.*【烹】①酒味(熔化)干酪酱. ②干酪煎肉丁. ③松脆干酪酥.

fons et o·ri·go [ˈfɔnz et əˈraigəu] 〔L.〕本源,根源.

font[1] [fɔnt] *n.* ①【宗】洗礼盘,圣水器. ②(煤油灯的)油壶. ③〔诗〕源泉.

font[2] [fɔnt] *n.* 美【印】(同一型号的)一副铅字,全副铅字(=fount). *a wrong ~* 非同一型号的铅字〔略 w. f.〕.

Fon·taine·bleau [ˈfɔntinbləu] *n.* 枫丹白露〔法国北部一城市〕.

font·al [ˈfɔntl] *a.* ①源泉的,本源的. ②洗礼的.

fon·ta·nel(le) [ˌfɔntəˈnel] *n.*【解】囟门.

food [fuːd] *n.* ①食物,食品,粮食,食料;养料. ②精神食粮,材料,资料. *animal [vegetable] ~* 肉[素]食. *canned ~* 罐头食品. *mental [intellectual] ~* 精神食粮. *non-staple [subsidiary] ~* 副食品. *spiritual ~* 精神食粮. *~ for poetry* 诗的素材. ***be [become] ~ for fishes*** 葬身鱼腹,淹死. ***be ~ for worms*** 死亡. ***~ and drink*** 饮食. ***~ for powder*** 炮灰,〔蔑〕兵士. ***~ for thought [meditation]*** 思考的材料. ~ **card [coupon]** 粮票,饭票. ~ **chain [cycle,** ~ **web**【生态】食物链]. ~ **office**〔英〕粮食管理局. ~ **poisoning** 食物中毒. ~ **pyramid**【生态】食物链塔状层次图. ~ **science** 食物营养学. ~ **stamp** (发给失业人口等免费或廉价的)食物券. ~***stuff*** 食品,粮食. **-less** *a.* 缺粮的,断炊的.

foo·fa·raw [ˈfuːfərɔː] *n.* 〔美俚〕①多余装饰品;(服装

等的)裙边；饰边．②大惊小怪．

fool[1] [fuːl] *n.* ①笨人，傻子，白痴．②受愚弄[欺骗]的人．③(已往王侯雇养的)小丑，弄臣．④有癖好的人．*Fool's haste is no speed.*〔谚〕欲速则不达．*a chess-playing* ~ 棋迷．*an April* ~ 愚人节被愚弄的人．***act [play] the*** ~ 当傻瓜，做蠢事，装傻样；扮演丑角，逗人乐．***All Fool's Day*** 愚人节〔四月一日〕．***be a*** ~ ***for one's pains*** 徒劳．***be a*** ~ ***to*** 比不上．***be*** ~ ***enough to do*** 笨到做…．***be no [nobody's]*** ~ 很精明．***be the*** ~ ***of fate*** 被命运愚弄．***A*** ~***'s bolt is soon shot.*** 蠢人往往一下子把箭射完〔指蠢人不善于把握时机地逐步运用力量，不善于节约精力、金钱等〕．***make a*** ~ ***of*** 愚弄．***make a*** ~ ***of oneself*** 闹笑话．***play the*** ~ ***with*** 欺瞒；使失败，弄坏．***go [be sent] on a*** ~***'s errand*** 去[被派去]作无谓奔走．— *vt.* ①愚弄；欺骗．②浪费，虚度．— *vi.* ①闹笑话；开玩笑；干傻事．②游手好闲；瞎弄．*Stop* ~*ing!* 别闹笑话了！*He is only* ~*ing.* 他不过是开玩笑罢了．***be badly*** ~***ed*** 上大当．~ ***about*** = ~ ***around***〔美口〕闲游，瞎干涉，多管闲事．~ ***away*** 浪费(时间、金钱等)．~ ***(sb.) into*** 骗人作…．~ ***(sb.) out of*** 骗取某人(财物等)．~ ***with*** 玩弄．— *a.*〔美口〕愚蠢的．~ **duck**【动】(北美出产的)赤鸭．~**hardy** *a.* 有勇无谋的，蛮干的．~ **hen**〔美〕松鸡．~**proof** *a.* ①〔俚〕傻瓜也明白[会干]的，极简单明了的．②有安全装置的．~**'s gold**【矿】黄铁矿，黄铜矿．~**'s paradise**(实际是荒唐无聊的)自以为非常幸福[有意义]的处境．

fool[2] [fuːl] *n.*〔英〕(煮熟的)糖水水果拌奶油．

fool·er·y [ˈfuːləri] *n.* 愚蠢的思想[谈吐、行动]．

fool·ish [ˈfuːliʃ] *a.* 愚蠢的；鲁莽的，可笑的，荒谬的．*Better a witty fool than a* ~ *wit.*〔谚〕宁做聪明的傻子，不做愚蠢的聪明人．***cut [make] a*** ~ ***figure*** 闹笑话．~ **powder**〔美俚〕海洛因．**-ly** *ad.* **-ness** *n.*

fool·oc·ra·cy [fuːˈlɔkrəsi] *n.* 愚人统治，愚人统治集团．

fools·cap [ˈfuːlzkæp] *n.* ①丑角帽；(罚不用功的学生戴的)圆锥形纸帽．②[ˈfuːlskæp] (约 13×16 英寸)大页书写纸．

fool's-pars·ley [ˈfuːlzˈpɑːsli] *n.*【植】毒欧芹．

foot [fut] *n. pl.* ***(feet*** [fiːt]***)*** ①脚，足．②步调，脚步．③〔集合词〕步兵．④(器物的)足部；(山)麓；帆的下缘．⑤底部，底座，最下部；压脚板；末尾．⑥英尺(=12 英寸，$\frac{1}{3}$ 码，0.3048 米)．★ 作长度单位时，前为数词，单数也可用作复数．例：two foot six = two feet six (inches)．⑦【韵】音步．⑧***(pl. foots)*** 渣滓，沉淀物；粗糖；油糟．⑨【动】跗节．⑩【植】花梗，发状根．*have a light* ~ 脚步轻．*have leaden [heavy] feet* 脚步沉重，行动迟缓．*the* ~ *of a bed* 床头的对面一端．〔*opp.* the head of a bed 床头；床的腿为 the legs of a bed〕．*the* ~ *of the list* 表列的下端．*the 42nd* ~ 步兵第42团．~ *and horse* 步兵与骑兵．*at the* ~ *of a hill* 在山脚．*at the* ~ *of a class* 全班的最后一名．*fleet [swift] of* ~ 行动敏捷，健步如飞．*Better the foot slip than the tongue trip.* = *Better to slip with the foot than with the tongue.*〔谚〕宁可失脚滑倒，不可随口失言．***at a*** ~***'s pace*** 用步行速度，常步．***at sb.'s feet*** 在某人脚下[门下，手下] (*sit at sb.'s feet* 拜某人为师)．***be carried out with one's feet foremost*** 被抬出去埋葬．***be sure of*** ~ 踏实．***betray [display, show] the cloven*** ~ 露马脚．***bring sb. to his feet*** 扶起某人．***carry [sweep, take] sb. off his feet*** 使人兴奋，使人狂热．***catch sb. on the wrong*** ~ 使人措手不及．***change*** ~ ***[feet]*** 换脚，换步．***drag one's feet*** ①拖着脚步走．②故意拖拉，迟缓误事．***drop [fall] on one's feet*** 运气好，没有跌着；安然脱险，幸免于难．***feel one's feet [legs, wing]*** 感到有把握．***feet of clay*** 泥足，外强中干的，不堪一击的 (*a colossus with feet of clay* 泥足巨人)．***find one's feet*** 开始站稳；能独立行动．***find [get, know, take] the length of sb.'s*** ~ 抓到某人的弱点．~ ***by*** ~ 一步一步；逐渐．~ ***to*** ~ 短兵相接．***have a*** ~ ***in the dish*** 有一份，获得立足点．***have cold feet*** 害怕，胆寒，畏缩，不敢上阵．***have [with] one*** ~ ***in the grave*** 风烛残年，离死不远．***have one's*** ~ ***into*** 插足．***have [put, set] one's*** ~ ***on the neck of sb.*** 压服某人．***have two left feet*** 笨极了．***jump [spring] to one's feet*** 突然站起，跃起．***keep one's feet*** 站稳．***lay sth. at sb.'s feet*** 把某物献在某人脚下．***lift off one's feet*** (被水等)冲[撞]倒．***measure another man's*** ~ ***by one's own last*** 以己度人．***miss one's*** ~ 失脚；踏空，走乱步子．***my [me]*** ~***!***〔口〕怪啦！胡说！去你的！***not to lift [move, stir] a*** ~ 一步也不动．***off one's feet*** 躺着，坐着，跌倒；不知所措；措手不及；不能控制自己．***on*** ~ 步行；在进行中 (*go on* ~ 走着去．*set a plan on* ~ 实施计划)．***on one's feet*** 站起；健康复原，经济独立，自立．***pull*** ~ 逃走．***put one's best*** ~ ***foremost [forward]*** 争先快走；全力以赴．***put [set] one's*** ~ ***down*** 立定脚跟；坚持立场；拿定主张．***put one's*** ~ ***in [into] it***〔口〕弄糟，闹笑话，引起麻烦．***put one's feet up***〔口〕双腿平搁起来休息．***raise sb. to his feet*** 扶起某人．***rise [spring, struggle] to one's*** ~ 站起．***rush sb. off his feet*** 使某人措手不及．***scrape one's feet*** 用脚擦地作声．***set*** ~ ***in*** 进入．***set*** ~ ***on*** 踏上．***set on*** ~ 着手．***set sb. [sth.] on his [its] feet*** 使某人[物]独立生存[存在]下去．***sling a nasty*** ~〔俚〕跳舞跳得到家．***sweep sb. off his*** ~ 使某人大为激动〔不能控制自己〕．***take to one's feet*** 走出，步行，走去．***trample [tread] under*** ~ 践踏，蹂躏；虐待．***under sb.'s*** ~ ***[feet]*** 屈服于人，唯命是从．***with both feet*** 强烈地，坚决地．***with one's feet foremost*** 死去．***with one's wrong*** ~ ***foremost*** 心情不好．— *vt.* ①踏在…上，在…上走，在…上跳；跳(舞)．②〔口〕结(帐)，付(款)．③给(袜子等)换底．④(鹰等)以爪捕捉．~ *the road* 走路．~ *the floor* 跳舞．~ *(up) an account* 结算帐目．~ *a bill* 付帐．— *vi.* ①步行；踏拍子；跳舞．②〔俚〕合计；共达．③(船等)前进．~ *up to $ 500.* 共计五百元．~ ***it***〔口〕走着去，跳舞．~ ***up***〔口〕凑成，凑足．~**and-mouth disease** (牛羊等的)口蹄疫．~**bath** 洗脚；脚盆．~**board** (马车、汽车等的)踏脚板；床靠脚一端的竖板．~**boy** 小听差．~**brake** 脚踏闸，脚踏式制动器．~**bridge** 人行小桥．~**-candle**【物】英尺烛光[烛光亮度]．~**drill**【军】徒手训练．~ **drop** 垂足病．~**fall** 脚步，脚步声．~ **fault** (网球)发球犯规；(排球)脚过中线．~**gear** 鞋袜．**F- Guards** (英国)近卫步兵连．~**hill** 山麓小丘，〔常 *pl.*〕山脉的丘陵地带．~**hold** 立足点，【军】据点．~**-in-mouth** *a.* 口不择言的；措词尖锐的．~**lights**〔*pl.*〕【剧】舞台上的脚光；舞台；演戏 (*appear before the* ~*lights* 上台演戏．*behind the* ~*lights* 在观众席上．*get across [over] the* ~*lights* 演出受欢迎．*smell of the* ~*lights* 象在做戏，装模作样．*smell the* ~*lights* 变成戏迷)．~**man** 步兵；(穿号衣的)马夫，男仆．~**mark** 足迹．~**note** ①*n.* (书中的)脚注．②*vt.* 为…作脚注．~**pace** ①常步，慢步．②【建】梯台．~**pad** ①(徒步的)拦路盗贼 (*cf.* highwayman)．②(软降落宇航器腿上防止在星球表面上陷入的)防陷足垫．~**page** 男仆．~ **passenger** 步行者，行人．~**path** ①步道，人行道．②小路．~**plate** (火车司机室内的)踏板，~**-pound**【物】英尺磅〔能的单位〕．~**-poundal**【物】英尺磅达〔功的单位〕．~**-pound-second** 英尺磅秒单位制．~**print** ①足迹，脚印．②宇宙飞船的预定着陆点．~**pump** 脚踏泵．~**race** 竞走．~ **rail**【矿】轨蹼，轨脚．~**rest** 搁脚板．~**rope**【海】(水手收帆时站的)脚缆，脚踏索，帆的下缘索．~ **rot** ①【植】根腐病．②【兽医】腐蹄病．~ **rule** 一英尺长的直尺．~ **soldier** 步兵．~**sore** *a.* 走痛了脚的．~**stalk**【植】叶柄；花梗；【动】肉茎．~**stall**【建】基脚；墩柱．~**step** 脚步；脚步声；足迹；【机】垫轴台，轴承架 (*follow [walk] in sb.'s* ~*steps* 步某人的后尘)．~**stock** = tailstock．~**stone** 基

石；墓基．～**stool** ①脚台，脚凳．②〔美〕地，大地．～-**sure** *a.* 脚步稳的，踏实的．～-**ton** 英尺吨〔能量单位〕．～**wall** 底帮，底壁，下盘；基础墙．～**warmer** 暖脚物．～**way** 人行道．～**wear** = foot gear. ～**well** (汽车中安设用脚操纵的脚闸、风门瓣等机件，驾驶者放腿脚的)搁脚处．～**work** ①【体】步法．②要跑腿的工作．～**worn** *a.* ①走累的．②被脚踏磨损的(～ *stairs* 磨损的楼梯)．

foot·age [ˈfutidʒ] *n.* 以英尺计的长度〔尺数〕；(影片等总长度的)英尺数．【矿】进尺．

foot·ball [ˈfutbɔːl] *n.* ①足球〔美国通常指橄榄球〕，足球运动，足球的球．②玩物，玩弄物；被踢来踢去的难题〔悬案〕．*American* ～ 美式足球，橄榄球．*Association* ～ 英式足球〔又称 soccer〕．*Rugby* ～ 橄榄球．*a* ～ *fiend* 〔美〕足球迷．***become a*** ～ ***of*** 变成玩弄品．***play*** ～ 踢足球；对难办的事采取踢皮球的态度．

foot·ball·er [ˈfutbɔːlə], **foot·ball·ist** [-ist] *n.* 足球〔橄榄球〕运动员．

foot·cloth [ˈfutˌklɔθ] *n.* (*pl.* **-cloths** [-ˌklɔːðz, -klɔːθs]) ①马披巾．②〔罕〕地毯；毯．

foot·ed [ˈfutid] *a.* ①有足的；有多足的．②有某种足或足型的〔用以构成有连字符的复合词〕．*four-*～ 四足的．

foot·er [ˈfutə] *n.* ①〔常用以构成复合词〕高…英尺的人．长…英尺的东西．②步行者．③〔英俚〕足球赛．*a six* ～ 身高六英尺的人．

foot·ing [ˈfutiŋ] *n.* ①立足处，立脚点．②立场，基础，地位；【建】底脚．③关系，交情．④合计，总额．⑤场地情况．⑥入会费，入社费，入学费．⑦【军】编制．*Mind your* ～. 当心脚下，别跌倒．*be on a friendly* ～ *with sb.* 跟某人关系好．***get [gain, obtain] a*** ～ 取得地位．***keep one's*** ～ 站稳；坚守立场．***lose [miss] one's*** ～ 跌交；丧失立场．***on a peace [war]*** ～ 按平时〔战时〕编制．***on an equal*** ～ 平等对待．***on one [a, the same]*** ～ ***with*** 以同等资格．***pay (for) one's*** ～ 缴入会费；纳费入伙．～ **course**【建】基础层．

foot·le [ˈfuːtl] *n.* 蠢话，傻事．—*vi.* ①说蠢话，做傻事．②浪费时间．

foot·less [ˈfutlis] *a.* ①无脚的．②无基础的，无支撑的．③〔诗〕人迹未到的．④〔口〕笨拙的，无能的，无益的．

foot·ling [ˈfutliŋ] *a.* 〔口〕①愚蠢的．②不关重要的；琐细的；微不足道的．

foot·lock·er [ˈfutlɔkə] *n.*【美军】士兵个人用品箱，床脚箱〔置于床脚的美士兵个人用品箱〕．

foot·loose [ˈfutˌluːs] *a.* 到处走动的；随心所欲的．

foot·sie, foot·sy [ˈfutsi] *n.* (*pl.* **-si·es**)〔儿〕脚儿．***play*** ～ ***(with)***〔口〕①(在桌下)柔情地碰碰腿儿〔膝〕．②调情；暗中勾搭，搞秘密交易．

foot·slog [ˈfutˌslɔg] *vi.* (**-gg-**) 在泥泞中行进．**-ger** *n.* 长途步行者；步兵．

foo·ty [ˈfuti] *a.* (**foo·ti·er; -i·est**) ①微不足道的，无足轻重的．②肯定很糟的，褴褛的．

foo·zle [ˈfuːzl] *vt., vi.* (尤指在高尔夫球中)笨拙地打(球等)；笨拙地做(事)；(把…)弄糟．—*n.* ①不高明的一击，笨拙的动作．②〔口〕笨人．

fop [fɔp] *n.* 纨袴子弟，花花公子．

fop·ling [ˈfɔpliŋ] *n.* 〔古〕= fop.

fop·per·y [ˈfɔpəri] *n.* 纨袴习气．

fop·pish [ˈfɔpiʃ] *a.* 浮华的，有纨袴子弟习气的．**-ly** *ad.* **-ness** *n.*

FOR, f.o.r. = free on rail【商】火车上交货(价格)．

for [强 fɔː，元音前常作 fɔr；弱 fə，辅音前常作 f，元音前常作 fr] *prep.* ①〔表示目标、去向〕向，往．*leave [sail]* ～ *London* 动身〔坐船〕到伦敦去．*passengers for Shanghai* 到上海去的旅客．*the train* ～ *Paris* 开往巴黎的火车．*He is getting on* ～ *forty.* 他快四十岁了．*Now* ～ *it!* 走吧！开动吧！*a change* ～ *the better* 好转．*a change* ～ *the worse* 恶化．②〔表示愿望、爱好、特长等〕倾向于，对于．*have a liking* ～ *music* 爱好音乐．*have respect* ～ *one's teachers* 尊敬老师．*long* ～ *freedom* 渴望自由．*an eye* ～ *beauty* 审美眼光．③〔表示目的〕为了．*a house* ～ *rent* 〔美〕房屋出租．*not* ～ *sale* 非卖品．*die* ～ *one's country* 为祖国牺牲．*go out* ～ *a walk* 出去散步．*struggle* ～ *existence* 生存竞争．*shout* ～ *help* 大声呼救．*send* ～ *a doctor* 叫人去请医生．*Oh,* ～ *a glass of water!* 啊，有一杯水就好了．④〔表示理由、原因〕因为．*My head aches* ～ *want of sleep.* 我因为睡眠不足而头痛．～ *fear of* 唯恐．⑤代，替，代表．*a substitute* ～ *butter* 奶油代用品．*speak* ～ *sb.* 代某人说话〔辩白〕．⑥〔表示等价、报酬、赔偿或比例关系〕交换．*I gave a dollar* ～ *it.* 我用一块钱弄到手的．*sell* ～ *a dollar* 一块钱卖掉了．*give blow* ～ *blow* 以打还打．*answer point* ～ *point* 逐点答复．*translate word* ～ *word* 逐字翻译．⑦〔表示时间、距离、数量等〕历经，达，计．～ *hours [days, years]* 有(好)几小时〔(好)几天，(好)几年〕．*the meeting lasted (*～*) an hour* 会议继续了一小时．*run (*～*) a mile* 跑一英里路．★在上述情形下，*for* 常可略去．⑧〔表示关联〕关于，说到．*He has no equal* ～ *running.* 讲到赛跑，他是无敌的．～ *my part* 至于我，讲到我．*So much* ～ *today* 今天就讲〔做〕这么多．⑨〔表示赞成，支持〕拥护，有利于 (*opp.* against)．*They are all* ～ *him.* 他们都支持他．*vote* ～ *sb.* 投某人的票．⑩〔表示身分等〕看作，当作，作为．*be hanged* ～ *a pirate* 被当作海盗绞死．*be mistaken* ～ *a Japanese* 被误认为是日本人．*They knew it* ～ *a fact.* 他们知道那是事实．*It was built* ～ *a pleasure boat.* 这条船是作为游艇建造的．⑪〔表示让步〕虽然，尽管．*F- all his wealth, I don't like him.* 尽管他那样有钱，我并不喜欢他．⑫〔表示与具体条件作比较〕比起来，考虑到，就…而言．*It is rather cold* ～ *April.* 拿四月来讲，天气算冷了一点．*clever* ～ *one's age* 拿年龄来说就算聪明的了．⑬〔表示对象〕属于…的，给…的．*a present* ～ *you* 送给你的礼物．⑭〔表示用途〕适于…的．*fit* ～ *food* 适于作食物．⑮〔与名词或代词等连用，后接动词不定式构成起主〔宾〕、定、状语作用的二元语核〕．*F- them to surrender would be impossible.* 要他们投降是不可能的．*make way for the car to pass* 给汽车让路．*The book is too difficult* ～ *me to read.* 这本书太艰深，我读不下去．*It is time* ～ *him to go.* 他该走了．***(as)*** ～ ***me*** 讲到我．***be*** ～ ***it*** ①赞成．②势必受罚．～ ***all*** 无论…怎样(*F- all you say, I still like him.* 不管你怎么说，我仍然喜欢他)．～ ***all I care*** 我管不着，与我无关．～ ***all I know*** 也许，或许．～ ***all that*** 虽然如此，还是．～ ***all time*** 永久．***F- crying out loud!***〔美口〕真想不到！见鬼！去你的吧！有这种事么！〔用于表示惊诧，不快〕．～ ***days (and days) on end*** 永远，老是．～ ***it*** ①应付的(手段，方法)．②因此．③快要发生麻烦，就要挨骂．④〔美〕(兵士)接到行动命令(*There is nothing* ～ *it but to wait.* 除等待外别无办法．*be worse* ～ *it* 因此更糟．*be in* ～ *it* 骑虎难下；势必要受罚)。～ ***one*** 至少有一个，举一个作例子〔用作插入语〕(*I,* ～ *one, object to it* 至少我是反对那样做的)．～ ***oneself*** 为自己；亲自；独自．～ ***one thing*** 第一〔表示列举〕；原因之一是〔用作插入语〕．—*conj.* 因为．*We can't go, for it is raining.* 天下雨，我们不去了．★用来说明理由，比 because 更为正式，但语气较弱，一般不用于句首，口语中也多不用．回答 why 引导的问题时，要用 because.

for- *pref.* ①表示"禁止"，"拒绝"，"蔑视"：*for*bear, *for*bid, *for*go. ②表示"破坏"：*for*do, *for*swear. ③表示"极度"，"过度"(= all over, thoroughly)：*for*gather, *for*lorn, *for*worn. ④= fore-: *for*cast.

for. = foreign; forestry.

fo·ra [ˈfɔːrə] *n.* forum 的另一复数形式．

for·age [ˈfɔridʒ] *n.* ①粮秣；饲料．②粮秣的搜索〔征发〕．***be on the*** ～ (牛马)正在找饲料，(兵)正在征发粮秣．—*vt., vi.* ①搜索〔征发〕粮秣．②给(马)吃草料．③〔古〕蹂躏，掠夺．～ *among papers* 乱翻文件．～

about [around] in a drawer 在抽屉里乱翻. ～ ***for oneself*** 自行采购(粮秣); 用现成食品当饭食; 自行谋生. ～ **acre** 饲料亩[牧场饲料作物的计算单位, 等于牧场总面积乘饲料作物所占百分比, 例如: 10 英亩×30% 密度 = 3 饲料亩]. ～ **cap** [英] 步兵便帽.

for·ag·er [ˈfɔridʒə] *n.* ①粮秣征发员. ②[*pl.*] 成散开横队的骑兵.

fo·ra·men [fəˈreimen] *n.* (*pl.* ***fo·ram·i·na*** [fəˈræminə]) 【动、植】孔. ～ **magnum** (昆虫的) 后头孔; (枕骨)大孔.

fo·ram·i·nate(d) [fəˈræminit(id)] *a.* [罕]有孔的; 有小孔的; 多孔的.

for·a·min·i·fer [ˌfɔːrəˈminifə, ˌfɔ-] *n.* (*pl.* ***fo·ram·i·nif·er·a*** [fəˌræmiˈnifərə]) 【动】有孔虫目. **fo·ram·i·nif·er·al, fo·ram·i·nif·er·ous** *a.*

for·as·much [fərəzˈmʌtʃ] *conj.* 由于, 鉴于(与 as 连用) (= since, considering that).

FORATOM = [F.] *Forum Atomique Européen* 欧洲原子能公司 (= European Atomic Forum).

for·ay [ˈfɔrei] *n., vt., vi.* 侵略, 掠夺; 摧残, 踩躏. *make [go on] a* ～ 进行袭击[劫掠].

forb [fɔːb] *n.* [美] 一种阔叶、开花的非禾本牧草; 任何非草本的药用植物.

for·bade [fəˈbeid], **for·bad** [-ˈbæd] forbid 的过去式.

for·bear[1] [fɔːˈbɛə] *vi.* (***-bore*** [fɔːˈbɔː]; ***-borne*** [fɔːˈbɔːn]) 忍耐, 容忍 (*with*); 克制, 节制, 戒 (*from*). —*vt.* 抑制, 节制; 忍住, 忍受, 忍耐. ～ *(from) complaining* 不发牢骚. ～ *to go into details* 不准备详细说. *I cannot* ～ *to go into details.* 我不得不详细说. *She could not* ～ *crying out.* 她禁不住叫喊出来. ～ *with sb. [sth.]* 容忍某人[某事]. ***bear and*** ～ [ˈfɔːbɛə] 忍了又忍.

for·bear[2] [ˈfɔːbɛə] *n.* = forebear.

for·bear·ance [fɔːˈbɛərəns] *n.* ①忍耐, 克制. ②【法】债务偿还期的延缓. ③放弃执行某些权利. *at the end of one's* ～ 忍无可忍. *F- is no (ac)quittance* [谚] 不催帐不等于取消帐.

for·bear·ing [fɔːˈbɛəriŋ] *a.* 能忍耐的; 宽容的. **-ly** *ad.*

For·bes [fɔːbz, ˈfɔːbis] *n.* 福布斯[姓氏].

for·bid [fəˈbid] *vt.* (***-bad*** [fəˈbæd], ***-bade*** [fəˈbeid]; ***-bid·den*** [fəˈbidn], ～) ①禁止, 不许. ②妨害, 阻止. *Cameras are forbidden.* 禁止拍照. *Parking forbidden!* 禁止停车! ～ *sb. the house* 不许某人进屋来. ～ *sb. to smoke* 禁止某人吸烟. *Time* ～*s.* 时间不许可. *High walls* ～ *all approach.* 高墙遮断, 难以接近. *The storm* ～*s us to proceed.* 暴风雨阻止我们前进. ***God [Heaven, The saints]*** ～! 但愿不这样! 决没有(那样的事) (*God* ～ *that he should injure you!* 他决不会害你的!).

for·bid·dance [fəˈbidəns] *n.* 禁止; 禁令.

for·bid·den [fəˈbidn] forbid 的过去分词. —*a.* 被禁止的. **F- city** 紫禁城. ～ **[prohibited] degrees** 【法】禁婚亲等. ～ **fruit** 【宗】禁果; 因被禁止反而更想弄到手的东西. ～ **ground [zone]** 禁区.

for·bid·ding [fəˈbidiŋ] *a.* 可怕的, 令人难亲近的; 凶险的. *a* ～ *countenance [look]* 严峻的面貌. **-ly** *ad.* **-ness** *n.*

for·bore [fɔːˈbɔː] forbear[1] 的过去式.

for·borne [fɔːˈbɔːn] forbear[1] 的过去分词.

for·by(e) [fɔːˈbai] *ad., prep.* [古, Scot.] 而且; 除…外. —*a.* 不同寻常的, 极好的.

force[1] [fɔːs] *n.* ①力, 势. ②脅力, 气力, 精力, 魄力. ③暴力, 压力; 兵力, 武力. ④[*pl.*] 部队, 军队, 兵力. ⑤势力, 威力; 【法】效力的约束, 实施. ⑥(语言、文字等的) 确切意义, 实质; 要点; 影响力, 说服力, 主动性. ⑦【物】…力; 势能. ～ *of character* 人格的力量. *the* ～ *of habit* 习惯势力. *the* ～*s of nature* 自然力. *the* ～ *of public opinion* 舆论的威力. *with the* ～ *of a thunderbolt* 以雷霆万钧之力. *a 12 force [12th-*～*] typhoon* 十二级台风. *the air* ～空军. *the armed* ～*s* 军队. *an assault* ～【军】突击队. *brutal* ～ 暴力. *centrifugal* ～ 离心力. *centripetal* ～ 向心力. *democratic* ～ 民主势力. *feudal* ～ 封建势力. *interatomic* ～ 原子间力. *the land* ～ 陆军. *magnetic* ～ 磁力. *the naval [sea]* ～ 海军. *the [police]* ～ [集合词]警察. *the productive* ～*s* 生产力. *the relation of* ～*s* 力量的对比. *the social* ～*s* 社会势力. *a striking* ～ 机动兵力. ***a*** ～ ***to be reckoned with*** 不可忽视的力量. ***by (main)*** ～ 用蛮力, 全靠气力; 凭暴力, 强迫. ***by (the)*** ～ ***of*** 由于, 迫于; 通过, 靠…的力量 (*by* ～ *of arms* 用武力. *by* ～ *of habit* 由于习惯. *by* ～ *of circumstances* 迫于环境. *by* ～ *of contrast* 通过对比). ***by [with]*** ～ ***and arms*** 用武力. ***cease to be in*** ～ 失效. ***come [enter] into*** ～ 实行, 生效. ***in*** ～ ①有效, 在有效期中. ②大举, 大批地, 大规模地. ***in full*** ～ 用全力; 发挥充分威力. ***in great*** ～ 大举, 大批地; 精力充沛地. ***join*** ～ ***with*** (军队)会师; (同人)联合, (与人)通力合作. ***of no*** ～ 无效. ***put in [into]*** ～ 施行, 实施. ***remain in*** ～ 在有效期中, 仍然有效. ***resort to*** ～ 诉诸武力. ***put up a show of*** ～ 示威. ***take by*** ～【军】夺取, 武力侵占. ***with all one's*** ～ 尽全力, 竭力. ***with much*** ～ 极有力地, 效力卓著地. —*vt.* ①强制, 迫使, 逼迫. ②强力夺取, 攻克. ③强行, 强加. ④推动. ⑤竭力提高, 抬高, 加快. ⑥勒索; 强奸. ⑦迫使(对手)出某张牌; 迫出(某张牌). ⑧(通过温室栽培等) 促成(植物) 早熟[发育, 生长]; 加速(学生的)学业. ～ *sb. to do [into doing, into an action]* 强迫某人做某事. *They were* ～*d to leave the town.* 他们被迫离开该城. ～ *an action*【军】迫使敌人作战. ～ *an entry* 强行进入. ～ *a passage* 强行通过. ～ *one's strength* 硬使劲. ～ *a smile* 强颜欢笑, 苦笑. ～ *one's voice* 提高嗓门. ～ *one's appetites* 勉强吃, 硬吃. ～ ***one's way into*** 闯进. ～ ***one's way through a crowd*** 由人群中挤过去. ～ ***sb.'s hand*** 逼使摊牌; 逼人过早行动. ～ ***the bidding*** (拍卖时)抬价. ～ ***the game*** (板球赛时)硬冒险. ～ ***the pace [running]*** (赛跑时)为使对手疲劳而尽力快跑. ～ **fan** 鼓风机. ～**-feed** *vt.* 强喂(食物), 强灌(食物)[尤指直插管灌送食物]; 强使接受. ～ **feed**【机】压力润滑, 压力进给. ～**-in-being** 可随时作战的军事力量. ～**-land** *vi.* 强迫降落; 强行登陆. ～**-out**【棒球】封死. ～ **pump** 压力泵, 压力水泵. **-less** *a.* 无力的, 较弱的.

force[2] [fɔːs] *n.* [北英]瀑布.

forced [fɔːst] *a.* ①强迫的, 强制的. ②用力的. ③勉强的, 不自然的. ～ *analogy* 牵强附会. *a* ～ *smile* 苦笑. *a* ～ *style* (文体)矫揉造作. ～ *tears* 假哭, 硬挤出的几滴眼泪. ～ **draught** (锅炉等的)鼓风, 压力通风. ～ **loan** 义务公债. ～ **landing** 强行登陆; (飞机)迫降. ～ **march** 强行军. ～ **oscillation [vibration]**【物】受迫振动[振荡]. ～ **quotations**【商】限价. ～ **sales** (为清偿债务而进行的)拍卖. **-ly** *ad.*

force de frappe [fɔrs də ˈfrɑːp] [F.] 打击力量[尤指法国的核打击[威慑]力量].

force·ful [ˈfɔːsful] *a.* 强有力的, 坚强的; 有说服力的. **-ly** *ad.* **-ness** *n.*

force ma·jeure [fɔːs mɑːˈʒəː] [F.] 不可抗力(如天灾等).

force·meat [ˈfɔːsmiːt] *n.* 加调料的肉馅; 五香碎肉 (= farcemeat).

for·ceps [ˈfɔːseps] *n.* (*pl.* ～, ***-ci·pes*** [-səpiːz]) ①镊子, 钳子. ②【动】(昆虫的)尾铗. ③【解】钳状体.

for·ci·ble [ˈfɔːsəbl] *a.* ①强有力的, 有说服力的. ②强暴的, 强迫的. ～ *detention* 扣留. *a* ～ *entry into* 强行闯入, 非法侵入. ～ *execution* 强制执行. ～**-feeble** *a.* 外强中干的, 貌似强大而实际虚弱的. **-bil·i·ty** [ˌfɔːsəˈbiliti] *n.* **-ness** *n.* **-bly** *ad.*

forc·ing [ˈfɔːsiŋ] *n.* ①强制, 强夺. ②【农】催熟栽培. —*a.* ①强迫的, 施加压力的. ②促成植物早熟的. ～ **bed**

温床. ～ **crops [culture]**【农】催熟作物[栽培]. ～ **house** 温室,温床. ～ **pump** = force pump.

for·ci·pate(d) [ˈfɔːsipeit(id)] *a.* 钳状的.

for·close [fɔːˈkləuz] *v.* = foreclose.

for·clo·sure [fɔːˈkləuʒə] *n.* = foreclosure.

Ford[1] [fɔːd] *n.* ①福特[姓氏]. ②**Henry** ～ 亨利·福特[1863—1947, 美国汽车制造厂商]. ③**G. R.** ～ 杰鲁·福特[美国第38任总统].

Ford[2] [fɔːd] *n.* ①福特牌汽车. ②[f-]时髦式样. **Ford·ize** *vt.* ①大量生产(标准化的产品). ②使(人员、生产方法等)标准化(以提高生产效率).

ford [fɔːd] *n.* 浅滩,津渡,可涉水而过的地方. — *vt., vi.* 涉(水). ～ ***over*** 涉水而过. **-able** *a.* 可以涉水而过的. **-less** *a.* 不能涉水而过的,没有浅滩的.

for·do [fɔːˈduː] *vt.* (***-did*** [fɔːˈdid]; ***-done*** [fɔːˈdʌn]) 毁坏;使疲乏[只用过去分词]. **for·done** *a.* [古]筋疲力尽的.

fore[1] [fɔː, fɔə] *a.* ①前面的 (*opp.* hind, back, aft). ②先前的. *the* ～ *part of an aircraft* 飞机的前部. — *ad.* 在前面, 在船头. — *prep., conj.* [方] 在前. — *n.* 前部;头;前桅;(马等的)前腿. ***at the*** ～ (信号旗)悬在前桅上;在最前. ***come to the*** ～ 发作,涌现出来;出人头地;惹人注意. ***to the*** ～ ①在前面,在显著地位. ②在场;立即有用;(钱等)在手边. ③活着. ～ **edge** (与书脊相对的)书的前页边. ～ **painting** (印在书的前页边上的)页边画饰.

fore[2] [fɔː, fɔə] *int.* (打高尔夫球时的叫声)前面的人让开!
[后面又有人要击球了].

fore- *pref.* ①表示"先","前","预": *fore*arm, *fore*cast, *fore*see. ②= *for-*: *fore*close.

fore-and-aft [ˈfɔːrəndˈɑːft] *a.* 【海】从船首到船尾的;纵向的. *a* ～ *sail* 纵帆 (*cf.* square sail). *a* ～*-rig* 纵帆装置.

fore-and-aft·er [ˈfɔːrəndˈɑːftə] *n.* 【海】①舱口盖纵梁. ②有纵帆装置的船.

fore·arm[1] [ˈfɔːrˌɑːm] *n.* 【解】前臂.

fore·arm[2] [fɔːˈɑːm] *vt.* 预先武装,使预作准备.

fore·bear [ˈfɔːbeə] *n.* [常 *pl.*] 祖先,祖宗.

fore·bode [fɔːˈbəud] *vt.* ①预示;预知. ②预感. — *vi.* ①预言. ②有预感.

fore·bod·ing [fɔːˈbəudiŋ] *n.* 预报,预示;(特指凶事的)预知,预感.

fore·body [ˈfɔːˌbɔdi] *n.* 船身前半部;水上飞机的前机身;弹体前部.

fore·brain [ˈfɔːˌbrein] *n.* 【解】①前脑. ②壮年人发达的脑部[包括间脑和大脑半球].

fore·cab·in [ˈfɔːˌkæbin] *n.* 前部船舱[通常是二等舱].

fore·cast [ˈfɔː-kɑːst] *vt.* (～, ～*ed*; ～, ～*ed*) 预测;预报(天气). — *n.* 预测;预报. *a weather* ～ 天气预报.

fore·cas·tle [ˈfəuksl] *n.* (轮船的)船首楼,(船首楼内的)水手舱. *a* ～ *deck* 船首楼甲板.

fore·close [fɔːˈkləuz] *vi.* 【法】(因超过限期等)取消赎取权. — *vt.* ①【法】取消(抵押人的)赎取权. ②逐出;排除. ③妨碍;结束,停止(讨论等). ④要求独占.

fore·clo·sure [fɔːˈkləuʒə] *n.* ①拒斥. ②【法】丧失赎取权.

fore·course [ˈfɔːkɔːs] *n.* 【海】前桅(最下一个)大横帆.

fore·court [ˈfɔːkɔːt] *n.* 前院.

fore·date [fɔːˈdeit] *vt.* 倒填(契据等的)日期 (= antedate).

fore·deck [ˈfɔːdek] *n.* 【海】前甲板.

fore·do [fɔːˈduː] *vt.* [古] = fordo.

fore·doom [fɔːˈduːm] *vt.* 注定…要遭遇不幸.

fore·fa·ther [ˈfɔːˌfɑːðə] *n.* [常 *pl.*] 祖先,祖宗;前人. **F-s' Day** [美](每年12月22日纪念英国清教徒于1620年在美洲登陆的)祖先纪念日.

fore·feel [fɔːˈfiːl] *vt.* (***-felt*** [-ˈfelt]; ***-felt***) 预感到.

fore·fend [fɔːˈfend] *vt.* = forfend.

fore·fin·ger [ˈfɔːˌfiŋgə] *n.* 食指.

fore·foot [ˈfɔːfut] *n.* (*pl.* ***fore·feet*** [ˈfɔː-fiːt]) ①(兽等的)前脚. ②【船】龙骨前端部.

fore·front [ˈfɔːfrʌnt] *n.* 最前部,最前线;(活动、趣味等的)中心. ***bring to [place in] the*** ～ 放在显著地位,使成为活动[注意]中心.

fore·gath·er [fɔːˈgæðə] *vi.* = forgather.

fore·gift [ˈfɔːgift] *n.* 【法】租赁押金,押租.

fore·go[1] [fɔːˈgəu] *vt., vi.* (***-went*** [-ˈwent]; ***-gone*** [-ˈgɔn]) 在前,居先,先行. ***the*** ～***ing statement*** 前面所述.

fore·go[2] [fɔːˈgəu] *vt.* (***-went*** [-ˈwent]; ***-gone*** [-ˈgɔn]) = forgo.

fore·go·er [fɔːˈgəuə] *n.* ①先行的人[物];带头的猎犬. ②先例. ③前人,前辈. ④祖先.

fore·gone [fɔːˈgɔn] forego[1] 和 forego[2] 的过去分词. — *a.* ①过去的; 早先的. ②预先决定的; 确定要发生的; (结局)必不可免的. *a* ～ *conclusion* 定论;不可避免的结果.

fore·ground [ˈfɔːgraund] *n.* (*opp.* background) ①(图画等的)前景. ②最显著的地位. *keep oneself in the* ～ 站在前面,处在最显著的地位.

fore·gut [ˈfɔːgʌt] *n.* 【解】前肠.

fore·hand [ˈfɔːhænd] *n.* ①前方. ②马体前部. ③(网球等的)正手打. — *a.* ①前方的; 预先的. ②正手打的. *a* ～ *payment* 预付款. *a* ～ *stroke* 正手一击.

fore·hand·ed [fɔːˈhændid] *a.* ①及时的;合时宜的. ②节俭的. ③[美]富裕的. ④(网球等的一击)正手打的. **-ly** *ad.* **-ness** *n.*

fore·head [ˈfɔrid, ˈfɔːhed] *n.* ①额,脑门. ②前部.

for·eign [ˈfɔrin] *a.* ①外国的;外交的. ②外国来[产]的;外省的,外地的;[美]他州的,本州管辖外的. ③别家工厂[公司,企业]的;他人的. ④【医】外来的;异质的. ⑤无关的,不相干的. *a* ～ *country [land]* 外国. *a* ～ *debt [loan]* 外债. *a* ～ *deposit* 国外存款. *the F- Office* (英国等的)外交部. ～ *languages* 外国语. ～ *students* 外国留学生. ～ *policy* 外交政策,对外政策. ～ *relations* 外交关系. ～ *trade* 国际贸易,对外贸易. ～ *affairs* 外交事务. *the F- Affairs Board* 外事局. *a* ～ *agency* 国外代理店. ～ *aid* 外援. ～ *capital* 外资. ～ *goods* 外国货. *a* ～ *visitor* 外宾. *a* ～ *car [line]* 别家公司的车辆[铁路]. ～ *body [substance]* 异物. ～ *protein* 异体蛋白. ～ *seeds* 混杂种子. ～ *to the question* 与本问题无关. ***the Minister for [of] F- Affairs = F- Minister*** 外交部长. ***the Ministry for [of] F- Affairs*** 外交部. ～**-born** *a.* 在外国出生的 (*the* ～*-born* 从外国来的移民). ～ **correspondent** 驻外记者. ～ **exchange** 外汇[外币、期票、汇票、支票、电汇、邮汇等的统称]. ～ **exchange control** 外汇管制. ～**-flag** *a.* (飞机等)在外国登记的,(船等)挂外国国旗的. ～ **protein**【生化】异体蛋白. ～ **mission** ①宗教使团[基督教在国外的传教机构]. ②驻外使团;出国谈判代表团. **F- Service** (美国国务院的)外事处. ～ **settlement** 租界,外国人居留地. **-ize** *vt., vi.* (使)外国化. **-ness** *n.*

for·eign·er [ˈfɔrinə] *n.* ①外国人. ②外人,陌生人. ③外国船;外来物,进口货物;(非本土的)外来动植物.

fo·reign·ism [ˈfɔːrinizm] *n.* ①外国的习语,外来语. ②外国习俗,外国作风[派头].

fore·judge[1] [fɔːˈdʒʌdʒ] *vt.* 【法】(由法庭判决)驱逐,逐出,剥夺(某种权利). **-(e)ment** *n.* 驱逐的判决.

fore·judge[2] [fɔːˈdʒʌdʒ] *vt.* 臆断;未经审问就判断.

fore·know [fɔːˈnəu] *vt.* (***-knew*** [fɔːˈnjuː]; ***-known*** [fɔːˈnəun]) 预知.

fore·knowl·edge [fɔːˈnɔlidʒ] *n.* 预知,先见之明.

for·el [ˈfɔrəl] *n.* ①(作书皮用的)羊皮纸. ②书套,书壳.

fore·la·dy [ˈfɔːˌleidi] *n.* (*pl.* ***-la·dies***) = forewoman.

fore·land [ˈfɔːlənd] *n.* ①(堤岸、墙壁的)前沿,前地. ②

地角. ③海岬;滨海地带 *(opp.* hinterland).
fore·leg [ˈfɔːleg] *n.* (兽的)前腿.
fore·limb [ˈfɔːlim] *n.*【解】前肢,上肢.
fore·lock[1] [ˈfɔːlɔk] *n.* 额发,额毛〔尤指马等的〕. ***take [seize] time [an opportunity, an occasion] by the ~*** 抓牢时机,乘机.
fore·lock[2] [ˈfɔːlɔk] *n.*【机】开口销,扁销. — *vt.* 用开口销[扁销]栓住.
fore·man [ˈfɔːmən] *n.* ①*(pl. -men)* 首席陪审员. ②工头,监工,领班.
fore·mast [ˈfɔːmɑːst] *n.*【海】前桅. *the ~ seaman [man, hand]* 前桅员;普通水手[水兵].
fore·milk [ˈfɔːmilk] *n.* 初乳.
fore·most [ˈfɔːməust] *a.* ①最初的,最前的. ②第一流的;主要的. — *ad.* 首先,第一. ***first and ~*** 首先,第一. ***head ~*** 轻率地.
fore·moth·er [ˈfɔːˌmʌðə] *n.* 女祖先.
fore·name [ˈfɔːneim] *n.* (姓前的) 名, 教名〔如 John Brown 中的 John〕.
fore·named [ˈfɔːneimd] *a.*〔美〕前面举出[提到]的.
fore·noon [ˈfɔːnuːn] *n.* 午前,上午. — *a.* 上午的, 午前的. ~ **watch**【海】上午八时至十二时的守望.
fore·no·tice [ˈfɔːˈnəutis] *n.* 预告.
fo·ren·sic [fəˈrensik] *a.* ①法庭的. ②公开辩论[讨论]的,论争的. ~ *ability [eloquence]* 辩才. — *n.* ①辩论练习. ②辩论学,辩论术. ~ **chemistry** 法律化学, 刑事侦破化学,化学破案术. ~ **medicine** 法医学. ~ **psychiatry** 法医心理分析学. **-cal·ly** *ad.*
fore·or·dain [ˌfɔːrɔːˈdein], **fore·or·di·nate** [fɔːrˈɔːdineit] *vt.* 预先注定.
fore·or·di·na·tion [ˌfɔːrɔːdiˈneiʃən] *n.* 预先注定.
fore·part [ˈfɔːpɑːt] *n.* ①前部. ②(时间的)前段.
fore·passed, fore·past [fɔːˈpɑːst, -ˈpæst] *a.*〔罕〕过去的;既往的.
fore·paw [ˈfɔːpɔː] *n.* (动物的)前爪.
fore·peak [ˈfɔːpiːk] *n.*【船】船首舱.
fore·plane [ˈfɔːplein] *n.* ①粗刨. ②【宇】前缘舵,前舵.
fore·quar·ter [ˈfɔːˌkwɔːtə] *n.* ①前槽肉〔牛、羊等腰板以上前半截的四分之一部分〕. ②〔*pl.*〕(马等的) 前身〔包括前腿〕.
fore·reach [fɔːˈriːtʃ] *vt.* ①(帆船)追过. ②赶上. ③超出. — *vi.* (帆船)凭惯性继续前进.
fore·run [fɔːˈrʌn] *vt.* *(-ran* [fɔːˈræn]; *-run)* ①在前跑, 先走. ②预报,预示. ③赶过,超过.
fore·run·ner [ˈfɔːˌrʌnə] *n.* ①先驱者;(提前赶到的)通报者. ②前兆. ③祖先.
fore·said [ˈfɔːˌsed] *a.*〔罕〕前述的; 上述的 (= aforesaid).
fore·sail [ˈfɔːseil, -sl] *n.*【海】(横帆船的)前桅帆.
fore·see [fɔːˈsiː] *vt.* *(-saw* [-ˈsɔː]; *-seen* [-ˈsiːn]*)* 预见到,预知,看穿. — *vi.* 有先见之明. **-able** *a.* 可预见到的. **-r** *n.* 预言者,有先见之明的人. **-ing·ly** *ad.* 有预见地.
fore·shad·ow [fɔːˈʃædəu] *vt.* 预示;预兆. *Dark clouds ~ a storm.* 乌云预示暴风雨.
fore·shank [ˈfɔːʃæŋk] *n.* ①(牛的) 上前腿. ②上前腿肉.
fore·sheet [ˈfɔːʃiːt] *n.*【船】前桅帆脚索. ②〔*pl.*〕前板, 艇首坐位.
fore·shock [ˈfɔːʃɔk] *n.* (大地震前的)预震.
fore·shore [ˈfɔː-ʃɔː] *n.* ①(高潮线和低潮线之间的) 前滩. ②海滩.
fore·short·en [fɔːˈʃɔːtn] *vt.*① (在绘画中) 按远近比例缩小(图形). ②省略,缩短.
fore·show [fɔːˈʃəu] *vt.* *(~ed; -shown* [-ˈʃəun]*)* 预示, 预告,预报.
fore·side [ˈfɔːsaid] *n.*〔罕、古〕前部;上部.
fore·sight [ˈfɔːsait] *n.* ①先见. ②深谋远虑. ③远景;【测】前视. ④(枪炮上的)瞄准器,准星.
fore·sight·ed [ˈfɔːsaitid] *a.* 有先见之明的; 深谋远虑的.
fore·skin [ˈfɔːskin] *n.*【解】包皮.
fore·speak [fɔːˈspiːk] *vt.* *(-spoke* [-ˈspəuk],〔古〕*-spake* [-ˈspeik]; *-spoken* [-ˈspəukn]〔古〕*-spoke; -speaking)*〔罕〕①预告;预言;预示. ②预先提出申请或要求;预约.
For·est [ˈfɔrist] *n.* 福雷斯特〔姓氏,男子名〕.
for·est [ˈfɔrist] *n.* ①森林,山林. ②(英国) 王家狩猎场. *a ~ fire* 森林火灾. *a ~ of masts* 林立的桅杆〔指大量的船只〕. — *vt.* 在…造林; 使长满树林, 使成为森林. ~ **fly**【幼】虱蝇. ~ **ranger** 林警,森林保护员. ~ **reserve**〔美〕保护林,保存林.
fore·stage [ˈfɔːˌsteidʒ] *n.* (幕前的)舞台前部.
for·est·al [ˈfɔristl] *a.* (有关)森林的.
fore·stall [fɔːˈstɔːl] *vt.* ①抢先,占先;先下手. ②阻止. ③垄断,屯积.
for·est·a·tion [ˌfɔrisˈteiʃən] *n.* 造林(法),植林.
fore·stay [ˈfɔːstei] *n.*【船】前桅支索.
fore·stay·sail [fɔːˈsteiseil,-sl] *n.*【海】前支索的三角帆.
For·est·er [ˈfɔristə] *n.* 福雷斯特〔姓氏〕.
for·est·er [ˈfɔristə] *n.* ①林务员. ②林中居民;林中禽兽. ③【动】(虎蛾科的)林蛾.
for·est·ry [ˈfɔristri] *n.* ①林学. ②林业. ③森林,森林地带.
fore·taste [ˈfɔːteist] *n.* ①试食,先尝,预尝到的滋味. ②预感. — *vt.* 先尝,试吃.
fore·tell [fɔːˈtel] *vt., vi.* *(-told* [-ˈtəuld]; *-told)* 预言,预示,预兆. **-er** *n.*
fore·thought [ˈfɔːθɔːt] *n.* ①事先的考虑,预谋. ②深谋远虑. — *a.* 预谋的,预先计划好的.
fore·thought·ful [ˈfɔˌθɔːtfl] *a.* 深谋远虑的;慎重的. **-ly** *ad.*
fore·time [ˈfɔːtaim] *n.* 已往,过去,往昔.
fore·to·ken [ˈfɔːtəukən] *n.* 预兆,征兆. — [-ˈtəukən] *vt.* 预示.
fore·told [fɔːˈtəuld] foretell 的过去式和过去分词.
fore·tooth [ˈfɔːtuːθ] *n.* *(pl. -teeth)* 门牙,前齿.
fore·top [ˈfɔːtɔp,-təp] *n.* ①前发,额发;(马的)额毛. ②【船】前桅楼;前桅平台.
fore-top·gal·lant [ˌfɔːtɔpˈgælənt] *a.* 在前桅中段以上的. ~ **sail** 前桅上桅帆.
fore·top·mast [fɔːˈtɔpmɑːst] *n.*【船】前桅的中段.
fore-top·sail [fɔːˈtɔpseil] *n.*【海】前桅中桅帆.
fore·type [ˈfɔːtaip] *n.* 前面的典型,原型,前例,范例.
for·ev·er [fəˈrevə] *ad.*〔美〕永远,不绝,不断. *go away ~* 一去不复返. *She's ~ complaining.* 她总是发牢骚. ★ 英国通常分写作 for ever. ~ ***and a day*** = ~ ***and ever*** = ~ ***and*** ~ =〔书〕~ ***and aye*** 永久,永远. — *n.* [the ~] 永远.
for·ev·er·more [fəˌrevəˈmɔː] *ad.* 永远〔语气比 forever 更强〕.
fore·warn [fɔːˈwɔːn] *vt.* 预先警告. *Forewarned is forearmed*〔谚〕警惕即警备.
fore·went [fɔːˈwent] forego 的过去式.
fore·wing [ˈfɔːwiŋ] *n.*【动】前翅.
fore·wom·an [ˈfɔːwumən] *n.* *(pl. -wom·en* [-ˈwimin]*)* ①女工头,女领班. ②女首席陪审员.
fore·word [ˈfɔːwəːd] 前言,序言.
fore·worn [fɔːˈwɔːn] *a.* 极疲倦的 (= forworn).
fore·yard [ˈfɔːjɑːd] *n.*【海】前桅的最下桅桁.
for·feit [ˈfɔːfit] *vt.* (因被罚而)丧失(所有权); (因犯罪等而)失去(职位、生命等);(因过劳等而)失掉(健康等). *~ one's life on the battlefield* 阵亡. *~ a motor licence* 汽车执照被没收. — *a.* 丧失了的,被没收了的. — *n.* ①

罚金;没收物. ②(权利、名誉,生命等的)丧失. ③〔*pl.*〕罚物游戏. ***be the ~ of one's crime*** (以生命等)抵罪.

for•fei•ture [ˈfɔːfitʃə] *n.* ①(地位、权利,生命等的)丧失. ②没收. ③没收物;罚金.

for•fend [fɔːˈfend] *vt.* ①〔古〕禁止;防止,避开. ②〔美〕保护. *God [Heaven] ~!* = God forbid.

for•fi•cate [ˈfɔːfikit, -keit] *a.* (某些鸟尾)分岔的.

for•gat [fɔːˈgæt] forget 的古体.

for•gath•er [fɔːˈgæðə] *vi.* ①聚会. ②偶然遇见 *(with)*. ③交往 *(with)*.

for•gave [fəˈgeiv] forgive 的过去式.

forge[1] [fɔːdʒ] *n.* ①铁工厂; 锻工车间. ②锻炉; 熔铁炉. ③(思想等的)锻炼. *a boiler ~* 锅炉锻工车间. *a portable ~* 轻便锻炉. —*vt., vi.* ①打(铁),锻制. ②锻炼. ③编造(故事等); 伪造(文书等). **-able** *a.* 可锻造的.

forge[2] [fɔːdʒ] *vi.* (坚定地)勉力前进. **~ *ahead*** (不停地)努力前进;(赛跑)努力赶上,领先.(*~ ahead with our work* 把我们的工作大力向前推进).

forg•er [ˈfɔːdʒə] *n.* ①伪造者. ②锻工.

for•ger•y [ˈfɔːdʒəri] *n.* ①伪造;伪造签字. ②(文件)伪造罪;伪造物,赝品.

for•get [fəˈget] *vt.* *(-got* [-ˈgɔt]*; -gotten* [-ˈgɔtn], 〔诗〕 *-got)* ①忘掉,忘记(*opp.* remember). ②忽略,疏忽掉. *Don't ~ me to your brother.* 别忘记代我问候你的兄弟. *~ one's keys* 忘带钥匙;忘记钥匙在那里. —*vi.* 遗忘,忘记. *F- about it.* 不要介意. ***forgive and ~*** 不念旧恶,不记仇. ***F- it.*** 〔美〕不用谢了,别再提了. ***~ oneself*** ①忘我. ②忘乎所以. ③奋不顾身. ④昏过去.

for•get•ful [fəˈgetful] *a.* *(opp.* mindful*)* ①健忘的. ②不留心的,疏忽的. ③〔古〕使人忘记的,易忘的. *be ~ of one's sleep and meals* 废寝忘食. **-ly** *ad.* **-ness** *n.*

for•ge•tive [ˈfɔːdʒətiv] *a.*【古】①能发明创造的. ②富有想象力的.

for•get-me-not [fəˈgetminɔt] *n.*【植】勿忘草(属).

for•get•ta•ble [fəˈgetəbl] *a.* ①易被忘记的. ②可以忘记的.

for•get•ter [fəˈgetə] *n.* 健忘者,容易忘记的人.

forg•ing [ˈfɔːdʒiŋ] *n.* ①锻造(法). ②锻件.

for•giv•a•ble [fəˈgivəbl] *a.* 可宽恕的.

for•give [fəˈgiv] *vt.* *(-gave* [-ˈgeiv]; *-giv•en* [-ˈgivn]*)* ①原谅,饶恕,宽恕. ②免除(债务等). *Pray ~ me!* 请原谅我吧! *You are forgiven.* 你得到宽恕了. *~ sb. his debts* 豁免某人的债务.

for•give•ness [fəˈgivnis] *n.* 饶恕,宽恕;宽大. *ask for ~* 请求宽恕. *be full of ~* 十分宽大.

for•giv•ing [fəˈgiviŋ] *a.* 宽大的;仁慈的. **-ly** *ad.* **-ness** *n.*

for•go [fɔːˈgəu] *vt.* *(-went; -gone* [-ˈgɔn]*)* ①摒绝,放弃;对…断念;谢绝. ②〔古〕从…离开.

for•got [fəˈgɔt] forget 的过去式及过去分词.

for•got•ten [fəˈgɔtn] forget 的过去分词. —*a.* 被忘却的. *a ~ man* 被遗忘的人〔如因失业而脱离原来的社会生活的人〕.

for•int [ˈfɔrint] *n.* 〔Hung.〕 福林〔匈牙利货币单位〕.

for•judge [fɔːˈdʒʌdʒ] *vt.* = forejudge.

fork [fɔːk] *n.* ①餐叉;肉叉;叉子;耙. ②树叉,木叉;分岔;分歧点,岔路;支流. ③【乐】调音叉. ④叉状闪电. ⑤(象棋中)同时可攻两个棋子的棋着. ⑥二者之间的选择. *a knife and ~* 一副刀叉. ***play (a good) knife and ~*** (因胃口好而)饱餐一顿. —*vi.*分歧,分叉. —*vt.* ①用叉叉起,用叉抛举(干草等);用耙耙. ②使成叉形. ③(象棋中)同时进攻(两个棋子). ④〔口〕交付,支付,放弃. ***~ out [over, up]*** 〔俚〕交出,支付. **~ dinner [luncheon]** (食物都已切好,只须用叉即可进食的)叉餐. **~lift** 叉式万能升降装卸车,铲车. **~tailed** *a.* (鸟)尾巴开叉的.

forked [ˈfɔːkt] *a.* 有叉的. *~ lightning* 叉状闪电. *three-~* 三叉的. **~ chain**【化】侧链. **~ tongue** 谎言,假话. **~-tongued** *a.* 不诚实的, 骗人的. **-ly** *ad.* **-ness** *n.*

fork•y [ˈfɔːki] *a.* ***(fork•i•er, fork•i•est)*** = forked. **forkiness** *n.*

for•lorn [fəˈlɔːn] *a.* ①绝望的;被遗弃的,孤独无助的;可怜的;凄凉的. ②〔诗〕被剥夺的 *(of)*. ***be ~ of hope*** 绝望. **~ hope** ①敢死队. ②冒险事业;没有成功希望的事业. ③渺茫的希望. **-ly** *ad.*

form [fɔːm] *n.* ①形状;形态,样子,外貌;【哲】形式 *(opp.* content*)*. ②人影,物影. ③格式;表格纸(=〔美〕blank). ④型;方式;种类. ⑤(人的)姿态,神气,精神;健康状态. ⑥态度;礼节;仪式. ⑦结构,组织. ⑧〔英〕条凳. ⑨(学校的)年级. ⑩【语法】形式,词形. ⑪【物】(晶)面式;【印】印版;【机、建】型,模壳. ⑫(野兔等的)窝,洞. *I see a ~ in the dark.* 我在黑处看见一个人影. *fill in [out] the ~* 填表. *an order ~* 定(货)单. *a telegraph ~* 电报纸. *attach importance to ~* 着重形式. *a matter of ~* 形式上的问题. *an established ~* 一定的方式. *bad ~* 失礼举动,粗鲁行为. *good ~* 〔英〕有礼貌的态度,端正的行动方式. *a ~ of address* 称呼. *the ~ of government* 政体. ***after the ~ of*** 照…的格式. ***be in (good) ~*** (运动员等)竞技状态良好. ***for ~'s sake*** 为了划一形式,形式上. ***minute ~s of life*** (微)生物. ***in due ~*** 正式地,照规定的格式. ***in ~*** 形式上. ***in great ~*** 精神饱满. ***in the ~ of*** 用…的形式. ***in [under] various ~s*** 用种种形式. ***lose one's ~ = out of ~*** (运动员)情绪失常. ***(run) true to ~*** 一如往常,一贯. ***take the ~ of*** 取…的形式,表现为. —*vt.* ①形成,养成,塑造. ②构成,成立,组织. ③作出,想出. ④【语法】构(词),造(句). ⑤结成(同盟). ⑥【军】排成;编成 *(up)*. *~ the dough into loaves* 把面粉团做成面包. *The House is not yet ~ed.* 议会还没有组成. *~ fours* 成四列. —*vi.* ①形成,产生. ②【军】排队. *~ into line* 排成队. *~ itself into* 成…形. *~ part of* 成为…的组成部分. *~ the character* 陶冶品性. **~ action**【法】诉讼手续[程序]. **~ class**【语】形式类,形(态)类. **~fitting** *a.* (衣服)贴身的. **~ genus**【动】形态属. **~ letter** 格式信件〔内容已印好,只需填写日期、收信人、地址等〕. **~piston, ~plunger**【机】模塞;阳模. **-ing** *n.* 成形,成型,模铸. **-less** *a.* 无形状的,无定形的.

form- *comb. f.* 表示【化】"甲酸","甲酰","甲醛": *form*aldehyde, *form*ate.

-form *suf.* 表示"具有…形式的,有…形状的": vermi*form*; uni*form*; multi*form*.

for•mal [ˈfɔːməl] *a.* ①正式的. ②礼节上的,仪式上的;郑重其事的. ③形态的,外形的;形式上的;拘泥形式的,刻板的. ④布置整齐的,有条理的. ⑤正规的,合乎规格的. ⑥【语言】规范化的,书面语的,正规的〔非俗语,俚语的〕. *a ~ receipt* 正式收据. *a ~ call* 正式访问. *a ~ manner* 郑重其事的态度. *~ logic* 形式逻辑. *a ~ resemblance* 外形上的类似. *~ obedience* 表面服从. —*n.* ①〔美〕须穿礼服的社交集会. ②〔口〕夜礼服. ***go ~*** 〔口〕穿夜礼服. **-ness** *n.*

form•al•de•hyde [fɔːˈmældihaid] *n.*【化】甲醛.

for•ma•lin [ˈfɔːməlin] *n.*【化】甲醛水溶液,福尔马林.

for•mal•ism [ˈfɔːməlizəm] *n.* 形式主义;拘泥形式.

for•mal•ist [ˈfɔːməlist] *n.* 拘泥形式的人;形式主义者. —*a.* 拘泥形式的,形式主义的. **-ic** [ˌfɔːməˈlistik] *a.* 形式主义的.

for•mal•i•ty [fɔːˈmæliti] *n.* ①拘泥形式,拘谨. ②礼节,俗套. ③〔*pl.*〕正式手续. *trivial formalities* 烦琐的礼节. ***go through [check in] formalities*** 办理(飞机等)的乘坐手续. ***without ~*** 不拘形式地.

for•mal•ize [ˈfɔːməlaiz] *vt.* ①使成正式. ②使具有形式,形式化. — *vi.* 拘泥形式. **-i•za•tion** [ˌfɔːməlai-

ˈzeiʃən] *n.* 形式化；正式化.

for·mal·ly [ˈfɔːməli] *ad.* ①正式地. ②遵照一定格式地. ③形式上.

for·mant [ˈfɔːmənt] *n.* 【语言】①共振峰. ②构形成分.

for·mat [ˈfɔːmæt, -mɑːt] *n.* ①(出版物的)开本，版式 (*cf.* folio). ②【自】(数据安排的)形式. ③(电视播送或硬币设计等的)组织[安排、布局]的总计划. —*vt.* 设计；构成；安排〔包括制作的全过程，但特别着重制成品的形式〕.

for·mate[1] [ˈfɔːmit] *n.* 【化】甲酸盐，甲酸酯.

for·mate[2] [ˈfɔːmeit] *vi.* 【空】飞机加入编队，编队飞行.

for·ma·tion [fɔːˈmeiʃən] *n.* ①构成，形成；设立；编制. ②组织，构造；形态；形成物，构造物；【军】编队，队形；兵团. ③【地】地岩层. 【生】社区；(植物)群系. *heat of* ~ 【化】形成热，生成热. *close* ~ 【军】密集队形. *dispersed [open]* ~ 【军】疏开队形. *fighting [battle]* ~ 【军】战斗队形. *rock* ~ 【地】岩层. *skirmish* ~ 【军】散兵线. ~ *flight [flying]* 【军】编队飞行. **-al** *a.*

form·a·tive [ˈfɔːmətiv] *a.* ①形成的，构成的. ②造型的. ③【语法】构词(用)的. *a* ~ *period* 发育期. *the* ~ *arts* 造型艺术. ~ *technique* 造形[型]技术，造形[型]工艺. — *n.* 构词要素〔指前缀、后缀等，= ~ element〕；用构词要素构成的词. ~ **cell** 【动】形成细胞，毛原细胞. ~ **period** 【生】形成期. ~ **tissue [layer]** 【生】形成组织[层].

forme [fɔːm] *n.* 【英印】印版.

form·er[1] [ˈfɔːmə] *n.* ①构成者，创造者. ②【机】模型，样板，成形[型]设备. ③【无】线圈架. ④中等学校的学生. *fifth* ~*s* 五年级学生.

for·mer[2] [ˈfɔːmə] *a.* ①以前的，从前的. ②在前的；〔美〕前任的. *in* ~ *times* 从前. *in the* ~ *case* 在前一例〔情况〕. *the* ~ 前者 (*opp.* latter). **-ly** *ad.*

for·mic [ˈfɔːmik] *a.* ①蚂蚁的. ②【化】甲酸的，蚁酸的. ~ **acid** 甲酸.

For·mi·ca [fɔːˈmaikə] 佛米卡〔一种做桌面等的抗热塑料薄板的商标名〕.

for·mi·car·y [ˈfɔːmikəri] *n.* 蚁巢，蚁山.

for·mi·cate [ˈfɔːmikeit] *vi.* 象蚂蚁一样爬行；群集.

for·mi·ca·tion [ˌfɔːmiˈkeiʃən] *n.* 【医】(皮肤上的)蚁走感.

for·mi·da·ble [ˈfɔːmidəbl] *a.* ①可怕的，可畏的. ②难以应付的；庞大的. *a* ~ *enemy* 强敌. *a* ~ *task* 难应付的工作. **-ness** *n.* **-bly** *ad.*

form·less [ˈfɔːmlis] *a.* 无形状的，无定形的. **-ly** *ad.*

For·mo·sa [fɔːˈməusə] *n.* 〔废〕"福摩萨"〔16 世纪葡萄牙殖民主义者对我国台湾省的称呼〕.

for·mu·la [ˈfɔːmjulə] *n.* (*pl.* ~*s, -lae* [-liː]) ①公式，程式；定则，方案. ②【医】配方，处方. ③(政治口号等的)提法，表述，套语，惯用语句. ④【宗】信仰表白书. ⑤【化】式；【数】公式. *a* ~ *for making soap* 肥皂制法[配方]. ~ *of integration* 积分公式. *a binominal* ~ 【数】二项式. *a legal* ~ 法律上的惯用语句. *a molecular* ~ 【化】分子式. *a structural* ~ 【化】结构式，构造式. — *a.* (赛车)方程式的(指赛车要符合规定的体积、重量及汽缸容量等). ~ **investing** 方程式投资〔按方程式计划进行的一种投资方法〕. ~ **translation** 【计】公式翻译，公式转换〔用以编写科技等计算程序的一种计算机语言〕.

for·mu·lar·i·za·tion [ˌfɔːmjuləraiˈzeiʃən] *n.* 公式化.

for·mu·lar·ize [ˈfɔːmjuləraiz] *vt.* = formulate.

for·mu·lar·y [ˈfɔːmjuləri] *n.* ①公式汇编. ②配方书，处方集，药典. ③有关宗教礼节[仪式]的书. — *a.* ①公式的. ②仪式上的. ③配方的.

for·mu·late [ˈfɔːmjuleit] *vt.* ①把…作成公式，用公式表示. ②对…作简洁陈述，有系统地表达. **-la·tion** [ˌfɔːmjuˈleiʃən] *n.*

for·mu·lism [ˈfɔːmjulizəm] *n.* 公式主义.

for·mu·list [ˈfɔːmjulist] *n.* 公式主义者.

for·mu·lis·tic [ˌfɔːmjuˈlistik] *a.* 公式主义(者)的.

for·mu·lize [ˈfɔːmjulaiz] *vt.* = formulate. **-za·tion** [ˌfɔːmjulaiˈzeiʃən] *n.*

for·myl [ˈfɔːmil] *n.* 【化】甲酰.

For·nax [ˈfɔːnæks] 【天】天炉(星)座.

for·ni·cate [ˈfɔːnikeit] *vi.* (未婚者之间或与未婚者)私通. **-tion** [ˌfɔːniˈkeiʃən] *n.* **-tor** *n.*

for·nix [ˈfɔːniks] *n.* (*pl.* ***for·ni·ces*** [-nisiːz]) 【解】穹窿，穹.

for·ra(r)d·er [ˈfɔrədə] *ad.* 〔英口〕更往前. ***get no*** ~ 不再前进.

for·rel [ˈfɔrəl] *n.* = forel.

for·sake [fəˈseik] *vt.* (***-sook*** [-ˈsuk]; ***-sak·en*** [-ˈseikən]) ①舍弃，放弃，丢弃. ②革除(旧风习等)；抛弃(坏习惯).

for·sak·en [fəˈseikən] forsake 的过去分词.

for·sook [fəˈsuk] *v.* forsake 的过去式.

for·sooth [fəˈsuːθ] *ad.* 〔反〕的确，真的，当然〔表示轻蔑、讥刺〕.

for·spent [fɔːˈspent] *a.* 〔古〕疲倦已极的.

for·stall [fɔːˈstɔːl] *v.* = forestall.

For·ster [ˈfɔːstə] *n.* 福斯特〔姓氏〕.

for·swear [fɔːˈswɛə] *vt.* (***-swore*** [-ˈswɔː]; ***-sworn*** [-ˈswɔːn]) ①发誓抛弃，断然放弃(坏习惯等). ②发誓否认，背(誓)，背弃(信义). *The old man forswore smoking.* 那老人下决心戒烟. ~ *an oath* 背弃誓言. — *vi.* 作伪证，发假誓. ~ ***oneself*** 发伪誓，作伪证.

for·sworn [fɔːˈswɔːn] forswear 的过去分词. — *a.* 发了假誓的，做了伪证的.

for·syth·i·a [fɔːˈsaiθjə] *n.* 【植】连翘(属).

fort [fɔːt] *n.* ①要塞，堡垒. ②〔美〕(从前和印第安人交易的)市集，(设有碉堡的)边界贸易站. ***hold the*** ~ ①守住堡垒. ②坚决不让步. ③处理日常事务；维持现状. — *vt.* 设要塞保卫. **F- Knox** 诺克斯堡〔美国联邦政府的黄金贮存地〕.

fort. = ①fortification. ②fortified.

for·ta·lice [ˈfɔːtəlis] *n.* 小碉堡，外堡；〔古、诗〕要塞.

Fort-de-France [fɔːt də ˈfrɑːns] 法兰西堡〔马提尼克岛首府〕.

forte [fɔːt] *n.* ①长处，拿手好戏. ②刀身的最强部〔自中央至刀柄〕(*opp.* foible). *Cooking is her* ~. 她擅长烹调.

forte [ˈfɔːti] *a.* 〔It.〕【乐】强音的 (*opp.* piano). — *ad.* 用强音，加强. — *n.* 强音部. ~ ***possible*** 最强. ~-**piano** 【乐】*ad.*, *a.* 强而转弱.

forth [fɔːθ] *ad.* ①向前，向前方. ②以后. ③向外，由隐而显. *burst* ~ (芽、蕾)绽开；(火山等)爆发. *stretch* ~ ~ *one's arms* 伸出胳臂. *sway back and* ~ 前后摇动. *put* ~ *leaves* 发芽. *from this time* ~ 今后，从此以后. ***and so*** ~ 等等. ***right*** ~ 立刻. ***so far*** ~ 到那儿为止，单就那些来说. ***so far*** ~ ***as*** … 到…的程度 (*so far* ~ *as you work* 你工作多少就…). — *prep.* 〔古〕出于，来自. *go* ~ *the house* 从屋里出去.

forth·com·ing [fɔːθˈkʌmiŋ] *a.* ①即将到来的，即将出现的. ②现有的，随时可得的. ③愿意帮助的，乐于供给消息的. *the* ~ *holidays* 即将到来的假日. *The funds are not* ~. 资金尚未筹得. — *n.* 来临，临近.

forth·right [fɔːθˈrait] *ad.* ①〔古〕立刻，径直地. ②直率地. *He told us* ~ *just what his objections were.* 他有什么不同的意见，都坦率地向我们讲了. — [ˈfɔːθrait] *a.* ①直接的. ②直率的. *It's sometimes difficult to be* ~ *and not give offence.* 又直率又不得罪人，这有时很难办到. — *n.* 〔古〕直路.

forth·with [ˈfɔːθˈwiθ] *ad.* 立刻. *Any member guilty of such conduct will be suspended* ~. 凡犯有类似错误的人，得立刻停止其会员资格. — *n.* 〔美俚〕必须立即执行的命令.

for·ti·eth [ˈfɔːtiiθ] *n., num.* 〔the ~〕 第四十(个); 四十分之一(的).

for·ti·fi·a·ble [ˈfɔːtifaiəbl] *a.* 宜于设防的, 可以弄巩固的.

for·ti·fi·ca·tion [ˌfɔːtifiˈkeiʃən] *n.* ①筑城, 筑垒, 设堡; 筑城学[术]. ②〔常 *pl.*〕 防御工事. ③堡垒, 要塞. ④(酒精、维生素)含量的增加, 强化.

for·ti·fi·er [ˈfɔːtifaiə] *n.* ①筑城者, 设防者. ②增强的人[物]; 强化物. ③〔谑〕(用强状剂泡的)含酒精饮料, 滋补酒.

for·ti·fy [ˈfɔːtifai] *vt.* ①在…设要塞, 在…建防御工事. ②加强(体力、结构等); 使(意志等)坚定. ③在(食物中)增加酒精[维生素等]的含量. *a fortified port* 军港. *a fortified town* 设防都市. *a fortified zone* 要塞地带. *powdered milk fortified with vitamins* 加有维生素的奶粉. — *vi.* 筑防御工事. ~ ***oneself*** 加强自己意志; 喝酒提神.

for·tis [ˈfɔːtis] *a.* 【语音】强音的〔指收紧发音器官肌肉而发出的, 如绝大多数清辅音性的爆破音〕. — *n.* 强音〔收紧发音器官肌肉发出的音〕.

for·tis·si·mo [fɔːˈtisiməu] *ad.* 〔It.〕【乐】用最强音, 极强〔略为 *ff.*〕 — *a.* 【乐】极强的.

for·ti·tude [ˈfɔːtitjuːd] *n.* 坚强意志[精神], 坚忍, 刚毅. *intestinal* ~ 坚忍不拔的精神. ***bear a calamity with*** ~ 毅然忍受灾祸.

for·ti·tu·di·nous [ˌfɔːtiˈtjuːdinəs] *a.* 坚忍不拔的, 刚毅的, 顽强的.

Fort-La·my [fɔːrlɑːˈmiː] *n.* 拉密堡〔乍得首都〕.

fort·night [ˈfɔːtnait] *n.* 〔主英〕 两星期 〔*cf.* sennight〕. *a ~'s holiday* 两个星期的休假. *Monday* ~ 两星期以前[以后]的星期一. *today [this day]* ~ 两个星期以前[以后]的今天.

fort·night·ly [ˈfɔːtˌnaitli] *a.* 〔主英〕 每两星期一次的. *a ~ review* 一种双周(评论)刊物. — *n.* 双周刊. — *ad.* 隔两周, 每两星期地.

For·tran, for·tran [ˈfɔːtræn] *n.* 【计】①公式变换 (= formula transformation). ②公式翻译, 公式译码(资料处理) (= formula translation). ③公式转换器, 公式翻译程序 (= formula translator).

for·tress [ˈfɔːtris] *n.* 要塞; 堡垒; 安全地带. *Flying F-* 〔美〕空中堡垒. *a floating* ~ 军舰. *an impregnable* ~ 难以攻陷的要塞. — *vt.* ①在…设置要塞. ②用要塞保卫.

for·tu·i·tism [fɔːˈtju(ː)itizəm] *n.* 【哲】偶然论.

for·tu·i·tist [fɔːˈtju(ː)itist] *n.* 偶然论者.

for·tu·i·tous [fɔːˈtju(ː)itəs] *a.* ①偶然的, 意外的. ②幸运的. **-ly** *ad.* **-ness** *n.*

for·tu·i·ty [fɔːˈtjuiti] *n.* ①偶然事件; 偶然机会. ②偶然性.

for·tu·nate [ˈfɔːtʃənit] *a.* ①幸运的, 侥幸的. ②带来幸运的. *a ~ man* 幸运的人. *a ~ star* 吉星. *the* ~ 幸运者. *be ~ in one's son* 幸而有个儿子. ***be born under a ~ star*** 生来有福. **-ly** *ad.*

for·tune [ˈfɔːtʃən] *n.* ①运气; 幸运; 命运. ②财产; 巨富; 〔古〕女财主, 女继承人. ③〔F-〕 司命运的女神. *F- favours the bold [brave].* 〔谚〕勇者成功. *F- is easily found, but hard to be kept.* 〔谚〕找到幸福容易, 维持幸福困难. *a man of* ~ 财主. *marry a* ~ 和有钱的女子结婚. ***be in good [bad]*** ~ 运气好 [坏]. ***by good*** ~ 幸好. ***come into a*** ~ 继承一笔财产. ***have a*** ~ 有财产. ***have ~ on one's side*** 走红运. ***have good [bad]*** ~ 运气好[坏]. ***have the ~ to do*** 幸而…. ***if ~ favours*** 如果运气好. ***make a*** ~ 发财. ***make one's*** ~ 成功立业, 发迹; 发财. ***push one's*** ~ 追求名利, 努力抬高自己的地位. ***seek one's*** ~ 找出路. ***spend a small ~ on*** *(books)* 〔口〕把一大笔钱花在(书)上. ***tell sb.'s ~s*** 为某人算命. ***tempt*** ~ 蔑视命运, 冒险. ***try one's*** ~ 碰运气. — *vt.* 〔古〕给…大宗财富, 给…带来幸运. — *vi.* 〔古、诗〕偶然发生; 偶然遇见 *(upon)*. *It ~d that ...* 偶尔. ~ **cookie** 占卜饼〔一种夹层饼, 其中夹有写着预言吉凶祸福或格言等的小纸片〕. ~ **hunter** 追求有钱女子的男子. ~ **hunting** 为了财产而追求有钱的女子. ~**teller** 算命卖卜者. ~**telling** 算命卖卜. **-less** 不幸的, 无财产的.

for·ty [ˈfɔːti] *num.* 四十, 四十个; 第四十. — *n.* ①〔*pl.*〕四十年代, 四十到四十九岁的时期. ②四十岁. ③【网球】三分. *Life begins at* ~. 〔谚〕人生始于四十. *a man of* ~ 四十岁的人. *After* ~ 四十岁以后. *in nineteen* ~ 在 1940 年. *in the nineteen forties* 在二十世纪四十年代〔略 1940's 或 1940s〕. ***like*** ~ 〔美口〕非常, 猛烈地. ***over [under]*** ~四十岁以上[以下]. ***Roaring Forties*** 大西洋南纬 40° 至 50° 之间风浪特大的海域. ***the Forties*** 苏格兰东北岸与挪威西南岸之间的海域〔因该区域水深 40 哼以上而得名〕. ~ **wink** 〔口〕小睡(特指午睡).

for·ty·ish [ˈfɔːtiiʃ] *a.* 近四十岁的, 四十岁左右的.

for·ty-eight·mo [ˈfɔrtiˈeitməu] *n.* 四十八开本, 四十八开的纸张[页面].

for·ty-five [ˈfɔːtiˈfaiv] *num.* 四十五, 四十五个. — *n.* ①45″ 口径手枪(常作 0.45, 意为 0.45 cm.) ②(每分钟)四十五转唱片 (常写作 45). ***the Forty-five*** 【英史】詹姆士二世党徒的 1745 年叛乱.

for·ty-nin·er [ˈfɔːtiˈnainə] *n.* 〔美〕1849 年涌往加利福尼亚州淘金的人.

fo·rum [ˈfɔːrəm] *n.* (*pl.* ***~s, fo·ra*** [-rə]) ①古罗马城镇的广场[市场]. ②论坛; 会议场; 法庭. ③座谈会, 讨论会; 评论; 评判; (广播、电视的) 专题讲话[座谈] 节目. ④制裁. *the ~ of conscience* 良心的制裁. *the ~ of public opinion* 舆论的评判. **the F-** 古罗马会议广场(遗址). ***the Forum*** 古罗马城大广场(遗址).

for·ward [ˈfɔːwəd] *ad.* ①向前, 前进 (*opp.* backward). ②【海】在船头, 向船头 (*opp.* aft). ③今后, 将来. ④出来, 出现, 表面化. *F-!* 【军】前进! *from this time* ~今后. *backward(s) and ~(s)* 来回地, 前前后后. ***carriage*** ~ 运费由收货人照付. ***date*** ~【商】预填日期, 填未来的日期〔如期票上所填若干日之后的日期〕. ***help*** ~ 促进. ***look*** ~ 向前看; 期待, 希望 (*look ~ to sb.'s visit* 等待某人来访). ***put*** ~ 提出 (计划、意见等). ***put [set] oneself*** ~ 出面, 挺身而出. ***rush*** ~ 冲向前. ***send*** ~ 打发; 发出. — *a.* ①前方的, 前面的. ②【海】船前部的. ③前进的; 进步的, 急进的. ④在时令前的, 过早的; 早熟的. ⑤热心的, 争先恐后的; 鲁莽的, 唐突的. ⑥【商】预约的, 预定的, 预先的, 期货的. *a ~ contract* 预约. *a ~ crop* 早熟作物. *a ~ march* 进军. *a ~ payment* 预付货款. *~ prices [rates]* 期货价格. *a ~ rally*【军】前方集结地区. *the ~ ranks.* 先头部队. *the ~ role* 带头作用. *a ~ school* 促进派, 急进派, 求进取的一派. *a ~ spring* 早来的春天. *a ~ pupil* 名列前茅的学生. ***be ~ in [with] one's work*** 工作有进展. ***be ~ to help*** 助人为乐. — *n.* ①(足球、篮球等的) 前卫, 前锋. ②期货; 远期外汇. — *vt.* ①促进, 助长; 促成, 推进(计划等); 促进(植物)发育 〔*cf.* force〕. ②转交(信件); 寄出(信件); 送到, 运送(货物). ③【装订】把(书帖)叠齐订好〔为粘贴封面作好准备〕. ~ *a plan* 推进一项计划. *Please ~ my mail to my new address.* 本人已迁居, 来信请转新址. *Please ~!* 请转交! ~ **buying** 购买期货. ~ **delivery** 〔商〕定期[来日]交货. ~ **echelon** 【美军】先头部队; 先遣指挥部. ~**-looking** *a.* 高瞻远瞩的, 进取的. ~ **pass** 【橄榄球】前进传球.

for·ward·er [ˈfɔːwədə] *n.* ①发运人(尤指报关行, 运输代理人, 运输代理行). ②【装订】把书帖订好(交付粘贴封面)的工人.

for·ward·ing [ˈfɔːwədiŋ] *n.* ①推进; 促进. ②寄送, 托运; 运输. ~ **agency** 运输行. ~ **agent** 运输商. ~

business 运输业. ~ **station** 转运站.

for·ward·ly [ˈfɔːwədli] *ad.* ①向前地;争先恐后地.②鲁莽地,唐突地. ③在前部.

for·ward·ness [ˈfɔːwədnis] *n.* 进取(心);急切,热心;早熟;鲁莽,唐突.

for·wards [ˈfɔːwədz] *ad.* = forward *(ad.)*.

for·wea·ried [fɔːˈwiərid] *a.* 〔古〕极疲倦的.

for·went [fɔːˈwent] forgo 的过去式.

for·why [fɔːˈwai, -ˈhwai] *ad.* 〔废、方〕为什么. — *conj.* 〔废〕因为.

for·worn [fɔːˈwɔːn] *a.* 〔古〕极疲倦的.

for·zan·do [fɔːˈtsɑːndəu] *a., ad.* = sforzando.

Fos·dick [ˈfɔzdik] *n.* 福斯迪克〔姓氏〕.

fos·sa [ˈfɔsə] *n.* (*pl.* ***fos·sae*** [ˈfɔsiː])【解】窝,凹. *the nasal* ~ 鼻窝.

fos·sate [ˈfɔseit] *a.*【解】凹的,有窝的.

foss(e) [fɔs] *n.* ①城壕,护城. ②【地】海渊. ③【解】= fossa.

fos·sette [fɔˈset] *n.* ①(齿冠等上的)小凹,小窝. ②酒窝,笑窝.

fos·sick [ˈfɔsik] *vi.* ①〔Aus.〕淘金. ②寻觅,搜求. ~ *for clients* 招揽顾客. — *vt.* ①采掘(金矿等). ②寻觅.

fos·sil [ˈfɔsl] *a.* ①从地下发掘出来的;化石的. ②属于旧时代的;陈腐的;不合时宜的. — *n.* ①化石. ②〔口〕旧事物,旧制度. ③老顽固,守旧者;习语中保存的旧词(如 to and fro 中的 fro). ~ **botany** 古植物学,植物化石学. ~ **fuels** (煤、石油、天然气等)矿物燃料. ~ **ivory** (古象的)化石象牙. ~ **oil** 〔美〕(石油的旧称)矿油. ~ **remains** (动物的)化石遗体.

fos·sil·ate [ˈfɔsileit] *vt.* = fossilize.

fos·sil·a·tion [ˌfɔsiˈleiʃən] *n.* = fossilization.

fos·sil·if·er·ous [ˌfɔsiˈlifərəs] *a.* 产化石的,含化石的.

fos·sil·ize [ˈfɔsilaiz] *vt.* ①使成化石. ②使(头脑等)陈腐,使僵化,使落伍. — *vi.* ①变成化石. ②僵化,陈腐,过时. ③〔口〕搜集化石标本. **-za·tion** [ˌfɔsilaiˈzeiʃən] *n.* 化石作用.

fos·si·lol·o·gy [ˌfɔsiˈlɔlədʒi] *n.* 化石学,古生物学.

fos·so·ri·al [fɔˈsɔːriəl] *a.*【动】掘土的,适于掘地的. ~ *animals* 掘土动物. ~ *claws* 适于掘土的爪.

Fos·ter [ˈfɔstə] *n.* 福斯特〔姓氏,男子名〕.

fos·ter [ˈfɔstə] *vt.* ①养育,抚育〔但并不在法律上认作继承人,与 adopt 有别〕. ②鼓励;扶植;促进(发育). ③怀抱(希望等). ~ *a spirit of righteousness* 发扬正气. ~ *a child* 收养一个小孩. ~ *an evil thought* 心怀恶意. ~ *the sick* 照料病人. ~ **brother [sister]** 在同一家庭中养育的(但不是同父母的)弟兄[姐妹]. ~ **child** 养子,养女. ~ **daughter** 养女. ~ **earth** 培养土. ~ **father** 养父. ~ **home** 寄养别人孩子的家庭. ~ **mother** 养母. ~**-mother** *vt.* 收养,抚养. ~ **parent** 养父母. ~ **son** 养子.

fos·ter·age [ˈfɔstəridʒ] *n.* ①养育,寄养. ②养子[女]身分. ③助长,鼓励,促进.

fos·ter·er [ˈfɔstərə] *n.* 养育者;鼓励者.

fos·ter·ling [ˈfɔstəliŋ] *n.* 养子,养女.

fou [fuː] *a.* 〔Scot.〕喝醉的.

fou·droy·ant [fuːˈdrɔiənt] *a.* ①闪电似的,使人眼花撩乱的,引起敬畏的. ②【医】急性的,暴发的. ~ **paralysis**【医】急性麻痹.

fouet·té [fweˈtei] *n.* 〔F.〕(芭蕾舞)单腿快速转身.

fou·gasse [fuːˈgɑːs] *n.* 〔F.〕【军】定向地雷.

fought [fɔːt] fight 的过去式及过去分词.

fought·en [fɔːtn] *a.* 〔古〕曾为战场的. *a* ~ *field* 古战场.

foul [faul] *a.* ①肮脏的;腐烂的;有恶臭的. ②(管道等)壅塞的;(船底等)粘满海藻、贝壳的;有触礁[撞碰]危险的;(水,空气等)污浊的. ③(绳子等)缠结难解的. ④(天气)恶劣的,不利航行的,逆风的;(疾病等)严重的,凶险的. ⑤卑鄙的,丑恶的;(言语等)下流的. ⑥丑陋的,难看的;讨厌的,令人作呕的. ⑦【体】违反规则的,犯规的,不正当的. ⑧【印】错误百出的. ⑨(船只)相撞;与…冲突 *(of)*. ~ *linen* (要洗的)脏衣. *a* ~ *smell [taste]* 恶臭的气味[味道]. ~ *breath* 臭气. *a* ~ *chimney* 阻塞不通的烟囱. *a ship* ~ *of a rock* 撞在岩石上的船. *a* ~ *deed* 恶劣的行为. *a* ~ *language* = *a* ~ *tongue* 下流话. *a* ~ *journey* 不愉快的旅行. ~ *murder* 用卑鄙的手段诱杀. ~ *weather* 恶劣的天气. *cut the* ~ *rope* 把纠缠着的绳子割开. ***be*** ~ ***with***给…弄脏. ***by fair means or*** ~ 不择手段地. ***get*** ~ (绳索)纠缠,缠住. ***in the teeth of a*** ~ ***wind*** 向着猛烈的逆风.— *ad.* ①碰撞地;争执不和地. ②不正当地,犯规地. ***fall [go, run]*** ~ ***of*** ①船只相撞. ②争吵. ***play sb.*** ~用卑鄙手段对待某人. — *n.* ①脏东西;逆境. ②碰撞;缠结. ③(在比赛中)犯规. ***claim a*** ~【体】声明对方犯规,表示胜利无效. ***through*** ~ ***and fair*** = ***through fair and*** ~ 在任何情形下,不管顺利或困难. — *vt.* ①污染,弄脏. ②使纠缠;使壅塞;阻碍. ③船只相撞,碰撞. ④(在比赛中)犯规. *It is an ill bird that* ~*s its own nest.* 〔谚〕家丑不可外扬〔原意为任何鸟都不肯把自己的窠弄脏〕. ~ *sb.'s name* 损坏某人名誉. ~ *one's hand with ...* 被…把手弄脏,因参与…而弄臭名誉. — *vi.* ①腐败,腐烂. ②(绳索、链条等)纠结,缠住;(管道、枪筒等)壅塞. ③船只碰撞. ④【体】犯规. ~ ***out*** ①〔美〕比赛中因犯规过多而被罚出场. ②【棒球】因击出的界外球被接住而出局. ~ ***up*** 〔美俚〕弄糟,搞坏. ~**-brood** (蜜蜂的)幼虫腐臭病〔由细菌引起,分为两种:一种叫欧腐病,一种叫美腐病〕. ~ **ball**【棒球】界外球. ~ **bill (of health)** 瘟疫流行地所发健康证书. ~ **coast** (暗礁多的)危险海岸. ~ **ground** (暗礁多的)危险海底. ~ **line** 犯规线,罚球线. ~**-mouthed [~-spoken, ~-tongued]** *a.* 说话不干净的,嘴巴臭的. ~ **play** ①【体】犯规. ②欺诈,卑鄙手段 *(opp. fair play)*. ~ **proof**【印】毛样. ~ **shot** (篮球)罚球;罚球所得的一分(= free throw). ~ **stroke** 犯规的击球. ~ *talk* 猥亵的谈话. ~ **tip**【棒球】触击球. ~**-up** 〔口〕①拙劣的工作. ②混乱,故障,乱七八糟. **-ly** *ad.* 下流地;粗鄙地;讨厌的. **-ness** *n.*

fou·lard [fuːˈlɑːd] *n.* 印花薄软绸;软绸手帕〔领带、领巾〕.

foul·ing [ˈfauliŋ] *n.* (水管、枪筒等中的)污垢.

fou·mart [ˈfuːmɑːt] *n.*【动】鸡貂.

found[1] [faund] find 的过去式和过去分词. — *a.* (文艺作品等)找到的,拾得的,拣到的,自然形态的〔不是创作的,而是由艺术家对天然物或已有的文字材料加工完成的〕. ~ **object** 拾得艺术品. ~ **poem** 拾得诗〔把现成的散文词句重新安排而成为诗的形式〕.

found[2] [faund] *vt.* ①为(建筑物等)打基础;建立,创办(学校等). ②树立,创(学说). ③以…为(论点、作品等)的根据;把(论点、作品等)建立在…的基础上 *(on, upon)*. ~ *a family* 建立家庭. ~ *a hospital [university]* 创办一所医院[大学]. *a novel* ~*ed on fact* 根据事实写成的小说. *well* ~*ed* 十分有根据的. *ill* ~*ed* 根据不可靠的. *laws* ~*ed on human experience* 以人类经验为根据的法律. ~ *one's claim on facts* 把自己的主张建立在事实材料的基础上.

found[3] [faund] *vt.* 铸造;熔铸. ~ *a bell* 铸钟. ~ *glass* 制玻璃. *a* ~*ing furnace* 铸造炉,熔炉. *metal* ~*ing* 金属熔铸.

found[4] [faund] *a.* 〔英〕(对房客等)不另加费供应的,已包括在价款[租金等]之内的〔通常置于句子末尾〕. *Room to let, laundry* ~. 房间出租,洗衣不另收费. — *n.* 不另外收费的供应品[服务等],(工资以外)另行供给的膳食[住宿等]. *Maid wanted, good salary and* ~. 征求女佣,高工资并供给食宿(等).

foun·da·tion [faunˈdeiʃən] *n.* ①建设,创设,创立. ②基础,根本;根据;地基,地脚. ③基金;捐款;用捐款创办

的事业；慈善机关；财团，基金会．④(编织品的)模型；(衣服的)衬里；帽心．*a stone* ～ 石基．*The* ～ *of the People's Republic of China was in 1949.* 中华人民共和国开国于1949年．*a frame* ～【机】架座，机架，地脚．***be on the*** ～ 由基金维持．***lay the*** ～ ***for [of]*** 给…打下基础．***strike at the*** ～ ***[root] of sth.*** 要毁灭某事物．***without*** ～ 无根据的．～ **cream** 粉底霜．～ **field** 种子田．～ **garment** 紧身褡，妇女胸衣．～ **hospital** 慈善医院．～ **member**〔英〕(团体等的)发起人，创办人，基本会员．～ **muslin** (上胶的)硬衬里细纱．～ **net** (上胶的)粗网眼纱．～ **school** 靠基金维持的学校．～ **stone** 基石；基础，根源．**-al** *a.* 基本的，基础的．**-er**〔英〕公费生．**-less** *a.*

found·er[1] [ˈfaundə] *n.* 奠基者，创立者，创办人．～**-member** (团体等的)创办人，发起人．～**s' shares**〔英〕(公司等的)发起人股份．

found·er[2] [ˈfaundə] *n.* 铸造工，翻砂工；铸件．

foun·der[3] [ˈfaundə] *vi.* ①【海】沉没．②失败，垮掉．③(土地等)陷落；掉进(泥淖等里) *(in)*；(房屋等)倒塌．④(马等)跸倒．⑤(马)患蹄叶炎．— *vt.* ①使沉没．②使摔倒，弄跛(马脚)；使倒塌，使垮掉．③破坏，损害．— *n.* (马的)蹄叶炎，胸肌风湿(= chest ～).

foun·der·ous [ˈfaundərəs] *a.* 泥泞的，易使人摔倒的(= foundrous). *a* ～ *road* 泥泞的道路．

found·ling [ˈfaundliŋ] *n.* 弃儿，拾来的小儿．～ **hospital** 育婴堂．

found·ress [ˈfaundris] 女奠基人，女创立者，女创办人．

found·ry [ˈfaundri] *n.* ①铸造，翻砂．②铸工厂；玻璃(制造)厂；铸工车间．*an iron* ～ 翻砂厂．*a glass* ～ 玻璃厂．*a type* ～ 铸字所．～ **goods** 铸件．～ **iron [pig]** 生铁．～ **proof**【印】(打纸型版前的)清样．～ **worker** 铸造工人，翻砂工人．

fount[1] [faunt] *n.* ①〔诗〕泉；源泉．②〔口〕(油灯上的)贮油罐；(自来水笔的)贮墨管．③〔美俚〕餐馆内出售苏打水、冰淇淋等的小卖部(= soda fountain).

fount[2] [faunt] *n.*〔英〕【印】(字体、大小都一样的)一套活字(= font[2]).

foun·tain [ˈfauntin] *n.* ①泉水，喷泉．②人造喷泉，人造喷泉装置，饮用喷泉(=drinking ～)；喷水池；喷水塔．③源泉，根源．④液体贮藏器(如贮墨器，油罐等)．⑤= soda ～. *a* ～ *of wisdom* 知识的源泉．*poison the* ～*s of trust* 损坏信用．***F- of Youth*** 青春泉，长生不老泉〔传说此泉在美洲和西印度群岛，饮此泉者有病治病，无病可返老还童〕．～**head** 水源；根源，本源 (*trace an error to its* ～*head.* 追究错误的根源)．～ **pen** 自来水笔．～ **shell** 大海螺．

four [fɔː] *num.* (基数)四，四个〔用作基数词可以单独表示数的概念；也可以同表示人或事物的词连用，起数量限定作用〕；第四〔用于表示章、节等词之后〕. *Six minus two equals* ～. 六减二等于四．～ *Chapters* 四章．*Chapter* ～ 第四章．— *n.* ①四人小组；(套在车上的)四匹马．②四的记号；(骰子的)四点；(钟点的)四时；四岁．③〔*pl.*〕四厘公债．④〔口〕四桨小艇；四桨小艇艇员；〔*pl.*〕四桨小艇竞赛．⑤〔*pl.*〕【军】四路纵队．⑥〔*pl.*〕【机】四汽缸发动机；四汽缸汽车．*a column of* ～*s* 四路纵队．*a child of* ～ 四岁的孩子．～*-and-twenty* = *twenty-*～ 二十四．***a coach and*** ～ 四匹马拉的大马车．***Form*** ～***s!***〔口令〕排成四列纵队！***Fours right [left]!*** (口令)排成四列向右〔左〕转！***in*** ～***s*** ①每组〔批〕四个．②一柄四叶．***on all*** ～***s*** ①匍匐，爬着．②完全一致的，完全吻合的 (*No simile runs on all* ～*s.* 任何比喻都有出入)．～ **ale**〔英古〕一夸脱四便士的啤酒．～**bagger**〔口〕(棒球中的)全垒打．～**-by-two** 擦枪布．～**colour** *a.*【印】四色的，四色版的，四色版印刷的〔指在印刷过程中用黄、红、蓝、黑四块分色印版表达出任何颜色〕．～**-colour problem**【数】四色难题〔指以四种颜色绘制地图、而不得让同一种颜色的地区相邻的数学难题〕．～**-cornered** *a.* 有四个角的；四方的；有四人参加的．～**-coupled** *a.* 有两对轮子的．～**-course** *a.* ①四样的，(叶等)四道的．②【农】四年轮作的．～**-cycle** *n.* (内燃机的)四冲程循环．～**-dimensional**, ～**dimensioned** *a.*【数】四维的．～**-eyes**〔美俚〕〔蔑〕戴眼镜的人，四眼先生；四眼田鸡．～**-flush** *vi.*〔美俚〕虚张声势，吹牛．～**flush**【牌】四张同花明牌、一张不同花暗牌的一手牌．～**flusher**〔美俚〕虚张声势的人，吹牛的人．～**-foot way**【英铁路】四英尺轨距．～**-footed** *a.* 四足的．～**-handed** *a.* 有四只手的；(游戏)四人玩的；四人一组的；【乐】(钢琴谱)二人合奏的．**F- Horsemen**【圣】(指战争、饥馑、瘟疫、死亡四大害的)四骑士．～ **hundred**〔也作 F- H-〕名士，名流〔前面加 *the*，原指纽约的四百知名人士，通指当地的名士、名流〕．～**-in-hand** ① *n.* 一人驾驶的四马马车；活结领带．② *a.* 四马拉的．③ *ad.* 一人驾驶四马马车．～**-leaf clover**【植】四叶苜蓿〔被看作幸运的象征〕．～**-letter** *a.*〔美〕庸俗的，下流的，黄色的．～**-letter word** 四字母忌讳词〔与性或大便有关、通常由四个字母构成的单音节的词，一般都忌讳不说〕．～**-o'clock** [fɔːrəˈklɔk]【植】紫茉莉；【动】食蜜鸟．～**-part** *a.*【乐】四部合唱的．～**pence**〔英〕四便士；(从前的)四便士银币．～**penny** ① *a.*〔英〕四便士的 (*a* ～*penny loaf of bread* 四便士一个的面包)．② *n.* (从前的)四便士银币；= ～-ale. ～**plex** 四单元住宅楼．～**ply** *a.* (羊毛等)四股的；(木材等)四层的．～**-poster** 四柱卧床．～**-pounder**【军】发射四磅炮弹的火炮；四磅重的面包(等)．～**score** *n., a.* 八十．～**-seater** 可坐四人的车辆．～**square** *a.* 方的；基础巩固的，坚定不移的；直率的．～**-star** *a.*〔美〕优良的，最上等的；〔美〕四星级军衔的(*a* ～*-star general*〔美军〕陆军四星上将)．～**-striper**〔美俚〕海军上校．～**-stroke cycle**【机】四冲程循环．～**-way** *a.* 四面皆通的 (～*-way pipe* 四通管)；由四人参加的．～**-wheel** *a.* 四轮的．～**-wheeler** 四轮出租马车．**-fold** *a., ad.* 四倍，四重．**-some** *n.* 四人一组；(游戏中，特指高尔夫球中的)双打；参加双打者．

four·chette [fuəˈʃet] *n.* ①(手套的)指叉．②【解】阴唇小带．

Four·drin·i·er [fuəˈdriniə] *n., a.* 佛氏造纸机(的)．

4-F [ˈfɔːrˈef] *n.*〔美〕选拔征兵制体检不合格者．

four·gon [furˈgɔːn] *n.*〔F.〕行李车．

Fou·rier [ˈfuriei] ①傅立叶〔姓氏〕．② **François Marie Charles** ～ 弗朗瓦斯·马利·沙利·傅立叶〔1772—1837，法国空想社会主义者〕．③ **Jean** ～ 让·傅立叶〔1768—1830，法国数学家，物理学家〕．～ **series**【数】傅立叶级数．

Fou·ri·er·ism [ˈfuriərizəm] *n.* 傅立叶(F.M. Charles Fourier)的空想社会主义，傅立叶主义．

Fou·ri·er·ist [ˈfuriərist], **Fou·ri·er·ite** [ˈfuriərait] *n.* 傅立叶主义者．

four·ra·gère [fuːrɑːˈʒɛə] *n.*〔F.〕【军】(军服的)彩色肩带(尤指某一部队全体的功勋肩带)．

four·teen [fɔːˈtiːn] *num.* 十四，十四个；第十四．— *n.* 十四的记号；十四岁，十四点钟，十五世纪．*in* ～ *forty* 在1440年．*in the* ～ *forties* 在十五世纪四十年代．

four·teenth [fɔːˈtiːnθ] *num.* 第十四(个)；十四分之一(的)．— *n.* 每月的第十四日．

fourth [fɔːθ] *num.* ①第四(个)．②四分之一(的)．— *n.* 每月的四日；【乐】四度音程，四度合音，第四音；〔*pl.*〕【商】四级品．*a* ～ *part* 四分之一．***the (glorious) F-*** = ***the F- of July*** 美国独立纪念日．～**-class** ① *a.* 第四类邮件的；邮包的．② *ad.* 以第四类邮件发送；以邮包发送．～ **dimension** (长、宽、高三维之外的)第四维〔在相对论中指时间〕．～**-dimensional** *a.* 第四维的．～ **estate**〔常用 F- Estate〕新闻界，报界．～ **market**〔美〕第四市场〔投资者之间直接进行的未挂牌证券的交易〕．**F- Republic** (法国)第四共和国(1947—1958)．**F- World** 第四世界(泛指资源贫乏的发展中

国家)。
fourth·ly [ˈfɔːθli] *ad.* 第四。
fou·ter, fou·tre [ˈfuːtə] *n.* 〔废〕无价值的东西〔强烈轻蔑语的婉转说法〕。
fo·ve·a [ˈfəuviə] *n.* (*pl.* ***fo·ve·ae*** [-ˌiː], ~*s*) ①【解】凹,窝。②中央凹 (= fovea centralis)。**fo·ve·al** [-əl], **fo·ve·ate** [-it, eit] *a.* **fo·ve·i·form** [-ifɔːm] *a.*
fo·ve·o·la [fəˈviələ] *n.* (*pl.* ***-lae*** [-ˌliː], ~*s*) 【解】小凹 (=foveole)。**fo·ve·o·late** [-lit, -leit], **fo·veo·lat·ed** [ˈfəuviəleitid] *a.*
fowl [faul] *n.* (*pl.* ~*s* 〔集合词〕~) ①鸡;家禽〔鸭,鹅,火鸡等〕;家禽肉。②〔前加定语〕…鸟;〔古、诗〕鸟。*a barndoor [barnyard, domestic]* ~ 鸡。~ *of the air* 飞鸟。*keep* ~*s* 养鸡。*fish, flesh, and* ~ 鱼,肉,鸡。*neither fish, flesh, nor* ~ 不伦不类的,非驴非马的。*game* ~ 猎禽。*guinea* ~ 【动】珍珠鸡。*sea* ~ 海鸟。*water* ~ 水鸟。*wild* ~ 野鸟。— *vi.* 捕鸟,打鸟。~ **cholera** 鸡霍乱,家禽霍乱症。~**-house** 鸡窝。~ **pest [plague]** 家禽的瘟症。~**-run** 〔英〕养鸡场。~ **variola** 家禽痘疮,家禽疮疹。
Fow·ler [ˈfaulə] *n.* 福勒〔姓氏〕。
fowl·er [ˈfaulə] *n.* 捕鸟者。
fowl·ing [ˈfauliŋ] *n.* 捕鸟,打鸟。~ **piece** 鸟枪,猎枪。
Fox[1] [fɔːks] *n.* ①福克斯人〔美国的一支印第安人〕。②福克斯语〔福克斯人、索克人等所操的阿尔衮琴语〕。
Fox[2] [fɔːks] *n.* ①福克斯〔姓氏〕。② **Charles James** ~ 查理·詹姆士·福克斯〔1749—1806,英国政治家〕。
fox [fɔks] *n.* ①狐;狐皮。②狡猾的人。③〔美俚〕大学新生。④【海】(多根绳子搓成的)绳索。*a white* ~ 白狐。~ *farming* 养狐业。*an old* ~ 老狐狸;老奸巨滑;狡猾的(老)人。~ ***and geese*** 〔棋戏〕狐入鹅群。~ ***and hounds*** 猎狗追狐(游戏)。***play the*** ~ 玩滑头,装假。***set a*** ~ ***to keep one's geese*** 引狼入室。***When the*** ~ ***preaches, take care of your geese.*** 〔谚〕狐狸在说教,当心鹅被盗。— *vi.* ①捕狐,猎狐。②用狡计,欺诈。③(书页等)变色,褪色;(啤酒等)变酸。— *vt.* ①使(书页等)生斑变色〔常用过去分词〕。②使(啤酒等)变酸。③〔口〕欺骗。④为(皮鞋)换面。⑤使醉。*be badly* ~*ed* (书页等)颜色变得很厉害。**Foxbat** 狐蝠〔北约指苏联米格25飞机的暗语。~**-bolt** 开尾螺栓。~ **brush** 狐尾。~ **earth** 狐穴。~**-fire** *n.* 狐火〔腐烂树木发出的磷火〕。~**-glove** 【植】毛地黄属,(中药)熟地。~ **grape** 【植】美国葽薁 (*Vitis Labrusca*) 〔产于北美洲南部〕。~**-hole** 【军】单人战壕,散兵坑。~**hound** 狐猩,捕狐的猎狗。~ **hunt** 猎狐。~ **hunter** 猎狐者。~**-pass** 〔美俚〕= faux pas. ~**'s sleep** 假睡;假装的漠不关心。~ **snake** 【动】黄背锦蛇 (*Elaphe Vulpina*)。~ **squirrel** 【动】黑松鼠 (*Sciurus niger*) 〔产于北美东部〕。~**tail** 狐尾;【植】狐尾状植物〔尤指看麦娘、狗尾草等〕,石松。~**tail lily** 独尾属。~**tail millet** 小米,谷子,粟。~ **terrier** 猎狐小狗〔目前多半养着玩〕。~**trot** ①*n.* (骑马的)快步;狐步舞(曲);〔F-〕通讯中用于代表字母 f 的词。② *vi.* 跳狐步舞。~ **wedge** 扩裂楔。~**wood** 褪色的木材。
foxed [fɔkst] *a.* ①(书页等)变了色的,生褐斑的。②(皮鞋)修过面的。③(啤酒等)变酸了的。④受骗的。
fox·ing [ˈfɔksiŋ] *n.* 鞋面皮;鞋面修补用皮。
fox·y [ˈfɔksi] *a.* (***fox·i·er; -i·est***) ①狐似的,狡猾的。②赤褐色的,狐色的。③变了色的,有褐斑的。④(啤酒等)酸的,有气味的。⑤〔美〕时髦的,迷人的,性感的。⑥(油画)红色过强的。**-i·ly** *ad.* **-i·ness** *n.*
foy [fɔi] *n.* 〔主 Scot.〕①告别宴会;饯行宴会;临别赠品。②秋收结束的会餐;打渔季节结束的会餐。
foy·er [ˈfɔiei] *n.* 〔F.〕①灶,炉。②(剧场、旅馆等的)门厅,休息室。
FP = ① fireplug. ② fully paid 全部付讫。③ floating policy 总保(险)单。④ foot-pound.
F.P. = ① field punishment 战地惩戒。② fireplug 消防栓。③ fission product 裂变产物。④ former pupil 从前的学生。
fp = ① freezing point 【物】冰点,凝固点。② foot-pound 英尺-磅 (功的单位)。③ foolscap 大页书写纸。
f.p. = ① feed pump 供给泵。② flash point 闪(燃)点。
FPA, fpa = free of particular average 【商】单独海损不赔。
FPC = fifth protein concentrate 蛋白鱼粉。
Fpc, F.P.C. 〔美〕= Federal Power Commission 【美】联邦动力委员会。
F.P.D. = fully paid 全数付讫。
f.p.m., fpm = feet per minute 英尺/分。
F.P.S. = Fellow of the Philological Society 〔英〕语文学会会员。
fps = 【物】① feet per second 英尺/秒 ② foot-pound-second 英尺磅秒单位制的。③ frames per second (电视图象的)每秒帧数。
Fr. = ① Father. ② France; French. ③ 〔G.〕*Frau.* ④ Friar. ⑤ Friday.
Fr = francium 【化】元素钫的符号。
fr. = ① fragment. ② franc(s). ③ frequent. ④ from.
Fra [frɑː] *n.* 〔It.〕兄弟〔用在教士姓名前,作称呼用〕。
fra·cas [ˈfrækɑː] *n.* (*pl.* ~ [ˈfrækɑːz]; ~*es* [-kəsiz]) 喧噪,吵闹。
frac·tion [ˈfrækʃən] *n.* ①小部分,碎片,片断。②一些,一点儿。③【化】(分)馏(部)分,级分。④【宗】圣餐面包分切式。⑤【数】分数。*a common [vulgar]* ~ 普通分数。*a compound [complex]* ~ 繁分数。*a mixed* ~ 带分数。*a decimal* ~ 小数。*a proper [improper]* ~ 真〔假〕分数。***a*** ~ ***closer*** 稍微靠近一点。***by*** ~***s*** 有余数的,不完全的。***crumble into*** ~***s*** 碎成片片。***in a*** ~ ***of a second*** 一秒钟的若干分之几,一转眼的工夫。***not a*** ~ ***of*** 一点也没有。***not by a*** ~ 一点也不。***to a*** ~ 〔口〕道道地地,百分之百地。
frac·tion·al [ˈfrækʃənl] *a.* ①零碎的,断片的。②【数】分数的,小数的,有零数的;不足买卖单位的。③【化】分馏的,分级的。*a* ~ *expression* 分数式。~ **column** 分馏塔,分馏柱。~ **currency** 辅币。~ **distillation** 【化】分馏 (作用)。~ **electric motor** 小马力电动机。~ **error** 相对误差,部分误差。~ **tower** =~ column.
frac·tion·al·ize [ˈfrækʃənəlaiz] *vt.* 把…分成分数;把…分成部分 (= fractionize)。**frac·tion·al·i·za·tion** [ˌfrækʃənəlaiˈzeiʃən] *n.* = frac·tion·i·za·tion.
frac·tion·ar·y [ˈfrækʃənəri] *a.* = fractional.
frac·tion·ate [ˈfrækʃəneit] *vt.* ①【化】使分馏。②把…分级,把…分成几部分。*a fractionating column* 分馏柱。*a fractionating tower* 分馏塔。**frac·tion·a·tion** [ˌfrækʃəˈneiʃən] *n.* 【化】分馏(法)。**frac·tion·a·tor** *n.* 【化】分馏器。
frac·tious [ˈfrækʃəs] *a.* ①倔强的。②易怒的;脾气不好的。③任性的。**-ly** *ad.* **-ness** *n.*
frac·tog·ra·phy [frækˈtɔgrəfi] *n.* 金属断面显微镜观察。**-phic** [ˌfræktəˈgræfik] *a.*
frac·ture [ˈfræktʃə] *vt., vi.* (使)破裂;(使)折断;(使)断裂。— *n.* ①破裂,折断,断裂。②裂痕,裂缝,裂面。③【医】挫伤,骨折。④【矿】断口;【地】断层。*a comminuted* ~ 粉碎骨折。*a compound* ~ 复合骨折。**frac·tur·a·tion** [ˌfræktʃəˈreiʃən] *n.* 【地】岩层断裂。
frac·tus [ˈfræktəs] *n.* 【气】(碎积云或碎层云的)碎云(类)。
frae [frei] *prep.* 〔Scot.〕从,自。
frae·num [ˈfriːnəm] *n.* (*pl.* ***frae·na*** [ˈfriːnə]) = frenum.
frag·ging [ˈfrægiŋ] *n.* 〔美军俚〕士兵(用手榴弹等杀伤性炸弹)杀伤军官的行为。
frag·ile [ˈfrædʒail] *a.* ①脆的,易碎的。②脆弱的,虚弱的。~ *health* 虚弱的体质。**-ly** *ad.* **-ness** *n.* = fragility.

fra·gil·i·ty [frəˈdʒiliti] *n.* ①脆弱;虚弱. ②脆性,脆度,易碎性.

frag·ment [ˈfrægmənt] *n.* ①碎屑,碎片,破片,断片. ②未完稿,断简残篇. ***lie in ~s*** 已成破片. ***reduce to ~s*** 弄碎. — *vi., vt.* (使)成碎片,(使)分裂.

frag·men·tal [frægˈmentl] *a.* = fragmentary.

frag·men·tar·y [ˈfrægməntəri] *a.* ①破片的,断片的. ②残缺不全的,不连续的. ③【地】碎屑质的,断岩的. ~ *memories* 片断的回忆. ~ *ejecta* 【地】喷屑. ~ **rocks** 【地】碎屑岩. **-tar·i·ly** *ad.* **-tar·i·ness** *n.*

frag·men·tate [ˈfrægmənteit] *vt., vi.* (使)成碎片,(使)碎裂.

frag·men·ta·tion [ˌfrægmenˈteiʃən] *n.* ①破碎,碎裂. ②【生】(染色体)断裂. *a ~ bomb* 杀伤炸弹. ~ **damage** 破片杀伤. ~ **effect** 破片杀伤效果. ~ **grenade** 碎裂手榴弹. ~ **shell** 杀伤炮弹.

frag·ment·ize [ˈfrægməntaiz] *vt., vi.* = fragmentate. **-zation** *n.*

fra·grance [ˈfreigrəns], **fra·gran·cy** [-si] *n.* 芳香,香气,香味.

fra·grant [ˈfreigrənt] *a.* 芬芳的,香的. **-ly** *ad.*

frail¹ [freil] *a.* ①脆弱的,虚弱的. ②意志薄弱的,不坚定的. ~ *happiness* 暂时的幸福. — *n.*〔美俚〕少女,少妇. **-ly** *ad.* **-ness** *n.*

frail² [freil] *n.* ①灯心草篓〔用以装无花果、葡萄干等〕. ②灯心草篓的容量〔约32、56或 75 磅〕.

frail·ty [ˈfreilti] *n.* ①脆弱,虚弱. ②意志薄弱. ③弱点,过失. *F-, thy name is woman.* 弱者,你的名字是女人〔莎士比亚剧作《汉姆莱特》中的名句〕.

fraise¹ [freiz] *n.* ①【军】(铁丝网或木桩构成的)障碍物. ②(16世纪欧洲流行的)皱领.

fraise² [freiz] *n.*【机】铣刀,绞刀,扩孔钻. — *vt.*【机】绞(孔),用绞刀扩大.

fraises des bois [freiz de ˈbwɑ]〔F.〕野生草莓.

frak·tur [frɑːkˈtuə] *n.* 德文尖角体的活字.

F.R.A.M. = Fellow of the Royal Academy of Music〔英〕皇家音乐院会员.

fram·a·ble [ˈfreiməbl] *a.* ①可构造的,可组织的,可制订的. ②可想象的. ③可装配框子的.

fram·b(o)e·si·a [fræmˈbiːziə] *n.*【医】雅司病,热带性类梅毒.

fram·boise [frɔːnˈbwɑːz] *n.*〔F.〕悬钩子白兰地酒.

frame [freim] *n.* ①机构;组织;系统. ②结构,框架,构架,骨架,骨骼. ③体格,身躯. ④精神状态,心情. ⑤【园艺】温床,阳畦;船的肋骨;【印】排字台,活字架;【机】架,座;【影】画面,镜头;【电视】帧. ⑥〔美俚〕桥牌比赛,职业拳击赛的一个回合,棒球的一局. ⑦〔美俚〕诬陷(=~-up). *backing* ~【摄】安片框. *cant* ~【船】斜肋骨. *a missile* ~【军】导弹弹体. *a pea* ~ 豌豆架. *square* ~【船】直肋骨. *the ~ of government* 政府机构. *a man of gigantic [massive]* ~ 体格魁梧的人. ***~ of axes***【数】座标系统. ~ ***of mind*** 心情,心境. ~ ***of reference*** **[reference ~]** ①【数、物】参考系(统),参考坐标[标架],坐标系(统),读数[计算]系统,空间座标,基准标架. ②观点,理论. ***out of*** ~ 纷乱,无秩序. ***sheriff's picture*** ~ 绞索. — *a.*〔美〕木造的,木结构的. ~ *building [dwelling, house]* 木造房屋. — *vt.* ①编制,组织. ②构造;给…装框子[装架子]. ③作出,拟定,想象,设计,计划. ④使适合 *(for)*. ⑤讲出,说出. ⑥〔口〕捏造(事件),陷害,诬陷. ⑦〔古〕举步走向 *(toward)*. *a lake ~d in woods* 树林环抱着的湖. ~ *a lie* 编谎话. ~ *a plan* 拟定计划. *be ~d*〔美〕陷入圈套. — *vi.* (计划等)有成功希望. ***be not ~d for*** 不适于;经不起;受不了. ~ ***to oneself*** 想象. ~ ***well*** 有才能,有希望 (*He ~s well in speaking.* 他有希望作演说家). ~ **aerial [antenna]**【无】框形天线. ~ **saw** 框锯. **~-up**〔美俚〕阴谋;诬害. **~work** 构架(工程),结构,框架;机构,组织. **-r** *n.* **-less** *a.*

fram·ing [ˈfreimiŋ] *n.* ①结构,组织,编制. ②框架;骨骼. ③计划,构想. ④【电视】图框配合;成帧,按帧调节光栅,调节帧频稳定图象.

franc [fræŋk] *n.* 法郎〔法国、比利时、瑞士等国的货币单位〕.

France¹ [frɑːns] *n.* ①法郎士〔姓氏〕. ②**Anatole** ~ 阿纳多勒·法郎士〔1844—1924,法国小说家,批评家〕.

France² [frɑːns] *n.* 法国,法兰西.

Fran·ces [ˈfrɑːnsis] *n.* 弗朗西丝〔女子名〕.

fran·chise [ˈfræntʃaiz] *n.* ①选举权;公民权,市民权,参政权;【史】(某种)豁免权. ②特许行使特权的地区;避难所. ③〔美〕(私人公司或社团所享有的)某种特许权. ④保险契约规定的免赔限度,免赔额. ⑤控制权,管辖范围. — *vt.* ①给…以特(许)权. ②赋与…以选举权[市民权、公民权、参政权]. **-chi·see** [ˌfræntʃaiˈziː] *n.* 大公司的联营店;获特许经营联营店者.

Fran·cis [ˈfrɑːnsis] *n.* 弗朗西斯〔男子名〕.

Fran·cis·can [frænˈsiskən] *a.*【宗】方济各会的. — *n.* 方济各会的修道士.

Fran·cis·co [frænˈsiskəu] *n.* 弗朗西斯科〔男子名,Francis 的异体〕.

fran·ci·um [ˈfrænsiəm] *n.*【化】钫.

Franck [frɑːŋk, fræŋk] *n.* ①弗朗克〔姓氏〕. ②**James** ~ 詹·弗朗克〔1882—1964,出生于德国的美国物理学家,诺贝尔奖金获得者〕.

Fran·co [ˈfrɑːŋkəu], **Francisco** 佛朗哥〔1892—1975,西班牙军人,国家元首(1939—1975)〕.

Fran·co- *comb. f.* 表示"法国(的)": the *Franco*-Prussian War 普法战争.

fran·co·lin [ˈfræŋkəulin] *n.*【动】鹧鸪.

Fran·co·phile, Fran·co·phil [ˈfræŋkəufail, -fil] *a.* 亲法国的. — *n.* 亲法分子.

Fran·co·phobe [ˈfræŋkəufəub] *a.* 厌恶法国的,恐惧[仇视]法国的. — *n.* 恐法(分子),仇视法国者. **Francophobia** [-fəubiə] *n.* 厌恶[仇视]法国,恐法病.

Fran·co·phone [ˈfræŋkəufəun] *n.* 说法语者(尤指通用两种以上语言的国家里). — *a.*〔常 f-〕说法语的.

Fran·co·phon·ic [ˌfræŋkəuˈfəunik] *a.*〔或 f-〕说法语的.

Fran·co·pho·nie [ˌfrænkəuˈfəuni] *n.*〔或 f-〕①〔集合词〕法语国家;说法语社会. ②法语国家[社会]文化;法语国家[社会]共同体.

franc-ti·reur [frɔːntiˈrœːr] *n.* (*pl.* ***francs-ti·reurs*** [frɔːntiˈrœːr])〔F.〕(法国非正规军的)义勇兵,游击队员.

fran·gi·bil·i·ty [ˌfrændʒiˈbiliti] *n.* ①脆弱,脆弱性. ②易脆性,脆度.

fran·gi·ble [ˈfrændʒəbl] *a.* ①脆弱的. ②易碎的. ~ **grenade**【军】烧夷瓶〔俗名 Molotov cocktail 或 gasoline bomb〕.

fran·gi·pane [ˈfrændʒipein] *n.* = frangipani.

fran·gi·pan·i [ˌfrændʒiˈpæni] *n.* ①【植】鸡蛋花,鸡蛋花属植物;从鸡蛋花提炼出的香料. ②杏仁酥.

Fran·glais [frɔːnˈglei] *n.*〔F.〕(法语中的)英语外来语〔尤指美语外来语〕.

Frank¹ [fræŋk] *n.* 弗兰克〔男子名〕.

Frank² [fræŋk] *n.* ①法兰克人〔古代日尔曼民族的一支〕. ②(近东各地的)西欧人. ③〔诗〕法兰西人.

frank [fræŋk] *a.* ①率直的,直言不讳的,坦白的. ②【医】症状明显的. *a ~ avowal of guilt* 坦白认罪. ***to be ~ with you*** 明白对你说,老实说〔插入语〕. — *n.* ①免费邮寄特权. ②免费寄发签字[印戳]. ③免费递送的邮件. — *vt.* ①免费邮寄. ②在(信件)上盖免费递送或邮资已付印戳. ③许…免费通行. ④特许自由出入. ⑤释放,豁免. **~ing-machine** 自动邮资盖印机.

Frank·en·setin [ˈfræŋkənstain] *n.* ①法兰肯斯坦〔英国女作家 Mary Wollstonecraft Shelley (1797—1851) 所

著小说中主人公，系一生理学家，曾制造一怪物，后为此怪物所毁灭〕。②作法自毙的人；毁掉创造者自己的事物；人形怪物。***a ~'s monster*** 自己所创造反而毁灭自己的恶魔；自找的烦恼。**-i·an** *a.*

Frank·fort [ˈfræŋkfət] *n.* ①(莱因河畔)法兰克福〔西德城市〕(= ~on the Main 或〔G.〕*Frankfurt am Main*)。②(奥得河畔)法兰克福〔东德城市〕(= ~ on the Oder 或〔G.〕*Frankfurt an der Oder*)。③〔f-〕= frankfurter. ~ **black** (铜板印刷用)黑色油墨。

frank·furt(er), frank·fort(er) [ˈfræŋkfət(ə)] *n.* 猪牛肉混合香肠。

frank·in·cense [ˈfræŋkinˌsens] *n.* 乳香。~ **oil**【化】蓝丹油。

Frank·ish [ˈfræŋkiʃ] *a.* ①法兰克人的，法兰克族的。②法兰克语的；法兰克文化的。③西欧人的。— *n.* 法兰克语。

Frank·lin, Franklyn [ˈfræŋklin] *n.* ①富兰克林〔姓氏，男子名〕。②**Benjamin** ~ 富兰克林〔1706—1790，美国政治家，科学家〕。~ **stove** 富兰克林炉〔一种壁炉状铸铁火炉〕。

frank·lin [ˈfræŋklin] *n.* ①(中世纪英国非贵族出身的)小地主。②〔主英〕拥有土地的富农。

frank·lin·ite [ˈfræŋklinait] *n.*【矿】锌铁矿，锌铁尖晶石。

frank·ly [ˈfræŋkli] *ad.* 率直地，坦白地，真诚地。~ ***speaking*** 老实说，坦率地说〔用作插入语〕。

frank·ness [ˈfræŋknis] *n.* 率直，坦白。

frank·pledge [ˈfræŋkpledʒ] *n.* ①【英史】十家连保制。②实施连保的十家。③实施连保的十家成员(指十二岁以上的男子)。

Franks [fræŋks] *n.* 弗兰克斯〔姓氏〕。

fran·se·ri·a [frɑːnˈsiəriə] *n.*【植】弗氏菊〔菊科植物，产于美国西部，以西班牙植物学家弗兰塞里 (*Antonio Franseri*) 命名〕。

fran·tic [ˈfræntik] *a.* ①狂乱的；疯狂的。②〔口〕厉害的，非常的。***be in a ~ hurry*** 急如星火。***be ~ with pain*** 痛得发狂，剧痛。**-(al)ly** *ad.* **-ness** *n.*

frap [fræp] *vt.* (用绳索等)捆牢，收紧。

frap·pé [ˈfræpei] *a.*〔F.〕冷却的，冰过的。— *n.* 冰镇冷饮，刨冰冷饮。*wine ~* 冰镇葡萄酒。

Fra·ser, Fra·zer [ˈfreizə] *n.* 弗雷泽〔姓氏〕。

frat [fræt] *n.* = fraternity.

fra·te [ˈfrɑːtei] *n.* (*pl.* ***fra·ti*** [ˈfrɑːti])〔It.〕= friar.

fra·ter[1] [ˈfreitə] *n.*〔废〕修道院食堂或斋堂。

fra·ter[2] [ˈfreitə, ˈfrɑːtə] *n.* ①(宗教团体或兄弟会的)兄弟；会友。②〔废〕托钵僧，修道士。

fra·ter·nal [frəˈtəːnl] *a.* ①兄弟的，兄弟般的，友爱的。②〔美〕兄弟会的，共济会的。*a ~ association [order, society]*〔美〕兄弟会，共济会。*~ affection [love]* 友爱。~ **twins**【生】异卵双生。**-ly** *ad.*

fra·ter·ni·ty [frəˈtəːniti] *n.* ①兄弟关系，友爱；博爱。②同行朋友，同人；会友，社友。③兄弟会，共济会。④〔美〕大学生联谊会〔美国男学生中略带秘密性的组织，女学生的此类组织则称Sorority，它们多以两个或三个希腊字母为其名称〕。⑤(动物)一次交配所生的全部幼畜。*freedom [liberty], equality and ~* 自由，平等，博爱。*the ~ of the Press* 报界同人。*the angling ~* 钓鱼的朋友。~ **house**〔美〕大学生联谊会会所。

frat·er·nize, frat·er·nise [ˈfrætənaiz] *vi.* ①亲如兄弟，亲近。②和敌兵[敌国国民]亲善(特指被占领国国民)。③〔美俚〕(第二次世界大战中及战后)士兵和敌国国民发生性行为。— *vt.* 使亲善，使亲如兄弟。**-za·tion** [ˌfrætənaiˈzeiʃən] *n.*

frat·ri·ci·dal [ˌfreitriˈsaidl, fræ-] *a.* 杀兄弟[姊妹]的；杀同胞的。*a ~ war [struggle]* 内战，自相残杀的战争。

frat·ri·cide [ˈfreitrisaid, ˈfræ-] *n.* ①杀兄弟[姐妹]的行为。②杀害兄弟[姊妹]者。

Frau [frau] *n.* (*pl.* ~*s*,〔G.〕***Frau·en*** [ˈfrauən])〔G.〕①夫人〔和英语 Mrs. 相当〕；妻。②〔口〕德国女人。

fraud [frɔːd] *n.* ①欺骗，欺诈；舞弊；欺诈行为，骗局。②骗子；伪品。*actual ~ = ~ in fact* 有意的欺骗。*constructive [legal] ~* 无意[合法]的欺骗。*pious ~* 善意的欺骗。***in ~ of = to the ~ of***【法】为了诈骗…。

fraud·u·lence [ˈfrɔːdjuləns], **fraud·u·len·cy** [-si] *n.* 欺骗性，欺诈。

fraud·u·lent [ˈfrɔːdjulənt] *a.* ①欺骗性的，欺诈的。②骗得的。**-ly** *ad.*

fraught [frɔːt] *a.*〔仅用作表语〕①〔古〕积载着…的，装着…的。②充满…的；隐藏着…的 (*with*)。*a policy ~ with danger* 充满危险的政策。*a ship ~ with precious wares* 满载着贵重货物的一条船。— *n.* 货物，装载物。

fräu·lein [ˈfrɔilain] *n.* (*pl.* ~*s*,〔G.〕~) ①〔G.〕小姐〔与英语 miss 相当〕。②〔口〕(德国)姑娘。③(英国人家庭中的)德国保姆[家庭教师]。

frax·i·nel·la [ˌfræksiˈnelə] *n.*【植】白鲜。

fray[1] [frei] *vt.* ①擦，磨；磨损(布边等)，擦破(绳子的末端)以致纤维散开。②使(关系、神经等)紧张。*Long wear had ~ed the cuffs of his old shirt.* 他那件旧衬衫穿的时间太久，袖口都磨破了。*The edge of the carpet was ~ed into a fringe.* 地毯的边缘被散编成一绺绺流苏。— *vi.* 被磨损，被擦断。— *n.* (织物等的)磨损处。

fray[2] [frei] *n.* ①吵闹；打架。②争论，辩论。***be eager for the ~***〔书〕希望发生事端，唯恐天下不乱。— *vt.*〔古〕吓唬，使惊恐。— *vi.*〔古〕吵架，打架。

fray·ing [ˈfreiiŋ] *n.* 织物磨损后落下的碎片，摩擦后落下的东西。

fra·zil [ˈfreizl] *n.* 河底所结的冰。

fraz·zle [ˈfræzl] *vt., vi.* ①磨损，磨破，(使)变破烂。②(使)疲倦。— *n.* ①磨破。②磨损的边缘。③疲倦。***be beaten to a ~*** 被打得死去活来。***be worn to a ~*** ①被穿破。②疲惫不堪。

fraz·zled [ˈfræzld] *a.* ①〔口〕穿破了的，磨损了的。②疲惫的。③〔美俚〕喝醉了的。

FRB= Federal Reserve Board [Bank]〔美〕联邦储备委员会[银行]。

FRC = ①Federal Radio Commission〔美旧〕联邦无线电委员会。②Foreign Relations Committee〔美〕外交委员会。

freak[1] [friːk] *n.* ①奇想，任性，异想天开。②反常行为，怪诞行为。③畸形的人[物]。④〔美俚〕吸毒成瘾者。⑤…爱好者，热心者。⑥嬉皮士，颓废分子；逃避现实的人。*human ~s* 畸形的人们。*a ~ of nature* 畸形的人[物]，天生的畸形。*~s of weather* 天气反常。*out of mere ~* 完全出于想入非非。— *a.* 反常的，奇特的。*~ shapes* 奇形怪状。*vi., vt.*〔仅用于 ~ out 成语中〕。~ ***out***〔俚〕①(因服毒品等而)产生幻觉[逃避现实]。②成为颓废派。③使处于极度兴奋中。④行动反常。**~-out** ①吸毒引起的幻觉。②通过吸毒逃避现实，通过吸毒逃避现实的人。③嬉皮士集会。④反常的行动。~ **show** (狂欢节余兴的)畸形人表演。**-ed** *a.* 有奇特斑纹[条纹]的。

freak[2] [friːk] *vt.* 使…上有斑点[条纹]。— *n.* 斑点，条纹。**-ed** *a.* 有斑点的，花的，有条纹的。

freak·ish [ˈfriːkiʃ] *a.* ①异想天开的。②捉摸不定的。③畸形的，反常的，奇特的。**-ly** *ad.* **-ness** *n.*

freck·le [ˈfrekl] *n.* 雀斑，斑点。— *vi., vt.* (使)生斑点，(使)生雀斑。

freck·ly [ˈfrekli] *a.* (***-li·er; -li·est***) 多雀斑的。

freak·y [ˈfriːki] *a.*〔美俚〕吸毒(者)的，逃避现实的。— *n.* 吸毒者。

Fre·da [ˈfriːdə] *n.* 弗丽达〔女子名 Winifred 的昵称〕。

Fred·er·ic(k), Fre·dric(k) [ˈfredrik] *n.* 弗雷德里克〔男子名〕。

Fred·er·i·c(k)a [ˌfredəˈriːkə] *n.* 弗雷德丽卡〔女子名〕。

free [friː] *a.* (***fre·er; fre·est***) ①自由的，自主的；自立的。*a ~ action* 自由行动。*~ competition* 自由竞争。*as ~*

as the wind 自由自在,行动自由. *You are* ~ *to go or stay.* 去留随你的便. ②自动的;任意的,奔放的;直率的,不客气的. *of one's own* ~ *will* 自发的,自动的. *I am* ~ *to confess.* 我直率地承认. ~ *spirit* 奔放不羁的精神. ③随意的,自如的;(文章等)流利的;不拘泥于文字的 (*opp.* literal). ~ *verse* 自由体诗歌. ~ *translation* 意译. *a* ~ *style of writing* 流畅的文体. ④不拘束的,随便的;大方的;不吝啬的. ~ *manners* 态度大方. *be* ~ *with [of] one's money* 用钱大方. ⑤空闲的 (*opp.* busy);(房屋、空间等)空余的. *Are you* ~? 你现在有空吗? *Have you any rooms* ~? 你有空房间吗? ⑥自由开放的,畅通无阻的. *a* ~ *port* 自由(贸易)港. *The way is* ~ *for an advance.* 此路通行无阻. ⑦免费的;免税的. *admission [admittance]* ~ 免费入场. ~ *medical care.* 公费医疗. *a* ~ *school* 免费学校. ~ *of charge(s)* 免费. *free goods* 免税品. ⑧免…的;无…的 (*from; of*). *an ice-*~ *harbour* 不冻港. *an interest-*~ *loan* 无息贷款. *a nuclear-weapon-*~ *zone* 无核武器区. ⑨【化】单体的,游离的;【植】分离的,离生的,特生的. ~ *nitrogen* 单体氮. ~ *oxygen* 游离氧. ~ *state* 游离状态. ⑩(土地等)易于耕作的;(石头等)易于凿取的. ⑪顺风的. ⑫【语言】(重音等)自由的,不固定的. ⑬丰富的,富足的. ~ *living* 优裕的生活. ⑭(线条等)优美的;(姿势等)潇洒的. ~ *lines and curves* 优美的线条和曲线. ~ *gestures and movements* 潇洒的手势和动作. ⑮(绳索等)未固定的;悬空的. *the* ~ *end of a rope* 绳子未系住的一端. ⑯在场者均参加的. *a* ~ *fight* 一场混战. ~ ***alongside ship***【商】船边交货〔略f. a. s.〕. ~ ***and easy*** 不拘仪式的,随便的. ~ ***from*** 无…的,不受…影响的 (*a day* ~ *from wind* 无风的日子). ~ ***of*** ①无…的,摆脱了…的;离开,在…外的(~ *of duty* 免税. ~ *of a burden* 无负担. *the sea* ~ *of ice* 无流冰的海. *The train was not* ~ *of the station yet.* 火车还没有离开车站). ②可自由进入并使用的 (*be* ~ *of a friend's house* 可自由使用朋友的房屋). ~ ***of all average***【商】一切海损不保在内. ~ ***on board***【商】船上交货〔略 f. o. b.〕. ~ ***on rail***【商】火车上交货〔略 f. o. r.〕 ***get*** ~ 获得自由 (*of*). ***give sb. a*** ~ ***hand*** 给与某人行动自由,听其自行处置. ***give [spend] with a*** ~ ***hand*** 随便花钱. ***have a*** ~ ***hand*** 有行动自由. ***have one's hands*** ~ ①可以自由行动. ②无事. ***make sb.*** ~ ***use of*** 使某人自由使用,使某人自由出入. ***make sb.*** ~ ***of the city*** 给某人市民权. ***make*** ~ ***with*** 随意使用. ***set*** ~ 释放,解放. — *ad.* ①自由地,无阻碍地. ②一帆风顺地. ③免费地. *Members are admitted* ~ 会员免费入场. *The yacht was sailing* ~ *over the sea.* 游艇在海上顺风行驶. — *vt.* 解放,释放,使自由;解救,使摆脱 (*from; of*);清除. ~ *the land from oppression* 把国家从压迫下解放出来. ~ *oneself from one's difficulties* 从困难中解脱出来. ~ **agent** 有自主权力的人;(可解约加入他队的)自由身职业运动员. ~ **air** 大气,大气层的空气. ~**-and-easy** 〔口〕可以自由抽烟的音乐会(在酒吧间的)聚餐;下流音乐厅〔酒馆〕. ~ **association**【心】自由联想〔让病人把所想到的不论什么念头和回忆,都毫无掩饰地说出来,以此发现和明确内心被压抑的内容〕. ~ **bench**【法】寡妇财产. ~**board**【船】干舷高度,干舷. ~**boot** *vi.* 做海盗,干抢劫勾当. ~**booter** 海盗,海盗似的冒险家. ~**booting** *a., n.* 干抢劫勾当(的);掠夺行为(的). ~**born** *a.* 生而自由的,自由民的,自由民生的. ~ **charge**【电】自由电荷. ~**-choice** *a.* 由牲口任意选择饲料的. **F- Churches** (由英国国教分离出来的)独立教会. ~**coinage**【经】自由铸造货币的制度. ~ **companion** (中世纪的)雇佣兵. ~**-drop** ① *n.* (不用降落伞的)自由空投(物). ② *vt.* 自由空投. ~ **education** 公费教育. ~ **energy**【物】自由能. ~ **enterprise** 私营企业自由竞争(论)〔美国资产阶级主张政府尽可能少地限制私营企业自由竞争的论点或做法〕. ~ **fall** ①(跳伞的)自由降落;降落伞张开以前的降落. ②(火箭等的)惯性运动. ~**-fire zone**【军】格杀区〔在该区内,任何移动的物体均将被轰击〕. ~ **flight** (火箭的)无动力飞行〔指燃料耗尽或断绝后的飞行〕. ~**-flight** *a.* 无动力飞行的. ~**-for-all** ① *n.* 自由参加的比赛;可以自由发表意见的争论;大吵大闹,打群架. ② *a.* 对任何人都开放的. ~**-for-aller** *n.* 〔英俚〕不择手段的谋取私利者. ~**-form** *a.* 形式[造型]自由的;线条不规则的;独创性的;反传统的;任意的. ~ **frequence**【物】固有频率,自然频率. ~ **goods** ①免税品. ②不需成本的原料〔空气、水等〕. ~**hand** *a.* 不用仪器而随手画出的 (*a* ~*hand drawing* 徒手画,写意画). ~ **hand** 自由行动. ~**handed** *a.* 不拘束的;慷慨的,用钱大方的. ~**hearted** *a.* 坦白的,爽朗的,大方的,感情用事的. ~**hold** 地产[职位等]的自由保有权,完全保有的地产. ~**holder** 不动产的所有人,世袭地的保有人. ~ **house** 可卖各种牌子酒的酒店. ~ **hydrogen**【化】有效氢,游离氢. ~ **labour** ①自由人的劳动(与奴隶劳动相对而言). ②〔集合词〕不属于工会的工人. ~ **lance** (中世纪的)自由骑士,游勇;自由行动者;(无固定职业,以卖文、卖艺为生的)自由作家[演员]. ~**-lance** ① *vi.* 做自由作家[演员]. ② *a.* 自由作家[演员]的. ~ **list** 免费入场名单,(期刊的)赠阅名单,免税品一览表. ~ **liver** 讲究吃喝玩乐的人. ~**-living** *a.* ①喜欢吃喝玩乐的. ②【生】独立生存的,非寄生的,非共生的. ~**load** *vi.* 利用别人慷慨而占便宜;吃白食. ~**loader** 利用别人慷慨而占便宜的人,揩油者,经常吃白食者. ~**loading** *a.* 利用别人慷慨而占便宜的. ~ **love** 非法同居;(不要婚姻和法律约束的)两性自由离合论. ~**man** (*pl.* **-men**) 自由民,享有市民特权的人,荣誉市民. ~ **market** 自由市场. ~**-martin** (同公牛孪生的)无生殖机能的小雌牛. ~**mason** (中世纪的)石工工会会员;〔F-〕共济会 (Free & Accepted Masons) 会员. **F-masonry** *n.* ①共济会规章[制度],共济会仪式,共济会成员. ②〔f-〕同病相怜. ~**minded** *a.* 无精神负担的. ~ **oscillation**【物】自由振动. ~ **press** 出版自由. ~ **radical**【原】自由基,游离基. ~**-return** *a.*【宇】自动重返大气层的. ~ **rider** 非工会会员但享受工会活动成果的工人. ~ **silver** 〔美〕银币的自由铸造. ~ **soil** 无奴隶制的地方;(美国南北战争前禁止蓄用奴隶的)自由地区,自由土地. ~ **speech** 言论自由. ~**-spoken** *a.* 直言不讳的,讲话坦率的. ~**standing** *a.* (雕刻、建筑物等)独立的,自力撑持的. **F- State** ①(美国南北战争前的)自由州,不蓄奴地区. ②爱尔兰自由邦. ~**stone** ① *n.* 易切石,软性石;核与肉容易分离的果实. ② *a.* (果实等)容易与核分离的. ~ **style**【游】自由式. ~**-swimming** *a.* (动物)能自由浮游的,能游泳的. ~**swinging** *a.* 大胆的,直率的,不考虑个人的. ~**thinker** 理性主义者;唯理论者,【宗】自由思想家. ~**thinking** *a.* 自由思想的(尤指宗教上). ~ **thought** (十八世纪不受传统宗教思想束缚的) 自由思想. ~ **throw**【篮球】罚球. ~**-tongued** *a.* 说话不当心的. ~ **trade** 自由贸易. ~ **trader** 自由贸易主义者;〔废〕走私者. ~ **university** 自由大学〔主要由学生们自己组织的独立大学或学院,学生可自由选课,不分班级〕. ~ **verse** (不受格律约束的) 自由诗. ~ **vibration**【物】自由振动. ~**way** ①快车道. ②不收养路费的公路. ~**wheel** *vi.* ①靠惯性滑行. ②随心所欲[放任自流]地生活[行动]. ~ **wheel** (自行车的)飞轮,【机】滑轮. ~**wheeling** ① *n.* 惯性滑行. ② *a.* 惯性滑行的;放任自流的,随心所欲的. ~**-will** *a.* 自由的,从心所欲的;自愿的,出乎自由意志的. ~ **will** 自愿,自由意志;【哲】自由意志论. ~**-wool** 净毛. ~ **zone** 堆放免付关税货物的地区.

free·bie, free·by [ˈfriːbi] *n.* (*pl.* **-bies**) 〔美俚〕①免费赠品〔如戏院赠票〕;不劳而获的东西. ②施与[接受]免费赠品者.

Freed·heim [ˈfriːdhaim] *n.* 弗里德海姆〔姓氏〕.

freed·man [ˈfriːdmən] *n.* (*pl.* **-men**) ①(由奴隶解放出

来的)自由民. ②法律上解除了约束的人.

free·dom [ˈfriːdəm] *n.* ①自由; 自主; 自由身分. ②〔使用等的〕自由权. ③直率; 放肆, 过分亲密. ④特权, 特许; 免除, 解脱 *(from)*. ⑤【物】自由度. ⑥(动作等的)优美, (生活的)优游闲适. *necessity and ~* 【哲】必然和自由. *the Four Freedoms* (1941 年美国总统罗斯福提出的所谓"言论自由、信仰自由、免于匮乏、免于恐惧"的)四大自由〔即 *~ of speech, ~ of worship, ~ from want, ~ from fear*〕. *~ of assembly* 集会自由. *~ of conscience* 信仰自由. *~ of the will* 意志自由. *~ of the air* 【军】空战主动权. *~ of the city* (赠与外宾的)荣誉市民权. *~ of the press* 出版自由. *~ of the seas* 【国际公法】战时中立国船只的自由航海权, 商船自由航海权. *~ from care* 放心. *~ from taxation* 免税. ***take [use] ~s with sb.*** 对某人放肆. ***with ~*** 自由地. **~-fighter** 争取自由的战士. **F- Ride** 〔亦作 f- r-〕〔美〕"自由乘客"运动〔为争取公民权利故意乘坐黑人白人同车同船的各种交通工具去南部各州, 要求废除车船种族隔离的示威运动〕. **F- Rider** 〔亦作 f- r-〕参加"自由乘客"运动的民权工作者.

free·ly [ˈfriːli] *ad.* ①自由地, 随意地. ②直率地, 不客气地. ③慷慨地, 豪爽地. ④免费地.

Free·man [ˈfriːmən] *n.* 弗里曼〔姓氏, 男子名〕.

free·ness [ˈfriːnis] *n.* ①自由. ②直率; 随意. ③大方. ④排水度.

free·si·a [ˈfriːʒiə, -siə] *n.* 【植】小苍兰属.

Free·town [ˈfriːtaun] *n.* 弗里敦〔塞拉利昂首都〕.

freeze [friːz] *vi.* ***(froze*** [ˈfrəuz]***; fro·zen*** [ˈfrəuzən]***)*** ①冷冻, 凝固, 结冰. ②冻僵, 冰冷. ③战栗, 颤抖; 〔美口〕木立不动. *It froze hard last night.* 昨夜冰冻得厉害. *I am simply freezing.* 我简直冻僵了. — *vt.* ①使冷冻, 使结冰, 使凝冻; 冷藏. ②使冻僵, 使冻伤, 使冻死. ③使沮丧. ④冻结(存款、工资、物价等). *~ ice cream* 制冰激淋. *~ sb. with a frown* 皱起眉头使某人沮丧〔吓退〕. ***~ [be frozen] to death*** 冻死. ***~ sb blood = make sb.'s blood ~*** 使某人毛骨悚然〔吓得不能动弹〕. ***~ (on) to*** 〔口〕①贴紧, 搂紧. ②抓紧. ***~ out*** ①冻干. ②〔口〕(用冷淡态度)使人无地自容, 逼走某人. ***~ over*** 全面结冰. ***~ together*** 冻结在一起. ***~ up*** ①(使)冻结. ②(态度等)变呆板〔冷淡, 僵硬〕. — *n.* ①结冰, 凝冻; 冻结. ②严寒期. **~-dry** *vt.* 【化】冷冻干燥, 冻干〔在高度真空内将冷冻状态的食物等干燥, 特别用以保存食物〕. **~-dryer** 冻干机. **~-etching** 冷裂法〔将标本速冻后割裂, 借以显示其内部立体结构以便观察〕. **~-frame** 【影, 电视】静止镜头.

freez·er [ˈfriːzə] *n.* ①制冰淇淋者, 冷藏工人. ②冷冻装置, 冷冻机, 冷藏车, 冷藏库, 电冰箱.

freez·ing [ˈfriːziŋ] *a.* ①凝冻的, 极冷的. ②使人打冷颤的; 极冷淡的. ③结冰的; 冷冻用的. *a ~ machine* 冷冻机. — *ad.* 冰冻一样地. *be ~ cold* 冰冻一样地冷. — *n.* 冻结, 结冰(作用). **~ drizzle** 冻毛雨. **~ mixture** 冷却剂, 冷冻混合物. **~ point** 【物】冰点, 凝冻点. **-ly** *ad.*

freight [ˈfreit] *n.* ①〔英〕船运货物, 运输〔美国兼指空运、陆运〕. ②货运. ③运费. ④〔美〕货运列车 (= ~ train). *~ rates* 运费率. *volume of ~* 货运量. ***by ~*** 〔美〕用普通货车运送. ***dead ~*** 空舱费. ***drag [pull] one's ~*** 〔美俚〕离开, 出发. ***~ forward*** 运费由提货人支付. ***~ paid*** 运费付讫. ***~ prepaid = advanced ~*** 运费先付. — *vt.* ①运送. ②装货于; 充满. ③出租〔租用〕(船、车). **~ agent** 运输行. **~ car** 〔美〕(一节)货车 (=〔英〕goods waggon). **~ engine** 货运机车〔注意其牵引力而不重视其速度〕. **~ house** 货栈, 堆栈. **~ liner** 〔英〕集装箱货运列车. **~ ton [tonnage]** 容积吨(数). **~ train** 〔美〕货运列车 (=〔英〕goods train).

freight·age [ˈfreitidʒ] *n.* ①货运. ②运费. ③运送的货物.

freight·er [ˈfreitə] *n.* ①租船人; 装货人, 货主; 承运人. ②货船, 运货机.

frem·i·tus [ˈfremitəs] *n.* 【医】震颤.

Fre·mont [friˈmɔnt] *n.* 弗里蒙特〔姓氏〕.

fre·na [ˈfriːnə] frenum 的复数.

French[1] [frentʃ] *n.* 弗伦奇〔姓氏〕.

French[2] [frentʃ] *a.* 法国的, 法兰西的; 法语的; 法国人的; 法国式的. — *n.* ①法语. ②〔the ~〕〔集合词〕法国人. ***pedlar's ~*** 窃贼的行话. **~ bean** 〔英〕菜豆. **~ bulldog** 法国牛头犬, 法国叭喇狗. **~ Canadian** ①法裔加拿大人. ②加拿大法语 (= Canadian French). **~ chalk** 滑石, 滑石粉. **~ Community** 法兰西共同体〔1958 年成立, 参加者有法国、中非共和国、乍得、刚果(布)、加蓬、马尔加什和塞内加尔等〕. **~ cuff** 法国双手铐. **~ curve** 曲线板, 曲线规. **~ doors** 法(式)双扇玻璃门. **~ dressing** 法式凉菜卤汁. **~ endive** 【植】菊苣嫩叶. **~ fry** 〔常用 f- fry〕【烹】炸得松脆的; 法(国)式土豆丝(片)〔俗称 ~ fries〕. **~ gray [grey]** 浅灰色. **~ heel** 法式高弯跟(女鞋). **~ horn** 【乐】法国号. **~ ice cream** 法式冰淇淋〔用鸡蛋和高脂肪奶油做成〕. **~ knot** 法式花芯刺绣针迹; 法式线结〔将线绕针数次而缝成的花式结. **~ leave** 不辞而别〔源出法国 18 世纪的习俗, 参加宴会的客人可不辞而别〕(*take ~ leave* 不辞而别). **~ letter** 〔英俚〕避孕套. **~man** ***(pl. -men)*** 法国人. **~ marigold** 【植】万寿菊. **~ pastry** 法式点心. **~ polish** 法国磨光漆. **~-polish** *vt.* 在…上法国漆. **~ Revolution** 法国大革命 (1789–1799). **~ roll** 花卷蛋糕. **~ roof** 法式屋顶. **~ seam** 【纺】来去(线)缝, 法式接缝. **~ telephone** 法式电话机〔早期电话机的一种〕. **~ toast** 蘸牛奶、鸡蛋后轻炸的面包片. **~ window** 双扇落地玻璃门〔一般通至阳台〕. **~ woman** *n.* ***(pl. -wo·men)*** 法国女人.

French·i·fy [ˈfrentʃifai] *vt.* 使法国化. **-fi·ca·tion** *n.*

French·less [ˈfrentʃlis] *a.* 不懂法语的.

French·y [ˈfrentʃi] *a.* ***(French·i·er; -i·est)*** ①法国式的. ②〔美俚〕轻松愉快的; 嘻笑作乐而不严肃的; 轻率的. — *n.* 〔口〕法国人. **French·i·ly** *ad.* **French·i·ness** *n.*

fre·net·ic [friˈnetik] *a.* ①非常激动的. ②发狂的 (= phrenetic). **-al** *a.* 〔古〕= phrenetic.

fren·u·lum [ˈfrenjuləm] *n.* (*pl.* ***~s, -la*** [-lə]) ①【解】小系带. ②【动】(昆虫的)翅缰.

fre·num [ˈfriːnəm] *n.* (*pl.* ***fre·na*** [ˈfriːnə], ***~s***) ①【解】系带. ②【动】(蔓足类的)系褶; (昆虫的)系带.

fren·zied [ˈfrenzid] *a.* 狂乱的, 狂暴的, 疯狂似的. *make ~ efforts* 拼命挣扎〔用力〕. *~ rage* 狂怒. **-ly** *ad.*

fren·zy [ˈfrenzi] *vt.* 〔主用被动语态〕使狂乱, 使发狂. *become frenzied* 发狂. *be frenzied with joy* 狂喜. — *n.* 狂乱, 疯狂似的激动. *drive sb. to ~* 使某人发狂. *in a ~* 发狂, 在狂乱中. *in the ~ of the moment* 在一时狂怒中. *work oneself into a ~* 渐渐狂暴起来. **-zi·ly** *ad.*

fre·on [ˈfriːɔn] *n.* 【化】氟里昂, 氟氯烷, 二氯二氟〔氟三氯〕甲烷〔商标名〕〔一种无色气体冷冻剂〕.

freq. = frequency; frequent; frequentative; frequently.

fre·quence [ˈfriːkwəns] *n.* = frequency.

fre·quen·cy [ˈfriːkwənsi] *n.* ①屡次, 频仍, 频繁. ②(脉搏等的)次数, 出现率; 频度; 【物】频率, 周率. *audio ~* 音频. *a high [low] ~* 高〔低〕频. *the ~ of earthquakes in Japan* 地震在日本的频繁发生. *mean [median] ~* 中频. *resonance [resonant] ~* 谐振频率, 共振频率. *ultrahigh ~* 超高频. *ultralow ~* 超低频. *very high ~* 甚高频. *very low ~* 甚低频. **~ band** 【无】频带, 波段. **~ changer [converter]** 【电】换频器, 变频器. **~ channel** 【电视】频道. **~ curve** 【统】频数曲线. **~ distribution** 【统】频数分布; 频率分布. **~ divider** 分频器. **~ meter** 【电】频率(周率)计. **~ modulation** 【电】调频, 频率调制; 调频播送. **~ selection** 【电】频

差法分辨.

fre·quent [ˈfriːkwənt] *a.* ①屡次的,常见的;频繁的. ②(脉搏等)急促的,快的. *a ~ caller [visitor]* 常客. *a ~ occurence* 经常发生的事情. *a coast with ~ lighthouses.* 灯塔密布的海岸. — [fri(ː)ˈkwent] *vt.* 常去,时常出入于. ②与…时常交际[来往]. *Tourists ~ the district.* 游客常去那个地方. *I know him, but I don't ~ him much.* 我认识他,但不常往来. *~ learned men [good company]* 与学者[正派朋友]交往. **-ly** *ad.*

fre·quen·ta·tion [ˌfriːkwenˈteiʃən] *n.* 常去,经常来往[出入].

fre·quen·ta·tive [friˈkwentətiv] *a.* 多次的,反复表示的. — *n.*【语法】反复动词〔如 chatter 是 chat 的反复动词〕(= ~ verb).

fre·quent·er [friˈkwentə] *n.* 常客,常来往的人.

frère [frɛr] *n.* 〔F.〕(*pl.* ~*s* [frɛr]) ①兄弟;团友,社友. ②(天主教的)修士.

fres·co [ˈfreskəu] *n.* (*pl.* ~*es*, ~*s*) ①(湿绘)壁画法. ②壁画. ***paint in ~*** 作壁画. — *vt.* 在…作壁画,用壁画法画出,作壁画.

fresh [freʃ] *a.* ①新产生的,新制的;新获得的;新近的,新到的. ②清新的;生气勃勃的,强健的,气色好的,鲜艳的,鲜嫩的. ③清洁的;清凉的. ④新鲜的,无咸味的(*opp.* salt); 未加盐(腌)的,生的. ⑤无经验的,不熟练的;新入学的,新进的(*opp.* old). ⑥〔俚〕微醉的;〔美俚〕莽撞的,放肆的,无礼的(尤指对异性). ⑦【气】疾(风);【海】迅速的. ⑧外加的,另外的,进一步的. ⑨(谈话等)有创见的,有启发性的. ⑩(母牛)开始有奶的,新近产犊的. *news ~ and ~* 最新消息. *~ flowers* 鲜花. *~ fish* 鲜鱼,生鱼. *~ fruit* 新鲜水果. *feel ~* 觉得清新[爽快]. *make a ~ start* 从新开始. *~ troops* 生力军. *a ~ hand* 无经验者,生手. *a ~ recruit* 新兵. *He's a bit ~* 他有点醉了. ***as ~ as paint [arose]*** 精神饱满的. ***be ~ in mind [memory]*** 记忆犹新. ***break ~ ground*** 开垦生荒地;着手新事业. ***~ from school [the country]*** 刚由学校[乡下]出来. ***F- paint!*** 油漆未干! ***get ~*** 〔美俚〕厚脸起来;变得无礼. ***green and ~*** 生的;不熟练的;幼稚的. ***in the ~ air*** 在户外. ***throw ~ light on*** 提供新情况. — *ad.* 刚,新,才. — *n.* ①(河流的)暴涨,泛滥. ②(流入咸水中的)淡水流. ③〔学俚〕新生. ④(一天、一年等的)开始. ***in the ~ of the morning*** 清晨. **~-blown** *a.* (花)刚开的. **~ breeze**【气】清劲风(五级风). **~-caught** *a.* 刚捕获的. **~-coined** *a.* (硬币)新铸造的. **~ gale**【气】强风(八级风). **~man** (*pl.* *-men*) 大学新生,一年级生;新手,生手. **~-run** *a.* (鱼)新由海中进到淡水中的. **~water** *a.* ①淡水的(*~water fish* 淡水鱼. *~water fishery* 淡水养鱼业. *a ~water lake* 淡水湖). ②只习惯于淡水航行的,无经验的,不熟练的. ③〔美俚〕内地的,不知名的(*~water college* 内地大学). **~water eel**【动】鳗鲡属. **-ness** *n.*

fresh·en [ˈfreʃn] *vt.* ①使新鲜. ②使清爽,使有精神;把(自己)盥洗一番(*up*). ③使变淡,去…的盐分. ④添(饮料). *The rest ~ed my spirit.* 我休息后精神饱满. — *vi.* ①变新鲜. ②变活泼. ③(风)变强. ④咸味变淡. ⑤(母牛)开始有奶,产犊. ***~ the way*** 增加船行速度. ***~ up*** ①弄新鲜,变新鲜. ②盥洗打扮. **-er** *n.* ①清凉剂(如饮料等). ②〔英俚〕新学生;新手.

fresh·et [ˈfreʃit] *n.* ①(因下雨、融雪而引起的)河水暴涨. ②流入海中的淡水流.

fresh·ly [ˈfreʃli] *ad.* ①新近;刚才. ②精神饱满地;气息清新地,活泼地.

Fres·nel [freiˈnel, F. freˈnɛl], **Augustin Jean** 弗瑞奈〔1788–1827, 法国物理学家〕. **~ mirrors**【光】弗瑞奈式镜.

fret[1] [fret] *vt.* ①使焦急,使烦恼. ②腐蚀,侵蚀,使消损,使磨损. ③侵蚀成…. ④(风等)使(水面)起浪. *a knife fretted with rust* 锈坏了的小刀. *~ oneself* 烦闷,焦急. *~ oneself ill* 急出病来. *~ oneself to death* 急死. *~ one's health away [out]* 烦坏了健康. — *vi.* ①焦急,烦恼. ②侵蚀. ③消损,磨损. ④(水面)起浪. *~ over mistake* 为错误而焦急. ***~ and fume*** 焦急. ***~ the bit*** (马)咬嚼子. ***~ away [out] one's life*** 在烦闷中过日子. — *n.* ①焦急,烦恼. ②腐蚀(处);磨损(处). ***in a ~ = on the ~*** 焦急,烦闷.

fret[2] [fret] *n.* (弦乐器指板上定音的)档子. — *vt., vi.* 把(弦)压在档子上.

fret[3] [fret] *n.*【建】回纹饰;网状饰物. — *vt.* 用回纹装饰. **~saw** 钢丝锯,线锯. **~work**【建】浮雕细工.

fret·ful [ˈfretful] *a.* ①焦急的, 烦恼的. ②(水面)起波纹的;(风)一阵阵的. **-ly** *ad.* **-ness** *n.*

fret·ty [ˈfreti] *a.* (*-ti·er; -ti·est*) ① = fretful. ②有回纹装饰的.

Freud [frɔid], **Sigmund** 弗洛伊德〔1856—1939, 奥国精神病学家〕.

Freud·i·an [ˈfrɔidjən] *a.* 弗洛伊德的, 弗洛伊德学说[学派]的,精神[心理]分析学的. — *n.* 弗洛伊德派,精神[心理]分析学家. **~ slip** 无意中泄露真实欲望的漏嘴. **-ism** *n.* 弗洛伊德学说[学派], 精神[心理]分析学.

Fri. = Friday.

fri·a·bil·i·ty [ˌfraiəˈbiliti] *n.* 脆性,易碎性.

fri·a·ble [ˈfraiəbl] *a.* 易(粉)碎的,脆的. *a ~ rock* 松散岩石.

fri·ar [ˈfraiə] *n.* (天主教的)男修士, 行乞修士. *The ~ preached against stealing and had a goose [pudding] in his sleeve.* 〔谚〕口里仁义道德, 心里男盗女娼. **~bird** 蜜鸟〔产于澳洲和西南亚,头部光光无羽毛〕. **~'s balsam** 安息香酊. **~'s lantern** 鬼火(= ignis fatuus).

fri·ar·y [ˈfraiəri] *n.* 男修道院. — *a.* 男修道院的;男修士的.

frib·ble [ˈfribl] *n.* ①无聊的人,轻佻的人. ②无聊的事,无聊的行为. — *vi.* 做无聊的事;浪费时间.

fric·an·deau [ˈfrikəndəu] *n.* (*pl.* ~*x* [-z]) 〔F.〕油焖[烤]小牛肉[其他肉类].

fric·an·do [ˈfrikəndəu] *n.* (*pl.* ~*es*) = fricandeau.

fric·as·see [ˌfrikəˈsiː] *n.* 〔F.〕油焖[油煎]原汁肉块. — *vt.* 油焖[油煎](原汁肉块).

fric·a·tive [ˈfrikətiv] *a.*【语音】摩擦的,由摩擦产生的. **~ consonants** 摩擦辅音. — *n.*【语音】摩擦音.

Frick(e) [frik] *n.* 弗里克〔姓氏〕.

fric·tion [ˈfrikʃən] *n.* ①摩擦,阻力. ②倾轧,冲突,不和(*between*). ③擦热皮肤. *moist ~*【医】湿擦. **~ ball, ~-ball** (轴承中的)滚珠. **~ band**【矿】摩阻带. **~ brake** 摩擦制动器, 摩擦刹车. **~ clutch** 摩擦离合器. **~ cone** 摩擦(锥)轮. **~ drive** 摩擦传动. **~ gear(ing)** 摩擦传动装置. **~ monger** 挑拨离间,制造不和的人. **~ tape** (导体外面包的)绝缘胶布;摩擦带.

fric·tion·al [ˈfrikʃənəl] *n.* 摩擦的,由摩擦而生的. **~ electricity** 摩擦电. **~ resistance** 摩擦阻力. **-ly** *ad.*

Fri·day [ˈfraidi] *n.* 星期五. *Black [Good] ~* 耶稣受难日〔复活节前的星期五〕. *Man F-* 忠仆〔F- 原为《鲁滨逊飘流记》中一个忠于鲁滨逊的仆人的名字〕. **-s** *ad.* 星期五,每星期五.

fridge [fridʒ] *n.* 〔主英口〕电冰箱,冷冻机.

fried [fraid] fry[1] 的过去式及过去分词. — *a.* ①油煎的. ②〔美俚〕喝醉了的. **~ cake** 油煎饼,炸面圈. **~ shirt** 〔美俚〕浆得笔挺的衬衫.

friend [frend] *n.* ①友人,朋友(*opp.* foe, enemy). ②〔称呼语〕朋友〔常作 *My ~*〕;〔英〕下议院议员间的称呼〔常作 *My honourable ~*〕;〔英〕法院律师间的称呼〔常作 My learned ~〕. ③自己人;支持者,赞助者, 同情者;助手,随从;〔*pl.*〕〔Scot.〕近亲,家属. ④【宗】公谊会 (the Society of friends) 教友. ⑤有帮助的事物[本质]. *A ~ in need is a ~ indeed.* 〔谚〕患难朋友才是真朋友. *Old ~s and old wine are best.* 〔谚〕陈酒味醇,老友情深. *The* *best of ~s must part.*〔谚〕天下无不散的筵席. *a boy [girl] ~* 男[女]朋友. *bosom [close, great, good, sworn] ~s* 好朋友,心腹朋友. *My shyness here are my best ~.* 我的腼腆在这里对我很有好处. ***a ~ at [in] court*** 有势力的朋友,好门路. ***be [make] ~s with*** 跟…要好,跟…做朋友. ***keep ~s with*** 跟…保持友好. ***make ~ again*** 言归于好,重修旧好. ***make ~s of*** 和…为友,引…为同党. ***part ~s*** 不伤感情地分手(*Let us part ~s.* 让我们好走好散). — *vt.*〔诗〕与…为友(= befriend).

friend·less [ˈfrendlis] *a.* 没有朋友的,无依无靠的. **-ness** *n.*

friend·ly [ˈfrendili] *a.* *(-li·er; li·est)* ①友好的;朋友似的,亲密的. ②有帮助的,互助的. *a ~ game [match]* 友谊赛. *a ~ nation* 友邦. *a ~ shower* 及时雨. *a ~ society*〔英〕互助会. *~ troops* 友军. ***be ~ to*** 赞成. ***be on ~ terms with = have ~ relations with*** 跟…友好. — *ad.* 友好地;朋友般地. **~ action [suit]** 目的在于解决疑点的友好诉讼. **-li·ly** *ad.* **-li·ness** *n.*

friend·ship [ˈfrendʃip] *n.* 友谊,友情;亲睦. *a ~ visit* 友好访问. ***strike up a ~*** 做起朋友来,建立友谊.

fri·er [ˈfraiə] *n.* = fryer.

Frie·sian [ˈfriːʒən] *a.* = Frisian.

frieze¹ [friːz] *n.* 起绒粗呢. —*vt.* 使(布上)起绒毛. **~ flannel** 棉毛法兰绒.

frieze² [friːz] *n.*【建】(柱的)中楣;带状装饰. **~ panel** 束腰板. **~ rail** 上腰板.

frig·ate [ˈfrigit] *n.* ①(十八、十九世纪装有大炮的)快速帆船. ②驱逐领舰. ③护卫舰,护航舰. **~ bird**【动】军舰鸟〔热带猛禽〕.

frig [frig] *vt.*〔俚、卑〕与(女子)发生性行为.

frig(e) [fridʒ] *n.*〔英口〕冰箱(=refrigerator).

frig·ging [frign] *a.*〔俚〕他妈的〔一个意义笼统的粗野的字眼〕(=damned).

fright [frait] *n.* ①恐怖. ②可怕的东西;难看的人. *a perfect ~* 极可怕、丑陋的人. ***die from [of] ~*** 吓死. ***get [have] a ~*** 大吃一惊. ***give a ~*** 使某人受惊. ***in a ~*** 在惊恐之下. ***take ~ at*** 因某事惊恐. — *vt.*〔诗〕= frighten.

fright·en [ˈfraitn] *vt.* 使惊惧,吓唬. *~ a child into fits* 把小孩吓得抽风〔不知人事〕. *~ sb. out of an evil practice* 吓掉某人的坏习惯. *~ sb. into submission* 吓某人服从. *~ sb. away* 把某人吓走. — *vi.* 惊恐,害怕. *I don't ~ easily.* 我不会轻易就害怕. ***be ~ed at*** 受…惊吓,看见…大吃一惊. ***be ~ed of***〔口〕害怕,对…感到恐惧(*The child has always been ~ of the dark.* 这孩子一直怕黑暗). ***be ~ed out of one's wits*** 被吓呆.

fright·ful [ˈfraitful] *a.* ①可怕的,令人毛骨悚然的. ②讨厌的,丑恶的. ③〔俚〕非常的. *have a ~ time* 真觉得不愉快. *a ~ bore*〔俚〕极讨厌的人. *a ~ scandal* 非常丢脸的事. **-ly** *ad.* ①可怕地. ②〔俚〕非常地. **-ness** *n.* ①恐怖;丑恶. ②(对占领地人民的)残暴政策.

frig·id [ˈfridʒid] *a.* ①寒冷的. ②冷淡的,生硬的. ③索然无味的. ④【医】(妇女)性欲冷淡的〔*cf.* impotent〕. *the ~ zones* 寒带. *a ~ manner* 冷淡的态度. **-ly** *ad.* **-ness** *n.*

Frig·id·aire [ˌfridʒiˈdeə] *n.*〔美〕电冰箱〔原为一种商标名称〕.

fri·gid·i·ty [friˈdʒiditi] *n.* ①寒冷;冷淡. ②索然无味. ③【医】(妇女)性欲冷淡.

frig·o·rif·ic [ˌfrigəˈrifik] *a.* 致冷的;冷冻的;冷却的.

frig·o·rim·e·ter [frigəˈrimitə] *n.* 低温计.

fri·jol(e) [ˈfriːhəul] *n.* (*pl.* *fri·joles* [-z])【植】豇豆. **~ refritos** 炒豆〔墨西哥和美国南部常吃的一种菜豆〕.

frill [fril] *n.* ①褶边. ②【摄】胶片边缘的绉褶. ③【动】壳皱. ④〔*pl.*〕〔俚〕摆架子;〔美〕虚饰. ④〔美俚〕女孩,妇女. ***put on ~s***〔俚〕摆架子,装腔作势. — *vi.* (胶片边缘)起皱褶. — *vt.* 在…上加褶边. **-ed** *a.* 有饰边的. **-er·y** *n.* 衣褶边.

frill·ies [ˈfriliz] *n. pl.*〔俚〕镶有褶边的裙子.

frill·y [ˈfrili] *a.* 镶褶边的.

fringe [frindʒ] *n.* ①(地毯等的)穗,须边,流苏;缘饰. ②(森林等最外面的)边缘;〔喻〕(知识等的)初步,皮毛. ③(动植物的)伞;缘缨. ④前刘海. ⑤【物】(光线中的)条纹. ⑥略知皮毛的人. ⑦= ~ benefit. *a ~ of (beard)* 一嘴(胡子). *the mere ~s of philosophy* 哲学的皮毛. *diffraction ~*【物】衍射条纹,绕射条纹. *interference ~*【物】干涉条纹. — *vt.* ①给…加穗饰. ②使成为缘饰;成为…的边缘. *houses fringing the road on either side* 点缀在路两边的房屋. — *a.*〔美〕①边缘的,外围的. ②次要的,附加的. **~ area**【无】线条区,电视接收边缘区,散乱边纹区,干扰区域. **~ benefit** (工资外的)补贴〔如年金、工资照付的假期、保险金等〕. **~ tree**【植】流苏树属植物(尤指美国流苏树). **-less** *a.* **-like** *a.*

fringed [frindʒd] *a.* = fringy. **~ gentian**【植】穗裂龙胆〔产于美国北部和加拿大〕. **~ polygala**【植】少叶远志〔产于北美东部〕.

fring·ing [ˈfrindʒiŋ] *n.*【无】①边缘现象,散射现象,边缘通量(的形成). ②彩色电视中同步不够时用转盘调整色帧. **~ reef**【地】靠近海岸而与海岸平行的珊瑚礁,裙礁,岸礁,边礁.

Fringlish [ˈfriŋglish] *n.*〔或 f-〕法国化英语,夹有法语的英语.

fring·y [ˈfrindʒi] *a.* *(fring·i·er; -i·est)* 穗状的,有穗状缘饰的.

frip·per·y [ˈfripəri] *n.* ①(衣服等)俗气的装饰;(文体等)拙劣的修饰. ②浮夸;无聊的东西.

Fris·bee [ˈfrizbiː] *n.*〔美〕〔或 f-; frisby〕飞盘〔塑料制圆盘形往来投掷的玩具,后发展成为运动器具〕.

Fris·co [ˈfriskəu] *n.*〔美口〕= San Francisco.

fri·sé [friˈzei] *n.* (家具包面用的)卷毛厚绒织物.

fri·sette [friˈzet] *n.*〔罕〕妇女额前卷发,前刘海.

fri·seur [friˈzəː] *n.*〔F.〕(为妇女理发的)理发师.

Fri·sian [ˈfriziən] *a.* ①弗里斯兰群岛的. ②弗里斯兰人的. ③弗里斯兰语的. — *n.* ①弗里斯兰人;弗里斯兰群岛人. ②荷兰北部古条顿人. ③弗里斯兰语〔与古英语有关系的弗里斯兰的西日耳曼语〕. **~ Islands** 弗里斯兰群岛〔北欧德国、荷兰及丹麦沿海一带的群岛〕.

frisk [frisk] *n.* ①(猫儿等)欢跃,蹦跳;快活的时刻. ②〔俚〕搜身. — *vi.* 欢跃,跳跳蹦蹦. — *vt.* ①(轻快地)摇动. ②〔俚〕搜查(身体). ③〔俚〕扒窃.

fris·ket [ˈfriskit] *n.*【印】夹纸框.

frisk·y [ˈfriski] *a.* *(frisk·i·er; -i·est)* 欢跃的,活泼的. **-i·ly** *ad.* **-i·ness** *n.*

fris·son [friˈsɔn] *n.* (*pl.* *~s* [-ˈsɔn])〔F.〕(由激动、恐惧或喜悦引起的)颤抖(尤指阅读惊险小说等引起的感觉).

frit [frit] *n.* 玻(璃)料;烧料. — *vt.* 烧结,用加热方法处理(玻璃料). **~ fly** 一种小蝇(小麦害虫).

frith [friθ] *n.* 河口,海口,海湾.

frit·il·lar·y [friˈtiləri] *n.* ①【植】贝母属. ②【动】豹纹蝴蝶.

frit·ter¹ [ˈfritə] *n.* ①油炸馅饼;〔*pl.*〕鲸油渣〔可作肥料〕. *apple ~s* 油炸苹果馅饼. *oyster ~s* 油炸牡蛎馅饼.

frit·ter² [ˈfritə] *vt.* ①剁碎,弄碎. ②(一点一点地)浪费掉 *(away)*. — *n.* 碎片.

fritz [frits] *n.*〔常 F-〕〔俚、贬〕德国人〔*cf.* John Bull〕;德国兵;德国飞机〔潜艇等〕. ***on the ~***〔美俚〕坏掉,不行了,有毛病. ***on the terrific ~*** 破烂不堪,要大大修理. — *vi.*〔美俚〕损坏〔仅用于下列成语〕: **~ out** (机器等)损坏,发生故障.

friv·ol [ˈfrivəl] *v.t, vi.* (〔英〕***-ll***)〔俚〕浪费时间 *(away)* 闲混,做无聊的事.

fri·vol·i·ty [friˈvɔliti] *n.* ①轻佻,轻浮. ②轻薄的话;无聊的举动.

friv·o·lous [ˈfrivələs] *a.* ①轻佻的. ②琐碎的,无意义的. **-ly** *ad.* **-ness** *n.*

fri·zette [friˈzet] *n.* = frisette.

friz, frizz[1] [ˈfriz] *n.* (*pl.* ***friz·zes***)卷曲,卷结,卷曲的东西(如头发). —*vt., vi.* (使)卷曲,(使)卷结,(使)起绒毛. **frizzing machine**【纺】卷结机,起球机.

frizz[2] [friz] *vi.* (油炸物时)吱吱吱地响.

friz·zle[1] [ˈfrizl] *n.* 卷发,小卷结,卷曲的状态. —*vt., vi.* = friz.

friz·zle[2] [ˈfrizl] *vt., vi.* (把肉等)炸焦,炸酥,炸得吱吱发响.

friz·zly, friz·zy [ˈfrizli, -zi] *a.* 卷结的,鬈发的.

fro[1] [frəu] *ad.* 向那边;向后. ***to and*** ~ 往复,来回,前前后后.

fro[2] [frə, frəu] *prep.* 〔英方〕 = from.

Fro [frəu] *n.* 〔美俚〕非洲发型(=Afro).

Fro·bish·er [ˈfrəubiʃə] *n.* 弗罗比舍〔姓氏〕.

frock [frɔk] *n.* ①(妇女、小儿的连衣裙式)长衣; ②长工作服; (船员的)毛绒卫生衣. ③僧袍. ④〔英〕长礼服式军服. ⑤〔英〕 = ~ coat. — *vt.* ①使穿长工作服〔礼服,长衣等〕. ②授与…圣职. ~ **coat** (男子)长礼服.

froe [frəu] *n.* 劈板斧〔柄与斧背成直角〕,锛.

Froe·bel [ˈfrəːbəl], **Friedrich** 弗勒贝尔〔1782—1852,德国教育家、幼稚园创办人〕.

Froe·bel·lism [ˈfrɔːbəlizəm] *n.* 弗勒贝尔的教育主张;弗勒贝尔式教育法.

frog [frɔg] *n.* ①蛙. ②关节窝;(马蹄底中部的)蹄楔. ③【铁路】辙叉,道岔. ④(腰皮带上的)挂剑圈,挂武器环. ⑤盘花饰扣. ⑥插花用底盘. ⑦(提琴弓上的) 紧弦螺母. ⑧〔F-〕〔贬〕= Frogeater. ~ ***in the throat*** 嘎嘎声. — *vi.* ①捉青蛙. ②〔美俚〕骗. ~**eater** 食蛙者;〔F-〕〔贬〕法国人. ~**fish**【鱼】躄鱼科的鱼;鮟鱇鱼. ~**hopper**【动】沫蝉,吹沫虫. ~ **hopping tactics**【军】跳进战术,跳岛战术. ~ **kick**【体】 蛙泳的蹬夹动作. ~**man** (*pl.* ***-men***) 蛙人;潜水员. ~**-march** *n., vt.* 蛙式抬运〔使犯人面朝下平伏,由四人提着四肢行走〕. ~**spawn**【植】红藻.

frog·gy [ˈfrɔgi] *a.* 多蛙的;蛙似的. — *n.* 〔儿〕蛙;〔F-〕〔俚、贬〕法国人.

Froh·man [ˈfrəumən] *n.* 弗罗曼〔姓氏〕.

frol·ic [ˈfrɔlik] *n.* ①嬉戏,玩乐. ②狂欢的聚会. — *vi.* ***(frolicked; -icking)*** 嬉戏,玩闹. — *a.*〔古、诗〕嬉戏的,快乐的. ~ **pad** 〔美俚〕夜总会,舞厅. **frol·ick·er** *n.*

frol·ic·some [ˈfrɔliksəm] *a.* 〔废〕嬉戏的,爱闹着玩的. **-ly** *ad.* **-ness** *n.*

from [强 frɔm; 弱 frəm, frm] *prep.* ①〔表示动作的起点〕从,自. *fall ~ the sky* 从天上落下. *jump (down) ~ a window* 从窗口跳下. *part ~ a friend* 跟朋友分离. *(re)move ~ one place to another* 从甲地迁到乙地. *set out ~ London* 从伦敦出发. *~ door [house] to door [house]* 挨门挨户. *~ place to place* 从一处到另一处,一处一处地. ②〔表示顺序的起点〕从. *count ~ one to ten* 从一数到十. *~ childhood* 从幼年时起. *~ now on* 从今以后. *~ 1st October* 从十月一日起. *~ that time onward* 从那时以后. *~ birth till death* 从生到死. *~ the beginning* 自始. *~ beginning to end* 自始至终. *~ time to time* 时时. ③〔表示变更、转变的原来状态〕从. *awake ~ a dream* 从梦中醒来. *recover ~ illness* 从病中恢复. *go ~ bad to worse* 愈来愈坏. ④〔表示距离、间隔〕 *away ~ home* 离开家. *five years ~ now* 今后五年. *be absent ~ school* 缺课. *rest ~ work* 工作后〔(暂时)搁起工作〕休息. *How far is it ~ here?* 离开这里多远? ⑤〔表示差异、区别、选择〕 *differ ~ others* 跟别的不同. *know right ~ wrong* 辨别是非. *distinguish good ~ bad* 区别好坏. *choose ~* 从…中选择. ⑥〔表示解除、除去、停止、阻碍、防止、阻止〕 *be expelled ~ school* 被学校开除. *take 3 ~ 10* 十减去三. *cannot refrain ~ laughing* 忍不住笑. *be prevented ~ coming in* 被阻止入内. *save oneself ~ falling* 使自己免于摔倒. ⑦〔表示出处、来源、根源、根据〕 *a letter ~ a friend* 朋友的来信. *quotations ~ Shakespeare* 引自莎士比亚的文句. *judge ~ sb.'s conduct* 根据某人的行为来判断. *People expect much ~ him.* 人们对他期望很大. *~ what I have heard* 根据我所听到的. ⑧〔表示原因、动机、理由〕 *die ~ cholera* 患霍乱而死. *act ~ a sense of duty* 出于责任感而行动. *suffer ~ influenza* 患流行性感冒. ⑨〔表示原料、材料〕 *make wine ~ grapes* 用葡萄酿酒. *Steel is made ~ iron.* 钢是生铁炼成的. ★在制造过程中,原料形状或性质不变的用 of, 例如: That bridge is made of steel. 那座桥是用钢造的. ⑩〔用于表示时间和地点的副词和前置词前〕从,自. *~ above [below]* 自上〔下〕. *~ within [without]* 从内〔外〕. *~ far and near* 从远处和左近. *choose a book ~ among these* 从这些书籍中选一册. *~ before the war* 自从战前. *speak ~ behind the door* 从门后说话. *~ over the sea* 从海外. *~ under the table* 从桌下. *~ of old* 自古以来. ~ ***way back*** 从很久以前. ~**-scratch** *a.* 白手起家的,从零开始的.

fro·mage [frɔːˈmaːʒ] *n.* 〔F.〕 = cheese.

frond [frɔnd] *n.* ①(羊齿,棕榈,海草等的)叶子. ②【植】叶状体,植物体. ③〔诗〕叶;棕榈复叶. **-age** *n.* 〔集合词〕叶丛,茂盛的叶.

fron·des·cence [frɔnˈdesns] *n.* ①【植】发叶过程,发叶状态,发叶期. ②叶子,叶丛. **-descent** *a.*

fron·dose [ˈfrɔndəus] *a.*【植】叶状体的;有叶的;多叶的.

frons [frɔnz] *n.*【动】(昆虫的)额.

front [frʌnt] *n.* ①前部,前面;正面;(剧场的)正面〔前面〕座位〔也可指全部观众席位〕(*opp.* back, rear). ②【军】前线;战线,战地;【政】阵线. ③(房屋的)正面,门面,方向;(道路、河、海等的)边;〔the ~〕〔英〕海滨人行道. ④(妇女的)额前头发;(衬衫的)硬衬胸;领结;(祭坛前面的)帷子(等). ⑤门面;相貌,模样儿;装模作样,厚脸皮;〔诗〕额. ⑥【语】舌前,硬颚;舌前音. ⑦【气】锋〔冷热空气团分界处〕. ⑧(企业、团体等的)挂名负责人,出面人物;幌子,掩护物. ⑨〔美〕现况,现状. ⑩〔美〕前面的那位〔指最近边的服务员,常于呼唤时用〕. *a question at the ~* 当前的问题. *the east ~* (房屋的) 东面. *a river ~* 河边. *the people's [popular] ~* 人民阵线. *the political ~* 政界现状. *a united ~* 统一战线. *~ armies* 方面军. *cold ~*【气】冷锋. ***be at the*** ~ 在前线. ***bring to the*** ~ 使出名. ***change*** ~ 改变看法〔态度〕,【军】变换方向. ***come to the*** ~ 出名;变得明显,引人注目. ***false*** ~ 假前发;骗人的企图. ~ ***to*** ~ 〔古〕面对面. ***get in*** ~ ***of oneself*** 〔美口〕赶紧. ***go to the*** ~ 上前线,出征. ***have the*** ~ *(to do)* 居然有脸,竟好意思…. ***head and*** ~ 主要部分. ***in*** ~ 在前方,在正对面;在人注意的地方. ***in*** ~ ***of*** 在…的前面. ***out*** ~ 在观众席上. ***present [put on, show] a bold*** ~ ***on*** 装出勇敢大胆的样子. ***put a bold*** ~ ***on*** 勇敢地对付. ***put up a*** ~ 设门窗;装饰门面. ***to the*** ~ 在场,还活着. ***up*** ~ ①在前面. ②预先. — *a.* ①前面的,最前的;正面的. ②【语音】舌前的. *the ~ row* 前排. *a ~ door* 前门. — *ad.* 在〔向〕前面. *Eyes ~!* (口令)向前看! — *vt.* ①面向;对抗. ②【语】把…发成舌前音,把(发音部位)移前. ③【军】向着(敌军等的)正面. ④装饰…的正面. ⑤把…附在前面 *(with)*. ⑥领导(乐队). *The hotel ~s the sea.* 饭店面临大海. *~ difficulties* 正视困难,不怕艰难. *Marble will ~ the building.* 大楼的正面将以大理石作装饰. — *vi.* ①面对 *(on)*. ②为…作掩护 *(for)*. *The house ~s on the sea.* 房屋面向大海. ~ ***for*** 〔美俚〕主办,后援,推荐,对…负责. ~**bencher** (英国下院的)前座议员,前排席位议员. ~**lash**〔美〕(对

不利的强烈反应所作的)对应反应(以便起抵销或中和作用). ~ **line** 前线,第一线. ~**-line** *a.* 前线的, 第一线的. ~ **man** (企业、团体的)挂名负责人, 出面人物. ~ **matter** 书籍正文前的材料〔序言、目录、用法说明等〕. ~ **office** ①(公司的)董事会, 理事会. ②(机关、企业中的)全体决策人员. ~ **page** ①(书的)标题页. ②(报纸)头版. ~**-page** ① *a.* 有在头版上登载价值的; 重要的,轰动的. ② *vt.* 把…登在头版上. ~ **room** 前屋(尤指起坐室). ~ **runner** ①比赛中领先者. ②遥遥领先者〔如赛马〕. ~ **view** 正面图,正视图.

front·age [ˈfrʌntidʒ] *n.* ①(房屋的)正面, 前面; 正面宽度; 面对方向,眼界. ②路边地, 河边地, 屋前空地. ③【军】扎营地. **-r** *n.* 临街[临河]空地的所有者.

fron·tal [ˈfrʌntl] *a.* ①前面的,正面的 (*opp.* back; rear). ②额部的,前额的. *a* ~ *attack* 正面攻击. — *n.* 额骨; 额前装饰物(如发带, 头帕); (祭坛前面的)帷子; (房屋的)正面,(门、窗上面的) 人字形小墙(檐), 三角楣. ~ **bone** 额骨. ~ **fog**〔气〕锋面雾. ~ **lobe**【解】额叶. **-ly** *ad.*

fron·tier [ˈfrʌntjə, ˈfrɔn-] *n.* ①边疆; 边界, 边缘. ②新开辟地,边地;〔美〕边疆城市. ③〔常 *pl.*〕(知识等的)尚待开发的领域. *the ~s of medicine [science]* 医学[科学]新领域. — *a.* ①边疆的. ②新垦地的, 边地的. ~ *guards* 边防战士. *a* ~ *town* 边疆城市. ~ **spirit**〔美〕开拓精神;进取精神.

fron·tiers·man [ˈfrʌntjəzmən] *n.* (*pl.* **-men**)〔美〕边疆居民;边疆开发者.

fron·tis·piece [ˈfrʌntispiːs, ˈfrɔn-] *n.* ①(书籍的) 卷首插画,〔罕〕扉页. ②【建】主立面,正门; (门、窗上面的)饰壁,人字形小墙(檐), 三角楣. ③〔俚〕脑门, 天庭. — *vt.* ①给(书)加进卷首插画. ②把…画入卷首插图.

front·less [ˈfrʌntlis] *a.* ①无前部的, 无正部的. ②〔古〕无耻的.

front·let [ˈfrʌntlit] *n.* ①额带, 额饰;【宗】额上护符; (兽类或禽类的)前额. ②祭坛前面帷子上的飘带.

fron·to·gen·e·sis [ˌfrʌntəuˈdʒenisis] *n.*【气】锋生(作用).

fron·tol·y·sis [frʌnˈtɔlisis] *n.*【气】锋消(作用).

fron·ton [ˈfrɔntɔn; 〔Sp.〕frəunˈtəun] *n.* ①回力球场. ②〔墨西哥〕回力球戏 (= jai alai).

frore [frɔː, frɔə] *a.*〔诗、古〕霜冻的; 极冷的.

frosh [frɔʃ] *n.*〔美口〕大学一年级生.

Frost [frɔst] *n.* ①弗罗斯特〔姓氏〕. ②**Robert Lee** ~ 罗伯特·弗罗斯特〔1875—1963, 美国诗人〕.

frost [frɔst, frɔːst] *n.* ①霜; 霜柱; 结霜, 冰冻, 严寒; 冰点以下的温度. ②(态度、感情等的)冷淡, 冷酷. ③〔俚〕(演剧、出版物宴会、旅行等的)失败; 扫兴. *a heavy [hard, severe]* ~ 酷寒. *ten degrees of* ~ 冰点下十度. *The dance turned out a* ~. 舞蹈节目完全失败. ***a dead*** ~〔俚〕彻底失败. ~ ***in the ground*** 地中霜柱, 地面冻结. ***Jack F-*** 霜精, 严寒. — *vt.* ①在…上覆以霜; 霜害(植物等);〔喻〕使意气沮丧. ②使(玻璃、金属等表面)无光泽, 使(头发)霜白; 在(糕饼等上)加糖霜. ③在(马蹄铁上)加钉防滑. — *vi.*〔罕〕①起霜, 受冻. ②(油漆的表面等)干成霜状. *It* ~*s.* 下霜. ~**bite** ① *n.* 冻伤, 霜害. ② *vt.* 冻伤, 使遭霜害. ~**bite boating**〔美〕冬季赛艇运动. ~**biter**〔美〕冬季赛艇运动用的赛艇. ~**biting** = ~bite boating. ~ **bitten** *a.* ①受霜害的; 被冻伤的; 生冻疮的 (*get one's limbs* ~ *bitten* 手脚全生冻疮). ②冷酷无情的,冷淡的. ~**-bound** *a.* ①(土地等)冰冻的. ②冷冰冰的,不热情的. ~**fish**【动】① = tomcod. ②初霜时节出现的几种鱼. ~**flower**【植】紫菀属. ~**-hardy** *a.* 抗寒的, 耐寒的. ~ **heave** (道路的) 冻胀, 冰冻隆胀. ~ **line**【气】霜线. ~ **snow** 冰晶. ~**work** (窗上冻结的)霜花; (银器等的)霜花纹装饰. **-less** *a.* 无霜的,无霜冻的.

frost·ed [ˈfrɔstid] *a.* ①霜盖着的; 冻结了的; 受了霜害的; 冻伤了的; (蔬菜等)经过快速冰冻的. ②(须、发等)变白了的; (糕饼)盖有霜状混合物的; (玻璃、金属等)霜状表面的,无光泽的,磨砂的. ③(态度等)冷淡的. *a* ~ *bulb* 磨砂灯泡. ~ *glass* 毛玻璃,磨砂玻璃. — *n.* (牛奶、糖浆、冰淇淋等做的)一种甜饮料.

frost·ing [ˈfrɔːstiŋ] *n.* ①糖霜〔糖、黄油、调料、水或其它汁、蛋青等的混合物, 用作糕点面上的盖浇物〕. ②(玻璃、金属等的)磨砂面. ③玻璃粉、油彩等的混合物〔作装璜用〕.

frost·y [ˈfrɔsti] *a.* ①霜冻的, 下霜的, 严寒的; 冻结的; 霜似的,霜白的. ②冷淡的, 无情的. ③(须、发等)白的、灰白的;〔喻〕年老的. *the* ~ *years of life* 老年. *a* ~ *smile* 冷笑. *give sb. a* ~ *stare* 冷冷地凝视某人. **-i·ly** *ad.* **-i·ness** *n.*

froth [frɔθ, frɔːθ] *n.* ①泡, 泡沫; 口边白沫. ②渣滓, 废物. ③浅薄的意见,空想,空谈. *a lot of verbal* ~ 花言巧语. ~ *at the mouth* 嘴角上的涎沫. — *vt.* ①使生泡沫. ②用轻松的东西装饰. — *vi.* 起泡沫. ~**-blower**〔英谑〕爱喝啤酒的人.

froth·y [ˈfrɔθi] *a.* ①起泡沫的; 多泡沫的. ②空虚的, 浅薄的. ③质料轻薄的. *a* ~ *orator* 空话连篇的演说者. **-i·ly** *ad.* **-i·ness** *n.*

Froude [fruːd] *n.* 弗鲁德〔姓氏〕.

frou·frou [ˈfruːfruː] *n.* ①(女子丝绸裙子等的)沙沙声. ②(能发沙沙声的)下摆垂饰; (女子服装上)过分多的装饰〔如穗边、丝带、褶边等〕. ③〔口〕过分精致.

frounce [frauns] *vt., vi.*〔废〕(使) 卷曲, (使)卷缩. — *n.*〔古〕虚夸的展示.

frow[1] [frau] *n.* ①荷兰[德国]妇女. ②妇女,妻子.

frow[2] [frəu] *n.* = froe.

fro·ward [ˈfrəuəd] *a.* ①难驾驭的; 桀骜不驯的. ②〔古〕不利的. **-ly** *ad.* **-ness** *n.*

frown [fraun] *n.* 皱眉, 蹙额. ~*s of fortune* 倒运. — *vi.* ①皱眉, 蹙额. ②皱眉头表示厌恶〔反对〕(*at; on; upon*). — *vt.* ①用皱眉蹙额对…表示不满. ②皱眉蹙额表示(不满). ~ *sb. into silence* 皱眉使某人闭嘴. ~ *one's displeasure* 皱眉表示不快. ~ ***down*** 用皱眉蹙额压制住(反对者等使不敢讲话).

frowst [fraust] *n.*〔英口〕屋内的闷热, 霉臭, 陈腐的气味. — *vi.*〔英〕闷居室内.

frowst·y [ˈfrausti] *a.*〔口〕闷热的,霉臭的.

frow·zy, -sy [ˈfrauzi] *a.* ①霉臭的; 难闻的; 闷热的. ②邋遢的. **frowz·i·ly** *ad.* **-i·ness** *n.*

froze [frəuz] freeze 的过去式.

fro·zen [ˈfrəuzn] freeze 的过去分词. — *a.* ①冰冻的. ②冻结的. ③冻僵[冻伤、冻死]了的. ④极冷的. ⑤冷淡的. ⑥〔美〕(事实、真理等)不可推翻的,不容否认的. ~ *bean curd* 冻豆腐. ~ *custard* 冰冻乳蛋糕. ~ *food* 冰冻食品. ~ *meat* 冻肉. ~ *plants* 冻伤的植物. *a* ~ *section* 冰冻切片. *a* ~ *stream* 冻了冰的河流. *the* ~ *zones* 寒带. ***the*** ~ ***limit***〔口〕令人无法容忍的限度. ~ **assets**【商】冻结资产. ~ **credits** 冻结债务. ~ **frame** (电影等的)静止镜头 (=freeze frame). ~ **loans** 呆帐. ~ **sleep**【医】冷眠疗法; 超低体温. ~ **sucker** 冰棍,棒冰. **-ly** *ad.* 冷淡地;〔美〕顽固地.

frs. = francs.

F.R.S., FRS = Fellow of the Royal Society〔英〕皇家学会会员.

frt. = freight.

fruc·tif·er·ous [frʌkˈtifərəs] *a.*【植】结果实的.

fruc·ti·fi·ca·tion [ˌfrʌktifiˈkeiʃən] *n.*【植】结实; 果实; 结实器官.

fruc·ti·fy [ˈfrʌktifai] *vi., vt.*【植】(使)结果实.

fruc·tose [ˈfrʌktəus] *n.*【化】果糖,左旋糖.

fruc·tu·ous [ˈfrʌktjuəs] *a.* = fruitful.

frug [fruːg] *n.* 扭摆舞〔摇摆舞的一种, 着重腰身, 头部, 肩臂的扭动,脚腿几乎不动〕. — *vi.* 跳扭摆舞.

fru·gal [ˈfru:gəl] *a.* 节俭的；俭朴的. ***be ~ of*** 节约. **-ly** *ad.*

fru·gal·i·ty [fru:ˈgæliti] *n.* 节俭；俭朴.

fru·giv·o·rous [fru:ˈdʒivərəs] *a.* 【动】食果实(为生)的.

fruit [fru:t] *n.* ①实，果实〔*cf.* berry, capsule, drupe, legume, nut, pome〕；水果. ★单数也可用作集合名词；复数指各种水果；作为食品时 fruit 是不可数名词. ②〔*sing., pl.*〕结果,效果；〔常 *pl.*〕产品，(…的)产物；收获；〔*pl.*〕收入，利益；〔古〕子孙；年幼的人；仔兽. ③〔美俚〕下流家伙，搞同性恋爱的男子；精神不正常的人. ④〔美俚〕容易受骗的人. *Forbidden ~ is sweet.* 〔谚〕禁果分外甜〔被禁止的东西更加吸引人〕. *fresh [dried] ~* 鲜[干]果. *preserved ~* 果脯. *bear ~* 结果实；发生效果. *the ~s of one's labour* 劳动果实. *the ~ of the body [loins, womb]* 子女. *the ~s of the earth [ground]* 土地的产物，农作物. ***eat the bitter ~ of one's own doings [making]*** 自食其果. ***Old ~!*** 〔英口〕喂，老兄！〔对好朋友的招呼〕. ***top one's ~*** 把好水果盖在坏水果上面，粉饰门面. — *vi., vt.* (使)结果实. ~ **bat** 【动】大蝙蝠亚目〔如：狐蝠〕. ~**bearer** 结果实的树. ~**cake** 嵌有水果［葡萄干等］的糕饼，水果蛋糕. ~ **cocktail [cup]** 糖水水果〔餐前或餐后小吃〕. ~ **fly** 实蝇科的小蝇；果蝇. ~ **juice** 水果汁. ~ **knife** 水果刀. ~-**machine** 〔口〕吃角子老虎〔即 slot machine, 因为滚筒上绘有各种水果，故名〕. ~ **piece** 水果的静物画［雕刻］. ~ **ranch** (大)果园. ~ **seeder** 水果去核器. ~ **sugar** 果糖. ~ **tree** 果树. ~**wood** (做家具、镶板等的)果木.

fruit·age [ˈfru:tidʒ] *n.* ①果实. ②果实产量；〔集合词〕水果. ③结果实，结子；结果，成果，产物.

fruit·ar·i·an [fru:ˈtɛəriən] *n.* 用果实当常食的人，果食主义者.

fruit·ed [ˈfru:tid] *a.* ①结有果实的. ②加水果调味的.

fruit·er [ˈfru:tə] *n.* ①水果装运船. ②果树. ③果树栽培者，果农.

fruit·er·er [ˈfru:tərə] *n.* 〔主英〕水果商.

fruit·er·ess [ˈfru:təris] *n.* 〔英〕女水果商.

fruit·ful [ˈfru:tful] *a.* ①果实累累的，多产的；肥沃的；丰饶的. ②效果好的，收益多的. *a session ~ in great measures* 重要议案多的议会. *a ~ occupation* 收入多的职业. *a ~ vine* 结得多的葡萄；多产的女人. **-ly** *ad.* **-ness** *n.*

fruit·ing body [ˈfru:tiŋ] 【生】子实体.

fru·i·tion [fru(:)ˈiʃən] *n.* ①结果实. ②成就，实现. ③享有，享受. *the ~ of one's studies* 研究的成果. ***be brought to ~ = come to ~*** (计划等)可以实现，有结果，有收获.

fruit·less [ˈfru:tlis] *a.* ①不结果实的. ②无效[结]果的；无益的. **-ly** *ad.* **-ness** *n.*

fruit·y [ˈfru:ti] *a.* ①果实状的；有水果香味的；(葡萄酒)有葡萄味的. ②丰腴的，(声音)圆润的. ③〔美俚〕(故事等)有趣味的. ④〔美俚〕猥亵的，粗俗的；精神不正常的；搞男性同性恋的；(男子)女模女样的.

fru·men·ta·ceous [ˌfru:menˈteiʃəs] *a.* 小麦[谷类]的；谷类[小麦]制的；似谷类[小麦]的.

fru·men·ty [ˈfru:mənti] *n.* 〔英〕牛奶麦粥.

frump [frʌmp] *n.* ①服装邋遢的女人. ②〔常 *pl.*〕〔英方〕情绪不好，不高兴. ③守旧者，老古董，老顽固.

frump·ish [ˈfrʌmpiʃ] *a.* ①(妇女)衣服邋遢的. ②〔古〕脾气坏的. **-ly** *ad.* **-ness** *n.*

frump·y [ˈfrʌmpi] *a.* = frumpish. **-i·ly** *ad.* **-i·ness** *n.*

Frun·ze [ˈfrunze] *n.* 伏龙芝〔苏联城市〕.

frus·ta [ˈfrʌstə] frustum 的复数.

frus·trate [frʌsˈtreit] *vt.* ①挫败(敌人)；破坏(计划等)，阻挠. ②使失败，使落空. ***be ~d in*** 在…方面归于失败；终成画饼. — [ˈfrʌstrit] *a.* ①〔古〕无益的，无效的. ②受挫折的；被破坏的；失败了的.

frus·tra·tion [frʌsˈtreiʃən] *n.* 挫折，失败，落空.

frus·tule [ˈfrʌstju:l] *n.* 【植】(硅)藻细胞.

frus·tum [ˈfrʌstəm] *n.* (*pl.* ~*s*, *-ta* [-tə]) ①【数】平截头体. ②【建】柱身. ~ *of a cone* 圆锥截体.

fru·tes·cent [fru:ˈtesnt] *a.* 【植】灌木的，灌木状[性]的.

fru·tex [ˈfru:teks] *n.* (*pl.* **-ti·ces** [-tisi:z]) 【植】灌木.

fru·ti·cose [ˈfru:tikəus] *a.* 【植】灌木的，灌木状的.

fry[1] [frai] *vt., vi.* ①用油煎，用油炸；烤；炒. ②〔美俚〕(使)被处电刑. ~ ***in one's own grease*** 作法自毙，自作自受. ~ ***the fat out of*** *(business men, etc.)* 【美政】使(实业家等)出钱. ***have other fish to ~*** 别有要事〔见 fish 条〕. — *n.* ①油炸物；〔英〕油炸杂碎. ②〔美〕油煎品聚餐[野餐]. ③〔口〕烦恼，愤激. *a fish ~* 备有油炸鱼的野餐会. ~**pan** 〔美〕= ~ing pan.

fry[2] [frai] *n.* 〔*sing., pl.*〕①鱼秧，鱼苗；小鱼. ②鱼苗群. ③小生物群[蜂、蛙等]. *small [lesser, young] ~* ①小鱼群. ②〔蔑〕小崽子，后生小子. ③零杂物件.

Fry(e) [frai] *n.* 弗赖伊[姓氏].

fry·er [ˈfraiə] *n.* ①做油炸食品的人. ②油炸锅. ③(适于)油炸的食品(如小鸡、鱼等).

fry·ing pan [ˈfraiiŋ pæn] *n.* 油炸锅. ***leap [jump] out of the ~ into the fire*** 跳出油锅落入烈火，境遇越来越糟.

FRZ = freeze.

FS = ①field service 野战勤务. ②Fleet Surgeon 海军军医.

F.S. = ①factor of safety 安全系数. ②finisher scutcher 【纺】末道清棉机.

F.S.A. = ①Farm Security Administration 〔美旧〕农户社会保险局. ②Federal Security Agency 〔美旧〕联邦社会保险署. ③Fellow of the Society of Arts 艺术学会会员.

FSCC = Federal Surplus Commodities Corporation 〔美旧〕联邦剩余商品公司.

F.S.E. = Fellow of the Society of Engineers 〔英〕工程学会会员.

FSH = follicle-stimulating hormone 【生化】卵泡刺激素.

FSLIC = Federal Savings and Loan Insurance Corporation 〔美〕联邦储蓄贷款保险公司.

F.S.S. = Fellow of the (Royal) Statistical Society 〔英〕(皇家)统计学会会员.

ft. = ①foot; feet. ②fort.

FTC = ①Federal Trade Commission 〔美〕联邦贸易委员会. ②Flying Training Command 〔英〕飞行训练司令部.

fth(m). = fathom 英寻〔测海深单位〕.

ft.-lb. = foot-pound 英尺-磅.

ft./s. = feet per second 英尺/秒.

fub·sy [ˈfʌbzi] *a.* 〔英方〕肥胖的，矮胖的.

fuch·sia [ˈfju:ʃə] *n.* ①【植】倒挂金钟属；灯笼海棠. ②紫红色. —*a.* 紫红色的.

fuch·sin(e) [ˈfu:ksin] *n.* 【化】(碱性)品红，洋红.

fu·ci [ˈfju:sai] fucus 的复数.

fuck [fʌk] *vt.* ①〔俚〕(男子)与…性交. ②欺骗. ③利用，占…的便宜. — *vi.* 〔俚〕性交. ~ ***about [around]*** 〔俚〕乱管闲事；胡闹. ~ ***a duck*** 〔俚〕他妈的；去你的. ~ ***it*** 〔俚〕①嗳呀，滚开. ②算了吧；别罗唆了. ~ ***off [up]*** 〔俚〕①走开. ②浪费时间. ③嘲弄；吊儿郎当. ④闯祸；搞糟；犯错误；使计划失败. ***F- you (charley)!*** 〔俚〕滚你的！— *n.* 〔俚〕①性交. ②些微，一点. ***I don't give a ~.*** 我才不管哩. — *int.* 〔俚〕他妈的！混帐！滚开！~**off,** ~**up** *n.* 〔俚〕①大错误. ②老犯错误的人.

fucked [fʌkt] *a.* 〔俚〕①受骗的，上当的. ②失败的，弄死了的. ~ ***out*** 〔俚〕精疲力竭的. ~ ***up*** 〔俚〕①混乱的，乱七八糟的. ②(不必要地)被弄复杂了的. ③因个人(生活)问题而陷于窘境的.

fuck·ing [ˈfʌkiŋ] *n.* 〔俚〕性交. — *a.* = fucky.

fuck·y [ˈfʌki] *a.* 〔俚〕①该死的. ②难做的,难完成的. ③低劣的,讨厌的,丑恶的. ④乱七八糟的.

fu·coid [ˈfjuːkɔid] *a.* 海草的,似海草的(尤指岩草). — *n.* 海草(尤指岩草,马尾藻属等的粗海藻).

fu·cus [ˈfjuːkəs] *n.* (*pl.* *~es, fu·ci* [ˈfjuːsai]) 【植】墨角藻属.

fud [fʌd] *n.* = fuddy-duddy *(n.)*

fud·dle [ˈfʌdl] *vt.* ①使醉. ②使迷糊. — *vi.* ①参加饮宴;常喝酒. ②大醉. *~ away* 醉中度日. *~ oneself* (因醉)昏迷. *~ one's cap [nose]* 大醉. — *n.* ①烂醉. ②糊涂,一团糟. *a ~ of dirty clothes* 一堆脏衣服. ***be on the ~*** 大醉.

fud·dy-dud·dy [ˈfʌdiˌdʌdi] *n.* 〔俚〕①爱唠叨的人,吹毛求疵的人. ②老派[守旧]的人; 老古董. — *a.* 保守的,古板的,老派的.

fudge [fʌdʒ] *n.* ①梦话,胡言; 捏造的话. ②(报纸中临时插入, 常用另一种颜色印出的)特载. ③奶油巧克力软糖. — *int.* 胡说! — *vt.* ①蒙混,捏造,骗 *(up)*. ②对…敷衍应付. — *vi.* ①胡说八道. ②弄虚作假. ③推诿 *(on)*. *~ on an exam* 考试作弊.

Fueh·rer [ˈfjuərə] *n.* 〔G.〕 = Führer.

Fu·e·gi·an [fuːˈeidʒiən] *a.* ①火地岛 (Tierra del Fuego) 的. ②火地岛(印第安)人的; 火地岛文化的. — *n.* 火地岛人.

fu·el [ˈfjuəl] *n.* ①燃料,柴炭. ★指燃料种类时为可数名词. ②刺激物. *atomic ~* 原子燃料. *gaseous [solid] ~* 气体[固体]燃料. *heavy ~* 柴油,燃料油. *jet ~* 喷气式发动机燃料. *liquid [wet] ~* 液体燃料. *~ alcohol* 燃料酒精,动力酒精. *~ capacity* 燃料容量. *~ economizer* 节油器. *~ gas* 燃气. *~ oil* 燃料油. *~ pump* 燃油泵. *~ ratio* 燃烧率. *~ ship* 油船. ***add ~ to the fire [flames]*** 火上加油. — *vt., vi.* (〔英〕 *-ll-*) (给…)加[供给]燃料, (给船等)上煤, (给…)加油. *~* **cell**, *~-***cell** 燃料电池〔可不断将一种燃料如氢的化学能直接转变为电能〕. *~* **gauge** 量油计,油规,油表. **-er** 使用特制混合燃料的赛车.

fu·el·(l)ing [ˈfju(ː)əliŋ] *n.* 加燃料, 加油. *a ~ station* 加油站,燃料供应站.

fug [fʌg] *n.* ①〔主英〕(室内的)闷浊或暖和空气. ②(室隅、桌下等的)尘土和垃圾. — *vi.* 呆在门窗关闭的房屋中. — *vt.* 使(房间等)空气闷浊. **-gy** *a.*

fu·ga·cious [fju(ː)ˈgeiʃəs] *a.* ①易逃逸的,难捕捉的; 瞬息即逝的, 一时的. ②【植】先落的, 早谢的. *~ leaves* 〔植〕早落叶. **-ly** *ad.* **-ness** *n.*

fu·gac·i·ty [fju(ː)ˈgæsiti] *n.* 挥发性; 逸性, 逸度.

fu·gal [ˈfjuːgəl] *a.* 【乐】赋格曲(性质)的. **-ly** *ad.*

-fu·gal *comb. f.* 表示"离开": centri*fugal*, febri*fugal*.

-fuge *comb. f.* 表示"驱逐"; "逃走"; "避开": febri*fuge*, re*fuge*, vermi*fuge*.

fug·gy [ˈfʌgi] *a.* ①空气闷浊的; 闷热的. ②爱住暖屋的.

fu·gi·tive [ˈfjuːdʒitiv] *a.* ①逃亡的. ②飘泊的, 流浪的. ③不固定的,一时的,(诗文)即兴的, 偶成的. *a ~ soldier* 逃兵. *~ colours* 易褪的颜色. *~ verses* 即兴诗. *~ essays* 随笔. *~ ideas* 偶感. *a ~ from justice* 逃犯. — *n.* ①逃亡者,亡命者,被放逐者. ②难以捕捉的东西. *~* **sorties** 〔军〕(飞离基地以躲避敌机攻击的)避战飞行. **-ly** *ad.* **-ness** *n.*

fu·gle [ˈfjuːgl] *vi.* 〔古〕担任示范兵,作为示范者演示; 作向导; 以身作则地指导. **-man** *n.* ①【军】示范兵. ②领导者; 示范者.

fugue [fjuːg] *n.* 〔F.〕 ①【乐】赋格曲〔一种多声部的乐曲,在五度上模仿并用复调方法发展主题〕. ②【心、医】浮客症,神游(症)〔患者患病时,行为似乎是正常的,但痊愈后,对其行为为失却记忆能力〕.

fugu·ist [ˈfjuːgist] *n.* (擅长)赋格曲的作曲家.

Füh·rer [ˈfjuərə] *n.* ①〔G.〕 元首〔纳粹党魁希特勒的称号〕. ②〔f-〕独裁者,暴君.

Fu·ji(san) [ˈfuːˈdʒiː(ˈsɑːn)], **Fu·ji·ya·ma** [ˌfuːdʒiˈjɑːmɑː] *n.* 〔Jap.〕 富士山〔日本〕.

Fu·ku·o·ka [ˌfuːkəˈəukə] *n.* 〔Jap.〕 福冈〔日本港市〕.

-ful *suf.* ①加在名词之后,构成形容词,表示"充满","…多的","赋有…性质的": shame*ful*, beauti*ful*. ②加在动词之后, 构成形容词, 表示"容易…的": forget*ful*. ③加在名词之后,构成名词,表示"满","容量": mouth*ful*.

Fu·la [ˈfuːlɑː] *n.* (*pl.* *~s, ~*) ①弗拉人〔西非黑人与高卡索瓦人混血血统的穆斯林牧民〕. ②弗拉语〔属尼日尔—刚果语〕(= Fulah, Ful).

Fu·la·ni [ˈfuːləni] *n.* (*pl.* *~s, ~*) = Fula〔尼日利亚北部一带用语〕.

Ful·bright [ˈfulbrait] *a.* 富布赖特奖学金的, 享有富布赖特奖学金的. — *n.* 富布赖特奖学金〔因美国阿肯色州参议员富布赖特 1946 年提出之法案而得名. 按该法案规定, 此奖金的基金大部是靠美国向国外推销剩余物资而来. 美国政府以之作为对外交换学者、教师等的奖学金〕.

ful·crum [ˈfʌlkrəm] *n.* (*pl.* *~s, -cra* [-krə]) ①【机】支点,支柱,支轴. ②【动】喙基骨,转节,舌骨,棘状鳞. ③【植】叶附属物. *a ~ bearing* 支点承座,刀口承.

ful·fil(l) [fulˈfil] *vt.* ①履行(条约,义务), 遵守, 执行(命令等). ②完成(计划等), 做完(工作). ③满(期). ④达到(目的); 应验(预言等); 满足(希望). ⑤使臻于完善; 〔~ oneself〕充分发挥潜在的能力. *~ one's duty* 履行义务. *~ one's promise* 兑现诺言. *~ one's expectations* 满足愿望. *~ a task ahead of schedule* 提前完成任务. *She succeeded in ~ing herself as an actress.* 她作为演员充分发挥了自己的才能. **-ment** *n.*

ful·gent [ˈfʌldʒənt] *a.* 〔诗〕光辉的, 灿烂的. **-ly** *ad.*

ful·gu·rate [ˈfʌlgjuəreit, ˈful-] *vi.* 闪耀, 闪烁. — *vt.* 【医】用电灼治疗. **-ration** *n.*

ful·gu·rat·ing [ˈfʌlgjuəˌreitiŋ] *a.* 【医】(病痛)突然剧烈发作的, 钻心的 (=fulgurant). *a ~ pain* 突如其来的剧痛.

ful·gu·rite [ˈfʌlgjuərait] *n.* 【地】闪电熔岩.

ful·gu·rous [ˈfʌlgjuərəs] *a.* 闪电似的, 满布闪电的; 闪光的.

ful·ham [ˈfuləm] *n.* 〔俚〕(赌博中作弊用的)灌过铅的骰子,假骰.

fu·lig·i·nous [fjuːˈlidʒinəs] *a.* ①充满烟灰的, 象烟灰的, 烟垢的. ②乌黑的, 阴暗的.

full[1] [ful] *a.* ①充满的, 装满的. ②充分的, 丰富的; 挤满的; (吃、喝等)尽兴的. ③(精神)饱满的. ④完全的, 完美的; (资格)正式的; 最高度的; (花)盛开的. ⑤又胖又圆的, (脸)丰满的; (衣服)宽松的, 多皱褶的. ⑥(光线)强烈的; (颜色)纯正的; (声音)洪亮的. ⑦(酒)醇厚的. ⑧同父同母的. ⑨详尽的, 完备的. *He that is ~ of himself is very empty.* 〔谚〕人若十分自恃, 必定十分无知. *F- Admiral* 〔美〕海军上将. *~ charge* 【军】全装(弹)药. *~ daylight* 大白天. *~ experience* 丰富的经验. *~ blood* 纯种; 同父母, 同胞. *a ~ figure* 又圆又胖的身材. *F- General* 〔美〕四星上将. *a ~ harvest* 丰收. *a ~ life* 经历丰富的一生. *a ~ man* 完人. *~ marks* 满分. *~ maturity* 完全成熟, 壮年. *a ~ meal* 丰盛的一餐. *a ~ member* 正式会员. *a ~ mile* 整整一英里. *~ pay* 全薪. *~ professor* 〔美〕正教授. *a ~ report* 详细的报告. *~ score* 【乐】总谱. *a ~ size* 原尺寸,原大. *~ speed* 全速. *~ speed [steam] ahead* 【海】全速前进. *a ~ stomach* 满腹. *~ strength* 全力; 【军】满员. *~ summer* 盛夏. *My heart is too ~ for words.* 我激动得说不出话来. *a ~ voice* 洪亮的嗓音. *a ~ bust* 丰满的胸部. *eat till one is ~* 吃饱肚子. ***as ~ as an egg is of meat*** = 〔美〕***as ~ as a tick*** 塞得满满的. ***at ~ length*** 手脚充分伸直地; 尽量详尽地. ***be ~ of*** 充满…(的). ***be ~ of one's own affairs = be ~***

of oneself 只为自己打算. ***be ~ of vigour and vitality*** 朝气蓬勃, 精力充沛. ***be ~ of years and honours*** 年高望重. ***~ to overflowing [the brim]*** 满得不能再满. ***~ up*** 〔俚〕①客满; 吃饱; 装满. ②激动得要流泪. ***in ~ activity [blast, chisel, play, swing]*** 正达到极点, 正起劲. ***in ~ feather [fig]*** 盛装; 穿着全套礼服; 精神饱满; 很有钱. ***turn (it) to ~ account*** 充分利用. — *n.* ①充分, 完全, 全部. ②极盛时, 极点. *I cannot tell you the ~ of it.* 我不能完全告诉你. ***at (the) ~.*** 在达到最高点, 在完满状态中. ***in ~*** 详细地(填写姓名等); 全部地 (*payment in ~* 全付, 付足). ***the ~ of the moon*** 满月时. ***to the ~*** 充分地, 十足地. — *ad.* ①充分地, 完全地. ②恰恰, 直接地. ③极其, 十分. *~ six miles* 整整六英里. *hit sb. ~ on the nose* 正打在某人鼻子上. ***~ and by*** 〔美〕扯满篷. ***~ as useful as*** 完全同…一样有用. ***~ fain*** 非常喜欢, 极想. ***~ many a*** 〔诗〕很多的. ***~ out*** 以最大能量, 最快地. ***~ soon*** 立即. ***~ well*** 很, 充分地. — *vt.* 把(衣服)裁宽大些, 把(裙子)缝出皱褶. — *vi.* 满; (衣服)宽大; 〔美〕(月)圆. ~ **age** 成年. ~**back** (足球)后卫, 后卫的位置. ~ **binding** (书籍的) 全皮装钉. ~**-blooded** *a.* ①多血质的, 精力旺盛的. ②情欲强烈的. ③非混血的, 纯种的. ④内容充实的, 有力的. ⑤真正的, 道地的. ~**-blown** *a.* (花)盛开的; 充分发展的, 成熟的; (帆)张满的 (*~-blown dignity* 神气活现. *a ~-blown power plant* 大型配套发电厂). ~**-bottomed** *a.* (船)底部宽阔的, 容量大的; (假发)长而垂到肩背的. ~ **brother [sister]** (同父母)亲兄弟[姊妹] (*opp.* half brother [sister]). ~ **dress** 礼服; (船只等)挂满旗. ~**-dress** *a.* 礼服的, (宴会等)应穿礼服的; 正式的; 大规模的 (*a ~-dress debate* 〔英〕议会的正式辩论. *a ~-dress operation* 大规模作战. *a ~-dress rehearsal* 正式排演, 彩排. *'~-dress talks* 正式会谈). ~**-face** ① *n.* (人的) 正面像; 黑体铅字. ②*ad.* 向正面, 面对面. ~**-faced** *a.* 圆脸的, 肥头肥脑的; 圆满无缺的; (月等)向正面的; 【印】黑体的. ~**-fledged** *a.* 羽毛丰满的; 发育充分的, 经过充分训练的; 有充分资格的. ~**-hand** 【牌】三张同点和两张同点的一组牌. ~**-hearted** *a.* 全心全意的, 诚恳的. ~ **house** ①客满, 满座. ② = ~**hand.** ~**-length** ① *a.* 全身的, 全长的; 标准长的, 未删节的; 大型的. ② *n.* 全身像. ~ **load** 满载. ~ **moon** 满月, 望月. ~**-mouthed** *a.* (牛等)牙齿齐全的; (狗等)大声的, (演讲)声音宏亮的; (文体等)刚劲的. ~ **name** (连名带姓的)全名. ~ **nelson** 【摔交】双肩下握颈翻, 里外肩下握颈翻. ~**page** *a.* 全页的, 整版的. ~ **sail** 【海】①帆数齐全. ②风帆尽张. ③全速(行驶). ~ **stop [point]** 句号, 句点. ~ **text** 全文. ~**-throated** *a.* 高声喧嚷的, 声音宏亮的. ~ **throat** 〔美口〕全力声援. ~ **tide** 全潮. ~**-time** *a.* 全部时间的, 专职的 (*~-time teacher* 专任教员). ~**-timer** 全日班学生〔*cf.* half-timer 选读生〕.

full[2] [ful] *vt.* 【纺】蒸洗, 漂洗〔使毛织品紧密〕; 缩绒, 缩呢. *~ing clay* 漂土, 漂泥. *a ~ing mill* 漂洗机.

full-bod·ied [fulˈbɔdid] *a.* ①身体丰硕的, 魁伟的. ②(指酒)醇厚的, 强烈的. *a ~ wine* 醇酒.

Ful·ler [ˈfulə] *n.* 富勒〔姓氏〕.

full·er[1] [ˈfulə] *n.* ①【冶】套柄铁锤, 套锤. ②用套锤锻成的槽(尤指马蹄铁上的槽). — *vt.* 用套锤锻制, 用套锤在…上开槽.

full·er[2] [ˈfulə] *n.* 【纺】蒸洗工, 缩绒工. ~**'s earth** 漂(白)土〔一种软质黄色泥, 可去衣上油渍〕.

full-fash·ioned [ˈfulˈfæʃnd] *a.* (袜子, 毛衣的)紧身的.

full·ness [ˈfulnis] *n.* ①满, 充满. ②成熟. ③充实, 丰富. ④(光的)强烈, (声音的)洪亮, (颜色的)纯度, 深度, 浓度; 【物】丰满度. ⑤丰满, 圆胖. ⑥发胀. *a ~ of sleeves* 宽袖. *a great ~ of face* 肥头大脸. ***in its ~*** 十分, 完全. ***in the ~ of one's heart*** 满腔热情; 无限感慨. ***in the ~ of time*** 在成熟的时候, 在预定的时候.

full-rigged [ˈfulˈrigd] *a.* ①(指船)桅帆众多齐备的. ②全副装备的; 装备齐全的.

full-scale [ˈfulˈskeil] *a.* ①照原物尺寸的, 足尺的. ②极大限度的; 完全彻底的; 全面的. *a ~ drawing* 与原物大小一致的图形. *~ warfare* 全面战争.

full·y [ˈfuli] *ad.* 充分地, 完全地; 足足; 至少. *be ~ paid up* 全部付讫. *~ refined wax* 精制石蜡. *It is ~ proved that.* …事实已充分证明…. *The journey will take ~ two hours.* 走这一趟足足要花两小时.

ful·mar [ˈfulmə] *n.* 【动】(北海)臭鸥, 管鼻鹱.

ful·mi·nant [ˈfʌlminənt] *a.* ①电闪雷鸣的, 轰鸣的. ②【医】(疾病)急性的, 爆发性的.

ful·mi·nate [ˈfʌlmineit] *vt.* ①使轰鸣, 使爆炸. ②怒骂, 怒喝. — *vi.* ①轰鸣. ②爆炸. ③(疾病)爆发. ④怒喝. — *n.* 【化】雷酸盐; 雷汞. *mercury ~* 雷酸汞. *silver ~* 雷酸银. **ful·mi·na·tion** [ˌfʌlmiˈneiʃən] *n.* ①猛烈爆发. ②严厉谴责.

ful·mi·nat·ing [ˈfʌmineitiŋ] *a.* ①爆炸发光的, 起爆的. ②呵斥的. ③(疾病) 暴发性的. ~ **cap** 雷帽, 雷汞爆管. ~ **compound** 【化】雷酸盐. ~ **powder** 雷爆(火)药(尤指雷粉).

ful·mi·na·tor [ˈfʌlmineitə] *n.* ①轰鸣者. ②怒喝者, 大声呵斥者; 谴责者.

ful·mi·na·to·ry [ˈfʌlmineitəri] *a.* ①轰鸣的, 爆炸的. ②怒喝的, 谴责的.

ful·mine [ˈfʌlmin] *vt., vi.* 〔罕、诗〕= fulminate.

ful·min·ic [fʌlˈminik] *a.* 爆炸性的. ~ ***acid*** 【化】雷酸.

ful·ness [ˈfulnis] *n.* = fullness.

ful·some [ˈfulsəm] *a.* (谄媚等) 因过分做作而显得可厌的, 令人作呕的. **-ly** *ad.* **-ness** *n.*

Ful·ton [ˈfultən] *n.* 富尔顿〔姓氏〕.

ful·vous [ˈfʌlvəs] *a.* 暗黄色的, 黄褐色的.

fu·made [fjuːˈmeid] *n.* 烟熏鲱鱼.

fu·mar·ic [fjuˈmærik] **acid** 【化】富马酸, 延胡索酸, 反式丁烯二酸, 紫槿酸.

fu·ma·role [ˈfjuːmərəul] *n.* 【地】(火山区的) 喷气坑, 气孔.

fu·ma·to·ri·um [ˌfjuːməˈtɔːriəm] *n.* (*pl.* ~***s***, ***-to·ri·a*** [~ˈtɔːriə]) 密封熏蒸所, 熏蒸器.

fu·ma·to·ry [ˈfjuːmətəri] *a.* 熏烟的. — *n.* 熏蒸室, 烟熏室.

fum·ble [ˈfʌmbl] *vi.* ①摸索, 乱摸 (*for; after*). ②笨手笨脚地摸弄. ③犯大错. ④失球, 接漏球. — *vt.* ①瞎摸, 笨手笨脚地做. ②失(球), 接漏(球). ~ ***about*** 瞎摸; 摸弄; 失错. ~ ***at [with] a lock*** 摸索着(对不准匙孔地)开锁. — *n.* ①摸索, 乱摸; 笨手笨脚的处理; 失错. ②失球, 接漏球. **-r** *n.* 摸索者, 笨手笨脚的人, 工作拙劣的人. **-bling** *a.*

fume [fjuːm] *n.* ①〔常 *pl.*〕烟气; 香气, 臭气; 熏烟; 水蒸气; 烟雾. ②激昂, 激怒. *~s of heat* 闷人的热气. ***be in a ~*** 愤怒; 怒气冲冲. ***put sb. in a ~*** 激怒某人. — *vt.* ①(用烟)熏. ②烘制(木材等). ③蒸发, 冒(烟、气等). ④烧(香). — *vi.* ①冒烟. ②(烟等)上升; 蒸发. ③发怒.

fumed [fjuːmd] *a.* 熏过的. ~ *oak* 氨熏橡木〔氨熏使橡木颜色变深〕.

fu·mi·gant [ˈfjuːmigənt] *n.* 熏蒸剂, 【医】熏剂.

fu·mi·gate [ˈfjuːmigeit] *vt.* ①(为杀虫等)用烟熏; 熏蒸消毒. ②烧(香). **-tion** [ˌfjuːmiˈgeiʃən] *n.* 熏蒸(消毒), 熏蒸法; 烧香. **-tor** *n.* 烟熏者; 烟熏器; 熏蒸消毒器.

fu·mi·to·ry [ˈfjuːmitəri] *n.* 【植】蓝堇属.

fum·y [ˈfjuːmi] *a.* 冒烟的; 发蒸气的; 烟雾状的.

fun [fʌn] *n.* ①嬉戏, 娱乐, 玩笑, 兴趣. ②有趣的人物[事物]. *be fond of ~* 爱闹着玩. *be full of ~* 很好玩, 极有趣. *Swimming is good ~.* 游泳很有趣味. *Skating is great ~.* 滑雪太有意思了. *Your friend is great ~.* 你的朋友真是个有趣的人. ***do not see the ~ of*** 不懂

得…的趣味,不以为有趣. ***for [in]*** ~ 开玩笑,不是认真的. ~ ***and games*** 〔口〕欢乐,开玩笑. ***for the ~ of it [the thing]*** 为了取笑,当作玩耍. ***have*** ~ 作乐,玩乐. ***like*** ~ ①〔口〕有力地;迅速地(*It sells like* ~. 很快就卖完). ②〔美俚〕(着重地表示否定或怀疑)不象是真的,不能相信;决不可能;完全不是(这样). ***make ~ of*** = ***poke ~ at*** 嘲弄,取笑. ***What ~!*** 多么有趣! — *vi.* 〔口〕开玩笑,说笑. — *a.* ①有趣的,奇妙的. ②供娱乐用的,为玩玩用的. ~**about** 游乐或赛车用小型汽车. **F- City** 游乐城〔纽约市的别号〕. ~ **fur** (供非正式场合穿着的)低廉毛皮[人造毛皮]外衣. ~ **house** 游乐园〔由各种玩乐设备组成的游乐场所〕.

fu·nam·bu·list [fju(:)ˈnæmbjulist] *n.* 走钢丝的杂技演员.

Fun·chal [funˈʃɑːl] *n.* 丰沙尔〔马德拉群岛首府〕.

func·tion [ˈfʌŋkʃən] *n.* ①功能,官能,机能,作用. ②〔常 *pl.*〕职务,职责. ③庆祝仪式;(盛大的)集会,宴会. ④【数】函数;与其他因素有密切关系的事. *The ~ of the ear is to listen.* 耳的功能是听. *the ~ of education* 教育的功能. *discharge one's ~s* 尽职. *the ~s and powers of the National Congress* 全国代表大会的职权. *a controllable* ~【火箭】遥控程序. *public [social]* ~ 招待会,文娱晚会,社交集会. *vital ~s* 生命机能. — *vi.* ①(器官等)活动,(机器等)运行,发挥作用. ~ *as teacher* 担任教师. *a sofa ~ing as a bed* 兼当床用的沙发. *The lathe doesn't ~ well.* 这台车床有毛病. ~ *digit [letter]* 【计】操作数码 [字码]. ~ **space**【数】函数空间. ~ **word**【语】(主要表示语法关系的)功能词.

func·tion·al [ˈfʌŋkʃənl] *a.* ①官能的,机能的. ②在起作用的;职务上的. ③【数】函数的. ④【建】从使用的观点设计[构成]的. ⑤有多种用途的;可改变用途的. ⑥可使用的,可操作的. ~ *disease* 官能病 (*opp.* organic disease). ~ *disorder* 机能紊乱. ~ *furniture* 实用的家具. ~ **illiterate** (看不懂与本职工作有关的指示、指令的)半文盲,职务文盲. ~ **shift**【语】词性转换. **-ism** *n.* 【心、建】机能主义〔心理学上指思想和行动的过程,是人的整个机体的反应;建筑学上指讲求实用,而不注重外观〕. **-ist** *n.* 机能主义者. **-ly** *ad.*

func·tion·ar·y [ˈfʌŋkʃənəri] *n.* 工作人员,职员,官员. *a petty* ~ 小职员. *a public* ~ 公务员.

func·tion·ate [ˈfʌŋkʃəneit] *vi.* = function (*vi.*).

func·tor [ˈfʌŋktə] *n.* ①起功能作用的东西. ②【数】函子;算符.

fund [fʌnd] *n.* ①资金,基金,专款. ②〔*pl.*〕〔the ~s〕(国家的)财源;〔英〕公债. ③〔*pl.*〕存款,现款. ④储备,蕴藏. ⑤特别基金管理机构. *a ~ of knowledge* 丰富的知识. *idle ~s* 游资. *public welfare ~s* 公益金. *a reserve* ~ 公积金. *a scholarship* ~ 奖学金基金. *a sinking* ~ 偿债基金. *~s for the living of troops* 军队的生活费. ***in ~s*** 有钱;有资本. ***out of ~s*** 缺钱. ***the (public) ~s*** 公债. — *vt.* ①换(短期借款)为长期公债. ②〔英〕投(资金)于公债. ③把…列作为基金[专款]. ④为…提供基金,储存(一笔钱款)以备付息. **~-holder** *n.* 公债持有人,证券持有人. **~-raiser** 基金筹措者. ~ **raising** 基金筹措. **~-raising** *a.* 基金筹措的.

fun·da·ment [ˈfʌndəmənt] *n.* ①臀部,肛门. ②基础,基本原理.

fun·da·men·tal [ˌfʌndəˈmentl] *a.* ①基础的,基本的,根本的,重要的;原始的,主要的. ②【物】基频的,基谐波的;【乐】基音的. *a ~ change* 根本变化. *a ~ function*【数】特征函数. *a ~ law* 根本法则,基本定律;基本法. *a ~ rule* 基本原则. — *n.* ①原理,原则;基本,根本,基础. ②【乐】基音;【物】基频,基谐波. ~ **bass**【乐】根音低音部,根音低音. ~ **frequency**【物】基频. ~ **particle**【物】基本粒子 (= elementary particle). ~ **star**【天】基本星. **-ism** *n.* 【宗】原教旨主义〔相信《圣经》所说的事情都是真实的,并认为这一点对基督教来说是最基本的〕. **-ist** ①*n.* 原教旨主义者. ② *a.* 原教旨主义的. **-ly** *ad.*

fun·da·men·tal·i·ty [ˌfʌndəmenˈtæliti] *n.* 基本性,根本状态;重要性.

fund·ed [ˈfʌndid] *a.* 成为有固定利息的长期借款的,以公债形式投资的. ~ **debt [liability]** (期限在一年以上的)长期借款.

fun·dus [ˈfʌndəs] *n.* (*pl.* ***fun·di*** [ˈfʌndai]) 〔L.〕【解】底,底部,基底. ~ *uteri* 子宫底.

fu·ner·al [ˈfjuːnərəl] *n.* ①葬礼;送丧行列 (= ~ procession);追悼会. ②〔喻〕不愉快的事,操心的事;有关系的事. *a state* ~ 国葬. *attend a* ~ 参加丧礼. — *a.* 葬礼的;出殡用的;出殡时的. *a ~ ceremony [service]* 丧礼. *a ~ director* 〔美〕丧葬承办人. *a ~ march* 丧礼进行曲. *a ~ oration* 悼词. *a ~ procession [train]* 送葬行列. *a ~ urn* 骨灰瓮. ***None of your ~!*** 那不是你的事〔与你无关〕. ***That's your ~.*** 那是你的事〔与我无关〕. ~ **home [parlor]** 殡仪馆.

fu·ner·ar·y [ˈfjuːnərəri] *a.* (有关)殡葬的. *a ~ urn* 骨灰瓮.

fu·ne·re·al [fju(:)ˈniəriəl] *a.* 丧葬似的;悲哀的;阴森的,严肃的. ~ *garments* 丧服.

fun·gal [ˈfʌŋgəl] *a.* = fungous.

fun·gi [ˈfʌndʒai, ˈfʌŋgai] *n.* fungus 的复数.

fungi- *comb. f.* 表示"真菌": *fungi*cide.

fun·gi·ble [ˈfʌndʒibl] *a.* 可代替的;【法】可互换的〔指可用一物代替他物偿债〕. — *n.*【法】(偿还债务时所用的)代替物.

fun·gi·cide [ˈfʌndʒisaid] *n.* 杀真菌剂.

fun·gi·form [ˈfʌndʒifɔːm] *a.* 真菌状的.

fun·gin [ˈfʌndʒin] *n.* 菌纤维素.

fun·giv·or·ous [fʌnˈdʒivərəs] *a.* 食真菌的.

fun·go [ˈfʌŋgəu] *n.* 飞球〔指打棒球的人自掷自打,让守野的人练习接球〕. *a ~ hit* 大飞球. *a ~ bat [stick]* 练习打球的棒.

fun·goid [ˈfʌŋgɔid] *a.* 似真菌的;有真菌特征的. — *n.* 真菌.

fun·gous [ˈfʌŋgəs] *a.* ①如真菌的;真菌状的;因真菌引起的. ②倏生倏灭的,忽然产生又迅速消失的.

fun·gus [ˈfʌŋgəs] *n.* (*pl.* ~***es***, ***fungi*** [ˈfʌŋgai]) ①真菌〔包括霉菌、酵母菌和伞菌等〕. ②突然发生的暂时现象. ③【医】海绵肿. — *a.* = fungous.

fu·ni·cle [ˈfjuːnikl] *n.* = funiculus.

fu·nic·u·lar [fju(:)ˈnikjulə] *a.* ①索状的,索带的;②用缆索运转的. ③【解】索的,脐带的,精索的. *a ~ machine* 吊重机. *a ~ polygon* 索多边形. *a ~ railway* 缆索铁道. — *n.* 缆车道(=~ railway).

fu·nic·u·lus [fju(:)ˈnikjuləs] *n.* (*pl.* ***-cu·li*** [-lai]) ①【解】索,脐带,精索. ②【植】珠柄. ③【动】白索. ④【生】菌丝索. ⑤〔罕〕细绳索.

Funk [fʌŋk] *n.* 芬克〔姓氏〕.

funk[1] [fʌŋk] *n.* 〔口〕①恐怖,惊慌. ②胆小鬼. ***be in a blue*** ~ 不胜惊恐;意志消沉. ***be in a*** ~ 畏缩,害怕. ***put sb. in [into] a*** ~ 使某人吓得要命. — *vi.*, *vt.* ①(使)害怕;(使)畏缩. ②怕(事). ~ *out of a fight* 怕打架而走开. ~ *a difficulty* 害怕困难,逃避困难. ~ **hole** 防空壕;逃避所. ~ **money** (转移国外以获取高利的)流动资金.

funk[2] [fʌnk] *n.* 〔美俚〕①刺鼻的味道,霉味. ②早期的爵士音乐. ③畸形艺术 (= ~ art). — *vt.* ①向…喷烟,以烟扰乱(某人);使闻到刺鼻的味道. ②吸(烟斗). — *vi.* ①抽烟,吸烟. ②发出刺鼻臭味. ~ **art** 畸形艺术,恶臭艺术〔以古怪、肮脏的物品拼凑成的一种所谓的"艺术作品"〕.

fun·ky[1] [ˈfʌŋki] *a.* 胆战心惊的;害怕的.

fun·ky[2] [ˈfʌŋki] *a.* 〔美俚〕①有恶臭的,刺鼻的. ②有早期爵士音乐味道的,朴质的. ③(模样或作风)古怪的.

④极好的.
fun·nel [ˈfʌnl] *n.* ①漏斗. ②漏斗形物，通风筒；【矿】通风井. ③(火车等的)烟囱. ④[美俚]酒鬼. — *vt.* ([英] *-ll-*) ①把…灌进漏斗. ②使成漏斗形. ③使汇集. — *vi.* ①成漏斗形，逐渐变窄[宽]. ②经过漏斗. ③汇集. ~ **cloud**【气】漏斗云. ~**form** *a.* 漏斗状的. ~**hood** 烟囱帽. ~**-shaped** *a.* 漏斗(状)的. ~**-tube** 漏斗管. **-like** *a.* 象漏斗的.
fun·nelled [ˈfʌnld] *a.* ①有漏斗的. ②漏斗状的. ③有…烟囱的[构成复合词]. *a two-~ steamer* 双烟囱轮船.
fun·nies [ˈfʌniz] *n. pl.* [美口]连环漫画；新闻漫画栏.
fun·ni·ly [ˈfʌnili] *ad.* 有趣地，好笑地，滑稽地；[口]奇怪地. ~ ***enough*** 说来真奇怪[插入语].
fun·ni·ment [ˈfʌnimənt] *n.* 笑话，滑稽动作.
fun·ny[1] [ˈfʌni] *a.* ①有趣的，好笑的，滑稽的. ②有病的，不舒服的. ③狡猾的，欺骗(性)的，可疑的，不光明的. ④[口]希奇的，古怪的. ⑤[美]粗野的，无礼的. *a ~ column* 漫画栏. *a ~ business* 怪事，不道德的行为. *a ~ thing* 古怪的事. *There is sth. ~ about it.* 那真有点蹊跷. ***a ~ way to behave*** 奇怪的行动. ***feel ~ = go all ~***(觉得)身体不对劲；(觉得)情形古怪. ***get ~ with*** [口]对人十分不敬. — *n.* ①滑稽人物. ②[常 *pl.*]滑稽连环漫画栏. ③笑话，有趣的故事. *make a ~* 说个笑话. ~**-bone** (受触时发麻的)肘部尺骨端. ~ **car** 一种比赛用的腊肠形汽车. ~ **farm** 精神病院. ~**man** (*pl.* *-men*)[美口]丑角，滑稽演员；爱说笑话的人. ~**-money** ①[美、加俚]膨胀的通货，滥发的货币. ②伪钞；收不回来的钱，对有倒闭危险的企业的投资. ~ **paper** 报纸的滑稽漫画和字谜栏. **-ni·ness** *n.*
fun·ny[2] [ˈfʌni] *n.* [英](比赛用)单人双桨小艇.
fun·ster [ˈfʌnstə] *n.* [美]爱逗人笑的人，幽默家，喜剧演员.
fur [fəː] *n.* ①毛，软毛；毛皮；[*pl.*]兽皮，皮货，毛皮制品，皮衣[裘]，毛皮手套(等). ★要与 leather [没有毛的皮革]区别. ②毛皮兽，软毛兽. ③【医】舌苔. ④(桃的)茸毛. ⑤锅垢，水锈. *a ~-puller* 剥皮匠. *a ~-trader* 毛皮商. *~ lining* 毛皮里子. ***~ and feather*** 禽兽. ***hunt ~*** 猎野兔. ***make the ~ fly*** 闹出乱子，引起争吵. ***stroke the ~ the wrong way*** 抚摸倒毛，惹怒人. — *vt.* ①用毛皮护覆，用毛皮给…镶里. ②使生水垢；除去(锅上的)水垢；使长舌苔. ③【建】给…钉上板条. *Hard water ~s the kettle.* 硬水使水壶生水垢. *become furred in influenza* 因感冒长了舌苔. — *vi.* 长舌苔；生水垢. ~ **piece** 皮领；皮披肩. ~ **seal** 海狗；海獭.
fur. = ①furlong. ②furnish(ed). ③further.
fu·ran [ˈfjuərən, fjuˈræn], **fu·rane** [ˈfjuərein] *n.*【化】呋喃，氧(杂)茂.
fu·ra·zol·i·done [ˌfjuərəˈzɔlidəun] *n.*【药】呋喃唑酮，痢特灵.
fur·be·low [ˈfəːbiləu] *n.* ①(女服的)裙褶，裙饰，边饰. ②[*pl.*]花哨庸俗的装饰. — *vt.* ①给…加裙褶[裙饰]. ②用花哨庸俗的装饰物装饰.
fur·bish [ˈfəːbiʃ] *vt.* ①研磨，磨光 *(up)*. ②刷新，翻新，修复，温习*(up)*.
fur·cate [ˈfəːkeit] *a.* 分叉的，叉形的. — *vi.* 分叉，分歧. **-d** *a.* 成叉形的.
fur·ca·tion [fəːˈkeiʃən] *n.* 分叉.
fur·cu·la [ˈfəːkjulə] *n.* (*pl.* *-lae* [-liː])【解、动】叉突；Y 腺；弹器；叉骨. **-r** *a.*
fur·cu·lum [ˈfəːkjuləm] *n.* (*pl.* *-la* [-lə]) = furcula.
fur·fur [ˈfəːfə] *n.* (*pl.* *~es* [-fəriːz]) 皮屑，头屑.
fur·fu·ra·ceous [ˌfəːfjuˈreiʃəs] *a.* ①糠的，似糠的；麸的；似麸的. ②多(头)皮屑的.
fur·fu·ral [ˈfəːfəræl] *n.*【化】糠醛；糠叉；呋喃(甲)叉.
fur·fu·ran [ˈfəːfəræn] *n.* = furan.
fu·ri·ous [ˈfjuəriəs] *a.* ①暴怒的，狂怒的. ②狂暴的，猛烈的. ③喧闹的. *be ~ with sb. [at sth.]* 对某人[某事]大发雷霆. *a ~ sea* 怒涛汹涌的海. ***run at a ~ pace*** 飞跑. ***grow fast and ~*** 疯狂起来. **-ly** *ad.* **-ness** *n.*
furl [fəːl] *vt., vi.* 卷收(风帆等)，收(伞)，拉拢(窗帘)；捲起，折起. *~ a flag* 叠好旗帜. *~ an umbrella* 收伞. *This umbrella doesn't ~ neatly.* 这把伞收不整齐. — *n.* ①卷，折，收拢. ②一卷东西.
fur·long [ˈfəːlɔŋ] *n.* 浪(英国长度单位，= $\frac{1}{8}$ 英里).
fur·lough [ˈfəːləu] *n.* (军人、官吏的)休假. — *vt.* ①给予休假. ②强迫…休假，使停职，暂时解雇. ***be on ~*** 在休假中. ***go home on ~*** 休假回国[家].
fur·me(n)·ty [ˈfəːməti, -mən-] *n.* = frumenty.
furn. = ①furnished. ②furniture.
fur·nace [ˈfəːnis] *n.* ①炉子，熔炉；高炉. ②极热的地方. ③磨炼，艰难. *an atomic [a nuclear] ~* 原子反应堆，核反应堆. *blast ~*【冶】鼓风炉，高炉. *an electric ~* 电炉. *electric-arc ~*【冶】电弧炉. *induction ~*【冶】感应炉. *open hearth ~*【冶】平炉. *a reverberating ~* 反射炉. ***be tried in the ~*** 受磨炼. — *vt.* 在炉中烧热(金属). ~ **coke** 冶金焦炭. ~ **heating** 暖气炉，暖房法. ~**man** 炉前工.
Fur·ness [ˈfəːnis] *n.* 弗尼斯[姓氏].
fur·nish [ˈfəːniʃ] *vt.* ①供给，供应，提供. ②装备，布置，装修(房屋). *~ sb. with sth.* = *~ sth. to sb.* 供给某人某种东西. *a well ~ed shop* 货物齐全的商店. *Furnished rooms to let.* 备有家具的房间出租. ***be ~ed with*** 备有. ~ ***out*** 补充；使完备[指房屋的设备]. **-er** *n.* 供给者；(承办家具陈设的)家具商. **-ing** *n.* [*pl.*]设备，家具；陈设品；[美]服饰品.
fur·ni·ture [ˈfəːnitʃə] *n.* [集合词]①家具，器具. ②设备，装修. ③附属品，内容 *(of)*. ④【印】空铅，填充材料. *~ and fixtures* 家具什物. *the ~ of one's mind* 知识，见闻，思想. *the ~ of one's pocket* 钱财. *the ~ of one's shelves* 书籍. ***remove ~*** (替人)搬家[指一种行业].
Fur·ni·val(l) [ˈfəːnivəl] *n.* 弗尼瓦尔[姓氏].
fu·ror [ˈfjuərɔː] *n.* [L.] ①狂怒. ②热烈的感谢[赞扬]. ③(对某事的)狂热. ***create a regular ~***(演出等)得到热烈的赞扬. ~ ***poeticus*** 诗迷，诗痴.
fu·ro·re [fjuːˈrɔːri] *n.* [It.] ①= furor. ②【乐】热烈，激情. ***make a ~*** 轰动一时.
fu·ro·se·mide [fjuəˈrəusəmaid] *n.*【药】速尿(灵)，腹氨酸，呋喃苯氨酸，利尿磺胺.
furred [fəːd] *a.* ①毛皮制的；用毛皮镶边的；用毛皮作衣服里子的. ②(野兽)有毛皮的. ③穿毛皮的，衣轻裘的. ④有舌苔的. ⑤钉上板条的.
fur·ri·er [ˈfʌriə] *n.* ①皮货商人. ②毛皮加工者. ③缝制[修补，改制]毛皮衣服的人.
fur·ri·er·y [ˈfəːriəri] *n.* ①[废]毛皮，皮货. ②皮货业；毛皮业.
fur·ring [ˈfəːriŋ] *n.* ①毛皮镶边，毛皮衬里. ②锅垢；③【建】垫高料，钉板条. ④【医】舌苔. ⑤船旁衬木，衬条. ~ **tile** 墙面磁砖.
fur·row [ˈfʌrəu] *n.* ①沟，犁沟，垄沟. ②耕地，农田. ③航迹；车辙，(脸上的)皱纹. *make deep ~s in the road* (车等)在路上留下深深的轮沟. ***draw a straight ~*** 老实地过日子. ***plough a lonely ~*** 孤独行动. — *vt.* ①(用犁)开(沟)，给(田)作垄. ②使起皱纹. ③[诗]破(浪)前进. *a brow ~ed with sorrows* 因忧患而布上皱纹的前额. *a ~ed field* 畦田. — *vi.* ①[古]犁地. ②起皱纹. ~ **drilling** 沟播. ~ **irrigation** 沟灌. ~ **opener** 开沟器. ~ **slice** 犁块. **-less** *a.* 无沟的，无皱纹的. **-y** *a.* 有沟的，多皱纹的.
fur·ry [ˈfəːri] *a.* ①毛皮的；毛皮制的；毛皮似的. ②穿毛皮的；镶毛皮的；衬毛皮的. ③水垢多的. ④有舌苔的. ⑤[美俚]可怕的；毛骨悚然的.
fur·ther [ˈfəːðə] [far 的两种比较级形式之一，另一形式为 farther] *a.* ①[表示距离和时间]更远的，较远的.

②〔表示程度〕更进一步的，深一层的．③更多的，此外的．*on the ~ side* 在那一边．~ *news* 续报．— *ad.* ①更远，更进一步．②而且．*I can walk no ~.* 我不能再走了．*inquire ~* 进一步探讨．*He said that he couldn't find it, and ~, that nobody would ever find it.* 他说他找不到那件东西，而且也不会有人找得到它．***for ~ details*** 至于详细情形(则请…)．~ ***on*** 再向前(进)．***till ~ notice*** 另候通知．***I'll see you ~ first.*** (那种事)我决不干〔~ 是 in hell 的委婉话〕．***to be ~ continued*** (未完)待续．***(to) go ~ and fare worse*** 越搞越糟(不如安于现状)．— *vt.* 促进，推动．~**ance** ['fəː-ðərəns] *n.* 助长，促进，推动．~**more** *ad.* 而且．~**most** *a.* 最远的(=furthest)．~**some** *a.* ①〔Scot.〕冒失的，鲁莽的．②〔古〕有利的，有帮助的，起促进作用的．

fur·thest ['fəːðist]〔far 的两种最高级形式之一，另一形式为 farthest〕*a.* 最远的．— *ad.* 最远地，最大程度地，最大限度地．

fur·tive ['fəːtiv] *a.* ①偷偷摸摸的，鬼鬼祟祟的．②偷来的．*a ~ glance* 偷看，窥．*a ~ look* 贼头贼脑的脸色．*be ~ in one's actions* 行动鬼祟．**-ly** *ad.* **-ness** *n.*

fu·run·cle ['fjuərʌŋkl] *n.*【医】疖．

fu·run·cu·lar [fjuə'rʌŋkjulə]，**fur·un·cu·lous** [fjuə'rʌŋkjuləs] *a.*【医】疖的．

fu·run·cu·lo·sis [fju,rʌŋkju'ləusis] *n.*【医】疖病．

fu·ry ['fjuəri] *n.* ①愤怒，狂怒．②(病状，天气等的)凶险，猛烈．③〔F-〕【罗神】复仇的三女神之一；〔*pl.*〕冤魂．④泼妇．***be haunted by the furies of*** 被…的冤魂纠缠．***fly into a ~*** 大怒．***in a ~*** 在狂怒中．***like ~***〔口〕猛烈地 (*work like ~* 猛干．*rain like ~* 下暴雨)．***the ~ of the elements*** 狂风暴雨．

furze [fəːz] *n.*【植】荆豆(属)．

fur·zy ['fəːzi] *a.* 荆豆茂盛的，象荆豆属植物的．

fu·sain [fjuː'zein] *n.* ①炭画笔．②炭笔画．③炭素．

fu·sar·i·um [fjuː'zæriəm] *n.*【生】镰刀霉．

fus·cin ['fʌsin] *n.*【生化】暗褐菌素．

fus·cous ['fʌskəs] *a.*【生】暗褐色的．

fuse[1] [fjuːz] *vt.* ①熔化．②熔合．③使(政党等)联合，合并，融合．— *vi.* ①熔化．②熔合．③(政党等)联合，合并，融合．④由于保险丝烧断而电路不通．*All the lights have ~d.* 由于保险丝烧断，电灯都灭了．— *n.*【电】保险丝，熔丝；熔断器．***have a short ~***〔美〕脾气急躁；容易发怒．***blow a ~*** 使保险丝熔断；〔口〕勃然大怒．~**-link** 熔线，熔断片，熔丝链．~ **wire** 作保险丝用的金属丝；保险丝，熔丝，熔(断)线．

fuse[2] [fjuːz] *vt.* 给…装信管，给…装导火线．— *n.* 信管；导火线，引线．*a non-delay [time] ~* 瞬发〔定时〕引信．

fused [fjuːzd] *a.* ①熔融的，熔凝的．②融合的，合并的．~ **quartz** 熔凝石英，熔凝水晶．~ **salt** 熔盐．

fu·see [fjuː'ziː] *n.* ①耐风火柴．②(铁路等的)带色闪光信号〔危险信号〕．③(钟表的)均力圆锥轮．④【宇】火箭发动机点火器．⑤雷管．⑥(马脚上的)骨瘤．

fu·se·lage ['fjuːzilɑːʒ] *n.* ①【空】飞机机身．②【宇】火箭的外壳；弹体，壳体．~ **cover** 机身外壳．

fu·sel ['fjuːzəl] **oil** *n.*【化】杂醇油．

fu·si·bil·i·ty [,fjuːzə'biliti] *n.* (可)溶性，熔度．

fu·si·ble ['fjuːzəbl] *a.* 可溶解的；易熔的．*a ~ alloy [metal]* 易熔合金〔金属〕．

fu·si·form ['fjuːzifɔːm] *a.*【生】纺锤状的；两端尖的；流线形的．

fu·sil ['fjuːzil] *n.* (旧式)燧发枪，明火枪．

fu·sil·ier, fu·si·leer [fjuːzi'liə] *n.*【史】燧发枪兵；〔*pl.*〕〔英〕明火枪团．

fu·sil·lade [,fjuːzi'leid] *n.* ①一齐射击，排枪．②一连串的猛烈批评．*a ~ of questions* 连珠炮似的质问．— *vt.* 以排枪射击，以排炮轰击．

fu·sion ['fjuːʒən] *n.* ①熔解，熔化；【物】(核)聚变，合成．②〔美〕融合；(政党等的)合并，联合．*the heat of ~* 熔化热．*the point of ~ = ~ point* 熔点．*atomic [nuclear] ~* 核聚变，核合成．*thermonuclear ~* 热核反应．~ **administration**〔美〕联合政府．~ **bomb** 热核弹，氢弹．~ **frequency** (电视中视觉的)停闪频率．~ **welding** 熔融焊，熔焊(接)．

fu·sion·ism ['fjuːʒənizəm] *n.* 党派大联合论．**fu·sion·ist** *n., a.*

fuss [fʌs] *n.* ①忙乱，激动；大惊小怪．②吹捧，过分体贴．③大惊小怪的人．④抗议；争吵．*Why all the ~?* 这值得大惊小怪么？~ ***and feathers*** 大吹大擂，夸示，炫耀．***get into a ~*** 焦急，忙乱．***kick up a ~***〔美俚〕制造麻烦〔如表示抗议等〕；骚乱〔如打架等〕．***make a ~ = make too much ~*** 小题大做，无事自扰．***make a ~ of sb.*** 对某人过分关心〔照料〕．***make a ~ over*** 大肆吹捧．***make a great ~ about nothing [trifles]*** 小题大做．— *vi.* ①忙乱，大惊小怪，小题大做，(不停地，东转西转地)忙忙碌碌 (*about; up and down*)．②奉承，过分关心；特别考究．③烦恼；抱怨；唠叨．④〔美俚〕追求女人．— *vt.* ①使无事自扰；使急躁．②〔美俚〕追求，与(女子)约会．~ ***around***〔美口〕无意义，无目的地忙乱．~**budget**〔口〕大惊小怪〔小题大做，终日忙忙碌碌〕的人，爱挑剔的人(尤指年老的泼妇)．~**pot** = ~-budget.

fuss·y ['fʌsi] *a.* ①爱大惊小怪的，爱小题大做的；过分操心的．②(衣着、字句等上)过分讲究的．***as ~ as a hen with one chick*** 在小事上瞎忙．**-i·ly** *ad.* **-i·ness** *n.*

fus·tet ['fʌstet] *n.*【植】黄栌．

fus·tian ['fʌstiən] *n.* ①粗斜纹布；纬起毛织物，纬起绒织物．②夸大的话，(文词的)浮夸．— *a.* ①粗斜纹布制的．②浮夸的，夸大的；无价值的．

fus·tic ['fʌstik] *n.*【植】黄颜树〔桑科〕；黄颜木；(黄颜木制成的)黄色染料．

fus·ti·gate ['fʌstigeit] *vt.* ①用棍子打．②猛烈抨击．

fus·ti·ga·tion [,fʌsti'geiʃən] *n.* **fus·ti·ga·to·ry** *a.*

fus·ty ['fʌsti] *a.* ①发霉的；陈腐的．②古板的；过时的．**-i·ly** *ad.* **-i·ness** *n.*

fut [fʌt] *n., ad.* = phut.

fut. = future.

fu·thark ['fuːθɑːk] *n.* 北欧古字母〔由起首六个字母 *f, u, p(th), a* (或 *o*)，*r, k* (或 *c*) 而得名〕(= futharc; futhorc; futhork)．

fu·tile ['fjuːtail,〔美〕-til] *a.* ①无用的，无益的．②(人)没出息的；轻浮的．③(事)不足道的，无关紧要的．**-ly** *ad.* **-ness** *n.*

fu·til·i·tar·i·an [,fjuːtili'tɛəriən] *a.* 悲观的，认为一切都是没有价值〔空忙一场〕的．— *n.* 悲观主义者．**-ism** *n.* 悲观主义，万事皆空论．

fu·til·i·ty [fju(ː)'tiliti] *n.* ①无用，无益．②无益的事．③轻浮的言行．

fut·tock ['fʌtək] *n.*【船】(艇上的)复肋材．

fu·tur·am·a [,fjuːtʃə'ræmə] *n.* 未来世界展示．

fu·tur·am·ic [,fjuːtʃə'ræmik] *a.* 未来型的，设计新颖的．

fu·ture ['fjuːtʃə] *n.* ①未来，将来．②前途，远景．③〔*pl.*〕【商】期货，期货交易．④〔俚〕未婚夫，未婚妻．⑤【语】将来时，将来式．~ *delivery* 期货交割．*have a ~* 有前途，将来有希望．*have no ~* 没有前途，前途无望．*deal in ~s* 作期货交易．***for the ~*** = in ~．***in (the) ~*** 将来，今后．★ in the ~ 比 in ~ 常用．***in the near [no distant] ~*** 在不久的将来．— *a.* 未来的，将来的；【语法】将来时的．*a ~ life* 来世．~ *ages [generations]* 后代，后世．~ **perfect**【语法】将来完成时．~ **shock** 未来休克〔对于迅速变化的客观环境的不能适应〕．**-less** *a.* 没有前途的，前途无望的．

fu·tur·ism ['fjuːtʃərizəm] *n.*【文艺】未来主义〔二十世纪初始于意大利的绘画、音乐、文学流派，抛弃传统手法,强调表现当代生活中机器代替一切的忙乱现象〕.

fu·tur·ist [ˈfjuːtʃərist] *n.* ①未来主义者,未来派文艺家. ②相信《圣经》预言会实现的基督教徒. ③未来学家. — *a.* 未来主义的,未来派的.

fu·tur·is·tic [ˌfjuːtʃəˈristik] *a.* ①未来的. ②未来派(艺术)的;未来主义的. **-ti·cal·ly** *ad.*

fu·tur·is·tics [ˌfjutʃuˈristiks] *n.* 未来学.

fu·tu·ri·ty [fjuːˈtjuəriti] *n.* ①未来,将来. ②未来性. ③〔*pl.*〕未来的事物,远景. ~ **industry** 未来工学〔未来的科技发展将会造成的工业〕. ~ **race** 优胜者(尤指赛马)早已排定的比赛.

fu·tu·rol·o·gy [fjuːtʃəˈrɔledʒi] *n.* 未来学〔研究未来科技发展及其对社会之影响的一门科学〕. **fu·tu·rol·o·gist** *n.* 未来学家.

fuze [fjuːz]〔美〕= fuse².

fu·zee [fjuːˈziː] *n.* = fusee.

fuzz [fʌz] *n.* ①微毛,细毛,茸毛,绒毛. ②〔美俚〕警察,侦探. — *vi.* 成绒毛状. — *vt.* ①使长绒毛. ②使模糊. ~**box**, ~**tone** (装在电吉他上的)嗡声箱,哑音器〔作用在于使乐音稍变粗哑〕.

fuzz·ball [ˈfʌzbɔːl] *n.*【植】马勃菌,牛屎菌.

fuzz·y [ˈfʌzi] *a.* ①有茸毛的,覆着细毛的,如茸毛的. ②不清楚的. *a ~ photo* 模糊的照片. **fuzzily** *ad.* **fuzziness** *n.*

FV, f.v. =〔L.〕*folio verso* 见本页背面 (= on the back of the page).

F.W.A. = Federal Works Agency〔美旧〕联邦工程局.

F.W.B. = four wheel brakes 四轮制动器.

F.W.D. = four wheel drive 四轮驱动.

Fwd Ech = Forward Echelon 先头梯队.

FX = Foreign Exchange 外汇.

F.Y. = Fiscal Year〔美〕财政年度.

-fy *suf.* 表示"弄成","变成","…化": beauti*fy*, magni*fy*.

fyce [fais] *n.* 小狗 (= feist).

FYI, fyi = for your information 供参考.

fyke [faik] *n.* 长袋鱼网 (= ~ net).

fyl·fot [ˈfilfɔt] *n.* 卍字形.

fytte [fit] *n.*〔古〕诗歌的一节.

fz. = fuze.

F.Z.S. = Fellow of the Zoological Society〔英〕动物学学会会员.

G

G, g [dʒiː] *(pl. G's, Gs, g's, gs* [dʒiːz]*)* 英语字母表的第七个字母. ①〔G〕G字形物. ②【乐】G调,G音. ③【物】〔g〕重力加速度 (acceleration of gravity) 的符号. ④〔G〕〔美〕学业成绩优良 (good) 的符号. ⑤〔g〕【心】普通〔一般〕智力(general intelligence)的符号. ⑥第七. ⑦〔G〕〔美俚〕一千美元. ⑧〔美〕〔G〕(电影) G级的,男女老少均可观看的. ⑨〔G〕【电】导电性 (conductance) 的符号. *G class* 第七级. *hard g* 发音为 [g] 的 *g*. *soft g* 发音为 [dʒiː] 的 *g*. ***G-1, G-2, G-3, G-4.***【军】(参谋本部下设的)人员部、情报部、作战与训练部及供给部. *G-77* 七十七国集团. **G flat** ($G^\flat$) 变G调. **G major** G大调. **G minor** G小调, **G sharp** ($G^\sharp$) 升G调.

G = ①generator. ②German. ③Germany. ④giga 十亿. ⑤Gossypium 棉属. ⑥grid. ⑦Gulf. ⑧【军】gun.

G. = ①German. ②George. ③ special gravity. ④Gulf.

g. = ① game. ② ga(u)ge. ③ gender. ④ genitive. ⑤〔美〕gold. ⑥grain. ⑦gram(s). ⑧grand. ⑨guide. ⑩guinea. ⑪gulf.

GA = gibberellic acid.

GA, G.A. = ①General Agent; General Assembly. ②General Average. ③General of the Army.

Ga =【化】gallium.

Ga. = ①Georgia. ② Gallic.

gab [gæb] *n.* ①〔主 Scot.〕废话,空谈,唠叨. ②【机】(偏心盘杆的)凹节. ③〔Scot.〕嘴. *Stop [stow] your ~!* 住嘴! *blow the ~* 泄露秘密,告密. *have the gift of (the) ~* 能说会道,有口才. — *vi.* 空谈,闲聊,唠叨. **gab session**〔美俚〕长时间的闲聊.

gab·ar·deen, gab·ar·dine [ˌgæbəˈdiːn, ˈgæbə-] *n.* ①【纺】斜纹呢,华达呢〔俗称轧别丁〕. ②(中世纪犹太人穿的)宽大长外套.

gab·ber [ˈgæbə] *n.* 唠叨的人;闲聊的人.

gab·ble [ˈgæbl] *vt.* 喋喋不休地讲;急促不清地说. — *vi.* ①唠叨. ②(鹅、鸭等)发出咯咯声. — *n.* ①急促不清的话;无意义的话. ②(鸡鸭等发出的)咯咯声. **-bler** *n.*

gab·bro [ˈgæbrəu] *(pl. ~s) n.*【地】辉长岩. **gab·bro·ic** [gæˈbrəuik] *a.*

gab·by [ˈgæbi] *a.*〔口〕爱说话的,多嘴的.

ga·belle [gæˈbel] *n.*〔F.〕〔古〕①税,国税. ②法国大革命前的盐税.

gab·er·dine [ˈgæbədiːn, ˌgæbəˈdiːn] *n.* ①工作服. ② = gabardine.

gab·er·lun·zie [ˌgæbəˈlʌnziː] *n.*〔Scot.〕乞丐.

Ga·be·ro·nes [ˌgɑːbəˈrəunəs] *n.* 加贝罗内斯〔博茨瓦纳首都〕.

gab·fest [ˈgæbfest] *n.*〔美口〕①长时间的闲谈. ②(社交中)非正式的聚谈.

ga·bi·on [ˈgeibiən] *n.* ①(盛土石用的)枝条筐. ②(筑堤、坝等用的)金属条筐.

ga·bi·on·ade [ˌgeibiəˈneid] *n.* 用盛装土石的筐垒成的堤〔墙〕.

ga·ble [ˈgeibl] *n.*【建】山墙,三角墙;三角形的建筑部分. ~ **end** 山墙端. ~ **roof**【建】人字屋顶,三角屋顶. ~ **window** 山墙窗;三角窗.

ga·bled [ˈgeibld] *a.* 有山墙的,人字形的.

ga·blet [ˈgeiblit] *n.*【建】花山头.

Ga·bon [F. gabɔ̃] *n.* 加蓬〔非洲〕.

Gab·o·nese [ˌgɑːbəˈniːz] *n.* 加蓬人.

Ga·boon [gəˈbuːn] *n.* = Gabon.

ga·boon [gəˈbuːn] *n.*〔方〕痰盂.

Ga·bri·el [ˈgeibriəl] *n.* ①盖布里尔〔男子名〕. ②【宗】(替上帝把好消息报告世人的天使)加百列. ③〔美俚〕爵士乐队中的)号手.

Ga·bun [gəˈbuːn] *n.* = Gabon.

ga·by [ˈgeibi] *n.*〔英方〕蠢货,傻瓜.

gad¹ [gæd] *n.* ①【矿】钢楔,小钢凿. ②〔方〕(赶牛用的)刺棒,棍. — *vt.* ①用刺棒刺. ②【矿】用钢楔凿碎或弄松(矿石).

gad² [gæd] *n.* 闲逛,游荡. — *vi.* ①游荡,闲荡 *(about, abroad, out)*. ②追求刺激. ③蔓延. *a gadding plant* 蔓生植物. *be on [upon] the ~* 游荡着.

gad[3], **Gad** [gæd] *int.* 〔古〕嘿! *By ~!* 天哪! 哎呀!

gad·a·bout [ˈgædəbaut] *n.* 游手好闲的人. — *a.* 游荡的; 游手好闲的.

gad·a·rene [ˌgædəˈriːn] *a.* 〔常 G-〕猛冲的; 急速的; 头朝下的.

gad·di [ˈgʌdi] *n.* 〔印〕①君主座席的垫子. ②〔喻〕王座, 王位, 宝座; 王权.

gad·fly [ˈgædflai] *n.* ①【动】虻, 牛虻. ②讨厌的人. ③强烈的刺激〔冲动〕.

gadg·et [ˈgædʒit] *n.* 〔口〕①小机件, 小配件; 小装置. ②新发明, 小玩意儿. ③〔喻〕诡计, 圈套.

gadg·e·teer [ˌgædʒəˈtiə] *n.* 制造小机件的人; 设计新玩意儿的人.

gadg·et·ry [ˈgædʒitri] *n.* ①小机件; 小玩意儿〔总称〕. ②专心琢磨新玩意儿; 爱搞小发明.

Ga·dhel·ic [gəˈdelik] *a., n.* = Goidelic.

ga·did [ˈgeidid] *n.* 鳕科 *(Gadidae)* 鱼.

ga·doid [ˈgeidɔid] *n.* 【鱼】鳕鱼. — *a.* 鳕科的, 似鳕的.

gad·o·lin·ite [ˈgædəlinait] *n.* 【矿】硅铍钇矿.

gad·o·lin·i·um [ˌgædəˈliniəm] *n.* 【化】钆.

ga·droon [gəˈdruːn] *n.* 圆模雕刻装饰; (银器上的)卵形凹凸刻纹. **-ing** *n.*

gad·wall [ˈgædwɔːl] *n.* *(pl. ~s, ~)* 【动】潦凫 *(Anas strepera)* 〔产于美洲北部淡水区〕.

gad·zooks [ˌgædˈzuːks] *int.* 〔常 G-〕〔古〕该死〔轻微的诅咒〕.

gae[1] [gei] *vi.* ***(gaed*** [geid]; ***gaen*** [gein]; ***gae·ing)*** 〔Scot.〕 = go.

gae[2] [gei] 〔Scot.〕 give 的过去式.

Gae·a [ˈdʒiːə] 【希神】盖娅〔大地女神〕.

Gael [geil] *n.* (苏格兰高地及爱尔兰等地的)盖尔人.

Gael·ic [ˈgeilik] *a.* 盖尔族的, 盖尔语的. — *n.* 盖尔语.

gaff[1] [gæf] *n.* ①鱼叉, 鱼钩, 钩竿. ②(爬电杆用的)攀钩; (肉铺的)挂钩. ③【海】桅斜桁. ④(装在斗鸡距上的)铁距. ⑤〔俚〕骗人的秘密机关; 欺骗, 愚弄, 花招. ⑥〔美俚〕苦难, 苦境, 刑罚; 嘲笑, 挖苦. ⑦= gaffe. ***blow the ~*** 〔俚〕泄露秘密. ***get [give] sb. the ~*** 〔美〕刺激某人. ***stand the ~*** 〔美俚〕忍受痛苦〔惩罚〕而毫不怯懦. — *vt.* 用鱼叉捕(鱼), 用鱼钩钓上来; 〔俚〕欺骗. **~-rigged** *a.* 主帆上有斜桁的. **~ sail** 【海】斜桁帆. **~-top sail** 【海】斜桁上帆.

gaff[2] [gæf] *n.* 〔英俚〕低级娱乐场, 低级戏院〔舞厅〕〔通常叫做 penny gaff〕.

gaffe [gæf] *n.* 〔F.〕过失, 不慎的言行, 出丑.

gaf·fer [ˈgæfə] *n.* ①〔贬、谑〕老头子〔对乡下老人的称呼, *cf.* gammer〕. ②〔英〕工头, 雇主. ③经理, 马戏团领班; (电影、电视的)照明电工. *G- Johnson* 约翰逊老头.

gag [gæg] *n.* ①塞口的东西, (牲畜的)口衔. ②对言论自由的压制; (议会)限制辩论时间, 终止辩论. ③【医】张口器. ④插科打诨, 逗乐. ⑤〔俚〕欺诈, 哄骗. *place [put] a ~ upon freedom of speech* 压制言论自由. — *vt.* ①塞住…的口; 【医】用张口器使(患者)张开口. ②压制…的言论自由, 限制…的发言. ③给(表演)加笑料. ④〔俚〕欺诈, 瞒. ⑤关闭(阀门等). — *vi.* ①〔俚〕插科打诨. ②窒息, 作呕. ③〔俚〕欺骗. ~ **bit** (驯马用的)衔铁. **~ law [rule]** 限制言论〔讨论〕自由的法令(尤指在立法机关里讨论某问题). **~man** *n.* 笑料的设计人, 插科打诨的演员. ~ **rein** 马缰.

ga·ga [ˈgɑːgɑː] *a.* ①糊涂的; 愚蠢的. ②狂热的. — *n.* 低级的观众.

gage[1] [geidʒ] *n.* ①抵押品, 担保品. ②(表示挑战扔下的)帽子〔手套等〕; 挑战, 挑衅. ***in ~ of ...*** 作为抵押. ***throw down a ~*** 挑战. — *vt.* 〔古〕以…作抵押; 以…打赌.

gage[2] [geidʒ] *n., vt.* ①〔美〕 = gauge. ②【海】吃水; (对于风及他船的)相对位置.

gage[3] [geidʒ] *n.* = greengage.

Gage [geidʒ] *n.* 盖奇〔姓氏〕.

gag·er [ˈgeidʒə] *n.* = gauger.

gag·ger [ˈgægə] *n.* ①箝住别人口的人, 塞口的东西. ②插科打诨的演员, 讲笑话的人. ③【机】铁骨. ④【交】校正轨距的工人.

gag·gle [ˈgægl] *n.* ①(鹅等的)一群. ②(杂乱的)一堆, 一簇. ③〔贬〕一群饶舌的妇女. *a ~ of reporters and photographers* 乱哄哄的一群记者和摄影师. — *vi.* (鹅等)嘎嘎地叫. — *vt.* 咯咯地叫出〔说出〕.

gag·ster [ˈgægstə] *n.* 开玩笑的人, 插科打诨的演员, 笑话的作者.

gahn·ite [ˈgɑːnait] *n.* 【矿】锌尖晶石.

Gai·a [ˈgeiə, ˈgaiə] = Gaea.

gai·ety [ˈgeiəti] *n.* ①愉快的神情, 欢乐的气氛. ②〔常 *pl.*〕狂欢, 乐事. ③(服装的)华美.

gai·ly [ˈgeili] *ad.* ①快活地. ②华丽地.

gain[1] [gein] *vt.* ①获得; 博得, 挣得; 赢得, 打胜(战争、官司). ②吸引; 争取…(到一边), 说服. ③(尤指通过努力)到达(目的地). ④增加, 增进; (钟、表等)走快 *(opp.* lose*)*. *~ one's living* 谋生. *~ the summit* 到达山顶. *My watch ~s five minutes a day.* 我的表每天快五分钟. — *vi.* ①得利, 得益. ②前进, 进步. ③增加, 增重, 增进. ④(钟、表等)走快. ~ ***by comparison [contrast]*** 比较〔对比〕之下显出其长处. ~ ***ground*** 进展, 占优势. ~ ***headway*** 前进. ~ ***in*** 获得, 增长(*~ in health* 增进健康. *~ in influence* 影响增长). ~ ***on [upon]*** ①蚕食, 侵入(*The sea gains on the land.* 海水侵入陆地). ②接近, 逼近, 赶上. ③占优势, 超过, 胜过(*The days are ~ing on the night.* 白天渐渐比夜晚长了). ④得欢心, 巴结上. ~ ***one's ends*** 达到目的. ~ ***one's point*** 贯彻自己意见. ~ ***over*** 说服, 拉拢过来. ~ ***speed*** 渐渐增加速度. ~ ***strength*** 力量增加; (风力等)渐强. ~ ***the ear of*** 得人倾听. ~ ***the wind*** 占他船的上风. ~ ***time*** ①(钟、表等)走得快. ②(用拖延等办法)争取时间. — *n.* *(opp.* loss*)* ①获利, 获得. ②得益, 利益. ③〔*pl.*〕收益, 利润; 报酬, 奖金. ④增大, 增加, 增进. ⑤【无】增益, 放大, 增量. *be blinded by the love of ~* 利令智昏. *Ill-gotten ~s never prosper.* 〔谚〕不义之财, 发不了家. *No ~s without pains.* 〔谚〕不劳则无获. *a ~ to one's happiness* 幸福的增进. ~ **control** 【无】增益调整. ~ **day** 盈余日〔地球自转一周所剩的时日〕.

gain[2] [gein] *n.* 【建】①(木料上或墙上的)腰槽. ②雄榫上的斜肩. — *vt.* 在…上开腰槽, 用腰槽联接.

gain·a·ble [ˈgeinəbl] *a.* 可得到的, 能赢得的.

gain·er [ˈgeinə] *n.* ①获得者, 得益者, 胜利者 *(opp.* loser*)*. ②【体】后滚翻花式跳水. ***come off a ~*** 结果获得胜利.

Gaines [geinz] *n.* 盖恩斯〔姓氏〕.

gain·ful [ˈgeinful] *a.* ①有利益的; 有报酬的. ②唯利是图的. **-ly** *ad.* **-ness** *n.*

gain·ings [ˈgeiniŋz] *n.* 〔*pl.*〕收入, 收益, 利益, 奖金, 奖品.

gain·less [ˈgeinlis] *a.* 无利可图的; 一无所获的, 没有进展的.

gain·ly [ˈgeinli] *a.* 优美的, 秀丽的.

gain·say [geinˈsei] *vt.* ***(-said*** [-ˈseid, -ˈsed]; ***-say·ing)*** 〔主要用于疑问句和否定句〕①否定, 否认. ②反驳, 反对. *There is no ~ing his honesty.* 他的诚实是不可否认的. — *n.* 否认, 矛盾. ***beyond ~*** 无可否认, 不容置疑.

Gains·bor·ough [ˈgeinzbərə] *n.* 盖恩斯伯勒〔姓氏〕.

(')gainst [geinst] *prep., conj.* 〔诗〕 = against.

gait[1] [geit] *n.* ①步态, 步法. ②(走、跑等的)速度. ***gang one's ain [own] ~*** 〔Scot.〕走自己的路, 我行我素. ***slacken one's ~*** 放慢步行速度. — *vt.* 训练(马的)步法.

gait^{2} [geit] *n.*【纺】穿经；花纹循环.

gai·ted [ˈgeitid] *a.* 有…步伐的. *heavy-*～ 步履沉重的.

gai·ter [ˈgeitə] *n.* ①鞋罩,绑腿. ②高帮松紧鞋,绑腿式长统靴. ***be ready to the last ～ button*** 有充分准备,已准备完毕.

Gait·skell [ˈgeitskəl] *n.* 盖茨克尔〔姓氏〕.

gal^{1} [gæl] *n.*〔俚〕= girl.

gal^{2} [gæl] *n.*【物】伽〔加速度单位〕.

Gal. = Galatian(s).

gal. =①gallery. ②gallon.

ga·la [ˈgɑːlə] *n.* ①庆祝,节日. ②〔古〕盛装. ③〔英〕运动盛会. — *a.* 节日的,欢乐的. *a ～ day* 庆祝日,节日. *a ～ dress* 节日服装,漂亮服装.

gal·a·bi·a, gal·a·bi·ya [ˈgæləˈbiə] *n.* 盖拉布衣〔阿拉伯国家的人特别是农民穿的长棉大褂〕.

ga·lac·ta·gogue [gəˈlæktəgɔg] *a.*【医】催奶的. — *n.* 催乳剂.

ga·lac·tic [gəˈlæktik] *a.* ①乳的,乳汁的;[医]催乳的. ②【天】银河的. ③极大的,巨额的. ～ **circle [system]**【天】银道圈[系]. ～ **cluster**【天】银河星团. ～ **noise**【无】银河(星系射电)噪声,银河系射频辐射. ～ **structure**【天】银河结构.

ga·lac·t(o) [gəˈlækt(ə)] *comb. f.* 表示"乳的": *galactose*.

gal·ac·tom·e·ter [ˌgælәkˈtɔmitə] *n.* = lactometer.

ga·lac·tor·rhe·a [gəˌlæktəˈriə] *n.*【医】乳溢.

ga·lac·tose [gəˈlæktəus] *n.*【化】半乳糖.

ga·lac·to·se·mi·a [gəˌlæktəˈsiːmiə] *n.*【医】半乳糖血.

ga·lac·to·side [gəˈlæktəsaid] *n.*【化】①半乳糖苷. ②半乳糖苷类.

ga·lah [gəˈlɑː] *n.*【动】凤头鹦鹉 *(Kakatoë roseicapilla)*〔产于澳洲,粉灰色,澳大利亚内陆到处可见,作观赏鸟〕.

ga·lan·gal [gəˈlæŋgl] *n.* ①【植】高良姜 *(Alpinia officinarum)*; 山奈 *(Kaempteria galanga)*. ②莎草属植物〔如高莎草 *(Cyperus longus)*〕.

gal·an·tine [ˈgælənˌtiːn] *n.* 〔F.〕(肉或鸡肉去骨加香料扎紧煮熟后做成的)冻肉卷.

ga·lan·ty show [gəˈlænti ˈʃəu] 影子戏.

gal·a·te·a [ˌgæləˈtiə] *n.* (作海魂衫童装用的)条纹花布.

Ga·la·tia [gəˈleiʃə] *n.* 加拉太〔小亚细亚中部一古国〕.

Ga·la·tian [gəˈleiʃən] *a.* 加拉太的,加拉太人的. — *n.* 加拉太人. ***The ～s***【圣】《加拉太书》.

gal·a·vant [ˈgæləvænt] *vi.* = gallivant.

ga·lax [ˈgeilæks] *n.*【植】加腊克斯 *(Galax aphylla)*〔产于美国东南部;为常绿灌木,开小白花,叶子有光泽,常用以编织花圈〕.

gal·ax·y [ˈgæləksi] *n.* ①〔the G-〕银河;银河系;〔*pl.*〕河外星系. ②人才荟粹,一群显赫的[出色的]人物;一系列光彩夺目的东西. *a ～ of talent [beauties]* 一群才子[美女].

gal·ba·num [ˈgælbənəm] *n.*【化】古蓬香脂,波斯树脂.

Gal·braith [gælˈbreiθ] *n.* 加尔布雷斯〔姓氏〕.

gale^{1} [geil] *n.* ①大风(尤指风速每小时在 30 至 60 英里的大风);暴风. ②〔口〕(感情等突发的)一阵. ③〔诗〕微风. *a fresh ～* 疾风. *a moderate ～* 强风. *a strong ～* 大风(九级风). *a whole ～* 烈风(十级风). *a ～ of wind* 一阵大风. *～s of laughter* 阵阵笑声.

gale^{2} [geil] *n.*【植】香杨梅.

gale^{3} [geil] *n.*〔英〕(租金的)定期交付. *a hanging ～* 租金欠交.

ga·le·a [ˈgeiliə] *n.* *(pl. -le·ae* [-liiː]*)* ①【植】盔瓣. ②【动】(昆虫的)外颚叶. ③【医】帽状头痛膜.

ga·le·ate(d) [ˈgeiliit(id)] *a.* 盔状的,戴盔的.

ga·lee·ny [gəˈliːni] *n.*【英动】珠鸡.

Ga·len [ˈgeilin] *n.* 盖伦〔男子名〕.

Ga·len [ˈgeilin] *n.* ①**Clandius ～** 克莱迪斯·盖伦〔130?—200?,古希腊名医〕. ②〔谑〕医生.

ga·le·na [gəˈliːnə] *n.*【矿】方铅矿.

Ga·len·ic [gəˈlenik] *a.* ①古希腊医生盖伦的,盖伦医说的. ②【药】草本制剂的.

ga·len·i·cal [gəˈlenikəl] *n.*【药】草本制剂. — *a.* = Galenic.

Ga·len·ism [ˈgeilənizəm] *n.* (古希腊名医)盖伦的医术,医学理论. **-ist** *n.* 奉行盖伦医学理论的人.

ga·len·ite [gəˈliːnait] *n.* = galena.

Ga·li·bi [gɑːˈliːbi] *n.* *(pl. ～s, ～)* 加利比人〔圭亚那的一支印第安人〕.

Ga·li·cia [gəˈliʃiə] *n.* ①加利西亚省〔西班牙西北部一省〕. ②加利西亚地区〔原为奥匈帝国领土,现分属波兰和苏联〕.

Ga·li·cian [gəˈliʃən] *a.* ①(西班牙)加利西亚地方的;加利西亚人的;加利西亚语的. ②(波兰)加利西亚地方的,加利西亚人的. — *n.* ①西班牙加利西亚人[居民]. ②西班牙加利西亚语的葡萄牙的方言. ③波兰的加利西亚人[居民].

Gal·i·le·an^{1} [ˌgæliˈli(ː)ən] *a.* (巴勒斯坦北部)加利利的. — *n.* ①加利利人[居民]. ②基督教徒. ***the ～*** 耶稣.

Gal·i·le·an^{2} [ˌgæliˈli(ː)ən] *a.* (意大利物理学家和天文学家)伽利略的. ～ **telescope** 伽利略望远镜.

Gal·i·lee [ˈgæləˌliː] *n.* 加利利〔巴勒斯坦北部的古罗马地名〕. ***Sea of ～*** 〔以〕太巴列湖(= Lake Tiberias).

gal·i·lee [ˈgæləliː] *n.*〔英〕(教堂的)门廊;(塔的)前厅,门厅.

Gal·i·le·o [ˌgæləˈliːəu], **Gal·i·le·i** 伽利略〔1564—1642,意大利物理学家和天文学家〕.

gal·i·ma·ti·as [ˌgæliˈmeiʃiəs, -ˈmætiəs] *n.* 胡说八道,胡言乱语.

gal·in·gale [ˈgæliŋgeil] *n.*【植】①(英国)高莎草. ②= galangal.

gal·i·ot [ˈgæliət] *n.* = galliot.

gal·i·pot [ˈgæliˌpɔt] *n.*【化】海松树脂.

gall^{1} [gɔːl] *n.* ①胆汁;胆囊,胆. ②苦物,苦味. ③恶毒,刻薄,怨恨. ④〔口〕厚脸,无耻. ***dip one's pen in ～*** 写恶毒文章. ***～ and wormwood*** 最令人厌恶的东西. ***have the ～ to do*** 〔美俚〕居然有脸做某事. ***in the ～ of bitterness*** 吃苦受难. ～ **bladder** 胆囊. ～**stone**【医】胆石.

gall^{2} [gɔːl] *n.* ①【植】(虫)瘿〔植物受到虫害等引起的瘤状物〕. ②五倍子,没食子. *Chinese ～* 五倍子. ～**fly**【动】五倍子虫. ～ **gnat [midge]**【动】瘿蚊. ～ **mite**【动】瘿螨. ～ **wasp**【动】瘿蜂.

gall^{3} [gɔːl] *n.* ①(马的)鞍伤,擦伤. ②瑕疵,缺点. ③苦恼,苦恼的原因. ④磨损的地方;(树丛等的)光秃处. — *vt.* ①擦伤,擦破;磨损. ②使烦恼,激怒. ③伤害(某人)感情,侮辱. —*vi.* ①被擦伤,被擦破,被磨损. ②【机】(因摩擦过度而)咬紧.

gall. = gallon.

Gal·la [ˈgælə] *n.* *(pl. ～s, ～)* ①盖拉人〔埃塞俄比亚南部和与索马里毗连的农、牧民〕. ②盖拉语.

Gal·la(g)·her [ˈgæləhə] *n.* 加拉赫〔姓氏〕.

gal·lant [ˈgælənt] *a.* ①服饰华丽的,堂皇的,壮丽的,雄壮的,雄伟的. ②勇敢的;豪侠的,有义气的. ③[gəˈlænt, ˈgælənt] 对女子殷勤的;好色的. *the honourable and ～ member* (英议会)军人身分的议员. *～ adventures* 艳遇,爱情奇遇. ***make a ～ show*** 装饰华丽. —*n.* ①豪侠. ②时髦人士. ③[gəˈlænt] 对妇女献殷勤的男人;情郎. — *vt.* ①向(女子)献殷勤. ②护卫,陪送(女子). — *vi.* 求爱,调情 *(with)*. ～ **show** = galanty show. **-ly** *ad.*

gal·lant·ry [ˈgæləntri] *n.* ①勇敢,豪侠;勇敢的言行. ②(对女子的)殷勤言行;对女子的尊崇. ③风流事件;淫荡.

Gal·la·tin [ˈgelətin] *n.* 加勒廷〔姓氏〕.

Gal·le [ˈgɑːlə], **Johann Gottfried** 约翰·戈特弗里德·

伽拉[1812—1910,德国天文学家,海王星的发现者].

gal·le·ass, gal·li·ass [ˈgæliˌæs] *n.* ((16-17 世纪航行于地中海的)有侧炮的)三桅军舰[通常用奴隶划桨].

gal·le·in [ˈgæliːin, ˈgæliːn] *n.*【化】棓因; 棓子色素.

gal·le·on [ˈgæliən] *n.* (15—18 世纪用做军舰或商船的)西班牙大帆船.

gal·ler·ied [ˈgælərid] *a.* ①有柱廊的,有看台的; 有画廊的; 有长廊的. ②有地下通道的; 有地道的.

gal·ler·y [ˈgæləri] *n.* ①看台,旁听席,(教堂、议院等的)边座,楼座; (剧场中票价最低的)廉价座,顶层楼座. ②观众,听众. ③回廊,走廊; 阳台; 游廊; 穿廊. ④美术馆,美术品陈列室; 画廊; [集合词]展出中的[收存中的]美术品. ⑤摄影室; (射击等的)练习室.【海】船尾看台. ⑥(要塞的)地道,地下通道; (水道工程的)暗渠;【矿】水平巷道,平巷,横坑道. *the distinguished guest's* ~ 贵宾席. *the press* ~ 记者席. *the public* ~ 旁听席. ***the National G-*** (伦敦的)国家美术馆. ***the rogues'*** ~ (警察部门等的)案犯照片栏. ***a*** ~ ***hit [shot, stroke]*** 卖弄技巧的表演,争取观众喝采的表演. ***bring down the*** ~ 博得满场喝采. ***play to the*** ~ 讨好观众的表演, 迎合低级趣味. — *vt., vi.* (在…)建筑长廊[游廊]; (在…)挖地道. ~ **forest** (沿海岸线生长而不向内陆伸展的)海边森林. ~-**gods** [美俚]顶楼观众. ~ **goer** 常去美术馆的人. **-ite** *n.* 顶层楼座的观众.

gal·let [ˈgælit] *n.* 碎石,石片. — *vt.* 把碎石嵌入….

gal·ley [ˈgæli] *n.* ①(古代用奴隶等划桨的)单层甲板大帆船; (古希腊、罗马的)军舰. ②军舰舰长用的大划艇; (船舰、飞机上的)厨房. ③【冶】长方形炉;【印】长方形活字盘,长条校样. ***be sent to the*** ~***s*** 被罚作划船苦工. ~ **proof**【印】长条(校样). ~ **range** (船)厨房炉灶. ~ **slave** ①划船的囚犯[奴隶]. ②[美俚]印刷商. ③= drudge. ~-**west** *ad.* [美俚]粉碎性地,彻底地,毁灭性地 (*knock* ~*-west* 彻底打败(对方),打得(对方)落花流水). ~**worm**【动】倍足纲的多足昆虫.

gal·li·am·bic [ˌgæliˈæmbik] *a.*【韵】抑抑扬扬格的. — *n.* 抑抑扬扬格的诗.

gal·li·ard [ˈgæljəd] *n.* ①愉快而勇敢的人. ②(十六、七世纪时流行的)轻快活泼的法国双人舞. — *a.* [古]愉快的,活泼的.

gal·li·ass [ˈgæliæs] *n.* = galleass.

Gal·lic [ˈgælik] *a.* ①高卢的,高卢人的. ②法国的,法国人的.

gal·lic[1] [ˈgælik] *a.* 虫瘿的,五倍子的,棓子的. ~ **acid** 棓酸; 五倍子酸, 鞣酸; 没食子酸; 镓酸.

gal·lic[2] [ˈgælik] *a.*【化】正镓的,三价镓的. ~ **compound**【化】正镓化合物.

Gal·li·can [ˈgælikən] *a.* ①= Gallic. ②法国天主教的; (1870年以前法国天主教徒中)主张限制教皇权力的. — *n.* ①法国天主教徒. ②【宗】教皇权力限制主义者. **-ism** *n.* (1862 年在法国掀起的)主张限制教皇权力的天主教自治运动.

Gal·li·ce, gal·li·ce [ˈgælisi(ː)] *ad.* [L.] 用法语; 法语化地.

Gal·li·cism, gal·li·cism [ˈgælisizəm] *n.* ①法语的成语性词语, 法语风格; 法语成语[表达方式]. ②法国习惯,法国思维方法.

Gal·li·cize, gal·li·cize [ˈgælisaiz] *vt., vi.* (使)法国化, (使)具有法国风.

gal·li·gas·kins [ˌgæliˈgæskinz] *n.* ①[*pl.*] (16—17 世纪用的)宽裤. ②(一般的)灯笼裤. ③[英方](打猎等用的)皮绑腿.

gal·li·mau·fry [ˌgæliˈmɔːfri] *n.* ①混合,杂凑. ②烧杂烩,炒什锦.

gal·li·na·cean [ˌgæliˈneiʃən] *n.*【动】鹑鸡类[鸡、鹧鸪等]. — *a.* = gallinaceous.

gal·li·na·ceous [gæliˈneiʃəs] *a.* ①家禽的. ②鹑鸡类的.

gall·ing [ˈgɔːliŋ] *a.* ①擦伤的,擦痛的. ②激怒的, 烦恼的. **-ly** *ad.*

gal·li·nip·per [ˈgælinipə] *n.* [美口]巨蚊; 叮咬人厉害的昆虫.

gal·li·nule [ˈgæliˌnjuːl, -ˌnuːl] *n.* 秧鸡科 *(Rallidae)* 动物(尤指鸸 *(Gallinula chloropus)*).

Gal·li·o [ˈgæliəu] *n.* ①【圣】迦流[亚该亚的总督,拒绝过问宗教争端]. ②[喻]躲避分外事的职员.

gal·li·ot [ˈgæliət] *n.* ①(旧时地中海的)一种帆桨并用的平底小快艇. ②单桅轻快的荷兰商船[渔船].

gal·li·pot[1] [ˈgælipɔt] *n.* ①陶制药罐. ②[古]药剂师.

gal·li·pot[2] [ˈgælipɔt] *n.* = galipot.

gal·li·um [ˈgæliəm] *n.*【化】镓. ~ **arsenide** 砷化镓[一种合成化合物,主要用作半导体材料].

gal·li·vant [ˌgæliˈvænt] *vi.* ①游荡,闲逛; 陪异性游荡. ②寻欢作乐; 找刺激.

gall·nut [ˈgɔːlnʌt] *n.* 五倍子,没食子.

Gal·lo- *comb. f.* 表示"法国的" (= Gallic 或 French): *Gallo-Briton* 法英的.

gal·lo·glass [ˈgæləuˌglæs] *n.* 古爱尔兰首长的武装随从,保镖.

Gal·lo·ma·ni·a [ˌgæləuˈmeinjə] *n.* 崇拜法国,法国迷.

gal·lon [ˈgælən] *n.* 加仑[液体 = 4 夸脱 (quarts), [英]固体 = 1/8 蒲式耳 (bushel)]. *the British imperial* ~ 英制加仑[=4.546 升]. *the wine [Winchester]* ~ 美制加仑[=3.7853 升].

gal·lon·age [ˈgælənidʒ] *n.* ①加仑量,加仑数. ②[美]汽油消费量.

gal·loon [gəˈluːn] *n.* ①细带,绦带. ②金银丝带,金银花边. **-ed** *a.*

gal·lop [ˈgæləp] *n.* ①(马四脚同时离地的)飞跑. ②骑马奔跑. ③[口]快步; 急驰,飞奔. *a canterbury* ~ 小跑. *a snail's* ~ [谑]慢吞吞地走. ***(at) a full*** ~ 飞跑,用最大速度. ***go at a*** ~ 用尽速力跑去. ***go for a*** ~ 去跑一趟; 骑马跑一阵. — *vt.* ①使(马等)飞跑. ②迅速运送. — *vi.* ①(马等)飞跑; (时间)飞驰. ②匆匆地说[读]. ③匆忙地做. ~ ***through [over] a book*** 急促地读书. ~ *through one's work* 急匆匆地把活儿做完. ~**ing consumption**【医】奔马痨, 急性肺结核. ~-**ing dominoes** [美俚]骰子.

gal·lo·pade [ˌgæləˈpeid] *n.* 四分之二拍的轻快横步舞(曲).

gal·lop·er [ˈgæləpə] *n.* ①骑马飞跑的人; 飞跑的马. ②【军】传令官,副官. ③【军】轻野炮,轻便炮车.

Gal·lo·phil(e) [ˈgæləufail] *n.* 爱好法国的人,亲法者. — *a.* 亲法的.

Gal·lo·phobe [ˈgæləufəub] *n.* 憎恶法国的人,恐法症者. — *a.* 恐法的,憎恶法国的.

Gal·lo·pho·bi·a [ˌgæləuˈfəubjə] *n.* 憎恶法国,恐法症.

gal·lous [ˈgæləs] *a.*【化】亚镓的.

Gal·lo·way [ˈgæləwei] *n.* ①加洛韦 [苏格兰西南部地名]. ②加洛韦马[一种产于该地体型小但强壮的马]; 加洛韦牛[一种产于该地黑毛的肉用牛].

gal·low·glass [ˈgæləuˌglæs] *n.* = galloglass.

gal·lows [ˈgæləuz] *n.* *(pl.* ~*es,* ~*)* ①绞刑架; 绞台. ②挂物架,(体操用的)铁杆架;【海】吊杆. ③绞刑,应受绞刑的人. ④[*pl.*] [方](裤子的)吊带,背带. ***cheat the*** ~ 逃脱绞刑,逃避死罪. ***come to [die on] the*** ~ 被绞死. ***have a*** ~ ***look*** = ***have the*** ~ ***in one's face*** 有被绞死的面相, 有不得善终的脸相. ***The*** ~ ***groans for him [you].*** 绞架在等着他[你]呢. — *a.* 该绞死的; 穷凶极恶的,坏透的; 非常的. ~ **bird** 应处绞刑的犯人; 穷凶极恶的人. ~ **bitts** [*pl.*]【海】甲板中央的双柱吊架. ~ **humo(u)r** [美]凄惨的幽默; 充满怨恨的幽默. ~ **look** 犯死罪的面相. ~-**ripe** *a.* 应处绞刑的. ~ **tree** 绞刑架,绞台.

Gal·lup [ˈgæləp] *n.* ①盖洛普[姓氏]. ②**George H.** ~

盖洛普〔美国公众舆论的统计家〕。~ **poll** (美国)盖洛普民意测验〔通过对一部分人进行典型调查以了解民意的方法〕。
gal·lus·es [ˈgæləsiz] *n.* 〔美方〕(裤子的)吊带,背带。
gal·ly [ˈgæli] *vt.* 〔主方〕吓唬,恐吓。
Ga·lois [gælˈwɑː], **Évariste** 伽罗瓦〔1811—1832,法国数学家〕。~ **equation** 伽罗瓦方程。~ **field** 有限域〔体〕,伽罗瓦域。~ **theory** 伽罗瓦理论。
ga·loot [gəˈluːt] *n.* ①〔美俚〕蠢货,傻瓜。②无经验的青年海员。
gal·op [ˈgæləp] *n.* = gallopade. — *vi.* 跳四分之二拍的轻快舞蹈。
ga·lore [gəˈlɔː, -ˈlɔə] *ad.* 多,许多,丰盛。***with beef and ale [beer]*** ~ 酒菜丰盛。— *n.* 〔罕〕丰富,充足。*in* ~ 丰富。
ga·losh [gəˈlɔʃ] *n.* 〔*pl.*〕(长统橡皮)套鞋。**-ed** *a.* 穿长统橡皮套鞋的。
gals. = gallons.
Gals·wor·thy [ˈgɔːlzwəːði, ˈgælzwəːði] ① *n.* 高尔斯沃西〔高尔斯华绥〕〔姓氏〕。②**John** ~ 约翰·高尔斯华绥〔1867—1933,英国小说家,剧作家〕。
Galt [gɔːlt] *n.* 高尔特〔姓氏〕。
Gal·ton [ˈgɔːltən] *n.* ①高尔顿〔姓氏〕。②**Sir Francis** ~ 高尔顿〔1822—1911,英国人类学、遗传学、气象学家〕。
ga·lumph [gəˈlʌmf] *vi.* 得意扬扬地走,昂首阔步地前进。
galv. = ①galvanic. ②galvanism. ③galvanized.
Gal·va·ni [gælˈvɑːni], **Luigi** 卢杰·贾法尼〔1737—1798,意解剖医学家,电流发现人〕。
gal·van·ic [gælˈvænik] *a.* ①以化学方法产生电流的。②触电似的;惊起的,激励的。③(笑等)不自然的。~ **battery [cell]** 原电池(组)。~ **belt** (医疗用)电带。~ **current** 直流,动电电流。~ **electricity** 动电。~ **pile** 电堆。~ **shock** 电休克。
gal·va·nism [ˈgælvənizəm] *n.* ①由原电池产生的电。②流电学。③【医】流电疗法。④有力,有劲。
gal·va·nist [ˈgælvənist] *n.* 流电学学家。
gal·va·nize [ˈgælvənaiz] *vt.* ①通电流于。②电镀,给(铁等)镀锌。③(用电)刺激,使兴奋,激励。*the ~d iron* 镀锌铁皮,白铁皮,马口铁。***be ~ to [into] life*** 受刺激而活跃起来。**-ni·za·tion** [ˌgælvənaiˈzeiʃən] *n.*
gal·va·niz·er [ˈgælvənaizə] *n.* ①电镀工;电镀器。②激励者。
gal·va·no- *comb. f.* 表示"电的","电流的"(= galvanic 或 galvanism): *galvano*meter, *galvano*plasty.
gal·van·o·graph [gælˈvænəgrɑːf] *n.* 【印】电铸版;电铸版印刷品。
gal·va·nog·ra·phy [ˌgælvəˈnɔgræfi] *n.* 电铸制版术。
gal·va·no·mag·net·ic [ˌgælvənəumægˈnetik] *a.* 电磁的。
gal·va·nom·e·ter [ˌgælvəˈnɔmitə] *n.* 电流计,电表。*a ballistic* ~ 冲击电流计。*Einthoven* ~ 弦线检流计。*a tangent* ~ 正切电流计。
gal·va·no·plas·tics [ˌgælvənəuˈplæstiks], **gal·va·no·plas·ty** [-ti] *n.* 电铸(制版法),电镀法。
gal·va·no·scope [ˈgælvənəuskəup] *n.* 验电(流)器,检流器。**-ic** *a.*
gal·ways [ˈgɔːlweiz] *n.* 〔*pl.*〕〔俚〕连鬓胡子。
Gal·we·gian [gælˈwiːdʒən] *a.* (苏格兰)加洛维区的;加洛维区人的。— *n.* 加洛维人,加洛维区居民。
gal·yak, gal·yac [ˈgæljæk] *n.* 羔皮。
gam¹ [gæm] *n.* ①【海】鲸鱼群。②(捕鲸船间的)交际性访问,联欢,〔美方〕(陆上的)联欢,聚会。— *vi.* ①(象鲸鱼一样)成群,聚拢,聚集。②(捕鲸船员)在海上交际,联欢。— *vt.* ①(在海上)与…联欢。②闲聊以消磨(时间)。
gam² [gæm] *n.* 〔美俚〕腿(尤指女人健美的腿)。
GAM = guided aircraft missile 机载导弹。
Ga·ma [ˈgɑːmə], **Vasco de** 伽马〔1469?-1524,葡萄牙航海家,首先经海路到达印度〕。
ga·ma grass [ˈgɑːmə] 【植】鸭茅状磨擦禾 *(Tripsacum dactyloides)* 〔产于美洲,为饲料草〕。
gamb, gambe [gæmb, gæm] *n.* (兽的)腿,胫。
gam·bade [gæmˈbeid], **gam·ba·do** [-ˈbeidəu] *n.* (*pl.* *~s, ~es*) ①(马的)跳跃。②奇怪举动,荒唐行为;戏谑,恶作剧。③长裹腿,长统靴。
gam·be·son [ˈgæmbisn] *n.* 中世纪软铠甲〔革制品或布中有填塞物的布制品〕。
Gam·bi·a [ˈgæmbiə] *n.* 冈比亚〔非洲〕。**-an** *n.* 冈比亚人。
gam·bi(e)r [ˈgæmbiə] *n.* 棕儿茶,黑儿茶。
gam·bit [ˈgæmbit] *n.* ①(国际象棋中牺牲一卒以取得优势的)起手着法。②(交易等的)开始,开场白。③策略,策划占人上风的一着。
gam·ble [ˈgæmbl] *vi.* ①赌,赌博。②投机;孤注一掷,冒险。— *vt.* ①赌输;以…打赌。②冒…的险。~ *at cards* 打纸牌。~ *in stocks [rice, gold]* 做股票〔大米、黄金〕投机。~ ***away*** 乱花,滥用;赌输掉。~ ***on*** 〔俚〕信任,靠牢。~ ***oneself out of house and home*** 赌得倾家荡产。— *n.* ①赌博,赌。②投机;冒险。***on the*** ~ 因赌;贪赌。**-some** *a.* 爱赌的;喜欢投机的。
gam·bler [ˈgæmblə] *n.* 赌钱者,赌徒;投机商人。
gam·bling [ˈgæmbliŋ] *n.* 赌博,投机,冒险。**~-den** *n.* 赌场。~ **hell [house]** 〔口〕赌窟。~ **joint** 赌场。
gam·boge [gæmˈbuːʒ] *n.* ①【化】藤黄胶脂。②橙黄色。
gam·bol [ˈgæmbəl] *n.* 欢跃,跳跃;嬉戏。— *vi.* (〔英〕 *-ll-*) 欢跃,跳跃;嬉戏。
gam·brel [ˈgæmbrəl] *n.* ①【动】(马等的)跗关节。②(肉店等的)挂肉钩架。③【美建】复斜屋顶〔又称 ~ roo 或 curb roof〕。
gam·bu·si·a [gæmˈbjuːʒə, -ʒiə] *n.* 【动】食蚊鱼 *(Gambusia affinis)*.
game¹ [geim] *n.* ①游戏;娱乐;戏谑;运动。②(运动、棋类等的)比赛,竞赛;(比赛中的)一盘,一场,一局;胜利;比分,得分,比赛成绩。③〔*pl.*〕比赛会,运动会。④游戏用具,比赛器具;比赛方式;比赛规则。⑤计划,事业。⑥花招,诡计,策略。⑦〔集合词〕猎物,野味;(鹊等的)群;野外游戏〔游猎、鹰狩等〕。⑧追求物,目的物。⑨胆量,勇气。⑩〔口〕行当,职业。*What a ~!* 多精采的比赛啊!多么有趣! *a close* ~ 接近的比分。*an advertising* ~ 广告竞争。*a* ~ *not worth the candle* 得不偿失。*How is the ~?* 胜负如何? *The ~ is 4 all [7 to 6, love three]*. 比赛成绩是4比4[7比6,0比3]。*The ~ is up [over]*. 无成功希望;一切都完了。*One careless move loses the whole ~*. 〔谚〕一着不慎,满盘皆输。*None of your ~s!* 别耍花招了! *That's a ~ two people can play.* 这一套你会我也会。*That's not the ~!* 那样干不对。*The same old ~!* 又是那一套老玩意儿!惯用伎俩! *winged* ~ 可猎鸟类。*big* ~【猎】巨兽〔狮、虎等〕;巨大的目标,冒险的事业。*fair* ~ 非禁猎的鸟兽;正当目的物;攻击的对象。*forbidden* ~ 禁猎的鸟兽。***ahead of the*** ~ 〔美口〕(特别在赌博中)处于赢家地位。***be on [off] one's*** ~ (马、选手等)竞技状态好〔不好〕。***fly at high*** ~ 胸怀大志。***fly at higher*** ~ 怀有更大的抱负;得陇望蜀。***force the*** ~ (板球等中)冒险快速得分。~ ***and*** ~ = ~ ***all*** 一比一。~ ***and (set)***【网球】比赛完结。***a ~ of chance*** 碰运气取胜的游戏。***a ~ of skill*** 凭技术取胜的游戏。***give the ~ away*** 露馅。***have a ~ with*** 蒙蔽,瞒骗。***have the ~ in one's hands*** 有必胜把握。***make ~ of*** 嘲笑,捉弄。***play a dangerous ~*** 干冒险玩意儿。***play a deep ~*** 背地捣鬼。***play a double ~*** 耍两面派。***play a good [poor] ~*** 赌法高明〔笨拙〕。***play a losing [winning] ~*** 作无〔有〕胜利希望的比赛;干明知无益〔有利〕的事。***play a waiting ~*** 待机下手。***play***

sb.'s ~ = *play the* ~ *of sb.* 无意中给别人占了便宜. ***play the*** ~ 按规则玩游戏;做事光明正大,守规矩. ***see through sb.'s*** ~ 看穿某人诡计. ***speak in*** ~ 说着玩,开玩笑. ***spoil the*** ~ 弄坏(事情). ***throw up the*** ~ 罢手,认输. — *a.* ①关于猎获物的,关于野味的. ②斗鸡似的;雄纠纠的,勇敢的,倔强的. ③对…有兴趣,爱. ~ *pie* 野味馅饼. ***be*** ~ ***for [to do] anything*** 对什么都有兴趣. ***die*** ~ 死斗,死拚;奋斗到底. — *vi.* 打赌,赌输赢. — *vt.* 赌输 (*away*). ~ **acts** 狩猎条例. **~-bag** *n.* 狩猎袋. ~ **ball** ①决胜负的一球. ②(送给球员或教练的)得胜纪念球. ~ **bird** 猎鸟,猎禽,法律许可捕猎的鸟类. **~cock** 斗鸡. ~ **fish** 供捕钓的鱼(尤指上钩时猛烈挣扎者). ~ **fowl** 斗鸡; 猎鸟. **~-keeper** 猎物看守人; 猎场看守人. ~ **land** 猎场. ~ **laws** 狩猎法. ~ **licence** ①许可狩猎;狩猎执照. ②买卖野味许可(证). ~ **plan** 精心策划的行动. ~ **preserver** 猎区经营者. ~ **room** 娱乐室. **~s master** 〔英〕体育[体操]教师. ~ **tenant** 猎场[渔场]承租人. ~ **theory** 策略运筹法[学],形势运筹学〔运用数学分析的方法去选择最好的策略以求在比赛、战争、商业等上缩小损失或转小胜为大胜的方法,也叫 theory of game〕.

game[2] [geim] *a.* 〔口〕跛的,瘸的;残废的,受伤的.

gam·e·lan [ˈgæmәlæn] *n.* 嘎麦兰〔印尼器乐大合奏,中有竹木琴,锣和其他打击乐器〕.

game·ly [ˈgeimli] *ad.* 雄赳赳地,兴致勃勃地.

game·ness [ˈgeimnis] *n.* 勇气,兴致勃勃.

games·man·ship [ˈgeimzmәnʃip] *n.* (运动、比赛中)制胜绝招,小动作.

game·some [ˈgeimsәm] *a.* 爱玩耍的,爱闹着玩的,快乐的. **-ly** *ad.* **-ness** *n.*

game·ster [ˈgeimstә] *n.* 赌棍,赌徒.

gam·e·tan·gi·um [ˌgæmiˈtændʒiәm] *(pl.* ***-gi·a*** [-ә]) 【植】配子囊.

gam·ete [gәˈmiːt] *n.* 【生】配子.

ga·me·to·cyte [gәˈmiːtәusait] *n.* 【生】配子母细胞.

ga·me·to·gen·e·sis [gәˌmiːtәuˈdʒenisis] *n.* 配子发生. **-gen·ic** [ˈ-dʒenik], **gam·e·tog·e·nous** [ˈgæmiˈtɔdʒinәs] *a.* **gam·e·tog·e·ny** [-ni] *n.*

ga·me·to·phore [gәˈmiːtәfɔː] *n.* 【植】配子托. **-phoric** *a.*

ga·me·to·phyte [gәˈmiːtәfait] *n.* 【植】配子体.

gam·ic [ˈgæmik] *a.* 【生】受精后方可发育的,受精的.

gam·i·ly [ˈgeimili] *ad.* 勇敢地;大胆地.

gam·in [ˈgæmin] *n.* 〔F.〕①流浪儿;顽童. ②妖冶的女人.

gam·ine [gæˈmiːn] *n.* 〔F.〕①女流浪儿;女顽童. ②妖冶的女人.

gam·i·ness [ˈgeiminis] *n.* 勇敢.

gam·ing [ˈgeimiŋ] *n.* 赌博. ~ **house** 赌场. ~ **table** 赌台.

gam·ma [ˈgæmә] *n.* ①希腊语的第三个字母〔Γ, γ = 〔英〕G, g〕;第三位的东西;【虫】γ 纹蛾;【天】(亮度居于第三位的)γ 星. ②〔*pl.*〕γ 量,微克(= 100 万分之一克). ③【物】伽马(磁场强度单位, $=10^{-5}$ 奥斯特). ④【摄】灰度(非线性)系数. ~ **decay** 【物】γ 衰变. ~ **globulin** γ 球蛋白. ~ **minus** 仅次于第三等. ~ **plus** 稍高于第三等. ~ **ray** 【物】①光(量)子. ②γ 射线. ~ **ray astronomy** γ 射线天文学. **~sonde** γ 探空仪.

gam·ma·di·on [gәˈmeidiɔn] *n. (pl.* ***-di·a*** [-diә]) (由 Γ 形成的)卐 字形,卍 字形.

gam·mer [ˈgæmә] *n.* 〔英〕乡下老太婆〔*cf.* gaffer〕.

gam·mex·ane [ˈgæmeksein] *n.* 【化】六氯化苯,六六六杀虫剂.

gam·mon[1] [ˈgæmәn] *n.*〔英口〕胡说八道;欺骗. — *int.* 胡说八道! — *vi.* 说瞎话;装假. — *vt.* 欺骗,愚弄. ~ ***and patter*** ①废话. ②隐语;行话.

gam·mon[2] [ˈgæmәn] *n.* 腊腿,熏腿;熏制五花肉. — *vt.* 把…制成腊肉. ~ ***and spinach*** 腊肉烧菠菜.

gam·mon[3] [ˈgæmәn] *n.* (西洋双陆棋戏中的)全胜〔即在对方未弃一子前即取得胜利〕; 连赢两盘. — *vt.* (以全胜[连赢两盘])击败,打败(对方).

gam·mon[4] [ˈgæmәn] *vt.* 【海】把(船首斜桅)缚在船头上.

gam·my [ˈgæmi] *a.* 〔英方〕跛的;残废的(尤指腿而言).

gam·o- *comb.f.* 表示 ①【生】"雌雄合体"; ②【植】"(器官的)结合": *gamo*genesis, *gamo*petalous.

gam·o·gen·e·sis [ˌgæmәuˈdʒenisis] *n.* 【生】有性生殖.

gam·o·pet·al·ous [ˌgæmәuˈpetәlәs] *a.* 【植】合瓣的.

gam·o·phyl·lous [ˌgæmәuˈfilәs] *a.* 【植】合被(片)的.

gam·o·sep·al·ous [ˌgæmәuˈsepәlәs] *a.* 【植】合萼的.

-gamous *comb. f.* 表示"…婚的","…性的": bi*gamous*, poly*gamous*.

gamp [gæmp] *n.* 〔英〕笨重的大伞.

gam·ut [ˈgæmәt] *n.* ①【乐】音阶; 长音阶; 全音域. ②〔喻〕整个领域,全体. *the complete* ~ *of the spectrum* 光谱波长的全区域. *the whole* ~ *of experience* 所有经验. *run the* ~ *of dissipation* 极端放荡. *run the* ~ *of emotions* 百感交集.

gam·y [ˈgeimi] *a.* ①猎物多的. ②有煮野味香味的. ③有胆量的,好斗的. ④下流的,猥亵的.

-gamy *comb. f.* 表示"…婚": bi*gamy*, poly*gamy*.

gan, 'gan [gæn] *v.* 〔古、诗〕gin[3] 的过去式.

Gan·da [ˈgændә] *n. (pl.* ***~s, ~***) ①干达人〔乌干达南部的农民〕. ②干达语〔属班图语系〕.

gan·der [ˈgændә] *n.* ①雄鹅. ②蠢汉. ③〔俚〕一看,一眼. ***see how the*** ~ ***hops*** 〔美口〕观望,看风使舵. ***take a*** ~ 看一看. — *vi.* 〔方〕漫步,游荡.

Gan·dhi [ˈgændiː] ①甘地〔印度姓氏〕. ②**Mohandas** ~ 莫汉达斯·甘地〔1869—1948, 印度民族主义领袖和社会改革家,有圣雄甘地之称〕. ②**Indira** ~ 英迪拉·甘地夫人〔1917— ,尼赫鲁之女, 担任印国大党领袖、政府总理等职〕.

Gan·dhi·ism [ˈgændiizәm] *n.* (印度甘地提出运用"非暴力抵抗"和"不合作运动"来实现民族解放的)甘地主义.

gan·dy [ˈgændi] **dancer** 〔俚〕(美国)铁路工段工人; 季节流动工.

ga·nef, ga·nof [ˈgɑːnәf] *n.* 〔美俚〕贼.

gang[1] [gæŋ] *n.* ①一队,一群; (盗贼等的)一帮; (儿童等的)一伙. ②(工具、机械等的)一套. ③〔美俚〕棒球队. ④〔美俚〕大量. *a* ~ *of thieves* 一帮贼. *a chain* ~ 系成一串的囚犯. *the* ~ *of four* 四人帮. — *vt.* ①把…编成班组. ②〔口〕合伙攻击. ③使成套. — *vi.* 〔美〕成群结队; 作伴 *(with)*. ~ ***up*** 〔美口〕成群结队; 勾结起来;聚集,集合. ~ ***up on [against]*** 〔美俚〕成群结队地对抗[攻击]. ~ ***up with*** 〔美俚〕同…联合起来一致行动. **~buster** 〔美俚〕打击流氓组织的执法人员. ~ **control** 【机】共轴控制. ~ **drill** 【机】排式钻床; 排式钻头. ~ **hook** 〔美〕(钓鱼竿的)联钩、串钩. **~land** 〔美俚〕盗贼充斥的街区; 黑社会. ~ **maintenance, ~master** 把头; 工长. ~ **mill** 框锯制材厂. ~ **milling** 多刀铣削,排铣. **~plough [plow]** 多铧犁. ~ **saw** 框锯,排锯. **~shag** 〔美俚〕爵士乐即席演奏会; 淫乱的聚会. ~ **socket** 联通插座. ~ **switch** 联动〔同轴〕开关. ~ **war** (歹徒之间的) 打群架; 火拼. **~-up** *n.* ①联合(以对付某人或某国). ②攻击.

gang[2] [gæŋ] *n.* = gangue.

gang[3] [gæŋ] *n.* 〔Scot.〕路,路程. — *vi.* 〔Scot.〕去,行走. ~ ***agley*** 〔Scot.〕(计划等)出差错. ~ ***one's ain gait*** 按自己的意思行事.

gang·board [ˈgæŋbɔːd] *n.* 【海】①(船首楼与船尾楼间的狭窄的)道板,(上甲板两侧的)过道. ②(上下船的)跳板,梯板.

gange [gændʒ] *vt.* 用细金属线加固(钓钩[钓线]).

gang·er [ˈgæŋә] *n.* 〔英〕把头,工头.

Gan·ges [ˈgændʒiːz] *n.* 恒河〔发源于喜马拉雅山,流经

印度和孟加拉〕.
gan·gli·a [ˈɡæŋɡliə] *n.* ganglion 的复数.
gan·gli·at·ed [ˈɡæŋɡliˌeitid] *a.* 有神经节的 (= gangliate).
gan·gling [ˈɡæŋɡliŋ] *a.* 瘦长的；身材难看的.
gan·gli·on [ˈɡæŋɡliən] *n.* *(pl.* *~s,* ***-gli·a*** [-gliə]) ①【解】神经节. ②【医】腱鞘囊肿. ③(活动、力量、兴趣等的)中心.
gan·gli·on·ate, gan·gli·on·at·ed [ˈɡæŋɡliəneit, -neitid] *a.* = gangliate.
gan·gli·on·ic [ˌɡæŋɡliˈɔnik] *a.* 神经节的.
gan·gly [ˈɡæŋli] *a.* = gangling.
gang·plank [ˈɡæŋplæŋk] *n.* 〔美〕 = gangboard.
gan·grel [ˈɡæŋɡrəl] *n.* 〔Scot.〕流浪汉；乞丐.
gan·grene [ˈɡæŋɡriːn] *n.* ①【医】坏疽. ②腐败,堕落. — *vi.* 生坏疽,腐烂. — *vt.* 使生坏疽,使腐烂.
gan·gre·nop·sis [ˌɡæŋɡreˈnɔpsis] *n.* 【医】走马疳,口颊坏疽.
gan·gre·nous [ˈɡæŋɡrinəs] *a.* 【医】坏疽性的.
gangs·man [ˈɡæŋzmən] *n.* *(pl.* ***-men)*** ①= ganger. ②= gangster.
gang·ster [ˈɡæŋstə] *n.* 〔美〕匪徒,歹徒,恶棍. **~dom** 〔集合词〕匪徒,歹徒,恶棍；黑社会. **-ism** *n.* 〔美〕歹徒的犯罪行为.
Gang·tok [ˈɡʌŋtɔk] *n.* 甘托克〔锡金首都〕.
gangue [ɡæŋ] *n.* 【矿】脉石,矿石中的杂质,矿物渣,尾矿.
gang·way [ˈɡæŋwei] *n.* ①通路. ②(剧场、音乐厅等座位间的) 过道. ③〔英〕下议院中划分前后座位的通道. ④(运输木材的)倾斜道. ⑤【矿】主巷道,主运输平巷；木桥. ⑥【船】舷门,舷梯,跳板 (= gangboard). ⑦(工地上临时搭建的)木板路. ***bring to the*** ~ (把水手)拉到舷门鞭打. ***members above [below] the*** ~ 英国议会下院中同其所属政党政策意见较一致[不甚一致]的议员. — *int.* 闪开！让路！ ~ **ladder** 舷梯.
gan·is·ter, gan·nis·ter [ˈɡænistə] *n.* ①【地】致密硅岩. ②【冶】硅石〔酸性炉衬料〕. ~ **brick** 硅砖. ~ **sand** 硅粉,石英砂.
gan·ja, gan·jah [ˈɡɑːndʒə] *n.* ①大麻. ②烟熏过的大麻叶和花 (尤指卷作香烟状作为麻醉药吸食的大麻叶和花) (= marijuana).
gan·net [ˈɡænit] *n.* ①【动】塘鹅. ②〔俚〕贪婪的人. **-ry** *n.*
gan·oid [ˈɡænɔid] *n.* 【鱼】硬鳞鱼,光鳞鱼. — *a.* (鱼)硬鳞的,光鳞的. *a* ~ *scale* 硬鳞.
gan·o·in [ˈɡænəuin] *n.* (鱼鳞的)闪光质,硬鳞质.
gant·let[1] [ˈɡɔːntlit] *n.* = gauntlet[1].
gant·let[2] [ˈɡɔːntlit] *n.* ①(已往军队中使犯人走在两排人当间受鞭打的)夹笞刑. ②交叉射击, 交叉火网. ③【铁路】(二线经过桥或隧道时的) 汇合的一段轨道, 套式轨道的套迭处. ~ *track* 套式轨道. ***run the*** ~ 受夹笞刑；受夹攻,遭受严格考验. — *vt.* 使(轨道等)套迭.
gant·line [ˈɡæntˌlain] *n.* 【海】桅顶吊索.
gan·try [ˈɡæntri] *n.* ①桶架. ②【机】龙门起重机；(起重机的)构台[门架]. ③【铁路】跨轨信号架. ④【宇】导弹拖车. ⑤火箭平台〔具有多层平台并可移动,用以吊竖火箭及发射前检修〕. ~ **crane** 高架龙门起重机, 跨线起重机.
Gan·y·mede [ˈɡænimiːd] *n.* ①【希神】甘尼米〔宙斯神的侍酒童子〕. ②〔谑〕侍酒少年, 侍者. ③【天】木星的第三卫星.
GAO = General Accounting Office 〔美〕总审计局.
gaol [dʒeil] *n.* 牢狱,监狱. *be sent to* ~ 入狱. ***deliver a*** ~ 提审监狱中的全部罪犯. ***in*** ~ 在押. — *vt.* 监禁,使…下牢,把…关进监狱. ★美国用 jail [dʒeil], 英国在正式文件中用 gaol, 一般文字中 gaol 与 jail 通用. **~-bird** 囚犯；惯犯；恶棍, 无赖. ~ **delivery** ①越狱,劫狱. ②【英法】提审囚犯出清监狱. ~ **fever** (从前在监狱中流行的)恶性伤寒. ~ **sentences** 徒刑.
gaol·er [ˈdʒeilə] *n.* 监狱看守.
gaol·er·ess [ˈdʒeiləris] *n.* 监狱女看守.
gap [ɡæp] *n.* ①(墙壁、篱笆等的)裂口,裂缝；豁口,缺口.【军】突破口. ②(意见的)龃龉,分歧；隔阂,距离,差距. ③山峡,隘口. ④间隙；【机】火花隙；【空】(双翼机的)翼隔. ⑤(文章等中的)脱漏, 中断；(知识等的)空白,缺陷. *a* ~ *in historical records* 史料的中断. *credibility* ~ 信用差距. *generation* ~ 代沟〔不同代的人之间的思想隔阂〕. *~s between teeth* 齿缝. *the* ~ *between imports and exports* 进出口差额. ***bridge [close, fill, stop, supply] a*** ~ 填补空白,弥补缺陷. ***stand in the*** ~ 首当其冲,挺身阻挡. — *vt.* 使豁裂,使生罅隙. — *vi.* 豁开. **~-filler** *n.* 【无】雷达辅助天线. **~-toothed** *a.* (由于缺牙)齿缝很大的.
Gap·a [ˈɡæpə] *n.* 地对空无线电导航飞行器.
gape [ɡeip] *n.* ①张口；打呵欠. ②张口呆看. ③豁口. ④【动】嘴裂,喙裂；口张时的阔度. ***the ~s*** (家禽的)张口病；〔谑〕打一阵呵欠. — *vi.* ①张大嘴；打呵欠. ②(地面等)开裂；裂开. ③目瞪口呆地凝视. ~ ***after [for]*** 渴望得到. ~ ***at*** 张口结舌地看,吃惊地呆看. **~-mouthed** *a.* 张开大嘴的. ~ **worm** (引起家禽患张口病的)线虫.
gap·er [ˈɡeipə] *n.* ①张口呆看的人. ②打呵欠的人. ③印度阔嘴鸟；张口蛤蜊. ④〔美俚〕镜子.
gape·seed [ˈɡeipsiːd] *n.* 〔英方〕注目；引起注意的人[事]. ***buy [seek, sow]*** ~ 〔讽〕在市场上闲逛, 在市场上呆看.
gapped [ɡæpt] *a.* 豁裂的,有缺口的.
gap·py [ˈɡæpi] *a.* 罅隙多的；有裂口的；脱节的.
gar [ɡɑː] *n.* *(pl.* *~, ~s)* 【动】①雀鳝. ②=needlefish.
GAR = guided aircraft rocket 机载导弹.
gar·age [ˈɡærɑːʒ, -ridʒ] *n.* 汽车库,汽车间；(汽车)修车场；飞机库. — *vt.* 把(汽车)开进车库[修理厂]. **~man** 汽车库工人, 汽车修理厂工人. ~ **sale** 车库买卖〔在卖主家进行的现场旧货出售, 因多在卖主家的车库前进行, 故名〕.
garb[1] [ɡɑːb] *n.* ①服装(尤指某一种人穿的服装)；装束. ②外表,外衣. *in clerical* ~ 牧师服,僧袍. *fantastic* ~ 奇装异服. *in the* ~ *of a sailor* 穿着水手服. *Hamlet in Chinese* ~ 中译本《汉姆莱特》. — *vt.* 〔常用被动语态或接 oneself〕穿,装扮. ~ *oneself as a sailor* 打扮成水手模样. *be elegantly ~ed* 衣着雅致.
garb[2] [ɡɑːb] *n.* 【徽】麦束.
gar·bage [ˈɡɑːbidʒ] *n.* ①残羹剩菜；丢弃的食物；〔美俚〕食品. ②废料, 脏东西. ③浮游于太空的失去作用的人造卫星[火箭]. ④无用的数据. *the* ~ *heap of history* 历史的垃圾堆. *literary* ~ 无聊读物. ~ **can [truck]** 垃圾箱[车].
gar·ban·zo [ɡɑːˈbænzəu, Sp. ɡɑːˈvɑːθəu, -səu] *n.* *(pl.* *~s)* 〔Sp.〕【植】鹰嘴豆,埃及豆,雏豆 (=chick-pea).
gar·ble [ˈɡɑːbl] *vt.* ①断章取义,任意窜改(原文等). ②无意中歪曲[混淆](事实,意思等). ③〔罕〕精选,筛选.
gar·board [ˈɡɑːbɔːd, -bəd] *n.* 【船】(贴近龙骨的)龙骨翼板〔又称 ~ strake〕.
Gar·ci·a [ɡɑːʃjə] *n.* 加西亚〔姓氏〕.
gar·çon [ɡarˈsɔ̃] *n.* *(pl.* *~s* [-sɔ̃]) 〔F.〕(旅馆中的) 男服务员；少年.
gar·dant [ˈɡɑːdənt] *a.* = guardant.
gar·den [ˈɡɑːdn] *n.* ①庭园；花园；菜园；果园. ②〔*pl.*〕公园,(动、植物)园；露天饮食店. ③〔*pl.*〕〔英〕(一排或数排房屋并种有树木的)…广场,…街. 土地肥沃的地区,精耕细作的土地. ④〔G-〕〔美〕新泽西州的别名. ⑤〔the G-〕伊壁鸠鲁 (Epicurus) 学派. *Everything in your garden is nice.* 你家园子里的一切都是好的〔反语,其真实含义为:"别把你家的一切都看得那么美！"〕. *a back* ~ 后花园. *botanical [zoological] ~s* 植[动]物园. *a kitchen*

~ 菜园. *a market* ~ 供应市场菜蔬、花果的农圃. *nursery* ~ 苗圃. *a public* ~ 公园. *Queen's G-* 女王广场. ***common or*** ~ 普通的,平凡的. ***G of Eden*** (《圣经》中所说亚当和夏娃所住的)伊甸园,没有罪恶的圣洁之地. ***lead sb. up [down] the ~ (path)*** 使迷惑,诱人误入歧途. ***the G- of the Gods*** (美国 Colorado Springs 市附近的) 奇岩园地带. — *a.* ①花园的, 果园的. ②花园似的,风光优美的. ③生长于园中的,在园中栽培的〔相对于野生的而言〕. ④普通的, 平凡的, 老一套的. — *vi.* 栽培花木,从事园艺. ~ *for pleasure* 栽培花木以自娱. — *vt.* 把…开辟为花园〔菜园、果园〕. ~ **apartments** 花园公寓〔周围有草坪或绿树荫封的公寓〕. ~ **balsam** 凤仙花 *(Impatients balsamian)*. ~ **city** 花园城市. ~ **cress**【植】独行菜 *(lepidium sativum)* 〔偶尔种作色拉用〕. ~ **engine** 庭园用小型抽水机. ~ **frame** 栽培植物用框架. ~ **glass** (罩植物用的)钟形玻璃罩. ~ **hiliotrope**【植】缬单 *(Valeriana officinalis)* 〔花极芳香,根味极辛烈,曾用作药草〕. ~ **party** 游园会. ~ **plant** 栽培植物. ~ **plot** 园地. ~ **seat** 庭园坐椅;〔英〕公共汽车顶层坐位. **G- State** 花园州〔美国新泽西州的别称〕. ~ **stuff** 蔬菜, 水果. **~-variety** *a.* 普通的,平凡的,老一套的.

Gar·den [ˈgɑːdn] *n.* 加登〔姓氏〕.

gar·dened [ˈgɑːdnd] *a.* 有花园的.

gar·den·er [ˈgɑːdnə] *n.* 园丁,花匠;菜农;园艺爱好者. *a jobbing* ~ 临时园林工人. *a nursery* ~ 苗圃经营者. *a market* ~ 菜农.

gar·de·ni·a [gɑːˈdiːniə] *n.*【植】栀子;〔G-〕栀子属.

gar·den·ing [ˈgɑːdniŋ] *n.* 园艺(学).

Gar·di·ner [ˈgɑːdnə] *n.* 加德纳〔姓氏〕.

Gard·ner [ˈgɑːdnə] *n.* 加德纳〔姓氏〕.

gar·dy·loo [ˌgɑːdiˈluː] *int.* 泼水啰!〔古时英国爱丁堡居民向窗外泼水而向行人发出的警告声〕.

gare·fowl [ˈgɛəfaul] *n.*【鸟】大海雀.

gar·fish [ˈgɑːfiʃ] *n.*【动】长嘴硬鳞的鱼(如颌针鱼).

gar·ga·ney [ˈgɑːgəni] *n.*【动】巡凫 *(Anas querquedula)*.

gar·gan·tu·an [gɑːˈgæntjuən] *a.* 庞大的, 巨大的〔该词源于 *Gargantua*, 他是法国讽刺作家拉伯雷 (*Rabelais*) 在其作品《巨人传》中所描写的一个食欲巨大的国王〕.

gar·get [ˈgɑːgit] *n.* (牛、猪等的)喉肿;乳房炎.

gar·gle [ˈgɑːgl] *vt.,vi.* ①漱(喉). ②(漱口时从喉底)发出(咕噜声). — *n.* ①含漱剂. ②漱口声,咕噜声.

gar·goyle [ˈgɑːgɔil] *n.* ①【建】(哥德式建筑上)怪形生物状的滴水嘴〔承霤口〕. ②奇形怪状的雕刻像. ③面貌古怪的人.

Gar·i·bal·di [ˌgæriˈbɔːldi], **Giuseppe** 加里波的〔1807—1888,意大利爱国者,将军〕.

gar·i·bal·di [ˌgæriˈbɔːldi] *n.* ①(女人、小儿用的)红色阔罩衫〔最初系仿照加里波的之红衫军所穿红色军服式样〕. ②〔美〕加利福尼亚红鱼. ③夹有酸栗果酱的饼干.

gar·ish [ˈgɛəriʃ] *a.* 耀眼的;(服装等)过于艳丽的,华丽而俗气的;(文章等)华美的,华而不实的. **-ly** *ad.* **-ness** *n.*

gar·land [ˈgɑːlənd] *n.* ①花环,花冠;【建】华饰;【海】索环. ②胜利和荣誉的象征. ③〔古〕诗歌选集. ***carry away [gain, win] the*** ~ 获胜,夺得锦标. — *vt.* ①给…饰以花环;给…戴上花环. ②把…做成花环.

Gar·land [ˈgɑːlənd] *n.* 加兰〔姓氏,男子名〕.

gar·lic [ˈgɑːlik] *n.* 蒜,大蒜. *a clove of* ~ 一瓣大蒜. ***be*** ~ ***for dessert*** 〔俚〕最不受欢迎的东西. **gar·lick·y** *a.* 大蒜一样的,有大蒜气味的;吃大蒜的.

gar·ment [ˈgɑːmənt] *n.* ①衣服,(尤指)外衣;外套;长袍. ②〔*pl.*〕服装;衣着. ③外观,外表;(物件的)包皮. — *vt.* 穿〔主用过去分词形式〕. *a lady ~ed in silk* 一位穿着绸衣服的女士. ~ **bag** 装衣服的塑料袋. **G-Center** 服装中心〔美国纽约曼哈坦区内服装工厂和时装商店林立的街区〕.

gar·ner [ˈgɑːnə] *n.* ①〔诗〕谷仓. ②蓄积,积累物. — *vt.* ①〔诗〕贮藏,积累. ②〔美口〕得…分〔票〕.

Gar·ner [ˈgɑːnə] *n.* 加纳〔姓氏〕.

gar·net[1] [ˈgɑːnit] *n.* ①〔矿〕石榴石. ②石榴红(色). **~-berry** *n.*【植】红醋栗. ~ **laser** 石榴石光激射器. **~-paper** 用石榴石细沙做的沙纸.

gar·net[2] [ˈgɑːnit] *n.*【船】装货用的滑车.

gar·ni [gɑːˈniː] *a.* (为食品)添配料的.

gar·ni·er·ite [ˈgɑːniərait] *n.*【矿】硅镁镍矿.

gar·nish [ˈgɑːniʃ] *n.* ①装饰品;(文章的)修饰;华丽的词藻. ②【烹】配菜,配头. — *vt.* ①装饰,文饰. ②给…加配菜,给…加配头. ③【法】= garnishee. ***swept and ~ed*** 扫除干净,布置一新.

gar·nish·ee [ˌgɑːniˈʃiː] *n.*【法】(接到扣押令的)第三债务人. ~ *order* 扣押令. — *vt.* 通知(受托人)扣押债务人的财产;向(第三债务人)下达扣押令;扣押(债务人的财产);扣发(债务人的工资).

gar·nish·er [ˈgɑːniʃə] *n.* ①装饰者. ②【法】通告扣押债权者.

gar·nish·ment [ˈgɑːniʃmənt] *n.* ①装饰,装饰品. ②【法】扣押债权的通知,(对第三者债务人发出的)出庭命令.

gar·ni·ture [ˈgɑːnitʃə] *n.* ①装饰品,摆设. ②服装,服饰. ③【烹】配头,配菜.

ga·rot(t)e [gəˈrɔt] *n., vt.* = garrotte.

gar·pike [ˈgɑːˌpaik] *n.*【鱼】雀鳝.

gar·ran [ˈgærən] *n.* = garron.

gar·ret[1] [ˈgærət, -rit] *n.* ①屋顶层,顶楼,阁楼,亭子间. ②〔俚〕头. *be wrong in the* ~ 头脑有毛病. *have one's ~ unfurnished* 头脑空虚,没学识. ***from cellar to ~ = from ~ to cellar [kitchen]*** 整幢房屋,屋里上上下下.

gar·ret[2] [ˈgærət, -rit] *vt.*【建】(用小石)填塞缝隙.

Gar·ret(t) [ˈgærət] *n.* 加勒特〔男子名〕.

gar·ret·eer [ˌgærəˈtiə] *n.* ①住顶楼的人. ②穷文人;亭子间作家.

gar·ri·son [ˈgærisn] *n.* ①守备队,卫戍部队,警备队,驻军. ②要塞,驻防地,卫戍区. ***be sent into*** ~ 奉派防守. ***go into*** ~去接防. ***in*** ~ 驻防,接防. ***on ~ duty*** 负责防守. — *vt.* 派兵驻守;把…派作守备队. ~ **artillery** 要塞炮兵. ~ **cap**【美军】①军便帽,船形帽(= overseas cap). ②军帽(= service cap). **G- finish** (赛马临近终点时优胜骑手从后面作的)终点冲刺. ~ **hospital** 卫戍医院. ~ **town** 有军队驻守的城镇.

Gar·ri·son [ˈgærisn] *n.* 加里森〔姓氏〕.

gar·ron [ˈgærən] *n.* 矮马.

gar·rot(t)e [gəˈrɔt] *n.* ①螺环绞刑〔西班牙的一种绞刑,行刑时旋紧,套于犯人颈上的螺钉〕;螺环绞具. ②(偷袭敌人时用以勒杀敌方哨兵等的) 绞颈索. ③勒杀抢劫. — *vt.* ①处…以螺环绞刑. ②(用绞颈索等)勒…的咽喉(使失去抵抗力). ③勒杀抢劫.

gar·rot·(t)er [gəˈrɔtə] *n.* 绞杀者;勒杀抢劫的强盗.

gar·ru·li·ty [gəˈruːliti] *n.* 饶舌,喋喋不休.

gar·ru·lous [ˈgæruləs] *a.* ①饶舌的,絮聒的,喋喋不休的. ②(鸟) 叽叽喳喳的;(流水) 潺潺不息的. **-ly** *ad.* **-ness** *n.*

gar·ter [ˈgɑːtə] *n.* ①〔*pl.*〕袜带. ★英国多半说 suspenders. ②〔英〕〔the G-〕嘉德勋章〔最高勋章〕,嘉德勋位. ③〔海俚〕〔*pl.*〕脚镣. *G- King of Arms* 英国勋章院的主管人. — *vt.* ①用袜带系紧. ②授给…嘉德勋位. ~ **belt** 吊袜带. ~ **snake** (美国无毒)花蛇. ~ **stitch** (织物的)平针织法,平针图案.

garth [gɑːθ] *n.* ①〔古〕庭院,花园;围场. ②修道院内的空地. ③为捕鱼而筑起的坝〔堰〕,鱼梁.

Garth [gɑːθ] *n.* 加斯〔姓氏,男子名〕.

Gar·y [ˈgɛəri] *n.* 盖里〔姓氏,男子名〕.

gas [gæs] *n.* *(pl. ~es* [ˈgæsiz]*)* ①气, 气体, 气态〔*cf.*

G

fluid; solid]. ②可燃气,煤气,沼气;【矿】瓦斯. ③【军】毒气(= poison gas); 毒瓦斯,(麻醉用的)笑气. ④煤气灯;〔美口〕汽油,(汽车等的)油门. ⑤〔俚〕空谈,吹牛. ⑥〔美俚〕令人愉快的人[事]; 使某人受到很大影响的人[事]. *Air is a mixture of ~es.* 空气是多种气体的混合物. *laughing ~* 笑气(即一氧化二氮). *marsh ~* 沼气. *natural ~* 天然气. *nerve ~* 神经毒气. *poison ~* 毒气. *a ~ projectile* 毒气弹. *tear ~* 催泪性毒气. *light the ~* 点亮气灯; 点燃煤气灶. ***step on the ~*** 〔美〕踏动(汽车的)加速器; 加速,赶紧,加油干. ***turn down the ~*** 扭小气灯. ***turn on the ~*** 开煤气; 〔口〕打开话匣子;吹牛. ***turn out [off] the ~*** 关掉煤气;〔口〕关掉话匣子, 停止吹牛. — *vi.* ①发散气体. ②给汽车加油. ③使用毒气. ④〔口〕空谈, 乱吹牛. — *vt.* ①供给…煤气,给…灌充煤气,给(汽车)加油. ②向…放毒气; 用毒气攻击[杀伤]. ③【纺】用煤气烧去[处理](布毛等). ④〔美口〕使获得快感,使开心,使兴奋. *be gassed* 中毒气. *~ the yarn* 烧去纱上的毛头. *~* ***up*** ①〔美口〕给汽车加油. ②〔美俚〕开着(汽车的)油门(以备随时开走). ~ **bacillus** 产气荚膜(梭状芽胞)杆菌,韦氏杆菌. ~**bag** (气球的)气囊;〔俚〕饶舌者,话匣子,废话连篇的人. ~ **black** 炭黑 (= carbon black). ~ **bomb [shell]** 毒气(炸)弹. ~ **bracket** 煤气灯管. ~ **burner** 煤气灶, 煤气灯; 煤气喷嘴, 煤气火焰. ~ **chamber** 死刑毒气室; (苹果等的)贮藏室. ~ **coal** (适于提炼煤气的)气煤. ~ **coke** 煤气焦炭. ~ **constant** 气体常数. ~ **current** 离子电流. ~**-eater** 耗油量大的汽车. ~ **engine** 内燃机,气体发动机. ~ **field** 天然气田. ~ **fire** 煤气取暖器. ~**-fired** *a.* 烧煤气的, 以煤气为燃料的. ~ **fitter** 煤气装置人;承装煤气的店家. ~ **fitting** 煤气装置工程; 〔*pl.*〕煤气装备. ~ **fixture** 煤气灯装置. ~ **furnace** 煤气发生炉,煤气炉. ~ **gangrene**【医】气菌坏疽. ~ **helmet [gas mask]** 防毒面具. ~**holder** 煤气库,煤气罐; 贮气柜[器]. ~**house** 煤气库; 〔喻〕贫民区; 〔美俚〕化学实验室. ~ **jet** 煤气喷嘴, 煤气火焰. ~**-laser** 气体激光器. ~ **law** 气体定律. ~**light** 煤气灯光;气灯. ~**lighter** 煤气点燃器;打火机. ~ **liquor** 煤气液,液化气. ~**lit** *a.* 以煤气灯照明的, 广泛使用煤气灯的. ~ **log** (煤气炉子的)燃烧嘴. ~ **main** 煤气总管. ~**man** 煤气工人;煤气收费员;【矿】通风员,瓦斯检查员. ~**mantle** 煤气网罩. ~ **meter** ①煤气表,气量计. ②贮气器,煤气罐 *(lie like a ~ meter* 乱撒谎). ~ **motor** 煤气(发动)机. ~ **oil** 瓦斯油,粗柴油. ~ **oven** 煤气灶. ~ **pipe**(煤)气管. ~ **plant**【植】白鲜*(Dictamnus albus)*〔开白色或浅红色花朵,芳香,炎热的夜晚则放出可燃气体〕. ~ **poker** *n.* 煤气点火棒. ~ **producer** 煤气发生炉. ~ **proof** *a.* 防毒气的, 不透气的. ~ **ring** (有环形喷火头的)煤气灶. ~ **station**〔美〕(汽油)加油站. ~ **stove** 煤气炉. ~**-tar** 煤焦油. ~**tight** *a.* 不透气的,气密的,密封的. ~ **turbine** 燃气轮机,燃气透平. ~ **well** 天然气井. ~**works** 〔*pl.*〕〔作 *sing.* 用〕①煤气厂. ②〔英俚〕下议院.

GAS = gasoline.

gas·a·ter·ia [ˌgæsəˈtiəriə] *n.* 〔美俚〕(汽车的) 自动加油站.

Gas·con [ˈgæskən] *n.* ①(以夸口著名的法国) 加斯科尼 *(Gascony)* 人. ②〔g-〕夸口的人,吹牛的人. — *a.* ①加斯科尼的,加斯科尼人的. ②〔g-〕夸口的,吹牛的. **-ism** *n.* 夸口,吹牛.

gas·con·ade [ˌgæskəˈneid] *n., vi.* 自夸,吹牛.

Gas·co·ny [ˈgæskəni] *n.* 加斯科尼〔法国西南部一地区〕.

gas·e·i·ty [gæˈsiːiti] *n.* 气态.

gas·e·lier [ˌgæsəˈliə] *n.* 枝形煤气吊灯.

gas·e·ous [ˈgæsiəs, ˈgeizjəs] *a.* ①气体的, 气态的. ②无实质的, 空虚的. ③过热的. ④〔美俚〕不可靠的. *~ density* 气体密度. *a ~ mixture* 气体混合物. *~ steam* 过热蒸汽. **-ness** *n.*

ga·ser [ˈgeizə] *n.*【物】γ射线激射器.

gash[1] [gæʃ] *n.* ①深长的伤口[切痕]. ②(地面等的) 裂缝. ③划开. — *vt., vi.* (在…上)划深长切口,划开.

gash[2] [gæʃ] *a.*〔英俚〕【海】多余的,备用的.

gash[3] [gæʃ] *a.*〔Scot.〕①衣冠楚楚的. ②伶俐的, 干净利落的.

gas·i·fi·a·ble [ˈgæsifaiəbl] *a.* 可气化的.

gas·i·fi·ca·tion [ˌgæsifiˈkeiʃən] *n.* 气化(作用).

gas·i·fi·er [ˈgæsifaiə] *n.* 气化器,燃气发生器.

gas·i·form [ˈgæsifɔːm] *a.* 气体的,气态的.

gas·i·fy [ˈgæsifai] *vt., vi.* (使)气化;(使)成为气体.

Gas·kell [ˈgæskəl] *n.* 加斯克尔〔姓氏〕.

gas·ket [ˈgæskit] *n.* ①【海】束帆索. ②【机】密封垫,密封片,垫圈,衬垫,填料.

gas·kin [ˈgæskin] *n.* ①〔*pl.*〕〔废〕(十六世纪前后的)灯笼裤; (打猎用的)皮绑腿. ②(马或其他蹄类动物的)后大腿.

gas·less [ˈgæslis] *a.* 无气体的,不用气体的.

gas·o·gene [ˈgæsədʒiːn] *n.* ①(小型)煤气发生器. ②(小型)汽水制造机.

gas·o·lier [ˌgæsəˈliə] *n.* = gaselier.

gas·o·line, gas·o·lene [ˈgæsəliːn, ˌgæsəˈliːn] *n.* 〔美〕汽油. ★英国叫 petrol. *gelatinized [jellied] ~* 凝固汽油 (= napalm). *a ~ bomb* 汽油弹. ~ **mileage** 汽车耗1加仑汽油平均所行的英里数.

gas·om·e·ter [gæˈsɔmitə] *n.* ①气量计; 煤气计算表. ②贮气器,煤气罐.

gas·om·e·try [gæˈsɔmitri] *n.* 气体计量.

gasp [gɑːsp] *vi.* ①喘,喘气; 透不过气. ②热望,切望*(after; for)*. — *vt.* 喘着气说,气吁吁地说 *(out)*. ~ ***one's life away*** = ~ ***out one's life*** = ~ ***one's last*** 死去. ~ ***up*** 咽气,断气. — *n.* 喘气; 屏息,透不过气. ***at one's last ~*** 奄奄一息. ***at the last ~*** ①奄奄一息. ②最后一刻,最后. ***prolong one's last ~*** 苟延残喘. ***to the last ~*** 到死.

gasp·er [ˈgɑːspə] *n.* ①喘气者. ②〔俚〕廉价香烟.

gasp·ing [ˈgɑːspiŋ] *a.* 气喘的,痉挛的,阵发性的. **-ly** *ad.*

gassed [gæst] *a.* 〔美俚〕喝醉酒的.

gas·ser [ˈgæsə] *n.* ①〔俚〕爱夸夸其谈的人,爱吹牛的人. ②天然气井. ③〔俚〕出类拔萃的人, 非常有趣的事.

Gas·ser [ˈgæsə] *n.* 加瑟〔姓氏〕.

gas·si·ness [ˈgæsinis] *n.* ①气态, 充满气体. ②爱说空话,夸夸其谈,吹牛.

gas·sing [ˈgæsiŋ] *n.* ①用煤气处理, 烧(布毛). ②毒气战;放毒气. ③〔俚〕瞎聊天. ④充气,放气,出气. ⑤起气泡,真空管中出现液体.

gas·sy [ˈgæsi] *a.* ①气体的, 气状的; 充满气体的. ②专好吹牛的,(话等)夸大的.

gaster-, gastero- *comb.f.* 表示"胃的": *gastero*poda.

gas·ter·o·pod [ˈgæstərəpɔd] *n.*【动】腹足纲软体动物〔如螺蛳等〕.

gastr-, gastri- *comb. f.*, 表示 "胃的": *gastr*ectomy, *gastr*itis.

gas·trae·a [gæsˈtriːə] *n.*【动】原肠祖,原肠幼虫.

gas·tral·gi·a [gæsˈtrældʒiə] *n.*【医】胃痛.

gas·trec·ta·sia [ˌgæstrekˈteiʒə] *n.* 胃扩张 (=gastrectasis).

gas·trec·to·my [gæsˈtrektəmi] *n. (pl. -mies)*【医】胃切除术.

gas·tric [ˈgæstrik] *a.* 胃的. ~ **fever** 胃热;(尤指)伤寒. ~ **juice** 胃液. ~ **ulcer** 胃溃疡.

gas·trin [ˈgæstrin] *n.*【生化】促胃液(激)素.

gas·tri·tis [gæsˈtraitis] *n.* 胃炎.

gastro- *comb. f.* 表示"胃的": *gastro*enteritis.

gas·tro·cam·e·ra [ˌgæstrəuˈkæmərə] *n.* 胃内摄影机.

gas·tro·col·ic [ˌgæstrəuˈkɔlik] *a.* 胃和大肠的；附于胃和大肠的．

gas·tro·derm [ˈgæstrəuˌdəːm] *n.* 内胚层(=endoderm)．

gas·tro·en·ter·it·ic [ˌgæstrəuinˈteritik] *a.* 胃肠的．

gas·tro·en·ter·i·tis [ˌgæstrəuˌentəˈraitis] *n.*【医】胃肠炎．

gas·tro·en·ter·ol·o·gy [ˌgæstrəuˌentəˈrɔlədʒi] *n.*【医】胃肠病学．**-o·gist** *n.*

gas·tro·in·tes·ti·nal [ˌgæstrəuinˈtestənl] *a.* 胃肠的．

gas·tro·lith [ˈgæstrəliθ] *n.*【医】胃结石．

gas·trol·o·ger [gæsˈtrɔlədʒə] *n.* 烹调学家，美食学家．

gas·trol·o·gist [gæsˈtrɔlədʒist] *n.* = gastrologer.

gas·trol·o·gy [gæsˈtrɔlədʒi] *n.* 烹调法〔学〕，美食学．

gas·tro·nome [ˈgæstrənəum], **gas·tron·o·mer** [gæsˈtrɔnəmə], **gas·tron·o·mist** [gæsˈtrɔnəmist] *n.* 善于烹调的人，考究饮食的人．

gas·tro·nom·ic(al) [ˌgæstrəuˈnɔmik(əl)] *a.* 烹调法的．*a* ~ *emporium*〔美俚〕餐馆；公寓．

gas·tron·o·my [gæsˈtrɔnəmi] *n.* 烹调法．

gas·tro·pod [ˈgæstrəpɔd] *n.* = gasteropod.

gas·tro·scope [ˈgæstrəskəup] *n.*【医】胃(窥)镜．

gas·trot·o·my [gæsˈtrɔtəmi] *n.*【医】胃切开术．

gas·tro·trich [ˈgæstrətrik] *n.*【动】腹毛类(*Gastrotricha*)动物．

gas·tro·vas·cu·lar [ˌgæstrəuˈvæskjulə] *a.*【动】①具消化及循环职能的．②具有消化及循环双重职能的器官的．

gas·tru·la [ˈgæstrulə] *n.* (*pl.* **-lae** [-liː])【动】原肠胚．

gas·tru·la·tion [ˌgæstruˈleiʃən] *n.*【医】原肠胚形成．

gat[1] [gæt] *n.*〔美俚〕左轮手枪．

gat[2] [gæt] *v.*〔古〕get 的过去式．

gat[3] [gæt] *n.* (山峡或沙洲间的)狭航道．

gate[1] [geit] *n.* ①大门，扉，篱笆门，门扇．②闸门；城门；洞门；隘口，峡道．③【冶】浇注道，浇口，切口；【无】门电路，选通电路，选通脉冲，启开脉冲，时间限制电路．④(运动会、展览会等的)门票收入；观众数；入场费．⑤〔英〕伦敦 Billingsgate, Newgate 等的略称．⑥锯架．⑦电影放映机镜头窗口．⑧〔俚〕解雇．*a folding* ~ 折叠门，活栅门．*a turnpike* ~ 征收通行税的关卡．*go [pass] through the* ~*(s)* 进门．*enter at a* ~ 从大门进去．*There was a* ~ *of thousands.* 观众数以千计．***at the*** ~***(s) of death*** 奄奄一息．***crash the*** ~〔俚〕擅自入场．***get the*** ~〔美〕被赶出，被解雇．***give sb. the*** ~〔美〕迫令退席；解雇．***keep the*** ~ 守门．***open a*** ~ ***to [for]*** 大开方便之门，给…以机会．***the*** ~ ***of horn*** 应验的梦兆，角门．***the*** ~ ***of ivory*** 不应验的梦兆，牙门〔据神话传说，应验的梦自角门入，不应验的梦自牙门入〕．— *vt.* ①在…装门．②(英大学)禁止(学生)外出．③用门控制．~ **bill**(英大学)迟到登记簿；迟到罚金．~**-crash** *vi.*〔俚〕无券入场，擅行入场．~ **-crasher**〔俚〕无券入场者，擅行入场的人．~**fold** 折叠插页．~**house** ①城门上面或旁边的屋子；门楼．②门房．③水电站闸门上的控制室．~**keeper** = ~**man** 看门人，门警，门房．~**-leg(ged) table** 折叠式桌子．~ **meeting** 收费的运动会．~ **money** 入场费．~**post** 门柱 (*between you and me and the* ~*post* 极秘密的，严守秘密的)．~**tender**〔美〕看守铁路平交道栏栅的人．~ **tower** 门楼．~**way** 门口，入口，通路；手段．**-less** *a.* 无门的．

gate[2] [geit] *n.* ①〔古〕街道，路〔一般作地名用，如 kirk*gate*〕．②〔方〕方式，方法．

Gates [geits] *n.* 盖茨〔姓氏〕．

gath·er [ˈgæðə] *vt.* ①集合，聚集；搜集．②摘，摘取，采集；征收(税等)．③蓄积；积累；增长．④皱(眉)；缝(衣褶)．⑤抱，围住，拉紧．⑥得出(印象、感想等)；推断，推测 (*that*)．⑦鼓起(勇气)；恢复(健康)；振作(精神)．⑧【火箭】导入，引入．~ *crops* 收庄稼．~ *flowers* 采花．~ *experience* 积累经验．~ *speed* 加速．~ *strength* 恢复体力．~ *taxes* 收税．~ *up one's tools* 收拾起工具．*The demand* ~*ed weight.* 要求渐渐增强了．~ *one's brows* 皱眉．— *vi.* ①聚集，蓄积；增长，增加．②皱，缩．③(疮)化脓，出头．④【海】逼近，接近(目标)．*The dusk is* ~*ing.* 暮色渐浓．***be*** ~***ed to one's fathers [people]*** 见老祖宗去．~ ***breath*** 喘过气来．~ ***colour*** 血气变好．~ ***flesh*** 长肉，发胖．~ ***ground*** 得势．~ ***head*** 化脓；(暴风雨等)力量增强．~ ***in*** 收获；〔口〕拾得．~ ***in upon*** (轮齿)咬合．~ ***one's energies*** 集中精力，尽力．~ ***one's wits*** 聚精会神．~ ***oneself up [together]*** 鼓起勇气，打起精神．~ ***out*** 选出．~ ***together*** 集合，集聚，收集．~ ***up*** 收集；总括(事件)；蜷缩(手、脚等)；集中力量；培拢．~ ***volume*** 增大，变大．~ ***way***【海】开动，开始移动．— *n.* ①聚集；收缩．②〔常 *pl.*〕衣褶，折裥．**-a·ble** *a.* 可收集的，可积聚的．**-er** *n.* 收集者．

gath·er·ing [ˈgæðəriŋ] *n.* ①聚集；集会．②搜集，采集；积聚，积累．③化脓；脓疮．④捐赠，捐款．⑤(印好后依页码次序折叠成的)毛书．⑥衣褶．*a social* ~ 社交聚会，联欢会．~ **coal** (使火终夜不熄的)封火煤．~ **cry** 战斗召集令．~ **ground** 水源地．

Gat·ling gun [ˈgætliŋ] 格林炮；格林式机枪〔美国 *R. J. Gatling* 所发明〕．

GATT = General Agreement on Tariffs and Trade 关税及贸易总协定．

gauche [gəuʃ] *a.*〔F.〕不善交际的；不灵活的；笨拙的；不机智的．**-ly** *ad.* **-ness** *n.*

gau·che·rie [ˌgəuʃəˈriː] *n.* ①笨拙．②笨拙举动．

Gau·cho [ˈgautʃəu] *n.* (*pl.* ~***s***) 高卓人〔南美洲草原地带的牧人，多系西班牙人和印第安人的混血种〕．

gaud [gɔːd] *n.* ①花哨而俗气的装饰品；不值钱的小玩意．②〔*pl.*〕庸俗的排场〔宴会、仪式〕．

gau·de·a·mus [ˌgaudeiˈɑːmuːs, ˌgɔːdiːˈeiməs] *n.* 尽情欢乐(尤指高等学校学生的作乐)．

gaud·er·y [ˈgɔːdəri] *n.* 浮夸的外观；华丽的服装．

gaud·y[1] [ˈgɔːdi] *a.* (衣服、装饰、文风)炫丽的，俗气的，华而不实的．**-i·ly** *ad.* **-i·ness** *n.*

gaud·y[2] [ˈgɔːdi] *n.*〔英〕(英国大学中每年举行一次的)宴会，招待会．

gauf·fer [ˈgɔːfə] *n., vt.* = goffer.

gauge [geidʒ] *n.* ①规，量规，量器，量计，表．②标准尺寸，标准规格，(金属片等的)厚度，(枪炮的)口径，(电线等的)直径．③容量，范围．④【建】葺脚(铺覆的瓦，石板等的外露部分)；(铁路的)轨距，(汽车等两侧车轮间的)轮距；【印】版面宽度．⑤(估计、判断等的)方法，手段，标准．⑥【纺】隔距．⑦【海】= gage[2]．★美国在航海用语以外亦拼作 gage. *an altitude* ~ 高度计．*a broad* ~ 宽轨．*a go* ~ 通过规．*a level* ~ 水准仪．*a marking* ~ (木工的)划线器．*a narrow* ~ 窄轨．*a no-go* ~ 不通过规．*a pressure* ~ 压力计．*a rain* ~ 雨量器．*a remote transmitting* ~ 遥测仪．*a screw pitch* ~ 螺距规．*a slide* ~ 游标卡尺．*the standard* ~ 标准轨距(=1.435米)．*a water* ~ 水位表，水标尺．*a wind* ~ 风速计．***get the*** ~ ***of*** 探测意向．***have the lee*** ~ ***of*** 在…的下风；较…不利．***have the weather*** ~ ***of*** 在…的上风；较…有利．***take the*** ~ ***of*** 估计，估价．— *vt.* ①测，量；估计，估价．②使成标准尺寸；使合标准．~ **block** 规矩块．~ **cock** 试水位旋塞．~ **glass** (锅炉)水位玻璃管，量液玻璃管．~ **group**【物】规范群．~ **lath**【建】挂瓦条．~ **lathe**【机】样板车床．~ **length** 标距，计量 ~ **line** 轨线；计量管．密度．~ **pile**【建】定位桩．~ **pressure** 表压．~**reel** *n.*【纺】纤度计．~ **stuff**【建】装饰石膏．~ **table** 计量表，校正表．**-a·ble** *a.* 可计量的，可测量的．

gaug·er [ˈgeidʒə] *n.* ①计量者；计量器．②(国内货物税的)收税官．

gaug·ing [ˈgeidʒiŋ] *n.* 规测，用规检验，测量，校准．~ **rod** 计量竿，探测杆，表尺．

Gaul [gɔːl] *n.* ①高卢〔领有今意大利北部、法、比、荷等国,属古罗马帝国一部分〕. ②高卢人. ③法国人.

Gau·lei·ter [ˈgauˌlaitə] *n.* 〔G.〕 ①(纳粹德国的)省长,地方长官. ②〔喻〕土皇帝,小暴君.

Gaul·ish [ˈgɔːliʃ] *a.* ①高卢的,高卢人的;高卢语的. ②法国人的. — *n.* 高卢语.

Gaull·ism [ˈgɔːlizəm] *n.* 戴高乐主义.

Gaull·ist [ˈgɔːlist] *n.* 戴高乐派. — *a.* 戴高乐主义的.

gault [gɔːlt] *n.*【地】重粘土. ~ **clay** 重粘土,泥灰质粘土. ~ **stage**【考古】(早白垩世晚期的)高尔特阶.

gaul·the·ri·a [gɔːlˈθiəriə] *n.*【植】冬绿树 *(Gaultheria procumbens)*, 平铺白珠树.

gaunt [gɔːnt] *a.* ①瘦削的,憔悴的. ②萧瑟的,荒凉的. **-ly** *ad.* **-ness** *n.*

gaunt·let¹ [ˈgɔːntlit] *n.* ①(铠甲的)铁护手; 臂铠. ②(骑马、击剑等用的)长手套;(防护手套;长手套的)腕部. ***take [pick] up the ~*** 应战;护卫. ***threw [fling] down the ~*** 挑战.

gaunt·let² [ˈgɔːntlit] *n.* = gantlet².

gaun·try [ˈgɔːntri] *n.* = gantry.

gaur [gauə] *n.* *(pl. ~, ~s)*【动】mouse *(Bibos gaurus)*〔印度野牛,为世界最大的牛〕.

gauss [gaus] *n.*【物】高斯〔磁感应强度单位, 磁通量密度单位〕. ~'s system of unit 高斯单位制. ~ **number** 高斯随机数. ~ **theorem** 高斯定理. **-age** *n.* 高斯数.

Gauss·i·an [ˈgausiən] *a.* 高斯的. ~ **curve**【统】高斯曲线.

gauze [gɔːz] *n.* ①(棉、丝等织成的)薄纱,罗纱布;网纱. ②薄雾. *wire* ~ 铁纱. ~ **room** 滤尘间.

gauz·y [ˈgɔːzi] *a.* 罗纱似的;轻薄透明的. *a ~ mist* 薄雾. **-i·ly** *ad.* **-i·ness** *n.*

ga·vage [gəˈvɑːʒ] *n.*【医】管饲法.

G **gave** [geiv] give 的过去式.

gav·el [ˈgævəl] *n.* ①〔美〕(法官、会议主席等用的)小槌;拍卖槌. ②石匠用的大槌. — *vi.* 敲小槌(催促通过议案、要求注意等). — *vt.* (用敲小槌)强行通过(议案等),要求(注意).

ga·vi·al [ˈgeiviəl] *n.*【动】①恒河鳄 *(Gavialis gangeticus)*. ②马来鳄 *(Tomistoma schlegeli)*.

ga·vot(te) [gəˈvɔt] *n.* (起源于法国农村的)加伏特舞(曲). — *vi.* 跳加伏特舞.

gawk [gɔːk] *n.* 笨人;腼腆的人. ***a ~'s errand*** 徒劳.— *vi.* 发呆地看着.

gawk·y [ˈgɔːki] *a.* 鲁钝的, 笨拙的, 腼腆的. — *n.* 笨人,腼腆的人. **-i·ness** *n.*

gay [gei] *a.* ***(~er; ~est)*** ①快乐的, 快活的(人、性格、举动等);轻快的,欢快的. ②华美的, 花哨的; 衣服漂亮的. ③〔婉〕淫荡的, 放荡的,〔俚〕同性恋爱的. ④〔美俚〕脸皮厚的,冒失的. ~ *colors* 鲜艳的颜色. *a ~ lady* 荡妇. ~ *quarters* 风化区. ~ *science* 诗,(特指)情诗. ***go ~*** = *lead a ~ life* 过放荡生活. — *n.* 同性恋爱者. ~ **cat**〔美卑〕小流氓, 盗匪的小喽啰, 新流浪人. ~ **dog**〔美俚〕纵情逸乐者,追求声色者. **-ness** *n.*

Gay [gei] *n.* 盖伊〔女子名〕.

gay·e·ty [ˈgeiəti] *n.* = gaiety.

Gay-Pay-Oo [ˈgeiˈpeiˈuː] *n.* 格伯乌〔1922–1935年间的苏联国家政治保安部〕.

gay·wings [ˈgeiˌwiŋz] *n.*【植】少叶远志 *(Polygala paucifolia)*〔产于美国南部和加拿大〕.

gaz. = gazette; gazetter.

ga·za·bo [gəˈzeibəu] *n.* *(pl. ~s, ~es)*〔美古俚〕人,家伙〔常用于贬意〕.

gaze [geiz] *vi.* (在感慨、惊异、欢喜下)盯看, 凝视; 注视 *(at, into, on, upon)*. ★ 在好奇、惊恐、愚钝、挑战、无礼等表现下时普通用 stare. ~ *at scenery* 注视景色. ~ *into the sky* 凝视天空. ~ ***after*** *sb.* 目送某人. ~ ***round*** 左顾右盼, 四处观望. — *n.* 凝视; 注视. ***at ~*** 盯着. ***fix one's ~ upon*** 盯着看. **-r** *n.* 凝视者.

ga·ze·bo [gəˈziːbəu] *n.* *(pl. ~s, ~es)* ①塔楼, 阳台,凉亭;信号台. ②〔美俚〕= gazabo.

gaze·hound [ˈgeizˌhaund] *n.*〔古〕锐目猎犬〔凭视力而不是嗅觉猎取野物的,如:灵提〕.

ga·zelle [gəˈzel] *n.*【动】瞪羚. ***~-eyed*** 眼睛象瞪羚似的.

ga·zette [gəˈzet] *n.* ①〔英〕公报;(牛津大学等的)学报. ②新闻纸,报纸;(作报纸名)…新闻,…报. *an official ~* 正式公报. *London G-* 伦敦公报. *appear [be] in the ~* = *be named in the ~; go into the ~; have one's name in the ~* 被宣告破产. — *vt.* 〔英〕公告; 在公报上发表; 正式任命. ***be ~d out*** 被公布辞职. ***be ~d to*** *(a post)* 在公报上被任命(担任某项职务).

gaz·et·teer [ˌgæziˈtiə] *n.* ①地名词典; 地名索引. ②〔古〕公报记者.

gaz·o·gene [ˈgæzədʒiːn] *n.* = gasogene.

gaz·pa·cho [gɑːzˈpɑːtʃəu; Sp. gɑːθˈpɑːtʃəu] *n.*〔Sp.〕西班牙凉菜汤〔西红柿、黄瓜片、胡椒、洋葱、油、醋等合烧成〕.

G.B. = Great Britain.

GB 一种神经性毒气的代号.

G.B.E. = Knight (Dame) Grand Cross of the Order of the British Empire 英帝国大十字最高级(女)勋爵士.

G.C. = George Cross〔英〕乔治十字勋章.

G.C.A., GCA = ground controlled approach【空】地面控制进场.

G.C.B. = Knight Grand Cross of the Bath〔英〕巴斯大十字最高级勋爵士.

G.C.D., GCD , g.c.d. = greatest common divisor【数】最大公约数.

G.C.F., GCF, g.c.f. = greatest common factor【数】最大公因子.

G.C.H. = Knight Grand Cross of the Hanoverian Order〔英〕汉诺威大十字最高级勋爵士.

G.C.M., g.c.m. = greatest common measure【数】最大公约数,最大公测度.

G.C.M.G. = Knight Grand Cross of St. Michael and St. George〔英〕圣迈克尔和圣乔治大十字最高级勋爵士.

GCR = ground control(led) radar 地面控制雷达.

G.C.R. = gas-cooled reactor 气(体)冷(却)式反应堆.

GCT = Greenwich Civil Time 格林威治民用时.

G.C.V.O. = Knight (Dame) Grand Cross of the Royal Victorian Order〔英〕维多利亚大十字最高级(女)勋爵士.

G.D. = ①Grand Duchess 大公爵夫人; 女大公爵. ②Grand Duchy 大公国;大公爵领地. ③Grand Duke 大公爵;大公.

Gd = ①gadolinium【化】钆. ②Guard 卫兵,警卫.

g/d = gram(me)s per denier 克/旦.

Gdansk, Gdańsk [gəˈdɑːnsk, Pol. gˈdaɲsk] *n.* 格但斯克〔旧称 Danzig 但泽〕〔波兰港市〕.

G.D.P. = Guanosine diphosphate【生化】= 磷酸乌甙.

GDR = German Democratic Republic 德意志民主共和国.

gds, gds. = goods〔*pl.*〕货物,商品.

Gdy·nia [gəˈdinjə] *n.* 格丁尼亚〔波兰港市〕.

GE, GEC = General Electric Company〔美〕通用电气公司.

Ge¹ = germanium【化】锗.

Ge² [ʒei] *n.* 热依语〔巴西南美印第安的一个语族名〕.

ge·an·ti·cli·nal [dʒiˌæntiˈklainl] *n.*【地】地背斜 (= geanticline). — *a.* 地背斜的,地背斜属性的.

ge·an·ti·cline [dʒiˈæntiklain] *n.*【地】地背斜.

gear [giə] *n.* ①【机】齿轮,(齿轮)传动装置,齿链; 排档. ②〔古〕衣服;甲胄与武器. ③家具;财物,动产. ④工具,用具；马具；船具；【火箭】起落架. ⑤〔英口〕胡说. ⑥〔英口〕行为，事件. *bevel* ~ 伞形齿轮. *bottom* ~ 低速档，末档. *helical* ~ 斜齿轮. *high* ~【机】高速档；〔口〕高速度. *hunting* ~ 打猎用具. *low* ~【机】低速档；〔口〕低速度. *magnetic* ~ 磁力离合器. *remote-control* ~ 遥控装置. *reverse* ~ 倒车档；反向齿轮. *steering* ~ 转向装置. *telemetering* ~ 遥测装置. *top* ~ 高速档，末档. ***get [put] into*** ~ = ***throw into*** ~ 开动机器；着手工作. ***get out of*** ~ = ***throw out of*** ~ 断开传动装置；使混乱. ***in*** ~ ①(机器)开得动，运转顺利；情况正常. ②(齿轮)搭上，联结上(发动机). ***in high*** ~ 开高速齿轮；热烈地进行. ***out of*** ~ ①(齿轮)脱开. ②(机器)开不动；情况混乱，出毛病. ***shift*** ~***s*** ①换档，变速. ②改变方式〔办法、调子〕. — *vt.* ①把齿轮装上(机器等)，使扣上齿轮；开动(机器等). ②给…装上马具 *(up)*. ③使适合 *(to)*. — *vi.* ①(齿轮)扣上 *(into)*；(机器)开动. ②适合，一致 *(with)*. ~ ***down*** 挂慢档，减小速度. ~ ***level*** 挂平档. ~ ***up*** 挂快档，增加速度；促进. ~**box** *n.* 齿轮箱，变速箱. ~ **case** 齿轮箱. ~**-driven** *a.* 齿轮传动的. ~**housing** *n.* 齿轮箱壳. ~ **lever** 变速杆. ~ **shaper** 插齿机，刨齿机. ~**shift**【机】变速，换档，变速装置. ~ **wheel**【机】齿轮.

gear·ing [ˈgiəriŋ] *n.* ①【机】传动装置，齿轮装置. ②传动，啮合. *feed* ~ 进刀传动装置. *link* ~ 联杆传动装置. *spiral* ~ 螺旋齿轮装置.

geck·o [ˈgekəu] *n.* *(pl.* ~*s,* ~*es)*【动】守宫，壁虎.

gee[1] [dʒiː] *n.* ①英语字母 G,g. ②〔美俚〕一千元. ③〔美俚〕人，家伙.

gee[2] [dʒiː] *int.* 〔美俚〕哎呀！ ~ ***whiz(z)*** 哎呀〔表示惊奇、兴奋等〕.

gee[3] [dʒiː] *int.* 〔驭马快走用语〕叽驾！ — ***vi., vt.*** 向右！*(opp.* haw) — *n.* = gee-gee.

gee[4] [dʒiː] *n.* "奇"导航系统〔英国的双曲线导航系统〕.

gee[5], **gee-gee** [dʒiː, ˈdʒiːdʒiː] *n.* 〔儿〕马.

geeho [ˈdʒiːˈhəu] = gee[3].

geek [giːk] *n.* 〔美俚〕①人，家伙. ②傻子. ③表演低级惊险节目的演员〔如咬下活鸡头、吞蛇等〕. 艺人，吞蛇(等)演员. ~ **show** 低级惊险节目的表演(如吞蛇等).

gee-pole [ˈdʒiːpəul] *n.* 橇的舵棍.

geese [giːs] *n.* goose 的复数.

gee·ser [ˈgiːzə] *n.* = geezer.

gee-up [ˈdʒiːˈʌp] *int.* = gee[3].

Ge·ez [giːˈez] *n.* (埃塞俄比亚的)古闪语 (= Ethiopic).

gee·zer [ˈgiːzə] *n.* 〔俚〕古怪的老头儿，老家伙；〔罕〕古怪的老太太.

ge·gen·schein [ˈgeigənʃain] *n.* 〔亦作 G-〕【天】对日照.

Ge·hen·na [giˈhenə] *n.*【犹史】(耶路撒冷附近的)希诺姆 *(Hinnom)* 谷；地狱；焦热地狱.

Gei·ger [ˈgaigə], **Hans** 盖革〔1882–1947，德国物理学家〕. ~ **counter**【物】(测定放射能的)盖革计数器. ~**-Müller counter**【物】盖革—弥勒计数器.

Gei·gers [ˈgaigəz] *n. pl.* 〔俚〕放射能微粒子.

gei·sha [ˈgeiʃə] *n.* *(pl.* ~*s)* 〔Jap.〕艺妓.

Geiss·ler tube [ˈgaisləˈtjuːb]【物】(真空放电实验用的)盖斯勒管〔H. Geissler (1814—1879) 为德国机械师，该管发明人〕.

geist [gaist] *n.* 〔G.〕灵魂，理智性；精神，时代精神.

gel [dʒel] *n.* 冻胶，凝胶(体). — *vi.* 成冻胶，胶化.

ge·län·de·läu·fer [gəˈlendəlɔifə] *n.* 〔G.〕越野滑雪者.

ge·län·de·sprung [gəˈlendəʃpruŋ] *n.* 〔G.〕【滑雪】越野飞跳.

ge·la·ti [dʒiˈlɑːtiː] *n.* 意大利果子露〔全脂牛奶加糖和明胶等调制成〕(=gelato).

gel·a·tin [ˈdʒelət*i*n], **gel·a·tine** [ˌdʒeləˈtiːn] *n.* ①胶；明胶；动物胶；胶质. ②凝胶体，果子冻. ③(舞台照明用的)彩色透明滤光板. *explosive [blasting]* ~【化】爆炸胶. ~ **paper** 照相软片片基. ~ **plate**【摄】干板. ~ **process**【印】胶板. **vegetable** ~ 植物胶，琼脂，洋菜.

ge·lat·i·nate [dʒiˈlætineit] *vt., vi.* (使)成为明胶，(使)成胶体.

ge·la·tin·i·form [ˌdʒeləˈtinifɔːm] *a.* 胶状的.

ge·lat·i·nize [dʒiˈlætinaiz] *vt.* ①使成明胶，使成胶状. ②【摄】涂明胶于. — *vi.* 成明胶，成胶状.

ge·lat·i·n(o)- *comb. f.* 表示"胶"：*gelatinoid, gelatinous.*

ge·lat·i·noid [dʒiˈlætinɔid] *a.* 似胶的；胶状的. — *n.* 胶状物质.

ge·lat·i·nous [dʒiˈlætinəs] *a.* ①凝胶的，含凝胶的. ②凝胶状的，胶冻状的，胶粘的.

ge·la·tion [dʒiˈleiʃən] *n.* ①冻结，凝结. ②凝胶化(作用)，胶凝(作用).

geld[1] [geld] *n.*【英史】(古代英国地主向君主缴纳的)贡赋(亦作 gelt, gheld).

geld[2] [geld] *vt.* *(*~*ed,* ***gelt*** [gelt]*;* ~*ed,* ***gelt****)* ①给…去势，阉割；割去…的卵巢. ②剥夺，减弱，删去(书等的)一部分内容. ~ *a book* 对一本书任意删削. **-er** *n.* 阉割者. **-ing** *n.* ①阉过的牲畜(尤指骟过的马). ②去势的人，太监.

gel·id [ˈdʒelid] *a.* 冰冷的，冻结的；冷淡的. **-lid·i·ty** [-ˈliːditi] *n.* **-ly** *ad.* **-ness** *n.*

gel·ig·nite [ˈdʒelignait] *n.* 葛里炸药〔由硝铵、硝酸、甘油和木浆混合制成〕；炸胶.

gel·se·mi·um [dʒelˈsiːmiəm] *n.*【植】①常绿钩吻 *(Gelsemium sempervirens)*. ②常绿钩吻根.

gelt[1] [gelt] geld[2] 的过去式及过去分词.

gelt[2] [gelt] *n.* ① = geld[1]. ②〔俚〕金钱.

GEM = ground effect machine 气垫车，气垫船.

gem [dʒem] *n.* ①宝石；宝物，珍宝；精华，佳作. ②【印】四点活字. ③〔美〕松饼，软面包. ④受尊重〔被喜爱〕的人. ⑤花苞，嫩芽. *a* ~ *of a boy* 宝贝男孩. ***G- of the mountains.*** 山中宝石〔美国爱达荷州的别名〕. — *vt.* 用宝石装饰，用宝石镶嵌. — *a.* (珠宝)最佳品质的. **-less** *a.* **-like** *a.*

Ge·ma·ra [gəmɑːˈrɑː] *n.* 《犹太教法典》(Talmud) 的注释篇.

gem·el [ˈdʒeməl] *a.* 双生的；成对的.

gem·i·nate [ˈdʒeminit] *a.*【生】双生的，成双的，成对的. ~ *fertilization* 对生受精. —[-neit] *vt., vi.* (使)加倍，(使)重复，(使)成对. **-na·tive** [ˌdʒemiˈneitiv] *a.*

gem·i·na·tion [ˌdʒemiˈneiʃən] *n.* ①加倍，重复. ②【语】辅音(字母)的重复.

Gem·i·ni [ˈdʒeminai] *n. pl.* 〔用作 *sing.*〕【天】双子座；双子宫〔黄道第三宫〕.

gem·ma [ˈdʒemə] *n.* *(pl.* ***-mae*** [-miː]*)*【植】叶芽，无性芽；【生】胞芽，(真菌的)芽孢.

gem·man [ˈdʒemən] *n.* 〔美黑人方言〕= gentleman.

gem·mate [ˈdʒemit] *a.* 有芽的，发芽繁殖的. —[-meit] *vi.* 发芽，发芽繁殖. **-ma·tion** [dʒeˈmeiʃən] *n.* **-ma·tive** [ˈdʒemeitiv] *a.*

gem·mif·er·ous [dʒeˈmifərəs] *a.* ①产宝石的. ②发芽的，发芽繁殖的.

gem·mip·a·rous [dʒeˈmipərəs] *a.* 发芽的，发芽繁殖的.

gem·ol·o·gy, gem·mol·o·gy [dʒeˈmɔlədʒi] *n.* 宝石学. **-mol·o·gist** *n.* 宝石学家.

gem·mu·la·tion [ˌdʒemjuˈleiʃən] *n.*【生】萌芽，生芽.

gem·mule [ˈdʒemjuːl] *n.* ①【植】= gemma. ②【动】胚芽；芽球.

gem·my [ˈdʒemi] *a.* 宝石多的；镶宝石的；光辉灿烂的.

ge·mot, ge·mote [giˈməut] *n.* (在诺曼人征服英国前的)英国早期自由民立法大会；自由民法庭.

gems·bok [ˈgemzbɔk] *n.* (南非的)大羚羊.

gem·stone [ˈdʒemˌstəun] *n.* 宝石.

ge·müt·lich [giˈmjuːtliʃ] *a.* 〔G.〕适意的；愉快的；舒服的；可亲的.

gen [dʒen] *n.* 〔英军俚〕情报 (= *gen*eral information).

— *vt., vi.* (给…)提供情报 (*up*).

Gen. = ①General. ②Genesis. ③Geneva; Genevan.

gen. = ①gender. ②genera. ③general(ly). ④generator. ⑤generic. ⑥genitive. ⑦genus.

-gen *suf.* 表示①【化】"产生": hydro*gen*, nitro*gen*. ②【植】"生长": acro*gen*, endo*gen*.

ge·nappe [ʒeˈnæp] *n.* 光滑绒线[纱线].

gen·darme [ˈʒɑːndɑːm] *n.* 〔F.〕 *(pl. ~s)* ①宪兵. ②〔美俚〕警察. ③山脊突岩.

gen·dar·me·rie, gen·darm·er·y [ʒɑːnˈdɑːməri] *n.* 〔F.〕 宪兵队.

gen·der[1] [ˈdʒendə] *n.* ①【语法】性. ②〔口〕性 (= sex). *the common [neuter]* ~ 通[中]性. *the masculine [feminine]*~阳[阴]性. *grammatical* ~ 语法的性. *natural* ~ 自然的性. **-less**【语法】无性的.

gen·der[2] [ˈdʒendə] *vt., vi.* 〔诗〕 = engender.

gene [dʒiːn] *n.*【生】遗传原质,基因. *dominant* ~ 显性基因. ~ **deletion**【生】基因删除. ~ **insertion**【生】基因插入. ~ **pool**【生】基因库.

geneal. = genealogy.

ge·ne·a·log·i·cal [ˌdʒiːnjəˈlɔdʒikəl] *a.* 家系的; 家谱的;系统的,系谱的. *a* ~ *table* 家谱; 系谱. *a* ~ *tree* 家系图;(动物等进化发育的)系统树. **-ly** *ad.*

ge·ne·al·o·gist [ˌdʒiːniˈælədʒist] *n.* 家系学者, 系谱学者.

gen·e·al·o·gize [ˌdʒiːniˈælədʒaiz] *vt.* 追溯…的系谱. — *vi.* 制定系谱.

ge·ne·al·o·gy [ˌdʒiːniˈælədʒi] *n.* ①家系, 血统; 系统. ②家谱. ③系谱学.

gen·e·ra [ˈdʒenərə] genus 的复数.

gen·er·a·ble [ˈdʒenərəbl] *a.* 可生殖的,可生育的.

gen·er·al [ˈdʒenərəl] *a.* *(opp.* special*)* ①一般的;综合的, 通用的. ②普通的, 广泛的, 通常的. ③全体的, 总的;全面的,普遍的;概括的,大概的,大体的,笼统的,简略的. ④【陆军】将官级的. ⑤〔用于职衔后〕总…, …长. *the* ~ *affair* 总务. *the* ~ *opinion* 一般舆论. *a* ~ *attack* 总攻击,全面进攻. ~ *knowledge* 一般知识,常识. *a* ~ *meeting* 大会,全会. ~ *principles* 原则, 总则, 通则. *a* ~ *outline* 大纲,概要. *the* ~ *programme* 总纲. *the* ~ *public* 公众,大众. ~ *readers* 一般读者. *the* ~ *welfare* 公共福利. *a* ~ *war* 全面战争. *a* ~ *rainfall* 普遍降雨. *a* ~ *secretary* 总书记. *the Attorney G-* (美国的)司法部长,(英国的)总检查长. *consul* ~ 总领事. *secretary-*~ 秘书长. ***as a ~ rule*** 原则上, 一般地说. ***for the ~ good*** 为公益. ***in a ~ way*** 一般说来. — *n.* ①〔英、美〕陆军[空军]上将,将军. ②战略[战术]家. ③【宗】会长, 团长,(救世军的)最高司令. ④〔the ~〕〔古〕一般,全体,全面 *(opp.* particular*)*;〔古〕一般人,庶民. ⑤〔主 *pl.*〕 通则,一般原则 *(opp.* particulars*)*. ⑥〔英口〕勤杂员. *G- of the air force*【美军】空军五星上将. *G- of the Armies*【美军】三军五星上将,三军元帅〔1919 年美国给珀辛 (J. J. Pershing) 授的特别军衔〕. *G- of the army* 【美军】 陆军五星上将. ***in ~*** 一般; 大体上 (*people in* ~ 普通老百姓). ***in the ~*** 概括地说; 全面; 普通. **G- American**〔美〕普通美语,美国普通话〔原指除新英格兰和南部各州绝大多数人外的美国其他地区人民所讲的美国英语,这说法现已很少用〕. ~ **anesthesia** 全身麻醉. ~ **armistice** 全面停战. **G- Assembly** 联合国大会; (美国的) 州议会. ~ **average**【保险】共同海损. ~ **cargo** 一般货物. ~ **computer** 通用计算机. ~ **concept [idea, notion]**【逻】普遍概念. ~ **course** 普通科. **G- Court** ①(美国殖民地时代行使有限司法权的) 州议会. ②美国新罕布什尔州和马萨诸塞州的)州议会. ~ **court-martial** 最高军事法庭. ~ **dealer**〔英〕杂货商. ~ **delivery**〔美〕留局待领邮件. ~ **editor** 总编辑. ~ **education** 普通教育. ~ **election** 普选. ~ **headquarters**【军】野战总司令部. ~ **hospital** 综合性(军)医院. ~ **line** 总路线. ~ **offensive** 全面进攻. ~ **officer** 将级军官. ~ **order**【军】一般命令; 卫兵守则. ~ **pardon** 大赦. ~ **paresis [paralysis]**【医】全身麻痹, 全瘫. ~ **post**〔主英〕①(邮件) 上午第一次的发送. ②职务的大变动. **G- Post Office** 邮政总局. ~ **practitioner** 普通医生〔各科病症均看,为专科医生之对〕. **~-purpose** *a.* 用途多的,通用的,万能的 (*~-purpose digital computer* 通用数字计算机). ~ **radiation** 连续辐射. ~ **semantics**【语】普通语义学. ~ **servant** 勤杂女工. **~ship** *n.* 将军的地位[身分]; 将帅的风度; 将才; 军略, 韬略. ~ **staff**【军】总参谋部. ~ **store [shop]** 百货店,百货公司. ~ **strike** 总罢工. ~ **term**【逻】全称名辞;【数】公项; 〔*pl.*〕 笼统的话.

gen·er·al·cy [ˈdʒenərəlsi] *n.* 将军的地位[任期,职权,军衔].

gen·er·al·is·si·mo [ˌdʒenərəˈlisiməu] *n.* *(pl. ~s)* 大元帅;最高统帅,总司令.

gen·er·al·ist [ˈdʒenərəlist] *n.* 知识渊博者,经验丰富的人,多面手. **-ism** *n.* 知识渊博;多面手,通才.

gen·er·al·i·ty [ˌdʒenəˈræliti] *n.* ①一般, 一般性, 普遍性; 通则. ②概括, 概要, 梗概. ③大部分,大多数. *come down from generalities to particulars* 从略说大概转到详述细节. *a rule of great* ~ 普遍性的法则. *the* ~ *of people* 一般人,多数人.

gen·er·al·i·za·tion [ˌdʒenərəlaiˈzeiʃən] *n.* ①一般化, 普遍化. ②概括,综合,总结;归纳; 法则化. ③广义; 概说,概念, 通则. *Don't be hasty in* ~. 不要急于笼统地下结论.

gen·er·al·ize [ˈdʒenərəlaiz] *vt.* ①使一般化. ②概括, 综合; 归纳. ③【美】强调…的基本特征 [一般性]. ④推广,普及. ~ *the use of video* 普及电视. ~ *a conclusion from a collection of facts* 从一大堆事实中归纳出结论. — *vi.* 形成概念,笼统地表达;延及全身.

gen·er·al·ly [ˈdʒenərəli] *ad.* ①大概,普通. ②通常,一般. ③广泛地,普遍地. ~ *speaking* 一般地说. *She is* ~ *here on Sunday.* 她星期天通常在这里. *It is* ~ *believed that ....* 普遍认为.

gen·er·ate [ˈdʒenəˌreit] *vt.* ①生殖,生育. ②产生,发生(光、热、电等). ③【数】生成,形成〔通过点、线、面的活动生成线、面、体〕. ④引起,招来; 酿成, 导致. **generating station [plant]** 发电厂〔站〕. **generating line**【数】母线,生成线.

gen·er·a·tion [ˌdʒenəˈreiʃən] *n.* ①生殖,生育;发生,产生. ②家族中的一代〔一世〕. ③代〔约 30 年〕,世代, 时代;同时代的人. ④【数】(面、体、线的)形成. ⑤完善化阶段,完善化方案,完善化的模型; 发展阶段. *a* ~ *ago* 约三十年前. *alternation of ~s*【生】世代交替. *the present* ~ 现代; 现代人. *the last [past]* ~ 上一代. *the first* ~ 第一代 (*the first* ~ *university students* 第一代大学生). *future ~s* 后代. *the beat* ~"垮掉的一代"〔美国青年中的颓废派〕. *the rising [coming]* ~ 下一代. ***for ~s*** 一连好几代,祖祖辈辈. ~ ***after*** ~ = ***from*** ~ ***to*** ~ 世世代代. ~ **gap** "代沟"〔不同辈份的人,如青年与老年在人生观、行为举止、习惯爱好和心理状态之间的差异〕.

gen·er·a·tive [ˈdʒenərətiv, -reit-] *a.* ①生产的,有生产力的. ②生殖的,有生殖力的. ③生成语法的. ~ **cell** 生殖细胞. ~ **force** *[power]* 发生力, 生殖力. ~ **fuel** 再生燃料. ~ **grammar**【语】生成语法,孳生语法. ~ **organs** 生殖器官.

gen·er·a·tor [ˈdʒenəreitə] *n.* ①产生者, 生殖者, 创始者. ②发电机, 发生器. ③【乐】基础低音. ④ = generatrix. *an A.C.* ~ 交流发电机. *a D.C.* ~ 直流发电机. *an electric* ~ 发电机. *a gas* ~ 煤气发生器. *an induction* ~ 感应发电机. *a shunt* ~ 分[并]激发电机. *a steam* ~汽锅,蒸汽发生器. *a thermo* ~ 温差电堆,热电

堆,热偶电池. *a timing* ～ 定时信号振荡器.

gen·er·a·trix [ˈdʒenəreitriks] *n. (pl.* **-tri·ces** [-trisiːz]*)* 【数】(产生线、面、体的)母点,母线,母面.

ge·ner·ic [dʒiˈnerik] *a.* ①【生】属的,类的. ②一般的,普通的 *(opp.* specific*)*. ③(商品)未注册的; 不受商标注册保护的. ④【语法】全称的,总称的. *a* ～ *name* 属名. *the* ～ *singular [plural]* 全称单数[复数]. *the* ～ *person* 全称人称〔one, you 等〕. — *n.* =*a* ～ *drug* 未注册的药品(如 aspirin). **-ness** *n.*

ge·ner·i·cal [dʒiˈnerikəl] *a.* = generic. **-ly** *ad.*

gen·er·i·type, gen·er·o·type [dʒiˈnerətaip] *n.* 【生】属典型种.

gen·er·os·i·ty [ˌdʒenəˈrɔsiti] *n.* ①宽大; 慷慨大方. ②〔*pl.*〕宽大[侠义]的行为,慷慨的行为. ③丰饶.

gen·er·ous [ˈdʒenərəs] *a.* ①宽大的, 大方的. ②丰盛的,丰富的. ③肥沃的; (色彩、酒味)浓的; 浓厚的,浓重的. *a* ～ *harvest* 丰收. *a* ～ *nature [spirit]* 宽大的性格. ～ *and selfless assistance* 慷慨无私的援助. *a* ～ *fare [table]* 丰盛的菜. ***be*** ～ ***with one's money*** 用钱大方. ***of*** ～ ***amount*** 大量的. ***of*** ～ ***size*** 十分大的. **-ly** *ad.* **-ness** *n.*

gen·e·sis [ˈdʒenisis] *n. (pl.* **gen·e·ses** [-siːz]*)* ①创始,发生; 起源. ②〔G-〕【圣】《创世纪》.

-genesis *comb. f.* 含有 genesis 意义的名词词尾: abio*genesis*, partheno*genesis*.

gen·et[1] [ˈdʒenit] *n.* ①【动】香猫,麝(香)猫. ②麝猫皮.

gen·et[2] [ˈdʒenit] *n.* = jennet.

ge·net·ic, ge·net·i·cal [dʒiˈnetik(əl)] *a.* ①遗传(学)上的. ②发生的,发展的; 创始的. ～ **code**【生】遗传密码. ～ **copying** 遗传复制. ～ **engineer** 遗传工程学家. ～ **engineering** 遗传工程. ～ **marker** 遗传标识. ～ **material**【生】遗传物质. ～ **relationship** 亲缘关系. ～ **system** 遗传系统. **-i·cal·ly** *ad.*

ge·net·i·cist [dʒiˈnetisist] *n.* 遗传学家.

ge·net·ics [dʒiˈnetiks] *n.* 遗传学.

ge·ne·va [dʒiˈniːvə] *n.* (荷兰)杜松子酒.

Ge·ne·va [dʒiˈniːvə] *n.* 日内瓦. *the* ～ *agreement* 日内瓦协议. *the* ～ *Conventions* 日内瓦公约. *Lake* ～ 日内瓦湖. ～ **bands** 日内瓦加尔文派牧师祭衣的白领带. ～ **Cross** 红十字. ～ **gown** 日内瓦加尔文派牧师穿的黑色宽袖长祭衣.

Ge·ne·van [dʒiˈniːvən], **Gen·e·vese** [ˌdʒeniˈviːz] *a.* ①日内瓦的,日内瓦人的. ②【宗】加尔文教派的. — *n.* ①日内瓦人. ②加尔文派教徒.

Ge·nève [F. ʒəˈnɛːv] *n.* 〔F.〕 = Geneva.

Gen·e·vese [ˌdʒinəˈviːz] *a., n.* 〔F.〕 = Genevan.

Gen·e·vieve [ˈdʒenəviːv] *n.* 吉纳维夫〔女子名〕.

Gen·ghis Khan, Jen·ghiz Khan [ˈdʒeŋgiz ˈkɑːn] *n.* 成吉思汗 〔1162—1227, 蒙古帝国的开国皇帝, 即元太祖〕.

ge·nial[1] [ˈdʒiːnjəl, -niəl] *a.* ①有利于生活和生长的; 温暖的,温和的; 宜人的,舒适的,愉快的. ②亲切的, 和蔼的,友好的. ③显示天才的. ④〔罕〕婚姻的; 生殖的,生产的. ⑤〔罕〕天生的,天然的. *a* ～ *climate* 温和的气候. ～ *instinct* 生殖本能. ～ *smiles* 亲切的微笑. ～ *sunshine* 和煦的阳光. **-ly** *ad.* **-ness** *n.*

ge·ni·al[2] [dʒiˈnaiəl] *a.* 【解】颏的.

ge·ni·al·i·ty [ˌdʒiːniˈæliti] *n.* ①温暖, 温和; 舒适. ②亲切,和蔼; 亲切的言行.

ge·ni·al·ize [ˈdʒiːniəˌlaiz] *vt.* 使适宜于动植物生长; 使宜人; 使温暖.

gen·ic [ˈdʒenik] *a.* 【生】基因的; 基因性的; 由基因引起的; 遗传的.

ge·nic·u·late(d) [dʒiˈnikjulit(id)] *a.* ①【生】有膝状关节的. ②(弯如)膝状的.

ge·nie [ˈdʒiːni] *n. (pl.* ～**s, *ge·ni·i*** [-niai]*)* = jinni.

ge·ni·i [ˈdʒiːniai] genius 和 genie 的复数.

ge·nis·ta [dʒiˈnistə] *n.* 【植】金雀花.

gen·i·tal [ˈdʒenitl] *a.* 生殖的; 生殖器的. *the* ～ *organs* 生殖器,外阴部. — *n.* 〔*pl.*〕(外)生殖器,外阴部. ～ **gland** 生殖腺.

gen·i·ti·val [ˌdʒeniˈtaivəl] *a.* 【语法】生格的, 所有格的.

gen·i·tive [ˈdʒenitiv] *a.*【语法】生格的,所有格的. *the* ～ *case* 生格,所有格〔英语所有格又叫 the possessive case〕. — *n.* 生格,所有格,属于生格[所有格]的词[词组].

genito- *comb. f.* 表示"生殖","生殖器": *genito*urinary.

gen·i·to·u·ri·nar·y [ˌdʒenitəuˈjuərinəri] *a.* 泌尿生殖器的. ～ *organs* 泌尿生殖器.

gen·ius [ˈdʒiːnjəs, -iəs] *n. (pl.* ～***es, ge·ni·i****)* [ˈdʒiːniai] ①天才,天资,天赋,天分,才华,创造能力. ②天才人物,才子,奇才. ③(时代)精神,思潮,倾向; (人种、语言等的)特征,特质; (某地方的)风气. ④*(pl.* genii*)* 〔常 G-〕守护神. ⑤神仙,恶魔; 对人有好或坏影响的人. *an infant* ～ 神童. *a man of* ～ 天才. *the* ～ *of modern civilization* 近代文明的特征. *be influenced by the* ～ *of* 受…风气所影响. *bear the impress of* ～ 带有天才的迹象. *have a* ～ *for poetry* 有诗才. ***one's evil*** ～ 附身恶魔; 给与坏影响的人. ***one's good*** ～ 护身神; 给与好影响的人. ～**loci** [ˈləusai] (某地的) 守护神; (某地的)风气.

genl. = general.

Gen·o·a [ˈdʒenəuə] *n.* 热那亚〔意大利港市〕.

gen·o·cide [ˈdʒenəusaid] *n.* 种族灭绝; 灭种的罪行. **-cid·al** [ˌdʒenəˈsaidl] *a.*

Gen·o·ese [ˌdʒenəˈiːz] *a.* 热那亚的; 热那亚人的. — *n. (pl.* ～*)* 热那亚人,热那亚市民.

ge·nome [ˈdʒiːnəum] *n.* 染色体组. **-nom·ic** [-ˈnəumik, -ˈnɔmik] *a.*

gen·o·type [ˈdʒenətaip] *n.* 【生】①基因型; 遗传型. ②属典型种,属模式种. **-typ·ic(al)** [-ˈtipik(əl)] *a.* **-typ·i·cal·ly** *ad.*

-genous *comb. f.* 表示"…生的","…发生的", "…生长的": nitro*genous*, auto*genous*.

Ge·no·va [ˈdʒenəuvɑ] 〔It.〕 = Genoa.

gen·re [ʒɑːŋr] *n.* 〔F.〕 ①(文艺作品的)类型,风格,流派,体裁. ②风俗画,世态画〔又作 ～ painting〕.

gens [dʒenz] *n. (pl.* **gen·tes** [ˈdʒentiːz]*)* ①(古罗马或古希腊的) 氏族. ②氏族 (尤指父系氏族). ～ **togata** 〔L.〕 古罗马公民.

Gen Serv = General Service【军】普通勤务.

gent [dʒent] *n.* 〔卑、谑〕男人,绅士; 人, 家伙〔是 gentleman 的缩略语〕. ～***s*** (店铺中)男宾部 *(*～*s' hairdresser* 男宾理发部*)*. ***the G-s*** 〔口〕男厕所.

gen·ta·mi·cin, gen·ta·my·cin [ˌdʒenˌtɑːˈmaisin] *n.* 【药】庆大霉素.

gen·teel [dʒenˈtiːl] *a.* ①有礼貌的,有教养的; 有上流社会特点的,适合上流社会的. ②〔口〕优雅的,文雅的,有品格的. ③时髦的; 〔反〕装绅士派头的,赶时髦的,摆架子的. ***do the*** ～ 装气派. ***live in*** ～ ***poverty*** 穷人摆阔. **-ly** *ad.* **-ness** *n.* **-ism** *n.* 〔书〕雅语〔如用 stomach 替代 belly〕.

gen·tes [ˈdʒentiːz] gens 的复数.

gen·tian [ˈdʒenʃiən] *n.* ①【植】龙胆属植物,龙胆. ②龙胆健胃剂. ～ **bitter** 龙胆苦味汁〔健胃剂〕. ～ **violet** 【化】龙胆紫.

gen·tile [ˈdʒentail] *n.* ①(犹太人眼中的)异邦人; 非犹太人 (尤指基督教徒). ②异教徒. ③〔美〕〔常 G-〕 非摩门教徒. ④【语法】说明民族[国籍]的词. — *a.* ①(犹太人眼中的)异邦人的,非犹太人的. ②异教徒的. ③非摩门教徒的. ④氏族的, 部落的; 民族的. ⑤【语法】说明民族[国籍]的. ～**dom** *n.* (犹太人眼中的)异邦; 异邦人; 异教徒.

gen·ti·lesse [ˈdʒentiles] *n.* 〔古〕良好的教养(尤指资产

阶级的文雅和礼貌).
gen·ti·li·tial [ˌdʒentiˈliʃəl] *a.* 国家的,民族的;部落的;家族的.
gen·til·i·ty [dʒenˈtiliti] *n.* ①名门,上流阶层. ②文雅,优雅;绅士气派. ③〔讽〕装绅士派头,充上流阶层. ④〔古〕出身高贵;绅士们. *shabby* ~ 摆阔气,硬要面子.
gen·tis·ic acid [dʒenˈtisik, -ˈtiz-]【化】龙胆酸.
gen·tle [ˈdʒentl] *a.* ①文雅的,有礼貌的. ②柔和的,轻柔的;(坡等)和缓的;不猛烈的,(药等)温和的. ③生长名门的,上流阶层的. ④驯服的,温顺的. ⑤〔古〕慷慨的,高尚的,豪侠的. ⑥有身分的;有带徽章资格的. *a ~ blow* 轻轻一击. *a ~ rain* 细雨. *a ~ smile* 温柔的微笑. *~ in action* 行动和缓. *~ and simple* 贵贱,上下各阶层. ***G- Reader (and Kind Heart)*** 敬爱的读者〔著者对读者的称呼〕. ***of ~ birth = of ~ blood*** 出身名门的. ***the ~ craft [art]*** 钓鱼;制鞋业. ***the ~ passion*** 恋爱. ***the G- People*** 〔美俚〕鼓吹非暴力主义的温和派. ***the ~ sex*** 女性 (*opp.* sterner sex). — *n.* 〔古〕绅士;(作鱼饵用的)蛆. — *vt.* ①使高贵. ②使文雅,使温和,使柔和. ③驯服(马等);抚弄,轻拍. ~ **breeze**【气】微风(三级风). **~folk(s)** *n.* 〔*pl.*〕有身分的人,上流人士. **~-hearted** *a.* 心肠软的. **~hood** *n.* 名门世族;绅士派头. **-ness** *n.*
gen·tle·man [ˈdʒentlmən] *n.* (*pl.* ***-men***) ①绅士;有身分的人,上流人士. ②〔男子尊称〕阁下. ③(中国旧时的)士大夫;【法】社会贤达〔证明文件上用语〕. ④(达官贵人的)随从,侍从. ⑤〔*pl.*〕(商业信函中的称呼)先生们(= Sirs 或 Dear Sirs). ⑥【英史】(非贵族但有使用家徽特权的)乡士〔有时略作 Gent, 附加名后表示身分〕. ⑦〔*pl.*〕男厕所. ⑧〔美〕议员. *a coloured* ~〔美讽〕有色绅士,黑人. *a country* ~ 乡绅,乡下地主. *a fine* ~ 时髦绅士;花花公子. *a walking* ~【剧】配角. ***a ~ at large*** 〔谑〕失业者,无职业者. ***a ~ in brown*** 〔谑〕臭虫. ***a ~ in waiting*** (英王的)侍从. ***a ~ of fortune*** 海盗;骗子;冒险家 (= adventurer). ***a ~ of the press*** 新闻记者. ***a ~ of the road [pad]*** 拦路强盗;游民,乞丐;出门兜揽生意的人. ***a ~ of the (long) robe*** 律师,教士. ***a ~ of the three outs*** 〔谑〕(无现钱、无袖肘、无信用的)三无绅士. ***a ~ of virtu*** 古董家,古玩专家. ***a ~'s [gentlemen's] agreement*** 君子协定. ***a ~'s ~*** 侍从,男仆. ***my ~*** 那家伙,此人. ***the ~ from …*** 〔美〕(从某州)选出的(众议院)议员. ***the ~ in black*** 恶魔. ***the old ~*** 〔谑〕恶魔. **~-at-arms'** *n.* (英国国王的)卫士. **~-farmer** *n.* (*pl.* ***gentlemen-farmers***) (占有土地,不劳动,只管经营、管理的)乡绅. **~like** *a.* = *gentlemanly*. ~ **ranker** 有军籍的绅士. **~-pensioner** =~-at-arms. **~ship** *n.* 绅士身分. ~ **usher** 〔英〕门役,拜谒者的引见人.
gen·tle·man·ly [ˈdʒentlmənli] *a.* 绅士的,绅士派头的. **-li·ness** *n.*
gen·tle·wom·an [ˈdʒentlwumən] *n.* (*pl.* ***-wom·en*** [-ˌwimin]) ①有身分的妇女,女士,贵妇人. ②(王室、贵族的)侍女,女仆. **~like** *a.* **-li·ness** *n.* **-ly** *a.*
gen·tly [ˈdʒentli] *ad.* ①文雅地,温柔地,有礼貌地. ②柔和地;轻轻地;渐渐地. ③出身高贵地,有教养地. *G-!* 慢点儿! *be ~ born* 出身名门的,有身分的. *smile ~* 嫣然一笑. *The road sloped ~ to the lake.* 路缓缓地向湖边倾斜下去.
gen·try [ˈdʒentri] *n.* ①贵族们,绅士们;〔英〕(仅次于贵族的)绅士阶级,上等人士;可以使用纹章的平民〔多为大地主〕. ②〔谑、蔑〕人们,伙伴. *evil ~s* 劣绅. ***the flash ~*** 盗贼们,流氓们. ***the ~ of the press*** 新闻界人士. ***the light-fingered ~*** 扒手们. ***the silk-stocking ~*** 富人,财主. ***these ~*** 〔蔑〕这些家伙.
gents [dʒents] *n.* gent 的复数.
ge·nu [ˈdʒiːnjuː, ˈdʒen-] *n.* (*pl.* ***gen·u·a*** [ˈdʒenjuwə])【解】①膝. ②膝状部分.
gen·u·flect [ˈdʒenju(ː)flekt] *vi.* ①曲膝,跪拜(尤指做礼拜时). ②屈服,屈从.
gen·u·flec·tion, gen·u·flex·ion [ˌdʒenju(ː)ˈflekʃən] *n.* 曲膝;屈服,屈从.
gen·u·flec·tor [ˈdʒenju(ː)flektə] *n.* 曲膝者;屈服者,屈从者.
gen·u·ine [ˈdʒenjuin] *a.* ①真正的 (*opp.* sham, counterfeit). ②坦率的,真诚的,真心诚意的. ③血统纯粹的,纯种的. *a ~ Rubens* 鲁本兹亲笔画. *a ~ signature* 亲笔签名. *a ~ writing* 真迹,墨宝. *a ~ skeptic* 十足的怀疑论者. *a ~ breed* 纯种. **-ly** *ad.* **-ness** *n.*
ge·nus [ˈdʒiːnəs] *n.* (*pl.* ***gen·er·a*** [ˈdʒenərə], ***~es***) ①种类,类;【生】属. ②【逻】类,类概念. ***the ~ Homo*** 人类.
-geny *suf.* 表示"起源","产生";"发展": anthropo*geny*, pro*geny*.
geo- *comb. f.* 表示"地球","土地": *geo*centric, *geo*logy.
geo [gjəu] *n.* 〔Scot.〕海湾.
Geo. = George.
ge·o·an·ti·cline [ˌdʒi(ː)əuˈæntiklain] *n.*【地】地背斜.
ge·o·cen·tric [ˌdʒi(ː)əuˈsentrik] *a.* 以地球为中心的 (*opp.* heliocentric);从地心出发计算[观察]的;地心的. *the ~ theory* 地球中心说,地心说. ~ **latitude** [*longitude*] 地心纬度[经度]. ~ **parallax** 地心视差. ~ **zenith** 地心天顶. **-al·ly** *ad.*
ge·o·cen·tric·ism [ˌdʒi(ː)əuˈsentrisizəm] *n.* 地球中心说.
ge·o·chem·is·try [ˌdʒi(ː)əuˈkemistri] *n.* 地球化学. **-i·cal** *a.* **-ist** *n.*
ge·o·chro·nol·o·gy [ˌdʒi(ː)əukrəˈnɔlədʒi] *n.* 地质年代学. **-chron·o·log·i·cal** [-ˌkrɔnəˈlɔdʒikl] *a.*
ge·o·chro·nom·e·try [ˌdʒi(ː)əukrəˈnɔmitri] *n.* 地球测时学. **-no·met·ric** [-krɔnəˈmetrik, -ˌkrəunə-] *a.*
ge·o·cide [ˈdʒi(ː)əusaid] *n.* 地球末日.
ge·o·co·ro·na [ˌdʒi(ː)əukəˈrəunə] *n.* 地华〔地球大气最外层,主要含氢〕.
geod. = geodesy; geodetic.
ge·ode [ˈdʒi(ː)əud] *n.*【地】晶洞,晶球,空心石核. **-od·ic** [dʒi(ː)ˈɔdik] *a.*
ge·o·des·ic [ˌdʒi(ː)əuˈdesik] *a.* ①大地测量学的. ②【数】(最)短线的. —*n.*【数】= ~ line. ~ **circle** 短程圆. ~ **line** 测地线;短程线.
ge·o·des·i·cal [ˌdʒi(ː)əuˈdesikəl] *a.* = geodesic.
ge·od·e·sy [dʒi(ː)ˈɔdisi] *n.* 大地测量学. *astronomical ~* 天文大地测量学.
ge·o·det·ic(al) [ˈdʒi(ː)əuˈdetik(əl)] *a.* = geodesic (*a.*). **-i·cal·ly** *ad.*
ge·o·det·ics [ˌdʒi(ː)əuˈdetiks] *n.* = geodesy.
ge·o·dy·nam·ic(al) [ˌdʒi(ː)əudaiˈnæmikəl] *a.* 地球动力学的.
ge·o·dy·nam·ics [ˌdʒi(ː)əudaiˈnæmiks] *n.* 地球动力学.
ge·o·e·lec·tric [ˌdʒi(ː)əuiˈlektrik] *a.*【物】地电的.
Geof·frey [ˈdʒefri] *n.* 杰弗里〔男子名〕.
geog. = geographer; geographic(al); geography.
ge·og·nos·tic(al) [ˌdʒiːɔgˈnɔstik(əl)] *a.* 地球构造学的. **-ti·cal·ly** *ad.*
ge·og·no·sy [dʒiˈɔgnəsi] *n.* 地球构造学.
ge·o·gram [ˈdʒi(ː)əugræm] *n.* 地球环境制图.
ge·og·ra·pher [dʒiˈɔgrəfə] *n.* 地理学者,地理学家.
ge·o·graph·ic(al) [ˌdʒiəˈgræfik(əl)] *a.* 地理学的,地理的. ~ **distribution** 地理分布. ~ **features** 地势. ~ **tatitude** 地理纬度. ~ **mile** 地理英里〔赤道上经度一分的长度,约 1,854 米〕. ~ **north** 正北. ~ **strategic point** 战略地点. **-i·cal·ly** *ad.*
ge·og·ra·phy [dʒiˈɔgrəfi] *n.* ①地理学. ②地理,地形,地势 (*of*). ③地志,地理书. ④(生产、建筑等的)配置,布局. *applied ~* 商业地理. *botanical ~* 植物分布学.

human ～ 人文地理学. *physical* ～ 地文学,自然地理. *political* ～ 政治地理学. *the* ～ *of Asia* 亚洲地理. 亚洲地形. *lessons in* ～ 地理课程.

ge·oid [ˈdʒiːɔid] *n.* 【地】①大地水准面. ②地球体,地球形.

geol. = geologic(al); geologist; geology.

ge·o·log·ic(al) [dʒiəˈlɔdʒik(əl)] *a.* 地质学的, 地质的. *a* ～ *survey* 地质调查. ～ **chronology** 地质年代学. ～ **section** 【地】地质剖面. **-i·cal·ly** *ad.*

ge·ol·o·gist [dʒiˈɔlədʒist] *n.* 地质学者,地质学家.

ge·ol·o·gize [dʒiˈɔlədʒaiz] *vi.* 研究地质(学); 搜集地质标本. — *vt.* 对(某地)作地质调查.

ge·ol·o·gy [dʒiˈɔlədʒi] ①地质学. ②(某一地区的)地质. ③地质学的著作. *economic* ～ 应用地质学. *historical* ～ 地史学. *structural* ～ 构造地质学.

geom. = geometer; geometric(al); geometry; geometrician.

ge·o·mag·net·ic [ˌdʒiːəumægˈnetik] *a.* 地磁的. ～ **storm** 地磁暴. **-netism** *n.* 地磁; 地磁学.

ge·o·man·cy [ˈdʒi(ː)əumænsi] *n.* 泥土占卜〔拿一把土撒在地上,按形成的形状进行占卜,或按在地上任意划的线或形状进行占卜〕. **-man·tic** [-ˈmæntik] *a.*

ge·o·me·chan·ics [ˌdʒi(ː)əumiˈkæniks] *n.* 地球力学,地质力学.

ge·om·e·ter [dʒiˈɔmitə] *n.* ① = geometrician. ②【动】尺蠖.

ge·o·met·ric [dʒiəˈmetrik] *n.* 有几何图形的东西.

ge·o·met·ric(al) [dʒiəˈmetrik(əl)] *a.* ①几何学的,几何图形的. ②按几何级数增长的. ～ **stairs** 弯曲的楼梯. ～ *ornaments* 几何图形装饰. ～ **mean** 【数】几何平均数, 等比中项 (中数). ～ **progression [series]** 几何级数,等比级数. ～ **projection** 几何投影. ～ **worm** 【动】尺蠖. **-ri·cal·ly** *ad.*

ge·om·e·tri·cian [ˌdʒiəuməˈtriʃən] *n.* 几何学者,几何学家.

ge·om·e·trid [dʒiˈɔmitrid] *n., a.* 尺蠖(的).

ge·om·e·trize [dʒiˈɔmitraiz] *vt.* 用几何图形表示, 使符合几何原理和定律. — *vi.* 研究几何学, 按几何学方法或原理工作.

ge·om·e·try [dʒiˈɔmitri] *n.* ①几何学. ②几何形状. ③几何学著作. *analytical* ～ 解析几何. *descriptive* ～ 图形几何,画法几何. *Euclidean* ～ 欧氏几何. *non-Euclidean* ～ 非欧几何. *plane* ～ 平面几何. *solid* ～ 立体几何. *spherical* ～ 球面几何.

ge·o·mor·phic [ˌdʒi(ː)əuˈmɔːfik] *a.* 地貌的; 地貌学的.

ge·o·mor·phol·o·gist [ˌdʒi(ː)əumɔːˈfɔlədʒist] *n.* 地貌学家.

ge·o·mor·phol·o·gy [ˌdʒiːəumɔːˈfɔlədʒi] *n.* 地貌学. **-pho·log·ic** [-ˌmɔːfəˈlɔdʒik]. **-pho·log·i·cal** *a.*

ge·oph·a·gy [dʒiˈɔfədʒi] *n.* 食土,食土癖.

ge·o·phone [ˈdʒi(ː)əufəun] *n.* 地音探听器,地震检波器.

ge·o·phys·ics [ˌdʒi(ː)əuˈfiziks] *n.* 地球物理学. **-i·cal** *a.* **-i·cal·ly** *ad.* **-i·cist** *n.*

ge·o·phyte [ˈdʒiːəfait] *n.* 地下芽植物.

ge·o·po·lit·i·cal [ˌdʒi(ː)əupəˈlitikəl] *a.* 地理政治论的,地缘政治学的. **-ly** *ad.*

ge·o·pol·i·ti·cian [ˌdʒi(ː)əuˌpɔliˈtiʃən] *n.* 地理政治论者,地缘政治学家.

ge·o·pol·i·tics [ˌdʒi(ː)əuˈpɔlitiks] *n.* 地理政治论,地缘政治学.

ge·o·pon·ic [ˌdʒi(ː)əuˈpɔnik] *a.* ①耕作的,农业的. ②〔谑〕乡间的,田园的.

ge·o·pon·ics [ˌdʒi(ː)əuˈpɔniks] *n.* ①耕作, 农业. ②〔谑〕乡间,田园.

ge·o·probe [ˈdʒiːəprəub] *n.* 地球探测火箭.

ge·o·ra·ma [ˌdʒiəˈrɑːmə] *n.* (由内面观赏的)内侧绘有世界地理实景的空心大圆球.

Geor·die[1] [ˈdʒɔːdi] *n.* 〔Scot.〕 = collier.

Geor·die[2] [ˈdʒɔːdi] *n.* George 的爱称.

George[1] [dʒɔːdʒ] *n.* 乔治〔姓氏, 男子名; 爱称 Geordie, Georgie, Dod, Doddy〕. *St.* ～ 英国的守护神. *St. G～'s day* 圣乔治日〔四月二十三日〕. ***By*** ～. 确实,实在〔发誓或感叹〕. ～ ***Cross [Medal]*** 乔治十字勋章〔英国王乔治六世 1940 年颁发的表彰英勇行为的勋章〕. ***Let*** ～ ***do it.*** 〔美俚〕让别人去干吧!

George[2] [dʒɔːdʒ] *n.* ①(英国嘉德勋章的两种图案之一)骑马降龙宝像. ②(英国有圣乔治像的)半克朗货币. ③〔g-〕褐色陶制大水壶. ④〔g-〕〔英俚〕(飞机的)自动驾驶仪. *a brown* ～ 褐色陶制容器.

George·town [ˈdʒɔːdʒtaun] *n.* ①乔治敦〔圭亚那首都〕. ②乔治敦〔开曼群岛(英)首府〕. ③美国华盛顿哥仑比亚特区内的住宅区.

George Town [ˈdʒɔːdʒ ˈtaun] 乔治市〔即 Penang 槟城〕〔马来西亚港市〕.

geor·gette [dʒɔːˈdʒet] *n.* 乔其绉纱(= ～ crepe).

Geor·gia[1] [ˈdʒɔːdʒjə] *n.* 乔治娅〔女子名〕.

Geor·gia[2] [ˈdʒɔːdʒjə] *n.* ①乔治亚〔一译佐治亚,美国州名〕. ②格鲁吉亚〔苏联加盟共和国名〕.

Geor·gian [ˈdʒɔːdʒjən] *a.* ①(英国)乔治一世至四世统治时期的; (英国)乔治五世统治时期的. ②(苏联)格鲁吉亚的,格鲁吉亚人的,格鲁吉亚语的. ③(美国)佐治亚州的,佐治亚州人的. — *n.* ①格鲁吉亚人; 格鲁吉亚语. ②佐治亚州人.

Geor·gi·(a)na [dʒɔːˈdʒiːnə] *n.* 乔治(亚)娜〔女子名〕.

geor·gic [ˈdʒɔːdʒik] *n.* 田园诗. ***The Georgics*** 《农事诗》〔古罗马诗人维吉尔 (Virgil) 所作的田园诗〕. — *a.* 农业(的).

Geor·gie [ˈdʒɔːdʒi] *n.* 乔吉〔George 的爱称〕.

ge·o·sci·ence [ˌdʒi(ː)əuˈsaiəns] *n.* 地球科学.

ge·o·sci·en·tist [ˌdʒi(ː)əuˈsaiəntist] *n.* 地球学家.

ge·o·space [ˈdʒi(ː)əuspeis] *n.* 地球空间(轨道).

ge·o·stat·ic [ˌdʒi(ː)əuˈstætik] *a.* 地压的;【建】耐地压的. ～ **curve** 地压曲线.

ge·o·stat·ics [ˌdʒiəuˈstætiks] *n.* 〔*pl.*〕〔用作单数〕刚体力学.

ge·o·sta·tion·ar·y [ˌdʒi(ː)əuˈsteiʃənəri] *a.* (人造卫星等)对地静止的,对地同步的. ～ **orbit** (人造卫星的)对地静止轨道.

ge·o·stra·te·gic [ˌdʒi(ː)əustrəˈtiːdʒik] *a.* 地理战略论的,地缘战略学的.

ge·o·strat·e·gist [ˌdʒi(ː)əuˈstrætidʒist] *n.* 地理战略论者,地缘战略学家.

ge·o·strat·e·gy [ˌdʒi(ː)əuˈstrætidʒi] *n.* 地理战略论,地缘战略学.

ge·o·stroph·ic [ˌdʒi(ː)əuˈstrɔfik] *a.* 【气】地转的,因地球自转引起的. ～ **current** 地转风气流. ～ **wind** 地转风. **-i·cal·ly** *ad.*

ge·o·syn·cli·nal [ˌdʒi(ː)əusinˈklainəl] *a.* 地向斜的, 地槽的. — *n.* = geosyncline.

ge·o·syn·cline [ˌdʒi(ː)əuˈsinklain] *n.* 【地】地槽, 地向斜.

ge·o·tax·is [ˌdʒi(ː)əuˈtæksis] *n.* 趋地性. **-tac·tic** [-ˈtæktik] *a.* **-tac·ti·cal·ly** *ad.*

ge·o·tec·ton·ic [ˌdʒi(ː)əutekˈtɔnik] *a.* 大地构造的. ～ **geology** 大地构造地质学. **-al·ly** *ad.*

ge·o·ther·mal [ˌdʒi(ː)əuˈθəməl], **ge·o·ther·mic** [ˌdʒi(ː)əuˈθəːmik] *a.* 地热的,有关地热的 (= geothermal). ～ **gradient** 【地】地温陡度〔每趋向地心 60 英尺,温度升高华氏一度〕. **-ally** *ad.*

ge·o·trop·ic [ˌdʒi(ː)əuˈtrɔpik] *a.* 向地性的. **-al·ly** *ad.*

ge·ot·ro·pism [dʒiˈɔtrəpizəm] *n.* 【生】向地性. *negative* ～负向地性,背地性. *positive* ～ 正向地性.

Ger. = German; Germany.

ger. = gerund.

G

ge·rah [ˈgiːrə] *n.* ①一种古希伯来银币. ②格拉[古希伯来衡器名,等于 1/20 谢克尔 *(shekel)*].
Ger·ald [ˈdʒerəld] *n.* 杰拉尔德[男子名].
Ger·al·dine [ˈdʒerəldiːn, ˈdʒerəldain] *n.* 杰拉尔丁[女子名].
ge·ra·ni·ol [dʒəˈreiniːɔːl] *n.*【化】拢牛儿醇.
ge·ra·ni·um [dʒiˈreinjəm, dʒəˈr-] *n.*【植】老鹳草属植物,天竺葵;[G.] 老鹳草属. ~ **oil** 草叶油.
Ger·ard [ˈdʒerɑːd, dʒəˈrɑːd] *n.* 杰勒德[姓氏,男子名].
ger·ber·a [ˈgəːbərə] *n.*【植】非洲菊 *(Gerbera jamesonii)*.
ger·bil, ger·bille [ˈdʒəːbl] *n.*【动】沙鼠亚科 *(Gerbillinae)* 动物;沙鼠.
ger·ent [ˈdʒiərənt] *n.* [罕] 有职有权者;经营管理者;统治者.
ger·e·nuk [ˈgeərəˌnuk, gəˈrenək] *n.*【动】长颈羚 *(Litocranius walleri* = giraffe antelope*)*.
ger·fal·con [ˈdʒəːˌfɔːlkən, -fɔːk-] *n.*【动】(冰岛产的)大隼.
Ger·hard [ˈgəːhɑːd] = Gerald.
ger·i·at·ric [ˌdʒeriˈætrik] *a.* 老年病学的,老年的,衰老的.
ger·i·a·tri·cian [ˌdʒeriəˈtriʃən] *n.* 老年病学家 (= geriatrist).
ger·i·at·rics [ˌdʒəriˈætriks] *n. pl.* [用作单数] 老年病学.
ger·i·at·rist [ˌdʒeriˈætrist] *n.* = geriatrician.
germ [dʒəːm] *n.* ①【生】幼芽,胚芽,胚原基. ②微生物,细菌,病菌,病原菌. ③起源,根源;萌芽. *the* ~ *of life* 生命的根源. ***be in*** ~ 处于萌芽状态,处在不发达阶段. — *vi.* [喻] 发芽,萌芽;发生. ~ **carrier** 带菌者. ~ **cell** 生殖细胞. ~**free** *a.* 无菌的;(实验动物)在无菌状态下生长的. ~ **layer** 胚层. ~**-plasm(a)** 种质. ~**-proof** *a.* 抗菌的. ~ **theory**【生】生源说;【医】病菌说,微生物说. ~**warfare** 细菌战争. ~ **weapon** 细菌武器.
Germ. = German; Germany.
Ger·man [ˈdʒəːmən] *a.* ①德意志的,德国的. ②日耳曼人的,德国人的. ③日耳曼语的,德语的. — *n.* ①德意志人,德国人;日尔曼人. ②日尔曼语,德语. ③[g-](一种复杂的)德国华尔兹舞,德国华尔兹舞舞会. *High* ~ 高地德语[现在的标准德语]. *Low* ~ 低地德语[包括 Frisian, Dutch, Flemish 等]. ~ **measles**【医】风疹. ~ **Ocean** 北海 = North Sea. ~ **sausage** 德国香肠,大腊肠. ~ **shepherd (dog)** 德国牧羊犬[也叫 (~) police dog]. ~ **silver** 锌白铜[镍、锌、铜的合金]. ~ **text** 德文式黑体字. ~ **wool** 细毛线.
ger·man [ˈdʒəːmən] *a.* ①同父母的,同祖父母的,同外祖父母的[常用连词符号附加在被修饰的名词后面]. ② [罕] = germane. *brothers [sisters]-*~ 胞弟兄[姊妹]. *cousins-*~ 嫡堂弟兄[姊妹].
ger·man·der [dʒəːˈmændə] *n.*【植】美洲石蚕;石蚕状婆婆纳[又叫 ~ speedwell].
ger·mane [dʒəːˈmein] *a.* ①(议论等)切题的,关系密切的. ②(比喻等)恰当的,贴切的 *(to)*. *a remark hardly* ~ *to the question* 同问题不大有关的话. **-ly** *ad.*
Ger·man·ic [dʒəːˈmænik] *a.* ①德意志的,德国的;德国人的,德语的. ②日耳曼人的,日耳曼语(系)的,条顿民族的. — *n.* 日耳曼语(系)[印欧语系中的重要分支,包括现代英语、德语、荷兰语、佛兰芒语、冰岛语、挪威语以及哥特语等].
Ger·man·ism [ˈdʒəːmənizəm] *n.* ①日耳曼[德意志]精神,日耳曼气质;日耳曼式,日耳曼倾向;日耳曼主义. ②日耳曼词语;德语习语,德语特色.
Ger·man·ist [ˈdʒəːmənist] *n.* ①德语学家,德意志文学专家,德意志主义者. ②日耳曼语学者,日耳曼文学专家.
ger·ma·nite [ˈdʒəːmənait] *n.*【矿】锗石.
ger·ma·ni·um [dʒəːˈmeiniəm] *n.*【化】锗. ~ **transistor** 锗晶体管.
Ger·man·ize [ˈdʒəːmənaiz] *vt.* ①使德意志化. ②把…译成德语. — *vi.* 具有德意志方式[习惯、态度]. **-i·za·tion** *n.*
Germano- *comb. f.* (= German): *Germano*phobia.
Ger·man·o·ma·ni·a [ˌdʒəːmənəuˈmeinjə] *n.* 崇拜德国,德国迷.
Ger·man·o·phil(e) [dʒəːˈmænəufail] *n., a.* 亲德派(的),德国崇拜者(的).
Ger·man·o·phobe [dʒəːˈmænəufəub] *n., a.* 恐惧和仇恨德国的人(的).
Ger·man·o·pho·bi·a [dʒəːˈmænəufəubiə] *n.* 恐德病,仇德狂.
Ger·ma·ny [ˈdʒəːməni] *n.* 德意志,德国. *East* ~ 东德[欧洲] (= the German Democratic Republic 德意志民主共和国). *West* ~ 西德[欧洲](= the Federal Republic of ~ 德意志联邦共和国).
ger·men [ˈdʒəːmen] *n.* ①【植】蕾,幼芽,子房. ②【动】生殖腺.
ger·mi·ci·dal [ˌdʒəːmiˈsaidəl] *a.* 杀菌(剂)的,有杀菌力的.
ger·mi·cide [ˈdʒəːmisaid] *n.* 杀菌剂.
Ger·mi·nal [ˈdʒəːminl] *n.* [F.] ①播种月[阳历 3 月 21 日至 4 月 19 日];法国革命历第7月. ②[g-] 树发芽时,春天.
ger·mi·nal [ˈdʒəːminl] *a.* ①胚种的,幼芽的. ②原始的,初期的. ~ *ideas* 原始观念. ~ **area** 胚盘. ~ **cell** 生发细胞. ~ **disc**【生】胚盘. ~ **furrow** 生殖槽. ~ **layer** 胚层,生发层. ~ **selection** 配子选择. ~ **vesicle** 胚胞. **-ly** *ad.*
ger·mi·nant [ˈdʒəːminənt] *a.* ①发芽的;有发育力的. ②开始的,发端的.
ger·mi·nate [ˈdʒəːmineit] *vi.* ①发芽,萌芽,发育. ②发生,发展. *Seeds* ~ *in the spring.* 种子在春天发芽. — *vt.* ①使发芽;使发育. ②使发生,使发展. *Seeds are* ~*d by warmth and moisture* 温暖的气候和水分促使种子发芽. **germinating ability [capacity]** (种子)发芽力. **germinating viability** 发芽势.
ger·mi·na·tion [ˌdʒəːmiˈneiʃən] *n.* 萌芽;发生. ~ **percentage** 发芽率.
ger·mi·na·tive [ˈdʒəːmiˌneitiv] *a.* 发芽的;有发育力的.
ger·mi·na·tor [ˈdʒəːmiˌneitə] *n.* ①使发芽[发育]的人[物]. ②种子发芽力测定器.
geront(o)- *comb. f.* 表示"老人","老年": *geronto*logy.
ger·on·toc·ra·cy [ˌdʒerənˈtɔkrəsi] *n.* ①老人政府;老人统治. ②[*pl.*] 老人组成的统治集团. **ge·ron·to·crat·ic** [dʒəˌrɔntəuˈkrætik] *a.*
ger·on·tol·o·gy [ˌdʒerənˈtɔlədʒi] *n.* 老年学,老年医学. **-to·log·i·cal** *a.* **-ogist** *n.* 研究老年医学的专家.
ge·ron·to·mor·pho·sis [dʒəˌrɔntəuˈmɔːfəsis] *n.*【医】特化进化.
Ger·ry [ˈgeri] *n.* 格里[姓氏,男子名].
ger·ry·man·der [ˈdʒerimændə] *vt.* [美] (为本党利益)不公正地改划(州、县等的选区);任意改划 (一地区的选区)以谋取利益. — *vi.* 不公正地划分选区. — *n.* 不公正地划分的选区.
gers·dorff·ite [ˈgerzˌdɔːfait] *n.*【矿】砷硫镍矿,辉砷镍矿.
Gersh·win [ˈgəːʃwin] *n.* 格什温[姓氏].
Ger·trude [ˈgəːtruːd] *n.* 格特鲁德[女子名].
Ger·ty [ˈgəːti] *n.* 格蒂[女子名 Gertrude 的昵称].
ger·und [ˈdʒerənd] *n.* ①【语法】(由动词加 -ing 形成的) 英语动名词. ②【语法】拉丁动名词. ~**-grinder** ①拉丁语教师. ②学究式的老师.
ge·run·di·al [dʒiˈrʌndiəl] *a.*【语法】动名词的. **-ly** *ad.*
ger·un·di·val [ˌdʒerənˈdaivəl] *a.*【语法】动形词的,动

词状形容词的. **-ly** *ad.*

ge·run·dive [dʒiˈrʌndiv] *a.* = gerundial. — *n.* ①【语法】拉丁动形词. ②(其它语言中)类似拉丁动形词的形式.

ges·ne·ri·a [gesˈniəriə] *a.* 【植】苦苣苔科的〔包括非洲紫苣苔 *(Saintpaulia ionantha)*; 大岩桐 *(Sinnigia speciosa)*〕.

ges·so [ˈdʒesəu] *n.* (绘画,雕刻用的)石膏粉.

gest(e) [dʒest] *n.* ①〔古〕武侠(故事)(尤指中世纪用韵文写的故事). ②英勇行为,冒险活动,奇遇.

ge·stalt [gəˈʃtælt] *n.* 〔G.〕 *(pl. ~en*[-ən]*)*【心】完形,经验的整体. **G- psychology** 形态心理学〔又译格式塔心理学,为现代欧美资产阶级心理学主要派别之一〕.

Ge·sta·po [geˈʃtɑːpəu] *n.* 〔G.〕盖世太保〔纳粹德国的秘密国家警察,源自德语的 *Ge*beime *Sta*at*po*lizei〕.

Ges·ta Ro·ma·no·rum [ˈdʒestəˌrəuməˈnɔːrəm] 《古罗马人记事》〔用拉丁文写出的一部十三、四世纪欧洲故事集〕.

ges·tate [ˈdʒesteit] *vt., vi.* ①(使)怀孕, 妊娠. ②酝酿,孕育.

ges·ta·tion [dʒesˈteiʃən] *n.* ①妊娠(期),怀孕(期). ②酝酿,孕育.

ges·tic [ˈdʒestik], **ges·tic·al** [-əl] *a.* 与身体动作有关的(尤指跳舞时).

ges·tic·u·late [dʒesˈtikjuleit] *vi.* 用姿势〔动作〕示意,打手势. — *vt.* 用姿势[动作]表达(意思).

ges·tic·u·la·tion [dʒesˌtikjuˈleiʃən] *n.* 用动作[姿势]示意,打手势.

ges·tic·u·la·tive [dʒesˈtikjuleitiv], **ges·tic·u·la·to·ry** [dʒesˈtikjulətəri] *a.* 打手势的,做手势的.

ges·tic·u·la·tor [dʒesˈtikjuleitə] *n.* 用姿势〔动作〕示意的人,打手势的人.

ges·ture [ˈdʒestʃə] *n.* ①姿势, 手势. ②〔古〕仪态,举止,样子. ③姿态,表示(尤指友好的表示). *a fine* ~ 雅量. *a warlike* ~ 耀武扬威,挑衅的姿态. — *vi., vt.* = gesticulate. ~ **language** 手势语.

Ge·sund·heit [gəˈzunthait] *int.* 〔G.〕为你的健康干杯!〔祝酒词〕;祝你健康!〔对刚打喷嚏的人的祝愿语〕.

get [get] *vt.* ***(got*** [gɔt]***; got,*** 〔美、古〕 ***got·ten*** [ˈgɔtn]***; getting)*** ①获得;赚得;赢得,博得,取得. ~ *a first prize* 获得头奖. ~ *a lot of money* 得到许多钱. ~ *more than one bargained for* 得到意外收获; 碰到意外不愉快的事. ~ *a living* 谋生. ~ *fame [credit, glory]* 获得名誉[信任, 荣誉]. ~ *knowledge* 获取知识. ②收到,接到. *Did you* ~ *my letter?* 你收到我的信了吗? ~ *a telegram* 接到一封电报. ③生(病),得(病),感染上(病);(毒品等)使上瘾. ~ *the measles* 出痧子. ~ *a film* 迷上一部电影. ④挨(打等);〔口〕受(罚),被判(刑). ~ *a blow on the head* 头上挨了一拳.〔口〕受罚,受苦;被判刑. ~ *three months* 被处徒刑三月. ~ *the sack* 〔口〕被解雇. ⑤买,定购. *Where did you* ~ *that hat?* 你在哪里买到这顶帽子的? ⑥拿;搞到,弄来. *Go* ~ *your exercise book.* 把你的作业本拿来. *G- me some food.* 给我弄点吃的来. ⑦抓住,捕捉. *The police got the thief.* 警察捉住了小偷. ⑧赶上,搭上(车、船等). *hurry to* ~ *train* 急着去赶火车. ⑨〔完成式 have got〕有. *I've got very little money.* 我没有多少钱. ⑩〔完成式后接不定式 have got to = have to〕得,该,不得不. *I've got to go to the doctor's.* 我得去看医生了. ⑪使达到(某种状态、地位、场所等),使产生(某种结果). ~ *the breakfast ready* 准备好早饭. ~ *the sum right* 把数目弄对. *add 2 and 2 to* ~ *4* 二加二等于四. ⑫使怀孕;(常用于动物)生,使生(仔). ~ *a woman with child* 使女人怀孕. ⑬说服,劝说. *I got him to do homework.* 我说服他去做功课. ⑭〔口〕理解, 了解; 暗记. *I can't* ~ *you.* 我不明白你的意思. ~ *the verse by heart* 把诗背熟. ⑮〔后接以过去分词作补足语的宾语〕使〔要〕…如何; 把…了. ~ *one's hair cut* 理发. ~ *one's coat mended* 修补上衣. *I got my arm broken.* 我把手臂弄断了. ~ *oneself elected* 使自己选上. ★参见释义⑪,有类似处. ⑯〔美〕迷人,吸引人,惹人欢喜. *The place doesn't* ~ *me altogether.* 这地方一点也不吸引我. *Her singing* ~*s me.* 她的歌唱迷住了我. ⑰〔口〕打,击中;使受伤,杀死. *The blow got him in the mouth.* 一拳打中他的嘴巴. *It* ~*s them in the end.* 终于弄死了他们. ⑱〔口〕吃;准备饭菜. ~ *lunch at the inn* 在旅馆吃中饭. ⑲使为难,问倒;使烦恼. *This problem* ~*s me.* 这问题难住我了. ⑳收听,(电话)接通. *Please* ~ *me Shanghai.* 请给我接通上海. ㉑【棒球】使对方球员下场. ㉒报复. *I'll* ~ *you yet!* 早晚要给你点颜色看看! — *vi.* ①得,成为…, 开始…起来. *It's getting dark [late, cold].* 天渐黑[晚,冷]起来. ~ *into rage* 生起气来. ~ *to be friends* 做起朋友来. *They got talking together.* 他们谈起话来了. *How did you* ~ *to know that I was here?* 你怎么知道我在这儿? *He soon* ~*s to like it.* 他不久就喜欢上它. ②到达;去;进去. *The train* ~*s here at one o'clock.* 火车一点钟到这里. ③〔与过去分词构成被动式〕被,受. ~ *beaten* 挨揍. ~ *caught in the rain* 遇上雨. ~ *drunk [hurt]* 喝醉[受伤]了. *He got laughed at [punished, scolded].* 他被人嘲笑[处罚,责备]. ④〔美方〕勉勉强强…,好容易…. *I got to come.* 我总算来了. ⑤〔俚〕赶快走开.(命令)去!滚!停止! *tell sb. to* ~ 叫某人立刻走开. ⑥获得财产,赚到钱. ~ ***about*** ①走动;旅行,往来. ②(消息等)传开. ③忙于工作,参加社会活动. ④(病后)下床活动了. ~ ***above oneself*** 变得自高自大. ~ ***abroad*** (消息等)传开. ~ ***across*** ①使通过. ②讲清楚,使人了解 (~ *sb. across the street* 带某人过马路. ~ *one's idea across to the audience* 使听众理解自己的想法). ~ ***after*** 〔美口〕①训诫,攻击. ②敦促,再三要求. ~ ***ahead*** 进步,获得成功 (~ *ahead with one's career* 事业有进展). ~ ***ahead and do it*** 〔美〕快干. ~ ***ahead of*** 赶过,胜过. ~ ***along*** ①过活,过日子. ②团结,和好相处 *(together; with)*. ③有起色,进步;成功. ④〔口〕〔主要用于祈使句〕走开,出去;胡说 (*How are you getting along [on]?* 你近来怎么样? ~ *along (well) together* 相处得很好. *Get along with you!* 〔口〕滚开!去你的!胡说!). ~ ***among*** 加入. ~ ***around*** 〔美〕①往来,走动. ②(消息等)传开. ③避开(法律等). ④参加社会活动;忙于工作. ⑤(用哄骗、奉承等)说服,影响,智胜(某人). ~ ***at*** ①到达;拿得到,够得着. ②抓住;看出,了解. ③〔口〕贿赂,收买(*The mayor has been got at.* 市长已受贿赂). ④〔俚〕挖苦,攻击;欺骗. ⑤意指. (*What are you getting at?* 你说这话是什么意思?). ~ ***away*** ①离开,逃脱;出发. ②把…送走. ~ ***away with (sth.)*** ①拿走,抢走,带走. ②〔俚〕卷(款)潜逃. ③避开责备、惩罚 (*The thief got away with my watch.* 那贼把我的手表偷走了). ~ ***away with it*** 侥幸成功;逃脱处罚. ***Get away [along, out] with you!*** 〔口〕滚开!去你的! ~ ***back*** ①取回. ②回来. ③送回. ④〔俚〕报复 *(on)* (~ *back one's own on sb.* 对某人进行报复). ~ ***back at*** 报复. ~ *back at sb. for doing sth.* 为某人所做某事对他实行报复. ~ ***behind*** ①落后. ②拖欠. ③看穿,看透 (~ *behind sb.'s tricks* 看穿某人诡计). ④回避. ⑤〔美〕支持,撑腰. ~ ***by*** ①走过,通过. ②〔美〕勉强混过去,侥幸成功. ~ ***clear of*** 脱离,摆脱,避开,还清(债务). ~ ***done with sth.*** 做完,结束. ~ ***down*** ①落下,降下;下车. ②写下. ③放下;咽下. ④使沮丧,使抑郁. ⑤开始认真对待,开始认真考虑 *(to)*. ~ ***down on*** 〔美〕产生恶感,开始不喜欢. ~ ***even with*** 〔俚〕报复 *(I'll* ~ *even with him sooner or later.* 我迟早要向他报复). ~ ***forward*** 进步;促进. ~ ***going*** ①〔美口〕开始,动手,采取行动. ②〔美俚〕离开,出去. ~ ***hep*** 〔美俚〕知道,熟悉起来;真相大白. ~ ***hold of*** 获得,找到;接触. ~ ***hold of the wrong end of the stick*** 根本弄

错,完全误解. ~ ***home*** ①回家,到家. ②达到目的. ③言语中肯. ~ ***in*** ①进入,到达. ②收(庄稼);收集(税收,捐款等). ③插入; 安排进…. ④请…来做. ⑤当选为议员 (~ *in on time* 准时到达. ~ *in for Chester* 当选为彻斯特选区议员. ~ *in the New Year goods* 进年货. ~ *in a word edgeways* 从旁插句话). ~ ***into*** ①进入;穿上. ②(酒劲)冲脑. ③成癖; 陷于. ④研究 (~ *into a mess [muddle, scrape]*〔口〕把事情搞糟. ~ *into positions*【军】进入阵地. ~ *into trouble* 陷入麻烦. *The wine got into his head.* 他酒力发作了). ~ ***in with*** ①和…好起来. ②【海】靠近. ~ ***it***〔口〕①懂得. ②挨骂,受处分. ~ ***it hot***〔口〕挨一顿痛骂,大受申斥. ~ ***it on***〔美俚〕兴奋,激动. ~ ***it right*** 正确理解,使人了解清楚. ~ ***left*** 失败,吃亏,上当. ~ ***next to*** ①知道(某事). ②结识(某人). ~ ***nowhere*** (使)无进展,(使)无效,(使)无成就 (*It will ~ you nowhere.* 这样不会对你有好处). ~ ***off*** ①下来,下车;脱下(衣服等). ②卖出(货物);发出(电报、信件等). ③〔口〕说(笑话). ④使入睡. ⑤出发,起飞;离去. ⑥逃脱,避开;免脱处罚[不幸、损失等]. ⑦〔美〕弄好;〔美俚〕弄错. ⑧〔美俚〕吸毒后感到飘飘然;处于快感中. (*tell sb. where he ~s off* 斥责某人). ~ ***off by heart*** 背诵. ~ ***off on the right [wrong] foot*** 出师顺利[不利]. ~ ***off one's chest*** 尽情倾诉,倾吐衷情. ~ ***off the air***〔美俚〕广播结束. ~ ***off to sleep*** 入睡. ~ ***off with***〔俚〕和异性亲热起来. ~ ***on*** ①上马,上车;穿上,安上. ②进步 *(with)*;繁荣,成功. ③过日子,生活;相好,相投 *(with, together)* (~ *on in the world* 发迹,出头. ~ *on in years* 上年纪. ~ *on like a house on fire* 进展迅速顺利. *have got 'em all on*〔口〕穿上最好的衣服,打扮得漂漂亮亮). ~ ***on for [to, toward]*** 靠近,接近,快要 (*It is getting on for midnight.* 快到半夜了. *He's getting on for seventy.* 他近七十岁了). ~ ***on the air***〔美〕开始广播[播音]. ~ ***on to***〔美〕①识破;理解,明白过来. ② 同…接触. ~ ***on sb.'s feet*** (尤指说话时)站起来;恢复. ~ ***on the move*** 开始活动. ~ ***one's [his, hers, yours, theirs]*** 得到应有的报酬,受到应得的惩罚 (*John will ~ his when his father learns that he did not attend school today.* 当约翰的父亲知道约翰今天逃学时,他准会挨骂). ~ ***one's skates on*** 赶快. ~ ***out*** ①走出,离开;摆脱;〔命令语气〕出去! (*G- out!* 滚!). ②泄漏,显露. ③取出;拔出;发现. ④说出,公布;出版;抛出(股票). ~ ***out of*** ①由…出来. ②逐渐放弃(恶习);避免. ③拔出;弄出. ④问出,打听出 (~ *out of control* 失去控制. ~ *out of one's duties* 逃避职责. ~ *out of hand* 控制不了,管不住了. *I could ~ nothing out of him.* 我从他嘴里什么也问不出). ~ ***outside of***〔俚〕吃,喝 (*The snake got outside of a frog.* 蛇吞下一只青蛙). ~***over*** ①越过,爬过(墙等). ②克服(困难). ③走完;完成. ④回避,逃避(法律、规则等). ⑤痊愈;复原. ⑥默认;原谅;断念;忘记过去;混过(时间). ⑦〔俚〕欺骗;消灭(证据等). ⑧〔俚〕说服,使了解. ~ ***rid of*** 摆脱,解脱;除去. ~ ***right down to cases***〔美口〕考虑基本问题. ~ ***round*** = ~ around. ~ ***round the table*** 使敌对各方坐下谈判. ***G- set!***【体】准备! ~ ***sth. down cold [pat]***〔美口〕完全了解,知道得一清二楚. ~ ***somewhere*** 使有成效,使有进展. ~ ***there***〔美〕成功,达到目的. ~ ***the weight of one's feet [legs]*** 坐下[躺下]休息. ~ ***through*** ①了结,办完. ②(使)通过(议案);及格. ③用完,花光. ④达到目的;成功 *(with)*;熬过(一段时期). ⑤打通(电话). ~ ***to*** ①到达,接触到. ②开始. ③〔美口〕收买. ~ ***to first base***〔美口〕成功. ~ ***together*** ①收集,积累. ②聚集,集会. ③〔口〕取得一致意见,同意. ~ ***under*** 镇压,控制. ~ ***under way*** 出发;出动,(船)开动. ~ ***up*** ①(使)起床,(使)起立;爬上;登上;骑上(马);逼近. ②(风等)变大;变烈;使(神经)兴奋[紧张]. ③飞出,跳出. ④准备,安排,组织;起草,编纂,出版. ⑤钻研. ⑥整理,修整,打扮,理发. ⑦增进(健康);演出(戏剧). ⑧〔对马吆喝〕走! ⑨玩弄(诡计等). ~ ***up and ~***〔口〕赶快走. ~ ***up and go*** 精力,魄力,主动精神 (*With his ~ up and go, he ought to be a success as a manager.* 以他的精力来说,他理当是一位成功的经理. ~ ***up early*** 早起;有进取心. ~ ***used to*** 惯于. ~ ***well*** 痊愈,复原. ~ ***wind of*** 听见,风闻. ~ ***wise to***〔美俚〕懂得,晓得. ~ ***with it***〔美俚〕赶上时髦,不落伍. — *n.* ①【畜】幼畜,(动物的)子. ②〔英俚〕私生子. ③(煤炭)产量. ④赢利;薪资. *What's your weeks ~?* 你的周薪多少? ~**-off** (飞机的)起飞. ~**-out** ①脱身;脱逃;〔美俚〕退路. ②亏盈相底 (*as all ~-out*〔美口〕极顶,最大程度). ~**-rich-quick** *a.* 想发横财的. ~**-together** ① *n.* (非正式的)会谈,会商;〔美〕联欢会;集会. ②*a.* 协议的;会商的;大群人的. ~**up** ①〔口〕装束,打扮,风度. ②式样,格式. ③(书籍的)装订. ④〔美〕野心,精力. ~**-up-and-go** *a.* 干劲十足的,有进取心的.

ge·ta [ˈgetə,-ɑː] *n.* *(pl.* ~, ~*s)*〔Jap.〕木屐.

get·at·a·ble [getˈætəbl] *a.* ①可到达的,可接近的,可获得的. ②能懂的. **-i·ty** *n.*

get·a·way [ˈgetəˌwei] *n.* ①〔口〕(盗贼等的)逃亡,逃走. ②(赛马、汽车的)起跑,开始. ③【空】最小飞行速度. *a car with a good ~* 一辆起动快的汽车. *make a [one's] ~* 逃走;【军】突围. ~ **day** (运动会等)赛会的最后一天.

Geth·sem·a·ne [geθˈsemәni] *n.* ①(耶路撒冷附近的)客西马尼园〔据传是耶稣被捕处〕. ②〔g-〕使人受精神折磨的地方[经验].

get·(t)a·ble [ˈgetəbl] *a.* 能得到的,能到手的.

get·ter [ˈgetə] *n.* ①获得者. ②(电子管的)收气剂;收气器. ③吸气剂,吸气器. ④采矿工,采煤工. ⑤采煤机. ⑥〔加〕毒饵.

Get·ty(s) [ˈgeti(z)] *n.* 格蒂(斯)〔姓氏〕.

Get·tys·burg [ˈgetizˌbəːg] *n.* 葛底斯堡〔美国城市〕. ~ **Address** (1863年美国总统林肯所作的)葛底斯堡演说〔其中有"民治,民有,民享" (by the people, of the people and for the people) 这一名句〕.

Ge·um [ˈdʒi(ː)əm] *n.*【植】水杨梅属;〔g-〕水杨梅.

Gev. = giga-electron-volt.

gew·gaw [ˈgjuːgɔː] *n.* 华而不实的东西,小玩意儿. — *a.* 外表好看的,华而不实的.

gey [gei] *a.*〔Scot.〕相当的;颇多的. — *ad.*〔Scot.〕十分,非常.

gey·ser[1] [ˈgaizə] *n.* ①间歇(喷)泉. ②〔英〕[ˈgiːzə] 水的(蒸汽)加热器,(浴室里的)热水锅炉.

gey·ser[2] [ˈgiːzə] *n.* = geezer.

gey·ser·ite [ˈgaizərait] *n.*【矿】硅华〔某种间歇(喷)泉周围的沉积物〕.

GFE = government furished equipment 政府提供的设备,官方设备.

G-film [ˈdʒiːfilm] *n.* G 级电影,男女老少均可观看的电影.

G-force [ˈdʒiːfɔːs] *n.* ①地心吸力. ②火箭或飞机改变速度时人体的反应力.

GFR = German Federal Republic.

G. G. = Grenadier Guards 英国近卫军步兵联队.

g. gr. = great gross【商】十二罗(= 1,728个).

GHA = Greenwich hour angle【海】格林威治时角.

Gha·na [ˈgɑːnə] *n.* 加纳〔非洲〕.

Gha·na·ian [gɑːˈneiən] *a.* 加纳的,加纳人的. — *n.* 加纳人.

ghar·ry [ˈgæri] *n.* (印度等地的)马车.

ghast·ful [ˈgɑːstful,ˈgæ-] *a.*〔古〕可怕的. **-ly** *ad.*

ghast·ly [ˈgɑːstli, ˈgæ-] *a.* ①鬼一样的,苍白的. ②恐怖的,可怕的. ③〔口〕糟透的,坏透的. ④极大的. *The dinner was ~.* 晚饭坏透了. *a ~ failure* 大失败. — *ad.* 鬼一样地,可怕地. **-li·ness** *n.*

gha(u)t [gɔːt] *n.* 〔印度英语〕①山路;〔*pl.*〕山脉(尤指印度南部沿海的山脉). ②(上下码头、浴场等的)石阶. ***a burning*** ~ 河旁边的火葬场.

gha·zi [ˈgɑːziː] *n.* ①(击败异教徒的)伊斯兰教勇士. ②(土耳其的)最高领袖〔给凯旋的苏丹或将军上的尊号〕.

ghee [giː] *n.* (做菜用的)印度酥油〔用水牛的乳制成〕.

gher·kin [ˈgəːkin] *n.* ①(一种做泡菜用的)小黄瓜. ②嫩黄瓜.

ghet·to [ˈgetəu] *n.* (*pl.* ~*s*, *-ti* [ˈgetiː]) ①(城市中)犹太居民区. ②(城市中因社会、经济压力而形成的)少数民族聚居区. ③〔美〕城市中的黑人. 波多黎各人等的集中居住区. — *vt.* = ghettoize. ~ **act** 种族隔离法.

ghet·to·ize [ˈgetəuaiz] *vt.* ①用压力使集中居住. ②使成为少数民族聚居区. **-i·za·tion** [ˌgetəuaiˈzeiʃən] *n.* 强迫集中居住.

ghet·to·lo·gist [geˈtɔlədʒist] *n.* 研究城市少数民族居住区情况的专家.

ghil·lie [ˈgiliː] *n.* ①活结无舌鞋. ②= gillie.

ghost [gəust] *n.* ①鬼,幽灵. ②灵魂. ③阴影;幻象. ④(光学和电视上的)双重图象,散乱的光辉,反常回波. ⑤【冶】鬼线. ⑥〔口〕(美术,文艺的)代笔人. ⑦微量,一点儿. *look like a* ~ 看起来象鬼一样. *look as if one had seen a* ~现出活见鬼的样子. *a* ~ *of a smile* 一丝丝微笑. ***give [yield] up the*** ~ 死. ***have not the*** ~ ***of a chance*** = ***have not a*** ~ ***of a show*** 〔美〕毫无希望. ***lay a*** ~ 把鬼撵跑,镇鬼. ***play*** ~ ***to sb.*** 替某人代笔. ***raise a*** ~ 使鬼魂出现,召鬼. ***the Holy G-*** 【宗】圣灵. ***when the*** ~ ***walks.*** 出鬼;〔俚〕(剧院)发薪水的时候. —*vi.* 〔美口〕替人代笔;(鬼一样)作祟. —*vt.* ①为某人代作(文章、作品等). ②象鬼一样出没于(某地). ~ **candle** (点在死者周围的)避邪烛. ~ **cell**【动】血影细胞. ~ **dance** 〔美〕(十九世纪北美印第安人的)鬼神舞. ~**like** *a.* 象鬼一样的. ~ **station** 鬼站〔已停用或无职工驻守的火车站〕. ~ **town** 〔美〕被遗弃城市的遗迹. ~ **word** 幽灵词〔因误读、误写而造出来的词,别字〕.

ghost·ly [ˈgəustli] *a.* ①鬼的;幽灵的,鬼一样的;朦胧的,可怕的. ②〔古〕灵魂的,精神上的,宗教上的. ③代人捉刀的. *our* ~ *enemy* 恶魔. *the* ~ *hour* 半夜. ~ **adviser [director, father]** 听忏悔的神父. ~ **comfort** (牧师对忏悔者或将死者的)精神安慰. **-li·ness** *n.*

ghost·write [ˈgəust-rait] *vi.* 受雇代为作文[作画] *(for)*. —*vt.* 为人代写(作品等).

ghost·writ·er [ˈgəustˌraitə] *n.* 捉刀人, 受雇作文[作画]的人.

ghost·y [ˈgəusti] *a.* 鬼的,幽灵的;鬼似的,幽灵似的.

ghoul [guːl, gaul] *n.* ①(东方神话中的) 食尸鬼. ②盗尸人. ③以恐吓人为乐的歹徒.

ghoul·ish [ˈguːliʃ] *a.* 食尸鬼似的;残忍的. **-ly** *ad.*

GHQ, G.H.Q.=general headquarters 统帅部,总司令部.

ghyll [gil] *n.* 〔英方〕 = gill[2].

GI,[1] G.I. [ˈdʒiːˈai] *n.* (*pl. GI's, G.I.'s*) 〔美口〕①(陆军)兵士. ②(发给士兵的) 军用品 (= government issue). — *a.* ①兵士的. ②军用的. ③符合军事法规的;要求严守军纪的. *an ex-GI* 退役军人. *GI shoes* 军鞋. — *vt.* ***(GI'd; GI'ing)*** 为准备接受军事检查而对(营房等)大扫除. — *ad.* 严格按照军事法规地. ~ **Jane [Jill, Joan]** 美国女兵. ~ **Joe** 〔俚〕美国兵;丘八(尤指第二次世界大战时的美国兵).

GI[2] = ①galvanized iron. ②gastrointestinal. ③general issue. ④government issue.

gi. = gill(s) 及耳(液量单位, =$\frac{1}{4}$ pint).

gi·ant [ˈdʒaiənt] *n.* ①巨人;大汉. ②巨兽;巨树,巨物. ③卓越人物. ***the G-'s Causeway*** 巨人堤道〔北爱尔兰安特里姆郡的岬,有上千的玄武岩小圆柱〕. — *a.* 巨大的;伟大的. *a* ~ *crab* 大蟹. ~ **gum** 杏仁桉. ~ **killer** 〔美〕重量拳击家,凶猛的拳击家. ~ **panda** 大熊猫. ~ **redwood** 【植】世界爷. ~ **star**【天】巨星. ~**('s) stride** (公园里的)旋转秋千. ~ **swing** 伏虎〔体育用具〕. ~**like** *a.* 巨人般的.

gi·ant·ess [ˈdʒaiəntis] *n.* 女巨人.

gi·ant·ism [ˈdʒaiəntizəm] *n.* ①巨大,庞大. ②【医】巨大畸形;巨大发育,巨大症.

giaour [ˈdʒauə] *n.* 邪教徒〔穆斯林对非伊斯兰教徒、基督教徒的蔑称〕.

Giauque [dʒiˈəuk] *n.* 吉奥克〔姓氏〕.

gib[1] [gib] *n.* 【机】凹字楔,扁栓,夹条. — *vt.* 用扁栓〔夹条〕固定.

gib[2] [gib] *n.* ①嗤嗤〔指所呼唤的猫〕. ②(阉过的)公猫.

Gib. = Gibraltar.

gib·ber [ˈdʒibə] *vi.* 急促不清楚地说话;(猴子)叽叽喳喳地叫. — *n.* = gibberish.

Gib·ber·el·la [ˌdʒibəˈrelə] *n.* 赤霉菌.

gib·ber·el·lic [ˌdʒibəˈrelik] **acid**【化】赤霉酸.

gib·ber·el·lin [ˌdʒibəˈrelin] *n.*【药】赤霉素.

gib·ber·ish[ˈdʒibəriʃ, ˈgib-] *n.* 急促而不清楚的话;无意义的声音.

gib·bet [ˈdʒibit] *n.* ①绞架. ②绞刑. ③(起重机的)臂. — *vt.* ①绞死, 吊死. ②把(某人)吊在示众架上;当众侮辱,使出丑. *die on the* ~ 被绞死.

gib·ble-gab·ble [ˈgiblˌgæbl] *n.* = gabble.

gib·bon [ˈgibən] *n.* 长臂猿.

Gib·bon(s) [ˈgibən(z)] *n.* 吉本(斯)〔姓氏〕.

gib·bose [ˈgibəus] *a.* = gibbous.

gib·bos·i·ty [giˈbɔsiti] *n.* ①凸状;隆起. ②驼背. ③【天】凸圆.

gib·bous [ˈgibəs] *a.* ①凸面的;隆起的. ②驼背的. ③【天】凸圆的. ④(月球、行星)光亮部分大于半圆的. *the* ~ *moon* 凸月. **-ly** *ad.*

Gibbs [gibz] *n.* 吉布斯〔姓氏〕.

gibbs·ite [ˈgibzait] *n.*【矿】水铝矿,三水铝矿.

gibe [dʒaib] *vt., vi.* 嘲笑 *(at)*. —*n.* 嘲笑. **gib·ing·ly** *ad.*

Gib·e·on·ite [ˈgibiənait] *n.*【圣】基遍人,贱民,苦力.

gib·er [ˈdʒaibə] *n.* 嘲笑者.

gib·let [ˈdʒiblit] *n.* (禽类的心、胗等)杂件.

Gi·bral·tar [dʒiˈbrɔːltə] *n.* ①直布罗陀. ②要塞地. ***the Straits of*** ~ 直布罗陀海峡. **-i·an** *n.* 直布罗陀的居民.

Gib·son[1] [ˈgibsn] *n.* 吉布森〔姓氏〕.

Gib·son[2] [ˈgibsən] *n.* 〔亦 g-〕吉布森鸡尾酒〔一种马提尼鸡尾酒,由艾酒、杜松子酒等混合而成〕. ~ **girl** 吉布森式女孩〔指美国插图画家吉布森 (C.D. Gibson, 1867—1944) 绘画中的十九世纪九十年代的美国女孩的形象〕.

gi·bus [ˈdʒaibəs] *n.* (歌剧中用的)折叠礼帽.

gid [gid] *n.* (羊的)回旋病.

gid·dap [giˈdæp] *int.* = giddyap.

gid·dy [ˈgidi] *a.* ①发晕的;眼花缭乱的. ②令人发晕的. ③急速旋转的. ④轻率的, 轻浮的. *a* ~ *girl* 轻浮的姑娘. *feel* ~ 发晕. *a* ~ *head* 轻率的人, 浮躁的人. *a* ~ *goat* 〔俚〕呆子. *a* ~ *round of pleasures* 接踵而至使人应接不暇的快乐. — *vi., vt.* (使)眩晕,(使)急速旋转. ~**-brained** *a.* 轻率的,浮躁的. ~**-go-round** 〔英口〕旋转木马 (= merry-go-round). **gid·di·ly** *ad.* **gid·di·ness** *n.*

gid·dy·ap [ˌgidiˈæp] *int.* 走吧! 快! 快! 驾! 〔对马的吆喝〕(= giddyup, giddap).

Gid·e·on [ˈgidiən] *n.* 吉迪恩〔男子名〕.

gie [ˈgiː, gi] *n.* 〔Scot.〕= give.

Giel·gud [ˈgi(ː)lgud] *n.* 吉尔古德〔姓氏〕.

Gif·ford [ˈgifəd] *n.* 吉福德〔男子名〕.

gift [gift] *n.* ①赠送;赠与权;赠品,礼物. ②天赋,才能,天资. *birthday* ~*s* 寿礼,生日礼物. *of many* ~*s* 多才

多艺. *Christmas* ～ 圣诞节礼品. *Gifts from enemies are dangerous.* 〔谚〕敌人的礼物是收不得的. ***a Greek*** ～ 图谋害人的礼物. ***at a*** ～ 白送 (*I wouldn't have [take] it at a* ～. 白送我也不要). ***by [of] free*** ～ 白送,免费赠送. ***Christmas G-!*** 〔美南部〕恭贺圣诞! ***Cordelia's*** ～ 妇女温柔的声音. ***have the*** ～ ***of (the) gab*** 能说会道. ***the*** ～ ***of tongues*** 学语言的天才. ***in sb.'s*** ～ = ***in the*** ～ ***of sb.*** 有赠与权. — *vt.* ①赠送,授予. ②天赋 (权利, 才能等). *be* ～*ed with talents* 有才能. ～**-book** *n.* 礼品书. ～ **coupon (certificate)** (百货公司等发的)礼券,赠券. ～**-enterprise** 附送赠品的买卖. ～ **horse** 馈赠的马, 〔转义〕价值有问题的礼物 (*Don't look a* ～ *horse in the mouth.* 〔谚〕送来的礼别挑剔). ～ **shop** 手工艺品店, 礼品店. ～**-wrap** *vt.* (以装璜花纸、丝绸等)包装(作礼品用的)商品.

gift·ed [ˈgiftid] *a.* 有天才的,天禀的.

gift·ie [ˈgifti] *n.* 〔Scot.〕才能,能力.

gig[1] [gig] *n.* ①旋转物. ②轻便二轮马车. ③小快艇,比赛快艇. ④【矿】轮子坡, 小水仓. ⑤两层罐笼, 吊桶. ⑥怪人. — *vi.* 〔常作 ～ it〕坐小快艇; 乘轻便二轮马车. ～ **lamps** 〔俚〕眼镜.

gig[2] [gig] *n.* 【纺】刺果起绒机 (= ～ mill).

gig[3] [gig] *n.* 鱼叉; (钓鱼用)排钩. — *vt.* ①用鱼叉叉(鱼). ②〔美〕戳;刺激,激励. — *vi.* 用鱼叉叉鱼.

gig[4] [gig] *n.* (军队、学校等的)记过. — *vt.* 给…以记过处分.

gig[5] [gig] *n.* 〔美俚〕①爵士音乐演奏会. ②演奏爵士音乐的职业. ③活儿.

giga- *comb.f.* 表示"京","千兆","十亿" (10^9): *gigacycle.*

gi·ga·cy·cle [ˈdʒigəˌsaikl] *n.* 千兆周.

giga-electron-volt [ˈdʒigə-iˈlektrɔn-vəult] *n.* 十亿〔千兆〕电子伏.

gi·ga·hertz [ˈdʒigəˌhəːts] *n.* 千兆赫(兹) 〔频率单位〕(= gigacycle).

gi·gan·te·an [ˌdʒaigænˈtiən, dʒaiˈgæntiən] *a.* 巨人似的;巨大的.

gi·gan·tesque [ˌdʒaigænˈtesk] *a.* 巨人似的, 适于巨人的;庞大的.

gi·gan·tic [dʒaiˈgæntik] *a.* 巨大的;庞大的;巨人似的. **-al·ly** *ad.* **-ness** *n.*

gi·gan·tism [ˈdʒaigæntizm] *n.* ①巨大, 庞大. ②【医】巨大症,巨大发育,巨大畸形 (= giantism).

gi·gan·tom·a·chy [ˈdʒaigænˈtɔməki] *n.* ① 〔G-〕【希神】巨人对天神的搏斗. ②巨人与巨人的战争; 巨人集团之间的战争;大国间的战争.

gi·ga·ton [ˈdʒigəˌtʌn] *n.* 十亿吨级〔热核武器爆炸力的计算单位,指相当于十亿吨级梯恩梯炸药的当量〕.

gig·git [ˈgigit] *vt.* 〔美〕赶快运 *(away).* — *vi.* 赶快去.

gig·gle [ˈgigl] *n., vi.* 吃吃地笑,痴笑. ～ **gas** 〔美俚〕笑气. ～ **smoke** 〔美俚〕大麻. ～ **soup [water]** 〔美俚〕酒. **gig·gly** *a.*

gig·let [ˈgiglet], **-lot** [-lət] *n.* 痴笑的女孩.

gig·man [ˈgigmən] *n.* *(pl.* ***-men)*** 马车主;市侩.

gig·man·i·ty [gigˈmæniti] *n.* 市侩阶层,庸夫俗子.

gig·o·lo [ˈdʒigələu] *n.* ①舞男. ②靠女人倒贴而生活的男子.

gig·ot [ˈdʒigət] *n.* (熟的)羊腿,鹿腿. *a* ～ *sleeve* 羊脚形袖子.

gigue [ʒiːg] *n.* 〔F.〕【乐】吉格舞曲〔尤指古曲音乐的组曲中的一个乐章〕.

Gi·la [ˈhiːlə] *n.* 【动】(美国西南部产的) 大毒蜥 (=～ monster).

Gil·bert [ˈgilbət] *n.* 吉尔伯特〔姓氏,男子名〕.

gil·bert [ˈgilbət] *n.* 【电】吉伯〔磁通势单位,等于 0.796 安匝〕.

Gilbert and Ellice Islands [ˈgilbət ənd ˈelis ˈailəndz] 吉尔伯特和埃利斯群岛〔西太平洋〕.

Gil·ber·ta [gilˈbəːtə] *n.* 吉尔伯塔〔女子名〕.

Gil·ber·ti·an [gilˈbəːtjən] *a.* 英国喜歌剧作家吉尔伯特 (Gilbert) 派的;滑稽的,诙谐的.

gild[1] [gild] *vt.* ***(～ed, gilt*** [gilt]; ***～ed, gilt)*** ①给…镀金,给…贴上金箔. ②使光彩夺目. ③修饰,虚饰. ④使有钱, 使阔气. *the sky* ～*ed by the morning sun* 被朝阳染成金色的天空. ～ ***the lily*** 作不恰当的修饰, 画蛇添足. ～ ***the pill*** 把不愉快的事情弄得使人容易接受;美化劣货;粉饰太平. ～ ***the refined gold*** 锦上添花, 多此一举.

gild[2] [gild] *n.* = guild.

Gil·da [ˈgildə] *n.* 吉尔达〔女子名〕.

gild·ed [ˈgildid] *a.* ①镀金的,涂金色的. ②修饰的,虚饰的. ③有钱的, 阔气的. *a* ～ *frame* 金色镜框. *a group of* ～ *youths* 一群纨绔子弟. ～ *vices* 阔佬们的消遣. ～ *vanities* 夸耀富贵的虚荣. **G- Chamber** 英国上议院. ～ **spurs** 金马刺〔爵士徽章〕.

gild·ing [ˈgildiŋ] *n.* ①镀金, 上金粉. ②镀金材料, 金箔,金粉. ③虚饰,粉饰. *chemical [electric]* ～ 电镀金. ～ **metal** 手饰铜.

Giles [dʒailz] *n.* 贾尔斯〔姓氏,男子名〕.

Gi·lhe·ney [giˈliːni] *n.* 吉利尼〔姓氏〕.

Gill[1] [dʒil] *n.* 〔有时 g-〕少女;女情人. *Every Jack has his* ～. 破锅不愁无烂盖,男人自有女人爱. *Jack and* ～ 青年男女.

Gill[2] [gil, dʒil] *n.* 吉尔〔女子名〕.

gill[1] [gil] *n.* ①〔常 *pl.*〕鱼鳃, (水生动物的)呼吸器. ②【植】层, 褶片; 菌褶. ③(鸡, 火鸡等的)垂肉, 颐下肉. ④〔常 *pl.*〕(人的)腮;〔美俚〕嘴巴. ***look blue [green, white, yellow] about the*** ～***s*** 血色不好〔面有菜色,面如土色,垂头丧气〕. ***look rosy about the*** ～***s*** 血色好. ***turn red in the*** ～***s*** 发怒. ***look white about the*** ～***s*** (因惊恐或患病而)脸色苍白. — *vt.* ①除去(鱼的)鳃和肚杂;除去(菌褶). ②用刺网捕(鱼). — *vi.* (鱼) 被刺网捕住. ～ **cleft [slit]** 鳃裂 (= visceral cleft). ～ **fungus** 伞菌. ～ **net** 【海】刺网.

gill[2] [gil] *n.* ①(树木茂盛的)峡谷. ②(峡谷中的)溪流.

gill[3] [dʒil] *n.* 及耳〔液量单位, =$\frac{1}{4}$ pint〕.

Gil·lett(e) [ˈgilit, ˈgilet] *n.* 吉勒特〔姓氏〕.

Gil·lian [ˈdʒiliən] *n.* 吉琳〔女子名 = Juliana.〕

gil·lie, gil·ly [ˈgiliː] *n.* ***(pl. gil·lies)*** ①(苏格兰高地的)游猎侍从;游猎向导. ②(旧时苏格兰高地的)氏族酋长侍从;男仆.

Gil·ling·ham [ˈgiliŋəm] *n.* 吉林厄姆〔姓氏〕.

gil·ly·flow·er [ˈdʒiliflauə] *n.* 【植】①紫罗兰花. ②桂竹香. ③麝香石竹. ④一种锥状苹果.

Gil·man [ˈgilmən] *n.* 吉尔曼〔姓氏〕.

Gil·mer [ˈgilmə] *n.* 吉尔默〔姓氏〕.

Gil·pin [ˈgilpin] *n.* 吉尔平〔姓氏〕.

gilt[1] [gilt] gild 的过去式及过去分词. — *a.* 镀金的, 涂金的; 金色的. — *n.* ①镀金材料, 镀金涂层. ②炫目的外表. ③〔口〕金钱. ***take the*** ～ ***off the gingerbread*** 剥去金箔,剥去美丽的外衣,把真相暴露出来. ***The*** ～ ***is off.*** 假象消失. ～**-edged** *a.* ①金边的. ②(证券等) 上等的. ③(演员等)阵容极强的,最好的 (*～-edged securities* 【商】信用可靠的证券,金边证券. *a ～-edged theatrical cast* 极佳的演员阵容). ～**head** *n.* 【动】鸟颊鱼.

gilt[2] [gilt] *n.* 小母猪.

gim·bal [ˈdʒimbəl] *n.* 〔常 *pl.*〕①(使罗盘等平衡的) 平衡环(= ～ring);常平架. ②【机】万向接头. ～ **error** 框架误差.

gim·baled [ˈdʒimbəld] *a.* 装有万向接头〔常平架〕的. ～ **engine** 换向发动机.

gim·crack [ˈdʒimkræk] *a.* 华而不实的. — *n.* 小玩意儿,华而不实的东西. **-crack·ery** [-krækəri] *n.* 〔集合词〕华而不实的东西.

gim·el [ˈgiml] *n.* 希伯来语的第三个字母.

gim·let [ˈgimlit] *n.* 手钻，手锥，螺丝锥．— *vt.* 用螺丝锥把(孔眼)钻透．— *a.* ①有钻孔能力的，锐利的．②有钻劲的．*eyes like ~s* 目光敏锐．**~-eyed** *a.* 目光锐利的．

gim·mal [ˈgiml, ˈdʒim-] *n.* 双连环；连环套．

gim·me [ˈgimi]〔俚〕= give me.

gim·mer [ˈgimə] *n.*〔英方〕①小母羊．②〔贬〕女人．

gim·mick [ˈgimik] *n.* ①〔口〕(轮盘赌具、魔术师道具等的)暗机关．②骗人玩意儿；鬼花招；〔俚〕产品广告噱头；竞选宣传伎俩．③巧妙的小机械；小发明；诀窍．— *vt.*〔口〕在…(轮盘赌、魔术道具等)上暗设机关．**-y** *a.* (赌具等)暗设机关的，(道具等)使用巧妙手法的．

gim·mick·ry [ˈgimikri] *n.*〔口〕①花招；伎俩．②耍花招；玩弄伎俩 (= gimmickery).

gimp[1] [gimp] *n.* ①(用以装饰衣服、窗帘等的)嵌心丝带．②经过加固的钓鱼丝．— *vt.* 用嵌心丝带装饰(衣服等)．

gimp[2] [gimp] *n.*〔美口〕精神，活力．

gimp[3] [gimp] *n.* 瘸子；跛行．— *vi.* 瘸着走，跛行．**-y** *a.* 跛的，瘸的．

gin[1] [dʒin] *n.* ①弹棉机，轧花机．②打桩机；三脚起重机．③陷阱；网，渔网．— *vt.* ①轧(棉)．②用陷阱(网)捕捉．*cotton ginning factory* 轧棉厂．**ginned cotton** 皮棉 (*cf.* unginned cotton 籽棉)．

gin[2] [dʒin] *n.* ①杜松子酒，荷兰酒．②〔美俚〕烈酒．**~ *and it*** 杜松子酒和苦艾酒混合的饮料．**~-fizz** 杜松子酒汽水．**~ mill**〔美俚〕低级酒店．**~-palace** 豪华的酒店．**~ rummy** 金罗美〔一种牌戏〕．

gin[3] [gin] *vi., vt.* ***(gan*** [gæn]; ***gun*** [gʌn]*)*〔古、诗〕开始．

gin·gel·li, gin·gel·ly [ˈdʒindʒili] *n.* = gingili.

gin·ger [ˈdʒindʒə] *n.* ①生姜，姜．②姜黄色；〔英俚〕(头发的)赤色，赤毛(人)．③〔口〕精神，气魄．*put some ~ into* 鼓起干劲来，加把劲．*There is no ~ in him.* 他没有勇气〔气魄、精神〕．— *vt.* ①使有姜味．②使有活力，鼓舞．**~ade** = ~ beer. **~ ale** 姜麦酒．**~ beer** 姜啤酒．**~ brandy** 姜汁白兰地．**~bread** ① *n.* 姜饼；华而不实的东西，俗气的装饰．② *a.* 华而不实的，俗气的．**~bread nut** 姜汁饼干．**~bread plum [tree]** 埃及棕榈．**~bread work** 华而不实的装饰．**~bread trap**〔口〕嘴．**~ cordial** 姜汁柠檬葡萄水．**~group**〔英〕(议员中的)鞭挞政府派．**~ nut** = gingerbread nut. **~ pop** = ~ ale. **~ race [root]** 姜根．**~snap** = ~ nut. **~ wine** 姜水甜酒．

gin·ger·ly [ˈdʒindʒəli] *a., ad.* 小心翼翼的〔地〕；兢兢业业的〔地〕．**-i·ness** *n.*

gin·ger·y [ˈdʒindʒəri] *a.* ①姜(似)的；辛辣的．②姜色的；〔英〕(头发)红的．③有精神的．

ging·ham [ˈgiŋəm] *n.* ①条格平布，方格花布．②〔口〕伞．— *a.* 方格花布做的．

gin·gi·li [ˈdʒindʒili] *n.* ①芝麻(= sesame)．②芝麻油．

gin·gi·val [dʒinˈdʒaivəl] *a.* 齿龈的，齿槽的，龈的．

gin·gi·vi·tis [ˌdʒindʒiˈvaitis] *n.*【医】龈炎．

ging·ko [ˈgiŋkəu] *n.* *(pl.* ***~es)*** ①【植】银杏，白果树．②〔G-〕银杏属．

gin·gly·mus [ˈdʒiŋgliməs] *n.* *(pl.* ***-mi*** [-mai]*)*【解】铰状关节，屈戌关节．

gink [giŋk] *n.*〔美俚〕怪人，家伙．

gink·go [giŋkgəu] *(pl.* ***~es)*** *n.*〔美〕= gingko.

gin·ner [ˈdʒinə] *n.* 机器轧棉工人．**-y** *n.* 轧花厂．

gin·seng [ˈdʒinseŋ] *n.* 人参．

gio [gjəu] *n.* = geo.

Gio·con·da, La [ˌlɑːdʒəukɔndə; 〔It.〕dʒəuˈkəundɑː] 蒙娜·丽莎〔意大利画家达芬奇的名画，通常叫做 Mona Lisa〕．

gio·co·so [dʒəuˈkəusəu] *a., ad.*【乐】谐谑的(地)，愉快的(地)，戏嬉的(地)．

gip [dʒip] *vt., vi.*〔美俚〕骗，诓骗．— *n.* 骗子．

gi·pon [dʒiˈpɔn, ˈdʒipɔn] *n.* = jupon.

gip·po [ˈdʒipəu] *n.*〔英俚〕肉汤；燉肉．

Gip·py [ˈdʒipi] *n.*〔英俚〕埃及兵；埃及香烟；吉普赛人．**~ tummy** (在热带国家旅游者患的)腹泻病．

gip·sy, gyp·sy [ˈdʒipsi] *n.* ①〔常 G-〕吉普赛人；〔G-〕吉普赛语．②象吉普赛人的人，黑脸妇女，顽皮〔动人〕的姑娘．③【海】绞绳筒，手推绞盘．— *a.* 吉普赛式的；流浪的．— *vi.* 过吉普赛式的生活，过流浪生活；野餐旅行．**~ bonnet** (妇女、小儿用的)宽边帽．**~ cab**〔美俚〕流动兜客的出租汽车．**~ caravan** 吉普赛式轿车．**~ leave**〔美俚〕不告而别．**~ moth**【动】舞毒蛾．**~ rose**【植】山葡萄．**~ table** 三脚小圆桌．**~ wheel** 锚链轮．**~ winch**【海】手推绞盘．**-hood** *n.* 吉普赛生涯，吉普赛人身分．**-dom** *n.* 吉普赛生涯；吉普赛人．**-fy** *vt.* 使吉普赛化．**-ish** *a.* 吉普赛人似的．**-ism** *n.* 吉普赛人的生活方式．

gi·raffe [dʒiˈrɑːf] *n.* *(pl.* ***~, ~s)*** ①【动】长颈鹿．②〔G-〕【天】鹿豹座．**-ish** *a.*

gi·ran·do·la, gir·an·dole [dʒiˈrændələ, ˈdʒirəndəul] *n.* ①多枝烛台．②旋射焰火．③旋转喷水嘴．④(周围镶有小宝石的)耳环．

Gi·rard [dʒiˈrɑːd] *n.* 吉拉德〔姓氏〕．

gir·a·sol(e) [ˈdʒirəˌsɔl, -ˌsəul] *n.* ①【矿】青蛋白石．②【植】菊芋．

gird[1] [gəːd] ***(~ed, girt*** [gəːt]; ***~ed, girt)*** *vt.* ①缠，束；佩(剑)．②装备；赋与(权力) *(with)*．③围绕，包围着 *(with)*．④〔~ oneself〕准备 *(for)*．*The climber ~ed himself with a rope.* 登山者以绳束腰．*a sea-girt island* 四面临海的岛屿．*to be girt with supreme power* 被赋与最高权力．*The soldiers girt themselves up for battle.* 士兵们准备投入战斗．**~ *on a sword*** [one's armour] 佩剑〔佩带甲胄〕．***~ oneself = ~ (up) one's loins*** 准备行动．—*vi.* 准备．

gird[2] [gəːd] *vi.* 嘲笑 *(at)*．— *vt.* 嘲笑．— *n.* 嘲笑．**-ing·ly** *ad.*

gird·er [ˈgəːdə] *n.*【建】纵梁，大梁，撑柱，撑杆，大型工字梁．*a framed ~* 构桁．**~ truss** 梁构桁架．**-less** *a.*

gir·dle[1] [ˈgəːdl] *n.* ①带，腰带．②环形物，围绕物．③【解】(支持四肢的)带．④【植】环形带，成带现象；环剥，环状剥皮．⑤【建】(抱)柱带．⑥〔美〕(女子的)紧身褡．⑦宝石与镶嵌底板接触处的边缘．*the pelvic [hip] ~* 骨盘带．*the shoulder ~* 上肢带．***have [hold] ... under one's ~*** 使服从，率领．***make [put] a ~ round*** 绕…一周；围绕．***under sb.'s ~*** 在某人控制下．***within the ~ of*** 被…环绕着的．— *vt.* ①用带束，拿带缠 *(round; in; about)*．②围，包围．③环剥(树皮)，剥去(树)的一圈皮．

gir·dle[2] [ˈgəːdl] *v.*〔Scot.〕= griddle. **~ cake**〔Scot.〕用浅锅烘的饼(= griddle-cake)．

gir·dler [ˈgəːdlə] *n.* ①把树咬成环槽的甲虫．②做腰带的人．③束缚〔围绕〕的人〔物〕．

girl [gəːl] *n.* *(opp.* boy*)* ①姑娘，女孩子，少女，未婚女子．②女儿．③女仆，保姆．④女职员，女店员；女演员．⑤〔口〕情人，女朋友．⑥〔和年龄无关只表示亲爱的称呼〕小姐，阿姊，阿姨．*a bachelor ~* 独身女子．*a chit [slip] of a ~* 黄毛丫头，瘦长的姑娘．*a fancy ~ [lady, woman]* ①情妇．②妓女．*a gaiety ~* 杂耍女艺人．*the ~s* (全家的)女儿们．*a shop ~* 女店员．*the principal [leading] ~* 女主角．*one's best ~* 情人．***a ~ about [of] the town*** 妓女．***my dear ~*** 亲爱的姑娘〔对妻的爱称〕．***old ~*** 老太婆〔对妇女或母马的爱称或蔑称〕．**~ Friday** 女事务员，能干的女助手．**~ friend** ①〔口〕未婚妻，女情人．②女性朋友．**~ guides**〔英〕女童子军．**~ scouts**〔美〕女童子军．

girl·cott [ˈgəːlkət] *n.*〔美口〕(妇女们)联合抵制(某人、某事物等)．

girl·hood [ˈgəːlhud] *n.* ①少女身分；姑娘时代．②〔集

合词]姑娘们.

girl·ie [ˈgəːli] *n.* ①〔爱〕姑娘,女人 ②〔俚〕妓女. — *a.* (杂志、电影)有裸体或半裸体女子图片〔镜头〕的.

girl·ish [ˈgəːliʃ] *a.* ①少女的; 少女似的. ②少女时期的. **-ly** *ad.* **-ness** *n.*

gir·ly [ˈgəːli] *a.* ①= girlish. ②= girlie(*a.*)

girn [ˈgəːn] *n., vi., vt.* 〔英方〕咆哮.

gi·ro [ˈdʒaiərəu] *n.* = autogiro.

Gi·ro [ˈdʒairəu] *n.* (西欧各国银行使用电子计算机处理的)邮政转帐服务.

Gi·ronde [dʒiˈrɔnd] *n.* (法国大革命时代的)吉伦特党.

Gi·ron·dist [dʒiˈrɔndist] *n.* 吉伦特党员; 稳健主义者. — *a.* 吉伦特党的; 稳健主义的.

girt[1] [gəːt] gird 的过去式及过去分词.

girt[2] [gəːt] *n.* = girth. — *vt.* ①束, 缠, 绕. ②用肚带束,给…束肚带. ③量…的围长. — *vi.* 围长为.

girth [gəːθ] *n.* ①(马等的)肚带. ②(树干, 人腰身的)围长;【建】围梁; 船壳围长. ③尺寸, 大小. *a man of large* ~ 粗腰身的人. *a tree 16 feet in* ~ 树身粗 16 英尺的树. — *vt.* ①围绕, 包围. ②给…上肚带, 给…紧肚带. ③给…量围长. —*vi.* 围长为.

gi·sarme [giˈzɑːm] *n.* (早期步兵使用的)战斧.

gis·mo [ˈgizməu] *n.* 〔俚〕= gizmo.

Gis·sing [ˈgisiŋ] *n.* ①吉辛〔姓氏〕. ②**George Robert** ~乔治·罗伯特·吉辛〔1857—1903, 英国小说家〕.

gist [dʒist] *n.* ①要点, 要旨. ②诉讼依据; 诉讼主因.

git [git] *vt.,vi.* 〔方〕= get.

git·tern [ˈgitəːn] *n.* 吉特恩〔类似吉他的一种古弦乐器〕.

give [giv] *vt.* ***(gave*** [geiv]; ***giv·en*** [ˈgivn]***)*** ①送给, 给. *I gave the boy a book. I gave a book to the boy.* 我给男孩一本书. ②授予, 赋予, 赐予(地位、头衔、名誉等). *The law ~s citizens the right to vote.* 该法律给公民选举的权利. *be ~n the title of* 被授予…称号. *G- a rogue rope enough and he will hang himself.* 〔谚〕坏人必自取灭亡. ③作出; 举出; 显示出; 载入; 提出, 表示出. ~ *an account* 说明. ~ *examples* 举例. ~ *a guess* 猜一猜. ~ *a suggestion* 提出建议, 建议. ~ *a try* 试一试. ~ *signs of an illness* 显示出病兆. *This word is not ~n in the dictionary.* 这个词没有载入字典. *The thermometer ~s 30° in the shade.* 在阴凉处温度计上是摄氏三十度. *gave him her confidence* 向他表示她的信任. ④致(谢), 转达(问候), 贺(喜); 提议为…干杯. ~ *thanks* 感谢, 致以感谢. *G- my love [compliments, regards] to your mother.* 请问候你的母亲. *I ~ you joy.* 恭喜恭喜. *I('ll) ~ you Mr. X.* 为恭贺X先生干杯吧. ⑤交付; 委托; 让出; 嫁出. ~ *the porter one's bag to carry* 把包交给搬行李工人提. ~ *a daughter in marriage* 把女儿嫁出去. ⑥卖与; 交换. *I will ~ it for 5 dollars.* 五块钱我就卖. *I will ~ 5 dollars for it.* 我出五块钱买. ⑦献身于, 致力于. ~ *one's mind to a matter* 为某件事费心. ~ *one's life to study* 为学问而献身. ⑧产生, 得出; 发, 生; 引起. *Trees ~ fruit.* 树结果子. *Cows ~ milk* 奶牛产奶. *4 divided by 2 ~s 2.* 二除四得二. ⑨说, 宣告; 发出. *Judgment was ~n against the plaintiff.* 作出原告败诉的裁决. ~ *a cry* 喊叫, 大叫一声. ~ *orders* 发出命令. *The umpire gave him out.* 裁判员宣告他出界. *The sun ~s lights.* 太阳发出光. ⑩作为…的源泉〔来源〕; 给(病人)服(药); 把(病)传染给; 为…生子女; 使…生子女. ~ *pleasure* 带来欢乐. *You have ~n me your cold.* 你把伤风传染给我了. *She gave him four sons.* 她给他生了四个儿子. *He gave her two daughters.* 他使她生了两个女儿. ⑪举行, 主办(音乐会, 宴会); 演出. ⑫施以(惩罚); 把…强加于. ⑬完成(一次具体的动作或努力) ~ *a kick [kiss, sly look, jump]* 踢, 吻, 睨视, 跳. ⑭假定, 假想〔主用过去分词〕. *Given health, I can finish the work.* 若是身体好, 我可以完成那项工作. ⑮被认为是, 被归于. *The pamphlet has been given to his pen.* 据说这册子是他写的. ⑯规定, 限定; 指定. *He gave us Sunday as our day of meeting.* 他指定星期日为我们的集会日. ⑰使接触到…; 使能够…; 使可见…. ~ *sb. to understand sth.* 使某人理解某事. *The window ~s the meadow.* 隔窗可见草地. ⑱牺牲, 失去. *She gave one eye in the accident.* 她在事故中失去一只眼睛. ⑲为…把电话接到…. *G- me the service desk, please.* 请接服务台. ⑳介绍. *Ladies and gentleman, I ~ you the Governor of Washington.* 女士们, 先生们, 我请华盛顿州州长和诸位见面. ㉑描述. ~ *the scenery of Beijing* 描述北京风光. — *vi.* ①捐助, 赠送. ~ *generously to charity* 慷慨捐助. ②(色)褪; (天气)变暖和; (冰等)融解. *The winter is giving.* 冬天(的寒冷)渐渐和缓了. *The frost did not ~ all day.* 霜终日不化. ③投降, 屈服, 让步. *The Iron Army never ~s.* "铁军"永不退却. ④(地等受压力)坍下, 凹下; (木器等)弯曲; (沙发等)有弹性; (螺钉等)松动. *The foundations are giving.* 地基陷下去了. *This sofa ~s comfortably.* 这个沙发的弹性好, 坐起来舒服. *His knees gave.* 他瘫了. ④干缩, 湿坏. ⑤面向, 通达. *a wicket giving into an avenue* 通到林荫路的小门. ⑥〔美俚〕发生, 进行. *He demanded to know what gave.* 〔美俚〕他要求知道发生了什么. ⑦适应, 顺应. *She gave to the motion of the horse.* 她适应马的动作. ~ ***a bit [piece] of one's mind*** 直言不讳. ~ ***about*** 分布; 传播(谣言). ~ ***and take*** 公平交换; 互让; 交换意见. ~ ***as good as one gets*** 回敬, 以牙还牙. ~ ***away*** ①让掉, 赠送; 分送, 分发. ②〔俚〕无意中泄漏(机密), 露马脚. ③出卖(朋友). ④(在结婚仪式中)将(新娘)引交新郎. ⑤放弃, 牺牲 (~ *away a good chance of success* 错过成功的良机). ⑥垮, 倒. ~ ***back*** ①归还; 返回, 报复. ②后退, 往后站; 凹陷. ~ ***down*** (牛等)使(奶)流出. ~ ***for*** 牺牲, 交换 (~ *one's life for the country* 为国牺牲). ~ ***forth*** 发出(气味、声音等); 发表, 公布. ~ ***in*** ①提出(文件等), 交上. ②屈服, 退让 *(to)*. ③宣布, 表示. ~ ***into*** (过道等)通向. ~ ***it to sb.*** 〔口〕痛骂, 狠揍. ~ ***lessons [instruction] in*** *(mathematics)* 教授(数学). ***G- me ...*** ①给我…. ②我愿…, 我比较喜欢 (*G- me liberty, or ~ me death.* 〔谚〕不自由, 毋宁死. *G- me the good old times!* 怀念从前. *G- me Bach and Mozart, not these modern composers.* 我喜欢巴哈和莫扎特, 不喜欢这些近代的作曲家). ~ ***off*** 放出, 发散(水蒸气等). ~ ***on [upon]*** (门、窗等)向着(~ *on (to) the garden* 通着花园). ~ ***oneself away*** 露马脚, 现原形. ~ ***oneself out to be [as]*** 自称为. ~ ***oneself over to*** 沉迷于(恶习等). ~ ***oneself to*** ①专心于, 迷恋 (~ *oneself to one's work body and soul* 一心一意埋头工作). ②沾染 (恶习等). ~ ***oneself up*** ①决心; 断念, 想开 *(for)*. ②埋头, 专心于 *(to)* (~ *oneself up to study* 专心读书). ③自首投降. ~ ***out*** ①分发. ②公布, 发表(~ *out the news* 公布消息). ③放出, 发出. ~ *out a good heat* 发出很大热量. ④精疲力竭. ⑤缺乏, 用尽 (*The water supply at last gave out.* 水的供给终于断绝了). ⑥=give. ~ ***over*** ①不再做, 停止做 *(doing)*. ②放纵. ③〔古〕宣布(病人)无可救药. ④托付, 委托. ⑤停息. (*She gave herself over to laughter.* 她纵声大笑. ~ *over a patient for dead* 认为病人无可救药. ~ *over trying to convince sb.* 不再想去说服某人. *The rain gave over.* 雨停了). ~ ***sb. best*** 承认某人的优点. ~ ***sb. his due [own]*** 公平对待某人. ~ ***sb. to understand that ...*** 使人确信…, 使人了解…. ~ ***sb. what for*** 〔口〕责骂某人, 痛打某人. ~ ***the devil his due*** 对坏人也要实事求是. ~ ***up*** ①放弃, 扔弃; 停止, 中止, 断绝 (~ *up smoking* 戒烟). ②对…断念; 对…放弃希望 (~ *sb. up for lost* 对某人已不抱任何希望了). ③引渡(罪人). ④投降; 自首 (*The enemy gave up.* 敌人投降了. *The criminal gave himself up.* 罪犯自首了). ⑤让与; (~ *up one's seat to the old* 给老人让座). ~ ***upon*** = ~on. ~ ***way*** ①坍

塌,垮下,毁坏;退让,屈服;让路,让步*(to)*。②划起(船)来,用力划。③(股票)跌价。④忍不住(*~ way to tears* 忍不住落泪)。***What ~s?***〔美俚〕出什么事了?— *n.* ①弹性;可弯性;可让性。②(精神、性格等的)适应性。③给予。*There is no ~ in a stone floor.* 石头铺的地面毫无弹性。

give-and-take [ˈgivənˈteik] *n.* ①公平交换;互让。②交换意见。— *a.* ①公平交换的;互让的。②交换意见的。

give·a·way [ˈgivəwei] *n.* ①泄露机密。②(招徕顾客的)赠品;(电台中的)有奖问答节目。

giv·en [ˈgivən] give 的过去分词。— *a.* ①一定的,特定的。②给予的,赠送的。③〔数学推理等的独立用法,表示条件〕已知的,假设的。④爱好的,喜欢的,习惯的*(to)*。⑤(文件等于…)签订的。*within a ~ period* 在一定期间内。*meet at a ~ time and place* 在约定的时间和地点会面。*G- X, it follows that ...* 已知 X, 则可推出…。*G- a protracted war, ...* 只要是长期战争,…。*I am not ~ that way.* 我不是干那种事的人。*be ~ romantically.* 生性浪漫。*G- under my hand and seal this 10th day of May 1980 in....* 一九八〇年五月十日在…亲笔签订。***be ~ to*** 喜欢,癖好(*be much ~ to reading and studying* 喜欢看书学习)。— *n.* (推理过程中的)已知事物。*It's taken as a ~.* 这被认为已知。**~ name** 教名,名字〔不包括姓氏〕。

giv·er [ˈgivə] *n.* 给的人,赠送者。*an alms ~* 施舍者。

giv·ing [ˈgiviŋ] *n.* 给予物,礼物。

giz·mo, gis·mo [ˈgizməu] *n.* 小物件,新玩意儿;小发明。

giz·zard [ˈgizəd] *n.* ①(鸟等的)砂囊,胗。②〔口〕喉咙,胃。***fret one's ~*** 苦恼。***stick in sb.'s ~*** 难被某人消化,不合某人口味。

Gjino·kast·ër [ˌgjiːnəuˈkɑːstə] *n.* 吉诺卡斯特〔阿尔巴尼亚城市〕。

GK. = Greek.

GL = gun laying (radar) set 炮瞄雷达。

Gl =【化】glucinum.

gla·bel·la [gləˈbelə] *n.* *(pl. -lae* [-i]*)*【解】眉间。**-r** *a.*

gla·brate [ˈgleibreit, -brit] *a.* ①无毛的,几乎无毛的,平秃的。②(老年或到成熟期时)变光秃的。

gla·bres·cent [gleiˈbresənt] *a.* 有点光秃的;变光秃的。

gla·brous [ˈgleibrəs] *a.* 无毛的,光滑的。

gla·cé [ˈglæsei] *a.*〔F.〕①(布、皮革等)光滑的,磨光的。②(水果)加糖霜的,糖渍的。③冰冻的。

gla·cial [ˈgleisjəl, ˈglæs-] *a.* ①冰的;冰状的。②冰河的,冰河时期的。③冰冷的,冷淡的。④象冰河运动般缓慢的。⑤【化】结晶状的。*a ~ wind* 凛冽的寒风。*a ~ stare* 冷冰冰的盯上一眼。*~ progress* 极缓慢的进展。**~ acetic acid** 冰醋酸。**~ deposits** 冰河堆积物。**~ epoch [era, period]** 冰河时期。**~-lake** 冰川湖。**~ meal** 冰河作用所形成的细石粉。**-ist** *n.* 冰河学家,冰河学者。

glac·i·ate [ˈglæsieit, ˈglei-] *vt.* ①使结冰,使冻结;使冰河化。②以冰[冰河]覆盖。③使受冰河作用。— *vi.* 被冰覆盖。**-d** *a.* 冰冻的;冰封的;【地】受冰河作用的。*(glaciated rock*【地】冰擦岩)。**-ation** *n.* 冰河作用,冰河化,冰蚀。

glac·ier [ˈglæsjə, ˈgleiʃə] *n.* 冰河,冰川。**~ avalanche**【地】冰崩。**~ plain** 冰川平原。

glac·i·er·et [ˌglæsjəˈret, ˌglei-] *n.* 小冰河,小冰川。

glac·i·ol·o·gy [ˌglæsiˈɔlədʒi, ˌglei-] *n.* ①冰河学,冰川学。②冰河造成的地理特征。

glac·is [ˈglæsis, ˈglei-] *n.* *(pl. ~es, ~* [ˈglæsiz]*)* ①缓斜坡;堡垒前的斜坡。②缓冲地区;缓冲国。

glad [glæd] *a.* ①〔用作表语〕高兴,欢喜,乐意。②令人高兴的,使人愉快的。③充满欢乐的;兴高采烈的。④(风光)明媚的,(景色)美丽的。*~ of heart* 欣然。***I am ~ of it.*** 那很好。*(I am very) ~ to see you.* 看到你很高兴。***I should be ~ to know ...***〔反、谑〕我倒想知道…。*a ~ spring morning* 春光明媚的早晨。*~ air [looks]* 笑容。*~ smile* 欣然微笑。*~ tidings* 好消息。***~ eye***〔口〕秋波;媚眼(*give the ~ eye* 送秋波,用眼色挑逗)。***~ hand*** (带有某种动机或虚情假意的)热情欢迎[打招呼]。**~-hand** *vt., vi.* 欢迎,招呼。**~hander**〔美口〕(虚情假意的)欢迎者[打招呼的人]。**~ rags**〔美俚〕盛装,夜礼服。**-ly** *ad.* **-ness** *n.*

glad·den [ˈglædn] *vt., vi.* (使)欢喜。

glade [gleid] *n.* ①林中空地[通道]。②沼泽地。

glad·i·ate [ˈglædieit, ˈgleidiit] *a.*【植】剑状的。

glad·i·a·tor [ˈglædieitə] *n.* ①(古罗马的)斗剑者,角斗士。②争论者。③格斗者(尤指职业拳击者)。

glad·i·a·to·ri·al [ˌglædiəˈtɔːriəl] *a.* ①斗剑(者)的,格斗(者)的。②争论(者)的。

glad·i·o·la [ˌglædiˈəulə], **glad·i·ole** [ˈglædiəul] *n.* = gladiolus.

glad·i·o·lus [ˌglædiˈəuləs] *n.* *(pl. ~es, -li* [-lai]*)* ①【植】唐菖蒲。②【解】胸骨中部。

gla·di·us [ˈgleidiəs] *n.* 古罗马军队的短剑。

glad·some [ˈglædsəm] *a.* 令人高兴的,快乐的,愉快的。*~ tidings* 喜讯。**-ly** *ad.* **-ness** *n.*

Glad·stone[1] [ˈglædstən] *n.* ①(由中部对开的)旅行提包〔又名 ~ bag〕。②(游览用)四轮双人马车。

Glad·stone[2] [ˈglædstən] *n.* ①格拉德斯通〔姓氏〕。②**William Ewart** 威廉·尤尔特·格拉德斯通〔1809—1898,英国政治家,于 1868—1894 年间四度任英国首相〕。

Glad·ys [ˈglædis] *n.* 格拉迪斯〔女子名〕。

glai·kit, glai·ket [ˈgleikit] *a.*〔主 Scot.〕愚蠢的;轻浮的;轻佻的。

glair [glɛə] *n.* ①(用于釉光或釉浆的)蛋白。②(用蛋白制成的)釉光,釉浆〔作装订书本等用〕。③蛋白状粘液。— *vt.* 在…涂蛋白。

glair·e·ous [ˈglɛəriəs], **glair·y** [-ri] *a.* 涂蛋白的,蛋白状的,蛋白质的。

glaive [gleiv] *n.*〔古、诗〕剑;(特指)阔剑。

glam·or [ˈglæmə] *n.*〔美〕= glamour.

glam·or·ize [ˈglæməraiz] *vt.* ①〔口〕使有魔力,使迷人。②美化,把…理想化。

glam·o(u)r [ˈglæmə] *n.* ①魔法,魔术;魔力。②魅力;(诗等的)迷人的神韵[意境]。***cast a ~ over*** 迷惑,使对…着迷。— *vt.* 迷惑,迷住。**~ boy**〔美〕美男子。**~ girl** 迷人的姑娘。

glam·o(u)r·ous [ˈglæmərəs] *a.* 富有魔力的,迷人的。

glance[1] [glɑːns] *n.* ①匆匆一看,一瞥,扫视;眼色。②一闪;闪光。③(炮弹等的)斜飞,侧过。④〔古〕约略提及,影射。*One ~ was enough.* 看一眼就够了。***at a ~ = at the first ~*** 一看就,一见就;初看。***cast hostile ~s upon*** 敌视,仇视。***exchange ~s*** 互相使眼色。***give [take] a ~ at [to, of, into, over]*** 对…匆匆一看,瞥一眼。***steal a ~ at*** 偷偷一看。***with a keen ~*** 以敏锐的一瞥。— *vi.* ①匆匆一看,一瞥,扫视 *(at; over)*。②约略提到;影射 *(at, over)*。③(枪弹等)擦过,掠过 *(aside; off)*。④闪耀,发光。— *vt.* ①(把眼睛等)向…晃一眼,扫视。②使反射,投射(光线)。③影射,暗示。***~ down [up]*** 朝下[朝上]一看,俯[仰]身一瞥。***~ (one's eyes) over [through]*** 粗略一看,浏览。

glance[2] [glɑːns] *n.*【矿】辉矿类。*lead ~* 方铅矿。*silver ~* 辉银矿。— *vt.* 使发光,磨光。**~ coal** 镜煤;无烟煤。**~ copper** 辉铜矿。

glanc·ing [ˈglɑːnsiŋ] *a.* ①粗略的,随便的。②偶尔的,间接的。**~ angle**【光】掠射角。**-ly** *ad.*

gland[1] [glænd] *n.* ①【解】腺。*a ductless ~* 无管腺。*the lacrimal ~s* 泪腺。*the salivary ~s* 唾腺。*the sweat [sudoriferous] ~s* 汗腺。*thyroid ~* 甲状腺。②【植】(分泌蜜等的)腺。

gland[2] [glænd] *n.* 【机】密封压盖，填料盖，密封套．*a labyrinth* ~ 迂回密封盖，曲折密封盖，迷宫式密封盖．*packing* ~ 压垫盖，填料盖．*a steam valve* ~ 汽阀压盖．

glan·dered [ˈglændəd] *a.* 【兽医】患鼻疽(病)的．

glan·ders [ˈglændəz] *n. pl.* 〔用作单〕【兽医】鼻疽病，马鼻疽．**-dered** [-dəd], **-der·ous** [-dərəs] *a.* 患鼻疽病的．

glan·des [ˈglændiːz] *n.* glans 的复数．

glan·di·fer·ous [glænˈdifərəs] *a.* 结坚果的．

glan·di·form [ˈglændifɔːm] *a.* ①腺状的．②坚果状的．

glan·du·lar [ˈglændjulə] *a.* ①腺的，含腺的，有腺的特征[功能]的．②天生的，固有的．③性的．*a* ~ *dislike for cat* 天生不喜欢猫．~ *relationship* 性关系．~ **cancer** 【医】腺癌．~ **fever** 传染性单核白血球增多 (= infectious mononucleosis)．~ **swelling** 【医】腺肿．**-ly** *ad.*

glan·dule [ˈglændjuːl] *n.* 【解】小腺．

glan·du·lif·er·ous [ˌglændjuˈlifərəs] *a.* 有小腺的．

glan·du·lous [ˈglændjuləs] *a.* = glandular. **-ness** *n.*

glans [glænz] *n.* (*pl.* **glan·des** [ˈglændiːz]) 【解】阴茎头；阴蒂头．~ **clitoridis** 阴蒂头．~ **penis** 龟头．

glare[1] [glɛə] *n.* ①闪耀，闪光；眩目的光，强烈的光．②显眼；炫耀；著名．③瞪眼．*the* ~ *of the footlights* 舞台上耀眼的灯光．***in the full ~ of publicity*** 非常显眼，在众目睽睽之下．— *vi.* ①发耀眼的光，发强烈的光，闪耀．②瞪 (*at; on; upon*) — *vt.* 用目光表示 (嫌恶，轻视)．③使反射．

glare[2] [glɛə] *n.* 〔美〕(冰等的) 平滑光亮的表面．— *a.* 亮晶晶的，光滑的．~ **ice** 光滑而发亮的冰．

glare·less [ˈglɛəlis] *a.* 不刺目的．

glar·ing [ˈglɛəriŋ] *a.* ①耀眼的，闪闪发光的．②瞪眼的，怒目而视的．③炫耀的，显眼的；突出的．④粗俗的，俗气的．~ *errors* 大错．*a* ~ *lie* 露骨的谎话．**-ly** *ad.* **-ness** *n.*

glar·y[1] [ˈglɛəri] *a.* = glaring.

glar·y[2] [ˈglɛəri] *a.* 〔美〕光滑的．

Gla·ser [ˈgleizə] *n.* 格莱泽〔姓氏〕．

Glas·gow [ˈglaːsgəu] *n.* 格拉斯哥〔英国城市〕．

glass [glaːs] *n.* ①玻璃；玻璃状物．②〔集合词〕玻璃制品，玻璃器具，料器；玻璃暖房 (= ~house)．③玻璃杯；一杯的量；酒．④镜子，望远镜，显微镜，晴雨表，温度表，砂漏，钟表的玻璃盖，玻璃框，车窗．⑤〔*pl.*〕眼镜．*crown* ~ 冕玻璃(硬性光学玻璃)．*cut* ~ 雕花玻璃，车玻璃．*flint* ~ 燧石玻璃(软性光学玻璃)．*frosted [mat]* ~ 磨沙玻璃，霜化玻璃．*ground* ~ 毛玻璃，磨口玻璃．*optical* ~ 光学玻璃．*organic* ~ 有机玻璃．*plate* ~ 板玻璃．*pyrex* ~ 派热克斯玻璃 (原商品名，一种耐热玻璃)．*spun* ~ 玻璃丝．*stained* ~ 彩画玻璃．*toughened* ~ 钢化玻璃，淬火玻璃．*wire(d)* ~ 嵌丝玻璃．*a* ~ *of wine [water]* 一杯酒[水]．*enjoy a* ~ *now and then* 时常喝酒．*look in the* ~ 照镜子．*The* ~ *is at fair.* 晴雨表上显示'天晴'．*dinner [table]* ~ 玻璃餐具．~ *and china* 料器和瓷器．***be fond of one's*** ~ 爱喝酒，爱杯中物．***clink ~es*** 碰杯．***flinch one's*** ~ 故意不把酒喝干．***have had a ~ too much*** 喝多了，喝醉了．***look through blue ~es*** 悲观地看事物．***look through green ~es*** 羡慕[妒忌]地看事物．***look through rose-coloured ~es*** 乐观地看事物．***raise one's ~ to*** 为某人的健康干杯．***under*** ~ 【园艺】在温室中．— *vt.* ①给…镶玻璃，用玻璃覆盖；把…装在玻璃器里．②使平滑如玻璃．③〔常作 ~ *oneself*〕映照，反映．④用望远镜了望．⑤使滞钝无光．~ *a window* 给窗户上玻璃．~*ed fruits* 密封于玻璃容器中的水果．*eyes ~ed by boredom* 因厌倦而滞钝无光的眼睛．*The flowers ~ themselves in the pool.* 花影映照在池中．— *vi.* ①成玻璃状，(目光等)变迟钝．②用望远镜了望．~**-arm** 容易发酸[麻木]的胳臂．~ **blower** 吹玻璃工人．~ **case** 玻璃橱柜．~ **cloth** 揩玻璃的布；玻璃纤维织布；涂有玻璃粉的织物；玻璃沙布．~ **culture** 温室栽培．~ **cutter** 划玻璃的人；划玻璃的刀．~ **dust** (研磨用的)玻璃粉．~ **eye** ①马眼黑内障病．②玻璃制假眼睛．③一片眼镜；〔*pl.*〕一副眼镜．~ **fibre** 玻璃纤维．~**-glaze** 玻璃釉．~**-glazed** *a.* 浓釉的．~**house** ①玻璃厂，玻璃店．②温室，玻璃房子．③〔英俚〕军事监狱．④〔口〕飞机驾驶员座位；装有玻璃天棚的摄影室 (*Those who live in ~houses should not throw stones.* 〔谚〕自己有短处就别揭别人的短处)．~ **jaw** 〔美俚〕拳击选手经不起打击的下颌．~**maker** *n.* 玻璃工匠，玻璃器皿工匠．~**making** *n.* 玻璃制造工艺〔工业〕．~**-man** *n.* 玻璃商人；装玻璃的工人；玻璃制造者．~ **paper** 玻璃沙纸，沙皮．~ **snake** 一种尾脆似玻璃的蛇蜥属 (*ophisaurus*) 动物．~**ware** 料器，玻璃器皿．~ **wool** 玻璃棉，玻璃绒，玻璃丝．~**work** ①玻璃制造业；玻璃制品．②〔常 *pl.*〕玻璃工厂．~**worm** *n.* 箭虫 (= arrowworm)．~**wort** *n.* 【植】欧洲海蓬子〔烧成灰可作玻璃原料〕；钾猪毛菜．**-less** *a.* 没有玻璃的，未装玻璃的．

Glass [glaːs] *n.* 格拉斯〔姓氏〕．

Glass·boro [ˈglæsbərə] *n.* 葛拉斯堡罗〔美国城市〕．

glass·ful [ˈglaːsful] *n.* 一杯的容量．

glass·ine [glæˈsiːn] *n.* 玻璃纸．

glass·y [ˈglaːsi] *a.* ①玻璃质的，玻璃状的．②(眼睛)呆滞的，没有神采的．③透明如玻璃的，平稳如镜的．*a* ~ *surface* 镜一样的平面．~**-eyed** *a.* 眼睛无神的；目光呆滞的．**-ily** *ad.* **-iness** *n.*

Glas·we·gian [glæsˈwiːdʒjən] *a.* 格拉斯哥的．— *n.* 格拉斯哥市民．

glau·ber·ite [ˈglaubərait] *n.* 【化】钙芒硝．

Glau·ber's salt [ˈglaubəz ˈsɔːlt] 【化】芒硝，结晶硫酸钠，〔口〕元明粉．

glau·co·ma [glɔːˈkəumə] *n.* 【医】青光眼，绿内障．**-tous** [-təs] *a.* (患)青光眼的．

glau·co·nite [ˈglɔːkənait] *n.* 【地】海绿石．

glau·cous [ˈglɔːkəs] *a.* ①淡灰蓝色的，淡灰绿色的．②【植】表面具白霜的．~ **gull** 【动】北极鸥〔产于北极〕．

glaum [glɔːm] *vt., vi.* 〔美俚，英方〕抢，夺，偷．

glaze [gleiz] *vt.* ①镶玻璃于，装玻璃于．②打光，擦亮；给…上釉；把…弄光滑．③在(油漆物上)涂透明[半透明]色料．④在(食物表面)浇糖浆．⑤使(眼睛)蒙上薄翳．⑥铺一层薄冰于．~*d bricks* 琉璃砖．~*d frost* 雨淞．~*d paper* 有光纸．~*d printing paper* 道林纸．~*d tiles* 琉璃瓦．— *vi.* ①变光滑；变明亮，变成薄膜状．②(眼光)变呆，变模糊．~ **in** 把…围在玻璃中，用玻璃盖上．— *n.* ①釉料；上光料．②光滑面，光滑层，薄冰层．③(眼光的)呆钝；(眼睛的)翳子．④上釉，上光．⑤【气】雨淞．⑥【烹】(浇在食物表面的)冻胶，糖浆．~ **wheel** 研磨轮，砑光轮．

glaz·er [ˈgleizə] *n.* 上釉工人，打光工人；上光机，轧光机．

gla·zier [ˈgleizjə] *n.* ①釉工；光布工．②装玻璃的人．*Is your father a* ~? [*Your father was a bad* ~.] 〔谑〕你老子是装玻璃的吗？[你老子是个蹩脚的装玻璃工．]〔意指：你怎么挡人光线呢，难道你的身体是玻璃的吗？〕．~**'s diamond** 划玻璃刀．**-ziery** *n.* 〔集合词〕①釉工．②装玻璃工．

glaz·ing [ˈgleiziŋ] *n.* ①玻璃装配(业)．②玻璃工艺；玻璃制品．③上釉．④釉；上光料．~ *calender* 【纺】轧光机，擦光机．

glaz·y [ˈgleizi] *a.* ①玻璃似的．②上过釉的．③(目光)无神的．

G.L.C. = Greater London Council 大伦敦市议会．

gleam [gliːm] *n.* ①闪光，微光．②(感情等的)闪现；短暂微弱的显现．③反光．*a* ~ *of hope* 一线希望．*a* ~ *of anticipation in his eyes* 他眼中闪烁着期待的目光．*the first ~s of day* 曙光．*the* ~ *of dawn in the east* 东方的晨曦．— *vi.* ①发微光，闪烁．②(感情等的) 闪现．— *vt.* 使发微光，使闪烁，隐约地显现．

gleam·y [ˈgliːmi] *a.* 发微光的,发闪光的.

glean [gliːn] *vt.* ①拾(落穗);收拾(遗留在田地的)庄稼. ②搜集(新闻、资料等). ③发现,查明. ~ *a field* 拾一块地上的残穗. — *vi.* 拾落穗;搜集新闻[资料]. **-er** *n.* 搜集人;拾落穗的人. **-ing** *n.* ①拾落穗;搜集. ②[*pl.*]搜集物;(资料、传闻等的)拾遗.

glebe [gliːb] *n.* ①教会附属地;圣职领耕地. ②[诗]土地,耕地. ③【矿】含矿地带.

glede [gliːd], **gled** [gled] *n.* 【动】鸢[产于欧洲].

glee [gliː] *n.* ①高兴,快乐,狂欢. ②【乐】(无伴奏的男声)合唱曲. ***full of*** ~ = ***in high*** ~ 欢天喜地. ~ **club** 合唱队.

gleed [gliːd] *n.* [方]一块燃烧着的煤.

glee·ful [ˈgliːful] *a.* 极高兴的,开心的;令人愉快的. ~ *news* 喜讯. ***in*** ~ ***mood*** 高高兴兴地. **-ly** *ad.* **-ness** *n.*

glee·man [ˈgliːmən] *n.* (*pl.* ***-men***) [古]吟游诗人.

Gleep [gliːp] *n.* 【原】低功率石墨实验性原子反应堆[graphite low energy experimental pile].

glee·some [ˈgliːsəm] *a.* = gleeful.

gleet [gliːt] *n.* ①【医】后淋,慢性淋病性尿道炎. ②(牲口等的)慢性鼻腔炎. — *vi.* 排出粘薄液体. **-y** *a.* 后淋的,淋病状的.

gleg [gleg] *a.* [Scot.] 警惕的;灵敏的;敏锐的.

glen [glen] *n.* 峡谷,幽谷. ~ **[G-] plaid** 格伦乌夸特方格呢[也叫 Glenurquhart plaid].

Glen(n) [glen] *n.* 格伦[姓氏,男子名].

Glen·da [ˈglendə] *n.* 格伦达[女子名].

Glen·gar·ry [glenˈgæri] *n.* (*pl.* ***-ries***) [有时用 g-] 苏格兰便帽(呈船形,帽后有二短飘带,系高地人所戴,=~ bonnet).

gle·noid [ˈgliːnɔid] *a.* 【解】(有)浅窝的,关节窝的. ~ **cavity** 关节腔.

gley [glei] *n.* 潜育层(土壤).

gli·a [ˈglaiə, ˈgliːə] *n.* 神经胶质 (= neuroglia). **-al** *a.*

gli·a·din [ˈglaiədin] *n.* 【化】麸朊;醇溶朊.

glib [glib] *a.* (***glib·ber, glib·best***) ①能说会道的,口齿流利的. ②(动作)轻巧的;浮浅的;随便的. ③[古]光滑的. *a* ~ *talker* 伶牙俐齿的谈话者. ~ *answers* 敏捷的回答. **-ly** *ad.* **-ness** *n.*

glide [glaid] *n.* ①滑行;滑动. ②流逝,消逝. ③【空】滑翔;【船】滑行台,滑道;【地】滑裂带. ④【语】滑音,滑移;【乐】滑音,延音. ⑤静悄悄的流水. — *vi.* ①流动,滑动;滑行. ②悄悄走,溜走. ③【空】滑翔. ④渐变,渐消(*into*). — *vt.* 使滑动,使滑行. ~ ***by [on]*** (时间等)悄悄过去[溜走]. ~**bomb** *vt., vi.* 下滑轰炸. ~ **bomb** 滑翔式炸弹. ~ **path** [空]①滑翔台. ②滑翔航道. ~ **slope** 滑翔斜率,滑翔道. ~ **vehicle** 滑翔导弹.

glid·er [ˈglaidə] *n.* ①滑行者,滑动物. ②【空】滑翔机;【海】滑行艇. ③(露台等处的)吊椅. ④【宇】滑翔导弹,可收回的卫星. *a* ~ *bomb* 滑翔式炸弹. ~ *troops* 滑翔部队. *a winged rocket-assisted* ~ 火箭加速滑翔机.

glid·ing [ˈglaidiŋ] *a.* 滑行的,滑翔的. *a* ~ *way of walking* 象滑行似的步伐. ~ **angle** 【空】下滑角. **-ly** *ad.*

glim [glim] *n.* ①[俚]灯火,蜡烛,灯笼. ②眼睛. ③模糊的感觉;微弱的迹象;少许,微量. ④一瞥,看一看. ***douse [dowse] the*** ~ [俚]熄灯.

glim·mer [ˈglimə] *n.* ①微光,薄光,闪光. ②模糊的感觉[概念];轻微的表露. ③少许,微量. ④【矿】云母(=mica). ⑤[*pl.*][俚]眼睛. *a* ~ *of hope* 一线希望. *have a* ~*ing of* 模模糊糊地知道. *a* ~ *of intelligence* 很少一点情报. — *vi.* ①发微光. ②朦胧出现. ***go*** ~***ing*** 渐渐消失.

glimpse [glimps] *n.* ①一瞥,瞥见(*at, of*). ②模糊的感觉;隐约的显现. ③[古]闪光. ***at a*** ~ 一瞥之间. ***catch [get] a*** ~ ***of*** 瞥见. ~***s of the truth*** 一孔之见. ***the*** ~***s of the moon*** ①夜间世界. ②世事,俗事. — *vt., vi.* 瞥见;[诗]闪现.

glint [glint] *vi.* ①闪耀,反射;发微光. ②(箭一样)飞出,掠过. ③窥视;闪现. — *vt.* 使发光,使闪光,使反射. — *n.* ①闪光;微光. ②短暂微弱的显露. ③(雷达的)回波起伏.

gli·o·ma [glaiˈəumə] *n.* (*pl.* ***-ma·ta*** [-mətə]) 【医】神经胶质瘤. **-ous** *a.*

glis·sade [gliˈsɑːd] *n.* ①(登山者沿覆雪斜坡)滑降. ②(芭蕾舞)横滑步. — *vi.* ①滑降. ②跳横滑步舞.

glis·san·do [gliˈsɑːndəu] *n.* (*pl.* ***-di*** [-di], ~***s***) 【乐】①级进滑奏,滑音,滑唱. ②有级进滑奏的乐段. — *a., ad.* 滑奏的[地],滑音的[地],滑唱的[地].

glis·sé [gliˈsei] *n.* [F.](芭蕾舞)横滑步.

glist [glist] *n.* ①闪耀. ②云母.

glis·ten [ˈglisn] *vi.* 发光,辉耀,闪烁;反光. — *n.* 闪光;反光;光辉.

glis·ter [ˈglistə] *n., vi.* [古] = glisten, glitter.

glitch [glitʃ] *n.* ①[美俚]晦气;过失;处置失当;小故障,小事故,小技术问题. ②假电子讯号. ③【天】(中子星)自转突快.

glit·ter [ˈglitə] *n.* ①光辉,灿烂. ②发光的小东西. — *vi.* ①闪烁,闪闪发光. ②华丽夺目,炫耀. *All is not gold that* ~*s.* [谚]闪闪发光者,未必尽黄金. ~ **ice** [Can.]【气】雨凇[雨水速冻而成的晶亮的冰]. ~ **rock** (由服饰华丽的男乐师演奏的)闪烁摇摆乐.

glit·ter·ing [ˈglitəriŋ] *a.* = glittery. **-ly** *ad.*

glit·ter·y [ˈglitəri] *a.* 晶亮的,灿烂的.

Gloag [gləug] *n.* 格洛格[姓氏].

gloam [gləum] *vi.* [主 Scot.] 暗下来,变朦胧. — *n.* [诗] = gloaming.

gloam·ing [ˈgləumiŋ] *n.* 黄昏,薄暮. *in the* ~ *of one's life* 在晚年.

gloat [gləut] *vi.* ①幸灾乐祸地注视;爱慕地凝视. ②得意地看[思索];贪婪地盯视 (*on; over; upon*). ~ ***on [upon]*** *a heap of treasure* 盯着一堆财宝. ~ ***over*** *sb.'s misfortune* 幸灾乐祸. — *n.* ①得意的注视;沾沾自喜. ②爱慕的凝视;垂涎. ③幸灾乐祸的观望. **-er** *n.*

gloat·ing [ˈgləutiŋ] *a.* 心满意足的. *a* ~ *smile* 得意的微笑. **-ly** *ad.*

glob [glɔb] *n.* (浓流体或半固体的)团块.

glob·al [ˈgləubəl] *a.* ①球面的,球状的;全球的. ②世界的. ③总体的,普遍的,综合的. *take a nonstop* ~ *flight* 作一次环绕世界一周的不着陆飞行. *a* ~ *system of communication* 全球通信系统. ~ *war* 全球战争. *the* ~ *sum* 总计(= total sum). ~ **village** 全球村[指将来电子交通传播发达、全球距离日益缩小,犹如一个村庄]. **-ly** *ad.*

glob·al·ism [ˈgləublizm] *n.* [美](看问题等着眼于全世界)全球性,全球观念;全球性干涉政策. **-ist** *a., n.* 赞成奉行全球性干涉政策的(人).

glo·bal·ize [ˈgləubəlaiz] *vt.* 使全球化;使成为世界范围,使在全世界应用. **-i·za·tion** [ˌgləubəlaiˈzeiʃən] *n.* 全球化.

glo·bate [ˈgləubeit] *a.* 球状的.

globe [gləub] *n.* ①球;球状物. ②[the ~] 地球;世界. ③天体. ④地球仪,天体仪. ⑤球形容器;灯罩,灯泡. ⑥【解】眼球. ⑦(象征王权的)小金球. *the terrestrial* ~ 地球. *a terrestrial* ~ 地球仪. *a celestial* ~ 天球仪. *the use of the* ~*s* (从前的)天文、地理仪器示教法. ***the whole habitable*** ~ 全世界. — *vt., vi.* (使)成球状. ~ **amaranth** 【植】千日红. ~ **artichoke** = cardoon. ~**fish** 【动】河豚. ~**flower** 【植】金莲花. ~ **lightning** 【气】球状闪电. ~**-mallow** 【植】球葵. ~**-trotter** [口](短期的)环球旅行家. ~**-trotting** ① *n.* (短期)环球旅行. ② *a.* 环球旅行的. ~ **valve** 【机】球(形)阀.

glo·big·er·i·na ooze [gləuˌbidʒəˈrainə uːz] 【地】抱球虫软泥.

glo·bin [ˈgləubin] *a.*【生】球蛋白,珠朊.
glo·boid [ˈgləubɔid] *a.* 球状的. — *n.* 球状体.
glo·bose [ˈgləubəus] *a.* 球状的,球形的.
glo·bos·i·ty [gləuˈbɔsiti] *n.* 球状,球形.
glob·u·lar [ˈglɔbjulə] *a.* ①球状的, 地球状的. ②世界范围的. ③由小球聚集成的; 有小球的. ④完整的. ~ *masses of fish eggs* 聚集成块的球状鱼卵. ~ **chart** 球面投影地图. ~ **projection** 球面投影法. ~ **proteins** 球蛋白. ~ **sailing**【海】球面航行. **-ly** *ad.* **-ness** *n.*
glob·u·lar·i·ty [ˌglɔbjuˈlæriti] *n.* 球状,球形.
glob·ule [ˈglɔbjuːl] *n.* ①小球. ②液滴,血球,药丸.
glob·u·lin [ˈglɔbjulin] *n.*【生化】球蛋白,球朊.
glob·u·lous [ˈglɔbjuləs] *a.* = globular.
glo·chid·i·ate [gləuˈkidiət] *a.*【植】有钩毛的.
glo·chid·i·um [gləuˈkidiəm] *n.* (*pl.* **-chid·i·a** [-ˈkidiə]) ①【植】钩毛. ②【动】河蚌幼虫; 瓣钩幼虫 (*Unionidae*).
glock·en·spiel [ˈglɔkənspiːl] *n.*【乐】①钟琴. ②钟组乐器,编钟.
glögg, glogg [glɔːg] *n.* 瑞典式热饮〔把酒、白兰地与糖和香料等温热,再加葡萄干和杏仁作配料〕.
glom [glɔm] *vt., vi.* 〔美俚〕= glaum.
glom·er·ate [ˈglɔmərit] *a.*【植、解】团集的.
glom·er·a·tion [ˌglɔməˈreiʃən] *n.* ①聚成团; 结成团块; 做成球状. ②团块; 球状物.
glo·mer·u·late [glɔˈmerjulit] *a.* 作团伞状的.
glom·er·ule [ˈglɔməruːl] *n.* ①【植】团伞序. ②= glomerulus.
glo·mer·u·lo·ne·phri·tis [gləuˈmerjələunefˈraitis] *n.*【医】血管球性肾炎.
glo·mer·u·lus [gləuˈmerjələs] *n.* (*pl.* **-li** [-lai])【医】血管小球,小球. **-u·lar** [-lə] *a.*
glon·o·in [ˈglɔnəuin] *n.* 硝化甘油, 甘油三硝酸酯 (= nitroglycerin).
gloom [gluːm] *n.* ①黑暗,幽暗,朦胧;〔诗〕幽暗处,背阴处. ②忧郁, 悲哀; 意气消沉. ③〔Scot.〕忧郁的面貌. *in the green ~s of the forest* 林中绿荫处. *A ~ fell over the household.* 全家黯然忧伤. **cast a ~ over** 使忧郁, 使阴暗. **chase one's ~ away** 解闷,消愁. **in the ~** 在幽暗中. — *vi.* ①变黑暗,变阴郁. ②变忧郁 (*over*). ③现愁容, 做苦脸 (*at; on*). — *vt.* ①使暗,使朦胧. ②使忧郁. ③忧伤地说.
gloom·y [ˈgluːmi] *a.* ①暗的, 黑暗的, 阴暗的. ②阴郁的,忧闷的; 令人沮丧的; 脾气不好的. ③没希望的,前途暗淡的. *take a ~ view of* 对…悲观. **-i·ly** *ad.* **-i·ness** *n.*
glop [glɔp] *n.* 〔美俚〕①软胶质物; 浓流体物. ②乏味的东西. **glop·py** [-i] *a.*
Glo·ri·a [ˈglɔːriə] *n.* 〔L.〕①(基督教用拉丁语 ~ 开始的)《荣耀颂》歌. ②《荣耀颂》的曲调. ③〔g-〕赞颂光荣. ④〔g-〕(神像等背后的)后光,光轮. ⑤〔g-〕丝毛交织薄绸. ~ ***in excelsis*** (用于赞美诗) 荣耀归于上帝. ~ ***Patri*** (用于赞美歌)荣耀归于圣父. ~ ***tibi*** (用于回答)荣耀归于您.
glo·ri·fy [ˈglɔːrifai] *vt.* ①赞美,崇拜. ②颂扬,夸赞. ③给予…光荣, 使增光. ④〔口〕装饰; 使(普通或低劣的东西)美观,美化,使有魅力, 使有吸力. ⑤使光辉灿烂, 使光彩夺目. *A large chandelier ~s the whole room.* 枝形大吊灯使整个房间光亮夺目. *a recipe for ~ing pancakes* 使薄煎饼好看的制法. ~ *oneself* 自夸. **-fi·ca·tion** [ˌglɔːrifiˈkeiʃən] *n.* ①赞美, 颂扬. ②美化. ③〔美口〕祝贺,庆祝.
glo·ri·ole [ˈglɔːriəul] *n.* (神像等背后的)光轮,后光.
glo·ri·ous [ˈglɔːriəs] *a.* ①光荣的; 荣耀的. ②壮丽的; 辉煌的, 灿烂的. ③〔口〕令人愉快的, 极好的. ④〔讽〕可怕的. ⑤有点儿醉的,酒后放纵的. *a ~ day* 光荣的日子; 好天气. *a ~ death* 光荣的牺牲. *~ fun* 非常有趣. *a ~ mess [muddle, row]* 乱七八糟. *a ~ view* 壮观, 绝景. ***have a ~ holiday [weekend]*** 过一个愉快的假日[周末]. ***the ~ Fourth*** 美国独立纪念日(7月4日). **-ly** *ad.*
glo·ry [ˈglɔːri] *n.* ①光荣,荣誉; (对神的)赞美. ②荣耀的事,可赞美的事,可夸耀的事. ③壮观,壮丽,美观. ④【宗】天上的荣光; 天国的荣誉. ⑤繁荣, 昌盛. ⑥兴致勃勃,得意扬扬. ⑦(神像等的)后光,光轮. ⑧日华, 月华; 日冕. *be in one's ~* 在极得意时. *cover oneself with ~* 满载荣誉, 取得辉煌胜利. ***Eternal ~ to*** …永垂不朽. ***go to ~*** 升天,死. ***return with ~*** 凯旋. ***send sb. to ~*** 〔谑〕送某人归天,处死. ***the old G-*** 美国国旗. — *vi.* 欢跃,狂喜; 自豪,得意. *~ in one's victory* 因胜利而得意扬扬. *~ in doing sth. [to do sth.]* 为做某事而自豪. ~ ***in honest poverty*** 甘守清贫. ~ ***in one's own disgrace*** 丢了脸还自鸣得意. ~ ***to do [in doing] sth.*** 为做某事而自豪. — *int.* 〔俚〕哎呀! 要命! 〔表示惊叹、欢喜,也说成 G- be!〕. **~-box** 〔澳、新西兰〕嫁妆箱[盒]. **~ hole** ①〔口〕放杂物的橱[抽屉、房间]. ②(玻璃熔化炉的)炉口; 观察孔,火焰窥孔.
Glos. = Gloucestershire.
gloss[1] [glɔs] *n.* ①(表面的)平滑,光泽,光彩. ②平滑的表面. ③虚饰,假象. *the ~ of varnished furnitures* 上漆家具的平滑表面 [光泽]. *a ~ of respectability* 装得道貌岸然. ***put [set] a ~ on*** 使…具有光泽,润饰…. — *vt.* ①给…加光泽, 给…上釉. ②掩饰; 掩盖 (*over*). — *vi.* 发光. *~ over one's faults* 掩盖错误. ~ **paint** 上光漆.
gloss[2] [glɔs] *n.* ①(书边或行间对难字难句的)注解,解释,评注. ②曲解. ③词汇表, 集注; 夹加于行间的注释性译文. — *vt.* ①注解, 注释; 评注. ②曲解; 搪塞. — *vi.* 作注释,写评注.
gloss. = glossary.
gloss-, glosso- *comb. f.* 表示①"舌": *gloss*algia. ②"语言": *glosso*logy.
glos·sa [ˈglɔsə] *n.* (*pl.* *~s, ~sae* [-siː])【解】舌;【动】(昆虫的)中唇舌.
glos·sal [ˈglɔːsəl] *a.* 舌的.
glos·sar·i·al [glɔˈseəriəl] *a.* 词汇的; 词汇表的. *a ~ index* 词汇索引.
glos·sa·ry [ˈglɔsəri] *n.* 难字[专业词,外来语]汇编, 集注, 词汇表. **-rist** [ˈglɔsərist] *n.* ①词汇表编辑者. ②书籍注释者.
glos·sa·tor [glɔˈseitə] *n.* 注释者, 评注者,注解者.
glos·sec·to·my [glɔˈsektəmi] *n.* 舌切除术.
glos·si·na [glɔˈsainə, glɔˈsiːnə] *n.*【动】舌蝇, 采采蝇 (= tsetse).
glos·si·tis [glɔˈsaitis] *n.*【医】舌炎.
glos·sog·ra·pher [glɔˈsɔgrəfə] *n.* = glossarist.
glos·so·la·li·a [ˌglɔsəuˈleiliə] *n.*【医】言语不清.
glos·so·pha·ryn·geal [ˈglɔsəuˌfærinˈdʒiːəl] *a.*【解】舌咽的.
glos·sot·o·my [glɔˈsɔtəmi] *n.*【解】舌切开术.
gloss·y [ˈglɔsi] *a.* ①有光泽的, 光滑的. ②虚饰的, 浮华的; 似是而非的. *a ~ surface* 光滑的表面. *~ deceit* 似是而非的欺骗. — *n.* ①〔口〕有光纸印刷的杂志. ②【摄】印在光纸上的相片. **-i·ly** *ad.* **-i·ness** *n.*
glost [glɔst] *n.* ①釉. ②上釉的瓷器.
glott-, glotto- *comb. f.* 表示"语言": *glotto*logy.
glot·tal [ˈglɔtl] *a.* ①【解】声门的. ②【语】自声门发出的. ~ **stop**【语】声门塞音.
glot·tis [ˈglɔtis] *n.* (*pl.* *~es, -ti·des* [-diːz])【解】声门.
glot·to·chro·nol·o·gy [ˌglɔtəukrəˈnɔlədʒi] *n.*【语】同源语言演变史学.
Glouces·ter [ˈglɔstə] *n.* ①格罗斯特〔英国格罗斯特郡的首府〕. ②格罗斯特干酪〔= ~ cheese〕. *single ~* (用脱脂乳制成的)次级干酪. *double ~* (用全脂乳制成的)

一级干酪.

Glouces·ter·shire [ˈglɔstəʃiə] *n.* 格罗斯特郡〔英国西南部的一郡〕.

glove [glʌv] *n.* ①手套(一般指五指分开的, *cf.* mitten). ②棒球手套; 拳击手套 (= boxing ~). *a pair of ~s* 一副手套. *Excuse my ~s.* (握手时的客套话) 对不起, 没有脱手套. ***be hand and [in] ~ with*** 与…合作, 与…亲密无间. ***bite one's ~*** 复仇. ***fit like a ~*** 恰恰相合. ***go for the ~s*** 孤注一掷. ***handle [treat] with (kid) ~s*** 灵活处理. ***handle without ~s*** 严厉对待. ***put on the ~s*** 〔口〕拳击. ***take off the ~s*** (争吵) 认真起来. ***take up the ~*** 应战. ***The ~s are off*** 认真起来. ***throw down the ~*** 挑战. ***without ~s*** =with the ~s off 毫不留情地. ***worth his fielder's ~*** 能干的. — *vt.* ①给…戴手套. ②作…的手套. ~ **box** ①手套箱. ②= ~ compartment. ③处理放射性物质的手套式密闭室. ~ **compartment** (汽车仪表盘上)存放零星杂物的凹处. ~ **fight** (戴手套的) 拳击 (*opp.* prize fight). ~ **money** 贿赂. ~ **sponge** 一种形似手套的劣质海绵. **-less** *a.* 不戴手套的. **-like** *a.* 象手套的.

glov·er [ˈglʌvə] *n.* 手套制造人;手套商.

Glov·er [ˈglʌvə] *n.* 格洛弗〔姓氏〕.

glow [gləu] *vi.* ①灼热; 发白热光; 燃烧 〔*cf.* blaze〕; 放光, 发热. ②(运动后)身体发热; (面色等)发红; (眼)发亮. ③(怒火等)燃烧, (感情等)洋溢. ④鲜艳夺目, 显示浓艳的颜色. ~ *with enthusiasm* 热情洋溢. ~ *with health* 脸色红润, 容光焕发. ~ *with pride* 得意扬扬. — *n.* ①白热, 灼热; 光辉. ②热烈, 激情, 喜悦. ③(色彩、印象等的)鲜明; (脸上的)红光, 红晕. *the ~ of sunset* 晚霞. *the ~ of happiness* 幸福的喜悦. ***all of a ~ = in a ~*** 〔口〕热烘烘; 红彤彤. ~ **discharge** 辉光放电. ~ **lamp** 辉光灯, 辉光放电管. ~ **watch** 夜光表. ~**worm** 萤火虫.

glow·er[1] [ˈgləuə] *n.* 【电】炽热体; 灯丝.

glow·er[2] [ˈglauə] *vi.* 怒视, 凝视(*at*). — *n.* 怒视, 凝视. **-ing·ly** *ad.*

glow·ing [ˈgləuiŋ] *a.* ①白热的; 通红的; 灼炽的. ②(色彩)鲜明的, 光辉的; 强烈的. ③热心的, 热烈的. ④脸色红润的, 容光焕发的. *give a ~ account of* 热烈赞赏. ~ *cheeks* 红润的两颊. ~ *colours* 光彩夺目的颜色. *a ~ example* 光辉榜样. *a ~ patriot* 热烈的爱国者. ~ **furnace** 淬火炉. **-ly** *ad.*

glox·in·i·a [glɔkˈsinjə] *n.* 【植】大岩桐; 〔G-〕大岩桐属.

gloze [gləuz] *vt.* ①护(短), 掩饰(错误) (*over*). ②〔古〕注解, 说明 (*on, upon*). —*vi.* ①谄媚. ②〔古〕评解, 说明. **gloz·ing·ly** *ad.*

GLR = gun laying radar 炮瞄雷达.

glu. = glutamic acid 【生化】谷氨酸.

glu·ca·gon [ˈglu:kəgɔn] *n.* 【生化】葡萄胱.

glu·ci·num [glu:ˈsainəm], **glu·cin·i·um** [glu:ˈsiniəm] *n.* 【化】鋍〔铍 beryllium 的别名〕.

glu·co·nate [ˈglu:kəneit] *n.* 【化】葡糖酸盐〔酯〕.

glu·co·ne·o·gen·e·sis [ˌglu:kəuniəˈdʒenisis] *n.* = glyconeogenesis.

glu·con·ic acid [glu:ˈkɔnik] 【化】葡萄酸.

glu·co·pro·tein [ˈglu:kəuˈprəuti:n, -ti:in] *n.* = glycoprotein.

glu·cose [ˈglu:kəus] *n.* 【化】葡萄糖, 右旋糖.

glu·co·side [ˈglu:kəsaid] *n.* 【化】葡萄糖甙, 糖甙, 配糖体.

glue [glu:] *n.* ①胶, 胶水. ②各种胶粘物. *stick like ~ to sb.* 缠住某人不放. — *vt.* ①粘上; 使粘牢. ②在…上涂胶水. ~ *two pieces of wood together* 把两片木头粘起来. ~ ***one's ears to*** 贴着耳朵听. ~ ***one's eyes on*** 盯着看. ~ **pot** 胶锅. ~ **water** 胶水.

glue·y [ˈglu(:)i] *a.* 胶的, 胶质的; 胶粘的.

glum [glʌm] *a.* 阴郁的, 闷闷不乐的, 愁容满面的. **-ly** *ad.* **-ness** *n.*

glu·ma·ceous [glu:ˈmeiʃəs] *a.* 【植】①有颖(片)的. ②颖(片)状的.

glume [glu:m] *n.* 【植】颖, 颖片. *an empty ~* 护颖. ~ **spot** 颖枯病. **-like** *a.*

glump·y [ˈglʌmpi] *a.* 〔口〕= glum.

glut [glʌt] *n.* ①吃得过多, 饱食. ②充斥; 供过于求. *a ~ of fruit* 水果太多了. —*vt.* ①使满足; 使吃饱; 使厌腻. ②使(市场)充斥. — *vi.* 狼吞虎咽. ~ *oneself with food* 吃得太饱. ~ *one's eyes* 看够, 大饱眼福. ~ *one's revenge* 出够了气. ~ *the market* 使存货过剩.

glu·ta·mate [ˈglu:təmeit] *n.* 【化】谷氨酸盐〔酯〕.

glu·tam·ic [glu:ˈtæmik] **acid** 【化】谷氨酸.

glu·ta·mine [ˈglu:təmi:n] *n.* 【化】谷酰胺.

glu·ta·thi·one [ˌglu:təˈθaiəun] *n.* 【生化】谷胱甘肽.

glu·te·al [glu:ˈtiəl, ˈglu:ti-] *a.* 【解】臀肌的, 近臀肌的.

glu·te·lin [ˈglu:təlin] *n.* 【化】谷朊.

glu·ten [ˈglu:tən] *n.* 【化】谷朊; 面筋, 麸质. ~ **bread** (供糖尿病人吃的)麸质面包, 面筋面包. ~ **flour** (大部分面粉已被除去的)麸质面粉.

glu·ten·ous [ˈglu:tnəs] *a.* 谷朊状的; 麸质多的.

glu·te·us [ˈglu:tiəs] *n.* (*pl.* ***glu·tei*** [glu:ˈti:ai]) 【解】臀肌.

glu·ti·nos·i·ty [ˌglu:tiˈnɔsiti] *n.* 粘质, 粘性.

glu·ti·nous [ˈglu:tinəs] *a.* 粘的; 粘质的; 【植】有粘液的. ~ *rice* 糯米. **-ly** *ad.* **-ness** *n.*

glut·ton[1] [ˈglʌtn] *n.* ①贪吃的人, 饕餮, 食量大的人. ②〔口〕对…入迷的人, 酷爱…的人. *a ~ of books* 手不释卷的人. *a ~ for work* 闲不住的人. *a ~ for punishment* 不怕挨打的拳击家.

glut·ton[2] [ˈglʌtn] *n.* 【动】狼獾.

glut·ton·ize [ˈglʌtənaiz] *vt.* 狼吞虎咽, 大吃. — *vi.* 吃得过多.

glut·ton·ous [ˈglʌtənəs] *a.* 贪吃的; 食量大的; 贪婪的. *be ~ of* 贪. **-ly** *ad.*

glut·ton·y [ˈglʌtəni] *n.* 暴饮暴食, 贪食.

gly. = 【化】glycine.

glyc·er·al·de·hyde [ˌglisəˈældihaid] *n.* 【化】甘油醛.

glyc·er·ate [ˈglisəreit] *n.* 【化】甘油酸盐.

gly·cer·ic acid [gliˈserik] 【化】甘油酸.

glyc·er·ide [ˈglisəraid] *n.* 【化】甘油酯. **-id·ic** [-ˈridik] *a.*

glyc·er·in(e) [ˈglisərin], **glyc·er·ol** [ˈglisərɔl] *n.* 【化】甘油, 丙三醇.

glyc·er·in·ate [ˈglisərineit] *vt.* 用甘油处理. **-i·na·tion** [ˌglisəriˈneiʃən] *n.*

glyc·er·yl [ˈglisəril] *n.* 【化】甘油基, 丙三基.

gly·cine [ˈglaisi:n] *n.* 【化】甘氨酸, 氨基醋酸.

glyc(o)- *comb. f.* 表示"糖原", "甘油": *glyco*genesis.

gly·co·coll [ˈglaikəkɔl] *n.* 【化】= glycine.

gly·co·gen [ˈglikəudʒen] *n.* 【化】糖原, 动物淀粉.

gly·co·gen·e·sis [ˌglaikəuˈdʒenisis] *n.* 【生化】糖原生成(作用).

gly·co·gen·ic [ˌglaikəuˈdʒenik] *a.* 【生化】生糖原的.

gly·col [ˈglaikɔl, -kəul] *n.* 【化】乙二醇; 〔口〕甘醇.

gly·col·(l)ic [glaiˈkɔlik] *a.* 乙二醇的. ~ **acid** 乙醇酸.

gly·col·y·sis [glaiˈkɔlisis] *n.* 糖解; 糖酵解. **-co·lyt·ic** [ˌglaikəuˈlitik] *a.*

gly·co·ne·o·gen·e·sis [ˌglaikəuniəˈdʒenisis] *n.* 【生化】糖原异生.

gly·co·pro·tein [ˌglaikəuˈprəutin, -ti:in] *n.* 【生化】糖朊; 糖蛋白.

gly·co·side [ˈglaikəˌsaid] *n.* 【生化】葡糖苷. **-sid·ic** [-ˈsidik] *a.*

gly·co·su·ri·a [ˌglaikəˈsjuəriə] *n.* 【医】糖尿病.

gly·cyr·rhi·za [ˌglisiˈraizə] *n.* 【植】甘草.
Glyn [glin] *n.* 格林〔姓氏〕.
gly·ox·al [glaiˈɔksæl] *n.* 【化】乙二醛.
glyph [glif] *n.* ①【建】束腰竖沟. ②雕像, 雕刻的文字. ③表达信息的符号〔加指路牌上的箭头号等〕. **-ic** *a.* 雕刻的.
glyph·o·graph [ˈglifəgrɑːf] *n.* 【印】电刻版. — *vt., vi.* 电刻. **-er** [gliˈfɔgrəfə] *n.* 电刻者. **-ic** [ˌglifəˈgræfik] *a.* 电刻版的.
glyph·og·ra·phy [gliˈfɔgrəfi] *n.* 电刻术.
glyp·tic [ˈgliptik] *a.* ①雕刻的; 雕刻宝石的. ②【矿】有花纹的. **-s** *n. pl.* 〔用作单数〕雕刻术; 宝石雕刻术.
glyp·to·dont [ˈgliptədɔnt] *n.* 【动】(古代动物)雕齿兽.
glyp·tog·ra·phy [glipˈtɔgrəfi] *n.* 宝石雕刻术; 宝石雕刻学.
GM = ①General Manager 总经理. ②General Motors Corporation 〔美〕通用汽车公司. ③guided missile 导弹.
G.M. =①good middling〔美〕三级棉. ②Grand Master (棋类)特级大师. ③George Medal 〔英〕乔治勋章.
gm. = gram(me) 克(重量单位).
G-man [ˈdʒiːmæn] *n.* *(pl.* *-men)* 美国联邦调查局(FBI) 的调查员,密探 (= *Government man*).
G.M.B.; g. m. b. = good merchantable brand 上好可销商品.
GMC = General Motors Corporation 〔美〕通用汽车公司.
G.M.C.=General Medical Council 〔英〕全国医学总会.
Gmc; Gmc. = Germanic.
GMT = Greenwich mean time 格林威治平时. 〔*cf.* GCT〕
gnar, gnarr [nɑː] *vi.* *(-rr-)* 〔罕〕咆哮,吼 (= gnarl).
gnarl[1] [nɑːl] *n.* (木材的)节,瘤. — *vt.* ①扭, 拗. ②使有节. —*vi.* 生节.
gnarl[2] [nɑːl] *vi.* = gnar(r).
gnarl·y [ˈnɑːli], **gnarled** [nɑːld] *a.* ①节多的,瘤多的, 扭曲的. ②脾气乖僻的. **-i·ness** *n.*
gnash [næʃ] *vt.* 切齿,咬(牙),啮. ~ *one's teeth* 咬牙切齿. — *vi.* (由于愤怒或痛苦而)咬牙. — *n.* 咬.
gnat [næt] *n.* ①〔英〕蚊子; 咬人的小昆虫. ②小烦扰, 琐碎的事. ***~'s heel*** 〔美〕极少量的. ***~'s whistle*** 〔美〕好东西. ***strain at a ~ and swallow a camel*** 小事拘谨而大事糊涂,见小不见大. **~-strainer** 见小不见大的人.
gnath·ic [ˈnæθik] *a.* 颚的,颌的. ~ **index** 颚指数〔鼻沟至后脑壳中缝的距离与后脑壳中缝至齿中缝的距离之比〕.
gnath·ism [ˈnæθizəm] *n.* 颚部突出.
gna·thite [ˈneiθait, ˈnæθait] *n.* 颚形附器,口器.
gna·th·i·tis [næˈθaitis] *n.* 【医】颌炎.
gna·thon·ic [næˈθɔnik] *a.* 〔罕〕讨好的,奉承的.
gnaw [nɔː] *vt.* *(~ed; ~ed, gnawn)* ①咬,啃; 咬断. ②使腐蚀; 侵蚀; 消耗. ③使苦恼, 折磨. — *vi.* ①咬, 啮, 啃 *(at, into)*. ②侵蚀, 消耗. ③折磨, 苦恼. *Anxiety and distress ~ed at his heart.* 焦虑和烦恼使他苦恼. ***~ away [off]*** 咬去. ***~ through*** 咬断,咬穿. **-er** *n.* 咬者; 蚀坏者; 啮齿类动物.
gnaw·ing [ˈnɔːiŋ] *n.* 咬, 不断的苦痛. —*a.* 咬的; 使人苦恼的. *a ~ animal* 啮齿动物. **-ly** *ad.*
GND = ground 地; 接地.
gneiss [nais] *n.* 【地】片麻岩. **-ic, -y** *a.*
gneiss·oid [ˈnaisɔid] *a.* 象片麻岩的,片麻岩状的.
gneiss·ose [ˈnaisəus] *a.* 片麻岩的.
gnoc·chi [ˈnɔkiː, ˈnɔː-; It. ˈnjɔukkiː] *n.* 形状不一的饺子〔土豆〕〔蘸酱油吃〕.
gnome[1] [nəum] *n.* 格言.
gnome[2] [nəum] *n.* ①(传说中居于地下保护财宝和矿藏的)地精,土地神. ②矮子,侏儒.
gno·mic(al) [ˈnəumik(əl)] *a.* ①格言的,用格言的,爱写格言诗的. ②【语法】(时态)表示永恒真理的. *gnomic poetry* (希腊的)箴言诗. **-mi·cal·ly** *ad.*
gnom·ish [ˈnəumiʃ] *a.* 地精的, 地精似的; 好戏要的.
gno·mon [ˈnəumɔn] *n.* ①(日晷的)晷针, 指时针. ②【数】磬折形〔自平行四边形的一角截去一较小平行四边形后的图形〕.
gno·mon·ic [nəuˈmɔnik] *a.* ①指时针的. ②【天】用日晷仪测时的. ③【数】磬折形的. ~ **projection [chart]** 心射切面投影(图).
gno·mon·ics [nəuˈmɔniks] *n. pl.* 〔用作单数〕日晷测时学; 日晷制造法.
gno·sis [ˈnəusis] *n.* 【宗】灵知,神秘的直觉.
Gnos·tic [ˈnɔstik] *a.* ①(相信神秘直觉说的早期基督教)诺斯替教派的,诺斯替派教徒的. ②〔g-〕有灵知的; 聪明的. — *n.* 诺斯替教徒.
Gnos·ti·cism [ˈnɔstisizəm] *n.*【宗史】诺斯替教.
GNP = gross national product 国民生产总值.
G.N.R. = Great Northern Railway 〔美〕大北铁路.
gnu [nuː, njuː] *n.* (*pl.* *~s,* 〔集合词〕~)【动】牛羚, 角马.
GO = General Orders 【军】一般命令; 卫兵守则.
go [gəu] *vi.* *(went* [went]; *gone* [gɔn]; 第二人称单数现在式〔古〕 ***go·est*** [ˈgəuist]; 第三人称单数现在式 ***goes*** [gəuz], 〔古〕 ***go·eth*** [ˈgəuiθ]*)* 〔*cf.* going 及 gone〕 ①去,走; 旅行; 前进. ~ *abroad* 出国. ~ *a walk* 去散步. ~ *by train [car, air, water]* 乘火车[汽车, 飞机,船]去. ~ *on foot* 走路去. ~ *on a journey* 去旅行. ~ *the same way* 向同一方向走. ~ *hunting [swimming, shopping, fishing, etc.]* 打猎 [游泳、买东西、钓鱼等]去. *Who ~es (there)?* (哨兵喝问用语) (是)谁? *Go.* (赛跑口令)跑! ~ *the shortest way* 走捷径. *You may ~ further and fare worse.* 〔谚〕走得越远,情形越坏. ②离去, 离开; 死; 垮, 坏; 放弃,停止存在, 消失. *It is really time for us to ~.* 我们该走了. *All hope is gone.* 一切希望都完了. *How goes the time?* 什么时候了? *Poor Tom is gone.* 可怜的汤姆死了. *First the sails and then the masts went.* 先是帆坏了,随后桅杆也断了. *The meat is ~ing.* 肉要坏了. *The bank may ~ any day.* 这家银行随时可能倒闭. *His sight is going.* 他的眼力不行了. *These slums have to ~.* 这些贫民窟必须拆除. ③处于…状态; 处于一般的状况. ~ *armed* 携带武器, 武装着. ~ *hungry* 挨饿. ~ *in rags* 衣衫褴褛. *She has gone six months with child.* 她怀孕六个月了. *forget how the song goes* 忘记歌是怎样唱的. *as things ~es* 从一般情况来看. ④流传, 流行; 通用. *as the saying ~es* 象俗话说的那样. *The story ~es that* 据说…. *It ~es as follows* 如下所说. *as [so] far as it ~es* 就现在来说. *The sovereign ~es throughout the British Isles.* 英镑在英伦诸岛通用. ⑤发生; 进展; 变为, 成为. *What's ~ing on?* 发生了什么事? *All things went well.* 一切都好. *How are things ~ing?* 形势怎么样了? ~ *mad* 发狂. ~ *blind* 变瞎. ~ *to pieces* 破碎,垮台. ⑥运转,运行; 起作用; 走动着. *The clock does not ~.* 钟不走了. *The car ~es by electricity.* 这车是用电开动的. *Her tongue ~es nineteen to the dozen.* 她喋喋不休说个没完. ⑦遵照…行动 *(by)*. *a good rule to ~ by* 应该遵守的良好规则. *What he says ~es.* 他说话算数. ⑧放置,装入,纳入; (算术的)除得. *Where are the forks to ~?* 叉子放在哪里? *The boots will not ~ into the bag.* 靴子装不进袋里去. *Six into twelve ~es twice.* 六除十二得二. *Six into five won't ~.* 六除五不能除. ⑨响,发音; (钟)报点. ~ *bang [crack]* 破裂[爆裂],砰[啪]地响. *It has just gone six.* 才敲过六点钟. ⑩(时间)消逝, 过去; (距离)走过, 经过. *The evening went pleasantly enough.* 晚上过得很愉快. *ten days to ~ before Easter* 还有十天到复活节. *There are eight miles to ~.* 还有八英里. ⑪归, 落入…手. *The prize*

went to his rival. 奖品落入对方手中去了. ⑫诉诸. ~ *to war* 诉诸武力,发动战争. ~ *to law* 诉诸法律,起诉. ⑬总共,合成. *How many ounces ~ to the pound?* 多少英两是一镑? *qualities that ~ to make a hero* 有助于造就一个英雄的品质. ⑭通到,到达;延伸至. *The road ~es to Rome.* 这条路通罗马. *His land ~es almost to the river.* 他的田几乎一直延伸到河边. *His knowledge fails to ~ very deep.* 他的知识不很精深. ⑮花费. *His spare money ~es on books.* 他多余的钱都花在买书上. ⑯卖,卖得(…价). *The house went cheap.* 这房子卖得很便宜. *The eggs went for 3s. a dozen.* 鸡蛋一打卖三先令. ⑰相配;(诗、歌词)有节奏;(与曲调)相配 *(to).* ⑱称为,叫做;冒(名). *He ~es by a name of Henry.* 他名叫亨利. ~ *under a false name* 用假名. ⑲有,备有〔主用现在分词形式〕. *There's sure to be some sort of dinner ~ing.* 肯定会有一顿饭吃吃的. ⑳招惹. *Don't ~ to trouble.* 不要惹麻烦. ㉑〔用以加强否定的命令语气〕. *Don't ~ and make a fool of yourself.* 别去干蠢事. ㉒〔美方〕想. *I didn't ~ to do it.* 我没有想做那样的事. ㉓〔用进行时态,后接不定式〕将要,打算. *It's ~ing to rain.* 快要下雨了. *We're ~ing to call a meeting to discuss it.* 我们准备开会讨论一下. ***as [so] far as it ~es*** 就现状来说;就其本身而言. ~ ***a long way in [towards]*** *(doing sth.)* 大有效力, 大大有用处 *(The president's statement went a long way towards reassuring the nation.* 总统的话在提高全国人民的信心方面收效甚大). ~ ***about*** ①四处走动,走来走去. ②着手(工作). ③(谣言等)流传. ④【海】掉转船头;【军】折回 (~ *about to do* 打算做. *Go about your business!* 走开,干你的事去! *A story is ~ing about that…* 风传…). ~ ***after*** 追求. ~ ***against*** 违背,反对;不利于 *(The case went against him.* 这案子作出了对他不利的裁决). ~ ***ahead*** 继续前进,取得进展. ~ ***all lengths*** 干到底. ~ ***all out*** = ~ ***all-out*** 全力以赴,鼓足干劲. ~ ***along*** 前进. ~ ***along with*** 陪[随]…一起去;赞同,同意. ***Go along with you!*** 〔口〕去你的! ~ ***and*** … 〔口〕去…,糊里糊涂地… *(I have gone and done it.* 我糊里糊涂就那样做了. *Go and be miserable!* 去受罪吧!). ~ ***around*** 〔美〕= ~ round. ~ ***at*** 〔口〕扑过去,攻击;兴冲冲开始干 (~ *at it hammer and tongs* 大干而特干). ~ ***away*** 离开;带走,拐逃 *(with).* ~ ***back*** ①回来;追溯到 *(to)*;回顾. ②走下坡路 *(The old tree is ~ing back.* 这棵老树不行了). ~ ***back of*** 〔美口〕调查,研究. ~ ***back on [from, upon]*** 破坏,背(约),背叛;〔美〕遗弃. ~ ***bad*** (食品、蛋等)坏掉. ~ ***before*** 走在前面;居先,超过. ~ ***behind*** ①调查,摸底;进一步斟酌. ②亏本. ~ ***between*** 做中间人. ~ ***beyond*** 超出,越过. ~ ***blooey*** 爆炸;出毛病. ~ ***by*** ①走过,过去. ②以…为根据(作判断). ③〔美〕顺道访问. ④受…所控制. ⑤称为,名叫 *(as time goes by* 随着时间的过去. *let an opportunity ~ by* 放过机会. *Years have gone by.* 经过多年. *I ~ by what I hear.* 我依据听到的作判断). ~ ***down*** ①下去,(价格等)下跌;(船只)沉没,(飞机)坠落,(日,月)落下;继续到 *(to)*;(风、浪等)平静下来;(潮、肿等)减退. ②被记下,被载入. ③倒下,垮台,破产. ④〔口〕咽下;被接受,受欢迎 *(with).* ⑤(英大学)退学,离校 (~ *down in history as a hero* 作为英雄留名史册. *The pill won't ~ down.* 这药丸无法下咽. *The film went down well with the audience.* 影片大受观众欢迎). ~ ***down hill*** 走下坡路. ~ ***dry*** 〔美〕禁酒. ~ ***easy*** 慢慢来,不紧张. ~ ***far*** 价值大,效力大;成功,大有前途. ~ ***far toward(s)*** 大大有助于. ~ ***flat out*** 全力以赴,鼓足干劲. ~ ***flooey*** = ~ blooey. ~ ***flop*** 失败. ~ ***for*** ①去拿,去找,去喊,去请,尽力求得. ②〔美〕拥护,支持,偏袒. ③被认为;适用于. ④〔口〕猛烈攻击,袭击;【剧】批评 *(It ~es for you too.* 这对你也是适用的. *A dog went for him.* 狗向他冲了过来. ~ *for a doctor* 去请医生. ~ *for each other in the papers* 在报上互相攻讦). ~ ***for little*** 被认为不大有用. ~ ***for much [nothing]*** 被认为大有用处[毫无用处]. ~ ***forth*** ①出发. ②发布;发表. ~ ***forward*** ①前进. ②发生. ~ ***free*** 被释放;被解放. ~ ***fut [phut]*** 〔俚〕(车胎等)破裂,泄气;失败,成泡影. ~ ***glimmering*** 〔口〕逐渐消灭,化为乌有. ~ ***halves [shares]*** 彼此一半,平分. ~ ***hang*** 不再被关心,被忘却. ~ ***hard with sb.*** 使某人为难. ~ ***home*** ①回家. ②击中,命中. ~ ***ill*** (事态)恶化. ~ ***ill with*** 对…不利. ~ ***in*** ①进入;放得进;参加. ②(纸牌赌博中)开价. ③天体被云遮盖. ④(钱)用于. ⑤(板球戏等)开始一局比赛. ~ ***in at*** 〔口〕激烈打击. ~ ***in for*** 〔口〕赞成,支持;寻求,追求,沉迷在…;参加 (~ *in for an examination* 参加考试. ~ *in for swimming* 热爱游泳. ~ *in for technical innovations* 搞技术革新). ~ ***in with*** 参加,加入. ***Going! Going! Gone!*** 要卖了! 要卖了! 卖掉了! 〔拍卖用语〕. ~ ***into*** ①(门等)通着;进入. ②加入;参与. ③查究. ④成为. ⑤说到,涉及. ⑥穿…的服装,(尤指)穿(孝). ⑦采取…态度,进入…状态 (~ *into action* 行动起来. ~ *into the army* 参军. ~ *into details* 深入细节. ~ *into mourning* 戴孝. ~ *into production* 投入生产. ~ *into a rage* 大发雷霆). ~ ***it*** 〔口〕① 使劲儿干,莽撞. ②放荡;挥霍. ~ ***it alone*** 单干. ~ ***it blind*** 〔口〕瞎干. ~ ***it strong on sth.*** 热烈赞许某事物. ~ ***near to do sth.*** 几乎做某事. ~ ***off*** ①经过,进行得 *(well, badly).* ②(枪)打出,(炸弹)爆炸;(话等)冒出. ③〔口〕(食物)变坏. ④睡着,昏过去. ⑤逃走,离去,走掉;(演员)退场,下. ⑥〔口〕(女儿)出嫁;渐渐忘怀;死;卖掉 *(Her voice is ~ing off.* 她的嗓子坏了. ~ *off into a faint* 昏过去. ~ *off into a fit of laughter* 哄然大笑. ~ *off into wild flights of fancy* 开始胡思乱想. ~ *off at high prices* 高价卖出). ~ ***off with*** 拿走,抢走,拐走. ~ ***on*** ①往前走;继续…下去 *(with; doing)*;日子过得 *(well, badly* 等). ②〔口〕胡作非为 *(shamefully* 等). ③责骂 *(at).* ④出场,上台. ⑤可穿用. ⑥发生. ⑦〔口〕接近. ⑧依据. ⑨受救济 *(He is four going on five.* 他四岁多快五岁了. *Go on with your work.* 接着干下去. ~ *on raining all day* 雨整天下个不停. ~ *on to say* 接着说. *These gloves won't ~ on.* 手套戴不上去). ***Go on!*** 〔口〕接下去!〔反〕别胡说啦! ~ ***on for*** 接近. ~ ***out*** ①出去,出国,(妇女)离家外出工作. ②(火、灯)熄,灭. ③退职,辞职;下台;不再流行;(衣着式样等)过时. ④出版. ⑤(时间)过去. ⑥出去交际. ⑦罢工. ⑧〔美〕垮下,倒塌. ⑨〔美〕参加选拔. ⑩向往,充满同情 (~ *out of one's mind* 发狂. ~ *out of print* 绝版). ~ ***out for*** 拼命取得. ~ ***over*** ①越过,渡过;转向 *(to)*,改变立场. ②温习,仔细检查. ③(车)翻倒. ④延期. ⑤〔美口〕很受欢迎,成功. ⑥走完. ~ ***over big*** 〔美口〕大受欢迎,大成功. ~ ***partners*** 共同出资. ~ ***round*** ①迂回走,四处走动. ②(传食物等)使人人分到. ③顺便访问. ④(带子)长得够绕一圈;足够分配. ~ ***slow*** 慢慢走;怠工. ~ ***so far as to say it*** = ~ ***the length of saying it*** 甚至说那样的话. ~ ***some*** 〔美口〕做了不少,得了不少. ~ ***(sb.) one better*** 〔美俚〕胜过某人. ~ ***steady*** 〔美俚〕成为关系相当确定的情侣. ~ ***the whole hog [figure]*** 全力以赴. ~ ***through*** ①通过,经过. ②修毕,受(考试等);经历,忍受. ③用光,荡尽. ④(书)突破(第…版). ⑤完成,贯彻 *(with).* ⑥仔细检查. ***Go to!*** 〔古〕去你的! ~ ***to*** ①相当于. ②付出. ~ ***to bat for*** 〔美口〕为人辩护判决. ~ ***together*** 陪同;相配;〔口〕恋爱. ~ ***too far*** 过火,走极端. ~ ***under*** 沉没;没落,破产;失败,屈服;〔美俚〕死. ~ ***up*** ①上升;〔英〕上大学,上城市去;腾贵;烧起来;爆炸. ②〔美〕破产;死;〔美〕失败;走向舞台正面的里头. ~ ***uphill*** 走上坡路. ~ ***upon*** ①据…来判断(行动). ②着手. ~ ***west*** ①死,上西天. ②(钱)完了. ~ ***with*** ①陪…同行;同…一致,同…调和;跟…谈恋爱. ②带有. ③领会,了解.

~ *without* 缺少；没有…而忍受过去. ~ *without saying* 不待说. ~ *wrong* ①走错路，误入歧途. ②出毛病，失败. *Here ~es.* 瞧，开始了. *leave ~ of* 松手放开. *let ~* ①松手，放开. ②释放. ③解雇. ④放弃；忘记. *let ~ with* 尽情地(说、叫喊等). *let oneself ~* 发脾气. *There you ~ again.* 你这一套又来了. *What ~es?* 〔美俚〕发生了什么事？— *vt.* 〔口〕①忍受；享受；买得走〔常用于否定结构〕. ②〔口〕打赌，叫牌，出价. ③承担责任. ④生产. *I will ~ you a shilling.* 我和你赌一个先令吧. *I can't ~ her music.* 她的音乐我听不下去. *I can't ~ the price.* 我出不起这价钱. — *n.* (*pl.* *~es*) ①去，进行. ②〔口〕事情(特指困难事情)，难关，约定的事情. ③〔the ~〕时髦. ④〔口〕精神，精力. ⑤〔口〕成功. ⑥拳击比赛；比赛. ⑦〔口〕(酒的)一杯；(食物的)一份. ⑧试一下；干一下；一口气. ⑨(英大学)学位考试. *a capital ~* 妙极了. *first ~* 〔口〕首先. *Here's a ~! = What a ~!* 这事真难办！ *a near ~* 侥幸逃脱难关. *a jolly [pretty, queer, rum] ~* 怪事. *It's no ~.* 〔口〕不行，没希望. *It is a ~.* 好吧，就这样决定. *He's plenty of ~ in him.* 他劲头十足. *itch to have a ~ at it* 跃跃欲试. ***at [in] one ~*** 一口气. ***be all [quite] the ~*** 〔口〕风行一时. ***be full of ~*** 精力充沛. ***come and ~*** 来往. ***from the word ~*** 〔美口〕从一开始. ***full of ~*** 精神旺盛. ***make a ~ of it*** 〔美〕成功，干好. ***on [upon] the ~*** ①在进行，在活动；刚要动身. ②衰微. ③有醉意. ***the little [great] ~*** (剑桥大学)学士学位预〔正〕考. — *a.* 好的，运行良好的；〔美口〕一切正常的，可以开始的；【宇航】可随时发射的. — *int.* (赛跑口令)跑. *On your mark! Get set! Go!* 各就各位！预备！跑！ ~ **condition**【宇】待飞，待发. ~-no-~ *n.* (宇宙飞船等)飞或不飞的最后决定；事情的最后决定. ~ **side**【机】通过端.

Go·a [ˈgəuə] *n.* ①果阿〔印度一地区〕. **go·a** [ˈgəuə] *n.*【动】藏原羚(藏黄羊) *(Procapra picticaudata)*〔产于我国西藏的一种棕灰色的长毛小羚羊〕. ~ **powder** (采自巴西 araroba 树上的)苛桠粉〔对皮肤病有特效〕.

goad [gəud] *n.* ①(赶家畜用的)刺棒. ②使痛苦〔烦恼〕之物；激励物，刺激物. — *vt.* ①用刺棒驱赶(家畜). ②激励，刺激，扇动；策动；唆使. ~ *sb. to do [into doing] sth.* 唆使某人做某事. ~ *sb. to [into] fury* 使某人发怒.

goaf [gəuf] *n.* = gob ②.

go-a·head [ˈgəuəˌhed] *a.* ①〔美口〕前进着的；进取的；有冒险精神的. ②可通行的. *a vigorous ~ company* 一个兴旺发达的公司. ~ *signal* 放行信号. — *n.* ①许可，放行信号. ②进取心；活力，精力.

goal [gəul] *n.* ①(赛跑等的)终点. ②(足球等运动的)球门；守门员. ③门球；门球得分. ④目的，目标；目的地. get [kick, make, score] a ~ 打进一个门球，得一分. *win by two ~s* 以两球获胜. *one's ~ in life* 人生目的. **~-directed** *a.* 有目的的，有用意的. **~keeper** (足球等运动的)守门员. ~ **line** (足球等运动的)门线. **~-mouth** (足球等运动的)球门区. ~ **post** (足球等运动的)门柱. ~ **post mast**【船】龙门架桅. **~tender** = ~ keeper.

goal·ee, goa·lie [ˈgəuli] *n.* 〔口〕= goal-keeper.

go-a·round [ˈgəu-əˌraund] *n.* ①回合；激烈争论. ②躲闪，拖延. ③回旋.

go-as-you-please [ˈgəuəzjuˈpliːz] *a.* 无拘束的，随意的.

goat [gəut] *n.* ①【动】山羊. ②〔the *G-*〕【天】山羊座；摩羯宫. ③坏人 (*opp.* sheep)；色鬼. ④〔俚〕替罪羊，牺牲品. ⑤【铁路】道岔扳子，转辙机. ***act [play] the (giddy) ~*** 胡闹. ***get sb.'s ~*** 使人发怒，使人焦急，触怒. ***ride the ~*** 加入秘密团体. ***separate the sheep from the goats*** 把好人和坏人区别开. ~ **antelope**【动】山羚羊〔特性介于山羊和羚羊之间的几种动物，如亚洲的苏门羊和斑羚〕. **~god**【希神】(人身羊足、头上有角的)畜牧神，潘神 = Pan. **~herd** 牧山羊人. **~skin** 山羊皮；山羊皮制品，羊皮囊. **~sucker**【动】夜鹰. **~'s wool** 不存在的东西. **-ish** *a.* ①山羊似的. ②好色的，淫荡的.

goat·ee [gəuˈtiː] *n.* 山羊胡子.

goat·fish [ˌgəutˈfiʃ] *n.* (*pl.* ~, ~*es*)【动】羊鱼科 *(Mullidae)* 鱼；羊鱼.

goat·ling [ˈgəutliŋ] *n.* (1—2岁的)小山羊.

goats·beard [ˈgəutsˌbiəd] *n.*【植】①缎升麻. ②波罗门参属 *(Tragopogon)* 植物.

goat's-rue [ˈgəutsˌruː] *n.*【植】①美洲灰叶 *(Tephrosia virginiana)*. ②山羊豆 *(Galega officinalis)*.

goat·y [ˈgəuti] *a.* = goatish.

gob[1] [gɔb] *n.* ①粘块〔如痰块〕. ②【矿】(填废坑用的)矿渣；矿内废石；采空区. ③〔*pl.*〕许多，大量. — *vi.* 吐；吐痰.

gob[2] [gɔb] *n.* 〔俚〕嘴. **~-stopper** 棒头糖.

gob[3] [gɔb] *n.* 〔美俚〕水兵.

go·ban(g) [gəuˈbæŋ] *n.* (日本用围棋盘下的)五子棋.

gob·bet [ˈgɔbit] *n.* ①〔古〕一片，一块(尤指生肉或食物)；一堆. ②一口(食物). ③(尤指在考试中供考生翻译或评论而摘录的)片段引文；乐章的片断.

gob·ble[1] [ˈgɔbl] *vt., vi.* ①狼吞虎咽. ②〔美俚〕急急抓住；任意花完 *(up)*. ③如饥似渴地阅读 *(up)*. **-r** *n.* 狼吞虎咽的人.

gob·ble[2] [ˈgɔbl] *vi.* 发出火鸡般的咯咯叫声. — *n.* (火鸡的)咯咯声. **-r** *n.* 公火鸡.

gob·ble·dy·gook [ˈgɔbldiˈguk] *n.* 〔俚〕浮夸、冗繁而费解的语言〔文章〕；官腔；官样文章 (= gobbledegook).

Gob·e·lin [ˈgəubəlin] *a.* 巴黎哥白林染织厂制双面挂毯的. — *n.* 哥白林厂制壁饰花毡. *the ~ tapestry* 壁饰花毡. ~ **blue** 暗青绿色.

gobe·mouche [ˈgɔbmuːʃ] *n.* (*pl.* ~*s* [-muːʃ])〔F.〕轻信小道消息的人.

go-be·tween [ˈgəubiˌtwiːn] *n.* ①掮客，媒人，中间人. ②【电】连接杆，连接环；中间节，中间网路.

go·bi [ˈgəubi] *n.* 〔the ~〕戈壁沙漠，戈壁滩.

go·bi·oid [ˈgəubiːˌɔid] *a.*【动】①虾虎鱼的. ②似虾虎鱼的. — *n.* 虾虎鱼.

gob·let [ˈgɔblit] *n.* 高脚杯；〔诗〕酒杯. ~ **cells**【医】杯状细胞.

gob·lin [ˈgɔblin] *n.* 妖魔，恶鬼. **-ry** *n.* 〔集合词〕鬼怪集团.

go·bo [ˈgəubəu] *n.* (*pl.* ~*s*, ~*es*) ①(摄影机的)透镜遮光片，(摄影机镜头周围的)遮光黑布. ②麦克风纯音片，麦克风话筒上排除杂音的遮布.

go·by [ˈgəubi] *n.* (*pl.* **-bies**, 〔集合词〕~)【动】(虾虎鱼科的)刺鳍鱼，刺虾虎鱼.

go-by [ˈgəubai] *n.* 〔口〕假装不见；不理. ***give sb. the ~*** 对某人冷淡.

GOC, G.O.C. = ①Gulf Oil Company〔美〕海湾石油公司. ②Government of Congo 刚果政府. ③Ground Observer Corps〔美〕地面观察队(勤务).

GOC(inC),G.O.C. (-in-C.) = General Officer Commanding (-in-Chief) 总指挥官.

go-cart [ˈgəukɑːt] *n.* ①小儿学步车；(折叠式)婴儿轻便车. ②手推车. ③早期的轻便马车. ④微型竞赛汽车(= kart).

god [gɔd] *n.* ①〔G-〕上帝，造物主. ②〔有时作 G-〕神；男神 (*opp.* goddess). ③神像，偶像；神化的人〔物〕；被极度崇敬的人〔物〕. ④〔*pl.*〕剧院顶层楼座观众. *G- help those who help themselves.* 〔谚〕天助自助者. *He that serves G- for money will serve the devil for better wages.* 〔谚〕为钱侍奉上帝，为更多的钱就会给魔鬼卖力. *When G- would destroy a man he first makes him mad.* 〔谚〕上帝毁灭人，先使他发狂. *Whom the ~s love die young.* 〔谚〕好人寿不长. ***a feast for the ~s*** 丰盛的酒席. ***a***

sight for the ~s 壮观. ***a (little) tin ~*** 受到过分尊敬的人,自命不凡的人. ***act of G-*** 【法】天灾,不可抗力. ***By (my) G-!*** 的的确确. ***for God's sake*** 看在上帝面上. ***G-! = Good G-! Great G-! My G-! Oh, G-!*** 天啊! 啊呀! *Thank G-! = G- be thanked!* 幸亏; 谢天谢地! ***G- bless me [my life, my soul, you, etc.]!*** (表示惊讶)啊呀! 喔唷! 吓我一跳! ***G- bless you [him]!*** 愿上帝保佑你[他]! ***G- damn you!*** 天杀的! 该死的! ***G- forbid!*** 上天不容! ***G- forfend*** 上天不容,决无此事. ***~ from the machine*** 意外的救星[源出古希腊戏剧中经常以机关推出的扮天神的角色]. ***G- grant ...!*** 但愿...! ***G help him!*** 唉,真可怜! ***G- knows when [where, why, what]*** 天晓得, 谁也不晓得. ***G- knows*** *(that)* 确确实实... ***G- speed you!*** 祝你一路平安! ***G- willing*** 如果情形允许的话. ***G- wot*** [古]天知道. ***So help me G-!*** 的的确确! 老天爷在上,决无半点假话! ***the ~ of day*** 太阳神 (Apollo, Phoebus). ***the ~ of fire*** 火神 (Vulcan). ***the ~ of heaven*** 天神(Zeus, Jupiter). ***the ~ of hell*** 地狱神 (Pluto). ***the G- of Host*** 【圣】万军之主耶和华. ***the ~ of love*** 爱神 (Cupid = the blind ~). ***the ~ of marriage*** 月下老人 (Hymen). ***the ~ of the sea*** 海神 (Poseidon, Neptune). ***the ~ of war*** 战神 (Ares, Mars). ***the ~ of wine*** 酒神 (Bacchus, Dionisus). ***the ~ of this world*** 魔王. ***make a ~ of one's belly*** 一味追求吃喝. ***on God's earth*** 世界上. ***under ~*** 就人间而言. ***with ~*** 和上帝一块; 死了. ***wrestle with G-*** 热忱祈祷. ***Ye ~s (and little fishes)!*** [口]怎么搞的! — *vt.* 神化, 把...崇拜为神. ~ *it* 做神, 俨然以神自居. **~-awful** *a.* 非常可怕的, 可憎的. **~ booster** [美俚]牧师. **~box** [美俚]教堂, 礼拜堂. **~child** 教子, 教女. **~daughter** 教女. **~-father** ①*n.* 教父; 洗礼时名字被用以命名的人. ②*vt.* 作...的教父. **~-fearing** *a.* 敬神的,虔敬的. **~-forsaken** *a.* 为神所抛弃的, 堕落的; 凄凉的, 邪恶的, 倒霉的. **~given** *a.* [偶用 g-]①天赐的. ②极受欢迎的; 恰当的; 应时的. **~head** 神性,神格; 神. **Godman** 基督; 神人. **~mother** 教母. **~ parent** 教父母. **~'s acre** 墓地 (尤指教堂墓地). **God's book** 圣经. **God's (own) cowntry** 天府之邦, 乐土,故乡,祖国. **God's earth** 全世界. **~send** 天赐; 意外得来的所需之物. **God's foolstool** [口] 大地, 地. **God's gift** 天赐. **God's image** 人体. **~son** 教子. **~speed** 成功, 幸运; 天惠 (*bid sb. ~speed* 祝某人成功; 祝某人一路平安). **God's plenty [quantity]** [口] 许多, 丰盛. **God's truth** 绝对真理. **-hood** *n.* 神性,神格. **-less** *a.* ①没有神的. ②不敬神的,不信神的. ③邪恶的. **-like** *a.* 神似的, 上帝般的; 庄严的; 神圣的. **-ship** *n.* 神道,神性,神位,神,上帝. **-ward(s)** *ad.* 向神,对神.

god·damn(ed) [ˈgɔdˈdæm(*d*)] *a.* ①该死的,讨厌的. ②十足的,完全的.

God·dard [ˈgɔdəd, ˈgɔdɑːd] *n.* 戈达德[姓氏].

god·dess [ˈgɔdis] *n.* ①女神. ②非凡的女子; 绝世美女. *the ~ of corn* 司五谷的女神 (Demeter, Ceres). *the ~ of heaven* 天后,天之女神 (Hera, Juno). *the ~ of hell* 地狱的女神 (Persephone, Proserpine). *the ~ of love* 爱的女神 (Aphrodite, Venus). *the ~ of the moon* 月的女神 (Artemis, Diana). *the ~ of war* 战争的女神 (Bellona). *the ~ of wisdom* 智慧的女神 (Athena, Minerva).

go·det [gəuˈdet] *n.* (填补、加固或放大衣服的)三角形布料.

go·de·ti·a [gəuˈdiːʃə] *n.* 【植】高代花.

go-dev·il [ˈgəudevl] *n.* ①拖木橇, 运石车. ②刮管器, 冲棍. ③油井爆破器,坠撞器.

God·frey [ˈgɔdfri] *n.* 戈弗雷[男子名].

god·less [ˈgɔdlis] *a.* ①没有神的. ②不信神的, 不虔诚的. ③邪恶的. **-ly** *ad.* **-ness** *n.*

god·like [ˈgɔdlaik] *a.* 如神的, 上帝般的; 神圣的, 庄严的.

god·ling [ˈgɔdliŋ] *n.* 【宗】小神祇.

god·ly [ˈgɔdli] *a.* 敬神的,信神的; [古]神圣的; 虔诚的. *the ~* [讽]善男信女. **-li·ness** *n.*

God·man [ˈgɔdmən] *n.* 戈德曼[姓氏].

Go·dol·phin [gəˈdɔlfin] *n.* 戈多尔芬[姓氏].

go·down [ˈgəudaun] *n.* (印度、菲律宾等地的)仓库.

God·win [ˈgɔdwin] *n.* 戈德温[姓氏].

god·wit [ˈgɔdwit] *n.* 【动】(塍鹬属中的) 长嘴涉水鸟.

go·er [ˈgəuə] *n.* ①去的人; 行人,路人. ②走动的人[车, 马, 钟表等]. ③常去...的人[常作 *comb. f.*] *a film ~* 经常看电影的人. *comers and ~s* 来往的人. *a good [poor] ~* 走得好[不好]的马[钟等].

Goe·the [ˈgəːtə], **Johann Wolfgang von.** 约翰·沃尔夫冈·歌德 [1749—1832, 德国诗人、剧作家、小说家、哲学家].

Goe·the·an, Goe·thi·an [ˈgəːtiən] *a.* 歌德的, 哥德派的,哥德风格的. — *n.* 德歌崇拜者.

goe·thite [ˈgəuθait, ˈgəːtait] *n.* 【矿】针铁矿.

gof·fer, go·fer [ˈgəufə] *n.* ①(衣服等的)襞, 皱褶. ②烫皱褶用的熨斗. — *vt.* 在...上作皱褶,在...上作出波纹, 作出浮花. *~ed cloth* 轧纹布, 拷花布. *~ed edges* (书籍的)锯齿状浮雕花边. *~ed paper* 皱纹纸.

go-ga(u)ge [ˈgəugeidʒ] *n.* 【机】过端量规,通过规.

go-get·ter [ˈgəuˈgetə] *n.* ①能干而有上进心的人. ②火箭自动制导的控制装置. — *a.* ①摇摆舞的, 跳摇摆舞小舞场的. ②最时髦的. ③活跃的,乱窜的,无节制的.

gog·gle [ˈgɔgl] *vi., vt.* 转动 [凸出] 眼珠; 瞪眼看, 斜眼看. — *n.* ①瞪眼, 转动眼珠. ②[*pl.*]遮风镜; [俚] 眼镜; 【机】护目镜. — *a.* (眼珠)突出的,转动的,瞪住的. **~-box** *n.* [英俚]电视机. **~-eye** *n.* 【动】弹突鱼类[如岩鲈]. **~-eyed** *a.* 眼睛转动的; 眼珠凸出的; 瞪眼的.

gog·let [ˈgɔglit] *n.* [印]冷水瓶.

go-go [ˈgəuˌgəu] *a.* ①摇摆舞的; 和跳摇摆舞的人有关的; 摇摆舞音乐唱片的; 摇摆舞厅的. ②[俚]活泼的; 有力的; 时髦的. ④赌博性投资的. — *n.* ①摇摆舞. ②赌博性投资(= ~ fund).

Go·gol [ˈgɔgəl], **Nikolai Vasilievitch** 果戈理[1809—1852,俄国小说家、剧作家].

Goi·del [ˈgɔidəl] *n.* 盖尔人; 讲凯尔特语的人.

Goi·del·ic [gɔiˈdelik] *a.* ①盖尔人的. ②盖尔语的. — *n.* (包括爱尔兰盖尔语、苏格兰盖尔语、曼岛语的)凯尔特语族.

go·ing [ˈgəuiŋ] go 的现在分词. — *a.* ①进行中的; 运转中的; 营业中的; 营业发达的. ②活着的, 存在的. ③现行的; 流行中的. *a ~ concern* 营业发达的商行[公司]. *the ~ prices* 时价. *the best novelist ~* 当今活着的最好小说家. *There is cold beef ~.* 有现成的冷牛肉. *the ~ rate* 现行率. ***~ and coming*** 逃脱不了 (*get sb. ~ and coming* 使某人无路可逃). ***~ strong*** [美]成功, 进行顺利. ***in ~ order*** 正常运转. ***get ~*** [口] = set ~. ***get sb. ~*** [俚]使某人激动,使某人发怒. ***~ (on)*** 接近,快到(某一年龄或时间) (*She is ~ on seventeen.* 她快十七岁了). ***keep ~*** 继续(运转,谈话); 维持. ***set ~*** ①使运转, 开动. ②实行. ③出发 (*set the clock ~* 开钟). — *n.* ①行走, 出行. ②出发, 动身. ③进展的情况; 工作 [行驶] 的方法 [速度]; 工作的条件. ④(走路、赛跑、开车等时)地面[路面]的状况. ⑤【建】(梯段的)级距; 级长. ⑥[常 *pl.*] 行为,举动. *heavy ~* 缓慢的进展. *rough ~* 困难的进程; (比赛运动中的)苦战. *a safe ~ and return* 平安出发与归来. *The ~ was very hard over this mountain road.* 在这山路上行走很吃力. ***go while the ~'s good*** 及时离开, 及时行动. **~ away** 出发过蜜月. **~-over** *n.* [美口] ①彻底检查, 彻底审查. ②申斥, 痛打. **~s-on** *n.* [口]①勾当, (坏) 举动,品行,(不良)行为[常与 such,

strange 等词连用〕. ②事件,发生的情况.
goi·tre, goi·ter [ˈgɔitə] *n.*【医】甲状腺肿. **-ed** *a.*
goi·trous [ˈgɔitrəs] *a.*【医】甲状腺肿的.
gok [gɔk] *vt.* ***(gokked, gok·king)***〔美俚〕完全懂得,彻底了解.
G.O.K. = God only knows〔美俚〕天晓得.
go-kart [ˈgəuˌkɑːt] *n.* 微型竞赛汽车.
Gol·con·da [gɔlˈkɔndə] *n.* ①戈尔康达〔印度南部古都,曾以出产金钢石著名〕. ②丰富的矿藏;大财源.
gold [gəuld] *n.* ①金,黄金;金币. ②财富;财宝;黄金一样贵重[富丽]的东西. ③金色,金黄色. ④包金,镀金;金粉,金线,金箔. ⑤(射箭的)金色靶心. ⑥金牌,金质奖章. *age of* ~ 黄金时代 *(= golden age). black* ~ 黑金,石油. *cloth of* ~ 金线织物. *dead* ~ 无光泽的金子. *fool's* ~〔美〕看来象黄金的矿,黄铁矿 (= iron pyrites). *greed of* ~ 黄金欲. *a heart of* ~ 一颗高贵的心. *She is pure* ~. 她纯洁无瑕. *a voice of* ~ 金嗓子,优美的声音. *the old* ~ 古金色,暗黄褐色. ***as good as*** ~ (小孩)很乖. ***be worth one's weight in*** ~ 非常有价值,非常有裨益. ***gild refined*** ~ 画蛇添足,多此一举. ***go off*** ~ 废除金本位. ***make a*** ~ 射中靶心. ***on a*** ~ ***basis*** 用金本位. — *a.* ①金的,金制的,含金的. ②金色的. ③金本位的. ~ **amalgam** 金汞膏. ~ **bank**〔美〕国立银行. ~ **bar** 金条. ~**-beater** 金箔工. ~ **beatle**【动】金甲虫. ~ **bloc** 金本位国家集团. ~**-brick** ①*n.*〔口〕假金砖,赝品,虚有其表的东西;〔美俚〕懒汉,(军队中)逃避工作的人. ②*vt.*〔美俚〕欺骗,以高价出售劣货. ③*vi.*〔军俚〕偷懒,不尽职,逃避工作,吊儿郎当. ~**bug** ① = ~ beatle. ②〔美俚〕主张金本位的人. ~ **bullion** 金块. ~ **certificate** 金券. **G- Coast** ①黄金海岸(非洲加纳的旧称). ②〔美口〕富豪住宅区. ~ **coin** 金币. ~ **content** 含金量. ~**-crest**【动】戴菊(鸟名). ~ **currency** 金本位货币. ~ **digger** ①金矿工人;淘金者. ②〔口〕以美色骗取男人钱财的女子. ~ **digging** 找金矿;淘金;淘金地带. ~ **dust** 砂金. ~ **exchange standard** 金汇兑本位制. ~ **fever** 淘金热. ~ **field** 采金地. ~**-filled** *a.* 镀金的,包金的. ~ **finch**【鸟】金翅雀. ~**fish** 金鱼. ~ **foil** 金箔. ~ **guarantee clause** 黄金保值条款. ~ **lace** 金线带. ~ **leaf** 金叶. ~ **medal** 金牌,金质奖章. ~ **mine** 金矿,金山;宝库. ~ **parity** 黄金平价. ~ **point** 黄金点〔相当于金的熔点或 1064.43℃〕. ~ **plate** 金制餐具;镀金的材料. ~ **record**〔美〕金唱片〔赠给大获成功的歌星的纪念性镀金唱片〕. ~ **reserve** 黄金储备. ~ **rush** 抢购黄金;涌往新金矿,淘金热. ~ **size** (贴饰金叶的)胶粘剂. ~ **standard** 金本位. ~ **star** 金星〔美军官兵阵亡的标志〕. ~**stone**【地】沙金石. ~**thread**【植】黄连属 (coptis) 植物〔尤指格林兰黄连 (coptis groenlandica)〕.
gol·darn [ˈgɔlˈdɑːn] *vt., a., ad.*〔美俚〕= damn, damned.
gold·en [ˈgəuldən] *a.* ①金色的,金黄色的. ②金的,金制的. ③产金的. ④(机会)贵重的,宝贵的;绝好的;(时代等)隆盛的. ⑤第五十周年的. ~ **age** 黄金时代;退休职工〔多作定语用〕. ~ **ager**〔口,也作 G- A-〕老人家,老大爷,老公公〔尤指六十五岁以上老人或上了年纪退休的老人〕. ~ **apple** ①【希神】(导致众女神争夺的)金苹果. ②西红柿,番茄. ③(英王加冕时所用象征王权的)宝珠. ~ **aster**【植】金菊属 (Chrysopsis) 植物. ~ **balls** 当铺招牌;当铺. ~ **bantan corn** 金黄短穗玉米. ~ **boy** 有名声的男子,有成就的男子. ~ **calf** 金犊〔古代以色列人崇拜的偶象〕;金钱崇拜. ~ **chain** = laburnum. **G- Delicious** (美国产苹果)金冠,黄元帅. ~ **eagle** 鹫 (Aquila chrysaëtos). ~**-eye**【动】鹊鸭,白鹅鸭. **G- Fleece** ①【希神】金羊毛〔传说 Jason 乘 Argo 号船只远征 Colchis 时带回的宝物〕. ②金羊毛骑士章〔西班牙等国最高勋位〕. **G- Gate** 金门〔美国旧金山入口处海峡名〕. ~ **girl** 有名声的女子,有成就的女子. ~ **glow**【植】金光菊 (Rudbeckia laciniata). ~ **goose** 金鹅〔希腊寓言中每天能产一金蛋的神鹅,其主人妄想一次取得全部金蛋,将鹅杀掉,结果一无所得〕. ~ **handshake** 退休金,退伍奖金. **G- Horn** (土耳其的)伊斯坦布尔港. ~ **hours** 幸福日子. ~ **jubilee** 五十周年,金婚礼. ~ **key** 贿赂. ~ **knop**〔英〕瓢虫. ~**mean** ①中庸(之道). ②= ~ section. ~**-mouthed** *a.* 雄辩的. ~ **number**【天】黄金数. ~ **opinions** 盛赞,高度评价. ~ **opportunity** 绝好的机会,良机. ~ **pheasant** 锦鸡. ~ **remedy** 灵药. ~ **retriever** 黄毛猎犬〔指任何一种猎取禽兽的厚黄毛猎犬〕. ~**rod** *n.*【植】(北美产的多年生)菊科植物,黄花. ~ **rule** 金箴〔语出圣经《马太福音》,指所谓推己及人的箴言〕. ~ **saying** 金玉良言. ~**seal**【植】白毛茛 (Hydrastis canadensis)〔产于美洲,原大量用于医药〕. ~ **section**【美术】黄金分割〔即矩形短边与长边之比等于长边与长短二边和之比〕. **G- State** 金山州〔美国加利福尼亚州的别名〕. ~ **syrup** 黄色糖浆. ~ **warbler**【动】金莺. ~ **wedding** 金婚〔结婚 50 周年纪念〕.
Golden [ˈgəuldən] *n.* 戈尔登〔姓氏〕.
Gold·i·locks [ˈgəuldiˌlɔks] *n.* ①金发姑娘〔民间故事中到三个狗熊家作客的小姑娘〕. ②〔g-〕有黄头发的人. ③金发状毛茛.
Golding [ˈgəuldiŋ] *n.* 戈尔丁〔姓氏〕.
gold·smith [ˈgəuldsmiθ] *n.* 金饰工;金首饰商. ~ **beetle**【动】金工甲虫.
Gold·smith [ˈgəuldsmiθ] *n.* ①戈德史密斯〔姓氏〕. ② **Oliver** 奥列弗·戈德史密斯〔1730?—1774,生于爱尔兰的英国剧作家,小说家〕.
go·lem [ˈgəulem] *n.* ①(十六世纪希伯来传说中的)有生命的假人. ②机器人.
Golf [gɔlf] 通讯中用于代表字母 g 的词.
golf [gɔlf] *n.* 高尔夫球. — *vi.* 打高尔夫球. ~ **club** ①高尔夫球棍. ②高尔夫球俱乐部. ~ **course [links]** 高尔夫球场. ~ **widow** 因丈夫迷恋高尔夫球而常独居的妇女. **-er** *n.* 打高尔夫球的人.
Gol·gi [ˈgəuldʒi] *n.* ①高尔基〔姓氏〕. ②**Camillo** ~〔1844–1926,意大利解剖学家与病理学家〕. ~ **apparatus**【生】高尔基体 (= Golgi body).
gol·gio·some [ˈgɔldʒiəsəum] *n.*【生】高尔基体.
Gol·go·tha [ˈgɔlgəθə] *n.* ①【宗】各各他〔耶稣被钉死的地方〕. ②〔g-〕墓地,受难地,殉教处.
gol·iard [ˈgəuljəd] *n.* 学生流浪诗人〔指中世纪晚期写拉丁文讽刺诗的流浪学生,常身兼行吟诗人和小丑〕. **-iar·dic** [-ˈjɑːdik] *a.*
Go·li·ath [gəˈlaiəθ] *n.* ①【圣】(非利士勇士)歌利亚;〔喻〕巨人. ②〔g-〕移动式大型起重机(= ~ crane). ~ **beetle**【动】(非洲产的)花金龟科大甲虫. ~ **heron**【动】(非洲产的)巨苍鹭.
Go·light·ly [gəˈlaitli] *n.* 戈莱特利〔姓氏〕.
gol·li·wog(g) [ˈgɔliwɔg] *n.* ①奇形怪状的黑面木偶. ②奇形怪状的人.
gol·ly¹ [ˈgɔli] *int.*〔口〕天哪!〔惊讶、发誓声,又作 By [my] ~!〕
gol·ly² [ˈgɔli] *n.* = golliwog.
go·losh(e) [gəˈlɔʃ] *n.* = galosh.
go·lup·tious [gəˈlʌpʃəs], **go·lop·tious** [gəˈlɔpʃəs] *a.*〔谑〕可口的,好吃的,使人高兴的.
G.O.M. = Grand Old Man〔英〕英国首相格莱斯顿 (Gladstone) 的尊称.
gom·been [gɔmˈbiːn] *n.*〔Ir.〕高利贷. ~**-man** *n.* 放高利贷者.
gom·broon [gɔmˈbruːn] *n.* 龚布龙陶瓷〔波斯产的一种白色半透明陶瓷〕.
gom·er·al, gom·er·el [ˈgɔmərəl], **gom·er·il** [-ril] *n.*〔Scot.〕蠢汉.

Go·mor·rah, Go·mor·rha [gəˈmɔrə] *n.* ①【圣】(古代的)蛾摩拉城〔因其居民罪恶深重而与 Sodom 城同时被神毁灭〕. ②罪恶的城市.

gom·pho·sis [gɔmˈfəusis] *n.*【动】嵌合.

go·mu·ti [gəuˈmuːti] *n.*【植】①桄榔 *(Arenga pinnata)*〔产于马来亚〕; 桄榔纤维. ②西谷椰子 *(Metroxylon sagu)*〔产于马来亚〕.

-gon *comb. f.* 表示"…角形": hexa*gon*, poly*gon*.

go·nad [ˈgəunæd] *n.*【生化】性腺,生殖腺,卵巢,睾丸. **-al, -i·al, -ic** *a.*

gon·a·do·tro·phin, [ˌgɔnədəuˈtrəufin], **gon·a·do·tro·pin** [ˌgɔnədəuˈtrəupin] *n.*【生化】促性腺激素.

gon·a·do·tro·pic [ˌgɔnədəuˈtrɔpik] *a.*【生化】促性腺的. ~ *hormone* 促性腺激素.

Gond [gɔnd] *n.* 龚德人〔印度中部的德拉维地族的一部〕.

Gon·di [ˈgɔndi] *n.* ①龚德语〔印度中部的德拉维地的方言群〕. ②该方言群的主要方言.

gon·do·la [ˈgɔndələ] *n.* ①(意大利威尼斯的) 平底狭长小船. ②大型平底船; 游览船. ③敞篷车. ④(飞船等的)吊舱; 吊篮. ⑤(设在商店中央的)商品陈列台. ⑥(运输混凝土的)带斥兜的卡车.

gon·do·lier [ˌgɔndəˈliə] *n.* (意大利威尼斯的) 平底船船夫.

Gond·wa·na·land [gɔndˈwɑːnəlænd] *n.* 冈瓦纳大陆〔假定性的大陆名称, 包括现今印度、澳大利亚、非洲、南美洲和南极洲,约在古生代时分离开来〕.

gone [gɔn, gɔːn] go 的过去分词. — *a.* ①过去的,已往的; …前的,以前的; 刚过完…的. ②垂死的,死了的. ③无望的; 无可挽救的. ④遗失了的; 衰败的. ⑤虚弱无力的,发晕的. ⑥用光了的. ⑦〔口〕入迷的, 一往情深的 *(on; upon)*. ⑧〔美俚〕怀孕的; 喝醉的. ⑨〔美俚〕极好的,第一流的. *dead and* ~ 死了. *past and* ~ 过去的,一去不复返的. *these ten years* ~ 以往的十年. *on Monday* ~ *five weeks* 五个星期以前的星期一. *be eight years* ~ 刚过八周岁. *a* ~ *feeling [sensation]* 虚飘飘的感觉,发晕的感觉. *She's six months* ~. 她怀孕六个月了. ***be dead*** ~ ***in love*** 深陷情网中. ***be far*** ~ ①(病,债、夜、骄傲、爱情、疲倦等) 到了很深程度. ②深深卷入某事. ***Be*** ~**!** 〔口〕走开. ***be*** ~ ***of [with]*** 变成,结果是 (*What has* ~ *of him?* 他结果怎样? 他情况怎样?) ***be*** ~ ***on sb.*** 倾心爱某人,迷恋某人. ***G- with the wind.*** 随风而逝, 往事如过眼云烟. 〔美国小说《飘》的原文名〕. ~ **case** 无可挽救的事; 没有希望的人. ~ **goose [gosling]** 〔美口〕 毫无希望的事; 无可挽救的人. **-ness** [ˈgɔnnis] *n.*

gon·ef [ˈgɔnif] *n.* 〔俚〕 = ganef.

gon·er [ˈgɔnə] *n.* 〔口〕无可挽救的人[物],失败者,落魄者; 临死的人.

Gon·er·il [ˈgɔnəril] 贡纳梨〔莎士比亚的《李尔王》中李尔的长女名,被作为冷酷、不孝的典型〕.

gon·fa·lon [ˈgɔnfələn] *n.* (中世纪意大利各城邦用的)旌旗.

gon·fa·lon·ier [ˌgɔnfələˈniə] *n.* 旗手; (中世纪意大利各城邦的)长官.

gon·fa·non [ˈgɔnfənən] *n.* ① = gonfalon. ②(悬于船等横杆上的)旗.

gong [gɔŋ] *n.* ①锣. ②皿形钟、铃. ③〔俚〕奖章,勋章,纪念章. ④(钟等用以报时的) 鸣钟弹簧. — *vi.* ①打锣. ②(交通警)鸣锣阻止汽车前进. ~ **buoy** 锣标〔装有铜锣的浮标〕. **-like** *a.*

Gon·go·rism [ˈgɔŋgərizəm] *n.* (西班牙诗人) 龚果拉 (Gongora, 1561–1627) 的风格; 文字交错缠结而华美瑰丽的风格.

gong·ster [ˈgɔŋstə] *n.* 〔俚〕用锣声指挥交通的警察.

go·nid·i·um [gəuˈnidiəm] *n.* *(pl.* ***-nid·i·a*** [-ˈnidiə]*)*【生】①藻(细)胞. ②微生子. **-i·al** *a.*

go·ni·om·e·ter [ˌgəuniˈɔmitə] *n.* ①角度计,测角计; 测向计. ②【无】天线方向性调整器.

go·ni·o·met·ric(al) [ˌgəuniəˈmetrik(əl)] *a.* 测角的,测角计的. **-cal·ly** *ad.*

go·ni·om·e·try [ˌgəuniˈɔmitri] *n.* 角度测定,测角(术); 测向(术).

go·ni·on [ˈgəuniˌɔn] *n.* *(pl.* ***-ni·a*** [-niə]*)*【解】下颌角点.

gon·na [ˈgɔnə] 〔美俚〕 = going to.

gono- *comb. f.* 表示"性的","生殖的": *gono*phore.

go·no·cho·rism [ˌgɔnəuˈkəurizəm] *n.*【生】雌雄异体.

gon·o·coc·cus [ˌgɔnəuˈkɔkəs] *n.* *(pl.* ***-coc·ci*** [-ˈkɔksai]*)*【微】淋球菌.

gon·o·cyte [ˈgɔnəsait] *n.*【生】生殖母细胞.

gon·of, gon·oph [ˈgɔnəf] *n.* 〔俚〕 = ganef.

gon·o·phore [ˈgɔnəfɔː] *n.* ①雌雄蕊柄; 生殖体. ②(软水母群的)无性繁殖芽体. **-phor·ic** [-ˈfɔːrik], **go·noph·o·rous** [gəˈnɔfərəs] *a.*

gon·o·pore [ˈgɔnəpɔː] *n.*【生】生殖孔.

gon·or·rh(o)e·a [ˌgɔnəˈriːə] *n.* 淋病.

gon·or·rh(o)e·al [ˌgɔnəˈriːəl] *a.* 淋病的,淋毒性的.

-gony *comb. f.* 构成名词,表示"…发生"; "…起源": cosmo*gony*, theo*gony*.

goo [guː] *n.* 〔美俚〕①雾; 粘性物质; 甜腻的东西. ②伤感,令人厌恶的自作多情. ③甜言蜜语.

goo·ber [ˈgu(ː)bə] *n.* (美国中部及南部)落花生〔又叫 ~ pea〕.

good [gud] *a.* *(**bet·ter*** [ˈbetə]; ***best*** [best]*)* *(opp.* bad*)* ①好的,良好的; 漂亮的,优美的. ②愉快的,幸福的. ③善良的,有品德的; 仁慈的,宽大的. ④技能好的,有本事的; 老练的; 有资格的 *(at)*. ⑤真正的; 健全的,无损伤的,完美的; 新鲜的. ⑥强壮的,结实的,坚牢的. ⑦有效的; 适当的,合适的; 正当的,有利的,有益的 *(for)*. ⑧有信用的,可靠的; 有根据的,真实的. ⑨可敬的; 〔反〕好(一个). ⑩充足的,十足的; 丰裕的; 肥沃的; 相当的. ⑪有趣的. ⑫亲密的. ⑬上流社会的; 有教养的. ⑭忠实的; 虔诚的. *a* ~ *few* 〔口〕相当多. *a* ~ *joke* 逗人乐的笑话. *a* ~ *match* 劲敌; 佳偶. *a* ~ *200 pounds* 足足二百磅. *a* ~ *year* 丰年. ~ *debts* 能收回的贷款. ~ *faith* 正直,诚实. ~ *form* 〔英〕正规礼节. ~ *land* 肥沃的土地. ~ *life* 道德的生活; 幸福的生活. ~ *looks* 美貌. ~ *luck* 幸运. ~ *money* 优良货币. ~ *nature* 好性格,温厚. *a* ~ *reason* 正当的理由. *a* ~ *saying* 名言. ~ *thing* 有利的交易,投机; 名言; 〔*pl.*〕好吃的东西. *my* ~ *sir [lady]* 〔讽〕我的老爷[太太]. *your* ~ *selves* 贵店,贵社. *I'll be* ~! 我以后不淘气了〔孩子对父母、老师悔过语〕. ***as*** ~ ***as*** ... 和…一样,事实上等于 (*He is as* ~ *as dead.* 他和死了一样). ***as*** ~ ***as a play*** 非常有趣. ***as*** ~ ***as gold*** ①(孩子)很乖的,规规矩矩的. ②极贵重的. ③十分可靠的 (*His promise is as* ~ *as gold.* 他的保证非常可靠). ***as*** ~ ***as one's word*** 守约, 践约. ***Be*** ~**!** 〔口〕 放乖些! ***be*** ~ ***at*** 善于… (*He is* ~ *at figures [painting, describing, etc.]*. 他善于计算[绘画,描写等]). ***be*** ~ ***enough to*** = ***be so*** ~ ***as to*** 请… (*Be* ~ *enough to shut the door.* 请把门关上). ***be*** ~ ***for*** ①值…,有支付…能力的. ②有效的,对…有用的 (*be* ~ *for a 100 dollars* 有支付一百元的能力). ***be*** ~ ***to*** ①适于 (*This water is* ~ *to drink.* 这水可喝). ②对…厚道 (*He has always been* ~ *to me.* 他对我总是很好). ***G- afternoon!*** [gudˌɑːftəˈnuːn] 您好吧! [ˈgudˌɑːftəˈnuːn] 再会〔午后用〕. ~ ***and*** 〔美〕非常,全然; 充分 (*He was* ~ *and mad.* 他完全疯了. *I'm* ~ *and ready.* 我充分准备好了). ~ ***and hard*** 〔美〕彻底. ***G- day!*** [gudˈdei] 您好! [ˈgudˈdei] 再见! ***G- evening!*** [gudˈiːvniŋ] 您好! [ˈgudˈiːvniŋ] 再会! ***G- for you [him].*** 〔美口〕干得好! 真运气! ***G- morning!*** [gudˈmɔːniŋ] 您好! 早安! [ˈgudˈmɔːniŋ] 再见! 〔午前用〕. ***G- morrow!*** 〔古〕 = Good morning. ***G- night!*** [gudˈnait] 晚安! 明天见! 再会! 〔夜晚用〕. ~ ***offices***

调停,调停人的作用;(有势力者的)影响. ~ ***Samaritan*** 厚道的外人. ~ ***turn*** 好意 (*One ~ turn deserves another.* 有好心应当有好报). ~ ***word*** 好话,推荐的话 (*say a ~ word for sb.* 替某人说好话). ***have a ~ mind to*** 相当想. ***have a ~ night*** 睡得好. ***have a ~ time (of it)*** 过得愉快,玩得高兴. ***hold ~ (for)*** 对…有效,对…适用. ***in ~ time*** 刚好,及时地;迅速地. ***make ~*** ①履行;证明. ②补偿,弥补;支付. ③维持,保持(地位等). ④〔美〕成功. ***do you~!*** 〔反〕这对你好处多着呢! ***not ~ enough to (do)*** 〔口〕没有…的价值;不值得做. ***Not so ~!*** 〔口〕糟透了! ***on ~ terms*** 相处得好,和睦. ***see ~ to do*** 认为做某事适当. ***too ~ to be true*** 哪有这么好的事. —*n.* ①善,善良,美德 (*opp.* evil, harm). ②利益,好处,幸福. ③〔the ~〕好人 (*opp.* the bad, the wicked). ④好事,好结果. *for our ~* 为我们好. *~ and evil* 善与恶. *What ~ is it? = What is the ~ of it?* 那有什么好处? *What is the ~ of the haste?* 急有什么用? ***after no ~*** 不怀好意,想干坏事. ***be some [much] ~*** 有点[极有]好处. ***come to ~*** 得好结果. ***come to no ~*** 结果不好. ***do ~ to*** 对…做好事;对…有益[有效]. ***do sb. ~*** 对某人有益. ***for ~ (and all)*** 永久地,一劳永逸地 (*I am going for ~ and all.* 我一去就不回了). ***for ~ or for evil*** 不论好坏. ***Much ~ may it do you!*** 〔反〕这对你好处多着呢! ***no ~*** 没用;〔美口〕不好,不行. ***to the ~*** ①有好处. ②【商】在贷方,纯益;净赚,多出来 (*We were 100 dollars to the ~.* 我们赚了100美元). ***up to no ~ = after no ~.*** —*ad.* = well. **G- Book**【宗】《圣经》. ~ **cheer** ①作乐,闹饮. ②美酒佳肴;大吃大喝. ③神采奕奕,意气风发,兴致勃勃. **G- Conduct Medal**【美军】品德优良奖章. ~ **fellow** 热诚而令人感到亲切的人. ~**-fellowship** *n.* 亲密,融洽;善于应酬. ~**-for-nothing, ~-for-nought** ① *a.* 无益的,无用的. ② *n.* 无用的人,饭桶. ~**-hearted** *a.* 好心肠的,仁慈的. ~**-humo(u)red** *a.* 心情好的,愉快的;脾气好的. ~ **Joe** 好好先生. ~**-looker** 〔俚〕美人. ~**-looking** *a.* 标致的,美貌的. ~**man** ①〔古〕家长,户主;丈夫,良人. ②先生〔次于 gentleman 的敬称, = mister, 用于人名前〕. ~**-natured** 性格好的,温厚的. ~**-neighbo(u)r** *a.* 睦邻的. ~**-neighbo(u)rhood, ~-neighbo(u)rliness, ~-neighbo(u)rship** 睦邻关系. ~ **neighbo(u)r policy** 睦邻政策. ~ **people** 仙女们. ~ **sense** 判断力强,机智. ~**-sized** *a.* 宽阔的;大的;相当大的;大号的. ~**-tempered** *a.* 性格好的,和蔼的. ~**time Charlie** 〔口〕逍遥派,无忧无虑、寻欢作乐的人. ~ **use** (语文的)标准用法. ~**wife** 〔Scot.〕夫人,主妇,太太〔次于 lady 的敬称, = mistress, 用于人名前〕. ~**-will** ①好意,友好,亲善 (*to*); 诚意,热心 (*an ambassador of ~ will* 亲善使节). ②【商】信誉,招牌.

good-by(e) [ˈgudˈbai] *int.* 再见! —[gudˈbai] *n.* 告别;告别辞. *have several ~s to say* 要到好几处告别. *kiss sb. ~* 吻别某人. *kiss sth. ~* 无可奈何地失去某物. *say ~ to sb.* 向某人告别. *wave ~* 挥手告别.

good·ish [ˈgudiʃ] *a.* 还好的.

good·ly [ˈgudli] *a.* ***(-li·er; -li·est)*** ①美丽的,优美的. ②好的,不错的. ③颇大的,颇多的. **-li·ness** *n.*

good·ness [ˈgudnis] *n.* ①善良;仁慈;善行,美德;优点. ②真髓;(食品的)养分;精华. ③〔作感叹词〕= God. *boil all the ~ out of coffee* 把咖啡的香味都煮跑了. ***for ~' sake*** 看在老天爷面上. ***G- knows!*** 天晓得!实实在在说. ***G- me!*** 天哪!啊呀!〔表示惊讶〕. ***have the ~ to (do)*** 有…的好意. ***in the name of ~*** 实实在在. ***Thank ~!*** 谢天谢地! ***wish to ~*** 希望,但愿 (*I wish to ~ that ...* 我非常想…).

goods [gudz] *n.* 〔*pl.*〕①商品,货物〔美国说 freight〕. ★不与数目字连用. ②动产. ③〔the ~〕〔美口〕本领;不负所望的人[物]. *capital ~* 生产资料. *consumer ~* 消费品. *damaged ~* 残损货品. *fancy ~* 化妆品,装饰品,时髦商品. *~ agent* 运输行. *~ in stock* 存货. *~ of first [second] order* 直接[间接]必需品. *green ~* 新鲜蔬菜;〔美俚〕伪造钞票. *printed ~* 印花布. *semi-finished ~* 半成品. *shaped ~* 定型制品. ***a piece of ~*** 〔贬〕人〔特指少女〕. ***by ~*** 用货车装运. ***catch sb. with the ~*** 人赃俱获. ***deliver the ~*** 交货;〔喻〕履行诺言,不负所望. ***get the ~ on sb.*** 〔美俚〕在某人身上发现罪证. ***~ and chattels***【法】私人财物,全部动产. ***have all one's ~ in the window*** 肤浅,华而不实,虚有其表. ***have the ~*** 有才干,有充分资格. ***He is the ~.*** 他就是合适的人. ***know one's ~*** 〔俚〕精通本行业务. ~**agent** 运货代理人. ~ **train** 货物列车〔美国说 freight train〕.

good·y[1] [ˈgudi] *n.* ①〔古〕〔常加在姓氏前〕(下层社会的)妇女,老妇人. ②〔美〕(哈佛大学)打扫宿舍的女人.

good·y[2] [ˈgudi] *n.* 〔主 *pl.*〕〔口〕①好吃的东西,糖果,甜食. ②特别吸引人的东西. ③英雄,好汉 (*opp.* baddy).

good·y[3] [ˈgudi] *a.* 〔口〕伪善的,假道学的. —*ad.* 伪善地,假道学地. —*n.* 伪善者,假道学. ~-~ ①*a.* 伪善的,假正经的. ② *n.* 伪善者,假君子.

good·y[4] [ˈgudi] *int.* 好啊〔孩子气地表示高兴〕!

Good·year [ˈgudjə(ː)] *n.* ①古德伊尔〔姓氏〕. ②**Charles ~** 查理·古德伊尔〔1800—1860, 发明硬橡皮的美国人〕.

goo·ey [ˈguːi] *a.* 〔美俚〕①黏的,甜腻的. ②过分伤感的.

goof [guːf] *n.* 〔美俚〕①傻瓜,糊涂虫. ②大错,疏忽. —*vi.* ①出大错. ②闲荡,混日子 (*off*). —*vt.* 弄糟;搞坏(事). ~ ***off*** 浪费时间,工作吊儿郎当. ~ ***up*** 把事情弄糟,出大错. ~**ball** 〔俚〕①兴奋剂;催眠药片;镇静剂. ②饭桶,神经失常的人〔也作 ~ **ball**〕. ~**-off** ①工作不负责任的人,吊儿郎当的人. ②休息时间.

goof·er [ˈguːfə] *n.* 〔美俚〕容易受骗的人,傻瓜.

go-off [gəuˈɔ(ː)f] *n.* 〔口〕出发;着手,开始. ***at one ~*** 一次,一举,一气. ***succeed (at) the first ~*** 一举成功.

goof·y [ˈguːfi] *a.* 〔美俚〕愚蠢的. **-i·ly** *ad.* **-i·ness** *n.*

goo·gly [ˈguːgli] *n.*【曲棍球,板球】曲球〔先转向一方,继而飞向另一方的球〕.

goo·gol [ˈguːgɔl] *n.* ①后面带有 100 个零的数〔常作 $10^{10^{10}}$〕; 10 的一百次方. ②巨大数目.

goo·gol·plex [ˈguːgɔlpleks] *n.*【数】$10^{10^{100}}$.

goo-goo[1] [ˈguːguː] *a.* 爱慕的,色情的. ~ **eyes** 媚眼.

goo-goo[2] [ˈguːguː] *n.* 〔美〕主张〔进行〕政治改良的人.

gook[1] [gu(ː)k] *n.* 〔美俚,蔑〕外国人〔尤指菲律宾人,太平洋群岛人,日本人等黄种人或棕种人〕.

gook[2] [gu(ː)k] *n.* 甜腻的东西 = goo. **-y** *a.*

goon [guːn] *n.* ①〔美俚〕蠢汉;古怪的人. ②(受雇恐吓工人的)打手,暴徒. ③粗鲁的人,无赖. ~ ***squad*** (破坏罢工的)打手队.

goo·ney [ˈguːni] **bird**【动】黝鹱 (Diomedea nigripes, goony bird).

goop[1] [guːp] *n.* ①举止粗鲁的孩子. ②〔俚〕笨蛋. ③平淡无趣的人.

goop[2] [guːp] *n.* 〔美俚〕胶状半流体. **-y** *a.*

goo·san·der [guːˈsændə] *n.*【动】秋沙鸭.

goose [guːs] *n.* ***(pl. geese*** [giːs]***)*** ①鹅;雌鹅 (*opp.* gander);鹅肉. ②*(pl. ~s)* (成衣铺的)弯把熨斗. ③呆头鹅,傻瓜. ④〔俚〕(鹅叫一样的)奚落声,倒彩. *The older the ~ the harder to pluck.* 〔谚〕年纪越大,越是一毛不拔. *The old woman is picking her geese.* 下雪了〔儿语〕. ***a wild ~ chase*** 徒劳的追求,无益的举动. *All his geese are swans.* ①夸大自己的长处. ②敝帚自珍. ***all right on the ~ = be sound on the ~.*** 〔美〕稳健,持正统观念. ***as silly [stupid] as a ~*** 蠢极了. ***cannot say bo [boh, boo] to a ~*** 〔口〕胆小怕事. ***chase the wild ~*** 徒劳的追求,无益的举动. ***cooked [gone] ~*** 无可救药

的人,没有希望的事. ***cook one's (own)*** ~ 自己害自己;毁掉自己的希望[机会,计划]. ***cook sb.'s*** ~ 〔俚〕干掉[杀死]某人;挫败某人的计划[希望]. ***get the*** ~ 〔俚〕被听众[观众]喝倒彩. ***give ... the*** ~ 〔美俚〕加快速度. ***the*** ~ ***that lays the golden eggs*** 摇钱树,财源. ***kill the*** ~ ***that lays the golden eggs.*** 杀鸡取卵;只顾眼前利益,不顾长远利益. ***like geese on a common*** 自由自在地闲逛. ***make a*** ~ ***of sb.*** 瞒骗某人,愚弄某人. ***shoe the*** ~ 徒劳无益,白费气力. ***swim like a tailor's*** ~ 〔谑〕沉下去. ***The*** ~ ***hangs [honks] high.*** 〔美俚〕前途有望,形势大好. ***turn geese into swans*** 把蠢鹅说成天鹅,言过其实. — *vt.* ①突然开大(汽车等的)油门;推动,促进. ②〔俚〕对(某人)发嘘嘘声〔表示反对〕. ~ **barnacle** 【动】茗荷儿(gooseneck barnacle). ~ **egg** 鹅蛋;〔美俚〕零分;〔美俚〕青肿块. ~ **flesh** 鸡皮疙瘩 (*I am* ~ *flesh all over.* 我浑身起鸡皮疙瘩). ~**foot** *n. (pl.* ~***foots)*** 【植】藜. ~**gog** *n.* 〔英口〕= gooseberry. ~ **grass** 【植】蟋蟀草,牛筋草. ~**herd** 牧鹅人. ~**neck** 鹅头颈;【机】鹅颈管[钩],S形弯曲管;台灯的活动灯架 (~*neck lamp* 有活动灯架的台灯). ~ **pimples** = ~ flesh. ~ **quill** 鹅毛管;鹅毛笔. ~ **skin** = ~ flesh. ~ **step** 正步,步法教练. ~**-step** *vi.* ①正步;进行步法教练. ②按上级命令行动.

goose·ber·ry [ˈguzbəri] *n.* 【植】①醋栗,鹅莓;茶藨子. ②醋栗果实;醋栗酒. ③(陪伴年轻女人到交际场所的)女伴. ***play*** ~ 社交场合少女的监护人;插在两个想单独在一起的人(如情侣)之间. ***play (up) old*** ~ ***with*** 击败;制止. ~ **fool** 醋栗果酱 (= jam).

goos·er·y [ˈguːsəri] *n.* ①养鹅场. ②〔集合词〕鹅群.

goos·ey[1], **goos·ie** [ˈguːsi] *n.* ①〔儿〕鹅. ②傻瓜.

goos·ey[2], **goos·y** [ˈguːsi] *a.* ①象鹅一样的,傻头傻脑的. ②神经质的.

GOP = Grand Old Party 美国共和党的别称.

go·pher[1] [ˈgəufə] *n.* ①(北美产的)地鼠,金花鼠;(美国南部)可以食用的龟;(无毒)穴居大土蛇 (= ~ snake). ②〔G-〕〔美俚〕明尼苏达州人. — *vi.* 〔美〕挖洞;拼命采掘.

go·pher[2] [ˈgəufə] *n.* ①【圣】制造诺亚方舟用的树木. ②【植】美洲香槐.

go·pher[3] [ˈgəufə] *n., vt.* = gof(f)er.

go·ral [ˈgɔːrəl] *n.* 【动】羚羊.

gor·bli·my, gor·bli·mey [gɔːˈblaimi] *int.* 〔英口〕哎呀! 糟了.

gor·cock [ˈgɔːkɔk] *n.* 红色雄松鸡.

Gor·di·an [ˈgɔːdiən] *a.* 古代弗吕加国王戈尔地雅斯(Gordius)的. ~ ***knot*** ①【希神】戈尔地雅斯难结〔按神谕,能解开此结者即可为亚细亚国王,后此结被亚历山大大帝解开〕;〔喻〕难解的结,难办的事,棘手问题. ②(问题或故事情节的)关键,焦点. ***cut the*** ~ ***knot*** 用大刀阔斧的方法解决困难问题,快刀斩乱麻. **g-worm** 【动】金线虫〔一种昆虫寄生虫〕.

Gor·don [ˈgɔːdn] *n.* ①戈登〔姓氏,男子名〕. ②**Charles George** 查理·乔治·戈登〔1833—1885,英国军人,曾协助满清政府镇压太平天国起义,后在远征 Sudan 中战死〕.

gore[1] [gɔː] *n.* 流出的血,血块.

gore[2] [gɔː] *n.* (衣服或帆上加缝的)三角形布条;衽,裆;三角形地带. — *vt.* 用三角形布条缝上;把…裁成三角形.

gore[3] [gɔː] *vt.* (用枪)刺破;(用角)牴伤;(礁石)撞通(船身).

gorge [gɔːdʒ] *vi.* 狼吞虎咽,拼命吃. — *vt.* 使吃饱;使塞足,使注满. ***be*** ~***d with*** = ~ ***oneself with*** 吃饱. — *n.* ①咽喉;胃;咽下物. ②峡,峡谷;【筑城】背面出入口;(代替钓钩的)吞饵. ③贪吃;饱吃. ④障碍物. *a full* ~ 一肚皮,满腹. ***cast [heave] the*** ~ ***at*** = ***cast up the*** ~ ***at.*** 见到…就吐;唾弃. ***one's*** ~ ***rises at ...*** 见了发呕,极端厌恶. ***raise [rouse, stir] the*** ~ 激怒.

gor·geous [ˈgɔːdʒəs] *a.* ①华丽的,豪华的. ②〔英口〕极好的,漂亮的. *He is perfectly* ~ *as Romeo.* 他演罗密欧演得真好. **-ly** *ad.* **-ness** *n.*

gor·ger·in [ˈgɔːdʒərin] *n.* 【建】柱颈.

gor·get [ˈgɔːdʒit] *n.* ①护喉甲胄. ②领子. ③(女子穿戴的)护颈胸布. ④(鸟、兽的)颈部杂色. ⑤【医】有槽导子. ~ **patch** 【军】领章.

Gor·gi·o [ˈgɔːdʒiəu] *n. (pl.* ~***s)*** 非吉普赛人〔吉普赛人用语〕.

Gor·gon [ˈgɔːgən] *n.* ①【希神】三个蛇发女怪之一〔人一见她即化为石〕. ②〔g-〕令人作呕的人[景象],丑妇. **-i·an** *a.*

gor·go·nia [gɔːˈgəuniə] *n.* 【动】柳珊瑚属.

gor·gon·ize [ˈgɔːgənaiz] *vt.* 使吓呆;睨视使化为石.

Gor·gon·zo·la [gɔːgənˈzəulə] *n.* (意大利米兰)葛更佐拉(村)白干酪,羊乳制的上等干酪.

gor·hen [ˈgɔːˌhen] *n.* 【动】牝山鸡,牝红松鸡;母松鸡.

Gori [ˈgɔːri] *n.* 哥里〔苏联城市〕.

go·ril·la [gəˈrilə] *n.* ①【动】大猩猩. ②〔美俚〕貌似大猩猩的人;丑恶的人. ③〔美俚〕凶手,打手.

gor·i·ly [ˈgɔːrili] *ad.* 血淋淋地,残忍地,骇人听闻地.

Gor·ki [ˈgɔːki], **Maxim** 马克西姆·高尔基〔1868—1936,苏联文学家〕.

gor·mand [ˈgɔːmənd] *n.* = gourmand.

gor·mand·ize, gor·mand·ise [ˈgɔːməndaiz] *vi.* 狼吞虎咽. — *vt.* 拼命吃,吞食. — *n.* 〔罕〕讲究饮食,大吃大喝.

gor·mand·iz·er, gor·mand·is·er [ˈgɔːməndaizə] *n.* 贪吃的人,讲究饮食的人.

gorm·less [ˈgɔːmlis] *a.* 〔英方〕智力迟钝的;愚蠢的.

gorse [gɔːs] *n.* 【植】荆豆.

gors·y [ˈgɔːsi] *a.* 荆豆(多)的.

Gor·ton [ˈgɔːtn] *n.* 戈顿〔姓氏〕.

go-round [ˈgəuraund] *n.* 〔美俚〕①争论激烈的会议. ②表演;轮班. ③周游一圈.

gor·y [ˈgɔːri] *a.* ①血淋淋的,沾满鲜血的. ②残酷的,流血的. ③骇人听闻的.

gosh [gɔʃ] *int.* 〔表示惊讶发誓,为 God 的变体〕. ***(by)*** ~ 天哪,啊呀!

gos·hawk [ˈgɔsˌhɔːk] *n.* 【动】苍鹰.

Go·shen [ˈgəuʃən] *n.* 【圣】歌珊地〔出埃及前以色列人所居住的埃及北部的肥沃牧羊地〕;〔喻〕丰饶之地,乐土.

gos·ling [ˈgɔzliŋ] *n.* ①小鹅. ②笨人,傻瓜;毛娃娃. ***shoe the*** ~ = shoe the goose. ~**-grass** = goose-grass.

go-slow [ˈgəuˈsləu] *a.* 故意拖延的. *a* ~ *strike* 怠工. — *n.* 怠工.

gos·pel [ˈgɔspəl] *n.* ①福音;【基督】〔G-〕新约圣经四《福音书》之一. ②真理,真实. ③主义,教理,信条. ④〔美〕黑人福音音乐〔一种黑人宗教音乐〕. *the G- according to St. John* 【圣】《约翰福音》. *go forth and preach G-* 宣传福音. *the* ~ *of efficiency* 效率主义. *the* ~ *of laissez faire* 放任主义. *the* ~ *of simple life* 简朴生活之道. *the* ~ *of soap and water* 清洁主义. *the* ~ *for the day* 圣餐式中所读的福音书章节. ***take sth. as [for]*** ~ 把…认为真理. ~ **oath** 手按《福音书》宣誓. ~ **pusher** ~ **shark** 〔美俚〕牧师. ~ **shop** 〔英蔑〕美以美派教堂. ~ **side** 教堂祭坛北侧. ~ **truth** 福音书中的真理,象福音一样真实的东西. — *a.* 福音的,传播福音的.

gos·pel·(l)er [ˈgɔspələ] *n.* 圣餐式中读《福音书》的人;福音宣传者,传道师. *a hot* ~ 热心的信徒,狂热的宣传者.

gos·po·din [gɔspɑˈdʒin] *n. (pl.* ***-da*** [-dɑː]) 〔Russ.〕…先生〔俄语尊称词〕.

gos·port [ˈgɔspɔːt] *n.* (飞机座舱间的)通话软管.

Goss(e) [gɔs] *n.* 戈斯〔姓氏〕.

gos·sa·mer [ˈgɔsəmə] *n.* ①游丝. ②薄纱,新娘面纱.

③纤细的东西；空幻的东西．④薄雨衣．— *a.* 轻而薄的，薄弱的；幻影似的．*a* ～ *justification* 站不住脚的辩解．**-ed, -y** *a.*

gos·san [ˈgɔsn] *n.*【矿】铁帽．

gos·sip [ˈgɔsip] *n.* ①街谈巷议，闲谈；闲话，流言蜚语．②碎嘴子，饶舌者．③漫笔，随笔．④〔古，英方〕密友．— *vi.* 聊天；说（别人的）闲话．*Going and lying go hand in hand.*〔谚〕说短道长，必然撒谎．～ **column**（报纸上的）闲话栏．**-er** = ～ **monger** *n.* 爱闲聊的人，搬弄是非者．**-ist** 闲话栏作家．**-y** *a.* 爱闲谈的；爱说闲话的；漫谈式的．

gos·soon [gɔˈsuːn] *n.*〔Ir.〕小伙子；服务员．

got [gɔt] get 的过去式及过去分词．

Gö·te·borg [ˈjeitəbɔːg] *n.* 哥德堡〔瑞典港市〕．

Goth [gɔθ] *n.* ①哥特人；哥特族〔古代日尔曼族的一支〕．②野蛮人；粗野的人．

Goth., goth. = Gothic.

Goth·am [ˈgəutəm] *n.* ①（英国传说中的）愚人村．②英国 Newcastle 市的别名．③[ˈgəuθəm]〔美〕纽约市的别名．***the wise men of*** ～ 愚人．

Goth·am·ite [ˈgəutəmait] *n.* ①愚人村的村民；愚人．②[ˈgəuθəmait]〔谑〕纽约人．

Goth·ic [ˈgɔθik] *a.* ①哥特人的，哥特族的；哥特语的．②〔有时作 g-〕中世纪的，野蛮的，粗鄙的．③【建】哥特式的．④【印】哥特体的，〔英〕黑体的．⑤〔有时作 g-〕哥特式小说体的．— *n.* ①哥特语．②【建】哥特式，尖拱式建筑．③【印】哥特体字，黑体字〔英国叫 black letter〕．～ **arch** 尖端拱门．～ **architecture** 哥特式建筑．～ **type** 黑体．**-al·ly** *ad.*

Goth·i·cism [ˈgɔθisizəm] *n.* ①哥特词语；哥特式倾向．②【建】哥特式建筑．③〔常作 g-〕野蛮，粗野．④【印】哥特体，黑字体．

Goth·i·cize [ˈgɔθisaiz] *vt.*〔常作 g-〕使具有哥特风，使哥特化．

Goth·ick [ˈgɔθik] *a.* 描写恐怖和凄凉体裁的；有可怖的中世纪气氛的．

Goth·ish [ˈgɔθiʃ] *a.* 野蛮的，粗野的．

go-to-meet·ing [ˈgəutəˈmiːtiŋ] *a.* ①常到教堂去的，虔诚的．②（衣服）节日穿的．③（举止等）极恰当的．

got·ta [ˈgɔtə]〔俚〕= (have) got to, (have) got a.

got·ten [ˈgɔtn] get 的过去分词．★ 英国除作 ill-gotten 应用外是古语，美国现在仍通用．*It has* ～ *to be quite late.* 太晚了．

got·up [ˈgɔtˈʌp] *a.* 做成的，人工的；假的．*a* ～ *affair* 故意造成的事件，圈套，鬼把戏．*a* ～ *match* 讲好了输赢的比赛．*hastily* ～匆忙做成的．— *n.*〔口〕一步登天的人，暴发户．

gouache [guˈɑːʃ] *n.*〔F.〕树胶水彩画法；树胶水彩画；树胶水彩画颜料．

Gou·da [ˈgaudə] *n.* 荷兰扁圆形干酪．

gouge [gaudʒ] *n.* ①凿，圆凿．②〔美口〕圆凿工艺；圆槽，凿孔；【地】断层泥．③〔美口〕欺诈；骗子．— *vt.* ①用圆凿打（眼）．②用大拇指抠出（眼珠子）．③〔美口〕欺诈．～ ***out*** 凿制（软木塞子等）；（用大拇指）抠出（眼珠）；挖开．

Gough [gɔf] *n.* 高夫〔姓氏〕．

gou·lash [ˈguːlæʃ] *n.* ①浓味蔬菜燉肉（又称 Hungarian goulash）．②【牌】重新分牌．

Gould(e) [guːld] *n.* 古尔德〔姓氏〕．

goup [guːp] *n.*〔美俚〕（巧克力糖浆之类的）粘液．

gou·ra·mi [ˈgurəmi, guˈrɑːmi] *n.* *(pl.* ～*(s))*【动】①丝足鱼，吻口鱼 *(Osphronemus goramy)*〔产于东南亚〕．②丝足鱼属的鱼．

gourd [guəd] *n.* ①【植】葫芦属植物，葫芦．②葫芦制成的容器．③葫芦形的细颈瓶．*the bottle [white-flowered]* ～ 葫芦．*the snake* ～ 蛇瓜．*the Spanish* ～ 南瓜．*the sponge [towel]* ～ 丝瓜．*the white* ～ 冬瓜．**-ful** *n.* 一葫芦的量．

gourde [guəd] *n.* 古德〔海地货币和硬币名〕．

gour·mand [ˈguəmənd] *n.* ①贪吃的人．②美食家，讲究饮食的人．**-ism** *n.* 美食主义．

gour·mand·ise [guəməːnˈdiːz] *n.*〔F.〕= gormandise.

gour·met [ˈguəmei] *n.* 讲究吃的人，食物品尝家．～ **powder** 味精．

goût [guː] *n.*〔F.〕①味道．②趣味，嗜好．③鉴赏力．

gout [gaut] *n.* ①【医】痛风．②〔古、诗〕（血的）滴，块．*rich [poor] man's* ～ 因营养过多[不足]而得的痛风．～ **fly**【动】麦秆蝇．

gout·y [ˈgauti] *a.* 象痛风病的；患痛风病的，因痛风而肿胀的．**-i·ly** *ad.* **-i·ness** *n.*

Gov., gov. = government; governor.

gov·ern [ˈgʌvən] *vt.* ①统治；统辖；执掌（政务等）．②支配，管理；左右，指挥，指导．③抑制，遏制，压制（感情等）．④运转（机械、船）；调节，控制．⑤【语法】（尤指动词或介词）支配（宾语）．*the* ～*ing class* 统治阶级．*a* ～*-ing body* 管理机构，（会议的）执行机构．*a* ～*ing principle* 指导原则[精神]．～ ***oneself*** 克制．— *vi.* 统治；控制，调节．

gov·ern·a·bil·i·ty [ˌgʌvənəˈbiliti] *n.* 统治的可能性．

gov·ern·a·ble [ˈgʌvənəbl] *a.* 可统治的，可支配的．

gov·ern·ance [ˈgʌvənəns] *n.* ①统治，管理，支配．②统治方式，管理方法．

gov·ern·ess [ˈgʌvənis] *n.* ①家庭女教师．②女统治者；女管理者；总督[州长]夫人．*a daily* ～ 每日来的家庭女教师．*a resident* ～ 在学生家中住宿的家庭女教师．*a nursery* ～ 保姆．— *vi.* 做家庭女教师；做保姆．～ **car [cart]**〔英〕面对面坐的轻便二轮马车．

gov·ern·ment [ˈgʌvənmənt] *n.* ①政治；政体；政权；管理，支配．②政厅；〔G-〕政府，〔英〕内阁．③行政管理区域．④【语法】支配．⑤政治学．⑥〔美〕〔*pl.*〕政府证券．*constitutional* ～ 立宪政治．*democratic* ～ 民主政治．*the local* ～ 地方政府．*form a G-*〔英〕组阁．～ **board**（交易所的）公债部．～ **bond** 公债．**G- House**（旧时英国殖民地等的）政府大厦，总督官邸．～**-in-exile** *n.* 流亡政府．～ **issue**〔美〕政府发给军人的供给品（如被服、装备等）〔略作 G. I.〕；（成批制成的）现成物品．～ **man** 官吏；支持政府者．～ **offices** 官厅，机关．～ **officials** 官吏，官员．～ **school** 公立学校．～ **securities [papers]**【商】政府证券[公债]．

gov·ern·men·tal [ˌgʌvənˈmentl] *a.* 统治的；政治上的；政府的，官设的．**-ism** *n.* 政府至上主义．**-ly** *ad.*

gov·ern·men·tese [ˌgʌvənmenˈtiːz] *n.* 官话，官腔．

gov·er·nor [ˈgʌvənə] *n.* ①统治者，管辖者．②地方长官，总督，县长，市长（等）；〔美〕州长；（要塞等的）司令官；〔英〕狱长．③〔英〕（组织、机构等的）主管人员（如银行总裁、学校董事等）．④〔英口〕父亲；头领；老板，〔称呼〕先生．⑤【机】节速器，调节器；【电】调节用变阻器，控制器．⑥（钓鱼的）假蚊钩．*the board of* ～*s* 理事会．*Look here, G-!* 喂，老板！*an electric* ～ 电气节速器．*a pendulum* ～【机】摆调节器．*a throttling* ～【电】节流调速器．～**-gen·er·al** *(pl.* ～*s-general)*〔英〕总督．～**-general-ship** 总督的职位[任期]．～**ship** 统治者的职位[任期]．

Govt., govt. = government.

gow [gau] *n.*〔美俚〕麻醉品（如鸦片等）．

gow·an [ˈgauən] *n.*〔Scot.〕【植】春白菊，英国普通雏菊．

Gow·er(s) [gɔə(z)] *n.* 高尔（斯）〔姓氏〕．

gowk [gauk] *n.*〔方〕①杜鹃，布谷鸟．②傻子．***give sb. the*** ～ 愚弄某人．

gown [gaun] *n.* ①长外衣，长袍；睡衣．②（教授、毕业生等穿的）大学礼服；教士服；法官服；文官服〔对军服而言〕．③〔the ～〕（穿着职业服装的）教士，法官（等）．④〔集合词〕大学的学生和教师．⑤（古代罗马市民的）外衣，罩袍；〔诗〕和平之衣．*an academic* ～ 大学礼服．*an evening* ～（女人）晚礼服．***arms and*** ～ 战争与和平．***in wig***

and ~ 穿着法官服. ***take [wear] the*** ~ 做教士,当律师. ***town and*** ~ (英国牛津和剑桥的)城镇居民和大学中的人. — *vt.* 〔主用 *p.p.*〕 穿长外衣,穿法衣,着大学礼服. *a* ~*ed war* 法庭上的争辩.

gowns•man [ˈgaunzmən] *n.* *(pl. -men)* ①穿长袍式礼服的人(如法官,教士,律师等). ②大学师生.

gow•ster [ˈgaustə] *n.* 〔美俚〕吸大麻的人;吸毒品者.

gox [gɔks] *n.* 气态氧 (= gaseous oxygen).

goy [gɔi] *n.* 非犹太人,异教徒.

goy•im [ˈgɔiim] *n.* 〔*pl.*〕 非犹太人.

GP = general audience, parental guidance suggested GP 级电影〔指适合一般观众观看,但建议父母对儿童观众加以指导的电影〕.

G.P., g.p. = ①general paresis 全身瘫痪. ②=〔英〕general practitioner 普通医生. ③= *Gloria Patria* (= Glory to the Father) 荣耀归于天父. ④ = Graduate in Pharmacy. 药学毕业生.

gp. = group.

g.p. = 【物】gauge pressure. 表压,计示压力.

GP bomb = general purpose bomb〔美〕普通炸弹,杀伤爆炸炸弹.

g.p.d. = 【纺】grams per denier.

g.p.d., gpd = gallons per day.

g.p.h. [m., s.] = gallons per hour [minute, second].

gpl = grams per litre.

gpmt. = 【美军】groupment.

G.P.O., GPO = General Post Office〔英〕邮政总局.

G.P.O. = General Post Office; Government Printing Office.

G.P.U., GPU [ˈdʒiː piːˈjuː, ˈgeiˌpeiˈuː] = Gay-Pay-Oo.

GQ. = general quarters【美军】战舰的战备状态.

G.Q.G. = Grand Quarter General.

GR. = 【军】①general reserve 总预备队. ②gunnery range 射击场.

Gr. = Grecian; Greece; Greek.

gr. = ①grade. ②grain(s). ③gram(me)(s). ④grammar. ⑤great. ⑥gross. ⑦group.

Gr. Br., Gr. Brit. = Great Britain 大不列颠.

G.R. ① = *Georgius Rex* (King George). ② = General Reserve.

Graaf•i•an [ˈgrɑːfiən] *a.* (荷兰解剖学家) 格拉夫 (R. de Graaf)的. ~ **follicle [vesicle]**【解】囊状卵泡.

grab [græb] *vt.* *(grabbed; grab•bing)* ①攫取,抓取; 抓住. ②抢夺,霸占. ③〔俚〕对…产生强烈的感情影响. ④〔美俚〕匆忙上(车). ~ *a bus* 赶搭公共汽车. — *vi.* ①抓住,抓牢 *(at, for, onto)*. ②急促行动. ③(马)后蹄踢着前蹄. ~ ***and keep*** 强取豪夺. ~ ***at*** 抓住不放. ~ ***hold of*** 抓紧. ~ ***off*** 〔美口〕抢得. — *n.* ①抓取,抢夺,不法所得. ②【机】抓扬机,挖掘机,抓斗,抓岩机,钻具打捞器. *make a* ~ *at a rope* 抓住绳索. ***have [get] the*** ~***on sb.*** 〔俚〕占得较…有利的地步,强过,胜过. ***up for*** ~***s***〔俚〕供人竞购(以售给出价最高者). ~**-all** *n.* 贪心汉;〔口〕杂物袋;(海岸附近的)固定渔网. ~ **bag,** ~ **box**〔美〕摸彩袋. ~ **hook** 起重钩. ~ **line,** ~ **rope** (船等) 作扶手用的绳子 (= guest-rope). ~ **sample**【化】定时取集的样品.

grab•ber [ˈgræbə] *n.* ①抢夺的人. ②贪心汉,唯利是图的人.

grab•ble [ˈgræbl] *vi.* ①摸索. ②匍匐,爬 *(for)*. — *vt.* 夺取.

grab•by [ˈgræbi] *a.* 贪婪的.

gra•ben [ˈgrɑːbən] *n.*【地】地堑,槽形断层. ~ **fault** 地堑断层.

Grace [greis] *n.* 格雷斯〔姓,女子名〕.

grace [greis] *n.* ①【宗】(神的)恩惠,恩典, 感化; 恩宠,慈悲;天惠,天恩;(对神的)皈依. ②【法】特权, 特赦权;【商】缓期,宽限. ③(动作,体态,结构等的)优美,优雅;(说话、举止)斯文,温雅;美德,美容;〔*pl.*〕风度,魅力. ④善意,恩赐; 情理,体面(感); 〔古〕宽厚, 仁慈. ⑤【宗】(饭前或饭后的)感恩祷告. ⑥【乐】装饰音. ⑦(英国牛津和剑桥大学)评议会的表决. ⑧〔G-〕阁下,夫人〔对公爵、公爵夫人、大主教等的尊称,前加 *His, Her, Your* 等〕. *an act of* ~ 恩典;(议会颁布的)大赦令. *I cannot with any* ~ *ask him.* 我没有脸去问他. *Every lover sees a thousand* ~*s in the beloved object.* 情人眼里出西施. ***airs and*** ~***s*** 装腔作势, 做作的派头. ***a saving*** ~ 可以弥补缺点的优点,可取之处. ***be in a state of*** ~【宗】蒙受天恩. ***by*** ~ ***of*** 承蒙,多承. ***days of*** ~ (票据付款的)宽限日期. ***fall from*** ~ 堕落, 犯罪; 失去天恩. ***good*** ~***s*** 好意, 友谊; 宠爱. ***have the*** ~ ***to (do)*** 有…的雅量,爽爽快快地…; 有勇气… *(have the* ~ *to apologize* 通情达理地道歉*)*. ***insinuate oneself into the good*** ~***s of sb.*** 巧妙地博得某人欢心. ***in sb.'s good [bad]*** ~***s*** 受某人照顾[白眼]. ***in this year of*** ~ 〔讥〕在基督教存在了这么久的现在尚且…. ***keep in sb.'s good*** ~***s*** 讨好,求宠. ***make one's*** ~***s*** 行礼. ***say*** ~ 做祷告. ***sue for*** ~ 请求照顾. ***the (three) Graces***【希神】司美丽、温雅、欢乐的三女神〔即 Aglaia, Euphrosyne 和 Thalia〕. ***the year of*** ~ 公元. ***with a bad [an ill]*** ~ 勉强地, 不情愿地. ***with a good*** ~ 高兴地, 欣然地. ***with an easy*** ~ 态度自若. — *vt.* ①装饰, 使优美 *(with)*. ②使增光,使有荣誉;惠赐. ③【乐】缀…以装饰音. *a character* ~*d by every virtue* 十全十美的人物. *Will you* ~ *our party with your presence?* 如蒙光临,不胜荣幸. ~ **cup** ①(感恩祷告后用的)祝酒杯. ②(宴会等的)最后一次祝酒. ~ **note(s)**【乐】装饰音. ~ **period** (缴保险费等的)宽限期.

grace•ful [ˈgreisful] *a.* ①优美的, 雅致的. ②得体的,适度的. *a* ~ *letter of thanks* 得体的感谢信. *as* ~ *as a swan* 姿态优美,举止端庄. **-ly** *ad.* **-ness** *n.*

grace•less [ˈgreislis] *a.* ①不优美的,不雅致的. ②粗俗的,粗鄙的. ③缺德的,邪恶的,堕落的. **-ly** *ad.* **-ness** *n.*

Gra•ci•a [ˈgreiʃiə] *n.* 格雷西亚〔女子名〕.

gra•ci•as [ˈgrɑːθiɑːs, -siː-] *int.* 〔Sp.〕 谢谢!

Gracie [ˈgreisi] *n.* 格雷西〔女子名, Grace 的昵称〕.

grac•ile [ˈgræsail] *a.* ①细长的,纤弱的. ②纤细优美的,苗条高雅的. **-ness** *n.*

gra•cil•i•ty [grəˈsiliti] *n.* ①细弱,纤弱;苗条. ②(文体的)简洁.

gra•ci•o•so [ˌgreiʃiˈəusəu, grɑːsi-; grɑːˈθjəusəu] *n.* 〔Sp.〕(西班牙喜剧中的)丑角;小丑.

gra•cious [ˈgreiʃəs] *a.* ①宽厚的,仁慈的;有礼貌的,谦和的;庄重的〔常指皇族人士,如 His ~ Majesty〕. ②亲切的,和蔼的; 态度自若的. ③优美的,雅致的; 高雅的,潇洒的. ④〔古〕幸运的,愉快的,神圣的. *It's* ~ *of you to come.* 承蒙光临. —*int.* 〔表示惊骇等〕天呀! ***Good [My]*** ~***! = G- Heaven [me, goodness]!*** 嗳呀! 天哪! **-ly** *ad.* **-ness** *n.*

grack•le [ˈgrækl] *n.*【动】鹩哥, 紫拟椋鸟 (Quiscalus quiscula)〔产于美洲〕.

grad [græd] *n.* 〔美口〕毕业生,校友 (graduate 的缩略).

grad. = gradient; graduate(d).

gra•date [grəˈdeit] *vi., vt.* ①(使) (色彩)渐次变浓〔变淡〕,(使…)显出层次来. ②顺次配列,(把…)分等级.

gra•da•tim [grəˈdeitim] *ad.* 〔L.〕 渐渐地, 徐徐地, 一步步地.

gra•da•tion [grəˈdeiʃən] *n.* ①分等, 分级. ②〔*pl.*〕 等级, 阶段. ③渐变; (颜色等的)层次;【美】浓淡法. ④【语】元音交替. **-al** *a.* 有次序的, 分等级的; 逐渐变化的. **-al•ly** *ad.*

grade [greid] *n.* ①等级, 级别; 阶段; 程度, 标准, 水平. ②〔美〕(中小学的)年级;某一年级的学生. ③〔*pl.*〕〔美〕小学校 (= ~ school). ④(学校考试的) 评分等级. ⑤〔主美〕坡度,斜坡,倾斜度. ⑥【畜】改良杂种. ⑦【语】元音交替. *a poor ~ of tea* 低级茶. ~ *A eggs* 甲级鸡蛋. *teach in the ~s* 做小学教师. ***at ~*** 〔美〕在同一水平面上. ***make the ~*** ①上陡坡. ②达到标准;成功. ***on the down ~*** 走下坡路,在衰败中. ***on the up ~*** 走上坡路,在兴盛中. ***up to ~*** 合格. — *vt.* ①定…的次序,定…的等级;给…分类;给…分级. ②〔美〕减缓(坡度);【地】均夷;使(色调)渐浓[渐淡]. ③给…记分数. ④【畜】通过杂交改良 *(up)*. — *vi.* ①属某种等级. ②(颜色等)渐次调和[变化]. ~ **crossing** 〔美〕(铁道、公路等的)平面交叉. ~ **label(l)ing** 〔美〕商品质量的标签说明. ~**mark** ① *n.* 表示货品等级的记号. ② *vt.* 在…上作货品等级的记号. ~ **school** 〔美〕小学. ~ **separation** 立体交叉〔指两条路以不同高度相交的交叉点〕. ~ **teacher** 〔美〕小学教师.

grad·er [ˈgreidə] *n.* ①分类者;分类机. ②〔美〕(小学校的)…年级生. *a fifth ~* 五年级生.

grade·ly [ˈgreidli] *a.* 〔英方〕①极好的,十足的. ②漂亮的,好看的. ③恰当的,真正的.

gra·di·ent [ˈgreidiənt] *a.* ①倾斜的. ②【动】步行的,能步行的. — *n.* ①〔英〕(道路的)倾斜度,坡度;坡路. ②【物】梯度,陡度;(温度、气压等的)变化率,梯度变化曲线.

gra·di·en·ter [ˈgreidjəntə] *n.* 倾斜测定器,倾斜计;水准仪,水平计.

gra·din [ˈgreidin], **gra·dine** [grəˈdi:n] *n.* ①阶梯的一级;阶梯座位的一排. ②【宗】祭坛后方的坛.

grad·ing [ˈgreidiŋ] *n.* ①【工】平地面,减少斜度. ②分品,分级,分段,校准. ③粒度.

gra·di·om·e·ter [ˌgreidiˈɔmitə], **gra·dom·e·ter** [grəˈdɔmitə] *n.* 倾斜仪,坡度测定仪.

grad·u·al[1] [ˈgrædʒuəl, ˈgrædjuəl] *a.* ①渐次的,逐渐的. ②渐进的;渐升[降]的;倾斜度小的. *a ~ slope* 缓坡,倾斜度不大的山坡. *the ~ increase of production cost* 生产成本的逐渐增加.

grad·u·al[2] [ˈgrædjuəl] *n.* 【天主】①弥撒圣歌〔圣餐后对唱的赞美诗 = ~ psalms〕. ②弥撒圣歌集. **-ly** *ad.* **-ness** *n.*

grad·u·al·ism [ˈgrædʒuəlizəm, -djuəlizəm] *n.* 渐进主义. **-al·ist** 渐进主义者(的) *n., a.* **-al·is·tic** *a.*

grad·u·ate [ˈgrædjueit] *vt.* ①〔美〕授与…学位,准予…毕业. ②给(量杯等)标上刻度;在(表,尺等上)分度. ③给(学生)分级. ④(用蒸发办法)使浓缩. *The university ~d 150 students last year.* 该大学去年有 150 名学生毕业. *She was [has been] ~d from* Beijing University *in the class of 1956.* 她是北京大学1956 届毕业生. *a ruler ~d in centimeters* 刻度为公分的尺. — *vi.* ①〔英〕大学毕业,取得学位 *(at)*,〔美〕毕业 *(from)*;取得资格 *(as; in)*. ②渐次变为 *(into)*;渐次消逝 *(away)*. — [ˈgrædʒuət, ˈgrædjuət] *n.* ①大学毕业生;〔美〕毕业生 *(of; in)*. ②【化】量筒,量杯. — *a.* ①得学士称号的,为大学毕业生设立的. ②刻度的,分等的. ~ **course** 〔美〕研究生课程. ~ **nurse** 受过正式训练的护士. ~ **students** 〔美〕研究生. ~ **school** 〔美〕研究院.

grad·u·at·ed [ˈgrædjueitid] *a.* ①分度的,刻度的. ②分等的. ③毕业了的. *a ~ glass* 刻度杯,量杯. ~ *taxation* 累进税.

grad·u·a·tion [ˌgrædjuˈeiʃən] *n.* ①毕业,授学位,得学位. ②毕业典礼,授学位典礼. ③〔*pl.*〕表示经纬度的线;刻度;分划,分度. ④分等级. ⑤浓缩. ~ **exercises** 〔美〕毕业典礼.

grad·u·a·tor [ˈgrædjueitə] *n.* 分度器;刻度器,刻度员.

gra·dus [ˈgreidəs, ˈgrædəs] *n.* ①诗韵辞典〔尤指写拉丁、希腊语诗歌用的格律〕. ②(由浅入深的)钢琴练习曲集.

Grae·cism [ˈgri:sizəm] *n.* = 〔英〕Grecism.

Grae·co- *comb. f.* 〔英〕= Greco-.

Graf [grɑ:f] *n.* *(pl.* ***Graf·en*** *[-n])* 〔G.〕(德国、奥地利、瑞典等国的)伯爵.

graf·fi·to [grəˈfi:təu] *n.* *(pl.* ***-ti*** *[-ti:])* (古墓、古墙上的)粗糙雕刻;现代在墙壁等处的乱涂. **graffiti pollution** 涂写污染〔指在公共场所乱涂乱写〕.

graf·fi·tist [grəˈfi:tist] *n.* (在公共场所的墙壁等处)乱涂乱写者.

graft[1] [grɑ:ft] *n.* ①接穗,嫁接;嫁接植物;嫁接法. ②【医】移植,移植片,移植物. ②〔美口〕贪污,受贿;(贪污所得的)赃品. ***take ~*** 贪污. — *vt., vi.* ①接枝,嫁接 *(in; into; on, upon)*. ②用嫁接法种植. ③【医】移植(皮、肉). ④〔美口〕贪污,受贿. ~ **copolymer** 接枝共聚物. ~ **hybrid** 嫁接杂种.

graft[2] [grɑ:ft] *n.* ①〔英〕一铲可以挖起的土的深度. ②弯口铁铲.

graft·age [ˈgrɑ:ftidʒ, ˈgræftidʒ] *n.* 【植】①嫁接,嫁接术. ②嫁接后的状态.

graft·er [ˈgrɑ:ftə] *n.* ①嫁接者,移植者. ②〔美口〕贪污分子,受贿者.

graft·ing [ˈgrɑ:ftiŋ] *n.* 嫁接法;【医】移植法. ~ **clay** 覆盖于接穗和砧木连接处的黏土.

Gra·ham(e) [ˈgreiəm] *n.* 格雷厄姆〔姓氏,男子名〕.

gra·ham [ˈgreiəm] *a.* 用未筛过的面粉制作的,全麦粉的. ~ **bread** 〔美〕(美国 S. Graham 创制的)营养黑面包. ~ **flour** 〔美〕(富有营养价值的)粗面粉,全麦面粉.

grail[1] [greil] *n.* ①杯;盘 (= platter). ②长期向往的事物. ***the [Holy] G-*** (中世纪传说中)耶稣在最后晚餐时所用的杯〔盘〕.

grail[2] [greil] *n.* = gradual psalms.

grail[3] [greil] *n.* 〔诗〕砾石,鹅卵石.

grain [grein] *n.* ①谷物,粮食〔英国叫 corn〕;谷类植物. ②谷粒,籽粒. ③(沙、金、盐等的)粒,颗粒;晶粒. ④些微,一点儿〔主要用于否定句〕. ⑤(木材、大理石等的)纹理;皮革的正面,粒面. ⑥脾气,特性,癖性. ⑦谷〔英美重量最低单位,略作 gr. = 64.8 毫克或 1/7,000 磅〕. ⑧胭脂虫;(用胭脂虫制的)红色染料;不褪色染料;〔古〕颜色,色调. ⑨〔*pl.*〕麦芽渣,酒糟. *a ~ distillery* 酒精厂. *a ~ of rice* 米粒;(瓷器上的)透明碎米花. *coarse ~* 粗粮,杂粮. *refined ~* 细粮. *(food) ~s* 粮食. *woods of fine [coarse] ~* 细[粗]纹木材. *There isn't a ~ of truth in what he said.* 他说的全不是真话. ***against the ~*** ①逆纹理. ②〔喻〕不合脾气地,违反意愿地. ***a ~ of mustard seed*** 发展前途极大的小东西. ***a ~ of wheat in a bushel of chaff*** 徒劳,毫无结果,无济于事. ***dye in ~*** 生染,用不褪色染料染. ***in ~*** 深红的;根深蒂固的;十足的;坏透的;天生的 *(knave [rogue] in ~* 生来的大坏蛋). ***with a ~ of salt = with some ~s of allowance*** 有保留地,不全信地,打上几分折扣(处理). ***without a ~ of …*** 一点也没有 *(a boy without a ~ of common sense* 一点道理都不懂的小男孩). — *vt.* ①把…作成细粒. ②把…漆[画]成木纹;使(皮等)表面粗糙. ③染透. ④刮去(皮上的)毛. — *vi.* 成为细粒. ~ **alcohol** 乙醇,酒精. ~ **elevator** 〔美〕谷塔,谷仓. ~**field** 庄稼(田)地. ~ **leather** 粒面向外的皮革. ~ **rust** 谷物锈病. ~**sick** (牛的)瘤胃扩张症. ~ **side** 皮革粒面. ~ **sorghum** 高粱. **-less** *a.* 没有谷粒的;没有纹理的.

grained [greind] *a.* 粒状的,有纹的. **-ness** *n.*

grain·er [ˈgreinə] *n.* ①脱毛器,刮毛刀;鞣皮剂. ②漆[画]木纹者;起纹器.

grains [greinz] *n. pl.* 〔作单数用〕双齿[多齿]鱼叉.

grain·y [ˈgreini] *a.* ①谷粒多的. ②粒状的,粒面的;木纹状的. ③有细粒的. **-i·ness** *n.*

graip [greip] *n.* 〔Scot.〕(叉肥料或掘马铃薯等用的)三齿[四齿]叉.

Gral·la·to·res [ˌgræləˈtɔ:ri:z] *n. pl.* 【动】涉禽类.

gral·la·to·ri·al [ˌgræləˈtɔ:riəl] *a.* 【动】涉禽类的.

gram[1] [græm] *n.* ①【植】鹰嘴豆. ②绿豆.

gram[2] [græm] *n.* 克〔重量单位,略作 g.〕. ~ **atom**【化】

克原子. ～ **calorie** 克卡〔热量单位〕. ～ **equivalent**【化】克当量. ～ **molecule**【化】克分子.
gram. = grammar; grammarian; grammatical.
-gram[1] *comb. f.* 表示"克": kilo*gram*.
-gram[2] *comb. f.* 表示"书写物","字": tele*gram*.
gra·ma, gram·ma [ˈgrɑːmə, ˈgræmə] *n.* 〔美〕【植】格兰马草 (= ～ grass).
gram·a·ry(e) [ˈgræməri] *n.* 〔英古〕魔术.
gra·mer·cy [grəˈməːsi] *int.* 〔古〕①多谢! ②天哪!
gram·i·ci·din [ˌgræmiˈsaidin] *n.*【药】短杆菌肽.
gram·i·na·ceous [ˌgræmiˈneiʃəs], **gra·min·e·ous** [grəˈminiəs] *a.* ①草的; 草似的. ②草多的; 草绿色的. ③禾木科的.
gram·i·niv·o·rous [ˌgræmiˈnivərəs] *a.* 吃草的,草食的.
gram·ma·log(ue) [ˈgræməlɔg] *n.* (速记中)用简略记号表示的字〔词〕.
gram·mar [ˈgræmə] *n.* ①语法; 语法学; 语法书. ②语法现象, (个人的)语法知识, 文理. ③(学术的)基本原理; 入门, 初阶. *general [philosophical, universal]* ～ 一般语法学. *historical* ～ 历史语法学. *His* ～ *is shocking.* 他的文句糟极了,他的文理极差. *a bad [good]* ～ 不正确的〔正确的〕说法. *a G- of Science* 《科学初阶》. ～ **school** ①〔英〕语法学校〔十六世纪以前以教拉丁文为主, 后变为中学, 教授语言、历史和自然科学等〕. ②〔美〕初级中学.
gram·mar·i·an [grəˈmɛəriən] *n.* 语法学者; 语法教师.
gram·mat·i·cal [grəˈmætikəl] *a.* 语法的, 语法上的; 合语法的. ～ *gender* 语法上的性. *a* ～ *sense* 字面的意义,语法上的意义. **-ly** *ad.* **-ness** *n.*
gram·mat·i·cize [grəˈmætisaiz] *vt.* 使合语法. — *vi.* ①讨论语法问题. ②卖弄语法知识.
gramme [græm] *n.* = gram[2].
gram·my [ˈgræmi] *n.*〔口〕= ①gramophone. ②grandmother.
Gram-neg·a·tive [ˈgræmˈnegətiv] *a.* 〔亦作 g-〕【医】革兰氏阴性的.
gram·o·phone [ˈgræməfəun] *n.* 留声机. *sing into the* ～ 灌唱片,灌音. **-phon·ic** [ˌgræməˈfəunik] *a.* **-i·cal·ly** *ad.*
Gram-pos·i·tive [ˈgræmˈpɔzətiv] *a.* 〔亦 g-〕【医】革兰氏阳性的.
gramps [græmps] *n.* 〔俚〕= grandfather.
gram·pus [ˈgræmpəs] *n.* ①【动】逆戟鲸, 鯱. ②〔口〕呼吸〔打鼾〕声音粗大的人. *blow [puff, snore] like a* ～ 鼾声如雷.
Gram's method [græmz ˈmeθəd] 革兰氏染色法〔研究细菌的一种染色法〕.
Gram stain [græm stein] *n.* 细菌染色液.
gran turismo [græn tuəˈrizməu] *n. (pl. **gran turismos**)* 〔It.〕(制造标准比得上赛车的)高级跑车.
gran·a·dil·la [ˌgrænəˈdilə] *n.*【植】西番莲属 *(Passiflora)* 植物的食用果实.
gran·a·ry [ˈgrænəri] *n.* 谷仓,粮仓; 产粮区. *a grand* ～ 天然粮仓; 鱼米之乡.
Gran Cha·co [ˈgrɑːn ˈtʃɑːkəu] 〔常与 the 连用〕(横贯阿根廷、玻利维亚、巴拉圭的)南美洲亚热带地区.
grand [grænd] *a.* ①盛大的,宏大的; 堂皇的, 雄伟的. ②〔口〕富丽的, 漂亮的, 豪华的. ③〔用于头衔〕最高的, 首要的; 伟大的, 杰出的; 崇高的, 尊贵的. ④(最)重要的, 重大的; 大的, 主要的 *(opp.* petit, petty, common*)*. ⑤总括性的, 全部的, 完全的. ⑥【乐】大合奏用的, 全…. ⑦〔口〕快乐的, 极好的. ⑧(亲属关系中)(外)祖…; (外)孙…. *a* ～ *air* 堂皇的气派, 堂堂仪表. *a* ～ *character* 崇高的人格. ～ *climax* 顶点, 最高潮. *a* ～ *committee* 英国下议院审议法律、贸易法案的两个常设委员会之一. ～ *entrance* 大门. *a* ～ *lady* 贵妇人. *a* ～ *man* 伟人; 名人. ～ *manner* = ～ style. *a* ～ *mistake* 大错误. ～ *question* 重大问题. ～ *relief* 高浮雕. ～ *sight* 壮观. *a* ～ *style* 庄重的文体. *the* ～ *total* 总计. *a* ～ *view* 壮丽的景色. *It will be* ～ *if you can come.* 你要是能来, 那就再好没有了. ***do the*** ～ 〔口〕装模作样, 摆架子. ***have a*** ～ ***time*** 过得极愉快. ***live in*** ～ ***style*** 过豪华生活. ***the G- National*** 英国利物浦每年举行一次的野外障碍赛马. ***the G- Old Man***【英史】英国首相格拉德斯通 (Gladstone) 的尊称. ***the G- Old Party*** 美国共和党的别称(略作 GOP). ***the*** ～ ***slam*** ①〔美俚〕(桥牌等的)满贯; (运动比赛等的)全胜. ②【棒球】满垒打, 本垒打, 也叫 ***～-slammer***. — *n.* ①大钢琴(= ～ piano). ②〔美俚〕〔单复同〕一千元 (钞票). ～**aunt** 叔祖母, 伯祖母, 姑婆, 舅婆, 姨婆. ～**baby** 小孙子, 小孙女(即婴孩期的 ～child). **G- Canal** ①中国大运河〔杭州—通县〕. ②意大利威尼斯主运河. **G- Canyon** 美国科罗拉多河流域的大峡谷. ～**child** *(pl.* ***～children)*** 孙子, 孙女, 外孙. **G- Cross** 英国大十字勋章. ～**daughter** 孙女, 外孙女. ～**dad**, ～**-dad** 〔口〕爷爷. ～**daddy** = grandfather. ～**-ducal** *a.* 大公的, 大公国的. ～ **duchess** 大公夫人; 大公爵夫人; 女大公爵. ～ **duchy** (大公辖下的)公国; 大公爵领地. ～ **finale** (戏剧、运动会等的)高潮性结尾. ～ **juror** 大陪审官. ～ **jury** 大陪审团〔由 12 人以上组成的审查罪案团体, 负责罪案的审查事项, 如证据充分, 则提请小陪审团审理〕. ～ **larceny**【法】①大盗窃案罪〔美国法定额各州不一, 一般为 25—60 美元, 为小盗窃罪 (petit larceny) 之对〕. ②(不拘数目, 不用武力, 人对人进行的)敲诈, 勒索. ～ **lodge** (共济会等秘密团体的) 总部. ～**ma**, ～**ma(m)ma** 〔口〕奶奶, 外婆. ～ **master** ①大师〔最高棋手等的称号〕. ②〔G-M-〕【英史】骑士团团长; (共济会等秘密团体分支组织的)领导人. **G- Monarch** 法国路易十四国王. ～**nephew** 侄孙, 侄外孙. ～**niece** 侄孙女, 侄外孙女. ～ **opera** 大歌剧〔无对白, 全部为歌唱〕. ～ **orchestra** 大型管弦乐队, 交响乐队. ～**pa**, ～**papa** 〔口〕爷爷, 外公. ～**parent** *n.* 祖父母, 外祖父母. ～ **piano** 大钢琴, 三角钢琴. ～ **right and left**【民间舞蹈】反向圆转〔两组成圆形交织, 作反向圆转〕. ～**sire** 〔古〕祖父; 祖先; 老者. ～**son** 孙子; 外孙. ～ **tour** ①教育旅行〔旧时英国贵族子弟到欧洲大陆旅行, 以完成自己的教育阶段〕. ②与此类似的旅行. ③有向导的参观〔如对建筑物等〕. ～**uncle** 伯祖父, 叔祖父, 外伯祖, 外叔祖. **-ness** *n.* 宏大; 壮观; 伟大; 堂皇; 庄严; 华丽.
gran·dam, gran·dame [ˈgrændæm, -dəm] *n.* 〔古〕祖母, 外祖母; 老太婆, 老妇人.
grande [grɑːnd] *a.* 〔F.〕重大的, 宏大的, 盛大的, 显要的. ～ **dame** 贵妇. ～ **passion** 寝食俱废的恋爱. ～ **toilette** 大礼服.
gran·dee [grænˈdiː] *n.* ①大公, (西班牙及葡萄牙的) 最高贵族. ②高官, 显贵.
gran·deur [ˈgrændʒə] *n.* ①宏伟庄严; 壮观. ②豪华, 富丽堂皇. ③伟大, 崇高. *full of power and* ～ 威武雄壮. *with* ～ 隆重的.
grand·fa·ther [ˈgrændˌfɑːðə] *n.* ①祖父, 外祖父. ②老大爷. ③祖先. *a great* ～ 曾祖父. ～ **clause** 〔美〕①老祖父条款〔规定南北战争前享有选举权的白人后代, 即使没有文化也有选举权〕. ②(某些法律中的)不追溯条款. ～**('s) clock** 有摆的座钟. **-ly** *a.* 祖父的, 祖父似的, 慈祥的.
gran·dil·o·quence [grænˈdiləkwəns] *n.* 夸大, 夸张.
gran·dil·o·quent [grænˈdiləkwənt] *a.* 夸张的, 夸大的. *Indeed, no eulogy could be more* ～ *than this.* 真是恭维备至. **-ly** *ad.*
gran·di·ose [ˈgrændiəus] *a.* ①雄伟的, 宏大的, 壮观的. ②铺张的, 夸大的, 浮夸的, 自以为是的, 沾沾自喜的. **-ly** *ad.*
gran·di·os·i·ty [ˌgrændiˈɔsiti] *n.* ①宏大, 辉煌; 堂皇. ②夸张; 铺张; 浮夸; 沾沾自喜.

gran·dio·so [grɑːnˈdjəusəu] *a., ad.* 〔It.〕【乐】雄伟地，壮丽地，崇高地.

grand·ly [ˈgrændli] *ad.* 宏伟地；堂皇地；盛大地；崇高地；华丽地.

grand mal [ˈgræn ˈmæl] 〔F.〕【医】癫痫大发作.

grand monde [ˌgrɑːn ˈmɔnd] 〔F.〕上流社会.

grand·moth·er [ˈgrænd̩ˌmʌðə] *n.* ①祖母，外祖母. ②老奶奶. ③女祖先. *a great* ～ 曾祖母. ***teach one's*** ～ ***(how) to suck eggs*** 教训长辈；班门弄斧. ***Tell that to your*** ～. 胡说. ***This beats my*** ～. 吓了一跳. — *vt.* 娇养，溺爱；悉心照料. ～ ***the cups*** 弄湿茶托以防杯滑. **-ly** *a.* 祖母似的，慈祥的，溺爱的，唠叨的.

grand prix [grɑːn ˈpri] 〔F.〕头等奖，最高奖.

grand siècle [grɑːn siˈekl] 〔F.〕古典时代，黄金时代〔尤指法国的十七世纪〕.

grand·stand [ˈgrændstænd] *n.* ①(体育场的)正面看台，大看台. ②坐在正面观众席上的观众. — *vi.* 〔口〕为博取观众喝彩而卖弄技巧. ～ **play** ①(比赛时为博取观众喝彩的)卖弄技巧. ②〔喻〕哗众取宠的言行；做作的举动. **-er** *n.* 为博取观众喝彩而卖弄技巧的运动员.

grange [greindʒ] *n.* ①〔英〕庄园；地主的住宅；〔古〕谷仓；(庄园、修道院的)附属农场. ②〔G-〕〔美〕格兰其〔成立于1867年的美国全国性保护田庄农民利益的秘密组织，正式名称为"农人协进会"〕.

grang·er [ˈgreindʒə] *n.* ①〔美〕"格兰其"成员，"农人协进会"会员. ②庄稼汉，农夫；农场管家.

grang·er·ism [ˈgreindʒərizəm] *n.* 转载别本书上的插图.

grang·er·ize [ˈgreindʒəraiz] *vt.* ①插入(由别本书上剪来的插图). ②从(书中)剪下插图. **-i·za·tion** *n.* **-iz·er** *n.*

gra·nif·er·ous [grəˈnifərəs] *a.* 结谷粒的，结颗粒状果实的.

gran·ite [ˈgrænit] *n.* ①花岗岩，花岗石. ②坚如磐石，坚韧不拔. *gneissic* ～ 片麻状花岗岩. ***as hard as*** ～ 象岩石一样坚硬的. ***bite on*** ～ 白费气力，徒劳无功. ***the G- City*** 苏格兰阿伯丁市的别名. ***the G- State*** 美国新罕布什尔州的别名. ～ **boys**〔美〕新罕布什尔州人(的绰号). ～**ware** 有花岗石斑纹的陶器；涂灰色珐琅的铁器.

gra·nit·ic [grəˈnitik] *a.* 花岗岩(似)的；由花岗岩形成的.

gra·nit·i·form [græˈnitifɔːm] *a.* 花岗石状的.

gran·it·oid [ˈgrænitɔid] *a.* 花岗岩状的；有花岗岩结构的.

gra·niv·o·rous [grəˈnivərəs] *a.* 食谷的，食种子的.

gran·nie, gran·ny [ˈgræni] *n.* ①〔口〕奶奶，外婆. ②老妈妈，老奶奶. ③婆婆妈妈的人；唠叨挑剔的人. ④〔美〕接生婆. ⑤=～'s knot. ***～'s knot*** 松8字结〔*cf.* reef knot〕. ***teach one's ～ (how) to suck eggs*** = teach one's grandmother (how) to suck eggs. — *a.* 祖母装的，松身密实装的. ～ **dress** (从颈部一直达到踝部的松身密实装，祖母装. ～ **glass** (外形类似过去老年妇女使用的)仿老式金丝眼镜. **G- Smith** 澳大利亚的绿苹果.

gran·o·lith [ˈgrænəliθ] *n.* 人造铺地石. **-ic** *a.*

gran·o·phyre [ˈgrænəfaiə] *n.* 【地】花斑岩，文象斑岩. **-phyr·ic** [-ˈfiərik] *a.*

grant [grɑːnt] *vt.* ①许可，答应，承认. ②授与，让渡，转让. ③假定，姑且承认. ～ *(sb.) a request* 接受(某人)要求. ～ *a pension* 给与退休金. *I* ～ *you.* 就算你对. *This ～ed, what next?* 就算这样，下文呢？ ***～(ing) that*** ... = ***～ed that*** ... 假定…，即使…. ***take it for ～ed*** 认为当然 (= accept as true). — *n.* ①许可；答应，承认. ②授与，让渡；转让证书. ③授给物，转让权；补助金. ***～ in aid (of)*** (…的)补助金. ***in*** ～ 【法】凭证件才能让渡的(财产). **～-aided** *a.* 受补助的 (*～-aided school* 接受公共基金资助的学校). **-a·ble** *a.* 可同意的，可授与的，可转让的. **-ed·ly** *ad.*

Grant [grɑːnt] *n.* ①格兰特〔姓氏，男子名〕. ②**Ulysses Simpson** ～ 尤利塞斯·辛普森·格兰特〔1822—1885，美国南北战争时北军总司令，第十八任总统〕.

gran·tee [grɑːnˈtiː] *n.* 【法】被授与者，受让人.

Gran·tham [ˈgrænθəm] *n.* 格兰瑟姆〔姓氏〕.

grant-in-aid [ˌgrɑːntinˈeid] *n.* (*pl.* ***grants-in-aid***)(中央对地方的)拨款；补助金，助学金.

grant·man [ˈgrɑːntmən] *n.* 申请补助费专家. **～ship** 懂得如何申请到补助费的本领.

gran·tor [grɑːnˈtɔː, ˈgræntə] *n.* 【法】授与者，让与者.

gran·u·lar [ˈgrænjulə] *a.* 颗粒状的，粒面的，由小粒形成的. ～ **lid** 【医】沙眼. ～ **structure** 【农】(土壤的)团粒结构. **-i·ty** [ˌgrænjuˈlæriti] *n.* 颗粒状；颗粒度；颗粒性. **-ly** *ad.*

gran·u·late [ˈgrænjuleit] *vt.* 使成颗粒，使成粒状；使表面粗糙，使表面成粒面. — *vi.* 形成颗粒，表面变粗糙. **～d glass** 麻面玻璃. **～d leather** 珠皮. **～d fertilizer** 颗粒肥料. **～d sugar** 砂糖.

gran·u·la·tion [ˌgrænjuˈleiʃən] *n.* ①形成颗粒，形成粒面；表面粗糙. ②【医】肉芽，颗粒；肉芽形成. ～ **tissue** 【病理】肉芽组织.

gran·u·la·tor [ˈgrænjuleitə] *n.* 砂糖成粒器；使形成颗粒的东西[人].

gran·ule [ˈgrænjuːl] *n.* ①颗粒，细粒. ②粒状斑点. ③【天】(日面的)米粒.

gran·u·lite [ˈgrænjulait] *n.* 【地】白粒岩，粒变岩. **-litic** [-ˈlitik] *a.*

gran·u·lo·cyte [ˈgrænjuləusait] *n.* 【医】粒性白血球. **-lo·cyt·ic** [-ləuˈsitik] *a.*

gran·u·lo·cy·to·pe·nia [ˌgrænjuləuˌsaitəˈpiːniə] *n.* 【医】粒细胞减少.

gran·u·lo·ma [ˌgrænjuˈləumə] *n.* (*pl.* ～*s*, ***-ma·ta*** [-mətə])【医】肉芽肿，肉芽瘤. **-tous** *a.*

gran·u·lo·ma·to·sis [ˌgrænjuləuməˈtəusis] *n.* 【医】肉芽肿症.

gran·u·lose [ˈgrænjuləus] *n.* 【化】淀粉糖. — *a.* = granular.

gran·u·lous [ˈgrænjuləs] *a.* 颗粒状的，有颗粒的.

gra·num [ˈgreinəm] *n.* 【生】叶绿粒体.

grape [greip] *n.* ①葡萄. ②葡萄色，深紫色. ③〔the ～〕葡萄酒. ④〔*pl.*〕(马脚上生的)葡萄疮；(牛的)结核病. ⑤【军】葡萄弹. ～ *juice* 葡萄汁. ***sour ～s*** 酸葡萄〔指可望而不可及的东西〕. ***the ～ = the juice of the ～*** 葡萄酒. ～ **brandy** 葡萄白兰地酒. ～ **cure** 葡萄疗法. ～**fruit** 【植】葡萄柚. ～ **hyacinth** 【植】麝香兰属(muscari)植物. ～ **ivy** 【植】菱叶白粉藤(Cissus rhombifolia)〔产于南美北部，为常见的园庭植物〕. **～-shot** 【军】葡萄弹. ～**stone** 葡萄核，葡萄种子. ～ **sugar** 葡萄糖. ～**vine** ①葡萄藤；葡萄树. ②〔美俚〕传闻；谣言；小道消息的流传；[秘密情报]的口头传递. ③一种花式滑冰的动作；一种摔交动作. **～vine telegraph** 小道消息的不胫而走.

grap·er·y [ˈgreipəri] *n.* 葡萄园；葡萄温室.

graph[1] [grɑːf] *n.* ①【数】曲线图；坐标图，图表. ②统计曲线. — *vt.* 用图表表示，把…绘入图表. ～ **paper** 图纸，坐标图纸，标绘图纸.

graph[2] [grɑːf] *n.* 胶版. — *vt.* 用胶版印刷.

graph[3] [grɑːf] *n.* 【语】①词的拼法. ②表示音素的最小字母单位.

-graph *comb. f.* 表示 ①"写、画、记录的用具"：phono*graph*, tele*graph*. ②"写[画、记录]的结果"：auto*graph*, photo*graph*.

graph·eme [ˈgræfiːm] *n.* 【语】①字母. ②(字母的)书写单位；(音素的)图形单位.

-graph·er *comb. f.* 表示"书写者"，"描绘者"，"记录者"：

photo*grapher*, biblio*grapher*.

graph·ic(al) [ˈgræfik(əl)] *a.* ①书写的,绘画的;印刷的,雕刻的. ②(叙述等)写实的,绘画似的,生动的. ③图的,图解的;用图表示的;用文字表示的. ~ *error* 笔误. ~ *method* 图解法. *the* ~ *arts* 书画刻印艺术. ~ **alg·bra** 图解代数学. ~ **formula**【化】图解式,结构式. **-ly** *ad.* **-ness** *n.*

graph·ics [ˈgræfiks] *n. pl.* 〔用作单数〕①(建筑或工程的)绘图学,制图学. ②图解计算,图式计算;(可用人工操作的)电子计算机图解法. ③【语】书法,字体.

graph·ite [ˈgræfait] *n.*【化】石墨,黑铅,炭精;铅笔粉. *colloidal* ~ 胶体石墨. ~ *electrode*【电】石墨电极. *live [dead]* ~ 含[不含]铀石墨. ~ **moderated reactor**【原】石墨减速反应堆.

graph·i·tize [ˈgræfitaiz] *vt.* ①使石墨化. ②在…内(或上)涂石墨,在…内充石墨. **-i·ti·za·tion** [ˌgræfitaiˈzeiʃən] *n.*

graph·i·toid [ˈgræfitɔid] *a.* 石墨状的.

graph·ol·o·gy [græˈfɔlədʒi] *n.* ①笔迹学. ②图解法.

graph·o·scope [ˈgræfəskəup] *n.* 电子计算机显示器.

graph·o·type [ˈgræfətaip] *n.* 白垩凸版.

-graph·y *comb. f.* 表示 ①"书法","写法","图示法": photo*graphy*. ②"志","记": geo*graphy*, biblio*graphy*.

grap·nel [ˈgræpnəl] *n.* ①小锚,四爪锚〔又叫 ~ *anchor*〕. ②(锚形)铁爪篙.

grap·pa [ˈgrɑːpɑː] *n.* 〔It.〕白兰地酒.

grap·ple [ˈgræpl] *vt.* ①抓住,捉牢. ②(用铁爪篙)钩住(敌船等). ③与…扭打,与…格斗. — *vi.* ①用铁锚〔铁钩〕钩住. ②揪扭,扭打;搏斗 *(with)*. ~ *an enemy* 与敌人格斗. ~ ***difficulties*** 与困难作斗争. ~ *with problems* 尽力解决问题. — *n.* ①抓机,抓斗. ②紧握;揪扭,扭打,格斗. ③ = grapnel. ***come to ~s with*** ①与…格斗. ②尽力从事[对付].

grap·pler [ˈgræplə] *n.* ①抓钩器,抓钩者. ②格斗者. ③〔俚〕手.

grap·pling [ˈgræpliŋ] *n.* = grapnel. ~ **iron** (打捞用的)抓机;(使船只泊下的)铁钩.

grap·to·lite [ˈgræptəlait] *n.*【动】笔石〔属于腔肠动物的一种化石〕. **-lit·ic** *a.*

grap·y [ˈgreipi] *a.* ***(grapi·er; grap·i·est)*** ①葡萄(似)的. ②由葡萄制成的,有葡萄(酒)味的. ③【医】生了葡萄疮的.

GRAS = Generally Recognized as Safe 一般安全〔美国食品药物管理局使用的检验标记,表示食品无害人体,安全可用〕.

grasp [grɑːsp] *vt.* ①抓住,握紧,抱住. ②领会,理解. ~ *the argument* 对论点有所了解. — *vi.* 抓牢,紧握. ***G-all, lose all.*** 〔谚〕样样抓,样样差;贪多必失. ~ ***at*** 去抓,攫取. ~ ***at a straw*** 捞救命稻草. ~ ***the nettle*** 迎着艰险上,挺身应付难局. — *n.* ①抓;把握,紧握. ②权力;统制,支配. ③理解;理解力. ④把手,柄,(剑等的)把. *a mind of wide* ~ 有多方面理解力的头脑. ***beyond one's*** ~ 手[能力]达不到,不能理解的,鞭长莫及. ***have a good*** ~ ***of*** 深刻了解. ***in the*** ~ ***of*** 在…掌握中. ***keep a firm*** ~ ***on*** 抓紧. ***within one's*** ~ 手[能力]达得到,能理解的.

gras·pa·ble [ˈgrɑːspəbl] *a.* 能理解的,可以懂的.

grasp·ing [ˈgrɑːspiŋ] *a.* ①抓的,握的. ②贪婪的. **-ly** *ad.* **-ness** *n.*

grass [grɑːs] *n.* ①草;牧草;牧草地,牧场;草地,草原. ②〔*pl.*〕【植】禾本科植物;〔*pl.*〕草叶;〔俚〕龙须菜,芦笋,莴苣,(色拉中的)生菜. ③草发绿时,春天. ④【矿】矿山地面,矿井地面. ⑤〔英俚〕(印刷厂的)临时排字工作,临时工作. ⑥【无】噪音细条,(雷达屏上的)"毛草". ⑦〔俚〕大麻〔北美产的毒品〕. ⑧闲居(处). *All flesh is* ~. 人尽如草,终必枯亡. ~ *family* 禾木科植物. *a* ~ *lamb* 牧放中生出的小羊. *a horse five years old next* ~ 来春五岁的马. *While the* ~ *grows the horse [steed] starves.* 〔谚〕远水不救近火. ***be at*** ~ = ***be out at*** ~ ①在牧放中. ②闲着(休假、失业等). ③【矿】离开矿井,在露天. ***between [betwixt]*** ~ ***and hay*** 〔美〕在儿童与成人之间的青少年. ***bring to*** ~ 把(矿)运出井外. ***come to*** ~ 走出矿井外. ***cut one's own*** ~ 〔口〕自食其力. ***cut the*** ~ ***from under sb.'s feet*** 妨碍某人;挫败某人. ***go to*** ~ ①(家畜)上牧场去. ②〔口〕歇工,休假;退休;死去. ③〔口〕被打倒*(Go to* ~*!* 去你的!见你的鬼!*)*. ***hear the*** ~ ***grow*** 极端敏感. ***hunt*** ~ 〔口〕一败涂地,被打倒. ***Come [Keep] off the*** ~. ①(布告)勿踏草地. ②谨慎小心. ***lay down in*** ~ (在地上)铺上草皮,使成草地. ***let no*** ~ ***grow under one's feet*** 不错过机会,说干就干. ***put [send, turn out] to*** ~ ①把…赶到牧场,放牧. ②辞退,解雇;强迫退休. — *vt.* ①用草覆盖;使长草,在…撒草种. ②使吃草,放牧. ③在草上晒;把…摊开在草地上. ④〔英〕打倒;把(鱼)钓上岸来;打落(飞鸟). ***be*** ~***ed down*** 用草盖着;埋在草下. ***be*** ~***ed over*** 完全被草盖上. — *vi.* ①(家畜)在牧场上吃草. ②长满草. ③〔美俚〕告密,当告密者. ~**-blade** 草叶. ~ **character** (汉语的)草书. ~ **cloth** ①亚麻布等. ②草编物. ~ **cutter** 割草机. ~ **green** 草绿色. ~**-green** *a.* ①草绿色的. ②绿草如茵的. ~ **hand** ①(汉语的)草书. ②〔英俚〕(印刷厂的)临时排字工. ~ **hopper** 蚱蜢,蝗虫. ~**land** 牧场;草地;草原. ~**plot** 草地. ~ **roots** ①草根. ②农牧地区;〔集合词〕农牧民. ③基础,根本;基层,基层群众 *(cadres at* ~ *roots level* 基层干部). ~**-roots** *a.* 〔美口〕农牧地区的,乡下的;农民的,来自民间的;基层的,基层群众的. ~ **skiing** 滑草(运动)〔长满青草或覆盖着稻草的斜坡上滑下的运动〕. ~ **snake** (无毒)青草蛇. ~ **snipe** 红胸滨鹬 (= pectoral sandpiper). ~ **tree** 草树〔百合科植物,澳大利亚产,树木短粗,木质,叶似草,有的还可产香树脂,经济价值很高〕. ~ **widow** 离了婚的女人,跟丈夫分居的女人. ~ **widower** 离了婚的男人,跟妻子分居的男人. ~**work** 〔英〕【矿】坑外作业. **-less** *a.* 不长草的,没有草的. **-like** *a.*

grass·y [ˈgrɑːsi] *a.* ①草深的,草多的. ②草似的,草绿色的. ③食草的. **-i·ness** *n.*

grat [græt] greet² 的过去式.

grate¹ [greit] *n.* ①炉格,炉篦,炉栅. ②火炉,壁炉. ③格栅,格子. ④【矿】篦条筛,固定筛. — *vt.* 在…上装炉格,在…上装格栅. **-d** *a.* 有格栅的,有炉格的. **-less** *a.* 无格栅的,无炉格的.

grate² [greit] *vt.* ①磨擦,轧. ②擦碎;磨损. ③使焦急,激怒. ~ *the teeth* 把牙磨得嘎嘎响. — *vi.* ①磨擦;轧,擦得嘎嘎嘎地响 *(against; on; upon)*. ②激怒,使人烦躁. *noises* ~*ing upon the ears* 刺耳的噪音.

G-rated [dʒiː-ˈreitid] *a.* (电影) G 级的,成年与儿童都适宜观看的.

grate·ful [ˈgreitful] *a.* ①感恩的,感谢的. ②愉快的,爽快的,可喜的. *a* ~ *letter* 道谢的信. *a* ~ *odo(u)r* 爽快的气味. ***be*** ~ ***to sb.*** 感谢某人*(for)*. ***make a*** ~ ***acknowledgement for*** 对…表示衷心的感谢. **-ly** *ad.* **-ness** *n.*

grat·er [ˈgreitə] *n.* ①摩碎[擦碎]东西的人[工具]. ②磨光机;擦菜板;粗齿木锉.

grat·i·cule [ˈgrætikjuːl] *n.* ①十字线,分度线,标线(片). ②【地】量板;(绘制地图用的)方格图.

grat·i·fi·ca·tion [ˌgrætifiˈkeiʃən] *n.* ①满足,喜悦;使人满足(喜悦)的事物. ②报酬,奖金. ③满足感. *Your praise gives me much* ~. 承您夸奖,十分高兴.

grat·i·fy [ˈgrætifai] *vt.* ①使满足. ②使喜悦,使高兴. ③〔古〕酬报,奖赏. *I was gratified to learn that your son had passed the entrance examination.* 得悉令郎已通过入学考试,我十分高兴. ~ *one's thirst for money* 满足金钱欲. **-fi·er** *n.* 使人感到满足的人[事物].

grat•i•fy•ing [ˈgrætifaiiŋ] *a.* 可喜的，令人满足的. ～ *results* 可喜的成绩. **-ly** *ad.*

grat•in [ˈgrætn] *n.* 〔F.〕 奶汁烤菜(法)；表面有一层焦花面包和干酪屑的食物；焦黄面包和干酪屑涂层.

grat•ing[1] [ˈgreitiŋ] *n.* ①格栅，格子；(船上作地板或透光用的)格子板，格子盖. ②【物】光栅. *diffraction* ～ 衍射光栅，绕射栅.

grat•ing[2] [ˈgreitiŋ] *a.* 刺耳的，使人烦躁的，讨厌的. —*n.* 摩擦，摩擦声. **-ly** *ad.*

gra•tis [ˈgreitis] *ad.* 免费. *sent the sample* ～ 免费赠送样品. *be admitted* ～ 受免费招待. ***free*** ～ ***for nothing*** 〔口、谑〕白送. —*a.* 〔多作表语〕免费的. *Entrance is* ～. 入场免费.

grat•i•tude [ˈgrætitjuːd] *n.* 感谢；谢意；礼物. *We can hardly express our* ～ *to you for your timely help.* 对于你们的及时帮助，我们很难表达我们的感激之情. ***devoid of all*** ～ 忘恩负义. ***in token of one's*** ～ 藉表谢意. ***out of*** ～ 出于感激. ***with*** ～ 感谢.

Grat•tan [ˈgrætn] *n.* 格拉顿〔姓氏〕.

gra•tu•i•tous [grəˈtju(ː)itəs] *a.* ①免费的；无偿的. ②无必要的；无故的，无理由的. ～ *service* [*help*] 免费服务[无偿援助]. ～ *blessing* 天恩. *a* ～ *liar* 无故扯谎的人. ～ **contract**【法】单方面受益的契约. ～ **utility**【经】自然效用. **-ly** *ad.* **-ness** *n.*

gra•tu•i•ty [grəˈtjuːiti] *n.* ①赏金，小费. ②【军】退伍金；养老金. *No gratuities accepted.* 不收小费.

grat•u•late [ˈgrætjuleit] *vt.* 〔古〕祝，贺.

grat•u•la•tion [ˌgrætjuˈleiʃən] *n.* 〔古〕祝贺；满足.

grat•u•la•to•ry [ˈgrætjuleitəri] *a.* 〔古〕祝贺的.

grau•pel [ˈgraupəl] *n.* 【气】霰；软雹.

Grau•stark [ˈgraustɑːk] *n.* 空想中的浪漫世界，高度浪漫主义的作品.

gra•va•men [grəˈveimen] *n.* (*pl.* ～*s*, *-va•mi•na* [-ˈveiminə]) ①不平，诉苦. ②【法】控诉理由. *the* ～ *of a charge* 控诉的要点.

grave[1] [greiv] *n.* ①坟墓；墓穴；墓碑；墓石. ②死；墓地；埋葬…的地方. ③〔英方〕菜窖. ***as secret*** [***silent***] ***as the*** ～ (对秘密)守口如瓶. ***beyond the*** ～ 死后，在阴间. ***dig one's*** ～ ***with one's teeth*** 为口腹伤生. ***dig one's own*** ～ 自掘坟墓. ***dread the*** ～ 怕死. ***find one's*** ～ ***in*** (*someplace*) 死在(某处). ～ ***of reputations*** 丢脸的地方(原因). ***have*** [***with***] ***one foot in the*** ～ 一只脚在棺材里，离死不远. ***in one's*** ～ 已死. ***make sb. turn in his*** ～ 做出使死者不安的事，说出使死者不安的话. ***on this side the*** ～ 在人世间. ***silent as the*** ～ ①没有一点声音；象坟墓那样寂静. ②一言不发，守口如瓶. ***sink into the*** ～ 死. ***sb. walking across*** [***on, over***] ***my*** ～ 有人在我坟头上走动〔无故打冷颤时的迷信说法〕. ～**clothes** 〔*pl.*〕尸衣，寿衣. ～**digger** 掘墓人；【动】埋葬虫. ～ **goods** 陪葬的贵重物品. ～ **robber** 盗墓者.

grave[2] [greiv] *a.* ①重大的，重要的；严重的. ②严肃的；认真的；庄重的；沉着的；沉重的. ③(颜色等) 朴素的. ④【语】低沉的，抑音的 (*opp.* acute). *a* ～ *international situation* 严重的国际局势. *look* ～ 面孔严肃. *a* ～ *man* 沉着的人. *as* ～ *as a judge* 板着面孔. —*n.*【语】抑音〔= ～ accent〕. **-ly** *ad.* **-ness** *n.*

grave[3] [greiv] *vt.* (～*d*; ～*d, graven*) 〔古〕雕，刻；铭记 (*in; on*). *be graven on one's heart* 铭记心上. —*vi.* 雕刻.

grave[4] [greiv] *vt.* 对(船底)作清洗并涂上沥青等涂料.

gra•ve [ˈgrɑːvei] *a., ad.* 〔It.〕【乐】沉重，庄重；极慢.

grav•el [ˈgrævəl] *n.* ①〔集合词〕砂砾，砾石. ②【地】砂砾层〔尤指含有金砂者〕. ③【医】尿砂. *auriferous* ～ 含金砾，金砂. *pay* ～ 有开采价值的砂金. ***scratch*** ～ 〔美口〕飞跑；为生活奔忙. —*vt.* (〔英〕*-ll-*) ①铺石子(在路上). ②〔口〕困住，使着慌. ③(因砂粒嵌入蹄内) 使(马)跛足. ④〔美口〕使发怒，激怒. ⑤〔废〕使(船)搁浅在沙滩上. ～ *a road* 以沙砾铺路. ***be gravelled for sth.*** 因为某事感到为难. ～**blind** *a.* 几乎失明的，快瞎的. ～ **pit** 碎石坑，碎石采掘场. ～ **road** 碎石路. ～**stone** 卵石. ～**-voiced** *a.* 声音粗哑的. ～ **walk** 砂砾小路. **-ly** *a.* 砂砾多的，铺砂砾的，由砂砾形成的；【医】尿砂的.

grav•en [ˈgreivən] *grave*[3] 的过去分词. —*a.* 雕刻的，铭记在心上的，不可磨灭的. ～ *image* 雕像，偶像.

Gra•ven•hurst [ˈgreivənhəːst] *n.* 格雷文赫斯特〔加拿大市镇；白求恩大夫故乡〕.

Grav•en•stein [ˈgrɑːvenˌstain] *n.* 伏花皮(晚熟)品种苹果.

grav•er [ˈgreivə] *n.* 雕刻刀，雕刻工具；〔古〕=engraver.

Graves[1] [grɑːv] *n.* (法国)格老弗白葡萄酒.

Graves[2] [greivz] *n.* 格雷夫斯〔姓氏〕.

graves [greivz] *n. pl.* = greaves.

grave•side [ˈgreivˌsaid] *n.* 墓边. —*a.* 在墓旁的；在墓旁发生的.

grave•stone [ˈgreivˌstəun] *n.* 墓石，墓碑.

grave•yard [ˈgreivˌjɑːd] *n.* 墓地. ～ **shift** [**watch**]【矿】(由午夜零时至上午八时的)末班作业；〔美口〕夜班.

grav•ics [ˈgræviks] *n.* 重力场学.

grav•id [ˈgrævid] *a.* 妊娠中的. **-vid•i•ty** [græˈviditi] *n.* **-ly** *ad.* **-ness** *n.*

gra•vim•e•ter [græˈvimitə] *n.* 【物】①重差计，比重计. ②引力测量计.

grav•i•met•ric [ˌgræviˈmetrik] *a.* (测定)重量的；重量分析的 (=gravimetrical). **-met•ri•cal•ly** *ad.*

gra•vim•e•try [græˈvimitri] *n.* 重量[密度]测定；重量分析法；重力测量学.

grav•ing[1] [ˈgreiviŋ] *n.* 雕刻品；〔古〕雕刻.

grav•ing[2] [ˈgreiviŋ] *n.* 船底的清洗和涂油. ～ **dock** 干船坞.

grav•i•sphere [ˈgrævisfiə] *n.*【宇】(太空中某一区域的)引力范围.

grav•i•tate [ˈgræviteit] *vi.* ①受重力作用，受引力作用，自然被吸引. ②沉淀；沉降. ③倾向 (*to; towards*). *If you all* ～ *to one side, you'll upset the boat.* 如果大家都移向一边，船就要翻了. *The population* ～*s towards the town.* 人口有集中都市的倾向. —*vt.* 使受重力吸引而移动，吸引.

grav•i•ta•tion [ˌgræviˈteiʃən] *n.* ①万有引力，地心吸力. 重力. ②引力作用；吸引力；下沉；(自然的)倾向，趋势. *the law of* ～ 引力定律. *terrestrial* ～ 地球引力，*universal* ～ 万有引力.

grav•i•ta•tion•al [ˌgræviˈteiʃənəl] *a.* 【物】万有引力的，地心吸力的. ～ **collapse**【物】引力坍陷. ～ **constant**【物】引力常数. ～ **field**【物】引力场，重力场. ～ **pull** (星球等对另一物体的) 引力作用. ～ **wave**【物】引力波，重力波. **-ly** *ad.*

grav•i•ton [ˈgrævitɔn] *n.*【物】引力子.

grav•i•ty [ˈgræviti] *n.* ①认真，严肃，庄重. ②重要性，严重性；危险性. ③重量. ④【物】重力，引力，地心吸力. ⑤【乐】(音调的)低沉. *acceleration of* ～ 重力加速度. *the centre of* ～ 重心，重点. *specific* ～ 比重. *null* [*zero*] ～ 失重. ***keep one's*** ～ 持重，不苟言笑. ～ **cell** 重力电池. ～ **feed** 自重供给，自重进料〔借自身的重力作用以供给燃料、原料等〕. ～ **knife** (朝下一摔即可启开的)重力弹簧刀. ～ **meter** 重差计，比重计. ～ **wave** (液体表面的)重力波；引力场变化波.

gra•vure [grəˈvjuə] *n.* ①照相凹版，照相凹版印刷术. ②照相凹版印刷品.

gra•vy [ˈgreivi] *n.* ①肉汁，肉卤. ②〔美俚〕非法所得的钱；容易挣得的钱；额外的收益. ***by*** [***good***] ～ 〔美口〕哎呀；好家伙！ ***dip in the*** ～ 〔美俚〕分肥，揩公家的油. ～ **boat** 上肉汁用的船形盘. ～ **soup** 肉羹. ～ **train** 〔美俚〕容易捞到钱的活儿，工作清闲而报酬优厚的职务.

gray [grei] 〔美〕= grey. ～ **diplomat** 〔美俚〕灰色外交家(指军舰). ～**-flanneled** *a.* 〔美俚〕广告商的, 广告业的. **G- Lady** 〔美〕红十字会义务女护士. ～**-legs** *n.* 〔美俚〕西点军官学校的全体学员. ～ **matter** ①(脑的)灰白质. ②〔美俚〕人脑; 智力, 主意, 点子(*loan sb.* ～ *matter* 给某人出主意).

Gray [grei] *n.* ①格雷〔姓氏, 男子名〕. ②**Thomas** ～ 托马斯·格雷〔1716—1771, 英国诗人, 其名作为《墓畔哀歌》〕.

gray·ling [ˈgreiliŋ] *n.* 【动】①茴鱼. ②眼蝶科灰色〔棕色〕蝴蝶.

Gray·son [ˈgreisn] *n.* 格雷森〔姓氏〕.

Graz [grɑːts] *n.* 格拉茨〔奥地利城市〕.

graze¹ [greiz] *vi.* ①喂草, 牧放; 吃草. ②〔谑〕吃饭. — *vt.* ①使吃青草, 放牧. ②在…放牧. ～ **cattle** 放牛. ～ **a field** 把一块地用作放牧的草场. — *n.* 放牧, 畜牧; 牧草. ***send sb. to*** ～ 赶出某人.

graze² [greiz] *vt.* ①轻擦; 擦破(皮肤). ②擦过, 掠过. — *vi.* 轻轻擦过(*along; against; by*). — *n.* ①擦过, 轻触. ②擦伤. ③【军】瞬发.

gra·zier [ˈgreizjə] *n.* 〔英〕畜牧业者.

gra·zier·y [ˈgreizjəri] *n.* 畜牧业.

graz·ing [ˈgreiziŋ] *n.* ①放牧, 放牧法. ②牧场; 牧草. ～**-land** *n.* 畜牧场; 放牧地.

gra·zi·o·so [ˌgrɑːtsiˈəusəu, grɑːˈtsjəusəu] *a., ad.* 〔It.〕【乐】优美; 幽雅; 柔和.

Gr. Br(it). = Great Britain 【地】①大不列颠(岛). ②英国.

grease [griːs] *n.* ①(炼出的)动物脂, 油脂; 【机】脂膏, 滑脂; (作颜料溶剂用的)脂油; 〔古〕脂肪. ②羊毛的脂肪成分; 未脱脂羊毛. ③【兽医】马踵炎. ④〔美俚〕黄油. ⑤〔美俚〕硝化甘油, 甘油炸药. ⑥〔俚〕贿赂. *axle* ～ 轴用润滑脂. *silicon* ～ 硅脂, 硅润滑油. *wool in the* ～ 未脱脂羊毛. ***Elbow ～ gives the best polish.*** 〔谚〕苦干出好活. ***fry [stew] in one's own*** ～ 自作自受. ***in*** ～ = ***in pride [prime] of*** ～ 打猎时禽兽正肥, 正好屠宰. ***melt one's*** ～ 使完了劲. — [griːz, griːs] *vt.* ①给…涂油, 搽油; 用油弄脏; 涂油润滑. ②贿赂. ③使(马)患踵炎症. ～ ***it in*** 〔美俚〕使飞机顺利着陆. ～ ***sb.'s palm [hand]*** 用金钱影响…; 贿赂, 收买. ～ ***the fat pig [sow]*** 管闲事. ～ ***the skids for*** 〔美口〕促使…垮台. ～ ***the wheels*** 给车轮上油; 行贿使事情好办. ～**ball** 〔美俚〕①意、西、希、葡等国人血统的美国人. ②皮肤润滑的人. ～ **box** (车轴上的)润滑油箱. ～**burner** 〔美口〕厨子〔尤指做油煎食品的厨子〕. ～**bush** = ～**wood.** ～ **cup** 【机】牛油杯, 滑脂杯. ～ **gun** ①【机】滑脂枪, 注油枪. ②〔美俚〕快速发射自动手枪; M3式手提机枪. ～ **heel** 马踵炎. ～ **monkey** 〔美俚〕机械工人〔尤指汽车或飞机的检修工〕. ～ **paint** (化妆用的)油彩. ～**proof** *a.* 防油脂的, 耐油脂的, 不吸收油脂的. ～**wood** ①【植】黑肉叶刺茎藜类植物. ②黑肉叶刺茎藜 (Sarcobatus vermiculatus) 〔产于美国西部沙漠地带, 常用作饲料〕.

greased [griːzd, griːst] *a.* ①〔美俚〕灌足酒的, 醉的. ②(马)患踵炎症的. ***like*** ～ ***lightning*** 风驰电掣地.

grease·less [ˈgriːslis] *a.* 没有油脂的. **-ness** *n.*

greas·er [ˈgriːzə] *n.* ①涂油〔上油〕工人; 擦拭工人. ②加润滑脂的器具. ③(轮船的)伙夫长. ④〔美俚〕贿赂者. ⑤〔美俚、蔑〕墨西哥、拉丁美洲人血统的美国人.

greas·y [ˈgriːsi, ˈgriːzi] *a.* ①多脂的, 油脂性的, 油腻腻的; (羊毛)未脱脂的. ②油滑的; 滑的; 泥泞的. ③【海】(天气)恶劣的, 阴沉的. ④会逢迎人的, 谄媚的. ⑤【兽医】患踵炎症的. *The road is* ～ [ˈgriːzi]. 路滑. *The candle is* ～ [ˈgriːsi]. 蜡烛一燃烧便滴下油脂. ～ **grind** 〔美俚〕用功的学生. ～ **pole** (游戏用的)滑棒. ～ **spoon** 〔美俚〕下等餐馆. **-ily** *ad.* **-iness** *n.*

great [greit] *a.* ①大的, 巨大的. ②很多的; 充足的, 十足的, 非常的. ③伟大的, 杰出的; 优异的, 显著的; 贵族的, 高尚的. ④重大的; 主要的; 长久的; 强烈的. ⑤〔口〕了不起的, 绝妙的, 非常愉快的, 令人满意的. ⑥精通的, 熟悉的, 熟练的. ⑦真正的, 名副其实的. ⑧(字母)大写的. ⑨〔口〕多么…〔用在其它形容词前面, 表示惊讶, 愤怒, 轻蔑等〕. *live to a* ～ *age* 活到很大年纪. *a* ～ *chair* 靠椅. *in* ～ *detail* 十分详尽地. *a* ～ *family* 名门望族. *the* ～ *house* 村中最大富豪. ～ *ladies* 贵妇人. *the* ～ *majority* 大部分, 大多数. *a truly* ～ *man* 真正的伟人. *a* ～ *occasion* 节日, 盛典; 重大时机. ～ *pain* 剧痛. *a* ～ *play* 盛大的演出. *have a* ～ *time* 过得很愉快. *That's* ～*!* 好得很! 真了不起! ～ *toe* 拇趾=big toe. *the* ～ *unpaid* 〔英谑〕〔集合词〕无俸法官. *the* ～ *unwashed* 〔谑〕(旧社会中的)穷苦老百姓, 下层社会. *a* ～ *while (ago)* 很久(以前). *a* ～ *word among scientists* 科学家爱用的一个词. *the* ～ *world* 上流社会, 贵族社会. ***be*** ～ ***at [in]*** 〔口〕善于; 精通 (*be* ～ *at tennis* 网球打得很好). ***be*** ～ ***on*** 〔口〕①对…很熟悉的. ②热中于…的 (*be* ～ *on science fiction* 爱读科学幻想小说, 科学幻想小说迷). ***be*** ～ ***with*** ①为某种感情所激动. ②〔英古〕怀孕的 (*be* ～ *with anger* 大为生气. *be* ～ *with child* 怀孕). ***G- Big*** 〔美俚〕很大, 巨大的. ***G- God!*** [Caesar! Heavens! Scott! Snake! Sun!] 啊呀; 〔表示惊叹、谴责、惋惜等〕. ***have a*** ～ ***mind to*** 想…得不得了. ***have a*** ～ ***notion to*** 常爱想…. ***no*** ～ ***matter*** 不重要; 无关紧要. ***no*** ～ ***scratch [shakes, thing,*** 〔美俚〕 ***shucks]*** 平常得很, 没有什么了不起. ***the G- Beyond*** 来生, 来世. ***the G- Day [Assize, Inquest]*** 【宗】世界末日大审判. ***the G- Depression*** (1929年资本主义世界的)大萧条. — *n.* ①全部, 全体. ②〔通常作 the ～〕大人物, 大事. ③〔美俚〕大师, 名家. ④〔*pl.*〕〔英俚〕牛津大学学士学位考试. 〔尤指古典文学和哲学的考试〕. ***a*** ～ ***of*** 〔美口〕大部分, 许多. ～ ***and small*** 大人物和小人物; 贵贱上下. ***in the*** ～ 总括. — *ad.* 〔口〕很好地, 成功地. *Things are going* ～. 事情进展顺利. ～ ～ **cats** 狮〔虎、豹等〕. ～ **ape** 类人猿〔如大猩猩(gorilla), 黑猩猩 (Pan satyrus) 等〕. ～ **auk** 大海鸟 (Pinguinas impennis) 〔原产于北大西洋, 一八四四年后已灭绝〕. ～**-aunt** = grandaunt. **G- Basin** 美国西部大盆地. **G- Bear** 【天】大熊座. **G- Beyond** 阴间, 彼岸. **G- Bible** 一五三九年 Coverdale 译的《圣经》. **G- Britain** 大不列颠. ～ **calorie** (热量单位) 大卡. **G- Charter** 【英史】大宪章. ～ **circle** 大圆〔尤指地球表面的大圆, 即球面或地球面上通过球心的平面切成的圆〕. ～**est common divisor [factor, measure]** 【数】最大公约数. ～ **coat** 厚大衣. **G- Dane** 丹麦猛犬, 丹麦种大猎犬. **G- Divide** ①大分水岭〔尤指大陆分水岭〕. ②分界线 (*cross the G- Divide* 死). ～ **forty days** 由复活节至升天节的四十日. ～ **game** ①高尔夫球. ②间谍活动. ～**hearted** *a.* 心胸开阔的, 宽宏大量的. ～ **go** 〔英俚〕①牛津大学文学士〔数学士〕的最终考试. ②文学士〔数学士〕的课程. ～ **gross** 大罗〔量词, 等于12罗〕. ～ **horned owl** 【动】猫鸮 (Bubo virginianus) 〔产于北美, 头上有两撮黑羽毛〕. ～ **hundred** 〔英〕一百二十. ～**-nephew** = grandnephew. ～**niece** = grandniece. ～ **power** 强国, 大国. ～**-power** *a.* 强国的, 大国的. ～**-power chauvinism** 大国沙文主义. ～ **pox** 〔美俚〕梅毒. ～ **primer** 【印】十八点活字. ～ **G- Society** ①大社会〔美国总统约翰逊提出的社会福利计划〕. ②社会整体. ～**-seal** 国玺; 御玺. **G- Seal** ①英国掌玺大臣. ②〔g- s-〕国玺. ～**uncle** = granduncle. **G- Wall** 中国的万里长城. **G- War** 第一次世界大战. **G- Week** = Holy Week. **G- White Way** 不夜街〔纽约市百老汇大街的剧院区〕. ～ **year** 柏拉图年〔等于25,800年〕.

great- *comb. f.* 用在由 grand 构成, 并表示亲属关系的复合词前, 表示更远一辈的亲属关系. *a* ～*-grandfather; a* ～*-grandson.*

great·en [ˈgreitən] *vt., vi.* (使)变得更加伟大[重大].
great-grand·child [ˌgreitˈgræntʃaild] *n.* (*pl.* *-children*) 曾孙,外曾孙. (= great-grandson). ②曾孙女,外曾孙女(= great-granddaughter).
great-grand·par·ent [ˌgreitˈgrændˌpɛərənt] *n.* ①曾祖,外曾祖 (= great-grandfather). ②曾祖母,外曾祖母(= great-grandmother).
great·ly [ˈgreitli] *ad.* ①大大地,非常地. ②崇高地.
great·ness [ˈgreitnis] *n.* ①大,巨大. ②高尚;伟大.
greave [griːv] *n.* 〔常 *pl.*〕胫甲,护胫.
greaves [griːvz] *n.* 〔*pl.*〕①油渣. ②【化】金属渣.
grebe [griːb] *n.*【动】䴙䴘.
Gre·cian [ˈgriːʃən] *a.* 希腊(式)的. ★除指建筑、容貌及成语外,一般用 Greek. — *n.* ①希腊人. ②希腊语学家. ～ **bend**〔英〕1870 年前后妇女中间流行的、上身微向前屈的步行姿势. ～ **knot**〔英〕(女人脑后的)发髻. ～ **nose** 悬胆鼻,鼻梁笔直的鼻子. ～ **profile** 鼻梁笔直的脸部侧面轮廓. ～ **slippers**〔英〕东方式的拖鞋. **-ize** *vt.* 使希腊化,使具希腊特征.
Gre·cism [ˈgriːsizəm] *n.* ①希腊词语,希腊习语. ②希腊文化,希腊精神.
Gre·cize [ˈgriːsaiz] *vt., vi.* (使)希腊化; (使)有希腊风格; (把…)译成希腊语.
Gre·co- *comb. f.* 表示"希腊": *Greco*-Roman.
Gre·co-Ro·man [ˈgriːkəuˈrəumən] *a.* 属希腊和罗马的,受希腊和罗马影响的.
gree[1] [griː] *n.* 〔废〕好意. *do* [*make*] ～ 〔古〕以德报怨.
gree[2] [griː] *n.* 〔Scot.〕优越;杰出;胜利.
gree[3] [griː] *vt., vi.* (使)同意.
Greece [griːs] *n.* 希腊〔欧洲〕.
greed [griːd] *n.* 贪心,贪婪.
greed·y [ˈgriːdi] *a.* ①贪吃的. ②贪心的,贪婪的 (*for; after; of*). ③渴望的, 热望的 (*of; for*). *be* ～ *of gain* [*honours*] 贪财[名]. *be* ～ *to do sth.* 渴望[急欲]做某事. **-i·ly** *ad.* **-i·ness** *n.*
Greek [griːk] *a.* ①希腊(人)的;希腊语的;希腊式的. ②【宗】东正教的;希腊正教的. ～ *architecture* 希腊式建筑. *gay* ～*s* 快活的人,游手好闲的人. *Greekless* ～ 只根据译本进行的希腊文学研究. — *n.* ①希腊人;希腊语;具有古代希腊人精神的人; 希腊正教会成员;〔美俚〕大学生联谊会会员. ②难懂的事. ③〔主俚〕骗子. *be all* ～ *to* 不懂 (*That's all* ～ *to me.* 我完全不懂). *When* ～ *meets* ～*, then comes the tug of war.* 〔谚〕两雄相遇,其斗必烈. ～ **calends** 从不,永不 (*She will do it on the* ～ *calends.* 她决不会这样做). ～ **Catholic** ①希腊正教会成员. ②做罗马天主教礼拜仪式的正教会成员. ～ **Church** 东正教会. ～ **cross** 四臂一样长的十字架. ～ **Fathers** 希腊正教会神父. ～ **fire** (从前海战时所用的)燃烧物. ～ **fret**【建】格子细工;回纹饰. ～ **gift** 别有用心的礼物. ～ **god** 美男子. ～**-letter** *a.* (大学)联谊会的 (*～-letter fraternity* 〔美〕用希腊语字母命名的联谊会).
Gree·l(e)y [ˈgriːli] *n.* 格里利〔姓氏〕.
green [griːn] *a.* ①绿色的, 青色的. ②未成熟的; 年青的;无经验的;易受骗的,天真的. ③未加工的,未处理过的; (木材等)未干的; (酒)不陈的; (鱼)未到产卵期的; (蟹)未到脱壳期的; 未训练过的. ④新的, 新鲜的; 活生生的. ⑤活泼的,精神旺盛的,青春的. ⑥(脸色)发青的,苍白的. ⑦〔口〕妒忌的. ⑧青葱的;无雪的,温暖的 (*opp.* white). ⑨就绪的, 顺利的. ⑩反对环境污染的,主张环境保护和维持生态平衡的. *a* ～ *eye* 妒忌的眼睛. *a* ～ *wound* 未愈合的伤口. *a* ～ *old age* 老当益壮. *a* ～ *winter* 温暖的冬天. ～ *cheese* 未熟的干酪. ～ *corn* (做菜用的)嫩玉米. ～ *crop* 青菜〔*cf.* white crop, root crop〕;绿肥. ～ *duck* 子鸭. ～ *feed* [*fodder*] 青饲料. ～ *glass* 瓶料玻璃. ～ *manure* 绿肥. ～ *recollections* 记忆犹新. *as* ～ *as grass* 幼稚,无经验. ～ *in earth* 刚埋葬不久. ～ *with envy* 十分妒嫉. *in the* ～ *wood* [*tree*] 在青春旺盛的时代. *keep the memory* ～ 永记不忘. — *n.* ①绿色,青色;草地;绿色物质,绿色颜料. ②〔英〕〔*pl.*〕蔬菜;〔*pl.*〕(装饰用的)青枝绿叶;绿叶花环. ③〔口〕青春,生气. ④绿色徽章;〔*pl.*〕绿色党,爱尔兰国民党. ⑤公有草地,草坪;高尔夫球(的)终打地区(=putting ～). ⑥〔美俚〕钱;低级的大麻叶(毒品);〔*pl.*〕性交. *Do you see any* ～ *in my eye?* 你以为我可欺吗? *in the* ～ 血气方刚的,少壮时代的. — *vt.* 使成绿色;〔俚〕欺骗. — *vi.* 〔罕〕成为绿色,变绿. ～ **algae**【植】绿藻门 (*Chlorophyta*). ～**back** 美钞. ～ **bag** ①旧时律师用以装文件的绿色布袋〔小箱〕. ②律师. ～ **bean** 青豆. ～ **belt** (环城)绿化地带. **G- Berets** "绿色贝雷帽"〔美国陆军的特种部队〕. ～**-blind** *a.* 绿色盲的. ～ **blindness** 绿色盲. ～ **book** (英、意等国政府内载供讨论的提议的)绿皮书;(华盛顿)的社交名册. ～ **brier** 绿蔷薇〔美国东部产〕. ～ **card**〔美〕绿卡〔发给墨西哥等国的入境临时作工许可证. ～ **charge** 未混合的火药. ～ **G- Cloth** ①英国宫廷事务部供应局. ②〔g- c-〕赌台. ～ **cross**【军】窒息剂(绿十字毒气). ～ **dragon**【植】龙根天南星 (*Arisaema dracontium*)〔产于美洲〕. ～ **drake**【动】蜉蝣. ～**-eyed** *a.* 绿眼睛的;嫉妒的 (*the ～-eyed monster* 嫉妒). ～**finch**【动】(欧洲产的)绿黄色雀科鸣鸟. ～ **fingers**〔英口〕园艺技能. ～**fly**〔英〕绿色蚜虫. ～ **foxtail**【植】狗尾草. ～**gage**【植】青梅子,青李子. ～**goods** ①新鲜货,蔬菜. ②〔美俚〕伪钞. ～**grocer**〔英〕蔬菜水果商人,菜贩. ～**grocery**〔英〕①蔬菜水果业. ②蔬菜水果店. ③〔集合词〕蔬菜,水果. ～ **hand** ①生手,没有经验的人. ②〔方〕园艺技能. ～**heart** *n.*【植】产于热带美洲的绿心硬木. ～**-horn** 生手;未经世故的人;容易上当的糊涂虫;〔口〕新到的移民. ～**keeper** 高尔夫球场看守人. ～ **lead ore**【矿】磷铅矿,水晶矿. ～**let** *n.* = vireo. ～ **light** (交通信号)绿灯;放行,准许 (*get the* ～ *light* 获准,准予通行. *give the* ～ *light to sb.* 给某人开绿灯,纵容某人). ～ **line**【军】轰炸线;敌我分界线. ～ **man**【海】新来水手. ～ **mold** 绿霉. ～ **monkey**【动】青猴 (*Cercopithecuo sabaeus*)〔产于非洲的长尾小猴,毛色微青〕. **G- Mountain Boys** 青山军〔美国独立战争中由艾丹·爱伦组织的佛蒙特士兵〕. **G- Mountain State** 美国佛蒙特州别名. ～ **onion** 大葱,青蒜. ～ **peak**【动】绿色啄木鸟. ～ **pepper**【植】灯笼椒,青菜椒 (*Capsicum frutescens var. fasciculatum*). ～ **power** 〔美〕金钱的力量. ～ **revolution** 绿色革命〔由于粮食作物新品种的发展和农业技术的改进,引起收成的极大增长〕. ～**-room** 演员休息室;(工厂内的)原料贮存室. ～**sand**【地】海绿石砂;【机】新取砂,湿砂〔铸造用〕. ～**shank**【动】青足鹬. ～ **sea**【海】冲击船首的巨浪. ～**sick** *a.*【医】患萎黄病的;【植】患缺绿病的. ～**sickness**【医】萎黄病,绿色贫血;【植】缺绿病. ～ **soap** 绿肥皂〔治皮肤病用的一种软皂〕. ～**stick**【医】旁弯骨折. ～**stick fracture**【医】半骨折;骨裂. ～**stone**【地】粗玄岩,绿岩,软玉. ～**stuff** 蔬菜;草木. ～**sward**草地,草皮. ～**tail** *n.*【动】步鱼. ～ **tea** 绿茶. ～ **thumb** 种植技能,园艺技能. ～ **turtle**【动】绿蠵龟 (*Chelonia mydas*). ～ **vitriol**【化】绿矾. ～**weed**【植】染料木. ～**wood** 新材,生材;绿林 (*go to the ～-wood* 落草,做绿林豪客).
Green [griːn] *n.* ①格林〔姓氏〕. ②**John Richard** ～ 约翰·里查·格林〔1837—1883,英国历史家〕. ③**Julian** ～〔1900—,美国小说家〕.
Green·a·way [ˈgriːnəwei] *n.* 格里纳韦〔姓氏〕.
green·er [ˈgriːnə] *n.* ①〔俚〕新来谋事的外国人. ②生手.
green·er·y [ˈgriːnəri] *n.* ①〔集合词〕绿叶,绿树. ②= greenhouse.
green·house [ˈgriːnhaus] *n.* ①玻璃暖房,温室. ②〔军

俚〕周围有玻璃的座舱;轰炸员舱. ～ **effect** (地球大气层吸收太阳红外辐射,引起地球表面增加的)温室作用.
green·ie [ˈgriːni] *n.* 〔美俚〕绿丸〔运动员为增加气力而在赛前服用的兴奋剂〕.
green·ing [ˈgriːniŋ] *n.* ①绿化. ②青皮苹果.
green·ish [griːniʃ] *a.* 带绿色的.
Green·land[1] [ˈgriːnlənd] *n.* 格林兰〔姓氏〕.
Green·land[2] [ˈgriːnlənd] *n.* 格陵兰(岛)〔丹麦〕. **-er** *n.* 格陵兰人. **-ish** *a.*
green·ling [ˈgriːnliŋ] *n.* 【动】六线鱼〔产于北太平洋〕.
green·ly [ˈgriːnli] *ad.* ①绿色地. ②新鲜地; 旺盛地. ③不熟练地.
green·ness [ˈgriːnnis] *n.* ①绿色. ②新鲜. ③未熟练.
green·ock·ite [ˈgriːnəˌkait] *n.* 【矿】硫镉矿.
Gree·nough [ˈgriːnəu] *n.* 格里诺〔姓氏〕.
Green·wich [ˈgrinidʒ] *n.* (伦敦)格林威治 〔英国伦敦东南一市镇,为本初子午线所经过的地方〕. ～ **mean time** 格林威治平时(略作 GMT). ～ **Royal Observatory** 格林威治天文台. ～ **time** 世界标准时. ～ **Village** (美国纽约市作家、艺术家等聚居的)格林威治村.
green·y [ˈgriːni] *a.* ***(green·i·er, green·i·est)*** 〔口〕 = greenish.
greet[1] [griːt] *vt.* ①向…致敬〔意〕,向…问好;迎接,欢迎. ②(景象、声音等)映入(眼帘),收入(耳中). ～ *a distinguished guest with loud applause* 以热烈的掌声欢迎贵宾. ～ *sb. by saying "Good morning!"* 向某人说"早上好!"致意问候. *be ～ed with hisses* 被嘘. *A roaring sound ～ed his ears.* 隆隆的响声传入他耳朵. *A surprising view ～ed her eyes.* 一个奇异的景象呈现在她眼前.
greet[2] [griːt] *vi.* ***(grat*** [græt]; ***grut·ten*** [grʌtn]***)*** 〔Scot.〕哭泣,悲伤.
greet·ing [ˈgriːtiŋ] *n.* ①敬礼. ②〔常 *pl.*〕问候话,欢迎辞. ～ **card** (生日、节日等的)贺片.
greg·a·rine [ˈgregərain, -ərin] *n.* 【动】簇虫 *(Gregarinida).* — *a.* 簇虫的 (= gregarinian).
gre·gar·i·ous [greˈgɛəriəs] *a.* ①【动】爱群居的, 群居(性)的; 【植】聚生的,簇生的. ②爱社交的,集体性的. **-ly** *ad.* **-ness** *n.*
gre·go [ˈgriːgəu, ˈgrei-] *n.* (地中海东岸诸国人民所穿的)有头巾的粗布短外衣; 粗布大外衣.
Gre·go·ri·an [greˈgɔriən] *a.* 罗马教皇格利高里的. — *n.* 格利高里圣歌. ～ **calendar** (现在通用的)阳历,西历. ～ **Chant** 以教皇格利高里为名的无伴奏齐唱圣歌. ～ **style** 新历. ～ **telescope** 反射望远镜〔苏格兰数学家约翰·格利高里发明的一种望远镜〕. ～ **tones** 格利高里圣歌曲调.
Greg·o·ry [ˈgregəri] *n.* 格利高里〔姓氏,男子名〕. **G-powder** 以大黄为主的泻药.
greige [greiʒ] *n.* ①本色布,本色纱. ②灰褐色. — *a.* 灰褐色的.
grei·sen [ˈgraizn] *n.* 【地】云英岩.
gre·mi·al [ˈgriːmiəl] *n.* 【宗】(主教做弥撒时披的)膝衣.
grem·lin [ˈgremlin] *n.* 〔英军俚〕①(二次大战中传闻常和飞机捣蛋的)小妖精. ②(使事情不能顺利进行的)小捣蛋鬼. ③冲浪新手.
Gre·na·da [grəˈneidə] *n.* 格林纳达〔拉丁美洲〕.
gre·nade [griˈneid] *n.* ①手榴弹〔通常称 hand-～〕; 枪榴弹〔又名 rifle-～〕. ②灭火弹; 催泪弹. ～**-discharger [launcher]** 枪榴弹发射器.
gren·a·dier [ˌgrenəˈdiə] *n.* ①掷弹兵. ②【动】长尾鳕科深海鱼. ③(南非)织布鸟属的鸟. ***G-s*** 英国近卫步兵第一团〔又称 **G- Guards**〕.
gren·a·dine[1] [ˈgrenədiːn] *n.* 五香小牛肉,五香鸡.
gren·a·dine[2] [ˈgrenədiːn] *n.* ①(做窗帘用的)薄纱; 紧拈细丝线. ②杂质品红.
gren·a·dine[3] [ˈgrenədiːn] *n.* 石榴汁.
Gren·fell [ˈgrenfel] *n.* 格伦费尔〔姓氏〕.
Gren·ville [ˈgrenvil] *n.* 格伦维尔〔姓氏〕.
Gresh·am [ˈgreʃəm] *n.* ①格雷沙姆(格雷欣)〔姓氏〕. ②**Thomas** ～ 托马斯·格雷欣〔1519—1570,英国财政学家〕. ～**'s law** 【经】格雷欣法则〔劣币驱逐良币的法则〕.
gres·so·ri·al [greˈsɔːriəl] *a.* 【动】(鸟类等的脚)适于步行的.
Gret·a [ˈgretə], **Gretch·en** [ˈgretʃən] *n.* 女子名〔Margaret 的爱称〕.
grew [gruː] grow 的过去式.
grey, 〔美〕 **gray** [grei] *a.* ①灰色的,灰白的,本色的. ②灰暗的,阴沉的,阴暗的. ③灰白头发的; 衰老的; 老练的,成熟的. ④古代的,古老的,太古的. ⑤【经】半黑市性质的. ⑥(人)匿名的,无法查明身分的. ⑦(教士)穿灰色衣服的. ⑧界限不明的, 介于两者之间的. ～ *experience* 老练. ～ *hair* 灰白头发. ～ *hairs* 〔喻〕老年. ～ *iron* 灰口铁. ～ *sister* = ～ friar sister. *the ～ past* 古代. — *n.* ①灰色,鼠色. ②灰色颜料; 灰色动物(特指马); 灰色衣服; 本色布. ③微明,黎明; 黄昏; 阴冷的光. ④〔黑人俚〕白人. *the ～ of the morning* 黎明. *be dressed in ～* 穿着灰色服装. ***in the ～*** (布)未加漂白. ***the (Scots) Greys*** (骑青灰马的英国)苏格兰龙骑兵第二团. — *vt., vi.* (使)变成灰色. ～ **area** 〔英〕灰区〔指就业率颇低,但并非低至可供政府特别补助的区域〕. ～**-back** *n.* 灰背类动物〔鸟类、鱼类、鲸类等中任何背带灰色者, 如小鲛、鳐类、鸭等〕. ～**beard** *n.* ①白胡子老人. ②石制大酒壶. ③【植】灰色地衣. ～ **cells** = ～ matter. ～ **cloth** 本色布. ～**coat** *n.* 〔英〕①穿灰衣服的人. ②(英国昆布兰郡的)义勇骑兵. ～ **collar** 灰领职工(指服务与维修性行业职工). ～ **drake** 【动】灰蜉蝣. ～ **eminence** 心腹人物; 暗中掌权的人 = eminence grise. ～**fish** 【动】绿鳕,星鲨. ～ **friar** 方济各会 (Franciscan) 修道士. ～ **goods** 本色布. ～ **goose** 【动】灰雁. ～**-haired,** ～**-headed** *a.* 白头的; 老的; 老练的 *(in)*; 古老的. ～ **hen** 【动】黑琴鸡. ～**lag** *n.* = ～ goose. ～ **mare** 比丈夫强的妻子, 雌老虎. ～ **matter** ①(脑的)灰质. ②头脑. ③智力. ～ **mullet** 【动】鲻鱼. ～ **sister** 方济各会女修道士. ～ **squirrel** 灰松鼠 *(Sciunis carolinensis)* 〔原产于美国〕. ～**stone** 【地】灰色火山岩, 玄武石. ～ **wacke** 硬砂岩, 杂砂岩. ～ **whale** 【动】灰鲸 *(Eschrichtins glancus)* 〔产于北太平洋,黑色带白斑〕. ～ **wolf** 【动】灰狼 *(Canis lubus)* 〔产于北半球北部, 特性是群出觅食〕.
Grey [grei] *n.* 格雷〔姓氏〕.
grey·cing [ˈgreisiŋ] *n.* 〔英口〕 = greyhound-racing.
grey·hound [ˈgreiˌhaund] *n.* ①(身体瘦长、善于赛跑的狗)灵猩. ②远洋快轮. ～ **racing** 赛狗,跑狗.
grey·ish [ˈgreiiʃ] *a.* 带灰色的.
grey·ly [ˈgreili] *ad.* 灰; 晦暗地.
grey·ness [ˈgreinis] *n.* 灰色,本色.
grib·ble [ˈgribl] *n.* 【动】蚀船虫,船蛆〔能在水下蛀坏船只的一种蛀虫〕.
grid [grid] *n.* ①格子,格栅. ②(蓄电池的)铅板. ③【无】栅级. ④铁道网; 【电】电力网; 〔英〕(全国) 高压输电网; 电(视)台网. ⑤〔美俚〕橄榄球场; 橄榄球. ⑥地图的坐标方格; (照相排字机的)字格. ⑦(烘烤面包等用的)铁篦子. ～ **bias** 栅偏压. ～ **circuit** 栅极电路. ～ **current** 栅(极电)流. ～ **leak** 【电】栅漏.
grid·der [ˈgridə] *n.* 〔美俚〕橄榄球运动员.
grid·dle [ˈgridl] *n.* ①(烤饼用的)烤盘. ②〔美〕薄烤饼 (= ～ cake). ③【矿】(选矿用的) 筛子, 大孔筛. — *vt.* ①用烤板烤. ②筛. ～**-hot** *a.* 刚出笼的,刚做成的.
gride [graid] *vi.* 嘎吱嘎吱地切〔刮、擦、轧〕 *(along; through).* — *n.* 擦刮声,轧轧声.
grid·i·ron [ˈgridˌaiən] ①(烧鱼肉等有柄的)烤架,铁丝格子. ②【海】格子船台,船架. ③(舞台上承受升降布景装置的) 梁格结构. ④栅形补偿摆 (= ～ pendu-

lum). ⑤格状物,格状结构. ⑥〔美俚〕美国国旗. ⑥〔美俚〕橄榄球场;橄榄球. ⑦(停货车等的)侧道〔= ~ siding〕;高压输电网. ***be on the*** ~ 受迫害,受苦. ***lay sb. on the*** ~嘲笑,取笑某人.

grief [gri:f] *n.* ①悲伤,忧伤,伤心事;〔美口〕困难,麻烦. ②痛苦,不幸,灾难. *bring sb. to* ~ 使受伤;使失败,使陷悲境. *come to* ~ 受伤;受欺负;出毛病,失败;遭难. *die of* ~ 气死. ***Good [Great]*** ~ 哎呀!〔表示惊奇,惊恐等的惊叹语〕. ***smile at*** ~ 不过度悲伤,达观.

grief-strick·en [ˈgri:fˌstrikn] *a.* 忧伤的;极为悲痛的;悲伤的.

griev·ance [ˈgri:vəns] *n.* ①不平,不满. ②抱怨,牢骚;冤苦悲叹. ③〔罕〕伤害;苦难. *nurse (hare) a* ~ *against sb.* 怀恨某人,不满某人. *pour out* ~ 诉苦. ***rip up old*** ~***s*** 重提旧怨.

grieve[1] [gri:v] *vt.* 使悲伤,使忧伤,使痛心. —*vi.* 悲伤,悲叹 *(at; for; over; about)*.

grieve[2] [gri:v] *n.* 〔方〕农场管理者,监工.

griev·ous [ˈgri:vəs] *a.* ①悲痛的,痛苦的. ②可叹的;痛心的. ③〔古〕极恶的. ④剧烈的,严重的,难忍的. *a* ~ *crime* 罪大恶极. *a* ~ *cry* 痛哭. *a* ~ *fault* 重大过失. ~ *news* 噩耗. ~ *pain* 剧痛. **-ly** *ad.*

griff [grif] *n.* = griffin[2].

griffe[1] [grif] *n.* 〔美〕黑白混血儿.

griffe[2] [grif] *n.*【建】虎爪饰〔用于立柱基础处的装饰〕.

grif·fin[1] [ˈgrifin] *n.* ①【希神】鹫头飞狮. ②看守者. ③(年青女子的)陪媪. ④【动】秃鹰类. ***the G-*** 伦敦的鹫头飞狮纪念碑.

grif·fin[2] [ˈgrifin] *n.* ①〔印〕新来的欧洲人,生手. ②〔美俚〕= griffe[1].

Grif·fin [ˈgrifin] *n.* 格里芬〔姓氏〕.

Grif·fith(s) [ˈgrifiθ(s)] *n.* 格里菲斯〔姓氏〕.

grif·fon [ˈgrifən] *n.* ①=griffin[2]. ②体格结实的比利时种小狗. ③粗毛短绒的长头猎狗. ~ **vulture** 秃头鹫.

grift [grift] *n.* 〔俚〕骗人行为. — *vt.* 〔俚〕诈骗.

grift·er [griftə] *n.* 〔俚〕赌棍,骗子,小偷.

grig [grig] *n.* 〔方〕①蟋蟀;蚱蜢. ②〔英〕小鳗. ③轻松愉快的人. ***as merry [lively] as a*** ~ 非常快活.

Gri·gnard reagent [gri:ˈnjɑ:d ri:ˈeidʒənt]【化】格林亚试剂.

gri·gri, gree·gree [ˈgri:gri] *n.* 〔美南部〕黑人的呪文〔崇拜物〕.

grill [gril] *n.* ①烤架,铁丝格子. ②炙烤的肉类食物. ③ = grill-room. ④ = grille. ***put sb. on the*** ~〔美〕严刑审讯某人. — *vt.* ①(在烤架上)炙烤. ②〔美〕使受酷热;用炙烤来折磨. ③〔美口〕(警察)严厉盘问. ④〔美橄榄球〕训练. ⑤用条花邮戳盖消(邮票). —*vi.* ①受烤,受炙. ②〔美口〕受严厉盘问. ~**room** *n.* 烤肉处;(供应烤肉的)小餐厅,小饭店.

gril·lage [ˈgrilidʒ] *n.* (软地上作建筑物基础的)格排垛,格床.

grille [gril] *n.* ①格栅,铁格子. ②(银行出纳台上的)格子窗. ③(养鱼的)孵卵器.

grilled [grild] *a.* ①装有栅格的. ②在烤架上烤的;焙的.

grilse [grils] *n.* *(pl.* ~*)*【动】幼鲑.

grim [grim] *a.* ①严厉的,冷酷的,残忍的. ②坚强的,不屈的. ③可怕的;讨厌的. ④不祥的,邪恶的. ~ *courage* 坚韧不拔的勇气. *a* ~ *smile [laugh]* 狞笑. *the* ~ *reality* 冷酷的现实. *a* ~ *war* 残酷的战争. ***hold on like*** ~ ***death*** 死不放手. **-ly** *ad.* **-ness** *n.*

gri·mace [griˈmeis] *n.* 愁眉苦脸;(做作出来的)怪相;鬼脸. ***make*** ~***s*** 作怪相. — *vi.* 皱着眉头,作怪相.

gri·mal·kin [griˈmælkin] *n.* ①老雌猫. ②心毒的老太婆.

grime [graim] *n.* 尘垢,灰尘;(道德上的)污点. — *vt.* (灰尘等)弄脏. **Grimes Golden** (晚秋品种)黄色苹果.

Grimm [grim], **Jakob Ludwig Karl** 雅可伯·路德维奇·卡尔·格林〔1785—1863〕, **Wihelm Karl** 威廉·卡尔·格林〔1786—1859〕〔两兄弟. 德国语言学家,童话作家〕.

grim·y [ˈgraimi] *a.* ***(grim·i·er; -i·est)*** 积满污垢的,肮脏的. **grim·i·ly** *ad.* **grim·i·ness** *n.*

grin [grin] *n.* (因苦痛或愤怒)龇牙咧嘴;露着牙齿笑. *sardonic* ~ 冷笑. ***on the (broad)*** ~ 笑嘻嘻,露齿而笑. —*vi.* 露出牙齿 *(with)*;露着牙齿笑 *(at)*. ~ ***and bear it*** 苦笑着忍受,逆来顺受. ~ ***like a cheshire cat*** 咧着嘴傻笑.

grind [graind] *vt.* ***(ground*** [graund],〔罕〕~***ed)*** ①磨碎;碾成 *(into)*;转动,推摇(磨等). ②磨快,磨光,磨薄. ③用手摇风琴演奏. ④折磨,虐待,使苦恼. ⑤〔口〕刻苦学习,苦心教授. ⑥咬牙;嘎吱嘎吱地擦. ~ *balls for bearings* 磨轴承滚珠. ~ *one's teeth* 磨牙齿,咬牙切齿. ~ *sb. in Latin* 教某人苦学拉丁语. — *vi.* ①碾;碾碎,磨碎;可磨. ②苦干,苦学*(at; for; up)*. ③摩擦得嘎嘎响. ④(跳舞时)扭摆屁股. *The truck ground to a stop.* 卡车嘎的一声刹住. *Though the mills of God* ~ *slowly, yet they* ~ *exceeding small.* 〔谚〕天网恢恢,疏而不漏. ~ *away at English studies* 刻苦钻研英语. ~ ***down*** 碾碎;折磨,虐待 *(be ground down by poverty* 受穷苦的折磨). ~ ***gerunds*** 〔美口〕在学校教书. ~ ***one's heel into*** 把脚跟踩进(砂等中). ~ ***out*** ①碾成. ②单调地演奏手摇风琴. ③苦吟(诗句). ~ ***the faces of the poor*** 压榨贫民. ~ ***up*** 碾成粉,擂碎. ***have an ax(e) to*** ~ 别有私图. — *n.* 碾,磨,碾声,磨声,摩擦声,研细的程度. ②苦差使,枯燥的工作;刻苦,用功. ③〔美〕刻苦用功的学生. ④〔美俚〕开玩笑,讥讽;开玩笑的人. ⑤〔英〕步行锻炼;越野障碍赛马〔赛跑〕. *a greasy* ~〔美俚〕埋头读书的学生. *the daily* ~〔口〕日常工作.

grin·de·li·a [grinˈdi:ljə, -ˈdi:liə] *n.*【植】胶草 *(Grindelia camporum)*〔茎和叶可作药用〕.

grind·er [graində] *n.* ①磨工. ②磨的上段;上磨扇;臼齿;〔*pl.*〕〔口〕牙齿. ③研磨机,粉碎机,磨床. ④〔口〕用功学生;为人作考试准备的教师. ⑤〔美方〕夹心面包. *cylindrical* ~ 外圆磨床. *high-precision* ~ 高精度磨床. *percussion* ~ 撞碎机. *swinging* ~ 摇摆研磨机. *universal internal* ~ 万能内圆磨床. ***take a*** ~ 把左手拇指按在鼻头上,用右手在胸前作出磨磨的样子以表示嘲笑. ~**'s asthma**【医】磨工气喘,因吸入灰屑所致的肺部疾患.

grind·er·y [ˈgraindəri] *n.* ①磨工车间. ②〔英〕革制品用具〔原料〕 ~ **warehouse** 皮鞋用具店.

grind·ing [ˈgraindiŋ] *a.* ①磨的,适合于磨的. ②折磨人的;难熬的. ~ *toothache* 难忍的牙痛. ~ *poverty* 赤贫. ~ *tyranny* 暴政. — *n.* 粉碎,研磨;磨擦;〔口〕填鸭式教. ~ **machine** 磨床. ~ **wheel** 砂轮. **-ly** *ad.*

grind·stone [ˈgraindstəun] *n.* 磨石;【机】砂轮形磨石. ***hold [keep] one's [sb.'s] nose to the*** ~ 不断折磨自己〔某人〕,使自己〔某人〕埋头辛苦地劳动.

grin·go [ˈgriŋgəu] *n.* *(pl.* ~*s)* 〔蔑〕外国佬(尤指在拉丁美洲的英国人和美国人).

grin·ner [ˈgrinə] *n.* 露着牙齿笑的人,龇牙咧嘴的人.

grin·ning [ˈgriniŋ] *a.* 露齿而笑的,龇牙咧嘴的. **-ly** *ad.*

grip[1] [grip] *n.* ①紧握,抓牢;握法;(互相道贺时的)亲密握手;(秘密团体等的)握手暗号. ②【机】柄,夹,把手. ③吸引力;掌握,支配,控制. ④理解力. ⑤〔美〕手提包,旅行包;〔美剧〕道具管理员,布景管理员. ⑥痉挛;流行性感冒. *cable* ~ 电缆扣. *vice* ~ 虎钳夹口. *wedge* ~ 楔形夹. *a bulldog* ~ 紧握不放. ***be at*** ~***s*** 互相揪着,搏斗. ***be at*** ~***s with*** 勉力对付 *(be at* ~*s with the subject.* 钻研问题). ***be in the*** ~ ***of*** 被…支配. ***come [get] to*** ~***s*** *(with)* 揪扭,扭在一起;开始努力对付. ***have a good [poor]*** ~ ***on a situation*** 善于

〔不会〕掌握形势. ***have a ~ on an audience*** 掌握听众心理,能吸引观众. ***lose ~ of one's audience*** 使听众扫兴. ***lose one's ~*** 放手. — *vt.* (*~ped,* 〔古〕 ***gript*** [gript]) ①握住,牢牢抓住; 吸住(注意力). ②(机器等)扣住,煞住. ③领会,了解,把握. ~ **brake** 手刹车.

grip² [grip] *n.* = grippe.

grip³ [grip] *n.* 〔英〕小阳沟.

gripe [graip] *n.* ①紧握,抓牢; 掌握; 支配. ②〔*pl.*〕〔口〕肠绞痛,腹绞痛. ③不平,愤怒. ④把手,柄. ⑤【机】离合器,制动器. ⑥船首添材,屈曲部前材; 〔*pl.*〕艇索,绊带. ***come to ~s*** 互相揪扭. ***in the ~ of*** 被抓牢; 在…掌握中的,在…把持下的. — *vt.* ①握紧,捉牢; 扭紧. ②使肠痛. ③〔美俚〕激怒,使苦恼,压迫. — *vi.* ①抓牢. ②肠痛. ③〔美俚〕诉苦,发牢骚. ④【海】逆风开行.

grip·er ['graipə] *n.* 〔美俚〕爱发牢骚的人.

grippe [grip, gri:p] *n.* 〔F.〕【医】流行性感冒.

grip·per ['gripə] *n.* ①握者. ②夹具; 【机】抓器,抓爪.

grip·ping ['gripiŋ] *a.* ①抓的,夹的. ②引人注意的,扣人心弦的. *a ~ story* 扣人心弦的故事. ~ **device** 【机】夹具,固定器. **-ly** *ad.* **-ness** *n.*

grip·ple [gripl] *a.* 〔英方〕吝啬的; 贪婪的.

grip·sack ['gripsæk] *n.* 〔美〕手提包,旅行包.

gript [gript] *v.* 〔古〕grip 的过去式及过去分词.

gri·saille [gri'zeil] *n.* 〔F.〕浮雕式灰色装饰画〔画法〕; (玻璃等上的)纯灰色画.

Gri·sel·da [gri'zeldə] *n.* ①格里塞尔达〔女子名〕. ②温顺的女人.

gris·eo·ful·vin [ˌgrizi:əu'fulvin] *n.* 【药】灰黄霉素.

gris·e·ous ['grisiəs, 'griz-] *a.* 灰色的(特指珠灰色的).

gri·sette [gri'zet] *n.* 〔F.〕(法国的)女工,女店员.

gris-gris ['gri:gri:] *n.* (*pl.* ~) 格哩格哩〔伏都教的一种符箓、咒文、咒语〕.

gris·kin ['griskin] *n.* 〔英〕(猪腰部的)五花肉.

gris·ly ['grizli] *a.* (相貌)可怕的; 〔口〕讨厌的. **-i·ness** *n.*

grist [grist] *n.* ①制粉用谷类; 谷粉; 酿造用麦芽; 一次所碾的谷; 一次所磨的粉. ②〔美〕大量,许多. ③有利的东西. ***All is ~ that comes to his mill.*** 〔谚〕到他磨里的东西全会变成粉,他善于利用一切机会〔事物〕. ***bring ~ to the mill*** 有利,能赚钱. ***~ to [for] sb.'s ~*** 对…有利的东西. **~mill** 磨坊.

gris·tle ['grisl] *n.* (牛等的)软骨. ***in the ~*** 骨头还软的,未成熟的.

gris·tly ['grisli] *a.* 软骨质的; 软骨状的; 由软骨形成的. **-tli·ness** *n.*

grit [grit] *n.* ①粗砂,砂砾,砂粒. ②=~stone. ③〔口〕刚毅,坚韧,勇气. *a hone of good ~* 优质磨石. *Americans of the true ~* 道地的美国人. ***hit the ~*** 〔美俚〕走路,跋涉. ***put (a little) ~ in the machine*** 破坏正常工作,捣乱. — *vi.* 发轧轧声. —*vt.* ①轧,研磨,摩擦. ②在…上铺砂砾. ~ *the teeth* 咬牙. **~stone** 粗(角)砂岩,天然磨石.

grits [grits] *n. pl.* 〔用作单或复〕①粗碾小麦〔谷类〕; 去壳但未碾制的燕麦. ②〔美〕玉米片; 玉米粥.

grit·ty ['griti] *a.* ①粗砂质的,砂多的; 砂砾的. ②刚强的,勇敢的,坚韧不拔的. **-ti·ly** *ad.* **-ti·ness** *n.*

griv·et ['grivit] *n.* 〔F.〕素领猴 (*Cercopithecus aethiops*) 〔一种产于非洲的长尾猴〕.

griz·zle¹ ['grizl] *vi.* 〔英口〕①烦恼,烦躁. ②(小孩)啼哭,使人烦躁的哭泣.

griz·zle² ['grizl] *vi., vt.* (使)成灰色. — *a.* 灰色的. — *n.* ①灰白头发,灰色假发. ②灰色,有灰色光斑的色调. ③灰色(或有灰白花斑的)图案〔动物〕. ④含硫次煤. ⑤烧得不透的砖,灰色次砖.

griz·zled ['grizld] *a.* ①灰色的,灰白的; 斑白的. ②灰白头发的.

griz·zly ['grizli] *a.* 灰色的,带灰色的; 灰色头发的. — *n.* ①灰熊(= ~ bear). ②【矿】格筛.

grm. = gram(s).

groan [grəun] *vi.* ①哼,呻吟,发呻吟声. ②苦恼,烦闷 (*beneath; under; with*). ③渴望 (*for*). — *vt.* 哼着说 (*out*); 用不满意的呻吟声反对. *~ing board* 摆满菜肴的桌子. ~ *under the heavy tax* 在重税下痛苦呻吟. *The shelf ~s with books.* 书架堆满书而嘎吱作声. ~ ***sb. down*** 发哼哼声阻止某人讲话. ~ ***inwardly*** 内心痛苦. — *n.* 呻吟,呻吟声; 哼声.

groat [grəut] *n.* ①(英国从前的)四便士银币. ②小额,少量. ***not care a ~*** 毫不介意. ***not worth a ~*** 一文不值.

groats [grəuts] *n.* 〔*pl.*〕去壳的谷粒; 去壳并弄成碎片的燕麦〔小麦,大麦等〕.

gro·cer ['grəusə] *n.* 食品商,杂货商. **~'s itch** (因长期接触螨类引起的)皮炎.

gro·cer·y ['grəusəri] *n.* ①〔美常用 *pl.*〕食品,杂货. ②食品杂货业. ③〔美〕食品杂货店; 〔美南部〕小酒馆.

gro·ce·te·ri·a [ˌgrəusə'tiəriə] *n.* (由顾客自行取货后到柜台付款的)食品杂货自助商店.

grog [grɔg] *n.* ①掺水烈酒. ②(喝掺水烈酒的)饮酒会. ③【冶】耐火材料,熟料,陶渣. *half and half ~* 酒水各半的淡酒. — *vi.* 喝掺水烈酒. — *vt.* 用热水注入(空酒桶)浸出一点酒. ~ **blossom** 酒糟鼻子. ~ **brick** 耐火砖. **~shop** *n.* 〔英〕(低级)小酒馆.

grog·ger·y ['grɔgəri] *n.* 〔古〕小酒馆.

grog·gy ['grɔgi] *a.* ①〔古〕喝醉酒的. ②不稳的,摇摇晃晃的. ③(马等)脚步不稳的; 踉踉跄跄的. ④〔美口〕头昏眼花的. **-gi·ly** *ad.* **-gi·ness** *n.*

grog·ram ['grɔgrəm] *n.* ①丝和马海毛〔羊毛〕的混纺的粗织物. ②丝毛混纺的衣服.

groin [grɔin] *n.* ①【解】腹股沟,鼠蹊. ②【建】穹棱,拱肋,交叉拱. ③= groyne (*n.*) — *vt.* ①使成穹棱,在…上盖拱肋. ②= groyne (*vt.*).

grok [grɔk] *vt., vi.* (***grokked, grok·king***) 〔美俚〕(由于移情作用而)透悉〔彻悟〕.

Gro·lier ['grɔ:liə] *a.* 法国十六世纪藏书家格罗里 (Grolier de Servières) 的. ~ **binding** 有金丝交错的美丽考究的装订.

grom·met ['grɔmit] *n.* ①【海】索眼,索环. ②金属孔眼. ③【机】垫圈; 【电】橡皮套管.

grom·well ['grɔmwəl, -wel] *n.* 【植】紫草 (*Lithospermum officinale*).

groom [grum, gru:m] *n.* ①马夫. ②新郎 (= bridegroom). ③英国王宫侍从官. ④〔古〕男仆. — *vt.* ①喂(马),刷(马). ②修饰,使整洁. ③〔美〕培训; 推荐(候选人). *an impeccably ~ed woman* 打扮得十分干净的妇女. *be ~ed as a presidential candidate* 被推荐作总统候选人. *be well [badly] ~ed* 修饰得整洁〔不整洁〕. — *vi.* 进行修饰. **~'s cake** (宝塔形的)结婚蛋糕.

grooms·man ['grumzmən] *n.* (*pl.* ***-men***) (在婚礼上)陪伴新郎者,伴郎,男傧相(又叫 bestman).

groove [gru:v] *n.* ①槽,沟; 车辙; 沟纹,纹道. ②常规,成规,惯例. ③最佳状态,得心应手的状态; 使人愉快的东西,适合能力和兴趣的职位; 合适的位置. ④【解】(器官、骨的)沟; 【印】(铅字末端的)槽; 【建】企口. *nail ~* 【解】甲沟. *oil ~* (润滑)油槽. *His mind works in a narrow ~.* 他心地狭隘. ***fall [get] into a ~*** 落入老一套,习惯于老一套. ***in the ~*** ①得心应手,处于最佳状态. ②(歌曲等)流行的; 完美的. ③合时,赶时髦. — *vt.* ①在…作槽; 在…挖沟. ②〔美俚〕灌(唱片). ③〔美俚〕高度欣赏; 使感到愉快. — *vi.* 〔美俚〕极度享受. **~d pulley** 【机】槽轮. **-less, -like** *a.*

groov·er ['gru:və] *n.* 挖槽者,挖槽工具,挖槽机.

groov·y ['gru:vi] *a.* ①沟的,槽的. ②常规的,千篇一律的. ③最佳状态的,〔美俚〕绝妙的. ④(歌曲等)流行的. **-i·ness** *n.*

grope [grəup] *vi.* ①(暗中)摸索. ②探索 *(after; for)*. ~ *about for information* 到处搜集情报. ~ *for a clue* 找线索. — *vt.* 用手摸索. ~ *one's way* 摸着走;摸索解决办法.

grop·ing·ly [ˈgrəupiŋli] *ad.* 摸索着;暗中摸索一样地.

gros·beak [ˈgrəusbiːk] *n.*【动】锡嘴雀;蜡嘴雀.

gro·schen [ˈgrəuʃən] *n.* *(pl. -schen)* ①格罗升〔奥地利货币和硬币名,等于一先令的1/100〕. ②格罗升〔德国曾使用过的一种币面价值多种的小银币〕.

gros de Lon·dres (或 ***lon·dres***) [grəu də ˈlɔːndrə]【纺】伦敦横棱绸.

gros de Naples [grəu də nɑːpl]〔F.〕(意大利那不勒斯产)厚重丝织物.

gros·grain [ˈgrəusgrein] *n.*【纺】厚斜纹绸,罗缎.

gross [grəus] *a.* ①粗壮的,肥大的;魁伟的. ②显著的;严重的;恶劣的. ③浓厚的,稠密的;茂盛的. ④粗劣的,粗糙的;油腻的. ⑤感觉迟钝的,不敏感的;(不用显微镜)肉眼看得见的. ⑥粗俗的,粗鲁的,下流的. ⑦总的,全体的;毛重的 *(opp.* net*)*. ⑧世俗的,肉体的. *a* ~ *blunder [error]* 严重的错误. *a* ~ *body* 肥壮的身体. ~ *darkness* 一团漆黑. *a* ~ *fog* 浓雾. ~ *income* 总收入. ~ *industrial output value* 工业总产值. ~ *losses* 毛损. ~ *proceeds* 总货价收入. ~ *profit* 毛利,总利润. ~ *sales* 销售总额. ~ *vegetation* 茂盛的草木. — *n.* ①总额,全部. ②〔*sing., pl.*〕罗 (=12 打). ***a great*** ~ 十二罗 (=1728个). ***a small*** ~ 十打 (= 120个). ***by the*** ~ 按罗;整批,全数;大量. ***in*** ~【法】绝对独立的. ***in (the)*** ~ ①大体上,一般地. ②批发,整批. — *vt.*〔口〕(未扣除各项费用之前)总共赚得. ~ **dynamics** 一般动力学. ~ **feeder** ①喜欢吃粗糙或油腻食物的人. ②大量耗用肥料的植物. ~ **national product** 国民总产值〔简称GNP〕. ~ **ton** ①长吨;英吨 (=2,240 磅). ②(船的)总吨位. ~ **weight** (包括容器、包装等在内的货物)毛重. **-ly** *ad.* **-ness** *n.*

gross·er [ˈgrausə] *n.*〔美俚〕赚钱的作品(如电影等).

gros·su·lar·ite [ˈgrɔsjulərait] *n.*【地】钙铝榴石.

Gros·venor [ˈgrəuvnə] *n.* 格罗夫纳〔姓氏〕.

grosz [grəuʃ] *n.* *(pl.* ***grosz·y*** *[-i])* 格罗希〔波兰货币名和硬币名,等于一兹罗提 *(zloty)* 的1/100〕.

grot [grɔt] *n.*〔诗〕= grotto.

Grote [grəut] *n.* 格罗特〔姓氏〕.

gro·tesque [grəuˈtesk] *a.* ①奇异的,奇形怪状的;怪诞的,可笑的. ②风格特殊的. — *n.* ①奇形怪状的人〔物,图形等〕;(文学、艺术上的)奇异风格;风格奇异的作品. ②〔英〕【印】粗黑体字〔美国称 gothic〕. **-ly** *ad.* **-ness** *n.*

gro·tes·quer·ie, gro·tes·quer·y [grəuˈteskəri] *n.* ①奇形怪状的东西. ②奇特,怪诞.

grot·to [ˈgrɔtəu] *n.* *(pl.* ~***es,*** ~***s)*** ①洞穴. ②(人工开挖的用于避暑或娱乐的)洞室.

grouch [grautʃ] *n.*〔美口〕①牢骚,怨气. ②脾气坏的人. — *vi.*〔美口〕闹别扭,发牢骚.

grouch·y [ˈgrautʃi] *a.* 脾气坏的,爱闹别扭的.

ground[1] [graund] grind 的过去式及过去分词. — *a.* 碾碎了的,磨过的,磨成粉的. ~ and polished piston【机】研磨活塞. ~ **glass** ①磨砂玻璃,毛玻璃. ②微粒玻璃,玻璃粉. ~ **rice** 米粉.

ground[2] [graund] *n.* ①地,地面;土地,地产;场;运动场,广场;〔*pl.*〕庭园,场地. ②底;水底,海底;【矿】脉石,母岩;矿区;〔*pl.*〕渣滓,沉淀物. ③基础;〔常 *pl.*〕理由,根据,原因;借口;立场,意见. ④地域,范围,面积;土壤. ⑤阵地. ⑥【美】底子;底色;〔*pl.*〕【建】底材;(铜版术)(涂在版面上的)防蚀剂. ⑦【电】接地;地线. ⑧【海】= groundage. *a classic* ~ 文物胜地,古迹. *fishing* ~*s* 渔场. *grazing* ~*s* 牧场. *a parade* ~ 练兵场,阅兵场. *a parking* ~ 停车场. *recreation* ~*s* 运动场. *weapons proving [testing]* ~*s* 武器试验场. *coffee* ~*s* 咖啡渣. *What* ~ *have you for thinking so?* 你有什么理由这样想? *The* ~ *here is stony.* 这里的地面多石. *a blue pattern on white* ~ 白地蓝花纹. ***above*** ~ 活着,在世上. ***beat over the old*** ~ 旧调重弹. ***be dashed to the*** ~ 一败涂地,遭受挫折. ***be off the*** ~站在一边,不妨碍. ***be on the*** ~ ①在场. ②在地上. ③在决斗. ***below*** ~ 死掉,被埋葬. ***bite the*** ~ 大败,倒下,死去. ***break fresh [new]*** ~ 开垦处女地,开辟新天地. ***break*** ~ ①耕田;破土,动工,开业. ②【海】开船. ***bring to the*** ~〔方〕埋葬. ***broken*** ~ 新开垦土地,凸凹不平之地. ***come [go] to the*** ~ 失败;灭亡. ***common*** ~ 共同立场,一致点 *(seek common* ~ *while reserving differences* 求同存异*)*. ***cover (the)*** ~ ①走完一段路程,旅行. ②包括,涉及(*The report covers much* ~. 报告涉及面很广). ③(工作)有所进展;充分地处理(某个题目). ***cut the*** ~ ***from under sb.'s feet*** 拆某人的台,破坏某人计划;使某人议论站不住脚. ***debatable*** ~ ①发生争执的土地. ②争论点. ***(down) to the*** ~〔口〕在各方面,彻底地. ***fall on stony*** ~ 无效,没有结果. ***fall to the*** ~ 坠地;失败,成画饼. ***forbidden*** ~ 禁区. ***from the*** ~ ***of one's [the] heart*** 出自心底,衷心地. ***from the*** ~ ***up*** ①从头开始,从基本点着手. ②〔美〕= down to the ~. ***gain [gather, get]*** ~ 占领阵地;占优势;流行;有进步,获得进展. ***gain*** ~ ***on [upon]*** ①压制,侵占. ②逼近,接近. ***gain*** ~ ***with sb.*** 同某人搞熟. ***get*** ~ ***of*** ①蚕食. ②优于. ③甩开(追者). ***get off the*** ~ ①飞起,进行顺利. ②(报刊等)开始发行,(事业等)着手干开,开始. ***give*** ~ = lose ~. ***go to*** ~ (狐狸)逃入地穴. ***Hit the*** ~***!***【军】卧倒! ***hold [keep, maintain, stand] one's*** ~ ①坚守阵地. ②坚持主张;站稳立场. ***jumping-off*** ~【军】进攻基地,据点,战略基地. ***kiss the*** ~ 匍伏;屈辱. ***lose*** ~ 退却,让步;失利;衰落. ***mop [wipe] the*** ~ ***with sb.***〔俚〕击倒某人,打某人打得一败涂地. ***on delicate*** ~ 处境微妙. ***on even*** ~ 在同样基础上. ***on firm*** ~ 处于安全地位. ***on one's own*** ~ 在行. ***on the*** ~***(s) of*** 由于,根据,以…为理由〔借口〕. ***raze to the*** ~ 夷为平地. ***run into the*** ~ ①做得过头,夸张. ②把事情弄糟. ***shift one's*** ~ 改变主张,改变立场. ***smell the*** ~ 船因水浅而失速;船擦底. ***suit down to the*** ~ 完全适合,完全令人满意. ***take*** ~ 占领阵地. ***take the*** ~ 搁浅. ***to*** ~ 进洞,躲起来. ***touch*** ~ ①船擦水底. ②触及实质性问题. ***tread on delicate*** ~ 接触微妙问题,碰到棘手问题. ***tread the*** ~ 步行,走路. ***worship the*** ~ ***sb. treads on*** 十分钦佩某人,拜倒在某人脚下. — *vt.* ①在…基础上树立,把(论据等)放在…基础上,给…打基础 *(on; in)*. ②教给…基本知识,使…受初步训练 *(in)*. ③把…放在地上,使落地;放下(武器). ④【电】使接地. ⑤【美】给…上底色. ⑥使搁浅. ⑦使停飞〔停驶等〕. ***be*** ~***ed on*** 以…为基础,根据. ***be well [ill]*** ~***ed in*** 在…方面很有〔没有〕基础〔根据〕. ~ *arms*放下武器,投降. *The boat was* ~*ed.* 船搁浅了. *I* ~*ed my argument on my own experience.* 我的论点是以自己的亲身经验为依据的. — *vi.* ①有基础. ②【海】搁浅;【空】着陆. ~**-air** *a.* 陆空的. ~**-air communication** 陆空通讯联络. ~ **alert**【空】地面待命,(军事机场的)戒备状态. ~ **antenna** 地面天线. ~ **ash**【植】白腊树幼树,白腊树手杖. ~ **bait** 投饵〔投到水底的鱼饵〕. ~ **bass**【乐】基础低音. ~ **beetle**【动】步行虫〔一种在山岩下生活的昆虫,夜出捕食其它小虫子〕. ~ **box** (花坛镶边或用作篱围用的)矮脚黄杨. ~**-breaker** 创始者,改进者. ~ **bridge** (沼地上)木棒铺成的路. ~ **cherry**【植】酸浆属 (Physalis) 植物〔如:灯笼果 (P. Peruviana);酸浆 (P. Alkekengi);毛酸浆 (P. Prainosa)〕. ~ **circle** (齿轮的)基圆. ~ **coat** 底涂层. ~ **colour** 底涂色. ~ **control**【空】地面控制,地面制导设备. ~ **control approach** (恶劣气候下由雷达引导的)地面控制进场. ~ **cover**【植】①地被植物. ②(森

林中幼树以外的)矮小植物. ～ **crew** 【空】地勤人员. ～ **echo** 地面回波. ～ **effect** (航空器接近地面飞行时升力增加的)地面效应. ～ **effect machine** 气垫船. [车]. ～ **fertilizer** 基肥. ～ **fir**【植】石松属 (Lycopodium) 植物〔如:卷柏状石松 (L. Selago) 和王柏 (L. Obscurum)〕. ～ **fire** 地面(对空)火力. ～**fish** 底栖鱼类. ～ **floor** ①〔英〕楼房底层 (=〔美〕first floor). ②有利地位,优先机会 (*get in on the ～ floor* 取得有利地位). ～ **fog** 靠近地面的晨雾. ～ **game**〔英〕猎兽[鹿、兔等]. ～ **gripper** = ～ crew. ～ **hemlock**【植】加拿大紫杉 (Taxus canadensis)〔产于美国东北〕. ～ **hog**【动】美国土拨鼠. ～ **hog day**〔美〕二月二日圣烛节〔传说土拨鼠于该日结束冬眠出洞〕. ～ **ivy**【植】欧亚活血丹. ～ **landlord**〔英〕房产地主. ～ **level** ①地平面. ②= ～ state. ～**line** 基线,地平线. ～ **link-up** 空降部队与地面部队的会合. ～ **loop**【空】地转〔飞机滑行时因失去控制而引起的猛烈旋转〕. ～**man** 球场管理员. ～**mass** *n.*【地】基质. ～ **meristem**【植】基本分生组织. ～ **mine** 海底水雷. ～ **net** 曳网,拖网. ～ **note**【乐】基音,基础低音. ～**nut**【植】①有可食块茎的植物;可食块茎. ②落花生. ～ **observer**【军】地面观察员,对空监视哨. ～ **pea** 落花生. ～ **pine**【植】扁叶石松. ～ **personnel** = ～ crew. ～ **plan** ①平面图;底层设计图. ②初步计划,根本计划. ～ **plane** (透视画中的)地平面. ～**-plane antenna** 水平极化天线. ～ **plate**【电】接地板. ～ **plum**【植】粗果黄芪 (Astragulus crassicarpus). ～ **rent** 地租. ～ **return**【电】地回路,地面反射. ～ **rule** ①【棒球】场(地)规则,【体】球场规则. ②为任何一项活动制定的一套规则. ～ **sea** (飓风和地震引起的)海啸. ～ **sheet** 铺在地上的防潮布. ～**(s) keeper** (运动场地、田庄、墓园等的)看管. ～**(s)man** = ～(s)keeper. ～ **speed**【空】(飞机的)对地速度. ～ **squirrel**【动】黄鼠属(Citellus) 动物. ～ **staff**〔英〕①= ground crew. ②全体职业板球运动员. ～ **state**【物】(原子的)基态. ～ **swell** ①= ～ sea. ②【地】地隆. ③数量、程度、力量等的突然大幅度增长. ～**-test** *vt.* 对(飞机、火箭等)作地面试验. ～**-to-air** = surface-to-air. ～**-to-**～ = surface-to-surface. ～ **torpedo** 海底水雷. ～ **troops** 地面部队. ～ **water** 地下水,潜水. ～ **wave**【电】地波. ～ **wire**【电】地线. ～**work** 基础,基本成分,基本原理. ～ **zero**【军】(核)爆心投影点;(炸弹的)着地点.

ground·age [ˈgraundidʒ] *n.*〔英〕船舶进港费,停泊费.

ground·ed [ˈgraundid] *a.* ①有基础的,根深蒂固的. ②【电】接地的. ～ **antenna** 接地天线. ～ **base** 基极接地. ～**-base transistor** 共基极晶体管. ～ **collector** 共集极接地. ～ **emitter** 发射极接地. ～ **grid** 接地栅极,抑制栅极. **-ly** *ad.* **-ness** *n.*

ground·er [ˈgraundə] *n.*【棒球】(沿地面跳滚的)滚地球 (= ～ ball).

ground·ing [ˈgraundiŋ] *n.* ①(画,刺绣等的)底子. ②基础训练;初步. ③【海】搁浅. ④【电】接地.

ground·less [ˈgraundlis] *a.* 没有根据的,没有理由的. **-ly** *ad.* **-ness** *n.*

ground·ling [ˈgraundliŋ] *n.* ①栖息地上[地下]的动物;栖息水底的鱼;匍匐植物. ②剧场中廉价座位的观众;缺乏鉴赏力的人. ③在陆地上生活[工作]的人 (*opp.* one in aircraft).

ground·sel[1] [ˈgraunsl] *n.*【植】千里光,金色千里光.

ground·sel[2] [ˈgraundsəl], **ground·sill** [-sil] *n.*【建】作基础的木材,木结构的最下部分,地槛.

group [gruːp] *n.* ①群;批,簇. ②集团,团体,小组. ③【化】基,团,组;(周期表的)属,族. ④(雕塑等的)群像. ⑤【地】界. ⑥(英、美的)空军大队. ⑦〔G-〕【宗】牛津团契. *a ～ of people* 一群人. *the grain ～* 谷类. *blood ～* 血型. ***a ginger ～*** 要求政府采取坚决行动的议员,起推动作用的政党骨干小组. ***a pressure ～***〔美〕(对国会等施加影响的)压力集团. ～ ***by*** ～ 分批地. ***in a ～ = in ～s*** 成群地. — *vt.* ①集合,使成一团 (*with*). ②组合,配合 (*together*). ③把…分类. —*vi.* 成群;聚集,类集. ～ **captain**〔英〕空军上校. ～ **commander** 空军大队长. ～ **formation**【军】大队编队(飞行). ～ **insurance** 集体人寿保险. ～ **leader** 小组长. ～**let**〔美〕小群. ～ **medicine** ①医生会同用药;集体制药. ②集体用药. ～ **mind**【心】团体心理. ～**psychology** 群众心理学. ～ **representation** 职业代表制〔不同于区域代表制〕. ～ **theory**【数】群论. ～ **therapy** [psychotherapy]【医】集体治疗,心理治疗〔把同病患者编组,指导他们互相诉说苦恼,互相批评,解除精神负担〕. ～**think** *n.* 小集团思想〔指集体内成员在思想观点上的一致〕. ～ **velocity**【物】波群速度. ～ **work** 社会团体福利工作〔组织社会团体开展文化娱乐等活动〕.

group·er [ˈgruːpə] (*pl.* ～*(s)*) ①【动】鮨科鱼. ②〔G-〕【宗】牛津团契成员. ③〔美俚〕参加集体淫乱活动的人.

grou·pie [ˈgruːpi] *n.*〔美俚〕追随歌星的青年女子;明星倾慕者.

group·ing [ˈgruːpiŋ] *n.* ①集团. ②【统】归组. *tactical* ～【军】战斗编组.

grouse[1] [graus] *n.* (*pl.* ～)【动】松鸡. *a black* ～ 黑琴鸡. *a hazel* ～ 榛鸡. *a red* ～ 红松鸡.

grouse[2] [graus] *vi.*〔英俚〕发牢骚,抱怨. —*n.* ①委屈,不平,牢骚话. ②爱发牢骚的人.

grous·er[1] [ˈgrausə] *n.* ①(拖拉机等的)履带齿片. ②(稳定钻机、船只等用的)临时桩.

grous·er[2] [ˈgrausə] *n.* 爱发牢骚的人.

grout[1] [graut] *n.* ①【建】薄胶泥,薄浆,石灰浆. ②〔英〕〔常 *pl.*〕渣滓. — *vt.*【建】给…灌浆. ～**ing machine** 水泥搅拌机.

grout[2] [graut] *vt., vi.* (猪)用鼻子拱(泥土等).

grout·y [ˈgrauti] *a.*〔方〕暴躁的,易怒的,脾气不好的;抑郁的,含怒的,不高兴的.

grove [grəuv] *n.* 小树林,树丛,园林. *an orange* ～ 一片小橘林. **-less** *a.* 无树林的.

grov·el [ˈgrɔvl] *vi.* ①趴,匍匐. ②卑躬屈节. ～ ***in the dust [dirt]*** 趴在地上;摇尾乞怜.

grov·el(l)·er [ˈgrɔvlə] *n.* ①趴着的人. ②卑躬屈节的人.

grov·el(l)·ing [ˈgrɔvliŋ] *a.* ①趴着的. ②奴颜婢膝的. **-ly** *ad.*

Grover [ˈgrəuvə] *n.* 格罗弗〔男子名〕.

Grove(s) [grəuv(z)] *n.* 格罗夫(斯)〔姓氏〕.

grov·y [ˈgrəuvi] *a.* 树丛的,林木的.

grow [grəu] *vi.* (***grew*** [gruː]; ***grown*** [grəun]) ①生长;成长,发育;发芽,茁长. ②长大,增加;变强. ③〔后接形容词、副词、成语等〕渐渐变得. ④形成,产生. *Great oaks from little acorns* ～.〔谚〕万丈高楼平地起. ～ *weary* 变疲乏. ～ *old [rich]* 变老[富]. — *vt.* 培育,栽培;培养,发展;使发达. ～ *a beard* 留胡子. ～ *roses* 种玫瑰. ～ ***down [downwards]*** 变小;减少. ～ ***in*** 增加 (～ *in beauty [strength, wisdom]* 增加美丽[力量、智慧]). ～ ***in [into]*** 长成. ～ ***on [upon]*** ①(感觉、习惯等)加深对…的影响 (*The smoking habit grew on me.* 我渐渐有烟瘾了). ②(书、画等)渐渐把人迷住,渐渐使人爱好 (*The picture ～s on him.* 他渐渐爱起那张画来). ～ ***out*** 出芽,发芽. ～ ***out of*** ①抛弃;戒除. ②长大而穿不上衣服. ③源出,来自,起因于 (～ *out of bad habits of his boyhood days* 戒除幼时的坏习惯. *The book grew out of a series of lecture.* 这书是由一系列讲稿编写而成的. *Soon, she grew out of her clothes.* 不久,她便长得高大而穿不上原先的衣服了). ～ ***together*** 长合,愈合. ～ ***up*** 长大,成人;发生,滋长. ～ ***up like mushrooms*** 象雨后春笋般地增长.

grow·a·ble [ˈgrəuəbl] *a.* 可种植的.

grow·er [ˈgrəuə] *n.* ①(以某种特殊方式生长的)…植物. ②种植者,栽培者,饲养者. *a fast [slow]* ～ 早熟[晚

熟]植物. *a cotton* ～ 棉农. *a livestock* ～ 饲养员.

grow·ing [ˈgrəuiŋ] *n.* 成长,发育,发达. — *a.* ①成长中的;发育中的;发育旺盛的;增长中的. ②促进发育的,适于生长的. ～ **pains** ①【医】发育性痛,发身期痛〔青少年的一种关节痛〕;发育期感情上的失去平衡. ②(企业等)早期发展过程中经历的困难. ～ **point**【植】生长点. ～ **season** 生长期. ～ **weather** 促进谷物生长的气候. **-ly** *ad.*

growl [graul] *n.* (动物,人,雷等的)低沉的怒吼,隆隆声;咆哮;不平. — *vi.* 嗥叫,咆哮 *(at)*;怒吼;鸣不平;(雷)发隆隆声. — *vt.* 咆哮着说,发牢骚地说 *(out)*.

growl·er [ˈgraulə] *n.* ①嗥叫的动物;咆哮的人. ②〔英俚〕四轮马车. ③小冰山. ④【电】短路线圈测试仪,电机转子试验装置. ⑤〔美俚〕啤酒罐. ***rush the*** ～〔美俚〕①带着酒具到酒店打酒. ②大量喝酒.

growl·er·y [ˈgrauləri] *n.* ①嗥叫(声);咆哮;轰鸣(声). ②发牢骚的地方,私室.

growl·ing [ˈgrauliŋ] *a.* 狺狺叫的,咆哮的;隆隆响的. **-ly** *ad.*

grown [grəun] grow 的过去分词. — *a.* ①已成长的,成熟的. ②被…长满的. *a well-*～ *tree* 生意盎然的大树. *a* ～ *man* 成年人. *a grass-*～ *place* 一处长满青草的地方. ～**-up** *n.* 成年人.

growth [grəuθ] *n.* ①生长,成长,发育,发展. ②栽培,培养. ③生长物,产物;【医】瘤,赘生物. ④【经】(资本价值与收益的)预期增长. *a* ～ *of weeds* 杂草丛生. *evil* ～*s* 弊病. ***of foreign*** ～ 外国培植的. ***of home*** ～ 本国培植的. ***of one's own*** ～ 自己栽培的. ***reach full*** ～ 充分发育,成熟. ～ **centre** 培训中心. ～ **factor**【生】生长因子,生长因素〔食品里促进正常发育的有机体〕. ～**fund** 发展基金(投资公司). ～ **industry** 发展特快的新行业. ～ **rate** 生长率,增长率.

groyne [grɔin] *n.*【建】防波堤,折流坝. — *vt.* 给(海滩等)筑防波堤.

grub [grʌb] *vt.* ①掘出(树根,树桩等),掘除 *(up, out)*. ②费力查出,找出(记录等). ③〔俚〕养活,供给吃住. — *vi.* ①挖地;(掘除树根等)开地. ②尽心查找 *(for)*. ③做苦工,孜孜从事 *(along, away, on)*. ④〔俚〕吃. ～ *up weeds* 根除杂草. ～ *about among records* 翻查记录. — *n.* ①【动】蛆蛴螬. ②做苦工的人,穷苦文人. ③邋遢人. ④〔俚〕食物. ⑤板球中的滚球. ～ **ax(e) [hoe, hook]** 鹤嘴锄. ～ **saw** 锯石头用的手锯. ～ **screw** 无头〔平头〕螺丝,木螺丝. **Grub Street** ①(伦敦的)格拉布街〔以前英国穷苦文人集居的街道,即现在的弥尔顿街〕. ②〔集合词〕穷文人;廉价小说. ～**street** *a.* 穷文人的,低级作品的.

grub·ber [ˈgrʌbə] *n.* ①掘树根的人〔工具〕;【农】碎土机. ②作苦工的人.

grub·by [ˈgrʌbi] *a.* ①生蛆的. ②污秽的,邋遢的. ③卑鄙的. **grub·bi·ly** *ad.* **grub·bi·ness** *n.*

grub·stake [ˈgrʌbsteik] *vt.* 〔美方〕(以分其所获物为条件)供给(探矿者)以资金、衣物、伙食. — *n.* ①(供给探矿者的)资金[物品]. ②贷款. **-r** *n.* 贷款者.

grudge [grʌdʒ] *vt.* ①羡慕,嫉妒. ②吝惜,不愿给. ～ *the time* 爱惜时间. *I* ～ *going.* 我不想去. *I* ～ *his going.* 我不愿意他去. — *vi.* ①嫉妒. ②〔古〕鸣不平. — *n.* 怨恨,妒嫉;恶意. ***bear [owe] sb. a*** ～ 对某人怀恨在心. ***hold [have] a*** ～ ***against sb.*** 怀恨某人.

grudg·ing [ˈgrʌdʒiŋ] *a.* 吝啬的,不愿的;勉强的;怀恨的. *a* ～ *praise* 勉强的赞扬. *be* ～ *of money* 吝啬,一钱如命. **-ly** *ad.*

grue [gruː] *vi.* 〔方〕(因害怕或寒冷而)发抖,战栗. — *n.* ①一阵战栗. ②可怕的性质[影响]. ③〔Scot.〕一点,一粒. ④〔Scot.〕薄浮冰,雪.

gru·el [gruəl,gruil] *n.* ①麦片粥,稀糊. ②〔英口〕严厉的惩罚. ***get [have, take] one's*** ～〔古〕受重罚;被击败;被处死. ***give sb. his*** ～〔口〕给予严重惩罚;击败;处死某人,干掉某人. — *vt.* (〔英〕***-ll-***) 重罚;使极度疲劳.

gru·el·(l)ing [ˈgruəliŋ] *n.* 痛打,惩罚. — *a.* 使极度疲劳的,激烈的.

Gru·en·ther [ˈgrʌnθə] *n.* 格仑瑟〔姓氏〕.

grue·some [ˈgruːsəm] *a.* 可怕的,令人毛骨悚然的. **-ly** *ad.* **-ness** *n.*

gruff [grʌf] *a.* ①态度生硬的,粗暴的;脾气坏的. ②声音粗哑的. ***as*** ～ ***as a bear*** 粗暴,粗卤. **-ly** *ad.* **-ness** *n.*

gruff·ish [ˈgrʌfiʃ] *a.* ①有点粗暴的,有点生硬的. ②(声音)有点粗哑的.

grum [grʌm] *a.* ***(grum·mer; grum·mest)***〔罕〕忧郁的,沉闷的.

grum·ble [ˈgrʌmbl] *vi.* ①鸣不平,发牢骚,诉委屈 *(at; about; over)*. ②咕哝,嘟囔. ③(雷等)隆隆响. — *vt.* ①抱怨 *(out)*. ②嘟囔地说出. ～ *one's complaint* 发牢骚. — *n.* ①不平;怨言. ②(雷等的)隆隆声. **grum·bly** *a.*

grum·bler [ˈgrʌmblə] *n.* 爱发牢骚的人.

grum·bling·ly [ˈgrʌmbliŋli] *ad.* 喃喃抱怨着,嘟嘟囔囔地.

grume [gruːm] *n.* ①【医】凝块. ②黏液.

grum·met [ˈgrʌmet, -it] *n.* = grommet.

gru·mous [ˈgruːməs] *a.* ①【植】成聚团颗粒的. ②象血块一样的;象黏液的.

grump [grʌmp] *n.* ①〔常 *pl.*〕一阵坏脾气,发火. ②脾气坏的人. — *vi.* 抱怨,嘀咕,发牢骚.

grump·ish [ˈgrʌmpiʃ] *a.* = grumpy.

grump·y [ˈgrʌmpi] *a.* 性情粗暴的,脾气坏的. **-i·ly** *ad.* **-i·ness** *n.*

Grun·dy [ˈgrʌndi] *n.* 〔常作 **Mrs. G-**〕心胸狭窄、拘泥礼俗、事事好挑剔他人的人〔原为 Tom Morton 所作喜剧 "Speed the Plough" (1798) 中的人物,其邻居 Dame Ashfield 事事怕她挑剔,以致谨小慎微〕. ***offend one's*** ～ 伤害一般人的感情. ***What will Mrs.*** ～ ***say?*** 别人会怎样说呢?

Grun·dy·ism [ˈgrʌndiizəm] *n.* (因害怕他人挑剔而谨小慎微的)拘泥礼节;因袭主义.

grun·ion [ˈgrʌnjən] *n.* ***(pl.*** ～***(s))***【动】叫嗓鱼 *(Leuresthes tenuis)*〔产于美国加利福尼亚海岸〕.

grunt [grʌnt] *vi.* ①(猪等)作咕噜声,喉鸣. ②发哼声,咕哝〔表示不满,不同意,疲劳等〕. — *vt.* 咕哝着说出 *(out)*. — *n.* ①(猪等的)哼声. ②咕哝,牢骚. ③〔美俚〕电气线路工助手. ④〔美俚〕猪肉. ⑤= grunter. ⑥〔美军俚〕步兵,海军陆战队〔越南战争中用语〕.

grunt·er [ˈgrʌntə] *n.* ①象猪一样哼的动物. ②【动】石鲈. ③哼哼的人,咕哝的人. ④〔美俚〕摔跤运动员.

grunt·ing [ˈgrʌntiŋ] *a.* 呼噜的,咕哝的. ～ **ox**【动】牦牛(= yak). **-ly** *ad.*

grunt·ling [ˈgrʌntliŋ] *n.* 小猪.

gru·yère [gruːˈjɛə] *n.* (瑞士)格里尔干酪.

gr. wt. = gross weight 毛重.

gryph·on [ˈgrifən] *n.* = griffin[1].

grys·bok [ˈgraisbɔk] *n.*【动】南非产灰色小羚羊.

Gs. = guilders.

gs. = guineas.

G.S. = ①General Secretary 总书记,秘书长. ②General Service 普通勤务. ③General Staff 总参谋部. ④Girl Scout〔美〕女童子军. ⑤ground speed.

g.s. = ①grandson. ②ground speed.

GSC = General Staff Corps【军】参谋团.

G.S.O. = General Staff Officer〔英〕(陆军)参谋部参谋.

G-string [ˈdʒiːstriŋ] *n.* ①【乐】小提琴的 G 弦. ②(系在腰上遮盖外阴部的)兜裆布〔为美洲印第安人和脱衣舞表演者所穿用〕.

G-suit [ˈdʒiːˌsjuːt] *n.* (飞行员或宇航员的)抗超重飞行衣,抗过载飞行衣(亦作 gravity suit 或 anti-G suit).

GSV = guided space vehicle 制导航天器.

G.T. = gross ton.

GT = Gran Turismo 高级跑车.
gt. = ①gilt. ②great. ③*gutta.*
g.t. = gilt top【印】天金.
Gt.Br.; Gt.Brit. = Great Britain ①大不列颠(岛). ②英国.
G.T.C., g.t.c. = good till cancelled, or countermanded【商】取消(定货)前有效.
gtd = guaranteed.
GTP = Guanosine triphosphate【化】三磷酸鸟苷.
gua·ca·mo·le [ˌgwɑːkəˈməulei] *n.* 色拉调味酱汁.
gua·cha·ro [ˈgwɑːtʃəˌrəu] *n.* *(pl. ~s)*【动】油鸱 *(Stealornis caripensis)*〔产于南美,为夜游飞禽,肉可食,油可点灯〕.
gua·co [ˈgwɑːkəu] *n.*【植】马兜铃属植物〔美洲热带地方所产的一种可治蛇毒的树〕.
Gua·da·la·ja·ra [ˌgwɑːdɑːlɑːˈhɑːrɑː] *n.* 瓜达拉哈拉〔墨西哥城市、西班牙城市和省名〕.
Gua·de·loupe [ˌgwɑːdəˈluːp] *n.* 瓜德罗普(岛)〔法〕〔拉丁美洲〕.
guai·ac [ˈgwaiæk] *n.*【植】①神圣愈疮木 (Guaiacum sanctum); 愈疮木 (Guaiacum officinale). ②= guaiacum.
guai·a·col [ˈgwaiəˌkəul,-ˌkɔl] *n.*【化】媾甲氧基苯酚,愈疮木酚.
guai·a·cum [ˈgwaiəkəm] *n.*【植】愈疮木属木材.
Guam [gwɑːm] *n.* 关岛〔西太平洋〕. **Guam·a·ni·an** [gwɑːˈmiən] *n.* 关岛人.
guan [gwɑːn] *n.*【动】冠雉〔产于中南美,以果类为食物〕.
gua·na [ˈgwɑːnɑː] *n.* = iguana.
gua·na·co [gwəˈnɑːkəu] *n.* *(pl. ~s)*【动】(南美安第斯山区野生的)红褐色美洲驼.
gua·nay [gwəˈnai] *n.*【动】冠鸬鹚 *(Phalacrocorax bougainvillii)*〔产于秘鲁和智利,该地鸟粪主要来源于这种鸟〕.
gua·neth·i·dine [guəˈneθidiːn] *n.*【药】胍乙啶.
guan·i·dine [ˈgwɑːnidiːn, -din] *n.*【化】胍. ~ **nitrate** 硝酸胍.
gua·nine [ˈgwɑːniːn] *n.*【化】鸟嘌呤,鸟尿环.
gua·no [ˈgwɑːnəu] *n.* ①(秘鲁产)海鸟粪,鸟粪石. ②鱼肥;人造氮肥. — *vt.* 在…上施鸟肥[鱼肥].
Guan·tá·na·mo [gwɑːnˈtɑːnɑːməu] *n.* 关塔那摩〔古巴城市〕.
guar [gwɑː] *n.*【植】瓜尔豆 *(Cyamopsis tetragonoloba)*〔产于美国西南部,作饲料用〕.
guar. = guarantee(d).
Gua·ra·ní [ˌgwɑːrɑːˈniː] *n.* ①*(pl. -nis, -ni)* 瓜拉尼人〔居住在巴拉圭河和大西洋之间的南美印第安人〕. ②瓜拉尼语. ③〔g-〕*(pl. -nis)* 瓜拉尼〔巴拉圭货币单位,等于100分〕.
guar·an·tee [ˌgærənˈtiː] *n.* ①保证;担保. ②保证人〔法律上用 guarantor〕. ③接受保证的人. ④抵押品,担保物. *Offer one's house as a ~* 以房屋作抵押. ***stand ~ for*** 做保人. — *vt.* ①保证,担保. ②〔口〕包,管保. *I ~ his success.* 我包他成功. ***be ~d against [from] loss*** 保证不受损失. ~ ***sb. against [from] a risk*** 保证某人不出危险. ~ **fund** 保证基金. ~ **engineer** 造船公司派在新船上进行观察,以便随时作机件修整的工程师.
guar·an·tor [ˌgænrənˈtɔː] *n.*【法】保证人.
guar·an·ty [ˈgærənti] *n.*【法】①保证;保证书. ②抵押品,担保物. ③= guarantor. — *vt.* = guarantee. ~ **money** 保证金. — *vt.* = guarantee.
guard [gɑːd] *n.* ①警卫;警戒;看守. ②防卫者;看守者;哨兵, 卫兵,[集合词]警卫队;〔the G-〕(英国等的)皇家禁卫军;【海】护航舰. ③防护装置;(车的)挡泥板;(枪的)保险;(刀、叉、剑等柄上的)护板. ④(击剑,拳击等的)防护姿势,防护术. ⑤〔英〕列车员 (=〔美〕conductor); (列车上的)司门员,制动手. ⑥(篮球、足球等的)卫、后卫. *the advance [rear] ~* 前[后]卫. *life ~* 救生员. *mud ~* 挡泥板. ***catch sb. off (his) ~*** 乘某人不备. ***come off ~***【军】离防,下防. ***drop [lower] one's ~*** 丧失警惕. ***get past sb.'s ~*** 冲破某人的防御. ***~ of honour*** 仪仗队. ***Imperial G-*** 警卫兵. ***keep [mount, stand] ~*** 站岗,守卫,放哨. ***keep sb. under close ~*** 把某人置于严密监视下. ***off one's ~*** 疏忽,不提防. ***on ~*** 值班,当班;提防着. ***on one's ~*** 警戒,提防. ***put [throw] sb. off his ~*** 使某人不提防. ***put [set] sb. on (his) ~*** 使某人提防. ***relieve [change] ~*** 接防站岗,换岗. ***row the ~*** 用小船在军舰周围巡逻. ***run the ~*** 偷过哨兵线. ***stand ~ over*** 派人看守. ***stand [be, lie] on [upon] one's ~*** 警戒,提防. ***the Life Guards***〔英〕禁卫骑兵第一、第二团. ***the Royal Horse Guards***〔英〕禁卫骑兵第三团. — *vt.* ①防守,警卫,守卫. ②看守,监视. ③给…加保护装置;对…进行校正检查. ④谨慎使用(言词等). ⑤【医】对…配用矫正剂. *~ a fortress* 防守要塞. *~ one's reputation* 维护自己的名誉. *The lunatic was carefully ~ed.* 对疯子严加看守. — *vi.* ①防卫,警惕,预防 *(against)*. ②警卫,看守. ③(击剑时)取守势. ~ *against disease* 预防疾病. ~ **boat** 警戒艇;巡逻艇. ~ **book** (钉线上衬有厚线条的)剪贴簿,相片簿. ~ **cell**【植】保护细胞. ~ **chain** 表链. ~ **duty**【军】警卫职务. ~ **flag**【军】(警戒舰的)值班旗. ~ **hair**【动】保护鬃毛. **~-house** =~room. ~ **mount** 卫兵交班礼. **~-officer**【军】联络官. **~-rail** (铁道)护轨;栏杆. ~ **ring** 护圈;防止戒指脱落的指环. **~room** ①卫兵室,警卫室. ②禁闭室. ~ **ship** 警戒舰. ~ **tent** 岗篷.
guard·ant [ˈgɑːdnt] *a.*【纹】兽面为正面而兽身为侧面的.
guard·ed [ˈgɑːdid] *a.* ①被保护着的. ②被看守着的. ③谨慎的. *a ~ answer* 谨慎的回答. *The warehouse is ~.* 库房有人看守. **-ly** *ad.* **-ness** *n.*
guard·ee [ˈgɑːdiː] *n.*〔英口〕衣冠楚楚的卫兵.
guard·er [ˈgɑːdə] *n.* 守卫者,卫兵;看守人[物].
guard·i·an [ˈgɑːdjən, -iən] *n.* ①保护者,保卫者,保管者,管理员. ②【法】监护人 *(opp.* ward*)*. ③方济各修道院院长. ④【英史】贫民救济委员. ⑤〔G-〕(用于报刊名)卫报. ~ ***ad litem*** (未成年被告的)诉讼监护人. — *a.* 守护的. ~ **angel** 守护天使. ~ **deity** 守护神. ~ **saint** 守护圣徒.
guard·i·an·ship [ˈgɑːdjənʃip] *n.* 保护,守护;监护人的职责[身分]. ***under the ~ of*** 在…保护下.
guard·less [ˈgɑːdlis] *a.* 无警戒的,无保护的.
guards·man [ˈgɑːdzmən] *n.* *(pl. -men)* ①卫兵,哨兵. ②〔英〕禁卫军官兵;〔美〕国民警卫队员.
Guar·ne·ri [gwɑːˈneriː]〔It.〕瓜奈里家族〔意大利克雷莫纳的小提琴制造家族〕.
Guar·ner·i·us [gwɑːˈneriəs] *n.* 瓜奈里小提琴.
Gua·te·ma·la [ˌgwætiˈmɑːlə] *n.* ①危地马拉〔拉丁美洲〕. ②危地马拉(城)〔危地马拉首都〕(=~ City).
Gua·te·ma·lan [ˈgwætiˈmɑːlən] *a.* 危地马拉的,危地马拉人的. — *n.* 危地马拉人.
gua·va [ˈgwɑːvə] *n.*【植】番石榴.
Guay·a·quil [ˌgwaiəˈkiːl] *n.* 瓜亚基尔〔厄瓜多尔港市〕.
gua·yu·le [gwɑːˈjuːl] *n.* ①【植】(美洲热带的)银胶菊. ②银菊胶〔银胶菊的脂,可作橡胶代用品〕.
gu·ber·na·to·ri·al [ˌgjuːbənəˈtɔːriəl] *a.* ①统治者的;地方长官的;总督的. ②〔美〕州长的.
guck [gʌk] *n.*〔俚〕浓胶黏性物质.
gud·dle [ˈgʌdl] *vt., vi.*〔Scot.〕(用手在溪边石缝里)摸(鱼). **-r** *n.*
gudg·eon[1] [ˈgʌdʒən] *n.* ①【动】鮈鱼〔作鱼饵用〕. ②容易受骗的人,傻子. ③饵,诱饵.

gudg•eon[2] [ˈgʌdʒən] *n.*【机】①耳轴. ②舵枢.
Gue•bre, Gue•ber [ˈgiːbə, ˈgei-] *n.* 拜火教徒.
guel•der-rose [ˈgeldəˈrəuz] *n.*【植】荚蒾, 绣球花(= snowball).
Guelph, Guelf [gwelf] *n.* 中世纪意大利的教皇党员〔参看 *Ghibelline*〕.
Guen•e•vere [ˈgwenəviə] *n.* 格纳维尔〔女子名〕.
gue•non [gəˈnəun] *n.*〔F.〕长尾猴属 *(Cercopithecus)* 动物〔包括青猴 *(C. sabaeus)*; 黑长尾猴 *(C. aethiops)*〕.
guer•don [ˈgəːdən] *n.*〔诗〕报酬, 奖赏. — *vt.*〔诗〕酬劳, 奖赏. **-less** *a.* 无报酬的.
gue•ri•don [ˈgeridən] *n.*〔F.〕作摆设的小桌子.
Guern•sey [ˈgəːnzi] *n.* ①(英国海峡中的)耿济岛 (Isle of ~). ②耿济种乳牛. ③〔g-〕黑色厚毛线衫.
guer•(r)il•la [gəˈrilə] *n.* ①游击队员;〔常 *pl.*〕游击队员. ②〔古〕游击战〔现多用 ~ war〕. *a ~ area* 游击区. *~ band* 游击队. *a ~ detachment* 游击支队. *~ forces* 游击队. ~ **strike** 未经工会同意的罢工. ~ **tactics** 游击战术. ~ **theatre** 流动剧团, 街头活报演出队. ~ **war [warfare]** 游击战. **-ism** *n.* 游击主义, 游击战.
guess [ges] *vt.* ①推测, 猜测. ②猜对, 猜中(谜等). ③〔口〕以为, 相信. *~ a riddle* 猜中谜语. *I ~ it's going to rain.* 我想天快下雨了. — *vi.* 猜 *(at)*; 推测. *~ at a riddle* 猜谜. *I ~ not.* 决不是那样. *I can't even ~ at what you mean.* 我猜不着你的意思. ***keep sb. ~ing*** 使人捉摸不定. — *n.* 推测. 猜测. ***at a ~ =by ~*** 依推测, 照估计. ***by ~ and by god [gosh]*** 凭瞎猜, 凭粗略估计. ***It's anybody's ~.*** 这是谁也拿不准的事. ***miss one's ~*** 推测错. ***My ~ is that...*** 我认为… ***One man's ~ is as good as another's.*** 猜测终究是猜测. **~-rope, ~-warp** *n.* = guest rope. ~ **stick**〔俚〕尺, 计算尺. ~ **who**〔美俚〕不认识的人. **~work** 推测.
gues(s)•ti•mate [ˈgestimit] *n.*〔美俚〕瞎猜, 瞎估计. — [-meit] *vt.*〔美俚〕瞎猜, 瞎估计.
guest [gest] *n.* ①客人, 宾客. ②旅客, 宿客, 顾客. ③客串演员, 特约演员. ④【动】寄生生物, 寄生虫;【植】寄生植物. *a distinguished ~* 贵宾. *a state ~* 国宾. *the ~ of honour* 正餐的主宾. *an unbidden ~* 不速之客. *house ~* 留宿的宾客. — *vt.* 招待, 款待. — *vi.* ①做客. ②〔美俚〕在无线电节目中客串演出. **~chamber** 客房. ~ **flag** 客旗〔挂在游艇上表示主人不在但有客人在船中的长方形白旗〕. **~house** 宾馆, 招待所, 高级寄宿舍. ~ **member** 特邀代表. ~ **mineral** 寄生矿物. ~ **night** (大学、俱乐部等)招待来宾的夜晚. ~ **players** 特邀选手. ~ **room** =~chamber. ~ **rope** ①扶手绳. ②(稳定拖船的)辅助缆索. ~ **speaker** 邀请来的演说者. ~ **worker** (在西德工作的)外籍工人. **-less** *a.* **-ship** *n.*
Guest [gest] *n.* 格斯特〔姓氏〕.
guest•ship [ˈgestʃip] *n.* 客人身分.
Gue•va•ra [geˈvɑːrɑː], **Ernesto** 格瓦拉〔1928—1967, 出生于阿根廷的拉丁美洲革命家. **-ist** 格瓦拉主义者〔主张以恐怖的游击战略推进革命〕.
guff [gʌf] *n.*〔美俚〕胡说, 瞎扯; 闲聊.
guf•faw [gʌˈfɔː] *n.* 哄笑, 大笑. — *vi.* 哄笑, 大笑. — *vt.* 大笑着说.
gug•gle [ˈgʌgl] *vi., n.* = gurgle.
Gui•an•a [giˈæne, gaiˈænə] *n.* 圭亚那〔拉丁美洲〕.
gui•chet [ˈgiːʃei] *n.*〔F.〕售票窗口; 格子窗口.
guid•a•ble [ˈgaidəbl] *a.* 可指导的.
guid•ance [ˈgaidəns] *n.* ①向导, 指引, 指导. ②导航, 制导. ③【机】导槽, 导板, 导管. *traffic ~* 交通管理. *vocational ~* 业务辅导. ***under sb.'s ~*** 在某人指导下. ~ **system**【宇】制导系统.
guide [gaid] *n.* ①引导, 指导. ②领路人, 导游者, 向导; 指导者, 指挥者. ③【军】向导舰;〔*pl.*〕基准兵, 标兵. ④〔英〕女童子军. ⑤规准, 指针. ⑥(旅行, 游览)指南; 入门书; 路标. ⑦【机】导轨, 导沟, 导杆;【电】导路; 导体; 导引物;【自】波导, 导向装置;【医】导子, 标. *a ~ fossil* 标准化石. *A G- To English Grammar*《英语语法入门》. ***G- center!***【军】向中看齐〔向中央基准兵看齐〕! ***G- left [right]!***【军】向左〔右〕看齐! — *vt.* ①引导. ②指导, 指挥; 支配(思想感情等), 左右(人的行为); 管理; 指示. ③教导, 辅导. *~ him in his studies* 辅导他学习. *~ the state* 治理国家. *be ~d by one's sense of duty* 在责任感支配下. ~ **bar [rod]**【机】导杆. ~ **bearing**【机】导引轴承. **~board** 路牌. **~book** 旅行指南, 参考手册. ~ **dog** 盲人引路犬. ~ **flag**【军】标旗, 指示旗. **~line** ①指导路线, 方针; 准则, 指标. ②指路绳. ③【印】样张, 样行, 标线. **~post** 路标. ~ **rope** 导绳. **~way**【机】导沟, 导向槽. ~ **word**【印】眉题(印在前页末尾的次页首词).
guided [ˈgaidid] *a.* 有领导的; 制导的. ~ **missile** 导弹. ~ **wave** 被导波, 循轨波.
guid•ing [ˈgaidiŋ] *n.* 导向, 定向; 制导, 导航; 导波, 控制. ~ **hole** 中导孔, 导孔. ~ **principles** 指导方针. ~ **rod** 标杆.
gui•don [ˈgaidən] *n.* ①队旗; 长标旗. ②旗手.
g(u)ild [gild] *n.* ①(互助性质的)协会; (中世纪的)行会, 同业公会, 基尔特. ②【植】依赖植物集团. *the ~ mentality [outlook]* 行会主义. ~ **socialism** 行会社会主义; 基尔特社会主义.
guil•der [ˈgildə] *n.* = gulden.
guild•hall [ˈgildˌhɔːl] *n.* ①(中世纪的)同业公会会所, 会馆. ②市政厅;〔the G-〕伦敦市政厅.
guilds•man [ˈgildzmən] *n.* (*pl.* **-men** [-mən]) 同业公会会员; 行会会员.
guile [gail] *n.* 狡猾; 诡计. **-less** *a.* 坦率的, 正直的.
guile•ful [ˈgailful] *a.* 狡诈的, 诡计多端的. **-ly** *ad.* **-ness** *n.*
Guillaume [giˈjəum], **Charles Edouard** 查利·吉永〔1861—1938, 法国物理学家, 曾获 1920 年诺贝尔物理奖金〕.
guil•le•mot [ˈgilimɔt] *n.*【动】海雀科的鸟, 海鸠.
guil•loche [giˈləuʃ] *n.*【建】扭索饰.
guil•lo•tine [ˌgiləˈtiːn, ˈgil-] *n.* ①断头台. ②【机】截切机, 闸刀. ③【物】截流器. ④【医】铡刀, 环状刀. *tonsil ~* 扁桃体铡除刀. ⑤(议会)中止辩论〔指在预定时间对议案等进行表决〕. — *vt.* ①把…送上断头台, 把…处斩刑. ②【医】用截切机截断. ③对(议案)中止辩论而付表决. ~ **amputation**【医】外科截断术.
guilt [gilt] *n.* ①罪, 罪过, 罪行. ②内疚, 有罪感. *The evidence proved his ~.* 证据已证明他有罪. ~ ***by association*** 牵连犯罪. ~ **complex**【心】犯罪情结〔老感到自己有罪的变态心理〕.
guilt•i•ly [ˈgiltili] *ad.* 有罪地; 有罪似地.
guilt•i•ness [ˈgiltinis] *n.* 有罪; 罪恶.
guilt•less [ˈgiltlis] *a.* ①无罪的, 无辜的. ②〔口〕不知的, 无经验的; 没有 *(of)*. *be ~ of writing poems* 不会作诗. *windows ~ of glass.* 没有玻璃的窗子. **-ly** *ad.* **-ness** *n.*
guilt•y [ˈgilti] *a.* ①有罪的; 犯了错误的. ②自觉有罪的; 内疚的. *a ~ behaviour* 犯罪行为. *have a ~ conscience* 自疚, 问心有愧. *wear a ~ look* 露出内疚的神色. ***be found ~*** 被判决有罪. ***be ~ of*** 犯…罪 *(be ~ of murder* 犯杀人罪). ***be inwardly ~*** 理亏心虚. ***~ of death***〔古〕应处死刑. ***plead not ~*** 不服罪.
guimp(e) [gimp, gæmp] *n.* (女用)带袖内衣.
Guin•ea [ˈgini] *n.* 几内亚〔非洲〕.
guin•ea [ˈgini] *n.* ①畿尼〔旧时英国金币, 合 21 先令〕. ②〔口〕= ~ fowl. **G- corn**【植】高粱, 蜀黍. ~ **fowl**【动】珍珠鸟. ~ **grains**【植】药用卡满龙种子(= grains of paradise). ~ **grass**【植】羊草. ~ **hen** ①雌珍珠鸟. ②= ~ fowl. ~ **pig**【动】豚鼠, 天竺鼠; 供料

学实验的人[物]. **G- worm** 麦地那龙线虫.

Guin·ea-Bis·sau [ˈginibiˈsəu] *n.* 几内亚比绍[非洲].

Guin·e·an [ˈginiən] *a.* 几内亚的,几内亚人的. —*n.* 几内亚人.

Guin·ness [ˈginis] *n.* (爱尔兰产)黑啤酒.

gui·pure [giːˈpjuə] *n.* 网络花边,凸纹花边.

guise [gaiz] *n.* ①态度,外观. ②伪装;借口. ③〔古〕服装,打扮. ***in [under] the ~ of*** 扮作;以…为幌子(*under the ~ of friendship* 假借友谊的名义. *in the ~ of a monk* 扮作和尚). —*vt., vi.* 〔英方〕伪装.

gui·tar [giˈtɑː] *n.* 六弦琴,吉他. *electric ~* 电吉他. —*vi.* 弹吉他. **-ist** [giˈtɑːrist] *n.* 弹吉他的人.

gui·tar·fish [giˈtɑːfiʃ] *n.* 【动】犁头鳐.

gu·lar [ˈgjuːlə, ˈguː-] *a.* 喉的,喉上的.

gulch [gʌltʃ] *n.* 〔美〕干谷,峡谷,冲沟(尤指金矿地的急流河床).

gul·den [ˈguldən] *n.* (*pl.* ~*s*, ~) 盾(荷兰货币单位).

gules [gjuːlz] *n., a.* 【纹章】红色(的).

gulf [gʌlf] *n.* ①(比 bay 大而深入陆地的) 海湾,内海,湾. ②深渊;深坑,鸿沟;漩涡,涡. ③(感情、意见等的)悬殊,分歧,隔阂 (*between*). ④〔诗〕深海. *a great ~ fixed* 歧异,不可逾越的鸿沟. *the ~ between rich and poor* 贫富之间的悬殊. ***the ~ below*** 地狱. ***the G-States*** 〔美〕墨西哥湾沿岸各州. ***the G- Stream*** 墨西哥湾流(由墨西哥湾向北流至大西洋的水流). —*vt.* 吞没,使深深卷入,卷进. ~**weed** 【植】果囊马尾藻.

gulf·y [ˈgʌlfi] *a.* 多漩涡的;多深坑的.

gull[1] [gʌl] *n.* 【动】鸥.

gull[2] [gʌl] *n.* ①〔古〕欺诈. ②容易受骗的人,笨蛋. —*vt.* 欺骗. *~ sb. into buying rubbish* 骗人买无用的东西. *~ sb. out of his money* 骗人钱.

Gul·lah [ˈgʌlə] *n.* (美国东南部的) 嘎勒族黑人;嘎勒英语.

gul·let [ˈgʌlit] *n.* ①【解】食道,咽喉,咽. ②海峡,水道. ③锯齿间空隙. ④【建】水落管,水槽.

gul·li·bil·i·ty [ˌgʌliˈbiliti] *n.* 易受欺骗.

gul·li·ble [ˈgʌlibl] *a.* 容易受骗的,容易上当的,轻信的. **-bly** *ad.*

gull·ish [ˈgʌliʃ] *a.* 笨的,呆的.

gul·ly[1] [ˈgʌli] *n.* ①沟渠,阴沟;(干涸的)沟壑,溪谷,涧谷. ②【建】集水沟,雨水口,檐槽. ③【板球】后方右侧场地. —*vt.* ①水流冲成(沟渠). ②在…开沟. ~ **drain** 【建】下水道. ~ **hole** 【建】沟渠;集水孔.

Gul·li·ver's [ˈgʌlivəz] **Travels** 《格列弗游记》〔英国作家 Jonathan Swift 的名作,其中有关于大人国和小人国的描写〕.

gul·ly[2] [ˈgʌli] *n.* 〔英方〕大刀.

gu·los·i·ty [gjuːˈlɔsiti] *n.* 贪婪;食欲过度.

gulp [gʌlp] *vt.* ①吞;狼吞虎咽地吃,一口吞下. ②抑制,忍住(眼泪等). —*vi.* ①吞下,狼吞虎咽. ②喘不过气来,哽塞. ~ ***down sobs*** 吞声饮泣. —*n.* ①吞咽. ②一口吞下的量,一大口. ***swallow at one ~*** 一口吞下,一饮而尽. **-ing·ly** *ad.*

gum[1] [gʌm] *n.* ①树胶,树脂. ②橡胶;〔美〕弹性树胶;橡胶树,产树胶的树. ③〔*pl.*〕〔美〕高统橡胶套鞋 (= ~ boots). ④〔美〕橡皮糖,口香糖 (= chewing ~). ⑤眼屎;病树的分泌物. —*vt.* ①在…涂树胶. ②用树胶粘合 (*down; together; up*). ③〔美俚〕欺骗. *~ down the flap of an envelope* 用胶黏好信封的盖口. *The boy's pocket was all gummed up with candy.* 这个男孩的口袋全被糖弄黏了. —*vi.* (果树因病) 分泌树液,(树)分泌树胶;结胶;发粘. ~ ***up*** ①黏合. ②〔美俚〕弄坏,搞乱. ~ **ammoniac** (= ammoniac) ① *n.* 氨草胶. ② *a.* 氨的,氨性的,含氨的. ~ **arabic** 阿拉伯树胶. ~ **boots** 〔美〕长统橡胶套鞋. ~ **dragon** = ~ tragacanth. ~**drop** 橡皮软糖. ~ **elastic** 弹性橡胶(即生橡胶). ~ **foot** 〔美俚〕便衣警察. ~ **resin** 【化】树胶脂. ~ **tragacanth** 【化】龙胶,黄蓍胶. ~ **tree** 【植】桉树,产橡胶的树 (*up a ~-tree* 不上不下,进退两难). ~**water** 阿拉伯胶溶液,胶水. ~ **wood** 橡胶树木料.

gum[2] [gʌm] *n.* 〔常 *pl.*〕齿龈;牙床. —*vt.* ①锉深(锯)齿. ②用牙床咀嚼. ***beat [bump] one's ~s*** 〔美俚〕唠叨,饶舌. ~**boil** 齿龈脓肿.

gum[3] [gʌm] *n.* 〔英方、俚〕上帝 (= God) (用于咒诅、发誓). ***By ~!*** 我敢向天发誓,确确实实. ***My ~!*** 天啊! 啊呀! (表示痛苦、悲哀或愤怒等)

gum·bah [guːmˈbɑː] 〔美俚〕老朋友,死党〔黑社会用语〕.

gum·bo [ˈgʌmbəu] *n.* (*pl.* ~*s*) ①【植】秋葵;秋葵荚. ②〔美〕浓汤. ③强黏土 (= ~ soil). ④〔G-〕〔美〕(路易斯安那州和西印度群岛的法国移民和黑人用的) 法语方言.

gum·ma [ˈgʌmə] *n.* (*pl.* ~*s*, ~*ta*) 【医】梅毒瘤;树胶状肿. **-tous** [-təs] *a.*

gum·mi·ness [ˈgʌminis] *n.* 树胶状,树胶质;黏性,黏着性.

gum·ming [ˈgʌmiŋ] *n.* ①结胶,胶合. ②【植】流胶症. ③【印】(在石版上)涂胶. ④树胶的采集.

gum·mite [ˈgʌmait] *n.* 【矿】脂铅铀矿.

gum·mo·sis [gəˈməusis] *n.* 【植】流胶;流胶病.

gum·mous [ˈgʌməs] *a.* 树胶质的,树胶状的.

gum·my [ˈgʌmi] *a.* ①树胶状的;树胶制的. ②含树胶的;胶黏的. ③(脚)树胶状肿的. ④〔美俚〕拙劣的,讨厌的. *~ bark* 分泌树胶的树皮. *~ ankles* 肿胀的足踝. ~ **tumour** 【医】梅毒瘤,树胶状肿.

gump [gʌmp] *n.* 〔方〕笨蛋.

gump·tion [ˈgʌmpʃən] *n.* ①〔口〕精明能干,通晓事理. ②事业心,进取精神. ③调合颜料的溶剂. **-less** *a.*

gump·tious [ˈgʌmpʃəs] *a.* 精力充沛的,非常能干的,机灵的.

gum·shoe [ˈgʌmˌʃuː] *n.* ①橡胶套鞋. ②〔*pl.*〕橡胶底帆布鞋. ③〔俚〕侦探. —*vi.* 〔美俚〕轻声走路,偷偷地走;侦察. —*a.* 〔美俚〕偷偷地进行的. ~ **man** 〔美俚〕侦探,警察.

gun [gʌn] *n.* ①炮,枪,猎枪;〔美口〕手枪. ②枪状物;〔美俚〕毒品注射器;(杀虫用)喷雾器. ③(信号枪、礼炮的)鸣放. ④〔美俚〕罪犯;扒手;强盗. ⑤〔谑〕烟斗. ⑥猎枪手. ⑦(引擎的)油门,风门. *a salute of twenty-one ~s* 二十一响礼炮. *When ~s speak it is too late to argue.* 〔谚〕大炮说话时,争辩已太迟. *an air ~* 汽枪. *a cement ~* 水泥喷枪. *electron ~* 【无】电子枪. *a heavy field ~* 重炮. *heavy mountain and field ~s* 山野重炮. *a machine ~* 机关枪. *a plasma ~* 等离子枪. *a spray ~* 【机】喷枪. *a squirt ~* 水枪. *a welding ~* 焊接喷灯,焊接喷枪. ***a big [great] ~*** 〔俚〕大人物,高级军官. ***as sure as a ~*** 不错,的确. ***beat [jump] the ~*** 〔俚〕(赛跑时)未听发令枪响就起跑,抢跑;行动过早. ***blow great ~s*** 刮大风. ***carry too many [the biggest] ~s*** (在议论、竞赛等中)占上风. ***give it the ~*** 开动,加快. ***go great ~s*** 快速有成效地干. ***~s and butter*** 既要大炮又要牛油的政策,军事与经济发展并重的政策. ***spike sb.'s ~*** 击败某人,挫败某人. ***stick [stand] to [by] one's ~ (s)*** 坚守阵地;固执己见. ***under the ~s*** 在严密监视下. —*vt.* ①〔美口〕向…开枪. ②〔美口〕开大(引擎、汽车等的)油门. *The guard was gunned down.* 卫兵被射倒. *~ the engine* 开大引擎的油门. —*vi.* 〔美口〕①拿枪射击;用枪打猎. ②开大油门前进. ~ ***for*** ①用枪搜索;捕杀. ②〔美俚〕寻求,争取. *That guy was gunning for a rise.* 那家伙在想办法升官. ~ **barrel** 枪筒;炮筒. ~**boat** 炮舰 (~*boat diplomacy* 炮舰外交). ~ **captain** (海军中的) 炮长. ~ **car** 铁道运炮车. ~ **carriage** 【军】炮车,炮架. ~ **case** ①猎枪套. ②〔英俚〕法官头巾. ~**cotton** 【军】火棉,强棉药. ~ **crew** 〔集合词〕炮手,机枪手. ~ **dog** 猎犬. ~**fight** ① *n.* 手枪格斗. ② *vi.*

(两人之间)用手枪格斗,枪战. ~**fighter** 用手枪格斗的人;(美国西部的)枪战能手. ~**fire** ①炮击,炮火. ②【军】号炮;号炮时. ~**flint** 枪机燧石. ~ **harpoon** 用射鲸炮发射的鱼叉. ~**house** 炮塔,炮室. ~**-howitzer** 加农榴弹炮. ~**-layer** 瞄准手,射击手. ~**lock** 炮机,枪机. ~**man** 带枪者;(罢工时的)带枪纠察员;〔美俚〕带手枪的歹徒;枪炮工人. ~ **metal** 炮铜〔铜锡锌合金〕. ~ **moll** 〔美俚〕带枪歹徒的女帮凶〔情妇〕. ~ **pit** 火炮掩体. ~**play** 手枪战〔如在歹徒警察之间发生的手枪战〕. ~**point** 枪口〔主要用在 *at gunpoint* (在枪口威胁下)这句短语里〕. ~**pointer** 方向瞄准手. ~**port** (军舰的)炮眼,炮门. ~**powder** ①黑色火药,有烟火药. ②中国珠茶(= ~powder tea). ~ **rack** 墙上的枪架. ~ **room** ①私宅中的藏枪室;枪炮陈列室. ②(英国军舰上的)下级军官住所. ~ **runner** 军火走私者. ~ **running** 军火走私. ~ **ship** 〔美军俚〕武装直升飞机. ~**shot** ①(自炮内射出的)炮弹. ②射击,炮击. ③(枪、炮的)射程(*within* ~*shot* 在射程内. *out of* ~*shot* 在射程外). ~**-shy** *a.* 怕枪炮声的,风声鹤唳的;(猎犬、马等)被枪炮声吓坏的. ~**sight** 瞄准器,标尺. ~**slinger** 〔俚〕带枪的歹徒,带枪的狗腿子. ~**smith** 枪炮工人. ~**stock** 枪托. ~**toting** *a.* 经常携带和使用枪枝的.

gung-ho [ˈgʌŋˈhəu] *a.* 〔美军俚〕同心协力的,雄心勃勃的,热烈的〔来自汉语"工业合作社"的简称"工合",二次大战中美国海军陆战队用语〕.

Gun·ite [ˈgʌnait] 古耐特 〔一种喷枪或水泥枪商标〕. — *n.* 〔g-〕喷枪,水泥枪.

gunk [gʌŋk] *n.* 〔俚〕油腻物,胶黏物质,浓糊状物质. ~**hole** (上有顶篷的)小船坞,小船停泊处. **-y** *a.*

gun·nage [ˈgʌnidʒ] *n.* (军舰的)火炮量.

gunned [gʌnd] *a.* 装备有大炮的;带枪的. *a ship heavily* ~ 装备多门火炮的船舰. *over-[under-]*~ 装备火炮过多〔不足〕的.

gun·nel[1] [ˈgʌnəl] *n.* = gunwale.

gun·nel[2] [ˈgʌnəl] *n.*【动】(北大西洋产的)锦鱼尉科鱼.

gun·ner [ˈgʌnə] *n.* ①炮兵,炮手,火炮瞄准手;飞机上的枪炮手. ②管理军械(库)的海军准尉. ③猎枪手. ***kiss [marry, be married to] the ~'s daughter*** 〔海军俚〕〔谑〕(水兵)被绑在大炮上鞭打.

gun·ner·a [ˈgʌnərə] *n.*【植】根乃拉草;〔G-〕根乃拉草属.

gun·ner·y [ˈgʌnəri] *n.* ①射击. ②射击技术,枪炮操作与射击法. ③〔集合词〕重炮,枪炮. ~ **jack [lieutenant]** 〔英俚〕炮术练习舰上的射击检查官. ~ **ship** 炮术练习舰.

gun·ning [ˈgʌniŋ] *n.* ①射击. ②打猎. ③用枪搜索捕杀. *go* ~ 去打猎.

gun·ny [ˈgʌni] *n.* ①粗黄麻布. ②黄麻麻袋. ~**-bag [sack]** 黄麻麻袋.

gun·sel [ˈgʌnsl] *n.* 〔俚〕①娈童〔指被人作为女性玩弄的男子〕. ②带枪的歹徒,带枪的狗腿子.

Gun·ter [ˈgʌntə] *n.* ①冈特〔姓氏〕. ②**Edmund** ~ 埃德蒙·冈特〔1581—1626,英国数学家〕. ***according to G-*** 〔美〕精确地. **Gunter's chain** 冈特氏测链〔长 66 英尺〕.

gun·ter [ˈgʌntə] *n.* ①【海、测】冈特氏尺规〔又叫 Gunter's scale〕. ②【海】中桅;中桅帆.

Gun·ther [ˈgʌnθə] *n.* 冈瑟〔姓氏〕.

gun·wale [ˈgʌnəl] *n.* 船舷的上缘. ~ ***down [to]*** 船舷和水面相平. ~ ***under*** 舷边没入水面以下.

gun·yah [ˈgʌnjə], **gun·yeh** [-je] *n.* 澳洲土人小屋.

gup [gʌp] 〔印度用英语〕闲话,闲谈;〔英口〕蠢话.

gup·py[1] [ˈgʌpi] *n.*【动】虹鳉鱼 *(Lebistes reticulatus)* 〔西印度胎生、观赏、食蚊小鱼〕.

gup·py[2] [ˈgʌpi] *n.* 有通气管的流线型潜艇〔是 *g*reater *u*nderwater *p*ropulsive *p*ower+*-y* 的缩略词〕.

gurge [gəːdʒ] *n.* 漩涡. — *vi.* (液体)形成漩涡.

gur·gi·ta·tion [gəːdʒiˈteiʃən] *n.* ①(液体的)涡旋;(波涛似的)沸腾;翻滚. ②沸腾声.

gur·gle [ˈgəːgl] *vi.* ①汩汩地流. ②(人高兴时从喉咙中)发咯咯声;(流水)作汩汩声. — *vt.* ①使发汩汩声. ②咯咯地发出(声响). ~ *one's delight* 发出咯咯的笑声. — *n.* ①汩汩声. ②咯咯声. ~*s of delight* 咯咯的笑声.

gur·goyle [ˈgəːgɔil] *n.* = gargoyle.

gur·jun [ˈgəːdʒʌn] *n.*【植】(东印度)陀螺状羯布罗香.

Gur·kha [ˈguəkə] *n.* ①(尼泊尔的)廓尔喀人. ②英国〔印度〕军队中的尼泊尔籍士兵. ~ **regiments** (英国陆军中)廓尔喀人组成的团.

gur·nard [ˈgəːnəd], **gur·net** [ˈgəːnit] *n. (pl.* ~*s,* 〔集合词〕~*)*【动】鲂鮄科海鱼,绿鳍鱼.

gur·rah [ˈgʌrə] *n.* (印度的)土瓮.

gur·ry [ˈgʌri] *n.* 鲸鱼的碎肉;鱼的碎肉.

gu·ru [ˈguruː] *n.* ①【印度教】个人的宗教教师〔指导〕. ②(受下级崇敬的)领袖,头目;〔美俚〕头面人物,权威.

Gus [gʌs] *n.* 格斯〔男子名〕〔Augustus 的爱称〕.

gu·san·o [guˈsɑːnəu] *n.* 〔古巴人用语〕虫豸,蛆虫〔指逃亡到美国的古巴人〕.

gush [gʌʃ] *n.* ①涌出,喷出,迸出. ②(感情的)冲动;洋溢的热情. ③洋洋洒洒的文章,滔滔不绝的讲话. *a* ~ *of enthusiasm* 热情迸发. *gas* ~【油】汽喷. — *vt.* ①涌出,喷出,迸出. ②洋洋洒洒地写,滔滔不绝地说. *The gaping wound* ~*ed forth [out] with blood.* 伤口大量出血. — *vi.* ①涌出,喷出,迸出. ②过分表露感情;洋洋洒洒地写,滔滔不绝地讲. ~ *over film stars* 不停地谈电影明星.

gush·er [ˈgʌʃə] *n.* ①迸出物. ②喷油井. ③容易动感情的人;滔滔不绝的说话者.

gush·ing [ˈgʌʃiŋ] *a.* ①涌出的,喷出的,迸出的. ②过分热情的,容易动感情的,滔滔不绝的. **-ly** *ad.* **-ness** *n.*

gush·y [ˈgʌʃi] *a.* ①迸发的,喷出的;流出的. ②过分多情的. **-i·ly** *ad* **-i·ness** *n.*

gus·set [ˈgʌsit] *n.* ①(用以填补、加固或放大衣服的)三角形布料. ②【机】角撑板,角板. ③楔形土地. — *vt.* ①在…缝三角形布料. ②给…装上角撑板.

gus·set·ed [ˈgʌsitid] *a.* ①缝有三角形布料的. ②装有角撑板的.

gus·sie, gus·sy [ˈgʌsi] *vt., vi.* (把…)打扮得花枝招展*(up)*.

gust[1] [gʌst] *n.* ①阵风;一阵狂风. ②(雨、火、烟、雹、声音等)突发的一阵;(感情)迸发. *a* ~ *of rage* 勃然大怒. *a* ~ *of rain* 一阵暴雨. *a* ~ *of wind* 一阵风.

gust[2] [gʌst] *n.* ①〔古〕味觉,味感. ②风味,嗜好. ***have a ~ of*** 嗜好,欣赏. — *vt.* 〔Scot.〕尝尝,享受.

Gus·ta [ˈgʌstə] *n.* 女名〔Augusta 的爱称〕.

gus·ta·tion [gʌsˈteiʃən] *n.* 尝味,味觉.

gus·ta·to·ry [ˈgʌstətəri] *a.* 味觉的. *the* ~ *bud* 味蕾. *the* ~ *cell* 味觉细胞. *the* ~ *nerve* 味觉神经.

Gus·ta·vus [gəsˈtɑːvəs] *n.* 古斯塔夫斯〔男子名〕.

gus·to [ˈgʌstəu] *n. (pl.* ~*s)* ①爱好,嗜好,趣味. ②热忱,兴致勃勃. ③〔古〕滋味. ④艺术风格. ***enjoy the full ~ of*** 〔古〕充分领略. ***with enormous*** ~兴致勃勃地,津津有味地.

gust·y [ˈgʌsti] *a.* ①阵风的;多阵风的,起大风的. ②迸发的. **-i·ly** *ad.* **-i·ness** *n.*

gut [gʌt] *n.* ①肠子,〔*pl.*〕内脏,〔口〕肚子;〔美俚〕香肠. ②〔*pl.*〕内容,内部的主要部分;本质,实质. ③〔*pl.*〕〔俚〕精神,毅力,耐久力,勇气,厚脸,无礼. ④(提琴、网球拍等的)肠线,(钓鱼钩上用的)丝线. ⑤狭水道,海岬,海峡;弯头,狭巷,狭道. *the blind* ~ 盲肠. *the large [small]* ~ 大〔小〕肠. *surgical* ~ 外科缝合用的羊肠线. ~ *ache* 肚子痛. *a* ~ *fighter* 顽强的对手. *a* ~ *issue [question]* 关键问题. ~ *language* 粗话. ***a man of***

[with] plenty of ~s 颇有胆量的人. ***get down to the ~s of a matter*** 触及问题的实质. ***hate sb.'s ~s***〔俚〕恨透了某人. ***have no ~s in sth.*** 毫无内容. ***have the ~s to do [say] sth.***〔美〕有做〔说〕某事的勇气. ***not fit to carry ~s to a bear*** ①太不中用. ②不能作食物. ***run sb. through the ~*** 折磨某人. ***spill one's ~***〔美俚〕告密,翻肠倒肚地全部说出. ***sweat one's ~s out*** 拼命干. ***tear the ~s out of sb.*** 耗尽某人精力. ***tear the ~s out of sth.*** 阉割精华,使化为乌有. — *vt.* ①取出(鱼等的)内肠. ②损毁(房屋等的)内部装置,抽去(书籍等的)主要内容. ③〔口〕狼吞虎咽. — *a.*〔美俚〕深有触感的,激起感情的;直觉的. ~ **course**〔美俚〕容易的课程. ~ **scrapper**〔美俚〕提琴师.

gut·buck·et [ˈgʌtbʌkit] *n.* 缓慢淫荡的四步爵士舞曲.

Gu·ten·berg [ˈguːtnbəːg], **Johannes** 古腾堡〔1400—1467,德国活版印刷发明人〕.

gut·less [ˈgʌtlis] *a.* 没有勇气的,懦怯的.

guts·y [ˈgʌtsi] *a.*〔俚〕有勇气的,有力量的.

gut·ta [ˈgʌtə] *n.* *(pl.* ***gut·tae*** [ˈgʌtiː]*)* ①滴,滴状物. ②【建】圆锥饰. ③【化】古塔胶,杜仲胶〔用于补牙或作绝缘体〕. ~**-percha** 杜仲胶,古塔胶. ~**-percha tree** 杜仲树.

gut·tate [ˈgʌteit] *a.* 滴状的; 有(彩色)斑点的. **gut·ta·tion** [gʌˈteiʃən] *n.*

gua·ta·tim [gəˈteitəm] *ad.*【处方】一滴一滴地(= drop by drop).

gut·ter [ˈgʌtə] *n.* ①水槽,檐槽. ②沟,边沟,街沟,明沟. ③【印】排版上的隔条;(装订)左右两页间的空白. ④贫民区,贫民窟. *caves* ~【建】天沟. *children of the* ~ 流浪儿. *vent* ~ 通风道. ***be born in the*** ~ 出身贫贱. ***lap the*** ~〔俚〕酩酊大醉. ***rise from the*** ~ 从微贱中发迹. ***take a child out of the*** ~ 收养穷苦小孩. — *vt.* ①在…开沟. ②为…装檐槽. ~ *a new building* 给新楼装导水槽. — *vi.* 流,淌蜡,(烛火)风中摇晃. ~ ***down [out]*** ①逐渐变弱熄灭. ②默默无闻地结束. ~**-bird** *n.* ①麻雀. ②声名狼藉的人. ~ **child** 流浪儿. ~ **film** 迎合低级趣味的电影. ~ **language**〔美俚〕脏话. ~**man** ①清除阴沟的人. ②摊贩. ~ **press** 迎合低级趣味的报纸. ~**snipe** 流浪儿,穷途末路的人.

gut·tle [ˈgʌtl] *vt., vi.* 狼吞虎咽. **-r** *n.* 贪吃者.

gut·tur·al [ˈgʌtərəl] *a.* ①喉的,咽喉的. ②【语】颚音的,喉音的. ③发出不愉快声音的. ~ *sounds* 喉音. *the* ~ *speech of the Germans* 德国人多喉音的说话. — *n.*【语】颚音,喉音〔如 g, k 等〕;颚音字母〔符号〕. **-ism** *n.* 颚音的性质〔习惯〕. **-ize** *vt.* 使发颚音,使颚音化. **-ly** *ad.* **-ness** *n.*

gut·ty [ˈgʌti] *a.* ①大胆的,生气勃勃的. ②感触很深的,挑动性的.

guy[1] [gai] *n.* ①〔英〕盖伊·福克斯(Guy Fawkes)的模拟像〔Guy Fawkes 为火药阴谋案的主犯,每年十一月五日焚烧其模拟像以示庆祝〕. ②怪人;服装奇异的人. ③〔美俚〕家伙,人,小伙子,朋友. *a little* ~ 矮子. *a queer* ~ 怪人. *a regular* ~ 虚有其表的人. *a right* ~〔美〕可靠的人. *a smart* ~ 自作聪明的人,精明的家伙. *a tough* ~ 硬汉. — *vt.* ①〔英〕把(某人)制成模拟像嘲弄. ②嘲笑,挖苦. ③糟蹋.

guy[2] [gai] *n.*〔俚〕逃走,逃亡. *do a* ~ 逃亡. *give the* ~ *to* 逃出,摆脱. — *vi.* 逃走.

guy[3] [gai] *n.*【海】支索,牵索,张索;【电】天线拉线. — *vt.* 用支索撑住,加固.

Guy [gai] *n.* 盖伊〔男子名〕.

Guy·a·na [gaiˈɑːnə,gaiˈænə] *n.* 圭亚那〔拉丁美洲〕. **-n** ① *n.* 圭亚那人. ② *a.* 圭亚那的.

guy·ot [giːˈəu] *n.* 海底平顶山,桌状山.

guz·zle [ˈgʌzl] *vi., vt.* 大吃大喝,吃光喝光. ~ *one's money* 大吃大喝花光金钱. **-r** *n.* 酒鬼,大吃大喝的人.

Gwen [gwen] *n.* 格温〔女子名〕〔Gwendolyn 的爱称〕.

Gwen·do·lyn [ˈgwendəlin] *n.* 格温多琳〔女子名〕.

G.W.R. = Great Western Railway.

gwyn·i·ad [ˈgwiniæd] *n.* (英国淡水湖产)鳟类小鱼.

gybe [dʒaib] *vi., vt.* (使)(帆)随风向自一舷移向他舷;将帆自一舷移向他舷以变更(船的航道)(= jibe). — *n.* ①帆的方向改变. ②航道的改变. ***jerk a*** ~ 伪造执照.

gym [dʒim] *n.*〔口〕①体育馆. ②体操,体育课. ~ **shoe** 球鞋,橡胶底运动鞋. ~ **suit** 运动衣.

gym·kha·na [dʒimˈkɑːnə] *n.* 运动会.

gym·na·si·a [dʒimˈneiziə] *n.* gymnasium 的复数.

gym·na·si·al [dʒimˈneiziəl] *a.* (德国或欧洲其他某些国家)大学预科的.

gym·na·si·arch [dʒimˈneiziɑːk] *n.* (古希腊的体育,竞技和学校的)监理官.

gym·na·si·ast [dʒimˈneiziæst] *n.* ①(德国等欧洲国家的)预科学生. ②运动家.

gym·na·si·um [dʒimˈneiziəm,gimˈnɑːziəm] *n.* *(pl.* ***gym·na·si·a*** [-ˈneiziə] 或 *~s)* ①体育馆,健身房. ②〔有时 G-〕(德国或欧洲其他某些国家的)大学预科,准备进大学的高级中学.

gym·nast [ˈdʒimnæst] *n.* 体操教员,体育家.

gym·nas·tic [dʒimˈnæstik] *a.* 体操的,体育的; 锻炼精神的. ~ *apparatus* 体操用具. — *n.* 锻炼课程. **-ti·cal·ly** *ad.*

gym·nas·tics [dʒimˈnæstiks] *n.*〔*pl.*〕①〔作单数用〕体育. ②〔作复数用〕体操.

gym·no *comb. f.*【生】表示"裸": *gymnosperm.*

gym·nos·o·phist [dʒimˈnɔsəfist] *n.* 古印度实行裸体的苦行者;裸体主义者.

gym·no·sperm [ˈdʒimnəuspəːm] *n.*【植】裸子植物 *(opp.* angiosperm*).* **-ous** *a.* **-y** *n.*

gym·no·tus [dʒimˈnəutəs] *n.* *(pl.* ***-ti*** [-tai]*)*【动】电鳗.

gymp [gimp] *n.* = gimp.

gyn- *pref.*〔用于元音前〕= gyno-: *gyn*archy.

G.Y.N. = gyn(a)ecology.

gyn·ae·ce·um [ˌgainiˈsiːəm, dʒai-] *n.* *(pl.* ***-ce·a*** [-ˈsiːə]*)* ①(古希腊、古罗马的)闺房,女眷内室. ②【植】= gynoecium.

gyn·ae·co- *comb.f.* 表示"女性","雌性": *gynaecology.*

gyn·(a)e·coc·ra·cy [ˌgainiˈkɔkrəsi,ˌdʒai-] *n.* 妇人政治;女权政治.

gy·n(a)e·col·o·gy [ˌgainiˈkɔlədʒi, ˌdʒai-] *n.* 妇科学.

gy·n(a)e·col·o·gist [-dʒist] *n.* 妇科医生.

gy·nan·der [gaiˈnændə, dʒai-] *n.*【生】雌雄嵌体.

gyn·an·dro·morph [giˈnændrəˌmɔːf, dʒai-] *n.*【生】雌雄嵌体. **-phic, -phous** *a.* **-phism, -phy** *n.*

gy·nan·drous [gaiˈnændrəs,dʒai-] *a.*【植】雌雄蕊合体的.

gyn·an·dry [giˈnændri, dʒai-] *n.*〔罕〕女性假两性畸形.

gyn·arch·y [ˈdʒinɑːki,ˈdʒai-] *n.* *(pl.* ***-arch·ies****)* 妇女执政,妇女政治.

gynec-, gyneco- *comb. f.* = gynaec-, gynaeco-.

gyn·e·coid [ˈgainikɔid,ˈdʒaini-] *a.* 妇女的, 女性的, 有女性特征的.

gyn·e·pho·bi·a [ˌgainiˈfəubiə,ˌdʒaini-] *n.* 恐女病.

gyn·i·at·rics [ˌgainiˈætriks,dʒai-] *n.*〔作单数用〕【医】妇科疗法.

gynic [ˈgainik,ˈdʒai-] *a.* 女子的,女性的 *(opp.* andric*).*

gyn·o- *comb. f.* 表示"女性的","雌性的": *gyno*phore.

gy·noc·ra·cy [gaiˈnɔkrəsi, dʒai-] = gyn(a)ecocracy.

gy·noe·ci·um [gaiˈniːsiəm,dʒai-] *n.* *(pl.* ***-ci·a*** [-siə]*)*【植】雌蕊群.

gyn·o·phore [ˈgainəufɔː, ˈdʒainəu-] *n.*【植】雌雄柄. **-phor·ic** *a.*

gyn·o·ste·gi·um [ˌgainəuˈstiːdʒiəm, ˌdʒai-] *n.*【植】合

蕊冠.

gyn·o·ste·mi·um [ˌgainəuˈstiːmiəm, ˌdʒai-] *n.* 【植】合蕊柱.

-gyn·ous *comb. f.* 表示"女": poly*gynous*.

gyp[1] [dʒip] *n.* 〔英〕(剑桥大学等的)校工.

gyp[2] [dʒip] *n.* 〔口〕〔英〕苦难. ***give sb.*** ~ 严厉地责备[处罚,击败]某人,使某人活受罪.

gyp[3] [dʒip] *n.* 〔俚〕欺骗,骗局,骗子. — *vt., vi.* 骗,欺骗. — *a.* 〔美俚〕①商业性的,旨在获取利润的. ②欺骗的,不诚实的. ~ **artist** 〔美俚〕骗子手. ~ **joint** 〔美俚〕骗钱的赌场[商店等].

gyps. = gypsum.

gyp·s(e)·ous [ˈdʒips(i)əs] *a.* 石膏状的,含有石膏的.

gyp·sif·er·ous [dʒipˈsifərəs] *a.* 含石膏的,产生石膏的.

gyp·site [ˈdʒipsait] *n.* 土石膏.

gyp·sog·ra·phy [dʒipˈsɔgrəfi] *n.* 石膏雕刻, 石膏雕刻术.

gyp·soph·i·la [dʒipˈsɔfilə] *n.* 【植】丝石竹属 *(Gypsophila)* 植物〔如满天星 *(G. paniculata)*〕.

gyp·sous [ˈdʒipsəs] *a.* = gypseous.

gyp·sum [ˈdʒipsəm] *n.* ①【矿】石膏. ②【农】石膏肥料. ③【建】灰泥板,灰胶纸柏板. — *vt.* ①给(农田)施石膏肥料. ②用石膏处理.

gyp·sy [ˈdʒipsi] *n.* 〔美〕 = gipsy.

gyr- *comb. f.* 表示"旋转","环": *gyr*ate.

gy·ral [ˈdʒaiərəl] *a.* ①旋转的,回旋的. ②【解】脑转的.

gy·rate [ˈdʒaiərit] *a.* 旋转的;【植】螺旋状的. —[ˌdʒaiəˈreit] *vi.* 旋转.

gy·ra·tion [dʒaiəˈreiʃən] *n.* ①旋转, 回旋. ②【动】螺层. **-al** *a.*

gy·ra·to·ry [ˈdʒaiərətəri] *a.* 旋转的.

gyre [ˈdʒaiə] *vi.* 〔诗〕 = gyrate. — *n.* ①线圈. ②= gyration.

gy·rene [ˌdʒaiəˈriːn] *n.* 〔美俚〕海军陆战队成员.

gyr·fal·con [ˈdʒəːfɔːlkən] *n.* 【动】矛隼 *(Falco ruslicolous)* 〔产于两极地带的一种巨雕〕.

gyro [ˈdʒaiərəu] *n.* *(pl.* ~*s)* ①= gyrocompass. ②= gyroscope. ③自转旋翼飞机(= autogyro). ~ **control** 【空】陀螺仪. ~ **horizon** 陀螺地平仪.

gy·ro- *comb. f.* 表示"环","回转": *gyro*magnetic, *gyro*scope.

gy·ro·com·pass [ˈdʒaiərəuˌkʌmpəs] *n.* 回转罗盘;陀螺罗盘.

gy·ro·cop·ter [ˈdʒaiərəuˌkɔptə] *n.* (只载一名乘客的)旋翼飞机.

gy·ro·dy·nam·ics [ˈdʒaiərəudaiˈnæmiks] *n.* 陀螺动力学.

gyr·o·dyne [ˈdʒaiərəudain] *n.* 旋翼式螺旋桨飞机.

gy·ro·graph [ˈdʒaiərəugrɑːf] *n.* 转数记录器.

gy·roi·dal [ˌdʒaiəˈrɔidl] *a.* 螺旋形的,回转的.

gy·ro·mag·net·ic [ˌdʒairəumægˈnetik] *a.* 【物】回转磁的.

gy·ro·pi·lot [ˈdʒaiərəuˌpailət] *n.* (陀螺)自动驾驶仪.

gy·ro·plane [ˈdʒaiərəuˌplein] *n.* 旋翼机.

gy·ro·scope [ˈdʒaiərəuˌskəup, ˈgaiə-] *n.* 陀螺仪,回转仪.
gy·ro·scop·ic [ˌdʒaiərəuˈskɔpik] *a.*

gy·rose [ˌdʒaiəˈrəus] *a.* 【植】前后屈曲的,波状的.

gy·ro·sta·bi·liz·er [ˈdʒairəuˈsteibəˌlaizə] *n.* 【海】陀螺稳定器.

gy·ro·stat [ˈdʒaiərəustæt, ˈgaiə-] *n.* 回转轮, 回转仪, 陀螺仪.

gy·ro·stat·ic [ˌdʒaiərəuˈstætik] *a.* 回转轮的, 回转仪的,陀螺仪的,旋转学的.

gy·ro·stat·ics [ˌdʒaiərəuˈstætiks] *n. pl.* 〔作单数用〕旋转学.

gy·rus [ˈdʒaiərəs] *(pl.* ***gy·ri*** [-rai]*)* *n.* 【解】脑回.

gyve [dʒaiv] *n.* 〔常 *pl.*〕〔古,诗〕脚镣;手铐. — *vt.* 把(某人)钉上镣;给(某人)戴上手铐.

H

H, h [eitʃ] (*pl.* **H's, Hs, h's hs** [ˈeitʃiz]) ①英语字母表的第八个字母. ②H 形物. *an H-beam steel* H 形钢条. *an H-Post* H 形电杆. ***drop one's h's*** 不发 h 音〔如伦敦方言中把 *hat* [hæt] 读作 *'at* [æt]〕. ~ ***hour*** 【军】发起攻击的时间;特定军事行动开始的时刻.

H =【电】henry;【化】hydrogen;【物】磁场密度 (intensity of magnetic field), 地磁水平分量 (the horizontal component of terrestral magnetism); (表示铅笔芯硬度的符号) = hard(ness); 〔俚〕 heroin.

H[1] =【化】protium. **H**[1+] = proton. **H**[2] =【化】deuterium. **H**[3] =【化】tritium.

h., H. = harbour; hard, hardness; heavy sea; height, high; hence; 【棒】hit(s); horns; hour(s); howitzer; humidity; hundred; husband.

H.A. = Heavy Artillery; High Altitude; Hockey Association.

h.a. 〔L.〕 = in this year 今年,本年度.

ha [hɑː] *int.* 哈! 〔表示惊愕、快乐、疑惑、踌躇等〕. — *vi.* "哈!"地叫一声. — *n.* "哈!"的一声.

ha. = hectare(s).

haaf [hɑːf] *n.* (苏格兰 Shetland 或 Orkney 诸岛附近的)深海渔场.

haar [hɑː] *n.* 〔Scot.〕 海雾,冷雾.

Ha·bak·kuk [ˈhæbəkək] *n.* ①【犹太教】哈巴谷〔公元前八世纪希伯来的一先知〕. ②【宗】(《旧约全书》中的)《哈巴谷书》〔记载哈巴谷的预言〕.

Ha·ba·na [Sp. aˈbana] *n.* 哈瓦那〔古巴首都〕(= Havana).

ha·ba·ne·ra [ˌhɑːbəˈnerə; Sp. ˌabaˈnera] *n.* ①哈巴涅拉舞〔类似探戈舞的一种动作缓慢的古巴舞蹈〕. ②哈巴涅拉舞曲.

hab. corp. = habeas corpus.

hab·da·lah [ˌhɑːvdɑːˈlɑː; Eng. hɑːvˈdɔːlə] 【犹太教】安息日结束仪式.

ha·be·as cor·pus [ˈheibjəs ˈkɔːpəs] 〔L.〕【法】①人身保护令〔要求把拘留或监禁的人及时送交法院处理的法令〕 (= a writ of habeas corpus). ②人身保护权. ***Habeas Corpus Act*** 人身保护法〔英王查理二世于 1679 年颁布实施〕.

hab·er·dash [ˈhæbədæʃ] *vi.* (男子)打扮,修饰.

hab·er·dash·er [ˈhæbədæʃə] *n.* ①〔英〕针线等缝纫用品商. ②〔美〕男子服饰用品商.

hab·er·dash·er·y [ˈhæbədæʃəri] *n.* ①男子服饰用品;缝纫用品. ②〔英〕针线等缝纫用品店[业]; 〔美〕男子服饰用品店[业].

hab·er·geon [ˈhæbədʒən] *n.* (中世纪武士穿的高领无

袖的)短锁子甲.

hab·ile [ˈhæbil] *a.* 〔书〕能干的;熟练的.

ha·bil·i·ment [həˈbilimənt] *n.* ①〔*pl.*〕服饰;装备. ②〔*pl.*〕(适合某一场合或职位穿着的)制服,礼服;〔谑〕衣服. **-ed** *a.* 穿着衣服[礼服等]的;盛装的.

ha·bil·i·tate [həˈbiliteit] *vi.* 具备资格(尤指德国大学中的教师资格等). — *vt.* ①〔美方〕对(矿山)投资和提供设备. ②给…穿衣. ③使合格;使有能力. **-ta·tion** [həˌbiliˈteiʃən] *n.* **-ta·tive** [həˌbiliˈteitiv] *a.*

hab·it [ˈhæbit] *n.* ①习惯,癖好. ②脾性,性情;(动植物的)习性,常态. ③体质,体格. ④举止,行为. ⑤〔古〕服装;法衣;骑装. ⑥毒瘾. *H- is second nature.* 〔谚〕习惯成自然. *early ~s* 早起的习惯. *the ~ of getting up late* 晚起的习惯. *sober ~s* 滴酒不尝的习惯. *a man of gouty ~* 易得痛风病的人. ***be in a [the] ~ of*** 有某种习惯[脾气],惯于. ***be off the ~*** 〔美俚〕①戒掉毒瘾. ②吸毒者未受毒品的影响,清醒着. ***break off a [the] bad ~ of*** 改掉坏习惯. ***fall [get] into a [the] ~ of*** 养成某种习惯. ***get sb. into the ~ of*** 使某人养成某种习惯. ***(do sth.) from force of ~*** 出于习惯势力(做某事). ***have a [the] ~ of = be in a [the] ~ of. ~ of body*** 体质. ***~ of mind*** 心情,性格. ***kick the ~*** 〔美俚〕戒掉嗜好〔尤指毒瘾〕. ***out of ~*** 出于习惯. — *vt.* ①装扮;穿着. ②〔古〕住在. *be ~ed in* 穿着…. **~-forming** *a.* 成习惯的;成癖的,使人上瘾的,使之成嗜好的 (*a ~-forming drug* 会使人上瘾的麻醉毒品).

hab·it·a·bil·i·ty [ˌhæbitəˈbiliti] *n.* 可居住性,适于居住.

hab·it·a·ble [ˈhæbitəbl] *a.* 可居住的,适于居住的. **hab·it·a·ly** *ad.* **-ness** *n.* = habitability.

hab·it·ant [ˈhæbitənt] *n.* 居住者,居民.

hab·i·tant [ˈhæbitɔ̃:ŋ] *n.* 〔F.〕加拿大、美国路易斯安那州的法裔农民〔也写作 habitan〕.

hab·i·tat [ˈhæbitæt] *n.* ①(动、植物生长的)自然环境〔地区〕. ②聚集处;住所,居住地. ③经常发现某种事物的地方. ④海底实验室人员居住的加压舱,海底实验室.

hab·i·ta·tion [ˌhæbiˈteiʃən] *n.* ①居住. ②〔书〕住所;住宅. ③聚居地. *a house fit for ~* 适于居住的房屋.

ha·bit·u·al [həˈbitjuəl] *a.* 日常的,平常的;惯常的,习惯的. *~ practice* 习惯的做法,惯技. *a ~ criminal* 惯犯. *a ~ cinema-goer* 经常看电影的人. *a ~ liar* 惯于说谎的人. **-ly** *ad.* **-ness** *n.*

ha·bit·u·ate [həˈbitjueit] *vt.* ①使习惯于. ②〔古〕常去. ***be ~d to (sth.)*** 惯于… (*He was ~d to hard work.* 他已经习惯于干重活). ***~ oneself (sb.) to (sth.)*** 使自己[某人]习惯于某事物. — *vi.* (吸毒)上瘾.

ha·bit·u·a·tion [heˌbitjuˈeiʃən] *n.* ①成为习惯. ②(对麻醉品等的)适应;毒瘾.

hab·i·tude [ˈhæbitju:d] *n.* 〔古〕 = habit ①②③.

ha·bit·u·é [həˈbitjuei] *n.* 〔F.〕①常客,熟客. ②有毒瘾的人.

hab·i·tus [ˈhæbitəs] *n.* (*pl.* ***hab·i·tus*** [-tu:s]) ①习惯,癖,嗜好;【植、动】习性. ②体型,体质.

H.A.C. = ①Hague Arbitration Convention. ②Honourable Artillery Company. ③Hughes Aircraft Corporation.

ha·chure [hæˈʃjuə] *n.* 〔F.〕(图上表示阴影的)影线;(地图上表示山岳的)蓑状线. — *vt.* 用蓑状线画.

ha·ci·en·da [ˌhæsiˈendə] *n.* 〔Sp.〕①(西班牙及中、南美的)大庄园,种植园,牧场,工厂,矿山. ②(上述农场或牧场里的)主要住宅.

hack[1] [hæk] *vt.* ①乱劈,乱砍. ②平(地),翻(地),耙(地),碎土播(种) (*in*). ③整修(篱笆、墙面等). ④(打橄榄球时)故意踢对方的外胫;(打篮球时)拉[打]对方的手. ④〔美方〕对付;宽容. ⑤胡乱删改. *~ in oat* 碎土播种燕麦. — *vi.* ①砍,劈. ②不断地干咳. ③〔英方〕说话结巴. ④(运动中)踢对方的手[脚]犯规. *~ a hacking cough* 不断的干咳. — *n.* ①劈,砍. ②劈或砍的工具,鹤嘴锄. ③【机】格架. ④砍痕,伤痕;(运动中)打手,踢胫. ⑤干咳. ⑥〔英方〕说话结巴. ⑦〔美方〕窘迫,困窘. ⑧(对海军军官的)营房拘禁. ***have sb. under ~*** 把某人拘禁在营房内. ***put sb. under ~*** 使某人张口结舌. ***take a ~ at*** 尝试. **~-file** 刀锉. **~ hammer** 劈石斧. **~saw** 弓锯,钢锯. **~watch** 航行表. **-er** *n.*

hack[2] [hæk] *n.* ①出租的马,骑用的马,役马;驽马,老马. ②出租马车;〔口〕出租汽车;出租马车的车夫,出租汽车司机. ③干苦活的雇工,受雇做乏味工作的文人;以赚钱为目的的劣等艺术家. ④〔美俚〕警察;监狱看守;看守人;(货物列车尾部的)守车. ⑤〔美〕唯命是听的政党工作人员. ⑥〔美俚〕娼妓. *a Grubstreet ~ = a ~ writer* 雇佣的穷文人. *political ~* 政治仆从. — *a.* ①出租的;用旧了的;(文人等)被雇佣的;雇佣文人做的. ③陈旧的,陈腐的. *a ~ job* 卖苦力的工作,苦工. — *vt.* ①出租(马等). ②雇(人)作苦工;雇(人)写文章. ③用旧,使变陈腐. — *vi.* ①用普通速度骑马〔尤指租用的马〕(*along*). ②〔口〕驾驶出租马车[汽车]. **~man** *n.* 出租汽车司机;出租马车的车夫. **~stand** *n.* 〔美〕出租汽车[马车]停车处. **~-work** *n.* (为了挣钱的)卖文工作;(为了卖钱的)劣等作品.

hack[3] [hæk] *n.* ①(鱼等的)晒架;晒砖场. ②饲草架. ③【猎】饲鹰板. ④【机】格架. ***be at ~*** (还未自己去猎过食物的小鹰)在饲养训练中. ***live at ~ and manger*** 过优裕的生活.

hack·a·more [ˈhækəmɔ:ə] *n.* (美西部驯马用的)马勒.

hack·ber·ry [ˈhækbəri] *n.* ①朴属植物〔产于美洲的树,其果实小如樱桃,可食用〕. ②朴树木,朴果.

hack·but [ˈhækbʌt] *n.* 一种老式手枪;一种火绳枪.

hack·but·eer, hack·but·ter [ˌhækbəˈti:ə, ˈhækbətə] *n.* 火绳枪射手,火枪手.

hack·er·y [ˈhækəri] *n.* (印度的)双轮牛车.

hack·ie [ˈhæki] *n.* 〔口〕出租汽车司机.

hack·le[1] [ˈhækl] *n.* ①(梳麻或生丝用的)刷梳;麻栉;(栉梳机的)针排. ②(雄鸡、雄孔雀颈上的)纤毛〔制蚊钩用〕,禽鸟颈毛. ③〔*pl.*〕(狗等)颈背部竖起的毛;〔喻〕脾气,暴怒. ④(钓鱼用的)蝇钩,假蚊钩. ***get sb.'s ~s up*** 使某人发怒. ***with one's ~s up*** 勃然大怒,怒得毛发倒竖. — *vt.* 梳理;为(假蚊钩)装上颈毛.

hack·le[2] [ˈhækl] *vt.* 乱砍,乱劈,剁碎,砍掉. — *n.* 锯齿形.

hack·ly [ˈhækli] *a.* 粗糙的,参差不齐的;锯齿状的.

hack·ma·tack [ˈhækmətæk] *n.* ①【植】(产于美国北部、加拿大等地的)落叶松 (=tamarack). ②【植】一种杨树 (= balsam poplar).

hack·ney [ˈhækni] *n.* ①普通乘用马或挽马;出租马. ②出租马车;出租汽车. ③作苦工的人. — *a.* ①出租的;被雇用的. ②陈腐的,平常的. — *vt.* ①出租(马、马车等). ②滥用,虐使;用旧,使变陈腐. **~ carriage [coach]** 出租马车.

hack·neyed [ˈhæknid] *a.* 陈腐的,平常的. *a ~ phrase [tune]* 陈词滥调. *a ~ comparision* 陈旧的比喻.

had [强 hæd; 弱 həd, əd] have 的过去式及过去分词. ***be had*** 受骗,上当;被利用. ***~ as good (do)*** 不如,宁可 (*~ as good study English instead of Russian* 宁可学英语而不学俄语). ***~ as lief [soon]*** 〔古〕〔书〕毋宁,宁可 (*I ~ just as lief [soon] stay out of the quarrel.* 我宁可置身争论之外). ***~ best (do)*** 最好 (*We ~ best go at once.* 我们最好马上走). ***~ better (do)*** 最好 (*You ~ better go.* 你还是走好). ***~ better have done*** …做了就最好了 (*You had better have gone already.* 你早就应该走了〔可惜没有走〕). ***~ better not (do)*** 最好不要 (*He ~ better not remain here.* 他还是不留在这里好). ***~ it not been for*** 若非,假使没有. ***~ like to*** 差不多,几乎就…了. ***~ need (to) (do)*** 应当 (*You ~ need to do your best.*

你应当尽最大的努力). ~ ***rather (do)*** 还是…的好. ~ ***rather ... than*** 宁可…也不愿;与其…宁可 (*I ~ rather undertake some purposeful labour than stay idly.* 我宁可做些有意义的劳动也不愿闲着). ~ ***sooner ... than*** 宁可…也不愿;比…更喜欢 (*He ~ sooner live in the countryside than in the city.* 他宁肯住在乡下,不愿住在城里).

ha·dal ['heidl] *a.* 超深渊的,大洋深处六千公尺以下水层的.

had·die ['hædi] *n.* 〔Scot.〕= haddock.

had·dock ['hædək] *n.* (*pl.* ~*s*, 〔集合词〕~)【动】(产于北大西洋的)小口鳕,黑线鳕.

hade [heid] *n.*【地】断层余角,伸角,伸向. — *vi.* 垂直倾斜.

Ha·des ['heidi:z] *n.* ①【希神】冥王哈得斯. ②〔h-〕〔口〕地狱,冥府.

hadj [hædʒ] *n.* = hajj.

hadj·i ['hædʒi(:)] *n.* = haji, hajji.

Had·ley ['hædli] *n.* 哈德利〔姓氏〕.

had·n't ['hædnt] = had not.

Ha·dow ['hædəu] *n.* 哈多〔姓氏〕.

had·ron ['hædrɔn]【物】强子. **-ic** [hæ'drɔnik] *a.*

hadst [强 hædst; 弱 hədst]〔古〕have 的单数第二人称过去式〔与主语 thou 连用〕.

hae [hei, hæ] *vt.* 〔Scot.〕有.

Haeck·el ['hekəl] *n.* ①海克尔〔姓氏〕. ②**Ernst Heinrich** ~厄恩斯特·海因里奇·海克尔〔1884—1919, 德国生物学家〕.

haem- *comb. f.* = haema-, haemat-, haemato-, haemo-, hem-, hema-, hemat-, hemato-, hemo-, 表示"血": *haemal, haematoma.*

haem(a) *comb. f.* = haem.

hae·mal ['hi:məl] *a.* ①血(液)的;血管的. ②位于心脏与大血管一侧的.

hae·mat·ic [hi:'mætik] *a.* 血的,血液的;多血的;对血液起作用的. — *n.* 补血剂,清血药. **hae·mat·ics** *n.* 血液学.

hae·ma·tin(e) ['hi:mətin] *n.* ①【生化】正铁血红素. ②【化】苏木因,氧化苏木精.

hae·ma·tite ['hi:mətait] *n.*【矿】赤铁矿,红铁矿.

haemato- *comb. f.* = hemato-.

hae·ma·to·blast [ˌhi:mətəu'blæst] *n.*【解】①血小板. ②成血细胞. **-ic** *a.*

haem·a·to·cele ['hi:mətəusi:l] *n.*【医】血囊肿,积血.

hae·ma·to·cyte ['hi:mətəusait] *n.*【解】血球,血细胞.

haem·a·tol·o·gy [ˌhi:mə'tɔlədʒi, 'hi:-] *n.* 血液学,血液病学.

hae·ma·to·ma [ˌhi:mə'təumə] *n.* (*pl.* ~*ta* [-tə], ~*s* [-z])【医】血肿.

haem·a·to·ther·mal [ˌhi:mətəu'θə:məl] *a.* 恒温动物的 (= homotothermal).

Hae·ma·tox·y·lin [ˌhi:mə'tɔksilin] *n.*【化】苏木精.

hae·ma·tox·y·lon [ˌhi:mə'tɔksilɔn] *n.* = logwood.

haem·a·tu·ri·a [ˌhi:mə'tjuəriə] *n.*【医】血尿(症).

haemo- *comb. f.* = hemo-.

hae·mo·cyte ['hi:məusait] *n.*【医】血球,血细胞.

hae·mo·dy·nam·ics [ˌhi:məudai'næmiks] *n.*【医】血流动力学.

hae·mo·glo·bin [ˌhi:məu'gləubin] *n.*【生化】血红蛋白,血红朊.

hae·mo·ly·sin [ˌhi:mu'laisin] *n.*【医】溶血素.

hae·mol·y·sis [hi:'mɔlisis] *n.* (〔*pl.*〕*-ses* [-si:z])【医】溶血(作用),血球溶解.

hae·mo·phil·i·a [ˌhi:məu'filiə] *n.*【医】血友病.

hae·mo·phil·i·ac [ˌhi:məu'filiæk] *n.*【医】血友病患者.

haem·or·rhage ['hemərid ʒ] *n.*【医】出血. *cerebral* ~ 大脑出血,脑溢血. *internal* ~ 内出血. —*vi.*【医】出血.

haem·or·rhag·ic [ˌhemə'ridʒik] *a.*

haem·or·rhoid ['hemərɔid] *n.* 〔*pl.*〕【医】痔疮. *external [internal]* ~*s* 外[内]痔.

hae·mo·sta·sia, hae·mosta'sis [ˌhi:məu'steizə, hi:'mɔstəsis] *n.*【医】止血(法).

hae·mo·stat ['hi:məustæt] *n.*【医】止血器;止血剂.

hae·mo·stat·ic [ˌhi:məu'stætik] *a.* 止血的,能够止血的. — *n.*【医】止血剂.

hae·mu·re·sis [ˌhi:mjuə'resis] *n.*【医】血尿 = haematuria.

hae·res ['hi:ri:z] *n.* (*pl.* **hae·re·des** ['hi:ri:di:z])【法】继承人 (=heir).

Haes [heiz] *n.* 黑斯〔姓氏〕.

haf·ni·um ['hæfniəm] *n.*【化】铪.

haft [hæft] *n.* (工具或武器的)柄,把. — *vt.* 给…装柄,为…配把.

hag[1] [hæg] *n.* ①女妖,母夜叉. ②女巫. ③凶相丑恶的老妇人. ④【动】八目鳗类鱼. ~**born** *a.* 女巫生的. ~**ridden** *a.* 为恶梦所扰的. ~**seed** *n.* 女巫的子女.

hag[2] [hæg]〔英方〕*n.* ①沼地,沼泽中的硬地. ②砍伐;标记出来以待砍伐的树木;〔集合词〕砍倒的树. — *vt.* 砍,劈.

Ha·gar ['heigɑ:] *n.* ①【圣】夏甲〔亚伯拉罕之妾,亚伯拉罕之妻萨拉出于妒嫉将其驱入沙漠〕. ②女子名.

hag·ber·ry ['hægberi] *n.* = hackberry.

hag·but ['hægbʌt] *n.* = hackbut.

hag·fish ['hægfiʃ] *n.* (*pl.* ~, ~*es*)【动】盲鳗〔一种口圆牙利的海鱼,能穿入其它鱼类体内并吞食之〕.

Hag·ga·da, Hag·ga·dah [hə'gɑ:də] *n.* (*pl.* ***-ga·doth*** [-'dəuθ]) ①【宗】〔常用 h-〕(犹太教法典中)解释某些戒律的)寓言、传说等;犹太教法典中载有上述传说的章节. ②逾越节在纪念出埃及的宴会上讲的《出埃及记》故事;载有上述故事及礼仪的书. **hag·gad·ic** [hə'gɑ:dik,-'gædik] *a.*

hag·ga·dist [hə'gɑ:dist] *n.* 犹太教法典中解释戒律的传说的著者[研究者]. **-dis·tic** [ˌhægə'distik] *a.*

Hag·gai ['hægeiai] *n.* ①【宗】哈该〔公元前六世纪希伯来一先知〕. ②《旧约全书》中的《哈该书》〔记载哈该的预言〕.

hag·gard ['hægəd] *a.* ①憔悴的,形容枯槁的;消瘦的. ②样子凶暴的. ③难驯服的,未驯服的,(鹰)成年被捕的. ~ *hawks* 野鹰. — *n.* 未驯服的鹰;悍鹰. **-ly** *ad.* **-ness** *n.*

Hag·gard ['hægəd] *n.* 哈格德〔姓氏〕.

hag·gis ['hægis] *n.* 一种苏格兰布丁〔把牛(羊)肉杂碎与麦片等放在羊肚中烹煮的食品〕.

hag·gish ['hægiʃ] *a.* 老丑妇似的,母夜叉似的,女巫似的.

hag·gle ['hægl] *vi.* (就价格、条件等)争论,争辩,讨价还价 *(about, over, for, with)*. ~ *over the price* 讨价还价,讲价钱. —*vt.* ①乱砍,乱劈. ②〔古〕(因争论)而烦恼;使疲惫. — *n.* 争论;讨价还价.

hagi- *comb. f.* "圣徒的","神圣的": *hagiarchy.*

hag·i·arch·y ['hægiɑ:ki] *n.* 圣徒[教士]统治;圣徒等级组织.

hagio- *comb. f.* = hagi-: *hagiology.*

Hag·i·og·ra·pha [ˌhægi'ɔgrəfə] *n.* 犹太教《圣经》的第三部分.

hag·i·og·ra·pher [ˌhægi'ɔgrəfə] *n.* ①犹太教《圣经》第三部分的作者. ②圣徒传记作者.

hag·i·og·ra·phist [ˌhægi'ɔgrəfist] *n.* = hagiographer.

hag·i·og·ra·phy [ˌhægi'ɔgrəfi] *n.* ①圣徒生平的写作与研究;圣徒传记. ②理想化的传记,偶像化的传记.

hag·i·o·graph·i·c(al) [ˌhægiə'græfik(əl)] *a.*

hag·i·ol·a·try [ˌhægi'ɔlətri] *n.* 圣徒崇拜. **hag·i·ol·a·ter** [-'ɔlətə] 圣徒崇拜者. *n.* **hag·i·ol·a·trous** [-'ɔlətrəs] *a.*

hag·i·ol·o·gy [ˌhægi'ɔlədʒi] *n.* ①圣徒传记文学;圣徒

传记研究. ②圣徒名单. **hag·i·o·log·i·c(al)** [ˌhægiəˈlɔdʒik(əl)] *a.* **hag·i·ol·o·gist** [ˌhægiˈɔlədʒist] *n.* 圣徒传记研究者.

hag·i·o·scope [ˈhægiəskəup] *n.* 中世纪教堂内壁上的窄窗〔由此可见主祭坛〕.

Hague [heig] *n.* 〔the ~〕海牙〔荷兰中央政府所在地〕. ~ **Tribunal** 海牙国际仲裁法庭.

hah [hɑː] *int., n.* = ha.

ha-ha¹ [hɑ(ː)ˈhɑː] *int.* 哈哈! 〔表示嘲笑等〕. — *n.* 哈哈的笑声; 〔美俚〕(对某人的)嘲笑. *give sb. the merry* ~ 嘲笑某人.

ha-ha² [ˈhɑːhɑː] *n.* (造在花园界沟里不遮挡视线的)隐篱, 暗墙 (= sunk fence).

hah·ni·um [hɑːiniːəm] *n.* 铧〔原子序数为105的人造放射性化学元素〕.

haick [heik] *n.* = haik.

Hai·fa [ˈhaifə] *n.* 海法〔以色列港市〕.

haik [ˈhaik] *n.* (阿拉伯人的)白布大罩衣.

hai·ku [ˈhaikuː] *n.* 〔Jap.〕①俳句〔由五、七、五共十七字组成的短诗〕. ②〔*pl.* ~ku〕俳句诗.

hail¹ [heil] *n.* ①雹, 冰雹. ②象雹子般落下的东西. *a ~ of blows [curses]* 一阵打击〔咒骂〕. *a ~ of bullets* 一阵弹雨. — *vt.* 使象雹子般落下. ~ *blows [curses] down on sb.* 给某人一顿痛打〔一通臭骂〕. — *vi.* 下雹; 冰雹般落下来. ~**stone** (一粒)冰雹. ~**storm** 下雹, 雹暴.

hail² [heil] *vt.* ①向…高呼, 为…欢呼; 向…欢呼致贺. ②招呼. ~ *sb. (as) King* 欢呼拥立某人为国王. ~ *a taxi* 叫出租汽车. — *vi.* 招呼; (向过往船只)打信号招呼. ~ ***from*** … ①(船)自…来. ②出生地是… (*She ~s from Shanghai.* 她是上海人. *~ from all corners of the country* 来自全国各地). — *n.* 高呼, 欢呼, 招呼; 欢迎. ***within*** ~ 在能听到呼叫的距离内〔尤指招呼船〕, 在近处. — *int.* 〔书、诗〕万岁! *All ~! = Hail to you!* 万岁! ***Hail Mary***! 【天主】万福马利亚! ***Hail Columbia*** 〔美俚〕①揍, 骂 (*give sb. Hail Columbia* 狠揍〔臭骂〕某人). ②喧闹. ~**-fellow** = ~**-fellow-well'-met'** ①*a.* 友好的, 很亲密的 (*be ~-fellow with everybody* 跟谁都很要好). ② *n.* 密友.

hail·er [ˈheilə] *n.* ①欢呼者; 打招呼者. ②(海军船舰等上的)手提扩音器 (= bullhorn).

hail·y [ˈheili] *a.* 雹子(一样)的; 夹有冰雹的.

hair [hɛə] *n.* ①〔集合词〕毛发, 头发, 汗毛. ②毛状物; 毛状金属丝; 毛发织物; 【植】茸毛. ③一丝丝, 些微. *grey ~s* 白发; 老年. *a fine coat of* ~ (马等)一身好毛. ***against the*** ~ 〔古〕违背本意, 不合本性. ***a ~ in one's neck*** 麻烦事. ***a ~ to make a tether of*** 〔Scot.〕小题大作. ***be not worth a*** ~ 一钱不值. ***both of a*** ~ 同类, 一丘之貉. ***bring sb.'s grey ~s (in sorrow) to the grave*** 使老人忧心至死. ***bush [head, shock] of*** ~ 浓浓的头发. ***by (the turn of) a*** ~ 差一点儿, 险些儿, 几乎. ***comb [stroke] sb.'s ~ for him*** 严责某人. ***do up one's*** ~ 梳头. ***fell of*** ~ 耷拉下来的头发, 发绺. ***get [have take] sb. by the short ~s*** 〔俚〕任意摆布某人, 完全操纵某人; 抓住某人辫子. ***get in sb.'s*** ~ 〔美俚〕触怒, 使烦恼. ***hang by a (single)*** ~ 千钧一发, 岌岌可危. ***have grey*** ~ 满头白发. ***have grey ~s*** 有些白头发. ***have one's ~ cut*** 剪发, 理发. ***in one's*** ~ 光着头. ***in the*** ~ ①毛向外的. ②兽皮有毛的. ***Judas*** ~ 红头发. ***keep your ~ on*** 〔俚〕保持镇静! 别发火! ***let one's (back) ~ down*** ①将头发散开. ②〔口〕举止随便, 不拘礼节. ③直言不讳. ***Let your ~ dry.*** 〔俚〕别那么神气, 别那么拿架子. ***lose one's*** ~ ①头变秃. ②发怒. ***make sb.'s ~ curl = make sb.'s ~ stand on end*** 使人毛骨悚然. ***not touch a ~ of sb.'s head*** 不动某人一根汗毛. ***not turn a ~ = without turning a*** ~ 不动声色, 镇定自若. ***put [turn] up one's*** ~ (少女成年后)梳拢头发. ***smooth [stroke] sb.'s ~ the wrong way = stroke sb. against the*** ~ 使某人恼怒. ***split ~s*** *(over sth.)* 作无益的细微分析, 无故挑剔. ***stroke sb. with the*** ~ 〔Scot.〕安抚. ***Take a ~ of the dog that bit you*** 〔谚〕以毒攻毒; 用酒解酒. ***tear one's [the]*** ~ 扯头发〔表示悲伤、焦急、忿怒〕. ***to (the turn of) a*** ~ 完全一样, 丝毫不差. ***wear one's (own)*** ~ 不戴假发. ~**ball** 毛球, 毛团〔常见于牛、猫等胃中的毛团块, 因牛、猫等爱舐毛而把毛吃入胃中, 渐聚之而成团〕. ~**breadth** ① *n.* 一发之差, 极微小的距离 (*by a ~-breadth* 一发之差, 间不容发. *within a ~breadth of sth.* 差一点就…). ② *a.* 一发之间的, 间不容发的 (*a ~-breadth escape* 九死一生, 死里逃生). ~**brush** 发刷, 毛刷. ~**clippers** 〔*pl.*〕发剪. ~**cloth** ①毛布〔马毛〔驼毛等〕与绒布的织物, 用于制家具套等〕. ②粗毛织衬衣. ~**cut** ①理发. ②发式. ~**cutter** 理发员. ~**do** 〔口〕①(女人的)梳发, 烫发. ②(女人)做头发, 头发梳法. ~**dresser** ①理发员. ②梳头者. ~**dressing** 理发, 梳头; 理发业 (*~dressing saloon* 理发馆). ~**dryer** 吹风器. ~**dye** 染发药水. ~ **felt** 毛毡. ~ **hygrometer** 毛发湿度计. ~**lace** 发带, 头带. ~**line** ①极细的线; 细缝; 细微的差别. ②(字画等的)纤细笔画. ③【纺】细线条, 线条精纺呢. ④头型轮廓, 发型轮廓. ⑤【军】瞄准线; 〔*pl.*〕光学仪器所用叉线 (*to a ~line* 精密地). ~ **net** 发网. ~ **oil** 发油. ~ **pencil** 画笔. ~**piece** *n.* ①男子的(遮秃)假发. ②女式假发. ~**pin** ① *n.* 发夹; 夹叉, 簪; 发夹状的东西; 道路的急转弯; 〔美俚〕女人, 女学生. ② *a.* U 字形的 (*a ~pin bend* 陡路上的; U 字形转弯的路). ~ **powder** 发粉. ~**-raiser** 令人吃惊的故事; 使人毛骨悚然的东西〔事情〕. ~**-raising** *a.* 〔口〕使人毛发竖起的, 恐怖的. ~ **restorer** 生发药. ~**s breath** = ~breath. ~ **seal** 海驴, 海豹. ~ **side** 【机】(皮带的)毛面. ~ **slide** 发夹. ~ **space** 【印】字间最小间隔. ~**-splitter** 专爱拘泥小节的人, 爱吹毛求疵的人. ~**splitting** *n., a.* 拘泥小节(的). 吹毛求疵(的). ~**spring** 【机】游丝; 细弹簧. ~**streak** 【动】窄尾小灰蝶〔一种翼上有细纹的蝴蝶〕. ~ **stroke** (字、画的)细笔画; 【印】细线. ~**tail** 带鱼. ~**-thin** *a.* 细如毛发的. ~ **trigger** 微火触发器. ~**-trigger** *a.* ①一触即发的, 即时的. ②一碰就坏的. ~**weaving** (尼龙)假发植入(术). ~**worm** = gordian worm. **-ed** *a.* 具有(某种)头发的 (*fair-~* 金发的. *short-~* 短发的). **-less** *a.* 无毛的, 无发的, 秃顶的. **-like** *a.* 毛发似的, 极细的.

hair·tic·i·an [hɛəˈtiʃiən] *n.* 〔美〕发型师.

hair·y [ˈhɛəri] *a.* ①毛发的, 多毛的, 毛厚的. ②发状的, 毛似的. ③〔美俚〕粗鲁的; 可怕的, 令人沮丧的. ④〔美俚〕(笑话等)陈腐不堪的. ~ ***about [at, in] the fetlocks [heel]*** 没有教养的, 没有礼貌的. ~**-chested** *a.* 粗壮的. ~**-heeled** [-hiːld] *a.* 〔俚〕没有教养的, 没有礼貌的. ~ **vetch** 【植】长柔毛野豌豆〔叶子带毛, 开小朵蓝花, 种植作饲料用〕. **hair·i·ly** *ad.* **hair·i·ness** *n.*

Hai·ti [ˈheiti] *n.* 海地〔拉丁美洲〕.

Hai·tian [ˈheiʃjən] *n.* ①海地人. ②海地人讲的法语(= Haitian Creole). — *a.* 海地的; 海地人的.

hajj [hædʒ] *n.* 【宗】(伊斯兰教的)麦加朝圣.

haj·ji, haj·i [ˈhædʒi(ː)] *n.* 哈吉〔曾赴麦加朝过圣的穆斯林的荣誉称号〕.

hake [heik] *n.* 【动】狗鳕, 无须鳕.

ha·keem [hɑːˈkiːm] *n.* (伊斯兰教国家的)大学者; 医生.

Ha·ken·kreuz [ˈhɑːkənkrɔits] *n.* 〔G.〕卐字〔德国纳粹党党徽〕.

ha·kim¹ [ˈhɑːkiːm] *n.* ①(伊斯兰教国家的)地方长官; 法官.

ha·kim² [hɑːˈkiːm] = hakeem.

Hak·ka [ˈhɑːkˈkɑː] *n.* 〔汉〕客家〔古代移居闽、粤等地的中原人的后裔〕; 客家人; 客家语.

Hak·luyt [ˈhæklu:t] *n.* ①哈克路特〔姓氏〕. ②**Richard** ～ 理查德·哈克路特〔1552?—1616，英国地理学及历史学家〕.

Ha·ko·da·te [ˌhækəuˈdɑ:ti] *n.* 函馆〔日本港市〕.

Ha·ko·ne [ˈhɑ:kəne] *n.* 箱根〔日本城镇；著名风景区〕.

hal- *comb. f.* (后接元音) = halo-: *hal*ite; *hal*ide.

Hal [hæl] *n.* 哈尔〔男子名，Henry 的昵称〕.

Ha·la·kha, Ha·la·cha [ˌhɑ:lɑ:ˈhɑ:, həˈlɑ:hə] *n.* (*pl.* **-la·khot, -la·chot** [-ˈhəut]) ①〔常用 h-〕犹太教法典异传(未载入圣经的戒律和教规). ②犹太教法典中载有上述戒律和教规的章节.

ha·la·khist, ha·la·chist [ˈhɑ:ləhist, həˈlɑ:hist] *n.* 犹太教法典异传的叙述〔编写〕者.

ha·la·ha(h) [həˈlɑ:lə] *n.* 赫拉勒〔沙特阿拉伯货币单位，等于 100 里亚尔〕.

ha·la·tion [həˈleiʃən] *n.* 【物】晕影；晕光作用.

hal·berd [ˈhælbə(:)d] *n.* 戟〔十五和十六世纪使用的一种枪钺合一的兵器〕.

hal·berd·ier [ˌhælbə:ˈdiə] *n.* 戟兵.

halbert [ˈhælbə(:)t] *n.* = halberd.

hal·cy·on [ˈhælsiən] *n.* ①【动】翠鸟，鱼狗. ②传说中的太平鸟〔巢居海上，冬至产卵时海波平静〕. — *a.* ①翠鸟的；翠鸟产卵期的. ②平静的. ③愉快的. ④富饶的. ～ ***days*** ①冬至前后十四日间海上平静的日子. ②宁静幸福的日子，太平时代.

Hal·dane [ˈhɔ:ldein] *n.* 霍尔丹〔姓氏〕.

hale[1] [heil] *a.* (尤指老人)强壮的，矍铄的. ～ ***and hearty*** 矍铄的，老当益壮的. **-ness** *n.*

hale[2] [heil] *vt.* 强拉，硬拖.

Hale(s) [heil(z)] *n.* 黑尔(斯)〔姓氏〕.

hal·er [ˈhɑ:lə] *n.* (*pl.* **-er·u** [-əru:], **～s**) 赫勒〔捷克货币名称，为 1/100 克朗〕.

half [hɑ:f] *n.* (*pl.* ***halves*** [hɑ:vz]) ①半，一半；一部分. ②半小时；半英里；半品脱；半价票；〔美〕半美元；半学年，一学期. ③(球赛的)半场，半局，半盘，半回合. ④(足球)中卫 (= halfback)；(运动中的)配手，合作者. ⑤(高尔夫球赛等)相同得分. ⑥(尤指打官司的)一方. ～ *past four* = 〔美〕～ *after four* 四点半钟. *[The]* ～ *of four is two.* 四的一半是二. ～ *and* ～ 一半一半，各半. *H- a loaf is better than none.* 〔谚〕面包半个别嫌少，总比没有面包好. *Never do things by halves.* 〔谚〕做事不可半途而废. *one* ～ 二分之一，一半. *one's better* ～〔谑〕妻子. *one's worse* ～〔谑〕丈夫. *The first blow [stroke] is* ～ *the battle.*〔谚〕良好的开端，就是成功的一半. *The* ～ *is more than the whole.* 〔谚〕过犹不及. *the other* ～ (穷人眼中的)有钱人；(有钱人眼中的)穷人. *too long by* ～ 长了一半. *two pounds and a* ～ = *two and a* ～ *pounds* 两磅半. *the summer* ～ 夏天开始的半学年. ***and a*** ～ 非常困难的 (*That is a job and a* ～. 那是非常困难的工作). ***by*** ～ ①只一半. ②〔反〕非常，极，过分(*too clever by* ～ 聪明过度). ***by halves*** 不完全(*do sth. by halves* 做事情半途而废，做事不彻底). ***cry halves*** 要求平分. ***cut in*** ～ = ***cut in(to) (two) halves*** 切成两半. ***divide sth. into halves*** 把…分成两半. ***go halves with sb. in sth.*** 与(某人)平分(某物). ***in*** ～ ***[halves]*** 成两半. ***not (the)*** ～ ***of*** 仅仅是次要部分，仅仅是小部分 (*That's not* ～ *of the story.* 那还仅仅是事情的一小部分〔严重的事还在后面呢〕). ***on (the) halves*** 平分，对分. ***see with*** ～ ***an eye*** 一看就明白. ***time and a*** ～ 在平时工资外另加 50%. ***to (the) halves*** ①到半途；不完全. ②〔美〕利益均分. ***with [have]*** ～ ***a mind [notion] to (sth.)*** 对…半心半意. — *a.* ①一半的. ②一部分的；不完全的. *a* ～ *share* 半份儿. *a* ～ *sheet of paper* 半张纸. ～ *a dozen* = *a* ～ *dozen* 半打，六个. ～ *an hour* = 〔美〕*a* ～ *hour* 半小时. ～ *knowledge* 一知半解，半瓶醋. *a* ～ *smile* 微笑，欲笑不笑. ～ *the number* 半数. *work* ～ *shift* 上半班. — *ad.* ①一半地. ②部分地，不完全地. ③相当地〔常与否定词连用，表示相反的意思〕. ～ *in doubt* 半信半疑. *Well begun is* ～ *done.* 〔谚〕开始良好等于一半成功. ～ *dead* 累得要命. ～ ***as much [many] again as*** 一倍半，多一半. ～ ***as much [many] as*** 只有一半，少一半. ～ ***green*** 半生的，半腌的. ～ ***shot*** 半醉的. ***I*** ～ ***wish*** ... 我很想. ***more than*** ～ 非常. ***not*** ～ ①一点也不 (*not* ～ *bad* 一点也不坏，相当好. *Her singing isn't* ～ *bad.* 她唱得很不坏). ②〔俚〕极其，非常 (*He didn't* ～ *swear.* 他骂得很凶. *Do you like beer?* — *Oh, not* ～! 你喜欢(喝)啤酒吗？— 喜欢极了！). **～-*and-*～** ① *n.* 两种成分各半的东西；淡烈两种啤酒各半的混合酒；奶油和全脂牛奶各半的混合物；混血儿. ② *a.* 两者各半的；不三不四的，不伦不类的. ③ *ad.* 等量地，各半地. **～back** *n.* (足球的)中卫. **～-baked** *a.* ①半生不熟的. ②不成熟的，思虑不缜密的(*～-baked ideas* 不成熟的意见. *a ～-baked scheme* 不周密的计划). ③浅薄的，无经验的(*a ～-baked youth* 初出茅庐的青年. *a ～-baked film critic* 半瓶醋的影评家). **～beak** *n.* 鱼箴科 (*Hemiramphidae*) 鱼〔一种下腭特别长的热带小海鱼〕. ～ **binding** 半精装. **～-blood** *n.* 同父异母，同母异父；杂种，混血儿. **～-blooded** *a.* 杂种的，混血的. ～ **blue**〔英〕(给次要运动员的)半蓝徽章. ～ **boot** 半高统靴. **～-bound** *a.* ①半精装的. ②【化】半化合的. **～-box** 无盖轴箱. **～-breadth** (船的)中轴距离. **～-bred** *a.* ①混血的，杂种的. ②教养不足的，粗野的. **～-breed** ① *n.* 杂种，混血儿〔尤指美洲印第安人与白种人的后代〕. ② *a.* 杂种的，混血的. ～ **brother** 异父〔异母〕兄弟. ～ **calf** 犊皮背精装. **～-caste** *n.*, *a.* 欧亚混血儿(的)；混血儿(的). **～-cell** 【化】半电池. ～ **cock** (枪)处于半击发状态，机头半张开 (*go off at* ～ *cock* = 〔美〕*go off* *～-cocked* 还没有开保险就发射；动手过早). **～-cocked** *a.* (枪)处于半击发状态的；行动过早的，仓促行事的. **～-cooked** *a.* 半熟的；〔美〕尚未成熟的. **～-cracked** *a.* 笨的，蠢的. ～ **crown** 半克朗〔英国旧银币名，合 2 先令 6 便士〕. ～ **deck** 商船上见习生的宿处. ～ **dollar** 〔美〕半元银币，五十分. **～-done** *a.* 半成的；不完全的；半熟的. ～ **eagle** 〔美〕(从前的)五元金币. **～-evergreen** *a.* 【植】半长青的. ～ **gainer** 【体】面对池反身直体跳水. **～-hardy** (植物等)能经受一般寒冷的，需要防低温〔霜雪〕的. **～-hearted** *a.* 无兴趣的，不热心的，半心半意的. ～ **hitch** (容易解开的)简单结子. **～-holiday** 半日假. **～-hour** ① *n.* 三十分钟，半小时. ② *a.* 半小时的，每半小时的. **～hourly** *a.*, *ad.* 每半小时的〔地〕. ～ **hunter** 双盖怀表. **～-length** ① *a.* 半身的. ② *n.* 半身像，半身画像. **～-life** 【原】半排出期〔放射性同位素从生物有机体中排出一半量的时间，也作 ～ life 或 ～ life period〕. **～light** 淡灰色光. ～ **line** 【数】半直线. **～-long** *a.* 【语】半长音的. **～-mast** ① *vt.* 下半(旗). ② *n.* 半旗位置 (*fly [hang, hoist] a flag at ～-mast* 下半旗. *～-mast high* 在半旗位置). ～ **measures** 姑息手段，折衷办法. **～-moon** 半月；半月形. ～ **mourning** 比黑色浅的(如灰、白、紫色的)丧服；穿浅色丧服时期. ～ **nelson** (摔交)扼颈 (*get a* ～ *nelson on sb.* 把某人完全压住). ～ **note**【乐】二分音符. ～ **nut** 【机】对开螺母，开缝螺母，闸瓣，闸瓦. ～ **pay** 半薪. **～-pay** *a.* 领半薪的 (*place sb. on the ～-pay list* 〔英〕令休职). **～penny** [ˈheipəni]① *n.* (*pl.* ***～pence*** [ˈheipəns], ***～pennies***) 半便士；〔口〕铜币. ② *a.* 半便士的；便宜的，没价值的 (*～-penny under the hat* 一种骗钱的下等赌博. *not a ～penny the worse* 毫不逊色，一点也不差. *three halfpence* 一便士半. *receive more kicks than ～pence* 〔口〕没有受奖反而更加倒霉. *turn up [come back] again like a bad ～penny* 来得不是时候). **～pennyworth** *n.* 半便士的东西；极少量. ～ **pint** ①十六分之一加仑. ②〔美俚〕个子矮小的人；微不足道的人. **～-price** *ad.* 半价. ～ **rest**

【乐】二分休止符. ~**-round** ① *a.* 半圆的, 半月形的. ② *n.* 半球. ~**-seas-over** *a.* ①【海】航行到半途的. ②〔口〕半醉的. ~ **sister** 异父〔异母〕姊妹. ~ **size** 上身短的(或身体矮小的)妇女的衣服尺寸. ~**-slip** 无上身衬裙. ~ **sole** 鞋前掌. ~**-sole** *vt.* 给(鞋)打前掌. ~ **sovereign** 半金镑〔英国旧币名, 等于旧币 10 先令〕. ~**-staff** *n., vt.* = ~-mast. ~ **step**【军】小步, 快步;【乐】半音(程). ~**-stuff** (造纸用) 半纸料. ~ **tide** 半潮〔满潮与退潮间的一半〕. ~**-timber(ed)** *a.*【建】(房屋等)半露木的. ~**-time** ①半工半薪. ②(比赛中的)半场休息时间 (*be on ~-time* 做半工支半薪. *What is the score at ~-time?* 上半场比分多少?) ~**-timer** 以一半时间做工的人;〔英〕半工半读的学生. ~ **tint** 中间色调; (水彩)薄涂. ~ **title** (书籍)印在扉页上的书名. ~**-tone** ① *n.*【印】照相铜版; 网目铜版; 中间色调;【乐】半音. ② *a.* 照相铜版的; 中间色调的 (*~ tone process* 网目铜版制版术). ~**-track** ① *n.* 半履带式, 半履带式车辆(尤指一种轻装甲车). ② *a.* 半履带式的. ~**-truth** *n.* 部分真实的陈述〔报导〕, 欺骗性的半真半假的陈述〔报导〕. ~ **volley** *n., vt.*【体】球一着地立即打出〔踢出〕. ~**way** ① *ad.* 半途; 不彻底地; 几乎, 快要 (*meet sb. ~way* 在半路迎接〔迎战〕某人; 迎合〔迁就〕某人. *meet trouble ~-way* 杞忧, 自寻烦恼. *I have ~way decided to go.* 我已差不多决定要去了.) ② *a.* 中间的, 半途的, 不彻底的 (*a ~-way house* 位于两城镇之间的旅店; 妥协方案, 折衷办法; 为吸毒者设立的戒瘾治疗中心; 为长期监禁或住院治疗者设立的重返社会训练所. *a ~way inn* 中途客栈. *~-way measures* 不彻底的办法, 折衷的办法 = half measures). ~**-wit** 笨蛋. ~**-witted** *a.* 鲁钝的, 迟钝的. ~**-yearly** *a., ad.* 每半年的〔地〕.

half·y [ˈhɑːfi] *n.* 〔美俚〕没有腿的残废人.

hal·i·but [ˈhælibət] *n.* (*pl.* ~*s,* 〔集合词〕~)【动】庸鲽, 大比目鱼.

hal·ide [ˈhælaid] *n.*【化】卤化物. — *a.* = haloid.

hal·i·dom [ˈhælidəm], **hal·i·dome** [ˈhælidəm, -dəum] *n.* 〔古〕圣物; 圣宝. ***by my*** ~ 誓必, 一定.

hal·i·eu·tic [ˌhæliˈjuːtik] *a.* 钓鱼的.

hal·i·eu·tics [ˌhæliˈjuːtiks] *n.* 钓鱼技术; 钓鱼论.

Hal·i·fax[1] [ˈhælifæks] *n.* ①哈利法克斯〔加拿大港市〕. ②哈利法克斯〔英国城市〕.

Hal·i·fax[2] [ˈhælifæks] *n.* 哈利法克斯〔姓氏〕.

hal·ite [ˈhælait] *n.*【化】石盐, 岩盐.

hal·i·to·sis [ˌhæliˈtəusis] *n.*【医】口臭.

Hal·i·ver [ˈhælivə] *n.* 〔美〕比目鱼肝油.

hall [hɔːl] *n.* ①〔常作 H-〕(政治团体、工会等的)本部, 总部, 办公大楼. ②会馆, 会场, 会堂; 展览厅; 娱乐场. ③〔常作 H-〕〔美〕(大学的)学部大楼, 教学大楼, 讲堂, 学生宿舍. ④〔英〕(大学的)大餐厅, 公共食堂. ⑤地主庄园的主要建筑, (已往王公贵族的)府第, 宅邸. ⑥门厅, 过道, 走廊. *a banquet* ~ 宴会厅. *a dance* ~ 跳舞厅. *a music* ~ 音乐堂. *a lecture* ~ 大讲堂. *a servants'* ~ 仆役室. *a taxi-dance* ~ 〔美〕有舞女伴舞的舞厅. ***H-of Fame*** ①纽约市纪念美国名人的纪念馆; 名人遗物收藏馆. ②杰出人物. ***~s of ivy*** 〔美〕高等学校. ***the City [Town] H-*** 市政厅. ***the H- of Mirrors*** (温莎宫的)镜厅. ***the Science H-*** 〔美〕科学大楼. ~**bedroom** 廊底小卧室〔尤指楼上走廊尽头间隔出来的小卧室〕. ~**man** ①门侍. ②〔美〕没有加入大学生联谊会的学生. ~**mark** ①*n.*(伦敦金业工会证明金银纯度的)检验印记; 质量证明; 标志, 特点. ②*vt.* 在…上盖检验印记. ~**stand** 衣帽架. ~ **tree** 柱式衣帽架(尤指大厅入口处者). ~**way** 〔美〕门厅, 过道.

Hall [hɔːl] *n.* 霍尔〔姓氏, 男子名〕.

hal·lah [ˈhɑːlə] *n.* (犹太人安息日和假日吃的) 白面包卷.

Hal·lam [ˈhæləm] *n.* 哈勒姆〔姓氏〕.

Hal·leck [ˈhælik] *n.* 哈利克〔姓氏〕.

hal·lel [hɑːˈleil, ˈhɑːlel] *n.* (犹太某些节日中诵咏的)《诗篇》第 113 到 118 篇.

hal·le·lu·iah, hal·le·lu·jah [ˌhæliˈluːjə] *n., int.* 哈利路亚〔犹太教和基督教的欢呼用语, 意为"赞美神"〕. ~**girl,** ~**lass** 〔谑〕救世军女工作人员.

Hal·ley [ˈhæli] *n.* 哈利〔姓氏〕.

Halley [ˈhæli] *n.* ①哈雷〔姓氏〕. ②**Edmund** ~ 埃德蒙德·哈雷〔1656—1742, 英国天文学家〕. ~**'s comet** 哈雷彗星.

hal·liard [ˈhæljəd] *n.* = halyard.

hal·lo(a) [həˈləu] *int.* 喂! 啊呀! — *n.* "喂"的一声, "啊呀"的一声. —*vt., vi.* 对…叫一声喂!

hal·loo [həˈluː] *int.* 喂! 嗨! 驰! 〔嗾狗声和引人注意的喊声〕. — *vt., vi.* 大声喊叫; 高声嗾使. — *n.* 高呼. ***Do not ~ until you are out of the wood(s).*** 〔谚〕未离险境, 别先高兴.

hal·low[1] [ˈhæləu] *vt.* 把…视为神圣; 尊敬; 把…献给神. — *n.* 圣人, 圣徒.

hal·low[2] [həˈləu] *int., v., n.* = halloo.

hal·lowed [ˈhæləud] *a.* ①(被视为)神圣的; 被尊为神圣的. ②受崇拜的. *the ~ traditions from the past* 神圣的古老传统. **-ly** *ad.* **-ness** *n.*

Hal·low·een [ˈhæləuˈiːn] *n.* 万圣节前夕〔指十月三十一日夜晚, 儿童可以纵情玩乐〕.

Hal·low·mas [ˈhæləumæs] *n.* 万圣节〔指十一月一日〕.

Hall·statt [ˈhɑːlstɑːt] *a.* 欧洲铁器时代早期的〔约公元前八世纪到四世纪〕. ~ **civilization** 欧洲铁器时代早期文化〔Hallstatt 系奥地利一村庄名, 该处曾有考古发现〕.

hal·lu·ci·nate [həˈluːsineit] *vt., vi.* (使)生幻觉.

hal·lu·ci·na·tion [həˌluːsiˈneiʃən] *n.* 幻觉, 错觉. **-na·to·ry** [-təri] *a.* 幻觉的, 妄想的.

hal·lu·ci·no·gen [həˈluːsinədʒen, ˌhæljuˈsinədʒen] *n.*【药】幻觉剂. —*a.* 引起幻觉的.

hal·lu·ci·no·sis [həˌluːsiˈnəusis] *n.*【医】幻觉病.

hal·lux [ˈhæləks] *n.* (*pl.* **-lu·ces** [-jusiːz])【解】拇趾, 大趾; 鸟的后趾.

halm [hɑːm] *n.* = haulm.

hal·ma [ˈhælmə] *n.* (棋盘有 256 目的)一种跳棋.

ha·lo [ˈheiləu] *n.* (*pl.* ~*(e)s*) ①(日月等的)晕, 晕圈. ②神像后的光环. ③荣光, 光辉. ④【解】乳晕, 乳头轮. — *vt.* 使有晕圈; 以光圈围绕 (*Rainbows ~ed the waterfalls* 彩虹给瀑布围上了光圈). — *vi.* 成晕圈.

halo- *comb. f.* (后接辅音) ①表示"盐": *halo*phyte. ②表示"卤": *halo*genide.

hal·o·bi·ont [ˌhæləuˈbaiɔnt] *n.*【动】(海中的)适盐生物.

hal·o·bi·os [ˌhæləuˈbaiɔs] *n.* 海洋生物.

hal·o·gen [ˈhælədʒen] *n.*【化】卤(素). ~ *acid* 氢卤酸.

hal·o·ge·nate [ˈhælədʒəneit] *vt.* ①卤化, 卤代. ②加卤, 卤合. **hal·o·ge·na·tion** *n.*

hal·o·gen·ide [ˈhælədʒənaid] *n.*【化】卤化物.

hal·o·ge·ton [ˈhælədʒətɔn, həˈlɔdʒitɔn] *n.*【植】盐生草 (*Halogeton glomeratus*) 〔产于美国西部〕.

hal·oid [ˈhælɔid] *a.*【化】卤(族)的; 含卤(素)的; 似海盐的. — *n.* 卤化物; 海盐.

hal·o·me·ter [hæˈlɔmitə] *n.*【化】盐量计.

hal·o·mor·phic [ˌhæləˈmɔːfik] *a.* (土壤)在中性环境(或碱性盐)中形成的. **-phism** *n.*

hal·o·phile [ˈhæləfail] *n.* 嗜盐生物, 适于在盐质环境中生长的动植物. **hal·o·phil·ic** [-ˈfilik], **ha·loph·i·lous** [həˈlɔfiləs] *a.*

hal·o·phyte [ˈhæləfait] *n.*【植】盐土植物.

hal·o·thane [ˈhæləθein] *n.*【化】卤(化)乙烷〔其气体可作吸入麻醉剂〕.

Hal·ste(a)d [ˈhɔːlstid, ˈhæːlsted] *n.* 霍尔斯特德〔姓氏〕.

H

halt[1] [hɔːlt] *n.* ①暂停前进,止步. ②休息;立定. ③(铁路)临时站;电车站. ***bring to a*** ~ 使停止. ***call [cry] a*** ~ 命令停止;命令立定 (*call a ~ to attacks* 命令停止进攻). ***come to a*** ~ =***make a*** ~ 停止. — *vi.* ①站住,立定,休息. ②停止;暂停前进. ~ *for a rest* (军队)停下来休息. — *vt.* ①止住,使停止. ②使驻扎. ~ *the troops for a rest* 命令军队停下来休息. *a ~ing place* 驻军地;休息地.

halt[2] [hɔːlt] *n., a.* 〔古〕跛(的). — *vi.* ①踌躇不前;吞吞吐吐地说. ②(韵文等)欠完整, 有缺点. ③〔古〕跛行. ~ *between two opinions* 拿不定主意. ~ *in one's speech* 讲话吞吞吐吐. *A poor argument ~s.* 论点拙劣,漏洞百出.

hal·ter[1] [ˈhɔːltə] *n.* ①(牛马等的)笼头, 韁绳. ②绞索; 绞刑. ③(女用)三角背心. ***come to the*** ~ 被处绞刑. ***put a ~ round one's own neck*** 自己套上绞索; 作茧自缚. ***stretch a*** ~ 受绞刑. — *vt.* ①给…套上笼头〔系上韁绳〕. ②绞死. ③束缚,抑制. **~-break** *vt.* 使(马)带惯笼头.

hal·ter[2] [ˈhɔːltə] *n.* 跛行者,踌躇者.

hal·ter[3] [ˈhɔːltə] *n.* ***(pl. ~es)*** (昆虫的)平衡棒, 平衡器.

halt·ing[1] [ˈhɔːltiŋ] *a.* 跛的. **-ly** *ad.* **-ness** *n.*

halt·ing[2] [ˈhɔltiŋ] *a.* 踌躇的;不完整的. *speak in a ~ way* 说话吞吞吐吐.

ha·lutz [hɑːˈluːts] *n.* ***(pl. ha·lutz·im*** [hɑːluːtˈsiːm]***)*** 哈鲁茨〔以色列农业居民点中最早移入的犹太拓荒者〕.

hal·vah, hal·va [hɑːlˈvɑː] *n.* 哈发糕〔用芝麻面和蜜糖作馅的点心,源出土耳其〕.

halve [hɑːv] *vt.* ①把…分成相等的两部分. ②使平均分担. ③将…减半. ④【建】把…开半对搭. ~ ***a hole with*** 【高尔夫球】和对方以同一打击数打进洞穴. ~ ***a match*** 【体】打成平手.

halves [hɑːvz] half 的复数.

halv·ing [ˈhɑːviŋ] *n.* 二等分;【建】半开胶合.

hal·yard [ˈhæljəd] *n.* 【海】扬帆绳,旗绳,升降索.

ham[1] [hæm] *n.* ①火腿; 〔*pl.*〕〔美〕火腿(夹心)面包. ②〔*pl.*〕膝腘;(兽类的)后踝; 腿臀. ③〔美俚〕表演过火的演员. ④〔俚〕爱做作的人. ⑤〔美〕无线电收发报业余爱好者. ***squat on one's ~s*** 蹲下. — *a.* ①过火的,做作的;蹩脚的. ②搞业余无线电收发报的. — *vt., vi.* (使)表演过火. **~-and-egger** *n.* 〔俚〕①普通人. ②不出众的拳击师. **~-and-eggery** *n.* 〔俚〕小饭店, 简易餐柜. **~-and-eggs** *a.* 日常的,普通的. **~-fisted, ~-handed** *a.* 〔主英〕①拳头很大的. ②〔俚〕笨拙的.

ham[2] [hæm] *n.* (旧时的)小镇;村庄.

Ha·ma [ˈhæmə] *n.* 哈马〔叙利亚城市〕.

ham·a·dry·ad [ˌhæməˈdraiəd] *n.* ①【希神】树精. ②(印度等地产的)一种眼镜蛇 (= king cobra). ③阿拉伯狒狒 *(Comopithecus hamadryas)* 〔产于阿拉伯和北非〕.

ha·mal [həˈmɑːl] *n.* (土耳其等中东国家的)搬运工人,搬行李的人.

Ha·man [ˈheimən] *n.* 海曼(哈曼)〔姓氏〕.

ha·mate [ˈheimeit] *a.* 【解】(骨)钩状的.

Ham·burg [ˈhæmbəːg] *n.* 汉堡〔西德港市〕. ②(欧洲种)红冠青脚鸡. ③= ~ steak. ~ **steak** 〔美〕①碎牛肉. ②牛肉饼,汉堡牛排〔碎牛肉煎成的圆饼〕. ③夹牛肉饼的面包片;汉堡包.

ham·burg·er [ˈhæmbəːgə] *n.* ①= Hamburg steak. ②被打得遍体鳞伤的拳击手. ***make ~ out of (sb.)*** 〔美俚〕把人打得一塌糊涂. ~ **steak** = Hamburg steak.

hames [heimz] *n.* 〔*pl.*〕马颈轭.

ham·fat·ter [ˈhæmfætə] *n.* 〔美俚〕拙劣的演员.

Ham·il·ton[1] [ˈhæmiltən] *n.* 汉密尔顿〔姓氏,男子名〕.

Ham·il·ton[2] [ˈhæmiltən] *n.* 汉密尔顿〔加拿大港市;百慕大群岛首府〕.

Ham·il·to·ni·an [ˌhæmilˈtəuniən] *a.* 【史】汉密尔顿主义的. — *n.* 【史】汉密尔顿的追随者.

Ham·il·to·ni·an·ism [ˌhæmilˈtəunjənizəm] *n.* 【史】汉密尔顿主义〔美国联邦党领导人汉密尔顿 (1757—1804)的政见,主张建立中央集权的联邦政府等〕.

Ham·ite [ˈhæmait] *n.* 含米特人〔分居于东非和北非的含族黑人〕.

Ham·it·ic [hæˈmitik] *a.* 含米特人的;含米特语族的;含米特语的. — *n.* 含米特语.

ham·let [ˈhæmlit] *n.* 村子;〔英〕(无教堂的)小村庄.

Ham·let [ˈhæmlit] *n.* ①汉姆雷特〔莎士比亚悲剧剧名和该剧主人公〕. ②〔喻〕优柔寡断的人. ~ ***without the Prince of Denmark*** = ~ ***with*** ~ ***left out*** 没有主人公的戏,去掉了本质的东西.

Ham·lin [ˈhæmlin] *n.* 哈姆林〔姓氏〕.

ham·mal [həˈmɑːl] *n.* = hamal.

ham·mam [ˈhæməm] *n.* 土耳其浴室,蒸汽浴室.

ham·mer [ˈhæmə] *n.* ①槌,铁锤,榔头. ②【机】唇锤,杵锤. ③(会议主席或拍卖人用的)小木槌. ④槌状物;(电铃的)小槌子,锣锤;【乐】音槌. ⑤(火器的)击铁. ⑥【体】链球. ⑦【解】(中耳的)锤骨. *a soldering* ~ 烙铁. *a steam* ~ 蒸汽锤. ~ *throwing* 掷链球. ***be [go] at it ~ and tongs*** 闹哄哄地激烈殴斗〔争辩〕. ***between (the) ~ and (the) anvil*** 腹背受敌,两面被夹攻. ***be [go, come] under the*** ~ 被拍卖. ***bring [send] sth. to the*** ~ 拿…去拍卖. ~ ***and tongs*** 〔口〕猛烈地,全力地,劲头十足地,以雷霆万钧之势. ***knight of the*** ~ 铁匠. ***up to the*** ~ 极好的,无可疵议的. — *vt.* ①锤击,锤薄;使锤成;把…锤进. ②(用拳头)痛打. ③〔口〕(用炮)猛轰;使惨败. ④〔英〕(交易所中敲榔头)宣布(某人、公司等)已无偿还能力. ⑤〔俚〕严厉批评,攻击. ⑤(辩论时)提出(有力理由等); 硬性灌输 *(home).* ~ *a box together* 钉成一个箱子. ~ *an idea into sb.'s head* 硬向某人灌输某种观念. *~ed finish of stone* 锤琢过的石材. — *vi.* 接连锤打. ***give sb. a good ~ing*** 痛打某人一顿. ~ ***at*** ①一再敲打. ②不断研究,埋头于…. ③接连说明. ~ ***away at*** 连连敲打; 刻苦钻研, 反复谈论 (~ *away at the same point* 老是强调同一观点). ~ ***down*** 用锤钉上. ~ ***in (to)*** 用锤敲进. ~ ***out*** ①锤薄; 锤平; ②苦心想出;推敲出. ③敲出(音调等). ④调整,消除. ~ **beam** 【建】椽尾(小)梁. ~**blow** 锤打,猛击. ~**cloth** *n.* 马车夫座位上的布篷. ~**fish** 【动】撞木鲛,双髻鲨. ~**-harden** *vt.* 用锤打紧(金属等). ~**head** ①锤头. ②【动】撞木鲛,双髻鲨. ③〔美俚〕笨蛋,傻子,白痴. ~**-headed** *a.* 有锤状头的;钝的. ~ **lock** 【摔交】把对方的手扭到背后. ~**man,** ~**smith** 锻工. ~ **throw** 【体】掷链球. ~ **toe** ①趾骨锤状变形. ②锤状趾.

ham·mer·ing [ˈhæməriŋ] *n.* 锤击. *cold* ~ 冷锻.

ham·mer·less [ˈhæməlis] *a.* ①无锤的. ②【军】内击铁的(指击铁在枪的内部). ~ *gun* 暗机枪.

ham·mock[1] [ˈhæmək] *n.* 吊床. *lash [sling] a* ~ 结绑〔吊挂〕吊床. ~ **chair** 帆布椅. **-like** *a.*

ham·mock[2] [ˈhæmək] *n.* =① hummock. ②美国南方肥沃的高地.

Ham·mond [ˈhæmənd] *n.* 哈蒙德〔姓氏〕.

ham·my[1] [ˈhæmi] *a.* 有火腿香味的.

ham·my[2] [ˈhæmi] *a.* 〔俚〕演技拙劣的;(把角色)演得过火的. **ham·mi·ly** *ad.* **ham·mi·ness** *n.*

Hamp·den [ˈhæmpdən] *n.* 汉普登〔姓氏〕.

ham·per[1] [ˈhæmpə] *vt.* 妨碍,阻挠,牵制. *be ~ed by a big, heavy overcoat* 为一件沉重的大衣所累. — *n.* ①【海】(平时不可少而暴风雨时则成累赘的)船具. ②阻碍物;足械. **-ed·ly** *ad.* **-ed·ness** *n.* **-er** *n.*

ham·per[2] [ˈhæmpə] *n.* 有盖提篮; 篮装食品〔礼品〕. — *vt.* 把(食品)装入篮内. *a ~ of wine* 一篮子酒.

Hamp·ton [ˈhæmptən] *n.* 汉普顿〔姓氏〕.

ham·shack·le [ˈhæmʃækl] *vt.* ①把(牛马等的)头用绳绑在前足上. ②束缚.

ham•ster [ˈhæmstə] n.【动】仓鼠.

ham•string [ˈhæmstriŋ] n.【解】腘旁腱;【动】(兽类的)后腿腱. —vt. (~ed, ham•strung [ˈhæmstrʌŋ]) ①割断…的腿筋;使残废. ②减弱…的活动能力.

ham•u•lus [ˈhæmjuləs] n. (pl. -li [ˈhæmjulai]) ①【解】钩. ②【动】钩形突;小钩.

Han [hæn] n. (pl. ~(s)) 〔中〕①【史】汉代 (= the ~ Dynasty). ②汉族,汉人. ③汉水.

han•a•per [ˈhænəpə] n. 文件筐.

Han•cock [ˈhænkɔk] n. 汉考克〔姓氏〕.

Hand [hænd] n. 汉德〔姓氏〕.

hand [hænd] n. ①手;(猴子等的)脚;(一般四足兽的)前脚. ②(钟表的)指针;(工具等的)把,柄. ③手状物;(香蕉等的)一扇;(烟叶的)一束. ④〔常 pl.〕握有;管理;支配;权力;(古代罗马法律中规定的)夫权. ⑤人手,职工,雇员;船员. ⑥支援,帮助,参加;插手,干预. ⑦技巧,手艺,手法. ⑧笔迹,书法;签名. ⑨方,侧;方面. ⑩答允;婚约. ⑪【牌】手中的牌;打牌人;牌戏的一盘. ⑫一掌之宽〔约 4 英寸,量马高度用〕. ⑬〔口〕拍手喝采. ⑭(摸皮革、织物等的)手感. a bench ~ 钳工. a ~ of banana 一扇香蕉. blind ~ 模糊不清的笔迹. the hidden ~ 看不见的势力,幕后操纵者. the last ~ 最后几笔,定稿前的润色. an old parliamentary ~ 精通议院事务的人. ~ of writ [write] 〔Scot.〕笔迹,字体. the minute [hour] ~ (钟表的)分[时]针. factory ~s 工人. an indicator ~ 指针. His ~ is in. 他在不断地练习. His ~ is out. 他不行. My ~s are tied. 我的权力极其有限. write a good ~ 写得一笔好字. ask for a girl's ~ 向女子求婚. A clean ~ wants no washing. 〔谚〕手上不沾污〔指罪恶、坏事等〕,不必多 刷. a cool ~ 冒失鬼. a crack [good, great] ~ 行 ,熟手. a dead ~【法】没有让渡权的所有主. extr ~s 临时工. a free ~ 放手处理的权力 (allow s a free ~ in his work 让某人放手工作). a fresh [green] ~ 生手. a good [poor] ~ at 巧[拙]于. a ~'s turn 小事 (not do a ~'s turn 易如反掌的事都不做). a nap ~ 一手好牌;有利的地位. a numb ~ 笨人. all ~s【海】全体船员;【口】全体人员. all ~s to the pump(s) 大家都来帮忙. an old ~ 内行,过来人. at first ~ 直接 (knowledge at first ~ 第一手知识). at ~ ①在手边,在近处. ②即将到来 (live close at ~ 住在附近. The autumn harvest is at ~. 秋收即将到来). at second ~ ①经过他人一道手的,第二手的;间接的. ②旧的,用过的. at the ~(s) of sb. = at sb.'s ~(s) ①在某人手下. ②出自某人之手 (suffer cruel exploitation at the ~s of the slaveholders 受奴隶主残酷剥削). bathe [dip] one's ~s in blood 双手沾满鲜血,成为杀人犯. bear [lend] a ~ (in) 参加. bear [lend] a ~ (with) 帮助,出一把力. be even ~s with sb. 〔Scot.〕向某人报复,同某人算帐. be out of sb.'s ~s 某人不能控制[处理,负责]. bite the ~ that feeds one 忘恩负义,恩将仇报. by ~ ①用手的,手工的;用手递交的. ②(婴儿)用牛奶抚养的 (bring up a child by ~ 亲手把孩子抚养成人;不用人奶喂大小孩. deliver a letter by ~ 信由专人递送. made by ~ 手工制的). by the ~s of 经…的手. by the left ~ ①贵族男子娶非贵族女子所生的;门第不相称的夫妇所生的. ②私生的. by the strong ~ 强制地. change ~s (财产等) 转换所有者,易手. check one's ~s in 拒绝做某事;认输. come to (one's) ~(s) 拿到手,收到. cross sb.'s ~ ①(用钱币)在某人手心中划十字〔指把钱币付给算命者〕. ②贿赂. die by one's own ~ 自杀. do not lift a ~ 不努力,不动手,不试一下;懒. eat [feed] out of sb.'s ~ 完全顺从某人,唯某人之命是从. fall [get] into sb.'s ~s [the ~s of sb.] 落到某人手里. fight ~ to ~ 短兵相接,肉搏. fold one's ~s 叉着手,袖手旁观. force sb.'s ~ (在作好准备前)强迫某人行动[表态]. from ~ to ~ 从甲手到乙手,传递. from ~ to mouth 做一天吃一天,现挣现吃,刚够糊口. gain [get, have] the upper ~ of 占优势,占上风. get a big ~ 〔美〕受到热烈鼓掌;大受欢迎. get ~ 得手,得势. get [have] one's ~ in ①使自己熟习. ②插手. ~ oneself in 控制自己. get sth. off one's ~s 摆脱某事,摆脱对某事的责任. give one's ~ on a bargain 保证履行契约. give one's ~ to sb. ①向某人伸出手. ②(女子)答应和某人结婚. give sb. a ~ 帮助某人. give sb. a [the] glad ~ 〔俚〕欢迎. grease the ~ of sb. 买通,向人行贿. ~ and foot 手脚一齐,完全地;尽力地 (bind sb. ~ and foot 把某人完全捆住). ~ and [in] glove with 亲密地;勾结着 (have all along worked ~ in glove with sb. 一直与某人狼狈为奸). Hands are full. 很忙. ~ in ~ ①手拉手. ②联合 (act ~ in ~ 联合行动). ~ over fist ①不费气力地,大量地. ②= ~ over ~. ~ over ~ ①(爬绳等时)一把一把往上. ②稳妥而迅速地 (前进). ~s down ①不费气力地,容易地. ②无疑地. Hands off! 请勿动手. Hands off …! 不许干涉(他)! Hands up! ①(要对方不抵抗的命令)举起手来! ②举手赞成. ~ to fist 〔口〕亲密的[地];齐心协力的[地]. ~ to ~ 逼近地. ~ under ~ 左右手替换着 (由绳子上降落). have a good ~ 有一手好牌. have a ~ in 干与,参与,插手. have a ~ like a foot 笨手笨脚. have an open ~ 慷慨. have long ~s 很有势力. have [hold, keep] (sb.) (well) in ~ 掌握,支配(某人). have one's ~s free ①空着手,无事干. ②可以自由行动. have one's ~s full 手头事很多,很忙. heavy on [in] ~ (马等)难驾驭;(人)难应付. hold ~s 手搀手. hold one's ~ 迟迟不下手. hold up one's ~s 举手(投降). in ~ ①现有,在手头. ②(工作)正在进行. ③控制住 (have the situation well in ~ 完全掌握着局势). in the ~s of … 在…掌握中;交托给. join ~s (with) ①同…携手,联合. ②同…合伙开店. ③同…结婚. keep a slack ~ 放松缰绳;漫不经心地管理. keep [have] one's ~ in 不断练习,使技能不荒疏. keep one's ~ [a firm ~] on 牢牢地控制着. kiss ~s [the ~] 吻君王的手〔一种礼仪〕. kiss one's ~ to 向…飞吻. lay (violent) ~s on oneself 自杀. lay ~s on [upon] sb. ①袭击某人. ②【宗】对…行按手礼. lay ~s on [upon] sth. 拿住,抓住;找到. lay one's ~ on the table = show one's ~. lie on sb.'s ~(s) ①(商品)在某人手中未脱手;(物件)在某人手中未用掉. ②(时间)使某人感到无聊. lift a [one's] ~ [against] 打,威胁. lift one's ~s 举手宣誓. light in ~ (马等)易于驾驭. lose the upper ~ 失去优势. make a ~ 成功;得利. Many ~s make light work. 〔谚〕人多好办事. marry with the left ~ 与门第比自己低的人结婚. off ~ 马上,立即,事前无准备地. off sb.'s ~s 脱手,卸脱责任. offer one's ~ ①伸出手来(准备握手). ②向女子求婚. offer [give] sb. the right ~ of fellowship ①同某人结交. ②同意某人入伙. on all ~s = on [at] every ~ 在各方面;一般. on either ~ 在两边中的任何一边. on ~ ①现有,在手头. ②〔美〕在近处,即将发生. ③〔美〕出席,到场. on sb.'s ~s 在某人手里;由某人负责照管 (She has many patients on her ~s. 她有许多病人要她照顾. Time hangs heavy on one's ~s. 时间慢得令人难过). on the left [right] ~ (of) 在…的左[右]边. on the mending ~ 在好转中. on the one ~, … on the other (~) 一方面…,另一方面. on the other ~ 从另一方面来说,相反,反之. one's right ~ 右手;得力助手. out of ~ ①即时. ②脱手;告终. ③难对付;难控制. overplay one's ~ ①过高地估计自己. ②做得过分. play a good ~ (牌)玩得精明. play a lone ~ 单干. play for one's own ~ 为自己的利益打算[行动]. play into sb.'s ~s = play into the ~s of sb. 因失算而使某人占了便宜.

play one's ~ for all it is worth 尽全力. *play one's ~ heavily* 做得过火. *pump sb.'s ~* 〔美〕使劲同某人握手. *Put not your ~ between the bark and the tree.* 〔谚〕少管闲事. *put one's ~ in [into] a hornet's nest* 惹祸,树敌. *put [set, turn] one's ~ to sth. [the plough]* 着手一项工作. *Put your ~ no further than your sleeve will reach.* 〔谚〕量入为出. *raise one's ~ against* = lift one's ~ against. *read sb.'s ~* 看某人的手相. *ready to one's ~* = under one's ~. *rub one's ~s* 因高兴而搓手. *serve sb. ~ and foot* 勤勤恳恳为某人服务. *set one's ~ to* ①着手,从事于. ②在…上面签字,批准,承认. *shake sb.'s ~* = shake ~s with sb., shake sb. by the ~ 同某人握手. *show one's ~* 摊牌;摆计划;表示态度. *sit on one's ~s* 〔美俚〕①(观众等)不鼓掌. ②(应当采取行动时)踌躇不前. *slack ~* 玩忽,不留心. *stay one's ~* 不作某事. *stay sb.'s ~* 使某人住手. *strengthen sb.'s ~(s)* 增强某人实力, 使某人得以采取强有力的行动. *strike ~s* 约定. *take a ~ in [at]* 参加,和…发生关系. *take in ~* ①处理;照料. ②控制;承担. ③尝试. *the upper ~* 优势. *throw in one's ~* 放弃,退出竞选. *throw up one's ~s* 绝望地放弃. *tip one's ~* 摊牌, 表明态度. *to ~* ①近在手边. ②收到,占有 (*your letter to ~ = yours to ~*【商】来函收到). *try one's ~ at* 试试. *under one's ~* 在手边,就可使用,来得及. *under one's ~ and seal* 经签名盖章. *upon ~* = on ~. *wash one's ~s* ①洗手. ②解手,上厕所. *wash one's ~s of* 不再管或负责某事;和…断绝关系. *wash one's ~s with invisible soap and impercepible water* 以无形的肥皂和水洗手〔意为由于紧张等而搓手〕. *win a lady's ~* 赢得某女子同意结婚. *with a bold ~* 大胆地. *with a firm ~* 坚决地. *with a free ~* ①慷慨地,不吝惜地. ②浪费地,无节制地. *with a heavy ~* ①粗手粗脚地,粗枝大叶地. ②高压地,严厉地. *with a high ~* 武断地,用高压手段. *with an iron ~* 严厉地,以铁腕. *with an iron ~ in a velvet glove* 外柔内刚地,口蜜腹剑地. *with a strong ~* 决断地,强硬地. *with clean ~s* 清白无罪地,廉洁地. *wring one's ~s over sth.* 为某事苦恼地绞扭着手. — *vt.* ①交付;传递给 (*to*). ②用手搀扶,用手帮助 (*to; into; out of; across; over*). ③【海】卷叠(风帆). ~ *a lady into a bus* 搀扶一位女士上公共汽车. ~ *a letter to her* 递给她一封信. ~ *sb. a surprise* 使某人大吃一惊. ~ ***a good line***〔美〕所有功课都考得很好. ~ ***around***〔美〕= ~ round. ~ ***back*** 交回. ~ ***down*** ①传下来. ②宣布(判决等) (~ *traditions down to us* 把传统传给我们). ~ ***in*** 交进;交上. ~ ***into*** 扶进,扶上车. ~ ***it to sb.*** 〔美俚〕承认某人的长处,给某人应得的荣誉. ~ ***off***【橄榄球】用手推开对手. ~ ***on (to sb.)*** 依次传递;传给后代. ~ ***out*** ①拿出来. ②分,分派. ③施舍. ~ ***over*** ①送交(当局等). ②移交,让与. (~ *sb. over to the police* 把某人送交警察). ~ ***round*** 顺次传递;分交. ~ ***up*** 交给,呈上;告密. ~**arm** (手)枪. ~ **ax [axe]** 手斧〔旧石器时代的一种石器〕(= broad hatchet). ~**bag** 手提包;旅行包. ~ **baggage** 手提行李. ~**ball** 手球,手球游戏;手触球犯规. ~**barrow** (前后二人推运的)平台车;手推车; (两边有柄的)抬物架. ~**bell**【乐】手摇铃. ~**bill** 传单,招贴,广告. ~**blown** *a.* 〔指玻璃器皿〕吹制的. ~**book** 手册,便览,指南;〔美〕赛马手册. ~ **brake** 手煞车. ~-**breadth** 一手之宽〔从二英寸半到四英寸〕,手掌宽. ~ **canter**【马术】缓跑,小跑. ~**car** 〔美〕铁路上所用手摇〔机动〕四轮小车. ~**cart** 手车,手推车. ~**clap** 拍手. ~**clasp** 握别,握手礼. ~ **computer** 手摇计算机. ~**craft** ①*n.* 手工,手工艺. ② *vt.* 用手工制作. ~**crafted** *a.* 手工的,手工艺的. ~**crank** 手动曲柄. ~**cuff** ① *n.* 〔常 *pl.*〕手铐. ② *vt.* 给…上手铐. ~ **drill**【机】手摇钻. ~**fast** ① *n.* 握手约;婚约;握紧,抓牢. ② *a.* 〔古〕握手定约的;订过婚约的. ③ *vt.* 〔古〕握手约定;使定婚约,使行定婚典礼. ~-**feed** *vt.* (*~-fed*) 用手喂. ~ **gallop** (马的)慢跑. ~ **glass** 有柄小镜;(阅读用)有柄放大镜. ~ **grenade** 手榴弹. ~**grip** ①紧握;握手. ②柄,把. ③〔*pl.*〕扭打;肉搏. (*come to ~grips* 开始搏斗). ~**gun** 手枪. ~**hold** ①把握;紧握. ②把手,把柄;(攀登时)可用手抓住的东西. ~-**in**-~ *a.* ①手牵手的,亲密的. ②并进的. ~-**jack** 手力起重器,手力千斤顶. ~-**knitted** *a.* 手编的. ~ **lamp** 手提灯. ~ **language** 手势语. ~ **level**【测】手持水平仪. ~ **line** 手钓丝. ~**loom** 手织机. ~-**luggage** 手提行李. ~**made** ①*a.* 手工的,手制的 (*opp.* machine-made). ② *n.* 手工制品. ~**maid**, ~**maiden** 〔古〕侍女,女仆,婢女;〔喻〕陪衬性的东西. ~-**me-down** ①*a.* 〔口〕现成的(常指价廉而劣等的); 用旧的. ②*n.* 〔口〕现成的衣服,旧衣服;旧事物. ~ **money** 定钱,保证金. ~-**off**【体】后卫传球组织进攻. ~ **organ** 手摇风琴. ~**out** ①施舍物;救济品. ②(政府、政界人物)交给新闻界发表的声明[报导]. ③(用作宣传、讲授的)小册子,传单,讲义. ~-**over** *a.* 移交的. (*~-over procedure* 移交手续). ~ **perforator** 三柱凿孔机. ~-**pick** ① *n.*【矿】手镐. ② *vt.* 用手选出;精心挑选,精选. ~-**picked** *a.* 精选的;〔美〕第一流的. ~**play** 互殴,扭打. ~**post** 路标. ~ **pump** 手压泵. ~**rail** 栏杆,扶手. ~-**reared** *a.* 一手养大的. ~-**receiver**【讯】手持受话器. ~-**running** *ad.* 〔方、口〕持续地,不中断地. ~**saw** 手锯,小锯. ~**'s-breadth** *n.* = ~-breadth. ~ **screw** ①手旋螺钉. ②木工用的夹子,夹钳. ~**scrub** = nail-brush. ~**s-down** *a.* ①唾手可得的,轻而易举的. ②无疑的. ~**set**【讯】送受话器,手机. ~**sewn** *a.* 手工缝制的. ~**shake** 握手. ~-**shaker** 善于打交道的人. ~**s-off** *a.* 不干涉的,不干预的,不插手的. ~-**sort** *vt.* 手拣,用手分类. ~**spike** 杠,推杆. ~**spring** (以手着地的)翻觔斗. ~ **staff** 连枷柄. ~**stand** *n.*【体】倒立. ~**'s turn** 一举手之劳的帮助 (*She did not do a ~'s turn.* 她一点忙也不帮). ~ **tape** 远距离皮卷尺. ~**taut**, ~-**tight** *a.*【海】用手劲尽量拉紧的. ~-**to**-~ *a.* ①短兵相接的,肉搏的. ②一个一个传下去的. ~-**to-mouth** *a.* 过一天算一天的; 勉强糊口的. ~ **trolley hoist** 手动架空绞车. ~ **truck** 手车,手推车. ~ **vice** 手钳. ~ **vote** 举手选举. ~**wheel** 手轮,操纵轮,驾驶盘,转向盘. ~-**work** 手工,精细工艺. ~-**worked** *a.* 手工制成的. ~ **woven** *a.* 手织的. ~ **writing** ①笔迹,手迹. ②手写稿 (*the ~ writing on the wall* 不祥之兆,灾祸的预兆). ~ **written** *a.* 手写的,用笔写的. ~-**wrought** *a.* = hand-worked.

h. and c. = hot and cold.

hand·ed [ˈhændid] *a.* ①惯用…手的. ②有…手的. ③有…人参加的. *right-~* 惯用右手的. *short-~* 人手不足的. *two-~* 有两只手的. *a three-~ game* 三人玩的游戏. ~-**down** *a.* 传下来的. -**ness** 惯用左手[右手].

Han·del [ˈhændl] *n.* ①汉德尔〔姓氏〕. ②**George Frederick** ~亨德尔〔1685—1759,生于德国的英国作曲家〕.

hand·ful [ˈhændful] *n.* ①一把,一握. ②少数,少量,一小撮. ③〔口〕难以控制的人[动物];麻烦的事.

hand·i·cap [ˈhændikæp] *n.* ①障碍,不利条件. ②(为使得胜机会均等,给强者以不利条件,给弱者以有利条件的)赛马或其它竞赛. ③(在强、弱手竞赛中)给弱者的有利条件,给强者的不利条件. — *vt.* ①妨碍,使不利. ②给(竞赛中强手)不利条件;使(竞赛中弱手)获得优待. *the handicapped* (身体或精神上有缺陷的)残废人.

hand·i·cap·per [ˈhændikæpə] *n.* ①在竞技中规定有利[不利]条件的人员. ②根据以往记录、竞技条件预测赛马胜负的新闻记者.

hand·i·craft [ˈhændikrɑːft] *n.* ①手工,手工艺. ②手工艺业. ③手工艺品. *a ~ worker* 手工业工人.

hand·i·crafts·man [ˈhændikrɑːftsmən] *(pl.* **-men** [-men]*)* *n.* 手工业者；手工艺人.

hand·i·cuff [ˈhændiˌkʌf] *n.* 用手打；〔*pl.*〕扭打.

hand·ie-talk·ie [ˈhændiˌtɔːki] *n.* 手提式步话机.

hand·i·ly [ˈhændili] *ad.* 巧妙地；敏捷地；便利地.

hand·i·ness [ˈhændinis] *n.* 巧妙；敏捷；轻便.

hand·i·work [ˈhændiwəːk] *n.* ①手工，工艺品（＝handwork）. ②（某人）亲手做的事情.

hand·ker·chief [ˈhæŋkətʃif] *n.* *(pl.* **~s, -chieves** [-tʃiːvz]*)* ①手帕. ②头巾，围巾. *a pocket* ~ 手帕. *a neck* ~ 围巾. ***throw the ~ to sb.***（游戏时）丢手帕给某人要他追自己；〔喻〕暗示看中某人.

han·dle [ˈhændl] *n.* ①柄，把手；曲柄；摇柄. ②（摸皮革、织物等的）手感. ③把柄，可乘之机，口实. ④〔口〕头衔，称号. ⑤（赛马等时投下的）赌金总额. *a crank* ~ 手摇曲柄. *a hammer* ~ 榔头柄. *a ~ to one's name*〔口〕头衔（如 Lord, Dr. 等）. *an operating* ~ 控制柄，操纵手摇柄. *a starting* ~ 起动曲柄. ***fly off [at] the ~***〔美口〕冒火，自制不住. ***give a ~ for [to]*** 使人有可乘之机，给人以口实. ***go off the ~***〔口〕死. ***the ~ of the face***〔谑〕鼻子. ***throw the ~ after the blade*** 赔，吃亏了又吃亏；坚持做无希望的事. ***up to the ~***〔美口〕彻底地. — *vt.* ①触，摸，抚，弄；掌握. ②处理；讨论（问题）；对待（人）；指挥（军队），统辖. ③〔美〕买卖，经营. ④驯养（马等）. ⑤〔美〕训练（拳击选手）. *~ sb. roughly* 虐待某人. *~ a subject* 讨论问题. — *vi.* ①用手搬运. ②操作；举动. *This car ~s easily.* 这车很灵活. *The troops ~d well.* 部队军纪很好. *H- with care!* 小心轻放！ ***~ without gloves [mittens]*** 严厉对待，毫不留情地对待. **~bar**〔常 *pl.*〕（自行车等的）把手.

han·dler [ˈhændlə] *n.* ①处理者，管理者. ②（赛马、警犬等的）训练者. ③【自】（信息）处理机.

hand·less [ˈhændlis] *a.* 没有手的；手笨拙的.

han·dling [ˈhændliŋ] *n.* ①处理，管理；操纵. ②装卸. *~ equipment* 辅助设备. *~ guy* 搬运索. *~ radius* 工作半径.

hand·sel [ˈhænsəl] *n.* ①贺礼，开张贺礼，新年赠品. ②定钱，保证金. ③第一笔营业收入. ④新上市的东西，初次用[吃]的东西；试样. — *vt.*（〔英〕**-ll-**）①给…送贺礼，庆祝…开业[落成]. ②给…付定钱. ③初次吃，第一次试用.

hand·some [ˈhænsəm] *a.* ①（一般指男子外貌）漂亮的，清秀的，俊俏的；（用于女人指体态）优美的，端庄的，温雅的. ②相当大的；（财产等）可观的. ③堂皇的，气派大的，美观的. ④慷慨的，大方的. ⑤〔美俚〕精巧的，高明的. ⑥〔古〕便利的，合适的；操纵灵便的. *a ~ contribution* 可观的捐款. *a ~ fortune* 不小的家产. *~ price* 相当大的价值. *~ treatment* 优待. ***H- is that [as] ~ does.***〔谚〕品德优美才算真美. **-ness** *n.*

hand·some·ly [ˈhænsəmli] *ad.* ①漂亮地，美观地，慷慨地，优厚地. ②【海】慢慢地，当心地，整齐地. ***come down ~***〔俗〕慷慨解囊，慷慨赠送.

hand·y [ˈhændi] *a.* ①手边的，近便的. ②便利的，得心应手的，便于使用的. ③手灵巧的，敏捷的. ④（船等）易驾驶的. ***as ~ as a pocket in a shirt***〔美口〕非常方便. ***come in ~*** 迟早有用. **~man** 手巧的人；干杂活的人. **~-talkie, ~-talky** = handie-talkie.

hand·y-dand·y [ˈhændiˌdændi] *n.*（儿童猜对方哪只手握着东西的）猜猜看游戏.

Han·ford [ˈhænfəd] *n.* 汉福德〔美国华盛顿州南部原子能研究重要中心〕.

hang [hæŋ] *vt.* *(hung* [hʌŋ], *~ed)* ①悬挂，垂吊（*to; on; from*）. ②〔过去式与过去分词为 ~ed〕绞死，吊死 ③贴（画等于墙上）；裱（壁纸）；（用画等）点缀（*with*）. ④安装（门铃、铰链等）. ④拖延（时日）；〔美〕使…悬而不决，搁置. ⑦〔诅咒语〕…该死，让…见鬼去. *Be ~ed! H- you! You be ~ed!*〔指人〕该死的家伙！ *H- it (all)!*〔指物〕岂有此理！真可恶！ *~ oneself* 自缢. *I'll be ~ed if I do so.*〔口〕我死也不会干那种事. *~ a scythe* 安镰刀把. *Never ~ a man twice for one offence*〔谚〕打了不罚，罚了不打. *be ~ed on the neck* 处以绞刑〔审判书用语〕. *~ the picture on the wall* 把图画挂到墙上. *~ the washing out* 把洗的衣服挂到外面. — *vi.* ①悬挂，垂吊. ②被吊死，被绞死. ③倾斜；倚靠；凭依. ④突出；使伸出；迫近（*over*）. ⑤附着，缠住. ⑥摇摆，晃动；徘徊；犹豫不决. ⑦（衣服等）随便披着（等）. *The picture was ~ing on the wall.* 图画挂在墙上. *Her hair was ~ing down.* 她的头发披散着. ***~ about*** 徘徊，荡来荡去；缠住不放；在附近逗留. ***~ around***【美】= ~ about. ***~ back*** 踌躇不前，退缩. ***~ behind*** 落在后面. ***~ by [on, upon] a thread [hair]*** 千钧一发，危在旦夕. ***~ by the eyelid*** 系得不牢，易于落下. ***~ by the wall*** 悬挂墙上不用；束之高阁. ***~ down*** 下垂. ***~ fire***（枪、炮）发火慢；发射不出；（行动、事态发展）延迟；耽误时间；犹豫不决. ***~ heavy on*** 使劳累，使受苦. ***~ in doubt*** 疑惑不决. ***~ in suspense*** 悬而未决. ***~ in the balance [wind]*** 安危未定；成败未决. ***~ it all!*** 见鬼！岂有此理！ ***~ it out***〔美〕怠工. ***~ loose*** 保持镇静，放松. ***~ off*** ①放. ②挂断电话. ③= hang back. ***~ on [upon]*** ①抱[握]住不放. ②坚持下去. ③赖着不走；继续存在. ④倚，靠. ⑤不挂断电话. ⑥渴望. ⑦有赖于，视…而定. ⑧专心地听. ***~ on by the eyebrows [eyelashes]*** 硬着头皮干下去，自找麻烦. ***~ on sb.'s lips [words]*** 听得入神；被某人的口才所迷. ***~ on sb.'s sleeve*** 倚赖某人. ***~ on to*** 紧紧握住，坚持下去（*I'll ~ on to it until I get another job.* 在未找到另外的工作以前，我要坚持干下去.） ***~ out*** ①把上身伸出（窗外）. ②〔俚〕住（*Where do you ~ out?* 你住在哪里？）③挂出门外[窗外]. ④〔美俚〕闲逛. ⑤拖延. ***~ out for*** 故意拖延以待良机. ***~ out the laundry [wash]***〔美俚〕空投伞兵. ***~ out the red flag*** 宣战. ***~ out the white flag*** 求降. ***~ over*** ①接近；挂在…上面. ②突出，伸出. ③迫近，临头，威胁，笼罩. ④被遗留. ***~ round***〔美〕= ~ about. ***~ one on***〔俚〕①向…猛击一拳. ②大醉. ***~ the head (down)***（羞得）低下头. ***~ the jury***〔美〕因陪审员意见不一而不能作出判决. ***~ the lip*** 撇嘴〔以表示轻蔑等〕. ***~ to*** 缠住，紧粘着. ***~ together*** ①团结一致，齐心协力. ②前后照应，首尾一致（*If we don't ~ together, we may all ~ separately.* 如果我们不团结一致，我们就会一个个被绞死. *His story does not ~ together.* 他的故事前后矛盾）. ***~ up*** ①挂，吊. ②弃置不问；拖延；中止；挂断电话. ③〔美〕抵押；赊帐. ***~ up a mark***【体】创新记录. ***~ up one's hat in sb.'s house*** 在别人家里久留不走. ***~ up the numbers*** 宣布比赛（尤指赛马）的结果. ***~ upon*** 靠，挨. ***(be) ~ on***〔口〕对…特别感兴趣. ***(be) hung over***〔美俚〕因宿醉而感觉不舒服的. ***(be) hung up [on]*** ①（因…而）精神不安的. ②对…上瘾的，迷上…的. ③被滞留. ④受挫折. ***let (things) go ~***〔口〕没关系. ***let it all ~ out***〔美黑人俚〕①让头发披散. ②无牵挂，无顾忌. — *n.* ①悬挂的样子. ②〔口〕用法，做法，诀窍. ③〔口〕大意，要点. ④（动作的）暂停. *the ~ of a machine* 机器的用法. ***get [see] the ~ of*** 摸清底细，懂得…的用法，知道…的诀窍，理解…. ***not care a ~***〔口〕毫不在乎. **~bird** *n.*【动】悬巢燕雀. **~dog** ① *n.* 卑鄙的人. ② *a.* 卑鄙的，下贱的，羞愧的（*~dog air [look]* 卑躬屈膝的样子，羞愧畏缩的样子）. **~fire** 迟发，滞火. **~ glider**（从悬崖等处滑下的）滑翔风筝，风筝状滑翔机. **~man** 绞刑吏，刽子手. **~nail**（手指上的）倒刺. **~out**〔俚〕（歹徒等的）聚集处，巢穴；经常去的地方；住处. **~over** ①〔美〕残剩物，遗留物. ②〔俚〕宿醉〔因饮酒过度引起的头痛、恶心等〕. **~tag**（商品上的）使用保养说明标签. **~-up**〔俚〕①障碍.

②大难题．③苦衷，(个人感情上的)疙瘩．～**wire** 炸弹保险丝．

han·gar [ˈhæŋə] *n.* 飞机棚，飞机库．*a ～ pilot*〔美俚〕只会胡吹而根本不会驾驶飞机的人．～ **deck** (航空母舰上的)飞机库甲板．

hang·er [ˈhæŋə] *n.* ①挂东西的人，糊墙的人．②吊[挂]着的东西 (尤指挂在皮带上的短剑)．③挂物的东西；挂钩；【机】吊架，吊轴承．④绞杀者，绞刑吏．⑤钩状笔划．⑥(旧时水手用的)短刀．⑦〔主英〕陡坡上的丛林．⑧〔美〕(挂在店内的)广告牌．～**-on** [ˈhæŋəˈɔn] *n.* (*pl.* ～*s-on* [ˈhæŋəzˈɔn]) 食客；随从．

hang·ing [ˈhæŋiŋ] *n.* ①悬挂，悬吊．②吊死，绞刑．③〔*pl.*〕悬挂物(如帘子，帷帐，壁纸；工作吊架等)．④斜坡，倾斜．— *a.* ①悬垂的，垂下的；悬挂用的．②应绞死的．③倾斜的，斜坡的．④未完的，未定的．⑤垂头丧气的．*a ～ affair [matter]* 可能导致绞刑的事．*a ～ crime* 死罪．*a ～ garden* 空中花园．～ **committee** (绘画展览会的)审查委员会．～ **indention**【印】除第一行外，余皆缩一字排．～ **paper**裱糊纸．～ **wall**【矿】上盘，顶板．

hank [hæŋk] *n.* ①(线、丝等绕成的) 圆环，束，绞．②一束〔一绞〕的长度〔棉线为 840 码，毛线为 560 码〕．③【海】纵帆前缘上的帆环．④优势，控制．***get [have] a ～ on [over, upon] sb.*** 控制某人．～ **for** ～ 两船平排着；〔罕〕平等地，同等地．***in a*** ～ 在困难中．

hank·er [ˈhæŋkə] *vi.* 切望，热望，追求 (*after; for*)．～**-ing** *n.* ～**-ing·ly** *ad.*

han·ky [ˈhæŋki] *n.* 〔口〕手帕．

han·ky-pan·ky [ˈhæŋkiˈpæŋki] *n.* 〔口〕①幻术，戏法．②欺诈，骗术，花招．③毫无意义的言行．***be up to some*** ～ 有点鬼鬼祟祟．***play ～ with sb.*** 欺骗某人．

Han·na [ˈhænə] *n.* 汉纳〔姓氏〕．

Han·nah [ˈhænə] *n.* 汉纳〔女子名〕．

Han·ni·bal [ˈhænibəl] *n.* 汉尼拔〔247—183 B.C.，迦太基名将〕．**-i·an** *a.*

Ha·noi [hæˈnɔi] *n.* 河内〔越南首都〕．

Han·o·ver, Han·no·ver [ˈhænəvə; Ger. haˈnəuvər] *n.* 汉诺威〔西德城市〕．***the House of*** ～ (英国的) 汉诺威王朝〔1714—1901，自 乔治一世至维多利亚女王〕．

Han·o·ve·ri·an [ˌhænəuˈviəriən] *a., n.* (英国)汉诺威 (Hanover) 王室的(成员)．

Hans [hænz] *n.* 汉斯〔男子名，Johannes 的昵称〕．

han·sa, hanse [ˈhænsə, hæns] *n.* 【史】①商业同业公会．②商业同业公会会费．**the Hanse** 汉萨同盟〔公元十三至十七世纪北欧城市结成的商业、政治同盟〕．

Han·sard [ˈhænsəd] *n.* 英国议会记录．

Han·sard·ize [ˈhænsədaiz] *vt.* 引证议会记录与(某人)对质．

han·se·at·ic [ˌhænsiˈætik] *a.* ①商业同业公会的．②〔H-〕汉萨同盟的．***the H- League*** 汉萨同盟 (= the Hanse)．

han·sel [ˈhænsəl] *n., v.* (〔英〕**-ll-**) = handsel.

Han·sen [ˈhænsn] *n.* 汉森〔姓氏〕．～**'s disease**【医】麻风 (= leprosy)．

Han·som [ˈhænsəm] *n.* 汉索姆〔姓氏〕．

han·som [ˈhænsəm] *n.* (车夫驾驶台在后的)单马双轮双座马车．

hant, ha'nt [hænt] *vt., vi., n.* 〔美方〕= haunt.

han't [heint] 〔口〕= have [has] not.

Hants. = Hampshire 〔英国汉普夏郡〕．

Ha·nu·ka, Ha·nuk·kah, Ha·nuk·ka [ˈhɑːnukɑː] *n.* 犹太圣节．

han·u·man [ˈhʌnumɑːn, ˈhɑːn-] *n.* ①瘤猴 (*Presbytis entellus*)〔产于东南亚，瘦小，长尾，食叶〕．②〔H-〕哈努曼〔印度神话中的猴神〕．

hap [hæp] *n.* ①〔古〕偶然；机会，幸运．②〔常 *pl.*〕意外事件．*good ～* 幸运．*by good ～* 侥幸．*～s and mishaps of life* 人生的祸福．— *vi.* 突然发生，偶然发生．

ha·pax le·go·me·non [ˈheipæks liˈgɔːmənɔn] (*pl.* **-na** [-nə]) 〔Gr.〕只用过一次的字句；罕用语．

hap·haz·ard [ˌhæpˈhæzəd] *n.* 偶然性，偶然的事；任意性．— *a., ad.* 偶然的[地]，随意的[地]；无计划的[地]．***at [by]*** ～ 偶然地；任意地．**-ly** *ad.* **-ness** *n.*

haph·ta·ra [ˌhɑːftɑːˈrɑː] *n.* (*pl.* **-ta·roth** [-ˈrəuθ]) 哈夫塔拉〔在犹太教安息日和假日做礼拜时念完《摩西五书》后所念的旧约圣经中的先知预言录〕．

hap·less [ˈhæplis] *a.* 不幸的，倒霉的．**-ly** *ad.* **-ness** *n.*

hapl(o)- *comb. f.* 表示"单"，"简单"：*haploid, haplosis*.

hap·log·ra·phy [hæpˈlɔgrəfi] *n.* 重复字母的漏写〔如把 convivial 漏写为 convial〕．

hap·loid [ˈhæplɔid] *a.* 【生】单元体的，单倍体的．— *n.* 单倍体．**-ic** *a.* **-y** *n.*

hap·lol·o·gy [hæpˈlɔlədʒi] *n.* 重复或类似音节的漏读〔如把 interpretative 读作 interpretive〕．

hap·lont [ˈhæplɔnt] *n.* 【生】单元体．

hap·lo·sis [hæpˈləusis] *n.* 【生】减半作用．

hap·ly [ˈhæpli] *ad.* 〔古〕①偶然地；侥幸地．②或许．

ha'·p'orth [ˈheipəθ] *n.* 〔英口〕= halfpennyworth.

hap·pen [ˈhæpən] *vi.* ①发生；〔口〕出现．②〔后接不定式〕偶然…，碰巧… (*to do*)．*Do you ～ to remember his name?* 你还记得他的名字吗？*If anything should ～ to me ...* 万一我有不幸…．*It (so) ～ed that ...* 偶然…，碰巧…．*No matter what [whatever] ～s* 不管发生什么事，不管出现什么情况．***as it ～s*** 碰巧．(*As it ～s, I have left the book at home.* 偏巧我(把书放在家里了)．***be likely to*** ～ 可能要发生．～ ***in*** 〔美〕偶然到…(来)．～ ***in with*** 偶然和…碰见．～ ***on [upon]*** 偶然看到[碰到，想到]．～ ***what may*** 无论发生什么事，不管怎样．

hap·pen·chance, hap·pen·stance [ˈhæpəntʃɑːns, ˈhæpənstəns] *n.* 偶然事件．

hap·pen·ing [ˈhæpəniŋ] *n.* 〔常 *pl.*〕①事件，偶然发生的事．②即兴表演；临时的演出(尤指意在激发观众情绪的滑稽表演)．

hap·pi·ly [ˈhæpili] *ad.* ①幸运地，幸福地．②快乐地．③巧合地，适当地．④〔古〕偶然．

hap·pi·ness [ˈhæpinis] *n.* ①幸福；〔古〕幸运．②愉快．③(用语等的)适当．*for the ～ of the greatest number* 为了最大多数人的幸福．

hap·py [ˈhæpi] *a.* ①幸福的，幸运的．②快乐的，愉快的．③感到满足的．④巧妙的，恰当的；可喜的．⑤〔口〕有点醉意的，飘飘然的；兴奋的．⑥(常用以构成复合词)喜欢…的；爱用…的；热衷于…的．*a ～ union* 幸福的结合〔婚姻〕．*He is as ～ as ～ can be.* 他再幸福没有了．*a ～ choice* 恰当的选择．*a ～ event* 可喜的事．*a ～ idea* 好主意，高见．*a ～ translation* 巧译、妙译．*trigger-～* 动不动爱扳枪机的；好斗的．*power-～* 权迷心窍的．*statistic-～* 热衷于统计数字的．***as ～ as the day is long = as ～ as a clam [king, lark]*** 非常幸福，非常快乐．***be ～ in*** (幸好)有… (*I was once ～ in a son.* 我也有过一个男孩子，可是…)．***be ～ in one's expressions*** 妙语风生．***be ～ in one's own degeneration*** 自甘堕落．***be ～ together*** (夫妇)和睦相处．***by a ～ chance*** 恰巧，正巧；顺顺当当．***hit [strike] the ～ mean [medium]*** 采取中庸之道，折衷．～**-go-lucky** *a.* 听天由命的，无忧无虑的．～ **land** 乐土．～ **hunting ground** (印第安人的心目中的)天堂．

Haps·burg [ˈhæpsbəːg] *n.* 哈普斯堡皇室〔奥地利皇室(1276—1918)，西班牙皇室(1516—1700)，神圣罗马帝国皇室(1438—1806)〕．

hap·ten [ˈhæpten], **hap·tene** [ˈhæptiːn] *n.* 【生，化】半抗原．**hap·ten·ic** [hæpˈtenic] *a.*

hap·tic(al) [ˈhæptik(əl)] *a.* 触觉的，与触觉有关的；感触的，能触知的．～ **lens** 眼白镜片〔覆盖眼白部分的隐形眼镜〕．

ha·ra·ki·ri [ˈhærəˈkiri] *n.* 〔Jap.〕切腹自杀.

ha·ram [ˈhɛərəm] *n.* = harem.

ha·rangue [həˈræŋ] *n.* ①(对公众集会作的)长篇大论的演说,慷慨激昂的长篇演说. ②高谈阔论;冗长的说教文章. ③叱责,训斥. — *vt., vi.* (向…)作长篇大论的演说;(向…)高谈阔论.

har·ass [ˈhærəs] *vt.* ①使烦扰,折磨. ②【军】扰乱,骚扰. *be ~ed by anxiety* 过着焦虑不安的苦日子. *be ~ed with debts* 苦于负债. **-able** *a.* **-er** *n.* **-ing** *a.* **-ingly** *ad.*

har·ass·ment [ˈhærəsmənt] *n.* ①折磨,骚扰. ②折磨人的东西;烦恼,忧虑.

har·bin·ger [ˈhɑːbindʒə] *n.* ①【史】(王室一行、军队等)派出打前站的人,先行官. ②通报者,先驱. ③预言者,预兆. *The robin is a ~ of spring.* 知更鸟是春天的报信人. — *vt.* 为…作先驱;预告,预示.

har·bo(u)r [ˈhɑːbə] *n.* ①海港,港口;港湾. ②〔喻〕避难所,藏身处. ③【军】坦克掩蔽场. *an air ~* 航空港. *a ~ barge* 码头驳船. *~ installations* 港口设施. *a ~ pilot* 领港员. *a natural ~* 天然港. *an artificial ~* 人工港. *a ~ of refuge* 避难港. ***give ~ to*** 窝藏(犯人). ***in ~*** 停泊中. ***make ~*** 入港停泊. — *vt.* ①隐匿,窝藏(罪犯等). ②怀抱(恶意). ③包含,聚藏. *~ malice against sb.* 对某人怀有恶意. — *vi.* ①躲藏,潜伏. ②停泊. **~age** *n.* 停泊处;避难处. **~ dues** 港务费. **~ master** 港务部长. **~ seal**【动】斑海豹 (*Phoca vitulina*)〔产于美国北大西洋沿岸海中〕. **-less** *a.* 无港的,无避难处的.

Har·court [ˈhɑːkət] *n.* 哈科特〔姓氏〕.

hard [hɑːd] *a.* ①硬的,坚固的 (*opp.* soft). ②(身体)结实的;(组织等)健全的. ③(问题、工作等)困难的,费力的;(人)难对付的 (*opp.* easy). ④难以忍受的;艰辛的. ⑤激烈的,猛烈的. ⑥(生活)刻苦的. ⑦严格的,严厉的. ⑧(人等)冷酷的,(天气)严酷的;(雇主等)刻薄的. ⑨(食物等)粗糙的,难吃的;发酸的. ⑩【语】发硬音的. ⑪(市价等)稳定的. ⑫确实的,不容怀疑的. ⑬(钱币)金属制的;(币制)可兑换成金子的. ⑭(水等)含无机盐的. ⑮(酒)烈性的,酒精成分高的. ⑯(声音等)刺耳的;(颜色等)刺目的. ⑰恶性难改的. ⑱【军】(导弹)可从地下发射并发射的;设于地下可防核攻击的. *a ~ bed* 硬板床. *a ~ bargain* 苛刻的交易. *~ common sense* 健全的理智. *a ~ customer* 挑剔的顾客. *~ dealing* 虐待. *~ drinker* 酒量大的人. *~ fact* 铁的事实. *a ~ fight* 恶斗,苦战. *~ food* 粗食 = ~ fare;固体食物;马料〔指谷类饲料, *cf.* fodder, mash〕. *a ~ knot* 死结. *~ labour* 苦工,苦役. *a ~ life* 困苦的生活. *~ liquor* 〔美〕烈酒. *a ~ saying* 难于理解的话;难于遵行的格言. *a ~ task* 困难的工作. *~ times* 市面萧条,不景气,艰难时世. *~ winter* 严冬. *~ words* 难于入耳的话. *H- words break no bones.* 〔谚〕直言无害. *~ work* 艰苦的工作,苦活. ***a ~ case*** ①难处理的事件. ②不堪救药的罪犯. ③〔美〕危重病人. ***a ~ nut to crack*** 难题. ***(as) ~ as a bone [brick]*** 极硬. ***(as) ~ as iron*** 坚如铁石,很严厉,很残酷. ***(as) ~ as nails*** ①结实,强健. ②冷酷无情. ***(as) ~ as the nether millstone*** 铁石心肠. ***at ~ edge*** 拼命,认真. ***be ~ on [upon] sb.*** 虐待某人;使某人难堪. ***be ~ up*** 〔口〕短缺,在急需中 (*be ~ up for money* 手头拮据). ***~ and fast*** ①严格规定的,刻板的,(规则等)一成不变的. ②(船)搁浅无法移动的. ***have ~ luck*** 倒霉. ***have a ~ time (of it)*** 难受,受苦,遭殃. ***in ~ condition*** 身体结实. ***learn sth. the ~ way*** 通过困难而学到某事. — *ad.* ①硬. ②拼命地,努力地. ③猛烈地,重重地. ④困难地,不容易地. ⑤接近地,立即地. ⑥〔美口〕非常,极. *try ~* 竭力一试. *think ~* 苦思. *drink ~* 暴饮. ***be ~ hit*** (感情等)受到沉重打击,很伤心. ***be ~ on [upon]*** 接近,紧跟着. (*be ~ on eighty* 快八十岁. *come in ~ upon sb.'s heels* 紧跟着某人进来). ***be ~ pressed*** 被催逼 (*be ~ pressed for money* 手头很紧. *be ~ pressed for time* 时间很紧). ***be ~ put to it*** 正在为难,陷于窘境. ***bear ~ on*** 拼命压迫. ***follow ~ after*** 紧紧跟着. ***go ~ with sb.*** 使某人为难[受苦]. ***~ by*** 在近旁. ***H- aport!***【海】左满舵! ***H- astarboard!***【海】右满舵! ***H- aweather! = H- up!***【海】转舵挡风! ***look [gaze, stare] ~ at*** 死盯着…. ***run sb. ~*** 紧追某人. ***take sth. ~*** 对某事耿耿于怀. — *n.* ①〔英〕硬海滩,登陆处. ②〔英俚〕(囚犯的)强迫苦役. *got two years ~* 被判处两年苦役. **~back** 精装书,硬书皮的书. **~bake** 〔英〕杏仁糖. **~-baked** *a.* 烤得硬的. **~ball** 棒球. **~-bitten** *a.* ①咬起来凶狠的. ②受到战争锻炼的,顽强的. **~board** 硬质纤维板. **~-boiled** *a.* ①(鸡蛋)煮得老的. ②(衣服等)浆硬的,挺括的. ③不动感情的,无情的,强硬的. **~bound** *a.* 硬书皮装订的. **~ cash** ①硬币. ②现金. **~ cider** 〔美〕含酒精的苹果汁. **~ chuck**【海】粗饼干. **~ coal** 硬煤,无烟煤. **~ copper** 冷加工铜. **~ copy** 清稿;复制件. **~-core** *a.* ①硬(果)心的,硬(木)髓的. ②(作品)赤裸裸黄色的. **~ core** ①(垫路基等的)碎砖石. ②(组织或运动中的)斗志最坚定的核心,铁杆分子. **~ court** 硬地网球场. **~cover** *a.* (书籍)精装的,硬书皮的. **~ currency** 硬通货,硬币 (*opp.* soft currency). **~-drawn** *a.*【机】冷拉的,冷抽的. **~ drug** 〔口〕成瘾毒品,麻醉品〔指一切能使人上瘾的和极有害于身心的毒品,如海洛因或古柯碱〕. **~-earned** *a.* 辛辛苦苦得到的;凭血汗挣得的. **~-faced, ~-favo(u)red, ~-featured** *a.* 面貌严厉的,其貌不扬的. **~ facing** 表面淬火,表面硬化. **~ finish** 墙上的油漆. **~-fisted** *a.* 双手坚硬有力的;吝啬的;强硬的. **~ goods** *n.* 〔*pl.*〕经久耐用品〔如汽车、家具等.亦作 ~**goods**〕. **~-grained** *a.* 木理细密的,坚硬的;(性格)固执的. **~hack** 绒毛绣线菊(= steeplebush). **~-handed** *a.* 双手牢靠有力的;用高压手段的. **~ hat** ①(建筑工人戴的)保护帽. ②建筑工人. ③持保守观点的建筑工程人员. ④真保守假激进的政客,形左实右派. **~head** *n.* ①精明而讲究实际的人. ②傻瓜. ③头上多刺和多骨头的鱼(尤指锯鲉、步鱼等). **~head sponge** 加勒比海粗纤维海绵〔产于加勒比海地区〕. **~-headed** *a.* 冷静的;讲究实际的;精明的;顽固的. **~-hearted** *a.* 无情的,冷酷的. **~ labo(u)r** (囚犯的)强迫苦役. **~-land** *vi., vt.* (使)硬着陆. **~ landing** (火箭的)硬着陆. **~-line** *n., a.* 强硬路线(的) (*take a ~-line on sth.* 就某事采取强硬路线). **~-liner** 主张强硬路线的人. **~ lines** 〔英〕运气不好. **~-lying money**【英海军】潜艇服役官兵的额外津贴. **~ maple** 糖槭,糖枫(= sugar maple). **~ money** 〔美〕= ~ **cash.** **~-mouthed** *a.* (马等)难以驾驭的;顽固的,倔强的. **~-nosed** *a.* ①(狗等)嗅觉不灵的. ②〔美〕顽固的;丑陋的. ③精明而讲究实际的. **~-of-hearing** *a.* 耳背,有点聋. **~ oscillation** 强振荡. **~ palate**【解】硬颚. **~pan** 〔美〕硬质地层,硬地;坚固的基础;隐藏着的真情 (*get down to the ~pan of a question* 把问题彻底弄清楚). **~ pencil** 硬铅笔. **~ rock** 剧烈摇摆乐. **~ rubber** 硬橡皮,硬质胶. **~ sauce** 甜奶油汁. **~ science** 硬科学,自然科学. **~scrabble** *a.* 辛苦劳动才能勉强维持生活的. **~ sell** 硬行推销. **~-sell** *a.* 硬行推销的. **~-set** *a.* ①窘迫的. ②安放牢固的. ③坚硬的;坚决的;顽固的. ④(鸡蛋)将要孵化的. ⑤(人)空腹的. **~ shadow** 清晰的影子. **~-shell(ed)** *a.* ①硬壳的. ②〔美俚〕坚持己见的,不妥协的,顽固的. **~ shower** 穿透射流,硬射流. **~ site** 地下场,地下设施. **~-spun** *a.* (纱线的)紧拈的. **~stand** 停机坪;停车场. **~-surface** *vt.* 在…上铺硬质路面. **~ surfacing** 表面硬化. **~tack** *n.* 硬饼干. **~tail** 鲹子. **~ tap** 出渣口凝结. **~top** 金属顶盖式汽车. **~-top** ①*n.* 有硬质路面的地区[道路]. ②*vt.* 给…铺硬质路面. **~ tube** 高真空电子管. **~-up** *a.* 〔口〕缺少;急需 (*I'm very ~-up just now.* 我现在手头很紧. *be ~-up for sth. to say* 想不出该说什么话). **~ware** 〔集合词〕

①五金器具；金属制品．②(计算机的)硬件；(电子仪器的)零件，部件；(导弹的)构件；机器；计算机．③电化教学设备〔指录音机、电唱机、闭路电视等〕．④(军队或警察的)武器装备；〔美俚〕重武器．~**wareman** 五金商人；五金工人．~**-wearing** *a.* (衣料等)耐穿的．~ **wheat** 硬粒小麦，硬质小麦．~**-won** 辛苦得来的 (*a* ~*-won victory* 来之不易的胜利)．~**wood** *n., a.* 硬木(的)，硬树木(的) (~*wood trees* 阔叶树〔*cf.* coniferous trees〕)．~**-worked** *a.* ①累透的．②陈腐的．~**working** *a.* 勤勉的，努力工作的．~**-wrought** *a.* 冷锻的．~ **X-rays** 高透力X射线．~ **zone** 硬化区．

hard·en [ˈhɑːdn] *vt.* ①使坚固，使变硬．②使锻练得坚强．使果断．③使变冷酷；使顽固．④(把导弹基地等用水泥等加固或设在地下)使不受爆炸〔热幅射〕之害．*a* ~*ed heart* 冷酷的心．~*(ed) steel* 淬火钢．*a* ~*ed offender* 惯犯．— *vi.* ①变硬，凝固．②变强硬；变果断．③变严厉；变冷酷．③(意见等)坚定；(行情等)看涨．~ *off* 使(幼苗)受冷而变得耐寒．**-ed** *a.* ①变硬的，已定型的．②(导弹等)有地下发射井的，可从地下发射的．

Hard·en [ˈhɑːdn] *n.* 哈登〔姓氏〕．

hard·en·a·bil·i·ty [ˌhɑːdənəˈbiliti] *n.* 可硬化性；可硬化度；【冶】可淬性．

hard·en·er [ˈhɑːdənə] *n.* ①锻工；锻件．②硬化剂．

hard·en·ing [ˈhɑːdəniŋ] *n.* ①硬化；【冶】淬火．②硬化剂．*air* ~气冷硬化．*case* ~ 表面硬化．~ *by cooling* 冷却硬化．~ *by hammering* 锤击硬化．~*process* 硬化法．*the* ~ *of arteries* 动脉硬化．~ *through*【机】淬透．

har·di·hood [ˈhɑːdihud] *n.* ①大胆；刚毅．②狂妄，傲慢．③健壮．

har·di·ly [ˈhɑːdili] *ad.* 大胆地；狂妄自大地．

har·di·ness [ˈhɑːdinis] *n.* ①强壮，结实；抗性，耐性．②大胆；勇气；傲慢．*winter* ~ 耐寒性．

Har·ding [ˈhɑːdiŋ] *n.* ①哈丁(哈定)〔姓氏〕．②**Warren** ~沃伦·哈定〔1865—1923，美国第二十九任总统(1921—23〕．

hard·ly [ˈhɑːdli] *ad.* ①几乎不，简直不．②不十分，才，仅．③严厉地，粗鲁地；苛刻地．④使劲地，拼命地；辛辛苦苦地．*It's* ~ *true.* 这不象是真的．*He will* ~ *come.* 他不大会来．*I need* ~ *say.* 几乎不须说．*He is* ~ *old enough.* 他稍微年轻了一点．*The battle was* ~ *contested.* 这场仗打得很凶．*live* ~ 日子过得苦．~ *earned* 苦挣来的；〔谑〕便便当当得来的．***deal*** ~ ***with*** 虐待．~ ***any*** 几乎没有．~ ***anybody (anything, anywhere)*** 简直没有什么人〔什么东西，什么地方〕(*I gain* ~ *anything.* 我几乎没得到什么)．~ ***ever*** 很少．~ ... ***when [before]*** 一…就…，刚…就… (*She had* ~ *reached there when it began to rain.* 她刚到那儿就下雨了)．***think [speak]*** ~ ***of*** 把…想得〔说得〕很坏．

hard·ness [ˈhɑːdnis] *n.* ①坚固．②冷酷无情．③苛刻．④困难．⑤硬性；硬度．⑥导弹基地防御核攻击的能力．*wear* ~ 抗磨力．

hards [hɑːdz] *n.* 〔*pl.*〕麻屑，毛屑 〔*cf.* noil〕．*flocks and* ~ 纤维屑〔塞缝隙用〕．

hard·ship [ˈhɑːdˌʃip] *n.* ①艰难，困苦；辛酸，苦难．②压制，虐待．*bear* ~ *without complaint* 任劳任怨．*undergo [go through] all kinds of* ~*s* 备尝辛酸．

har·dy[1] [ˈhɑːdi] *a.* ①强壮的，能吃苦的，耐劳的．②大胆的，勇敢的．③鲁莽的；蛮干的．④(植物)耐寒的．*half* ~【园艺】冬季须防霜雪的．***the*** ~ ***annual*** 耐寒的一年生植物；〔谑〕(议会、报纸)每年提出的老问题．

har·dy[2] [ˈhɑːdi] *n.* (锻工用的)一种方柄凿．~ *hole* 铁砧插模孔．

Har·dy [ˈhɑːdi] *n.* ①哈迪(哈代)〔姓氏〕．②**Thomas** ~ 托马斯·哈代〔1840—1928，英国小说家〕．

hare [hɛə] *n.* (*pl.* ~*s*, 〔集合词〕~) ①野兔．②怪人，傻瓜．③〔英俚〕坐车不买票的人．***as mad as a March*** ~ 疯狂得象三月(交尾期)里的野兔．~ ***and hounds*** 兔子与猎犬〔一种儿童游戏，"兔子"在前面撒纸屑跑，"猎犬"在后追逐〕．***First catch your*** ~ ***(then cook him).*** 〔谚〕先捕兔后烹调；勿谋之过早．***hold [run] with the*** ~ ***and run [hunt] with the hounds*** 两面讨好．***hunt [run] the wrong*** ~ 估计错误，错怪某人．***make a*** ~ ***of sb.*** 愚弄某人．***start a*** ~ 在讨论中提出枝节问题．— *vi.* 飞跑．~ *away* 逃走，逃跑．~ *off* 〔英口〕跑开．~**bell**【植】钓钟柳．~**brained** *a.* 轻率的，浮躁的．~**-hearted** *a.* 胆小的．~**lip** *n.* 兔唇，豁嘴．

har·em [ˈhɛərem] *n.* ①(伊斯兰教国家的)闺房，后宫．②〔集合词〕妻妾婢女等的总称．③【动】〔集合词〕(与一只雄兽配偶和聚居的)一群雌兽．

har·i·cot [ˈhærikəu] *n.* ①〔主英〕扁豆 (= ~bean)．②浓味羊肉炖蔬菜．

hark [hɑːk] *vi.* 〔主要用于祈使句〕听．*H-(ye)!* 听！*H-away [off, forward]!* 〔命令猎犬〕去！— *vt.* 〔古〕听．~ ***after*** 追随．~ ***back*** (猎狗)循原路重找嗅迹；回到原处，回到本题 (*He* ~*ed back to the subject.* 他回到了本题)．~ ***to [at]*** 〔口〕听 (*Just* ~ *to [at] him!* 听他说！)．

hark·en [ˈhɑːkən] *vi.* 侧耳倾听 *(to)*，给予注意．

harl, harle [hɑːl] *n.* 羽毛上的细毛．

Har·lem [ˈhɑːləm] *n.* 哈莱姆〔美国纽约市的一个区，居民大都为黑人〕．**-ite** *n.* 哈莱姆人．

har·le·quin [ˈhɑːlikwin] *n.* ①(英国哑剧或意大利喜剧中)头戴面具和身穿各种颜色衣服的角色．②丑角；滑稽角色．③五颜六色．— *a.* 滑稽的，五颜六色的．~ **bug**【动】菜蝽蟓〔一种食白菜等的昆虫〕．~ **snake**【动】珊斑蛇〔美洲的一种珊瑚色的蛇〕．

har·le·quin·ade [ˌhɑːlikwiˈneid] *n.* (哑剧中)丑角出场的一幕，以丑角为主的戏；滑稽表演．

Har·ley [ˈhɑːli] *n.* 哈利〔姓氏，男子名〕．~ **Street** [ˈhɑːlistriːt] (伦敦的)哈利街〔多名医居住〕．

har·lot [ˈhɑːlət] *n.* 妓女，娼妓．— *a.* 娼妓的；卖淫的．

har·lot·ry [ˈhɑːlətri] *n.* ①卖淫．②〔集合词〕妓女．

Har·low [ˈhɑːləu] *n.* 哈洛〔男子名〕．

harm [hɑːm] *n.* 损害，伤害；危害．*no* ~ *done* 没有人受伤，一切平安无事．*There is no* ~ *in trying.* 不妨试试．*mean [think] no* ~．并没有恶意 ***come to*** ~ 遭不幸，受害．***do sb.*** ~ = ***do*** ~ ***(to) sb.*** 损害某人．***do no*** ~ 无害．***keep out of*** ~***'s way*** 保持安全，避免损伤．***Harm set,*** ~ ***get.*** = ***Harm watch,*** ~ ***catch.*** 〔谚〕害人终害己．— *vt.* 损害，伤害，危害．

har·mat·tan [ˌhɑːməˈtæn, hɑːˈmætən] *n.* (每年11月至次年3月由非洲内陆吹向大西洋海岸的)燥风，哈马丹风．

harm·ful [ˈhɑːmful] *a.* 有害的．**-ly** *ad.* **-ness** *n.*

harm·less [ˈhɑːmlis] *a.* ①无害的；没有恶意的．②没有受到伤害的．*(as)* ~ *as a dove* 温和得象鸽子．*escape* ~ 安全逃脱．**-ly** *ad.* **-ness** *n.*

har·mon·ic [hɑːˈmɔnik] *n.* ①【乐】泛音；和声．②〔*pl.*〕【数】谐函数，调和函数．③【物】谐波，谐音．— *a.* ①和睦的，融洽的．②【数】调和的．③【乐】和声的，悦耳的．④【物】谐波的．~ **analysis**【物】傅里叶级数学；【数】调合分(解)析，调波分析．~ **function**【数】调和函数．~ **interval**【乐】音程．~**mean**【数】调和平均(值)，调和中项．~ **motion**【物】谐运动．~ **oscillator**【电】谐(波)振(荡)器．~ **progression [series]**【数】谐级数，调和级数．~ **tone**【乐】泛音．**-ical** *a.* **-ically** *ad.*

har·mon·i·ca [hɑːˈmɔnikə] *n.* ①【乐】口琴 (= mouth organ.) ②玻璃键琴 (= musical glasses.) ③一种打击乐器．

har·mon·i·cal [hɑːˈmɔnikəl] *a.* = harmonic.

har·mon·i·con [hɑːˈmɔnikən] *n.* ①harmonica 的单数．②= orchestrion.

har·mon·ics [hɑːˈmɔniks] *n.*【乐】和声学．

har·mo·ni·ous [hɑːˈməunjəs, -niəs] *a.* ①悦耳的．②和谐的；融洽的；和睦的．③调和的，相称的．*a* ~ *family* 和睦的家庭 **-ly** *ad.* **-ness** *n.*

har·mo·nist [ˈhɑːmənist] *n.* ①和声学家,作曲家;演奏者. ②诗人. ③使和谐协调者,调停者. ④【宗】福音书的对照研究者.

har·mo·ni·um [hɑːˈməunjəm] *n.* 小风琴.

har·mo·ni·za·tion [ˌhɑːmənaiˈzeiʃən] *n.* 调和,一致.

har·mo·nize [ˈhɑːmənaiz] *vt.* ①使调和,使一致;使和睦,调停. ②【乐】给(曲调等)配和声. — *vi.* ①调和;融洽 *(with)*;相称 *(with)*. ②成为谐调. ~ *in feeling* 感情融洽. **-r** *n.* 使和谐协调的人.

har·mo·nom·e·ter [ˌhɑːməˈnɔmitə] *n.* 和声计,和声表.

har·mo·ny [ˈhɑːməni] *n.* ①调和;融洽;适应. ②【乐】谐调,和声(学). ③【宗】四福音对照书. ***be in ~ with*** 与…协调一致. ***be out of ~ with*** 与…不协调一致. ***live in ~*** 和睦相处.

Harms·worth [ˈhɑːmzwə(ː)θ] *n.* 哈姆斯沃斯[姓氏].

har·ness [ˈhɑːnis] *n.* ①马具,挽具. ②〔古〕甲胄,铠甲. ③跳伞员、摩托驾驶员的全套衣帽装备. ④【纺】综絖;(提花机上的)通丝. ⑤〔美俚〕警察制服;工作装备. ***die in ~ = die with ~ on one's back*** 在工作中死去,殉职. ***get back into ~*** 重新回去工作. ***in double ~*** 已婚的. ***in ~*** 做日常工作;受约束. ***single ~*** 〔谑〕光棍生活. ***work [run] in double ~*** (两匹马或牛)同时拉车;两人合作;(夫妇)双双工作. — *vt.* ①给…套上马具[轭具];使做固定的工作. ②利用(瀑布、风等),治理. ③〔古〕给…穿铠甲. ~ *a waterfall* 利用瀑布作动力. ~ **bull,** ~ **cop,** ~ **dick** 〔美俚〕穿制服的警察,外勤巡警. ~ **hitch** 攀踏结[绳结的一种]. ~ **horse** ①挽马. ②(赛马中)拖两轮车比赛的马. ~ **race** 挽车赛马[快马或蹓蹄马拖着单人二轮马车的跑马赛]. **-er** *n.* **-less** *a.* **-like** *a.*

Har·old [ˈhærəld] *n.* 哈洛德[男子名].

harp [hɑːp] *n.* ①竖琴. ②竖琴状的东西. ③[the H-]【天】天琴座. ④〔美俚〕爱尔兰人. ***hang one's ~ [~s] on the willows*** 乐极生悲. — *vi.* ①弹竖琴. ②唠叨地反复讲 *(on; upon)*. ~ ***on the same string*** 老调重弹. ~ ***on one's troubles*** 唠唠叨叨地诉苦. ~ **antenna** 【无】扇形天线. **-less** *a.* **-like** *a.*

harp·er [ˈhɑːpə] *n.* 弹竖琴的人,竖琴师.

Har·per [ˈhɑːpə] *n.* 哈珀[姓氏].

harp·ings, harp·ins [ˈhɑːpiŋz, -inz] *n. pl.* 船首部外侧腰板;造船用的临时牵条.

harp·ist [ˈhɑːpist] *n.* = harper.

har·poon [hɑːˈpuːn] *n.* (捕鲸等的)鱼叉,标枪. — *vt.* 用鱼叉叉(鲸鱼). ~ **gun** *n.* 捕鲸炮,发射鱼叉的炮.

harp·si·chord [ˈhɑːpsikɔːd] *n.* 【乐】大键琴[钢琴的前身]. **-ist** *n.* 奏大键琴者.

har·py [ˈhɑːpi] *n.* ①[H-]【希、罗神】鸟身女怪. ②残忍贪婪的人. ③恶妇人. ~ **eagle** (中、南美的)角鹰.

har·que·bus [ˈhɑːkwibəs] *n.* (旧时的)火绳枪.

har·ri·dan [ˈhæridən] *n.* 凶恶的老妇;鬼婆,丑婆.

har·ri·er[1] [ˈhæriə] *n.* ①猎兔狗. ②[*pl.*][集合词]打猎队中的猎人和猎狗. ③越野赛跑者.

har·ri·er[2] [ˈhæriə] *n.* ①侵略者,掠夺者;蹂躏者. ②鹞[一种捕食昆虫和小动物的鹰].

Har·ri·et(t), Har·ri·ot [ˈhæriət] *n.* 哈丽特[女子名, Henrietta 的异体].

Har·ri·man [ˈhærimən] *n.* 哈里曼[姓氏].

Har·(r)ing·ton [ˈhæriŋtən] *n.* 哈灵顿[姓氏].

Har·ris [ˈhæris] *n.* 哈里斯[姓氏].

Har·ri·s(s)on [ˈhærisn] *n.* 哈里森[姓氏].

Har·ris tweed [ˈhæris twiːd] *n.* (苏格兰哈利斯地区产的)一种手织呢;哈利斯牌呢.

Har·rod [ˈhærəd] *n.* 哈罗德[姓氏].

Har·ro·vi·an [həˈrəuvjən] *a.* 哈罗 (Harrow) 的,哈罗公学的. —*n.* 哈罗居民;哈罗公学学生[毕业生].

har·row[1] [ˈhærəu] *n.* 耙. ***under the ~*** ①(田等)耙过的. ②在困苦中,为难. — *vt.* ①用耙耙(地). ②弄伤,抓伤. ③使苦恼,折磨. ~ *(up) a field* 耙地松土. ~ *(up) one's feelings* 伤感情. — *vi.* (地)被耙松. **-er** *n.*

har·row[2] [ˈhærəu] *vt.* 〔古〕掠夺,抢劫. **-ment** *n.*

Har·row [ˈhærəu] *n.* ①哈罗[英国伦敦西北面的一个市镇]. ②哈罗公学[培养英国上层阶级子弟的一所中学= ~ School].

har·row·ing [ˈhærəuiŋ] *a.* 悲惨的,折磨人的. **-ly** *ad.*

har·rumph [həˈrʌmpf] *vi.* ①作赫噜声[清清嗓子的声音,尤指故意大声地清嗓子]. ②提抗议;埋怨. — *n.* 清嗓子的动作[赫噜声].

har·ry [ˈhæri] *vt.* ①掠夺,蹂躏. ②折磨,使苦恼. ③驱走. — *vi.* 作骚扰性的攻击,掠夺.

Har·ry [ˈhæri] *n.* ①[男子名]哈里[Henry 的昵称]. ②恶魔,恶鬼[常说作 old H-]. ③胡闹的青年人;伦敦佬[常略作 'Arry]. ***by the Lord ~*** 一定. ***play old ~ with*** 使混乱.

harsh [hɑːʃ] *a.* ①粗糙的;荒芜的,不毛的. ②(表情等)生硬的;(声音)刺耳的;刺目的. ③严厉的,苛刻的. *a ~ climate* 恶劣的气候. *a ~ cloth* 粗布. *a ~ contrast* 不调和的对照. *~ land* 荒芜的土地. *~ to the taste* 味涩. **-ly** *ad.* **-ness** *n.*

hars·let [ˈhɑːslit] *n.* = haslet.

hart [hɑːt] *n.* ***(pl. ~s,*** [集合词] ***~)*** 公鹿[尤指五岁以上的雄赤鹿]. *a ~ of grease* 〔古〕(正好宰食的)壮鹿. *a ~ of ten* 有十枝角的公鹿.

Hart(e) [hɑːt] *n.* 哈特[姓氏].

hart(e)·beest [ˈhɑːt(i)biːst] *n.* 【动】(南非)狷羚.

Hart·ford [ˈhɑːtfəd] *n.* 哈特福德[美国城市].

Hart·mann [ˈhɑːtmən] 哈特曼[姓氏].

harts·horn [ˈhɑːtshɔːn] *n.* ①鹿角;鹿茸. ②〔俗〕氨水,阿摩尼亚 = spirit of ~ [因早先用作嗅盐的碳酸铵从鹿角炼取].

hart's-tongue [ˈhɑːtstʌŋ] *n.* 【植】①荷叶蕨. ②水龙骨科的一种植物.

har·um-scar·um [ˈhɛərəm ˈskɛərəm] *a.* 轻率的,莽撞的. — *ad.* 轻率地,莽撞地. — *n.* 冒失鬼;轻举妄动.

ha·rus·pex [həˈrʌspeks] *n.* ***(pl. -pi·ces*** [-pisiːz]***)*** (古代罗马根据祭神牺牲的肠进行占卜的)肠卜师.

Harv. = Harvard.

Har·vard [ˈhɑːvəd] *n.* ①(美国)哈佛大学 (= ~ University). ②哈佛大学学生[毕业生]. **~man** 哈佛大学毕业生.

har·vest [ˈhɑːvist] *n.* ①收获;收割. ②收获物;产量,收成. ③收获期. ④结果;报酬. *abundant [bumper, good, rich] ~s* 丰收. *bad [poor] ~* 歉收. *~ festival* 收获节. *a peak ~* 最高产量. ***reap the ~ of one's diligence*** 勤有功,勤勉获成果. ***make a long ~ for [about] a little corn*** 小题大做. ***owe sb. a day in the ~*** 受某人的恩惠. — *vt.* ①收获(谷物等);在…收割;获得(成果等). ②定时杀死(受保护的野生动物)以保持生态平衡. — *vi.* 收获,收割. ~ **bug** 【动】恙螨. ~ **fly** 〔美〕蝉,秋蝉 (= cicada). ~ **home** ①收割完毕. ②庆祝收获完成的节日. ③收获完成时唱的歌. ~ **louse** = ~ bug. **~-man** ①收割庄稼的人;收获季节的帮工. ②【动】盲蛛. ~ **mite** 恙螨,沙蚤 (= chigger). ~ **month** 收割月[九月]. ~ **moon** 秋分前后的满月. ~ **mouse** ***(pl. ~ mice)*** (构巢于谷草中的)欧洲田鼠. ~ **tick** = ~ bug.

har·vest·er [ˈhɑːvistə] *n.* ①收获者,收割庄稼的人. ②收割机. ~ **thresher** 自动收割脱粒机.

Har·vey [ˈhɑːvi] *n.* ①哈维[姓氏,男子名]. ②**William** ~威廉·哈维[1578—1657,英国医生,解剖学家,血液循环的发现者].

has [强 hæz; 弱 həz, əz, z] have 的第三人称单数、现在式.

has-been [ˈhæzbin] *n.* 〔口〕曾经时兴的东西;曾风流一时的人物. *It is better to be a ~ than a never-was.* 〔谚〕

宁可昙花一现，不能没没无闻. — *a.* 〔美口〕过时的，从前的.

ha·sen·pfef·fer [ˈhɑːzenfefə] *n.* 〔G.〕腌泡汁炖兔肉.

hash [hæʃ] *n.* ①切碎的食物(尤指肉丁和土豆丁). ②拼凑起来的东西；大杂烩. ③重申，复述，推敲. ④〔Scot.〕傻瓜. ⑤〔美俚〕传闻. ⑥〔美俚〕麻醉品. ***make a ~ of*** 〔口〕弄糟. ***settle sb.'s ~*** 使某人服贴，使某人哑口无言；收拾某人. — *vt.* ①切细. ②弄糟. ③反复推敲. ***~ out*** 〔美口〕长时间讨论后解决. ***~ over*** 〔俚〕重新考虑；详细讨论，长时间讨论. **~head** 〔美俚〕吸毒者. **~ house** 〔美俚〕廉价小餐馆. **~ mark** 军役袖章，军役袖章上的斜条. **~-slinger** 〔美俚〕(小餐馆的)服务员. **~-up** 〔俚〕改写的作品.

hash·eesh, hash·ish [ˈhæʃiːʃ] *n.* 海吸希〔印度大麻制成的麻醉品〕.

hash·er [ˈhæʃə] *n.* ①〔美俚〕侍者. ②厨师，厨师下手.

hash·er·y [ˈhæʃəri] *n.* 〔美俚〕廉价小餐馆.

Has·i·dim [ˈhæsidim; *Heb.* hɑːˈsiːdim] *n.* 〔*pl.*〕(*sing.* ***Has·id*** [ˈhæsid; ˈhɑːsid]) 【宗】虔敬派信徒〔犹太神秘教的一个教派〕. **Ha·sid·ic** [-ˈsidik] *a.* **Has·i·dism** *n.* 【宗】虔敬派.

has·let [ˈheizlit] *n.* (猪和其它动物的)内脏.

has·n't [ˈhæznt] = has not.

hasp [hɑːsp] *n.* ①搭扣. ②【纺】(亚麻或黄麻的)纱绞〔长度为 3,600 码〕. — *vt.* 用搭扣扣上.

has·sel [ˈhæsəl] *n.* = hassle *(n.)*

has·sle [ˈhæsl] *n.*〔口〕激烈争论，争吵.

has·sock [ˈhæsək] *n.* ①蒲团，膝垫. ②草丛. ③〔美俚〕(棒球的)垒〔尤指本垒〕.

hast [强 hæst，弱 həst, əst, st] 〔诗、古〕have 的第二人称单数现在式〔与 thou 连用〕.

has·ta la vis·ta [ˈɑːstɑː lɑ ˈviːstɑ] 〔Sp.〕再见！(= See you again!).

hasta lue·go [ˈɑːstɑː ˈlwegəu] 〔Sp.〕再见！(= See you later!).

hasta ma·ña·na [ˈɑːstɑː mɑːˈnjɑːnɑː] 〔Sp.〕再见！明天见！(= See you tomorrow!).

has·tate [ˈhæsteit] *a.* 【植】(叶子)戟状的.

haste [heist] *n.* ①急速，紧迫，仓促. ②轻率. *Fool's ~ is no speed.* 〔谚〕傻瓜紧张，白忙一场. *Marry in ~ and repent at leisure.* 〔谚〕草率结婚事后悔恨. *More ~, less [worse] speed.* 〔谚〕欲速则不达. *H- makes waste.* 〔谚〕忙乱易错. ***in ~*** 急忙地；仓促地. ***in hot ~*** 火急. ***make ~*** 赶紧. ***make ~ slowly*** 慢慢快起来，开头别太快. ***make ~ to [and] (do sth.)*** 赶快(做某事). — *vi.* 赶紧，匆忙. *~ away* 赶忙走掉. — *vt.* 〔古〕使快，催促. ***~ away*** 赶快去.

has·ten [ˈheisn] *vt.* ①使加紧，催促. ②促进. — *vi.* 赶紧，赶快. *~ home* 急忙回家. *~ to sb.'s assistance* 赶去救助某人. *~ to the destination* 赶到目的地去. *~ to the scene* 赶到现场.

hast·i·ly [ˈheistili] *ad.* 急速地；轻率地，慌忙地.

hast·i·ness [ˈheistinis] *n.* 急速，轻率，慌忙.

Has·tings [ˈheistiŋz] *n.* ①黑斯廷斯〔姓氏〕. ②海斯汀斯〔英国地名〕. **Battle of ~** 海斯汀斯战役〔诺曼第的威廉击败英王哈罗德二世的一战〕.

hast·y [ˈheisti] *a.* ①急速的. ②性急的，急躁的. ③仓促的；轻率的. *a ~ conclusion* 草率的结论. **~ pudding** 〔美〕玉米粥；〔英〕面糊，麦片糊.

hat [hæt] *n.* ①帽子〔一般是指有边的〕，礼帽. ②红衣主教的红帽；红衣主教的职权〔地位〕. *bowler ~* 礼帽. *cocked ~* 卷边三角帽；折成三角的信. *gipsy ~* 妇女、儿童戴的宽边帽. *leaf ~* 斗笠. *matinee ~* 看日场戏戴的普通女帽；避免在剧院妨碍别人视线的特制女帽. *red [scarlet] ~* 红衣主教的帽子；红衣主教. *silk [stove-pipe, tall] ~* 大礼帽. *His ~ covers his family.* 他是光棍一条. ***as black as one's ~*** 纯黑的. ***at the drop of a [the] ~*** 〔美〕立即，毫不犹豫地. ***bad ~*** 〔俚〕坏蛋，卑鄙的人. ***be in a [the] ~*** 进退两难. ***bet one's ~*** 孤注一掷. ***black ~*** 〔澳俚〕新来的移民. ***by this ~*** 〔口〕我拿一切担保！千真万确！毫无疑问. ***get into the ~*** 进退两难. ***go round with the ~*** = ***make the ~ go round.*** 募捐. ***hang one's ~ on sb.*** 依靠某人. ***hang up one's ~ in sb.'s house*** 在别人家里久留不走，长期居住. ***~ in hand*** 卑躬屈节，必恭必敬 (*A man's ~ in hand never did him any harm.* 对人恭敬于己无害). ***~s off to sb.*** 钦佩某人. ***have a brick in one's ~*** 〔俚〕喝醉. ***knock into a cocked ~*** 打得不成样子，驳得体无完肤. ***I'll bet a ~.*** 保证没错. ***I'll eat my [old Rowley's] ~.*** 我决不，一定不会. ***My ~!*** 〔俚〕啊呀！嘿！ ***my ~ to a half penny! = by this ~! pass [send] round the ~*** 募捐. ***raise [take off] one's [the] ~ to*** 向…脱帽致敬. ***talk through one's ~*** 〔俚〕说大话，吹牛. ***throw [have, toss] one's ~ in the ring*** 准备加入比赛〔竞选、战斗〕. ***touch one's ~ to*** 碰帽边向…致敬. ***under one's ~*** 〔口〕秘密的. — *vt.* 〔口〕给…戴上帽子. **~band** 帽圈〔指帽边上的一圈丝带〕. **~block** 帽型. **~box** *n.* 帽盒. **~-in-hand** *a.* 对人恭敬的；卑躬的. **~ money** 【海】(货主送给船长的)酬金. **~peg** 供挂帽用的钉. **~pin** *n.* 妇女帽针. **~rack** ①帽架. ②瘦弱的动物. **~rail** (墙上的)帽挂. **~stand** (可移动的)帽架. **~ tree** 衣帽架. **~ trick** ①用帽子变的魔术. ②巧妙的一着. ③(在板球、足球等运动中)一人进三球或连得三分.

hat·a·ble [ˈheitəbl] *a.* = hateable.

hatch[1] [hætʃ] *vt.* ①孵化，孵. ②创造，使发生. ③图谋，策划. *~ chickens* 孵小鸡. *~ a plot* 搞阴谋. *~ a theory* 创立理论. ***Don't count the chickens before they are ~ed.*** 〔谚〕蛋尚未孵出别数鸡，别太指望未有把握之事. — *vi.* (蛋)孵化；(小鸡)出壳. ***~ out*** 想出计划，结果变成. ***~ up*** 〔美〕发明，设计，计划. *Five chickens ~ed yesterday.* 昨天孵出了五只小鸡. — *n.* ①(小鸡等的)一窝. ②孵化. ***~es, catches, matches and dispatches*** 〔谑〕(报纸上的)出生、订婚、结婚及死亡栏.

hatch[2] [hætʃ] *n.* ①【船】入孔，升降孔，舱口；舱口盖. ②(大门上的)便门，小门，短门. ③(水闸的)闸门；鱼栏. *an escape ~* 应急出口. ***a booby ~*** 〔美俚〕囚车，监牢；疯人院. ***down the ~*** 一饮而尽，干杯. ***under ~es*** ①【海】受禁闭. ②在困苦中，受压制. ③死. **~way** 【海】舱口，升降口.

hatch[3] [hætʃ] *vt.* 在…上画影线. — *n.* 影线〔表示阴影的细密平行线条〕.

hatch·el [ˈhætʃəl] *n.* 【纺】梳麻针排. — *vt.* (〔英〕***-ll-***) (用梳麻针排)梳理.

hatch·er [ˈhætʃə] *n.* ①孵卵的动物. ②孵卵器. ③阴谋家.

hatch·er·y [ˈhætʃəri] *n.* ①(特指鱼和家禽的)孵卵处. ②大型幼猪养殖场.

hatch·et [ˈhætʃit] *n.* 短柄小斧. ***bury the ~*** 休战，媾和. ***dig [take] up the ~*** 宣战，开战. ***throw [fling, sling] the ~*** 吹牛. ***throw the helves after the ~*** ①连受损失. ②完全放弃. ③一不做二不休，绝望挣扎. **~ face** 尖脸；面孔瘦削的人. **~ job** 〔口〕人身攻击；恶毒诽谤. **~ man** 〔口〕①被雇用的刺客，打手. ②走卒，走狗. ③〔美俚〕破坏他人(尤指竞选人)名誉的作家〔演说者等〕. **-try** *n.* 大刀阔斧的削减.

hatch·ing [ˈhætʃiŋ] *n.* 【机】(制图)晕渝，影线.

hatch·ment [ˈhætʃmənt] *n.* (挂在死者门前或墓前的)丧徽.

hate [heit] *n.* 怨恨；嫌恶. — *vt.* ①恨，憎恶. ②嫌. ③〔口〕不愿，不喜欢. *~ sb.'s guts* 〔美俚〕恨透某人. *~ the sight of* 讨厌看到. *I ~ troubling [to trouble] you.* 我真不想打搅你. **~monger** 煽动仇恨者(尤指对少数民族煽动仇恨者).

hate·a·ble [ˈheitəbl] *a.* 可恨的,讨厌的,该受怨恨的.
hate·ful [ˈheitful] *a.* 可恨的,讨厌的;〔罕〕表示敌意的. **-ly** *ad.* **-ness** *n.*
hate·less [ˈheitlis] *a.* 不憎恨的;不讨厌的.
hat·er [ˈheitə] *n.* 怀恨者.
hat·ful [ˈhætful] *n.* 一帽子的容量,许多.
hath [强 hæθ; 弱 həθ, əθ]〔古〕have 的第三人称单数现在式.
Hath·or [ˈhæθɔː] *n.* (埃及神话中牛头人身的)司爱情及欢乐的女神,爱神. ~ **column**【建】(柱头雕有牛头人身像的)爱神柱. **-ic** *a.* 爱神的;【建】爱神柱的.
hat·less [ˈhætlis] *a.* 不戴帽子的.
ha·tred [ˈheitrid] *n.* 仇恨,憎恨,憎恶,敌意,恶意. ***have a ~ for [of]*** 憎恶…. ***in ~ of*** 憎恨.
hat·ter[1] [ˈhætə] *n.* 制[修]帽人;帽商. ***as mad as a ~*** 〔口〕疯狂,发狂;大怒〔原为 as mad as an atter〕.
hat·ter[2] [ˈhætə] *n.*〔澳〕隐居者.
hat·ti [ˈhæti], ***hat·ti·she·rif*** [ˈhætiʃeˈriːf] *n.*〔Turk.〕(旧时由土耳其皇帝颁布的不可更改的)敕命.
Hat·tie [ˈhæti] *n.* 哈蒂〔女子名, Harriet(t) 的昵称〕.
hat·ting [ˈhætiŋ] *n.* ①制帽;制帽法[业]. ②制帽材料. ③脱帽礼.
Hat·ty [ˈhæti] *n.* 海蒂〔女子名, Harriet, Harriot 的爱称〕.
hau·ber·geon [ˈhɔːbədʒən] *n.* habergeon 的废体.
hau·berk [ˈhɔːbəːk] *n.* (中古时代的)锁子甲.
haugh [hɔː, hɑːx, hɑːf] *n.*〔Scot.〕河边冲积地.
haugh·ty [ˈhɔːti] *a.* ①傲慢的,骄傲的. ②〔古〕崇高的,高贵的. **-ti·ly** *ad.* **-ti·ness** *n.*
haul [hɔːl] *vt.* ①(用力)曳,牵,拖. ②拖运. ③使降落,降(旗) *(down)*. ④【海】使(船)改变航向. ⑤硬拖,硬拉;把(某人)押交法庭等处盘问[审讯];拘捕. ~ *a boat* 拖船. ~ *coal* (用车等)装运煤. ~ *timber* 拖运木材. — *vi.* ①曳,牵,拉 *(at; upon)*. ②(船、风)改变方向. ③〔喻〕改变主意. ***~ down one's flag [colours]*** 屈服,投降. ***~ in*** 拉进. ***~ in with***【海】使船靠近. ***~ off*** ①改变船的航行以躲避某物. ②退却,撤退. ③〔口〕打人前先缩回手臂. ***~ on [to, upon] the wind = ~ the wind***【海】抢风驶船. ***~ over the coals*** 申斥,谴责. ***~ round***【海】风向逐渐改变;因避危险而迂回航行. ***~ up*** ①船迎风行驶. ②拖上来. ③停止. ***~ sb. up***〔口〕责问某人. — *n.* ①拖,拉,强曳. ②拖运;拖运量;拖运路程. ③一网打得的鱼,捕获物. *long ~s by water* 长距离水路运输. ***make [get] a fine [good] ~*** 打了一大网鱼;捞了一笔. **~back** 拉回,拉线. **~ing winch** 绞车,绞盘.
haul·a·bout [ˈhɔːləbaut] *n.* (供)煤船.
haul·age [ˈhɔːlidʒ] *n.* ①拖曳;拖运. ②牵引量;牵引力. ③拖运费. ~ *business* 搬运业. ~ *motor* (电)机车. ~ *rope* 拖缆. *the road ~ industry* 公路货运业.
haul·er [ˈhɔːlə] *n.*〔美〕= haulier.
haul·ier [ˈhɔːljə, -liə] *n.*〔英〕①拖运者;运输工. ②货物承运人. ③拉线. ④绞车,起重机.
haulm [hɔːm] *n.* ①麦秸,稻草,豆秸. ②苫屋顶用的干草. ③(草等的)一枝茎,一秆.
haul·yard [ˈhɔːljəd] *n.* = halyard.
haunch [hɔːntʃ] *n.*〔常 *pl.*〕①(人的)腿臀部. ②(动物的)腰腿. ③【建】拱腋,梁腋,柱帽. *squat on one's ~es* 蹲着.
haunt [hɔːnt] *vt.* ①常去,常到(某地);缠住(某人). ②(鬼魂等)反复出没于,缠住(某人). ③(思想等)萦绕;(疾病等)缠(身). *be ~ed by fears* 老是提心吊胆. *~ one [one's memory]* 萦回脑际. *The house is said to be ~ed.* 据说这屋有鬼. — *vi.* ①经常出没,逗留. ②(鬼魂等)作祟. — *n.* ①常到的地方;(动物等的)栖息处;(罪犯等的)巢穴. ②〔方〕幽灵,鬼. *the ~s of one's schooldays* 学生时代常去的地方. *a ~ of fashion* 讲时髦的地方. *busy ~s of men* 人群熙攘的地方. *the ~s of criminals* 罪犯的巢穴. *the ~s of vice and crime* 罪恶的渊薮. **-er** *n.* 常到的人;常出现的鬼.
haunt·ed [ˈhɔːntid] *a.* ①闹鬼的,鬼魂经常出没的. ②反复出现的. ③令人烦恼的.
haunt·ing [ˈhɔːntiŋ] *a.* 萦绕心头的,无法甩脱的. *the ~ music* 难以忘怀的音乐. **-ly** *ad.*
Haupt·mann [ˈhaupmaːn], **Gerhart** 霍普曼〔1862—1946,德国剧作家,小说家、诗人〕.
Hau·sa, Hau·ssa [ˈhausə] *n. (pl. ~(s))* ①(非洲)豪萨人;〔the ~〕豪萨族. ②豪萨语.
hau·sen [ˈhauzn, ˈhɔːzn] *n.*〔G.〕= beluga.
haus·tel·lum [hɔːsˈteləm] *n.* *(pl. -tel·la [-ə])*【动】吸喙(蝇口器). **haus·tel·late** [-it, ˈhɔːstileit] *a.*
haus·to·ri·um [hɔːsˈtɔːriəm] *n. (pl. -ri·a [-ə])*【植】吸器. **haus·to·rial** [-əl] *a.*
haut·bois [ˈhəubɔi] *n. (pl. ~ [ˈhəubɔiz])* = hautboy.
haut·boy [ˈhəubɔi] *n.* ①【乐】双簧管 (= oboe). ②【植】麝香草莓.
haute cou·ture [əut kuˈtjuːr]〔F.〕①妇女时装设计师;[商店]妇女时装大师设计制作的服装. ②妇女时装新式样.
haute cui·sine [əut kwiːˈziːn]〔F.〕名厨的烹饪;佳肴,名菜.
haute é·cole [ˌəut eiˈkɔːl] *n.*〔F.〕①高超的骑术,花式骑术. ②马的特技训练法,高级驯马.
hau·teur [əuˈtəː] *n.*〔F.〕傲慢.
haut goût [həu ˈguː] *n.*〔F.〕①芳香,香味;〔喻〕风味. ②强烈的气味;调味很浓的菜. ③臭气.
haut monde [əu ˈmɔ̃ːnd]〔F.〕上流社会.
Ha·van·a Ha·van·na(h) [həˈvænə] *n.* ①哈瓦那〔古巴首都〕. ②古巴烟草;用古巴烟草制成的雪茄烟.
have [强 hæv; 弱 həv, əv, v; (在不定式"to"之前) hæf].〔词形变化〕(1)现在式: *I [you, we, they]* ***have***, *he [she, it]* ***has***, (口语略作) ***I've, you've, we've, they've, he's, she's, it's.*** (2)过去式: *I [you, he, she, it, we, they]* ***had***, (省略形) ***I'd, you'd, he'd, she'd, we'd, they'd.*** (3)否定省略形: ***haven't, hasn't, hadn't.*** (4)现在分词: ***having.*** (5)过去分词: ***had.*** (6)〔古〕现在式: *(thou)* ***hast*** *(he, she, it)* ***hath;*** 过去式: *(thou)* ***hadst.*** *vt.* ①有,持有,具有,含有. *How much money do you have?* 你有多少钱? *How many days have May?* 五月有几天? *I had no news of him.* 我没有他的消息. ②知道,了解,懂得. *She has your idea.* 她了解你的意思. *He has only a little Latin.* 他只懂一点点拉丁文. *You ~ me, ~ you not?* 晓得了吗,怎么样?〔出自莎士比亚 *Hamlet*〕. *H- you got [Do you ~] any idea where he lives?* 你知道他住在哪里吗? ③吃;喝;吸(烟);洗(澡). *Will you ~ a cigarette?* 抽一支烟吧? *~ some food* 吃点东西. *~ some water* 喝点水. *What will you ~?* 你要吃什么? *~ a bath* 洗澡. ④受,拿,取得. *May I ~ this one?* 我能拿这个吗? *She've had three letters from her friend.* 她已经收到朋友的三封来信. *~ a lesson* 受教. ⑤接受,忍受,容许〔多用于否定句〕*I won't ~ it.* 我受不了. ⑥体验;享受;经受,遭受,碰到. *~ a bad headache* 头痛得厉害. *We had a pleasant holiday.* 我们假日玩得很痛快. ⑦使[让、叫]某人做某事〔做某事用不带 to 的不定式来表示〕. *H- him come early.* 让他早点来. ⑧使[在]某方面出现某状态〔某状态多用过去分词等结构来表示〕. *~ one's hair cut* (请人)理发. *I had my purse stolen.* 我的钱包被人偷掉了. ⑨从事,进行,作(某事) *Shall we ~ a swim?* 我们游泳吗? ⑩表明,说,主张. *as Mr. Jones has it* 据琼斯先生所说. ⑪〔和带 to 的不定式连用〕必须,不得不. *Man ~ to eat.* 人要吃饭. ⑫显示,表现. *~ no fear* 不怕. *~ the courage to do sth.* 显示出敢做某事的勇气. ⑬〔英俚〕欺骗;〔口〕打败,胜过. *I ~ been had.* 我受骗了. *You've no reply to that; he has you here.* 你对此一言不答,你在这里是认输了.

H

⑭生育. ~ *a baby* 生孩子. ★(a) ①和②义在否定句与疑问句中,在英国通常不用助动词 do, 用③—⑧义造句时通常用 do; 但有时也可用两种构造而意义不变: *Had you [Did you have] any rain during your journey?* 你路上遇到雨吗? 有时意义稍有不同: *Have you time to do it?* 你(现在)有时间做它吗? *Do you have much time for your work?* 你工作的时间(经常)很多吗? (b) ⑪义在否定句与疑问句中,有时可用 do, 有时可不用 do: *Have you to do this?* (= Must you do this?) *Do you have to do this?* 〔美〕你非做这事不可吗? 〔英〕你经常都得做这事吗? (c) have + noun 通常等于同一义的动词: *have a dance* = dance (跳舞); *have a dream* = dream (做梦); *have a drink* = drink (喝). *have a smoke* = smoke (抽烟). (d) ③⑤⑨义在翻译时,须变通运用: ~ *a talk* 谈一谈. ~ *a try* 试一试. ~ *a class* 上课. ~ *a meeting* 开会. ~ *a game* 玩一盘. ~ *hospitable entertainment* 受到厚待. *I won't ~ it* 我(忍)受不了. ~ *a cold* 感冒. ~ *a fever* 发烧. — *v. aux.* ①〔现在完成式〕*I ~ [I've] written it.* 我把它写完了. *He has [He's] gone.* 他去了. *I ~ [I've] been there.* 我去过那里. *H- you done it?* 你做完那件事了吗? *Yes, I ~.* 是,做完了. *No, I haven't.* 不,还没有完. *He has not [hasn't] gone there.* 他还没有到那里去. *Hasn't he gone yet?* 他还没去吗? *No, he hasn't.* 是,还没去. ②〔过去完成式〕*I had [I'd] finished my breakfast when he came.* 他来的时候我已经吃过早饭了. *Had he done it?* 他(那时)已经把那事做好了吗? *Yes, he had.* 是的,已经做好了. *No, he hadn't.* 不,还没有. ③〔未来完成式〕*I shall ~ read it by the time you turn up tomorrow morning.* 你明早来时我就念完了. ④〔表示虚拟语气〕*If it had not been (= Had it not been) for ...* 要不是因为[幸而有]…. 或 *Had I* (= If I had) *only known it, ...* 只要我晓得的话…. ⑤〔与 got 连用,成 have got, 主英口,意为"有" = have〕: *I've [haven't] got it.* 我[没]有. *H- you got any?* 你有吗? ★(1) 与过去分词结合构成完成式; 这时 have, has, had 等通常发弱音. (2) 英国用完成式的地方,美国则常单用过去式: *I just got here* (= I ~ just got here). 我刚到. ~ ***a bad time*** 很倒霉. ~ ***a bun on*** 〔美〕喝醉. ~ ***a good time*** 过得快乐. ~ ***and hold*** 【法】保有,永远领有. ~ ***at*** 袭击; 谴责. ***H- done!*** 停止! ~ ***everything one's own way*** 样样照自己的意思做; 为所欲为. ~ ***had it*** 〔俚〕①吃够了苦,受到致命打击. ②(人)已过时. ③无希望,命已注定. ~ ***it*** ①胜利. ②〔口〕被打,挨骂. ③说,主张. ④死(*The ayes[noes] ~ it.* 赞成[反对]的占多数. *Let him ~ it* 让他倒霉去. *Rumour has it that ...* 有谣言说…; 传闻…. *He will ~ it that ...* 他坚持说,他硬说…). ~ ***it (all) over sb.*** 胜过某人. ~ ***it coming*** 〔美口〕活该倒霉. ~ ***it in for sb.*** 〔口〕对某人怀有仇恨,想对某人报仇. ~ ***it on sb.*** 〔美〕比(某人)强,胜过(某人). ~ ***it out*** 达成谅解; 解决掉; 得出结果. ~ ***it out of sb.*** 对某人报仇; 使某人受罚. ~ ***it out with sb.*** 与某人较量以解决争端; 与某人决一雌雄; 同某人讲明白. ~ ***much to do with*** 与…很有关系,与…有许多共同之处. ~ ***nothing for it but*** 只得,只好; 唯有. ~ ***nothing to do with*** 与…毫无关系,与…并无共同之处. ~ ***on*** ①穿着; 戴着. ②有事,有约会; 计划做. ③〔口〕欺瞒,骗,使人上钩. ~ ***one's eye on ...*** 注意,注视. ~ ***one's sleep out*** 睡够. ~ ***only to ... to ...*** 只要…就能… (*You ~ only to go on and then turn right to find the store.* 你只要往前走,再向右拐,就能找到那店). ~ ***(got) sb. (stone) cold*** 〔俚〕击败某人,控制某人. ~ ***sb. down*** 请某人到乡下作客. ~ ***sb. in*** ①请某人来家. ②叫某人来家干活. ~ ***sb. on toast*** 〔英俚〕骗. ~ ***sb. up*** ①请某人到城市作客. ②对某人起诉,控告某人. ~ ***sth. back*** 收回某物,把某物要回去. ~ ***sth. in*** 屋里备有某物. ~ ***sth. out*** 把某物弄出来(~ *a tooth out* 拔掉一颗牙). ~ ***to do with*** 同…有关系. ***Let sb. have it*** 〔俚〕①惩罚某人. ②和某人讲明自己对他的看法. — *n.* ①〔常 *pl.*〕〔口〕有产者,有钱人; (天然资源多的)富国. ②〔英俚〕欺诈,诈骗. *the ~s and the ~-nots* 有钱人和穷人; 富国和穷国.

have·lock [ˈhævlɔk] *n.* (垂在帽子后面保护头颈的)遮阳布.

Have·lo(c)k [ˈhævlɔk] *n.* 哈夫洛克〔姓氏,男子名〕.

ha·ven [ˈheivən] *n.* ①港口; 船舶抛锚处. ②避难所; 安息所. — *vt.* ①把(船)开进港. ②使(船)避难; 为…提供避难所,掩护. **-er** *n.* 港务长. **-less** *a.* **-ward** *ad.*

have-not [ˈhævnɔt] *n.* 〔常 *pl.*〕穷人; 穷国. *"have-not" power* 缺乏天然资源的强国.

have·n't [ˈhævnt] = have not.

ha·ver[1] [ˈheivə] *vi.* 〔主英〕①胡说八道,唠叨. ②犹豫不决,摇摆不定. — *n.* 〔常 *pl.*〕〔主 Scot.〕胡说八道,无聊的话.

ha·ver[2] [ˈhævə] *n.* 野生燕麦.

ha·ver[3] [ˈhɑːvə] *n.* (*pl.* ***ha·ver·im*** [-ˈveirim]) 伙伴; 同事.

hav·er·sack [ˈhævəsæk] *n.* 行军〔旅行〕帆布背包; 干粮袋.

hav·il·dar [ˈhævildɑː] *n.* (旧时印度兵的)中士.

hav·ing [ˈhæviŋ] *n.* 所有; 〔*pl.*〕所有物,财产.

hav·oc [ˈhævək] *n.* ①(自然力、暴动等造成的)大破坏,浩劫; 蹂躏,摧残. ②大混乱,大骚动. ***cry ~*** 预告灾难将临; 命令(军队)掳掠破坏; 鼓动暴乱. ***make ~ of, play [raise] ~ among*** = work ~ with 对…大肆破坏; 使陷入大混乱. — *vt.* (***hav·ocked; hav·ock·ing***) 严重破坏,使糜烂. — *vi.* 毁灭.

haw[1] [hɔː] *n.* ①【植】山楂; 山楂的果实. ②〔古〕篱; 围地; 花园; 墓地.

haw[2] [hɔː] ①(马、狗等的)第三眼睑,瞬膜. ②〔常 *pl.*〕瞬膜炎.

haw[3] [hɔː] *n.* 支吾声; 呃,嗯〔表示踌躇、疑问等〕. — *vi.* 说话支支吾吾; 发出呃〔嗯〕声. *hem [hum] and ~* 支支吾吾,闪烁其词; 嗯嗯呃呃地说. — *int.* 呃! 〔话顿住时的发声〕.

haw[4] [hɔː] *int.* 〔美〕豁! 〔吆喝马等向左转声〕. — *vt.* 使(马)向左转. — *vi.* (马等)向左转.

Ha·wai·i [hɑːˈwaiiː] *n.* 夏威夷〔美国州名〕.

Ha·wai·ian [hɑːˈwaii-ən] *a.* 夏威夷的; 夏威夷人〔语〕的. *the ~ Islands* 夏威夷群岛. — *n.* 夏威夷人〔语〕. ~ **guitar** 夏威夷吉他.

haw·finch [ˈhɔːfintʃ] *n.* 【动】(欧、亚洲的)蜡嘴雀 (= grosbeak).

haw-haw [ˈhɔːˈhɔː] *int., n., vi.* 啊啊! 哈哈! 哈哈大笑,哄笑 (= ha-ha).

hawk[1] [hɔːk] *n.* ①鹰,隼. ②贪心汉; 凶狠的人; 骗子. ③(政治上的)鹰派,主战派. *doves and ~s* 鸽派和鹰派. *Hawks will not pick ~s' eyes out.* 〔谚〕同类不相残. ***know a ~ from a handsaw [her(o)nshaw]*** 还算有判断力,还有点见识. — *vi.* ①放鹰,用鹰打猎. ②(鹰一样地)袭击,猛扑(*at*); (鹰一样地)翱翔,盘旋. — *vt.* (象鹰一样地)捕捉,攫取. **~-eyed** *a.* 眼光敏锐的,(象鹰眼那样)明察秋毫的. ~ **monitor** [**~-moth**]【动】天蛾. **~-nosed** *a.* 鹰钩鼻的. **~'s-beard**【植】还阳参属(*Crepis*) 植物. **~sbill** 玳瑁. **~weed**【植】山柳菊属(*Hieracium*) 植物〔包括桔黄山柳菊 (*H. aurantiacum*)〕. **-like** *a.*

hawk[2] [hɔːk] *vi.* ①大声清嗓. ②咳嗽. — *vt.* 咳出. ~ *up phlegm* 把痰咳出来. — *n.* 咳痰声,清嗓声.

hawk[3] [hɔːk] *vt.* ①叫卖兜售. ②散布(消息等),传播(谣言等).

hawk[4] [hɔːk] *n.* (泥水工用的带柄方形)灰浆板.

Hawk(e) [hɔːk] *n.* 霍克〔姓氏〕.

hawk·er[1] [ˈhɔːkə] *n.* ①放鹰打猎者. ②驯鹰者.

hawk·er[2] [ˈhɔːkə] *n.* 叫卖的商贩,小贩. *No ~s!* 小贩禁止入内!

Hawk·eye [ˈhɔːkai] *n.* 〔美〕衣阿华 (Iowa) 州的别名; 〔*pl.*〕衣阿华州人. *the ~ State* 衣阿华州.

hawk·ing [ˈhɔːkiŋ] *n.* 养鹰术;放鹰术,放鹰打猎术.

Haw·kins [ˈhɔːkinz] *n.* 霍金斯〔姓氏〕.

hawk·ish [ˈhɔːkiʃ] *a.* ①似鹰的,鹰嘴般的. ②(政治上)有鹰派味道的.

hawk·shaw [ˈhɔːkʃɔː] *n.* 〔口〕侦探,密探.

hawse [hɔːz] *n.* ①【海】锚链孔; 有锚链孔的船首部分. ②船首与锚间的水平距离. ③双锚停泊时锚链的位置. *a clear [an open] ~* 顺畅无结的锚链. *a foul ~* 缠结不顺的锚链. ~ **bag** 锚链孔塞. ~**hole** 锚链孔 (*come in through [at] the ~hole* 水兵出身). ~**pipe** 【船】锚链筒.

haw·ser [ˈhɔːzə] *n.* 【海】(供系船、下锚用的)粗绳,大索,钢缆. ~ **bend** 单索花结〔绳结的一种〕. ~**-laid** *a.* 左捻三根三股索的.

haw·thorn [ˈhɔːθɔːn] *n.* 【植】山楂.

Haw·thorn(e) [ˈhɔːθɔːn] *n.* ①霍索恩(霍桑)〔姓氏〕. ②**Nathaniel** ~ 纳·霍桑〔1804—1864,美国小说家〕.

hay[1] [hei] *n.* ①干草; (喂牲畜的)饲草. ②成果, 酬报. ③小额款项. ④〔美俚〕床. ***between [betwist] grass and ~ [~ and grass]*** (成人与儿童之间的) 青少年. ***hit the ~*** 〔美俚〕上床睡觉. ***look for a needle in a bundle [bottle] of ~*** 草捆中找针;大海捞针;徒劳无益. ***make ~ of*** ①将…割晒成干草. ②使混乱,弄乱(头发等)(*of*). ***make ~ out of*** 使对自己有利. ***Make ~ while the sun shines.*** 〔谚〕太阳好,就晒草;乘机行事;抓紧时机. ***not ~*** 〔美俚〕为数可观的一笔钱;相当大的数目. ***roll in the ~*** 〔口〕求爱; 调情. — *vt.* ①割晒(干草). ②给…喂干草. ③使成割制干草的草地. — *vi.* 制成干草; 割草晒干. ~**box** 干草箱〔保温用〕. ~**burner** *n.* 〔俚〕马(尤指第二流的赛马). ~**cock** 〔英〕干草堆,(圆锥形)草堆. ~ **fever** 【医】花粉热, 枯草热. ~**field** (牧草)打草场. ~**fork** 干草叉. ~ **knife** 割草刀. ~**-loft** 干草棚, 秣棚. ~**maker** ①翻晒干草的人; 干草机. ②〔俚〕猛击一拳. ~**making** ①翻晒干草. ②对现有机会的利用. ~**mow** ①干草堆. ②干草顶棚. ~**rack** ①干草饲料槽. ②干草车的装草架;有装草架的大车. ~**-rick** 〔英〕 = ~stack. ~**ride** *n.* 〔美〕 乘垫有干草的大车郊游. ~**seed** ①干草种; 干草(尘)屑. ②〔美俚〕乡下佬 (*He hasn't got the ~ seed out of his hair yet.* 他才从乡下出来). ~**seed center** (远离大都市的)农村. ~**stack** 干草堆. ~**wire** ① *n.* 〔美〕捆干草的铁丝,乱铁丝. ② *a.* 〔美俚〕疯狂的;混乱的;杂乱无章的;匆忙拼凑成的 (*go ~wire* 发疯; 出故障, 出毛病. *The radio went ~wire.* 无线电出了毛病).

hay[2] [hei] *n.* 一种乡村舞蹈.

Hay [hei] *n.* 海〔姓氏〕.

Hay·dn [ˈhaidn], **Franz Joseph** 海顿〔1732—1809, 奥地利作曲家〕.

Hayes [heiz] *n.* 海斯〔姓氏,男子名〕.

Haynes [heinz] *n.* 海恩斯〔姓氏〕.

Hays [heiz] *n.* 海斯〔姓氏〕.

Hay·ti [ˈheiti] *n.* = Haiti.

hay·ward [ˈheiwəd] *n.* (教区、村镇、庄园等的)家畜围篱管理员.

Hay·wood [ˈheiwud] *n.* 海伍德〔姓氏〕.

ha·zan [ˈhɑːzn; hɑˈzɑːn] *n.* ***(pl. ha·zan·im*** [-ˈzɑːnim]***)*** (犹太人教堂)合唱指挥;领唱者 (= hazzan).

haz·ard [ˈhæzəd] *n.* ①碰巧,机会;偶然的事. ②孤注一掷,冒险. ③危险;公害;事故,意外. ④(用骰子玩的)游戏〔赌博〕. ⑤(网球场中)可得分的开球;【台球】使球触他球后落入袋中的击法;【高尔夫球】障碍地带. ⑥〔英方〕马车停车场. *health ~* 对健康的危害. ***a losing ~*** (台球戏中)打出的球和他球相撞后落入袋中. ***at all ~s*** 不顾一切危险;务必. ***at [by] ~*** ①在危急中. ②胡乱地,随便地. ***at the ~ of*** 拚着. ***a winning ~*** (台球戏中)打出的球和他球相撞后使他球落入袋中. ***be on the ~*** 在危险中,受到威胁. ***run the ~*** 冒险,冒险一试. — *vt.* ①使遭受危险. ②冒…的危险; 冒险一试. *~ a guess* 作无把握的揣测. *~ one's life* 冒生命危险.

Haz·ard [ˈhæzəd] *n.* 哈泽德〔姓氏〕.

haz·ard·ous [ˈhæzədəs] *a.* ①危险的, 冒险的. ②凭运气的. *~ chemicals* 危险的化学品. *a ~ climb* 冒险的攀登. **-ly** *ad.* **-ness** *n.*

haze[1] [heiz] *n.* ①霾,烟雾,霭;朦胧. ②疑惑; 思想糊涂; 暧昧. ***in a ~*** 在雾中,渺茫 (*with one's minds in a ~* 糊里糊涂地). ***no ~ of doubt*** 没有怀疑表现. — *vt.* ①使雾笼罩,使朦胧. ②使糊涂. — *vi.* ①起雾; 变朦胧. ②变糊涂. **-less** *a.*

haze[2] [heiz] *vt.* ①【海】罚…做苦工, 折磨. ②〔美俚〕欺侮,戏弄(大学新生). ③骑马放牧〔驱赶〕.

ha·zel [ˈheizl] *n.* ①【植】榛,榛子,榛实,榛木. ②淡褐色(尤指眼睛). — *a.* ①榛树的,榛木制的. ②(眼睛等)淡褐色的. ~ **hen [grouse]** 松鸡 (*Tetrastes bonasia*) 〔产于欧洲〕. **-ly** *a.* ①榛多的. ②淡褐色的.

ha·zel·nut [ˈheizlnʌt] *n.* 榛子.

Haz·litt [ˈheizlit, ˈhæzlit] *n.* 黑兹利特〔姓氏〕.

ha·zy [ˈheizi] *a.* ①多烟雾的,烟雾弥漫的. ②朦胧的,模糊的. ③〔美俚〕喝醉的. **haz·i·ly** [ˈheizili] *ad.* **haz·i·ness** [ˈheizinis] *n.*

H.B., HB = hard black 硬黑〔表示铅笔芯软硬度的符号〕.

H.B.M. = His [Her] Britannic Majesty('s) 英国皇家的.

H-bomb [ˈeitʃbɔm] *n.* 氢弹 (= hydrogen bomb).

H.C. = ①high conductivity 高电导性. ②Holy Communion 【宗】圣餐. ③ House of Commons 〔英〕下(议)院.

H.C.F. = Honorary Chaplain to the Forces 〔英〕荣誉随军牧师.

h.c.f. = highest common factor 最大公约数, 最大公因子.

HD = ①Harbor Defense 港口防务. ②heavy-duty 关税重的;重型的;经得起损耗的.

hdbk. = handbook.

hdkf. = handkerchief.

hdqrs. = headquarters.

HE = high explosive 烈性炸药.

He = 【化】元素 helium 的符号.

H.E. = ①His Eminence 阁下〔天主教中对红衣主教的尊称, 间接提及时用〕. ②His [Her] Excellency 阁下〔间接提及时的尊称〕.

he[1] [常 hiː; 弱 iː, hi, i] *pro.* ***(pl. they)*** 〔人称代名词、第三人称、单数、男性、主格;所有格为 his, 宾格为 him, 物主代名词为 his〕他, 那个男人. *He who [that]* …者,…的人. *He would.* 〔美〕那家伙就可能那样做;那家伙就是那种人〔含有憎厌的意思〕. *He that talks much errs much* 〔谚〕言多必失. — *n.* ***(pl. hes, he's*** [hiːz]***)*** 男人;〔口〕雄,公. *Is it a he or a she?* (婴孩)是男的还是女的? (动物)是公〔雄〕的还是母〔雌〕的? ~**-man** ***(pl. -men)*** 〔美口〕健美男子;健壮而充满男性气概的人.

he[2] [hiː] *int.* 嘻! 〔常重复作 he! he! 表示嘲笑〕.

he[3] [hei] *n.* 希伯来文的第五个字母.

he- *comb. f.* 表示"雄","公": *he*-goat.

head [hed] *n.* ①头,头部,首. ②头脑, 才能; 智力,想象力,理解力. ③前部,上部; 顶端,尖突部;船首; (书页等的)天头;(桌位的)首席;弹头. ④首脑,首长,领导. ⑤个人,人数;(牲畜的)匹数,头数. ⑥条目, 项目, 头绪; 要点;标题. ⑦(有头像的)硬币正面 (*opp.* tail); (有头像的)邮票. ⑧(河的)源头;(疮、疖等的)脓头. ⑨(水站等的)蓄水高度,水位差,水头,落差,压力; 势头. ⑩海角;

岬。⑪头状物体；鹿角；【植】顶梢；谷穗；头状花序；头状叶丛。⑫危机；极点，绝顶；结论。⑬〔口〕(宿醉引起的)头痛。⑭酒沫，泡沫；〔英〕(浮在牛乳表面的)奶油。⑮〔口〕脑袋，生命；嘴。⑯〔俚〕(舰船上的)厕所。⑰【矿】水平巷道，煤层中开拓的巷道。⑱【机】盖，帽。⑲【语】中心成分。⑳【乐】音符的符头。㉑〔俚〕麻醉药品吸食者；主张种植麻醉药品作物者。a clear [cool] ~ 明智的[冷静的]头脑。hot ~ 急性；急性的人。level ~ 头脑清醒的人。strong ~ 酒量大的人。wise ~ 聪明人；自作聪明的人。a wooden ~ 笨蛋，木头人。Two ~s are better than one. 〔谚〕集思广益，三个臭皮匠胜过诸葛亮。the H- 〔俚〕校长。twopence per [a] ~ 每客两便士。20 ~ of cattle 二十头牛〔单复数相同〕。crowned ~(s) 君主，国王，王后。a deer of the first ~ 初生角的鹿。the ~ of a lake (河流注入处的)湖口。scare ~ 〔美〕醒目的报纸标题。Shut your ~! 住口！**a big ~ and little wit** 脑袋大而智力有限。**above the ~s of** *(an audience)* 深奥得使(听众)不能理解。**addle one's ~** 搞得头昏脑胀，绞尽脑汁。**an old ~ on young shoulders** 少年老成。**at the ~ of** 以…为首，在…的前面。**beat sb.'s ~ off** 打得某人头破血流；使某人焦头烂额。**beat [put, get] sth. out of sb.'s ~** 使某人忘记某事；使某人对某事断念(*Do get this idea out of your ~.* 抛弃这种念头吧)。**be unable to make ~ or tail of sth.** =**make neither ~ nor tail of sth.** **Better be the ~ of an ass than the tail of a horse.** 〔谚〕宁为鸡首，不为牛后。**break Priscian's ~** 犯语法错误。**bring matters to a ~** 使事态陷于危机。**bury one's ~ in one's hand** 用双手抱头(表示痛苦等)。**bury one's ~ in the sand** 闭眼不看眼前的危险，采取鸵鸟政策。**buy sth. over sb.'s ~** 比某人出更高的价格抢购某物。*(down)* **by the ~** ①【海】船头比船尾吃水深。②〔俚〕稍醉。**by the ~ and ears** = **by ~ and shoulders** ①粗暴地。②(身材、气度)相当高的 (*taller by the ~ and shoulders* (身材)高得多；〔喻〕(能力等)高超得多)。**carry [hold] one's ~ high** 趾高气扬。**come into [enter] one's ~** 想起，想到。**come to a ~** ①(疮、疖等)化脓。②(时机、事件等)成熟；逼近严重关头，达到顶点。**come under the ~ of** 归入…部，属于…项下。**cost sb. his ~** 断送某人性命。**cut [make] shorter by the ~** 砍头。**drag by (the) ~ and ears** ①粗暴地拖。②勉强扯进 (*drag sb. out by ~ and ears* 蛮横地把某人拖出。*drag the anecdote by the ~ and ears into one's conversation* 硬把那件趣闻扯进谈话里)。**draw to a ~** = come to a ~。**eat one's ~ off** ①(家畜等)能吃不能做；(人)好吃懒做。②失业；无所事事。**fling [throw] oneself at sb.'s ~ [at the ~ of sb.]** (女子)勾引某人，接受某人求婚。**from ~ to foot [heel]** 从头到脚，全身；完全。**gather ~** ①(疮、疖等)化脓。②(时机、事情等)成熟。③(风等)增强。**get a ~** 醉得第二天还没有醒酒。**get into one's ~** (酒劲)冲上头。**get [take] it into one's ~** 凭空想到，主观认为，硬想。**get [have] swelled [the big] ~** 自以为了不起。**give a ~** 〔口〕使头痛，引起头痛。**give ... his [her, its] ~** 放松缰绳；让某人自由行动。**give one's ~ for the washing** 俯首受辱。**go about with one's ~ in the air** 自高自大，摆架子。**go off one's ~, go out of one's ~** 发疯，发狂。**go to one's [the] ~** ①酒劲冲上头。②使兴奋；使自高自大。**hang [hide] one's ~** (羞愧得)把头垂下。**hang over sb.'s ~** (危险、灾难)临头。**have a good ~ for** 有…的才能。**have a ~**【医】酒后头痛。**have a (good) ~ on one's shoulders** 有见识；有能力。**have a hard ~** 坚定；头脑顽固。**have a ~ like a sieve** 记忆力很差。**have a long ~** 有远见。**have one's ~ in a tar barrel** 〔美〕陷入困境。**have one's ~ screwed on the right way** 头脑清醒，有判断力。**~ and ears** 全身(陷于) *(in)*。**~ and front** 顶点；本质，要点。**~ and shoulders above** 高出一个头，远远超过。**~ first [foremost]** ①头朝下，倒栽葱。②不顾前后，冒冒失失。**~ of hair** 头发 (*He has a red ~ of hair* 他有一头的红头发)。**~ on** 把船头朝前；迎面地。**~ over ears** 深深地陷入。**~ over heels, heels over ~, Heads I win, tails you lose.** 正面我赢，反面你输〔掷钱币打赌时说，意指无论怎样，我不吃亏〕。**~(s) or tail(s)** 你要正面还是反面〔掷钱币打赌〕？**Heads up!** 〔口〕注意！小心！**~ to ~** 头对头，交头接耳。**hide one's diminished ~** 失势退隐。**keep one's ~** 镇定，不慌不忙。**keep one's ~ above ground** 活着。**keep [hold] one's ~ above water** ①未淹没。②不负债。**knock ~** 叩头。**knock sb. on [in] the ~** 打某人的头部；杀掉某人，消灭某人。**knock sb.'s ~ off** 轻易胜过某人。**knock their ~s together** 强迫争议双方接触和谈；用武力制止两人争吵。**laugh [run, scream] one's ~ off** 狂笑[奔走，呼叫]不已。**lay [put] ~s together** 一起策划；共同商量。**lie** *(the blame)* **on sb.'s ~** 把(过失等)归罪于某人。**lift (up) one's ~** 振作，欣喜。**lose one's ~** ①被砍头，丧命。②着慌，不知所措。**loss of ~** 水头抑损，(水)位(抑)损。**make ~** ①前进。②武装反抗。**make ~ against** 抵抗；制止。**make neither ~ nor tail of** 对某事莫名其妙。**make sb.'s ~ sing** 把某人打得头昏耳鸣。**not right in one's [the] ~** 神经失常。**off (out of) one's ~** 过于兴奋；精神失常。**one's ~ is full of bees** 想入非非，异想天开。**on one's [sb.'s] ~** ①倒立着 (*stand facts on their ~s* 颠倒黑白)。②〔口〕易如反掌地 (*can do sth. on one's ~* 做某事不费吹灰之力)。③是…的责任 (*Be it on your ~!* 那由你负责！)。**open one's ~** 〔美俚〕开口，说。**out of one's ~** 精神错乱。**out of one's own ~** 自己想出来的，独出心裁的。**over ~ and ears in debt [love]** 身负重债[深陷爱情中]。**over sb.'s ~** ①出人头地；被晋升至某人之上。②使人不能理解。③不同人商量(而越级上告等)。**Pope's ~** 长柄扫帚。**put a ~ on sb.** 殴打某人；使某人住口。**put one's ~ in [into] a noose** 自己把头套在绞索中，自投罗网。**put one's ~ into the lion's mouth** 轻入险地，冒大险。**put sth. into [out of] one's ~** 使人想起[忘记]某事。**ram sth. into sb.'s ~** 对某人填鸭式地灌输某事。**raw ~ and bloody bones** (死亡的象征)骷髅头和交叉骨；吓唬小孩的妖怪。**run one's ~ against a wall** 碰壁。**scratch one's ~** 搔头皮，对某事迷惑不解。**screw one's ~ on tight** 保持清醒头脑，精明。**show one's ~** 出现，到场。**soft in the ~** 傻里傻气。**stake one's ~ on** 以生命打赌。**stand on one's ~** 为人古怪。**take sth. into one's ~** 突然想起，心血来潮。**take the ~** 领头，执牛耳。**talk sb.'s ~ off** 啰啰嗦嗦，谈得使人生厌。**turn sb.'s ~** 使某人感到骄傲，使某人头脑发热。**turn sth. over in one's ~** 再三思忖，反复考虑。**trouble one's ~ about sth.** 为某事伤脑筋。**turn ~ over heels** 翻筋斗，颠倒，倒转。**use one's ~** 动脑筋。**wash an ass's ~** 徒劳无益。**weak [touched] in the ~** 脑子笨的。**win by a ~** (赛马时)以一个马头的距离获胜。**work one's ~ off** 苦干，不停地工作。— *vt.* ①站在…的前头，率领，牵头；打破(记录等)。②阻拦，妨碍；反抗。③为(箭等)安头；使构成顶部；在…上加标题。④把头对着；溯(源)；〔美〕使(车、船等)向着某处行驶。⑤用头顶(球)。⑥砍伐(树等)的顶枝；收割(庄稼)；切去(鱼)头〔砍去人头用 behead〕。~ *the list* 名列第一。~ *all records* 打破所有记录。~ *a fish* 切掉鱼头。~ *a nail* 制钉头。— *vi.* ①前进，出发；驶往 *(for)*。②(果实、麦穗等)成头状物，结实，抽穗。③(疮、疖等)出脓头。④(河流等)发源。**be ~ed for** = **~ for**。**~ back** ①绕至前方。②阻止。**~ down** 截去树梢，摘心，掐尖。**~ for** 走向，向…方向前进。**~ into** 〔美〕开始，着手。**~ off** ①上前拦截(车辆、羊群等)，使之转变方向或退回。②阻止某事；使某人不做某事 (*I ~ed him off [from] making a speech.* 我打

断了他演说的念头). ~ ***the ball*** (踢足球时)顶球. ~ ***up*** ①指挥,当主管. ②给…加盖子. — *a.* ①头的,头部的. ②主要的,首席的. **~ache** 头痛;头痛的事 (*cause [give]a ~ache* 叫人头痛). **~achy** *a.* 头痛的,有头痛病的;使人头痛的. **~band** ①头带,束发带. ②印在书页顶端的花饰;嵌在书脊上下两端的布片 (*~band receiver* 头戴式耳机). **~-block**【矿】井口挡车器;柱帽. **~board** 床头板,床头架. **~chair** (牙医诊所、理发店等内的)有头靠的椅子. **~cheese** (猪头、脚、舌等做成的)碎肉冻[香肠]. ~ **cold** 伤风(感冒). ~ **count** 人口调查. ~ **doctor**〔俚〕精神病医生. **~dress** 头巾,头饰;发式. **~fast, ~ fast** 船首系索. **~fish**【动】翻车鲀(=ocean sunfish). **~frame**【矿】井架. ~ **gate** (运河、水渠的)闸门;总闸. **~gear** 头饰,帽子,安全帽;马首挽具. **~-hunter** ①割取敌人的头作战利品的人. ②物色人材的人. ~ **lamp** (汽车等的)前灯;桅灯;(矿工头上的)照明灯. **~land** ①岬. ②地头,畦界. **~light** ① = ~lamp. ②(机翼上的)雷达天线. **~linesman** 足球赛的巡边员. **~lock**【摔交】用手臂把对方的头擒住. **~long** *ad., a.* ①头向前地[的];倒栽葱地[的]. ②急速地[的]. ③轻率地[的],鲁莽地[的]. ④〔古〕险峻地[的] (*rush ~long into danger* 鲁莽冒险). **~man** ①首领,酋长. ②工头,领班,组长. ③刽子手. **~master**〔英〕校长. **~mistress** 女校长. ~ **money** ①人头税. ②旧时按斩首或捕获成绩给与的赏金. ③(移民等的)入境税. **~most** *a.* 最前面的,领头的. **~note** (书的)眉批,顶注;批注. ~ **office** 总社;总店;总局. **~-on** *a.* 迎头的;(冲突等)正面的. **~-page** 扉页. **~phone** 头戴送受话器,耳机. **~piece** *n.* ①胄,盔,帽子,头巾. ②才智. ③【印】(书的)扉页;(章节开头的)花饰. ④ = ~phone. **~pin**【体】(九柱戏的)前角柱. ~ **pressure** 排出压力. **~quarter** ① *vi.* 设总部. ② *vt.* 在…设总部;把…放在总部中. **~quarters** *n.*〔*sing., pl.*〕①指挥部,司令部,大本营. ②总署;总局;总店. ③当局. **~race** (水车的)引水槽(*opp.* tailrace). ~ **register** (声音的)高音区. **~rest** (牙医诊所、理发店坐椅的)头靠. **~room** *n.*【建】(门口、水渠等的)净空,净空高度. **~sail** 前帆〔船首斜桅三角帆总称〕. **~sea** 逆浪,顶头浪. **~set** = ~phone. **~ship** 首领地位,首领的资格[权威]. **~shop** ①时装店. ②〔俚〕麻醉毒品店. **~shrinker** ①割取敌人头颅使其干缩以作战利品者. ②〔俚〕精神病医生. ~ **smut** 黑穗病. **~spring** 水的源头;根源. **~-stand** 三角顶,三角倒立(杂技). ~ **start** (赛跑起跑时的)让步,抢先. **~stall** 马笼头. **~stock** 车头箱,车床头. **~stone** ①墓石. ②【建】墙基石. **~stream** (大河的)源流. **~strong** *a.* 倔强的,任性的,刚愎的. ~ **teacher**〔美俚〕公立中、小学校长. ~ **tone** 头腔音〔由头腔发出的共鸣音〕. ~ **voice**【音】头声. **~waiter** *n.* 侍者领班. **~wall**【建】山墙. **~waters**〔*pl.*〕河源,水源. **~way** ①前进;进展. ②【海】航行速度;【矿】进展. ③【建】净空,净空高度〔由地面至拱顶等的空间〕;【交】(同一路线同一方向上两车之间的)时间间隔. **~wind** 逆风,顶头风. **~word** ①章节前的标题;词目. ②【语法】复合词的主要部分. **~work** ①脑力工作;思维. ②【建】(拱心石上作成动物头等的)拱顶装饰. ③(足球的)头球技术. ~ **worker** 脑力劳动者.

head·ed [ˈhedid] *a.* ①有头的;有标题的;(植物等)结成头的. ~ *bolt* 有头螺栓. ~ *paragraph* 加有标题的段落. ②〔常用来组成复合词〕有…头的. *a cool-~ businessman* 头脑冷静的实业家. *a round-~ screw* 圆头螺丝.

head·er [ˈhedə] *n.* ①制造钉头[工具头]的人[机械]. ②〔口〕刽子手,断头机;割穗机. ③【机】通水管,通汽管,集管;(锅炉的)联管箱. ④【建】露头砖,露头石;半端梁搁栅. ⑤〔口〕头朝下一跳[跌落]. ⑥(足球的)头顶球. *take a ~ off a ladder* 从梯子上倒栽下来.

head·ing [ˈhediŋ] *n.* ①标题,题名;题词,信纸上端所印文字. ②斩首;(鱼)去头;(植物的)打尖,摘心. ③【建】露头. ④【矿】平巷,横坑道. ⑤【海、空】(罗盘上指示的)航向;方向;磁向. ⑥(足球的)用头顶球. ⑦〔*pl.*〕【矿】精矿,选矿所得重质部分. ⑧【植】抽穗. ~ **stage** (植物的)抽穗(期).

head·less [ˈhedlis] *a.* ①无头的;割去头的. ②无人领导的. ③无头脑的,愚笨的.

head·line [ˈhedlain] *n.* ①(报刊新闻等的)大字标题;(书籍的)页头标题. ②〔*pl.*〕新闻广播摘要. *banner ~s* 通栏大字标题. ***go into ~s*** 被报纸用大字标题登出. ***hit [made] the ~s in the press*** 成为报纸的头条新闻. — *vt.* ①加标题于. ②大肆宣传. ③演出中担任(要角). **-r** *n.* ①(报馆的)标题编辑. ②(戏单中用大字写出其姓名的)红角,明星. ③名人;要事,要闻.

heads·man [ˈhedzmən] *n.* ①刽子手. ②捕鲸船指挥. ③【英矿】运煤工.

head·y [ˈhedi] *a.* ①顽固的,任性的;猛烈的. ②轻率的,鲁莽的. ③(酒等)易使人醉的;易使人兴奋的. ④〔口〕头脑清楚的. **-i·ly** *ad.* **-i·ness** *n.*

heal [hiːl] *vt.* ①医治,治愈(病伤等);使恢复健康. ②使恢复;使和解. *Time ~s most troubles.* 时间会消除烦恼. *~ the war wounds* 医治战争创伤. — *vi.* (病)痊愈,恢复健康. ***~ up [over]***(伤口)愈合. **~-all** 万灵药,百宝丹. **-able** *a.*可治愈的. **-er** *n.* ①治疗的人(尤指试图通过祈祷或信仰治病的人). ②治疗物(*Time is a great ~er.*〔谚〕时间是治愈感情创伤的良药).

heal·ing [ˈhiːliŋ] *a.* ①痊愈中的,恢复健康的. ②医治用的. *a ~ ointment* 药膏. *the ~ art* 医术. — *n.* 治疗(法). **-ly** *ad.*

health [helθ] *n.* ①健康;健康状态;卫生. ②昌盛,兴旺;生命力. ③(祝健康的)干杯. *H- is better than wealth.* = *Good ~ is above wealth.*〔谚〕健康胜于财富. *Here is to your ~!* = *To your ~!* (敬酒时用语)祝您健康! *public ~* 公共卫生. *public ~ work* 保健工作. *a ~ centre [station]* 保健站. *~ certificate* 健康证明书. *the board of ~* 卫生局[科]. ***broken in ~*** 体弱多病. ***drink (to) sb.'s ~ = drink a ~ to sb.*** 举杯祝某人健康. ***in a delicate state of ~***〔婉〕有喜,有孕. ***in (good) ~*** 健康. ***in poor ~*** 不健康. ***inquire after sb.'s ~*** 问安,问候. ***not ... for one's ~*** 为了物质利益;另有目的 (*He is not here for his ~.* 他到这里来另有目的). ***out of ~*** =in poor ~. ***propose the ~ of sb.*** 提议为某人的健康干杯. ***recover [resume] one's ~*** 恢复健康. ~ **food** 营养食品,滋补品. **~-giving** *a.* 增进健康的. **~-guard**〔英〕检疫官. ~ **physicist** 辐射防护物理学家. ~ **physics** 有害辐射防护学,辐射防护物理学. ~ **resort** 休养地. ~ **salts**【医】轻泻剂. ~ **service** 公共医疗事业. ~ **spa** 减肥中心. ~ **visitor** 巡回医务人员.

health·ful [ˈhelθful] *a.* ①保健的,有益于健康的. ②健康的,健全的. **-ly** *ad.* **-ness** *n.*

health·y [ˈhelθi] *a.* ①健康的,健壮的;有益于健康的. ②健全的,卫生的. ③大量的;旺盛的. *a ~ appearance [colour]* 健康的脸色. *~ reading for the young people* 有益青年的读物. **-i·ly** *ad.* **-i·ness** *n.*

Hea·ly [ˈhiːli] *n.* 希利〔姓氏〕.

heap [hiːp] *n.* ①(一)堆,堆积. ②〔口〕许多,大量. ③〔美俚〕(破旧)汽车;炼焦堆. *go to ~s of places* 到各处. ***a ~ of = ~s of*** 许多的,大量的. ***a ~ of time*** 多时. ***be knocked [struck] all of a ~***〔口〕一下子被吓倒;慌作一团. ***fall all of a ~*** 咕咚地倒下. ***~s of time*** 充裕的时间. ***~s of times*** 多次,屡次. ***in a ~ = in ~s*** 成山,成堆,累累. ***top [bottom] of the ~***〔口〕获胜者[失败者]. — *vt.* ①把…堆成一堆,堆积,堆起 (*up; together*);积累. ②大量地给,滥给;拚命添加. ③装满,灌满. *a ~ed spoonful* 满满一调羹. *~ insults on sb.* 对某人百般侮辱. *~ praise upon* 大肆宣扬[颂扬].

~ *titles and honours on a conqueror* 对征服者滥给头衔和勋章. **-ing** *a.* 成堆的.

heaps [hiːps] *ad.* 〔口〕非常,极其. *feel ~ better* 感觉好多了.

hear [hiə] ***(heard*** **[həːd]*)*** *vt.* ①听,听见,听取. ②得知,闻知,听说. ③注意听,倾听;听(课、歌剧等). ④【法】审问;听(证人)陈述. ⑤允许;服从,照准. *I heard a loud noise.* 我听见一声巨响. *I heard that he was ill.* 我听说他有病. *He was heard to groan [groaning].* 人家听见他在呻吟. *They are heard to have come over.* 听说他们已经来了. ~ *and examine the reports (of)* 听取和审查(…的)报告. ~ *a case* 审理案件. ~ *a boy's lesson* 检查孩子的功课. — *vi.* ①听,听见,听说. ②得知 *(of, about)*. ③〔美〕承认. *So I ~.* 听说就是这样. *You will ~ of [about] this.* 等着瞧吧!〔意指这件事还不算完〕. ***H- and tremble!*** 好好听着,好好记住! ***~ from*** 得到…的消息,得到…的信 (*I ~ from her now and then.* 我常常收到她的信). ***H-! H-!*** 听哪,听哪!说得好!〔表示赞成,常用作反语〕. ***~ of*** 听到…的事,听到…的话. ***~ (more) of*** 关于…的事还未结束. ***~ say [tell] (of)*** 听人讲起 (*Have you ever heard tell this matter?* 你听人说起过这件事吗?). ***~ sb. out*** 听某人把话讲完. ***make oneself heard*** 把意见等说给人听. ***never [not] ~ of [to]*** (通常与 will 或 would 同用)不听从,不愿考虑. **-able** *a.* 听得见的,中听的.

heard [həːd] hear 的过去式及过去分词.

hear·er [ˈhiərə] *n.* 听的人;旁听者.

hear·ing [ˈhiəriŋ] *n.* ①听(动作或过程). ②听力,听觉. ③发言机会. ④审问. ⑤听得见的范围. ⑥〔美〕意见听取会. *Her ~ is not very well.* 她耳朵不好. *at the ~ of the news.* 听到消息以后. ***gain [get] a ~*** 获得发言〔申诉〕机会. ***give sb. a (fair) ~*** 让某人申诉. ***hard of ~*** 耳朵不灵. ***in sb.'s ~*** 在某人听得见的地方. ***out of [beyond] ~*** 在听不见的地方. ***within ~*** 在听得见的地方. ~ **aid** 助听器. ~ **examiner,** ~ **officer** 〔美〕(组织意见听取会的)政府特派调查员.

heark·en [ˈhɑːkən] *vi.* = harken.

Hearn [həːn], **Lafcadio** 赫恩〔1850—1904, 加入爱尔兰籍的日本作家,即小泉八云 (Koizumi Yakumo)〕.

hear·say [ˈhiəsei] *n., a.* 风闻(的),传闻(的),道听途说(的). *I speak not from ~.* 我可不是根据传闻这样讲的. ~ **evidence** 【法】传闻证据〔指证人根据传说提供的证据〕. ~ **rule** 【法】传闻证据否定法.

hearse [həːs] *n.* ①灵车. ②〔古〕棺架,棺台. ③【天主】条案形蜡烛排架. — *vt.* 用灵车装运;埋葬.

Hearst [həːst] *n.* 赫斯特〔姓氏〕. ~ **Newspaper Group** (美国)赫斯特报系.

hearst·ling [ˈhəːstliŋ] *n.* 〔美口〕赫斯特报系的人.

heart [hɑːt] *n.* ①心脏,心. ②胸,胸部;心胸,心地,心肠,胸怀. ③感情,热情,爱情;灵魂;良心. ④勇气,胆力;勇士. ⑤精神,气质;心境,心情. ⑥中心,核心;精华,要点,本质. ⑦意中人,情人;心爱的人,宝贝儿. ⑧〔主英〕(土地的)肥沃程度. ⑨心脏形的东西. ⑩【牌】红桃,红心;〔*pl.*〕一组红桃花样的纸牌;一种设法不拿到红桃的纸牌游戏. *a broken ~* 心碎,绝望. *abundance of the ~* 感情充沛. *athletic [athlete's] ~* 因运动过度所致的心脏肥大. *a big ~* 胸襟宽广,心胸开阔. *a false ~* 居心险诈,虚伪. *a free ~* 胸怀坦白,无忧无虑. *a hard ~* 冷酷,残忍. *a kind [soft, sympathetic, warm] ~* 好心肠,善良的心. *a light ~* 无忧无虑,快乐. *a single ~* 单纯质朴,一心一意. *a stout ~* 勇敢,果敢. *a ~ of flint [stone]* 铁石心肠. *a ~ of gold = a tender ~* 温柔的心肠,好心肠. *The girl is all ~.* 那姑娘很温柔. *a man of ~* 有情感的人. *one's dear [sweet] ~* 情人. *a true ~* 真正的勇士. *an affair of the ~* 恋爱. *Every ~ knows its own bitterness.* 〔谚〕各人苦恼自己知. *Faint ~ never won fair lady.* 〔谚〕胆怯者赢不到美人. *Nothing is impossible to a willing ~.* 〔谚〕有志者事竟成. *The ~ that once truly loves never forgets.* 〔谚〕真正的爱情,永远不变心. *What the ~ thinks the tongue speaks.* 〔谚〕言为心声. *When the ~ is afire, some sparks will fly out at the mouth.* 〔谚〕心里有什么,嘴上藏不住;心直口快. ***a change of ~*** ①改变主意. ②变心,变节. ③改邪归正;【宗】改宗,皈依. ***a ~ of oak*** 刚强的人,果断的人. ***after one's (own) ~*** 符合自己的心意,正中下怀. ***at ~*** 在感情深处,内心里. ***at the bottom of one's ~*** 内心上. ***be enthroned in the ~s*** 念念不忘. ***be of good ~*** 心情舒畅. ***be sick at ~*** ①苦闷,愁苦,悲观. ②〔婉〕厌恶,恶心. ***bless my [your] ~!*** 我的天哪!好家伙! ***break sb.'s ~*** 使某人很伤心,使某人悲痛欲绝. ***break the ~ of sth.*** 度过最困难的时刻. ***bring sth. home to sb.'s ~*** 〔多用被动结构 be brought 或用 come, go 等〕使某事为某人深知,使某事为某人深受感动. ***cross one's ~*** 在胸口画十字(表示说的是真话). ***cry [weep] one's ~ out*** 痛哭,哭得死去活来. ***cut [touch] sb. to the ~*** 触及某人痛处. ***do sb.'s ~ good*** 使某人高兴. ***devour one's ~ = eat one's ~ out*** 因伤心而消瘦,忧伤过度. ***find it in one's ~ to (do)*** 〔常用于否定句中〕意欲(做…),忍心(做…) (*She could not find it in her ~ to leave him.* 她不忍心离开他). ***follow the dictates of one's ~*** 按照自己的爱好. ***from one's ~ = from the bottom of one's [the] ~*** 自心底,衷心. ***gain [have] sb.'s ~*** 取得某人的欢心,获得某人宠爱. ***gather ~*** 鼓起勇气,打起精神. ***give ~ to sb.*** 鼓励某人. ***give one's ~ to sb.*** 爱上某人. ***go to sb.'s ~ [the ~]*** 使某人伤心;说中心病. ***go to [get to] the ~ of matter*** 抓住要点. ***harden sb.'s ~*** 使某人心肠变硬. ***have a ~*** 〔口〕发发慈悲,做做好事. ***have a soft [warm] spot in one's ~ for sb.*** 爱上某人. ***have sth. at ~*** 把某事放在心上,对某事深切关心. ***have no ~*** *(to do sth.)* 不想,无意于. ***have one's ~ in*** 专心一意. ***have [bring] one's ~ in one's mouth = One's ~ leaps into one's mouth [throat]*** 吓一大跳. ***have one's ~ in one's work*** 专心工作. ***have the [one's] ~ in the right place*** 真心实意,好心好意. ***have the ~ to do [say]*** 〔常用于否定句中〕有勇气做〔说〕;忍心做〔说〕. ***~ and soul [hand]*** 全心全意地,热心地. ***imprint on sb.'s ~*** 铭刻某人心中. ***in (good) ~*** ①精神抖擞的,情绪高昂的. ②(土地)肥沃的. ***in one's ~ (of ~s)*** 在内心深处;秘密地. ***in the fullness of one's ~*** 满腔热情地. ***in the inmost [secret] recesses of the ~*** 在心坎里. ***in the ~ of*** 在…中心. ***in the pride of one's ~*** 自豪,得意. ***keep a good ~*** 不丧失勇气. ***lay one's ~ bare*** 倾吐衷情. ***lay sth. to ~*** 把(忠告、责备等)记在心里;认真考虑. ***learn [get, have] sth. by ~*** 熟记. ***lie [lie heavy] at sb.'s ~ = weigh upon sb.'s ~.*** ***lie near sb.'s ~*** 受到某人的深切关怀. ***lose ~*** 沮丧,扫兴. ***lose one's ~ to*** 爱上. ***make sb.'s ~ bleed*** 使某人非常痛心. ***make sb.'s ~ leap*** 使某人大吃一惊. ***move [stir, touch] sb.'s ~*** 打动某人的心. ***My ~s!*** 【海】勇敢的伙伴们! ***near [nearest] (to) one's ~*** 非常关怀的;重大的,贵重的. ***not to have the ~ to do [say] sth.*** 没有勇气做〔说〕;不忍心做〔说〕. ***one's ~ gives a leap*** 吓一跳. ***one's ~ is broken*** 心碎,非常伤心. ***one's ~ sinks (low within one) =*** 〔口〕***one's ~ sinks in (to) one's boots [heels]*** 心灰意懒,消沉;惊恐不安. ***one's ~ stands still*** (因惊吓)愣住. ***one's ~ warms towards sb.*** 一直想念某人,喜欢某人. ***open [pour out, uncover] one's ~ to sb.*** 向某人倾吐衷情. ***out of ~*** ①没精神,没精打采. ②(土地)贫瘠的. ***pluck up one's ~*** 鼓起勇气,打起精神. ***put one's ~ into sth.*** 热心…,一心一意去…. ***put sb. out of ~*** 使某人失去勇气〔心灰意懒〕. ***read sb.'s ~*** 看出某人心意. ***reverberate [ring]***

in one's* ~** 言犹在耳. ***search one's [the]* ~** 反省. ***set one's* ~ *at rest [ease] 安心,放心. ***set one's [sb.'s]* ~ *on (doing) sth.*** 使自己[某人]下决心做某事. ***set one's [the]* ~ *on [upon] sth.*** 全神贯注做某事. ***speak to the* ~** 说动人心. ***shut one's* ~ *to fear* = *steal one's* ~ *against fear*** 一点不怕;横下心来. ***steal sb.'s* ~** 赢得某人欢心. ***take* ~ = *pluck up one's heart. take* ~ *of grace*** 鼓起勇气. ***take sth. to* ~** 对某事痛心,对某事介意. ***take sth. [sb.] to one's* ~** 〔口〕对某事[某人]表示喜爱,喜欢某事[某人]. ***take the* ~ *out of sb.* = *tire sb.'s* ~ *out*** = put sb. out of ~. ***wear [carry] one's* ~ *on [upon] one's sleeve*** 心直口快,过于直率. ***wear sb. [sth.] in one's* ~** 忠于某人[某事]. ***weigh upon sb.'s* ~** 压在某人心上. ***win sb.'s* ~** = gain sb.'s ~. ***with a* ~ *and a half*** 高兴(做). ***with a heavy* ~** 心情沉重,闷闷不乐. ***with a light* ~** 高高兴兴,轻松愉快. ***with all one's* ~ = *with one's whole* ~** 诚心诚意,真心地. ***with half a* ~** 勉勉强强地,半心半意地. — *vt.* 将…记在心中. ~ *a warning* 记住警告. **~ache** 心痛;伤心. **~ attack** 心力衰竭,心脏病发作. **~beat** ①心跳,心搏. ②感情. ③〔喻〕中心,动力. **~ block**【医】心传导阻滞. **~('s)-blood** 生命必需的血液;生命. **~break** ①*n.* 悲伤,悲痛. ②*vt.* 使心碎. **~breaking** 令人悲痛的,使人心碎的. **~broken** 悲伤绝望的. **~burn** ①【医】胃灼热,心口灼热. ② = ~burning. **~burning** 不平,不满;妒忌. **~ cherry** 心形樱桃〔甜樱桃的一个变种〕. **~ disease** 心脏病. **~ failure** 心力衰竭;心脏停跳. **~felt** *a.* 深深感觉到的,衷心的. **~-free** *a.* 无拘无束的;无所依恋的. **~land** 心脏地带,中心地带. **~-lung machine** (用于心脏手术的)人工心肺机. **~man** 接受心脏移植手术者. **~-rending** *a.* 令人悲痛的,令人伤心的. **~-searching** *n.* 内心的反省,对自己感情的检查. **~-sease, ~'s-ease** *n.* ①内心平静. ②【植】三色堇. **~sick** *a.* 愁眉苦脸的,闷闷不乐的. **~some** *a.* ①精神振作的;令人振奋的. ②欢乐的,愉快的,活泼的. **~sore** ①*n.* 悲伤,痛心. ②*a.* 悲伤的,痛心的. **~stirring** *a.* 振奋人心的. **~-stricken, ~struck** *a.* 痛心的. **~string** *n.* 〔常 *pl.*〕深情,心弦(*break one's ~-strings* 使伤心. *pull at [touch] one's ~-strings* 打动心弦). **~throb** ①心跳,心悸. ②〔俚〕〔常 *pl.*〕柔情;感伤;爱人,情人. **~-to-~** 坦白的,开诚布公的;亲切的. **~ urchin**【动】猬团目(*spatangoida*)动物. **~warming** *a.* 暖人心房的,鼓舞人心的. **~-whole** *a.* ①专心一意的;真诚的. ②勇敢的,不沮丧的. ③情窦未开的;无所眷恋的. **~-wood**【植】心材. **~worm**【动】犬恶丝虫(*Dirofilaria imsictis*)〔为蚊子所传布,寄生于血液中,尤其在狗、猫等的心脏中〕.

heart·ed [ˈhɑːtid] *a.* 〔常用来构成复合词〕有…心的,心…的. *faint-~* 心软的. *kind-~* 仁慈的. *stone-~* 铁石心肠的.

heart·en [ˈhɑːtn] *vt.* 振作(精神),鼓励,激励(*up; on*). *~ing news* 令人振奋的消息. — *vi.* 振作起来(*up*).

hearth [hɑːθ] *n.* ①壁炉地面. ②炉边;〔喻〕家庭. ③【冶】(平炉的)炉床;(高炉的)炉膛,炉缸. ***~ and home*** 家园. **~rug** 炉边地毯. **~stone** ①炉石;磨石. ②炉边;家庭.

heart·i·ly [ˈhɑːtili] *ad.* ①诚恳地,亲切地. ②热情地,劲头十足地. ③胃口很好地;(吃、喝)痛快地. ④完全,非常. *be ~ glad* 十分高兴. *eat ~* 饱餐一顿,吃得津津有味. *set to work ~* 积极开始工作. *thank sb. ~* 衷心感谢某人.

heart·i·ness [ˈhɑːtinis] *n.* 诚恳,热心.

heart·less [ˈhɑːtlis] *a.* ①无情的,残酷的. ②无精打采的. **-ly** *ad.* **-ness** *n.*

heart·y [ˈhɑːti] *a.* ①衷心的,诚恳的;恳切的;热诚的. ②精神饱满的,强健的. ③营养丰富的;丰盛的;丰饶的. ④强烈的,猛烈的. ⑤胃口好的. *a ~ appetite* 好胃口. *a ~ welcome* 热情欢迎. ***hale and* ~** (年老而)精神矍烁的. — *n.* ①(英国大学的)运动员. ②〔古〕朋友,伙伴(尤指水手). *My hearties!*【海】伙伴们! 弟兄们!

heat [hiːt] *n.* ①热;热力;热度;热量. ②体温;发烧. ③(气候的)高温,暑气. ④【冶】熔炼的炉次;装炉量;一炉(钢、铁等). ⑤(赛跑等的)一场[盘、轮];预赛,竞赛;一次努力. ⑥(战斗、争论、讲演等)最激烈的阶段;强烈的感情;愤怒. ⑦(辣椒等的)辣味. ⑧(母兽交尾期的)发情. ⑨〔美俚〕威逼,压力;警察;(警察对罪犯的)侦察,逼供,穷追. ⑩〔美俚〕手枪;炮火,枪弹射击. ⑪〔美俚〕喝醉. ⑫激情. ⑬浓香. *an intense ~* 酷热. *black ~* 暗热〔未发光时的热〕. *latent ~* 潜热. *radiant ~* 辐射热. *red ~* 赤热. *sensible ~*【物】显热. *specific ~*【物】比热. *white ~* 白热〔发光时的热〕;激情. *a ~ of steel* 一炉钢. *a dead ~* 不分胜负的赛跑. *the final ~* 决赛. *preliminary ~s* = trial ~s 预赛. *prickly ~* 痱子,汗疹. ***a dead* ~** (竞赛中)并列名次. ***at a* ~** 一口气地,一气呵成. ***at* ~** (母兽等)在交尾期. ***at a white* ~** 白热地,极端激动地. ***give sb. the* ~** 〔美俚〕开枪击毙某人. ***have a* ~ *on*** 〔美俚〕喝醉酒. ***in [on]* ~** = at ~. ***in the* ~ *of*** 在(辩论等)最激烈的时候. ***put the* ~ *on sb.*** 逼某人干活[付款];使某人为难. ***The ~'s on.*** 〔美俚〕警察正在穷追罪犯. ***turn on the* ~** 〔美俚〕①出死劲干,拚命工作. ②责备,谴责. ③激起热情. ④开枪射击. ⑤穷追罪犯. — *vt.* ①给…加热;使…温暖. ②使激动,刺激. *a room ~ed by stove* 用火炉取暖的房间. — *vi.* ①变热;变暖. ②(食物等)发热变质. ③激动,发怒. *Water ~s slowly.* 水是慢慢变热的. **~ barrier** 热障(= thermal barrier). **~ bump** 热疖子. **~ capacity**【物】热容量. **~ engine** 热力机(*a ~ engine plant* 火电厂). **~ exchanger** 热交换器. **~ exhaustion** 中暑. **~ flash**(原子爆炸等所产生的)强热. **~ island** 热岛〔城市中由于街道和建筑物密集而特别炎热的区域〕. **~lightning** 闪电(尤指夏夜无雷声的热闪). **~proof** *a.* 耐热的(= ~resistant). **~ prostration** = ~ exhaustion. **~ pump** 热泵. **~ rash** 栗粒疹,痱子,汗疹(=miliria). **~ resisting alloy** 耐热合金. **~-set** *vt.* 对(塑料、织物上的(皱褶等)进行热定形. **~ sink** 吸热设备,冷源;散热片. **~spot** ①雀斑,酒刺. ②热觉点. **~-stroke** 中暑. **~-treat** *vt.*【冶】对…作热处理. **~ treatment** 热处理. **~ unit** 热(量)单位. **~ value** 发热值. **~ wave** ①热浪,热波. ②热浪期.

heat·ed [ˈhiːtid] *a.* ①热的;加热的. ②激昂的,兴奋的. *a ~ argument* 激烈的争论. *the ~ term* 〔美〕夏季. **-ly** *ad.* **-ness** *n.*

heat·er [ˈhiːtə] *n.* ①加热的人;加热器,散热器;暖房装置. ②〔美俚〕手枪. ③〔美俚〕雪茄烟. *gas ~* 煤气炉. **~ tube** 旁热式电子管.

heath [hiːθ] *n.* ①【植】欧石南属常青灌木;石南. ②石南丛生的荒野,荒地. *one's native ~* 出生地,幼年生长的地方. **~ aster**【植】菊科植物〔俗名石楠菊,产于北美〕. **~ bell** 欧石南属的花;钓钟柳. **~berry** 岩高兰之类. **~bird**【动】黑松鸡,黑山鸡;(尤指)黑琴鸡. **~cock** 雄松鸡. **~ family** 杜鹃花科. **~ fowl** = ~-bird. **~ hen** ①黑琴鸡(= gray hen). ②【动】草原鸡(*Tympanuchus cupido cupido*)〔产于美国新英格兰,已绝种〕.

hea·then [ˈhiːðən] *n.* (*pl.* **~s,** 〔集合词〕 ***the* ~**) ①(不信基督教、伊斯兰教、犹太教等的)异教徒;多神教信仰者. ②不信教的人;未开化的人,野蛮人. — *a.* ①信异教的. ②不信教的;野蛮的. **-dom** 异教国;〔集合词〕异教徒;异教的风俗信仰;〔古〕异教. **-ism** *n.* 异教;异教教义,偶像崇拜;野蛮. **-ise, -ize** *vt., vi.* (使)信奉异教. **-ry** *n.* ① = ~ism. ②异教徒;异教民.

hea·then·ish [ˈhiːðəniʃ] *a.* ①异教的,异教徒的. ②野蛮的,未开化的. **-ly** *ad.* **-ness** *n.*

heath·er [ˈheðə] *n.* ①【植】石南属植物. ②石南属植物

丛生的荒野. *set the ～ on fire* 煽起骚动. *take to the ～* 〔Scot.〕做土匪,落草为寇. — *a.* = heathery.

heath·er·y [ˈheðəri] *a.* ①石南的; 石南丛生的; 似石南的. ②杂色的. ～ **mixture**【纺】混色毛纱. ～ **tweed**【纺】杂色花呢. **heath·er·i·ness** *n.*

heath·y [ˈhi:θi] *a.* = heathery.

heat·ing [ˈhi:tiŋ] *a.* ①加热的; 供热的. ②刺激的. *a ～ drink* 暖身的饮料. *a ～ apparatus* 供暖装置. ～ *pipe* 暖气管. *a ～ system* 暖气系统. — *n.* ①加热;供暖;(建筑物的)暖气装置. ②白炽,灼热. ～ **pad** 电热敷垫. ～ **zone** 加热区,加热段.

heat·ron·ic [hi:ˈtrɔnik] *a.* 【物】高频(率)电介质加热的.

heaume [həum] *n.* (古代套在头盔上的)连颈重盔,大盔.

heave [hi:v] *vt.* *(～d 或 hove* [həuv]) ①举,举起. ②使鼓起,使胀起,挺起(胸部). ③(吃力地)发出(叹声、呻吟声). ④〔口〕投掷,扔. ⑤【海】(用绳)拉起;卷起;使(船)开动. ⑥【地】使平错,使隆起. ～ *a heavy box* 举起一个沉重的箱子. ～ *an anchor* 起锚. ～ *a brick* 扔砖头. ～ *a sigh* 叹息. — *vi.* ①举,升起,胀;(浪、地面)起伏. ②喘息;呕吐. ③努力,操劳. ④【海】曳,卷 *(at)*; (船)开动前进. ～ *on the rope* 拉绳子. *heaving waves* 汹涌起伏的波涛. ～ ***(ship) ahead***【海】收着曳索使(船)前进. ***H-away [ho]!*** (水手起锚时的呼叫声)用力拉呀!加劲卷呀! ～ ***down*** (使)船倾倒一边以进行清理,维修等. ～ ***in sight*** (船)进入视野. ～ ***out*** ①将船的龙骨露出水面进行维修. ②扯起(风帆、旗子等). ～ ***the lead***【海】投水砣测水的深度. ～ ***the sphere***〔美棒球〕投球. ～ ***to*** 顶风停船. ～ ***up*** ①起锚. ②呕吐. — *n.* ①举起,扛起. ②胀起,隆起;波动,起伏. ③呕吐. ④【摔交】右手勒住对方右肩的摔法. ⑤【地】平错. ⑥〔the ～s〕(马的)喘病. ～ *of the sea* 海波.

heave-ho [ˈhi:vˈhəu] *n.* 〔口〕免职,开除. ***get the (old) ～*** 被免职,被开除. ***give sb. the (old) ～*** 免某人的职,开除某人. — *vi., vt.* 〔美俚〕用力提起(物品).

heav·en [ˈhevən] *n.* ①天,天空 (*opp.* earth)〔散文通常用 *pl.*〕. ②天堂,天国,极乐世界,乐园;极快乐的事. ③〔H-〕上帝,神;〔*pl.*〕诸神. *the starry ～s* 星空. *the eye of ～* 太阳. *It's ～ to go angling.* 钓鱼是一大乐事. ***By H-!*** 老天在上! ***go to ～*** 升天,死. *H- be praised!* = *Thank H-!* 谢天谢地! ***Good [Gracious, Great] ～s!*** 天哪! 嗳呀!〔表示惊愕,谴责,非难〕. ～ ***and earth*** 宇宙,万物;天哪〔惊叫声〕. ***H- forbid [forfend]!*** 上天不容,决无此事. ***H- (only) knows*** 只有天晓得! 千真万确,向天发誓. ～ ***of ～s*** = the seventh ～. ～ ***on earth*** 人间天堂. ***H-'s vengeance is slow but sure.*** 〔谚〕天网恢恢,疏而不漏. ***in ～*** ①在天上的;已死的. ②〔用以加强语气〕究竟,到底 (*Where in ～ were you?* 你当时究竟在哪里?) ***move ～ and earth*** 竭尽全力*(to do)*. ***nigger ～*** 〔美俚〕(戏院等)楼座最高部分. ***the seventh ～***【宗】七重天,极乐世界. ***The ～ opens.*** 下起倾盆大雨. ***to ～(s)*** 极度地. ***under ～***〔用以加强语气〕究竟,到底. ～**-born** *a.* 天生的;天赋的. ～**-dust**〔美俚〕可卡因,古柯鹹. ～**-kissing** *a.* 摩天的,高耸云霄的. ～**-reacher** 牧师〔尤指讲道时常常作望天姿势的〕. ～**-sent** *a.* 天赐的,极巧的. ～**ward** *a., ad.* 向天上的[地];向天空的[地]. ～**wards** *ad.* 向天上,向天空.

heav·en·li·ness [ˈhevənlinis] *n.* 神圣,尊严;秀美;十全.

heav·en·ly [ˈhevənli] *a.* ①天的,天空的. ②神圣的;至上的;天国的. ③超凡的;超绝的;〔口〕漂亮的;可爱的. *the ～ bodies* 天体. ～ *beings [angels]* 天使. *a ～ mind* 虔诚的心. *H- Twins*【天】双子星座. *What ～ peaches!* 多可爱的美人! — *ad.* ①极,无比的. ②借天神之力. ***The ～ City*** ①乐土,天堂. ②新耶路撒冷. ～**-minded** *a.* 虔诚的,圣洁的.

heav·er [ˈhi:və] *n.* ①举起[移动]重物的人[工具];举起物. ②【海】(卷起船缆的)杠杆. ③重量. ④〔美俚〕(棒球的)投手. ⑤叉簧;钩键;小铁梃.

heav·i·ly [ˈhevili] *ad.* ①重重地,沉重地. ②缓慢地;迟钝地. ③猛烈地,厉害地. ④沮丧地,灰溜溜地. ⑤沉闷地;〔古〕悲伤地. ⑥暴虐地. *a ～ wooded area* 树木浓密的地区. *a ～ guarded fortress* 戒备森严的堡垒. *a ～ loaded truck* 重载的卡车. *suffer ～* 受到沉重打击.

heav·i·ness [ˈhevinis] *n.* ①重,沉重. ②悲哀,抑郁,痛苦. ③迟钝,不活泼;疲倦. ～ *of movement* 动作的笨拙.

heav·ing [ˈhi:viŋ] *n.* 举起,拿起,扔去. ～ **line**【海】扔到岸上以便将轮船系住的大铁索. ～**-line bend**【海】丁香结,酒瓶结.

Heav·i·side [ˈhevisaid] *n.* ①海维赛德〔姓氏〕. ② **Oliver ～** 奥列弗·赫维赛〔1850—1925, 英国物理学家〕.

Heav·i·side layer [ˈhevisaid ˈleiə]【无】海维赛德层,海氏层,E电离层〔高出地面100公里反射电波的大气层,亦作 Kennelly-～ layer〕.

heav·y¹ [ˈhi:vi] *a.* (马)患哮喘病的.

heav·y² [ˈhevi] *a.* ①重的 *(opp.* light*)* 有重量的;重型的;装备重型武器的. ②大的;大量的,多的;(交通等)拥挤的,稠密的. ③有力的,沉重的;猛烈的,狂暴的;厉害的,严重的. ④困难的,繁重的,不易对付的. ⑤沉闷的,难忍耐的;悲惨的,忧郁的. ⑥迟钝的,笨重的;单调的,乏味的,(文章等)冗长的;(声音等)深沉的. ⑦(天气)阴沉的;多云的;低压的. ⑧(食物等)难消化的;(面包等)没发酵好的;(酒等)烈性的. ⑨粗的;粗糙的;粗壮的. ⑩(道路等)难行走的;(土地)难耕作的. ⑪(眼皮)重垂的;欲睡的,困倦的. ⑫(剧中角色)庄重的,严肃的;悲剧的. ⑬(妇女)怀孕的. ⑭(思想等)深邃的. ⑮〔美俚〕极好的. ⑯〔美俚〕老于世故的. *a ～ blow* 沉重的打击. *a ～ bomber* 重型轰炸机. *a ～ brigade* 装备重武器的旅. ～ *artillery* 重炮(兵). ～ *industry* 重工业. *a ～ crop* 大丰收. *a ～ drinker* 酒喝得多的人. *a ～ eater* 大肚汉,食量大的人. *a ～ fate* 悲惨的命运. *a ～ fire* 猛烈的炮火. ～ *food* 难消化的食物. *a ～ heart* 沉重的心情. ～ *money [sugar]* 大笔钱. *a ～ sea* 波涛汹涌的海面. ～ *news [tidings]* 噩耗,坏消息. *a ～ road* 泥泞的道路. *a ～ sky* 阴沉的天气. *a ～ sleep* 酣睡. *a ～ smoker* 烟抽得多的人. *a ～ snowfall* 大雪. ～ *soil* 难耕的土地. *a ～ style* 枯躁冗长的文体. *a ～ task [work]* 繁重的工作. *a ～ wine* 烈酒. ***have a ～ hand*** 笨手笨脚. ～ ***with child*** 怀孕,大肚子. ～ ***with fruit*** 果实累累. ～ ***with sleep*** 睡意正浓. — *ad.* = heavily. ★现在多用于复合词或成语. *Time hangs ～ on one's hands.* 时间过得又慢又无聊,度日如年. ***lie [sit, weigh] ～ at [on, upon]*** (工作、肠胃等)负担过重. ***lie [sit] ～ on one's [the] stomach*** (食物)滞积胃中,不消化. — *n.* ①〔*pl.*〕重物(尤指重型车辆、重轰炸机、重炮). ②【剧】庄重角色,演庄重角色的演员. ③严肃的报纸. ④〔*pl.*〕重工业. ⑤〔*pl.*〕重骑兵队. ⑥〔美俚〕(影、剧中的)强盗,恶棍. ⑦〔美俚〕重量级拳击选手. ***come the ～ over sb.*** 对某人摆架子. ***do the ～*** 〔俚〕自高自大,摆架子. ***the Heavies*** 〔英〕龙骑兵团. ～**-armed** *a.* 装备重武器的,重装甲的. ～**-bedded**【地】厚层的. ～**-browed** *a.* 眉头紧蹙的. ～**-buying** *a.* 大量购入的. ～**cake** 〔美俚〕一心寻找女生做朋友的男大学生. ～ **casting** 大型铸件. ～ **click** 〔美俚〕(票房收入的)爆满. ～ **current** 强电流,大电流. ～**-duty** ①重载的,重型的;耐用的. ②关税重的. ～**-footed** *a.* 脚步沉重的,笨手笨脚的. ～ **fuel** 柴油,重燃(料)油. ～**-handed** *a.* ①拙劣的. ②高压的,暴虐的. ～**-headed** *a.* 头部大而沉重的;迟钝的. ～**-hearted** *a.* 抑郁的;悲伤的. ～ **hour** 忙时. ～ **hydrogen**【化】重氢,氘(=deuterium). ～**-laden** *a.* 负重载的;心情沉重的. ～ **metal** ①重金属. ②〔俚〕巨炮(弹). ③〔俚〕劲敌. ④〔俚〕伟人. ～ **(merchant) mill** 大型轧钢厂. ～ **oxygen**【化】重氧. ～ **repair** 大修. ～ **ring**【机】承力环. ～**set** *a.* 身体强壮的;身材矮胖的. ～**-spar**

【化】重晶石. ～ **water**【化】重水. ～**weight** ①身体特重的人. ②【体】重量级拳击[摔交]运动员[体重 175 磅以上]. ③[美口]有影响的人,要人. ～ **wet** [英俚]麦芽酒.

Heb. = Hebrew; Hebrews.

heb·do·mad [ˈhebdəmæd] *n.* 七天,【圣】一周; 成七的一组.

heb·dom·a·dal [hebˈdɔmədl] *a.* 一周的; 每星期的.

heb·dom·a·dar·y [hebˈdɔmədəri] *a.* = hebdomadal.

He·be [ˈhiːbi] *n.* ①【希神】青春女神[在奥林匹斯山替众神斟酒的女神]. ②女侍应员,酒吧间的女招待.

he·be·phre·ni·a [ˌhiːbiˈfriːniə] *n.* 【医】青春期痴呆. **he·be·phren·ic** [-ˈfrenik] *a.*

He·ber [ˈhiːbə] *n.* 希伯[姓氏].

heb·e·tate [ˈhebiteit] *vt., vi.* (使)变迟钝. — *a.* ①愚笨的. ②【植】具钝尖头的.

he·bet·ic [hiˈbetik] *a.* 青春期的,发生于青春期的.

heb·e·tude [ˈhebiˌtjuːd] *n.* 愚钝; 感觉迟钝.

He·bra·ic [hi(ː)ˈbreiik] *a.* 希伯来人的; 希伯来语的. **-i·cal·ly** *ad.*

He·bra·ism [ˈhiːbreiizəm] *n.* ①希伯来语词[表达方式]. ②希伯来人的特点[道德, 精神, 做法等]. ③希伯来教.

He·bra·ist [ˈhiːbreiist] *n.* ①希伯来语语文学家; 精通希伯来语的人. ②希伯来教徒. ③有希伯来思想道德的人. **-is·tic** *a.*

He·bra·ize [ˈhiːbreiaiz] *vt., vi.* (使) 希伯来化; (使)成希伯来语.

He·brew [ˈhiːbruː] *n.* ①希伯来人,[美]犹太人. ②希伯来语. ③[口]难听懂的话. *modern* ～ 现在以色列通用的犹太语. *the Epistle to the ～s*【圣】《希伯来人书》. *It's ～ to me.* 那我一点也不懂. — *a.* ①希伯来人的. ②希伯来语的. ～**wise** *ad.* 照希伯来文写法自右至左.

Heb·ri·des [ˈhebridiːz] *n. pl.* [the ～] 赫布里底群岛[英国].

Hec·a·te [ˈhekəti] *n.*【希神】海克提[司天地及冥界的女神,后世认为系巫术、魔法女神].

hec·a·tomb [ˈhekətəum, -tuːm] *n.* ①(古希腊的)大祭(尤指一次宰一百头牛的大祭). ②大牺牲,大屠杀.

heck[1] [hek] *n.* [英口] = hell [用以加强语气或咒骂]. *a ～ of a lot of money* 好多好多钱. *What the ～?* (你讲的)什么鬼玩意?

heck[2] [hek] *n.* [英方](河里阻拦鱼游向的)鱼栏.

heck·le [ˈhekl] *vt.* ①梳理(亚麻等). ②质问(当众演说的候选人等). — *n.* 梳理 (= hackle); 【纺】针排.

heck·ler [ˈheklə] *n.* 质问者.

hec·tare [ˈhektɑː, ekˈtɑː] *n.* 公顷[=100 公亩或2.471 英亩,合 15 市亩].

hec·tic [ˈhektik] *a.* ①(因患肺病等)发烧的, 消耗热的; 有病态潮红的. ②患热病的; 患肺痨病的. ③[口]紧张的,闹哄哄的; 兴奋的,狂热的. *a ～ fever* 消耗热. ～ *spots* (肺病患者脸颊上的)潮红. *have a ～ time* 非常激动,热闹了一阵. — *n.* ①肺病热,消耗热; 肺病热患者. ②【医】潮红. **-ti·cal·ly, -ly** *ad.* **-ness** *n.*

hecto- *comb. f.* 表示"一百": *hectograph, hectometre.*

hec·to·cot·y·lus [ˌhektəˈkɔtləs] *n.* *(pl.* **-y·li** [-ai]) 【动】化茎腕,交接腕.

hec·tog = hectogram(me).

hec·to·gram(me) [ˈhektəugræm] *n.* 百克[重量单位].

hec·to·graph [ˈhektəugrɑːf] *n.* 【印】胶版誊写法. — *vt.* 用胶版誊写法印刷.

hectol. = hectolitre.

hec·to·li·ter, [Eng.] **-tre** [ˈhektəuliːtə] *n.* (容量单位)百升,公石(=1 市石).

hec·tom. = hectometre.

hec·to·me·tre, [Am.] **-ter** [ˈhektəumiːtə] *n.* (长度单位)百米.

hec·to·new·ton [ˈhektəunjuːtn] *n.* 【物】(力的单位)百牛顿.

hec·tor [ˈhektə] *n.* 威吓者, 虚张声势的人. — *vt., vi.* 吓唬; 欺负; (向…)虚张声势. ～ *sb. into [out of]* 威吓某人做[不做]….

Hec·tor [ˈhektə] *n.* ①赫克托[男子名]. ②荷马史诗《伊利亚特》中一勇士名.

hec·to·watt [ˈhektəuwɔt] *n.* (功率单位)百瓦.

Hec·u·ba [ˈhekjubə] *n.* 海丘巴[荷马史诗《伊里亚特》中特洛依国王普里安之后].

he'd [hiːd] = he had; he would.

hed·dles [ˈhedlz] *n.* [*pl.*]【纺】综片,综线,综丝. — *vt.* 使(经线)穿过综眼.

he·der [ˈheidə] *n.* *(pl.* ***ha·dar·im*** [hɑːˈdɑːrim]) 犹太儿童宗教学校.

hedge [hedʒ] *n.* ①(用灌木等构成的)树篱,(树枝等编成的) 篱笆, (石头、草皮等垒成的) 隔墙. ②障碍物,界限. ③(赌博中的) 赌两面, 两方下注. ④模棱两可的话. ⑤(在交易所中买进现货卖出期货或反之以避免损失的)套头交易. *a dead ～* 用树枝编成的篱笆, 柴垣. *a quickset ～* 由活树围成的树篱. *a ～ of stones* 石头堆成的围墙. ***A ～ between keeps friendship green.*** [谚]君子之交淡如水. ***be on the ～*** 要两面态度, 骑墙. ***be on the right side of the ～*** 主意打对了. ***come down on the wrong side of the ～*** 打错了主意. ***hang in [on] the ～*** (诉讼)悬而未决. ***make a ～*** 赌两面. ***not grow on every ～*** 稀少. ***over ～ and ditch*** 抄小路. ***sit on (both sides of) the ～*** = be on the ～. ***take a sheet off a ～*** 公然窃取. ***the only stick left in one's ～*** 剩下的唯一办法. — *vt.* ①用树篱围住[隔开]; 围护,防范. ②设障碍于, 妨碍. ③两方下注以避免(赌博、冒险等的)损失. ④躲闪,推诿,搪塞. ～ *a field* 用树篱围起田地. ～ *a question* 对问题避不作答. — *vi.* ①作树篱,修树篱. ②赌两面,(在交易所)做套头交易. ③躲闪,规避,推诿. ④做事留后路,说话留余地. ～ ***in [round] with*** 用…围住. ～ ***off*** ①用篱笆隔起来. ②两面下注. ～ ***out*** 用篱笆隔断. — *a.* ①树篱的,树篱下的,树篱旁的. ②偷偷摸摸的,名声不好的; 低劣的. ～ **bill** 长柄镰. ～**-born** *a.* 出身卑贱的. ～**hog** *n.* ①【动】猬; [美]豪猪. ②【军】刺猬弹[反潜用的深水炸弹]; 铁丝网,环形筑垒阵地. ③容易发怒的人,难对付的人. ④【植】野毛茛. ～**hop** *vi.* [美]掠地飞行,极低空飞行,[俚]跳栏飞行. ～**hopper** 掠地飞行的飞机[驾驶员]. ～ **hyssop** 【植】金黄水八角 *(Gratiola aurea)* [产于美国缅因州到佛罗里达州一带]. ～ **marriage** ①秘密结婚. ②不合法的结婚. ～ **priest** [英]无知的低级教士. ～**-row** 一排栽成树篱的灌木. ～ **school** (爱尔兰等地的)露天学校, 野外学校, 低级学校. ～ **sparrow** 【动】篱雀. ～ **writer** 穷文人,卖文者,寒士.

He·djaz [hiːˈdʒæz] *n.* = Hejaz.

he·don·ic [hiːˈdɔnik] *a.* ①享乐的. ②享乐主义的, 享乐主义者的. **-i·cal·ly** *ad.* ～**s** ①享乐主义的学说. ②【心】关于欢乐主义的学说.

he·don·ism [ˈhiːdənizəm] *n.* 享乐主义; 【心】欢乐主义 **he·don·ist** 欢乐主义者,享乐主义者. **he·do·nis·tic** *a.* [-ˈnistik] 欢乐说的,享乐主义的.

-hedral [ˈhiːdrəl] *suf.* 表示"…边的", "…面的": *polyhedral.*

-hedron [ˈhiːdrən] *suf.* 表示"…边形", "…面形": *polyhedron.*

hee·bie-jee·bies [ˈhiːbiˈdʒiːbiz] *n.* [常作 the ～][俚]神经紧张; 颤抖.

heed [hiːd] *vt.* 注意到, 留心. ～ *a warning* 注意到警告. — *vi.* 注意, 留意. — *n.* 注意, 留意. *Take ～ (and you) will surely speed.* [谚]谨慎是迅速之本. ***give [pay] ～ to*** 注意,留心. ***take ～ to [of]*** 注意, 提防. ***take no ～ of*** 不注意. **-ful** *a.* 注意的,留心的 *(of).*

heed·less [ˈhiːdlis] *a.* ①不注意的，不留心的；不顾…的 *(of)*. ②心不在焉的. **-ly** *ad.* **-ness** *n.*

hee·haw [ˈhiːhɔː] *vi., n.* ①驴叫(声). ②傻笑，大笑.

heel[1] [hiːl] *vt.*【海】使(船)倾斜 —*vi.* (船)倾侧 *(over)*. ～ *to port [starboard]* 船向左[右]舷倾斜. — *n.* (船的)倾斜(度).

heel[2] [hiːl] *n.* ①踵，脚后跟. ②〔*pl.*〕(四足动物的)后脚；后脚脚跟；蹄后部. ③(鞋、袜等的)后跟. ④踵状物〔如提琴的弓把，高尔夫球杓头弯曲部，梯子的底脚等〕. ⑤〔美俚〕小偷；卑劣的人，告密者，叛徒；食客，寄生虫. ⑥〔*pl.*〕剩余(物)，残余(物). ⑦〔美俚〕越狱；从作案地点逃跑. *the* ～ *of Italy.* 意大利的东南部. *the iron* ～ 铁蹄，专横统治. *wear high* ～*s* 穿高跟鞋. ***at* ～ = *to heel*** 跟在后面. ***close at* ～** 紧跟着. ***at [on, upon] sb.'s* ～*s*** 紧跟着某人. ***betake oneself to one's* ～*s*** 溜之大吉. ***bring sb. to* ～** 使某人跟着来；使某人就范. ***clap [lay, set] sb. by the* ～*s*** 给某人钉脚镣，把某人逮捕下狱；制服某人. ***come to* ～** 服从(规则)，跟着(别人转)；〔美〕追逐异性；〔喊狗〕跟着来！***cool [kick] one's* ～*s*** 久等，等得不耐烦. ***cop a* ～** 〔美俚〕逃跑，越狱. ***dig in one's* ～*s* = *dig one's* ～*s in*** 站稳脚步，坚持自己的立场. ***down at (the)* ～** ①(鞋)穿掉后跟的. ②(人)不修边幅的，邋里邋遢的. ***drag one's* ～*s*** ①拖着脚步走. ②迟缓误事，拖拖拉拉. ***follow on [upon] the* ～*s of*** 紧跟在后面. ***follow sb. to* ～** 亦步亦趋地追随某人. ***get [have] the* ～*s of*** 赶过，胜过. ***H-!*** (喊狗声)跟来！ **～ *and toe*** 正常地行走. **～*s over head* = *head over* ～*s*** ①头朝下，颠倒. ②完全地，深深地. ***keep to* ～*!* = *H-!*** ***kick up its* ～*s*** (马)溜腿. ***kick up one's* ～*s*** ①〔俚〕蹦蹦跳跳，狂欢. ②伸直腿死去，翘辫子. ***lay in by the* ～*s* = *lay sb. (fast) by the* ～*s*** 束缚某人手脚；逮捕某人下狱. ***make a* ～** 踢. ***neck and* ～*s*** 全身. ***on the* ～*s of* =** at sb.'s ～s. ***out at (the)* ～*s*** 袜跟[鞋跟]穿得露出脚跟的；衣衫褴褛的；穷相毕露的. ***over head and* ～*s in love*** 一往情深. ***raise [lift up] the* ～ *against sb.*** 凌辱某人. ***set one's* ～ *on [upon]*** 压制，践踏. ***show one's* ～ = *show a clean pair of* ～*s* = *take to one's* ～*s*** 溜掉，逃之夭夭. ***take it on* ～ *and toe*** 〔美俚〕溜掉. ***the* ～ *of Achilles* = *Achilles'* ～** 致命弱点，要害. ***to* ～** 追随，紧跟. ***tread on sb.'s* ～*s*** 踏着某人的脚迹前进；紧随某人之后. ***trip [strike, throw] up sb.'s* ～*s*** 用脚把人绊倒. ***turn on one's* ～*s*** 急向后转. ***turn up one's* ～*s*** 死，翘辫子. ***turn [tumble] up sb.'s* ～*s*** 〔口〕踢倒某人；杀死某人. ***under the* ～ *of*** 被蹂躏；受虐待. ***with the* ～*s foremost [forward]*** 成僵尸. — *vt.* ①给(鞋)钉后掌；给(斗鸡)上铁距；【高尔夫球】用杓后跟击(球)；(足球)用脚后跟传(球). ②(用脚后跟)践踏. ③紧跟，追赶. ④对…施加压力，催促. ⑤〔美俚〕供给(钱)；提供(武器). ～ *a pair of shoes* 给鞋钉掌. ～ *a cigarette butt out* 踩灭烟头. ～ *sb. upstairs* 跟着某人上楼. — *vi.* ①在后紧跟，快跑. ②用脚后跟跳舞；(足球)用脚后跟向后传球，【高尔夫球】用杓后跟打球. **～*in*** 【园艺】在根部培土暂植. **～ *out*** (足球)用脚后跟向后传球. **～*-and-toe*** *a.* 【体】(步伐)后脚脚尖还未离地前脚脚跟即已着地的 (*get on the* ～*-and-toe*〔美〕赶，加快. ～*-and-toe walking*【体】竞走). **～ball** (鞋匠上光用的)硬蜡和煤烟混合物；(拓碑文的)油烟. **～piece** 鞋后跟，踵状物. **～plate** 鞋盘，盘钉〔钉在鞋跟上以护鞋耐磨的铁片〕. **～post** ①马房(或牛栏)间隔柱. ②门柱. **～tap** ①鞋跟皮. ②杯中残酒 (*No* ～*taps!* 干杯，一饮而尽).

heeled [hiːld] *a.* ①有鞋后跟的；(斗鸡)带有铁矩的. ②〔美俚〕带着手枪的. ③〔美俚〕有钱的. *well* ～ ①(用手枪等)武装齐全的. ②有充分金钱的.

heel·er [ˈhiːlə] *n.* ①绱鞋后跟的人. ②善踢的斗鸡. ③〔美俚〕唯唯诺诺的小政客.

heel·ing [ˈhiːliŋ] *n.* (船的)倾侧. ～ *error* 【海】倾斜自差.

heel·less [ˈhiːllis] *a.* 没有后跟的.

H.E.F. = high energy fuels 高能燃料.

heft [heft] *n.* ①〔美、英方〕重量，体重. ②〔喻〕势力，影响. ③〔美口〕大半，大部分. — *vt.* 举起试测…的重量；〔美口，英方〕举起. — *vi.* 重达. *a box* ～*ing 5 pounds* 重达5磅的盒子.

heft·y [ˈhefti] *a.* ①〔口〕重的. ②〔口〕强健的，肌肉发达的. ③异常大的. *a* ～ *blow* 很重的一击. *a* ～ *majority* 压倒多数. *a* ～ *child* 壮大的婴儿. *a* ～ *book* 一本很重的书. — *n.* 体壮力大的人；〔美拳击〕重量级拳击选手. **-i·ly** *ad.* **heft·i·ness** *n.*

he·gar·i [hiˈgæri,-ˈgɛər-] *n.* 【植】谷粒芦粟〔产于苏丹，其茎多汁液，多叶；直穗；粟粒带灰色〕.

He·gel [ˈheigl], **George Wilhelm Friedrich** 黑格尔〔1770—1831，德国哲学家〕.

He·ge·li·an [heiˈgiːljən] *a.* 黑格尔哲学的，黑格尔学派的. — *n.* 黑格尔派哲学家，黑格尔哲学的信徒.

He·ge·li·an·ism [heiˈgiːljənizəm] *n.* 黑格尔哲学.

heg·e·mon·ic(al) [ˌhi(ː)giˈmɔnik(əl) Am.ˌhedʒi-] *a.* 霸权的，统治的.

he·ge·mo·nism [ˌhi(ː)giˈmɔnizəm Am.ˌhedʒi-] *n.* 霸权主义.

heg·em·o·nist [ˌhi(ː)giˈmɔnist Am.ˌhedʒi-] *n.* 霸权主义者.

he·gem·o·ny [hi(ː)ˈgeməni, Am. hiːˈdʒeməni] *n.* 霸权，霸权主义.

Heg·i·ra [ˈhedʒirə] *n.* ①【宗】(公元622年)穆罕默德由麦加到麦地那的逃亡〔此年即定为伊斯兰教纪元〕. ②〔h-〕逃亡.

he-goat [ˈhiːgəut] *n.* 公山羊. ***milk a* ～ *into a sieve*** 徒劳无功，做不会成功的事.

he·gu·men [hiˈgjuːmen] *n.* 【东正教】修道院长，寺院长.

heh[1] [hei] *n.* = he[3].

heh[2] [hei] *int.* 嗨！〔表示惊异、质问〕.

Hei·del·berg [ˈhaidlbəːg] *n.* 海德堡〔德国地名〕. ～ **jaw**【人类】史前人的颚骨. ～ **man** 海德堡人，欧洲史前人种.

heif·er [ˈhefə] *n.* ①(未生过小牛的)小母牛；母牛. ②〔美俚〕女人.

heigh [hei] *int.* 嗨！〔表示注意、质问、鼓舞、高兴等〕.

heigh-ho [ˈheiˈhəu] *int.* 嗨嗬！〔表示疲劳、丧胆、惊愕、高兴等〕.

height [hait] *n.* ①高，高度；身高；海拔. ②〔常 *pl.*〕高地，山丘. ③高贵，卓越. ④绝顶，顶点；【圣】天. ⑤〔罕〕显贵，高的社会地位. *What's your* ～*?* 你多高？ *I'm five feet in* ～. 我身高五英尺. *the* ～ *above (the) sea level* 海拔. *in the* ～ *of fashion* 极时髦. *in the* ～ *of summer* 在盛夏. ～ *of one's power* 权力的极点. *on the* ～ 高地上的. *the* ～ *of folly* 笨透. ***at its* ～** 正盛，正在绝顶；正起劲. ***in* ～** 以高计. **～ *of land*** 〔Canad.〕分水界；〔口〕流域. **～-to-paper**【印】铅字标准高度〔在说英语国家是0.9186英寸〕.

height·en [ˈhaitn] *vt.* ①升高，增高；提高，加高 (*opp.* lower). ②加强，加深，加剧；增大. ③使高尚；使显著，使突出. ④给(描写、故事)添加细节；给(绘画)加浓色彩. — *vi.* ①升高；增加. ②(颜色等)变深.

heil [ˈhail] 〔G.〕*vt.* 向…欢呼，向…呼万岁. — *n.* 嗨！万岁〔表示欢呼的喊声〕！

hein [ɑːn] *int.* 〔F.〕啊！嗯！

Hei·ne [ˈhainə], **Heinrich** 海因里希·海涅〔1797—1856，德国诗人〕.

hei·nous [ˈheinəs] *a.* 可恨的，极凶恶的. *a* ～ *crime* 滔天大罪. **-ly** *ad.* **-ness** *n.*

heir [ɛə] *n.* 后嗣，嗣子 *(to)*；继承人. ～ *at law*【法】法定继承人. ～ *in tail*【法】直系继承人. *legal [right]*

～【法】合法继承人. ～ *of the [one's] body* 嫡生子〔女〕. *the* ～ *to the crown [throne]* 王位继承人. ***cut off one's ～ with a shilling*** 用象征性的一先令取消继承者的继承权. ～ **apparent** 〔*pl.*〕(*～s apparent*)【法】法定继承人,有确定继承权的人. ～ **collateral**【法】旁系继承人. ～ **presumptive,** 〔*pl.*〕～**s presumptive**【法】假定继承人〔虽有继承权但其继承权可因近亲之出生而消失的人〕. — *vt.* 继承.

heir·dom [ˈɛədəm] *n.* = heirship.

heir·ess [ˈɛəris] *n.* 嗣女,女继承人.

heir·less [ˈɛəlis] *a.* 无后嗣的;无继承人的.

heir·loom [ˈɛəluːm] *n.* ①【法】相传动产〔随不动产转移产权的动产〕. ②祖传宝物,传家宝.

heir·ship [ˈɛəʃip] *n.* 继承权;承继,世袭.

heist [haist] *vt.* ①〔方〕举起. ②〔美俚〕持凶器行劫,劫夺;偷. — *n.* 持凶器行劫,劫夺;偷窃. **-er** *n.* 持械抢劫者,劫夺者,偷窃者.

Hejaz [hiːˈdʒæz] *n.* 汉志〔阿拉伯西部伊斯兰教国,与 Nejd 合称 Saudi Arabia〕.

He·ji·ra [ˈhedʒirə] *n.* = Hegira.

hek·tare [ˈhektɑː] *n.* = hectare.

hekto- *pref.* = hecto-.

hek·to·gram(me) [ˈhektəgræm] *n.* = hectogram(me).

hek·to·lit·er [ˈhektəlitə] *n.* = hectoliter.

hé·las [eiˈlɑːs] *int.* 〔F.〕哎呀! 哎哟!

held [held] hold 的过去式和过去分词.

hel·den·ten·or [ˈheldənteˈnəuə] *n.* 英雄男高音, 华格纳歌剧男高音〔指适于演唱歌剧作曲家华格纳 (*Wagner*) 的歌剧的男高音〕.

Hel·en [ˈhelən] *n.* ①海伦〔女子名〕. ②【希神】美女海伦〔为斯巴达王 *Menelaus* 的王后,因她被 *Paris* 所拐去引起 *Troy* 战争〕.

Hel·e·na [ˈhelinə, heˈliːnə] *n.* 海伦娜〔女子名〕.

he·li- [ˈheli] *comb. f.* 〔后接元音〕 = helio-: *heli*anthus.

he·li·a·cal [hiːˈlaiəkəl] *a.* 太阳的;与太阳同时升落的. ～ ***rising [setting] (of a star)***【天】(星的)偕日升〔偕日落〕. **-ly** *ad.*

he·li·an·thus [ˌhiːliˈænθəs] *n.* 【植】向日葵属植物;〔H-〕向日葵属.

he·li·borne [ˈhelibɔːn] *a.* 由直升飞机运载〔输送〕的. ～ *tactics* 直升飞机战术. ～ *troops* 由直升飞机运送的部队.

he·li·bus [ˈhelibʌs] *n.* (作为大都市交通工具的)公共直升飞机.

hel·i·cal [ˈhelikəl] *a.* 螺旋状的,螺旋线的. ～ **gear**【机】斜齿轮. **-ly** *ad.*

hel·i·ces [ˈhelisiːz] helix 的复数.

hel·i·ci·ty [heˈlisiti] *n.*【物】螺旋性.

hel·i·cline [ˈheliklain] *n.* 螺旋形坡道.

hel·i·co·gyre [ˈhelikəudʒaiə], **hel·i·co·gyro** [-u] *n.* 螺旋桨旋翼直升飞机.

hel·i·coid [ˈhelikɔid] *a.* 螺状的,螺旋状的. — *n.*【数】螺旋面,螺旋体. **-al** *a.*

Hel·i·con [ˈhelikən] *n.* ①【希神】(文艺九女神 Muses 住的)赫利孔山. ②诗思的灵感源泉. ③〔h-〕黑里康大号〔一种套在肩上吹的低音大号〕.

hel·i·co·ni·a [ˌheliˈkəuniə] *n.*【植】海里康属 (*Heliconia*) 植物.

Hel·i·co·ni·an [ˌheliˈkəuniən] *a.* 赫利孔山的. **the ～ maids** 文艺九女神 (= Muses).

hel·i·copt [ˈhelikɔpt] *vt., vi.* = helicopter (*vt., vi.*).

hel·i·cop·ter [ˈhelikɔptə] *n.* 直升飞机. — *vt.* 用直升飞机载送. ～ *sb. aboard the ship* 用直升飞机把某人送到船上. — *vi.* 乘直升飞机. ～ **carrier** 直升飞机母舰. **-ist** 直升飞机驾驶员. ～**manship** 驾驶〔乘坐〕直升飞机来往.

hel·i·drome [ˈhelidrəum] *n.* 直升飞机机场.

hel·i·home [ˈhelihəum] *n.* 直升汽车屋〔直升飞机与住屋汽车结合而成〕.

helio- [ˈhiːliə] *comb. f.* 〔后接辅音〕表示"太阳": *helio*centric, *helio*graph.

he·li·o·cen·tric [ˌhiːliəuˈsentrik] *a.* 以太阳为中心的;以日心测量的 (*opp.* geocentric). **the ～ theory** 地动说,日心说.

he·li·o·cen·tric·ism [ˌhiːliəuˈsentrisizəm] *n.* 地动说,日心说.

he·li·o·chrome [ˈhiːliəukrəum] *n.* 天然色照片, 彩色照片. **he·li·o·chro·mic** *a.*

he·li·o·chro·my [ˈhiːliəukrəumi] *n.* 天然色照相术,彩色照相术.

he·li·o·gram [ˈhiːliəugræm] *n.* 回光信号,日光反射信号器发射的信号.

he·li·o·graph [ˈhiːliəugrɑːf] *n.* ①日光反射信号器,回光仪. ②太阳照相机. ③【天】日光仪;日光光度计. ④【印】日光胶版. — *vt.* ①用日光反射信号器传达(信号). ②用太阳照相机拍摄. **-er** *n.* 使用回光仪〔太阳照相机〕的人.

he·li·o·gra·phy [ˌhiːliˈɔgrəfi] *n.* ①日光反射信号法. ②【印】日光胶版术. ③【天】太阳面记述. **he·li·o·graph·ic** *a.* [-ˈgræfik]

he·li·o·gra·vure [ˈhiːliəugrəˈvjuə] *n.*【印】照相凹版(术).

he·li·o·gy·ro [ˈhiːliəuˌdʒaiərəu] *n.* 直升飞机.

he·li·ol·a·try [ˌhiːliˈɔlətri] *n.* 太阳崇拜.

he·li·ol·o·gy [ˌhiːliˈɔlədʒi] *n.* 太阳研究,太阳学.

he·li·om·e·ter [ˌhiːliˈɔmitə] *n.*【天】量日仪.

He·li·os [ˈhiːliɔs] *n.*【希神】赫利俄斯〔太阳神〕.

he·li·o·scope [ˈhiːliəskəup] *n.* 太阳望远镜;回照器.

he·li·o·sis [ˌhiːliˈəusis] *n.* (*pl.* ***-ses*** [-siːz]) ①【医】日射病,中暑. ②【植】日射病黑斑.

he·li·o·stat [ˈhiːliəustæt] *n.*【天】定日镜.

he·li·o·tax·is [ˈhiːliəuˈtæksis] *n.*【生】趋日性.

he·li·o·ther·a·py [ˌhiːliəuˈθerəpi] *n.*【医】日光疗法.

he·li·o·trope [ˈhelijətrəup] *n.* ①【植】向日性植物;天芥菜属植物. ②天芥菜花的气味〔颜色〕. ③淡紫色. ④回光仪,日光反射信号. ⑤【地】鸡血石.

he·li·ot·ro·pin(e) [ˌheljəˈtrəupin] *n.*【化】天芥菜精.

he·li·ot·ro·pism [ˌhiːliˈɔtrəpizəm] *n.*【植】向日性,趋日性. *positive* ～ (茎叶的)向日性. *negative* ～ (茎叶的)背日性.

he·li·o·type [ˈhiːliəutaip] *n.* 胶版(画).

he·li·ox [ˈhiːljɔks] *n.* (供深水呼吸用的)氦氧混合剂. 〔含98%的氦和2%的氧〕.

he·li·o·zo·an [ˌhiːliəuˈzəuən] *n.*【动】太阳虫目 (*Heliozoa*) 动物. **he·li·o·zo·ic** [-ik] *a.*

hel·i·pad [ˈhelipæd] *n.* = heliport.

hel·i·port [ˈhelipɔːt] *n.* 直升机场,临时直升飞机降落点.

he·li·um [ˈhiːljəm, -liəm] *n.*【化】氦. ～**-4** 氦4〔氦的最常见同位素〕.

he·lix [ˈhiːliks] *n.* (*pl.* ***hel·i·ces*** [ˈhelisiːz], *～es* [ˈhiːliksiz]) ①螺旋线. ②【解】耳轮. ③【建】螺旋(线)饰. ④【动】蜗牛,蜗牛属动物. *normal* ～【机】正交螺旋线. *pan-cake* ～ 扁平螺旋线圈.

hell [hel] *n.* ①地狱,阴间. ②苦境,罪恶之地;极大的痛苦,虐待. ③赌窟. ④恶魔;黑暗势力. ⑤垃圾箱. ⑥大混乱,毁坏. ⑦训斥,咒骂. ⑧〔用以加强语气或咒骂〕胡闹,见鬼. *hungry as* ～ 饿得要命. *living* ～ = *a* ～ *on [upon] earth* 人间地狱,活地狱. ***a ～ of a ...*** ①极度的;可怕的,糟糕的. ②极好的 (*a ～ of a life* 人间地狱. *a ～ of a mess* 一塌糊涂. *a ～ of an actor* 一个糟糕〔出色〕的演员). ***all ～ let loose*** 一团糟. ***as ～*** 〔口〕很,非常的,极端的;可怕的. ***be ～ for*** 对…极度关心;竭力坚持. ***be ～ on*** 〔美俚〕对…十分严格;对…十分有害;使…非常痛苦. ***beat ～*** ①令人吃惊. ②超过一

切. ***blast [knock] ～ out of sb.*** 痛打某人. ***catch [get] ～*** 〔美俚〕挨训斥,受惩罚. ***give sb. ～*** 痛斥某人,狠狠揍某人一顿. ***go through ～*** 赴汤蹈火. ***Go to ～!*** 滚蛋! 见鬼去吧! ***have a [the] ～ of a time*** 〔口〕①经历一段非常可怕的生活. ②玩得很痛快. ***H-!*** 见鬼! 混蛋! ***～ and gone*** 极远的;不可挽回的. ***～ and [or] high water*** 任何困难. ***H- breaks loose.*** 喧闹起来,闹得天翻地覆. ***the ～ you say*** 那真叫人吃惊. ***～ to pay*** 痛责, 严厉惩罚, 后果不堪设想. ***in ～*** 〔用以加强语气〕究竟,到底(*What in ～ are you doing?* 你究竟在干什么). ***just for the ～ of it*** 〔美俚〕就是为了捣乱,只是为了好玩. ***like ～*** ①〔俚〕极猛烈,拚命,不顾死活地 (*run like ～* 拚命跑). ②哪有这种事,绝不会. ***make one's life a ～*** 过地狱一样的生活. ***move ～*** 想尽办法, 无所不用其极. ***play [kick up] ～ and Tommy*** 〔口〕破坏得一塌糊涂;堕落. ***play ～ with*** ①破坏, 糟蹋. ②伤害, 肃清, 消灭. ***raise ～*** 〔俚〕喧闹,怒斥. ***smell ～*** 受罪,吃苦头. ***suffer ～*** 遭受很大的痛苦. ***the ～*** 见鬼去 (*get the ～ out of here* 滚出去); ***The ～ of it is ....*** 〔美俚〕妙就妙在…;糟就糟在…. ***to beat ～*** 〔美俚〕〔作状语用〕又快又猛地. ***to the ～ = the ～.*** ***what the ～*** ①〔用以加强语气或咒骂〕(*What the ～ do you want?* 你究竟要什么?) ②〔表示无所谓, 不在乎〕(*What the ～, I may as well go tomorrow instead.* 没什么,我明天去也可以). — *vi.* ①放荡地欢闹. ②(车辆)急驰. ～ ***around*** 混日子;爱出入下等酒吧间. ～ **bender** ①(北美俄亥俄流域产的)大鲵鱼. ②〔美俚〕喧闹的人;鲁莽人. ～**-bent** *a., ad.* 〔俚〕固执的[地],拚命的[地],不顾一切的[地]. ～**box** 印刷所的坏铅字箱. ～**broth** 〔古〕巫士行邪术调制的羹汤. ～ **buggy** 〔军俚〕坦克. ～**cat** 巫婆;泼妇. ～**dive** *vi.* 【空】俯冲轰炸. ～**diver** 俯冲轰炸机. ～**fire** (惩罚罪人的)地狱火. ～**-fired** *a., ad.* 极度的[地]. ～**-for-leather** ①*a., ad.* 拚命的[地],又快又猛的[地]. ② *n.* 不顾一切,慌忙. ～**hole** 〔口〕令人厌恶的地方,下流场所. ～**hound** (神话中的)地狱看门狗;恶魔,恶鬼一样的人. ～**kite** 穷凶极恶的人,残酷的人. ～**'s bells** ①〔表示惊诧〕喔唷! ②〔表示愤慨、不耐烦等〕见鬼! ～ **ship** (对水手进行虐待的)地狱船. **-ward** *a., ad.* 向着地狱的[地]. **-like** *a.*

he'll [hi:l] = he will; he shall.

Hel·las [ˈheləs] *n.* 〔诗〕希腊.

hel·le·bore [ˈhelibɔ:, -bɔə] *n.* ①【植】菟葵; 嚏根草属植物. ②【药】藜芦.

Hel·lene, Hel·le·ni·an [ˈheli:n, heˈli:niən] *n.* 古希腊人,希腊人.

Hel·len·ic [heˈli:nik] *a.* ①希腊的, 希腊人的. ②古希腊文化的; 古希腊语的. — *n.* (印欧语系之一的)古希腊语.

Hel·len·ism [ˈhelinizəm] *n.* ①希腊语风; 古希腊文化. ②对古希腊文化的崇拜. ③古希腊人文主义. ④希腊国民性.

Hel·len·ist [ˈhelinist] *n.* ①用希腊语的人. ②希腊语言学家;希腊文化研究者[崇拜者]. ③【圣】以希腊语为母语的人(尤指犹太人). ④十五世纪在欧洲帮助复兴古典文艺的拜占庭希腊人.

Hel·len·is·tic [ˌheliˈnistik] *a.* ①希腊语言使用者的. ②希腊语言的;希腊语言学家的. ③古希腊建筑式的;古希腊艺术风格的. **-ti·cal·ly** *ad.*

Hel·len·ize [ˈhelinaiz] *vt., vi.* (使)希腊化. **Hel·len·i·za·tion** *n.*

hell·er[1] [ˈhelə] *n.* 〔俚〕= hellion.

hel·ler[2] [ˈhelə] *n.* ①德国的黄铜币;奥地利的青铜币. ② = haler.

hel·ler·i [ˈhelərai] *n.* 【动】剑尾鱼 (= swordtail).

hell·gram·mite, hell·gra·mite [ˈhelgrəmait] *n.*【动】美洲翅虫 (*Corydalis cornuta*) 的幼虫.

hel·lion [ˈheliən] *n.* 〔口〕坏人,恶棍;爱恶作剧的人.

hell·ish [ˈheliʃ] *a.* ①地狱(似)的; 魔鬼(似)的,凶恶的. ②〔口〕讨厌的,可憎的. **-ly** *ad.* **-ness** *n.*

hel·lo [ˈheˈləu, heˈləu] *int.* 喂! 〔用以唤起注意,回答电话或表示问候、惊奇等〕. — *vi., vt.* (向…)喊一声,"喂". — *n.* 表示问候等的声音. *Say ～ to your mother = Tell your mother "～" for me.* 代我问候你母亲. *H- ! This is Mr. Carter speaking.* (在电话中说)喂! 我是卡特. ～ **girl** 〔美口〕女电话接线员.

helm[1] [helm] *n.* ①【船】舵柄;舵轮;舵机. ②(国家、企业等的)机要部门,领导. *the clique at the ～ of the war* 战争指导集团. ***Down with the ～!*** 转舵背风开! ***ease the ～*** 将舵转回中央位置. ***H- alee*** 转舵背风开! ***put the ～ up [down]*** 转舵迎风[背风]. ***take the ～ of state*** 掌握政权. ***Up with the ～!*** 转舵迎风开! — *vt.* 掌(舵);指挥,掌握.

helm[2] [helm] *n.* 头盔. — *vt.* 给…戴上头盔. ～ **cloud** 〔英方〕(暴风雨时的)盖山乌云.

hel·met [ˈhelmit] *n.* ①头盔;钢盔. ②防护帽;遮阳帽;飞行帽. ③发动机罩. ④盔状花冠[花萼]. ⑤〔美俚〕警察. *a gas ～* 防毒面具. *a safety ～* (建筑工人等戴的)安全帽. — *vt.* 给…戴上头盔. **-ed** *a.* ①头盔状的. ②戴头盔的.

Helm·holtz [ˈhelmhəults], **H. L. F. Von** 冯·赫姆霍尔兹〔1821—1894,德国生理学家及物理学家〕.

hel·minth [ˈhelminθ] *n.* 【动】蠕虫,肠虫.

hel·min·thi·a·sis [ˌhelminˈθaiəsis] *n.* 【医】蠕虫病,肠虫病.

hel·min·thic [helˈminθik] *a.* ①蠕虫的, 肠虫的. ②驱虫的,驱蠕虫的. — *n.* 驱虫剂,打蠕虫药.

hel·min·thoid [helˈminθɔid] *a.* 虫状的,似蠕虫的.

hel·min·thol·o·gy [ˌhelminˈθɔlədʒi] *n.* 蠕虫学.

helms·man [ˈhelmzmən] *n.* 舵手.

he·lo·phyte [ˈheləfait] *n.* 沼生植物.

Hel·ot [ˈhelət] *n.* ①赫洛特〔古代希腊斯巴达人的奴隶〕. ②〔h-〕奴隶,农奴.

hel·ot·i·sm [ˈhelətizəm] *n.* ①(古代斯巴达的赫洛特)奴隶制度. ②奴隶身分;奴役现象. ③【生】菌藻共生.

hel·ot·ry [ˈhelətri] *n.* ①农奴阶级; 奴隶制度. ②奴隶地位;农奴地位.

help [help] *vt.* (～*ed*, 〔古〕 ***holp*** [həulp]; ～*ed*; 〔古〕 ***holp·en*** [ˈhəulpən]) ①帮助,援助; 救,救济. ②治疗;补救. ③促进,助长. ④〔与 cannot, can 连用〕避免;抑制,阻止;忍耐. ⑤盛(饭),添(菜),劝(酒). ⑥〔婉〕侵吞,窃用. ⑦〔口〕分配. *God [Heaven] ～s those who ～ themselves.* 〔谚〕天助自助者. *H- me (to) lift it.* 请帮助我把它抬起来. *So ～ me (God).* (用于誓语)愿上帝助我〔因为我在说实话〕;我敢对天发誓. *God ～ him!* 可怜! 可怜虫! *I can't ～ it.* 没有办法. *It can't be ～ed. = There is no ～ for it.* 实在没有办法. —*vi.* ①帮助. ②有用,有帮助. ③开饭,上菜. *Don't be longer than you can help.* 请不要呆得太久. *Every little ～s.* 〔谚〕点点滴滴,全有助益. *H-! H-!* 救人啦! ***cannot ～ being...*** 不免要成为…. ***cannot ～ ...ing*** =〔美口〕***cannot ～ but (do)*** 不得不… (*I could not ～ laughing.* 我忍不住不笑). ***～ a lame dog over a stile*** 帮助人度过难关. ***～ sb. forward [on]*** 搀扶着某人前进; 使某人获得进步. ***～ oneself to*** ①自由取食. ②任意占用 [取用] (*H- yourself to the cake.* 请随便吃糕饼). ***～ sb. down*** 把某人搀扶下来. ***～ sb. in [into]*** 搀扶某人进入. ***～ sb. off with*** 帮某人脱去. ***～ sb. on with*** 帮某人穿上. ***～ sb. out*** 帮忙某人完成工作;补助(费用). ***～ sb. over*** 帮忙渡过;帮忙越过;帮助打胜. ***～ sb. through*** 帮助某人完成. ***～ sb. to*** ①给某人进食. ②帮助某人得到. ***～ sb. up*** 把某人扶起;扶某人攀登上去. — *n.* ①帮助; 援助; 救济; 挽救方法; 补救; 医治. ②〔单数与不定冠词连用〕助手,帮手,帮忙的人[物]. ③〔口〕(菜的)一份,(酒的)一杯. ④〔美〕佣人,仆人. *a lady ～* 女仆. *a mother's ～* 家庭保姆. *the ～* 女仆,保姆. *There is no ～ for it.* 无

法可想. ***be of*** ~ 有用,有益. ***be of much [no, some] ~ to sb.*** 对某人很有[没有,有些]帮助. ***by the ~ of …*** 得…的帮助. ***cry for*** ~ 求援;求救. ***lay off*** ~ 辞退佣人. ***with the ~ of*** 在…的帮助下.

help·er [ˈhelpə] *n.* ①帮手,助手. ②起救助作用的东西.

help·ful [ˈhelpful] *a.* 有帮助的,有益的,有用的 *(to).* **-ly** *ad.* **-ness** *n.*

help·ing [ˈhelpiŋ] *a.* 帮助人的,辅助的. *a ~ verb* 助动词. *be ready to give [lend, reach out] a ~ hand* 乐意助人. — *n.* ①帮助,支援. ②(食物的)一份,一杯. *a second ~* 第二杯. *Have some more ~.* 再来一点. **-ly** *ad.*

help·less [ˈhelplis] *a.* ①无帮助的,未受到帮助的. ②孤弱的,无依无靠的. ③无能的,无用的. ***be ~ with mirth*** 笑得打滚,笑破肚皮. **-ly** *ad.* **-ness** *n.*

help·mate, help·meet [ˈhelpmeit, -miːt] *n.* ①合作者;良伴,伴侣. ②配偶,妻子[丈夫].

Hel·sing·fors [ˈhelsiŋfɔːz] = 〔芬〕Helsinki.

Hel·sin·ki [ˈhelsiŋki] *n.* 赫尔辛基〔芬兰首都〕.

hel·ter-skel·ter [ˈheltəˈskeltə] *ad.* 手忙脚乱地,慌慌张张地,狼狈地,混乱地. — *a.* 手忙脚乱的,混乱的. — *n.* ①慌张,狼狈. ②乱七八糟的表演.

helve [helv] *n.* (工具的)柄(尤指斧柄). ***throw the ~ after the hatchet*** ①〔谚〕赔了夫人又折兵〔接连遭受损失〕. ②全部放弃. ③孤注一掷,一不做二不休. — *vt.* 给(斧等)装柄.

Hel·ve·tia [helˈviːʃə] *n.* 海尔维希〔瑞士的拉丁语名称〕.

Hel·ve·tian, Hel·vet·ic [helˈviːʃiən, -vetik] *n.* (古代瑞士)海尔维希族人. — *a.* 海尔维希族人的;瑞士(人)的.

hem[1] [hem] *n.* (布、衣服的)褶边;折缝. — *vt.* ①给…缝边;给…镶边. ②围住,关进 *(in; about; round).* ③接界. ~ ***(sb.) out*** 排斥,逐出(某人). — *vi.* 做折边.

hem[2] [hem, hm, mm] *int.* 哼;〔表示踌躇、讽刺、唤起注意或清嗓咳痰时的发声〕. — *n.* 哼声;清嗓咳痰声. — *vi.* 发哼哼声;咳嗽. ~ ***and haw*** 〔美〕结结巴巴地说;嗯嗯呃呃〔表示说话时踌躇;或在寻找恰当的字〕.

hem(a)- *comb. f.* = hemo-.

he·ma·cy·tom·e·ter [ˌhiːməsaiˈtɔmitə, ˌhemə-] *n.* 血球计数器.

he·mag·glu·ti·nate [ˌhiːməˈgluːtineit, ˌhemə-] *vt.* 【医】使血球凝集. **-na·tion** *n.*

he·mag·glu·ti·nin [ˌhiːməˈgluːtinin,ˌhemə-] *n.* 【医】血球凝集素.

he·mal [ˈhiːməl] *a.* = haemal.

he·male [ˈhiːˈmeil] *n.* 〔口〕= he-man.

hemat- *comb. f.* = hemato-: *hemat*ic.

he·ma·te·in [ˌhiːməˈtiːin, ˌhemə-] *n.* ①【生化】正铁血红表. ②【化】苏木因,氧化苏木精.

he·ma·ther·mal [ˌhiːməˈθəːml,hemə-] *a.* 恒温动物的 (= homoiothermal).

he·mat·ic [hiːˈmætik] *a.* = haematic.

hem·a·tin [ˈhemətin] *n.* = haematin.

hem·a·tin·ic [ˌheməˈtinik] *n.* 【医】补血剂. — *a.* 血红素的,有关血红素的.

hem·a·tite [ˈhemətait] *n.* = haematite.

hemato- *comb. f.* 表示"血": *hemato*ma, *hemato*poiesis.

hem·a·to·blast [ˈhemətəuˌblæst] *n.* 【解】血小板,成血细胞. **-blas·tic** [-ˈblæstik] *a.*

hem·a·to·cele [ˈhemətəsiːl] *n.* = haematocele.

hem·a·to·crit [ˈhemətəkrit] *n.* ①血流比容计,血球容量计. ②(用血球容量计测出的)血球密度 (= hematocrit reading).

hem·a·to·cyte [ˈhemətəsait] *n.* = haematocyte.

hem·a·to·gen·e·sis [ˌhemətəuˈdʒenisis] *n.* = hematopoiesis. **-to·gen·ic** [-ˈdʒenik], **-to·ge·net·ic** [-dʒiˈnetik] *a.*

hem·a·tog·e·nous [ˌheməˈtɔdʒinəs] *a.* ①成血的. ②(细菌等)由血流所扩散的.

he·ma·tol·o·gy [ˌheməˈtɔlədʒi, hemə-] *n.* 血液学. **-log·ic** [-təˈlɔdʒik], **-to·log·i·cal** *a.* **he·ma·tol·o·gist** *n.* 血液学家.

he·ma·to·ma [ˌheməˈtəumə] *n.* 【医】血肿 (= haematoma.)

he·ma·toph·a·gous [ˌheməˈtɔfəgəs] *a.* 食血为生的,血养的.

hem·a·to·poi·e·sis [ˌhemətəupɔiˈiːsis] *n.* 【医】血生成. **hem·a·to·poi·et·ic** [-ˈetik] *a.*

he·ma·to·ther·mal [ˈhemətəuˌθəːml] *a.* 恒温动物的 (= homoiothermal).

he·ma·tox·y·lin [ˌhiːməˈtɔksilin] *n.* = haematoxylin.

hem·a·to·zo·on [ˌhemətəuˈzəuɔn] *n.* *(pl.* ***-zo·a*** [-ə]*)* 血寄生虫. **hem·a·to·zo·ic** [-ik], **hem·a·to·zoal** *a.*

he·ma·tu·re·sis [ˌhiːməˈtjuərisis] *n.* 【医】=hematuria.

he·ma·tu·ri·a [ˌhiːməˈtjuriə] *n.* 【医】血尿.

heme [hiːm] *n.* 【生化】血红素,亚铁原卟啉.

hem·el·y·tron, hem·el·y·trum [heˈmelitrɔn, -trʌm] *n.* *(pl.* ***-tra*** [-trə]*)* 【动】半鞘翅〔异翅亚目昆虫的前翅〕.

hem·er·a·lo·pi·a [ˌhemərəˈləupiə] *n.* ①【医】昼盲(症). ②夜盲(症) (= night blindness). **hem·er·a·lo·pic** [-ˈlɔpik] *a.*

hemi-, *pref.* 表示"半": *hemi*anopsia, *hemi*cycle.

-hemia *suf.* = -emia.

hem·i·a·nop·si·a [ˌhemiəˈnɔpsiə] *n.* 【医】偏盲.

he·mic [ˈhiːmik] *a.* 关于血的 (= haematic).

hem·i·chor·date [ˌhemiˈkɔːdeit] *a.* 半索亚门动物的. — *n.* 半索亚门动物.

hem·i·cra·ni·a [ˌhemiˈkreiniə] *n.* 【医】偏头痛.

hem·i·cy·cle [ˈhemiˌsaikl] *n.* ①半圆形. ②半圆形建筑物;半圆形斗技场.

hem·i·dem·i·sem·i·qua·ver [ˌhemiˌdemiˈsemikweivə] *n.* 〔主英〕【乐】六十四分音符.

hem·i·el·y·tron [ˌhemiˈelitrɔn] *n.* 半鞘翅 (=hemelytron).

hem·i·he·dral [ˌhemiˈhiːdrəl] *a.* 【化】(晶体)半面的. ~ *form* 半面晶形.

hem·i·hy·drate [ˌhemiˈhaidreit] *n.* 【化】半水合物,半水化物.

hem·i·me·tab·o·lous [ˌhemimiˈtæbələs] *a.* 【动】半变态的 (= hemimetabolic). **-tab·o·lism** *n.*

hem·i·mor·phic [ˌhemiˈmɔːfik] *a.* 【物】异极的,异极晶形的.

hem·i·mor·phite [ˌhemiˈmɔːfait] *n.* 【矿】异极矿.

he·min [ˈhiːmin] *n.* 【生化】氯高铁血红素.

Hem·ing [ˈhemiŋ] *n.* 赫明〔姓氏〕.

Hem·ing·way [ˈhemiŋwei] *n.* ①海明威〔姓氏〕. ② **Ernest** ~ 欧内斯特·海明威 〔1899—1961,美国小说家〕.

hem·i·o·la [ˌhemiˈəulə] *n.* 【乐】3:2 的比率;五度的;五度音程关系;三倍的 (= hemiolia).

hem·i·par·a·site [ˌhemiˈpærəsait] *n.* ①【动】半寄生虫. ②【植】半寄生(植)物. **-par·asit·ic** [-ˈsitik] *a.*

hem·i·ple·gia [ˌhemiˈpliːdʒiə] *n.* 【医】半身不遂,偏瘫.

He·mip·te·ra [hiˈmiptərə] *n.* 【虫】半翅目.

he·mip·ter·an [hiˈmiptərən] *n.* 半翅目 *(Hemiptera)* 昆虫〔包括床虱 (臭虫)、虱、蚜虫等〕. **he·mip·ter·oid** [-rɔid], **he·mip·ter·ous** [-rəs] *a.*

hem·i·sphere [ˈhemisfiə] *n.* ①(地球或天球的)半球. ②半球地图,半球模型. ③半球上的所有国家[人民]. ④【解】大脑半球 (= cerebral ~). ⑤(活动、知识等的)范围,领域. *the Eastern [Western] H-* 东[西]半球. *Magdeburg ~s* 【物】马德堡半球〔气压实验用具〕. *a ~ of special knowledge* 专业知识的范围.

hem·i·spher·ic(al) [ˌhemiˈsferik(əl)] *a.* 半球的.

hem·i·sphe·roid [hemiˈsfiərɔid] *n.* 半球体.
hem·i·stich [ˈhemistik] *n.* (诗的)半句,半行;不完全行.
hem·i·ter·pene [ˌhemiˈtəːpiːn] *n.*【化】半萜.
hem·i·trope [ˈhemitrəup] *a.*【地】半体双晶的 (= hemitropic). — *n.*【地】半体双晶.
hem·line [ˈhemlain] *n.* ①(裙子、衣服等的)底边,贴边. ②上述底边离地的高度.
hem·lock [ˈhemlɔk] *n.* ①〔英〕铁杉;毒芹;毒胡萝卜;毒胡萝卜精〔毒药〕. ②〔美〕(北美)梅树 (= ~ spruce). ~ **parsley** 川芎属植物(尤指芎䓖).
hem·mer[1] [ˈhemə] *n.* 哼哼作声的人[机器].
hem·mer[2] [ˈhemə] *n.* ①缝边的人. ②(缝纫机的)翻边装置.
hemo- *comb. f.* 表示"血": *hemo*lysin, *hemo*philia.
he·mo·blast [ˈhiːməblæst] *n.* = hematoblast.
he·mo·chro·ma·to·sis [ˌhiːməˌkrəuməˈtəusis] *n.* 血色素沉着病,血色沉着病.
he·mo·cy·a·nin [ˌhiːməˈsaiənin] *n.*【生化】血蓝蛋白.
he·mo·cyte [ˈhiːməsait] *n.* 血细胞,血球.
he·mo·cy·tom·e·ter [ˌhiːməusaiˈtɔmitə] *n.* 血球计数器,血球计.
he·mo·di·al·y·sis [ˌhiːməudaiˈælisis] *n.* 血渗析,血透析.
he·mo·dy·nam·ics [ˌhiːməudaiˈnæmiks] *n.*【医】血流动力学.
he·mo·flag·el·late [hiːməuˈflædʒileit] *n.*【医】血内鞭毛虫,血鞭虫.
he·mo·glo·bin [ˌhiːməuˈgləubin] *n.*【生化】血红蛋白 (= haemoglobin).
he·mo·glo·bin·u·ri·a [ˌhiːməˌgləubiˈnjuəriə]【医】血红蛋白尿. **he·mo·glo·bin·u·ric** *a.*
he·moid [ˈhiːmɔid] *a.* 血状的.
he·mo·lymph [ˈhiːməlimf] *n.*【医】血淋巴.
he·mo·ly·sin [ˌhiːməˈlaisin] *n.*【医】溶血素 (= haemolysin).
he·mol·y·sis [hiːˈmɔləsis] *n.* (*pl.* **-ses** [-siːz]) 溶血(作用),血球溶解. **he·mo·lyt·ic** [ˌhiːməˈlitik] *a.*
he·mo·lyze [ˈhiːməlaiz] *vi., vt.* (**-lyz·ed; -lyzing**) 使溶血,引起(血球)溶解.
he·mo·phil·i·a [ˌhiːməˈfiliə] *n.*【医】血友病 (= haemophilia).
he·mo·phil·i·ac [ˌhiːməˈfiliæk] *n.* 血友病患者.
he·mo·phil·ic [ˌhiːməˈfilik] *a.* ①血友病的;患血友病的. ②(某些细菌的)嗜血性的.
he·mo·phyle [ˈheməfil, -fail] *n.* = haemophyle.
he·mop·ty·sis [hiˈmɔptisis] *n.*【医】咯血.
hem·or·rhage [ˈheməridʒ] *n.* ①【医】出血 (=haemorrhage). ②〔美俚〕番茄汁. *cerebral* 脑溢血. ***have a*** ~〔美俚〕大怒,大发脾气,大为愤慨. — *vi.*【医】出血.
hem·or·rhoid [ˈhemərɔid] *n.*〔常 *pl.*〕【医】痔 (= haemorrhoid). *internal [external]* ~*s* 内[外]痔.
hem·or·rhoid·ec·to·my [ˌhemərɔiˈdektəmi] *n.* (*pl.* **-mies**)【医】痔切除术.
he·mo·sta·sia [ˌhiːməˈsteiʒiə] *n.*【医】止血(= haemostasia, hemostasis).
he·mo·sta·sis [hiˈmɔstəsis] *n.* (*pl.* **-ses** [-siːz])【医】①止血. ②止血法.
he·mo·stat [ˈhiːməstæt] *n.* 止血器(尤指止血钳,止血剂).
he·mo·stat·ic [ˌhiːməˈstætik] *a.* 能够止血的. — *n.* 止血剂 (= haemostatic).
he·mo·tox·in [ˌhiːməˈtɔksin] *n.* 红血球毒素〔能杀灭红血球的一种毒素〕. **he·mo·tox·ic** [-ˈtɔksik] *a.*
hemp [hemp] *n.* ①【植】大麻;大麻纤维. ②纤维,长纤维的植物. ③〔the ~〕由大麻制成的麻醉药 (= bhang). ④〔谑〕绞索; *gambo* ~ 洋麻. *Indian* ~ 黄麻. ~ **agrimony** 大麻叶泽兰 (*Eupatorium cannabinum*) 〔产于欧洲,原用于医药〕. ~ **hook** 砍麻刀. ~ **nettle**【植】鼬瓣花属 (*Galeopis*) 植物〔尤指黄鼬瓣花 (*Galeopsis tetrahit*), 原产欧洲〕. ~ **palm** 棕榈. ~**seed**【植】大麻子.
hemp·en [ˈhempən] *a.* 大麻(似)的;大麻制的. *a ~ collar* 绞首索.
hem·stitch [ˈhemstitʃ] *n.*【纺】花饰线迹,抽丝线迹,(布边抽丝后做成的)花边;结穗缘饰. — *vt.* 用抽丝法做(花边),在…上用抽丝法刺绣.
Hen. = Henry.
hen [hen] *n.* ①母鸡. ②雌禽;雌鱼[虾、蟹等]. ③〔俚〕(嘴碎或爱管闲事的)女人,长舌妇. *a ~ sparrow* 雌麻雀. *a ~ crab* 雌蟹. *a wet [an old]* ~〔美俚〕讨厌的人,泼妇. *a ~ on* 策划中的阴谋 (*There's a ~ on.* 其中有阴谋). ***A ~ is on.*** 有人正策划阴谋. ***as mad as a wet*** ~〔美俚〕非常生气. ***like a ~ on a hot girdle*** 象热锅上的蚂蚁,坐立不安;极为难受. ***like a ~ with one chicken*** 大惊小怪,无事忙. ***sell one's ~s on a rainy day*** 亏本出售. —*vi.* (**-nn-**)〔美俚〕(女人)聊天;散播流言蜚语. ~**-and-chickens**【植】屋顶长生花. ~ **battery** 备有分隔产卵箱的鸡舍. ~**coop** 鸡窝;〔美俚〕女生宿舍. ~**cote** 鸡棚. ~ **fruit**〔俚〕鸡蛋. ~ **harrier**【动】鸡鹞. ~**-hearted** *a.* 胆小的. ~ **house** ①家禽的笼舍. ②〔美俚〕军官俱乐部. ~ **party**〔俚〕妇女聚会. ~**roost** 鸡窝. ~ **track** 潦草难认的字. ~**-wife** *n.* 养鸡女人.
hen·bane [ˈhenbein] *n.*【植】天仙子,莨菪 (=hyoscyamus).
hen·bit [ˈhenbit] *n.*【植】宝盖草 (*Lamium amplexicaule*).
hence [hens] *ad.* ①〔古〕由是,从此;今后,此后. ②因此,所以,本来[其后动词常略去不用]. *five years ~* 五年之后. *go [pass] ~* 死. *H- with him!* 把他带走! *H- (comes) the name ...* 因此有…之名. — *int.*〔诗〕去. *Hence! [Go ~!]* 出去,走开.
hence·forth, hence·for·ward [ˈhensˈfɔːθ; ˈhensˈfɔːwəd] *ad.*〔书〕从今以后,今后.
Hench [hentʃ] *n.* 亨奇[姓氏].
hench·man [ˈhentʃmən] *n.* (*pl.* **-men**) ①亲信,心腹;(政治上的)支持者,仆从,捧场者. ②〔废〕侍从.
hendeca- *comb. f.* 表示"十一": *hendeca*gon.
hen·dec·a·gon [henˈdekəgən] *n.* 十一角形,十一边形.
hen·dec·a·he·dron [henˌdekəˈhiːdrən] *n.* (*pl.* **~s; -dra** [-drə]) 十一角体. **-a·he·dral** *a.*
hen·dec·a·syl·la·ble [henˌdekəˈsiləbl] *n.* 十一音节诗句. **-a·syl·lab·ic** [-siˈlæbik] *a., n.*
Hen·der·son [ˈhendəsn] *n.* 亨德森[姓氏].
hen·di·a·dys [henˈdaiədis] *n.*【修】重言法,重名法〔用 and 连接两名词以代替一名词及一形容词的修辞法: death and honour (= honourable death). cups and gold (= golden cups)〕.
hen·e·quen, hen·e·quin [ˈhenikin] *n.* (墨西哥产)黑纳金树;黑纳金树叶的纤维.
Hen·ley [ˈhenli] *n.* 亨里[姓氏].
hen·na [ˈhenə] *n.* ①【植】指甲花,散沫花 (*Lawsonia inermis*). ②散沫花染料〔可染指甲、头发、眼皮〕. ③棕红色. — *a.* 棕红色的. — *vt.* 用散沫花染料染(指甲等).
hen·ner·y [ˈhenəri] *n.* 家禽饲养场,养鸡场.
hen·ny [ˈheni] *a., n.* 羽毛象母鸡的(雄鸡).
hen·o·the·ism [ˈhenəθiizəm] *n.* (信仰多神中有一个主神的)单一神教.
hen·peck [ˈhenpek] *vt.* (妻)管制(丈夫).
hen·pecked [ˈhenpekt] *a.*〔口〕怕老婆的.
Hen·ri·et·ta [ˌhenriˈetə] *n.* 亨丽埃塔[女子名].
Hen·ry [ˈhenri] *n.* ①亨利[姓氏,男子名]. ②**O.** ~ 奥·亨利 (1862—1901) 美国短篇小说家〔真实姓名为 William Sydney Porter〕.

hen•ry [ˈhenri] *(pl. -ries, ~s)*【电】亨(利)〔电感单位，略作 H〕.

hent [hent] *vt. (hent; hent•ing)*〔古〕①抓住. ②领悟，理解. — *n.*〔古〕①抓住；领悟，理解. ②理解了的事物；观念；意图.

he•or•to•lo•gy [ˌhiːəˈtɔlədʒi] *n.* 宗教节日学.

HEOS = highly eccentric orbit satellite 高偏心轨道卫星.

hep[1] [hep] *n.* 野蔷薇的果实.

hep[2] [hep] *a.*〔美俚〕①懂得世故的. ②对…熟悉的，对…通晓的，对…有欣赏能力的 *(to)*. *be ~ to movies* 电影通. *put sb. ~ to* 教某人了解…. **~-cat** ①知情人. ②〔美〕爵士音乐〔摇摆舞音乐〕迷；爵士音乐大师.

hep[3] [hep] *int.* 嗜〔使步伐整齐的口令声〕.

he•par [ˈhiːpɑː] *n.* ①【解】肝. ②肝脏色的物质.

hep•a•rin [ˈhepərin] *n.*【药】肝素〔一种抗凝血药〕.

hep•a•rin•ize [ˈhepərinaiz] *vt.*【医】用肝素治疗.

hepat- *comb. f.* 表示"肝": *hepat*itis.

hep•a•tec•to•my [ˌhepəˈtektəmi] *n. (pl. -mies)*【医】肝切除术.

he•pat•ic [hiˈpætik] *a.* ①肝的，对肝有影响的. ②肝状的，肝色的. ③欧龙牙草的. *the ~ artery* 肝动脉. — *n.*【植】欧龙牙草.

he•pat•i•ca [hiˈpætikə] *n. (pl. ~s, -cae [-siː])*【植】獐耳细辛属植物.

hep•a•ti•tis [ˌhepəˈtaitis] *n.*【医】肝炎. *infectious [serum] ~* 传染性〔血清〕肝炎.

hep•a•ti•za•tion [ˌhepətaiˈzeiʃən] *n.*【医】肝样变.

hepato- *comb. f.* = hepat: *hepato*sis.

hep•a•to•fla•vin [ˌhepətəuˈfleivin] *n.*【药】核黄素.

hep•a•to•sis [ˌhepəˈtəusis] *n.*【医】肝痛，肝病.

Hep•burn [ˈhebəːn] ①赫伯恩〔姓氏〕. ② **James Curtis ~** 赫伯恩〔1815—1911，美国传教士，医生，语言学家，*Hepburn* 式日本语罗马字拼法创始人〕.

He•phaes•tus [hiˈfiːstəs]【希神】赫斐斯塔斯〔火和锻冶之神〕.

Hep•ple•white [ˈheplhwait] *n.* ①海普怀特〔姓氏〕. ②**George ~** 乔治·海普怀特〔?—1786，英国家具设计师〕. —*a.* (家具)海普怀特式的〔以纤细轻巧为其特征〕.

hepta- *comb. f.* 表示"七": *hepta*d, *hepta*gon.

hep•ta•chord [ˈheptəkɔːd] *n.* 七弦琴；【乐】七声音阶.

hep•tad [ˈheptæd] *n.* ①七个，成七的一组，成七的一套. ②【化】七价物，七价元素，七价基.

hep•ta•glot [ˈheptəglɔt] *a., n.* 用七种语言写的(书).

hep•ta•gon [ˈheptəgən] *n.* 七角形，七边形. **-al** *a.*

hep•ta•hed•ron [ˈheptəˈhedrən] *n. (pl. ~s, -dra [-drə])* 七面体. **-hed•ral** [-rəl] *a.*

hep•tam•er•ous [hepˈtæmərəs] *a.*【植】(花)七瓣的 (= 7-merous).

hep•tam•e•ter [hepˈtæmitə] *n.* 七韵步的诗. — *a.* (诗)七韵步的.

hep•tane [ˈheptein] *n.*【化】庚烷.

hep•tar•chy [ˈheptɑːki] *n.* ①〔常 H-〕【英史】(七至八世纪不列颠的盎格鲁和萨克逊人的)七王国. ②七头政治. ③【生】七原型. **-chic, -i•cal** *a.*

hep•ta•stich [ˈheptəstik] *n.* 七行诗.

Hep•ta•teuch [ˈheptətjuːk] *n.*【圣】《旧约全书》的头七卷.

hep•ta•va•lent [ˈheptəˌveilənt] *a.*【化】七价的.

hep•tode [ˈheptəud] *n.*【无】七极管.

hep•tose [ˈheptəus] *n.*【化】庚糖.

heptr =【空】helicopter.

her〔常 həː；弱əː, hə, ə〕*pro.* ①〔she 的宾格〕她. ②〔*she* 的所有格〕她的. ③〔古、诗〕〔作反身代名词用〕= herself. ④〔口〕〔作表语用〕= she. *Give it to ~.* 把这个给她. *I am sorry about her leaving.* 我对她的离去很感遗憾. *It's ~, sure enough.* 一定是她. *Her sister sews better than ~.* 她姐姐比她缝衣服的手艺高. *She sat ~ down by the fire.* 她在炉火旁边坐下.

her. = heraldic; heraldry.

He•ra [ˈhiərə] *n.*【希神】赫拉〔天后，主神宙斯 (Zeus) 之妻〕.

Her•a•cles, Her•a•kles [ˈherəkliːz] *n.* = Hercules.

Her•a•cli•tus [ˌherəˈklaitəs] 赫拉克利特〔535?—475 B.C.?，希腊哲学家〕.

her•ald [ˈherəld] *n.* ①(旧时的)传令官. ②(英国中世纪司宗谱纹章的)纹章官. ③通报者；使者；先驱，预兆. *The cuckoo is a ~ of spring.* 杜鹃是春天的先驱. ***the Heralds' College***〔英〕宗谱纹章院. — *vt.* ①传达，通告. ②预告，预示…的到来. ③欢呼. *The song of birds ~s the approach of spring.* 百鸟齐鸣报春到.

he•ral•dic [heˈrældik] *a.* ①传令官的. ②纹章官的. ③纹章学的. **-di•cal•ly** *ad.*

her•ald•ry [ˈherəldri] *n.* ①宗谱纹章官的职位〔职权〕；宗谱记录法. ②纹章学；〔集合词〕纹章，家徽. ③〔诗〕(仪式等的)壮观，豪华.

herb [həːb] *n.* ①草，草本植物. ②茎叶可作药品、食品、香料等的植物；香草，药草. ③牧草. *No ~ will cure love.*〔谚〕相思病无药可医. *the ~ of grace* 芸香. *medicinal ~s* 药草，草药. **~ beer** 草药制的饮料. **~ doctor** 草药医生. **~ Paris** 轮叶王孙 *(Paris quadrifolia)*〔一种百合科植物〕. **~ Robert**【植】罗伯特氏老鹳草 *(Geranium robertianum)*. **~ tea, ~ water** (草药煎成的)汤药. **-less** *a.* 缺乏草本植物的.

her•ba•ceous [həːˈbeiʃəs] *a.* ①草本的；草质的. ②(颜色、纹理、形状等)似绿叶的，叶状的. *a ~ border* (花园沿边)种草本植物的花坛. *a ~ root [stem]* 草质根〔茎〕.

herb•age [ˈhəːbidʒ] *n.* ①〔集合词〕草本植物 (尤指牧草). ②(草的)茎叶. ③【法】(在他人土地上的)放牧权.

herb•al [ˈhəːbəl] *a.* 草本植物的，草本植物制的. — *n.* ①草药书. ②〔古〕草本志；草本植物志. ③植物标本. **-ist** *n.* ①草本植物学家. ②草药采集人；种草药的人. ③草药商. ④草药医生.

her•bar•i•um [həːˈbɛəriəm] *(pl. -ri•a [-riə], ~s) n.* ①植物标本集. ②植物标本箱；植物标本室. ③蜡叶标本.

Her•bart [ˈhəːbɑːt] ①赫巴特〔姓氏〕. ② **Johann Friedrich ~** 约翰·弗里德里克·赫巴特〔1776—1841，德国哲学家，教育家〕.

Her•bart•i•an [ˈhəːbɑːtiən] *a.* 赫巴特(学派)的.

Her•bart•i•an•ism [həːˈbɑːtiənizəm] 赫巴特的教育说.

herb•ar•y [ˈhəːbəri] *n.* ①= herbarium. ②草本植物园，药草园.

Her•bert [ˈhəːbət] *n.* 赫伯特〔姓氏，男子名〕.

her•bi•cide [ˈhəːbisaid] *n.*【生化】除莠剂. **-dal** *a.*

her•bif•er•ous [həːˈbifərəs] *a.* 生草的.

her•bi•vore [ˈhəːbivɔː] *n.*〔F.〕食草动物.

her•biv•o•rous [həːˈbivərəs] *a.* ①吃草的. ②身体粗大而肠子细长的. *~ animals* 食草动物.

her•bo•ri•za•tion [ˌhəːbəraiˈzeiʃən] *n.* 植物采集，药草收集.

her•bo•rize [ˈhəːbəraiz] *vi.* 采集植物〔药草〕.

herb•y [ˈhəːbi] *a.* ①草的，草本的. ②草多的，长满草的.

Her•cu•le•an [ˌhəːkjuːˈljən] *a.* ①【希、罗神】赫尔克里斯的，大力神的. ②力大无比的. ③费力的，非常困难的. *a ~ labour* 艰巨的劳动. *a ~ warrior* 魁梧的战士.

Her•cu•les [ˈhəːkjuliːz] *n.* ①【希、罗神】赫尔克里斯，大力神〔主神宙斯之子，力大无比的英雄〕. ②〔h-〕大力士. ③〔the ~〕【天】武仙座. *a regular ~* 大力士. **~'s choice** 宁可吃苦，不愿享乐. ***the Pillars of ~ = ~s' Pillars*** 世界的尽头；直布罗陀海峡两岸的悬岩. **~ beetle** 大金龟子〔南美大甲虫〕. **~ powder** 矿山炸药. **~s'-club** *n.*【植】①多刺楤木 *(Aralia spinosa)*

〔产于美国东部，即土当归属〕. ②美国南部刺椒 *(Zanthoxylum clava-herculis)*.

herd[1] [hə:d] *n.* ①兽群,牛群,猪群. ②〔the ～〕〔蔑〕群众,民众. ***ride ～ on*** ①骑在马上放牧(畜群). ②监督、管束 *(ride ～ on the children* 管束小孩子们). —*vt.* 把…赶在一块. —*vi.* 成群,群集 *(with; together)*. ～ **book** 家畜血统记录. ～ **instinct**【心】群居本能.

herd[2] [hə:d] *n.* 牧人. 〔通例用作复合词: cow*herd*, shep*herd*, swine*herd*〕. —*vt.* 看管(家畜),放牧.

herd·er [ˈhə:də] *n.* ① =herdsman. ②〔美俚〕监狱看守.

her·dic [ˈhə:dik] *n.* 赫狄克式马车〔由 P. Herdic 发明,为二轮或四轮的低矮马车,座位在两边,门在背后〕.

herd's-grass [ˈhə:dzgrɑ:s] *n.* ① = redtop. ②= timothy.

herds·man [ˈhə:dzmən] *(pl. -men) n.* ①〔英〕牧人. ②畜群所有者. ③〔the H-〕【天】牧夫座 (= Boötes).

here [hiə] *ad.* ①在这里; 到这里; 向这里〔*cf.* there〕. ②在这一点上; 这时. ③【宗】在这个世界上, 在尘世间. ④这里〔用于唤起注意或加强语气, 用在名词之后〕. *H- I am.* 我来了,我到了. *H- I come, honey.*〔美口〕喂. *H- it is.* ①在这里. ②这是给你的. *H-'s sth. for you.* 这一点点东西是送你的. *My friend ～ knows it.* 我这里的朋友懂得它. ***belong ～*** 此地人,当地人. ***～ and now*** 就在此时此地. ***～ and there*** 各处; 零零落落地. ***～ below*** 在尘世间. ***H- goes!***〔口〕啊,开始吧! 这就动手吧! ***～, there and everywhere*** 到处. ***H- is to you!= H- is to your health!*** 祝您健康! 敬您一杯! ***～ today and gone tomorrow*** 行踪不定,飘忽无常. ***H- you are.***〔口〕①你要的[找的]东西在这里呢. ②(你)已经到了. ***look [see] ～***〔口〕听我说. ***neither ～ nor there***〔口〕与本题无关,没有什么,不中肯. ***same ～***〔口〕彼此彼此,我也一样. ***this ～ [ere] man***〔卑〕= ***this man ～***. (这儿的)这个人,就是这个人. —*n.* 这里; 这一点. ***from ～*** 从这里. ***in ～*** 在这里,在这一点上. ***near ～*** 在这附近. ***up to ～*** 到这里. —*int.* ①〔唤人注意的话〕喂! ②〔点名时的回答〕到! 有!

here·a·bout(s) [ˈhiərəbaut(s)] *ad.* 在这附近.

here·af·ter [hiərˈɑ:ftə] *ad.* ①今后, 以后, 此后. ②在来世. —*n.* ①将来. ②【宗】来世.

here·at [hiərˈæt] *ad.*〔古〕由是,因此.

here·a·way(s) [ˈhiərəˈwei(z)] *ad.* 在这附近.

here·by [ˈhiəˈbai] *ad.* ①兹,特此; 以此〔公文、布告等用语〕. ②〔废〕附近. *Notice is ～ given that …* 特此布告. *I ～ resign my office.* 特此辞职.

he·re·des [həˈri:di:z] *n.* heres 的复数.

he·red·i·ta·bil·i·ty [hiˌreditəˈbility] *n.* =heretability.

he·red·i·ta·ble [həˈreditəbl] *a.* = heritable.

her·e·dit·a·ment [ˌheriˈditəmənt] *n.* ①【法】世袭财产; 不动产. ②继承.

he·red·i·tar·i·an [hiˌrediˈtɛəriən] *n.* 遗传论者, 信奉遗传说的人.

he·red·i·tar·i·ly [hiˈrediterili] *ad.* 世袭地; 遗传地.

he·red·i·tar·y [hiˈreditəri] *a.* ①遗传的,遗传性的. ②【法】世袭的. ～ *characters* 遗传特征. ～ *diseases* 遗传病. *a ～ enemy* 世仇. *a ～ feud* 宿怨. ～ *friendship* 世交. ～ *property* 世袭财产.

he·red·i·tism [hiˈreditizəm] *n.* 遗传学.

he·red·i·ty [hiˈrediti] *n.* ①遗传; 遗传性. ②遗传性特征. ③继承; 传统.

Her·e·ford [ˈherifəd] *n.* ①(英国)赫勒福德郡. ②赫勒福德种牛. —*a.* 赫勒福德牛的.

here·from [hiəˈfrɔm] *ad.* 由此.

here·in [ˈhiərˈin] *ad.* 此中; 于此, 据此看来. *H- lies the answer.* 答案就在这里. *by the clauses ～* 根据(本约)所列条款.

here·in·a·bove [ˌhiərinəˈbʌv] *ad.* 在上文.

here·in·af·ter [ˈhiərinˈɑ:ftə] *ad.* 在下文,以下. ～ *called Buyer* 以下统称买方.

here·in·be·fore [ˈhiərinbiˈfɔ:] *ad.* 在上文,以上.

here·in·be·low [ˈhiərinbiˈləu] *ad.* 在下文.

here·in·to [ˈhiərˈintu] *ad.* 到这里面.

here·of [hiərˈɔv] *ad.* ①关于这个. ②本, 此. *upon the receipt ～* 据此收条. *more ～ later* (关于这一点) 详见后文.

here·on [hiərˈɔn] *ad.* = hereupon.

he·res [ˈhiəri:z] *n. (pl.* ***he·re·des*** [hiˈri:di:z]*)*【法】继承人.

here's [hiəz] = here is. *Here's to you!* 干杯, 祝你成功! 祝你愉快! 〔祝酒词〕.

he·re·si·arch [həˈri:ziɑ:k] *n.* 异教祖师; 异教首领.

her·e·sy [ˈherəsi] *n.* ①异教,异端. ②左道邪说; 信奉异端邪说. ***be guilty of ～*** 犯异端邪说罪. ***fall into ～*** 陷入旁门左道.

her·e·tic [ˈherətik] *n.* ①异教徒. ②持有非正统见解的人; 信奉邪说的人. —*a.* = heretical.

he·ret·i·cal [hiˈretikəl] *a.* 异教的,异端的. **-ly** *ad.*

here·to [ˈhiəˈtu:] *ad.*〔古〕到此时; 到此地; 至此; 关于这个. *annexed ～* 并入于此.

here·to·fore [ˌhiətəˈfɔ:] *ad.* 前此,以前,迄今为止.

here·un·der [hiərˈʌndə] *ad.* ①在下面,在下(文). ②依此. *articles enumerated ～* 下列商品.

here·up·on [ˌhiərəˈpɔn] *ad.* ①于是. ②关于这.

here·with [hiəˈwið] *ad.* ①同此,并此〔信中用语〕. ②以此方法. *enclosed ～* 并此附上. *I am sending you ～ a cheque.* 现附上支票一张.

her·i·ot [ˈheriət] *n.*【英法】租地继承税〔指依据英国封建时代法律规定,佃农死时向地主交纳的钱款或实物〕.

her·it·a·ble [ˈheritəbl] *a.* ①被继承的; 可继承的. ②被遗传的; 可遗传的. **-i·ta·bil·i·ty** *n.* 遗传率, 遗传力. **-a·bly** *ad.*

her·it·age [ˈheritidʒ] *n.* ①世袭财产. ②(长子)继承权. ③继承物; 遗产; 传统. ④(犹太教圣经中所说的)上帝的选民.

her·i·tance [ˈheritəns] *n.*〔古〕= inheritance.

her·i·tor [ˈheritə] *n. (fem. -tress* [-tris]*)* 继承人.

herl [hə:l] *n.* ①(做假蚊钩的) 蚊羽细毛. ②用细羽毛做成的假蚊钩.

Her·man(n) [ˈhə:mən] *n.* 赫尔曼〔男子名〕.

her·maph·ro·dite [hə:ˈmæfrədait] *n.* ①阴阳人, 两性人. ②两性体; 【动】雌雄同体; 【植】雌雄同株. —*a.* 具有两性的,具有相反性质的. ～ **brig**【海】双桅帆船.

her·maph·ro·dit·ic(al) [hə:ˌmæfrəˈditik(əl)] *a.* 雌雄同体〔同株〕的; 具有相反两种性质的. **-i·cal·ly** *ad.*

her·maph·ro·dit·ism [hə:ˈmæfrədaitizəm] *n.* 两性体,雌雄同体〔同株〕.

her·me·neu·tic(al) [ˌhə:miˈnju:tik(əl)] *a.* (圣经) 解释(学)的; 释经学的. —*n.*〔*pl.*〕释经学; 圣经注解学.

HERMES = Heavy Element Radioactive Material Electromagnetic Separator 重放射性同位素电磁分离器.

Her·mes [ˈhə:mi:z]【希神】赫耳墨斯〔为众神传信并掌管商业、道路的神〕.

her·met·ic(al) [hə:ˈmetik(əl)] *a.* ①〔H-〕海尔梅斯神的〔埃及神 Thoth 的希腊名称为 Hermes Trismegistus, 据说为炼丹术始祖〕. ②炼金术的, 奥妙的. ③密闭的, 密封的. *the H- art [philosophy, science]* 炼金术. ～ **sealing**【冶】熔接密闭.

her·met·i·cal·ly [hə:ˈmetikəli] *ad.* 密封地,密闭地; 牢牢地.

her·mit [ˈhə:mit] *n.* ①隐者, 逸士. ②(加有葡萄干、核桃、香精的)小甜饼. ③【动】独居性动物. ④【动】(热带森林中的)蜂鸟. *a false ～* 寄居蟹的一种. ***go ～***〔美〕过孤独的生活. ～ **crab**【动】寄居蟹. ～ **thrush**【动】

北美隐居鸫 *(Hylocichla guttata)*. ~ **warbler**【动】森莺 *(Dendroica occidentalis)*〔产于北美西部，头部黑黄色，灰背〕.

her·mit·age [ˈhəːmitidʒ] *n.* ①隐士住处，茅庐，僻静的住处；修道院. ②隐士生活. ③〔H-〕法国南部产的一种红葡萄酒. ④〔H-〕苏联列宁格勒的一所博物馆.

hern[1] [həːn] *n.* 〔英方〕苍鹭 = heron.

hern[2], **her'n** [həːn] *pro.* 〔方〕 = hers, her own.

her·ni·a [ˈhəːnjə] *n. (pl. ~s, -ni·ae* [-niiː]*)* 【医】疝，突出.

her·ni·al [ˈhəːnjəl] *a.* 疝的.

her·ni·ar·y [ˈhəːnjəri] *a.* (治)疝的.

her·ni·ate [ˈhəːnieit] *vi.* 【医】形成疝. **-ni·a·tion** *n.*

her·ni·or·rha·phy [ˌhəːniˈɔːrəfi] *n. (pl. -phies)* 【医】疝缝术.

hern·shaw [ˈhəːnʃɔː] *n.* 〔方〕【动】苍鹭.

he·ro [ˈhiərəu] *n. (pl. ~es)*. ①英雄，豪杰，勇士. ②(古代神话中的)神人，半神的勇士. ③(小说等的)男主角，男主人公〔*fem.* heroine〕. ~ ***of the quill*** 著名作家，文坛健将. ~ ***of the spigot***〔谑〕酒鬼. ***make a ~ of*** 赞扬，捧，使英雄化. ~ **sandwich** "英雄"三明治〔夹着各种冷肉、奶酪和蔬菜的面包卷〕. ~ **worship** 英雄崇拜；对个人的盲目崇拜. **~-worship** *vt.* 把…当作英雄崇拜. **~-worship(p)er** 英雄崇拜者.

Her·od [ˈherəd] 【圣】(以残暴著称的犹太国王)希律王. ***out-herod*** ~ 比希律王更希律王，比希律王还要残暴.

He·rod·o·tus [hiˈrɔdətəs] 希罗多德〔公元前 484?—425?，纪元前 5 世纪希腊历史学家，有历史之父之称〕.

he·ro·ic [hiˈrəuik] *a.* ①英雄的，勇士的；神人的，超人的. ②英勇的，壮烈的；强大的，崇高的；冒险的，果断的. ③(语言)夸张的，高雅的，〔诗〕歌颂英雄的；史诗般的. ④(声音)宏大的，(雕像等)大于实物的. ⑤(措施等)冒险的；(药物)剂量大的，猛烈的. ~ *conduct [deeds]* 英雄行为. *a ~ drug* 烈性麻醉品. ~ *measures* 冒险的措施. ~ *medicine* 烈性的药；剂量大的药. ~ *poetry* 英雄诗，史诗. ~ *size [on a ~ scale]* 大于实物的尺寸. ***the ~ age*** 古希腊的"英雄时代". — *n.* ①英雄诗，史诗. ②〔*pl.*〕夸张的言行. ③咬文嚼字，文诌诌. ***go into ~s*** 过于夸张. ~ **couplet** 英雄偶句诗体〔互相押韵，含有抑扬音步的两行诗. 乔叟首先在英诗中采用〕. ~ **line**, ~ **metre**, ~ **verse** 英雄诗体. ~ **tenor** 英雄男高音，华格纳歌剧男高音.

he·ro·i·cal [hiˈrəuikəl] *a.* = heroic*(a.)* **-ly** *ad.*

he·ro·i·com·ic(al) [hiˌrəuiˈkɔmik(əl)] *a.* (诗、故事等)滑稽史诗体的，壮烈而滑稽的〔一种以史诗体来歌颂卑微或滑稽事物的讽刺性文体〕.

he·ro·i·fy [hiˈrəuifai] *vt.* 使英雄化.

her·o·in [ˈherəuin] *n.* 【药】海洛因，二乙酰吗啡.

her·o·ine [ˈherəuin] *n.* ①女英雄. ②烈女，烈妇. ③半神式的女英雄. ④(小说等中的)女主角，女主人公.

her·o·ism [ˈherəuizəm] *n.* ①英雄气概，英雄行为，英雄品质. ②英雄主义.

her·o·ize [ˈhiərəuaiz] *vt.* 把…英雄化. — *vi.* 以英雄自居.

her·on [ˈherən] *n. (pl. ~(s))*【动】苍鹭.

her·on·ry [ˈherənri] *n.* 苍鹭的巢穴.

her·ons·bill [ˈherənzbil] *n.*【植】牻牛儿苗属 (Erodium) 植物.

her·pes [ˈhəːpiːz] *n.* 【医】疱疹. ~ **simplex**【医】单纯疱疹. ~ **zoster**【医】带状疱疹.

her·pet·ic [həːˈpetik] *a.* 【医】疱疹性的.

her·pe·tol·o·gy [ˌhəːpiˈtɔlədʒi] *n.* 爬虫学.

Herr [hεə] *n. (pl. Her·ren* [ˈhɛrən]*)* 〔G.〕 ①先生〔与英语 Mr. 相当〕. ②德国绅士. *Meine Herren* 各位(先生)，诸位(先生).

Her·ren·volk [ˈhɛrənfɔlk] *n.* 〔G.〕 统治民族.

Her·rick [ˈherik] *n.* 赫里克〔姓氏〕.

her·ring [ˈheriŋ] *n. (pl. ~s,* 〔集合词〕 *~)* 鲱鱼，鲭白鱼. *a red ~ = kippered ~* 熏鲱鱼. ***as dead as a ~*** 死得象鲱鱼一样僵硬. ***be packed as close as ~s*** 挤得象罐头里的鲱鱼. ***draw a red ~ across the path [track, trail]*** 扯些不相干的事转移别人的注意力. ***like ~s in a barrel*** 挤在一起. ***neither fish, flesh, nor good red ~*** 非驴非马，不伦不类；不相干的东西. ***shotten ~*** 产过卵的鲱鱼，废物. ***the king of the ~s*** 月鱼. ~ **gull**【动】(北大西洋产的)大海鸥. **~-pond** ①海洋. ②〔谑〕北大西洋.

her·ring·bone [ˈheriŋbəun] *n.* ①【建】(砖、石头等砌成)鲱骨(式)；人字形. ②【纺】海力蒙(衣服)，人字呢(衣服). — *a.* 鲱骨状的；人字形的. — *vt.* 把…作成人字形，在…上作交叉缝式；在…上作矢尾形(接合). — *vi.* ①作成人字形；作交叉缝式，作矢尾形接合. ②【滑雪】滑橇尖向外作人字形爬坡. ~ **bridging** 人字撑. ~ **earth**【电】鱼骨形接地. ~ **gear** 人字形齿轮，双螺旋齿轮. ~ **pavement**【建】人字式(铺砌)路面. ~ **stitch**【纺】人字形缝，缝成人字形的图案. ~ **tooth** 人字齿，双螺旋齿.

hers [həːz] *pro.* 〔she 的物主代词〕她的，她的东西，她的家属〔有关的人〕. *Is that his or ~?* 那是他的还是她的? *H- is better than mine.* 她的比我的好. *Give my best wishes to her and ~.* 问候她和她的家人〔爱人、朋友等〕. *This seems to be a hat of ~.* 这好象是她的帽子. ***his and ~*** 丈夫和妻子；男男女女.

Her·schel(l) [ˈhəːʃəl] *n.* ①赫谢尔〔姓氏，男子名〕. ② **Sir John William** ~ 小约翰·威廉·赫谢耳〔1792—1871，英国天文学家、哲学家〕. ③**Sir William** ~老赫谢耳〔1738—1822，英国天文学家小赫谢耳之父，天王星的发现者〕. ④天王星的别名. ⑤【物】赫谢耳〔光源的辐射亮度单位〕.

her·self [həːˈself, həˈself] *pro. (pl. themselves)* ①〔作反身代词〕她自己. *She ought to be ashamed of ~.* 她应当感到羞愧. *She killed ~.* 她自杀了. ②〔加强语气〕她本人，她亲自. *She said it ~.* 她自己说的. *H- an orphan, she understood the situation.* 她本身是个孤儿，理解这情况. ***be [become, come to] ~*** (情绪、健康)处于正常情况 *(She is not quite ~ today.* 她今天有些反常〔不舒服〕. *She has come to ~.* 她已复原了，她已恢复正常). ***(all) by ~*** 她独自地；她独立地.

Her·sey [ˈhəːsi] *n.* 赫西〔姓氏〕.

Hert·er [ˈhəːtə] *n.* 赫脱〔姓氏〕.

hertz [həːts] *n.*【电】赫，赫兹〔频率单位；周/秒〕.

Hertz [həːts], **Hein·rich Ru·dolph**, 赫兹〔1857—1894，德国物理学家〕.

Hertz·i·an [ˈhəːtsiən] *a.* 赫兹的. ~ **wave** 赫兹电波〔德国物理学家 H. Hertz 所发现的电磁波〕.

Her·ze·go·vi·na [ˌhεətsəgəuˈviːnə] *n.* 黑塞哥维那〔南斯拉夫一地区〕.

he's [常 hiːz; 弱 hiz, iz] = he is; he has.

Hesh·van [heʃˈvɑːn, Eng. ˈheʃvən] *n.* 〔Heb.〕 犹太历二月.

hes·i·tance, hes·i·tan·cy [ˈhezitəns] *n.* 踌躇，犹豫 (= hesitation).

hes·i·tant [ˈhezitənt] *a.* ①踌躇的，犹豫的. ②吞吞吐吐的. **-ly** *ad.*

hes·i·tate [ˈheziteit] *vi.* ①犹豫，踌躇；不愿. ②含糊，支吾. ③口吃. ~ *about joining the expedition.* 他对于是否参加远征队犹豫不决. ~ *between fighting and submitting* 或战或降，踌躇不决. ~ *to take such a big risk.* 不愿冒这样大的险. ~ *in speaking* 说话吞吞吐吐. *They ~d at nothing to gain their ends.* 他们不惜一切来达到目的. *If there is anything you want, please don't ~ to ask me.* 你要是需要什么，请别客气问我要好了. *I don't ~ to say that* 长话短说〔开门见山〕. ***He who ~s is lost.*** 〔谚〕当断不断，必受其患.

hes·i·tat·ing·ly [ˈheziˌteitiŋli] *ad.* 踌躇地，犹豫地，含糊地.

hes·i·ta·tion [ˌheziˈteiʃən] *n.* ①踌躇，犹豫. ②含糊. ③口吃. ***have no ~ in saying*** 毫不踌躇地说. ***without ~*** 毫不踌躇地，立即.

hes·i·ta·tive [ˈhezitətiv] *a.* 踌躇的. **-ly** *ad.*

Hes·per [ˈhespə] *n.* 〔诗〕 = Hesperus.

Hes·pe·ri·an [hesˈpiəriən] *a.* 〔诗〕西方的，西方国家的. — *n.* 西方国家的人.

Hes·per·ides [hesˈperidiːz] *n. pl.* ①【希神】看守金苹果乐园的四姊妹. ②〔作 sing. 用〕金苹果园.

hes·per·i·din [hesˈperidin] *n.* 【化】桔皮苷.

hes·per·i·di·um [ˌhespəˈridiəm] *n. (pl. **-di·a*** [-ə]*)* 柑桔属植物的果实〔如桔或柠檬〕，柑果，柠檬果.

hes·per·or·nis [ˌhespəˈrɔːnis] *n.* 【古生】黄昏鸟〔美洲大陆产〕.

Hes·per·us [ˈhespərəs] *n.* 【天】金星，长庚星.

Hess [hes] *n.* 赫斯〔姓氏〕.

Hes·se, Hes·sen [ˈhesi, -sn] *n.* 黑森〔德意志联邦共和国州名〕.

Hes·sian [ˈhesiən] *a.* (德国)黑森州的. — *n.* ①黑森人. ②〔美〕美独立战争时英军中的德国雇佣兵；雇佣兵；为金钱而听人使唤的人；流氓. ③〔h-〕打包麻布. **~ boots** (黑森士兵穿的)膝前有饰縫的长靴. **~ fly** 麦蝇〔麦的害虫，似蚊〕.

hess·ite [ˈhesait] *n.* 【矿】蹄银矿.

hes·so·nite [ˈhesənait] *n.* 【矿】钙铝榴石 (=essonite).

hest [hest] *n.* 〔古〕 = behest.

Hes·ter [ˈhestə] *n.* 赫丝特〔女子名，Esther 的异体〕.

Hes·ti·a [ˈhestiə] *n.* 【希神】赫斯提〔灶神或炉神〕.

het[1] [het] *a.* 〔美，英方〕 = heated. ***~ up*** 兴奋，激动，勃然大怒.

het[2]**, heth** [het] *n.* 希伯来文的第八个字母.

hetae·ra [hiˈtiərə] *n. (pl. **-rae*** [-riː]*)* = hetaira.

he·tae·rism [hiˈtiərizəm] *n.* = hetairism.

he·tai·ra [hiˈtairə] *n. (pl. **-rai*** [-rai]*)* ①(古代希腊的)妾；妓女，艺妓. ②依靠美色获取财富、社会地位的女子. **-ric** *a.*

he·tai·rism [hiˈtairizəm] *n.* ①【考古】(同部族内的)乱婚；杂婚. ②公开蓄妾.

heter(o) *-comb. f.* 表示"异"，"异型"，"其他"〔元音前用 heter-〕: *heterogen.*

het·er·o [ˈhetərəu] *a.* 〔美俚〕向异性的，非同性爱的. — *n.* 非同性恋者.

het·er·o·aux·in [ˌhetərəuˈɔːksin] *n.* 【化】吲哚乙酸，异茁长素.

het·er·o·cer·cal [ˌhetərəˈsɔːkl] *a.* 【动】歪尾的〔尤指鲨鱼〕.

het·er·o·charge [ˈhetərəutʃɑːdʒ] *n.* 【物】混杂电荷.

het·er·o·chro·mat·ic [ˌhetərəukrəuˈmætik] *a.* ①异色的，有异色的；包含不同颜色的；多色的. ②【生】异染色质的.

het·er·o·chro·ma·tin [ˌhetərəuˈkrəumətin] *n.* 【生】异染色质.

het·er·o·chro·mo·some [ˌhetərəuˈkrəuməsəum] *n.* 【生】异染色体 (= sex chromosome).

het·er·o·chro·mous [ˌhetərəuˈkrəuməs] *a.* 【生】异色的，不同色的.

het·er·o·clite [ˈhetərəuklait] *n.* ①【语法】不规则的词(尤指名词). ②违反一般规则的人〔事〕. — *a.* 不规则的，变态的. ***~ nouns [verbs]*** 不规则名词〔动词〕.

het·er·o·cot·y·lus [ˌhetərəuˈkɔtləs] *n. (pl. **-y·li*** [-ai]*)* = hectocotylus.

het·er·o·cy·cle [ˈhetərəusaikl] *n.* 【化】杂环.

het·er·o·cy·clic [ˌhetərəuˈsaiklik] *a.* 【化】杂环型的.

het·er·o·cyst [ˈhetərəusist] *n.* 【生】异形细胞.

het·er·o·des·mic [ˌhetərəuˈdesmik] *a.* 【物】杂键的.

het·er·o·dox [ˈhetərəudɔks] *a.* ①异端的；异教的. ②违反共认标准的.

het·er·o·dox·y [ˈhetərəudɔksi] *n. (pl. **-dox·ies**)* ①异端. ②异教；异说.

het·er·o·dyne [ˈhetərəudain] *n.* 【无】外差法. — *a.* 【无】外差法的，成拍的. — *vt., vi.* (使)成拍，(使)致差，(使…)混合. **~ oscillator** 外差振荡器. **~ receiver** 外差式收音机.

het·er·oe·cism [ˌhetəˈriːsizəm] *n.* 【植】转主寄生(现象).

het·er·o·ga·mete [ˌhetərəugəˈmiːt] *n.* 【生】异形配子.

het·er·og·a·mous [ˌhətəˈrɔgəməs] *a.* ①【生】由异形配子生殖的 *(opp.* isogamous*)*. ②【植】有异性花的 *(opp.* homogamous*)*.

het·er·o·gen [ˈhetərəudʒen] *n.* 【生】异基因.

het·er·o·ge·ne·i·ty [ˌhetərəudʒiˈniːiti] *n.* ①【生】异质性. ②【化】不均匀性. ③【数】不纯一性.

het·er·o·ge·ne·ous [ˈhetərəuˈdʒiːniəs] *a.* ①异种的，异类的. ②异质的，不纯的，成分复杂的 *(opp.* homogeneous*)*. ③【数】非齐次〔性〕的，参差的，不纯一的. ④【化】不均匀的，多相的. ***a ~ light*** 杂色光. **-ly** *ad.*

het·er·o·gen·e·sis [ˌhetərəuˈdʒenisis] *n.* 【生】异型有性世代交替；突变.

het·er·o·ge·net·ic [ˌhetərəudʒiˈnetik] *a.* 【生】异源的.

het·er·og·e·nous [ˌhetəˈrɔdʒinəs] *a.* 【生，医】异源的，异种的，异体的.

het·er·og·o·ny [ˌhetəˈrɔgəni] *n.* ①【生】世代交替 (= alternation of generations). ②【植】花柱异长 (= heterostyly). ③形体变异学 (=Allometry). **-o·nous** [-nəs] *a.*

het·er·o·graft [ˈhetərəuˈgrɑːft] *n.* 【医】异质移植物.

het·er·og·ra·phy [ˌhetəˈrɔgrəfi] *n.* 【语】①同一字母的不同发音. ②同一词的非标准拼法.

het·er·og·y·nous [ˌhetəˈrɔdʒinəs] *a.* (蜜蜂、蚁等)有生殖和不生殖两种雌性的.

het·er·o·lec·i·thal [ˌhetərəuˈlesiθəl] *n.* 【生】异卵黄.

het·er·ol·o·gous [ˌhetəˈrɔləgəs] *a.* ①【生】异素的，异种的. ②【医】异种的，异质的；异要素的. ③不齐的；不等的；不同的. **-o·lo·gy** [-ˈrɔlədʒi] *n.*

het·er·ol·y·sis [ˌhetəˈrɔlisis] *n.* 【生化】①异种溶解. ②异种血解；异族溶解. **-o·lyt·ic** [-əˈlitik] *a.*

het·er·o·me·tab·o·lism [ˌhetərəumiˈtæbəlizəm] *n.* 【动】不全变态. **-o·met·a·bol·ic** [-ˌmetəˈbɔlik], **-o·me·tab·o·lous** [-miˈtæbələs] *a.*

het·er·o·mor·phic [ˌhetərəuˈmɔːfik] *a.* ①【生】异形的，异态的；【虫】完全变态的. ②【化】多晶(型)的. ③【物】复形性的.

het·er·o·mor·phism [ˌhetərəuˈmɔːfizəm] *n.* ①【生】异态性，异态现象. ②【化】多晶(型)现象. ③【物】复形性，复型性.

het·er·o·mor·phy [ˈhetərəuˌmɔːfi] *n.* 【生】异态性，异态现象.

het·er·on·o·mous [ˌhetəˈrɔnəməs] *a.* ①受外界支配的，他治的，不自治的. ②【生】异律的 *(opp.* autonomous*)*；发展规律不同的，不同于一般形态的，形态互异的.

het·er·on·o·my [ˌhetəˈrɔnəmi] *n.* ①他治，不自治，无自由权〔自决权〕的状态. ②【生】异律 *(opp.* autonomy*)*.

het·er·o·nym [ˈhetərənim] *n.* ①同形异音异义词〔如读音为 [led] 的 lead (铅)和读音为 [liːd] 的 lead (领导)〕. ②(两种语言中的)对译同义词.

het·er·on·y·mous [ˌhetəˈrɔniməs] *a.* ①同形异音义词的；同形异音义词性的. ②不同名称的〔指一对关连词〕. ③(视平行线焦点外)影像交叉的. *Son and daughter are ~.* 儿子和女儿是名称不同的一对关连词. **-y·mous·ly** *ad.*

het·er·op·a·thy [ˌhetəˈrɔpəθi] *n.* 【医】对症疗法，对抗

疗法；反应性异常.

het·er·o·phil [ˈhetərəfil] *a.*【生】(红血球的) 嗜异染性的.

het·er·oph·o·bi·a [ˌhetərəuˈfəubiə] *n.* 异性恐怖症.

het·er·oph·o·ny [ˌhetəˈrɔfəni] *n.*【乐】离开同音的声部；(一个声部外所加的) 装饰音声部；(非复调的) 多声部.

het·er·o·pho·ri·a [ˌhetərəuˈfəuriə] *n.*【物】隐斜视.

het·er·o·phyl·lous [ˌhetərəuˈfiləs] *a.*【植】具异形叶的. **-phyl·ly** *ad.*

het·er·o·phyte [ˈhetərəufait] *n.*【植】异养植物. **-phyt·ic** [-ˈfitik] *a.*

het·er·o·plas·ty [ˈhetərəuˌplæsti] *n.*【医】异质成形术. **-plas·tic** *a.*

het·er·o·ploid [ˈhetərəuplɔid] *a.*【生】异倍体的. **-ploi·dy** *n.*

het·er·o·po·lar [ˌhetərəuˈpəulə] *a.*【物】异极的.

het·er·o·po·lar·i·ty [ˌhetərəupəuˈlæriti] *n.*【物】异极性.

het·er·op·ter·ous [ˌhetəˈrɔptərəs] *a.*【动】①半翅的；异翅的. ②异翅目的 (= hemipterous).

het·er·o·sex·u·al [ˌhetərəuˈseksjuəl] *a.* ①异性爱的 *(opp.* homosexual*)*. ②不同性别的. *a* ～ *flock of ducklings* 一群雌雄夹杂的小鸭. ～ *twins* 孪生兄妹，孪生姐弟. — *n.* 异性爱者.

het·er·o·sex·u·al·i·ty [ˌhetərəuˌseksjuˈæliti] *n.* 异性爱.

het·er·o·sis [ˌhetəˈrəusis] *n.*【遗传】杂种优势. **-ot·ic** *a.*

het·er·o·sphere [ˈhetərəusfiə] *n.*【气】非均质层. **-o·spher·ic** [-ˈsfɛərik] *a.*

het·er·os·po·rous [ˌhetəˈrɔspərəs, ˌhetərəuˈspɔːrəs] *a.*【植】具异形孢子的.

het·er·o·sty·ly [ˈhetərəuˌstaili] *n.*【植】花柱异长. **-o·sty·lous** *a.*

het·er·o·tax·i·a, het·er·o·tax·is, het·er·o·tax·y [ˌhetərəuˈtæksiə, -sis, -si] *n.*【医】内脏异位；【地】地层变位. **-o·tac·tic, -o·tac·tous, -o·tax·ic** *a.*

het·er·o·thal·lic [ˌhetərəuˈθælik] *a.*【植】雌雄异株的；异宗配合的. **-thal·lism** *n.*

het·er·o·tope [ˈhetərəutəup] *n.*【化】异(原子)序元素；(同量)异序(元)素.

het·er·o·to·pi·a [ˌhetərəuˈtəupiə] *n.*【医】异位 (= heterotopy). **-o·top·ic** [-əˈtɔpik] *a.*

het·er·o·troph [ˈhetərəutrɔf] *n.*【生】异养生物.

het·er·o·troph·ic [ˌhetərəuˈtrɔfik] *a.*【微】异养的〔指细菌只能从有机物中获得养料，不能从无机物中取得蛋白和醣〕.

het·er·o·tro·phy [ˈhetərəuˌtrɔfi] *n.*【微】异养.

het·er·o·typ·ic [ˌhetərəuˈtipik] *a.*【微】异型的 (= heterotypical).

het·er·o·zy·go·sis [ˌhetərəuzaiˈgəusis] *n.*【生】①杂合现象. ②异型接合性.

het·er·o·zy·gote [ˌhetərəuˈzaigəut] *n.*【生】异型接合体，异型接合子；杂合体，杂合子.

het·er·o·zy·gous [ˌhetərəuˈzaigəs] *a.*【生】杂合的.

het·man [ˈhetmən] *n.* *(pl.)* ①波兰旧时司令官. ②哥萨克兵的将官.

het·ra·zan [ˈhetrəzæn] *n.*【药】海群生.

Het·ty [ˈheti] *n.* 海蒂〔女子名，Henrietta 的爱称〕.

heu·land·ite [ˈhjuːləndait] *n.*【矿】片沸石.

heu·ris·tic [hjuəˈristik] ①(教学、研究等) 启发(式)的. ②(计算机解题)探索法的. ～ *method of teaching* 启发式教学法. **-s** *n.* ①启发式教学法，启发式的艺术 [应用]. ②【计】直观推断，试探法. **-ally** *ad.*

HEW = (Department of) Health, Education, and Welfare〔美〕卫生教育和福利部.

hew [hjuː] *vt.* *(～ed; hewn* [hjuːn], *～ed)* ①(用斧等) 砍，劈，剁，伐. ②砍倒 *(down)*. ③砍成，切成；剁；砍开，开辟. ～ *out a tomb in the rock* 凿岩成墓. — *vi.* ①砍，劈，剁，伐. ②坚持，遵守，恪守*(to)*. ～ ***asunder*** = ～ ***to pieces***. ～ ***away*** 砍去，斩去. ～ ***one's way*** 开路，辟路；排难前进. ～ ***to pieces*** 剁碎.

hew·er [ˈhjuːə] *n.* 砍伐者；采煤工人. ～***s of wood and drawers of water*** 劈柴挑水的人，做苦活的人〔出自圣经〕.

Hew·lett [ˈhjuːlit] *n.* 休利特〔姓氏〕.

hewn [ˈhjuːn] hew 的过去分词. — *a.* 粗削的. ～ **squares**【林】披方. ～ **stone** 粗削石，毛石. ～ **timber**【林】披材.

hex [heks] *vt.* 〔美方〕①施魔法于…. ②给…招来坏运气；使倒霉. ③迷惑. — *vi.* 施魔法. — *n.* ①巫婆，术士. ②不吉祥的人[物]. ③魔力.

hex(a)- *comb.f.* 表示"六"〔在元音前用 hex-〕: *hexad, hexagon.*

hex·a·chlo·ro·cy·clo·hex·ane [ˈheksəˌklɔːrəuˌsaikləˈheksein] *n.*【药】六氯环已烷，六六六.

hex·a·chlo·ro·eth·ane [ˌheksəˌklɔːrəuˈeθein] *n.*【化】六氯乙烷 (= hexachlorethane).

hex·a·chlo·ro·phene [ˌheksəˈklɔːrəfiːn] *n.*【药】六氯酚〔用于香皂等内作防臭剂〕.

hex·a·chord [ˈheksəkɔːd] *n.*【乐】六声音阶.

hex·ad, hex·ade [ˈheksæd, ˈhekseid] *n.* ①六；六个；成六的一组. ②【化】六价元素，六价物，六价基. ③【物】六重轴.

hex·a·dec·i·mal [ˌheksəˈdesiməl] *a.* 十六进制的.

hex·a·em·er·on [ˌheksəˈemərɔn] *n.* ①【圣】"创世"的六天；《创世纪》有关"创世"的六天的纪述. ②有关"创世"的论说 (= hexahemeron).

hex·a·gon [ˈheksəgən] *n.* 六角形，六边形. **-al** *a.*

hex·a·gram [ˈheksəgræm] *n.* 六线形，六芒星形〔✶〕.

hex·a·hed·ral [ˈheksəˈhedrəl] *a.* 六面体的，有六面体的.

hex·a·he·dron [ˌheksəˈhedrən] *n.* *(pl.* ～*s, -dra* [-drə]*)* 六面体. *a regular* ～ 立方体，正六面体.

hex·a·hem·er·on [ˌheksəˈhemərɔn] *n.* = hexaemeron.

hex·a·hy·drate [ˌheksəˈhaidreit] *n.*【化】六水合物.

hex·a·hy·dric [ˌheksəˈhaidrik] *a.*【化】六羟的，六元的. *a* ～ *alcohol* 六元醇，六羟基醇.

hex·am·er·ous [hekˈsæmərəs] *a.* (花瓣)有六基数的 (=6-merous).

hex·am·e·ter [hekˈsæmitə] *n.* 六韵步；六韵步诗体. — *a.* = hexametric.

hex·a·meth·yl·ene·tet·ra·mine [ˌheksəˌmeθəliːnˈtetrəmiːn] *n.*【化】六甲撑四胺，乌洛托品.

hex·a·met·ric [ˌheksəˈmetrik] *a.* 六音步的，由六韵步组成的.

hex·a·mine [ˈheksəmin] *n.*【化】六胺；【药】乌洛托品.

hex·ane [ˈheksein] *n.*【化】已烷.

hex·ang·u·lar [hekˈsæŋgjulə] *a.* 六角的.

hex·a·pla [ˈheksəplə] *n.* 用六国语言对译的书.

hex·a·ploid [ˈheksəplɔid] *a.*【生】有六倍体的. — *n.*【生】六倍体.

hex·a·pod [ˈheksəpɔd] *a.* 有六足的. — *n.* 六足动物 (尤指昆虫).

Hex·ap·o·da [hekˈsæpədə] *n.* 〔*pl.*〕【动】六足类，昆虫纲.

hex·ap·o·dy [hekˈsæpədi] *n.* 六音步诗句.

hex·a·stich [ˈheksəstik] *n.* 六行诗，六节诗.

hex·a·style [ˈheksəstail] *a.*【建】有六柱的，六柱式的. — *n.* 正面有六柱的建筑物.

hex·a·syl·la·ble [ˈheksəˈsiləbl] *n.* 六音节(语).

Hex·a·teuch [ˈheksətjuːk] *n.*【宗】《旧约全书》的头六卷.

hex·a·va·lent [ˈheksəveilənt] *a.*【化】有六价的.

hex·en·be·sen [ˈheksənbeizn] *n.*【植】扫帚病，丛枝病 (= witches' broom).

hex·e·rei [ˌheksəˈrai] *n.* 巫术.

hex·ode [ˈheksəud] *n.*【无】六极管.

hex·one [ˈheksəun] *n.*【化】异己酮 (= methyl isobutyl ketone) —*a.* 由蛋白质水解而成为每一分子中含六个碳原子的有机碱类.

hex·o·san [ˈheksəsæn] *n.*【化】聚己糖(类).

hex·ose [ˈheksəus] *n.*【化】己糖(类).

hex·yl [ˈheksil] *n.*【化】①己基. ②六硝炸药，六硝基二苯胺.

hex·yl·res·or·cin·ol [ˌheksilreˈzɔːsinəul] *n.*【化】己基间苯二酚.

hey [hei] *int.* 嗐! 嘿! 〔表示惊愕、喜悦、疑问或唤起注意〕. ***Hey for …!*** …好呀! 〔对某人或某物表示赞美〕. ***Hey presto!*** 嗐，说变就变! 〔魔术师语〕; 嗐，奇怪!

hey·day[1] [ˈheidei] *int.* 啊呀! 〔表示喜悦，惊异〕.

hey·day[2] [ˈheidei] *n.* ①全盛期. ②〔古〕高兴. *in the ~ of youth* 在青春时期，年轻力壮. *in the ~ of his vigour* 在他精力最旺盛时期.

Hey·mans [ˈhaimɑːns] *n.* 海曼斯〔姓氏〕.

Hey·ward [ˈheiwəd] *n.* 海沃德〔姓氏〕.

Hey·wood [ˈheiwud] *n.* 海伍德〔姓氏〕.

Hf =【化】hafnium.

hf. = half.

h.f., H.F. = high frequency; height finding;【印】heavy face; home forces.

hfbd = half-bound.

h-f-c. = high-frequency current.

hf. cf = half-calf.

H.G = High German; His [Her] Grace; 〔英〕Home Guard; Horse Guards.

hg. = hectogram; heliogram; hemoglobin.

Hg =【化】hydrar gyrum (= mercury).

HGH = human growth hormone 人体生长刺激素.

hgt. = height.

hgwy = highway.

H.H.,HH = His [Her] Highness; His Holiness.

hhd., hhd = hogshead.

HHD = doctor of humanities.

HH(H) = (铅笔) double-(treble-) hard.

H hour [ˈeitʃˌauə] *n.*【军】①预定发起进攻时刻. ②特定军事行动开始时刻.

HI =【物】hazard index.

H.I. = Hawaiian Islands;【物】high-intensity; 〔美〕human interest.

hi [hai] *int.* 嗨! 〔表示问候或用以唤起注意〕.

hi·a·tus [haiˈeitəs] *n.* *(pl.* **~(es)***)* ①裂缝，罅隙. ②脱文; 漏字. ③【地】间断. ④中断，拖宕. ⑤【逻】(论证的)连锁中断. ⑥【语音】两个字[音节]中同一元音连续出现时发音的短促停顿〔如 *he entered* 和 *reenter* 中的 '*e*'〕.

Hi·a·wa·tha [haiəˈwɔːθə] *n.* 哈瓦沙〔美国诗人 *Longfellow* 的长诗 *'The Song of Hiawatha'* 中的印第安英雄〕.

hi·ba·chi [hiˈbɑːtʃiː] *n.* *(pl.* ~*)* 〔Jap.〕(日本) 木炭火盆.

hi·ba·ku·sha [hiˈbɑːkuːʃə] *n.* 〔Jap.〕原子爆炸余生者 (指 1945 年广岛及长崎原子弹爆炸余生者).

hi·ber·nac·u·lum [ˌhaibəˈnækjuləm] *n.* *(pl.* ***-u·la*** [-lə]*)* ①(植物的) 越冬芽. ②(植物的) 离体冬芽. ③(动物的)越冬巢; (冬眠动物的)冬眠场所. ④人工冬眠装置.

hi·ber·nal [haiˈbəːnl] *a.* 〔书〕冬天的; 寒冷的. *~ annual plants* 越冬一年生植物.

hi·ber·nant [ˈhaibənənt] *a.* (动物)冬眠的.

hi·ber·nate [ˈhaibəneit] *vi.* ①冬眠; 蛰居; 越冬. ②避寒. **-na·tion** *n.*

Hi·ber·ni·a [haiˈbəːnjə] *n.* 〔诗〕爱尔兰〔拉丁语名〕. **-ni·an** [haiˈbəːnjən] *a.* ①爱尔兰(人)的. ②*n.* 爱尔兰人.

Hi·ber·ni·cism [haiˈbəːnisizəm] *n.* 爱尔兰的特点〔性格、语言现象、风俗〕.

Hi·bis·cus [haiˈbiskəs] *n.*【植】木槿属; 〔h-〕木槿，芙蓉.

hic [hik] *int.* 嘻嗝! 〔打嗝声，尤指酒醉时的打嗝声〕. —*n.* = hiccup.

hic·cough [ˈhikəp] *n., vi., vt.* = hiccup.

hic·cup [ˈhikəp] *n.* 打嗝，打呃. —*vi.* 打嗝; 作打呃声. —*vt.* 打着呃说出 *(out)*.

hic ja·cet [ˈhik ˈdʒeiset] 〔L.〕①…长眠于此〔墓碑语，略作 H.J.〕. ②碑铭; 墓志铭.

hick[1] [hik] *n.* 〔美俚〕乡下佬. —*a.* 〔美俚〕乡下佬(似)的.

hick[2] [hik] *vi.* = hiccup *(vi.)*.

hick·ey [ˈhiki] *n.* *(pl.* ***~s -ies****)* ①〔口〕器械，小机件，小装置，新玩意儿. ②弯管器. ③(电气设备的)螺纹接合器. ④〔口〕疙瘩，粉刺，小脓疱.

Hick·ok [ˈhikɔk] *n.* 希科克〔姓氏〕.

hick·o·ry [ˈhikəri] *n.* ①【植】山核桃属植物. ②山核桃木; 山核桃木手杖[鞭条].

Hicks [hiks] *n.* 希克斯〔姓氏〕.

hid [hid] *hide*[1] 的过去式及过去分词. —*a.* 隐藏的; 神秘的.

hi·dal·go [hiˈdælgəu] *n.* *(fem.* ***-ga****)* 西班牙下级贵族.

hid·den [ˈhidn] *hide*[1] 的过去分词. —*a.* 隐藏的; 秘密的; 神秘的. *a ~ danger* 隐患. *a ~ meaning* 言外之意. *a ~ microphone* 窃听器. *~ property* 埋藏的财物，隐财. *a ~ traitor* 内奸. ~ **tax** 间接税.

hide[1] [haid] *vt.* *(****hid*** [hid]; ***hid·den*** [ˈhidn], ***hid****)* ①藏，隐藏. ②隐瞒，掩饰; 使不知道，向…守秘密 *(from)*. ③包庇. *~ oneself* 躲藏. *~ one's feelings* 掩饰感情. *~ one's head [face]* 把脸藏起来，羞得躲起来. —*vi.* 隐藏，潜伏. ***one's light under a bushel*** 不露锋芒. ***~ out*** 〔美〕隐藏，埋伏. ***~ the face*** 转过脸去. ***~ the face from*** 假装不见，转面不顾. ***~ up*** 〔俚〕包庇. —*n.* (对野兽摄影或打猎用的) 隐藏处. **~-and-seek** *n.* 捉迷藏. **~ away** *n.* 隐蔽所; 偏僻的小餐馆. **~out** *n.* 隐藏; 躲藏处.

hide[2] [haid] *n.* ①兽皮，皮革. ②〔口〕(人的)皮肤; 〔俚〕厚脸皮. *a green [raw] ~* 生皮. ***bat ~s*** 〔美俚〕钞票. ***dress [tan] sb.'s ~*** 鞭打某人. ***have a thick ~*** 脸皮厚. ***have the ~ to do sth.*** 厚颜无耻地做某事. ***~ and hair*** 连毛带皮; 〔美〕完全. ***(neither) ~ nor hair*** 什么也没有; 无影踪. ***save one's own ~*** 避免受罚[受害、受伤]; 保全性命. ***tan sb.'s ~*** 把某人打一顿. —*vt.* ①剥(皮). ②鞭打.

hide[3] [haid] *n.* 〔英〕够养活一家人的土地面积〔约为 60—120 英亩〕.

hide-and-seek [ˈhaidənˈsiːk] 〔美〕**hide-and-go-seek** [-ˈgəuˈsiːk] *n.* 捉迷藏; 蒙混，躲闪. ***play (at) ~ (with)*** (同…)捉迷藏; 〔喻〕与躲躲闪闪的人[物]打交道.

hide·a·way [ˈhaidəwei] *n.* 〔口〕①隐藏处，隐退的地方. ②偏僻的小酒吧间[娱乐场所]. —*a.* 隐蔽的，隐藏的.

hide·bound [ˈhaidbaund] *a.* ①偏狭的，气量狭窄的. ②(动物)因营养不良而瘦骨嶙峋的; (树木)因树皮太紧而影响生长的. ③墨守成规的; 死板的.

hid·e·ous [ˈhidiəs] *a.* 可怕的; 骇人听闻的; 丑恶的，讨厌的. **-ly** *ad.* **-ness** *n.*

hide·out [ˈhaidaut] *n.* 〔口〕(匪盗等的)巢穴，窝，隐匿处，躲藏处.

hid·ey-hole [ˈhaidihəul] *n.* = hideaway.

hid·ing[1] [ˈhaidiŋ] *n.* ①隐匿，躲藏. ②躲藏处. ***be [remain] in ~*** 躲藏着. ***come out of ~*** 从躲藏处出

来. ***go into*** ～ 躲藏起来. ～**-place** 躲藏处，储藏处. ～ **power** (油漆等的)遮盖力，覆盖力，披覆力.

hiding² [ˈhaidiŋ] *n.* 〔口〕鞭打，痛打. ***give sb. a good*** ～ 痛打某人.

hi·dro·sis [haiˈdrəusis] *n.* ①排汗(尤指大量出汗). ②【医】汗病.

hi·drot·ic [haiˈdrɔtik] *a.* ①与发汗有关的. ②使发汗的，促使发汗的. — *n.* 发汗药.

hid·y-hole [ˈhaidihəul] *n.* = hideaway.

hie [hai] *(～ing, hy·ing) vt.* 使赶紧；催促〔常与反身代词同用〕. *He hied himself to the theatre.* 他赶紧去剧场. — *vi.* 〔诗〕赶往 *(to)*. *Hie thee!* 赶快! *Hie on!* 〔嗾狗〕去!

hi·e·mal [ˈhaiiməl] *a.* 冬季的；似冬天的，寒冷的.

hi·er·arch [ˈhaiərɑːk] *n.* ①大主教；祭司长. ②统治集团首领. **-al** *a.*

hi·er·ar·chic(al) [ˌhaiəˈrɑːkik(əl)] *a.* ①僧侣统治(集团)的. ②统治集团的. ③等级(制度)的. **-cal·ly** *ad.*

hi·er·ar·chism [ˈhaiərɑːkizəm] *n.* 僧侣政治；僧侣制度.

hi·er·ar·chy [ˈhaiərɑːki] *n.* ①僧侣统治集团，僧侣统治. ②统治集团. ③等级制度. ④【宗】天使团，天使的级别. ⑤【动、植】(纲、目、科、属等的)分类等级. ⑥【计】分层，层次. ～ *of power* 权力等级. *data* ～【计】数据层次. ～ *of memory*【计】分级存储器系统.

hi·er·at·ic [haiəˈrætik] *a.* ①僧侣的，(文字)僧侣所用简体的〔指古埃及僧侣所用的一种简化象形文字〕. ②神圣的. — *n.* 〔the ～〕 = ～ **writing** 僧侣所用简化文字.

hier(o)- *comb. f.* 表示"神圣的"，"僧侣的"：*hierocracy*.

hi·er·oc·ra·cy [ˌhaiəˈrɔkrəsi] *n.* 僧侣统治；僧侣统治制度. **-o·crat·ic** *a.*

hi·er·o·dule [ˈhaiərədjuːl] *n.* (古希腊神庙的)圣役〔由奴隶充当〕.

hi·er·o·glyph [ˈhaiərəglif] *n.* ①象形文字，图画文字；秘密文字. ②〔谑〕潦草难解的字.

hi·er·o·glyph·ic [ˌhaiərəˈglifik] *a.* ①象形文字的；用象形文字写成的. ②符号的，有神秘意味的，象征的. ③〔谑〕潦草难解的. — *n.* ①象形文字. ②〔常 *pl.*〕象形文字绘写法. ③〔常 *pl.*〕难解的符号，潦草难解的文字.

hi·er·o·glyph·i·cal [ˌhaiərəˈglifikəl] *a.* = hieroglyphic. **-ly** *ad.*

hi·er·ol·a·try [ˌhaiəˈrɔlətri] *n.* 圣徒〔圣物〕崇拜 (= hagiolatry).

hi·er·ol·o·gy [ˌhaiəˈrɔlədʒi] *n.* ①古埃及象形文字的研究. ②(一个民族的)宗教传说，宗教文学，圣典文学.

hi·er·o·phant [ˈhaiərəfænt] *n.* ①【宗】(解释秘义的)圣师. ②(古代希腊等的)祭司长.

hi·fa·lu·tin [ˌhaifəˈluːtn] *a.* 夸张的，夸大的 (= highfalutin).

hi-fi [ˈhai ˈfai] *n.* ①高保真度(= high-fidelity). ②具有高保真度的收音机〔录音机、留声机〕. — *a.* 高保真度的.

Hig·gin·son [ˈhiginsn] *n.* ①希金森〔姓氏〕. ②**Thomas Wentworth** ～ 托马斯·温·希金森〔1823—1911，美国作家〕.

hig·gle, hig·gle-hag·gle [ˈhigl, ˈhigl-ˈhægl] *vi.* 讨价还价；讲条件；争执.

hig·gle·dy-pig·gle·dy [ˈhigldiˈpigldi] *a., ad.* 极紊乱的〔地〕；乱七八糟的〔地〕. — *n.* 混乱.

high [hai] *a.* ①高的〔指物，形容人的身高用 tall〕；高处的；高地的. ②高级的，高等的，高位的，重要的. ③高尚的，崇高的；高贵的. ④昂贵的，奢侈的. ⑤主要的，严重的，重大的. ⑥高度的；剧烈的；很大的，非常的；偏激的；极度的，极端的；(色)浓的；高声调的，尖声的. ⑦高傲的，盛气凌人的. ⑧(精力等)旺盛的；(兴致等)方酣的；(时间、季节)正盛的；恰好到时的. ⑨(食物，尤指肉、野味)有气味的，开始变质的. ⑩〔美俚〕醉了的，被麻醉品麻醉了的. ⑪【地】高纬度的，远离赤道的. ⑫【语音】(舌位)高的. ⑬【机】(齿轮)以最高速度转动的. *the* ～ *tower* 高塔. *a* ～ *mountain* 高山. *The building is 40 feet* ～. 楼高 40 英尺. ～ *feeding* 美食，佳餚. ～ *flying [flight]* 高空飞行. ～ *gear* (汽车)高速挡. ～ *latitudes* 高纬度地方. *a* ～ *character* 崇高的人格. *a* ～ *manner* 傲态. ～ *cost of living* 高昂的生活费用. *the* ～ *street* 正街，大街〔*cf.* 〔美〕main street〕. *a* ～ *crime* 重大罪行. ～ *explosives* 烈性炸药. *a* ～ *voice* 尖嗓门. *a* ～ *folly* 大蠢事. *a* ～ *Tory* 极端的保守党员. ～ *noon* 正午；〔喻〕顶峰，尖端. *a* ～ *flavour* 开始变质的味道，馊味. *He is pretty* ～. 他醉得很凶. ～ *summer* 盛夏. ***get*** ～ ***hat*** (= ***wear a*** ～ ***hat***). ***have a*** ～ ***old time*** (～ ***jinks***) 玩得痛痛快快，过一段极愉快的时间. ***have a*** ～ ***opinion of sb.*** 推崇〔佩服〕某人. ***have a*** ～ ***sense of*** *(duty)* 具有高度的(责任)感. ～ ***and dry*** ①(船)搁浅. ②陷于困境，孤立无援. ③(人)落后，过时. ～ ***and low*** 各种身分的人，高低贵贱的人. ～ ***and mighty*** 地位高的；〔口〕趾高气扬，神气活现. ～ ***on*** 热心于，热衷于. ～, ***wide and handsome*** 〔美口〕无忧无虑地，充满自信地. ***in*** ～ ***favour with*** 非常满意. ***in*** ～ ***terms*** 称赞. ***of*** ～ ***antiquity*** 老早以前的，远古时候的. ***on the*** ～ ***horse*** = ***ride the [a]*** ～ ***horse*** 摆架子. ***talk in*** ～ ***language*** 说大话，吹牛皮. ***wear a*** ～ ***hat*** 〔美〕摆架子. ***with a*** ～ ***hand*** 用高压手段. — *n.* ①高气压；高气压地带. ②(纸牌中的)王牌. ③〔美口〕最高水平〔纪录〕，高额数字. ④高位，高处；高地. ⑤〔美〕中学. ⑥〔the H-〕〔英口〕大街，正街(=High Street，尤指牛津的大街). ⑦〔the h-〕=～ table. ⑧〔美〕=～ school. ⑨(齿轮的)高速度转动. *barometric* ～【气】高气压. *hit an all-time* ～ 创历史上最高纪录. ***from (on)*** ～ 从天上. ～ ***and mighties*** 大人物. ***How is that for*** ～? 〔俚〕好不奇怪? ***on*** ～ 在高空；在天上. ***the Most High***【宗】上帝. — *ad.* ①高. ②奢侈地. ③高价地. *climb* ～ 登高，上游. *bid* ～ 出高价. *fly* ～ 高飞. *live* ～ 过得奢侈. ～ ***and low*** 各处，上上下下 (*search* ～ *and low* 到处搜寻). ***pay*** ～ 付高价. ***play*** ～ 大赌；出大牌. ***run*** ～ ①潮急，浪大. ②兴奋，激动；(语言)粗暴. ③涨(价). ～**-altitude** *a.* 高空的 (*a pilotless* ～*-altitude military reconnaisance plane* 军用无人驾驶高空侦察机，～*-altitude sickness* 高山症). ～ **analysis** 〔作定语用〕(肥料)高成分的(指含有百分之二十以上的植物养料). ～**-angle** *a.* 高射界的；高角的. ～ **area**【天】高气压圈. ～ **art** 纯艺术. ～**ball**〔美〕①*n.* 掺有苏打水、姜汁酒的威士忌；指示火车全速前进的信号；速度很快的火车. ②*vi.* 〔俚〕高速前进. ～ **barrier** 〔美运〕高栏. ～ **beam** 车前灯的远距离光束，高光束，上方光束. ～**binder** 〔美俚〕下流政客；骗子；无赖汉，暗杀者. ～ **birth** 名门. ～**-blooded** *a.* 血统纯正的，性质优良的. ～ **bloomery** (炼熟铁的)原始高炉. ～**blower** 鼻息粗烈的马. ～**-blown** *a.* 意气扬扬的，自高自大的. ～**born** *a.* 出身高贵的. ～**boy** 〔美〕高脚抽屉柜. ～ **bred** *a.* 出身高贵的，品格高尚的；纯种的，血统纯正的. ～ **brass** 优质黄铜. ～ **brightness** 最大亮度. ～**brow** ①*n.* 〔美俚〕知识分子；(自以为)有学识的人，有教养的人. *(opp.* lowbrow*)*. ②*a.* 〔蔑〕卖弄学问的，自炫博学的. ～**-browed** *a.* 额头宽大的，有教养的，炫耀学问的. ～**browism** *n.* 自命不凡，炫耀学问. ～**-capacity** ①爆炸弹头. ②大电容，大容量. ～**chair** 婴儿高脚椅. **H- church**【宗】高派教会. ～ **churchman** 高派教会教徒. ～**class** *a.* 高级的，高等的. ～ **cockalorum** ①〔美俚〕要人，大老板；自命不凡的人. ②〔英〕(儿童玩的)跳背游戏. ～ **colour** 深色. ～**-coloured** *a.* 深色的；生动的；(脸色)红润的. ～ **comedy** 高雅的喜剧. ～ **command** 统帅部，最高指挥部；(机关中的)最高领导班子. ～ **commissioner** 高级专员(尤指英联邦各国相互派驻的大

使级代表). **H- Court (of Justice)** 〔英〕高等法院. **~ day** 节日,假日. **~-energy particle** 【原】高能粒子. **~-energy physics** 高能物理学. **~ fidelity** ①(收音,录音设备等的)高保真度. ②具有高保真度的收音机、录音机或留声机. **~flier, -flyer** ①高飞的人[鸟];好高骛远的人. ②极端分子;说大话的人;有手腕的人;极会挥霍的人. ③【英史】(17—18世纪的)高派教会人士,保守党员. **~-flown** *a.* ①好高骛远的;高超的. ②夸张的. **~flying** *a.* ①高飞的. ②骄傲的,自命不凡的. **~ frequency**【无】高频(率),高周率〔略作 H. F.〕. **~ furnace** 竖炉. **H- German** (现为标准德语的)高地德语. **~-grade** *a.* 高级的,优质的,上等的 (*~-grade steel* 优质钢). **~grown** 长满高大植物的. **~-handed** *a.* 高压的,横暴的 (*~-handed measures* 高压手段). **~ hat** ①高帽. ②〔美〕自大的人;冒充绅士的人. **~-hat** ① *n.* 〔俚〕势利鬼,自命不凡的人. ② *a.* 骄傲的,私利的;时髦的,贵族派头的. ③*vi., vt.* (对…)摆架子;盛气凌人地对待(人),冷淡待(人). **~-hearted** *a.* 勇敢的;果敢的. **~-heeled** *a.* (鞋)高跟的. **~ hurdle** 〔美〕(田径)高栏. **~ jinks [jinx]** 热闹的玩乐;喧闹. **~ jump** 跳高. **~-keyed** *a.* 感情紧张的;敏感的,兴奋的,高音调的. **~-level** *a.* ①高级官员的,高级官员作出的. ②高级的. **~light** ① *vt.* 在…上投上强光;强调,使显著;【美剧】派给…当主角. ② *n.* (画中受光最多的)明亮部分;〔常*pl.*〕(演出等的)精彩场面,精采节目;(报纸中的)特讯,要闻;要点. **~ liver** 生活奢侈者,挥霍无度者. **~-lows** *n. pl.* 有绊皮靴. **~-mettled** *a.* 猛烈的,兴高采烈的. **~-minded** *a.* 品格高尚的;〔古〕高傲的,傲慢的. **~-muckamuck, ~-muckety-muck** *n.* 〔美俚〕大人物;神气活现的人. **~ necked** *a.* (衣服)高领的. **~-octane** *a.*【化】辛烷值的. **~-pitched** *a.* ①音调高的,尖声的. ②坡度陡的,(屋顶等)倾斜度大的. ③紧张的;极敏感的. ④高尚的. **~ place** 山顶祭坛〔闪族人早期信奉宗教时进行宗教活动的场所〕. **~ polymer**【化】高分子. **~-powered** *a.* 十分强大的;极有权势的;大功率的. **~precision** *a.* 高精密度的,高准确度的. **~-priced** 高价的,昂贵的. **~ priest** 祭司长(尤指犹太教的祭司长). **~-pressure** ① *a.* 高压的;强买强卖的;急迫的,硬干的. ② *vt.* 〔口〕强制,逼使,对…施加压力;强行推销. **~-principled** *a.* 原则性高的;操守高洁的. **~-proof** *a.* 酒精含量高的. **~ profile** 高姿态,明确的立场. **~-ranking** *a.* 高级的 (*a ~-ranking official* 高级官员). **~ relief** 隆(浮)雕;隆(浮)雕刻品. **~-rise** ① *a.* (建筑物的)高耸的,多层楼房的. ②*n.* 高大建筑物,多层高楼. **~road** 大路,公路;最容易[美好]的途径 (*the ~-road to ruin* 灭亡之道). **~-roller** 〔美俚〕肆意挥霍的人;狂赌的人. **~-rolling** *a.* 肆意挥霍的,豪华的. **~ school** 〔美〕中学 (*a junior [senior] ~ school* 初[高]中);〔英〕大学预科. **~ seas** 公海. **~ sign** 暗号. **~-sounding** *a.* 夸大的;动听的;高调的. **~-speed** *a.* 高速的,高速度的 (*~-speed photography* 快速照相术. *~-speed steel*【冶】高速钢,锋钢). **~-spirited** *a.* ①勇敢的,有精神的. ②易激动的;易发怒的,脾气大的. **~ spirits** 高兴,快乐. **~-stepper** ①蹄步高抬的马;有派头的人. ②〔美俚〕生活奢华的人. **~ spot** ①显著点,特点. ②名胜,古迹. **~-strung** *a.* 紧张的,敏感的,易兴奋的. **~ style** 最时髦的服装. **~ table** (英大学餐厅中)校长、导师等的餐桌〔俗称 the high〕;〔英〕(正式宴会中的)主宾席. **~-tail** *vi.* 迅速撤退,迅速逃走 (*~-tail it off with sb.* 同某人一起迅速逃走). **~ tea** 〔英〕(下午五、六时之间的)正式茶点. **~ teens** 十六至十九岁的青少年. **~-temper steel** 激硬化钢. **~-temperature steel** 耐热钢. **~-tension** *a.* 高(电)压(的). **~-test** ①经过严格试验的;高级的. ②(汽油)沸点低的 (*~-test gasoline* 高度挥发性汽油). **~ tide** 高潮. **~ time** ①并不为晚的时候;不早不晚恰当时. ②〔俚〕兴高采烈的时候〔亦作 **~ old time**〕. **~-toned** *a.* ①调子高的;〔谑〕崇高的,高尚的;〔讽〕唱高调的. ②〔口〕漂亮的,时髦的;〔口〕优良的,优秀的. **~ treason** 叛逆,叛逆罪. **~-up** *n.* 社会地位高的人. **~ water** 高潮;高水位;昌隆. **~-water mark** ①高潮线,满潮标. ②高水位线. ③最高点,绝顶. **~ wine** 酒精成分很高的蒸馏酒. **~ wire** (走钢丝演员表演用的)高空钢丝绳. **~-wire** *a.* 走高空钢丝绳的;危险的. **~-wrought** *a.* 极度紧张的,非常激动地. **~-yield** *a.* 产量很高的;(核武器等)将大量放射性尘埃放入空气的.

high•er [ˈhaiə] *a.* 〔high 的比较级〕较高的;高等的. *~ command*【军】= high command. *~ criticism* 圣经考证学. *~ education* 高等教育. *~ mathematics* 高等数学. ***on a ~ plane*** 在更高水准上. **~-up** *n.* 〔美口〕领导,上司;要人.

high•est [ˈhaiist] *a.* 〔high 的最高级〕最高的. *the ~ bidder* (拍卖时)出价最高的人. *the ~ good* 至善. *the ~ possible price* 最高价格. — *n.* 最高者;最高地位. ***the H-*** 至高无上者,上帝(= the most High). ***in the ~*** 【宗】在至高之处的天堂. — *ad.* 最高地.

high•fa•lu•tin(g) [ˈhaifəˈluːtin,-tiŋ] *a.* 夸张的,夸大的. — *n.* 夸张的话,大话.

high-jack [ˈhaidʒæk] *vt.* 〔口〕①抢劫(违禁品等);拦路抢劫(车、人等). ②劫持(飞机),绑架. ③强逼.

high-jack•er [ˈhaidʒækə] *n.* 抢劫者;劫持飞机者.

high•land [ˈhailənd] *n.* ①高地,高原. ②〔the Highlands〕苏格兰高地. — *a.* ①高原的. ②〔H-〕苏格兰高地的. **~ fling** 苏格兰高地舞.

high•land•er [ˈhailəndə] *n.* ①高地人,山地人. ②〔H-〕苏格兰高地人;苏格兰高地联队士兵.

high•ly [ˈhaili] *ad.* ①高,高度地. ②很,非常. ③称赞地. ④高贵地. ⑤按高额. *a ~ gifted actor* 很有天才的演员. *be ~ paid* 薪水[工资]高. *~ amusing* 非常有趣的. *~ original* 很有独特性的. *to feel oneself ~ flattered* 自觉非常荣幸. ***speak ~ of*** 赞扬,推奖. ***think ~ of*** 尊重. **~-strung** *a.* = high-strung.

high•ness [ˈhainis] *n.* ①高,高度;高位;高价;高尚. ②〔H-〕殿下. *His [Her, Your] H-* 殿下.

hight[1] [hait] *a.* 〔古、诗〕所谓…的,被称为…的;名字叫做…的. *a maide ~ Elaine* 名叫埃莱恩的少女.

hight[2] [hait] *n.* 〔废〕= height.

high•ty-tigh•ty [ˌhaitiˈtaiti] *a.* ①轻浮的;反复无常的. ②傲慢的,骄傲的. ③易怒的,脾气大的;怒气冲冲的. — *n.* ①轻率. ②傲慢. —*int.* 哎呀!〔表示傲慢或忿怒〕(= hoity-toity).

high•way [ˈhaiwei] *n.* ①公路,大路 (*opp.* byway). ②交通干线;正路,直路. ③(达到目的的)途径. *a ~ to success* 成功之道. *ocean ~s* 海洋航路. *~ traffic* 公路交通. *~s and byways* 干道和支路. *the king's ~* 天下的公路. ***go on the ~ = take (to) the ~*** 作拦路的强盗. ***the silent H-*** 静寂的大路(指英国泰晤士河). **~-man** 拦路强盗,响马.

H.I.H., HIH = His [Her] Imperial Highness 殿下〔间接提及时用〕.

hi•jack [ˈhaidʒæk] *vt.* = 〔口〕high-jack.

hi•jack•ee [ˌhaidʒæˈkiː] *n.* 劫持事件的受害者;被劫持者.

hi•jack•er [ˈhaidʒækə] *n.* 〔口〕= highjacker.

hi•jinks [ˈhaiˈdʒiŋks] *n.* = high jinks.

hij•ra(h) [ˈhidʒrə] *n.* = hegira.

hike [haik] *vi.* 〔口〕①步行;作长途徒步旅行,行军;散步. ②飞起,扬起,飘起 (*up*). ③〔美俚〕在高空检修电线. **~ *out*** 露营. — *vt.* ①拉起,使升起. ②猛提(价格). 〔美俚〕涂改(支票以提高票面金额). — *n.* ①徒步旅行;散步;行军. ②提高,增加. *go on [take] a ~* 作徒步旅行,去散步. *a pay ~ plan* 加薪方案.

hik•er [ˈhaikə] *n.* ①徒步旅行者. ②〔美俚〕高空电线检修工.

hi·la [ˈhailə] hilum 的复数.

HILAC = heavy-ion linear accelerator 重离子直线加速器.

hi·lar [ˈhailə] *a.* ①【解】门的; 脐的. ②【植】种脐的; (淀粉)脐点的.

hi·lar·i·ous [hiˈlɛəriəs] *a.* ①愉快的; 热闹的. ②有趣的,妙的. **-ly** *ad.* **-ness** *n.*

hi·lar·i·ty [hiˈlæriti] *n.* 欢乐,高兴;热闹,狂欢.

Hil·a·ry[1] [ˈhiləri] *n.* 希勒里〔男子名〕.

Hil·a·ry[2] [ˈhiləri] *a.* 圣希勒里节日(1月13日)时候的. ***the ~ term [sitting]*** ①旧时英国高等法院开庭期〔1月13日—31日〕. ②牛津大学及都柏林大学的春季学期.

Hil·da [ˈhildə] *n.* 希尔达〔女子名〕.

Hil·de·brand [ˈhildəbrænd] *n.* 希尔布兰特〔男子名〕(G. = battle sword).

Hil·de·gard(e) [ˈhildəgɑːd] *n.* 希尔德加德〔女子名〕.

hil·ding [ˈhildiŋ] *n.* 〔古〕卑贱者. — *a.* 〔古〕卑贱的.

Hill [hil] *n.* 希尔〔姓氏〕.

hill [hil] *n.* ①小山〔英国通常指 2000 英尺以下的山丘〕; 〔*pl.*〕丘陵. ②土堆,土墩. ③(道路的)斜坡. ④【军】高地. ⑤〔美〕〔H-〕美国国会 (= Capitol H-). ⑥(植物根部的)土墩,小堆. ⑦成堆种植的作物. *an artificial ~* 假山. *H- 305* 三〇五高地. *a ~ of corn* 玉米堆. *a potential ~* 【物】位垒,势垒. ***a ~ of beans*** 〔口〕少量; 小事; 不值钱的东西. ***go over the ~*** 〔美俚〕越狱; 〔军俚〕开小差; 偷偷地迅速离开. ***go up [down] a ~*** 上〔下〕山. ***~ and dale*** (矿山、炭坑等)上〔下〕坡; 坑窪起伏的地方. ***over the ~*** ①度过难关,度过危机. ②上了年纪的; 走下坡路的. ***the gentleman on the ~*** 〔美〕国会议员. ***up ~ and down dale*** ①上山下坑; 到处; 彻底, 完全. ②猛烈地; 坚忍不拔地. — *vt.* 把…堆成小山; 培土于(树木周围) *(up)*. **~billy** *n.* 〔美口〕南部山区居民; 粗人, 乡下人. **~man** *n.* 山区居民; 印度山地居民. **~ myna** 【动】鹩哥 (*Eulabes religiosa*) 〔产于亚洲, 能学人语〕. **~side** *n.* (小山)山腰,山坡. **~ station** (印度等地的)山中避暑地. **~top** *n.* (小山)山顶.

Hill·man [ˈhilmən] *n.* 希尔曼〔姓氏〕.

hil·lo(a) [hiˈləu] *int., n., v.* 〔古〕= hollo, holla, halloo.

hill·ock [ˈhilək] *n.* 小丘. **-y** [-i] *a.*

hill·y [ˈhili] *a.* ①多小山的; 多丘陵的, 多斜坡的. ②似小山的; 峭峻的. **hill·i·ness** *n.*

hilt [hilt] *n.* (刀等的)柄,把. ***fight ~ to ~*** 短兵相接, 个对个作战. ***(up) to the ~*** 十分, 彻底 (*be proved to the hilt* 被彻底证明). — *vt.* 给(刀等)装上把.

Hil·ton [ˈhiltən] *n.* 希尔顿〔姓氏〕.

hi·lum [ˈhailəm] ***(pl. -la*** [-lə]***)*** *n.* ①【植】种脐. ②(淀粉粒的)脐点. ③【医】门脐.

him [him, 弱 im, əm] *pro.* ①〔he 的宾格〕 他. ②〔口〕〔用作表语〕 = he. ③〔古〕〔强势, 反身用法〕 = himself. *That's ~.* 〔口〕那正是他. ④〔用于 than 之后〕 = he. *Him and his wife were sitting by the fire.* 他和他老婆坐在炉火旁边〔现代标准英语须在前面用 He〕. *He sat ~ by the fire.* 他在炉火边上坐下来. *His wife is taller than ~.* 他妻子比他高.

H.I.M., HIM = His [Her] Imperial Majesty 陛下〔间接提及时用〕.

Hi·ma·la·ya(s) [ˌhiməˈleiə(z)] *n.* 喜马拉雅山(脉). **Hi·ma·la·y·an** [-ən] *a.* 喜马拉雅山脉的.

hi·mat·i·on [hiˈmætiɔn,-ən] *n.* ***(pl. -mat·i·a*** [-ˈmætiə]***)*** 古希腊人所穿的长方形外衣.

him·self [himˈself, 弱 im-] *pro.* 〔*he* 的反身代词或用作加强语气〕 ***(pl. themselves)*** 他自己, 他亲自, 他本人. ①〔作反身代词〕 *He cut ~.* 他割伤了自己. *He gave ~ much trouble.* 他自找苦吃. ②〔加强语气〕 *He ~ says so.* = *He says so ~.* 他本人是那样说的. *I saw him ~.* 我看见他本人了. *H- unhappy, he understood the situation.* 他本人很不幸,所以理解这种情况. ③〔人称代词代用语〕 *I can do it better than ~.* 我比他本人可以做得更好一些〔在 *better than* 之下为主语〕. *One of the party and ~ saw it.* 那群人中的一个人和他本人都看见的. *H- will be there.* 他会亲自去的〔现代标准英语须在前面用 He〕. ***be [become, come to] ~*** (情绪、健康)处于正常情况 (*He is not quite ~ today.* 他今天有些反常, 他今天不舒服. *He is ~ again.* 他复原了,他恢复了正常). ***beside ~*** 发狂,疯癫. ***(all) by ~*** 独自,独立. ***for ~*** 为自己; 自个儿.

Hind. = Hindi; Hindu; Hindustan; Hindustani.

hind[1] [haind] *a.* ***(~er; ~(er)most)*** 后面的, 后边的. ★一般用 hinder, 对 fore 说时用 hind. *the ~ legs [limbs]* (兽的)后腿. *~ wheels* 后轮. ***on one's ~ legs*** 采取坚决或独立的立场. **~brain** 【解】后脑. **~gut** 【解】后肠. **~quarter** *n.* (牛、羊、猪等的)后腿肉. **~ quarters** (四腿动物的)两条后腿.

hind[2] [haind] *n.* ***(pl. ~s,*** 〔集合词〕***~)*** ①(特指 3 岁以上的)红色雌鹿. ②红鮨鱼.

hind[3] [haind] ①〔古〕雇农; 乡下人. ②(英格兰北部和苏格兰)有经验的农场工人; 农场管理人.

hin·der[1] [ˈhində] *vt.* 妨害,妨碍; 阻止,阻挠. *~ sb. from coming* 阻止某人来. — *vi.* 妨害,阻碍.

hind·er[2] [ˈhaində] hind 的比较级. — *a.* 后面的, 后方的. *the ~ gate* 后门. *the ~ part of a ship* 船的后部.

hind·er·most, hind·most [ˈhaindəməust, ˈhaindməust] hind 的最高级. — *a.* 最后的. ***The devil takes [catches] the ~.*** 〔谚〕迟者遭殃.

Hin·di [ˈhinˈdiː, ˈhindiː] *a.* 印度北部的. — *n.* 印地语.

Hind·ley [ˈhaindli, ˈhindli] *n.* 欣德利〔姓氏〕.

Hin·doo [ˈhinˌduː] = Hindu.

Hin·doo·stan·ee, Hin·doo·sta·ni [hinduˈstæni] *a. n.* = Hindustani.

hin·drance [ˈhindrəns] *n.* ①妨害, 障碍. ②起妨碍作用的人[物]. ***without let or hindrance*** 不受干涉的,通行无阻地; 自由地,为所欲为地.

hind·sight [ˈhaindsait] *n.* ①(步枪的)照尺. ②(对事件等的)事后聪敏, 事后的认识 (*opp.* foresight). *realize with ~* 事后才懂得…. ***knock [kick] sb.'s ~ out = knock [kick] the ~ off sb.*** 〔美口〕压服某人,使某人畏缩.

Hin·du [ˈhinduː] *n.* ①印度人. ②信奉印度教的人. — *a.* ①印度教的. ②印度人的. **-ism** *n.* 印度教. **-ize** [ˈhinduaiz] *vt.* 使改信印度教,使受印度教影响.

Hin·du·stan·i [ˌhinduˈstɑːni] *n.* ①兴都斯坦人, 印度斯坦人. ②兴都斯坦语,印度斯坦语. — *a.* ①兴都斯坦的,印度斯坦的. ②兴都斯坦人的,印度斯坦人的. ③兴都斯坦语的,印度斯坦语的.

hinge [hindʒ] *n.* ①铰链, 折叶. ②铰合部, 蝶铰. ③枢纽; 枢要,中枢,要点; 关键,转折点. ④(集邮册上粘邮票用的)透明胶水纸. ⑤〔美俚〕一瞥. *the ~ of the knee* 膝关节. ***get [take] a ~*** 看一看. ***off the ~s*** ①铰链脱落; 脱节. ②失常; (精神)错乱. — *vt.* ①用铰链接合, 给(门等)安铰链. ②使…以(…)为转移〔依据〕. *~ one's action on* 以…为行动准绳. — *vi.* ①(门等)装有蝶铰. ②随着蝶铰转动; 〔喻〕看…而定, 依…为转移 *(on; upon)*. *My acceptance will ~ upon the terms.* 我接受与否将依条件而定. **~ joint** ①【解】屈戌关节. ②【机】铰链接合. **hinging post** 门柱. **-less** *a.* 无铰链的, 不用铰链的.

hinged [hindʒd] *a.* 有铰链的,用铰链的.

hin·ny[1] [ˈhini] *n.* 驮騠, 驴骡〔公马和母驴所生的种间杂种〕.

hin·ny[2], **hin·nie** [ˈhini] *n.* 〔Scot.〕宝贝儿 (= honey).

hint [hint] *n.* ①暗示. ②提示,线索. ③微量,少许,点滴. *a ~ of spice* 一丁点儿香料. *Hints for housewives.* 家庭主妇须知〔作标题或书名〕. ***drop [give, let fall] a***

～ 给人暗示. ***take a*** ～ 接受别人的暗示，领悟. — *vt.* 暗示. *He ～ed vaguely [broadly] that he might be late.* 他隐约地[明白地]暗示他可能迟来. — *vi.* 暗示 *(at)*. ～ *at one's anxiety* 暗示自己很着急.

hin·ter·land [ˈhintəlænd] *n.* ①腹地，内地. ②〔*pl.*〕穷乡僻壤. ③可依赖港口供应的内地贸易区；物资供应地区.

hip[1] [hip] *n.* ①臀部. ②【解】髋，髋部. ③【动】(昆虫的)基节. ④【建】屋脊. ⑤〔*pl.*〕〔美俚〕不利结局. ***catch [have, get, take] sb. on the*** ～ 制服某人，压倒某人. ***down in the*** ～ ***[～s]*** 马臀骨受伤；垂头丧气，无精打采. ***on [upon] the*** ～ 〔罕〕处于不利地位. ***shoot from the*** ～ 鲁莽地讲话[行事]. ***smite sb.*** ～ ***and thigh*** 使某人惨败. ***sth. on the*** ～ 〔美谑〕后裤袋中的东西(指扁平的小酒瓶). — *vt.* ①使(家畜)扭脱股关节；用屁股撞. ②【建】使作成四坡屋顶. ～ **bath**, 坐浴，半身浴；坐浴浴盆. ～**bone** 坐骨，髋骨，无名骨. ～ **boot** (消防队员或渔夫所穿)长到大腿的长靴. ～ **disease** 股关节症，髋关节症. ～ **fire** 【军】坐射. ～ **gout** 坐骨神经痛. ～ **joint** 【解】髋关节. ～ **roof** 【建】四坡屋顶. ～**shot** *a.* 髋骨位置不正的；股关节脱节的.

hip[2], **hyp** [hip] *n.* 〔口〕病态的忧郁，情绪低沉 (＝ hypochondria). — *vt.* ***(-pp-)*** 使忧郁.

hip[3] [hip] *n.*【植】蔷薇果 (＝ hep[1]).

hip[4] [hip] *int.* (集体的)喝采[欢呼]声〔一般仅用于: *Hip! Hip! hurrah!* 嗨！嗨！万岁！〕.

hip[5] [hip] *a.* 〔美俚〕①熟悉内情的，市面灵通的；赶时新的. ②聪明的，机灵的. ③〔美〕颓废派的，嬉皮派的. ***I'm*** ～. 〔美俚〕别噜苏了！我懂了！ ～ **capitalism** 满足"嬉皮"派需要的资本主义工商业. ～ **chick** 〔美俚〕熟悉时新东西的女学生. ～**-hugger** *a.* (裤子) 紧裹臀部的. ～**-huggers** 紧裹臀部的裤子.

hip·parch [ˈhipɑːk] *n.* (古希腊)骑兵司令.

hipped[1] [hipt] *a.* ①臀部…的. ②(牲畜等) 股关节脱节的. ③(屋顶)有斜脊的. *broad [narrow]* ～ 臀部宽[窄]的. *a* ～ *roof* 四坡屋顶.

hipped[2] [hipt] *a.* ①〔英口〕忧郁的；沮丧的. ②〔美俚〕热衷于…的，迷恋于…的*(on)*. *feel* ～ 觉得郁闷. ③〔俚〕被激怒的. ～ *on movies [golf]* 电影[高尔夫球]迷.

hip·pi·at·rics [ˌhipiˈætriks] *n. pl.* 〔作 sing. 用〕马医学〔兽医学的一门〕.

hip·pie [ˈhipiː] *n.* 〔俚〕嬉皮士，希比派，嬉皮派〔六十年代美国青年中出现的颓废派青年的称呼. 他们对社会怀有某种不满，但以奇装异服、蓄长发、吸毒等来发泄〕. **-dom** 〔集合词〕嬉皮士世界，颓废派.

hip·pish [ˈhipiʃ] *a.* 有点忧郁的.

hipp(o)- *comb. f.* 表示"马"〔元音前用 hipp-〕: *hippo*campus.

hip·po [ˈhipəu] *n.* 〔俚〕河马 (＝ hippopotamus).

hip·po·cam·pus [ˌhipəˈkæmpəs] *n.* ***(pl. -pi*** [-pai]***)*** ①【希神】(马头鱼尾的) 怪兽. ②【动】海马. ③【解】(脑内的)海马状突起.

hip·po·cras [ˈhipəkræs] *n.* (欧洲中世纪的)姜汁补身葡萄酒.

Hip·poc·ra·tes [hiˈpɔkrətiːz] 希波克拉底 (公元前460—360?)，古希腊的名医，世称医学之父.

Hip·po·crat·ic [ˌhipəuˈkrætik] *a.* (古希腊医师) 希波克拉底的；希波克拉底学派的.

Hip·po·crene [ˌhipəuˈkriːni(ː), ˈhipəkriːn] *n.* 【希神】赫利孔 (Helicon) 山的灵泉；诗的灵感.

hip·po·drome [ˈhipədrəum] *n.* ①(古希腊、罗马战车和马车的)竞技场，赛马场. ②马戏场.

hip·po·griff, hip·po·gryph [ˈhipəgrif] *n.*【希神】半鹰半马的有翅怪兽.

hip·po·pot·a·mus [ˌhipəˈpɔtəməs] *n.* ***(pl.*** ***～es, -mi*** [-mai]***)*** 【动】河马.

hipps [hips] *n.* hip[2] 的复数.

hip·py[1] [ˈhipiː] *n.* ＝ hippie. ～**dom** 美国颓废派，颓废派行为. ～**hood** 美国颓废派身分，颓废派风度.

hip·py[2] [ˈhipi] *a.* 臀部大的.

hip·ster [ˈhipstə] *n.* ①消息灵通人士，赶时髦的人. ②机灵的人. ③美国颓废派成员. ④爵士音乐迷.

hir·a·ble [ˈhaiərəbl] *a.* 能租用的，能雇用的.

hi·ra·gan·a [ˌhirəˈgɑːnə] *n.* 〔Jap.〕 (日语字母的草书) 平假名.

Hi·ram [ˈhaiərəm] *n.* 海勒姆〔男子名〕.

hir·cine [ˈhəːsain] *a.* ①山羊的；象山羊的. ②羊膻味重的. ③好色的.

hire [ˈhaiə] *n.* ①租金；酬金；工钱. ②租借，雇用. *motor-cars on* ～ 〔英〕 ＝ *automobiles for* ～ 〔美〕出租汽车. *let out (sth.) on* ～ 出租. *pay for the* ～ *of* 付租费. *work for* ～ 做雇佣工作. ***for [on]*** ～ 供租用*(books for* ～书籍出租*)*. — *vt.* ①租用，赁借；雇，雇用. ②出租*(out)*. ～ *oneself out as a hack writer* 做雇佣文人. ～ *oneself out to* 投靠. ～ ***on*** 找到职业. ～ ***out ... (by the hour)*** (按钟头)出租. ～ **purchase [system]** 〔英〕分期付款销货法.

hire·ling [ˈhaiəliŋ] *a.* 做雇佣工作的. — *n.* ①佣工；〔蔑〕为钱劳动的人. ②租用物.

hir·er [ˈhaiərə] *n.* 雇主；租借者.

hir·ing [ˈhaiəriŋ] *n.* 雇用，租赁. — *a.* 雇用的，租赁的. ～ **hall** (美国航运业等举办、挨次介绍登记者就业的) 职业介绍所，失业工人待雇所.

hi-rise [ˈhairaiz] *n.* ＝ high rise.

Hi·ro·shi·ma [ˌhirəˈʃiːmə] *n.* 广岛〔日本市、县名〕.

hir·sute [ˈhəːsjuːt] *a.* (动物达到发情期时)毛多的；有粗毛的；有须的. **-ness** *n.*

hir·su·tu·lous [həːˈsjuːtjələs] *a.* 毛稀少[很短]的.

hir·u·din [ˈhirudin] *n.* 【生化】水蛭素.

Hir·u·din·e·a [ˌhiruˈdiniə] *n.* 〔*pl.*〕【动】蛭纲.

hi·ru·di·noid [hiˈruːdnɔid] *a.* 水蛭的；似水蛭的.

hi·run·dine [hiˈrʌndin,-dain] *a.* 燕的；似燕的. — *n.* 燕科鸟.

his [hiz, 弱 iz] *pro.* ①〔he 的所有格〕他的. ②〔he 的物主代词〕他的东西. ③〔古〕〔置于男子名后作所有格〕他的. *in Henry the Fourth* ～ *time* 在亨利四世时代. *This book is* ～, *not mine.* 这本书是他的，不是我的. *himself and* ～ 他(自己)和他的家属.

his(')n [hizn] *pro.* 〔古，方〕 ＝ his, his own.

His·pa·ni·a [hisˈpeiniə,-ˈpɑː-] *n.* ①〔诗〕西班牙 (＝ Spain). ②古罗马时代西班牙和葡萄牙地区的拉丁名.

His·pan·ic [hisˈpænik] *a.* ①西班牙的；西班牙和葡萄牙的. ②拉丁美洲的. ～ *America* 拉丁美洲.

His·pan·i·cism [hisˈpænisizəm] *n.* (英语上下文中出现的)西班牙语语言现象〔指词、短语等〕.

his·pa·ni·dad [ispaniˈdad] *n.* 〔Sp. 常作 H-〕(在拉丁美洲推行的)西班牙文明至上主义.

his·pa·nism [ˈhispənizəm] *n.* 〔常作 H-〕①＝hispanidad. ②来源于西班牙语的语言特点.

Hispano- *comb. f.* 表示"西班牙": *Hispano*-Gallican.

His·pa·no-Gal·li·can [ˈhispənə-ˈgælikən] *a.* 西班牙—法国的.

his·pid [ˈhispid] *a.* 有鬃的，有刺的，硬毛多的.

hiss [his] *vi.* ①(鹅、蛇、蒸气等)发嘶嘶声. ②发嘘嘘声表示反对[鄙视]. *A ball* ～*ed by.* 子弹嘶地一声飞过. ～ *for silence* 发嘘声要大家别讲话. — *vt.* ①发嘶嘶声表示，嘶嘶地说出. ②对…发嘘嘘声〔表示反对，鄙视〕，用嘘嘘声轰赶. ～ *an actor* 对演员发嘘声. ～ ***sb. off [away, down]*** 把某人嘘走. — *n.* 嘘音，嘶嘶的啸声；拖长的[s]声.

hist[1] [sːt, hist] *int.* 〔古〕嘶嘶！嘘！〔促起注意或制止人讲话的发声〕. — *vt.* 向…发嘘声.

hist[2] [hist] *n.*, *v.* 〔方〕 ＝ hoist.

hist. ＝ histology; historian; historical; history.

his·tam·i·nase [hisˈtæmineis, ˈhistəmineis] *n.*【生化】组胺酶.
his·ta·mine [ˈhistəmiːn,-min] *n.*【生化】组胺. **-ta·min·ic** [-ˈminik] *a.*
his·ti·dine [ˈhistidiːn,-din] *n.*【生化】组氨酸.
his·ti·o·cyte [ˈhistiəsait] *n.*【生】组织细胞. **-o·cyt·ic** [-ˈsitik] *a.*
histo- *comb. f.* 表示"组织": *histo*genesis.
his·to·chem·is·try [ˌhistəuˈkemistri] *n.* 组织化学. **-i·cal** [-ikl] *a.* **-i·cal·ly** *ad.*
his·to·gen [ˈhistəudʒən] *n.*【植】组织原.
his·to·gen·e·sis [ˌhistəuˈdʒenisis] *n.*【生】组织发生. **-ge·net·ic** [-dʒəˈnetik] *a.* **-ge·net·i·cal·ly** *ad.*
his·to·gram [ˈhistəugræm] *n.*【统】(次数)矩形图,直方图.
his·toid [ˈhistɔid] *a.*【医】①常规组织状的. ②仅从一种组织发展而来的.
his·tol·o·gy [hisˈtɔlədʒi] *n.* ①【生】组织学;(生物的)组织机构. ②研究组织学的论文.
his·tol·y·sis [hisˈtɔlisis] *n.*【生】组织溶解. **-to·lyt·ic** [ˌhistəˈlitik] *a.*
his·tone [ˈhistəun] *n.*【生化】组蛋白.
his·to·pa·thol·o·gy [ˌhistəupəˈθɔːlədʒi] *n.* 组织病理学.
his·to·phys·i·ol·o·gy [ˌhistəuˈfiziˈɔlədʒi] *n.* 组织生理学.
his·to·plas·mo·sis [ˌhistəuplæzˈməusis] *n.*【医】荚膜组织浆菌病.
his·to·ri·an [hisˈtɔːriən] *n.* ①历史学家. ②年代史编者,编史家.
his·to·ri·at·ed [hisˈtɔːrieitid] *a.* (书页每段开头、每页的边或手稿等)用人[动物]的图像装饰的,有图案的.
his·tor·ic [hisˈtɔrik] *a.* ①历史上有名的,有历史意义的. ②历史上的(= historical) *a(n)* ~ *town* 历史名镇. *a(n)* ~ *event* 历史事件. *the* ~ *[historical] present*【语法】历史现在时态〔指用现在时态叙述过去的事件,以达到描写生动的目的〕. *a(n)* ~ *spot* 史迹,古迹. ~ *times* 有史时期 (*opp.* prehistoric times).
his·tor·i·cal [hisˈtɔrikəl] *a.* ①史学的;有关历史的. ②历史的,历史上的;过去的. ③有根据的,真实的,非杜撰的 (*opp.* legendary). ④依据历史发展叙述的. ⑤历史上著名的〔现在一般用 *historic*〕. ⑥【语法】历史现在时态的. ~ *science* 历史学. *the* ~ *method* 历史的方法. ~ *studies* 历史研究. *a(n)* ~ *novel* 历史小说. *the* ~ *period* 历史阶段. *a(n)* ~ *personage* 历史人物. *the* ~ *present*【语法】= the historic present. *a(n)* ~ *treatise* 史论. ~ **geography** 历史地理学. ~ **linguistics** 历史语言学. ~ **materialism** 历史唯物主义. ~ **school** 历史学派. **-ly** *ad.* 在历史上,从历史观点上说.
his·tor·i·cism [hisˈtɔrisizəm] *n.* ①历史主义. ②历史发展天定论. ③对历史传统的崇拜.
his·to·ric·i·ty [ˌhistəˈrisiti] *n.* 历史性,真实性.
his·tor·i·cize [hisˈtɔːrisaiz] *vt.* 使具历史真实性,赋与…以历史意义. — *vi.* 运用史料.
his·to·ried [ˈhistərid] *a.* 历史上有名的,有历史的,有来由的;作为历史记载的. *a richly* ~ *land* 历史悠久的国家.
his·to·ri·ette [ˌhistɔːriˈet] *n.*〔F.〕史话,小史.
his·to·ri·og·ra·pher [ˌhistɔːriˈɔgrəfə] *n.* 历史家;史官,史料编纂者.
his·to·ri·og·ra·phy [ˌhistɔːriˈɔgrəfi] *n.* 编史工作,历史编纂学. **-o·gra·phic(al)** *a.*
his·to·ry [ˈhistəri] *n.* ①历史,历史学. ②沿革,来历;(个人的)履历,经历. ③对过去事件的记载;大事记. ④对形成未来的进程有影响的事件[思想]. ⑤过去的事. ⑥历史剧. *a case* ~ 病例,典型例证. *Ancient [Medieval, Modern] H-* 古代[中古、近代]史. *natural* ~ 博物学,自然史. *This sword has a* ~. 这剑有来历. *She has a* ~. 她的身世有难言之隐. *temperature* ~ 温度变化过程. *time* ~ 时间关系曲线图. ***H- repeats itself.***〔谚〕历史往往重演. ***make*** ~ 影响历史进程,做名垂青史的大事.
his·to·ther·a·py [ˈhistəuθerəpi] *n.*【医】组织疗法.
his·tri·on·ic(al) [ˌhistriˈɔnik(əl)] *a.* ①演员的,戏剧上的;戏剧性的. ②〔蔑〕象做戏似的,装腔作势的,虚伪的. ③面部肌肉的. — *n.* ①演员. ②〔*pl.*〕戏剧表演;舞台艺术. ③〔*pl.*〕戏剧似的言行;装腔作势. ~ **muscles**【解】表情肌. **-i·cal·ly** *ad.*
his·tri·on·i·cism, his·tri·on·ism [ˌhistriˈɔnisizəm, ˈhistriənizəm] *n.* 戏剧性,舞台效果.
hit [hit] *vt.* ***(hit; hitting)*** ①(箭、子弹等)打,打击,命中 (*opp.* miss). ②碰撞,使碰撞. ③偶然碰见,遇见;(搜寻后)找到,发现;想到. ④袭击,打击,使遭受. ⑤抨击,批评;伤…的感情. ⑥猜对,说中,戳穿(真相). ⑦适合,投合;要求,请求. ⑧达到,完成(指标);〔美俚〕到达,到…去;出现于(报刊等);搜寻(猎踪). ⑨【体】(板球等)得(分);【棒球】打出(安全打)〔打出能使击球者跑到第一垒的一击〕. ⑩精确地反映,原样复制. ⑪〔美俚〕埋头干;沉溺于. ⑫大口大口地吃[喝]. ⑬出发,上路. ~ *one's head against the door* 头撞在门上. ~ *it right* 正中,命中. *You've* ~ *it.* 你猜对了. ~ *one's fancy* 正中下怀. *H- the ground!* 卧倒! ~ *a likeness* 逼真地复制[绘制]原物. ~ *the town* 到达镇上. ~ *the job*〔美俚〕埋头工作. ~ *sb. for a loan* 向某人借钱. ~ *a new high* (物价等)上涨到新高峰. *The new train can* ~ *100 m. p. h.* 新火车时速可达 100 英里. *The report has hit the papers.* 那篇通讯已经见报. — *vi.* ①打,打击 (*at*); 命中. ②说中,猜对. ③偶然碰上,碰见 (*against, on, upon*). ④忽然想起,偶然想到 (*on, upon*). ⑤(在内燃机汽缸内)点火. ~ *upon a good idea* 灵机一动,忽然想到一个妙主意. *The army* ~ *at dawn.* 军队拂晓时出击. *His head* ~ *against the wall.* 他的头撞到墙上. ~ ***(...) against*** 撞击;把…碰到. ~ ***at*** 批评,嘲笑. ~ ***for***〔美〕向…出发. ~ ***horses together*** 齐心协力. ~ ***it*** ①说对;猜对;达到目的. ②〔美〕飞快地走. ~ ***it off*** 性情相投;〔口〕相处得很好 (*with; together*). ~ ***it up*** 坚持前进. ~ ***off*** ①〔讽〕逼真地描画,模仿. ②当场作(诗). ③打掉. ④(板球等)得分. ⑤适合,与…融洽 (*with*). ~ ***on [upon]*** 碰见;发现;想出(好办法),想到. ~ ***on all [six] cylinders*** 汽缸全部点火;〔喻〕拚命工作;性能良好. ~ ***one's stride*** 全力以赴. ~ ***out*** 抨击,猛烈打击 (*at*). ~ ***sb. below the belt*** (拳击)犯规行为;〔喻〕利用不正当手段打击某人,乘某人之危打击他. ~ ***sb. between the eyes*** 使某人有强烈的印象. ~ ***sb. when he is down*** 乘人之危,落井下石. ~ ***sb. where it hurts*** 打中要害,触到某人痛处. ~ ***the [one's] books***〔美俚〕用功. ~ ***the bottle*** 酗酒. ~ ***the breeze [pike, trail]***〔美俚〕旅行;流浪,漂泊. ~ ***the bull's-eye***〔美俚〕说到问题的本质. ~ ***the ceiling [roof]***〔美俚〕勃然大怒. ~ ***the clock***〔美〕打上班[下班]记时钟;在上班签到簿上签名. ~ ***the deck***〔美俚〕起床工作. ~ ***the gong [pipe]***〔美俚〕吸鸦片烟. ~ ***the gow***〔美俚〕吸食麻醉品. ~ ***the hay [sack]***〔美俚〕上床睡觉. ~ ***the headlines***【美体】出名,成为头条新闻. ~ ***the high spots*** ①上街;上夜总会. ②做事马虎. ③简略介绍. ~ ***the jackpot***〔美俚〕大获成功,走运. ~ ***the mark [target]*** 击中目标,打中要害. ~ ***the (right) nail on the head*** 命中;中肯. ~ ***the road***〔美俚〕上路,出发. ~ ***the spot*** (尤指食品,饮料)提神解乏,使满足. ~ ***the stands*** 上市,开始发售. ~ ***the tone of society*** 善于交际. ~ ***up*** ①催促;加速. ②〔美〕乞求. ③(板球等)得(分). ~ ***upon a stratagem*** 计上心来. — *n.* ①打击;命中,击中. ②碰撞. ③演出[尝试]的成功;轰动一时的人物;风行一时的东西. ④批评;讽刺 (*at*);俏皮话;⑤【棒球】安全打;(棒球等的)得分. ⑥好运气. ⑦一剂麻醉毒品,一口大麻烟.

a lucky ~ 偶中,幸中. *a clever* ~ 巧妙的一击;一句巧妙的俏皮话. *His novel was a great* ~. 他的小说大受欢迎. *clear* ~【棒球】绝好的安全打,快打. *fair* ~ 好球. **~ or miss** ①不顾胜败地;冒险地. ②漫无目的地. ***look to [mind] one's ~s*** 抓机会;关心自己的利益. ***make a [capital, great, magnificent, tremendous] ~*** 博得好评,很受欢迎,很成功. ***silent ~*** 〔美〕受欢迎的无声影片. ***smash ~*** 〔俚〕成功的演出. **~-and-miss** *a.* 有时打中而有时又打不中的;碰巧的. **~-and-run** *a.* ①闯祸后逃逸的〔通常指汽车司机在造成车祸后逃跑〕. ②(打棒球时)打了就跑的,击球跑垒的 (*a ~-and-run victim* 被已逃跑的汽车压死的人). **~-and-runner** 闯祸后逃走的汽车司机. **~ man** *n.* 职业凶手. **~-or-miss** *a.* 冒险的;不论成功与否的. **~ parade** (歌曲等的) 最流行的一批,流行唱片目录. **~-runner** 〔美〕= **~-and-runner.** **~-skip** = hit-and-run ①.

hitch [hitʃ] *vi.* ①被挂住,被钩住. ②一颠一簸地移动,跛行,蹒跚. ③〔美俚〕搭便车 (= hitchhike). ④〔口〕和好,协调. ⑤〔美俚〕结婚 (*up*). *My dress ~ed on a nail.* 我的衣服被钉子挂住了. — *vt.* ①拴住,系住,钩住,套住(牛马). ②急拉,猛拉;扯起;拉进,收进(故事中). ③〔美俚〕要求搭(车),搭便车去(旅行等)(=hitchhike). ④〔美俚〕使结婚. ~ *a rope over [round] the bough* 用索子套住树枝. ~ *a ride back to school* 搭便车返校. ***be ~ed = ~ oneself*** 结婚. ***~ horses together*** 把马系在一起;〔美〕和好,一致行动. ***~ one's waggon to a star*** 好高骛远,野心勃勃. ***~ up*** ①扯起. ②(把马等)拴在(车上). ③〔美俚〕使结婚. — *n.* ①系,拴,套,钩. ②起;停止,急止. ③障碍,顿挫. ④【海】索结,结索,索眼. ⑤〔美军俚〕服役期. ⑥蹒跚. ⑦〔美俚〕搭便车旅行. *His three-year ~ is not yet completed.* 他的三年兵役还没有满. ***without a ~*** 无障碍地,一帆风顺地. **~ing post** 拴马栓. **~hike** ① *vi.* 〔美口〕搭乘他人便车旅行. ② *vt.* 叫住(过路车等)要求免费搭乘;搭乘便车去(旅行等);获得(得到免费搭车)的机会. ③ *n.* 免费搭车. **~hiker** 〔美〕沿途搭乘他人汽车旅行的人.

Hitch·cock [ˈhitʃkɔk] *n.* 希契科克〔姓氏〕.

hith·er [ˈhiðə] *ad.* 〔古〕向此处. — *a.* 这里的,这边的,附近的. ***~ and thither*** = 〔美〕 ***~ and yon*** 到处,向各处,忽东忽西. ***on the ~ side (of …)*** ①在这一边. ②(年龄)不到…岁. *on the ~ side of sixty* 不到六十岁.

hith·er·most [ˈhiðəməust] *a.* 最近的.

hith·er·to [ˌhiðəˈtuː] *ad.* 迄今;到目前为止.

hith·er·ward(s) [ˈhiðəwəd(z)] *ad.* 〔罕〕 = hither *ad.*

Hit·ler [ˈhitlə], **Adolf,** 阿道夫·希特勒〔1889—1945,德国纳粹头目〕.

Hit·ler·i·an [hitˈliəriən] *a.* 希特勒的,希特勒式的,希特勒统治的.

Hit·ler·ism [ˈhitlərizəm] *n.* 希特勒主义.

Hit·ler·ite [ˈhitlərait] *n.* 希特勒主义者,纳粹党徒. — *a.* 希特勒主义者的,纳粹党徒的.

hit·ter [ˈhitə] *n.* ①打击者,击中者. ②【机】铆钉枪.

Hit·tite [ˈhitait] *n.* ①赫梯人〔小亚细亚东部和叙利亚北部古代部族〕. ②赫梯语. — *a.* ①赫梯人的. ②赫梯语的.

hive [haiv] *n.* ①蜂巢,蜂房,蜂箱. ②蜂群. ③蜂巢状物. ④热闹场所;熙攘的人群. *a ~ of industry* 繁忙的工厂区. — *vt.* ①使(蜂)入蜂箱,贮(蜜)于蜂箱中. ②贮备,积蓄. ③使(人)安居家中. — *vi.* ①(蜂)进蜂箱,栖巢中. ②同栖聚居. ***~ off*** (养蜂)分封;〔喻〕从团体中分出来成为独立的(自治的)部分. **~ nest** 鸟的群栖巢.

hives [haivz] *n. pl.* 〔用作 sing. 或 pl.〕【医】荨麻疹;〔英〕哮吼,喉炎.

hi·ya [ˈhaijə] *int.* 〔美俚〕你好! (= How are you?).

H.J., HJ = here lies 〔拉丁语 *his jacet* 的略语〕…长眠于此.

hk. = 【纺】hank.

HKA = Hong Kong Airways 香港航空公司.

hl. = hectolitre(s).

H.L., HL = House of Lords.

H.L.I. = 【英军】Highland Light Infantry.

hm. = hectometre.

h'm [hm] *int.* = hem², hum.

H.M., HM = His [Her] Majesty.

H.M.A.S. = His Majesty's Australian Ship. 澳大利亚舰船.

HMG = heavy machine gun.

H.M.S. = His [Her] Majesty's Service [Ship]. 英国舰船〔公函〕.

H.M.T. = His Majesty's Trawler. 英国拖网船.

Ho = 【化】holmium.

H.O., HO = ① Head Office 总部,总店. ②Home Office (英国)内政部.

ho [həu] *n.* = whore.

ho(a) [həu] *int.* ①嗬!〔唤起注意或表示惊讶、满足、喜悦〕. ②站住!〔止马声〕. ***ho! ho! ho!*** 哈!哈!哈!〔嘲笑声〕. ***ho! there*** 喂! ***What ho!*** 嗬,什么! ***(Westward) ho!*** 【海】向(西)去啊!

hoa·gy, hoa·gie [ˈhəugi] *n.* (*pl.* **-gies**) = herosandwich.

hoar [hɔː,hɔə] *a.* ①(头发)灰白的,白色的. ②有灰白头发的. ③〔方〕发霉的. — *n.* ①灰白色;白发. ②白霜 (= ~frost).

hoard [hɔːd] *n.* ①窖藏的财宝,密藏的东西. ②(食品的)贮藏,贮藏物. ③(知识等的)宝库. *a ~ of money* 积蓄. — *vt.* ①积蓄;贮藏;囤积 (*up*). ②把…隐藏在心;心怀. ~ *gold* 积聚黄金. ~ *revenge* 怀恨. — *vi.* 贮藏;囤积.

hoard·er [ˈhɔːdə] *n.* 贮藏者;囤积者.

hoard·ing¹ [ˈhɔːdiŋ] *n.* ①贮藏;囤积;(货币的)埋藏. ②〔*pl.*〕贮藏物;囤积物.

hoard·ing² [ˈhɔːdiŋ] *n.* ①〔英〕(空地、修建场所的)临时围篱,板围. ②广告牌. ③(古代用木头搭在城墙外的)守望台.

hoar·hound [ˈhɔːhaund] *n.* = horehound.

hoarse [hɔːs] *a.* (嗓子)嘶哑的,沙哑的;刺耳的. *as ~ as a raven* 声音沙哑. *talk oneself ~* 把嗓子说哑. **-ly** *ad.* **-ness** *n.*

hoars·en [ˈhɔːsn] *vt.* 使(嗓子)嘶哑. — *vi.* (嗓子)变嘶哑.

hoarstone [ˈhɔːstəun] *n.* 灰色古石;〔英〕(特指史前的)界标石.

hoar·y [ˈhɔːri, ˈhɔəri] *a.* ①灰白的;(因年老)头发变白的,白发的. ②陈旧的,古老的. ③【植、动】生满灰白毛的. *a ~ head* 须发斑白的头. *the ~ antiquity* 远古. ~ *ruins* 古代遗迹. **~ marmot** 【动】花白旱獭 (*Marmota caligata*) 〔发现于北美洲〕. **hoar·i·ly** *ad.* **hoar·i·ness** *n.*

hoar·y-head·ed [ˈhɔːrihedid] *a.* 白发苍苍的.

ho·at·zin [həuˈætsin] *n.* 【动】(南美产、幼鸟翼上有爪、能攀树的)何爱青鸟 (*Opisthocomus hoazin*), 麝雉.

hoax [həuks] *n.* 欺骗,愚弄,戏弄;骗术,骗局. — *vt.* 欺骗,戏弄.

hoax·er [ˈhəuksə] *n.* 欺骗者,戏弄者.

hob¹ [hɔb] *n.* ①(壁炉一侧的) 锅架,开水壶架. ②【机】滚(铣)刀,螺旋铣刀;元阳模;蜗(轮)杆;螺(旋)杆. ③平头钉. ④投环戏的标棍;用石头打落棒头钱的游戏. — *vt.* ①给…钉平头钉. ②【机】滚铣.

hob² [hɔb] *n.* ①〔英方〕淘气鬼. ②〔口〕捣乱,恶作剧;破坏. ***play [raise] ~*** ①恶作剧,捣乱. ②歪曲 (*with*) (*play ~ with facts* 歪曲事实).

hob-and-nob [ˈhɔbənˈnɔb] *a.* 亲密的.

Ho·bart [ˈhəubɑːt] *n.* ①霍巴特〔姓氏,男子名〕. ②霍巴特〔澳大利亚港市〕.

Hobbes [hɔbz] *n.* ①霍布斯〔姓氏〕. ② **Thomas ～** 托马斯·霍布斯〔1588—1679,英国哲学家〕.

Hobbes·i·an [ˈhɔbziən] *a.* 英国哲学家霍布斯的，霍布斯哲学理论的. — *n.* 霍布斯哲学理论的鼓吹〔追随〕者.

Hob·bism [ˈhɔbizəm] *n.* 霍布斯的哲学理论.

Hob·bist [ˈhɔbist] — *a., n.* ＝Hobbesian.

hob·ble [ˈhɔbl] *vi.* ①蹒跚，跛行 *(along; about).* ②(说话、行动)疙疙瘩瘩；(诗)不流畅. — *vt.* ①使跛行. ②将(马的)两只脚拴在一起. ③阻碍. — *n.* ①跛行；韵律不全的诗. ②马的脚绊. ③〔口、方〕困境. ***be in [get into] a (nice) ～*** 陷入进退两难. **～bush** *n.* 【植】桤叶荚蒾 *(Viburnum alnifolium).* ～ **skirt** 膝以下窄狭的裙子. **hobblingly** *ad.*

hob·ble·de·hoy [ˈhɔbldiˈhɔi] *n.* 青少年；(笨拙的)小伙子.

hob·by[1] [ˈhɔbi] *n.* ①业余爱好；嗜好，兴趣. ②(小孩玩的)竹马，木马. ③〔罕〕小马. ***mount [ride] a [one's] ～ (to death)*** 沉溺在业余的嗜好中(不可自拔),反复说〔做〕自己喜欢做的事(以致令人生厌). **-ist** *n.* 有业余爱好的人.

hob·by[2] [ˈhɔbi] *n.* (用以猎捕小鸟的)小隼.

hob·by·horse [ˈhɔbihɔːs] *n.* ①木马，摇马，竹马；玩具马. ②〔罕〕业余爱好，嗜好. ③爱反复讲的话题. *Every man has his ～.* 〔谚〕人各有所好. ***mount [ride] a [one's] ～*** ＝ mount [ride] a [one's] hobby.

hob·gob·lin [ˈhɔbˌgɔblin] *n.* ①妖怪，小鬼；淘气鬼. ②令人厌恶的东西，怪物.

hob·nail [ˈhɔbneil] *n.* ①(钉在靴底上的)平头钉. ②穿钉有平头钉靴子的人，乡下佬. — *vt.* 在(鞋底等上)钉平头钉. ～ **liver** 【医】(肝硬变引起的)鞋钉肝，门静脉性肝硬变. **-ed** *a.* (鞋底)钉有平头钉的；土头土脑的 *(hobnailed liver* ＝ hobnail liver*).*

hob·nob [ˈhɔbnɔb] *vi.* ①共饮，开怀对饮. ②恳谈；亲切交往 *(with; together).* — *n.* 聚会，恳谈. — *ad.* 随意地.

ho·bo [ˈhəubəu] *n.* ***(pl. ～(e)s)*** 〔美俚〕①(随季节流动各地的)流动工人. ②(白坐火车到处流浪的)无业游民，流浪汉. ～ **belt** 〔美〕加州的香橼栽培区. ～**limited**〔美俚〕车务员宽待游民的火车. — *vi.* 过流浪生活. **-ism** *n.* 流浪生活.

ho·boe [ˈhəubəu], **ho·boy** [ˈhəubɔi] *n.* ＝ hautboy.

Hob·son [ˈhɔbsn] *n.* 霍布森〔姓氏〕. ～**'s choice** 无选择余地〔源自英国 16—17 世纪的租马房经营者托马斯·霍布森,该马房规定租马的顾客不许挑选〕.

hock[1] [hɔk] *n.* ①【动】(有蹄类的)跗关节 (＝ ～ joint). ②(猪的)腿肉，肘子. — *vt.* 割断蹄筋使成残废.

hock[2] [hɔk] *n.* ①典当，抵押. ②〔美俚〕监牢. — *vt.* 典当，抵押. ***in ～*** ①在典当中；借着债. ②〔美俚〕在坐牢. ***out of ～*** ①已赎出(典当物). ②已不欠债. ～ **shop** 〔美俚〕当铺.

hock[3] [hɔk] *n.* 〔英〕(德国)莱茵白葡萄酒.

hock·er [ˈhɔkə] *n.* 典当者.

hock·ey [ˈhɔki] *n.* 曲棍球；曲棍球球棒. *field ～* 曲棍球. *ice ～* 冰上曲棍球，冰球. ～ **stick** 曲棍球棒.

Hock·ing [ˈhɔkiŋ] *n.* 霍金〔姓氏〕.

ho·cum [ˈhəukəm] *n.* ＝ hokum.

ho·cus [ˈhəukəs] *n.* ①欺骗. ②蒙汗药酒. — *vt.* (〔英〕 ***-ss-***) ①欺骗. ②加麻醉剂(在酒中)；麻醉. ③在…中掺假.

ho·cus-po·cus [ˈhəukəsˈpəukəs] *vt., vi.* ***(-s(s)-)*** 〔俚〕哄骗，戏弄. — *n.* ①(变戏法人转移观众注意力的)咒语〔手法〕. ②转移注意力的言语〔行动〕. ③欺骗. ***play ～*** 玩弄欺骗手法.

hod [hɔd] *n.* ①灰浆桶，砖泥斗. ②煤斗. ～ **carrier** 泥瓦活小工.

ho·dad, ho·dad·dy [ˈhəudæd, ˈhəuˌdædi] *n.* 常去冲浪海滩假充会冲浪的人，冒牌冲浪运动员.

hod·den, hod·din [ˈhɔdn] *n.* 〔Scot.〕手织粗呢. — *a.* 穿着手织粗呢衣服的；土里土气的. ～ **gray [grey]** 黑白毛交织的手织粗呢.

Ho·dei·da [həuˈdeidə] *n.* 荷台达〔阿拉伯也门共和国港市〕.

Hodge[1], **hodge** [hɔdʒ] *n.* 〔英〕乡下人，庄稼汉.

Hodge[2] [hɔdʒ] *n.* 霍奇〔男子名, Roger 的爱称〕.

Hodge·kin [ˈhɔdʒkin] *n.* 何杰金〔姓氏〕. ～**'s disease** *n.* 【医】何杰金氏病〔淋巴肉芽肿〕.

hodge·podge [ˈhɔdʒpɔdʒ] *n.* ＝ hotch-potch.

Hodg·son [ˈhɔdʒsn] *n.* 霍奇森〔姓氏〕.

hod·i·er·nal [ˌhɔdiˈəːnl] *a.* 现在的，今天的；今世的.

hod·man [ˈhɔdmən] *n.* ***(pl. -men*** [-men]***)*** ①灰泥砖瓦搬运工 ＝ (hod carrier)，小工，苦工. ②代笔穷文人.

hod·o·graph [ˈhɔdəgrɑːf] *n.* 【数】速矢端线；【物】速端曲线.

hod·om·e·ter [hɔˈdɔmitə] *n.* 车程计，路程计，计距器，轮转计 (＝ odometer).

hod·o·scope [ˈhɔdəskəup] *n.* 荷多仪；【宇】辐射计数器；【物】描迹器.

hoe [həu] *n.* 锄头；灰耙. *back ～* 反向铲，倒铲. *Dutch ～* 一种锹. *trench ～* 挖沟机. — *vt., vi.* 用锄除(草等)，用锄(松土等)；挖掘. ***a hard [tough] row to ～*** 艰苦生活，困难的工作. ***a new row to ～*** 〔美〕新任务. ***～ a big row*** 〔美〕干大事. ***～ another row*** 〔美〕着手新工作. ***～ one's own row*** 干自己的事，自扫门前雪. ***～ your potatoes*** 〔美〕别管闲事. **～cake** 〔美〕玉米饼. **～down** 〔美俚〕①一种农村舞. ②喧闹的舞会〔宴会〕. ③吵闹，争论；闹事，打群架. ～ **teeth** 梳形矿耙齿.

Hof·man(n) [ˈhɔfmən] *n.* 霍夫曼〔姓氏〕.

Hof·stad·ter [ˈhɔfstætə, ˈhɔfstɑːtə] *n.* 霍夫施塔特〔姓氏〕.

hog [hɔg] *n.* ①猪〔尤指阉过的、重120磅以上的肉用猪〕；阉过的公猪；猪肉；【动】杂食性动物. ②〔口〕贪婪、卑鄙、粗野、龌龊的人. ③〔英方，常拼作 hogg〕尚未剪毛的羊羔；从羊羔身上剪下的毛. ④〔美俚〕火车头. ⑤【海】船底扫除帚. ⑥【机】弯拱；纸浆桶搅拌器. ⑦鲁莽的骑〔驾〕车者. *～-raisers' association* 〔美〕养猪业公会(＝〔英〕pigbreeder's association). ***a ～ in armo(u)r*** 穿漂亮衣服而局促不安的人；动作笨拙的人. ***as [like] a ～ on ice*** 〔美〕(象猪在冰上那样)处境困难. ***bring one's ～s to the wrong market*** 〔口〕走错了门路；找不适当的人〔场合〕提出要求. ***drive one's ～s to market*** 〔俚〕大声打鼾. ***go (the) whole ～*** 彻底干，干到底. ***live [eat] high on [off] the ～*** 〔美口〕生活得很阔气，过奢侈的生活. ***～ Latin*** ＝ pig Latin. ***～ mane*** 剪短的马鬣. ***make a ～ of oneself*** 贪吃，馋嘴. ***on the ～*** 〔美俚〕分文没有. ***play the ～*** 独吞独揽，行为卑鄙. ***raise more ～s and less hell*** 〔美〕多干活，少闯祸. — *vi.* ①(船等象猪背一样)中部拱起. ②〔口〕横冲直撞. — *vt.* ①剪短(马鬣等). ②【海】扫除(船底). ③使(船底)中部拱曲. ④鲁莽地骑(车)〔驾驶(车)〕. ⑤【无】扰乱(别人播送). ⑥〔美俚〕贪婪地抢夺，抢占(全部或大部)；〔美俚〕剽窃(别人的著作等). **～back** 拱起的背；象猪背一样向上拱起的东西；陡峻的拱地，陡峻的山脊. ～ **cholera** 猪霍乱. ～ **deer** 豚鹿 (＝ axis). **～fish** 猪头鱼；鲜红鱼 (Lachnobaimus maximus)〔产于美国东南沿海〕. **～-killing** 〔美方〕喧闹的聚会. **～leg** 〔美方〕左轮手枪. **～let** 〔美〕小猪. **～man** 养猪人. **～-nut**＝pignut. ～ **peanut**【植】同株二型豆 *(Amplicarpaea monoica)*〔产于北美洲东部〕. **～pen** 〔美〕猪圈. **～'s-back** ＝ ～back. **～'s fennel** 前胡属植物. **～skin** 猪皮，猪皮做的东西. ～ **still** 【化】蒸馏塔. **～wash** ①猪食，泔脚. ②废话；空洞的作品. **～weed** 劣草〔如美洲豚草〕. **～wild** *a.* 〔俚〕无约束的，混乱的，过于兴奋而狂乱的.

ho·gan [ˈhəugɔːn] *n.* 印第安人草屋〔多指北美印第安人

纳瓦霍 (Naraho) 族用泥和树枝盖的小屋〕.

Ho·garth [ˈhəugɑːθ] *n.* ①霍格斯〔姓氏〕. ②**William** ~ 威廉·霍格斯〔1697—1764,英国绘画家和雕刻家〕.

Hog·ben [ˈhɔgbən] *n.* 霍格本〔姓氏〕.

Hogg [hɔg] *n.* 霍格〔姓氏〕.

hog·ger·el [ˈhɔgərel] *n.* = hogget ①.

hog·ger·y [ˈhɔgəri] *n.* ①养猪场, 猪棚. ②猪群. ③猪一样的举动.

hog·get [ˈhɔgit] *n.* ①满一岁的羔羊〔小猪, 小马〕. ②= hogshead.

hog·gin [ˈhɔgin] *n.* (筛过的)夹砂砾石,含砂砾石.

hog·ging [ˈhɔgiŋ] *n.* 弯曲,扭曲;挠度;凸起.

hog·gish [ˈhɔgiʃ] *a.* 猪似的;肮脏的;卑鄙的;贪婪的;食量大的. **-ly** *ad.* **-ness** *n.*

hog·ma·nay, -ney [ˈhɔgməˈnei] *n.* 〔Scot.〕 ①大年夜,除夕. ②年夜饭;(给孩子的)年节礼物.

hog·nose [ˈhɔgnəuz] *n.* (北美)猪鼻蛇〔又作 ~ snake〕.

hogs·head [ˈhɔgzhed] *n.* ①(容量约 63—140 美制加仑的)大桶. ②液量单位〔52.5 英制加仑 (= 198.75 升); 63 美制加仑 = 238.5 升〕.

hog·tie [ˈhɔ(:)gtai] *vt.* ***(-ti·ed; -ty·ing, -tie·ing)*** ①缚住…的手脚,绑住…的四肢. ②〔口〕使动弹不得〔束住手脚不能进行有效的活动〕.

Ho·hen·zol·lern [ˈhəuəntsələn] *n.* ①霍亨索伦王室〔德国普鲁士王室(1701—1918)〕. ②霍亨索伦州〔普鲁士一州名〕.

Ho·ho·kam [ˈhəuˈhəukɑːm] *a.* 〔美考古〕霍荷卡姆文化的. ~ **culture** 霍荷卡姆文化〔美国西南部 *Gila* 河流域史前的沙漠文化,该文化有大地洞室、陶器、骨贝装饰品及火葬遗址〕.

ho-hum [ˈhəuˈhʌm] *int.* 喝哼!〔表示无聊、不感兴趣、疲倦等的感叹词〕.

hoi(c)k [hɔik] *vt.* 〔方〕 = hoist.

hoick(s) [hɔik(s)] *int.* 嗬嚏〔驱赶猎犬声〕.

hoi·den [ˈhɔidn] *n.* = hoyden.

hoi pol·loi [ˌhɔipəˈlɔi] 〔Gr.〕 ①〔常冠以 the〕民众;群众. ②老百姓,每个人. ③〔美俚〕有钱有势的人,名流.

hoise [hɔiz] *vt.* ***(hoised, hoist*** **[hɔist]*; hois·ing)*** 〔古〕= hoist. ***be hoist with one's own petard*** 〔古〕搬起石头砸自己的脚.

hoist [hɔist] *n.* ①扯起,绞起,升起. ②升举器,起重机,升降机,吊车. ③【海】(帆、旗升起后的)高度;一排信号旗;桅杆中部. ④〔俚〕推,托,举. *air* ~ 气动葫芦,气吊,气压起重机. *carriage* ~起重车,卷扬机. *give sb. a* ~ (如爬墙等)把某人往上一推. — *vt.* 升,扯起,举起(旗帜等). — *vi.* 升起来,扯起来. ~ ***down*** 扯下. ~**hole,** ~**-way** (货物)起卸口;(升降机)通路.

hoist·er [ˈhɔistə] *n.* ①起重机,卷扬机;【矿】提升机,绞车. ②起重机〔提升机〕的司机.

hoist·ing [ˈhɔistiŋ] *n.* 起重,提升. ~ **cable** 钢丝绳. ~ **drum** 绞车滚筒. ~ **jack** 千斤顶.

hoi·ty-toi·ty [ˈhɔitiˈtɔiti] *a.* ①轻浮的;反复无常的. ②傲慢的,骄傲的. ③易怒的,脾气大的;怒气冲冲的. — *n.* 轻率,傲慢. — *int.* 哎呀!〔表示傲慢或忿怒〕.

hoke [həuk] *vt.* ***(hoked; hok·ing)*** 〔俚〕①以虚情假意对待;搪塞,敷衍. ②勉强拼凑〔通常与 *up* 连用〕. — *n.* 〔俚〕=hokum. **hok·ey** *a.* 〔俚〕假的,做作的.

ho·k(e)y·po·k(e)y [ˈhəukiˈpəuki] *n.* 〔俚〕①(沿街叫卖的)廉价冰淇淋. ②= hocuspocus.

Hok·kai·do [həˈkaidəu] *n.* 北海道〔日本〕.

ho·kum [ˈhəukəm] *n.* ①〔俚〕(影剧中)逗人笑或惹人落泪的惯用手法,噱头. ②欺骗,无聊的话;无聊的主张.

Hol·arc·tic [hɔˈlɑːktik] *a.* 【动】(大陆动物地区之一)全北区的.

HOLC, l ol : = Home Owner's Loan Corporation 〔美〕房主贷款公司.

hold[1] [həuld] *vt.* ***(held*** [held]; ***held, hold·en*** [ˈhəuldən]) ①(用手、手臂等)拿住,握住,抓住,夹住. ②有,拥有,保存(财产);掌握;占据,保持(地位等);担任(职务等). ③包含,收容;容纳,装着. ④控制,保持…的状态;支持,托住;压住,止住;吸住(注意等). ⑤〔美〕拘押;扣留;保留;使负(责任等). ⑥怀有,持有(见解等);认为,相信,想;判决. ⑦举行,开(会). ⑧依法占有,用契约约束. ⑨【乐】延长(发音). ~ *a pen* 拿钢笔. ~ *the baby in one's arms* 抱孩子. *have and* ~ 保有. ~ *a pipe between the teeth* 嘴里啣着烟斗. *Lightly won, lightly held.* 〔谚〕得来容易丢失得快. ~ *the first position (among …)* 占第一位. *This room can* ~ *fifty people.* 这个房间可以容纳五十人. *The pail* ~*s milk.* 桶内装着牛奶. ~ *the door open* 让门开着. ~ *oneself in readiness* 准备着. ~ *one's breath* 屏息. *H-your hand!* 住手! *H-!* = *H- hand!* 停止. *A fever held him for a week.* 他发烧一个星期了. ~ *one to be a fool* 拿人当傻瓜. *I* ~ *it my duty to inform [tell] you.* 我认为我有责任通知你. *There is no* ~*ing him.* 弄他不过,制不了他. ~ *a discussion* 开讨论会. ~ *an examination* 举行考试. ~ *sb. guilty* 判定某人有罪. *be held at the station house* 被拘留在警察局. — *vi.* ①抓着,握着;保持(*on, to*). ②持久,耐久;支持得住. ③继续,继续进行,持续. ④合用,可适用,(条约等仍然)有效. ⑤享有,保有土地〔财产、权利等〕*(of; from)*. ⑥停止〔常用于命令式〕. *The rope* ~*s.* 绳子吃得住〔不会断〕. *Winter still* ~*s.* 冬天还没有过去. *The rule does not* ~ *(good) in this case.* 这规则在这种情况下不适用. ***be neither to*** ~ ***nor to bind*** 非常激动,无法抑制. ***cry*** ~ 命令停止. ~ ***a candle to the devil*** 助纣为虐,为虎作伥. ~ ***(oneself) aloof*** 不接近别人,清高超然. ~ ***[keep] at arm's length*** 冷淡待人. ~ ***back*** ①踌躇,退缩不前. ②阻止;抑制,压住;扣住 *(from)*,保守秘密,隐瞒. ~ ***by*** 赞成(主张);坚持(目的、见解等). ~ ***(sb.) captive*** 俘虏,拘捕. ~ ***cheap*** 瞧不起,不重视. ~ ***dear*** 看重,珍视. ~ ***demonstration against*** 举行游行示威反对. ~ ***down*** ①垂下. ②压制;牵制;阻止,忍耐;压低(物价等);缩减. ③〔美口〕维持,保有;保持(职位). ~ ***everything [it]*** 〔美口〕停止,等一下. ~ ***fast [to]*** 坚持. ~ ***for*** 适用,适于. ~ ***forth*** ①提出;提供;发表(意见). ②〔蔑〕滔滔不绝地演说. ~ ***from doing sth.*** 忍住不作某事. ~ ***good [true]*** *(for)* 有效;适用;有理. ~ ***hard!*** 〔用于命令式〕停止! 别忙! 等一等! ~ ***in*** 抑制;忍住. ~ ***in abhorrence [abomination]*** 厌恶,痛恨. ~ ***in balance*** 使不稳定,使悬而不决. ~ … ***in esteem [honour, regard, respect]*** 尊重,尊敬. ~ ***in memory*** 记住. ~ ***in one's temper*** 忍气吞声. ~ … ***in place [position]*** 使…保持固定位置. ~ ***[keep] in play*** 使劳动,使有事做. ~ ***in pledge*** 抵押. ~ ***in trust*** 保管. ~ ***it good*** *(to do)* 以为(做…)是好的. ~ ***off*** ①使离开,使不接近. ②抵抗(进攻等). ③延缓,拖延. (*The rain still* ~*s off.* 雨还下不来). ~ ***on*** ①拉住,抓牢. ②继续;坚持下去. ③(打电话时)不挂断;〔口〕等一等,停住. ④(交易中)煞价钱. ⑤(暴风)吹个不停. ~ ***on like grim death*** 死不松手. ~ ***on one's way*** 不顾干扰地继续前进. ~ ***on to*** 盘据,赖着不走. ~ ***(one's) fire*** 不表示态度. ~ ***one's ground[own]*** 固守阵地,一步不退,坚持. ~ ***one's hand [hands]*** 谨慎,留余地. ~ ***one's hand high*** 骄傲. ~ ***one's horses*** 〔美〕停止,等待 (~ *your horses* 不要忙). ~ ***one's noise [peace, tongue]*** 保持沉默. ~ ***one's nose*** 用手掩鼻. ~ ***out*** ①伸出;提出,主张. ②制止,阻止. ③支持,维持. ④不退让,坚持到底. ⑤〔美俚〕保留一部分分赃时被隐匿的钱. ~ ***out against*** 经受得住,顶得住. ~ ***out on sb.*** 不让某人了解情况,隐瞒. ~ ***over*** ①将…延迟. ②保存. ③期满后继续任职;期满后继续占有. ④加以(恐吓). ⑤胜过,优于. ~ ***power over*** 有支配…的权利. ~ ***sb. responsible for*** 使某人对…负责. ~ ***strike against*** 举行罢工反对. ~ ***talks***

with 同…举行会谈. ~ ***the bag*** 受害(详见 bag 条). ~ ***the fort*** ①固守堡垒，打退敌人的进攻. ②毫不示弱. ③继续干活. ~ ***the rein*** 掌权；执政；支配. ~ ***the stage*** ①继续活跃在舞台上. ②引起观众注意. ~ ***to*** 赞成，坚持. ~ ***together*** (使)团结在一起，(使)结合在一起. ~ ***true*** 适用. ~ ***up*** ①举起；展示；举出(做榜样)，揭露出(给人嘲笑). ②〔口〕阻止，使停滞，使停顿；〔命令〕停止！③〔美〕拦劫. ④支持住；持久；忍住. ⑤【猎】放慢步子. ⑥(晴天)继续，〔美〕(雨)停. ~ ***up one's hands*** 举起双手表示不抵抗，投降. ~ ***up one's head*** 抬着头，打起精神. ~ ***up the work*** 停工. ~ ***water*** ①(容器)不漏水. ②(论点)站得住脚，说得有理有据. ③(欲停船时)制住桨. ~ ***with*** 赞成，同意；和…抱同一意见. — *n.* ①握住；掌握；保持. ②支撑点，可攀〔踏〕的东西；线索，端绪. ③威力，势力；理解力. ④容器. ⑤监禁，监牢；城砦；避难所. ⑥【物】同期，同步. ⑦【乐】延长号，延音. ⑧(拳击，摔交等中的)擒拿法. ⑨保留，预约；关于延迟的通知. ⑩〔美〕(导弹的)延迟倒数，延期发射. ***(be) in ~s*** 揪着，扭着. ***catch [claw, get, lay, seize, take] ~ of*** 抓住，掌握. ***have a ~ on [over]*** 对…有把握力〔支配力，威力，作用〕. ***get [have] ~ of the wrong end of the stick*** 完全误解. ***keep ~ of [on]*** 握紧. ***lay ~ of [on]*** 到手，得到；掌握. ***let go [leave, lose] ~ of sth.*** 放松手，放弃. ***maintain [relax] its ~ over …*** 抓牢〔放松〕对…的控制. ***no ~s barred***〔口〕没有清规戒律的约束. ***put a ~ on*** 预约 (*put a ~ on a library book* 向图书馆预约借一本书). ~**all** 帆布袋，工具袋. ~**back** ①妨碍，牵制；障碍物. ②(马车上的)煞车. ③暂时停顿；暂时被扣下的东西(如工资等). ~**down** (费用等的)缩减. ~ **furnace [hearth]**【冶】混合炉，保温炉. ~**out** ①伸出，延续；提供；坚持；不让步. ②拖签合同者〔资本主义国家职业运动员对老板讨价还价的举动〕；拒不参加者，拒不达成协议者，坚持不合作者. ~**over**〔口〕①残存的人，遗物. ②任期已满仍然继续任职的人员. ③比赛或演出后继续参加的人员. ④留级的学生. ⑤〔俚〕宿醉. ~ **up** ①(交通)堵塞. ②拦劫，抢劫. ③〔口〕要高价，敲竹杠.

hold² [həuld] *n.*【船】货舱，底层舱. ~ *capacity* 货舱容量. *break out the* ~ 开始卸货. *stow the* ~ 装舱. ~**man** 舱内装卸工人.

hold·en [ˈhəuldən]〔古〕hold 的过去分词.

hold·er [ˈhəuldə] *n.* ①持(票)人；(土地、权利等的)所有人，货主. ②烟嘴；(笔)杆. ③台；座，架；夹；储存器. *a ~ of an office* 负责人. *a record ~* 记录保持人. *a share ~* 股票持有人. *a bit [drill] ~*【机】钻套. *a cigarette ~* 烟嘴. *a pen ~* 笔杠. *a gas ~* 装气罐，贮气室. *a lamp ~* 灯座. *a mirror ~* 镜架. ~**-on** *n.* (船上的)铆工.

hold·fast [ˈhəuldfɑːst] *n.* ①紧缠，紧握. ②钩子，钉子，夹钳. ③【动】吸附器官. ④【植】固着器. ***lose one's ~*** 放松，控制不住.

hold·ing [ˈhəuldiŋ] *n.* ①把握；支持. ②持有，享有，所有，财产. ③〔常 *pl.*〕所有物；保有股份；租借地，保有地；所有权. ④【体】持球，非法抱人〔撞人〕. *~s in a business company* 在某公司中的股份. ~ **attack**【军】牵制攻击. ~ **company** 控股公司. ~ **current**【电】维持电流. ~ **device**【机】夹具. ~ **pattern** (飞机在机场上空等待腾出跑道时的)椭圆形盘旋. ~ **temperature** 保温温度. ~ **time** (电话)占用时间.

hole [həul] *n.* ①洞，穴，孔；(衣服等上的)破洞；伤口；漏洞；窝，坑；水流的深凹处，(河道的)缓流注. ②(兽的)洞穴，窝巢；陋屋，狭小阴暗的地方〔房子〕；监狱中的隔离牢房. ③〔口〕陷阱；绝境. ④缺陷，缺点. ⑤【物】空穴，空子. ⑥高尔夫球的穴；高尔夫球得分. ⑦〔美〕铁路的支线. ⑧大型导弹地下井. ⑨〔美〕小湾，小港. ***a ~ in one's coat*** 缺点，瑕疵. ***a ~ in the road***〔美口〕村庄. ***a poky ~*** 非常闭塞的地方，穷乡僻壤. ***a square peg in a round ~*** 不适宜担任某项工作的人(见 peg 条). ***every ~ and corner*** 每个角落，到处. ***find a ~ to creep out*** 在困境中找出路，寻找脱身之计. ***in a devil of a ~*** 处境非常困难. ***in a ~*** 陷入绝境，为难. ***in the ~***〔口〕经济困难，负债；(在纸牌中)得一负点. ***leave a ~ to creep out*** 留后路. ***like a rat in a ~*** 象坑中的老鼠一样跑不脱，瓮中之鳖. ***make a ~ in*** ①开洞. ②花费过多. ***make a ~ in the water*** 跳水自尽. ***make ~*** 钻油井. ***pick a [~s ~] in*** 对…吹毛求疵；批评，责备. ***pick a ~ in sb.'s coat*** 找某人的岔子. ***the nineteenth ~***〔谑〕高尔夫球俱乐部的酒吧间. — *vt.* ①穿(孔)，打(洞)，开(隧道等)；挖(坑等). ②把…赶入洞中；把(高尔夫球)打入穴中. — *vi.* ①掘洞；钻进洞中. ②把高尔夫球打进穴中. ~ ***out*** (*in four*) (四击)将高尔夫球打入穴内. ~ ***up*** ①蛰居洞中. ②躲藏. ③安置…在避难处〔躲藏处〕. ④监禁. ~**-and-corner** *a.* 秘密的，偷偷摸摸的. ~ **card** 牌面朝下的牌；隐藏的优点. ~**-gauge** 内量规，内测微计. ~**proof** *a.* (衣服等)不会破洞的；(法律等)没有漏洞的.

hole·r [ˈhəulə] *n.* ①挖洞者. ②(高尔夫球场等)有若干洞穴的场所〔常与数字连用〕.

hole·y [ˈhəuli] *a.* 有孔的，多洞的.

hol·i·but [ˈhɔlibət] *n.* = halibut.

hol·i·day [ˈhɔlədi, ˈhɔlidei] *n.* ①节日，假日，休息日. ②〔英 *pl.*〕休假. ③〔古〕圣日(= holy day). ***be home for the ~*** 放假回家. ***blind man's ~***〔谑〕黄昏. ***busman's ~*** 照样做日常工作的休假. ***highdays, ~s and bonfire nights***〔谑〕节日，休假日. ***make [take]*** (*a week's*) ~ 休假(一星期). ***official ~s*** 法定假日. ***on ~*** 在休假中，在度假. ***Roman ~*** 以观看别人受苦为乐的娱乐. — *a.* 节日的，节日适用的；愉快的，活泼的. ~ *clothes [attire]* (节日穿的)盛装. ~ *mood [spirit]* 欢悦的心情. — *vi.*〔主英〕度假，休假. ~ **English** 一本正经的英语. ~**-maker** 度假者. ~ **speeches [terms, words]** 冠冕堂皇的话，好听的话，奉承话. ~ **task**〔英〕学生的假期作业. **-er** *n.* 度假者.

hol·i·days [ˈhɔləˌdeiz] *ad.*〔美〕在假日，每逢假日.

ho·li·er-than-thou [ˈhəuliəðənˈðau] *a.* 假装神圣的；自以为是的.

ho·li·ly [ˈhəulili] *ad.* 虔诚地；神圣地.

ho·li·ness [ˈhəulinis] *n.* ①【宗】神圣；清净，纯洁. ②〔H-〕陛下，宗座〔对罗马教皇等的尊称，常与 His 或 Your 连用〕.

ho·lism [ˈhəulizm] *n.*【哲】整体论. **ho·list** *n.* 整体论者. **ho·lis·tic** *a.* **ho·lis·ti·cal·ly** *ad.*

hol·la [ˈhɔlə, hɔˈlɑː] *int., n., vi., vt.* = hollo(a).

Hol·land [ˈhɔlənd] *n.* ①荷兰〔正式名称是 *the Netherlands*〕. ②〔h-〕〔常 *pl.* 但作 *sing.* 用〕荷兰麻布，洁白亚麻细布，窗帘棉布；〔*pl.*〕荷兰杜松子酒(= ~ gin). **-er** ①荷兰人；荷兰船. ②〔h-〕(造纸)打浆机.

hol·lan·daise [ˌhɔlənˈdeiz] *a.* 荷兰式的. — *n.* 蛋黄奶油酸辣酱(= ~ sauce).

hol·ler [ˈhɔlə] *n.* ①呼叫，呼救. ②〔美〕盗贼受害人的控诉. ③(美国黑人随口哼的)劳动号子. — *vt.* 喊出. — *vi.* ①叫喊，大喊大叫. ②诉苦，抱怨.

Holler·ith [ˈhɔuləriθ] *n.*【计】利用凿孔把字母信息在卡片上编码的一种方式〔以美国发明人赫尔曼·霍尔瑞斯(Herman Hollerith, 1860—1929)命名〕. ~**code** 霍尔瑞斯编码. ~ **constant** 霍尔瑞斯常数. ~ **type machine** 霍尔瑞斯型计算机.

Hol·lis [ˈhɔlis] *n.* 霍利斯〔姓氏，男子名〕.

hol·lo(a) [ˈhɔləu] *int.* 喂！— *vi.* 喂喂地叫. — *vt.* 向…发"喂"声. — *n.* 喂喂的叫声.

hol·low [ˈhɔləu] *vt.* 使成凹形，使成空洞，挖空 (*out*). *river banks ~ed out by rushing water* 被流水掏空的河岸. — *vi.* 变空. — *n.* ①凹地，穴，洞坑. ②山谷. *the ~ of the* *hand* 手心. — *a.* ①空的,中空的. ②空虚的,不诚实的,虚伪的. ③(声音)瓮塞的,空洞的;沉重的. ④空腹的,饥饿的. ~ *cheeks* 凹陷的双颊. ~ *eyes* 凹陷的眼睛. ~ *pleasures* 空幻的快乐. ~ *compliments* 应酬话. *a* ~ *pretence* 虚伪的借口. ~ *promises* 空洞的诺言. ~ *race [victory]* (因对手弱)没有意思的赛跑[胜利]. ~ *square* 【军】空方阵. ~ *words* 空话. — *ad.* 〔口〕完全,彻底. ***beat sb. (all)*** ~ 打垮某人,把某人打得惨败. **~-drill steel** 【冶】空心钻钢. **~-eyed** *a.* 眼睛凹陷的. **~-hearted** *a.* 不真诚的,虚伪的. ~ **spar** 红柱石. **~-ware** *n.* 〔集合词〕凹形器皿(尤指凹形银器). **-ly** *ad.* **-ness** *n.*

hol·lo·ware [ˈhɔləuˌwɛə] *n.* = hollowware.

hol·ly [ˈhɔli] *n.* ①【植】冬青属植物. ②(圣诞节时装饰用的)冬青枝. ***English*** ~ 圣诞树.

Hol·ly [ˈhɔli] *n.* 霍莉〔女子名〕.

hol·ly·hock [ˈhɔlihɔk] *n.* 【植】蜀葵.

Hol·ly·wood [ˈhɔliwud] *n.* ①好莱坞〔美国电影业中心〕. ②美国影片. ③美国电影工业,美国电影界. — *a.* ①好莱坞(式)的. ②〔美俚〕(衣服等)艳丽的,花哨的,(人)做作的. **-ish** *a.* 好莱坞(式)的. **-ize** *vt.* 使好莱坞化. **-er** *n.* 好莱坞地方的人. **-i·an** *a.* **-i·an·a** [-iənə] *n.* 关于好莱坞生活与历史的书籍、报纸等.

holm [həum] *n.* 【植】①圣栎 (= ~oak). ②〔方〕冬青属植物.

Holman [ˈhəulmən] *n.* 霍尔曼〔姓氏〕.

holm(e) [həum] *n.* 〔英方〕①河边低地. ②河中(或近陆地)的小岛. ★英国地名带有 holm(e) 一字的很多: Priest*holm*, Willow *H-*.

Holme(s) [həum(z)] *n.* ①霍姆(斯)〔姓氏〕. ②**Sherlock** ~ 夏洛克·福尔摩斯〔英国作家柯南道尔 (Sir Arthur Conan Doyle) 笔下的大侦探〕;〔转义〕名侦探;有解答疑难和推理力的人. **-i·an** ① *n.* 福尔摩斯迷. ② *a.* 福尔摩斯式的.

hol·mi·um [ˈhɔlmiəm] *n.* 【化】钬.

holm·oak [ˈhəumˈəuk] *n.* 【植】圣栎.

holo- *comb. f.* 表示"完全": *holo*gram, *holo*hedral.

hol·o·blas·tic [ˌhɔləuˈblæstik] *a.* 【胚】全裂的〔指某些有小卵黄的卵细胞〕.

hol·o·caust [ˈhɔləkɔːst] *n.* ①(焚烧全兽祭神的)燔祭. ②大屠杀. ③大破坏,浩劫.

Hol·o·cene [ˈhɔləusiːn] *a.* 【地】全新统的,全新世的. —*n.* 【地】全新世.

ho·lo·crine [ˌhɔləukrin] *a.* 【动】全泌的.

ho·lo·en·zyme [ˌhɔləuˈenzaim] *n.* 【生化】全酶.

hol·o·gram [ˈhɔləugræm] *n.* 【物】全息图,全息照片,综合衍射图.

hol·o·graph [ˈhɔləugrɑːf] *n.* 亲笔文件〔证件〕;手书. — *a.* 亲笔写的. — *vi.* 拍摄全息照片.

hol·o·graph·ic, hol·o·graph·i·cal [ˌhɔləuˈgræfik(əl), ˌhəulə-] *a.* ①亲笔写的 (= holograph). ②全息照相的,与全息照相有关的.

ho·log·ra·phy [həˈlɔgrəfi] *n.* (不用透镜而用激光的)全息照相术;全息学.

hol·o·he·dral [ˌhɔləuˈhiːdrəl] *a.* 【物】全面的;全对称晶形的.

hol·o·he·drism [ˌhɔləuˈhiːdrizəm] *n.* 【物】全对称性.

hol·o·hed·ron [ˌhɔləuˈhedrən] *n.* 【地】全面体.

hol·o·me·tab·o·lism [ˌhɔləumiˈtæbəlizm] *n.* 【医】完全变态 (= complete metamorphosis). **hol·o·me·tab·o·lous** *a.*

hol·o·mor·phic [ˌhɔləuˈmɔːfik] *a.* 【物】(晶体)对当的.

hol·o·par·a·site [ˌhɔləuˈpærəsait] *n.* 【动】全寄生物. **hol·o·par·a·sit·ic** [-sitik] *a.*

hol·o·phone [ˈhɔləufəun] *n.* 声音全息记录器.

hol·o·phote [ˈhɔləufəut] *n.* 全光反射装置,(灯塔等的)全射影.

hol·o·phras·tic [ˌhɔləuˈfræstik] *a.* 以单词表示全句的,以单词表示短语的〔如命令句 Go!〕.

hol·o·phyt·ic [ˌhɔləuˈfitik] *a.* 【生】全植(物)营养的.

hol·o·plank·ton [ˌhɔləuˈplæŋktən] *n.* 【动】终生浮游生物.

hol·o·scope [ˈhɔləuskəup] *n.* 全息照相机. **-scop·ic** [ˌhɔləuˈskɔpik] *a.* 全面观察的,一览无遗的.

hol·o·thu·ri·an [ˌhɔləuˈθjuəriən] *n.* 海参类动物,海参. — *a.* 海参类动物的,海参的.

hol·o·type [ˈhɔləutaip] *n.* 【分类】①全型. ②完模标本. **hol·o·typ·ic** [-ˈtipik] *a.*

hol·o·zo·ic [ˌhɔləuˈzəuik] *a.* 【生】全动物营养的.

holp [həulp] *v.* 〔古〕help 的过去式.

hol·pen [ˈhəulpən] 〔古〕help 的过去分词.

Hol·stein (-Frie·sian) [ˈhɔlstain(ˈfriːʒən)] *n.* (荷兰)霍尔斯坦种乳牛〔体形大,有黑白斑,原产荷兰 Friesland〕.

hol·ster [ˈhəulstə] *n.* 手枪皮套.

holt[1] [həult] *n.* 〔诗〕杂木林;林丘.

holt[2] [həult] *n.* 兽穴(尤指水獭的巢穴).

Holt [həult] *n.* 霍尔特〔姓氏〕.

Hol·tham [ˈhəulθəm] *n.* 霍萨姆〔姓氏〕.

ho·lus-bo·lus [ˈhəuləsˈbəuləs] *ad.* 〔口〕一起,一口,一下子. *gulp sth. down* ~ 一口把东西吞下.

ho·ly [ˈhəuli] *a.* ①神圣的;神的,供神用的;献身于神的. ②圣洁的;至善的. ③虔诚的;崇敬的;宗教的. ④〔口〕令人生畏的,可怕的;厉害的,非常的. ~ *rites* 宗教仪式. ~ *ground* 圣地. *a* ~ *place* 灵场. *the* ~ *place* 圣殿,大殿. *a* ~ *man* 虔诚的信徒. ~ *love* 纯真的爱. *a* ~ *terror* 难以对付的家伙,无法无天的小家伙. ~ *cow [smoke]!* 天哪!〔表示惊讶、强调的感叹语〕. — *n.* 神圣的东西,圣堂. *the Holiest* 至圣者(指上帝或基督)(=the ~ of the holiest). *the Holy of Holies* 犹太神殿中的至圣所;神圣的地方. **H- Alliance** 【史】(1815—1816 俄、普、奥三国君主订立的)神圣同盟. ~ **Ark** 犹太教教堂里保存经文的柜子. **H- Bible** 【宗】圣经. ~ **bread [loaf]** 圣餐用的面包. **H- City** 圣城(如耶路撒冷、麦加、罗马). **H- Communion** 【宗】圣餐礼. ~ **day** 宗教节日. ~ **day of obligation** ①天主教徒参加弥撒日. ②天主教的领圣餐日. **H- Father** 【宗】圣父;罗马教皇. **H- Ghost** 【宗】圣灵. **H- Grail** 圣杯〔传说耶稣在最后的晚餐所用的杯〕. ~ **Joe** 〔美俚〕传教师;信徒;〔美口〕(陆军的)随军牧师. **H- Land** 【宗】圣地(指巴勒斯坦). **H- office** (天主教的)宗教法庭. **H- One** 上帝;基督. ~ **orders** 圣职,牧师的职位. **H- Roman Empire** 【史】神圣罗马帝国. **H- Saturday** 【宗】耶稣复活节前一周的星期六. **H- Son** 【宗】圣子耶稣. **H- Spirit** = **H- Ghost** 【宗】圣灵. **H- Thursday** ①【宗】耶稣升天节. ②耶稣受难节前一周的星期四. **~tide** 〔古〕宗教季节;祭祀日;斋期. ~ **water** 【天主】圣水;【佛】净水. **H- Week** 复活节前的一周. **H- Writ** 基督教圣经.

ho·ly·stone [ˈhəulistəun] *n.* 【海】(磨甲板的)沙石. — *vt.* 用沙石磨(甲板).

hom·age [ˈhɔmidʒ] *n.* ①【史】效忠宣誓礼,效忠. ②顺从,臣服. ③尊敬. ***do [pay]*** ~ ***to*** 对…表示敬意;服从.

hom·a·lo·graph·ic [ˌhɔmələˈgræfik] *a.* = homolographic.

hom·bre [ˈɔmbre] *n.* 〔Sp.〕人.

hom·burg, H- [ˈhɔmbəːg] *n.* 翘边帽.

home [həum] *n.* ①家,家庭;家庭生活;〔美〕住宅. ②本国,故乡;(活动的)中心地,根据地,大本营;(动植物的)栖息地,原产地;(思想等的)发祥地. ③疗养所;休息所;收容所,养育院(等). ④【体】(径赛的)终点;(棒球的)本垒. *the Smith* ~ 〔美〕史密斯的住宅〔=〔英〕Mr. Smith's house〕. ***a*** ~ ***from*** ~ 象家一样自在和舒适的地方,旅客之家. ***at*** ~ ①在家;在家接待客人 (*She* *is not at ~ today.* 她今日不会客)。②在故乡，在本地，在本国 (*opp.* abroad.) ③安适，自在 (*be [feel] at ~* 觉得安适，无拘束。*Make yourself at ~.* 请随便，别客气)。④精通 (*in; on; with*) (*be at ~ in French* 法语很好)。***one's long [last, narrow] ~*** 坟墓。***set for ~*** 向根据地返回。***sit at ~*** 闲居，不活动。— *a.* ①家庭的，家乡的，本地的。②本国的，本国产的；内地的，国内的。③中要害的，严厉的。*the H- Counties* 伦敦附近各郡〔如 Essex, Kent 等〕。*the H- Department [office]* 〔英〕内务部。*a happy ~ life* 幸福的家庭生活。*the ~ market* 国内市场。*H- minister* 内务部长。*~ office* 总机构(如总公司、总店等)。*~ question* 中要害的质问。*~ rule* 地方自治。***a ~ truth*** 使人难堪的事实；逆耳忠言；老生常谈。***be ~ free*** 遥遥领先，稳操胜券。***~ and dry*** 达到目的；安全。— *ad.* ①在家，在本国；回家，回国；【棒球】回本垒。②全，深，尽量；(议论等)彻底；痛切，切实。*carry ~* 拿回家。*Is he ~ yet?* 他回家了么？*see sb. ~* 送某人回家。*He was ordered ~.* 他已奉命回国。*write ~ to the government* 写信给本国政府。***bring ~ to sb.*** ①使某人认识，使某人相信 (*bring ~ to him the importance of modernization drive* 使他认识四化的意义)。②证实某人有某罪 (*bring a fraud ~ to sb.* 证实某人犯诈骗罪)。***bring oneself (come, get) ~*** 收回损失；恢复原来地位。***come ~*** ①回家，回国。②使人沉痛地感到 (*Curses (like chickens) come ~ to roost.* 〔谚〕害人终害己)。***drive ~*** ①讲明白，使人理解。②胜利完成，顺利结束。***drive [knock] the nail ~*** 把钉子钉牢；〔喻〕坚持到底。***get ~*** 到家，回到；命中。***go ~*** ①回家，回国。②〔口〕死，回老家，上西天。③(忠告等)刻骨铭心。***hit [strike] ~*** 击中要害；触及痛处。***look at ~*** 扪心自问。***nobody ~*** 疯疯癫癫。***nothing to write ~ about*** 〔口〕无聊的，平凡的。***press ~*** 极力主张。***push the bolt ~*** 把门闩闩上；关上炮闩。***romp ~*** 赛马时轻易获胜。***row the stroke ~*** 把船桨划到底。***scrape ~*** 费了大劲才达到目的。***swear ~*** 破口大骂。***take ~ to oneself*** 深刻领会。***thrust a dagger ~*** 全刀刺入。— *vi.* ①回家。②(动物)回巢穴，回出生地区。③(飞机)归航，按信号暗示回场；【火箭】(自动)导航，自动寻的。④安下家，居住。— *vt.* ①把…放在家中，把…送到家中。②给…住处。③【火箭】使自动寻的。*~ in on (target)* (火箭)依靠导航系统自动飞向（目标)。~ **base** ①根据地；本站。②【棒球】本垒。~**bird** 深居简出的人。~**body** *n.* (*pl.* **-bod·ies**) 家庭至上者；深居简出者，以家庭为生活中心的人。~**born** *a.* 土生土长的。~**bound** *a.* ①回家的，回家乡的，回国的，(船)回头开的。②不出家门的，闭居在家的。~**bred** *a.* 家内饲养的；国产的；粗野的。~-**brew** ①家里酿的酒(尤指啤酒)。②当地培育的人[物]。~-**brewed** ① *a.* (酒)家里酿的。② *n.* 家内酿的酒。~-**coming** *n.* ①回老家，回国。②〔美〕返校节。~-**ec** *n.* (美国学生用语) = ~ economics. ~ **economics** 持家学，家政学。~-**farm** 供应大庄园或供自用的农场。~-**felt** *a.* 痛切感到的。~ **freight** 返程运费。~ **front** ①大后方。②作为一国战争力量组成部分的民用工业。~**grown** *a.* (瓜果、蔬菜等)的本国出产的，当地消费的；土生的。**H- Guard** 英国国民军成员。~ **help** 家务女佣。~**keeper** 怕出门的人。~**keeping** *a.* 家居不外出的。~**land** 本国，故国；〔H-〕英国本国。~**made** *a.* 自己制的，手工的；本国制的。~ **maker** 持家的妇女，主妇。~-**owner** (住)房主。~ **plate** = ~ **base**. ② ~ **range** 【生态】巢区〔动物(每日或季节)活动范围〕。~**room** (学校的)班级会议室〔点名，听报告等的场所〕。~ **rule** 地方自治。~ **run** (棒球)本垒打。~**sick** *a.* 想家的，患怀乡病的。~**sickness** 思家病，怀乡病。~ **signal** (火车)进站信号。~**spun** ① *a.* 家里纺的，家里做的；简朴的，粗陋的；朴实的，平凡的，不做作的。② *n.* 土布；手工纺织呢，手织大衣呢。~-**stead** ① *n.* (包括附近田地在内的)家宅，宅地；祖传的住宅；〔美、加拿大〕(分给定居移民)居住和耕种的土地。② *vt., vi.* (使)得到[占有]宅地。~**steader** ①占有宅地的人。②分得土地的定居移民。~**stretch** (赛跑)从最后的拐弯到终点间的一段跑道；最后阶段的工作。~-**thrust** 致命的一戳；说中要害的批评。~**town** 故乡，家乡。~ **work** 课外习题，家庭作业；家庭工作；(讨论等以前的)准备工作。**-less** *a.* 无家可归的；无饲主的。**-like** *a.* ①象家一样舒适、亲切的。②(饭菜等)简单而有益健康的。**-ward** *a., ad.* 向家(的)，向家乡(的)，向本国(的)。**-wards** *ad.* 向家，向家乡，向本国。

Home [həum, hju:m] *n.* 霍姆(休姆)〔姓氏〕。

home·ly [ˈhəumli] *a.* ①家庭的，家常的。②朴实的，不做作的。③象在家一样的，不拘束的。④〔美〕不漂亮的，不好看的。*quite a ~ sort of body* 极朴实的人。*~ as a mud fence* 〔美〕面孔极丑的。**home·li·ness** *n.*

ho·me·o *pref.* 表示"同"：*homeo*chromatic.

ho·me·o·chro·ma·tic [ˌhəumiəukrəˈmætik] *a.* 【生】同色的。

ho·me·o·mor·phism [ˌhəumiəuˈmɔ:fizm, ˌhɔmiə-] *n.* 【化】异质同晶(现象)。**ho·me·o·mor·phous** [-fəs] *a.*

ho·me·o·path [ˈhəumjəpæθ] = homoeopath.

ho·me·o·path·ic [ˈhəumiə*u*ˈpæθik] *a.* =homoeopathic.

ho·me·op·a·thist [ˌhəumiˈɔpəθist] *n.* = homoeopathist.

ho·me·op·a·thy [ˌhəumiˈɔpəθi] *n.* = homoeopathy.

ho·me·o·sta·sis [ˌhəumiəuˈsteisis] *n.* 【生理】①体内平衡。②(社会群体的)自我平衡。**ho·me·o·stat·ic** [-ˈstætik] *a.*

ho·me·o·ther·mal [ˌhəumiə*u*ˈθə:məl] *a.* = homoiothermal.

ho·me·o·typ·ic [ˌhəumiə*u*ˈtipik] *a.* 【生】同型的；(生殖细胞核的)成熟后第二次分裂的。

ho·mer[1] [ˈhəumə] *n.* 侯马〔①希伯来早期干体量具名，相当于$6^{1}/_{4}$普式耳。②希伯来液体量具名，相当于58加仑〕。

hom·er[2] [ˈhəumə] *n.* ①【棒球】本垒打〔打出可跑完一圈回到本垒的球〕。②传书鸽，通信鸽。③【空】归航信标机，归航台。④自动引导导弹。*a heat-~* 有热感应自动引导弹头的导弹。— *vi.* 【棒球】击出本垒打。

Ho·mer[1] [ˈhəumə] *n.* 霍默〔姓氏，男子名〕。

Ho·mer[2] [ˈhəumə] *n.* 荷马〔纪元前 10 世纪前后的希腊盲诗人，*Iliad* 及 *Odyssey* 的作者〕。***H- sometimes nods.*** 〔谚〕智者千虑，必有一失。

Ho·mer·ic [həuˈmerik] *a.* ①荷马的；荷马式的，荷马史诗的。②英勇的，巨大的。~ **battle** 英勇的战斗。~ **laughter** 放声大笑〔源出荷马史诗中所写的诸神的大笑〕。~ **verse** 六音步的诗。

hom·ey [ˈhəumi] *a.* 〔美口〕①家庭似的，象家里一样安适自在的。②温暖的，舒适的。

hom·i·ci·dal [ˌhɔmiˈsaidl] *a.* 杀人的；有杀人癖性的。~ *mania* 杀人狂。

hom·i·cide [ˈhɔmisaid] *n.* ①杀人(行为)，杀人罪。②杀人者。*justifiable ~* 【法】有正当理由的杀人。

hom·i·let·ic(al) [ˌhɔmiˈletik(əl)] *a.* 说教(式)的，布道的；教训性质的。**-i·cal·ly** *ad.*

hom·i·let·ics [ˌhɔmiˈletiks] *n.* 〔*pl.* 用作单数〕说教术，布道术。

hom·i·list [ˈhɔmilist] *n.* 说教者，布道者。

hom·i·ly [ˈhɔmili] *n.* ①布道。②使人厌烦的说教。

hom·ing [ˈhəumiŋ] *a.* ①回家的，有归还习性的。②【空】归航的；导航的。—*n.* 归来，(信鸽等的)归还性能；【空】归航，导航；【宇】自动引导。*radar ~* 雷达自动引导。~ **beacon** 无线电归航信标。~ **device** 导归器。~ **equipment** 自动瞄准[导航]装置，寻的装置。~ **instinct** 归巢本能。~ **missile** 自动寻的导弹。~ **pigeon** 通信鸽。~ **torpedo** 自动导的水雷。

hom·i·nid [ˈhɔminid] *n.* ①【动】人科 (*Hominidea*)。②

原人，原始人类．— *a.* 人科的．

hom·i·ni·ze [ˈhɔminaiz] *vt.* ①使(机械等)人性化．②利用(世界)为人类服务．**-ni·za·tion** [ˌhɔminaiˈzeiʃən] *n.*

hom·i·noid [ˈhɔminɔid] *n.*【动】类人猿 *(Hominoidea)*．— *a.* 类人猿的；人的；类人的；象人的．

hom·i·ny [ˈhɔmini] *n.* 〔美〕玉米粥；玉米片．

ho·mo [ˈhəuməu] *n., a.* 〔美俚〕 = homosexual.

ho·mo [ˈhəuməu] *n. (pl.* ***hom·i·nes*** [ˈhɔmini:z]*)* 〔L.〕人〔学名〕；〔H-〕人类．***H- sapiens*** [ˈseipinz] 人类．

homo- *comb. f.* 表示"同"，"似"〔通常用在希腊系语词前 *(opp.* hetero-)〕: *homo*centric, *homo*geneous.

hom·o·cen·tric [ˌhɔməuˈsentrik] *a.* 同中心的．

ho·mo·cer·cal [ˌhɔməuˈsə:kl] *a.* (鱼的)正尾的；等形的．

ho·mo·charge [ˈhɔməutʃɑ:dʒ] *n.*【物】纯号电荷．

ho·mo·chro·mat·ic [ˌhɔməkrəuˈmætik] *a.* 单色的，只有单色的 (= homochromous).

ho·mo·des·mic [ˌhɔməuˈdesmik] *n.*【物】纯键．— *a.*【物】纯键的．

ho·mo·dyne [ˈhɔməudain] *n.*【物】零差，零拍．

ho·moe *pref.* = homeo.

ho·moe·cious [ˈhəumjəuʃəs] *a.* (寄生虫的)单种宿主寄生的．

ho·moe·o·path [ˈhəumjəupæθ] *n.*【医】顺势疗法医师．

ho·moe·o·path·ic [ˌhəumjəuˈpæθik] *a.*【医】顺势疗法的．**-i·cal·ly** *ad.*

ho·moe·op·a·thist [ˌhəumiˈɔpəθist] *n.* = homoeopath.

ho·moe·op·a·thy [ˌhəumiˈɔpəθi] *n.* 顺势疗法，类似疗法 *(opp. allopathy)*.

ho·mo·e·rot·i·cism [ˌhəuməuiˈrɔtisizəm] *n.* = homosexuality. **ho·mo·e·rot·ic** *a.*

ho·mog·a·my [həˈmɔgəmi] *n.* ①【植】具有同性花；雌雄(蕊)同熟．②【生】同配生殖 (*opp.* heterogamy)；同族结婚．**ho·mog·a·mic, ho·mog·a·mous** *a.*

ho·mog·e·nate [həˈmɔdʒineit] *n.*【医】均浆．

hom·o·ge·ne·i·ty [ˌhɔməudʒeˈni:iti] *n.* ①同种；同质；同性．②【数】齐性，均匀；同一性，均衡性．

hom·o·ge·ne·ous [ˌhɔməuˈdʒi:njəs] *a.* ①同种的，同质的，同性的，相似的．②纯一的，均质的；均匀的．③【数】齐性的，齐次的．~ **alloy** 均质合金．~ **light** 单色光．~ **ray** 单色射线．~ **integral equation** 齐次积分方程．**-ly** *ad.* **-ness** *n.*

hom·o·gen·e·sis [ˌhɔməuˈdʒenisis] *n.*【生】纯一生殖．

hom·o·ge·net·ic [ˌhɔməudʒiˈnetik] *a.* = homogenous.

ho·mog·e·nize [həˈmɔdʒənaiz] *vt.* ①使均匀．②使均质，用高压高速搅拌．~*d milk* 均质牛奶．**hom·og·e·ni·za·tion** [həˌmɔdʒənaiˈzeiʃən] *n.*

ho·mog·e·ni·zer [həˈmɔdʒinaizə] *n.* 均质器，均化器，高速搅拌器．

ho·mog·e·nous [həˈmɔdʒinəs] *a.*【生】同质的〔指因遗传而构造相似的〕；纯系的；同源的．

ho·mog·e·ny [həˈmɔdʒini] *n.*【生】同构发生，同源发生．

ho·mog·o·ny [həˈmɔgəni] *n.* = homostyly. **ho·mog·o·nous** [-nəs] *a.*

ho·mo·graft [ˈhɔməugrɑ:ft, ˈhɔmə-] *n.*【医】同种移植片；自体移植片．

hom·o·graph [ˈhɔməugrɑ:f] *n.* 同形异义词，同形词〔如 seal 为海豹，又为图章〕．**-ic** *a.*

ho·moi·o·ther·mal [həuˌmɔiəuˈθə:məl] *a.*【动】恒温动物的 (= homoiothermic.)

ho·mo·lec·i·thal [ˌhɔməuˈlesiθəl] *a.*【动】均卵黄的．

hom·o·log [ˈhɔmələg] *n.* = homologue.

ho·mol·o·gate [hɔˈmɔləgeit] *vt.* *(-gat·ed; -gat·ing)* ①赞同，认可．②【法】正式确认，批准．— *vi.* 〔罕〕同意．**ho·mol·o·ga·tion** *n.*

ho·mo·log·i·cal [ˌhɔməˈlɔdʒikəl, ˌhɔmə-] *a.* = homologous. **ho·mo·log·i·cal·ly** *ad.*

ho·mol·o·gize [hɔˈmɔlədʒaiz] *vt.* ①使相应，使一致，使相同．②表示与…同系．— *vi.* 同系，同源．

ho·mol·o·gous [hɔˈmɔləgəs] *a.* ①同源的．②【生】异体同型的．③【化】同系列的；同属列的；同周期的．④【医】同源的．⑤【医】 = homoplastic. ~ **bodies** 同族体．~ **organs** 同源器官〔如人肺与鱼鳃〕．~ **series**【化】同系列．

hom·o·lo·graph·ic [ˌhɔmələˈgræfik] *a.*【测】等面积的．

hom·o·logue [ˈhɔmələg] *n.* ①【化】同系物．②【生】(细胞)同源染色体，对等．③相应物．

ho·mol·o·gy [hɔˈmɔlədʒi] *n.* ①相应，符合；关系相同．②【化】同系(现象)．③【生】同源．④【数】透射；同调．

ho·mo·mor·phism [ˌhɔməˈmɔ:fizm] *n.* ①同形．②【生】同型性〔指器官或有机体〕．③【植】同形体〔大小〕〔如雌蕊和雄蕊〕．④【动】成幼同型(= homomorphy)．⑤【数】同态．**ho·mo·mor·phic, ho·mo·mor·phous** *a.*

hom·o·nym [ˈhɔmənim] *n.* ①同音异义词〔如 bear 与 bare；广义的 homonym 包含狭义的 homophone 和 homograph〕；同形异义词；同音同形异义词．②异人同名．③【生】异物同名．

hom·o·nym·ic, ho·mon·y·mous [ˌhɔməˈnimik, hɔˈmɔniməs] *a.* 同音〔同形〕异义的；同名的；双关的．

ho·mo·phile [ˈhəuməufail] *n., a.* = homosexual.

hom·o·phone [ˈhɔməfəun] *n.* ①同音字母〔c 与 s，c 与 k 等〕．②同音异义词〔狭义的 homophone 相当于狭义的 homonym；广义的还包含 homograph 一义〕．

hom·o·phon·ic [ˌhɔməˈfɔnik] *a.* ①【乐】同音的；同音歌唱的；单旋律歌曲的；单音调乐曲的．② = homonymous.

ho·moph·ɔ·ny [hɔˈmɔfəni] *n.* ①【语】同音异义．②【乐】同音；齐唱〔奏〕；单旋律歌曲．

ho·mo·plas·tic [ˌhɔməˈplæstik] *a.*【生】①同型的，相似的．②同种的．**-plas·ti·cal·ly** *ad.*

ho·mo·pla·sy [-plæsi] *n.*【生】异体同功．

hom·o·po·lar [ˌhɔməˈpəulə] *a.*【电】同极的，单极的．~ *generator* 单极发电机．**-i·ty** [-ˈlæriti] *n.*

ho·mop·ter·ous [hɔˈmɔptərəs] *a.* (昆虫)同翅类的．

ho·mo·sex·u·al [ˌhəuməuˈseksjuəl] *a.* 同性恋爱的．— *n.* 同性恋爱者．

ho·mo·sex·u·al·i·ty [ˌhəuməuˌseksjuˈæliti] *n.* 同性恋爱；同性的性行为．

ho·mo·sphere [ˈhɔməsfiə] *n.*【气】均质层．**ho·mo·spher·ic** [-ˈsferik] *a.*

ho·mos·po·rous [hɔˈmɔspərəs] *a.*【植】具同形孢子的；仅产生一种孢子的．

ho·mo·sty·ly [ˈhɔməstaili] *n.*【植】花柱同长．**ho·mo·sty·lous** *a.*

ho·mo·tax·is [ˌhɔməˈtæksis] *n.*【地】排列类似．**ho·mo·tax·i·al** [-ˈtæksiəl] *a.*

ho·mo·thal·lic [ˌhɔməˈθælik] *a.*【动】同宗配合(现象)的．**-thal·lism** *n.*

ho·mo·ther·mal [ˌhɔməˈθə:məl] *a.* = homoiothermal (= homothermic).

ho·mo·trans·plant [ˌhɔməˈtrænsplɑ:nt] *n.* = homograft. **-trans·plan·ta·tion** [ˌhɔmətræsplɑ:nˈteiʃən] *n.*【医】同种移植；自体移植．

hom·o·type [ˈhɔmətaip] *n.*【生】同型；等模标本．

ho·mo·zy·go·sis [ˌhɔməzaiˈgəusis] *n.*【生】①纯质性．②纯合基因．**ho·mo·zy·got·ic** [-ˈgɔtik] *a.*

ho·mo·zy·gote [ˌhɔməˈzaigəut] *n.*【生】同型结合子〔体〕，纯合子〔体〕．**-zy·gous** *a.*

Homs [həums] *n.* ①胡姆斯〔叙利亚城市〕．②胡姆斯〔利比亚港市〕．

ho·mun·cule, ho·mun·cle [həˈmʌŋkju:l, -kl] *n.* = homunculus.

ho·mun·cu·lus [həuˈmʌŋkjuləs] *n.* *(pl.* ***-li*** [-lai]*)* 矮

子,侏儒.

hom·y [ˈhəumi] *a.* = homey.

hon [hʌn] *n.* =〔美〕honey.

Hon., hon. = Hono(u)rary; Hono(u)rable.

hon·cho [ˈhɔːtʃəu] *n.*〔美俚〕头头,老板.

Hond. = Honduras.

Hon·du·ran [hɔnˈdjuərən] *a.* 洪都拉斯的; 洪都拉斯人的; 洪都拉斯文化的. — *n.* 洪都拉斯人.

Hon·du·ras [hɔnˈdjuərəs] *n.* 洪都拉斯〔拉丁美洲〕.

hone[1] [həun] *n.* ①细磨刀石. ②【机】磨孔器. — *vt.* ①(在细磨刀石上)磨. ②磨孔使放大.

hone[2] [həun] *vi.*〔方〕①咕噜,抱怨. ②渴望.

hon·est [ˈɔnist] *a.* ①诚实的; 正直的,耿直的; 坦率的,坦白的,正派的,公正的. ②可敬的,有好名声的. ③〔古〕可靠的,善良的; 贞节的. ④(金钱)用正当手段获得的. ⑤(酒等)真正的,纯正的. ⑥朴实的,普通的. *an ~ man* 正直的人. *an ~ woman* 贞节的女人. *an ~ living* 正正派派的生活. *the ~ truth* 原原本本的事实. *~ goods* 真货. *~ food* 普通饭菜. ***be ~ with*** 对…说老实话. 同…规规矩矩来往. ***be quite ~ about it*** 老实说〔常用作插入语〕. ***earn [turn] an ~ penny*** 用正当手段挣钱. ***H- Injun*** [ˈindʒən]!〔俚〕没错! 真的!〔作状语用〕. **~-to-God, ~-to-goodness** *a.* 真正的,道地的.

hon·est·ly [ˈɔnistli] *ad.* 老老实实,正正当当; 老实说.

hon·es·ty [ˈɔnisti] *n.* ①老实; 诚实; 公正. ②〔古〕贞节; 廉耻. ③【植】缎花属植物. *H- is the best policy.* 诚实是上策. *~ of purpose* 认真.

hone·wort [ˈhəunˌwəːt] *n.*【植】北柴胡 *(Cryptotaenia canadensis)*〔发现于美国东部〕.

hon·ey [ˈhʌni] *n.* ***(pl. ~s, honies)*** ①蜂蜜; 蜜. ②甘美,甜蜜. ③宝贝儿〔称呼用〕; 漂亮姑娘; 使人非常愉快〔满意〕的东西. *virgin ~* 生蜜. *my ~* 亲爱的. — *a.* ①蜂蜜似的. ②〔古〕心爱的. — *vt.* (***~ed*** 或 ***honied***) ①加蜜等使甜. ②说甜言蜜语; 奉承. — *vi.* 说甜言蜜语; 奉承. ~ ***up to sb.*** 向…灌迷汤. ~ **bag** (蜜蜂体中的) 蜜囊. ~ **bear**【动】蜜熊 (kinkajou) 和懒熊 (sloth bear) 的俗称. **~bee** 蜜蜂. **~bun, ~bunch** *n.*〔口〕宝贝,亲爱的〔多用作亲昵称呼语〕. **~comb** ① *n.* 蜜蜂窝; 蜂窝状物;【冶】蜂窝状沙眼; (反刍动物的)蜂巢胃. ② *vt.* 使成蜂窝状; 渗透进…的各个部分; 削弱,把…弄得百孔千疮; 破坏(团结等). **~-cooler**〔美俚〕(对女子的)奉承; 用奉承赢得女子信任的男子. **~dew** ①(蚜虫等分泌的) 甘汁,蜜露,树蜜. ②甜味烟草. **~ dew melon** 香蜜瓜. ~ **eater** 蜜雀 *(meliphagidae)*〔产于澳大利亚〕. **~fogle,** *vt.*〔美俚〕用甜言蜜语欺骗. ~ **guide** 指蜜鸟 *(Indicatoridae)*〔产于亚非和东印度群岛,据说可引领人、兽找蜂窝,待蜂房被取走后去啄食蜜蜂幼虫〕. **~lipped** 嘴甜的,甜言蜜语的. ~ **locust**【植】美洲皂荚. **~moon** ① *n.* 婚后第一月,蜜月,新婚旅行(期间),蜜月旅行. ② *vi.* 度蜜月*(at; in)*. **~mooner** 度蜜月者. **~-mouthed** *a.* = ~ lipped. ~ **pot** (蜜蚁的) 贮蜜囊. **~sucker** ① = ~ eater. ②长吻袋貂 *(Tarsipes spenceri)*〔产于澳大利亚〕. **~suckle**【植】忍冬属. **~-sweet** *a.* 甜如蜜的,极甜的. **~-tongued** *a.* = ~lipped. ~ **wag(g)on**〔美俚〕①垃圾车,粪车. ②手提户外马桶.

hon·eyed [ˈhʌnid] *a.* 多蜜的; 甜如蜜的. *~ words* 甜言蜜语.

hong [hɔŋ] *n.*〔Chin.〕(中国、日本的)行,商行.

Hong Kong, Hong·kong [hɔŋˈkɔŋ, ˈhɔŋˈkɔŋ] 香港.

hon·ied [ˈhʌnid] honey 的过去式和过去分词. — *a.* = honeyed.

hon·ies [ˈhʌniz] honey 的复数.

honk [hɔŋk] *n.* ①雁叫声; 类似雁叫声. ②汽车喇叭声. — *vi.* ①(雁) 叫. ②汽车喇叭响. — *vt.* ①揿喇叭表示. ②〔口〕揿(喇叭). **~-out**〔美俚〕失败.

honk·ie, honk·y [ˈhɔŋki] *n.*〔美俚〕〔蔑〕白人.

honk·y-tonk [ˈhɔŋkitɔŋk] *n.*〔美俚〕有舞场的低级酒馆. — *a.* ①低级酒吧的. ②(地区)有很多低级酒吧的.

Hon·o·lu·lu [ˌhɔnəˈluːluː] *n.* 火奴鲁鲁(又译檀香山)〔美国港市〕.

hon·or [ˈɔnə] *n., vt.*〔美〕= honour.

Ho·nor·a [həuˈnɔːrə] *n.* 霍诺拉〔女子名. (L. =honor), 爱称 Nora(h)〕.

hon·or·a·ble [ˈɔnərəbl] *n.*〔美〕= honourable.

hon·o·rar·i·um [ˌɔnəˈrɛəriəm] *n.* ***(pl. ~s, -rar·i·a [-ə])*** 报酬(金),谢礼(金)〔指习惯上或礼貌上不便收取或定出价目的酬金,如润笔、对医师的酬谢等〕.

hon·or·ar·y [ˈɔnərəri] *a.* ①名誉的,名誉上的; 义务的. ②荣誉的,光荣的. ③(债务等)道义上的,信用的. ④纪念性的. *an ~ degree* 名誉学位. *an ~ member* 名誉会员. *an ~ secretary* 义务秘书〔不领取报酬〕. *an ~ president* 名誉董事长〔没有具体职权〕. *~ debts* (虽无法律强制性但道义上必须偿还的)欠债. *an ~ ode* 赞歌. — *n.* ①名誉团体. ②名誉学位; 获名誉学位者. ③〔古〕= honorarium.

Ho·no·ri·a [həuˈnɔːriə] *n.* = Honora.

hon·or·if·ic [ɔnəˈrifik] *a.* 尊敬的,表示敬意的. *an ~ title* 敬称. — *n.* ①尊称. ②【语】敬语〔用于某些东方语言,尤指日语和汉语中所用者,如汉语中的令(郎)、贵(姓)、大(名)等〕.

hon·or·is cau·sa [hɔˈnɔːrisˈkɔːsə]〔L.〕为名誉起见 (= for the sake of honour).

hon·o(u)r [ˈɔnə] *n.* ①荣誉,光荣; 名誉,面子,体面. ②节操,廉耻,正直; 道义; 贞操. ③尊敬,敬意. ④高位,高官;〔His H-, Your H-〕阁下〔英国主要用于尊称地方法官,美国用于尊称一般法官〕. ⑤荣典,叙勋; 徽章,勋章;〔*pl.*〕敬礼式. ⑥荣幸,优惠,优待. ⑦〔*pl.*〕(大学中的)优等成绩; 给优等生开设的高级课程;〔英〕优等成绩奖金. ⑧纸牌中价值最高的牌〔如 A, K, Q, J, 及 10〕. ⑨(高尔夫球的) 先打权. ⑩荣幸〔客套语〕. ⑪光荣的人,光荣的事〔与不定冠词连用〕. *business ~* 商业信用. *a debt of ~* (无字据的)信用借款. *H- and profit lie not in one sack.*〔谚〕荣誉和私利,决不在一起. *May I have the ~ of your company at dinner?* 敬备菲酌,恭请光临. *His H- the Judge* 法官阁下. *pass with ~ in mathmatics* 数学考试成绩优异. *an ~'s degree* 优等学位. *a sense of ~* 荣誉感,廉耻心. *funeral [last] ~s* 葬礼. *The ~s rest with him.* 集荣誉于一身,他获得很大成功. *military ~s* 军葬礼; 军礼. ***a roll of ~*** 阵亡烈士名单. *an affair of ~* 决斗. ***be on one's ~ to do sth.*** = ***be in ~ bound to do sth., be bound in ~ to do sth.*** 道义上必须做某事. ***come off with ~*** 光荣地完成. ***compromise one's ~*** 累及名誉. ***do ~ to*** 给…带来荣誉,对…表示敬意. ***do the ~s (of the house)*** 作主人招待宾客,尽地主之谊. ***for (the) ~ of***【商】为顾全…的信用起见. ***guards of ~*** 仪仗队. ***give [pay] ~ to*** 向…致敬. ***give one's word of ~*** 用名誉担保. ***go in for ~s***〔大学用语〕考取优等. ***graduate [pass] with ~s*** 优等毕业〔考试成绩优等〕. ***hold sb. in ~*** 敬重某人. ~ ***bright***〔口〕誓必,一定; 以名誉担保. ***in ~*** 道义上. ***in ~ of*** 向…表示敬意,为祝贺…,为纪念…. ***maid of ~*** ①官女. ②〔美〕女傧相. ***make ~s to sb.*** 向某人致敬. ***on [upon] one's (word of) ~*** 以名誉担保. ***pledge one's ~*** 用名誉担保. ***point of ~*** 有关体面的事. ***put sb. on his ~*** 信任某人会重视他的名誉. ***save one's ~*** 保全面子. ***the code [law] of ~*** ①公认的行为准则. ②决斗惯例. ***the ~'s list*** 受勋者名单. ***the ~ of war*** 给与战败军队的优待〔如允许其保留武器、旗帜等〕. ***with ~s easy*** 优势均等. — *vt.* ①尊敬; 尊重; 给与荣誉,给与…的光荣; 以…为荣; 向…授勋 *(with)*; 礼遇. ②接受;【商】承认如期付款,承兑(票据),兑现. *~ a debt in advance* 提前还债. *~ one's promise* 实践诺言. **~-bound** *a.* 为荣誉不得不做

的．～ **guard** 仪仗队．～**s course**（大学中的）独立研究课程〔通过后即得优等学位〕．～ **roll** 荣誉名册．～ **system**（学校的）无监考考试制；（监狱的）无看守监禁制．～**s system**（大学的）优等生制度．

hon·o(u)r·a·ble [ˈɔnərəbl] *a.* ①可敬的，高尚的；正直的，廉洁的；有名誉的，光荣的；体面的．②〔H-〕阁下〔英国用以尊称阁员、高等法院推事、殖民地行政官、宫中女官、伯爵以下的贵族子弟等；美国用于尊称国会议员及州议员等；略作 Honble, Hon.〕．*an ～ discharge* 荣誉退役．*an ～ duty* 名誉职位．*an ～ mention* 褒奖；表扬．*win ～ distinctions* 立下光荣的功劳．***the H- gentleman*** *[member]* = *my H- friend* 英国下议员在议场中对其它议员的称呼．***the Most H-*** 侯爵、巴斯勋爵、枢密顾问官名字前用的尊称〔略 Most Hon.〕．***the Right H-*** 枢密顾问官、伯爵以下贵族、伦敦市长名字前用的尊称〔略 *Rt. Hon.*〕．

hon·o(u)r·a·bly [ˈɔnərəbli] *ad.* 受尊敬地，体面地；正当地．

hon·o(u)r(s)·man [ˈɔnə(z)mæn] *n.* 大学毕业考试的优等生．

Hon·shu [ˈhɔnʃuː] *n.* 本州〔日本〕．

hooch [huːtʃ] *n.* 〔美俚〕①烈酒．②非法酿造和出售的劣酒．

Hood [hud] *n.* 胡德〔姓氏〕．

hood[1] [hud] *n.* ①头巾；（连在外套上的）兜帽．②（大学制服后以其颜色表示学位及学校的）垂布．③（马或鹰的）头罩．④车盖，车篷；烟囱帽，灯盖；炮塔顶篷；〔美〕（汽车的）引擎罩；打字机的罩子；【海】天窗盖，舱口盖．⑤【建】帽盖，出簷．⑥【动】羽冠．⑦（雷达荧光屏的）遮光板．— *vt.* ①用头巾包；使（马、鹰等）戴头罩；给…加罩．②覆盖，隐蔽．**-less** *a.*

hood[2] [hud] *n.* 〔美俚〕 = hoodlum.

-hood *suf.* ①〔前接一般名词〕表示"身分"，"资格"：king*hood*. ②〔前接形容词〕表示境遇，状态，性质：false*hood*. ③〔前接一般名词〕表示具有特殊性质的集体：neighbour*hood*, priest*hood*.

hood·ed [ˈhudid] *a.* ①戴头巾的；有头罩的；头兜状的．②顶饰羽冠的．③（眼镜蛇等）颈部因胁骨运动而膨胀的．④头部颜色与身体其他部分迥然不同的．～ **crow**【动】灰鸦 *(Corvus cornix)*〔产于欧洲，灰背，灰胸，黑头，黑翼，黑尾〕．～ **seal** 冠海豹 *(Cystophora cristata)*〔产于北大西洋，其雄者头部有可膨胀的钩状袋〕．

hood·ette [ˈhuːdet] *n.* 女流氓，女阿飞，女强盗．

hood·lum [ˈhuːdləm] *n.* 〔美俚〕强盗，流氓，恶棍，阿飞．**-ism** *n.*

hood·man [ˈhudmə] *n.* 〔古〕（捉迷藏游戏中的）蒙眼人．

hood·man-blind [ˈhudmənblaind] *n.* 〔古〕捉迷藏（= blindman's buff）．

hoo·doo [ˈhuːduː] *n.* ①〔美口〕不吉利的人，不祥之物．②〔美口〕倒楣，恶运．③ = voodoo*(n)*. ④（因受侵蚀而形成的）一种天然怪岩柱．— *vt.* 使遭恶运，使倒楣．

hood·wink [ˈhudwiŋk] *vt.* ①使（马）带上眼罩．②欺瞒，蒙蔽；隐蔽．*Stop your ～ing.* 别装了，别装样子．**-a·ble** *a.* **-er** *n.* 欺骗者，骗子．

hoo·ey [ˈhuːi] *n., int.* 〔美俚〕胡说，废话．

hoof [huːf] *n.* *(pl.* *～s,* 〔罕〕 ***hooves*** [huːvz]*)* ①蹄；〔谑〕（人的）脚．②有蹄类动物．*a cloven ～* 分趾蹄．***beat [pad] the ～*** = ***be upon the ～***〔俚〕走．***～-and-mouth disease*** = foot-and-mouth disease. ***give sb. the ～*** 叫某人滚蛋．***on the ～***（牛、马等）活着的，尚未屠宰的．***see sb.'s ～ in*** 在…中看出某人势力〔影响〕．***show the (cloven) ～***（魔鬼）露出爪趾，显出原形．***under the ～*** 被践踏．— *vt.* ①走．②踢；用蹄踏．— *vi.* ①走．②踢；踏．③跳舞．***be ～ed*** 被踢开；〔口〕被踢脱（差事等）．～ ***it***〔美口〕①步行．②逃走，跑掉．③表演跳舞．～ ***out*** 踢出．～**-and-mouth disease** 口蹄疫（= foot-and-mouth disease）．～**beat** 蹄声．～**bound** *a.* 兽蹄因病而感到疼痛紧缩的．～**pad** 蹄垫．～**pick**（剔去蹄下石片等物用的）蹄签．～**print** 蹄印．～**let** 小蹄．

hoofed [huːft] *a.* 有蹄的．

hoof·er [ˈhuːfə] *n.* ①步行者．②〔美俚〕木屐舞〔踢跶舞〕舞女．③〔美俚〕黑人．

hoo-ha [ˈhuːˌhɑː; 做感叹词用时，huːˈhɑː] *n.* 〔主英口〕吵闹，骚乱，骚动．— *int.* 呼哈！〔表吃惊、兴奋等的嘲弄性感叹词〕．

hook [huk] *n.* ①钩，铁钩；吊钩（= pothook）；针钩；镰刀；〔俚〕锚．②圈套，陷阱．③钩状物；河湾；钩状岬；【动、植】钩状器官；【乐】钩符（♪）；【拳】肘弯击，钩击；（高尔夫球中的）左曲球．④〔美俚〕妓女．⑤〔美俚〕手，手指．⑥〔美俚〕麻醉药（尤指海洛因）．*a belt ～* 皮带扣．*a bill ～* 钩刀．*a fish ～* 钓钩．*a telephone ～* 电话机钩键．***angle with a silver ～*** 行贿．***by ～ or (by) crook*** 想方设法，千方百计，不择手段．***drop [go, pop, slip] off the ～s***〔俚〕①发狂．②死．***get one's ～s into***〔美口〕占据，占有；惩罚．***get sb. off the ～***〔美俚〕使某人摆脱危境；解除某人的困难或义务．***get the ～***〔美俚〕被解雇．***～, line, and sinker***〔美俚〕完全地，全部地．***on one's own ～***〔俚〕独力地，独自地．***on the ～*** ①陷入圈套；受拘束，难摆脱．②拖延．***take [sling] one's ～***〔俚〕逃亡．***with a ～ at the end*** 有保留的同意．— *vt.* ①用钩挂 *(in; on; up)*；用钓钩钓；用钩针织；钩住，钓着．②（牛）用角尖挑．③引（人）上钩，欺骗．④〔俚〕偷，扒．⑤【拳】用肘弯侧击；【高尔夫球】使球向左弯．— *vi.* ①弯成钩形；钩住．②用角挑．③【高尔夫球】球向左弯．～ ***in*** 钩进；钩住．～ ***it***〔美俚〕逃走，快跑〔叫人逃走时的警告语〕．～ ***Jack***〔美〕偷懒，逃学．～ ***on*** 钩在一起；用钩子挂；钩上．～ ***up*** ①用钩子钩住；【机】接上．②【无】〔口〕联播．～ **and eye** 风纪扣．～ **and ladder** 云梯救火车〔有长梯子，折卸天花板用的钩子及其他设备的救火车〕．～**-bill** 鹦鹉；鹦鹉类的鸟．～**nose** ①钩鼻．②〔美俚〕犹太人，守财奴．～**-nosed** *a.* 钩鼻的．～**shop**〔美俚〕妓院．～ **shot**（篮球）单手勾手投篮．～**-up** *n.* ①【无】试验线路，电路耦合，接续图．②联播电台．③联合，同盟．～**-up wire** 架空电线．～**worm** 钩虫．～**worm disease** 钩虫病．～**wrench**【机】钩形扳手．**-let** *n.* 小钩子．

hook·(a)h [ˈhukə, -kɑː] *n.* 水烟筒．

hooked [hukt] *a.* ①钩状的．②有钩的．③钩织成的．④〔美俚〕吸毒成瘾的．⑤着迷于…的 *(on)*．⑥〔俚〕已婚的．*a ～ nose* 钩鼻．*a ～ rug* 钩针编织的地毯．**-ness** *n.*

hook·er[1] [ˈhukə] *n.* ①荷兰双桅渔船．②爱尔兰海岸单桅渔船．③旧船；废舰．

hook·er[2] [ˈhukə] *n.* ①【橄榄球】扭夺时的中心选手．②〔俚〕引人上钩者；娼妓．③一大杯威士忌酒．

hook·er[3] [ˈhukə] *n.* 【纺】码布机．

Hook·er [ˈhukə] *n.* 胡克〔姓氏〕．

hook·ey [ˈhuki] = hooky[2].

hook·y[1] [ˈhuki] *a.* 钩多的；钩状的．— *vt.* 〔美俚〕扒窃．

hook·y[2] [ˈhuki] *n.* 〔美俚〕旷课，逃学；逃学者．***play ～*** 逃学．

hoo·li·gan [ˈhuːligən] *n.* 〔俚〕阿飞，无赖，小流氓．**-ism** *n.* 无赖行为；流氓习性．

hoop[1] [huːp] *n.* ①箍．②箍状物；（孩子玩的）铁环，（马戏团供演员穿过的）大铁圈；〔*pl.*〕（旧时衬裙摆用的）裙环；鲸骨圈；戒指．③（篮球的）篮，篮圈；（槌球戏中的）弓形小门．***go through the ～ [～s]*** 受磨炼．***put sb. through the ～*** 使某人受折磨．***roll one's ～*** ①顺利向前．②稳妥办事．③〔美俚〕只管自己的事．***trundle a ～ along*** 滚铁环．— *vt.* ①在（桶等）上加箍；用箍围绕．②包围；拥抱．～ **iron**（做桶箍的）带钢；铁箍．

~**man** 篮球运动员. ~**skirt** 有裙环的女裙. ~ **snake** 环箍蛇〔美洲民间传说中尾含在嘴里全身作环状的蛇〕.
hoop[2] [hu:p] *vi.* 百日咳患者咳嗽时发唬唬声;唬唬地叫. — *n.* 鹄鸣声;(百日咳患者的)呼呼声. **hoop·ing cough**【医】百日咳.
hoop·er [ˈhu:pə] *n.* 箍桶人.
hoop·la [ˈhu:plɑ:] *n.* ①〔口〕极度兴奋;喧闹. ②大吹大擂的宣传;大话. ③投环套物游戏.
hoop·poe [ˈhu:pu:] *n.*【动】戴胜科鸟.
hoo·ray [huˈrei] *int., n., vt., vi.* = hurrah.
hoos(e)·gow [ˈhu:sgau] *n.* 〔美俚〕①监狱. ②警卫室. ③厕所.
hoosh [hu:ʃ] *n.* 〔俚〕一种浓汤.
Hoo·sier [ˈhu:ʒə] *n.* 〔美〕印第安纳州人. ***the ~ State*** 印第安纳州的别名.
hoot [hu:t] *vi.* ①(表示不满或嘲笑的)唬唬大叫. ②作猫头鹰叫声. ③〔英〕(汽笛、汽车喇叭等)嘟嘟;喵喵.— *vt.* ①用唬唬声表示(轻蔑、不赞成等). ②哄赶. ~ ***down*** (把某人)哄下台. ~ ***out [away, off]*** 哄走. ~ ***with laughter*** 狂笑. — *n.* ①猫头鹰叫声,汽笛声,汽车喇叭声,表示不满的叫声. ②极少量. ***not care a ~ [two ~s]*** 毫不在乎. ***not worth a ~*** 毫无价值. ~ **owl**【动】角枭(尤指大枭).
hootch [hu:tʃ] *n.* = hooch.
hoot·chy-koot·chy [ˌhu:tʃiˈku:tʃi] *n.* ***(pl. -koot·chies)*** 屁股舞;肚皮舞〔某些资本主义国家妇女跳的色情舞〕(= cooch; hootchiekootchie).
hoot·en·an·ny [ˈhu:tənæni] *n.* ①〔方〕(忘记或叫不上名称的)新玩意儿. ②(非正式的)民间歌舞表演会.
hoot·er [ˈhu:tə] *n.* 汽笛.
Hoot·on [ˈhu:tən] *n.* 胡顿〔姓氏〕.
hoots [hu:ts] *int.* 〔Scot.〕唬;〔表示不满或不赞成〕.
hoove [hu:v] *n.* (动物的)臌胀症.
Hoo·ver[1] [ˈhu:və] *n.* ①胡佛〔姓氏〕. ②**Herbert Clark** ~胡佛〔1874—1964,美国第三十一任总统1929—1933〕.
Hoo·ver[2] [ˈhu:və] *n.* 一种真空吸尘器. — *vt.* 用吸尘器扫除.
hooves [hu:vz] hoof 的复数.
hop[1] [hɔp] *vi.* ①(人)独脚跳,(鸟、蛙等)齐足跳;跳跃;跛行. ②〔口〕跳舞. ③〔口〕(飞机)作短途飞行,起飞. ④〔俚〕(忽然)走掉,走开 *(off)*. — *vt.* ①跳过;使(球)跳. ②〔美〕跳上(火车、飞机等);搭乘. ③〔口〕飞过,飞越. ***be hopping mad*** 〔美口〕气得跳起来,大怒. ~ ***it*** 〔口〕赶紧走开. ~ ***off*** (飞机)起飞. ~ ***on [all over]*** 〔俚〕责骂. ~ ***the twig [stick]*** 〔俚〕①逃避债务. ②忽然死掉. ~ ***to it*** 开始作某事. — *n.* ①单足跳;弹跳. ②〔俚〕舞会. ③飞行;(长距离飞行中的)一段航程;④短途旅行;免费搭乘. ***catch on the ~*** 出其不意地,正当其时地;忙乱地. ~, ***step [skip] and jump***【体】三级跳. ***on the ~***〔口〕到处奔忙. ~**scotch** 小儿(独脚)跳踢石子的游戏,"造房子"游戏,"踢房子"游戏,"跳方"游戏. ~**-toad** ①〔儿〕蛤蟆. ②〔美俚〕痛饮.
hop[2] [hɔp] *n.* ①【植】蛇麻草,忽布. ②〔*pl.*〕(用以使啤酒等带苦味的)蛇麻子. ③〔美俚〕一种麻醉药(尤指鸦片). ④瘾君子,有毒瘾的人. ***full of ~s*** 〔美俚〕(麻醉品药性未过而)胡说着. — *vt.* ①在…中加蛇麻子,用蛇麻子加味. ②用麻醉毒品刺激 *(up)*. ③超额增大(发动机)的功率;超额增大(车辆)发动机的功率. — *vi.* 种蛇麻子,采蛇麻子. ***be hopped up*** 〔美俚〕兴奋的;抽鸦片烟抽得昏昏沉沉的,(发动机)被超额加大功率的. ~**bind,** ~**bine** 蛇麻草蔓. ~ **clover** 黄花苜蓿〔干燥后象忽布〕. ~ **field** 蛇麻草田. ~ **fiend**〔美俚〕吸毒鬼. ~**fly** 蛇麻草蚜虫. ~ **garden** 蛇麻草园. ~**head** 〔美俚〕吸毒鬼. ~**horn beam** ①苗榆属 *(Ostrya)* 植物〔产于北美,尤指美洲铁木 *(O-virginiana)*〕. ②美洲铁木树材. ~**joint** 〔美俚〕低级酒店;鸦片馆. ~ **picker** 采蛇麻草的人,采蛇麻草机. ~ **pillow** 蛇麻草做芯子的枕头〔据说可促进睡眠〕. ~ **pocket** (可装168磅的)蛇麻草袋. ~ **pole** 蛇麻草的支柱;细长个子.
Hope [həup] *n.* 霍普〔姓氏,女子名〕.
hope [həup] *n.* ①希望 *(opp* despair*)*;(有信心的)期望,愿望 *(opp.* fear*)*. ②寄予希望的人〔物〕. *cherish [entertain] the ~ that* 抱着…的希望. *live up to the ~s of* 不辜负…的期望. *H- deferred maketh the heart sick.* 〔谚〕希望不实现,心碎亦可怜. *H- is a good breakfast, but a bad dinner.* 〔谚〕事前希望真美妙,事情失败成苦恼. *If it were not for ~, the heart would break.* 〔谚〕人靠希望而生. *The result exceeds my ~s.* 结果出乎我意外. *Where there is life, there is ~.* 〔谚〕有生命就有希望. *He is the ~ of his school.* 他是学校的希望. ***anchor [lay, pin, set] one's ~ in [on]*** 寄希望于. ***beyond [past] (all) ~*** 毫无希望,不可挽救. ***dash [shatter] sb.'s ~s*** 粉碎某人的希望. ***elevate [raise] sb.'s ~s*** 增强某人的信心. ***forlorn ~*** ①渺茫的希望,空想. ②孤注一掷的举动,绝望的事. ③敢死队. ***give up (resign) all ~*** 放弃一切希望. ***in ~s of = in the ~ of [that]*** 希望着,期待着. ***in vain ~*** 抱着不能实现的希望,幻想地. ***lose all ~*** 失掉一切希望. ***one's last ~*** 最后的希望. ***There is a ray of ~.*** 仍有一线希望. ***without any ~ of*** 毫无…的希望. — *vt.* 希望,期待 *(that; to do)*. ~ *to see you soon* 希望能再见到你. *It is ~d that ...* 希望能…,可以指望…. — *vi.* ①希望,期望. ②〔古〕信赖,相信 *(in)*. *I ~ so.* 但愿如此. *I ~ not.* 希望不至如此. *H- for the best, prepare for the worst.* 〔谚〕作最好的打算,作最坏的准备. ~ ***against*** ~ 存万一的希望,妄想 (*He ~s against ~ that no one would know the open secret.* 他痴心妄想,但愿谁也不会知道这个公开的秘密). ~ **box [chest]** 〔美俚〕女子的嫁妆,装嫁妆的箱子.
hope·ful [ˈhəupful] *a.* ①有希望的,有前途的. ②抱着希望的. ***a ~ outlook*** 有希望的前途. ***be [feel] ~ of [about]*** 对…抱希望〔持乐观态度〕. — *n.* 有希望成功的人,有希望被选上的人. ***a presidential ~*** 可望当上总统的人. ***a young ~*** 有希望的青年〔常用为反语〕. **-ly** *ad.* **-ness** *n.*
hope·ful·ly [ˈhəupfuli] *ad.* ①抱有希望地. ②可以指望 (= it is hoped).
hope·less [ˈhəuplis] *a.* 没有希望的;绝望的. *a ~ case* 不治之症;绝症病人;不堪造就的人. ~ *grief* 绝望的悲伤. **-ly** *ad.* **-ness** *n.*
hop·er [ˈhəupə] *n.* 希望者.
Hop·kin(s) [ˈhɔpkin(z)] *n.* 霍普金(斯)〔姓氏〕.
Hop·kin·son [ˈhɔpkinsn] *n.* 霍普金森〔姓氏〕.
hop·lite [ˈhɔplait] *n.* (古希腊的)装甲步兵.
hop-o'-my-thumb [ˈhɔpəmaiˈθʌm] *n.* 矮子.
hop·per[1] [ˈhɔpə] *n.* ①单足跳者;跳虫(如跳蚤、干酪蛆等). ②(磨粉机等的)漏斗,送料斗,加料斗;(卸除垃圾、废土等的)底卸式船〔车〕;贮水槽. ③(钢琴键盘后)抬举小木槌的机件. ~ **barge** (船底有漏斗的)垃圾搬运船. ~ **car**【铁路】底卸式货车. ~**grass** 〔方〕蚱蜢,蝗虫.
hop·per[2] [ˈhɔpə] *n.* = hop-picker.
hopping [ˈhɔpiŋ] *a.* ①忙碌的,繁忙的. ②从一处到另一处的;到处奔忙的. ~ ***mad*** 〔口〕大怒,狂怒.
hop·ple [ˈhɔpl] *n.* (牛、马等的)脚拴. — *vt.* ①把(牛、马等)的双脚拴起来. ②给(人)带上脚镣;妨碍…的自由.
hop·py [ˈhɔpi] *a.* 有蛇麻子味的.
hop·sack·ing [ˈhɔpsækiŋ] *n.*【纺】①席纹粗黄麻袋布. ②板司呢,席纹呢 (= hopsack).
hor. = horizon(tal); horology.
ho·ra [ˈhɔ:rə, ˈhəurə] *n.* ①霍拉舞〔罗马尼亚等地一种轻快活泼的民间舞〕. ②霍拉舞曲.
Hor·ace [ˈhɔrəs] *n.* ①霍勒斯〔男子名〕. ②贺拉斯〔公元前65—8年,罗马诗人,拉丁语原名为 Quintus

Horatius Flaccus〕.

Ho·rae [ˈhɔːriː] *n.* 〔*pl.*〕【希神】(掌管季节时序的) 季节三女神.

ho·ral [ˈhɔːrəl] *a.* ①每一小时的. ②时间上的.

ho·ra·ry [ˈhɔːrəri] *a.* ①每小时的. ②时间上的, 表示时间的. ③持续一小时的.

Ho·ra·tian [hɔˈreiʃiən] *a.* (罗马诗人)贺拉斯 (Horace) (式)的, 贺拉斯的诗歌的; 有贺拉斯风格的.

Ho·ra·ti·o [hɔˈreiʃiəu] *n.* 霍雷肖〔男子名〕.

horde [hɔːd] *n.* ①蒙古游牧部落. ②游牧民族; 游牧部落. ③〔蔑〕人群, 群. *a ~ of flies* 一大群苍蝇. *a gypsy ~* 吉普赛人部落. *the Golden H-* 金帐汗国. — *vi.* 成群; 结成部落而居.

Hor·deum [ˈhɔːdiəm] *n.* 【植】①大麦属. ②〔h-〕大麦属植物(包括大麦、元麦等).

hore·hound [ˈhɔːhaund] *n.* ①普通夏至草 (*Marrubium vulgare*). ②夏至草. ③夏至流浸膏〔治咳嗽药〕. ④唇形科植物.

ho·ri·zon [həˈraizn] *n.* ①地平; 地平线; 地平圈. ②地平仪, 水平仪. ③【地】地层, 层位. ④眼界, 视界; 范围, 见识. *apparent ~*【气】视地平. *artificial [false] ~* 人造地平. *celestial ~*【气】天球地平. *the ~ of knowledge* 知识范围. *radar ~* 雷达地平, 雷达作用距离. *~ of soil* 土层. *true ~*【气】真地平. *visible ~*【气】可见地平. *Science gives us a new ~.* 科学使我们大开新的眼界. *widen one's ~* 开阔眼界. ***on the ~*** 在地平线上, 刚冒出地平线.

hor·i·zon·tal [ˌhɔriˈzɔntl] *a.* ①地平的, 地平线的. ②水平的 (*opp.* vertical, perpendicular); 卧式的. ③同一行业的; 相同地位的. ④【植】(枝条)平层的. *a ~ axis* 水平轴, 横轴. *a ~ bar*【体】单杠. *the ~ line* 地平线, 水平线. *a ~ plane* 水平面. *a ~ engine* 卧式发动机. *a ~ rudder*【海、空】水平舵, 升降舵. *a ~ range* 广度. *a ~ union* (不同工业内同行业的)跨部门同业工会 (*opp.* vertical union). — *n.* 水平线; 水平面; 水平物. ***out of the ~*** 不成水平的. **-ly** *ad.* **-i·ty** *n.* 水平状态〔性质, 位置〕.

hor·mone [ˈhɔːməun] *n.*【生化】荷尔蒙, 激素, 内分泌. **hor·mo·nal, hor·mon·ic** [-ˈmɔnik] *a.*

hor·mon·ol·o·gy [ˌhɔːməˈnɔlədʒi] *n.* 内分泌学.

horn [hɔːn] *n.* ①(牛、羊、鹿等动物的)角, 触角; (动物头上的)角状羽毛; 触须. ②〔美俚〕鼻子. ③角质, 角质物, 角制物; 角状物, 角状容器. ④(角制)号角; 喇叭; (作为管乐器的)号, 管. ⑤警报器, 扬声器, 角状扩声器. ⑥(新月的)钩尖, (铁砧的)尖角, (马鞍的)鞍头. ⑦海湾的分叉; 河流的支流; 岬, 海角; 半岛;【地】角峰. ⑧【空】操纵杆. ⑨防卫武器; 力量; 光荣. ⑩魔鬼头上的角. ⑪〔*pl.*〕其妻与人通奸的人头上所生的角〔譬喻说法, 如汉语中的"绿帽子"〕. ⑫〔the -〕〔美俚〕电话. *a fog ~* 雾笛. *an English ~*【乐】英国管. *a French ~*【乐】法国号. *a shoe ~* 角质鞋拔. *a bull ~* 强力扬声器. ***a ~ of abundance [plenty]*** 丰满角〔希腊神话中主神宙斯所用的山羊角, 角中的乳永远倒不完〕; 丰裕的象征 (= cornucopia). ***blow [toot] one's own ~*** 自吹自擂. ***come out at the little end of the ~*** 吹牛失败; 说大话没有兑现. ***draw [haul, pull] in one's ~s*** 退缩, 撤退; 克制自已; 软化下去. ***lift up one's ~*** 趾高气扬; 盛气凌人. ***lock ~s*** ①(牛等)用角挑斗. ②难分难解地搏斗. ***lower one's ~*** 卑躬屈膝; 降低身份. ***on [between] the ~s of a dilemma*** 进退两难. ***put [denounce] sb. to the ~***【史】宣布(某人)不受法律保护. ***show one's ~s*** 露出凶相. ***take a ~*** 喝一杯酒. ***take the bull by the ~s*** 不畏艰险. ***wind the ~*** 吹号角, 吹喇叭; (昆虫)嗡嗡叫, 吱吱叫. — *vt.* ①在…上装角. ②把…做成角状. ③(动物)用角抵触〔刺挑〕. ④把(牛角)截去; 截短(牛角). ⑤【船】使(船的框架)与其龙骨成直角. ⑥(妻)使(丈夫)头上生角(当王八). *~ **in***〔美俚〕闯入, 侵入, 干涉. — *a.* 角制的, 角质的 (= horny). *~ **antenna*** 喇叭形天线. *~**bar*** 马车的横木. *~**beam***【植】鹅耳枥属树. *~**bill***【动】犀鸟科鸟; 犀鸟. *~**blende***【矿】角闪石. *~**book*** ①角帖书〔纸页上印有文字, 其上盖有透明角片的儿童识字书籍. ②初级论文. *~ **fly***【动】角蝇 (*Haematobia irritano*)〔可咬牛皮肤的一种吸血蝇〕. *~**-mad*** *a.* 大怒的. *~**pipe*** ①号角〔一种单簧管乐器〕. ②(英国水手跳的)号笛舞; 号笛舞曲. *~ **pox*** 水痘. *~**rimmed*** *a.* (眼镜)角质架的. *~**-rims***〔俚〕角质边的眼镜. *~ **silver*** 角银矿 (= cerargyrite). *~**stone***【矿】角岩. *~**-swoggle*** *vt.*〔美俚〕欺骗, 瞒. *~**-tail***【动】树蜂科 (*Siricidae*) 动物. *~**work*** ①〔集合词〕角制品; 角细工. ②(防御用的)角堡. *~**worm***【动】天蛾幼虫.

Horn [hɔːn] 合恩〔南美洲最南端的一岛名〕. ***Cape ~*** 合恩角.

Horn·by [ˈhɔːnbi] *n.* 霍恩比〔姓氏〕.

horned [hɔːnd, ˈhɔːnid] *a.* 有角的; 角状的. *the ~ moon*〔诗〕半月. *~ **bladderwort***【植】具角狸藻. *~ **grebe***【动】角䴙䴘. *~ **lizard*** = *~ toad.* *~ **owl***【动】枭. *~ **pout***【动】角鲶. *~ **puffin***【动】角目鸟. *~ **toad***【动】角蟾. *~ **violet***【植】簇生堇菜. *~ **viper***【动】角蝰 (*Cerastes cornutus*)〔产于北非〕.

horn·er [ˈhɔːnə] *n.* ①制角工人. ②吹号角者. ③〔俚〕服海洛因的人.

hor·net [ˈhɔːnit] *n.*【动】大黄蜂. ***arouse [stir up] a nest of ~s*** 捅马蜂窝, 惹来敌人〔反对者〕. ***arouse [bring, raise] a ~'s nest about one's ears*** 树敌招怨, 惹麻烦.

horn·fels [ˈhɔːnfels] *n.* 〔*sing., pl.*〕【矿】角页岩.

horn·ful [ˈhɔːnful] *n.* 满满一角杯.

horn·i·ness [ˈhɔːninis] *n.* 角质, 硬质.

hor·ni·to [hɔːˈniːtəu] *n.* (*pl.* **-tos** [-təuz])【地】溶岩滴丘.

horn·less [ˈhɔːnlis] *a.* 无角的; 无号角的. *a ~ sheep* 无角羊.

horn·y [ˈhɔːni] *a.* ①角的; 角制的. ②角状的, 角质的, 有角的. ③坚硬如角的; 粗硬起老茧的. ④〔美俚〕好色的, 猥亵的. ⑤〔古〕半透明的. *a ~ hand* 粗硬的手. *the ~ coat* (眼睛的)角膜. *~**-handed*** *a.* 手上长有老茧的.

horol. = horologe; horology.

hor·o·loge [ˈhɔrəlɔdʒ] *n.* 计时仪; 钟表, 日晷. **-loger** [-ˈrɔlədʒə], **ho·rol·o·gist** [-ˈrɔlədʒist] *n.* 钟表制造者; 钟表学家; 钟表商. **-log·ic(al)** [-ˈlɔdʒik(əl)] *a.* 钟表的, 钟表学的.

hor·o·lo·gi·um [hɔrəˈləudʒiəm] *n.* (*pl.* **-gi·a** [-dʒiə]) ①=horologe. ②〔the H-〕【天】时钟座.

ho·rol·o·gy [hɔˈrɔlədʒi] *n.* ①钟表学; 钟表制造术. ②测时法.

hor·o·scope [ˈhɔrəskəup] *n.* ①星占. ②算命天宫图. *cast a ~* 以占星术算命. **-scop·ic(al)** [-ˈskɔpik(əl)] *a.*

ho·ros·co·py [hɔˈrɔskəpi] *n.* ①星占(占星术算命者所说的人诞生时的)星位, 星相.

hor·ren·dous [hɔˈrendəs] *a.* 可怕的. **-ly** *ad.*

hor·rent [ˈhɔrənt] *a.*〔诗〕汗毛直竖的, 毛骨悚然的.

hor·ri·ble [ˈhɔrəbl, -ribl] *a.* ①可怕的, 令人毛骨悚然的. ②〔口〕讨厌的, 可恶的. *a ~ murder* 令人发指的谋杀罪行. *~ weather* 讨厌的天气. — *n.*〔常 *pl.*〕衣着古怪的人. **-ness** *n.* **hor·ri·bly** *ad.*

hor·rid [ˈhɔrid] *a.* (*superl.* *~est*) ①可怕的. ②〔口〕讨厌的, 可恶的. ③〔古〕粗糙的, 粗硬的. *What a ~ nuisance!* 真讨厌! **-ly** *ad.* **-ness** *n.*

hor·rif·ic [hɔˈrifik] *a.* 可怕的.

hor·ri·fy [ˈhɔrifai] *vt.* ①使恐怖, 使毛骨悚然. ②〔口〕使反感, 使厌恶. *be horrified at* 一想起…就不寒而慄. *be horrified to hear the news* 听到消息十分惊讶. **-fi·ca·tion** *n.* **-ing** *a.*

hor·rip·i·late [hɔ'ripileit] *vt., vi.* (使)毛发竖立,(使)起鸡皮疙瘩.

hor·rip·i·la·tion [hɔ,ripi'leiʃən] *n.* (由于寒冷、恐怖等引起的)毛发竖立;鸡皮疙瘩.

hor·ror ['hɔrə] *n.* ①战栗,恐怖;可怕的事物. ②嫌恶,痛恨. ③讨厌的人[事]. ④〔口〕非常丑恶,糟糕的东西. *He was filled with ~ at the sight.* 他看见那种光景就吓得发抖. *the Chamber of H-s* 恐怖陈列室〔原指伦敦*Tussaud's* 蜡像陈列馆〕. *He is a perfect ~.* 他是一个十分讨厌的家伙. *That coat is a ~.* 〔口〕那件大衣难看透了. ***have a ~ of sth.*** 对某事极厌恶. ***the ~s*** 〔口〕战栗,打冷颤(尤指发酒疯). ~ **fiction** 恐怖小说. ~-**stricken,** ~-**struck** *a.* 吓得发抖的,受惊吓的.

hors [hɔː] *ad., prep.* 〔F.〕 在外,在…之外. ~ ***concours*** [kɔ̃ːŋ'kur] (展览品)不参加竞赛评奖的. ~ ***de combat*** [də'kɔ̃ːmbaː] 失却战斗力的. ~ ***d'œuvre*** ['dɔːvr] 餐前小吃;〔转义〕无关重要的事.

horse [hɔːs] *n.* *(pl. ~s,* 〔集合词〕 *~)* ①马(尤指长大的公马),马科动物. ②〔集合词〕骑兵. ③象马的东西,有脚的架子(如衣架,手巾架等); 脚搭; (体操用)木马; 〔口〕(象棋中的)马. ④〔美俚〕(考试作弊用的)夹带. ⑤【矿】夹块,夹石;【地】夹层. ⑥【海】(卷帆时水手的)搭脚索,铁杆. ⑦〔美俚〕粗汉,笨蛋. ⑧〔美俚〕碎牛肉. ⑨〔美俚〕一千美元. ⑩〔美俚〕恶作剧. ⑪马力. *hold a ~* 执住马嘴. *light ~* 轻骑兵. *A good ~ cannot be of a bad colour.* 〔谚〕马好色也正. *A good ~ should be seldom spurred.* 〔谚〕好马不宜多加鞭. *a long ~* 直跳木马. *a side ~* 横跳木马. *Never swap [swop] ~s while crossing the stream.* 〔谚〕行到河中别换马. *When two ride on one ~, one must sit behind.* 〔谚〕两人同骑一匹马,总有一个坐后头. *You may take a ~ to the water, but you cannot make him drink.* 〔谚〕你可带马到水边,却不能强迫它喝水. ***a dark ~*** (赛马中出现的)冷门马; 实力难测的竞争者; 竞争中出人意料的获胜者. ***a ~ of another [different] colour*** 完全另外一回事. ***a ~ of the same colour*** 那是一回事. ***a ~ on sb.*** 〔俚〕针对某人的恶作剧. ***ask a ~ the question*** 要求马赛跑时拼命. ***back the wrong ~*** (赛马时)下错赌注; 支持失败的一方. ***be on one's high ~*** 趾高气扬. ***change ~*** 换马, 换班子, 调换主持人. ***come off one's high ~*** 放下架子. ***eat like a ~*** 吃得多. ***flog a dead ~*** ①鞭打死马,徒劳. ②企图把已经讨论过并已被搁置的旧事重提. ***from the ~'s mouth*** 〔美俚〕(消息等)来自可靠方面. ***hitch ~ (together) = put up one's ~s together*** 〔古〕同心协力; 情投意合; 结婚. ***hold one's ~*** 〔俚〕忍耐,镇静,不冲动. ***~ and foot*** 骑兵和步兵, 全军; 全力以赴地. ***~ and ~*** 齐头并进,并驾齐驱. ***H- Guards*** 〔英〕近卫骑兵队. ***iron ~*** 〔口〕火车头; 自行车;【军】坦克. ***(it is) enough to make a ~ [cat] laugh*** 太可笑了. ***lock [shut] the barn [stable door] after the horse is stolen*** 贼去关门. ***look a gift ~ in the mouth*** 对礼物挑剔. ***mount [ride] the high ~*** 〔口〕 趾高气扬, 耀武扬威. ***on ~ of ten toes = on foot's ~*** 〔谑〕骑两脚马, 徒步. ***outside of a ~*** 〔口〕 骑在马上. ***pay for a dead ~*** 为死马花钱,花冤枉钱. ***play ~*** ①(儿童游戏)骑竹马. ②〔美俚〕胡闹. ***play ~ with sb.*** ①嘲笑某人,愚弄某人. ②无礼对待某人. ***play ~ with sth.*** 〔美俚〕搞乱次序,造成混乱. ***proud ~*** 〔诗〕矫健的马,骏马. ***put the cart before the ~*** 本末倒置. ***roll up ~ and foot = roll up ~, foot and guns*** 使全军覆没. ***spur a willing ~*** 鞭打好好干活的马,给以不必要的刺激. ***take ~*** 骑马去; (母马)交尾. ***take the ~*** (母马)受孕. ***talk a ~'s hind leg off = talk the hind leg off a ~*** 滔滔不绝地谈. ***talk ~*** 说大话,吹牛. ***the flying [winged] ~*** 【希神】(诗神缪斯所骑的)飞马. ***the war ~*** 战马; 老兵,老手. ***To ~!*** (命令)上马! ***work for a dead ~*** 从事徒劳的工作. ***work like a ~*** 苦干,实干. — *vt.* ①给人[车]备马; 骑上(马). ②〔古〕使(某人)平躺放在木马或人背上鞭挞; 鞭挞. ③〔口〕猛推. ④【海】虐待. ⑤〔美〕嘲弄,愚弄. — *vi.* ①骑马. ②〔美〕作弄人,拿人开玩笑. ③〔卑〕性交. ~ ***around*** 〔俚〕起哄,胡闹. — *a.* ①马的. ②马拉的, 骑〔套〕着马的. ③(同类中)大而粗硬的. ~-**and-buggy** *a.* 〔美〕 过时的,老式的. ~**back** ①*n.* 马背; 隆起的条状地带. ② *ad.* 在马背上. ~**bean**【植】马蚕豆. ~ **block** 骑马墩. ~ **box** ①〔英〕 (运马用的) 有篷货车. ②〔谑〕 教堂的条凳席. ~**boy** 马夫. ~**breaker** 驯马师. ~**car** 〔美〕铁路马车; 运马车. ~ **chestnut** 七叶树属植物, 欧洲七叶树. ~**cloth** (盖在马身上或装饰马用的)马衣, 马被. ~ **collar** 马颈圈 *(grin through a ~ collar* 〔古〕把头从马颈圈伸出来互作鬼脸的游戏;〔喻〕硬充滑稽). ~ **coper,** ~ **couper,** ~ **dealer** 马贩子. ~ **doctor** 〔口〕马医, 兽医; 蹩脚医生. ~-**faced** *a.* 马脸的; 脸长而难看的. ~**feathers** *n.* 〔*pl.*〕梦话,胡说八道. ~**flesh** ①马肉. ②马〔集合词〕. ~-**fly** 虻,马蝇. ~**foot** ①【植】款冬. ②【动】鲎. ~ **gear** 马具; 马力装置. ~ **gentian**【植】莛子藨属 *(Triosteum)* 植物. ~**hair** ①马毛,马鬃. ②马毛呢. ~ **hide** ①马皮. ②马革. ~ **latitudes** 〔*pl.*〕【气】 回归线无风带. ~**laugh** 哄笑, 纵声大笑. ~**leech** 蚂蝗; 贪心汉; 榨取者 *(daughters of the ~leech* 贪得无厌的人们). ~ **mackerel**【鱼】竹筴鱼; 金枪鱼. ~**man** 养马的人; 骑手,骑师; 骑兵. ~**manship** 马术. ~ **marine** 骑马水兵 (指不存在的东西); 外行 *(Tell it [that] to the ~ marines!* 鬼才会相信!) ~ **master** *n.* 驯马师; 租马商. ~ **mastership** 御马术. ~**mint** *n.* 【植】 香蜂草属 *(monnardra)* 植物〔尤指梦菲薄荷 *(m. punctata)*〕. ~ **opera** 〔美俚〕西部"牛仔"影片〔广播剧、电视剧〕. ~ **pistol** 马枪. ~**play** *n., vi.* 恶作剧,胡闹. ~ **pond** 饮马池; 洗马池. ~**power**【机】马力. ~**pox** 马痘. ~ **race [racing]** 赛马. ~**radish** 【植】 辣根. ~ **rake** 马拉集草机, 马拉耧耙. ~ **sense** 〔口〕起码常识. ~-**shit** ①马粪. ②〔俚〕 胡说. ~**shoe** ①*vt.* 给(马)钉掌. ② *n.* 马蹄铁; 马蹄形的东西 *(a ~shoe magnet* 蹄形磁铁. *a ~shoe nail* 蹄钉. *a ~shoe crab* 鲎). ③U形的. ~**tail** ①马尾. ②【植】木贼属. ~-**trade** *vi.* 精明地讨价还价. ~ **trade** ①马的交易. ②讨价还价后互相让步的交易. ~ **trader** 马贩,马商. ~**whip** ① *n.* 马鞭. ② *vt.* 用马鞭鞭打. ~ **woman** 女骑手; 女养马人.

horse·less ['hɔːslis] *a.* ①无马的. ②无需马的; 自动的. *An automobile was formerly called a ~ carriage.* 汽车原来被叫做不用马拉的车子.

hors·ey ['hɔːsi] *a.* = horsy.

Hors·ley ['hɔːsli] *n.* 霍斯利〔姓氏〕.

hor·som. 〔处方〕睡觉时 (= at bed time).

horst [hɔːst] *n.* 【地】地垒.

hors·y ['hɔːsi] *a.* ①马的; 马似的. ②爱马的; 爱赛马的; 热心改良马匹的. **hors·i·ly** *ad.* **hors·i·ness** *n.*

hort., hortic. = horticultural; horticulture.

hor·ta·tion [hɔː'teiʃən] *n.* 劝告; 奖励.

hor·ta·tive ['hɔːtətiv] *a.* 劝告性的; 忠告性的. **-ly** *ad.*

hor·ta·to·ry ['hɔːtətəri] *a.* = hortative.

Hor·tense [hɔː'tens] *n.* 霍顿斯〔女子名〕(L. = gardener).

hor·ti·cul·ture ['hɔːtikʌltʃə] *n.* 园艺(学). **-tur·al** *a.* 园艺(技术)上的. **-tur·ist** 园艺家.

hor·tus sic·cus ['hɔːtəs 'sikəs] 〔L.〕 ①(压干的) 植物标本(集). ②一堆枯燥的事实.

ho·san·na [həu'zænə] *n.* 【宗】和散那〔赞美上帝的用语〕.

hose [həuz] *n.* *(pl. hose(s),* 〔古〕 ***ho·sen*** [həuzn]) ①长筒袜. ②(旧时男子穿的) 紧身裤, 短裤. ③水龙带, 软管,胶皮管; 蛇管. ④叶鞘. *half ~* 短袜. — *vt.* ①使穿长筒袜. ②用胶皮管浇水. ③〔美俚〕向…拍马屁,用甜言蜜语笼络. ~ **cart** (消防队的) 水管车. ~**man**

消防人员. ~**pipe** 水龙软管. ~**-tops** [*pl.*] 无脚部的长筒袜.

Ho·se·a [həu'ziə] *n.* ①(纪元前8世纪希伯来先知)何西阿. ②《旧约全书》中的《何西阿书》.

Ho·sier ['həuzjə] *n.* 霍西尔[姓氏].

ho·sier ['həuʒə] *n.* 经售男袜、内衣和针织品商人,袜商.

ho·sier·y ['həuʒəri] *n.* ①[集合词]男袜; 男用针织品. ②针织品生意;针织厂.

hosp. = hospital.

hos·pice ['hɔspis] *n.* [F.] ①(特指教会、僧侣办的)旅客招待所. ②救济院,济贫院.

hos·pi·ta·ble ['hɔspitəbl] *a.* ①善于招待的, 款待周到的;殷勤的,好客的. ②(气候、环境)宜人的,适宜的. ③易于接受的. *a ~ reception* 热情的招待. *a mind ~ to new ideas* 善于接受新思想的人. **-ness** *n.* **-bly** *ad.*

hos·pi·tal ['hɔspitl] *n.* ①医院; 兽医院. ②[古] 旅客招待所. ③慈善收养院. ④(钟表、钢笔等小物件的)修理商店. ⑤公立学校[此意仅作专有名词用,如 Christ's H-]. *a clearing ~* 兵站医院. *a field ~* 野战医院. *an infectious ~* 传染病医院. *an isolation ~* 隔离病院. *lock ~* [英] 性病医院,花柳病医院. *a lying-in [maternity] ~* 产科医院. *magdalen ~* 妓女教养院. *a mental ~* 精神病医院. ***be in ~*** 住院. ***go to [enter] ~*** 入院. ***out of ~*** 出院. ***walk the ~s*** (医科学生)到医院实习. ~ **bed** 医院床[可以升降活动的床]. ~ **fever** 医院热[以前在医院里流行的一种斑疹伤寒病]. ~**man** [美] 海军医务兵. **H- Saturday [Sunday]** [英]医院募捐的星期六[日][星期六在街头募捐,星期日在教堂募捐]. ~ **ship** 医疗船,运送伤病员的船. ~ **train** 运送伤病员的列车.

hos·pi·tal·ism ['hɔspitəlizəm] *n.* ①医院制度. ②长期住医院给病人带来的不良影响. ③长期孤儿院生活的不良影响.

hos·pi·tal·i·ty [ˌhɔspi'tæliti] *n.* ①(对客人的)亲切招待,款待,[*pl.*] 殷勤. ②(气候,环境等的)宜人,适宜. *partake of ~* 受人款待.

hos·pi·tal·i·za·tion [ˌhɔspitəlai'zeiʃən] *n.* ①住院治疗. ②[美口](保证偿付住院费的)住院保证单 (=hospitalization insurance).

hos·pi·tal·ize ['hɔspitəlaiz] *vt.* 把…送入医院治疗.

hos·pi·tal·(l)er ['hɔspitələ] *n.* ①慈善收养院职员. ②医院牧师. ③[军]就医的人. ***Knight H-*** 中世纪在耶路撒冷建立的十字军骑士团救护成员.

host¹ [həust] *n.* [常 H-]【宗】圣饼,圣餐用面包.

host² [həust] *n.* ①主人 (*opp.* guest). ②(广播、电视的)节目主持人. ③旅馆老板. ④【生】寄主,宿主. ⑤【物】晶核, 基质. *a ~ country* 东道国. ***count [reckon] without one's ~*** 不考虑某些重要因素 [未与主要有关人员协商]作计划; 无视困难和反对 (*You are counting without your ~.* 你是在打如意算盘). ***play ~ to*** 作东,招待. — *vt.* 主办(宴会等); 款待. ~ **plant** 【生,植】宿主,寄主. ~**-specific** *a.* 【生】寄生于特殊宿主上的.

host³ [həust] *n.* ①一大群,许多. ②[古] 军队. *a ~ of friends* 一大群朋友. *a ~ of troubles* 许许多多麻烦. ***be a ~ in oneself*** 能以一当十; 一人能做很多人的事. ***the ~(s) of heaven*** ①【宗】天使军. ②日月星辰. ***the Lord [God] of H-s*** 【圣】万军之主,上帝.

hos·tage ['hɔstidʒ] *n.* 人质; 抵押品. ***be held in [as an] ~*** 被扣作人质. ***give ~ to fortune*** ①听天由命. ②有家室之累. ~ ***to fortune*** 随时会失去的人[物](尤指妻子、孩子、珍宝). **-ship** 充当人质,被抵押状态.

hos·tel ['hɔstəl] *n.* ①[英] 大学宿舍. ②[美] (招待徒步旅行青年等的)招待所 (=youth ~). ③[英古]旅馆.

hos·teler ['hɔstələ] *n.* ①招待所管理员; [古] 旅馆的主人. ②住招待所的青年旅行者.

hos·tel·ry ['hɔstəlri] *n.* [英古] 旅馆,客栈.

host·ess ['həustis] *n.* ①女主人. ②旅馆女老板. ③[美] (餐馆、列车、飞机等的)女服务员,女侍应生. ④(舞厅里的)舞女. *an air-~* 飞机上的女服务员,空中小姐. — *vt.* 在…作女主人; 作女主人招待.

hos·tile ['hɔstail] *a.* ①敌人的,敌方的. ②怀有敌意的,敌对的 (*to*), 不友善的. *a ~ army* 敌军. *~ feeling* 敌意. *a ~ looks* 显示敌意的面色. *~ to reform* 反对改革. *assume [take] a ~ attitude* 抱敌对态度. *be ~ to* 敌视. *~ operations* 敌对行动. — *n.* ①【美史】敌视白人的印第安人. ②敌对分子. **-ly** *ad.*

hos·til·i·ty [hɔs'tiliti] *n.* ①敌意, 敌视. ②敌对行为, 反抗行为; [*pl.*] 战争行动; 战斗. *feelings of ~* 敌意. *an act of ~* 敌对行为. *naval hostilities* 海战. *open [suspend] hostilities* 开[休]战. *the outbreak of ~* 战事的爆发. *the renewal [resumption] of hostilities* 恢复敌对行动.

hos·tler ['ɔslə, 'hɔslə] *n.* ①[古] = ostler. ②机车[机器]的维修人.

hot [hɔt] *a.* ①热的 (*opp.* cold). ②(味道)刺激性的, 辣的,辛辣的;【猎】野兽的气味强烈的;(色彩)强烈的,给人热感的(如红、黄等). ③热烈的,激动的;猛烈的,激烈的;热情的,热心的;急躁的,发火的. ④淫秽的;色情的;性欲强的,(动物) 正当交尾期的. ⑤(爵士音乐) 节奏快的;[美俚]吵闹的,即兴的;兴奋之余自由演奏的. ⑥时新的,流行的,热门的;最近的,刚到的,刚做好的;才出锅的,才出炉的,(菜等)热腾腾的;(公债等)才发行的;[美俚] 刚偷来的,非法得来的;危险的. ⑦杰出的,极好的;(选手)强有力的;(演技等)优秀的. ⑧[俚]极走运的;正在劲头上的; 竞技状态极佳的. ⑨(游戏)接近目的物的;差一点就(猜中)的. ⑩通高压电的;【原】放射性强的. ⑪紧随的,接近的;被通缉的. ⑫[俚] 荒诞的,不可信的. *be piping [steaming] ~* 酷热, 闷热. *Strike the iron while it is ~.* [谚] 趁热打铁, 趁机行事. *a ~ battle* 激战. *~ blush* 红脸. *a ~ place in the battle* 激战地. *~ words* 激烈话. *a ~ argument* 激烈辩论. *~ idea* [美] 极好的主意. *Pepper is ~.* 胡椒是辣的. *~ temper* 暴燥的脾气. *a ~ scent or trail* 猎物气味强烈或有强烈臭味的路径[打猎用语]. *in ~ pursuit* 紧追. *a ~ wire* 高压电线. ***all ~ and bothered*** [俚]骚动中的. ***at its [the] hottest.*** 在最激烈的一点上. ***be ~ on sb.'s trail*** 穷追某人. ***be ~ on [for]*** 热中于,热心. ***be ~ under the collar*** [俚] 发怒. ***drop sth. like a ~ potato [chestnut]*** [口] 急忙扔掉. ***get ~*** ①变热,发热. ②激动,发怒. ③[俚]使劲干. ④接近. ***get into ~ water*** [口]遭到麻烦,惹来麻烦. ***get [catch] it ~*** [口] 被大骂一顿. ***give it sb. ~ = let sb. have it ~*** [口]痛骂某人,痛打某人. ***go ~ and cold (all over)*** (因害怕等)感到一阵子热一阵子冷. ~ ***and heavy*** 猛烈; 极力, 拼命. ~ ***and ~*** (食物)才出锅的,才出炉的. ~ ***and strong*** 猛烈地,激烈地. ~ ***from the press*** 刚印好的. ~ ***off the wire*** 电报[电话]刚刚打来的. ***in ~ blood*** 发怒,激昂. ***in ~ haste*** 火急. ***make the place too ~ for sb. = make it too ~ to hold sb.*** 使某人呆不下去. ***not so ~*** 不太好, 不太杰出. ***sizzling ~*** 火烫一样的热; 充满愤怒. ***the ~s*** [美俚] 爱情,性欲. — *vi.* [英] 变热; 变得激动; 骚动起来 (*up*). — *vt.* [英] 使热 (*up*); 刺激,使骚动. — *ad.* ①热; 热烈地,猛烈地. ②愤怒地. ③趁热. ***blow ~ and cold*** 无定见,犹豫不决. ***come ~ on sb.'s heels*** 紧跟某人来. ~ **air** [俚] 空话, 浮夸的文章. ~**-air artist** [俚] 吹牛大王. ~ **atom** 热原子 [具有放射核的原子]. ~**bed** 温床 (*a ~bed of war* 战争的策源地). ~ **blast** 【冶】热鼓风. ~**blood** 易激动者,轻举妄动者. ~**-blooded** *a.* ①热血的;易激怒的; 血气方刚的; 情欲旺盛的. ②(马) 英国种的, 阿拉伯种的. ③(家畜) 良种的. ~**box** (火车上的)过热轴承箱. ~**-brained** *a.* = hotheaded. ~ **cake** 烤饼 (*go [sell] like ~ cakes* (货物)很快地卖光). ~ **cell** 【原】热室, 高放射线物质工作屏蔽室. ~**cha** ['hɔttʃɑː] [美俚]

爵士音乐. ～ **chair** 〔美俚〕电椅. ～ **chow** 〔美口〕热腾腾的食物. **hot charging**【冶】热装料. ～ **cockles** 蒙眼猜人游戏. ～ **cooling** 沸腾冷却. ～ **corner** ①(垒球)第三垒. ②〔美俚〕战场[政治]上的关键地方. ～ **cross bun** 十字霜糖面包(尤指基督教四旬斋日所吃者). ～ **dog** ① *n.* 〔口〕小红肠,热狗,红肠面包;〔美俚〕最佳运动员. ② *a.* 〔美俚〕极好的. ～**dog** *vi., vt.* (在作冲浪或滑雪运动时)卖弄(花式动作). ～ **dogging** 吃热狗. ～**flash** 经绝期阵发性发热感. ～**foot** ① *ad.* 急急忙忙地. ② *vi.* 急急忙忙地走. ③ *n.* 〔*pl.* ～***foots***〕暗中将火柴放在别人鞋中点燃的恶作剧;心灵的刺激,震惊. ～**-galvanization** 热镀锌. ～ **gas welding** 气焊. ～ **gospel(l)er** 狂热的清教徒,奋兴派牧师. ～**head** 性急的人. ～**-headed** *a.* 性急的,鲁莽的. ～**house** ① *n.* 温室;陶器干燥室. ② *a.* 温室中生长的,人工的,过份纤弱的. ～**iron** 铁水. ～ **laboratory** 强放射性物质研究实验室. ～ **landing** 高速降落. ～ **light** 热光,电视广播室中最重要的灯光. ～ **line** ①"热线"(尤指苏美两国政府首脑间的直接通话线). ②直接联系的途径. ③广播现场提出的问题. ～ **material** 强放射性物质. ～ **money** ①赃款;偷来的钱. ②(为牟利)由一国转移至另一国的流动资金. ～ **pants** 〔美〕(妇女穿在外面的)冬季短裤. ～ **pack** ①【医】热敷. ②(制罐头的)快装法. ～ **pepper** ①辣胡椒. ②辣胡椒树. ～ **pilo** 〔美空俚〕优秀的战斗机驾驶员. ～ **place** 〔美俚〕地狱. ～ **plane** 〔美空俚〕起飞降落极快的飞机. ～ **plate** ①煤气炉;电炉. ②餐厅出售的热食. ③保温盘;烤盘. ～ **pot** 〔英〕马铃薯炖牛[羊]肉. ～ **potato** 难题,棘手的问题. ～**-press** ① *vt.* 热压. ② *n.* 热压机. ～ **pups** ＝～ dog. ～ **rod** 〔俚〕①(旧车拆卸改装的)减重高速汽车. ②＝～ rodder. ～ **rodder** 〔俚〕减重高速汽车驾驶者. ～ **rodding** 驾驶减重高速汽车. ～**-roll** *vt.* 【冶】热轧. ～ **seat** ①〔美俚〕电椅. ②尴尬处境. ～ **shoe** 热靴〔摄影机上的闪光灯插座〕. ～**-short** 加热就脆的,热脆性的. ～ **shortness** 热脆性. ～**shot** ①(运送易腐物品等的)快车,快船,快机. ②大人物,飞黄腾达的野心家;艺高而自负的人. ～ **sketch** 〔美俚〕漂亮女人[女学生]. ～ **spot** 〔美俚〕①麻烦地点,潜在的危险地区. ②电椅. ③低级下流的夜总会. ④辐射最强处,过热点. ～ **spring** 温泉. ～ **spur** ① *n.* 性急的人. ② *a.* ～ **squat** 〔美俚〕电椅;被处电刑. ～ **strip** 热轧带钢. ～**stuff** 〔俚〕①好手,专家. ②意志坚强的人. ③脾气暴躁的人;好色的人. ④大胆的举动,引起轰动的事物. ～**tap**【冶】(钢锭的)热帽. ～ **tear** 缩裂,热裂. ～**-tempered** *a.* 暴躁的,易激怒的. ～ **war** 热战〔"冷战"之对〕. ～ **water** ①热水. ②困境. ～**-water bag,** ～**-water bottle** 热水袋. ～**-water heating** 暖气设备. ～ **well** 温泉. ～**-wire** ① *a.* 【电】热线式的,热电阻线的. ② *vt.* 短路打(火)〔发动汽车时不用车匙,使汽车的电线短路以发动引擎〕. ～ **wire** 〔美俚〕(好)消息. ～**-working**【冶】热加工. **-ly** *ad.* **-ness** *n.*

hotch·pot [ˈhɔtʃˌpɔt] *n.* 【法】财产混同〔指将各项产业合并,以便在继承人中平分〕.

hotch·potch [ˈhɔtʃpɔtʃ] *n.* ①(蔬菜、土豆、肉等煮的)浓汤;杂烩. ②混杂物;杂乱的一堆东西. ③＝hotchpot.

Ho·tel [həuˈtel] 通讯中代表 h 的词.

ho·tel [həuˈtel] *n.* 旅馆,旅社. *a(n)* ～ *car* 〔美〕带餐车的卧车. *American plan* ～ 美国式旅馆,膳宿合并计算法. *European plan* ～ 欧洲式旅馆,膳宿费分别计算. *temperance* ～ 禁酒旅馆. ***His Majesty's*** ～ 〔谑〕监狱. ***the sheriff's*** ～ 〔俚〕监狱. — *vt.* 使住旅馆〔通常说 ～ it〕. ～ **car** 带餐室的卧车. ～**keeper** 旅店老板. ～**-keeping** 旅店业.

hôt·el [əuˈtel] *n.* 〔F.〕官邸;(富人或显要人士的)公馆. ～ **de ville** [dəˈviːl] 〔F.〕市政府. ～ **Dieu** [djəː] 〔F.〕医院.

ho·tel·ier [həuˈteliei] *n.* 旅馆老板;旅馆经理.

hot·sy-tot·sy [ˈhɔtsiˈtɔtsi] *a.* 〔美俚〕好的;壮观的;精采的.

Hot·ten·tot [ˈhɔtntɔt] *n.* ①(西南非洲)霍屯督族;霍屯督人. ②霍屯督语.

hou·dah [ˈhaudə] *n.* ＝ howdah.

Hou·din·i [huːˈdiːni] *n.* 霍迪尼〔姓氏〕.

hough [hɔk] *n., vt.* 〔英〕＝ hock[1].

hound[1] [haund] *n.* ①狗;猎狗. 〔英〕〔the ～s〕猎狐的一群猎狗. ②撒纸追逐的"狗免赛跑"游戏中扮演猎狗的人. ③【动】角鲨,星鲨,弓鳍鱼. ④卑鄙的人. ⑤〔构成复合词〕有…迷[瘾]的人. *the* ～ *of hell* ＝ *Cerberus. an autograph* ～ 爱请人在纪念册上签名题字的人. *a jazz* ～ 爵士音乐迷. *a publicity* ～〔美俚〕爱在报上露名的人,喜欢自吹自擂的人. ***a tea*** ～〔美俚〕爱交际的人,爱同女人交际的男子;女人腔的男子. ***follow (the)*** ～***s*** ＝ ***ride to*** ～***s*** 骑马纵狗打猎. ***hare and*** ～***s*** 撒纸追逐的"狗免赛跑"游戏. ～***s of law*** 缉捕员. ***ride before [past] the*** ～***s*** 骑马纵狗打猎;抢光;先下手. — *vt.* ①用猎狗打猎;追逐;迫害. ②唆使,煽动 *(on)*;使追逐 *(at)*. ***be*** ～***ed out of*** 从…中被赶出. ～ ***out*** 挑唆;煽动.

hound[2] [haund] *n.* 〔*pl.*〕【船】桅肩.

hound's-tongue [ˈhaundzˈtʌŋ] *n.* 【植】倒提壶属 *(cynoglossum)* 植物.

hour [ˈauə] *n.* ①小时,钟头. ②时间,时刻. ③一小时的行程;一小时的工作量. ④〔*pl.*〕固定时间(尤指工作时间);课时;【宗】天主教的定时祈祷,祈祷文. ⑤…点钟. ⑥死期,末日. ⑦(…)时,时代. ⑧〔the ～〕目前,现在. ⑨【天】赤经十五度. ⑩〔H-〕【希神】掌管季节、时序等的女神. *An* ～ *in the morning is worth two in the evening.* 〔谚〕一日之计在于晨. *half an* ～ ＝〔美〕*a half* ～ 半小时. *a quarter of an* ～ 一刻钟. *every* ～ *or two* 每一二小时. *What is the* ～? 现在几点钟了? *The* ～ *is 11:15.* 十一点一刻了. *school* ～*s* 上课时间. *office* ～*s* 办公时间. *business* ～*s* 营业时间. *dark* ～*s* 艰苦的时刻. *The darkest* ～ *is that before the dawn.* 〔谚〕黎明之前天最黑. *golden* ～*s* 幸福的日子. *The city is two* ～*s away [distant].* 该城离此两小时路程. *One's* ～ *has come [struck].* 末日已到,命数已尽. *my boyhood's* ～*s* 我的童年时代. *The clock struck the* ～. 钟响报时. *combat flying* ～【军】战斗飞行小时. ***after*** ～***s*** 办公[营业]时间以后. ***at a good*** ～ 恰巧,正好,侥幸. ***at all*** ～***s*** 随时. ***at the eleventh*** ～ 在最后时刻,在危急关头. ***by the*** ～ 按钟点. ***for*** ～***s (and*** ～***s)*** 好几小时. ***for*** ～***s together*** 一连好几小时. ～ ***after*** ～ 一小时又一小时,连续地. ***in a good [happy, lucky]*** ～ 在幸运的时刻. ***in an evil [ill]*** ～ 在不幸的时刻. ***in the*** ～ ***of need*** 紧急的时候. ***keep bad [late]*** ～***s*** 迟出迟归,晚起晚睡. ***keep good [early, regular]*** ～***s*** 早睡早起;早出早归. ***make long*** ～***s*** 长时间地工作. ***news to this*** ～ 〔美〕(无线电广播的)最后消息. ***of the*** ～ 目前的,现在的,紧急的 *(the question of the* ～ *目前的问题)*. ***off*** ～***s*** 业余时间. ***on the*** ～ 准时地;按整小时地. ***out of*** ～***s*** 在上班时间之外. ***serve the*** ～ 随波逐流;趋炎附势. ***the dead*** ～***s*** 半夜三更,夜深人静. ***the inevitable*** ～ 死期. ***the long*** ～***s*** 午夜十一、二点. ***the rush*** ～***s*** 交通拥挤时间,高峰时间. ***the short*** ～***s*** 午夜以后两、三点. ***the small [wee]*** ～***s*** 半夜一、二、三点. ***the trying*** ～ 艰难困苦的时刻. ***the unearthly*** ～ 太早,早得厉害,早得不象话. ***to an*** ～ 恰好 *(three days to an* ～ *恰好三天)*. ～ **angle** 【天】时角. ～ **circle**【天】时圈;子午线. ～**glass** 沙漏,水漏. ～ **hand** (钟表的)时针,短针. ～ **plate** (钟、表的)字盘.

hou·ri [ˈhuəri] *n.* ①伊斯兰教天堂中的美女. ②妖艳的美人.

hour·ly [ˈauəli] *a.* 每小时的,每小时一次的;时时,常

常. 一 *ad.* 每小时一次;时时,随时.

House [haus] *n.* 豪斯〔姓氏〕.

house [haus] *n. (pl.* ~s [ˈhauziz]*)* ①房屋, 住宅; 住家;一家,一户. ②家,家庭;家务. ③家族;王朝. ④建筑物,馆;商号,社,所,机构;〔美〕旅馆;戏院. ⑤〔集合词〕观众,听众;演出的场次. ⑥(英国式大学)宿舍;全体寄宿生. ⑦房间,室. ⑧(牲畜、家禽等的)栏,房,棚;(仪器)罩. ⑨(大学等的)校董会(会议);宗教团体;修道院. ⑩〔the H-〕议会;议院〔特指下院〕;〔集合词〕议员. ⑪〔口〕伦敦证券交易所. ⑫〔美俚〕妓院. ⑬(牛津大学的)基督学院 (Christ Church College). ⑭〔英俚〕救贫院. *An Englishman's* ~ *is his castle.* 〔谚〕英国人的家是他的堡垒,非请不得擅入. *Burn not your* ~ *to rid it of the mouse.* 〔谚〕不要为了驱鼠而焚烧房屋;勿因小失大. *the* ~ *of David* 大卫王室. *Johnson H-* 〔英〕=〔美〕*the Johnson* ~ 约翰逊宅. *a business* ~ 商店. *H- Full* = *Full H-* 【剧】客满. *a hash* ~ 〔美〕小饭馆. *a rogue* ~ 〔口〕监牢. *The* ~ *rose to its feet.* 全场起立. *The second* ~ *starts at 9.* 第二场9时开演. *thin* ~ 观众稀少. *the White H-* 〔美〕白宫. *Name not a halter [rope] in his* ~ *that hanged himself.* 〔谚〕房里有人吊死,千万别提绳子. ***as safe as*** ~***s [a*** ~***]*** 十分安全. ***be in possession of the H-*** 在议会中发言. ***bow down in the H- of Rimmon*** [ˈrimən] 为妥协以达到一致行动而牺牲自己的原则〔源出《圣经》《列王纪》〕. ***bring down the*** ~ 博得满场喝采. ***bring the*** ~ ***about one's ears*** 在家中成为众矢之的. ***(burn) like a*** ~ ***on fire*** 燃烧得又快又猛. ***carry the*** ~ 博得满场喝采. ***clean*** ~ ①打扫房屋. ②内部清洗 (= ~ clean). ***count the*** ~ 计算出席人数. ***eat sb. out of*** ~ ***and home*** 把某人吃穷. ***enter the H-*** 当选为议员. ***from*** ~ ***to*** ~ 挨家挨户. ***give sb. a lot of*** ~ 〔美俚〕给某人很多鼓励. ~ ***and home*** 家〔加强语气的说法〕. ~ ***of assignation*** 妓院. ***H- of Burgesses*** 〔美〕州众议院. ~ ***of call*** ①职业介绍所, 荐头行. ②常去的场所(如酒店等). ~ ***of cards*** 小孩子用纸牌搭成的房子;不牢靠的计划. ***H- of Commons*** 〔英〕众议院,下院. ~ ***of correction*** 教养院,改造所. ***H- of Delegates*** 〔美〕州参议院. ~ ***of detention*** 拘留所. ~ ***of God*** 教堂. ~ ***of ill fame*** 妓院. ***H- of Lords*** 〔英〕贵族院,上院. ~ ***of refuge*** 难民收容所;养育院. ***H- of Representatives*** 〔美〕众议院. ***iron*** ~ 〔美俚〕监牢. ***keep a good*** ~ 待客周到. ***keep*** ~ 料理家务;当家. ***keep*** ~ ***with*** 和…同住. ***keep open*** ~ ***[doors, table]*** 好客, 随时欢迎来客. ***keep the [one's]*** ~ 呆在家中不外出. ***make [keep] a H-*** (英下院)使出席议员达法定人数40人. ***make sb. free of one's*** ~ 让某人自由使用自己的房子. ***move*** ~ 搬家. ***on the*** ~ 〔美俚〕主人开销的,免费的. ***play*** ~ "做家家"〔儿童假装大人做家务〕. ***public*** ~ ①公共会堂. ②〔英〕酒馆. ***put [set] one's*** ~ ***in order*** 整理家务;进行必要的改革. ***the big house*** 〔美俚〕(州或联邦的)监狱. ***the dark*** ~ 〔婉〕坟墓. ***the half-way*** ~ ①两市镇间的客店. ②妥协. ***the*** ~ ***that Jack built*** ①〔谑〕重复的故事. ②〔俚〕监狱. ***the narrow*** ~ 坟墓. ***the pudding*** ~ 〔俚〕胃,肚子. ***the semidetached*** ~ 与别家共一道墙的独立住宅. ***the third*** ~ 〔美〕"第三院",国会外的实力派,院外活动集团. 一 [hauz] *vt.* ①供给…房子住[用];收容,接待,留宿. ②覆蔽,庇护, ③收藏. ④【建】嵌入;【海】安置(炮台);收好(桅木). ⑤给(机器、齿轮)装外罩. ~ *one's books* 收藏书籍. —*vi.* ①住. ②躲藏 *(up)*;到达安全处所. ~ **agent** 〔英〕房地产经纪人. ~ **arrest** 本宅软禁〔受软禁者不准离开家〕. ~**boat** 可供住家的船, 水上住宅; 宽敞的游艇. ~**-bound** *a.* 因故不能离的;家居不外出的. ~**boy** = ~man. ~**breaker** 为抢劫而侵入他人住宅者;〔英〕拆房屋的人. ~**breaking** 为抢劫而侵入住宅;〔英〕拆房屋. ~**broken,** ~**broke** *a.* ①(猫、狗等)经训练有家居卫生习惯的. ②有管教的,有礼貌的. ~**bug** 臭虫. ~ **cat** 家猫;〔美〕老是住在家里的人. ~**clean** ① *vi.* 大扫除;清洗,清理. ②*vt.* 打扫;改革. ~**cleaning** ①房屋清扫,大扫除. ②清洗,清理(人员). ~**coat** *n.* ①妇女在家穿的宽敞便服. ② = dressing gown. ~ **counsel** 公司的顾问律师. ~ **detective** 百货公司或旅馆雇用的私家侦探. ~ **dinner** (俱乐部等为会员举办的)晚宴. ~ **doctor** 住院医生. ~ **dog** 看家狗. ~**dress** (家务) 女便服. ~ **duty** 房捐. ~**famine** 房荒. ~**father** ①男舍监. ②一家之父. ③社团的男性领袖. ~ **flag** 【海】(商船的)公司旗. ~ **flannel** (用作抹布的) 粗绒布. ~**fly** 家蝇. ~**guest** 在家过夜的来客. ~**holder** 户主. ~ **hunting** 找房子. ~**keep** *vi.* 〔美口〕自立门户;主持家务. ~**keeper** ①主妇;女管家. ②房屋管理人. ~**-keeping** ①家务管理,家政. ②(企业中) 房屋的管理 *(go* ~*keeping* 组织家庭*)*. ~**leek** 【植】长生草属植物. ~**lights** (剧场的)观众席照明灯. ~**line** 【航】三股左旋扭成的小捆绳子. ~**maid** 女仆. ~**maid's knee** (因常常跪着劳动而引起的)膝盖骨囊炎. ~**-man** *n. (pl.* -*men)* ①男仆; 旅馆勤杂工. ②保镖. ~**-master** ①主人,户主,家长. ②〔英〕(学校宿舍的)舍监. ~ **match** 〔英〕(学校中的)舍际友谊赛. ~**mate** 同住者. ~**mistress** ①女主人,主妇. ②女舍监. ~ **moss** 〔美俚〕在家具下〔地板上〕积聚的灰尘. ~**mother** 照管学生宿舍的女管家. ~ **mouse** *(pl.* ~ *mice)* 家鼠. ~ **organ** 给职员和顾客看的店刊. ~ **party** 招待客人过夜的别墅招待会;享受别墅招待的全体宾客. ~ **physician** 住院内科医生. ~**phone** (旅馆等不接外线的)内线电话. ~ **plant** 室内盆栽植物. ~**-proud** *a.* 关心家事的;讲究家庭摆设的. ~**-raising** 盖房会〔农村中邻里来帮忙盖房子的聚会〕. ~ **rent** 房租. ~**-renter** 租屋的人. ~**room** ①(家内的)卧室;放东西的地方. ②住宿 *(I would not give it* ~ *room.* 屋子窄,我不要那种东西*)*. ~ **shoes** 拖鞋. ~ **sparrow** = English sparrow. ~ **staff** 全体住院医生. ~ **surgeon**住院外科医生. ~**-to-**~ *a.* 挨户的 *(a* ~*-to-*~ *visit* 挨户访问*)*. ~**top** 屋顶 *(cry [declare, preach, proclaim] sth. upon [from] the* ~*-top(s)* 广泛宣扬*)*. ~**wares** *n. pl.* 家用器皿(尤指厨房用具). ~**warming** 新屋落成宴, 暖房酒. ~**wife** ① [ˈhauswaif] *(pl.* ~*wives)* 主妇. ②[ˈhʌzif] *(pl.* ~*-wifes* [ˈhʌzifs], ~*wives* [ˈhʌzivz]*)* 针线盒. ~**wifely** *a.* 家庭主妇的,主妇似的;节俭的,会当家的. ~**wifery** [ˈhausˌw(a)ifəri] 家政,家事. ~**work** 家务劳动〔烹饪、缝纫等〕.

house·ful [ˈhausful] *n.* 满屋,一屋子. *a* ~ *of guests* 满屋子客人.

house·hold [ˈhaushəuld] *n.* ①〔集合词〕全家人;(包含佣人在内的)眷,家属,家里人;家庭,户. ②家务. ③〔the H-〕〔英〕王室. ④〔英〕〔*pl.*〕次等面粉. *the king of the* ~ 婴儿. *the number of* ~*s* 户数. ***the Imperial [Royal] H-*** ①皇室,王室. ②〔集合词〕宫内官. 一 *a.* ①家庭的,家内的,一家的. ②〔*H-*〕王室的. ③家常的, 普通的. ~ *affairs* 家务. ~ *furniture* 家具. ~ *expenses* 家庭开支. ~ *wares* 家用器具. ~ **art** 持家艺术. ~ **effects** 家具,家庭用具. ~ **gods** (古罗马的)家庭守护神;家庭必需品;传家宝. ~ **franchise [suffrage]** 户主选举权. ~ **management** = ~ art. ~ **stuff** 〔古〕家具,家产. **H-troops** (王室)近卫队. ~**word** 家常话,家喻户晓的用语.

house·hold·er [ˈhaushəuldər] *n.* ①占有房子的人,住户. ②户主.

hou·sel [ˈhauzl] *n.* 〔废〕【宗】圣餐; 圣餐物 (特指面包),圣体 (=eucharist). 一 *vt.* 〔废〕对…施圣餐.

house·less [ˈhauslis] *a.* ①无家的. ②无房屋的.

house·let [ˈhauslit] *n.* 小房子.

hous·ing[1] [ˈhauziŋ] *n.* ①供给住宅. ②〔集合词〕房屋;住宅. ③掩护,庇护;避难所. ④【机】壳;套. ⑤【建】柄穴, 炉套. ⑥【海】桅脚. *bearing* ~ 轴承箱. *fan* ~ 风

扇壳. *valve* ~ 阀室. ~ *project* 住房建筑计划. *a* ~ *shortage* 房荒. *a* ~ *box*【机】轴箱. **open** ~〔美〕黑人与白人自由混合居住.

hous·ing² [ˈhauziŋ] *n.* 马服;〔常 *pl.*〕马饰,鞍褥.

Hous·man [ˈhausmən] *n.* 豪斯曼〔姓氏〕.

Hous·ton [ˈhuːstən, ˈhaustən] *n.* 豪斯顿〔姓氏〕.

hous·to·ni·a [huːsˈtəunia] *n.*【植】北美茜草属 *(Rubia)* 植物〔开蓝、白或紫花〕.

hove [həuv] heave 的过去式及过去分词.

hov·el [ˈhɔvəl] *n.* ①陋室,放杂物的小房间. ②茅舍,棚舍. ③窑的圆锥形外壳.

hov·el(l)·er [ˈhɔvələ] *n.* 无执照的领港员.

Hov·ell [ˈhəuvəl] *n.* 霍维尔〔姓氏〕.

hov·er [ˈhɔvə] *vi.* ①翱翔, 盘旋 *(about; over)*. ②徘徊 *(about; near)*. ③踌躇,徬徨. ④(直升飞机)停悬. — *vt.* 伏窝孵化. — *n.* 翱翔;徘徊. **~ing act**【国际法】①禁止外国船只在领海逗留法. ②规定三海里领海外的外国船只检查办法的法律.

hov·er·barge [ˈhɔvəbɑːdʒ] *n.* 大型气垫游艇.

hov·er·craft [ˈhɔvəkrɑːft] *n.* 水陆两用垫式航行器;气垫船.

hov·er·lin·er [ˈhɔvəˈlainə] *n.* 巨型核动力气垫船.

hov·er·plane [ˈhɔvəplein] *n.*〔英〕= helicopter.

hov·er·train [ˈhɔvətrein] *n.* 气垫火车.

Ho·vey [ˈhəuvi] *n.* 霍维〔姓氏〕.

how [hau] *ad.* ①怎样,怎么 (= in what manner); 用什么手段、方法 (= by what means)〔疑问副词和连接副词两用〕. *H- does he do it?* 他是怎样做的? *Ask him* ~ *he does it.* 问问他是怎样做的. *H- did it happen?* 事情怎么发生的? *He does not know* ~ *to swim.* 他不知道怎样游泳. ②情况如何 (= in what state)〔指身体健康等状况〕. *H- is she?* 她(身体)怎样? *H- goes it with you?* 你好么? *How are things in your school?* 你们学校的情况怎么样? ③价钱多少(= in what price)〔指金钱价值〕. *H- is wheat today?* 今天小麦市价怎样? *Find out* ~ *the exchange is.* 查明汇率多少. ④几何,多少 (=to what extent)〔指数量、程度,多和形容词或副词连用,用作疑问副词或连接副词〕. *H- many are there?* 有多少? *H- much do you want?* 你要多少? *H- old is he?* 他多大年纪? *I wonder* ~ *old he is.* 不晓得他是几岁. *H- fast are we running now?* 我们现在跑的速度怎么样? *H- often do you go there?* 你多久去那里一次? *H- damager is the car?* 车子损坏得如何? ⑤以为如何〔多用于征询意见〕. *H- do you like it?* 你觉得它怎么样? 喜欢它吗? *H- would it be to do it tomorrow?* 明天干这件事怎么样? ⑥怎么会,为什么?〔表现惊异的通俗用法〕. *H- can you talk such nonsense?* 你怎么会这样胡说八道? *H- is it that you've come so early?* 你怎么来得这么早? *H- happens it that you are late?* 你怎么迟到了? ⑦怎样(= the way in which)〔关系词〕. *This is* ~. 〔口〕就是这样. *So that's* ~ *it is!* 原来如此! *I don't see* ~. 〔口〕我看不行. *This is* ~ *it happened.* 事情就是这样发生的. ⑧= that〔用于间接陈述〕. *I told him* ~ (=that) *I had read in the papers.* 我告诉他我是在报上看见的. ⑨尽可能 (= as best)〔关系词〕. *Do it* ~ (= as best) *you can.* 你尽可能做做看. ⑩多么〔用作感叹词以修饰形容词、副词或动词〕. *H- absurd!* 多么荒唐! *H- fluently he speaks!* 他说得多流利啊! *H- he snores!* 他的鼾声多大啊! ***all you know*** ~〔俚〕尽你所能. ***and*** ~〔美口〕〔用于加强语气〕当然啰! 那还用说! 可不是! ***Here's*** ~**!** 敬你一杯! 祝你健康! ***H- about …?*** (你以为)…如何? …怎么样? *(H- about going for a walk?* 去散散步怎么样? *How about you let me worry about this?* 你让我来操这份心好不好?) ***H- are you?*** ①你身体怎样? ②〔招呼用语〕你好! ***H- come …?***〔美口〕怎么会的? *(H- come you never visit us anymore?* 你怎么不再来看我们?) ***H- do you do?*** 你好!〔初次见面时用语,对方要用同样的话回答〕. ***H- goes it …?*** …的情况怎样? ***H- is that for …?***〔口〕好不…! 多么…! *(H- is that for impudent [impudence]!* 多么放肆!) ***H- much?*** ①(价钱)多少? ②什么?〔要求对方重讲一遍时用, =〔英〕What?〔美〕H-〕. ***H- now?***〔古〕这是怎么回事? 嗳哟! ***H-'s about [for]?***〔美俚〕= H- about. ***H- so?*** 怎么会这样的? 为什么? ***How's that?*** ①那是怎么一回事? ②什么? ***(= How much?*** ②**)**. ③【板球】(问裁判)击球手出局了吗? ***H- the deuce [devil, dickens, ever, on earth] …?*** 到底怎么回事? ***H- then*** ①这是什么意思? ②后来怎样? 还有什么? — *n.* 方法. *She explained all the* ~*s and whys of the issue.* 她详尽说明了问题的情况及原由.

how. = howitzer.

How·ard [ˈhau-əd, ˈhauəd] *n.* 霍华德〔姓氏,男子名〕.

how·be·it [ˈhauˈbiːit] *conj.*〔古〕虽说,虽然. — *ad.*〔古〕尽管如此;仍然.

how·dah [ˈhaudə] *n.* 象轿;驼轿〔驮在象或骆驼背上可供数人乘坐的凉亭状座位〕.

how·die, how·dy [ˈhaudi] *n.*〔Scot.〕接生婆.

how-do-you-do,how-de-do,how-d'ye-do[ˈhaudəjuˈduː, ˈhaudˈduː, ˈhaudiˈduː] *n.*〔口〕讨厌、尴尬的局面〔前面常加 fine, pretty, nice 等形容词〕. *Here's a pretty [nice]* ~. 这可太糟了! 这真叫人为难.

how·dy [ˈhaudi] *int.*〔方〕你好! (=How do you do?)

Howe [hau] *n.* 豪〔姓氏〕. *E* ~ 豪(1819—1867),美国缝纫机发明人.

how·e'er [hauˈɛə] *ad., conj.* = however.

How·ell(s) [ˈhauəl(z)] *n.* 豪厄尔(斯)〔姓氏,男子名〕.

how·ev·er [hauˈevə] *ad.* ①无论如何, 不管怎样. ②可是,仍然. ③〔英俚〕究竟. *We have not yet won;* ~, *we shall try again.* 我们没有取胜, 不过我们还要再试一下. *H- tired you may be, you must do it.* 不管怎样累, 你也得做. *We must do something, on* ~ *humble a scale.* 我们得做点事,不论如何微不足道. *H- did you manage it?* 你究竟怎样处理的? — *conj.* ①不管用什么方法. ②〔古〕虽然. *Arrange your hours* ~ *you like.* 你爱怎么安排时间就怎么安排.

how·itz·er [ˈhauitsə] *n.* 榴弹炮.

howl [haul] *vi.* ①(狗,狼等)嚎,嗥叫. ②(风等)怒号,怒吼. ③(人悲痛时的)号叫,哀号,嚎啕大哭. ④狂笑;狂闹,欢闹. *They* ~*ed with laughter.* 他们高声狂笑. — *vt.* ①吼叫着说出; 喝住. ②把…喝下台 *(down; out; away)*. ~ *the speaker off the platform* 把演说者哄下台. ~ *defiance at the enemy* 吼叫着向敌人挑战. — *n.* ①嚎叫, 吠声. ②怒号; 叫声. ③狂笑,嚎哭. ④【无】啸声,嗥鸣,颤噪效应.

howl·er [ˈhaulə] *n.* ①咆哮者; 哭叫的人. ②【动】吼猴〔产于南美〕. ③〔口〕愚蠢可笑的错误;大笑话. ④【无】嗥鸣器. *commit a* ~ 铸成大错. ***come a*** ~ 遭到失败.

howl·et [ˈhaulit] *n.*〔古、方〕枭 (= owlet).

howl·ing [ˈhauliŋ] *a.* ①咆哮的; 嚎叫的. ②荒僻的, 凄凉的. ③〔俚〕非常的, 极端的. *a* ~ *lie* 弥天大谎. *a* ~ *shame* 奇耻大辱. *a* ~ *success* 巨大的成功. *a* ~ *swell* 骄横的人. *a* ~ *wilderness* 野兽咆哮的荒野. — *n.*【无】啸声,嗥鸣; 颤噪效应. *acoustic* ~ 音响啸声. ~ **monkey**【动】吼猴〔发现于中南美,长尾,啼声如吼叫〕.

how·so·ev·er [ˌhausəuˈevə] *ad.* 无论如何,不管怎样.

how-to [ˈhauˈtuː] *a.*〔口〕介绍基础知识的. *a* ~ *book* 基础知识书,入门书.

hoy¹ [hɔi] *int.* 嗬! 喂!〔唤喊或驱赶家畜等的呼声〕.

hoy² [hɔi] *n.* 沿海岸航行的短航程独桅小船.

hoy·den [ˈhɔidn] *n.* 顽皮姑娘. — *a.* 顽皮姑娘的.

hoy·den·ish [ˈhɔidniʃ] *a.* 顽皮女孩似的,带男孩气的.

Hoyle [hɔil] *n.* ①霍伊尔〔姓氏〕. ②*Edmond* ~ 埃德蒙·霍伊尔〔1672—1769, 英国纸牌戏规则书著者〕. ③霍伊

尔所著纸牌游戏书. ***according to*** ~ ①按照规则的[地]. ②公正的[地].
Hoyt [hɔit] *n.* 霍伊特〔姓氏,男子名〕.
H.P., HP, h.p., hp = ①half pay. ②horsepower. ③high-pressure. ④horizontal plane.
H-particle 质子.
HPRR = high-performence research reactor. 高性率研究反应堆.
H.Q., h.q., HQs, Hq = Headquarters.
HQMC = 〔美〕Headquarters, Marine Corps.
HR = homogeneous reactor. 均匀反应堆.
H.R. = ①【纺】hank roving 粗纱支数. ②Home Rule. ③House of Representatives.
hr. = hour(s).
h.r., hr【棒球】= home run(s).
H.R.H., HRH = His [Her] Royal Highness.
hrs. = hours.
H.S. = ①High School. ②【医】〔L.〕*hora somni* 〔睡眠时〕.
H.S.E. = 〔L.〕*hic sepultus est* (=here lies buried 葬此).
H.S.H = His [Her] Serene Highness.
H.T. = ①Hawaiian Territory. ②heat treat. ③high tension.
ht. = ①height. ②heat.
h.t. = high tenacity.
HUAC = House Un-American Activities Committee. 非美活动调查委员会.
hua·ra·ches [həˈrɑːtʃiːz, 〔Sp.〕wɑːˈrɑːtʃes] *n. pl.* 条带鞋帮拖鞋.
hub[1] [hʌb] *n.* ①【机】(轮)毂,旋翼叶毂. ②中心,中枢. ③(电器面板上的)电线插孔. ④【机】衬套;套壳;中轴壳. *a ~ of industry [commerce]* 工业[商业]中心. *the ~ of the universe* 宇宙的中心,世界的中心. ***from ~ to tire*** 〔美〕完全,从头到尾. ***the H-*** 〔美〕波士顿市的别名. ***up to the ~*** 深深陷入,给…完全缠住. **~cap** ①(车轮的)毂盖. ②〔美俚〕骄傲自大的人.
hub[2] [hʌb] *n.* 〔口〕丈夫〔husband 的缩写〕.
hub·a-hub·a, hub·ba-hub·ba [ˈhʌbəˈhʌbə] *int.* 〔美口〕好极好极! 赞成赞成! 赶快!
Hub·bard [ˈhʌbəd] *n.* 哈伯德〔姓氏〕.
Hub·bard squash [ˈhʌbəd skwɔʃ] 古巴瓜〔一种坚硬的冬季南瓜,瓜皮发绿或发黄,瓜肉呈黄色〕.
Hub·ble [ˈhʌbl] *n.* 哈勃〔姓氏〕. **~('s) constant**【天】哈勃常数〔天文学计量单位,根据哈勃定律计算行星运行速度时使用〕.
hub·ble-bub·ble [ˈhʌblbʌbl] *n.* ①沸腾声. ②吵闹声,骚动. ③水烟筒.
hub·bub [ˈhʌˌbʌb], **hub·ba·boo, hub·bu·boo** [ˈhʌbəbuː] *n.* 吵闹声;喧哗.
hub·by [ˈhʌbi] *n.* 〔口〕= hub[2].
Hu·bert [ˈhjuːbə(ː)t] *n.* 休伯特〔姓氏〕.
hu·bris [ˈhjuːbris] *n.* 狂妄自大. **hu·bris·tic** *a.*
huck·a·back [ˈhʌkəbæk] *n.*【纺】(质地浮松,表面粗糙的棉或亚麻织物,作毛巾用或揩布用的)浮松布.
huck·le [ˈhʌkl] *n.* 髋部,臀部,屁股,(羊、鹿的)腰部. **~-backed** *a.* 驼背的. **~berry** ***(pl. -ries)***【植】①美洲越桔;卵叶越桔. ②美洲越桔子;卵叶越桔子;乌饭树的紫黑浆果. **~bone** 髋骨;(四足兽的)距骨.
huck·ster [ˈhʌkstə] *n.* ①叫卖小贩;行商. ②〔美〕代人写广播[电视]商业广告者;大吹大擂推销商品的人. ③唯利是图的人;受雇佣者. *a political ~* 政治贩子. — *vt.* ①叫卖,零售. ②和…讨价还价. ③吹嘘. *~ one's service* 打零活. — *vi.* 讨价还价.
HUD [hʌd] *n.* 〔美〕房屋及城市发展部〔美国政府于1965年设立的一个部门,全名为 Department of Housing and Urban Development〕.
hud·dle [ˈhʌdl] *vt.* ①乱挤,胡乱堆集. ②把…卷作一团 *(into; up; together)*. ③草率从事 *(up; through)*;胡乱穿上 *(on)*. ④把…隐藏起来. *~ a job through* 匆匆忙忙地做完一件工作. *~ oneself up = be ~d up* 把身体缩成一团. — *vi.* ①群集,拥挤 *(together)*. ②卷缩 *(up)*. ③碰头商议. ④[橄榄球]赛前球员列队(等候开车信号). *~ over one's duty* 潦草塞责. *~ together for warmth* 挤在一块取暖. *~ up in a corner* 挤在角落里. — *n.* ①(杂乱的)一团,一堆,一群. ②拥挤,混乱. ③〔美俚〕(秘密)会议;(足球运动员比赛中)碰头商讨战术;【橄榄球】赛前队员列队. *all in a ~* 乱七八糟. *~ upon ~* 成一团,成一堆. ***go into a ~ with sb.*** 〔美俚〕同某人秘密商议. ***in a ~*** 〔美俚〕在开会.
Hu·di·bras·tic [ˌhjuːdiˈbræstik] *a.* (英国诗人 *Samuel Butler* 讽刺诗)滑稽式英雄体的;讽刺而滑稽的.
Hud·son [ˈhʌdsn] *n.* ①赫德森〔男子名〕. ②**Henry ~** 亨利·哈得逊〔1576—1611?,英国航海家;美国哈得逊湾(Hudson Bay)的发现者〕. ***the ~ Bay*** 哈得逊湾〔在北美东北部〕. ***the ~ River*** 哈得逊河〔美国纽约州的河〕.
Hue, Hué [hjuːˈei] *n.* 顺化〔越南港市〕.
hue[1] [hjuː] *n.* ①色,色彩,色调;(意见等的)特色. ②样子,形式. *the ~s of the rainbow* 虹的色彩. *politicians of various ~s* 形形色色的政客.
hue[2] [hjuː] *n.* 〔只用于 ~ and cry 短语中〕喊叫声. ***a ~ and cry*** ①追捕犯人时的叫声;通缉令. ②大声呼喊;(表示反对的)叫嚷. *(raise a ~ and cry over [against]* 对…大喊大叫(表示反对). *make a ~ and cry* 大嚷大叫起来).
hueb·ne·rite [ˈhjuːbnərait] *n.*【矿】钨锰矿.
hued [hjuːd] *a.* 有某种色调的;有某些种色彩的.〔多组成复合词〕. *rosy-~* 玫瑰色的. *dark-~* 黑色的.
huff [hʌf] *vt.* ①吹胀,提高…的价格. ②吓唬. ③激怒. *~ sb. into silence* 吓得某人不敢讲话. *~ sb. out of the room* 把某人吓出屋外. *~ sb. to pieces* 拚命欺负某人. — *vi.* ①吹气,喷气. ②激怒. ③吓唬. — *n.* 发怒. *in a ~* 怒冲冲地. *get into a ~* 发怒.
huff-duff [ˈhʌfˈdʌf] *n.* 〔俚〕无线电高频测向仪.
huff·ish [ˈhʌfiʃ] *a.* ①自大的,傲慢的. ②怒冲冲的,不高兴的. **-ly** *ad.* **-ness** *n.*
huff·y [ˈhʌfi] *a.* ***(huff·i·er; -i·est)*** = huffish. **huff·i·ly** *ad.* **huff·i·ness** *n.*
hug [hʌg] *vt.* ①紧抱,拥抱,搂抱. ②(熊用前腿)抱住. ③抱有,坚持(信仰、偏见等). ④〔多用反身〕使庆幸,使得意. ⑤【海】靠(海岸)航行;(行人、车辆等)靠近…走. *~ cherished beliefs* 坚持所抱的信念. *The ship was hugging the shore.* 船靠岸航行. ***~ oneself on [for, over]*** 沾沾自喜,窃喜. — *n.* ①拥抱. ②(熊用前腿的)紧抱. ③(摔交中的)抱住. ***give sb. a big ~*** 紧抱住(某人). **~-me-tight** *n.* 〔美〕(女子的)紧身短马甲.
huge [hjuːdʒ] *a.* 巨大的,庞大的,极大的. *a ~ mountain* 大山. ***a ~ gate***【美剧】门票的巨大收入. **-ly** *ad.* **-ness** *n.*
huge·ous [ˈhjuːdʒəs] *a.* 〔谑〕= huge.
hug·ger-mug·ger [ˈhʌgəmʌgə] *n.* ①混乱. ②〔古〕秘密. — *a.* ①混乱的. ②秘密的. — *ad.* ①混乱地. ②秘密地. — *vt.* 替…守秘密;压下…不作声张 *(up)*. — *vi.* ①胡乱地干. ②秘密行动;密议.
hug·ger·y [ˈhʌgəri] *n.* 〔英〕①律师抢生意的活动. ②高级法院律师要求低级法院律师寄送诉讼事实摘要.
Hug·gins [ˈhʌginz] *n.* 哈金斯〔姓氏〕.
Hugh [hjuː] *n.* 休〔男子名〕.
Hughes [hjuːz] *n.* 休斯〔姓氏〕.
Hu·go [ˈhjuːgəu] *n.* ①雨果〔男子名 Hugh 的异体〕. ②**Victor Mavie ~** 维克多·雨果〔1802—1885,法国小说家,剧作家〕.
Hu·gue·not [ˈhjuːgənɔt] *n.*【史】胡格诺派教徒〔十六、十七世纪法国的加尔文派教徒〕. **-ic** *a.* **-ism** *n.* 胡格诺派

的教义.

huh [hʌ] *int.* 哼!〔表示轻蔑、吃惊或疑问的感叹词〕.

hui•sa•che [ˈhjuːiːsɑːtʃi] *n.* 【植】金合欢 *(Acacia farnesiana)* 〔产于得克萨斯和墨西哥〕.

hu•la [ˈhuːlə], **hu•la-hu•la** [ˈhuːləˈhuːlə] *n.* ①(波利尼西亚)呼拉圈舞;(夏威夷)草裙舞. ②呼拉圈舞曲,草裙舞曲. ~ **hoop** 呼拉圈〔原商标名,一种套在身上游戏用的圈〕. ~ **skirt** 草裙.

hulk [hʌlk] *n.* ①笨重的大船. ②废船船体;〔*pl.*〕【史】用作监牢等的废船. ③巨大笨重的人〔物〕. ④(房屋等的)残骸, 外壳. — *vi.* 〔英方〕①愈来愈显得巨大 *(up)*. ②笨重地移动. **-ing** *a.* 庞大的;笨重的.

hulk•y [ˈhʌlki] *a.* = hulking.

Hull¹ [hʌl] *n.* 赫尔〔姓氏〕.

Hull² [hʌl] *n.* 赫尔〔英国港市〕.

hull¹ [hʌl] *n.* ①(果实等的)外壳; 豆荚. ②浆果的花萼. ③薄膜, 膜片; 被覆物; 〔*pl.*〕衣服. — *vt.* 脱…的壳, 去…的皮. ~ **barley** 给大麦去皮. ~*ed rice* 糙米. **-er** *n.* 脱皮机,脱壳机.

hull² [hʌl] *n.* 【海】船体,船壳;【空】(水上飞机的)机身;(飞艇的)艇身. ~ ***down*** (船)远在只见船桅不见船身的地方;(坦克等)藏在能观察到敌人并能向其射击的隐蔽处. — *vt.* (用鱼雷、炮弹等)打穿(船身). — *vi.* 漂流.

hul•la•ba•loo [ˌhʌləbəˈluː] *n.* 喧哗,吵闹. ***make [raise] a*** ~ 大吵大嚷.

hul•lo(a) [ˈhʌˈləu] *int., vi., vt.* = hello.

hum¹ [hʌm] *vi.* ①(蜜蜂等)嗡嗡叫. ②(在嘴里)咕咕哝哝,磕磕巴巴;哼;哼曲子. ③〔口〕(事业等)变得有生气;忙碌;活跃起来. ④〔俚〕发出恶臭. *My head ~s.* 头发昏. —*vt.* ①哼(歌曲). ②哼歌哄(小孩等). ~ *a child to sleep* 哼着歌哄孩子入睡. ~ ***along*** (汽车等)一路发出嗡嗡声前进. ~ ***and ha [haw]*** (无词可答而)支支吾吾,结结巴巴;〔喻〕踌躇,犹豫. ***make things*** ~〔口〕使有活气,使兴旺. — *n.* ①嗡嗡声;哼哼声;嘈杂声. ②〔俚〕恶臭. — *int.* 哼!〔表示轻蔑、踌躇、怀疑等〕.

hum² [hʌm] *n., vt.* 〔口〕欺骗.

hu•man [ˈhjuːmən] *a.* ①人的, 人类的 *(opp.* divine, animal). ②凡人皆有的, 显示人类特点的. ③有人性的,通人情的. ~ *affairs* 人事. *a* ~ *being [creature]* 人. *the* ~ *race* 人类. *To err is* ~. 〔谚〕人皆有过. ~ *torpedo* 人控鱼雷. — *n.* 〔口、谑〕人; 〔the H-〕人类. ***less than*** ~ 没人性,不合人道. ***more than*** ~ 超人一等. ~ **engineering** ①(特指工业、企业内的) 人事管理. ②(专门研究人与机械设备的关系的) 人机工程学. ~ **geography** 人文地理学. ~ **nature** 人性. **-like** *a.* **-ness** *n.*

hu•mane [hjuːˈmein] *a.* ①有人情的, 人道的, 仁慈的. ②(指学科)高尚的,文雅的. ~ *feelings* 慈悲心. *a man of* ~ *character* 性格温雅的人. ~ **killer** 牲口无痛宰杀机. ~ **learning** 古典文学. **H- Society** ①〔英〕拯救溺水者协会. ②慈善协会. ③保护动物协会. ~ **studies** 人文学科. **-ly** *ad.* **-ness** *n.*

hu•man•ise [ˈhjuːmənaiz] *vt., vi.* = humanize.

hu•man•ism [ˈhjuːmənizəm] *n.* ①人道主义, 人本主义, 人文主义. ②人文学;〔h- 或 H-〕(文艺复兴期的)古典文学研究. **hu•man•ist** *n.* 人性学者;人道主义者,人文主义者,人本主义者;〔h- 或 H-〕(文艺复兴期的)古典文学研究家. **hu•man•is•tic** [ˌhjuːməˈnistik] *a.* ①人情的,人性研究的. ②人文学的,人文主义的,人本主义的,人道主义的.

hu•man•i•tar•i•an [hju(ː)ˌmæniˈtɛəriən] *n.* ①人道主义者. ②慈善家,博爱主义者. — *a.* ①人道主义者的. ②慈善家的;博爱主义者的. **-ism** *n.* ①博爱主义. ②人道主义;人性论. ③【宗】基督凡人论.

hu•man•i•ty [hju(ː)ˈmæniti] *n.* ①人类;(许多)人. ②人性,人情,人道,人性论;〔*pl.*〕人的属性;人类. ③仁爱;〔*pl.*〕慈善行为. ④文史哲学,人文学. *justice and* ~ 仁义. **the humanities** ①古典文学(尤指希腊、拉丁文学). ②人文学科〔通常包括语言、文学、哲学等〕.

hu•man•ize [ˈhjuːmənaiz] *vt.* ①赋与…人性,使人格化;使适应人体特性. ②使变得博爱仁慈;使通人情. *The milk has been ~d.* 这种牛奶业已经过加工,类似人乳. — *vi.* 成为人;变得通人情. **hu•man•i•za•tion** *n.* 赋与人性,人格化. **-r** *n.*

hu•man•kind [ˈhjuːmənˈkaind] *n.* 人类,人.

hu•man•ly [ˈhjuːmənli] *ad.* ①从人的角度; 以人的方法; 采用人的手段. ②在人的知识和能力范围内. ③充满人情地. *H- speaking, he cannot recover.* 以人力来说,他的病是好不了的. *It is not ~ possible.* 这是人力所做不到的〔这在人情上是不可能的〕.

hu•man•oid [ˈhjuːmənɔid] *a.* (形状或举动)近似人的. — *n.* ①近似人的动物(尤指古人猿). ②(科学幻想小说中的)星球人.

hu•mate [ˈhjuːmeit] *n.* 【化】腐殖酸盐,腐殖酸酯.

hum•ble [ˈhʌmbl] *a.* ①恭顺的, 谦卑的, 谦逊的 *(opp.* insolent, proud). ②下贱的 *(opp.* noble), (动、植物等)低级的,不值钱的. ③粗陋的; 微末的. *a* ~ *cottage* 寒舍. ~ *fare* 粗淡的饮食. *a man of* ~ *origin* 出身微贱的人. *a* ~ *occupation* 卑下的职业. ***eat*** ~ ***pie*** 忍辱含垢, 低声下气地道歉. ***in my*** ~ ***opinion*** 鄙见以为. ***your*** ~ ***servant*** 〔信末谦恭的自称〕你的恭顺的仆人,晚,职. — *vt.* ①压下(某人的锐气等),使丧失(威信等);贬低. ②使谦卑. ~ *sb.'s pride* 压某人的气焰,使某人丢脸. ~ *one's enemy* 挫敌人锐气. ~ *oneself* 自卑,低声下气. **~bee** *n.* 〔英〕= bumblebee. ~ **pie** 〔古〕(狩猎后赏给仆从吃的)用鹿内脏做馅的煎饼. **-ness** *n.* **hum•bly** *ad.*

Hum•boldt [ˈhʌmbəult] ①**Baron [Friedrich Heinrich] Alexander ~, von,** 亚历山大•亨伯特〔1769—1859,德国博物学家,旅行家及政治家〕. ②**Baron [Karl] Wilhelm,** 威廉•亨伯特〔1767—1835,德国语言学家及外交家,系亚历山大•亨伯特之兄〕.

hum•bug [ˈhʌmbʌg] *n.* ①瞒骗,欺诈. ②谎言,空话,奉承话; 用来骗人的东西. ③骗子; 吹牛的人. ④〔英〕一种薄荷糖. — *vt.* 诈骗,瞒骗. ~ *sb. into buying rubbish* 骗人买坏货. ~ *sb. out of his money* 诈骗某人钱财. — *vi.* 行骗. — *int.* 胡说八道! **-ger** *n.* 欺骗者,骗子.

hum•bug•ger•y [ˈhʌmbʌgəri] *n.* 欺骗,欺诈.

hum•ding•er [hʌmˈdiŋgə] *n.* 〔美俚〕非常好的人〔物〕.

hum•drum [ˈhʌmdrʌm] *a.* 平常的;单调的,无聊的. — *n.* ①单调,无聊. ②无聊的话. ③无聊的人. — *vi.* 单调地动作. **-ness** *n.*

Hume [hjuːm] *n.* ①休姆〔姓氏〕. ②**David** ~ 大卫•休谟〔1711—1776,苏格兰的史学家、哲学家〕.

hu•mec•tant [hjuːˈmektənt] *n.* 【化】保湿剂〔如甘油〕. — *a.* 润湿(剂)的.

hu•mer•al [ˈhjuːmərəl] *a.* ①肱骨的, 近肱骨的. ②肩的,近肩的. — *n.* (天主教教士做弥撒时用的)披肩 (= ~ veil).

hu•me•rus [ˈhjuːmərəs] *n.* *(pl.* **-ri** [-rai]) 【解】肱骨.

hu•mic [ˈhjuːmik] *a.* ①腐殖的. ②从腐殖质中提取的. ~ **acid** 【化】腐殖酸,黑腐酸. ~ **coal** 【地】腐殖煤.

hu•mid [ˈhjuːmid] *a.* 湿的,湿气重的. **-ly** *ad.* **-ness** *n.*

hu•mid•i•fi•er [hju(ː)ˈmidifaiə] *n.* 增湿器,湿润器.

hu•mid•i•fy [hju(ː)ˈmidifai] *vt.* 使湿润. **hu•mid•i•fi•ca•tion** [hjuːˌmidifiˈkeiʃən] *n.*

hu•mid•i•stat [hjuːˈmidistæt] *n.* 恒湿器,湿度调节器.

hu•mid•i•ty, hu•mid•ness [hju(ː)ˈmiditi, -ˈmidnis] *n.* 湿气; 【物】湿度. *absolute* ~ 【物】绝对湿度. *relative* ~ 【物】相对湿度.

hu•mi•dor [ˈhjuːmidɔː] *n.* ①(防止烟草变干的)保润盒;保湿器. ②装有保湿器的烟草贮藏室.

hu•mi•fy [ˈhjuːmifai] *vt.* 使成腐殖质. **hu•mi•fi•ca•tion** [ˌhjumifiˈkeiʃən] *n.* **hu•mi•fied** *a.*

hu·mil·i·ate [hju(:)ˈmilieit] *vt.* 使丢脸,使蒙羞,屈辱,使出丑. *The country was ~d by defeat.* 该国因战败而受辱. ~ *oneself* 丢脸,出丑. **hu·mil·i·at·ing** *a.* 丢脸的,耻辱的,献丑的. **-i·a·tion** [-ˈeiʃən] *n.* 丢脸; 蒙羞,屈辱. **hum·il·i·a·tor** *n.* 羞辱者.

hu·mil·i·ty [hju(:)ˈmiliti] *n.* ①谦恭,谦让. ②〔*pl.*〕谦让的行为.

hu·mi·ture [ˈhju:mitʃə] *n.* 温湿度〔华氏度数与相对湿度之和的一半〕.

hum·mel [ˈhʌməl] *a.* 〔Scot.〕(牛、鹿等)没有角的.

hum·mer [ˈhʌmə] *n.* ①用鼻哼唱的人; 发嗡嗡声的东西. ②=hummingbird. ③〔美俚〕= humdinger.

hum·ming [ˈhʌmiŋ] *a.* ①发嗡嗡声的, 哼着唱的. ②〔口〕忙碌的,活跃的,精力旺盛的;(酒)起泡的;(敲打等)猛烈的. *a ~ knock on the head* 在头上猛敲一下. — *n.* 低唱; 哼唱; 嗡嗡声, 蜂音. ~**bird**【动】蜂鸟, 蜂鸟科的鸟. ~ **top** 响簧陀螺.

hum·mock [ˈhʌmək] *n.* ①小圆丘, 圆冈. ②(冰原上的)冰丘; 波状地. ③沼泽中的高地.

hu·mor [ˈhju:mə] 〔美〕= humour.

hu·mor·al [ˈhju:mərəl] *a.*【医】体液的. ~ *disorders* 体液失调. ~ **pathology** 体液病理学.

hu·mor·esque [ˌhju:məˈresk] *n.*【乐】诙谐曲.

hu·mor·ist [ˈhju:mərist] *n.* 〔美〕=humourist. **-is·tic** *a.*

hu·mor·ous[ˈhju:mərəs] *a.* ①有幽默感的,诙谐的. ②可笑的,轻佻的; 喜剧的. ③〔古〕湿性的; 体液的. *a ~ writer* 幽默作家. **-ly** *ad.* **-ness** *n.*

hu·mour [ˈhju:mə] *n.* ①幽默,诙谐,幽默感. ②幽默的东西〔言词、文章等〕. ③(生来的)脾气, 性情, 气质; (一时的)兴致,心情,情绪. ④(眼球的)玻璃状液体; (旧时生理学所说动物的)体液; (植物的)汁液. ⑤古怪的幻想; 遐想. ⑤〔*pl.*〕有趣的节目. *a sense of ~* 幽默感. *Every man has his ~.* 〔谚〕各人有各人的脾气. *a man of ~* 富有幽默感的人. *a man of sanguine ~* 性情乐观的人. *aqueous [vitreous]*【解】水样 (玻璃状) 液. *black ~* 黑色幽默〔六十年代美国新兴的一个文学流派〕. *dry ~* 绷着脸说的笑话. ***in bad ~*** 不高兴. ***in good ~*** 高兴. ***in no ~ for*** … 不高兴…, 无心…. ***in the ~ for*** …高兴…, 有意…. ***out of ~*** 不高兴. ***please sb.'s ~*** 迎合某人. ***put sb. in [into] a bad ~*** 使人生气. ***the cardinal ~s*** 〔古〕四体液〔即 blood, phlegm, choler, melancholy, 据说能决定人的性格〕. *aqueous [vitreous]* ***when the ~ takes me*** 我高兴的时候. — *vt.* ①迎合,迁就,纵容. ②使自己适应于…; 顺着…办; 灵活处理〔掌握〕. *It's not wise to ~ a small child.* 纵容小孩子可不好. *Don't force the lock, you must ~ it.* 别出死力开锁,得试着点儿开. **-ed** *a.* 〔用以构成复合词〕脾气…的 (*good ~ed* 性情好的). **-ist** *n.* 幽默家,幽默作家; 滑稽家,丑角. **-less** *a.* 不幽默的,不滑稽的,无趣味的. **-some** *a.* 幽默滑稽的; 古怪的.

hump [hʌmp] *n.* ①(驼)峰,(驼子的)驼背,(某些动物背部的)隆肉. ②小圆丘; 〔英俚〕山脉; 海岸凸出部. ③【铁路】驼峰调车场. ④〔the H-〕(二次大战时英美飞行员用语)喜马拉雅山. ⑤〔英〕沮丧,忧郁. ⑥危急关头,困难时期,难关. *a camel with two ~s* 双峰骆驼. ***get a ~ on*** ①赶紧. ②苦干. ***get sb. on the ~*** 使某人大费力气. ***get [have] the ~*** 难过. ***give sb. the ~*** 使人难过. ***hit the ~*** 〔美俚〕越狱; 开小差. ***live on one's (own) ~*** 自食其力. ***on the ~*** 大费精力. ***over the ~*** 〔美俚〕工作完成过半,已完成工作中最困难部分; (服苦役等)已度过一半时间. — *vt.* ①使弓起(背); 使成驼背. ②〔俚〕使忧郁. ③〔口〕使自己努力干〔~ oneself〕. ④〔澳俚〕把…背在背上. — *vi.* ①隆起. ②急速移动,飞跑. ③〔美俚〕努力. ~**back** ①驼背,弓背; 驼子. ②【动】座头鲸. ~**backed** *a.* 驼背的.

humped [hʌmpt] *a.* 有隆肉的,驼背的.

humph [hʌmf] *int.* 哼! 〔表示怀疑,不满,轻蔑等〕. — *vi.* 发"哼"声. — *n.* 哼的一声.

Hum·phr(e)y [ˈhʌmfri] *n.* 汉弗莱〔姓氏,男子名〕.

Hump·ty-Dump·ty [ˈhʌmptiˈdʌmpti] *n.* ①矮胖子. ②倒下去就起不来的人; 损坏后无法修复的东西.

hump·y[1] [ˈhʌmpi] *a.* ①有隆肉的; 有驼峰的. ②隆肉状的; 驼峰状的.

hump·y[2] [ˈhʌmpi] *n.* 〔澳〕小棚屋.

hu·mus [ˈhju:məs] *n.* 〔L.〕 腐殖质. ~ **soil** 腐殖土. **-like** *a.*

Hun., Hung. = Hungarian; Hungary.

Hun [hʌn] *n.* ①匈奴人,匈奴族. ②〔h-〕〔喻〕野蛮人,(艺术品等的)任意破坏者. ③〔蔑〕德国丘八〔欧战时用语〕.

hunch [hʌntʃ] *n.* ①肉峰,隆肉. ②(饼等的)厚片,大块. ③推. ④〔美口〕预感,第六感觉. *have a ~ that* …, 总觉得…. — *vt.* ①弓(背等); 使隆起,使成弓状 *(up)*. ②推. — *vi.* ①向前移动. ②弯成弓状,隆起. ~**back** 驼背; 驼子. ~**backed** *a.* 驼背的.

hunch·y [ˈhʌntʃi] *a.* = humped.

hun·dred [ˈhʌndrəd] *num.* 百, 一百个; 一百人 〔物〕. *a [one] ~* 一百. *five ~ (and) fifty-four* 五百五十四. *some ~ persons* 约一百人. *two ~* 二百. ★伴随数词或数量形容词时复数不加 s; 另外, hundred 后有零头时, 英语须插用 and, 美语常略. — *n.* ①一百的记号〔100 或 C〕. ②〔*pl.*〕数以百计; 许多. ③一百个一组,一百个人〔物〕一组. ④【体】百米〔码〕赛跑; 〔英〕一百镑; 〔美〕一百元; 一百岁. ⑤【英史】郡的分区; 【美史】县的分区. *several ~(s) of persons* 几百人. *some ~s of students* 几百个学生. *nine ~ hours* 上午九点〔常写作 0900 hours〕. *in* nineteen ~ 在一九〇〇年. *in the nineteen ~s* 在二十世纪(即一九〇〇至一九九九年). *~s of examples* 许多例子. *~s of millions of the working people* 亿万劳动人民. *The old man lived to a ~.* 那位老人活到一百岁. ***a cool ~*** 〔口〕百镑巨款; 巨款. ***a great [long] ~*** 一百二十. ***a ~ and one*** 许多 (*in a ~ and one ways* 千方百计). ***a [one] ~ percent*** 百分之百; 全然,完全. ***a ~ to one*** 百分之九十九; 很有可能地. ***by the ~, by ~s*** 数以百计,大批地. ***~s and thousands*** 撒在糕饼上做装饰的蜜饯〔小糖果〕. ***~s of*** 好几百,许许多多. ***~s of thousands of*** 几十万,无数. ***in the ~*** 每百,百分中的. ***like a ~ of bricks*** 〔口〕以压倒的势力, 来势猛烈地. ***ninety-nine out of a ~*** 百分之九十九,几乎全部. ***the (upper) four ~*** (美国的)四百家族; 名流,上层. — *a.* 许多,很多. *I have a ~ things to do.* 我有很多事情要做. ***not a ~ miles away*** 〔谑〕离得不怎么远. **H- Days** ①【法史】(拿破仑再次称帝的)百日天下〔1815年3月20日—6月28日〕. ②【美史】(由罗斯福召开的)百日特别国会〔1933年 3月9日—6月16日,会上通过多项重要的社会福利法案〕. **~-percent** *a.* 百分之百的; 彻底的,十足的. **~-percenter** ①极端民族主义分子. ②(政治上的)盲从分子; 极端分子. **~-percentism** 极端民族主义. **~'s place**【数】百位. **-fold** *a., ad., n.* 一百倍,一百重.

hun·dredth [ˈhʌndrədθ] *num.* ①第一百,第一百个,第一百号. ②百分之一. *six ~s* 百分之六. —*a.* 第一百的,第一百个的. ***old H-***【宗】《旧约全书》中的《诗篇》第一百篇.

hun·dred·weight [ˈhʌndrədweit] *n.* 英担〔〔英〕=112磅(又叫 long ~); 〔美〕= 100 磅(又叫 short ~)〕(略 cwt. 或 hwt.).

hung [hʌŋ] hang 的过去式及过去分词.

Hung. =Hun.

Hun·gar·i·an [hʌŋˈgɛəriən] *a.* 匈牙利的; 匈牙利人的; 匈牙利语的. — *n.* ①匈牙利人. ②匈牙利语.

Hun·ga·ry [ˈhʌŋgəri] *n.* 匈牙利〔欧洲〕.

hun·ger [ˈhʌŋgə] *n.* ①饿,饥饿. ②食欲. ③渴望,热望 *(for, after)*. *H- is the best relish [sauce].* 〔谚〕饥者易为食. *die from [of] ~* 饿死. *a ~ for learning*

求知欲. ～ *after kindness* 渴望得到照顾. — *vt.* 使饥饿;使因饿而… (*into; out of*) *try to* ～ *sb. into submission* 企图断粮迫使某人屈服. —*vi.*①饥饿. ②渴望 (*after; for*). ～ **cure** 饥饿疗法. ～ **march** 反饥饿游行. ～ **marcher** 参加反饥饿游行的人. ～ **strike** ① *n.* 绝食(尤指狱中的抗议行动). ② *vi.* 举行绝食抗议, 进行绝食斗争.

hun·gri·ly [ˈhʌŋgrili] *ad.* 饥饿似地; 渴望地. *go at [to] it* ～ 争先恐后地干起来.

hun·gri·ness [ˈhʌŋgrinis] *n.* 饥饿; 渴望; (土地的)贫瘠.

hun·gry [ˈhʌŋgri] *a.* (*-gri·er; -gri·est*) ①饥饿的, 空腹的; 饥饿似的; (工作)引起饥饿的; 〔罕〕促进食欲的. ②渴望…的 (*for; after*). ③(土地)贫瘠的, (土地)不毛的; (年成)饥馑的. ④贫乏的. *be* ～ *for knowledge* 渴望求知. *She was [felt]* ～. 她饿了. ～ *times* 荒年. *a power-*～ *politician* 有权力欲的政客. *a* ～ *look* 饥色, 菜色. ***as*** ～ ***as a hawk [hunter, wolf]*** 非常饥饿. ***go*** ～ 挨饿. ***the H- Forties*** 【英史】饥饿的四十年代(1840—49).

hunk[1] [hʌŋk] *n.* 〔口〕肉峰; 厚片, 大片, 大块. *a* ～ *of bread and cheese* 一大片干酪面包. ～ *of cable* 电缆盘. ～*s of iron* 铁块.

hunk[2] [hʌŋk] *a.* = hunky[2].

hunk[3] [hʌŋk] *n.* 〔美俚、贬〕= hunky[1].

hun·ker[1] [ˈhʌŋkə] *n.* ①〔H-〕纽约民主党保守派的一员. ②保守派; 守旧派.

hun·ker[2] [ˈhʌŋkə] *vi.* 蹲下. — *n.*〔*pl.*〕臀部, 屁股. ***on one's*** ～***s*** 蹲下.

hunks [hʌŋks] *n.* 〔*sing., pl.*〕心肠坏的人; 贪鄙小人, 守财奴, 吝啬鬼.

hunk·y[1] [ˈhʌŋki] *n.* (*pl. hunkies*) 〔美俚、贬〕来自中欧或东欧的人(尤指匈牙利人).

hunk·y[2] [ˈhʌŋki] *a.* 〔美俚〕①很好的, 不错的. ②相等的, 两相抵消的. *feel oneself all* ～ 感到已经恢复正常. *get* ～ *with sb.* 同某人不分胜负.

hunk·y-do·ry [ˈhʌŋkiˈdɔːri] *a.* = hunky[2].

Hun·nish [ˈhʌniʃ] *a.* ①匈奴的, 匈奴似的. ②野蛮的.

Hunt [hʌnt] *n.* 亨特〔姓氏〕.

hunt [hʌnt] *vt.* ①(用狗马等)追猎, 猎取; 在…狩猎. ②搜索 (*up; out*); 追捕, 追获. ③驱赶, 骚扰, 迫害. ～ *big game* 猎捕猛兽. ～ *ivory* 猎取象牙. ～ *the hounds* 用猎犬狩猎. ～ *one's horse all winter* 一冬天都骑马狩猎. ～ *a county* 在该郡狩猎, 搜索该郡的猎物. — *vi.* ①打猎. ②(兽类等)猎食. ③探求, 搜寻 (*after; for*). ④【电】摆动, 振荡. ⑤(机器等)不规则地动. ～ *for [after] a lost book* 找一本丢失的书. ～ *high and low for sth.* 到处搜寻某物. ～ ***and peck*** 看一个键按一个字的打字方法. ～ ***counter*** (猎狗)逆着猎物臭迹追. ～ ***down*** 穷追; 追捕; 搜寻. ～ ***for [about]*** 追猎; 搜寻. ～ ***out*** 搜寻出. ～ ***up*** 搜索, 搜出. — *n.* ①打猎; 打猎队; 猎区; 猎人会. ②探求, 搜索. *a* ～ *ball* 猎人舞会. ***be on a*** ～ ***for*** 寻找, 找. ***have a*** ～ ***for*** 搜求. ***still*** ～ 暗中活动. ～ **away** *n.* 〔澳〕牧羊犬. ～ **box** = ～ing box. ～**-the-slipper** 找拖鞋〔室内游戏〕.

hunt·er [ˈhʌntə] *n.* ①猎人〔英国骑马猎狐兔的人不叫～, 叫做 *huntingman*〕; 猎狗; 猎马; 猎食其他动物的野兽. ②〔罕〕探求者, 追求者. ③(有金属盖保护表面的)猎表, 双盖表 (=～ing watch). ***as hungry as a*** ～ 非常饥饿的. ～ **green** 草绿色. ～**-killer** *a.* (舰队)为搜寻敌方潜艇而编组的. ～**'s moon** 狩猎季节的满月〔即收获季节后的满月〕.

Hunt·er [ˈhʌntə] *n.* 亨特〔姓氏〕.

hunt·ing [ˈhʌntiŋ] *n.* ①打猎, (尤指)狐猎. ②搜索, 追寻. ③【电】摆动, 寄生振荡; (同步电动机的)速度偏差; (自动控制系统的)寻求平衡. *leak* ～【电】泄漏点寻觅, 测漏. ～ **boot** 猎靴. ～ **box** 猎舍. ～ **cap** 猎帽. ～ **case** 猎用表的表盒. ～ **crop** 猎鞭. ～ **field**, ～ **ground** 猎场. ～ **horn** 猎号. ～ **knife** 猎刀. ～**man** 〔英〕猎狐[兔]爱好者. ～ **watch** 猎用表.

Hunt·ing·don·shire [ˈhʌntiŋdənʃiə] 亨廷顿郡〔英国中东部郡名, 又名 Huntingdon, Hunts〕.

Hun·ting·ton [ˈhʌntiŋtən] *n.* 亨廷顿〔姓氏〕.

hunt·ress [ˈhʌntris] *n.* ①女猎人. ②雌猎马.

hunts·man [ˈhʌntsmən] *n.* 〔英〕猎人; 管猎狗的人. ～**-ship** *n.* 打猎术.

hunts·man's-cup [ˈhʌntsmənzˌkʌp] *n.* 瓶子草属植物; 猪笼草 (=pitcherplant).

hur·dle [ˈhəːdl] *n.* ①〔英〕疏篱, 树枝编成的篱笆. ②〔*pl.*〕(赛马或赛跑用)栏架, 跳栏. ③【化】栅格. ④障碍, 困难. ⑤【史】(送犯人到刑场的雪橇状)囚笼, 囚车. ***the high [low]*** ～***s*** 【体】高 [低] 栏赛跑. — *vt.* ①用疏篱围住 (*off*). ②跳过(栏). ③突破(难关). — *vi.* 跳栏; 跨越障碍. ～ **race** 跳栏赛跑.

hur·dler [ˈhəːdlə] *n.* ①跳栏运动员. ②编篱笆的人.

hurds [həːdz] *n. pl.* 粗亚麻, 麻屑, 毛屑 (=hards).

hur·dy-gur·dy [ˈhəːdiˈgəːdi] *n.* (*pl.* ***-gur·dies***) ①绞弦琴. ②手摇风琴 (=barrel organ).

hurl [həːl] *n.* 猛投, 猛掷. — *vt.* ①猛投, 猛掷. ②猛推, 推翻. ③吐(恶言), 激烈地说(出). ～ *threats [abuse] at sb.* 恶狠狠地威胁[责骂]某人. ～ *a spear at* 向(野兽等)投掷标枪. — *vi.* ①猛投, 猛掷. ②猛推, 猛撞. ③〔美俚〕(垒球中的)投球. ～ ***oneself at [upon] the enemy*** 猛攻敌人. ～**bat** *n.* (曲棍球的)打球棒.

hurl·er [ˈhəːlə] *n.* 投掷者; (棒球的)投球员.

Hur·ley [ˈhəːli] *n.* 赫尔利〔姓氏〕.

hurl·ey [ˈhəːli] *n.* = hurly[1].

hurl·ing [ˈhəːliŋ] *n.* ①投掷. ②爱尔兰式棒球.

Hurl·ing·ham [ˈhəːliŋəm] *n.* 英国马球总会.

hurl·y[1] [ˈhəːli] *n.* 爱尔兰棒球戏; 爱尔兰棒球的球棒.

hurl·y[2] [ˈhəːli] *n.* 骚乱, 喧闹.

hurl·y-burl·y [ˈhəːliˈbəːli] *n.* 骚乱, 喧闹.

Hu·ron [ˈhjuərən] *n.* ①(北美易洛魁人中的)休伦族; 休伦族人; 休伦语. ②(北美)休伦湖 (=Lake ～).

Hur·rah, hur·ray [huˈrɑː, huˈrei] *int.* 万岁! 好哇! *H- for the King!* 国王万岁! — *n.* ①欢呼声. ②激动. ③纷争. — *vi., vt.* (向…)呼万岁, 欢呼. ～**'s nest** 〔美俚〕大混乱的场所, 乱糟糟的东西.

hur·ri·cane [ˈhʌrikən, -kin] *n.* ①飓风, 十二级风. ②飓风般猛烈的东西; (愤怒或其他感情等的)爆发. ③〔H-〕〔英〕飓风式战斗驱逐机. *a* ～ *of blows* 一阵猛烈的打击. *a* ～ *of applause* 暴风雨般的鼓掌. ～ **bird** 军舰鸟. ～ **deck** 〔美〕(客轮的)最上层甲板, 飓风甲板. ～ **globe** (灯、烛等的)防风罩. ～ **lamp** 防风灯. ～ **lantern** 防风灯笼.

hur·ri·coon [ˈhəːrəkuːn] *n.* 侦测飓风汽球.

hur·ried [ˈhʌrid] *a.* 仓卒的, 慌忙的; 草率的. **-ly** *ad.* **-ness** *n.*

hur·ri·er [ˈhʌriə] *n.* 匆忙的人; 催促者.

hur·ry [ˈhʌri] *n.* ①匆忙; 仓促, 慌忙. ②〔口〕需要匆忙行动的理由〔用于否定、疑问句中〕. ③混乱, 骚动. *Don't go yet — there is no* ～. 别走——不必忙. *Why all this* ～? 为什么这样急匆匆的? *Is there any* ～ *about it?* 有必要这样匆匆忙忙吗? ***in a*** ～ ①匆忙, 慌忙. ②急于要; 〔口〕愿意地. ③〔口〕容易地, 立即(*be in a* ～ *to leave* 急着要走. *It's not to be understood in a* ～. 这不是一下子就能理解的. *I shall not do it again in a* ～. 我可不乐意再干这事了). ***in no*** ～ 不急于…; 不愿意; 不容易. ***no*** ～ 不忙, 不必着急. ***not … in a*** ～ 并不是很快就可…, 并不是容易. — *vt.* ①催促, 使加快 (*up; on; along; away; into; out*). ②急派, 急忙运去; 匆忙移开, 忽忙拿走. *He refused to be hurried.* 他不要人催. *soldiers hurried to the front* 急运前线的部队. — *vi.* 赶急, 赶快, 仓促. ～ ***along*** 赶快走. ～ ***away [off]*** 匆匆离去; 使赶快去. ～ ***back*** 赶紧折回. ～ ***on*** (*with*) 赶紧办理. ～ ***over*** 赶快办完. ～ ***through***

匆匆赶完. ～ **up** 催促,赶紧;赶快,快点 *(H- up! You will be late.* 赶快!你要来不及了. *～-up wagon* 急修车,抢险车). **～-scurry, ～-skurry** [ˈhʌriˈskʌri] ①*ad., a.* 慌慌张张. ② *n.* 躁急,慌张. ③ *vi.* 慌忙乱窜,手忙脚乱地干.

Hurst [həːst] *n.* 赫斯特〔姓氏〕.

hurst [həːst] *n.* ①(海、河的)沙岸. ②有树林的山岗;树林,小丘.

hurt [həːt] *vt. (hurt)* ①伤害,刺痛. ②使痛心,使伤感情,使不快. ③损害,危害. *Another glass won't ～ you.* 再喝一杯也无妨. *a ～ book* 一本受到损坏的书. *She ～ my feelings.* 她伤了我的感情. — *vi.* ①惹起痛苦;伤害,伤痛. ②危害,有害. ③〔方〕需要. *My leg still ～s.* 我的脚还在痛呢. *My shoe is too tight; it ～s.* 我的鞋太紧了,挤脚痛. ***feel ～*** 感觉不快. ***～ oneself = get ～*** 受伤,负伤. — *n.* 伤害;(精神的)苦痛. ***do ～ to*** 伤害,损害.

hurt·ful [ˈhəːtful] *a.* 有害的,造成伤痛的 *(to)*. **-ly** *ad.* **-ness** *n.*

hur·tle [ˈhəːtl] *vi.* ①猛烈碰撞;发出碰撞声. ②猛烈飞出去,嘘一声射出去. — *vt.* ①猛掷,猛射. ②〔古〕猛烈碰撞,使猛烈冲撞. ～ ***at*** 嘘一声射向;向…猛烈冲击. — *n.* 碰撞;碰撞声.

hur·tle·ber·ry [ˈhəːtlberi] *n. (pl. -ries)* ①越桔,欧洲越桔树;笃斯越桔树;欧洲越桔子;笃斯越桔子 (whortleberry). ②=huckleberry.

hurt·less [ˈhəːtlis] *a.* 〔古〕无害的;未受伤的.

hus·band [ˈhʌzbənd] *n.* ①丈夫 *(opp.* wife). ②〔英〕管家. ③〔古〕节俭的管理人. ④船舶管理人(=ship's ～). ***～'s tea*** 〔谑〕丈夫泡的茶〔又淡又冷〕. — *vt.* ①节俭地使用[经营]. ②〔古〕耕(地),栽培(植物). ③〔诗、谑〕使有丈夫;〔罕〕做…的丈夫. **-age**【海】船舶管理费〔商船船主付与其商务代表的酬金〕. **～man** 〔古〕庄稼人. **-like** *a.* 善于管理农活的. **-ly** *a.* ①节俭的. ②农夫的,耕作的. ③丈夫的,丈夫般的.

hus·band·ry [ˈhʌzbəndri] *n.* ①农业,耕作. ②〔古〕家政;节俭,节约. *animal ～* 畜牧业. *bad ～* 不会当家. *good ～* 会当家.

hush [ʃiː,hʌʃ] *int.* 嘘! 别响! — [hʌʃ] *n.* ①静寂;沉默. ②秘而不宣. *in the ～ of deep night* 深夜静悄悄. — *vt.* ①使静下来,使沉默. ②压下…不声张,掩盖. *～ her fears* 使她安静下来不再害怕. *～ the scandal up* 把丑事掩盖住不声张. — *vi.* ①静下来,沉默. ②秘而不宣. ～ ***up*** 掩盖,秘而不宣. ***H- up!*** 别作声! ～ **boat,** ～ **ship** 伪装军舰. ～ **money** 封住嘴的贿赂.

hush·a·by [ˈhʌʃəbai] *int.* 乖乖睡! — *vt.* 哼摇篮曲使(哄小儿入睡).

hush-hush [ˈhʌʃˈhʌʃ] *a.* 〔俚〕秘密的,秘而不宣的. *a ～ report* 秘密报告. — *n.* 秘密气氛,(政治、战略等方面的)机密. — *vt.* 勒令秘而不宣,禁止声张,封锁(新闻).

husk [hʌsk] *n.* ①外皮,壳,荚;〔美〕玉米包皮;茧衣. ②(无用的)外皮,无价值的部分. ③支架. ④牛瘟. — *vt.* ①剥去…的外皮,去…的荚. ②用粗嗄声讲(话). — *vi.* 声音变嗄.

husk·ing [ˈhʌskiŋ] *n.* ①〔美〕剥玉米包皮. ②〔美〕农家碾米会〔指邻舍、亲友边碾米边聊天的聚会,又叫 ～-bee〕. *a rice ～ machine* 碾米机.

husk-to·ma·to [ˈhʌsktəˈmɑːtəu] *n. (pl. -toes)* =ground-cherry.

husk·y [ˈhʌski] *a.* ①壳的,壳似的;壳多的. ②(嗓音)嗄声的,干哑的. ③〔俚〕粗鲁的;结实的,强健的. — *n.* 〔口〕强壮结实的人. **-i·ly** *ad.* **-ness** *n.*

Hus·ky [ˈhʌski] *n.* ①爱斯基摩人,爱斯基摩语. ②〔h-〕爱斯基摩狗.

hus·sar [huˈzɑː] *n.* ①轻骑兵. ②十五世纪的匈牙利轻骑兵,轻骑兵〔以制服华丽著称〕.

hus·sif [ˈhʌzif] *n.* 针线盒(= housewife²).

Huss·ite [ˈhʌsait] *n.* (十五世纪捷克爱国者及宗教改革家)胡斯〔*John Huss* (1369—1415)〕的拥护者,胡斯运动派成员. **Huss·it·ism** *n.* 胡斯运动;胡斯主义.

hus·sy [ˈhʌsi, ˈhʌzi] *n.* ①轻佻的女子,荡妇. ②鲁莽的女子.

hus·tings [ˈhʌstiŋz] *n. [sing., pl.]* ①【英史】(1872 年以前)候选人在国会发表竞选演说的讲坛;竞选讲坛. ②选举手续. ③〔英〕地方法院.

hus·tle [ˈhʌsl] *vt.* ①硬挤,乱推,挤进 *(into)*,挤出 *(out of)*. ②硬逼,逼使 *(into)*. ③〔口〕使匆匆做成. ④强夺;欺骗. ⑤强卖;在(某地)竭力推销. *～ sb. into doing sth.* 强使某人作某事. *～ sth. out of the way* 排除障碍物. — *vi.* ①乱挤,乱推,挤过去;奔忙. ②〔口〕努力快做. ③骗钱;诱赌;(妓女)拉客. — *n.* ①挤;推. ②努力. ③设骗局. ***Get a ～ on!*** 快干! 使劲干.

hus·tler [ˈhʌslə] *n.* ①乱挤乱推者(尤指扒手同伙). ②(非法买卖等的)好手;骗子;妓女. ③能干人.

hut [hʌt] *n.* ①小屋,茅舍,棚屋. ②【军】临时营房. ③〔美俚〕牢房. — *vt., vi.* (使)住临时营房[小屋].

hutch [hʌtʃ] *n.* ①(盛物)箱;橱;碗架. ②(动物、家禽的)笼,舍;兔箱. ③〔美方〕(渔夫的)小棚屋. ④【矿】铁车;洗矿槽;跳汰机筛下室;沉积槽底的矿砂. — *vt.* ①把…装在箱内. ②【矿】用洗矿槽洗.

hut·ment [ˈhʌtmənt] *n.* ①【军】设营. ②临时营房. ③住临时营房.

Hutt [hʌt] *n.* 赫特〔姓氏〕.

hüt·te [ˈhjutə] *n.* 〔G.〕小舍,临时小屋.

hutz·pah [ˈhuːtspə, -pɑː] *n.* = chutzpah.

Hux·ley [ˈhʌksli], *n.* ①赫克斯利〔姓氏〕. ② **Thomas Henry** ～ 汤姆斯·亨利·赫胥黎〔1825—1895,英国生物学家〕. ③**Andrew Fielding** ～ 安德鲁·菲尔丁·赫克斯利〔1918—　英国生理学家. 1963 年与 A. L. Hodgkin 和 Sir J. C. Eccles 合得诺贝尔医药奖〕.

huz·za, huz·zah [huˈzɑː] *int., n., vi., vt.* = hurrah.

H.V. = high voltage.

hv = heavy.

HVAR = high velocity aircraft rocket. 机载高速火箭.

HW = Handford Works 汉福特原子厂.

HWL = 【纺】heat-fast, water-fast, light-fast 耐烫,耐洗,耐晒.

H.W.(M.), HWM, h.w.(m.) = high-water(mark). 高水位线,高潮线.

hwt. = hundredweight (又略作 cwt.).

hwy. = highway.

Hy. = Henry.

hy·a·cinth [ˈhaiəsinθ] *n.* ①【植】风信子. ②紫蓝色. ③【矿】红锆石.

hy·a·cin·thine [ˌhaiəˈsinθain] *a.* ①似风信子的. ②紫蓝色的. ③楚楚可怜的,美丽的.

Hy·a·des, Hy·ads [ˈhaiədiːz,ˈhaiədz] *n.* 〔*pl.*〕【天】(金牛宫中的)毕(宿)星团.

hy·ae·na [haiˈiːnə] *n.* = hyena.

hy·a·line [ˈhaiəlin] *a.* ①玻璃的. ②〔诗〕透明的,玻璃〔水晶〕一样的. — *n.* ①透明物;〔诗〕碧空,镜面一样的海. ②【生化】透明朊;【解】玻璃质. ～ **cartilage**【解】透明软骨. ～ **membrane disease** 透明膜(毛根)病.

hy·a·lite [ˈhaiəlait] *n.* 【矿】玻璃蛋白石.

hy·al(o)- *comb. f.* 表示"玻璃(状)的","透明的"〔元音前用 hyal-〕: *hyal*ite、*hyalo*plasm.

hy·a·loid [ˈhaiəlɔid] *a.* 透明的,玻璃状的. ～ **membrane**【解】玻璃状体膜.

hy·a·lo·plasm [ˈhaiələˌplæzəm]【生】透明质,胞基质.

hy·al·u·ron·ic [ˌhaiəljuˈrɔnik] *a.* ～ **acid**【生化】透明质酸.

hy·al·u·ron·i·dase [ˌhaiəljuˈrɔnideis] *n.*【生化】透明质酸酶.

hy·brid [ˈhaibrid] *n.* ①【生】杂种,杂交种;混血儿.②(由两种来源的东西组成的)混合物;受过两种不同文化传统教育的人;(由不同语言中的词组成的)混合词.④【无】混合波导联结;等差作用;桥结岔路.— *a.* 杂种的;混合的;混合语的. *a* ~ *animal* 杂种动物. ~ **computer** (模拟、数字)混合型计算机. ~ **parameter**【数】杂系参数. ~ **type**【无】混合型,桥接岔路型,差动式. ~ **vigo(u)r**【生】杂种优势. **-ism** *n.* ①杂种,混血,杂交(现象). ②混合性,杂种性,混杂作用.

hy·brid·ist [ˈhaibridist] *n.* 杂种繁殖者.

hy·brid·i·ty [haiˈbriditi] *n.* 杂种性.

hy·brid·ize [ˈhaibridaiz] *vi., vt.* (使)产生杂种,(使)杂交;(使)混成. **hy·brid·iz·a·ble** *a.* 能产生杂种的;能杂混的. **hy·brid·iza·tion** *n.*

hy·bris [ˈhaibris] *n.* = hubris.

hyd. = ①hydraulics. ②hydrostatics.

hy·da·thode [ˈhaidəθəud] *n.*【植】排水器〔皮表水分排泄的器官〕.

hy·da·tid [ˈhaidətid] *n.*【医】包虫囊.

Hyde [haid] *n.* 海德〔姓氏〕.

Hyde Park [ˈhaidˈpɑːk] (伦敦的)海德公园. *a* ~ *orator* 鼓动群众的演说家.

Hy·der·a·bad [ˈhaidərəbɑːd] *n.* 海得拉巴〔印度、巴基斯坦的两个同名城市〕.

hydr- *comb. f.* 〔用于元音或以 h 开始的词前〕= hydro-.

hydr. = hydraulics.

hy·dra [ˈhaidrə] *n.* *(pl.* ~*s, -drae* [-driː]*)* ①〔H-〕【希神】九头蛇〔斩去一头会生出二头〕. ②难以一下根绝的祸害;大患,不断产生困难的问题. ③【动】水螅,水蛇. ④〔H-〕【天】长蛇座. ~**-headed** *a.* ①多头的;多分支的,多中心的. ②难根绝的;困难重重的.

hy·drac·id [haiˈdræsid] *n.*【化】氢酸,含氢酸.

hy·dra·go·gue [ˈhaidrəgɔg] *n.*【药】利尿剂,水泻剂. — *a.* 利尿的,驱水的.

hy·dran·ge·a [haiˈdreindʒiə] *n.* 绣球花属(即八仙花属)的一种植物.

hy·drant [ˈhaidrənt] *n.* 消防龙头;配水龙头,给水栓,取水管.

hy·dranth [ˈhaidrænθ] *n.*【动】水螅体.

hy·drar·gy·rism [haiˈdrɑːdʒirizəm] *n.*【医】汞中毒.

hy·drar·gy·rum [haiˈdrɑːdʒirəm] *n.*【化】汞.

hy·drar·thro·sis [ˌhaidrɑːˈθrəusis] *n.*【医】关节积水.

hy·drase [ˈhaidreis] *n.*【生化】水化酶.

hy·dras·tine [haiˈdræstiːn, -tin] *n.*【化】白毛茛碱,(北美)黄连碱.

hy·dras·tis [haiˈdræstis] *n.*【植】白毛茛.

hy·drate [ˈhaidreit] *n.*【化】水合物. ~ *cellulose* 水合纤维素. — *vt., vi.* (使)成水合物;(使)水合.

hy·drat·ed [ˈhaidreitid] *a.*【化】含水的. ~ **alumina** 氢氧化铝.

hy·dra·tion [haiˈdreiʃən] *n.*【化】水合(作用). ~ **heat** 水合热. ~ **water** 结合水.

hydraul. = hydraulic(s).

hy·drau·lic [haiˈdrɔːlik] *a.* ①水力的,液力的;用水发动的. ②液压的,水压的. ③水力学的. ④【建】水硬的. ~ **brake** 水压制动机,水力闸;闸式水力测功器. ~ **cement** 水硬水泥. ~ **crane** 水力起重机. ~ **drop** 水力落差. ~ **engine** 水力机,水压机,水力发动机. ~ **engineering** 水利工程. ~ **lift** 水力起重机. ~ **lime** 水硬石灰. ~ **motor** 水力电动机. ~ **press** 水压机. ~ **power plant** 水电厂. ~ **pump** 水力泵. ~ **ram** 水力夯锤,压力扬汲机. ~ **test** 水压试验. ~ **transport** ①水力运输. ②液压输送. **-li·cal·ly** *ad.*

hy·drau·li·cian [ˌhaidrɔːˈliʃən] *n.* 水力学家.

hy·drau·lics [haiˈdrɔːliks] *n.* 水力学.

hy·dra·zide [ˈhaidrəzaid] *n.*【化】酰肼.

hy·dra·zine [ˈhaidrəziːn, -zin] *n.*【化】肼;联氨.

hy·dra·zo·ate [ˌhaidrəˈzəueit] *n.*【化】叠氮化物.

hy·dri·a [ˈhaidriə] *n.* *(pl.* *-ae* [-iː]*)* 古希腊、古罗马的水罐.

hy·dric [ˈhaidrik] *a.*【化】(含)氢的.

-hydric *comb. f.* 表示"含酸式氢","含羟基": mono*hydric.*

hy·dride [ˈhaidraid], **hy·drid** [-rid] *n.*【化】氢化物.

hy·dro [ˈhaidrəu] *n.* ①〔口〕水上飞机 (= hydroplane). ②〔英俚〕水疗处,接待水疗病人的旅馆 (=hydropathic establishment). ③〔美口〕水力电;〔*pl.*〕水力发电厂.— *a.* = hydroelectric.

hy·dro- *comb. f.* 表示"水","氢化的","氢的": *hydro*dynamic, *hydro*carbon.

hy·dro·a·cous·tic [ˈhaidrəuəˈkuːstik] *a.* 液压声能的;水底传音的.

hy·dro·ae·ro·plane [ˈhaidrəuˈɛərəplein] *n.* = hydroairplane.

hy·dro·air·plane [ˈhaidrəuˈɛəplein] *n.* 水上飞机.

hy·dro·bi·ol·o·gy [ˈhaidrəubaiˈɔlədʒi] *n.* 流体生物学.

hy·dro·bomb [ˈhaidrəuˈbɔm] *n.* 空投水雷.

hy·dro·bro·mic [ˈhaidrəuˈbrəumik] *a.* ~ **acid**【化】氢臭酸,溴化氢.

hy·dro·car·bon [ˈhaidrəuˈkɑːbən] *n.* 碳氢化合物,烃.

hy·dro·ceph·a·lous, hy·dro·ce·phalic [ˈhaidrəuˈsefələs, ˈhaidrəusiˈfælik] *a.*【医】脑积水的.

hy·dro·ceph·alus [ˈhaidrəuˈsefələs] *n.*【医】脑积水,水脑.

hy·dro·chlo·ric [ˈhaidrəuˈklɔrik] *a.*【化】氯化氢的. ~ **acid** 盐酸,氢氯酸.

hy·dro·chlo·ride [ˈhaidrəuˈklɔraid] *n.*【化】氢氯化物,盐酸化物,盐酸盐.

hy·dro·cli·mate [ˈhaidrəuˈklaimit] *n.* 水中生物的物理及化学环境(如水温、酸度等).

hy·dro·corti·sone [ˈhaidrəuˈkɔːtisəun] *n.*【生化】皮质醇;【药】氢化可的松 (=cortisol).

hy·dro·crack [ˈhaidrəukræk] *vt.*【化】加氢裂化,氢化裂解. **-er** 氢化裂解器.

hy·dro·cy·an·ic [ˈhaidrəusaiˈænik] *a.*【化】氰化氢的. ~ **acid** 氢氰酸.

hy·dro·dy·nam·ic [ˈhaidrəudaiˈnæmik] *a.* ①水力的;水压的. ②流体动力学的.

hy·dro·dy·nam·ics [ˈhaidrəudaiˈnæmiks] *n.* 流体动力学.

hy·dro·e·lec·tric [ˈhaidrəu-iˈlektrik] *a.* 水力发电的. *a* ~ *power station* 水力发电站. **-tric·i·ty** *n.*

hy·dro·ex·trac·tor [ˈhaidrəu-iksˈtræktə] *n.* 脱水机.

hy·dro·flu·or·ic [ˈhaidrəuflu(ː)ˈɔrik] *a.*【化】氟化氢的. ~ **acid** 氢氟酸.

hy·dro·foil [ˈhaidrəufɔil] *n.* ①(空翼船上的)水翼. ②水翼船.

hy·dro·form·ing [ˈhaidrəufɔːmiŋ] *n.*【化】临氢重整过程,生氢.

hy·dro·gel [ˈhaidrədʒel] *n.*【化】水凝胶.

hy·dro·gen [ˈhaidridʒən] *n.*【化】氢. ~ **bomb** 氢弹. ~ **bond**【化】氢键. ~ **ion**【化】氢离子. ~ **oxide** 氧化氢,水. ~ **peroxide** 过氧化氢. ~ **sulphide** 硫化氢.

hy·dro·gen·ate, hy·dro·gen·ize [haiˈdrɔdʒineit, -naiz] *vt.*【化】使氢化,使与氢化合,使还原. **hy·dro·gen·a·tion, hy·dro·gen·i·za·tion** *n.* 加氢(作用).

hy·dro·gen·i·um [ˌhaidrəuˈdʒiːniəm] *n.*【化】金属氢.

hy·dro·gen·ol·y·sis [ˌhaidrəudʒəˈnɔləsis] *n.*【化】氢解作用.

hy·drog·e·nous [haiˈdrɔdʒinəs] *a.*【化】氢的,含氢的.

hy·dro·graph [ˈhaidrəgræf] *n.* ①自记水位计,流量速度计算仪. ②水文图,水文曲线.

hy·drog·ra·pher [haiˈdrɔgrəfə] *n.* 水文学家,水文地理学家.

hy·drog·ra·phy [haiˈdrɔgrəfi] *n.* ①水文学，水文地理学. ②水道图；水道测量术. **-pher** *n.* 水文学家，水文地理学家. **-phic(al)** *a.* 水路的；水道测量术的. **-phi·cal·ly** *ad.*

hy·droid [ˈhaidrɔid] *n.*【动】螅体. — *a.* 螅体的，螅状的.

hy·dro·ki·net·ics [ˈhaidrəukaiˈnetiks] *n.* 流体动力学.

hy·drol·o·gy [haiˈdrɔlədʒi] *n.* 水文学，水理学.

hy·drol·y·sate [haiˈdrɔliseit, -zeit] *n.*【化】水解产物. (=hydrolyzate).

hy·drol·y·sis [haiˈdrɔlisis] *n.*【化】水解(作用).

hy·dro·lyte [ˈhaidrəlait] *n.*【化】水解质.

hy·dro·lyt·ic [ˌhaidrəˈlitik] *a.*【化】水解的.

hy·dro·lyze [ˈhaidrəlaiz] *vt., vi.* ***(-lyz·ed; -lyz·ing)*** 水解，进行水解. **hy·dro·lyz·a·ble** *a.*

hy·dro·mag·net·ics [ˌhaidrəumægˈnetiks] *n. pl.* 〔动词用单数〕磁流体动力学(= magnatohydrodynamics). **hy·dro·mag·net·ic** *a.*

hy·dro·man [ˈhaidrəmæn] *n.* 液压操作器，水力控制器.

hy·dro·man·cy [ˈhaidrəumænsi] *n.* 水卜〔一种以水进行占卜的迷信活动〕. **hy·dro·mancer** [-sə] *n.* 用水占卜的术士.

hy·dro·ma·ni·a [ˈhaidrəuˈmeinjə] *n.*【医】投水狂，自溺狂.

hy·dro·me·chan·ics [ˈhaidrəumiˈkæniks] *n.* 流体力学.

hy·dro·me·du·sa [ˈhaidrəumiˈdjuːsə, -ˈduː-; -zə] *n.* *(pl. -sae* [-siː]*)* 水螅水母类.

hy·dro·mel [ˈhaidrəməl] *n.* 蜂蜜酒〔蜂蜜加水发酵后制成〕.

hy·dro·met·al·lur·gy [ˌhaidrəuˈmetləːdʒi] *n.* 湿法冶金学[术].

hy·dro·me·te·or [ˌhaidrəuˈmiːtiə] *n.*【气】水汽凝结体.

hy·drom·e·ter [haiˈdrɔmitə] *n.* 液体比重计.

hy·dro·met·ric(al) [ˌhaidrəuˈmetrik(əl)] *a.* (液体)比重计的；测定比重的.

hy·drom·e·try [haiˈdrɔmitri] *n.* 液体比重测定(法).

hy·dro·mor·phic [ˌhaidrəuˈmɔːfik] *a.*【植】具有适于水生的结构特性的.

hy·dro·mo·tor [ˈhaidrəuˈməutə] *n.* 射水发动机，液压马达，油马达.

hy·dro·naut [ˈhaidrəunɔːt] *n.*【美海军】深潜器驾驶员.

hy·dro·naut·ics [ˌhaidrəuˈnɔːtiks] *n.* 海洋工程学.

hy·dro·ne·phro·sis [ˌhaidrəuniˈfrəusis] *n.*【医】肾盂积水膨出.

hy·dro·ni·um [haiˈdrəuniəm] *n.*【化】水合氢离子 (=～ ion).

hy·dro·path·ic [ˌhaidrəuˈpæθik] *a.* 水疗法的. *a* ～ *establishment* 水疗处，水疗旅馆. ～ *treatment* 水疗法. — *n.* 〔口〕水疗处，水疗旅馆.

hy·drop·a·thist [haiˈdrɔpəθist] *n.* 水疗医生.

hy·drop·a·thy [haiˈdrɔpəθi] *n.*【医】水疗法.

hy·dro·phane [ˈhaidrəufein] *n.*【地】水蛋白石. **hy·droph·a·nous** [haiˈdrɔfənəs] *a.*

hy·dro·phile [ˈhaidrəufail] *n.* 亲水(性).

hy·dro·phil·ic [ˌhaidrəuˈfilik] *a.*【化】亲水的.

hy·droph·i·lous [haiˈdrɔfiləs] *a.* ①=hydrophytic. ②水媒的.

hy·dro·phobe [ˈhaidrəufəub] *n.* ①【化】疏水物；疏水胶体. ②患恐水病的人[动物].

hy·dro·pho·bi·a [ˌhaidrəuˈfəubjə] *n.*【医】恐水病，畏水；狂犬病，瘈咬病. **-bic** *a.* 恐水病的，狂犬病的；患恐水病的.

hy·dro·phone [ˈhaidrəfəun] *n.* 水听器；水中听音器；水中地震检波器；漏水检查器.

hy·dro·phyte [ˈhaidrəufait] *n.* 水生植物.

hy·dro·phyt·ic [ˌhaidrəuˈfitik] *a.*【植】水生的.

hy·drop·ic [haiˈdrɔpik] *a.*【医】水肿的，浮肿的.

hy·dro·plane [ˈhaidrəuplein] *n.* ①水上飞机. ②水面滑走快艇. ③(潜水艇的)水平舵. ④(水上飞机的)水翼. — *vi.* ①乘水上飞机. ②作水上滑行. ③(汽车车轮)在湿路上打滑，车轮空转.

hy·dro·pneu·mat·ic [ˌhaidrəunjuːˈmætik] *a.* 液压气动的.

hy·dro·pneu·mat·ics [ˌhaidrəunjuːˈmætiks] *n.* 液压气动学.

hy·dro·po·nic [ˌhaidrəuˈpɔnik] *a.* ①溶液培养(学)的；水栽法的. ②溶液培养出来的.

hy·dro·po·nics [ˌhaidrəuˈpɔniks] *n.* 溶液栽培法；水栽法〔现在有时指一种为宇宙飞行员提供新鲜食用植物的方法〕.

hy·drop·o·nist [haiˈdrɔpənist], **hy·dro·pon·i·cist** [ˈhaidrəuˌpɔnisist] *n.* 溶液栽培专家.

hy·dro·pow·er [ˈhaidrəupauə] *n.*【电】水力发出的电.

hy·dro·press [ˈhaidrəpres] *n.* 液压机.

hy·drop·s(y) [ˈhaidrɔpsi] *n.*【医】积水，水肿(=dropsy). ～ **abdominis**【医】腹(膜积)水.

hy·dro·qui·none [ˌhaidrəukwiˈnəun] *n.*【化】氢醌；对苯二酚.

hy·dros. = hydrostatics.

hy·dro·scope [ˈhaidrəuskəup] *n.* ①验湿器；水气计. ②深水望远镜，深水探视仪. ③水力测试器；压力测试器. **-pic** *a.* 吸湿的；湿度计的.

hy·dro-ski [ˈhaidrəuˌskiː] *n.* 水橇〔飞机可借以在水上或雪上起落的雪橇或水翼〕.

hy·dro·skim·mer [ˈhaidrəuˈskimə] *n.* 〔美〕水面滑行艇〔航行于水面上的气垫船〕.

hy·dro·sol [ˈhaidrəˌsɔl, -ˌsɔːl] *n.*【化】水溶胶.

hy·dro·space [ˈhaidrəˌspeis] *n.* ①大洋水域(尤指作为科学考查的对象者). ②水下空间.

hy·dro·sphere [ˈhaidrəusfiə] *n.*【气】水界，水圈.

hy·dro·stat [ˈhaidrəustæt] *n.* 汽锅保险，防爆装置；警水器.

hy·dro·stat·ic(al) [ˌhaidrəuˈstætik(əl)] *a.* 流体静力(学)的；静水(学)的. ～ **balance** 比重器，比重秤. ～ **lubricator** 水压滑润器. ～ **press** 水压机. ～ **pressure** 流体静压，静水压力.

hy·dro·stat·ics [ˌhaidrəuˈstætiks] *n.* 静水力学，流体静力学.

hy·dro·sul·fate, hy·dro·sul·phate [ˌhaidrəuˈsʌlfeit] *n.*【化】硫酸氢盐，硫酸化物.

hy·dro·sul·fide, hy·dro·sul·phide [ˌhaidrəuˈsʌlfaid] *n.* 氢硫化物.

hy·dro·sul·fite, hy·dro·sul·phite [ˌhaidrəuˈsʌlfait]【化】*n.* 连二亚硫酸盐；连二亚硫酸钠.

hy·dro·sul·fu·rous [ˌhaidrəuˈsʌlfurəs] *a.* ～ **acid**【化】连二亚硫酸(=hyposulfurous acid).

hy·dro·tax·is [ˌhaidrəuˈtæksis] *n.*【生】向水性. **hy·dro·tac·tic** [-ˈtæktik] *a.*

hy·dro·ther·a·peu·tic [ˈhaidrəuˌθerəˈpjuːtik] *a.* 水疗法的.

hy·dro·ther·a·py [ˈhaidrəuˈθerəpi] *n.* 水疗法.

hy·dro·ther·mal [ˈhaidrəuˈθəːməl] *a.* 热液的，热水(作用)的. ～ **deposit** 热液矿床.

hy·dro·tho·rax [ˈhaidrəuˈθɔːræks] *n.*【医】胸膜积水，水胸.

hy·dro·tim·et·er [ˌhaidrəuˈtimitə] *n.* 水硬度计.

hy·dro·treat [ˈhaidrəutriːt] *vt.*【化】对…作氢化处理.

hy·dro·trop·ism [ˌhaidrəuˈtrɔpizəm] *n.*【植】向水性.

hy·drous [ˈhaidrəs] *a.* ①【化】水合的，水化的；水状的. ②含水的.

hy·dro·vane [ˈhaidrəuvein] *n.* (飞机的)着水板.

hy·drox·ide [haiˈdrɔksaid, -sid] *n.*【化】氢氧化物.

hy·drox·y [hai'drɔksi] *a.*【化】羟(基)的.
hy·drox·yl [hai'drɔksil] *n.*【化】羟基.
hy·drox·yl·a·mine [hai,drɔksili'mi:n, -'æmin] *n.* 羟胺,胲.
hy·drox·yl·ate [hai'drɔksileit] *vt.* ***(-at·ed; -at·ing)***【化】羟化,羟代. **hy·drox·yl·ation** *n.*
hy·dro·zin·cite [,haidrəu'ziŋkait] *n.*【矿】水锌矿.
hy·dro·zo·an [,haidrəu'zəuən] *a.*【动】水螅纲的.— *n.* 水螅纲动物(如:水螅、软水母).
hy·dyne ['haidain] *n.* 美国的一种火箭发动燃料.
hy·e·na, hy·ae·na [hai'i:nə] *n.* ①【动】鬣狗. ②残酷的人,贪婪的人,阴险的人.
hyeto- *comb. f.* 表示"雨","下雨": *hyeto*graphy. *hyeto*logy.
hy·e·to·graph ['haiitəugrɑ:f] *n.* 平均雨量分布图;雨量计.
hy·e·tog·ra·phy [,haii'tɔgrəfi] *n.* 雨量分布学;雨量图法.
hy·e·tol·o·gy [,haii'tɔlədʒi] *n.* 降水量学,雨学.
hy·e·tom·e·ter [,haii'tɔmitə] *n.* 雨量表,雨量计.
Hy·fil ['haifil] *n.* 海菲尔〔一种玻璃纤维的商标名〕.
Hy·ge·ia [hai'dʒi(:)ə] *n.*【希神】司健康的女神.
hy·ge·ian [hai'dʒi:ən] *a.* ①健康的,医药卫生的. ②〔H-〕健康女神的. — *n.* 传授[提倡]卫生术的人.
hy·giene ['haidʒi:n] *n.* 卫生学;健康法. *school* ~ 学校卫生.
hy·gi·en·ic(al) [hai'dʒi:nik(əl)] *a.* ①卫生学的. ②卫生的,有益健康的. *a* ~ *laboratory* 卫生实验所. **-i·cal·ly** *ad.*
hy·gi·en·ics [hai'dʒi:niks] *n.* 卫生学,健康法.
hy·gi·en·ist ['haidʒi:nist] *n.* 卫生学家.
hy·gro- *comb. f.* 表示"湿","湿气": *hygro*meter, *hygro*scopic.
hy·gro·graph ['haigrəugrɑ:f] *n.* 湿度计,湿度自计器.
hy·grol ['haigrɔl] *n.*【化】胶状汞,汞胶液,胶态汞.
hy·grol·o·gy [hai'grɔlədʒi] *n.* 湿度学.
hy·grom·e·ter [hai'grɔmitə] *n.* 湿度表.
hy·gro·met·ric [,haigrəu'metrik] *a.* ①测湿的. ②吸湿性的.
hy·grom·e·try [hai'grɔmitri] *n.* 测湿法.
hy·gro·phyte ['haigrəfait] *n.* = hydrophyte.
hy·gro·scope ['haigrəuskəup] *n.* 测湿器.
hy·gro·scop·ic [,haigrəu'skɔpik] *a.* ①吸湿的;收湿的. ②湿度器的;可用湿度器计量的.
hy·gro·stat ['haigrəustæt] *n.* 恒湿器,湿度检定箱,测湿计.
hy·gro·ther·mo·graph [,haigrəu'θə:məgrɑ:f, -græf] *n.* 温湿计.
hy·ing ['haiiŋ] hie 的另一种现在分词形.
hy·la ['hailə] *n.*【动】①雨蛙属动物;雨蛙. ②〔H-〕雨蛙属.
hy·le ['hai,li:] *n.*【哲】实质,物质.
hy·lic ['hailic] *n.*【哲】实质的,物质的.
hy·loph·a·gous [hai'lɔfəgəs] *a.* 食木的〔如某些昆虫〕.
hy·lo·the·ism [,hailə'θi:izəm] *n.*【哲】物神论,泛神论.
hy·lo·zo·ism [,hailə'zəuizəm] *n.*【哲】万物有生论,物活论.
Hy·men ['haimen] *n.* ①【希神、罗神】司婚姻之神. ②〔h-〕结婚;婚礼的诗歌.
hy·men ['haimen] *n.*【解】处女膜.
hy·me·ne·al [,haime'ni(:)əl] *a.* 婚姻的. ~ *rites* 结婚仪式. — *n.* ①结婚之歌. ②〔*pl.*〕婚礼,婚姻.
hy·me·no- *comb. f.* 表示"膜": *hymeno*ptera, *hymeno*pterous.
Hy·me·nom·y·ce·tes ['haiminəumai'si:tiz] *n.*【微】伞菌类.
Hy·me·nop·ter·a [,haimi'nɔptərə] *n.*【动】膜翅目.
hy·me·nop·ter·an [,haimi'nɔptərən] *n.*【动】膜翅目昆虫〔包括蜜蜂、胡蜂、蚁类等〕. — *a.* 膜翅目的 (= hymenopterous).
hymn [him] *n.* ①【宗】赞美诗,圣歌. ②赞歌. — *vt., vi.* (为…)唱赞歌. ~ **book** 赞美诗集.
hym·nal ['himnəl] *n.* 赞美诗集 (=hymnbook) — *a.* 赞美诗的;使用赞美诗的.
hym·nar·i·um [him'nɛəriəm] *n.* ***(pl. -nar·i·a*** [-riə]***)*** 赞美诗集.
hym·nist, hym·no·dist ['himnist, 'himnədist] *n.* 赞美诗作者.
hym·no·dy ['himnədi] *n.* ①〔集合词〕赞美诗. ②唱赞美诗. ③写作赞美诗. ④赞美诗研究.
hym·nog·ra·pher [him'nɔgrəfə] *n.* = hymnist.
hym·nol·o·gy [him'nɔlədʒi] *n.* ①赞美诗学. ②作赞美诗. ③〔集合词〕赞美诗. **hym·no·log·ic** *a.*
hy·oid ['haiɔid] *a.* 舌骨的. — *n.*【解】舌骨 (=the ~ bone).
hy·o·scine ['haiəsi:n] *n.*【化】天仙子碱.
hy·os·cy·a·mine [,haiə'saiəmi:n, -min] *n.*【化】天仙子胺.
hy·os·cy·a·mus [,haiə'saiəməs] *n.*【植】天仙子,韭沃斯〔一种茄科有毒植物〕.
hyp[1] [hip] *n.*【物】亥普〔衰减单位, =1/10 奈培〕.
hyp[2] [hip] *n.*〔古〕= hypochondria.
hyp. = ①hypotenuse. ②hypothesis. ③hypothetical.
hyp- *pref.* = hypo-.
hyp·a·byss·al [,hipə'bisl] *a.*【地】半深成的,浅成的.
hy·pae·thral [hi'pi:θrəl, hai-] *a.* 露天的,无屋顶的(指古典式建筑和院子).
hy·pan·thi·um [hi'pænθiəm, hai-] *n.* ***(pl. -thi·a*** [-ə]***)***【植】隐头花序. **hy·pan·thi·al** *a.*
hy·pal·la·ge [hai'pæləgi:] *n.*【修】换置法〔如将 apply water to the wound 说成 apply the wound to water 之类〕.
hype [haip] *vt.* ***(hyped; hyp·ing)*** ①〔俚〕用药剂刺激,用麻醉剂注射使兴奋〔一般与 *up* 连用〕. ②大肆宣传. — *n.* 〔美俚〕①吸毒成瘾的人. ②广告. ③被广泛宣传的人〔事〕. ④花招,骗局. **-r** 宣传人员.
hy·per- *pref.* 表示"超出","过于","极度": *hyper*sensitive, *hyper*oxide.
hy·per·ac·id [,haipə(:)'ræsid] *a.* 胃酸过多的.
hy·per·ac·id·i·ty [,haipə(:)rə'siditi] *a.*【医】酸过多,胃酸过多.
hy·per·ac·tive [,haipə(:)'ræktiv] *a.* 极度活跃的(尤指活跃得反常的). **hy·per·ac·tiv·i·ty** [-æk'tiviti] *n.*
hy·per·ae·mi·a [,haipə(:)'ri:miə] *n.*【医】充血. **hy·per·ae·mic** *a.*
hy·per·aes·the·si·a [,haipəris'θi:zjə] *n.* 知觉过敏,感觉过敏. **hy·per·aes·thet·ic** *a.*
hy·per·bar·ic [,haipə(:)'bærik] *a.* ①超气压的;超比重的. ②超气压处理室的(指用作处理各种疾病实验的充氧室). **hy·per·bar·ism** *n.*
hy·per·ba·ton [hai'pə:bətɔn] *n.* ***(pl. ~s, -bata*** [-bətə]***)***【修】倒装法〔为加强文义而颠倒词序,一般是主语和谓语的次序,例如 Happy is he!〕.
hy·per·bo·la [hai'pə:bələ] *n.* ***(pl. ~s, ~e*** [-li:]***)***【数】双曲线.
hy·per·bo·le [hai'pə:bəli] *n.*【修】夸张法.
hy·per·bol·ic(al)[1] [,haipə(:)'bɔlik(əl)] *a.*【数】双曲线的. **-i·cal·ly** *ad.*
hy·per·bol·ic(al)[2] [,haipə(:)'bɔlik(əl)] *a.* 夸张法的.
hy·per·bo·lism [hai'pə:bəlizəm] *n.* ①用夸张法. ②夸张的陈述.
hy·per·bo·lize [hai'pə:bəlaiz] *vt., vi.* ***(-liz·ed; liz·ing)*** 对…大肆夸张,夸大.
hy·per·bo·loid [hai'pə:bəlɔid] *n.*【数】双曲面.
hy·per·bo·re·an [,haipə(:)bɔ:'ri:ən] *a.* ①〔H-〕【希神】

住在北方乐土的. ②极北的;非常寒冷的. ③北国人的. — *n.* 〔H-〕. ①【希神】住在北方乐土的人. ②北国人,住在极北方的人.

hy·per·cat·a·lec·tic [ˌhaipə(:)kætˈlektik] *a.* (诗行的)超音节的(指在一行诗末音节后尚有的一两个音节).

hy·per·charge [ˈhaipətʃɑːdʒ] *vt.* 对…增加压力; 加压过重.

hy·per·crit·ic [ˌhaipə(:)ˈkritik] *n.* 苛刻的批评家.

hy·per·crit·i·cal [ˌhaipə(:)ˈkritikəl] *a.* 吹毛求疵的,过分苛刻的. **-ly** *ad.*

hy·per·crit·i·cism [ˌhaipə(:)ˈkritisizəm] *n.* 苛刻的批评.

hy·per·du·li·a [ˌhaipədjuːˈlaiə, -duː-] *n.* 【天主】对圣母的最高崇敬,特殊崇敬.

hy·per·e·las·tic [ˌhaipəriˈlæstik] *a.* 【物】超弹性的.

hy·per·e·mi·a [ˌhaipə(:)ˈri(:)miə] *n.* = hyperaemia. **hy·per·e·mic** *a.*

hy·per·es·the·sia [ˌhaipərisˈθiːzjə] *n.* = hyperaesthesia. **hy·per·es·thet·ic** *a.*

hy·per·eu·tec·tic [ˌhaipərjuˈtektik] *a.* 【物】高级低共溶体的.

hy·per·eu·tec·toid [ˌhaipərjuˈtɛktɔid] *n.* 【物】高级低共熔体;过共析. ~ *steel* 过共析钢.

hy·per·fo·cal distance [ˌhaipə(:)ˈfəukl] 【摄】无穷大焦距.

hy·per·frag·ment [ˌhaipə(:)ˈfrægmənt] *n.* 【物】含超裂片.

hy·per·gly·ce·mi·a [ˌhaipəglaiˈsiːmiə] *n.* 【医】高血糖. **hy·per·gly·ce·mic** [-mik] *a.*

hy·per·gol [ˈhaipə(:)gɔl] *n.* 【空】自燃式火箭燃料; 用自燃料的推进系统.

hy·per·gol·ic [ˌhaipə(:)ˈgɔlik, -ˈgɔːl-] *a.* (火箭的)自行着火的,自燃的.

hy·per·in·fla·tion [ˌhaipəinfˈleiʃən] *n.* 过度膨胀.

hy·per·in·su·lin·ism [ˌhaipə(:)ˈinsəlinizm] *n.* 【医】胰岛机能亢进;胰岛素过多.

hy·per·ker·a·to·sis [ˌhaipə(:)ˌkerəˈtəusis] *n.* (*pl.* *-toses* [-siːz]) 【医】①角化过程(症). ②眼角膜细胞增多. **hy·per·ker·a·tot·ic** [-ˈtɔtik] *a.*

hy·per·ki·ne·sia, hy·per·ki·ne·sis [ˌhaipə(:)kaiˈniːʒiə, ˌhaipə(:)kaiˈniːsis] *n.* 【医】运动过度. **hy·per·ki·net·ic** *a.*

hy·per·mar·ket [ˌhaipəˈmɑːkit] *n.* 特级市场; 巨型超级市场.

hy·per·me·ter [haiˈpəːmitə] *n.* 诗体中多余的音节. **-met·ric(al)** [ˌhaipəːˈmetrik(əl)] *a.*

hy·per·me·tro·pi·a [ˌhaipə(:)miˈtrəupiə] *n.* 【医】远视 (*opp.* myopia). **hy·per·me·trop·ic** [-ˈtrɔpik] *a.*

hy·perm·ne·sia [ˌhaipəmˈniːziə] *n.* 【医】记忆增强.

hy·per·on [ˈhaipə(:)rɔn] *n.* 【物】超子.

hy·per·ope [ˈhaipə(:)rəup] *n.* 远视者.

hy·per·o·pi·a [ˌhaipə(:)ˈrəupiə] *n.* = hypermetropia.

hy·per·os·to·sis [ˌhaipərɔsˈtəusis] *n.* (*pl.* *-ses* [-siːz]) 【医】骨肥厚. **hy·per·os·tot·ic** [-ˈtɔtik] *a.*

hy·per·ox·i·a [ˌhaipə(:)ˈrɔksiə] *n.* 【医】体内氧过剩.

hy·per·ox·ide [ˌhaipə(:)ˈrɔksaid] *n.* 【化】过氧化物.

hy·per·phys·i·cal [ˌhaipə(:)ˈfizikl] *a.* ①超肉体的; 超物质的; 超自然的. ②与肉体分开的; 与物质分开的. **hy·per·phys·i·cal·ly** *ad.*

hy·per·pi·tu·i·ta·rism [ˌhaipəpiˈtjuːətərizm, -ˈtuː-] *n.* 【医】①垂体机能亢进. ②由此而引起的巨大发育〔巨大畸形〕. **hy·per·pi·tu·i·tar·y** [-təriː] *a.*

hy·per·plane [ˈhaipəplein] *n.* 【数】超平面.

hy·per·pla·si·a [ˌhaipə(:)ˈpleiʒiə] *n.* 【医】增生, 增殖,数量性肥大.

hy·per·pne·a [ˈhaipəˈniːə, -pəp-] *n.* 呼吸增强, 喘息 (=hyperpnoea). **hy·per·pne·ic** *a.*

hy·per·py·rex·i·a [ˌhaipəpaiˈreksiə] *n.* 【医】高烧,体温过高. **hy·per·py·ret·ic** [-ˈretik] *a.*

hy·per·quan·ti·za·tion [ˈhaipə(:)ˌkwɔntiˈzeiʃən] *n.* 【物】超量子化.

hy·per·sen·si·tive [ˌhaipə(:)ˈsensitiv] *a.* 过敏的, 过敏性的. **-ness** *n.*

hy·per·son·ic [ˌhaipə(:)ˈsɔnik] *a.* 高超音速的〔指超音速五倍以上者〕. ~ **transport** 超高音速飞机〔缩写作 HST〕.

hy·per·sthene [ˈhaipəːsθiːn] *n.* 【矿】紫苏辉石.

hy·per·syn·chro·nous [ˌhaipə(:)ˈsiŋkrənəs] *a.* 【物】超同步的.

hy·per·ten·sion [ˌhaipəːˈtenʃən] *n.* ①【医】高血压. ②过度紧张.

hy·per·ten·sive [ˌhaipə(:)ˈtensiv] *a.* 高血压的. — *n.* 高血压患者.

hy·per·therm [ˈhaipə(:)θəːm] *n.* 【医】人工发热器.

hy·per·thy·roid [ˈhaipə(:)ˈθairɔid] *a.* 甲状腺机能亢进的. — *n.* 甲状腺机能亢进患者. **-ism** *n.* 【医】甲状腺机能亢进.

hy·per·ton·ic [ˌhaipə(:)ˈtɔnik] *a.* ①【医】张力亢进的. ②【化】高渗性. **hy·per·to·nic·i·ty** [-təˈnisiti] *n.*

hy·per·tro·phy [haiˈpəːtrəfi] *n.* ①【医】肥大. ②过度膨胀,过度增大. — *vt., vi.* (使)变得异常肥大. **-trophied, -troph·ic** *a.*

hy·per·ve·loc·i·ty [ˈhaipə(:)viˈlɔsiti] *n.* 超高速,特超声速(指宇宙飞船或核粒子等的运动速度).

hy·per·ven·ti·la·tion [ˌhaipə(:)ˌventiˈleiʃən] *n.* 【医】换气过度. **hy·per·ven·ti·late** [-ˌeit] *vi., vt.*

hy·per·vi·ta·min·o·sis [ˌhaipə(:)ˌvaitəmiˈnəusis] *n.* 【医】维生素过多症.

hyp·es·the·si·a [ˌhipisˈθiːʒə] *n.* 感觉减退(尤指触觉减退). **hyp·es·the·sic** [-ˈθiːsik], **hyp·es·thet·ic** [-ˈθetik] *a.*

hy·pe·thral [hiˈpiːθrəl] *a.* = hypaethral.

hy·pha [ˈhaifə] *n.* (*pl.* *-phae* [-fiː]) 【植】菌丝. **-phal** *a.*

hy·phen [ˈhaifən] *n.* ①【印】连字号〔即"-"〕. ②谈话中音节间的短暂休止. — *vt.* 用连字号连接.

hy·phen·ate [ˈhaifəneit] *vt.* ①用连字号连接;把…用连字号移行. ②用连字号写〔抄、印〕. — *n.* 〔美〕归化的美国移民(=hyphenated American).

hy·phen·at·ed [ˈhaifəneitid] *a.* ①用连字号连接的. ②〔美〕(公民)归化的;关于归化的美国公民的〔因归化的美国公民常被称为 German-Americans, Irish-Americans 等,原国籍与"美籍"之间用连字号连接,用时含有贬意〕. ~ **American** 归化的美国公民. ~ **words** 复合词.

hy·phen·a·tion [ˌhaifəˈneiʃən] *n.* ①用连字号的连接. ②连字号.

hyp·na·gog·ic [ˌhipnəuˈgɔdʒik] *a.* ①催眠的,使瞌睡的. ②(睡眠)似醒非醒状态的.

hyp·no- *comb.f.* 表示"睡眠","催眠术"〔元音前用 hypn-〕: *hypno*genesis, *hypno*therapy.

hyp·no·a·nal·y·sis [ˌhipnəuəˈnælisis] *n.* 催眠精神分析.

hyp·no·gen·e·sis [ˌhipnəuˈdʒenisis] *n.* 催眠. **hyp·no·ge·net·ic** [-dʒeˈnetik] *a.*

hyp·noid [ˈhipnɔid] *a.* 似睡的,似入睡的(=hypnoidal).

hyp·nol·o·gy [hipˈnɔlədʒi] *n.* 睡眠学,催眠学.

hyp·no·pom·pic [ˌhipnəuˈpɔmpik] *a.* 半睡醒状态.

Hyp·nos [ˈhipnɔs] *n.* 【希神】睡神.

hyp·no·sis [hipˈnəusis] (*pl.* *-ses* [-siːz]) *n.* 催眠(状态);催眠术,催眠术研究.

hyp·no·ther·a·py [ˌhipnəuˈθerəpi] *n.* 【医】催眠疗法.

hyp·not·ic [hipˈnɔtik] *a.* ①催眠的; 有催眠性的. ②易受催眠的; 受催眠术影响的. — *n.* ①催眠药. ②在催眠状态中的人;易受催眠的人. **-i·cal·ly** *ad.*

hyp·no·tism [ˈhipnətizəm] *n.* 催眠(术);催眠状态;催眠术研究.
hyp·no·tist [ˈhipnətist] *n.* 催眠术师.
hyp·no·tize [ˈhipnətaiz] *vt.* ①对…施催眠术;使入催眠状态. ②〔俚〕使着迷,使精神恍惚. ③使着迷. **-tizer** *n.* = hypnotist. **-ti·za·tion** *n.*
hy·po[1] [ˈhaipəu] *n.*【化】五水合硫代硫酸钠〔hyposulfite of soda 之略,摄影定像用〕,大苏打,海波〔俗称〕.
hy·po[2] [ˈhaipəu] *n.*〔美口〕①=hypochondria. ②=hypochondriac *(n.)*.
hy·po[3] [ˈhaipəu] *n.* ①皮下注射(=hypodermic injection). ②刺激. ③吸毒成瘾的人. — *vt.* 给…以刺激.
hy·po- *pref.* 表示①"在…下". ②【化】"低下","次","亚"〔元音前用 hyp- *(opp.* hyper-)〕: *hypo*glycemia, *hypo*chlorous.
HYPO =high-power water boiler 大功率沸腾式反应堆.
hy·po·blast [ˈhaipəblæst] *n.*【生】内胚层,下胚层;【植】基芽. **-tic** *a.*
hy·po·bran·chi·al [ˌhaipəuˈbræŋkiəl] *a.*【动】鳃下的.
hy·po·caust [ˈhaipəkɔːst] *n.* ①(古罗马的)炕. ②罗马式火炕供暖装置.
hy·po·cen·ter, hy·po·cen·tre [ˈhaipəusentə] *n.* (核爆的)震源.
hy·po·chlo·rite [ˌhaipəuˈklɔːrait] *n.*【化】次氯酸盐.
hy·po·chlo·rous [ˌhaipəuˈklɔːrəs] *a.*【化】次氯酸的. ~ *acid*【化】次氯酸.
hy·po·chon·dri·a [ˌhaipəuˈkɔndriə] *n.*【医】忧郁症,臆想症,疑病症(指病态的自拟患病).
hy·po·chon·dri·ac [ˌhaipəuˈkɔndriæk] *a.* ①忧郁症的,臆想症的,疑病症的. ②【解】季肋部的. — *n.* 忧郁症患者,臆想症患者,疑病症患者.
hy·po·chon·dri·a·cal [ˌhaipəukɔnˈdraiəkəl] *a.* = hypochondric ①. **-ly** *ad.*
hy·po·chon·dri·um [ˌhaipəuˈkɔndriəm] *n.* *(pl.* **-dri·a** [-ə]*)* ①【医】忧郁症,臆想症,疑病症. ②【解】季肋部.
hy·po·co·ris·tic [ˌhaipəukəˈristik] *a.*【语】爱称的,表示亲爱的.
hy·po·cot·yl [ˌhaipəˈkɔtl] *n.*【植】(下)胚轴.
hy·poc·ri·sy [hiˈpɔkrəsi] *n.* 伪善,虚伪.
hyp·o·crite [ˈhipəkrit] *n.* 伪善者,虚伪的人. ***play the*** ~ 装伪君子.
hyp·o·crit·ic(al) [ˌhipəˈkritik(əl)] *a.* 伪善(者)的,言不由衷的. **-i·cal·ly** *ad.*
hy·po·cy·cloid [ˌhaipəuˈsaiklɔid] *n.*【数】圆内旋轮线,内摆线.
hy·po·derm [ˈhaipədəːm] *n.* ①皮下组织. ②=hypoblast.
hy·po·der·mal [ˌhaipəuˈdəːməl] *a.* ①【植】皮下的;【动】真皮的. ②表皮下的.
hy·po·der·mi·a [ˌhaipəuˈdəːmiə] *n.*【医】皮下组织.
hy·po·der·mic [ˌhaipəuˈdəːmik] *a.* ①皮下的,皮下组织的. ②皮下注射用的. ③刺激性的. — *n.* 皮下注射;皮下注射器. ~ **canal** 皮下管. ~ **injection** 皮下注射. ~ **medication** 皮下注射治疗. ~ **needle** 皮下注射针头,安上针头的皮下注射器. ~ **syringe** 皮下注射器. **-mi·cal·ly** *ad.*
hy·po·der·mis [ˌhaipəuˈdəːmis] *n.* ①【植】下皮;下胚层. ②【动】下皮;(昆虫的)真皮.
hy·po·eu·tec·tic [ˌhaipəuju(ː)ˈtektik] *a.*【冶】亚共晶的.
hy·po·eu·tec·toid [ˌhaipəuju(ː)ˈtektɔid] *a.*【冶】亚共析的. ~ **steel** 亚共析钢.
hy·po·gas·tric [ˈhaipəuˈgæstrik] *a.* 腹下部的,下腹的.
hy·po·gas·tri·um [ˈhaipəuˈgæstriəm] *n.* *(pl.* **-tria** [-striə]*)*【解】腹下部,下腹.
hy·po·ge·al [haipəuˈdʒiːəl] *a.* ①地中的,起于地中的;地下的. ②【植】地下生的〔如花生、松露〕;(尤指)(子叶)留土的. ③【动】(打洞、生活、成长于)地下的〔如某些昆虫、动物等〕(=hypogean).
hy·po·gene [ˈhaipədʒiːn] *a.*【地】地面下形成的,深成的;上升的. ~ **rocks** 深成岩. ~ **water** 上升水.
hy·pog·e·nous [haiˈpɔdʒinəs] *a.*【植】在下着生的〔如某些羊齿植物叶背面着生的孢子〕.
hy·po·ge·ous [ˌhaipəuˈdʒiːəs] *a.* = hypogeal.
hy·po·glos·sal [ˌhaipəuˈglɔsl] *a.* 舌下的. — *n.* 舌下神经.
hy·po·gly·ce·mi·a [ˌhaipəuglaiˈsiːmiə] *n.*【医】低血糖.
hy·pog·na·thous [haiˈpɔgnəθəs] *a.*【动】下颚突出的,下口式的.
hy·pog·y·nous [haiˈpɔdʒinəs] *a.*【植】①(花被,雄蕊)下位的. ②有下位排列部分的. ~ **flowers** 下位花. **-ny** [-ni] *n.*
hy·poid gear [ˈhaipɔid]【机】偏轴伞齿轮.
hy·po·ki·ne·sis [ˌhaipəukiˈniːsis] *n.*【医】运动减退(=hypokinesia). **hy·poki·net·ic** [-ˈnetik] *a.*
hy·po·lim·ni·on [ˌhaipəuˈlimniɔn] *n.* 深水缺氧层.
hy·po·ma·ni·a [ˌhaipəuˈmeiniə] *n.*【医】轻躁狂. **hy·po·man·ic** [-ˈmænik] *a.*
hy·po·nas·ty [ˈhaipəˌnæsti] *n.*【植】偏下性. **hy·po·nas·tic** [-ˈnæstik] *a.*
hy·po·ni·trite [ˌhaipəuˈnaitrait] *n.*【化】连二次硝酸盐.
hy·po·ni·trous [ˌhaipəuˈnaitrəs] *a.* ~ **acid**【化】连二次硝酸.
hy·po·phos·phate [ˌhaipəuˈfɔsfeit] *n.*【化】连二磷酸盐.
hy·po·phos·phite [ˌhaipəuˈfɔsfait] *n.*【化】次磷酸盐.
hy·poph·y·sis [haiˈpɔfisis] *n.* *(pl.* **-ses** [-siːz]*)* *n.*【解】垂体.
hy·po·pi·tu·i·ta·rism [ˌhaipəupiˈtju(ː)ətərizm] *n.*【医】①垂体机能减退. ②垂体机能减退症〔如儿童发育减慢,性腺活动减弱等〕. **hy·po·pi·tu·i·tar·y** [-təri] *a.*
hy·po·pla·si·a [ˌhaipəuˈpleizjə] *n.* ①【医】发育不全. ②细胞灭生(现象). **-plas·tic** [-ˈplæztik] *a.*
hy·po·py·on [haiˈpəupiɔn] *n.*【医】眼前房积脓.
hy·po·scope [ˈhaipəskəup] *n.* 蟹眼式望远镜.
hy·po·sen·si·tize [ˌhaipəuˈsensitaiz] *vt.* *(-tiz·ed;-tiz·ing)* 使(对抗菌素的)敏感度减退. **hy·po·sen·si·ti·za·tion** *n.*
hy·pos·ta·sis [haiˈpɔstəsis] *n.* *(pl.* **-ses** [-siːz]*)* ①【哲】本质,实在. ②【宗】三位一体之一,基督人格. ③【医】坠积性充血. ④【化】沉渣,液底沉淀. ⑤【生】下位.
hy·po·stat·ic(al) [ˌhaipəuˈstætik(əl)] *a.* ①【哲】本质的,实在的,实体的. ②沉下的. ③下位的. ~ **union**【宗】基督的位格结合(神人合一). **-i·cal·ly** *ad.*
hy·pos·ta·tize [haiˈpɔstətaiz] *vt.* *(-tiz·ed; -tiz·ing)* ①【哲】把…视为实存;使实体化. ②把个人的存在归于…;使人格化. **-ti·za·tion** [haiˌpɔstətiˈzeiʃən] *n.*
hy·po·style [ˈhaipəustail] *a.*【建】多柱式建筑的. — *n.* 多柱式建筑.
hy·po·sul·fite, hy·po·sul·phite [ˌhaipəuˈsʌlfait] *n.*【化】①连二亚硫酸盐. ②= hydrosulfite. ③sodium thiosulfate 的误称.
hy·po·sul·fu·rous [ˌhaipəusəlˈfjuərəs] *a.* ~ **acid**【化】连二亚硫酸.
hy·po·tax·is [ˌhaipəuˈtæksis] *n.*【语法】(句法中)从属结构,主从关系(如主句与从句等). **hy·po·tac·tic** [-ˈtæktik] *a.*
hy·po·ten·sion [ˌhaipəuˈtenʃən] *n.*【医】低血压,血压过低. **hy·po·ten·sive** *a.*
hy·pot·e·nuse [haiˈpɔtinjuːz] *n.*【数】弦,斜边.
hypoth. = ①hypothesis. ②hypothetical.
hy·po·thal·a·mus [ˌhaipəuˈθæləməs] *n.* *(pl.* **-mi** [-mai]*)*

【医】丘脑下部，下丘脑. **hy·po·tha·lam·ic** [-θəˈlæmik] *a.*

hy·poth·ec [haiˈpɔθik] *n.* 【法】(不转移财产所有权的)抵押权，担保权. ~ **bank** 劝业银行.

hy·poth·e·car·y [haiˈpɔθikeri] *a.* 【法】抵押的；由抵押而获得的.

hy·poth·e·cate [haiˈpɔθikeit] *vt.* (以不转移占有权的方式)抵押(财产). **-ca·tion** *n.* ①抵押. ②押船契约；担保契约. ③对抵押财产的索赔权. **-ca·tor** *n.*

hy·po·ther·mal [ˌhaipəuˈθəːməl] *a.* ①不冷不热的，温热的. ②体温过低的. ③(某些矿床的)在300°C以上温度下产生的.

hy·po·ther·mi·a [ˌhaipəuˈθəːmiə] *n.* 体温过低.

hy·poth·e·sis [haiˈpɔθisis] *n.* *(pl.* **-ses** [-siːz]*)* ①假设；假说. ②【逻】前提.

hy·poth·e·size [haiˈpɔθisaiz] *vi., vt.* 假设，假定.

hy·po·thet·ic(al) [ˌhaipəuˈθetik(əl)] *a.* ①假设的. ②【逻】有前提的 *(opp.* categorical). **-cal·ly** *ad.*

hy·po·thy·roid [ˈhaipəuˈθairɔid] *a.* 【医】甲状腺机能减退的. —*n.*【医】甲状腺机能减退的人. **-ism** *n.* 甲状腺机能减退.

hy·po·ton·ic [ˌhaipəuˈtɔnik] *a.* ①【医】张力减退的. ②【化】低渗性的. **hy·po·to·nic·i·ty** [-təˈnisiti] *n.*

hy·po·xan·thine [ˌhaipəuˈzænθiːn, -θin] *n.* 【生化】次黄嘌呤.

hy·pox·i·a [haiˈpɔksiə] *n.* 【医】缺氧症.

hyp·so- *comb. f.* 表示"高度": *hypso*meter.

hyp·sog·ra·phy [hipˈsɔgrəfi] *n.* ①地形测绘学. ②等高线法. ③测高学，测高法. ④表示不同高度的地形图.

hyp·som·e·ter [hipˈsɔmitə] *n.* ①沸点测高计. ②(树木的)三角法测高计.

hyp·som·e·try [hipˈsɔmitri] *n.* 测高术. **hyp·so·met·ric** [ˌhipsəuˈmetrik] *a.*

hy·ra·coid [ˈhairəkɔid] *n.* = hyrax. —*a.* 蹄兔的.

hy·rax [ˈhairæks] *n.* *(pl.* ~**es**, **-ra·ces** [-rəsiːz]*)*【动】非洲蹄兔，岩狸.

Hyr·ca·ni·a [həˈkeiniə] *n.* 赫卡尼亚〔古波斯和马其顿王国的一个省名〕. **Hyr·ca·ni·an** *a., n.* 赫卡尼亚地方的(人).

hy·son [ˈhaisn] *n.* 熙春茶〔中国绿茶的一种〕.

hy·spy [ˈhaispai] *n.* (游戏)躲猫，捉迷藏.

hys·sop [ˈhisəp] *n.* 【植】海索草；海索草属植物.

hys·ter·ec·to·my [ˌhistəˈrektəmi] *n.*【医】子宫切除术.

hys·ter·e·sis [ˌhistəˈriːsis] *n.* ①【物】磁滞. ②【物】滞后现象[作用]；迟滞性. ③平衡阻碍. **hys·ter·et·ic** [-ˈretik] *a.*

hys·te·ri·a [hisˈtiəriə] *n.* ①【医】癔病；(特指女人的)歇斯底里. ②病态的兴奋.

hys·ter·ic [hisˈterik] *a.* ①癔病的；歇斯底里的. ②病态感情[兴奋]式的. —*n.* 歇斯底里患者；〔*pl.*〕发歇斯底里；发狂. *go off (fall) into ~s* 发歇斯底里.

hys·ter·i·cal [hisˈterikəl] *a.* 癔病的，歇斯底里的；患癔病的. **-ly** *ad.*

hys·ter·o- *comb. f.* 表示"子宫": *hystero*tomy.

hys·ter·oid, hys·te·roi·dal [ˈhistərɔid, ˌhistəˈrɔidl] *a.* 【医】癔病似的.

hys·ter·ol·o·gy [ˌhistəˈrɔlədʒi] *n.* 【医】子宫学.

hys·ter·on-prot·e·ron [ˈhistərɔnˈprɔtərɔn] *n.* 〔G.〕①【修】逆序法；次序倒转. 〔如 I die, I faint, I fall〕. ②【逻】倒逆论法.

hys·ter·ot·o·my [ˌhistəˈrɔtəmi] *n.* 【医】子宫切开术.

hys·tri·co·mor·phic [ˌhistrikəˈmɔːfik] *a.* 【动】豪猪形啮齿动物(包括豪猪、豚鼠、大耳鼰鼠等)的.

hyte [hait] *a.* 〔古，方〕疯狂的.

hy·ther·graph [ˈhaiθəgrɑːf] *n.* 【气】温湿图，温度与湿度关系图.

Hz = hertz.

I

I, i [ai] *(pl.* ***I's, i's*** [aiz]*)* ①英语字母表第九字母. ②罗马数字I. ③(I) I 字形的物体，工字形物体. *I-bar* 工字钢，工字条. *I-beam* 工字梁，工字铁条. ***dot the i's and cross the t's.*** 给字母 i 加点，给字母 t 加短横；点横不丢；一丝不苟；一板一眼地细讲.

I [ai] *pro.* *(pl.* ***we****)* 〔人称代词、第一人称、单数、主格 *(poss. adj.* ***my****; obj.* ***me****; poss. pro.* ***mine****)*〕我. *It is I.* 是我〔口语也用 It's me〕. *It is I who am to blame.* 应当负责任的是我. *Am I not ...?* 我难道不是…？(口语通常说作〔美〕*Ain't I?*〔英〕*An't [Aren't] I?*) *You and I.* 你和我(英语习惯，除特殊情况外，一般不说 I and you [he, she]). —*n.* *(pl.* ***I's*** 或 ***Is****)* ①自我. ②极端自私的人，说话老是"我怎么怎么"的人. ③[the I]【哲】自我意识. *You shouldn't use too many ~'s in writing.* 写文章写信时不要老用我怎么怎么的字眼.

I., i. = ①island(s). ②Idaho. ③Independent. ④Iowa. ⑤incisor. ⑥interest. ⑦intransitive. ⑧isle(s). ⑨【化】iodine.

-i- *comb. f.* 多用于拉丁语词源的复合词中: curv*i*linear, omn*i*vorous; cune*i*form, French*i*fy.

-i [-ai] 拉丁语系名词的复数后缀: alumn*i* (< alumn*us*), foc*i* (< foc*us*).

-ia ①拉丁、希腊语名词后缀: hyster*ia*, milit*ia*. ②国名后缀: Austral*ia*. ③希腊、拉丁语名词的复数形: paraphernal*ia*, regal*ia*. ④与人名有关系的花名: dahl*ia*, wistar*ia*. ⑤动植物分类上的复数形: Cryptomer*ia*.

Ia. = Iowa.

i.a. = 〔L.〕*in absentia* 缺席.

IAAF = International Amateur Athletic Federation 国际业余田径联合会.

IADL = International Association of Democratic Lawyers 国际民主法律工作者协会.

IAEA = International Atomic Energy Agency (联合国)国际原子能机构.

IAF = International Astronautical Federation 国际星际航空联合会.

I·a·go [iːˈɑːgəu] *n.* ①埃古〔莎士比亚剧作《奥赛罗》中的反面人物〕. ②阴险奸猾的人.

-ial *suf.* 表示"具有…性质的"；"属于…的": ceremon*ial*.

IAMAP = International Association of Meteorology and Atmospheric Physics 国际气象和大气物理协会.

i·amb [ˈaiæmb] *n.* = iambus.

i·am·bic [aiˈæmbik] *a.* (英诗)短长格的，抑扬[弱强]格的. —*n.* ①短长格；抑扬格. ②〔常用复〕短长[抑扬]格的诗.

i·am·bus [aiˈæmbəs] *n.* *(pl.* ***-bi*** [-bai], ***-buses****)*【韵】短

长格，抑扬格。

I·an [iən] *n.* 伊恩〔男子名，John 的异体〕。

-ian *suf.* = -an: Christ*ian*, reptil*ian*.

-i·an·a *suf.* = -ana.

IAP = international airport 国际机场。

IAR = 〔美〕Institute for Atomic Research.

iar·o·vi·za·tion [ˌjɑːrəvaiˈzeiʃən] *n.* = vernalization.

iar·o·vize [ˈjɑːrəvaiz] *vt.* (用人工方法)使(植物)提早开花结实 (=vernalize)。

IAS = ①Institute of Aeronautical Sciences 〔美〕航空科学学院。②indicated airspeed【空】指示空速。

-i·a·sis *suf.* 表示"病"，"病态"：elephant*iasis*.

IATA = International Air Transport Association 国际航空运输协会。

i·at·ric(·al) [iˈætrik(əl), ai-] *a.* 医学的，医疗的，医生的，药物的。

-i·at·rics *comb. f.* 构成名词，表示医学分科：ped*iatrics*.

i·at·ro·chem·is·try [aiˌætrəˈkemistri] *n.*【医】医疗化学。

i·at·ro·gen·ic [aiˌætrəˈdʒenik] *a.* 由治疗引起的〔尤指由医生的话引起病人的臆测性症候〕。

-i·a·try *comb. f.* 构成名词，表示医治法：psych*iatry*.

IAZ = inner artillery zone 高射炮防空禁区。

ib. = 〔L.〕*ibidem.*

I·ba·dan [iˈbædən] *n.* 伊巴丹〔尼日利亚城市〕。

I·be·ria [aiˈbiəriə] *n.* 伊比利亚〔西班牙半岛的古名〕。

I·be·ri·an [aiˈbiəriən] *a.* (包含西班牙、葡萄牙二国在内的)伊比利亚(半岛)的；伊比利亚人的；伊比利亚语的。— *n.* 伊比利亚语。

i·bex [ˈaibeks] *n.* (*pl.* ~*es*, ***ibices*** [ˈibisiːz]) (阿尔卑斯山的)野山羊。

Ib·i·bi·o [ˌibiˈbiːəu] *n.* (*pl.* ~*(s)*) ①伊比比欧人〔尼日利亚东南部人〕。②伊比比欧语。

ibid. = 〔L.〕*ibidem.*

i·bi·dem [iˈbaidem] *ad.* 〔L.〕在同书，在同章，在同句，在同处，同上，同前〔略 *ib*, *ibid*〕。

-i·bil·i·ty *suf.* 表示"可能性"：feas*ibility*.

i·bis [ˈaibis] *n.* (*pl.* ~*(es)*)【动】鹮，朱鹭；鹮科的涉禽。*the sacred* ~ (古埃及的)灵鸟。

-i·ble *suf.* 表示"可"，"能"，"得"，"堪"〔与 *-able* 同义，但除拉丁系形容词外少用〕：divis*ible*, permiss*ible*.

IBM =① intercontinental ballistic missile 洲际弹道导弹。②International Business Machines Corporation 〔美〕国际商用机器公司。

I·bo [ˈiːbəu] *n.* (*pl.* ~*(s)*) ①伊博人〔尼日利亚东南部的非洲人〕。②伊博语。

IBRD = International Bank for Reconstruction and Development (联合国)国际复兴(与)开发银行。

Ib·sen [ˈibsen], **Henrik** 亨利·易卜生〔1828—1906，挪威剧作家，以社会问题剧 (*problem play*) 形式对社会作批评、讽刺〕。

Ib·sen·ism [ˈibsənizəm] *n.* ①挪威戏剧家易卜生提倡的戏剧创作方法。②(提倡演社会问题戏剧的)易卜生主义。

Ib·sen·ist [ˈibsənist] *n.* 易卜生主义者。

Ib·sen·ite [ˈibsənait] *n.* ①易卜生的崇拜者。②模仿易卜生的剧作家。— *a.* 易卜生的，具有易卜生或其剧作特点的。

IC = ①integrated circuit【无】集成电路。②interior communications 内部通讯联络。

I.C. = *Iesus Christus* (= Jesus Christ); inductance-capacitance; Issued Capital.

i.c. = ionization chamber; between meals【医】(处方)在两餐之间。

i/c = in charge; internal combustion.

-ic¹ *suf.*〔构成形容词〕①表示"…的"，"…似的"，"…性的"：bas*ic*, poet*ic*. ②表示"与…有关的"：Asiat*ic*, volcan*ic*. ③表示"由…产生的"，"由…引起的"：photograph*ic*, symphon*ic*. ④表示"由…组成的"，"含有…的"：alcohol*ic*, dactyl*ic*. ⑤表示"原子价较高的"〔指与 -ous 结尾的词相比〕：ferr*ic*, sulphur*ic*.

-ic² *suf.*〔构成名词〕①表示"学术"，"艺术"：arithmet*ic*, log*ic*, mus*ic*. ②表示"具有某种性质或特征"：class*ic*, crit*ic*. ③表示"呈现出…"，"受…影响"：rust*ic*. ④表示"产生"：anaesthet*ic*.

ICA = International Cooperative Alliance (联合国)国际合作社联盟。

-i·cal *suf.* 构成形容词，表示"…的"，"…似的"：chem*ical*, mus*ical*.

-i·cal·ly *suf.* 构成与 -ic, -ical 相应的副词：poet*ically*, com*ically*.

ICAO = International Civil Aviation Organization (联合国)国际民用航空组织。

I·car·i·an [aiˈkeəriən] *a.* (象神话中的 Icarus 飞得过高、致使其蜡翼为太阳融化那样)过分冒险的。

ICARUS = intercontinental aerospacecraft range unlimited system 航程无限的洲际宇宙火箭。

Ic·a·rus [ˈaikərəs] *n.*【希神】(蜡翼人)伊卡洛斯〔建筑师 Daedalus 之子，以蜡翼飞上天空，但因飞得过高，蜡翼为太阳融化，坠海而死〕。

ICBM = intercontinental ballistic missile 洲际弹道导弹。

ICC = ①International Chamber of Commerce 国际商会。②Interstate Commerce Commission 〔美〕州际商务委员会。

ice [ais] *n.* ①冰，冰块。②〔英〕雪糕，冰淇淋 (= ice cream)；〔美〕冰凉饮料〔点心〕。③冰状物，糖衣。④(态度)冷淡。⑤〔美俚〕钻石。⑥贿赂。*eat an* ~ 吃一块雪糕。*two strawberry* ~*s* 两杯冰杨梅。*water* ~ 冰糕。***be made of*** ~ 冷若冰霜。***be on [over] thin*** ~ 如履薄冰，处境极为艰险。***break the*** ~ 起头；打破沉闷，开口。***cut no [little]*** ~ 〔美口〕不起作用，无效。***find [get] one's*** ~ ***legs*** 开始学会滑冰。***have one's brains on*** ~ 〔口〕保持冷静。***on*** ~ ①〔美俚〕储备，贮存。②在监狱中。③有获胜〔成功〕的把握。***open*** ~ (不妨碍航行的)散冰。***put ... on*** ~ ①把…暂时搁起，把…遗忘。②杀死…。③有把握将…握在手中。***skate on [over] thin*** ~ = ***be on thin ice. straight off the*** ~ 立刻；(食品等)新鲜的。— *vt.* ①冰冻；使成冰。②用冰覆盖，用冰封冻 (*over*)。③加糖衣(在糖果上)。④〔美俚〕谋杀，凶杀 (*out*)。⑤〔美俚〕(社交上)忽视，排斥 (*out*)。*The pond was* ~*d over.* 池子给冰封起来了。~ *wine* 冰一冰酒。***be*** ~***d up*** (船)被冰冻结起来了。~ ***the decision [game]*** 〔美口〕保证胜利。~ ***up*** 用冰填满。— *vi.* 结冰 (*up*, *over*)。~ **age** ①【地】冰期；冰河时代。~ **ax(e)** (登山用的)破冰斧。~ **bag** 冰袋〔医用〕。~**berg** ①冰山；流冰。②不怕冷的人；感情上冷冰冰的人。③表面上呈现的东西，(事物全貌的)一小部分。~**berg lettuce**【植】冰山形莴苣〔一种卷叶莴苣，叶子不大不小，在顶部紧密地聚成圆形〕。~**blink** (冰原上的)反光。~**boat** 冰上滑行船；破冰船。~**bound** *a.* 被冰封锁着的，被冰封冻着的。~**box** 冰箱；〔美俚〕严寒地带；〔美俚〕单人牢房。~**breaker** ①破冰船；碎冰器。②基本收费，(出租汽车的)首里收费。~**cap** 冰盖；冰冠。~ **chest** = ~box 冷箱，冰库。~ **coating** 敷冰；结冰。~**-cold** *a.* 极冷的，冰冷的。~ **cream** 冰淇淋。~**-cream** *a.* 乳白色的。~**fall** ①冰布(冰川陡峭部分)。②冰崩。~ **field** (两极地方的)冰原。~**floe** (海上)大浮冰。~**foot** (两极地方的)冰壁。~**-free** *a.* 不冻的 (*an* ~*-free port* 不冻港)。~ **glass** 冰花状玻璃。~ **hockey** 冰球，冰上曲棍球。~**house** 冰室，冰窖；制冰场所；(爱斯基摩人的)冰屋。~**jam** ①流冰壅塞。②阻塞，僵局。~**khana** 冰上汽车比赛。~ **machine** 制冰机。~**man** 〔美〕制冰的人；卖冰的人；

冰上旅行家；善于在冰上行走的人。~ **milk** 冻奶油糕。~ **needle**【气】冰针。~**-out**（水面冰块）融化。~ **pack** 浮冰群；〔美〕冰袋。~ **pantomime** = ~ show。~**-paper**（制图用）透明纸。~ **pick**（餐桌上用的）碎冰锥。~ **plant**【植】冰叶日中花。~ **rink** 滑冰场。~ **run** 冰橇滑行路。~ **sheet**（长期覆盖着陆地的）大冰原。~ **shelf** 冰棚；（两极地方的）陆缘冰。~ **show** 冰上表演。~ **skate**〔常 *pl.*〕（冰鞋下的）冰刀。~**-skate** *vi.* 溜冰。~ **sucker** 棒冰，冰棍。~**-tray**（冰箱内）制冰块的盘子。~**-up** 全面结冰。~ **water**〔美〕冰水；雪水。~ **yacht** 冰上快艇。

-ice *suf.* 构成名词，表示"状态"，"性质"：just*ice*, serv*ice*.

Ice. = Iceland; Icelandic.

iced [aist] *a.* 用冰封着的，加了糖衣的。~**-water** 冰过的水。

Icel. = Iceland; Icelandic.

Ice·land [ˈaislənd] *n.* 冰岛〔欧洲〕。~ *moss*【植】（可供食用的）地衣。~ *spar*【矿】冰洲石（双折射透明方解石）。

Ice·land·er [ˈaisləndə] *n.* 冰岛人。

Ice·lan·dic [aisˈlændik] *a.* 冰岛的；冰岛人的；冰岛语的；冰岛文化的。— *n.* 冰岛语（北日耳曼语）。

ICFTU = International Confederation of Free Trade Unions 国际自由工会联合会。

Ich·a·bod [ˈikəbɔd] *n.* 伊卡博德〔男子名〕。

ich·neu·mon [ikˈnjuːmən] *n.*【动】①獴。②姬峰（= ~-fly）。

ich·nite [ˈiknait] *n.*【地】化石足迹。

ich·n(o)- *comb. f.* 表示"痕迹"，"足迹"：*ichno*graphy.

ich·no·graph [ˈiknəugrɑːf] *n.* 平面图。

ich·nog·ra·phy [ikˈnɔgrəfi] *n.* 平面图法。**-no·graph·i·c(al)** *a.*

ich·no·lite [ˈiknəlait] *n.* = ichnite.

ich·nol·o·gy [ikˈnɔlədʒi] *n.*【地】化石足迹学，足迹学。**ich·no·log·i·cal** *a.*

i·chor [ˈaikɔː] *n.* ①【希神】（诸神血管中的）灵液。②【医】腐液，创液，脓水。

i·chor·ous [ˈaikərəs] *a.*【医】腐液的，脓水的。

ich·thy·ic [ˈikθiːik] *a.* 鱼的；有鱼的特性的。

ich·thy(o)- *comb. f.* 表示"鱼类的"，"象鱼的"〔元音前用 *ichthy-*〕：*ichthyo*logy.

ich·thy·og·ra·phy [ikθiˈɔgrəfi] *n.* 鱼类志，鱼族学，鱼论。

ich·thy·oid [ˈikθiɔid] *a.* 象鱼的，鱼状的。— *n.* 鱼形脊椎动物。

ich·thy·ol [ˈikθiɔl] *n.*【药】鱼石脂，鱼石脂磺酸铵。

ich·thy·ol·a·try [ˌikθiˈɔlətri] *n.* 鱼神崇拜。

ich·thy·o·lite [ˈikθiəlait] *n.* 鱼化石。

ich·thy·ol·o·gist [ˌikθiˈɔlədʒist] *n.* 鱼类学家，鱼学研究者。

ich·thy·ol·o·gy [ˌikθiˈɔlədʒi] *n.* ①鱼类学。②鱼类研究。

ich·thy·oph·a·gous [ˌikθiˈɔfəgəs] *a.* 食鱼的。

ich·thy·oph·a·gy [ˌikθiˈɔfədʒi] *n.* 以鱼为食。

ich·thy·or·nis [ikθiˈɔːnis] *n.*【动】鱼鸟。

ich·thy·o·saur [ˈikθiəsɔː] *n.* (*pl.* ~*ia*)【古生】鱼龙。

ich·thy·o·saur·us [ˌikθiəˈsɔːrəs] *n.* (*pl.* ~*es*) = ichthyosaur.

ich·thy·o·sis [ˌikθiˈəusis] *n.*【医】鱼鳞癣。**ich·thy·ot·ic** *a.*

ICI = Imperial Chemical Industries〔英〕帝国化学工业公司。

-i·cian *suf.* 构成名词，表示"精通者"，"（专）家"，"能手"：mus*ician*, phys*ician*.

i·ci·cle [ˈaisikl] *n.* 冰柱，冷冰冰的人。**-d** *a.*

i·ci·ly [ˈaisili] *ad.* 冰似地，冰冷地，冷淡地。

i·ci·ness [ˈaisinis] *n.* 冰冷，冰冷的状态。

Ic·ing [ˈaisiŋ] *n.* ①（糕点的）糖霜，酥皮。②【空】飞机外身的霜冻。

ICJ = International Court of Justice（联合国）国际法院。

Ickes [ˈikis] *n.* 伊基斯〔姓氏〕。

i·ck·le[1] [ˈikl] *n.*〔英方〕= icicle.

ick·le[2] [ˈikl] *a.*〔儿〕= little.

ick·y [ˈiki] *a.* (*ick·i·er, ick·i·est*) ①非常讨厌的。②粘得难过的。③太甜的，多愁善感得使人腻烦的。**-i·ly** *ad.* **-i·ness** *n.*

ICM = intercontinental missile 洲际导弹。

i·con [ˈaikɔn] (*pl.* ~*s* [-z], *i·co·nes* [-kəniːz]) *n.* ①人像；肖像；画像；雕像；（学术书的）插画。②【宗】圣像。③偶像，崇拜对象。④【逻】类似记号〔表现〕。**-ize** *vt.* 把…作为偶像，盲目崇拜。

i·con·ic(al) [aiˈkɔnik(əl)] *a.* ①人像的；圣像的；偶像的；偶像般的。②老一套的，风格固定的。

i·con(o)- *comb. f.* 表示"像"：*icono*latry.

i·con·o·clasm [aiˈkɔnəˌklæzəm] *n.* ①偶像破坏；圣像破坏。②对传统观念的攻击。

i·con·o·clast [aiˈkɔnəklæst] *n.* ①反对崇拜圣像的人。②反对崇拜偶像的人。③攻击传统观念的人。**i·con·o·clas·tic** [aiˌkɔnəˈklæstik] *a.* **i·con·o·clas·ti·cal·ly** *ad.*

i·co·nog·ra·pher [ˌaikɔˈnɔgrəfə] *n.* 肖像学者，肖像研究家。

i·co·nog·ra·phy [ˌaikɔˈnɔgrəfi] *n.* ①肖像画法。②肖像学，肖像研究。③插画，图解。**i·con·o·graph·i·c(al)** *a.*

i·co·nol·a·ter [ˌaikɔˈnɔlətə] *n.* 圣像〔偶像〕崇拜者。

i·co·nol·a·try [ˌaikɔˈnɔlətri] *n.* 圣像〔偶像〕崇拜。

i·co·nol·o·gy [ˌaikɔˈnɔlədʒi] *n.* ①【宗】圣像学；偶像学。②圣像；偶像（总称）。③象征性表现；象征主义。— **i·con·o·log·i·cal** [aiˌkɔnəˈlɔdʒikl] *a.* **i·co·nol·o·gist** *n.*

i·co·nom·e·ter [ˌaikəˈnɔmitə] *n.*【摄】反光镜；【测】测距镜；测影仪；录象器；取景器。

i·con·o·scope [aiˈkɔnəskəup] *n.*【物】光电摄象管，光电析象管。*image* ~ 移象光电摄象管。

i·co·nos·ta·sis [ˌaikəˈnɔstəsis] *n.* (*pl.* *-ses* [-ˌsiːz]) （东正教）圣障，圣壁。亦作 **i·con·o·stas** [aiˈkɔnəˌstæs].

i·co·sa·he·dron [ˈaikəusəˈhedrən] *n.* (*pl.* ~*s* 或 *-ra* [-rə])【数】二十面体。

ICRC = International Committee of the Red Cross 红十字国际委员会。

ICRP = International Commission on Radiological Protection 国际放射性辐射防护委员会。

-ics *suf.* 构成复数名词。①〔用作单数或复数〕表示"…学"，"…术"：kinet*ics*, phys*ics*. ②〔用作复数〕表示（特定的）"实践"，"活动"，"体系"，"性质"：acrobat*ics*, mechan*ics*.

I.C.S. = Indian Civil Service; International Correspondence School(s)〔美〕国际函授学校（网）。

I.C.T. = inflammation of connective tissue; Institute of Clay Technology; International Critical Tables.

ic·ter·ic [ikˈterik] *a.*【医】黄疸的。

ic·ter·us [ˈiktərəs] *n.* ①【医】黄疸。②【植】叶黄病。

ic·tus [ˈiktəs] *n.* (*pl.* ~*(es)*) ①（诗中的）强音，扬音。②【医】暴发病；搏动；冲击。~ *solis* 日射病，中暑（= sunstroke）。

ICU = intensive care unit 特别医疗单位。

I.C.W. = Inter-American Commission of Women; interrupted continuous wave【无】断续等幅波。

i·cy [ˈaisi] *a.* (*i·ci·er; -ci·est*) ①冰封着的，冰多的。②冰似的，冰冷的。③冷淡的，生疏的。*the* ~ *North* 冰天雪地的北方。*an* ~ *welcome* 冷淡的欢迎。*an* ~ *wind* 寒风。

ID = identification 台名识别〔电台或电视台暂时中断广播以宣布台名〕。

ID, I.D. [ˈaidiː] *n.* *(pl. ID's, I.D.'s)* 身分证 (= ID card, I.D. card).
Id. = Idaho.
id. = 〔L.〕 *idem.*
I'd [aid] 〔口〕 = I had; I would; I should.
id [id] *n.*【生】遗传基质;本能冲动.
I.D. = Infantry Division; inside diameter; Intelligence Department.
-id[1] *suf.* ①表示"…(姑)娘": Dana*id.* ② 表示"…流星": Leon*id*【天】狮子座流星. ③用作叙事诗的题名: Aene*id.*
-id[2] *suf.*【动】用作科属动物的名词、形容词: arachn*id.*
-id[3] *suf.* 用以形成原为拉丁语名词的名词: chrysal*id*, pyram*id.*
-id[4] *suf.* 由拉丁语动词、名词作成表示状态的形容词: hor*rid*, flu*id*, sol*id.*
-id[5] *suf.* 〔美〕 = -ide.
I·da [ˈaidə] *n.* 艾达〔女子名〕.
IDA = International Development Association (联合国)国际开发协会.
Ida. = Idaho.
-i·dae [iˈdiː] *suf.*【动】表示"…科": Fel*idae.*
I·da·ho [ˈaidəhəu] *n.* 爱达荷〔美国州名〕.
I·da·ho·an [ˈaidəˌhəuən] *a.* 爱达荷州的. — *n.* 爱达荷州人.
-ide *suf.*【化】表示"…化合物": brom*ide*, carb*ide*, ox*ide.*
IDDD = International Direct Distance Dialing 国际直通长途电话.
i·de·a [aiˈdiə] *n.* ①主意;念头;思想;计划,打算;意见. ②想象,模糊想法. ③【哲】理念,理性概念,观念;【心】表象. ④【乐】主题,乐句,音型. *Eastern [Western] ~s* 东方[西方]思想. *the general ~ of an article* 文章大意. *a good ~* 好主意. *a man of ~s* 足智多谋的人. *An ~ struck me.* 我想出了一个主意. *conceive an ~* 起念头. *full of ~s* 主意多. *Such an ~ never occurred to me.* 我从来没有这样想过. *the ~ of such a thing!* 多糊涂的想法! *the young ~* 小孩子的想法. *What is your ~?* 你的意见怎样? *I have no ~ (as to) what you mean.* 我摸不清你的意思. *absolute ~*【哲】绝对观念. *a fixed ~* 固定观念,固执的想法. ***an ~ outline of [about]*** 关于…的设想. ***in ~*** 想象上 *(opp.* in reality). ***put ~s in sb.'s head*** 使某人存奢望,使某人得意忘形. ***run away with the ~*** 不加考虑地附和某种意见,轻率地下结论. ***That's the ~.*** 〔口〕对了,就是这意思! 这行! 这我同意! ***the big [grand, great] ~*** 〔美〕(往往表示讽刺)高见,好主意. ***What's the big ~?*** 〔美〕有何高见? ***The ~!*** 〔口〕什么! 这! 糊涂! 〔表示愤怒、惊异、轻蔑〕. ***upon an ~*** 心生一计. ***What an ~!*** 〔口〕什么话! 多么荒唐! **~ man** 谋士. **~phobia** 惧思考症.
i·de·aed, i·de·a'd [aiˈdiəd] *a.* 有某种看法的,主意多的.
i·de·al [aiˈdiəl] *a.* ①理想的,典型的. ②观念的;想象的;空想的;不切实际的. ③唯心论的;理想主义的. *an ~ place for a holiday* 度假的理想场所. *~ happiness* 想象中的幸福. — *n.* 理想;典型,模范;空想的事物;【数】理想子环,理想数. *beau ~* 十全十美的理想. ***the Ideal and the Real*** 理想与现实. ***That is only an ~.*** 那仅仅是空想. **~ point**【数】理想点,假[伪]点. **-ly** *ad.*
i·de·a·less [aiˈdiəlis] *a.* 缺乏理想的,没有主意的.
i·de·al·ism [aiˈdiəlizm] *n.* ①理想主义. ②【哲】唯心论,唯心主义,观念论 *(opp.* materialism). *historical ~* 历史唯心主义. *objective ~* 客观唯心主义. *subjective ~* 主观唯心主义.
i·de·al·ist [aiˈdiəlist] *n.* ①唯心主义者,唯心论者. ②理想主义者;空想家. — *a.* ①唯心主义的. ②理想主义的;空想家的,唯心论的. *the ~ conception of history* 唯心史观.
i·de·al·is·tic [aiˌdiəˈlistik] *a.* ①理想主义者的,空想家的. ②唯心主义者的. ③唯心论的. **-ti·cal·ly** *ad.*
i·de·al·i·ty [ˌaidiˈæliti] *n.* 理想;空想;想象力.
i·de·al·ize [aiˈdi(ː)əlaiz] *vt., vi.* 使理想化,使合于理想. **i·de·al·i·za·tion** *n.*
i·de·ate [aiˈdi(ː)eit] *vt.* 想象;思考. —*vi.* 形成观念. — [aiˈdiːit] *n.*【哲】与观念相应的客体.
i·de·a·tion [ˌaidiˈeiʃən] *n.* 心理作用,观念作用;观念化.
i·dée fixe [ide ˈfiks] 〔F.〕 固定的观念;成见.
i·dem [ˈaidem] *n., pro., a.* 〔L.〕 同著者; 同上,同前〔略 id.〕. ***~ quod*** 同….
i·den·tic [aiˈdentik] *a.* ① = identical. ②(外交)相同文件的. *an ~ action* 相同行为. *an ~ note* 相同文件〔照会〕.
i·den·ti·cal [aiˈdentikəl] *a.* 同一的;同样的;【数】恒等的 *(with)*;【生】同卵的. *on the ~ day* 在同一天. *the ~ person* 同一人. *an ~ conception*【逻】同一概念. *~ twins*【生】同卵双生 *(cf.* fraternal twin). *~ equation*【数】恒等式,全等式. **~ proposition**【逻】同一命题,同一关系〔主、谓语在内涵和外延上一致的命题: *That which is mortal is not immortal.* 凡是会死的就不是永生的〕. **-ly** *ad.* 同一;同样.
i·den·ti·fi·a·ble [aiˈdentifaiəbl] *a.* 可视为相同的;可证明为同一的. **i·den·ti·fi·a·bly** *ad.*
i·den·ti·fi·ca·tion [aiˌdentifiˈkeiʃən] *n.* ①认出,识别,鉴定,验明(罪人正身等). ②【心】自居作用. ③身分证. ④【数】粘合,同化. *target ~ bomb*【军】目标识别炸弹. **~ card [paper]** 身分证. **~ disk [tag]** (士兵的)证章. **~ lamp** 标灯. **~ plate** (汽车)牌照.
i·den·ti·fy [aiˈdentifai] *vt.* ①使等同于…,使成为一致,把…看做一致 *(with).* ②把…鉴定为同一人 [同一物],验明(正身),鉴别,辨认,识别;【生】确定…在分类学上的位置. *~ the payee of a check* 验明支票的取款人. *~ handwriting* 鉴定笔迹. *~ a corpse* 验尸. *~ class status* 划分阶级成分. ***~ oneself with*** 参加到…中去;和…打成一片 *(He identified himself with the masses wherever he went.* 他每到一地,就和那里的群众打成一片).
i·den·ti·ty [aiˈdentiti] *n.* ①同一,一致;同一性. ②本体;正身;个性. ③【逻】同一性. ④【数】恒等(式). *an ~ card* 身分证,居民证. *an ~ disk [tag]* (士兵的)证章. *systems suited to its national ~* 符合自己民族特点的制度. *national ~* 民族面貌. *the principle of ~*【逻】同一律. *establish [prove] one's ~* 证明身分. *mistaken [false] ~* 认错人. *no matter what their ~* 无论什么人. *sink one's ~* 隐瞒历史. **~ crisis**【心】个性转变期〔尤指青春期一段心绪不宁的时间〕.
id·e·o·gram, id·e·o·graph [ˈidiəugræm, ˈidiəugrɑːf] *n.* ①会意〔表意〕文字. ②表意符号(如 5, +, =). *a Chinese ideograph* 汉字.
id·e·o·graph·ic(al) [ˌidiəuˈgræfik(əl)] *a.* 会意的,表意文字的,表意符号的. **-i·cal·ly** *ad.*
id·e·og·ra·phy [ˌidiˈɔgrəfi, ˌaid-] *n.* 会意文字学;表意文字的应用,表意符号的运用.
i·de·o·log·ic(al) [ˌaidiəˈlɔdʒik(əl)] *a.* 思想(体系)上的. 意识形态的;空论的. **-i·cal·ly** *ad.*
i·de·ol·o·gist [ˌaidiˈɔlədʒist, id-] *n.* 理论家;思想家;空想家.
i·de·ol·o·gize [ˌaidiˈɔlədʒaiz] *vt.* ***(-giz·ed, -giz·ing)*** ①作思想分析. ②改变成某一种思想.
i·de·o·logue [ˈaidiːəulɔg] *n.* 〔F.〕 思想家,理论家,空想家.
i·de·ol·o·gy [ˌaidiˈɔlədʒi, id-] *n.* ①观念学. ②思想体系,思想意识. ③观念形态,意识形态,思想方式. ④空想,空论.
i·de·o·mo·tor [ˌaidiəˈməutə, ˈidi-] *a.*【心】观念运动的.
i·de·o·phone [ˈaidiəfəun, ˈidiə-] *n.*【语】摹拟音;象音成份〔许多非洲语言的一种表意法,借助一种重复的声音去创造行为、事物的形象〕.

ides [aidz] *n.* 〔*pl.*〕古罗马历 3, 5, 7, 10 每月中的第 15 日以及其他各月中的第 13 日.

id est [id ˈest] 〔L.〕即,那就是〔= that is (to say) 略作 i.e.〕.

id•ge•nus•om•ne [idˈdʒiːnəsˈɔmni] 〔L.〕 = all of that kind.

id•i•o- *comb. f.* 表示"特殊的","特有的","本身的": *idio*morphic.

id•i•o•blast [ˈidiəˌblæst] *n.* 【生】异细胞. **-blas•tic** *a.*

id•i•o•chro•mat•ic [ˌidiəukrəˈmætik] *a.* (矿物等)自色的.

id•i•o•cy [ˈidiəsi] *n.* ①白痴. ②极端愚蠢的言行.

id•i•o•e•lec•tric [ˌidiəiˈlektrik] *a.* 非导体的;【物】摩擦生电的.

id•i•o•e•lec•trics [ˌidiəiˈlektriks] *n.* 非导体.

id•i•o•gram [ˈiːdiəgræm] *n.* 【生】染色体组型,染色体模式图.

id•i•o•graph [ˈidiəgrɑːf] *n.* ①个人特有的署名. ②商标.

id•i•o•graph•ic [ˌidiəˈgræfik] *n.* ①个人署名的;商标的. ②具有特点的,独特的,个别的.

id•i•o•lect [ˈidiəulekt] *n.* 【语】个人习语,个人语型.

id•i•om [ˈidiəm] *n.* ①习语,成语. ②惯用语法,某种语言的特性. ③方言,土语. ④(某一作家独特的)表现方法;(音乐、美术等的)风格.

id•i•o•mat•ic(al) [ˌidiəˈmætik(əl)] *a.* ①成语的;符合语言习惯的. ②成语丰富的,用很多成语的. ③富有习语性质的. ④(某团体或个人)特有的,独特的. **-i•cal•ly** *ad.* **-i•cal•ness, -tic•i•ty** *n.*

id•i•o•mor•phic [ˌidiəˈmɔːfik] *a.* 【矿】自形的,自发的,整形的.

id•i•o•path•i•c [ˌidiəˈpæθik] *a.* 【医】突发性的. **-i•cal•ly** *ad.*

id•i•op•a•thy [ˌidiˈɔpəθi] *n.* 【医】突发性的疾病.

id•i•o•phone [ˈidiəufəun] *n.* 【乐】意狄欧风〔一种非膜质的打击乐器〕.

id•i•o•plasm [ˈidiəplæzəm] *n.* 【生】异胞质. **-mat•ic, -mic** *a.*

id•i•o•syn•cra•sy [ˌidiəˈsiŋkrəsi] *n.* ①(人的)特质,特性,个性. ②(著者)特有的风格. ③【医】特(异反)应性;特异体质,特异素. **-crat•ic** *a.*

id•i•ot [ˈidiət] *n.* 白痴;〔口〕傻子. ~ **board [card]**〔俚〕(电视演员的)提词板〔牌〕. ~ **box**〔俚〕电视机. **~-proof** *a.* 简单易解的,容易操作的,可靠的(= foolproof).

id•i•ot•ic(al) [ˌidiˈɔtik(əl)] *a.* 白痴(一样)的;愚蠢的. **-i•cal•ly** *ad.*

id•i•ot•ism [ˈidiəutizəm] *n.* ①白痴行为. ②〔古〕白痴. ③〔废〕= idiom.

IDL = international date line 国际日期变更线,日界线.

i•dle [ˈaidl] *a.* ①懒惰的,吊儿郎当的. ②空闲的;【机】空转的. ③没用的,无益的,无效的;【物】无功的;无根据的. ~ *worms* 懒虫. *I- folks lack no excuses.*〔谚〕懒人不愁无借口. *have one's hands* ~手空着,没事. *the* ~ *rich* 有闲阶级. ~ *compliment* 应酬话,虚礼. ~ *hours* 闲时. *it is* ~ *to say that* … 说…是没有用的. *an* ~ *dream* 痴心妄想. *an* ~ *rumour* 毫无根据的谣言. ***be at an*** ~ ***end*** 闲着无事,赋闲. ***eat*** ~ ***bread*** = eat the bread of idleness 吃闲饭. ***lie*** ~ 被搁置;一事不做. ***run*** ~ (机器)空转. ***stand*** ~ 袖手旁观. —*vt.* 空费,虚度(岁月). ~ ***away one's time [life]*** 虚度时光〔一生〕. — *vi.* 懒,不做事;闲混,闲逛 *(about)*;(机器)空转 *(over)*. ~ **capacity** 储备容量;备用电容. ~ **circuit** 空载电路. ~ **current** 无效电流. ~ **frequency** 中心频率;未调制的频率. ~ **funds [money]**【经】游资. ~ **motion** 空转. ~ **roll** 传动轧辊,随转轧辊. ~ **space** 余隙空间. ~ **time** 空载时间,停机时间. ~ **unit** 闲置设备. ~ **wheel**【机】惰轮,空转轮,调紧皮带轮.

i•dle•ness [ˈaidlnis] *n.* ①懒惰;坐食. ②赋闲无事,失业. ③无益,无效. *busy* ~ 整天无事忙. *I- is the mother [parent, root] of all evil [sin, vice].*〔谚〕懒惰为万恶之源. *I- rusts the mind.*〔谚〕怠惰使头脑迟钝. ***eat the bread of*** ~ 坐吃. ***live in*** ~ 游手好闲.

i•dler [ˈaidlə] *n.* ①懒人;游手好闲者. ②不当班的海军士兵. ③【机】惰轮,空转轮,调紧皮带轮. ④【铁路】空车.

i•dlesse [ˈaidles] *n.* 〔古、诗〕= idleness.

i•dly [ˈaidli] *ad.* 懒惰地;空闲地;无用地.

I•do [ˈiːdəu] *n.* 简化世界语〔指 1907 年在法国发表的世界语改革方案〕.

i•do•c rase [ˈaidəukreis, ˈidəu-] *n.* = vesuvianite (符山石,维苏威石).

i•dol [ˈaidl] *n.* ①偶像. ②被崇拜的人[物]. ③【逻】谬论,谬见. ④幻像;幽灵. ***make an*** ~ ***of sb.*** 崇拜[迷信]某人.

i•do•la [aiˈdəulə] *n.* idolum 的复数.

i•dol•a•ter [aiˈdɔlətə] *n.* 偶像崇拜者;盲目崇拜者.

i•dol•a•tress [aiˈdɔlətris] *n.* 偶像的女崇拜者,女盲目崇拜者.

i•dol•a•trize [aiˈdɔlətraiz] *vt., vi.* ***(-triz•ed, -triz•ing)*** 盲目崇拜,实行偶像崇拜.

i•dol•a•trous [aiˈdɔlətrəs] *a.* 崇拜偶像的;盲目崇拜的. **-ly** *ad.* **-ness** *n.*

i•dol•a•try [aiˈdɔlətri] *n.* *(pl.* ***-tries)*** ①偶像崇拜. ②盲目崇拜;过分尊崇.

i•dol•ism [ˈaidlizəm] *n.* ①= idolatry. ②〔古〕谬见;错误推理.

i•dol•ize [ˈaidəlaiz] *vt.* 把…当偶像崇拜,盲目崇拜,醉心于. ~ *the ancients* 复古. —*vi.* 崇拜偶像. **-i•za•tion** *n.*

i•do•lum [aiˈdəuləm] *n.* *(pl.* ***-la*** [-lə]*)* ①幻想,观念. ②【逻】谬论,谬见.

i•dyl(l) [ˈidil, ˈaidil] *n.* ①即景诗,田园诗. ②(适合田园诗的)民间传说,田园风景. ③【乐】田园乐曲,牧歌.

i•dyl•lic [aiˈdilik, iˈdilik] *a.* ①田园诗的,牧歌的. ②质朴宜人的,生动逼真的.

i•dyl(l)•ist [ˈaidilist] *n.* 田园诗人,田园乐曲[牧歌]作者.

i•dyl(l)•ize [ˈaidilaiz] *vt.* 使(生活)成田园诗;使成为牧歌.

I.E. = ①Indo-European 印欧语系(的). ②Indian Empire 〔旧〕印度帝国. ③= industrial engineering 工业工程学.

-ie *suf.* = -y² ①表示"小";"小而可爱": beaut*ie*, dear*ie* fair*ie*. ②表示"具有…性质的人(或物)": soft*ie*. ③表示"…职业的人": book*ie*.

i.e. [ˈaiˈiː] 〔L.〕= *id est* 那就是;即 (= that is to say).

IEA = International Energy Agency 国际能源机构.

-i•er *suf.* = -eer: brigad*ier*, glaz*ier*.

if [if] *conj.* ①〔表示条件〕倘若,如果. *If you are tired, we will sit down.* 如果你疲倦了,我们就坐下吧. *Return* ~ *undelivered.* 无法投递请退回原处. ~ *weather permits,* … 如果天气好的话,…〔常略作 I.W.P.〕. ②〔表示假设〕要是,假设: *If I knew, I would say.* 我要知道,我就说了. *If I were a bird, I could fly.* 假使我是只鸟,我就会飞了. *If he had tried, he would have succeeded.* 如果他当初试验过,他本来是会成功的. ★在书面用语中主语与动词次序颠倒, *if* 即可略去: *Were I in your place,* … = *If I were in your place,* …; *Should I find it,* … = *If I should find it,* … ③〔表示让步〕虽然,即使. *If he is little, he is strong.* 他年纪虽小,气力倒大. *I will do it* ~ *it kills me. [If I die for it]* 我拚命也要干. *His manner,* ~ *patronizing, was not unkind.* 他的态度,虽然是以恩人自居,然而并不粗暴. ④〔口〕是否,是不是〔常用于 ask, see, try, doubt, learn, wonder 等词之后〕. *Ask* ~ *he* *is at home*. 问他在不在家。*I don't know* ~ *he is here*. 我不知道他是不是在这里。⑤…的时候总是…，一…就。*If I feel any doubt, I ask*. 我一有疑惑就问。⑥〔条件句表示愿望、感叹。用过去时态的虚拟语气〕要是…多好：*If I only knew!* 要是我知道多好！〔可惜不知道〕。*If I haven't lost my watch!* 我的表不丢多好！〔句前常可加用 *I'm blessed* 等〕。***as*** ~ 活象 (*as* ~ *he had seen it* 活象他见过似的)。~ ***a day [an inch etc.]*** 无论如何应该是…；至少有… (*He is seventy* ~ *(he is) a day (old)*. 他该有七十岁了。*The enemy is 2000 strong* ~ *a man*. 敌人至少有二千人。*I've come three miles* ~ *(I've come) a yard*. 我走了该有三英里了)。~ ***and when*** ①= if. ②= when. ~ ***any*** 即使有也(极少) (*There is little* ~ *any hope*. 希望极少)。~ ***anything*** 甚至可能，或许甚至。~ ***it were not for*** = ~ ***it had not been for*** 若不是…的话。~ ***necessary*** 如有必要。~ ***not*** 要是不，即使不。~ ***only*** ①只要。②要是…就好 (*If only it cleers up, we'll go*. 只要天一晴，我们就去。*If only he arrives in time!* 他要是能及时赶到就好了！) ~ ***possible*** 如果可能。~ ***so*** 如果这样。~ ***so be that*** = if. ~ ***you please [will]*** ①请。②〔谑〕如何〔问人意向〕。***What (matters it)*** ~ ***I fail!*** 失败算什么〔*cf.* what〕。***What (would happen)*** ~ ***you should fail!*** 你要是失败了怎么办〔那就糟了〕！ — *n*. 条件，设想。*Dash these* ~*s!* 让这一大堆"如果"见鬼去吧！*There is no* ~ *in the case*. 这里没有假定的余地。*Your argument seems to have too many* ~*s*. 你的论据似乎假设太多。~ **clause**【语法】条件从句。~ **statement** 计算机用条件语句。

IFC = International Finance Corporation (联合国)国际金融公司。

IFF = identification: friend or foe【军】敌我识别器，敌我识别系统。

if·fy [ˈifi] *a*. 〔口〕可怀疑的；不确定的；偶然性的；有条件的。

IFJ = International Federation of Journalists 国际新闻工作者联合会。

I.F.S. = Irish Free State〔旧〕爱尔兰自由邦。

-i·fy *suf*. = -fy: intens*ify*, solid*ify*.

IG = ①Indo-Germanic 印欧语系(的)，会印欧语系语言的人。②Inspector General 监察长。

Ig·bo [ˈiːgbəu] *n*. = Ibo.

IGD = Inspector General's Department 总监署。

I.G.H.Q. = Industrial Group Headquarters 工业组织管理局(英国原子能管理局)。

ig·loo, ig·lu [ˈigluː] *n*. (*pl*. ~*s*) ①爱斯基摩(Eskimo)人居住的外壳用硬雪块砌成的圆顶小屋。②圆顶建筑。③手提透明塑胶保护罩。

ign. ①= ignition. ②〔L.〕unknown.

ig·ne·ous [ˈigniəs] *a*. ①火的，似火的。②【地】火成的。~ *magma* 岩浆。~ *rock* 火成岩。

ig·nes·cent [igˈnesnt] *a*. ①爆成火焰的。②碰击而冒火星的。— *n*. 碰击而冒火星的物质。~ *stones* 打火石。

ig·nis fat·u·us [ˈignis ˈfætjuəs] (*pl*. ***ig·nes fat·u·i*** [ˈigniːz ˈfætjuai])〔L.〕①鬼火，磷火。②虚幻的希望〔目标〕。

ig·nit·a·ble, ig·nit·i·ble [igˈnaitəbl] *a*. 可发火的，易燃的。**-a·bil·i·ty, -nit·i·bil·i·ty** *n*.

ig·nite [igˈnait] *vt*. ①点火，点燃；使燃烧。②使灼热。③使兴奋，使激动。— *vi*. 点火，发火，燃烧。

ig·nit·er, ig·nit·or [igˈnaitə] *n*. ①点火器；传火药，点火剂；点火者。②引爆装置。

ig·ni·tion [igˈniʃən] *n*. ①点火，着火，燃烧；【化】灼热。②【机】发火装置。~ **charge** 点火药。~ **point**【物】燃点。~ **temperature** 着火温度。

ig·ni·tron [ˈignitron] *n*.【无】点火管；引燃管；放电管。

ig·no·ble [igˈnəubl] *a*. ①卑鄙的；可耻的，不体面的。②卑贱的，出身微贱的。**ig·no·bil·i·ty** [ˌignəuˈbiliti], **-ness** *n*.

ig·no·bly [igˈnəubli] *ad*. 卑贱地；卑鄙地。*be* ~ *born* 出身微贱。

ig·no·min·i·ous [ignəˈminiəs] *a*. 可耻的，不光彩的，丢脸的；卑鄙的。*an* ~ *treaty* 屈辱性条约。**-ly** *ad*. **-ness** *n*.

ig·no·min·y [ˈignəmini] *n*. ①耻辱，污辱，不名誉。②无耻行为，丑行。

ig·no·ra·mus [ˌignəˈreiməs] *n*. 没有知识的人；愚人。

ig·no·rance [ˈignərəns] *n*. 无知，缺乏教育，愚昧；不知道。*I- of the law excuses no one*. 〔谚〕不懂法律不能作为免罪的口实。*Where* ~ *is bliss, 'tis (it is) folly to be wise*. 〔谚〕难得糊涂〔该糊涂就得糊涂〕。***from*** ~ 出于无知。***be in*** ~ ***of sth***. 不知某事。***live in a state of*** ~ 浑浑噩噩地生活。***plead*** ~ 声言不知。

ig·no·rant [ˈignərənt] *a*. 无学识的，无知的，愚昧的；由无知引起的。*an* ~ *person* 无知的人。~ *behaviour* 愚蠢行为。***be*** ~ ***of*** 不了解。**-ly** *ad*.

ig·no·ra·ti·o e·len·chi [ˌignəˈreiʃiəu iˈleŋkai]〔L.〕【逻】用歪曲对方论点的手法驳斥对方。

ig·nore [igˈnɔː] *vt*. ①忽视，不理，不顾；抹煞(建议)。②【法】驳回。

ig·no·tum per ig·no·ti·us [igˈnəutəm pəː igˈnəuʃiəs]〔L.〕解释得比原来需要解释的事物更难懂，以其昏昏使人昭昭。

Ig·o·rot [ˌi(ː)gəˈrəut] *n*. (*pl*. ~*s*) (菲律宾)伊哥洛人；伊哥洛语。

i·gua·na [iˈgwɑːnə] *n*. 鬣蜥〔西印度、南美所产大蜥蜴〕。

i·guan·o·don [iˈgwɑːnədɔn] *n*.【古生】禽龙〔古代大蜥蜴〕。

IGY = International Geophysical Year 国际地球物理年。

i.h.p. = indicated horsepower 指示马力。

ih·ram [iˈrɑːm] *n*. ①朝圣服〔穆斯林披着到麦加朝圣的双片白布〕。②穿朝圣服者必须遵守的约法规章。

IHS = Jesus.

Ike [aik] *n*. Isaac 的爱称。

ike [aik] *n*. = iconoscope.

i·ke·ba·na [ˈiːkeˈbɑːnɑː] *n*. 〔日〕插花艺术。

i·key [ˈaiki] = iky.

i·kon [ˈaikɔn] *n*. = icon.

i·ky [ˈaiki]〔俚〕*a*. 狡猾的，厚颜无耻的，狂妄的。— *n*. ①犹太人；高利贷者。②当铺。

Il =【化】illinium.

il- *pref*. 〔用于以字母 l 开始的词之前，表示否定〕：*il*logical.

-il *suf*. = -ile: civ*il*.

i·lang-i·lang [ˈiːlɑːŋ ˈiːlɑːŋ] *n*. ①伊兰伊兰树。②伊兰伊兰香精。

-ile *suf*. ①作形容词后缀：ag*ile*, fut*ile*. ②作名词后缀：miss*ile*, text*ile*.

il·e·ac, il·e·al [ˈiliæk, ˈiliəl] *a*. ①回肠的。②有关回肠的。

il·e·i·tis [ˌiliˈaitis] *n*.【医】回肠炎。

il·e·os·to·my [ˌiliːˈɔstəmi] *n*.【医】回肠造口术。

il·e·um [ˈiliəm] *n*.【解】回肠。

il·e·us [ˈiliəs] *n*.【医】肠梗阻绞痛。

i·lex [ˈaileks] *n*. (*pl*. ~*es*)【植】①圣栎。②冬青属植物。

il·i·ac [ˈiliæk] *a*.【解】肠骨的，髂的。

Il·i·ad [ˈiliəd] *n*. ①(描写特洛伊战争的英雄史诗)《伊利亚特》。②荷马式的叙事诗。③一系列史诗般的战绩。***an*** ~ ***of woes*** 一连串的不幸。

il·i·um [ˈiliəm] *n*. (*pl*. ***il·i·a*** [ˈiliə])【解】肠骨，髂骨。

ilk [ilk] *a*. 〔Scot.〕相同的，同一的。— *pro*. 〔Scot.〕每一。— *n*. 〔口〕家族，同类。*Hitler and his* ~ 希特勒之流。*liquidate all those not of his* ~ 排斥异己。***of that*** ~ 同名的，同姓的，同地的；同族的，同类的 (*Ross of that* ~ 罗斯地方的罗斯家 (= Ross of Ross))。***that*** ~ 〔口〕那一家族，那一等级，那一伙。

ill [il] *a.* (*worse* [wəːs]; *worst* [wəːst]) ①〔用作表语〕有病的. ★英国此义作定语时是用 sick. 美国无论作表语或作定语通常均用 sick. ②〔用作表语〕难过的,不高兴的,不痛快的. ③〔用作定语〕不健康的,恶劣的,有害的,不幸的. ④困难的,麻烦的. ⑤拙劣的,笨拙的. *be mentally* ~ 有精神病. *He that is* ~ *to himself will be good to nobody.* 〔谚〕不能自爱,焉能爱人. *The sight made me* ~. 这种景象使我难受. *It's an* ~ *wind that blows nobody good.* 〔谚〕世上没有对人人都不利的事. *Ill news runs apace.* 〔谚〕恶事传千里. ~ *deeds* 恶劣行为,坏事. ~ *nature* 劣根性. *of* ~ *repute* [*fame*] 名声不好. ~ *health* 不健康. ~ *fortune* [*luck*] 不幸. ~ *will* [*blood*] 怨恨,恶意. ~ *breeding* 教养不好. ~ *management* 管理不善. *It is* ~ *to be defined.* 很难对它下定义. ***be*** ~ ***to please*** 很难讨好. ***be*** ~ ***of*** [***with***] (*pneumonia*) 患(肺炎). ***be taken*** ~ 害病. ***do sb. an*** ~ ***turn*** 害某人. ***fall*** [***get***] ~ 患病,染疾. ***meet with*** ~ ***success*** 终于失败. ***take in*** ~ ***part*** 误会,动气. — *ad.* (***worse; worst***) ①坏,恶劣;拙劣,笨. ②不完全,不充分,几乎不. *behave* ~ 行为不好. ~ *got,* ~ *spent* 悖入悖出. *It* ~ *becomes him to speak so.* 他不应该这样说. *I can* ~ *afford it.* 这我办不到. *use sb.* ~ 残酷地驱使,虐待. *It would go* ~ *with him.* 他要吃亏的. ***be*** ~ ***accord with*** 和…很不相称[不一致]. ***be*** ~ ***at ease*** 不安. ~ ***off*** 困苦,家境不好. ***speak*** ~ ***of*** 说…的坏话. ***take sth.*** ~ 误会,动气(*Don't take it* ~ *of him.* 你别为他生气). ***think*** ~ ***of*** 误会. — *n.* ①恶,凶;罪恶. ②〔*pl.*〕不幸,灾难;病痛. *do* ~ 为害. *the* ~*s of life* 人生的艰难困苦. *bodily* ~*s* 疾病. *the* ~*s that flesh is heir to* 人生不能避免的痛苦,命运的打击. ***for good or*** ~ 好歹. ***work*** ~ 作恶. ~**-adapted** *a.* 不协调的. ~**-advised** *a.* 没脑筋的,鲁莽的. ~**-affected** *a.* 怀抱不平的,不服气的. ~**-being** 病态;不幸;贫穷(*opp.* well-being). ~**-boding** *a.* 凶兆的,不吉的. ~**-bred** *a.* ①无教养的,教养不良的,粗鲁的. ②(动物等)劣种的. ~**-conditioned** *a.* 情况糟的;心地坏的;病态的. ~**-considered** *a.* 考虑欠周的;不适当的;不明智的. ~**-defined** *a.* 意思[态度]不明确的;不清楚的;不确定的. ~**-disposed** *a.* ①怀敌意的,存心不良的. ②对…不友好的;对…不利的(*toward*). ~**-effect** 对…产生恶劣影响. ~**-equipped** *a.* 装备不良的. ~**-fated** *a.* 招致不幸的;注定要倒霉的. ~**-favo(u)red** *a.* (容貌)丑的,不漂亮的;使人不快的. ~**-fed** 营养不良的. ~**-feeling** *n.* 敌意,仇视. ~**-fortune** 倒霉. ~**-founded** *a.* 无事实根据的;理由不充分的. ~**-gotten** *a.* 非法得到的(~*-gotten gains* 不义之财). ~ **heath** 不健康. ~**-humo(u)red** *a.* 不高兴的; 坏脾气的. ~**-judged** *a.* 没有脑筋的,愚昧的,决断失当的. ~**-looking** *a.* ①不吸引人的;丑陋的. ②凶相的. ~**-mannered** *a.* 没礼貌的,粗鲁的. ~**-matched** *a.* = ill-sorted. ~**-natured** *a.* 怀着恶意的;性情坏的. ~**-omened** *a.* 凶兆的,不吉利的. ~**-sorted** *a.* 搭配失当的,极不相称的(*an* ~*-sorted pair* 不相配的一对夫妻). ~**-spent** *a.* 乱花掉的,花钱浪费的. ~**-starred** *a.* = ill-fated. ~**-suited** *a.* 不合适的;不适应的. ~**-tempered** *a.* = ill-humo(u)red. ~**-timed** *a.* 不合时宜的,不适时的(*Your remark is* ~*-timed.* 你这话说得不是时候). ~**-treat,** ~**-use** *vt.* 虐待. **ill-treatment,** ~ **usage,** ~**-usage** 虐待,滥用,糟塌. ~**-wisher** *n.* 幸灾乐祸的人.

Ill. = Illinois.

ill. = ①illuminate, illumination. ②illustrate, illustration.

I'll [ail] 〔口〕 = I shall; I will.

il·la·tion [iˈleiʃən] *n.* 【逻】①推论,推理;演绎(法). ②结论;演绎的结果.

il·la·tive [iˈleitiv] *a.* ①演绎的,推论的. ~ *conjunctions* 推论连接词〔如 *then, therefore* 等〕. **-ly** *ad.*

il·laud·a·ble [iˈlɔːdəbl] *a.* 不值得赞美的.

il·le·gal [iˈliːgəl] *a.* 不法的,非法的. *an* ~ *operation* 堕胎(罪). **-ly** *ad.*

il·le·gal·i·ty [ˌili(ː)ˈgæliti] *n.* 违法;犯规;非法行为.

il·le·gal·ize [iˈliːgəlaiz] *vt.* 使非法,宣布…为非法.

il·leg·i·bil·i·ty [iˌledʒiˈbiliti] *n.* 难以辨认;字迹模糊;印刷模糊.

il·leg·i·ble [iˈledʒəbl] *a.* 难以辨认的,字迹[印刷]模糊的.

il·leg·i·bly [iˈledʒəbli] *ad.* 难以辨认地,字迹[印刷]模糊地.

il·le·git·i·ma·cy [ˌiliˈdʒitiməsi] *n.* ①非法,违法. ②不合理,不合逻辑. ③不符合惯例. ④私生.

il·le·git·i·mate [ˌiliˈdʒitimit] *a.* ①非法的,违法的. ②不合理的,不合逻辑的. ③不符合惯例的. ④私生的. — *n.* 没有合法身分的人(指私生子). — [ˌiliˈdʒitimeit] *vt.* 宣布…为非法. **-ly** *ad.*

il·le·git·i·ma·tion [ˌiliˌdʒitiˈmeiʃən] *n.* ①认为非法. ②认为[宣布为]私生子.

il·lib·er·al [iˈlibərəl] *a.* ①缺乏教育的,无教养的. ②吝啬的,气量狭窄的;思想偏狭的. **-ly** *ad.*

il·lib·er·al·i·ty [iˌlibəˈræliti] *n.* ①缺乏教育,无教养. ②吝啬,气量狭窄,思想偏狭.

il·lic·it [iˈlisit] *a.* 违法的,违禁的,不正当的. *have* [*maintain*] ~ *relations with a foreign country* 里通外国. ~ *intercourse* 私通,通奸. ~ *sale* 私卖. **-ly** *ad.* **-ness** *n.*

il·lim·it·a·ble [iˈlimitəbl] *a.* 无限的,广阔无边的,不可计量的. *the* ~ *ocean* 浩渺无边的海洋. **-bil·i·ty, -ness** *n.* **-bly** *ad.*

il·lin·i·um [iˈliniəm] *n.* 【化】钷〔现名 promethium 钷〕.

Il·li·nois [ˌiliˈnɔi(z)] *n.* 伊利诺斯(美国州名). **-an** [-zən] *a.* **-i·an** [-ziən] *a.* **Il·li·noi·an** [ˌiliˈnɔiən] *a.* 伊利诺斯州的;伊利诺斯州人的. — *n.* 伊利诺斯州人.

il·liq·uid [iˈlikwid] *a.* ①非现金的;不能立即兑现的. ②无流动资金的. **-di·ty** [-diti] *n.*

illit = illiterate.

il·lite [ˈilait] *n.* 【地】伊利石;伊利水云母.

il·lit·er·a·cy [iˈlitərəsi] *n.* ①失学;未受教育;文盲. ②(语言)错误. *wipe out* ~ 扫除文盲.

il·lit·er·ate [iˈlitərit] *a.* ①不识字的,未受教育的,文盲的. ②缺乏语言[文学]方面知识的. ③语言错误的: *an* ~ *letter* 语言错误百出的信. — *n.* 失学者,文盲. **-ly** *ad.* **-ness** *n.*

ill·ness [ˈilnis] *n.* 病,不健康(*opp.* health). *suffer from a serious* ~ 害重病;病的很厉害. *triumph over* ~ 战胜疾病; ~*es of women* 各种妇女病.

il·log·ic [iˈlɔdʒik] *n.* 不合逻辑,缺乏逻辑.

il·log·i·cal [iˈlɔdʒikəl] *a.* 缺乏逻辑的,不合逻辑的,说不通的,无条理的,无意义的. **-ly** *ad.* **-ness** *n.*

il·log·ical·i·ty [ˈilɔdʒiˈkæliti] *n.* 不合逻辑,矛盾.

il·lo·ty·cin [ˌiləˈtaisin] *n.* 【药】(商品名)红霉素.

illth [ilθ] *n.* = ill-being.

il·lume [iˈljuːm] *vt.* 〔诗〕照亮;启发.

il·lu·mi·na·ble [iˈljuːminəbl] *a.* 可被照明的.

il·lu·mi·nance [iˈljuːminəns] *n.* 【物】照度,施照度.

il·lu·mi·nant [iˈljuːminənt] *a.* 照明的,发光的. — *n.* 发光物;照明剂.

il·lu·mi·nate [iˈljuːmineit] *vt.* ①照亮,照明. ②使光辉灿烂. ③〔英〕装置照明,装饰. ④说明(问题等);启发,启蒙. ⑤(用饰字、饰画)装饰. ⑥使受辐射照射. — *vi.* ①照亮. ②进行辐射照射.

il·lu·mi·nat·ed [iˈljuːmiˌneitid] *a.* ①照明的;装有照明装饰的;受到启发[启蒙]的;加有彩饰的. ②〔美俚〕喝醉了的. *a well-*~ *room* 照明良好的房间. *an* ~ *car* 彩车,花车. *an* ~ *manuscript* 金泥写本,彩饰真迹写本.

il·lu·mi·na·ti [ˌiluːmiˈnɑːtiː] *n.* (*pl., sing.* **-na·to** [-təu]) ①自称天才的人们,自认聪明过人的人们. ②〔I-〕光明会〔十八世纪主张自然神论和共和主义的秘密社团〕. ③

〔I-〕主张宗教开明的社团.
il·lu·mi·nat·ing [iˈljuːmiˌneitiŋ] *a.* 照亮的,照明的;启发的,说明的. ~ *attachments* 照明设备. ~ *effect* 照明效果. ~ *engineering* 照明工程(学). ~ *flare (projectile)*【军】照明弹.
il·lu·mi·na·tion [iˌljuːmiˈneiʃən] *n.* ①照明,光照;照(明)度;〔常用 *pl.*〕灯饰. ②启发,启蒙. ③(手写本的)彩饰. *stage* ~ 舞台照明. **il·lu·mi·na·tive** *a.*
il·lu·mi·na·tor [iˈljuːmineitə] *n.* ①照明者. ②发光体,照明装置;灯饰装置. ②启发者. ③装饰书稿的人.
i·llu·mine [iˈljuːmin] *vt.* 照亮;启发;使发亮. — *vi.* 明亮起来.
il·lu·min·ism [iˈluːminizm] *n.* (历史上的)光明会教义;启蒙主义. **-ist** *n.*
illus. = illustrated; illustration.
il·lu·sion [iˈluːʒən, iˈljuː-] *n.* ①幻影;幻觉;妄想,幻想;错觉. ②(妇女用)透明面纱. *an optical* ~ 视错觉. ***be under no ~ about [as to] sth.*** 对某事不存幻想. **-al, -a·ry** *a.* **-ism** *n.* ①物质世界幻觉说. ②引起错觉的艺术手法. **-ist** *n.* 物质世界幻觉论者;幻想家;魔术师.
il·lu·sive [iˈluːsiv] *a.* 幻影的,幻觉的;错觉上的,迷惑人的. **-ly** *ad.* **-ness** *n.*
il·lu·so·ry [iˈluːsəri] *a.* = illusive. **-i·ly** *ad.*
illust. = illustrated; illustration.
il·lus·trate [ˈiləstreit] *vt.* ①(用例子、图解等)说明;举例证明. ②加上插图[图解]. *an ~d book [newspaper]* 有插画的书籍[报纸]. —*vi.* 举例.
il·lus·tra·tion [ˌiləsˈtreiʃən] *n.* 说明,例证,实例;图解,插画. ***in ~ of*** 作为…的例证.
il·lus·tra·tive [ˈiləstreitiv] *a.* ①说明性质的. ②作为…例证的,能阐释…的 *(of)*. *a simile ~ of a subject* 说明问题的比喻. **-ly** *ad.*
il·lus·tra·tor [ˈiləstreitə] *n.* 说明者;插图画家.
il·lus·tri·ous [iˈlʌstriəs] *a.* ①卓越的;杰出的;有名的,著名的. ②辉煌的,灿烂的. ~ *accomplishments* 杰出的成就. ~ *deeds* 辉煌的事绩. **-ly** *ad.* **-ness** *n.*
il·lu·vi·al [iˈluːviəl] *a.*【地】淀积层的;与淀积层有关的;淀积(作用)的;与淀积(作用)有关的.
il·lu·vi·ate [iˈluːvieit] *vi.*【地】经受淀积作用.
il·lu·vi·a·tion [iˌluːviˈeiʃən] *n.*【地】淀积作用.
il·lu·vi·um [iˈluːviəm] *n. (pl. ~s, -via* [-ə]*)*【地】淀积层.
il·ly [ˈili] *ad.* 〔口〕坏,恶劣地. *be ~ prepared* 准备不充分. — *a.* = ill.
Il·lyr·i·an [iˈliəriən] *a.* ①(古代亚得里亚海东岸地区)伊利里亚的;伊利里亚人的;伊利里亚文化的. ②伊利里亚语〔一般认为属印欧语系〕. — *n.* 伊利里亚人.
il·men·ite [ˈilminait] *n.*【矿】钛铁矿.
ILO = ①International Labo(u)r Organization (联合国)国际劳工组织. ②International Labo(u)r Office (联合国)国际劳工局.
I.L.P. = Independent Labour Party. 〔英〕独立工党.
Il·se [ˈilzə] *n.* 女名〔*Elizabeth* 的爱称〕.
'im = him.
I.M. = Isle of Man 曼岛〔英国〕.
I'm [aim] 〔口〕= I am.
im- *pref.* 用于以 b, m, p 开始的词前. ①表示"向…内";"在…上";"向…": *im*bed, *im*migrate. ②表示"否定": *im*moral, *im*patient.
im·age [ˈimidʒ] *n.* ①像,肖像,画像;偶像. ②影象,图像. ③相象的人(或物);翻版. ④形象,典型. ⑤形象化的描绘. ⑥【语】形象化的比喻,象喻. ⑦【心】概念,意象;心象. *graven* ~ 雕象. ~ *frequency* 图象频(率);镜频. *real* ~【物】实象. *television* ~ 电视图象. *virtual* ~【物】虚象. *God's* ~ 人体. *He is the ~ of his father.* 他活象他父亲. *the spitting ~ of* 同…完全一样的人[物]. *speak in ~s* 用比喻讲;说话形象化. *thinking in terms of ~s* 形象思维. — *vt.* ①作…的像;使…成像. ②反映. ③想象. ④形象地描画;用比喻描写. ⑤象征. ~ **converter**【电】光电变换器;光电图象变换管;图象变换器;变象管. ~ **dissector**【电】析象管. ~ **orthicon**【电】超正析(摄)象管,移象正析(摄)象管. **-less** *a.* 缺少形象的.
im·age·a·ble [ˈimidʒəbl] *a.* 可以描摹的.
im·age·ry [ˈimidʒəri] *n.* ①〔集合词〕像,肖像,画像,雕像. ②意象. ③【修】比喻;形象化的描述.
i·mag·i·na·ble [iˈmædʒinəbl] *a.* 可以想象得到的. ★常与最高级形容词或 *all, every, no* 等连用,以加强语气. *try every means* ~ 用一切想得出的方法. *the greatest difficulty* ~ 几乎想象不到的困难. *the best thing* ~ 再好没有的东西. **imaginably** *ad.*
i·mag·i·nal [iˈmædʒinl] *a.* 想象的,有关想象的;【动】成虫的.
i·mag·i·nar·y [iˈmædʒinəri] *a.* ①想象中的,假想的 *(opp.* actual*)*. ②【数】虚数的. *an ~ enemy* 假想敌人. ~ *number* 虚数. ~ *root* 虚根. ~ *unit* 虚数单位,$\sqrt{-1}$ 符号 *i*. **i·mag·i·na·ri·ly** *ad.* **i·mag·i·na·ri·ness** *n.*
i·mag·i·na·tion [iˌmædʒiˈneiʃən] *n.* ①想象,想象力,创造力. ②妄想;空想. ③想象出来的事物. *have a good [poor]* ~ 想象力好[差];〔谑〕很会[不会]说谎.
i·mag·i·na·tive [iˈmædʒinətiv] *a.* 想象的;富于想象力的. **-ly** *ad.* **-ness** *n.*
i·mag·ine [iˈmædʒin] *vt., vi.* ①想象,设想;猜想,推测. ②〔古〕企图. *Just ~!* 想想看! *I cannot ~ who the man is.* 我想不出这个人是谁. *I- yourself (to be) on a desert island.* 设想你处在一个荒岛上.
im·ag·ism [ˈimədʒizəm] *n.* 意象主义〔一种文学上的流派〕.
im·ag·ist [ˈimədʒist] *n.* 意象主义者,意象派. — *a.* = imagistic.
i·ma·go [iˈmeigəu] *n. (pl. **imagines*** [iˈmeidʒiniːz] 或 *~es)* ①【动】成虫. ②【心】像,意象.
i·mam, i·maum [iˈmɑːm] *n.* ①(伊斯兰教的)阿訇. ②〔*I-*〕伊玛姆〔伊斯兰教国家元首的称号或指伊斯兰教教长〕.
i·mam·ate [iˈmɑːmeit] *n.*【宗】①伊斯兰教长国. ②教长职权.
i·ma·ret [iˈmɑːret] *n.* (土耳其的)小客店,香客客店.
im·bal·ance [imˈbæləns] *n.* 不平衡,失调.
im·balm [imˈbɑːm] *vt.* = embalm.
im·be·cile [ˈimbisail, -siːl] *a.* 低能的;愚笨的. — *n.* 低能儿;愚蠢的人. **-ly** *ad.*
im·be·cil·i·ty [ˌimbiˈsiliti] *n.* ①低能,愚笨. ②愚蠢的言行.
im·bed [imˈbed] *vt.* = embed.
im·bibe [imˈbaib] *vt.* ①吸收(养分等),吸进(空气等). ②〔口〕喝. ③吸收(思想等). — *vi.* 喝;吸收,接受.
im·bi·bi·tion [ˌimbiˈbiʃən] *n.* ①【化】吸液. ②吸入,吸收. **-al** *a.*
im·bit·ter [imˈbitə] *vt.* ①使变苦,加苦味于. ②使更痛苦;使恶化. ③使激怒;使怨恨 (= embitter).
im·bod·y [imˈbɔdi] *vt.* ①使肉体化,体现,使具体化. ②使形体可触知(或可见). ③使组成整体. ④化零为整,拼凑,收录 (= embody).
im·bos·om [imˈbuzəm -ˈbuːzəm] *vt.* ①把…藏于胸怀内;拥抱;怀抱. ②围护;包围;遮掩 (= embosom).
im·bow·er [imˈbauə] *vt.* 用凉亭遮掩 (= embower).
im·bri·cate [ˈimbrikeit] *vt., vi.* (使)叠盖;(使)成鳞状. — [ˈimbrikit] *a.* ①【动】叠瓦状的;鳞状的. ②重叠的.
im·bri·ca·tion [ˌimbriˈkeiʃən] *n.* 叠瓦状;鳞甲花样〔构造〕. **-ca·tive** *a.*
im·bro·gli·o [imˈbrəuliəu] *(pl. ~s)* *n.* 〔It.〕纷乱,(时局的)纠纷;(戏剧的)复杂情节;思想的混乱,误解,纠葛.
im·brown [imˈbraun] *vt.* 使成褐色 (= embrown).

im·brue [imˈbruː] *vt.* (尤指以血)玷污. ～ *one's hands with [in] blood* 犯杀人罪. **-ment** *n.*
im·brute [imˈbruːt] *vt., vi.* (使)堕落到和禽兽一样,(使)变残忍.
im·bue [imˈbjuː] *vt.* ①使吸入(水分等);浸染. ②使感染,使蒙受;鼓吹;灌注. *He is ～d with new ideas.* 他受了新思想的感染.
im·burse [imˈbəːs] *vt.* ①把…放入钱袋. ②偿还,付. ③在经济上支持.
IMCO = Intergovernmental Maritime Consultative Organization (联合国)政府间海事协商组织.
IMF = International Monetary Fund (联合国)国际货币基金组织.
im·id·az·ole [ˌimiˈdæzəul, -əˈzəul] *n.* 【化】咪唑,异吡唑.
im·ide [ˈimaid, -id] *n.* 【化】吡唑.
im·i·do [ˈimidəu, iˈmiːdəu] *a.* 【化】(酰)亚胺的.
im·ine [ˈimiːn, -in; iˈmiːn] *n.* 【化】亚胺.
im·i·no [ˈiminəu, iˈmiːnəu] *a.* 【化】亚胺的.
imit. = imitation; imitative.
im·i·ta·bil·i·ty [ˌimitəˈbiliti] *n.* 可模仿.
im·i·ta·ble [ˈimitəbl] *a.* 可模仿的;值得模仿的. *simple and ～ virtues which are within every man's reach* 人人都能办到的简单而值得模仿的美德.
im·i·tate [ˈimiteit] *vt.* ①仿效,模仿;学样;摹拟. ②仿造;伪造;假充,冒充. ～ *the virtues of great and good men* 仿效伟大善良人们的美德. ～ *the strokes of model Chinese calligraphy* 临摹字帖的笔法. *Wood is often painted to ～ stone.* 木料制品常被人们涂以油漆冒充石料制品.
im·i·ta·tion [ˌimiˈteiʃən] *n.* ①模仿,仿效;学习. ②仿造;仿造品;赝品. ③【生】拟态. ～ *leather* 人造革. ～ *wool* 人造毛. *Beware of ～s.* 谨防假冒. *an ～ of marble* 人造大理石. ***in ～ of*** 模仿. ～ **milk** 人造牛奶.
im·i·ta·tive [ˈimitətiv] *a.* ①模仿的,仿效的. ②爱模仿的. ③仿制的,伪造的. ④【生】拟态的. ***be ～ of sb.*** 仿效某人. ～ *arts* 模仿艺术〔指绘画、雕刻〕. ～ *music* 拟声音乐. ～ *words* 拟声词〔如 *hiss, moo, tinkle* 之类〕. **-ly** *ad.* **-ness** *n.*
im·i·ta·tor [ˈimiˌteitə] *n.* 模仿者;仿造者.
im·mac·u·la·cy [iˈmækjuləsi] *n.* 洁净,纯洁;无瑕.
im·mac·u·late [iˈmækjulit] *a.* 洁净的,纯洁的;洁白的;〔常谑〕毫无瑕疵的;无缺点的;【生】纯色的,无斑点的. *an ～ shirt* 洁白的衬衫. *an ～ text* 完全正确的版本. ***I- Conception***【宗】(关于圣母玛利亚的) 纯洁受胎说,圣灵怀胎说. **-ly** *ad.* **-ness** *n.*
im·mane [iˈmein] *a.* ①〔古〕巨大的;无限的,广大的. ②残酷的;野蛮的.
im·ma·nen·ce, -nen·cy [ˈimənəns, -si] *n.* 内在,固有;内在性,固有论.
im·ma·nent [ˈimənənt] *a.* ①内在的,固有的. ②意识之内的. ③【宗】存在于宇宙万物之内的(指上帝). ～ *cause* 内因 (*opp.* transcendent cause). *an ～ factor* 内在的因素. **-ly** *ad.*
im·ma·nent·ism [ˈimənəntizm] *n.* ①【哲】内在论,认识固定论. ②【神】上帝无所不在论.
im·ma·nent·ist [ˈimənəntist] *n.* 内在论者.
Im·man·u·el [iˈmænjuəl] *n.* 伊曼纽尔〔男子名〕〔Heb. = God with us〕.
im·ma·te·ri·al [ˌiməˈtiəriəl] *a.* ①非物质的,无形的. ②不重要的,不足取的,琐细的. *It is quite ～ to me.* 那对我无所谓.
im·ma·te·ri·al·ism [ˌiməˈtiəriəlizəm] *n.* 非物质论.
im·ma·te·ri·al·ist [ˌiməˈtiəriəlist] *n.* 非物质论者〔英国崇奉贝克莱的主观唯心主义的人〕.
im·ma·te·ri·al·i·ty [ˈiməˌtiəriˈæliti] *n.* ①非物质性,无形物. ②不重要.
im·ma·te·ri·al·ize [ˌiməˈtiəriəlaiz] *vt.* 使无实体,使无形.
im·ma·ture [ˌiməˈtjuə] *a.* ①未成熟的. ②未完成的,不完全的,粗糙的. ③【地】幼年的,未成年的. ～ *fruit* 尚未成熟的果实. *an ～ essay* 不成熟的论文. ～ *death* 夭折. **-ly** *ad.* **-ness** *n.*
im·ma·tu·ri·ty [ˌiməˈtjuəriti, -ˈtuər-, -ˈtʃuər-] *n.* 不成熟;生硬;不圆熟;幼稚 (= immatureness).
im·meas·ur·a·ble [iˈmeʒərəbl] *a.* 无法计量的;无穷尽的;巨大的,广大的. **-bil·i·ty** *n.* **-bly** *ad.*
im·meas·ur·a·ble·ness [iˈmeʒərəblnis] *n.* 无法计量;无限;广阔无垠.
im·me·di·a·cy [iˈmiːdiəsi] *n.* 直接;直接性;刻不容缓.
im·me·di·ate [iˈmiːdjət, -dʒət] *a.* ①直接的;最接近的. ②即时的,立即的. ③当前的,现在的. ④直觉的. ～ *delivery*【商】即交. ～ *payment*【商】即付. ～ *reply* 立即答复. ～ *shipment*【商】即装. *our ～ plans* 当前计划. *an ～ cause* 直接原因,近因. *in the ～ future* 在最近的将来. ～ *information* 第一手消息. *one's ～ neighbour* 紧邻. *one's ～ superior* 顶头上司,上一级领导. ～ *perception* 直觉. ～ **constituent**【语】直接构成要素. **-ness** *n.*
im·me·di·ate·ly [iˈmiːdjətli] *ad.* ①马上,立即. ②直接地,紧密地. ～ *in the vicinity* 就在附近. — *conj.* 〔英〕一…(就…) (= as soon as). *I told him ～ he came.* 他一来我就告诉他了.
im·med·i·ca·ble [iˈmedikəbl] *a.* 医不好的,无法治疗的.
Im·mel·mann (turn) [ˈimilˌmɑːn, -mən]【空】伊麦尔曼式筋斗翻转〔因德国飞行员 M. 伊麦尔曼而得名: 飞机作半筋斗翻转后还原〕.
im·me·mo·ri·al [ˌimiˈmɔːriəl] *a.* 无法追忆的;太古的,极古的. *from time ～* 远古以来. **-ly** *ad.*
im·mense [iˈmens] *a.* ①无限的,无穷尽的;巨大的,广大的. ②〔俚〕极好的,极妙的. *an ～ amount* 巨额的. *an ～ ocean* 无边的海洋. *The performance was ～.* 演出很成功. **-ly** *ad.* 无限地,大大地;〔口〕非常,很. **-ness** [iˈmensnis], **-si·ty** [iˈmensiti] *n.* 巨大,广大;无限,无限空间;巨物.
im·men·su·ra·ble [iˈmenʃurəbl] *a.* = immeasurable.
im·merge [iˈməːdʒ] *vi.* ①浸入. ②专心,埋头. *There is no need to ～ further into this topic.* 不必再钻进这个题目里了. — *vt.* 〔古〕 = immerse.
im·merse [iˈməːs] *vt.* ①沉浸. ②给…施浸礼〔基督教中的一种仪式〕. ③〔主要用于 ～ *oneself* 或被动语态〕使埋头,使一心一意地…;卷入,陷入. *be ～ed in difficulties* 陷入重重困难中. ～ *oneself among the masses* 深入群众中. ～ *oneself [be ～d] in study* 埋头研究.
im·mersed [iˈməːst] *a.* ①浸入的,沉入的. ②【宗】行浸礼的. ③【生】陷入的. ④【植】沉水(生长)的.
im·mers·i·ble [iˈməːsibl] *a.* (某些电气用品)可置于水中的.
im·mer·sion [iˈməːʃən] *n.* ①沉浸,浸没. ②【宗】浸礼. ③【天】掩始. ④专心. ～ *in study* 埋头研究. ～ *in thought* 沉思. ～ **freezer** 浸液致冷器. ～ **heater** 浸入式加热器. ～ **lens**【物】浸没透镜.
im·mesh [iˈmeʃ] *vt.* 网捕;使缠住;使陷入网中 (= enmesh).
im·me·thod·i·cal [ˌimiˈθɔdikəl] *a.* 不规则的,无秩序的,杂乱的. **-ly** *ad.*
im·met·ri·cal [iˈmetrikəl] *a.* 无韵律的.
im·mie [ˈimiː] *n.* 〔口〕玛瑙弹球,玻璃弹子.
im·mi·grant [ˈimigrənt] *a.* (从外国)移来的,移民的,侨民的 (*cf.* emigrant). — *n.* ①(来自外国的)移民,侨民. ②从异地移入的动物〔植物〕. *European ～s in America.* 住在美国的欧洲侨民.
im·mi·grate [ˈimigreit] *vi.* 移居外国,迁移 (*opp.* emigrate) — *vt.* 使移居,移(民).

im·mi·gra·tion [ˌimiˈgreiʃən] *n.* ①移居；移民出境. ②移民总称. *the ~ law* 移民法. *an ~ officer* 入境检查员.

im·mi·nence, im·mi·nen·cy [ˈiminəns, -si] *n.* 急迫；迫近的危险[祸患]，燃眉之急.

im·mi·nent [ˈiminənt] *a.* 迫切的，危急的，逼近眼前的，临头的. *A storm is ~.* 暴风雨即将来临. **-ly** *ad.*

im·min·gle [iˈmiŋgl] *vt., vi.* ***(-gled, -gling)*** = intermingle.

im·mis·ci·ble [iˈmisəbl] *a.* 不能混和的，不溶混的. **-bil·i·ty** *n.* **-bly** *ad.*

im·mis·sion [iˈmiʃən] *n.* 注入，注射.

im·mit·i·ga·ble [iˈmitigəbl] *a.* 不能调解的，不能缓和的，不能减轻的. **-bly** *ad.*

im·mix [iˈmiks] *vt., vi.* 混合，混杂，卷入，搀和. **-ture** [-tʃə] *n.*

im·mo·bile [iˈməubail] *a.* ①不动的，不机动的，固定的. ②不变的，静止的. **-bil·i·ty** [ˌiməuˈbiliti] *n.*

im·mo·bi·lize [iˈməubilaiz] *vt.* ①使不动，使固定. ②使(部队、车辆)不能调动. ③收回(硬币)使不流通. ④(用夹板等)使(肢、关节)不动. **-za·tion** [iˌməubilaiˈzeiʃən] *n.*

im·mod·er·ate [iˈmɔdərit] *a.* 无节制的，过度的，过分的(放纵等). **-ly** *ad.* **-ness** *n.*

im·mod·er·a·tion [iˌmɔdəˈreiʃən] *n.* 无节制；放肆，过度，极端.

im·mod·est [iˈmɔdist] *a.* ①不谦虚的，不礼貌的；不正派的；无节制的. ②莽撞的，卤莽的，不客气的，放肆的. **-ly** *ad.*

im·mod·es·ty [iˈmɔdisti] *n.* ①不谦虚，不礼貌，不正派，无节制. ②莽撞，卤莽，不客气；放肆.

im·mo·late [ˈiməuleit] *vt.* ①宰杀…作祭品. ②牺牲. ③杀戮，毁灭. **-la·tion** *n.* **-la·tor** *n.* 被当作祭品的人.

im·mo·ral [iˈmɔrəl] *a.* ①不道德的，道德败坏的，邪恶的. ②不正派的，猥亵的. **-ly** *ad.*

im·mor·al·ist [iˈmɔːrəlist] *n.* 不道德的人(尤指鼓吹不道德行为者).

im·mo·ral·i·ty [ˌiməˈræliti] *n.* ①不道德，道德败坏. ②不道德的行为，伤风败俗的行为.

im·mor·tal [iˈmɔːtl] *a.* ①不死的；不灭的. ②永生的，不朽的. ③〔口〕永久的. ④神的. — *n.* ①不死的人[物]. ②〔*pl.*〕(古希腊，罗马神话中的)诸神. ③不朽的作家. ④〔I-〕法国科学院院士；〔I-s〕古代波斯万人近卫军成员. *the I- Bard* 不朽的诗人〔指莎士比亚〕. *the Forty Immortals* 法国科学院 40 人委员会成员. [ˌimɔˈtæliti] **-tal·i·ty** *n.*

im·mor·tal·ize [iˈmɔːtəlaiz] *vt.* 使不朽，使不灭；使传诸永远. **-i·za·tion** *n.*

im·mor·tal·ly [iˈmɔːtəli] *ad.* 不朽地，永久地；〔口〕非常，很. *be ~ green* 万年常青. *be ~ glad* 很高兴.

im·mor·telle [ˌimɔːˈtel] *n.* (坟墓上插用的)灰毛菊、银苞菊等，(花干后色和形状不变的)菊科植物.

im·mo·tile [iˈməutl] *a.* 不动的，固定的，不能移动的.

im·mov·a·bil·i·ty [iˌmuːvəˈbiliti] *n.* 不动(性)，不变(性)，固定(性).

im·mov·a·ble [iˈmuːvəbl] *a.* ①稳定的，固定的. ②(精神、决心等)不可动摇的；不屈的；坚定的；冷静的，呆板的. ③(节日等)固定不变的；【法】(财产)不动的 (*opp.* movable, personal). *~ property* 不动产. — *n.* 固定不动[不变]；〔常用 *pl.*〕【法】不动产. **-bly** *ad.* **-ness** *n.*

im·mune [iˈmjuːn] *a.* ①【医】免疫(性)的. ②有免疫力的，可避免的. ③免除(税等)的. ④不受影响的，无响应的. *be ~ against attack* 免受攻击. *be ~ from smallpox* 不受天花感染. *~ from taxation [taxes]* 免税. — *n.* 免疫者. ~ **agglutinin** 免疫凝集素. ~ **body** = antibody. ~ **serum** 免疫血清.

im·mu·ni·ty [iˈmjuːniti] *n.* ①(税等的)免除 (*from*)；豁免. ②免疫力，免疫性 (*from*). *acquired ~* 后天免疫性. *active ~* 自动免疫性. *diplomatic ~* 外交豁免权. *the noise ~* 【无】抗扰度，抗扰性，抗噪音度.

im·mu·nize [ˈimju(ː)naiz] *vt.* 使免疫；使免除 (*against*). *be ~d from disease* 有免疫力. *Vaccination ~s people against smallpox.* 种牛痘可以免患天花. **-ni·za·tion** *n.*

im·mu·no·chem·is·try [iˈmjuːnəuˈkemistri] 免疫化学. **-chem·i·cal** [-ikl] *a.*

im·mu·no·flu·o·res·cence [iˈmjuːnəufluːəˈresəns] *n.* 【医】萤光免疫检验法. **-cent** *a.*

im·mu·no·ge·net·ics [iˈmjuːnəudʒiˈnetiks] *n.* 〔*pl.*〕〔动词用单数〕免疫遗传学. **-net·ic** *a.*

im·mu·no·gen·ic [iˌmjuːnəuˈdʒenik] *a.* 产生免疫性的. **-gen·i·cal·ly** *ad.*

im·mu·no·glob·u·lin [iˈmjuːnəuˈglɔbjulin] *n.* 【生化】免疫球蛋白.

im·mu·nol·o·gy [ˌimjuˈnɔlədʒi] *n.* 【医】免疫学.

im·mu·no·re·ac·tion [iˈmjuːnəuriˈækʃən] *n.* 免疫反应.

im·mu·no·ther·a·py [iˈmjuːnəuˈθerəpi] *n.* 【医】免疫疗法.

im·mure [iˈmjuə] *vt.* ①禁闭，监禁. ②〔~ oneself〕使隐居，使足不出户. ③把…镶在墙上；把…埋在墙里. *~ oneself in books* 埋头读书. ~**ment** *n.*

im·mu·ta·bil·i·ty [iˌmjuːtəˈbiliti] *n.* 不变性，不易性.

im·mu·ta·ble [iˈmjuːtəbl] *a.* 不可改变的；永远不变的. **-bly** *ad.* **-ness** *n.*

Im·o·gen [ˈimədʒen] *n.* ①伊莫金(女子名). ②莎士比亚作品辛白林 (*Cymbeline*) 中的女主人公〔贞节的典型〕.

Im·o·gene [ˈiməˌdʒiːn] *n.* = Imogen ①.

imp [imp] *n.* ①顽童，小淘气. ②〔口〕小鬼，鬼娃娃. ③〔古〕孩子，后代. — *vt.* ①移植羽毛以修补(鹰的翅膀或尾巴). ②在…上装翅膀. ③加强，增大，补充.

imp. = imperative; imperfect; imperial; implement; imported; *imprimatur* (= let it be printed); 〔美〕improvement.

Imp. = imperator.

im·pact [ˈimpækt] *n.* 碰撞；冲击(力)；(火箭的)降落〔着陆〕；【军】弹着；影响，效力. *the point of ~* 弹着点. *~ head* 动压头，动压力值. *~ load* 突加负载. *~ pressure* 动压力，碰撞压力. *~ strength* 冲击韧性；(抗)冲击强度. *~ test* 冲击试验. — [imˈpækt] *vt.* ①装填，填入 (*in, into*)；压紧；塞满. ②冲击，碰撞. ~ **crater** 撞击火山口；陨石坑.

im·pact·ed [imˈpæktid] *a.* ①压紧的，嵌入的，嵌塞的，阻生的. ②人口稠密的；十分拥挤的；因人口剧增而使当地公用事业不敷需要的. *an ~ area* 人口稠密地区，〔美〕"受冲击区"(因人口剧增而造成公用事业紧张). *an ~ tooth* 阻生的牙.

im·pac·tion [imˈpækʃən] *n.* ①装紧，压紧. ②撞击. ③【医】阻生；嵌入，嵌塞. *food ~* 食物嵌塞.

im·pair [imˈpɛə] *vt.* ①损害，损伤. ②减少，削弱. *~ one's health* 损害健康. **-ment** *n.*

im·pa·la [imˈpɑːlə, -ˈpælə] *n.* ***(pl. -la, -las)*** 【动】黑斑羚 (*Aepyceros melampus*)〔产于中非和南非〕.

im·pale [imˈpeil] *vt.* ①刺穿，钉住. ②把…钉在尖桩上处死，把…绑在桩上折磨. ③使无法可想，使绝望；使尴尬. ④【纹】把(两个纹章)连扣在一个盾牌上. ⑤〔罕〕用栅围住. **-ment** *n.*

im·pal·pa·ble [imˈpælpəbl] *a.* ①摸不着的；细微的. ②难以了解的；难以识别的. *~ distinctions of meaning* 意义上的细微区别. **-bil·i·ty** *n.* **-bly** *ad.*

im·pal·u·dism [imˈpæljudizəm] *n.* 【医】疟，瘴.

im·pa·na·tion [ˌimpəˈneiʃən] *n.* 圣体圣餐合一说.

im·pan·el [imˈpænl] *vt.* = empanel.

im·par·a·dise [imˈpærədais] *vt.* ①使登天堂；使无比快乐. ②使成乐园.

im·par·i·ty [imˈpæriti] *n.* 不等，不匀称；不同，差异.

im·park [imˈpɑːk] *vt.* ①围(鹿等)在园内. ②围(地)作

公园[猎苑]. **-ka·tion** [ˌimpɑːˈkeiʃən] *n.*
im·part [imˈpɑːt] *vt.* ①给予,把…分给,传授*(to)*. ②告诉,通知 *(to)*. *~ news to sb.* 将消息通知某人. **-ment, -ta·tion** *n.*
im·par·tial [imˈpɑːʃəl] *a.* 公平的;无私的,无偏见的. **-i·ty** [ˈimˌpɑːʃiˈæliti] *n.* **-ly** *ad.*
im·part·i·ble [imˈpɑːtibl] *a.* 不能分割的,不可分的. **-bil·i·ty** *n.* **-bly** *ad.*
im·pass·a·ble [imˈpɑːsəbl] *a.* ①不可通行的,不可逾越的. ②不可流通的. **-bil·i·ty** [-ˈbiliti] *n.* **-bly** *ad.* *~ roads* 不通行的道路.
im·passe [æmˈpɑːs, im-] *n.* ①死路,死胡同. ②绝境;僵局. *reach an ~* 陷入僵局.
im·pas·si·ble [imˈpæsəbl] *a.* ①不觉疼痛的;麻木的,无感觉的. ②不能伤害的. ③泰然自若的, 无动于衷的. **-bil·i·ty** *n.* **-ness** *n.* **-bly** *ad.*
im·pas·sion [imˈpæʃən] *vt.* 激起…的热情,使感动,使感激. **-ed** *a.* 感动的; 充满热情的, 热烈的 (*an ~ed speech* 热烈的发言).
im·pas·sive [imˈpæsiv] *a.* ①无感情的,冷淡的. ②呆钝的. ③冷静的. ④无感觉的;无意识的. **-ness, -vi·ty** *n.* **-ly** *ad.*
im·paste [imˈpeist] *vt.* ①使成糊状. ②用浆糊封住[粘贴]. ③【绘】涂浓厚色彩于…上.
im·pas·to [imˈpɑːstəu] *n.* (在画上)厚涂颜料色彩.
im·pa·tience [imˈpeiʃəns] *n.* ①不耐烦,急躁. ②渴望,切望. *He awaited her answer with ~.* 他焦急地等待她的答复.
im·pa·ti·ens [imˈpeiʃiˌenz, -ʃənz] *n.* 【植】风仙花属 *(Impatiens)* 植物.
im·pa·tient [imˈpeiʃənt] *a.* ①急躁的, 急切的. ②对…不耐烦, 对…忍耐不住 *(of, with)*. ③急想, 渴望〔后接不定式〕. ④〔古〕不合的,不许的. *be ~ of any interruptions* 对任何干扰都不耐烦. *be ~ with children* 对孩子急躁. *~ for the arrival of May Day* 切望五一节的到来. *be ~ to get about one's business* 急于抓业务.
im·pav·id [imˈpævid] *a.* 〔古〕无惧的,无畏的. **-ly** *ad.*
im·pawn [imˈpɔːn] *vt.* ①典当,抵押. ②立誓,许诺.
im·pay·a·ble [imˈpeiəbl] *a.* ①金不换的, 极贵重的,无价的. ②〔口〕超越一般限度的;异常的.
im·peach [imˈpiːtʃ] *vt.* ①责问,弹劾,检举,告发. ②责难,指责,不信任,怀疑. *~ sb. with (of) a crime* 控告某人犯罪. *be ~ed for treason* 被告发犯有叛国罪. **-a·ble** *a.* **-ment** *n.*
im·pearl [imˈpəːl] *vt.* ①使形成珍珠;使形成珠状物. ②用珍珠装饰.
im·pec·ca·ble [imˈpekəbl] *a.* ①不会做坏事的;不容易做坏事的. ②无缺点的,无瑕疵的. — *n.* 不会作坏事的人;毫无缺点的人. **-bil·i·ty** *n.* **-bly** *ad.*
im·pec·cant [imˈpekənt] *a.* 无罪的;无缺点错误的;无咎的. **-can·cy** [-kənsi] *n.*
im·pe·cu·ni·ous [ˌimpiˈkjuːnjəs] *a.* 没有钱的;贫穷的. **-ni·os·i·ty** [ˌimpiˌkjuːniˈɔsiti], **-ness** *n.* 无钱;贫穷. **-ly** *ad.*
im·ped·ance [imˈpiːdəns] *n.* 【物】阻抗. *acoustic ~* 声阻抗.
im·pede [imˈpiːd] *vt.* 妨碍,阻碍,阻止: *~ sb.'s progress* 妨碍某人的进步. *The muddy roads ~ our journey.* 我们的旅游被泥泞的道路阻挠了.
im·ped·i·ment [imˈpedimənt] *n.* ①妨碍,阻碍 *(to)*; 障碍物. ②法定婚姻的障碍. ③〔*pl.*〕= *impedimenta*. ④口吃〔又作 *~ in speech*〕. ***throw ~s in the way*** 阻碍进行.
im·ped·i·men·ta [imˌpediˈmentə] *n.* 〔*pl.*〕①行李. ②妨碍行进的负重,包袱. ③【军】辎重.
im·ped·i·men·tal [imˌpediˈmentl], **im·ped·i·men·ta·ry** [-təri] *a.* 妨碍的,阻碍的. *causes ~ to success* 阻碍成功的原因.
im·pel [imˈpel] *vt.* ***(impelled; impel·ling)*** ①推动,推进;激励. ②驱使,迫使,使不得不. *~ sb. to do sth.* 推动某人做某事. *impelling force* 推进力. *What motives impelled him to do so?* 是什么动机促使他这么干? *feel impelled to speak* 觉得不得不说.
im·pel·lent [imˈpelənt] *a.* 推动的,推进的,促使的.
im·pel·ler [imˈpelə] *n.* ①推进者,推动器. ②【电】转子;转叶片. ③【机】叶轮. *an air ~* 空气叶轮. *an ~ shaft* 叶轮轴.
im·pend [imˈpend] *vi.* ①悬挂,吊(在上头) *(over)*. ②(事件,危险等)逼近;即将临头. *We went indoors because rain ~ed.* 我们进屋里去,因为就要下雨了. **-pend·ence, -cy** [-ˈpendəns, -si] *n.* **-ent** *a.* = impending.
im·pend·ing [imˈpendiŋ] *a.* 吊在头上的;逼近的,即将到来的,紧急的. *an ~ danger* 逼在眉睫的危险.
im·pen·e·tra·bil·i·ty [imˌpenitrəˈbiliti] *n.* ①不可入,不能贯穿;【物】不可入性. ②不可测知;不可解. ③无情,冷酷.
im·pen·e·tra·ble [imˈpenitrəbl] *a.* ①进不去的;难贯穿的;【物】不可入性的. ②看不透的, 不可测知的,费解的. ③不动心的,不接受的,顽固的. *~ by a bullet* 子弹打不穿的. *~ darkness* 漆黑. *an ~ mystery* 费解的秘密. *a mind ~ by [to] new ideas* 不接受新思想的顽固头脑. **-ness** *n.* **-bly** *ad.*
im·pen·e·trate [imˈpenitreit] *vt.* 穿,深深戳进;渗透.
im·pen·i·tence [imˈpenitəns], **im·pen·i·ten·cy** [-si] *n.* 不悔悟;顽固.
im·pen·i·tent [imˈpenitənt] *a., n.* 不悔悟的(人);顽固的(人). **-ly** *ad.*
imper(at). = imperative.
im·per·a·ti·val [imˌperəˈtaivəl] *a.* 【语】祈使语气的.
im·per·a·tive [imˈperətiv] *a.* ①命令的,强制的,专横的. ②不可避免的,绝对必要的,迫切的,紧急的. ③【语】祈使的. *an ~ manner* 专横的态度. *~ mood* 祈使语气. *~ sentence* 祈使句. *It is ~ that we should [it is ~ for us to] act at once.* 我们必须马上行动. *an ~ duty* 紧急任务. *~ necessity* 迫切需要. — *n.* ①命令;规则;必须做的事. ②【语】祈使语气, 祈使语气动词. **-ly** *ad.* **-ness** *n.*
im·pe·ra·tor [impəˈrɑːtɔː] *n.* 〔L.〕①(古罗马的)大将军,凯旋将军. ②皇帝,元首.
im·per·a·to·ri·al [imˌperəˈtɔːriəl] *a.* (古罗马)大将军的,皇帝的. **-ly** *ad.*
im·per·cep·ti·ble [ˌimpəˈseptəbl] *a.* ①感觉不到的,觉察不到的 *(to)*. ②细微的,微妙的. *Color is ~ to the touch.* 颜色是感觉不到的. **-bil·i·ty** [-ˈbiliti], **-ness** *n.* **-bly** *ad.*
im·per·cep·tive [ˌimpəˈseptiv] *a.* 无知觉的; 无知觉力的. **-ness** *n.*
im·per·cip·i·ent [ˌimperˈsipiənt] *a.* = imperceptive.
im·per·ence [ˈimpərəns] *n.* = impudence.
imperf. = imperfect; imperforate.
im·per·fect [imˈpəːfikt] *a.* ①不完全的,有缺点的. ②不完整的, 未完成的. ③法律上不能实施的. ④减弱的,缩小的. ⑤【语】未完成体的. *~ combustion* 不完全燃烧. *~ grain* 不饱满的谷粒. *the ~ tense* 【语】未完成时. — *n.* 【语法】未完成体. *~* **fungus** 半知菌. **-ly** *ad.* **-ness** *n.*
im·per·fect·i·ble [ˌimpəˈfektəbl] *a.* 不可能完善的.
im·per·fec·tion [ˌimpəˈfekʃən] *n.* 不完全,不足;缺点.
im·per·fec·tive [ˌimpəˈfektiv] *a.* 【语法】(俄语等动词的)未完成体的. — *n.* ①未完成体. ②未完成体动词.
im·per·fo·rate [imˈpəːfərit] *a.* ①无(气)孔的;不穿孔的. ②(邮票)无齿孔的. ③【解】无孔的,闭锁的. — *n.* 无齿孔邮票.
im·pe·ri·a [imˈpiəriə] imperium 的复数.

im·pe·ri·al [im'piəriəl] *a.* ①帝国的,皇帝[皇后]的. ②合皇帝身分的,庄严的. ③[英][常 I-] 英帝国(制定)的. ④超级的,特等的. ⑤英国度量衡法定标准的; 22×32英寸的(纸). *an ~ household* 皇室. *an ~ envoy* 钦差大臣. *the ~ examinations* (封建社会的)科举. *~ politics* 英国政治. *~ preference* [英]国内特惠关税. *~ taxes* [英]国税. *the ~ gallon* 英国加仑(=4.546升). —*n.* ①写字纸[[英]22×30或32英寸;[美]23×31英寸]. ②特等品,特大(号)物品. ③一小绺须[因拿破仑三世曾留此须而得名]. ④帝俄时代的金币[1745年第一次发行等于10卢布;从1897年到1917年等于15卢布]. ⑤公共马车顶,放在车顶上的箱子. ⑥【史】神圣罗马皇帝的拥护者.

im·pe·ri·al·ism [im'piəriəlizəm] *n.* 帝国主义.

im·pe·ri·al·ist [im'piəriəlist] *n.* ①帝国主义者. ②皇帝的支持者;帝制拥护者. ③[I-]【史】神圣罗马皇帝的拥护者. —*a.* 帝国主义的.

im·pe·ri·al·is·tic [im,piəriə'listik] *a.* ①帝国主义的,帝国主义者的. ②赞成帝国主义的. **-ti·cal·ly** *ad.*

im·pe·ri·al·ize [im'piəriəlaiz] *vt.* ①使成帝国. ②使帝国主义化.

im·per·il [im'peril] *vt.* ***(im·per·il(l)ed; im·per·il(l)-ing)*** 危害,使陷于危险.

im·pe·ri·ous [im'piəriəs] *a.* ①专横的;傲慢的. ②迫切的,紧要的. *an ~ manner* 自高自大的样子. *~ need* 紧急的需要. **-ly** *ad.* **-ness** *n.*

im·per·ish·a·ble [im'periʃəbl] *a.* 不灭的,不朽的,永久的. **-bil·i·ty** *n.* **-bly** *ad.*

im·pe·ri·um [im'piəriəm] *n.* *(pl.* ***-ri·a*** [-riə]*)* *n.* [L.] 最高权力;主权;统治权;司法权;裁判权. *~* ***in imperio*** 政府中的政府,帝国中的帝国,主权内的主权.

im·per·ma·nence [im'pə:mənəns], **im·per·ma·nen·cy** [-si] *n.* 非永久(性),暂时(性).

im·per·ma·nent [im'pə:mənənt] *a.* 非永久的,暂时的.

im·per·me·a·ble [im'pə:mjəbl] *a.* ①不能通过的. ②不能透过的,不可渗透的. *The passage became absolutely ~.* 过道完全不通了. *~ to water* 不透水的. **-bil·i·ty** [im,pə:mjə'biliti] *n.*

im·per·mis·si·ble [,impə'misəbl] *a.* 不允许的,不许可的. **-bil·i·ty** *n.*

impers. = impersonal.

im·per·scrip·ti·ble [,impə'skriptəbl] *a.* 没有文件证明的;非官方的,非正式的.

im·per·son·al [im'pə:snl] *a.* ①非个人的,和个人无关的. ②不具人格的;一般性的. ③【语法】非人称的. *~ forces* 非人力. *an ~ verbs* 【语法】非人称动词. *~ pronouns* 非人称代词. —*n.*【语法】非人称动词;非人称代名词. **-i·ty** [im,pə:sə'næliti] *n.* 与个人无关,非人格性;非人格性的东西. **-ly** *ad.*

im·per·son·al·ize [im'pə:snəlaiz] *vt.* ***(-iz·ed, -iz-ing)*** 除去个性;使非人格化,使…不特指.

im·per·son·ate [im'pə:səneit] *vt.* ①使人格化,体现. ②模仿,扮演,假冒. —*a.* 被人格化了的,体现…的.

im·per·son·a·tion [im,pə:sə'neiʃən] *n.* 使人格化;体现;扮演;模仿;假冒.

im·per·son·a·tive [im'pə:səneitiv] *a.* 扮演的,模仿的.

im·per·son·a·tor [im'pə:səneitə] *n.* 扮演者,模仿者.

im·per·son·i·fy [,impə'sonifai] *v.* = personify.

im·per·ti·nence [im'pə:tinəns], **im·per·ti·nen·cy** [-si] *n.* ①无礼,鲁莽,傲慢. ②不适当,弄错. ③离题,不得要领. ④鲁莽的言行.

im·per·ti·nent [im'pə:tinənt] *a.* ①无礼的,鲁莽的,傲慢的. ②不适当的,不恰当的. ③离题的,不得要领的. *an ~ youth* 傲慢的青年. *adduce ~ facts in support of a theory* 罗列不恰当的事实支持某一学说. **-ly** *ad.*

im·per·turb·a·ble [,impə(:)'tə:bəbl] *a.* 沉着的,冷静的. **-bil·i·ty** ['impə(:),tə:bə'biliti], **-ness** *n.* **-bly** *ad.*

im·per·tur·ba·tion [,impə:tə'beiʃən] *n.* 沉着,冷静.

im·per·vi·ous [im'pə:vjəs] *a.* ①不可渗透的,穿不过的,透不过的. ②不受干扰的,不受影响的. ③对(批评等)无动于衷的,不接受的. *an ~ desert* 无人能通过的沙漠. *be ~ to all reason* 不通情理. **-ly** *ad.* **-ness** *n.*

im·pe·ti·go [,impi'taigəu] *n.*【医】脓疱病.

im·pe·trate ['impitreit] *vt.* ***(-trat·ed, -trat·ing)*** ①求得. ②[罕]恳求;哀求. **-tra·tion** *n.*

im·pe·tig·i·nous [,impi'tidʒinəs] *a.* 脓疱病的;如脓疱病的.

im·pet·u·os·i·ty [im,petju'ɔsiti] *n.* 激烈,猛烈;急躁;急性病.

im·pet·u·ous [im'petjuəs] *a.* ①激烈的,猛烈的. ②激动的;急躁的;冲动的,轻举妄动的,鲁莽的. *an ~ charge* 猛袭. *an ~ wind* 狂风. *an ~ youth* 急躁的青年. **-ly** *ad.* **-ness** *n.*

im·pe·tus ['impitəs] *n.* ①动量,动力. ②推动,促进. ***give [lend] an ~ to*** 推动,刺激,促进. ***with great ~*** 用大力.

impf. = imperfect.

imp. gal. = imperial gallon.

im·pi ['impi] *n.* *(pl.* *~es, ~s)* (南非)卡菲尔 *(Kaffir)* 人的武装队或其他南方武装部队.

im·pi·e·ty [im'paiəti] *n.* ①不虔诚,不信神. ②不恭敬,不孝. ③不恭敬的言行,邪恶的言行.

imp·ing ['impiŋ] *n.* 接枝;接穗.

im·pinge [im'pindʒ] *vi.* ①冲击,撞击 *(on, upon, against)*. ②侵害;侵犯. ③(密切)接触. *Rays of light ~ upon the retina.* 光线射到网膜上. *~ on [upon] one's authority* 侵犯某人权限. —*vt.* (气体等)撞击. **-ment** *n.*

im·pi·ous ['impiəs] *a.* ①不信神的,邪恶的. ②不恭敬的,不孝的. **-ly** *ad.*

imp·ish ['impiʃ] *a.* 小鬼似的;顽皮的. **-ly** *ad.* **-ness** *n.*

im·plac·a·ble [im'plækəbl] *a.* ①难宽恕的;难和解的,仇恨深的;毫不留情的. ②不能改变的. *an ~ enemy* 死敌. ***have an ~ hatred for ...*** 对…深恶痛绝. **-bil·i·ty** [-'biliti], **-ness** *n.* **-bly** *ad.*

im·pla·cen·tal, im·pla·cen·tate [,implə'sentl, -teit] *a.* (哺乳动物)无胎盘的(=aplacental).

im·plant [im'plɑ:nt] *vt.* ①植,栽进. ②【医】移植. ③注入,灌输,牢固树立. —['implɑ:nt] *n.* ①移植片,移植物. ②【医】(插入体内治癌症等用的)植入管.

im·plan·ta·tion [,implɑ:n'teiʃən] *n.* ①种植. ②插入;灌输,鼓吹. ③【医】皮下注射.

im·plau·si·ble [im'plɔ:zəbl] *a.* 难以置信的,不象有理的. **-bil·i·ty** *n.* **-bly** *ad.*

im·plead [im'pli:d] *vt.* 控告. —*vi.* 起诉.

im·ple·ment ['implimənt] *n.* [常用 *pl.*] ①工具;器具. ②[Scot.]【法】履行(契约等). *agricultural [farm] ~s* 农具. *household ~s* 家具,日用器具. *~s of warfare* 武器. —*vt.* ①给…供给器具. ②执行,履行(契约);落实(政策);贯彻,实施;使生效. ③把…填满;补充. *~ our foreign policy* 执行外交政策.

im·ple·men·tal [,impli'mentl] *a.* ①器具的,作器具用的. ②起作用的,有帮助的.

im·ple·men·ta·tion [,implimen'teiʃən] *n.* 执行,履行;贯彻,落实.

im·ple·tion [im'pli:ʃən] *n.* 满,充满.

im·pli·cate ['implikeit] *vt.* ①使纠缠,缠绕. ②令生关系,使牵连. ③影响[用于被动语态]. ④含有…的意思. *be ~d in ...* 和…有牵连[有连带关系]. *This confession ~s numerous officials in the bribery scandal.* 这一供认会使许多官员牵连到受贿的丑事中. —['implikit] *n.* 包含(暗指)的东西.

im·pli·ca·tion [,impli'keiʃən] *n.* ①牵连,牵涉,纠缠. ②含蓄,含意,言外之意. ③【数】蕴涵,蕴含. ④本质,实质. ⑤[常 *pl.*] 推断,结论. ***by ~*** 含蓄地,用寓意,

暗中. *agree by* ~ 默契.

im·pli·ca·tive [im'plikətiv;'implikeitiv] *a.* ①含蓄的,意外之意的. ②牵连的. **-ly** *ad.*

im·plic·it [im'plisit] *a.* ①含蓄的,不讲明的. ②内含的,隐含的 *(opp.* explicit*)*. ③绝对的,盲目的. *an* ~ *agreement* 默契,暗暗同意. *an* ~ *answer* 含蓄的答复. ~ *obedience* 盲从. ~ ***confidence in*** 盲目相信. ~ **differentiation**【数】隐微分法. ~ **function**【数】隐函数. **-ly** *ad.*

im·plied [im'plaid] *a.* 含蓄的,隐含的,不言而喻的,言外的 *(opp.* expressed*)*. *an* ~ *consent* 默许. **-ly**[-aiidli] *ad.*

im·plode [im'pləud] *vi., vt.*【物】①(使)爆聚,(使)内向爆炸;(使)压破. ②【语】用内破裂音发(音).

im·plore [im'plɔ:] *vt.* 恳求,乞求,哀求. ~ *sb. for sth.* 为某事恳求某人. ~ *sb. to do sth.* 央求某人做某事. **-ra·tion** [ˌimplɔ:'reiʃən] *n.*

im·plor·ing [im'plɔ:riŋ] *a.* 恳求的,乞求的,哀求的. **-ly** *ad.*

im·plo·sion [im'pləuʒən] *n.* ①【物】爆聚,内向爆炸 *(opp.* explosion*)*. ②【语】内破裂.

im·plo·sive [im'pləusiv] *a.* 内破裂形成的. — *n.* 内破裂音. **-ly** *ad.*

im·plu·vi·um [im'plu:viəm] *n. (pl.* ***-vi·a*** [-viə]*) n.* (古代罗马房屋院内的)蓄水池.

im·ply [im'plai] *vt.* ①含蓄,包含;含有…的意思. ②暗示,暗指. *Silence often implies consent.* 沉默常常表示同意. *Do you realize what his words* ~*?* 你领会他说话的含意吗? *Do you* ~ *that ...?* 你的意思是不是说…?

im·po ['impəu] *n.* 〔俚〕= imposition, impot.

im·pol·der [im'poldə] *vt.* 从海边围垦(土地),把…变成耕地.

im·pol·i·cy [im'pɔlisi] *n.* 失策,不明智.

im·po·lite [impə'lait] *a.* 没礼貌的,失礼的,粗鲁的. **-ly** *ad.* **-ness** *n.*

im·pol·i·tic [im'pɔlitik] *a.* 失策的,不得当的,不高明的. **-ly** *ad.*

im·pon·der·a·ble [im'pɔndərəbl] *a.* ①无重量的,极轻的. ②不可称量的,无法估计的. *be of* ~ *weight* 重量称不出. — *n.* ①无重量的东西,不可量物. ②〔*pl.*〕无法估量的事物〔影响、作用〕. **-bil·i·ty** [imˌpɔndərə'biliti], **-ness** *n.*, **-bly** *ad.*

im·pone [im'pəun] *vt.* ***(-pon·ed, -pon·ing)*** 〔废〕保证;赌,打赌,作赌注.

im·port [im'pɔ:t, 'impɔ:t] *vt.* ①输入;进口;引进 *(opp.* export*)*. ②意味,表明,说明. ③对…有重大关系. ~ *sth. from a country* 从某国输入某物. ~ *sth. into a country* 把某物输入某国. ~*ed goods* 进口货. ~ *personal feelings into a discussion* 把个人感情带进讨论中. *I should like to know what his action* ~*s.* 我倒想知道他的行动用意何在. *It* ~*s us to know ...* 知道…对我们有重大关系. *questions that* ~ *us nearly* 和我们有切身关系的问题. —*vi.* 有(重大)关系. *It* ~*s little whether we are early or late.* 我们早点迟点没什么关系. —['impɔ:t] *n.* ①输入,进口,引进;〔主 *pl.*〕进口货. ②意义,含义. ③重要(性). ~ *duties* 进口税. *an* ~ *surplus* 入超. *an* ~ *quota* 进口限额. *the* ~ *of his remarks* 他说话的含意. *a matter of great* ~ 大事情.

im·port·a·ble [im'pɔ:təbl] *a.* 可进口的.

im·por·tance [im'pɔ:təns] *n.* ①重要性. ②重要地位,显著,有力. ③骄傲,自大. *a matter of great* ~ 重大事情. *a matter of no* ~ 无关紧要的事. *a position of* ~ 重要地位. *be conscious of one's* ~ 自己觉得了不起,自高自大. *speak with an air of* ~ 带着傲慢的态度讲话. ***attach*** ~ ***to*** 重视.

im·por·tant [im'pɔ:tənt] *a.* ①重要的,重大的. ②大量的,许多,大的. ③优越的,显著的;有权力的. ④自恃自大的. *an* ~ *figure [person]* 要人. *look* ~ 了不起似的. **-ly** *ad.*

im·por·ta·tion [ˌimpɔ:'teiʃən] *n.* 输入,进口,引进 *(opp.* exportation*)*; 进口货,输入品.

im·port·er [im'pɔ:tə] *n.* 进口商,进口者 *(opp.* exporter*)*.

im·por·tu·nate [im'pɔ:tjunit] *a.* 强求的,缠扰不休的,讨厌的. ②坚持的,迫切的. **-ly** *ad.*

im·por·tune [im'pɔ:tju:n] *vt.* ①向…硬要,向…强求,死乞白赖地要求. ②纠缠. ③(妓女)拉客. ~ *sb. for sth.* 向某人强求某物. — *vi.* 强求;纠缠不休. — *a.* = importunate. **-ni·ty** [-niti] *n.*

im·pose [im'pəuz] *vt.* ①征收(税等),使…负担. ②强派(工),把…强加给. ③把(次品等)硬卖给;以…欺骗 *(upon, on)*. ④【印】把…拼版,装版. ⑤〔古〕放置. ~ *a tax upon [on] sb.* 向某人征税. ~ *one's opinion upon sb.* 把意见强加于某人. ~ *a false article upon [on] sb.* 拿假货卖给人. ~ *hands on sb.*【宗】对某人按手. — *vi.* ①利用 *(on, upon)*. ②欺骗 *(on, upon)*. ③施加影响 *(on, upon)*. ~ *upon sb.'s kindness* 趁人心软. *I am not to be* ~*d upon.* 我是不会上当的.

im·pos·ing [im'pəuziŋ] *a.* ①给人印象深刻的. ②(建筑物等)堂皇的,雄伟的,使人赞叹的. *an* ~ *appearance.* 仪表堂堂. *an* ~ *building* 壮丽的大楼. *an* ~ *figure* 大人物,要人.

im·po·si·tion [ˌimpə'ziʃən] *n.* ①征税,课税;税,负担. ②强加,强迫接受. ③〔英〕(处罚学生的)惩罚作业〔略: impo, impot〕. ④欺瞒,哄骗. ⑤〔罕〕置放,安放;【宗】按手礼. ⑥【印】拼版,装版.

im·pos·si·bil·i·ty [imˌpɔsə'biliti] *n.* 不可能;不可能的事.

im·pos·si·ble [im'pɔsəbl] *a.* ①做不到的,不能做的,不可能的. ②不会有的,不会发生的;不能相信的;〔口〕(帽子等)奇形怪状的. ③〔口〕不能忍受的,讨厌的. *an* ~ *fellow* 讨厌的家伙. *an* ~ *event* 不可能发生的事件. *an* ~ *story* 不能相信的故事. *Nothing is* ~ *to a willing mind.* 〔谚〕天下无难事,只怕有心人. *an* ~ *task* 不可能的工作. ~ ***of execution*** 无法实行. ***next to*** ~ 几乎是不可能的. ***not*** ~ 并非不可能. ***try to do the*** ~ 想做做不到的事;缘木求鱼. ~ **art** 概念"艺术"〔侧重反映艺术家在创作过程中产生的概念的一种"艺术",又称 conceptual art〕.

im·pos·si·bly [im'pɔsəbli] *ad.* 办不到地,不可能地;无法可想地. *not* ~ 多半,或许.

im·post[1] ['impəust] *n.* ①税,进口税,关税. ②〔俚〕【赛马】强马所负担的重量. —*vt.*〔美〕类分(进口商品,以便征税).

im·post[2] ['impəust] *n.*【建】拱墩,拱基.

im·pos·t(h)ume [im'pɔstju:m] *n.* 〔古〕①脓肿. ②腐败,道德败坏.

im·pos·tor [im'pɔstə] *n.* 冒名顶替者;骗子.

im·pos·ture [im'pɔstʃə] *n.* 冒名顶替;欺骗,诈骗行为;以诈骗为生.

im·pot ['impɔt] *n.* ①〔英俚〕= imposition. ②impo.

im·po·tence ['impətəns], **im·po·ten·cy** [-si] *n.* ①无力,衰弱;无能. ②无效,无法可想. ③【医】阳萎. *We have reduced the enemy to* ~. 我们已经使敌人丧失战斗力.

im·po·tent ['impətənt] *a.* ①无力的,虚弱的;软弱无能的,不起作用的. ②【医】阳萎的. *an* ~ *conclusion* 虎头蛇尾. *in* ~ *fury* 干着急. — *n.* 虚弱者;阳萎者. **-ly** *ad.*

im·pound [im'paund] *vt.* ①(将家畜)关在栏中;拘禁(人等). ②蓄(水等). ③充公,没收.

im·pov·er·ish [im'pɔvəriʃ] *vt.* ①使穷困. ②使枯竭. ~*ed health* 虚弱无力的健康状况. *an* ~*ed existence* 平淡无味的生存. ~*ed rubber* 失去弹性的橡皮. ~*ed soil* 贫瘠的土壤. **-ment** *n.*

im·pow·er [imˈpauə] *vt.* empower 的废体.

im·prac·ti·ca·ble [imˈpræktikəbl] *a.* ①不能实行的,做不到的,不现实的. ②难对付的,顽梗的(人等). ③不能用的,不能通行的(道路等). *an* ~ *scheme* 不能实行的计划. **-bil·i·ty** [-ˈbiliti], **-ness** *n.* **-bly** *ad.*

im·prac·ti·cal [imˈpræktikəl] *a.* ①不实用的,不实际的. ②不能实行的,做不到的. **-ly** *ad.* **-i·ty** [imˌpræktiˈkæliti], **-ness** *n.*

im·pre·cate [ˈimprikeit] *vt.* 咒,诅咒,祈求降(祸) *(upon)*. ~ *evil upon sb.* 祈求降祸某人. **-ca·tion** [ˌimpriˈkeiʃən] *n.* **-ca·to·ry** *a.*

im·pre·cise [ˌimpriˈsais] *a.* 不精确的;不精密的;不确定的;含糊的. **-ly** *ad.* **-sion** [-ˈsiʒən] *n.*

im·preg [ˈimpreg] *n.*【建】树脂浸渍木材.

im·preg·na·ble[1] [imˈpregnəbl] *a.* 难攻破的;坚固的,坚定的. *an* ~ *argument* 破绽毫无的议论. *an* ~ *belief* 坚定不移的信念. *an* ~ *bulwark* 坚不可摧的堡垒. ~ *virtue* 坚贞不屈的情操. **-bly** *ad.* **-bil·i·ty** [imˌpregnəˈbiliti], **-ness** *n.*

im·preg·na·ble[2] [imˈpregnəbl] *a.* 有受精[怀孕]可能的.

im·preg·nate [ˈimpregneit] *vt.* ①使受精,使怀孕. ②使充满,使饱和 *(with)*. ③渗透,灌注,注入 *(with)*. *water* ~*d with salt* 饱含盐的水. — [imˈpregnit] *a.* 怀孕的;渗透的;饱和的. **-na·tion** [ˌimpregˈneiʃən] *n.* 怀孕,受精;饱和;注入;【矿】围岩中的浸染矿床;【化】渗透. **-tor** *n.*, **-to·ry** *a.*

im·pre·sa [imˈpreizə] *n.*〔废〕箴言;箴言牌.

im·pre·sa·ri·o [ˌimpreˈsɑːriəu] *n.* *(pl.* ~*s)*〔It.〕(歌剧团、乐团等的)演出主办人;经理,导演,指挥.

im·pre·scrip·ti·ble [ˌimprisˈkriptibl] *a.* 不受法令约束的;不可剥夺的;不可侵犯的.

im·press[1] [imˈpres] *vt.* *(*~*ed* 或〔古〕*im·prest)* ①盖印;在…打上记号. ②使铭记,使记住;使深深感到. ③传递,发送. ④【电】给(线路)加电压. *He did not* ~ *me at all.* 他没有给我留下丝毫印象. *an* ~*ed current* 外加电流. ~ *a mark (up)on a surface* = ~ *a surface with a mark* 在表面上打记号. *an* ~*ed stamp* 盖了戳的邮票. ~ *an official letter with one's seal* = ~ *one's seal on an official letter* 在公函上盖印. ***be favourably [unfavourably]*** ~***ed*** 中意[不中意],得到好的[不好的]印象. ***be*** ~***ed by [with]*** 深感;为…所感动. — *vi.* 引人注意,哗众取宠. — *n.* ①盖印;铭刻;印记,记号. ②印象,痕迹;特征. *bear the* ~ *of* 带有…的特征.

im·press[2] [imˈpres] *vt.* *(*~*ed* 或〔古〕*im·prest)* ①强制…服兵役. ②征用. ③(在辩论中)引用,利用. —[ˈimpres] *n.* = impressment.

im·press·i·ble [imˈpresəbl] *a.* 可印的,可铭刻的;容易感动的,敏感的. **-bil·i·ty** [imˌpresiˈbiliti] *n.* **-bly** *ad.*

im·pres·sion [imˈpreʃən] *n.* ①印象,感觉;感想,模糊的观念. ②意见,想法. ③影响,效果. ④盖印,印记,压痕. ⑤【印】印刷,印数,印次,第…版,印制品;(雕版等的)印图. ⑥(牙齿的)印模. *First* ~ *are half the battle [are most lasting].*〔谚〕最初的印象最重要[最深刻]. *be under the* ~ *that* 有…这样的想法. *give one's* ~*s of* 陈述自己的意见. *make an* ~ *on sb.* 给某人印象,使某人感动. *make no* ~ *on sb.* 对某人无影响. *a first* ~ *of 200,000 copies* 初版二十万册. *the second* ~ *of the second edition* 再版第二次印刷.

im·pres·sion·a·ble [imˈpreʃənəbl] *a.* 易感的,敏感的,易受影响的;可以打上记号的;可塑的. **-bil·i·ty** [imˌpreʃənəˈbiliti] *n.*

im·pres·sion·al [imˈpreʃənəl] *a.* 印象的,基于印象的;印象派的.

im·pres·sion·ism [imˈpreʃənizəm] *n.* 印象主义,印象派〔十九世纪七十年代兴起的在绘画、文艺方面的一种流派. 代表人物绘画方面如西班牙画家毕加索. 音乐方面如法国作曲家德彪西〕.

im·pres·sion·ist [imˈpreʃənist] *n.* ①印象主义者,印象派艺术家. ②(专门摹仿名人以取悦观众的)摹仿演员. — *a.* 印象主义的,印象派的.

im·pres·sion·is·tic [imˌpreʃəˈnistik] *a.* 印象的,印象主义的,印象派的. **-ti·cal·ly** *ad.*

im·pres·sive [imˈpresiv] *a.* 给人深刻印象的,令人难忘的,令人感动的. *an* ~ *ceremony* 给人深刻印象的典礼. **-ly** *ad.* **-ness** *n.*

im·press·ment [imˈpresmənt] *n.* 强迫服役;征用,强征. *the* ~ *of soldiers* 强制征兵.

im·pres·sure [imˈpreʃə]〔古〕(= impression).

im·prest[1] [ˈimprest] *n.* (政府基金的)预付款;预付公务费. — *a.*【会计】预付的,借支的.

im·prest[2] [imˈprest] *v.*〔古〕impress[1,2] 的过去式和过去分词.

im·pri·ma·tur [ˌimpriˈmeitə] *n.*〔L.〕①(主指天主教的)出版牌照. ②(官方审查后的)出版许可. ③认可,批准.

im·pri·mis [imˈpraimis] *ad.*〔L.〕最初,首先.

im·print [imˈprint] *vt.* ①盖(印);印刷. ②刻上(记号),标出(特征). ③使铭记,使铭感. ~ *a letter with a postmark* 信件上盖上邮戳. ~ *one's personality on one's writing* 在作品里表现出个性. *ideas forever* ~*ed on one's mind* 永远铭刻于心. —[ˈimprint] *n.* 盖印,刻印;痕迹;特征;印象;(书籍的)版权标记. *the printer's [publisher's]* ~ = The ~. (书籍版权页上关于出版者、印刷者及发行年月日的)版本说明.

im·print·ing [imˈprintiŋ] *n.*【心】铭记〔动物生命早期即起作用的一种学习机制〕.

im·pris·on [imˈprizn] *vt.* ①关押,监禁. ②束缚,限制. **-ment** *n.* 关押;束缚 (*be sentenced to one year's imprisonment* 被判一年徒刑).

im·prob·a·bil·i·ty [imˌprɔbəˈbiliti] *n.* 不大可能,不大可能有的事. *Don't worry about such improbabilities as earthquakes.* 不必为象地震这类罕见的事情而担心.

im·prob·a·ble [imˈprɔbəbl] *a.* ①未必有的,不大可能发生的;罕见的. ②【物】不可几的,非概然的. *an* ~ *story* 不可信的故事. *Rain is* ~ 不象有雨的样子. *It is* ~ *that he will come.* 他不见得会来. **-a·bly** *ad.* *not* ~ 或许.

im·pro·bi·ty [imˈprəubiti] *n.* 不正直,不诚实;邪恶.

im·promp·tu [imˈprɔmptjuː] *ad., a.* 即席地[的],临时地[的],无准备地[的]. *an* ~ *speech* 即席演说. *speak* ~ 即席演讲. — *n.* 即席之作;即席演说;即兴演奏.

im·prop·er [imˈprɔpə] *a.* ①不适当的,不合适的;非正常的. ②不正确的,错误的. ③不道德的;亵渎的,不合礼仪的,下流的. *a remark* ~ *to the occasion* 不合时宜的话. *put sth. to an* ~ *use* 误用. ~ *language* 无礼的话. *an* ~ *person* 下流的人. ~ **fraction**【数】假分数,可约分数. ~ **function**【数】非正常函数. ~ **integral**【数】广义积分,非正常积分. **-ly** *ad.* **-ness** *n.*

im·pro·pri·ate [imˈprəuprieit] *vt.* ①把(教会财产)交俗人保管. ②把(教会财产)据为己有. —[-priit] *a.* 变成私人所有的. **-a·tion** [imˌprəupriˈeiʃən] *n.* **-a·tor** *n.* 保管教会财产的俗人.

im·pro·pri·e·ty [ˌimprəˈpraiəti] *n.* ①不适当,不合式;不正当. ②用词错误. ③不得体的举止,不正当的行为.

im·prov·a·ble [imˈpruːvəbl] *a.* 能改良的,可以改进的. **-bil·i·ty** [imˌpruːvəˈbiliti] *n.* **-bly** *ad.*

im·prove [imˈpruːv] *vt.* ①改良,改善,增进. ②利用,活用. ③增高(土地等的)价值. *The farm tool is not good enough, I am going to* ~ *it.* 这农具不好,我要加以改进. ~ *oneself in English* 提高自己的英语水平. ~ *the occasion [opportunity, shining hour]* 利用机会. ~ *every moment* 爱惜每一刻光阴. ~ ***away [off]*** 想改良反而搞

坏. — *vi.* 变好；增加，升值. *The situation is improving.* 情形逐渐好转. *an ~d variety* 育成品种. *~ [upon] on* 改良.

im·prove·ment [im'pru:vmənt] *n.* ①改良，改进，增进；进步. ②利用，活用. ③〔美〕(增高房屋、土地等价值的)装修，改良措施. ④更优秀的人，更进步的人. *~ of soil*【农】土壤改良. *This letter is an ~ upon [on] your last.* 这封信比你上次的好.

im·prov·er [im'pru:və] *n.* ①改良者，改进者；改进物. ②见习生，学徒.

im·prov·i·dence [im'prɔvidəns] *n.* 目光短浅；不顾将来；不经济，不节约.

im·prov·i·dent [im'prɔvidənt] *a.* ①目光短浅的；不顾将来的. ②不经济的，不注意节约的. **-ly** *ad.*

im·prov·i·sa·tion [ˌimprəvai'zeiʃən] *n.* ①即席创作，即席演奏[演唱]. ②临时凑合的东西，即兴作品. **-al** *a.*

im·prov·i·sa·tor [im'prɔvizeitə] *n.* 即兴诗人；即席演奏[演唱]者.

im·pro·vi·sa·to·re [ˌimprɔˌvizɑ'tɔ:re] *n.* 〔It.〕(*pl.* ***-ri*** [-ri]) = improvisator.

im·prov·i·sa·to·ri·al, -to·ry [imˌprɔvizə'tɔ:riəl, ˌimprə'vaizətəri] *a.* ①即席的，即兴的. ②临时凑合的.

im·prov·i·sa·tri·ce [ˌimprɔˌvizɑ'tri:tʃe] *n.* 〔It.〕(*pl.* ***-ci*** [-tʃi:]) 女即兴诗人，女即席演奏[演唱]者.

im·pro·vise ['imprəvaiz] *vt.* ①即席创作，即席演奏[演唱]. ②临时准备，临时凑成. *an ~d makeshift* 临时凑合的办法. *an ~d operating room* 临时简易手术室. *~ a bed on a sofa* 把沙发作为临时铺[床].

im·pro·vis·er ['imprəvaizə] *n.* 即兴诗人，即席演奏[演唱]者.

im·pru·dence [im'pru:dəns] *n.* ①轻率，鲁莽. ②轻率[鲁莽]的行为[言论]. *commit an ~* 犯错误. *have the ~ to* 竟轻率地.

im·pru·dent [im'pru:dənt] *a.* 轻率的，粗心大意的. **-ly** *ad.*

im·pu·dence ['impjudəns] *n.* ①厚颜无耻；冒失，无礼. ②厚颜无耻[冒失，无礼]的言行. *have the ~ to do* 竟厚着脸皮做. *None of your ~!* 别那么不要脸.

im·pu·dent ['impjudənt] *a.* 厚颜无耻的；冒失的；无礼的. *an ~ young rascal* 蛮横的小流氓. *be ~ enough to (do) ... = so ~ as to (do) ...* 竟然无耻到(干，做)…. **-ly** *ad.*

im·pu·dic·i·ty [ˌimpju'disiti] *n.* 无耻；放肆.

im·pugn [im'pju:n] *vt.* 责难，攻击；指摘(声明、行为、性质等). **-a·ble** *a.* 可责难的，可攻击的，可反对的. **-ment** *n.*

im·pu·is·sance [im'pju(:)isns] *n.* 无能，虚弱，无力. **-is·sant** *a.*

im·pulse ['impʌls] *n.* ①冲动；【物】冲量；推进力；脉冲；【医】冲动，搏动. ②鼓舞，刺激；一时高兴，兴奋. *a man of ~* 感情用事的人. *act from ~* 凭一时冲动行事. *be seized with a sudden ~ to do sth.* 一时情不自禁地做某事. *feel an irresistible ~* 觉得情不自禁. *give an ~ to* 刺激，促进. ***on the ~ of the moment*** 由一时高兴. — *vt.* 推动. *~* **buyer** 一时冲动的买主. *~* **buying** (不考虑价格、质量或效用)只凭一时的高兴购物. *~* **turbine**【机】冲动式透平.

im·pul·sion [im'pʌlʃən] *n.* ①冲动；推进. ②刺激，鼓舞. ③冲力；推动力.

im·pul·sive [im'pʌlsiv] *a.* ①冲动的；刺激的；被一时感情所驱使的，任性的. ②【物】瞬动的，冲击的. *an ~ force* 冲力，推进力. **-ly** *ad.* **-ness** *n.*

im·pu·ni·ty [im'pju:niti] *n.* 不受惩罚，无罪；无事，不受损失. ***with ~*** 不受惩罚地，泰然地.

im·pure [im'pjuə] *a.* ①不纯的，掺假的. ②混杂的. ③不纯洁的，不道德的，下流的. ④(语言)不规范的. *the ~ air of towns* 城市里空气不纯洁. *~ motives* 不纯的动机. *~ language* 下流话. **-ly** *ad.* **-ness** *n.* 不纯 (*~ness acceptor*【无】(半导体中)受主杂质).

im·pu·ri·ty [im'pjuəriti] *n.* 〔常用 *pl.*〕①不纯，不洁. ②下流，不道德，不贞节，杂质. *impurities in food* 食物中的杂质. *political impurities* 政治渣滓；牛鬼蛇神.

im·put ['imput] *n.* = input *n.*

im·put·a·ble [im'pju:təbl] *a.* 可归罪于…的，可归因于…的 (*to*). *The oversight is not ~ to him.* 这一疏忽不能怪他. **-bil·i·ty** [imˌpju:tə'biliti] *n.* **-bly** *ad.*

im·pu·ta·tion [ˌimpju(:)'teiʃən] *n.* ①归罪，责怪，转嫁罪责. ②毁谤；污名. *cast an ~ on sb.'s character* 诋毁某人人格.

im·put·a·tive [im'pju:tətiv] *a.* 可归罪的，可责怪的，(罪责)被归于某人的. **-ly** *ad.*

im·pute [im'pju:t] *vt.* 把…归咎于；把…归因于；把…推给；把…转嫁于 (*to*). *~ one's poverty to bad luck* 把贫穷归咎于坏运气. *~ one's failures to one's misfortune* 失败怪命运不好.

impv. = imperative.

in [in] *prep.* ①〔表示地点、场所、位置〕在…中，在…内，在…上. *live ~ London* 住在伦敦. *~ the distance* 在远处. *~ the house* 在家中. *~ town* 在城里；〔英〕在伦敦. *~ bed* 在床上，睡着. *~ class* 在上课. *~ the street [train]* 〔英〕在大街[火车]上. ★ 美国用 on the street [train]. ②〔表示时间〕在…之内；在…后，过…后；〔美〕…中，…来. *~ the daytime* 在白天. *~ (the) spring* 在春天. *~ two months* 在两个月内；过两个月后. *~ those days* 在当时. *~ a few days* 几天以后；几天之内. *~ a moment [an instant, a minute]* 立刻，马上. *the coldest day ~ ten years* 十年来最冷的日子. *I haven't seen him ~ [for] years.* 〔美〕我好多年没有见他了. *a man ~ his thirties* 一个三十几岁的男子. ③〔表示状态、情况〕处在…中，在…状态中. *be ~ good health* 健康. *~ haste* 急着，忙着. *~ a circle* 围成圆圈. *~ arms* 武装着. *be ~ (the) fashion* 正流行着，是时髦的. *be ~ liquor* 喝醉了. *~ progress* 在进行中，开始. ④〔表示服装、打扮〕穿着，戴着，带着. *a wolf ~ sheep's skin* 披着羊皮的狼. *a woman ~ white* 穿白衣服的女人. *~ uniform* 穿着制服. *~ spectacles* 戴着眼镜. *~ a top hat* 戴着大礼帽. *~ irons* 带着镣铐. ⑤〔表示范围、领域、方面〕在…之内，在…方面. *~ my opinion* 我的意见是，据我想. *~ one's power* 在力所能及的范围内，尽力. *Victory is ~ sight.* 胜利在望. *be blind ~ one eye* 瞎了一只眼睛. *~ politics* 在政治方面. *the latest thing ~ loud speakers* 〔口〕最新式的扬声器. *~ all respects* 在各方面. *be strong [weak] ~ English* 英语很好[不好]. *China is rich ~ products.* 中国物产丰富. *nine ~ ten* 十之八九. *not one ~ ten* 十不得一. *vary ~ colour [length, number, size, weight]* 颜色[长度、数目、大小、重量]不一. ⑥〔表示职业、活动〕从事于，参加着. *~ an amateur play* 参加业余演出. *~ rice* 〔美〕经营米业. *~ trade* 经商. *~ the army* 在军队中(服役). ⑦〔表示传达信息的方式或使用的工具、材料等〕以，用. *written ~ pencil* 用铅笔写的. *paint ~ oils* 画油画. *speak [talk] ~ English* 用英语交谈. *~ a few words* 三言两语，简而言之. *a telegram ~ cipher* 密码电报. *a book ~ cloth* 布面精装书. *have the money ~ gold* 持有的款项是黄金. ⑧〔表示地位、方式、方法、形式〕用…，以…，按照…，依…，符合于…. *~ this way* 用这个办法. *~ an advisory capacity* 以顾问的身分. *~ this manner* 照这样. *~ foreign style* 照外国式样. *arrange ~ alphabetic order* 按字母顺序排列. *buy ~ instalments* 以分期付款方式购买. *Do everything ~ the interests of the people.* 一切行动都要符合人民利益. ⑨〔表示目的、原因、动机〕为着…，作为…. *~ pursuit* 追逐. *speak ~ reply* 回答说. *~ honour of his safe return* 为庆祝他的安全归来. *cry out ~ alarm* 吓得叫喊起来. *rejoice ~ one's recovery* 因为病好了而高兴.

⑩〔表示性质、能力〕包含在…之中. *There is some good ~ him.* 他有一些可取的地方. *as far as ~ me lies* 在我能力所及的限度内. *I didn't think he had it ~ him.* 我没有想到他有这个本事. *Sound ~ body, sound ~ mind.* 健全的精神寓于健全的体魄. ⑪〔表示过程〕在…当儿,在…过程中. *be killed ~ action* 阵亡. *the machine ~ assembling* 在装配中的机器. *~ crossing the river* 在渡河的当儿. ⑫〔表示同位关系〕在…上,在…身上. *lose a great scholar ~ Dr. X* 失去 X 博士这位大学者. *I have found a friend ~ Juliet.* 我找到了朱丽叶这位朋友. *You made a mistake ~ asking him.* 你求他就错了. ***be ~ it*** 〔口〕从事, 参加在内(*They had a good time, but I was not ~ it.* 他们玩得很高兴,可是我没有参加). ***be ~ it up to the neck*** 深陷,沉迷. ***~ as [so] much as*** 因为,由于. ***~ bad*** 〔美〕正在倒霉,关系不好. ***~ good*** 〔美〕受欢迎,关系好. ***~ itself*** 本身,实质上. ***~ that*** 〔古〕因为,由于. ***~ twos and threes*** 三三两两地. — *ad.* ①朝里,向内,在内. *a coat with a furry side ~* 有皮里子的外衣. *Come ~, please.* 请进来. *The horses are ~.* 马(在车上)套着. *When ale is ~, wit is out.* 〔谚〕酒喝多了,智力少了. ②在家. *Is he ~?* 他在家么? *have sb. ~ for dinner* 请某人到家里来吃饭. ③到达,来到;得到. *The train is ~.* 火车到了. *Summer is ~.* 夏天来了. *be a 100 pounds ~* 得到〔赚得〕100 镑. ④当政,当选,掌握政权. *The Conservatives are ~.* 保守党当政. ⑤流行,时髦. *Tomatoes are ~.* 番茄上市了. *Those hats are ~.* 那种帽子很流行. ⑥在狱中. *What offence is Tom ~ for?* 汤姆是因什么罪名坐牢的? ⑦成功,取胜. *The actor was ~.* 演员获得成功. ⑧一致. *fall ~ with sb.'s plan* 同某人的计划一致. ⑨(火等)燃烧着;(灯)亮着. *Keep the fire ~.* 让火燃烧着不灭. ⑩油井正出油. *The well has come ~.* 这口油井出油了. ***all ~*** 〔美俚〕累极了. ***be ~ for*** 遭受,不得不受;参加(考试、竞争). ***be ~ for it*** 〔口〕①欲罢不能,骑虎难下. ②难免受罚;深陷困境. ***be [keep] ~ with sb.*** 跟…亲近;【海】接近…,使接近. ***day ~, day out*** 一天又一天. ***week ~, week out*** 一周又一周. ***year ~, year out*** 年复一年. ***have it ~ for sb.*** 〔口〕怀恨某人. ***~ and ~*** 同种交配,近亲交配. ***~ and out*** 迂曲,作之字形;忽隐忽现,进进出出,里里外外. ***In with it!*** 把它装进去吧! ***In with you!*** 〔口〕进去吧! ***put a notice ~*** 在报上登广告. — *a.* ①朝内的,在里面的 (*opp.* out). *an ~ patient* 住院的病人. *the ~ side* 【板球】攻方. ②到站的,抵港的. *an ~ train* 到站列车. ③在朝的,执政的. *the ~ party* 执政党. ④流行的,时髦的. *the ~ thing to do* 流行的事情,时髦的做法. ⑤赚进的. *be ~ a million dollars* 赚进一百万美元. — *n.* 〔常用 *pl.*〕①在朝派,执政党,知情者: *the ins and the outs* 执政党与在野党,在朝派和在野派. *know all the ins and outs of a problem* 知道问题的详情. ②【体】(板球或棒球)攻球的一方. *He was bowled before he had been ~ five minutes.* 他攻球未到五分钟便被迫退场了. ③〔美口〕入口;门路. ④〔美俚〕(与大人物的)特殊关系,提携. *enjoy some sort of ~ with the manager* 在一定程度上得到经理的赏识.

in [in] *prep.* 〔L.〕= in (*prep.*). ***~ ab·sen·ti·a*** [æbˈsenʃiə] 缺席,当…不在时. ***~ ae·ter·num*** [iːˈtəːnəm] 永久,永远. ***~ ar·ti·cu·lo mor·tis*** [ɑːˈtikjuləu ˈmɔːtis] 临终时. ***~ cam·e·ra*** [ˈkæmərə] 在(法官)私人房间内,秘密;【法】秘密审判. ***~ con·tu·ma·ci·am*** [ˌkɔntjuˈmeiʃiæm] 蔑视法庭. ***~ es·se*** [ˈesi] 实际存在 (*opp.* in posse). ***~ ex·ten·so*** [iksˈtensəu] 全部,详细,十足. ***~ ex·tre·mis*** [iksˈtriːmis] 临终时. ***~ fla·gran·te de·lic·to*** [fləˈgrænti diˈliktəu] 在犯罪当场,在现行中. ***~ for·ma pau·per·is*** [ˈfɔːmə ˈpɔːpəris] 作为穷人(免收讼费). ***~ li·mi·ne*** [ˈlimini] 开头. ***~ lo·co*** [ˈləukəu] 在相当处所,在一定地点. ***~ loco ci·ta·to*** [ˈləukəu saiˈteitəu] 在前面引文内. ***~ lo·co pa·ren·tis*** [ˈləukəupəˈrentis] 替代父母,以父母立场. ***~ medi·as res*** [ˈmiːdiæs ˈriːz] 在〔从〕事物中心;从中途(发生的重大事件)(说起). ***~ me·mo·ri·am*** [miˈmɔːriæm] 为纪念,献给…之灵;祭文,辋诗. ***~ nu·bi·bus*** [ˈnjubibʌs] 在云中,含糊,不明. ***~ per·pe·tu·um*** [pəˈpetjuəm] 永久. ***~ pos·se*** [ˈpɔsi] 可能地,潜在的 (*opp.* in esse). ***~ pro·pri·a per·so·na*** [ˈprəupriə pəˈsəunə] 亲自,自行 (*opp.* by proxy). ***~ pu·ris nat·u·ral·i·bus*** [ˈpjuːris nætʃuˈrælibʌs] 赤裸,全裸. ***~ re*** [ˈriː] 按…的讼诉事件;关于,说到. ***~ si·tu*** [ˈsaitjuː] 在原来位置,在自然地位. ***~ sta·tu pu·pil·la·ri*** [ˈsteitjuː pjuːpiːˈlɑːri] 以被保护人身分;以学徒〔学生〕身分. ***~ sta·tu quo*** [ˈsteitjuː ˈkwəu] 照原样,维持现状. ***~ ter·ro·rem*** [təˈrɔːrem] 作为警告. ***~ to·to*** [ˈtəutəu] 全部,整体. ***~ vit·ro*** [ˈvaitrəu] 在(生物)体外;在试管内.

In = 【化】indium.

in. = ①inch(es). ②income.

in-¹ *pref.* 在带有"停止"意义的动词前 = in, on; 在带有"运动"意义的动词前 = into, against, towards. ★ ①在 l 前作 il-; 在 b, m, p 前作 im-; 在 r 前作 ir-: *im*press, *ir*radiate. ②常与古法语中的 *en-*, *em-* 并存: *in*quire, *en*quire.

in-² *pref.* 无,非. ★在 l 前作 il-; 在 b, m, p 前作 im-; 在 r 前作 ir-: *il*logical, *im*moral, *ir*rational.

-in¹ *suf.* 表示"属于…的"〔系希腊、拉丁语形容词及其派生名词的后缀〕: ru*in*.

-in² *suf.* 【化】① = -ine. ②化学制品〔药品〕等的后缀: aureomyc*in*.

-in³ *suf.* 〔口、方〕= -ing: go*in* = going.

in-¹ *comb. f.* 〔常与名词组成形容词修饰语〕表示"在…之中"、"正当…"等: in-car 装置于汽车内的; in-career 在职的; in-city 市内的; in-home 家中的; in-process 生产中的; in-state 〔美〕本州的. ★此种组合的重读音通常落在 in- 上,同时保留原名词的重读音, 如 in-city [ˈinˈsiti]; 但作为 out- 的对应词时,重读音只落在 in- 上,如 in-state students 中的 in-state [ˈinsteit].

in-² *comb. f.* 〔常与名词组成名词词组〕表示"最新的"、"新式的"、"独有的": in-jargon 流行术语; in-language 现代语言; in-thing 新近流行的东西; in-word 新口头禅. ★此种组合的重读音落在 in- 上, 如 in-crowd [ˈinkraud].

-in *comb. f.* 〔置于动词后组成名词〕表示"示威行动"、"集会"等: sit-in 静坐示威; kneel-in 黑人进入种族隔离教堂参加礼拜; ride-in 黑人乘坐种族隔离汽车; stall-in 故意阻塞交通; smoke-in 争取吸大麻合法化; be-in (颓废派的)社交集会; eat-in 聚餐会; study-in 学习会.

-ina *suf.* ①构成女性名称: Czar*ina*, Georg*ina*. ②构成乐器名称: concert*ina*.

I·na [ˈainə] *n.* 艾娜〔女子名〕.

in·a·bil·i·ty [inəˈbiliti] *n.* 无能,无力;无能为力.

in·ac·ces·si·ble [ˌinækˈsesəbl] *a.* ①达不到的;进不去的. ②不能见到的;不能接近的. ③得不到的. **-si·bil·ity** [ˈinækˌsesəˈbiliti] *n.* **-bly** *ad.*

in·ac·cu·ra·cy [inˈækjurəsi] *n.* 误差;不精确,不准确,不精确的东西,错误. *avoid the ~ in the use of words* 避免用字不准确.

in·ac·cu·rate [inˈækjurit] *a.* 不精密的;不准确的;错误的. **-ly** *ad.* *an ~ account* 不准确的报表.

in·act. *a.* =【物】inactive.

in·ac·tion [inˈækʃən] *n.* 不活动;不活跃;怠惰,懒散;迟钝.

in·ac·ti·vate [inˈæktiveit] *vt.* ①使不活动. ②撤消(部队,政府机构等). ③【化】使钝化,减除…的活性;使不旋光.

in·ac·tive [inˈæktiv] *a.* ①不活动的,不活跃的;迟钝的;懒散的. ②没事做的;暂停不用的. ③【化】钝性的;【物】不旋光的;无放射性的. ④【军】非现役的. ⑤

【医】静止性的. *an* ~ *fleet* 后备舰队. *an* ~ *machine* 一台停用的机器. *an* ~ *reserve* 已退役后备队. ~ *tuberculosis* 非活动性结核. **-ly** *ad.* **-ness** *n.* **-tiv·i·ty** [ˌinækˈtiviti] *n.*

in·a·dapt·a·ble [ˌinəˈdæptəbl] *a.* ①不能适应的,无适应性的. ②不可改编的. **-bil·i·ty** [ˌinəˌdæptəˈbiliti], **-a·tion** [ˌinədæpˈteiʃən] *n.*

in·ad·e·qua·cy [inˈædikwəsi] *n.* *(pl.* **-cies***)* ①不充分;不适当. ②【医】官能不足,机能不全. *renal* ~ 肾机能不全.

in·ad·e·quate [inˈædikwit] *a.* 不适当的;不充足的. *be* ~ *to do sth.* 不适宜作某件事. *be* ~ *to (for) a purpose* 不能达到目的. ~ *equipment* 不充足的设备. **-ly** *ad.*

in·ad·mis·si·ble [ˌinədˈmisəbl] *a.* 不能答应的, 不能允许的, 难承认的. ~ *behavior* 不能允许的行为. **-bil·i·ty** [ˈinədˌmisəˈbiliti] *n.* **-bly** *ad.*

in·ad·vert·ence, in·ad·vert·en·cy [ˌinədˈvəːtəns, -si] *n.* 粗心大意,疏忽,错误. *Mistakes proceed from* ~. 错误出自粗心大意.

in·ad·vert·ent [ˌinədˈvəːtənt] *a.* ①疏忽的; 漫不经心的. ②出于无心的,非故意的,无意中的. **-ly** *ad.*

in·ad·vis·a·ble [ˌinədˈvaizəbl] *a.* 不可取的,不妥当的;不明智的;不慎重的. **-bili·ty** *n.*

in·af·fa·ble [inˈæfəbl] *a.* 不和蔼的.

in·al·ien·a·ble [inˈeiljənəbl] *a.* 不可剥夺的; 不可分割的;不能转让的. ~ *rights* 不可剥夺的权利. *an* ~ *part of the territory* 不可分割的领土. **-a·bil·i·ty** [inˌeiljənəˈbiliti] *n.* **-a·bly** *ad.*

in·al·ter·a·ble [inˈɔːltərəbl] *a.* 不能变更的, 不变的. **-bil·i·ty** [inˌɔːltərəˈbiliti] *n.* **-bly** *ad.*

in·am·o·ra·ta [inˌæməˈrɑːtə] *n.* 〔It.〕女爱人,女情人,情妇.

in·am·o·ra·to [inˌæməˈraitəu] *n.* 〔It.〕男爱人,男情人.

in-and-in [ˈinəndˈin] *a., ad.* 同种交配的[地],近亲交配的[地]. ~ *breeding* 同种[近亲]繁育.

in-and-out [ˈinəndˈaut] *a.* (证券)短期买卖的.

in·ane [iˈnein] *a.* ①空的,空虚的. ②空洞的,无意义的. *make an* ~ *remark* 言之无物. — *n.* 〔*the* ~〕空洞无物,无限空间. **-ly** *ad.*

in·an·i·mate [inˈænimit] *a.* ①无生命的, 死的. ②无生气的, 没精打采的. *an* ~ *object* 无生物. ~ *nature* 无生物界. *an* ~ *conversation* 沉闷的谈话. **-ly** *ad.*

in·an·i·ma·tion [inˌæniˈmeiʃən] *n.* 无生命; 不活动,不活泼,无生气.

in·a·ni·tion [ˌinəˈniʃən] *n.* ①无内容,空虚. ②【医】营养不足,虚弱.

in·an·i·ty [iˈnæniti] *n.* ①空虚, 空洞. ②无知, 愚妄; 〔常 *pl.*〕无聊的话, 无聊的事. *irrelevant inanities* 无关痛痒的废话.

in·ap·par·ent [ˌinəˈpærənt] *a.* 不明显的. (*opp.* apparent).

in·ap·peas·a·ble [ˌinəˈpiːzəbl] *a.* 难劝解的,难说服的,难满足的.

in·ap·pel·la·ble [ˌinəˈpeləbl] *a.* (判决等)不得申诉[上诉]的.

in·ap·pe·tence, -cy [inˈæpitəns, -si] *n.* 食欲不振, 无胃口;欲望缺乏.

in·ap·pli·ca·ble [inˈæplikəbl] *a.* 不能应用的,不适用的, 不合适的. *The principle is* ~ *to the case.* 这个原则对这件事不适用. **-bil·i·ty** [inˌæplikəˈbiliti] *n.* **-bly** *ad.*

in·ap·po·site [inˈæpəzit] *a.* 不适合的,不恰当的,不相干的;不对题的. **-ly** *ad.*

in·ap·pre·ci·a·ble [ˌinəˈpriːʃəbl] *a.* 小得难以觉察的,微不足道的. **-bly** *ad.*

in·ap·pre·ci·a·tion [ˌinəˌpriːʃiˈeiʃən] *n.* 不正确评价,不欣赏.

in·ap·pre·ci·a·tive [ˌinəˈpriːʃjətiv] *a.* ①不欣赏…的 *(of).* ②评价不正确的,缺乏眼光的. ~ *criticism* 妄评. **-ly** *ad.*

in·ap·pre·hen·si·ble [ˌinæpriˈhensəbl] *a.* 难了解的,难领会的,不可理解的.

in·ap·pre·hen·sion [ˌinæpriˈhenʃən] *n.* 缺乏理解力.

in·ap·pre·hen·sive [ˌinæpriˈhensiv] *a.* ①缺乏理解力的. ②未意识到的;未觉察到危险的. **-ly** *ad.*

in·ap·proach·a·ble [ˌinəˈprəutʃəbl] *a.* 难接近的; 无可比拟的.

in·ap·pro·pri·ate [ˌinəˈprəupriit] *a.* 不适当的,不相宜的. ~ *remarks* 不当的言辞. ~ *to the season* 不合时宜. **-ly** *ad.* **-ness** *n.*

in·apt [inˈæpt] *a.* ①(对)…不适当的,不合适的 *(for).* ②拙劣的,无能的;(在某方面)不熟练的 *(at). an* ~ *analogy [quotation]* 不恰当的比喻[引用]. **-ly** *ad.* **-ness** *n.*

in·apt·i·tude [inˈæptitjuːd] *n.* ①不适当, 不合适. ②拙笨,无能,不熟练.

in·arch [inˈɑːtʃ] *vt.*【园艺】接枝.

in·arm [inˈɑːm] *vt.* 〔诗〕拥抱.

in·ar·tic·u·late [ˌinɑːˈtikjulit] *a.* ①发音不清楚的,口齿不清的. ②哑口无言的,说不出的,无法言喻的. ③不会表达内心思想的. ④【动】无关节的. *almost* ~ *with excitement* 激动得几乎说不出话来. ~ *misery [pain]* 哑子吃黄连. ~ *animals* 无关节动物. **-ly** *ad.* **-ness** *n.*

in·ar·ti·fi·cial [ˌinɑːtiˈfiʃəl] *a.* ①非人造的, 天然的. ②单调的,拙劣的,不熟练的. **-ly** *ad.* **-i·ty** *n.*

in·ar·tis·tic(al) [ˌinɑːˈtistik(əl)] *a.* 非艺术的;无艺术性的,无艺术修养的. **-ti·cal·ly** *ad.*

in·as·much [ˌinəzˈmʌtʃ] *ad.* 〔与 as 连用,起连接词作用〕因为, 由于;〔古〕只要. *Inasmuch as we have no money, it is no good thinking about a holiday.* 因为我们没有钱,所以考虑休假是没有用的.

in·at·ten·tion [ˌinəˈtenʃən] *n.* 不注意;漫不经心,疏忽.

in·at·ten·tive [ˌinəˈtentiv] *a.* 不注意的; 漫不经心的;疏忽的. **-ly** *ad.* **-ness** *n.*

in·au·di·ble [iˈnɔːdəbl] *a.* 听不见的. **-bil·i·ty** [inˌɔːdəˈbiliti] *n.* **-bly** *ad.*

in·au·gu·ral [iˈnɔːgjurəl] *a.* 就职(仪式)的;开幕的,开始的. *an* ~ *address* 就职演说;开幕词. *an* ~ *ceremony* 就职典礼,成立典礼,开幕典礼. *an* ~ *lecture* (教授)就职讲义. — *n.* 〔美〕就职演说,就职典礼.

in·au·gu·rate [iˈnɔːgjureit] *vt.* ①为(新官员,教授等)举行就职典礼. ②开始;举行(开业、落成、成立等)仪式. ③创始; 开幕, 开张. ~ *a new era* 创新纪元. ~ *a president* 举行总统就职典礼. *The Export Commodities Fair was* ~*d yesterday.* 出口商品交易会昨天开幕了. *the inaugurating general meeting* 成立大会. — *vi.* 致开幕[就职]词.

in·au·gu·ra·tion [iˌnɔːgjuˈreiʃən] *n.* 就职典礼;〔美〕总统就职典礼;开幕仪式,落成典礼,开通典礼,成立典礼;开张,开始. **I- Day** 美国总统就职日.

in·au·gu·ra·tor [iˈnɔːgjureitə] *n.* 主持就职仪式者;开创者,创始人.

in·au·gu·ra·to·ry [iˈnɔːgjurətəri] *a.* = inaugural.

in·aus·pi·cious [ˌinɔːsˈpiʃəs] *a.* 不吉祥的,不利的. **-ly** *ad.* **-ness** *n.*

in·be·ing [ˈinbiːiŋ] *n.* 内在的事物;本质,本性.

in·board [ˈinbɔːd] *a.*【空】内侧的;【海】船内的,舱内的;靠近船中线的 (*opp.* outboard); 内纵的. ~ *cabin* 内侧舱室. ~ *profile* 舱内纵剖面图. — *ad.*【海】在船内;在舱内;向内侧.

in·board-out·board [ˈinbɔːdˈautbɔːd] *a.*【船】(小艇的)舷内—舷外动力装置的. — *n.* 有舷内—舷外动力装置的小艇.

in·born [ˈinˈbɔːn] *a.* 生来的, 天赋的, 天生的, 先天的 (*opp.* acquired).

in·bound [ˈinbaund] *a.* (船舶)开回本国的；归航的(*opp.* outbound)；入境的，入站的.

in·break [ˈinbreik] *n.* 入侵.

in·breathe [ˈinˈbriːð] *vt.* 吸入；〔喻〕灌输(思想等)，启发.

in·bred [ˈinˈbred] *a.* ①生来的，先天的. ②近亲繁殖的. ③选种产生的. *the* ～ *line* 近交系.

in·breed [ˈinˈbriːd] *vt.* (*-bred, -breed·ing*) ①〔罕〕使在内部形成〔发展〕. ②【生】使(动物)近亲繁殖. — *vi.* ①进行近亲繁殖. ②(由于社会与文化联系极为局限而)变得文雅过度.

in·breed·ing [ˈinˈbriːdiŋ] *n.* ①【生】近亲繁殖，同系交配. ②(知识等)限于狭隘范围.

inc. = inclosure; including; inclusive; income; 〔常 I-〕incorporated 注册; increase.

In·ca [ˈiŋkə] *n.* ①印加人(印卡人)〔南美印第安人的一个部落〕. ②印加帝国国王(或贵族成员). **-n** *a.*

in·ca·bloc [ˈiŋkəˌblɔk] *n.* (手表内的)防震装置. — *a.* (手表等)防震的.

in·cal·cu·la·ble [inˈkælkjuləbl] *a.* ①不可胜数的，无数的；极大的. ②难预测的；靠不住的，无定的. **-bil·i·ty** [inˌkælkjuləˈbiliti] *n.* **-bly** *ad.*

in·ca·les·cent [ˌinkəˈlesnt] *a.* 〔罕〕渐热的. **-cence** *n.*

in·can·desce [ˌinkænˈdes] *vt., vi.* (使)白热化，(使)遇热发光.

in·can·des·cence, -cy [ˌinkænˈdesns, -si] *n.* 白炽，白热.

in·can·des·cent [ˌinkænˈdesnt] *a.* ①白热的，白炽的，发白热光的. ②辉煌的. ～ **lamp** 白炽灯(*an* ～ *filament* 白热灯丝(霓虹灯丝)). ～ **particle** 发光粒子. ～ **sand flow**【地】热沙流.

in·can·ta·tion [ˌinkænˈteiʃən] *n.* 咒语，咒符，妖术，念咒.

in-cap [ˈinkæp] *n.* 〔美军俚〕智能麻醉剂〔一种使人失去智能的化学药剂〕.

in·ca·pa·ble [inˈkeipəbl] *a.* ①无能的，没有用的. ②不会…的 *(of)*. ③【法】没有资格的. ～ *of doing sth.* 无能力做某事. *an* ～ *officer* 无能的官吏. ～ *of telling a lie* 不会扯谎. *be drunk and* ～ 醉烂如泥，酩酊大醉. — *n.* 没有能力的人. **-bil·i·ty** [inˌkeipəˈbiliti] *n.* **-bly** *ad.*

in·ca·pa·cious [ˌinkəˈpeiʃəs] *a.* ①无能的，无知的；狭小的；容积不大的. ②〔古〕有智力缺陷的. *a silly and* ～ *person* 笨拙无能的人.

in·ca·pac·i·tant [ˌinkəˈpæsitənt] *n.* = in-cap.

in·ca·pac·i·tate [ˌinkəˈpæsiteit] *vt.* ①使无能力，使残废. ②【法】使无资格. ～ *sb. from singing* 使某人不能歌唱. *be* ～*d from voting* 被剥夺选举权. **-ta·tion** [ˈinkəˌpæsiˈteiʃən] *n.* **-ta·tor** *n.* = in-cap.

in·ca·pac·i·ty [ˌinkəˈpæsiti] *n.* ①无能力. ②【法】无资格；【医】官能不全. ～ *for work [to work, for doing work]* 不能工作. *renal* ～ 肾机能不全.

In·cap·a·ri·na [inˌkæpəˈriːnə] *n.* 廉价蛋白食品〔用棉籽、玉米及高粮面、酵母粉等合制而成. 拉美尤用于防止蛋白质缺乏症〕.

in·cap·su·late [inˈkæpsəleit] *vt.* (*-lat·ed, -lat·ing*) = encapsulate.

in·car·cer·ate [inˈkɑːsəreit] *vt.* ①禁闭，监禁. ②【医】钳闭. **-a·tion** [inˌkɑːsəˈreiʃən] *n.*

in·car·di·nate [inˈkɑːdineit] *vt.* (*-nat·ed, -nat·ing*) ①【天主】(使圣职人员)隶属于同一主教管区. ②提升…为红衣主教. **-na·tion** [inˌkɑːdiˈneiʃən] *n.*

in·car·na·dine [inˈkɑːnədain, -din] *vt.*【诗】使成肉色〔或血红色〕. — *n., a.* 肉色(的)，淡红色(的)；血红色(的).

in·car·nate [ˈinkɑːneit] *vt.* ①赋予…以形体，使成…的化身. ②使具体化，体现，实现(理想等). — *a.* [ˈinkɑːnit] ①实体化的，成为人形的，化身的. ②具体化的，体现的. ③肉色的，红色的；玫瑰红的. *a devil* ～ 魔鬼的化身. *God* ～ 神的化身. *Liberty* ～ 自由的具体表现.

in·car·na·tion [ˌinkɑːˈneiʃən] *n.* 肉体化，化身，体现；【医】肉化. *The leading dancer is the* ～ *of grace.* 演主角的舞蹈家简直是美的化身. **-al** *a.*

in·case [inˈkeis] *vt.* = encase.

in·cau·tious [inˈkɔːʃəs] *a.* 不慎重的，轻率的；不注意的. **-ly** *ad.* **-ness** *n.*

in·cen·di·a·rism [inˈsendjərizəm] *n.* 放火，纵火；挑拨，煽动.

in·cen·di·ar·y [inˈsendjəri] *a.* ①放火的，纵火的，燃烧的. ②煽动性的. *an* ～ *fire* 人放的火. *an* ～ *bomb [bullet]* 燃烧弹. *an* ～ *speech* 煽动性的演说. — *n.* ①纵火者；燃烧弹；可易燃物. ②煽动者.

in·cense[1] [ˈinsens] *n.* ①(焚香时可产生香气的)香；香发出的烟. ②巴结，奉承. *a stick of* ～ 一根香，一柱香. ***burn [offer]*** ～ ***to*** 向…烧香；向…献媚. — *vt.* 对…烧香，用香熏. — *vi.* 供香，上香. ～ **burner** 香炉. ～ **cedar**【植】拟肖楠属植物〔产于北美洲西部〕.

in·cense[2] [inˈsens] *vt.* 使发怒，激怒. *be* ～*d at sb.'s words [conduct]* 对某人的言论〔行为〕感到愤慨. *be* ～*d against [by, with] sb.* 对…发怒.

in·cen·so·ry [ˈinsensəri] *n.* 有盖香炉.

in·cen·tive [inˈsentiv] *a.* 刺激性的，鼓励性质的. ～ *pay* (增产)奖金；*be* ～ *to further study* 鼓励进一步研究. — *n.* 刺激；鼓励，动机；诱因. *much* ～ *(many* ～*s) to work hard* 很多努力工作的动机. ～ **wage** (增产)奖励工资. **-ly** *ad.*

in·cept [inˈsept] *vt.* ①接收(入会)；【生】摄取. ②〔古〕开始. — *vi.* ①(在英国剑桥大学)取得硕士〔博士〕学位. ②就职.

in·cep·tion [inˈsepʃən] *n.* ①开始，发端. ②(英国剑桥大学)硕士〔博士〕学位的取得. *at the (very)* ～ *of* 在…的开头.

in·cep·tive [inˈseptiv] *a.* 起头的，开端的；【语法】表示动作开始的. ～ *verbs*【语法】开始动词，起动动词. — *n.*【语法】表示开始的动词〔短语〕. **-ly** *ad.*

in·cep·tor [inˈseptə] *n.* ①开始人，发端者. ②在英国剑桥大学取得硕士〔博士〕学位的人.

in·cer·ti·tude [inˈsəːtitjuːd] *n.* ①无把握，不肯定，怀疑. ②不安全，不稳定.

in·ces·san·cy [inˈsesnsi] *n.* 持续不断的状态，不间断性.

in·ces·sant [inˈsesnt] *a.* 不停的，不断的. *a week of* ～ *rains* 连续下了一个星期的雨. **-ly** *ad.* **-ness** *n.*

in·cest [ˈinsest] *n.* 乱伦.

in·ces·tu·ous [inˈsestjuəs] *a.* 乱伦的；犯乱伦罪的. **-ly** *ad.* **-ness** *n.*

inch[1] [intʃ] *n.* ①英寸〔旧译时略作 in.〕. ②少量，少额，少许. ③〔*pl.*〕身长，身段，个子. *an* ～ *of rain* 一英寸的雨量. *Give him an* ～ *and he'll take an ell.* 〔谚〕他得寸进尺. *not yield an* ～ 寸步不让. *an* ～ *of cold steel* 尖刀的一戳. *a man of your* ～*es* 象你一样高的人. ***by*** ～***es*** 一点一点地，渐渐 (*die by* ～*es* 渐死，就要死. *kill by* ～*es* 慢慢地折磨死). ***every*** ～ 完全地，彻底地 (*He is every* ～ *a local despot* 他彻头彻尾是个土皇帝). ***gather up one's*** ～***es*** 直站起来. ～ ***by*** ～ = ***by*** ～***es.*** ***to an*** ～ 丝毫不差地，精密地. ***within an*** ～ ***of*** 差点儿，几乎. ***within an*** ～ ***of one's life*** 差点儿丧命. ***by*** ～ ***of candle*** 通过拍卖. — *vt.* 使渐进，使渐动；使一点一点地移动. ～ *one's way forward* 慢慢前进. — *vi.* 渐进，一步一步前进. ～ *along a ledge on a cliff* 在悬岩的突出部分匍匐而进.

inch[2] [intʃ] *n.* 〔Scot.〕小岛.

inched [intʃt] *a.* 长…英寸的；刻有英寸的. *a 4-*～ *hook* 四英寸长的钩子.

inch·er [ˈintʃə] *n.* 口径〔长、直径等〕是…英寸的东西. *a six-incher* (口径)六英寸口径的炮.

inch·meal [ˈintʃmiːl] *ad.* 慢慢地，一步一步地，一点一

点地. ***by*** ～ = inchmeal.

in·cho·ate [ˈinkəueit, -kəuit] *a.* ①才开始的; 初步的. ②未完成的,不发达的. **-ly** *ad.* **-ness** *n.*

in·cho·a·tion [ˈinkəueiʃən] *n.* 开始;初期,初步.

in·cho·a·tive [inˈkəuətiv] *a.* ①开始的. ②【语法】表示开始的. — *n.*【语法】表示开始的动词[短语].

inch·worm [ˈintʃwəːm] *n.*【动】尺蠖(虫).

in·ci·dence [ˈinsidəns] *n.* ①发生;影响;着落;(税的)负担;影响范围;发生率. ②【空】(机翼)倾角,安装角. ③【数】关联,接合. ④【物】入射,入射角,角. *the* ～ *of the tax* 税款的负担. *the* ～ *of taxation* 征税的范围. *the* ～ *of disease* 患病的范围. ～ *wire* 倾角线. ～ *numbers*【数】关联数. *the angle of* ～ 入射角. *the plane of* ～ 入射(平)面.

in·ci·dent [ˈinsidənt] *n.* ①(政治性)事故;事变. ②偶发事件,某事件的附随事件,小事件. ③(剧情的)枝节,(小说的)插话. ④【法】财产所附带的权利[义务]. ***without*** ～ 平安无事. — *a.*〔多作表语用〕①易起的,易有的;附随的. ②【法】附带的 (*to*). ③入射的 (*upon*). *diseases* ～ *to childhood* 幼年容易得的疾病. ～ (*with one another*)【数】(互相)关联. ～ *rays* 入射线.

in·ci·den·tal [ˌinsiˈdentl] *a.* ①容易发生的. ②附带的,伴随的,非主要的. ③偶然的. *the dangers* ～ *to a soldier's career* 军人生涯中容易发生的危险. ～ *colours* [*images*] 残色[附带发生的色彩感觉]. ～ *expenses* 杂费. ～ *music*【乐】(剧、影片、诗朗诵等的)配音,配乐. *an* ～ *acquaintance* 萍水相逢的人. *an* ～ *remark* 偶然中漏出的话. — *n.* 附带事件;〔*pl.*〕杂项,杂费. ～ **music**【乐】(剧、影片、诗朗诵等的)配音,配乐.

in·ci·den·tal·ly [ˌinsiˈdentli] *ad.* ①附带地,偶然地. ②顺便说一句〔口语中另换话题的用语〕.

in·cin·er·ate [inˈsinəreit] *vt., vi.* (把…)烧成灰,烧掉,焚化. **-a·tion** *n.* 焚化. **-a·tor** *n.* 焚化者;(垃圾的)焚化炉;火葬炉.

in·cin·der·jell [inˈsindədʒel] *n.* 凝固汽油〔混有凝固剂的汽油,用以制造燃烧弹等〕.

in·cip·i·ent [inˈsipiənt] *a.* 开始的,刚出现的,初期的. *an* ～ *cause* 远因. *an* ～ *disease* 初发的病. *the* ～ *light of day* 曙光. **-ence, -en·cy** *n.* **-ly** *ad.*

in·ci·pit [ˈinsipit] *n.*〔L.〕(本文自此)开始〔中世纪时抄本开端用语〕.

in·cise [inˈsaiz] *vt.* ①切入,切开. ②雕刻.

in·cised [inˈsaizd] *a.* ①切入的;雕刻的;用锐器切入而做成的. ②(叶子)缺裂的. *an* ～ *leaf* 缺裂的叶子. ～ *wound*【医】刀伤,割伤,切伤.

in·ci·sion [inˈsiʒən] *n.* ①切入;【医】切开. ②【植】(叶的)缺刻. ③雕刻.

in·ci·sive [inˈsaisiv] *a.* ①切入的,锐利的. ②尖锐的,深刻的,透彻的. ③【解】切牙的,门牙的. *an* ～ *criticism* 尖锐的批评. *an* ～ *teeth* = incisor. **-ly** *ad.* **-ness** *n.*

in·ci·sor [inˈsaizə] *n.*【解】门齿;切牙 (= ～ teeth).

in·cit·ant [inˈsaitənt] *a.* 刺激的,兴奋的. — *n.* ①刺激因素. ②【医】兴奋剂,提神药.

in·ci·ta·tion [ˌinsaiˈteiʃən] *n.* 刺激,激励,煽动;刺激物;动机,诱因.

in·cite [inˈsait] *vt.* ①激励;刺激. ②煽动,唆使. *Insults* ～ *resentment.* 侮辱激起愤恨. ～ *a crowd to riot* 煽动群众暴动.

in·cite·ment [inˈsaitmənt] *n.* = incitation.

in·ci·vil·i·ty [ˌinsiˈviliti] *n.* ①无礼貌,粗野. ②不礼貌的言行.

in·ci·vism [ˈinsivizəm] *n.* 无视公民义务;缺乏爱国心.

incl. = inclosure; including; inclusive.

in·clear·er [ˈinkliərə] *n.* 票据交换员.

in·clear·ing [ˈinkliəriŋ] *n.*〔英〕(票据交换后所收入的)应付票据总额.

in·clem·en·cy [inˈklemənsi] *n.* ①(天气的)险恶,凛烈,酷寒. ②冷酷无情.

in·clem·ent [inˈklemənt] *a.* ①(天气、气候)险恶的,酷烈的,狂暴的;寒冷的. ②(人)无情的,严酷的.

in·clin·a·ble [inˈklainəbl] *a.* ①倾向于…的;赞成…的. ②可使倾斜的. *be* ～ *to sth.* 倾向于某事.

in·cli·na·tion [ˌinkliˈneiʃən] *n.* ①倾斜;点头,鞠躬. ②斜坡,倾度;【数】倾角;【天】(轨道的)交角. ③倾向;嗜好. ④爱好的事物. ⑤体质的倾向;斜角. ～ *of an orbit*【天】轨道交角. *express one's consent with an* ～ (*of the head*) 点头表示同意. *an* ～ *to stoutness* 容易发胖的体质. ***against one's*** ～ 违反着本意. ***follow one's own*** ～ 随心所欲. ***have an*** ～ ***for*** 爱好,欢喜. **-al** *a.*

in·cline [inˈklain] *vt.* ①弄斜,使倾斜,使偏向. ②低(头),屈(身). ③使(某人)倾向于,使(某人)有意思(做某事)〔常用被动态〕. ～ *a post against the wall* 把柱子靠墙斜立着. ～ *one's ear to sb.* 侧耳倾听某人讲话. ～ *one's head in greeting* 低头致意. *His attitude did not* ～ *me to help him.* 他的态度使我不想帮助他. *be* ～*d to go by air* 想要[倾向于]坐飞机去. *Are you* ～*d for a walk?* 你想散步吗? — *vi.* ①倾斜. ②低头,屈身. ③爱好,赞同. ④易于…,有…的倾向. ⑤近似. ⑥【军】侧转前进. ～ *toward the speaker to hear more clearly* 斜着身子向发言人靠近,以便听得更清楚些. ～ *to traditional way* 喜爱传统的做法. *The leave* ～ *to dark.* 树叶绿得发黑. *purple inclining to red* 近似红色的紫色. *Right* ～! 半面向右转走! — *n.* 斜面;坡度.

in·clined [inˈklaind] *a.* ①倾斜的;成斜坡的;【数】与线或平面成角的. ②倾向于…的〔同不定式连用〕. ～ **plane**【数】斜面.

in·cli·nom·e·ter [ˌinkliˈnɔmitə] *n.* 倾角仪;磁倾计;倾斜仪.

in·close [inˈkləuz] *vt.* = enclose.

in·clo·sure [inˈkləuʒə] *n.* = enclosure.

in·clud·a·ble [inˈkluːdəbl] *a.* 可以包括在内的.

in·clude [inˈkluːd] *vt.* (*opp.* exclude) ①包住,关住. ②包含,包括;算入,计入. *The nutshell* ～*s the kernel.* 果壳裹住果仁. *all charges* ～*d* 包括一切费用[连一切费用在内]. *There were ten present including* [*not including*] *myself.* 连我在内[除我而外]共有十人出席. *The farm* ～*s 160 acres.* 这个农场有160英亩. *He* ～*s everything in his survey.* 他事事调查,巨细无遗.

in·clud·ed [inˈkluːdid] *a.* ①包入的,包有的,包含的. ②【植】内藏的,不伸出的.

in·clud·i·ble [inˈkluːdəbl] *a.* = includable.

in·clu·sion [inˈkluːʒən] *n.* ①包含,含有. ②参杂;杂质;内涵物. ③【逻】包摄;【医】包涵物;【矿】包体;【冶】夹杂物. ～ **body**【医】包涵体.

in·clu·sive [inˈkluːsiv] *a.* (*opp.* exclusive) ①包围住的,范围广的. ②包括…的;…也算入的(*of*). ③一切开支包括在内的. *an* ～ *list* 详表. *from Jan. 1st to 31st* ～〔略 *incl.*〕从1月1日至31日〔1日与31日在内 (*cf.*〔美〕*Jan. 1st through 31st*)〕. *an* ～ *fee* (旅馆)连伙食一切包括在内的费用. *a party of ten,* ～ *of the host* 主客共计十人的聚会. ～ *of* 包含. **-ly** *ad.* **-ness** *n.*

in·co·er·ci·ble [ˌinkəuˈəːsəbl] *a.* 难强制的,不能压制的.

in·cog. [inˈkɔg] *a., ad., n.*〔口〕= incognita, incognito.

in·cog·i·ta·ble [inˈkɔdʒitəbl] *a.*〔罕〕不可想象的;不可思议的;难以置信的.

in·cog·i·tant [inˈkɔdʒitənt] *a.* 没有思虑的;轻率的,不顾及他人的.

in·cog·ni·ta [inˈkɔgnitə] *n.* (*pl.* ～**s, -te** [-tei]) 改用假名的女人;化装出行的女人. *She went to Paris* ～. 她化装到巴黎去(了). — *a.* (女人)改用假名的,化装出行的.

in·cog·ni·to [inˈkɔgnitəu] *a., ad.* 化装的[地];用假名的[地]. *travel* ～ 微行,微装出游. — *n.* (*pl.* ～**s, -ti**

[-ti:]) 微装出游的人;用假名的人. *drop one's* ～ 说出自己的真正身分.

in·cog·ni·za·ble [inˈkɔgnizəbl] *a.* 不能认识的,不可知.

in·cog·ni·zant [inˈkɔgnizənt] *a.* 没有认识到的, 没意识到的 *(of)*. **-zance** *n.*

in·co·her·ence [ˌinkəuˈhiərəns], **in·co·her·en·cy**[-si] *n.* 支离破碎;不连贯. *the* ～ *of speech* 语无伦次.

in·co·her·ent [ˌinkəuˈhiərənt] *a.* 支离破碎的, 七零八落的,东扯西拉的;不连贯的, 前后矛盾的; 无条理的,不相干的. **-ly** *ad.*

in·co·he·sive [ˌinkəuˈhi:siv] *a.* 无粘聚力的; (势力等)易分裂的,散的.

in·com·bus·ti·bil·i·ty [ˈinkəmˌbʌstəˈbiliti] *n.* 不燃性.

in·com·bus·ti·ble [ˌinkəmˈbʌstəbl] *a.* 不能燃烧的. — *n.* 不燃物. **-bly** *ad.*

in·come [ˈinkəm] *n.* (定期)收入,所得,收益. *an earned [unearned]* ～ 劳动[不劳]所得. *draw a large* ～ 收入很多. ***live with one's*** ～ 量入为出. ～ **account [statement]** 损益计算书,收益帐. ～ **tax** 所得税.

in·com·er [ˈinˌkʌmə] *n.* ①进来者; 外来移民; 新来者. ②后继者,替手. ③侵入者,闯入者.

in·com·ing [ˈinˌkʌmiŋ] *n.* *(opp.* outgoing) ①进来, 到来. ②〔*pl.*〕收入,岁入. *the* ～ *of spring* 春天的到来. ～*s and outgoings* 收支. — *a.* ①进来的, 回来的. ②接着来的; 继任的. ③(利益等)正在产生的, (自然) 增殖的. ④(居民等)移来的. *the* ～ *mayor* 继任市长. ～ *profits* 即将取得的利润. *the* ～ *tide* 涨潮.

in·com·men·su·ra·ble [ˌinkəˈmenʃərəbl] *a.* ①不能按同一标准衡量的, 无共同尺度的. ②不能比较的 *(with)*; 悬殊的 *(with)*. ③【数】不能通约的,无公度的. ～ *numbers* 不可通约数. — *n.* 【数】无理数; 悬殊的东西. **-bil·i·ty** *n.* **-bly** *ad.*

in·com·men·su·rate [ˌinkəˈmenʃərit] *a.* ①= incommensurable. ②不相称的,不适当的,不相对应的 *(to; with)*. *His abilities are* ～ *to [with] the task he has been given.* 他的能力同给予他的工作不相适应. **-ly** *ad.*

in·com·mode [inkəˈməud] *vt.* 使不便,妨碍; 打扰, 使为难. *One is seriously* ～*d at theatres by ladies' hats.* 戏院中女人的帽子最妨碍人了.

in·com·mo·di·ous [ˌinkəˈməudjəs] *a.* ①不舒服的; 不方便的.②小得无回旋余地的. *an* ～ *little bedroom* 一间窄小不堪的卧室. **-ly** *ad.* **-ness** *n.*

in·com·mu·ni·ca·ble [ˌinkəˈmju:nikəbl] *a.* ①不能传达的, 无法表达的. ②沉默寡言的, 孤僻的. **-bil·i·ty** [ˌinkəˌmju:nikəˈbiliti], **-ness** *n.* **-bly** *ad.*

in·com·mu·ni·ca·do [ˌinkəˌmju:niˈkɑ:dəu] *a.* 被禁止接触外界的,(尤指犯人)被单独监禁的.

in·com·mu·ni·ca·tive [ˌinkəˈmju:nikətiv] *a.* 不爱说话的,沉默寡言的,不爱交际的. **-ly** *ad.* **-ness** *n.*

in·com·mut·a·ble [ˌinkəˈmju:təbl] *a.* 不能交换的; 不能变换的. **-bil·i·ty** *n.* **-bly** *ad.*

in·com·pact [ˌinkəmˈpækt] *a.* 不紧密的,松散的; 不结实的. **-ly** *ad.* **-ness** *n.*

in·com·pa·ra·ble [inˈkɔmpərəbl] *a.* 无比的, 无双的; 不能比较的 *(with; to)*. *a woman of* ～ *beauty* 绝代佳人. **-bly** *ad.*

in·com·pat·i·ble [ˌinkəmˈpætəbl] *a.* ①不相容的, 难两立的, 矛盾的 *(with)*. ②【医】配伍禁忌的. ③不能溶合成一体的. *She asked for a divorce because they were utterly* ～. 她请求离婚,因为他们完全合不来. ～ *colours* 不调和的色彩. **-bil·i·ty** [ˈinkəmˌpætəˈbiliti] *n.* **-bly** *ad.*

in·com·pe·tence, -ten·cy [inˈkɔmpitəns, -si] *n.* ①无能, 不熟练. ②不适当, 不胜任, 不够格. ③法律上无资格. ④【医】关闭不全, 机能不全. *He lost his job because of* ～. 因为不能胜任, 他失掉了(工作)职位.

in·com·pe·tent [inˈkɔmpitənt] *a.* ①无能的, 不熟练的. ②不适当的, 不胜任的, 不够格的. ③法律上无资格的. *be* ～ *as a teacher* 不适宜当教员. *be* ～ *to teach [for teaching]* 不能教书. — *n.* ①无能者. ②不胜任者. ③法律上无资格的人. **-ly** *ad.*

in·com·plete [ˌinkəmˈpli:t] *a.* 不完全的,未完成的,不完备的. ～ *combustion* 不完全燃烧. ～ *reaction* 【化】不完全反应,可逆反应. **-ly** *ad.* **-ness** *n.*

in·com·ple·tion [ˌinkəmˈpli:ʃən] *n.* 不完全, 未完成, 不完备.

in·com·pli·ant [ˌinkəmˈplaiənt] *a.* 不服从的; 不让步的; 不柔顺的. **-ance, -an·cy** *n.* **-ly** *ad.*

in·com·pre·hen·si·ble [ˌinkɔmpriˈhensəbl] *a.* ①不能理解的,费解的; 莫测高深的. ②〔古〕广大无边的, 无限的. — *n.* 无限物,无限者. **-bil·i·ty** *n.* **-bly** *ad.*

in·com·pre·hen·sion [inˌkɔmpriˈhenʃən] *n.* 不了解, 缺乏理解.

in·com·pre·hen·sive [inˌkɔmpriˈhensiv] *a.* ①理解不深的, 没有理解力的. ②范围狭的, 包含得很少的. **-ly** *ad.* **-ness** *n.*

in·com·press·i·ble [ˌinkəmˈpresəbl] *a.* 不能压缩的; 不易压缩的; 坚硬的; 不屈的. *an* ～ *fluid* 不可压缩流体. **-bil·i·ty** [ˈinkəmˌpresəˈbiliti] *n.* 不可压缩性.

in·com·put·a·ble [ˌinkəmˈpju:təbl] *a.* 不能计算的, 数不清的.

in·con·ceiv·a·ble [ˌinkənˈsi:vəbl] *a.* ①不能想象的; 不可思议的; 不可理解的. ②〔口〕难于相信的,惊人的. **-bil·i·ty** [ˈinkənˌsi:vəˈbiliti] *n.* **-bly** *ad.*

in·con·cin·ni·ty [ˌinkənˈsiniti] *n.* 不适合, 不协调. **-cin·nous** *a.*

in·con·clu·sive [ˌinkənˈklu:siv] *a.* 不确定的; 不充分的; 不得要领的; 不能使人信服的; 无确定结果的; 无效的. *an* ～ *discussion* 没有结果的讨论. **-ly** *ad.*

in·con·clu·sive·ness [ˌinkənˈklu:sivnis] *n.* 不确定, (证据)不充分; (议论)不得要领; 不能使人信服; 无确定结果; 无效.

in·con·den·si·ble [ˌinkənˈdensəbl] *a.* 不能凝缩的 (= incondensable). **-bil·i·ty** *n.*

in·con·dite [inˈkɔndit] *a.* ①(文体等)拙劣的, 生硬的. ②无礼貌的, 粗鲁的.

in·con·form·i·ty [ˌinkənˈfɔ:miti] *n.* 不一致, 不符合 *(to, with)*.

in·con·gru·ent [inˈkɔŋgruənt, ˌinkənˈgru:ənt] *a.* 不相合的,不一致的, 不适当的, 不相称的. **-ence** *n.* **-ent·ly** *ad.*

in·con·gru·i·ty [ˌinkɔŋˈgru(:)iti] *n.* ①不调和, 不一致; 不相称. ②不协调的事物.

in·con·gru·ous [inˈkɔŋgruəs] *a.* ①不适当的; 不适宜的,不合理的. ②不调和的, 不相称的, 不一致的 *(with)*; 【数】不等的 (*opp.* congruous). **-ly** *ad.* **-ness** *n.*

in·con·nu [ˌinkəˈnu:] *n.* *(pl.* **-nus, -nu**) 【动】白北鲑 *(Stenodus mackenziti)* 〔产于北美西北和亚洲东北〕.

in·cons·cient [inˈkɔnʃənt] *a.* 无意识的; 失去知觉的; 漫不经心的.

in·con·sec·u·tive [ˌinkənˈsekjutiv] *a.* 不连续的; 不连贯的,无顺序的. **-ly** *ad.* **-ness** *n.*

in·con·se·quence [inˈkɔnsikwəns] *n.* ①不连贯, 前后不符,矛盾. ②不重要.

in·con·se·quent [inˈkɔnsikwənt] *a.* ①不合逻辑的, 不连贯的, 前后不符的; 矛盾的. ②不重要的,无价值的. **-ly** *ad.*

in·con·se·quen·tial [inˌkɔnsiˈkwenʃəl] *a.* ①无意义的,不重要的. ②不连贯的, 前后不一的, 不合逻辑的. **-i·ty** *n.* **-ly** *ad.*

in·con·sid·er·a·ble [ˌinkənˈsidərəbl] *a.* 不值得考虑的,无足轻重的,些微的. **-bly** *ad.*

in·con·sid·er·ate [ˌinkənˈsidərit] *a.* ①不替别人着想的,不体谅别人的. ②考虑不周的, 粗心的,轻率的. ～

remarks 轻率的语言. ～ *children* 鲁莽的孩子. **-ly** *ad.* **-ness** *n.*

in·con·sid·er·a·tion [ˈinkənˌsidəˈreiʃən] *n.* ①不替别人着想,不会体谅人. ②考虑不周,粗心,轻率.

in·con·sist·ence [ˌinkənˈsistəns], **in·con·sist·en·cy** [-si] *n.* ①不一致,不协调;前后矛盾,不一贯. ②不一致的事物,自相矛盾的言行.

in·con·sis·tent [ˌinkənˈsistənt] *a.* ①不一致的,不调和的 *(with)*. ②前后矛盾的,不合逻辑的. ③反复无常的. ～ **equation**【数】不相容方程,矛盾方程. **-ly** *ad.*

in·con·sol·a·bil·i·ty [ˌinkənˌsəuləˈbiliti] *n.* 无可安慰,无可慰藉 (= inconsolableness).

in·con·sol·a·ble [ˌinkənˈsəuləbl] *a.* 无可安慰的,无可慰藉的. **-bly** *ad.*

in·con·so·nance [inˈkɔnsənəns] *n.* 不调和,不和谐,不一致.

in·con·so·nant [inˈkɔnsənənt] *a.* 不调和的,不和谐的,不一致的 *(to, with)*. *be* ～ *with* 与…不调和. *be* ～ *to the ear* 刺耳. **-ly** *ad.*

in·con·spic·u·ous [ˌinkənˈspikjuəs] *a.* ①不显眼的,不引人注目的. ②【植】(花)小而色淡的. **-bly** *ad.* **-ness** *n.*

in·con·stan·cy [inˈkɔnstənsi] *n.* ①反复无常,易变;无规则. ②轻浮,无信义.

in·con·stant [inˈkɔnstənt] *a.* ①反复无常的,易变的;无规则的. ②轻浮的,无信义的. **-ly** *ad.*

in·con·sum·a·ble [ˌinkənˈsjuːməbl] *a.* 烧不尽的;用不完的;消耗不了的;【经】非消费性的. **-a·bly** *ad.*

in·con·test·a·bil·i·ty [ˌinkənˌtestəˈbiliti] *n.* 不可争,无可争辩.

in·con·test·a·ble [ˌinkənˈtestəbl] *a.* 不能争辩的,无怀疑余地的,否定不了的. ～ *evidence* 铁证. **-bly** *ad.*

in·con·ti·nence [inˈkɔntinəns], **in·con·ti·nen·cy** [-si] *n.* ①无节制〔尤指纵欲〕;无抑制. ②不能保持. ③【医】大小便失禁.

in·con·ti·nent[1] [inˈkɔntinənt] *a.* ①无节制的,不能抑制的. ②不能保持的. ③【医】大小便失禁的. **-ly** *ad.*

in·con·ti·nent[2] [inˈkɔntinənt] *ad.* 〔古〕立即. **-ly** *ad.*

in·con·trol·la·ble [ˌinkənˈtrəuləbl] *a.* 不能控制的. **-bly** *ad.*

in·con·tro·vert·i·ble [ˌinkɔntrəˈvəːtəbl] *a.* 无可辩驳的,颠扑不破的,不容置疑的. **-bly** *ad.*

in·con·ven·ience [ˌinkənˈviːnjəns] *n.* ①不方便,不自由. ②为难之处,麻烦的事. *if it is no* ～ *to you* 如果对你方便的话. *put sb. to* ～ 使某人感到不便〔为难〕. — *vt.* 使感不便,使为难,使麻烦. *I hope I do not* ～ *you.* 我希望我不会打搅你. *Do not* ～ *yourself for my sake.* 请不必为我麻烦.

in·con·ven·ient [ˌinkənˈviːnjənt] *a.* 不方便的,引起不方便的;麻烦的. *if it is not* ～ *to you* 如果你方便的话. **-ly** *ad.*

in·con·vert·i·ble [ˌinkənˈvəːtəbl] *a.* ①不能变换〔转换〕的. ②不能换成硬币的,不能兑换外汇的. ～ *notes [paper-money]* 不能兑换成硬币的纸币. **-bil·i·ty** [ˌinkənˌvəːtiˈbiliti] *n.* **-bly** *ad.*

in·con·vin·ci·ble [ˌinkənˈvinsəbl] *a.* 不能说服的. **-ci·bil·i·ty** *n.* **-bly** *ad.*

in·co·or·di·nate [ˌinkəuˈɔːdinit] *a.* ①不配合的. ②不同格的;不同等的.

in·co·or·di·na·tion [ˌinkəuɔːdiˈneiʃən] *n.* ①不配合,不协调. ②不同格,不同等.

incor(p). = incorporated 注册.

in·cor·po·ra·ble [inˈkɔːpərəbl] *a.* ①可以结合的. ②可合为一体的. ③可以混合的. ④可以加入公司、社团的. ⑤可以具体化的.

in·cor·po·rate[1] [inˈkɔːpəreit] *vt.* ①结合,合并,收编. ②使成为法定组织;〔美〕使成为有限公司;使注册. ③使混合. ④使加入. ⑤〔罕〕使具体化,体现. *be* ～*d a member of a learned society* 被吸收为学会成员. ～ *new ideas into a book* 把新思想收入书内. — *vi.* ①合并;混合 *(with)*. ②成为社团,组成公司. *The mill* ～*d with others.* 这家厂子与别家合并了. — [-pərit] *a.* ①法定组织的. ②〔罕〕合并的,结合起来的;具体化了的.

in·cor·po·rate[2] [inˈkɔːpərit] *a.* 无形(体)的;精神上的,心灵上的.

in·cor·po·rat·ed [inˈkɔːpəreitid] *a.* ①合并的;结合的,联合的. ②组成法人组织的.

in·cor·po·ra·tion [inˌkɔːpəˈreiʃən] *n.* ①结合;合并;编入. ②团体,结社;法人,公司.

in·cor·po·ra·tive [inˈkɔːpəritiv, -pəˈreit-] *a.* ①合并的;结合的. ②成为法人组织的.

in·cor·po·ra·tor [inˈkɔːpəreitə] *n.* 合并者,社团成员,公司创办人.

in·cor·po·re·al [ˌinkɔːˈpɔːriəl] *a.* ①非物质的,精神的;无实体的,无形的. ②【法】无形体的. ～ *capital*【经】无形资本. *an* ～ *hereditament*【法】无形遗产. **-ly** *ad.*

in·cor·po·re·i·ty [ˌinkɔːpəˈriːiti] *n.* ①非物质性;无实体,无形体. ②*(pl.* **-ties***)* 无实体物.

in·cor·rect [ˌinkəˈrekt] *a.* ①错误的,不正确的;不妥当的. ②原稿未经妥善校正的. **-ly** *ad.*

in·cor·rect·ness [inkəˈrektnis] *n.* ①不正确. ②(尤指)不适当. ③不真实;不准确;错误;有缺点.

in·cor·ri·gi·bil·i·ty [inˌkɔridʒəˈbiliti] *n.* 难以纠正;不能改正;不能改进;不能改造〔尤指习惯成自然,或指儿童已养成坏习惯难以改正〕(= incorrigibleness).

in·cor·ri·gi·ble [inˈkɔridʒəbl] *a.* 难以纠正的;不可改造的,不可救药的;固执的,难弄的. — *n.* 无可救药的人,不改悔的人. **-bly** *ad.*

in·cor·rupt [ˌinkəˈrʌpt] *a.* ①纯洁的,正直的,廉洁的;不能收买的. ②(版本等)无差错的,无改动的.

in·cor·rupt·i·ble [ˌinkəˈrʌptəbl] *a.* ①不会腐蚀的,不易败坏的. ②不能收买的,廉洁的. — *n.* 不易腐蚀的东西. **-bil·i·ty** *n.* **-bly** *ad.*

in·cor·rup·tion [ˈinkəˌrʌpʃən] *n.* 〔古〕不腐,不朽;廉洁.

incr. = increased; increasing.

in·cras·sate [inˈkræsit] *a.*【生】增厚的. — *vt.* ①使浓厚. ②【药】浓缩. **-a·ble** *a.*

in·crease [inˈkriːs] *vt.* 增加,增大,增多;增强,增进 (*opp.* decrease). ～ *speed* 增加速度. ～ *one's pace* 放快脚步. ～ *one's efforts* 更加努力. — *vi.* 增加;繁殖;〔诗〕(月亮)渐渐变大,渐圆. ～ *in number* 数目增加. ～ *in power* 权力增大. ～ *with years* 逐年增加. — [ˈinkriːs] *n.* 增加,繁殖;增加量,增大额;〔古〕农产品,作物. *an [the]* ～ *of money* 钱数增加. ～ *in the population* 人口的增长. ***be on the*** ～ 不断增加,正在增加.

in·creas·ing [inˈkriːsiŋ] *a.* 增加的,增大的. ～ **return**【经】收获递增.

in·creas·ing·ly [inˈkriːsiŋli] *ad.* 不断增加地,日益,格外,越来越. *be* ～ *prosperous and strong* 日益繁荣富强.

in·cre·ate [ˌinkriˈeit, ˈinkrieit] *a.* 非创造出来的〔指神灵之类〕.

in·cred·i·ble [inˈkredəbl] *a.* ①不可相信的. ②〔口〕不可思议的;惊人的;未必可能的. *with* ～ *speed* 用惊人的速度. **-bil·i·ty** *n.* **-bly** *ad.*

in·cre·du·li·ty [ˌinkriˈdjuːliti] *n.* 不相信,怀疑.

in·cred·u·lous [inˈkredjuləs] *a.* 不轻易相信的;表示怀疑的 *(of; about)*;奇怪的. *an* ～ *smile* 含有疑意的微笑. **-ly** *ad.*

in·cre·mate [ˈinkrimeit] *vt.* 火葬.

in·cre·ment [ˈinkrimənt] *n.* 增额,增值,增长;【数】增量;利润. *unearned* ～【经】自然增值. ～ *value duties* 增值税.

in·cre·men·tal [ˌinkriˈmentl] *a.* ①增加的,增大的,增

长的. ②增额的. ③【数】增量的.
in·cre·men·tal·ism [ˌinkriˈmentlizəm] *n.* (政治和社会改革方面的)渐进主义.
in·cres·cent [inˈkresnt] *a.* 增加的,成长的;〔尤指〕(月的)渐盈的.
in·cre·tion [inˈkriːʃən] *n.* 内分泌,内分泌物(= internal secretion). **-tion·ar·y, -to·ry** *a.*
in·crim·i·nate [inˈkrimineit] *vt.* 归罪于,使负罪;控告. ～ *oneself* 自陷法网. **-na·tion** *n.* **-na·tor** *n.* **-na·to·ry** *a.*
in·croach [inˈkrəutʃ] *vt.* = encroach.
in·cross [ˈinkrɔːs] *n.* 品种内异系交配体. — *vt.* = inbreed.
in·crowd [ˈinkraud] *n.* 小圈子,小集团;(小圈子里的)熟人;小集团成员.
in·crust [inˈkrʌst] *vt., vi.* = encrust.
in·crus·ta·tion [ˌinkrʌsˈteiʃən] *n.* ①用外皮包覆,结硬壳. ②硬壳,外皮,外壳,疮痂. ③渣壳,水锈,水垢. ④镶嵌;镶嵌物;(建筑物的)表面装饰;镶嵌细工. ⑤(风俗、习惯等的)逐渐形成.
in·cu·bate [ˈinkjubeit] *vi.* ①孵卵;孵化. ②沉思. ③【医】(病)潜伏. — *vt.* ①孵卵;(人工)孵化. ②保育(早产婴儿). ③培养(细菌). ④仔细考虑,想(办法),策划.
in·cu·ba·tion [ˌinkjuˈbeiʃən, ˌiŋ-] *n.* ①孵卵,孵化;培育. ②策划,图谋,企图. ③【医】潜伏期. ④深思熟虑. *artificial* ～ 人工孵化. ～ **period** 潜伏期.
in·cu·ba·tion·al [ˌinkjuˈbeiʃənəl, ˌiŋ-] *a.* ①孵卵的,孵化的. ②【医】潜伏的,潜伏期的.
in·cu·ba·tive [ˈinkjubeitiv] *a.* 孵卵的;潜伏期的.
in·cu·ba·tor [ˈinkjubeitə] *n.* ①孵卵器;孵卵员. ②细菌培养器. ③早产婴儿保育箱.
in·cu·ba·to·ry [ˈinkjubeitəri] *a.* = incubative.
in·cu·bus [ˈiŋkjubʌs] *n.* (*pl.* **-bi** [-bai], ～*es*) ①恶梦;梦魇. ②沉重的负担,梦魇般的精神压力[压迫者].
in·cu·des [iŋˈkjuːdiːz] incus 的复数.
in·cul·cate [inˈkʌlkeit] *vt.* 反复灌输;谆谆劝导. **-ca·tion** *n.* **-ca·tor** *n.*
in·culp·a·ble [inˈkʌlpəbl] *a.* 无过的;无可责难的;无罪的.
in·cul·pate [ˈinkʌlpeit, inˈkʌl-] *vt.* ①使负罪,控告. ②连累(某人)受罪. **-to·ry** *a.*
in·cul·pa·tion [ˌinkʌlˈpeiʃən] *n.* ①归罪,控告. ②连累.
in·cult [inˈkʌlt] *a.* 〔罕〕①未开垦的. ②粗野的,粗鲁的.
in·cum·ben·cy [inˈkʌmbənsi] *n.* ①(主指牧师的)任职,任期,职权. ②义务,职责.
in·cum·bent [inˈkʌmbənt] *a.* ①靠在[压在]上面的. ②有义务的,成为责任的,义不容辞的 (*on, upon*). ③在职的. ④弯垂下来的. ⑤(地层)重叠的,叠覆的,上覆的. *It is* ～ *(up)on us to do so.* 这样做是我们义不容辞的责任. — *n.* 〔英〕教区牧师;〔美国政府或团体,学术机构中〕任职者.
in·cum·ber [inˈkʌmbə] *vt.* = encumber.
in·cum·brance [inˈkʌmbrəns] *n.* = encumbrance.
in·cu·nab·u·lum [ˌinkjuˈnæbjuləm] *n.* (*pl.* **-la** [-lə]) ①〔常用复〕初期,黎明期,摇篮时代. ②〔特指十六世纪前的〕古版本书,古代的作品. **-r** *a.*
in·cur [inˈkəː] *vt.* (*in·curred; in·cur·ring*) 招致,承受,惹起. ～ *danger* 遭受危险. ～ *hatred* 惹人仇恨. ～ *a mountain of debt* 承受巨大债务.
in·cur·a·ble [inˈkjuərəbl] *a.* 医治不好的;不能矫正的. — *n.* 〔常 *pl.*〕医不好的病人. *an* ～ *disease* 不治之症. **-bil·i·ty, -ness** *n.* **-bly** *ad.*
in·cu·ri·os·i·ty [inˌkjuəriˈɔsiti] *n.* ①不关心,无好奇心;不爱追根究底. ②引不起兴趣.
in·cu·ri·ous [inˈkjuəriəs] *a.* ①〔古〕不注意的,不关心的;不感兴趣的,不爱追根究底的. ②〔主要与 not 连用〕乏味的,没兴趣的. *a not* ～ *anecdote* 有趣的逸事. **-ly** *ad.*
in·cu·ri·ous·ness [inˈkjuriːəsnis] *n.* 无好奇心;无探索意;无兴趣;淡漠.
in·cur·rence [inˈkəːrəns] *n.* 蒙受,招致.
in·cur·rent [inˈkəːrənt] *a.* 流入的〔尤指水流入的〕. *the* ～ *canals of sponges* 海绵吸水管.
in·cur·sion [inˈkəːʃən, Am. -ʒən] *n.* ①侵入,侵略;袭击. ②(河水等)流入,进入.
in·cur·sive [inˈkəːsiv] *a.* 攻入的,侵入的,袭击的;流进来的.
in·cur·vate [ˈinkəːveit] *vt., vi.* (使)弯曲,(使)向心弯曲. — *a.* 弯曲的,向内弯曲的. **-va·tion** *n.*
in·curve[1] [ˈinˈkəːv] *vt., vi.* (使)弯曲,(使)向内弯曲. **-d** *a.*
in·curve[2] [inˈkəːv] *n.* 【棒球】内曲球.
in·cus [ˈiŋkes] *n.* (*pl.* ***-cu·des*** [iŋˈkjuːdiːz]) 〔L.〕【解】砧骨.
in·cuse [inˈkjuːz] *vt.* 在(硬币面上)压印. — *a.* 有压印的,压铸的. — *n.* (硬币等)压铸;压铸成的花样.
Ind [ind] 〔古、诗〕= India;〔废〕= the Indies.
Ind. = ①India; Indian. ②Indiana.
ind. = ①independent. ②index. ③indicative. ④industrial. ⑤indigo.
in·da·ba [inˈdɑːbɑː] *n.* ①(南非本地人的)会议. ②〔口〕重要会议.
in·da·mine [ˈindəmiːn, -min] *n.* 【化】吲达胺.
In·dan·threne [inˈdænθriːn] *n.* 阴丹士林染料;标准还原蓝.
in·dan·throne [inˈdænθrəun] *n.* 【化】(阴丹士林的正式名称)靛蒽醌.
in·debt·ed [inˈdetid] *a.* ①负债的 (*to*). ②受过人恩惠的,感激的. *be* ～ *to sb. for 100 dollars* 欠某人 100 元. *He was* ～ *to her for nursing him through pneumonia.* 他感激她护理好他的肺炎. *She is* ～ *to the library for most of her information.* 她的学识多数是从这个图书馆得来的. *I am* ～ *to you for kindness.* 谢谢您的好意. **-ness** *n.*
in·de·cen·cy [inˈdiːsnsi] *n.* ①粗鄙,猥亵,下流;下流言行. ②〔口〕不适当,不合适.
in·de·cent [inˈdiːsnt] *a.* ①粗鄙的,猥亵的,下流的. ②〔口〕不适当的,不合适的. ～ *language* 下流话. *leave in* ～ *haste* 灰溜溜地[很不光彩地]急忙离开. **-ly** *ad.*
in·de·cid·u·ous [ˌindiˈsidjuəs] *a.* 【植】常绿的,不落叶的 (*opp.* deciduous).
in·de·ci·pher·a·ble [ˌindiˈsaifərəbl] *a.* ①(密码等)破译不出的. ②(字迹等)难辨读的,模糊的,难懂的.
in·de·ci·sion [ˌindiˈsiʒən] *n.* 不决定,无决断力,优柔寡断,犹豫不决.
in·de·ci·sive [ˌindiˈsaisiv] *a.* ①非决定性的. ②不决定的;无决断力的,优柔寡断的,犹豫不决的. ③不明确的,模糊的. **-ly** *ad.* **-ness** *n.*
indecl. = indeclinable.
in·de·clin·a·ble [ˌindiˈklainəbl] *a.* 【语法】无格的变化的,无语法形态变化的. — *n.* 不变词〔名词、代名词、形容词以外的词〕. **in·de·clin·a·bly** *ad.*
in·de·com·pos·a·ble [ˌindiːkəmˈpəuzəbl] *a.* 不能分解的,难分解的;不腐败的.
in·dec·o·rous [inˈdekərəs] *a.* 不合礼节的;不正派的;不规矩的;低级趣味的;不体面的. **-ly** *ad.*
in·dec·o·rous·ness [inˈdekərəsnis] *n.* 不合礼节;不正派;不规矩;低级趣味;不体面.
in·de·co·rum [ˌindiˈkɔːrəm] *n.* ①不合礼节;不正派;不规矩;低级趣味,不体面. ②失礼的言行.
in·deed [inˈdiːd] *ad.* ①实际上,真正地. *He is* ～ *a great man.* 他实在是一个伟人. ②〔加强语气〕确实,实在. *I shall be very glad* ～. 那我真太高兴啦. *I- yes!*

= *Yes, ~!* 不错，真的！③〔表示让步〕当然，固然. *There are ~ exceptions.* 当然有例外. ④〔表示同意或反语〕真的，真是. *Who is this Mr. James? — Who is he, ~!* 这个詹姆斯先生是谁？—〔同感〕是谁呀！真的！〔我也不知道的意思〕；〔反〕你问谁，真是！〔奇怪，你还不知道〕. ⑤〔表示疑问〕当真. *There's a big fire raging. — Indeed?* 起大火了. — 真的吗？⑥〔表示进一层的意思〕甚至. *There are many good people in our school, ~ in the whole society.* 在我们学校里好人很多，其实整个社会都是这样.

indef. = indefinite.

in·de·fat·i·ga·ble [ˌindiˈfætigəbl] *a.* 不疲倦的；不屈不挠的. **-bil·i·ty** [ˈindiˌfætigəˈbiliti] *n.* **-bly** *ad.*

in·de·fea·si·ble [ˌindiˈfi:zəbl] *a.* 难废除的，不能取消的. **-bil·i·ty** [ˈindiˌfi:zəˈbiliti] *n.* **-bly** *ad.*

in·de·fect·i·ble [ˌindiˈfektəbl] *a.* ①不易损坏的，不败的；永存的，不朽的. ②完美的，无缺点的. **-bil·i·ty** [ˈindiˌfektəˈbiliti] *n.* **-bly** *ad.*

in·de·fen·si·bil·i·ty [ˌindiˌfensəˈbiliti] *n.* ①难防御，难保护. ②难辩解；难辩护；难宽恕.

in·de·fen·si·ble [ˌindiˈfensəbl] *a.* ①难防御的，难保护的. ②难辩解的；难辩护的. ③难宽恕的. *an ~ position* 难以防御的阵地. *~ behaviour* 难以宽恕的行为. *an ~ argument* 站不住脚的论点. **-bly** *ad.*

in·de·fin·a·bil·i·ty [ˌindiˈfainiˈbiliti] *n.* 难限定，难确定；难下定义.

in·de·fin·a·ble [ˌindiˈfainəbl] *a.* 难限定的，难确定的；难下定义的. — *n.* 难以下定义的事物. **-bly** *ad.*

in·def·i·nite [inˈdefinit] *a.* (*opp.* definite) ①模糊的，不明确的，不确定的. ②无定限的，无限期的. ③【语法】不定的. *a strike of ~ duration* 无限期罢工. *an ~ answer* 含糊其词的回答. *the ~ article* 不定冠词〔a, an〕. *~ pronouns* 不定代名词. ④【植】(雄蕊)无定数的. ***for an ~ time*** 无限期地. ***in an ~ manner*** 模模糊糊地，不明确地. *~* **integral**【数】不定积分，无定积分. **-ly** *ad.*

in·def·i·nite·ness [inˈdefənitnis] *n.* ①无定限；〔尤指〕无准限；意思不精确；含糊；轮廓不分明，不明显；无把握；不确定. ②【植】(雄蕊的)无定数. ③【语法】不定(冠词).

in·de·his·cent [ˌindiˈhisnt] *a.*【植】不裂的. *~ fruits* 闭果. **-cence** *n.*

in·del·i·ble [inˈdelibl] *a.* 不能消除的，擦不掉的；持久的. *~ ink* 去不掉的墨渍. *an ~ pencil* 笔迹难擦掉的铅笔. **-bil·i·ty** [inˌdeliˈbiliti] *n.* **-bly** *ad.*

in·del·i·ca·cy [inˈdelikəsi] *n.* ①粗俗，淫猥，下流. ②下流的举动，粗俗的事物.

in·del·i·cate [inˈdelikit] *a.* ①粗俗的. ②淫猥的，下流的. *~ words* 粗俗的话. **-ly** *ad.*

in·dem·ni·fi·ca·tion [inˌdemnifiˈkeiʃən] *n.* ①保护，保障. ②赦免. ③赔偿，补偿.

in·dem·ni·fy [inˈdemnifai] *vt.* ①保护，保障 (*against, from*). ②赔偿，补偿 (*for*). ③使免于受罚. *~ sb. from [against] harm* 保证某人不受损害. *~ sb. for the loss incurred* 赔偿某人所受损失.

in·dem·ni·ty [inˈdemniti] *n.* ①保护，保障. ②损失赔偿，补偿. ③赔偿金；(对战胜国的)赔款. ④免罚，赦免. *~ insurance* 损失补偿保险. *a letter of ~* 赔偿保证书. *a war ~* 战争赔款.

in·de·mon·stra·ble [inˈdemənstrəbl, indiˈmɔns-] *a.* 不能证明的；无证明必要的，(道理)自明的. **-bly** *ad.*

in·dene [ˈindi:n] *n.*【化】茚〔制造合成树脂的原料〕.

in·dent[1] [inˈdent] *vt.* ①把…刻成锯齿状，使犬牙交错. ②使弯入，使凹进. ③一式二份〔多份〕地起草文件〔合同等〕. ④【印】把(每段的首行)缩排二字；【商】用双联订单订货. ⑤【英陆军】征用(物资). — *vi.* 刻上齿痕；首行缩排二字；订约；【英陆军】进行征发；分发双联订单〔委托书等〕. *~ upon sb. for goods* 向某人订货. — *n.* ①齿痕，缺刻. ②双联订单；契约；购买委托书. ③〔英〕征用令. ④【印】缩排. *order goods by means of an ~* 用订单订货.

in·dent[2] [inˈdent] *vt.* 在…上压凹痕；压印(图案等). — [ˈindent] *n.* 凹痕.

in·den·ta·tion [ˌindenˈteiʃən] *n.* ①呈锯齿形；缺刻. ②海岸线凹入处. ③(印刷或书写中每段首行开端的)空格. ④凹痕. *~ hardness*【物】压痕硬度.

in·dent·ed [inˈdentid] *a.* ①锯齿状的，犬牙交错的；【印】首行缩排的. ②(学徒)有定期契约的. *an ~ coastline* 犬牙交错的海岸线.

in·den·tion [inˈdenʃən] *n.*【印】(行首)缩进；打缺刻；缺刻；凹入，锯齿形.

in·den·ture [inˈdentʃə] *n.* ①合同，契约. ②〔*pl.*〕定期服务契约；师徒合同. ③【法】(盖有骑缝章的)证书；(商业上的传票等)凭单. ④打缺刻；缺刻；成员；凹凸不平. ***take up [be out of] one's ~s*** 服务期满，学徒期满，契约期满. — *vt.* 立合同决定；用契约束缚(学徒).

in·de·pend·ence [ˌindiˈpendəns] *n.* ①独立，自主，自立 (*of; on*). ②足够维持闲居生活的收入. ③独立心，自恃心. *national ~* 民族独立. **I- Day** 美国独立纪念日〔7月4日〕.

in·de·pend·en·cy [ˌindiˈpendənsi] *n.* ①独立，自主，自立. ②独立国，独立省. ③〔I-〕【宗】独立派运动，公理会教义.

in·de·pend·ent [ˌindiˈpendənt] *a.* ①独立的，自主的，自治的，有主见的. ②自食其力的，收入足够维持闲居生活的. ③愿意独立的，独立不羁的，自尊心强的. ④〔I-〕【宗】独立派的. ⑤【政】无党无派的. ⑥单独的，不承担义务的，不接受外援的. ⑦【语法】主要的，独立的. ⑧【数】无关的，独立的，无党无派的. *an ~ manner* 不愿受约束的样子. *an ~ voter* 无党派选民. *an ~ attack*【军】单独进攻. *an ~ grocer* 独立经营的杂货商. *an ~ clause* (主从复合句中的)主句. *an ~ state* 独立国. *~ thinking* 独立思考. *an ~ income* 可过富裕生活的收入. ***be ~ of*** ①独立于…之外的，不受…支配的 (*be ~ of control* 不受控制. *an objective law ~ of man's will* 不以人们意志为转移的客观规律). ②与…无关的，不倚赖…的 (*be ~ of each other* 互无关系. *be ~ of one's parents* 不倚赖父母. *be ~ of doctors* 同医生无缘). — *n.* ①独立自主的人. ②无党派人士. ③【宗】〔I-〕独立派教徒，公理会教徒. *~* **functions**【数】独立函数. *~* **variable**【数】自变数〔量〕.

in·de·pend·ent·ly [ˌindiˈpendəntli] *ad.* 独立地，自主地；自由地，任意地. *~ of* 同…无关地，不取决于…地.

in-depth [ˈinˈdepθ] *a.* 认真作出的；详细的；深入的；彻底的. *an ~ study* 深入的研究.

in·de·scrib·a·ble [ˌindiˈskraibəbl] *a.* ①难于描述的，形容不出的. ②模糊的，不明确的. *~ beauty* 无法形容的美丽. *an ~ sensation* 一种莫名其妙的感觉. — *n.* 〔*pl.*〕〔俚〕裤子. **-bil·i·ty** [ˈindisˌkraibəˈbiliti] *n.* **-bly** *ad.*

in·de·struct·i·ble [ˌindiˈstrʌktəbl] *a.* 不能破坏的，毁灭不了的；牢不可破的. **-bil·i·ty** [ˈindisˌtrʌktəˈbiliti] *n.* *the -bility of matter* 物质的不灭性. **-bly** *ad.*

in·de·ter·mi·na·ble [ˌindiˈtə:minəbl] *a.* ①(问题、争执)不能决定的，不能解决的. ②无法确定的，不能查明的. **-bly** *ad.*

in·de·ter·mi·na·cy [ˌindiˈtə:minəsi] *n.* 不确定；不明确，犹豫不决 (= indetermination). *~* **principle** = uncertainty principle.

in·de·ter·mi·nate [ˌindiˈtə:minit] *a.* ①不确定的，不定的，模糊的. ②【语】无确定音值的. ③【植】总状的，花被与花苞分隔而未被覆盖着的. ④无结果的，未决定的，仍有疑问的. ⑤【数】不确定的，未定元的. *an ~ result* 不明确的结果. *an ~ vowel* 中性元音. *an ~ sen-*

tence【法】无定期徒刑. ～ *analysis* 不定解析［分析］. *an* ～ *problem*【数】不定问题. ～ *cleavage*【动】不定裂,不定形卵裂. **-ly** *ad.* **-ness** *n.*

in·de·ter·mi·na·tion [ˌindiˌtəːmiˈneiʃən] *n.* ①不确定,不明确,模糊. ②优柔寡断,犹豫不决.

in·de·ter·min·ism [ˌindiˈtəːminizəm] *n.* ①【哲】非决定论,非定命论,意志自由论. ②难以预测,不可预言.

in·de·ter·min·ist [ˌindiˈtəːminist] *n.* 非决定论者. — *a.* 非决定论的;非决定论者的.

in·dex [ˈindeks] *n.* *(pl.* **-es, -di·ces** [-disiːz]*)*. ①索引. ②指标,标准,标志. ③食指 (= ～ finger). ④指数. ⑤【印】指标,示指,参见号. ⑥(刻度盘上的)指针;【机】(铣床)分度(头). ⑦〔the I-〕【天主】禁书目录. *card* ～*es* 卡片索引. *Style is an* ～ *of the mind.* 风格是心灵的反映. *the cost of living* ～ 生活费指数. *a price* ～ 物价. *an* ～ *pin [plate]* 指度针[盘]. *a fixed* ～ 固定瞄准器. — *vt.* ①为…加索引;把…编入索引;指明,指出. ②〔美口〕按生活指数调整(价格). — *vi.* 加索引. ～ **crime**〔美〕指数罪案〔联邦调查局每年分类罪案报告中所列的严重罪案〕. ～ **error** 指数误差,指标误差,仪标误差. **I- Expurgatorius**〔L.〕【宗】(书中部分内容应予删节的)禁书目录. ～ **fossil**【地】标准化石. ～ **head** 分度头,分度器. **I- Librorum Prohibitorum**〔L.〕【宗】绝对禁书目录. ～ **number** 指数. ～ **of refraction**【物】折射指数. ～ **signal** 指引信号,指示信号. **-er** *n.* 编索引的人. **-i·cal** *a.* **-less** *a.* 无索引的.

In·di·a[1] [ˈindjə, -diə] *n.* 印度〔亚洲〕. ～ **cotton** 印度花布. ～ **ink** ①墨. ②墨汁. ～**man** *n.* 印度航线班轮(早年英国来往于印度和英国之间的商船,尤指英国东印度公司的大型商船). ～ **paper** ①摹拓纸. ②圣经纸,字典纸. ～ **rubber** 橡皮;橡胶;橡胶套鞋.

In·di·a[2] [ˈindiə] *n.* 通信中用以代表字母 i 的词.

In·di·an [ˈindjən, -diən] *a.* ①印度的;印度人的;印度文化的. ②西印度群岛的,西印度群岛文化的;印第安人的,印第安文化的. ③玉米做的. — *n.* ①印度人. ②印第安人 (= American ～ 或 Red ～). ③印第安语. ④过去长期住在印度的欧洲人(尤指英国人). ⑤〔the I-〕【天】印度人座. ⑥〔口〕= ～ corn. ～ **agency** (美国及加拿大的) 印第安事务厅. ～ **agent** (美国及加拿大的)印第安事务官. ～ **bread** ①玉米面包. ②=tuckahoe.【体】火棒,瓶状棒. ～ **corn**〔英〕玉蜀黍, 玉米,苞米. ～ **file** 一路纵队. ～ **gift**〔口〕送出后企图对方退回的礼物,期待对方还礼的礼物. ～ **giver**〔口〕送礼给人以后又索回的人;企图对方还礼而送礼的人. ～ **hay**〔美俚〕大麻. ～ **hemp** ①磁麻 *(Apocynum cannabium)*〔产于美洲. 印第安人用其纤维结绳,用其根作药〕. ②大麻 (= hemp). ～ **ink** = India ink. ～ **licorice** = jequirity. ～ **mallow**【植】苘麻 *(Abutilon theophrasti)*. ～ **meal**〔英〕玉米粉. ～ **millet** 食用高粱. ～ **Mutiny** 印度反英暴动〔1857—1858年印度士兵反对英国殖民政策的暴动〕. ～ **ocean** 印度洋. ～ **paintbrush**【植】扁萼花属 *(Castilleja)* 植物〔尤指红扁萼花 *(C. coccinea)*〕. ～ **pipe** 水晶兰 *(Monotropa uniflora)*〔产于北半球〕. ～ **pudding** 玉米奶油布丁. ～ **red** ①印度红〔北美印第安人用以表示战争的涂料〕. ②【化】三氧化铁,氧化正铁. ～ **sign** 妖符,不祥的东西〔主用于 ***to have*** (或 ***put***) ***the*** ～ ***sign on*** 短语中〕. ～ **states and Agencies** 印度半独立诸国和管理区. ～ **summer** ①晚秋的晴暖气候,小阳春. ②宁静愉快的晚年. ～ **Territory** 印第安人保留地〔美国的印第安人居住地区〕. ～ **tobacco**【植】路辈利草(祛痰菜) *(Lobelia inflata)*〔一种一年生有毒植物,产于美国东部〕. ～ **turnip**【植】印度天南星 *(Arisaema triphyllum)* 或其根〔也叫 Jack-in-the-pulpit〕. ～ **weed** 烟草. ～ **wrestling** ①扳腕子. ②拽推比试〔两人右足相抵,右手相握,以强使对方身体失去平衡为止〕.

In·di·an·a [ˌindiˈænə] *n.* 印第安纳〔美国州名〕.

In·di·an·an, In·di·an·i·an [ˌindiˈænən, ˌindiˈæniən] *n.* 印第安纳州人. — *a.* 印第安纳州的;印第安纳州人的.

In·di·an·ap·o·lis [ˈindiəˈnæpəlis] *n.* 印第安纳波利斯〔美国城市〕.

In·di·an·ize [ˈindjənaiz, -diə-] *vt.* 使印度人化,使印度化. **In·di·an·i·za·tion** *n.*

In·dic [ˈindik] *a.* ①印度的. ②印度—伊朗语族的〔包括印度、巴基斯坦、斯里兰卡过去和现在所讲的多种语言的〕.

indic. = indicating; indicative.

in·di·can [ˈindikæn] *n.*【化】尿蓝母.

in·di·cant [ˈindikənt] *a.* 指示的. — *n.* 指示物;【医】病征.

in·di·cate [ˈindikeit] *vt.* ①指示,表示;指出. ②【医】表明(症状、原因),需要(治疗方法等);象征,暗示,预示. ③简单陈述. *Snow* ～*s the coming of winter.* 下雪表示冬天的到来. ～ *assent* (用脸色、动作、或态度)表示同意. ～**d horse-power**【机】指示马力 (略 i. h. p.). ～**d power**【机】指示功率. ～**d work**【机】指示功.

in·di·ca·tion [ˌindiˈkeiʃən] *n.* ①指示,指出,表示. ②象征,征兆,迹象. ③【医】指示法,适效,指征,适应症. ④指示器表示的量(或度数). *There is every* ～ *(no* ～*) that we shall have an earthquake.* 所有的[没有]迹象表明,将要发生(一次)地震.

in·dic·a·tive [inˈdikətiv] *a.* ①【语法】陈述的,直陈的. ②指示…的,表示…的 *(of)*. *the* ～ *mood* 陈述语气. *Is a high forehead* ～ *of great mental power?* 前额高表示智慧高吗? — *n.*【语法】陈述语气. **-ly** *ad.*

in·di·ca·tor [ˈindikeitə] *n.* ①指示者;指示物;标识. ②【化】指示剂. ③【机】指示器,示功器. *an* ～ *card [diagram]* 示功图. *revolution* ～ 转速计. *speed* ～ 速度计.

in·dic·a·to·ry [inˈdikətəri] *a.* 指示的,表示的 *(of)*.

in·di·ca·trix [ˌindiˈkeitriks] *n.* ①【数】指标;指示量;指示线,特征曲线. *spherical* ～ *of scattering* 球面散射指示量. *curvature* ～ 曲率指示线. ②光率体. ～ *of optical diaxial crystal* 二轴晶光率体.

in·di·ces [ˈindisiːz] index 的复数.

in·di·ci·a [inˈdiʃiə] *n.* indicium 的复数.

in·di·ci·um [inˈdiʃiəm] *n.* *(pl.* ***in·di·ci·a*** [inˈdiʃiə]*)* ①征候,表示;记号. ②〔美〕(大宗邮件上盖的)邮资总付邮戳.

in·dict [inˈdait] *vt.*【法】控告,告发,对…起诉. ～ *sb. for theft* 控告某人犯有盗窃罪. ～ *sb. as a thief* 指控某人为窃贼. *He was* ～*ed on a charge of theft.* 他因犯盗窃罪被起诉. **-ion** [inˈdikʃən] *n.*

in·dict·a·ble [inˈdaitəbl] *a.* 可以起诉[告发]的;应起诉的,应告发的. *an* ～ *offence* 刑事罪. *an* ～ *offender* 刑事犯. *an offence not* ～ 不论罪.

in·dict·ee [ˌindaiˈtiː] *n.*【法】被告.

in·dict·er, in·dict·or [inˈdaitə] *n.*【法】起诉人,原告.

in·dic·tion [inˈdikʃən] *n.* ①(罗马史)定额征税法〔罗马皇帝康士坦丁制订的以十五年为一期的征收定额财政税的制度〕. ②十五年定额税. ③十五年纪期. ④十五年纪期中的任何一年. ⑤〔古〕宣告,公布.

in·dict·ment [inˈdaitmənt] *n.* ①控告,起诉,告发. ②诉状,起诉书. *bring in an* ～ *against sb.* 控告某人. *a bill of* ～ 起诉书[状子].

in·die [ˈindi] *n.*〔美俚〕独立经营的电影院〔广播电台、电视台〕.

In·dies [ˈindiz] *n.*〔*pl.*〕〔the I-〕东印度群岛 (= the East Indies); 西印度群岛 (= the West ～).

in·dif·fer·ence [inˈdifrəns], **in·dif·fer·en·cy** [-si] *n.* ①不关心,不计较,冷淡 *(to, towards)*. ②不重要,不在乎. ③中立,中性. ④【语法】任凭关系〔no matter how 或 whatever 等引导的从句所表示的结构〕. *show* ～ *to personal affairs* 不计较个人的事. *a matter of* ～ 无关紧

要的事. ***with*** ~ 冷淡地，满不在乎地（*face death with supreme* ~ 置生死于度外）.

in·dif·fer·ent [in'difrənt] *a.* ①漠不关心的，冷淡的，不感兴趣的. ②公平的，中立的，不偏袒的. ③平凡的. ④无关重要的，无足轻重的，满不在乎的. ⑤【物】中性的，惰性的. ⑥【生】未分化的. ~ *to hardships and dangers* 置困难危险于度外. *an* ~ *judge* 铁面无私的法官. *remain* ~ *in a dispute* 对争论保持中立. *an* ~ *book* 质量不高的书. *an* ~ *performance* 水平不高的演出. *meet with* ~ *success* 获得不大的成功. *be in* ~ *health* 健康状况不佳. *It is quite* ~ *to me whether you go or not.* 你去不去，我都无所谓. ~ *equilibrium*【物】随遇平衡. *the* ~ *gas* 惰性气体. *a* ~ *point* 中性点. ***be*** ~ ***to*** 对…不关心（*be* ~ *to the sufferings of the others* 不关心别人的痛苦）. — *n.* （对政治、宗教等）冷淡的人.

in·dif·fer·ent·ism [in'difərəntizəm] *n.* （对宗教的）冷淡主义；冷淡态度；【宗】信教无差别论；冷淡；无差别. **in·dif·fer·ent·ist** *n.* 冷淡主义者.

in·dif·fer·ent·ly [in'difrəntli] *ad.* ①不关心地，冷淡地，漫然，漠然. ②无差别地；无可无不可地；普通地；差得很地〔常同 *but, very* 等词连用〕. *look on* ~ *at a match* 冷淡地参观比赛. *play but* ~ 玩得相当糟糕.

in·di·gence, in·di·gen·cy ['indidʒəns, -si] *n.* 贫穷，穷困.

in·di·gene ['indidʒi:n] *n.* 当地人；土生的动物〔植物〕.

in·dig·e·nous [in'didʒinəs] *a.* ①本土的，土生土长的. ②生来的；为…所固有的 *(to)*. *use* ~ *raw materials* 就地取材. *an* ~ *population* 土著居民. *feelings* ~ *to human beings* 人类固有的感情. **-ly** *ad.* **-ness** *n.*

in·di·gent ['indidʒənt] *a.* 贫困的；贫穷的. **-ly** *ad.*

in·di·gest·ed [ˌindi'dʒestid, ˌindai'dʒestid] *a.* ①难消化的，不消化的. ②考虑未成熟的，杂乱的，条理不清的，生硬的.

in·di·gest·i·ble [ˌindi'dʒestəbl, ˌindai'dʒestəbl] *a.* ①不消化的，难消化的. ②难理解的，难领略的. **-bil·i·ty** ['indiˌdʒestə'biliti] *n.* **-bly** *ad.*

in·di·ges·tion [ˌindi'dʒestʃən, ˌindai'dʒestʃən] *n.* ①消化不良，胃弱. ②杂乱，生硬，难理解. *suffer from* ~ 患消化不良症. *have an attack of* ~ 患消化不良.

in·di·ges·tive [ˌindi'dʒestiv, ˌindai'dʒestiv] *a.* 消化不良的，不消化的.

in·dign [in'dain] *a.* 〔废、诗〕①不值得的，无价值的. ②耻辱的，丢脸的.

in·dig·nant [in'dignənt] *a.* 愤怒的，愤慨的. *be* ~ *at a false accusation* 对诬告愤愤不平. *be* ~ *with a cruel person* 对凶残的人感到愤慨. **-ly** *ad.*

in·dig·na·tion [ˌindig'neiʃən] *n.* 愤怒，愤慨，义愤. *arouse the* ~ *of the people* 激起人民的愤怒. *an* ~ *meeting* 声讨大会.

in·dig·ni·ty [in'digniti] *n.* 轻蔑，侮辱；侮辱的言行. *be subjected to indignities* 受辱. *put an* ~ *upon sb.* [*treat sb. with* ~] 侮辱某人.

in·di·go ['indigəu] *n.* (*pl.* ~*s*, ~*es*) ①靛蓝，靛青；靛蓝类染料. ②一种深蓝色. ③【植】能产生靛蓝的植物. *the Chinese* ~ 草本靛青. *the Indian* ~ 木本靛青. *the* ~ *plant* 木蓝. ~ **blue** ①= indigotin. ②靛蓝〔光谱七色之一〕. ~**blue** *a.* 靛蓝色的. ~ **snake**【动】①森王靛蛇 (*Drymarchon corais couperi*)〔出现于美国南卡罗来纳到德克萨斯间的低地〕. ②褐牛蛇(= bull snake).

in·di·goid ['indigɔid] *a.* 靛类的. — *n.* 靛类染料.

in·di·go·sol ['indigəusɔl] *n.*【化】溶靛素(染料).

in·di·got·ic [ˌindi'gɔtik] *a.* 靛蓝的，靛青的.

in·dig·o·tin [in'digətin] *n.*【化】靛.

in·di·rect [ˌindi'rekt, -dai-] *a.* ①间接的，第二手的；迂回的；曲折的. ②不直截了当的，不坦率的，不诚实的. *an* ~ *answer* 侧面回答. ~ *descent* 旁系. ~ *fire*【军】间接射击. *an* ~ *route* 迂回的路，绕行的路. *make an* ~ *reference to sb.* 间接提到某人. ~ *methods* 不正当的手段. ~ **discourse [narration, speech]** 间接引语. ~ **evidence**【法】间接证据. ~ **lighting** 间接照明，无影照明. ~ **object**【语法】间接宾语. ~ **passive**【语法】间接被动时态. ~ **tax** 间接税. **-ly** *ad.* **-ness** *n.*

in·di·rec·tion [ˌindi'rekʃən] *n.* ①间接，迂回. ②不诚实，欺骗. ***by*** ~ 拐弯抹角地，兜着圈子，间接地.

in·dis·cern·i·ble [ˌindi'sə:nəbl] *a.* 觉察不出的；难辨别的. **-bly** *ad.*

in·dis·cerp·ti·ble [ˌindi'sə:ptəbl] *a.* 不能溶解的，不会溶解的. **-ti·bil·i·ty** ['indiˌsə:ptə'biliti] *n.*

in·dis·ci·pline [in'disiplin] *n.* 无纪律，缺乏训练. **-plin·a·ble** *a.* 〔罕〕难驾驭的；训练不好的.

in·dis·creet [ˌindis'kri:t] *a.* 欠慎重的，轻率的；不得体的. *Is it* ~ *to ask you the reason?* 问问理由可以吗? **-ly** *ad.*

in·dis·crete [ˌindis'kri:t] *a.* 不分开的；紧凑的.

in·dis·cre·tion [ˌindis'kreʃən] *n.* 欠考虑，不慎重，轻率；轻率的言行. *have the* ~ *to do sth.* 居然轻率地做某事. *commit a grave* ~ 生活极不检点(尤指男女关系).

in·dis·crim·i·nate [ˌindis'kriminit] *a.* ①不加区别的，不分青红皂白的. ②任性的，杂乱的. *an* ~ *reader* 乱读书的人. *be* ~ *in making friends* 乱交朋友. *deal out* ~ *blows* 乱打一气. **-ly** *ad.* **-ness** *n.*

in·dis·crim·i·nat·ing ['indisˌkrimineitiŋ] *a.* 不加区别的，无选择的 (= undiscriminating). **-ly** *ad.*

in·dis·crim·i·na·tion ['indisˌkrimi'neiʃən] *n.* ①不加区别，无选择，混淆. ②任意；任性.

in·dis·crim·i·na·tive [ˌindis'kriminətiv] *a.* 不加区别的.

in·dis·pen·sa·ble [ˌindis'pensəbl] *a.* ①不可缺少的，必需的，重要的 (*to; for*). ②不能撇开的，责无旁贷的. *Air and water are* ~ *to life.* 空气和水是生命所必需的. *an* ~ *obligation* 不可推卸的责任. **-bil·i·ty, -ness** *n.* **-bly** *ad.*

in·dis·pose [ˌindis'pəuz] *vt.* ①使厌恶，使不愿. ②使不适合，使不适当，使不能. ③使不舒服. *Illness* ~*s a man for enjoyment.* 疾病使人不想娱乐.

in·dis·posed [ˌindis'pəuzd] *a.* ①不舒服的，有病的. ②厌倦的，不愿的. *I am* ~ *with a cold.* 我因为伤风感到不舒服. *He is* ~ *to go.* 他不愿去. *be* ~ *towards sb.* 讨厌某人.

in·dis·po·si·tion [ˌindispə'ziʃən] *n.* ①不舒服，小病. ②不想，厌恶.

in·dis·pu·ta·ble [ˌindis'pju:təbl] *a.* 不可争辩的，无可置疑的. **-bil·i·ty, -ness** *n.* **-bly** *ad.*

in·dis·sol·u·ble [ˌindi'sɔljubl] *a.* ①难溶解的；不能分解的；不能分离的. ②坚固的；永久不变的. *an* ~ *friendship* 牢不可破的友谊. **-bil·i·ty** *n.* 不溶解性；不分解性；不变性，永久性. **-bly** *ad.*

in·dis·tinct [ˌindis'tiŋkt] *a.* 不清楚的，模糊的；朦胧的，不确定的. ~ *memories* 模糊的记忆. ~ *speech* 暧昧不明的话. **-ly** *ad.* **-ness** *n.*

in·dis·tinc·tion [indis'tiŋkʃən] *n.* 不清楚，模糊；不确定，难辨认；同等，同格.

in·dis·tinc·tive [ˌindis'tiŋktiv] *a.* 不显著的，无特色的；无差别的. **-ly** *ad.*

in·dis·tin·guish·a·ble [ˌindis'tiŋgwiʃəbl] *a.* ①难区别的，不能辨别的. ②无特征的. **-bly** *ad.* **-ness** *n.*

in·dis·trib·u·ta·ble [ˌindis'tribjutəbl] *a.* 不可分配的；不可散布的.

in·dite [in'dait] *vt.* 〔罕〕著作，写(诗、文等). ~ *a speech (poem)* 写演讲稿(诗). **-ment** *n.* **-r** *n.* 撰述人，作者.

in·di·um ['indiəm] *n.*【化】铟.

in·di·vert·i·ble [ˌindai'və:təbl] *a.* 不能引开的，难使转向的；难使分心的. **-bly** *ad.*

individ. = individual.

in·di·vid·u·al [ˌindiˈvidjuəl] *a.* ①单一的,个别的,单独的. ②个人的,个体的. ③特殊的,特有的,独特的 (*opp.* general, universal). *give ~ attention [instruction]* 给予个别注意[教导]. *each ~ person* 各个人. *an ~ style of speaking* 独特的谈话风格. *a set of ~ tea cups* (花色等)各不相同的一套茶杯. — *n.* 个人 (*opp.* society, family) 个体,独立单位;〔俚〕人. *a disagreeable ~* 讨厌的家伙. *an agreeable ~* 好人. *a private ~* 私人,个人. *representative ~s* 代表人物.

in·di·vid·u·al·ism [ˌindiˈvidjuəlizəm] *n.* ①个人主义,利己主义. ②个性,独特性. ③(资本主义政府对私营工商企业的)不干涉主义,自由放任主义.

in·di·vid·u·al·ist [ˌindiˈvidjuəlist] *n.* 个人主义者,利己主义者. — *a.* 个人主义的; 个人主义者的. *an ~ careerist* 个人主义野心家.

in·di·vid·u·al·is·tic [ˌindiˌvidjuəˈlistik] *a.* 个人主义的,个人主义者的. *~ heroism* 个人英雄主义.

in·di·vid·u·al·i·ty [ˌindiˌvidjuˈæliti] *n.* ①个体;个人;独立存在. ②个人的特征,个性. ③〔*pl.*〕个人的趣味(或嗜好). *a man of marked ~* 个性特别的人.

in·di·vid·u·al·ize [ˌindiˈvidjuəlaiz] *vt.* ①使各不相同,使个体化;使个性化,使有个人特色. ②一一列举,分别详述. *His peculiar style strongly ~s his work.* 他的特殊文体使他的作品带有显著的个性. **-i·za·tion** [ˌindiˌvidjuəlaiˈzeiʃən] *n.*

in·di·vid·u·al·ly [ˌindiˈvidjuəli] *ad.* ①以个人资格. ②个性上,个别地,各自地,独特地. *traits ~ different* 各不相同的特征.

in·di·vid·u·ate [ˌindiˈvidjueit] *vt.* 使个体化,使具体化,使有个性,使具特色. **-a·tion** *n.* 个性化;个别化.

in·di·vis·i·bil·i·ty [ˈindiˌviziˈbiliti] *n.* 不可分性.

in·di·vis·i·ble [ˌindiˈvizəbl] *a.* ①不可分割的. ②【数】除不尽的. — *n.* 不能分割的东西;极微分子,微量. **-bly** *ad.*

In·do- [ˈindəu] *comb. f.* 表示"印度","印度种".

In·do-Ar·y·an [ˈindəuˈæriən; -jən] *a.* ①印度—雅利安族的; 印度—雅利安语的. ②= indic. — *n.*〔罕〕讲印度语支的一种语言的印度人.

In·do-Chi·na [ˈindəuˈtʃainə] *n.* 印度支那〔亚洲〕.

In·do-Chi·nese [ˈindəu-tʃaiˈni:z] *n.* 印度支那人. — *a.* 印度支那的;印度支那人的.

in·do·cile [inˈdəusail] *a.* 难驯服的,倔强的.

in·do·cil·i·ty [ˌindəuˈsiliti] *n.* 难驯服,倔强.

in·doc·tri·nate [inˈdɔktrineit] *vt.* ①教训. ②灌输. *~ sb. with an idea [a belief]* 给某人灌输某种思想[信仰]. **-na·tion** [inˌdɔktriˈneiʃən] *n.*

In·do-Eu·ro·pe·an [ˈindəuˌjuərəˈpi(:)ən] *a.* 印欧语系的. — *n.* 印欧语系;说印欧语系语言的人.

In·do-Ger·man·ic [ˈindəudʒə:ˈmænik] *a., n.* = Indo-European.

In·do-Hit·tite [ˈindəuˈhitait] *n.* ①印度—赫提语系〔包括印欧语和安纳托利亚语〕. ②印欧语和赫提语的母语〔赫提语被认为是印欧语系的一个语族〕.

In·do-I·ra·ni·an [ˈindəuiˈreiniən] *a.* 印度—伊朗语族的. — *n.* 印度语和伊朗语的母语.

in·dole [ˈindəul] *n.*【化】吲哚;氮(杂)茚.

in·dole·a·ce·tic [ˈindəuliəˈsi:tik] **acid**【化】吲哚基醋酸.

in·dole·bu·tyr·ic [ˈindəulbju:ˈtirik] **acid**【化】吲哚丁酸.

in·do·lence [ˈindələns] *n.* ①懒惰,不积极. ②【医】不痛,小痛.

in·do·lent [ˈindələnt] *a.* ①懒惰的,不积极的. ②【医】不痛的,小痛的. *an ~ cyst* 无痛囊肿. **-ly** *ad.*

in·dom·i·ta·ble [inˈdɔmitəbl] *a.* 不可屈服的,不屈不挠的;大无畏的;不气馁的. *an ~ spirit* 一往无前的精神,大无畏的精神. *an ~ will* 百折不回的毅力. *an ~ struggle* 不屈不挠的斗争. **-bly** *ad.*

In·do·ne·sia [ˌindəuˈni:zjə] *n.* 印度尼西亚〔亚洲〕.

In·do·ne·sian [ˌindəuˈni:ʃən, -ʒən] *n.* 印度尼西亚人;印度尼西亚语. — *a.* 印度尼西亚的;印度尼西亚人的;印度尼西亚语的.

in·door [ˈindɔ:] *a.* (*opp.* outdoor) ①屋内的,室内的. ②呆在家里的. ③〔英〕救济院内的. *~ games* 室内游戏. *~ antenna* 室内天线. *an ~ child* 呆在家里的孩子. *~ relief* 救济院内的救济品.

in·doors [ˈinˈdɔ:z] *ad.* 在屋里. *go ~* 到屋里. *keep [stay] ~* 呆在家里,不外出.

in·do·phe·nol [ˌindəuˈfi:nəul, -nɔ:l] *n.*【纺】靛酚.

in·dor·sa·tion [ˌindɔ:ˈseiʃən] *n.* = endorsement.

in·dorse [inˈdɔ:s] *vt.* = endorse.

in·dor·see [ˌindɔ:ˈsi:] *n.* = endorsee.

in·dox·yl [inˈdɔksl] *n.*【化】吲哚酚,吲羟.

in·dra [ˈindrə] *n.*〔印度神话〕因陀罗〔印度神话中印度教的主神.雷神及雨神的神格化〕.

in·draft, in·draught [ˈindrɑ:ft] *n.* ①引入,吸入. ②向内的气流或水流. ③〔古〕引诱,魅力.

in·du·bi·ta·ble [inˈdju:bitəbl] *a.* 不容置疑的;明确的. **-bil·i·ty** [inˌdju:bitəˈbiliti], **-ness** *n.* **-bly** *ad.*

induc. = induction.

in·duce [inˈdju:s] *vt.* ①劝诱,诱导,敦促. ②引导,导致. ③【逻】归纳 (*opp.* deduce). ④【电】感应. *~ sb. to do sth.* 劝诱某人做某事. *Nothing shall ~ me to go.* 我怎么都不去. *~ abortion* 人工流产,引产. *weakness ~d by starvation* 因贫困引起的衰弱. *~d current* 感应电流. *~ radioactivity* 感应放射性. *~d velocity* 诱导速度. *inducing current* 施感电流.

in·duce·ment [inˈdju:smənt] *n.* ①诱导,劝诱. ②诱因,动机. ③【法】提出主张事项前的陈述说明. *have many ~s [much ~] to do sth.* 很想作某事.

in·duc·er [inˈdju:sə] *n.* ①诱导者,劝诱者. ②【化】诱导物. ③【机】(离心式鼓风机、压缩机泵的)进口段. ④【电】电感器,诱导体.

in·duct [inˈdʌkt] *vt.* ①(通过仪式)使就职 (*to, into, as*). ②使正式入会;征调…入伍 (*to, into*). ③使初步入门,介绍(知识等). ④引入,引导. ⑤【电】感应,感生. *~ sb. to an office of mayor* 使某人就任市长. *~ sb. into a seat* 引人就座.

in·duct·ance [inˈdʌktəns] *n.*【电】电感,感应现象;感应系数;(发动机)进气. *~ bridge* 电感电桥.

in·duct·ee [ˌindʌkˈti:] *n.* 就任者;入会者;〔美〕应征(入伍)者.

in·duc·tile [inˈdʌktail] *a.* ①没有延性的,不能拉长的. ②难塑造的,不易弯曲的. ③不顺从的,难驾驭的.

in·duc·tion [inˈdʌkʃən] *n.* ①引入,诱发,诱导(作用). ②【逻】归纳法,归纳推理 (*opp.* deduction). ③就职,就职典礼;入会,入伍. ④【电】感应,感应现象. ⑤〔古〕导言,序幕. ⑥首次经验,入门. ⑦吸入. *make an ~ from* 由…归纳出来的. *mutual ~* 互感应. *self ~* 自感应. *air ~* 吸气. *~* **centre** 征兵中心. *~* **coil**【电】感应线圈,电感线圈. *~* **field**【电】感应磁场,感应电场. *~* **furnace**【冶】感应电炉. *~* **heating**【电】感应加热. *~* **motor**【电】感应电动机,异步电动机. *~* **pipe** 进口管. *~* **stroke**【机】吸入冲程. *~* **valve**【机】吸入阀,进气门. **-less** *a.* 无感应的.

in·duc·tive [inˈdʌktiv] *a.* ①引入的,诱导的 (*to*). ②【逻】归纳的,归纳法的 (*opp.* deductive). ③【电】感应的,电感的. ④导论的,绪论的. *~ reasoning* 归纳推理. *an ~ method* 归纳法. *an ~ coil* 有感线圈,电感线圈. *the ~ capacity* 电感容量,电容. *~ coupling* 电感耦合. *the ~ reactance*【电】感抗. **-ly** *ad.* **-ness** *n.*

in·duc·tiv·i·ty [ˌindʌkˈtiviti] *n.* 诱导性;【电】诱导率,感应率,介电常数,电容率.

in·duc·tor [inˈdʌktə] *n.* ①引导者，授职人．②【电】感应器，感应体，感应物，电感线圈，电感器．③手摇磁石发电机．④【化】诱导物．
in·duc·to·syn [inˈdʌktəsin] *n.*【无】感应式传感器．
in·due [inˈdjuː] *vt.* = endue.
in·dulge [inˈdʌldʒ] *vt.* ①纵情，沉迷，沉溺．②放任，纵容，娇养．③使满足，使快乐．④迁就．⑤【商】容许延期付款．⑥【天主】赦免，恕罪；赋予特权．～ *one's appetite for sweets* 特别爱吃甜食．～ *oneself in smoking* 纵情抽烟．～ *a child* 纵容孩子．～ *the company with a song* 唱歌给大家助兴．*It is sometimes necessary to* ～ *a sick child.* 迁就一个生病的小孩，有时是必要的．— *vi.* ①〔口〕酗酒，嗜酒．②纵情，沉迷，沉溺．*Will you* ～? 喝一杯吧！～ *in dreams* 爱空想．
in·dul·gence [inˈdʌldʒəns] **in·dul·gen·cy** [-si] *n.* ①纵情，沉迷，沉溺．②放任，纵容，娇养．③嗜好，着迷的事物．④恩惠；(天主教的) 免罪；赦免．⑤【商】付款延期．⑥【英史】信教自由．*the Declaration of I-*【英史】信教自由令．
in·dul·gent [inˈdʌldʒənt] *a.* 纵容的，放纵的；宽容的，溺爱的．*an* ～ *father* 溺爱的父亲．*be* ～ *to sb.* 对某人宽容．**-ly** *ad.*
in·du·line, in·du·lin [ˈindjuˌliːn, -lin] *n.*【纺】引杜林染料；对氮蒽蓝．
in·dult [inˈdʌlt] *n.*【天主】罗马教皇的特许．
in·du·na [inˈduːnə] *n.* 非洲东南部祖鲁 (Zulu) 人的族长．
in·du·pli·cate [inˈdjuːplikit, -ˈduː-] *a.*【植】(花叶的) 内向镊合状的．
in·du·rate [ˈindjuəreit] *vt.* ①使硬化，使坚硬．②使无感觉，使无情，使顽固．③使坚固，使巩固．— *vi.* 变硬；巩固起来．— [ˈindjuərit] *a.* ①硬化的．②冷酷的．③顽固的．
in·du·ra·tion [ˌindjuəˈreiʃən] *n.* 硬化；冷酷；顽固．
in·du·ra·tive [ˈindjuərətiv] *a.* 变硬的；无情的．
In·dus [ˈindəs] *n.* ①印度河．②【天】印第安座．
in·du·si·um [inˈdjuːziəm, -ˈduː-; -ʒiː-] *n.* (*pl.* **-si·a** [-ə]) ①【解、动】胚被；幼虫膜．②【植】柱头下毛圈；囊群盖．**-si·al** [-əl] *a.*
in·dus·tri·al [inˈdʌstriəl] *a.* ①工业的，产业的，实业的．②工业上用的．③工业高度发展的．④从事工业的．⑤工人的．⑥勤奋努力而得到的．～ *alcohol* 工业用酒精．～ *diamond* 工业用钻石．～ *arts* 工艺劳作〔美国中小学的一门课程〕．*an* ～ *nation* [*state*] 工业国．*an* ～ *town* 工业城市．*the* ～ *classes* 工人阶级．*an* ～ *reserve army* 工业后备军．～ *workers* 产业工人．～ *training* 职业训练．～ *welfare* 职工福利．*an* ～ *crop* 因勤劳而得的收获．— *n.* ①产业工人，工业工人．②工业公司．③【商】工业股票．～ **archaeology** 工业考古学〔对过去技术发达时代，尤指产业革命后各个阶段的研究〕．～ **disease** 职业病．～ **park** 工业区．～ **relations** 劳资关系．**I- Revolution** (十八世纪六十年代在英国开始的) 工业革命，产业革命．～ **school** ①中等工业技术学校．②(“顽劣”青少年被送入改造的) 教养学校．～ **store** 员工福利商店．～ **union** 同一工业内跨行业的职工工会．**-ly** *ad.*
in·dus·tri·al·ism [inˈdʌstriəlizəm] *n.* 工业〔产业〕主义．
in·dus·tri·al·ist [inˈdʌstriəlist] *n.* 工业主义者；实业家．
in·dus·tri·al·i·za·tion [inˌdʌstriəlaiˈzeiʃən] *n.* 工业化．*intense* ～ 高度工业化．*bring about* ～ 实现工业化．
in·dus·tri·al·ize [inˈdʌstriəlaiz] *vt., vi.* (使) 工业化．
in·dus·tri·ous [inˈdʌstriəs] *a.* 勤恳的，刻苦的．*an* ～ *and simple style of work* 艰苦朴素的工作作风．**-ly** *ad.* **-ness** *n.*
in·dus·try [ˈindəstri] *n.* ①勤劳，勤奋，刻苦．②工业，产业，实业，事业．③〔集合词〕资方．④有组织的劳动，经常的工作〔努力〕．*heavy* [*light*] ～ 重〔轻〕工业．*the automobile* ～ 汽车工业．*the sugar* ～ 制糖业．*the shipping* ～ 航海业．*the broadcasting* ～ 广播事业．*the beauty* ～ 美容业．～**-education marriage** 工教结合．
in·dwell [ˈinˈdwel] *vi., vt.* (**in·dwelt** [ˈinˈdwelt]; **in·dwell·ing**) 内在，存在于…之中．
in·dwell·er [ˈinˌdwelə] *n.* 内在的精神〔力量、原则〕．
in·dwell·ing [ˈinˈdweliŋ] *a.* 存在于内心〔灵魂〕中的．
-ine *suf.* ①〔构成名词或形容词〕表示“…属的”，“…似的”，“…性质的”: can*ine*, serpent*ine*, mar*ine*. ②〔由科学术语中专有名词构成形容词〕表示“含…的”，“…成的”: alkal*ine*, saturn*ine*. ③〔构成名词〕表示女性的名字〔称呼〕: hero*ine*. ④〔构成抽象名词〕表示 带有技术、处置、行为等抽象意义: discipl*ine*, doctr*ine*. ⑤〔构成名词〕表示【化】“六节的杂环”，“生物碱”: caff*eine*. ⑥构成由意大利语表示小的 *-ino*, *-ina* 转化而来的名词: mandol*ine*, figur*ine*.
in·earth [inˈəːθ] *vt.* 〔古〕把…置于土中；埋葬，葬，埋．
in·e·bri·ant [inˈiːbriənt] *a., n.* = intoxicant.
in·e·bri·ate [iˈniːbrieit] *vt.* ①使醉；灌醉．②使兴奋，使发呆．*be* ～*d by success* 因成功而高兴．— [iˈniːbriit] *a.* 喝醉的．— *n.* 酒鬼，酒徒．
in·e·bri·a·tion, in·e·bri·e·ty [iˌniːbriˈeiʃən, ˌini(ː)ˈbraiəti] *n.* ①酩酊大醉．②高兴，如痴如醉．
in·ed·i·ble [inˈedibl] *a.* 不适于食用的，不能吃的．～ *oil* 非食用油．**-bil·i·ty** [inˌediˈbiliti] *n.*
in·ed·it·ed [inˈeditid] *a.* 未经编辑的；未出版的．*an* ～ *document* 不曾发表过的文件．
in·ed·u·ca·ble [inˈedjukəbl] *a.* 不可教育的．
in·ef·fa·ble [inˈefəbl] *a.* ①不可言喻的，不可名状的，说不出的．②不能说的，应当避讳的．～ *joy* 说不出的高兴．**-bil·i·ty** [ˌiniˌfeiˈbiliti] *n.* **-bly** *ad.*
in·ef·face·a·ble [ˌiniˈfeisəbl] *a.* 不能消除的，抹不掉的．*an* ～ *impression* 消灭不了的印象．**-a·bil·i·ty** [ˌiniˌfeisəˈbiliti] *n.* **-bly** *ad.*
in·ef·fec·tive [ˌiniˈfektiv] *a.* ①无效的，不起作用的．②不动人的，缺乏艺术性的．③效率低的，无能的．**-ly** *ad.* **-ness** *n.*
in·ef·fec·tu·al [ˌiniˈfektjuəl] *a.* 无效的，不灵验的，徒劳无益的．**-ly** *ad.* **-ness** *n.*
in·ef·fi·ca·cious [ˌinefiˈkeiʃəs] *a.* 无效力的，无实效的，疗效不好的．**-ly** *ad.* **-ness** *n.*
in·ef·fi·ca·cy [inˈefikəsi] *n.* 无效力，无疗效．
in·ef·fi·cien·cy [ˌiniˈfiʃənsi] *n.* 无效；无能，不称职．
in·ef·fi·cient [ˌiniˈfiʃənt] *a.* 无效力的，无能力的，效能差的，不称职的．**-ly** *ad.*
inel. = inelastic.
in·e·las·tic [ˌiniˈlæstik] *a.* ①无弹力的，无伸缩性的．②无适应性的，不能变通的，僵硬的，不弯曲的．～ **collision**【物】非弹性碰撞．
in·e·las·tic·i·ty [ˌinilæsˈtisiti] *n.* ①无弹性，无伸缩性．②无适应性，不能变通．
in·el·e·gance, -gan·cy [inˈeligəns, -si] *n.* ①粗俗，生硬，不雅，不精致．②粗俗的东西．
in·el·e·gant [inˈeligənt] *a.* 不雅的；粗俗的，生硬的，粗糙的．**-ly** *ad.*
in·el·i·gi·ble [inˈelidʒəbl] *a.* 不可取的，不合格的，无被选资格的．*be* ～ *for the position* 无资格任职．— *n.* 不合格的人．**-bil·i·ty** [inˌelidʒˈbiliti] *n.* **-bly** *ad.*
in·el·o·quent [inˈeləkwənt] *a.* 不雄辩的，无说服力的；言语不流畅的；无口才的．**-quence** *n.* **-ly** *ad.*
in·e·luc·ta·ble [ˌiniˈlʌktəbl] *a.* 难避免的，不可避免的；必然发生的．**-bil·i·ty** [ˌiniˌlʌktəˈbiliti] *n.* **-bly** *ad.*
in·el·ud·i·ble [ˌiniˈluːdəbl] *a.* 逃脱不了的，躲避不了的．**-bly** *ad.*
in·e·nar·ra·ble [ˌiniˈnærəbl] *a.* 难以描述的，无可名状的．
in·ept [iˈnept] *a.* ①愚昧的，愚蠢的．②不适当的，不适

合的. ③无能的,不称职的. ～ *remarks* 不恰当的语言. **-ly** *ad.* **-ness** *n.*

in·ept·i·tude [iˈneptitjuːd] *n.* 不适当; 不称职; 愚笨; 无能.

in·e·qua·ble [inˈekwebl] *a.* 不一样的,不均匀的,不公允的.

in·e·qual·i·ty [ˌini(ː)ˈkwɔliti] *n.* ①不平等,不平均,不平衡,不等量. ②不相同,互异. ③变动,变化,高低,起伏. ④【数】不等式;【天】均差. ⑤(平面等的)不平坦. ⑥不胜任. *an ～ of temperature* 温度上的变化. *the ～ of the climate* 气候上的变动. *～ in size* 大小不同. *the ～ between the rich and the poor* 贫富不均. *one's ～ to a task* 不胜任.

in·e·qui·lat·er·al [iniːkwiˈlætərəl] *a.* 不等边的. *an ～ triangle* 不等边三角形.

in·eq·ui·ta·ble [inˈekwitəbl] *a.* 不公平的, 不公正的, 偏私的. **-bly** *ad.*

in·eq·ui·ty [inˈekwiti] *n.* 不公平,不公正.

in·e·qui·valve [inˈiːkwəvælv] *a.* 【动】(壳的)不等瓣的.

in·e·rad·i·ca·ble [ˌiniˈrædikəbl] *a.* 难以根除的,根深蒂固的. **-bly** *ad.*

in·e·ras·a·ble [ˌiniˈreisəbl] *a.* 不能涂抹的, 消除不了的.

in·er·ra·ble [inˈerəbl] *a.* 不会错的,绝对正确的. **-bil·i·ty** [inˌeræˈbiliti] *n.* **-bly** *ad.*

in·er·ran·cy [inˈerənsi] *n.* 无错误,绝对正确.

in·er·rant [inˈerənt] *a.* = inerrable.

in·er·rat·ic [ˌiniˈrætik] *a.* 非反复无常的,有规律的,固定的. ～ *stars* 固定的星球.

in·ert [iˈnəːt] *a.* ①【物】无自动力的, 无活动力的. ②【化】惰性的,非活性的. ③不活泼的,无生气的; 迟钝的. ④【医】无作用的, 无效的, 中性的. *Stone is an ～ mass of matter.* 石头是一块无生命的物体. ～ **gas** 惰性气体. ～ **matter** 惰性物质. ～ **type**【生】安定型,不活泼型. **-ly** *ad.* **-ness** *n.*

in·er·tia [iˈnəːʃiə] *n.* ①【物】惯性,惯量. ②不活动, 不活泼, 迟钝, 惰性. ③【医】无力. *the force of ～* 惯性, 惰性. *the law of ～* 惯性定律. *the moment of ～* 转动惯量,惯性矩. ～ **governor**【机】惯性调速器. ～ **selling** 惯性推销〔把商品寄给并未订货但有可能购买的顾客,如不退货即向其收账〕. **-less** *a.* 无惯性的,无惯量的.

in·er·tial [iˈnəːʃəl] *a.* 【物】惯性的, 惯量的. ～ **guidance [navigation]**【空、海】惯性制导. ～ **space** 惯性空间, 惯性作用区〔假设有固定座标的地球上空的一部分,用以计算导弹、宇宙飞船等的航道〕.

in·es·cap·a·ble [ˌinisˈkeipəbl] *a.* 必然发生的, 逃避不了的,不可避免的. *an ～ duty* 推卸不了的责任. **-bly** *ad.*

in·es·sen·tial [ˈiniˈsenʃəl] *a.* ①不重要的; 非必需的. ②无实质的,非物质的. — *n.* 可有可无的东西. **-i·ty** *n.*

in·es·ti·ma·ble [inˈestiməbl] *a.* ①难以估计的. ②极贵重的,无价的. *an ～ service* 非常宝贵的贡献. **-bly** *ad.*

in·ev·i·ta·ble [inˈevitəbl] *a.* ①不可避免的, 不可逃避的; 必然的. ②合情合理的, 逼真的. ③〔口〕照例的, 照常的. *the ～ hour* 死期. *with his ～ camera* 照常带着照相机. *the ～* 必然的事情, 不可避免的命运. **-bil·i·ty** [inˌevitəˈbiliti], **-ness** *n.* **-bly** *ad.*

in·ex·act [ˌinigˈzækt] *a.* ①不精确的, 不准确的. ②不严格的,不仔细的. **-ly** *ad.* **-ness** *n.*

in·ex·act·i·tude [ˌinigˈzæktitjuːd] *n.* 不精确,不准确. *a terminological ～* 〔谑〕谎言.

in·ex·cit·a·ble [ˌinikˈsaitəbl] *a.* 不会激动的,不易感动的,冷静的.

in·ex·cus·a·ble [ˌiniksˈkjuːzəbl] *a.* ①无法辩解的. ②难以原谅的,不可宽恕的. **-bil·i·ty, -ness** *n.* **-bly** *ad.*

in·ex·e·cu·ta·ble [inˈeksikjuːtəbl] *a.* 不能实行的, 难以办到的.

in·ex·er·tion [ˌinigˈzəːʃən] *n.* 不努力;不尽力.

in·ex·haust·i·ble [ˌinigˈzɔːstəbl] *a.* ①用不完的, 无穷尽的. ②不知疲倦的,精神好的. **-bil·i·ty** [ˈinigˌzɔːstəˈbiliti] *n.* **-bly** *ad.*

in·ex·haus·tive [ˌinigˈzɔːstiv] *a.* ①〔古〕= inexhaustible. ②不详尽的,不彻底的. **-ly** *ad.*

in·ex·ist·ent [ˌinigˈzistənt] *a.* ①不存在的, 不成立的. ②〔古〕内在的; 固有的,先天的. **-ence** *n.*

in·ex·o·ra·ble [inˈeksərəbl] *a.* ①无情的,铁面无私的. ②不可动摇的, 不屈不挠的. *an ～ law* 不可抗拒的规律. *an ～ struggle* 坚决的斗争. **-bil·i·ty** *n.* **-bly** *ad.*

in·ex·pe·di·ence, -cy [ˌiniksˈpiːdjəns, -si] *n.* 不适当; 不明智; 不得计.

in·ex·pe·di·ent [ˌiniksˈpiːdiənt, -djənt] *a.* 不适当的; 不明智的; 不得计的. **-ly** *ad.*

in·ex·pen·sive [ˌiniksˈpensiv] *a.* 花费不多的, 廉价的. **-ly** *ad.* **-ness** *n.*

in·ex·pe·ri·ence [ˌiniksˈpiəriəns] *n.* 无经验,不熟练.

in·ex·pert [ˌineksˈpəːt] *a.* 不熟练的,不老练的,业余的. *n.* 生手. **-ly** *ad.* **-ness** *n.*

in·ex·pi·a·ble [inˈekspiəbl] *a.* ①(罪过)不能抵偿的, 不能赎的. ②(仇恨等)不能和解的, 极深的. **-ness** *n.* **-bly** *ad.*

in·ex·plain·a·ble [ˌiniksˈpleinəbl] *a.* 不可解释的, 难说明的.

in·ex·pli·ca·ble [inˈeksplikəbl] *a.* 无法说明的, 费解的, 莫名其妙的. *There are many things which are ～ by science.* 有很多事科学还无法解释. **-bil·i·ty** [inˌeksplikəˈbiliti] *n.* **-bly** *ad.*

in·ex·plic·it [ˌiniksˈplisit] *a.* 模糊不清的; 含糊的. **-ly** *ad.* **-ness** *n.*

in·ex·plo·sive [ˌiniksˈpləusiv] *a.* 不爆炸的,不破裂的.

in·ex·press·i·ble [ˌiniksˈpresəbl] *a.* 表达不出的,说不出的,难形容的. *a scene of ～ beauty* 难以描绘的美景. — *n.* 〔*pl.*〕〔古〕裤子. **-bil·i·ty** *n.* **-bly** *ad.*

in·ex·pres·sive [ˌiniksˈpresiv] *a.* ①缺乏表情的, 无表情的; 无深意的. ②不表白自己的, 沉默的. ③〔古〕= inexpressible. *an ～ face* 毫无表情的面孔. **-ly** *ad.* **-ness** *n.*

in·ex·pug·na·ble [ˌiniksˈpʌgnəbl] *a.* 攻不破的, 难推翻的; (议论等)确定不移的. *～ hatred* 难解除的仇恨. **-bly** *ad.*

in·ex·ten·si·ble [ˌiniksˈtensəbl] *a.* 不能扩张的,伸展不了的.

in·ex·tin·guish·a·ble [ˌiniksˈtiŋgwiʃəbl] *a.* 不能消灭的; 压制不住的. **-bly** *ad.*

in·ex·tir·pa·ble [ˌiniksˈtəːpəbl] *a.* 不能根除的, 不能根绝的.

in·ex·tri·ca·ble [inˈekstrikəbl] *a.* ①解不开的. ②纠缠不清的; 不能解决的. ③不能解脱的, 不能解救的. *an ～ knot* 解不开的结子. *～ confusion* 纠缠不清的混乱. *an ～ maze* 无法解脱的困境. **-bil·i·ty** [inˌekstrikəˈbiliti] *n.* **-bly** *ad.*

I·nez [ˈiːnez] *n.* 伊内兹〔女子名, Agnes 的异体〕.

inf. = ①infantry. ②infinitive. ③information. ④〔L.〕 *infra.*

in·fall [inˈfɔːl] *n.* ①侵入,侵略. ②合流,汇合. ③流入.

in·fal·li·ble [inˈfæləbl] *a.* ①一贯正确的; 不会犯错误的. ②确实可靠的. *an ～ memory* 不会错的记忆. *an ～ remedy* 肯定有效的药方; 可靠的补救办法. — *n.* 一贯正确的人,可靠的事物. **-bil·i·ty** [inˌfæləˈbiliti] *n.* (*His Infallibility* 罗马教皇〔尊称〕. *papal infallibility* 【天主】教皇不谬性[说]). **-bly** *ad.*

in·fa·mize [ˈinfəmaiz] *vt.* 使声名狼藉.

in·fa·mous [ˈinfəməs] *a.* ①名誉极臭的, 声名狼藉的. ②伤风败俗的,无耻的,不名誉的. ③【法】(因犯重罪)被褫夺公权的;〔美〕被剥夺法律上作证权的. ④很差的,低劣的. *an ~ swindler* 臭名昭著的骗子. *~ behaviour* 丑行. *an ~ crime*〔英〕丧失廉耻罪;〔美〕(罚作苦役以上的)重罪. *an ~ dinner* 质量极坏的一顿饭. **-ly** *ad.*

in·fa·my [ˈinfəmi] *n.* ①臭名昭著,声名狼藉. ②出丑,丑行. ③【法】(因犯重罪而)丧失公权. *hold sb. up to ~* 使某人出丑.

in·fan·cy [ˈinfənsi] *n.* ①婴儿期,幼时,幼年时代. ②【法】未成年. ③初期,摇篮时代,幼年期. *in one's* [its] *~* 在摇篮时代.

in·fant [ˈinfənt] *n.* ①婴儿,幼儿〔未满七岁〕. ②【法】未成年人〔二十一岁以下〕. ③生手. — *a.* ①幼儿的;幼小的,幼稚的,初期的. ②【法】未成年的. ③婴儿〔幼儿〕用的. *~ diseases* 小儿病. *~ civilization* 初期文化. *~ fruit* 未熟的水果. *an ~ industry* 新建的工业. *~ food* 幼儿食物. **~s' school** *n.*〔英〕幼儿园.

in·fan·ta [inˈfæntə] *n.* (西班牙、葡萄牙的)公主 (*opp.* infante)〔尤指帝王的长女〕.

in·fan·te [inˈfænti] *n.* (西班牙、葡萄牙的)王子〔尤指帝王的次子,不能继承王位〕.

in·fan·ti·cid·al [inˌfæntiˈsaidl] *a.* 杀婴儿的,杀幼儿的;杀婴罪的.

in·fan·ti·cide [inˈfæntisaid] *n.* 杀害婴儿;杀婴罪;杀婴犯.

in·fan·tile [ˈinfəntail] *a.* ①婴儿的,幼儿的;婴儿期的,幼儿期的. ②适合于婴儿〔幼儿〕的,幼稚的,孩子气的. ③早期的,初期的. *~ diseases* 小儿病. *~ mortality* 婴儿死亡率. *~ paralysis*【医】婴儿麻痹,小儿麻痹,脊髓灰质炎.

in·fan·ti·lism [inˈfæntilizəm] *n.* ①【医】幼稚型,婴儿型. ②【心】幼稚病,幼稚行为.

in·fan·tine [ˈinfəntain, -tin] *a.* 幼稚的;婴儿的;稚气的;孩子的.

in·fan·try [ˈinfəntri] *n.* ①〔集合词〕步兵. ②步兵团. *~ tactics* 步兵战术. *light ~* 轻步兵. **-man** *n.* (*pl.* **-men**) 步兵.

in·farct [inˈfɑːkt] *n.*【医】(血管)梗塞.

in·farc·tion [inˈfɑːkʃən] *n.*【医】血块的构成 (= infarct).

in·fare [ˈinˌfɛə] *n.*〔方〕婚礼招待会,婚宴〔一般于婚礼次日举行〕.

in·fat·u·ate [inˈfætjueit] *vt.* ①使冲昏头脑,弄糊涂. ②使迷恋,使错爱. *be ~d with pride* 被骄傲冲昏头脑. *be ~ with sb.* 迷恋某人. — *a.* = infatuated. — *n.* 变得昏头昏脑的人;迷恋者.

in·fat·u·at·ed [inˈfætjueitid] *a.* 变得昏头昏脑的;迷恋着的,跟…打得火热的 (*with a woman*). **-ly** *ad.*

in·fa·tu·a·tion [inˌfætjuˈeiʃən] *n.* 昏头昏脑;迷惑,迷恋.

in·fea·si·ble [inˈfiːzəbl] *a.* 不能实行的,办不到的. **-bil·i·ty** [inˌfiːzəˈbiliti] *n.*

in·fect [inˈfekt] *vt.* ①传染;散布病毒;侵染. ②使受影响,感染. *the ~ed area* [*zone*] 传染病流行区〔地带〕. *His courage ~ed the followers.* 他的勇气激励了后来人. ***be ~ed with*** 感染,沾染上.

in·fec·tion [inˈfekʃən] *n.* ①传染,感染,侵染. ②传染病,染毒物. ③影响;感染.

in·fec·tious [inˈfekʃəs] *a.* ①传染的,传染性的. ②易传染的;易感染的. ③有坏影响的,有损害的. *an ~ laugh* 有感染力的一笑. *~ disease* 传染病. *an ~ hospital* 传染病院. *~ water* 带菌水. *~* **hepatitis**【医】传染性肝炎. *~* **mononucleosis**【医】传染性单核白血球增多. **-ly** *ad.* **-ness** *n.*

in·fec·tive [inˈfektiv] *a.* ①传染性的,易传染的. ②影响别人的,感染别人的. **-ness** *n.*

in·fec·tiv·i·ty [ˌinfekˈtiviti] *n.* 传染性;易传染.

in·fe·cund [inˈfekənd, -ˈfiːk-] *a.* 不结子的,不妊的;不毛的. **-di·ty** *n.*

in·fe·li·cif·ic [inˌfiːliˈsifik] *a.* 引起不幸的.

in·fe·lic·i·tous [ˌinfiˈlisitəs] *a.* ①不幸的,不吉的. ②不适当的,不贴切的. *an ~ marriage* 不幸的婚姻. **-ly** *ad.*

in·fe·lic·i·ty [ˌinfiˈlisiti] *n.* ①不幸,不吉. ②不适当的事物;不恰当的言行. *There is so much ~ in the world.* 人世间有很多不幸的事.

in·fer [inˈfəː] *vt.* (**in·ferred; infer·ring**) ①推理,推论,推断. ②猜想,臆测. ③表示,意味着,暗示,含有…的意思. *~ a motive from an effect* 从效果推知动机. *What am I to ~ from your remarks?* 你说的话究竟是什么意思呢? *Your silence ~s consent.* 你沉默就是表示同意. — *vi.* 作出推论.

in·fer·a·ble [inˈfəːrəbl] *a.* 可推断的,可推论的,可推想而知的.

in·fer·ence [ˈinfərəns] *n.* ①推理,推论;推断,结论,论断;含蓄,含意. ②推断的结果;(逻辑上的)结论. *speak from ~* 推测说. *draw* [*make*] *an ~ from ...* 根据…下结论. *the deductive* [*inductive*] *~* 演绎〔归纳〕推理.

in·fer·en·tial [ˌinfəˈrenʃəl] *a.* 推理的,推论的;推理上的,推论上的. *~ procedure* 推论上的程序. **-ly** *ad.*

in·fe·ri·or [inˈfiəriə] *a.* (*opp.* superior) ①(位置在)下部的,下面的. ②(身分)低下的,下级的. ③(质量等)低劣的,次的,普通的,差的,劣势的. ④【植】下位的,下生的. ⑤【解】在下的,在其他器官之下的. ⑥【军】阶级低的. ⑦【印】排〔抄〕在字母下的. ⑧【天】行星在地球轨道内侧的,在地球与太阳之间的. *~ limit*【机】下限,最小尺寸. *the ~ court* 下级法院. *Woman is ~ to man in running.* 妇女跑不过男子. *~ goods* 低档货. *an ~ enemy* 劣势敌人. *~ by comparison* 相形见绌. *be ~ to sb.* 不及某人. *~ wings* 后翅. *an ~ officer* 下级军官. *~ figures* 下附数字(如 H_2 中下附的 2). *~ conjunction*【天】下合. *~ planet* 内行星. — *n.* 晚辈,下级(的人);劣者;【印】下角码. ***be sb.'s ~ in*** 在…上不及某人. **-ly** *ad.*

in·fe·ri·or·i·ty [inˌfiəriˈɔriti] *n.* 下位,下部;下级;次级,低级,劣等 (*opp.* superiority). *have a sense of pride and not of ~* 有自豪感而不应当有自卑感. *~* **complex [feelings]**【心】自卑情结;自卑感〔指心理上的一种病态〕.

in·fer·nal [inˈfəːnl] *a.* ①阴间的,地狱的. ②地狱般的,恶魔似的,穷凶极恶的. ③〔口〕坏透的,可恨的,该死的. *~ regions* 地狱,阴间. *an ~ deed* 残暴行为. *~* **machine**【军】定时炸弹,饵雷,诡雷. **-i·ty** *n.*

in·fer·no [inˈfəːnəu] *n.* (*pl.* *~s*) ①地狱;阴森恐怖的地方,可怕的东西. ②〔the I-〕《地狱篇》〔但丁所作《神曲》的第一部〕.

in·fe·ro·an·te·ri·or [ˌinfiˌrəuænˈtiəriə] *a.* 下前方的.

in·fer·ra·ble, in·fer·ri·ble [inˈfəːrəbl, -ribl] *a.* = inferable.

in·fer·tile [inˈfəːtail] *a.* ①不毛的,瘠瘦的,不肥沃的. ②不结果实的;不生育的. **-til·ity** [ˌinfəˈtiliti] *n.*

in·fest [inˈfest] *vt.* ①(指老鼠、害虫、盗贼等)大批出没,成群出现. ②在…上寄生于. *be ~ed with pirates* 海盗横行. *warehouses ~ed with rats* 老鼠横行的仓库. *fleas ~ing cats* 寄生于猫身上的跳蚤.

in·fes·ta·tion [ˌinfesˈteiʃən] *n.* ①(老鼠、害虫、盗贼)大批出没,侵扰,蔓延. ②(昆虫)传染.

in·feu·da·tion [ˌinfjuˈdeiʃən] *n.* 赐与封地,采邑授与.

in·fi·del [ˈinfidəl] *a.* ①不信宗教的;异教徒的;不信仰的. — *n.* ①不信宗教的人. ②异教徒. **-ize** *vt., vi.* (使)不信宗教.

in·fi·del·i·ty [ˌinfiˈdeliti] *n.* ①不信神,无宗教信仰. ②不信基督教. ③背信,不忠诚. ④(夫妇间的)不忠实,不忠实行为. *conjugal ~* 私通,不守贞节.

in·field [ˈinfiːld] *n.* ①宅边田地;可耕地. ②(棒球或垒球球场的)内场;内野,全体内野手 (*opp.* outfield). ③

椭圆形跑道内的运动场地.

in·field·er [ˈinfiːldə] *n.* (棒球等的)内野手.

in·fight·ing [ˈinfaitiŋ] *n.* ①(拳击中的)接近战,贴近对打,近身殴斗. ②混战,乱打. ③暗斗. *deadly ~ among the politicians* 政客间的勾心斗角.

in·fil·trate [inˈfiltreit] *vt.* ①使渗入,透过 *(through, into)*; 使浸润. ②【军】渗透,通过;侵袭. *~ the tissue with a local anaesthetic* 用局部麻醉剂浸入组织. *an infiltrating column* 渗透纵队. — *vi.* 渗入,混进. — *n.* 渗入物.

in·fil·tra·tion [ˌinfilˈtreiʃən] *n.* ①渗入;【医】浸润. ②【军】渗透,通过;渗透活动. ③【化】渗滤. *advance by ~* 渗透前进. *an ~ force* 渗透部队.

in·fil·tra·tor [ˈinfiltreitə] *n.* 渗入者.

infin. = infinitive.

in·fi·nite [ˈinfinit] *a.* (*opp.* finite) ①无限的,无穷的,广大无边的. ②无数的,许许多多的. ③【语法】非限定的,不受人称、数、时态限制的〔如动词不定式、动名词〕. ④【数】无穷(大)的,无尽的. *~ space* 无限空间. *an ~ sums of money* 巨额款项. *an ~ decimal* 无尽小数. *an ~ series* 【数】无穷级数,无限级数. — *n.* ①无限物. ②【数】无穷(大);无尽. ③〔the ~〕无限,无穷. ④〔the I-〕【宗】造物主,神. ***an ~ of*** 〔古〕无限的,无限量的. **-ly** *ad.* **-ness** *n.*

in·fin·i·tes·i·mal [ˌinfiniˈtesiməl] *a.* ①无限小的,无穷小的,极小的,极微的. ②细微末节的. — *n.*【数】无限小,无穷小,微元. *~* ***calculus*** 微积分. *~* ***geometry*** 微分几何. **-ly** *ad.*

in·fin·i·ti·val [inˌfiniˈtaivəl] *a.*【语法】不定式的.

in·fin·i·tive [inˈfinitiv] *a.*【语法】(不受人称、数、时态限制的)动词不定式的. — *n.*【语法】动词不定式〔I can go, I want to go 等中的 go, to go 等〕. *~* ***nexus*** 【语】不定式二元语核〔特指 for ... to 这种结构形式〕.

in·fin·i·tude [inˈfinitjuːd] *n.* 无限,无穷;无限量,无穷数;无限的范围. *the ~ of outer space* 无限的外层空间.

in·fin·i·ty [inˈfiniti] *n.* ①= infinitude. ②【数】无穷大〔符号为 ∞〕. ③大量,大宗. *an ~ of things* 极多的东西. ***at ~*** 在无限远的距离上. ***to ~*** 直到无限.

in·firm [inˈfəːm] *a.* *(-er, -est)* ①虚弱的,带病的. ②优柔寡断的,懦弱的. ③不巩固的,不牢固的,薄弱的. *be ~ with age* 衰老的. *~ of purpose* 意志薄弱的. **-ly** *ad.* **-ness** *n.*

in·fir·ma·ry [inˈfəːməri] *n.* 医院;(学校、工厂等的)医务室;诊所.

in·fir·mi·ty [inˈfəːmiti] *n.* ①虚弱,衰弱. ②疾病,病症. ③优柔寡断,懦弱;弱点,缺点. *I- often comes with old age.* 虚弱常随年老而来. *infirmities of old age* 老年体弱,老年的病症.

in·fix [inˈfiks] *vt.* ①把…插入,把…嵌入. ②使深印入(脑海),渗入. ③【语法】插入中缀. *The idea was ~ed in students' minds.* 这种概念已经深深地印入学生们的脑海中. — [ˈinfiks] *n.*【语法】中缀,中加成分.

in·flame [inˈfleim] *vt.* ①使烧燃,使炽热. ②激怒;煽动,刺激. ③加剧,使火上加油. ④【医】使红肿,使发炎. *be ~d with rage* 激怒. *~d eyes* 红肿的眼睛. *The hills were ~d with autumnal tints.* 秋色染山一片红. — *vi.* ①着火,燃烧. ②激怒. ③发炎.

in·flam·ma·bil·i·ty [inˌflæməˈbiliti] *n.* 易燃性,可燃性;易激动.

in·flam·ma·ble [inˈflæməbl] *a.* ①易燃的. ②易激动的,易激怒的. — *n.* 可燃物. **-ness** *n.* **-bly** *ad.*

in·flam·ma·tion [ˌinfləˈmeiʃən] *n.* ①着火,发火,燃烧. ②激动. ③【医】红肿,炎症. *the ~ of the lungs* 肺炎.

in·flam·ma·to·ry [inˈflæmətəri] *a.* ①刺激性的,煽动性的. ②【医】炎性的,易红肿的. *~ speeches* 煽动性演说. *an ~ fever* 炎症热.

in·flat·a·ble [inˈfleitəbl] *a.* 可膨胀的. — *n.* 可充气物品.

in·flate [inˈfleit] *vt.* (*opp.* deflate) ①使膨胀;【机】给…打气. ②使(通货)膨胀,抬高(物价). ③使骄傲;使得意. *~ the paper currency* 滥发纸币. *be ~d with pride* 扬扬得意. — *vi.* 进行充气;膨胀.

in·flat·ed [inˈfleitid] *a.* ①充了气的. ②(语言等)夸张的,言过其实的. ③(通货)恶性膨胀的;(价格)飞涨的,暴涨. ④【植】肿胀的,扩大了的. *~ stem* 空心而张大的茎. *an ~ tyre* 充气轮. *an ~ style* 夸张的文体. *the ~ value of land* 土地价格.

in·flat·er [inˈfleitə] *n.* = inflator.

in·fla·tion [inˈfleiʃən] *n.* (*opp.* deflation) ①膨胀. ②【经】通货膨胀;信用膨胀;(物价)暴涨. ③自负;夸张. ④【工】(气体、空气的)补给,打气,充气,胀气. *runaway ~* 如脱缰之马的通货膨胀. *~* **inlet**【机】充气进口. *~* **pressure**【机】充气压力,气胀压力. **-ism** *n.* 通货膨胀政策〔现象〕. **-ist** ① *n.* 通货膨胀政策的支持者. ② *a.* 支持通货膨胀政策的.

in·fla·tion·ar·y [inˈfleiʃənəri] *a.* 膨胀的;通货膨胀的;由膨胀引起的;由通货膨胀引起的. *the ~ policies* 通货膨胀政策. *~* **spiral** (通货、物价、工资等的)螺旋形膨胀.

in·flat·or [inˈfleitə] *n.* ①充气者. ②充气机;打气筒;增压泵.

in·flect [inˈflekt] *vt.* ①使弯曲,使屈折. ②【语】使变音,使转调. ③【语法】使词发生屈折变化. — *vi.*【语法】发生屈折变化.

in·flec·tion [inˈflekʃən] *n.* = inflexion.

in·flec·tive [inˈflektiv] *a.* ①屈折的,弯曲的. ②【语】变音的,转调的;【语法】词有屈折变化的.

in·flex·i·ble [inˈfleksəbl] *a.* ①不可弯曲的. ②不屈服的,刚直的;坚强的,坚定的. ③不变的,固定的. *an ~ rule* 硬性的规定. *an ~ tactics* 呆板的战术. *an ~ will* 坚强的意志. **-bil·i·ty** [inˌfleksəˈbiliti] *n.* **-bly** *ad.*

in·flex·ion [inˈflekʃən] *n.* ①弯曲. ②变音,转调. ③【语法】屈折形式,屈折变化. ④【数】拐折,回折,拐点,回折点. **-less** *a.* 无屈折变化的.

in·flex·ion·al [inˈflekʃənəl] *a.* ①弯曲的. ②抑扬的. ③有屈折变化的. *an ~ language* 有屈折变化的语言. **-ly** *ad.*

in·flict [inˈflikt] *vt.* ①加以(打击等);使受(痛苦、损失等). ②处以刑罚,加刑. *~ a wound (up)on sb.* 使人受伤. *~ heavy casualties* 使蒙受重大伤亡. *~ harm on* 陷害. *~ oneself [one's company] (up)on sb.* 使某人受累,打搅某人. *~ the death penalty upon the murderer* 处杀人犯以死刑. **-a·ble** *a.* **-ion** *n.*

in·flict·er [inˈfliktə] *n.* 加害者,科罚者,处罚者(= inflictor).

in-flight [ˈinˈflait] *a.* 飞行中的. *~ movies* 飞机上放映的电影.

in·flo·res·cence [ˌinflɔ(ː)ˈresns] *n.* ①开花;开花期. ②【植】花序. ③花簇;花朵. ④带附属体的花轴. *the definite [indefinite] ~* 有限[无限]花序. **-cent** *a.*

in·flow [ˈinfləu] *n.* ①流入,流注. ②流入物. ③内流,吸入;吸风. *an ~ of bank deposit* 银行存款的增加.

in·flow·ing [ˈinfləuiŋ] *a.* 流入的,注入的. — *n.* = inflow.

in·flu·ence [ˈinfluəns] *n.* ①影响,感化 *(on; upon)*. ②势力,权势. ③有影响的人物[事物],有权势的人. ④感应. *exercise ~ on [upon] sb.* 影响某人,对某人施加影响. *have ~ on [upon] sb.* 对某人有影响. *a man of great ~* 很有权势的人. *backstair ~* 潜在势力,后台势力. *exercise one's ~ in sb.'s behalf* 为某人尽力. *have ~ over [with] sb.* 有左右某人的能力. *petticoat ~* 女性的作用[影响]. *through the ~ of* 靠…的力量. *use one's ~ for sb.* 为某人尽力[活动]. *within sb.'s sphere of ~* 在某

人势力范围内. *an ~ in the politics* 在政界有势力的人. ***under the ~ of*** ①受…的影响 (*He is under the ~ of drink.* 他醉了). ②受…的感化. — *vt.* ①影响. ②感化;左右,改变. ③〔婉〕贿赂, 运动, 收买. ④〔美口〕加(酒)于饮料中. *The weather ~s crops.* 天气影响收成. *~ sb. for good* 与人为善,使人受良好影响.

in·flu·ent [ˈinfluənt] *a.* 流入的; 能流动的. — *n.* ①流入. ②流入物; 流体, 液体. ③支流. ④【生态】一种生物对其他生物的影响.

in·flu·en·tial [ˌinfluˈenʃəl] *a.* ①有影响的. ②有势力的,有权力的. *~ action* 感应作用. *an ~ man* 有力人物. **-ly** *ad.*

in·flu·en·za [ˌinfluˈenzə] *n.* ①【医】流行性感冒〔略 flu.〕. ②(马、猪等的)流感.

in·flux [ˈinflʌks] *n.* ①流入,注入;汇集(指人或物) (*opp.* efflux), 到来, 充斥. ②注入口, 河口. *the ~ of foreign goods* 外货充斥.

in·fo. [ˈinfəu] 〔口〕 = information.

in·fold [inˈfəuld] *vt.* = enfold.

in·form[1] [inˈfɔːm] *vt.* ①告诉, 报告, 通知〔把某事告某人中,某人为直接宾语,某事为of的宾语〕. ②使活跃,使充满 (*with*), 赋予活力. ③〔罕〕教导. *~ sb. of sth.* 把某事告诉某人. *Please ~ us how to find his house.* 请告诉我们他的家在哪里. *be rightly [wrongly] ~ed* 得到正确[错误]的知识[情报]. *be ~ed of* 听得,知道. *I beg to ~ you that ...,* …特此奉告. *~ oneself of* (由调查中)知道. *Keep sb. ~ed of ...* 向人不断报告…. *be well ~ed about sth.* (对某事)了如指掌; (对某事)消息灵通. *Breath ~s the body.* 呼吸使身体有活力. — *vi.* 告发, 密告 (*against*). *~ against [on] an agent* 告发一名间谍.

in·form[2] [inˈfɔːm] *a.* 〔古〕不成形的,无形状的.

in·for·mal [inˈfɔːməl] *a.* ①非正式的,简略的. ②不拘礼节[形式]的; 口语的. *an ~ visit* 非正式访问. *~ proceedings* 简略手续. *an ~ style* (日常使用的)语体. **-ly** *ad.*

in·for·mal·i·ty [ˌinfɔːˈmæliti] *n.* ①非正式; 不拘礼节[形式]. ②变通的行动.

in·form·ant [inˈfɔːmənt] *n.* ①通知者, 通报者, 报告者; 密告者. ②(分析当地语音、国语等时的)标准发音者.

in·for·mat·ics [ˌinfəˈmætiks] *n. pl.* 〔用作单数〕信息学.

in·for·ma·tion [ˌinfəˈmeiʃən] *n.* ①通知, 通报, 报告. ②报导,消息,情报. ③资料,知识,学识. ④【自】信息,数据. ⑤【法】起诉, 告发. *acting on ~ received* 〔警察作证时用的话〕据报导. *ask for ~ about [concering, on] sth.* 打听关于某事的消息. *For fuller ~, please contact ....* 欲知详情, 请与…联系. *~ concering the enemy* 敌情. *a man of wide ~* 博学多闻的人. *a mine of ~* 知识宝库. *official ~* 官方消息. *pry for ~* 刺探情报. ***firsthand ~*** 第一手资料. ***For Your I- Only*** 仅供参考. ***get in [collect, gather] ~ (up) on*** 增加…的知识, 搜集…的情报. ***lay [lodge] ~ against sb.*** 告发某人. *~* **bureau** 情报局. *~* **desk** 问讯处. *~* **engineering** 信息工程学. *~* **officer** 情报员. *~* **science** ①资料学. ②【自】信息学. *~* **supermarket** 计算机服务中心;自动问讯处. *~* **theory** 信息论 (= theory of ~). **-al** *a.*

in·form·a·tive [inˈfɔːmətiv] *a.* 提供情报的,报告消息的;增进知识的; 有教益的. *an ~ book* 资料丰富的书. *an ~ talk* 有助益的谈话. **-ly** *ad.* **-ness** *n.*

in·form·a·to·ry [inˈfɔːmətəri] *a.* = informative.

in·formed [inˈfɔːmd] *a.* 有学识的,见闻广的,有情报根据的. *an ~ mind* 博学多闻的人. *a well-~ man* 消息灵通的人. *be well-~ [ill-~] as to ...* 深深[不怎么]知道…. *~ public opinion* 明达的舆论. *~ sources* 消息灵通人士.

in·form·er [inˈfɔːmə] *n.* ①通知者,通报者. ②告密的人,密探. *a common [professional] ~* 专业密探. ***turn ~ on sb.*** 告发某人.

in·fra [ˈinfrə] *ad.* (*opp.* supra) 〔L.〕 在下,在以下. *see ~ p. 40* 参看 40 页以下, *vide ~* 见下,参看下文. *~ dig* = *~* ***dignitatem*** 减低威严的,有失身分的.

in·fra- *pref.* 表示"在下","在下部": *infra*structure.

in·fract [inˈfrækt] *vt.* 〔罕〕破坏法律,违法;背信. **-or** *n.*

in·frac·tion [inˈfrækʃən] *n.* 破坏法律,违法,背信.

in·fra·dyne [ˈinfrədain] *n.* 【无】低外差法.

in·fra·hu·man [ˌinfrəˈhjuːmən] *a.* ①低于人类的〔尤指类人猿的〕. ②似人类的,类人猿的.

in·fra·lap·sar·i·an [ˌinfrəlæpˈsɛəriən, -ˈsær-] *n.* 堕落而后拯救论者〔加尔文教派的一个分支,说什么上帝等人类堕落之后再来拯救〕. — *a.* 堕落而后拯救论的; 堕落而后拯救论者的. **-sar·i·an·ism** *n.* 堕落而后拯救论.

in·fran·gi·ble [inˈfrændʒibl] *a.* 不可破的, 不能分离的; 不能违反的, 不可侵犯的. *an ~ promise* 不能违反的契约. **-bil·i·ty** [inˌfrændʒiˈbiliti], **-ness** *n.* **-bly** *ad.*

in·fra·nics [inˈfræniks] *n.* 红外线电子学.

in·fra·red [ˈinfrəˈred] *a.* 【物】红外线的; 红外区的; 产生红外辐射的; 对红外辐射敏感的. *an ~ detector* 【军】红外线探测器. *~ maser* 红外激射器. *~ photography* 红外照相术. *~ radiation* 红外辐射. *~ rays* 红外线. *an ~ seeker* 红外线寻的制导导弹(或其弹头). *~ vidicon* 红外摄象管. — *n.* 红外线; 红外区.

in·fra·son·ic [ˌinfrəˈsonik] *a.* 【物】亚声的,次声的〔声频低于人耳所能听到的〕.

in·fra·sound [ˌinfrəˈsaund] *n.* 亚声,次声,不可听音.

in·fra·spe·cif·ic [ˌinfrəspiˈsifik] *a.* 同物种的〔如亚种〕.

in·fra·struc·ture [ˈinfrəˈstrʌktʃə] *n.* ①下部基础〔尤指社会、国家赖以生存和发展的,如道路、学校、电厂、交通、通讯系统等基本设施〕. ②【军】永久性基地, 永久性防御设施. **-tur·al** *a.*

in·fre·quence, -cy [inˈfriːkwəns, -si] *n.* 很少发生, 稀罕.

in·fre·quent [inˈfriːkwənt] *a.* 稀罕的,少见的;偶然的. *not ~* 常常发生的. **-ly** *ad.*

in·fres·sion [inˈfreʃən] *n.* 【经】膨胀形衰退 (指物价上涨但收入不变甚至削减的状况).

in·fringe [inˈfrindʒ] *vt.* 破坏(法律等), 侵犯(权利等), 违反(协议等). *Be careful not to ~ the rights of other people.* 当心不要侵犯别人的权利. — *vi.* 侵犯 (*on; upon*). *Don't ~ on (upon) sb.'s privacy.* 不要侵犯某人. **-ment** *n.*

in·fruc·tu·ous [inˈfrʌktjuəs] *a.* ①不结果的, 不毛的. ②徒劳的,无效果的.

in·fun·dib·u·la [ˌinfʌnˈdibjulə] *n.* infundibulum 的复数.

in·fun·dib·u·lar [ˌinfʌnˈdibjulə], **-late** [-lit] *a.* 【植】①= infundibuliform. ②有漏斗状器官的.

in·fun·dib·u·li·form [ˌinfənˈdibjulifɔːm] *a.* 漏斗状的.

in·fun·dib·u·lum [ˌinfənˈdibjuləm] *n.* (*pl.* **-la** [-lə]) 【解】漏斗状器官.

in·fu·ri·ate [inˈfjuərieit] *vt.* 激怒, 使发怒. ***be ~d at*** 对…极为愤怒. — *a.* 狂怒的. **-a·tion** *n.* **-ly** *ad.*

in·fu·ri·at·ing [inˈfjuəriˌeitiŋ] *a.* 万分激怒的, 令人发怒的. **-ly** *ad.*

in·fus·cate [inˈfʌskit, -keit] *a.* 烟褐色的〔指昆虫翅〕(= infuscated).

in·fuse [inˈfjuːz] *vt.* ①注入; 灌注, 灌输. ②鼓舞, 激发; 使充满. ③泡(茶); 浸渍; 泡(药). *~ the mind [sb.] with new hope* 用新的希望激励某人. *~ new blood* 注入新鲜血液. *~ tea* 沏茶.

in·fus·er [inˈfjuːzə] *n.* ①鼓吹者. ②注入器;浸渍器;茶壶.
in·fu·si·ble[1] [inˈfjuːzəbl] *a.* 能注入的,能灌输的.
in·fu·si·ble[2] [inˈfjuːzəbl] *a.* 不溶性的,难溶化的. **-bil·i·ty** [inˌfjuːzəˈbiliti] *n.*
in·fu·sion [inˈfjuːʒən] *n.* ①注入; 灌输. ②注入物. ③泡制;浸渍. ④浸液;【医】输注. *saline* ～ 盐水输注. ～ *of tea* 泡茶,沏茶. *fresh* ～*s*【医】新鲜浸剂.
in·fu·sion·ism [inˈfjuːʒənizəm] *n.*【神】灵魂投胎论. **-ist** *n.*
in·fu·sive [inˈfjuːsiv] *a.* 趋于灌输的,可灌输的.
In·fu·so·ri·a [ˌinfjuːˈzɔːriə] *n.* 〔*pl.*〕【动】纤毛虫纲.
in·fu·so·ri·al [ˌinfjuˈsɔːriəl, -ˈzɔː-] *a.* 滴虫的,含滴虫的,有滴虫特性的.
in·fu·so·ri·an [ˌinfjuːˈzɔːriən] *n.* 纤毛虫. — *a.* = infusorial.
-ing[1] *suf.* 构成动名词或名词. ①表示"动作": danc*ing*, hunt*ing*. ②表示"职业": bank*ing*, garden*ing*. ③表示"材料": rail*ing*, cloth*ing*. ④表示"动作的结果"、"产物": paint*ing*, build*ing*. ⑤表示"动作的对象": sew*ing*, wash*ing*. ⑥表示"配合": colour*ing*, feather*ing*.
-ing[2] *suf.* 构成现在分词. ①〔用作形容词〕: charm*ing*. ②〔用作介词、副词〕: dur*ing*, notwithstand*ing*. ③〔用作半被动性分词〕: cook*ing* apples.
-ing[3] *suf.* 构成名词. ①加于父名后作子名: Bill*ing* (= son of Bill). ②表示"…类物", "…状物", "作成物": farth*ing*, geld*ing*.
in·gath·er [inˈgæðə] *vt., vi.* 〔古〕①聚集, 收集. ②收获,收割. **-ing** [ˈinˌgæðəriŋ] *n.*
in·gem·i·nate [inˈdʒemineit] *vt.* 重申;反复讲.
in·gen·er·ate [inˈdʒenərit] *a.* 〔古〕天生的, 固有的. — [inˈdʒenəreit] *vt.* 〔古〕产生于内,产生,生出.
in·gen·ious [inˈdʒiːnjəs] *a.* ①机灵的, 足智多谋的, 有独创性的. ②精巧制成的, 巧妙的. *an* ～ *mind* 机灵的头脑. *an* ～ *machine* 精巧的机器. **-ly** *ad.* **-ness** *n.*
in·gé·nue [ænʒeiˈnjuː, F. ɛ̃ʒeiˈnjuː] *n.* (*pl.* ～*s* [-ˈnjuːz]) 〔F.〕天真的姑娘;扮演天真姑娘的女演员.
in·ge·nu·i·ty [ˌindʒiˈnjuːiti] *n.* ①机灵,机智,独创性. ②独出心裁,设计新颖; 巧妙, 精巧. *I- in varying tactics depends on mother wit.* 运用之妙,存乎一心.
in·gen·u·ous [inˈdʒenjuəs] *a.* 直率的,坦白的,老实的; 天真的. **-ly** *ad.* **-ness** *n.*
In·ger·soll [ˈiŋgəsɔl] *n.* ①英格索尔〔姓氏〕. ②**Robert Green** ～ 罗伯特·格林·英格索尔〔1833—1899,美国法学家,律师,不可知论的倡导者〕.
in·gest [inˈdʒest] *vt.* 咽下,摄取,吸收. **-i·ble** *a.* 可摄取的. **-ive** *a.* 有关(食物等的)摄取的,供吸收的. **-ion** *n.* ①咽下,吸收. ②【机】空气〔气体,液体〕的吸入.
in·ges·ta [inˈdʒestə] *n.* 〔*pl.*〕营养物,食物.
in·gle [ˈiŋgl] *n.* 〔Scot.〕①炉火;火焰. ②壁炉,火炉. ～**-nook** *n.* 〔英〕炉边,壁炉旁的角落. ～**side** 炉边,炉旁.
in·glo·ri·ous [inˈglɔːriəs] *a.* ①不光彩的,不体面的,可耻的. ②〔古〕无名的,湮没无闻的. **-ly** *ad.*
in·go·ing [ˈinˌgəuiŋ] *a.* ①进来的, 进入的 (*opp.* outgoing). ②洞察的, 深入的. *the* ～ *administration* 上台的政府. *an* ～ *particle* 入射粒子. *an* ～ *tenant* 新的租户. *an* ～ *tide* 涨潮. *an* ～ *writer* 洞察入微的作家. — *n.* ①进入. ②〔英〕新租户付给房东的装修费; 商号受盘人付出的款子.
in·got [ˈiŋgət] *n.*【冶】铸模;铸块,锭. ～ *bar* 铸块. ～ *dogs* [*tongs*] 锭钳. ～ *iron* 锭铁, 低碳钢. ～ *metal* 金属锭,铸金属. ～ *pit* 均热炉. ～ *slab* 扁钢锭.
in·graft [inˈgrɑːft] *vt.* = engraft.
in·grain [inˈgrein] *vt.* ①【纺】使原纱(或原料)染色. ②使全部渗透,使根深蒂固(= engrain). *be deeply* ～*ed in the mind* 在头脑中根深蒂固. — *a.* ①由染色原纱〔原料〕制成的. *an* ～ *towel* 提花毛巾. ②遍体渗透的; 根深蒂固的. *an* ～ *criminal* 惯犯. — *n.* ①原纱〔原料〕染色;染色原纱织物. ②固有的品质,本质.
in·grained [inˈgreind, ˈingreind] *a.* 根深蒂固的. ～ *habits* 积习,根深蒂固的偏见.
In·gram(s) [ˈiŋgrəm(z)] *n.* 英格拉姆(斯)〔姓氏〕.
in·grate [inˈgreit] *n.* 忘恩负义的人. — *a.* 〔古〕忘恩的.
in·gra·ti·ate [inˈgreiʃieit] *vt.* 使迎合,使讨好,使巴结. ～ *oneself with sb.*, ～ *oneself into sb.'s favour* 讨好某人. **-a·tion** *n.*
in·gra·ti·at·ing [inˈgreiʃieitiŋ] *a.* ①讨好的, 迎合的. ②吸引人的, 迷人的. *an* ～ *smile* 迷人的微笑. **-ly** *ad.*
in·grat·i·tude [inˈgrætitjuːd] *n.* 忘恩负义. ～ *to one's parents* 对父母不孝.
in·gra·ves·cence [ˌingrəˈvesns] *n.* (病势)加重,恶化.
in·gra·ves·cent [ˌingrəˈvesnt] *a.* (病势)日愈恶化〔加重〕的.
in·gre·di·ent [inˈgriːdiənt] *n.* ①(混合物的)组成部分,成分,要素. ②【化】拼份,拼料.
in·gress [ˈingres] *n.* (*opp.* egress) ①进入; 入口, 进路; 进入权; 内移. ②【天】初切. *a means of* ～ 入口. ～ *of groundwater*【建】地下水侵入. **-ion** *n.* 进入.
in·gres·sive [inˈgresiv] *a.* ①与进入有关的. ②【语法】动作〔情况〕的开始的 (= inceptive).
Ing·rid [ˈiŋgrid] *n.* 英格丽德〔女子名〕.
in-group [ˈingruːp] *n.* 内部集团,自己人集团.
in·grow·ing [ˈinˌgrəuiŋ] *a.* 向内生长的;(指甲)生进肌肉内的.
in·grown [ˈingrəun] *a.* ①向内生长的. ②天生的, 生来的. *an* ～ *toenail* 长入肉内的足趾甲(尤指向肉内).
in·growth [ˈinˌgrəuθ] *n.* ①向内生长. ②长进肌肉内的东西.
in·gui·nal [ˈiŋgwinl] *a.* 【解】腹股沟的. *the* ～ *canal*【解】腹股沟管. *the* ～ *glands*【解】腹股沟淋巴结.
in·gulf [inˈgʌlf] *vt.* 吞没, 席卷 (= engulf). *battlefields* ～*ed in smoke and strewn with debris* 浓烟滚滚,瓦砾遍地的战场. **-ment** *n.*
in·gur·gi·tate [inˈgəːdʒiteit] *vt., vi.* 狼吞虎咽,大吃大嚼. **-ta·tion** [inˌgəːdʒiˈteiʃən] *n.*
in·hab·it [inˈhæbit] *vt.* 居住; 栖息. ～ *a city* 住在城市. **-a·ble** *a.* 适于居住〔栖息〕的. **-er** *n.* 居住〔栖息〕者.
in·hab·it·an·cy [inˈhæbitənsi] *n.* (暂时性的)居住; 住处.
in·hab·it·ant [inˈhæbitənt] *n.* ①居民,住户,常住居民. ②栖息的动物.
in·hab·i·ta·tion [inˌhæbiˈteiʃən] *n.* 居住; 栖息; 住宅,住处.
in·hab·it·ed [inˈhæbitid] *a.* 有人居住的,有人烟的; 住着的;(屋子)在使用(或租用)的. *an* ～ *island* 有人居住的岛. *be thickly* [*thinly*] ～ 人烟稠密〔稀少〕的. ～ *satellite* 载人卫星.
in·hal·ant [inˈheilənt] *a.* 吸入的. — *n.* 被吸入的药物或其它东西.
in·ha·la·tion [ˌinhəˈleiʃən] *n.* 吸入;吸入物,吸入剂;吸入法.
in·ha·la·tor [ˈinhəleitə] *n.* ①【医】吸入器. ②口罩呼吸器,防毒面具 (= respirator).
in·hale [inˈheil] *vt.* ①吸入. ②〔美俚〕吃(小餐),喝(咖啡、汤等). ～ *fresh air* 吸入新鲜空气. — *vi.* 吸气. *Inhale! Exhale!* 吸气! 呼气! *Do you* ～ *when you smoke?* 你抽烟时是否把烟深深吸入肺部?
in·hal·er [inˈheilə] *n.* ①吸入者; 吸入器. ②【化】吸气器,滤气器. *ether* ～【医】醚吸入器.
in·har·mon·ic [ˌinhɑːˈmɔnik] *a.* 不和谐的,不协调的,冲突的.
in·har·mo·ni·ous [ˌinhɑːˈməunjəs, -niəs] *a.* ①不和谐的,不协调的,嘈杂的. ②不和睦的, 冲突的. **-ly** *ad.*

-ness *n.*

in·har·mo·ny [inˈhɑːməni] *n.* 不和谐,不协调,冲突.

in·haul [ˈinˌhɔːl] *n.*【海】①引索. ②卷帆索(= inhauler).

in·here [inˈhiə] *vi.* 固有,具有(性质等) *(in)*; (权利)属于(人),原有 *(in)*; 含有(意义).

in·her·ence, -en·cy [inˈhiərəns, -si] *n.* 内在(性), 固有(性),基本属性.

in·her·ent [inˈhiərənt] *a.* 内在的,固有的, 生来的 *(in)*. *~ stability*【空】固有稳定性. *the power ~ in the office of President* 总统一职所具有的权力. *Weight is an ~ quality of matter.* 重量是物质固有的特性. *He has an ~ love of beauty.* 他天生爱美. **-ly** *ad.*

in·her·it [inˈherit] *vt.* ①继承(传统、遗产、权利等). ②经遗传而得(性格、体质等). *She ~s her mother's looks and her father's temper.* 她承受了母亲的相貌和父亲的脾气. *~ a fortune* 继承财产. — *vi.* 接受遗产;成为继承人. *Astronomy ~s from astrology.* 天文学的前身是占星术.

in·her·it·a·ble [inˈheritəbl] *a.* ①可继承的; 有继承权的. ②可遗传的. **-bili·ty** [inˌheritəˈbiliti] *n.*

in·her·it·ance [inˈheritəns] *n.* ①继承,承受. ②遗传;遗传性,遗传质. ③遗产;继承物,遗赠. ④天赋. ⑤继承权,世袭权. *criss-cross ~*【生】交叉遗传. *receive sth. by ~* 由继承而获得某物. *~ tax* 〔美〕遗产税,继承税〔英国称 death-duty 或 estate tax〕.

in·her·i·tor [inˈheritə] *n.* 继承人;嗣子,后继者.

in·her·i·tress, in·her·i·trix [inˈheritris, -triks] *n.* (*pl.* **-tri·ces** [-traisiːz]) 女继承人.

in·he·sion [inˈhiːʒən] *n.* = inherence.

in·hib·it [inˈhibit] *vt.* ①抑制; 约束. ②禁止, 阻止. ③【宗】使停止教权. *~ wrong desires* 抑制邪念. *~ sb. from doing sth.* 禁止某人做某事.

in·hib·it·er, in·hib·i·tor [inˈhibitə] *n.* 禁止者, 抑制者;抑制因素〔尤指【化】抑制剂;阻化剂〕.

in·hi·bi·tion [ˌinhiˈbiʃən] *n.* ①禁止, 阻止. ②【心】压制,抑制(作用). ③【英法】诉讼停止命令. ④【宗】教权停止命令. ⑤【化】阻化. *central ~*【医】中枢抑制.

in·hib·i·to·ry [inˈhibitəri] *a.* 禁止的; 抑制的, 阻止的. *~ nerve*【生理】抑制神经.

in·ho·mo·ge·ne·i·ty [ˈinˌhɔməudʒeˈniːiti] *n.*【生】不同质,非纯系,不同源.

in·ho·mo·ge·ne·ous [ˌinhəuməˈdʒiːniəs, -hɔmə-] *a.* ①【生】不同质的;非纯系的,不同源的. ②不均匀的,不纯一的. ③【数】非齐次的. *~ coordinates* 非齐次坐标.

in·hos·pi·ta·ble [inˈhɔspitəbl] *a.* ①不好客的,冷淡的,不亲切的. ②不适于居住的,荒凉的. **-ness** *n.* **-bly** *ad.*

in·hos·pi·tal·i·ty [ˈinˌhɔspiˈtæliti] *n.* 冷淡,不亲切.

in-house [ˈinhaus] *a.* 由本机构内部产生的, 机构内部的.

in·hu·man [inˈhjuːmən] *a.* ①非人的, 不近人情的. ②残忍的,野蛮的,无人性的. **-ly** *ad.*

in·hu·mane [ˌinhju(ː)ˈmein] *a.* 不近人情的, 薄情的; 残忍的,无人道的. **-ly** *ad.*

in·hu·man·i·ty [ˌinhju(ː)ˈmæniti] *n.* ①无情,残忍,野蛮. ②残忍行为.

in·hu·ma·tion [ˌinhju(ː)ˈmeiʃən] *n.* 埋葬,土葬.

in·hume [inˈhjuːm] *vt.* 埋葬,土葬.

in·im·i·cal [iˈnimikəl] *a.* ①有敌意的,敌视的 *(to)*. ②不利的, 有害的. *nations ~ to one another* 互相敌视的国家. *circumstance ~ to success* 不利于成功的情况. **-ly** *ad.*

in·im·i·ta·ble [iˈnimitəbl] *a.* 不可仿效的, 不可比拟的;无比的,无双的. **-bil·i·ty** [iˌnimitəˈbiliti] *n.* **-bly** *ad.*

in·im·i·ta·ble·ness [iˈnimitəblnis] *n.* 不可仿效,不可比拟,无比,无双.

in·i·on [ˈiniən] *n.*【解】枕骨隆突.

in·iq·ui·tous [iˈnikwitəs] *a.* 不公正的; 不法的, 不义的,不公平的,邪恶的. **-ly** *ad.*

in·iq·ui·tous·ness [iˈnikwətəsnis] *n.* 不公正; 不法; 不义;不公平;邪恶.

in·iq·ui·ty [iˈnikwiti] *n.* ①不公正,不法,不义. ②不义行为,罪恶,罪过.

init. = initial.

in·i·tial [iˈniʃəl] *a.* 最初的,开始的;原始的;初期的,初发的. *the ~ boiling point*【化】初馏点〔第一滴馏物滴下时的温度〕. *the ~ cost [expenditure]* 开办费. *the ~ difficulties* 开始的困难. *the ~ issue of a magazine* 杂志的创刊号. *~ line*【数】极轴. *~ prosperty* 初步繁荣. *the ~ stage* 初期, 开始阶段. *~ vacuum* 预真空. *~ velocity*【物】初速, 初速度. *an ~ letter* 词首字母. *an ~ signature* 仅用姓名词首字母的签名. *an ~ word* 词首字母缩略词(如 NATO). — *n.* 词首字母,词首大写字母;〔*pl.*〕姓名中的大写字母〔如 John Smith 中的 J. S.〕. — *vt.* ***(-l(l)ed, -l(l)ing)*** 在…上记上姓名的词首字母,用词首字母在…上署名;【政】草签,临时签署(条约等). *an initialled handkerchief* 记有姓名第一字母的手帕. **I- Teaching Alphabet** 初学英语拼音字母〔英国詹姆斯、皮特曼创造的一套拼音字母,计 44 个字,和读音一致, 用以教初学者〕. **-ism** 词首字母缩略词. **-ly** *ad.* 起初,开始.

in·i·ti·ate [iˈniʃieit] *vt.* ①开始;着手;创始,发动;【物】起爆. ②启发,启蒙,使入门. ③引进, 正式介绍. ④提议, 倡议. *~ a reform* 着手改革. *~ the attack* 开始攻击. *~ pupils into the elements of grammar* 把基本语法教给学生. *~ sb. into a secret* 把秘密传授给某人. *~ sb. into a club* 正式介绍某人加入俱乐部. *the ~d* (集体的)入会者. *~ a constitutional amendment* 提出宪法修正案. — [iˈniʃiit] *a., n.* 被传授初步知识的(人); 新入会的(人).

in·i·ti·a·tion [iˌniʃiˈeiʃən] *n.* ①开始, 创始; 起爆. ②教导, 指点, 启发. ③正式加入; 入会仪式, 入党仪式. *vorticity ~* 涡流的产生. *~* **fee** 〔美〕入会费.

in·i·ti·a·tive [iˈniʃiətiv] *a.* 起始的, 初步的, 创始的. *~ spirit* 主动精神. — *n.* ①第一步,发端;着手,创始,倡议;主动精神,创始力. ②〔the ~〕(立法机关对新法案的)动议权;(公民的)创制权. ③【军】(先发制人的)主动性. *subjective ~* 主观能动性. ***have the ~*** 掌握主动权. ***on one's own ~*** 主动地. ***take the ~*** 带头,采取主动.

in·i·ti·a·tor [iˈniʃieitə] *n.* ①开始者;创始者,倡议者. ②教导者,传授者. ③引药,引发剂,起爆药. ④激磁机. *play the role of an ~* 起带头作用.

in·i·ti·a·to·ry [iˈniʃiətəri] *a.* ①起始的, 发端的, 初步的;启蒙的. ②入会的,入社的,入党的.

in·ject [inˈdʒekt] *vt.* ①注入,注射. ②注满. ③插入(意见等). ④把…射入(轨道). ⑤【机】喷射,引射 *(into)*. *~ penicillin into the blood-stream* 把青霉素注入血液. *~ hypodermically* 皮下注射. *~ a remark into the conversation* 插嘴.

in·jec·tion [inˈdʒekʃən] *n.* ①注射. ②注射剂,注射液,针药,灌肠(药). ③充满, 注满. ④【医】充血. ⑤【机】喷射. ⑥【宇】(卫星等的)入轨,射入轨道,射入轨道的时间[地点]. *hyperdermic [subculaneous] ~* 皮下注射. *an ~ in the buttock* 注射臀部的一针. *fuel ~* 燃料喷射,注油. *~ pump* 喷射泵,喷油泵. *an ~ cylinder* 压射缸. *an ~ grid*【电】注频栅极. *~* **molding** 喷射造型法, 喷射模塑法. *~***molded** *a.* 喷射造型法的,喷射模塑法的.

in·jec·tor [inˈdʒektə] *n.* ①注射者; 注射器, 针管. ②【机】喷射器,喷注器,喷雾器,喷头. *an exhaust steam ~* 排气喷射器. *a spray ~* 射流式喷嘴. *~* **razor** 弹射式剃须刀.

in·ju·di·cial [ˌindʒu(ː)ˈdiʃəl] *a.* ①不依照法律形式的,不符合法官身分的. ②= injudicious.

in·ju·di·cious [ˌindʒu(ː)ˈdiʃəs] *a.* 判断欠妥的,不明智的,不慎重的. ~ *remarks* 欠考虑的言语. **-ly** *ad.* **-ness** *n.*

In·jun, in·jun [ˈindʒən] *n.* 〔美俚〕印第安人. ***get up one's*** ~ 〔美俚〕发怒. ***play one's*** ~ 逃匿.

in·junct [inˈdʒʌŋkt] *vt.* 〔口〕禁止.

in·junc·tion [inˈdʒʌŋkʃən] *n.* 命令,责戒;【法】指令,禁令. *lay ~s upon [on] sb. to do sth.* 命令某人做某事.

in·junc·tive [inˈdʒʌŋktiv] *a.* ①命令的, 训诫的, 教训的,指令的. ②【法】禁令的.

in·jur·ant [ˈindʒurənt] *n.* 有害的东西.

in·jure [ˈindʒə] *vt.* ①损害,毁坏. ②伤害(感情,自尊心等). *He ~d his left hand in a fire.* 他在火灾中伤了左手. *be badly ~d on both legs in a traffic accident* 在车祸中两腿受了重伤. ~ *sb.'s pride [feelings]* 伤害别人的自尊心[感情].

in·jured [ˈindʒəd] *a.* 受伤的; 受损害的; 损伤感情的. *the* ~ 受伤者. ~ *looks* 受冤屈的样子. *the ~ party* 被害者. *in an ~ voice* 用愤怒的声音. *with an ~ air* 带着生气的样子.

in·jur·er [ˈindʒərə] *n.* 毁坏者,加害者,伤害者.

in·ju·ri·ous [inˈdʒuəriəs] *a.* ①有害的. ②侮辱的, 诽谤的. *a climate ~ to health* 有害健康的气候. ~ *words* 中伤的言论.

in·ju·ry [ˈindʒəri] *n.* ①损害,毁坏,伤害. ②伤害的行为. ③受伤处. *suffer severe injuries* 受重伤. ***add insult to*** ~ 伤害之外又加侮辱. ***be an ~ to*** 伤害…, 危害…,对…有害. ***do sb. an ~ = do an ~ to sb.*** 伤害某人.

in·jus·tice [inˈdʒʌstis] *n.* ①不公正,非正义,不公平,权利侵害. ②不公正的行为. *do sb. an* ~ 使某人受屈,冤枉某人.

ink [iŋk] *n.* ①墨水;(印刷用的)油墨. ②(乌贼分泌的)墨液. ③〔俚〕咖啡;廉价酒. *China [Chinese, India, Indian]* ~ 墨,墨汁. *indelible [marking, permanent]* ~ 不变墨水. *invisible [secret, sympathetic]* ~ 密写墨水. *printing* ~ 油墨. *writing* ~ 墨水. *as black as* ~ 漆黑的. *sling* ~ 〔俚〕做职员;当作家,卖文为生. ***before the ~ is dry*** 墨迹未干;立即. ***spill printer's*** ~ 付印. — *vt.* ①用墨水写;涂油墨; 用墨水弄墨,用墨水沾污. ②〔美〕签名(在…上). ~ *one's fingers* 墨水弄脏手指. ***~ in [over]*** 用墨水描 (~ *in a drawing* 在铅笔底线上用墨水加描). ~ ***out*** 用墨水涂去. ~**bag** (乌贼的)墨囊. ~**-berry** *n.* 【植】①光滑冬青 (*Ilex glabra*) 〔产于北美东部〕. ②光滑冬青果. ③= pokeweed. ~**-blot test**【心】墨迹测验. ~ **bottle** 墨水瓶. ~**fish** *n.* 墨鱼, 乌贼. ~ **holder** 墨水瓶; (自来水笔的)贮墨管. ~**horn** (旧时的)角制墨水瓶 (*smell of ~horn* 有学者派头的,学究气的;卖弄学问的). ~**pad** 印台. ~ **pencil** 复写用颜色铅笔. ~**pot** 墨水瓶. ~ **recorder** 笔写记录器. ~ **sac** = ~ bag. ~**slinger**〔美〕作家,办事员,记录员. ~**-stand** ①= ~ well. ②墨水台. ~**stone** ①【矿】水绿矾. ②砚. ~**well** (桌上)墨水池. ~**writer** (电报)印字机. **-less** *a.* 没有墨水的,没有墨汁的.

ink·er [ˈiŋkə] *n.* 【印】印版上的油墨辊;(电报)印字机.

ink·i·ness [ˈiŋkinis] *n.* 墨黑,漆黑.

in·kle [ˈiŋkl] *n.* 〔罕〕①亚麻带子. ②编亚麻带子用的线或纱.

ink·ling [ˈiŋkliŋ] *n.* ①暗示细微的迹象. ②微微觉得,模糊的想法. *get an ~ of* 微微明白. *give an ~ of* 给人一些暗示. *have an ~ of* 略有所知.

ink·y [ˈiŋki] *a.* ***(ink·i·er; -i·est)*** 涂有墨水的; 给墨水弄污的; 漆黑的. *an ~ handkerchief* 沾了墨水的手帕. ~ *darkness* 一片漆黑. ~ **cap** 【植】墨水盖鬼伞〔鬼伞类 (*Coprinus*) 蘑菇,其顶盖液化成墨汁〕.

in·lace [inˈleis] *vt.* ***(-laced; -lac·ing)*** = enlace.

in·laid [ˈinˈleid] inlay 的过去式和过去分词. — *a.* 镶嵌的,嵌有花样的. *an ~ table* 镶嵌花的桌子. ~ *work* 镶嵌工艺.

in·land [ˈinlənd] *a.* ①内地的, 内陆的. ②国内的. *an ~ duty* 内地税. ~ *navigation* 内河航行. *the ~ sea* 内海. *an ~ town* 内地城市. ~ *commerce [trade]* 国内贸易. ~ *exchange* 国内汇兑. ~ *mails* 〔英〕国内邮件 (=〔美〕domestic mails). ~ *revenue* 〔英〕国内税收 (=〔美〕internal revenue). ~ *telegraph* 国内电报. — [inˈlænd] *ad.* 在内地,向内地. *go ~* 到内地去. — [ˈinlənd] *n.* 内地,国内.

in·land·er [ˈinləndə] *n.* (生长在)内地的人.

in·land·ish [ˈinləndiʃ] *a.* 本地的;内地的.

in-law [ˈinlɔː] *n.* 〔口,常用 *pl.*〕姻亲.

in·lay [ˈinˌlei, inˈl-] *vt.* ***(-laid*** [ˈinˈleid]***; -lay·ing)*** ①镶嵌,镶入;镶(以) (*with*). ②用镶嵌物装饰,插入(页、卡片等). *ivory inlaid with gold* 镶金象牙. — [ˈinlei] *n.* ①镶嵌物;镶嵌工艺;镶嵌所用材料. ②(作接穗用的)接芽(= ~ graft). ③【医】嵌体;内置法,嵌入法. **-er** *n.* 镶嵌者.

in·let [ˈinlet] *n.* ①进口,入口. ②【电】引入,输入,输入线. ③水湾, 小港. ④插入物, 镶嵌物. *an ~ chamber* 【机】进气室. ~ *and outlet channels* (水库的)进出渠道. ~ *eye* 进气孔. *an ~ passage* 【军】进路. — *vt.* ***(inlet, inletting)*** ①引进. ②嵌入,插入.

in·li·er [ˈinlaiə] *n.* 【地】内窗层,内围层,内露层.

in·ly [ˈinli] *ad.* 〔诗〕在内;在心中,暗中;从心里.

in·ly·ing [ˈinlaiiŋ] *a.* 在内的,内部的.

in·mate [ˈinmeit] *n.* ①同居人〔尤指同院病人、同狱犯人、或住在同一收容所的人〕. ②居民. *be the ~ of* 同住在. *be the ~ of sb.'s heart* 留在某人心中.

in·mesh [inˈmeʃ] *vt.* = enmesh.

in-mi·grant [ˈinˈmaigrənt] *a.* 外地迁来的.— *n.* 外地迁入者;(动物的)引进品种.

in-mi·grate [ˈinˈmaigreit] *vi.* (由外地)移来, 迁入. **-tion** *n.*

in·most [ˈinməust] *a.* 最内部的;最深入的;秘藏心中的. *one's ~ feelings [thoughts]* 内心深处的感情[思想].

inn [in] *n.* ①小旅馆,客栈,小饭店, 小酒馆. ②〔古、诗〕住宅,住处. *keep an ~* 开旅馆. *put up at an ~* 住客栈. *the Inns of Chancery* 法学院〔原为英国伦敦法学协会管理下的法科学生宿舍〕. *the Inns of Court* 法律协会〔英国伦敦具有授予律师资格权的四个法学团体: *Inner Temple, Middle Temple, Lincoln's Inn* 及 *Gray's Inn*〕.— *vi.*住旅馆. ~**holder,** ~**keeper** *n.* 客栈老板,小旅馆老板.

in·nards [ˈinədz] *n.* 〔口〕①内脏. ②内部结构, 内部机构.

in·nate [ˈineit] *a.* 生来的,天生的,先天的,遗传的,固有的. *sb.'s ~ courtesy* 某人天生的温文有礼. *an ~ defect* 固有的缺点. *an ~ gift* 天赋,资质. **-ly** *ad.* **-ness** *n.*

in·ner [ˈinə] *a.* ***(superl. ~most, inmost)*** ①内部的 (*opp.* outer). ②思想的, 精神的; 内心的, 秘密的. *the ~ circle* 核心集团. *an ~ room* 内室. *I- Temple* (见 inn 条). *the ~ life of man* 人的内心活动,人的精神生活. *an ~ meaning* 深意. *one's ~ thoughts* 内心深处的思想. ~ *world* 内心世界. — *n.* ①内部, 里面. ②接近靶心部分,射中接近靶心部分的一发. ~ **cabinet** 核心内阁. ~ **circle** 核心集团. ~ **city** 内城区〔多为穷人居住,相对于中产阶级居住区与郊区而言〕. ~**-city** *a.* 内城的;贫民区的. ~**-directed** *a.* 有主见的; 有自己理想与目标的,不随俗的. ~ **flux** 【机】内烟道. ~ **grid** ①控制栅极,控制电极. ②调制电极. **I- Light**【宗】灵光〔教友派认为是上帝在一个人的灵魂中产生的指引力量〕. ~ **man** ①灵魂,精神 (*opp.* outer man). ②〔谑〕肚子,胃口 (*refresh [satisfy] one's ~ man* 吃饱肚子). ~ **part [voice]**【乐】中声部. ~**sole** = insole. ~ **space** ①思想中的潜意识部分. ②水下空间, 海洋深处. ③抽象画的质量[深度]. ~**spring mattress** 弹簧垫子. ~

tube 内胎. **-most** *a.* = inmost.

in·ner·vate [ˈinəːveit, iˈnəː-] *vt.* ①使受神经支配. ②刺激.

in·ner·va·tion [ˌinəːˈveiʃən] *n.*【解】支配; 神经分布; 神经兴奋作用[过程].

in·nerve [iˈnəːv] *vt.* ①鼓舞. ②= innervate.

In·ness [ˈinis] *n.* ①英尼斯〔姓氏〕. ②**George** ~ 乔治·英尼斯〔1825—1894, 美国画家〕.

in·ning [ˈiniŋ] *n.* ①〔单复数相同〕(棒球,板球的)一局,盘, 回合. ②海滩荒地的围垦,〔*pl.*〕围垦的土地. ③〔*pl.*〕轮到显身手的机会; 任职期间; 当权时期. *Our team made 307 runs in its first ~.* 我们队在第一局获 307 分. ***get one's ~s*** 碰到好机会,走运. ***have a good long ~s*** 一直走运;长寿. ***have an ~s*** 轮到击球; 参加某项活动. ***have the ~(s)*** 当权,执政.

in·no·cence [ˈinəsns],〔古〕**in·no·cen·cy** [-si] *n.* ①无罪;清白. ②单纯,天真无邪. ③无知, 头脑简单. ④无罪的人,清白无辜的人. ⑤【医】良性. ***assume [put on] an air of injured ~*** 装出无辜受累的样子.

in·no·cent [ˈinəsnt] *a.* ①清白的; 无罪的, 无辜的. ②〔口〕缺…的,无…的 *(of)*. ③天真无邪的;单纯的. ④头脑简单的,无知的. ⑤无恶意的, 无害的. ⑥【医】良性的. *be ~ of a crime* 无罪. *an ~ child* 天真的孩子. *an ~ tumour* 良性瘤. *a wall ~ of paint* (未抹墙面的)毛墙. — *n.* ①无辜的人;天真无邪的人. ②头脑简单的人,笨蛋. ***do the ~*** 装糊涂. ***massacre [slaughter] of the ~s*** ①屠杀婴儿. ②〔英俚〕(议会趁会期快满而作出的)撤销某些议案的决定. ***the (Holy) Innocents' Day***【宗】屠杀无辜婴儿纪念日〔12 月 28 日〕. ~ **passage** (船舶在航行中遇险时)未经主权国同意在其港口停泊的权利,无害通过(权). **-ly** *ad.*

in·no·cu·i·ty [ˌinəˈkjuːiti] *n.* ①无害,无毒. ②不关痛痒,乏味.

in·noc·u·ous [iˈnɔkjuəs] *a.* ①无害的,无毒的. ②无关痛痒的,乏味的. *an ~ drug* 无毒的药品. *~ generalities* 不关痛痒的泛泛之谈. **-ly** *ad.* **-ness** *n.*

in·nom·i·nate [iˈnɔminit] *a.* 无名的; 匿名的. *~ bone*【解】髋骨.

in·no·vate [ˈinəuveit] *vi.* 刷新, 革新, 改革 *(in; on; upon)*. — *vt.* 创始.

in·no·va·tion [ˌinəuˈveiʃən] *n.* 创新,革新,改革; 新设施, 新方法, 新发明. *technical ~* 技术革新. *a vitally important ~ in industry* 一项具有重大意义的工业上的革新. **-al** *a.* 革新的,富有革新精神的.

in·no·va·tive, in·no·va·tory [ˈinəuveitiv, -təri] *a.* 革新的,创新的;富有革新精神的.

in·no·va·tor [ˈinəuveitə] *n.* 革新者,改革者. *a technical ~* 技术革新者.

in·nox·ious [iˈnɔkʃəs] *a.* 无害的,无毒的. **-ly** *ad.* **-ness** *n.*

Inns·bruck [ˈinzbruk] *n.* 因斯布鲁克〔奥地利东部的城市〕.

in·nu·en·do [ˌinjuˈendəu] *n.* *(pl. ~es)* ①暗示,讽刺,影射. ②【法】文件中的附注句. *attack by ~* 旁敲侧击;含沙射影. — *vi.* 使用暗讽;【法】加注说明. — *vt.* 用暗讽表现[表达].

in·nu·mer·a·ble [iˈnjuːmərəbl] *a.* 无数的,数不清的. **-bly** *ad.*

in·nu·mer·ous [iˈnjuːmərəs] *a.* = innumerable.

in·nu·tri·tion [ˌinju(ː)ˈtriʃən] *n.* 缺乏营养,营养不良.

in·nu·tri·tious, -tive [ˌinju(ː)ˈtriʃəs, -tiv] *a.* 缺乏营养的;营养不良的.

in·ob·serv·ance [ˌinəbˈzəːvəns] *n.* 不留心, 玩忽; (对习惯法律等)不遵守.

in·ob·serv·ant [ˌinəbˈzəːvənt] *a.* 不注意的, 玩忽的, 违反的.

in·oc·u·la·ble [iˈnɔkjuləbl] *a.* ①接种的,预防注射的,移植(细菌)的. ②接枝的,接芽的. ③灌输(思想)的.

in·oc·u·lant [iˈnɔkjulənt] *n.* = inoculum.

in·oc·u·late [iˈnɔkjuleit] *vt.* ①【医】给…接种,给…注射预防针,移植(细菌). ②【植】嫁接; 播种. ③注入,灌输(思想). *~ sb. for [against] smallpox* 给…种痘. *be ~d against smallpox* (接受)种痘. *~ sb. with new ideas* 给某人灌输新思想.

in·oc·u·la·tion [iˌnɔkjuˈleiʃən] *n.* ①【医】接种; 预防注射;(细菌等的)移植. ②感染,灌输(思想等). ③【植】接枝, 接芽;嫁接. ④【冶】加孕育剂法. *artificial ~* 人工接种. *protective ~* 预防注射.

in·oc·u·la·tive [iˈnɔkjuleitiv] *a.* 接种的,种痘的.

in·oc·u·la·tor [iˈnɔkjuleitə] *n.* 接种者; 注射者; 接枝者.

in·oc·u·lum [iˈnɔkjuləm] *n.* 〔*pl.* **-u·la**〕 接种体, 接种物,种菌 (= inoculant).

in·o·dor·ous [inˈəudərəs] *a.* 没有气味的,没有香味的.

in·offen·sive [ˌinəˈfensiv] *a.* 无害的; 不讨厌的; 没有恶意的. **-ly** *ad.* **-ness** *n.*

in·of·fi·cious [inəˈfiʃəs] *a.* ①不尽职责的, 无义务观念的, 不遵守道义的. ②【法】不履行道德上的义务的〔如无理地剥夺子女或妻子正当的继承权〕. *an ~ testament [will]* 违反义务观念的遗嘱〔无理剥夺继承人的继承权的遗嘱〕.

in·op·er·a·ble [inˈɔpərəbl] *a.* ①【医】不能施行手术的, 不宜动手术的. ②不能实行的, 行不通的. *an ~ cancer* 不宜动手术的癌.

in·op·er·a·tive [inˈɔpərətiv] *a.* ①不起作用的. ②(法律、规章等)不生效的. **-ness** *n.*

in·o·per·cu·late [ˌinəuˈpəːkjulit] *a.* 无囊盖的, 无盖的.

in·op·por·tune [inˈɔpətjuːn] *a.* 不合时宜的, 不适当的,不凑巧的. *at an ~ time* 不合时机. **-ly** *ad.* **-ness** *n.*

in·or·di·nate [iˈnɔːdinit] *a.* ①紊乱的, 不规则的. ②无限制的,过度的. ***keep ~ hours*** 过着无规律的生活,熬夜. **-ly** *ad.*

inorg. = inorganic.

in·or·gan·ic [ˌinɔːˈgænik] *a.* ①【化】无机的; 无机物的. ②无生物的. ③无组织体系的, 人造的, 无特性的,无活力的. *~ sphere*【地】无生物界. *~ chemistry* 无机化学. *~ matter* 无机物. **-cal·ly** *ad.*

in·or·gan·i·za·tion [inˌɔːgənaiˈzeiʃən] *n.* 缺乏组织, 无组织;无组织状态.

in·or·nate [ˌinɔːˈneit, inˈɔːnit] *a.* 不加修饰地;(文体等)朴素的.

in·os·cu·late [iˈnɔskjuleit] *vi., vt.* ①(使)(血管等)接合 *(with)*;(使纤维等)缠合. ②(使)密切结合. **-tion** *n.*

in·o·sine [ˈinəsiːn] *n.*【生化】次黄嘌呤核甙, 肌甙. ~ **monophosphate** [ˈmɔnəuˈfɔsfeit] 一磷酸肌甙,肌甙酸.

in·o·sin·ic [ˌinəˈsinik] *a.*【生化】次黄嘌呤核甙的. ~ **acid**【生化】次黄嘌呤核甙酸,肌甙酸.

in·o·si·tol [iˈnəusitəul, -tɔːl] *n.*【生化】肌醇; 环已六醇 (= inosite).

in-pa·tient [ˈinˌpeiʃənt] *n.* 住院病人.

in-per·son [ˌinˈpəːsən] *a.* 亲身的;在场的.

in per·so·nam [ˌin pəˈsəunæm]【法】对人〔指判决的对象〕.

in pet·to [iːn ˈpetəu]〔It.〕秘密地, 不公开地〔指教皇指派红衣主教,但尚未提名〕.

in·phase [ˈinfeiz] *a.*【电】(交流)同位相的, 同相的.

in·pour·ing [ˈinpɔːriŋ] *n., a.* 注入(的), 倾入(的).

in·put [ˈinput] *n.* ①【电】【自】输入; 输入端. ②输入电路, 输入信号, 输入功率[电压]. ③放入物, 投入的资金. — ***(in·putted; in·put·ting)*** *vt., vi.* 把(数据等)输入计算机.

in·quest [ˈinkwest] *n.* ①【法】(有陪审员列席的)审讯;验尸. ②公审庭;陪审团; 验尸团. ③判决, 调查判决报告. ④查询,调查. *the great [last] ~*【宗】世界末日的大审判.

in·qui·e·tude [in'kwaiitjuːd] *n.* 不安,焦虑.

in·qui·line ['inkwilain, -lin] *n.* 【动】寄食昆虫, 寄食动物. **-lin·ism** [-linizm] *n.*

in·quire [in'kwaiə] *vt.* ①打问,打听,问〔向某人打问某事时,某人前用介词 of, 所问某事为直接宾语〕. ②调查 *(out)*. ③〔古〕质问. ～ *a matter of sb.* 向某人打听一件事. ～ *of sb. how to proceed with the work* 问某人怎样进行这个工作. ～ *of one's friend what one should do* 问朋友自己该怎么办. ～ *sb.'s telephone number* 问某人的电话号码. — *vi.* 询问,查问;调查 *(into)*〔问某人某事时,某人前用介词 of, 所问某事前则用 of, about, concerning 等〕. *He* ～*d of her about her homework.* 他问她家庭作业做得如何. ～ *into the deployment of the enemy troop* 调查敌军的兵力部署情况. ～ *about trains to London* 打听去伦敦的火车. ～ ***after*** 问候(病人等) *(May I* ～ *after your health?* 你好吗?) ～ ***for*** ①询问(行市、商品、地点等) (～ *for a new book* 问问有没有新书). ②要见 (～ *for the manager* 求见经理). ～ ***into*** 调查;探索. ～ ***out*** 问出,查出.

in·quir·er [in'kwaiərə] *n.* 询问的人,探究者, 调查者.

in·quir·ing [in'kwaiəriŋ] *a.* ①爱追根究底的. ②好奇的. *an* ～ *look* 诧异的样子. **-ly** *ad.*

in·quir·y [in'kwaiəri] *n.* ①询问, 质问; 追究. ②调查, 审查. ～ *agency* (工商)调查所, 征信所. ～ *office* 问讯处, 问事处. *hold an official* ～ 进行正式调查. *make a searching* ～ 追究, 探究. *make inquiries* 质问, 询问, 调查,探访 *(about; into)*. *on [upon]* ～ 调查之后(的结果). *make inquiries of sb. about sth.* 向某人询问某事. *hold an* ～ *into a case* 对一桩案子进行调查.

in·qui·si·tion [ˌinkwi'ziʃən] *n.* ①调查, 审查. ②【法】讯问, 审理; 调查〔审查〕报告书. ③〔the I-〕(中世纪天主教审判异端的)宗教法庭. ④(对于被认为是危险分子的)恣意镇压, 严厉刑罚. **-al** *a.*

in·quis·i·tive [in'kwizitiv] *a.* 好问人的, 好研究的; 好盘根究底的; 好奇的. — *n.* 好询问的人, 爱打听别人事情的人. **-ly** *ad.* **-ness** *n.*

in·quis·i·tor [in'kwizitə] *n.* ①审问者, 检察官. ②〔I-〕(中世纪天主教的)宗教法庭法官. ③讯问器. *the Grand I-* 宗教法庭庭长. *the I- General* (西班牙的)宗教法庭庭长.

in·quis·i·to·ri·al [inˌkwizi'tɔːriəl] *a.* ①审问官(似)的, 宗教法官(似)的. ②有关审问的, 有关调查的. ③打听别人事情的. **-ly** *ad.*

in rem [in 'rem] 【法】对物〔指判决的对象是物或财产〕.

in·road ['inrəud] *n.* ①(突然)袭击, (突然)侵犯 *(upon, on, into)*. ②损害, 侵犯 *(into, on)*. *make* ～*s into a small country* 侵犯一个小国家. *make* ～ *into sb.'s life* 干预某人的生活. *make* ～*s (up)on sb.'s health* 使某人的健康受到损害.

in·rush ['inrʌʃ] *n.* 涌入, 闯入; 流入. *an* ～ *of fresh air* 新鲜空气的流入. *the spring* ～ *of tourists* 旅游者随春天大批涌来.

I.N.S. = International News Service〔美〕〔旧〕国际新闻社.

ins. = ①inches. ②insulated. ③insurance.

in sae·cu·la sae·cu·lo·rum [in 'sekjulə sekju'lɔːrəm]〔L.〕永远永远.

in·sal·i·vate [in'sæliveit] *vt.* (细嚼)把唾液混入(食物). **-tion** [inˌsæli'veiʃən] *n.* 【医】混涎作用, 和涎作用.

in·sa·lu·bri·ous [ˌinsə'ljuːbriəs] *a.* (气候、环境等)对身体有害的, 不利于健康的. *live in an* ～ *environment* 在不利于身体健康的环境里生活.

in·sa·lu·bri·ty [ˌinsə'ljubriti] *n.* 不利于健康, 不卫生.

in·sane [in'sein] *a.* *(-san·er; -est)* ①精神错乱的, 精神病的; 疯狂的. ②精神病患者的, 为疯人开设的. ③非常愚蠢的. *an* ～ *asylum [hospital]* 精神病院, 疯人院. *go* ～发疯. *the* ～ 精神病患者, 疯子. *a perfectly* ～ *idea* 极端荒谬的想法. **-ly** *ad.* **-ness** *n.*

in·san·i·tar·y [in'sænitəri] *a.* 不卫生的, 有害健康的.

in·san·i·ty [in'sæniti] *n.* ①疯狂, 癫狂; 精神错乱, 精神病. ②非常愚蠢, 荒谬. ③蠢事.

in·sa·ti·a·ble [in'seiʃəbl] *a.* 不知足的, 贪得无厌的. *an* ～ *hunger for knowledge* 渴望知识. *be* ～ *in learning* 学而不厌. **-bil·i·ty** [inˌseiʃjə'biliti], **-ness** *n.* **-bly** *ad.*

in·sa·ti·ate [in'seiʃiit] *a.* = insatiable. **-ly** *ad.* **-ness, -ti·e·ty** *n.*

in·scape ['inskeip] *n.* 内在的特性, 内在的特质.

in·scribe [in'skraib] *vt.* ①写, 记. ②雕, 刻. ③登记(姓名, 证券等). ④题献, 题赠. ⑤牢记, 铭记. ⑥【数】使(图形)内接. ～*d securities* 记名证券. *an* ～*d stock*〔英〕记名股票〔公债〕. ～ *sb.'s name on a monument* 把某人的名字刻在纪念碑上. ～ *one's name in a book* 把名字写在书里面. *This book I* ～ *to ....* 谨将本书献给…. ～ *sth. on the memory* 铭记心上. *an* ～*d circle* 内接圆. **-a·ble** *a.* ①可刻〔雕〕的. ②可题写的. **-a·ble·ness** *n.* **in·scrib·er** *n.*

in·scrip·tion [in'skripʃən] *n.* ①记入. ②碑文; 铭刻; (赠书上的)题词, 署名. ③编入名单, 注册,〔英〕(公债等的)登记. *an* ～ *on a tombstone* 墓志铭, 碑文. **-al, -tive** *a.*

in·scroll [in'skrəul] *vt.* 把…载于卷册, 把…记录下来.

in·scru·ta·ble [in'skruːtəbl] *a.* 莫测高深的, 不可思议的, 费解的. *an* ～ *smile* 莫名其妙的微笑. **-bil·i·ty** [inˌskruːtə'biliti], **-ness** *n.* **-bly** *ad.*

in·seam ['insiːm] *n.* (裤管或衣袖的)内缝; 手套毛边内缝.

in·sect ['insekt] *n.* ①虫, 昆虫. ②微贱的人, 小人. *a destructive* ～ 害虫. — *a.* ①昆虫的. ②卑劣的. ～ *pests [vermin]* 虫害. ～ *powder* 除虫药粉. ～ *wax* 白蜡.

in·sec·tar·i·um [ˌinsek'tɛəriəm] *n.* (*pl.* ***in·sec·tar·ia*** [ˌinsek'tɛəriə]) 养虫室, 昆虫馆.

in·sec·tar·y ['insektəri] *n.* = insectarium.

in·sec·ti·cide [in'sektisaid] *n.* 杀虫剂. *farm* ～ 农业杀虫剂, 农药. *spray* ～ 喷射杀虫剂. **-cid·al** *a.* 除虫的 *(inseccidal oil* 杀虫油).

in·sec·ti·fuge [in'sektifjuːdʒ] *n.* 驱虫剂; 除虫药.

in·sec·tile [in'sektail] *a.* ①虫的; 昆虫的, 似昆虫的 (= insectival). ②有虫的.

In·sec·tiv·o·ra [ˌinsek'tivərə] *n.* 〔*pl.*〕【动】食虫目.

in·sec·ti·vore [in'sektivɔː] *n.* 食虫动物〔植物〕.

in·sec·tiv·o·rous [ˌinsek'tivərəs] *a.* 以虫类为食的, 食虫的. *the* ～ *animals [plants]* 食虫动物〔植物〕.

in·sec·to·cu·tion [inˌsektə'kjuːʃən] *n.* 通电杀虫.

in·sec·tol·o·gy [ˌinsek'tɔlədʒi] *n.* 经济昆虫学〔研究昆虫在经济方面对人类所起的作用〕〔*cf.* entomology〕.

in·se·cure [ˌinsi'kjuə] *a.* *(-cur·er; -est)* 不安全的, 不牢靠的; (诺言等)靠不住的; (地面、冰等)易坍陷的. *an* ～ *promise* 不可靠的诺言. *an* ～ *investment* 不太保险的投资. **-ly** *ad.*

in·se·cu·ri·ty [ˌinsi'kjuəriti] *n.* 不安全, 不牢靠; 不安定; 易崩坏. *a sense of* ～ 不安全感.

in·sem·i·nate [in'semineit] *vt.* ①播(种), 栽. ②使受孕, 授精.

in·sem·i·na·tion [inˌsemi'neiʃən] *n.* ①播种. ②受孕, 授精. *artificial* ～ 人工授精.

in·sem·i·na·tor [in'semineitə] *n.* 人工授精操作者.

in·sen·sate [in'senseit, -sit] *a.* ①无知觉的, 无生命的; 无感情的. ②残忍的, 无情的. ③愚钝的, 没有理智的. *mute* ～ *things* 哑然无言的生物. **-ly** *ad.* **-ness** *n.*

in·sen·si·ble [in'sensəbl] *a.* ①无感觉的, 麻木不仁的; 昏迷不省的. ②感觉迟钝的, 不敏感的. ③不关心的, 漫不经心的. ④冷淡的, 无情的. ⑤难看出的, 缓慢的. *be* ～ *to [of] pain* 不感觉疼痛, 不感觉痛苦. *be knocked* ～

被打得人事不省. *fly* ~ 昏过去. *hands* ~ *from cold* 冻得麻木了的手. *be* ~ *of one's danger* 不知道自己面临的危险. *by* ~ *degree* 极慢地. **-bil·i·ty, -ness** *n.* **-bly** *ad.*

in·sen·si·tive [inˈsensitiv] *a.* 感觉迟钝的, 不敏感的, 无感觉的 (*to*). **-ly** *ad.* **-ness, -tiv·i·ty** *n.*

in·sen·ti·ent [inˈsenʃənt] *a.* 无知觉的,无感觉的; 无生命的,无情感的. **-ence, -ti·cy** *n.*

insep. = inseparable.

in·sep·a·ra·ble [inˈsepərəbl] *a.* 分不开的, 不可分离的. ~ *friends* 分不开的朋友. *an* ~ *prefix* 【语法】非分离性前缀〔dis-, un- 等独立时即无意义〕. — *n.*〔*pl.*〕不可分的事物;好友. **-bly** *ad.* **-bil·i·ty** *n.*

in·sep·a·ra·ble·ness [inˈsepərəblnis] *n.* 不可分离 (= inseparability).

in·sep·a·rate [inˈseparit] *a.* 不分开的, 不分离的, 相连的.

in·sert [inˈsəːt] *vt.* ①插进,夹入. ②写进,记入;刊登. ③(缝纫中)镶, 补. *insert a key in [into] a lock* 把钥匙插进锁中. ~ *a word in a line* 插一个字到行里. ~ *an advertisement in a newspaper* 在报上登广告. — *vi.*【医】(肌肉)附着. — [ˈinsəːt] *n.* ①插入物, 嵌入物. ②补垫. ③电报头. ④〔*pl.*〕金属型芯, 嵌入物. ⑤插页;【影】插入画面.

in·sert·ed [inˈsəːtid] *a.*【生】着生的.

in·sert·er [inˈsəːtə] *n.* 插入物, 插件. *data* ~ 数据输入器.

in·ser·tion [inˈsəːʃən] *n.* ①插入; 记入; 刊登. ②插入物; 插入句; 插入广告; 插绣, 补绣. ③【动、植】着生(点). ④【电】嵌入, 介入. ⑤【医】(肌肉的) 附着. *the* ~ *of muscle* 肌附着,肌止端. **-al** *a.*

in-ser·vice [ˈinˈsəːvis] *a.* 在职期间进行的, 使用中进行的.

in·ses·so·ri·al [ˌinseˈsɔːriəl] *a.* (某些鸟的)适于栖止的.

in·set [inˈset] *vt.* *(inset; insetted; inset·ting)* 嵌入,插入(插图等). —[ˈinset] *n.* ①插入物;插入广告;插页, 插图. ②镶边. ③水道;(潮水)流入.

in·sheathe [inˈʃiːð] *vt.* *(-sheath·ed, -sheath·ing)* 插入鞘;用鞘覆盖 (= ensheathe).

in·shoot [ˈinʃuːt] *n.*【棒球】内射球.

in·shore [ˈinˈʃɔː] (*opp.* offshore) *a.* 近海岸的; 向陆的. ~ *currents* 沿岸流. ~ *fishing [fishery]* 近海渔业. ~ *patrol*【军】沿海巡逻. *an* ~ *wind* 向陆风. — *ad.* 沿海,靠近海岸. ~ *of* 比…靠近海岸.

in·shrine [inˈʃrain] *vt.* = enshrine.

in·side [ˈinˈsaid] (*opp.* outside) *n.* ①内部, 内面. ②(道路的)内侧;(跑道的)内道,内圈. ③内容,内心,内情;内幕情报〔消息〕. ④[inˈsaid] (公共马车等的) 车内乘客;车内座位. ⑤期中. ⑥〔口〕内脏, 肠胃. *the* ~ *of the hand* 手心. *the* ~ *of a sidewalk* 人行道内侧. *The CIA from Inside*《美国中央情报局内幕》. *know the* ~ *of sb.* 了解某人内心. *know the business from* ~ 完全了解这一行业. *the* ~ *of a week* 星期一至星期五. *feel a pain in one's* ~ 感觉肚子痛. — [ˈinsaid] *a.* ①里面的, 内部的, 在屋里的. ②内幕的, 秘密的. ③在室内工作的. ~ *address* 信纸上的姓名, 地址〔信封上姓名地址之对〕. ~ *diameter* 内径. ~ *facts* 内幕, 秘密. ~ *information* 内部情报. *For I- Circulation Only* 内部传阅. ~ *knowledge [story]* 内情,内幕. *an* ~ *man* 内勤人员. — [inˈsaid] *ad.* 在内, 在内部, 在里面. *There is nothing* ~. 里面什么也没有. — *prep.* 在…之内,在…里面. *step* ~ *the gate* 跨进门内. *return* ~ *a month* 一月之内回来. ~ ***of***〔口〕①在…以内. ②(时间上)少于(~ *of a mile* 不到一英里. ~ *of a week* 少于一个星期). ~ ***out*** ①从里面翻到外面. ②彻底地(*turn everything* ~ *out* 翻箱倒柜. *know a matter* ~ *out* 对一件事彻底了解). ***on the*** ~ 从里面, 在里面(*The door locked on the* ~. 门反锁着). ~ **job**〔美口〕内部自己人作的案,有内应关系作的案. ~ **track** ①运动场跑道的内圈. ②有利地位, 好机会.

in·sid·er [inˈsaidə] *n.* ①组织或团体内部的人. ②了解内幕者,知内情的人.

in·sid·i·ous [inˈsidiəs] *a.* ①阴险的, 狡猾的; 暗中为害的. ②在不知不觉之间加剧的. *an* ~ *enemy* 阴险的敌人. ~ *wiles* 奸计. *the* ~ *approach of age* 不知不觉就老了. **-ly** *ad.* **-ness** *n.*

in·sight [ˈinsait] *n.* ①洞察力; 直觉, 悟力; 眼光; 见识. ②【心】顿悟. *a man of deep* ~ 有深远见识的人. *gain [have] an* ~ *into sb.'s mind* 看透某人心思.

in·sight·ful [ˈinˌsaitful] *a.* 有见识的,有眼光的; 显出洞察力的.

in·sig·ni·a [inˈsigniə] *n.* (*pl.* ~*(s)*; *sing.* ***in·sig·ne*** [-niː]) ①勋章; 国徽. ②(权威、尊严、荣誉的)标帜〔如王冠,帝王的宝杖,军人的领章, 肩章等〕. *the* ~ *of an order* 勋章. *a red collar* ~ 红领章.

in·sig·nif·i·cance [ˌinsigˈnifikəns] *n.* ①无意义; 不足道; 无价值; 不重要. ②低微,可鄙.

in·sig·nif·i·can·cy [ˌinsigˈnifikənsi] *n.* ①= insignificance. ②微不足道的人〔东西〕.

in·sig·nif·i·cant [ˌinsigˈnifikənt] *a.* ①无意义的; 不足取的; 琐碎的; 无价值的. ②小的, 低微的, 可鄙的. ~ *talk* 废话. ~ *things* 微不足道的东西. *waste time on* ~ *points* 时间花在琐碎事情上. ~ *people* 小人物. ~ *town* 小小的城镇. **-ly** *ad.*

in·sin·cere [ˌinsinˈsiə] *a.* 不诚实的,无诚意的; 虚假的, 伪善的. **-ly** *ad.*

in·sin·cer·i·ty [ˌinsinˈseriti] *n.* 不诚实,无诚意; 伪善; 不诚实的言行.

in·sin·u·ate [inˈsinjueit] *vt.* ①使潜入,巧妙地进行,慢慢插入 *(into)*. ②暗讽,暗示. ~ *doubts into sb.'s mind* 使某人慢慢产生疑虑. ~ *oneself into sb.'s favour* 巧妙地巴结上某人, 巧妙地向人献媚求宠. ~ *oneself into the crowd* 暗暗地挤进人群. ~ *one's doubt of this action* 暗示对于这一行动的怀疑. — *vi.* 暗示,含沙射影. ~ *that sb. is dishonest* 暗示某人不诚实. **-a·tive, -a·to·ry** *a.*

in·sin·u·at·ing [inˈsinjueitiŋ] *a.* ①暗示(式)的. ②献媚的, 讨好的. *make an* ~ *remark* 暗讽. *speak in an* ~ *voice* 低声下气地说. *an* ~ *smile* 肉麻的微笑. **-ly** *ad.*

in·sin·u·a·tion [inˌsinjuˈeiʃən] *n.* 慢慢进去; 巧妙巴结; 暗示. *attack by* ~ 含沙射影地攻击. *make* ~*s* 含沙射影.

in·sin·u·a·tor [inˈsinjueitə] *n.* ①献媚者. ②暗示者, 暗讽者.

in·sip·id [inˈsipid] *a.* ①没有味道的; 不好吃的. ②乏味的,无风趣的,无生气的. ~ *food* 淡而无味的食品. ~ *conversation* 枯燥无味的谈话. **-ly** *ad.* **-ness** *n.*

in·si·pid·i·ty [ˌinsiˈpiditi] *n.* 无味; 枯燥,平淡.

in·sip·i·ence [inˈsipiəns] *n.*〔古〕缺乏才智, 愚钝. **-ent** *a.*

in·sist [inˈsist] *vi.* ①硬要,坚持 *(on, upon)*. ②坚决要求,定要. *I will have another glass if you* ~. 你硬要劝我,我只好再喝一杯. *I* ~ *on his innocence.* 我坚认他无罪. *I* ~ *on being present.* 我一定要出席. ~ *on a point* 强调一点. *He* ~*s on going with you.* 他坚持要和你一起去. — *vt.* 坚决主张;坚决认为;坚决要求 *(that)*. *I* ~ *that he is innocent.* 我坚决认为自己无罪. *I* ~ *that you shall be present.* 务必请您到场.

in·sist·ence, -ten·cy [inˈsistəns, -si] *n.* 坚持, 强调, 极力主张. ~ *(up)on strict obedience* 强调要严格服从.

in·sist·ent [inˈsistənt] *a.* 坚持的,逼人注意的; 显眼的, 显著的. *an* ~ *demand* 迫切的要求. *an* ~ *rhythm* 动人的旋律. **-ly** *ad.*

in·sist·er [inˈsistə] *n.* 固执的人,坚持者.

in·snare [inˈsnɛə] *vt.* = ensnare.

in·so·bri·e·ty [ˌinsəuˈbraiəti] *n.* 无节制，饮酒过度，酗酒.

in·so·cia·ble [inˈsəuʃəbl] *a.* 不爱社交的，不会交际的，孤僻的，不讨人喜欢的. **-bil·i·ty** *n.* **-bly** *ad.*

in·so·far [ˌinsəuˈfɑː -sə-] *ad.* 到如此程度〔通常与 as 连用〕. ~ *as* 在…限度内，在…的范围内 (*I shall do what I can* ~ *as I am able.* 我力所能及的都要去做. *I- as possible, our examples will be drawn from Chinese.* 在可能范围内，例证均引自汉语).

in·so·late [ˈinsəuleit] *vt.* 曝晒.

in·so·la·tion [ˌinsəuˈleiʃən] *n.* ①曝晒. ②日光浴. ③【医】中暑，日射病. ④【气】日射，日射率.

in·sole [ˈinsəul] *n.* 鞋内底；鞋垫.

in·so·lence [ˈinsələns] *n.* ①傲慢，横蛮. ②傲慢的态度，侮辱性的言行.

in·so·lent [ˈinsələnt] *a.* 傲慢的，横蛮无礼的. **-ly** *ad.*

in·sol·u·ble [inˈsɔljubl] *a.* ①不能解决的；难解释的. ②不溶解的，不溶化的. **-bil·i·ty** *n.* **-bly** *ad.*

in·sol·u·ble·ness [inˈsɔljublnis] *n.* ①难解决；难解释. ②不溶解，不溶化.

in·solv·a·ble [inˈsɔlvəbl] *a.* = insoluble.

in·sol·ven·cy [inˈsɔlvənsi] *n.* 无力偿付债务，破产.

in·sol·vent [inˈsɔlvənt] *a.* 无力偿付债务的，破产的. — *n.* 无力偿还债务者，破产者.

in·som·ni·a [inˈsɔmniə] *n.*【医】失眠；失眠症.

in·som·ni·ac [inˈsɔmniæk] *a.* 患失眠症的. — *n.* 患失眠症的人.

in·som·ni·ous [inˈsɔmniəs] *a.* 失眠的，患失眠症的.

in·so·much [ˌinsəuˈmʌtʃ] *ad.* ①到这样的程度，如此地 (*as, that*). *The rain fell in torrents,* ~ *that we were ankle-deep in water.* 大雨滂沱，水深没膝. ②因为，由于〔与 as 连用，= inasmuch as〕.

in·so·nate [ˈinsəuneit] *vt., vi.* (使)受声波(尤指超高频声波)的作用. **-na·tion** *n.*

in·sou·ci·ance [inˈsuːsjəns] *n.* 〔F.〕漫不经心，满不在乎. ***in·sou·ci·ant*** *a.* 〔F.〕

in·soul [inˈsəul] *vt.* = ensoul.

INSP, insp. = inspect; inspection; inspector.

in·span [inˈspæn] *vt., vi.* (*-spanned; -span·ning*) 〔南非用的英语〕把(牛、马等)套到车上，套(车).

in·spect [inˈspekt] *vt.* 检阅；检查；审查；视察. ~ *troops* 阅兵. ~ *school* 视察学校. **-a·bil·i·ty** *n.* **-a·ble** *a.* **-ing·ly** *ad.*

in·spec·tion [inˈspekʃən] *n.* ①检查，检验；审查. ②检阅，视察，参观. *bottom* ~ 船底检查. *close* ~ 严格检查. *full* ~ 全船检查. *a house-to-house* ~ 挨户检查. *medical* ~ 检疫；检查身体；卫生检查. ~ *arms*【军】验枪姿势；(口令用语)验枪. *an* ~ *door* (军舰上减速器的)窥孔盖. *an* ~ *hole*【冶】观察孔，检验孔. ~ *tools*【冶】检验工具，控制工具. ***for (your kind)*** ~ 祈查阅(为感). ***I- declined!*** 谢绝参观. ***make an*** ~ ***of*** 视察 (*make an* ~ *of a university* 视察一所大学). ***on the first*** ~ 一看之后.

in·spec·tor [inˈspektə] *n.* 检查员，监察员，检阅者；视察员. *an* ~ *of ordnance*【军】军械检验员. *an* ~ *of weights and measures* 度量衡检查员. *an* ~ *of hull* 船身检查员. *a police* ~ 警察巡官. *an* ~ *of schools* = *a school* ~ 督学. ~ ***general*** *n.* 监察长；【美军】检阅总监 (*the I- General of the Army [Navy]* 美国陆[海]军监察长. *the I- General's Department* 监察署). **-al, -i·al** *a.* **-ship** *n.* 检查员[监察员]的地位[职权].

in·spec·tor·ate [inˈspektərit] *n.* ①检查员[监察员]的地位[职责]. ②〔总称〕视察人员，视察团. ③检查员(监察员等)的管辖区域.

in·spec·to·scope [inˈspektəskəup] *n.* 一种用 X 光透视检查违禁品的器械.

in·spec·tress [inˈspektris] *n.* 女检查员，女监察员.

in·sphere [inˈsfiə] *vt.* (*-sphered, -spher·ing*) = ensphere.

in·spi·ra·tion [ˌinspəˈreiʃən] *n.* ①吸气；【机】进气 (*opp.* expiration). ②【宗】神的启示；(诗人的)灵感. ③鼓舞，激励，感化. ④〔口〕灵机，妙想. ⑤(上级的)指示，授意，鼓动. *have a sudden* ~ 灵机一动. *draw [get]* ~ *from* 从…得到启发. *The poem is a pure* ~. 这首诗纯粹是灵感之作. *the governmental* ~ *of a report* 按政府意旨所作的报告. **-al** *a.* **-ism** *n.* 灵感论，神秘直觉说. **-ist** *n.* 灵感论者.

in·spi·ra·tor [ˈinspəreitə] *n.* 呼吸器；喷汽注水器，注射器.

in·spir·a·to·ry [inˈspaiərətəri] *a.* 吸气的；吸入的.

in·spire [inˈspaiə] *vt.* ①吸，吸气 (*opp.* expire). ②注入，灌注. ③使生灵感，使感悟，感动. ④鼓舞，激励，激发. ⑤指示，授意. ~ *sb. with courage* = ~ *courage into sb.* 鼓起某人勇气. ~ *a new thought into sb.* 将新思想灌输给某人. — *vi.* ①吸入. ②赋予灵感.

in·spired [inˈspaiəd] *a.* ①受到灵感的. ②被人授意的，受鼓动的. *an* ~ *poet* 有灵感的诗人. *the* ~ *writings* 圣书. *an* ~ *article* 由别人授意而写成的文章. ~ *views* 体现长官意志的意见.

in·spir·ing [inˈspaiəriŋ] *a.* 鼓动的，激励的，勇壮的. *an* ~ *sight* 振奋人心的光景. ~ *activity* 鼓舞人心的活动. *The music is* ~. 这音乐激动人心.

in·spir·it [inˈspirit] *vt.* 振奋，激发，激励. ~ *sb. to an action (to do sth.)* 鼓励某人采取行动(做某事). **-ing** *a.*

in·spis·sate [inˈspiseit] *vt., vi.* ①(使)浓缩，(使)浓厚，(使)强烈. ②(使)(心情)沉重. ~*ing the gloom of the room atmosphere* 使房子里的空气变得更加阴沉. **-d** *a.* **-tion** *n.* 浓厚化；【化】蒸浓法. **-tor** *n.* 【化】蒸浓器.

Inst. = Institute; Institution.

inst. = instant; instrumental.

in·sta·bil·i·ty [ˌinstəˈbiliti] *n.* 动摇性，不稳定性；不坚决，反复无常，三心二意. *the* ~ *of human affairs* 人事沧桑.

in·sta·ble [inˈsteibl] *a.* 动摇的，不安定的；不坚定的，易变的，反复无常的 (= unstable).

in·stal(l) [inˈstɔːl] *vt.* (*in·stalled*) ①任命，使就(职)，把…安插到(*in*). ②安置，使坐，使入席. ③安装(机器)，设置. ~ *a college president* 任命学院院长. ~ *sb. in an office* 把某人安插在办公室里. ~ *sb. in a deck chair* 让某人坐在甲板上的躺椅上. *be* ~*ed in a seat* 在座位上坐定. ~ *a heating system* 装设暖气设备.

in·stal·lant [inˈstɔːlənt] *n.* 任命者.

in·stal·la·tion [ˌinstɔːˈleiʃən] *n.* ①就职，就任；就职礼. ②装置，设备. ③安装；设置；安置. ④军事设施. *a heating* ~ 暖气设备. *an* ~ *diagram*【机】装置图. *an ammunition* ~ 弹药补给机关，弹药库. *military* ~*s* 军事设施.

in·stall·er [inˈstɔːlə] *n.* 安装者.

in·stal(l)·ment [inˈstɔːlmənt] *n.* ①分期付款中的每期应付款，摊付金. ②(从书杂志等的)一部，一期，(小说等)分期连载的一部分. ③〔古〕= installation. *monthly* ~ 每月摊付的款项. *pay by [in]* ~*s* 分期付款. *appear in* ~*s* 分期发表[出版]. ~ ***plan [system]*** 〔美〕分期付款购货法 (*buy on the* ~ *plan* 用分期付款办法购买).

in·stance [ˈinstəns] *n.* ①事例，例证，实例，场合. ②情况. ③要求，建议. ④【法】诉讼手续. ***in this [your]*** ~ 在这种[你的]情况下. ***at the*** ~ ***of*** 因…之请，由于…的主张[建议]. *one* ~ *out of many* 许多例子中的一个. *cite [give, produce] an* ~ 举例. *a court of first* ~ 初审庭，预审庭. ***in the first*** ~ 最初，首先；在第一审时. ***in the last*** ~ 最后，在终审时. ***for*** ~ 例如. — *vt.* 举…为例，引以为例，举例证明.

in·stan·cy [ˈinstənsi] *n.* ①紧急，急迫. ②即时，瞬间. ③坚持.

in·stant [ˈinstənt] *a.* ①迫切的,紧急的. ②当月的,本月的〔商业或正式文件中使用,一般略为inst.〕. ③立即的,直接的. ④食物已配制好的. *be in ~ need of help* 急需帮助. *the 3rd of this ~ June* 这一个六月的三号. *your letter of the 10th ~* 本月十日尊函. *an ~ response* 立即回答. *~ coffee* 速溶咖啡. — *n.* 瞬间,时刻,即时. *at that ~* 在那时候,在那瞬间. *I went that ~.* 我立刻就走了. *this ~* 立刻,马上. ***for an ~*** 一瞬间 (*I couldn't answer for an ~.* 我一时答不上来). ***in an ~*** 立刻,马上(*I'll be with you in an ~.* 我立刻就来). ***on the ~*** 立即,即时 (*march off on the ~* 马上出发). ***the ~*** *conj.* = as soon as 一…(就) (*The ~ we heard the alarm, we fell in for action.* 我们一听到警报, 就立即集合准备战斗). ~ **replay** 即时重播〔以录相带录下体育动作,于动作完成后即可用慢动作重播〕. ~ **reply** 可立时放送的录象.

in·stan·ta·né [ˌɛ̃ːnstænˈtɑːnei] *n.* 〔F.〕 ①快照. ②简报.

in·stan·ta·ne·ous [ˌinstənˈteinjəs] *a.* 即刻的,瞬间的. *an ~ bomb* 瞬发炸弹. *~ death* 即刻死去. *an ~ effect* 速效. *~ exposure* 自动快速曝光. *an ~ photograph* 快照. *an ~ response* 即刻的反应. *~ velocity* 【物】瞬时速度. **-ly** *ad.* **-ness** *n.*

in·stan·ter [inˈstæntə] *ad.* 马上,立刻.

in·stan·ti·ate [inˈstænʃieit] *vt.* 用具体例证说明. **-a·tion** [inˌstænʃiˈeiʃən] *n.*

in·stant·ly [ˈinstəntli] *ad.* 立即,即刻. — *conj.* 一…就. *I telegraphed ~ I arrived there.* 我一到了那里就打电报.

in·star[1] [ˈinˈstɑː] *n.* (虫)龄〔幼虫两次蜕皮之间的虫期〕.

in·star[2] [inˈstɑː] *vt.* (*-star·red, -star·ring*) ①嵌星,饰以星. ②〔古〕把…摆成星状.

in·state [inˈsteit] *vt.* 任命,使就任;安置,设置.

in sta·tu quo [in ˈsteituː kwəu] 〔L.〕 维持现状.

in·stau·ra·tion [ˌinstɔːˈreiʃən] *n.* ①恢复,修复,更新. ②〔古〕设立,建立.

in·stau·ra·tor [ˈinstɔːreitə] *n.* ①复兴者,重建者. ②创立者,设立者.

Inst. C. E. = Institution of Civil Engineers 〔英〕土木工程师学会.

in·stead [insˈted] *ad.* 代替,顶替. *come another day ~* 改天再来吧. *Give me this ~.* 请改拿这个给我. *~ **of*** 代替,而不是 (*I'll go ~ of you.* 我愿代你去. *I gave him advice ~ of money.* 我给了他忠告而没有给他钱).

in·step [ˈinstep] *n.* ①脚背. ②盖上脚背的鞋面和袜面部分. ③【动】蹠.

in·sti·gate [ˈinstigeit] *vt.* 教唆,煽动,唆使;挑起,发动(战争),策划. *~ sb. to do sth.* 唆使某人做某事. *~ a rebellion* 煽动叛乱. *~ a strike* 煽动罢工. **-ga·tor** *n.* 唆使者,煽动者.

in·sti·ga·tion [ˌinstiˈgeiʃən] *n.* 鼓动,煽动;刺激;刺激物. *at [by] the ~ of sb.* 在某人的鼓动下.

in·stil(l) [inˈstil] *vt.* ①滴注. ②慢慢灌输. *~ ideas into sb.'s mind* 把思想灌输到某人脑中.

in·stil·la·tion [ˌinstiˈleiʃən] *n.* ①滴注;【医】滴注法. *rectal ~* 【医】直肠滴注法. ②注入;灌输. ③滴注物,滴剂,浸润物.

in·stil(l)·ment [inˈstilmənt] *n.* 滴注.

in·stinct [ˈinstiŋkt] *n.* ①本能,才能,直觉. ②生性,天性,天才. *Suckling is an ~ in mammals.* 哺乳是哺乳动物的本能. *act on ~* 凭直觉行动. *by ~* 凭本能,本能地. *Birds learn to fly by ~.* 鸟儿学飞系由于本能. ***have an ~ for*** 生来就有…的本能,有…的才能. — [inˈstiŋkt] *a.* 充满的 (*with*). *be ~ with life* 充满生气.

in·stinc·tive [inˈstiŋktiv] *a.* 生来的,天性的;本能的;直觉的. **-ly** *ad.*

in·sti·tute [ˈinstitjuːt] *n.* ①协会,学会;学院,专科大学;(学院附设的)研究所. ②〔美〕讲习会,(短期)训练班. ③会址,院址,校址,所址. ④原则,规则,惯例. ⑤〔*pl.*〕(给初学者用的法律、医学等的)浅说,(公认的)基本原理. *an ~ of technology* 理工学院. *a farmers' ~* 〔美〕农民讲习所. *a teachers' ~* 〔美〕教师训练班. — *vt.* ①设,设立;制定. ②实行,创立,开始. ③任命,【宗】授…以圣职. *~ a government* 组织政府. *~ an inquiry into* 开始调查. *~ an action at law* 提起法律诉讼. *~ a suit against sb.* 对某人提起诉讼. *~ sb. into [to] a parish* 任命教区牧师.

in·sti·tu·tion [ˌinstiˈtjuːʃən] *n.* ①设立,创设,制定. ②惯例,制度,规定. ③学会,协会;院,会,社,馆,所;机关;社会事业机构(指学校、医院、教会等). ④会址,校址,院址,所址. ⑤【宗】授职;授职礼. ⑥〔口〕名人,名物. *a public ~* 公共机关(指医院、学校). *a training ~ for* 训练班. *He is quite an ~.* 他是个很有名的人.

in·sti·tu·tion·al [ˌinstiˈtjuːʃənəl] *a.* ①惯例的,规定的,制度上的. ②公共机构的,社会事业性质的〔尤指慈善事业机构〕. ③〔美〕(广告)主要为建立公司产品声誉而创招牌的. *in need of ~ care* 需要慈善事业机构照顾. **-ly** *ad.*

in·sti·tu·tion·al·ism [ˌinstiˈtjuːʃənəlizm] *n.* ①社会事业机构. ②社会慈善机构的救济. ③尊重社会事业和传统制度的政策.

in·sti·tu·tion·al·ize [ˌinstiˈtjuːʃənəlaiz] *vt.* (*-ized, -iz·ing*) ①使制度化;使成为习惯;把…看作制度. ②使成惯例;使成为制度;使成为风俗习惯. ③把…送交专门机构治疗〔拘留〕. **-za·tion** *n.*

in·sti·tu·tion·ar·y [ˌinstiˈtjuːʃəˌnəri] *a.* ①学会的,协会的,团体的. ②创始的,制定的,规定的 (= institutional). ③【宗】授予圣职的;圣餐制度的.

in·sti·tu·tive [ˈinstitjuːtiv] *a.* 设立的;(法律等的)制定的;惯例的;制度的;机关的.

in·sti·tu·tor [ˈinstitjuːtə] *n.* ①设立者,创立者,制定者. ②〔美〕授任圣职者.

Inst. M. E. = Institute of Marine Engineers 〔英〕轮机工程师学会.

Inst. N. A. = Institution of Naval Architects 〔英〕造船(工程)师学会.

instr. = instructor; instrument; instrumental.

in·struct [inˈstrʌkt] *vt.* ①教,教授,教导. ②通知,向…提供事实情况. ③命令,指示. *~ sb. in English* 教某人英语. *be ~ed when to start* 得到出发时间的通知. *~ sb. to do sth.* 命令某人做某事. **-i·ble** *a.*

in·struct·ed [inˈstrʌktid] *a.* ①受教育的. ②被委派的,得到指示的. *~ delegates* 委派的代表. **-ly** *ad.* **-ness** *n.*

in·struc·tion [inˈstrʌkʃən] *n.* ①教育,教导. ②教训,教诲. ③〔*pl.*〕指令,训令,指示,细目. *give sb. ~s to do sth.* 命令某人做什么. *an ~ book* 说明书. *maintenance ~s* 维护说明. *operating ~s* 业务〔工作〕须知,操作规程. ***ask for ~*** 请示. ***give ~ in*** 教授. ***give ~s to*** 训令. ***receive in ~*** 接受指导. ~ **deck** 【计】指令卡片组. ~ **repertoire [set]** 【计】指令系统.

in·struc·tion·al [inˈstrʌkʃənəl] *a.* 教授的,教训的,教育的. *for ~ purpose* 用于教育目的. ~ **display** 示教显示器. ~ **film** 教学影片. ~ **television** 教学电视〔缩写为 ITV〕.

in·struc·tive [inˈstrʌktiv] *a.* 有教育意义的,有启发的,有益的. *an ~ film* 科学普及片. *~ lessons* 有益的教训. **-ly** *ad.* **-ness** *n.*

in·struc·tor [inˈstrʌktə] *n.* 教导者,教员;〔美〕(大学)讲师. *an ~ in history* 历史教员. *a political ~* 政治指导员. *an assistant ~* 助教. **-ship** *n.* 讲师职位.

in·struc·tress [inˈstrʌktris] *n. fem.* ①〔军〕女教师. ②女讲师.

in·stru·ment [ˈinstrumənt] *n.* ①仪表,仪器〔*cf.* tool, implement〕. ②乐器 (= musical ~). ③【法】证件,证

券,文件. ④手段,工具. *airborne* ~*s* 航空仪表. *all-purpose* ~*s* 万能仪表. *end* ~*s* 敏感元件. *nautical* ~*s* 航海仪器. *optical* ~ 光学仪器. *precision* ~*s* 精密仪器. *surgical* ~*s* 外科器械. *stringed* ~*s* 弦乐器. *wind* ~*s* 管乐器. *an* ~ *of credit* 商业证券. *negotiable* ~ 流通票据,可转让证券. *the* ~ *of ratification* 批准书. ~*s of production* 生产工具. *act as sb.'s* ~ 做某人傀儡. *be the* ~ *of sb.'s death* (误)致某人死亡. — *vt.* ①用仪器装备. ②给乐器编(曲),为管弦乐队编(曲). ③向…提交法律文件. ~ **board [panel]** 仪表板. ~ **flight [flying]** 【空】仪表(引导)飞行,盲目[无线电导航]飞行. ~ **landing** 盲目[无线电导航]着陆,仪表(引导)降落.

in·stru·men·tal [ˌinstruˈmentl] *a.* ①仪器的,器械的,器具的〔*cf.* vocal〕. ②乐器(上)的,为乐器谱曲的,用乐器演奏的. ③作为手段[工具]的,有帮助的,起作用的. ④【语法】工具格的. ~ *drawing* 器械画. ~ *errors* 仪器误差,仪表误差. *an* ~ *ensemble* 器乐重奏曲. ~ *music* 器乐. ~ *parts* 器乐部. *be* ~ *to a purpose* 对目的有帮助. ~ *in improving the qualities of our products* 有助于提高我们产品的质量. ~ **case** 【语法】工具格. **-ist** ① *n.* 器乐演奏者;工具主义者. ②*a.* 主张工具主义的,根据工具主义的.

in·stru·men·tal·ism [ˌinstrəˈmentlizm] *n.* 【哲】工具主义〔实用主义的一种理论〕.

in·stru·men·tal·i·ty [ˌinstrumenˈtæliti] *n.* 手段,媒介,工具,帮助. ***by [through] the*** ~ ***of*** 靠…,借助于…,以…做为手段.

in·stru·men·tal·ly [ˌinstruˈmentəli] *ad.* 用仪器地;用乐器地;机械地,间接地.

in·stru·men·ta·tion [ˌinstrumenˈteiʃən] *n.* ①装设仪器;使用仪器;【自】检测仪表;测试设备. ②用乐器演奏谱曲,作曲法〔*cf.* orchestration〕. ③乐器研究;仪器制造学. ④手段.

in·sub·or·di·nate [insəˈbɔːdnit] *a.* ①不服从的,反抗的. ②地位不低[劣]的. — *n.* 不服从的人,反抗者. **-ly** *ad.*

in·sub·or·di·na·tion [ˈinsəˌbɔːdiˈneiʃən] *n.* 不服从,反抗.

in·sub·stan·tial [ˌinsəbˈstænʃəl] *a.* 无实体的;不实在的;幻想的;不坚固的;脆弱的. **-tial·i·ty** [-ʃiːˈæliti] *n.*

in·suf·fer·a·ble [inˈsʌfərəbl] *a.* 难忍受的;受不了的. **-bly** *ad.*

in·suf·fi·cience [ˌinsəˈfiʃəns] *n.*〔罕〕= insufficiency.

in·suf·fi·cien·cy [ˌinsəˈfiʃənsi] *n.* ①不够,不足,不充分;不适当. ②机能不全〔尤指心阀闭锁不全〕. *the* ~ *of provisions* 粮食不足. *cardiac* ~ 心机能不全.

in·suf·fi·cient [ˌinsəˈfiʃənt] *a.* 不够的,不足的,不充分的;不适当的. **-ly** *ad.*

in·suf·flate [inˈsʌfleit] *vt.* ①吹进,吹上;喷注. ②【医】把(粉剂,气体等)吹入人体〔尤指肺部〕. ③【宗】对(受洗者)吹气以驱除妖魔〔一种仪式〕.

in·suf·fla·tion [ˌinsəˈfleiʃən] *n.* 吹入,吹上;吹入剂,吹入法. *mouth-to-mouth* ~ 对口吹气法. *oxygen* ~ 注氧法.

in·suf·fla·tor [ˈinsəfleitə] *n.* 吹入器;吹粉器;(使指纹显出的)指纹吹粉器;吹药器.

in·su·lar [ˈinsjulə] *a.* ①海岛的,岛国的,岛形的. ②岛民的,象岛民的. ③具有岛民特性的,偏狭的. ④孤立的,隔绝的,象岛似的. ⑤在岛上居住的,位于岛上的. ⑥【医】岛屿状的,散开的;【解】胰岛的,脑岛的. *an* ~ *climate* 海岛性气候. *an* ~ *fortress* 孤立无援的要塞.

in·su·lar·ism [ˈinsjulərizəm] *n.* = insularity.

in·su·lar·i·ty [ˌinsjuˈlæriti] *n.* 岛国性质;(思想、观点等的)偏狭性.

in·su·late [ˈinsjuleit] *vt.* ①隔离,使孤立. ②【物】使绝缘;使绝热. ③使成岛. *an* ~*d life* 孤独的生活. ~*d body* 被绝缘体. *(an)* ~*d wire* 【电】绝缘线. *insulating tape* 胶带.

in·su·la·tor [ˈinsjuleitə] *n.* ①隔离者. ②隔离物,隔振子,隔电子. ③【物】绝缘物,绝缘体,绝缘子;绝热体. *glass* ~ 玻璃绝缘体. *thermal [heat]* ~ 热绝缘体. *porcelain* ~ 瓷瓶,瓷绝缘子.

in·su·la·tion [ˌinsjuˈleiʃən] *n.* ①隔离,孤立. ②【物】绝缘;绝热. ~ *board* 隔音[绝热]板. ~ *material* 绝缘材料. ~ *resistance* 【电】绝缘电阻. *sound* ~ 声绝缘,隔声. *thermal* ~ 热绝缘,保温层. ~ *workshop* 保温车间.

in·su·lin [ˈinsjulin] *n.* 【生化】胰岛素. *bovine* ~ 牛胰岛素. *histone* ~ 组朊胰岛素. *man-made synthetic* ~ 人工合成胰岛素. *total synthetic crystalline* ~ 完全人工合成结晶胰岛素. ~ **shock** 【医】胰岛素休克.

in·sult [ˈinsʌlt] *n.* ①侮辱,凌辱. ②〔古〕攻击,袭击. ③损害. *enviromental* ~*s* 环境对人体的危害. ***add*** ~ ***to injury*** 伤害之外又加侮辱. ***offer an*** ~ ***to*** ... 侮辱…. ***put up with [swallow (down), pocket, take] an*** ~ 忍受侮辱. ***remark or action that*** ~***s*** 侮辱的言行. ***sit down under*** ~***s*** 甘受侮辱. — [inˈsʌlt] *vt.* 侮辱.

in·sult·ing [inˈsʌltiŋ] *a.* 侮辱的,无礼的. *use* ~ *language* 使用侮辱性语言. **-ly** *ad.*

in·su·per·a·ble [inˈsjuːpərəbl] *a.* ①不能克服的,难以越过的. ②不可战胜的,无敌的. *an* ~ *barrier* 无法逾越的障碍. ~ *heroes* 无敌的英雄. **-bil·i·ty** *n.* **-bly** *ad.*

in·sup·port·a·ble [ˌinsəˈpɔːtəbl] *a.* ①难堪的,难忍的,不能忍受的. ②无根据的,无理由的. ~ *charges* 无理的指责. **-bly** *ad.*

in·sup·press·i·ble [ˌinsəˈpresəbl] *a.* 难制服的,压抑不住的. **-bly** *ad.*

in·sur·a·bil·i·ty [inˌʃuərəˈbiliti] *n.* 可以保险,应当保险.

in·sur·a·ble [inˈʃuərəbl] *a.* 可以保险的,应当保险的. ~ *interest* 被保险利益. ~ *property* 可以接受保险的财产. **-a·bil·i·ty** *n.*

in·sur·ance [inˈʃuərəns] *n.* ①安全保障. ②保险,保险业. ③保险单(通称 ~ policy). ④保险费〔通称 permium〕. ⑤保险额. *provide* ~ *against floods* 为防洪提供安全措施. *accident* ~ 意外事故保险. *fire* ~ 火灾保险. *labour* ~ 劳动保险. *life* ~ 人寿保险. *marine* ~ 海上保险,水险. *term* ~ 定期保险. *whole [straight] life* ~ 终身保险. *an* ~ *agent* 保险代办所. *an* ~ *man* 保险推销员. ~ *business* 保险(事)业. *an* ~ *company* 保险公司. — *a.* 〔美俚〕(篮球赛等)稳胜对方的,胜券在握的.

in·sur·ant [inˈʃuərənt] *n.* 被保险人,受保人.

in·sure [inˈʃuə] *vt.* ①保险;给…保险. ②保障,为…提供保证. ~ *sb.'s property against fire* 给某人财产保火险. ~ *oneself [one's life] for £5,000* 给某人保寿险五千镑. ~ *sth. against loss at sea.* 给某物办海上保险. ~ *success* 保证成功. — *vi.* 投保,承保. ~ *against death* 保寿险. *the* ~*d* 被保险人,受保户. *an* ~*d letter* 保价信.

in·sur·er [inˈʃuərə] *n.* 承保人;保险公司.

in·sur·gence [inˈsəːdʒəns] *n.* ①起义,暴动,叛变行动.

in·sur·gen·cy [inˈsəːdʒənsi] *n.* ①起义,暴动,叛变行动[性质、状态]. ②= insurgence.

in·sur·gent [inˈsəːdʒənt] *a.* ①起义的,造反的,暴动的. ②(波涛)汹涌澎湃的. ~ *troops* 叛军. — *n.* 起义者,造反者,暴动者;〔美〕(政党的)反党分子. **-ly** *ad.*

in·sur·mount·a·bil·i·ty [ˌinsə(ː)ˌmauntəˈbiliti] *n.* 不可克服,难以逾越.

in·sur·mount·a·ble [ˌinsə(ː)ˈmauntəbl] *a.* 不可克服的,难以逾越的. **-bly** *ad.*

in·sur·rec·tion [ˌinsəˈrekʃən] *n.* 起义,叛乱,造反,暴动. *armed* ~ 武装起义. *rise in* ~ 起义,暴动. **-ist** *n.* 起义者,叛乱者.

in·sur·rec·tion·al [ˌinsəˈrekʃənəl] *a.* 起义的，叛乱的.
in·sur·rec·tion·ar·y [ˌinsəˈrekʃənəri] *a.* 起义的，叛乱的. — *n.* 起义者，叛乱者.
in·sus·cep·ti·ble [ˌinsəˈseptəbl] *a.* ①无感觉的，不受感动的；不易受…影响的 *(of, to)*. ②不容许…的. *a mind ~ to flattery* 不受奉承的人. *a disease ~ of medical treatment* 不能医治的病. *The clause is ~ of another interpretation.* 这一条文不能有其他解释. **-bil·i·ty** *n.* **-bly** *ad.*
in·swept [ˈinˌswept] *a.* (汽车等)前端窄狭的，流线型的.
in't [int] 〔古、诗〕= in it.
int. = ①interjection. ②intransitive. ③interest. ④interim. ⑤interior. ⑥internal. ⑦international. ⑧interpreter.
in·tact [inˈtækt] *a.* 〔作表语用〕未经触动的，未受损的，原封不动的，完整无损的. *keep [leave] sth. ~* 使某物保持原样，让某物原封不动. *keep our friendship ~.* 让我们的友谊地久天长. **-ness** *n.*
in·ta·gliat·ed [inˈtæljeitid] *a.* 凹雕的.
in·tagl·i·o [inˈtæliəu, -ˈtɑː-] *n.* *(pl. ~s, in·tagl·i* [inˈtɑːljiː]*)* 凹雕〔*cf.* relief, relievo〕；凹雕玉石〔*cf.* cameo〕. *~ printing* 凹板印刷. — *vt.* 凹雕.
in·take [ˈin-teik] *n.* ①吸入，纳入，收纳. ②进水口(*opp.* outlet)；输入端，(矿井的)进风巷道，通风孔. ③吸气，进气. ④【医】摄入量，摄取. ⑤纳入(数)量；【物】输入能量；【矿】进风量. ⑥〔英方〕(从沼泽等圈入的)围地，垦地. ⑦被收纳的东西，被吸收到团体[组织]里的人. *an ~ guide* 吸气导管. *~ of food* 食物摄取. *an ~ tower* 进水塔.
in·tan·gi·ble [inˈtændʒəbl] *a.* ①触摸不到的，无实体的，无形的. ②不可捉摸的，难以确定的，模糊的. *~ value* 无形价值. *an ~ asset* 无形财产. *~ ideas* 难以明白的概念. — *n.* 无形的东西，不可捉摸的东西. **-bil·i·ty** *n.* **-bly** *ad.*
in·tar·si·a [inˈtɑːsiə] *n.* 镶嵌细工〔尤指意大利文艺复兴时代象牙、金属等〕.
in·te·ger [ˈintidʒə] *n.* ①【数】整数 *(opp.* fraction*)*. ②完整的东西，整体.
in·te·ger vi·tae [ˈintidʒə ˈvaitiː] 无过失的；正直的.
in·te·gra·ble [ˈintigrəbl] *a.* ①可汇总的，可并合的. ②可聚合的，可并拢的. ③可得出总计的. ④可取消种族隔离的. ⑤【数】可求积分的.
in·te·gral [ˈintigrəl] *a.* ①完全的；缺一不可的，主要的. ②【数】整的，积分的. *an ~ steel plant* 综合钢铁厂. *an ~ part of* … 的一个主要部分. *an ~ whole* 整体. *~ equation* 积分方程. — *n.* 全体，整体；【数】积分. *definite ~* 定积分. *double ~* (二)重积分. *indefinite ~* 不定积分. *~* **calculus**【数】积分(学). **-i·ty** *n.* 完整性. **-ly** *ad.*
in·te·grand [ˈintigrænd] *n.*【数】被积函数，被积式.
in·te·grant [ˈintigrənt] *a.* = integral. *an ~ part* (构成)要素. — *n.* 成分，组成部分，要素.
in·te·graph [ˈintigrɑːf] *n.* 积分仪，积分描图仪，积分曲线仪，积分器.
in·te·grate [ˈintigreit] *vt.* ①使成整体，使并入，使一体化，使结合起来. ②〔英〕取消(学校的)种族隔离，使(黑人等)不受歧视. ③表示(面积、温度等的)总和. ④【数】求…的积分. *~ theory with practice* 理论联系实际. *~ the Negroes in this school.* 这个学校取消了对黑人的种族歧视. — *vi.* 与…结合起来，成一体 *(with)*. *A ~s with B.* A与B结合起来，AB成为一体 — [ˈintigrit] *a.* 完整的，完全的.
in·te·grat·ed [ˈintigreitid] *a.* 完整的，完全的. *an ~ iron and steel works* 钢铁联合企业. *an ~ oil company* 大型石油(联合)公司. *~* **circuit**【无】集成电路，积分电路. *~* **mill** 全能工厂，综合工厂. *~* **school** 兼收白人与黑人子弟的学校.
in·te·gra·tion [ˌintiˈgreiʃən] *n.* ①结合；综合；一体化. ②【心】整合(作用). ③【数】积分(法) *(opp.* differentiation*)*. ④【经】(产业的)集中. ⑤〔美〕取消种族隔离；给以种族上的平等待遇. *~ by parts*【数】部分积分法.
in·te·gra·tion·ism [ˌintiˈgreiʃənizəm] *n.* 取消种族隔离主义. **-ist** *n.*, *a.* 主张取消种族隔离主义者(的).
inte·gra·tive [ˈintigreitiv] *a.* 综合的，整[一]体化的；可以并合的；可以结合的；【数】可求积分的.
in·te·gra·tor [ˈintigreitə] *n.* ①综合者. ②【数】求积器，积分仪. ③【无】积分电路 (= *~* circuit).
in·teg·ri·ty [inˈtegriti] *n.* ①诚实，正直. ②完全，完整. *a man of ~* 正直的人. *moral ~* 骨气，气节. *people of unyielding ~* 硬汉. *territorial ~* 领土完整. ***in its ~*** 完整，原封未动.
in·teg·u·ment [inˈtegjumənt] *n.* ①(动植物的)覆盖物(如皮肤，皮膜，壳荚，果皮，珠被等). ②一般覆盖物. **-a·ry** *a.* 外皮的，外皮般的.
in·tel·lect [ˈintilekt] *n.* ①理智，才智，智力. ②(集合的或个别的)明智者，有才智的人. ③〔古、俚〕〔*pl.*〕理性. *a man of ~* 有才智的人. *the ~(s) of the age* 当代有才智的人士，当代的知识界.
in·tel·lec·tion [ˌintiˈlekʃən] *n.* 理解，智力活动.
in·tel·lec·tive [ˌintiˈlektiv] *a.* ①理性的，智力的. ②有理智的，聪明的.
in·tel·lec·tu·al [ˌintiˈlektjuəl] *a.* ①智力的，理智的. ②用脑筋的，需智力的. ③理性的，凭理智行事的，打动别人理智的. *the ~ powers [faculties]* 智能. *an ~ process* 理智作用. *the ~ class* 知识分子阶层. *~ employments [pursuits]* 脑力工作. — *n.* 知识分子. *highly qualified ~s* 高级知识分子. **-ism** *n.* 智力活动；【哲】唯理智论. **-ist** *n.* 过分强调智力活动的人；唯理智论者. **-ly** *ad.*
in·tel·lec·tu·al·is·tic [ˌintiˌlektjuəˈlistik] *a.*【哲】唯智论的，唯智主义的.
in·tel·lec·tu·al·i·ty [ˈintiˌlektjuˈæliti] *n.* 理智，理智性.
in·tel·lec·tu·al·ize [ˌintiˈlektjuəlaiz] *vt.* 赋与理智，使有理智，使理智化. — *vi.* 推理，思考. **-al·i·za·tion** *n.* 理智化.
in·tel·li·gence [inˈtelidʒəns] *n.* ①智力，智慧，才智，聪明. ②通知，消息. ③情报，谍报，情报机构. ④(导引)信息，(瞄准)信号. ⑤【宗】〔常 *pl.*〕神、天使. *~ quotient* 智商，智力商数 (略作 I. Q.)〔心理学家进行智力测验的术语〕. *an ~ test* 智力测验. *exchange a look of ~* 递眼色. *give ~ of* 通知. *receive ~ of* 接到通知. *~ agent* 情报员. *~ bureau [department]* 情报局，情报处. *~ centre* 情报所，情报中心. *~ data* 情报资料. *~ office* 情报处[局]；〔美〕职业介绍所. *~ officer* 情报部将校. *communications ~*【军】电信侦察. *current ~*【军】动态情报. *the Supreme I ~* 上帝. *~* **signal**【火箭】信息，信号.
in·tel·li·genc·er [inˈtelidʒənsə] *n.* ①报导者，通信员. ②情报员；间谍.
in·tel·li·gent [inˈtelidʒənt] *a.* ①理解力强的，有才智的，聪明的，明智的. ②可执行部分电脑工作的. *an ~ child* 聪明的孩子. *~ answers to questions* 对问题聪明的答复. *an ~ reader* 聪明的读者. **-ly** *ad.*
in·tel·li·gen·tial [inˌteliˈdʒenʃəl] ①智力的，理智的. ②传送情报的. *~ channels* 情报的渠道.
in·tel·li·gent·si·a [inˌteliˈgentsiə], **in·tel·li·gent·zi·a** [-ˈdʒen-] *n.* 知识分子. *the ~* 〔通常为集合词单数〕知识分子，〔总称〕知识界.
in·tel·li·gi·bil·i·ty [inˌtelidʒəˈbiliti] *n.* ①可理解性. ②可理解的事物.
in·tel·li·gi·ble [inˈtelidʒəbl] *a.* ①可以理解的，易于了解的，明白的. ②【哲】只能用智力了解的，概念的. *~ speech* 明快的言语. *~ pronunciation* 清晰的发音. *make*

oneself ～讲得使人了解. **-bly** *ad.*

In·tel·sat [ˈintelsæt] *n.* ①国际电信卫星组织. ②国际通信卫星.

in·tem·per·ance [inˈtempərəns] *n.* ①无节制,放纵;过度,激烈. ②暴饮,酗酒.

in·tem·per·ate [inˈtempərit] *a.* ①无节制的, 放纵的; 过度的,激烈的. ②喝酒过度的,酗酒的. ③(气候等)酷烈的. ～ *ambition* 狂妄的野心. ～ *language* 狂言. ～ *habits* 酒癖. *an* ～ *man* 酒徒. ～ *wind* 烈风. *an* ～ *zone* 热[寒]带 *(opp. temperate zone)*. ～ *weather* 恶劣的天气. **-ly** *ad.*

in·tend [inˈtend] *vt.* ①想,打算 *(to do)*. ②企图. ③打算使…成为. ④意思是,意指. *I* ～ *to go home.* 我想回家. *I* ～*ed an ode.* 我打算写一首颂歌. *I* ～ *it as a stop-gap.* 我想拿它凑数. *Was this* ～*ed?* 这是故意的吗? *He* ～*s no harm.* 他没有恶意. *The gift was* ～*ed for you.* 这个礼物是要送给你的. *What do you* ～ *by your words?* 你说这些话是什么意思呢?

in·tend·ance [inˈtendəns] *n.* ①监督, 管理. ②行政管理部门.

in·tend·an·cy [inˈtendənsi] *n.* ①监督人[管理人]的职责. ②监督[管理]人员. ③(殖民主义者在南美的)监督管辖区.

in·tend·ant [inˈtendənt] *n.* ①监督人,管理人;经理. ②【史】(法、西、葡封建王朝的)州长. ③(殖民主义者在南美的)地方行政长官.

in·tend·ed [inˈtendid] *a.* ①预期的, 打算中的. ②有意的,故意的. ③已订婚的. *bring on* ～ *results* 带来预期的结果. *an* ～ *insult* 蓄意的侮辱. *one's* ～ *wife* 未婚妻. — *n.* 〔口〕〔加用物主代名词〕已订婚的人. *my* ～ 我的未婚妻[夫].

in·tend·ing [inˈtendiŋ] *a.* 〔主英〕预期的; 未来的; 将来的.

in·tend·ment [inˈtendmənt] *n.* ①〔古〕目的; 目标; 企图. ②(法律的)含义.

in·ten·er·ate [inˈtenəreit] *vt.* **(-at·ed; -at·ing)** 〔罕〕使变柔软. **-a·tion** *n.*

intens. = ①intensified. ②intensifier. ③intensive.

in·tense [inˈtens] *a.* **(-er; -est)** ①激烈的,强烈的;紧张的. ②热烈的, 热情的, 认真的. ③【摄】(底片)明暗度强的. *an* ～ *light* 强烈的灯光. ～ *cold* 严寒. ～ *heat* 酷热. ～ *pain* 剧痛. *the* ～ *sun* 烈日. *an* ～ *person* 热情认真的人. *an* ～ *life* 奋发图强的生活. ～ *study* 认真的研究. **-ly** *ad.* **-ness** *n.*

in·ten·si·fi·ca·tion [inˌtensifiˈkeiʃən] *n.* ①使强烈,加强,强化. ②【摄】加厚 *(opp.* reduction*)*.

in·ten·si·fi·er [inˈtensifaiə] *n.* ①【摄】增厚剂;【物】增强剂;【机】增强器. ②照明装置;【电】增辉电路. *spark* ～【机】火花增强器.

in·ten·si·fy [inˈtensifai] *vt.* ①使强烈,加强;加剧. ②【摄】加厚(底片阴纹). — *vi.* 强化,变猛烈.

in·ten·sion [inˈtenʃən] *n.* ①强度, 紧张, 加强. ②专心致志, 努力. ③【逻】内包. ④【数】内涵. *(opp.* extension*)*. ⑤【农】集约经营.

in·ten·si·ty [inˈtensiti] *n.* ①(思想、感情的)强烈,激烈. ②强度. ③【摄】(底片的)明暗度. *go mad at the* ～ *of one's grief.* 因为过度悲伤而发疯. ～ *of illumination* 照度,光照强度. *bombardment* ～ 炮火强度. *current* ～【电】电流强度. *labour* ～ 劳动强度. *luminous* ～ 光度. *radiant* ～【物】辐射强度.

in·ten·sive [inˈtensiv] *a.* ①加强的; 集中的; 深入细致的,彻底的. ②【语】加强词义的. ③【农】精耕细作的, 集约的. ④【逻】内包的. ⑤【医】渐进的. *an* ～ *bombardment* 密集炮击. *an* ～ *study* 彻底的研究. ～ *reading* 精读 (*opp.* extensive reading 泛读). ～ *adverb* 强义副词(如 very, awfully, terribly 等). ～ *agriculture [farming]* 细耕农业, 集约农业. ～ *(and careful) cultivation* 精耕细作. — *n.* ①加强器; 加强剂. ②【语】强义词[前缀]. ～ **culture** 集约耕作. ～ **inoculation** 【医】渐进接种. **-ly** *ad.* **-ness** *n.*

in·tent [inˈtent] *n.* ①意图; 目的. ②意义,含义. *criminal* ～【法】犯罪意图. *use one's leisure time to good* ～ 有益地利用空闲时间. *with good [malicious]* ～ 好[恶]意地. *with murderous* ～ *behind one's smiles* 笑里藏刀. *with* ～ *to defraud* 存心欺诈. ***to all*** ～***s and purposes*** 无论从哪一点来看,事实上,实际上 (*The revised edition is to all* ～*s and purposes a new book.* 修订本简直是本新书). — *a.* ①目不转睛的, 集中的;热心的. ②专心致志的,坚决的. *an* ～ *look* 凝视. *an* ～ *person* 热心的人. *be* ～ *on one's work* 一心一意地工作. **-ly** *ad.* **-ness** *n.*

in·ten·tion [inˈtenʃən] *n.* ①意向; 意图,目的; 打算. ②〔口〕〔*pl.*〕结婚的意图. ③意义, 意旨. ④【逻】概念. ⑤【医】愈合. *a person of good* ～*s* 好心人. *by* ～ 故意. *have no* ～ *of doing* 无意做…. *She began to worry that her boy friend's* ～*s might not be serious.* 她开始担心她的男朋友打算结婚不是认真的. *the* ～ *of a clause* 条文的意旨. *heal by first* ～【医】第一期愈合. *heal by second* ～【医】第二期愈合. *with good* ～*s* = *with the best of* ～*s* 好心好意地,诚心. ***with the*** ～ ***of*** 打算…, 以…为目的. ***without*** ～ 无意中,不是故意地.

in·ten·tion·al [inˈtenʃənəl] *a.* 有意(识)的,故意的 *(opp.* accidental*)*. **-ly** *ad.*

in·ten·tioned [inˈtenʃənd] *a.* 有意的,故意的. ★ 前面常加连字符号 (-) 与其它词在一起形成复合词: *well-*～ 善[好]意的. *maliciously(ill)-*～ 恶意的,蓄意的.

in·ter [inˈtəː] *vt.* 埋葬. ～ *a dead body into the earth* 把尸首埋起来.

in·ter [ˈintə] *prep.* 〔L.〕在中间, 在内, 互相. ～ ***alia*** [ˈintə ˈeiliə] 除了别的事物以外, 尤其. ～ ***nos*** [ˈnəus] 莫对别人讲, 秘密地. ～***se*** [-ˈsiː] 秘密; 在同品种之间(交配). ～ ***vivos*** [ˈvaivəus]【法】在生存者当中.

inter- *comb. f.* 表示"在…中","在…间","在…内";"相互": *interact, interˈcity.*

in·ter·act[1] [ˌintərˈækt] *vi.* 相互作用, 相互影响. **-active** *a.*

in·ter·act[2] [ˈintərækt] *n.* = ***entr'acte.***

in·ter·act·ant [ˌintəˈæktənt] *n.* 相互作用物〔尤指化学反应物〕.

in·ter·ac·tion [ˌintərˈækʃən] *n.* ①相互作用, 相互影响. ②【空】干扰. ～ *of electrons*【物】电子的相互作用. *jet-shock* ～ 射流-激波干扰.

in·ter·ac·tive [ˌintəːˈæktiv] *a.* 相互作用的, 相互影响的.

in·ter·a·li·a [ˌintəˈeiliə] *ad.* 〔L.〕在其它的事物之中; 首先,尤其.

in·ter·a·li·os [ˌintəˈeiliəus] 〔L.〕在其余的人中, 在其他的人中.

in·ter-Al·lied [ˌintə(ː)rəˈlaid] *a.* (第一次大战时)协约国间的.

in·ter-A·mer·i·can [ˌintərəˈmerikən] *a.* 美洲国家之间的. ～ *Development Bank* 泛美开发银行.

in·ter·blend [ˌintə(ː)ˈblend] *vt., vi.* **(**～**ed, -blent)** 混合; 相混.

in·ter·bor·ough [ˈintə(ː)ˈbʌrə] *a.* (各)自治村镇之间的,(各)独立区之间的. — *n.* 自治村镇之间的交通工具〔地铁、电车等〕.

in·ter·brain [ˈintəbrein] *n.* 间脑〔脊椎动物前脑的后部〕(= diencephalon).

in·ter·breed [ˌintəˈbriːd] *vt., vi.* = hybridize.

in·ter·ca·lar·y [inˈtəːkələri] *a.* ①(历法)闰的. ②插入的,添加的,夹层的. *an* ～ *day* 闰日(二月二十九日). *an* ～ *month* 闰月. *an* ～ *year* 闰年(二月). *an* ～ *plate* 加插板. ～ *strata*【地】夹层.

in·ter·ca·late [inˈtəːkəleit] *vt.* ①设置(闰日[闰月]等).

②插入；添加．**-la·tion** *n.*

in·ter·cede [ˌintə(:)ˈsi:d] *vi.* ①调停，调解．②代为请求，说情．～ *with the teacher for sb.* 为某人向老师说情．

in·ter·cel·lu·lar [ˌintə(:)ˈseljulə] *a.*【生】(细)胞间的．～ *space* 胞间隙．～ *substance* 胞间质．

in·ter·cept [ˌintə(:)ˈsept] *vt.* ①拦截，截击(敌军)，截断(光、热、水等)，阻止，中止．②窃听，侦听．③交切，相交，交叉．④【数】(在两点或两线间)截取．～ *a messenger* 阻拦信使．～ *a forward pass* 阻止前进．— *n.* ①拦截，截击．②窃听，侦听．③【数】截距，截段．～ *heading*【军】截击航向．*an* ～ *mission*【军】截击任务．*an* ～ *officer*【军】截击军官．*an* ～ *station*【军】侦听台．～ *of a line [plane]* 线[面]的截距．**-tive** *a.*

in·ter·cept·er, in·ter·cep·tor [ˌintə(:)ˈseptə] *n.* ①拦截者，阻止者．②【空】遮断器；阻止器；扰流板．③【军】截击机，拦击机；拦截器；拦截导弹．④截击机雷达台，窃听器．～ *plate* 翼缝扰流板．

in·ter·cep·tion [ˌintə(:)ˈsepʃən] *n.* ①拦截；截击；遮断，阻止；截取．②窃听，侦听；【空】雷达侦察．*long-range* ～【空】远距离雷达侦察．*blind* ～【空】(用仪表)盲目拦截．*ground-controlled* ～【军】地面控制截击(设备)．

in·ter·ces·sion [ˌintəˈseʃən] *n.* ①调解，说情．②【宗】代人祈祷．***make an ～ to A for B*** 向某甲为某乙说情．***through sb.'s*** ～ 经某人调解．**-al** *a.*

in·ter·ces·sor [ˌintəˈsesə] *n.* ①调解者，说情者．②【宗】代理主教．

in·ter·ces·so·ry [ˌintəˈsesəri] *a.* 调解的，说情的；代人祈祷的．

in·ter·change [ˌintə(:)ˈtʃeindʒ] *vt.* ①交换，互换．②交替(位置等)．③使更迭发生；轮流进行．～ *civilities* 相互问候．～ *gifts* 互赠礼品．～ *cares with pleasures* 有苦有乐．～ *labour and repose* 劳逸兼顾．～ *letters* 互通信件．～ *opinions [view]* 交换意见．— *vi.* 交替发生；交换位置．— [ˈintə(:)tʃeindʒ] *n.* ①交换，交替．②【建】互通式立体交叉，道路立体枢纽．*an* ～ *of personnel* 人事更迭．

in·ter·change·a·ble [ˌintə(:)ˈtʃeindʒəbl] *a.* 可交换的，可更替的；可互换的．**-bil·i·ty, -ness** *n.* **-bly** *ad.*

in·ter·cit·y [ˌintəˈsiti] *a.* 城市间的，市际的．*an* ～ *bus* 市际公共汽车．

in·ter·class [ˈintə(:)klɑ:s] *a.* 年级之间的．*an* ～ *basketball tournament* 年级之间进行的篮球赛．

in·ter·clav·i·cle [ˌintəˈklævikl] *n.*【解】锁间骨；(龟的)锁间骨甲．**-vic·ular** [-kləˈvikjulə] *a.*

in·ter·col·lege [ˌintəˈkɔlidʒ] *a.* = intercollegiate.

in·ter·col·le·gi·ate [ˌintə(:)kəˈli:dʒiit] *a.* 大学[学院]间的．*an* ～ *regatta* 院际[校际]船赛．

in·ter·co·lo·ni·al [ˌintə(:)kəˈləunjəl] *a.* 殖民地间的．

in·ter·co·lum·nar [ˌintə(:)kəˈlʌmnə]【建】*a.* 柱间的．

in·ter·co·lum·ni·a·tion [ˈintə(:)kəˌlʌmniˈeiʃən] *n.*【建】分柱法．

in·ter·com [ˈintə(:)kɔm] *n.* (军舰、飞机等内的)通讯装置，内部通讯联络系统．

in·ter·com·mu·nal [ˌintəˈkɔmjunl] *a.* 社团之间的，社会团体间所共有的．

in·ter·com·mu·ni·cate [ˌintə(:)kəˈmju:nikeit] *vi.* 互通；互相联系，互相通信．*intercommunicating rooms* 互通的房间．*intercommunicating set* 内部互通电话机．

in·ter·com·mu·ni·ca·tion [ˌintə(:)kəˌmju:niˈkeiʃən] *n.* 互相联系，互相通信；内部通信联络．

in·ter·com·mun·ion [ˌintə(:)kəˈmju:njən] *n.* ①【宗】各教派间共同举行的圣餐．②各教派之间的思想感情交流．

in·ter·com·mu·ni·ty [ˌintə(:)kəˈmju:niti] *n.* 公用，共有，共同参加．— *a.* 共同体间的，共通性．

in·ter·con·nect [ˌintə(:)kəˈnekt] *vt., vi.* (使)互相联系．*be closely* ～ 相互紧密地联系在一起．

in·ter·con·nec·tion [ˌintə(:)kəˈnekʃən] *n.* 相互联系．

in·ter·con·ti·nen·tal [ˌintəˌkɔntiˈnentl] *a.* 洲际的；(飞机、火箭导弹等的)可跨洲飞行的．*an* ～ *(ballistic) missile* 洲际(弹道)导弹．*an* ～ *ballistic rocket* 洲际弹道火箭．

in·ter·con·ver·sion [ˌintə(:)kənˈvə:ʃən] *n.*【化】互变(现象)．

in·ter·con·ver·ti·ble [ˌintə(:)kənˈvə:təbl] *a.* 可互相转换的．**-bil·i·ty** *n.* **-bly** *ad.*

in·ter·cool·er [ˌintə(:)ˈku:lə] *n.*【机】中间冷却器．

in·ter·cos·tal [ˌintə(:)ˈkɔstl] *a.* ①【解】肋间的．②【植】生于叶脉间的．～ *muscles* 肋间筋．～ *nerves* 肋间神经．— *n.*【解】肋间肌．**-ly** *ad.*

in·ter·course [ˈintə(:)kɔ:s] *n.* ①交际，来往；相互关系．②精神上的交换，神交，灵交．③【生】交合 *commercial [trade]* ～ 通商，商业关系．*diplomatic* ～ 外交往来．*friendly* ～ 友好往来，交际．*social* ～ 社交．*have [hold]* ～ *with sb.* 和某人交际．*illicit* ～ 私通．*sexual* ～ 性交．

in·ter·crop [ˌintəˈkrɔp] *vt., vi.* ***(-crop·ped, -crop·ping)*** 间作，间种．— [ˈintəkrɔp] *n.* 间种作物．

in·ter·cross [ˌintə(:)ˈkrɔs] *vt., vi.* ①(使)交叉．②(使)杂交．— *n.* 异种交配；杂种．

in·ter·crys·tal·line [ˌintə(:)ˈkristəlain] *a.* 晶粒间的．～ *fracture*【地】晶间破裂．～ *rupture*【物】(晶)粒间断裂．

in·ter·cul·tur·al [ˌintə(:)ˈkʌltʃərəl] *a.* 在不同文化的人们中间的．

in·ter·cur·rent [ˌintə(:)ˈkʌrənt] *a.* ①在过程中发生的，介入的．②【医】间发的；介入的，并发的．*an* ～ *disease* 间发病．**-ly** *ad.*

in·ter·de·nom·i·na·tion·al [ˌintədiˌnɔmiˈneiˌʃənl] *a.*【宗】在各教派之间的；各教派共有的；涉及不同教派的．

in·ter·den·tal [ˌintə(:)ˈdentl] *a.* ①齿间的．②【语音】齿间音的，舌齿音的〔如 [θ]〕．

in·ter·de·part·men·tal [ˌintə(:)diˌpɑ:tˈmentl] *a.* 部门之间的．**-ly** *ad.*

in·ter·de·pend [ˌintə(:)diˈpend] *vi.* 互相依赖，互相依存．

in·ter·de·pend·ence, in·ter·de·pend·en·cy [ˌintə(:)diˈpendəns, -si] *n.* 互相依赖，互相依存．

in·ter·de·pend·ent [ˌintə(:)diˈpendənt] *a.* 互相依赖的，互相依存的．**-ly** *ad.*

in·ter·dict [ˌintə(:)ˈdikt] *vt.* ①禁止，制止．②【军】闭锁，阻断(敌人通路)．③【宗】停止教权．～ *sb. from doing sth.* 禁止某人做某事．～ *sth. to sb.* 禁止某人使用某物．— [ˈintə(:)dikt] *n.* ①禁止，制止．②禁令．③【宗】停止教权的命令．*lay a town under an* ～ 停止某一城市的宗教活动．**-tor** *n.* 禁止者．

in·ter·dic·tion [ˌintə(:)ˈdikʃən] *n.* ①禁止；制止．②【军】闭锁，阻断．*a barrage of* ～ 封锁火力．～ *fire* 远距离拦阻射击．**-to·ry** *a.*

in·ter·dig·i·tate [ˌintə(:)ˈdidʒiteit] *vt.* 两手手指交叉锁住．

in·ter·dis·ci·pli·nar·y [ˌintə(:)ˈdisiplinəri] *a.* 涉及两种以上训练的；涉及两门以上学科的．*an* ～ *approach to cultural history* 有关文化史的多方面探讨．

in·ter·est [ˈintrist, ˈintərist] *n.* ①利害关系，利害；〔常 *pl.*〕利益．②关心，趣味；感兴趣的事，兴趣；爱好，好奇心．③重要性；势力；影响；援引，引线．④利息．⑤权利；股份，所有权；事业；财产．⑥行业．*the public* ～*s* 公众利益．*It is to your* ～ *to give up smoking.* 戒烟对你有好处．*know one's own* ～*s* 很精明，会打算．*look after one's own* ～*s* 顾自己利益．*take the* ～*s of the whole into account* 顾全大局．*vested* ～*s* 既得利益．*feel [have, take] an* ～ *in sth.* 对某事感兴趣．*feel [have, take] no* ～ *in sth.* 对某事不感兴趣．*it is of* ～ *to note that* 值得注意的是；饶有

兴趣的是. *place of* ~ 名胜. *a matter of considerable* ~ 相当重要的事. *a matter of little* ~ 不大重要的事. *have* ~ *with sb.* 对某人产生影响. *lose one's* ~ *with sb.* 对某人失去影响. *through* ~ 通过别人的援引. *annual* ~ 年利. *daily* ~ 日息. *compound* ~ 复利. *simple* ~ 单利. *buy an* ~ *in* 作…的股东,买…的股票. *the business* ~ 商业界. *the landed* ~ 地主. *the money* ~ 金融业者. *the shipping* ~ 航运界. ***in the* ~*(s) of*** 为了…的利益,为了. ***lose*** ~ 不再感兴趣,不再引起兴趣. ***make*** ~ ***with sb.*** (从利害关系出发)施加影响于某人. ***take (an)*** ~ ***in*** 对…感兴趣. ***sink one's own*** ~***s*** 不考虑自己的利益. ***with*** ~ ①带着兴趣(*hear it with* ~ 津津有味地听). ②附利息;加重(*return a blow with* ~ 加重还击). ③通过某种关系(*obtain a position with* ~ 通过某种关系取得职位). — *vt.* 使发生兴趣,使关心,使注意;使生关系,使有份儿. *be* ~*ed in sth.* 对某事有兴趣. *Can I* ~ *you in a game of golf?* 你有兴趣和我打高尔夫球吗? ~ *oneself in an enterprise* 为某项事业奔走. ~ *sb. in an enterprise* 使某人加入某项事业. *the person* ~*ed* 关系人. ~**-free** *a.* 无息的 (*an* ~*-free loan* 无息贷款). ~ **group** 利益集团.

in·ter·est·ed [ˈintristid] *a.* ①对…感兴趣的,有趣味的 *(in)*. ②有关系的,有份儿的,有利害关系的. ③为私利打算的,偏私的. *be* ~ *in music* 爱好音乐. ~ *spectators* 感兴趣的观众. *with an* ~ *look* 带着感兴趣的样子. *the* ~ *parties* 有关的当事人. *the person* ~ 关系人. ~ *motives* 不纯洁的动机. ~ *witness* 偏心的证人. **-ly** *ad.* **-ness** *n.*

in·ter·est·ing [ˈintristiŋ] *a.* 引起兴趣的,有趣的. *in an* ~ *condition [situation]* 〔英〕有孕,有喜. ~ *conversation* 有趣味的谈话. **-ly** *ad.*

in·ter·face [ˈintə(:)ˌfeis] *n.* 分界面,两个独立体系的相交处. — *vt.* *(-faced, -fac·ing)* 把界面缝合.

in·ter·fa·cial [ˌintə(:)ˈfeiʃəl] *a.* ①界面的,面际的. ②界面角的. ~ **angle**【地】面交角. ~ **tension**【物】面际张力.

in·ter·faith [ˈintə(:)ˌfeiθ] *a.* 在信仰不同的人之间的,涉及各种信仰者的.

in·ter·fere [ˌintəˈfiə] *vi.* ①(利害、要求等)抵触,冲突 *(with)*. ②干涉,干预;调停,排解. ③妨碍,打扰. ④有害于. ⑤【物】干扰. ⑥(马等行走、奔跑时)一脚碰在另一脚上. ⑦(橄榄球赛中)阻挡,犯规撞人. ⑧【法】对发明专利权提起诉讼. *interests interfering with each other* 互相冲突的利害关系. ~ *in private concerns* 干涉他人私事. *Don't* ~ *with him.* 别打扰他. *I shall go tomorrow, if nothing* ~*s.* 如果没有妨碍,我明天就走. *Sedentary habits often* ~ *with health.* 长坐不动的习惯往往有害于身体.

in·ter·fer·ence [ˌintəˈfiərəns] *n.* ①冲突,抵触. ②干涉,干预. ③妨碍,打扰,阻碍物. ④【物】干扰;干涉. *linguistic* ~ 本族语对外语学习的干扰. *stop* ~ *from outside* 制止外来干涉. ***run*** ~ ***for*** (橄榄球赛中)保护(带球者)以防对方抢球. ~ **colours** 干涉色. ~ **wave** 干涉波.

in·ter·fe·ren·tial [ˌintəfəˈrenʃəl] *a.*【物】干涉的,干扰的.

in·ter·fer·ing [ˌintəˈfiəriŋ] *a.* 干涉的,多管闲事的;互相冲突的;干扰的.

in·ter·fer·om·e·ter [ˌintəfiˈrɔmitə] *n.*【物】干涉仪,干扰计. **-met·ric** [-fiərəˈmetrik] *a.* **-e·try** *n.*

in·ter·fer·on [ˌintə(:)ˈfiərɔn] *n.*【生化】干扰素.

in·ter·fer·tile [ˌintəˈfə:tail] *a.* 可混种繁殖的,可杂交的. **-til·i·ty** [-fəˈtiliti] *n.*

in·ter·flow [ˌintə(:)ˈfləu] *vi.* 合流,互通. — [ˈintə(:)fləu] *n.* 合流,互通. *the* ~ *of commodities between the urban and rural areas* 城乡之间的商品交流.

in·ter·flu·ent [inˈtə:fluənt] *a.* 交流的,流在中间的.

in·ter·fluve [ˈintə(:)flu:v] *n.*【地】河间地;江河分水区.

in·ter·fold [ˌintəˈfəuld] *vt., vi.* 折叠.

in·ter·fuse [ˌintə(:)ˈfju:z] *vt.* 使渗入;使混入;混合;使充满. — *vi.* 混合,融合.

in·ter·fu·sion [ˌintə(:)ˈfju(:)ʒən] *n.* 渗入;混合,融合.

in·ter·ga·lac·tic [ˌintəgəˈlæktik] *a.*【天】存在于星系际的,发生于星系际的. ~ *space* 星系际空间.

in·ter·gen·er·a·tion·al [ˌintə(:)ˌdʒenəˈreiʃənl] *a.* 存在于两代[数代]人之间的.

in·ter·gla·cial [ˌintəˈgleisjəl] *a.*【地】形成于两个间冰期间的;发生于两个间冰期间的.

in·ter·grade [ˌintə(:)ˈgreid] *vi.* *(-grad·ed; -grad·ing)* 渐次变形,逐渐融合. — [ˈintə(:)greid] *n.* 间渡. **-da·tion** [-greiˈdeiʃən] *n.*

in·ter·group [ˈintə(:)ˈgru:p] *a.* 集团之间的;涉及集团之间的〔尤指不同种族之间的〕.

in·ter·growth [ˈintə(:)grəuθ] *n.*【物】共生,交互生长.

in·ter·im [ˈintərim] *n.* ①暂时,临时. ②临时协定. ③〔the I-〕【史】(宗教改革时的)临时敕令. *in the* ~ 在间歇的当儿,在过渡期间. — *a.* 临时的,暂时的,期中的. *an* ~ *dividend* (未决算前的)期中股利. *an* ~ *government* 过渡政府. *an* ~ *council* 临时议会, *an* ~ *report* 中期报告,临时性报告. *an* ~ *trial* 临时试验;期中试验. *an* ~ *certificate* 临时证件.

in·te·ri·or [inˈtiəriə] *a.* ①内的;内部的,室内的 *(opp.* exterior*)*. ②内地的. ③国内的 *(opp.* foreign*)*. ④内面的,内心的,秘密的. ~ *guards*【军】内卫兵. *operate on* ~ *lines*【军】内线作战. *an* ~ *city* 内城. ~ *trade* 国内贸易. *an* ~ *cabinet* 秘密内阁. — *n.* ①内部,内景. ②内地. ③内务,内政. ④内心,本性. *the* ~ *of a house* 室内. *travel in the* ~ 内地旅行. *the U.S. Department of the I-* 美国内政部 (英国为 Home office). *the Minister of the I-* (法德意等国的)内政部长. *the Secretary of the I-* 〔美〕内政部长. ~ **angle**【数】内角. ~ **decoration** ①室内装饰,室内摆设. ②室内装饰术,室内装饰业. ~ **decorator** 室内装饰家(工人,师父). **-ly** *ad.*

in·te·ri·or·ize [inˈtiəriəraiz] *vt.* *(-iz·ed, -iz·ing)* 使(观念、道德标准等)深入内心. **-i·za·tion** [inˌti:əriəraiˈzeiʃən] *n.*

interj. = interjection.

in·ter·ja·cent [ˌintə(:)ˈdʒeisənt] *a.* 处在中间的.

in·ter·ject [ˌintə(:)ˈdʒekt] *vt.* 突然插入,插话,插嘴说. ~ *a question* 突然插入问题.

in·ter·jec·tion [ˌintə(:)ˈdʒekʃən] *n.* ①突然的叫声,感叹. ②【语法】感叹词〔如 oh, ah, alas 等〕. ③插入,插入物.

in·ter·jec·tion·al [ˌintə(:)ˈdʒekʃənl] *a.* 叫声的,感叹的;感叹词的;插入的,插入语的. **-ly** *ad.*

in·ter·jec·tor [ˌintə(:)ˈdʒektə] *n.* 插入者,插入物.

in·ter·jec·to·ry [ˌintə(:)ˈdʒektəri] *a.* = interjectional.

in·ter·lace [ˌintə(:)ˈleis] *vt.* 使交织,使组合,使交错 *(with)*. ~*d branches* 交错的树枝. *be* ~*d with another thing* 与另一事物交织在一起. ~*d scanning*【电视】飞跃扫描,隔行扫描. — *vi.* 交织,交错,夹杂. *interlacing arches*【建】交叉拱门.

in·ter·lace·ment [ˌintəˈleismənt] *n.* 组合,交加,交杂,交织.

in·ter·lam·i·nate [ˌintəˈlæmineit] *vt.* *(-nat·ed; -nat·ing)* ①插于薄片间. ②置于交错薄片间. **-na·tion** *n.*

in·ter·lard [ˌintə(:)ˈlɑ:d] *vt.* ①以肥肉等加于(待煮的食物). ②使混杂,在…中插入不相干的东西. ~ *one's speech with foreign words* 在讲话中夹杂外国词儿. **-ment** *n.*

in·ter·lay [ˌintəˈlei] *vt.* *(-laid* [-leid]*;-lay·ing)* 置于其中.

in·ter·lay·er [ˈintə(:)ˌleiə] *n.*【建】夹层,间层;【物】界层,隔层.

in·ter·leaf [ˈintəˌli:f] *n.* *(pl. -leaves)* ①中间层,夹层. ②夹入书页中的空白纸. ③夹页上印〔写〕的东西. — *vt.* = interleave.

in·ter·leave [ˌintə(ː)ˈliːv] *vt.* *(-left)* ①使隔行;使交织;交替,交插. ②在…插入空白纸;在(书页)间装订衬纸. ③【电视】隔行(扫描).

in·ter·line, in·ter·line·ate [ˌintə(ː)ˈlain, ˌintə(ː)ˈliniːeit] *vt.* ①写在…的行间,印在…的行间. ②隔行书写,隔行印刷. ③在(衣服)面子和里子之间加内衬. ~ *notes on pages* 在版面的行间加上注释. ~ *a translation in a text* 在正文的行间插入译文. *a proof* ~*d with corrections* 在行间加有修改的校样. ~ *a garment with an inner lining* 衣服里面加上内衬. **-a·tion** *n.*

in·ter·lin·e·ar [ˌintə(ː)ˈliniə] *a.* ①写在[印在]行间的. ②一本书用不同的文字隔行对照印出的. ~ *notes* 行间注释. *a Latin text with an* ~ *translation* 一本逐行对照翻译的拉丁原文书. **-ly** *ad.*

In·ter·lin·gua [ˌintəˈliŋgwə] *n.* 拉丁国际语〔以拉丁语所派生的语言为主创造的一种文字,便于国际上使用,尤其在科技方面〕.

in·ter·lin·ing [ˈintəˈlainiŋ] *n.* ①衣服衬里. ②衣服里衬布料.

in·ter·link [ˌintə(ː)ˈliŋk] *vt.* 把…互相联系起来. — *n.* 连环.

in·ter·lock [ˌintə(ː)ˈlɔk] *vt., vi.* (使)连结,(使)连锁. ~*ing branches* 交错的树枝. ~*ing device* 连锁装置. ~*ing director* 兼任经理. ~*ing directorate* 连锁董事会〔董事会中有几个成员由某几个人共同兼任以便使企业经营协调,统一控制〕. ~*ing signal* 连锁信号. — *n.* 连结,连锁,连锁装置.

in·ter·lo·cu·tion [ˌintə(ː)ləuˈkjuːʃən] *n.* 对话,会话,交谈.

in·ter·loc·u·tor [ˌintə(ː)ˈlɔkjutə] *n.* *(fem. -tress, -trice, trix)* ①对话者,参加交谈的人. ②美国滑稽戏中由白人扮演黑人和引人发笑的配角.

in·ter·loc·u·to·ry [ˌintə(ː)ˈlɔkjuˈtəri] *a.* ①对话的,对话体的;插在对话中的. ②插入的,插话的. ③【法】(判决等)在诉讼期间宣告的,非最后的. ~ *wit* 对话中插入机智话(打趣话). *an* ~ *divorce decree* 宣布离婚判决书.

in·ter·lope [ˌintə(ː)ˈləup] *vi.* ①侵犯他人权利. ②闯入,干涉. ③无执照营业.

in·ter·lop·er [ˈintə(ː)ləupə] *n.* (为营利而)干涉他人事务者;无执照营业者.

in·ter·lude [ˈintə(ː)luːd, -ljuːd] *n.* ①幕间;幕间插入的戏. ②插曲;【乐】间句. ③穿插,间歇;穿插事件. ~*s of bright weather* 间隔的晴朗天气. *a forest with* ~*s of open meadow* 夹有空旷草地的森林.

in·ter·lu·nar [ˌintəˈluːnə] *a.* 【天】无月期的〔指残月后与新月前之间看不见月亮的四天〕.

in·ter·knit [ˌintəˈnit] *vt., vi.* *(-knit·ted, -knit; -knit·ting)* 编合,交缠,缠结.

in·ter·mar·riage [ˌintə(ː)ˈmæridʒ] *n.* ①异族〔不同宗教,不同人种间的〕通婚. ②近族(近亲)通婚.

in·ter·mar·ry [ˌintə(ː)ˈmæri] *vi.* ①(同种族、家族,同宗教、阶级间)内部通婚. ②近族通婚. ③【法】结婚.

in·ter·med·dle [ˌintə(ː)ˈmedl] *vi.* 干涉(他人事情),管闲事,多嘴 *(in; with)*. **-r** *n.*

in·ter·me·dia [ˌintə(ː)ˈmiːdjə] intermedium 的复数.

in·ter·me·di·ar·y [ˌintə(ː)ˈmiːdjəri] *a.* ①中间的,居间的. ②中间人的;媒介的,调解人的. — *n.* ①中间人,调解人. ②媒介,媒介物;手段,工具. ③中间形态;中间阶段. ~ *business* 牙行. *through the* ~ *of* 经…的手.

in·ter·me·di·ate [ˌintə(ː)ˈmiːdjət] *a.* 中间的,居间的. *the* ~ *class* (船的)特别三等. *an* ~ *compound* 中间化合物,中间体. — *n.* 中间物;中间分子,中间人;【化】中间体;期中考试;中间试验. — *vi.* 起调解作用;起媒介作用 *(between)*. ~ *culture* 补植. ~ *elements* 中间分子. ~ **frequency**【无】中频. ~ *forces* 中间力量. ~ **host**【生】中间宿主. ~**-range [medium-range] ballistic missile** 中程弹道导弹〔略 IRBM〕. ~ **zone**【军】中间阵地〔地带〕. **-ly** *ad.* 在中间. **-ness, -di·a·cy** *n.* 调解.

in·ter·me·di·a·tion [ˌintə(ː)ˌmiːdiˈeiʃən] *n.* 调解.

in·ter·me·di·a·tor [ˌintə(ː)ˈmiːdjətə] *n.* 中间人,调解人.

in·ter·me·din [ˌintəˈmiːdn] *n.* 【医】(垂体)中叶激素.

in·ter·me·di·um [ˌintə(ː)ˈmiːdiəm] *n.* *(pl. -dia, ~s)* 中间体,媒介物.

in·ter·ment [inˈtəːmənt] *n.* 埋葬,葬礼.

in·ter·me·tal·lic [ˌintə(ː)miˈtælik] *a.* 金属间的,金属间化合的.

in·ter·mez·zo [ˌintə(ː)ˈmetzəu] *n.* *(pl. ~s* [-z], *-mez·zi* [-ˈmetzi]*)* 幕间演出;【乐】间奏曲.

in·ter·mi·gra·tion [ˌintə(ː)maiˈgreiʃən] *n.* 相互迁移.

in·ter·mi·na·ble [inˈtəːminəbl] *a.* 无限的,无止境的;冗长的. *the I-* 无限的实在. **-ness** *n.* **-bly** *ad.*

in·ter·min·gle [ˌintə(ː)ˈmiŋgl] *vt.* 使搀和,使混合 *(with)*. ~ *one thing with another* 把一种东西和另一种东西搀和起来. — *vi.* (与…)混合 *(with)*. ~ *with sth.* 和某种东西混合起来.

in·ter·mis·sion [ˌintə(ː)ˈmiʃən] *n.* 中止,中断,间歇;(学校的)课间休息〔*cf.*〔英〕recess, break〕;(戏剧的)幕间休息〔*cf.*〔英〕interval〕. **without** ~ 不停地,不间断地. **-mis·sive** *a.*

in·ter·mit [ˌintə(ː)ˈmit] *vi.* 一时停止,(发烧疼痛等)中止,间断,(脉搏等)间歇. *The fever* ~*s.* 一会儿发烧,一会儿不发烧. — *vt.* 使间断,使中断. ~ *one's efforts* 暂停努力.

in·ter·mit·tence [ˌintə(ː)ˈmitəns] 中断,间断;间歇性,周期性.

in·ter·mit·tent [ˌintə(ː)ˈmitənt] *a.* 间断的,断断续续的;周期性的. *an* ~ *discharge* 间歇放电. ~ *fever*【医】间歇热. ~ *fighting* 打打停停的战斗. ~ *jet* 脉动式喷气发动机. ~ *noise* 断断续续的闹声. ~ *oiling*【机】间歇油润. ~ *reaction*【化】间歇反应. *an* ~ *spring* 间歇泉. *the* ~ *yield*【农】隔年收获. — *n.*【医】= intermittent fever. **-ly** *ad.*

in·ter·mix [ˌintə(ː)ˈmiks] *vt., vi.* (使)混杂;(使)混合. *Coal seams* ~*ed with iron ore.* 煤层和铁矿混杂一起.

in·ter·mix·ture [ˌintə(ː)ˈmikstʃə] *n.* 混合;混合物.

in·ter·mo·lec·u·lar [ˌintə(ː)məˈlekjulə] *n.* 分子间的.

in·ter·mon·tane [ˌintəˈmɔntein] *a.* 山的,山间的. *an* ~ *lake* 山间湖.

in·tern[1] [inˈtəːn] *vt.* 拘禁(俘虏等);扣留(船只等). *These soldiers were* ~*ed in a neutral country until the war was over.* 这些士兵被拘留在一个中立国,直到战争结束. — [ˈintəːn] *n.* = internee.

in·tern[2] [ˈintəːn] *n.* = interne. — *vi.* 做实习医生.

in·ter·nal [inˈtəːnl] *a.* ①内的,内部的 *(opp.* external*)*. ②国内的,内政的. ③体内的,内服的. ④内在的,本质上的,固有的. ⑤主观的,内心的,精神的. ~ *organs* 内脏. *the* ~ *parts of the body* 身体的内部. ~ *resistance*【物】内阻力,内电阻. ~ *structure* 内部构造. ~ *debts* 内债. ~ *navigation* 内河航行. ~ *trade* 国内贸易. ~ *revenue* 国内税收. *an* ~ *trouble* 内乱. *an* ~ *war* 内战. ~ *remedies* 内服药. ~ *bleeding* 内出血. ~ *injuries* 内伤. ~ *secretion* 内分泌. *for* ~ *use* 内用(药). ~ *evidence* 内证. ~ *monologue* 内心独白. ~ *peace* 内心的平静. *the* ~ *world* 主观世界. — *n.* ①〔*pl.*〕内脏,内部器官. ②本质,本性. ~ **carotid artery** 颈内动脉. ~ **ear** 内耳. ~ **gauge** 塞规. ~ **medicine** 内科学. ~ **respiration**【生】内呼吸;组织呼吸. ~ **rhyme** (诗歌中的)词间韵,行间韵. **-ly** *ad.*

in·ter·nal-com·bus·tion [inˈtəːnl-kəmˈbʌstʃən] *a.* 【机】内燃的. ~ *engine* 内燃机.

in·ter·nal·i·ty [ˌintə(ː)ˈnæliti] *n.* 内在,内在性.

in·ter·nal·ize [inˈtəːnəlaiz] *vt.* *(-ized; -iz·ing)* 使变成内部的;使…成为个人品性的一部分〔尤指把他人的态

度,想法等变成自己的思想方式〕. **-i·za·tion** *n.* 内在化.

in·ter·nat. = international.

in·ter·na·tion·al [ˌintə(:)ˈnæʃənəl] *a.* 国际(上)的,国际间的;世界的;〔I-〕国际工人协会的;〔I-〕国际信号的. *an ~ conference* 国际会议. *an ~ court* 国际法庭. *~ games [matches]* 国际运动比赛. *an ~ official record*【体】世界公认最高纪录. *~ copyright* 国际著作权. *an ~ treaty* 国际条约. *~ waters* 国际航路,公海. *the I- Working Men's Association* 国际工人协会〔普通单称 *International*〕. *hoist an ~ "B"* 悬挂国际信号旗B. — *n.* ①国际运动比赛参加者. ②取得一国国籍而长期侨居他国的人. ③〔I-〕国际工人协会;(社会主义)国际(组织). ④〔the I-〕=Internationale. *the First I-* 第一国际〔1864—1876〕. *the Second I-* 第二国际〔1889—1914〕. *the Third I-* 第三国际〔Communist International 简称 Comintern, 1919—1943〕. **I- Bank for Reconstruction and Development** 国际复兴开发银行. **~ candle**【物】国际烛光. **I- chamber of Commerce** 国际商会. **~ date line** 日界线,国际日期变更线(= date line). **I- Development association** 国际开发协会. **I- Finance Corporation** 国际金融公司. **I- Geophysical Year** 国际地球物理年. **I- Monetary Fund** 国际货币基金组织. **~ law** 国际法. **~ private law** 国际私法. **I- Phonetic Alphabet** 国际音标. **~ pitch** 音乐会的音高标准〔较通常标准略高〕. **~ unit(s)** (测定维生素成份、效果等的)国际单位. **-ly** *ad.*

in·ter·na·tio·nale [ˌintənæʃəˈnɑ:l, intənæʃənəl; F. ɛ̃tɛrnasjɔnal] *n.* 〔F.〕 ①〔***L' I-*, the *I-***〕《国际歌》. ②(前)(社会主义)国际(组织)〔法〕.

in·ter·na·tion·al·ism [ˌintə(:)ˈnæʃənəlizəm] *n.* 国际主义 (*opp.* nationalism);国际性.

in·ter·na·tion·al·ist [ˌintə(:)ˈnæʃənəlist] *n.* 国际主义者;国际法学家;〔美〕国际派. — *a.* 国际主义的. **-ic** *a.* 国际主义的.

in·ter·na·tion·al·i·za·tion [intəˌnæʃənəlaiˈzeiʃən] *n.* 国际化;国际共管.

in·ter·na·tion·al·ize [ˌintə(:)ˈnæʃənəlaiz] *vt.* 使国际化;把…置于国际共管之下.

in·terne [ˈintə:n] *n.* 〔美〕实习医生.

in·ter·ne·cine [ˌintə(:)ˈni:sain] *a.* ①自相残杀的,两败俱伤的;血腥的. ②(集团内部)互相冲突的. *~ war* 大血战.

in·tern·ee [ˌintə:ˈni:] *n.* (战争时期的)被扣留者;【军】拘留民,拘留犯.

in·ter·neu·ron [ˌintəˈnjuərɔn, ˈ-nuər-] *n.* (= internuncial neuron).

in·ter·nist [ˈintənist, ˈtə:-] *n.* 内科医生 (*opp.* surgeon).

in·tern·ment [inˈtə:nmənt] *n.* 拘留;收容. ***an ~ camp*** 〔英〕俘虏收容所〔美 detention camp〕.

in·ter·node [ˈintəˌnəud] *n.* ①【动,解】神经纤维内部的节间(结间). ②【植】节间. **-nod·al** *a.*

in·ter·nos [ˈintə(:)ˈnəus] 〔L.〕只限于咱俩之间〔不得外传〕(=between ourselves). *I don't believe in his sincerity; but this is ~.* 我看他没有什么诚意;不过,这一点是不能对外人讲的.

in·tern·ship [ˈintə:nʃip] *n.* ①实习医生的职务. ②实习医生的实习期.

in·ter·nun·cial [ˌintə(:)ˈnʌnʃəl] *a.* 在中间的,联系的. **~ neuron**【解】联系感觉神经和运动神经的神经细胞.

in·ter·nun·ci·o [ˌintə(:)ˈnʌnʃiəu] *n.* (*pl.* *~s*) ①信使,使节,中间人. ②罗马教皇的公使代表.

in·ter·o·ce·an·ic [ˈintə(:)rˌəuʃiˈænik] *a.* 海洋间的.

in·ter·o·cep·tor [ˌintərəuˈseptə] *n.* 内感受器,内受(纳)器. **-tive** *a.*

in·ter·of·fice [ˌintəˈɔ:fis, -ˈɔf-] *a.* 本机关办公室之间的.

in·ter·os·cu·late [ˌintəˈɔskjuleit] *vi.* ***(-lated; -lating)*** ①相互联系,互相接触. ②【生】具有共同性. **in·ter·os·cu·lant** [-lənt] *a.* **-la·tion** *n.*

in·ter·page [ˌintə(:)ˈpeidʒ] *vt.* 把…印入[插入]书页间.

in·ter·pel·lant [ˌintə:ˈpelənt] *a.* 质问的.

in·ter·pel·late [ˌintə:ˈpeleit] *vt.* (在议会中就政府政策等等向有关人)质问. **-la·tion** *n.* **-la·tor** *n.*

in·ter·pen·e·trate [ˌintə(:)ˈpenitreit] *vt.* 贯通;渗透. — *vi.* 互相贯通,互相渗透. **-tra·tion** *n.* 互相贯通;【建】交截细工. **-tra·tive** *a.*

in·ter·per·son·al [ˌintəˈpə:sənl] *a.* ①人与人之间的. *~ relationships* 人与人之间的关系. ②人与人之间的关系的,涉及人与人之间的关系的. **-ly** *ad.*

in·ter·phase [ˈintə(:)feiz] *n.* 【动】(细胞的)分裂期间.

in·ter·phone [ˈintə(:)fəun] *n.* (办公室等)内部电话;内部通讯装置;对讲(电话)机;内线自动电话机.

in·ter·plan·e·tar·y [ˌintə(:)ˈplænitəri] *a.* 星际间的,行星际的. *~ navigation* 星际导航. *~ travel* 星际航行.

in·ter·plant [ˌintə(:)ˈplɑ:nt] *vt.* ①【农】间作,套种. ②在…间插栽幼树.

in·ter·play [ˈintə(:)ˈplei] *n.* 相互作用;相互影响. *the ~ of light and shadow* 光影交错. — *vi.* 相互作用,相互影响.

in·ter·plead [ˌintə(:)ˈpli:d] *vi.* ***(-pleaded, -plead, -pled; -pleading)***【法】(提出债权要求者)互相诉讼. **-er** *n.* 互相诉讼,互相诉讼者.

In·ter·pol [ˈintə(:)pəul] *n.* 国际刑警组织〔全称: International Criminal Police Organization〕.

in·ter·po·late [inˈtə:pəuleit] *vt.,vi.* ①窜改(文稿). ②增添,插入. ③【数】插值,内插,内推. **-la·tion** [inˌtə:pəuˈleiʃən] *n.* ①窜改. ②插入,插入物. ③【数】插值法,内插法,内推法. **-la·tor** *n.* 窜改者,插入者.

in·ter·pol·y·mer [ˈintə(:)ˈpɔlimə] *n.* 【化】互聚物,共聚物. **-po·lym·er·i·za·tion** *n.* 共聚作用.

in·ter·pos·al [ˌintə(:)ˈpəuzl] *n.* = interposition.

in·ter·pose [ˌintə(:)ˈpəuz] *vt.* ①放入,插入. ②提出(异议). ③【影】使一镜头迅速替换(另一镜头). *~ oneself* 插手,干与. *~ one's authority* 利用自己职权干涉. — *vi.* ①插进来,干预. ②调解. ③插嘴.

in·ter·po·si·tion [inˌtə:pəˈziʃən] *n.* ①插入;干涉;调停,提出异议. ②插入物.

in·ter·pret [inˈtə:prit] *vt.* ①说明,解释. ②翻译,口译. ③把…理解为,把…看作. ④(根据自己的解释)演奏,表演. *~ a dream* 圆梦. *~ sb.'s laughter as an insult.* 把某人的笑声看作是耻辱. — *vi.* 解释;口译. **-a·ble** *a.* 可以解释的.

in·ter·pre·ta·tion [inˌtə:priˈteiʃən] *n.* ①解释,说明. ②翻译. ③表演,演奏. *put a favourable ~ on* 对…作有利的解释. *signal ~* 信号译释. *What is the ~ of this poem?* 这首诗的译文是什么意思?

in·ter·pre·ta·tive [inˈtə:prəteitiv] *a.* = interpretive. **-ly** *ad.*

in·ter·pret·er [inˈtə:pritə] *n.* (*fem.* ***-pret·ress***) ①解释者;判断者;译员;口译者. ②【军】情报判读员. ③【自】翻译器;翻译程序. **-ship** 翻译人员的职务[身分].

in·ter·pre·tive [inˈtə:pritiv] *a.* 解释的;翻译的;说明的. **-ly** *ad.*

in·ter·ra·cial [ˌintə(:)ˈreiʃəl] *a.* 不同人种间的;不同种族间的 (= interrace).

in·ter·ra·di·al [ˌintə(:)ˈreidiəl] *a.* 射线间的;半径之间的. **-ly** *ad.*

in·ter·reg·num [ˌintə(:)ˈregnəm] *n.* ***(pl. ~s, -na*** [-nə]***)*** ①(旧王死后新王尚未即位的)空位期;(政府改组期间的)政权空白期. ②间歇,中断.

in·ter·re·late [ˌintə(:)riˈleit] *vt., vi.* ***(-lated, -lating)*** (使)相互联系. **-lat·ed** *a.* **-lat·ed·ness** *n.*

in·ter·re·la·tion [ˈintə(:)riˈleiʃən] *n.* 相互关系,相互联系(性). **-ship** *n.* 相互关系.

in·ter·rex [ˈintəˌreks] *n.* *(pl.* ***in·ter·reges*** [-ˌriːdʒiːz]*)* 摄政王.

in·ter·rog. = interrogation, interrogative.

in·ter·ro·gate [inˈterəgeit] *vt.* 讯问, 质问, 审问. ～ *a prisoner* 讯问囚犯. — *vi.* 提出问题.

in·ter·ro·ga·tion [inˌterəˈgeiʃən] *n.* ①讯问, 质问, 审问. ②【语法】疑问句. ③问号〔?〕. *an* ～ *mark [point, note]*【语法】疑问号.

in·ter·rog·a·tive [ˌintəˈrɔgətiv] *a.* 讯问性的, 表示疑问的; 质问的. *an* ～ *adverb* 疑问副词. *an* ～ *pronoun* 疑问代词. — *n.* 疑问词. **-ly** *ad.*

in·ter·ro·ga·tor [inˈterəgeitə] *n.* ①讯问者, 质问者, 审问者. ②【无】询问器, 问答机. *airborne* ～ 飞机用询问器. *low-power* ～ 低功率询问器.

in·ter·rog·a·to·ry [ˌintəˈrɔgətəri] *a.* 表示疑问的, 讯问的, 质问的. *an* ～ *tone* 质问的口气. *the* ～ *method (of teaching)* 问答式(教授法). — *n.* ①疑问, 讯问, 质问, 审问; 〔*pl.*〕【法】书面质问. ②表示询问的符号[信号]. **-to·ri·ly** *ad.*

in·ter·rupt [ˌintəˈrʌpt] *vt.* ①阻止; 妨碍; 遮断. ②打断(别人的话等); 中断; 打搅. ③截断. ～ *a view* 遮住视线. *Don't* ～ *me.* 别打扰我. *He* ～*ed college to serve in the army.* 他中断大学的学业到军队服役. ～ *sb. in his work* 打搅某人工作. *May I* ～ *you to comment on that last remark?* 对不起, 刚才这句话是什么意思请讲讲. ～ *an electric current* 截断电流. — *vi.* 打扰, (别人谈话时)插嘴.

in·ter·rupt·ed [ˌintəˈrʌptid] *a.* 被遮断的, 被阻止的, 不通的, 中断的. ～ *screw* 断纹螺丝. **-ly** *ad.*

in·ter·rupt·er, in·ter·rupt·or [ˌintəˈrʌptə] *n.* ①打断者, 阻碍者, 障碍物. ②【电】断续器, 断流器. *an* ～ *gear*【机】断续齿轮. *a periodic* ～【电】周期性断续器. *a primary* ～【电】原电路断续器.

in·ter·rup·tion [ˌintəˈrʌpʃən] *n.* ①打断; 中断; 停止. ②断绝, 断路. ③插话, 打岔. ④障碍物, 遮断物. ⑤中断期, 休止期. ～ *of communication* 交通中断. *service* ～ 业务中断. *without* ～ 无间断, 继续. *alternating current* ～ 交流电流断路.

in·ter·rup·tive, in·ter·rup·to·ry [ˌintəˈrʌptiv, ˌintəˈrʌptəri] *a.* ①遮断的, 中断的, 阻碍的. ②打断的, 打扰的.

in·ter·scho·las·tic [ˌintəskəˈlæstik] 学校之间的. ～ *athletics* (中等学校的)校际比赛.

in·ter·sect [ˌintə(ː)ˈsekt] *vt.* 横断, 横切, 和…相交. *The line AB* ～*s the line CD at E.* 直线 AB 与直线 CD 相交于 E 点上. — *vi.* 相交, 交叉. *The lines AB and CD* ～ *at E.* 直线 AB 与直线 CD 相交于 E 点上.

in·ter·sec·tion [ˌintə(ː)ˈsekʃən] *n.* ①横断, 横切; 交叉, 相交. ②【数】交集. ③交点, 交叉线, 十字路口. ④逻辑乘法.

in·ter·sec·tion·al [ˌintə(ː)ˈsekʃənl] *a.* ①交点的; 形成交点的. ②地区之间的. ～ *football games* 区际足球赛.

in·ter·serv·ice [ˌintə(ː)ˈsəːvis] *a.*【军】军种间的.

in·ter·sex [ˈintəseks] *n.* ①【生】间性, 雌雄间体. ②不分性别.

in·ter·sex·u·al [ˌintəˈseksjuəl] *a.* ①两性之间的. ②具有间性特征的. ③不分性别的, 男女平等的. ～ *rivalry* 间性对抗.

in·ter·sol·u·bil·i·ty [ˌintəˌsɔljuˈbiliti] *n.*【化】互溶性, 互溶度.

in·ter·space [ˈintə(ː)ˈspeis] *n.* ①空间, 空隙〔指场所、时间〕, 间隙. ②星际. — [ˌintəˈspeis] *vt.* *(-spaced; -spacing)* ①在…之间留出空间. ②在…之间填补空间.

in·ter·spe·cif·ic [ˌintə(ː)spiˈsifik] *a.*【生】种间的.

in·ter·sperse [ˌintə(ː)ˈspəːs] *vt.* ①散布; 散置 *(between, among)*. ②点缀, 装饰. ～ *peach trees among the willows* 桃柳相间. ～ *a book with pictures* 使书图文并茂.

in·ter·sper·sion [ˌintə(ː)ˈspəːʃən] *n.* 散布, 散置; 点缀, 装饰.

in·ter·sput·nik [ˌintəˈsputnik] *n.* 苏联全球卫星通讯系统.

in·ter·sta·di·al [ˌintə(ː)ˈsteidiəl] *n.*【地】间冰段.

in·ter·stage [ˌintə(ː)ˈsteidʒ] *a.* 级间的, 级际的. ～ **coupling**【无】级间耦合.

in·ter·state [ˌintə(ː)ˈsteit] *a.* 〔美〕各州间的, 州际的. **I- Commerce Commission** 〔美〕州际商务委员会.

in·ter·stel·lar [ˈintə(ː)ˈstelə] *a.*【天】星际的. ～ *aeronautics* 星际航行. ～ *space* 星际空间.

in·ter·stice [inˈtəːstis] *n.* 间隙, 空隙, 裂缝.

in·ter·sti·tial [ˌintə(ː)ˈstiʃəl] *a.* ①裂缝间的; 空隙的; 在裂缝间的. ②【解】细胞(组织)间的, 间质的. ③【物】填隙的. ～ *cells* 间质细胞. ～ *tissue* 间质组织. ～ *alloy* 填隙式合金. ～ *structure* 填隙式结构. — *n.*【物】填隙, 填隙子. ～ **cell-stimulating hormone** 间质细胞(激)素. **-ly** *ad.*

in·ter·tex·ture [ˌintə(ː)ˈtekstʃə] *n.* 交织, 交织物.

in·ter·tid·al [ˌintə(ː)ˈtaidl] *a.* 潮间(地)带的.

in·ter·till [ˌintə(ː)ˈtil] *vt.* ①中耕. ②在作物的畦行间耕作. ～*ed crops* 中耕作物. **-age** *n.* 中耕; 间作.

in·ter·trib·al [ˌintə(ː)ˈtraibl] *a.* 部落间的.

in·ter·trop·i·cal [ˌintə(ː)ˈtrɔpikl] *a.* 南北回归线之间的, 夏至冬至线之间的.

in·ter·twine [ˌintə(ː)ˈtwain] *vt., vi.* (使)缠结, (使)缠绕在一起.

in·ter·twist [ˌintə(ː)ˈtwist] *vt., vi.* 捻合; 缠结.

in·ter·u·ni·ver·si·ty [ˈintə(ː)ˌjuːniˈvəːsiti] *a.* 大学间的. *an* ～ *match* 大学校际比赛.

in·ter·ur·ban [ˌintə(ː)ˈəːbən] *a.* 城市间的. *an* ～ *bus* 市际公共汽车. *an* ～ *railway* 城市之间的铁路. — *n.* 城市间的交通路线[车辆].

in·ter·val [ˈintəvəl] *n.* ①(空间方面的)间隔; 空隙. ②(时间方面的)间隔, 间歇; 工间休息, 幕间休息. ③【军】(各小队间的)间隔. ④【乐】音程. ⑤【数】区间. ⑥〔美〕= intervale. *an* ～ *of five metres* 相隔五米. *after a year's* ～ 隔一年后. *I- -10 Min.* 休息十分钟〔常用于演出节目单中〕. *in the* ～*s of business* 在工作空隙时间. *There is a two hour's* ～ *to the next train.* 下一班火车还要过两个小时. ***at*** ～***s*** 时时; 处处; 偶尔. ***at*** ～***s of*** 每隔…〔就时间、场所说〕. ***at long*** ～***s*** 间或. ***at regular*** ～***s*** 每隔一定时间[距离]. ***at short*** ～ 常常. ***in the*** ～***s*** 不一会儿, 不久. ***lucid*** ～ ①狂人神志清醒的时期. ②阴天太阳偶然出现的时候. ③在暴风雨似的事件中平静的时期; 生活平静的时刻.

in·ter·vale [ˈintə(ː)veil] *n.* 〔美〕(丘陵间的)低地, 平地; (适于耕作的)河滩地.

in·ter·val·(l)ic [ˌintə(ː)ˈvælik] *a.* ①间隔的, 间歇的, 幕间的, 工间的. ②悬殊的. ③【乐】音程的.

in·ter·var·si·ty [intə(ː)ˈvɑːsəti] *a.* 〔英〕= interuniversity.

in·ter·vene [ˌintə(ː)ˈviːn] *vi.* ①插进, 介入〔介于时间或空间当中〕. ②调停. ③干预, 干涉. ④【法】(第三者为保护个人权利)参加诉讼. ～ *between two objects* 夹在两件东西当中. *the years that* ～*(d)* 其中有几年. *I shall come if nothing* ～*s.* 如果没有别的事, 我就来. ～ *in a dispute* 调停争端. ～ *between two people quarrelling* 在两个争吵者之间进行调解. ～ *in the internal affairs of other countries* 干涉他国内政. **-r, -ven·or** *n.* 干涉者, 介入者, 调停者.

in·ter·ven·ient [ˌintəˈviːnjənt] *a.* 干预的; 介入的, 调解的. — *n.* 干涉者; 调解人; 插入物.

in·ter·ven·tion [ˌintə(ː)ˈvenʃən] *n.* ①插进, 介入. ②调解, 排解. ③干涉, 干预, 妨碍. *armed* ～ = ～ *by arms* 武装干涉.

in·ter·ven·tion·ist [ˌintə(ː)ˈvenʃənist] *n.* 内政干涉者,

武装干涉者，主张在国际事务中进行干涉的人. — *a.* ①干涉的，干涉者的. ②进行干涉的，主张进行干涉的. **-tion·ism** *n.* 干涉主义.

in·ter·ver·te·bral [ˌintə(ː)ˈvəːtibrəl] *a.* 椎骨间的. ~ **disk**【解】椎间盘. **-ly** *ad.*

in·ter·view [ˈintəvjuː] *n.* ①接见；会见；会谈；协商. ②(记者的)访问；访问记. ③口头审查. *have [hold] an ~ with sb.* 会见某人. *give [grant] an ~ to sb.* 接见某人. *job ~* 对申请工作者的口头审查. — *vt.* 接见；会见；(记者)访问. **-ee** *n.* 被会见者；被接见者；被采访者. **-er** *n.* 会见者；接见者；采访者.

in·ter vi·vos [ˌintə(ː) ˈviːvəus] *ad.* 〔L.〕 在生存者之间.

in·ter·vo·cal·ic [ˌintə(ː)vəuˈkælik] *a.* 【语】两元音间的〔指辅音〕.

in·ter·volve [ˌintə(ː)ˈvɔlv] *vt., vi.* 卷进；缠绕；(使)互卷，(使)互相盘绕.

in·ter-war [ˈintə(ː)ˈwɔː] *a.* 两次战争之间的.

in·ter·weave [ˌintə(ː)ˈwiːv] *vt.* ***(-wove*** [-ˈwəuv], ***~d; -woven*** [-ˈwəuvən] 或 ***~d; -weaving;)*** 使交织，织进；使交错编织；使紧密结合，使混杂. *~ truth with fiction* 真伪混杂. — *vi.* 交织，混杂.

in·ter·wind [ˌintə(ː)ˈwaind] *vt., vi.* ***(-wound***[-ˈwəund]***)*** (使)互相盘绕，(使)互卷.

in·ter·zon·al [ˌintə(ː)ˈzəunəl] *a.* 地带之间的.

in·tes·ta·cy [inˈtestəsi] *n.* 无遗嘱，无遗嘱死亡.

in·tes·tate [inˈtesteit] *a.* 没有留下遗嘱的；不能根据遗嘱处理的. *die ~* 没有遗嘱就死了. — *n.* 无遗嘱死亡者.

in·tes·ti·nal [inˈtestinl] *a.* ①内部的；生活在内部的. ②肠的；在肠内的. *the ~ canal* 肠腔，肠. *~ catarrh*【医】肠炎. ~ **fortitude** 持久力；勇气. **-ly** *ad.*

in·tes·tine [inˈtestin] *a.* 内部的；国内的. *~ war* 内战. — *n.* 〔常 *pl.*〕【解】肠. *the large [small] ~* 大[小]肠.

in·thral(l) [inˈθrɔːl] *vt.* ***(-thral·led; -thral·ling)*** 迷惑，迷；擒，俘虏，〔罕〕使做奴隶，奴役 (= enthral(l)).

in·throne [inˈθrəun] *vt.* = enthrone.

in·ti·ma [ˈintimə] *n.* ***(pl. -mae*** [miː], ***-mas)***【解】内膜.

in·ti·ma·cy [ˈintiməsi] *n.* ①亲密，亲近，友好. ②〔婉〕私通，亲热. ③〔*pl.*〕亲昵行为. *be on terms of ~* 亲密.

in·ti·mate[1] [ˈintimit] *a.* ①亲密的，亲近的；密切的. ②直接的，完全的，详细的. ③内部的，内心深处的，本质的. ④个人的，私人的. ⑤私通的. *an ~ friend* 亲密的朋友. *be on ~ terms with sb.* 同某人关系密切. *an ~ knowledge of life* 熟悉生活. *one's ~ feelings* 心内感觉. *~ reflections* 内省. *the ~ structure of matter* 物质的内部结构. *one's ~ affairs* 私事. *an ~ diary* 私人日记. *be ~ with a woman* 同某妇人有不正当的性关系. — *n.* 亲密的朋友，知己. **-ness** *n.*

in·ti·mate[2] [ˈintimeit] *vt.* ①宣布，通知，通告，明白表示. ②暗示，提示. *~ one's approval of a plan* 表明同意某项计划. **-ly** *ad.*

in·ti·ma·tion [ˌintiˈmeiʃən] *n.* ①告知，通知，通告. ②【法】正式宣告，正式宣布. ③暗示，提示.

in·time [ænˈtiːm] *a.* 〔F.〕 亲切的 (= intimate).

in·tim·i·date [inˈtimideit] *vt.* ①恫吓，恐吓. ②威逼某人做某事 *(into)*. *This cannot ~ us.* 这吓不倒我们. *~ sb. into doing sth.* 胁迫某人做某事. **-da·tor** *n.* **-da·to·ry** *a.*

in·tim·i·da·tion [inˌtimiˈdeiʃən] *n.* 威胁，恐吓. *surrender to ~* 屈服于威胁. *atomic ~* 原子恫吓.

in·ti·mist [ˈintimist] *a.* 描绘内心思想和感情的. — *n.* 描绘内心的作家[画家].

in·tim·i·ty [inˈtimiti] *n.* ①秘密，亲密. ②本质，本性.

in·tinc·tion [inˈtiŋkʃən] *n.*【宗】(圣餐的)面包浸酒.〔系一种宗教浸礼仪式. 把圣餐的面包浸入酒中，然后分给参加受圣餐的每人两片〕.

in·tine [ˈintiːn, -tain] *n.* (= endospore).

in·ti·tle [inˈtaitl] *vt.* ***(-tled, -tling)*** = entitle.

in·tit·ule [inˈtitjuːl] *vt.* 给(法令等)命名，加标题于….

Intl. = International.

in·to [元音前读 ˈintu，句尾主读 ˈintuː，辅音前读 ˈintə] *prep.* ①〔表示动向〕向内，到…里. *go ~ a room* 走进屋里. *come ~ the garden* 来到园里. *look ~ the box* 看箱子里头. *peer ~ the darkness* 探望暗处. *throw sth. ~ the fire* 把某物扔进火里. *get ~ trouble* 遇到麻烦. *inquire ~ a matter* 对某事进行调查. ②〔表示时间〕进入[继续]到. *look ~ the future* 展望未来. *pass out of childhood ~ manhood* 从童年进入成年. *work far [well] ~ the night* 工作到深夜. ③〔表示变化状态，结果〕转入，变成，聚成，迫使 *(opp.* out of*)*. *turn water ~ ice* 使水变成冰. *build China ~ a culturally advanced socialist country* 把我国建设成为高度文明的社会主义国家. *translate English ~ Chinese* 把英语翻译成汉语. *burst ~ tears* 突然哭起来. *collect them ~ heaps* 把它们聚集起来. *be flogged ~ submission* 被迫屈服. ④〔表示撞击〕. *bumper ~ a door* 撞在门上. *run ~ a tree* 碰(撞)在树上. ⑤〔表示从事工作、活动等〕. *enter ~ dictionary making* 从事词典编纂工作. *go ~ teaching* 投入教学工作. ⑥【数】乘〔a×b 读作 a into b = a multiplied by b〕；除〔a÷b 读作 b into a = a divided by b〕. ⑦〔方〕= in. *He fought ~ the Revolution.* 〔美〕他参加过独立战争. ⑧〔美俚〕深深卷入于；对…有很大兴趣；欠…的债.

in·toed [ˈintəud] *a.* 脚趾向内弯曲的.

in·tol·er·a·bil·i·ty [inˌtɔlərəˈbiliti] *n.* 不堪；难忍；难受 (= intolerableness).

in·tol·er·a·ble [inˈtɔlərəbl] *a.* 不堪的；难忍的；难受的. **-bly** *ad.*

in·tol·er·ance [inˈtɔlərəns] *n.* ①不容纳异说[意见、信仰]，偏狭；固执. ②【医】不耐(性)〔对某些药物的过敏反应〕.

in·tol·er·ant [inˈtɔlərənt] *a.* 偏狭的，气量狭窄的；忍受不住的，不耐…的. *~ of* 不能容忍的，不耐…的. *plants ~ of shade* 不耐阴的植物. *be ~ of great heat* 不耐高温. — *n.* 不容忍的人；偏狭的人. **-ly** *ad.*

in·tomb [inˈtuːm] *vt.* = entomb.

in·to·nate [ˈintəuneit] *vt., vi.* = intone.

in·to·na·tion [ˌintəuˈneiʃən] *n.* ①音的抑扬. ②语调，声调. *a falling [rising] ~* 降[升]调. ③【乐】发声，转调. ④【宗】吟诵，咏唱；(圣歌等的)起始句. ~ **pattern**【语】调型. **-al** *a.*

in·tone [inˈtəun] *vt.* ①吟诵，咏唱(圣歌、祷文等). ②唱(圣歌等的)起始唱句. ③给…一种特殊音调. — *vi.* ①吟诵，咏唱. ②发出拖长的声音. **-r** *n.* 吟诵者，咏唱者.

in·tor·sion [inˈtɔːʃən] *n.*【植】(茎的)螺旋形盘绕，弯曲，绕缠.

in·tort [inˈtɔːt] *vt.* 〔罕〕〔常用于过去分词〕向内扭结.

in to·to [inˌˈtəutəu] *ad.* 〔L.〕 完满地，完全地，总的看来，总共地.

In·tour·ist [ˈintuərist] *n.* 苏联国际旅行社.

in·tox·i·cant [inˈtɔksikənt] *n.* 麻醉品；〔尤指〕酒精饮料. — *a.* 使醉的，麻醉的，沉醉的.

in·tox·i·cate [inˈtɔksikeit] *vt.* ①使醉. ②使陶醉. ③使中毒. *become ~d from wine* 喝醉了酒. *be ~d by [with] one's success* 陶醉于自己的成就. *be ~d with joy* 欣喜若狂. **-ca·tion** *n.*

in·tox·i·cat·ing [inˌtɔksiˈkeitiŋ] *a.* ①醉人的. *an ~ beverage* 酒类. ②令人陶醉的. **-ly** *ad.*

intr. = intransitive.

in·tra- *comb. f.* 表示"内"，"在内"，"内部"〔主用于学术用语〕: *intracellular, intramural, intravenous.*

in·tra·cel·lu·lar [ˌintrəˈseljulə] *a.* 细胞内的；发生于个体细胞内的.

in·tra·cit·y [ˌintrəˈsiti] *a.* 市内的.

in·trac·ta·ble [in'træktəbl] *a.* ①倔强的，难处理的．②难操作的，难加工的．③难治疗的；难对付的．*an* ～ *child* 难管教的孩子．*an* ～ *metal* 难加工的金属．～ *pain* 难消除的疼痛．**-bil·i·ty, -ble·ness** *n.* **-bly** *ad.*

in·tra·cu·ta·ne·ous test [ˌintrəkju:'teiniəs]【医】皮内试验．

in·tra·der·mal [ˌintrə'də:ml] *a.* 皮内的；皮层内的．

in·tra·dos [in'treidɔs] *n.*【建】拱腹(线)．

in·tra·mo·lec·u·lar [ˌintrəmə'lekjulə] *a.* 作用于分子内的；存在于分子间的；发生于分子内的．**-ly** *ad.*

in·tra·mu·ral [ˌintrə'mjuərəl] *a.* ①城墙内的；城市内的；建筑物内的；大学内的．②【解】(器官)壁内的．*an* ～ *railway* 市内铁路．～ *sports* 校内运动．～ *strife* 内部倾轧．**-ly** *ad.*

in·tra·mus·cu·lar [ˌintrə'mʌskjulə] *a.* 位于肌肉的；肌肉注射的．**-ly** *ad.*

intrans. = intransitive.

in·tran·si·gence [in'trænsidʒəns] *n.* 拒绝调解，不让步，不妥协 (= intransigency).

in·tran·si·gent [in'trænsidʒənt] *a.* 拒绝调解的，不让步的，不妥协的．— *n.* 不妥协的人〔尤指政治上的〕．**-gent·ly** *ad.*

in·tran·si·tive [in'trænsitiv] *a.*【语法】不及物的．*an* ～ *verb*【语法】不及物动词．— *n.*【语法】不及物动词．**-ly** *ad.*

in·trant ['intrənt] *n.* = entrant.

in·tra·psy·chic [ˌintrə'saikik] *a.* 存在于头脑中的；存在于灵魂中的，出现于头脑[灵魂]中的 (= intrapsychical). **-chi·cal·ly** *ad.*

in·tra·spe·cif·ic [ˌintrəspi'sifik] *a.*【动】种内的．

in·tra·state [ˌintrə'steit] *a.* 州内的〔尤指美国的一州内的〕．

in·tra·tel·lu·ric [ˌintrəte'ljuərik] *a.* ①地内形成的，位于地内的；出现于地内的．②地中岩浆期的．

in·tra·u·ter·ine [ˌintrə'ju:tərin] *a.* 子宫内的．～ **(conceptive) device** 子宫内安放的避孕环〔缩写为 IUD〕．

in·trav·a·sa·tion [inˌtrævə'seiʃən] *n.*【医】内沉，内渗，进入血管或淋巴管的异物．

in·tra·ve·hi·cle [ˌintrə'vi:ikl] *a.* 宇宙航行器内的．

in·tra·ve·nous [ˌintrə'vi:nəs] *a.*【医】静脉内的，静脉注射的．～ *drip* 静脉滴注．～ *injection* 静脉注射．**-ly** *ad.*

in·tra·zon·al [ˌintrə'zəunl] *a.*【植】隐域的．

in·treat [in'tri:t] *vt., vi.* = entreat 的古变体．

in·trench [in'trentʃ] *vt., vi.* = entrench.

in·trep·id [in'trepid] *a.* 刚毅的，勇猛的，无敌的，无畏的．**-id·i·ty, -ness** *n.* **-ly** *ad.*

Int. Rev. = Internal Revenue.〔英〕国内税收．

in·tri·ca·cy ['intrikəsi] *n.* ①纷乱，错综，复杂．②〔*pl.*〕错综复杂的事物．

in·tri·cate ['intrikit] *a.* ①缠结的，错综的，复杂的．②精致的．*an* ～ *piece of machinery* 复杂的机器．*an* ～ *plot* 情节复杂．*an* ～ *problem* 复杂的问题．**-ly** *ad.* **-ness** *n.*

in·tri·g(u)ant ['intrigənt] *n.* 阴谋者；奸夫．

in·tri·g(u)ante [ˌintri'gænt] *n.* 女阴谋者，淫妇．

in·trigue [in'tri:g] *n.* ①阴谋，密谋；诡计．②私通；勾结．③(戏剧、小说等的)纠葛，伏线．*political* ～*s* 政治阴谋．— *vi.* ①计划阴谋，密谋 *(against)*．②私通 *(with)*．～ *against one's friends* 阴谋陷害朋友．～ *with a woman* 同某女人私通．— *vt.* ①用诡计取得；〔古〕哄骗．②〔新闻用语〕使发生兴趣，使着迷，使好奇．*The news* ～*d all of us.* 这新闻引起了大家的兴趣．

in·trigu·er [in'tri:gə] *n.* 阴谋家；私通者．

in·trigu·ing [in'tri:giŋ] *a.* ①阴谋的；与阴谋有关的．②引起兴趣的，有魅力的．*an* ～ *smile* 动人的微笑．*a most* ～ *piece of news* 最引人兴趣的消息．**-ly** *ad.*

in·trin·sic [in'trinsik] *a.* *(opp.* extrinsic*)* ①内在的；本来的；真正的，实在的．②【解】内部的，体内的．～ *energy*【物】内能．～ *qualities* 本质．～ *value* 实价，内在的价值．～ **factor**【生化】内因子〔使胃吸收维生素 B_{12} 的胃液〕．

in·trin·si·cal [in'trinsikəl] *a.* = intrinsic. **-ly** *ad.* **-ness** *n.*

int·ro- *comb. f.* 表示"在内"，"向内"：*intro*spect; *intro*vert.

introd; intro. = introduction; introductory.

in·tro·duce [ˌintrə'dju:s] *vt.* ①引导，带领．②介绍．③使开始经验[体验]．④推广，采用，引进．⑤提出(议案等)．⑥以…作为文章、讲话的开头．⑦插入．⑧开始．～ *a guest into the parlour* 领客人进客厅．*Allow me to* ～ *Dr. Li (to you).* 请允许我(向你)介绍这位李大夫．～ *a freshman to campus life* 向新生介绍校内生活．～ *oneself* 自我介绍．～ *a person to town life* 让某人开始城市生活．～ *a new fashion* 采用新式样．*Space science has* ～*d many new words.* 宇宙科学采用许多新词汇．～ *a bill into Congress* 向大会提出提案．～ *a motion* 提出动议．～ *a humorous note in a speech* 先讲几句幽默话作为演讲的开场白．～ *a subject with a short preface* 用短序开始讨论一个问题．～ *an electric wire into a conduct* 把电线插入导管内．～ *a probe into a wound* 把探针插进伤口里．～ *a talk with an anecdote* 开始讲述轶事．**in·tro·duc·i·ble** *a.*

in·tro·duc·er [ˌintrə'dju:sə] *n.* 介绍人，推荐人；引进者；提出者；导引器．

in·tro·duc·tion [ˌintrə'dʌkʃən] *n.* ①引导；传入．②介绍．③推广，采用；引进．④(育种)引种．⑤序，导言，绪言；【乐】前奏，序奏．⑥初步，入门(书)，概论．*The word is a recent* ～. 这个词是新传来的词．*a letter of* ～ 介绍信．～ *of better strains of seeds* 良种的采用．*An I- to Chemistry* 《化学入门》．

in·tro·duc·tive [ˌintrə'dʌktiv] *a.* = introductory.

in·tro·duc·to·ry [ˌintrə'dʌktəri] *a.* 介绍的；导言的，绪言的；预备的．～ *address* 介绍辞；开会辞．～ *note* 按语．～ *remarks* 绪言，开场白．**-ri·ly** *ad.* **-ri·ness** *n.*

in·tro·gres·sion [ˌintrə'greʃən] *n.*【生】基因渗入．**-sive** [-'gresiv] *a.*

in·tro·it [in'trəuit, 'introit] *n.*【天主】祭文〔祭司在主持祭祀时所唱的赞美诗等〕；【英国国教】圣餐仪式前所唱的歌．

in·tro·ject [ˌintrə'dʒekt] *vt.*【医】(精神分析学方面的用词)吸取，摄取．**-tion** *n.*

in·tro·mis·sion [ˌintrəu'miʃən] *n.* ①送入，插入．②允许进入，进入．

in·tro·mit [ˌintrəu'mit] *vt.* ***(～-mit·ted; ～-mit·ting)*** ①送入，插入．②允许进入，进入．**-mit·tent** *a.*

in·trorse [in'trɔ:s] *a.*【植】内向的，向心的〔指花药〕*(opp.* extrorse*)*. **-ly** *ad.*

in·tro·spect [ˌintrəu'spekt] *vt., vi.* 对思想感情等进行反省．

in·tro·spec·tion [ˌintrəu'spekʃən] *n.* 内省，反省．**-ist** ① *a.* 内省的，反省的．② *n.* 内省者，反省者．

in·tro·spec·tive [ˌintrəu'spektiv] *a.* 内省的，反省的．**-ly** *ad.* **-ness** *n.*

in·tro·ver·si·ble [ˌintrəu'və:səbl] *a.* 可向内翻的，可向内弯的．

in·tro·ver·sion [ˌintrəu'və:ʃən] *n.* ①内曲，内翻．②内向，反省．③【心】内倾，内向性 *(opp.* extroversion*)*.

in·tro·ver·sive [ˌintrəu'və:siv] *a.* ①内曲的，内翻的．②内向的，内省的．③【心】内倾的．

in·tro·vert [ˌintrəu'və:t] *vt.* ①使内翻，使向内弯．②使(思想)内向，使内省．③【动】使(器官)向里翻．～ *sth. inward* 使某物向里弯．～ *one's attention upon oneself* 使注意力内向．— *vi.* 进行内省；成为内弯的．— ['intrəvə:t] *n.* ①【心】内向型性格的人．②内弯[内翻]的东西．— *a.* = introverted *(opp.* extrovert*)*.

in·tro·vert·ed [ˌintrəuˈvəːtid] *a.* 有内向的特征的；有内向性格的；内弯性的，内翻的．

in·tro·ver·tive [ˌintrəuˈvəːtiv] *a.* = introversive.

in·trude [inˈtruːd] *vt.* ①硬把自己挤进 *(into)*；把观点等强加他人．②【地】使侵入其它地层．～ *oneself into a meeting* 闯进会场．～ *one's opinions upon sb.* 把自己的意见强加于人．～ *liquid magma into solid rocks* 把糊浆灌到岩层中去．～*d rocks*【地】侵入岩．— *vi.* 闯进 *(upon)*；打扰，入侵．～ *upon sb.'s privacy* 闯入某人的私室．*I hope I am not intruding.* 我希望我不致打搅你．

in·trud·er [inˈtruːdə] *n.* ①闯入者，侵入者；爱管闲事的人，好干涉的人．②夜盗；【空】轰炸机．

in·tru·sion [inˈtruːʒən] *n.* ①闯入，侵入；干涉，打扰，妨碍．②【地】侵入；侵入岩(浆)．

in·tru·sive [inˈtruːsiv] *a.* *(opp.* extrusive*)* ①闯进的；侵入的．②【地】侵入岩形成的．*the* ～ *sound*【语音】插入音．～ *body*【地】侵入岩体．～ *rocks*【地】侵入岩．**-ly** *ad.* **-ness** *n.*

in·trust [inˈtrʌst] *vt.* = entrust.

in·tu·bate [ˈintjubeit] *vt.*【医】把管子插进(喉头等)．

in·tu·ba·tion [ˌintjuˈbeiʃən] *n.*【医】插管，插管法．

in·tu·it [inˈtju(ː)it] *vt., vi.* 直观，由直觉知道．**-a·ble** *a.*

in·tu·i·tion [ˌintju(ː)ˈiʃən] *n.* 直感，直觉知识，直感事物．**-ist** ① *n.* 直观论者，直觉主义者．② *a.* 直观论的，直觉主义的．

in·tu·i·tion·al [ˌintju(ː)ˈiʃənl] *a.* 直觉的；直观的．**-ist** *n., a.* = intuitionist.

in·tu·i·tion·al·ism [ˌintjuːˈiʃənəlizəm] *n.* = intuitionism.

in·tu·i·tion·ism [ˌintjuːˈiʃənizəm] *n.*【哲】直观主义，直观论．

in·tu·i·tive [inˈtju(ː)itiv] *a.* 直觉的；直观的．*an* ～ *truth* 直观真理．**-ly** *ad.* **-ness, -tiv·ism** 直观论；直觉主义．**-tiv·ist** *n., a.* = intuitionist.

in·tu·mesce [ˌintju(ː)ˈmes] *vi.* 膨胀，肿起；扩大．

in·tu·mes·cence [ˌintju(ː)ˈmesns] *n.* ①膨胀；肿大；扩大．②肿胀物．③(油漆等遇热时的)泡沸．

in·tu·mes·cent [ˌintju(ː)ˈmesnt] *a.* ①膨胀的；肿起的；扩大的．②(油漆等遇热时)泡沸的．

in·tus·sus·cept [ˌintəssəˈsept] *vt.* ①摄吸营养．②吸取，接收．③使肠子套叠．④使反折．

in·tus·sus·cep·tion [intəsəˈsepʃən] *n.* ①(营养的)摄取；(思想等的)吸收，接受．②【生】内填，内滋．③缩入；反折；【医】肠套叠．

in·twine [inˈtwain] *vt., vi.* = entwine.

in·twist [inˈtwist] *vt.* = entwist.

in·u·lase [ˈinjuleis] *n.*【化】菊粉酶．

in·u·lin [ˈinjulin] *n.*【化】菊粉．

in·unc·tion [inˈʌŋkʃən] *n.* ①涂油．②【医】涂擦，涂擦法．③软膏；〔*pl.*〕涂擦剂．

in·un·dant [inˈʌndənt] *a.* 涨溢的，泛滥的．

in·un·date [ˈinəndeit] *vt.* 淹没，泛滥；使充满．*be* ～*d with water* 充满了水．*a place* ～*d with visitors* 参观者络绎不绝的地方．**-da·tion** *n.* 洪水，泛滥．**-da·tor** *n.* **-da·to·ry** *a.*

in·ur·bane [ˌinəːˈbein] *a.* 粗野的，不礼貌的，粗鄙的．**-ban·i·ty** *n.*

in·ure [iˈnjuə] *vt.* 〔常用被动语态〕使习惯于；锻炼．*be* ～*d to cold* 使身体耐寒．～ *oneself to hardship* 使自己能吃苦耐劳．— *vi.*【法】生效，适用；有助于．～ *to the prosperity and welfare of the nation* 有利于全国国民的繁荣与福利．**-ment** *n.*

in·urn [inˈəːn] *vt.* 把(骨灰)装入瓮内；埋葬．～ *ashes of the dead into an urn* 把骨灰放入缸内．

in u·ter·o [in ˈjuːtərəu] *ad.*〔L.〕在子宫内，未诞生，在诞生前，在未来．

in·u·tile [inˈjuːtail] *a.* 无益的，没有用的．**-ly** *ad.*

in·u·til·i·ty [ˌinjuˈtiləti] *n.* ①无益，无用．②无用的人，废物．*talk inutilities* 说废话．

inv. = ①invented; inventor. ②invoice.

in va·cu·o [in ˈvækjuːəu] *ad.*〔L.〕在空处，在真空中．

in·vade [inˈveid] *vt.* ①侵入，侵略(他国)，侵犯(权利)．②蜂拥而入，挤满．③打扰．④(疾病、声音等)袭来，侵袭．*The town was* ～*d by a crowd of tourists.* 这个城市拥进了一群游客．～ *sb.'s privacy* 打扰某人．*a body* ～*d by disease* 受到疾病侵入的身体．— *vi.* 进行侵略．

in·vad·er [inˈveidə] *n.* 侵略者；侵入者；侵犯者；侵入物．

in·vag·i·nate [inˈvædʒineit] *vt.* ①摄吸，吸取．②使内陷；把…收入鞘内；使(管、器官等)内缩；使反折．(= intussuscept). — *vi.* 反折；入鞘；凹入．

in·vag·i·na·tion [inˌvædʒiˈneiʃən] *n.* ①内陷；入鞘；反折．②反折处；内陷[入鞘]部分．③【医】肠套叠．

in·va·lid[1] [ˈinvəlid] *a.* ①有病的，病弱的，伤残的．②病人用的．～ *soldiers* 伤兵．*an* ～ *chair* 病人用椅．*an* ～ *diet* 病号菜饭．— *n.* 病人，病弱者，病号，伤病军人．*a resort of* ～*s* 伤病员疗养地．— [ˌinvəˈliːd] *vt.* ①使病弱；使伤残．②把…作为伤病员处理．*be* ～*ed for life* 成终身病人．*be* ～*ed home* 被作为伤病员送回家．*be* ～*ed out of the army* 因伤病而奉命退伍．— *vi.* ①失去健康．②因伤病而退伍．

in·val·id[2] [inˈvælid] *a.* ①无用的；不能成立的．②【法】无效的，作废的．～ *arguments* 站不住脚的论点．～ *cheques* 无效的支票．～ *claims* 无效的要求．～ *contracts* 无效的契约．*declare a marriage* ～ 宣布结婚无效．**-ly** *ad.*

in·val·i·date [inˈvælideit] *vt.* 使无效，使失效．

in·val·i·da·tion [inˌvæliˈdeiʃən] *n.* 无效；失效．

in·va·lid·ism [ˈinvəlidizəm] *n.* 病弱，虚弱，伤残．

in·va·lid·i·ty [ˌinvəˈliditi] *n.* ①无效力．②(因病残而)丧失工作能力．

in·val·u·a·ble [inˈvæljuəbl] *a.* 无法估价的，无价的；非常贵重的．*an* ～ *treasure* 无价之宝．**-bly** *ad.* **-ness** *n.*

in·var [inˈvɑː] *n.*【冶】因钢，因瓦(铁镍)合金，不胀钢，恒范钢．

in·var·i·a·ble [inˈvɛəriəbl] *a.* 无变化的；不变的；一律的．— *n.*【数】不变量，常数．**-bil·i·ty, -ness** *n.* 不变性．**-bly** *ad.* 不变地；永恒地；常常．

in·var·i·ant [inˈvɛəriənt] *a.* 不变的，无变度的；一定的，恒定的．— *n.*【数】不变式；不变量．**-i·ance** *n.*

in·va·sion [inˈveiʒən] *n.* ①侵入，侵略．②侵害，侵犯．③【医】发病，发作．*an* ～ *of locust* 蝗虫的侵袭．*cultural* ～ 文化侵略．*an* ～ *of disease* 疾病的侵入．*make an* ～ *upon* 侵入，袭击．～ *of sb.'s privacy* 非法干预某人的私事．

in·va·sive [inˈveisiv] *a.* 侵略性的，侵害的；侵袭的．**-ness** *n.* 侵略性，侵袭性．

in·vec·tive [inˈvektiv] *a.* 诽谤的，责骂的．— *n.*〔*pl.*〕骂人的话．*a stream of coarse* ～*s* 一连串下流的骂人话．*utter* ～*s against sb.* 痛骂某人．**-ly** *ad.* **-ness** *n.*

in·veigh [inˈvei] *vi.* 痛骂，猛烈攻击 *(against)*．～ *against bureaucracy* 指责官僚主义．

in·veigh·er [inˈveiə] *n.* 咒骂者，攻击者．

in·vei·gle [inˈviːgl, -ˈvei-] *vt.* 诱惑，诱骗，诱陷．～ *sb. into (doing) sth.* 诱骗某人做某事．～ *sb. out of sth.*〔口〕骗取某人东西．**-ment** *n.*

in·vei·gler [inˈviːglə, -ˈvei-] *n.* 诱骗者，诱陷者，诱惑者．

in·ve·nit [inˈveinit] *v.* *(pl.* ***in·ve·ne·runt*** [ˌinviˈniərənt]*)*〔L.〕〔第三人称单数〕(某某)作，创制．

in·vent [inˈvent] *vt.* ①发明，创作，创制．②捏造，虚构．*Morse* ～*ed the telegraph* 摩尔斯发明电报．～ *an excuse* 捏造借口．**-er, -or** *n.* 发明者，创制者．

in·ven·tion [inˈvenʃən] *n.* ①发明，创造．②新发明；发明的东西．③创造力，发明才能．④捏造，虚构．⑤〔古〕发见．⑥【乐】创意曲．*Necessity is the mother of* ～．〔谚〕需要是发明之母．*make an* ～ 发明；杜撰．*a registered* ～

注过册的新发明.

in·ven·tive [in'ventiv] *a.* 发明创造的, 有发明能力的, 能独出心裁的, 有创造力的. ～ *powers* 发明创造的能力. **-ness** *n.* 有发明创造能力; 独创性; 独创能力. **-ly** *ad.*

in·ven·to·ry ['invəntri] *n.* ①(财产等的)清单, 报表; (商品的)目录. ②盘存, 存货. *an aircraft* ～【军】编制内飞机总数. *physical* ～【商】实地盘存. ～ *control* (计算机的)编目控制. ～ *liquidating*【商】减少存货. *make [take, draw up] an* ～ *of* 编制…的目录, 开列…的清单. — *vt.* 编制(商品等的)目录, 开清单, 盘存. **-to·ri·al** [-'tɔriəl] *a.* **-to·ri·al·ly** *ad.*

in·ve·rac·i·ty [ˌinvə'ræsiti] *n.* ①不诚实; 虚伪. ②*(pl. -ties)* 谎言, 欺骗.

in·ver·ness [ˌinvə'nes] *n.* ①长披风, 带护肩的斗篷 (= I- ['invənes] cape [cloak, coat]).

in·verse [in'və:s] *a.* 相反的; 逆的; 翻转的, 倒转的. *an* ～ *network* 倒置(电)网络. ～ *time* 逆时, 反时. *an* ～ *transistor* 换接晶体管. — *n.* 反面; 反量, 倒数. *be an* ～ *measure of a number of* 是同…成反比. *'Evil' is the* ～ *of 'good'*. '恶'是'善'的反面. — *vt.* 使倒转, 使成反面. ～ **function**【数】反逆函数. ～ **proportion**【数】反比例. ～ **ratio**【数】反比, 逆比.

in·verse·ly [in'və:sli] *ad.* 相反地. ～ *as the square of* 与…的平方成反比. ～ *proportional to* 成反比.

in·ver·sion [in'və:ʃən] *n.* ①倒转, 反转, 逆转; 倒置, 转换. ②倒置物, 颠倒现象. ③【语法】倒装法, 语序倒置法; (语言的)卷舌. ④【数】反演. ⑤【乐】(和音、主题等的)转回. ⑥【化】转化. ⑦【机】(四杆机构的)机架变化. ⑧【医】内翻. ⑨【精神病学】同性恋. ⑩【气】逆温, 逆增. ⑪【生】(染色体的)倒位. ⑫【电】(直流电转成交流电的)换流; 【自】反相. ～ *of relief*【地】地形倒置. ～ *point* 转化点. ～ *hybrid* 倒位杂种. *the* ～ *layer* 逆温层.

in·ver·sive [in'və:siv] *a.* 反向的, 倒转的.

in·vert [in'və:t] *vt.* ①翻过来, (上下, 前后)倒置, 反转. ②【乐】转回. ③【化】转化. ～ *a glass* 把茶杯扣起来. — ['invə:t] *n.* ①【建】仰拱. ②性欲颠倒的人. ③颠倒了的事物. — ['invə:t] *a.*【生化】转化的. ～ *sugar* 转化糖.

in·vert·ase [in'və:teis] *n.*【生化】转化酶, 蔗糖酶.

in·ver·te·brate [in'və:tibrit] *a.* ①【动】无脊骨的, 无脊椎的. ②无骨气的, 软弱无能的. — *n.* ①无脊椎动物. ②没骨气的人.

in·vert·ed [in'və:tid] *a.* 反转的; 倒转的; 倒置的; (电压)反接的. ～ *arch*【建】仰拱. ～ *blockade* 空中封锁. ～ *engine*【机】倒缸发动机. ～ *flight*【军】倒飞. ～ **comma** 引号 (= quotation mark). ～ **mordent**【乐】逆波音.

in·vert·er [in'və:tə] *n.*【电】①换流器; 倒相器, 倒换器. ②变换电路. ③反相旋转换流器.

in·vert·i·ble [in'və:tibl] *a.* ①可颠倒的, 可反转的. ②【化】可转化的.

in·vest [in'vest] *vt.* ①使穿; 使带(勋章等). ②授与, 赋予. ③使带有(某种性质等). ④【军】包围. ⑤投资, 投入(时间、精力等). ～ *sb. with a decoration* 给某人戴上奖章. ～ *sb. with full power* 把全权授与某人. ～ *sb. in an office* 任命某人担任某职务. *be* ～ *with mystery* 使带有神秘色彩. *The enemy* ～*ed the city.* 敌人包围了那个城市. ～ *money in stocks* 投资购买股票. ～*ed capital* 投入资本. — *vi.* ①投资 *(in)*. ～ *heavily in sth.* 对某事大量投资. ②〔口〕买进 *(in)*. ～ *in a hat* 买帽子.

in·ves·ti·gate [in'vestigeit] *vt.* 研究, 调查; 审查. *Scientists* ～ *the nature.* 科学家研究自然. ～ *a murder* 审查杀人案件. — *vi.* 研究, 调查. ～ *into an affair* 调查一件事情.

in·ves·ti·ga·tion [inˌvesti'geiʃən] *n.* ①研究, 调查; 审查. ②研究论文, 调查报告. *make an* ～ *on [of, into] sth.* 对某事进行调查研究. *The matter is under* ～. 这事正在调查中.

in·ves·ti·ga·tive, in·ves·ti·ga·to·ry [in'vestigeitiv, -gətəri] *a.* 研究的, 调查的, 爱调查研究的.

in·ves·ti·ga·tor [in'vestigeitə] *n.* 研究者, 调查者, 侦查员.

in·ves·ti·tive [in'vestitiv] *a.* ①投资的, 有投资能力的, 有投资可能的. ②授权[任命]的.

in·ves·ti·ture [in'vestitʃə] *n.* ①〔英〕授职(仪式); 授权. ②(性格等的)赋予. ③服装, 装饰. ④(封建时代的)封地仪式.

in·vest·ment [in'vestmənt] *n.* ①投资; 投资额; (时间、资本等的)投入; 投入资金的东西. ②授职(仪式); 授权. ③包围, 封锁. ④覆盖. *make an* ～ *in* 投资. ～ **bank** 投资银行. ～ **fund** 投资信托, 投资公司〔投资于证券者〕. ～ **company [trust]** 投资信托公司. ～ **letter stock** 投资信股; 未登记股票 (= letter stock).

in·ves·tor [in'vestə] *n.* ①投资者. ②授权者. ③包围者, 围攻者.

in·vet·er·a·cy [in'vetərəsi] *n.* (成见、仇恨、习惯等的)根深蒂固.

in·vet·er·ate [in'vetərit] *a.* 根深蒂固的, 长期形成的, 积重难返的. *an* ～ *conservative* 顽固不化的保守派. *an* ～ *disease* 宿疾, 老毛病. *an* ～ *enemy* 不共戴天的仇敌. *an* ～ *habit* 积习. *an* ～ *smoker* 烟瘾很大的人. **-ly** *ad.*

in·vid·i·ous [in'vidiəs] *a.* ①引起反感的, 令人厌恶的. ②招嫉妒的, 招猜忌的. ～ *remarks* 不中听的话. ～ *distinctions* 使人反感的差别. ～ *position* 招人猜忌的地位. **-ly** *ad.* **-ness** *n.*

in·vig·i·late [in'vidʒileit] *vi.* 〔英〕监考; 〔罕〕监视. **-la·tion** *n.* **-la·tor** *n.*

in·vig·or·ate [in'vigəreit] *vt.* 提神, 使强壮; 鼓舞, 激励. ～ *the national spirit* 振奋民族精神.

in·vig·or·at·ing, -a·tive [in'vigəreitiŋ, -tiv] *a.* 提神的, 爽快的, 令人鼓舞的. *an* ～ *climate* 令人心旷神怡的气候. ～ *news* 鼓舞人心的消息.

in·vig·or·a·tion [inˌvigə'reiʃən] *n.* 增益精力; 滋补; 鼓舞.

in·vig·or·a·tor [in'vigəˌreitə] *n.* 激励者; 补药.

in·vin·ci·bil·i·ty [inˌvinsi'biliti] *n.* 无敌.

in·vin·ci·ble [in'vinsəbl] *a.* 无敌的; 战无不胜的. *an* ～ *army* 常胜军. ～ *ignorance* 无法可想的愚蠢. **-ci·ble·ness** *n.* = invincibility **-bly** *ad.*

in vi·no ve·ri·tas [in 'vi:nəu 'veritæs, -'vainəu-] 〔L.〕酒醉吐真言.

in·vi·o·la·bil·i·ty [inˌvaiələ'biliti] *n.* 不可侵犯, 神圣; 不可违背.

in·vi·o·la·ble [in'vaiələbl] *a.* 神圣的, 不可侵犯的; 不可违背的. *an* ～ *promise* 不可违背的诺言. *an* ～ *heavens* 不可违背的上苍. **-bly** *ad.*

in·vi·o·late [in'vaiəlit], **-d** [-leitid] *a.* 不受侵犯的; 神圣的, 无污点的. *keep one's faith* ～ 坚持信仰. **-vio·la·cy, -ness** *n.* **-ly** *ad.*

in·vis·cid [in'visid] *a.* 非粘滞性的; 无韧性的; 不能展延的.

in·visi·ble [in'vizəbl] *a.* ①看不见的, 无形的. ②不显眼的, 微小得看不出的. ③不露面的, 谢绝来客的. ④未列在公开帐目上的, 统计表上看不出的. ～ *cap* (传说中的)隐身帽. ～ *spectrum*【物】不可见光谱. ～ *mending* 织补. ～ *to the naked eye* 肉眼看不见. *keep oneself* ～ *in his room* 躲在屋内不露面. ～ *assets* 帐外资产. — *n.* 看不见的人[物]. 〔the ～〕【宗】幽冥世界, 冥界; 〔the I-〕神, 上帝. **I- Empire** 无形帝国〔美国三K党活动初期的别称〕. ～ **export** 无形输出. ～ **green** 深绿. ～ **import** 无形输入. ～ **ink** 密写墨水〔经热气或药品作用方显字迹的墨水〕. ～ **supply** (农家未出售的)余粮总量. ～ **transactions** 无形交易(指非具体

商品的交易,如航运、保险、旅游等). **-bil·i·ty, -ness** *n.* **-bly** *ad.*

in·vi·ta·tion [ˌinviˈteiʃən] *n.* ①招待,邀请;请帖. ②吸引,诱惑. *accept [decline] an* ~ 接受[谢绝]邀请. *admission by* ~ *only* 凭柬入场. *an* ~ *tournament* 邀请赛. *at the* ~ *of sb.* 应某人邀请. *The* ~*s are out.* 请帖已发出.

in·vi·ta·tion·al [ˌinviˈteiʃənl] *a.* 邀请的,应邀参加的. *an* ~ *art exhibit* 一件应邀参加展出的美术作品.

in·vi·ta·to·ry [inˈvaitətəri] *a.* 邀请的,招待的.

in·vite [inˈvait] *vt.* ①招待,邀请. ②请求,征求. ③引起,吸引. *an* ~*d guests* 来宾. *be* ~*d out* 应邀,被邀请. ~ *sb. in* 邀请某人到家里. ~ *oneself* 不请自到. ~ *sb. to consider* 请求某人考虑. *Questions are* ~*d.* 欢迎提问题. ~ *tenders* 招(人投)标. ~ *war* 引起战争. *Every scene* ~*s the ravished eye.* 场场引人入胜. — [ˈinvait] *n.* 〔口〕招待;邀请. **-e** *n.* 被招待者,被邀请者. **-r** *n.* 招待者,邀请者.

in·vit·ing [inˈvaitiŋ] *a.* 引人注目的,吸引人的. **-ly** *ad.* **-ness** *n.*

in vi·vo [in ˈviːvəu] 〔L.〕在活微生物中出现的.

in·vo·cate [ˈinvəukeit] *vt., vi.* 〔罕〕祷求,祈求,祈灵.

in·vo·ca·tion [ˌinvəuˈkeiʃən] *n.* ①祈祷;祈求. ②召唤魔鬼,符咒,咒语. ③(法权的)行使,(法规、条文等的)援引;发动.

in·vo·ca·tion·al [ˌinvəuˈkeiʃənl] *a.* 祈求的;祈祷的,恳求的.

in·voc·a·to·ry [inˈvɔkətəri] *a.* 祈祷的,恳求的.

in·voice [ˈinvɔis] *n.* ①【商】发票,装货清单. ②货物的托运. ~ *specification* 发票明细单. *receive a large* ~ *of goods* 接受大宗商品的托运. — *vt., vi.* 开(…的)发票,开(…的)清单. ~ **book** *n.* 进货簿;发票存根.

in·voke [inˈvəuk] *vt.* ①祈求(神灵)保佑,乞灵于,用符咒召唤. ②吁请,乞求. ③行使(法权等),实行. ④援引(法规、条文等). ⑤引起,产生. ~ *evil spirits* 召唤恶魔. ~ *the power of the law* 请求依法支持. ~ *sb.'s help* 恳求某人帮助. ~ *economic sanctions* 实行经济制裁. ~ *the veto in the meeting* 在会议中行使否决权. ~ *an article of the U.N. Charter* 援引《联合国宪章》条文. ~ *new problems* 引起一些新问题. **-r** *n.* 祈求者.

in·vol·u·cel [inˈvɔljusel] *n.* 【植】小总苞,小叶苞. **-cel·late** *a.*

in·vo·lu·crate [ˈinvəluːkrit, -kreit] *a.* 【植】有总苞的;有花被的;有蒴苞的.

in·vo·lu·cre [ˈinvəluːkə] *n.* ①【解】外皮,包膜. ②【植】花被,蒴包,总苞.

in·vo·lu·crum [ˌinvəˈluːkrəm] *n.* = involucre (*pl.* ***involucra*** [ˌinvəˈluːkrə]). **-lu·cral** *a.*

in·vol·un·tar·y [inˈvɔləntəri] *a.* ①无意识的,不自觉的. ②非故意的,偶然的. ③非自愿的,不随意的 (*opp.* voluntory). *Sneezing is* ~. 打喷嚏是不自觉的. *an* ~ *confession* 不打自招的供状. ~ *homicide* 【法】过失杀人(罪). ~ *muscles* 【解】不随意肌. **-tar·i·ly** *ad.* **-tar·i·ness** *n.*

in·vo·lute [ˈinvəluːt] *a.* ①纷乱的,错综复杂的. ②【植】内卷的. ③内旋的;螺状的. ~ *teeth [gear]* 【机】渐开线齿轮. — *n.* 【数】渐伸线,渐开线,切展线. — [ˌinvəˈluːt] *vi.* ①内卷,卷起. ②恢复原状. ③消失,消散.

in·vo·lu·tion [ˌinvəˈluːʃən] *n.* ①卷入,纠缠;错综复杂. ②【数】乘方. ③【生】退化;内转 (*opp.* evolution). ④【医】萎缩,退化,复旧. ⑤复杂的句型. *senile* ~ 老年性退化.

in·volve [inˈvɔlv] *vt.* ①包缠,卷缠. ②拖累,连累,使陷入,使卷入(旋涡). ③包围,围住,笼罩 (*in, with*). ④包括,涉及,引起,包含;含有…的意义. ⑤〔主用被动式〕使埋头,使专注. ⑥【数】把某数字乘方. *be* ~*d in trouble* 陷入烦恼. *Clouds* ~ *the mountain top.* 云雾笼罩山头. *The real meaning of his remark is* ~*d in ambiguity.* 他这句话的真正意思很难捉摸. ~ *much difficulty* 带有许多困难. *This* ~*s an increase of the national debt.* 这样就难免使国债增加. *be* ~*d in working out a plan* 专心一意地制订计划. ~ *a number to the fifth power* 把某数字五乘方. ***become*** ~***d in*** 卷入,陷入. ***be*** ~***d in*** 被包入;被卷入旋涡,被连累(*be* ~*d in war* 被卷入战争旋涡. *be* ~*d in debt* 债台高筑. *be* ~*d in disaster* 陷入不幸). ***get*** ~***d with*** 给…缠住.

in·volved [inˈvɔlvd] *a.* ①卷入的,陷入的. ②(财政上)困难的. ③复杂的;混乱的,晦涩的. ④有关的,所包含的. ~ *phraseology* 晦涩的措词. *an* ~ *sentence* 复杂的句子. *all governments* ~ 各有关政府. *the various academic questions* ~ 涉及到的各种学术问题.

in·volve·ment [inˈvɔlvment] *n.* ①包缠,缠绕;包含,含有. ②牵连的事务,复杂的情况. ③财政困难.

invt. = inventory.

in·vul·ner·a·ble [inˈvʌlnərəbl] *a.* ①不会受伤害的,刀枪不入的. ②无可辩驳的. ~ *arguments* 无懈可击的[攻不破的]论点. **-bil·i·ty** *n.* **-bly** *ad.*

in·ward [ˈinwəd] (*opp.* outward) *a.* ①内面的,内部的;向内的. ②内地的. ③内心上的,亲密的,熟悉的. ④(声音)低沉的,暗自说着的. ⑤本来的,本质上的. ⑥【商】进口的,输入的,引进的. ~ *correspondence* 来信. *an* ~ *curve* 内弯. *the* ~ *organs of the body* 身体内部的器官. *an* ~ *voyage* 归航. ~ *Asia* 亚洲的腹地. ~ *happiness* 内心的喜悦. ~ *struggle* 精神上的斗争. ~ *nature of a thing* 事物的本质. *speak in an* ~ *voice* 说话的声音低沉. ~ *charges* 入港费. *an* ~ *entry* 进口申请书. *an* ~ *manifest* 进口货清单. ~ *processing* 运进加工. — *n.* ①(物体的)内部;内心. ②〔*pl.* 常例作[ˈinərdz]〕〔口〕内脏. (作食品的)肠,胃. *a pain in the* ~*s* 肚子痛. ③〔*pl.*〕〔英〕进口税,进口货. — *ad.* ①向内,向内心. ~ *bound* 【海】向内行驶. *slope* ~ 向内倾斜. ②向着内心,进入心灵. **-ly** *ad.* ①在内,在内部;内里,向内,向中心 (*bleed* ~*ly* 内出血). ②在心灵深处;思想上;精神上 (~*ly resentful* 内心不满的). ③暗自地 (*speak* ~*ly* 自言自语). **-ness** *n.* ①真相,真意;本性,本质. ②心性,灵性. ③思想感情的深度,诚挚.

in·wards [ˈinwədz] *ad.* ⇒ inward (*ad.*)

in·weave [inˈwiːv] *vt.* (***-wove*** [-wəuv], ***-weaved; -woven-*** [-ˈwəuvn], ***-wove, -weaven*** [-wiːvn]) 使织入,使交织.

in·wrap [inˈræp] *vt.* = enwrap.

in·wreathe [inˈriːð] *vt.* = enwreathe.

in·wrought [ˈinˈrɔːt] *a.* ①织有(花纹)的,绣有…的,嵌有…的 (*with*). ②纺织品中织入花纹的,加花纹的 (*in, on*). ③与…紧密配合的. *skirts* ~ *with patterns* 织有图案的裙子.

I·o [ˈaiəu] *n.* ①【希神】爱莪〔主神宙斯的情人,后为宙斯之妻 Hera 施法变为母牛〕. ②【天】木星的第二卫星.

Io = 【化】ionium.

I/O = Input/Output【自】输入/输出.

IOC = International Olympic Committee 国际奥林匹克委员会.

IOCS = input-output control system. 输入-输出控制系统.

i·od- *comb. f.* 表示"碘": *iodate.*

i·o·date [ˈaiədeit] *vt.* 用碘处理;向…加碘. — *n.* 【化】碘酸盐. **-da·tion** *n.*

i·od·ic [aiˈɔdik] *a.* 碘的;含碘的;五价碘的. ~ **acid** 碘酸.

i·o·dide, i·o·did [ˈaiədaid, -did] *n.* 碘化物. ~ *of potassium* 碘化钾.

i·o·di·nate [ˈaiədineit] *vt.* (***-nated; nat·ing***) 【化】碘化;用碘处理. **-na·tion** *n.*

i·o·dine, -din [ˈaiədiːn, -din] *n.* ①【化】碘. ②〔口〕碘酊. *an* ~ *number* 碘值. ~ *preparation* 碘剂. *tincture of*

～【药】碘酊.
i·o·dism [ˈaiədizm] *n.*【医】碘中毒.
i·o·dize [ˈaiədaiz] *vt.* 用碘[碘化物]处理;使含碘. ～*d salt* 加碘食盐[加有少量的碘化钠或碘化钾].
i·o·do- *pref.* = iod-.
i·o·do·form [aiˈɔdəfɔːm] *n.*【化】碘仿,三碘甲烷.
I·o·dol [ˈaiədəul] *n.* 碘末防腐剂[商标名.碘的黄色晶状粉末,用作消毒剂].
i·o·dom·e·try [ˌaiəˈdɔmitri] *n.*【化】碘量滴定法. **-tric** [-dəuˈmetrik] *a.*
i·o·do·pro·tein [ˌaiədəuˈprəutin, -prəutiːin] *n.*【化】碘蛋白.
i·o·dop·sin [aiəˈdɔpsin] *n.* 视紫蓝质,视青紫素.
i·o·dous [aiˈəudəs,ˈaiədəs] *a.* 亚碘的.
I. of W. = Isle of Wight [英] 怀特岛.
IOJ = International Organization of Journalists 国际新闻工作者协会.
i·o·lite [ˈaiəˌlait] *n.* (= cordierite).
IOM = Isle of Man 马恩岛[英国].
I·o moth [ˈaiəu mɔθ]【动】大蚕蛾 *(Automeris io)* [产于北美,后翅上有眼状斑,其幼虫的毛有毒,能蜇人].
i·on [ˈaiən,ˈaiɔn] *n.*【物】离子. *positive [negative]* ～ 正[负]离子. ～ **engine** 离子发动机. ～ **exchange** 离子交换(作用). ～ **exchange resin** 离子交换树脂. ～ **exclusion** 离子摈斥. ～ **implantation** 离子注入技术[制造半导体的一个程序]. ～ **rocket** 离子火箭.
-ion *suf.* 构成名词. ①表示行为的过程,结果. ②表示状态[情况]: translat*ion*, condemnat*ion* fus*ion*, conscript*ion*, correct*ion*.
I·o·ni·a [aiˈəuniə] *n.* 爱奥尼亚[位于小亚细亚西岸,包括爱琴海的岛屿,公元前十一世纪曾为古希腊工商业和文化中心之一].
I·o·ni·an [aiˈəunjən,-niən] *a.* 爱奥尼亚(人)的;【建】爱奥尼亚式的. — *n.* 爱奥尼亚人,爱奥尼亚语. *the* ～ *mode*【乐】爱奥尼亚音阶法. ～ **Islands** 爱奥尼亚岛屿[小亚细亚西岸]. ～ **Sea** (希)爱奥尼亚海.
I·on·ic [aiˈɔnik] *a.* 爱奥尼亚的,爱奥尼亚人的; 爱奥尼亚音步的;【建】爱奥尼亚式的. ～ *capital* 爱奥尼亚式的柱顶. — *n.* 爱奥尼亚语; [*i*-]【印】一种粗字面铅字. ～ **dialect** 爱奥尼亚方言. ～ **foot** 爱奥尼亚音步.
i·on·ic [aiˈɔnik] *a.* 离子的. ～ *bond [link]*【化】电子键. **-i·ty** *n.* 离子性,电离度.
i·o·ni·um [aiˈəuniəm] *n.*【化】锾(天然存在的放射性元素,钍的同位素).
i·on·i·za·tion [ˌaiənaiˈzeiʃən] *n.*【物】电离(作用); 离子化. ～ *by impact [light]* 碰撞[光感]电离. ～ *constant* 电离常数. *an* ～ *gauge* 电离压力[真空]计. ～ *layer* 电离层. *photo* ～ 光致电离. ～ **chamber** 电离室.
i·on·iz·a·bil·i·ty [ˌaiənaizəˈbiliti] *n.* 电离度.
i·on·ize [ˈaiənaiz] *vt.* 使电离,使电离成离子. — *vi.* 电离. **-r** *n.* 电离剂[器].
i·on·o·gen [aiˈɔnədʒən] *n.* 电解质,电解物;可离子化的基团. **-gent·ic** [-ˈdʒentik] *a.*
i·on·o·me·ter [aiˈəunəmiːtə] *n.* ①离子计,离子测定仪. ②射线强度计.
I·o·none [ˈaiənəun]【化】"紫罗(兰)酮"[商标名]. — *n.* [*i*-] 紫罗(兰)酮[制香水的一种原料].
i·on·o·phone [aiˈɔnəfəun] *n.*【无】离子扬声器.
i·on·o·pho·re·sis [ˌaiɔnəˈfɔrəsis] *n.*【化】电离电泳作用.
I·on·o·sonde [aiˈɔnəsɔnd] *n.*【无】电离层探测装置.
i·on·o·sphere [aiˈɔnəsfiə] *n.*【物】电离层. **-spher·ic** *a.*
IOS = International Organization for Standardization (联合国)国际标准化组织.
i·o·ta [aiˈəutə] *n.* ①希腊语的第九个字母[即 I, ι = i]. ②微小,一点. *have not an* ～ *of* 没有一点儿…. *not change by an* ～ 丝毫不变.
i·o·ta·cism [aiˈəutəsizəm] *n.* ①过多使用"i"(希腊字母 iota) 字母. ②对其他元音加 [iː] 音的倾向[尤其希腊语如此].
IOU, I.O.U. [ˈaiəuˈjuː] *n.* 借据 [由 I owe you 的读音缩略转义而成].
-iour *suf.* 表示"…的人": pav*iour*, sav*iour*.
-ious *suf.* 表示"具有…特质的","充满…的": delic*ious*, fur*ious*, prec*ious*, prodig*ious*, relig*ious*.
I.O.W. = Isle of Wight [英] 怀特岛.
I·o·wa [ˈaiəwə] *n.* 衣阿华[美国的州名]. **-wan** ①*a.* 衣阿华州的,衣阿华州人的. ② *n.* 衣阿华州人.
IP = initial point 起点.
IPA = ①International Phonetic Association 国际语音学协会. ②International Phonetic Alphabet 国际音标.
ip·e·cac, ip·e·cac·u·an·ha [ˈipikæk, ˌipiˌkækjuˈænə] *n.* ①【植】吐根. ②吐根的根茎和根;吐根制剂.
Iph·i·ge·ni·a [iˌfidʒiˈnaiə] *n.*【希神】(迈锡尼王阿伽门农的女儿)伊芙琴尼亚.
IPI = International Press Institute 国际新闻学会.
ip·o·moe·a [ˌipəˈmiːə,ˌaipəˈmiːə] *n.*【植】番藷属 *(Ipomoea)* 植物[包括圆叶牵牛(紫花牵牛); 番藷(白薯,山芋,地瓜)].
I.P.R. = Institute of Pacific Relations [美] 太平洋学会.
ips, i.p.s. = inches per second 每秒英寸[…英寸/秒].
ip·se dix·it [ˈipsi ˈdiksit] *(pl.* ***ip·se dix·its)*** [L.] 武断的话;亲口所述 (=he himself said it).
ip·si·lat·er·al [ˌipsiˈlætərəl] *a.* (身体的)同一侧的; 影响身体的同一侧的. **-ly** *ad.*
ip·sis·si·ma ver·ba [ipˈsisimə ˈvəːbə] [L.] 作者的原话(= the very word).
ip·so fac·to [ˈipsəu ˈfæktəu] [L.] 照那个事实,根据事实本身.
ip·so ju·re [ˈipsəu ˈdʒuəriː] [L.] 根据法律本身,依法律.
IPU = ①Inter-Parliamentary Union 各国议会联盟. ②International Peasant Union 国际农民联合会.
IQ, I.Q. = intelligence quotient 智商,智力商数[心理学家进行智力测验的术语].
i.q. = [L.] *idem quod* 同… (= the same as).
IR = infrared.
Ir = iridium【化】元素铱的符号.
Ir. = Ireland; Irish.
ir- [iə] *pref.* [用于以 r 开始的字前面]. ①表示"不","非"如: *ir*replaceable, *ir*responsible, *ir*respective. ②表示"进入","在内"如: *ir*regation, *ir*ruption.
I·ra [ˈaiərə] *n.* 艾拉[男子名].
IRA, I.R.A. = Irish Republican Army 爱尔兰共和军.
i·ra·cund [ˈairəkʌnd] *a.* [古] 易怒的; 暴躁的. **-di·ty** *n.*
i·ra·de [iˈrɑːdi] *n.* ①(穆斯林)教徒的统治者的法令[教令]. ②【史】土耳其皇帝的敕令.
I·rak [iˈrɑːk] *n.* = Iraq.
I·ra·ki [iˈrɑːki] *n., a.* = Iraqi.
I·ran [iˈrɑːn] *n.* 伊朗[亚洲].
Iran. = Iranian.
IRANAIR = Iranian Airways 伊朗航空公司.
I·ra·ni·an [iˈreinjən] *a.* 伊朗的,伊朗人的,印欧语系的[包括波斯语,普什图语,阿韦斯塔语,库尔德斯坦语等] — *n.* 伊朗人;伊朗语系.
Iraq [iˈrɑːk] *n.* 伊拉克[亚洲].
I·ra·qi [iˈrɑːki] *n.* *(pl.* ～*s)* 伊拉克 *(Iraq)* 人; 伊拉克人讲的阿拉伯语. — *a.* 伊拉克的; 伊拉克人的; 伊拉克人讲的阿拉伯语的.
i·ras·ci·ble [iˈræsibl] *a.* 易怒的,性情暴躁的. **-bil·i·ty** **-ble·ness** *n.* **-bly** *ad.*
i·ra·ser [iˈreisə] = infra-red amplification by stimulated emission of radiation 红外激射(器); 红外激光.

i·rate [aiˈreit] *a.* 愤怒的,发怒的,激怒的. **-ly** *ad.* **-ness** *n.*

I.R.B. = Irish Republican Brotherhood. 爱尔兰共和兄弟会.

IRBM = intermediate range ballistic missile 中程弹道导弹.

IRC = International Red Cross 国际红十字会.

ir·dome [ˈiədəum] *n.*【物】可通过红外线的整流罩,红外穹门.

ire [ˈaiə] *n.* 〔诗〕怒火,忿怒. **-ful·ness** *n.*

Ire. = Ireland.

ire·ful [ˈaiəful] *a.* 〔诗〕发怒的,忿怒的. **-ly** *ad.*

Ire·land [ˈaiələnd] *n.* 爱尔兰.

I·rene [aiˈri:ni,ˈairi:n] *n.* ①艾琳〔女子名〕. ②【希神】和平的女神.

i·ren·ic(al) [aiˈrenik(əl)] *a.* 促进和平的,和平的,爱好和平的. ~ *means* 和平的手段. **-i·cal·ly** *ad.*

i·ren·i·con [aiˈreniˌkən] *n.* = eirenicon.

i·ren·ics [aiˈreniks, aiˈri:niks] *n. pl.* 〔动词用单数〕(基督教各教派)和睦相处论〔促进基督教各教派在神学观点的分歧上和平相处的主张或做法〕;和平相处神学.

I·re·ton [ˈaiətn] *n.* 艾尔顿〔姓氏〕.

Ir·i·an [ˌiəriˈɑ:n] 伊里安〔"新几内亚"的印尼语名称〕.

i·rid [ˈairid] *n.*【植】鸢尾科植物.

i·ri·da·ceous [ˌairiˈdeiʃəs] *a.*【植】鸢尾科的.

ir·i·dec·to·my [ˌiəriˈdektəmi, ˌaiəri-] *n.* *(pl.* **-mies** [-mi:z]*)*【医】虹膜切除术.

ir·i·des [ˈiəriˌdi:z,ˈaiəri-] iris 的复数.

ir·i·des·cence [ˌiriˈdesns] *n.* ①【气】虹彩. ②彩虹色.

ir·i·des·cent [ˌiriˈdesnt] *a.* ①【气】虹彩的. ②彩虹色的. ③【纺】闪光的,闪色的. ~ *cloud* 虹彩云. ~ *fabric* 闪光织物,闪色织物. **-ly** *ad.*

i·rid·ic [iˈridik, ai-] *a.* ①铱的;含铱的. ②含四价铱化合物的. ③虹膜的.

i·rid·i·um [iˈridiəm] *n.*【化】铱.

ir·i·dos·mine [ˌiəriˈdɔzmin,ˌaiəri-; -ˈdɔs-mi:n] *n.*【矿】铱锇矿 (= iridosmium).

I·ris [ˈaiəris] *n.* ①艾丽斯〔女子名〕. ②【希神】(为诸神报信的)彩虹女神.

i·ris [ˈaiəris] *n.* *(pl.* **-es;** ***i·ri·des*** [ˈaiəridi:z]*)* ①【解】(眼球的)虹膜. ②虹;虹状物;虹彩,彩虹色. ③【物】膜片,可变光阑,(照相机的)光圈 (= ~ diaphragm). ④【植】鸢尾属植物,鸢尾,蝴蝶花. ⑤【矿】彩虹色石英. ~ **diaphragm**【摄】光圈. ~ **in**【电视】圈入. ~ **out**【电视】圈出.

i·ris·at·ed [ˈaiəriseitid] *a.* 虹彩的,彩虹色的.

i·ris·a·tion [ˌairiˈseiʃən] *n.*【气】虹彩.

i·rised [ˈaiərist] *a.* 彩虹色的.

I·rish [ˈaiəriʃ] *a.* 爱尔兰的;爱尔兰人的;爱尔兰语的. *too (bloody)* ~! 当然! — *n.* ①爱尔兰语. ②〔*the* ~〕爱尔兰人. ③〔口〕怒火. *get one's* ~ *up*〔美〕发怒,大发脾气. ~ **bridge** (横过路面的)石砌明水沟. ~ **bull** 自相矛盾的说法. ~ **coffee** 爱尔兰咖啡〔咖啡加威士忌和奶油的饮料〕. ~ **daisy**【植】蒲公英. ~ **diamond** 水晶. ~ **Free State** (1922—1937) 爱尔兰自由邦. ~ **Gaelic** 爱尔兰居尔特语. ~ **hurricane**〔俚〕海上风平浪静时细雨蒙蒙. ~**man** *n.* *(pl.* ~**men***)* 爱尔兰人. **-man's dinner**〔美〕绝食. **-man's promotion [rise]** 明升暗降. **-man's sidewalk**〔美〕人行道. ~ **marathon**【美体】接力赛跑. ~ **moss**【植】角叉菜. ~ **nightingale**〔俚〕男高音歌唱者. ~ **point (lace)** 爱尔兰手工花边. ~ **potato**〔美〕马铃薯〔又叫 white potato, 即普通的白马铃薯,同 sweet potato 区别而言〕. ~ **setter** 黑褐色长毛猎狗. ~ **stew** 马铃薯洋葱煮羊肉. ~ **terrier** 爱尔兰㹴犬. ~ **welcome**〔俚〕欢迎随时光临的邀请. ~ **wolfhound** 爱尔兰大猎狗. ~**woman** *n.* *(pl.* ~**women***)* 爱尔兰妇女. **-ism** *n.* 爱尔兰习语,爱尔兰风土人情. **-ry** *n.* ①〔集合词〕爱尔兰人. ②爱尔兰人性格.

I·rish·ize [ˈaiəriʃaiz] *vt.* 使爱尔兰化,使具有爱尔兰风格.

i·ri·tis [aiəˈraitis] *n.*【医】虹膜炎.

irk [ə:k] *vt.* 〔书〕使苦恼,使厌倦. *It* ~*s me to lie.* 我讨厌说假话.

irk·some [ˈə:ksəm] *a.* 讨厌的,令人厌倦的,使人厌烦的. **-ly** *ad.* **-ness** *n.*

Ir·kutsk [ə:ˈkutsk, iəˈkutsk] *n.* 伊尔库次克〔苏联亚洲的城市〕.

IRO = International Refugee Organization 国际难民组织.

i·ron [ˈaiən] *n.* ①铁. ②铁器,铁制品;小刀,尖刀;熨斗,烙铁. ③〔俚〕(牛羊身上打的)烙印. ④脚镣,手铐;马镫. ⑤(高尔夫球)铁头球棒. ⑥〔俚〕手枪,小枪. ⑦铁剂,含铁补药. ⑧铁色. ⑨(坚忍不拔的)毅力,意志. *cast* ~ 铸铁. *pig* ~ 生铁. *scrap* ~ 废铁. *wrought* ~ 熟铁,锻铁. *Strike while the* ~ *is hot.* 〔谚〕趁热打铁. *an electric* ~ 电熨斗. *an electric soldering* ~ 电烙铁. *fire* ~*s* 炉子的生火用具. *a smoothing* ~ 熨斗. *put sb. in* ~*s* 给某人系上脚镣手铐. *a barking [shooting]* ~ 手枪. *a man of* ~ 铁汉,意志坚强的人;铁面无私的人. ~ *or gold* 毅力或金钱. *muscles of* ~ 非常结实的肌肉. *rule with a rod of* ~ 用高压手段统治. ***as hard as*** ~ 铁一样坚硬. ***fresh from (off) the*** ~***s*** 崭新的;刚从学校出来的. ***have (too) many*** ~***s in the fire*** 揽在手里的事过多. ***in*** ~***s*** 带着脚镣手铐;【海】帆船掉不过头来. ***the*** ~ ***hand in the velvet glove*** 面善心狠. ***put all*** ~***s [every*** ~***] in the fire*** 使用一切手段〔方法〕. — *a.* ①铁的,铁制的. ②铁似的,坚强的,顽强的;巩固的;坚忍不拔的. ③严格的;冷酷无情的. ~ *dross [dust, filings]* 铁屑. *an* ~ *constitution* 健壮的体格. *an* ~ *will* 坚强的意志. — *vt.* ①烫(衣服等). ②给…上脚镣手铐. ③给…装铁具. — *vi.* ①烫衣服. ②(衣服等)被烫平. ~ **out** ①烫平;用铁滚轧平. ②〔美〕使和解,调停. ③压平(物价). ④〔美俚〕杀掉. ⑤消除 (~ *out misunderstandings* 消除误解). ~ **age** ①(神话)黑铁时代. ②(人类的)颓废时期,末世. *the I-Age*【考古】铁器时代. ~**bark** *n.*【植】①桉树属 *(Eucalyptus)* 植物. ②桉树属木材. ~**bound** *a.* ①包铁的. ②坚硬的;严厉的. ③岩石围绕的,险阻的. ***I- Chancellor***【史】铁血宰相〔指德国首相俾士麦〕. ~**channel** 槽钢. ~**clad** ① *a.* 装甲的〔现在多用 *armoured*〕;〔美〕严格的,无可推诿的(誓约等) (*an* ~*clad note*〔口〕有担保的期票. *an* ~*clad proof* 铁证). ② *n.* 装甲舰. ~ **curtain** 铁幕. ~**fisted** *a.* 吝啬的;残忍的. ~ **foundry** 翻砂厂,铸铁厂,铸铁车间. ~ **glance**【矿】镜铁矿. ~**-gray,** ~**-grey** *a.* 铁灰色,灰白色. ~ **hand** 严厉的手段,严刑峻法. ~**handed** *a.* 铁腕的,严厉的,用高压手段的. ~ **hat**〔美俚〕礼帽. ~**-hearted** *a.* 无情的,铁石心肠的. ~ **horse**〔口〕火车头,机车. ~ **house**〔美俚〕监狱. ~ **lung** 铁肺〔人工呼吸器〕. **I- maiden** 铁女〔旧刑具名〕. ~ **man** ①钢铁工人;〔美俚〕体力坚强的运动选手,铁汉. ②〔美俚〕银元. ~**-master** 铁工厂老板. ~ **melting furnace**【冶】化铁炉,溶铁炉. ~**monger**〔英〕铁器商,五金商. ~**mongery**〔英〕铁器类,五金制品类;铁器店,五金店. ~**mo(u)ld** ① *n.* (布等上的)铁锈迹;墨水斑点. ② *vt., vi.* (使)弄上锈迹〔墨水迹〕;(使)生锈. ~ **ore** 铁矿. ~ **pony**〔美俚〕摩托车. ~ **pyrite** 黄铁矿 (= pyrite). ~ **rations**【军】(非有命令不得食用的)应急干粮. ~ **rule** 苛政. ~ **rust** 铁锈. ~ **sand** 铁砂. ~**side** ①勇敢果断的人. ②〔I-〕〔常 *pl.*〕【英史】克伦威尔铁甲军. ③〔常 *pl.*〕铁甲舰. ~**smith** 铁匠,锻工. ~**stone** ①【矿】铁石,含铁矿石,菱铁矿. ②(英国产)坚硬的白色瓷器〔又名 ~stone china〕. ~**ware** 铁器,五金制品. ~**weed**【植】斑鸠菊属 *(Vernonia)* 植物. ~**wire** 铁丝. ~**wood**〔美〕

木质坚硬的树；坚质木材 (*a black ~wood* 野橄榄树). ~**work** ①铁工. ②铁制品. ③(建筑物、船舶等的)铁制部分. ~**worker** ①钢铁工人，铁器工人. ②铁桥构架工. ~**works** *n.* 〔*sing., pl.*〕钢铁厂.

i·ron·er [ˈaiənə] *n.* ①熨衣工. ②轧布机；砑光机；碾压机.

i·ron·ic(al) [aiəˈrɔnik(əl)] *a.* ①冷嘲的，反语的；讽刺的. ②令人啼笑皆非的. ~ *remarks* 冷言冷语. *an* ~ *smile* 冷笑. **-i·cal·ly** *ad.*

i·ron·ing [ˈaiəniŋ] *n.* ①熨烫. ②〔集合词〕要烫的衣服；烫过的衣服. ~ **board [table]** 熨衣台.

i·ron·ist [ˈaiərənist] *n.* 讽刺家，冷嘲者.

I·ron·side [ˈaiən-said] *n.* 艾恩赛德〔姓氏〕.

i·ro·ny[1] [ˈaiərəni] *n.* ①反语；讽刺，讥讽. ②【修】反语法. *the* ~ *of fate [circumstances]* 命运的嘲弄. *Socratic* ~ 苏格拉底式的佯装无知法.

i·ron·y[2] [ˈaiəni] *a.* 铁的；铁似的；含铁的.

Ir·o·quoi·an [ˌirəˈkwɔiən] *a.* 易洛魁语系的. — *n.* ①易洛魁人〔北美的一个印第安部族〕. ②易洛魁语.

Ir·o·quois [ˈirəkwɔi, ˈirəkwɔiz] *n.* 易洛魁人. — *a.* 易洛魁族的，易洛魁人的.

ir·ra·di·ance, ir·ra·di·an·cy [iˈreidiəns, -si] *n.* ①发光；射出光线. ②光辉，灿烂. ③启示. ④【物】辐照度.

ir·ra·di·ant [iˈreidiənt] *a.* 发光的；光辉的，灿烂的.

ir·ra·di·ate [iˈreidieit] *vt.* ①照耀；发光. ②使明白，启发，阐明. ③放射，扩散，送出. ④用X射线、紫外线或日光等照射；【物】辐照. *a face ~d by [with] a smile* 喜气洋洋的脸. ~ *the mind* 启发心窍. ~ *a subject* 摆清问题. ~ *energy* 发送出能量. *~d foods* 紫外线食品〔受紫外线照射使含有丙种维他命的食品〕. — *vi.* 发光，变得光辉灿烂. — *a.* 有放射力的，发光的. **ir·ra·di·a·tive** *a.* **ir·ra·di·a·tor** *n.* 【物】辐射器.

ir·ra·di·a·tion [iˌreidiˈeiʃən] *n.* ①照耀；发光. ②阐明，启发. ③【物】光渗；照光，辐照. ④【医】照射. ⑤扩散. ~ *damage* 辐射损伤. ~ *sickness* 【医】辐射病. ~ *of excitation* 【医】兴奋扩散.

ir·ra·di·ca·ble [iˈrædikəbl] *a.* 无法根除的.

ir·ra·tion·al [iˈræʃənəl] *a.* ①无理性的. ②不合理的；荒谬的. ③【数】无理的. ~ *conduct* 荒唐的行为. *an* ~ *expression* 无理式. *an* ~ *equation* 【数】无理方程式. *an* ~ *function* 无理函数. *an* ~ *number* 无理数. — *n.* ①无理性的生物. ②无理数. **-ly** *ad.* **-ness** *n.*

ir·ra·tion·al·ism [iˈræʃənəlizəm] *n.* 【哲】①非理性思想，不合理性的信仰(行为). ②非(反)理性主义. **ir·ra·tion·al·ist** *n.*

ir·ra·tion·al·i·ty [iˌræʃəˈnæliti] *n.* ①非理性；不合理. ②不合理的事.

ir·ra·tion·al·ize [iˈræʃənəlaiz] *vt.* 使无理性；使不合理.

Ir·ra·wad·dy [ˌirəˈwɔdi] *n.* 伊洛瓦底江〔缅甸〕.

ir·re·al·iz·a·ble [iˈriəlaizəbl] *a.* ①不能实现的，不能达到的. ②不能兑成现金的.

ir·re·claim·a·ble [ˌiriˈkleiməbl] *a.* 不能恢复的，不能取回的；不能开垦的；不能矫正的. **-bly** *ad.*

ir·rec·og·niz·a·ble [iˈrekəgnaizəbl] *a.* 不能认识的，不能辨认的；不能承认的.

ir·rec·on·cil·a·ble [iˈrekənsailəbl] *a.* ①不能和解的. ②不可调和的 *(to, with)*. *be* ~ *to [with] sb.* 同某人势不两立. ~ *enemies* 死敌. ~ *as fire and water* 如水火不相容. — *n.* 不能和解的人；(政治上的)死硬派；〔*pl.*〕不能调和的思想〔信仰等〕. **-bil·i·ty** *n.* **-bly** *ad.*

ir·re·cov·er·a·ble [ˌiriˈkʌvərəbl] *a.* 不能恢复的；不能挽回的；医治不好的；不能收回的(贷款等). ~ *losses* 无法弥补的损失. **-bly** *ad.*

ir·re·cu·sa·ble [ˌiriˈkju:zəbl] *a.* 回绝不了的，不可抛弃的，不可拒绝的. **-bly** *ad.*

ir·re·deem·a·ble [ˌiriˈdi:məbl] *a.* ①不能赎回的. ②(公债、纸币等)不能偿还的；不能兑成现金的. ③难矫正的；不能恢复[医治、补救]的. ~ *bank-note* 不兑现纸币. — *n.* 定期偿还公债〔指到期之前不能偿还〕. **-bly** *ad.*

ir·re·den·ta [ˌiriˈdentə] *n.* (根据历史或居民的种族)应属甲国而被乙国统治的地区.

ir·re·den·tism [ˌiriˈdentizəm] *n.* 领土收复主义，民族统一主义.

ir·re·den·tist [ˌiriˈdentist] *n.* (指十九世纪意大利的)领土收复主义者，民族统一主义者. — *a.* ①领土收复主义的，民族统一主义的. ②住在收复地区的；关于有待收复地区居民的.

ir·re·duc·i·ble [ˌiriˈdju:səbl] *a.* ①不能降低[削减]的. ②【医】难回复的，难复位的. ③【数】不能化简的，不能约的，既约的. ~ *equation* 不可约方程. ~ *fraction* 既约分数. ~ *minimum* 最小值. **-bil·i·ty** *n.* **-bly** *ad.*

ir·re·flex·ive [ˌiriˈfleksiv] *a.* 【物】漫反射的，反自反的. ~ *relation* 【逻】反(非)自反关系.

ir·ref·ra·ga·ble [iˈrefrəgəbl] *a.* 不能驳倒的，不可争辩的，不能否认的. **-bil·i·ty** *n.* **-bly** *ad.*

ir·re·fran·gi·ble [ˌiriˈfrændʒibl] *a.* ①不能违犯的. ②【光】不可折射的. **-bly** *ad.*

ir·ref·u·ta·ble [iˈrefjutəbl] *a.* 无可辩驳的，不能反驳的，驳不倒的. *an* ~ *fact* 无可辩驳的事实. **-bil·i·ty** *n.* **-bly** *ad.*

irreg. = irregular; irregularly.

ir·re·gard·less [ˌiriˈgɑ:dlis] *a., ad.* 〔非正式用语〕= regardless.

ir·reg·u·lar [iˈregjulə] *a.* ①不规则的，无规律的. ②非正规的；非正式的；法律上无效的. ③不合常规的，不正当的. ④不整齐的；参差不一的. ⑤【语法】不规律变化的. ⑥〔美〕(商品)等外的，有小缺陷的. *be* ~ *in one's attendance* 不时缺席. *an* ~ *curve* 不规则曲线；曲线板. *an* ~ *liner* 不定期航船. ~ *menstruation* 月经不调. *an* ~ *physician* 无照开业的内科医生. ~ *troops* 非正规军. ~ *conduct* 不正当的行为. *an* ~ *coast line* 曲折的海岸线. ~ *teeth* 不整齐的牙齿. ~ *verbs* 不规则动词. *slightly* ~ *shirts* 略有缺陷的衬衫. — *n.* ①非正规的人[物]. ②〔常 *pl.*〕非正规兵. ③〔美〕〔常 *pl.*〕等外品. **-ly** *ad.*

ir·reg·u·lar·i·ty [iˌregjuˈlæriti] *n.* ①不规则，无规律. ②非正规，非正式. ③不正规的事物，违法乱纪，非法行为. ④不整齐，参差不一. ⑤【语法】不规则变化. ⑥例外. ~ *of attendance* 有时缺席. *internal* ~ 【物】内在紊乱. *operating* ~ 工作事故.

ir·rel·a·tive [iˈrelətiv] *a.* (与…)无关系的 *(to)*；不相干的. **-ly** *ad.*

ir·rel·e·vance, ir·rel·e·van·cy [iˈrelivəns, -si] *n.* ①不恰当；无关系；不相干，不对题. ②缺乏时代性.

ir·rel·e·vant [iˈrelivənt] *a.* ①不恰当的；(与…)无关系的；不相干的 *(to)*，不对题的. ②缺乏时代性的，落后于潮流的. *What he said is* ~ *to the matter.* 他所说的和事实本身毫无关系. **-ly** *ad.*

ir·re·liev·a·ble [ˌiriˈli:vəbl] *a.* 不能解救的；不治的；不能减轻的；不可刻成浮雕的.

ir·re·li·gion [ˌiriˈlidʒən] *n.* 无宗教；轻视宗教，无宗教信仰，反对宗教. **-ist** *n.* 无宗教信仰者，反对宗教者.

ir·re·li·gious [ˌiriˈlidʒəs] *a.* ①无宗教的，不信[敌视]宗教的. ②违反宗教的，亵渎的，不敬神的. **-ly** *ad.*

ir·rem·e·a·ble [iˈremiəbl, -ˈri:mi-] *a.* 〔古〕一去不复返的，有去无回的.

ir·re·me·di·a·ble [ˌiriˈmi:diəbl] *a.* ①医治不好的. ②不可挽回的，不可弥补的，难改正的. *an* ~ *disease* 不治之症. ~ *faults* 无可挽救的过失. **-ble·ness** *n.* **-bly** *ad.*

ir·re·mis·si·ble [ˌiriˈmisibl] *a.* ①不能原谅的，不可宽恕的. ②不能避免的，必须承担的. **-bly** *ad.*

ir·re·mov·a·ble [iriˈmu:vəbl] *a.* ①不能移动的；不能

清除的. ②不能罢免的, 不能撤职的. **-bil·i·ty** *n.* **-bly** *ad.*

ir·rep·a·ra·ble [iˈrepərəbl] *a.* 不能修补的; 不能恢复的,不能挽回的,不能弥补的. *an* ~ *loss* 无可弥补的损失. **-ness** *n.* **-bly** *ad.*

ir·re·peal·a·ble [ˌiriˈpiːləbl] *a.* ①执行(决议)的,维护(法令)的. ②不能放弃的,无法否定的.

ir·re·place·a·ble [ˌiriˈpleisəbl] *a.* ①不能恢复原状的. ②不能替代的,失掉了就无法弥补的.

ir·re·plev·i·a·ble [ˌiriˈpleviəbl] *a.* 【法】不准保释的; (物件)被扣押的; 不能收回的.

ir·re·press·i·ble [ˌiriˈpresəbl] *a.* 压制不住的, 约束不了的. — *n.* 控制不住的人. **-bil·i·ty** *n.* **-bly** *ad.*

ir·re·proach·a·ble [ˌiriˈprəutʃəbl] *a.* 无可指摘的, 无缺点的,无过失的. **-bil·i·ty** *n.* **-bly** *ad.*

ir·re·sist·i·ble [ˌiriˈzistəbl] *a.* ①不可抗拒的, 压制不了的, 非常坚强的. ②具有非常的魅力的. *an* ~ *force* 【法】不可抗力. *She saw an* ~ *skirt in the store window.* 她看见商店的橱窗里有一条叫人着迷的裙子. **-bil·i·ty** *n.* **-bly** *ad.*

ir·res·o·lu·ble [iˈrezəljubl] *a.* 不可分解的; 不能溶化的,不能解决的.

ir·res·o·lute [iˈrezəljuːt] *a.* 无决断的,犹豫不决的,优柔寡断的,踌躇不定的; 动摇的. **-ly** *ad.* **-ness** *n.*

ir·res·o·lu·tion [ˈiˌrezəˈljuːʃən] *n.* 无决断,优柔寡断; 无定见.

ir·re·solv·a·ble [ˌiriˈzɔlvəbl] *a.* ①不能分解的,不能分离的. ②不能解决的.

ir·re·spec·tive [ˌirisˈpektiv] *a.* 不顾[不考虑,不问](…)的*(of)*. ~ *of a person* 不顾某人. ~ *of the consequences* 不顾后果. ~ *of age* 不问年龄大小. ~ *as to whether … or* …不问其是否…. **-ly** *ad.*

ir·re·spir·a·ble [ˌirisˈpaiərəbl] *a.* 不适于呼吸的.

ir·re·spon·si·ble [ˌirisˈpɔnsəbl] *a.* ①不承担责任的, 不需负责任的. ②无责任感的; 不负责任的; 不可靠的. *It is very* ~ *of him not to answer my letter.* 不回复我的信是他太不负责任. — *n.* 不承担责任的人, 无责任心的人. **-bil·i·ty, -ness** *n.* **-bly** *ad.*

ir·re·spon·sive [ˌirisˈpɔnsiv] *a.* ①不回答的. ②没有反应的*(to)*. **-ly** *ad.* **-ness** *n.*

ir·re·ten·tion [ˌiriˈtenʃən] *n.* ①不能保持, 无把持力. ②【医】(小便的)失禁.

ir·re·ten·tive [ˌiriˈtentiv] *a.* 不能保持的,无保持力的; 不能保留的.

ir·re·trace·a·ble [ˌiriˈtreisəbl] *a.* 难查出的, 不能探索的,无法描绘的. **-bly** *ad.*

ir·re·triev·a·ble [ˌiriˈtriːvəbl] *a.* 不能弥补的,不能挽救的,不能恢复的. *an* ~ *loss* 无可弥补的损失. **-bil·i·ty** *n.* **-bly** *ad.*

ir·rev·er·ence [iˈrevərəns] *n.* ①不虔诚; 不尊敬. ②无礼; 傲慢. ③不敬的行为[言语]. *be held in* ~ 丢丑. *They did* ~*s to the teachers.* 他们对老师很不尊敬.

ir·rev·er·ent [iˈrevərənt] *a.* ①不虔诚的; 不尊敬的. ②无礼的. **-ly** *ad.*

ir·rev·er·en·tial [ˌirevəˈrenʃəl] *a.* = irreverent.

ir·re·vers·i·ble [ˌiriˈvəːsəbl, -sib-] *a.* ①不可逆的,不能翻转的,不能倒置的,不能倒退的. ②【法】不能取消的,不能改变的. ~ *cycle* 【机】不可逆循环. ~ *process* 【物】不可逆过程. ~ *reaction* 【化】不可逆反应. *the* ~ *decisions of the court* 不可撤消的法院判决. **-bil·i·ty** *n.* 不可逆性. **-bly** *ad.*

ir·rev·o·ca·ble [iˈrevəkəbl] *a.* ①不能取消的, 不可废止的. ②不能改变的; 不能挽回的. ~ *letter of credit* 不可撤销信用证. *make an* ~ *decision* 做出不可变更的决定. *speak* ~ *words* 讲了决定性的言语. **-a·bil·i·ty, -ness** *n.* **-bly** *ad.*

ir·ri·den·ta [ˌiriˈdentə] *n.* = irredenta.

ir·ri·ga·ble [ˈirigəbl] *a.* 可灌溉的.

ir·ri·gate [ˈirigeit] *vt.* ①灌溉. ②【医】冲洗(伤口). ③滋润, 使清新. *a land* ~*d by many streams.* 有不少河流灌溉的土地. ~ *the desert* 灌溉荒地. — *vi.* ①进行灌溉. ②〔美俚〕饮酒过度.

ir·ri·ga·tion [ˌiriˈgeiʃən] *n.* 灌溉; 水利. ②【医】冲洗(法), 〔*pl.*〕冲注洗剂. *bring the farmland under* ~ 使农田水利化. *an* ~ *canal [channel]* 灌溉渠. *an* ~ *project* 灌溉计划. **-al** *a.* **-ist** *n.* 灌溉者,水利专家.

ir·ri·ga·tor [ˈirigeitə] *n.* 【农】①灌溉者; 灌溉设备[用具]. ②【医】冲洗器.

ir·rig·u·ous [iˈrigjuːəs] *a.* 〔古〕①潮湿的, 水分充分的. ②灌溉的.

ir·ri·ta·ble [ˈiritəbl] *a.* ①易怒的, 急躁的. ②【医】易激动的, 过敏性的. **-bil·i·ty**[-ˈbiliti], **-ness** *n.* **-bly** *ad.*

ir·ri·tant [ˈiritənt] *a.* 刺激的, 有刺激性的; 引起发炎的. ~ *gas* 【军】刺激性毒气. — *n.* 刺激, 刺激品, 刺激剂.

ir·ri·tate [ˈiriteit] *vt.* ①激怒,使发怒,使急躁. ②刺激, 使兴奋. ③使不舒服,使发炎,使疼痛. — *vi.* 起使人不愉快的影响[效果].

ir·ri·tat·ed [ˌiriˈteitid] *a.* ①被激怒的, 生了气的. ②(皮肤等)变粗的; 发红的; 因刺激而发炎的. *be* ~ *at [by, against, with]* 因…而发怒[着急].

ir·ri·tat·ing [ˈiriˌteitiŋ] *a.* ①惹人生气的, 使人不愉快的. ②【医】起刺激作用的. *He brought us many* ~ *news.* 他带给我们许多令人沮丧的消息. **-ly** *ad.*

ir·ri·ta·tion [ˌiriˈteiʃən] *n.* ①激怒, 愤怒, 生气, 焦躁. ②【医】刺激, 兴奋, 疼痛, 发炎. ③刺激物. *mechanical* ~ 机械性刺激.

ir·ri·ta·tive [ˈiriteitiv] *a.* 使人发怒的, 使人不快的; 刺激性的.

ir·ro·ta·tion·al [ˌirəuˈteiʃənl] *a.* 【物】无旋的. ~ *motion* 无旋运动.

ir·rupt [iˈrʌpt] *vi.* ①突然侵入,突然闯入 *(into)*, 猛然发作. ②【生态】(动物的)激增繁殖. **-tion** *n.* **-tive** *a.*

IRSC = International Radium Standard Commission 国际镭标准委员会.

IR seeker = infrared seeker 红外搜索器.

ir·tron [ˈəːtrɔn] *n.* 【天】类星星系,红外光射电源.

Ir·vin [ˈəːvin] *n.* 欧文〔姓氏,男子名〕.

Ir·ving [ˈəːviŋ] *n.* ①欧文〔姓氏,男子名〕. ②**Washington** ~ 华盛顿·欧文〔1783—1859,美国作家〕.

Ir·win [ˈəːwin] *n.* 欧文〔姓氏,男子名〕.

is [强 iz; 弱(在浊音后) z, (在清音后) s] be 的第三人称,单数,现在时,陈述语气.

is. = island; isle.

Isa. = Isaiah.

I.S.A. = International standard atmosphere 国际标准大气(压).

I·saac [ˈaizək] *n.* ①艾萨克〔男子名〕. ②【圣】以撒〔希伯来族长,犹太人的始祖亚伯拉罕和萨拉的儿子〕.

Is·a·bel [ˈizəbel] *n.* 伊莎贝尔〔女子名, Isabelle, Isabella 的异体〕.

Is·a·bel·la [ˌizəˈbelə] *n.* 伊莎贝拉〔女子名, Bella 的爱称〕.

is·a·bel·line [ˌizəˈbelin] *a.* 灰黄色的.

is·a·cous·tic [ˌaisəˈkuːstik] *a.* 【物】等音强的; 与等音强有关的.

i·sa·go·ge [ˈaisəˌgəudʒi] *n.* (对研究一门科学的)序言, 概论. **-gog·ic** [-ˈgɔdʒik] *a.*

I·sa·iah [aiˈzaiə] *n.* ①(公元前七、八世纪希伯来大预言家)以赛亚. ②(《圣经·旧约》中的)《以赛亚书》. ③艾赛亚〔男子名〕.

i·sal·lo·bar [aiˈsæləbɑː] *n.* 【气】等变压线. **-ic** *a.* ~*ic chart* 等变压图.

i·sa·tin [ˈaisətin] *n.* 【纺】靛红,吲哚满二酮.

ISBN = International Standard Book Number 国际标准书号.
ISC = International Sericultural Commission 国际蚕丝业委员会.
Is·car·i·ot [is'kεəriət]【宗】①以色加略人〔指出卖耶稣的犹大〕. ②叛徒.
is·ch(a)e·mi·a [is'ki:miə] *n.*【医】局部缺血, 局部贫血. **-mic** *a.*
is·chi·ad·ic, -at·ic [ˌiski'ædik, -'ætik] *a.* ①【解】臀部的, 坐骨(神经)的. ②【动】坐节的; (昆虫的)侧板的.
is·chi·um ['iskiəm] *n.* *(pl.* ***is·chi·a*** ['iskiə]) ①【解】坐骨. ②【动】坐节; (昆虫的)侧板.
-ise[1] *suf.* 构成名词, 表示"状态"、"性质" *(cf.* -ice): exerc*ise*, fran*ise*.
-ise[2] *suf.* = -ize.
-ish[1] *suf.* 构成形容词, 表示 ①"…的", "…民族的", "…语的": Engl*ish*, heathen*ish*. ②"…似的", "…气的", "患…的": fiend*ish*, fool*ish*, fever*ish*. ③"…一样的": child*ish*, monk*ish*. ④"微…的": cold*ish*. ⑤〔口〕"左右": 4:30 *-ish* 四点半左右; come at ten*ish* next Monday 下星期一十点左右来; I'll call on you dinner*ish*. 我大约在吃饭前后来找你.
-ish[2] *suf.* 构成动词: abol*ish*, fin*ish*, pun*ish*.
Ish·er·wood ['iʃə(:)wud] *n.* 伊舍伍德〔姓氏〕.
Ish·ma·el ['iʃmeiəl] *n.* ①【圣】(亚伯拉罕的庶子) 以实玛利. ②被社会唾弃的人.
Ish·ma·el·ite ['iʃmiəlait] *n.* ①【圣】以实玛利的后裔. ②被社会唾弃的人. **-it·ish** *a.*
i·sin·glass ['aiziŋglɑ:s] *n.* ①鱼胶. ②【地】白云母薄片.
I·sis ['aisis] *n.*【埃神】司生育与繁殖的女神.
isl. *(pl. isls)* = island; isle.
Is·lam ['izlɑ:m,-læm,-ləm] *n.* ①伊斯兰教, 回教. ②〔集合词〕伊斯兰教信徒, 穆斯林. ③伊斯兰教国家, 伊斯兰世界.
Is·lam·a·bad [is'lɑ:məbɑ:d] *n.* 伊斯兰堡〔巴基斯坦首都〕.
Is·lam·ic, Is·lam·it·ic [iz'læmik, ˌizlə'mitik] *a.* 伊斯兰教的, 穆斯林的.
Is·lam·ism ['izləmizəm] *n.* 伊斯兰教教义〔习俗〕; 回教.
Is·lam·ite ['izləmait] *n.* 伊斯兰教徒, 穆斯林.
Is·lam·ize ['isləmaiz,'iz-] *vt., vi.* *(-iz·ed, -izing)* 使皈依伊斯兰教, 使改信伊斯兰教. **-i·za·tion** *n.*
is·land ['ailənd] *n.* ①岛, 岛屿. ②岛状物; 孤立的地区; 孤立的组织. ③【船】航空母舰或船只的上层建筑〔如舰桥、舰台等〕. ④〔美〕大草原中的森林地带. ⑤(街道中的)交通安全岛, 让车地点; 路岛 (=traffic safety island). ⑥【解】岛; 脑岛; 胰岛. ⑦(喷气式飞机中的) 导管固定部. *a floating* ~ 浮岛. ~ *territories* 属岛. *an* ~ *of resistance*【军】孤立支撑点. *a pedestrian* ~ (交叉口处的) 行人安全岛. *a safety [street]* ~ (路中) 安全岛. *blood* ~ 血岛. ***~s of Langerhans***【医】胰岛. ***Islands of the Blessed [Blest]***【希神】极乐岛, 福人岛. — *a.* 岛的, 岛国的. *an* ~ *empire* 岛国. — *vt.* ①使成岛状. ②使孤立. ③象岛屿一样分布在. *a prairie* ~*ed with grooves* 树丛象岛屿分布着的大草原. **~-hopping** *n.*【军】越岛作战. ~ **hopping strategy**【军】越岛作战战术. ~ **platform** (火车站上的) 岛式站台. ~ **universe** 岛宇宙〔以前 external galaxy 的称呼〕. **-less** *a.* 无岛屿的.
is·land·er ['ailəndə] *n.* 岛民; 岛上居民.
isle [ail] *n.* (小)岛. ★在诗或散文中通常作地名用, 如 Isle of Wight, British Isles 等. — *vt.* 使成岛; 使隔离. — *vi.* 住在岛上. **Isles of the Blessed** = Islands of the Blessed.
is·let ['ailit] *n.* ①小岛; 岛状地带, 孤立地点. ②【解】胰岛. ***~s of Langerhans*** = islands of Langerhans.
Isls., isls. = islands.
ism ['izəm] *n.* 主义, 学说, 制度. *an age of* ~*s* 主义、学说多的时代. *various* ~*s of modern literature and art* 当代文艺的各种流派.
-ism [-izəm] *suf.* 构成抽象名词, 表示①"主义", "学说", "信仰", "制度": marx*ism*, atom*ism*. ②"行为", "行动": critic*ism*, vandal*ism*. ③"状态": barbar*ism*. ④"特征", "特性": colloquial*ism*. ⑤"病态": alcohol*ism*.
Is·ma·i·li·a [ˌizmai'li:ə] *n.* 伊斯梅利亚〔埃及城市〕.
Is·ma·il·i·an [ˌismei'iliən] *n.* (穆斯林) 伊斯迈里派教徒.
is·n't ['iznt]〔口〕= is not.
I.S.O. = Imperial Service Order〔英〕帝国服役勋章.
i·so- *comb. f.* 构成科技性质的名词或形容词. ①表示"等", "同": *iso*cheim, *iso*chore, *iso*chronism, *iso*morphic, *iso*tope. ②表示"同分异构", "异构".
i·so·a·cet·y·lene [ˌaisəuə'setili:n] *n.*【化】异乙炔.
i·so·ag·glu·ti·na·tion [ˌaisəuəglu:tə'neiʃən] *n.* 同种凝集反应, 同族凝集现象.
i·so·ag·glu·ti·na·tive [ˌaisəuə'glu:tiəneitiv] *a.* 同种凝集的, 同族凝集的.
i·so·ag·glu·ti·nin [ˌaisəuə'glu:tiənin] *n.* 同种凝集素, 同族凝集素.
i·so·an·ti·bod·y [ˌaisəu'æntibɔdi] *n.* *(pl. -bodies)*【医】异抗体, 同族抗体.
i·so·an·ti·gen [ˌaisəu'æntidʒən] *n.*【医】异抗原, 同种抗原.
i·so·bar ['aisəubɑ:] *n.* ①【气】等压线. ②【化】同量异位素.
i·so·bar·ic [ˌaisəu'bærik] *a.* ①【气】等压线的. ②【化】同量异位的. ~ *line* 等压线. ~ *surface* 等压面. ~ *nucleus* 同量异位核. ~ *spin* 同位旋.
i·so·bath ['aisəuˌbɑ:θ] *n.* 等(水)深线.
i·so·bu·tyl·ene [ˌaisəu'bju:tli:n] *n.*【化】异丁烯 (= isobutene).
i·so·cheim ['aisəuˌkaim] *n.*【气】冬季等温线, 等冬温线. **-al** *a.*
i·so·chor, i·so·chore ['aisəuˌkɔ:] *n.*【物】等体积线, 等容线. **-ic** *a.*
i·so·chro·mat·ic [ˌaisəukrəu'mætik] *a.*【物】等色的, 单色的, 一色的.【摄】正色的.
i·soch·ro·nal, -nic, -nous [ai'sɔkrənl, -nik, -nəs] *a.* ①等时的. ②发生于相等间隔时间内的. ~ *oscillation* 等时振荡. **-ly** *ad.* **-nism** *n.*【物】等时性.
i·soch·ro·nize [ai'sɔkrəˌnaiz] *vt.* *(-nized, -niz·ing)* 使等时, 使发生在相等间隔时间内.
i·soch·ro·ous [ai'sɔkrəuəs] *a.* 等色的, 同色的.
i·so·cli·nal, i·so·clin·ic [ˌaisəuklainl, -klinik] *a.* 等斜倾的, 等斜的. ~ *fault*【地】等斜断层. ~ *valley*【地】等斜谷. ~ *lines on a map* 地图上的等斜线. — *n.*【物】等磁倾线, 等斜线. **-ly** *ad.*
i·soc·ra·cy [ai'sɔkrəsi] *n.* *(pl. -cies)* 平等参政权, 平等参政权制度.
i·so·cy·a·nate [ˌaisəu'saiəneit] *n.*【化】异氰酸盐.
i·so·cy·a·nine [ˌaisəu'saiəni:n,-nin] *n.*【纺】异花青.
i·so·cy·clic [ˌaisəu'saiklik,-'siklik] *a.*【化】等节环(型)的, 同素的,〔尤指〕碳环型的 (= carbocyclic).
i·so·di·a·met·ric [ˌaisəuˌdaiə'metrik] *a.* 等直径的, 等轴的.
i·so·di·a·phere [ˌaisəu'daiəfiə] *n.*【物】等超额中子核素.
i·so·di·mor·phism [ˌaisəudai'mɔ:fizm] *n.*【化】同二晶(现象). **-phous** [-fəs] *a.*
i·so·dose ['aisəuˌdəus] *a.*【物】等剂量的, 等剂量线的.
i·so·dy·nam·ic [ˌaisəudai'næmik] *a.*【物】等力的; 等能的. ~ *line*【物】等(磁)力线.
i·so·e·lec·tric [ˌaisəui'lektrik] *a.*【物】等电位的, 零电

位差的. ~ *point*【物】等电离点.

i·so·e·lec·tron·ic [ˌaisəuilekˈtrɔnik] *a.* 等电子的. **-i·cal·ly** *ad.*

i·so·eu·gen·ol [ˌaisəuˈjuːdʒinɔl] *n.*【化】异丁子香酚.

i·so·ga·mete [ˌaisəuˈgæmit, -gəˈmiːt] *n.*【生】同形配子. **-met·ic** [-ˈmetik] *a.*

i·sog·a·my [aiˈsɔgəmi] *n.*【生】同配生殖. **-mous** [-məs] *a.*

i·so·gen·e·sis [ˌaisəuˈdʒenisis] *n.*【生】同源.

i·sog·e·nous [aiˈsɔdʒənəs] *a.*【生】有同源的. **-e·ny** [-ni] *n.*

i·sog·e·ny [aiˈsɔdʒəni] *n.*【生】同源.

i·so·ge·o·therm [ˌaisəuˈdʒiəθəːm] *n.* 等地温线. **-al** *a.*

i·so·gloss [ˈaisəuglɔs] *n.*【语】①同言线, 同语线, 等语线, (方言地图上的)同言线. ②某特定地区的语言特点.

i·so·gon [ˈaisəugɔn] *n.* ①等角多角形. ②【气】同风向线. ③【物】等(磁)偏线.

i·sog·o·nal [aiˈsɔgənl] *a.*【数】等角的. ~ *transformation* 等角变换.

i·so·gon·ic [ˌaisəuˈgɔnik] *a.* ①等偏角的. ②【物】等偏角的; 等(磁)偏的; 等偏线的. — *n.* 等(磁)偏线.

i·sog·o·ny [aiˈsɔgəni] *n.* (有机体各部的)对称发育.

i·so·gram [ˈaisəugræm] *n.*【气】等值线(图).

i·so·graph [ˈaisəugrɑːf] ①【空】等线图. ②【自】(解微分方程用的)求根仪. **-ic** *a.*

i·so·gyre [ˈaisəudʒaiə] *n.*【物】同消色线.

i·so·he·dral [ˌaisəuˈhiːdrəl] *a.*【物】等面的.

i·so·hel [ˈaisəuhel] *n.* (地图上的)等日照线.

i·so·hy·dric [ˌaisəuˈhaidrik] *a.*【化】等氢离子的. ~ *solutions* 等氢离子溶液.

i·so·hy·et [ˌaisəuˈhaiət] *n.*【气】等雨量线. **-al** *a.*

i·so·lan·tite [ˌaisəuˈlæntait] *n.*【无】爱索兰太特〔陶瓷高频绝缘材料, 状如滑石〕.

i·so·late [ˈaisəleit] *vt.* ①隔离, 使孤立. ②【电】绝缘. ③【化】使离析. ④【微】使(细菌)分离; 使与种群隔离. *an* ~*d patient* 被隔离的病人. ~ *oneself from all society* 隐居. — *n.*【微】分离菌; 隔离种群. ~**d point**【数】孤立点, 孤点.

i·so·la·tion [ˌaisəuˈleiʃən] *n.* ①隔离, 分离; 孤立, 单独. ②封锁交通. ③【电】绝缘. ④【化】离析(作用). *fight in* ~ 孤军作战. — *a.* 孤立主义的, 孤立主义者的. ~ **hospital** 隔离医院. *an* ~ *booth* 隔音室. ~ **ward** 隔离病室. **-ism** *n.* 孤立主义. **-ist** *n.* 孤立主义者, 孤立派.

i·so·la·tor [ˈaisəleitə] *n.* ①隔离者, 隔离物; 孤立者. ②【电】绝缘体(= insulator).

i·so·lead [ˈaisəuliːd] *n.*【军】等提前量曲线 (= ~ curve).

i·so·lette [ˌaisəˈlet] *n.* 〔〔F.〕isolette, 商标名〕不足月婴儿人工抚育器.

i·so·leu·cine [ˌaisəuˈluːsiːn, -sin] *n.*【化】异亮氨酸.

i·so·line [ˈaisəulain] *n.* = isogram.

i·sol·o·gous [aiˈsɔləgəs] *a.*【化】同构异素的. **-logue, -log** [-səˌlɔːg, -ˌlɔg] *n.*

i·so·mag·net·ic [ˌaisəumægˈnetik] *a.* ①等磁的. ②等磁力点的. ~ *lines on a map* 地图上的等磁线. — *n.* 等磁线.

i·so·mer [ˈaisəumə] *n.*【化】同分异构体;【物】同质异能素. ~ *of nucleus* 原子核的同质异能素. *an optical* ~ 旋光异构体.

i·so·mer·ic(al) [ˌaisəuˈmerik(əl)] *a.*【化】同分异构的, 同质异能的. ~ *change* 异构变化. *an* ~ *nucleus* 同质异能核. **-cal·ly** *ad.*

i·som·er·ism [aiˈsɔmərizəm] *n.* 同分异构性; 同质异能性. *core* ~ 原子核心同质异能性.

i·som·er·i·za·tion [aiˌsɔməraiˈzeiʃən] *n.*【化】异构化(作用).

i·som·er·ous [aiˈsɔmərəs] *a.* ①等分数的. ②【植】等基数的;【动】(昆虫)等附节的. ③【化】= isomeric.

i·so·met·ric [ˌaisəuˈmetrik] *a.* ①【化、物】等轴的; 立方的; 等轴晶的. ②等体积的, 等容积的 (= cubic). ③等比例的; 等角的, 等距离的; 等径的. ~ *system*【物】立方系, 立方晶系. ~ *drawing* 等角图; 等距画法. ~ *projection* 等角投影. — *n.* 等容线 (= ~ line). ~ **exercise** 静力锻炼肌肉运动〔如以手推墙等〕.

i·so·met·ri·cal [ˌaisəuˈmetrikəl] *a.* = isometric(*a.*). **-ly** *ad.*

i·so·met·rics [ˌaisəuˈmetriks] *n.*【体】静力锻炼法. (*cf.* isometric exercise).

i·so·me·tro·pi·a [ˌaisəumiˈtrəupiə] *n.*【医】(两眼的)折光相等.

i·som·e·try [aiˈsɔmitri] *n.* ①度量相等. ②【地】等高.

i·so·morph [ˈaisəumɔːf] *n.*【生】同态体, (类质)同晶型体.

i·so·mor·phic [ˌaisəuˈmɔːfik] *a.* ①同晶型的. ②【生化】同形的, 同态的 (= isomorphous).

i·so·mor·phism [ˌaisəuˈmɔːfizəm] *n.* ①【生】同态性, 同形性, 同态现象. ②【化】(类质)同晶型(现象). ③【数】同构.

i·so·mor·phous [ˌaisəuˈmɔːfəs] *a.*【物、化】同晶的, 同晶型性, 同态的, 类质同象的, 类质同晶型的. ~ *crystal* 同形晶体. ~ *pair* 同形偶. ~ *replacement* 同形置换. ~ *substitution* 同形替换.

i·so·ni·a·zid [ˌaisəuˈnaiəzid] *n.*【药】异烟肼(雷米封)〔肺结核药〕.

i·son·o·my [aiˈsɔnəmi] *n.* 法律平等; 权利平等; 特权平等.

i·so·oc·tane [ˌaisəuˈɔktein] *n.* 异辛烷.

i·so·path·ic [ˌaisəuˈpæθik] *a.*【医】同源疗法的.

i·sop·a·thy [aiˈsɔpəθi] *n.* 同源疗法.

i·so·phane, -phene [ˈaisəufein, -fiːn] *n.*【气】(植物生长阶段中)同时开花线, 同时线; 等物候线.

i·so·phyl·lous [ˌaisəuˈfiləs] *a.* 等叶的.

i·so·phyl·ly [ˈaisəuˌfli] *n.*【植】等叶式.

i·so·pi·es·tic [ˌaisəupaiˈestik] *a.* 示等压的. — *n.* 等压线 (= isobar).

i·so·pleth [ˈaisəupleθ] *n.*【气】等值线.

i·so·pod [ˈaisəpɔd] *n.* 等足目(*Isopoda*)动物. — *a.* 等足目动物的 (= isopodan).

i·so·pre·na·line [ˌaisəuˈprenəli(ː)n] *n.*【药】异丙基肾上腺素.

i·so·prene [ˈaisəupriːn] *n.*【化】异戊二烯.

i·so·pro·pyl [ˌaisəuˈprəupil] *n.*【化】异丙基.

i·sop·te·rous [aiˈsɔptərəs] *a.*【动】(昆虫)等翅目的.

i·so·pulse [ˈaisəupʌls] *n.*【无】衡定脉冲.

i·sos·ce·les [aiˈsɔsiliːz] *a.*【数】(三角形)等腰的, 等边的. *an* ~ *triangle* 等腰三角形.

i·sos·cope [ˈaisəuskəup] *n.*【自】同位素探伤仪.

i·so·seis·mal, i·so·seis·mic [ˌaisəuˈsaizməl, -mik] *a.* ①等震的. ②等震线的. — *n.* 等震线.

is·os·mot·ic [ˌaisɔsˈmɔtik] *a.* (= isotonic).

i·so·spon·dy·lous [ˌaisəuˈspɔndiləs] *a.*【动】等椎类鱼的, 与等椎类(鱼)有关的.

i·so·spore [ˈaisəuspɔː] *n.*【生】同形孢子.

i·so·spo·rous [ˌaisəuˈspɔːrəs] *a.* 孢子同型的 (= homosporous).

i·so·spo·ry [ˈaisəuˌspɔːri] *n.*【生】孢子同型.

i·sos·ta·sy [aiˈsɔstəsi] *n.* ①压力均衡. ②【地】地壳均衡. *the theory of* ~ 地壳均衡说.

i·so·stat·ic [ˌaisəuˈstætik] *a.* 均衡的. ~ *compensation*【地】均衡补偿.

i·so·ste·mo·ny [ˌaisəuˈstiːməni] *n.*【植】同基数雄蕊式. **-nous** *a.*

i·so·there [ˈaisəuˌθiə] *n.*【气】等夏温线. **-er·al** [aiˈsɔθirəl] *a.*

i·so·therm [ˈaisəuθəːm] *n.*【气】等温线,恒温线.

i·so·ther·mal [ˌaisəuˈθəːməl] *a.* 等温的;等温线的. ～ *atmosphere* 等温大气. — *n.* 等温线, 恒温线. *a reduced* ～ 对比等温线.

i·so·tone [ˈaisəutəun] *n.* ①【物】等中子(异位)数;【化】同中子异荷素. ②等渗性,等压性,等张性.

i·so·ton·ic [ˌaisəuˈtɔnik] *a.* ①【化】等中子异位的. ②等张的,等渗压的. ～ *concentration*【化】等渗(等压)浓度. ～ *muscle*【医】等张肌. **-i·cal·ly** *ad.* **-nic·i·ty** [-ˈnisiti] *n.*

i·so·tope [ˈaisəutəup] *n.*【化、物】同位素.

i·so·top·ic [ˌaisəuˈtɔpik] *a.* 同位素的. ～ *abundance ratio* 同位素丰度比. ～ *spin* 同位旋. **-al·ly** *ad.*

i·sot·o·py [aiˈsɔtəpi] ①【数】合伦. ②【物、化】同位素学.

i·so·tron [ˈaisəutrɔn] *n.*【物】同位素分析器.

i·so·trope [ˈaisəuətrəup] *n.*【物】均质,各向同性,各向同性晶体.

i·so·trop·ic, i·sot·ro·pous [ˌaisəuˈtrɔpik, aiˈsɔtrəpəs] *a.* 各向同性的. ～ *scattering* 各向同性散射.

i·sot·rop·ism [aiˈsɔtrəpizəm] *n.*【物】各向同性(现象).

i·sot·ro·py [aiˈsɔtrəpi] *n.* 各向同性(现象),无向性,均质性.

i·so·type [ˈaisəutaip] *n.* ①适应于不同地区生活的动物〔植物〕. ②反映统计数字的象征性图表.

Ispy [ˈaiˈspai] *n.* ①捉迷藏. ②一种文字游戏.

Isr. = Israel.

Is·ra·el [ˈizreiəl] *n.* ①以色列〔亚洲〕. ②〔总称〕以色列人,犹太人;〔喻〕【宗】上帝的选民.

Is·rae·li [izˈreili] *n.* 以色列人, 犹太人. — *a.* 以色列的,犹太的;以色列人的,犹太人的.

Is·ra·el·ite [ˈizriəlait] *n.* ①古以色列人; 犹太人. ②【宗】上帝的选民. — *a.* 古以色列(人)的,犹太(人)的.

Is·ra·el·it·ic [ˌizriəˈlitic], **Is·ra·el·it·ish** [ˈizriəlaitiʃ] *a.* 以色列人的,犹太人的.

Is·sei [ˈiːsˈsei] *n.* *(pl.* ～*s)* 第一代移居美国的日本人.

is·su·a·ble [ˈiʃu(ː)əbl] *a.* ①可发表的; 可发行的. ②可争辩的,可辩论的;可辩护的. **-bly** *ad.*

is·su·ance [ˈiʃu(ː)əns] *n.* ①发行,颁布. ②配给.

is·su·ant [ˈiʃu(ː)ənt] *a.* ①〔罕〕发表的; 发行的. ②【纹】只能见上部的. *a lion* ～ 半身狮子.

is·sue [ˈiʃuː] *n.* ①出口;河口. ②结果, 结局; 成绩. ③收获,收益. ④颁布, 发行; 发行额; 发行物. ⑤流出,(血,水等的)涌出;【病】出血,流脓. ⑥【法】子孙,子女. ⑦论点;争论问题;商讨;【法】争点,争端. *bring sth. to a successful* ～ 使某事圆满结束. *decide the* ～ *of the battle* 决定战役胜败. *a bank of* ～ 发行银行. *a new* ～ (纸币等的)新发行; (书报等的)新版; (军需品等的) 新发给. *items of* ～ (军队的)补给品. *monetary* ～ 货币放行. *the* ～ *of an order* 命令的颁布. *the latest* ～ 最近一期报刊. *an* ～ *of blood* = *a bloody* ～ 出血,流血. *die without* ～ 死后无子孙. *a major* ～ *of principle* 大是大非的问题. *a minor [side]* ～ 枝节问题. *debate an* ～ 讨论问题. *distinguish right from wrong on* ～*s of major importance* 分清大是大非. *the burning* ～ *of the day* 燃眉之急的问题. ***at*** ～ 不一致, 不相容;【法】在争论中; 待裁决的 (*be at* ～ *with sb.* 与某人意见不一致. *point at* ～ 争点). ***bring an*** ～ ***to a close*** 把问题解决. ***face the*** ～ 正视事实,认真对待事实. ***force an*** ～ 强迫对方表示态度. ***in*** ～ 在争论中. ***in the*** ～ 结局, 到头来. ～ ***of fact*** 事实上的争点. ～ ***of law*** 法律上的争点. ***join*** ～ ***(with)*** 对…持异议,和…争持;【法】诉讼双方一同提出争持焦点请求裁决. ***make an*** ～ ***of sth.*** 把某事当作问题, 反对…. ***put to the*** ～ 使对问题便于作出决定. ***raise a new*** ～ 提出新论点. ***ride off on a side*** ～ 专谈枝节问题. ***take*** ～ ***with sb.*** 反对某人, 同某人争持. — *vi.* ①出, 流出, 涌出, 发出. ②生,起;得…结果. ③(报刊等的)发行,发布. ④提出抗议,进行辩护. ⑤【法】传代,传下. *The students* ～*d out into the streets.* 学生涌到街上. *Blood* ～*d from the cut.* 血从伤口流出. *smoke issuing from a chimney* 从烟囱里涌出的烟. *The oversight* ～*d in heavy losses.* 疏忽造成重大损失. ～ *forth [out]* 出来,跳出,进出. ～ *from* 生自…, 是…的子孙. — *vt.* ①使流出,放出. ②发行(邮票等);发布(命令);发行(书刊), 出版. ③发给,配给. ～ *an order* 发布命令. ～ *ammunition to troops* 发弹药给军队.

is·sue·less [ˈisjuːlis] *a.* ①无子女的. ②无结果的. *an* ～ *effort* 徒劳. ③无可争辩的.

is·su·er [ˈisju(ː)ə] *n.* 发行者,出版者.

-ist[1] *suf.* 构成名词, 表示①动作的实践者: antagon*ist*, tour*ist*. ②"…主义者", 信仰者: athe*ist*, imperial*ist*, social*ist*. ③"专业人员": pian*ist*, botan*ist*, dent*ist*, flor*ist*.

-ist[2] *suf.* 构成形容词,表示"具有…特性的": dilettant*ist*.

Is·tan·bul [ˌistænˈbuːl] *n.* 伊斯坦布尔〔旧称君士坦丁堡〕.

Isth., isth. = isthums.

isth·mi·an [ˈisθmiən] *a.* ①地峡的. ②〔I-〕希腊科林斯(Corinth) 地峡的;巴拿马地峡的. *the I- Canal* 巴拿马运河. — *n.* 地峡地带居民. ***I- Games*** 科林斯地峡运动大会〔古希腊四大竞技之一, 其盛大仅次于 *Olympic Games*〕.

isth·mus [ˈisməs,ˈisθməs] *n.* *(pl.* ～*es)* ①地峡,地颈,土腰. ②〔the I-〕巴拿巴地峡; 苏伊士地峡. ③【解】峡,器官峡,管峡. ～ *of thyroid* 甲状腺峡.

-is·tic [ˈistik], **-is·ti·cal** [-tikəl] *suf.* 构成形容词,如: real*istic*, art*istic*.

is·tle [ˈistli] *n.* 龙舌兰纤维(从中、南美出产的龙舌兰科植物提制而成,用以制绳索、网、篮等编制物).

ISV = International Scientific Vocabulary 国际通用科技词汇.

it[1] [it] *n.* 〔英口〕意大利苦艾酒.

it[2] [it] *pro.* *(sing. nom.* ***it****; obj.* ***it****; poss.* ***its****; pl. nom.* ***they****; obj.* ***them****; poss.* ***their****)* 它, 这. ①指已说过的东西〔指无生命的东西, 也可指不分性别的幼儿、动物〕. *Is this the peony? No, it is the tree-peony.* 这是芍药吗? 不, 这是牡丹. *He took a stone and threw it.* 他拾起一块石头, 把它扔了出去. *The child lost its way.* 这孩子迷路了. ②〔指心中记着或成为问题的人物、事情和行为〕. *Go and see who* ～ *is.* 去看看是谁? *It's me.* 〔口〕是我 (= It is I.). *Oh, it's you!* 哦,是你呀! *It's the girls having their rehearsal.* 是女同学在排戏. *It's the wind shaking the window.* 是风刮得窗户响. ③〔用作无人称动词的主语, 或表示天气、时日、距离、状态、情况、事体、温度、问候语等〕. *It rains.* 下雨了. *It is cold.* 天冷. *It is a long way to the sea.* 离海很远. *It is five minutes' walk.* 要走五分钟. *Is* ～ *well with you?* 你身体好吗? *We had a splendid time of* ～. 那时候我们真快乐. *There* ～ *is, do what you like.* 好罢,你高兴怎样就怎样办. *run for* ～ 逃走. ④〔预用 it 代表其后所说的事实上的主语〔宾语〕〕. *It is right to do so.* 这样做是对的. *It is no use trying.* 试也无用. *It is certain that we shall succeed.* 我们是一定会成功的. *It is a nuisance, this delay.* 这样拖延,实在是讨厌. *I don't think it worthwhile taking such trouble.* 我想不值得费这么大的事了. ⑤〔作先行代词,用于表示强调的句型中〕. *It is the factory that we have been wanting to visit.* 这就是我们一直想访问的工厂. *It was here that I first met him.* 这就是我初次与他见面的地方. *It is I that am fortunate.* 幸运的是我〔句中动词应和 I 的人称数相一致〕. ⑥〔用于作及物动词用的名词之后作宾语〕. *cab* ～ 坐车去. *foot* ～ 走. *lord* ～ 摆架子. *queen* ～ 扮演女王; 玩女王派头. ⑦〔口语中 用作某种动词的含糊的宾

语〕. *as ill luck will have* ~ 偏偏不巧. *fight* ~ *out* 打到底. *get with* ~ 振作精神. *Go* ~ *while you are young.* 趁你还年轻就努力干罢. *have* ~ *one's own way I have done* ~ 我搞糟了. *keep at* ~. 坚持下去! **as ~ is [was]** 事实上, 既然如此 (*As* ~ *is, we can hardly get to the station by 6 o'clock.* 事实上,我们六点钟以前是很难赶到车站的.) **as ~ were** 似乎, 可以说是 (*This book gives, as* ~ *were, a picture of the evil old society.* 这本书可以说是罪恶的旧社会的一幅图景). —*n.* ①〔俚〕绝妙的人; 理想的东西; 登峰造极. *In a lilac sun bonnet she was* ~. 她戴着一顶紫色遮阳帽, 漂亮极了. *For barefaced lying you are really* ~. 以无耻造谣而论, 你真算得上天下第一. ★作此义解时, 通常写作斜体并加重发音. ②〔口〕性的魅力. *have* ~ 有性感. ③〔美俚〕傻瓜, 笨蛋. ④(瞎子摸鱼游戏中的)瞎子. ⑤〔俚〕讨厌的人. *He is a perfectly* ~. 他太讨厌了. ⑥〔常作 I-〕自大的人, 自负者. ⑦〔英口〕= *Italian vermouth.*

It., Ital. =①*Italian.* ②*Italic.* ③*Italy.*

ITA = Independent Television Authority. 〔英〕独立电视局.

it·a·col·u·mite [ˌitəˈkɔljumait] *n.* 【地】(淤积岩层中的)晶莹小颗砂石.

it·a·con·ic acid [ˌitəˈkɔnik]【化】甲叉丁二酸,衣康酸,乌头二酸.

I·tal·ia [iˈtɑːljɑː] *n.* 〔It.〕意大利(= Italy).

I·tal·ian [iˈtæljən] *a.* 意大利的; 意大利人的; 意大利语的; 意大利文化的. — *n.* 意大利人; 意大利语. ~ **cloth** 【纺】意大利棉毛呢, (英国制)黑色直贡呢. ~ **East Africa** 意大利从前的东非殖民地. ~ **hand** ①暗中干预,不露痕迹的操纵. ②= ~ handwriting. ~ **handwriting** 意大利字体〔现今英法意所通行的书写体〔*cf.* Gothic〕. ~ **iron** 圆筒形烫斗〔用以烫皱花边〕. ~ **sonnet** = petrarchan sonnet. ~ **warehouse** 意大利杂货店. ~ **warehouseman** 意大利杂货商.

I·tal·ian·ate [iˈtæljəneit] *a.* 意大利形式〔外貌, 风格〕的. — *vt.* 使意大利化 (= Italianize).

I·tal·ian·ism [iˈtæljənizəm] *n.* 意大利式; 意大利精神〔气质〕; 意大利腔; 意大利语调; 对意大利特色的爱好.

I·tal·ian·ize [iˈtæljənaiz] *vt., vi.* 意大利化.

I·tal·ic [iˈtælik] *a.* ①【印】意大利字体的, 斜体的. ②〔I-〕古代意大利(人)的, 意大利语族的. ~ *type* 斜体活字. — *n.* ①〔主 *pl.*〕斜体字〔*cf.* Roman〕. ②〔I-〕意大利语族. *in* ~*s*用斜体. *I quote the passage; the* ~*s are mine.* 我引用这一节,着重点是我加上的.

i·tal·i·cise, -cize [iˈtælisaiz] *vt.* 用斜体字印刷; 在字下划线表示(排斜体). **-ci·za·tion** [iˌtælisaiˈzeiʃən] *n.*

I·tal·i·cism [iˈtælisizəm] *n.* (= Italianism).

I·tal·i·ot, I·tal·i·ote [iˈtæliət, iˈtæliəut] *n.*【史】意大利南部古希腊殖民地居民. — *a.* 意大利南部古希腊殖民地的.

It·a·ly [ˈitəli] *n.* 意大利〔欧洲〕.

ITC = Infantry Training Centre 步兵训练中心.

itch [itʃ] *n.* ①痒; 〔the ~〕【医】疥癣. ②热望, 渴望. *have an* ~ *for…* 心里很想…. *the barber's* ~ 须癣. *the grocer's* ~ 脓疱性湿疹.— *vi.* ①痒, 发痒. ②渴望, 极想. *I scratched him where he* ~*ed.* 我搔他的痒处. ~ *for a try* 跃跃欲试. *My fingers* ~ *to box his ears.* 我手痒, 很想打他的耳光. ~ **mite**【动】疥癣虫, 痒螨.

itch·ing [ˈitʃiŋ] *a.* ①痒的. ②渴望着的, 焦急着的. *be* ~ *to do sth.* 渴望做某事. ***have an* ~ *palm*** 〔口〕贪财. ***have an* ~ *ear*** 想听闲话.

itch·y [ˈitʃi] *a.* ***(itch·i·er; -i·est)*** 生疥癣的; 发痒的; 渴想中的. **itch·i·ness** *n.*

-ite *suf.* 构成名词, 表示①"…的居民", "…的后代", "…分子", "…党员", "…主义者": Israel*ite*, Trotsky*ite*. ②〔学术用语〕(a) 岩石、矿物的名称: dolom*ite*, haemat*ite*. (b) 化石名称: ammon*ite*, trilob*ite*, (c) 盐类名称: selen*ite*, sulf*ite*. (d) 炸药名称: cord*ite*, dynam*ite*. (e) 商标名称: ebon*ite*, vulcan*ite*.

i·tem [ˈaitəm, ˈaitem] *n.* ①条, 条款, 项目, 品目, 细目. ②(新闻的)一条, 一则; (戏剧的)节目. *business* ~ 营业项目. ~ *by* ~ 逐条. *end* ~*s* 成品. *local* ~*s* 地方新闻. — *ad.* 〔逐条列举时开头用〕又, 同上. ~ **veto** 提案部分项目否决权〔美国某些州州长的职权之一〕.

i·tem·ize [ˈaitəmaiz] *vt.* 〔美〕分条开列, 详细列举. ~ *a bill* 分别开帐. *an* ~*d account* 细帐.

it·er·ance, it·er·an·cy [ˈitərəns, -si] *n.* 反复, 重复, 重复申说.

it·er·ate [ˈitəreit] *vt.* ①反复, 重复, 重复地说. ②叠代. **-a·tion** [ˌitəˈreiʃən] *n.* ①反复, 重复地说. ②叠代法, 叠演. **-a·tive** *a.* 反复的, 重复的; 叠代的, 叠接的.

Ith·a·ca [ˈiθəkə] *n.* ①伊萨卡岛〔爱奥尼亚群岛之一, 位于希腊西部爱奥尼亚海中, 为希腊神话中 Ulysses 的故乡〕. ②伊萨卡城镇〔美国〕. **-a·can** *a.*

ith·er [ˈiðə] *a., pro.* 〔Scot.〕= other; either.

I·thu·ri·el [iˈθjuəriəl] *n.* (Milton 著《失乐园》中的)负责搜捕魔鬼的天使. ~***'s spear*** 验证真伪的可靠物.

itin. = itinerant; itinerary.

i·tin·er·a(n)·cy [iˈtinərə(n)si, aiˈt-] *n.* ①巡回. ②流动团体〔组织〕. ③牧师轮流巡回制度.

i·tin·er·ant [iˈtinərənt] *a.* 巡回的, 流动的. — *n.* 巡回者(如巡回传教士; 巡回法官; 行商). ~ *peddlers* 行商. *an* ~ *judge* 巡回法官. *an* ~ *library* 流动图书馆.

i·tin·er·ar·y [aiˈtinərəri, iˈt-] *n.* ①旅行指南. ②旅行日记. ③旅行日程. ④旅程, 路线. — *a.* 巡回的, 流动的; 旅行的; 旅行途中的, 巡回中的. *an* ~ *map* 路线图. *an* ~ *pillar [column]* 路标.

i·tin·er·ate [iˈtinəreit, aiˈt-] *vi.* 巡回, 巡游; 巡回裁判. *an itinerating library* 流动图书馆. **-a·tion** *n.* = itineracy.

-i·tion *suf.* 构成名词, 表示"动作"、"状态": defin*ition*, exped*ition*.

-i·tious *suf.* 构成形容词: ambi*tious*, expedi*tious*.

-i·tis *suf.* 表示"炎(症)": bronch*itis*, gastr*itis*.

-i·tive *suf.* 构成形容词及名词: appos*itive*, pun*itive*.

it'll [ˈitl] = it will; it shall.

ITO = International Trade Organization 国际贸易组织.

-i·tous *suf.* 构成形容词: calam*itous*, felic*itous*.

its [its] *pro.* 〔it 的所有格〕它的, 其. *the plan and* ~ *realization* 计划及其实施.

it's [its] ①= it is. ②= it has.

it·self [itˈself] *pro.* *(pl.* ***themselves)*** ①它自己, 它本身〔作为反身代词〕. *The dog is stretching* ~. 这条狗在伸懒腰. *The baby tripped and hurt* ~. 这娃娃摔倒跌伤了. ②自身, 本身〔也用以加强语气〕. *At last the house* ~ *fell down.* 房子终于自己倒了. *Doing is* ~ *learning.* 干本身就是学习. *Even the well* ~ *was empty.* 甚至连井也是空的. ***by* ~** 单独地, 孤零零地; 独立的. ***in* ~** 实质上, 本身. ***of* ~** 自行, 自然而然的.

ITT = International Telephone and Telegraph Corporation〔美〕国际电话电报公司.

ITTF = International Table Tennis Federation 国际乒乓球联合会.

it·ty-bit·ty [ˈitiˈbiti] *a.* 〔口〕不大点儿〔儿语摹仿〕(= itsybitsy).

ITU = International Telecommunication Union (联合国)国际电信联盟.

ITV = ①industrial television 工业电视. ②instructional television 教学电视. ③Independent Television 〔英〕独立电视公司〔英国商业电视网〕.

-ity *suf.* 构成抽象名词, 表示"性质"、"状态"、"程度": calam*ity*, pur*ity*, solubil*ity*.

IU, I.U. = international unit(s)【生、药】国际单位.
IUCD = IUD.
I.U.D. = intrauterine device 子宫内(避孕)器具.
-i·um *suf.* 构成名词 ①表示化学元素的拉丁名字: sod*ium*, ion*ium*. ②表示正离子: ammon*ium*, carbon*ium*.
IUPAC = International Union of Pure and Applied Chemistry 国际理论和应用化学联合会.
IUPAP = International Union of Pure and Applied Physics 国际理论和应用物理联合会.
IUS = International Union of Students 国际学生联合会.
I.V. = ①initial velocity 初速度.
i.v. = increase value 增值.
I·van [aivən] *n.* ①伊凡〔男子名, John 的异体〕. ②伊凡三世〔1440—1505, 世称俄国大公, 在位期间 1462—1505〕. ③伊凡四世〔1530—1584, 世称伊凡雷帝, 1547—1548年在位的俄国第一个沙皇〕.
IVBA = International Volleyball Association 国际排球联合会.
I've [aiv] = I have.
-ive *suf.* 构成形容词, 表示①"…的", "与…有关的", "具有…性质的": nat*ive*, substant*ive*. ②"倾向于…活动的": amus*ive*, creat*ive*.
Ives [aivz] *n.* ①艾凡斯〔男子名〕. ②Charles Edward ~ 查理世·爱德华·艾凡斯〔1874—1954, 美国作曲家〕. ③James M. ~ 詹姆斯·姆·艾凡斯〔1824—1895, 美国印刷术创始人之一〕.
i·vied [ˈaivid] *a.* 常春藤覆盖着的.
i·vo·ry [ˈaivəri] *n.* ①象牙; (河马、独角鱼的)牙齿. *artificial* ~ 人造象牙. *fossil* ~ 古代巨象的象牙化石. ②象牙色, 乳白色. ③〔*pl.*〕象牙雕制品, 仿象牙制品. ④牙质(= dental ~). ⑤厚光纸. ⑥〔常 *pl.*〕〔俚〕牙齿; 骰子; 台球; 弹子; 钢琴键. ***show one's ivories*** 龇牙咧嘴. ***solid*** ~〔美俚〕头脑迟钝的人. ***wash one's ivories*** 〔口〕喝酒. — *a.* ①象牙制成的, 似象牙的. ②象牙色的, 乳白色的. ~ **black** 象牙墨〔象牙烧制的黑色颜料〕. ~**-billed woodpecker** 蓝黑色的白尖嘴啄木鸟. ~**-dome** *n.*〔俚〕笨蛋. ~ **nut** 象牙椰子, 植物象牙 (= vegetable ~). ~ **palm** 象牙椰子树. ~ **paper** (艺术上用的) 带象牙光泽的厚光纸. ~ **tower** 象牙之塔. ~**-towered** *a.* 关在象牙之塔内的. ~ **white**, ~ **yellow** 乳白色. ~**-white** *a.* 乳白色的.
Ivory Coast [ˈaivəriˈkəust] 象牙海岸〔非洲〕.
i·vy [ˈaivi] *n.*【植】常春藤. *the English* ~ 常春藤. *the Boston* ~【植】爬山虎. *the grand* ~ 连钱草. — *a.* ①学院的, 学究式的. ②纯理论的, 抽象的; 无实用意义的. — *vt.* 用常春藤点缀〔覆盖〕, 使长满常春藤. ~ **buttercup** 常春藤毛茛. **I- League** ①(美国东北部八个名牌大学的) 常春藤联合会. ②属于该组织的名牌大学或其师生. ③名牌大学派头. ~**-leaved** *a.* 常春藤(叶)的. ~**-leaved crowfoot** 常春藤毛茛.
I.W. = interrupted wave; Isle of Wight;【化】isotopic weight.
i·wis [iˈwis] *ad.*〔古〕当然; 确实地.
IWS = International Wool Secretariat 国际羊毛书记处.
I.W.T. = Inland Water Transport〔英〕内河航运.
I.W.W., IWW = Industrial Workers of the World〔美〕世界产业工人组织.
IX = ion exchange 离子交换.
-ix *suf.* -or 型阳性名词的阴性型后缀: executr*ix*.
ix·i·a [ˈiksiə] *n.*【植】①〔I〕鸢尾属. ②加州藜芦.
Ix·i·on [ikˈsaiənz] *n.*【希神】伊克塞翁〔帖撒里国王〕. ~**'*s wheel*** 地府旋轮〔Ixion 因为向赫拉 (Hera) 求爱, 受神惩罚, 被绑在永远旋转的地狱车轮上〕.
ix·tle [ˈikstli, ˈis-] *n.* = istle.
I·yar [iːˈjɑː, ˈiːjɑː] *n.*〔Heb.〕(犹太历)八月.
-i·za·tion *comb. f.* 构成与 -ize 型动词相应的名词: civil*ization*, organ*ization*.
-ize *suf.* ①构成及物动词, 表示 ⓐ"使成为", "使变成", "使…化": civil*ize*, national*ize*. ⓑ"使变成…状", "产生…": crystall*ize*, hypothes*ize*. ⓒ 象…似地从事活动, "照…法处理": calvan*ize*, bowdler*ize*. ⓓ"作…处理", "使渗透", "使与…结合": dramat*ize*, iod*ize*, oxid*ize*. ②构成不及物动词, 表示"成为", "变成", "…化": apostat*ize*, sympath*ize*; ★-ize 与 -ise 英美尚无一定用法, 但美语中多用 -ize. 下列数语则英美均用 -ise: advertise, comprise, devise, revise, surprise.
Iz·mir [izˈmiə] *n.* 伊兹密尔〔即士麦那 (Smyrna), 土耳其海港〕.
Iz·ves·ti·a [izˈvestjə] *n.* 《消息报》(苏联政府报纸).
iz·zard [ˈizəd] *n.*〔古, 方〕字母 z. *from A to* ~ 自始至终, 彻底地.
iz·zat [ˈizət] *n.*〔Ind.〕名誉, 荣誉; 自尊心; 自大.

J

J, j [dʒei] *(pl. J's, j's, Js, js* [dʒeiz]*)* ①英语字母表第十字母. ★J, j 原为 I, i 的异体字母, 17 世纪才开始确定 j 为辅音字母, i 为元音字母. ②第十. ③【数】与 y 轴平行的单位矢量. ④ J 字形物体[记号]〔如 J 字形螺钉或 J 字形钩等〕. ⑤J 字母在语音上通常发的塞擦音 (j). ⑥【数】虚数 $\sqrt{-1}$. *a J (-pen)* 宽尖钢笔尖. — *a.* ①J 或 j 的. ②J 形的. ③第十的.
J. = ①Journal. ②Judge. ③Justice.
J.j. = ①【牌】Jack. ②【物】joule. 焦耳.
ja [jɑː] *ad.*〔G.〕= yes.
Ja. = January.
J.A., JA = ①Joint Account (数人)共有的(银行存款等)帐户. ②Judge Advocate 军法官; 军法检查官. ③Joint Agent 联合代理人.
ja·al goat [ˈdʒeiəlgəut, ˈjɑːl-]【动】(埃塞俄比亚, 上埃及等地产的)长角野山羊.
jab [dʒæb] *vt.* ①刺, 戳. ②捅; 猛碰. ~ *one's elbow into sb.'s side* 用胳膊肘猛碰别人的腰部. ~ *a wild hog with a spear* = ~ *a spear into a wild hog* 用长矛猛刺野猪. — *vi.* 刺, 戳, 刺进 (into); 猛击(at). ~ ***a right*** 〔美拳击〕挥右拳猛击. ~ ***a vein*** 〔美俚〕进行麻醉品注射. — *n.* 〔口〕①猛戳, 刺进;【军】连续戳. ②猛碰;【拳】短促有力的戳击. ③〔美俚〕皮下注射. *receive a* ~ *in the arm* 〔口〕在臂上打一针〔接种〕. ~**-off** *n.*〔美俚〕麻醉药的皮下注射; 注射麻醉药后发生的作用.
Ja·bal·pur [ˌdʒʌbəlˈpuə] *n.* 贾巴尔普尔〔印度中央邦的城市〕.
jab·ber [ˈdʒæbə] *n.* ①急促不清的话. ②无意义的话; 莫名其妙的话. — *vi.* ①急急忙忙地说. ②闲聊. ③

(猿猴等)吱吱喳喳地叫. — *vt.* 急促不清地说. **-er** *n.* 说话莫名其妙的人,说话荒唐的人.

jab·ber·wock·y [ˈdʒæbəwɔki] *n.* 无聊的话[文章]— *a.* 莫名其妙的.

jab·i·ru [ˈdʒæbiruː] *n.* 【动】①(美国南部和南美的)林鹳(= wood ibis). ②非洲凹嘴鹳 (= *Ephippiorhynchus senegalensis*).

jab·o·ran·di [ˌdʒæbəˈrændi] *n.* 毛果芸香 (= *Pilocarpus jaborandi*)〔产于南美,是芸香科植物的叶干,内含生物碱〕.

ja·bot [ʒæˈbəu, F. ʒabo] *n.* ①镶在女服胸前的皱褶花边,胸饰. ②十八世纪男子穿的衬衫领子前的皱褶花边.

JAC = Joint Aircraft Committee 飞机制造联合委员会.

J.A.C. = Junior Association of Commerce 青年商会.

Jac. = Jacob; Jacobus.

ja·cal [hɑːˈkɑːl] *n.* (*pl.* **-ca·les** [-ˈkɑːleis], ~*s*) (墨西哥和西南美的)木桩小茅屋〔用木桩涂泥作墙的茅屋〕.

jac·a·mar [ˈdʒækəmɑː] *n.* 【动】鹟䴕〔产于中南美,为食鱼鸟〕.

ja·ça·na, ja·ca·na [ˌʒɑːsəˈnɑː] *n.* 【动】水雉〔产于热带和亚热带〕.

jac·a·ran·da [ˌdʒækəˈrændə] *n.* 【植】兰花楹属(*Jacaranda*)植物.

j'accuse [ʒəˈkuːz] 〔F.〕①我控诉. ②强烈控诉,强烈谴责.

jac·inth [ˈdʒæsinθ] *n.* ①【矿】红锆石; 橘红色的宝石. ②橘红色.

jack[1] [dʒæk] *n.* ①〔常 J-〕杰克〔男子名,也作 John 的俗称或昵称〕. ②〔J-〕普通人,男子,家伙,小伙子. ③水手,水兵,海员 (= Jack-tar). ④伐木工;杂役,打杂工. ⑤(烤肉等用的)铁叉;脱靴器. ⑥〔J〕(纸牌中的)杰克〔在国王 (King) 和王后 (Queen) 之下〕. ⑦赢得的大量赌注. ⑧【机】起重机;千斤顶;(支柱等)支撑物. ⑨【电】插座,插口;塞孔; 弹簧开关. ⑩【机】传动装置;动力油缸. ⑪(标志国籍的)船首旗;公司旗. ⑫公驴;幼雄鲑鱼;寒鸦. ⑬〔美〕长耳大野兔 (= jack rabbit). ⑭(滚球游戏中作靶子的)小白木球; (抛石游戏中所用的)小石块 (金属片). ⑮〔美〕(夜间打猎或捕鱼用的)篝灯. ⑯〔美俚〕金钱. ⑰苹果酒; 白兰地酒. ⑱【矿】打眼机;安全防风灯罩. ⑲【矿】闪锌矿. ⑳(跳水前弯身的)一种跳水法. ㉑(时钟的)钟锤. *automobile* ~ 汽车千斤顶. *bridging* ~ 【电】并联塞孔,桥接塞孔. *cheap J-* 小贩. *hydraulic* ~ 液压千斤顶. *oil* ~ 油压千斤顶. *ratchet* ~ 棘轮起重器. *screw* ~ 螺旋撑杆;螺旋千斤顶. *tripod* ~ 三脚起重器. *A good J- makes a good Gill [Jill]* 〔谚〕夫善使妻贤. *All shall be well, J- shall have Gill [Jill].* 〔谚〕有情人皆成眷属. *All work and no play makes J- a dull boy.* 〔谚〕用功不玩耍,弄得孩子会变傻. *before you can [could] say J- Robinson* 转瞬间,突然,说时迟那时快. *climb like a steeple* ~ 善于爬山. *Every J- shall have his Gill [Jill].* 〔谚〕人必有偶. ***J- among the maids*** 讨好妇女的男子. ***every man ~, every ~ one [man]*** 人人,每个人. ***J- and Gill [Jill]*** 少年和姑娘;男人和女人. ***J- at a pinch*** 临时拉来帮忙的人. ***J- in the water*** 〔俚〕码头脚夫. ***J- Johnson*** 【军】重型炮弹. ***J- of all trades*** 什么事都能干的人,万能博士,三脚猫. ***J- of all trades and master of none.*** 行行皆通,样样稀松. ***J- of [on] both sides*** 骑墙派. ***J- of straw*** ①稻草人. ②无资产者. ③寄生者. ***make one's ~*** ①达到目的. ②赚大钱. ***not a ~*** 一个也不. ***the Union J-*** 英国国旗. — *a.* (动物)雄的,公的. —*vi.* 用篝灯打猎[捕鱼]. — *vt.* ①(用起重机)起,举,扛. ②增加,抬高(物价等). ③放弃,停止(工作,计划等). ④申诉,责备,规劝 (*up*). ⑤夜间用篝灯捕(鱼)[猎(兽)]. ⑥〔美俚〕拔(枪等) (*out*). ~ (*up*) *a car* 把汽车顶起. ~ (*up*) *expenditure* 增加开支. ***be ~ed up*** 〔口〕败事,完蛋; 筋疲力尽. **Jack-a-dandy** *n.* 花花公子. **Jack-a-Lent** (*pl.* ***Jack-a-Lents***) *n.* ①四旬斋期游戏中被击的小玩偶. ②小人物. ~**ass** ①公驴. ②笨蛋,傻瓜. ~**assery** 愚蠢的行为. ~**bean**【植】洋刀豆(**caravalia ensifornis**)〔产于美国南部,作饲料用,籽可食〕. ~**boots** *n. pl.* 过膝的长统靴. ~**dish** *n.* 鱼〔土名儿,尤指白斑狗鱼 (*Esor lucius*)〕. ~ **engine** 辅助发动机. **Jack Frost** 〔霜寒的拟人化名称〕霜精,严寒. ~**fruit** *n.* 【植】①波罗蜜树〔产于东印度〕. ②波罗蜜树果实. ③波罗蜜树木材. ~**hammer** *n.* 槌击凿岩机; 气锤. ~ **Horner** 自负的小孩子. **Jack-in-office** *n.* (*pl.* ***Jacks-in-office***) 自命不凡的小官吏,作威作福的芝麻官,摆官架子的人. ~**-in-the-box** *n.* (*pl.* ***~-in-the-boxes, ~s-in-the-box***) ①(打开盖子即有玩偶跳起的)玩偶匣. ②(能放出多种玩意的)盒子焰火. ③【机】差动齿轮[装置]. **Jack-in-the-Green** *n.* (*pl.* ***Jack-in-the-Greens, Jacks-in-the-Green***) 花屋中的人 (西俗五月一日用冬青和鲜花扎成小屋,人居其中上街游行). ~**-in-the-pulpit** *n.* 【植】美国黄花菖蒲. **Jack Ketch** 〔英〕绞刑吏. ~**knife** ①*n.* 大折刀; (跳入水中以前)弯身跳水法. ② *vt.* 用大折刀切. ③ *vi.* (跳水等时)弯身. ~ **ladder** 【船】木踏板绳梯. ~**lamp** 安全灯. ~**leg** *a., n.* ①技术不高明的(人);外行的(人). ②不诚实的(人);不择手段的(人). ③权宜之计的(行动). ~**light** ①【猎】 *n.* (用以引诱鱼或猎物的)篝火. ② *vt.* 用篝火[灯]引猎(兽类); 用篝火等诱捕(鱼类). ~**-o'-lantern** ①磷火. ②行踪不定的人. ③使人迷惑的事物. ④〔美〕南瓜灯. ~ **pine** 【植】短叶松 (*Pinns banksiana*) 〔产于加拿大和美国北部,针叶短而成对排列〕. ~ **plane** 【机】粗刨,大刨. ~ **post** 【机】轴柱. ~**pot** *n.* ①【牌】(要有一对杰克以上的好牌才能赢的)赌注. ②积累的赌注. ③〔口〕(彩票等的)头奖; (可在任何冒险事业中取得的)最大成功. ④〔美〕困境. (*hit the ~pot* 〔俚〕赢得大笔赌注; 获得极大成功, 运气非常好). ~ **pudding** 〔古〕丑角. ~ **rabbit** 【动】(北美)长耳大野兔. ~ **rafter** 【建】小椽. ~**screw** 【机】螺旋起重器. ~**shaft** *n.* 副轴,变速机传动轴. ~**snipe** 【动】小鹬. ~ **Sprat** 矮子,侏儒. ~ **staff** 舰首旗竿. ~**stay** ①【机】撑杆. ②【船】天幕边索; 支索; 舰首旗杆; (汽艇用)分隔索. ~ **tar, J- Tar** 水手; 水兵. ~ **towel** 环状毛巾 (= roller towel).

jack[2] [dʒæk] *n.* ①(中世纪步兵的)无袖皮上衣. ②〔古〕装酒的皮囊.

jack[3] [dʒæk] *n.* ①(东南亚等地产的)面包树. ②面包树果实.

jack- [dʒæk] *comb. f.* 〔构成名词〕①表示"雄性",如: *jack*ass 公驴. ②表示"大",如: *jack*boot 长统靴. ③表示"男孩或人",与连字号"-"组合在一起,如 *jack*-in-the-box 玩偶匣(打开盖子即有玩偶跳起).

jack·al [ˈdʒækɔːl] *n.* ①【动】豺类. ②爪牙,走狗. ③骗子,诈骗者. ***~ from [of] the same lair*** 一丘之貉. ***play the ~ to the tiger*** 为虎作伥. — *vi.* 作爪牙,当走狗 (*for*).

jack·a·napes [ˈdʒækəneips] *n.* ①〔古〕驯服的猴子. ②傲慢无礼而又专横的人. ③顽劣孩子.

jack·a·roo, jack·e·roo [ˌdʒækəˈruː] *n.* 〔澳俚〕(牧羊场来的)新牧童.

jack·daw [ˈdʒækdɔː] *n.* ①【动】穴鸟,寒鸦 (*corvus monedula*)〔产于欧洲的一种类似乌鸦的黑鸟〕. ②= grackle. ***~ in peacock's feathers*** 乌鸦披着孔雀毛; 鸦学彩凤.

jack·et [ˈdʒækit] *n.* ①短上衣,外套. ②包书纸,护封; 公文套; 唱片套; 弹壳. ③(动物的)皮毛; (马铃薯等的)皮. ④【机】盒,罩,套,外壳. ⑤(软木)救生衣. *cylinder* ~ 汽缸套. *life (-saving)* ~ 救生圈. *potatoes boiled in their ~s* 连皮煮的马铃薯. ***dust [lace, swinge, thrash, trim] sb.'s ~*** 殴打某人. ***Pull down your ~!*** 〔口〕安静些. ***send in one's ~*** 辞职不干. ***warm sb.'s ~*** 惩罚某人,辱骂某人. — *vt.* ①给…穿短上衣; 给…盖上罩子[套子等]; 给…包上护封. ②〔口〕打. *a steam ~ed* *kettle* 双重蒸煮锅.

jack·et·ing [ˈdʒækitiŋ] *n.* ①【机】套. ②〔口〕殴打,鞭打.

jack·ing [ˈdʒækiŋ] *n.* ①【纺】(走锭纺纱机的)走车牵伸;迭层轧光揉布工艺. ②用篝灯打猎[捕鱼].

jacks [dʒæks] *n. pl.* 〔动词用单数〕抓子游戏.

jack·smelt [ˈdʒæksmelt] *n.*【动】似银汉鱼 *(Atherinopsis californiensis)* 〔产于太平洋〕.

Jack·son[1] [ˈdʒæksn] *n.* 杰克逊〔地名: ①美国密西西比州的首府. ②美国密执安州南部的城市. ③美国田纳西州城市〕.

Jack·son[2] [ˈdʒæksn] *n.* 杰克逊〔姓氏, 男子名〕. ①**Andrew** ~ 安德鲁·杰克逊〔1767—1845,美国将军,于1829—1837 任美国第七任总统〕. ②**Helen Maria Hunt** ~ 海伦·玛丽安·亨特·杰克逊〔1830—1885, 本姓 Fiske, 美国女小说家〕. ③**Robert Houghwout** ~ 罗伯特·霍伍特·杰克逊〔1892—1954,美国法学家〕.

Jack·so·ni·an [dʒækˈsəuniən] *a.* (美国第七任总统) 杰克逊的; 与杰克逊有关的; 杰克逊政策的, 与杰克逊政策有关的. — *n.* 杰克逊的追随者.

jack·stone [ˈdʒækstəun] *n.* ①抓子游戏的子儿. ②〔*pl.*〕〔动词用单数〕= jacks.

jack·straw [ˈdʒækstrɔː] *n.* ①稻草人 (= straw man). ②(抽杆游戏用的)细木杆[塑料杆等].

jack·y [ˈdʒæki] *n.* ①= Jack Tar. ②〔英〕杜松子酒.

Ja·cob [ˈdʒeikəb] *n.* 雅各〔《圣经》中人名,有好几个,其中一个是犹太人的祖先之一, 即以色列; 另一个是耶稣的门徒〕. ~**'s ladder** ①【圣】(雅各在梦中见到的)天使上下的天梯. ②【海】(有木或铁制踏板的) 绳梯. ③【植】花葱. ④(吊桶的)循环链. ~**'s staff** ①香客杖. ②(测量器的)支架; 测高器; 测距器. ~**'s tears**【植】薏苡.

Jac·o·be·an [ˌdʒækəˈbi(ː)ən] *a.* ①英国詹姆士一世的,詹姆士一世时代 (1603—1625)的. ②(家具) 黑橡木色的. — *n.* ①詹姆士一世时代的作家[诗人、外交家等]. ②= Jacobite. ~ ***determinant***【数】函数行列式.

Jac·o·bin [ˈdʒækəbin] *n.* ①【宗】多明我教派修道士. ②【史】(1789 年法国革命时代的)雅各宾党人〔因其俱乐部会址设在巴黎雅各宾修道院举行而得名〕. ③激进民主派成员. ④〔j-〕【动】毛领鸽. **-ic(al)** *a.* 雅各宾党(人)的. **-ism** *n.* 雅各宾主义;激进民主主义.

Jac·o·bite [ˈdʒækəbait] *n.* ①英王詹姆士二世退位以后的拥戴者, 或要求詹姆士二世的后裔继承王位者. ②美国小说家亨利·詹姆士 (Henry James) 的崇拜者. **-bit·ic, -bit·i·cal** *a.*

ja·co·bus [dʒəˈkəubəs] *n.* 英国詹姆士一世时代铸制的金币〔约合 20 先令〕(= unite).

jac·o·net [ˈdʒækənit] *n.* ①白色薄棉布; 医用防水细纱布. ②一面轧光的染色棉布.

J

jac·quard [dʒəˈkɑːd] *n.* 〔常作 J-〕①【纺】提花机 *(=* ~ loom). ②提花织物 (= ~ weave). **J-loom** 提花机〔法国人 Jacquard (1752—1834)发明的衣布织机〕.

Jac·que·line [ˈdʒækliːn] *n.* 杰奎琳〔女子名〕.

Jac·que·ric [ʒækˈriː,F. ʒakri] *n.* 〔F.〕①1358年法国的扎克雷农民起义. ②〔j-〕农民起义.

jacta est alea [ˈdʒæktə estˈeiljə] 〔L.〕骰子已经掷出〔凯撒(Caesar)越过卢比孔 (Rubicon) 河欲与庞培 (Pompey) 决战时讲的话〕; 木已成舟,事已决定.

jac·ta·tion [dʒækˈteiʃən] *n.* ①夸大. ②【医】= jactitation.

jac·ti·ta·tion [ˌdʒæktiˈteiʃən] *n.* ①【医】辗转不安;四肢或肌肉的抽动. ②〔古〕自夸,自吹. ③【法】诈称(为某人的配偶). ~ *of marriage* 冒称配偶罪.

jac·u·late [ˈdʒækjuleit] *vt.,vi.* 投掷. **-la·tion** *n.*

jade[1] [dʒeid] *n.* ①玉,翡翠. ②翡翠色. — *a.* ①玉制的. ②翡翠色的. ~**green** 绿玉色. ~ **plant** 乔木状青锁龙 *(crassula arborescens)* 〔产于南非和亚洲〕. ~**stone** 硬玉.

jade[2] [dʒeid] *n.* ①劣马, 驽马, 老马, 疲备不堪的马. ②〔贬〕荡妇,女流氓. ③〔谑〕女人. — *vt., vi.* (使)疲倦; (使)劳累.

jad·ed [ˈdʒeidid] *a.* ①精疲力竭的. ②(因过饱或过多)腻烦的. *a* ~ *appetite* 败坏的胃口. **-ly** *ad.* **-ness** *n.*

jade·ite [ˈdʒeidait] *n.* 硬玉,翡翠.

j'adoube [ʒɑːˈduːb] 〔F.〕我把棋子摆摆正〔下棋的人用手碰到并不想移动的棋子时向对方打招呼的话 = I adjust〕.

jae·ger[1] [ˈjeigə] *n.* (纯毛织)雅茄呢;雅茄呢做的服装.

jae·ger[2] [ˈjeigə] *n.* ①【动】贼鸥. ②猎人,穿猎人服装的保镖. ③〔主 J-〕(旧德国或奥地利军队中的)狙击兵.

Jaf·fa [ˈdʒæfə] *n.* 雅法〔巴勒斯坦西部港口〕. ~ **orange** 雅法桔.

Jaff·na [ˈdʒæfnə] *n.* 贾夫纳〔斯里兰卡的港口〕.

jag[1] [dʒæg] *n.* ①〔古〕织品上的V字形凹口[尖裂缝]. ②锯齿状缺口的突出部. *a* ~ *of rock* 一块突出的岩石. — *vt.* ①在…上刻 V 形凹口. ②把…撕成锯齿状,把…切得参差不齐. ③在(衣服)上开叉[穿饰孔]. *a jagged rent in cloth* 一块布上撕成锯齿状的裂口. — *vi.* ①刺,戳. ②颠簸地移动.

jag[2] [dʒæg] *n.* ①〔方〕(马的)一驮之量. ②〔美俚〕狂饮,酒席. ③〔口〕(感情等的)突发(时期),一阵. *have a* ~ *on* 酩酊大醉. *a crying* ~ 大哭一阵. *a laughing* ~ 一阵大笑.

Jag [dʒæg] *n.* 〔口〕美洲虎牌小汽车 (= Jaguar).

J.A.G. = Judge Advocate General. 〔美〕军法处长.

Jag·an·nath [ˈdʒʌgəˌnɑːt, -nɔːt] *n.* = Juggernaut.

JAGD = Judge Advocate General's Department 〔美〕军法署.

jä·ger [ˈjeigə] *n.* = jaeger[2].

jag·ged [ˈdʒægid] *a.* 锯齿状的, 有缺口的, 参差不齐的, 粗糙的,凸凹不平的. *a* ~ *rock* 巉岩. **-ly** *ad.* **-ness** *n.*

jag·ger·y [ˈdʒægəri] *n.* 棕榈糖;粗糖.

jag·gy [ˈdʒægi] *a.* ***(-gi·er; -gi·est)*** = jagged.

jag·uar [ˈdʒægwɑː] *n.*【动】美洲虎.

jag·ua·run·di [ˌdʒægwəˈrʌndi] *n.* 小豹猫〔产于美洲的热带和亚热带,短腿长尾细身子,毛呈灰色〕.

Jah [dʒɑː] **Jah·ve(h), Jah·we(h)** [ˈjɑːvei] *n.* =Jehovah.

jai a·lai [ˈhailai, ˌhaiəˈlai] *n.* 〔Sp.〕回力球〔一种与手球相似的球类活动,流行于拉丁美洲〕.

jail [dʒeil] 〔美〕 *n., vt.* = gaol. ~**bait** ①与其有性行为即构成强奸罪的未成年女子. ②性感女郎. ③任何会为之下狱的诱惑. ~**bird** 囚犯,惯犯. ~**break** 越狱. ~ **delivery** ①劫狱,用暴力释放囚犯. ②把囚犯带去法庭受审出空监狱. ~**house** 监狱.

jail·er, jail·or [ˈdʒeilə] *n.* 监狱看守(= gaoler).

jail·er·ess [ˈdʒeləris] *n.* 监狱女看守.

Jain [dʒain], **Jai·na** [dʒainə] *a.* (印度的)耆那教的,耆那教徒(式)的. — *n.* 耆那教教徒.

Jain·ism [ˈdʒainizəm] *n.* 耆那教〔印度非婆罗门教的一派,其教义与佛教有些相同,主张苦行与戒杀〕.

Ja·kar·ta [dʒəˈkɑːtə] *n.* 雅加达 (= Djakarta) 〔印度尼西亚首都(=Djakarta)〕.

jake[1] [dʒeik] *n.* ①〔贬〕粗鲁的乡下人,家伙.

jake[2] [dʒeik] *a.* 〔美俚〕对的, 好的, 令人满意的. *Everything is* ~ *with me* 万事如意.

jake[3], **jakey** [dʒeik, ˈdʒeiki] *n.* 〔俚〕牙买加姜汁酒〔在禁酒时代作为饮料〕. ~ **leg** 由于饮酒而引起的麻痹症.

jakes [dʒeiks] *n.* 〔古、方〕屋外厕所,茅坑.

JAL = Japan Air Lines 日本航空公司.

jal·ap [ˈdʒæləp] *n.*【植】①药喇叭〔球根牵牛〕. ②药喇叭的根制做的泻药.

jal·a·pin [ˈdʒæləpin] *n.*【化】紫茉莉苷.

Ja·lis·co [hɑːˈliskə] *n.* 哈利斯科〔墨西哥太平洋岸的州,首府为瓜达拉哈拉〕.

ja·lop·(p)y [dʒəˈlɔpi] *n.* 〔美俚〕 ①破旧的汽车[飞机].

②车辆.

jal·ou·sie [ˈʒælu(:)zi:] *n.* 【建】百叶窗.

jam[1] [dʒæm] *n.* ①拥挤，阻塞. ②(机器等因拥塞)轧住，停顿. ③【无】干扰，失真. ④〔美口〕困境，窘境；和警察等口角. ⑤〔美俚〕一举手之劳的事情. *a ~ of logs in a river* 挤满一河的木材. *a traffic ~* 交通拥挤，交通阻塞. ***be in [get into] a ~*** 处于[陷入]困境. —*vt.* ①(把…)挤进，塞进. ②使(机器等)轧住，使卡住，使塞满. ③轧伤，压碎. ④【无】干扰. ⑤使(通道等)堵塞. *~ one's clothes into a suitcase* 把衣服塞进箱子里. *The bus was ~med full.* 公共汽车挤得很满. *The driver ~s the brakes on.* 司机刹住车. *a ship ~med in ice* 被夹在冰里的船. —*vi.* ①塞满，拥挤；挤进. ②楔紧；(机器等)轧住不动. ③〔美俚〕改奏即兴爵士音乐活跃空气，参加爵士音乐演奏会. ④【无】干扰. *The gearing ~med* 齿轮装置卡住. *~ into the lift* 挤进电梯. *The brakes ~med.* 刹车失灵了. ~ **nut**【机】锁紧螺母，防松螺母. **~-packed** *a.* 包装扎实的，塞紧的，挤得水泄不通的. ~ **session** 〔美俚〕爵士音乐即席演奏会；一群演奏者为自己举行的非正式演奏会. ~ **welding**【机】对接焊.

jam[2] [dʒæm] *n.* ①果酱. ②〔俚〕奢侈；酒席，好菜. *real ~* 〔俚〕美好的东西，好菜，使人痛快的事. —*vt.* ①给…涂上果酱. ②制成果酱. *jamming sugar* 果酱用糖. ***~ tomorrow*** 可望而不可得的好事.

Jam. = Jamaica; James.

Ja·mai·ca [dʒəˈmeikə] *n.* 牙买加〔拉丁美洲国家，英联邦的成员，首都金斯顿〕. ~ **rum** 牙买加甜酒.

Ja·mai·can [dʒəˈmeikən] *a.* 牙买加的，牙买加人的. —*n.* 牙买加人.

jamb(e) [dʒæm] *n.* ①【建】门窗侧壁；侧柱；〔*pl.*〕壁炉两旁的墙. ②【矿】矿柱；矿脉中的土石层.

jam·ba·lay·a [ˌdʒʌmbəˈlaiə] *n.* ①〔大米与虾米、牡蛎、火腿、鸡肉等烹调而成的〕什锦饭. ②杂烩，混合物.

jam·beau [ˈdʒæmbəu] *n.* (*pl.* ***-beaux*** [-bəuz]) (中世纪的)胫甲〔护胫铠甲〕.

jam·bo·ree [ˌdʒæmbəˈri:] *n.* 〔口〕①大喝大闹；大型娱乐会，庆祝会. ②大集会；全国〔国际〕的童子军大会. ③有多种娱乐的节目单.

James [dʒeimz] *n.* ①詹姆斯〔姓氏，男子名〕. ②(《圣经》中的)《雅各书》.

Jame·son [ˈdʒeimsn, ˈdʒimsn] *n.* 詹姆森〔姓氏〕.

James·town [ˈdʒeimztaun] *n.* 詹姆斯敦. 〔①圣赫勒拿岛首府. ②1607 年英国在美洲建立的第一个殖民地居地，在弗吉尼亚州詹姆士河的河口处. ③美国纽约西南部的城市〕.

jam·mer [ˈdʒæmə] *n.* ①【无】干扰发射机，干扰发射台. ②【机】U 型钢丝芯撑，簧丝芯撑.

jam·ming [ˈdʒæmiŋ] *n.* 【无】①收报时的干扰；人为干扰. ②扰乱台，干扰台. ③抑制. *spot ~* 局部干扰. ~ **intensity** 干扰强度.

Jam·mu [ˈdʒʌmu:] *n.* 查谟〔城市，位于亚洲查谟和克什米尔的西南〕.

Jam·mu and kash·mir [ˈdʒʌmu: ən kæʃˈmiə] *n.* 查谟和克什米尔〔在亚洲，一部分属于印度，一部分属于巴基斯坦〕.

jam·my [ˈdʒæmi] *a.* ①粘上果酱的. ②〔英〕使人愉快的，适意的.

jam-pack [ˈdʒæmˈpæk] *vt.* 塞满，挤满，充满. *~ the basket with all kinds of fruit* 用各种水果把篮子装满. *Vacationists ~ed the trains.* 火车里装满了休假的人.

Jam·shed·pur [dʒʌmʃedˈpuə] *n.* 贾姆谢普尔〔印度的钢铁工业城市，位于东北部的比哈尔邦〕.

Jan. = January.

Ja·ná·ček [ˈdʒænəʃek], **Leoš** 利奥斯·杰纳谢克〔1854—1928，捷克作曲家〕.

Jane [dʒein] *n.* ①简(女子名)〔Joan(n) 的异体〕. ②〔蔑、美俚〕姑娘，女学生. *a G.I. ~* 女兵. ~ ***Doe*** 〔美〕法律诉讼中隐匿真名的女方.

Jan·eite [ˈdʒeinait] *n.* 英国小说家简·奥斯汀 (Jane Austin)的崇拜者.

Ja·net [ˈdʒænit] *n.* 珍妮特〔女子名，Jane 的昵称〕.

jan·gle [ˈdʒæŋgl] *vi.* ①(铃等)发出刺耳的声音. ②〔古〕吵架，争论. —*vt.* ①乱摇铃使发出刺耳声. ②吵吵闹闹地讲. ③使…心烦意乱. *The whine of the motors ~d her nerves.* 马达的轰鸣吵得她心烦意乱. —*n.* ①吵闹，口角. ②刺耳的声音. ③空谈.

Jan·is·sary [ˈdʒænisəri] *n.* = Janizary.

jan·i·tor [ˈdʒænitə] *n.* (*fem.* ***-tress***) ①看门人，守门人. ②照管一座房屋或办公室的工人. **-i·al** *a.*

Jan·i·zar·y [ˈdʒænizəri] *n.* ①【史】14—19 世纪土耳其苏丹的近卫步兵. ②土耳其士兵. ③〔喻〕亲信，拥护者；亲信部队的成员.

jan·nock [ˈdʒænək] *a.* 〔英方〕老实的，诚实的；真心的；爽直的.

Jan·u·ar·y [ˈdʒænjuəri] *n.* 一月. *in ~* 在一月里. *on ~ 10* 一月十日. *on the evening of ~ 15.* 一月十五日晚.

Ja·nus [ˈdʒeinəs] *n.*【罗神】看守门户的两面神. **~-faced** *a.* 脸朝两面的；虚伪的，口是心非的.

Jap [dʒæp] *a.*, *n.* 〔常贬〕= ①Japan. ②Japanese.

Ja·pan [dʒəˈpæn] *n.* 日本，日本国〔亚洲〕. *the ~ Current* 日本海流，黑潮. *the Sea of ~* 日本海. ~ **allspice** 蜡梅. ~ **cedar**【植】柳杉. ~ **china** 日本产陶器. ~ **clover**【植】鸡眼草(*lespedeza striata*)〔美国西南种植作为干饲料〕. ~ **cypress** 扁柏. ~ **earth** 日本阿仙药染料. ~ **ink** 墨. ~ **medlar** 枇杷. ~ **wax** 日本蜡.

ja·pan [dʒəˈpæn] *n.* ①日本漆；亮漆. ②日本式漆器. ③日本式物品〔如日本瓷器、日本丝等〕. *~ black* 黑漆. —*vt.* ①给…涂漆. ②使平滑光亮. *japanned leather* (黑色)漆皮. —*a.* ①日本漆器的，具有日本漆器特征的. ②涂了日本漆的. ~ **cabinet** 漆饰五屉柜. ~ **ware** 漆器.

Jap·a·nese [ˌdʒæpəˈni:z] *a.* ①日本的；日本人的. ②日语的. —*n.* 〔*sing.*, *pl.*〕①日本人. ②日语. *a ~* 一个日本人. *the ~* 〔集合词〕日本人. ~ **andromeda**【植】马醉木 (*Pieris japonica*)〔一种常绿植物〕. ~ **iris**【植】花菖蒲 (*Iris kaempferi*). ~ **ivy** 爬山虎 (= Boston ivy). ~ **lantern** 灯笼 (= Chinese lantern). ~ **oyster**【动】日本长蛎 (*Ostrea gigas*). ~ **persimmon** ①【植】亚洲柿树 (*Diospyros kaki*). ②柿子. ~ **plum** 李 (*Prunus salicina*)〔原产于中国〕. ~ **quince**【植】①贴梗海棠树 (*Chaenomeles lagenaria*). ②贴梗海棠. ~ **rose** 蔷薇；〔俚〕山茶. ~ **spurge**【植】富贵草 (*Pachysandra terminalis*)〔一种种于草坪的常绿草〕. ~ **tissul** 薄纸.

Jap·a·nesque [ˌdʒæpəˈnesk] *a.* 日本式的.

Ja·pan·ism [dʒəˈpænizəm] *n.* ①日本精神〔性格〕. ②日本迷. ③日语语法. ④日本研究.

Jap·a·ni·za·tion [ˌdʒæpənaiˈzeiʃən] *n.* 日本化.

Jap·a·nize [ˈdʒæpənaiz] *vt.* 使日本化，使成日本式.

ja·pan·ner [dʒəˈpænə] *n.* (油)漆工.

Japano- *comb.f.* 义为"日本": *Japano*phile.

Jap·a·nol·o·gy [ˌdʒæpəˈnɔlədʒi] *n.* 日本学，日本事物的研究. **-nol·o·gist** *n.* 研究日本的学者，日本学专家.

Jap·a·no·phile [ˈdʒæpənəufail] *n.* 亲日派，亲日分子.

Ja·pan·o·phobe [dʒəˈpænəufəub] *n.* 憎恶日本的人.

Jap·a·no·pho·bi·a [dʒæpənəuˈfəubiə] *n.* 憎恶日本，恐日病.

jape [dʒeip] *vi.* 说笑话，戏谑，嘲弄. —*vt.* 〔罕〕开…的玩笑，嘲弄. —*n.* ①笑话，笑柄. ②嘲弄；愚弄.

Ja·pheth [ˈdʒeifeθ] *n.*【圣】雅弗〔诺亚 (Noah) 三个儿子中的幼子〕.

Ja·phet·ic [dʒeiˈfetic] *a.* ①雅弗 (Japheth) 的. ②印

欧(Indo-European) 的〔旧称〕.

Ja·pon·ic [dʒəˈpɔnik] *a.* ①日本的;日本人的;日本特有的. ②日语的.

ja·pon·i·ca [dʒəˈpɔnikə] *n.*【植】日本榅桲,日本山茶.

Ja·ques [ˈdʒeikwiz] *n.* 詹奎兹〔莎士比亚所著剧本《如愿》(As You Like It) 中的犬儒学派哲学家〕.

jar[1] [dʒɑː] *vi.* ①发出刺耳的声音,轧轧作响. ②给人烦躁[痛苦]的感觉,刺激 (*on*);(发出刺耳声地)撞击 (*on, upon, against*). ③震动,震荡;(不和谐地)反响,回荡. ④(意见,行动等)不一致,冲突,激烈争吵 (*with*). ~ *on sb.* 给某人不快之感. ~ *on sb.'s nerves [ear]* 刺激某人神经(耳朵). *Their opinions* ~ *with others.* 他们的意见和我们不一致. *It* ~*s with the surroundings.* 同周围环境不调和. — *vt.* ①使震动,使摇动. ②使发出刺耳的声音. ③给…不愉快的感觉;刺激神经等. *He was badly* ~*red by the blow.* 这个打击使他的神经受到很大的刺激. *The wind* ~*red the whole house.* 风吹得全屋轧轧地响. — *n.* ①刺耳的声音,轧轧声. ②剧烈的震动. ③(精神上、肉体上)受到的刺激[打击]. ④冲突;不和,口角,争执. ⑤(节奏等)突然中止. *a hit of a* ~〔俚〕意外的震动. *family* ~*s* 家庭口角. *get a* ~ 受刺激. *be at a* ~ 在争执中.

jar[2] [dʒɑː] *n.* ①(圆柱形、大口的)罐子,坛子,瓶子. ②一罐[坛、瓶]的量. ③【电】电瓶,蓄电池壳. ④【电】加耳〔电容量单位,=1/900 微法〕. *a bell* ~ 钟罩. *a* ~ *of oil* 一罐油. *two* ~*s of honey* 两坛蜂蜜. *accumulator* ~ 蓄电池容器. *battery* ~ 蓄电地壳,蓄电池容器,电池槽,电瓶. *Vacuum* ~ 真空瓶,真空干燥器.

jar[3] [dʒɑː]〔古〕旋转. ★今仅用于短语 ***(up)on the [a]*** ~ (门)半开着,微开着.

jar·di·nière [ˌʒɑːdiˈnjɛə] *n.*〔F.〕①花盆架;(装饰用的)花盆,花瓶. ②花果叶花纹. ③肉食的配头〔由几种蔬菜分别切开煮熟制成〕;炒素.

jar·gon[1] [ˈdʒɑːgən] *n.* ①行话;黑话,隐语. ②难懂的话,莫名其妙的话. ③南腔北调的混合语〔如 Pidgin English, lingua franca 等〕. ④奇特粗俗的语言[方言],土话. ⑤(鸟等)叽叽喳喳的叫声. *critics'* ~ 评论家的专用语. *law* ~ 法律界行话. — *vi., vt.* = jargonize. **-ic, -is·tic** *a.*

jar·gon[2], **jar·goon** [ˈdʒɑːgɑːn, dʒɑːˈguːn] *n.* 晶体锆灰色,非晶体锆黑色.

jar·go·nel(l)e [ˌdʒɑːgəˈnel] *n.* (法国)早熟种黄梨.

jar·gon·ize [ˈdʒɑːgənaiz] *vi.* ①讲难懂的话[行话、隐话、黑话]. ②用行话[黑话等]写文章. — *vt.* ①用难懂的话[行话、隐话、黑话]讲或写. ②使成为难懂的话.

jarl [jɑːl] *n.*【史】古代北欧的首领,贵族.

jar·o·vize [ˈjɑːrəvaiz] *vt.* 使春化;使加速开花结果 (= vernalize). **-vi·za·tion** *n.* 春化作用,春化处理.

jar·rah [ˈdʒærə] *n.* 红柳桉树 (Eucalyptus marginata)〔产于澳大利亚,红心,木质坚硬〕.

jar·ring [ˈdʒɑːriŋ] *a.* ①刺耳的. ②不和谐的. — *n.* ①刺耳声. ②振动. ③冲突,倾轧,争执. **-ly** *ad.*

jar·v(e)y [ˈdʒɑːvi] *n.* ①〔英口〕出租马车车夫. ②(爱尔兰的)轻便二轮马车车夫.

Jar·vis [ˈdʒɑːvis] *n.* 贾维斯〔男子名〕.

JAS = Journal of the Aeronautical Science〔美〕《航空科学学报》〔期刊名称〕.

Jas. = James.

ja·sey [ˈdʒeizi] *n.*〔英口〕假发(尤指毛线做的假发).

jas·min(e) [ˈdʒæsmin] *n.* ①【植】素馨;茉莉. ②类似素馨的植物〔如栀子等〕. ③素馨[茉莉]香水. ④淡黄色. *the American* ~ 圆叶茑萝. *the Arabian* ~ 茉莉. *the winter (flowering)* ~ 迎春(花).

Ja·son [ˈdʒeisn] *n.* ①贾森〔男子名〕. ②【希神】伊阿宋〔忒萨利亚王子,曾率领一支勇敢的队伍乘 Argo 号船到海外寻找金羊毛,在 Medea 的帮助下,终于成功〕.

Jas·per [ˈdʒæspə] *n.* 贾斯珀〔男子名〕.

jas·per [ˈdʒæspə] *n.* ①【矿】碧玉. ②墨绿色. ③【圣】宝石.

Jas·pers [ˈjɑːspəs] *n.* *Karl Jaspers* 卡尔·雅斯帕尔斯〔1883—1969, 德国哲学家〕.

jas·pil·ite, jas·pi·lyte [ˈdʒæspəlait] *n.*【矿】(含有赤铁矿类似碧玉的)硅质岩石.

jas·sid [ˈdʒæsid] *n.*【植】浮尘子科 *(Jassidae)* 动物.

jato, JATO [ˈdʒeitəu] = jet-assisted takeoff【空】①助飞. ②助飞器,起飞加速器. ~ *unit* 助飞装置,起飞加速装置. *reverse* ~ 反向助飞器,喷气刹车.

jaun·dice [ˈdʒɔːndis] *n.* ①【医】黄疸;黄疸症〔如肝炎〕. ②妒忌,猜忌;偏见. — *vt.* ***(-diced; -dic·ing)*** ①使产生黄疸. ②使妒忌,使猜忌,使成偏见.

jaun·diced [ˈdʒɔːndist] *a.* ①害黄疸病的. ②有偏见的,有猜忌心的,嫉妒心重的. *take a* ~ *view of sth.* 用持有偏见的眼光来看待某事.

jaunt [dʒɔːnt] *vi.* 作短途游览. ~*ing car* (爱尔兰的)轻快二轮马车. — *n.* 短途游览.

jaun·ty [ˈdʒɔːnti] *a.* ①〔古〕斯文的. ②时髦的,时兴的. ③快活的,轻快的,活泼的;洋洋得意的;满怀信心的. — *n.*〔英俚〕舰船纠察队长,运输船纠察长. **-ti·ly** *ad.* **-ti·ness** *n.*

Jav. = Java(nese).

Ja·va [ˈdʒɑːvə] *n.* ①爪哇〔印度尼西亚的大岛,面积 130,510 平方公里〕. ②爪哇咖啡. ③〔俚〕〔常 j-〕咖啡. ④爪哇鸡. ~ **canvas** 刺绣(用)十字布. ~ **cotton** 木棉. ~ **man** 爪哇猿人. ~ **Sea** 爪哇海〔太平洋的一部分〕. ~ **sparrow** 文鸟.

Ja·van [ˈdʒɑːvən] *a., n.* = Javanese.

Jav·a·nese [ˌdʒævəˈniːz] *a.* ①爪哇的;爪哇人的. ②爪哇语的. — *n.*〔*sing., pl.*〕①爪哇人. ②爪哇语.

jav·e·lin [ˈdʒævlin] *n.* 标枪,投枪. ~ **formation**【军】(轰炸机的)标枪队形. ~ **throw(ing)**【体】掷标枪. ~ **thrower** 标枪投手.

jav·e·li·na [ˌhɑːviˈliːnə] *n.*〔美〕西貒〔野猪〕(=peccary).

jaw [dʒɔː] *n.* ①颌,颚. ②〔*pl.*〕上下颚,口部,口腔. ③〔*pl.*〕(峡谷、通路等的)狭口,咽喉. ④〔机〕爪,虎钳牙;叉头,〔*pl.*〕夹片. ⑤〔*pl.*〕危险境遇. ⑥〔口〕嚼舌头,说废话;讲道,训人. *the lower [upper]* ~ 下[上]颌. *His* ~ *dropped.* 他的下巴脱下来了. *the* ~*s of danger* 险境. *be snatched from the* ~*s of death* 从死亡的绝境中被抢救出来. *get into [out of] the* ~*s of death* 陷入[逃脱]险境. ***all*** ~ 刺刺不休,一篇空话. ***Hold your*** ~*!* 住嘴! 别唠叨了! ***lantern*** ~ 尖瘦的嘴脸. ***wag one's [the]*** ~***(s)*** 喋喋不休. — *vt.*〔俚〕向…唠叨;唠唠叨叨地训斥. — *vi.*〔俚〕唠叨;唠唠叨叨地责备. ~**breaker** ①〔口〕难发音的字. ②〔美俚〕一种圆的硬糖. ③【矿】颚形碎石[矿]机. ~**-breaking** *a.* 极难发音的. ~ **crusher** 颚式破碎机,虎口碎矿机. ~ **plate** 颚板.

jaw·bone [dʒɔːˈbəun] *n.* ①颚骨,牙床骨. ②〔美俚〕借贷;借到的款子. ③〔美俚〕(财务上的)信用. — *vi.*〔美俚〕①耐心地讲道理以达到赊买[借贷等]目的. ②赊卖给人;借贷给人. — *vt.*〔美俚〕①赊买,借到. ②利用职权企图压服(某人),利用权势对…施加压力. — *ad.*〔美俚〕凭信用地. *buy* ~ 赊买;分期付款购买.

jay [dʒei] *n.* ①【动】樫鸟. ②〔口〕爱唠叨的傻瓜. ③〔美俚〕花花公子;乡下佬;呆汉,容易受骗的人. ④中蓝色. ***scalp sb. for a*** ~ 愚弄某人. ~**bird** *n.*【动】樫鸟〔~的方言变体〕.

Jay [dʒei] *n.* ①杰伊〔姓氏,男子名〕. ②John ~ 约翰·杰伊〔1745—1829,美国政治家和法学家〕.

jay·cee [ˈdʒeiˈsiː] *n.*〔美〕①国际青年会 (Junior Chamber, International) 会员. ②美国青年会 (United States Jaycee) 会员〔源出 J. C. 二字母的发音〕.

jay·gee [ˈdʒeiˈdʒiː] *n.*〔美〕海军中尉.

jay·hawk·er [ˈdʒeiˌhɔːkə] *n.* ①〔美俚〕(南北战争时期)废除农奴派的游击队员. ②强盗;袭击者,掠夺者. ③

〔口〕〔J-〕堪萨斯州人. *the J- State* 〔美〕堪萨斯州.

jay·hawk·ing [ˈdʒeihɔːkiŋ] *n.* 〔美俚〕盗窃; 掠夺.

jay·vee [ˈdʒeiˈviː] *n.* 〔美〕大学运动队二队(或其成员). 〔源出 junior versity 开首二字母 j 和 v 的发音〕.

jay·walk [ˈdʒeiˌwɔːk] *vi.* 〔美口〕(不遵守交通规则)乱穿马路. *No ~ing!* 不要乱穿马路! **-er** *n.* 乱穿马路的人.

jazz [dʒæz] *n.* ①爵士音乐, 爵士舞(曲). ②〔美俚〕爵士音乐风格〔刺激、兴奋、活泼、放纵〕; 活泼放纵. ③浮华而不实的行为; 陈腔滥调的废话. — *a.* ①爵士音乐的. ②不调和的; (色彩等)花哨恶俗的. *a ~ garden* 有舞池的咖啡馆. *a ~ hound* 舞迷. — *vt.* ①把…奏成爵士音乐. ②在…中加入爵士音乐风味; 使有刺激性, 使活泼*(up)*. ③〔美俚〕加快…的速度. — *vi.* ①奏爵士乐; 跳爵士舞. ②游荡 *(around)*. ~ **band** 爵士乐队. ~ **buff** 爵士音乐迷. ~**man** 〔*pl.* **-men**〕 爵士音乐演奏者. ~ **music** 爵士音乐. **-ist** *n.* 爵士音乐爱好者. **-y** *a.* ①有爵士音乐特征的. ②〔美俚〕活泼放纵的. **-i·ly** *ad.* **-i·ness** *n.*

J.B. = John Bull.

J.C. = ①Jesus Christ. ②Julius Caesar. ③jurisconsult.

J.C.B. = 〔L.〕 Juris Civilis Baccalaureus 民法学士 (= Bachelor of Civil Law).

J.C.D., JCD = ①〔L.〕 *Juris Canonici Doctor*(= Doctor of Canon Law) 教会法博士. ②〔L.〕 *Juris Civilis Doctor* 民法学博士 (=Doctor of Civil Law).

J.C.R. = Junior Combination Room; Junior Common Room 〔英〕大学三年级学生公共休息室.

JCS = Joint Chiefs of Staff 〔美〕参谋长联席会议.

jct. = junction.

JD = ①〔L.〕 Jurum Doctor (=Doctor of Laws) 法学博士. ②juvenile delinquency (or delinquent) 少年罪犯.

Je. = June.

jeal·ous [ˈdʒeləs] *a.* ①妒忌心重的, 吃醋的; 出于妒忌的. ②猜疑的, 留意提防的. ③爱惜的, 注意的, 戒备的. ④【宗】〔罕〕(上帝)要求绝对忠实和崇敬的. *a ~ wife* 一个爱妒忌的妻子. *be ~ of sb.'s fame* 妒忌某人的名声. *a ~ guardian* 谨慎的保护人. *with ~ care* 小心翼翼. *a citizen ~ of [for] his rights* 珍惜自己权利的公民. *a ~ rage* 怨愤. ~ **glass** 不透明玻璃. **-ly** *ad.* **-ness** *n.*

jeal·ous·y [ˈdʒeləsi] *n.* ①妒忌, 猜忌. ②小心提防, 谨慎戒备.

Jean [dʒiːn] *n.* 吉恩〔①男子名, John 的异体. ②女子名, Joanna 的异体〕.

jean [dʒein] *n.* ①【纺】三页细斜纹布. ②〔*pl.*〕(三页细斜纹蓝布做的)工作服, 工装裤.

Jeanne [dʒiːn] *n.* 珍妮〔女子名, Joan(n) 的异体〕.

Jean·(n)ette [dʒiˈnet] *n.* 珍妮特〔女子名, Jeanne 的昵称〕.

Jeans [dʒiːnz] *n.* ①琼斯〔姓氏〕. ②**Sir James (Hopwood)** ~ 詹姆士·琼斯〔1877—1946, 英国数学家, 物理学家, 天文学家〕.

Jeb(b) [dʒeb] *n.* 杰布〔姓氏〕.

je·bel [ˈdʒebl] *n.* 〔Ar.〕山, 高山〔时常作阿拉伯地方名字用〕. *J- Druze (Druse)* (叙利亚的)德鲁兹山.

jee [dʒiː] *int.*, *n.* 驾! 〔驭马用语"向右走!"、"向前走!"之意〕 —*vt.*, *vi.* (使)(马)向前[右]走. (= gee).

jeep [dʒiːp] *n.* ①吉普车; 小型越野汽车. ②【军】小型护航航空母舰 (= ~ carrier). ③有线电视系统. ④新兵. ⑤轻型侦察机. *TV ~* (实况转播的)电视车. — *vi.* 坐吉普旅行. — *vt.* 用吉普车运输.

jee·pers [ˈdʒiːpəz] *int.* 天呀! 〔表示惊讶、强调等的适度感叹词〕.

jeer[1] [dʒiə] *n.* 嘲笑, 戏弄. — *vi.*, *vt.* 嘲笑, 戏弄 *(at)*. **-ing·ly** *ad.*

jeer[2] [dʒiə] *n.* 〔常 *pl.*〕【海】升降帆的滑车索.

jeer·er [ˈdʒiərə] *n.* 嘲笑者, 戏弄者. ***J-s must be content to taste of their own broth.*** 〔谚〕嘲笑人者必被人笑.

Jeff [dʒef] *n.* Jeffrey 的爱称.

Jef·fers [ˈdʒefəz] *n.* ①杰弗斯〔姓氏〕. ②**John Robinson** ~ 约翰·鲁滨逊·杰弗斯〔1887—1962, 美国诗人〕.

Jef·fer·son [ˈdʒefəsn] *n.* ①杰斐逊〔姓氏〕. ②**Thomas** ~ 汤姆斯·杰斐逊〔1743—1826, 美国政治家, 第三任总统, 独立宣言的起草人〕. ~ **City** 杰斐逊城〔美国密苏里州的首府〕. ~ **Day** 杰斐逊诞辰纪念节〔4月13日, 在美国某些州为法定假日〕. **-so·ni·an** [ˌdʒefəˈsəuniən] ① *a.* 杰斐逊特性的; 杰斐逊思想的, 杰斐逊民主的. ② *n.* 杰斐逊追随者. **-so·ni·an·ism** *n.* 杰斐逊主义.

Jeff·rey(s) [ˈdʒefri(z)] *n.* 杰弗里(斯)〔姓氏, 男子名, Jeff 为其昵称〕.

je·had [dʒiˈhɑːd] *n.* = jihad.

Je·ho·vah [dʒiˈhəuvə] *n.* 【宗】(对上帝的称呼) 耶和华.

Je·ho·vist [dʒiˈhəuvist] *n.* = Yahwist.

Je·hu [ˈdʒiːhjuː] *n.* ①【圣】耶和〔以色列国王, 相传为莽撞的御车者. ②〔j-〕〔俚〕出租马车车夫; 出租汽车司机. ③〔谑〕莽撞的车夫[司机]. ***drive like ~***. 〔美口〕开飞车.

je·june [dʒiˈdʒuːn] *a.* ①缺乏营养的; (土地等)贫瘠的. ②(内容等)空洞的; 枯燥无味的. ③幼稚的, 不成熟的. *a ~ diet* 缺乏营养的食物. *a ~ narrative* 枯燥无味的叙述. *a ~ behavior toward others* 孩子气的待人态度. **-ly** *ad.* **-ness** *n.*

je·ju·nec·to·my [ˌdʒidʒuːˈnektəmi] *n.* ***(pl. -mies)*** 【医】空肠切除术.

je·ju·num [dʒiˈdʒuːnəm] *n.* ***(pl. -na*** [-nə]***)*** 【解】空肠.

Je·kyll [ˈdʒiːkil, ˈdʒekil] *n.* 杰基尔〔姓氏〕.

Je·kyll and Hyde [ˈdʒekil ənd ˈhaid] 有两种面目的人, 具双重人格的人〔原为英国小说家斯蒂文生故事中的一个人物, 他服用自配的药物, 使自己时而变恶, 时而变善〕. *lead a Jekyll and Hyde existence.* 过双重人格的生活.

jell [dʒel] *vi.* 〔美口〕①凝成胶状, 结冻. ②(意见, 计划等)定形, 具体化, 变明确. — *vt.* ①使成胶状, 使结冻. ②使定形, 使具体化, 使明确. *plans that haven't ~ed yet.* 没有定形的计划. — *n.* 果子冻; 肉冻; 胶状物.

jel·la·ba [dʒeˈlɑːbɑː] *n.* = djellaba.

jel·lied [ˈdʒelid] *a.* ①成胶状的, 胶粘的, 胶质的. ②外涂胶状物的. ③拌有果子冻的. ~ **gasolene** 胶凝汽油, 凝汽油剂.

jel·li·fy [ˈdʒelifai] *vt.*, *vi.* ①(使)成胶状. ②(使)变松懈, (使)变软弱. **-fi·ca·tion** *n.* 胶凝; 冻结; 凝结.

Jell-O [ˈdʒeləu] *n.* 〔美〕(商标名)吉露牌果子冻〔作甜食吃〕; 〔j-〕果子冻.

jel·ly [ˈdʒeli] *n.* ①(透明)冻(胶), 胶状物. ②果子冻, 肉冻. ③畏惧, 优柔寡断. ④〔美俚〕不费力的事, 不花钱得来的东西. ***beat sb. to [into] a ~*** 痛打某人. — *vt.* ①使成为胶质; 使冻. ②在…上加胶冻物. — *vi.* ①结冻, 凝结, 成胶状. ②〔美俚〕闲逛聊天. ~ **baby** = ~ bean. ~**-bag** 做果酱时滤果汁用的袋. ~ **bean** *n.* 豆形胶质软糖. ~**fish** ①【动】水母, 海蜇. ②〔美俚〕无骨气的人; 优柔寡断的人. ~**graph** 胶版. ~ **roll** *n.* 涂果子冻的薄卷饼.

jem·a·dar [ˈdʒemədɑː] *n.* 〔Ind.〕 ①印度军队中的尉官. ②印度警官. ③仆人头目. ④(印度用的英语)〔口〕打扫工.

jem·my [ˈdʒemi] *n.* ①= jimmy. ②〔英〕羊头肉.

Je·na [ˈjeinə] *n.* 耶拿〔德意志民主共和国城市〕.

je ne sais quoi [ʒə nə seiˈkwɑː] 〔F.〕 ①难以描绘和表达的东西[事件]. ②我不知道是什么 (= I do not know what).

Jen·ghiz Khan, Jen·ghis Khan [ˈdʒengisˌkɑːn] 成吉思汗〔1162—1227, 元朝第一个开国皇帝〕. (= Genghis Khan).

Jen·kin(s) [ˈdʒenkin(z)] *n.* 詹金(斯)〔姓氏〕.

Jen·ner(s) [ˈdʒenə(z)] *n.* ①詹纳 (斯)〔姓氏〕. ②**Edward** ～ 爱德华·詹纳〔1749—1823,英国医生,种痘法的首创人〕. ②**William** ～ 威廉·詹纳〔1815—1898,英国医生〕.

jen·net [ˈdʒenit] *n.* ①一种西班牙产的小马. ②母驴.

Jen·ni·fer [ˈdʒenifə] *n.* 詹妮弗〔女子名〕.

Jen·nings [ˈdʒeniŋz] *n.* 詹宁斯〔姓氏〕.

Jen·ny [ˈdʒeni] *n.* 詹妮〔女子名〕.

jen·ny [ˈdʒeni] *n.* ①【机】移动起重机, 移动吊车. ②【纺】(同时可织几条线的)旧式纺纱机. ③雌鸟; 母驴; 某些雌性动物. ～ **ass** 母驴. ～ **wren** 雌鹪鹩〔俗名"巧妇鸟"〕.

jeop·ard [ˈdʒepəd] *vt.* 〔美〕 = jeopardize.

jeop·ard·ize, jeop·ard·ise [ˈdʒepədaiz] *vt.* 使受危险〔危害〕,危及. ～ *one's life* 冒生命危险.

jeop·ard·y [ˈdʒepədi] *n.* ①危难, 危险. ②【法】有罪受刑的可能性. ③刑事案件中被告的处境. *be in* ～ *of one's life* 处于生命危险中. *guarantee against double* ～ 对同一罪犯不受双重审判的保障.

je·quir·i·ty [dʒiˈkwiriti] *n.* ***(pl. -ties)***【植】①相思豆,红豆 (= jequirity bean). ②相思子 (= *Abrus precatorius*).

Jer. = Jeremiah; Jeremy; Jerome; Jersey.

jer·bo·a [dʒəːˈbəuə] *n.* 【动】跳鼠〔后腿特长〕.

jer·e·mi·ad [ˌdʒeriˈmaiəd] *n.* 哀诉; 哀史, 悲哀的故事.

Jer·e·mi·ah [ˌdʒeriˈmaiə] *n.* ①杰里迈亚〔男子名, Jerry 为其昵称; Jeremy 的异体〕. ②【宗】耶利米〔公元前六、七世纪时希伯来的大预言家〕. ③【宗】(《圣经·旧约》中的)《耶利米书》. ④对于前途抱悲观主义的人.

Jer·e·my [ˈdʒerimi] *n.* 杰里米〔男子名〕.

Jer·i·cho [ˈdʒerikəu] *n.* ①耶利哥〔死海以北的古城〕. ②〔口〕非常遥远的地方. ***from*** ～ ***to June*** 非常遥远地. ***Go to*** ～! 滚蛋! ***stay [tarry] in*** ～ ***until one's beard is grown*** 静待时机.

jerk[1] [dʒəːk] *n.* ①急促而猛烈的动作; 猛地一拉〔一推、一扭、一扔等〕. ②【医】(因反射动作引起的)肌肉挛缩. ③〔*pl.*〕(因受感动引起的)四肢或脸部的抽搐. ④【体】举重的挺举. ⑤〔美俚〕笨蛋,傻瓜; 微不足道的人. *a knee* ～ 膝反射. *physical* ～*s* 〔口〕体操. ***get a*** ～ ***on*** 卖力干,赶紧干. ***in a*** ～ 立刻,马上. ***pull with a*** ～ 猛地一扯. ***put a*** ～ ***to [into] it*** 使劲干, 努力干. — *vt.* ①猛拉,猛推,猛撞,猛扭. ②急促说出, 突然说出. ③〔俚〕在冷饮店里供应(苏打水、冰淇淋等). ～ *a fish out of the water* 猛地从水里拉出一条鱼. — *vi.* ①急拉,猛推,猛撞. ②颠簸地行进. ③痉挛. *The door* ～*ed open.* 门突然开了. ～ ***chin music*** 多嘴. ～ ***out one's words*** 脱口说出.

jerk[2] [dʒəːk] *vt.* 把(牛肉)切成薄片晒干. ～*ed beef* 牛肉干. — *n.* = jerky[2].

jer·kin [ˈdʒəːkin] *n.* ①(十六、十七世纪时)一种无袖紧身皮茄克; 短上衣. ②女用背心.

jerk·wa·ter [ˈdʒəːkwɔːtə] *n.* 〔美〕铁路专用支线. — *a.* ①铁路专用支线上的. ②〔口〕不重要的, 微小的, 乡下的. *a* ～ *town* 铁路上的小镇. *a* ～ *train* 慢车. *a* ～ *person* 无足轻重的人.

jer·ky[1] [ˈdʒəːki] *a.* ***(jerk·i·er; -i·est)*** ①急拉的; 急跳的; 急动的. ②痉挛性的. ③颠簸的,不平稳的. ④愚蠢的, 笨拙的. ⑤拗口的,佶屈聱牙的. *a* ～ *vehicle* 颠簸的破车辆. *a* ～ *mind* 疯子. **-i·ly** *ad.* **-i·ness** *n.*

jer·ky[2] [ˈdʒəːki] *n.* 肉片干,牛肉干.

jer·o·bo·am [ˌdʒerəˈbəuəm] *n.* 大酒杯〔尤其盛香槟酒的酒杯〕.

Je·rome [dʒəˈrəum] *n.* 杰罗姆〔姓氏, 男子名, Jerry 为其昵称〕.

jer·que [dʒəːk] *vt.* 〔英〕检查(船中有无私货). **-r** *n.* 船舶检查员,水上稽查员.

jer·ri·can [ˈdʒerikæn] *n.* = jerrycan.

Jer·(r)old, Jer·ald [ˈdʒerəld] *n.* 杰罗尔德〔男子名, Gerald 的异体〕.

jer·ry[1] [ˈdʒeri] *a.* 草率了事的,偷工减料的,马虎应付的. ～**-build** *vt.* 偷工减料地建造. ～ **builder** *n.* 偷工减料的营造商. ～ **building** 偷工减料的建筑工程. ～**-built** *a.* 偷工减料地建造的,用贱料草草建成的. ～**can** 五加仑的大汽油〔水〕罐 (= jerrican).

jer·ry[2] [ˈdʒeri] *n.* 〔英俚〕夜壶,尿罐.

Jer·ry [ˈdʒeri] *n.* ①杰丽〔女子名, Geraldine 的昵称〕. ②〔英俚〕德国兵,德国人.

jer·ry·man·der [ˈdʒerimændə] *v., n.* = gerrymander.

Jer·sey [ˈdʒəːzi] *n.* 泽西岛〔英吉利海峡中最大的岛〕. ～ *City* 泽西城〔美国新泽西州东北部的海港城市〕.

jer·sey [ˈdʒəːzi] *n.* ***(pl.*** ～***s)*** ①〔J-〕泽西种乳牛. ②【纺】平针织物. ③针织紧身内衣; 卫生衫, 运动衫.

Je·ru·sa·lem [dʒeˈruːsələm] *n.* 耶路撒冷〔巴勒斯坦古城,犹太教、基督教和伊斯兰教的圣地〕. *The New* ～ 天堂,乐园. ～ **artichoke** ①【植】北美菊芋(洋姜) (*Helianthus tuberosus*). ②洋姜. ～ **cherry**【植】冬珊瑚 (*Solanum Pseudo-capsicum*), 毛叶冬珊瑚 (*Solanum capsicastrum*). ～ **cricket**【动】耶路撒冷蟋蟀〔产于美国西部干燥地区〕. ～ **oak**【植】总状花藜 (*chenopodium botrys*)〔产于美国北部和加拿大〕. ～ **thorn**【植】①扁叶轴木 (*Parkinsonia aculeata*)〔产于美洲热带地区〕. ②滨枣,刺马甲子 (= christ's thorn).

Jer·vis [ˈdʒɑːvis, ˈdʒəːvis] *n.* 杰维斯〔姓氏〕.

Jes. = Jesus.

Jes·per·sen [ˈjespəsn, ˈdʒes-], **Otto** ～ 奥托·叶〔杰〕斯帕森〔1860—1943,丹麦语言学家,尤以英语见长〕.

jess [dʒes] *n.* 猎鹰的脚带. — *vt.* 给(鹰)系上脚带.

jes·sa·mine [ˈdʒesəmin] *n.* = jasmin(e).

Jes·se [ˈdʒesi] *n.* ①杰西〔男子名, Jess 为其昵称〕. ②【宗】耶西〔以色列王大卫的父亲之名〕. ～ **tree**【宗】耶稣的家谱. ～ **window** 画有耶稣家谱的玻璃窗.

jes·se, jes·sie, jes·sy [ˈdʒesi] *n.* 〔美俚〕辱骂; 殴打. ***catch*** ～ 〔美俚〕受责骂; 被殴打. ***give sb.*** ～ 〔美俚〕痛责某人; 殴打某人.

Jes·si·ca [ˈdʒesikə] *n.* 杰西卡〔女子名〕.

Jes·sie [ˈdʒesi] *n.* 杰西〔女子名〕.

jest [dʒest] *n.* ①玩笑,笑话, 俏皮话. ②戏谑, 诙谐; 打趣. ③笑柄. ***Better lose a*** ～ ***than a friend***〔谚〕宁肯少说笑话, 决不得罪朋友. ***be a standing*** ～ 经常被嘲笑的对象. ***break [drop] a*** ～ 说笑话. ***in*** ～ 开玩笑地(*speak half in* ～, *half in earnest* 半真半假地讲). ～***ing apart***〔作插入语用〕说正经的. ***make a*** ～ ***of sb.*** 愚弄某人. — *vi.* ①取笑,嘲弄 (*at*). ②开玩笑, 打趣 (*with*). *Please don't* ～ *with me.* 请别和我开玩笑. ～ *at sb.* 嘲笑某人. — *vt.* 对…开玩笑,嘲笑. ～**book** *n.* 笑话书. **-ful** *a.*

jest·er [ˈdʒestə] *n.* ①爱说笑话的人. ②小丑,(中世纪的)弄臣.

jest·ing [ˈdʒestiŋ] *n.* 笑话; 滑稽,诙谐. — *a.* 开玩笑的,爱说笑话的,滑稽的. **-ly** *ad.*

Je·su [ˈdʒiːzjuː] *n.* 〔古〕= Jesus (尤用于呼格).

Jes·u·it [ˈdʒezjuit] *n.* ①【天主】耶稣会会士. ②阴险的人,虚伪狡诈的人. *the* ～*s* 耶稣会. ～**s' [～'s] bark**【植】金鸡纳树皮,金鸡纳皮. **-ic(al)** *a.* **-i·cal·ly** *ad.*

Jes·u·it·ism [ˈdʒezjuitizəm] *n.* ①耶稣会的教义. ②〔j-〕狡猾,阴险.

Jes·u·it·ize [ˈdʒezjuitaiz] *vt.* ***(-iz·ed, -iz·ing)*** ①使成为耶稣会员. ②使变狡猾,使变阴险.

Jes·u·it·ry [ˈdʒezjuitri] *n.* = Jesuitism.

Je·sus [ˈdʒiːzəs] *n.* ①杰西〔男子名〕. ②【宗】耶稣〔基督教的创始人〕. *the society of* ～ (天主教的)耶稣会. ***knock the*** ～ ***out of sb.*** 把某人打得昏头昏脑. — *int.* 天哪! 岂有此理!〔表示怀疑、不满、失望、惊恐、痛苦,甚

至辱骂，有时也说 ~ Christ!〕．~ **Christ** 耶稣基督．

jet[1] [dʒet] *n.* ①【矿】煤玉，黑色大理石．②乌黑发亮的颜色．— *a.* ①煤玉制的，黑色大理石制的．②乌黑发亮的．*her ~ hair* 她那一头乌油油的秀发．~**-black** *a.* 乌黑发亮的，黑玉色的．**jet·ted** *a.* 用黑玉装饰的．

jet[2] [dʒet] *n.* ①喷射，喷出；【物】喷注，气流；射流．②喷口，喷嘴；喷射器．③【空】喷气式发动机；喷气式飞机．④喷出物；〔喻〕喷流似的涌出物．*an electron ~* 电子束，电子流．*a plasma ~* 等离子流．*a nozzle ~* 汽嘴．*travel by ~* 乘喷气式飞机旅行．*talk in a ~*．滔滔不绝地谈话．*a ~ of water sent up by a fountain* 喷泉中喷出的水束．***at a single ~*** 一想就懂．***at the first ~*** 由于一时的冲动．— *vt.* ①喷射出(水流等)．②用喷气式飞机载送．— *vi.* ①喷射．②乘坐喷气式飞机．③飞速移动．— *a.* ①喷气式(发动机)推进的．②用喷气式飞机的．③迅速的，飞快的．~**airplane** = ~ plane．~ **blower**【机】喷气鼓风机．~**boat** 喷气快艇．~ **burner** 喷射口，火口．~ **engine** 喷气发动机，空气喷气发动机．~ **generator**【物】喷注发生器，液哨(超生波发生器)．~ **lag** (乘喷气式飞机高速飞行引起的)生理节奏失调；(连续几次航行后的)疲累；时差感；飞行时差反应．~**liner** 喷气客机(尤指班机)．~**plane** 喷气式飞机．~**port** 喷气式飞机机场．~**powered** 喷气动力的．~**-propelled** *a.* 喷气发动机推动的，喷气式发动机推动的．~**-propeller** 喷气式推进器，喷气式螺旋桨．~ **propulsion**【空】喷气推进．~ **pump**【机】喷射泵．~ **set** 喷气机旅行界〔乘喷气客机到处旅行的富翁阶层〕．~ **setter** 乘喷气飞机到处旅行的富人．~ **stream** ①急流，喷流．②【空】喷射气流，喷流．~**vane** 喷气导流控制片，燃气舵．

jet·bead [ˈdʒebi:d] *n.*【植】鸡麻属〔灌木，花为四瓣，呈白色；果似小珠，发亮而呈黑色〕．

je·té [ʒəˈtei] *n.* 〔F.〕(芭蕾舞)越步．

je·ton [ˈdʒetn] *n.* 公用电话，自动计费器．

jet·sam [ˈdʒetsəm] *n.* ①船舶遇难时投弃的货物〔船上的装备〕．②沉入海底或冲到岸上的废弃货物〔设备〕．③废弃的东西．**flotsam and ~** ①飘浮海面或冲到岸上的船只残骸或其货物．②流离失所者，流浪者，被毁掉的人．③零碎物，无价值的东西．

jet·ti·son [ˈdʒetisn] *n.* ①(紧急情况下的)投弃货物．②抛弃，放弃．— *vt.* ①(在紧急情况下)向海中投弃(货物等)．②扔弃(累赘物品)．③(飞机等在飞行时)投弃(炸药，辅助装备、燃料等)．

jet·ty[1] [ˈdʒeti] *a.* ①煤玉似的．②乌黑发亮的．

jet·ty[2] [ˈdʒeti] *n.* ***(pl. -ties)*** ①防波堤．②码头．③【建】建筑物的突出部．— *vi.* ***(-tied; -ty·ing)*** 突出，伸出．

jeu [ʒə:] *n.* ***(pl. jeux*** [ʒə:(z)]***)*** 〔F.〕①游戏，娱乐．②【乐】演奏．~ ***de mots*** [F.ˈʒə:dəˈməu] 双关话，俏皮话．~ ***d'es·prit*** [F. ˈʒə:desˈpri:] 机智的话，妙语．

jeune fille [F.ʒœn fij] 〔F.〕年轻女子，小姐．

jeune pre·mier [F. ʒœn prəˈmje] 〔F.〕扮演少年主角的男演员．

jeu·nesse do·rée [F. ʒœnes dɔre] 〔F.〕阔少爷，花花公子．

jeux [ʒə:(z)] jeu 的复数．

Jev·ons [ˈdʒevənz] *n.* ①杰文斯〔姓氏〕．②William Stanley ~ 威廉·斯坦利·杰文斯〔1835—1882，英国经济学家和逻辑学家〕．

Jew [dʒu:] *n.* ①犹太人，犹太教徒．②〔贬〕高利贷者；守财奴；奸商．*an unbelieving ~* 疑心重的人．*the wondering ~* 流浪的犹太人，流浪者．***(as) rich as a ~*** 大财主．***go to the ~s*** 〔俚〕向高利贷者借钱．***Tell that to the ~s.*** 鬼相信那种话．***worth a ~'s eye*** 〔古〕极为贵重．— *vt.* 〔j-〕①〔俚〕欺骗．②〔口〕杀价购买 (*down*)．~**-baiter** 迫害犹太人者．~**-baiting** 迫害犹太人．**-dom** ①〔集合词〕犹太人；犹太人的世界．②犹太教．

jew·el [ˈdʒu:əl] *n.* ①宝石，宝玉．②宝石饰物，镶有宝石的装饰品．③贵重的人〔物〕．④手表中的宝石轴承．*a ~ of a boy* 宝贝孩子．— *vt.* ***(jewel(l)ed; jewel(l)ing)*** ①用宝石装饰．②把宝石轴承镶进(手表中)．~**weed**【植】(北美产)凤仙花属 *(Impatiens)* 植物．**-like** *a.*

Jew·el(l) [ˈdʒu:əl] *n.* 朱厄尔〔女子名〕．

jew·el·(l)er [ˈdʒu:ələ] *n.* 宝石匠；宝石商，珠宝商．~**'s bar** 贵金属工艺品的坯子．

jew·el·lery, jew·el·ry [ˈdʒu:əlri] *n.* ①珠宝类．②珠宝饰物．

Jew·ess [ˈdʒu:is] *n.* 犹太妇女．

Jew·ett [ˈdʒu:it] *n.* ①朱伊特〔姓氏〕．②**Sarah Orne ~** 萨拉·奥恩·朱伊特〔1849—1909，美国女小说家〕．

jew·fish [ˈdʒu:ˌfiʃ] *n.* ***(pl.~(es))***【鱼】暖海鱼属〔如大海鲈 *(= Stereolepis gigas)* 或石斑鱼 *(= Epinephelus itajara)*〕．

Jew·ish [ˈdʒu(:)iʃ] *a.* 犹太人的；犹太人似的，犹太人作风的．*the ~ calendar* 犹太历〔希伯来人用的阴阳合历〕．— *n.* = Yiddish. **-ly** *ad.* **-ness** *n.*

Jew·ry [ˈdʒuəri] *n.* ①〔集合词〕犹太人；犹太民族．②犹太人居住区域．

Jew's-ear [ˈdʒu:ziə] *n.*【植】黑木耳．

Jew's-harp, Jews'-harp [ˈdʒu:zhɑ:p] *n.* (咬在牙齿上用手弹的)口拨琴．

Jez·e·bel [ˈdʒezəbl] *n.* ①耶西别〔古代以色列国王亚哈的妻子，残忍淫荡〕．②〔j-〕无耻放荡的女人，胭脂虎．

jg, j.g. = 【美海军】junior grade.

jiao [dʒau] *n.* 〔Chin.〕(中国辅币单位)角．

jib[1] [dʒib] *n.* ①【机】吊机臂，挺杆，绞辘；人字起重机的桁．②【矿】截盘．~ **crane** 摇臂吊车，旋臂吊车．~ **door** (与墙同样高矮和同样颜色的)隐门．

jib[2] [dʒib] *n.*【海】船首三角帆．***cut off sb.'s ~*** 打断他人谈话．***the cut of one's ~*** 相貌，仪表．— *vt.* 使(帆、桁等)从一边转到另一边．— *vi.* 船帆等从一边转到另一边．~ **boom**【海】第二斜桅．~**-headed** *a.* 刀刃成三角帆形的；【海】三角的〔指纵帆〕．

jib[3] [dʒib] *vi.* ①(马等)退缩，横跑，后退．②(人)踌躇不前．~ ***at*** 对…表示踌躇，讨厌 (~ *at hard work* 不愿做艰苦的工作)．

jib·ba(h) [ˈdʒibə] *n.* (穆斯林男子穿的)长布袍．

jib·ber [ˈdʒibə] *n.* 后退的马；踌躇不前的人．

jibe[1] [dʒaib] *vi.* (帆)从一舷转至他舷．— *vt.* 使调换方向，使改变航道．

jibe[2] [dʒaib] *n., vt., vi.* 嘲笑，嘲弄．**-r** *n.* 嘲笑者，嘲弄者．

jibe[3] [dʒaib] *vi.* 〔美口〕与…一致；符合 *(with)*．*accounts that don't ~* 与实际开支不符的帐目．

JIC = ①Joint Intelligence Committee〔美〕联合情报委员会．②joint intelligence center〔美〕联合情报中心．

Jid·da(h) [ˈdʒidə] *n.* 吉达〔沙特阿拉伯红海沿岸的海港城市〕．

jiff, jif·fy [dʒif, ˈdʒifi] *n.* 〔口〕一会儿．***in a ~*** 马上，立刻．***wait (half) a ~*** 稍等一下．

jig [dʒig] *n.* ①捷格舞〔一种轻松快速的三拍子舞〕；捷格舞曲；快步舞(曲)．②(诱饵在水中上下跳动的)冰下鱼钩．③【矿】筛选机，跳汰机；跳汰选矿法．④【机】夹具；钻模；装配架；模具，规尺，样板．⑤【无】衰减波群．*an assembly ~* 装配架．*reaming ~* 铰孔夹具．***in ~ time*** 马上，极快地．***on the ~*** 战战兢兢地．***The ~ is over [up]*** 〔俚〕一切都完了．***whistle ~s to a milestone*** 对牛弹琴．—*vt., vi.* ①跳(捷格舞)；(使)跳跃．②(使)(上下前后急剧)跳动．③用特种钓鱼钩钓(鱼)．④【矿】筛(矿)．⑤【机】用夹具加工(工件等)．~ **borer** 钻模镗床，座标镗床．~ **plate** 夹具模；钻板模．~ **point** 基点．~ **welding** 焊接夹具．~ **washer** 跳汰洗矿机．

jig·ger[1] [ˈdʒigə] *n.* ①开跳汰机的工人；【矿】筛矿器，跳汰

机. ②跳捷格舞的人. ③【机】小滑车,盘车,辘轳. ④【海】补助帆;一种小帆船. ⑤〔俚〕小巧复杂的东西,小玩意. ⑥【无】减幅振荡变压器;可变耦合变压器. ⑦〔美〕(混合饮料用的 $1\frac{1}{2}$ 盎司)量杯;一量杯的酒. ⑧【高尔夫球】小头铁球棒. ~ **mast** (四桅船的)后桅;(小艇的)船尾小桅.

jig·ger^{2} [ˈdʒigə] *n.* = chigoe, chigger.

jig·gered [ˈdʒigəd] *a.* 〔口〕'damned' 的委婉语. *Well, I'm ~!* 不会罢! *I'll be ~ if* …哪有…的事.

jig·ger·y-pok·er·y [ˈdʒigəriˈpəukəri] *n.* 〔口〕阴谋,诡计;欺骗;秘密活动;诈骗.

jig·gle [ˈdʒigl] *vt., vi.* (使)轻轻摇晃[跳动]. — *n.* 〔美〕轻轻的摇晃[跳动].

jig·gly [ˈdʒigli] *a.* 摇晃的,不稳定的.

jig·saw [ˈdʒigsɔː] *n.* 〔美〕锯曲线机,钢丝锯,竖锯. *a war of ~ pattern* 【军】犬牙交错的战争态势. — *vt.* ①用锯曲线机锯. ②使互相交错搭接. ~ **puzzle** (玩具)益智分合板,拼板玩具.

ji·had [dʒiˈhɑːd] *n.* ①【宗】穆斯林的护教战争,圣战;宗教讨伐. ②维护信仰[主义、政策等]的运动 (*for*); 反对某项主义[政策、学说、信仰等]的运动 (*against*). *a ~ against a new doctrine* 反对新教义的运动.

Jill [dʒil] *n.* =Gill (*opp.* Jack). ①吉尔〔女子名〕. ②〔罕〕少女,妇女〔尤指情人〕.

jil·lion [ˈdʒiljən] *n.* 〔美俚〕巨量.

jilt [dʒilt] *n.* 任意遗弃情人的女子. — *vt.* (女子)任意遗弃(情人).

jil·tee [dʒilˈtiː] *n.* 〔美〕被遗弃的人.

Jim [dʒim] *n.* 吉姆〔男子名,James 的略称或昵称〕.

jim·ber·jawed [ˈdʒimbədʒɔːd] *a.* 下颚突出的.

Jim Crow [ˈdʒimˈkrəu] 〔美〕①〔贬〕黑人. ②对黑人的种族岐视 (=Jim Crowism). ③〔j- c-〕【机】弯轨机. *the Jim Crow car* 黑人专用火车(或电车).

Jim-Crow, jim-crow [ˈdʒimˈkrəu] *a.* ①〔贬〕黑人的. ②歧视黑人的. ③黑人专用的. *a Jim-Crow school* 黑人专用学校. *Jim-Crow Law* 歧视黑人的法律. —*vt.* 歧视(黑人).

jim-dan·dy [ˈdʒimˈdændi] *n.* 〔口〕出色人物,优秀人物;讨人喜欢的东西. — *a.* 〔口〕优秀的,头等的,非常讨人喜欢的.

jim·jams [ˈdʒimdʒæmz] *n. pl.* 〔俚〕①(因酒精中毒引起的)震颤性谵妄. ②〔常与 the 连用〕极度紧张不安.

Jim·mie [ˈdʒimi] *n.* =Jimmy.

Jim·my [ˈdʒimi] *n.* 吉米〔男子名,James 的昵称〕.

jim·my [ˈdʒimi] *n.* ①〔美〕(盗贼用的)撬门棍. ②【机】短撬棍. ③煤车. — *vt.* (用撬棍)撬,撬开. *The burglar jimmied a window.* 盗贼撬开了一扇窗.

jim·son weed [ˈdʒimsnwiːd] 【植】曼陀罗〔一年生的有毒草本植物,叶带臭味,花似喇叭,呈黄色或淡紫色,果有刺〕.

jin^{1} [dʒin] *n.* = jinni.

jin^{2} [dʒin] *n.* 〔Chin.〕斤 (=0.5 公斤).

jing·bang [ˈdʒiŋˈbæŋ] *n.* 〔俚〕团体;群众;许多. *the whole ~* 全体,统统.

jin·gle [ˈdʒiŋgəl] *n.* ①(小铃、钱币等的)丁当声;发丁当声的东西. ②诗的简单韵律;韵律简单的字句[音节]. ③(爱尔兰或澳洲的)二轮有顶马车. — *vt., vi.* ①(使)丁当响. ②(使)(诗句和音乐等)具有简单而又引人注意的韵律[节奏]. *The bells ~d.* 铃声丁当. *~ the keys* 把钥匙弄得丁零当郎直响. ~ **bell** ①门铃;装在雪橇上的铃铛. ②(通知船速的)信号铃. ~ **jangle** ① *n.* 丁当声;〔美俚〕钱. ② *vi.* 发出丁当声. **jin·gly** *a.* 丁当响的;简单押韵的.

jin·gled [ˈdʒiŋgld] *a.* 〔美俚〕喝醉的.

jin·go^{1} [ˈdʒiŋgəu] *n.* (*pl. ~es*) 侵略主义者,沙文主义者,武力外交政策论者. **-ism** *n.* 侵略主义,沙文主义,武力外交政策. **-ist** *n.* 侵略主义者,沙文主义者.

jin·go^{2} [ˈdʒiŋgəu] *int.* ***by (the living) ~*** 啊呀! 天哪! 〔表示快乐、惊异或加强语气〕.

jin·go·is·tic [ˌdʒiŋgəuˈistik] *a.* 侵略主义的,侵略分子的. **-cal·ly** *ad.*

jink [dʒiŋk] *vi.* ①闪开,急忙避开,急转. ②〔俚〕(飞机)颠簸飞行(躲避高射炮火等). — *vt.* 避开,躲开. — *n.* ①闪开,急忙回避. ②〔*pl.*〕喧闹的游戏. *give the ~s* 巧妙避开. *high ~s* 大吵大闹的嬉戏.

jinn [dʒin] *n.* jinni 的复数〔一般把此词当作单数,并加了一个复数形式 *jinns*〕.

jin·nee, jin·ni [dʒiˈniː] *n.* (*pl. jinn*) (伊斯兰教中的)神灵.

J.I.N.R. = Joint Institute for Nuclear Research 〔苏联〕联合核研究所.

jin·rik·(i)·sha, jin·rick·sha [dʒinˈrikʃə], **jin·rick·shaw** [dʒinˈrikʃɔː] *n.* 人力车,黄包车.

jinx [dʒiŋks] *n.* 〔美口〕①不吉祥的人[物]. ②倒霉,坏运气. *a ~ day* 不吉利的日子. ***break [smash] the ~*** (运动比赛)连败之后转向胜利. — *vt.* 使倒霉;破坏.

ji·pi·ja·pa [ˌhiːpiːˈhɑːpə] *n.* 【植】①巴拿马草 (*Carludovica palmata*) 〔产于中南美,叶子可编草帽〕. ②巴拿马干草. ③巴拿马帽 (=Panama hat).

JIS = Japanese Industrial Standard 日本工业规格,日本工业标准.

jit·ney [ˈdʒitni] *n.* ①〔美俚〕五分硬币,镍币. ②(票价五分的)小型公共汽车,收费低廉的公共汽车. ③便宜货,次等品. — *vt., vi.* 乘坐公共汽车(去). ~ **bag** 〔美俚〕手提小皮包. ~ **circuit** 〔美〕郊区的廉价戏. ~ **dance** 〔美〕五分钱跳一次的公开舞会.

jit·ter [ˈdʒitə] *vi.* 〔口〕紧张不安,烦躁不安;战战兢兢,颤抖. — *n.* 〔*pl.*〕〔美俚〕极度的紧张不安. *have the ~s* 极度紧张不安;战战兢兢.

jit·ter·bug [ˈdʒitəbʌg] *n.* ①神经紧张不安的人. ②吉特巴舞〔随爵士音乐节拍跳的快速舞〕. ③跳吉特巴舞的人. ④爵士舞曲迷. — *vi.* 跳吉特巴舞.

jit·ter·y [ˈdʒitəri] *a.* 〔美俚〕神经极度紧张不安的.

jiu·jit·su, jiu·jut·su [dʒjuːˈdʒitsuː] 〔Jap.〕 *n.* = jujitsu.

Ji·va·ro [ˈhiːvɑːrəu] *n.* ① (*pl. ~(s)*) 黑瓦洛人〔厄瓜多尔南部和秘鲁北部的一个印第安部族的成员〕. ②黑瓦洛语.

jive [dʒaiv] *n.* ①(节奏快速、活泼的)爵士音乐. ②爵士音乐中的专业术语;吸毒者等用的黑话. ③〔美俚〕花言巧语;蠢话,废话. — *vi.* ①奏爵士乐. ②〔美俚〕用花言巧语欺骗;干无益的蠢事. — *vt.* ①奏(爵士乐);随着爵士音乐跳(舞). ②欺骗,取笑.

JJ. = Judges; Justices.

JL = Journal; July.

JMP = 〔Chin.〕Jen Min Pi 人民币〔现用 RMB〕.

Jn = June; junior; Junction.

Jno. [dʒɔn] = John.

Jo [dʒəu] *n.* 乔〔Joseph, Josephine 的简称〕.

Jo. = Joel; John; Joseph; Josephine.

jo [dʒəu] *n.* (*pl. ~es*) 〔Scot.〕情人.

joad [dʒəud] *n.* 〔美〕(随农业季节而劳动的)流动工人.

Joan(n) [dʒəun] *n.* 琼〔女子名〕.

Jo·an·na [dʒəuˈænə] *n.* 乔安娜〔女子名,Joan 的异体〕.

Job [dʒəub] *n.* ①乔布〔男子名〕. ②约伯〔《圣经》中的人物,以忍艰耐劳著称〕. ③《旧约圣经》中的《约伯记》(=the book of ~). *the patience of ~* 极度的忍耐. *It would try the patience of ~.* 那就太气人了. **~'s comforter** 增加别人痛苦的安慰者,对别人的悲痛假安慰真刺激的人. **~'s dock** 医院. **~'s news** 噩耗,坏消息. **~'s post** 传恶耗者,报讯者. **~'s pound** 监狱. **~'s tears** 【植】①〔动词用单数〕薏苡(回回米) (*coix lacryma-jobi*) 〔一种一年生热带草本植物,籽可食〕. ②薏苡米珠.

job^{1} [dʒɔb] *n.* ①工作,活计. ②零活,散工,包工. ③

任务，职责，作用. ④加工的物品〔原料〕；结果；产品. ⑤〔美口〕职业，职位，地位. ⑥犯罪的行为（尤指偷盗）；损人的事；假公济私的事，贪污行为. ⑦〔口〕事件，情况，事情. ⑧〔口〕费力的事. ⑨〔俚〕人，女人. ⑩〔口〕汽车. *make a thorough ~ of it* 把这件事做彻底. *a man paid by the ~* 计件工. *odd ~s* 零活，杂务. *It is your ~ to be on time.* 你有责任按时来. *This is a put-up ~.*〔俚〕这是骗局，这是阴谋. *a queer ~* 蹊跷. *a fat ~* 肥缺. *be out of a ~* 失业. *look out for a ~* 找工作. *have a ~ as a typist* 担任打字员的职务. *His poem is a superb ~.* 他的诗是一部出色的作品. *The theft must have been an inside ~.* 这一窃案一定是内部人干的. *a good ~* 舒服的工作. *a bad ~* 吃力不讨好的事. *have a hard ~ to do sth.* 做某事很吃力. *It was a real ~ to talk over that noise.* 要压过那样的吵闹声讲话真费劲. *a straight ~*（没有拖车的）载重汽车. ***by the ~*** 包做，计件. ***do a ~ on sb.*** 〔俚〕整掉某人，损毁某人. ***do sb.'s ~ for him, do the ~ for sb.*** ①代某人做事. ②〔俚〕送掉某人的命 *(This will do his [the] ~ for him.* 这会送掉他的命). ***~s for the boys***〔口〕酬劳支持者的肥缺，美差. ***just the ~*** 恰好要的东西. ***keen of a ~***〔口〕很想工作. ***lie down on the ~*** 敷衍了事. ***make a good ~ of*** 办好；处理好. ***make the best of a bad ~*** 设法收拾残局；尽量减少损失. ***nose a ~ in everything*** 到处看到有利可图. ***on the ~***〔俚〕(努力)工作着. ***put up a ~ on sb.***〔美〕捉弄某人，欺骗某人. —*vi.* ①作零工，作包工，打杂. ②假公济私，营私舞弊. ③做股票经纪. —*vt.* ①承包，分包(工程等)；(临时)雇用. ②临时租用，出租(车、马等). ③代客买卖(股票等)，批发(商品等). ④用假公济私的手腕处理. ⑤〔美俚〕除掉，搞垮. ⑥〔美俚〕欺骗，欺诈. *~ sb. out of his money* 骗走某人的钱. *a jobbing house*〔美〕批发庄. ***~ about*** 做散工. ***~ sb. into a post*** 用营私舞弊的手段使某人就任，卖官鬻爵. ***~ off*** 赚钱卖出；非法处分. ***~ out*** 把巨大的工作分包出去. **~ action**（警察等的）临时性罢工示威. **~ analysis** 企业工种分析学〔研究各工种的操作、劳动条件、工人技术水平等〕. **~ case**【印】铅字盒. **~ commuting** 远途往返上班活动. **J- Corps** 就业团(计划)〔美国政府为无业青年搞的就业训练计划〕. **~ holder** ①有职业者. ②〔美〕公务员. **~ hopping** 为求经济利益而改行，跳厂，跳槽. **~ hunter**〔美〕找事的人，求职者. **~ lot** ①(货物的)搭配花色批发. ②随便搭配花色批发(尤指货质低劣者). **~ master** 出租车〔马〕的人. **~ printer** 承印零星印件的印刷商. **~ printing** 零星小商品印刷〔如印刷信封上端的文字、传单、请帖等〕. **~-splitting** 一工分做制〔现代资本主义企业把全日工改为两个半日工的办法〕. **~ work** ①包工；散工. ②零件印刷.

job² [dʒɔb] *n., vt., vi.*〔方〕= jab.

jo·ba·tion [dʒəuˈbeiʃən] *n.*〔口〕冗长的训诫，谴责.

job·ber [ˈdʒɔbə] *n.* ①散工，零工，包工. ②〔英〕租车人，租马人. ③〔英〕股票经纪人. ④假公济私的人. ⑤批发商.

job·ber·nowl [ˈdʒɔbəˌnəul] *n.*〔口〕笨蛋，蠢汉. —*a.* 愚蠢的.

job·ber·y [ˈdʒɔbəri] *n.* 假公济私；徇私舞弊.

job·less [ˈdʒɔblis] *a.* ①无职业的；失业的. ②与失业有关的. *the ~* 失业者. **-ness** *n.*

Jo·cas·ta [dʒəuˈkæstə] *n.*【希神】伊俄卡斯达〔因命运捉弄，竟成为其子奥狄浦斯之妻，发觉后即自尽身死〕.

Jock [dʒɔk] *n.*〔英〕〔军俚〕苏格兰(尤指高地)的士兵.

jock¹ [dʒɔk] *n.* = jockey *(n.)*.

jock² [dʒɔk] *n.* = jockstrap.

jock·ey [ˈdʒɔki] *n.* ①职业赛马骑师. ②〔古〕马商. ③驾驶员；(机器等的)操作者. ④〔英〕小伙子，下属，帮手. ⑤薄膜. ⑥【机】连接装置. —*vt.* ①骑(马)参加比赛；驾驶(汽车等)，操作(机器). ②欺骗，欺诈. ③移动. *~ sb. into doing sth.* 骗某人做某事. *~ sb. into a trap* 诱骗某人落入圈套. *~ sb. out of sth.* 诈取某人某物. —*vi.* ①当职业赛马骑师. ②运用手段谋利. ***~ for position*** ①(赛马时)挤其他骑师以占有利位置. ②运用手段谋利. **~ cap**（有尖帽舌的）赛马骑师帽. **J- Club** ①(英国的)赛马总会. ②〔j- c-〕赛马俱乐部. **~ pulley**【机】导轮. **~ rollers** 张力辊.

jock·o [ˈdʒɔkəu] *n.*【动】黑猩猩.

jock·strap [ˈdʒɔkstræp] *n.* ①(男运动员的弹性织物)下体护身. ②〔俚〕运动员〔贬称，亦作 jock〕.

jo·cose [dʒəˈkəus] *a.* 开玩笑的，诙谐的，滑稽的. **-ly** *ad.* **-ness** *n.*

jo·cos·i·ty [dʒəuˈkɔsiti] *n.* ①滑稽，诙谐，戏谑. ②〔*pl.*〕诙谐的言行.

joc·u·lar [ˈdʒɔkjulə] *a.* ①诙谐的，滑稽的，好开玩笑的. ②打趣的，寻乐的. **-ly** *ad.*

joc·u·lar·i·ty [ˌdʒɔkjuˈlæriti] *n.* ①滑稽，诙谐. ②滑稽的言行.

joc·und [ˈdʒɔkənd] *a.* 欢乐的，快活的. **-ly** *ad.*

jo·cun·di·ty [dʒəuˈkʌnditi] *n.* ①欢乐，快活. ②〔*pl.*〕欢乐〔快活〕的言行.

Jodh·pur [dʒɔdˈpuə] *n.* 乔德普尔〔印度贾拉斯坦邦的城市〕.

jodh·pur [ˈdʒɑːdpə] *n.* ①〔*pl.*〕骑马裤. ②短马靴.

Joe [dʒəu] *n.* ①乔〔男子名，Joseph 的昵称〕. ②〔美口〕〔j-〕(对不相识者的称呼)家伙. ③美国兵〔=G. I. Joe〕. ④= Joe Miller. ⑤〔j-〕〔英俚〕四便士的银币. ⑥〔j-〕〔Scot.〕情人=jo. ⑦〔j-〕〔美俚〕咖啡. ***a good ~***〔美〕讨人喜欢的家伙. **~ Miller** 滑稽书，笑话集；陈套滑稽. *I don't see the J- Miller of it.* 我觉得这没有什么逗乐的. ***Not for ~!***〔俚〕决不干！决不是！—*a.*〔美俚〕知内情的. ***get ~ to sth.*** 了解某事内情. ***Put sb. ~*** 使某人得知内情. **~ Blow [Doakes]** 老百姓. **~ college**〔美口〕男大学生.

Jo·el [ˈdʒəuel] *n.* ①约耳〔男子名〕. ②约耳〔古代希伯来预言者〕. ③(《旧约圣经》中的)《约耳书》.

joe-pye weed [ˌdʒəuˈpai-wiːd] *n.*〔美〕紫花，紫菀草.

jo·ey [ˈdʒəui] *n.* ①〔澳〕小袋鼠；小动物. ②〔英俚〕三便士硬币.

jog¹ [dʒɔg] *vt.* ①轻推，轻撞；轻摇. ②唤起（记忆），提醒. ③使(马)缓步前进. ④【印】使(纸张)整齐，把(纸张)垛齐. *~ sb. with one's elbow to get his attention* 用肘轻推某人以引起他的注意. *~ sb.'s memory* 唤起某人注意. —*vi.* ①颠簸地移动. ②磨磨蹭蹭地走. ③缓慢而平稳地进行. ④熬时间. *The bus ~ged along.* 那辆公共汽车上下颠簸地行驶. *~ a few miles on horseback* 骑马慢慢地走几英里. *Matters ~ along.* 事情按部就班地进行. *We must ~ along [on] somehow.* 我们得一步步干下去. *Time keeps ~ging on.* 时间不断地磨蹭掉. —*n.* ①轻推；轻摇，轻撞. ②慢步，缓行. **~ trot** ①慢步，缓行. ②单调的进程，常规.

jog² [dʒɔg] *n.* ①〔美〕(线、面上的)参差不齐，凹凸不平. ②突然的转向. —*vi.* ①凹进，凸出. ②突然转向.

jog·gle¹ [ˈdʒɔgl] *vt., vi.* 轻轻摇动. —*n.* 轻轻颠摇.

jog·gle² [ˈdʒɔgl] *n.*【建】啮合扣；接榫. —*vt.* 啮合；榫接. **~ joint** 啮合接；肘接；榫接.

Jog·ja·kar·ta [ˌdʒɔgjəˈkɑːtə] *n.* 日惹〔印度尼西亚城市〕.

Jo·han·nes [dʒəuˈhænis] *n.* 约翰尼斯〔男子名，John 的别称〕.

jo·han·nes [dʒəuˈhæniz] *n. (pl. ~nes)* 葡萄牙十八、十九世纪的金币.

Jo·han·nes·burg [dʒəuˈhænisbəːg] *n.* 约翰内斯堡〔南非(阿扎尼亚)城市〕.

Jo·han·nis·ber·ger [dʒəuˈhɑːnisbəːgə] *n.*（德国 Johannisberg 产）高级白葡萄酒.

John [dʒɔn] *n.* ①约翰〔男子名〕；使徒约翰〔耶稣十二门徒之一〕；(新约《圣经》中的)《约翰福音》. ②〔美俚〕〔i〕盥洗室，〔j-〕厕所. ③〔俚〕〔j-〕男子〔尤指容易受骗的人〕. ④〔美俚〕〔j-〕嫖客. ～ **Barleycorn** 粮食酒，啤酒〔拟人化的称呼〕. ～ **Bull** 约翰牛〔英国或英国人的绰号〕. ～ **Bullism** 英国人的品质〔性格、精神〕. ～ **Chinaman** 〔贬〕典型中国人. ～ **Citizen** 普通人，老百姓. ～ **Company**〔口〕【史】东印度公司. ～ **Doe**【法】在不动产收回诉讼中对不知真实姓名的当事人的称呼 (*opp.* Richard Roe). ～ **Dory**【动】海鲂. ～ **Hancock**〔美俚〕亲笔签名. ～ **Henry** ①美国歌谣中的传奇式英雄. ②亲笔签名. **～-o'-Groat's (-House)** 苏格兰的最北端 (*from ～-o'-Groat's to Land's End* 英国全国). ～ **Q. Public,** ～ **Q.,** ～ **Q. Citizen**〔美〕普通人，一般群众. ～ **the Apostle**【宗】使徒约翰〔耶稣最爱的弟子〕. ～ **the Baptist**【宗】施洗的约翰.

john•boat [ˈdʒɔnbəut] *n.* (一种在内河行驶的) 平底小船.

John•ny, John•nie [ˈdʒɔni] *n.* ①约翰尼〔男子名，John 的昵称〕. ②〔美俚〕= John. ③〔口〕〔j-〕家伙；纨袴子弟. ④〔j-〕(住院病人穿的)短袖无领罩衫. **johnnycake**〔美〕玉米饼；〔澳〕麦面饼. **～-come-lately**〔美〕新来者，生手，暴发户. ～ **Crapaud,** ～ **Crapeau**〔口〕法国人. **～-jump-up**【植】美洲紫罗兰；〔美〕野生三色紫罗兰. ～ **Newcome [Raw]** 生手，新兵. **～-on the-spot**〔口〕① *n.* 召之即来者. ② *a.* 召之即来的. ～ **Reb**【美史】联邦士兵〔拟人化称呼〕.

Johns [dʒɔnz] *n.* 约翰斯〔姓氏〕.

John•son [ˈdʒɔnsn] *n.* ①约翰逊〔姓氏〕. ②**Samuel** ～ 塞缪尔·约翰逊〔1709—1784，英国文学家，词典编纂家〕. ～ **grass**【植】阿拉伯高粱 (*Sorghum halepense*)〔产于美国南部，作牧草、饲料用〕. ～ **noise**【无】约翰逊噪声，热(激)噪声.

John•son•ese [ˌdʒɔnsəˈniːz] *n.* 塞缪尔·约翰逊的文体〔文风〕.

John•so•ni•an [dʒɔnˈsəunjən, -niən] *a.* 约翰逊 (Samuel Johnson) (风格)的；矫揉造作的，夸张的.

Johns•ton [ˈdʒɔnstən, ˈdʒɔnsn] *n.* 约翰斯顿〔姓氏〕.

Jo•hore [dʒəuˈhɔː] *n.* 柔佛〔马来联邦之一〕.

Jo•hore Bah•ru [dʒəuˈhɔː ˈbaːruː] *n.* 新山〔柔佛邦的首府，在新加坡对面〕.

joie de vi•vre [F. ʒwa dˈviːvr]〔F.〕生活之欢乐，尽情享受生活之乐趣.

join [dʒɔin] *vt.* ①接合，连接，使结合. ②参加，加入，作(团体等的)成员；和(某人)作伴. ③回(原岗位)，归(队). ④联合；使结交，使联姻. ⑤会合，合流. ⑥〔口〕毗连，接近. ～ *two points by a straight line* 用直线把两点连起来. *J- us in a walk.* 和我们一起走走. ～ *battle* 参战. ～ *the army* 参军. ～ *the Party* 入党. ～ *sb. in the discussion* 同某人一起讨论. ～ *one's ship* 回到船上. *The brook ～s the river.* 小川同河流汇合. *His house ～s mine.* 他的家就在我家的隔壁. — *vi.* ①结合，联合 (*with; to*). ②参加，加入 (*in; with*). ③毗连，接近. *My mother ～s with me in congratulating you.* 我的母亲跟我一道向你祝贺. *In this point I ～ with you.* 这一点我跟你一致. ～ *in a conversation* 参加谈话. ～ ***forces with*** ①军队会师. ②同…合作，同…联合. ～ ***hands with*** ①同…联合. ②同…合伙开店. ③同…做夫妻. ～ ***issue***【法】共同起诉；进行辩论. ～ ***[take] issue with sb. on sth.*** 就某事与某人争论. ～ ***the colours*** 服兵役. ～ ***the (great*** 或 ***silent) majority*** 死. ～ ***up***〔口〕①参军，入伍. ②联合起来. — *n.* ①连接；结合. ②接合处，接合点，接合线，接合面. *You can hardly see the ～ in the coat.* 你几乎看不出那件外衣的接缝.

join•der [ˈdʒɔində] *n.* ①连接；接合；汇合；联合. ②【法】联合诉讼；原告或被告的联合，共同诉讼；对另一方提出的争论之点的接受.

join•er [ˈdʒɔinə] *n.* ①结合者；结合物. ②细木工，小木匠. ③〔美口〕加入许多俱乐部和社团的人.

join•er•y [ˈdʒɔinəri] *n.* ①细木工技术〔行业〕. ②细木工的制作物.

join•ing [ˈdʒɔiniŋ] *n.* 连接，结合；接缝. ***～-up in parallel***【电】并接. ***～-up in series***【电】串接.

joint [dʒɔint] *n.* ①接合，榫接合处，接合点. ②【解】关节. ③【植】节. ④【电】接头. ⑤【建】接缝. ⑥(硬皮书面的)折合线；两条钢轨的连接物. ⑦【地】节理. ⑧(用来烤食的)大块肉；带骨的腿肉. ⑨〔美俚〕下流场所(指赌窟，小酒店等)，热闹场所. ⑩〔美俚〕(大麻叶烟的)吸用场所，吸毒窝；大麻叶烟. *air-tight* ～【机】气密接合. *ball and socket* ～ 球窝关节. *Charcotis* ～ 爱科式关节〔神经原性关节病〕. *expansion* ～ 伸缩(接)缝. *finger* ～ 手指关节. *knee* ～ 膝关节. *rivet* ～【机】铆(钉接)合. *water-tight* ～【机】水密结合. *an eating* ～〔美俚〕小饭馆. *a hop* ～〔美俚〕鸦片烟馆. ***out of*** ～ ①脱节，脱榫，脱臼. ②纷乱. ③不协调. ④不满. ***put sb.'s nose out of*** ～ 使某人丢脸；推翻某人的计划. ***put one's foot [arm, knees] out of*** ～ 使足[臂、膝]脱臼. ***the ～ in sb.'s armour*** 要害，致命的弱点. — *a.* ①连接的，结合的. ②联合的，共同的；同时的. ③合办的，共有的. ④连带的. *a ～ association* 联合会. ～ *authors* 合著者. *a ～ communiqué* 联合公报. *a ～ declaration [statement]* 联合声明. ～ *exercise [manoeuvre]* 联合演习. ～ *owners* 有共同所有权的物主. *a ～ pipe* 接合管. *a ～ property* 共有的财产. *a ～ protest* 共同抗议. *during their ～ lives* 〔法律用语〕当他们都活着的时候. *in our ～ names* 连名. *a ～ state-private enterprise* 公私合营企业. ～ *responsibility [liability]* 连带责任. — *vt.* ①使在接口处连接，接合. ②使有接头. ③从接口处分开，自关节处切断；把(肉)切成带骨的大块. ④【建】用油灰涂(接缝). ⑤焊接. — *vi.* ①贴合. ②【植】生节；长骨节. ～ **account** (银行存款等的) 联合帐户. ～ **action** ①联合行动〔战斗〕. ②【法】共同诉讼. **～-chair**【建】接轨垫板. **J- Chiefs of Staff**〔美〕国防部参谋长联席会议. ～ **committee** (议会两院或几个组织的)联合委员会. ～ **pin** 连接销. ～ **resolution** (议会两院的)共同决议. ～ **return** 夫妇合报的所得税申报书. ～ **session [convention]** (议会两院的)联席会议. ～ **stock** 合股. **～-stock company [corporation]** 股份公司. **～weed**【植】海滨假蓼 (*Polygonella articulata*). **～worm**【动】禾节虫，禾茎广肩小蜂.

joint•ed [ˈdʒɔintid] *a.* 有接缝的；有节的，有关节的.

joint•er [ˈdʒɔintə] *n.* ①接合人；接合物；接合器. ②(泥工用的)抹子. ③(木工用的)长刨. ④【农】三角犁.

joint•ing [ˈdʒɔintiŋ] *n.* ①焊接；连接；接合. ②填料，垫料封泥. ～ *rule* (石工用的)长标尺，接榫规.

joint•less [ˈdʒɔintlis] *a.* 无接缝的；无关节的.

joint•ly [ˈdʒɔintli] *ad.* 联合地，连带地，共同地. ～ *and severally [separately] liable* 连带和单独负责.

joint•ress [ˈdʒɔintris] *n.*【法】享有寡妇产权的妇女.

join•ture [ˈdʒɔintʃə] *n.* ①【法】(丈夫生前指定的)由妻子继承的遗产；寡妇所得财产. ②〔罕〕连接，接合，接合处. — *vt.* 指定身后由(妻子)继承财产；使(妻子)继承遗产.

joist [dʒɔist] *n.*【建】①搁栅；小梁；(地板等的)托梁. ②工字钢 (=～ steel). — *vt.* 为…架搁栅；为…装托梁. ～ **ceiling** 搁栅平顶. ～ **shears** 型钢剪切机. ～ **steel** 工字钢，梁钢.

joke [dʒəuk] *n.* ①笑话，戏谑，诙谐. ②笑柄，笑料. ③容易的事，易如反掌的事. ④不足取的东西，无实质性价值的东西；空话. *A ～ never gains an enemy but often loses a friend.*〔谚〕戏谑永远不能化敌为友，反而常常失去朋友. *carry [push] the ～ too far* 玩笑开得太过分了. *It is all a ～.* 这完全是笑话. *It is no ～.* 可不是开玩笑

的事. *for a* ～ 当作笑话,开玩笑. *say sth. in a* ～ 是开玩笑说的. *be [become] the standing* ～ *of the company* 成了朋友间的笑柄. *That test was a* ～. 那个测验太容易了. *turn everything into a* ～ 把任何事情都当儿戏. ***a practical*** ～ 恶作剧. ***be but a*** ～ 只不过开开玩笑,完全是句空话. ***crack [cut, make] a*** ～ 说笑话. ***have one's*** ～ 开玩笑. ***joking apart [aside]*** 〔口〕且别开玩笑;言归正传. ***make a*** ～ ***about sb. [sth.]*** 拿某人[某事]开玩笑. ***play a*** ～ ***on sb.*** 取笑某人,欺骗某人. ***put the*** ～ ***on sb.*** 〔美〕开某人玩笑. ***The*** ～ ***is on him.*** 玩笑开在他身上了,结果他当了傻瓜. — *vi.* 说笑话;开玩笑. *Now you must be joking.* 你是说笑罢. — *vt.* ①和…开玩笑,取笑,愚弄. ②以说笑话取得(赏赐等). ～**book** 幽默小说.

jok·er [ˈdʒəukə] *n.* ①滑稽角色,诙谐者. ②〔俚〕人,家伙,东西. ③〔J-〕【牌】百搭〔可代替任何一张牌或作王牌〕. ④〔美〕非法酒店;非法酒吧. ⑤〔美〕(为使法案失效而插入的)伏笔. ⑥隐蔽的障碍[挫折];没有预料到的因素.

jok·ing [ˈdʒəukiŋ] *a.* 开玩笑的. *This is no* ～ *matter.* 这不是开玩笑的事. **-ly** *ad.*

jo·kul, *jökull* [ˈjəukul] *n.* (冰岛终年积雪的)雪山.

jo·ky [ˈdʒəuki] *a.* 爱开玩笑的.

jol·li·fi·ca·tion [ˌdʒɔlifiˈkeiʃən] *n.* 欢乐,欢宴,(节日)庆祝.

jol·li·fy [ˈdʒɔlifai] *vt.* 〔口〕使欢乐,使高兴, — *vi.* 寻欢,作乐(尤指喝酒).

jol·li·ness [ˈdʒɔlinis] *n.* 愉快,高兴.

jol·li·ly [ˈdʒɔlili] *ad.* 愉快地,高兴地.

jol·li·ty [ˈdʒɔliti] *n.* 欢乐;欢庆;欢宴.

jol·ly [ˈdʒɔli] *a.* ①愉快的,快活的,有趣的,兴高采烈的. ②〔口〕极愉快的,令人高兴的. ③〔口〕大大的. ④微醉的. *a* ～ *companion* 有趣的伙伴. *as* ～ *as a sandboy* 兴高采烈. *We're having* ～ *weather.* 天气宜人. *a* ～ *fool* 大傻瓜. *What a* ～ *mess I am in!* 这个事情真糟. *the* ～ *god* 酒神. ***a*** ～ ***dog about town*** 〔俚〕快活的游人. ***grow*** ～ (因喝醉而)高兴. — *ad.* 〔英口〕非常,很. *a* ～ *good fellow* 大好人. *all* ～ *fine* 好极了. *be so* ～ *green* 非常天真. *have a* ～ *bad time of it* 糟透了. *It is a* ～ *good job that you came.* 〔口〕你来了真好极了. *I'll be* ～ *glad to help you.* 我很高兴帮助你. *take* ～ *good care* 特别当心. *You will* ～ *well have to do sth.* 你非得去做某事. — *n.* ①寻欢作乐. ②〔美〕奉承,逢迎. ③ = ～ boat. ④〔英俚〕皇家陆战队兵士;水兵. ***a tame*** ～ 民兵,义勇兵. ***get one's jollies*** 作乐. — *vt.* ①〔口〕(用哄、捧等方式)使高兴,使愉快*(along; up)*. ②开…的玩笑,戏弄. — *vi.* 开玩笑. ～ *with sb.* 同某人开玩笑. ～ **boat** (附属于大船上的)单座艇. ～ **fellow** ①快活人;有趣的伙伴. ②酒徒. ③〔俚〕贼. **J- Roger** (饰有白色骷髅等的)海盗[黑]旗. ～**-up** ①〔俚〕非正式的舞会,跳舞. ②〔俚〕酒宴;豪饮.

jolt [dʒəult] *vt.* ①使颠簸,摇晃. ②(拳击中)猛击(对手). ③使吃惊,使慌乱;使(精神)受刺激. ④(粗暴地)突然干涉. — *vi.* (车辆等)颠簸;摇晃. — *n.* ①(车辆的)摇晃,颠簸. ②突然的猛击〔尤指拳击〕;一击. ③震惊,引起震惊的事情. ④意外的挫折. ⑤〔美俚〕(麻醉药的)注射. ⑥少量(可提神的东西). *With a tremendous* ～ *the car started* 汽车狠狠摇晃一下才起动了. *The news gave me quite a* ～. 这消息使我大吃一惊. *pour a* ～ *of whisky* 倒一点威士忌提提神. ***pass a*** ～ 猛然一击. ～**-waggon** *n.* 〔美方〕农家牛车. **-ingly** *ad.*

jolt·er·head [ˈdʒəultəhed] *n.* 大傻瓜.

jolt·y [ˈdʒəulti] *a.* 摇晃的,颠簸的.

Jon [dʒɔn] *n.* 乔恩〔男子名,Jonah 和 Jonathan 的略称〕.

Jon(a). = Jonathan.

Jo·nah [ˈdʒəun] *n.* ①乔纳〔男子名〕. ②约拿〔《圣经》中希伯来的预言者〕. ③带来不幸的人,灾星,(为避免带来不幸而)被牺牲的人. ④(《旧约圣经》中的)《约拿书》. ⑤〔美俚〕爵士音乐迷. ～**'s gourd** ①蓖麻. ②朝生暮死的东西. ～ **trip** 不幸的航程;不成功的计划. **-esque** *a.*

Jo·nas [ˈdʒəunəs] *n.* = Jonah.

Jon·a·than [ˈdʒɔnəθən] *n.* ①乔纳森〔男子名,Jon 为其昵称〕. ②典型的美国人〔亦作 Brother ～〕. ③〔美〕一种红皮的晚秋苹果. ④约拿单〔《圣经》中索尔 *(Saul)* 的长子,大卫 *(David)* 的好朋友〕.

Jones [dʒəunz] *n.* 琼斯〔姓氏〕.

jon·gleur [ʒɔːŋˈgləː] *n.* 〔F.〕 中世纪法国和英国的游吟诗人.

jon·quil [ˈdʒɔŋkwil] *n.*【植】(水仙属)长寿花. ～ *colour* 淡黄色.

Jon·son [ˈdʒɔnsn] *n.* 琼森〔姓氏〕.

Jor·dan¹ [ˈdʒɔːdn] *n.* 乔丹〔姓氏〕.

Jor·dan² [ˈdʒɔːdən] *n.* ①约旦〔亚洲〕. ②〔the ～〕约旦河. ～ **almond** ①杏仁〔大量用于糖果中〕. ②彩色糖衣杏仁. **-ian** *a.* 约旦的.

jor·dan [ˈdʒɔːdn] *n.* 〔废〕便壶,尿罐(=chamber pot).

jor·na·da [hɔrˈnɑːdə] *n.* 〔Sp.〕 ①一天的旅程. ②(美南部、墨西哥的)荒漠地带.

jo·rum [ˈdʒɔːrəm] *n.* 大杯;一满杯(量).

Jos. = Joseph; Josiah.

Jo·seph [ˈdʒəuzif] *n.* ①约瑟夫〔男子名〕. ②约瑟〔《圣经》中人物,一指雅各 *(Jacob)* 的第十一个儿子;一指玛利亚 *(Mary)* 之夫〕. ③正派男子,讨厌女人的男子. ③〔j-〕十八世纪妇女骑马时穿的大氅. ***～'s coat*** 【植】苋菜 *(=Amaranthus tricolor)*.

Jo·se·phine [ˈdʒəuzifiːn] *n.* 约瑟芬〔女子名〕.

Josh [dʒɔʃ] *n.* 乔希〔男子名,Joshua 的昵称〕.

josh [dʒɔʃ] *n.* 〔美俚〕揶揄,嘲笑,戏弄. — *vt., vi.* 〔美俚〕(无恶意地)戏弄,哄骗,(和…)开玩笑. **-er** *n.* 开玩笑的人,戏弄者.

Josh·u·a [ˈdʒɔʃwə] *n.* ①乔舒亚〔男子名〕. ②约书亚〔《圣经》中人物,古代以色列人首领摩西的继承者〕. ②《约书亚书》〔旧约《圣经》中的一卷〕. ～ **tree**【植】短叶丝兰 *(=Yucca brevifolia)*〔产于美国西南部〕.

jos·kin [ˈdʒɔskin] *n.* 〔俚〕乡巴佬,笨人.

joss [dʒɔs] *n.* (中国的)神像,菩萨. ～ **house** *n.* (中国的)寺,庙;神龛. ～ **paper** (中国祭祀用的)钱纸,锡箔. ～ **stick** (中国祭神用的)香.

joss·er [ˈdʒɔsə] *n.* ①〔澳〕牧师. ②〔英〕家伙;傻子.

jos·tle [ˈdʒɔsl] *vt.* ①(用肘)推,挤,撞;贴近. ②惹,刺激,使激动. ③与…竞争,与…争夺. *He* ～*d his way through a crowd.* 他从人群中挤过去. ～ *sb. away [from, out of]* 把某人推开. *Many cars lay jostling each other at the parking lot.* 许多汽车在停车场上紧紧挨着. *The thought* ～*d her complacency.* 这种想法使她不安. —*vi.* ①拥挤,推撞;贴近. ②竞争,争夺. ～ *against sb.* 推撞某人. *The crowd* ～*d into the theater.* 人群挤进了戏院. ～ ***with each other*** 互相倾轧. ～ ***with sb. for sth.*** 同某人争抢某物. — *n.* 拥挤,推撞. **-r** *n.* 推撞者;〔美〕扒手.

jot [dʒɔt] *n.* ①(字母的)一点,一划. ②〔通例用否定结构〕一点儿,少量. *not care a* ～ *about* ... 对…毫不在乎. *not one* ～ *or little* 一丝一毫也不(有时亦作 not a ～). — *vt.* 匆匆记下 *(down)*. ～ *down ones license number* 匆匆记下某人的执照号.

jo·ta [ˈhəutə] *n.* (西班牙)阿拉贡双人舞.

jot·ter [ˈdʒɔtə] *n.* ①匆匆记下某事的人. ②(作备忘录用的)小笔记本,小本子.

jot·ting [ˈdʒɔtiŋ] *n.* 简短的笔记,略记.

Jo·tun(n) [ˈjɔːtun] *n.* (北欧神话中)巨人族的一员. ～**-heim** [-heim] 巨人之家.

Joule [ˈdʒuːl, dʒəul] *n.* ①朱尔〔姓氏〕. ②**James P.** ～ 焦耳〔1818—1889,英国物理学家〕.

joule [dʒaul, dʒuːl] *n.*【物】焦耳(能量和功的单位).

jounce [dʒauns] *vi.* (车辆等)摇晃,震动,颠簸. — *vt.* 使震动,使摇晃,使颠簸. — *n.* 震动,摇晃;颠簸.
jouncy [ˈdʒaunsi] *a.* 摇晃的,颠簸的.
jour. = journal; journalist; journeyman.
jour de fête [F. ʒur də fɛt] 〔F.〕节日.
jour·nal [ˈdʒəːnl] *n.* ①日记,日志;【海】航海日记. ②【会计】分类帐,日记帐. ③日报;定期刊物,杂志. ④〔the Journals〕(立法机关、委员会等的)议事录. ⑤【机】轴颈. *a monthly* ~ 月刊. *thrust* ~【机】止推轴颈. *yellow* ~ 黄色新闻. ~ **box**【机】轴颈箱.
jour·nal·ese [ˌdʒəːnəˈliːz] *n.* (草率、低劣的)新闻笔调.
jour·nal·ism [ˈdʒəːnəlizəm] *n.* ①新闻工作,新闻写作,新闻编辑,报刊出版;新闻出版界. ②〔集合词〕报刊,报刊文章;(有别于学术专著的)报刊通俗文章. ③新闻学. *yellow* ~ = yellow journal.
jour·nal·ist [ˈdʒəːnəlist] *n.* ①新闻工作者,报刊编辑,报刊撰稿人,记者;报刊经营者. ②记日记的人. *yellow* ~ 黄色记者. **-is·tic** *a.* **-is·ti·cal·ly** *ad.*
jour·nal·ize [ˈdʒəːnəlaiz] *vt.* 把…记入日记[日记帐、日志]. — *vi.* ①记日记. ②记日记帐. ③从事报刊工作[事业].
jour·ney [ˈdʒəːni] *n.* ①(通常指陆上的)旅行〔*cf.* voyage〕;路程,旅程. ②历程;道路. *a two days'* ~ 两天的路程. *A pleasant* ~ *to you!* = *I wish you a good [happy]* ~*!* 祝你一路顺风. *life's* ~ 人生的历程. *the* ~ *to success* 成功之道. ***be (away) on a*** ~ 在旅行中(不在家). ***break one's [the]*** ~ ***at*** ... 在…中途下车. ***cheat the*** ~ 消磨旅途的寂寞. ***get to one's*** ~***'s end*** 到达目的地. ***go [start, set out] on a long*** ~ 出发作长途旅行. ***go on one's last*** ~ 死. ***make [take, undertake] a*** ~ 旅行. — *vi.* 旅行. ~ *by land* 陆上旅行. ~ *on foot* 徒步旅行. **-man** *(pl.* **-men**, *fem.* **-wo·man)** ①(由学徒工升成的)工匠. ②雇工,短工,计日工. ③(工厂)技工. ④被雇者. **-work** 短工,散工;临时的工作.
joust [dʒaust] *n.* ①(骑士等的)马上枪术比武. ②〔*pl.*〕比赛. ③斗争. — *vi.* ①骑马进行枪术比武. ②参加比赛.
Jove [dʒəuv] *n.* ①【罗神】= Jupiter. ②〔诗〕木星. ***by*** ~*!*〔英〕哎哟! 天哪! 好家伙!
jo·vi·al [ˈdʒəuvjəl, -viəl] *a.* ①〔J-〕【罗神】主神朱庇特的(= jovian). ②〔J-〕【天】木星的. ③快活的,高兴的,愉快的. **-ly** *ad.*
jo·vi·al·i·ty [ˌdʒəuviˈæliti] *n.* ①快活,高兴,愉快. ②〔*pl.*〕愉快的话,快活的行为.
Jo·vi·an [ˈdʒəuviən] *a.* ①【罗神】主神朱庇特(Jupiter)的;朱庇特似的. ②雄伟的,威风凛凛的. ③【天】木星的.
Jow·ett [ˈdʒauit, ˈdʒəuit] *n.* ①乔伊特〔姓氏〕. ②**Benjamin** ~ 本杰明·乔伊特〔1817—1893,英国古典学者,柏拉图著作翻译家〕.
jowl [dʒaul] *n.* ①颚;颚骨;下颚;下巴. ②颊;猪的颊肉. ③(牛、禽类的)喉袋,垂肉;(鸟的)嗉囊. ④鱼头及头边部分. ***cheek by [with]*** ~ 亲热;和…靠近.
Joy [dʒɔi] *n.* 乔伊〔女子名〕.
joy [dʒɔi] *n.* ①快乐,高兴. ②乐事,乐趣. ③喜庆,欢乐. ④最大的幸福. *be filled with [be full of]* ~*s* 非常高兴. *I wish [give] you* ~ *of your success.* 我祝贺你的成功,恭喜恭喜. *in* ~ 快活,高兴. *jump [leap] for* ~ 欢喜得跳起来,欢欣鼓舞. *shouts of* ~ 欢呼. *sing and dance for [with]* ~ 高兴得载歌载舞. *to one's great* ~ 使人特别高兴的是. *share* ~*s and sorrows of life* 同甘共苦. *There was great* ~ *in the city.* 城内一片欢腾. *Joys shared with others are more enjoyed.* 〔谚〕与众同乐,其乐无穷. — *vi.* 欢欣,高兴. ~ *in sb.'s success* 为某人的成功而高兴. — *vt.*〔诗〕使高兴,享受. ~**bells** *n.*〔*pl.*〕(教堂中通报喜庆事件的)报喜钟,庆祝钟. ~**house**〔美俚〕妓院. ~**-juice**〔美俚〕酒. ~**pop** *vi.*〔美俚〕逢场作戏地吸毒. ~**-powder**〔美俚〕吗啡. ~ **ride**〔口〕驾车兜风〔尤指偷车以高速胡乱行驶〕. ~ **rider** 驾车兜风的人. ~ **riding** 驾车兜风. ~**-smoke** 逢场作戏的吸毒. ~**stick**〔俚〕飞机操纵杆;操纵方向的装置.
joy·ance [ˈdʒɔiəns] *n.*〔古〕快乐,喜悦.
Joyce [dʒɔis] *n.* 乔伊斯〔姓氏,女子名〕.
joy·ful [ˈdʒɔif*u*l] *a.* ①快乐的,快活的,高兴的. ②令人开心的,使人喜悦的. *a* ~ *countenance* 喜笑颜开. *a* ~ *event* 喜事. ~ *tidings* 喜讯. **-ly** *ad.* **-ness** *n.*
joy·less [ˈdʒɔilis] *a.* 不愉快的,不高兴的. **-ly** *ad.* **-ness** *n.*
joy·ous [ˈdʒɔiəs] *a.* = joyful. **-ly** *ad.* **-ness** *n.*
J.P. = Justice of the Peace 兼理一般司法事务的地方官,治安官.
Jp. = jet propulsion 喷气推进.
JPL = Jet Propulsion Laboratory 〔美〕喷气推进实验所.
Jr., jr. = ①journal. ②junior.
J.S. = ①Judgment Summons〔英〕判决债务传票. ②judicial separation 法院判决的夫妇分居.
JST = Japan Standard Time 日本标准时间.
Jt.-ed. = Joint-editor 合编者(之一).
ju·ba [ˈdʒuːbə] *n.* (美国黑人的)朱巴舞〔以手帕等加强舞蹈节奏〕.
jub·bah [ˈdʒubə] *n* 〔Ar.〕裾巴〔穆斯林男女均穿的宽敞外衣〕.
ju·be [ˈdʒuːbi] *n.*【建】(教堂的)圣坛隔栏;圣殿屏廊.
ju·ber·ous [ˈdʒuːbərəs] *a.*〔美方〕怀疑的,犹豫的.
ju·bi·lance, -cy [ˈdʒuːbiləns, -si] *n.* 欢呼,兴高彩烈,喜气洋洋.
ju·bi·lant [ˈdʒuːbilənt] *a.* 欢呼的;喜气洋洋的,欢欣鼓舞的. **-ly** *ad.*
ju·bi·la·rian [ˌdʒuːbiˈlɛəriən] *n.* 五十周年纪念的庆祝者.
ju·bi·la·te [ˈdʒuːbileit] *vi.* 欢呼,欢欣.
Ju·bi·la·te [ˌdʒuːbiˈlɑːti] *n.* ①【宗】复活节后的第三个星期日. ②《旧约圣经》中的《诗篇》第一百篇(的乐曲)〔即 the Old Hundred(th)〕.
ju·bi·la·tion [ˌdʒuːbiˈleiʃən] *n.* 欢呼;喜悦;庆祝(胜利).
ju·bi·lee [ˈdʒuːbiliː] *n.* ①〔J-〕(古代犹太)五十年节〔每五十年举行一次庆祝解放和复兴的节日〕. ②(天主教的)大赦年. ③(结婚等)五十周年纪念;二十五周年纪念. ④欢乐的节日. ⑤欢乐. ⑥〔美〕(歌唱未来幸福时日的)黑人民歌. *the silver* ~ 二十五周年纪念. *the golden* ~ 五十周年纪念. *the diamond* ~ 六十周年纪念. *The Diamond J-* 英国维多利亚女王统治六十周年纪念(一八九七年). *We had a big* ~ *to celebrate the victory.* 我们举行盛大的纪念以祝贺胜利. *They abandoned themselves to* ~. 他们沉醉在狂欢之中. ~ **port** 1897 年英国女皇维多利亚即位六十周年纪念时酿造的葡萄酒. ~ **singer** 唱黑人民歌的美国黑人歌手. ~ **song**〔美〕黑人民谣,黑人灵歌.
ju·che [ˈtʃuːtʃei] *n.*〔Kor.〕自主.
Jud. = Judges; Judgment; judicial; Judith.
Ju·dae·a, Ju·de·a [dʒuːˈdiːə] *n.* 犹地阿〔古代罗马统治下的巴勒斯坦南部地区〕.
Ju·dae·o-, Ju·de·o- [dʒuːˈdiəu] *comb. f.* 表示"犹太的"如: *Judae*ophile.
Ju·dae·o·phile [dʒuːˈdiəufail] *a.* 对犹太人亲善的.
Ju·dah [ˈdʒuːdə] *n.* ①朱达〔男子名〕. ②犹大〔《旧约圣经》中犹太人十二列祖之一〕. ③巴勒斯坦南部古王国.
Ju·da·ic(al) [dʒu(ː)ˈdeiik(əl)] *a.* ①犹太人的;犹太民族的;犹太文化的. ②犹太教的.
Ju·da·ism [ˈdʒuːdeiizəm] *n.* ①【宗】犹太教. ②对犹太风俗[仪式等]的遵奉. ③犹太人的文化、社会和宗教信仰. ④全体犹太人.

J

Ju·da·ist [ˈdʒuːdeiist] *n.* 犹太教信徒；尊崇犹太风俗的人.

Ju·da·ize, Ju·da·ise [ˈdʒuːdeiaiz] *vt.* 使犹太化；使信仰犹太教. — *vi.* 犹太化，信奉犹太教. **-z(s)a·tion** *n.* **-z(s)er** *n.*

Ju·das [ˈdʒuːdəs] *n.* ①犹大〔耶稣的门徒，出卖耶稣者〕. ②(伪装亲善的)叛徒. ③〔j-〕(门、墙上的)监视孔，窥视孔 (= ~ window). **~-colo(u)r** (胡须等的)红色. **~-colo(u)red** *a.* 红色的. **~ kiss** 假亲热，口蜜腹剑，阴险的背叛. **~ tree**【植】紫荆 (cercis 的俗称).

Judd [dʒʌd] *n.* 贾德〔姓氏〕.

jud·der [ˈdʒʌdə] *vi.* 摇动；振动；颤动. — *n.* 颤抖，震动声.

Jude [dʒuːd] *n.* ①裘德〔男子名〕. ②《犹大书》〔《圣经·新约》中的篇名〕.

Ju·den·het·ze [ˈjuːdənhɛtsə] *n.* 〔G.〕迫害犹太人(=Jew-baiting).

Judg. = Judges.

judge [dʒʌdʒ] *n.* ①审判员，法官，推事. ②〔J-〕最高审判者〔指神，上帝〕. ③(纠纷等的)评判者；(比赛等的)裁判员. ④鉴定人，鉴赏家. ⑤【史】士师〔犹太所罗国王以前的统治者〕. ⑥〔J-〕〔*pl.*〕(《旧约圣经》中的)《士师记》(=the Book of Judges). *an associate ~, a side ~* 陪审员. *an examining [preliminary] ~* 第一审判员. *as grave [sober] as a ~* 象法官那样庄重，非常严肃. *act as ~ at the race* 在赛跑中担任裁判员. *a good ~ of horses* 善于识马的人. *He is no ~ in such matters.* 他对这些事是外行. ***be no ~ of*** 不能鉴定. — *vt.* ①判决；审理；审判. ②裁判；评定；裁决. ③鉴定；识别；评价. ④断定，认为. ⑤〔古〕批评，指责. *~ works of art* 评价艺术品. *It was ~d better to set out at once.* 认为立刻出发比较好. — *vi.* ①下判断，作出裁判. ②作评价. *~ by [from] appearances* 由外观上判断. *judging from the fact* 由事实上推测. *~ between two combatants* 在两个竞技者之间裁决胜负. **J- Advocate** 总军法官；军法检查官. **J- Advocate General** 军法署署长. **J- Advocate General's Department** 军法署，军法处. **~-made** 由法官[判决]创造的 (*the ~-made law*【法】判例法).

judg(e)·mat·ic(al) [dʒʌdʒˈmætik(əl)] *a.* 〔口〕眼光敏锐的，考虑周到的，明智的. **-i·cal·ly** *ad.*

judg(e)·ment [ˈdʒʌdʒmənt] *n.* ①审判，裁判，判决. ②由判决所确定的债务；确定债务的判决书. ③鉴定，评价，判断. ④判断力，见识；精明. ⑤意见，看法；批评，指责. ⑥公正，正义〔《圣经》中用语〕. ⑦〔J-〕【宗】上帝的最后审判(日)(=the Last J- 或 J- Day). ⑧天罚，报应. *a ~ against the plaintif* 裁定原告败诉的判决. *a ~ for the plaintif* 裁定原告胜诉的判决. *a ~ of acquittal* 宣判无罪. *a ~ of conviction* 宣判有罪. *sit in ~ on a case* 审判一件案子. *a ~ creditor* 判决确定的债权人. *a ~ debt* 判决确定的债务. *an error of ~* 判断错误. *form a ~ upon facts* 根据事实作出判断. *a man of sound ~* 判断力健全的人. *a man without ~* 无判断力的人. *disturb the ~* 令人迷惑. *exercise [use] one's ~* 运用判断力. *show good ~* 判断力强. *in my personal ~* 根据我个人的见解. *on one's own ~* 按照自己的意见，独断. *private ~* 一己之见〔特指宗教上不同传统的见解〕. *It is a ~ on you for getting up late.* 这是你睡懒觉的报应. ***Daniel come to ~.*** 好一个丹尼尔，好公正的清官〔现在一般用作讽刺语〕. ***give [pass, render] ~ (up) on sb.*** 对某人下判决，定案. ***~ by default***【法】缺席判决. **J- Day**【宗】上帝的最后审判(日)(=the Last J-). ***~ reserved***【法】审讯后延缓判决. **~ seat** ①裁判员席. ②法院. ***to the best of one's ~*** 根据本人认识所及.

judge·ship [ˈdʒʌdʒˌʃip] *n.* 法官地位；法官职权；法官任期.

ju·di·ca·ble [ˈdʒuːdikəbl] *a.* ①可裁判的；可审判的. ②应受审判的.

ju·di·ca·tive [ˈdʒuːdikətiv] *a.* 审判的，判决的；司法的；法院裁决的.

ju·di·ca·to·ry [ˈdʒuːdikətəri] *a.* 审判的，司法的. — *n.* 法院；审判制度.

ju·di·ca·ture [ˈdʒuːdikətʃə] *n.* ①司法. ②司法权. ③审判员的职权[职务、地位]. ④审判制度. ⑤审判员，法院. *the Supreme Court of J-* 〔英〕最高法院.

ju·di·cial [dʒu(ː)ˈdiʃəl] *a.* ①司法的，审判上的. ②审判员的；法官的；法院的；法院判决的[规定的]. ③法官似的，符合法官身份的. ④考虑周到的；慎重的；公平的，公正的. ⑤【宗】上帝审判的. *~ affairs* 司法. *a ~ assembly* 审判大会. *the ~ bench* 〔集合词〕法官. *~ circles = the ~ world* 司法界. *the ~ departments* 司法部门. *the J- Department (Office)* 司法部. *~ gravity* 象审判员那样严肃. *a ~ pestilence* 天降瘟疫. *a biography ~ in purpose* 一本批判性的传记. *a man with a ~ mind* 内心公正的人. **~ chemistry** 法医化学. *~ functions* 司法职能. **~ murder** 合法但不公正的死刑判决. **~ police** 法警. **~ power** 司法权. **~ precedent** 判例. **~ proceedings** 审判程序；诉讼手续 (*take ~ proceedings against sb.* 对某人起诉). **~ sale** 法院判决的拍卖. **~ separation** 法院判决的夫妇分居. **-ly** *ad.*

ju·di·ci·ar·y [dʒu(ː)ˈdiʃiəri] *a.* 法院的；审判员的；司法的. *~ proceedings* 审判程序. — *n.* ①司法部. ②〔集合词〕审判员. ③法院系统，法院制度.

ju·di·cious [dʒu(ː)ˈdiʃəs] *a.* 有见识的，明智的；合机宜的；审慎的. **-ly** *ad.* **-ness** *n.*

Ju·dith [ˈdʒuːdiθ] *n.* 朱迪丝〔女子名〕.

ju·do [ˈdʒuːdəu] *n.* ***(pl. ~(s))*** 〔Jap.〕日本柔术，日本柔道〔日本的一种摔跤运动〕.

ju·do·ka [ˈdʒuːdəukɑː] *n.* (日本)柔术家，柔道家.

Jud·son [ˈdʒʌdsn] *n.* 贾德森〔姓氏，男子名〕.

Ju·dy [ˈdʒuːdi] *n.* 朱迪①〔女子名〕. ②英国木偶戏《笨拙与朱迪》(Punch and Judy) 中的女主角 (Punch) 之妻.

jug[1] [dʒʌg] *n.* ①(有把手、小口、用以盛水或酒等的)大壶，罐，盂；陶制啤酒壶. ②罐中物，壶中物. ③〔俚〕监牢. ④〔美俚〕银行，保险箱. ⑤〔俚〕一瓶威士忌酒. — *vt.* ①将(兔肉等)燉煨〔通常用过去分词〕. ②把…装进壶[罐]中. ③〔俚〕关押，监禁. *jugged hare* 用土锅燉的野兔肉. **~ band** 〔美〕瓶罐乐队〔以口琴、卡苏为乐器，以敲打瓶、罐、搓板、水桶等加强节奏效果的小民乐队或小爵士乐队〕. **~-handled** *a.* ①不匀称的. ②单方面的；片面的.

jug[2] [dʒʌg] *n.* (特指夜莺等的)叫声. — *vi.* 模仿夜莺等啭鸣，发出夜莺般的鸣声.

ju·gal [ˈdʒuːgəl] *a.* ①【解】颧骨的. ②面颊的. **~ bone** 颧骨.

ju·gate [ˈdʒuːgeit] *a.*【生】(鳞翅目昆虫)具翅轭的.

jug·ful [ˈdʒʌgful] *n.* ①满壶，满罐. ②非常多. *not by a ~* 〔俚〕一点也不，决不.

Jug·ger·naut [ˈdʒʌgənɔːt] *n.* ①【印度教】讫里什那 (Krishna)神像；〔喻〕世界的主宰. ②〔常用 j-〕可怕的，不可抗拒的力量. ③〔常用 j-〕使人盲目崇拜和牺牲的事物 (=~ car). **~ car** 讫里什那神车〔据说讫里什那为 Vishnu 的化身，每年都用车载此神像举行巡行仪式，许多人相信被神像车辗死即可升天，因而不惜投身车下〕.

jug·gins [ˈdʒʌginz] *n.* 〔俚〕傻瓜.

jug·gle [ˈdʒʌgl] *vi.* ①(用球、小刀、盘子等)玩杂耍；变戏法. ②要花招. ③歪曲，窜改；欺骗 (*with*). *~ with balls* 耍球. *~ with history* 歪曲历史. *~ with sb.* 耍弄某人. *~ with words* 玩文字游戏. — *vt.* ①耍(球、小刀、盘子等)；耍弄. ②用戏法变出；欺骗，诈取. ③歪曲，窜改，颠倒(事实等). ④对…抓[握]不住[牢]. *~ a fan into a bird* 把扇子变成鸟. *~ money out of sb.* = *~ sb. out of his money* 骗取某人的钱. *~ sb. into doing sth.* 骗

某人做某事．～ *sth. away* 耍花招骗取某物．～ *black and white* 混淆黑白．～ *the figures* 窜改数字．— *n.* ①变戏法，玩杂耍，魔术．②耍花招，欺诈，欺骗．
jug·gler [ˈdʒʌglə] *n.* ①玩杂耍的人；魔术师．②骗子．*a ～ with words* 诡辩家．
jug·gler·y [ˈdʒʌgləri] *n.* ①魔术．②花招，把戏．③欺诈，欺骗．
jug·head [ˈdʒʌghed] *n.* 〔美俚〕笨蛋，傻瓜．
Ju·go-Slav, Ju·go·slav [ˈju:gəuˈslɑ:v] *a.* 南斯拉夫(人)的(＝Yugoslav)．— *n.* 南斯拉夫人．
Ju·go-sla·vi·a, Ju·go·sla·vi·a [ˈju:gəuˈslɑ:vjə] *n.* 南斯拉夫(＝Yugoslavia)．
Ju·go·sla·vi·an [ˈju:gəuˈslɑ:vjən] *n.* 南斯拉夫人(＝Yugoslavian)．— *a.* 南斯拉夫的；南斯拉夫人的．
jug·u·lar [ˈdʒʌgjulə] *a.* ①【解】喉的，颈的；颈静脉的．②(鱼)喉部有腹鳍的；(鳍)在喉部的．— *n.*【解】颈静脉．*the ～ vein* 颈静脉．
jug·u·late [ˈdʒʌgjuleit] *vt.* ①割断…的喉咙；扼杀，勒死．②【医】(采用极端措施)阻止(病的)恶化．
ju·gum [ˈdʒu:gəm] *n.* (*pl.* **-ga** [-gə], ～*s*)【生】腕锁；(翅)轭．
juice [dʒu:s] *n.* ①(菜蔬、果实、植物等的)汁、液、浆．②〔*pl.*〕体液．③精，精髓，精力．④〔美俚〕电，电流，汽油，液体燃料，硝化甘油．⑤〔俚〕酒(尤指威士忌酒)；冷饮．⑥(舞台等的)照明员，灯光员．⑦〔俚〕非法之财，油水；高利；薪水，收入．⑧高利贷款．⑨〔俚〕权势，地位．*fruit ～* 果子汁．*grape ～* 葡萄汁．*meat ～* 肉汁．*the ～s* 体液．*duodenal ～(s)* 十二指肠液．*gastric ～(s)* 胃液．*the ～ of life* 生命的活力，元气．～*d rehearsal* 电视节目预演．***full of ～*** 充满活力；盛气凌人．***give her ～*** 〔美俚〕①设法使事情进行顺利．②开快(汽车的)速度．***stew in one's own ～*** 自作自受．***tread [step] on the ～*** 加速，促进．— *vt.* ①〔口〕从…中榨汁．②在…中加汁．～ *a cow* 挤牛奶．～ ***up*** 使有精力，使活跃．～ **dealer**〔俚〕放印子钱的人．**J-'s-harp** 口拨琴(＝Jew's-harp)．～**head**〔美俚〕酒鬼．～ **joint**〔美俚〕①果汁摊．②酒吧间，夜总会．③(禁酒法废止前的)秘密酒馆．～ **peddler**〔美口〕电力公司．**-less** *a.* 无汁的．
juic·er [ˈdʒu:sə] *n.* ①榨汁器．②〔美俚〕一贯酗酒的人．③〔美俚〕(舞台等的)照明员，灯光员．
juic·y [ˈdʒu:si] *a.* ①多汁的．②(天气)多雨的，阴湿的．③〔口〕有趣的，津津有味的；刺激性强的．④(色调)鲜润的，绚烂的．⑤油水多的，报酬多的．⑥有力的，活力充沛的．⑦微醉的．*a ～ contract* 有利可图的合同．*a ～ pear* 汁水多的梨．*a ～ road* 道路泥泞．*a ～ bit of gossip about sb.* 关于某人的有声有色的小道消息．*a ～ kick* 猛踢．**-i·ly** *ad.* **-i·ness** *n.*
ju·jit·su [dʒu:ˈdʒitsu:] *n.* 〔Jap.〕柔术，柔道〔日本的一种拳术和摔跤术〕．

J

ju·ju [ˈdʒu:dʒu:] *n.* ①物神〔西非某些部族用语〕．②符咒；魔力．
ju·jube [ˈdʒu:dʒu(:)b] *n.* ①【植】枣子；枣树；枣属植物；枣酱．②枣味〔枣状〕胶糖．
ju·jut·su [dʒu:ˈdʒitsu:, -ˈdʒʌt-] *n.* 〔Jap.〕＝ jujitsu.
juke [dʒu:k] *vt.* 用假动作诱使(对方球员)离位．
juke·box, juke box [ˈdʒu:kbɔks] *n.* 〔美口〕(在酒吧间、餐馆等投入硬币就自动演唱的)自动电唱机．
juke joint [ˈdʒu:k dʒɔint] *n.* 〔美〕备有自动电唱机的小餐馆或小舞厅．
Jul. ＝ July.
ju·lep [ˈdʒu:lep] *n.* ①(服药用的)糖水；药制饮料．②威士忌〔白兰地〕酒加糖和薄荷的冷饮．③含香草的冷饮．
Jules [dʒu:lz] *n.* 朱尔斯〔男子名，Julius 的异体〕．
Jul·ia [ˈdʒu:ljə] *n.* 朱莉亚〔女子名〕．
Jul·ian [ˈdʒu:ljən, -liən] *n.* 朱利安〔男子名〕．— *a.* (古罗马独裁者)儒略·恺撒(*Julius Caesar*)的．～ ***calendar*** 儒略历〔即当前用的阳历〕．
Ju·li·an·a [dʒu:liˈɑ:nə] *n.* 朱莉安娜〔女子名〕．
ju·li·enne [ˌdʒu:liˈen] *n.* 〔F.〕菜丝汤．— *a.* (将蔬菜)切成丝的．*green beans ～* 青豆丝．～ *potatoes* 土豆丝(马铃薯丝)．
Ju·li·et [ˈdʒu:ljət, -liət] *n.* ①朱丽叶〔女子名〕．②莎士比亚悲剧《罗米欧与朱丽叶》中的女主角．～ **cap** 朱丽叶女帽〔带在后脑的帽子，常作新娘婚礼服的一部分〕．
Ju·li·ett [ˈdʒu:liet] 通讯中用以代表字母 j 的词．
Jul·ius [ˈdʒu:ljəs] *n.* 朱利叶斯〔男子名〕．
Ju·ly [dʒu(:)ˈlai] *n.* 七月〔略作 Jul., Jl., Jy.〕．
Ju·ma·da [dʒuˈmɑ:də]〔Ar.〕回历年中的五月或六月．
jum·bal [ˈdʒʌmbəl] *n.* ＝ jumble.
jum·ble[1] [ˈdʒʌmbl] *n.* 环形甜薄饼．
jum·ble[2] [ˈdʒʌmbl] *vt.* 搞乱，使混杂(*up*; *together*)．— *vi.* 搞乱，混杂乱成一团．— *n.* ①混乱，杂乱；混乱的一堆．②〔英〕旧杂品义卖；旧杂货义卖品．～ **sale** 旧杂货拍卖．～ **shop**〔英〕廉价杂品店．
jum·bly [ˈdʒʌmbli] *a.* 混乱的，乱七八糟的．
jum·bo [ˈdʒʌmbəu]〔口〕*n.* (*pl.* ～*s*) ①体大而笨拙的人〔动物、物件〕；大型喷气式客机；庞然大物．②〔J-〕(伦敦动物园的)大象．③大受欢迎的人．④钻车；移动式钻机台；高炉渣口冷却器．— *a.* 巨大的，特大的．～ *jet* 大型喷气式客机．
jum·buck [ˈdʒʌmbʌk] *n.* 〔澳〕羊．
jump [dʒʌmp] *vi.* ①跳，跳跃，跳起；弹跳，跳动．②(用降落伞从飞机里)跳出．③猛烈地移动；积极行动，奔忙，活跃．④跳过，越过；越级提升．⑤(物价等)猛增，暴涨．⑥(结论)匆匆作出；(话题，主张等)突然改变．⑦随随便便(注意力等)无目的地转移；(工作等)任意更动．⑧欣然接受(*at*)，急切投入(*in*, *into*)．⑨一致，符合．⑩(电影中的映象)歪跳，颠倒．⑪(桥牌中的)跳级叫牌．～ *from seat* 从坐位上跳起来．～ *to one's feet* (由坐着)一跃而起．～ *for [with] joy* 欢跃．～ *at once* 立即行动．*The whole town is ～ing.* 全镇一片活跃．～ *over a page or two* 跳过一两页．*Gold Shares ～ed yesterday.* 昨天黄金股票猛涨．*The steel output is ～ing.* 钢产量正在猛增．～ *at [to] a conclusion* 匆匆作出结论，轻率断定．～ *from one topic to another* 从一个话题跳到另一个话题．～ *from job to job* 盲目地调换工作．～ *to another employment* 另有高就．～ *at the job* 抢着接受任务．～ *at the chance* 急切地抓住机会．*Good [Great] wits will ～ together.* 〔谚〕智者所见略同．*Her opinions ～ with mine.* 她的意见和我一致．*His tastes and his means do not ～ together.* 他的爱好跟他的收入不相称．— *vt.* ①跳过，越过．②使跳跃，使颤动．③使惊起．④跳上，跳下，搭上．⑤突然离开(轨道等)，擅离(职)．⑥使(物价等)猛涨；使(人)连升职位〔级别〕．⑦(报刊中)把(文章一部分)转入他页．⑧【电】跨接，跳线．⑨【地】把(岩石)冲击打眼．⑩〔口〕猛攻，叱责．⑪(打桥牌时)跳级叫高．⑫(赛跑，开车)抢在…前出发；抢先于…．⑬〔俚〕(因欠债等)逃离，逃亡．⑭非法侵占(采矿权等)．⑮(在煎锅中)摇动着煎煮．～ *a section* 跳过一节．～ *a fence* 跳过篱笆．～ *a baby up and down on one's knees* 把孩子抱在膝上上下颠动．～ *a horse across a ditch* 纵马跃过小沟．～ *sb. out of chair* 使某人吃惊得从椅子上跳起．～ *a bus* 跳上公共汽车．*The train ～ed the rail [track].* 火车出轨了．～ *ship* 离职弃船．～ *town* 逃离城市．*They ～ their prices to offset heavy expenditures.* 他们提高物价来抵销庞大的开支．*The college ～ed him from instructor to full professor.* 大学突然把他从讲师提升为正教授．～ *the green light* 抢绿灯〔在红灯转换以前把车开过去〕．～ *a claim* 霸占土地〔矿权等〕．***be ～ed into doing sth.*** 被骗去做某事．～ ***down sb.'s throat*** 〔口〕驳得某人哑口无言，问住．～ ***in the lake*** 〔口〕离开不再讨厌．～ ***in with both feet*** 全力以赴．～ ***like parched peas*** 横蹦乱跳．～ ***off*** ①【军】突然出动攻击．②开始．～ ***on [all over]*** ①严词责备．②突然袭击．～***(one's)***

bail 在保释后逃亡. ~ *out of one's skin* 惊喜若狂,大吃一惊. ~ *sb. out* 叱责某人. ~ *the broom* 结婚. ~ *over the broomstick* 姘居. ~ *the gun* 〔美〕仓促行动;【体】未闻号令声偷跑. ~ *the queue* 加塞儿,不按次序排队. *J- to it!* 〔俚〕赶快; ~ *up and down* 跳上跳下. — *n.* ①跳跃;跳跃运动;一跳的距离;(需要跳越的)障碍. ②惊跳;〔the ~s〕震颤;心神不定. ③(物价等的)暴涨,猛增. ④(系列的)中断;矿脉的断层;急转. ⑤(空航途中的)短程. ⑥(起步,出发时)抢先. ⑦【印】〔口〕(报刊文章的)转页,转版. ⑧【自】跳变,转移. ⑨〔俚〕(爵士音乐等的)急奏. ⑩【建】大放脚的梯级. ⑪跳伞. ⑫(象棋中)吃对方子的一着. *the broad [long]* ~ 跳远. *the high* ~ 跳高. *the pole* ~ 撑杆跳. *give sb. a* ~ 使某人吓一跳. *The prices takes a* ~. 物价暴涨. *at a* ~ 一跃. *on one's last* ~ *from New York to San Francisco* 从纽约到旧金山的航空途中最后一段短程. *a forced* ~ 被迫跳伞. ***at a full*** ~ 全速. ***be all of a*** ~ 胆战心惊. ***get [have] the*** ~ ***on*** 抢在…之前行动. ***keep the enemy on the*** ~ 使敌人疲于奔命. ***on the*** ~ 〔口〕来回奔忙;在忙碌中. ***on the keen*** ~ 赶快. — *a.* (爵士音乐中)急拍子的. *a* ~ *tune* 急奏曲. ~ **area** (降落伞的)降落地. ~ **ball** (篮球的)跳球. ~ **cut(s)** (影片)跳割. ~**ed-up** *a.* ①暴发的,刚发财的. ②自大的;无耻的. ~ **function**【数】跃变函数. ~ **if not** (计算机中的)条件转移. ~ **instruction**【计】转移指令,跳越指令. ~**-off** *n.* (赛跑或进攻的)开始. ~ **seat** (轿车等前后座之间的)折迭式小座位. ~ **shot** (篮球)跳起投篮. ~ **suit** ①跳伞服;修车技工工作服. ②妇女连身裤紧身便服. ~ **wire**【电】跨接线. **-a·ble** *a.*

jump·er[1] [ˈdʒʌmpə] *n.* ①跳跃者;跳跃的选手;跳伞者;(送货车上)递送包件的人. ②跳虫〔如蚤等〕;经过训练能跳越障碍的马. ③【电】跳线,跨接线. ④长凿子,(钟表的)棘爪,制轮爪,掣子. ⑤(儿童)雪橇. ⑥(船的)桅间牵索. ⑦【地】冲击钻杆;跳动器械. ~ **stay** (船的)横牵索.

jump·er[2] [ˈdʒʌmpə] *n.* ①工作服. ②(妇女穿的)无袖连衣裙〔布拉吉〕;〔英〕妇女的宽上衣. ③〔*pl.*〕(孩童的)连衫裤.

jump·ing [ˈdʒʌmpiŋ] *n.* 跳动,跃变. — *a.* 跳跃的,用于跳跃的. ~ **bean** 跳豆〔墨西哥灯台草的种子,因寄生幼虫,故能跳动,也称 Mexican ~ bean〕. ~**-disease**【医】痉跳病. ~ **jack** (用线牵动的)娃娃玩具. ~ **mouse**【动】北美林跳鼠. ~ **net** 救生网〔用于接救从楼上跳下来的人〕. ~**-off** (铁路等的)中间小站. ~**-off place** ①偏僻的地方. ②旅行的终点,下车处. ③山穷水尽的地步. ④起点,出发站. ~ **pole** (撑竿跳用的)撑竿. ~ **sheet** 〔英〕(失火时接住从楼上跳下的人用的)接跳布.

jump·y [ˈdʒʌmpi] *a.* ***(-p·i·er; -p·i·est)*** ①跳跃的,急剧变化的. ②心惊肉跳的,神经质的. **-i·ly** *ad.* **-i·ness** *n.*

Jun. = ①June. ②Junior.

Junc, junc. = junction.

jun·co [ˈdʒʌŋkəu] *n.* *(pl.* ~*s)*【动】雪鹀.

junc·tion [ˈdʒʌŋkʃən] *n.* ①接合,连接,连络. ②接合点,交叉点,(河流的)汇合处,(铁道的)联轨点. ③【电】中继线. ④【物】接头,结. *We effected a* ~ *of our two armies.* 我们使自己的两支军队会师了. *make a* ~ 取得联络,连接起来. ~ **box** 接线盒,套管;联轴器. ~ **diode** 面结型二极管. ~ **efficiency** 中继效率. ~ **group** 中继电阻,中继线群. ~ **laser** 面结型激光器. ~ **line [rail]** 联轨线. ~ **service** 短程通信. ~ **station** 联轨站,枢纽站,换车站. ~ **transistor** 结式(面结型)晶体管.

junc·ture [ˈdʒʌŋktʃə] *n.* ①接合,连结,接缝,接合点;交界. ②时机,关头. ③【语】连音. *an important* ~ *in a man's career* 人生历程中的重要关键. *at this* ~ 在这个时候. *in the present critical* ~ *of things* 在目前这一危急关头下.

June [dʒu:n] *n.* ①琼〔女子名〕. ②六月〔略作 Jun., Je.〕. ~ **beetle [bug]** (美国北部的)六月甲虫;(美国南部的)无花果虫.

Ju·neau [ˈdʒu:nəu] *n.* 朱诺〔美国阿拉斯加州的首府〕.

june·ber·ry [ˈdʒu:nberi] *n.* ***(pl. -ries)***【植】①唐棣属 *(Amelanchier)* 植物. ②唐棣属植物的果实.

jun·gle [ˈdʒʌŋgl] *n.* ①(热带的)丛林,密林,莽丛. ②〔the J-〕〔俚〕(伦敦证券交易所内的)西非洲矿业股票市场;西非洲矿业股票交易人. ③〔美俚〕(无业游民的)露营地,集合处;城市中人口稠密的居民区〔工业区〕. ④一堆混乱的东西;错综复杂的事. ⑤为生存而残酷斗争的地方. ~ *warfare* 丛林战. ~ **fever** 丛林热. ~ **fowl** 原鸡〔东印度的野鸡,雄的称 ~ cock, 雌的称 ~ hen〕. **J-Gym** 一种儿童攀爬器具(包括杆、梯子等)的商标名称;〔j- gym〕儿童攀爬器具. ~ **justice** 弱肉强食;私刑. ~ **law** 弱肉强食原则.

jun·gli [ˈdʒʌŋgli] *n.* 印度丛林居民. — *a.* ①住在印度丛林地带的. ②印度丛林居民的. ③土头土脑的,粗野的.

jun·gly [ˈdʒʌŋgli] *a.* ①丛林的,丛林地带的. ②象丛林的;丛林地带居民的.

jun·ior [ˈdʒu:njə] *a.* ①较年幼的,较年小的 *(opp.* senior) 〔常略为 Jr. 或 Jun., 加在姓名之后,指兄弟二人中的弟弟或由于父子同名在儿子姓名后加上 J-〕. ②资历较浅的;日期较后的. ③由青少年组成的,专为青少年准备的. ④(美国四年制大学或中学中的)三年级的;低年级的. *be* ~ *to sb.* 比某人年少. *John Smith, J- [Jn., Jun.]* 小约翰·史密斯. *Smith* ~ 指同级中较幼的史密斯. ~ *members of the staff* 年资较低的职工. *a* ~ *partner* 地位较低的伙伴. *a* ~ *readers* 青少年读物. *the* ~ *class* 三年级. — *n.* ①年少者. ②低班生;等级较低者;晚辈. ③(美国四年制大学或中学的)三年级生. ④少女衣服尺寸. *He is my* ~ *by three years.* = *He is three years my* ~. = *He is three years* ~ *to me.* 他比我小三岁. ~ **college** ①〔美〕初级大学〔指一二年制大学〕. ②〔美俚〕监狱. ~ **high school** 〔美〕初级中学. **J- League** 〔美〕女青年会〔多为有闲妇女组成,开展慈善活动等〕. ~ **miss** ①(十三至十五、六岁的)少女. ②苗条妇女和少女的衣服尺寸. ~ **school** 〔美〕小学. ~ **varsity** (大学院校的)体育代表队二队.

jun·ior·i·ty [ˌdʒu:niˈɔriti] *n.* ①年少,较年幼者的身份. ②晚辈〔下级〕的身份〔处境〕.

ju·ni·per [ˈdʒu:nipə] *n.*【植】桧属植物,红松. *the* ~ *tamarisk* 华北柽柳(又名三春柳或红柳). *the Chinese* ~ 桧. *the common* ~ 欧洲刺柏.

junk[1] [dʒʌŋk] *n.* ①(肉等的)大块,厚片. ②(填缝隙用的)旧绳絮. ③〔古〕(船上用的)醃牛肉. ④〔口〕零碎废物〔烂铁、旧罐等〕;废物堆. ⑤〔俚〕麻醉品,毒品〔鸦片、海洛因等〕. ⑥便宜货,假货;废话,哄骗. ⑦抹香鲸头部的脂肪组织. *a* ~ *of mutton* 一大块羊肉. — *vt.* ①把…当作废物丢掉. ②把…分成块. ~ **bottle** 深色厚玻璃瓶. ~ **dealer** 废品商,废旧船具商人. ~ **heap** 〔美俚〕破旧汽车. ~ **jewelry** 〔口〕不值钱的服饰珠宝. ~ **mail** 三等邮件〔指大量邮寄的广告、宣传品、通知单、征求意见单,征求订户单〕. ~ **man** 旧货商,废品商. ~ **market** 废旧货市场. ~ **price** 赔本价钱. ~ **shop** 废品店;旧船具店. ~ **yard** 废品清理场;破旧汽车堆积场.

junk[2] [dʒʌŋk] *n.* (中国的)平底帆船,舢板船. *a motorized* ~ 机帆船. ~ **man** 帆船船工.

junk[3] [dʒʌŋk] *n.* 毒品〔尤指海洛因〕.

Jun·ker [ˈjuŋkə] *n.* 〔G.〕①容克〔音译;意为普鲁士地主贵族之子〕;德国贵族地主. ②专制的德国军官. ①容克地主的特性〔政策等〕. ②〔集合词〕容克地主. **-dom** *n.* **-ism** *n.* 容克地主的精神.

jun·ker [ˈdʒʌŋkə] *n.* 〔美俚〕①吸毒者. ②破旧得不能使用的汽车.

jun·ket [ˈdʒʌŋkit] *n.* ①冻奶食品;乳酥. ②宴会,欢聚;

〔美〕野餐。③游览；(以视察为名)利用公费的旅行。— *vi.* ①设宴请客，举行野餐。②旅游，游山玩水；用公费旅行。— *vt.* 宴请，设宴招待。

junk·ie, junk·y [ˈdʒʌŋki] *n.* (*pl.* ***junk·ies***) 〔俚〕吸毒者(尤指吸食海洛因者)。

Ju·no [ˈdʒuːnəu] *n.* ①【罗神】(主神朱庇特的妻子)朱诺；天后；司婚姻的女神。②气派高贵的美人。

Ju·no·esque [ˌdʒuːnəuˈesk] *a.* (妇女)象朱诺般雍容华贵的。

jun·ta [ˈdʒʌntə] *n.* (*pl.* *~s*) 〔Sp.〕①执政团〔指革命或政变后控制政府的政治集团；秘密团体〕。②(西班牙、拉美、意大利等国的)立法〔行政等〕机构。③秘密政治集团，小集团；派系。*a military ~* 发动政变后上台的军政府。

jun·to [ˈdʒʌntəu] *n.*(*pl.* *~s*) = junta③。

Ju·pi·ter [ˈdʒuːpitə] *n.* ①【罗神】(主神)朱庇特。②【天】木星。③〔美〕一种中程弹道导弹的名字。***by ~!*** 〔古〕哎哟！天哪！好家伙！**~ Fulgur [Fulminator]** 雷神。**~ Pluvius** 雨神。

ju·pon [ˈdʒuːpɔn, dʒuːˈpɔn] *n.* 铠甲罩衣，铠甲衬衣。

Ju·ra [ˈdʒuərə] *n.* 【地】侏罗纪，侏罗系(=Jurassic period [system])。

ju·ra [ˈdʒuərə, ˈjuːrə] *n.* 〔L.〕*jus*[1] 的复数。

ju·ral [ˈdʒuərəl] *a.* ①法制的；法律上的。②关于权利义务的。**-ly** *ad.*

ju·rant [ˈdʒuərənt] *a.* 【法】立誓的；宣誓的。

Ju·ras·sic [dʒuəˈræsik] *a.* 【地】侏罗纪〔系〕的。— *n.* 【地】侏罗纪〔系〕(=~ period [system])。

ju·rat[1] [ˈdʒuəræt] *n.* ①(Chinque Ports 地方的)市政长官。②(Channel Islands 地方的)名誉法官。

ju·rat[2] [ˈdʒuəræt] *n.* 【法】宣誓证明文件(或说明书)〔说明宣誓时的时间、地点和在场人的文件，作为宣誓书附件〕。

ju·ra·to·ry [ˈdʒuərətəri] *a.* 【法】宣誓的；以誓言表达的。

Jur. D. = 〔L.〕*Juris Doctor* (=Doctor of Law)。

ju·rel [huːˈrel] *n.* 【动】鲹。

ju·rid·i·c(al) [dʒuəˈridik(əl)] *a.* ①审判上的，司法上的；法院的。②法律上的，合法的。**~ association** 社团法人。**~ days** 法院开庭日。**~ person** 法人。**-cal·ly** *ad.*

ju·ris·con·sult [ˈdʒuəriskənˌsʌlt] *n.* = jurist。

ju·ris·dic·tion [ˌdʒuərisˈdikʃən] *n.* ①裁判权；司法；司法权。②管辖权；管辖范围；权限。***be under the ~ of sb.*** 在某人管辖〔权限〕之下。***exercise [have] ~ over sb.*** 对某人有裁判权。**-al** *a.*

jurisp. = jurisprudence。

ju·ris·pru·dence [ˌdʒuərisˈpruːdəns] *n.* ①法学，法理学。②法学的分支(如民法、刑法、行政法等)。③法律体系。④(民法中的)法院审判规程，判决录。*medical ~* 法医学。

ju·ris·pru·dent [ˌdʒuərisˈpruːdənt] *a.* 精通法律的。— *n.* 法律学家。**-den·tial** *a.* **-den·tial·ly** *ad.*

ju·rist [ˈdʒuərist] *n.* ①法理学家；法律著述家。②法科学生。③法律专家；法官；律师。

ju·ris·tic(al) [dʒuəˈristik(əl)] *a.* ①法律的，法律上的；法学的。②法学家的；法理学的。*a ~ act* 法律行为。*a ~ fact* 法律承认的事实。*~ theory* 法律理论。**-ti·cal·ly** *ad.*

ju·ror [ˈdʒuərə] *n.* ①陪审员；(展览会、竞赛等的)评审委员，评奖人。②(表示忠诚等的)宣誓人。*a grand ~* 大陪审委员团中的一员；大陪审员。

ju·ry[1] [ˈdʒuəri] *n.* 【法】①陪审团。②(展览会、竞赛等的)全体评审员，评奖人。③舆论的裁决。*common [petty, trial] ~* 【法】普通陪审团，小陪审团。*coroner's ~* 【法】验尸陪审团。*grand ~* 【法】大陪审团。*packed ~* 〔口〕被买通的陪审团。*special ~* 【法】特别陪审团。***hang the ~*** 〔美〕(律师等通过不正当手段施加影响)使陪审团由于意见分歧而无法作出决定。**~ box** 陪审席。**~-fixer** 〔美俚〕收买〔胁迫〕陪审员的人。**~man** 陪审员。**~-woman** 女陪审员。

ju·ry[2] [ˈdʒuəri] *a.* 【海】(船上)应急用的，暂时的。*a ~ anchor* 应急锚。*~ repairs* 临时应急的修理。**~ mast** 【海】应急桅杆。**~-rigged** *a.* 【海】临时配备的。**~ rudder** 【海】应急舵。**~ strut** 应急支柱。

jus[1] [dʒʌs] *n.* (*pl.* ***jur·a*** [ˈdʒuərə]) 〔L.〕①法；法律，法律制度。②法律的原则；法律保证的权力〔权利〕。***~ ad rem*** 对物权。***~ canonicum*** (宗教改革前的)教堂法，寺院法(=canon law)。***~ civile*** 民法。***~ criminale*** 刑法。***~ gentium*** ①古罗马侨民法。②国际法(=international law)。***~ in re*** 物权。***~ natural [naturale]*** 自然法。***~ sanguinis*** 血统主义〔以父母国籍决定子女国籍的规定〕。***~ scriptum*** 成文法。***~ soli*** 出生地主义〔以出生地决定国籍的规定〕。

jus[2] [F. ʒy] *n.* 〔F.〕汁液；肉汁，浆汁。*roast beef au ~* 有汁烤牛肉〔菜单用语〕。

jus, just = justice。

jus·sive [ˈdʒʌsiv] *a.* 【语法】表示命令的。— *n.* 【语法】表示命令的词〔格、语气等〕。

just[1] [dʒʌst] *a.* ①公正的，正直的；公平的，正义的。②恰当的；适当的；应得的。③正当的，合法的。④合理的，有充分根据的。⑤精确的，正确的。*a ~ man* 正直的人。*a ~ decision* 公正的裁决。*a ~ price* 公平的价格。*a ~ punishment* 应受的惩罚。*a ~ praise* 应得的赞扬。*a ~ claim [title]* 正当的要求〔权利〕。*a ~ opinion* 合理的意见。*~ suspicions* 有理由的怀疑。*~ weights* 精确的砝码。*a ~ balance of colours* 色彩协调。*a ~ report* 真实的报导，正确的报告。— *ad.* ①正好，恰好，正要。②刚才，方才，刚刚。③只不过；仅仅。④差一点，好不容易。⑤〔口〕真正，实在，非常。⑥请，试着…看！〔用于祈使语气中〕。⑦直接，就。*It is ~ six (o'clock).* 现在正好六点钟。*It is ~ on six (o'clock).* 马上就要六点钟了。*I was ~ going when he came in.* 他进来时我正要走。*This is ~ the point.* 问题就在这里。*We ~ missed the train.* 我们正好没有赶上火车。*He has ~ come.* 他才来。*He is only ~ of age.* 他刚刚成年。*She is not ~ a singer.* 她不仅是一位歌唱家。*~ a taste* 只是尝了尝。*I'm ~ teasing you.* 我只不过给你闹着玩。*~ east of the church* 就在教堂的东面。*~ there* 就在那里。*I ~ managed to get there in time.* 我好不容易才及时赶到那里。*I only ~ caught the last bus.* 我刚好赶上末班公共汽车。*Every one was so happy that time ~ flew.* 人人都很快活，所以日子象飞一样地过得极快。*Do you like beer? — Don't I, ~!* 你爱喝啤酒吗？—不爱？！爱喝极啦！*Did he cry? — Didn't he, ~!* 他哭吗？—不哭？！哭得可厉害呢！*~ splendid!* 好极了。*J- look at this picture.* 看一看这幅画吧。*J- shut the door, will you?* 关一关门，好吗？*J- fancy [think of] the terrible result.* 想想那种可怕的后果吧！*J- come in.* 请进来吧。***~ about*** 正是…附近，几乎。***~ after*** 在…之后就。***~ as*** ①正象。②正在…的时候。***~-as-good articles*** 代用品。***~ as it is [they were]*** 恰好如此，照原样。***~ as ..., so ...*** 正象…一样，…也。***~ as you please*** 随您的意。***~ in time*** 恰巧，正好赶上。***J- (like) my luck!*** 啊呀，又是倒霉！***~ now*** 刚才；正在。***~ so*** 正是那样。***~ the same*** 完全一样。***~ the thing*** 适合的东西，很合用。***~ then*** 正在那时。***~ the opposite [reverse], ~ the other way about*** 恰恰相反。***not ~ ... but*** 不仅…而且…。***only ~ enough*** 勉强过得去。**-ly** *ad.* **-ness** *n.*

just[2] [dʒʌst] *n., vi.* = joust。

jus·te-mi·lieu [F. ʒystəmiljø] *n.* 〔F.〕中庸之道(=golden mean)。

jus·tice [ˈdʒʌstis] *n.* ①正义，公道；公正，公平。②正确；妥当，确实。③正当(理由)，合法。④审判，司法。⑤审判员，法官，(治安)推事；〔英〕高等法院法官；〔美〕最高法院法官. ⑥〔J-〕正义女神. *have a sense of* ～ 有正义感. *deny sb.* ～ 对某人不公平. *social* ～ 社会正义. *treat sb. [sth.] with* ～ 秉公对待某人[某事]. *Both sides have some* ～ *in their claims.* 双方的要求都有些理由. *examine [inquire] the* ～ *of a complaint* 审查控诉是否正当. *administer* ～ 执法,行使审判职权. *a court of* ～ 法院. *the Department of J-* 〔美〕司法部. *the* ～*s* (全体)法官. *Mr. J- X* 〔美〕某某法官先生. *Lord J- X* 〔英〕某某法官阁下. **bring sb. to** ～ 把某人缉拿归案,依法处分某人. **do** ～ **to** ①公平评判;公平对待 (*To do him* ～, *we must say that he is honest.* 说句公道话,他是诚实的). ②酷肖,极象,逼真 (*The photograph has done you* ～. 这张照片很象你本人). ③欣赏,大吃,饱食 (*do* ～ *to a meal* 饱餐一顿). **do oneself** ～ 充分发挥自己的本领. **in** ～ **to sb.** 为了对某人公平起见. **poetic(al)** ～ (只有在小说、诗歌中才能见到而在现实生活中却很难遇到的)理想的赏罚严明. **temper** ～ **with mercy** 宽严相济;恩威并施. **J- of the Peace** 治安推事. **Justice's** ～ 执法不当的审判〔讽刺治安推事往往以一己之见代替法律〕.

jus·tice·ship [ˈdʒʌstisʃip] *n.* 法官[治安推事]的身份[资格、地位、职务].

jus·ti·ci·a·ble [dʒʌsˈtiʃiəbl] *a.* 可交法院审判的.

jus·ti·ci·ar [dʒʌsˈtiʃiɑː] *n.* ①【英史】(从十一世纪诺曼第人入侵直到十三世纪金雀花王朝初期的)首席政法官. ②高等法院法官.

jus·ti·ci·ar·y [dʒʌsˈtiʃiəri] *n.* ①＝justiciar. ②法官的裁判权. — *a.* 司法上的,法官职务上的.

jus·ti·fi·a·ble [ˈdʒʌstifaiəbl] *a.* ①可证明为有理的,正当的,无可非议的. ②情有可原的,可辩护的. ～ *abortion* 正当堕胎〔因怀孕将危及母亲健康者〕. ～ *homicide* 有正当理由的杀人〔因为自卫或是阻止暴行〕. **be (seem) hardly** ～ 说不过去. **be the least** ～ 最要不得的,最不应该的. **-bil·i·ty** *n.* **-bly** *ad.*

jus·ti·fi·ca·tion [ˌdʒʌstifiˈkeiʃən] *n.* ①认为正当,证明为正当;正当的理由,辩护,辩明. ②无咎,无过失;【神学】释罪〔由于义所当然,犯罪可不受谴责〕. ④【印】(活字的)整理,装版. *in* ～ *of one's behavior* 为自己的行为辩护. *attack sb. without* ～ 毫无理由攻击某人. *for sb.'s* ～ 为了证明某人无咎. *What's your* ～ *for being so late?* 你来得这样迟有何理由? ～ **by faith** 【神学】因为信仰耶稣而可释罪.

jus·ti·fi·ca·tive, jus·ti·fi·ca·tory [ˈdʒʌstifikeitiv, -təri] *a.* 认为正当的;辩护性的,辩解的.

jus·ti·fi·er [ˈdʒʌstifaiə] *n.* ①辩解者;证明者;释罪者. ②【印】整版工人. ③【印】空铅,隔条.

jus·ti·fy [ˈdʒʌstifai] *vt.* ①证明…有道理,为…辩护. ②为…提供法律根据,宣誓证明(自己)有财力作保. ③【神学】对…释罪. ④【印】整(版),装(版),调整(铅字)的间隔使全行排满. *designs that are economically justified* 经济上合算的设计. *I hope I am justified in saying that ....* 我以为我可以说…. ～ *oneself for one's conduct* 证明自己的行为是正当的. — *vi.* ①【法】提出充分法律证据,证明合法. ②证明自己财力上有资格作保证人[保释人]. ③【印】整版,装版;(铅字)各行长度正合适.

Jus·tin [ˈdʒʌstin] *n.* 贾斯廷〔男子名〕.

Jus·ti·na [dʒəsˈtiːnə, -tai-] 贾斯廷娜〔女子名〕.

jus·tle [ˈdʒʌsl] *v., n.* ＝ jostle.

Jus·tus [ˈdʒʌstəs] *n.* 贾斯特斯〔男子名〕.

jut [dʒʌt] *vi.* 突出;伸出 (*out, forth, up*). — *vt.* 使突出;使伸出. — *n.* ①突出;伸出. ②突出部分,伸出部分.

Juta [ˈdʒuːtə] *n.* 朱塔〔姓氏〕.

jute [dʒuːt] *n.* 【植】①黄麻属植物,黄麻;长蒴黄麻. ②黄麻纤维. *Chinese* ～ 苘麻,青麻.

Jute [dʒuːt] *n.* 朱特人〔古代居住在北欧日德兰半岛的日耳曼人一部落集团〕;〔*pl.*〕朱特族.

jut·ty [ˈdʒʌti] *n.* (*pl.* **-ties**) ＝ jetty.

juv. ＝ juvenile.

ju·ve·nes·cence [ˌdʒuːviˈnesns] *n.* ①返老还童,变年轻. ②少年时期,从婴儿期向青年时期的过渡.

ju·ve·nes·cent [ˌdʒuːviˈnesnt] *a.* ①返老还童的,变年轻的. ②年轻的,从婴儿期向青年时期过渡的.

ju·ven·ile [ˈdʒuːvinail] *a.* ①青少年的,年少的. ②适于青少年的,供青少年用的. ③幼稚的. *a* ～ *adult* 将成年的少年. ～ *books* 少年读物. ～ *literature* 儿童文学. ～ *behaviour* 幼稚的行为. — *n.* ①青少年. ②少年读物. ③演少年的演员. ④羽毛未丰的鸟,雏鸟;(供竞赛用的)两岁的马. ～ **court** 少年法庭. ～ **delinquency** 少年犯罪. ～ **delinquent** 少年罪犯. ～ **hormone** (昆虫)返幼激素. ～ **lead** ①青少年扮演的主角. ②扮演青少年的主角演员. ～ **officer** 主管少年犯罪的警官.

ju·ve·nil·i·a [ˌdʒuːviˈniliə] *n.* ①(某作家、画家等)青少年时代的作品(集). ②少年文艺读物.

ju·ve·nil·i·ty [ˌdʒuːviˈniliti] *n.* ①年少,年幼. ②幼稚,幼稚的言行[思想等]. ③〔集合词〕少年人.

ju·ve·noc·ra·cy [ˌdʒuːviːˈnɔkrəsi] *n.* 由年轻人管理的国家.

ju·vie, ju·vey [ˈdʒuːvi] *n.* 〔美俚〕①少年罪犯,失足青少年. ②少年罪犯教养所.

jux·ta- *comb. f.* 表示"次","近","并": *juxta*position.

jux·ta·pose [ˈdʒʌkstəpəuz] *vt.* 使并置,使并列.

jux·ta·po·si·tion [ˌdʒʌkstəpəˈziʃən] *n.* 并置,并列.

JV ＝ junior varsity.

jwlr. ＝ jewel(l)er.

J.X. ＝〔L.〕*Jesus Christus* (＝ Jesus Christ) 耶稣基督.

Jy. ＝ July.

K

K,k [Kei] (*pl.* **Ks, K's; ks, k's** [keiz]) ①英语字母表第十一字母. ②K字形物体[记号]. ③一个序列中的第十一〔若J略去则为第十〕. ④【数】与Z轴平行的单位矢量. ⑤【化】元素钾(Potassium)的符号〔由拉丁名Kalium而来〕. ⑥〔K〕【气】积云(cumulus)的符号. ⑦〔K〕【数】常数(constant)的符号. ⑧代表数字"千"(10^3). *a salary of $14k* ＝ a salary of $14,000 一万四千美元的薪金. ⑨计算机的存储单位,相当于1024二进位组. *a computer memory of 64k* 存储量为64k的计算机. **K-series** (光谱线的)K系列. **K-shell** K层,K电子层,K壳层. — *a.* ①K形的. ②第十一的〔若J略去,则为第十的〕.

K., k. ＝ ①【电】capacity. ②karat, carat. ③【物】Kelvin. ④kilo. ⑤kilogram(me). ⑥king. ⑦knight. ⑧【海】knot. ⑨kope(c)k(s). ⑩krona, kronor. ⑪krone, kroner, kronen.

K-a corps 〔美〕为送信、看门、打斗而训练的一群警犬.

KA, ka ＝ kiloampere.

ka [kɑː] *n.* 〔Egy.〕【宗】(古埃及人或偶像的)灵魂,鬼魂,阴灵.

ka. = *kathode*, cathode.

Kaa·ba [ˈkɑːbə] *n.* = Caaba.

kab [kæb] *n.* 开普 (= cab)〔古希伯来粮食等干物的量具名,相当于二夸脱〕.

kab·(b)a·la [ˈkæbələ,kəˈbɑːlə] *n.* = cab(b)ala.

ka·bob [kəˈbɔb] *n.* = kebab.

ka·boo·dle [keˈbuːdl] *n.* = caboodle.

ka·bu·ki [ˌkɑːbuˈki] *n.* 〔Jap.〕歌舞伎〔创始于 17 世纪的日本传统剧种〕.

Ka·bul [ˈkɔːbl] *n.* 喀布尔〔阿富汗首都〕.

Ka·byle [kəˈbail] *n.* ①卡拜尔人〔北非阿尔及利亚或突尼斯的柏柏尔族之一〕. ②卡拜尔语.

kad·dish [ˈkɑːdiʃ] *n.* 【犹】珈底什〔每日作礼拜时或为死者祈祷时唱的赞美诗〕.

ka·di [ˈkɑːdi] *n.* = cadi.

kaf [kɑːf, kɔːf] *n.* 〔Heb.〕希伯来语的第十一个字母"ב, כ"〔相当于英语的 k〕.

kaf·fee·klatsch [ˈkɑːfeiˌklɑːtʃ,ˈkɔːfiːˌklætʃ] *n.* 〔美〕咖啡会〔一种非正式聚会,如家庭妇女白天聚在一起边喝咖啡边聊天〕(亦作 kaffee klatsch).

Kaf·(f)ir [ˈkæfə] *n.* ①异教徒〔阿拉伯人对不信伊斯兰教的人的蔑称〕. ②(南非洲说班图语的)卡菲尔人;卡菲尔语. ③〔*pl.*〕〔英〕南非洲矿山股票. ④〔k-〕一种高粱 (=～ corn).

kaf·fi·yeh [kɑːˈfiːjə] *n.* 阿拉伯人的头巾.

kaf·tan [ˈkæftən] *n.* = caftan.

ka·go [ˈkɑːgəu] *n.* 〔Jap.〕日本轿子.

Ka·go·shi·ma [ˌkɑːgəˈʃiːmə] *n.* 鹿儿岛〔日本港市〕.

kai·ak [ˈkaiæk] *n.* = kayak.

kail [keil] *n.* = kale.

kail·yard [ˈkeiljɑːd] *n.* = kaleyard.

kai·nite [ˈkain(a)it] *n.* 【矿】钾盐镁矾.

kai·ser [ˈkaizə] *n.* ①皇帝. ②〔K-〕神圣罗马帝国的皇帝. ③〔K-〕第一次世界大战前德国和奥国的皇帝. ④〔K-〕行使绝对权威的人;独裁者. **-dom** *n.* 皇帝的地位〔权力、统治区〕. **-ism** *n.* 独裁政治.

kai·ser·in [ˈkaizərin] *n.* (德国等的)皇后.

ka·ka [ˈkɑːkə] *n.* (新西兰产的)卡卡鹦鹉.

ka·ka·po [ˌkɑːkəˈpəu] *n.* (*pl.* ～*s*)【动】鸮鹦 (*Strigops habroptilus*)〔新西兰的一种鹦鹉〕.

ka·ke·mo·no [ˌkækiˈməunəu] *n.* (*pl.* ～*s*)〔Jap.〕(挂在墙上的)字画,条幅.

ka·ki [ˈkɑːkiː] *n.* (*pl.* *-kis*)〔Jap.〕①亚洲柿树. ②柿子 (= Japanese persimmon).

ka·kis·toc·ra·cy [ˌkækiˈstɔkrəsi] *n.* 坏人政府,恶人政治.

kal. = kalends; calends.

ka·la-a·zar [ˌkɑːlɑːɑːˈzɑː] *n.* 【医】黑热病.

Kal·an·cho·e [ˌkælənˈkəui] *n.* 【植】高凉菜属.

kale [keil] *n.* ①【植】羽衣甘兰. ②〔Scot.〕青菜,蔬菜;菜汤. ③〔美俚〕钞票,钱 (= ～ seed). **～yard** *n.* 〔Scot.〕菜园. **～yard school** 菜园派〔19 世纪末叶用苏格兰方言描写生活的一派作家〕.

ka·lei·do·phone [kəˈlaidəfəun] *n.* 【物】发音体振动显像仪.

ka·lei·do·scope [kəˈlaidəskəup] *n.* ①万花筒. ②万花筒般千变万化的情景. *the* ～ *of life* 变化莫测的人生.

ka·lei·do·scop·ic(al) [kəˌlaidəˈskɔpik(əl)] *a.* 万花筒(一样)的,千变万化的. **-i·cal·ly** *ad.*

kal·ends [ˈkæləndz] *n.* 〔*pl.*〕= calends.

Ka·le·va·la [ˌkɑːləˈvɑːlɑː] 《英雄的国土》〔芬兰史诗名,由 Elias Lönnrot 根据民间传说编写,1835 年初版〕.

kal·ian [kɑːˈljɑːn] *n.* 伊朗的水烟筒.

ka·lif, ka·liph [ˈkælif] *n.* = caliph.

Ka·li·man·tan [ˌkɑːliˈmɑːntɑːn] *n.* 加里曼丹〔旧称婆罗洲 (Borneo),为亚洲一大岛,构成印度尼西亚的四个省〕.

ka·li·um [ˈkeiliəm] *n.* 【化】钾.

kal·mi·a [ˈkælmiə] *n.* 山月桂属 (*Kalmia*) 植物〔北美的一种长绿灌木,如山月桂〕.

Kal·much, Kal·muk [ˈkælmʌk] *n.* ①卡尔美克人〔高加索东北部和新疆北部的蒙古族人〕. ②卡尔美克语 (= Kalmyk).

ka·long [ˈkɑːlɔŋ, ˈkæ-] *n.* 【动】狐蝙蝠〔以果实为食,产于马来群岛的一种大蝙蝠〕.

kal·pa [ˈkælpə] *n.* 〔Sans.〕【宗】劫〔根据印度教的宇宙论,宇宙从创始到毁灭的一个周期,约四十三亿二千万年〕.

kal·pak [ˈkælpæk] *n.* 羊皮帽,黑毡帽 (= calpace, calpack).

kal·so·mine [ˈkælsəmain] *n.*, *vt.* = calcimine.

ka·ma·la [kəˈmeilə, ˈkæmələ] *n.* 〔Sans.〕①【植】粗糠柴 (*Mallotus philippinensis*)〔东印度一种树〕. ②咖马拉〔粗糠柴蒴果腺毛制成的轻细粉末,用作红色染料和驱虫药〕.

Kam·chat·ka [kæmˈtʃætkə] *n.* 堪察加半岛〔位于苏联的鄂霍次克海和白令海之间〕.

kame [keim] *n.* (冰川溶化时淤积起来的含有砾子的)小沙丘.

ka·me·rad [ˌkæməˈrɑːt] *int.* 伙计!〔第一次世界大战时,德国兵表示投降时的用语〕— *vi.* 投降.

Ka·mi [ˈkɑːmi] *n.* (*sing.*, *pl.*)〔Jap.〕神.

ka·mi·ka·ze [ˌkɑːmiˈkɑːzi] *n.* 〔Jap.〕〔K-〕(第二次世界大战末期日本空军中驾驶满载炸弹之飞机作自杀性攻击的)神风(突击)队队员. ②神风队所使用的飞机.

Kam·pa·la [kɑːmˈpɑːlə] *n.* 坎帕拉〔乌干达首都〕.

kam·pong [ˈkɑːmpɔːŋ] *n.* 〔Ma.〕(马来亚的)小村庄;茅屋群.

kamp·tu·li·con [kæm*p*ˈtjuːlikən] *n.* 橡皮地毯.

Kam·pu·che·a [kɑːmˈpuːtʃiə] *n.* 柬埔寨〔亚洲〕(= Cambodia).

kam·seen, kam·sin [kæmˈsiːn] *n.* = Khamseen, Khamsin.

Kan., Kans. = Kansas.

ka·na [ˈkɑːnə] *n.* (*pl.* ～*s*)〔Jap.〕假名〔日语字母,由汉字简化而成〕.

Ka·na·ga·wa [kəˈnɑːgəwə] *n.* 神奈川〔日本县名〕.

Ka·nak·a [ˈkænəkə] *n.* (夏威夷及南洋群岛的)卡内加人.

ka·na·my·cin [ˌkænəˈmaisin] *n.* 【药】卡那霉素.

Ka·na·rese [ˌkɑːnəˈriːz] *a.* (印度)卡纳拉 (Kanara) 地区的;卡纳拉人的;卡纳拉语的. — *n.* (*pl.* ～) ①卡纳拉人. ②= Kannada.

Ka·na·za·wa [kəˈnɑːzəwə] *n.* 金泽〔日本港市〕.

Kan·da·har [ˌkændəˈhɑː] *n.* 坎大哈〔阿富汗城市〕.

Kan·dy [ˈkændi] *n.* 康提〔斯里兰卡城市〕.

Kane [kein] *n.* 凯恩〔姓氏〕.

kang [kɑːŋ] *n.* 〔Chin.〕炕.

kan·ga·roo [ˌkæŋgəˈruː] *n.* (*pl.* ～*s*; 集合词 ～)【动】大袋鼠. ～ **closure** (英国议会下院的)限制议事法跳议法,抽议法〔规定议会或委员会主席有权决定几个修正案中何者应进行辩论,何者予以搁置〕. ～ **court** 〔美口〕(非法的或不按法律程序的)非正规法庭;(囚犯在狱内举行的)模拟法庭. ～ **rat** 鼷〔大洋洲产,也称 rat ～〕;美洲有袋啮齿类动物.

kan·ji [ˈkændʒi] *n.* (*pl.* ～(*s*))〔Jap.〕日本汉字.

Kan·na·da [ˈkɑːnədə] *n.* 卡纳达语〔印度迈索尔邦及其附近印度南部地区讲的一种主要的德拉维德语〕.

Ka·no [ˈkɑːnəu] *n.* 卡诺〔尼日利亚城市〕.

ka·noon [kɑːˈnuːn] *n.* (波斯和阿拉伯五六十根弦的)齐特拉琴.

Kan·pur [kɑːnˈpuə] *n.* 坎普尔〔印度北方邦的城市〕.

K

Kans. = Kansas.
Kan·san [ˈkænzən] *a.* (美国) 堪萨斯州的; 堪萨斯州人的. — *n.* 堪萨斯州人.
Kan·sas [ˈkænzəs] *n.* 堪萨斯〔美国州名〕.
Kant [kænt], **Immanuel** 伊曼纽尔·康德〔1724—1804, 德国哲学家〕.
kan·tar [kɑːnˈtɑː] *n.* 坎塔尔〔穆斯林国家的重量单位, 从 100 磅到 700 磅不等〕.
Kant·i·an [ˈkæntiən,-tjən] *a.* 康德的; 康德哲学的. — *n.* 康德学派的人,康德主义者. **-ism** *n.* = Kantism.
Kant·ism [ˈkæntizəm] *n.* 康德哲学,康德主义.
Kant·ist [ˈkæntist] *n.* 康德派哲学家,康德主义者.
Ka·nu·ri [kɑːˈnuəri] *n.* ①*(pl. ~(s))* 卡努里人〔尼日利亚北部及其附近地区的穆斯林〕. ②卡努里语〔卡努里人讲的尼罗-撒哈拉语〕.
kao·liang [ˌkauˈliæŋ] *n.* 〔Chin.〕 高粱 (= sorghum).
ka·o·lin(e) [ˈkeiəlin] *n.* 高岭土,瓷土 (= china clay).
ka·o·lin·ite [ˈkeiəlinait] *n.* 【矿】高岭石.
ka·o·lin·ize [ˈkeiəlinaiz] *vt.* 使高岭土化.
ka·on [ˈkeiɔn] *n.* 【物】*K* 介子.
Ka·pell·meis·ter [kæˈpelmaistə] *n.* 〔*sing., pl.*〕〔G.〕〔蔑〕合唱团(管弦乐队的)指挥. ~ **music** 一般性的音乐,没有创造性的音乐.
kaph [kɑːf, kɔːf] *n.* = kaf.
ka·pok [ˈkeipɔk] *n.* 木棉.
kap·pa [ˈkæpə] *n.* ①希腊语的第十个字母 "K, κ". ②(遗传学上的)卡巴粒.
ka·put [kəˈput] *a.* 〔俚〕〔仅作表语用〕 ①坏了的,过时了的. ②完蛋了的,彻底失败了的.
Ka·ra·chi [kəˈrɑːtʃi] *n.* 卡拉奇〔巴基斯坦港市〕.
Kar·a·ite [ˈkɛərəait] *n.* 【犹】圣经派信徒〔该派于八世纪成立于中东,不接受犹太法学博士的教义或犹太法典,只信仰圣经〕. **Kar·a·ism** *n.* 【犹】圣经派教义.
Ka·ra-Kal·pak [kɑːˌrɑːkɑːlˈpɑːk] *n.* ①卡拉卡巴克人〔苏联乌兹别克的土耳其族人〕. ②卡拉卡巴克语.
kar·a·kul [ˈkærəkəl] *n.* ①中亚卡拉库尔羊. ②宽尾羊羔皮〔用此意时一般拼为 caracul〕.
kar·at [ˈkærət] *n.* = carat.
ka·ra·te [kəˈrɑːti] *n.* 〔Jap.〕 空手道〔一种徒手自卫拳术,源自日本冲绳岛〕.
Ka·re·li·an [kəˈriːliən,-ˈriːljən] *a.* ①(苏联)卡累利阿的; 卡累利阿人的. — *n.* ①卡累利阿人〔属芬兰族,居于卡累利阿和芬兰东部〕. ②卡累利阿语〔卡累利阿人讲的芬兰语〕.
Ka·ren [ˈkɑːren, Am. kəˈren] *n.* ①克伦〔女子名〕. ②(缅甸的)克伦人; 克伦语.
Karl [kɑːl] *n.* 卡尔〔男子名, Charles 的异体〕.
Kar·lo·vy Var·y [ˈkɑːləvi ˈvɑːri] 卡罗维发利〔捷克斯洛伐克城市〕.
kar·ma [ˈkɑːmə] *n.* 〔Sans.〕 ①【宗】羯磨〔梵文译音〕,业〔决定来世命运的所作所为〕. ②因果报应,因缘.
ka·ross [kəˈrɔs] *n.* (南非用兽皮制的)披肩; 皮褥; 皮毯.
ka(r)·roo [kəˈruː] *n.* *(pl. ~s)* ①南非干燥台地. ②【地】无水亚粘土草原.
karst [kɑːst] *n.* 【地】水蚀石灰岩地区; 岩溶. ~ **cave** 水蚀石灰洞〔喀斯特〕.
kart [kɑːt] *n.* ①小型汽车; 小型车子. ②微型赛车.
kar·tell [kɑːˈtel] *n.* = cartel.
kar·y·o- [ˈkæriəu] *comb. f.* 表示"核": *karyogamy, karyolysis*.
kar·y·og·a·my [ˌkæriˈɔgəmi] *n.* 【生】核配(合).
kar·y·o·ki·ne·sis [ˌkæriəukaiˈniːsis] *n.* 【生】有丝分裂; 核分裂.
kar·y·o·lymph [ˈkæriəlimf] *n.* 【生】核液.
kar·y·ol·y·sis [ˌkæriˈɔlisis] *n.* 【生】核溶解. **-y·o·lit·ic** *a.*
kar·y·om·i·to·sis [ˌkæriəuˈmaitəusis] *n.* 【生】(细胞核的)有丝分裂.
kar·y·on [ˈkæriən] *n.* 【生】细胞核,核.
kar·y·o·plasm [ˈkæriəuplæzəm] *n.* 【生】核质,核浆.
kar·y·o·some [ˈkæriəsəum] *n.* 【生】染色质核仁,核粒.
kar·y·o·tin [ˌkæriˈəutin] *n.* 【生】染色质,染色体,染色粒 (= chromatin).
kar·y·o·type [ˈkæriətaip] *n.* 【生】染色体组型. **-typic** [-ˈtipik], **-typical** *a.*
kas·bah [ˈkɑːzbɑː] *n.* = casbah.
ka·sha [ˈkɑːʃə] *n.* 荞麦粥; 麦粥.
ka·sher [ˈkɑːʃə] = kosher.
Kash·mir [ˈkæʃmiə] *n.* 克什米尔.
Kash·mir·i [kæʃˈmiəri] *n.* ①克什米尔语. ②*(pl. ~(s))* 克什米尔人.
Kash·mir·i·an [kæʃˈmiriən] *a.* 克什米尔的,克什米尔人的,克什米尔语的. — *n.* 克什米尔人.
kash·rut(h) [kɑːʃˈruːt,ˈkɑːʃrut] *n.* (犹太教)饮食教规.
Ka·shu·bi·an [kæˈʃjuːbiən] *n.* 卡舒比语〔波兰北部所说的一种近似波兰语的西斯拉夫方言〕.
ka·so·lite [ˈkæsəlait] *n.* 【矿】硅铅铀矿.
kat [kɑːt] *n.* = khat.
Ka·tab·a·sis [kəˈtæbəsis] *n.* ①【希腊史】"大败退"〔据希腊历史学家色诺芬 (Xenophone) 所写《希腊远征波斯记》*(the Anabasis)* 记载,追随波斯王塞鲁士 (Cyrus) 的希腊雇用军战败后大举向海边撤退,史称"大败退"〕. ②〔k-〕*(pl. -ses [-siːz])* (军队的)撤退.
kat·a·bat·ic [ˌkætəˈbætik] *a.* (风等)下降的, 下吹的 *(opp.* anabatic). ~ **wind** 【气】下降风,下吹风.
ka·tab·o·lism [kəˈtæbəlizəm] *n.* 【生】分解代谢〔catabolism 的异体〕.
ka·ta·ka·na [ˈkætəˈkɑːnə] *n.* 〔Jap.〕(日语字母楷书)片假名.
Ka·tan·ga [kəˈtæŋgə] *n.* 加丹加〔扎伊尔沙巴地区 (Shaba) 的旧名〕.
Ka·ta·ther·mom·e·ter [ˌkætəθəˈmɔmitə] *n.* 冷却温度表,冷却率温度表.
Kate [keit] *n.* 凯特〔女子名, Catherine 的昵称〕.
ka·tha·rev·ou·sa [ˌkɑːθɑːˈrevuːsɑː] *n.* (符合古希腊语用法的)现代希腊语; 地道希腊语.
Kath·ar·ine, Kath·er·ine, Kath·ryn [ˈkæθərin, ˈkæθrin] *n.* 凯瑟琳〔女子名, Kitty 为其昵称, Catherine 的异体〕.
ka·thar·sis [keˈθɑːsis] *n.* = catharsis.
Kath·leen [ˈkæθliːn] *n.* 凯瑟琳〔女子名, Catherine 的异体〕.
kath·ode [ˈkæθəud] *n.* = cathode.
kat·i·on [ˈkætaiən] *n.* = cation.
Kat·man·du [ˈkɑːtmɑːnˈduː] *n.* 加德满都〔尼泊尔首都〕.
ka·ty·did [ˈkeitidid] *n.* 蝈蝈儿〔纺织娘〕 (= catydid).
katz·en·jam·mer [ˈkætsnˌdʒæmə] *n.* ①喧闹. ②坐立不安; 沮丧. ③剧烈的头疼〔尤指因宿醉引起者〕.
Kauf·man(n) [ˈkɔːfmən], **Angelica,** 安吉利卡·考夫曼〔1741—1807,瑞士女画家〕.
kau·ri [ˈkauriː] *n.* 〔Maori〕【植】①南方贝壳杉 *(Agathis australis)* 〔产于新西兰〕. ②南方贝壳杉木. ③贝壳松脂,栲树脂.
ka·va [ˈkɑːvə] *n.* ①卡瓦胡椒 *(Piper methystium)* (= ~ pepper). ②卡瓦酒 (= kavakava).
ka·vass [kəˈvæs] *n.* ①(土耳其显贵的)卫士. ②(土耳其的)武装警察.
kay·ak [ˈkaiæk] *n.* ①爱斯基摩独木舟〔一种独人的小划子,木船体外面裹以海豹皮〕. ②(用帆布或塑料制的)小划子.
Kay(e) [kei] *n.* 凯〔女子名, Catherine 的昵称〕.
kay·o [ˈkeiˈəu] *n.* *(pl. ~s)* 〔美俚〕【拳】击倒(= K.O., knock-out). — *vt.* 〔美俚〕【拳】击倒. **-ed** *a.* 被拳击

倒的.

ka·za·chok [kɑːzɑːˈtʃɔːk] *n.* *(pl.* ***-zach·ki*** [-zɑːtʃˈkiː]*)* = kazatsky.

Ka·zak(h) [kɑːˈzɑːk] *n.* 哈萨克人;哈萨克族.

Ka·zak(h)·stan [ˌkɑːzɑːkˈstɑːn] *n.* 哈萨克〔苏联哈萨克加盟共和国,亚洲,首都阿拉木图〕.

Ka·zan [kəˈzɑːn] *n.* 喀山〔苏联鞑靼自治共和国首都〕.

ka·zat·sky, ka·zat·ski [kəˈzɑːtski] *n.* *(pl.* ***-skies****)* 〔Russ.〕(由一名男演员独舞的)哥萨克舞(= kazatska).

ka·zoo [kəˈzuː] *n.* 小笛〔一种玩具乐器〕.

KB = King's bishop (国际象棋中与"王"同列配置的)象.

K.B. =①King's Bench 英国高等法院. ②Knight Bachelor 英国古代最低级爵士.

k·bar [ˈkeibɑː] *n.* 千巴〔气压或声压单位〕(= kilobar).

K.B.E. = Knight Commander of the British Empire 〔英〕不列颠帝国高级勋位爵士.

K.C., KC = ①King's Counsel 英国王室法律顾问. ②Knight Commander 英国(第二等的)高级爵士. ③Knight(s) of Columbus 〔美〕(天主教)慈善会(成员). ④King's College 〔英〕皇家学院.

kc. = kilocycle(s).

kcal. = 【物】kilocalorie(s).

K.C.B. = Knight Commander of the Bath 〔英〕巴士高级勋位爵士.

K.C.I.E. = Knight Commander of the Indian Empire 〔英〕印度帝国高级勋位爵士.

K.C.M.G. = Knight Commander of St. Michael and St. George 〔英〕圣迈克尔和圣乔治高级勋位爵士.

K.C.S.I. = Knight Commander of the Star of India 〔英〕印度星级勋位高级爵士.

K.C.V.O. = Knight Commander of the Royal Victorian Order 〔英〕皇室维多利亚勋章高级爵士.

K.D., k.d. = knocked down 【商】拆开的, 卸开的,分解的.

K.E. = kinetic energy 【物】动能.

ke·a [ˈkeiə] *n.* 【动】(新西兰产的)食肉鹦鹉.

Kean(e) [kiːn], **Edmund** 埃德蒙·基恩〔1787—1833,英国男演员〕.

Keats [kiːts], **John** 约翰·济慈〔1795—1821,英国诗人〕.

ke·bab [kəˈbɑːb] *n.* ①〔常 *pl.*〕烤腌(羊)肉串. ②(肉串上的)肉块.

keb·bok, keb·bock [ˈkebɔk] *n.* 〔Scot.〕干酪,乳酪.

Ke·ble [ˈkiːbl], **John** 约翰·基布尔〔1792—1866,英国公理会牧师和诗人,牛津运动的创始人〕.

Kech·ua [ˈketʃwɑː] *n.* = quechua. — **kech·uan** *a.*, *n.*

Ke·chu·ma·ran [ˈketʃuməˈrɑːn] *n.* = quechumaran.

keck [kek] *vi.* ①作呕,恶心. ②表示[感觉]厌恶 *(at)*. ③(鸟)咯咯地叫.

keck·le [ˈkekl] *vi.*, *n.* = cackle.

ked·dah [ˈkedə] *n.* 捕象陷阱.

kedge [kedʒ] *n.* 小锚(又称 kedge-anchor). — *vt.*, *vi.* ①抛锚移(船). ②(使)船跟着锚抛去的方向移动.

ked·ger·ee [ˌkedʒəˈriː] *n.* (印度的)鸡蛋葱豆饭;欧洲用鱼和米、蛋作的食品.

ke·ef [kiːˈef] *n.* ①(吸毒后产生的)迷糊状态. ②(有上述作用的)麻醉品.

keek [kiːk] *vi.* 〔Scot., 英方〕偷看,窥视;侦查.

keel[1] [kiːl] *n.* ①(船等的)龙骨. ②〔诗〕船. ③(动物的)龙骨脊,脊棱;(植物的)龙骨瓣 *false* ~【船】副龙骨,保险龙骨. ***on an even*** ~ ①船首船尾在同一水平上的,[地],平稳的(地). ②稳定的(地). ③均衡的(地). ④神志清楚的(地). — *vt.* ①给(船等)装龙骨. ②把(船等)翻过来(以便修理), 使(船)倾覆. ③〔诗〕以龙骨破(浪)前进. — *vi.* (船等)翻身,倾覆. ~ ***over*** ①翻身,倾覆,颠倒. ②〔口〕突然昏倒. ~**blocks** *n.*【船】龙骨墩. ~**boat** *n.* 内河运货船. ~**haul** *vt.* ①把(某人)用绳子缚在船底拖曳(作为惩罚). ②严厉斥责. ~ **line** *n.*【船】首尾线,龙骨线. ~ **piece** 龙骨件材. ~ **surface** 飞机垂直安定的翼面.

keel[2] [kiːl] *n.* ①(运煤的)平底船(尤指运煤的驳船). ②一驳船的煤. ③〔英〕煤的重量单位(= 21.2 长吨).

keel[3] [kiːl] *n.* (给木材等做记号的)红色颜料,代赭石.

ke(e)·lson [ˈkelsən] *n.*【船】内龙骨.

keen[1] [kiːn] *a.* ①锐利的,锋利的 *(opp.* dull*)*;(言语等)刺人的. ②敏锐的,敏捷的. ③厉害的,强烈的,激烈的. ④泼辣的,热心的,渴望的. ⑤〔美俚〕漂亮的;愉快的;极好的. *a razor with a* ~ *edge* 刀口锋利的剃刀. *a* ~ *scent* 刺鼻的气味. *be* ~ *of hearing [sight]* 听觉[视觉]敏锐. ~ *eyes* 锐眼. *a* ~ *intelligence* 聪慧过人. *a* ~ *observer* 敏锐的观察者. *a* ~ *critic* 尖锐的批评家. *a* ~ *north wind* 凛烈的北风. *a* ~ *sense of justice* 强烈的正义感. *a* ~ *appetite* 强烈的食欲. ~ *desire* 强烈的欲望. *a* ~ *golfer* 热爱高尔夫球的人. *be* ~ *on stamp collecting* 喜欢集邮. ~ *prices* 极低廉的价格. ***be dead*** ~ ***on sth.*** 〔口〕非常喜爱. ***be*** ~ ***about*** 喜爱,迷着. ***be*** ~ ***on*** 〔口〕喜爱,渴望. ***be*** ~ ***to*** 非常想 *(I am* ~ *to go to the cinema.* 我非常想去看电影*)*. ***(as)*** ~ ***as mustard*** 极热心的. **-ly** *ad.* **-ness** *n.*

keen[2] [kiːn] *n.* 〔爱尔兰〕号哭,恸哭;(号哭着唱出的)挽歌. — *vt.*, *vi.* 为安慰(死者)而号哭,恸哭.

keen·er [ˈkiːnə] *n.* 〔爱尔兰〕哭丧者(尤指以哭号为职业的人).

keep [kiːp] *vt.* ***(kept*** [kept]***)*** ①拿着,保持;保存,保留;保管;把守(门等);保守(秘密等). ②保护,防护,防守. ③履行;遵守. ④庆祝,过(节),过(年),举行(仪式). ⑤扶养;雇用. ⑥饲养. ⑦备有,经售. ⑧经营,开设,管理. ⑨继续沿着…走. ⑩整理,料理. ⑪记住;记载,记入. ⑫挽留,留住;拘留. ⑬使…保持着(某种状态)〔用此义时在宾语后加补足语〕. ⑭制止,防止;妨碍;隐瞒. ⑮留在(房屋等)内;保持在(座位等)上不动. ~ *a stick in one's hand* 手里拿着一根棍子. *You may* ~ *the magazine as your own.* 你把那本杂志当作自己的东西留下来好啦(不必还). *The bank* ~*s money for people.* 银行替人保管存款. ~ *a fortress [town] against the enemy* 防守要塞[城市]抵御敌人. *Who* ~*s the goal?* 谁守球门? ~ *a promise* 守约. ~ *the rules* 守规则. ~ *early hours* 早睡早起. ~ *late hours* 晚睡晚起. ~ *a secret* 守秘密. ~ *one's word* 履行诺言;说话算话. ~ *one's birthday* 做生日,祝寿. ~ *Chinese New Year* 过春节. *have a wife and family to* ~ 要养家. ~ *chickens* 养鸡. ~ *a motorcar* 自备汽车. *Do you* ~ *postcards here?* 你们这里有明信片吗? ~ *a school* 办学校. ~ *(a)shop* 开店. ~ *the middle of the road* 一直沿着路中间前进. ~ *house* 管理家务. ~ *a fact in mind* 心里记住一件事. ~ *accounts [books]* 记帐. ~ *a diary* 记日记. *What* ~*s him here, I wonder?* 我不知道他呆在这里干什么? *I won't* ~ *you long.* 我不会耽搁你很久. ~ *sb. in custody* 扣留某人. ~ *a razor sharp* 使剃刀经常锋利. *Cold bath* ~*s me in good health.* 冷水浴使我健康. ~ *the window open* 把窗子开着. ~ *the tears from one's eyes* 忍住眼泪. *He* ~*s nothing from me.* 他什么事都不瞒我. ~ *a child away from the fire* 让孩子离火远一点. ~ *sb. from hurting himself* 提防某人受伤. *Illness kept me from coming yesterday.* 我昨天因病没有来. ~ *one's bed* 卧床不起. ~ *the house* 足不出户. — *vi.* ①继续,保持,维持. ②〔口〕逗留;住在;呆. ③〔口〕(店等)开着,(学校)上课. ④继续不断〔用此义时常接动词 + ing〕. ⑤(食物等)保持不坏. ⑥拖,搁. ⑦保持某种路线〔方向、活动〕. *K- dry!* 切勿受潮. *K- silent!* 别作声,保持肃静! *Where do you* ~? (尤指剑桥大学)你住在哪里? *School* ~*s till four o'clock.* 学校上课到四点钟. *K- smiling* 别悲观,常常笑笑吧. *The baby kept crying all night.* 婴儿哭了一夜. *These fish will* ~ *overnight.* 这些鱼过夜不会坏. *The matter will* ~ *until tomorrow.* 问题拖到明天再讲. *Traffic* ~*s to the right.* 车

K

辆等靠右边走. ~ *check on* 检查,监督. ~ ***a firm [tight] hand [rein] on sb.*** 紧紧地控制某人. ~ ***at*** ①纠缠(*They kept at me with their appeals for subscriptions.* 他们硬要我捐款). ②坚持地做. ~ ***at it*** 〔口〕使劲,加油干. ~ ***away*** 不给挨近;避开,离开. ~ ***back*** ①退缩. ②隐瞒. ③阻止. ④留住. ~ ***bad [good] company*** 跟坏[好]人交往. ~ ***dark*** 保守秘密,不泄密. ~ ***down*** ①压住; 镇压, 压服. ②【印】用小活字排印. ③缩减. ④保留(食物等). ⑤一直坐着,一直睡着. ~ ***from*** ①避开 (~ *from talking* 避而不谈). ②禁止(~ *sb. from smoking* 禁止某人抽烟). ③隐瞒(~ *sth. (back) from sb.* 对某人隐瞒某事). ④抑制 (*He couldn't* ~ *from crying.* 他禁不住哭了). ~ ***hold of*** 抓住不放. ~ ***in*** ①扣留, 下课后罚学生留校. ②压住,控制. ③【印】排紧. ④让(火)烧着. ⑤闭门不出. ~ ***in with sb.*** 与某人友好相处. ~ ***it up*** 〔口〕加紧做; 坚持做下去. ~ ***off*** ①防止, 不让接近, 避开(敌人等). ②不接近 (*K- off the grass.* (牌告)勿踏草地). ~ ***on*** ①穿[戴]着不脱. ②继续 *(doing)* (~ *on blowing one's nose* 一直在擤鼻子). ★ ~ on ... ing 表示动作的反复, ~ ... ing 表示状态的继续. ~ ***on at*** ①继续干. ②纠缠. ③责骂不休. ~ ***one's bones green*** 不衰老. ~ ***one's head*** 不激动, 保持冷静. ~ ***oneself to oneself*** 不与人往来, 不交际, 离群索居. ~ ***out*** ①把…关在门外, 不使入内 (*Danger. K- out.* 危险. 切勿入内). ②阻止, 挡住(~ *out sunlight* 遮住阳光). ③【印】疏排. ④不参加,不卷入. ~ ***out of*** 置身于…之外 (~ *out of sb.'s affair* 不过问某人的事). ~ ***sb. shady*** 〔美口〕蒙蔽某人, 不让某人了解事实真相. ~ ***sb. underfoot*** 控制某人. ~ ***to*** 坚持, 遵守, 不违背(*K- to every promise you have made.* 一切诺言都必须坚守不渝. *K- to your task till you've finished.* 坚持工作,直到做完为止). ~ ***sb. advised [conversant, posted] on sth.*** 使某人了解某事. ~ ***sb. busy*** 不让某人闲着. ~ ***sb. going*** ①用金钱帮助某人. ②维持某人生活. ~ ***sb. going in sth.*** 供给某人以某物. ~ ***to oneself*** ① *vi.* 不交际, 不与人往来. ② *vt.* *[sth.]* 保守秘密. ~ ***under*** 压住,控制 (*The firemen managed to* ~ *the fire under.* 火势总算被救火员控制住了). ~ ***up*** ①支持,维持;保持. ②继续,持续;停歇. ③不为(病等)所屈,能支持. ④【印】用大写正体排印. ~ ***up with [on]*** 跟上(人、时势等),不落后 (~ *up with the situation* 跟上形势). — ***n.*** ①保持,保养;管理. ②生活资料,衣食;饲料. ③【史】中世纪城堡的最牢固的部分, 城堡的高楼;堡垒;要塞,坚固据点. ④监牢,监狱. *be worth one's* ~ 值得保存[饲养]. *earn one's* ~ 挣生活费. *the castle* ~ 城堡的高楼. ***for ~s*** 〔口〕①分胜负(*play for ~s* 为了分输赢而游戏). ②〔口〕永远地 (*settle the controversy for ~s* 一劳永逸地解决这一纠纷. *The fight is on for ~s.* 斗争永远不断. *You may have the book for ~s.* 这本书你拿去好了,不必归还). ***in bad [low]*** ~ 保存得不好. ***in good [high]*** ~ 保存得好.

keep·er [ˈkiːpə] *n.* ①看守人;看护人;猎场看守人; 动物园的饲养员. ②管理人,保管人〔英国常用作官职名〕. ③(商店客栈等的)所有者,经营者. ④衔铁,永磁衔铁. ⑤【机】保位物; 止动螺帽, 锁紧螺母; 夹子, 夹头, 卡箍. ⑥履行者,遵守者;记录员. ⑦耐藏的水果[蔬菜]. *a park* ~ 〔美〕运动场管理员; 〔英〕猎场管理员. *a shop* ~ 店主. ~*of magnet* 保磁用衔铁. *oil* ~ 油承. *a* ~ *of his words* 说话算数的人. *a good [bad]* ~ 耐藏的[不耐藏的]物品. *the K- of the Exchange and Mint* 〔英〕造币局局长. *the K- of the King's Conscience* (作国王国务上行为负责人的)大法官. *the K- of the Privy Seal* 〔英〕御玺官. *the Lord K- (of the Great Seal)* 〔英〕国玺官. **-less** *a.* **-ship** *n.*

keep·ing [ˈkiːpiŋ] *n.* ①保持,保有,保留; 〔*pl.*〕保留物. ②管理,看守,保管. ③供养,饲养. ④一致; 协调. *This stamp is worth (the)* ~. 这枚邮票值得保存. *in safe* ~ 保管得好. *The papers are in my* ~. 文件由我在保管. *the* ~ *of one's family* 抚养全家. *loose* ~ 散放饲养. ***in ~ with*** 和…一致, 与…协调. ***out of ~ with*** 和…不一致,与…不协调. — *a.* ①适于贮藏的. ②坚贞的. ~ *apples* 耐贮藏的苹果. *a* ~ *husband* 忠实的丈夫. ~ **room** 〔美〕起居室,内客厅.

keep·sake [ˈkiːpseik] *n.* 纪念品; (精装)纪念本.

kees·hond [ˈkeisˌhɔnd] *n.* 荷兰狮毛狗.

kees·ter [ˈkiːstə] *n.* = keister.

keet [kiːt] *n.* 【动】珍珠幼鸟.

kef [kef, keif] *n.* = keef.

kef·fi·yeh [kəˈfiːə] *n.* = kaffiyeh.

keg [keg] *n.* ①小桶〔容量通常少于 10 加仑〕. ②桶〔钉子的重量单位 = 100 磅〕.

keis·ter, kees·ter [ˈkiːstə] 〔俚〕①手提皮箱, 小提包, 挎包. ②屁股.

Keith [kiːθ] *n.* 基斯〔姓氏,男子名〕.

keg·ler, kegel·(l)er [ˈkeg(ə)lə] *n.* (板球等的)击球员.

keit·lo·a [ˈkaitləuə,ˈkeit-] *n.* 【动】犽犀 *(keitloa)* 〔南非所产的两角犀〕.

Ke·lao [kəˈlau] *n.* 仡佬族;仡佬族人.

Kel·land [ˈkelənd] *n.* 凯兰〔姓氏〕.

Kel·ler [ˈkelə] *n.* ①凯勒〔姓氏〕. ②**Helen Adams** ~ 海伦·凯勒〔1880—1968,美国盲哑女作家〕.

Kel·l(e)y [ˈkeli] *n.* 凯利〔姓氏,男子名〕.

Kel·logg [ˈkelɔg] *n.* 凯洛格〔姓氏〕.

kel·ly, Kel·ly [ˈkeli] **green** (浓厚的)黄绿色.

ke·loid [ˈkiːlɔid] *n.* 【医】瘢痕瘤,瘢痕疙瘩.

kelp [kelp] *n.* ①巨藻;海草; 大型褐藻. ②海草灰〔从中可提取碘〕.

kel·pie, kel·py [ˈkelpi] *n.* 〔Scot.〕(传说中能诱人自溺的)马形水怪.

kel·son [ˈkelsn] *n.* 【船】内龙骨.

Kelt [kelt] *n.* = Celt.

kelt [kelt] *n.* (产卵后的)鲑鱼[鳟鱼].

kel·ter [ˈkeltə] *n.* = kilter.

Kelt·ic [ˈkeltik] *a., n.* = Celtic.

Kel·vin [ˈkelvin] *n.* ①凯尔文〔男子名〕. ②**Lord William Thomson** ~ 威廉·汤姆逊·凯尔文〔1824—1907,英国物理学家〕. ~ **effect** 【无】集肤效应. ~ **scale** 【物】开氏温标.

Ke·mal·ism [kəˈmɑːlizəm] *n.* 基马尔主义〔土耳其共和国第一任总统 Kemal (1881—1938)所提倡的政治主张. 基马尔旧译凯末尔〕.

Ke·mal·ist [kəˈmɑːlist] *n.* 基马尔主义者. — *a.* 基马尔主义的,基马尔式的.

Kem·ble [ˈkembl] *n.* 肯布尔〔姓氏,男子名〕.

kemp [kemp] *n.* ①〔英方〕(在收割庄稼竞赛时所获的)冠军. ②粗羊毛. — *vi.* (在收割庄稼时)争取冠军.

kempt [kempt] *a.* 干净的,整洁的,收拾得干净利落的.

Ken. = Kentucky.

ken[1] [ken] *n.* ①眼界, 视野; 景象. ②知识范围, 见地. *beyond [out of, outside] one's* ~ 在知识范围之外. *in one's* ~ 在知识范围之内. — *vt., vi.* **(~*ned*** [-d] 或 ***kent)*** ①〔Scot.〕认识;知道. ②〔古〕看出.

ken[2] [ken] *n.* 〔俚〕(盗贼等的)巢穴,窝.

ke·naf [kəˈnæf] *n.* ①洋麻, 槿麻 *(Hibiscus cannabinus)* 〔亚洲热带植物,似黄麻〕. ②洋麻[槿麻]纤维.

kench [kentʃ] *n.* (腌制鱼或皮革的)长方形大腌箱.

Ken·dal (green) [ˈkendl] *n.* ①(英国)肯达耳绿色粗呢. ②肯达耳绿.

Ken·dall [ˈkendl] *n.* 肯德尔〔姓氏,男子名〕.

Ken·nan [ˈkenən] *n.* 凯南〔姓氏〕.

Ken·ne·dy [ˈkenidi] *n.* 肯尼迪〔姓氏〕. ~ **Round** 〔常用 K- round〕肯尼迪回合〔美国总统肯尼迪 1962 年发起的对西欧共同市场之间的谈判, 目的是打破六国关税壁垒以扩大美国出口〕.

K

ken·nel[1] [ˈkenl] *n.* ①狗窝;〔*pl.*〕养狗场. ②(狐等棲身的)洞. ③一群猎狗,一群野兽. ④鄙陋的小矮房,陋室. *go to* ～ (狐等)藏到洞中. — *vt., vi.* (〔英〕*-ll-*) ①(使)住在狗窝内;(使)呆在窝内;(使)钻进狗窝. ②(使)(人)住进陋室.

ken·nel[2] [ˈkenl] *n.* 阴沟,路旁的下水道.

Ken·nel·ly [ˈkenəli] *n.* 肯内利〔姓氏〕.

Ken·nel·ly-Heav·i·side layer [ˈkenəliˈhevisaid ˈlɛə] *n.*【无】肯涅利——海维赛层,E电离层(= E-layer).

Ken·neth [ˈkeniθ] *n.* 肯尼思〔男子名〕.

ken·ning [ˈkeniŋ] *n.* ①〔Scot.〕知道,认识. ②微量;痕迹. ②〔古,诗〕隐喻表达法〔一般用复合词作比喻,如以"whale-path"(鲸路)喻"大海","oar-steed"(划马)喻"船"〕.

Ken·ny [ˈkeni] *n.* 肯尼〔姓氏〕. **K- method [treatment]** 肯尼疗法〔早期用热裹和锻炼身体治疗小儿麻痹症的方法,为澳大利亚护士伊丽莎白·肯尼所创〕.

ke·no [ˈkiːnəu] *n.* (*pl.* ～*s*) 叠纸牌赌博.

ke·no·sis [kiˈnəusis] *n.*【神】(基督的)对神性的放弃.

ke·not·ic [-ˈnɔtik] *a.*

ken·o·tron [ˈkenətrɔn] *n.*【无】高压整流二极管. ～ **rectifier** 二极管整流器.

kens·peck·le [ˈkenspekl] *a.* 明显的,容易发现的,引人注意的.

Kent[1] [kent] *n.* 肯特〔姓氏,男子名〕.

Kent[2] [kent] *n.* 肯特郡〔英格兰东南端〕.

kent [kent] *v.* ken[1] 的过去式及过去分词.

Kent·ish [ˈkentiʃ] *a.* 英国肯特郡的. ～ **fire** (观〔听〕众表示不耐烦或抗议时)长时间有节奏的鼓掌. ～ **man** 麦特威(Medway)河以西的肯特人,西肯特人〔*cf.* man of Kent 东肯特人〕. ～ **rag** 肯特郡产坚硬砂质石灰岩.

kent·ledge [ˈkentlidʒ] *n.*【船】压载用的生铁.

Ken·tuck·i·an [kenˈtʌkiən] *a.* 肯塔基州的,肯塔基州人的. — *n.* 肯塔基州人.

Ken·tuck·y [kenˈtʌki] *n.* 肯塔基〔美国州名〕. ～ **coffee tree**【植】加拿大皂荚 (*Gymnocladus dioica*)〔产于美国东部,籽可作咖啡代用品〕.

Ken·ya [ˈkiːnjə,ˈkenjə] *n.* 肯尼亚〔非洲〕. **-n** ①*a.* 肯尼亚的,肯尼亚人的. ②*n.* 肯尼亚人.

Ken·yon [ˈkenjən] *n.* 凯尼恩〔姓氏〕.

ke·os [ˈkeiɔs] = kea.

ke·pi [ˈkeipiː,ˈkepiː] *n.* (有平圆顶及水平帽沿的)法国军帽.

Kep·ler [ˈkeplə], **Johann** 约翰·开普勒〔1571—1630,德国天文学家,物理学家〕. ～**'s laws** 行星运动三定律. **-ian** *a.* J. 开普勒的.

Kep·pel [ˈkepəl] *n.* 凯珀尔〔姓氏〕.

kept [kept] keep 的过去式及过去分词. — *a.* 被收买的,受人供养的;受人控制的. *the* ～ *press* 御用报纸. *a* ～ *woman* 情妇,外室.

ker- [kəː]〔象声词〕*comb. f.* 表示强烈的砰击,撞击声,如: *ker*plunk (击水的砰声).

Ker·a·la [ˈkerələ] *n.* 喀拉拉〔印度邦名〕.

ke·ram·ic [kiˈræmik] *a.* = ceramic.

ke·ram·ics [kiˈræmiks] *n.* = ceramics.

ker·a·tec·to·my [ˌkerəˈtektəmi] *n.* (*pl.* *-mies*)【医】角膜切除术.

ker·a·tin [ˈkerətin] *n.*【生化】角蛋白,角朊.

ker·a·ti·tis [ˌkerəˈtaitis] *n.*【医】角膜炎.

ker·a·t(o)- *comb. f.* 表示"角","角质": *kerato*plasty.

ker·a·tog·e·nous [ˌkerəˈtɔdʒənəs] *a.*【解】引起角质组织生长的.

ker·a·toid [ˈkerəˌtɔid] *a.* 角状的;角质的.

ker·a·to·plas·ty [ˈkerətəuplæsti] *n.* (*pl.* *-ties*)【医】角膜成形术.

ker·a·tose [ˈkerətəus] *a.* 角质的. — *n.* 角质物.

ker·a·to·sis [ˌkerəˈtəusis] *n.* (*pl.* *-ses* [-siːz])【医】①皮肤的角质生长〔如疣〕. ②角化症.

ker·a·tot·o·my [ˌkerəˈtɔtəmi] *n.* (*pl.* *-mies*)【医】角膜切开术.

kerb [kəːb] *n.*〔英〕①(街道的)路边镶边石. ②井栏(= curb) *on the* ～ 场外交易,交易所收场后的买卖. ～ **drill** (行人横穿马路演习的)简便规章. ～ **market** 场外证券市场. ～**stone**〔英〕= curbstone. ～ **weight** (无人无货的汽车)空载重量.

ker·chief [ˈkəːtʃif] *n.* (*pl.* ～*s*, *-chieves*) ①(妇女的)头巾;围巾. ②〔诗〕手巾,手帕. **-ed** *a.* 包着头巾的,围着围巾的.

Ke·res [ˈkerəs] *n.* (*sing., pl.*) ①克勒斯人〔新墨西哥的七个印第安人村庄的居民〕. ②克勒斯语(= Keresan).

kerf [kəːf] *n.* ①(斧、锯等的)劈痕,截口;【机】(气割的)切缝. ②切割下之物. — *vt.* 在(木材等)上锯切口.

ker·fuf·fle [kə(ː)ˈfʌfəl] *n.* 混乱,骚动,动乱.

ker·mes [ˈkəːmi(ː)z] *n.* ①虫胭脂,胭脂虫粉. ②(胭脂虫寄生的)胭脂虫栎(= ～ oak). ③【矿】硫氧锑矿.

ker·mess, ker·mis [ˈkəːmes, ˈkəːmis] *n.* ①(荷兰、比利时等国的)露天集市;露天狂欢. ②〔美〕热闹的义卖集市[游艺].

Ker·mit [ˈkəːmit] *n.* 克米特〔姓氏,男子名〕.

Kern [kəːn] *n.* ①克恩〔姓氏〕. ②**Jerome** ～ 杰罗姆·克恩〔1885—1945,美国作曲家〕.

kern[1] [kəːn]〔英方〕*vt., vi.* 结(果实). — *n.* (果实的)核;仁;颗粒.【物】～ **oscillation** 核振荡.

kern[2]**, kerne** [kəːn] *n.* ①(古爱尔兰的)轻步兵. ②爱尔兰农夫,乡下人.

ker·nel [ˈkəːnl] *n.* ①(果实的)核,仁. ②谷粒,麦粒. ③内核,核心,要点. ④【原】原子实,原子核. ⑤【数】(积分方程的)影响函数核. ⑥【机】模芯. ⑦【电】(带电导体中)零磁场强度线. *the* ～ *of the question* 问题的核心,问题的要点. —*vt.* 把…包在核内. ～ **sentence**【语法】(生成语法中的)核心句. **-(l)ed** *a.* 有核[仁]的.

ker·nic·ter·us [kəːˈniktərəs] *n.*【医】核黄疸.

kern·ite [ˈkəːnait] *n.*【地】四水硼砂.

ker·o·gen [ˈkerədʒən] *n.*【矿】油母质,油原. ～ **shale** 油页岩.

ker·o·sene, ker·o·sine [ˈkerəsiːn] *n.* 煤油,火油(= ～ oil). *a* ～ *lamp*〔美〕煤油灯.

ker·plunk [kəːˈplʌŋk] *ad.* (击水的)扑通声.

Kerr [kɑː, kəː] *n.* 克尔〔姓氏〕.

ker·ri·a [ˈkeriə] *n.*【植】棣棠属 (*kerria*) 植物〔尤指棣棠花 (*kerria japonica*)〕.

Ker·ry [ˈkeri] *n.* 克里〔男子名〕.

ker·sey [ˈkəːzi] *n.* (英国)克瑟手织窄面斜纹呢;〔*pl.*〕克瑟斜纹呢织品.

ker·sey·mere [ˈkəːzimiə] *n.* 斜纹细毛料,开士米毛料(= cassimere).

ke·ryg·ma [kəˈrigmə] *n.*【宗】①宣讲福音. ②宣讲中强调福音的要旨. **ker·yg·mat·ic** [ˌkerigˈmætik] *a.*

kes·trel [ˈkestrəl] *n.*【动】茶隼.

ketch [ketʃ] *n.*【海】双桅船.

ketch·up [ˈketʃəp] *n.* 番茄沙司,番茄酱.

ke·tene [ˈkiːtiːn] *n.*【化】①乙烯酮. ②烯酮.

ket(o)- *comb. f.* 表示"酮": *ketone*, *keto*genic.

ke·to·gen·e·sis [ˌkiːtəuˈdʒenisis] *n.*【化】生酮作用. **ke·to·gen·ic** *a.*

ke·tol [ˈkiːtəul, -tɔːl] *n.*【化】乙酮醇.

ke·tone [ˈkiːtəun] *n.*【化】酮. ～ **body**【化】酮体. **ke·ton·ic** *a.*

ke·to·ne·mi·a [ˌkiːtəuˈniːmiə] *n.*【医】酮血症.

ke·to·nu·ri·a [ˌkiːtəuˈnjuəriə] *n.*【医】酮尿.

ke·tose [ˈkiːtəus] *n.* 酮糖.

ke·to·sis [kiːˈtəusis] *n.*【医】酮病.

ke·to·ster·oid [ˌkiːtəuˈstiərɔid] *n.* 酮类固醇.

Ket·ter·ing [ˈketəriŋ] *n.* 凯特灵〔姓氏〕.

ket·tle [ˈketl] *n.* ①(烧水用的)水壶,水锅. ②小汽锅. ③【地】锅穴 (= ~ hole). *A watched ~ never boils.* 〔谚〕看着的水壶永不开〔性急也无用〕. ***a (pretty) ~ of fish*** ①困境,窘境,尴尬的境地. ②要处理的事情. ~ **holder** *n.* (锅把的)布套.

ket·tle·drum [ˈketldrʌm] *n.* (打击乐器中的)铜鼓. **-mer** *n.* 击鼓人.

kev, Kev [kev] *n. (sing., pl.)* 千电子伏特.

kev·el [ˈkevəl] *n.* 【海】缆耳,盘绳栓. ★小型的称作cleat.

Kew(Gardens) [kjuː] *n.* 伦敦西郊国立植物园.

kew·pie [ˈkjuːpiː] *n.* (有手有卷发的圆脸蛋)洋娃娃.

Kew·pie doll [ˈkjuːpiː dɔl] 丘比洋娃娃〔商标名〕.

key[1] [kiː] *n.* ①钥匙. ②要害,关口,要冲. ③关键,线索;秘诀;解法. ④(外国书的)直译本,图例,题解,图解,解释. ⑤【乐】调,主音调;(思想、表现等的)基调,调子. ⑥(上钟表发条等的)钥匙;【机】楔,栓,销子. ⑦【电】电键,电钥. ⑧【建】板条间灰泥,初涂;拱顶石,冠石. ⑨〔常 *pl.*〕(钢琴等的)键,(打字机的)键盘. ⑩〔*pl.*〕精神权威(尤指教皇权). ⑪【植】翅果. *false [skeleton] ~* 配制的钥匙. *master ~* 万能钥匙. *turn the ~* 转动钥匙;开锁. *Aden, the ~ to the Middle East* 亚丁—中东的咽喉. *a ~ to one's success* 成功的秘诀. *the ~ to a riddle* 谜底. *the ~ to the code* 电码索引. *a high [low] ~* 高昂[低沉]的调子. *all in the same ~* 千篇一律. *a chromatic ~* 钢琴等的黑键. *a natural ~* 钢琴等的白键. ***get [have] the ~ of the street*** 被关在屋外;流浪街头. ***hold the ~s of*** 支配,控制. ***in a minor ~*** 用低调;带着阴郁的情绪. ***lay[put] the ~ under the door*** 闭门而去. ***the golden [silver] ~*** 贿金. ***the House of Keys*** 英国萌岛 (Isle of Man) 的下院. ***the king's [queen's] ~s*** 警察破门捕人时所用的器具. ***the power of the ~s*** 教皇的权威. ***under lock and ~*** 郑重保管. — *vt.* ①锁上;插上(栓等) *(in; on)*. ②【乐】调整…的调子,给…调音. ③【建】用拱顶石装饰 *(in)*. ④键控,发(报). ⑤为…提供解决的线索[答案]. ⑥用动植物特征分类表鉴定(生物标本). ⑦使(绘画等)具有某种色调[色彩]. *~ a piano* 调整钢琴的音调. *~ the strings* 调弦. — *vi.* 使用钥匙. ~ ***off [out]*** 【电】切断. ~ ***on*** 【电】接通. ~ ***up*** ①使升调门;使紧张,鼓舞. ②提出(要求等). — *a.* 主要的. *the ~ industries* 主要工业,基本工业. *a ~ man* 要人,核心人物 *(cf. ~ man)*. *a ~ point* 要点. *a ~ position*据点;要职. ~ **atom** 【物】钥原子. ~ **bed** 【地】标准层. ~ **board** ①*n.* (钢琴、打字机等的)键盘;挂钥匙的板. ③*vi.* 操作键盘字排字机. ③*vt.* 向(自动键盘)进料,操纵(自动开关). ~ **cabinet** 电话控制盒. ~ **club** 钥匙俱乐部〔西方私人夜总会,成员自带钥匙〕. ~ **colour** 基本色. ~ **diagram** 概略原理图,解说图. ~ **drawing** 解释图;索引图. ~-**frame** (电)键架. ~ **fruit** 【植】翅果〔如枫树、榆树等果实〕. ~ **groove** 链槽. ~**hole** ① *n.* 锁眼;栓孔;钥匙孔 *(listen at [spy through] the ~ hole* 由锁眼里面偷听[看]). ② *a.* 透露内情的 *(a ~hole reporter* 报道内幕的记者). ~ **instruction** 【计】引导指令. ~ **light** 主灯光,基本灯光. ~**man** 要人,骨干分子,中心人物. ~ **metal** (有色金属)母合金. ~ **modulation** 键控调制. ~ **money** (房地产经济人索取的)额外小费,顶费,挖费. ~ **note** ①*n.*【乐】主调音,基音;主旨,要旨,基调 *(give the ~note to* 决定…的主要方针. *strike (sound)the ~note of* 揣摩[试探]…的主要动向). ②*vt.* 〔美〕在(会议等场合)发表施政方针;给…定下基调. ~-**noter** *n.* 定基调的人,作主要讲话的人. ~ **pattern** 卍字花纹. ~ **punch** 键控穿孔器. ~ **ring** 钥匙圈. ~ **seat** = ~way. ~ **sender** 电键发送器. ~**sending** 电键选择[拨号]. ~ **signature** 【乐】调号. ~ **source** 密码索引,密码本. ~**stone** ①【建】拱顶石,冠石,塞缝石. ②【无】梯形失真(光栅). ③要旨,根本原理. ~**way** *n.* 【机】键槽,销座;锁槽. ~ **well** 关键井;基准井;基准钻孔;注入井,加压油井,控制井.

key[2] [kiː] *n.* 礁,暗礁 (= cay, quay).

keyed [kiːd] *a.* ①带键的〔如键盘乐器〕. ②【建】用拱顶石加固的. ③定调的;调子…的〔常用以构成复合词〕. ④使调子和谐一致的.

key·er [ˈkiːə] *n.* ①【无】电键器;键控器;调制器;控制器. ②定时器,计时器.

Keyes [kiːz, kaiz] *n.* 凯斯〔姓氏〕.

Keynes [keinz] *n.* ①凯恩斯〔姓氏〕. ②**John Maynard ~** 约翰·梅纳德·凯恩斯〔1883—1946,英国经济学家和作家〕.

Keynes·i·an [ˈkeinziən] *a.* 凯恩斯理论的;符合凯恩斯理论的. — *n.* 凯恩斯主义者. **-an·ism** *n.*

Key·stone [ˈkiːstəun] *a.* 吉斯通式的〔指类似吉斯通电影公司拍的庸俗喜剧无声片,如描绘一群愚蠢无能的警察 (Keystone Kops) 疯狂追捕的场面〕. **K- State** 宾夕法尼亚州的浑名.

K.G. = Knight of the Garter〔英〕嘉德勋爵士.

kg. =①keg(s). ②kilogram(me)(s).

K.G.B., KGB = 〔Russ.〕***Komitet Gosudarstvennoi Bezopasnosti*** *(= Committee of State Security)* 克格勃〔苏联国家安全委员会〕.

kg-m = kilogram-meter, 公斤-米,千克-米.

Kgs. = Kings (O.T.)〔《旧约全书》中的《列王纪》〕.

Kha·ba·rovsk [xɑːˈbɑːrəfsk] *n.* 哈巴罗夫斯克〔即伯力〕〔苏联城市〕.

kha·di [ˈkɑːdi] *n.* 印度土布(= khaddar).

khaf [hɑːf, hɔːf] *n.* 希伯来语第十一个字母 *(kaf)* 的变体.

kha·ki [ˈkɑːki] *a.* ①土黄色的. ②卡其布的. — *n. (pl. ~s)* ①卡其布. ②土黄色. ③〔*pl.*〕卡其布军服,卡其布裤子. ***be in ~*** 是军人. ***get into ~*** 参军,入伍. ~ **election** 〔英〕利用紧张局势博取多数人投票的选举.

kha·lif(a) [kɑːˈliːfə] *n.* = caliph.

kha·li·fat(e) [ˈkɑːlifæt] *n.* = caliphate.

Khal·khas [ˈkælkɑz] *n.* 柯尔克孜族;柯尔克孜族人.

kham·sin [ˈkæmsin, kæmˈsiːn] *n.* 喀新风〔埃及的一种干热南风〕.

khan[1] [kɑːn, kæn] *n.*【史】可汗〔古代土耳其、鞑靼、蒙古、突厥各族最高统治者的尊称〕. ②汗〔古代中亚,阿富汗等国统治者和官吏的尊称〕.

khan[2] [kɑːn, kæn] *n.* (土耳其等地供旅行者停宿的)简陋驿店,商栈.

khan·ate [ˈkɑːneit, ˈkæn-] *n.* 可汗的领土,汗国.

khaph [hɑːf, hɔːf] *n.* = khaf.

kha·pra beetle [ˈkɑːprə]【动】谷斑皮蠹 *(Trogoderma granarium)* 〔伤害谷物的一种毁灭性害虫,原生于南亚和东南亚〕.

Khar·kov [ˈkɑːkɔf] *n.* 哈尔科夫〔苏联城市〕.

Khar·t(o)um [kɑːˈtuːm] *n.* 喀土穆〔苏丹首都〕.

khat [kɑːt] *n.* 阿拉伯茶 *(Catha edulis)* 〔产于非洲和阿拉伯,鲜叶可嚼或泡茶〕.

khed·ah [ˈkedə] *n.* 捕象陷阱 (= keddah).

khe·dive [kəˈdiv] *n.* 埃及总督〔1867—1914 年土耳其驻埃及代表的尊称〕.

khet, kheth [het] *n.* = het.

khi [kai] *n.* = chi〔希腊语字母表第 22 字母〕.

Khmer [kəˈmeə] *n.* ①高棉人. ②高棉语.

Khoi·san [ˈkɔisɑːn] *n.* (南非)克瓦桑语族〔包括霍屯督语 *(Hottentot)* 和布须曼语 *(Bushman)*〕.

Khond [kɔnd] *n.* 孔德人〔印度中东部德拉维德各部落的居民〕.

Khor·ram·shahr [ˌkɔːrəmˈʃɑː] *n.* 霍拉姆沙赫尔〔伊朗港市〕.

Kho·war [ˈkəuwɑː] *n.* 高瓦尔语〔巴基斯坦西北部使用

的一种印度—伊朗语〕.

Khrush·chev [kruːʃ'tʃɔːf], **N. S.** 赫鲁晓夫〔1894—1971,曾任苏联部长会议主席(1958—1964)〕.

khud [kʌd] *n.* 〔Hind.〕悬崖,绝壁;峡谷. *a ~ stick* 爬山杖.

khus·khus ['kʌskəs] *n.* (印度)须芒草茎〔可做扇子〕(= cuscus).

kHz = kilohertz.

Ki. = Kings.

KIA = killed in action 阵亡.

ki·ang [kiː'æŋ] *n.* (内蒙古、西藏的)骞驴 *(Equus kiang)*.

kib·ble[1] ['kibl] *n.* (凿井用的)铁吊桶.

kib·ble[2] ['kibl] *vt.* 把…磨成粗粒;把…压成碎块. *~d biscuits* 压碎的饼干 — *n.* (磨成粗粒[压成碎块]的)食物[狗食等].

kib·butz [ki'buːts, -'buts] *n.* *(pl. **-but·zim** [ˌkiːbuː'tsiːm])* (以色列)集居区〔尤指集体农场〕.

kib·butz·nik [ki'buːtsnik] *n.* (以色列)集居区居民;集体农场农民.

kibe [kaib] *n.* 〔古〕冻疮(尤指脚后跟的冻疮). ***gall [tread on] sb.'s ~s*** 触及某人痛处,伤害某人感情.

ki·bit·ka [ki'bitkə] *n.* 〔Russ.〕①(鞑靼人的)圆顶帐篷. ②(俄国)有篷顶的乡下雪车.

kib·itz ['kibits] *vi.* 〔口〕(牌戏旁观者等)多嘴,乱出主意;多管闲事. — *vt.* (看牌戏等时)对(牌戏等)乱出主意. *~ a card game* 看玩纸牌时乱出主意.

kib·itz·er ['kibitsə] *n.* (观看牌戏等时)乱出主意的人,多管闲事的人.

kib·lah ['kiblɑː] *n.* 〔Ar.〕穆斯林朝觐的方向〔即朝着麦加殿堂的方向〕.

ki·bosh ['kaibɔʃ] *n.* 〔俚〕胡说. ***put the ~ on*** 使彻底失败,挫败,制服 (*Another such injury will put the ~ on his athletic career.* 再受一次这样的伤,就会使他的运动事业告吹).

kick[1] [kik] *vt.* ①踢. ②【机】朝…反冲,(枪炮等)向…后坐. ③〔美俚〕拒绝(求婚者);申斥;解雇. ④戒除(毒瘾). ⑤(足球)踢球(得分). ⑥使(汽车)加速. *~ the ball back* 把球踢回去. *~ the car into higher gear* 给汽车挂快档. *The gun ~ed his shoulders.* 枪因后坐力的作用撞上他的肩膀. *~ goal* 踢进一球得分. — *vi.* ①踢. ②(枪炮等)后坐;【机】反冲;(仪表指针)急冲,突跳. ③〔口〕反对,反抗;发牢骚. ④【板球】反跃 *(up)*. ⑤〔俚〕死. *That horse ~s.* 那匹马老爱踢. *~ **about*** = ~ around. *~ **against [at]*** 向…踢;反对,反抗,拒绝 (*~ against [at] harsh treatment* 对虐待表示抗议). *~ **around*** 〔口〕①仗势欺人. ②到处流浪;经常改变行业. ③从各个角度考虑[调查,讨论等]. ④海阔天空地随便聊. *~ **back*** ①踢回;反冲;〔口〕突然退缩. ②〔美俚〕退赔(赃物). ③交付(租金、佣金、酬金等). *~ **in*** ①破门而入. ②〔俚〕死. ③〔美〕捐(款),捐助;清还. *~ **off*** ①踢脱(鞋等). ②(足球)中线开球;开始(某种活动). ③〔俚〕翘辫子,死. *~ **oneself*** 严厉自责. *~ **out*** ①踢出. ②踢足球出界. ③〔口〕逐出,解雇,开除. *~ **sb. downstairs*** 把某人踢下楼;撵走,赶出. *~ **sb. upstairs*** 把某人踢上楼;明升暗降. *~ **the bucket*** 〔俚〕翘辫子,死去. *~ **the clouds [wind]*** 被绞死. *~ **up*** 踢起(灰尘);引起(骚动). *~ **up a dust [fuss, row, shindy, shine]*** 〔俚〕引起骚扰. *~ **up its heels*** (马)溜腿. *~ **up one's heels*** ①高兴得跳起来. ②活跃一阵. ③〔俚〕翘辫子,死去. — *n.* ①踢;踢伤. ②反冲;反应力,反击力;(枪炮等的)后坐力;(赛跑等的)冲刺力. ③〔口〕反对,拒绝;牢骚. ④踢足球;踢足球的人. ⑤〔口〕(酒等的)刺激;极度的兴奋[快感]. ⑥〔英俚〕六便士硬币. ⑦〔俚〕戏闹;猛烈出击. ⑧〔俚〕提高. ⑨〔the ~〕〔俚〕解雇,撤职. *a death-bed [dying, last] ~* 垂死挣扎. *give a ~ at* 踢一踢. *The bruise was caused by a ~.* 这伤痕是脚踢的. *I have no ~ against that.* 我对于那一点并无异议. *a bad ~* 足球踢得糟的人. *a good ~* 踢足球的好手. *get a big ~ out of ...* 〔美俚〕从…得到极大的快感[愉快]. *a whiskey with lots of ~ in it* 劲儿很足的威士忌酒. *There is not much ~ in the cocktail.* 这种鸡尾酒没有多少劲儿. *two and a ~* 二先令六便士. *a demand for a salary ~* 要求增加工资. *have no ~ left* 〔口〕无力反抗,无反击力. ***a ~ in one's gallop*** 〔俚〕异想天开. ***a ~ in the pants [teeth]*** 意想不到的挫折. ***get the ~*** 〔俚〕被解雇. ***give sb. the ~*** 免某人职,解雇某人. ***(get) more ~s than halfpence*** 未受优待反遭虐待,很费力气而很少获利,得不偿失. ***on a ~*** 〔美俚〕正在迷恋. ***off a ~*** 不再迷恋. **~back** ①〔口〕强烈的反应. ②〔俚〕佣金[酬金、回扣等]的支付. ③佣金,酬金,回扣. **~ball** 儿童垒足球〔垒球规则的足球游戏〕. **~-it centre** (美国)戒毒中心. **~off** *n.* ①(足球)开球. ②(战役或运动等)开始;首回. **~on** (自动寻线机)跳出. **~out** *n.* ①(足球中的)踢球出界. ②〔口〕撵走;撤职,解雇. **~ pleat** 运动褶裙. **~ sorter** 〔口〕振辐分析器,选分仪. **~stand** 自行车或摩托车支架;撑脚架. **~ starter** (摩托车等的)反冲式起动器. **~ transformer** 脉冲变压器. **~ turn** 活动[转动]撑架. **~up** 〔口〕骚乱;吵闹,鼓噪.

kick[2] [kik] *n.* (玻璃瓶等的)凹底.

Kick·a·poo ['kikəˌpuː] *n.* *(pl. ~(s))* ①克卡普人〔墨西哥阿尔衮琴印第安人部落的人〕. ②克卡普语.

kick·er ['kikə] *n.* ①踢的人. ②爱踢的马. ③〔口〕爱唱反调的人,发牢骚者. ④(枪炮中的)送弹装置. ⑤【宇】喷射器;抛掷器. ⑥〔俚〕未料到的困难;隐藏的难点. ⑦〔俚〕出乎意料的结局;突然的转折. ⑧〔俚〕(游艇等艇身之外的)辅助发动机.

kick·shaw ['kikʃɔː] *n.* ①佳肴;特别讲究的菜. ②华而不实的小玩意儿.

kid[1] [kid] *n.* ①小山羊;小羚羊. ②小山羊皮;(食用)小山羊肉;〔*pl.*〕小山羊皮手套[皮鞋]. ③〔口〕孩子,少年,儿童. — *a.* ①小山羊皮制的. ②较幼的. *my ~ brother (sister)* 我的小弟弟(妹妹). *a ~ prof* 〔美俚〕年轻教授[讲师] *the ~ lay* 抢夺[偷]外出购物的儿童的钱〔盗贼用语〕. — *vi., vt.* (山羊,羚羊等)产(仔). **~-glove(d)** *a.* 温和的;过分讲究的;考虑周到的 (*~glove(d) methods* 软的手段). **~ gloves** 羔皮手套 (*handle with ~ gloves* 〔口〕小心而巧妙地处理[对待];作圆通处理). **~skin** 羊羔皮〔制鞋、手套用〕. **~(s') stuff** 〔俚〕适合于孩子的东西;极简单容易的东西.

kid[2] [kid] *n.* 嘲弄;欺骗. — *vt.* ①欺骗;愚弄. ②取笑,戏弄. *It's the truth; I wouldn't ~ you.* 这是真的,我不骗你. —*vi.* 戏弄,取闹 *(around)*. *No ~ding.* 别开玩笑.

kid[3] [kid] *n.* (水手盛食物的)小木桶.

Kidd [kid] *n.* 基德〔姓氏〕.

Kid·der·min·ster ['kidəminstə] *n.* (英国基德明斯特市所产两面花纹颜色相反的)双面提花地毯.

kid·die ['kidi] *n.* = kiddy.

kid·dle ['kidl] *n.* 鱼梁;鱼簖〔捕鱼的一种工具〕.

kid·dush [ki'duːʃ, 'kiduʃ] *n.* 【犹】吉都什〔节日和安息日(星期六)前夕举行的祝福仪式〕.

kid·dy, ['kidi] *n.* *(pl. -dies)* 〔口〕小家伙,小孩〔kid 的昵称〕. *~* **car** 小孩玩的三轮脚踏车.

kid·nap ['kidnæp] *vt.* (〔英〕*-pp-*) 诱拐(小孩等);绑架.

kid·nap·ee ['kidnæpi] *n.* 〔美〕被绑架的人,肉票.

kid·nap·per ['kidnæpə] *n.* 拐子;绑架者.

kid·ney ['kidni] *n.* ①【解】肾. ②(动物的)腰子〔供食用〕. ③脾气,性格. *a man of that ~* 那一种脾气的人. *a man of the right ~* 脾气好的人. *artifical ~* 人工肾. **~basin** 腰盘. **~beans** 菜豆;肾形豆. **~ machine** = artifical ~. **~ ore** 肾状矿石. **~ potato** 卵形马铃薯. **~-shaped** *a.* 肾形的. **~ stone** 【医】肾结石.

kid·ol·o·gy [ki'dɔlədʒi] *n.* 儿童心理学.

kief [kiːf] *n.* = keef.

kiel·ba·sa [kiːlˈbɑːsə] *n.* (*pl.* **-si** [-siː], ~*s*) 〔Pol.〕波兰熏肠.

Kiel [kiːl] *n.* 基尔〔德意志联邦共和国港市〕. ~ **Canal** 基尔运河.

kier [kiə] *n.* (漂白、染色用的)煮布锅.

kie·sel·guhr, kie·sel·gur [ˈkiːzlguə] *n.* 【地】硅藻土.

kie·ser·ite [ˈkiːzərait] *n.* 【地】硫镁矾,水镁矾.

Ki·ev [ˈkiːev] *n.* 基辅〔苏联城市〕.

kif [kif] *n.* = kef.

Ki·ga·li [kiˈgɑːli] *n.* 基加利〔卢旺达首都〕.

kike [kaik] *n.* 〔俚、蔑〕犹太人.

Ki·kon·go [kiːˈkɔŋgəu] *n.* ①刚果人〔即班图人〕. ②刚果语〔即班图语〕.

Ki·ku·yu [kiˈkuːjuː] *n.* ①(*pl.* ~(*s*)) 吉库尤人〔肯尼亚从事农业生产者〕. ②吉库尤语〔吉库尤人讲的班图语〕.

kil. = kilometre(s).

kil·der·kin [ˈkildəkin] *n.* ①基德尔钦〔英国旧容量单位,等于 16—18 加仑,即 1/2 桶 (barrel)〕. ②(装液体等的)小桶.

kil·erg [ˈkiləːg] *n.* 【物】千尔格〔功的单位〕.

Kil·i·man·ja·ro [ˈkilimənˈdʒɑːrəu], **Mount** 乞力马扎罗山〔非洲最高峰,高 19,321 英尺〕.

kill[1] [kil] *vt.* ①杀死,弄死;屠宰,屠杀. ②扼杀,毁掉. ③消磨(时间). ④中和;抵销. ⑤否决(议案等);(断然)拒绝(申请等). ⑥涂掉,删去. ⑦(网球等中的)杀(球). ⑧〔口〕使着迷,使感到有趣. ⑨煞住,使停住,使(机器等)停止运转;切断(电流). ⑩耗尽;喝光,吃光. ⑪使(声音)降低〔消失〕. ⑫使筋疲力尽. 喝光. *be ~ed in action* 阵亡,战死沙场. *The frost ~ed the seedings.* 严霜把幼苗冻坏了. ~ *sb.'s appetite* 使某人倒胃口. *The news ~ed their hopes.* 这消息使他们的希望破灭. ~ *time* 消磨时间. *The wallpaper ~s the furniture.* 家具给糊墙纸衬得不好看了. ~ *a bill* 否决议案. ~ *a petition* 毅然拒绝申请. *The editor ~ed the local item.* 编辑把地方新闻删去了. *The funny play nearly ~ed me.* 这个有趣的剧几乎把我笑死了. ~ *a live circuit* 截断通电电路. ~ *an engine* 使发动机停火. ~ *one's hunger* 充饥. ~ *the pain* 止痛. *They ~ed a bottle of wine.* 他们把一瓶酒喝完了. — *vi.* ①杀,杀害;被杀死. ②(植物等)被弄死;(家畜等)适于屠宰. ③产生不可抗拒的效果. *Thou shalt not ~.* 不可杀人. *These flowers ~ easily.* 这些花很容易枯死. *The ox ~ well.* 牛的出肉率高. ***be dressed [got up] to ~*** 着意打扮以求迷人. ~ ***down*** 杀死;冻死. ~ ***off [out]*** 杀光,消灭. ~ ***oneself to*** 〔接不定式〕〔美口〕费九牛二虎之力去(…). ~ ***or cure*** 孤注一掷,好歹 (*I'll try it, ~ or cure.* 不论吉凶祸福,我都要试一试). ~ ***two birds with one stone*** 〔谚〕一石二鸟,一举两得. ~ ***with kindness*** 爱之适以害之,宠坏. ***to ~*** 〔俚〕过分地,过度地. *dance to ~* 拼命地跳舞). — *n.* ①杀死,杀伤. ②(被打死的)猎获物. ③(网球等的)杀球. ④被击毁的敌机〔敌舰、敌潜艇等〕. *mass ~ weapons* 大规模杀伤武器. *a plentiful ~* 丰富的猎获物. ***be in at the ~*** ①猎物被杀时在场. ②事情结尾时在场. **~-devil** ①假饵. ②〔方〕一种甜酒;劣质廉价饮料. **~joy** *n.* 扫兴的人〔物〕. **~time** *n.* 用来消磨时间的事,消遣.

kill[2] [kil] *n.* 〔美方〕水路,小河〔常用作地名: Schuylkill, Catskill〕.

kill·deer [ˈkildiə] *n.* (*pl.* ~(*s*)) 【动】双胸斑沙鸻 (*Charadrius vociferus*) 〔北美所产一种小鸟,叫声又高又尖〕.

killed [ˈkild] *a.* ①被杀死的;被屠宰的. ②【冶】镇静的. ③【化】饱和了的. ④断开的. ⑤(疫苗等)不再有传染力的. ~ *lines* 断线. ~ **lime** 消石灰,失效石灰. ~ **steel** 优质钢,镇静钢.

kil·ler [ˈkilə] *n.* ①杀人者,凶手. ②逆戟鲸(=~ whale). ③杀死…的药剂〔东西〕,宰杀的器具. ④〔口〕迷人的人〔物〕. ⑤【无】限制器,抑制器,瞄准器. ⑤待屠宰的牲畜. *a humane ~* 使动物无痛苦的屠宰机. *a submarine ~* 防潜舰艇. *a weed ~* 除草药. *a noise ~* 噪声抑制器. *a robot ~* 雷达自动瞄准器. *a spot ~* 亮点消除器,余辉消除器. *That flowered hat is a real ~.* 那顶花帽真漂亮. ~ **boat** 捕鲸船. ~ **satellite** 拦截卫星.

kil·lick [ˈkilik] *n.* ①小锚,石锚. ②做锚用的石块.

kil·li·fish [ˈkilifiʃ] *n.* (*pl.* ~(*es*)) 【动】鳉科 (*Cyprinodontidae*) 鱼;底鳉.

kill·ing [ˈkiliŋ] *a.* ①致死的. ②使人疲乏的. ③〔口〕吸引人的,迷人的. ④〔口〕滑稽的. *a ~ disease* 致命的病. *a ~ work* 令人精疲力竭的工作. *a ~ caricature* 笑死人的漫画. — *n.* ①杀害,屠杀. ②(一次行猎的)猎获品. ③(交易等)赚的一笔大钱;突然获得的大成功: *make a ~ on silk deal* 做丝绸生意赚大钱. **-ly** *ad.* 〔口〕吸引人地,迷人地.

kil·lock [ˈkilək] *n.* = killick.

Kil·mer [ˈkilmə] *n.* 基尔默〔姓氏〕.

kiln [kiln] *n.* 窑. — *vt.* 在窑里烧制〔烘干〕. **~-dry** *vt.* 在窑内烘干. **~man** *n.* 烧窑工人.

kil·o- *comb. f.* 表示"千": *kilo*watt.

Ki·lo [ˈkiːləu] *n.* 通讯中用以代表字母 k 的词.

ki·lo [ˈkiːləu] *n.* ①公斤,千克 (= kilogram). ②公里,千米(= kilometer). ~ **bomb** 【军】轻燃烧弹,重一公斤的燃烧弹.

ki·lo [ˈkiːləu] (*pl.* ~*s*) *n.* = kilogramme, kilometre, kilolitre. &c.

kil·o·am·pere [ˈkiləuˌæmpeə] *n.* 千安培.

kil·o·bar [ˈkiləuˌbɑː] *n.* 千巴〔汽压单位〕.

kil·o·cal·o·rie [ˈkiləuˌkæləriː] *n.* 大卡,千卡〔热量单位〕.

kil·o·cu·rie [ˈkiləuˌkjuəri] *n.* 【原】千居里〔放射性强度单位〕.

kil·o·cy·cle [ˈkiləuˌsaikl] *n.* 【无】千周;千赫(兹).

kil·o·e·lec·tron-volt [ˈkiləuiˈlektrɔnˈvəult] *n.* 【原】千电子伏特.

kil·o·gram(me) [ˈkiləugræm] *n.* 公斤,千克.

kil·o·gram-me·tre, 〔美〕 **-ter** [ˈkiləgræmˈmiːtə] *n.* 【物】公斤米,千克米〔功的单位〕.

kil·o·hertz [ˈkiləuˌhəːts] *n.* (*pl.* **-hertz**) 千赫.

kil·o·li·ter, 〔英〕 **-tre** [ˈkiləuliːtə] *n.* 千升.

kil·o·me·ter, 〔英〕 **-tre** [ˈkiləuˌmiːtə] *n.* 千米,公里. **-met·ric, -ri·cal** *a.*

kil·o·par·sec [ˈkiləuˌpɑːˌsek] *n.* 【天】千秒差距.

kil·o·stere [ˈkiləustiə] *n.* 千立方米.

kil·o·ton [ˈkiləuˌtʌn] *n.* 千吨〔核爆力单位〕.

kil·o·var [ˈkiləuvɑː] *n.* 【电】千乏,无效千伏安.

kil·o·volt [ˈkiləuvəult] *n.* 【电】千伏(特).

kil·o·volt-am·pere [ˈkiləuˌvəultˈæmpeə] *n.* 千伏(特)安(培).

kil·o·watt [ˈkiləuwɔt] *n.* 【电】千瓦(特). **~-hour** 【电】千瓦(特)(小)时〔略作 K.W.H.〕. **~-meter** 千瓦计,电力计.

Kil·pat·rick [kilˈpætrik] *n.* 基尔帕特里克〔姓氏〕.

kilt [kilt] *n.* ①(苏格兰高地男子穿的)褶迭短裙〔通常用格子呢制做〕. ②(妇女和儿童穿的)苏格兰式短裙. —*vt.* 〔Scot.〕①卷起,捋起(裙等) (*up*). ②使(衣服)有直褶.

kil·ter [ˈkiltə] *n.* 〔美俚〕(身心等的)良好状态. *in ~* 情形好,舒服. *out of ~* 情形不好,不舒服.

kilt·ie [ˈkilti] *n.* (*pl.* ~*s*) 穿苏格兰高地短裙的人〔兵〕.

kim·ber·lite [ˈkimbəlait] *n.* 【地】角砾云橄岩,金伯利岩.

kim·chi [ˈkimtʃi] *n.* 〔Kor.〕朝鲜咸菜.

ki·mo·no [kiˈməunəu] *n.* (*pl.* ~*s*) 〔Jap.〕①和服. ②和

K

服式女晨衣。

kin [kin] *n.* ①〔集合词〕亲属，亲戚。②亲属关系。③家族，门第。④性质相似的东西；地位〔职业〕相近的人。*What ~ is he to you?* 他和你是什么关系？ *He comes of good ~.* 他出身好。*We are near of ~.* 我们是近亲。 — *a.* ①有亲属关系的。②同类的，同质的。*He is ~ to me.* 他是我的亲属。*We are ~.* 我们是亲属。**be ~ to** ①是…的亲戚。②类似，近于。**count ~ with** 〔Scot.〕①和…算亲属关系，和…是近亲。②和…比血统〔门第〕。**more ~ than kind** 亲戚不亲。**near of ~** 近亲。**next of ~** 【法】最近的亲族。**of ~** 有亲属关系（*They are not of ~.* 他们没有亲属关系）。**-less** *a.* 无家属〔亲属〕关系的。**-ship** *n.* 家属〔亲属〕关系；象家属〔亲属〕的密切关系。

-kin *suf.* 表示"小"：lamb*kin*, prince*kin*.

kin- *comb. f.* = kine.

kin·aes·the·si·a [ˌkinisˈθiːʒə] *n.* 【心】动觉（= kinesthesia, kinaesthesis）. **kin·aes·thet·ic** [-ˈθetik] *a.*

ki·nase [ˈkaineis, ˈkineis] *n.* 【生化】激酶。

kin·chin [ˈkintʃin] *n.* 〔俚〕小孩〔盗贼隐语〕。**the ~ lay** 〔盗贼俚〕抢〔偷〕外出购物小孩的钱。

kind[1] [kaind] *a.* ①厚道的，仁慈的，仁爱的；和蔼的。②亲切的。③〔古〕相爱的，充满柔情的。④容易处理的；(毛)柔软的；(矿石)易采的。 *be ~ to* 对…厚道。 *be so kind as to (do)* = *be ~ enough to (do)* 请…。*It is very ~ of you.* 谢谢你的好意。*It is very ~ of you to come.* 难得你来。*He has a ~ word for everybody.* 他对任何人说话都很恳切。*Your ~ attention will oblige.* 请您费心，拜托拜托。*Give my ~ regards to ....* 请代我向…问好。*with ~ regards* 祝好，致敬礼〔信尾用语〕。*stone ~ for dressing* 容易加工的石头。

kind[2] [kaind] *n.* ①种；类；属；〔贬〕帮，伙。②性质，本质。③实物，商品；同样的东西。④〔古〕天性；家族，世系。⑤〔古〕方式，方法。⑥【宗】圣餐用品，圣体〔指面包及葡萄酒〕。*that ~ of bread* 那一种面包。*the human ~* 人类。*the cat ~* 猫属。*many different ~s of things [stamps]* 许多不同种类的东西〔邮票〕。*He is not the ~ of person to lie.* 他不是那种说谎的人。*Hitler and his ~* 希特勒之流。*differ in ~, not merely in degree* 不仅程度不同，性质也不同。*act after one's ~* 按自己的一套作法办理。**a ~ of** ①一种，一类（*He is a ~ of fool.* 他是一种傻瓜。 *a of gentleman* 绅士一类的家伙）。②几分；稍稍（*have a ~ of feeling that ...* 有点感觉到…）。**all ~s of** 各种各样的。**in a ~** 有几分，在某种程度上。**in ~** ①用实物（*pay in ~* 用实物缴纳）。②以同样的方法(回敬)（*be repaid in ~ for one's rudenes* 以无礼回报无礼）。③性质上（*differ in ~* 性质上不同）。**~ of** 〔口〕有点儿；有几分（*I ~ of thought he would come.* 我有点儿感到他要来）。★ ~ of 常被说作 kind o', kind a' [ˈkaində], kinder [ˈkaində], 主要在形容词前，有时在动词前用作状语：*That's ~ o' good.* 那个还好。*He acted kinder ugly.* 他干得有点儿丢脸。*He ~ o' [kinder] laughed.* 他有点儿要笑。**nothing of the ~** 毫不相似，决不是那样（*I shall do nothing of the ~.* 我决不做这种事）。**of a ~** ①同一种类的(*Things of a ~ come together.* 物以类聚)。②徒有其名的；蹩脚的（*coffee of a ~* 徒有其名的咖啡）。**something of the ~** 那一类的东西。**these ~ of men** = **men of this kind** 〔口〕这样的人。**the worst ~** 〔美口〕极其，非常（*He loves this picture the worst ~.* 他极爱这张画）。

kind·a [ˈkaində] 〔口〕= kind of.

kin·der·gar·ten [ˈkindəˌgɑːtn] *n.* 幼儿园。**-er** = **kin·der·gart·ner** ①幼儿园老师〔保育员〕。②幼儿园的儿童。

kind-heart·ed [ˈkaindˈhɑːtid] *a.* 厚道的，仁慈的，富于同情心的。**-ly** *ad.* **-ness** *n.*

kin·dle [ˈkindl] *vt.* ①点燃，照耀。②煽动，鼓舞，激发。*~ an audience* 煽动听众。*~ sb. with [to] passion* 激发某人的感情。 — *vi.* ①着火，烧起来。②发亮；照耀。③兴奋，激动。*Her eyes ~d with excitement.* 她兴奋得两眼闪闪发光。

kin·dling [ˈkindliŋ] *n.* ①点火，燃烧。②〔常 *pl.*〕引火物；〔美〕引火柴（= ~ wood）. *His wagon was smashed into ~ wood.* 他的货车撞得稀烂。~ **point** 着火点，燃点。~ **temperature** 着火温度。

kind·ly [ˈkaindli] *a.* ①厚道的，亲切的；有同情心的，体贴的。②(气候等)温和的，宜人的；适于…的。③〔古〕自然的，天然的，天性的。④土生土长的。*a ~ heart* 慈悲心肠。*a ~ weather* 宜人的气候。*~ soil for crops* 适于耕作的土地。*the ~ fruits of the earth* 土地上生长的丰富果实。—*ad.* ①厚道地，亲切地；有同情心地，体贴地。②诚恳地，衷心地。③请〔客套语〕。④自然地，容易地。*be ~ treated* 受到亲切接待。 *Thank you ~.* 衷心地感谢你。*K- refrain from smoking.* 请勿吸烟。**take (sth.) ~** ①善意地解释(事物)。②诚恳地接受（忠告等）。**take ~ to** 自然而然地爱上了。 **-li·ly** *ad.* **-li·ness** *n.*

kind·ness [ˈkaindnis] *n.* ①厚道，亲切。②友好的态度〔行为〕，好意。*out of ~* 出于好意。*Will you do me a ~?* 你能帮我一下忙么？

kin·dred [ˈkindrid] *n.* ①宗族。②亲属〔亲戚〕关系；血缘关系。③〔集合词〕亲属；血缘族〔遗传学用语〕。④类似，同质 (*with*). *claim ~ with sb.* 声称与某人有亲戚关系。— *a.* ①亲属的；亲戚的；宗族的。②类似的，同种的，同源的，同性质的。*~ languages* 同源的语言。*~ tribes* 同族的部落。

kine[1] [kain] *n.* 〔*pl.*〕〔古〕母牛；牛。

kine[2] [ˈkini] *n.* = kinescope.

kine- *comb. f.* 表示"运动"：*kine*matic, *kine*tic.

kin·e·ma [ˈkinimə] *n.* 〔英〕= cinema.

ki·ne·mat·ic (al) [ˌkainiˈmætik(əl)] *a.* 【物】运动学(上)的。~ **design** 机动设计。**-i·cal·ly** *ad.*

ki·ne·mat·ics [ˌkainiˈmætiks] *n.* 【物】运动学。

kin·e·mat·o·graph [ˌkainiˈmætəgrɑːf] *n., vt., vi.* = cinematograph. **-y** *n.* **-ic** *a.*

ki·ne·mo·me·ter [ˌkainiˈmɔmitə] *n.* 【物】流速计〔表〕；感应式转速表，灵敏转速计。

kin·e·photo [ˈkainifəutə] *n.* 显象管录象，屏幕录象。~ *equipment* 屏幕录象设备。

kin·e·scope [ˈkiniskəup, ˈkaini-] *n.* ①(电视)显像管。②显象管录象；电视屏幕纪录片。 — *vt.* 拍摄(电视节目)的屏幕纪录片。*colour ~* 彩色显象管。~ **grid** 显象管控制栅极。~ **recorder** 屏幕录象机〔录象装置〕。~ **recording** 屏幕录象。

ki·ne·si·at·rics [kaiˌniːsiˈætriks] *n.* 【医】运动疗法〔用作单数〕。

ki·ne·sics [kiˈniːsiks, kai-] *n. pl.* 〔动词用单数〕人体动作学，举止神态学〔研究姿势、表情等非语言的人体动作与人际沟通的关系的一种科学〕。**ki·ne·sic** [-ˈnesik] *a.*

ki·ne·si·ol·o·gy [kaiˌniːsiˈɔlədʒi, ki-] *n.* 【医】人体运动学。

-kinesis *comb. f.* 表示"运动"：karyo*kinesis*.

ki·ne·si·the·ra·py [kaiˌniːsiˈθerəpi] *n.* 【医】运动疗法。

kin·es·the·si·a, -sis [ˌkainisˈθiːʒə, -sis] *n.* 【医】运动觉。 **kin·es·thet·ic** [-ˈθetik] *a.*

ki·net·ic [kaiˈnetik] *a.* ①【物】动力(学)的，运动的。②活动的，活跃的，能动的，有力的。*~ friction* 动摩擦。*the ~ molecular theory* 分子运动论。*~ theory of heat [gases]* 热〔气态〕运动论。*a man of ~ energy [force]* 精力充沛的人。 ~ **art** 动态艺术〔指部分设计成动态并配以音响、照明等的雕塑艺术〕。~ **energy** 动能。~ **friction** 动摩擦。

ki·net·ics [kaiˈnetiks] *n. pl.* 〔动词用作单数〕动力学。

K

ki•net•in [ˈkainətin] *n.*【植】激动素.

kinet•o- *comb. f.* 表示"运动": *kineto*graph, *kineto*scope.

ki•ne•to•graph [kaiˈniːtəgrɑːf] *n.* (早期的) 活动电影摄影机. **-er** *n.* **-ic** *a.*

ki•ne•to•phone [kaiˈniːtəˌfəun, kiˈniː-] *n.* (早期的)有声电影机.

ki•net•o•plast [kiˈniːtəˌplæst] *n.*【医】动基体.

ki•ne•to•scope [kaiˈniːtəskəup] *n.* (早期的) 活动电影放映机.

kin•folk(s) [ˈkinfəuk(s)] *n.* *(pl.)* 亲戚,亲属 (=kinsfolk).

king [kiŋ] *n.* ①王,国王,君主 *(opp.* subject*)*; (部落的)首领,魁首. ②(某界)巨子,…大王. ③王一样的东西. ④ (纸牌中的)老 K (国王); (国际象棋的)王; (西洋跳棋的)王棋. ⑤〔K-〕【宗】上帝,耶稣. ⑥(水果、植物等中)最上等品. ⑦〔The K-s〕(«旧约圣经»中的)«列王纪». *the K- of England* 英国国王. *a ~ of the Indians* 印第安人的首领. *an oil ~* 石油大王. *a pirate ~* 海盗头目. *a fur ~* 毛皮巨商. *a railway ~* 铁路大王. *the ~ of beasts* 百兽之王. *the ~ of birds* 鸟王 (指鹰). *K- of day* 太阳. *~ of fish* 鲸. *the ~ of gases.* 芥气. *the ~ of metals* 金. *the ~ of middles* 〔美〕【拳】中量级拳击选手. *the ~ of the jungle* 虎. *the ~ of the countryside* 土皇帝. *the ~ of the sea* 〔谑〕鲱鱼. *the ~ of pears* 上等品种的梨. *tragedy ~* 在悲剧中扮演主角的男演员. ***a K- Log*** 有名无实的君王,放任而无权的君王. ***a ~ of shreds and patches*** 专事抄袭的小文人. ***a K-stork*** 暴君. ***go up K- Street*** 〔澳〕破产. ***Kings go mad and the people suffer for it.*** 〔谚〕国王发狂,百姓遭殃. ***Kings have long arms [hands].*** 〔谚〕国王手长,百姓理短. ***more royalist than the ~*** 比国王还国王. ***The K- can do no wrong.*** 〔谚〕国王不会犯错误〔指国王无权,实权在内阁〕. ***turn King's [Queen's, State's] evidence*** 供出对同犯不利的证据. — *vi.* ①做国王. ②统治. — *vt.* 立…为王. *~ it* 做国王,统治; 称王称霸 *(over)*. **K- at [of] Arms** 英国主管纹章的长官. **~bird**【动】极乐鸟. **~bolt**【机】中心立轴; (汽车转向关节)主销; 大螺丝. **K- Charles's spaniel** 黑褐色长耳小狗. **~ cobra** 眼镜蛇 (眼镜王蛇) *(Naja harmah)*. **~crab** 鲎 (= horseshoe crab). **~craft** 统制者的统治权术. **~cup**【植】鳞茎毛茛; 驴蹄草. **~fish** ①食用大海鱼. ②〔美口〕头子,首领. **~fish•er** 翠鸟,鸩,鱼狗. **K- James Version** = Authorized Version. **K- Lear** ①«李尔王»〔莎士比亚悲剧名〕. ②该剧的主角李尔王〔传说中的英国国王〕. **~maker** *n.* ①〔谑〕(总统竞选时)候选人手下的竞选工作人员; 左右候选人选择的重要人物. ② 国王拥立者. **K- of Bliss [Glory, Heaven]** 神,基督. **K- of Kings** 神,上帝. **K- of the Castle** (小儿游戏中的)山寨大王. **~ oscillator** 主振荡器. **~pin** ①(滚球) 中柱. ②〔口〕首要人物,中心人物,领袖. ③ = ~bolt. **~ post**【建】人字架上的中柱,中柱,桁架中柱;【船】吊杆柱. **~-post truss**【建】单柱桁架. **~ salmon** 大鳞大麻哈鱼 **~-size(d)** *a.* ①特大的,特长的. ②不寻常的. **~ snake**【动】王蛇 *(Lampropeltis getulus)* 〔产于美国南部〕. **~truss**【建】 有中柱的桁架,单柱桁架. **~wood** ①(巴西) 西阿拉黄檀木. ②西阿拉黄檀树 *(Dalbergia cearensis)* **-King's Bench** 英国高等法院. **King's blue** = cobalt blue. **King's colour** 英军的团旗. **King's [Queen's] Council** 英国王室法律顾问. **King's [Queen's] English** 标准英语. **King's [Queen's] evidence**【法】刑事案件的揭发证词〔通常由同案犯提供〕. **King's evil** 瘰疬〔旧时认为此病经国王一触即可痊愈的迷信〕. **King's head** 〔俚〕邮票. **King's highway** ①水陆交通干线. ②行为的大道,正道. **King's picture [portrait]** 〔英俚〕钱. **King's pipe** 伦敦船坞内的焚毁炉. **King's silver** 纯银. **King's weather** 适合庆典时的晴朗天气. **King's yellow** = orpiment. **-less** *a.* 无国王的; 无政府状态的. **-let** ①小王,小国的王. ②【动】戴菊鸟. **-like** *a.* 国王似的. **-ling** 小王. **-ship** *n.* ①王位; 王权; 王尊. ②国王统治; 君主政体. ③陛下〔有时用作对君王的称谓,前面加 his〕.

king•dom [ˈkiŋdəm] *n.* ①王国. ②〔K-〕【宗】天国,神政. ③领域. ④界(指自然三界之一). *the United K-* (大不列颠与北爱尔兰)联合王国. *the ~ of God [heaven]* 天国. *the ~ of science* 科学领域. *The mind is the ~ of thought.* 头脑是思想的王国. *the animal [vegetable, mineral] ~* 动[植、矿]物界. ***come into one's ~*** 〔俚〕发迹,因继承财产而成为富翁; 飞黄腾达, 获得权力. ***~ come*** 〔口〕来世, 天国(*go to ~ come* 死. *send sb. to ~ come* 送某人上西天).

King•lake [ˈkiŋleik] *n.* 金莱克〔姓氏〕.

king•ly [ˈkiŋli] *a.* ①国王的; 君主地位的. ②国王似的; 适合国王身分的. ③君主政体的. *the ~ power* 王权. *a ~ crown* 王冠. *a ~ bearing* 君王的风度. — *ad.* 国王似地. **-li•ness** *n.*

Kings•ton [ˈkiŋstən] *n.* ①金斯敦〔牙买加首都〕. ②金斯敦〔诺福克岛首府〕. ③金斯敦〔圣文森特首府〕.

kink [kiŋk] *n.* ①(线、绳、索、头发等的)纽结,绞缠. ②乖僻,偏执; 怪想法,狂念. ③奇方妙法. ④(背、颈等处的)痉挛,抽筋. ⑤(计划的设想或机器设计等方面的)缺陷. — *vt., vi.* (使)纠结,(使)绞缠. **~-cough** *n.*【医】百日咳.

kin•ka•jou [ˈkiŋkədʒuː] *n.*【动】(中、南美产的)蜜熊.

kin•kle [ˈkiŋkl] *n.* ①(头发等的) 卷曲; 小纽结. ②〔喻〕模糊的暗示. —*vt., vi.* (使)卷曲,(使)纽结. **-d** *a.* 卷曲的,有小纽结的.

kink•y [ˈkiŋki] *a.* ①绞缠的; (头发)卷曲的. ②〔俚〕不正当的. ③〔英〕性情乖僻的,古怪的. *~ thread* 绞缠的线. **~-haired** *a.* 卷发的.

kin•ni•ki•nic(k) [ˌkinikiˈnik] *n.* (北美印第安人用树叶和树皮制成的)烟草代用品.

ki•no[1] [ˈkiːnəu] *n.* *(pl. ~s)* 桉树胶 (= ~ gum).

ki•no[2] [ˈkiːnəu] *n.* *(pl. ~s)* 电影院 (= cinematograph).

Kin•sey [ˈkinzi] *n.* 金西〔姓氏〕.

kins•folk [ˈkinzfəuk] *n.* 〔*pl.*〕〔集合词〕家属; 亲戚; 亲属. (亦作 *~s*).

Kin•sha•sa [kinˈʃɑːsə] *n.* 金沙萨〔扎伊尔首都〕.

kin•ship [ˈkinʃip] *n.* 亲属关系,亲戚关系.

kins•man [ˈkinzmən] *n.* ***(pl. -men)*** 男亲属.

kins•wom•an [ˈkinzˌwumən] *n.* ***(pl. -wom•en*** [-ˌwimin]*)* 女亲属.

kin•tal [ˈkintl] *n.* = quintal.

ki•osk [kiˈɔsk] *n.* ①(土耳其和波斯式的)凉亭,亭子. ②(车站、广场等处的)书报摊,音乐台,广告亭,公共电话间.

Kio•to [ˈkiəutəu] *n.* Kyoto.

Ki•o•wa [ˈkaiəuwɑː, -əwə] *n.* ①*(pl. ~(s))* 凯欧瓦人〔美国俄克拉何马州印第安人〕. ②凯欧瓦语.

kip[1] [kip] *n.* (没有鞣制过的)生幼兽皮〔小牛皮,羔羊皮〕.

kip[2] [kip] *n.* 〔俚〕旅店,客栈;床. — *vi.* 〔俚〕①睡觉; 住客栈. ②逃学.

kip[3] [kip] *n.* ***(pl. ~(s))*** (老挝货币单位)基普.

kip[4] [kip] *n.* 基普〔重量单位,相当于1,000 磅〕.

Kip•ling [ˈkipliŋ] *n.* ①基普林〔姓氏〕. ②**Rudyard ~** 拉迪亚德·基普林〔1865—1936,英国作家,诗人〕.

kip•per [ˈkipə] *n.* ①(产卵期或产卵后的) 雄鲑〔鳟鱼〕. ②熏〔腌〕鲑鱼〔鳟鱼〕. ③〔俚〕人,家伙. — *vt.* 腌制〔熏制、晒干〕(鲑、鲱等鱼).

Kir•by [ˈkəːbi] *n.* 柯比〔姓氏,男子名〕.

Kir•(g)hiz [ˈkəːgiz] *n.* ***(pl. ~(es))*** ①吉尔吉斯人. ②吉尔吉斯语.

Kir•(g)hi•zia [kəːˈgiːziə], **Kir•ghi•zia** [kəːˈgiːʒiə] *n* 吉尔吉斯〔苏联加盟共和国名〕. **-n** *a.*

ki•ri [ˈkiri] *n.* 〔Jap.〕(日本)泡桐树.

kirk [kəːk] *n.* 〔Scot.〕教会. **~man** ①苏格兰教会的

信徒．②〔Scot.〕教士，教徒．～-**session** 苏格兰教会基层理事会．

kir·mess [ˈkəːmis] *n.* kermess, kermis 的变体．

kirn [kəːn, kiən] *n.*〔Scot., 英方〕①收获节．②收获完毕的最后一捆．

kirsch·was·ser [ˈkiəʃvɑːsə] *n.*〔G.〕樱桃酒．

kir·tle [ˈkəːtl] *n.* ①女长袍；外裙．②〔古〕男外衣．

Ki·san·ga·ni [ˌkiːsənˈgɑːniː] *n.* 基桑加尼〔扎伊尔城市〕．

Ki·shi·nev [ˈkiʃinef] *n.* 基什尼奥夫〔苏联城市〕．

kish·ke [ˈkiʃkə] *n.* = derma (= kishka).

Kis·lev [ˈkislef] *n.*〔Heb.〕(犹太历)三月．

kis·met [ˈkismet] *n.*〔Turk.〕〔常 K-〕命运，天命〔亦作 kismat〕．

kiss [kis] *n.* ①吻．②〔诗〕(微风等的)轻拂，轻触，轻抚．③【台球】球与球的接触．④蛋白小甜饼；小糖果．⑤〔儿〕(奶、茶等上浮的)泡泡．*give a* ～ 接个吻．*snatch [steal] a* ～ 偷吻．***blow [throw] a*** ～ ***at [to] sb.*** 向某人飞吻 (= ～ ***one's hand to sb.***). ***Judas*** ～ 阴险的背叛，口蜜腹剑．— *vt.* ①吻．②〔诗〕(微风等)轻拂轻触，轻抚．～ *the baby on the cheek* = ～ *the baby's cheek* 吻婴儿的颊．～ *sb. goodby(e)* 吻别某人．～ *sth. goodby(e)* 无可奈何地失掉[去掉]某物．*The breeze* ～*ed the face* 轻风拂面．— *vi.* ①接吻．②轻触，轻抚．③【台球】(球与球的)接触．～ *and be friends* 接吻复归于好．*make glasses* ～ 碰杯．～ ***away*** ①吻掉(眼泪等)．②为女人花费金钱．～ ***hand [the hand]*** 吻(国王的)手〔一种正式的致意或大臣等就任时的仪式〕．～ ***off***〔俚〕拒绝；(无理地)把…解雇，开除．～ ***one's hand to sb.*** 向某人飞吻．～ ***the Bible [the book]*** 吻《圣经》宣誓．～ ***the canvas [resin]***〔美俚〕(在职业性拳击中)被击倒．～ ***the dust*** ①屈服．②被杀．～ ***the ground*** ①俯伏在地．②受辱．～ ***the hare's foot*** 迟到．～ ***the post*** 吃闭门羹．～ ***the rod*** 受罚．～-**in-the-ring** *n.*〔男女青年围成环状而相互追逐的〕追吻游戏．～-**me-quick** *n.* ①垂于额前的卷发．②(戴在头部后的)小罩帽．③【植】野生三色紫罗兰[虎耳草]．～ **of death** 表面上友好实际上坑害人的行为．～ **of life** (口对口的)人工呼吸；起死回生的措施．～**off** *n.*〔俚〕(特指粗暴无理的)解雇；开除．

kiss·er [ˈkisə] *n.* ①接吻者．②〔俚〕嘴；嘴唇；脸，面孔．

kiss·ing [ˈkisiŋ] *a.* ①接吻的．②轻触的，轻抚的．③关系亲密的．*be on* ～ *term with* … 同…交情不错．～ **bug** ①咬嘴唇、面孔等的害虫(如锥鼻虫)．②好接吻的人，想接吻的愿望 (*She's got the* ～ *bug.* 她有想接吻的意思)．～ **cousin [kin]** ①可以互行接吻礼的亲戚．②〔俚〕关系融洽的人，可以相容的事．～ **crust** (烘烤时面包与面包接触处形成的)面包软壳．～ **gate**〔英方〕(只能通过一人的)小门．～ **kind** = ～ **cousin.**

Kis·sin·ger [ˈkisəndʒə] *n.* 基辛格〔姓氏〕．

kist[1] [kist] *n.*〔Scot., 英方〕箱子；盒；柜子．

kist[2] [kist] *n.* = cist.

kit[1] [kit] *n.* ①〔方〕木桶；(盛鱼、黄油等的)小桶．②成套工具[用具、物件、器材、设备]；整套配件．③【军】士兵的个人装具．④工具箱；工具袋；用具包；(旅行等的)行装．⑤〔口〕全部；一群(人)；一套东西．*shoemaker's* ～ 一套鞋匠用具．～ *inspection*【军】装备检查．*a travel* ～ 一套旅行用物件．*a riding* ～ 骑马的行装．*a tropical* ～ 用于热带地区的装具．*a first aid* ～ 急救药箱．*a spare parts* ～ 备用零件箱．*a tool* ～ 工具箱．***(the whole)*** ～ ***and boodle [caboodle]*** 全部人马[全套东西]．— *vt.* 装备．～ **bag** ①长形帆布用具袋．②【军】(士兵个人的)长形帆布装具袋．

kit[2] [kit] *n.* (从前跳舞教师用的)小提琴．

kit[3], **kitt** [kit] *n.* ①小猫(= kitten)．②小狐；软毛小动物；软毛小动物的毛皮．

Ki·ta·kyu·shu [ˈkiːtɑːˈkjuːʃuː] *n.* 北九州〔日本港市〕．

Kit-Cat [ˈkitkæt] *n.* ①十八世纪英国辉格党人俱乐部的成员．②〔kit-cat〕小于半身但包括双手的画象 (= ～ portrait)．～ **Club**【英史】在詹姆士二世时辉格党的政治家们建立的俱乐部．

kitch·en [ˈkitʃin] *n.* ①厨房，灶间．②〔集合词〕炊事人员．③(便于携带的)全套炊具．*an army field* ～ 军用野外炊具．— *a.* ①厨房的．②在厨房工作的．③(语言)粗俗的，不雅的．*a* ～ *help* 厨房帮手．～ **cabinet** ①厨柜．②(〔常用 K- C-〕美国第七任总统杰克逊的)私人顾问团；政府首脑的私人顾问团〔参谋团、智囊团〕．～ **garden** 菜园．～ **maid** 帮厨女工．～ **match** 用于点煤气炉的粗头火柴．～ **midden**【考古】贝冢，贝丘．～ **physic** 滋补身体的食物；美味．～ **police** ①帮厨的士兵．②(犯过失士兵的)帮厨勤务．～**sink** ①*n.* 厨房中的洗涤盆〔水池〕；搬不动的东西；乱七八糟的东西；〔喻〕(绘画、戏剧等中)极端现实主义的东西 (*everything but the* ～*sink* 可以想象到的一切)．②*a.* (剧本等)表现西方现代生活中肮脏情景的．～ **stuff** ①供烹饪用的食物〔尤指菜蔬〕．②厨房的下脚〔尤指从锅上弄下的油垢〕．～**unit**〔英〕(兼做洗涤盆、厨柜的)一套厨房设备．～**ware** 厨房用具．

kitch·en·er [ˈkitʃinə] *n.* ①厨师，厨房总管．②〔英〕(烧饭用的)铁炉．

kitch·en·ette [ˌkitʃiˈnet] *n.* 小厨房．

kite [kait] *n.* ①【动】鸢．②骗子；流氓，光棍．③风筝．④轻型飞机；风筝式飞机；〔美俚〕飞机．⑤〔*pl.*〕【海】(微风时使用的)最高的轻帆．⑥【商】抵用票据，空头支票 ⑦〔美俚〕信．***draw in a*** ～ 收风筝．***fly [send up] a*** ～ ①放风筝．②试探舆论．③开空头支票．④〔美〕(从狱中)非法寄出信件；(为告贷或求助而)寄航空信．***fly one's own*** ～ 图谋私利．***go fly a*** ～〔美俚〕滚开．***higher than a*** ～〔美俚〕①极高．②大醉．— *vi.*〔口〕①(象风筝一样)上升，飞起．②【商】用空头支票骗钱．— *vt.* ①使(物价等)上涨．②【商】用空头支票骗(人)．～-**airship** 系留气艇．～ **balloon [sausage]** (用于军事观测)圆柱形系留气球．～ **camera** 俯瞰图照相机．～-**flying**〔美〕(以事后便于否认的方式)胡乱发布政治新闻〔旨在试探舆论〕．～**mark** (英国标准化协会的)规格说明标志．

kith [kiθ] *n.* ①亲属．②〔古〕朋友，相识，邻居．～ ***and kin*** 亲属；朋友．

kithe [kaið] *vt., vi.* ***(kithed, kith·ing)***〔Scot., 英方〕①以行动表示，证明．②〔废〕以语言表示，宣布，公布．

kit-kat [ˈkitkæt] *n.* = kit-cat.

ki·tool [kiˈtuːl] *n.* = kittul.

kitsch [kitʃ] *n.*〔G.〕迎合低级趣味的拙劣作品．-**y** *a.*

kit·ten [ˈkitn] *n.* ①小猫．②小的哺乳动物．③顽皮姑娘．***have (a litter of)*** ～**s**〔口〕发怒；烦恼；兴奋．— *vi., vt.* (猫)产(仔)．～**ball**〔美〕垒球．

kit·ten·ish [ˈkitniʃ] *a.* ①小猫似的；嬉耍的，活蹦乱跳的．②忸怩作态的．-**ly** *ad.* -**ness** *n.*

kit·ti·wake [ˈkitiweik] *n.*【动】三趾鸥；海鸥．

kit·tle [ˈkitl] *a.*〔Scot.〕①烦躁的，容易激动的．②敏捷的，灵巧的．③多变的，无常的．④难应付的，难驾驭的．～ *cattle* 难驾驭的牛；难对付的人〔事〕．— *vt.* ①逗(人)笑；使快活．②使困惑，使为难．

Kit·tredge [ˈkitridʒ] *n.* 基特里奇〔姓氏〕．

kit·tul [kiˈtuːl] *n.* (东印度的)棕榈[棕树]．

Kit·ty [ˈkiti] *n.* 基蒂〔女子名，Catherine 的昵称〕．

kit·ty[1] [ˈkiti] *n.*〔儿〕小猫．

kit·ty[2] [ˈkiti] *n.* ①(纸牌戏中的)全部赌注．②(从每人赌注中抽出的)头钱．③〔口〕凑集的金钱[物品]；共同的资金〔尤指小额集存的储蓄〕．

kit·ty-cor·nered [ˈkitiˌkɔːnəd] *a., ad.* = cater-cornered.

Ki·tu·ba [kiːˈtuːbə] *n.* 吉土巴语〔刚果河下游及其支流一带所讲的商业语言，由刚果语、凌加拉语 (*lingala*) 和法语混合而成〕．

Kit·we [ˈki:twei] *n.* 基特韦〔赞比亚城市〕.

ki·va [ˈki:və] *n.* 基瓦〔美国印第安人举行宗教仪式、开会、工作、休息等用的大圆屋〕.

ki·wi [ˈki:wi:] *n.* ①【动】鹬鸵，几维〔新西兰产的一种不能飞行的鸟〕. ②〔军俚〕不飞行的空军军官，地勤军官. ③〔K-〕〔口〕新西兰人.

KKK, K.K.K. = Ku Klux Klan〔美〕三 K 党.

KKt = King's Knight（国际象棋中与“王”并列配置的）马.

kl. = kilolitre(s).

Kla·math [ˈklæməθ] *n.* *(pl. ~(s))* ①克拉马斯人〔美国俄勒冈州南部的北美印第安人〕. ②克拉马斯语.

Klan [klæn] *n.*〔美〕① = Ku Klux Klan. ②三K党分部. **~sman** *n.* *(pl. -men)* 三K 党党员.

klatch, klatsch [klætʃ] *n.*（非正式的）聚会，谈话会.

Klaus [klaus] *n.* 克劳斯〔男子名〕.

klax·on [ˈklæksn] *n.* 电警笛；电喇叭；高音气笛.

Klee·nex [ˈkli:neks]“克里奈克斯”〔一种用作面巾纸的薄页纸商标名〕. — *n.*〔有时用 k-〕一张面巾纸.

kleig [kli:g] *n.* = klieg.

klepht [kleft] *n.* ①（十五世纪希腊被土耳其并吞后上山坚持斗争的）希腊爱国者. ②（希腊等地的）山贼.

klep·to·ma·ni·a [ˌkleptəuˈmeiniə] *n.* 偷盗癖.

klep·to·ma·ni·ac [ˌkleptəuˈmeiniæk] *n.* 有偷盗癖的人.

klep·to·scope [ˈkleptəuskəup] *n.*【军】潜望镜.

klieg [kli:g] *n.* **~ eyes**（由于强烈光线的照射而引起的）眼结膜炎. **~ light**（摄电影用）溢光灯，强烈弧光灯.

Kline test [klain]【医】克氏梅毒试法.

klip·das [ˈklipdæs] *n.*〔S. Afr.〕野兔，兔蹄.

klip·spring·er [ˈklipˌspriŋə] *n.* *(pl. -ers, -er)* 山羚 *(Oreotragus oreotragus)*〔产于东非和南非〕.

klong [klɔ:ŋ] *n.*〔Thai.〕（泰国的）运河，水道.

kloof [klu:f] *n.*〔南非〕深谷，峡谷.

klys·tron [ˈklaistrən] *n.*【电】速（度）调（制）（电子）管，调（制）速（度）管. **~ oscilator** 速调管振荡器.

km. = ①kilometre(s). ②kingdom.

KMT = Kuomintang.

kn., kn = knot.

knack [næk] *n.* ①诀窍，窍门；（练习而得的）技巧；妙法. ②需要技巧的工作. ③花巧，花样. ④（言语、行为等的）习惯，癖. ⑤玩具，小玩意. ***have one's own ~ in ...*** 对…有独到之处. ***There's a ~ in it.*** 这里面有窍门.

knack·er [ˈnækə] *n.* ①收买和屠宰废马的人；收买老病家畜〔家畜尸体〕的人. ②收买废屋、废船的人. ③〔方〕老病无用的家畜〔尤指马〕. ***go to the ~s***（马）被屠宰. **-y** *n.*〔英〕废马屠宰场；家畜尸体处理场.

knack·wurst [ˈnɑ:kˌwə:st; G. ˈknɑ:kˌvuəʃt] *n.* 熏腊肠.

knack·y [ˈnæki] *a.* 巧妙的；机灵的.

knag [næg] *n.* ①木节，木瘤. ②（挂物用的）木钉.

knag·gy [ˈnægi] *a.* 节多的；疙瘩多的.

knap[1] [næp] *vt.*〔方〕①敲打，碰撞，打（火石等）. ②打碎；砸碎（石头等）. ③猛咬；啃. ④喋喋不休地讲，闲聊. — *n.*〔方〕猛击；敲.

knap[2] [næp] *n.*〔方〕小山的顶；小山.

knap·per [ˈnæpə] *n.* 敲碎（石头等）的人；破碎器；碎石槌.

knap·sack [ˈnæpsæk] *n.*（军用或旅行用）背包.

knap·weed [ˈnæpwi:d] *n.*【植】矢车菊属植物.

knar [nɑ:] *n.* 木瘤，木节.

knave [neiv] *n.* ①流氓，无赖. ②〔古〕仆人. ③（纸牌中的）杰克 *(Jack)*. **~ [vogue] in grain** 大坏蛋，无赖透顶的人. **~ of hearts** ①讨好女人的人. ②（纸牌中的）红心杰克.

knav·er·y [ˈneivəri] *n.* 流氓行为，无赖行为；诈骗；恶作剧.

knav·ish [ˈneiviʃ] *a.* 无赖的；骗人的，奸诈的. **-ly** *ad.* **-ness** *n.*

knead [ni:d] *vt.* ①揉，捏（面粉、陶土等）；捏做（面包、陶器等）. ②按摩（肌肉等）. ③陶冶（性情），锻炼（性格）. *~ and shape one's children to one's thought* 按照自己的思想培养塑造子女. — *vi.* 揉，捏.

knee [ni:] *n.* ①膝，膝盖，膝头，膝关节. ②（长裤、长袜等的）膝部. ③（马、犬等的）腕骨；（鸟类的）胫骨. ④膝状物；【机】弯头（管），膝（形）杆；架合角铁；（铣床的）升降台；【建】扶手弯头，曲材；（木船用的）肋材. ⑤曲线的弯曲处. ⑥（用膝的）碰击. *at one's mother's ~s* 在母亲膝下，幼小时候. ***bend [bow] the ~ before [to] sb.*** 向某人屈膝，屈服于. ***bow the ~ to Baal*** 崇拜偶像. ***bring sb. to his ~s*** 迫使某人屈服. ***draw up the ~s*** 伸直膝盖. ***drop (on) to one's ~s*** 跪下. ***fall on a ~*** 屈下一膝. ***fall on one's ~s*** 跪下. ***get ~ to ~ with sb.*** 同某人促膝谈心. ***give [offer] a ~ to sb.***（在拳击中）当助手；支持，帮忙. ***go down on one's ~s*** 跪下. ***gone at the ~s***〔俚〕（马）衰老. ***go on one's ~s*** 跪着，卑躬屈膝地. ***on bended ~s*** 屈膝跪着. ***on the ~s of the gods*** 人力所不及的；尚未可定〔知〕的. ***rise on the ~s*** 站起来. — *vt.* *(~d)* ①用膝盖碰. ②用弯头〔弯管〕接合. ③〔口〕使（裤子的）膝部凸出. **~ action**【机】膝（形）杆动作；膝（形）杆作用（*~ action suspension*【机】独立悬挂）. **~ and ~ column**（铣床的）升降台. **~ brace**【机】隅撑，角撑. **~ breeches** 短裤. **~cap** ①【解】膝盖骨. ②护膝. **~-deep** *a.* 深到膝的，没膝的；深陷在…中的 *(in)*. **~-high** *a.* 高到膝盖的（*~-high to a duck [grasshopper, mosquito]* 很小的，微不足道的，无聊的）. **~-hole**（写字台等）容纳膝部的地方（*a ~ hole desk* 左右有抽屉的写字台）. **~ iron** 隅铁. **~ jerk**【医】膝反射（= patellar reflex.）**~ joint** ①【解】膝关节. ②【机】弯头接合，肘接，臂接. **~pad** 护膝. **~pan**【解】膝盖骨. **~ piece** 膝甲〔护膝铠甲〕. **~ pipe** 曲管. **~ point**（曲线）弯曲点. **~ roof** 覆斜屋顶. **~sprung** *a.*（马由于屈肌腱的收缩）把膝向前弯的. **~ swell**（风琴的）膝板，增音器. **~ tool** 膝形刀. **~ voltage**（曲线）膝处电压.

kneel [ni:l] *vi.* *(**knelt** [nelt], 或 ~ed)*, 跪下，跪着 *(before; to, down)*. — *n.* 跪的动作〔姿态〕 **-ing·ly** *ad.*

kneel·er [ˈni:lə] *n.* ①跪垫. ②跪台. ③跪拜的人.

kneel-in [ˈni:lin] *n.*〔美〕祈祷示威〔黑人进入白人教堂参加礼拜以示对种族隔离政策的抗议〕.

knell [nel] *n.* ①钟声，丧钟声. ②凶兆 *(of)*. — *vt.*〔古〕①敲丧钟. ②敲丧钟报丧. — *vi.* ①敲丧钟，发丧钟声. ②发出不吉利的声音. ***sound [toll] the death ~ for [of] sth. [sb.]*** 给某物〔人〕敲丧钟，宣告某物〔人〕死亡.

knelt [nelt] kneel 的过去式及过去分词.

Knes·set [ˈkneset] *n.*（以色列）议会.

knew [nju:] know 的过去式.

Knick·er·bock·er [ˈnikəbɔkə] *n.* ①（最初到美国纽约的）荷兰移民的子孙；荷兰籍纽约人；纽约人. ②〔k-〕〔*pl.*〕（在膝下扎起的）灯笼裤.

knick·ers [ˈnikəz] *n.*〔*pl.*〕①〔口〕= knickerbockers. ②（女用）扎口短裤.

knick·knack [ˈniknæk] *n.* 小家具；小玩意；小摆设；小装饰品.

knick·knack·er·y [ˈnikˌnækəri] *n.*〔集合词〕小家具类；小玩具类；小摆设类；小装饰品类.

knife [naif] *n.* *(pl. **knives** [knaivz])* ①小刀；餐刀；菜刀. ②〔诗〕短刀，匕首. ③【机】（切断器的）刃部；（机器上的）刀具〔刀片〕. ④〔*the ~*〕【外】手术刀. *a folding ~* 折刀. *a ~ and fork*（吃西餐用的）一副刀叉. *a pocket ~*（可折合的）小刀. *a table ~* 餐刀. ***before you can [could] say ~***〔口〕说时迟那时快；一眨眼；突然. ***cut like a ~***（风等）冷得刺骨. ***get [have] a [one's] ~ into sb.*** 对某人报复，猛烈攻击某人，同某人过不去. ***go [pass] under the ~***〔口〕动外科手术，开刀. ***have a horror***

of the ~ 怕动外科手术. ***play a good ~ and fork*** 吃得津津有味;饱餐一顿. ***sharpen one's ~ for sb.*** 准备惩罚[攻击]某人. ***That one could cut it with a ~…*** 十分明显的, 非常压抑的. ***under the ~*** 〔口〕动外科手术. ***war to the ~*** 血战,鏖战. —*vt.* ①拿小刀切;拿尖刀戳. ②〔口〕秘密打击,用阴险手段击败,背叛. ③刀切似地穿过. ④用括刀涂(颜料等). —*vi.* (刀似地)劈开,穿过. ~ **board** ①磨刀板. ②【史】公共马车顶上的长座位. ~ **edge** ①刀口,刀刃. ②锋利的边缘. ③(门框、舱门等的)刃形边缘. ④【机】(天平等的) 刀形支承. **~-edged** 锋利的,锐利的. ~ **grinder** ①磨刀工人. ②磨刀装置;磨刀石;砂轮. ~ **machine** 磨刀机. ~ ***money*** (中国古时的)刀币. ~ **rest** (餐)刀架. ~***smith*** 小刀匠. ~ **switch**【电】刀形开关,闸刀开关.

knife·point [ˈnaifpɔint] *n.* 刀尖. ***at ~*** 在(刀尖)威胁下.

knight [nait] *n.* ①(欧洲中世纪的)骑士;武士,勇士(尤指打仗或比武时作贵妇人侍从或斗士的人). ②(古罗马的)骑士〔奴隶主集团中的一个阶层的成员〕;(古希腊雅典的)第二等级公民. ③〔英〕爵士〔得用 Sir 的称号,其夫人可称为Dame, 民间称为Lady〕. ④【英史】郡选议员. ⑤(政治、社交、慈善团体的) 会员,社员,团员;某一事业[主义等]的忠诚拥护者. ⑥〔谑〕专家,大家. ⑦(国际象棋中的)马. ~ *of fortune* 〔婉〕冒险家. ~ *of the brush* 美术家,画家. ~ *of the cleaver* 〔谑〕肉商. ~ *of the cue* 打台球的. ~ *of the green cloth* 爱玩牌的人,牌迷,赌徒. ~ *of the hammer* 打铁工人,铁匠. ~ *of the lady* 妇女的保护人;情夫. ~ *of the pen [pencil, quill]* 文人,耍笔杆的. ~ *of the pestle (and mortar)* 药剂师. ~ *of the post* 【英史】以作假见证为职业的人. ~ *of the road* ①拦路贼. ②无业游民. ③流动推销员. ~ *of the Round Table* (亚瑟王的)圆桌骑士. ~ *of the Rueful [Woeful] Countenance* 愁颜骑士〔指唐·吉诃德〕. ~ *of the whip* 〔谑〕马车夫. ~ *of the whipping-post* 〔谑〕骗子. *K- without Fear and without Reproach* 见义勇为的骑士. *Knights of Columbus* 【天主】哥伦布骑士团〔罗马天主教的一个所谓"国际互助慈善"团体名,成立于 1882 年〕. *Knights of Labour* 【美史】(1869 年成立的秘密工会)劳动骑士团. *Knights of Pythias* 派西亚斯骑士团〔所谓"互助慈善"团体名,成立于 1864 年. 派西亚斯,公元前四世纪希腊哲学家〕. *Queen's ~* (国际象棋中) 和"王后"同列配置的"马". —*vt.* 把…封为骑士[爵士]. **~age** 骑士,爵士;骑士[爵士]名录;骑士[爵士]的地位. ~ **bachelor** 英国古代最低级爵士. ~ **commander** 英国第二等高级爵士. **~-errant** *n.* ***(pl. ~s-errant)*** ①(中世纪的)游侠骑士. ②侠客,好汉. **~-errantry** 骑士风度;侠义行为. **~head** *n.* (船首斜桅的)支撑杆. **~hood** ①骑士[爵士]资格[地位、身分]. ②骑士精神,骑士道,侠义. ③骑士,爵士. **K- Hospitaler** (1096—1099 前后的)十字军救护团团员. **~-('s) service**【史】以服兵役为条件对土地享有的占有权. **K- Templar** ***(pl. Knights Templars)*** ①圣殿骑士团骑士〔十二世纪侵略性的十字军参加者以"保护圣墓"名义而建立的军事宗教团体的成员〕. ②(共济会中一个宗派)"互助慈善"团的成员. **-ly** ①*a.* 骑士[爵士](般)的;侠义的;由骑士[爵士]组成的. ②*ad.* 骑士般地,侠义地.

knish [keˈniʃ] *n.* 克尼什烙薄面卷〔一种肉(干酪)馅烤(煎)薄面卷〕.

knit [nit] *v.* ***(knitted*** 或 ***knit)*** *vt.* ①编织,编结;针织;把(毛线等)织成(衣服). ②使皱起,使皱紧. ③拼合(碎片等),粘合;接合(折骨等). ④(由于共同利益等)使(家族等)联合. ⑤使(论点等)紧密,使(文章等)紧凑〔多用过去分词〕. ~ *wool into stockings* 织毛线袜. ~ *stocking out of wool* 用毛线织袜. ~ *timbers* 拼接木材. *Mortar ~s bricks together* 灰泥把砖粘合在一起. *be ~ together by common interests [marriage]* 因共同利益[婚姻关系]而结合起来. ~ *one's brows* 皱眉. *a closely ~ argument* 严密的论点. *a well-~ frame* 结实的体格. —*vi.* ①编织,编结,针织. ②(折骨等)接合,结合. ③(眉头)皱起,皱紧. ④(植物)生长,结果实;(蜂)蜂拥,成群. *She often knits while reading.* 她看书的时候常编织东西. *The broken bones ~ (together).* 折骨接合起来了. *Her brows ~ in thought.* 她皱眉深思. ~ ***in*** 编入,织进. ~ ***up*** ①编结成,织补. ②结束(议论等). ③结合. —*n.* ①编织,针织;编结. ②编织品,编织衣物. ~ *goods* 编织品,针织品,卫生衣类. *a ~ goods mill* 针织厂. ~ **wear** *n.* 针织品. (*woollen ~* 羊毛织物.)

knit·ter [ˈnitə] *n.* ①编织者, 编织工人. ②针织机, 编织机.

knit·ting [ˈnitiŋ] *n.* ①编织, 针织. ②编织物; 针织品. ③接合, 结合; 联合. ***attend [mind, get down to, stick close to, tend to] one's ~*** 各人自扫门前雪. ~ **machine** 编织机,针织机. ~ **needle** 织针,毛衣针.

knives [naivz] knife 的复数.

knob [nɔb] *n.* ①疖, 瘤, 疙瘩; 〔俚〕头. ②球形突出物;(树干等的)节;(棒等的)圆顶. ③门拗,门把,拉手,球形捏手. ④【机】旋钮,按钮,调节器. ⑤(旗竿、桅杆上的)雕球饰,顶华. ⑥(砂糖等的)团粒,团块. ⑦〔美〕圆丘;〔*pl.*〕丘陵地带. ***with ~s on*** 〔俚〕尤其突出地,更加. — *vt.* ①使有球形突出物在…上生节(长瘤). ②给(门等)装球形捏手. ③(琢石时)将(多余石块)敲掉. — *vi.* 鼓起,突出. ~ **insulator** 【电】瓷柱. **~kerrie** (旧时南非本地人用作武器的) 圆头棍. ~ **lock** 一种弹簧锁.

knob·ble [ˈnɔbl] *n.* 节子,瘤子,疙瘩.

knob·bly [ˈnɔbli] *a.* = knobby.

knob·by [ˈnɔbi] *a.* ①节多的. ②疙瘩多的. ③小圆丘多的. ④〔美俚〕(服装等)时髦的,流行的,漂亮的. ⑤小球形的. ⑥(问题等)棘手的,使人困惑的. **knob·biness** *n.*

knob·stick [ˈnɔbstik] *n.* ①(= knobkerrie.) ②〔英〕罢工时上工的工人,工贼.

knock [nɔk] *vt.* ①敲,打,击; 敲掉,去掉. ②使碰撞; 撞倒;凿打(洞等). ③〔英俚〕使震惊,给…强烈印象. ④〔美口〕找…岔子,对…挑剔,糟蹋. ~ *one's head against the door* 以头撞门,头撞到门上. ~ *the wall down* 把墙拆除. ~ *a hole in a wall* 在墙上凿一洞. ~ *in a nail* 敲进一枚钉子. *What ~s me most is his ignorance.* 使我大吃一惊的是他的无知. —*vi.* ①敲,打,击 *(at, on)*. ②碰,撞. ③(机器发生毛病)发出爆击声. ④〔美俚〕找岔子,说坏话. ⑤奔忙,忙乱. *Who is ~ing?* 谁在敲门? ~ *into sb.* 撞在某人身上. ~ ***about [around]*** ①接连敲打;乱打,乱敲. ②殴打,虐待;(浪等)冲打(船只). ③〔口〕流浪,漂遊,到处漫游. ~ ***against*** ①碰撞;同…冲突. ②偶然遇见. ~ ***at*** 敲(门、窗等)(~ *at an open door* 多此一举. ~ *at the wrong door* 找错了门路). ~ ***away*** 敲下,敲掉. ~ ***back*** 〔俚〕一口喝掉. ~ ***civ(v)ies into shape*** 〔美〕训练新兵. ~ ***down*** ①打倒,撞倒. ②(拍卖时)敲槌卖出. ③〔俚〕请求 (~ *sb. down for a song* 要求某人唱歌). ④〔俚〕使减价. ⑤打败,驳倒. ⑥拆除; 拆卸(~ *down a machine* 拆卸机器). ⑦〔俚〕获得(收入、薪金等);揩油,贪污. ⑧〔美俚〕介绍. ~ ***for a loop [goal]*** 〔美俚〕①猛击,打昏;用酒灌醉. ②破坏. ③使人吃惊. ~ ***for admittance*** 敲门求见. ~ ***head*** 叩头. ~ ***home*** (把钉子等)敲牢,钉到头;彻底打击. ~ ***in [into]*** 打进,敲进;(英大学)迟到后敲门进去. ~ ***(sb.) into a cocked hat*** 把(某人)的计划破坏. ②把(某人)打得鼻青脸肿. ③把(某人)驳得体无完肤. ④超越,胜过(某人). ~ ***sb. into the middle of next week*** 打败,痛击(某人). ~ ***it off*** 〔美俚〕住口! 别再吵了! ~ ***off*** ①敲落,敲掉,把…击倒 (~ *sb. off his feet* 把某人打倒在地). ②中止(工作)(~ *off (work) for lunch at noon* 正午停工吃午饭). ③即席作

(诗文等)(~ *off a few lines* 匆匆写上几句)。④减低(价格),减少(速度)(~ *off ten per cent for cash* 如付现金可减价一成)。⑤〔美俚〕杀死;压倒。~ ***(sb.) on the head*** ①把(某人)打昏过去,打死。②破坏(某人的计划等)。 ~ ***oneself out*** 把自己弄得筋疲力竭。 ~ ***out*** ①打出,敲出。②敲空(~ *out a pipe* 敲出烟斗中的烟灰)。③(拳击中)彻底打倒,使屈服(~ *out an enemy plane* 打落一架敌机)。④使失去效能,使无用;破坏。⑤急速做好,匆匆拟出(计划等)(~ *out an idea* 匆匆想出个主意)。⑥【无】脱模。~ ***over***〔俚〕①弄倒,打翻。②屈服;死。③〔美〕(警察)袭击,逮捕,搜查。~ ***over a drink***〔美俚〕喝杯酒。 ~ ***sb.'s head off*** 轻易胜过某人。~ ***the bottom [stuffing tar] out of*** 敲掉(箱子等的)底;打破(规则等),推翻(学说等),彻底弄明白。~ ***the breath out of sb.'s body*** 使某人大吃一惊。~ ***the spots off [out of] sb.*** ①痛打某人,痛击某人。②大大超过某人。~ ***together*** ①使碰撞;颤抖着相碰(*K- their heads together* 让他们的头撞一撞〔有时指以武力强制两个打架的人停手〕)。②拼凑;赶造,赶建。~ ***to pieces*** ①打碎。②推翻(论点)。~ ***under***(向…)投降(*to*)。~ ***up*** ①敲起,叫起(熟睡中的人)。②(在板球赛中)很快得分。③〔英口〕(使)筋疲力尽。④赶做,赶造,赶安排(~ *up a meal* 匆匆做好一顿饭。~ *up a hen-house* 赶搭起一个鸡窝)。⑤(装订)弄齐(纸)边。⑥〔美俚〕使受孕。~ ***up against***=~ against. — *n.* ①敲,打击,(狠狠)一击;敲门(声)。②不幸;挫折;艰苦;困苦。③(机器等发出的)爆(击)声,爆击。④〔美俚〕吹毛求疵,找碴儿。⑤〔英俚〕(板球赛中的)盘,局,回合。⑥【无】敲击信号。⑦〔英俚〕拍卖时互相勾结压价的商人集团;有压价人捣鬼的拍卖。*a* ~ *at [on] the door.* 敲门声。*a* ~ *on the head* 头上捱了一拳。*a* ~*test engine* 测爆机。*The engine is* ~*ing badly.* 引擎的爆击声响得厉害。*stand [take] the* ~*s* 忍受指摘。***get the*** ~〔口〕①被辞退,被解雇。②喝醉。***take the*** ~〔俚〕①经济上受到沉重打击;拮据,手头紧。②喝醉。~**about** ①*a.* 吵闹的,喧嚣的;〔口〕流浪的;(衣服)结实的。② *n.* 武打戏的表演[演员];结实的东西;狠斗;流浪汉;快帆船。~**-down** ①*a.* 击倒的;压倒的;能拆开的,折迭式的;(拍卖)价格最低的。② *n.* 打倒;打倒的一击;〔俚〕强烈的酒;互殴,乱斗;可拆散的东西;〔美俚〕介绍;降低。~**-down(-and)-drag-out** *a.* (拳击中)打倒而被拖出的,你死我活的,残酷无情的。~**ed-down** *a.* (家具等)未装配的。~**-knee**【医】膝内翻症;〔*pl.*〕内翻膝。~**-kneed** *a.* 膝内翻的。~ **meter** 爆震计。~**out** ① *a.* 拳击猛烈的,打倒的;在拍卖时互相串通用廉价买得的;使昏迷的 (~*-out drops*〔俚〕(放在饮料中的)迷药;蒙汗药);引人注目的,轰动一时的。② *n.* (拳击)把对手打倒的一击;打倒;彻底的击败;(拍卖时)互相串通的压价收买;〔俚〕轰动一时的东西,引人注目的人。~ **rating** 爆击率。 ~**-reducer**【化】抗震剂。~ **wurst** = knackwurst.

knock·er [ˈnɔkə] *n.* ①敲的人,来访者。②门扣,门环。③〔口〕吹毛求疵的人;顽固的悲观主义评论家。***up to the*** ~〔俚〕①完全地,十分地(*be ready up to the* ~ 作好了充分准备)。②健康正常(*do not feel up to the* ~ 感觉身体不够好)。~**-up** *n.*〔英〕喊醒工人起来工作的人。

knoll[1] [nəul] *n.* 圆丘,土墩。

knoll[2] [nəul] *n., vt., vi.*〔英方,古〕= knell.

knop [nɔp] *n.* ①(门上的)圆形把手;扣子,拉手。②【建】蕾形饰,顶华。③(树干等的)节,花芽。

knot [nɔt] *n.* ①结,绳结,结节;(装饰用的)花结,蝴蝶结。②(婚姻等的)结合。③(树木或木材上的)节疤;(人或动物身上的)硬块,节,瘤。④一小群,一小队,一小簇。⑤紧缩,收缩;紧缩感。⑥难事,难题,麻烦事;(问题的)要点;(戏剧、小说的)情节的症结。⑦【海】节(=浬/小时),浬,海里。⑧(工人扛物用的)垫肩,头垫(= Porter's ~)。*a figure-of-eight* ~ "8"字结。*a fool's [granny's] knot* 打得不牢固的结。*a reef* ~ 平结,方结。*a true lover's [true-love]* ~ (象征忠贞爱情的)同心结,鸳鸯结。*make [tie] a* ~ *in a rope* 把绳子打个结。*loosen [undo, untie] a* ~ 把结解开。*the marriage [nuptial]* ~ 婚姻[夫妇]关系。*stand about in* ~*s* 三五成群地站着。*the* ~ *of the matter* 问题的症结。*His stomach was all in* ~*s.* 他的胃收缩成一团。*a matter full of legal* ~*s* 充满法律纠葛的事。*a* ~ *in a gland*【医】腺瘤,腺节。*She can do [make, steam] 35* ~*s.* 那艘船时速35海里。*a shoulder* ~ 肩章。***a Gordian*** ~ ①难解的结;难办的事;棘手的问题。②(问题或故事情节等的)焦点,关键。***at the rate of*** ~***s***〔口〕非常快,迅速。***cut the (Gordian)*** ~ 快刀斩乱麻。***get into*** ~***s*** 困惑不解。***seek a*** ~ ***in a rush [bulrush]*** 想平地起风波。***tie in*** ~***s***〔口〕使人迷惑不解,使人糊涂不堪。***tie oneself (up) in(to)*** ~***s*** 陷入苦境。— *vt.* ①把…打结;把…连结;捆扎,包扎。②使密切结合。③使纠结。④皱(眉)。⑤打结成(缕)。~ *a parcel safely* 把小包扎紧。— *vi.* ①打结;成结;作花结。②纠集,纠缠。③形成硬块。④打结成缕。~ **grass** *n.*【植】两耳草;软花属植物。~**hole** *n.* (木板或树上的)节孔。~**root** *n.*【植】甘露子,草石蚕。**-less** *a.* 无结的。**-like** *a.* 似结的。

knot·ted [ˈnɔtid] *a.* ①打结的。②全是结子的。③纠缠的;错综复杂的。④费解的,令人困惑的;棘手的。

knot·ter [ˈnɔtə] *n.* ①打结的人[物]。②解结的人[物]。

knot·ting [ˈnɔtiŋ] *n.* 结形花边。

knot·ty [ˈnɔti] *a.* ①有节的,有结的;节疤多的。②纠纷的,棘手的。*a* ~ *rope* 多结的绳子。*a* ~ *passage* 难懂的一段文字。~ **pine** 多结松木〔供内部装饰和做某些家具用〕。**-ti·ly** *ad.* **-ti·ness** *n.*

knot·work [ˈnɔtwəːk] *n.* 缀饰;编结工艺。

knout [naut] *n.* 皮鞭〔沙俄所用刑具〕;〔the ~〕笞刑。— *vt.* 鞭打,对…处笞刑。

know [nəu] *v.* ***(knew*** [njuː], ***known*** [nəun]***)*** *vt.* ①知道;了解,懂得。②相识,认识;结识。③能区别,能分辨,能识别。④熟悉,精通,记牢。⑤体验,尝受,经历。⑥〔古〕与(女性)发生性关系。 ~ *the facts* 知道[了解]事实。*Do you know English?* 你懂英语吗? ~ *for certain that …* 确实知道。*the importance of* ~*ing oneself* 知己的重要性,自知之明的重要性。*Do you* ~ *how to play chess?* 你会下棋吗? *The man has gone nobody* ~*s where.* 谁也不知道那个人到哪里去了。*Who* ~*s if it may be so?* 也许是这样的。*(as) you* ~*, don't you* ~〔用作插入语〕你也知道,你是知道的。*We all knew him to be honest.* 我们都以为他是老实的。*I never* ~ *such a man.* 我从来不认识这样一个人。*I* ~ *him to speak to.* 我不深知他,只是见面打打招呼罢了。*I* ~ *of him, but I do not* ~ *him personally.* 我知道他,但不认识他。*I knew him at once.* 我立刻认出他来。*I knew him for an American.* 我看出他是个美国人。*I would* ~ *her even in a crowd.* 就是在人群中,我也能认出她来。~ *right from wrong* 分辨是非。*He doesn't know a friend from an enemy.* 他不分敌友。*I don't* ~ *him from Adam.* 我简直不晓得他是谁。~ *one's lines by heart* 背熟自己的台词。*I have told you I don't know how many times not to touch it.* 我对你说不要碰它,不知多少次了。~ *sb. by name* 只知道某人的名字;能说出某人的名字。~ *sb. by sight* 同某人只是面熟。~ *truth through practice* 通过实践认识真理。*He has known better days.* 他过过好日子。*He never knew fear.* 他从来不知道害怕。*His wrath knew no bounds.* 他怒不可遏。— *vi.* 知道,了解,懂得。*Do you* ~ *of that matter?* —*Yes, I* ~. 你知道那件事吗?—我知道。*The best method I* ~ *of.* 我所知道的最好的方法。*I* ~ *of its being so.* 我知道是如此的。***all one*** ~***s***〔口〕力所能及的一切;尽全力(地)(*He will do all he* ~*s* 他会拼命干的)。***before you*** ~ ***where you are***〔口〕立即,马上。***don't I*** ~ ***it***〔口〕就算我知道〔表示无可奈何的同意〕。

for all [aught] I ~ 就我所知(*For all I ~, the matter may have been settled.* 据我所知，这事也许早解决了). ***God [Goodness, Heaven, Lord, the Lord] knows!*** 天晓得！谁知道！(*God ~s that it is true.* 这绝对是真的. *God [Heaven] ~s where he fled.* 谁知道他跑到哪里去了. *He is always busy with God knows what.* 谁知道他整天在忙啥东西). ***I ~ what.*** 我有一个新的想法[建议]. ***I knew it.*** 我早知道那件事要发生. ***I want to ~.***〔美口〕哎呀，唷〔表示惊讶等〕. ***I wouldn't ~.***〔美〕我不知道. ***~ a thing or two, ~ black from white, ~ chalk from cheese, ~ how many beans make five, ~ one's way about, ~ what's what*** 精明，有经验，有判断力，明事理，洞悉世态人情. ***~ about [of]...*** 知道关于…的情况. ***~ all the answers***〔口〕①聪明伶俐. ②自称无所不知的人，知识里手. ***~ better (than that, than to do)*** 明白事理(而不至于…)(*I ~ better than to do such a thing.* 我决不会蠢到去干那样的事). ***~ one's goods [onions, stuff]***〔美〕精通某事［某问题］，有充分的专门知识. ***~ one's business*** 精通自己干的一行. ***~ one's own mind*** 有自己的想法，果断. ***~ the time of day*** 消息灵通；能见机行事. ***~ what one is about*** 一切能应付裕如. ***To ~ everything is to ~ nothing.***〔谚〕样样都懂，样样不通. ***What do you ~?***〔口〕真想不到. ***What do you ~ about this [that]?***〔口〕你看怪不怪？真没有想到. ***Who ~s?***〔口〕怎么知道呢？说不定. ***You never ~ what you can do till you try.***〔谚〕下手尝试，才知自己有几分本事. — *n.*〔口〕知晓，知情〔仅用于成语〕. ***be in the ~*** 了解内情. ***not in the ~*** 不明真相. ***those in the ~***〔口〕消息灵通人士. **~-all, ~-it-all** ① *n.*〔口〕自称无所不知的人，知识里手；〔反〕万事通. ② *a.* 自称无所不知的，万事通的. **~-how** *n.*〔口〕专门技能，知识，窍门(*the ~-how of atomic bomb* 制造原子弹的技术). **~-nothing** *n.* ①无知的人. ②不可知论者. ③【美史】(十九世纪反对外来移民、天主教徒等的)一种秘密党派成员. **~-nothingism** *n.* ①不可知论；(对一切事物均答不知的)不知道主义，一问三不知. ②〔k-〕【美史】(十九世纪反对外来移民等的)秘密党派的排外主义.

know·a·ble [ˈnəuəbl] *a.* 可知的，可认识的；易知的. — *n.*〔常 *pl.*〕知道的事. *~s and unknowables* 知道的和不知道的. **-bil·i·ty** *n.* 可知性.

know·ing [ˈnəuiŋ] *a.* ①知道的，有知识的；有见识的. ②机敏的，机警的，聪明的. ③老练的，世故的，狡猾的. ④故意的，成心地. ⑤心照不宣地，会意的. ⑥自以为无所不知的. ⑦〔口〕时髦的，漂亮的. *a ~ scholar* 饱学之士. *a ~ dog* 机警的狗. *a ~ look* 会意的一瞥. *the ~ one* 万事通，自以为无所不知的人. — *n.* 知道；认识. ***There is no ~*** …无法知道(*There is no ~ when he will come.* 无法知道他什么时候来). 无法知道. **-ly** *ad.* ①故意地. ②会意地. ③老练地. **-ness** *n.*

knowl·edge [ˈnɔlidʒ] *n.* ①知识；学识，学问. ②了解，理解；消息. ③认识. ④〔古〕学科. ⑤〔古〕性关系. *book ~* 书本知识. *K- is power.*〔谚〕知识就是力量. *practical ~* 实际的知识. *secondhand ~* 第二手知识，传授来的知识. *working ~ of French* 法语知识学到能应用的地步. *I have no ~ of London.* 我对伦敦毫无所知. *It is within your ~ that* …这是你所知道的. *The ~ of our victory caused great joy.* 我们获得胜利的消息传来，万众欢腾. *perceptual ~* 感性认识. *logical [rational] ~* 理性认识. *the theory of ~*【哲】认识论. *branches of ~* 学科. *carnal ~* 性交. ***come to sb.'s ~*** 被某人知道. ***common [general] ~*** 众所周知，常识. ***grow out of (sb.'s) ~*** 被忘掉了. ***have some [a general, a thorough] ~ of*** 懂得一点［懂得一个大概，精通］. ***not to my ~*** 我知道并不是那样. ***out of all ~*** (变得)认不出来，无法辨认. ***to my ~*** 据我知道. ***to sb.'s certain ~*** 据某人确知. ***to the best of my ~*** 据我所知，就我所知而论(= so far as I know). ***Too much ~ makes the head bald.***〔谚〕知识太多老得快. ***without sb.'s ~*** 不通知某人，背着某人. **~-box** *n.* ①〔俚〕头. ②〔美俚〕校舍. **~ factory**〔美〕学校(尤指高等院校)；教育机构.

knowl·edge·a·ble [ˈnɔlidʒəbl] *a.*〔口〕有知识的；精明的. *a ~ question* 有见地的问题. *a ~ student* 有头脑的学生.

known [nəun] know 的过去分词. — *a.* 大家知道的；知名的；已知的. *a nationally ~ writer* 全国知名的作家. ***be it ~ that*** …特此通告. ***be ~ as = be ~ by the name of*** …通称，叫做. ***be ~ for*** …因…而著名. ***be ~ to*** …为…所知. ***make ~*** 发表，公布. ***make oneself ~ to sb.*** 向某人作自我介绍. ***make sth. known to sb.*** 向某人公布某事. **~ number**【数】已知数. **~ quantity**【数】已知量.

Knox [nɔks] *n.* 诺克斯〔姓氏〕.

Knt. = knight.

knuck·le [ˈnʌkl] *n.* ①指关节，指节. ②〔通常 *pl.*〕铜指节套(= ~ duster，又称 brass ~s). ③(小牛、猪等的)膝关节，脚圈；肘，蹄. ④【机】钩爪，关节；铰结，肘形接；【船】船尾棱缘；【建】(屋顶等的)脊. *a coupler ~* 车钩关节. *a universal joint ~*【机】万向接头关节. ***get a rap on [over] the ~s*** 挨骂，受申斥. ***give sb. a rap on [over] the ~s*** 责骂某人，申斥某人. ***near the ~***〔口〕(笑话等)近似猥亵的，接近海淫的. — *vt.* 用指关节打［压，碰，擦］. — *vi.* (儿童弹玻璃弹子时)以指关节贴地(*down*). **~ down** ①开始认真工作；干劲十足地干(*~ down for an hour and finish* 认真干一个小时把…干完). ②(向…)投降(*to*)(= ~ under). **~ under to sb.**〔口〕(向某人)认输，屈服. **~ ball**【棒球】指节球，指关节球〔把指尖叩在球面上投的球，也叫 knuckler〕. **~bone** *n.* ①指关节骨；(牛羊等的)蹠骨. ②〔*pl.*〕用蹠骨玩的游戏；(小牛等的)肘骨肉. **~-duster** 指关节保护套〔套在四指关节上的铜套，握拳时铜套向外，作打人的武器〕. **~head**〔口〕傻瓜，笨蛋. **~joint** ①骨关节. ②【机】铰结，肘形接. **~ pin** 关节销. **~ tooth** 圆顶齿.

knuck·ler [ˈnuklə] *n.* = knuckle ball.

Knud·sen effect [ˈnu:dsən]【物】克努曾作用.

knurl [nə:l] *n.* ①(树木等的)硬节，瘤. ②小的隆起物；金属表面上的小粒；(硬币边上的)小凸边压花；【机】压花，滚花. ③(打字机上使滚筒转动的)圆形按钮［旋钮］. ④〔Scot.〕矮小结实的人. — *vt.* 在(硬币等的边上)作小凸边；【机】在…上滚花. **-ing** *n.*【机】滚花. **-y** *a.* 多节的；滚花的.

knurr, knur [nə:] *n.* ①(树木等的)节疤. ②〔英〕木球〔球戏用〕.

knut [nʌt] *n.*〔谑〕纨袴子弟，花花公子(= nut).

K.O., k.o. = knock-out.

ko·a [ˈkəuə] *n.*〔Haw.〕【植】寇阿相思树(*Acacia koa*)〔产于夏威夷，为建筑和家具用材，树皮可用于鞣皮〕.

ko·a·la [kəuˈɑ:lə] *n.*【动】考拉〔大洋洲无尾熊〕.

ko·an [ˈkəuɑ:n] *n.*【佛】心印，以心传心〔佛教禅宗沉思中的重要一环，以一种简短而不合逻辑的问题，使思想脱离理性的范畴〕.

kob [kɔb] *n.*【动】非洲水羚(*Kobus kob*)〔产于东南非〕.

Ko·be [ˈkəubi] *n.* 神户〔日本城市〕.

Ko·ben·havn [ˌkə:bənˈhaun] 哥本哈根〔丹麦文写法〕.

kob·old [ˈkɔbəuld] *n.*【德神】帮助做家务的小精灵；(矿山等的)地下精灵.

Koch [G. kɔx], **Robert,** 罗伯特·科赤〔1843—1910，德国细菌学家，医学家，结核菌、霍乱菌发现者〕.

ko·dak [ˈkəudæk] *n.* ①手提照相机. ②〔K-〕〔美〕柯达〔柯达公司的照相机和照相材料的商标名〕. ③小型照相机拍的照片. — *vi., vt.* 用手提照相机拍(照片).

ko·di·ak bear [ˈkəudi:æk]【动】科迪亚克棕熊(*Ursus*

K

middendorffi)〔产于科迪亚克岛及其邻近地区，体重可达 1,500 磅〕.

ko·el [ˈkəuəl] *n.* 鬼布谷〔产于印度、东印度群岛及澳大利亚的一种类似杜鹃的鸟〕.

Koest·ler [ˈkestlə] *n.* 凯斯特勒〔姓氏〕.

K. of C. = Knight(s) of Columbus〔美〕(天主教)慈善会(成员).

Koh·i·noor, Koh-i-noor [ˈkəuinuə] *n.* ①皇冠钻石〔英国皇冠上一颗重 108 克拉的印度大金钻石〕. ②〔k-〕出类拔萃的东西.

kohl [kəul] *n.* (阿拉伯妇女涂眼圈的)眼圈墨.

kohl·ra·bi [ˈkəulˈrɑːbi] *n.*【植】球茎甘蓝.

koi·ne [kɔiˈnei, ˈkɔinei, -niː] *n.* 〔K-〕①柯因内语〔希腊罗马时代东地中海等希腊语国家的共同语〕. ②共同语.

ko·ji [ˈkəudʒi] *n.*【微】日本麴.

ko·kan·ee [kəuˈkæniː] *n.* (*pl.* **-ees, -ee**) 红大麻花鱼(*Oncorhynchus nerka kennerlyi*)〔产于美国西北部〕.

kok-sa·ghyz, kok-sa·gyz [ˈkəuksæˈgiːz] *n.*【植】橡胶草,青胶蒲公英(*Taraxacum kok-saghyz*)〔苏联的一种蒲公英,从其根部可提炼橡胶〕.

ko·la [ˈkəulə] *n.* = cola. ~ **nut** (非洲)可拉果.

ko·lin·sky [kəuˈlinski] *n.* 亚洲貂,西伯利亚貂. ~ **skins** 元皮.

Kol·khoz [kɔlˈhɔz] *n.* 〔Russ.〕(苏联的)集体农庄.

Köln [G. kœln] *n.* 科隆〔德意志联邦共和国城市〕.

ko·lo [ˈkəuləu] *n.* (*pl.* **~s**) 科洛舞〔塞尔维亚的一种民间舞蹈〕.

Kom·in·tern [ˈkɔmintəːn] *n.* = Comintern.

kom·man·da·tu·ra [kəˌmændəˈturə] *n.* 军事管制总部〔尤指第二次世界大战后苏联等国在欧洲城市所设的此类机构〕.

Ko·mo·do dragon [kəˈməudəu] *n.*【动】科莫多巨蜥(*Varanus komodoensis*)〔产于印尼科莫多岛，全长 9 英尺,当今地球上最长的蜥蜴〕.

Kom·so·mol [ˌkɔmsəˈmɔl] *n.* 〔Russ.〕共产主义青年团.

Kom·so·molsk [ˌkɔmsəˈmɔlsk] *n.* 共青城〔苏联城市〕.

Kon·go [ˈkɔŋgəu] *n.* (*pl.* **~(s)**) ①(安哥拉和刚果的)班图人. ②班图语.

ko·nim·e·ter [kəuˈnimitə] *n.* 尘度计, 计尘器〔测量空气浮尘量用〕.

kon·i·ol·o·gy [ˌkəuniˈɔlədʒi] *n.* 空气中的灰尘; 微尘学.

kon·i·scope [ˈkɔniskəup] *n.* 检尘器.

kon·zern [G. kɔnˈtsɛən] *n.* 〔G.〕【经】康采恩.

koo·doo [ˈkuːduː] *n.* (*pl.* **~(s)**) (南非产)条纹羚羊(= kudu).

kook [kuːk] *n.* 〔美俚〕傻子; 怪人; 狂人.

kook·a·bur·ra [ˈkukəbəːrə] *n.*【动】笑鸡(*Dacelo gigas*)〔一种澳大利亚翠鸟〕.

kook·y, kook·ie [ˈkuːkiː] *a.* 〔美俚〕傻的, 古怪的; 发狂的. **kook·i·ness** *n.*

Koord [kɔːd, kuəd] *n.* = Kurd.

Koo·te·nay [ˈkuːtnei] = Kutenai.

kop [kɔːp] *n.* 〔南非〕山, 山岳.

kop. = kope(c)k.

ko·pe(c)k [ˈkəupek] *n.* (苏联辅币名)戈比〔100 戈比 =1 卢布〕.

koph [kɔːf] *n.* 希伯来语第十九个字母.

kop·je, kop·pie [ˈkɔpi] *n.* (南非的)小山, 丘陵.

kor [kɔː] *n.* 侯尔〔希伯来早期量具名. 作干体量具相当于 6¹/₄普式耳; 作液体量具相当于 58 加仑〕(= homer).

Ko·ran [kɔˈrɑːn] *n.* (穆斯林的)《古兰经》,《可兰经》. **-ic** *a.*

Kor·do·fan·i·an [ˌkɔːdəˈfæniən] *n.* 科尔多凡语〔非洲语言中的刚果—科尔多凡语系的一个语族, 有五个语支〕.

Ko·re·a [kəˈriə, kɔ(ː)ˈriə] *n.* 朝鲜〔亚洲〕. *the Democratic People's Republic of* ~ 朝鲜民主主义人民共和国〔略作 DPRK〕.

Ko·re·an [kəˈriən] *a.* 朝鲜的; 朝鲜人的; 朝鲜族的; 朝鲜族人的; 朝鲜语的. — *n.* 朝鲜人; 朝鲜族; 朝鲜族人; 朝鲜语.

Korn·berg [ˈkɔːnbəg] *n.* 科恩伯格〔姓氏〕.

Kor·sa·koff's psychosis [syndrome] [ˈkɔːsəˌkɔːfs]【医】柯萨可夫氏精神病〔由于酒精中毒, 维生素缺乏等引起的精神病, 表现为多发性神经炎、失去记忆和不辨方向等〕.

ko·ru·na [kəuˈruːnɑː] *n.* (*pl.* **~s, ko·run**) ①克朗〔捷克货币名称, 等于 100 赫勒 (*Hallers*)〕. ②克朗币〔硬币〕.

kos [kəus] *n.* (*pl.* **kos**) 科斯〔印度的长度名, 长度由 1.5—3 英里, 各地不一〕.

ko·sher [ˈkəuːʃə] *a.* ①【犹】(按犹太教食规)清洁可食的; 供应清洁可食食物的. ②按犹太教传统食谱烹调的. ③〔俚〕可以的; 正当的; 正确的. — *n.* ①按犹太教食规清洁可食的食品. ②〔口〕合法的卫生食品. 犹太教食品. — *vt.* 使(食物)清洁可食.

ko·to [ˈkəutəu] *n.* (*pl.* **~s**) 〔Jap.〕(日本的)十三弦古筝.

ko(w)·tow [ˈkəuˈtau] *n.* 〔Chin.〕叩头, 磕头. — *vi.* ①叩头, 磕头. ②拍马屁, 奉承 (*to*).

kot·wal [ˈkɔtwɑːl] *n.* 〔Hind.〕(印度的)警察局长; 行政长官.

kot·wa·li [ˈkəutwɑːli] *n.* 〔Hind.〕(印度的)警察局.

kou·miss [ˈkuːmis] *n.* ①(中亚地区牧民用马乳或骆驼乳做的)乳酒. ②(欧美人的)牛奶酒.

Kour·bash [ˈkuəbæʃ] *n.* = Kurbash.

KP, K.P. = kitchen police.

Kp = king's pawn (国际象棋中"王"前面的)兵.

KR = king's rook (国际象棋中与"王"同列配置的)车.

Kr =【化】krypton.

kr =【物】kiloroentgen.

kr. =① krona. ②krone.

kraal [krɑːl] *n.* ①(南非当地居民有栅栏防护的)村庄; 村中居民. ②(南非的)羊栏, 牛栏. — *vt.* 把(家畜)关进栏内.

kraft [ˈkrɑːft] *n.* 牛皮纸 (= ~ paper).

krait [krait] *n.* 〔Hind.〕(产于南亚和东南亚的) 孟加拉毒蛇.

kra·ken [ˈkrɑːkən] *n.* (相传常在挪威海中出现的)海怪.

Kra·ków [ˈkrækau; Pol. ˈkrɑkuːf] *n.* 克拉科夫〔波兰城市〕.

kra·ter [ˈkreitə, ˈkrɑː-] *n.* 搀和器〔古希腊把酒和水搀和在一起的一种双柄大口罐〕.

K ra·tion [ˈkei ˈræʃən] *n.* (美军三包一天分、内有肉、饼干、香肠等的) K 种口粮袋, 应急口粮.

Krebs [krebz] *n.* 克雷布斯〔姓氏〕.

Kreis·ler [ˈkraislə] *n.* 克赖斯勒〔姓氏〕.

krem·lin [ˈkremlin] *n.* 〔Russ.〕①(俄国的)城堡. ②〔the K-〕(莫斯科的)克里姆林宫; 苏联政府. — *a.* 〔K-〕克里姆林宫的; 苏联政府的.

Krem·lin·ol·o·gy [ˈkremlinˈɔlədʒi] *n.* 〔口〕(西方国家的)苏联政策研究. **-ol·o·gist** *n.* 苏联政策研究专家.

kre·o·sote [ˈkriəsəut] *n.* = creosote.

krep·lach [ˈkreplɑːk, -lək] *n.* 〔*pl.*〕三角馄饨.

kreut·zer, kreu·zer [ˈkrɔitsə] *n.* 〔G.〕克娄泽〔13 世纪至 19 世纪中叶德国和奥地利通行的一种铜币〕.

Krieg·ie [ˈkriːgi] *n.* 〔G.〕战俘.

krieg·spiel [ˈkriːgspiːl] *n.* 〔G.〕(用作盘上战术指挥训练的)军棋游戏.

krill [kril] *n.* (*pl.* **krill**)【动】磷蝦.

krim·mer [ˈkrimə] *n.* 克里米亚黑(灰)色羊羔皮.

kris [kris] *n.* 马来西亚人的波纹刀刃短剑 (= crease, creese).

K

Krish·na [ˈkriʃnə] *n.*【印度神】(象征丰收和幸福的)牧牛神讫里什那. **-ism** *n.* 牧牛神崇拜.
Kriss Krin·gle [ˈkris ˈkriŋgl]【宗】= Santa Claus.
Kroll [krəul] *n.* 克罗尔〔姓氏〕.
kro·na [ˈkrəunə] *n.* ①*(pl.* ***-nor*** [-nɔː]*)* (瑞典的货币单位)克朗. ②*(pl.* ***-nur*** [-nə]*)* (冰岛的货币单位)克朗.
kro·ne[1] [ˈkrəune] *n.* *(pl.* ***-r*** [-nεə]*)* (丹麦、挪威的货币单位)克朗.
kro·ne[2] [ˈkrəunə] *n.* *(pl.* ***-nen*** [-nən]*)* ①旧德国金币. ②旧奥国银币.
Kron·s(h)tadt [ˈkrɔnʃtæt] *n.* 喀琅施塔得〔苏联港市〕.
Kroo, Kru [kruː] *n.* 克鲁人〔利比里亚沿海岸具有熟练技术的黑种人水手〕. — *a.* 克鲁人的.
Kroo·boy [ˈkruːbɔi] *n.* 克鲁人.
Kroo·man [ˈkruːmən] *n.* *(pl.* ***-men****)* = Krooboy.
Kro·pot·kin [krəuˈpɔːtkin], **Prince Pëtr Aleksyeevich** 克鲁泡特金〔1842—1921, 俄国地理学家、无政府主义者〕.
K.R.R. = King's Royal Rifles〔英〕皇家步枪队.
Kru [kruː] *n.* = Kroo.
krul·ler [ˈkrʌlə] *n.* = cruller.
krumm·horn, krum·horn [ˈkrumhɔːn, ˈkrʌm-] *n.* 变号〔一种古双簧乐器〕.
Krupp [krʌp], **Alfred** 克鲁伯〔1812—1887, 德国军火制造商〕.
Krutch [kruːtʃ] *n.* 克鲁奇〔姓氏〕.
kryp·tol [ˈkriptɔl] *n.* 粒状碳〔电极粒状物〕, 碳棒; 硅碳棒.
kryp·ton [ˈkriptɔn] *n.*【化】氪.
Ks. = Kansas.
Kshat·ri·ya [ˈkʃætriə] *n.* 刹帝利〔印度四大封建种姓的第二种姓(武士或贵族)〕.
Kt = knight (国际象棋中的)马.
kt = karat 开〔黄金成色单位〕.
kts = knots per hour 节(海里/小时)〔复数〕.
Kua·la Lum·pur [ˈkwɑːlə ˈlumpuə] 吉隆坡〔马来西亚首都〕.
Ku·blai Khan [ˈkuːblai ˈkɑːn] *n.* 忽必烈〔1216?—1294, 元世祖, 中国元朝皇帝, 成吉思汗之孙〕.
ku·chen [ˈkuːkən, -hən] *n.*〔G.〕糕点〔德国早餐点心〕.
Ku·ching [ˈkuːtʃiŋ] *n.* 古晋〔马来西亚港市〕.
ku·dos [ˈkjuːdɔs] *n.*〔口〕名誉, 光荣, 荣誉.
ku·du [ˈkuːduː] *n.* *(pl.* *~(s)* *)* = koodoo.
kud·zu [ˈkudzuː] *n.*【植】(产于中国和日本的)葛 *(Pueraria thunbergiana)*.
Ku·fic [ˈkjuːfik, ˈkuː-] *a.* 古阿拉伯字母表〔使用于巴比伦南部地区使用〕(= Cufic).
Kui·by·shev [ˈkwibiʃev] *n.* 古比雪夫〔苏联城市〕.
Ku Klux [ˈkjuːˈklʌks, kuː-] ①Ku Klux Klan 之略. ②(用私刑迫害黑人和进步工人的美国恐怖组织) 三 K 党党徒 (= Ku Kluxer).
Ku Klux·er [ˈkjuː ˈklʌksə] *n.* 三 K 党成员.
Ku Klux Klan [ˈkjuː ˈklʌksklæn, kjuː-] *n.* 三 K 党.
Ku Klux·ism [ˈkjuː ˈklʌksizəm] 三 K 党主义.
kuk·ri [ˈkukri] *n.* (印度廓尔喀人用的)曲刀.
ku·lak [kuːˈlɑːk] *n.* *(pl.* ***kulaki*** [ˈkuːlɑːki]*)*〔Russ.〕富农.
Kul·tur [kulˈtuə] *n.*〔G.〕①文明, 文化〔与英语 culture 相当〕. ②〔讽〕德国文化〔指沙文主义, 军国主义, 恐怖主义等〕. ③德国纳粹分子等统治下的社会组织〔制度〕.
kul·tur·kampf [kulˈtuːəkɑːmpf] *n.*〔G.〕(1873—1887 年罗马天主教会和德国政府之间围绕教育和教职任命权进行的)文化斗争.
Ku·ma·mo·to [ˈkuːməˈmautəu] *n.* 熊本〔日本城市〕.
ku·mis(s) [ˈkuːmis] *n.* = koumiss.
küm·mel [ˈkuməl] *n.*〔G.〕茴香甜酒.
kum·mer·bund [ˈkʌməbʌnd] *n.* 腰围, 腹带, 腹套 (= cummerbund).
kum·quat [ˈkʌmkwɔt] *n.*【植】金钱桔 (= cumquat).
kunz·ite [ˈkuntsait] *n.*【地】紫锂辉石.
Kuo·min·tang [ˈkwəuminˈtæŋ] *n.*〔Chin.〕〔the ~〕(中国)国民党.
Kur·bash [ˈkuəbæʃ] *n.* (旧时土耳其、埃及用作抽打犯人的)皮鞭. — *vt.* 鞭笞.
Kurd [kəːd] *n.* 库尔德人〔主要居住在伊朗库尔德斯坦和高加索南部的穆斯林游牧民族〕.
Kurd·ish [ˈkəːdiʃ, kuədiʃ] *a.* 库尔德人的; 库尔德语的; 库尔德文化的. — *n.* 库尔德语.
Ku·ril(e) Islands [kuˈriːl ˈailəndz] 千岛群岛.
Kur·o·shi·o [kuˈrəuʃiːˈəu] *n.* (从台湾东面的菲律宾海流向日本的)暖流 (= Japan current).
kur·ra·jong [ˈkəːrədʒɔːŋ, -dʒɔŋ] *n.*【植】异叶瓶木 *(Brachychiton populneum)*〔澳大利亚树名, 其枝根可以织网和席〕.
kur·saal [ˈkuəzɑːl] *n.*〔G.〕(德国温泉、海水浴场等处的)娱乐馆.
Kurt [kəːt, kuət] *n.* 库尔特〔男子名, Conrad 的昵称〕.
kurt(o)- *pref.* 表示"鼓起", "凸出": *kurtosis*.
kur·to·sis [kəːˈtəusis] *n.*【统】峭度. ~ *of frequency curve* 频率曲线峰态.
ku·ru [ˈkuːru] *n.*【医】苦鲁病〔发现于新几内亚东部高原的一种中枢神经系统退化症〕.
ku·ruş [kuˈruːʃ] *n.* *(pl.* ***ku·rus****)* 库鲁〔土耳其货币名, 等于 1/100 土镑, 亦称里拉〕.
Kusch [kuʃ] *n.* 库施〔姓氏〕.
Ku·te·nai, Ku·te·nay [ˈkuːtnei] *n.* ①库特内人〔居住美国蒙大拿和爱达荷两州以及加拿大哥伦比亚省的印第安人〕. ②库特内语.
Ku·wait [kuˈweit] *n.* ①科威特〔亚洲〕. ②科威特〔科威特首都〕.
Ku·wai·ti [kuˈweiti, kəˈwaiti] *a.* 科威特的; 科威特人的. — *n.* 科威特人.
kv. = kilovolt(s).
KVA, KVa, kva = kilovolt-ampere 千伏安.
kvas(s) [kvɑːs] *n.*〔Russ.〕葛瓦斯〔一种类似啤酒的清凉饮料〕.
kw. = kilowatt(s).
Kwa [kwɑː] *n.* 克瓦语〔非洲西部和北部讲的尼日尔—刚果语族的一个语支〕.
kwa·cha [ˈkwɑːtʃɑː] *n.* *(pl.* ***kwa·cha****)* 克瓦查〔赞比亚和马拉维的货币名称〕.
Kwa·ki·u·tl [ˌkwɑːkiːˈuːtl] *n.* ①夸丘特尔人〔加拿大不列颠哥伦比亚省的一个印第安人部落的居民〕. ②夸丘特尔语.
kwa·shi·or·kor [ˌkwɑːʃiːˈɔːkɔə] *n.* 夸休可尔症〔由于食物缺乏蛋白和热量引起的一种儿童营养不良病, 症状是个儿矮小、水肿、腹部突出, 发现于非洲〕.
kwh., KWH, K.W.H., kw-h, kw-hr = kilowatt-hour 千瓦小时.
ky. = Kentucky.
ky·ack [ˈkaiæk] *n.* (美国西部挂在鞍子两边的)皮包〔帆布包〕.
ky·ak [ˈkaiæk] *n.* = kayak.
ky·a·nite [ˈkaiənait] *n.* = cyanite.
ky·an·ize [ˈkaiənaiz] *vt.* 给(木材)注入升汞, 用升汞溶液(给木材)防腐.
kyat [kjɑːt] *n.* 元〔缅甸货币名, 等于 100 分 *(pyas)*〕.
Kyd [kid] *n.* 基德〔姓氏〕.
kyle [kail] *n.* 海峡.
ky·lin [ˈkailin, ˈkiːlin] *n.*〔Chin.〕【动】麒麟〔雄的谓之麒, 雌的谓之麟〕.
ky·lix [ˈkailiks, ˈkiliks] *n.* *(pl.* ***ky·li·kes*** [-kiːz]*)* 双柄杯〔古希腊用的大口酒杯〕.
ky·lo(e) [ˈkailəu] *n.*【动】(苏格兰高地产)长角牛犊.
ky·mo·gram [ˈkaiməugræm] *n.*【医】记波图.

K

ky·mo·graph [ˈkaiməugrɑːf, -ˌgræf] *n.*【医】记波器，描波器。**-ic** *a.*
ky·mo·gra·phy [kaiˈmɔgrəfi] *n.* 记波照相术，记波法。
Kym·ric [ˈkimrik] *a., n.* = Cymric = Welsh.
Kym·ry, Kym·ri [ˈkimri, ˈkimriː] *n.* *(pl.* ***-ry, -ri, -ries)*** = Cymry.
Kyo·to [kiˈəutəu] *n.* 京都〔日本城市〕。
ky·pho- *pref.* 表示"向前弯曲": *kypho*scoliosis, *kyph*osis.
ky·pho·sco·li·o·sis [ˈkaifəuˌskɔliˈəusis] *n.*【医】脊柱后侧凸。
ky·pho·sis [kaiˈfəusis] *n.*【医】脊柱后凸，驼背。**ky·phot·ic** [kaiˈfɔtik] *a.*
Kyr·i·e e·le·i·son [ˈkiriˌei iˈleiiˌsəun]〔Gr.〕【宗】恳求主怜悯我们〔希腊正教和天主教用作弥撒的起始语；英国圣公会用作对十诫的回答语〕。
kyte [kait] *n.*〔Scot.〕胃，肚子。*fill one's* ~ 饱腹。
Kyu·shu [ˈkjuːˈʃuː] *n.* 九州〔日本〕。

L

L, l [el] ***(pl. L's, l's*** **[elz]*)*** ①英语字母表第十二字母。②L形物；【机】L字管；L形建筑物。③第11〔连J计算时为第12〕。④〔the L〕〔美口〕elevated railroad 高架铁路(*ride on the L* 坐高架电车。*an L station* 高架铁路车站)。⑤(罗马数字的)50〔*LV* = 55. *LXIV* = 64. *CXL* = 140〕。⑥〔L.〕【物】潜热(latent heat)的符号。***the three L's***【海】三L〔指 lead(测铅)的用法，latitude(纬度)的知识，及严密的 look-out(守望)〕。**L-beam, L-iron** 不等边角钢。**L-cathode** 金属多孔阴极，L型阴极。**L-square** 直角板。
L, £ = 〔L.〕*libra* (=pound).
L., l. = ①lady. ②lake. ③lambert. ④land. ⑤large. ⑥Latin. ⑦latitude. ⑧law. ⑨league. ⑩left. ⑪ledger. ⑫length. ⑬liberal. ⑭〔L.〕*libra(e)*. ⑮licentiate. ⑯light. ⑰line. ⑱link. ⑲lira, lire. ⑳litre(s). ㉑lodge. ㉒lord. ㉓lost. ㉔low. ㉕lumen.
L.A. = ①Law Agent 法律代理人。②Legislative Assembly〔美〕州的两院制议会。③Library Association〔英〕图书馆协会。④Local Agent (房地产保险公司)驻地方代理人。
La =【化】lanthanum.
La. = Louisiana.
la[1] [lɑː] *n.*【乐】长音阶全音阶的第六音，A音的唱名。
la[2] [lɔː, lɑː] *int.*〔古，方〕啊呀！看哪！〔用以加强语气或表示惊愕。〕~ ***me!***〔俚〕啊呀！
LAA, L.A.A. = light antiaircraft 轻型高射炮；轻型高射炮兵。
laa·ger [ˈlɑːgə] *n.* ①(用货车等围成的)野营。②【军】车阵；(用各种车辆围成的)临时防御阵地；装甲车停车处。— *vi.* ①围成车阵。②驻扎在车阵内。— *vt.* 把(车辆等)围成车阵〔临时阵地〕。
lab. [læb] *n.*〔口〕= ①labo(u)r. ②laboratory.
Lab. [læb] = ①Labour Advisory Board 劳工咨询委员会。②Laborite 工党党员。③Labrador 拉布拉多半岛〔加拿大〕。
lab·a·rum [ˈlæbərəm] ***(pl. lab·a·ra*** **[-rə]*)*** *n.* 拉伯兰旗〔①罗马帝国后期的军旗。②(罗马天主教的)教旗〕。
lab·da·num [ˈlæbdənəm] *n.*【化】劳丹脂，半日花脂〔作香料用〕。
lab·e·fac·tion [ˌlæbiˈfækʃən] *n.* 动摇；衰弱；朽败；崩溃，覆灭。
la·bel [ˈleibl] *n.* ①纸条，贴条，标签，签条。②称号，绰号。③标记，符号。④(词典中用的)说明性略语。⑤(有胶水的)邮票〔印花税票〕。⑥【建】披水石。⑦〔古〕布条，带子；封文件的丝带。*attach a* ~ *on* ... 在…上加标签。*union* ~〔美〕(证明产品确是工会会员制成或销售的)工会标签。*acquire the* ~ *of* 得了…的绰号。— *vt.* (〔英〕***-ll-***) ①贴标签于，用签条标明。②把…叫做，把…列为。③(用放射性同位素)使(元素或原子)示踪；(用示踪原子)使(化合物等)示踪。~ *a trunk for Paris* 给箱子贴上运往巴黎的标签。*The bottle is* ~*(l)ed "Poison"*. 瓶上标明"有毒"。~ *sb. (as) a turncoat* 把某人叫做叛徒。
la·belled [ˈleibld] *a.* 加有标记的；示踪的。~ **atom** 示踪原子。
la·bel·lum [ləˈbeləm] *n.* ***(pl. la·bel·la*** **[ləˈbelə]*)***【植】唇瓣。
la·bi·a [ˈleibiə] *n.* labium 的复数。~ **majora** [məˈdʒɔurə]【解】大阴唇。~ **minora** [miˈnɔːrə]【解】小阴唇。
la·bi·al [ˈleibiəl] *a.* ①嘴唇的，唇状的。②【语】唇音的。— *n.* ①风琴管。②唇音〔[b] [p] [m] 等〕。**-ism** *n.* 唇音的特征；发唇音的倾向，好发唇音。**-i·ty** *n.* **-ly** *ad.*
la·bi·al·ize [ˈleibiəlaiz] *vt.* ①用唇发音。②使唇音化。**-i·za·tion** [ˌleibiəlaiˈzeiʃən] *n.*
la·bi·ate [ˈleibieit] *a.* ①唇形的。②【植】唇形科的。③【动】有唇形物的。— *n.*【植】唇形科植物。~ **corolla** 唇形花冠。
la·bile [ˈleibail] *a.* ①易变化的；【物、化】不稳定的。②【电】滑动的，不安定的。~ **gene**【生】易变基因。~ **oscillator** 易变振荡器。~ **shower** 晶霰。~ **state**【化】不稳定态；易变态。
la·bi·o- *comb. f.* 表示"唇的"；"唇和…的"：*labio*dental.
la·bi·o·den·tal [ˌleibiəuˈdentl] *a.*【语音】用唇齿发音的。— *n.* 唇齿音〔[f]、[v]等〕。
la·bi·o·na·sal [ˌleibiəuˈneizl] *a.*【语音】唇鼻音的〔如 m〕。— *n.* 唇鼻音。
la·bi·o·ve·lar [ˌleibiəuˈviːlə] *a.*【语音】唇软颚音的〔如 w〕。— *n.* 唇软颚音。
la·bi·um [ˈleibiəm] *n.* ***(pl. -bi·a*** **[-biə]*)*** ①〔*pl.*〕【解】唇；阴唇。②【动】(无脊椎动物的)唇状部分；(昆虫的)下唇。③【植】(唇形花冠的)下唇瓣。
la·bor [ˈleibə] *n., v.*〔美〕= labour. **L- Day** 美国劳动节〔九月的第一个星期一，相当于欧洲的 May Day〕。**L- Department**〔美〕劳动部。
lab·o·ra·to·ri·al [ˌlæbərəˈtɔːriəl] *a.* 实验(室)的。**-ly** *ad.*
la·bo·ra·to·ry [ləˈbɔrətəri, ˈlæbərətəri] *n.* ①实验室，化验室，研究室。②炉房。③化学工厂；药厂。④实验课。*a chemical* ~ 化学实验室。*an express* ~ 快速化验室。*a hygienic* ~ 卫生试验所。~ *rats* 实验用鼠。~ *sole* 炉底，炉床。~ **course** 实验学科。~ **school** 为学生实习而设的大学实验学校。
la·bo(u)red [ˈleibəd] *a.* 费力做成的；费力的，吃力的。
la·bo·ri·ous [ləˈbɔːriəs] *a.* ①费力的，麻烦的。②勤勉的。③(文体等)不流畅的。*a* ~ *task* 吃力的工作〔任

务]. **-ly** *ad.* **-ness** *n.*

la·bor·ite [ˈleibərait] *n.* ①工党党员或支持者. ②[L-]英国工党党员; 工党支持者 (=Labourite).

la·bour [ˈleibə] *n.* ①劳动. ②努力,苦干. ③工作; 活计. ④工人 (*opp.* capital; management); [集合词]劳工,工人阶级,体力劳动者 (*opp.* professional). ⑤[L-](英国或英联邦成员国的)工党. ⑥[*pl.*]世事,俗务. ⑦分娩,临产阵痛. ⑧【海】船只的剧烈摇动. *forced* ~ 强迫劳动. *free* ~【史】自由民的劳动;美国未加入工会者的劳动. *hard* ~ 劳役,苦役. *mental* ~ 脑力劳动. *manual [physical]* ~ 体力劳动. *~-consuming processes* 重体力劳动作业. *wage* ~ 雇佣劳动. *cheap* ~ 廉价劳动力. ~ *and capital* 劳资双方. ~ *aristocrats* 工人贵族. *skilled* ~ 熟练劳动. *surplus* ~【经】剩余劳动. *the Minister of L- and National Service* [英] 劳工大臣. *the ministry of L- and National Service* [英] 劳工部. *unskilled* ~ 不熟练工人. *the L- vote* 支持工党的选票. *His ~s are over.* 他的一生结束了. *a woman in* ~ 临产的妇女. *difficult* ~ 难产. *natural* ~ 顺产. *~ of love* 不取报酬自愿承担的工作, 义务劳动,社会工作. *~ of Sisyphus = Sisyphean* ~ 沉重而无结果的工作. *lost* ~ = ~ *lost* 徒劳. ~ *leader* 工会领袖. *(the) L- Leader* 工党领袖. *~ of Hercules = Herculean ~(s)* 需要极大努力的工作. — *vi.* ①工作; 劳动. ②努力(争取)(*for*); 出力. ③分娩; 产前阵痛. ④(船只)剧烈摇动; 颠簸; 困难地前进. *~ at a task* 埋头工作; 辛苦地干. *~ after wealth* 忙于赚钱. *~ for bread* 挣饭吃. *~ at a problem* 绞尽脑汁地做一道难题. *I ~ed to understand him.* 我努力想了解他. *The wheels ~ed in the sand.* 车轮在沙中空转(无法前进). *The ship ~ed in the heavy seas.* 船在大海中吃力地前进. — *vt.* ①使劳动; 出力做. ②详细论述. ③使疲倦; 麻烦. ④[古]耕种. ⑤开(矿). *I'll not ~ the point.* 这一点我就不详细谈了. ~ *the reader with unnecessary detail* 以不必要的细节来困惑读者. ***~ for breath*** 觉得呼吸困难. ***~ on [along] the way*** 勉强前进. ***~ one's way*** 克服困难前进. ***~ under*** 在…下耗费精力[感到困难]. ***~ under a delusion*** 想错, 误解. **L- Bureau** 劳动局. ~ **camp** ①(对犯人实行强制劳动的)劳动营. ②流动工人营地. ~ **content** 【经】(商品成本中的) 加工费. ~ **cost** 人工成本. ~ **court** 劳资争议法庭. ~ **dispute** 劳资争议. ~ **exchange** ①物物平等交换, 产品交换. ②职业介绍所; [英] 劳工介绍所. ~ **force** 劳动力. ~ **insurance** 劳动保险. ~ **market** 劳动市场. ~ **movement** 工人运动. ~ **organization** 工人组织. ~ **pains** 产前阵痛. ~ **relations** 劳资关系. **~-saving** *a.* 省力的, 减轻劳动的. ~ **turn over** (工人雇入、解雇、转业等变动的)工人移动率. ~ **union** 工会.

la·boured [ˈleibəd] *a.* = labored.

la·bo(u)r·er [ˈleibərə] *n.* 工人; 劳工,劳动者. *a free* ~ 自由劳动者. *a hired farm* ~ 雇农. *a long-term* ~ 长工. *a seasonal* ~ 短工.

la·bo(u)r·ing [ˈleibəriŋ] *a.* ①劳动的. ②费力的, 辛苦的. ③(船)剧烈颠簸的. *a ~ man* 工人, 劳动者. *the ~ class(es)* 工人阶级. *the ~ people* 劳动人民. ***take the ~ oar*** 担任最困难的工作. **-ly** *ad.*

la·bo(u)r·ism [ˈleibərizəm] *n.* 工党 [工会] 的主义[政策].

la·bo(u)r·ist [ˈleibərist] *n.* [英] [L-] 工党党员 (=Labo(u)rite).

la·bo(u)r·some [ˈleibəsəm] *a.* 吃力的.

la·bra [ˈleibrə, ˈlæbrə] *n.* labrum 的复数.

Lab·ra·dor [ˈlæbrədɔː] *n.* 拉布拉多 [北美哈德逊湾与大西洋间的半岛]. ~ **current** (加拿大)拉布拉多(冷)洋流 [从巴芬 (Baffin) 海湾经拉布拉多和纽芬兰流入墨西哥湾流的北极寒流]. ~ **retriever** 拉布拉多猎犬[能衔回猎物的猎犬].

lab·ra·dor·ite [ˈlæbrədɔːrait] *n.* 【地】富拉玄武岩; 拉长石.

la·bret [ˈleibret] *n.* (某些原始民族用的)嘴唇装饰物[指介壳、骨片等].

lab·roid [ˈlæbrɔid, ˈleibrɔid] *a.* 【动】咽颌亚目 *(Pharyngognathi)* [包括隆头鱼科和鹦嘴鱼科]的. — *n.* 咽颌亚目的鱼.

la·brum [ˈleibrəm] *n.* *(pl.* **-bra** [-brə]*)* 【动】上唇, 外唇.

la·bur·num [ləˈbəːnəm] *n.* 【植】金链花; 金链花属[毒豆属]植物.

lab·y·rinth [ˈlæbərinθ] *n.* ①迷宫, 曲径. ②(事件等的)错综复杂, 纠纷; 曲折; 难事. ③【解】(内耳的)迷路. *bony* ~ 骨迷路. *membranous* ~ 膜迷路.

lab·y·rin·thi·an [ˌlæbəˈrinθiən], **lab·y·rin·thic** [-ik], **lab·y·rin·thine** [-ain] *a.* ①迷宫的, 迷宫似的. ②曲折的, 错综复杂的.

lac[1] [læk] *n.* 【化】虫胶, 紫胶, 虫脂. ~ **insect** 【动】紫胶虫.

lac[2] [læk] = lakh.

L.A.C., LAC = ①leading aircraft(s)man [英] 空军二等兵. ②London Athletic Club [英]伦敦田径俱乐部.

lac·co·lite, lac·co·lith [ˈlækəlait, ˈlækəliθ] *n.* 【地】岩盖. ~ **mountain** 岩盖山.

lace [leis] *n.* ①(鞋)带子, 系带. ②花边, 饰边; 饰带, 丝带, 缎带; 辫带. ③(带有装饰图案的)精细网织品, 透孔织品. ④(加在咖啡或食物中的) 少量烈性酒. *shoe* ~ 鞋带. *a dress trimmed with ~s* 有花边的服装. *gold ~s* (外交官、海军等的服装所饰的)金边. — *vt.* ①结(鞋)带, 用带子系紧. ②在…上穿带子; 交织, 刺绣. ③镶花边于, 加条纹于. ④[口] 鞭打. ⑤给…搀酒; 搀合, 混合. ~ *one's waist in* 用带束腰. *be tight-~d* 腰束得太紧. *coffee ~d with brandy* 加白兰地的咖啡. — *vi.* ①结带子; 用带子系紧. ②[口] 打, 鞭打. *These boots ~.* 这靴子是结带的. ~ ***into*** [口] 打, 鞭打; 斥骂. ~ ***sb.'s coat [jacket]*** [俚] 鞭打某人. ~ ***up*** 用带子束 [结]紧. ~ **boots** 穿带长统靴. **~-curtain** *a.* ①矫饰的. ②模仿中产阶级的, 极想成为中产阶级的. ~ **frame** 花边制造机. ~ **glass** 有花边状图案的玻璃器皿. **~man** 花边商人. ~ **paper** 花边纸. ~ **pillow** 编织花边时放在膝上的垫子. **~-ups** [口] 绑带的鞋子[袜子]. **~wing** 【动】脉翅目昆虫. **~work** 【纺】网眼针织物, 花边针织物. **-less** *a.* 没有带子的; 不镶花边的. **-like** *a.* 带子般的, 花边状的.

laced [leist] *a.* ①有带子的, 结带子的. ②镶着花边的. ③(花)有彩色条纹的. ④(咖啡等)加有酒的.

Lac·e·dae·mo·ni·an [ˌlæsidiˈməunjən, -niən] *a.* ①古代斯巴达的, 古代斯巴达人的, 古代斯巴达文化的. ②语言简洁的. — *n.* 古代斯巴达人.

lac·er·a·ble [ˈlæsərəbl] *a.* 划得破的, 容易撕碎的.

lac·er·ate [ˈlæsəreit] *vt.* ①撕碎, 划破, 割裂(软组织等). ②使痛心, 使苦恼. — [ˈlæsərit] *a.* ①撕碎了的, 划破了的. ②【植】(叶子等)撕裂状的. ③精神深受创伤的; 悲痛的. **-ly** *ad.*

lac·er·a·tion [ˌlæsəˈreiʃən] *n.* ①撕裂, 划破. ②伤口, 裂口. ③痛苦, 悲痛, 苦恼. **-a·tive** *a.*

La·cer·ta [ləˈsəːtə] *n.* 【天】蝎虎(星)座.

la·cer·til·i·an [ˌlæsəˈtiliən] *a.*, *n.* 【动】= saurian.

lach·es [ˈleitʃiz] *n.* 【法】懈怠, 玩忽职守.

Lach·e·sis [ˈlæksis] *n.* 【希神】命运三女神之一.

Lach·ry·ma Chris·ti [ˈlækrəmə ˈkristi] *n.* (意大利产)浓烈甘美的红葡萄酒[原意为基督的泪].

lach·ry·mal [ˈlækriməl] *a.* 泪的; 满是泪水的; 泌泪的. — *n.* [*pl.*] 泪腺. ~ **canal** 【解】泪管. ~ **gland** 【解】泪腺. ~ **sac** 【解】泪囊.

lach·ry·ma·tion [ˌlækriˈmeiʃən] *n.* 流泪.

lach·ry·ma·tor [ˈlækriˌmeitə] *n.* 催泪剂, 催泪物, (尤指)催泪毒气.

lach·ry·ma·to·ry [ˈlækrimətɔːri] *a.* 泪的; 催泪的.

L

— *n.* 泪壶〔古罗马人墓中发现的细颈小瓶,据说是送葬人接眼泪的小壶〕. ～ **gas**【军】催泪毒气. ～ **shell [bomb]**【军】催泪弹.

lach·ry·mose [ˈlækriməus] *a.* ①落泪的;爱流泪的. ②催泪的,悲哀的. **-ly** *ad.*

lac·i·ly [ˈleisili] *ad.* 花边状[式]地,带状[式]地.

lac·i·ness [ˈleisinis] *n.* 带状;花边状.

lac·ing [ˈleisiŋ] *n.* ①结带;镶花边;编丝. ②衣服系带,鞋带;花边;【电】花线. ③(咖啡等中加用的)调味酒. ④(花瓣、羽毛等上的)条纹. ⑤〔口〕鞭打,殴打;【拳】猛击.

la·cin·i·ate [ləˈsiniit] *a.* ①有穗的,有穗边的. ②【植】条裂的,锯齿状的.

lack [læk] *vi.* 缺乏,不够,不足〔主要用现在分词形式 lacking〕. *Money is ～ing.* 钱不够. *Nothing is ～ing for your comfort.* 你的舒适设备,应有尽有了. —*vt.* ①缺乏,不够,不足. ②需要. *The vote ～s five of being a majority.* 得票数差五票不足多数. *It ～s 10 minutes of seven.* 现在是七点差十分. *That fellow ～s common sense.* 那个家伙缺乏理智. *What do you ～?* 你要买点什么?〔旧时小贩叫卖声〕. ★下列例句中的 lacking 可作介词看待: Lacking (without) any better idea, adopt mine. 没有更好的主意,就采用我的主意吧. — *n.* ①缺乏,不足. ②缺少的东西,需要的东西. *the ～ of sleep* 睡眠不足. ***for [by, from, through] ～ of*** 因缺乏…,因无…. ***have no ～ of*** 不(缺)乏.

lack·a·dai·si·cal [ˌlækəˈdeizikəl] *a.* ①若有所思的,感伤的. ②装腔作势的. ③无精打采的,懒洋洋的. **-ly** *ad.* **-ness** *n.*

lack·a·day [ˈlækədei] *int.* 〔古〕悲哉! 哀哉!

lack·er [ˈlækə] *n., vt.* = lacquer.

lack·ey [ˈlæki] *n.* *(pl. ～s)* ①(穿制服的)仆人,仆从. ②走狗. — *vt.* ①侍候,服侍. ②奉承,谄媚.

lack·lus·tre, 〔美〕**-ter** [ˈlækˌlʌstə] *a.* ①(眼睛等)没有光泽的. ②毫无生气的. — *n.* ①无光泽. ②缺乏生气.

La·comb [ləˈkəum] *n.* ①勒科姆种〔加拿大勒科姆实验站培养的一种白猪〕. ②〔常 l-〕勒科姆白猪.

la·con·ic(al) [ləˈkɔnik(əl)] *a.* (文章、说话等)简洁的,简短的;精练的. **-i·cal·ly** *ad.*

la·con·i·cism, lac·o·nism [ləˈkɔnisizəm, ˈlækənizəm] *n.* ①(语句的)简短,简洁. ②简练的语句;警句.

lac·quer [ˈlækə] *n.* ①(涂在金属上的)漆. ②真漆;(中国、日本等地产的)天然漆. ③硝基漆,清喷漆. ④漆器. — *vt.* 在…涂漆. ～ **plant [tree]** 漆树. ～ **ware** 漆器.

lac·quer·er [ˈlækərə] *n.* 漆工.

lac·quer·ing [ˈlækəriŋ] *n.* ①上漆. ②漆涂层.

lac·quey [ˈlæki] *n., vt.* = lackey.

lac·ri·mal [ˈlækriməl] *a., n.* = lachrymal.

lac·ri·ma·tion [ˌlækriˈmeiʃən] *n.* = lachrymation.

lac·ri·ma·tor [ˈlækrimeitə] *n.* = lachrymator.

lac·ri·ma·to·ry [ˈlækrimətɔːri] *a., n.* =lachrymatory.

lac·ri·mose [ˈlækriməus] *a.* = lachrymose.

la·crosse [ləˈkrɔs] *n.* 曲棍网兜球(运动)〔曲棍上附有一网兜,把球兜着设法投入对方球门中〕.

lact- *comb. f.* 〔用于元音前〕= lacto-.

lac·tam [ˈlæktæm] *n.*【化】内酰胺.

lac·ta·ry [ˈlæktəri] *a.* 〔古〕乳的;产乳白浆汁的.

lac·tase [ˈlækteis] *n.*【生化】乳糖酶.

lac·tate [ˈlækteit] *vi.* ①出奶,分泌乳汁. ②喂奶,授乳. — *n.*【化】乳酸盐. *calcium ～* 乳酸钙.

lac·ta·tion [lækˈteiʃən] *n.* ①乳汁的分泌. ②授乳,哺乳. ③授乳期.

lac·te·al [ˈlæktiəl] *a.* ①乳的,乳汁的;乳状的. ②含有乳状液的,输送乳状液的. ③乳糜管的. *the ～ gland*【解】乳腺. —*n.*〔*pl.*〕【解】乳糜管(=～ vessels). **-ly** *ad.*

lac·tes·cence [lækˈtesns] *n.* ①乳汁状;乳汁色. ②乳汁的形成. ③【植】乳汁的分泌.

lac·tes·cent [lækˈtesnt] *a.* ①成为乳汁状的. ②产乳汁的. ③【植】分泌乳汁的.

lac·ti- *comb. f.* = lacto-.

lac·tic [ˈlæktik] *a.* 乳的;乳汁的;得自乳汁的. ～ **acid**【化】乳酸. ～ **fermentation**【微】乳酸发酵.

lac·tif·er·ous [lækˈtifərəs] *a.* ①输送乳汁的;产生乳汁的. ②【植】分泌乳状汁的. *the ～ duct*【解】输乳管.

lac·to- *comb. f.* 表示"乳";"乳酸";"乳糖"〔元音前用 lact-〕: *lacto*bacillus.

lac·to·ba·cil·lus [ˌlæktəubəˈsiləs] *n.* *(pl. -cil·li [-ai])*【微】乳杆菌,乳酸杆菌.

lac·to·fla·vin [ˌlæktəuˈfleivin] *n.*【生化】核黄素(= riboflavin).

lac·to·gen·ic [ˌlæktəˈdʒenik] *a.* 催乳的,刺激乳腺分泌的. ～ **hormone** 催乳激素.

lac·tom·e·ter [lækˈtɔmitə] *n.* 乳比重计,乳汁计.

lac·tone [ˈlæktəun] *n.*【化】内酯.

lac·to·prene [ˈlæktəpriːn] *n.*【化】聚酯橡胶,乳胶〔人造橡胶〕.

lac·to·pro·te·in [ˌlæktəuˈprəutiːn, -prəutiːin] *n.*【生化】乳蛋白(质).

lac·tose [ˈlæktəus] *n.*【化】乳糖.

la·cu·na [ləˈkjuːnə] *n.* *(pl. -s, -nae [-niː])* *n.* ①空隙;(知识面等的)空白;(文章中等的)脱漏,缺文. ②【解】腔隙,陷窝. ③【植】(孢粉)空隙,气胞. ④【地】缺失(地层);洼地. *blood ～* 血腔隙.

la·cu·nar [ləˈkjuːnə] *a.* 有花格平顶的(=lacunal). — *n.* *(pl. ～s, lac·u·nar·i·a [ˌlækjuˈneriə])*【建】①花格平顶. ②花格平顶的凹板.

la·cu·nose [ləˈkjuːnəus] *a.* ①多孔的,多空隙的. ②多空白的;脱漏多的.

La·cus [ˈlækəs] *n.*【天】(月面上的)湖.

la·cus·tri·an [ləˈkʌstriən] *a.* = lacustrine. —*n.* (尤指史前时代的)湖上居民.

la·cus·trine [ləˈkʌstrain] *a.* ①湖泊的. ②生活[栖息]在湖上[中]的. ③【地】湖中形成的. ～ *dwellings* (史前)湖上村落. *the ～ age* (史前)湖上生活时代. ～ *fishes* 湖鱼. ～ *plants* 湖沼植物. ～ *deposits*【地】湖成冲积物. *a ～ plain*【地】湖成平原. ～ *soil*【地】湖积土.

lac·y [ˈleisi] *a.* *(lac·i·er; -i·est)* ①有花边的,有带子的. ②花边状的,带子状的. **-i·ly** *ad.* **-i·ness** *n.*

lad [læd] *n.* ①少年,小伙子. ②〔俚〕情人. ③〔口〕伙伴,老朋友. ④〔英〕管赛马房的马夫. ⑤〔俚〕放荡鬼. *a ～ in his teens* 十几岁的小伙子. *my ～s* (表示亲密的称呼)哥儿们,弟兄们. *one of the ～s*〔口〕自己人. *He's a bit of a ～.* 那家伙有点放荡.

lad·a·num [ˈlædənəm] *n.* 〔L.〕= labdanum.

lad·der [ˈlædə] *n.* ①梯子. ②梯状物;〔喻〕(进身的)阶梯,成功的手段. ③〔英〕(袜子抽丝而形成的)梯形裂缝(=～-like hole). *a Jack ～*【船】木踏板绳梯. *a scaling ～* 云梯. *climb a rung of the social ～* 社会地位增高. ～ *of success* 发迹的阶梯. ***climb up the ～*** 往上爬,官运亨通. ***get one's foot on the ～*** 开始,着手. ***get up [mount] a ～*** ①上梯. ②〔俚〕被处绞刑,被吊死. ***He who would climb the ～ must begin at the bottom.*** 〔谚〕千里之行始于足下. ***Jacob's ～*** ①【圣】天梯. ②〔口〕陡梯. ③【海】绳梯,软梯. ④从乌云中照射出来的一道太阳光. ⑤【植】花葱. ***kick away [down, over] the ～ by which one rose*** 过河拆桥. ***see through a ～*** 看出显而易见的东西. — *vi.* ①〔英〕(袜子)抽丝. ②成名,走红. ～ *to the top of one's profession* 爬到本行业的最高峰. —*vt.* ①用梯子爬(墙等). ②在…架设梯子. ③使(袜子)发生抽丝现象. ～ *a wall* 用梯子爬墙. ～ *a water tower* 在水塔上架梯子. **～-back** *a.* (椅子等)背

L

部有梯格式横档的. ～**company** 云梯救火队. ～**-proof** *a.* 〔英〕(袜子等)不抽丝的. ～ **stitch** 梯形(图案)刺绣法. ～ **truck** 云梯救火车. **-less** *a.* **-like** *a.*

lad·die [ˈlædi] 〔主 Scot.〕少年, 年青人; 小伙子; 〔俚〕老兄.

lade [leid] *vt.* ***(lad·ed; lad·ed, lad·en*** [ˈleidn]***)*** ①装载, 把…装到[装进](车、船内); 使担负〔主用 ***p.p.***〕. ②汲出(船水). ③塞满, 把…压倒. ～ *a ship with cargo* 把货物装载于船上. ～ *water out of a boat* 从船里戽出水. — *vi.* ①装货. ②汲取液体.

Lade·fo·ged [ˈlædifəugid] *n.* 拉迪福吉德〔姓氏〕.

lad·en[1] [ˈleidn] lade 的过去分词. —*a.* ①装着货的; 结满果实的. ②有精神负担的,心情沉重的,苦恼的. *trees ～ with fruit* 果实累累的树. *camels laden with bundles of silk* 载着一捆捆丝的骆驼. *a heart ～ with sorrow* 忧心忡忡.

lad·en[2] [ˈleidn] *vt., vi.* = lade.

la-di-da [ˈlɑːdiˈdɑː] *a.* 〔口〕装腔作势的; 装模作样的; 故作文雅的. — *n.* 〔口〕①装腔作势的人; 装模作样的人; 故作文雅的人. ②装腔作势; 矫揉造作. — *int.* 臭德性! 〔表示对装腔作势,浮华作风的嘲笑〕.

la·di·fy [ˈleidifai] *vt.* ①使成为贵妇人; 把…称为夫人; 把…看作贵妇人. ②使适合贵妇人的身分〔口味〕. **la·di·fied** *a.* 有贵妇人风度的.

La·din [ləˈdiːn] *n.* ①拉登语〔奥地利蒂罗尔省南部讲的莱脱—罗曼斯方言〕. ②说拉登语的当地人.

lad·ing [ˈleidiŋ] *n.* ①装载; 汲取. ②船货, 货物. ③重量,压力. *a bill of ～* 装货凭单; 提(货)单.

La·di·no [ləˈdiːnəu] *n.* ①拉地诺语〔土耳其和一些其它地中海国家的西班牙犹太人讲的一种西班牙方言〕. ② ***(pl. -nos)*** 〔拉美〕混血儿.

la·dle [ˈleidl] *n.* ①长柄杓子. ②【机】铸杓; 铸桶; 铁〔钢〕水包. — *vt.* ①(用杓子)舀, 戽. ②〔口〕给与, 赠送. ～ ***in*** 舀进; 混入,掺入. ～ ***out*** 舀出; 端出; 提供.

la·dle·ful [ˈleidlful] *n.* 一满杓.

La·do·ga [ˈlɑːdəgə] *n.* (苏联列宁格勒东北方的)拉多加湖.

la·drone [ləˈdrəun] *n.* 强盗〔西班牙语地区用语〕.

la·dy [ˈleidi] *n.* ①贵妇; 淑女. ②〔L-〕夫人, 小姐〔英国拥有某些爵位的贵族妻女的尊称〕. ③〔常 *pl.*〕女士(们)〔用作称呼语〕. ④女主人〔仅用于 ～ of the house 一语〕; 太太,小姐〔仆人对主妇的称呼〕. ⑤情妇; 妻子; 未婚妻. ⑥〔*pl.* 用作 *sing.*〕女厕所〔=ladies' room〕. ⑦〔用作定语〕女性. ⑧〔L-〕【宗】圣母. ⑨〔L-〕女王. *Ladies and gentlemen* 女士们, 先生们! *a ～ aviator* 女飞行家. *a ～ doctor* 女医生. *a ～ dog* 〔谑〕母狗. *be not quite a ～* 不大象个贵妇人. *extra [walking] ～* 跑龙套的女演员. *fancy ～* ①情妇. ②妓女. *fine ～* ①上流妇女. ②硬装作贵妇人的女子. *Ladies first!* 〔口〕(男子让路时说的) 女士们请先走! *Our L-* 圣母马利亚 (= the Virgin Mary). *Our Sovereign ～* 〔古,诗〕女王. *the first ～ (of the land)* 〔美〕总统〔元首〕夫人. *the leading ～* 担任主角的女演员. *the old ～* 老妇人; 〔俚〕母亲; 妻子. *one's good ～* 妻子; 老婆. *the Old L- in [of] Threadneedle Street* 英格兰银行〔别称〕. *young ～* ①(未出嫁的)青年女子. ②〔口〕爱人. **ladies' gallery** (英国下议院的)妇女旁听席. **ladies' man** = ～'s man. **ladies' room** 公共女厕所,女盥洗室. **ladies'-tresses** = ～'s-tresses. ～**beetle** = ～**bird** = ～**bug**【动】瓢虫. **L- Bountiful** "帮得忙"太太〔英国剧作家法夸尔喜剧中人物,泛指摆慈善样子给人看的资产阶级妇女〕. ～ **chair** 两人用手交叉搭成的座架〔抬运伤员用〕. ～ **chapel** 大教堂内的圣母堂. **L- Day**【宗】①报喜节(3月25日). ②〔英〕春季结帐日(3月 25日). ～**finger**〔美〕①指形糕饼. ②〔*pl.*〕【美拳】拳头. ～**fish** *n.* ***(pl. fish, fishes)***【动】海鲢 *(Elops saurus)*〔产于热带海洋〕. ～**help**〔英〕(作为家属待遇的)女帮工. ～**hood** ①贵妇的身分〔品格〕. ②〔集合词〕太太们,小姐们. ～**-in-waiting** (皇后或公主的)亲随, 宫廷女侍. ～**-killer** 专门勾引女子的人. ～**kin** 小女孩; 〔爱〕小姐. ～**like** *a.* ①贵妇人似的; 优雅的, 温柔的. ②(男子)带女人腔调的. ～**love** 情妇. **L- Mayoress**〔英〕伦敦市长夫人. ～ **of easy virtue** 放荡的女子; 淫妇,妓女. ～ **of letters**〔谑〕女文学家. ～ **of one's heart** 意中人. ～ **of pleasure** 妓女. ～ **of the bedchamber**〔英〕宫廷女侍. ～ **of the evening** 妓女. ～ **of the frying pan**〔谑〕女厨子. ～**'s companion** 女用手提包; 针线包. ～**'s maid** 侍女. ～**'s man** 喜欢在妇女中厮混献殷勤的男子. ～**'s-slipper**【植】杓兰(属). ～**'s-smock**【植】①草地碎米荠,酢浆草. ②布谷鸟剪秋罗; 〔美〕石芥花. ～**'s-thumb**【植】春蓼 *(Polygonum persicaria)*〔一种一年生植物〕. ～**'s-tresses**【植】绶草属 *(Spiranthes)*. ～**'s-wind** 软风, 微风. ～**ship** ①夫人〔贵妇〕的身分〔品格〕. ②〔常 L-〕〔英〕夫人, 小姐〔对有 Lady 头衔的妇女的尊称〕. (*your [her] Ladyship* 太太, 小姐.)

la·dy·fy [ˈleidifai] *vt.* = ladify.

La·e [ˈlɑːei] *n.* 莱城〔新几内亚首都〕.

lae·o·trop·ic [ˈliːətrɔpik] *a.* 左转的〔如螺纹和腹足纲的软体动物〕.

lae·vo- *comb. f.* = levo-.

La Fa·yette [ˌlɑːfaiˈet] *n.* ①拉法埃脱〔男子名〕. ②**Marquis de ～** 马奎斯·德·拉法埃脱〔1757—1834 法国将军,政治家. 美国独立战争时,曾率领法军援助美军〕.

La Fon·tain [lɑːfɔːnˈtein] *n.* **Jean de** 拉封登〔1621—1695 法国诗人,寓言作家〕.

LAFTA = Latin-American Free Trade Association 拉丁美洲自由贸易协会.

lag[1] [læg] *vi.* ①延迟,逗留,落后; 慢条斯理地走. ②未充分发展. ③【电】滞后. ④慢慢地减少, 变弱, 松懈. ～ *behind* 落后. ～ *in phase*【电】相位滞后. *Interests ～s in such matters.* 对这类事的兴趣慢慢地减少了. — *vt.* ①落后于; 【电】滞后于. ②〔废〕使落后. — *n.* ①迟延; 减速; 滞后, 落后, 逗留. ②(两件事之间)相隔的时间. ③(牲畜等的)落后者,掉队者. *go forward without ～* 毫不延迟地进行. *the ～ of the tide* 迟潮时间. *a time ～* 时间滞差,时滞. *a time ～ of two months* 迟两个月的时间. — *a.* ①迟的,慢的. ②最后的.

lag[2] [læg] *n.* ①桶板. ②(锅炉等的)外套,防护套; (纺织)绞板. — *vt.* 给…加上外套. ～ **bolt [screw]** 方头木螺钉,方头尖螺丝.

lag[3] [læg] *vt.* 〔俚〕①把…关进牢里; 把(犯人等)押送去做苦役. ②〔英俚〕逮捕. — *n.* 〔俚〕囚犯; 前科犯. ②服刑期间,苦役期间. *an old ～* 惯犯.

lag·an [ˈlægən], **lag·end** [ˈlægənd] *n.*【法】(海船发生事故时)系以浮标投入海中的货物.

lag b'O·mer [ˌlɑːg ˈbəumə] 犹太八月节〔犹太历 8月18日〕.

la·ger [ˈlɑːgə] *n.* 贮藏啤酒〔一种淡啤酒, 酿成后贮藏数月,澄清后饮用,又作 ～ beer〕.

lag·gard [ˈlægəd] *a.* 迟缓的, 落后的. — *n.* ①迟钝的人,慢吞吞的人. ②市价落后有价证券. **-ly** *ad.*

lag·ger[1] [ˈlægə] *n.* ①落伍者,落后者; 落后的事物. ②停滞的经济指数.

lag·ger[2] [ˈlægə] *n.* 〔俚〕囚犯,惯犯.

lag·ging[1] [ˈlægiŋ] *n.* 落后, 迟延. — *a.* 慢的, 落后的. ～ **circuit** 滞后电路. ～ **device**【电】滞相装置. ～ **edge**【电】(脉冲的)下降边. **-ly** *ad.*

lag·ging[2] [ˈlægiŋ] *n.* ①(锅炉等的)外套, 防护套, 罩壳. ②加套; 横板; 护壁板. ③【建】套板; 横挡板; 支拱板条.

la·gniappe, la·gnappe [lænˈjæp] *n.* 〔美〕(送给顾客的)小赠品.

lag·o·morph [ˈlægəmɔːf] *n.*【动】兔形目 *(Lagomorpha)*〔兔、野兔等〕. **-ic** *a.*

la·goon, la·gune [ləˈguːn] *n.* 环礁湖; 咸水湖; 泻湖.

La·gos [ˈleigɔs] *n.* 拉各斯〔尼日利亚首都〕.

La Gua·i·ra [Sp. lɑˈgwairɑ] *n.* 拉瓜伊拉〔委内瑞拉港市〕.

lah-di-dah, lah-de-dah [ˈlɑːdiˈdɑː] = la-di-da.

La·hore [ləˈhɔː] *n.* 拉合尔〔巴基斯坦城市〕.

LAI =〔It.〕*Linee Aeree Italiane* 意大利航空公司.

la·ic [ˈleiik] *a.* ①俗人的〔与僧侣相对而言〕. ②外行的(=laical). — *n.* 俗人;外行人.

la·i·cize [ˈleiisaiz] *vt.* ①使还俗; 使世俗化;将(公职等)交给俗人去办. ②将(公职等)让外行担任. **la·i·ci·za·tion** [ˌleiisaiˈzeiʃən] *n.*

la·i·cism [ˈleiisizəm] *n.* 政权还俗主义〔反对教权主义,限制教会的政治权力和影响的政策和原则〕.

laid [leid] lay[1] 的过去式及过去分词. ~ *out*〔美俚〕负伤的;昏过去的,昏厥的;喝醉的. ~**-back** *a.* 松弛的;自在的;从容不迫的. ~ **paper** 直纹纸;夫士纸.

laigh [leih] *a., ad.*〔Scot.〕低的,低矮的.

lain [lein] lie[1] 的过去分词.

lair[1] [lɛə] *n.* ①兽窝,兽穴,兽窟. ②〔英〕(送家畜至市场时路上给家畜休息用的)围栏. ③(人的)休息处,常去处;躲藏处.〔Scot.〕墓地;〔古〕床. *the pirate's* ~ 海盗的巢穴. — *vi.* (兽)进窝,在洞里睡. —*vt.* ①把(兽等)赶进窝里; 把(家畜等)关进围栏里. ②把…作为洞穴;给…设洞穴.

lair[2] [lɛə] *n.*〔Scot.〕泥潭,泥沼. — *vt.* 使陷入泥潭. — *vi.* (在泥水中)打滚.

Laird [lɛəd] *n.* 莱尔德〔姓氏〕.

laird [lɛəd] *n.*〔Scot.〕地主. **-ly** *ad.* **-ship** *n.*

lais·ser-faire, lais·sez-faire [ˈleiseiˈfɛə] *n.*〔F.〕放任,不干涉主义;自由放任主义〔尤指资本主义国家对工商业的政策〕. — *a.* 放任(主义)的. ~ *capitalism* 自由资本主义.

lais·sez-al·ler [ˈleiseizælei] *n.*〔F.〕自由,放任.

lais·sez-pas·ser [ˈleiseipæˈsei] *n.*〔F.〕通行证,护照.

la·i·ty [ˈleiiti] *n.*〔集合词〕①(与教士、僧侣等相对的)俗人. ②(与专家相对的)外行.

La·ius [ˈlaijəs] *n.*【希神】(被儿子奥狄浦斯杀死的底比斯国王)拉伊俄斯.

Lake [leik] *n.* 莱克〔姓氏〕.

lake[1] [leik] *n.* ①湖;(公园等中的)池塘,小湖. ②(贮油等的)池. *The Great L-* 大西洋. *The Great L-s* 北美洲五大湖. *the Lakes* (英国北部的)湖泊地区. ***Go jump in the ~!***〔美俚〕别来麻烦!滚开!不要吵! **L- Country, L- District** = the Lakes. ~ **dweller** (尤指史前的)湖上居民. ~ **dwelling** (尤指史前时代建造在木桩上的)湖上桩屋. ~**front** 湖边平地. ~**let** 小湖. **L- Poets, L- School** 湖畔派〔十八世纪末十九世纪初以华滋华斯为首的一种浪漫主义诗歌流派〕. **L- State** 大湖洲〔美国密执安州的别称〕. **L- Success** 成功湖〔在纽约近郊,1952 年以前为联合国秘书处所在地〕. ~ **trout**【动】灰红点鲑 *(Salvelinus namaycush)*〔产于北美洲深水湖中〕.

lake[2] [leik] *n.* ①【化】色淀;沉淀染料. ②胭脂红. ~ **colour** 色淀染料. ~ **oil** 琥珀油.

lake[3] [leik] *vi.* 血球溶解. — *vt.* 使(血液)发生血球溶解.

lak·er [ˈleikə] *n.* ①湖鱼〔尤指鳟鱼〕. ②湖船〔尤指北美洲五大湖上的船〕.

lakh [lɑːk] *n.*〔Ind.〕①十万(特指十万卢比). ②巨额,无数.

lak·y[1] [ˈleiki] *a.* ①湖的; 湖水的. ②多湖的. ③湖状的.

lak·y[2] [ˈleiki] *a.* 胭脂红色的.

lak·y[3] [ˈleiki] *a.*【医】(血液中)部分红血球已崩坏的,泄色的.

lall [læl] *vi.*【语音】①[l]发音不正确. ②将[r]音读成[l]音. **lal·la·tion** [læˈleiʃən] *n.*

Lal·lan [ˈlælən] *a.*〔Scot.〕苏格兰东南部低地的. — *n.* ①苏格兰东南部低地. ②苏格兰东南部低地方言(= Lallans).

L'Al·le·gro [læˈleigrəu] 快活人〔原为弥尔顿一首诗的题目〕.

Lam. = Lamentations【圣】《哀歌》.

lam[1] [læm] *vi., vt.*〔俚〕(用棍子等)打,鞭打,笞责 *(out; into)*.

lam[2] [læm] *vi., n.*〔美俚〕逃走,潜逃. ***on the*** ~ 在潜逃中 (*a convict on the* ~ 在逃犯). ***take it on the*** ~ 潜逃,远走高飞.

la·ma[1] [ˈlɑːmə] *n.* (西藏、蒙古的)喇嘛. **-ism** *n.* 喇嘛教. **-ist** *n.* 喇嘛教徒.

la·ma[2] [ˈlɑːmə] *n.*【动】= llama.

La·mar [ləˈmɑː] *n.* 拉马尔〔姓氏,男子名〕.

La·marck [ləˈmɑːk], **Jean Baptiste Pierre Antoine de Monet, Chevalier de** 拉马克〔1744—1829, 法国博物学家,进化论者〕. **-i·an** ①*a.* 拉马克学说的. ②*n.* 拉马克学派的人. **-ism** *n.* 拉马克的进化论[学说].

la·ma·ser·y [ˈlɑːməsəri] *n.* 喇嘛庙.

lam·as·ter [ˈlæməstə] *n.*〔美俚〕= lamister.

Lamb [læm] *n.* ①拉姆〔姓氏〕. ②**Charles** ~ 查尔斯·兰姆〔1775—1834,英国散文家,批评家〕.

lamb [læm] *n.* ①羔羊, 小羊; 小羚羊. ②羔羊肉;羔羊皮. ③象羔羊般柔弱[温和、天真烂漫]的人. ④〔俚〕容易上当的人〔尤指在证券交易方面〕. ⑤好宝宝, 小乖乖〔对孩子的爱称〕. ⑥〔the L-〕【宗】耶稣. *my* ~ 好宝宝. ***a fox [wolf] in ~'s skin*** 伪君子,伪善者. ***as well be hanged [hung] for a sheep as (for) a*** ~ 一不做二不休. ***like a*** ~ ①驯顺地, 乖乖地. ②天真烂漫地;容易上当地. ***the ~ of God*** 神的羔羊,耶稣. — *vt.* ①生(小羊). ②照顾(产期母羊). —*vi.* 生小羊. ~**kill** = sheep laurel. ~**kin** 小羊羔;小家伙,小鬼〔有时用作对儿童的爱称〕. ~**like** *a.* ①羔羊似的,怯弱的,温和的. ②天真烂漫的. ~**skin** ①羔羊皮〔尤指带羊毛的〕. ②羔皮革;羊皮纸. ③仿羔羊皮织物;纬面缎纹绒布. ~**'s-quarters**【植】藜 *(Chenopodium album)*〔一种一年生野草,有时作野草食用〕. ~**'s wool** 羔毛〔极柔软的高级羊毛〕;加糖水苹果丁的甜啤酒.

lam·bast(e) [læmˈbeist] *vt.* ①〔俚〕鞭打,狠揍. ②严厉申斥.

lamb·da [ˈlæmdə] *n.* ①希腊语第十一个字母〔Λ, λ 与英语字母 L 相当〕. ②微升〔百万分之一升〕. ③λ 粒子(= ~ particle). ~ **hyperon** λ 超子.

lamb·da·cism [ˈlæmdəsizəm] *n.* ① L 字使用过多. ② = lallation.

lamb·doid [ˈlæmdɔid] *a.* 似希腊语第十一个字母(Λ)的〔尤指联结枕骨和头顶骨的骨缝〕.

lam·ben·cy [ˈlæmbənsi] *n.* ①(光、火焰等的)轻轻摇曳,微微闪跃. ②柔光. ③(诙谐等的)巧妙.

lam·bent [ˈlæmbənt] *a.* ①(火焰等)在燃烧中,轻轻摇曳的, 闪烁的. ②(眼睛等)微亮的;发柔光的. ③(诙谐等)巧妙的. **-ly** *ad.*

Lam·bert [ˈlæmbə(ː)t] *n.* ①兰伯特〔姓氏〕. ②【物】朗伯〔亮度单位〕.

Lam·beth [ˈlæmbəθ] *n.* ①伦敦朗伯斯区. ②伦敦坎特伯雷大主教官邸 (=~ Palace); 该宫邸所在地. ③坎特伯雷大主教的地位[职位].

lam·bre·quin [ˈlæmb(r)əkin] *n.* ①(门窗等上部的)垂饰; (橱柜的)帘幕. ②(瓷器边缘上的)扇形彩色图案. ③(中世纪骑士铁盔上的)饰罩,覆巾.

lame[1] [leim] *a.* ***(lam·er, lam·est)*** ①跛的,瘸的,残废的. ②僵痛的. ③有缺点的;(论据等)站不住脚的;不中用的. ④(诗)不合韵律的. *be ~ of [in] one leg* 跛一条腿的. *go ~* 变成瘸子. *walk ~* 跛行,一瘸一拐地走. *a ~ excuse* 站不住脚的辩解. *a ~ imitation* 低劣的仿制品. *~ verses* 蹩脚的诗. ***help a ~ dog over a stile*** 帮助人度过难关. — *vt.* ①使跛,使残废,把…弄残废. ②使不中用. *be ~d for life* 终身残废. — *vi.* 跛行. — *n.* ①古板守旧

的人；落后分子．②消息不灵的人，不知情况〔内情〕的人．～**brain**〔口〕蠢人，笨蛋，傻瓜．～**brained** *a.* 蠢，笨，傻．～ **duck** ①残废者；不中用的人〔物〕．②〔美〕（任期快满未再当选而暂时留守的）即将去职的官员〔议员〕．③〔美〕不能再竞选连任的总统．④无力履行财政债务的股票投机者．**-ly** *ad.* **-ness** *n.*

lame² [leim] *n.* ①（金属）薄板，薄片．②〔*pl.*〕（古代护身甲上的）重叠金属片．

la·mé [lɑːˈmei] *n.* 〔F.〕金银线织物．

la·med [ˈlɑːmid] *n.* 希伯来语第十二个字母．

la·mel·la [ləˈmelə] *n.* ***(pl. -lae*** [-iː], ***~s)*** ①薄片，薄层，薄板，薄结构．②【解】同心板骨；【动】鳃瓣，壳层；【植】菌褶；栉片．**-r** *a.* 片状的；层状的．**-ly** *ad.*

lam·el·late [ˈlæməleit, ləˈmeleit] *a.* ①包含薄片层的，排成薄片层形的，似薄片层的．②＝lamelliform.

la·mel·li·branch [ləˈmelibræŋk] *n.* 【动】瓣鳃纲斧足类 *(Pelecypoda)* 软体动物〔如蛤、蠔等〕．— *a.* 瓣鳃纲斧足类软体动物的（＝lamellibranchiate).

la·mel·li·corn [ləˈmelikɔːn] *a.* 【动】①鳃角的．②鳃角类（甲虫）的〔包括小金虫和蜣螂等〕．— *n.* 鳃角类甲虫．

la·mel·li·form [ləˈmelifɔːm] *a.* 薄片形的，薄片状的，片状的，鳞状的，鳃状的．

la·mel·li·ros·tral [ləˌmeliˈrɔstrəl] *a.* 【动】扁嘴类的〔如野鸭、鹅等水禽〕（＝lamellirostrate).

la·mel·lose [ləˈmeləus, ˈlæmələus] *a.* ＝ lamellate. **-los·i·ty** [-ˈlɔsiti] *n.*

la·ment [ləˈment] *n.* ①悲叹，哀悼，恸哭．②哀歌，挽歌，悼词．—*vi.* 悲叹，哀悼．～ *for a friend over his death* 哀朋友的故去．— *vt.* ①哀悼，痛惜．②悲叹．～ *the death of a hero* 为英雄逝世而哀悼．～ *one's folly* 悔恨自己的愚笨．*We ～ed his absence.* 我们对他的缺席深感遗憾．

lam·en·ta·ble [ˈlæməntəbl] *a.* ①可悲的，可叹的．②哀伤的，悲哀的．③（作品，制作物等）质量低的；不象样的．**-bly** *ad.*

lam·en·ta·tion [ˌlæmenˈteiʃən] *n.* ①悲叹；哀悼；痛哭．②〔*L-s*〕（旧约《圣经》中的）《哀歌》．

la·ment·ed [ləˈmentid] *a.* 被哀悼的．***the late ～*** 死者（特指亡夫）．**-ly** *ad.*

la·ment·ing [ləˈmentiŋ] *a.* 悲伤的，悲哀的．**-ly** *ad.*

la·mi·a [ˈleimiə] *n.* ***(pl. ~s, -ae*** [-miː]) ①【希罗神】半人半蛇吸血女怪．②妖妇．

lam·i·na [ˈlæminə] *n.* ***(pl. -nae*** [-niː], ***~s)*** ①（金属或动物组织的）薄片，片层，薄层；迭层，层状体．②【植】叶片．**-l, -ry** *a.* ＝ laminar.

lam·i·na·ble [ˈlæminəbl] *a.* 可辗薄的；可切成薄片（层）的．

lam·i·nar [ˈlæmənər] *a.* 由薄片或层状体组成的，薄片状的；层状的．～ *flow* 【物】片流，层流．

lam·i·nate [ˈlæmineit] *vt.* ①把（金属等）辗压成薄板．②把…切〔分〕成薄片．③用薄片迭成．④用薄板覆盖．⑤粘合（薄片）．—*vi.* 变〔分〕成薄板〔薄片〕．—[ˈlæminit] *n.* 薄片制品；层压板．— [ˈlæminit] *a.* ＝ laminated.

lam·i·nat·ed [ˈlæmineitid] *a.* 由薄片迭成的；层状的．～ **chain** 分片链．～ **coal** 页煤．～ **core**【电】迭片铁心．～ **plastics**【化】层压塑料．～ **wood** 层积木，胶合板．

lam·i·na·tion [ˌlæmiˈneiʃən] *n.* ①层压；迭合．②【电】叠片，铁心片．③迭片结构；层压结构．④【地】纹理．⑤＝ lamina.

lam·i·nec·to·my [ˌlæmiˈnektəmi] *n.* ***(pl. -mies)***【医】椎板切除术．

lam·i·ni·tis [ˌlæmiˈnaitis] *n.* 【兽医】蹄叶炎．

lam·ish [ˈleimiʃ] *a.* ①有点瘸的．②不怎么完善的．

lam·is·ter [ˈlæmistə] *n.* 〔美俚〕＝ lamster.

Lam·mas (Day) [ˈlæməs] *n.* 八月一日收获节．***at later [latter]*** ～ 决不会再有的〔因为一年只一个 8 月 1 日〕．

lam·mer·gei·er, lam·er·gey·er [ˈlæməgaiə] *n.* 【动】髭兀鹰 *(Gypaetus barbatus)*〔产于欧亚的一种大鹰〕．

lamp [læmp] *n.* ①灯．②灯泡．③电子管．④（智慧等的）明灯；思想的指导．⑤〔诗〕（明亮的）天体〔日、月、星〕．⑥〔*pl.*〕〔俚〕眼睛，炬火．*an amber* ～（表示交通危险而悬挂的）黄色信号灯．*an amplifying* ～【电】放大管．*an arc* ～ 弧光灯．*a blackout* ～ 防空灯．*a crater* ～ 凹孔放电管；点源录影灯．*a daylight* ～ 日光灯．*a dim* ～ 磨砂灯泡．*a discharge* ～ 放电灯，放电管．*an electric* ～ 电灯．*a kino* ～ 显像管．*an oil*（〔美〕*kerosene)* ～ 煤油灯．*an ultraviolet* ～ 紫外线灯．～ *of heaven* 发亮的天体〔日、月、星〕．～ *of Phaebus* 太阳．*Aladdin's* ～ 阿拉丁的神灯，如意灯．***hand [pass] on the*** ～ 助长知识的发达〔文化的进步〕〔出自古希腊的火炬接力赛跑〕．***rub the*** ～ 很容易地实现自己的计划〔象摩擦阿拉丁神灯一般〕．***smell of the*** ～ 带有（在灯下）苦心构思的痕迹．— *vt.* ①〔诗〕照亮．②〔美俚〕看，看到．～**black** ①灯黑色，灯烟色．②油烟．～ **bulb** 电灯泡．～ **burner** 灯口．～ **chimney**（煤油灯用）玻璃灯罩．～ **holder**（插电灯泡的）灯座．～**-hour** 电灯时．～**house**（仪器上的）光源．～**light** 灯火，灯光．～**-lighter**（已往街灯的）点灯者（*like a ～lighter* 很快地，迅速地)．～**post** 灯杆，路灯柱．～**shade** 灯罩．～ **shell**【动】酸浆介〔一种带壳的海内蠕形动物〕．～ **stand** 灯台．～**wick** 灯心．**-less** *a.*

lam·pa·de·pho·ri·a [ˌlæmpədiˈfɔːriə] *n.*（古希腊的）火炬接力赛跑（＝lampadedromy).

lam·pas¹ [ˈlæmpəs] *n.* 【兽医】腭嵴红肿（＝lampers).

lam·pas² [ˈlæmpəs] *n.* 〔F.〕彩花细锦缎〔全丝、全棉或丝棉交织〕．

lam·pi·on [ˈlæmpiən] *n.*（马车上装饰用）彩色小油灯．

lam·poon [læmˈpuːn] *n.* 讽刺文〔诗〕．— *vt.* 写讽刺诗〔文〕讽刺．**-er, -ist** *n.* 讽刺作家．

lam·prey [ˈlæmpri] *n.* 【动】七鳃鳗，八目鳗．

lam·pro·phyre [ˈlæmprəfaiə] *n.* 【地】煌斑岩．

Lamp·son [ˈlæm*p*sn] *n.* 兰普森〔姓氏〕．

lam·ster [ˈlæmstə] *n.* 〔美俚〕潜逃者，逃亡者；逃犯，逃兵．

la·na·i [lɑːˈnɑːi] *n.*（上有顶棚的）夏威夷式阳台，晒台．

la·nate [ˈleineit] *a.* 【植、动】绵状的；具绵状毛的；面上有细绒〔细毛〕的．

Lan·ca·shire [ˈlæŋkəʃiə] *n.* 兰开夏〔英国郡名〕．

Lan·cas·ter [ˈlæŋkəstə] *n.* ①兰开斯特〔英、美城市〕．②【英史】兰开斯特王朝〔1399—1461〕．

Lan·cas·tri·an [læŋˈkæstriən] *a.* ①兰开夏郡的．②兰开斯特城的．③【英史】兰开斯特王朝的．— *n.* ①兰开夏郡人．②兰开斯特城的居民．③【英史】（尤指玫瑰战争中）拥护兰开斯特王朝的人．

Lance [lɑːns] *n.* 兰斯〔男子名，Lancelot 的昵称〕．

lance [lɑːns, -æ-] *n.* ①标枪，长矛．②〔*pl.*〕枪骑兵，持长矛骑马的战士．③矛状器具；捕鲸枪；【军】撞杆〔旧时装填大炮弹药的杆〕．④【医】柳叶刀，双刃小刀．*oxygen* ～ 氧气切割枪，氧气切割嘴．***break a ～ with sb.*** 和某人比赛〔争论〕．— *vt.* ①用矛刺穿．②【医】用柳叶刀割开．③投，掷．— *vi.* 急速前进．～ **corporal**（英国陆军中代理下士而薪俸并不增加的）一等兵．～ **fish**【动】＝ launce. ～ **sergeant**【英军】代理中士〔由下士暂时代理的中士〕．

lance·let [ˈlɑːnsəlit] *n.* 【动】蛞蝓鱼，文昌鱼．

Lan·ce·lot [ˈlɑːnsələt] *n.* 兰斯洛特〔①男子名．②亚瑟王 *(King Arthur)* 故事中圆桌骑士之一〕．

lan·ce·o·lar [ˈlænsiələ], **lan·ce·o·lat·e(d)** [ˈlɑːnsiəlit(id)] *a.* ①矛尖状的．②【植】（叶）披针形的．

lanc·er [ˈlɑːnsə] *n.* ①持标枪的人．②枪骑兵．③〔*pl.*〕特种四人对舞(quadrille)（舞曲）．

lan·cet [ˈlɑːnsit, læn-] *n.* ①【医】柳叶刀；刺血针；口针. ②【建】矛尖状装饰；尖拱 (= ~ arch)；尖头窗 (=~ window).

lan·cet·ed [ˈlɑːnsitid] *a.*【建】矛尖状装饰的；有尖拱的；有尖头窗的.

lan·ci·form [ˈlænsifɔːm] *a.* 矛(尖)状的；标枪状的.

lan·ci·nate [ˈlænsineit] *vt.* (*-nat·ed; -nat·ing*) 刺；扎；撕裂〔现除医学外罕用〕. *a ~ pain* 刀绞般的疼痛. **lan·ci·na·tion** [ˌlænsiˈneiʃən] *n.*

Lancs. = Lancashire.

land [lænd] *n.* ①陆地，地面. ②土地，田地；农田；〔*pl.*〕所有地，地产. ③国土，国，国家；领土；地方；(…的)世界；地带，境界. ④台阶. ⑤采掘段. ⑥(枪炮的)阳堂线. ⑦〔美口〕老天爷！(=Lord). ⑧(刀刃的)厚度；刃棱面；(纹间)表面. ⑨平台. *a ~ campaign* [*warfare*] 陆战. *go by ~* 从陆路去. *arable ~* 适于耕作的土地. *open barren ~* 开荒. *coal ~* 煤田. *green ~* 牧场. *~ reclamation* 开垦荒地. *waste ~* 荒地. *work* [*go*] *on the ~* 务农. *Do you have much ~ in France?* 你在法国有很多地皮么？*own houses and ~s* 拥有房地产. *come home from foreign ~s* 从外国归来. *from all ~s* 来自各国. *home* [*native*] *~* 祖国. *throughout the ~* 全国各地. *in the ~ of dreams* 在梦乡. *in the ~ of the living* 在人世，在现世. *Back to the ~!* 回故乡去！(文学上)回到田园生活！*back ~s* 穷乡僻壤. *bad ~s* ①易受侵蚀、不堪耕作的干旱土地. ②〔B- L-〕美国西部这类荒地. *the ~ of cakes* 糕饼国〔指苏格兰〕. *the L- of Flowers* 花卉之乡〔美〕〔佛罗里达州的别名〕. *the ~* [*L-*] *of Nod* 睡乡. *the ~ of Promise* [*Covenant*]【圣】应许的乐土〔指上帝应许赐给亚伯拉罕子孙的迦南乐土〕. *the ~ of stars and stripes* 星条旗之国〔指美国〕. *the ~ of the bone-dry free* 〔讽〕没有喝酒自由的国家〔指实施禁酒法时期的美国〕. *the ~ of the golden fleece* 金羊毛之国〔澳大利亚的别号〕. *the ~ of the leal* 天堂. *the ~ of the Rose* 玫瑰之国〔指英国〕. ***clear ~*** 清除土地上的树木等 (以备耕种). ***clear the ~*** (船只)离岸出海. ***close with the ~*** 接近陆地. ***Dixie L-*** ①【史】美国南方实行奴隶所有制的各州. ②美国南方各州. ***good ~*** 〔美口〕天啊！好家伙！糟糕！***how the ~ lies*** ①【海】在什么方位？②形势如何？情况如何 (*find out how the ~ lies* 摸清情况). ***~ flowing with milk and honey***【圣】乳与蜜流河的国土；富裕的福地. ***L- ho!*** 看到陆地啦！〔海员在航海中发现陆地时的欣喜喊声.〕***lay* [*shut in*] *the ~***【海】远出海中不见陆地. ***lie along* [*keep in with*] *the ~*** 沿岸航行. ***make (the) ~*** 看见陆地，到岸. ***My L-!*** = good ~! ***no man's ~*** ①【史】无主地. ②【军】无人地带，真空地带. ***on ~*** 在陆地上. ***see ~*** ①看到陆地. ②行将达到目的. ***see how the ~ lies*** 观察形势. ***set (the) ~*** 测陆地的方向. ***sight the ~*** = make (the) ~. ***the ~ of the living*** 人世，现世. ***the lay* [*lie*] *of the ~*** ①【海】海岸的方向，陆地的位置. ②事物的情况. ***touch* [*reach*] *~*** (从海上)逃到陆上；〔喻〕得到稳固的立足点. — *vt.* ①使上陆，使登岸；使(飞机)着陆，使降陆. ②自船〔飞机〕上卸下；将(捕到的鱼等)拉上岸〔船〕. ③使到达，把…送到. ④〔口〕捞到，获得. ⑤打. ⑥使处于. ⑦(骑师)使(马)进入决胜点(跑得第一名). *The pilot ~ed the aeroplane.* 驾驶员使飞机着陆. *The ship ~ed its passengers.* 船让旅客登岸. *The detective ~ed the criminal.* 侦探捕获了犯罪. *~ a prize* 得奖. *This ~ed me in great difficulties.* 这使我非常为难了. *be nicely ~ed* 〔反语〕一筹莫展，毫无办法. *~ a man with coat that doesn't fit* 给人穿不合身的上衣. — *vi.* ①上岸，登陆 (*at*)；(飞机)着陆. ②【无】接地. ③到达. ④陷入. ⑤(马)跑得第一名. ⑥(罪犯等)落网. *The passengers ~ed.* 旅客都已上岸. *The thief ~ed in jail.* 罪犯被捕入狱. ***~ on*** 〔俚〕申斥，批评. ***~ on one's* [*both*] *feet*** 逢凶化吉. **~ agency** 〔英〕地产管理(处)；〔美〕土地买卖代办所. **~ agent** 〔英〕地产经理人，土地管理人；〔美〕地产经纪人. **~-air** *a.*【军】①地对空的. ②陆空联合的. **~ bank** 〔美〕(专营地产抵押业务的)地产银行. **~-based** *a.* 在陆地上有基地的，岸基的. **~ breeze** 陆风〔自陆地吹向海上的微风〕. **~ carriage** 陆运. **~ casing**【机】下套管. **~ clearance**【机】周刃隙角. **~ contract** 房地产转让分期付款契约. **~ crab** 陆栖蟹. **~fall** ①远洋航行后初见陆地，接近陆地(*make a bad ~fall* 未按预计时间靠岸. *make a good ~fall* 按预计时间靠岸). ②【空】着陆. ③地崩. ④土地所有权的突然获得. **~fill** 填埋洼地垃圾，垃圾垫土. **~ force(s)** 陆军. **~form** 地形. **~ girl** 〔英〕(战时代替男子作农业劳动的) 青年农民妇女. **~-grabber** ①霸占土地者. ②〔爱〕驱逐佃户而收买〔承租〕其土地的人. **~-grant** *a.* 被拨给土地的〔指美国获得政府拨给土地的大学，条件是必须开授有关农业和机械技术课程〕. **~ grant** 〔美〕(为建设铁路或给大学的)拨赠土地. **~holder** ①土地所有者. ②土地租用人. **~ hunger** 土地占有热；领土扩张热. **~-jobber** 地产投机商；地皮掮客. **~lady** ①(旅馆等的) 女店主. ②女地主；女房东. **~law** 土地法. **~line** 陆上通讯〔运输〕线. **~locked** *a.* ①(湖等)被陆地包围着的(*a ~ locked country* 内陆国家). ②【动】(鲑等)生活在与海洋隔绝的淡水中的. **~lord** ①地主 (*the ~lord class* 地主阶级. *the despotic ~lord* 恶霸地主). ②(旅馆等的)店主；房东. **~lordism** 地主所有制. **~lubber** ①没有出过海的；不习惯海上生活的人. ②外行水手. **~mark** ①界标. ②【海】陆标. ③(一生中或历史上的)突出事件，划时期的事件. ④(有特殊历史价值或艺术价值的)地面文物；受保护的文物建筑. **~mass** 大陆块，大片陆地. **~ measure** ①地积制. ②地积单位〔如英亩、公顷等〕. **~ mine** ①地雷. ②第二次世界大战中用降落伞投下的薄壳炸弹. **L- of the Midnight Sun** 午夜太阳国〔指挪威〕. **L- of the Rising Sun** 日出之国〔指日本国〕. **~ office** 土地管理局〔处理和登记国家的土地买卖事宜〕. **~-office business** 〔口〕兴旺的生意，买卖兴隆. **~owner** 土地拥有者；地主. **~ownership** 土地拥有者的身分〔地位〕. **~owning** *a.*, *n.* 拥有土地的(人). **~ patent** 土地证. **~ plaster** 石膏肥料. **~-poor** *a.* 有地无钱的〔指拥有大量土地、但因土地税高和产量低而缺现款者〕. **~ power** ①陆军(实力). ②陆军强国. **~ rail** = corncrake. **~ reform** 土地改革. **~ rover** 轻便汽车〔英制工农业用吉普车型〕. **~ scurvy**【医】紫癜. **~'s end** ①(一国或一地的) 末端地区. ②〔L- End〕美国最西端小村. **~ service** 陆军兵役. **~ shark** ①(专骗登陆水手的)码头骗子. ②抢土地者. **~-side** 犁侧板，耕沟壁. **~skip** 〔废〕landscape 的变体. **~slide** 〔主美〕① = landslip. ②〔美〕(选举的)大胜利；压倒的优胜 (*the momentum of a ~slide* 排山倒海之势). **~slip** 〔英〕山崩；崩塌；塌方. **~ swell** (海岸附近的)巨浪. **~tax** 土地税. **~ tie**【建】着地拉杆. **~ waiter** 海关人员. **~wash** ①波浪对海岸的冲击. ②高潮线. **~way** *n.* 陆路；陆路交通. **~ wind** =~ breeze. **~worker** 农夫.

lan·dau [ˈlændɔː] *n.* ①(车顶后半可折叠放下的)一种旧式小汽车. ②(顶盖分为前后两半，可分别开阖的)四轮马车. **~let, ~lette** 小型车顶折叠式马车.

land·ed [ˈlændid] *a.* ①有土地的，地主方面的. ②土地的；地产的，不动产的. ③(运到)陆地上的；上了岸的. *the ~ classes* 地主阶级. *the ~ interest* 地主方面的利益. *a ~ estate* = *~ property* 地产. *newly ~ fish* 刚卸到岸上的鱼.

lan·der [ˈlændə] *n.* ①【矿】司罐工人，把钩工人. ②(宇宙飞行)着陆器，着陆舱. ③(输送金属用的)斜槽.

L. & G. = loss and gain 损益.

land·grave [ˈlændgreiv] *n.* ①伯爵领主〔中世纪德国拥有土地的伯爵〕. ②某些德国王公的称号. **-gra·vi·ate** [-ˈgreiviit] *n.* 伯爵领主的职位〔权力，领地〕.

-gra·vine [-grəˌviːn] *n.* 女伯爵领主;伯爵领主的夫人.

land·ing [ˈlændiŋ] *n.* ①登陆;着陆,降落;下车. ②登陆处;(飞机)着陆地;码头;(车站的)月台. ③【建】楼梯平台;梯台;【林】集材场,贮木场;【矿】装卸台. ④【无】(电子的)沉陷,沉淀. *make [effect] a* ~ 登陆;着陆. *make a forced* ~ 强迫降落,迫降. *make a safe* ~ 安全降落. *make a soft* ~ 软着陆. ***Happy*** ~! 祝旅途平安〔送行者向上飞机的人告别语〕. ~ **account**【商】起货报告. ~ **book**【商】起货清单. ~ **certificate**〔美〕登陆证. ~ **charges**〔*pl.*〕 起货费. ~ **craft** 登陆艇. ~ **field [ground]** 着陆地,飞机场. ~ **force** 登陆部队,陆战队. ~ **gear**【空】起落装置,起落架. ~ **net** (用以抄取上钩的鱼的)抄网. ~ **party** 登陆(分遣)队. ~ **place** 登陆处,码头;着陆地. ~ **run** 降落滑行距离. ~ **ship** 登陆舰. ~**-ship-tank** 登陆艇〔略作 L. S. T.〕. ~ **skid**【空】起落橇. ~ **speed** (最低)着陆速度. ~ **stage** 趸船,栈桥. ~ **station**【空】降落站. ~ **strip** ①(飞机场的)起落跑道. ②可着陆地区. ~ **T,** ~ **tee**【空】(指示飞机着陆的)T形着陆标志,T字布. ~ **wire** = anti-lift wire. ~ **waiter** = landwaiter.

länd·ler [ˈlentlə] *n.* ①兰德勒舞〔奥地利农村的一种民间舞蹈,慢节奏,三拍子〕. ②兰德勒舞曲.

land·less [ˈlændlis] *a.* 无土地的;无不动产的;无陆地的.

land·oc·ra·cy [lændˈɔkrəsi] *n.* 〔谑〕大地主阶级. **land-o·crat** 地主阶级分子.

Lan·don [ˈlændən] *n.* 兰登〔姓氏〕.

Lan·dor [ˈlændɔː] *n.* ①兰道〔姓氏〕. ②**Walter Savage** ~ 沃尔特·萨维奇·兰道〔1775—1864, 英国散文家,诗人〕.

land·scape [ˈlændskeip] *n.* ①风景, 景致. ②山水画,风景画, 风景摄影. ③【地】景观, 地形. ④眼界,前景展望. *a* ~ *of snow* 雪景. *a* ~ *in oil* 风景油画. —*vt.* 美化(自然环境等). — *vi.* ①做自然环境美化工作. ②做庭园设计师. ~ **architect** 环境美化专家. ~ **architecture** 园林建筑学. ~ **gardener** 园艺美化家. ~ **gardening** 造园法. ~ **painter** 风景画家, 山水画家. ~ **painting** 风景画(法).

land·scap·ist [ˈlændˌskeipist] *n.* ①风景画家. ②庭园设计师.

Land·seer [ˈlænsiə] *n.* 兰西尔〔姓氏〕.

lands·man [ˈlændzmən] *n.* ***(pl. -men*** [-mən]***)*** ①陆居人;未出过海的人;(无经验的)新水手. ②本国人,同胞.

land·sturm [ˈlɑːndʃturm] *n.* ①〔G.〕(战时)全国总动员〔宣布征召六十岁以下全部男子〕. ②战时后备军.

land·ward [ˈlændwəd] *ad.* 向陆地 (=landwards). — *a.* 面向陆地的. ~ *wind* 海风.

land·wehr [G.ˈlɑːntveə] *n.* 〔G.〕(受过训练的)后备役人员.

Lane [lein] *n.* 莱恩〔姓氏,男子名〕.

lane [lein] *n.* ①小路, 小巷. ②(行列间的)通路. ③航道; 空中走廊; 规定的单向行车道. ④【体】跑道. ⑤〔the L-〕(伦敦的剧院区)特鲁利街 (= Drury Lane). *a blind* ~ 死路,死胡同. *the inside [outside]* ~ 内〔外〕车道. ***It is a long*** ~ ***that has no turning.***〔谚〕路必有弯;山穷水尽还有路. ***the red*** ~ 喉咙. ~ **route** 外洋航线(= ocean ~).

lang. = language.

lang·bein·ite [ˈlæŋbainait] *n.*【化】无水钾镁矾.

Lange [ˈlæŋə] *n.* 兰格〔姓氏〕.

Lang·land [ˈlæŋlənd] *n.* ①兰兰〔姓氏〕. ②**William** ~ 威廉·兰兰〔1332?—1400,英国诗人〕.

lang·lauf [ˈlɑːŋˌlauf] *n.*〔G.〕越野滑雪. **-er** 越野滑雪者.

Lang·ley [ˈlæŋli] *n.* ①兰利〔姓氏〕. ②**Samuel Pierpont** ~ 塞缪尔·皮尔庞特·兰利〔1834—1906, 美国天文学家,物理学家和航空学先驱者〕.

lang·ley [ˈlæŋli] *n.* ***(pl.*** ~***s)***【物】兰〔能通量单位〕.

Lang·muir [ˈlæŋmjuə] *n.* 兰米尔〔姓氏〕.

Lan·go·bard [ˈlæŋɡəuˈbɑːd] *n.* (意大利北部)伦巴第人. **-ic** ①*a.* 伦巴第的;伦巴第语的;伦巴第文化的. ②*n.* 伦巴第语.

lan·gouste [lɑːŋˈguːst] *n.* 〔F.〕【动】龙虾 (= spiny lobster).

lang·syne [ˈlæŋˈsain] *ad., n.* 〔Scot.〕 很久以前;往昔.

Lang·ton [ˈlæŋtən] *n.* 兰顿〔姓氏〕.

lan·guage [ˈlæŋgwidʒ] *n.* ①语言;(某民族, 某国的)国语;语调,措词. ②(谈话者或作者所使用的)言语,语风,文风,文体. ③专门用语,术语. ④(动物的)叫声;(动作,手势等所表示的)表意语. ⑤【自】机器代码(= machine ~). ⑥〔俚〕粗话,骂人的话;坏话. ⑦态度, 立场. ⑧〔古〕民族;某国国民. *a common* ~ 共同的语言. *a dead* ~ 死语言. *a foreign* ~ 外国语. *a living* ~ 活语言. *long* ~ (与符号语言相对的) 通用语言. *oral [spoken]* ~ 口语. *the Chinese* ~ 汉语. *written* ~ 书面语. *high* ~ 夸张的言词. *in his own* ~ 按他自己的说法. *with a great command [an easy flow] of* ~ 口若悬河. *legal* ~ 法律用语. *medical* ~ 医学用语. *parliamentary* ~ 议会辞令;有礼貌的话. *the* ~ *of diplomacy* 外交辞令. *the* ~ *of the science* 科学用语. *finger [gesture, sign]* ~ 手势语. *the* ~ *of flowers* 花语〔如以 lily 象征纯洁等〕. *the* ~ *of the eyes* 目语, 眉目传情. *billing gate* ~ = ~ *of the fish-market* 下流的粗话. *in strong* ~ 用激烈的下流话. *use (bad [foul, warm])* ~ *to sb.* 谩骂某人. ***in fourteen*** ~***s*** 〔美俚〕非常. ***speak the same*** ~ 说共同的语言, 信仰和观点相同. ~ ***arts*** 中小学的语文课程. ~ **master** 语言教师.

langue d'oc [ˌlɑːŋgəˈdɔk] *n.* 〔F.〕 ①中世纪法国南部方言. ②现代的普罗旺斯语 (=modern Provençal).

langue d'o·il [ˌlɑːŋgəˈdɔil] *n.* 〔F.〕 ①中世纪法国北部方言. ②现代法语 (=modern French).

lan·guet, lan·guette [ˈlæŋgwit] *n.* 小舌, 舌状物;起舌状作用的东西.

lan·guid [ˈlæŋgwid] *a.* ①疲倦的. ②(天气) 阴沉的;(市面等)不兴旺的,萧条的. ③无精打采的, 不活泼的;不高兴的,不情愿的. ④缓慢的. **-ly** *ad.* **-ness** *n.*

lan·guish [ˈlæŋgwiʃ] *vi.* ①衰弱, 疲倦. ②(草木等)凋萎. ③烦恼;焦思,渴望 *(for)*. ④憔悴;潦倒. ⑤(兴趣等)减弱,减少. ⑥作出楚楚动人的伤感之态〔倦态等〕. *My interest in the subject has greatly* ~*ed.* 我对这一问题的兴趣大大减退了. *All business* ~*es.* 百业萧条. *The leaves* ~*ed in the drought.* 天旱使树叶枯萎. ~ *for home* 因为思家而憔悴. ~ *for years in a dungeon* 长年苦尝铁窗风味. — *n.* ①憔悴. ②惹人怜爱的感伤模样〔倦态等〕;脉脉含情. **-er** *n.* **-ment** *n.*

lan·guish·ing [ˈlæŋgwiʃiŋ] *a.* ①衰弱下去的. ②焦思的,忧郁的. ③(疾病等) 长期拖延的. ④故作感伤〔倦态〕而引人怜爱的;脉脉含情的. **-ly** *ad.*

lan·guor [ˈlæŋgə] *n.* ①(温暖气候等引起的)疲倦;倦怠. ②意气消沉;郁闷. ③〔常 *pl.*〕柔情. **-ous** *a.* **-ously** *ad.*

lan·gur [ˌlʌŋˈguə] *n.*【动】 龄猴 *(Presbytis)* 〔东南亚一种长尾猴〕.

lan·iard [ˈlænjəd] *n.* = lanyard.

la·ni·ar·y [ˈlæniəri] *a.*【解】(牙)适于扯裂东西的;(犬)牙的. — *n.*【解】短刀形犬牙.

La·nier [ləˈniə] *n.* 拉尼尔〔姓氏〕.

la·nif·er·ous, la·nig·er·ous [ləˈnifərəs, ləˈnidʒərəs] *a.* 有细毛的,羊毛状的.

lan·i·tal [ˈlænitæl, -təl] *n.* 人造羊毛.

lank [læŋk] *a.* ①瘦的, 细长的. ②(草等)长而柔软的. ③(头发)长而无卷曲的. **-ly** *ad.* **-ness** *n.*

Lan·kes·ter [ˈlæŋkistə] *n.* 兰基斯特〔姓氏〕.

lank·y [ˈlæŋki] *a.* ***(lank·i·er; -i·est)*** 瘦长的, 细长的. **-i·ly** *ad.* **-i·ness** *n.*

lan·ner [ˈlænə] *n.*【动】 南非隼 (尤指狩猎用的这种雌鹰).

lan·ner·et [ˌlænəˈriːt] *n.* 【动】南非雄隼.
Lan·ny [ˈlæni] *n.* 兰尼〔男子名, Lawrence 的昵称〕.
lan·o·lin(e) [ˈlænəli(ː)n] *n.* 羊毛脂.
la·nose [ˈleinəus] *a.* = lanate.
Lan·sing [ˈlænsiŋ] *n.* 兰辛〔姓氏〕.
lans·que·net [ˈlænskənet] *n.* ①(16—17 世纪德国的)雇佣兵. ②沙弥斗罗汉〔源出德国的一种牌戏,庄家与闲家各分一牌比大小〕.
lan·ta·na [lænˈteinə, -ˈtɑː-] *n.* 【植】马缨丹属 *(Lantana)* 〔生长于美洲热带和亚热带〕.
lan·tern [ˈlæntən] *n.* ①提灯; 灯笼; 街灯. ②幻灯(= magic ~). ③(灯塔的)灯火室. ④【建】天窗灯笼式屋顶. ⑤【机】油环,套环. *a Chinese* ~ 灯笼. *a dark* ~ (仅一孔漏光的)暗灯. *a* ~ *procession* 提灯游行. *a signal* ~ 信号灯. *The Feast of Lanterns* (中国的)上元节,灯节,元宵节. *Lantern-and-candle light!* 小心火烛〔伦敦更夫的呼声〕. *the parish* ~ 〔方〕月亮. —*vt.* ①供给…以灯火; 给…配上提灯. ②把…吊死在街灯柱上. ~ *a lighthouse* 给灯塔点上灯火. ~ *a fishing boat* 给渔船配上提灯. **~-and-candle man** 伦敦更夫. ~ **fish** 【动】灯笼鱼. ~ **fly** 【动】白蜡虫. ~ **jaw** 突出的下巴. **~-jawed** *a.* 下巴突出的,双颊深陷的. ~ **pinion [wheel]** 灯笼式小齿轮. ~ **ring** (泵的)套环. ~ **slide** 幻灯片. ~ **tree** 【植】红百合木 *(Crinodendron hookerianum)* 〔智利产的一种树,美国南部有时用该树作装饰品〕.
lan·tha·nid(e) [ˈlænθəˌnid, -ˌnaid] *n.* 【化】镧化物, 镧族元素. ~ **series** 【化】镧系〔即稀土元素〕.
lan·tha·num [ˈlænθənəm] *n.* 【化】镧.
lant·horn [ˈlæntən] *n.* 〔废〕lantern 的变体.
Lan·tian man *n.* 【人类】蓝田(猿)人.
la·nu·go [ləˈnjuːgəu, -ˈnuː-] *n.* (婴儿的)胎毛; (昆虫身上的)细毛; 柔毛. **la·nu·gi·nous** [-dʒinəs], **la·nu·gi·nose** [-dʒinəus] *a.*
lan·yard [ˈlænjəd] *n.* ①【军】(发射火炮等用的)牵索,拉火绳. ②(船上系物用的)短绳. ③(挂在水手脖子上的)系刀绳,小绳. ④勋带.
Lao [lau, ˈlɑːəu] *a., n.* *(pl.* ~*(s))* = Laotian.
La·oc·o·ön [leiˈɔkəuɔn] *n.* ①【希神】拉奥孔〔特洛伊的祭师,因警告特洛伊人不要中木马计而触怒天神,连同其二子被巨蟒缠死〕. ②(表现拉奥孔父子垂死时与巨蟒奋勇搏斗的)拉奥孔雕像. ③英勇搏斗者.
La·od·i·ce·an [ˌleiəudiˈsiən] *a., n.* (对政治、宗教等)不热心的(人),冷淡的(人).
La·os [ˈlauz] *n.* 老挝〔亚洲〕.
La·o·tian [leiˈəuʃən] *a.* 老挝的; 老挝人的; 老挝文化的. — *n.* ①老挝人,寮人. ②老挝语.
lap[1] [læp] *n.* ①膝; 〔喻〕怀抱, 境遇. ②(衣服的)下摆,裙兜,衣兜. ③〔诗〕(山间的)凹地, 山坳; (书等的)面. ④养育所,休息处. ⑤〔古〕耳朵. ⑥【体】(跑道的)一圈; 一段行程; 工作阶段. ⑦重叠部分; 重叠量; 【机】余面. ⑧【建】(瓦的)互搭,搭接. ⑨(滚筒上绳索的)一圈; 【纺】棉卷,毛卷. ⑩掌管,范围. *have a baby on one's* ~ 把孩子放在膝上. *hold a child in [on] one's* ~ 把孩子抱在膝上. ***drop [dump] the whole thing in [into] sb.'s*** ~ 把事情都推在某人身上. ***Everything falls into sb.'s*** ~. (某人)事事顺利. ***(be [lie]) in the ~ of the gods*** 在神的掌握之中, 结果尚难预料. ***in Fortune's ~ = in the ~ of Fortune*** 走运,运气好. ***in nature's*** ~ 在大自然的怀抱里. ***in the ~ of future*** 未来的事情,尚在未知之数. ***in the ~ of luxury*** 极尽奢华. ***sit in the ~ of*** 倒在…怀抱里. ***throw oneself into the ~ of*** 投入…的怀抱, 投靠. —*vt.* ***(lapped*** [ˈlæpt]; ***lap·ping*** [ˈlæpiŋ]*)* ①包围,包住. ②折叠,重叠,搭叠. ③把…抱在膝上; 把…爱护地怀抱着. ④【纺】使 (经过梳梳的棉花)成卷. ⑤赛跑时比(某人)领先…圈; 跑完(全程等). ~ *oneself in a blanket* 用毯子裹住身体. *She was lapped in luxury.* 她生活奢侈. ~ *a wrist in a bandage* 用纱布包住手腕. ~ *the course* 跑完全程. ~ *roof-slates* 迭盖石板瓦. — *vi.* ①被包住,围起. ②部分重叠,搭接; 并排. ③伸出,突出,露出. ④跑完全程. *Joy lapped over her.* 她沉浸于欢乐中. ~ ***over*** 重叠. *(His reign ~s over into the sixteenth century.* 他的统治延至十六世纪). ~ **belt** (汽车座位上系在腰部的)安全带. ~ **board** *n.* 膝板〔放在膝上当桌子用的平板〕. ~ **dissolve** 〔电影、电视〕叠化〔一个镜头未完,另一个镜头重叠出现,然后原镜头逐渐消逝的摄影手法〕. ~ **dog** 叭儿狗. ~ **joint,** **~-joint,** ~**ped joint** 搭接(处). **~-joint flange** 松套法兰. ~ **robe** 围毯,膝毯〔坐车、坐雪橇和看户外运动等盖在膝上使下身保暖的毯子〕. **~stone** 皮匠放在膝上的垫石〔铁〕. **~-strap** (飞机乘客系在腰部的) 安全带. ~ **time** 【体】跑一圈的时间. **~ful** *a.* 一满兜.
lap[2] [læp] *n.* ①舐; 舐一次的分量; 一舐. ②(波浪的)拍打声. ③〔俚〕淡饮料. ***take a ~ at*** 舐一下. — *vt.* ①舐,舐食. ②拼命吃[喝]. ③爱听(奉承话). ④(波浪)拍打. *Cats ~ water.* 猫舐水. *The sea ~s the base of the cliff.* 海浪拍打悬崖的底部. — *vi.* ①舐, 舐食. ②(波浪)拍打. ~ ***up [down]*** ①(贪婪地)舐光,喝干. ②欣然接受; 热烈倾听.
lap[3] [læp] *n.* (磨宝石等的)磨盘, 研磨机. — *vt., vi.* 用磨盘磨; 研磨,磨光.
lap·a·rot·o·my [ˌlæpəˈrɔtəmi] *n.* *(pl.* ~*s)* 【医】剖腹术.
La Paz [lɑː ˈpæz] 拉巴斯〔玻利维亚首都, 政府所在地, 法定首都是苏克雷 (Sucre)〕.
la·pel [ləˈpel] *n.* 〔主 *pl.*〕(西服上衣的)翻领.
lap·i·cide [ˈlæpisaid] *n.* 石工.
lap·i·dar·i·an [ˌlæpiˈdeəriən] *a.* = lapidary *a.*
lap·i·dar·ist [ˈlæpiˈdeərist] *n., a.* = lapidary.
lap·i·dar·y [ˈlæpidəri] *n.* ①玉石[宝石]工. ②玉石[宝石]工艺. ③玉石[宝石]鉴识家; 宝石商. — *a.* ①玉石[宝石]雕刻的; 与玉石雕刻有关的. ②铭刻在石上的. ③(文字等)有碑铭风格的, 简洁优雅的. ~ *inscriptions* 碑文. ~ **style** 【修】碑文体.
lap·i·date [ˈlæpideit] *vt.* 〔古〕用石头投掷,用石头砸死.
lap·i·da·tion [ˌlæpiˈdeiʃən] *n.* ①投石击毙刑. ②投掷乱石.
la·pid·i·fy [ləˈpidifai] *vt., vi.* 〔古〕(使)变成石头. **-dific(al)** *a.* **-i·fi·ca·tion** [-ˌpidifiˈkeiʃən] *n.*
la·pil·li [ləˈpilai] *n.* lapillus 的复数.
la·pil·lus [ləˈpiləs] *n.* *(pl.* ***la·pil·li*** [-lai]*)* 【地】火山砾.
lap·in [ˈlæpin; F. lapɛ̃] *n.* 〔F.〕兔; 兔的毛皮.
lap·is laz·u·li [ˌlæpis ˈlæzjulai] 〔L.〕①【地】天青石,青金石. ②天青石色.
La·place [lɑːˈplɑːs], **Pierre Simon, Marquis de** 拉普拉斯〔1749—1827,法国天文学家、数学家〕.
Lap·land [ˈlæplænd] *n.* 拉普兰〔北欧地名, 包括挪威、瑞典、芬兰北部及苏联西北部科拉 (Kola) 半岛的一个地区〕.
Lap·land·er [ˈlæplændə] *n.* 拉普(兰)人.
La Pla·ta [ləˈplɑːtə] 拉普拉塔〔阿根廷港市〕.
Lapp [læp] *n.* ①(分布在挪威、瑞典、芬兰和苏联北部的)拉普(兰)人. ②拉普(兰)语.
lap·pet [ˈlæpit] *n.* ①(衣、帽等的)垂片, 垂饕, 垂饰. ②耳垂,(火鸡等颈部的)垂肉. ③= lapel.
Lap·pic, Lap·pish [ˈlæpik, ˈlæpiʃ] *a.* 拉普兰的, 拉普兰人的. — *n.* 拉普兰语.
lapse [læps] *n.* ①时间的消逝[推移,间隔]. ②缓流. ③错失, 过失, 小错. ④行为失检, 偏离正道; 堕落. ⑤废除; 【法】(权利等的)丧失, 消失. ⑥(气温,气压等的) 骤降,下降. ⑦【物】垂直梯度. *after a ~ of five years* 事隔五年之后. ~ *of time* 时光的流逝, 一段时间. *with the ~ of time* 随着时间的过去. *the ~ of a stream* 溪水的缓流. *a ~ of attention* 一时疏忽. *a ~ of memory* 记错. *a*

~ *of the pen* 笔误. *a* ~ *of the tongue* 失言. [*a* ~ *into crime* 犯罪. *a moral* ~ 道德败坏. *a* ~ *from respectability* 有失体面. *a* ~ *from virtue* 堕落,违背道德的行为. — *vi.* ①(时间)悄悄流逝 (*away*). ②退步 (*away; back*); 坠落;犯罪,陷入,堕入. ③【法】(权利、任期等)终止,失效;【法】转归 (*to*). ④塌陷. ~ *backward* 落后. ~ *into ruin* 塌陷成一片废墟. ~ *into vice* 陷入罪恶活动,变坏. ~ *from good manners* 行为渐渐变坏. *The conversation* ~*d.* 谈话停止了. *The tenure of the office has* ~*d.* 任期届满. — *vt.* 使失效,废止. ~ *a policy* 废止一项政策. ~ **rate**【气】(与高度成比例的)气温直减率,递减率.

lap•sus [ˈlæpsəs] *n.* 〔L.〕 ***(pl.*** ~ [-sjuːs]***)*** 失误;错误;差错. ~ ***ca•la•mi*** [ˈkæləmai] 笔误,写错. ~ ***lin•guae*** [ˈliŋgwai] 失言;口误. ~ ***me•mo•riae*** [miˈmɔːrii] 记错.

La•pu•ta [ləˈpjuːtə] *n.* 飞岛,拉普他岛〔英国作家江奈生·斯威夫特 (Jonathan Swift) 所著《格列佛游记》中的一个飞岛,岛上居民多幻想而不务实际〕.

La•pu•tan [ləˈpjuːtən] *n.* 飞岛居民,拉普他岛人. — *a.* 拉普他人的,拉普他人似的;不切实际的,异想天开的,荒唐不经的.

lap•wing [ˈlæpwiŋ] *n.*【动】凤头麦鸡,田凫.

lar [lɑː] *n.* ***(pl.*** ~***es*** [ˈlɛəriːz], ~***s)*** ①〔常 *pl.*〕(古罗马人崇拜的)家神,护家神. ②***(pl.*** ~***s)***【动】(马来群岛的)白掌猿 (= ~ gibbon).

lar•board [ˈlɑːbəd] *n.*【海】左舷〔为避免与 starboard (右舷)混淆,现一般用 port 一词代替〕. — *a.* 左舷方面的. — *ad.* 朝左舷方面.

lar•ce•ner, lar•ce•nist [ˈlɑːsinə, ˈlɑːsinist] *n.* 盗窃犯,窃贼,侵占犯.

lar•ce•nous [ˈlɑːsinəs] *a.* ①偷窃的;构成偷窃[侵占]罪的. ②犯偷窃[侵占]罪的. **-ly** *ad.*

lar•ce•ny [ˈlɑːsni] *n.*【法】窃盗罪;非法侵占他人财产.

larch [lɑːtʃ] *n.* ①【植】落叶松属. ②落叶松木材.

lard [lɑːd] *n.* 猪油. — *vt.* ①在…涂上猪油. ②嵌(腌肥肉片)到(牛肉、鸡肉)中. ③润色(文章等),点缀(谈话等). ~ *a boned chicken* 用腌肉片塞填去骨鸡. ~ *one's conversation with Latin words* 在会话中引用拉丁语. ~ **beetle**【动】火腿皮蠹. ~**-bucket**〔美俚〕胖子. ~ **fruit**【植】猪油果(也称油渣果,油瓜). ~**head**〔美俚〕蠢人. ~**like** *a.*

lar•da•ceous [lɑːˈdeiʃəs] *a.* ①猪油(似)的. ②【医】豚脂样的,含淀粉样蛋白的.

lard•er [ˈlɑːdə] *n.* ①藏肉所,食品库. ②家中贮存的食品.

Lard•ner [ˈlɑːdnə] *n.* 拉德纳〔姓氏〕.

lar•don [ˈlɑːdən], **lar•doon** [lɑːˈduːn] *n.* (烹调前嵌在肉中的)肥咸肉[腊肉]片.

lard•y [ˈlɑːdi] *a.* ***(lard•i•er; lard•i•est)*** ①含猪油的;脂肪多的,肥的. ②猪油似的,涂猪油的. ~**-dar•dy** *a.* 〔英俚〕装模作样的;怪模怪样的;装得娇弱无力的.

la•res [ˈlɛəriːz] *n.* lar 的复数. ~ ***and penates*** ①(古罗马人崇拜)护家神. ②家珍,家宝.

lar•gac•til [lɑːˈgæktil] *n.*【药】氯普马嗪 (=chlorpromazine).

lar•gan•do [lɑːˈgɑːndəu] *a., ad.* 〔It.〕 = allargando.

large [lɑːdʒ] *a.* ①(体积,空间,数量,规模等)大的,巨大的;(权限等)广泛的. ②(心胸)宽广的,度量大的;(眼界等)开阔的,(见识等)广博的. ③(艺术风格等)奔放的,气魄宏大的;夸张的. ④【海】顺风的. *a* ~ *calibre gun* 大口径炮. *a* ~ *garden* 大花园. *a* ~ *room* 大房间. ~ *and small sizes* 大小尺寸. *be* ~ *of limbs* 大手大脚. *a* ~ *family* 多子女的家庭. *a* ~ *number* 大批(= ~ numbers). *a* ~ *population* 人口众多. *a* ~ *farmer* 富农. *a* ~ *merchant* 巨商. *have a* ~ *discretion* 有广泛的决定权. ~ *powers* 大权. ~ *units* 大兵团. *a* ~ *heart* 宽宏大量. *a man of* ~ *views* 见识广博的人. ~ *tolerance* 胸怀宽大. ★ *large* 在口语中不象 big 那样常用,也不象 great 那样含有"伟大","壮大"的意义. ***as*** ~ ***as life*** ①和原物一样大小. ②〔谑〕亲自,千真万确 (*There he was as* ~ *as life.* 他本人就在那里). — *n.* 大〔仅用于下列习语〕. ***at*** ~ ①自由,随便;拉杂地,零乱地. (*He scatters imputations at* ~. 他乱讲坏话). ②未被捕,逍遥自在 (*Is the prisoner still at* ~*?* 犯人还未归案么?). ③全体;普遍;一般 (*the people at* ~ 一般人民). ④充分,详细 (*talk at* ~ 详细讲). ⑤未决定 (*leave the matter at* ~ 让事件无着落). ⑥无固定职位[任所]的 (*a gentleman at* ~ 无职宫廷官吏;〔谑〕无一定职业的人. *an ambassador at* ~ 〔美〕无任所大使). ⑥〔美〕(非某一选区而是)全州选出的 (*a Congressman at* ~ 州选议员). ⑦笼统地 (*arrangements made at* ~ 笼统作出的安排). ***in (the)*** ~ ①大规模地. ②一般地. — *ad.* ①大,大大地. ②详细地. ③夸大地. ④【海】顺风地 (*sail* ~ 顺风航行). ***by and*** ~ 从全体看来. ***talk*** ~ 吹牛,说大话. ~ **calorie** 大卡,千卡. ~**-eyed** *a.* ①大眼的. ②大针孔的. ③睁大眼睛的. ~**-handed** *a.* 大手大脚的;大方的,慷慨的. ~**-hearted** *a.* 慷慨的,富于同情心的,正直的. ~**-minded** *a.* 气量大的;宽宏大量的;思想开通的. ~**mouth (black) bass**【动】大口黑鲈. ~**-scale** *a.* ①(地图等的)大比例的. ②大规模的;大面积的;巨型的 (~*-scale business operations* 大规模的经营). ~**-tonnage product** 大量产品.

large•ly [ˈlɑːdʒli] *ad.* ①大量地. ②主要地. ③慷慨地. *build* ~ 大兴土木. *His failure is* ~ *due to timidity.* 他的失败主要是由于胆小. *give* ~ 慨然捐助.

large•ness [ˈlɑːdʒnis] *n.* ①巨大;广大. ②伟大. ③慷慨. ④广博. *have* ~ *of mind* 思想开通,襟怀坦白.

lar•gess(e) [ˈlɑːdʒes, ˈlɑːdʒis] *n.* ①慷慨的赏赐[援助];赏赐物. ②〔古〕慷慨. ③本性. ***cry*** ~ 讨赏钱.

lar•ghet•to [lɑːˈgetəu] *a., ad.* 〔It.〕【乐】稍缓慢,稍宽广. — *n.*【乐】小广板.

larg•ish [ˈlɑːdʒiʃ] *a.* 稍大的.

lar•go [ˈlɑːgəu] *a., ad.* 〔It.〕【乐】缓慢,宽广. — *n.*【乐】广板.

lar•i•at [ˈlæriət] *n., vt.* 〔美〕= lasso.

lar•ine [ˈlærin, -rain] *a.*【动】①鸥科的,鸥亚科的. ②鸥的;似鸥的.

lark[1] [lɑːk] *n.*【动】云雀;百灵科鸣禽. *a meadow* ~〔美〕象寒鸦的小鸟. ***as cheerful [gay, happy] as a*** ~ 非常快乐. ***If the sky falls, we shall catch*** ~***s.*** 〔谚〕天垮了正好捉云雀,杞忧无益. ***rise [be up] with the*** ~ 早起. — *vi.* 捉云雀.

lark[2] [lɑːk] 〔口〕 *n.* 嬉戏,戏谑,玩笑,玩乐. *What a* ~*!* 真有趣! ***be up to sb.'s*** ~***s*** 在开某人的玩笑. ***for a*** ~ 当作玩笑. ***have a*** ~ ***with sb.*** = ***have*** ~***s with sb.*** 开某人玩笑. — *vi.* ①嬉戏,闹着玩. ②骑马越野. ***Stop*** ~***ing about!*** 别开玩笑了! — *vt.* ①取笑,愚弄. ②骑(马)越野;骑马跳越.

Lar•kin [ˈlɑːkin] *n.* 拉金〔男子名〕.

lark•spur [ˈlɑːkspəː] *n.*【植】飞燕草.

lark•y [ˈlɑːki] *a.* ***(lark•i•er; lark•i•est)*** 爱耍闹的;嬉戏的.

larn [lɑːn] *vt., vi.* 〔俚,谑〕= learn.

lar•ri•gan [ˈlærigən] *n.* 〔美〕(伐木工人穿的)长统鹿皮靴.

lar•ri•kin [ˈlærikin] *n.* 〔澳俚〕恶棍,无赖. — *a.* 吵闹的.

lar•rup [ˈlærəp] *vt.* ①〔方〕打,鞭打. ②彻底击败. — *vi.* 垂着头懒散地走. — *n.* 一击.

Lar•ry [ˈlæri] *n.* 拉里〔男子名, Lawrence 的昵称〕.

lar•va [ˈlɑːvə] *n.* ***(pl. -s, -vae*** [-viː]***)*** ①【动】幼虫;幼体. ②〔废〕鬼,妖怪.

lar•val [ˈlɑːvəl] *a.*【动】幼虫的;幼体的;幼虫期的;幼虫形的,幼体形的.

lar•vi•cide [ˈlɑːvisaid] *n.* 杀幼虫剂. **-vi•cid•al** *a.*

la·ryn·gal [lə'riŋgəl] *a.*【语音】喉音的. — *n.* 喉音.

la·ryn·ge·al [ˌlærin'dʒi(:)əl, læ'rindʒiəl] *a.* ①【解】喉的. ②【医】侵犯喉头的; 医喉的. ③【语音】喉音的. — *n.*【语音】喉音. **-ly** *ad.*

la·ryn·ges [lə'rindʒi:z] *n.* larynx 的复数.

lar·yn·gic [lə'rindʒik] *a.* = laryngeal.

lar·yn·gi·tis [ˌlærin'dʒaitis] *n.*【医】喉炎.

lar·yn·g(o)- *comb. f.* 表示"喉的","喉部和…的": *laryng*itis, *laryngo*scope.

lar·yn·gol·o·gy [ˌlæriŋ'gɔlədʒi] *n.*【医】喉科学. **la·ryn·go·log·i·cal** [ləˌriŋgə'lɔdʒikl] *a.* **lar·yn·gol·o·gist** *n.* 喉科医师.

la·ryn·go·pha·ryn·ge·al [ləˌriŋgəufə'rindʒiəl, -dʒəl] *a.* 咽喉的.

la·ryn·go·phone [lə'riŋgəfəun] *n.* 喉头送话器.

la·ryn·go·scope [lə'riŋgəskəup] *n.*【医】喉镜.

lar·yn·got·o·my [ˌlæriŋ'gɔtəmi] *n.*【医】喉切开术.

lar·ynx ['læriŋks] *n.* *(pl. ~es, la·ryn·ges*[lə'rindʒi:z]*)*【解】喉.

la·sa·gna [lə'zɑ:njə] *n.*【烹】烤宽面条〔上浇肉末番茄汁〕(=lasagne).

las·car ['læskə] *n.* ①(旧时欧洲轮船上的)印度水手. ②(旧时英国陆军中的)印度炮兵.

las·civ·i·ous [lə'siviəs] *a.* ①淫荡的, 好色的. ②色情的,猥亵的. **-ly** *ad.* **-ness** *n.*

lase [leiz] *vi.* *(lased; las·ing)* 发射[放射, 产生]激光, 光激射.

la·se·con ['leisəkɔn] *n.* 激射光转换器.

la·ser ['leizə] *n.* 激光,受激发射光,莱塞; 激光器,光激射器 (= light amplification by stimulated emission of radiation)〔由以上各词首字母组成的缩略词〕. *a ~ space-to-ground voice link* 激光空对地通话联系. *glass ~* 玻璃光激射器. ~ **bounce** 激光反射. ~ **gun** 激光枪. ~ **rod** 激光棒. ~**tracking** 激光跟踪. **-ing** = lasing. ~**-bomb** *vt.* 以激光炸弹轰击.

lash[1] [læʃ] *n.* ①鞭打,鞭挞,抽打;〔*the* ~〕鞭笞刑. ②鞭子 (尤指鞭子上的皮条). ③(波浪等的)冲击, (雨水等的)击打. ④讽刺; 严厉的谴责. ⑤(狗等的)摇尾. ⑥眼睫毛. ⑦【机】游隙,余隙,空隙. *the ~ of storm* 风暴的冲击. *back ~*【机】齿隙. *work under the whip ~* 在鞭笞下工作,被强迫劳动. ***under the ~*** 受体刑; 遭痛骂. — *vt.* ①打,鞭打. ②(波浪等)冲击; 急打. ③激起,煽动. ④骂,讽刺, 挖苦; 严厉谴责. ⑤(狗等)愤激地摇(尾巴). *The waves ~ the shore.* 波浪冲击海岸. *~ sb. into a fury* 激得某人大怒. — *vi.* ①鞭打. ②(风、波浪等)冲打. ③讽刺; 痛骂. ④(马等) 踢 *(out)*. ~ ***back at*** 猛烈反击. ***come ~ down*** (雨)下得很大. ~ ***down the silverware***【美体】稳拿银杯〔尤指在帆船竞赛中〕. ~ ***out*** ①猛打; (马)乱踢. ②大骂, 抨击. ③大量生产〔印制〕.

lash[2] [læʃ] *vt.* 用绳〔链等〕捆绑. ~**-up**〔口〕①应急办法,应急物. ②安排,布置.

lash·er ['læʃə] *n.* ①鞭打者; 责骂者. ②〔英方〕拦河坝,堰; 从堰上泄出的水; (堰下容纳泄出水的)蓄水池.

lash·ing ['læʃiŋ] *n.* ①鞭打; 非难,申斥. ②〔*pl.*〕捆绑. ③捆绑用的绳子. ④〔英方〕许多,大量 *(of)*.

Lash·io ['lɑ:ʃjəu] *n.* 腊戌〔缅甸城市〕.

lash·kar ['læʃkɑ:] *n.* = lascar.

las·ing ['leisiŋ] *n.* 激光作用. — *a.* 产生激光的.

Las·ki ['læski] *n.* 拉斯基〔姓氏〕.

Las Pal·mas [lɑ:s 'pɑ:lməs] 拉斯帕尔马斯〔加那利岛上一港口〕.

L-as·par·a·gi·nase [ˌelæspə'rædʒəneis] *n.*【药】左旋天门冬酰胺酶〔用于阻断白血病等癌细胞生长〕.

lass [læs] *n.* ①少女, 小姑娘 (*opp.* lad). ②情人. ③〔Scot.〕使女.

Las·salle [lə'sæl], **Ferdinand** 拉萨尔〔1825—1864, 一度为德国工人运动的领导人〕.

Las·salle·an [lə'sæliən] *n.* 拉萨尔派成员. *the ~s* 拉萨尔派〔十九世纪六十至七十年代德国工人运动中的机会主义派别〕. **-ism** *n.* 拉萨尔主义.

las·sie ['læsi] *n.*〔Scot.〕①少女,小姑娘. ②情人.

las·si·tude ['læsitju:d] *n.* ①疲倦,疲乏. ②厌倦, 无精打采.

las·so ['læsəu] *n.* *(pl. ~(e)s)* (一端有活结、用以捕捉牛马等的)套索. — *vt.* 用套索捕捉. **-er** *n.* 使用套索的人.

last[1] [lɑ:st] *a.* (*opp.* first) ①最后的, 末尾的; 最后剩下的. *We will defend our motherland to the ~ drop of our blood.* 我们愿为保卫祖国流尽最后一滴血. *for the ~ time* 最后一次. *~ but one [two]* 倒数第一[二]. *the ~ spurt* 最后的努力. *the ~ train* 末班火车. ②临终的. *in one's ~ moments* 临死时. ③紧接前面的, 刚过去的. *in the ~ few months* 在最近几个月. *~ month [week]* 上月[星期]. *the month [week] before ~* 上上个月[星期]. *in January ~* 去年一月. *on Sunday ~* 上星期天. *~ night* 昨晚. *this day ~ year* 去年今日. ④最近的,最新流行的,最时髦的. *the ~ thing in hats* 最时髦的帽子. ⑤最上的. *a paper of the ~ importance* 极端重要的文件. ⑥最糟糕的, 最坏的. *the ~ crime* 最恶劣的罪行. ⑦决定性的, 结论性的, 权威性的. *He has said the ~ word on the matter.* 他对于这一问题提出了决定性意见. *the ~ explanation*结论性的解释. ⑧极少可能的; 最不适当的. *He is the ~ man to do it.* 他决不会干那件事. *That is the ~ thing to try.* 那种事不值得去试. *the ~ man I expected to see* 我决没有料想会见面的人. *the ~ man I want to see* 我最不想见的人. *The ~ thing they want is …* 他们最不乐意的事是. ⑨〔加强语气用〕每一的. *every ~ square inch of good land* 每一平方英寸的良田. *Tell me every ~ word.* 把每句话一五一十地告诉我. *The lecture won't start until every ~ person is seated.* 直到每一个人就座以后,演讲才开始. ⑩最低的. *the ~ boy in the class* 班上倒数第一的男孩. *the ~ prize* 最低的奖赏. ★ last 和 latest 的区别: (1) 表现连续事物的'最末'事物时, 一般用 last: *the last number of the Spectator* 《旁观者》(周刊)的最后一期. (2) 表现尚未完结的连续事物时,一般用 latest 或 last: *the latest [last] installment of the story* 本期连载小说. ***put the ~ hand to*** 完成. ***the ~ great change*** 长眠, 死. ***the ~ cry*** 最新流行品. ***the ~ days [times]*** (人的)临终; 世界的末日. ***the ~ (news) I heard…*** 据最近的消息. ***to the ~ man*** 到最后一人. — *ad.* ①最后. *L- came the students* 最后来的是学生. *Who spoke ~?* 谁最后讲的话? ②上一次,最近一次. *I ~ met him in London.* 我最近一次在伦敦遇见他. *Since I saw you ~.* 自上次见你之后. ③最后一点, 总起来说. *and ~, I'd like to consider the economic aspects* 最后我想考虑一下经济方面的情况. ~ ***but not least*** 最后但不是最不重要的一点. ~ ***of all*** 最后. — *n.* ①最后, 临终. *from first to ~* 自始至终. *I was at his bedside at the very ~.* 一直到他临终我都守在他的床边. *the night before ~* 前夜. ②最近的人[物]. *as I said in my ~* 象我在前函中说的. *I received your ~ in June.* 我在六月收到你最后一封信. *The ~ out will please shut the door.* 最后出去的人请关门. ③动作[行为]的最后一次. *look one's ~ at* 朝…看最后一次. ④〔美〕末尾. *the ~ of the week* 周末. *the ~ of the month* 月底〔不一定是最后一天〕. ***at ~*** 终于(*At ~, man has reached the moon.* 人类终于到达了月球). ***at long ~*** 好容易才. ***breathe [gasp] one's ~*** 断气,死. ***hear the ~ of*** 最后听到. ***see the ~ of*** 最后一次看见. ***the ~ of pea-time***〔美〕最后阶段, 终点. ***the ~ of the mohicans*** "最后的莫希干人"〔原为美国作家 J. M. Coope 所著小说的名称,指某种衰亡没落人物最后的残存者〕. ***to [till] the ~*** 直到最后, 至死, (军队)苦战

到最后一兵一卒 (*hold on to the* ~ 坚持到底). ~ **day**【宗】最后审判日,世界末日. ~ **ditch** 最后一道防线; 最后的依靠 [手段] (*fight to the* ~ *ditch* 打到底). ~**-ditch** *a.* 拼死抵抗的, 无后退余地的, 最后挣扎的 (~*-ditch struggle* 拼死斗争). ~ **hurrah** 最后的努力 [尝试]. **L- Judg(e)ment**【宗】①(世界末日时上帝对人类的)最后审判. ②(上帝对人类的) 最后审判日. ~**-minute** *a.* 最后一分钟的, 紧急关头的. ~ **name** 姓. ~ **quarter** 下弦(月). ~ **rites**【宗】①(为死者举行的)最后仪式. ②为临终者举行的圣礼. ~ **sleep** 长眠, 死. ~ **straw** 使人不能忍受的最后一击; 使人不支而垮下的因素. **L- Supper**【宗】(耶稣被害前夕和十二门徒共进的)最后晚餐. ~ **word** ①(起裁决性作用的)最后一句话; 定论; 最后决定权. ②完美的事物. ③〔口〕最新式样; 最先进的品种.

last² [lɑːst] *vi.* 继续; 持久, 耐久, 经久. *The storm will not* ~ *long.* 暴风雨不会持续很久. *if my health* ~*s* 如果我的健康许可. *Our money will* ~ *till we get home.* 我们的钱足够到家了. *The festival* ~*ed two weeks.* 节日持续了两星期. *This cloth* ~*s well.* 这种布很耐穿. *This cloth will not* ~ *long.* 这布不经穿. — *vt.* 够用, 使得以维持; 经受住. *This watch will* ~ *me a lifetime.* 这只表够我用一辈子. ~ *out* 支持到底, 维持到最后 (*Will this coal* ~ *out the winter?* 这点煤能够烧一冬吗?). — *n.* 持久力, 精力.

last³ [lɑːst] *n.* 鞋楦头. — *vt.* 用鞋楦头来调整. ***stick to one's*** ~ 安分守己, 不管闲事 (*Let the cobbler stick to his* ~. 让人人各守本分).

last⁴ [lɑːst] *n.* 拉〔英国重量及容量单位, 约 4,000 磅〕. *a* ~ *of wool* 1 拉羊毛 (=4,368 磅). *a* ~ *of corn* 1 拉麦 (=80蒲式耳).

Las·tex [ˈlæsteks] *n.* 橡皮线, 松紧线〔商标名〕.

last·ing [ˈlɑːstiŋ] *a.* 耐久的, 持久的. *a* ~ *peace* 持久的和平. — *n.* 斜纹呢. **-ly** *ad.* **-ness** *n.*

last·ly [ˈlɑːstli] *ad.* 最后; 终于. *L-, I must point out that* … 最后, 我必须指出….

Lat. = Latin.

lat. = latitude.

lat [lɑːt] *n.* ***(pl. lats, la·ti)*** (拉脱维亚的货币单位)拉特.

La·ta·ki·a [ˌlætəˈkiː(ː)ə] *n.* ①拉塔基亚〔叙利亚港市〕. ②(拉塔基亚附近产的)一种上等烟草 (= ~ tobacco).

latch¹ [lætʃ] *n.* ①闩, 插销. ②碰锁, 弹簧锁. ③【机】档器, 掣子, 活门. *guard* ~ 保护锁键. *The door is on the* ~. 门上了闩. ***off the*** ~ 活栓开着. ***on the*** ~ 活栓扣着. — *vt., vi.* 用碰锁锁上(门等), 用插销扣上(门等). *Will the door* ~*?* 门锁得上么? ~**key** (住所大门)弹簧锁钥匙 (*win one's* ~*key* 取得出入大门的钥匙, 可以自由进出[行动]). ~**key child** 父母为双职工的孩子. ~**key voter** 〔蔑〕住在旅馆里的选民. ~ **lock** 弹簧锁. ~**string** (由门外拉开活栓锁的) 栓锁带 (*draw in the* ~*string for* 〔美〕不许自由出入. *hang out the* ~*string for* 允许自由出入).

latch² [lætʃ] *vi.* 获得; 抓住; 占有; 理解 *(on to)*.

latch·et [ˈlætʃit] *n.* 〔古〕鞋带.

late [leit] *a.* ***(later, latter; latest, last)*** ①迟, 晚. ②晚期的, 后期的. ③晚近的, 新近的, 近时的. ④已去世的, 已故的. ⑤前任的; 卸任不久的. *a* ~ *comer* 迟到者. *be two minutes too* ~ *for the train* 来晚了两分钟没有赶上火车. *be* ~ *for school [work]* 上学[上班]迟到. *be* ~ *from school [an office]* 迟迟从学校[办公室]回来. *a* ~ *Customer* 晚来顾客. *a* ~ *dinner* 晚上的正餐. *a* ~ *marriage* 晚婚. *a* ~ *worker* 通常工作很晚的人. *at a* ~ *hour* 在很晚的时候. *in one's* ~ *years* 晚年. *in the* ~ *afternoon* 傍晚. *in the* ~ *seventies* 七十年代后期. *in the* ~ *20th century* 二十世纪末叶. ~ *crops* 晚熟作物. ~ *spring* 暮春. *one's* ~ *residence* 故居. *the* ~ *belligerents* 前不久的交战国. *the* ~ *earthquake* 最近的地震. *my* ~ *husband* (寡妇用语)亡夫. *the* ~ *Professor Li* 已故的李教授. *the* ~ *prime minister* 前总理[首相]. ***keep*** ~ ***hours*** 迟睡迟起. ***of*** ~ 近来. ***of*** ~ ***years*** 近年来. — *ad.* ①迟; 过迟, 来不及. ②晚; 到深夜. ③以前是, 原先是. ④不久前; 最近. *as* ~ *as 1945* 迟在 1945 年. *Better* ~ *than never* 〔谚〕不怕慢, 只怕站; 晚做总比不做好. *come* ~ 来迟. *It is never too* ~ *to learn.* 〔谚〕活到老, 学到老. *ripen* ~ 晚熟. *early and* ~ 从早到晚. *early or* ~ = sooner or later. ~ *in 1960's* 在二十世纪六十年代后期. *work* ~ *into the night* 工作到深夜. *his own room,* ~ *his uncle's* 他自己的屋子, 以前是他叔父住的. *Mr. Smith,* ~ *of London* 最近住在伦敦的史密斯先生. *I saw her as* ~ *as yesterday.* 直到昨天我还看见过她. ***sit up*** ~ 深夜不睡. ~ **fee** (英国邮局在规定时间之后投递邮件所收的)过时补加费. ~ **gate** 后闸门. **L- Greek** (二世纪末至六世纪用的)后期希腊语. **L- Latin** (二世纪至六世纪用的)后期拉丁语. ~**-model** *a.* 新型的. **-ness** *n.*

lat·ed [ˈleitid] *a.* 〔诗〕迟来的, 姗姗来迟的, 迟到的.

la·teen [ləˈtiːn] *a.* (地中海上帆船用的)三角帆的. — *n.* 三角帆 (= ~ sail); 三角帆船. ~**rigged** *a.* 装有三角帆的.

late·ly [ˈleitli] *ad.* 近来, 最近. ★英国口语中的否定句, 疑问句多用 lately, 肯定句则用其他说法: *I haven't seen him* ~. *Have you seen him* ~*? I saw him recently [a short time ago].*

lat·en [ˈleitn] *vi., vt.* (使)变迟, (使)晚生长.

la·ten·cy [ˈleitənsi] *n.* ①隐伏, 潜伏, 潜在. ②潜伏物, 潜在因素.

La Tène [lɑː ˈten]【考古】拉特尼文化〔公元前约 600 年到公元约 100 年间存在于中欧的一种铁器时代文化, 特征为武器及用具上附有铜、金、釉彩等装饰〕.

la·tent [ˈleitənt] *a.* 存在但看不见的; 潜伏的; 潜在的. — *n.* 隐约的指印, 潜指印. ~ **ambiguity**【法】潜在含糊性〔指法律文件文字本身清楚, 但由于外在证据而使其产生一种以上含义〕. ~ **bud**【植】潜伏芽, 休眠芽. ~ **deed**【法】秘密保存二十年以上的证件. ~ **force** 潜力. ~ **heat**【物】潜热. ~ **image**【摄】(底片上已拍摄, 但尚未显影的) 潜像 [影]. ~ **period**【医】潜伏期. ~ **root**【数】潜伏〔本征, 特征〕根. **-ly** *ad.*

lat·er [ˈleitə] *a.* (late 的比较级)更[较]迟的; 更后的. — *ad.* 在后, 过后. *I will see you* ~. = *See you* ~. 再见. *no* ~ *than* 不迟于. ~ ***on*** 过后, 以后. ***sooner or*** ~ 早晚, 迟早(总有一天).

lat·er·ad [ˈlætəˈræd] *ad.*【解】向侧面地.

lat·er·al [ˈlætərəl] *a.* ①横的, 侧面的, 旁边的; 横向的. ②【语音】边音的, 旁流的, (舌)边的. ~ *buds* 生在侧面的蓓蕾, 旁蕾. *a* ~ *branch (of a family)* 旁系(亲属). ~ *pressure*【物】旁压力. *a* ~ *root* 侧根. *a* ~ *view* 侧面图. — *n.* ①侧部的东西, 侧向生长的东西. ②【电】支线. ③横材. ④【矿】走向平巷;【建】横向排水沟. ⑤【语音】边音, 旁流音. ~ **action**【军】侧翼推进. ~ **coordinate** 横座标. ~ **guidance** 俯仰制导, 相控盲目降落装置. ~ **inversion** 图象水平装置. ~ **line**【动】(鱼及两栖类的)侧线 (感官). **-ly** *ad.*

lat·e·ral·i·ty [ˌlætəˈræliti] *n.* 对一个侧面的偏重〔如惯用右手〕; 偏向一侧状态.

lat·er·al·ize [ˈlætərəˌlaiz] *vt.* 使向侧面.

Lat·er·an [ˈlætərən] *n.* ①(罗马的) 拉特兰大教堂. ②拉特兰宫.

lat·er·ite [ˈlætərait] *n.*【地】红土, 砖红壤, 铁矾土.

lat·er·i·za·tion [ˌlætəriˈzeiʃən] *n.*【地】红土化作用.

lat·er·ize [-əraiz] *vt.* ***(-iz·ed, -iz·ing)*** 使红土化.

lat·est [ˈleitist] *a.* (late 的最高级)最迟的, 最后的; 最近的, 最新的. *the* ~ *fashion* 最新式样. *the* ~ *news* 最后消息. *the* ~ *thing* 新奇的东西, 最新发明品. ***at (the)*** ~ 至迟.

la·tex [ˈleiteks] *n.* *(pl. ~es, lat·i·ces* [ˈlætisiːz]*)*【植】橡浆,乳液,树乳,胶乳.

lath [lɑːθ] *n.* *(pl. ~s* [lɑːθs]*)*【建】板条,板桩. *a ~ and-plaster shed* (木架)板条,灰面屋. *a ~ painted to look like iron* 虚张声势的胆小鬼. *a ~ cutter* 割板机. *a measuring ~* 测量标杆. ***as thin as a ~*** 骨瘦如柴. — *vt.* 给…钉板条;用板条覆盖[衬里]. ~ **house**【园艺】遮光育苗室.

lathe [leið] *n.*【机】车床,镟床 (= turning-~). *an automatic ~* 自动车床. *an automatic turret ~* 自动六角车床. *a boring ~* 镗床. *a drill ~* 钻孔车床. *a programme-controlled vertical ~* 程序控制立式车床. *a screw-cutting ~* 旋螺丝车床. *a tool-maker ~* 工具车床. *a universal ~* 万能车床. *a vertical ~* 立式车床. *a ~ turner* 车工. *a ~ dog* 车床夹头. — *vt.* 用车床加工.

la·thee, la·thi [ˈlɑːti] *n.* (印度人作武器的)铁箍棒.

lath·er[1] [ˈlɑːðə] *n.* ①肥皂泡,泡沫. ②(马等的)汗沫. ③〔喻〕激动,焦躁. *make a ~ on sb.'s face* 在某人脸上涂肥皂沫. ***be (all) in a ~*** 满身是汗;〔口〕激动. ***A good ~ is half a shave.*** 〔谚〕好的基础是成功的一半. — *vi.* ①涂肥皂沫;发泡沫. ②(马)流汗. — *vt.* ①在…上涂肥皂沫. ②使某人焦急[紧张] *(up)*. ③〔俚〕狠狠地打. *~ one's face before shaving* 刮脸前先在脸上涂上肥皂沫.

lath·er[2] [ˈlɑːðə] *n.* 钉板条工人.

lath·er·y [ˈlæðəri] *a.* 泡沫造成的;泡沫覆盖的;起泡沫的.

lath·ing [ˈlɑːθiŋ] *n.* ①钉板条. ②〔集合词〕板条.

lath·y [ˈlɑːθi] *a.* ***(lath·i·er; -i·est)*** 板条似的;狭长的.

lati- *comb. f.* 表示"宽的","阔的": lat*i*tude.

lat·i·ces [ˈlætisiːz] *n.* latex 的复数.

lat·i·cif·er·ous [ˌlætiˈsifərəs] *a.* 产生橡浆[乳液]的,含有橡浆的;分泌橡浆的.

lat·i·fun·di·um [ˌlætiˈfʌndiəm] *n.* *(pl. -dia* [-diə]*)* 大庄园,大领地,大地产.

lat·i·mer·i·a [ˌlætiˈmiəriə] *n.*【动】矛尾鱼 *(Latimeria chalumnae)*〔产于南非东海岸,特别是莫桑比克海峡〕.

Lat·in [ˈlætin] *a.* ①拉丁的;拉丁语的;拉丁人的. ②天主教的. *the ~ peoples* 拉丁民族. — *n.* ①拉丁语,拉丁字母表. ②拉丁人(尤指拉丁美洲人);古罗马人. ③罗马天主教徒. *Old ~* (公元前 75 年以前的)古代拉丁语. *Classical ~* (公元前 75 年至公元 175 年间的)古典拉丁语. *Late ~* (公元 175—600 年的)后期拉丁语. *Medieval [Middle] ~* (约公元 600—1500 年的)中世纪拉丁语. *Modern [New] ~* (公元 1500 年以后的)近代拉丁语. *Low [Vulgar] ~* (公元 175 年前后)民间拉丁语,俗拉丁语. *dog monk's ~* 不纯正的[半通不通的]拉丁语. *thieves' ~* 盗贼用黑话. ~ **America** 拉丁美洲. ~ **American** 拉丁美洲人. ~ **Church** (以拉丁语作礼拜仪式的)罗马天主教. ~ **cross** 纵长十字. ~ **Quarter** (巴黎的)拉丁区. ~ **rite**【宗】罗马天主教的礼拜仪式. ~ **school**, ~ **grammar school** (以拉丁语及希腊语为主科的)古典文科中学. ~ **square**【统】拉丁方.

Lat·in·ate [ˈlætineit] *a.* 拉丁语的;从拉丁语派生的;近似拉丁语的 (= Latinic).

la·ti·ne [ləˈtainiː] *ad.* 〔L.〕在拉丁语内,用拉丁文写.

Lat·in·ism [ˈlætinizəm] *n.* ①拉丁语风,拉丁语[词,成语等]. ②拉丁性质.

Lat·in·ist [ˈlætinist] *n.* 拉丁语学家;罗马文化研究家.

La·tin·i·ty [ləˈtiniti, læ-] *n.* ①拉丁语的使用[写作]. ②拉丁语风. ③拉丁语法.

Lat·in·ize [ˈlætinaiz] *vt.* ①把…译成拉丁语. ②使拉丁化. ③使(信条、教义)罗马天主教化,使符合天主教的仪式[习惯等]. ④使有拉丁语特征. — *vi.* ①有拉丁语特征. ②有天主教影响的表现. **-i·za·tion** *n.*

La·ti·no [læˈtiːnəu, lə-] *n.* *(pl. ~s)* 拉丁美洲人.

lat·ish [ˈleitiʃ] *a., ad.* 稍迟的[地],稍晚的[地].

lat·i·tude [ˈlætitjuːd] *n.* ①纬度 *(opp.* longitude*)*. ②【天】黄纬. ③〔*pl.*〕(以纬度而论的)地区,地方,地域. ④(见解、思想、行动的)自由. ⑤〔罕〕范围,活动余地;〔罕〕宽度. ⑥【摄】胶片曝光时间的有效范围[伸缩限度]. *high [low] ~s* 高[低]纬度地方,离赤道远[近]的地方. *thirty degrees north [south] ~* 北[南]纬三十度. ***be allowed some ~*** 被允许有若干自由. ***out of one's ~*** 越出自己的本行[知识]以外 (*He is out of his ~.* 他在干外行事). ***understand sth. in its proper ~*** 充分理解某事.

lat·i·tu·di·nal [ˌlætiˈtjuːdinl] *a.* 纬度的.

lat·i·tu·di·nar·i·an [ˌlætiˌtjuːdiˈnɛəriən] *a.* 自由主义的,放任主义的;放纵的;不拘泥于教义的. — *n.* 自由主义者;不拘泥于教条的人. **-ism** *n.* (宗教信仰上的)自由主义.

lat·ke [ˈlɑːtki] *n.* *(pl. ~s)* 土豆饼〔特指用生土豆磨碎制成〕.

la·tri·a [ləˈtraiə] *n.*【天主】专对天主的礼拜.

la·trine [ləˈtriːn] *n.* 作成沟形或坑形的厕所,公共厕所.

-la·try *comb. f.* 表示"崇拜": ido*latry*, Mario*latry*.

lat·ten, lat·tin [ˈlætən, ˈlætin] *n.* ①金属薄板,镀锡铁片. ②黄铜片,类似黄铜的合金片.

lat·ter [ˈlætə] *a.* ①后面的,末了的,末尾的 *(opp.* first*)*. ②〔the ~〕(二者中)后者的,〔用作 *pro.*〕后者 *(opp.* the former*)*. ③近来的,晚近的. ④〔古〕最后的,末期的. *the ~ half of the month [year]* 下半月[年]. *Of the two the ~ is better than the former.* 二者中后者比前者好. *in these ~ days* 近来,现今. *one's ~ end* 某人的结局,死. **~-day** *a.* 近来的,晚近的;现代的. **-ly** *ad.* 〔罕〕近来,后来.

lat·ter·most [ˈlætəməust] *a.* (排列在)最后的.

lat·tice [ˈlætis] *n.* ①格子. ②【物】点阵;网络. ③【建】格构. *crystal ~* 晶体;【物】点阵,晶格. *a ~ frame* 格子框架. — *vt.* ①把…制成格子状. ②用格子覆盖[装饰]. ~ **bridge** 格构桥. ~ **girder** 格构大梁,花格大梁. ~ **network** X 形(电)网络. ~ **points** 格点,网点. ~ **tower**【无】(支持天线的)格架塔. ~ **window** 格子窗. **~work** *n.* ①格子. ②格子细工,格子花样.

lat·ticed [ˈlætist] *a.* 制成格子的;装有格子的. *a ~ door [window]* 装格子的门[窗].

lat·ti·ci·nio [ˌlætiˈtʃiːnjəu] *n.* 〔It.〕不透明乳白玻璃〔常以线条形式构成玻璃器皿上的装饰〕.

Lat·ti·more [ˈlætimɔː] *n.* 拉铁摩尔〔姓氏〕.

Lat·vi·a [ˈlætviə] *n.* 拉脱维亚〔苏联加盟共和国名,正式名称为 Latvion Soviet Socialist Republic〕. **-n** *a.* ①拉脱维亚(人)的. ②拉脱维亚语的. — *n.* ①拉脱维亚人. ②拉脱维亚语.

la·uan [ləˈwɑːn] *n.*【植】(菲律宾产的)柳安树;柳安木料.

laud [lɔːd] *vt.* 赞美,称赞. *~ sb. to the skies* 对某人备加赞颂. — *n.* ①赞美,称赞. ②〔*pl.*〕赞美歌;颂歌,颂乐.

laud·a·ble [ˈlɔːdəbl] *a.* 值得称赞的. *~ feats* 可称颂的功绩[杰出事迹]. **-a·bil·i·ty** [ˌlɔːdəˈbiliti] *n.*

laud·a·num [ˈlɔdnəm]【药】鸦片酊.

lau·da·tion [lɔːˈdeiʃən] *n.* 赞美,称赞.

laud·a·tive [ˈlɔːdətiv], **-to·ry** [-təri] *a.* 赞美的,称赞的.

laugh [lɑːf] *n.* ①笑,笑声. ②令人发笑的事. ③嘲笑,取乐;〔*pl.*〕玩笑,逗乐. *He gave a loud ~.* 他大笑一声. *She laughed a hearty ~.* 她放声大笑. *The joke raised a ~.* 这笑话引起一阵大笑. *sardonic ~* 狞笑,冷笑. *What a ~ to say that!* 说出那种话来真可笑! *give sb. the ~ for his folly* 因为某人的愚蠢行为而嘲笑他. *beat sb. for ~s* 打某人一顿取乐. ***break into a ~*** 突然笑起来. ***get [have] the ~ at [of, on] sb.*** 反过来笑某人,轮到某人受嘲笑. ***have a good [hearty] ~*** 笑得痛快. ***have the ~ on one's side = get [have] the ~ at [of, on] sb. holy ~*** 狂笑,神经质的大笑. ***with***

a ～ 笑着，一笑． — *vi.* ①大笑；发笑．②(自然物等)呈现令人欢快的形态．*Green pines* ～ *in the breeze.* 青松迎风欢笑．*The hill* ～*s with verdure.* 山上一片青葱，欣欣向荣．— *vt.* ①以笑表示．②笑得使…．*He* ～*ed his dissent.* 他笑着表示不同意．～ *a reply* 以笑作答．～ *oneself to death* 笑得要死．～ *sb. out of his belief* 笑得某人失去信心．***burst out*** ～***ing*** 放声大笑．***He*** ～***s best who*** ～***s last.***〔谚〕最后笑的人笑得最好．***He who*** ～***s at crooked men should need walk very straight.***〔谚〕要笑别人驼背，自己就要挺起胸膛走路．***It is enough to make a cat [horse]*** ～．太可笑了．***L- and grow fat.***〔谚〕心宽体胖．***L-, and the world will*** ～ ***with you.***〔谚〕你如果乐观，世界将陪着欢笑．～ ***at*** ①因…而发笑 (～ *at a joke* 听了笑话而发笑)．②嘲笑 (*We* ～*ed at his fancy.* 我们嘲笑他异想天开)．③付之一笑，不以为意 (～ *at difficulties* 对困难一笑置之)．～ ***away*** ①付之一笑，笑着不理．②笑着消磨(时间) (～ *away all one's apprehensions* 对自己的一切忧虑付之一笑)．～ ***down*** 用笑声来打断[拒绝]．～ ***in [up] one's sleeve*** 暗暗发笑，窃笑．～ ***in sb.'s face*** 当面嘲笑某人．～ ***off*** ①一笑置之．②以笑来排除(怒气、窘境等) (～ *off sb.'s suspicions* 以嬉笑排除某人的疑心)．～ ***oneself into convulsions [fits]*** 笑破肚皮．～ ***on the wrong side of one's mouth [face]*** 笑脸变成哭脸，由得意变成失意．～ ***out*** 哄笑．～ ***out one's consent*** 含笑表示同意．～ ***out of court*** 付之一笑．～ ***over*** 笑着谈论 (～ *over a letter* 笑着谈论一封信)．

laugh·a·ble [ˈlɑːfəbl] *a.* 可笑的，有趣的．

laugh·a·bly [ˈlɑːfəbli] *ad.* 可笑．*look* ～ *archaic* 样子古老得可笑．

laugh·ing [ˈlɑːfiŋ] *a.* ①笑的，笑着的，笑着似的．②可笑的．*This is no* ～ *matter.* 这可不是什么好笑的事．— *n.* 笑．*hold one's* ～忍住笑．～ **gas**【化】笑气．～ **hyena**【动】笑猿，斑猿．～ **jackass**【动】笑鸿．～**stock** 笑柄 (*make a* ～*-stock of oneself* 丢人，出洋相)．**-ly** *ad.*

laugh·ter [ˈlɑːftə] *n.* ①笑，笑声．②〔古〕好笑的事．***burst into*** ～ 放声大笑．***die with*** ～笑得要死．***Homeric*** ～ 宏亮[健康]的笑声〔原指荷马史诗中天上诸神的大笑声〕．***roar with*** ～ 哄堂大笑．

Laugh·ton [ˈlɔːtn] *n.* 劳顿〔姓氏〕．

launce [lɔːns, læns, lɑːns] *n.*【动】玉筋鱼 (= sand eel)．

launch[1] [lɔːntʃ, lɑːntʃ] *vt.* ①使(船)下水．～ *a ship from a shipyard* 使船从船坞下水．②发射；投出；提出，发出．③(把孩子等)送出；使独立谋生．④开办，创办；发动，发起；开展．～ *a man-made [an artificial] satellite* 发射人造卫星．～ *an airplane* 使飞机起飞．～ *a spear* 投矛．～ *a torpedo* 发射鱼雷．～ *into space a sputnik-ship* 向宇宙发射卫星飞船．～ *one's child in [into] the world* 把子女送到社会上．～ *sb. in [into] business* 使某人进入商界．～ *a new enterprise* 创办新企业．～ *a fierce attack* 开始猛攻．～ *a mass movement* 开展群众运动．～ *a campaign of abuse* 开始互骂．～ *threats against sb.* 对某人发出威胁．— *vi.* ①起飞，下水．②投入．③开始，着手进行．*A bird* ～*ed off.* 鸟飞走了．～ *into a strong rebuke* 激烈斥责．～ *on one's study* 开始学习．～ *upon the production of cars* 开始生产汽车．～ ***out*** ①船下水．②出航 (～ *out on a journey* 首途旅行)．③开始 (～ *out in a new scheme* 开始新的计划)．④挥霍．～ ***out into*** ①乘船出海；投身…(界)．②开始，着手．③挥霍 (～ *out into extravagance* 大肆挥霍)．— *n.* 发射，下水．～ *of a new liner* 新(定期)客轮[班机]下水[首航]．～ **airplane** 火箭运载机．～ **pad** (火箭等的)发射台．～ **vehicle** 运载火箭；活动发射装置．～ **window** 发射时限〔指条件适合发射宇宙飞船的一段时期〕．

launch[2] [lɔːntʃ, lɑːntʃ] *n.* 汽艇，游艇．*a motor* ～ 摩托艇．

launch·er [lɔːntʃə, lɑːntʃə] *n.* ①弹射器；弹弓；石弩．②(安装在步枪上的)手榴弹发射器．③(导弹、宇宙飞船等的)发射装置．

launch·ing [ˈlɔːntʃiŋ, ˈlɑːntʃiŋ] *n.* ①发射．②起飞；(船等)下水；下水典礼．③开办．*battery* ～ (导弹的)齐射．*zero-length* ～ (火箭)原地发射，垂直发射．～ **pad** = launch pad．～ **site** 发射场，发射场的全部设备．～ **tube** (水雷等的)发射管．～ **ways** (船的)下水滑道．

laun·der [ˈlɔːndə, ˈlɑːndə] *vt.* ①洗(衣等)．②(洗后)烫(衣等)．③〔美俚〕贪污，侵吞；(把款项等)非法转移〔如秘密通过外国银行汇到国外等〕．— *vi.* ①洗烫衣物．②经洗；耐烫．*This fabric* ～*s well.* 这种织品经洗耐用．— *n.*【矿】槽洗机，流槽．**-a·bil·i·ty** *n.* **-a·ble** *a.* **-er** *n.*

Laun·der·ette [ˌlɔːndəˈret, ˌlɑːn-] *n.*〔美〕自动洗衣店的招牌；〔l-〕自动洗衣店〔设有由顾客自行操作的自动洗衣机〕．

laun·dress [ˈlɔːndris, ˈlɑːndris] *n.* 洗烫衣物的女工．

Laun·dro·mat [ˈlɑːndrəˌmæt, ˈlɔːn-] *n.*〔美〕自动洗衣店的招牌；〔l-〕自动洗衣店．

laun·dry [ˈlɔːndri] *n.* ①洗衣．②洗衣房，洗衣店．③要洗的东西，洗好的东西．***hang out the*** ～〔军俚〕空投伞兵．～ **list** ①交付洗衣店的待洗衣服清单．②〔喻〕一大张清单[名单，项目单等]．～ **machine** 洗衣机．～**-man** 洗衣工人． ～**woman** *(pl.* ***-wom·en)*** = laundress．

Lau·ra [ˈlɔːrə] *n.* 劳拉〔姓氏〕．

Lau·ra·sia [lɔːˈreiʒə, -ʃə] *n.*【地】劳亚古大陆〔被认为是古代曾存在的大陆名，包括北美洲和欧亚大陆，约在古生代末期分离开来〕．

lau·re·ate [ˈlɔːriit] *a.* ①戴桂冠的．②有戴桂冠资格的，卓越的．③(桂冠)用月桂树造的．— *n.* ①戴桂冠的人．②〔L-〕桂冠诗人 (= Poet L～)．③奖金[荣誉]获得者．— *vt.* ①使戴桂冠，授以荣誉．②授以桂冠诗人的称号．～**ship** 桂冠诗人的称号[身份]．

lau·re·a·tion [ˌlɔːriˈeiʃən] *n.* 授以桂冠[荣誉]．

Lau·rel [ˈlɔrəl] *n.* 劳雷尔〔女子名〕．

lau·rel [ˈlɔrəl] *n.* ①【植】月桂树，月桂树叶，月桂属植物．②(表示荣誉的)桂冠；〔*pl.*〕光荣，荣誉；【美体】(比赛的)胜利．***look to one's*** ～***s*** 小心保持荣誉．***rest on one's*** ～***s*** 安于已得名誉，安于小成，吃老本．***win [gain, reap] one's*** ～***s*** 博得名声．— *vt.* ①使戴桂冠．②给以荣誉．

lau·rel(l)ed [ˈlɔrəld] *a.* 戴桂冠的；获得荣誉的．

Lau·rence [ˈlɔrəns] *n.* 劳伦斯〔姓氏，男子名〕．

Lau·ren·ti·an [ˈlɔːrenʃiən] *a., n.* ①【地质】劳伦系(的)．②(加拿大等 St. Lawrence 河附近的)劳伦系岩石层．

lau·ric acid [ˈlɔːrik æsid]【化】月桂酸；十二(烷)酸．

Lau·rie [ˈlɔ(ː)ri] *n.* 劳丽〔女子名，Laura 的昵称〕．

lau·rus·ti·nus [ˌlɔrəsˈtainəs] *n.*【植】(南欧产)一种高大的常绿灌木 (= laurestinus)．

lau·ryl alcohol [ˈlɔːril ˈælkəhɔl]【化】十二(烷)醇．

Lau·sanne [ləuˈzæn] *n.* 洛桑〔瑞士城市〕．

lav [læv]〔美口〕盥洗室 (= lavatory)．

la·va [ˈlɑːvə] *n.*【地】熔岩；火山岩；〔*pl.*〕火山岩层．*aqueous* ～ 泥流岩．

la·va·bo [ləˈveibəu] *n.* *(pl.* ～***es***, ～***s)*** ①【宗】洗手礼．②行洗手礼时用《诗篇》．③洗手礼手巾[水盘]．④洗手所；〔*pl.*〕盥洗室．

lav·age [ləˈvɑːʒ, ˈlævidʒ] *n.*【医】灌洗；洗出法；洗胃；灌肠．

la·va-la·va [ˈlɑːvəˈlɑːvə] *n.*〔Samoan〕(南太平洋岛屿特别是萨摩亚群岛居民穿的)花腰布；短裙．

lav·a·liere, lav·a·lier [ˌlɑːvəˈliə, ˈlævə-] *n.* 项链上的垂饰 *(= lavallière)*．

la·va·tion [læˈveiʃən] *n.*【医】= lavage．

lav·a·to·ry [ˈlævəˌtəri] *n.* ①盥洗室；厕所．②洗脸盆；

【宗】洗礼盆.
lave[1] [leiv] *vt., vi.* 〔诗〕洗;(波浪)冲刷(河岸).
lave[2] [leiv] *n.* 〔Scot.〕遗留物,剩余物.
lave·ment [ˈleivmənt] *n.* 【医】灌洗;洗出法.
lav·en·der [ˈlævində] *n.* ①【植】薰衣草. ②薰衣草的花[叶,茎]. ③淡紫色. ***lay (up) in*** ~ ①小心保存(以备日后使用). ②送进当铺. ③禁闭,关进监狱. — *a.* ①薰衣草的. ②淡紫色的. — *vt.* 夹薰衣草(在衣间),用薰衣草熏香. ~ **water** 薰衣草香水.
la·ver[1] [ˈleivə] *n.* ①〔古〕盥洗用具(如盆等). ②(犹太教祭司用的)铜质洗涤盆. ③【宗】洗礼盘;洗礼水.
la·ver[2] [ˈleivə] *n.* ①【植】紫菜属的一种,甘紫菜. ②【植】石莼属的一种.
lav·er·ock [ˈlævərək] *n.* 〔Scot.〕云雀.
lav·ish [ˈlæviʃ] *vt.* 大量地乱用,浪费;挥霍;滥花;慷慨地给与. ~ *care upon one's children* 溺爱儿女. ~ *money on sth.* 在某事上乱花钱. ~ *praises on sb.* 乱捧某人. — *a.* ①过分大方的,慷慨的;大量的. ②过于丰富的,过度的,浪费的. *be* ~ *of money* 用钱大手大脚的. ~ *hospitality* 过于好客. **-ly** *ad.* **-ment, -ness** *n.*
La·voi·sier [ˌlɑːvwɑˈzjei], **A. L.** 拉瓦锡〔1743—1794,法国化学家,氧发现者〕.
Law [lɔː] *n.* 劳〔姓氏〕.
law[1] [lɔː] *n.* ①法律,法令;法典. ②法学;诉讼;司法界;律师(界),律师职务. ③(事物或科学的)法则,规律;定律,定理. ④(生活中或各种娱乐游戏的)惯例;规则;(宗教)戒律. ⑤(行猎时给与所猎猎物,比赛时给与弱方的)宽让时间[距离]. ⑥〔美俚〕(the ~) 司法人员;警察;监狱看守. *abide by the* ~ 守法. *break the* ~ 犯法. *contract* ~ 契约法. *deal with sb. according to* ~ 依法处理某人. *domestic* ~ 国家法. *Draconian* ~*s* 古雅典执政官德拉科的法律;〔喻〕严竣的法律. *subjective* ~ 财产法. *the blue-sky* ~ 〔美〕无信用股票取缔法. *maintain* ~ *and order* 维持法律和秩序. *be learned in the* ~ 精通法学. *read [study]* ~ 学法律. *follow [practice]* ~ 做律师 (= go in for ~). *the* ~ *of the land* 国法. *go to* ~ *against sb.* 跟某人打官司. *a* ~ *of nature* (= a natural ~) 自然规律. *the jungle* ~ 丛林的法律,弱肉强食原则. *the L- of Nature [Reason]* 天理. *Where they saw chance, we see* ~. 从他们过去所看到的偶然性中,我们发现了规律. *Boyle's* ~ 【物】波义耳定理. ~ *of conservation of energy* 能量守恒定律. ~ *of mass action* 质量作用律;分量作用定律. ~ *of motion* 运动三定律. ~ *of parity* 宇称定律. ~ *of relativity* 相对论. ~ *of social development* 社会发展规律. ~ *of the unity of opposites* 对立统一规律. ~ *of universal gravitation* 万有引力定律. ~ *of zero or unity* 【统】零一律. *Ohm's* ~ 【电】欧姆定律. *the* ~ *of painting* 绘画法. *the* ~*s of the chase* 狩猎规则. *blue* ~*s* 清教徒式的严酷法律. *club* ~ 暴力[大棒]政治;俱乐部规章. ~ *of honour* 行为法则;决斗惯例. ***a [the]*** ~ ***of the Medes and Persians*** 不可更改的法律. ***be a*** ~ ***to [unto] oneself*** 照自己的意思去做,独断独行. ***be at*** ~ 在诉讼[审判]中. ***be bad*** ~ 违背法律. ***be beyond the*** ~ 在法律范围以外. ***be bred to the*** ~ 被训练成律师[法官]. ***be good*** ~ 符合法律. ***be outside the*** ~ 不合法. ***be within the*** ~ 合法. ***contend at*** ~ 诉讼,打官司. ***give (the)*** ~ ***to sb.*** 对某人发号施令. ***go to*** ~ ***with sb.*** = ***have [take] the*** ~ ***of sb.*** 控告某人. ***lay down the*** ~ 发号施令. ***strain [stretch] the*** ~ 枉法,曲解法律. ***take the*** ~ ***into one's own hands*** (= have the ~ in one's own hands) 随意处罚,滥用法律. — *vi., vt.* 〔俚〕起诉,控告. ~**-abid·ing** *a.* 守法的. ~**book** 法律学课本;法律学书籍,法典. ~**breaker** 违法分子,犯法者. ~**-breaking** 违法,犯法;违法的. ~**court** 法庭. ~ **French** 诺曼第法语. ~**giver** 立法者,法典制定人. ~**giving** ①*n.* 立法,制定法典. ②*a.* 立法的. ~**hand** (英国旧时)写法律文件的一种书法. **L- Lord** 〔英〕上院执掌司法的议院. ~**maker** 立法人;协助制定法律者〔尤指立法委员〕. ~**making** 立法;协助制定法律 ~**man** *(pl. -men)* 执法者〔尤指美国联邦法院执行官、司法官、警察等〕. ~ **merchant** 商业惯例,商法. ~ **monger** 讼棍. ~ **office** 〔美〕法律事务所. ~ **officer** 司法官;检察长〔次长〕. **L- of Moses** = mosaic ~. ~ **of nations** = international ~. ~ **of parsimony** 【哲】最经济规律. ~ **stationer** ①法律书籍商. ②法律文件代书人. ~**suit** 诉讼(案件) (*bring in [enter] a* ~*-suit against sb.* 对某人起诉). ~ **term** ①法律用语. ②法庭开庭期.
law[2] [lɔː] *int.* 〔英俚〕天哪! 嗳呀!
Lawes [lɔːz] *n.* 劳斯〔姓氏〕.
law·ful [ˈlɔːfəl] *a.* 合法的;法定的;守法的. *a* ~ *act* 合法行为. *a* ~ *age* = ~ *years* 法定年龄,成年. ~ *goods* 【法】中立国船只装载的货物. *a* ~ *day* (法院)开庭日;(法律上规定的)营业日. **-ly** *ad.* **-ness** *n.*
lawk(s) [lɔːk(s)] *int.* 〔俚, Lord 的讹用〕嗳呀! 糟了!
law·less [ˈlɔːlis] *a.* ①无法律的,不能实施法律的. ②不法的,违法的,无法无天的. *a* ~ *man* 不法之徒. ~ *passions* 无法控制的情欲. ~ *practices* 违法行为.
lawn[1] [lɔːn] *n.* ①上等细麻布. ②英国国教主教的职位. ~ **sleeves** ①上等细(麻)布袖. ②主教的职位.
lawn[2] [lɔːn] *n.* ①草地,草坪,草场. ②〔诗〕林间空地. ~ **bowling** 滚球戏. ~ **mower** 刈草机,刈草人. ~ **party** 〔美〕游园会. ~ **ten·nis** 草地网球.
lawn·y[1] [ˈlɔːni] *a.* 细麻布做的,细麻布一样的.
lawn·y[2] [ˈlɔːni] *a.* 草地(多)的;草地一样的.
Law·rence [ˈlɔrəns] *n.* ①劳伦斯〔姓氏〕. ②**E. O.** ~ 劳伦斯〔1901—1958,美国物理学家,回旋加速器的发明人〕. ③**David Herbert** ~ 戴维·赫伯特·劳伦斯〔1885—1930,英国小说家〕.
law·ren·ci·um [lɔːˈrensiəm,lɑː-] *n.* 【化】铹.
laws [lɔːz] *int.* = law[2].
law·yer [ˈlɔːjə] *n.* ①律师. ②法律家. ***a forecastle*** ~ 〔美俚〕经常爱争论[抱怨、议论]的人. ***a good*** ~ 懂法律的人. ***a Jack-leg*** ~ 〔美〕讼棍. ***a philadelphia*** ~ 〔美〕很精明的人;狡猾的人. **a poor** ~不懂法律的人. ***enough to puzzle a philadelphia*** ~ 〔美〕太错综复杂使人难于弄明白的. ***He is no*** ~. 他不懂法律.
Law·son [ˈlɔːsn] *n.* 劳森〔姓氏〕.
lax[1] [læks] *a.* ①(肠)宽松的,易通便的,腹泻的. ②松弛的;质地松的. ③不严格的,马虎的;不精密的;含糊的. ④【植】(花簇)疏松的. ⑤【乐】弛缓的,不紧张的 *(opp.* tense*)*. ⑥【语音】(元音)松弛的. ~ *morals* 行为放荡. ~ *discipline* 松懈的纪律. ~ *vowels* 【语音】松元音. — *n.* 泻肚,下痢. **-ly** *ad.* **-ness** *n.*
lax[2] [læks] *n.* 【动】(挪威、瑞典的)鲑.
lax·a·tion [lækˈseiʃən] *n.* ①松弛,弛缓. ②【医】轻泻.
lax·a·tive [ˈlæksətiv] *a.* ①通大便的;有轻度腹泻的. ②放松的;放肆的. — *n.* 【药】轻泻剂. **-ly** *ad.* **-ness** *n.*
lax·i·ty [ˈlæksiti] *n.* ①轻泻(性). ②松弛. ③(纺织品等的)疏松. ④粗心,疏忽.
lay[1] [lei] ***(laid)*** *vt.* ①放,搁,摆. ~ *oneself down* 躺下. ②安排;预备;布置. ~ *a fire* 准备生火. ~ *an ambush* 设下埋伏. ~ *a snare [trap]* 设下陷阱. ~ *mines* 布雷,埋雷. ~ *the table for breakfast* 摆食具预备开早饭. ③铺设;敷设;砌砖. ~ *a pavement* 铺装路面. ~ *a railroad track* 铺铁路轨道. ~ *the foundations of* 奠定…的基础. ④产卵,生蛋. ~ *eggs* 下蛋,产卵. ⑤涂饰,涂覆. ~ *a wall with paint* 用油漆涂墙. ~ *plaster on the wall* 在墙上涂灰泥. ⑥使负担;抽税,加处罚. ~ *a burden on sb.* 把负担加在某人身上. ~ *duties on imports* 对进口货抽税. ⑦打倒. ~ *sb. low* 打败某人. *The storm laid the crops.* 暴风吹倒了庄稼. ⑧镇压,使静下来. *A city is laid in the dust [in ashes, in ruins].* 全城化为灰烬[废墟].

L

water the street to ~ *the dust* 街上洒水压灰。⑨归罪，嫁祸。~ *the blame on sb.* 责怪某人。~ *a fault to sb.'s charge [at sb.'s door]* 归咎于某人。⑩想出，拟定。~ *one's plans* 拟定计划。⑪提出，提示；申述(主张等)。~ *claim to sth.* 对某物提出所有权要求。~ *an indictment* 提起公诉。~ *the question before a committee* 把问题提交委员会。⑫规定(损害数量)。~ *the damage at £100.* 确定损失为一百英镑。⑬打赌，下赌注。~ *a [bet] wager* 下赌注。*I* ~ *five dollars he will not come.* 我赌五块钱他不会来。⑭(将故事等的场面)放在(某地)。*The scene of the tale is laid in London.* 故事发生在伦敦。⑮埋，葬；平息；消除；平服。~ *sb.'s doubts* 打消某人的疑虑。⑯使处于某种状态[地位]。~ *bare a scheme* 揭露阴谋。~ *sb. under (an) obligation (to)* 使某人对…承担义务。⑰打，砍。~ *one's axe to the tree* 用斧头砍树。⑱(扭)绞；搓；编。~ *a hedge* 把树枝编成树篱。~ *(up) a rope* 搓绳。⑲【军】瞄准(炮)。— *vi.* ①生蛋。*The hens don't* ~ *in this cold weather.* 这样冷的天气鸡不生蛋。②打赌；保证。~ *on a horse race* 赌跑马。③准备 *(for)*。④【海】就位。~ *aft* 到船尾就位。⑤拚命干。*The sailors laid to their oars.* 水手们用力划桨。~ ***a (one's) course*** ①(船朝某一方向)直驶。②制订计划。~ ***a ship aboard*** 把船紧逼敌船(以便越舷进攻)。~ ***about*** ①向四面八方攻击，奋战。②努力奋斗，尽全力。③作准备。~ ***aside*** ①留起，保存，贮蓄。②搁开，放在一边，留出 (~ *aside a day for golf* 打一天高尔夫球)。③放弃，丢弃 (*He was laid aside six months by an accident.* 他因事故已停止工作六个月了)。~ ***asleep*** 埋葬；使一命呜呼。~ ***at*** 对准…打过去，攻击。~ ***away*** ①保存，留起，贮蓄。②[美]埋葬。~ ***back*** ①使向后。②放回，送回。~ ***before*** 拿出，提出。~ ***by*** ①= ~ aside. ②【海】= ~ to. ~ ***down*** ①放下。②铺设(铁路)，建造(船等)。③拟定(计划等)。④贮藏(酒等)。⑤确定，规定。⑥扔弃，放弃 (*The enemy laid down their arms.* 敌人放下武器投降。~ *down one's life for the country* 为国牺牲。~ *down one's commission* 辞职)。⑦支付；下赌注。⑧在(田里)栽 (~ *down a field in grass* 在田里栽牧草)。⑨写下，记下，画下。~ ***eyes on*** 看见，发现。~ ***fast (by the heels)*** 拘束；监禁。~ ***field to field*** 不断地增加所有地[财产]。~ ***for*** 准备(占领、攻击等)；埋伏着等待。~ ***great store upon*** 重视。~ ***hands on*** ①抓住，逮住。②得到，找到。③袭击，伤害。④行按手礼。~ ***hands on oneself*** 自杀。~ ***heavy odds that*** 坚决主张，确实声明。~ ***in*** ①贮藏。②[俚]吃。③修剪(树篱等)。~ ***in for*** 申请；设法购买；企图获得。~ ***(an) information against*** 告发。~ ***into*** [俚]痛打；痛斥。~ ***it on (thick)*** [俚] = ~ ***it on with a trowel*** [俚]乱夸赞，乱恭维。~ ***off*** ①暂时解雇；[美]解雇，辞退 (=[英] stand off)。②停止(工作等)；[美]休息，休养。③区分，划分(土地)。④【海】(使)离开(海岸、他船)；【船】放大样。⑤[美]脱(衣服)。~ ***off your lid*** [美]不要自大，别摆架子。~ ***on*** ①加给。②袭击，攻击。③安装 (*Is gas laid on?* 安装煤气了吗？)。③抽，征(税等)。④涂(颜料等)。⑤使(狗)跟踪追赶(猎物)。⑥下，发(命令)；挥鞭等。~ ***one's account with*** 把…算在里头；指望，期待。~ ***one's bones*** 被埋葬，死。~ ***one's cards on the table*** [美]摊牌，把一切都说出来。~ ***oneself open to*** 暴露在，蒙受 (~ *oneself open to suspicion* 遭受嫌疑)。~ ***oneself out*** 煞费苦心，竭力 (*They laid themselves out to entertain us.* 他们为了款待我们煞费苦心)。~ ***oneself out for*** 作准备，决心。~ ***one's hopes on*** 指望，期待。~ ***one's plans*** 准备，布置。~ ***open*** ①切开，割开。②揭开；暴露；揭穿。~ ***out*** ①消费，使用；投资。②展开，铺开(以便使用)；暴露出来。③布置，安排，设计(花园等)。④准备入殓安葬。⑤[俚]打倒，[美俚]打昏。~ ***over*** ①= overlay. ②[美俚]展期，延期。③中途下车。④胜过，力量超过。~ ***to*** ①【海】把船停下；船顶着风停止。②把(功，过)归于。③努力干。④打。~ ***to heart*** 非常挂心，铭记在心。~ ***(sb.) to rest [sleep]*** ①使睡，使休息。②埋葬，葬。~ ***together*** 聚集，聚拢；比较。~ ***(sb.) under restraint*** 拘束某人。~ ***up*** ①贮蓄。②留着不用；搁置。③使卧床不起。④将船只拆卸进坞。~ ***upon*** [古]勒索。~ ***violent hands on sb.*** 对某人下毒手，杀某人。~ ***wait for*** 埋伏着等待。~ ***waste*** 破坏，使荒废。— *n.* ①位置；方向；地理形势。*the* ~ *[lie] of the land* 地形；形势，局势，事态。②绳索的股数[拧法]；(裁剪)铺放。③分红，分配渔获品。④方针，计划；[俚]工作，职业，生意。*start a new* ~ 开始新的工作。⑤[美]代价，价格。*sell sth. at a good* ~ 以高价售出。⑥层，隐蔽处。⑦下蛋。*be in full [good]* ~ (经常地，正常地)下蛋。***on the*** ~ (黑话)(小偷、扒手等)下手，作案。***the kid [kinchin]*** ~ (黑话)偷窃[抢夺]出外购物的儿童的财物。**~about** [主英口]游手好闲，二流子，无业游民。**~away plan** 逐月付款的累积购买法。**~-by** ①(河道中的)泊[错]船处。②铁路侧线，旁轨。③(公路上的)停[错]车处。④【农】(作物种植中的)最后一遍田间操作。~ **day**【海】(租船契约所允许的)装卸货物日期，停泊日数[过期应缴纳延期费]。~ **figure** ①人体活动模型。②傀儡般的人物。**~off** ①解雇。②(临时)解雇期。③关闭；停歇。④停止活动[比赛]时期。**~out** ①布局；设计；安排；陈设。②版面编排。③一套器具[工具、衣服等]。④[美口]事态，情况。⑤[美]地形，坐落[指建筑物及四周环境]。**~over** *n.* 中途的短暂停留。**~shaft**【机】副轴；中间轴；水平轴。**~stall** [英]垃圾堆。**~up** (篮球)上篮，切入篮[篮下跳起单手投篮]。

lay[2] [lei] *a.* ①一般信徒的，俗人的，凡俗的 *(opp.* clerical*)*。②无经验的，外行(人)的 *(opp.* professional*)*。③【纸牌】非主牌的，普通牌的。~ **analyst** 非专业的心理分析学家。~ **brother** (在修道院内干勤杂工的)俗人修士。**~man** ①俗人；平信徒。②门外汉，外行。~ **reader** ①【宗】(圣公会主持礼拜的)俗人司仪。②外行[非专业人员]的读者，一般读者。

lay[3] [lei] *n.* ①民歌，民谣；短诗。②歌曲；曲调；音乐的旋律；鸟的啼啭。

lay[4] [lei] lie[1] 的过去式。

Lay·ard [lɛəd] *n.* 莱亚德[姓氏]。

lay·er [ˈleiə] *n.* ①放置者，铺设者，计划者。②【赛马】(一般)赌客。③产卵的鸡。④【军】瞄准手。⑤层；阶层；地层；涂层。⑥【植】压条；倒伏庄稼。⑦敷设轨。⑧垫片；层板；夹层；膜。*a brick* ~ 砌砖者。*a mine* ~ 布雷舰艇。*a bad [good]* ~ 生蛋少[多]的鸡。*a* ~ *of rock* 一层岩石。*boundary* ~ 边层。*carburized* ~ 渗炭层。*turberlent* ~ 紊流附面层。*~s and backers* (赛马等的)赌客。— *vt.* ①分层砌。②用压条法繁殖。— *vi.* 庄稼倒伏。~ **cake** [美]多层奶油蛋糕。~ **age**【植】压条。

lay·ette [leiˈet] *n.* [F.] 婴儿的全套用品[如衣服、被褥、洗涤用具等]。

lay·ing [ˈleiiŋ] *n.* ①布置；层积；铺设。②(炮的)瞄准。③搓绳；搓绳法。④最初所涂底层。⑤产卵期；产卵数；一次孵的蛋。***the*** ~ ***on of hands***【宗】按手礼。

la·zar [ˈlæzə, ˈlei-] *n.* 恶疾病人[尤指麻疯病人]。~ **house** 麻疯医院。**-like** *a.*

laz·a·ret, laz·a·ret·to [ˌlæzəˈret, -ˈretəu] *n. (pl.* ~*s)* ①传染病医院(特指麻疯医院)。②检疫所；检疫船。③【海】(近船尾的)贮藏室。

Laz·a·rus [ˈlæzərəs] *n.* ①【圣】浑身生疮的拉撒路。②[常作 l-]麻疯乞丐；穷人。~ *and Dives* 穷人和富人。

laze [leiz] *vt., vi.* 偷懒；混日子。~ *away one's life* 混过一辈子。~ *time away* 蹉跎岁月。— *n.* ①懒散。②混过去的时间。

la·zi·ly [ˈleizili] *ad.* 偷懒地，懒洋洋地，吊儿郎当地。

la·zi·ness [ˈleizinis] *n.* 懒惰；偷懒。

laz·u·li [ˈlæzjulai] *n.* = lapis lazuli. **-ne** *a.*

laz·u·lite [ˈlæzjuˌlait] *n.*【地】天蓝石。**laz·u·lit·ic**

[ˌlæzjuˈlitik] *a*.

laz·u·rite [ˈlæzjuˌrait] *n*.【地】天青石,青金石.

la·zy [ˈleizi] *a*. ***(-zi·er; -zi·est)*** ①懒惰的,没精打采的. ②慢吞吞的. ③令人懒散的. *a* ～ *boy [beggar, dog]*〔口〕懒鬼. *a* ～ *stream* 缓流. *a hot*, ～ *summer* 夏日炎炎正好眠. ～**back** 马车座位的靠背. ～**bed**〔英〕马铃薯培植床. ～**bones**, ～**boots**〔口〕懒骨头. ～ **eight**【空】8 字形飞行法. ～ **eye (blindness)**【医】(一目)弱视 (= amblyopia). ～ **guy**【船】吊杆稳索. ～ **jack**【机】屈伸起重机. **L- susan** (餐桌上便于自取食物的)旋转盘. ～ **tongs**【机】(用以钳取远处东西的)惰钳,伸缩钳. **-ish** *a*. 懒散的,懒洋洋的.

laz·za·ro·ne [ˌlæzəˈrəuni] *n*. 〔It.〕***(pl. -ro·ni*** [-niː]***)*** (意大利拿不勒斯街头的)以行乞和做杂工度日的流浪者.

LB, L.B. = 〔L.〕 *Literarum Baccalaureus* 文学士 (= Bachelor of Letters 或 Bachelor of Literature).

lb. = 〔L.〕 *libra(e)* (= pound(s)) 磅.

lb.ap. = pound, apothecaries 药衡磅.

lb.av. = pound, avoirdupois 常衡磅.

lb.in. = pound-inch 磅-英寸.

lbs. = 〔L.〕 *librae* 磅 (= pounds).

lb.t. = pound troy. 金衡磅.

LC = ①Library of Congress 〔美〕国会图书馆. ②landing craft 登陆艇. ③left centre (舞台的)中心部左方.

L.C. = ①Lord Chancellor 〔英〕大法官. ②Lower Canada 下加拿大〔魁北克省的旧称〕.

l.c. = ①lower case【印】小写字母盘 ②〔L.〕 *loco citato* 在前面引文中.

L/C, l/c = letter of credit【商】信用状.

L.C.C. = London County Council〔英〕伦敦郡议会.

LCI = Landing Craft, Infantry〔美〕步兵登陆艇.

L.C.J. = Lord Chief Justice〔英〕高等法院院长.

L.C.L. = less-than-carload (铁路运输中的)零担的.

L.C.M., LCM = lowest (or least) common multiple【数】最小公倍数.

LCP = landing craft, personnel 人员登陆艇.

LCT = landing craft, tank 坦克登陆艇.

LD = ①lethal dose【医】致死剂〔药〕量. ②line of departure【军】进攻出发线. ③long distance 长途电话通讯;长途电话局(或交换机);长途话务员.

L.D. = ①Lady Day【宗】报喜节. ②Doctor of Letters 文学博士. ③Low Dutch 低地荷兰语. ④〔L.〕 *Laus Deo* (= Praise be to God)【宗】荣誉属于上帝. ⑤left door 左(侧)门. ⑥London Docks〔英〕伦敦船坞.

Ld. = ①Limited. ②Lord.

ldg. = loading.

L-do·pa [elˈdəupə] *n*.【药】左旋多巴〔= levodopa 治帕金森综合症〕.

Ldp., Lp. = Ladyship; Lordship. **Ldry** = Laundry.

L.D.Tel. = long-distance telephone 长途电话.

LE = ①low explosive 低级炸药. ②labo(u)r exchange 实物交换,产品交换;职业介绍所;〔主英〕(劳工部的)劳工介绍所.

-le *suf*. 附在动词之后,表示"动作的小幅度重复": hobb*le*, pratt*le*, wigg*le*.

lea[1] [liː] *n*.〔主诗〕草地,牧场.

lea[2] [liː] *n*.【纺】缕,小绞〔棉纱长 120 码;麻纱长 300 码;毛纱长 80 码〕.

leach [liːtʃ] *n*. ①沥滤. ②(采灰汁用的)滤灰,灰汁;滤汁. ③沥滤器,滤灰槽. —*vt*., *vi*. 滤,用水漂;溶化,溶解. **-able** *a*.

leach·y [ˈliːtʃi] *a*. (土壤)有气孔的;能渗透的.

Lea·cock [ˈliːkɔk] *n*. 利科克〔姓氏〕.

lead[1] [led] *n*. ①铅,铅制器. ②【海】测铅,测深锤,水砣. ③〔*pl*.〕(铺屋顶的)铅皮;铅皮屋顶;【印】插铅,铅条. ④铅笔心. ⑤子弹,枪弹. *white* ～ 铅白,碱式碳酸铅. *work* ～ (鼓风炉产含银)粗铅. *yellow* ～ 铅黄,氧化铅. *an ounce of* ～ 一颗子弹. ***arm the*** ～ 注兽脂入测深锤底部凹处〔以便粘起泥沙而了解海底情况〕. ***as dull as*** ～ 色泽象铅一样灰暗的;非常鲁钝的. ***cast [heave] the*** ～【海】用水砣〔测锤〕测深. ***get the*** ～ 饮弹,中弹. ***pump*** ～ ***into sb***.〔口〕向某人扫射. ***swing the*** ～〔军俚〕装病,偷懒. —*vt*. ①用铅覆盖,塞铅. ②用铅条固定住. ～*ed glass* 铅条玻璃. ③加铅〔铅的化合物〕于. ～ *gasoline* 加铅汽油,乙基化汽油. ④【印】排空铅,(在行间)插铅条. — *vi*. ①用水砣〔测锤〕测深. ②被铅覆盖;被铅塞住. ～ **acetate**【化】醋酸铅;乙酸铅. ～ **arsenate**【化】砷酸铅;砷酸气铅. ～ **colic**【医】铅毒疝. ～**-covered** *a*. 镀铅的,铅包的. ～**-free** *a*. 无铅的. ～ **glass** 铅玻璃. ～ **hardening** 铅浴淬火. ～ **line**【海】测锤绳. ～ **pencil** 铅笔. ～**-pipe [cinch]**〔美俚〕①轻而易举的事. ②肯定的事情. ～ **poisoning**【医】铅中毒. ～ **swinging**〔英俚〕偷懒;逃避工作. ～ **tetraethyl** 四乙铅 (= tetraethyl ～). ～ **wool [yarn]**【建】(接铅管用的)铅毛. ～**work** 铅衬;铅制品. ～**works** 制铅工厂,铅矿熔炼厂. **-less** *a*.

lead[2] [liːd] *vt*. ***(led*** [led]***)*** ①领导,引导,带领. ②搀,牵. ③领头,压倒,占首位,居第一;【体】领先. ④率领,指挥,领导,主持. ⑤引导某人做某事;诱使某人做某事〔接不定式〕. ⑥过某种生活〔日子〕. ⑦使…过某种生活. ⑧超前瞄准射击(飞机,飞鸟等). ⑨【拳击】先向对手打一拳. ⑩【牌】先出牌. ～ *sb*. *by the nose* 牵着某人的鼻子走. ～ *a horse by the bridle* 牵着马的缰绳. *He* ～*s his class in English*. 英语方面他在全班数第一. ～ *a happy [miserable] life* 过幸福〔悲惨〕生活. ～ *sb*. *a dog's life* 使某人过着受折磨的日子. ～ *a case* (律师)主持一个案件. ～ *a campaign* 指挥一场战役. ～ *an army* 带领一支军队. ～ *a fashion* 开风气. ～ *the procession* 走在仪仗队前头. ～ *the choir* 指挥合唱队. ～ *the singing* 领唱. ～ *the way* 引路,领路. ～ *sb*. *astray* 把某人引入歧途. ～ *sb*. *into a trap* 引某人落入圈套. *What led you to think so?* 是什么使得你这样想的呢? *Chance led him to London*. 偶然的机会导致他到伦敦来. *The pipes* ～ *the water into the fields*. 这些管道把水引到田里. *This path will* ～ *you to the station*. 你走这条路可以到火车站. — *vi*. ①响导,引导. ～ *in the charge* 冲锋在前. ②(道路等)通到. ③导致;引起 (*to*). ④领先,打头,居首位. ⑤【牌】(先)出牌. *All roads* ～ *to Rome*〔谚〕条条道路通罗马. *This road* ～*s to the river*. 这条路通往河边. *Oxford led by two lengths*. 牛津队在赛艇中占先两个艇身. *Who* ～*s?* 谁先出牌. ～ ***away*** 带走;引诱,诱入. ～ ***back*** ①带回. ②按搭档所出花色出牌. ～ ***for the prosecution*** (律师)主持诉讼. ～ ***nowhere*** 不会有什么结果. ～ ***off*** ①开始,开头,牵头 (～ *off the debate* 领头辩论). ②领走 (*The students were led off the school by the teacher*. 老师带着学生离开了学校). ～ ***on*** ①引领…继续前进. ②引诱,诱使. ～ ***out*** ①开始,领头,领舞伴 (离开座位)起舞. ～ ***out of*** 直通. ～ ***to*** 通向,导致. ～ ***up to*** 渐渐诱入,把话题渐渐引到…;【牌】设法引出. — *n*. ①领导,指导;指导地位,首位;榜样. ②领先,优势;领先的程度〔距离,时间等〕. ③领先者;领唱者;主角. ④(新闻等的)导言,引子,按语;在前的重要消息. ⑤管道;导线;【矿】矿脉. ⑥【乐】序曲,前奏. ⑦线索,提示,暗示. ⑧拳击的第一拳;牌戏中先出的牌,出牌权. ⑨牵引带〔如牵狗的带〕. *take the* ～ *in* 领导,带头,居首位. *With him in the* ～, *all the others followed suit*. 在他带动下,别的人也都跟上来了. *follow the* ～ *of sb*. 跟着某人走,效法某人. *give sb*. *a* ～ ①带头,以身作则. ②给某人提示. *gain [have] the* ～ *in a race* 在赛跑中领先. *have a* ～ *of ten metres over the other runners* 比其他赛跑的人领先十米. *hold a safe* ～ 遥遥领先. *The story starts off with a* ～. 故事用一段引子开始. *play the* ～ *in a* *film* 在一部影片中担任主角. *the juvenile* ~ 青年主角. *phase* ~ 相位超前. *a hot* ~ 很好的线索. *provide* ~*s for further research* 为进一步的研究提供了线索. ***have a long ~ on*** 遥遥领先. ***return the ~***【牌】跟牌,(在下一轮)出搭档者所出花色的牌. — *a.* ①领头的,领先的. ②最重要的,头条的,以显著地位刊载的. *a* ~ *bomber* 领队轰炸机. *a* ~ *horse* 带头[领先]的马. *a* ~ *editorial* 主要[头版]社论. *a* ~ *headline* 头条标题. ~ **angle** 超前角,导前角. ~**-in** ①【无】引入线〔英国也叫 down-~〕. ②介绍,开场白. ~ **network** 超前网络;强制四端网络. ~ **number** 导数. ~**off** 开始,开端;打出的头一拳;先发球者. ~ **screw** 导螺杆,丝杆. ~ **time** (制造业)投产准备阶段. ~**-up** 导致物. **-a·ble** *a.* 能被领导的;能被指挥的.

lead·en [ˈledn] *a.* ①铅制的,铅质的. ②铅灰色的. ③沉重的,沉闷的. ④钝的;质量差的;低廉的. ~ *sky* 铅灰色的天空. *a* ~ *pipe* 铅管. ~ *limbs* 沉重无力的手脚. ~ *rules* 麻烦的规则. *a* ~ *sword* 钝刀. ~**-eyed** 无光的眼睛. ~**-foot·ed** *a.* 缓慢的,慢条斯理的.

Lead·en·hall [ˈlednhɔːl] *n.* 伦敦肉类市场.

lead·er [ˈliːdə] *n.* ①领导(人),领袖,首领,首长. ②乐队指挥;领唱者;首席小提琴手;第一女高音. ③主要辩护人,首席律师. ④(报刊的)社论. ⑤向导船,先头舰;领机;先导马. ⑥【机】导杆,导管;【建】水落管;排水沟;引线,导火线;【矿】露头,导脉;【机】主轮. ⑦【植】主干,顶枝. ⑧【印】指引线. ⑨【影】(叙事)字幕. ⑩【商】吸引客人的特价品. ⑪【数】首项,领项. ⑫【解】腱,筋. ⑬【经】主要指数[指标](= leading indicator). *the* ~ *of the Opposition* (资本主义国家的)在野党[反对党]领袖. *a destroyer* ~【军】驱逐领舰. *a* ~ *plane*【空】长机. ***a blind ~ of the blind*** 盲人领盲人. ***community*** ~ 社会活动家. ***floor*** ~〔美〕政党的国会领袖. ***follow my*** ~ (一种儿童游戏)学领袖. ~ ***of praise*** 〔Scot.〕教堂唱诗班的领导人. ~**less** *a.* 无领袖的,无领导的. ~ **mill** 精整轧机. ~ **writer** 社论作者;〔英〕社论委员〔美国叫做 editorial writer〕.

lead·er·ette [ˌliːdəˈret] *n.* (报纸等的)短评;(新闻纪事等前的)编者按语.

lead·er·ship [ˈliːdəʃip] *n.* ①领导,指导. ②领导人员. ③领导能力;领导权. *collective* ~ 集体领导. *the* ~ *and the led* 领导者与被领导者.

lead·ing¹ [ˈlediŋ] *n.* ①铅制覆盖物. ②空铅,铅条,铅皮. *the* ~ *of a stained-glass window* 有色玻璃窗的铅框.

lead·ing² [ˈliːdiŋ] *n.* ①领导,指导. ②引导. *a man of light and* ~ 权威,大家,有真才实学的人. ~ *of water to arid lands* 把水引到旱地去. — *a.* ①指导的,领导的. *a* ~ *cadre* 领导干部. ②主要的;主导的;扮演主角的;第一位的. *the* ~ *topics of the hour* 当前最主要的话题. *a* ~ *part* 主角. *a* ~ *lady [man]* 演主角的女[男]演员. ~ **aircraftman**〔英〕空军上等兵. ~ **article** ①〔英〕社论. ②【商】(吸引顾客的)特价品. ~ **business** 主要角色. ~ **case**【法】典型案件. ~ **coefficient**【数】首项系数. ~ **current**【电】超前电流. ~ **edge** (飞机翼的)前缘. ~ **fossil**【地】标准化石. ~ **light** (社会团体中)有影响的人物. ~ **motive** ①主要动机. ②【乐】主导主题,主导旋律. ~ **note** = ~ tone. ~ **question**【法】诱导性的提问. ~ **rein** 驾驭马的缰绳. ~ **seaman**〔英〕海军一等水兵. ~ **staff** 附在牛鼻环上的棒头. ~ **strings**〔*pl.*〕(带幼儿学走路的)引带;〔喻〕指导,管教 (*be in ~ strings* 不能独立;还在学步;为他人所操纵). ~ **tone**【乐】导音. ~ **wind** 顺风.

lead·plant [ˈledˌplɑːnt] *n.* 〔美〕【植】灰毛紫穗槐 (*Amorpha canescens*).

leads·man [ˈledzmən] *n.* (*pl.* **-men** [-men])【海】测铅手,测深员. ~**'s platform** 测深台.

lead·wort [ˈledˌwəːt] *n.*【植】白花丹属 (*Plumbago*)〔尤指欧洲蓝茉莉 (*P. europaea*)〕.

lead·y [ˈledi] *a.* 似铅的;铅制的.

leaf¹ [liːf] *n.* (*pl.* ***leaves***) ①叶;〔集合词〕叶子;茶叶,烟叶. ②花瓣. ③(书刊等的)一张(两面). ④金属薄片,箔. ⑤【建】叶饰. ⑥(门等的)页扇. ⑦(可折叠的)活动桌面;(办公桌等的)桌盖. ⑧(飞机的)天窗. ⑨(步枪的)瞄准尺;【机】小轮齿. ⑩〔英方〕帽边. ⑪(汽车等片弹簧的)簧片. *shed leaves* (树)落叶. *a rose* ~ 一片玫瑰花花瓣. ***come into*** ~ 长叶,发芽. ***in*** ~ 生叶子的,叶茂盛的. ***leaves without figs*** 空谈,口惠而实不至. ***take a ~ out of sb.'s book*** 模仿某人. ***the fall of the*** ~ 落叶时;秋天. ***turn over a new*** ~ 翻开新的一页;革面洗心,过新生活. — *vi.* ①生叶,长叶. ②〔美〕翻书页. *The trees are beginning to* ~ *out.* 树木正在开始长叶. ~ *through a book* 把书翻阅一遍. — *vt.* 翻…的书页. ~ **blade** 嫩叶;叶片. ~ **bridge** 跳桥. ~ **bud** 叶芽. ~**-cast** 落叶病. ~ **fat** (猪)板油. ~ **hopper**【动】叶蝉. ~ **insect**【动】蛸. ~ **lard** (板油炼出的)上等猪油. ~ **miner**【动】潜叶虫〔其幼虫生存于叶脉和叶茎内〕. ~ **mo(u)ld**【农】腐叶堆[土];叶霉病. ~ **rust** (谷类等的)叶锈病. ~ **spot**【植】叶斑. ~**spring** 弹簧板[片]. ~**stalk**【植】叶柄. ~ **valve** 簧片阀. **-ed** *a.* 有叶的. **-less** *a.* 无叶的.

leaf² [liːf] *n.* 〔英军俚〕休假.

leaf·age [ˈliːfidʒ] *n.* 〔集合词〕(树)叶;叶丛;叶饰.

leaf·let [ˈliːflit] *n.* ①小叶,嫩叶. ②复叶的一片. ③叶状器官. ④传单;广告,仿单,散叶印刷品. — *vt.* 向…散发传单. ~ *a rally* 在群众大会上散发传单.

leaf·y [ˈliːfi] *a.* (***leaf·i·er; -i·est***) ①叶多的,叶茂盛的. ②叶状的,叶子覆盖着的. ③阔叶的,叶子做成的. *the* ~ *month of June* 树叶茂盛的六月. *a* ~ *plant* 阔叶植物. *a* ~ *shade* 树荫.

league¹ [liːg] *n.* ①同盟,联盟,盟约. ②社团,联合会,竞赛联合会. ③(蒙古的)盟. ④种类,类型. *the L- of Nations* (1914—1946 年的)国际联盟. *the Communist Youth L- of China* 中国共产主义青年团. *the Communist L-* 共产主义者同盟. ***the L-***〔史〕神圣同盟(= the Holy L-). ***be in*** ~ 联合[团结]起来干某事[反对某人] *(to do; against sb.)*. ***be in the ~ of*** 与…是同类型的人〔常用否定结构〕(*He just [simply] isn't in your* ~. 他和你根本不是同类型的人). ***in ~ with*** 与…同盟[联合、有好感];同…勾结[沆瀣一气] (*She may have been in ~ with the thieves.* 她可能同盗窃犯勾结). —*vt., vi.* (使)结盟;(使)联合[团结]. *They were* ~*ed together by a tacit treaty.* 他们根据默契关系联合起来了. *The nations* ~*ed together to stop the war.* 这些国家结成联盟来制止战争. ~**match** 联赛. ~ **table**〔英〕对照表,比较表.

league² [liːg] *n.* 里格〔长度名;在英美约为三英里或三海里〕.

lea·guer¹ [ˈliːgə] *n.* 结盟者,盟员;同盟者[国].

lea·guer² [ˈliːgə] *n.* 〔古〕围攻;围攻部队[阵营]. — *vt.* 〔古〕包围.

leak [liːk] *n.* ①漏洞,漏罅,裂缝. ②漏;漏水,漏气,漏出,渗漏;泄漏. ③漏出物;【电】漏电,漏泄电阻. ④〔俚〕撒尿. *a* ~ *detector* 检漏器. *a* ~ *in the boiler* 锅炉的裂缝. *A small* ~ *will sink a great ship.* 〔谚〕小患不治成大灾. *spring [start] a* ~ 出漏洞,生漏缝. *stop [plug] a* ~ 塞漏洞. *officially inspired* ~*s* 官方故意透露的消息. *do [have, take] a* ~〔俚〕撒尿. — *vi., vt.* ①(使)漏,(使)渗. ②(使)漏出,使泄漏. *The roof* ~*s.* 屋顶漏水. ~ ***off*** 漏泄. ~ ***out*** 漏出;泄漏. ~**hunting** 检漏,测漏. ~**-proof** *a.* 不漏的,密闭的.

leak·age [ˈliːkidʒ] *n.* ①漏,漏出. ②泄露. ③漏出物,漏出量. ④【商】漏损率;漏损量. *cause a* ~ 引起渗漏. *a* ~ *of information* 走漏消息. ~ **conductor** 线路闭雷器. ~ **current**【电】漏泄电流. ~ **test** 密封性试验.

Lea·key [ˈliːki] *n.* 利基〔姓氏〕.

leak·y [ˈliːki] *a.* (***leak·i·er; -i·est***) ①漏的,有漏洞的.

②〔口〕容易泄漏秘密的. ③小便失禁的. *a ~ person [vessel]* 不守秘密的人. **-i•ness** *n.*

leal [liːl] *a.* 〔Scot.〕〔诗〕忠实的, 诚实的. *the land of the ~* 天国.

lean¹ [liːn] *vi.* *(~ed* [lent, liːnd], 〔英〕*leant)* ①倾斜, 倾侧; 躬屈, 弯斜. ②倚靠; 依靠, 依赖. ③(思想等)倾向; 偏向; 偏袒. *The pillar ~s to the north.* 柱子朝北倾斜. *~ against the wall* 倚墙. *~ on a stick* 拄着手杖. *~ on the table* 倚靠在桌子上. *~ on [upon] sb. for support* 靠某人支持. *~ backward* 向后仰. *~ forward* 探过身去. *~ out of the window* 身子探出窗外. *~ over a book* 低头看书. *I rather ~ to [toward] your view.* 我倒比较倾向你的见解. — *vt.* ①使倾斜. ②使…倚靠. *~* ***off*** 〔口〕停止倚靠〔主要用命令式〕. *~* ***on [upon]*** ①靠在. ②倚赖. ③【军】据险(固守)(*The enemy ~ed upon the river.* 敌人据河而守). *~* ***over backward*** 〔口〕(为纠正偏向而)采取极端相反的态度, 矫枉过正. *~* ***to one side.*** 倾向一方. — *n.* 倾斜; 偏差. *a wall with a slight ~* 稍微有点倾斜的墙. **~-to** ① *n.* 单坡屋顶的小房子, 披屋. ② *a.* 【建】单坡的. **-ing** 倾斜, 倾向.

lean² [liːn] *a.* ①瘦的, 瘠瘦的. ②贫乏的, 贫弱的(才能等); 枯燥无味的(文章等). ③瘠薄的, 不毛的. ④没收成的. ⑤利益少的, 不合算的. ⑥营养少的, 脂肪少的, 瘦的(肉). *as ~ as a rake* 骨瘦如柴. *~ coal* 【矿】贫煤. *a ~ year* 凶年. *~ work* 没有利益的工作. *a ~ diet* 粗食. — *n.* 瘦肉. **-ly** *ad.* **-ness** *n.*

lean•ing [ˈliːniŋ] *a.* 倾斜的. *the L- Tower of Pisa* 比萨斜塔. — *n.* 倾斜; 倾向.

leant [lent] lean¹ 的过去式和过去分词的异体词.

leap [liːp] *vi.* *(leapt* [lept], *leaped* [liːpt]) 〔现在除成语外, 普通用 jump〕①跳跃, 跃起; 跳越; 迅速行动. ②(胸部等)跳动. ③交尾. *~ for [with] joy* 雀跃. *~ on a horse* 跳上马. *~ over a fence* 跳过篱笆. *Look before you ~.* 〔谚〕三思而后行. *My heart ~s up when I behold the rainbow in the sky.* 我一看到天空的虹, 我的心就扑通地跳. *one's heart ~s into one's mouth* (因惊恐)心剧烈跳动. *~ at a chance [an opportunity]* 抓住机会. *~ from one topic to another* 从一个话题跳到另一个话题. *~ to conclusions* 匆匆作出结论. *~ to the eye* 涌现在眼前, 历历在目. — *vt.* ①跳过, 跳越. *~ a wall* 跳墙. ②使跳过. *~ a horse over a fence* 使马跳过篱笆. *~* ***at*** 扑向; 跳起来〔急切地〕接受, 抢着抓住 (*~ at a proposal* 欣然接受提议). *~* ***out of one's skin*** 得意忘形. — *n.* ①跳跃; 飞跃, 跃进; 跳跃的高度〔距离〕. ②交尾. *take a ~ over an obstacle* 越过障碍物. *a ~ of seven metres* 七米的跃距. ***a ~ in the dark*** ①冒险的行动, 轻举妄动. ②死. ***by ~s and bounds*** 飞跃地, 突飞猛进地. ***in one ~*** 一跃. ***reach at a single ~*** 一蹴而就. ***with a ~*** (收入等)突然增加等. ***with ~s and bounds*** 有飞跃的发展; 飞跃地, 迅速地. **~ day** 闰日〔指 2 月 29 日〕. **~-frog** ① *n.* 跳背游戏; 蛙跳(游戏). ② *vi.* 作蛙跳动作; (车辆等) 忽前忽后地行进. ③ *vt.* 闪过; 越过, 跃过; 【军】使两支部队交互跃进; 互相增进. **~frogging tactics** 蛙跳战术. **~ year** 闰年.

leap•er [ˈliːpə] *n.* 跳跃者.

leapt [lept] leap 的过去式及过去分词.

Lear [liə] *n.* ①利尔〔姓氏〕. ②*Britain* 岛的传说中的王; 莎士比亚剧作《李尔王》中的主人公.

learn [ləːn] *vt.* *(learned* [-t, -d], *learnt)* ①学; 学到, 学会; 习得. ②记住. ③听到, 知道, 弄清楚, 了解到. ④〔俚〕教. *~ English* 学英语. *~ (how to) ride* 学骑马. *~ the lines of a play* 背台词. *I ~ it from [of] him.* 我是从他那里听来的. *~ the news of…* 接到…的消息. *This will ~ you to keep out of mischief.* 这将教训你不要再捣蛋了. — *vi.* ①学, 学会. ②听到, 知道, 认识到. *~ fast* 学得快. *~ like a parrot* 鹦鹉学舌般地背诵. *I ~ed of his death only yesterday.* 我昨天才听说他去世. ***I am [have] yet to ~ the truth.*** 我还不知道真相呢〔带怀疑对方的口气〕. ***It is ~ed that …*** 据悉. ***~ by [from] experience = ~ to one's cost*** 学乖. ***~ by heart*** 记住. ***~ by rote*** 死记, 机械地学会. ***Soon ~t, soon forgotten.*** 〔谚〕学得快, 忘得快〔强记容易忘却〕. ***We regret to learn that …*** (函电等习用语) 惊悉…. **-a•ble** *a.*

learn•ed [ˈləːnid] *a.* ①有学问的; 博学的; 精通某门学问的; 〔英〕精通法律的. ②学术上的; 学问上的; 需要经过学习研究的; 有(高深)学问的. *a ~ man* 学者. *the ~* 学者〔总称〕. *my ~ friend [brother]* 〔英〕阁下〔律师在下议院或法庭上对同事的敬称〕. *a ~ periodical* 学术期刊. *a ~ society* 学会. *the ~ profession* 需要学问的职业〔尤指律师、医生、牧师等职业〕. *~ skills* 学到的技术. *a ~ language* 学术语言〔尤指拉丁语〕. *a ~ word* 高深〔学者使用〕的词; 学来的词. ***be ~ in the law*** 精通法律. **-ly** *ad.*

learn•er [ˈləːnə] *n.* 学习者; 初学者. *an advanced ~* 程度较高的学习者; 进修者.

learn•ing [ˈləːniŋ] *n.* 学, 学习; 学问, 学识; 专门知识. *good at ~* 善于学习. *a man of ~* 学者. ***New ~*** 新学问, 新科学〔尤指十六世纪在英国传播的宗教改革学说及用希伯来文及希腊文对于《圣经》的考证研究〕.

learnt [ləːnt] learn 的过去式及过去分词.

lease¹ [liːs] *vt.* ①出租(土地). ②租借(土地). — *n.* ①租契, 租约. ②租借权. ③租借物. ④租借期限. ***a ~ of life*** 寿命. ***a perpetual ~*** 永久租借权. ***give sb. a new ~ of life*** 使某人重新振作起来. ***hold on [by] ~*** 租借. ***put out to ~*** 出租. ***(take) a new ~ of life*** 得庆更生. ***take on ~*** 租借.

lease² [liːs] *n.* 【纺】分经, 分绞. — *vt.* 使分经, 使分绞. **~-back** 回租〔出售产业同时长期租用该产的作法, 也称 sale and ~-back〕. **~hold** ① *a.* 租来的, 借来的. ② *n.* 租得物; 租借期 (*a life ~hold* 租借地终身保有权). **~hold•er** 租借人. **~-lend, L~-Lend** *n., a., vt.* = lend-lease. **leas•a•ble** *a.* **-less** *a.* **-r** *n.*

leash [liːʃ] *n.* ①(系狗的)皮带, 皮条. ②(打猎用语)三只(狗、兔等); 成三的一组. ③(织机篾上经线穿过的)综束, 综把, 吊环. ④束缚, 控制. *a ~ of hounds* (拴在一起的)三只狗. *a ~ of days* 一连三天. ***hold [have] in ~*** 用皮带系住(狗); 束缚, 控制. ***slip the ~*** 猎狗挣脱皮带; 摆脱束缚. ***strain at the ~*** 猎狗想挣脱皮带; 努力争取自由. — *vt.* ①用皮带系上. ②束缚, 控制.

leas•ing [ˈliːziŋ] *n.* 〔古〕虚言, 谎话.

least [liːst] *a.* (little 的最高级, 比较级为 less 或 lesser) ①最小的, 最少的 (*opp.* most). ②最不重要的, 地位最低的. ③〔美方〕年纪最小的; (动、植物) 最小种类的. *the ~ distance* 最小的距离. *the ~ number* 最小数. *the ~ squares* 【数】最小平方, 最小二乘方. *the last but not the ~* 最后的但并非最不重要的. *sb.'s ~ one* 某人最小的孩子. — *ad.* 最小, 最少. *the ~ angry man* 丝毫没有脾气的人. *Young people are the ~ conservative.* 青年人最不保守. *~* ***of all*** 尤其是, 最不 (*I like that ~ of all.* 我最不爱那个). ***not the ~*** ①(最小的)一点…也没有 (*There is not the ~ wind today.* 今天一点风也没有). ②〔强调 not〕不少, 非常, 很 (*There's not the ~ danger.* 危险可不少呢). — *n.* 最小, 最少, 最少量, 最小限度. *Of two evils, the ~ should be taken.* 两害相权取其轻. *That's the ~ of my anxieties.* 那是我最不担心的. ***at (the) ~*** 至少, 起码 (*The trip will take three days at ~.* 这一趟旅行最少得走三天). ***at the very ~*** 〔用以加强语气〕= at (the) ~. ***in the ~*** 一点, 丝毫. ***not in the ~*** 一点也不 (*I am not in the ~ afraid of it.* 那我一点也不怕). ***The ~ said, the soonest mended*** = Least said, soonest mended; The ~ said the better. 〔谚〕话越少越好. ***to say the ~ (of it)*** 至

少可以这样说，退一步讲。~ **common denominator**【数】最小公分母。~ **common multiple**【数】最小公倍数。~**ways**〔方〕，~**wise**〔口〕*ad.* 至少，无论如何。

leat [liːt] *n.* 〔英方〕磨坊专用水渠。

leath·er [ˈleðə] *n.* ①皮，皮革。②革制品；〔美口〕皮鞋；皮带；〔俚〕（板球、足球等用的）球，台球棒的头；〔*pl.*〕（骑马用）皮短裤，皮绑腿；〔美俚〕皮包，皮夹子。③〔俚〕皮肤。④狗耳的下垂部分。⑤〔the ~〕〔美俚〕拳击中的一击。*American* ~〔英〕油布，漆布；人造革。*enamel* ~ 漆皮。*heavy* ~ 原革。*imitation* ~ 漆布。*patent* ~ 漆皮。*mountain* ~ 石棉。***hell-bent for*** ~ 非常快，极快。***lose*** ~〔俚〕擦破皮肤。***(There is) nothing like*** ~〔谚〕自夸自赞〔相传一皮匠认为护城利器莫过于皮革，故云〕。— *vt.* 制成皮；蒙上皮，钉皮；〔口〕（用皮带等）抽打。— *a.* 皮革的，皮革制的。~ **and prunella** 衣着外表的差异；无关紧要的事情。~**back**【动】棱皮龟 *(Dermochelys coriacea)*〔它的体重可达 1,200 磅，是龟中最大者〕。~**board**（做鞋底用的）再生革。~**bound** *a.* 皮面精装的。~**cloth** 漆布，油布。~**-head** ①〔俚〕笨蛋。②〔美俚〕守夜人，巡警。③〔L-〕美国宾夕法尼亚州人。~ **hunting**〔俚〕（板球的）防守。~**jack·et** ①【动】无腹鳍刺鲀。②〔英〕长脚蝇的蛆。~**neck**〔美俚〕海军陆战队士兵。~ **welting** 鞣革。~**wood**【植】沼泽革木 *(Dirca palustris)*〔产于北美〕。

leath·er·et(te) [ˌleðəˈret] *n.* 人造革。

leath·ern [ˈleðəːn] *a.* 皮革的，似皮革的；革制的，革质的。

leath·er·oid [ˈleðəˌrɔid] *n.* ①勒塞洛伊德〔一种绝缘纸皮的商标名〕。②人造革，绝缘纸皮；薄钢纸。

leath·er·y [ˈleðəri] *a.* ①似革的，革质的。②强韧的。

leave[1] [liːv] *vt.* ***(left)*** ①离开，脱离；退出；辞去；遗弃；放弃，停止（某事）。②剩下；遗留；留下；遗赠。③听任；让某人做某事；留置不动。④交付；委托。⑤使…处于某种状态〔后接分词等〕。⑥使…成某状态而离去。⑦（从旁）走过去［经过，通过］。~ *Japan for France* 离日赴法。~ *medicine for art* 放弃医学改学艺术。~ *school* 离校〔指毕业或退学〕。*Winter will ~ us soon.* 冬天即将过去。~ *a card on sb.* 留名片给某人。~ *a deep impression on our minds* 在我们心里留下了深刻的印象。~ *her at home* 把她留在家里。~ *no room [scope] for doubt* 不容置疑。*Six from seven ~s one.* 七减六剩一。*To be left till called for.*（邮件等）留局待领。*Nothing was left to accident.* 没有一件事是靠运气的。*L- him go.* 让他走吧。*L- him to do as he likes.* 某人爱做什么，就让他做什么。~ *sth. undone* 放着某事不做。~ *the work until tomorrow* 把工作留到明天去做。*He left a widow and two children.* 他死时留下遗孀和两个孩子。*He left her £ 500.* 他遗给她五百镑。*I left my book in the car.* 我把书丢在汽车里了。~ *a sum in the bank* 存款在银行里。~ *sb. in charge of the matter* 委托某人负责办理此事。~ *sb. sth.* (~ sth. with sb.) 把某物交给某人。*L- this (up) to me.* 把这事交给我。~ *the door open* 让门开着。*Nothing was left undone.* 要做的都做了。*I left my father quite well an hour ago.* 一小时前我离开父亲时，他还是好好的。~ *the park on the left* 靠公园左手走过去。— *vi.* ①离去；走掉；动身，出发。②〔古〕停止。*It's time for us to ~* = It's time we left. 我们该走了。*I am leaving for Shanghai tomorrow.* 我明天动身到上海去。***be (nicely) left*** 被骗，上当。***be well left*** 得大量遗产。***get left*** ①被遗弃。②被打败。~ ***about*** 把东西丢下不管。~ ***alone*** 丢下不管，不理会（*L- him alone.* 别管他。*L- alone the books* 别动书。）。~ ***behind*** ①遗留（*He has left a sweet memory behind.* 他留芳百世）。②留下（~ *one's book* 忘记把书带去）。③追过，超过（*I left him far behind.* 我把他远远丢在后面）。~ ***go [loose] of sth.*** 〔口〕松手放掉（某物），放弃（某物）。~ ***[loose] hold of*** 放手，松手。~ ***in the air*** 搁置，使悬而不决。~ ***it at that [as it is]*** 〔俚〕就那么好了。~ ***much to be desired*** 还有待改进。~ ***no means untried*** 用尽方法。~ ***nothing to be desired*** 完美无缺。~ ***off*** ①戒除，停止（*begin where one's father left off* 继承父业）。②不再穿，不再用。~ ***sb. cold [cool]*** 使人扫兴。~ ***oneself wide open*** 〔美〕暴露在打击之下。~ ***out*** ①省去，删去。②遗漏。③不考虑；没有考虑。④〔美〕离开。⑤忘记；忽视。~ ***out of account [consideration]*** 不去注意，置之度外。~ ***over*** ①留下，剩下。②展期，延期。~ ***severely alone*** 尽量不干涉，不发生关系，敬而远之。~ ***sb. (out) in the cold*** 〔口〕不睬某人。~ ***sb. the bag to hold*** 把麻烦事推给某人。~ ***sb. to himself [to his own devices, to sink or swim]*** 听其自然，让它自生自灭。~ ***sb. unmoved*** 对某人毫无影响。~ ***sth. as it is*** 听其自然。~ ***the track*** 〔美〕出轨。~ ***undone***（应做的事）不去做。~ ***unpaid***（应付款项）不付。~ ***well [enough] alone*** = let well [enough] alone. ~ ***word*** 留言。— *n.*【台球】（前一人击球后）遗留下来的球的位置。**-r** *n.* 离开的人〔常指学校的毕业生〕。

leave[2] [liːv] *n.* ①许可，同意。②告假，休假；假期。*I beg ~ to inform you of it.* 特此奉告。*I take ~ to consider the matter settled.* 请原谅我认为这件事情已经解决。*a ~ of absence* 准假〔一般指时间较长的假〕；假期；休假。*a ticket of ~* 假释许可证。*break [overstay] one's ~* 超过假期。*go home on ~* 请假回家。*sick ~* 病假。***by [with] your*** ~〔口〕请原谅，对不起。***get one's*** ~ 被免职。***have [go on]*** ~ 请准假。~ ***off*** 休假许可。~ ***out*** 外出许可。***neither with your*** ~ ***nor by your*** ~ 不管你喜欢不喜欢，不管你怎么讲。***on*** ~ 请假中，在休假。***refuse*** ~ ***to*** 拒不允许。***take French*** ~ 不告而别，溜之大吉。***take*** ~ ***of one's senses*** 发狂。***without*** ~ 擅自。***without a 'by [with] your*** ~' 〔俚〕未经许可地，擅自。~**-breaker** 超假的人。

leave[3] [liːv] *vi.*（植物）生叶，长叶。

leaved [liːvd] *a.* 有…叶的，…叶的〔构成复合词〕。*a broad-~ tree* 阔叶树。*a four-~ clover* 四个叶子的三叶草。*a two-~ screen* 二折屏风。

leav·en [ˈlevən] *n.* ①酵母，麯，发酵剂。②潜在作用，影响力。③气味，色调。*the old ~*（难革除的）旧习气，陋习，陋规。— *vt.* 使发酵；发生影响；使带…气味。

leaves [liːvz] *n.* leaf 的复数。

leav·ing [ˈliːviŋ] *n.* ①〔*pl.*〕剩余物，残余。②剩余。*the ~s of meals* 剩余的饭菜。

leave-tak·ing [ˈliːvˌteikiŋ] *n.* ①告辞，告别。②告别辞。*His ~ was brief.* 他的告别辞很简短。

leav·y [ˈliːvi] *a.* leafy 的古体。

Leb·a·nese [ˌlebəˈniːz] *a.* 黎巴嫩的，黎巴嫩人的。— *n.* 黎巴嫩人。

Leb·a·non [ˈlebənən] *n.* 黎巴嫩。

Le·bens·raum [ˈleibənsˌraum] *n.* 生存空间〔德国法西斯作向外侵略借口的反动理论〕。

Leb·ku·chen [ˈleibˌkuːhən] *n.* 蜜饯果饼〔一种德国式糕饼〕。

lech [letʃ] *vi.* 〔俚〕好色；贪求 *(for; after)* — *n.*〔俚〕①淫欲，色欲。②淫棍，色鬼。

lech·er [ˈletʃə] *n.* 淫棍，好色的人。

lech·er·ous [ˈletʃərəs] *a.* ①好色的，淫荡的。②色情的，挑逗性的。

lech·er·y [ˈletʃəri] *n.* 色欲；好色，淫荡。

lec·i·thin [ˈlesiθin] *n.*【生化】卵磷脂。

lec·i·thin·ase [ˈlesiθiˌneis] *n.*【生化】卵磷脂酶。

lec·tern [ˈlektə(ː)n] *n.* ①（教堂中的）读经台。②（演讲台上的）小台架。

lec·tion [ˈlekʃən] *n.* ①（礼拜时）诵读的经文。②（同一著作不同版本的）异文。

lec·tion·ar·y [ˈlekʃənəri] *n.*【宗】（为全年礼拜时诵读用的）经文选。

lec·tor [ˈlektə] *n.* ①【宗】（教堂做礼拜时的）读经人。②

【天主】读经人〔四个最低等级中的第三等级．其他三个等级：一．祭司助手，二．被摩人，四．看门人〕．③讲师．

lec·ture [ˈlektʃə] *n.* ①讲义，讲演，讲话 *(on)*．②教训，训斥．*attend a* ～ 听报告；上课．*deliver [give] a* ～ 讲课，讲演．*a curtain* ～ 枕边训话，妻子私下对丈夫的责备．*read sb. a* ～ 教训某人一顿．— *vi.* 讲授，讲演．～ *on chemistry* 讲授化学．— *vt.* ①向…演讲，给…讲课．②训导，训斥．～ **room** 讲堂．～**ship** ①讲师的职位[资格、身分]．②(大学的)讲座．～ **theater [theatre]** 阶式讲堂．～ **tour** 演讲[讲学]旅行．

lec·tur·er [ˈlektʃərə] *n.* ①讲演者．②(大学、学院中的)讲师；训导者．

LED = ①large electronic display 大电子显示器．②light emitting diode 发光二极管．

led [led] lead² 的过去式及过去分词．— *a.* 受指导的，受控制的；被牵着走的．*a* ～ *captain* 善于拍马的人．*a* ～ *farm* 〔Scot.〕主人远居他地的农庄．*a* ～ *horse* 备用马．～ ***by the nose*** 受别人支配，被人操纵，仰人鼻息．

Le·da [ˈliːdə] *n.* 【希神】勒达〔斯巴达王后，与化为天鹅的宙斯交接而生了引起特洛伊战争的海伦〕．

le·der·ho·sen [ˈleidəˌhəuzən] *n.* (阿尔卑斯山民的)皮短裤．

ledg. = ledger.

ledge [ledʒ] *n.* ①壁架．②【地】(岩石突出的)岩架；岩礁；暗礁．③【矿】矿脉．**-d** *a.* 有壁架的；有突出物的；有暗礁的．

ledg·er [ˈledʒə] *n.* ①总帐，分类帐，底账．②(坟墓的)台石．③【建】(脚手架)横木，卧材．④底饵．～ **bait** 底饵[固定鱼饵]．～ **blade** 【纺】剪毛机上的固定刀片．～ **board** ①托梁横木；板条．②(栅栏的)横顶板；栏杆的扶手．～ **line** ①【乐】加线．②附有底饵的钓丝．～ **tackle** 能使钓饵沉于水底的鱼具．

Lee [liː] *n.* ①李〔姓氏，男子名，女子名〕．②**Rober Edward** ～ 罗伯特·爱德华·李〔1807—1870，美国南北战争时南军总司令〕．

lee [liː] *n.* ①保护，庇护．②【海】下风，背风面 *(opp.* windward, weather side*)*．③庇护所；避风处．④【地】背冰川面．***on [under] the*** ～ 在背风处．— *a.* 背风的．*the* ～ *side* 蔽面，背风面．～**board** 【船】边的横漂抵板．～ **shore** 下风岸；〔喻〕危险的境地 *(on a* ～ *shore* 在困难[危险]中)．～ **tide** 背风潮．

leech¹ [liːtʃ] *n.* ①【动】水蛭，蚂蟥，(特指)医用蛭．②榨取他人脂膏者，吸血鬼，重利盘剥者，高利贷．③〔古〕医师．***stick to sth. [sb.] like a*** ～ 钉住[缠住]不放．— *vt.* ①用水蛭吸血．②榨取干净，吸尽血汗．～ *sb. white* 把某人的精力[钱财等]榨取干净．～**craft** 〔古〕医术．

leech² *n.* 【船】帆的纵缘．

Leeds [liːdz] *n.* 利兹〔英国城市〕．

leek [liːk] *n.* 【植】青蒜，韭葱．***eat [swallow] the*** ～ 忍受耻辱．***not worth a*** ～ 毫无价值．

leer¹ [liə] *n.* 斜瞅，睨视，横目．— *vi., vt.* (愤恨、轻蔑地)斜眼瞅，瞟 *(at; upon)*．

leer² [liə] *n.* 【化】(玻璃的)退火炉．

leer·y [ˈliəri] *a.* ***(leer·i·er; -i·est)*** 〔口〕①机警的，狡猾的．②对…怀有戒心 *(of)*．*a* ～ *old bird* 老滑头．

lees [liːz] *n.* 〔*pl.*〕(葡萄酒等的)渣滓；沉积物；残渣．*drain [drink] a cup to the* ～ ①喝干．②备尝辛酸．*the* ～ *of life* 残年．*There are* ～ *to every wine.* 〔谚〕有酒就有酒渣．

leet¹ [liːt] *n.* 【英史】(封建领主设的)民事法庭或该法庭的管辖范围．

leet² [liːt] *n.* 〔Scot.〕候选人名单．*a short* ～ 最后一选的候选人名单．

Leeu·wen·hoek [ˈleivənˌhuːk], **A. van** ～列文虎克〔1632—1723，荷兰博物学家，显微镜创制者〕．

lee·ward [ˈliːwəd, ˈluːəd] *a.* 【海】下风的，在下风处的．— *ad.* 在下风，向下风．— *n.* 下风，背风面．**-most** *a.* 〔古〕最下风的．**-ly** *a.* 易向下风漂流的．

Lee·ward Islands [ˈliːwəd] *n.* 背风群岛〔西印度小安的列斯群岛的北部〕．

lee·way [ˈliːwei] *n.* ①【海】风压〔船在进行中被冲向下风〕；风压差，风压角〔进路与航路间的角〕；【空】偏流〔因风力造成飞行上的偏差〕．②时间的损失，落后．③〔口〕灵活性；余裕，余地．***have*** ～ 有回旋余地；〔口〕有充裕时间．***have much [a great deal of]*** ～ ***to make up*** 要花大力才能赶上．***leave some*** ～ 留有余地．***make*** ～ ①漂离航道．②离开预定航道．***make up (for)*** ～ ①赶上；弥补(损失)．②摆脱困难．***retain a certain*** ～ 保持相当的灵活性．

left¹ [left] leave 的过去式及过去分词．～ *on base* 【棒球】(攻守换班时)留在垒上．

left² [left] *a.* ①左的，左边的，左侧的．②左翼的；〔L-〕左派的．***have two*** ～ ***hands*** 非常笨拙．～ ***field*** 【棒球】左外垒．— *ad.* 向左；在左边．*Eyes* ～! 向左看齐！*L- dress!* 向左看齐！*L- face [turn]!* 向左转！*L- wheel* 左转弯走！— *n.* ①左，左面，左侧；〔美〕(船的)左舷．②〔常作 L-〕(议长席左侧的)议员；急进党，左派；(哲学、宗教的)革新派，急进派．③【军】左翼；【棒球】左外垒．*on the* ～ *of* 在…的左面．*keep to the* ～! 靠左边走！***over the*** ～ ***(shoulder)*** 倒过来说，恰恰相反．～**field** 〔美口〕活动中心以外的地区[范围]，局外人圈子．～**-hand** *a.* ①左手的，左边的；用左手的．②勉强的，不合理的．*(a* ～*-hand marriage* 门户不相当的婚姻)．③非法的．～**-handed** *a.* ①用左手的．②惯用左手的．③笨拙的．④可疑的，暧昧的；不诚实的；居心叵测的 *(a* ～*-handed compliment* 假恭维)．⑤门户不相当的，地位不相称的(婚姻)．⑥〔古〕不吉利的．⑦向左旋转的，反时针的 *(a* ～*-handed screw* 左转螺丝)．— *ad.* 用左手．*write* ～*-handed* 用左手写字．～**-hander** ①左撇子，用左手的人．②(在拳击中)用左手的一击；意外的打击．～ **heart** 心左半侧〔包括左心室和左心房，向肺部以外的全身输送血液〕．～**-leaning** *a.* 左倾的．～**-mind·ed** *a.* 〔美〕古怪的．～**most** *a.* 最左的，极左的．～ **wing** (政党等的)左翼．～**-wing** *a.* 左翼的，急进的．～**winger** 左派．

left·ism [ˈleftizəm] *n.* 〔有时 L-〕左派观点[主张、运动]．

left·ist [ˈleftist] *a.* 〔L-〕左派的．— *n.* 左派的人．

left-lug·gage [ˈleftˈlʌgidʒ] *n.* 寄存行李．*a* ～ *office* 行李寄存处．

left-off [ˈleftˈɔ(ː)f] *a.* (衣服等)弃置不用的，脱下不穿的．

left·o·ver [ˈleftˌəuvə] *n.* 剩余物〔如剩菜〕．— *a.* 剩余的；未用完的；吃剩的．

left·ward(s) [ˈleftwəd(z)] *a.* 左面的，左侧的．— *ad.* 向左面，在左手．

left·y [ˈlefti] *n.* 〔俚〕①左撇子，用左手的人．②左派的人，左倾的人．— *a., ad.* = ～-handed.

leg [leg] *n.* ①腿；(猪、羊等)供食用的腿．②(桌椅等的)腿脚；支架，支柱；支管．③三角形底部以外的侧边．④(裤子等的)腿部，袜统；靴统；脚管．⑤假腿．⑥〔英俚〕骗子．⑦(板球中)击球员左后方场地．⑧【海】抢风直驶的一段航程；旅程的一段．⑨〔古〕后脚一弯的行礼，屈膝礼．⑩喷道．⑪【电】引线，支线；多相变压器的铁心柱；(多相系统的)相．⑫(牌戏等上下两局中的)一局，一盘．***a*** ～ ***of the law*** 警察；律师；执法人员．***as fast as one's*** ～***s could carry one*** 开足马力，拼命跑．***be all*** ～***s (and wings)*** ①又瘦又长，长手长脚．②【海】樯又多又高．***be off one's*** ～***s*** 跌倒；站不住；(因走路，站立或工作过久而)筋疲力尽．***be run off one's*** ～***s*** 破产．***change the*** ～ (马)改换步调．***dance sb. off his*** ～***s*** 使某人跳舞跳得筋疲力尽．***fall on [upon] one's*** ～***s [feet]*** 跌下但未跌倒；侥幸度过困境．***feel [find] one's*** ～***s*** ①(婴儿)开始能行走[站起]．②对自己的能力开始有了自信心．***find [get] one's ice*** ～ 学会滑冰．***get a*** ～ ***in*** 〔口〕得到…的信任．***get one's*** ～ ***over the***

traces〔美〕违反党或组织的利益. *get [set] sb. on his* ～*s* ①使某人恢复健康. ②使某人经济自主. *get up on one's hind* ～*s*〔口〕气势汹汹，盛气凌人. *give sb. a* ～ *up* ①扶人上马. ②帮助某人度过困难. *hang a* ～ 裹足不前；犹豫不决. *have a bone in one's* ～ 不善行走，难于行走. *have (got) by the* ～〔美〕使处于困难地位. *have* ～*s* 走得快；出名出得快；有忍耐力. *have not a* ～ *to stand on* (言论等)没有根据，站不住脚. *have one's* ～ *over the harrows* 不受管制，拒绝服从. *have [put, stretch] one's* ～*s [feet] under sb.'s mahogany* 受某人款待〔指请吃饭〕. *have the* ～*s of* 比…跑得快. *in high* ～ 非常高兴. *keep one's* ～*s* 立定脚跟；不跌倒. *keep on [upon] one's* ～*s* 一直站着. ～ *and* ～ 双方得分相等，平分秋色. ～ *before wicket* (板球)击球员违反规则用腿截球. *lose one's* ～*s*〔俚〕喝得东倒西歪，喝醉. *make a* ～〔古〕弯膝行礼，打千儿. *on [upon] one's* ～*s* ①站着〔尤指演说时〕. ②病后能下床走动. ③发达的，富裕的. *on [upon] one's last* ～*s* 奄奄一息；快要结束. *pull sb.'s* ～〔口〕愚弄某人，嘲弄某人. *put [set] one's best* ～ *first [foremost, forward]*〔口〕全力以赴. *run off one's* ～*s* 累得精疲力尽，疲于奔命. *run sb. off his* ～*s* 使某人筋疲力尽. *shake a* ～ ①〔口〕跳舞. ②〔美俚〕赶紧. *shake a loose [free]* ～ 过放荡生活，放荡. *show a* ～〔口〕起床. *show* ～〔美俚〕逃跑. *stand on one's own* ～*s* 不依赖他人，自立. *stretch one's* ～*s* 散步，遛遛腿. *stretch one's* ～*s according to the coverlet* 适应环境，量入为出. *take to one's* ～*s* 逃走，溜之大吉. *talk the hind* ～ *off a donkey [horse]* 唠叨不休. *try it on the other* ～〔俚〕使用另一办法〔最后一着〕. *walk [trot] sb. off his* ～*s* 使人走累. — *vi.* ①〔口〕走，徒步走；跑. ②(为…)奔走，卖力 *(for)*. ③用腿抵住运河隧洞壁推船通过. — *vt.* 用腿抵壁把船推过运河隧洞. ～ *it* 走着去；跑；逃走(*L- it as fast as you can.* 快快跑吧!). ～ **art** 曲线美照片；裸体照片. ～ **bail**〔谑〕逃走 (*give* ～ *bail* 逃跑，越狱). ～**-bye**【板球】触身得分〔球触及击球人手以外的身体任何部分而使对方得分〕. ～**-guard** (运动员的)护腿. ～**iron** ① *n.* 脚镣. ② *vt.* 用脚镣锁住. ～**man** ①〔美〕采访记者. ②(机关办公室的)外勤，跑腿人. ～**-of-mut·ton** *a.* 羊腿状的〔尤指羊腿状衣袖或三角状帆〕. ～**-pull** 欺骗；恶作剧，嘲弄. ～**-rest** (病人等用的)脚凳. ～**room** (轿车或剧院等座位的)放脚处. ～ **show** 大腿戏. ～**work**〔口〕跑外工作，外勤，跑腿儿活；新闻采访工作. **-less** *a.* 无腿的. **-like** *a.*

leg. =① legal. ② legate. ③ legato. ④ legislature.

leg·a·cy [ˈlegəsi] *n.* ①【法】(动产的)遗赠；遗产. ②传代物；传统，遗教. *inherit a* ～ 继承遗产. *a* ～ *of hatred [ill-will]* 宿恨，世仇. *a rotten* ～ 烂摊子. ～**-hunter** 为争得遗产而钻营奉承的人.

le·gal [ˈliːɡəl] *a.* ①法律(上)的. ②法定的，合法的，正当的. ③【宗】按照摩西律法的. *one's* ～ *status* 合法地位. *the* ～ *profession* 律师业. *a* ～ *adviser* 法律顾问. *a* ～ *fare* 法定运费. — *n.* ①法定权利. ②依法必须登报的声明. ③〔*pl.*〕储蓄银行〔信托公司〕可以用来投资的证券. ～ **cap** 律师公文纸〔$8\frac{1}{2}$英寸宽，13 (或 14)英寸长，带边纸的白纸〕. ～ **holiday** 法定假日. ～ **limit** (汽车等的)法定速限. ～ **list** (储蓄银行等的)合法投资. ～ **person** 法人. ～ **remedy** 法律的制裁. ～ **reserve** (银行等的)法定准备金. ～ **separation** (夫妻的)合法分居. ～ **tender** 合法货币〔指可以用来偿债而债主必须接受的货币〕. **-ly** *ad.*

le·gal·ese [ˌliːɡəˈliːz] *n.* 晦涩的公文，法律用语.

le·gal·ism [ˈliːɡəlizəm] *n.* ①墨守法规，条文主义；文牍主义. ②【宗】信奉律法〔与信奉福音相对〕.

le·gal·ist [ˈliːɡəlist] *n.* ①墨守法规者，条文主义者；法律学家. ②【宗】律法主义者. **-ic** *a.* **-i·cal·ly** *ad.*

le·gal·i·ty [li(ː)ˈɡæliti] *n.* ①合法性；法律性. ②守法主义. ③【宗】墨守律法. ④〔*pl.*〕法律上的义务.

le·gal·i·za·tion [ˌliːɡəlaiˈzeiʃən] *n.* 合法化；批准，法律上认可.

le·gal·ize [ˈliːɡəlaiz] *vt.* 法律认可，使合法，合法化.

le·gate[1] [liˈɡeit] *vt.* 作为遗产让与，遗赠. *give and* ～ 作为遗产让与.

leg·ate[2] [ˈlegit] *n.* ①罗马教皇的使节. ②使节，国使. ～**ship** 使节的职权〔任期〕.

leg·a·tee [ˌlegəˈtiː] *n.*【法】遗产承受人，受遗赠人.

leg·a·tine [ˈlegətain] *a.* ①教皇使节的；国使的. ②国使职权规定的.

le·ga·tion [liˈɡeiʃən] *n.* ①使节的派遣；使节所负的使命. ②公使馆；公使馆全体人员. ③使节的职位〔职权〕.

le·ga·to [leˈɡɑːtəu] *a., ad.*〔It.〕【乐】连奏.

le·ga·tor [liˈɡeitə] *n.* ①遗赠人. ②立遗嘱人.

leg·end [ˈledʒənd] *n.* ①传说；神话. ②伟人传. ③(奖章、纪念牌等的)铭文，题跋. ④地图的图例，插图的说明. ⑤〔the L-〕【宗】圣徒故事集 (= the Golden L-).

leg·end·ar·y [ˈledʒəndəri] *a.* 传说(中)的，传奇(中)的；传说〔传奇〕似的. — *n.* ①传说集；【宗】圣徒传. ②传说编纂者.

leg·end·ry [ˈledʒəndri] *n.* 传说集.

leg·er·de·main [ˈledʒədəˈmein] *n.* (变)戏法；骗术；花招.

leg·er line [ˈledʒə]【乐】加线〔五线谱的上加线或下加线〕.

le·ges [ˈliːdʒiːz, ˈleigeis] *n.*〔L.〕*lex* 的复数.

leg·ged [ˈlegid, legd] *a.* ①〔用作构词成分〕：有腿的. ②有…腿的. *a long-*～ *man* 腿长的人. *a four-*～ *animal* 四足动物.

leg·ger [ˈlegə] *n.* ①= legman. ②用腿抵住运河隧洞壁把船推过去的人. ③织袜统机；织袜统工人. ④(屠宰场等处)加工腿肉的工人.

leg·ging [ˈlegiŋ] *n.*〔主 *pl.*〕绑腿；(幼儿用的)细腿毛线裤.

leg·go [ˈlegəu] *int.*〔英俚〕放开！(= let go).

leg·gy [ˈlegi] *a.* *(-gi·er; -gi·est)* ①(特指小孩、小马等)腿细长的，细腿的. ②【植】茎长的. ③露腿的.

Leg·horn [ˈlegˈhɔːn] *n.* ①来亨〔意大利地名〕. ②〔或 l-〕[leˈɡɔːn] 来亨鸡. ③〔l-〕[ˈleghɔːn, leˈɡɔːn] 意大利麦杆缏，意大利麦缏草帽 (= ～ hat).

leg·i·ble [ˈledʒəbl] *a.* 可以辨认的，易读的(笔迹)，字迹清楚的. **-bil·i·ty** *n.* **-ness** *n.* **-bly** *ad.*

le·gion [ˈliːdʒən] *n.* ①古罗马军团〔约有三千至六千步兵，辅以骑兵〕. ②军团，大批部队. ③众多，大批，无数. ④〔L-〕= American L-, Foreign L- 等的简称. *a* ～ *of followers* 大批追随者. *Their name is Legion [legion].* 他们很多. *the American [British]* ～ 美国〔英国〕军团〔退伍军人组织〕. **L- of Hono(u)r** 法国勋级会荣誉军团〔1802年拿破仑为表彰有功勋者而成立的荣誉团体名〕. **L- of merit** 军功勋章〔美国政府向本国或外国军人颁发的勋章〕.

le·gion·ar·y [ˈliːdʒənəri] *a.* ①(古罗马)军团的；军队的. ②退伍军人协会的. ③很多的. — *n.* ①古罗马军团的兵. ②退伍军人协会会员. ～ **ant** 行军蚁〔美国热带一种成群结队吞食其前进路上的昆虫和动物的蚂蚁 = army ant〕.

le·gion·aire [ˌliːdʒəˈneə] *n.* ①军团的一员. ②〔常 L-〕美国军团(美国退伍军人组织)成员. ③ 外籍军团〔由外国人组成的军队中 (如过去法国在北非的殖民军中的外籍军团)〕的一员.

Legis. = ①legislation. ②legislature.

leg·is·late [ˈledʒisˌleit] *vi.* 制定法律，立法. — *vt.*〔美〕依法律…. ～ *sb. out of an office*〔美〕按法定手续免某人的职.

leg·is·la·tion [ˌledʒisˈleiʃən] *n.* ①立法. ②〔集合词〕法规. ③立法机构的审议事项. *paternal* ～ 家长式的(限

制公民自由的)繁琐立法.

leg·is·la·tive [ˈledʒisˌleitiv] *a.* 立法的; 有立法权的; 立法部门的. *(cf.* administrative, executive, judicial*)*. *a ~ bill* 法案. *the ~ body* 立法机关. *~ power* 立法权. *the L- Bureau* 法制局. — *n.* 立法权; 立法机关. ~ **assembly** 〔常作 L- Assembly〕①美国各州的两院制议会. ②两院制议会的下院. ③一院制立法议会. ~ **council** 〔常作 L- Council〕①英国议会的上院. ②(英国殖民地或美国领地的)一院制议会. ③美国州议会的常设委员会.

leg·is·la·tor [ˈledʒisˌleitə] *n.* 立法者; 议员; 立法机关的成员. **-ial** *a.* **-ship** *n.*

leg·is·la·ture [ˈledʒisˌleitʃə] *n.* 立法机关, 立法部, 议会; 〔美〕(特指)州议会.

le·gist [ˈliːdʒist] *n.* 法律学家.

le·git [ləˈdʒit] 〔美俚〕 *a.* ①合法的, 守法的. ②(戏剧、剧院等)正统的. — *n.* 正统剧; 正统剧院. ***on the ~*** 正当的; 在合法范围之内.

le·git·i·ma·cy [liˈdʒitiməsi] *n.* ①合法性; 正统性. ②嫡系; 嫡出; 正统.

le·git·i·mate [liˈdʒitimit] *a.* ①合法的, 正常的. 正当的. ②正统的. ③嫡系的, 嫡出的. ④(感情等)真实的. *a ~ claim* 正当要求. *a ~ inference* 合理的推断. *~ drama* 正统戏. — [-meit] *vt.* ①使合法; 认为正当; 认为正统. ②承认(庶子)为嫡出. **-ly** *ad.* **-ma·tion** [-ˈmeiʃən] *n.*

le·git·i·ma·tize [liˈdʒitiməˈtaiz] *vt.* ***(-tiz·ed, -tiz·ing)*** = legitimize.

le·git·i·mism [liˈdʒitimizəm] *n.* 正统主义.

le·git·i·mist [liˈdʒitimist] *n.* 正统王朝拥护者. — *a.* 正统王朝拥护者的.

le·git·i·mize [liˈdʒitiˌmaiz] *vt.* ***(-mized, -miz·ing)*** ①使合法化, 宣布合法化; 〔尤指〕使合法; 予以法律保障〔地位〕; 官方〔正式〕认可; 授权. (对非婚生子)给予合法地位. ②证明…有理. **-za·tion** *n.*

le·gong [ˈleigoːŋ] *n.* 〔Balinese〕 黎弓舞〔巴厘的一种传统女双人舞〕.

leg·ume [ˈlegjuːm] *n.* 【植】①豆科植物. ②豆荚. ③(食用)豆. *~s bacteria.* 根瘤细菌.

le·gu·men [liˈgjuːmən] *n.* ***(pl. legumina*** [-minə]***)*** = legume.

le·gu·min [liˈgjuːmin] *n.* 【生化】豆球朊.

le·gu·mi·nous [leˈgjuːminəs] *a.* 【植】①荚的, 有荚的; 生豆的. ②豆科的. *~ crops* 豆科作物. *~ plants* 豆科植物.

Le Ha·vre [ləˈhɑːvr] 勒阿弗尔〔法国港市〕.

Leh·mann [ˈleimən] *n.* 莱曼〔姓氏〕.

le·hu·a [leiˈhuːɑː] *n.* 【植】夏威夷桃金娘树; 这种树的木材或花.

lei[1] [ˈleii] *n.* ***(pl. ~s)*** (夏威夷人戴在颈上的)花环.

lei[2] [lei] *n.* leu 的复数.

Leib·nitz [ˈlaibnits], **Gottfried Wilhelm von** 莱布尼茨〔1646—1716, 德国哲学家、数学家〕.

Lei·ca [ˈlaikə] *n.* 【摄】莱卡照相机〔商标名〕.

Leices·ter [ˈlestə] *n.* ①莱斯特〔英国城市〕. ②莱斯特郡〔英国郡名〕(= ~ shire). ③莱斯特羊 (= ~ sheep).

Leigh [liː] *n.* 利〔姓氏, 男子名〕.

Leigh·ton [ˈleitn] *n.* 莱顿〔姓氏〕.

Le(i)·la [ˈliːlə] *n.* 莉拉〔女子名〕.

Leip·zig [ˈlaipzig] *n.* 莱比锡〔东德城市〕.

leish·man·i·a·sis [ˌliʃməˈnaiəsis] *n.* 【医】利什曼(原虫寄生)病; (尤指)黑热病.

leis·ter [ˈliːstə] *n.* (三齿)鱼叉. — *vt.* 叉鱼.

leis·ure [ˈleʒə; Am. ˈliːʒə] *n.* ①空闲, 闲暇, ②悠闲, 安逸. *wait sb.'s ~* 等到某人有空时. *a life of ~* 悠闲的生活. ***at ~*** ①在闲暇中, 有空〔常作表语〕. ②从容不迫地〔常作状语〕. ③失业〔作定语或表语〕. ***at one's ~*** 有空时, 方便时 (*Drop in to see me at your ~* 有空时请到我这里来). — *a.* 闲暇的, 有空的, 有闲的 (阶级等). **-less** *a.* 无空闲的.

lei·sured [ˈleʒəd; Am. ˈliːʒəd] *a.* 有闲空的; 悠闲自在的. *the ~ classes* 有闲阶级.

lei·sure·ly [ˈleʒəli; Am. ˈliːʒəli] *a.* 从容不迫的, 悠闲的. — *ad.* 从容不迫地, 慢慢地, 悠然, 悠闲地. *work ~* 悠闲地工作. **-ness** *n.*

Leith [liːθ] *n.* 利斯〔姓氏〕.

leit·mo·tif, leit·mo·tiv [ˈlaitməuˌtiːf] *n.* 【乐】①主导旋律, 主导主题. ②中心思想〔主题〕.

lek [lek] *n.* 列克〔阿尔巴尼亚货币名, 等于 100 昆塔 *(quintar)*〕.

Le·land [ˈliːlənd] *n.* 利兰〔姓氏, 男子名〕.

LEM = ①lunar excursion module 月球探测飞船. ②laser energy monitor 激光能量监控器.

Lem·an [ˈlemən] *n.* 莱曼〔姓氏〕.

le·man [ˈlemən] *n.* 〔古〕爱人, 情人, 奸夫, 情妇.

lem·ma[1] [ˈlemə] *n.* ***(pl. ~ta*** [-tə], ***~s)*** ①【逻、数】(辅)助定理, 引(定)理, 预备定理. ②(诗等的)主题, 题目. ③(词典的)词目. ④(图画等上的)题词.

lem·ma[2] [ˈleme] *n.* 【植】(禾本科小穗的)外稃.

lem·ming [ˈlemiŋ] *n.* 【动】(北极的)旅鼠.

lem·nis·cus [lemˈniskəs] *n.* ***(pl. -nis·ci*** [-ˌniszai]***)*** 【解】丘系, 蹄系.

lem·on [ˈlemən] *n.* ①柠檬; 柠檬树. ②= lemon yellow. ③〔美俚〕无聊的人〔物〕, 没有价值的东西, 叫人失望的人〔物〕. ***hand sb. a ~*** 〔口〕欺骗某人, 把不值钱的东西卖给某人. ***The answer's a ~.*** 〔俚〕你这个(可笑的)建议, 无法回答〔理解〕. — *a.* 柠檬的, 柠檬味的; 柠檬色〔黄〕的, 柠檬制的. ~ **balm** 【植】蜜蜂花 *(melissa officinalis)* 〔一种叶带香味的多年生薄荷, 可用作食物和药物的香料〕. ~ **butter (sauce)** ①柠檬黄油. ②柠檬黄油汁. ~ **day lily** 【植】金针菜. ~ **drop** 柠檬硬糖. ~ **kali** 柠檬汽水. ~ **squash** 〔英〕鲜柠檬苏打水. ~ **squeezer** 柠檬压榨器. ~ **yellow** 柠檬色〔黄〕, 柠檬黄颜料. **-ish, -like** *a.*

lem·on·ade [ˌleməˈneid] *n.* 柠檬汽水.

lem·on·y [ˈleməni] *a.* 柠檬的, 有柠檬香味的.

lem·pi·ra [lemˈpiːrɑː] *n.* ***(pl. -ras)*** 伦皮拉〔洪都拉斯货币名〕.

le·mur [ˈliːmə] *n.* 【动】狐猴.

Le·na [ˈliːnə] *n.* ①莉娜〔女子名, Helena 的昵称〕. ②(苏联)勒拿河.

lend [lend] *vt.* ***(lent*** [lent]***)*** ①借给, 贷与, 出借 (*opp.* borrow). ②借助, 提供. ③使(自己)适合. ④添加. *~ money at interest* 取息贷款. *This fact ~s probability to the story.* 从这个事实看来, 这个故事好象是真的. — *vi.* 贷款. ***~ a (helping) hand with [in]*** 帮助, 帮忙. ***~ assistance [aid] to*** 帮助. ***~ itself to*** 对…有用〔适合〕. ***L- me your ears.*** 请听我说吧. ***~ one's countenance to*** 赞成; 支持. ***~ one's name to*** 让人用自己的名义. ***~ one's turn*** 让位子. ***~ oneself to*** 给…卖命. ***~ out*** 借出(书等). ***~ sb. a box on the ear*** 打某人一记耳光. — *n.* (短期)贷款. *take a ~ of* 〔英俚〕通融一下. **-a·ble** *a.*

lend·er [ˈlendə] *n.* 出借人, 贷方; 贷款者.

lend·ing [ˈlendiŋ] *n.* ①借给, 贷与. ②借出物, 贷出物; 租借物; 附属物; 〔*pl.*〕借来的衣服. — *a.* 贷出的. ~ **library** ①收费图书馆. ②〔英〕公共图书馆; 图书馆的借书处. ~ **stock** 【商】抵押品.

lend-lease [ˈlend ˈliːs] *vt.* 根据租借法案供给. — *a.* ①由租借法批准的. ②批准租借法的. — *n.* 平等租借交换. *the Lend-Lease Act* (1941 年美国制订的)租借法.

length [leŋθ] *n.* ①长, 长度, 长短. ②(时间的)长短, 期间. ③(赛艇的)一艇的长度; 一马的长度. ④程度, 范围. ⑤【板球】球程; 投至适当距离的球. ⑥【语】音长. ⑦一段, 一节. *a dress ~, a ~ of cloth* 一段衣料. *a ~*

of pipe [tubing] 一节管子. *The boat won by three ~s.* 这只艇以三艇长之差得胜. *a (good) ~ ball* 球程准确的球. ***at arm's ~*** 在手臂伸得到的地方, 疏远 (*keep sb. at arm's ~* 不与接近, 敬而远之). ***at full ~*** ①冗长地; 充分地, 详细地 (*give all the facts at full ~* 提供详细的材料). ②全身平伸地 (*lie at full ~* 挺直身体躺着). ***at great ~*** 冗长地, 罗罗唆唆地. ***at ~*** ①最后, 终于, 好容易才. ②充分地, 详细地 (*speak at great ~* 详细讲了好久). ***at some ~*** 相当详尽地. ***cannot see beyond the ~ of one's nose*** 鼠目寸光. ***draw out to a great ~*** 拖得很久, 占去很长时间. ***fall [measure] all one's ~*** 直挺挺地倒下. ***find [get, have, know] the ~ of sb.'s foot*** 了解某人的弱点. ***go (to) all ~s [any ~] = go to great ~s*** 什么事都做得出; 不遗余力. ***go (to) the ~ of (doing)*** 甚至于, 不惜. ***go the whole ~ of it.*** 彻底干; 干到底. ***~ of (sb.'s) days [life]*** 某人的寿命. ***measure one's (own) ~*** 跌倒在地. ***of some ~*** 相当长. ***over [through] the ~ and breadth of*** 到处, 四面八方. ***work at arm's ~*** 在不利的条件下工作.

length·en [ˈleŋθən] *vt.* 延长, 伸长, 拉长. *~ a vowel* 【语音】拖长元音音长. — *vi.* 变长; 延伸; 转为 *(into)*. *Summer ~s (out) into autumn.* 夏去秋来. *The days are ~ing.* 白天长起来了. *The shadows ~.* 天色渐黑; 年纪渐老; 死期已近. *~ out* 过分延长.

length·ways [ˈleŋθˌweiz] *ad.* 纵长地.

length·wise [ˈleŋθˌwaiz] *ad., a.* 纵长地[的].

length·y [ˈleŋθi] *a.* ***(length·i·er; -i·est)*** ①过长的, 漫长的. ②冗长的, 罗唆的 (演说、文章等). **-i·ly** *ad.* **-i·ness** *n.*

le·ni·ence, -en·cy [ˈliːniəns, -si] *n.* ①宽大, 宽厚, 怜悯. ②宽大的行为. *a policy of ~* 宽大政策. *excessive ~* 宽大无边.

le·ni·ent [ˈliːnjənt] *a.* ①宽大的, 宽厚的, 怜悯的. ②〔古〕减轻痛苦的, 缓解的. **-ly** *ad.*

Lenin [ˈlenin], **Vladimir Ilich** 列宁〔1870—1924, 无产阶级革命导师〕.

Len·in·grad [ˈleningræd, -grɑːd] *n.* 列宁格勒〔旧名 St. Petersburg〕.

Len·in·ism [ˈleninizəm] *n.* 列宁主义.

Len·in·ist [ˈleninist] *n.* 列宁主义者. — *a.* 列宁主义的.

le·nis [ˈliːnis, ˈlei-] *a.* 【语音】弱 (辅音) 的〔发音时肌肉松弛, 如浊连续音〕. — *n.* 弱辅音.

len·i·tive [ˈlenitiv] *a.* 有缓和作用的, 止痛的. — *n.* 【药】止痛剂, 缓和剂.

len·i·ty [ˈleniti] *n.* ①宽大; 慈悲. ②宽大的处理.

le·no [ˈliːnəu] *n.* 【纺】①纱罗织法〔经纱双股扭织〕. ②纱罗织物, 通花布.

lens [lenz] *n.* *(pl. ~es)* ①透镜; 一组透镜. ②【解】(眼球的)晶体. ③【摄】(照相机的)镜头. ④凸透镜状物件; 汽车的灯玻璃. ⑤【矿】透镜状油矿; 扁豆状矿体. *a concave [convex] ~* 凹面[凸面]镜. *an electron ~* 电子透镜. *a biconcave [biconvex] ~* 双凹 [双凸] 面透镜. *the power of a ~* 透镜的焦强. *~* **louse** 〔美影俚〕抢镜头的人. *~***man** *(pl. -men)* 〔美口〕摄影师. *~ **shyness*** 〔美影俚〕新演员在摄影机前的畏怯心理, 怯场. *~* **turret** (摄影机或电视机上的)透镜旋转台.

lent [lent] lend 的过去式及过去分词.

Lent [lent] *n.* ①(基督教的)四旬斋, 大斋期〔指复活节前的四十天〕. ②〔*pl.*〕〔英〕(剑桥大学)春季赛艇会. *~* **lily** ①〔英〕= daffodil. ②= Madonna lily. *~* **term** 〔英〕春季学期.

-lent *suf.* 表示"充满…的"; "富于…的"; "以…为特征的": pesti*lent*, vio*lent*.

len·ta·men·te [ˌlentəˈmentei] *ad.* 【乐】缓慢地.

len·tan·do [lenˈtɑːndəu] *ad., a.* 【乐】渐慢.

Lent·en [ˈlentn] *a.* ①四旬斋的; 大斋期的. ②四旬斋时举行的; 适合于四旬斋的; 简朴的, 简陋的; 没有肉食的; 严肃的. *~ clothing* 朴素的衣服. *a ~ face* 阴沉的脸. *~ fare* 斋, 素菜. *a ~ pie* 无肉斋饼.

len·tic [ˈlentik] *a.* 【生态】静水的; 生活于静水(如湖泊、池塘等)中的.

len·ti·cel [ˈlentisəl] *n.* 【植】皮孔. **len·ti·cel·late** [ˌlentiˈselit] *a.*

len·tic·u·lar [lenˈtikjulə] *a.* ①双凸透镜状的. ②透镜的. ③(眼球的)晶(状)体的. ④【地】透镜状的, 扁豆状的. ⑤【摄】凹凸式(胶片)的. *~ film* (电影的) 凹凸式胶片. *~ sand* 【地】透镜状地层.

len·tic·u·late [lenˈtikjuˌleit] *vt.* ***(-lat·ed, -lat·ing)*** 使成为凹凸式胶片〔加上特殊滤色器可摄出带自然色的照片〕. **len·tic·u·la·tion** *n.*

len·tic·u·lated [lenˈtikjuleitid] *a.* = lenticular.

len·ti·form [ˈlentiˌfɔːm] *a.* = lenticular.

len·tig·i·nous [lenˈtidʒinəs] *a.* ①雀斑的, 斑点的. ②长雀斑的, 长斑点的 (= lentiginose).

len·ti·go [lenˈtaigəu] *n.* ***(pl. len·tig·i·nes*** [lenˈtidʒiˌniːz]***)*** 斑点;【医】雀斑.

len·til [ˈlent*i*l] *n.* 【植】小扁豆(属).

len·tisk [ˈlentisk] *n.* 【植】乳香黄连木.

len·tis·si·mo [lenˈtisiˌməu] *a., ad.* 【乐】非常缓慢.

len·ti·tude [ˈlentitjuːd] *n.* 〔古〕缓慢; 懒散.

len·to [ˈlentəu] *ad., a.* 〔It.〕【乐】徐缓地[的]; 柔和地[的].

len·toid [ˈlentɔid] *a.* 透镜状的.

l'en·voi, l'en·voy [ˈlenvɔi] *n.* 〔F.〕(诗, 文的)结束语, 尾声.

LEO 【物】 = low enrichment ordinary water reactor 低浓缩普通水反应堆.

Le·o [ˈli(ː)əu] *n.* ①利奥〔男子名〕. ②【天】狮子座; 狮子宫. *~* **minor** 【天】小狮(星)座.

Le·on [ˈli(ː)ən] *n.* 利昂〔男子名, Leo 的异体〕.

Lé·on [ˈleiɔn] *n.* 莱昂〔姓氏〕.

Le·o·na [liːˈəunə] *n.* 利昂娜〔女子名〕.

Leon·ard [ˈlenəd] *n.* 伦纳德〔姓氏, 男子名〕.

Leo·nar·do da Vin·ci [liəuˈnɑːdəudəˈvintʃi] *n.* (达)芬奇〔1452—1519 意大利文艺复兴时期伟大画家, 雕刻家, 建筑学家〕.

Le·o·nar·desque [ˌliːənɑːˈdesk] *a.* (意大利画家) (达) 芬奇式[风格]的.

le·one [liːˈəun] *n.* 利昂〔塞拉利昂货币名, 等于 100 分 (cents)〕.

Le·o·nid [ˈli(ː)ənid] *n.* ***(pl. ~s, ~es*** [-iːz]***)*** 【天】狮子座流星.

le·o·nine [ˈliːənain] *a.* ①狮子 (似) 的. ②雄壮的; 勇猛的.

Le·o·nor·a [ˌli(ː)əˈnɔːrə] *n.* 利奥诺拉〔女子名, Eleanor 的异体〕.

leop·ard [ˈlepəd] *n.* 【动】豹. *an American ~* = jaguar. *a hunting ~* = cheetah. *a snow ~* = ounce[2]. *Can the ~ change his spots?* 本性难移. *~* **spot** 豹斑〔常指一方在另一方地域内的分散据点, 在地图上标色不同, 状如豹斑〕.

leop·ard·ess [ˈlepədis] *n.* 【动】母豹.

le·o·tard [ˈliːəˌtɑːd] *n.* (杂技和舞蹈演员等穿的)高领长袖紧身衣; 紧身衣.

lep·er [ˈlepə] *n.* ①麻疯病人. ②别人避之唯恐不及的人. *~* **colony** (孤岛等的) 麻疯病人隔离区. *~* **house** 麻疯病人收容所.

lep·i·do- [liˈpidəu] *comb. f.* 表示"鳞": *lepido*pterous.

le·pid·o·cro·cite [ˌlepidəuˈkrəusait] *n.* 【矿】纤铁矿.

le·pid·o·lite [liˈpidəˌlait, ˈlepidəˌlait] *n.* 【矿】锂云母.

Lep·i·dop·ter·a [ˌlepiˈdɔptərə] *n.* 〔*pl.*〕【动】鳞翅目(昆虫), 蝶类.

lep·i·dop·ter·al [ˌlepiˈdɔptərəl] *a.* 【动】鳞翅目(昆虫)的, 蝶类的.

lep·i·dop·ter·an [ˌlepiˈdɔptərən] *n.* 【动】鳞翅目

(Lepidoptera) 昆虫〔包括蝶和蛾〕.

lep·i·dop·ter·ist [ˌlepiˈdɔptərist] *n.* 鳞翅目昆虫学家.

lep·i·dop·ter·ous [ˌlepiˈdɔptərəs] *a.* = lepidopteral.

lep·i·do·si·ren [ˌlepidəuˈsairən] *n.* 【动】美洲肺鱼 *(Lepidosiren paradoxa)* 〔产于南美沼泽等死水中〕.

lep·i·do·sis [ˌlepiˈdəusis] *n.* *(pl.* ***lepidoses*** [ˌlepiˈdəusiːz]*)* 动物鳞片的排列和特质.

lep·i·dote [ˈlepiˌdəut] *a.*【生】有鳞片的.

lep·o·rid [ˈlepərid] *n.* *(pl.* ***le·por·i·dae*** [liˈpɔːriˌdiː]*)* 【动】兔科. *(Leporidae)*. — *a.* 兔科的.

lep·o·rine [ˈlepəˌrain,-rin] *a.* 野兔的; 如野兔的.

lep·re·chaun [ˈleprəˌkɔːn, -ˌkɑːn] *n.* (爱尔兰传说中帮主妇做事的勤奋的)小妖精.

lep·ro·sa·ri·um [ˌleprəˈsɛəriəm] *n.* *(pl.* ***-ri·ums, -ri·a*** [-ə]*)* 麻风病院; 麻风病人隔离区〔收容所〕.

lep·rose [ˈleprəus] *a.*【生】多鳞的; 鳞状的.

lep·ro·sy [ˈleprəsi] *n.* ①【医】麻风病. ②极坏的作用, 有危害性的事物. *moral* ~ 道德败坏.

lep·rous [ˈleprəs] *a.* ①麻风的; 似麻风的; 患麻风的. ②不洁净的, 丑恶的. ③鳞状的, 有鳞被的. **-ly** *ad.* **-ness** *n.*

lep·to- [ˈleptə] *comb. f.* 表示"小","细","薄": *leptocephalic.*

lep·to·ce·phal·ic [ˌleptəusiˈfælik] *a.* 头盖骨狭小的.

lep·to·ceph·a·lus [ˌleptəˈsefələs] *n.* *(pl.* ***-li*** [-lai]*)* 【动】叶状幼体.

lep·to·dac·tyl [ˌleptəuˈdæktil] *a., n.*【动】脚趾细长的(禽类或兽类).

lep·to·dac·ty·lous [ˌleptəˈdæktləs] *a.* 有细长趾的〔如某些鸟类〕.

lep·ton[1] [ˈleptɔn] *n.* *(pl.* ***lep·ta*** [-tə]*)* ①雷普塔〔古希腊小硬币名〕. ②雷普塔〔希腊现行货币名, 等于一德拉克马 *(drachma)* 的 1/100〕.

lep·ton[2] [ˈleptɔn] *n.*【物】轻粒子, 轻子. ~ *number* 轻子数. **-ic** *a.*

lep·to·some [ˈleptəsəum] *n.* 体格细长的人, 瘦弱型的人. — *a.* 体格细长的, 瘦弱型的.

lep·to·spire [ˈleptəˌspaiə] *n.*【医】钩端螺旋体.

lep·to·spi·ro·sis [ˌleptəuspaiˈrəusis] *n.*【医】钩端螺旋体病. **lep·to·spi·ral** [-ˈspairəl] *a.*

Ler·mon·tov [ˈljermɔntɔf], **Mikhail Yurevich** 莱蒙托夫〔1814—1841 俄国诗人, 小说家〕.

le roi le veut [ləˈrwɑːləˈvəː]〔F.〕国王对此同意.

le roi s'avisera [-sɑːˈviːzərɑː]〔F.〕国王将加考虑〔委婉的拒否用语〕.

Les·bi·an [ˈlezbiən, -bjən] *a.* ①(古希腊)勒斯波斯岛 (Lesbos) 的. ②女性同性爱的. ~ **love** (女性间的)同性爱. —*n.* ①勒斯波斯岛的居民. ②搞同性爱的女子. **-ism** *n.* 女性间的同性爱关系〔行为〕.

lèse-ma·jes·té [ˈleizˈmæʒestei] *n.*〔F.〕= lese majesty.

lese maj·es·ty [ˈliːzˈmædʒisti] *n.*【法】欺君罪, 叛逆罪.

le·sion [ˈliːʒən] *n.* ①损害, 损伤. ②【医】(机体、器官等的)损害. *focal* ~ 病灶损害. *periodontal* ~ 牙周损害. — *vt.* 损害, 对…造成损伤〔损害〕.

Les·ley, Les·lie [ˈlezli, ˈlesli] *n.* 莱斯莉〔女子名〕.

Les·lie [ˈlezli, ˈlisli] *n.* 莱斯利〔姓氏, 男子名〕.

Le·sot·ho [ləˈsəuthəu] *n.* 莱索托〔非洲〕.

les·pe·de·za [ˌlespiˈdiːzə] *n.*【植】胡枝子属 *(Lespedeza)*〔一年生或多年生植物, 用以改良土壤和作为牲畜饲料〕.

less [les] *a.*〔little 的比较级之一〕①更小的, 较小的; 更少的, 较少的. ②较次的, 较劣的, 较不重要的; 身分较低的. *an article of* ~ 更小的东西. *find* ~ *difficulty with one's work* 觉得工作困难较少. *Your shadow hasn't grown any* ~. 你一点也没有瘦. *an article of* ~ *weight* 更轻的东西. *Eat more vegetable and* ~ *meat.* 多吃蔬菜少吃肉. *He spends* ~ *time at work than at play.* 他工作上的时间比游玩时间少. ~ *but better* 少而精. *L- noise, please!* 请静一点. *More haste,* ~ *speed.*〔谚〕欲速则不达. *try to make* ~ *mistakes* 尽量少犯错误. *an article of* ~ *value* 更不值钱的东西. *a matter of* ~ *importance* 次要的事情. *James the L-* 副手杰姆斯, 打下手的杰姆斯. ★表示数量意义时, fewer 比 less 普通: *Fewer people study Latin today than formerly.* 现在学拉丁文的人比从前少了. ***far*** ~ 远不及. ***little*** ~ 少一点. ***little*** ~ ***than*** 相差无几. ***more or*** ~ 多少, 或多或少, 若干. ***no*** ~ ***than*** ①正好…, 至少…, 有…那么多 (*He has no* ~ *than three daughters.* 他有三个女儿之多). ②原来就是, …那样的 (*He was no* ~ *(a person) than the mayor.* 他原来就是市长). ***nothing*** ~ ***than*** = no ~ than (*We expected nothing* ~ *than an attack.* 受攻击是预料到的). — *ad.* ①较少, 更少. ②没有…那样. *be* ~ *known* 不大著名. *He is* ~ *fat than he was.* 他不及过去胖了. *The heat has grown* ~ *intense.* 没有先前那样热了. *Eat* ~, *drink* ~ *and sleep more.* 少吃少喝多睡觉. *Speak* ~ *and listen more.* 少讲多听. ***no*** ~ ... ***than*** 不下于, 和…同样 (*He is no* ~ *clever than his brother.* 他跟他的兄弟一样聪明). ***none the*** ~ = ***not the*** ~ = ***no*** ~ 仍旧, 依然 (*He has faults, but I like him none the* ~. = *I like him none the* ~ *for his faults.* = *He has faults; none the less, I like him.* 他有缺点, 但我仍旧喜欢他). ***not*** ~ ***than*** 不少于; 至少 (*Each party shall consist of not* ~ *than ten.* 每组至少由十人组成). ***not*** ~... ***than*** 在…方面不下于 (*The pupil was not* ~ *famous than his master.* 学生同老师齐名). ***nothing*** ~ ***than*** 完全一样 (*He is nothing* ~ *than a thief.* 他简直是个贼). ***sth.*** ~ ***than*** 较…少几分. ***still [even, much]*** ~〔附在否定句后〕更不用说, 何况 (*We fear no death, still* ~ *difficulties.* 我们死都不怕, 何况困难). — *prep.* 少掉; 不足; 减去. *a year* ~ *three days* 一年差三天. *Five* ~ *three leaves two.* 五减三剩二. — *n.* 较少, 更小. *expect to see* ~ *of sb.* 不想多见某人. *He is* ~ *of a fool than he looks.* 他不象看上去那样笨. *He will not take* ~. 他不肯少拿〔坚持要那么多〕. *in* ~ *than a year* 在不到一年的时间里. *L- of your nonsense.* 少说废话. *L- than twenty of them remain now.* 他们剩下的现在还不到二十人. ***any the*** ~ 更少一点, 更小一些 (*He did not work any the* ~ *for his illness.* 他虽有病在身, 工作却没有少做). ***in*** ~ ***than no time*** 立刻, 马上. ***nothing*** ~ ***than*** 同样, 正好是, 恰恰是. **~-than-carload** *a.* (铁路运输中的)零担的. **~-than-truckload** *a.* 卡车零担的.

-less *suf.*〔附在名词或动词之后〕①构成形容词, 表示"无","缺","没有": end*less*, home*less*, leaf*less*. ②构成副词, 表示"不": doubt*less*.

les·see [leˈsiː] *n.*【法】承租人, 租户.

less·en [ˈlesn] *vt.* ①缩小, 减少; 减轻. ②贬低; 轻视, 看不起. — *vi.* 变小, 变少, 减少.

less·er [ˈlesə] *a.*〔little 的比较级之一〕①更小的, 更少的; 较小的. ②【乐】= minor. *a* ~ *nation* 小国. *a* ~ *power* 弱国. **L- Bear**【天】小熊座. ~ **panda**【动】小熊猫 *(Ailurus fulgens)*.

Le·ssing [ˈlesiŋ], **Gotthold Ephraim** 莱辛〔1729—1781 德国诗人, 批评家〕.

les·son [ˈlesn] *n.* ①功课. ②一节课, (教科书中的)一课. ③〔*pl.*〕课程. ④教训, 训诫; 惩戒. ⑤【宗】日课. *hear sb. his* ~ 听人温习功课. *L- Three* 第 3 课. *give* ~*s in music* 教音乐. *object* ~ 实物教学; 明显的实例. ***be a*** ~ ***to*** 对…是一个教训. ***give a*** ~ ***to sb.*** = give sb. a lesson 教训某人, 申斥某人. ***learn one's*** ~ 得到教训. ***read sb. a*** ~ 教训某人一顿. ***take [have]*** ~***s in English from sb.*** 跟某人学英语. — *vt.* ①教课. ②教训, 训斥.

les·sor [leˈsɔː] *n.*【法】出租人.

lest [lest] *conj.* ①唯恐, 免得〔引出状语从句〕. ②〔用在 fear, afraid 等词的后面, 引出名词从句〕= that. *He fled* ~ *he (should) be arrested.* 他唯恐被捕于是就逃跑了. *I was afraid* ~ *he should come too late.* 我怕他来得

太迟。

Les·ter [ˈlestə] *n.* 莱斯特〔姓氏,男子名〕.

let[1] [let] *vt.* ①容许,让,听任;使得。②假设,假定。③出借,出租。④使流出;泄漏,放出;让通过。⑤(把工作等)让人承包,承办。*Don't* ~ *this happen again.* 别让这种事情再发生了。*L- me try.* 让我试一下。*L- nobody lag behind.* 别让任何人落后。*L- them do their worst.* 让他们尽量作恶吧! *L- us [Let's] go at once.* 我们马上走吧! *L- ∠ABC be an angle of ninety degrees.* 假设 ∠ABC 为直角。*He* ~ *it be known that…* 他对人说…。*L- him do it.* 让他去做吧。~ *sb. through* 让某人通过。*Please* ~ *me know.* 请告诉我。*We* ~ *him go.* 我们放他走了。~ *(out) a sigh* 叹一口气。*The water is* ~ *into the tank.* 让水流入水箱。*This pair of boots* ~ *(in) water.* 这双靴子漏水。*House [Room] to L-.* 房屋[房间]召租。~ *one's house* 出租房屋。— *vi.* 租出,被人借用中。*The house* ~*s for 100 dollars a month.* 这所房子月租一百元。*The room* ~*s well.* 这个房间租价高[不易租出]。~ ***alone*** ①不理,不管,放任 (*L- him alone to do it.* 任他自己去做罢)。②更不用说(*I can't speak French,* ~ *alone Russian.* 我连法语也不会讲,更不用说俄语了。*He knows Latin and Greek,* ~ *alone English.* 他懂拉丁文和希腊语,英语更不在话下)。~ ***be*** 不管,听任 (*L- her be.* 别打扰她)。~ ***blood*** 【医】放血,流血。~ ***by*** 让人过去 (*L- me by, please.* 借光,让让路)。~ ***down*** ①放落,放下 (~ *down the blinds* 放下百叶窗)。②抛弃,使失望 (~ *him down* 使他失望)。③损坏威信,下面子,搞臭。~ ***drive at*** … 向…打出,向…投掷。~ ***fall [drop, slip]*** ①落下,倒下。②不当心泄露,无意中说出。③【数】画(垂线等)。~ ***fly*** ①发射,投射。②骂。~ ***fly at*** 发射,射出。***L- George do it.*** 〔美俚〕让别人干吧。~ ***go*** ①放开;释放。②发射。③放任不管。④拳打,辱骂。⑤辞退。~ ***go hang*** 放任,不管。~ ***in*** ①放入(~ *in some fresh air* 打开门窗透透新鲜空气。~ *sb. in* 让某人进来)。②插入,嵌入。③〔俚〕欺骗。④使受损失,陷入…。~ ***in on*** 〔美〕告诉,告知。~ ***into*** ①放进。②嵌进。③告诉,告知 (~ *sb. into a secret* 告诉某人秘密)。④〔俚〕打击,殴打;责骂。~ ***it go at that*** 谈论到此为止。~ ***loose*** 放掉,释放;放任。***L- me see.*** 让我想想看。~ ***off*** ①放(枪,花炮等);说出(俏皮话等)。②宽恕,从轻处理 (~ *sb. off lightly* 从轻发落)。③漏出,放出(水、瓦斯等)。④免除(约束、工作、责任等)。~ ***on*** 〔口〕①泄密。②假装。~ ***oneself go*** 尽情(做某事);忘乎所以。~ ***out*** ①放出。②泄漏。③放宽,放大,放长。④出租(车马等)。⑤〔美口〕放学;散场。⑥打,踢,骂 (*at*)。⑦〔美俚〕解雇。~ ***pass*** 不追究,原谅,宽恕。~ ***ride*** 不管,放任自流。~ ***slide*** 〔美〕不关心,放过。~ ***slip*** ①解开,放走。②无意中说出。③错过(机会等)。~ ***sb. down easily [gently]*** 给某人留面子〔不加深究〕。~ ***sb. have it*** 〔美俚〕殴打某人,让某人吃苦头。~ ***things go hang*** = ~ ***things slide*** 随它去,不管它,听其自然。~ ***up*** 〔口〕停止,中止;(风雨等)减弱。~ ***up on*** 〔口〕宽大对待。~ ***us say*** 比方说,假定说。~ ***well [enough] alone*** (已经够好了)就让它去,不要画蛇添足。— *n.* 〔英口〕出租;租出的房屋。*get a* ~ *for the room* 为这房间找到租户。

let[2] [let] *vt.* ***(let·ed, let)*** 〔古〕阻碍,防害。— *n.* ①〔古〕障碍,阻碍。②(网球等)球触网。***without*** ~ ***or hindrance*** 毫无障碍。

-let *suf.* ①表示"小": ring*let*, stream*let*. ②表示"在…上佩带的饰品": ank*let*, arm*let*.

Le·ta [ˈliːtə] *n.* 莉塔〔女子名〕.

letch [letʃ] *vi., n.* = lech.

let·down [ˈletˌdaun] *n.* 〔美〕(速度,努力等的)下降,减少。②松劲。③〔口〕失望;令人失望的事物。

le·thal [ˈliːθəl] *a.* 致死的,致命的,杀伤性的。*a* ~ *chamber* 煤气屠杀室。*a* ~ *dose* 致死(药)量〔略 LD〕。~ *gas* 致死性毒气。~ *weapons* 凶器。— *n.* = ~ gene. ~ **gene** 致死基因,致死因子,致死因素〔也称 ~ factor〕. **-i·ty** *n.* 致死性,杀伤力;致死率。**-ly** *ad.*

le·thar·gic(al) [leˈθɑːdʒik(əl)] *a.* ①昏睡(状态)的,嗜眠的,瞌睡的。②无气力的,不活泼的;冷漠的。*a* ~ *sleep* 昏睡。**-gi·cal·ly** *ad.*

leth·ar·gize [ˈleθəˌdʒaiz] *vt.* ***(-giz·ed, -giz·ing)*** 使昏睡;使无气力。

leth·ar·gy [ˈleθədʒi] *n.* ①嗜眠症。②沮丧;冷漠,不活泼;无生气。

Le·the [ˈliːθi(ː)] *n.* ①【希神】忘河〔人饮其水,就忘却过去〕。②[l-] 忘却。**le·the·an** [liˈθiːən] *a.* ①忘河的。②使人忘却过去的。

Le·ti·tia [liˈtiʃiə] *n.* 利蒂希娅〔女子名〕.

l'é·toile du nord [letˈwɑdyˈnɔː] 〔F.〕 北极星。

let's [lets] = let us.

Lett [let] *n.* ①列特人〔波罗的海东岸,尤其是拉脱维亚的一个民族〕。②列特语。

let·ted [ˈletid] ①〔废〕 let[1] 的过去时和过去分词。②let[2] 的过去时和过去分词的异体。

let·ter[1] [ˈletə] *n.* 出租人。

let·ter[2] [ˈletə] *n.* ①字母,文字。②【印】活字,铅字。③书信。④〔*pl.*〕文学,学问;〔*pl.*〕读写初步知识。⑤〔常 *pl.*〕证书,许可证。⑥字面(意义),形式。⑦〔美〕运动服上的字母标志。*teach a child his* ~*s* 教孩子识字。*black* ~古代英国哥特式黑体字。*white* ~ 罗马体活字。*a man of* ~*s* 文人。*art and* ~*s* 文学艺术。*the commonwealth [republic] of* ~*s* 文坛。*the profession of* ~*s* 著作界。*in* ~ *and in spirit* 形式精神都,在形式和内容上。*the* ~ *of the law* 法律条文,法律字面上的意义。***be slow at one's*** ~***s*** 读书进步慢。***by*** ~ 以书信形式 (*inform sb. by* ~ 写信通知某人)。***call*** ~***s*** 呼号。***drop*** ~ 〔美〕托人由一地带到另一地付邮的信件。~ ***worship*** 拘泥字句。***night*** ~ 夜间无线电报。***to the*** ~ ①严格按照字句,彻头彻尾,不折不扣。②详细知道;了如指掌。***win one's*** ~ 当上运动选手。— *vt.* 写[刻,印]上文字[字母];标上字母分类;加标题。— *vi.* ①写上字母。②【美体】当上选手。~ **balance** (邮局中称信的)信秤。~ **board** 【印】铅字盘。~ **bomb** 邮件爆炸物,书信炸弹。~ **book** 书信发文簿。~**bound** *a.* 拘泥字句的。~ **box** 信筒;信箱。~ **card**〔英〕邮简。~ **carrier** 邮递员。~ **case** (携带用)文件夹。~ **drop** 投信口。~**form** ①字母型式〔尤指字母的设计、发展中所呈现的形状〕。②信笺。~ **founder** 铸铅字的人。~**gram** 书信电报〔较普通电报为慢〕(*a day* ~ *gram* 昼间书信电报〔当天送达〕。*a night* ~*gram* 夜间书信电报〔次日送达〕)。~**head** 笺头〔印在信纸上端的人名或商行的名称、地址等〕。②印有上述笺头的信笺。~ **lock** 字码锁。~**man**〔美〕(得奖的)运动员。~ **missive** 传达上级命令、任命、许可、邀请的函件。~ **[~s] of marque [and reprisal]** 武装私人船舶捕押敌船的许可证。~ **paper** 信纸,信笺。~**per·fect** *a.* ①【剧】台词记得很熟的。②(文件、校样等)完全正确的。~**press** 【印】①〔主英〕有插图的书中正文。②活版印刷。~**set** 【印】文字版面的胶印。③书信复写器。~ **sheet** 邮简。~**s of administration** 【法】遗产管理委任状。~**s of business** (英国国王发出的)召开教会高级人士会议通知书。~**s of credence** (=~s credential) (外交)国书。~**s of recall** (外交)召回使节的公文。~**s patent** 专利特许证。~**s testamentary** 【法】遗嘱执行状〔法院向遗嘱执行人发的证书〕。~ **weight** ①镇纸,纸压。②= ~ balance. ~ **writer** ①写信者;书信代书人。②尺牍。③书信复写器。

let·tered [ˈletəd] *a.* ①识字的,有文化的。②有学问的。③有文字的,印有字母的。

let·ter·er [ˈletərə] *n.* 字母[文字]刻写人。

let·ter·ing [ˈletəriŋ] *n.* ①手写字,印刷字,雕刻字。②

写字,印字,刻字.

Let·tic [ˈletik] *a., n.* = Lettish.

Let·tish [ˈletiʃ] *a.* 列特人的; 列特语的. — *n.* 列特人, 列特语.

et·tre de ca·chet [letr də kɑːˈʃei] ***(pl. let·tres de ca·chet)*** 〔F.〕密信;〔尤指〕(法国革命前国王不通过法律手续发出的)秘密逮捕令.

let·tuce [ˈletis] *n.* ①【植】莴苣. ②〔美俚〕钞票.

let·up [ˈletˌʌp] *n.* 〔美口〕停止, 中止; 休息. *He jaws with no ~.* 他没完没了地讲. *It rained without ~.* 雨下个不停.

le·u [ˈleu] *n.* ***(pl. lei*** [lei]***)*** (罗马尼亚的货币单位)列伊.

leu·c(o)- *comb. f.* 表示"白色";"无色": *leucocyte, leucorrh(o)ea.*

leu·c(a)e·mi·a [ljuːˈsiːmiə] *n.* = leuk(a)emia.

leu·cine [ˈluːsiːn, -sin] *n.*【化】白氨酸.

leu·cite [ˈluːsait] *n.*【地】白榴石.

leu·co·cyte [ˈljuːkəˌsait] *n.* = leukocyte.

leu·co·cy·th(a)e·mi·a [ˌljuːkəusaiˈθiːmiə] *n.* =leuk(a)emia.

leu·co·cy·to·sis [ˌljuːkəsaiˈtəusis] *n.* =leukocytosis.

leu·co·my·cin [ˈljuːkəˌmaisin] *n.*【药】白霉素.

leu·co·plast(id) [ˈljuːkəuplæst(id)] *n.*【植】白色体,白色粒.

leu·cor·rh(o)e·a [ˌljuːkəˈriːə] *n.* = leukorrhea.

leu·cot·o·my [ljuˈkɔtəmi] *n.*【医】脑白质切除术.

leu·k(a)e·mi·a [ljuːˈkiːmiə] *n.*【医】白血病. **leu·ke·mic** [-mik] ① *a.* 白血病的. ② *n.* 白血病患者. **leu·ke·moid** [-mɔid] *a.*

leuk(o)- *comb. f.* = leuc(o)-.

leu·ko·cyte [ˈljuːkəˌsait] *n.* 白血球, 白血细胞. **leu·ko·cyt·ic** *a.* **leu·ko·cyt·oid** *a.*

leu·ko·cy·to·blast [ˌljuːkəˈsaitˌblæst] *n.* 白血球细胞形成核. **-ic** [-ˈblæstik] *a.*

leu·ko·cy·to·sis [ˌljuːkəsaiˈtəusis] *n.*【医】白血球增多. **leu·ko·cy·tot·ic** [-ˈtɔtik] *a.*

leu·ko·der·ma [ˌljuːkəˈdəːmə] *n.*【医】角斑; 角白膜斑.

leu·ko·dys·tro·phy [ˌljuːkəˈdistrəfi] *n.*【医】脑白质病.

leu·ko·pe·ni·a [ˌljuːkəˈpiːniə] *n.*【医】白血球减少. **leu·ko·pe·nic** *a.*

leu·ko·poi·e·sis [ˌljuːkəpɔiˈiːsis] *n.*【医】白血球生成. **leu·ko·poi·etic** [-ˈetik] *a.*

leu·kor·rhe·a [ˌljuːkəˈriːə] *n.*【医】白带过多. **-l** *a.*

leu·ko·sis [ljuːˈkəusis] *n.* = leuk(a)emia.

lev [lef] *n.* ***(pl. le·va*** [ˈlevə]***)*** 列弗〔保加利亚货币名,等于 100 斯托丁基 *(stotinki)*〕.

Lev. = Leviticus.

Le·val·loi·si·an [ˌlevəˈlɔiziən] *a.* 列瓦洛期文化的〔指旧石器时代中期文化. 列瓦洛是法国地名, 该地出土的文物特点为片状工具〕.

Le·vant [liˈvænt, lə-] *n.* ①地中海东部沿岸诸国和岛屿.〔包括叙利亚、黎巴嫩、巴勒斯坦等〕. ②= ~ morocco. ③〔l-〕地中海上的强烈东风. ~ **morocco** (装钉书籍用的)优质山羊鞣皮. **-ine** *a., n.* 地中海东部沿岸诸国和岛屿的(人).

le·vant [liˈvænt] *vi.* 〔英〕躲债逃匿.

le·vant·er[1] [liˈvæntə] *n.* ①(地中海上的)强烈东风. ②〔L-〕地中海东部沿岸诸国和岛屿的人.

le·vant·er[2] [liˈvæntə] *n.* 〔英〕逃亡者; 躲债逃匿的人.

le·va·tor [liˈveitə] *n.* ***(pl. lev·a·to·res*** [ˌlevəˈtɔːriːz], ***le·va·tors)*** ①【解】提肌. ②【医】脑骨碎片镊子.

lev·ee[1] [ˈlevi] *n.* ①(国王等起床后的)接见. ②〔英〕(国王专对男臣举行的)早朝; 接见; (法国宫廷的)早朝. ③〔美〕总统招待会. ④专为某人举行的招待会.

lev·ee[2] [ˈlevi] *n.* ①〔美〕(河中泥沙形成的)冲积堤. ②天然堤. ③码头. — *vt.* 筑堤.

lev·el [ˈlevl] *n.* ①水平仪,水准仪;水准测量. ②水平线,水平面;水平状态;平面,平地. ③水平, 水准; 水位; 标准; 高度; 层次; 级; 等级. ④【物】能级,电平;【矿】主平巷. *4,000 metres above sea ~* 海拔四千米. *the ~ of the sea* = (the) sea ~. (标准)海面. *the rise and fall of water ~* 水位的升降. *a normal blood-sugar ~* 正常血糖量标准. *above [below] the general ~* 在一般水准以上[以下]. *at eye ~* 齐眼睛那么高. *high ~ bombing* 高空轰炸. *the ground ~*【物】基级. *at the grass-roots ~* 在基层. *social ~s* 社会地位. *the government at all ~s* 各级政府机关. *top-~ talks* 最高级会谈. *the ~ of a gun* 瞄准线. *the ~ of vision* 视线. *take a ~* 作水准测量. *a dead ~* 平面,平地;单调;【矿】空层,备用层. ***bring sb. to his ~*** 打掉某人的傲气. ***find [seek] one's (own) ~*** 找到相称的位置 (*Water tries to find its ~.* 水往低处流). ***~ to ~ administration*** 分级管理. ***land on the street ~*** 〔美口〕失业. ***on a ~ with sb.*** 和某人同一水准; 和某人同等 (地位). ***on the deal ~*** 〔美口〕极正直的,极诚实的. ***on the ~*** 〔美口〕①公平地, 公正地. ②老实说, 实实在在 (*On the ~ I am awfully disappointed.* 老实说我完全失望). ***rise to higher ~*** 水平提高. — *a.* ***(~er; ~est;*** 〔英〕 ***~ler; ~lest)*** ①水平的,平坦的. ②同高度的;程度[水平,级别]相同的;【电】等位的;【乐】平调的. ③平稳的; 冷静的. ④平直的. ⑤均匀的; 平均分布的; 保持一定水平[状态]的; 恒定的. *~ ground* 平地. *make a surface ~* 使表面变平. *a ~ race* 势均力敌的赛跑. *sing [speak] in ~ tones* 用平板的声音唱[说]. *keep a ~ head in a crisis* 在危险时刻保持冷静的头脑. *give sb. a ~ look* 平直地看某人一眼. *keep a workshop at a ~ temperature* 保持车间恒温. ***be ~ with sb.*** 跟某人相齐; 跟某人同等. ***do one's ~ best*** 〔口〕竭尽全力. — *ad.* ①水平地,平坦地. ②准确, 一直. ③和…成水平, 同样高. ④和…不分优劣, 势均力敌地. *The missile went ~ to its mark.* 火箭准确打中目标. *fill a basin ~ with the brim* 把盆装满到盆边. *draw ~ with sb.* 同某人拉平 — *vt.* ①使成水平; 使平坦; 弄平; 平整. ②使同等; 拉平; 废除. ③推倒, 夷平. ④对准, 瞄准. ⑤测定高度. ⑥使(声音, 色调等)平板. *~ down the ground* 铲平地面. *~ up the ground* 填平地面. *~ a speech to the capacity of the audience* 按听众水平演讲. *~ all social distinctions* 消除一切社会差别. *~ a gun at the enemy* 把枪瞄准敌人. *~ a satire against sb.* 针对某人进行讽刺. — *vi.* ①用武器瞄准; 对准 *(at)*. ②用水平仪测量高度. ③【空】(着陆时) 水平飞行. ④拉平. ⑤坦率地对待. *I'll ~ with you.* 我将对你开诚布公. *~ the enemy stronghold in the dust = ~ the enemy stronghold to [with] the ground* 把敌人的堡垒夷平. ***~ off*** ①弄平,整平. ②达到同一水平; (物价等)稳定. ③(飞机降落前)水平飞行. ***~ up [down]*** 提高[降低]成同一水准,提高[降低]成一样,扯平,平整. ~ **crossing** 〔英〕(道路) 平面交叉点,道口,岔口. ~ **curve** = contour line. ~ **compensator** 分层补偿器. ~ **control** (信号)电平调整,级位控制. ~ **flight** 水平飞行. ~ **gauge** 水平仪;水位计. ~ **headed** *a.* 稳健的,头脑冷静的. ~ **indicator** 液面指示器;电平指示器. ~ **meter** 电平表, 电平测量器. ~ **of significance**【统】有效 (位) 水平 (= significance ~). **~-peg** *vi.* 〔英〕保持平衡, 保持均势. ~ **pressure** 扯平压力.

lev·el(l)·er [ˈlevələ] *n.* ①把事物弄平[使事物相等, 消除差别]的人[物]. ②水准测量员; 校平器, (钢板) 矫平机. ③平等主义者. ④〔L-〕(英国十七世纪的)平均主义者.

lev·el·(l)ing [ˈlevəliŋ] *n.* 测平, 校平; 平整(土地); 水准测量. *a ~ instrument [mechanism]* 水准仪. *a ~ machine* (道路)整平机;【冶】钢板矫平机. ~ **pole [rod, staff]** 水准(标)尺.

Le·ver[1] [ˈliːvə] *n.* 利弗〔姓氏〕.

le•ver² [ˈliːvə, Am. ˈlevə] *n.* ①杆,杠. *a ball* ~ 浮球杆. *a brake* ~ 闸杆. *a control* ~ 控制杆. *a throttle* ~ 节流杆. *a timing* ~ 定时杆. ②手段. *Pity is a* ~ *for quickening love.* 怜悯是加速爱情的手段. — *vt., vi.* 用杠杆撬动;撬开 *(along; up)*. *control* ~ 用杆操纵.

le•ver•age [ˈliːvəridʒ] *n.* ①杠杆作用. ②杠杆装置;杠杆机构. ③臂比,杠杆率;扭转力矩. ④达到目的的手段;势力;影响.

lev•er•et [ˈlevərit] *n.* 一岁的小兔.

lev•i•a•ble [ˈleviəbl] *a.* 可征收的(税等),得课税的(货物等).

le•vi•a•than [liˈvaiəθən] *n.* ①〔L-〕(《圣经》中象征邪恶的)海中怪兽. ②大船;巨型远洋舰;大海兽;庞然大物. ③势力大的人,大人物. ④〔L-〕《利维坦》〔英国十七世纪著作家霍布斯论国家组织的著作〕;权力集中的(君主)国家.

lev•i•er [ˈleviə] *n.* 强征人(尤指征税人).

lev•i•gate [ˈlevigeit] *vt.* ①粉碎,弄成粉;弄成糊. ②磨光,磨细. ③澄清,洗净;洗矿. **-ga•tion** [ˌleviˈgeiʃən] *n.*

lev•in [ˈlevin] *n.* 〔古〕电光.

Le•vi's [ˈliːvaiz] *n. pl.* 牛仔裤〔商标名,写作 levis〕.

lev•i•tate [ˈleviteit] *vt., vi.* (使)轻轻浮起,(使)飘浮空中. **-ta•tion** [ˌleviˈteiʃən] *n.* 悬浮,漂浮,浮置.

Le•vite [ˈliːvait] *n.* ①【圣】利未人,利未人的子孙. ②〔俚〕犹太人.

Le•vit•ic(al) [liˈvitik(əl)] *a.* 利未人的,利未族的.

lev•i•ty [ˈleviti] *n.* ①轻率,轻浮,轻薄. ②变化无常. ③〔罕〕轻.

le•vo- *comb. f.* 表示"向左的,左旋的": *levo*glucose, *levoro*tation.

le•vo•do•pa [ˌlevəuˈdəupə] *n.* 【药】=L-dopa.

le•vo•glu•cose [ˌliːvəuˈgluːkəus] *n.* 【化】左旋葡萄糖.

le•vo•gy•rate [ˌliːvəuˈdʒaireit] *a.* = levorotatory, levogyrous.

le•vo•ro•ta•tion [ˌliːvəurəuˈteiʃən] *n.* 【物】左旋.

le•vo•ro•ta•to•ry [liːvəˈrəutəˌtɔːri] *a.* ①左旋的,反时针方向转动的. ②使偏正光面,向左方旋转的〔如某些水晶等物〕.

lev•u•lin [ˈlevjulin] *n.* 【化】多缩左旋糖.

lev•u•lose [ˈlevjuˌləus] *n.* 【化】左旋糖,果糖.

Lev•y [ˈliːvi, ˈlevi] *n.* 利维〔姓氏〕.

lev•y [ˈlevi] *vt.* ①征收;索取. ②征集,征用. ③(动员)发动战争. ④【法】扣押. 索取. ~ *a fine [tax] on sb.* 向某人征收罚金〔税款〕. ~ *a ransom on sb.* 向某人索取赎金. ~ *troops* 征集军队. ~ *war against [upon]* ... 对…开战. — *vi.* ①征税,抽款. ②扣押财产. ~ ***black-mail upon*** 讹诈,敲诈. ~ ***on*** 扣押. — *n.* ①征税;派款;征收额. ②召集,征集,募集;征募兵额. *a capital* ~ 资本课税. *a* ~ *in kind* 征用实物. *green levies and veteran soldiers* 新兵和老兵. ~ *en masse* 〔F.〕= ~ in mass (战时)全民总动员.

lewd [luːd] *a.* ①好色的,淫猥的. ②〔古〕粗野的,卑鄙的,邪恶的. **-ly** *ad.* **-ness** *n.*

Lew•es [ˈlu(ː)is] *n.* 刘易斯〔姓氏〕.

Lew•is [ˈlu(ː)is] *n.* ①刘易斯〔姓氏,男子名,Louis 的异体〕. ②**Sinclair** ~ 辛克莱·刘易斯〔1885—1951 美国作家,获 1930 年诺贝尔文学奖〕.

lew•is [ˈlu(ː)is], **lew•is•son** [ˈluːisən] *n.* 【机】起重爪;吊楔;地脚螺栓.

lew•is•ite [ˈluːəˌsait] *n.* 【化】路易式毒气.

lex [leks] *n.* (*pl.* ***leges*** [ˈliːdʒiːz]) 〔L.〕法律. ~ ***loci*** [ˈləusai] 地方法律. ~ ***non scripta*** [nɔnˈskriptə] 不成文法. ~ ***scripta*** 成文法. ~ ***talionis*** [ˌtæliˈəunis] 同害惩罚法〔以其人之道还治其人的办法〕.

lex. [leks] = lexicon.

lex•eme [ˈleksiːm] *n.* 【语】词素,词位,词汇单位. **lex•em•ic** [-ˈsiːmik] *a.*

lex•i•cal [ˈleksikəl] *a.* ①词汇的. ②词典编纂上的. **-ly** *ad.*

lexicog. = ①lexicographer. ②lexicography.

lex•i•cog•ra•pher [ˌleksiˈkɔgrəfə] *n.* 词典编纂者.

lex•i•co•graph•i•cal [ˌleksikəˈgræfikəl] *a.* 词典编纂上的. ~ ***order*** 字母次序.

lex•i•cog•ra•phy [ˌleksiˈkɔgrəfi] *n.* 词典编纂(法),词典学.

lex•i•col•o•gy [ˌleksiˈkɔlədʒi] *n.* 【语】词汇学. **lex•i•co•log•i•cal** [-kəˈlɔdʒikl] *a.* **lex•i•col•o•gist** *n.*

lex•i•con [ˈleksikən] *n.* ①(尤指希腊语、希伯来语或拉丁语的)词典. ②特殊词汇,专门词汇.

lex•ig•ra•phy [lekˈsigrəfi] *n.* (以一个符号代表一个词的)符号文字.

lex•is [ˈleksəs] ***(pl. lex•es)*** *n.* 词,词汇.

ley [lei] *n.* 牧草地.

Ley•den [ˈleidn, ˈlaidn] *n.* 莱顿〔荷兰城市〕. ~ ***jar [bottle, vial]*** 【物】(在 Leyden 发明的)莱顿电瓶.

leze majesty [liːz] = lese majesty.

LF = low frequency【无】低频.

L/F = ledger folio 分类帐页.

lf = left fielder (棒球)左场(手).

l.f. = light face【印】细体铅字.

l.f.c. = low-frequency current 低频电流.

L.F.TK = light fast tank 轻型快速坦克.

L.G. = ①Life Guards〔英〕近卫(骑兵)团. ②Low German 低地德语.

l/g = grams per litre 克/升.

L.G.O.C. = London General Omnibus Company〔英〕伦敦通用公共汽车公司.

l.h. = left hand【乐】左手.

L.H.A. = Lord High Admiral〔英旧〕海军大臣.

L.H.D. = *Litterarum Humaniorum Doctor* (= Doctor of Humane letters) 希腊、拉丁古典文学博士.

L.H.T. = Lord High Treasurer〔英旧〕财政大臣.

L.I. = ①Long Island 长岛. ②Light Infantry 轻步兵. ③【物】low-intensity 低强度的.

Li = 【化】lithium. **li.** = link.

li [liː] *n.* (*pl.* ~)〔Chin.〕(中国里程单位)里.

li•a•bil•ity [ˌlaiəˈbiliti] *n.* ①责任,义务. ②〔*pl.*〕负债,债务 *(opp.* assets*)*. ③倾向;易于…的倾向〔性质〕. ④不利条件. *hold no* ~ *for damages* 不负赔偿责任. *limited [unlimited]* ~ 有限〔无限〕责任. ~ *for military service* 有服兵役义务. *assets and liabilities* 资产与负债. *meet one's liabilities* 偿还债务. ~ *to disease* 弱不禁风. ~ *to error* 容易犯错误. *Poor handwriting is a* ~ *in getting a job.* 拙劣的书法是求职的不利条件.

li•a•ble [ˈlaiəbl] *a.* ①(对…)应负(法律)责任的,有义务的. ②应受的,应服从的. ③有…倾向的,易…的,易陷于…的,易害…的;〔口〕大概,多半,很可能. *be* ~ *for a debt* = *be* ~ *to pay a debt* 有偿还债务责任. *be* ~ *to the law* 应服从法律. *be* ~ *to the penalty* 该受罚. *be* ~ *to tax* 应付税. *be* ~ *to catch cold* 容易伤风. *Difficulties are* ~ *to occur* 容易出问题. *He is* ~ *to fits of temper* 他动不动就发脾气. *He is* ~ *to come today.* 他今天很可能会来.

li•aise [liːˈeiz] *vi.* *(-ais•ed, -ais•ing)*〔主英口〕与…建立联系,连络 *(with)*.

li•ai•son [li(ː)ˈeizɑːn, -zn] *n.* 〔F.〕 ①【语音】连音〔指法语中词尾的无声辅音与后面一词的词头元音连结所成的发音;英语中指 r 与后面一词的词头元音连结所成的发音〕. ②【烹】加浓料〔使汤等浓厚用的鸡蛋等物〕. ③私通. ④【军】联络. ~ *officer* 联络官.

li•a•na [liˈɑːnə], **li•ane** [liˈɑːn] *n.* 【植】藤本植物,蔓生植物. ~ **rubber** 藤胶.

liang [ljɑːŋ] *n.* 〔Chin.〕(中国衡量单位)两.

li·ar [ˈlaiə] *n.* 说谎的人. *Show me a ～, and I will show you a thief.*〔谚〕说谎是偷窃的开始.

Li·as [ˈlaiəs] *n.*【地】①里阿斯统(早侏罗世). ②〔l-〕蓝色石灰岩. **Li·as·sic** [laiˈæsik] *a.*

lib [lib] = liberation. *women's* ～ 妇女解放(运动). ～**ber** 解放运动者 (*a women's* ～*ber* 妇女解放运动者).

lib. = ①liberal. ②library; librarian. ③〔L.〕*liber* (= book). ④〔L.〕*libra* (= pound).

li·ba·tion [laiˈbeiʃən] *n.* ①(倒酒在地上祭神的)奠酒; 祭奠用的酒. ②〔谑〕饮酒,酒.

Lib·by [ˈlibi] *n.* ①莉比〔女子名,Elizabeth 的昵称〕. ②利比〔姓氏〕.

li·bel [ˈlaibəl] *n.* ①诽谤文;【宗】诽谤的诉状. ②【法】诽谤,诽谤罪. ③侮辱,对人不公平. *sue sb. for* ～ 控告某人犯诽谤罪. *The greater the truth, the greater [worse] the* ～.〔谚〕事情越真实,诽谤越厉害〔相当于"道高一尺,魔高一丈"〕. *This photograph is a* ～ *on her.* 这张照片简直是诽谤〔把她照得太难看了〕. — *vt.* (〔英〕*-ll-*) ①污蔑,诽谤. ②【法】发表诽谤…的文件; 进行文字诽谤. ③【海事和教会法】提出书面控告; 控诉. ④对…作不好看的描画; 对…不够公平. — *vi.* 诽谤.

li·bel(l)·ant [ˈlaibələnt] *n.* ①诽谤者. ②(向海事或宗教裁判所起诉的)控告人.

li·bel(l)·ee [ˌlaibəˈliː] *n.* ①被诽谤者. ②(在海事或宗教裁判所中的)被控告者.

li·bel(l)·er, li·bel(l)·ist [ˈlaiblə, ˈlaiblist] *n.* 诽谤者.

li·bel(l)·ous [ˈlaibələs] *a.* ①诽谤的. ②爱中伤的. **-ly** *ad.*

li·ber [ˈlaibə, ˈliːbɛə] *n.* (*pl.* ***li·bri*** [ˈlaibrai, ˈliːbriː]) 〔L.〕书册; 簿册〔尤指契据登记簿〕.

lib·er·al [ˈlibərəl] *a.* ①自由人的; 不受束缚的. ②大方的; 慷慨的. ③心胸宽大的,思想开明的; 公正的,没有偏见的. ④丰富的,充足的. ⑤自由的,不拘泥于字义的,广泛的(解释等). ⑥自由主义的; 〔L-〕自由党的. *He is* ～ *of [with] his money.* 他用钱大方. *a* ～ *table* 丰盛的饭菜. ～ *ideas* 开明的思想. *a* ～ *translation* 意译. — *n.* ①思想开明的人. ②自由主义者. ③〔L-〕自由党党员,支持自由党的人. ～ **arts** 文科〔原意为自由人应具有的学识〕. ～ **education** 文科教育〔相对于职业教育,专门技术教育而言; 原意为自由人应受的教育〕. ～**-minded** *a.* 气量宽宏的; 思想解放的. **L- Party**〔英〕自由党. **L- Unionist**〔英〕自由统一党员. **-ly** *ad.* **-ness** *n.*

lib·er·al·ism [ˈlibərəlizəm] *n.* 自由主义. **lib·er·al·ist** *n., a.* 自由主义者(的). **lib·er·al·is·tic** [ˌlibərəˈlistik] *a.* 自由主义的.

lib·er·al·i·ty [ˌlibəˈræliti] *n.* ①思想开明; 气量大; 公平; 豪爽,磊落. ②大方,慷慨; 礼物. ③丰富,丰满.

lib·er·al·ize [ˈlibərəlaiz] *vt.* ①使自由化; 使自由主义化. ②放宽限制. ③解除官方控制. **-ization** *n.*

lib·er·ate [ˈlibəreit] *vt.* ①解放,释放; 解除; 使脱离. ②【化】释出,放出;【物】使(力)起作用. ③〔俚〕偷,劫掠〔尤指对于被打败的敌人〕. ～ *the mind from prejudice* 解除心中偏见. *John* ～*d two cameras.* 约翰打游击打到了两个照相机. **-d** 被解放了的 (*the* ～*d area* 解放区).

lib·er·a·tion [ˌlibəˈreiʃən] *n.* ①释放,解放. ②【化】释出,放出,析出(作用). *the Chinese People's L- Army* 中国人民解放军. *the* ～ *of heat* 放热. **-ism** *n.* 政教分立主义. **-ist** *n.* 政教分立主义者. *a.* 政教分立主义者的.

lib·er·a·tor [ˈlibəˌreitə] *n.* 解放者,释放者.

Li·ber·i·a [laiˈbiəriə] *n.* 利比里亚〔非洲〕.

Li·ber·i·an [laiˈbiəriən] *a.* 利比里亚的; 利比里亚人的; 利比里亚文化的. — *n.* 利比里亚人.

lib·er·tar·i·an [ˌlibəˈtɛəriən] *n.* ①【哲】意志自由论者. ②鼓吹公民充分自由权的人. — *a.* 意志自由论者的; 鼓吹公民充分自由权的. **-ism** *n.* 意志自由论; 公民拥有充分自由权论.

li·ber·té, é·ga·li·té, fra·ter·ni·té [libɛrˈtei egɑːliˈtei frɑːtɛrniˈtei]〔F.〕自由、平等、博爱〔法国一七八九年资产阶级革命的口号〕.

li·ber·ti·ci·dal [liˌbəːtiˈsaidl] *a.* 扼杀自由的.

li·ber·ti·cide [liˈbəːtisaid] *n.* ①扼杀自由. ②扼杀自由者. — *a.* = liberticidal.

lib·er·tine [ˈlibə(ː)tain, -tiːn] *n.* ①浪子,放荡的人. ②【宗】自由思想家. ③古罗马获得自由的奴隶. — *a.* 放荡的; 自由思想的. *a chartered* ～〔谑〕天下公认的浪子.

lib·er·tin·ism [ˈlibətinizəm] *n.* ①放荡,放纵. ②【宗】自由思想.

lib·er·ty [ˈlibəti] *n.* ①自由(权). ②解放,释放. ③〔*pl.*〕特许权; 特权〔自治权,选举权,参政权等〕. ④〔英〕自由地区,特许区域; (管)辖区; (某种)范围. ⑤放肆,无礼,不客气; 冒昧,擅自行动. ⑥【哲】意志自由. ⑦【海】(短时间)上岸许可〔较长时间为 leave〕. ～ *of action* 行动的自由. ～ *of choice* 选择的自由. ～ *of conscience* (= religious ～) 宗教〔信仰〕自由. *natural* ～ 天赋自由权. *Give me* ～*, or give me death.* 不自由,毋宁死. *the liberties of the city of London* 伦敦市的特权. ～ *of a prison* 犯人放风地段. *be guilty of a* ～ 放肆无礼. *Excuse my liberties.* 请原谅我的冒昧. ～ *in one's translation* 翻译不够忠实. *You may have the* ～ *of this room.* 你可以随时使用这个房间. ***at*** ～ ①自由,随意 (*at* ～ *to air one's views* 可以自由发表意见). ②(人、东西)闲着 (*I am very busy now, but I'll be at* ～ *presently.* 我现在很忙,不久就有空了). ***get one's*** ～ 获得自由,得到释放. ***set sb. at*** ～ 释放某人; 恢复某人的自由. ***take liberties with*** ①跟…无礼; 调戏(妇女) (*Don't take liberties with a stranger.* 别同陌生的人无礼). ②损害 (*take liberties with one's health* 糟蹋身体). ③歪曲,任意改变 (*take liberties with a text* 任意更改原文. *take liberties with grammar* 不顾语法规则). ***take the*** ～ ***of doing [to do]*** 冒昧行事. **L- Bell** "自由钟"〔美国费城独立厅的大钟,一七七六年七月四日鸣该钟宣布独立〕. ～ **cap** = cap of liberty. ～ **hall** 便厅〔指客人可以在此自由自在、不拘礼节的房间〕. ～ **man**〔英〕获准上岸的水手. ～ **pass**【军】外出许可,外出许可证. **L- Ship** "自由轮"〔美国第二次世界大战期间大量建造的一种万吨商船〕.

li·bid·i·nal [liˈbidnəl] *a.* libido 的,性欲的. **-ly** *ad.*

li·bid·i·nous [liˈbidinəs] *a.* 好色的,淫荡的. **-ly** *ad.* **-ness** *n.*

li·bi·do [liˈbaidəu] *n.* 性的本能,性欲;【心】"利比多"〔弗洛伊德心理分析学说中的精神动力,实际即是性的本能〕.

Li·bra [ˈlaibrə] *n.*〔L.〕【天】天平座; 天平宫.

li·bra [ˈlaibrə] *n.*〔L.〕(*pl.* ***-brae*** [-briː]) ①磅〔略 lb.〕. ②[ˈliːbrɑ] 镑〔略 £〕.

li·braire [liˈbrɛə] *n.*〔F.〕书店;〔古〕图书馆.

li·brar·i·an [laiˈbrɛəriən] *n.* ①图书馆长,图书管理员. ②图书馆管理学专家. ～**ship** 图书馆长〔图书管理学专家〕的职位〔资格〕.

li·brar·y [ˈlaibrəri] *n.* ①图书馆,书库; 藏书楼; 藏书. ②丛书,文库. *a circulating* ～ 流动图书馆. *a free* ～ 免费图书馆. *reference* ～ (书不外借的)参考图书馆. *have a* ～ *of 5,000 volumes* 藏书五千册. *Everyman's L-*〔英〕人人文库〔丛书〕. ***a walking*** ～ 活字典,博学家. ～ **edition** 图书馆版〔开本较大,装订较坚固的布面精装本〕. **L- of Congress** 国会图书馆〔美国于 1800 年建立的国家图书馆〕. ～ **science** 图书馆学. ～ **steps** 图书馆用(可折迭的)小梯.

li·brate [ˈlaibreit] *vi.* ①摆动. ②保持平衡.

li·bra·tion [laiˈbreiʃən] *n.* ①振动,摆动; 平衡. ②【天】天平动. *optical* ～ 光学天平动. ～ *of the moon* 月球的天平动.

li·bra·to·ry [ˈlaibrətəri] *a.* 摆动的,振动的; 保持平衡的.

li·bret·tist [liˈbretist] *n.* (歌剧的)脚本作者.

li·bret·to [li'bretəu] *n.* *(pl.* ~*s, -ti* [-ti:]) 歌剧脚本.
Li·bre·ville [ˌli:brə'vi:l] *n.* 利伯维尔〔加蓬首都〕.
li·bri ['laibrai] *n.* liber 的复数.
li·bri·form ['laibrəˌfɔ:m] *a.* 【植】韧型的.
Lib·ri·um ['libriəm] *n.* 〔或 l-〕【药】利眠宁 (= chlordiazepoxide).
Lib·y·a ['libiə] *n.* 利比亚〔非洲〕.
Lib·y·an ['libjən, -biən] *a.* 利比亚的; 利比亚人的. —*n.* 利比亚人.
lice [lais] *n.* louse 的复数.
li·ce·i·ty [lai'si:əti] *n.* 合法.
li·cence, li·cense ['laisəns] *n.* ①许可,特许; 许可证,特许证,执照. ②放纵, 放肆; (文艺、美术、音乐等的)奔放, 不羁, 破格. *a* ~ *to sell spirits* 出售酒类的许可. *give full* ~ *to do sth.* 授权放手做某事. *Have I your* ~ *to remove the fence?* 你让我拆除这篱笆么? *a* ~ *to practise medicine* 行医执照. *apply for a driving* ~ 申请驾驶执照. *grant a marriage* ~ 颁发结婚证书. *special* ~ (坎特伯雷大主教所发)结婚特别许可证. *The invading troops displayed the most unbridled* ~. 入侵军队胡作非为到了极点. ***under*** ~ 领有执照. —*vt.* 批准,许可; 发许可证[执照]. ~ ***sb. to practise as a doctor*** 批准某人作开业医生. ~ **fee** 牌照费. ~ **plate [tag]** (汽车等的)牌照.
li·cenced, li·censed ['laisənst] *a.* 得到许可的,领有执照的; 公认的. *a* ~ *house* 有执照的酒店[妓院]. ~ *premises* 特准卖酒的店家[地区]. *a* ~ *satirist* 公认的讽刺家.
li·cen·cee, -see [ˌlaisən'si:] *n.* 被许可的人,领有执照[许可证]的人; 特许酒店.
li·cen·cer, li·cen·ser, li·cen·sor ['laisənsə] *n.* 认可者,发许可证[执照]者. *a* ~ *of plays [films, the press]* 剧本[电影、出版物]检查官.
li·cen·sure ['laisənʃə, -ˌsuə] *n.* 许可证的发给〔如营业执照等〕.
li·cen·ti·ate [lai'senʃiit] *n.* ①硕士. ②(大学或学会等认可的) 有开业资格的人. ③无牧师资格而被允许传道的人.
li·cen·tious [lai'senʃəs] *a.* ①放肆的; 放荡的,淫荡的. ②〔罕〕不顾规则的,破格的(文体等). **-ly** *ad.* **-ness** *n.*
li·cet ['laiset] 〔L.〕(这是)准许[合法]的.
lich [litʃ] *n.* 〔Scot. 英方〕死尸; 尸体.
li·chee ['li:ˌtʃi:] *n.* = litchi.
li·chen ['laikən] *n.* ①【植】地衣. ②【医】苔癣. —*vt.* 使生满地衣.
li·chened ['laikend] *a.* 生着[盖满]地衣的.
li·chen·in ['laikənin] *n.* 【化】地衣淀粉.
li·chen·ol·o·gy [ˌlaikə'nɔlədʒi] *n.* 【植】地衣学.
li·chen·ous ['laikinəs] *a.* ①生满地衣的. ②苔癣病的.
lich·gate ['litʃgeit] *n.* 〔英〕有屋顶的公墓入口〔可暂时停放棺材等待主持牧师等到来〕.
licht [likt] *a., ad., n., vi., vt.* 〔Scot.〕light 的异体.
Li·ci·an ['liʃiən] *a.* 利西亚的; 利西亚人的; 利西亚语的. 〔利西亚,西南亚细亚地中海的古国〕. —*n.* ①利西亚人. ②利西亚语.
lic·it ['lisit] *a.* 合法的,正当的. **-ly** *ad.*
lick [lik] *vt.* ①舐; 舐吃. ②(波浪、火焰等)触及,蔓延,吞没,掠过. ③〔口〕鞭打; 打败,胜过. ~ *a saucer clean* 把碟子舐干净. *The flames* ~*ed up everything there.* 火焰吞没了那里的一切. *I cannot* ~ *a fault out of him.* 我无论怎样打都改不了他的缺点. *That man deserves to be well* ~*ed.* 那个人应当被人狠狠揍一顿. *This* ~*s me.* 我弄不清楚这是怎么回事. —*vi.* ①象舐东西一样蔓延; (波浪)轻轻拍打. ②胜过, 赢得, 高速行进. *go off as hard as one can* ~ 赶快跑走. ~ ***(all) creation*** = ~ ***everything*** 〔俚〕胜过一切; 无可比拟. ~ ***into shape*** 使象样; 教养; 锻炼. ~ ***off [away]*** 舐吃; 舐尽. ~ ***one's lips [chops]*** 切盼,馋涎欲滴. ~ ***sb.'s boots [feet, shoes, spittle]*** 巴结某人,奉承某人. ~ ***the dust*** 被杀; 屈服. ~ ***up*** 舐光; (火焰)烧光. —*n.* ①舐,一舐. ②一舐的量,少量,些许. ③〔美〕野兽跑去舐盐的盐渍地 (= salt lick). ④〔俚〕重打,痛殴. ⑤〔口〕速度,速力. ⑥〔俚〕轮到的机会. ⑦〔美俚〕(即兴插入的)爵士音乐装饰乐句. *put on a* ~ *of paint* 涂上一层薄漆. *big* ~*s* 〔美、澳〕费力的工作. *at a great* ~ = *(at) full* ~ 急忙. ***give a*** ~ ***and a promise*** (把工作)马马虎虎做好〔约定以后再去完成〕. ***give sb. a*** ~ ***with the rough side of one's tongue*** 对某人出言粗鲁,出恶言伤害某人. ***put in best [big, solid]*** ~***s*** 尽最大努力,苦干. **-spit(tle)** 马屁精,奉承者.
lick·er·ish ['likəriʃ] *a.* ①讲究吃的; 贪吃的; 狼吞虎咽的. ②渴望的. ③好色的,淫荡的. **-ly** *ad.* **-ness** *n.*
[1]**lick·e·ty-split** ['likəti'split] *ad.* 〔口〕极为迅速地.
[1]**lick·ing** ['likiŋ] *n.* ①舐. ②〔口〕狠狠的一顿打; 〔俚〕惨败. ***get a good*** ~ 被痛打. ***give sb. a good*** ~ 痛打某人. ***take the*** ~ 遭惨败.
Lick Ob·ser·va·to·ry 李克天文台〔美国加利福尼亚州汉密尔顿山顶上〕.
lic·o·rice ['likəris] *n.* = liquorice.
lic·tor ['liktə] *n.* (古罗马的) 执法吏〔肩荷象征刑法的束棒, 在行政长官前面喝道, 并执行捕捉人犯等事的小吏〕.
lid [lid] *n.* ①盖子; 〔美俚〕帽子. ②眼睑 (= eyelid). ③【动】= operculum. ④制止,取缔. ⑤〔美俚〕一小包大麻烟〔约一盎司〕. *clamp[clap] a* ~ *on gambling* 取缔赌博. ***blow one's*** ~ 发脾气,勃然大怒. ***blow the*** ~ ***off sth.*** 揭盖子,把丑事公开出来. ***flip one's*** ~ 〔美俚〕①大发脾气. ②失去理智. ③放声狂笑. ***keep down the*** ~ = ***keep the*** ~ ***on*** 隐瞒罪恶. ***put the*** ~ ***on*** ①〔英俚〕结束. ②〔美俚〕禁止,取缔. ③胜过一切,冠绝. ***sit on the*** ~ 压制; 镇压. ***take the*** ~ ***off*** 揭盖子,揭露丑事. ***the*** ~ ***is on*** 事情完蛋了,无话可说了. ***with the*** ~ ***off*** 开着盖儿; 使丑事暴露于众. —*vt.* 给装盖子,盖盖子.
li·dar ['laidə] *n.* ①激光雷达. ②激光定位器. ③光探测和测距.
lid·ded ['lidid] *a.* ①有盖子的,盖着的. ②长着…眼睑的; 眼睑呈…状的. *with heavy-*~*eyes* 眼皮重垂着.
Lid·del(l) ['lidl, li'del] *n.* 利德尔〔姓氏〕.
lid·less ['lidlis] *a.* ①无盖的. ②无眼睑的. ③〔诗〕(眼睛)睁着的; 注视的.
Li·do ['li:dəu] *n.* ①丽都〔意大利威尼斯附近一个小岛,为著名的游乐地〕. ②〔l-〕海滨浴场; (露天)游泳池〔尤指远洋客轮上的〕.
lie[1] [lai] *vi.* ***(lay*** [lei]; ***lain*** [lein]; ***ly·ing)*** ①躺, 横卧〔过去分词不常用, *I have lain down* 可改作 *I have been lying down*〕. ~ *face downward* 俯卧. ~ *in bed* 睡觉. ~ *on a bed* 躺在床上. ~ *on one's back* 仰卧. ~ *on one's side* 侧卧. ②〔常带表语〕(静止不动地)呆着. ~ *idle* 不活动; (资金)呆滞. ~ *motionless* 呆着不动. ~ *sick* 卧病. ③(东西)被平放. *Let it* ~. 让它在那里(别动). *Snow* ~*s thick on the fields.* 田野里铺着厚厚一层雪. *The book* ~*s open on the table.* 那本书摊在桌上. *The land* ~*s waste.* 土地荒废了. ④东西被存放. *the fund lying at the bank* 存在银行的基金. ⑤被埋葬. ~ *in the cemetery* 葬在公墓. ⑥在,位于. *Japan* ~*s (to the) east of China.* 日本位于中国以东. *The house* ~*s high.* 这房子座落在高处. ⑦(抽象事物)存在, 在于, 有(…关系). *How* ~*s the land?* 情况如何. *The choice* ~*s between death and dishonour.* 在死亡与受辱之间任择其一. *The difficulty* ~*s here.* 困难就在这里. ⑧(风景等)展现,伸展. *A bright future* ~*s ahead.* 前途光明. *the landscape lying before us* 在我们面前展现的风景. *The path* ~*s along the coast.* 路线沿着海岸展开. ⑨(船只)停泊; (部队)驻扎; (猎鸟等)蹲着. ~ *at anchor* (抛锚)停泊着. ⑩处于某种状态. *Don't leave your books lying about.* 别把你的

书四处乱扔. *His plans* ~ *hidden.* 他的计划还不清楚. *How do they* ~ *to each other?* 他们之间的关系怎样? ⑪【法】成立,可受理. *The appeal does not* ~. 控诉不成立. ***as far as in me*** ~***s*** 尽我的力量. ~ ***about*** 散在. ~ ***against*** 靠在. ~ ***along*** 躺成大字形,尽量伸直手脚;【海】因侧风歪朝一边. ~ ***along the land [shore]*** 沿岸航行. ~ ***at sb.'s door*** (责任)在某人. ~ ***at one's heart*** …挂在心上;老是思慕着. ~ ***at the mercy of*** 处在…操纵之下,被…支配着. ~ ***back*** 向后靠. ~ ***by*** ①躺在…边上. ②近在手边,由…保管着. ③放在一旁,没有使用. ④休息. ⑤【海】= ~ to. ~ ***[keep] close*** 躲着,挤在一块. ~ ***dead*** 〔美〕躲着,隐藏着. ~ ***doggo*** 〔口〕隐伏不动. ~ ***down*** ①躺下. ②〔口〕躺在睡椅上休息 (~ *down on the job* 不干活,磨洋工). ③屈服;盲从 (*take it lying down* 俯首帖耳地屈服). ~ ***down under*** 甘受(侮辱等). ~ ***heavy [hard] (up) on*** 压迫,使痛苦. ~ ***in*** ①(分娩后)坐月子. ②(原因、本质等)在于,存在于 (*The case* ~*s in a nutshell.* 这件事情用一句话就可以说明了). ~ ***in sb.*** ①集中在,全在 (*All their hopes* ~ *in him.* 他们的希望全在他身上). ②依…而定,系于;…能做得到. ~ ***in the way*** 妨害,阻碍. ~ ***in wait for*** 埋伏着等待. ~ ***low*** ①伏卧. ②隐蔽,不露声色. ③死. ④受屈辱. ~ ***off*** ①(船)稍微离开(陆地或他船). ②〔俚〕(赛跑中)初跑时控制速度. ③暂时停止工作,歇一歇. ~ ***on [upon]*** ①落在…的肩上(*It* ~ *on us to lick illiteracy.* 扫除文盲是我们的责任). ②依赖 (~ *on the result* 要看结果如何). ③成为…的负担,压迫. (~ *heavy on one's conscience* 良心非常难受. ~ *heavy on one's stomach* (食物)滞积胃中). ~ ***open*** 开着,暴露着. ~ ***over*** ①事情暂时搁置,缓办 (*Let the matter* ~ *over until next month.* 把这个问题留到下月再解决吧). ②(支票等)过期未付. ~ ***to*** (船)顶风停住;集中全力在…(*The crew lay to their oars.* 船员拼命划桨). ~ ***under*** 蒙受,遭到. ~ ***up*** ①卧床;病倒(不能出门). ②退隐. ③(船)入坞. ~ ***with*** ①和…发生性关系. ②(责任、义务、决定权等)在于… (*It* ~*s with you to decide.* 该由你决定). — *n.* ①位置,状态. ②巢,穴,窝. ③(高尔夫球的)球位. ④〔英口〕躺;休息. *go and have a* ~ 去躺一下. **~abed** 睡懒觉的人. **~-down** 小睡,小憩. **~-in** ①〔口〕睡懒觉. ②卧地示威.

lie[2] [lai] *n.* ①谎言,谎话. ②虚伪,欺诈; 假象. *L-s have short legs.* 〔谚〕谎言终究要败露. *act a* ~ (用实际行动)骗人. *a black* ~ 用心险恶的谎话. *a white* ~ 无恶意的谎话. *His promise was a big* ~. 他的诺言是个大欺骗. *worship a* ~ 盲目崇拜错误的事物. *He would not take the* ~. 他不服气别人说他撒谎. ***a*** ~ ***(made) out of (the) whole cloth*** = ***a*** ~ ***with a latchet*** 说得天花乱坠的谎话. ***give sb. the*** ~ 指责某人说谎. ***give the*** ~ ***to*** 当面拆穿…的谎话;证明虚伪,和…相矛盾. ***live a*** ~ 过欺骗人的生活. ***nail a*** ~ ***to the counter*** 揭穿弄虚作假[谎言]. ***swap*** ~***s*** 〔美口〕讲空话,闲谈,胡扯. ***the big*** ~ ①弥天大谎. ②编造谎言并大肆宣传的骗人手段. — *vi., vt.* ***(lied; lying)*** 说谎;欺骗;迷惑. ~ *oneself out of trouble* 聊以自慰. ~ *sb. into doing sth.* 骗某人去做某事. ~ *sb. out of his money* 骗某人钱财. ~ ***away*** 骗取(名誉等),骗去. ~ ***in one's teeth [throat]*** 〔古〕无耻地瞪着眼[当面]撒谎. ~ ***like a gas-meter*** 乱撒谎. ~ **detector** 〔美〕测谎器.

Lieb·frau·milch [ˈliːbfrauˌmilk; G. ˈliːpfrauˌmilkh] *n.* 〔G.〕圣母酒〔一种来茵区白葡萄酒〕.

Lie·big [ˈliːbig], **J. Baron von** 李比希 〔1803—1873, 德国化学家〕.

Liech·ten·stein [ˈliktənˌstain] *n.* 列支敦士登〔欧洲〕.

lied [liːd] *n.* ***(pl. lied·er*** **[-ə])** 〔G.〕歌曲,浪漫曲〔主要指十九世纪德国的浪漫曲〕.

Lie·der·kranz [ˈliːdəˌkrɑːnts] *n.* 〔G.〕①【商标】歌王干酪. ②男声合唱团. ③一组歌曲.

lief [liːf] *ad.* 欣然,乐意地. ~ ***or loath*** 不管愿意不愿意. ***would [***〔古〕***had] as*** ~ ***…*** *(as)* 宁…(不…);(与其…)不如… (*I would [had] as* ~ *go there as anywhere.* 我宁愿到那里也不到别处). ***would [had] liefer … than …*** 宁…不…,与其…不如… (*I would liefer die than surrender.* 我宁愿死也不投降). — *a.* 〔古〕①乐意的,情愿的. ②亲爱的.

Li·ège [liˈeiʒ] *n.* 列日〔比利时城市〕.

liege [liːdʒ] *n.* ①君主,王侯. ②〔the ~s〕臣民,家臣. — *a.* ①君主的, 至上的. ②臣民的; 君臣关系的. *my* ~*!* (称呼)陛下! *a* ~ *lord* 君主. ~ *subjects* 臣民. ③忠诚的. **-man** ①臣民. ②忠实的部下.

li·en[1] [ˈli(ː)ən] *n.* 【法】扣押权,留置权. ***have a*** ~ ***on*** 对…有留置权. ***have a prior*** ~ ***on*** 对…有先取权.

li·en[2] [ˈlaien] *n.* 〔L.〕【解】脾 (=spleen). **-al** *a.* 【医】脾炎的.

li·e·ni·tis [ˌlaiəˈnaitis] *n.* 【医】脾炎.

li·er [ˈlaiə] *n.* 躺卧者.

li·erne [liːˈəːn] *n.* 【建】枝肋.

lieu [ljuː] *n.* 处所. ***in*** ~ ***of*** 代,代替.

Lieut. = Lieutenant.

Lieut. Col. = Lieutenant Colonel 〔英〕陆军[海军陆战队]中校;〔美〕陆军[空军、海军陆战队]中校.

Lieut. Comdr. = Lieutenant Commander 〔英、美〕海军少校.

Lieut. Gen. = Lieutenant General 〔英〕陆军[海军陆战队]中将;〔美〕陆军[空军、海军陆战队]中将.

Lieut. Gov. = Lieutenant Governor (省或地区的)代理总督,副总督;〔美〕副州长.

lieu·ten·an·cy [〔英陆军〕 lefˈtenənsi, 〔英海军〕 ləˈt-; 〔美〕 ljuːˈt-] *n.* 陆军中尉[海军上尉等]的职位[任期].

lieu·ten·ant [〔英陆军〕 lefˈtenənt, 〔英海军〕-ləˈt-; 〔美〕 ljuːˈt-] *n.* ①副官. ②〔英〕陆军中尉,海军上尉. ③〔美〕海军上尉. *deputy* ~ 〔英〕副郡长. *a first* ~ 〔美〕陆军[空军]中尉,海军上尉. *a second* ~ 〔中、美〕陆军[空军]少尉;〔英〕陆军少尉[空军少尉叫 *pilot officer*]. *a* ~ *of junior grade* 〔美〕海军中尉. *a sub-*~ 〔英〕海军中尉. *an acting sub-*~ 〔英〕海军少尉. ~ **colonel** 陆军中校. ~ **commander** 海军少校. ~ **general** 陆军中将. ~ **governor** 〔英〕代理总督,副总督;〔美〕代理州长,副州长.

lieve [liːv] *ad., a.* = lief.

life [laif] *n.* ***(pl. lives*** **[laivz])** ①生命,性命. ②一生;寿命;【原】(亚原子粒子的)生命期;使用期限,耐久性. ③人生,人事;世间,尘世. ④生计,生活. ⑤传记. ⑥〔集合词〕生物. ⑦实物;原物(大小). ⑧生命力;精神,生气;弹性;精华,主要力量. ⑨被保险者. ⑩无期徒刑. *Many lives were lost.* 死了不少人. *sacrifice [give, lay down] one's* ~ *for the country* 为国牺牲. *There is no* ~ *on the moon.* 月球上没有生命. *the average* ~ *of a nation* 一国人口的平均寿命. *the* ~ *of an artificial satellite* 人造卫星的寿命. *the* ~ *of the present Government* 现内阁的寿命. *While there is* ~ *there is hope.* 〔谚〕一息尚存,希望不灭;留得青山在,不怕没柴烧. *a* ~ *of struggle* 战斗的一生. *a matter of* ~ *and death* 生死攸关的事情. *devote one's whole* ~ *to the study of science* 一辈子献身于研究科学. *high [low]* ~ 上层[下层]生活. *lead [live] a happy* ~ 过幸福生活. *political* ~ 政治生涯. *struggle for* ~ 生存竞争. *way of* ~ 生活方式. *begin* ~ *as a worker* 工人出身. *enter upon* ~ 踏进社会. *get on in* ~ 立身处世. *see much of* ~ 见过不少世面. *see nothing of* ~ 没见过世面. *The L- of Plato* 《柏拉图传》. *animal* ~ 动物. *bird* ~ 鸟类. *forest* ~ 林中生物. *insect* ~ 昆虫. *plant* ~ 植物. *a* ~ *class* 人体写生课. *a still* ~ 静物画. *as large as* ~ 象实物那样大. *The portrait is drawn from (the)* ~. 这幅像是写生的. *The portrait is drawn to the* ~. 这幅像画得唯妙唯肖. *full of* ~ 生气勃勃.

add [give] ～ *to an article* 增加文章的生气. *the* ～ *of the society* 社会的中心人物. *The batsman was given a* ～. 击球员获得新机会. *a bad* ～ 估计活不到平均寿命的人. *a good* ～ 估计会超过平均寿命的人. *my dear* ～ 我的命根子. *If found guilty, he will get* ～. 如果证实有罪,他将被判处无期徒刑. *the* ～ *of a bow* 弓的弹力. ***a future*** ～【宗】来生. ***all one's*** ～ 一辈子,毕生,终生. ***anything for a*** ～ 只要能安宁,什么都行. ***as much as one's*** ～ ***is worth*** 〔口〕性命攸关. ***attempt the*** ～ ***of sb.*** 企图弄死某人. ***be settled in*** ～ 生活得到安顿. ***Bless my*** ～ = Bless me. ***bother [harass, nag, plague, worry] the*** ～ ***out of sb.*** 跟某人纠缠不休. ***breathe [infuse] (a) new*** ～ ***into*** = give new ～ to 给予生气, 赋予生机. ***bring to*** ～ 使苏醒, 使复活. ***carry [take] one's*** ～ ***in one's hands*** 手里提着脑袋过日子,过冒险生活. ***choke the*** ～ ***out of sb.*** 把某人闷死. ***come to*** ～ 苏醒过来. ***depart (from) this*** ～ 离开人间,逝世. ***escape with bare*** ～ 仅以身免,死里逃生. ***escape with*** ～ ***and limb*** 仅以身免,死里逃生. ***eternal*** ～【宗】永生. ***expectation of*** ～ (=〔美〕～ ***expectancy***) 估计寿命. ***fight for dear*** ～ 死拼,作殊死战. ***flee [run] for dear [one's]*** ～ 拼命跑走. ***for*** ～ ①终身. ②为逃[保]命. ***for one's*** ～ = ***for dear [very]*** ～ ①为逃[保]命. ②拼命. ***for the*** ～ ***of me*** 即使要我的命,无论如何(也不…等). ***from (the)*** ～ 从原物,用原物做范本. ***get a chance in*** ～ 得到出头[发迹]的机会. ***have the time of one's*** ～ 〔俚〕过着一生中最快乐的时期. ***How's*** ～ 〔口〕你近来生活好么? ***I'll bet my*** ～ 我敢打赌. ***in*** ～ ①生前, 活着的时候 (*late in* ～ 在晚年). ②完全, 全然 (*anything in* ～ (无论)什么都. *nothing in* ～ 决没有,毫不). ***insure one's*** ～ 保人寿险. ***lay down one's*** ～ 抛弃生命,牺牲生命. ***lead a fast*** ～ 过放荡的生活. ***lead sb. a dog's*** ～ 使某人过悲惨的生活. ***lead [live] a double*** ～ 过双重人格的生活,搞两面派. ～ ***for*** ～ 以命偿命. ***lose one's*** ～ 死. ***make one's own*** ～ 自己谋生. ***not on your*** ～ 〔口〕决不,绝不可能. ***on my*** ～ =upon my ～. ***pawn one's*** ～ 以生命保证. ***raise [recall] to*** ～ 使苏醒,使复活. ***ride for dear*** ～ 拼命奔驰. ***safe in*** ～ ***and limb*** 安全无恙. ***see*** ～ ①交游广. ②见世面. ***seek the*** ～ ***of*** = attempt the ～ of. ***sell one's*** ～ ***dearly*** 奋勇杀敌,负伤阵亡. ***small*** ～ (肖像)比真人略小的尺寸. ***take [get] a new [fresh] lease of*** ～ 死里逃生. ***take one's (own)*** ～ 自杀. ***take one's*** ～ ***in both hands and eat it*** 过惊涛骇浪的冒险生活. ***take sb.'s*** ～ 干掉某人. ***the*** ～ ***of Riley*** 〔美俚〕放纵的生活. ***the*** ～ ***of the party*** 社交场合中的中心人物. ***the*** ～ ***of the world to come*** = ***the other [future]*** ～ 来世. ***this*** ～ 现世. ***to the*** ～ 大小和实物一样,逼真. ***true to*** ～ 逼真,栩栩如生. ***upon ['pon] my*** ～ 拼着这条命,誓必. **～-and-death, ～-or-death** *a.* 生死攸关的,极重要的. ～ **annuity** 终身年金. ～ **assurance** 〔英〕= ～ insurance. ～ **belt** 救生带. ～**blood** ①〔诗〕生命必需的血液,鲜血;〔喻〕生命线,命脉;力量的泉源. ②嘴唇[眼睑]的痉挛. **～boat** 救生艇. ～ **buoy** 救生圈. ～ **cycle** 【生】①生活周期. ②与上述类似的周期,生命周期. ～ **estate** 非世袭的终身财产. ～ **expectancy** 估计寿命, 平均寿命. **～-force** 生命力. **～-giv·ing** *a.* ①给与生命的. ②提神的. **～guard** ①〔*Life-Guards*〕〔英〕近卫骑兵旅. ②近卫兵. ③(机车上的)排障器. ④〔美〕(游泳场的) 救生员 (= ～ savers). ～ **history** ①【生】生活史; 生活周期. ②人生历程. ～ **insurance** 〔美〕人寿保险. **～in·terest** 终身财产所有权. **～jacket** 救生衣. **～-kiss** 口对口人工呼吸. ～ **line** ①救生索; (潜水员的)通报绳. ②命脉, 生命线. **～long** *a.* 终身的, 毕生的,一生的. **～manship** 虚张声势以达到目的的手法. ～ **member** 终身会员. ～ **net** (消防队用的)救生网. ～ **office** 人寿保险业; 人寿保险公司办事处. ～ **peer** 一代贵族. ～ **peerage** 一代贵族的爵位. ～ **preserver** ①救生用具; 浮衣. ②〔英〕护身用具[手枪、带刀手杖、棍棒等]. ～ **raft** 救生筏. **～saver** ①救命的人. ②〔美〕救生员. ③〔俚〕应急的东西. **～saving** ①*a.* 救生的. ②*n.* 救生[尤指救护溺水者免于溺毙]. ～ **science** 〔常 *pl.*〕生命科学[所指包括生物学,医学,人类学,社会学]. **～-size(d)** *a.* 同原物[自身]一样大的. ～ **span** = ～ time. **～-spring** 生命的源泉. **～-strings** 〔*pl.*〕生命线. ～ **style** 生活作风, 生活方式. **～-support system** (宇航员等的)生命维持系统. ～ **table** = mortality table. **～time** ①一生,终生. ②【原】寿命. **～-work** 毕生事业; 一生中最重要的工作. ～ **zone** 生物带. **-like** *a.* 逼真的,栩栩如生的.

life·less [ˈlaiflis] *a.* ①无生命的;〔尤指〕从未曾有过生命的. ②无生气的. ③已死的. ④无生物的. ⑤呆板的,单调沉闷的;不活跃的. ***a*** ～ ***planet*** 无生物行星. **-ly** *ad.* **-ness** *n.*

lif·er [ˈlaifə] *n.* ①无期徒刑. ②无期徒刑犯. ③职业军人.

lift [lift] *vt.* ①举起,使升起,提起,抬起;提高;提升. ②使高尚;鼓舞. ③运送,搬运;空运 (= airlift). ④偷窃,偷去;抄袭,剽窃. ⑤起出,拔起;掘出;拔营. ⑥(把板球等)向高空击去. ⑦〔美〕清偿; 赎出,赎取(典押物). ⑧解除,撤除,撤消. ～ *that parcel down the shelf* 把那包东西从架上拿下来. ～ *weights* 举重. *Mount Qomolangma* ～*s its cone into the clouds.* 珠穆朗玛峰顶高耸入云. ～ *the tariff* 〔美〕提高税率. *His wallet was* ～*ed.* 他的皮夹子被人扒走了. ～ *a passage from the book* 从书中剽窃一段文字. ～ *a mortgage* 偿付抵押债款. ～ *the ban on* 解除对…的禁令. ～ *the curfew.* 撤消宵禁. —*vi.* ①被提高,升起. ②消散. ③水涨船高,(船)乘浪升高. ④(地面)隆起. ⑤耸立. *The window will not* ～.(往上提起的)窗子开不开. *The fog* ～. 雾消散. ～ ***off***【空】起飞. ～ ***one's hat*** (把帽子从头上拿起一下)脱帽致敬. ～ ***sb.'s face*** 用美容术伸平面皱,为某人整容. ～ ***up*** 提起来,上升. ～ ***up a cry*** 高声大叫. ～ ***up one's [the] eyes [face]*** 仰望,注视;祈祷. ～ ***up one's [the] feet*** 快去援救. ～ ***(up) one's [the] hand*** ①(举手)起誓. ②祈祷. ～ ***(up) one's [the] hand against*** 反叛,攻击,压制. ～ ***up one's head*** 抬头; (因自信,得意等)昂起头来;狂喜. ～ ***up one's [the] heel*** 不以礼相待. ～ ***up with pride*** 得意扬扬. — *n.* ①举起;抬高;提升,搬起. ②高昂的姿态. ③情绪昂扬,精神振奋. ④(一次)举重量,起重量;【矿】(一次)采掘量. ⑤【机】扬力,(水泵)扬程;【空】升力,浮力. ⑥〔英〕电梯;吊车;升降机 (=〔美〕elevator). ⑦起重机;千斤顶. ⑧鞋后跟皮的一层. ⑨土地的隆起, 小丘. ⑩(雾等的)消散. ⑪帮助, 帮忙, 照顾. *a* ～ *in cost* 费用[成本]提高. *walk with the proud* ～ *of one's head* 昂首阔步. *a* ～ *of sheet steel* 一次吊起的钢板. ***give sb. a*** ～ 给某人以鼓励;帮某人的忙;在半路上让某人搭自己的车;扶某人上车. ***a dead*** ～ (不用起重机等机械)用人力硬搬;〔喻〕费力的艰巨任务. **～boy** 〔英〕= ～man. ～ **bridge** 升降吊桥. ～ **cable**, ～ **wire** 【空】升力线,升力索. **～-drag ratio** 【空】升阻比,(空)气动(力)性能. ～ **hammer** 落锤. ～ **irrigation** 抽水灌溉. **～man** *n.* 〔英〕开电梯的工人. **～-off** 【空】保险伞下降;(飞机、导弹等的)起飞; 发射(时刻),起离(时刻),初动. ～ **pump** 【机】扬水泵,提升泵. ～ **truck** 起重机车[车辆];自动装卸车.

lift·er [ˈliftə] *n.* ①起重者. ②升降机,起重机. ③推料机. ④升降杆,推杆. ⑤电磁铁的衔铁. ⑥～ **winch** 起重绞车.

lift·ing [ˈliftiŋ] *n.* 举起;吊起;上升. ～ **area** 升力面积. ～ **body** 【空】宇宙和高空飞行两用机[可重返大气层并自行着陆]. ～ **gear** 起重机. ～ **jack** 千斤顶;起重吊车. ～ **pins** 推杆;造型机顶杆. ～ **ring** 提圈. ～ **screw**

螺旋起重机;升力螺旋桨.

lig·a·ment [ˈligəmənt] *n.* *(pl.* ～*s,* ～*a* [-mentə]*)* ①系带. ②【解】带,韧带.

lig·a·men·tal, ～tar·y, ～tous [ˌligəˈmentl, -ˈmentəri, -ˈmentəs] *a.* 带状的,韧带(似)的.

li·gan [ˈlaigən] *n.* = lagan.

lig·and [ˈligənd, ˈlaigənd] *n.* 【化】配合基[体],向心配合(价)体.

lig·ase [ˈligˌeis] *n.* 【生】连接酶.

li·gate [ˈlaigeit] *vt.* 绑扎;【医】结扎(血管等).

li·ga·tion [laiˈgeiʃən] *n.* ①绑扎. ②【医】结扎;缚法;结扎线,缚线.

lig·a·ture [ˈligətʃuə] *n.* ①绑扎,结扎. ②带子;绷带;【医】结扎线;缚线. ③连系物. ④【印】连字〔如 æ, fi 等〕;连字符号(-),连字弧线. ⑤【乐】连结线,连音. — *vt.* 绑扎,结扎.

li·geance [ˈlaidʒəns; Am. ˈli-] 效忠;忠心〔如臣对君,人民对政府等〕.

li·ger [ˈlaigə] *n.* (雄狮和雌虎生的)狮虎.

light[1] [lait] *n.* ①光,光线;光明,亮光 *(opp.* darkness*).* *Hang the picture in a good* ～. 把那幅画挂在能看清楚的地方. ②发光体,光源;灯,信号灯;灯塔;天体. *a blackout* ～ 防空灯. *ancient* ～*s* 保护光线不受挡住的权利. *the greater* ～ 太阳. *the lesser* ～ 月亮. ③〔俚〕(舞台的)脚光. *before the* ～*s* 在舞台上;登台演出. ④日光;白昼;黎明. *Let's leave before the* ～ *fails.* 我们要在天黑以前离开. *L- is breaking.* 天已破晓. *The attack was on at the first* ～. 天一亮,进攻就开始了. ⑤窗;天窗;取光孔;(温室的)玻璃屋顶[墙壁];【法】光线不受(邻居)阻碍权. *a room with* ～*s on three sides* 三方都有光线进来的房间. ⑥明白,显露;启发,说明;教化. *new* ～*s on a question* 说明问题的新线索. ⑦见解,见识;眼光. *see sb. in a new* ～ 用新眼光看待某人. ⑧光;〔诗〕视力;眼神;〔*pl.*〕〔俚〕眼睛. ⑨名家,权威;明星. *the guiding [shining]* ～ 显赫人物. *the leading* ～*s of diplomacy* 外交界头面人物. *the literary* ～*s of the day* 当代文豪. ⑩【宗】荣光,福祉. *the inner* ～ 灵光. ⑪(绘画中的)明亮部分,投光部分. ～ *and shade* ①明暗. ②强烈的对比. *the high* ～ *of a picture* 画的强光部分. ⑫火花,点火物. *a box of* ～*s* 〔英〕一盒火柴. *put a* ～ *to the fire* 点火. *strike a* ～ 擦火柴. *Will you give me a* ～*?* 借个火儿. ⑬【法】采光权(= ancient ～s). ⑭〔*pl.*〕智能. *do one's best according to one's* ～*s* 尽力而为. ***A*** ～ ***breaks in upon sb.*** 某人恍然大悟. ***be [go] out like*** ～〔美俚〕①醉得不省人事. ②被打昏;昏睡. ***between the*** ～***s*** 在黄昏时. ***between two*** ～***s*** 在夜里;乘黑夜. ***bring to*** ～ 暴露,揭露. ***by the*** ～ ***of nature*** 本能地,自然而然地. ***cast [shed, show, throw, turn] light on [upon] sth.*** 阐明. ***come to*** ～ 显露,出现. ***expose sth. to the*** ～ ***of day*** 把某事暴露在光天化日之下. ***fast*** ～ 耐光. ***get in sb.'s*** ～ 挡人光线,妨碍人. ***get out of the*** ～ 不妨碍. ***give a [the] green*** ～ 开绿灯,准许前进. ***give*** ～ ***on [upon]*** 使…明白,使明显. ***in a good [bad]*** ～ 在看得清楚[不清楚]的地方. ***in*** ～ 被光线照着. ***in the*** ～ ***of*** ①以…的模样. ②按照,根据. ③当作… (*view his conduct in the* ～ *of a crime* 把他的行为当作犯罪看). ～ ***of one's eye [eyes]*** 心爱的人,掌上明珠. ～ ***of sb.'s countenance*** 〔谑〕照顾,恩惠,好意. ***man of*** ～ ***and leading*** 权威,大家. ***place [put] in the clearest*** ～ 阐述得非常清楚. ***place [put] sb. [sth.] in a different*** ～ 对某人[某事]另有一种看法. ***place [put] sb. [sth.] in a false*** ～ 使人误解某人[某事];把某人[某事]说得面目全非. ***place [put] sb. [sth.] in a favourable*** ～ 把某人[某事]说得特别好. ***put out [quench] sb.'s*** ～ 杀死某人,送某人归天. ***put out the*** ～熄灯. ***see a [the] red*** ～ 觉察到危险. ***see*** ～ 理会. ***see [view] sth. in a different*** ～ 从另一种观点来看某事. ***see sth. in its true*** ～ 对某事有正确的见解. ***see sth. in the same*** ～ 对某事有同样的看法. ***see the*** ～ ***(of day)*** ①(人)出生,出世. ②领悟. ***set*** ～ ***to*** 点火. ***shut one's*** ～ ***off*** 死. ***stand [be] in one's own*** ～ ①背光. ②损害自己的利益. ***stand [be] in sb.'s*** ～ ①挡住某人的光线. ②妨碍某人前程. ***switch [turn] off the*** ～***s*** 关电灯. ***switch [turn] on the*** ～***s*** 开电灯. ***white*** ～ ①白昼的光. ②公正的判断. — *vt.* ***(light·ed*** [ˈlaitid] ***lit*** [lit]***)*** ①点火,点燃. ～ *a cigarette* 点着香烟. ②照亮,照耀. ③使发亮,光润,使春风满面. ④用灯照亮道路. ～ *sb. to bed* 点灯带人去睡. — *vi.* ①点火,点着(火). *He fished out a cigarette and lit up.* 他摸出一支烟来点着了. ②变亮;(眼睛)发亮,满面春风. ～ ***into*** 攻击;责备. ～ ***out for*** 〔美口〕逃往. ～ ***up*** ①点火,点灯;弄亮,照亮;点香烟. ②变快活;有喜色. — *a.* *(opp.* dark*)* ①发光的,明亮的. *It's beginning to get* ～. 天亮了. ②浅色的,淡色的. *a* ～ *blue* 浅蓝色. ～ **adaptation** 光适应. ～ **blues** 剑桥大学的选手、啦啦队. ～ **buoy** 【海】灯浮标. ～ **due [duty]** 灯塔税. **a** ～ **evening** 薄暮. ～**fast** *a.* 耐光的〔尤指颜色〕. ～**-fastness** 耐光. ～**house** 灯塔. ～**house tube** 【无】灯塔管. ～ **meter** 曝光表,照度计. ～ **pen** 【电】光笔. ～**proof** *a.* 不透光的. ～ **quantum** 【物】= photon. ～**ship** 灯船,灯塔船. ～**show** (伴随摇摆舞音乐暗示迷幻效果的)光影闪烁表演. ～**s out** ①熄灯号(铃). ②就寝时间. ～**-struck** *a.* 【摄】漏过光的. ～**tight** *a.* 防光的,不透光的. ～ **tracer** 曳光弹. ～ **trap** ①蛾灯,光捕虫器. ②暗室进出口的避光装置. ～ **wave** 【物】光波. ～**wood** 易燃的木头;轻材,多脂材. ～**-year** 【天】光年.

light[2] [lait] *a.* *(opp.* heavy*)* ①轻的. *as* ～ *as a feather* 轻如鸿毛. ～ *industry* 轻工业. ②少量的,轻微的,微弱的. ～ *applause* 微弱的掌声. *a* ～ *frost* 微霜. ～ *losses* 轻微的损失. *a* ～ *meal* 吃得不多的一餐饭. *a* ～ *mistake* 小错. *a* ～ *rain* 小雨. ③容易消化的,清淡的. ～ *beer* 淡啤酒. ～ *food* 清淡的食物. *a* ～ *sleep* 微睡. *a* ～ *soup* 清汤. ④无积载的,装货少的. ～ *traffic* 轻量交通. *the* ～ *watermark* 船不装货时的吃水线. ⑤轻快的;轻装的;轻便的. *a* ～ *bomber* 轻轰炸机. *a* ～ *car* 轻便汽车. *a* ～ *cruises* 轻巡洋舰. *a* ～ *machine-gun* 轻机关枪. *300* ～ *cavalry [horse]* 三百轻骑兵. ⑥容易的,轻松的. ～ *illness* 轻病. ～ *punishment* 不重的惩罚. ～ *work* 轻活. ⑦嗓音柔和的. ⑧分量不足的. *a* ～ *coin* 分量不足的钱币. *give* ～ *weight* 克扣分量. ⑨轻松愉快的. *a* ～ *heart* 轻松愉快的心情. *be* ～ *of heart* 心情轻松愉快. ～ *literature* 轻松文学. ～ *music* 轻音乐. ～ *reading* 轻松读物. ⑩轻率的,轻浮的,轻薄的. *a* ～ *woman* 轻佻的妇女. *as* ～ *as a butterfly* 轻佻,轻率. ～ *conduct* 轻浮的举动. ～ *opinions* 轻率的意见. *person of* ～ *character* 轻薄的人. ～*est word* 毫无意义的话. ⑪松脆的,易碎的,疏松的. *a* ～ *cake* 松软的蛋糕. ～ *sand* 松砂. ～ *soil* 轻质土,砂土. ⑫易醒的. *a* ～ *sleeper* 睡不踏实的人. ⑬【建】精巧的,优美的. ～ *architecture* 精巧的建筑. ⑭【语音】弱音的. *a* ～ *syllable* 弱音音节. ⑮不重要的,琐碎的. ～ *conversation* 随便的闲聊. ⑯晕眩的. *He was a bit* ～ *after the illness.* 病后他有点头晕. ⑰轻快的,灵巧的. *be* ～ *on one's feet* 脚步轻快. *have a* ～ *hand* 手灵巧. ～ *movement* 轻快的行动. ⑱人手不足的,缺少人员的. ～ ***in hand*** (马等)容易驾驭的,(人)容易相处的. ～ ***in the head*** ①头晕,眼花. ②头脑简单,愚蠢. ***L- gains make heavy purses.*** 〔谚〕因小失大. ～ ***of belief*** = ～ ***of ear*** 耳朵软,轻信. ～ ***of fingers*** 手脚不干净,有偷窃癖. ***make*** ～ ***of*** 轻视,小看 (*make* ～ *of the danger* 不把危险放在心上). ***set*** ～ ***by*** 轻视. ***sit*** ～ ***on*** (工作等)对…负担不重 (*Her years sit* ～ *on her.* 她年事虽长,但不见老). — *ad.* 轻地,轻快地;轻装地. *L- come,* ～ *go.* = Lightly come, lightly go. *sleep* ~ 睡得不熟. *travel* ~ 轻装旅行. ~ **air** 软风〔一级风〕. ~**-armed** *a.* 【军】轻武器装备的. ~ **artillery** 轻型火炮, 轻炮兵. ~ **bob** 〔英〕轻步兵. ~ **bread** (美国南部) 用酵母发酵的白面包. ~ **breeze** 轻风〔二级风〕. ~ **chain** 【生】轻(多肽)链. ~**-duty** *a.* (机器等) 轻型的; 可用轻型机械做成的. ~ **engine** 没有挂列车的机车. ~**er-than-air** (飞船等) 轻于空气的. ~**-face** *n., a.* 【印】白体活字(的). ~**-fingered** *a.* ①手指灵巧的. ②有窃盗癖的 (*a* ~*-fingered gentleman* 〔谑〕扒手). ~**footed** *a.* 走路轻快的; 轻盈的 (= 〔诗〕 ~foot). ~**-foot·ed·ly** 走路轻快地. ~**footedness** 走路轻快. ~**-hand·ed** *a.* ①手上没有什么[多少]东西的. ②人手不足的. ③手巧的, 手法高明的. ~**-headed** *a.* ①头昏眼花的. ②轻率的; 轻浮的. ~**-hearted** *a.* 无忧无虑的, 心情愉快[轻松]的. ~ **heavyweight** (拳击等的)轻重量级运动员〔体重为 161—175 磅〕. ~**-heeled** 〔古〕①步子轻快的. ②放纵的, 淫荡的. ~ **horse,** ~**-horseman** 轻骑兵. ~ **housekeeping** 轻的家务活. ~**-mind·ed** *a.* 不严肃的; 轻浮的. ~**-o'-love** *(pl.* ~*-o'-loves)* 荡妇. ~ **opera** 轻歌剧. ~**plane** 轻型飞机〔尤指私人小飞机〕. ~**-skirts** 〔作单数用〕轻浮的妇女. ~ **verse** (幽默讽刺的) 打油诗. ~ **water** 【原】普通水〔与重水相对而言〕. ~**-weight** ①*n.* 标准重量以下的人[动物]; 轻量级选手; 不重要的人; 不够坚强的人, 不能胜任的人. ② *a.* 轻量的; 平均重量以下的; 不重要的.

light[3] [lait] *vi.* ***(lit*** [lit] 或 ~***ed)*** ①〔古〕下马, 下车; 停落. ②鸟歇在树上. ③偶然遇见; 偶然得到. ④〔方〕突然发生. *The bird lit on a branch.* 小鸟歇在枝头. — *vt.* 【海】拉起(绳索等), 移动(风帆等). ~ ***into*** 〔美俚〕责备, 攻击, 骂. ~ ***(up)on*** 偶而碰见, 发现. ~ ***on one's feet [legs]*** 双脚落地; 幸免; 侥幸成功. ~ ***out*** 〔美俚〕逃走, 溜掉.

light·en[1] [ˈlaitn] *vt.* ①照亮, 点亮; 点火. ②弄明白, 启发. ③使春风满面, 使(眼睛)发亮. ④使(绘画)色调轻柔明朗. — *vi.* ①发亮, 变亮. ②打闪. *A full moon* ~*ed our path.* 一轮明月照亮了我们的道路. *It thundered and* ~*ed.* 雷电交作.

light·en[2] [ˈlaitn] *vt.* ①减轻(负担); 缓和, 减少. ②使轻松, 使高兴. — *vi.* 变轻; 变轻松, 舒畅起来. ~ *a ship of her cargo* 减轻船载.

light·er[1] [ˈlaitə] *n.* ①点火者; 点火器. ②打火机; 引燃器. *spark* ~ 点火器.

light·er[2] [ˈlaitə] *n.* 驳船. — *vt.* 用驳船运.

light·er·age [ˈlaitəridʒ] *n.* ①驳运费. ②驳船运送[装卸]. ③驳运船.

light·er·man [ˈlaitəmən] *n.* ***(pl. -men)*** 驳船工人.

light·ing [ˈlaitiŋ] *n.* ①照明; 照明设备; 舞台灯光. ②点火, 发火. ③(画中的)明暗分布. ~**-up time** 行驶车辆的规定开灯时间.

light·ish [ˈlaitiʃ] *a.* ①(颜色)稍淡的. ②重量稍差的; 载货少的.

light·less [ˈlaitlis] *a.* ①无光的, 暗的. ②不发光的.

light·ly [ˈlaitli] *ad.* ①轻轻地. ②轻易地, 容易地, 不费力地; 轻捷地. ③泰然自若地; 淡然地; 清淡地. ④轻率地. ⑤轻松地, 轻快地; 愉快地. ⑥轻蔑地. *He wears his seventy years* ~. 他简直看不出有七十岁. *get off* ~ 轻易逃脱. *L- come,* ~ *go.* 〔谚〕悖入悖出, 来得容易去得快. *take bad news* ~ 对坏消息不以为意. *behave* ~ 轻举妄动. *Don't take it* ~ 不可等闲视之. *give up sth.* ~ 轻易放弃某物. *leap* ~ *over a ditch* 轻轻跳过小沟. *think* ~ *of sb.'s achievements* 轻视某人的成绩. *punish* ~ 从轻处罚. ~ *cooked* 烹调得很清淡.

light·ness[1] [ˈlaitnis] *n.* ①轻. ②敏捷, 机敏. ③精巧, 优美. ④轻率; 轻浮. ⑤愉快, 轻松. ⑥清淡; 易消化.

light·ness[2] [ˈlaitnis] *n.* ①明亮, 光亮度. ②(色调的)清淡.

light·ning [ˈlaitniŋ] *n.* ①闪电, 电光. ②意外的幸运. ③〔美俚〕劣等威士忌酒. *chain [forked]* ~ 叉状闪电. *heat [summer]* ~ (夏季的)无声闪电, 热闪. *sheet* ~ 片状闪电. *The* ~ *has struck a house.* 雷电击倒了一座房子. *chained* ~ 〔美俚〕下等酒. *forty-rod* ~ 〔美俚〕下等烈性酒. ***a*** ~ ***before death*** 回光返照. ***a*** ~ ***attack*** 突然袭击, 闪电袭击. ***at [like, with] (greased)*** ~ 闪电似的, 风驰电掣地, 一眨眼. — *vi.* 闪电. ~ **arrester [conductor, rod]** 避雷针. ~ **beetle [bug]** 〔美〕萤火虫. ~ **strike** 闪电式罢工. ~ **war** 闪击战.

lights [laits] *n. pl.* (供食用的)兽类肺脏.

light·some[1] [ˈlaitsəm] *a.* ①轻快的, 敏捷的. ②愉快的; 无忧无虑的. ③轻薄的; 轻浮的. **-ly** *ad.* **-ness** *n.*

light·some[2] [ˈlaitsəm] *a.* ①发光的, 辉耀的. ②明亮的; 不暗的.

lign·al·oes [laiˈnæləuz, lig-] *n.* 沉香木.

lig·ne·ous [ˈligniəs, -njəs] *a.* 木的, 木质的; 木头似的.

lig·n(i)- *comb.f.* 表示"木": *lignify.*

lig·ni·fy [ˈligniˌfai] *vt.* ***(-fi·ed, -fy·ing)*** 使…木质化, 木质化, 变为木. **-fi·ca·tion** [ˌlignifiˈkeiʃən] *n.*

lig·nin [ˈlignin] *n.* 【化】木质素.

lig·nite [ˈlignait] *n.* 【矿】褐煤 (= brown coal).

lig·no- *comb. f.* = lign(i).

lig·no·caine [ˈlignəˌkein] *n.* 【药】利多卡因, 赛鲁卡因〔又称 lidocaine, xylocaine, 局部麻醉及抗心律紊乱药〕.

lig·no·cel·lu·lose [ˈlignəuˈselju̇ˌləus] *n.* 【化】木质纤维素. **lig·no·cel·lu·los·ic** [-ˈləusik] *a.*

lig·nose [ˈlignəus] ①= liguin. ②含有硝酸甘油和木质纤维的炸药.

lig·num vi·tae [ˈlignəmˈvaiti:] ①= guaiacum. ②愈创树的特硬木材〔商业上的俗称〕.

lig·ro·in(e) [ˈligrəuin] *n.* 【化】挥发油, 轻石油, 石油醚, 粗汽油, 里格若英 (= benzine).

lig·u·la [ˈligjulə] *n.* ***(pl. -lae*** [-ˌli:], ***-las)*** 【动】(昆虫的)唇舌.

lig·u·late [ˈligjulit] *a.* 【植】舌状的; 有叶舌的. ~ *corolla* 舌状花冠.

lig·ule [ˈligju:l] *n.* 【植】叶舌; 舌状; 舌状花冠.

lik·a·ble [ˈlaikəbl] *a.* 可爱的, 讨人喜欢的; 亲切的, 和蔼的. **-ness** *n.*

like[1] [laik] *vt.* ①喜欢, 爱好. *He* ~*s vegetables.* 他喜欢蔬菜. *I* ~ *apples better than pears.* 苹果和梨比较起来, 我更爱吃苹果. ②希望, 想要, 喜欢, 愿意做某事〔后接不定式或动名词〕. *I should much* ~ *to come.* 我很想来. *He doesn't* ~ *to smoke [smoking].* 他不喜欢吸烟. ③希望[欢迎]某人做某事〔后接带 to 的不定式, 在美国口语中可接不定式二元语核, 即 for … 加带 to 的不定式结构〕 *I* ~ *people to tell the truth.* 我希望人们说实话. *I* ~ *for him to come soon.* 我欢迎他马上来. ④使某人感到适宜[惬意]. *Lobsler doesn't* ~ *me.* (吃)龙虾对我的健康不合适. ⑤对某事物有某种感觉〔观感〕. *How do you* ~ *this poem?* 你觉得这首诗怎么样? *I* ~ *your imprudence.* 我看你就是脸皮厚. — *vi.* ①喜欢, 愿意, 希望. ②〔方〕赞同. *Do as you* ~. 你喜欢怎么做就怎么做. *You may take as you* ~. 你可以任意拿. ***if you*** ~ 如果你喜欢的话 (*You may come if you* ~. 高兴的话请过来. *I am shy if you* ~. 〔重读 shy〕(如果你要那么说)就算我怕见人吧〔但实际并不怕见人〕; 〔重读 I〕那就说我怕见人吧〔但不能说别人也这样〕). ***I*** ~ ***that!*** 你倒说得出! 说得倒好! ~ ***it or not*** 〔插入语〕不管你喜欢不喜欢. — *n.* 〔*pl.*〕嗜好. *one's* ~*s and dislikes* 好恶, 爱憎.

like[2] [laik] *a.* ***(more like; most like;*** 〔诗〕 ***lik·er, lik·est)*** ①相象的, 相似的, 类似的; 同类的, 同样的, 同等的. ~ *figure* 【几】相似形. ~ *terms* 【数】同类项. *two men of* ~ *pursuits and tastes* 志趣相同的两个人. *I cannot cite a* ~ *instance.* 我一时举不出类似的例子. *in* ~ *manner* (用)同样 (方式). *on this and* ~ *occasions* 在这

种场合和类似的场合。②相似,类似〔用作表语〕. *The two sisters are very ~.* 这姐妹俩非常相象. *Things which seem to be ~ may be different.* 看来相同的东西实际可能不同. ③〔方,古〕可能,大概〔用作表语〕. *'Tis ~ that he's gone mad.* 他大概是疯了. *It is ~ we shall see him no more.* 恐怕不会再见到他了. *It's ~ to happen again.* 说不定又要来一下. ④〔古〕简直, 几乎要. *I am ~ to cry whenever I think of my love.* 我每想到自己的情史,简直要痛哭起来. ***L- father, ~ son.*** 有其父必有其子〔文中前一 like 为关联词,后一 like 为指示词〕. — *prep.* ①象…那样,和…一样. *a thing ~ that* 象那样的东西. *swim ~ a fish* 象鱼那样游泳. *Don't talk ~ that.* 讲话不要象那个样子. ②(表面、外观、内容等) 与…相似. *Your necklace is just ~ mine.* 你的项链和我的项链很相似. *The wind in the trees made a sound so much ~ the sea.* 林中风声响动, 和海水声极其相似. ③能表明…特征. *It is ~ him to forget our appointment.* 把我们的约会忘掉,这正是他的行径. ④有…征候;有…希望〔姿态〕. *It doesn't look ~ rain.* 不象要下雨的样子. *The snow looks ~ lasting.* 这场雪看样子要继续下的. *You sound ~ a professor.* 您讲话很有教授风度. ⑤想要做某事〔前面通常用动词 feel, 后面用名词或动名词形式〕*I feel ~ a ride in my new sports car.* 我想乘坐我新买的赛跑汽车行驶一趟. *I didn't feel ~ going out for dinner.* (当时)我不想到外面去吃饭. ⑥〔非规范用法〕诸如…等,象…等等〔=as, such as〕. *There are numerous hobbies you might enjoy, ~ photography or painting.* 大家可以享用的文娱活动有许多许多,如摄影和绘画等等. ***~ a book*** 详细地;准确地; 严谨地 (*He speaks ~ a book.* 他讲话用词严谨. *I can read his mind ~ a book.* 我对他的心事了如指掌). ***~ anyting*** 非常, 极其; …得不成样子 (*The maid wanted ~ anything to try on her mistress's clothes.* 这位女仆很想把女主人的衣服穿起来试试看). ***~ nothing on earth*** 世间稀有的. ***nothing ~*** ①没有什么比…更…〔nothing 用作名词〕(*There is nothing ~ a cold drink of water when one is thirsty.* 渴的时候什么东西也比不上一杯凉水). ②丝毫〔哪方面〕都不象…那样…(*It was nothing ~ what we expected.* 事情一点也不象原来所期望的那样). ***nothing ~ [near] as [so] …as*** 远远不象…那样…(*This is nothing ~ as good as that.* 这个远远不如那个那样好). ***something ~*** ①几乎, 差不多,有几分象. ②大约. ③了不起的…; 象样的… (*It looks something ~ this.* 看来跟这个差不多. *It cost us something ~ $1,000.* 我们在这方面约花了一千美元. *He is something ~ an orator.* 他是一位了不起的讲演家). ★根据现代多数词典对词性划分的情况,本词典关于 like 一词的条目, 凡词后带有宾语的均作为介词处理, 用作名词的定语或作表语用的则均作形容词处理. — *ad.* ①象…,和…一样地. ②〔口〕多半,恐怕. ③〔口〕似乎, 宛如, 简直. *I thought ~ you.* 我想的和你一样. ***(as) ~ as not*** 〔口〕大概, 十之八九 (*He will come, as ~ as not.* 他多半会来). ***~ anything [blazes, crazy, fun, mad, one o'clock, the devil]*** 〔俚〕极,非常, 猛烈地 (*be brave ~ anything* 勇敢非常). ***very ~ = ~ enough*** 多半是的,很可能如此. — *conj.* 〔美口〕好象,如同. *I cannot do it ~ you do.* 我不能做得象你那样. *Now swing your bat ~ I do.* 来, 照我的样子挥动球棒. — *n.* ①相似的人〔物〕; 同样的人〔物〕. ②【高尔夫球】分数相同的一击. *Hitler and his ~* 希特勒之流. *I shall never do the ~ again.* 我决不再那样搞了. *We shall never see his ~ again.* 我们再也看不到他那样的人了. ***and such [the] ~ = or the ~*** 等等,诸如此类. ***L- attracts [draws to] ~.*** 〔谚〕物以类聚. ***L- cures ~.*** 〔谚〕以毒攻毒. ***L- for ~.*** 以牙还牙. ***L- knows ~.*** 〔谚〕英雄识英雄. ***Requite [return] ~ for ~.*** 一报还一报,即以其人之道还治其人之身. ***the ~ of it*** 那一类的东西. ***the ~s of me*** 〔口〕 象我这样 (不行) 的人. ***the ~s of you*** 〔俚〕象你这样了不起的人. **-mind·ed** *a.* 有同样思想的,志同道合的.

-like *suf.* 〔附在名词之后,构成形容词或副词〕表示"…一样","象…": lily*like*, woman*like*.

like·a·ble [ˈlaikəbl] *a.* = likable.

like·li·hood, like·li·ness [ˈlaiklihud, -nis] *n.* ①可能(性). ②【数、统】似然,似真. ③〔古〕希望,前途. *There is no ~ of his coming again.* 他不见得会再来了. *a young man of great ~* 很有前途的青年. ***in all ~*** 十之八九, 多半.

like·ly [ˈlaikli] *a.* ***(more ~, most ~, like·li·er; -li·est)*** ①很可能的. ②很象真事的; 象是可信的,好象可靠的. ③适当的,恰好的;有希望的. ④〔方〕漂亮的,吸引人的. *be ~ of success* 可能成功. *He is not ~ to come = It is not ~ (that) he will come.* 他不见得来. *Such a case is possible, but not ~.* 这种情况是可能的,但不见得会发生. *his most ~ halting place* 他很可能会停歇的地方. *It is ~ they will win.* 他们很可能要赢. *It is ~ to be cold there.* 那里可能很冷. *It is ~ to rain.* 象要下雨. *That's a ~ story!* 说得倒象! 象煞有介事! *a ~ house* 适当的房子. *a ~ spot to build on* 有希望〔适合〕大兴土木的地方. *a ~ young man* 有前途〔希望〕的青年. — *ad.* 〔英国常加 *very; most*〕 多半,大概,有可能. *I shall most [very] ~ see you again.* 我一定能再见到你. ***as ~ as not*** (= mostly [very] ~) 很可能, 说不定 (*He'll forget all about it as ~ as not.* 他说不定〔很可能〕会把这件事情忘得一干二净). ***~ enough*** 恐怕,也许.

lik·en [ˈlaikən] *vt.* ①比作 *(to)*. ②〔罕〕使象,弄得象….

like·ness [ˈlaiknis] *n.* ①相似,类似 *(between; to)*. ②像,肖像,画像. ③外表,表面现象. *a bad ~* 不很象的肖像. *a flattering ~* 比本人还要好看的像. *a good ~* 很象的肖像. *a living ~* 栩栩如生的肖像. ***in the ~ of*** 貌似,假装 (*an enemy in the ~ of a friend* 伪装成朋友的仇敌). ***take sb.'s ~*** 给某人画像〔照相〕.

like·wise [ˈlaikwaiz] *ad.* ①同样地,一样地. ②也,而且.

li·kin [ˈliːkiːn] *n.* 〔Chin.〕(十九世纪中叶至二十世纪三十年代的中国货物过境税)厘金.

lik·ing [ˈlaikiŋ] *n.* 兴趣,嗜好. ***be to sb.'s ~*** 合某人的意,合某人的胃口. ***have a ~ for*** 喜欢. ***on (the) ~*** 实习的;试用的. ***take a ~ to [for]*** 开始喜欢…,爱上….

li·ku·ta [liˈkuːtɑː] *n.* ***(pl. ma·ku·ta*** [mɑː-]***)*** 里库塔〔扎伊尔货币名,等于 1/100 扎伊尔〕.

li·lac [ˈlailək] *n.* ①【植】丁香花属;丁香花,紫丁香. ②淡紫色. — *a.* 淡紫色的.

lil·i·a·ceous [ˌliliˈeiʃəs] *a.* 【植】百合科的.

lil·ied [ˈlilid] *a.* ①多百合花的;百合花覆盖的. ②〔诗〕百合花似的;洁白的.

Lil·ien·thal [ˈliljənθɔːl] *n.* 利连索尔〔姓氏〕.

Lil·(l)i·an [ˈliliən] *n.* 莉莲〔女子名, Elizabeth 的昵称〕.

lil·li·bul·le·ro [ˈlilibəˈliərəu] *n.* ①英国勒里不利罗〔1688 年政变时流行的一首讽刺爱尔兰天主教歌曲的部分迭句〕. ②上述歌曲.

Lil·li·put [ˈliliˌpʌt] *n.* (英国作家 Swift 作小说《格列佛游记》中的)小人国.

Lil·li·pu·tian [ˌliliˈpjuːʃiən, -ʃjən] *a.* ①小人国的; 小人国人的. ②矮小的;卑陋的,心胸狭窄的. — *n.* ①小人国人. ②〔l-〕小人,矮子.

Lil·on·gwe [ˈlilɔːŋkwi] *n.* 利隆圭〔马拉维首都〕.

lilt [lilt] *vi., vt.* ①欢唱,快活地唱. ②轻快地跳动. — *n.* ①轻快的歌曲. ②(诗等的)韵律; 节. ③轻快的动作.

Lil·y [ˈlili] *n.* 莉莉〔女子名〕.

lil·y [ˈlili] *n.* ①【植】百合属; 百合,百合花. ②纯白的东西;纯洁的人;〔常 *pl.*〕洁白美丽的颜色. ③〔常 *pl.*〕= fleur-de-lis. ④〔美俚〕女人腔调的男子. ***gild [paint] the ~*** 在百合花上镀金〔擦粉〕;画蛇添足. ***lilies and roses*** 美观. ***the ~ of the valley (pl. lilies of the***

valley)【植】欧铃兰 *(convallaria majalis)*. — *a.* 百合(花)的;洁白的;纯洁的. ～ **iron** 头上装有倒钩的鱼叉. ～**-livered** *a.* 胆怯的;胆小的〔词出莎士比亚悲剧《麦克佩斯》〕. ～ **pad** 浮在水面上的睡莲叶子. ～**-white** ① *a.* 纯白的;〔美〕纯白种运动派的. ② *n.*〔美〕排斥黑人的纯白种运动派成员.

lim. = limit.

Li•ma[1] [ˈliːmə] *n.* 利马〔秘鲁首都〕. ～ **bean** (美洲)利马豆,白扁豆.

Li•ma[2] [ˈlimə] 通讯中用以代表字母 l 的词.

lim•a•cine [ˈliməˌsain, ˈlaimə-; -sin] *a.* 蛞蝓的;似蛞蝓的 (= limaciform).

li•man [liˈmɑːn] *n.* 河口,江河入海处的港湾.

limb[1] [lim] *n.* ①肢,手足;翼,翅膀. ②大树枝. ③分支;突出物;(河的)支流. ④(句中的)从句. ⑤骨干;爪牙. ⑥顽童. ～ *of the devil [hell]* = ～ *of satan, the devil's [fiend's]* ～ (坏人的)爪牙;顽童. ～ *of the bar [law]* 警察,律师. ***out on a*** ～ 〔口〕处于危险境地. ***pull [tear] sb.*** ～ ***from*** ～ 撕裂某人肢体. ***rest one's tired*** ～***s*** 使疲倦的四肢休息. — *vt.* ①割断…的四肢,肢解. ②砍树枝. **-less** *a.* 无肢的;无翼的;无枝叉的.

limb[2] [lim] *n.* ①(日、月等天体的)边缘. ②(四分仪等的)分度弧. ③【植】瓣片;萼簷;冠簷.

lim•bate [ˈlimbeit] *a.* 边缘明显的〔如颜色与主体不同〕.

lim•bec(k) [ˈlimˌbek] *n.*〔古〕= alembic.

limbed [limd] *a.*〔常用以构成复合词〕有…肢[分枝,翼]的. *long-*～ 有长肢[枝、翼]的. *short-*～ 有短肢[枝、翼]的.

lim•ber[1] [ˈlimbə] *a.* ①柔软的;可塑的;易弯曲的. ②轻快的,敏捷的. ～ *terms* 可变通的条件. — *vt.* 使柔软. — *vi.* 柔和一下身体,(比赛前)做做预备运动 *(up)*.

lim•ber[2] [ˈlimbə] *n.* (炮车的)拖车. — *vt., vi.* 把炮系在拖车上.

lim•bers [ˈlimbəz] *n.*〔*pl.*〕(船底龙骨两侧的)污水道,污水孔.

lim•bo[1] [ˈlimbəu] *n.* ***(pl.*** ～***s)*** ①【宗】地狱的外缘〔善良的非基督徒或未受洗礼者的灵魂归宿处〕. ②监牢,拘禁. ③丢弃废物的地方;易被疏忽的地方. ④中间过渡状态[地带].

lim•bo[2] [ˈlimbəu] *n.* 林勃舞〔西印度群岛一种特技舞蹈〕.

Lim•burg•er [ˈlimbəːgə] *n.* (比利时)林堡干酪.

lim•bus [ˈlimbəs] *n.* ***(pl. -bi*** [-bai]***)*** (色差较大的)明显边缘.

lime[1] [laim] *n.* ①石灰. ②粘鸟胶. *caustic [quick, unslaked]* ～ 生石灰. *slaked [slack]* ～ 熟石灰. ～ *and water* 石灰水. ～ *process* 灰退法〔用石灰去皮革上的毛〕. ～ *soil* 钙质土. — *vt.* ①用石灰处理;撒石灰;浸在石灰水中. ②涂粘鸟胶,用粘鸟胶捕捉;诱陷. ～**burner** 烧石灰工人. ～ **glass** 石灰玻璃. ～ **kiln** 石灰窑. ～**light** ①(旧时用燃烧石灰的办法照明舞台的)石灰光,灰光灯;舞台照明,聚光灯;舞台上照明部分. ②众人注目的中心 (*be fond of the* ～*light* 爱引人注意,爱出风头. *come into [take] the* ～*light* 变成人们注意的中心. *in the* ～*light* 引人注目. *a tendency to seek* ～*light* 风头主义). *throw* ～ *light on* 阐明,使真相毕露;把光集中在…;使显著,使成注目中心. ～ **pit** 石灰石坑,石灰窑. ～**stone** (石)灰石. ～ **sulfur [sulphur]** 石(灰)硫(黄)混合杀虫剂. ～ **twig** ①涂有粘鸟胶的树枝. ②罗网,陷阱. ～**water** 石灰水.

lime[2] [laim] *n.*【植】椴属;欧椴.

lime[3] [laim] *n.*【植】酸橙. ～ **juice** 酸橙汁. ～**juicer** 〔俚〕①英国佬;英国水兵. ②英国船.

lime•ade [ˈlaimˈeid] *n.* 酸橙汁,柠檬水.

li•men [ˈlaimen] *n.*【心】阈限.

lim•er•ick [ˈlimərik] *n.* (按 aabba 押韵的)五行打油诗.

li•mes [ˈlaimiːz] *n.* ***(pl. limites*** [limitiːz]***)*** 境界.

Lim•ey [ˈlaimi] *n.* = lime-juicer.

li•mic•o•line [laiˈmikəˌlain,-lin] *a.*【动】栖居岸边的〔尤指涉禽类〕.

li•mic•o•lous [laiˈmikələs] *a.*【动】生活于泥中的.

lim•i•nal [ˈliminl] *a.*【心】阈限的.

lim•it [ˈlimit] *n.* ①界限,界线;边界. ②极限,限度;限制. ③〔*pl.*〕范围,范域. ④限价;限额;赌注限额;猎物限额. *place* ～*s on the number of men* 限制人数. *set a* ～ *to* … 对…加以限制. *the danger* ～ 危险线;极点. *reach the* ～ *of one's patience* 忍无可忍了. ～ *value*【数】极限值. *the age* ～ *for enlistment* 入伍的年龄限制. *There is a* ～ *to everything.* 凡事都有限度. ***be the*** ～ 太过分,叫人无法容忍. ***go beyond [over] the*** ～ 超过限度. ***go the*** ～ 运动赛完全局[全场]. ***go to any*** ～ 竭尽全力. ***off*** ～***s*** 〔美〕(军人)禁入地区 (*Off* ～*s to all unauthorized personnel.* 闲人免进). ***on*** ～***s*** 〔美〕(军人)活动地区. ***reach the*** ～ ***of one's resources*** 山穷水尽. ***the inferior*** ～ ①最迟的限期. ②最小的限额. ***the*** ～ 〔口〕使人无法容忍的人[物],到了绝顶的事物. ***the*** ～ ***man*** 在赛跑时受最大让步的运动员. ***the superior*** ～ ①最早的限期. ②最大的限额. ***That's the*** ～. 这算到头了,不能再容忍了. ***to the (utmost)*** ～ 到极点 (*strain oneself to the* ～竭尽全力). ***within*** ～***s*** 适当地,在一定范围之内. ***within the city*** ～***s*** 在市内. ***within the*** ～***s of*** 在…的范围之内. ***without*** ～ 无限制地,无限地. — *vt.* ①限制,限定. ②减少. ～ *the number to fifty* 把数目限制到五十. ～ *the expenses* 节省开支. **-a•ble** *a.*

lim•i•tar•y [ˈlimitəri] *a.* 有限制的;受到限制的.

lim•i•ta•tion [ˌlimiˈteiʃən] *n.* ①限制. ②界限;极限;限度;局限性;限制因素. ③【法】(诉讼)时效,有效期限. *a* ～ *on imports* 进口限制. *an arms* ～ 军备限制. *Each man has his* ～*s.* 人各有所不能. *know one's own* ～*s.* 有自知之明. *owing to the* ～ *of space* 限于篇幅.

lim•i•ta•tive [ˈlimiteitiv] *a.* 限定的,有限制的.

lim•it•ed [ˈlimitid] *a.* ①有限的,有限制的;【政】(君主权力)受宪法限制的. ②〔美〕乘客名额有限制的,速度快的,停站少的. ③智力[能力等]有限的. *a* ～ *war* 有限战争. ～ *number* 少数. *a* ～ *express (train)* 特别快(车). *a* ～ *mail* (定额)特别邮车. *They possess a rather* ～ *intelligence.* 他们的知识面相当狭窄. ～ *monarchy* 君主立宪政体,有限君主制. — *n.* 高级快车. ～ **(liability) company** 〔英〕股份有限公司〔用在公司名字之后时,作 Limited, 或略作 Ltd. 美国叫 incorporated company〕. ～ **policy** 有限制的保险证书. ～ **service**【军】(人员)不适合担任战斗任务;(装备,器材)不适用于战区. **-ly** *ad.* **-ness** *n.*

lim•it•er [ˈlimitə] *n.* ①限制物. ②限制器,限动器,限幅器. *speed* ～ 限速器.

lim•it•ing [ˈlimitiŋ] *a.* 限制(性)的,有限制力的,起限定作用的〔不涉及性质的各种定语如: several, four 等〕. ～ **factor** 限制因素〔对有机物的生活或对人口数量、分布起限制作用的客观环境〕. ～ **quantity** 影响量.

lim•it•less [ˈlimitlis] *a.* 无界限的,无限制的;无限期的;一望无际的.

lim•i•trophe [ˈlimitrəuf] *a.* 位于边界上的,边界接壤的. *two* ～ *countries* 相邻的两国.

li•miv•o•rous [laiˈmivərəs] *a.*【动】食泥的〔如蚯蚓〕.

lim•mer [ˈlimə] *n.*〔英俚〕流氓,恶棍;不正经的女人.

limn [lim] *vt.* ①描画;勾划. ②描写;生动地叙述.

limn•er [ˈlimnə] *n.* 画师,画匠;描述者.

lim•net•ic [limˈnetik] *a.*【生】生活于湖沼的.

lim•nol•o•gy [limˈnɔlədʒi] *n.* 湖沼学.

li•mo [ˈlimәu] *n.*〔口〕= limousine.

lim•o•nene [ˈliməˈniːn] *n.*【化】苧烯.

li•mo•nite [ˈlaiməˌnait] *n.*【矿】褐铁矿.

lim•ou•sine [ˈlimu(ː)ziːn] *n.* 轿车;大型高级轿车;接送旅客的交通车. ～ **liberal** 〔美讽〕大轿车自由主义者

〔指富有的自由主义者〕.

limp[1] [limp] *vi.* ①一瘸一拐地走. ②慢腾腾地进行. ③(诗)韵律〔抑扬〕紊乱. — *n.* ①跛行. ②挣扎着慢慢前进. ③(诗的)韵律紊乱. **-ing·ly** *ad.* 一瘸一拐地.

limp[2] [limp] *a.* ①柔软的,易曲的. ②柔弱的,无生气的. ③(装订)软面的. ~ *as a doll* [*rag*] 无精打采的. **-ly** *ad.* **-ness** *n.*

lim·pet [ˈlimpit] *n.* ①【动】蝛,帽贝. ②牢牢抱住某物〔官职等〕不舍的人;恋栈者. ③水下爆破弹 (= ~ mine). ***stick like a*** ~ 纠缠不休.

lim·pid [ˈlimpid] *a.* ①清澈的,透明的. ②明朗的,清晰的. ③平静的,无忧无虑的. **-pid·i·ty** [-ˈpiditi] *n.* **-ly** *ad.* **-ness** *n.*

limp·kin [ˈlimpkin] *n.*【动】秧鸡 (*Aramus vociferus*)〔产于美国弗罗里达州与西印度群岛〕.

limp·sy, limp·sey [ˈlimpsi] *a.* (***-si·er, -si·est***)〔方〕软弱无力的.

lim·u·lus [ˈlimjuləs] *n.* (*pl.* ***-li*** [-ˌlai])【动】鲎 (= horseshoe crab).

lim·y [ˈlaimi] *a.* (***lim·i·er; -i·est***) ①含石灰的;石灰质的;石灰似的. ②涂有粘鸟胶的;粘的. **-i·ness** *n.*

lin. = ①lineal. ②linear.

lin·a·ble [ˈlainəbl] *a.* 可作线状排列的;能划线的.

lin·ac [ˈlainæk] =【物】linear accelerator.

lin·age [ˈlainidʒ] *n.* ①(原稿等的)行数. ②(稿费的)行数计酬法.

lin·al·o·ol [liˈnæləˌəul, -ˌɔːl; ˌlinəˈluːl] *n.*【化】里哪〔芫荽〕醇,沉香(萜)醇.

linch·pin [ˈlintʃˌpin] *n.* ①车辖,制轮楔. ②关键. *the ~ upon which success or failure depends* 成败的关键.

Lin·coln [ˈliŋkən] ①林肯〔姓氏,男子名〕. ②**Abraham** ~ 林肯〔1809—1865, 美国第十六任总统,1862 年颁布奴隶解放令〕. ③〔美〕林肯牌大轿车〔福特汽车厂产的名牌豪华汽车〕. ~ **green**【纺】林肯绿呢. **~'s Inn** (英国四法学协会之一的)林肯法学会.

Lin·coln·i·an [liŋˈkəuniən] *a.* 美国林肯总统的,关于林肯总统的.

lin·co·my·cin [ˌliŋkəˈmaisən] *n.*【药】林肯霉素〔链霉素的一种〕.

Lin·da, Lyn·da [ˈlində] *n.* 琳达〔女子名〕.

lin·dane [ˈlinˌdein] *n.*【化】六氯化苯,林丹.

Lind·bergh [ˈlindbəːg] *n.* 林德伯格〔姓氏〕.

lin·den [ˈlindən] *n.*【植】椴属;欧椴;美洲椴;菩提树.

Lind·say [ˈlindzi] *n.* 林赛〔姓氏〕.

line[1] [lain] *n.* ①线;绳索;钓丝;测深度用绳,卷尺. *a fishing ~* 钓鱼线. *be clever with rod and ~* 会钓鱼. *hang the clothes on the ~* 把衣服挂在绳子上. ②(诗文的)一行;短信;〔*pl.*〕短诗;〔*pl.*〕罚课〔罚学生抄写拉丁诗百行等〕. *just a ~ to tell you that ...* 迳启者. ③路线,铁路线;航线;交通线,铁轨. *a belt ~* 环行线电车路;环行铁路. *a blockade ~* 封锁线. *an air ~* 航空线. *a ~ of supply*【军】补给线. *the down* [*up*] *~* 火车的下〔上〕行线. *the main ~ of a railway* 铁道干线. ④排,行列;【陆军】两列横队;整列的战舰;阵形. *attack in ~* 横队进攻. *draw up in* [*form into*] *~* 排成二列横队. *the ~ abreast* [*ahead*] 航队横〔纵〕列. ⑤(英陆军的)正规军;(美军的)战斗部队,前线部队. ⑥条纹;皱纹;掌纹. *a face covered with deep ~s of care* 满面愁容. ⑦家系,血统,朝代;门第. *a direct ~* 直系. *relations in the female ~* 母系亲属. ⑧界线. *a dividing ~* 分界线. *go* [*step*] *over the ~* 越界,超越限度. ⑨方面,范围;擅长,专门;行业. *It is not in my ~ to interfere.* 干涉不是我干的. *Cards are not in my ~.* 打牌不是我的拿手〔嗜好〕. *Geology is his particular ~.* 地质学是他的专长. *What ~ (of business) are you in?* 你从事的是哪门行业? *I am in the farm side ~.* 我经营的是农村副业. ⑩(商品的)种类,存货. *a full ~ of winter wear* 各种冬装,一应俱全. *the best-selling ~ in scarf* 最畅销的一种围巾. ⑪形状,外形,轮廓. *have good ~s in one's face* 面孔的轮廓很好. ⑫方针,路线,方法. *guiding ~* 方针. *the general ~* 总路线. *the proletarian revolutionary ~* 无产阶级革命路线. ⑬〔*pl.*〕【剧】台词. *memorize one's ~s* 记诵台词. ⑭〔*pl.*〕结婚证书 (= marriage ~s). ⑮【数】线,直线;【无】扫描线 (=scanning ~);【乐】乐谱的线;〔*pl.*〕【船】船体线图. *a curved ~* 曲线. *a straight ~* 直线. *an undulating ~* 波状线. *~ of centres* 联心线. *ruled ~s* 格子线. ⑯ *the ~* 赤道. ⑰情报,迹象,消息. *give sb. a ~ on sth.* 对某人透露一点有关某事的情况. *try to get* [*have*] *a ~ on sth.* 想打听到某事. ⑱(长度单位)十二分之一英寸. ⑲缰绳. ⑳金属线;电线;线路;管;管道作业线. *Hold the ~, please.* (电话)请等一等. *L- busy.* (电话)〔美〕占线,有人在打〔英国说 Number engaged〕. *an extension ~* (电话)分机. *a main ~* (电话)中继线. *a sewage ~* 下水管道,污水管道. *a telegraph ~* 电报线路. *an assembly ~* 装配线. *a production ~* 生产线. ㉑战线,前线. *fight behind the enemy ~s* 在敌后作战. *the first ~ of defence* 第一道防线. ㉒〔*pl.*〕(英军的)一排营帐. *inspect the ~s* 巡视营房. ㉓命运,运气. *Hard ~s!* 倒霉! ***all along the ~*** 在全线,在每一点上;到处. ***be in ~*** ①成直线,排成一行. ②有希望. ③符合,依照. ***be in one's ~*** ①擅长. ②合胃口. ***be out of one's ~*** ①不擅长. ②不合胃口. ***below the ~*** 在水准以下. ***bring* [*get*] *into ~*** 使成一排;使一致;使合作 (*with*). ***by* (*rule and*) *~ = by ~ and level*** 准确地,精密地;正确地. ***come* [*fall*] *into ~*** ①排齐. ②一致,协力,合作 (*with*). ***cross the ~*** (船)通过赤道〔通常举行庆祝〕. ***down the ~*** ①往市中心去. ②完全地 (*back sb. down the ~* 完全支持某人). ***draw a ~ between ...*** 区别清楚. ***draw the* [*a*] *~*** 划界线 (*One must draw the ~ somewhere* 忍耐也有个限度. *know when* [*where*] *to draw a ~* 不越轨,知道分寸). ***draw up in* [*into*] *~*** 排队. ***drop* [*send*] *a ~* [*a few ~s*]** 写封短信. ***form into ~*** 排成一行. ***give sb. ~ enough*** 先纵后擒〔原意为鱼吞饵后暂将钓丝放长,然后钓起〕. ***go up the ~*** 到前线去. ***have sb. on a ~*** ①愚弄某人,跟某人开玩笑. ②操纵某人. ***hew to the ~*** 循规蹈矩,服从纪律. ***hit the ~***〔美〕①(橄榄球赛中)带球冲过对方防线. ②勇敢果断地行事. ***hold the ~*** ①(打电话时)等着不挂断. ②坚持下去. ***in a ~*** 成一行,排队. ***in ~ for***〔美〕即将得到,取得胜算. ***in ~ with*** 和…成一直线;〔美〕和…一致,符合. ***keep to* [*take*] *one's own ~*** 干自己的本行;坚持自己的原则. ***lay* [*put*] *it on the ~*** ①付钱. ②坦率地说,提供证据. ***~ upon ~*** 得一进二地,一步接一步地(推进). ***muff one's ~s***【剧】接不上台词. ***no hard and fast ~ can be drawn between ... and ....*** …和…是不能截然分开的. ***on a ~*** 同等的,同等地. ***on the ~*** ①(挂)在不高不低的地方. ②模棱两可. ③立即,马上. ④处于危险状态. ⑤沦为妓女. ***on the same ~*** 以同样方式. ***on this ~*** 按此方针. ***out of ~*** ①不成一直线. ②不一致,不协调. ***ride the ~***〔美〕骑马赶回离群的牲畜. ***shoot a ~***〔俚〕吹牛,说大话. ***sign on the dotted ~s*** 在虚线上署名;全部接受. ***take a strong ~*** 干得起劲;采取强硬手段. ***take the air ~*** 走直线,走最短的路. ***the bread ~*** 失业者领取免费面包的长蛇阵. ***the ~ of beauty*** 美的线条, S 形线条. ***the ~ of conduct*** 行为的准则. ***the ~ of duty*** 值勤,公务 (*be wounded in the ~ of duty* 因公负伤). ***throw a good ~*** 会钓鱼. ***toe the ~*** ①准备起跑. ②服从纪律. ***under the ~*** 在赤道上. — *vt.* ①画线,画轮廓;用线画分. ②起皱纹. *a face ~d with age* 因年老起了皱纹的脸. ③排成一行;沿…排列. *a road ~d with trees* 两旁种着树的路. *People ~ the streets to welcome.* 人们夹道欢迎. ④(给演员)勾脸. ⑤派工作 (*to*). — *vi.* 排齐,排队. ***~ off*** 用线

划开. ~ ***out*** ①标出,划线标明. ~ *out the route on the map* 在地图上把路线标示出来. ②把…排成行;【植】列植. ③用线条标明…需要删去. ④迅速移动. *The plane ~d out east.* 飞机向东直飞而去. ⑤放声高唱. *He ~d out a few songs upon request.* 他在大家请求之下唱了几个歌. ~ ***through*** 划掉,(一笔)勾消. ~ ***up*** 整顿(机械等); 排成一列; 使(兵士)排齐; 整顿阵容. ~ **back·er** (橄榄球)前锋. ~ **chief** 机场外场保养组组长. ~ **drawing** 线条画〔如钢笔画、铅笔画等〕. ~ **drive** 【棒球】平直球,直球. ~ **engine** 直列式发动机. ~**engraving** 线雕;线雕画. ~ **firing** 【军】横队射击. ~-**haul** *n.* 长途运输. ~ **lamp** 呼叫灯,号灯. ~ **loop** 电话回路. ~ **man** ①护路工,养路工. ②【电】线务员,线路工人. ③【军】架线兵. ④(橄榄球)前锋. ⑤【测】执线人. ~**men's climber** 脚扣〔电工上电杆时套在鞋上的钩状物〕. ~ **of battle** (军队或军舰的)战列,战斗队形. ~ **of beauty** 美的线条. ~ **of conduct** 行为的准则. ~ **of credit** (银行对某客户的)贷款最高限额. ~ **officer** 前线军官. ~ **of scrimmage** (橄榄球假想的)前锋抢球线. ~ **of sight** ①视线,瞄准线〔也叫 ~ of vision〕. ②【无、电视】视线〔发射天线至地平线之间的直线距离〕. ~-**of-sight** *a.* 视线的,瞄准线的. ~-**of-sight reception** 视距信号接收. ~ **production** 流水作业. ~ **radio** 有线载波通信. ~ **selector** 终接器,寻线器. ~ **shaft** 总轴,天轴,机轴,动力轴. ~ **shafting** 传动轴系. ~ **shooter** 吹牛的人. ~ **shooting** 吹牛. ~**sman** ①【电】线务员,线路工人. ②护路工,养路工. ③(球类比赛中的)巡边员. ④〔英〕正规军陆军士兵,列兵. ~ **speed** 线速度. ~ **squall** 【气】线飑. ~ **tape** 卷尺. ~-**to-ground** ①线路对地的. ②线路接地. ~ **unit** 接线盒. ~-**up** ①一排人〔尤指排队受检查的嫌疑犯〕. ②(抱有相同兴趣或宗旨的)一组人; (用途相同的)一批东西. ③(比赛时)球员的阵容.

line² [lain] *vt.* ①镶(衣服)里子;裱褙;衬里. ②填塞. ~ *a coat with fur* 用皮子给大衣衬里. *a study ~d with books* (四壁)摆满书的书房. ~ ***one's pocket(s) [purse]*** 〔口〕填塞私囊,中饱. ~ ***the inside*** 〔俚〕填肚皮,吃饱.

line³ [lain] *vt.* 交尾.

lin·e·age¹ [ˈliniidʒ] *n.* 血统,世系,门第.

lin·e·age² [ˈlainidʒ] *n.* = linage.

lin·e·al [ˈliniəl] *a.* ①直系的,正统的. ②嫡系的,世袭的; 祖先传来的. ③世系的, 属同一世系的. ④线的, 线状的;用线的. ⑤= linear. ⑥战斗部队的. *a ~ ascendant [descendant]* 直系尊属后裔,子孙. **-ly** *ad.*

lin·e·a·ment [ˈliniəmənt] *n.* 〔常 *pl.*〕面貌;轮廓;特征.

lin·e·ar [ˈliniə] *a.* ①线的,直线的. ②长度的. ③【数】一次的,线性的. ④【动、植】线状的;细长的. ⑤由线条组成的,以线条为主的,强调线条的. ~ *amplification* 直线放大. *a ~ equation* 一次方程式. *a ~ leaf* 长叶片. ~ *arts* 线条艺术. ~ **accelerator** 【物】直线性加速器. ~ **algebra** 【数】线性代数. ~ **distortion** 【无】线性失真. ~ **measure** ①测量长度. ②长度单位制〔尤指 12 英寸 = 1 英尺等单位制〕. ~ **perspective** 直线透视. ~ **programming** 【数】线性规划.

lin·e·ar·i·ty [ˌliniˈæriti] *n.* 线性,直线性.

lin·e·ar·ize [ˈliniəˌraiz] *vt.* *(-iz·ed, -iz·ing)* 直线〔线性〕化. **-i·za·tion** [ˌliniəraiˈzeiʃən] *n.* 线性化.

lin·e·ate [ˈliniːit, -ˌeit] *a.* 有线的;标线的;有条纹的.

lin·e·a·tion [ˌliniˈeiʃən] *n.* ①画线,标线. ②轮廓. ③一列线.

lin·en [ˈlinin] *n.* ①亚麻布,亚麻线. ②〔*pl.*〕亚麻布类; 〔集合词〕亚麻布制品〔衬衫、被单等〕. ③= ~ paper. ***shoot one's ~*** (放下手)露出袖口. ***wash one's dirty ~ in public [at home]*** 家丑外扬〔不外扬〕. — *a.* 亚麻的,亚麻布制的;亚麻色的. ~ **closet** (放床单、桌布等的)亚麻织品衣橱. ~ **draper** 〔英〕亚麻布制品商. ~ **paper** 布纹纸.

lin·en·ette [ˌliniˈnet] *n.* 【纺】充亚麻织物.

lin·e·o·late [ˈliniəˌleit] *a.* 【生】有细条纹的.

lin·er¹ [ˈlainə] *n.* ①(固定航线的)定期班;班机. ②画线者. ③画线的工具. ④(棒球中的)直球,平球.

lin·er² [ˈlainə] *n.* ①制衬里〔衬垫等〕的人;装衬里〔衬垫等〕的人. ②衬里;【机】衬垫,套圈,衬套. *a bearing ~* 轴瓦.

line·y [ˈlaini] *a.* ***(lin·i·er, lin·i·est)*** = liny.

ling¹ [liŋ] *n.* 【动】鳕科鱼;长身鳕鱼.

ling² [liŋ] *n.* 【植】石南.

-ling *suf.* ①附在名词后构成名词,表示"小","不重要","低劣": duck*ling*, prince*ling*. ②附在名词、形容词、副词后构成名词,表示"…的人[物]": dar*ling*, nurs*ling*, shalve*ling*, under*ling*. ③〔古、方〕附在名词或形容词后构成副词,表示"方向","状态": dark*ling*, flat*ling*, side*ling*.

linga, lingam [ˈliŋgə, ˈliŋgəm] *n.* ①【宗】男性生殖器像〔印度为湿婆神 Siva〕. ②〔梵语语法〕男性.

Lin·ga·la [liŋˈgɑːlə] *n.* 林格拉语〔刚果西部使用的一种混合班图语〕.

ling·cod [ˈliŋˌkɔd] *n.* ***(pl. -cod, -cods)*** 【动】蛇齿单线鱼〔北太平洋中的一种大鱼〕.

lin·ger [ˈliŋgə] *vi.* 逗留;停竚;徘徊;缠绵不去;拖延. — *vt.* 挨过,拖延(时间). ~ ***on a subject*** 踌躇考虑;絮絮不休地说一件事. ~ ***out one's life*** 苟延残喘. ~ ***over one's work*** 磨洋工.

lin·ge·rie [ˌlænʒəˈriː, ˈlæn-] *n.* 〔F.〕亚麻布制品〔妇女、小孩的内衣,睡衣之类〕.

lin·ger·ing [ˈliŋgəriŋ] *a.* 逡巡的,拖延的;踌躇的. *a ~ disease* 缠绵不去的病. *cast a ~ look behind* 踌躇地回头一看. **-ly** *ad.*

lin·go [ˈliŋgəu] *n.* ***(pl. ~es)*** 〔蔑〕听不懂的话〔指外国话、术语等〕;隐语.

ling·on·ber·ry [ˈliŋənˌberi] *n.* ***(pl. -ries)*** = cowberry.

lingu- *comb. f.* 表示"舌","语言": *lingu*ist, *lingu*late.

lin·gua [ˈliŋgwə] *n.* ***(pl. -guae*** [-gwiː]***)*** ①舌;下咽头. ②语言. ~ **fran·ca** ①佛兰卡语〔意大利、法兰西、阿拉伯、希腊、西班牙等国语言的混合语,通行于地中海各港〕. ②(国际商业上通用的)混合语.

lin·gual [ˈliŋgwəl] *a.* ①舌的,舌状的,舌旁的. ②【语音】舌音的. ③= linguistic. — *n.* 舌音;舌音字母〔t, d, l, n, s 等〕. **-ly** *ad.*

Lin·gua·phone [ˈliŋgwəfəun] *n.* 【商标名】灵格风〔英国一家把各国语言教材灌制成唱片和录音带的制造商的商标名称〕. *the ~ English course* 灵格风英语教程. *the ~ method* 灵格风教授法.

lingui- *comb. f.* = lingu-.

lin·gui·form [ˈliŋgwifɔːm] *a.* 舌形的,舌状的.

lin·gui·ne [liŋˈgwiːniː] *n.* 宽面条.

lin·guist [ˈliŋgwist] *n.* ①语言学家. ②通多种外国语的人.

lin·guis·tic(al) [liŋˈgwistik(əl)] *a.* 语言的;语言学的. ~ **atlas** 方言地图,语言地图. ~ **form** 语言形态〔如词素、单词、单语、句子等〕. ~ **geographer** 语言地理学家. ~ **geography** 语言地理学. ~ **stock** ①基础语,母语〔母语及其所派生出来的亲属语言和亲属方言〕. ②讲上述语言或方言的本地人. **-al·ly** *ad.*

lin·guis·ti·cian [ˌliŋgwisˈtiʃən] *n.* 语言学家.

lin·guis·tics [liŋˈgwistiks] *n.* 语言学. *comparative ~* 比较语言学. *general ~* 一般语言学.

lin·gu·late [ˈliŋgjulit, -lait] *a.* 舌形的,舌状的.

linguo- *comb. f.* = lingu-.

lin·hay [ˈlini] *n.* 〔方〕= linn(e)y.

lin·i·ment [ˈlinimənt] *n.* 【药】搽剂,擦剂.

linin [ˈlainin] *n.* 【生】核丝.

lin·ing [ˈlainiŋ] *n.* ①(衣服等的)衬里,里子;衬料. ②〔古〕内容. ③装衬里〔衬套等〕. ④【机】衬,衬套,套筒,衬垫;(汽机的)气套. ⑤【建】隔板.

link¹ [liŋk] *n.* ①环；链环。②(编织物的)链圈眼。③(链状物中的)一节；(多节香肠等的)一节；单节小香肠。④承前启后的人[物]；环节；联系。⑤【机】连杆，滑环；链节。⑥【化】键，键合。⑦(测量用长度单位)令〔=7.92英寸〕。⑧〔*pl.*〕(衬衫袖口的)链扣(= cuff ~s)。⑨【无】通讯线路；网络节；固定接线。⑩【电】熔丝。⑪〔*pl.*〕〔方〕河道弯曲处。*draw* ~ 牵引连杆。*drive* ~ 传动杆。*all-round* ~*s, radio relay* ~ 无线电中继线路。*One ~ broken, the whole chain is broken.* 〔谚〕一环断，全链断。*The chain is no stronger than its weakest ~ = The strength of a chain is its weakest ~.* 〔谚〕一环软弱，全链不强。***the missing*** ~ 短缺的环节；全部推论[材料]中还不能衔接之处；设想存在于人类与类人猿之间的过渡生物；联系；环接；握(手)，搭(手臂)。— *vi.* 连结；联合。~ ***up with*** 和…同盟，和…提携；结亲。~ **lever** 提环杆。~**man** ①【橄榄球，足球等】(中锋与后卫间的)联络员。②(广播、电视辩论节目中的)调停员。③中间人，中介。~**-motion** 【机】连杆运动。~ **mounting** 插环。~ **receiver** 【无，讯】中继接收机，接力接收机。~ **rod** (副)连杆。~**s-and-**~**s machine** 双反面针织机，回复机。~**up** 连结，联合，会合。~ **verb** = linking verb. ~**work** ①环节联结物〔如链条〕。②【机】联动齿轮系统，联动装置，链系。

link² [liŋk] *n.* 火把，火炬。~**boy,** ~**man** 拿火炬的人。

Link trainer [ˌliŋkˈtreinə] *n.* 林克式地上飞行练习装置。

link·age [ˈliŋkidʒ] *n.* ①联系；连锁；联动；连接。②【化】键合。③链系，联动装置。④【电】耦合；磁链；匝连。*brake* ~ 制动联动装置。

link·ing [ˈliŋkiŋ] *n.* 耦合，结合，咬合；联系；连接。~**-up ship** 联络舰。~**-up station** 中继电台。~ **verb** 联系动词〔其后可接用作表语的一些动词，如 be, get, seem, become 等〕。

Link·la·ter [ˈliŋkˌleitə] *n.* 林克莱特〔姓氏〕。

links [liŋks] *n.* 〔*pl.*〕①〔Scot.〕(海边高低起伏的)砂丘。②〔亦可用作单数说作 a links〕高尔夫球场。~**land** = links ①. ~**man** 〔美〕打高尔夫球的人。

linn [lin] *n.* 〔Scot.〕①瀑布；瀑布下的水潭。②溪谷，绝壁。

Linn. = ①Linnaeus. ②Linnean.

Lin·n(a)e·an [liˈni(ː)ən] *a.* 【生】瑞典博物学家林奈的；按照林奈命名法的。

Lin·nae·us [liˈni(ː)əs], **Carolus** 林奈〔1707—1778，瑞典博物学家，瑞典原名为 Karl von Linné〕。

lin·net [ˈlinit] *n.* 【动】朱顶雀，红雀。

lin·n(e)y [ˈlini] *n.* 〔英方〕农家棚屋。

lino. = linotype.

li·no [ˈlainəu] *n.* = linoleum. ~**cut** *n.* ①亚麻油毡浮雕(版)。②油毡浮雕的印刷图样。

li·no·le·ate [liˈnəuliˌeit] *n.* 【化】亚油酸盐。

lin·o·le·ic acid [ˌlinəˈliːik] 【化】亚油酸。

lin·o·le·nate [ˌlinəˈliːneit] *n.* 【化】亚麻酸盐(或酯)。

lin·o·le·nic acid [ˌlinəˈliːnik] 【化】亚麻酸。

li·no·le·um [liˈnəuljəm] *n.* 亚麻油(地)毡，漆布。

lin·o·type [ˈlainəˌtaip] *n.* ①行型活字铸造机[排版机]。②行型活字；行型活字印刷品。— *vi.* 操纵行型活字铸造机。— *vt.* 用行型活字铸造机排版。

lin·sang [ˈliŋsæŋ] *n.* 【动】林狸〔产于澳大利亚等地〕。

lin·seed [ˈlinsiːd] *n.* 亚麻子[仁]。~ **cake** 亚麻子饼。~ **meal** 亚麻子饼粉。~ **oil** 亚麻子[仁]油。

lin·sey(-wool·sey) [ˈlinziˈwulzi] *n.* ①【纺】亚麻羊毛交织物。②混杂物；梦话，胡话。

lin·stock [ˈlinstɔk] *n.* (古时放炮用的)火绳杆。

lint [lint] *n.* ①皮棉(= ~ cotton)。②(作绷带用的)软麻布。③棉绒。

lin·tel [ˈlintl] *n.* 【建】楣；壁炉横梁。

lint·er [ˈlintə] *n.* ①剥绒机。②〔*pl.*〕棉籽绒，棉短绒。

lint·white [ˈlintˌwait] *n.* = linnet.

lin·y [ˈlaini] *a.* (***lin·i·er; -i·est***) ①象一根线的；细弱的。②由线条构成的；多线条的，多纹路的，多皱纹的。

li·on [ˈlaiən] *n.* ①狮子。②勇猛的人，慓悍的人。③名流，名人。④〔*pl.*〕名胜〔过去参观伦敦的人必去看伦敦塔的狮子〕。⑤〔L-〕【天】狮子座；狮子宫；【徽】狮印，狮子纹章。*A ~ at home, a mouse abroad.* 〔谚〕在家象狮子，出外成老鼠。*The ~ is not so fierce as he is painted.* 〔谚〕传闻往往失实。***a ~ in the way [path]*** 途中的障碍，拦路虎。***as bold [brave] as a ~*** 勇猛如狮。~ ***and unicorn*** (捧英国皇室徽章的)狮子和独角兽。***make a ~ of sb.*** 使某人红极一时。***put [run] one's head into the ~'s mouth*** 轻入险境，冒险。***see the ~s*** 〔英〕游览名胜。***show sb. the ~s*** 〔英〕带领某人游览名胜。***the (old) British L-*** 英国的别称。***the ~'s share*** 最大最好的份额〔语出《伊索寓言》〕。***the ~'s skin*** 表面的威武。***twist the ~'s tail*** (尤指美国记者)说英国坏话。~**heart** ①勇士。②〔L-〕英王理查一世。~**hearted** *a.* 勇猛的，大胆的。~**-hun·ter** *n.* ①猎狮者。②专事巴结社会名流的人。~**hood,** ~**ship** 社会名流的地位。**-like** *a.*

li·on·cel [ˈlaiənˌsel] *n.* 幼狮；小狮子。

Li·o·nel [ˈlaiənl] *n.* 莱昂内尔〔男子名〕。

li·on·ess [ˈlaiənis] *n.* 母狮。

li·on·et [laiənit] *n.* 小狮子。

li·on·ism [ˈlaiənizəm] *n.* ①专事巴结名流的行为。②【医】(麻疯病者后期的)狮面症状。

li·on·ize [ˈlaiənaiz] *vt.* ①捧人，捧为名流。②〔英〕游览名胜；导游名胜。— *vi.* ①巴结名流。②〔英〕游览名胜。**-r** *n.* 专事巴结名流的人。**-iz·a·tion** *n.*

L.I.P. = life insurance policy 人寿保险单。

lip [lip] *n.* ①嘴唇。②唇状物；(杯、壶等的)口，边；【植】唇瓣；(管乐器的)管唇。③〔俚〕无理[礼]的回答；冒昧的话，无礼。④〔美〕律师。*an upper ~* 上唇。*an under [a lower] ~* 下唇。*be as close as the ~s are to the teeth = be closely related as ~s and teeth* 唇齿相依。*I heard it from his ~s.* 我听他亲口讲的。*She never opened her ~s.* 她从来不开口。*Don't give me any ~!* 别讲这种荒唐话！不要这么无礼！*None of your ~!* 〔俚〕别放肆！***be steeped to the ~s in*** 深陷…之中。***bite one's ~*** (为压制感情)咬紧嘴唇。***button up one's ~*** 〔美俚〕住嘴，保守秘密。***carry [have, keep] a stiff upper ~*** 倔强，固执；坚持下去。***curl the [one's] ~*** 撇嘴〔表示轻蔑或讨厌〕。***escape [pass] sb.'s ~s*** (话)无意中说漏嘴。***from the ~s outward*** 不假思索地；敷衍地。***hang on sb.'s ~s*** 被某人的话迷住，听得入神。***hang one's ~*** 沮丧。***lick [smack] one's ~s*** (馋得)舐嘴唇；垂涎三尺。***make (up) a ~*** (因不平、生气等而)撅嘴。***on sb.'s ~s*** (话)就在嘴边。***on the ~s of*** ①在…中间流传。②出诸…之口，挂在…嘴上。***part with dry ~s*** 没有接吻即分手。***pass one's ~s*** ①被某人吃掉[喝完]。②被某人冲口说出。***put [lay] one's finger to one's ~s*** 把手指搁在嘴唇上〔叫人沉默时的手势〕。***refuse to open one's ~s*** 拒不开口。***rush to one's ~s*** (话)一齐涌到嘴边。***seal sb.'s ~s*** 封住某人嘴巴，禁止某人说话。***shoot out one's ~s*** 蔑视地撅嘴。***Zip your ~s!*** 〔美俚〕闭嘴！— *vt.* ①用嘴唇接触；〔诗〕吻。②(波浪)冲刷(海岸)。③轻轻地说；〔俚〕唱；〔美俚〕吹奏。④把高尔夫球打到穴边而未进去。— *vi.* ①(吹奏管乐器时)用嘴唇。②(水)潺潺地响。— *a.* ①唇的。②口头上的。③唇音的。~ *consonant* 唇辅音。~ *comfort* 空口安慰。~**-deep** *a.* 口头上的，无诚意的。~ **language** (聋哑者用嘴唇形状表示语声的)唇话，视话。~ **microphone** (戴在讲话人嘴唇上的)唇式传声器。~ **print** 唇印〔嘴唇留下的印痕，据说人各不同〕。~ **read** *vt., vi.* (~**-read** [-red], ~ ***reading***) 观唇辨意〔如聋哑人根据讲话者的唇动去理解其意〕。~ **reader** 善于观唇辨意的人〔如聋哑者〕。~ **salve** ①润唇(防裂)油膏。②拍马屁，奉承。~ **service** 空口答应〔应酬话〕，口惠。

~**stick** 口红，唇膏。~**-sync** *vt., vi., n.* 对口形〔使口的动作与录音讲话等的声音一致，如电影配音等〕。~**-worship** 口是心非的崇拜。

li·pase [ˈlaipeis, ˈlipeis] *n.*【化】脂(肪)酶。

lip·id [ˈlipid, ˈlaipid] *n.*【化】脂类 (= lipide).

lip·(o)- *comb. f.* 表示"脂肪的": *lipo*lysis, *lipo*tropic.

li·pog·ra·phy [liˈpɔgrəfi] *n.* (书写时)字母或词的脱漏，漏写。

li·poid [ˈlipɔid, ˈlaipɔid] *a.*【生化、化】类脂的 (= lipoidal). — *n.* 类脂物，类脂化合物。

li·pol·y·sis [liˈpɔlisis] *n.* 脂解(作用)。 **lip·o·lyt·ic** [ˈlipəˈlitik] *a.*

li·po·ma [liˈpəumə, lai-] *n.* *(pl. -po·ma·ta* [-tə], *-pomas)*【医】脂肪瘤。**-tous** *a.*

lip·o·phil·ic [ˌlipəˈfilik] *a.* 亲脂的；嗜肥的。

lip·o·pro·tein [ˌlipəˈprəutiːn, -ˈprəutiːin] *n.*【生】脂蛋白。

lip·o·trop·ic [ˌlipəˈtrɔpik] *a.*【生化】抗脂(肪)的，减少脂肪积聚的。**li·pot·ro·pism** [liˈpɔtrəpizm] *n.*

lipped [lipt] *a.* ①有唇的〔常作复合词，如 tight-~ 嘴唇紧闭的；嘴紧的〕。②有嘴的(壶、杯等)。③【植】= labiate.

lip·pen [ˈlipn] *n., vt., vi.* 〔主 Scot.〕信任；信托。

lip·per [ˈlipə] *n.*【海】①涟漪；细浪。②浪花，水花。

lip·ping [ˈlipiŋ] *n.* ①【解】(骨的)唇形变。②(吹管乐器时的)嘴形，唇形。

Lip(p)·man(n) [ˈlipmən] *n.* 李普曼〔姓氏〕。

lip·py [ˈlipi] *a.* *(-pi·er, -pi·est)* 〔俚〕无礼的；傲慢的。**lip·pi·ness** *n.*

Lip·ton [ˈliptən] *n.* 利普顿〔姓氏〕。

liq. = ①liquid. ②liquor.

liq·uate [liˈkweit] *vt.*【冶】熔解，熔析。**li·qua·tion** *n.*

liq·ue·fa·cient [ˌlikwəˈfeiʃənt] *a.* 液化的；使成为液体的；促使液化的。— *n.* 液化素，解凝剂。

liq·ue·fac·tion [ˌlikwiˈfækʃən] *n.* 液化(作用)。

liq·ue·fi·er [ˈlikwiˌfaiə] *n.* ①液化器。②液化器操作工。

liq·ue·fy [ˈlikwifai] *vt., vi.* (使)液化。**liq·ue·fi·a·ble** *a.*

li·ques·cent [liˈkwesnt] *a.* 可液化的，融解的。**li·quescence** *n.*

li·queur [liˈkjuə] *n.* ①(饭后饮用的)甜露酒。②(饮甜露酒的)小酒杯 (= ~ glass). — *vt.* 用甜露酒调味。

liq·uid [ˈlikwid] *n.* ①液体。②【语】流音〔如 [l], [r]〕。— *a.* ①液体的，液态的，流动的。②清澄的，透明的。③易变的，不稳定的。④流畅的，流利的；柔和的，清脆的。⑤【语】流音的。⑥【经】流动的，易变为现金的。~ *diet [food]* 流质食物。~ *phase* 液相。~ *state* 液态。~ *sky* 明朗的天空。~ *opinions* 易变[多变]的意见。~ *assets*【商】流动资产。~ *capital* 流动资本。~ **air** 液态空气。~ **crystal** 液晶(体)。~ **fire** 液体燃烧剂。~ **measure** *n.* ①液量单位〔如 gill, pint, quart, gallon 等；*cf.* dry-measure〕。②液体测量器。~ **oxygen** 液态氧。**-ly** *ad.* **-ness** *n.*

liq·uid·am·bar [ˈlikwidˌæmbə] *n.* ①【植】胶皮糖香树 *(Liquidambar styraciflua)* 〔产于亚洲和北美〕。②胶皮糖香液。

liq·ui·date [ˈlikwideit] *vt.* ①清理，清算(破产的公司等)；了结；清偿(债务等)。②除掉，消灭，杀掉；结束。③(拿证券、资产等)换成现款。— *vi.* 清算；破产。

liq·ui·da·tion [ˌlikwiˈdeiʃən] *n.* ①(公司等的)清理，清算；(债务的)清偿，了结；(资产等的)变现。②清除，消灭；取消；杀掉。*go into* ~ (公司等)破产，停业清理。~ **sale** 停业清理大拍卖。

liq·ui·da·tion·ism [ˌlikwiˈdeiʃənizəm] *n.* 取消主义。**-tionist** *n., a.* 取消主义者[的]。

liq·ui·da·tor [ˈlikwideitə] *n.* 清算人。

liq·uid·i·ty [liˈkwiditi] *n.* ①液性。②流动性，流畅。

liq·uid·ize [ˈlikwidaiz] *vt.* 使成液体，使液化。

liq·ui·fy [ˈlikwifai] *vt., vi.* = liquefy.

liq·uor [ˈlikə] *n.* ①液，液体。②【药】溶液；液剂。③煮汁，煎汁。④(特指蒸馏制成的)酒。*meat* ~ 肉汁。~ *traffic* 酒的非法买卖。*malt* ~ 啤[麦]酒类 *[ale, beer, porter* 等*]*. *spirituous* ~ 烧酒；烈性酒。*vinous* ~ 葡萄酒。***be fond of*** ~ 喜欢喝酒。***be in*** ~ = ***be (the) worse for*** ~ 喝醉。***carry one's*** ~ ***like a gentleman*** 毫无醉意。***take [have] a*** ~ ***[~-up]*** 〔俚〕喝酒提神。***under the influence of*** ~ 有点醉，微醉。— *vt., vi.* 泡浴；浸在液体中；上油(在鞋子等上)；〔俚〕喝酒 *(up)*. ~ **head** 醉汉。

liq·uo·rice [ˈlikəris] *n.*【植】甘草属，甘草。~ **stick** 〔美俚〕单簧管。

li·quor·ish[1] [ˈlikəriʃ] *a.* ①= lickerish. ②嗜酒的。**-ly** *ad.* **-ness** *n.*

li·quor·ish[2] [ˈlikəriʃ] *n.* = liquorice.

li·ra [ˈliərə] *n.* *(pl. lir·e* [-ri], *~s)* (意大利货币单位)里拉。

lir·i·pipe [ˈliəriˌpaip] *n.* (教士服等的)长披巾，长披肩。

Li·sa [ˈliːzə, ˈlaizə] *n.* 莉萨〔女子名，Elizabeth 的昵称〕。

Lis·bon [ˈlizbən] *n.* 里斯本〔葡萄牙首都〕。

lisle [lail] *n.* ①(法国 Lisle 出产的坚牢的)莱尔棉线。②莱尔线织物。

lisp [lisp] *vi., vt.* ①咬着舌头发音〔如将 s, sh [ʃ], z 等音读作 th [θ, ð]〕。②(孩子似地)口齿不清地说。*She ~s.* 她说话口齿不清。— *n.* ①咬舌头，口齿不清。②咬舌头发出的声音；(树叶、流水等的)沙沙声。

lis pen·dens [lisˈpendenz] *n.* 〔L.〕【法】未决的诉讼，悬案。

lisp·ing·ly [ˈlispiŋli] *ad.* 咬着舌头地，口齿不清地。

lis·som [ˈlisəm] *a.* ①柔软的。②轻快的，灵活的，敏捷的。**-ly** *ad.* **-ness** *n.*

list[1] [list] *n.* ①清单，目录，表，一览表；名单。②(交易所中)全部上市证券。③= ~ price. *an active* ~ 现役军人名册。*a black* ~ 黑名单。*a casualty* ~ 伤亡名单。*an export* ~ 出口商品清单[目录]。*a packing* ~ 装箱单。*a reading* ~ 阅读书目。*a reserved* ~ 后备役军人名单。*a retired* ~ 复员军人名单。*a shopping* ~ 购物清单。***be struck off the*** ~ 被除名。***close the*** ~ 截止征募。***draw up [out] a*** ~ 造表。***head [lead] the*** ~ 名列第一。***make a*** ~ = draw up a ~. ***on the*** ~ 在名册中。***on the sick*** ~ 害着病。***pass first on the*** ~ 以第一名通过考试。***stand first on the*** ~ 居首位，名列前茅。— *vt.* ①登记；记入目录中，记入表中，列入名单[簿]中。②征募，列入军籍。— *vi.* ①入伍。②列入价目表。*~ed securities*【美商】上市证券。~ **price** (商品)目录价格，价目单上定价〔出售时根据不同情况打折扣或增加各种附加费用〕。

list[2] [list] *n.* ①布边，布头，布条。②狭条；(木板上截下的)木条。③田埂。④【建】边饰；扁带饰。⑤〔*pl.*〕(中世纪竞技场的)围栏，栅栏；竞技场，运动场；竞争场所。⑥(马背中央等处的)深色条纹。***enter the ~s against*** 向…挑战；应战，出战。— *vt.* ①给…装布边。②把(布条等)拼成一块。③从木板上截下边条。④犁地。

list[3] [list] *vt., vi.* 〔诗〕听，倾听。

list[4] [list] *vt., vi.* *(listed,* 〔古〕 ***list; listed.*** *3rd sing.* ***list, listeth)*** 中…的意，称…的心；希望，想 *(to do)*. *He did as him* ~. 他按他自己的意思做了。

list[5] [list] *vi., vt.* (船等)倾斜。— *n.* 倾斜(性)。*That ship has a* ~ *to port [a port* ~*]*. 那条船向左倾斜。

list·el [ˈlistl] *n.*【建】扁带饰。

lis·ten [ˈlisn] *vi.* ①听。②听从，服从 *(to)*. ③听上去，听起来。~ *with strained ears* 竖起耳朵听。*L- to me.* 听我说。*We ~ed but we heard nothing.* 我们听着，但什么也没听见。~ *to reason* 服从道理。~ *to temptation* 甘受诱惑。*It doesn't* ~ *reasonable.* 〔美口〕这听上去并不适当。~ ***for*** 倾耳听，等着听 (~ *for an answer* 侯

复). ～ **in** ①收听,监听. ②偷听,窃听. — *n.* 听,倾听. *Please have a ～ to this.* 请听听这个吧. **on the ～** 注意地听着.

lis·ten·er [ˈlisnə] *n.* ①听者;收听者. ②〔俚〕耳朵. ～-**in** *(pl. -in)* ①收听者. ②监听者,偷听者. **-ship** 听众(人数).

lis·ten·ing [ˈlisniŋ] *n.* 倾听. — *a.* ①收听的,留心的,注意的. ②助听的. ～ **button** 耳塞助听器. ～ **gear** 听音器. ～-**in** 收听无线电. ～-**in device**【军】潜听装置. ～-**in line** 监听线;听话线. ～ **post**【军】听音哨;(一般的)情报监听处. ～ **station**【军】雷达〔无线电〕侦察接收站;监听站.

Lis·ter [ˈlistə] *n.* 李司忒〔1827—1912,英国外科医生〕. ～**ism**【医】李司忒消毒法. ～**ize** *vt.*【医】施行李司忒消毒法.

lis·ter¹ [ˈlistə] *n.* (农机)双壁开沟犁.

list·er² [ˈlistə] *n.* 造表人,编目人.

lis·ter·ine [ˈlistəriːn] *n.* 防腐溶液.

list·ing [ˈlistiŋ] *n.* ①造表,编目. ②表册上的项目〔如房地产中间人关于待售房产的记载〕. ③表册.

list·less [ˈlistlis] *a.* 冷淡的;懒洋洋的,无精打采的,倦怠的. **-ly** *ad.* **-ness** *n.*

lit [lit] *light* 的过去式及过去分词. — *a.* ①照亮的,点着的. ②〔美俚〕喝醉了的,被毒品麻醉了的. **be ～ up** 〔俚〕喝醉了;被毒品麻醉了.

lit. ＝ ①literally. ②literary. ③literature. ④litre.

lit·a·ny [ˈlitəni] *n.* ①【宗】启应祷文. ②(枯燥、重复的)连续不断的说明〔叙述〕. *the L-* (英国教会《公祷文》中的)启应祈文.

Lit. B., Lit B ＝ Litt. B.

li·tchi [ˈliːˌtʃiː] *n.*【植】荔枝树;荔枝.

lit-crit [ˈlitˈkrit] *n.* 文学批评,文学评论.

Lit. D., Litt. D. ＝〔L.〕Lit(t)erarum Doctor (＝Doctor of Literature) 文学博士.

-lite *comb. f.* 表示"石","矿物","岩石","化石": chryso*lite,* hya*lite* oo*lite.*

li·te·pen·den·te [ˈlaitiːpenˈdentiː]〔L.〕在宙理中.

li·ter [ˈliːtə] *n.*〔美〕＝ litre.

lit·er·a·cy [ˈlitərəsi] *n.* 识字,能读能写;有学问 *(opp.* illiteracy*). a ～ campaign* 扫盲运动. *a ～ class* 扫盲班.

lit·erae hu·ma·ni·o·res [ˈlitəriː hjuˌmeiniˈɔːriːz]〔L.〕①人文学科. ②希腊罗马古典语文研究.

lit·er·al [ˈlitərəl] *a.* ①文字的,文字上的. ②字面上的,逐字逐句的. ③没有夸张的,朴实的,原原本本的. ④呆板的,平庸的,乏味的. ⑤字母的,用字母代表的. *the ～ arithmetic* 代数学. *a ～ translation* 逐字逐句直译. *a ～ interpretation* 字面解释. *the ～ truth* 原原本本的实情. — *n.*【印】错排,文字上的错误. ***in the ～ sense of the word*** 照字面的意思;实在,真正 (*In the ～ sense of the word, I hear nothing.* 我听是实在没有听到〔但可能看到过〕). ～ **contract**【法】成文契约,书面契约. **-i·ty** [-ˈræliti] 直译;实际,精确. **-ness** *n.*

lit·er·al·ism [ˈlitərəlizəm] *n.* 拘泥字义〔文字〕;直译;【美】直写主义. **-ist** *n.* 拘泥字义〔文字〕者;直译者;直写主义者.

lit·er·al·ize [ˈlitərəˌlaiz] *vt.* *(-iz·ed, -iz·ing)* ①照字面解释. ②对…逐字逐句翻译. **-za·tion** *n.*

lit·er·al·ly [ˈlitərəli] *ad.* ①照字义,逐字地. ②确实,真正,完全. ③差不多,简直. *The city was ～ destroyed.* 城市差不多全毁了. *In the race he ～ "flew" round the track.* 他在赛跑中简直象飞似地绕着跑道跑.

lit·er·a·ri·ly [ˈlitərərili] *ad.* 文学上,学问上,学术上.

lit·er·ar·i·ness [ˈlitərərinis] *n.* 文学性,文艺性.

lit·er·ar·y [ˈlitərəri] *a.* ①文学的,文学上的. ②通文学的;喜欢文学的;以写作为职业的. ③书本上的;书面语的. ～ *columns* (报纸等的)文艺栏. *a ～ image* 文学形象. ～ *works [writings]* 文学作品. *a ～ executor* 遗稿保管人. *a ～ man* 文学家,学者,作家. ～ *property* 著作权,版权. ～ *pursuits* 文字生涯. *quite a ～ person* 擅长文学的人. ～ *style* 书面体.

lit·er·ate [ˈlitərit] *a.* ①有学问的,有文化的;能写能读的 *(opp.* illiterate*).* ②精通文学的;会写作的. — *n.* 识字的人;有学问的人. **-ly** *ad.*

lit·er·a·ti [ˌlitəˈrɑːtiː, -ˈreitai] *n.* 〔*pl.*〕*(sing.* **-tus** [-təs]*)* 〔L.〕文学家;文人学士.

lit·e·ra·tim [ˌlitəˈreitim] *ad.*〔L.〕逐字地;按照原文.

lit·er·a·tion [ˌlitəˈreiʃən] *n.* 用字母代表声音或词.

lit·er·a·tor [ˈlitəˌreitə] *n.* 文人;作家.

lit·er·a·ture [ˈlitəritʃə] *n.* ①文学,文学作品. ②文献. ③文学研究;著作业,著作. ④〔口〕(广告、宣传用的)印刷品. ⑤(为乐器演奏用的)一组乐曲. ⑥〔古〕学识,学问. *English ～* 英国文学. *light ～* 大众〔通俗〕文学. *polite ～* 纯文学. *mathematical ～* 数学文献. *a person of infinite ～* 学识广博的人.

lit·e·ra·tus [ˌlitəˈrɑːtəs] *n.*〔L.〕literati 的单数.

lith- *comb. f.* ＝ litho-.

-lith *comb. f.* ①表示"石","人造石": aero*lith*, grano*lith*, mega*lith*. ②表示"结石": uro*lith*. ③表示"矿石","岩石": licco*lith*.

Lith. ＝ Lithuania(n).

lith., litho., lithog. ＝ lithograph(y).

lith·arge [ˈliθɑːdʒ, liˈθɑːdʒ] *n.*【化】①密陀僧,一氧化铅. ②正方铅矿.

lithe [laið] *a.* ①柔软的. ②敏捷的,轻快的. **-ly** *ad.* **-ness** *n.* **-some** *a.* ＝ lithe.

lith·i·a [ˈliθiə] *n.* ①【化】氧化锂. ②【医】结石病. ～ ***water*** 锂盐矿水.

lith·i·as·is [liˈθaiəsis] *n.*【医】结石病. *renal ～* 肾结石.

lith·ic [ˈliθik] *a.* ①石的. ②【化】锂的. ③【医】结石的.

lith·i·um [ˈliθiəm] *n.*【化】锂.

lith·o- *comb. f.* 表示"石","岩石","结石": *litho*graph, *litho*sphere.

lith·o·graph [ˈliθəˌgrɑːf] *n.*【印】石〔平〕版,石〔平〕版画. — *vt.* 石印,用平版印刷.

li·thog·ra·pher [liˈθɔgrəfə] *n.* 石印〔平版印刷〕工人.

lith·o·graph·ic [ˌliθəˈgræfik] *a.* ①平版画的;石印的,平版印刷品的. ②平版印刷(术)的. **-i·cal·ly** *ad.*

li·thog·ra·phy [liˈθɔgrəfi] *n.* 石印〔平版印刷〕术;平版印刷品.

lith·oid, -al [ˈliθɔid, -l] *a.* 石质的,石状的.

li·thol·o·gy [liˈθɔlədʒi] *n.* ①【地】岩性学;岩性. ②【医】结石学. **-log·ic(al)** *a.* **-log·i·cal·ly** *ad.*

lith·o·marge [ˈliθəˈmɑːdʒ] *n.*【地】密高岭土.

lith·o·me·te·or [ˌliθəˈmiːtiə] *n.*【气】大气尘粒.

lith·on·trip·tic [ˌliθənˈtriptik] *a.*【医】溶结石的;碎结石的. — *n.*【药】溶石药,碎石药.

lith·o·phyte [ˈliθəˌfait] *n.*【植】岩表植物〔如地衣〕,石生植物. **-o·phyt·ic** [-ˈfitik] *a.*

lith·o·pone [ˈliθəˌpəun] *n.* 锌钡白.

lith·o·print [ˈliθəuprint] *vt.* 用照相胶印法印刷.

lith·o·sphere [ˈliθəˌsfiə] *n.*【地】岩石圈,陆界.

li·thot·o·my [liˈθɔtəmi] *n.*【医】膀胱切开取石术,膀胱石切除术. **-tom·ic, -tom·i·cal** [ˌliθəˈtɔmikl] *a.* **li·thot·o·mist** *n.* (膀胱)切石专家. **-o·mize** *vt.* 做膀胱切石手术.

li·thot·ri·ty [liˈθɔtriti] *n.*【医】碎石术.

Lith·u·a·ni·a [ˌliθju(ː)ˈeinjə, -niə] *n.* 立陶宛.

Lith·u·a·ni·an [ˌliθju(ː)ˈeiniən] *a.* 立陶宛的,立陶宛人〔语〕的. — *n.* 立陶宛人;立陶宛语.

lit·i·ga·ble [ˈlitigəbl] *a.*【法】可诉讼的.

lit·i·gant [ˈlitigənt] *a.* 有关诉讼的. *the parties ～* 诉讼当事人. — *n.* 诉讼当事人.

lit·i·gate [ˈlitigeit] *vt., vi.* 诉诸法律,打官司;争论.

lit·i·ga·tion [ˌlitiˈgeiʃən] *n.* 诉讼,起诉.

li·ti·gious [liˈtidʒəs] *a.* ①好诉讼的，爱打官司的；爱争论的。②可诉讼的，可争论的。**-ly** *ad.* **-ness** *n.*

lit·mus [ˈlitməs] *n.*【化】石蕊。~ **paper**【化】石蕊试纸。~ **test** 石蕊试验；〔喻〕简单而具有决定性的试验。**-less** *a.* 中性的。

li·to·tes [ˈlaitəuti:z] *n.*【语】曲意法，间接表达法，反语法〔如将 little 用作 not, rather 用作 very much indeed; 又如用 no small 代 great, not bad 代 very good〕。

li·tre [ˈli:tə] *n.*（容量单位）升。

Lit·sea [ˈlitsiə] *n.*【植】(樟科中的)木姜子属。

Litt. B. =〔L.〕*literarum Baccalaureus* (= Bachelor of Letters 或 Bachelor of literature) 文学士。

Litt. D. =〔L.〕*Literarum Doctor* (= Doctor of Letters 或 Doctor of Literature) 文学博士。

lit·ten [ˈlitn] *a.*〔古〕点燃的。

lit·ter [ˈlitə] *n.* ①担架，舁床；轿舆。②(兽类睡眠用的)褥草，垫圈。③枯枝层，落叶层。④七零八碎的东西，杂乱。⑤(猪等)同胎生下的小崽。~ *bearers* 担架兵。*a ~ of little pigs* 一窝小猪。~ *of weeds* 枯草层。***be in*** ~ (狗、猪等)临产。***in a*** ~ (房间等)乱七八糟，杂乱。—*vt.* ①铺褥草。②乱丢(东西)。③弄乱(房间等) *(with)*。④(猪等)产仔。— *vi.* ①(家畜等)产仔。②乱丢东西，乱丢废物[垃圾等]。~ **bag** 废物袋〔如在汽车中置备，供丢弃废物〕。~**-bin** 废物箱。~**bug** 公共场所乱扔废纸废物的人。

lit·ter·ae hu·mani·o·res [ˈlitəri: hjuˌmeiniˈɔ:ri:z] = literae humaniores.

lit·té·ra·teur [ˌliterəˈtə:] *n.*〔F.〕文学家；文人。

lit·ter·i·ness [ˈlitərinis] *n.* 杂乱。

lit·ter·y [ˈlitəri] *a.* ①褥草的；满是稻草的。②杂乱的；不整洁的。

Lit·tle [ˈlitl] *n.* 利特尔〔姓氏〕。

lit·tle [ˈlitl] *a.* ***(less*** 或 ***lesser; least;***〔俚、方〕***-tler; -tlest)*** ★ less, lesser, least 通例是与 more, most 相对应的用语，表示数量、程度方面的小，亦可代替表示形体小的 smaller, smallest. 又：little 除"小"的意义之外，还含有可怜、轻蔑等的感情。习惯上只说 great and little, big and little, great and small, large and small, 不说 large and little, big and small. ①*(opp.* big) 小，小的；年轻的，年纪小的，可爱的。*a ~ dog* 小狗。*a ~ drop [a ~ glass] of whisky* 一小滴[一小杯]威士忌酒。*the ~ Smiths* 斯密士(家)的孩子们。*my ~ man [woman]* 小弟弟[姑娘]。*a nice ~ thing* 可爱的小家伙。*our ~ life* 我辈短促的生命〔人生如寄之意〕。②*(opp.* great) 孩子似的，孩子气的；琐细的，小的，吝啬的，心地狭窄的。*L- things amuse ~ minds.* 小孩欢喜小东西。*sb.'s ~ game* 孩子似的[可笑的]举动[手法]。*a ~ thing* 小事。*a ~ mind [soul]* 狭小的气量。③〔表示数量等的否定用法，无冠词〕*(opp.* much) 只有少许[一点点]，没有多少。*There is but ~ hope.* 没有多少希望。*I have ~ hope, if any = I have ~ or no hope* 简直没有希望。④〔表示数量等的肯定用法，加冠词〕〔*cf.* a few〕有一点。*There is a ~ hope.* 有一点希望。*a ~ time [while] ago* 片刻之前，刚才。*I will go a ~ way with you.* 我陪你走一段路。*A ~ care would have prevented it.* 稍微当心一点，这种事情就不会发生。★有时纯属礼貌上的形式，无表示微少的意义，只作 some 的代用语。例：*Let me give you a ~ mutton.* 让我给你(一点)羊肉。*May I have a ~ money?* 给我(点)钱好吗？*A ~ more [less] sugar, please.* 请给我多[少]来一点糖。*only a ~ wine* 只一点点酒。*I gave him the ~ money that I had. = I gave him what ~ money I had.* 我把所有的一点点钱统统给了他。***but*** ~ 只一点点 (*I have but ~ money.* 我只有一点点钱)。***go but a ~ way to*** 差得远，不够。***make ~ of*** ①不重视，轻视，不以为意。②难了解，不领会。~ ***ones*** 孩子们〔加用 our, her 等〕。~ ***or no*** 简直没有，几乎没有。***no*** ~ (= not a ~) 不少，很多。***very*** ~ 很少；一点也没有 (*He has very ~ sense.* 他没有常识。*He takes very ~ trouble about his work.* 他做事一点也不用心)。— *n.* ①〔肯定用法，表示程度、数量的〕小，少。*Every ~ helps.*〔谚〕点点滴滴都起作用。*know a ~ of everything* 什么都懂一点。*the ~* 不重要[无足轻重]的人。*A ~ is better than none.* 聊胜于无。②〔否定用法，无冠词〕一点点，少许，些许。*He has seen ~ of life.* 他不懂世故。*L- remains to be said.* 简直没有甚么可以讲了。*I got but [very, rather] ~ out of it.* 我简直没有从这当中得着什么。***a ~ at a time*** 每次少许。***after a ~*** 过了一会儿。***by ~ and ~ = ~ by ~*** 一点一点地，慢慢地，逐渐地。***for a ~*** 一会儿，不久。***from ~ up***〔美〕从幼年起。***in ~*** 小规模的，小型的。~ ***or nothing*** = ~ ***if anything*** 简直没有，几乎没有。***not a ~*** 不少，相当多。***quite a ~***〔美口〕大量，许多，丰富。***the ~ = what ~*** 仅有的一点 (*He did the ~ that [what ~] he could.* 他尽到了他仅有的微力)。— *ad.* ①〔肯定用法，加冠词 a〕一点，稍，略。*I speak English a ~.* 我稍能说一点英语。*Wait a ~.* 等一下。*He is a ~ better today.* 他今天好一点了。②〔否定用法，无冠词〕毫不，一点也不；几乎不，简直不〔主要和 know, imagine, dream, think, guess 等词连用〕。~ *known writers* 不大出名的作家，无名作家。*He ~ knows.* 他不知道。~ ***better [less] than*** 和…一样，和…没有差别，半斤八两。~ ***more than*** 和…一样[无差别]。~ ***short of*** 简直是，几乎。***set ~ by*** 轻视。***think ~ of*** 不重视，不在乎。**L- Bear**【天】= Ursa minor. ~**-ease**【史】使人立卧不得的牢笼。~ **finger** 小指 (*twist [wrap] around one's ~ finger.* 轻而易举地控制[施影响于]他人)。**L- Fox**【天】= Vulpecula. ~ **go**〔英〕(剑桥大学)学士学位的小考[预考]。~ **hours** ①夜半一二点钟。②[L- Hours] (天主教的)日间例行祷告课[即晨祷，三时课，午祷，九时课等]。~ **Joe**〔美俚〕骰子中的四点。~ **leaf**【植】小叶病。**L- League** 少年棒球协会。**L- Leaguer** 少年棒球协会会员。~ **magazine** 小杂志〔一种刊登试验性文艺作品的非商业性而且发行有限的小杂志〕。~ **Mary**〔口〕肚子。~ **neck**【动】小颈幼贝〔产于美国，通常生吃，也叫 ~ neck clam〕。~ **office** (天主教的) 小礼拜。~ **people** (民间迷信中的)小精灵。**L- Rhody** 美国罗得岛州的别称。**L- Rock** (美国)小石城。**L- Russian** 小俄罗斯人〔乌克兰人的旧称〕。~ **slam**【桥牌】小满贯。~ **theatre** ①(大学或艺术团体等实验演出用的) 小剧场。②小剧场演出的戏剧。~ **woman** ①懂事的小女孩。②〔美俚〕妻子。

lit·tle·ness [ˈlitlnis] *n.* ①小。②少量，些许。③褊狭，吝啬，卑鄙。

Lit·tle·ton [ˈlitltən] *n.* 利特尔顿〔姓氏〕。

lit·tlish [ˈlitliʃ] *a.* 有点儿小的。

lit·to·ral [ˈlitərəl] *a.* 海滨的；沿岸的；沿海的 *(opp.* pelagic)；【生】栖息在沿岸浅海中的。~ *fauna* 沿岸动物区系。*the ~ province* 沿海省份[地区]。— *n.* 沿(海)岸地区。**-ly** *ad.*

li·tur·gic(al) [liˈtə:dʒik(əl)] *a.* 礼拜仪式的。**-cal·ly** *ad.* 按照礼拜仪式的。

lit·ur·gist [ˈlitədʒist] *n.* ①使用(或主张使用)礼拜仪式者。②礼拜仪式方面的权威。

lit·ur·gy [ˈlitə(:)dʒi] *n.* ①礼拜仪式。②[the L-] (英国教会的)《公祷文》；(希腊正教的)圣餐仪式。

litz wire [ˈlits ˌwaiə]【电】编织线，绞合线。

liv·a·bil·i·ty [ˌlivəˈbiliti] *n.* ①(家禽、牲畜等的)存活率。②适于居住。

liv·a·ble [ˈlivəbl] *a.* ①(房子、气候等)可以[适合]居住的。②(生活条件，工作条件等)有生活价值的。③(人)易于相处的，能与之共同生活的。**-ness** *n.*

live[1] [liv] *vi.* ①生存；活着〔现常用 be alive 或 be living〕。②生活，过日子，过活；做人，处世。③居住。④生

活得很愉快、高兴；在生活中得到享受. ⑤一直活到；(事物)继续发展[存在]；(船等)度过危险. ⑥(人物形象等)栩栩如生,生动如真；留在别人的记忆中. *L- and let* ~. 〔谚〕自己活也让别人活. *He ~s what he teaches.* 他言行如一. *He ~s [is living] in France.* 他住在法国. *~ under the same roof* 住在一幢房子里. *She ~d and died a virgin.* 她终身没有结婚. *I have ~d today.* 我今天过得很高兴. *L- and learn.* 〔谚〕活到老，学到老. *~ to be a hundred* 活到一百岁. *The ship ~d in the storm.* 这船没有在风浪中沉没. *make a historical character ~* 把历史人物描写得非常生动. *His memory ~s.* 他活在人的心中. — *vt.* ④过(…的生活)；度过. ②(在自己的生活中)表现,实行,实践. ***(as sure) as I ~*** 的的确确 (*He is dead, as I ~.* 他确实死了). ***He ~s long that ~s well.*** 〔谚〕活得好就是活得久. ***~ a double life*** 过双重(人格)生活. ***~ a lie*** 过虚伪的生活. ***~ above [beyond] one's income [means]*** 生活和收入不相称,入不敷出. ***~ by*** ①靠…为生 (*~ by one's hands* 自食其力. *~ by one's fingers' ends* 靠手艺过活). ②住在…附近. ***~ by oneself*** 独居. ***~ carefully*** 俭省地[有节制地]过日子. ***~ down*** 靠以后的行为洗清污名等. ***~ from hand to mouth*** 做一天吃一天地过日子. ***~ hard*** 过勤苦生活. ***~ in*** ①住进. ②(雇员等)住在东家 (*opp.* ~ out). ***~ in ease*** 过得逍遥自在. ***~ in [within] oneself*** 孤独地生活. ***~ in the past*** 靠着缅怀往昔过日子〔意味着目前生活不如意等〕. ***~ it up*** 〔俚〕狂欢；纵情作乐. ***~ off*** ①住在…之外. ②以…为生. ***~ on [upon]*** ①以…为主食 (*~ on rice* 以米为主食). ②靠…生活 (*~ on sixpence a day* 每天花六便士维持生活). ③继续活着. ***~ on forever*** 万古长青. ***~ on the cross*** 〔俚〕以偷窃为生；行为不正. ***~ out*** ①(雇员等)外宿,住在外面. ②活过,多活(一定期间) (*~ out another month* 又多活一个月). ***~ rough*** 过苦日子. ***~ single*** 过独身生活. ***~ through*** 度过 (*~ through an economical crisis* 度过经济危机). ***~ to oneself*** 过孤独的生活. ***~ up to*** 量…过日子；实行(主义等)；生活得无愧于,配得上,够得上；达到预期标准 (*~ up to expectations* 终于取得预期的东西[事业的成功等]). ***~ well*** ①过有道德生活. ②过优裕生活. ***~ with sb.*** ①和某人同居. ②寄住在某人处 (*~ with sb. in peace* 和某人和平共处). ***where sb. ~s*** 〔美俚〕某人的要害 (*The word goes right where I ~.* 这话正刺中我的要害). **~-forever** 景天属植物.

live² [laiv] *a.* ①活的，有生命的 (*opp.* dead). *a ~ fish* 活鱼. *a ~ fence* 树篱. ②〔谑〕〔常接在 real 之后〕真的,活生生的. *a real ~ mountain* 真正的山. *There's a real ~ burglar under my bed!* 我床下面真有一个窃贼. ③活泼的,有精神的,生气勃勃的. *a ~ man* 精力旺盛的人. *~ eyes* 炯炯有神的眼睛. *the ~ murmur of a summer's day* 夏天的虫声. ④目前大家感觉兴趣的,当前的. *a ~ issue [question]* 尚在争论中的问题. ⑤(机器等)能开动的；传动的,动力发动的. *a ~ axle* 传动轴. ⑥燃烧着的. *~ coals* 燃烧着的炭. *a ~ hatred* 怒火中烧. ⑦装着炸药的实弹,有作用,充电的. *a ~ bomb* 未爆炸的炸弹. *~ shell shooting* 实弹射击. ⑧未使用过的；(岩石等)未采掘的；原状的. *~ feathers* 由活鸟身上拔下来的羽毛. *a ~ match* 没擦过的火柴. ⑨正在使用着的；(球等)正在玩的. *a ~ machine* 可以使用的机器. *a ~ runway* 现用跑道. ⑩(稿子等)尚未排版的. ⑪(空气)清新的；(颜色)鲜艳的. *~ air* 空气新鲜. ⑫(参加)实况播送的. *It was a ~ broadcast, not a recording.* 那是实况转播,不是录音. — *ad.* 在(表演)现场,从(表演)现场,实况地. *The trial was broadcast ~ from the courtroom.* 审判情况是从审判室实况转播的. **~ account** 【商】流水帐. **~ bait** (钓鱼用的)活饵. **~-box** 放在河中使鱼虾保持新鲜的箩筐[栅栏]. **~ centre** 【机】活顶尖，活顶针. **~ firing** 实际发射. **~ graphite** 含铀块石墨. **~ load** 【机】动(力)负载，活载荷；工作负载，有效负载. **~ lode** 可采矿脉. **~ oak** 【植】①栎属〔尤指弗吉尼亚栎 (*Quercus virginiana*)〕. ②= Encina (木叶栎). ③栎木. **~ parking** 司机等候在车内的车辆停放. **~ pick-up** 【电视】实况录象；播送室内实况广播. **~ quartz** 含矿石英. **~ room** 交混回响室. **~ steam** 新汽〔直接从锅炉出来的高压蒸气,与"废气"相对而言〕. **~ steam valve** 进气阀. **~ stock** *n.* 家畜，牲畜 (*a ~ stock farming* 畜牧). **~ studio** 具有较好混响装置的播音室. **~ time** 实况转播时间. **~ wire** ①通电的电线. ②生龙活虎般的人.

live•a•ble [ˈlivəbl] *a.* = livable.

-lived [-livd, -ˈlaivd] *comb. f.* 表示"寿命…的"；"生活…的"：*long-*lived, *short-*lived.

live•li•hood [ˈlaivlihud] *n.* 生活,生计. *means of ~* 生活资料. ***earn [get, gain, make] a ~*** 谋生. ***earn an honest ~*** 规规矩矩地挣钱生活. ***pick up a scanty ~*** 过苦日子.

live•li•ly [ˈlaivlili] *ad.* 活泼地,生气勃勃地；快活地,热闹地；生动地,鲜明地.

live•li•ness [ˈlaivlinis] 活泼,快活,热闹,繁华；生动,鲜明；强烈. *a certain ~* 〔军俚〕猛烈的炮火.

live•long [ˈlivˌlɔŋ] *a.* 漫长的；整个的；完全的. *the ~ day* 一整天. *the ~ night* 漫漫长夜.

live•ly [ˈlaivli] *a.* ①活泼的,精神旺盛的,充满生气的；愉快的,活跃的. ②(舞蹈等)轻快的；(球等)弹性好的. ③(船)行驶轻快的,驾驶灵便的. ④(色彩等)鲜明的,强烈的. ⑤(描写等)逼真的,生动的. ⑥(感情等)强烈的,热烈的. ⑦振奋的,提神的. ⑧〔谑〕惊心动魄的,使人提心吊胆的. *a ~ description* 生动的描写. *a ~ imagination* 丰富的想象力. *a ~ discussion* 热烈的讨论,激烈的辩论. *a ~ sense of gratitude* 深厚的谢意. *make it [things] ~ for sb.* 使某人紧张[为难]. ***as ~ as a grip*** 非常快活. ***have a ~ time*** 大为慌乱[活跃]一阵 (*The enemy had a ~ time during the battle.* 敌人在战火中大为慌乱). ***take a ~ interest in*** 对…抱有强烈兴趣. — *ad.* 生气勃勃地,精力充沛地；活生生地；鲜明地.

liv•en [ˈlaivən] *vt., vi.* (使)活跃起来,(使)愉快；变得愉快；振奋起来〔常与 *up* 连用〕. **-er** *n.*

liv•er¹ [ˈlivə] *n.* ①【解】肝脏. ②(食用)肝. ③赤褐色. *a hot ~* 热情. *a lily [white] ~* 怯懦,胆小. **~ oil** (鱼)肝油. **~ wing** ①(煮熟的鸡的)右膀. ②〔谑〕(人的)右腕. **~ colour** 肝色,赤褐色. **~ complaint** 肝病. **~ extract** 【药】肝浸膏,肝精. **~ fluke** 【医】肝吸虫. **~ leaf** 【植】獐耳细辛属；地钱属 (= hepatica). **~ spot** 【医】肝斑〔指皮肤上的雀斑、痣等斑块,旧时以为由肝机能上的毛病所引起〕. **~wort** 【植】欧龙牙草. **~wurst** 【烹】(肝泥灌制的)肝肠.

liv•er² [ˈlivə] *n.* 生活者；居住者. *a clean ~* 洁身自好的人. *a close ~* 吝啬的人,守财奴. *an evil ~* = *a fast [loose] ~* 浪子,放荡的人. *a free [high] ~* 考究享受[吃喝玩乐]的人；生活奢侈的人. *a good ~* 品德好的人；考究饮食的人；〔方〕生活优裕的人. *a hearty ~* 贪吃的人. *the longest ~* 【法】活得最久的受益人.

liv•er•ied [ˈlivərid] *a.* 穿特殊制服的,穿号衣的.

liv•er•ish [ˈlivəriʃ] *a.* ①肝色的. ②有肝病的. ③脾气坏的,易怒的.

Liv•er•pool [ˈlivəˈpuːl] *n.* 利物浦〔英国港市〕.

Liv•er•pud•li•an [ˌlivəˈpʌdliən] *a., n.* 利物浦的(人).

liv•er•y¹ [ˈlivəri] *a.* ①象肝的. ②有肝病征象的.

liv•ery² [ˈlivəri] *n.* ①(侍从、仆人穿的) 特别制服,号衣. ②伦敦各种行会会员的制服；伦敦同业工会会员. ③〔古〕侍从,仆从. ④〔诗〕鸟等的服装,装束. ⑤(马的)日粮；(人的)口粮,配给粮食. ⑥= ~ stable. (马的)马房. ⑦【法】财产所有权的让渡 (批准书). ⑧各种车辆出租行. *the ~ of spring* 春天的服装. *the ~ of grief [woe]*

丧服. ~ *and bait* 马的口粮. ***at*** ~ (马)付饲料〔或费用〕托人代养(着) (*keep a horse at* ~ 领饲料代人养马;付饲料托人养马;出租马). ***in*** ~ 穿着制服. ***out of*** ~ 不穿制服,穿着便衣. ***sue (for) one's*** ~ (继承人)向法院申诉要求让渡财产. ***take up one's*** ~ 入同业公会. ***the*** ~ ***of sb.'s opinion*** 借用某人的意见. ~ **coach** 出租马车. ~ **company** 伦敦市同业公会〔因从前同业会会员穿规定制服〕. ~ **man** ①(伦敦的)同业公会会员. ②出租马车的人. ③〔古〕(穿特殊制服的)侍从,仆从. ~ **stable** (出租车马的)马车行,马房.

lives [laivz] *n.* life 的复数.

liv·id [ˈlivid] *a.* ①铅色的,青灰色的. ②(被打伤而呈现)青黑色的. ③〔英口〕怒冲冲的. *a face* ~ *with rage* 气得发青的脸. *a* ~ *face* 苍白的脸,死灰色的脸. *a* ~ *hue* 带青色. ~ *hatred* 刻骨痛恨. **-ly** *ad.* **-ness** *n.*

li·vid·i·ty [liˈviditi] *n.* 铅色,青灰色;(被打伤而呈现的)青黑色.

liv·ing [ˈliviŋ] *a.* ①活着的,生存着的;有生命的;在活动中〔起作用〕的;在使用中的. ②活泼的,生动的;生气勃勃的,旺盛的;强烈的,猛烈的. ③天然的,自然状态的;未开采过的. ④栩栩如生的,逼真的. ⑤(维持)生活的;(适于)居住的. ⑥〔口〕(加强语气词) = very. ⑦生活的,维持生活的. ~ *beings* 生物. *the greatest* ~ *poet* 现在活着的第一流诗人. ~ *coals* 燃烧着的煤块. *a* ~ *language* 活的语言. ~ *water* 活水. *a* ~ *faith* 强烈的信仰. *a* ~ *gale* 烈风. *a* ~ *rock* 天然岩石. *He is the* ~ *image of his father.* 他活象他的父亲. ~ *conditions* 生活条件. *the* ~ *area* 适于居住的地方. *scare the* ~ *daylights out of sb.* 把某人吓得半死. ~ *likeness* 逼肖的画像. ~ *picture* (由活人扮演的)活画. ~ *pledge* 资产抵押. *the* ~ 生者,现存者. *the* ~ *theatre* 舞台剧〔与电影及电视相对而言〕. ***within*** ~ ***memory*** 在世人记忆中的. — *n.* ①生活;生计;生存. ②〔英〕教士的俸禄. ③〔古〕财产. *high* ~ 奢华的生活. *good* ~ 讲究(吃喝)的生活. *plain* ~ *and high thinking* 生活朴素思想高超. *the art of* ~ 生活的艺术. *the cost of* ~ 生活费用. *the standard of* ~ 生活水平. ***earn [get, make] one's*** ~ 谋生. ***in the land of the*** ~ 活着的,现存的. ***make a good*** ~ 过安乐生活. **L- Buddha** (喇嘛教的)活佛. ~ **death** 活受罪〔指生活境遇〕;活地狱. **~-in** (被雇者)住在东家,供住. **~-out** (被雇者)住在外面,不供住. ~ **room** ①起居室. ②= ~ space. ~ **space** ①生存空间. ②(房屋的)可居住面积. ~ **unit** (公寓)套房. ~ **wage** 生活工资. ~ **will** 要求在病入膏肓,已成废物时不必用人工方法勉强延长生命的书面声明. **-ly** *ad.* **-ness** *n.*

Liv·ing·ston [ˈliviŋstən] *n.* 利文斯顿〔姓氏〕.

Liv·ing·stone [ˈliviŋstən] *n.* 利文斯通〔姓氏〕.

li·vre [ˈlivə; *F.* liːvr] *n.* 里弗尔〔法国十九世纪前货币名,原相当于一磅银子,后为法朗所代替〕.

l.i.w. = lost in weight 重量不足〔损耗〕.

lix·iv·i·ate [likˈsiviˌeit] *vt.* ***(-at·ed, -at·ing)*** = leach. **-i·a·tion** *n.*

lix·iv·i·um [likˈsiviəm] *n.* ***(pl. -i·ums, -i·a*** [-ə]***)*** 【化】浸滤液,灰汁;碱汁.

liz·ard [ˈlizəd] *n.* ①【动】蜥蜴. ②一种家养的杂色金丝雀. ③〔L-〕〔美〕亚拉巴马州的别号;〔Lizards〕亚拉巴马州人. *a house* ~ 守宫,壁虎. ~ **fish** 【动】歧须鮠科 *(synodontidae)* 的鱼.

Liz·zie [ˈlizi] *n.* 莉齐〔女子名, Elizabeth 的昵称〕.

liz·zie [ˈlizi] *n.* 〔美俚〕廉价的破旧汽车;早期的福特牌汽车. *a* ~ *label* 〔美俚〕汽车上的标记;旧汽车的标记. *a* ~ *stiff* 〔美俚〕坐破旧汽车到处移动的流动工人〔流浪者〕.

L.J. = Lord Justice 〔英〕上诉法院法官.

Lju·blja·na [ˈljuːbljɑːnɑː] *n.* 卢布尔雅那〔南斯拉夫城市〕.

LL. = ①Late Latin 后期拉丁语. ②Low Latin (公元二世纪的)民间拉丁语,俗拉丁语.

ll. = lines.

'll = will, shall (如 she'll, I'll 等).

lla·ma [ˈlɑːmə] *n.* 【动】美洲驼,无峰驼.

lla·no [ˈlɑːnəu] *n.* *(pl.* ~*s)* 南美洲的大草原.

LL. B., LLB = 〔L.〕 *Legum Baccalaureus* (= Bachelor of Laws) 法学士.

LL. D., LLD = 〔L.〕 *Legum Doctor* (= Doctor of Laws) 法学博士.

Llew·el·lyn [lu(ː)ˈwelin] *n.* 卢埃林〔男子名〕.

LL. JJ. = Lords Justices 〔英〕上诉法院法官(复数).

L(l)oyd [lɔid] *n.* 劳埃德〔男子名〕.

Lloyd's [lɔidz] *n.* (伦敦经营海上保险及船舶检查注册的)劳埃德商船协会. ***A 1 at*** ~ ①(在劳埃德商船协会注册的)第一级(船). ②最好的,第一流的. ~ **list** 劳埃德协会海报. ~ **Register** 劳埃德船舶年鉴 (= ~ Register of British and Foreign Shipping).

L.LT. = London Landed Terms 伦敦起卸货条例.

LM ①【宇】 = lunar module 登月舱. ②= low middling 〔美〕七级白棉.

lm = 【物】 lumen.

LMF = liquid metal fuel 液态金属燃料.

LMG = light machine gun 轻机枪.

L.M.S. ①London Missionary Society【宗】伦敦传教会. ②London Midland and Scottish Railway 〔英〕伦敦——米德兰——苏格兰铁路.

LMT = local mean time 地方平均时.

L.N.E.R. = London North-Eastern Railway 〔英〕伦敦东北铁路.

LNG = liquefied natural gas 液化天然气.

lo [ləu] *int.* 〔古〕看哪! 瞧! *Lo and behold!* 嗳哟,你瞧! 〔叙述惊人的事情前的用语.〕

loach [ləutʃ] *n.* 【动】泥鳅.

load [ləud] *n.* ①装载,担子;负担;工作(负荷)量. ②车船等的)装载量;一驮,一车,一飞机. ③【电、机】(机械等的)负载(量),负荷(量);发电量. ④充填,装药,装弹. ⑤〔*pl.*〕许多,大量,一大堆. ⑥〔俚〕使人喝醉的量. ⑦【生】(不利)负荷〔指有害基因的存在〕. *a* ~ *of care* 精神负担. *a* ~ *of debt* 债务的负担. *be ever ready to bear a heavy* ~ *on one's shoulders* 勇于挑重担. *a cart* ~ *of furniture* 一货车家具. *a* ~ *of hay* 一堆干草. *We have to make three* ~*s of the cargo.* 我们得把货物分成三批装运. *genetic* ~ 【生】遗传负荷〔指有害基因的存在〕. *the breaking* ~ 最大载荷. *the capacity* ~ 满载. *the dead [static]* ~ 恒载,静(荷)载,自重. *the live [moving, mobile]* ~ 活负载,动荷载. *the peak* ~ 最大负载,峰负载. *the permissible* ~ 容许负载. *the rated* ~ 额定载荷. *the safe* ~ 安全负载. *the working* ~ 资用负载. ~*s of friends* 大批朋友. ~*s of time* 充裕的时间. *a teaching* ~ *of twenty hours a week* 每星期二十小时的讲课任务. ***be a*** ~ ***off one's mind*** 如释重负. ***get a*** ~ ***of*** 〔美俚〕仔细听;注意看. ***have a*** ~ ***on*** 〔美俚〕喝醉. ***lay not all the*** ~ ***on the lame horse*** 〔谚〕别把担子都放在跛马身上;别把希望完全寄托在不中用的人身上. ***take a*** ~ ***off one's feet*** 〔美俚〕坐下休息. ***take a*** ~ ***off sb.'s mind*** 解除某人思想负担,使某人放心. — *vt.* ①把货装到(船、车等)上;装(货). ②装满,使负担. ③把子弹装到(枪里);把胶片装入(照相机). ④用铅加重(骰子、手杖等);用低劣物质等搀入. ⑤(人寿保险)加收额外保险费. ~ *cargo into the hold* 把货装进船舱. *a heart* ~*ed with care* 心事重重. *a table* ~*ed with delicacies* 桌上摆满山珍海味. *air* ~*ed with carbon* 充满碳气的空气. ~ *one's stomach with food* 吃得太多. ~ *sb. with praise* 极力称赞某人. *I am* ~*ed.* 我的枪已上好子弹. ~ *a camera with film* 给照相机装胶卷. *This wine has been* ~*ed.* 这种酒是搀了水的. — *vi.* ①(在枪里)装弹药;装料. ②

(车、船等)装货; 上船,上车. *Load!* 【军】装子弹! *The ship is ~ing for Shanghai.* 这船正装货运往上海. *They ~-ed into the boat.* 他们上船了. ***be ~ed down with***〔美〕= ***be ~ed up with*** 装着…;存有(某种股票等). ***~ down*** 装载甚重. ***~ed for bear***〔俚〕①有充分准备. ②生气;准备打架. ***~ the dice against sb.*** 对某人使用加重骰子;使用不正当手段占人便宜. ~ **displacement**【海】满载排水量. ~ **draught,** ~ **draft**【海】满载吃水. ~ **factor**【电】负载因数,负载系数. ~ **line** 满载吃水线. ~ **shedding** (为防电站超载而实行的)分区停电. ~ **water line** = ~ line.

load·age [ˈləudidʒ] *n.* 装载量.

load·ed [ˈləudid] *a.* ①载重的;有负荷的,装着货的,有含意的. ②装着子弹的; 灌过铅的; 搀有杂质的;加有填料的. ③〔美俚〕喝醉了的. ④〔美俚〕富有的,钱很多的. ⑤吃饱了的. *a ~ question* 另有意义的问题. ~ *cane* 铅头杖. ~ *dice* (容易掷出六点的)铅心骰子. ~ *rubber* 填料橡胶. ~ *wine* 搀过的酒. *a ~ stomach* 吃得很饱的肚子.

load·er [ˈləudə] *n.* 装货的人;载货设备;装弹机;装填者,(尤指跟猎人)装弹药的人.

load·ing [ˈləudiŋ] *n.* ①装货. ②装载量;重量;载荷;(船只等的)货载. ③填充物,填料. ④额外人寿保险费. ~ *and unloading* 装卸. ~ *charges* 装货费. ~ *days* 装货期限. ~ **coil**【电】加感线圈. ~ **waveguide**【无】加载波导.

load·star [ˈləudstɑː] *n.* ①【天】北极星. ②目标;指导原则.

load·stone [ˈləudstəun] *n.* ①天然磁石. ②吸引人的东西.

loaf[1] [ləuf] *n.* ***(pl. loaves)*** ①一个面包〔通常重 1,2,4 磅〕. ②面包形糖块(=sugar ~);面包形菜肴、食品等〔如一个菜心〕. ③〔英口〕脑袋. *Half a ~ is better than no bread.*〔谚〕半个面包比没有面包好. *The ~ has risen in price.* 面包涨价了. *a white ~*(高级)白面包. *a brown ~* 黑面包. *a ~ of cheese* 长方形大块干酪. *Use your ~!* 用脑袋想想! ***loaves and fishes*** 私利; 眼前的利益;不很正当的利益,油水.

loaf[2] [ləuf] *vi., vt.* 混日子;游荡. ~ ***away*** 虚度 (*Don't ~ away your time.* 别虚度光阴). ~ ***on***〔美〕在某人处做食客. ~ ***on a job*** 干活磨磨蹭蹭. ~ ***through life*** 游荡一辈子. — *n.* 混日子. ***have a ~*** 游手好闲. ***on the ~*** 在游荡,混日子.

loaf·er [ˈləufə] *n.* ①游手好闲的人,二流子,无业游民. ②平底便鞋,懒人鞋. ~ *way* 二流子习气. **-ish** *a.*

loam [ləum] *n.* ①肥土,沃土;壤土. ②(制砖等的)粘砂土. — *vt.* 用肥土填〔覆盖〕.

loam·y [ˈləumi] *a.* ***(-i·er; -i·est)*** 肥土似的,含肥土的.

loan[1] [ləun] *n.* ①出借,借出,贷. ②借出物;资金;公债,贷款. ③外来语 (= ~ word); 外来风俗习惯. *Will you favour me with [May I have] the ~ of this book?* 我可以把你的这本书借用一下么? *domestic [foreign] ~* 内〔外〕债. *public [government] ~* 公债. *~ for consumption* 消费贷款. ***ask for the ~ of*** 请求借用…. ***have the ~ of*** 借. ***~ on personal guarantee*** 保证贷款. ***~ on personal security*** 信用贷款. ***~ on security*** 担保贷款. ***on ~*** 出借;借. — *vt., vi.*〔美〕借贷,借出 (*out*). ~ **collection** 借用展品〔为举行展览而借用的画、古董等〕. ~ **holder** 债券持有人;(押款的)受押人. ~ **myth** 外来神话. ~ **note** 借据. ~ **office** 贷款处;当铺;公债募集处. ~ **shark**〔口〕高利贷者. ~**shift** 已经部分同化的外来词〔例: smearcase 原词是 *schmierkäse*〔G.〕〕. ~ *syndicate* 借款财团. ~ **translation** 仿造语 (= calque). ~**word** 外来语.

loan[2] [ləun], **loan·ing** [ˈləuniŋ] *n.*〔Scot.〕①小路. ②挤牛奶的场地.

loan·a·ble [ˈləunəbl] *a.* 可借出的.

loan·ee [ləuˈniː] *n.* 借入者,债务人.

loan·er [ˈləunə] *n.* ①出借者,租出者. ②借用物〔汽车、无线电、打字机等〕,出租物.

loath [ləuθ] *a.* 厌恶,讨厌;不愿 (*to do; that*). ***(be) ~ for him to go*** 不愿意他去. ***nothing ~*** 很愿意,很高兴.

loathe [ləuð] *vt., vi.* 讨厌,厌恶;〔口〕不欢喜. ~ *the sight of food* 看见吃的东西就恶心.

loath·ful [ˈləuðful] *a.*〔罕〕= loathsome.

loath·ing [ˈləuðiŋ] *n.* 厌恶,憎恨.

loath·li·ness [ˈləuðlinis] *n.* 厌恶.

loath·ly [ˈləuðli] *a.* ①〔古〕= loathsome. ②不愿意地.

loath·some [ˈləuðsəm, ˈləuθ-] *a.* 令人讨厌的;可厌的;叫人恶心的. **-ly** *ad.* **-ness** *n.*

loath·y [ˈləuði] *a.* = loathsome.

loaved [ləuvd] *a.*〔英〕(卷心菜等)结成球的.

loaves [ləuvz] *n.* loaf 的复数.

lob[1] [lɔb] *vi.* ①慢慢地走〔跑、动〕 (*along*). ②【网球】吊高球;【板球】扔得慢而低. — *vt.* ①吊高球. ②〔古〕使垂下. — *n.* ①笨重的人, 傻大个儿. ②【网球】高球;【板球】下手球.

lob[2] [lɔb] *n.* = lugworm.

lo·bar [ˈləubə] *a.* 【医】(肺)叶的;【植】浅裂片的. ~ *pneumonia* 大叶肺炎.

lo·bate, lo·bat·ed [ˈləubeit, -id] *a.*【植】有裂片的;分裂的.【动】有叶状膜的,有蹼的.

lo·ba·tion [ləuˈbeiʃən] *n.* 叶状;形成叶状;叶片.

lob·by [ˈlɔbi] *n.* ①门廊,门厅,过厅. ②(英国下院的)会客室,休息室;(表决时分别投票的)投票厅 (= division ~). ③〔美〕(出入议院休息室用收买等手段左右法案的)院外活动集团.— *vi., vt.* ①〔美〕(在会议室中)运动议员, 收买议员; 运动通过议案. ②暗中运动. ~**man** (戏院、剧场等的)收票员. **-ing, -ism** *n.*〔美〕(国会的)院外活动;游说,疏通. **-er, -ist** *n.* 院外活动集团的成员;进行疏通的人;说客.

lobe [ləub] *n.* ①耳垂. ②【植】裂片;圆裂片;滚裂片. ③【无】波瓣,瓣. ④【解】(肺、脑、肝等的)叶. ⑤【机】凸角. ⑥(气球的)舵囊,气袋. ~ **chamber** 翼室.

lo·bec·to·my [ləuˈbektəmi] *n.*【医】叶〔肝、脑、肺或甲状腺的一叶〕切除术.

lobed [ləubd] *a.* ①= lobate. ②【植】浅裂的;圆裂的;分裂的.

lo·be·li·a [ləuˈbiːljə] *n.*【植】半边莲属.

lo·be·line [ˈləubiˌliːn, -lin] *n.*【药】洛贝林〔呼吸中枢兴奋药〕,山梗菜硷,山梗烷醇酮.

Lo·bi·to [ləuˈbiːtəu] *n.* 洛比托〔安哥拉港市〕.

lob·lol·ly [ˈlɔblɔli] *n.* ①稠麦片粥. ②〔方〕泥坑. ③粗人;乡下人. ④火炬松;火炬松木 (= ~ pine). ~ **boy [man]** 打杂的帮工;军医助手,看护兵.

lo·bo [ˈləubəu] *n.*【动】(美国西部产)大灰狼.

lo·bot·o·mized [ləuˈbɔtəˈmaizd] *a.* 迟钝的〔好象是切除了前额脑叶似的〕.

lo·bot·o·my [ləuˈbɔtəmi] *n.* = leucotomy.

lob·scouse [ˈlɔbˌskaus] *n.* 肉、菜、硬饼干混烹的一种海员饮食.

lob·ster [ˈlɔbstə] *n.* ①大螯虾; 大螯虾肉. ②龙虾 (= spiny [spini]); 龙虾肉. ③〔蔑〕英国兵. ④笨人,傻子;容易受骗的人. ***red as a ~*** 虾一样红的(脸等). ~**-eyed** *a.* 眼睛凸出的. ~ **pot [trap]** 捕虾篓. ~ **shift [trick]**〔美口〕(报馆人员的) 夜班采访; 夜班. ~ **tail** ①甲壳类动物的尾巴. ②甲壳类动物的尾肉. ~ **thermidor**【烹】蘑菇龙虾.

lob·u·lar [ˈlɔbjulə] *a.* 有小裂片的, 有小叶的; 小裂片〔小叶〕状的.

lob·ule [ˈlɔbjuːl] *n.* ①【植】小裂片;腹片. ②【解】小叶.

lob·worm [ˈlɔbˌwəːm] *n.* = lugworm.

loc. = ①location. ②local.

lo·cal [ˈləukəl] *a.* ①地方的，当地的，本地的。②局部的。③乡土的，狭隘的，片面的。④【邮】本市的，本地的；【铁路】区间的。⑤【数】轨迹的。*a* ～ *adverb* 表示地点的副词(如 here, there 等)。*a* ～ *custom* 地方习惯。*a* ～ *name* 地名。～ *news* 本地新闻。*a* ～ *station* 地方电台。～ *anaesthesia* 局部麻醉。*a* ～ *point of view* 偏狭的见解。～ **colour** (文艺作品的)乡土色彩，地方色彩。～ **court** 地方法院。～ **examinations** 〔英〕地方考试。～ **exchange** 市内电话局。～ **government** 地方政府；地方自治。～ **option [veto]** 当地居民抉择权。～ **oscillation** 【物】本机振荡。～ **preacher** 【宗】被允许在当地讲道的教友。～ **strain** 局部应变。～ **stress** 【物】局部应力。～ **time** 【无】地方时。～ **war [operations]** 局部战争。— *n.* ①(报纸上的)本地新闻。②本地居民；本地律师；本地教士；本地医生。③慢车。④工会支部。⑤〔英〕= ～ examination(s)。⑥〔*pl.*〕本地球队。⑦〔英口〕本地酒店，附近的小酒店[馆]。⑧在一定地区使用的邮票。

lo·cale [ləuˈkɑːl] *n.* (事故等发生的)现场，地点，场所。***in whatever*** ～***s*** 在任何场合下。

lo·cal·ism [ˈləukəlizəm] *n.* ①地方风俗。②土话，方言，土音。③乡土观念，地方主义；地方性。④思想闭塞，心胸狭隘。

lo·cal·i·ty [ləuˈkæliti] *n.* 地点，位置，场所，方向；地区；(植物的)产地；环境。*a description of* ～ 关于地点的记载。*one's bump [sense] of* ～ 对于场所的记忆力。*the* ～ *of a crime* 犯罪地点。

lo·cal·iz·a·ble [ˈləukəlaizəbl] *a.* 能地方化的，可以定域的。**-a·bi·li·ty** 【物】可局限性，可定域性。

lo·cal·i·za·tion [ˌləukəlaiˈzeiʃən] *n.* ①定位，定域。②局限。③地方化。*fault* ～ 探伤；障碍部位测定。

lo·cal·ize, lo·cal·ise [ˈləukəˌlaiz] *vt.* ①使局限于某一地方[局部]；使(军队)分驻各地。②定位，定域。③地方化，添地方色彩。④集中(注意等) *(upon)*。⑤找出(部位、原因、地点等)。⑥〔美〕写本地新闻。— *vi.* 局限，集中。

lo·cal·iz·er [ˈləukəˌlaizə] *n.* 【海】定位器，定位信标。

lo·cal·ly [ˈləukəli] *ad.* ①在地方上。②局部地，在局部上。③在本地。

Lo·car·no [ləuˈkɑːnəu] *n.* 洛迦诺〔瑞士城市〕。

lo·cate [ləuˈkeit] *vt.* ①〔美〕设置在…；确定…的位置；位于，在〔用被动语态〕。②住(在某处)。③说出来源；找出，探出(痛处等)。④【法】出租(土地等)。⑤〔美〕设计，计划。— *vi.* 〔美口〕居住，住下来。

lo·cat·er [ˈləukeitə] *n.* 〔英〕= locator.

lo·ca·tion [ləuˈkeiʃən] *n.* ①定位；【铁路】定线；〔美〕测量，设计。②位置，场所，地点。③拍摄外景；外景拍摄地。④(房屋、土地等的)出租。⑤非洲土著居住的城郊。*a* ～ *beacon* 定位标灯。*fault* ～ 障碍点测定。*be on* ～ 正在拍外景。*a good* ～ *for* 定…的好地方。

loc·a·tive [ˈlɔkətiv] *a.* 【语法】表示位置的。— *n.* 【语法】位置格 (= ～ case)；位置格的词。

lo·ca·tor [ˈləukeitə] *n.* ①定位器；探测器；无线电定位器，雷达。②勘定地界者。*an echo* ～ 回声[回波]勘定器。*a fault* ～ 探伤仪，故障探测器。

loc. cit. = 〔L.〕 *loco citato* 在上述引文中。

loch [lɔk, lɔx] *n.* 〔Scot.〕①滨海湖。②海湾。

lo·chi·a [ˈləukiə, lɔˈkiə] *n.* 【医】恶露，产褥排泄。

lo·ci [ˈləusai] *n.* locus 的复数。

lock[1] [lɔk] *n.* ①锁，闩，栓。②(运河等的)船闸。③制轮楔。④【机】气闸，气塞，锁气室。⑤【军】枪机。⑥锁住，固定。⑦〔俚〕拘留所。⑧〔英〕性病医院(= ～ hospital)。⑨【自】同步。⑩结合，固着。⑪(摔跤的)揪扭。⑫煞车。*off the* ～ 未锁。*on the* ～ 锁着。*trick* ～ (对字的)密码锁。～ *the stable door after the horse has been stolen* 贼走关门。***be at [on, upon] the*** ～ 〔方〕在窘困中。～***, stock and barrel*** 全部；完全。***under*** ～ ***and key*** 锁着，妥为保藏。— *vt.* ①锁，锁上。②收藏起来，秘藏。③抱紧，挽住；揪扭。④(使资本等)固定。⑤使固定。⑥用水闸止住；使通过水闸 *(up; down)*。⑦卡住，塞住。⑧将曲面印版装在轮转印刷机滚筒上。～ *a secret in one's heart* 严守秘密。*be* ～*ed in a fight* 打得难分难解。*be* ～*ed in contemplation* 陷入沉思。*The ship was* ～*ed fast in ice.* 这条船被冰封住。*The gears are* ～*ed.* 齿轮卡住了。— *vi.* ①锁住。②紧闭，不动。③抱住，揪扭，嵌进。④(船)通过水闸；造水闸。～ ***away*** 锁起来。～ ***down*** 让船开出水闸。～***horns*** 争论 *(over)*。～ ***in [into]*** 关起来；锁在里面。～ ***in synchronism*** 进入同步。～ ***on*** 用雷达波束自动跟踪(目标)。～ ***oneself in*** 把自己关在里面，闭门谢客。～ ***out*** ①关在外面。②(资本家)封闭工厂。～ ***up*** ①上锁，锁住。②监禁。③收藏(文件等)。④固定(资本)。～**-away** 〔英〕长期证[债]券。～ **bolt** 【机】锁紧螺栓。～**-chain** 锁车轮链条。～**fast** *a.* 〔Scot.〕锁牢的。～ **gate** 闸门。～**-in** 〔美〕①关进。②占领并封锁建筑物的示威行动。～**jaw** 【医】牙关紧闭症，咀嚼肌痉挛；破伤风。～ **keeper** 闸门管理员。～**master** (运河)船闸看管人。～**nut** 【机】①防松螺母。②对开螺母(= ～ nut)。～**-on** ①(雷达的)自动跟踪。②(潜艇等之间)密封通道的接通。～**out** ①锁定，闭锁。②停工，闭厂〔厂主对付罢工的一种方法〕。③排斥教员；将学生关在课室外。④【海】(水下舷窗的)锁定；封锁。～**sman** = ～keeper. ～**smith** 锁匠。～ **step** 连锁步伐〔队列行进时步伐完全一致；固定不变的方式[安排]。～ **stitch** 双线连锁缝纫法。～**up** ①锁，闭，锁住。②(学校等晚上的)关门时间。③拘留所，监狱。④资本的固定，固定资本。**-less** *a.* 无锁的；无船闸的。

lock[2] *n.* [lɔk] ①一绺卷发；〔*pl.*〕头发。②(干草、羊毛等的)小量，一把，一撮。

lock·age [ˈlɔkidʒ] *n.* ①水闸结构(材料)。②水闸通行税。③(水闸中的)水位高度。④水闸通过。

Locke [lɔk] *n.* ①洛克〔姓氏〕。②**John** ～ 洛克〔1632—1704，英国哲学家〕。

Lock·er [ˈlɔkə] *n.* 洛克〔姓氏〕。

lock·er [ˈlɔkə] *n.* ①上锁的人；(英国海关的)仓库管理人。②(公共更衣室等中可锁起来的)小橱，抽屉，小室。③冷藏间。④(船上的)橱柜，库房。⑤(车轮上的)锁具，锁扣装置。*a shot* ～ 【海】弹药库。*a chain* ～ 锚链舱。***Davy Jone's*** ～ 海底；水手的坟墓 (*be in [go to] David Jone's* ～ 葬身海底)。***not a shot in the*** ～ 身上没有一文钱。～ **paper** 冷藏包装纸。～ **room** (体育馆、游泳地、工厂等的)更衣室。

lock·et [ˈlɔkit] *n.* (挂在表链等下面装相片等用的)小金盒。

Lock·hart [ˈlɔkət, ˈlɔkhɑːt] *n.* 洛克哈特〔姓氏〕。

Lock·i·an [ˈlɔkiən] *a.* (英国)洛克 (Locke) (哲学)的，洛克学派的。

lo·co[1] [ˈləukəu] *n.* ① = ～ weed. ② = ～ disease. ③患疯草病的动物。④疯子。— *a.* 〔俚〕发疯的，精神错乱的。— *vt.* ①用疯草毒害。②〔俚〕使发疯，使发狂。～ **disease** 【医】疯草病〔马、牛、羊食疯草后引起的一种神经病〕。～**weed** 疯草〔黄芪属 *(Astragalus)* 和棘豆属 (Oxytropis) 植物，产于北美洲西部，牛、羊、马食之引起疯草病〕。**-ed** *a.* ①(动物)患疯草病的。②(人)发疯的，发狂的。**-ism** *n.* = ～ disease.

lo·co[2] [ˈləukəu] *n.* 〔美俚〕火车头，机车 (locomotive 的缩写)。

lo·co- *comb. f.* 表示"从一处到另一处"：*loco*motion.

lo·co ci·ta·to [ˈləukəu siˈteitəu] 〔L.〕在上述引用文中〔略作 loc. cit. 或 l. c.〕。

lo·co·fo·co [ˌləukəuˈfəukəu] *n.* 〔美〕①摩擦火柴；摩擦点火的雪茄。②〔L-〕一八三五年纽约民主党激进派(成员)；〔废〕民主党人。

lo·co·mo·bile [ˌləukəˈməubi(ː)l] *n.* 自动机车。— *a.* 自动推进的。

lo·co·mote [ˌləukəˈməut] *vi.* 移动;走动;行进.
lo·co·mo·tion [ˌləukəˈməuʃən] *n.* ①运动,移动,位移;运动力,移动力,运转力. ②旅行.
lo·co·mo·tive [ˌləukəˈməutiv] *n.* ①火车头,机车. ②〔*pl.*〕〔俚〕脚. ③能行动的动物. ④节奏逐渐快起来的集体欢呼. *Use your ~s!* 走呀! — *a.* ①运动的,运转的,移动的. ②有运动力的,起运动作用的. ③机动的. ④〔谑〕旅行的;爱旅行的. *a ~ person* 〔谑〕常常旅行的人. *in these ~ days* 在当今旅行方便的时代中. ~ **engine** 机车,火车头. ~ **engineering** 机车工程. ~ **faculty [power]** 运动能力,移动力. ~ **oil** 汽缸油. ~ **organs** 脚. ~ **tender** 煤水车.
lo·co·mo·tor [ˌləukəˈməutə] *a.* 运动的,移动的,运动器官的. ~ *ataxia [ataxy]* 【医】运动失调病,脊髓痨. — [ˈləukəməutə] *n.* 有运动力的人[物];移动发动机.
lo·co·mo·to·ry [ˌləukəˈməutəri] *a.* = locomotor.
loc·u·lar [ˈlɔkjulə] *a.* 【生】有细胞的;有小室的.
loc·u·late [ˈlɔkjulit, -leit] *a.* = locular.
loc·u·li·ci·dal [ˌlɔkjuliˈsaidl] *a.* 【植】室背[胞间]开裂的.
loc·u·lus [ˈlɔkjuləs] *n.* *(pl.* **-li** [-ˌlai]*)* 【动、植】小腔;小室〔如子房、花药等〕;子囊腔 (= locule).
lo·cum [ˈləukəm] *n.* 〔口〕= locum tenens.
lo·cum te·nens [ˈləukəm ˈtiːnenz] *(pl. ~ tenentes)* 代理牧师;代理医师.
lo·cus [ˈləukəs] *n.* *(pl.* ***lo·ci*** [ˈləusai]*)* ①场所,地点,所在地. ②【数】轨迹. ③【生】(染色体的)位点,基因座. ④(书籍,文献等中的某一)文句,章节,段落.
locus ci·ta·tus [ˈləukəs siˈteitəs] 〔L.〕引述的文句[章节]等.
lo·cus clas·si·cus [ˈləukəs ˈklæsikəs] 〔L.〕常受人引用的文句[章节].
lo·cus in quo [ˈləukəs inˈkwəu] 〔L.〕现场,当场.
lo·cus si·gil·li [ˈləukəs siˈdʒilai] 盖印处,签名盖章处〔略 L. S.〕.
locus stan·di [ˈləukəsˈstændai] (公认的)正式地位;参加权;(可到法院[议会]中为某一问题争辩的)陈述权.
lo·cust [ˈləukəst] *n.* ①蝗虫;蚱蜢. ②〔美〕蝉. ③破坏者;贪吃的人. ④【植】洋槐,刺槐;洋槐[刺槐]的木材. ⑤【植】角豆树. ⑥〔美俚〕警棍. *oriental migratory ~* 东亚飞蝗. ~ **bean** 【植】角豆. ~ **tree** 【植】刺槐.
lo·cu·tion [ləuˈkjuːʃən] *n.* ①特别的说话方式;语风;语法. ②惯用语,成语,短语.
L.O.D. = Little Oxford Dictionary 小牛津词典.
lode [ləud] *n.* ①矿脉;丰富的蕴藏. ②〔英方〕水路,(沼泽的)排水沟. ③天然磁石 (= loadstone).
lo·den [ˈləudn] *a.* 【纺】①罗登(缩绒厚)呢〔全毛或与驼毛交织,能防水〕. ②罗登(缩绒厚)呢色〔深橄榄色〕.
lode·star [ˈləudˌstɑː] *n.* = loadstar.
lode·stone [ˈləudˌstəun] *n.* = loadstone.
Lodge [lɔdʒ] *n.* 洛奇〔姓氏〕.
lodge [lɔdʒ] *n.* ①(森林、猎场等的)看守小屋;(学校、工厂等的)门房,传达室. ②〔古〕小屋,草屋;(北美印第安人的)小屋,帐篷;其中的居住者. ③(海狸、獭等的)巢穴,窝. ④(共济会、秘密结社、工会等的)支部会员们;支部会员聚会处;支部. ⑤〔美〕大学生联谊会,大学女生联谊会. ⑥〔英〕(剑桥大学)院长住宅. ⑦(游览区的)小旅馆. *the grand ~* (共济会等支部的)干事,理事. — *vi.* ①暂住,寄宿. ②(箭、枪等)竖立;(子弹等)停留,进入. ③(庄稼等)倒伏. ④猎物逃入丛中. ~ *at an inn* 住旅馆. ~ *with sb.* 寄住某人家中. *A bullet ~d in his thigh.* 子弹打进他的大腿里. — *vt.* ①留宿,使住宿. ②存放,寄存. ③把(子弹等)打入,射进,打在. ④(风)吹倒,使倒伏. ⑤提出(报告、抗议等). ⑥授与. ⑦(将猎物)赶进巢穴. *The hotel is well [ill]-~d* 这旅馆设备好[不好]. ~ *money in a bank [with a person]* 把钱存在银行里[寄存在某人处]. ~ *a protest against sb.* 向人提出抗议. ~ *a complaint against sb. with the authorities concerned* 向有关当局对某人提出控诉. ~ *information against* 告密. ~ *power in [with, in the hands of] sb.* 把权力交给某人.
lodg·er [ˈlɔdʒə] *n.* 寄宿者,房客. ***take in ~s*** 接受房客[寄宿者].
lodg(e)·ment [ˈlɔdʒmənt] *n.* ①住处,寄宿处;立足点. ②【军】占领;占领后的紧急防御工事;据点. ③(担保品等的)交存,寄存;存款,贮蓄;贮存. ④提出. ⑤沉积(物);沉积处. *a ~ area* 滩点占领区;空降作战初期占领区. *the ~ of a protest* 抗议的提出. *a ~ of dirt inside the radio* 收音机内的积尘. ***effect [find, make] a ~*** ①占领阵地,获得据点. ②占牢固的地位. ③征服人心.
lodg·ing [ˈlɔdʒiŋ] *n.* ①住宿,寄宿. ②住处,寄宿处. ③〔*pl.*〕出租的房间,公寓. ④存放处. ⑤(庄稼等的)倒伏. *ask for a night's ~* 借宿一晚. *board and ~* 膳宿,包吃包住. *dry ~* 不供伙食的寄宿舍. ***take up one's ~s*** 决定住处,投宿. **~-house** 公寓 (*a common ~-house* 〔英〕包住不包吃的公寓).
lod·i·cule [ˈlɔdiˌkjuːl] *n* 【植】浆片,鳞片.
Lódź, Lodz [luːʒ] *n.* 罗兹〔波兰城市〕.
lo·ess [ˈləuis] *n.* 【地】黄土. **~-child, ~-doll** 黄土结核,料姜石. **-al, -i·al** *a.*
Loe·we [ˈləui] *n.* 洛伊〔姓氏〕.
L of C = Lines of Communication 交通线.
lo-fi [ˈləufai] *a.* 保真度不高的,非保真的;灵敏度不高的.
LOFT = low frequency radio telescope 低频射电[无线电]望远镜.
loft [lɔ(ː)ft] *n.* ①(屋顶下的)顶楼,阁楼. ②(堆干草等用的)厩楼. ③(讲堂、教堂等的)楼厢. ④〔美〕(仓库、商业建筑物等的)顶层. ⑤鸽房;鸽群. ⑥【高尔夫球】打高球;(高尔夫球棒端的)高击斜面. *a fixed [mobile] ~* 固定[移动]鸽房. —*vt.* ①贮存在阁楼上;加造阁楼. ②放(鸽子)进鸽房,在鸽房里养鸽子. ③(把高尔夫球)高打出去. ④把…向(空间)发射. ⑤跳过(障碍物). — *vi.* 【高尔夫球】打高球.
loft·er [ˈlɔ(ː)ftə] *n.* 【高尔夫球】(打高球用的)高击棒.
loft·ing [ˈlɔftiŋ] *n.* 放样;理论模线的绘制. ~ **iron** = lofter.
lofts·man [ˈlɔftsmən] *n.* *(pl.* **-men***)* (造船或造飞机的)放样员. *a mould ~* 放样工人.
loft·y [ˈlɔ(ː)fti] *a.* ***(loft·i·er, -i·est)*** ①极高的,巍峨的. ②高尚的,崇高的. ③骄傲的,傲慢的. *a ~ mountain* 高山. ~ *aims* 崇高的目的. ~ *contempt [disdain]* 藐视. *speak in a ~ strain* 说大话. **-i·ly** *ad.* **-i·ness** *n.*
log[1] [lɔg] *n.* ①原木,圆木,干材. ②测程仪,计程仪. ③航海日志;(飞行员的)航行日志;旅行日记. ④〔英〕裁缝店日工的工作时间表. ⑤【机】记录表. *clear ~* 干材. *heave [throw] the ~* 用测程仪测船速. *sail by the ~* 靠测程仪测船位航行. *a rough ~* 航海日志草稿. *a smooth ~* 誊清的航海日志. *a performance ~* (机器等的)运转情况记录(簿). *a well ~* 钻井记录. ***as easy as falling [rolling] off a ~*** 〔美〕极容易. ***in the ~*** 未经斧削过的. ***keep the ~ rolling*** 〔美〕使工作高速度地进行下去. ***Roll my ~ and I'll roll yours*** 〔谚〕互相帮忙;互相吹嘘. ***sleep like a ~*** 睡得很死. ***split the ~*** 〔美〕分析,解释. — *vt.* ①(把树)砍倒. ②锯成圆材;拖(木头). ③把…记入航海[飞行]日志;把…输入电子计算机 *(in)*. ④航行;飞行;以…的时速飞行[航行]. — *vi.* 采伐树木. **~book** = ~ *(n.)* ③. ~ **cabin** (用圆木搭建的)小木屋. ~ **chip** 【海】(测程仪的)测程板. **~jam** ①浮木阻塞. ②工作障碍. ~ **line** 【海】测程仪线. ~ **reel** 【海】测程仪线络车. **~wood** ①【植】洋苏木树 *(Haematoxylon campechianum)* 〔产于中美和西印度群岛,枝带刺,开小黄花〕. ②洋苏木木料[染料].
log[2] [lɔg] *n.* = logarithm.
log[3] [lɔg] *vt.* 向…提供补给品. — *n.* 补给品的发放,补给品发放的日子.

LOG, log = logarithum.
log. = logic.
Lo·gan [ˈləugən] *n.* 洛根〔姓氏，男子名〕.
log·an [ˈlɔgən] *n.* 摇石 (= ~ stone).
lo·gan·ber·ry [ˈləugənbəri] *n.* 【植】罗甘莓〔blackberry 和 raspberry 的杂交种〕.
lo·ga·ni·a [ləuˈgeiniə] *a.* 【植】马钱科 (*loganiaceae*) 的.
log·a·oe·dic [ˈlɔːgəˈiːdik, -lɔg-] *a.* (扬抑格和扬抑抑格交混或抑扬格和抑抑扬格交混的)混合音步诗律的. —*n.* 混合音步诗.
log·a·rithm [ˈlɔgəriθəm] *n.* 【数】对数. *common ~s* 常用对数. *general ~s* 普通对数. *natural ~* 自然对数. *the table of ~s* 对数表.
log·a·rith·mic [ˌləugəˈriθmik, -iðm-] *a.* 对数的. *~ function* 对数函数. *a ~ scale* 计算尺. *~ series* 对数级数. *the ~ table* 对数表. **-cal·ly** [-kəli] *ad.* 用对数.
loge [ləuʒ] *n.* 〔F.〕①小屋，摊棚. ②(剧场中的)包厢，前座. ③(房间等)隔开的一小块地方.
log·ged [lɔgd] *a.* ①在水中泡重了的(圆材). ②低湿的，浸透的(土地).
log·ger [ˈlɔgə] *n.* ①伐木工，锯木工. ②圆材装载机；圆材拖车. ③【物，机】测井仪；(参数自动分析)记录器.
log·ger·head [ˈlɔgəhed] *n.* ①笨人，傻子. ②捕鲸船船尾圆柱. ③铁球棒. ④【动】= ~ shrike. ⑤【动】= ~ turtle. ***at ~s with sb.*** 和某人相争，同某人不和. ***fall [get, go] to ~s*** 争吵起来. **~ shrike** 【动】螭龟. **~ turtle** 【动】红海龟.
log·gi·a [ˈlɔdʒə, ˈlɔdʒiə] *n.* (*pl.* *~s, log·gi·e* [-dʒiei]) 【建】凉廊.
log·ging [ˈlɔgiŋ] *n.* ①伐木事业；伐木量. ②载入值班簿〔航行日志〕；记录；存入. ③记下调谐位置. ④【地】录井，测井. *~ clearing* 集材. *a ~ railway* 森林(运送木材)铁路.
log·gy [ˈlɔgi] *a.* = logy.
log·i·a [ˈlɔgiə] *n.* 〔*pl.*〕(*sing. logion*) (宗教家的) 名言集；〔L-〕(《圣经》上所无的)耶稣语录.
log·ic [ˈlɔdʒik] *n.* ①逻辑，论理学. ②推理〔方法〕；逻辑性，条理性. ③威力，压力，强制(力). *deductive [inductive] ~* 演绎〔归纳〕逻辑. *dialectical ~* 辩证逻辑. *formal ~* 形式逻辑. *a gangster ~* 强盗逻辑，恶徒的歪理〔言行〕. *mathematical ~* 数理逻辑. *pure ~* 纯粹逻辑. *He is not governed by ~.* 他没有逻辑性. *That is not ~.* 那不合逻辑. *the irresistible ~ of facts* 事实的不可抗拒的威力. *the ~ of events [war]* 事件〔战争〕的强制力. *His ~ is shaky.* 他的推理站不住脚. ***chop ~*** 诡辩. **~ core** 【自、数】逻辑磁心.
-logic, -logical *suf.* 〔构成与 -logy 结尾的名词相应的形容词〕表示"…学的": bio*logical*, philo*logical*.
log·i·cal [ˈlɔdʒikəl] *a.* ①逻辑的，逻辑上的；逻辑学上的. ②合乎逻辑的. ③逻辑上必然的. *~ constants* 逻辑常词〔常项〕. *~ necessity* 逻辑的必然性. *a ~ argument* 条理分明的论证. *a ~ process* 合理的程序；合乎逻辑的〔必然的〕过程. *the ~ result* 必然的结果. **-ly** *ad.* **-ness** *n.* **~ positivism** 逻辑实证主义. **~ empiricism** 逻辑经验主义.
log·i·cal·i·ty [ˌlɔdʒiˈkæliti] *n.* 逻辑性.
lo·gi·cian [ləuˈdʒiʃən] *n.* 逻辑学家，论理学家.
lo·gie [ˈləugi] *n.* (演戏用的)假珠宝.
log·i·on [ˈlɔgiɔn] *n.* logia 的单数.
-lo·gist *suf.* 表示"某一学科的专家，学者，研究者": antho*logist*, bio*logist*.
lo·gis·tic [ləuˈdʒistik] *n.* ①【逻、数】逻辑斯蒂，符号〔数理〕逻辑；计算术. ②【军】后勤(学). — *a.* 【军】后勤学的；后勤的 (= logistical). **-al·ly** *ad.*
lo·gis·tics [ləuˈdʒistiks] *n.* 【军】后勤学；后方勤务. *a ~ base* 后勤基地. *~ department* 后勤部.
log·nor·mal [ˈlɔgˈnɔːməl] *a.* 【数】对数正态的. **-mal·i·ty** [ˌlɔgnɔˈmæliti] *n.* **-ly** *ad.*
log·o- *comb. f.* 表示"词"，"语": *logo*gram, *logo*graph.
lo·go [ˈlɔgəu] *n.* = logotype.
log·o·gram [ˈlɔgəugræm] *n.* ①语标，词符〔如用 $ 表示 dollar 之类〕；略字〔如用 s. 表示 shilling 之类〕. ②速记符号. **-mat·ic** *a.*
log·o·graph [ˈlɔgəugrɑːf] *n.* ① = logogram. ② = logotype.
log·o·griph [ˈlɔgəgrif] *n.* 字谜〔如字母移位，回文，换音变词等游戏〕.
lo·gom·a·chy [lɔˈgɔməki] *n.* ①对言语〔文词〕的争执；口角；舌战. ②〔美〕字谜游戏.
lo·gom·e·ter [lɔˈgɔmitə] *n.* ①【电】电流比(率)计；比率表. ②对数计算尺.
log·or·rhe·a [ˌlɔgəˈriːə] *n.* 【医】多言癖.
Log·os [ˈlɔgɔs] *n.* ①【哲】逻各斯，理性；理念. ②【神】(三位一体的第二位)基督或上帝的话，道.
log·o·type [ˈlɔgəutaip] *n.* ①【印】成语铅字，连合活字. ②(广告等用的)标识〔语句〕.
log·roll [ˈlɔgrəul] *vi.* 〔美〕①互相帮助 (滚木头). ②互相捧场. ③做水上踩滚木游戏. — *vi.* 互投赞成票促使提案通过.
log·roll·ing [ˈlɔgrəuliŋ] *n.* 〔美〕①滚木头，搬运木材. ②支援，互助，合作. ③互相吹嘘. ④水上踩滚木游戏.
-logue *suf.* ①表示"谈话"，"写作": dia*log(ue)*, cata*log(ue)*. ②表示"学者"，"专家": sino*logue*.
lo·gy [ˈləugi] *a.* (*-gi·er; -gi·est*) 〔美〕①举动迟钝的，笨的. ②弹性不足的.
-lo·gy *suf.* ①表示"…学"，"…论": philo*logy*. ②表示"语"，"词": tauto*logy*.
loid [lɔid] *n.* 〔俚〕撬锁塑料片〔小偷用来拨开弹簧锁舌的〕.
loin [lɔin] *n.* ①〔*pl.*〕【解】腰；耻骨区；生殖器官. ②(牛、羊等的) 腰肉. ***a fruit [child] of one's ~s*** 自己生的孩子. ***be sprung from sb.'s ~*** 是某人所生. ***gird up one's ~s*** 束紧腰带，准备行动. **~-cloth** 腰带.
loir [ˈlɔiə] *n.* 【动】(欧洲产)大睡鼠.
Loire [lwɑːr] *n.* 罗亚河〔法国第一大河〕.
Lo·is [ˈləuis] *n.* 洛伊丝〔女子名〕.
loi·ter [ˈlɔitə] *vi.*, *vt.* 游手好闲，闲逛；耽搁；混日子；混掉(时间) (*away*).
loi·ter·er [ˈlɔitərə] *n.* 闲混的人，混日子的人.
loi·ter·ing·ly [ˈlɔitəriŋli] *ad.* 游手好闲地，懒散地，吊儿郎当地.
Lo·ki [ˈləuki] *n.* 【北欧神】洛基〔不断制造纠纷、祸害的神〕.
loll [lɔl] *vi.* ①懒洋洋地躺〔靠〕；闲荡. ②(头等)下垂. ③(舌头等)伸出 (*out*). *~ against a wall* 懒散地靠在墙上. *~ in a chair* 懒洋洋地靠在椅上. *~ about the streets* 在街上闲荡. — *vt.* ①垂下；伸出 (*out*). ②(把头、手脚等) 懒洋洋地靠着. ③吊儿郎当地混日子 (*away*). **-ingly** *ad.*
lol·la·pa·loo·sa, lol·la·pa·loo·za [ˌlɔləpəˈluːzə] *n.* 〔美俚〕非常出色的人〔物〕.
Lol·lard [ˈlɔləd] *n.* 【英宗史】(十四世纪的) 威克利夫 (John Wyclif) 派教徒. **Lol·lard·ism, Lol·lard·ry** *n.* 威克利夫主义.
lol·li·pop [ˈlɔliˌpɔp] *n.* 〔常 *pl.*〕①【英俚】钱. ②棒糖；糖果. ③〔英〕拦车棒〔一根长棍上钉有一个大圆牌，用来在过街处拦阻车辆通过，让小学生放学时安全走过街道〕.
lol·lop [ˈlɔləp] *vi.* ①跳跳蹦蹦地走. ②= loll, lounge.
lol·ly [ˈlɔli] *n.* (*pl.* *-lies*) 〔英方〕①钱. ②硬糖果.
lol·ly·gag [ˈlɔliˌgæg] *vi.* (*-gag·ged, -gag·ging*) 〔美口〕浪费时间；闲游浪荡.
lol·ly·pop [ˈlɔlipɔp] *n.* = lollipop.
Lom·bard [ˈlɔmbəd, ˈlʌmbəd] *n.* ①【史】伦巴族人〔日

耳曼民族之一〕; 伦巴族人后裔. ②(意大利的) 伦巴第人. ③从事金融业的伦巴第人; 放债者, 银行家. ④〔l-〕银行,当铺. — *a.* = Lombardic. ~ **loan** 英格兰银行给商业银行的证券抵押贷款. ~ **Street** 伦巴第人街, 伦敦的银行街; 金融市场, 金融界; 伦敦的金融中心.

Lom·bar·dia [ˌlɔmbəˈdiə] *n.* = Lombardy.

Lom·bar·dic [lɔmˈbɑːdik] *a.* 伦巴第族的; 伦巴第(人)的; 伦巴第式的. — *n.* 伦巴第草写体.

Lom·bar·dy [ˈlɔmbədi] *n.* 伦巴第〔意大利一地区〕.

Lom·bro·si·an [lɔmˈbrəuziən] *a.* 隆布洛索犯罪学理论的〔隆布洛索是意大利的犯罪学家, 他的学派认为犯罪者是明显的隔代遗传类型〕.

Lo·mé [ləuˈmei] *n.* 洛美〔多哥首都〕.

lo·ment [ˈləument] *n.* 【植】节荚 (= lomentum). **-a·ceous** [-mənˈteiʃəs] *a.*

Lon., long. = longitude.

Lon·don [ˈlʌndən] *n.* ①伦敦〔姓氏〕. ②伦敦〔英国首都〕. *the Greater* ~ 大伦敦〔包括市区及郊区〕. ~ **ivy** 伦敦的烟雾. ~ **particular** 〔口〕伦敦特有的大雾. ~ **pride** 虎耳草属植物的一种. ~ **smoke** 暗灰色. **-er** 伦敦人. **-ism** 伦敦式; 伦敦腔. **-ize** *vt.* 使成伦敦式, 使伦敦化.

Lon·don·der·ry [ˌlʌndənˈderi] *n.* 伦敦德里〔英国港市〕.

lone [ləun] *a.* ①寂寞的. ②无人烟的, 人迹稀少的; 孤寂的. ③〔谑〕独身的, 寡居的. ④孤独的; 无伴的. *a* ~ *flight* 单独飞行. *the L- Star State* 得克萨斯州〔别称〕. ~ **hand** ①独行其是的人. ②(牌戏中的)头家. ~ **wolf** = loner.

lone·ly [ˈləunli] *a.* **(-li·er; -li·est)** ①寂寞的. ②幽静的; 孤独的, 孤单的. ③荒凉的, 人迹稀少的. **-li·ness** *n.*

lon·er [ˈləunə] *n.* 〔口〕独来独往的人, 性格孤癖的人.

lone·some [ˈləunsəm] *a.* ①幽静的; 寂寞的; 孤独的. ②凄凉的, 人迹稀少的. *feel* ~ 寂寞. — *n.* 自己(一人). ***by [on] one's*** ~ 独自地; 单独地; 靠自己的力量. **-ly** *ad.*

Long [lɔŋ] *n.* 朗〔姓氏〕.

long[1] [lɔŋ] *vi.* 渴想, 极想, 渴望 (*for*, 〔古〕*after; to do*).

long[2] [lɔŋ] *a.* (**-er** [ˈlɔŋgə]; **-est** [ˈlɔŋgist]) ①长, 长的. *a* ~ *way* 远距离. *a* ~ *way off* 离得很远. *It is five feet* ~. 这有五英尺长. ②个子高的. *a* ~ *man* 高个子的人. ③长久的, 长期的. *a* ~ *friendship* 长期的友谊. *a* ~ *memory* 长久不忘的好记性. *a* ~ *note* 远期票据. *It will be* ~ *before we know the truth.* 很久以后真相才会大白. *It will not be* ~ *before we know the truth.* 不久真相就会大白. *Now we shan't be* ~*!* 〔口〕这回就好啦! ④冗长的, 拖长的. *Don't be* ~ *about it!* 别慢吞吞的. *She is* ~ *in coming.* 她姗姗来迟. ⑤…以上, 足足. *three* ~ *hours* 足足三小时. *a* ~ *mile* 一英里以上. ⑥达到远方的. *have a* ~ *arm* (为了扩张势力)把手伸得老远. *take a* ~ *view of the matter* 从长远考虑这事. ⑦〔诗〕长音的, 重读的; 【语音】长音(节)的. ⑧【商】行情看涨的, 做多头的. *be on the* ~ *side of the market* 做多头. ⑨长于…的. *be* ~ *on understanding* 理解力强. ⑩众多的, 充足的, 大的. *Corn is in* ~ *supply.* 谷物供应充足. *fetch* ~ *prices* 售得高价. *have a* ~ *family* 有很多子女. *read a* ~ *list of books* 读很多书. ***as broad as it is*** ~ 反正都一样. ***as*** ~ ***as*** ①长达…, 达…之久 (*as* ~ *as five years* 长达五年之久). ②只要. ***as*** ~ ***as one's arms*** 极长. ***at (the)*** ~***est*** 至多. ***be*** ~ ***in ...ing*** 很不容易… (*Spring is* ~ *in coming.* 春天好不容易才来). ***before (very)*** ~ 不(需很)久. ***by a*** ~ ***chalk [shot, way]*** = ***by*** ~ ***chalks*** 〔口〕在很大程度上, 远远, …得多. ***make a*** ~ ***arm*** 把手伸得老远. ***make a*** ~ ***guess*** 作大致估计. ***not by a*** ~ ***chalk [shot]*** 绝不; 差得远. ***one's*** ~ ***home*** 坟墓 (*go to one's* ~ *home* 死). — *ad.* ①长久; 久已. *The opportunity was not* ~ *(in) coming.* 机会不久就来了. *He will not be* ~ *for this world.* 他不会活得久了. *I have* ~ *been meaning to write.* 我早就想写信了. *It was* ~ *before he recovered.* 他的病好久才痊愈. ②始终. *all day [night]* ~ 整天[夜]. *all one's life* ~ 一辈子. ③遥远地. *a* ~*-travelled person* 曾到远处旅行的人. ***any*** ~***er*** (不)再 (*I shall not wait (any)* ~*er.* 我不再等了). ***how*** ~***?*** 多久 (*How* ~ *have you been here?* 你来了多少时候?). ~ ***after*** 很久之后. ~ ***ago [since]*** 老早[以前]. ~ ***before*** 老早以前. ***no*** ~***er*** 已不, 不再. ***So*** ~***!*** 〔口〕再见! ***so*** ~ ***as*** 只要 (*Stay so* ~ *as you like.* 只要你喜欢尽管呆在这儿好啦). — *n.* ①长期间. *It will not take* ~. 这不需要很多时间. ②〔the L-〕= ~ vacation. ③〔*pl.*〕【商】看涨的人, 做多头的人 (*opp.* shorts). ④【语音】长元音; 长音节; 长辅音. ⑤(服装的)长尺寸; 〔*pl.*〕长裤. ***for*** ~ 长久. ~***s and shorts*** ①诗〔尤指古希腊的和古拉丁的〕. ②【建】长短砌合. ***the*** ~ ***and the short of it is that ...*** 要点, 梗概, 总之. ~**-ago** ① *a.* 从前的, 往时的. ② *n.* 〔the ~〕往时, 古昔. ~**-awaited** *a.* 期待已久的. **L- Beach** (美国)长滩. ~**-bill** 长嘴的鸟(尤指沙锥鸟, 鹬). ~**-boat** (放在大船上的最大的)大艇. ~**-bow** 大弓 (*draw [pull] the* ~*-bow* 吹牛). ~**-cherished** *a.* 长期渴望的. ~**-cloth** 细棉布. ~**-clothes** 〔*pl.*〕褪褓. ~**-dated** *a.* 远期的. ~**-day** *a.* 【植】长日照的. ~**-distance** *a.* ①长途的, 长距离的 (*a* ~*-distance bomber* 远程轰炸机). ②长途电话的. **long distance** ①长途电话; 通讯. ②长途电话机[交换机]; 长途话务员. ~ **division** 【数】长除法. ~ **dozen** 十三个. ~**-drawn (-out)** *a.* 拉长的 (~*drawn sigh* 长叹). ~**-eared** *a.* ①有长耳朵的. ②驴子似的; 笨的. ~ **face** 不愉快的脸色. ~ **field** 【板球】离击球员最远的外场. ~**green**〔美俚〕钞票. ~**hair** 〔美口〕① *a.* 知识分子(气味)的〔尤指爱好古典音乐的〕(=~haired). ② *n.* 知识分子〔尤指爱好古典音乐的〕. ③ *n.* = hippie. ~**hand** 普通写法 (*opp.* shorthand). ~**head** 长头人. ~**-head·ed** *a.* ①头颅长的. ②聪明的, 有远见的. ~**hop** 长途飞行. ~**-horn** ①〔美〕长角牛. ②得克萨斯州人〔绰号〕. ③(探测飞机的)测音器. ~**-horned beetle** 【动】天牛科 (*cerambycidae*) 甲虫. ~**-horned grasshopper** 【动】长角螽斯. ~ **hours** 夜晚十一、二点钟, 午夜 (*opp.* small hours). ~ **house** (美洲易洛魁人和其他印第安部落的)议事厅. ~ **hundred** 一百二十; 一百多. ~ **hundredweight** 长担, 英担〔等于 112 磅〕. **L- Island** (纽约附近的)长岛. ~ **johns** 〔口〕长内衣裤. ~ **jump** 跳远. ~ **leaf pine** 【植】长叶松 (*Pinus palustris*) 〔产于美国南部, 木质硬而沉, 经济价值很高〕. ~**-legged** *a.* 长腿的. ~**-lived** *a.* 长寿的. ~ **measure** = linear measure. ~ **moss** = Spanish moss. ~**-nine** 〔美〕廉价雪茄烟. ~**-off** 【板球】掷球员左后方的守场员. ~**-on** 【板球】掷球员右后方的守场员. **L- Parliament** 【英史】长期议会〔1640 年 11 月 3 日开幕, 1653 年被克伦威尔驱散, 1659 年重开, 1660 年解散〕. ~ **pig** 食人生番嘴里的牺牲品. ~ **play** 慢转唱片, 密纹唱片. ~**-play·ing** *a.* (唱片的) 慢转的〔$33^1/_3$ 转速〕. ~**-play·ing record** 慢转密纹唱片. ~ **prim·er** 五号与六号间的铅字. ~**-range** *a.* 远程的; 长期的 (*a* ~*-range fire* 远程射击. *a* ~*-range missile* 远程导弹. *a* ~*-range research* 深入的研究). ~ **robe** 律师服装. ~**-run** *a.* 长远的. ~ **shillings** 〔口〕优厚的工资. ~**shore** *a.* 沿岸工作的. ~ **shore-man** 码头搬运工人; 近海渔民; 〔口〕海滨零杂工人. ~**-short story** 较长的短篇小说, 中篇小说. ~ **shot** 没有希望当选的候选人. ~**-sight·ed** *a.* ①眼力好的; 有眼光的, 有先见之明的. ②远视的. ~**some** *a.* 〔方〕漫长的; 过长的; 冗长的. ~**-spur** 【动】铁爪鹀〔产于北极地带及北美大平原〕. ~**-standing** *a.* 长期间的, 长年累月的 (*a*~*-standing policy* 传统政策). ~ **stop** 〔英〕用来抑制[阻挡, 阻止]的人或物. ~**-suf·fering** ① *a.* 能忍耐的, 坚忍的. ② *n.* 坚忍. ~ **suit** ①【牌戏】(手上的

牌中）张数多的那一花色．②长处，胜过别人的东西．~-**term** *a.* ①长期的；时间持续很长的．②(资本、借贷等的)涉及较长期限的〔半年以上〕．~-**tested** *a.* 久经考验的．~**time** *a.* 长期的．~-**timer** ①在某地住过很久的人；长期从事某项工作的人．②长期徒刑犯．**L- Tom** 远程大炮．~ **ton** 长吨〔英制等于 2,240 磅〕．~-**tongued** *a.* 长舌的，话多的，饶舌的．~ **vacation** ①大学暑假．②法院夏季休庭．~ **wave**【无】长波．~-**wave** *a.* 长波的．~**ways,** ~**wise** *ad.* = lengthwise. ~-**wind•ed** *a.* ①气长的．②喋喋不休的，冗长的．**-ly** *ad.* **-ness** *n.*

-long *suf.* 表示"向"，"在"：end*long*, side*long*.

lon•gae•val [lɔnˈdʒiːvəl] *a.* = langeval.

lon•gan [ˈlɔŋgən] *n.* 【植】龙眼树 (*Euphoria longana*)；龙眼．

lon•ga•nim•i•ty [ˌlɔːŋgəˈnimiti] *n.* 忍受(伤痛)；坚忍，忍耐．

longe [lʌndʒ] *n.* ①练马长绳．②使用练马绳练马．— *vt.* (*-longed; -longe•ing, -long•ing*) 用练马绳训练马的各种步态．

lon•ge•ron [ˈlɔndʒərən] *n.* 〔常 *pl.*〕【空】(飞机的)纵梁，大梁．

lon•ge•val [lɔnˈdʒiːvəl] *a.* 〔罕〕长寿的．

lon•gev•i•ty [lɔnˈdʒeviti] *n.* ①长寿．②长期供职，资历．~ **pay** 〔美〕年资附加工资．

lon•ge•vous [lɔnˈdʒiːvəs] *a.*【罕】长寿的．

Long•fel•low [ˈlɔŋˌfeləu] *n.* ①朗费罗〔姓氏〕．②**Henry Wadsworth** ~亨利·沃兹沃思·朗费罗〔1807—1882，美国著名诗人〕．

lon•gi•corn [ˈlɔndʒiˌkɔːn] *a.* 有长角的；具长触角的〔如某些甲虫〕．

long•ies [ˈlɔːŋiːz] *n.* 〔*pl.*〕〔美口〕= long johns.

long•ing [ˈlɔŋiŋ] *n.* 渴望，热望 (*for*)．— *a* 渴望的．**-ly** *ad.*

long•ish [ˈlɔŋiʃ] *a.* 稍长的，略长的．

lon•gi•tude [ˈlɔndʒitjuːd] *n.* ①经度，经线〔*cf.* latitude〕．②【天】黄经．*the meridian of* ~ 黄经圈．③〔谑〕长，长度．

lon•gi•tu•di•nal [ˌlɔndʒiˈtjuːdinl] *a.* ①经度的，经线的．②纵的，纵向的．~ *mass*【物】纵质量．*a* ~ *section* 纵剖面．**-ly** *ad.*

Long•man [ˈlɔŋmən] *n.* 朗曼〔姓氏〕．

Lon•go•bard [ˈlɔŋgəuˌbɑːd] *n.* (*pl.* **-bards, Lon•go•bar•di** [-ˈbɑːdi]) **-ic** *a.* =Lomdard *n.*

Long•street [ˈlɔŋstriːt] *n.* 朗斯特里特〔姓氏〕．

longue ha•leine [F. lɔ̃g alɛn] 〔F.〕长期努力．*a work of [de] longue haleine* 需要长期努力的工作[著作]．

lon•guette [lɔːŋˈget] *n.* (长及小腿肚的)长裙，长连衫裙．

lon•gueur [F. lɔ̃ˈgœːr; E. lɔːŋˈgə] *n.* 〔F.〕(小说、乐曲等的)冗长而枯燥无味的部分．

lon•i•ce•ra [ləuˈnisərə] *n.*【植】〔L-〕忍冬属；忍冬，金银花．~ *distillate* 金银花露．

Lons•dale [ˈlɔnzdeil] *n.* 朗斯代尔〔姓氏〕．

loo[1] [luː] *n.* 一种纸牌赌博．

loo[2] [luː] *n.* 〔英口〕便所．

loo•by [ˈluːbi] *n.* 笨人，蠢汉．

Loo•choo (Islands) [ˈluːˈtʃuː] *n.* 琉球 (= Ryukyu Islands).

Loo•choo•an [ˈluːˈtʃuːən] *a.* 琉球的；琉球人的．— *n.* 琉球人．

loo•ey, loo•ie [ˈluːi] *n.* 〔美军俚〕中[少]尉．

loo•fa(h) [ˈluːfə] *n.* = luffa.

look [luk] *vi.* ①看，注视，盯 (*at*)．*Look!* 你瞧！看哪！*We* ~*ed but saw nothing.* 我们看是在看，可是什么也没有看见．②〔带有表语〕显得，好象．~ *sick* 显得有病的样子．*He does not* ~ *his age.* 他看上去不象是有这个年纪的人．*He* ~*s very tired.* 他好象很疲倦．*He* ~*s every inch a worker.* 他没有一处不象工人．*It* ~*s as though we should have a storm.* 好象要有暴风雨．*It* ~*s like rain.* 看来要下雨．~ *happy* 喜形于色．③留心，注意；弄清，查明．*L- (to it) that they do not escape.* 当心别让他们逃跑了．*L- if it is right.* 查查对不对．④(房屋等)朝着，面向；(事实、情况等)倾向…，倾向… *The house* ~*s (to the) south.* 这房子朝南．*Conditions* ~ *toward war.* 局势趋向战争．⑤预期．*I did not* ~ *to meet you here.* 我没有想到在这里遇见你．— *vt.* ①用眼色表示，用态度表示．*He* ~*ed his consent [thanks].* 他用眼睛表示了同意[谢意]．②瞧，注视，打量．~ *sb. into silence* 瞪着某人不敢作声．~ *sb. full in the face* 盯着某人的面孔细看．~ *sb. out of countenance* 瞧得人局促不安．~ *sb. up and down* 上上下下打量某人．~ ***about (one)*** 四下里看；观察形势；戒备，警戒；计划行动．~ ***about for*** 四下寻找．~ ***after*** ①回头看；目送．②寻求，渴望．③注意，照管，照应，看守．~ ***ahead*** 考虑未来，预先作好准备．***L- ahead, Sir!***【海】看前面．~ ***alive*** 当心；快些！~ ***around*** 〔美〕= ~ round. ~ ***as if*** 看起来好象，似乎，好象．~ ***at*** ①看，查看 (*The girl is pretty to* ~ *at.* 这个姑娘好看)．②考虑，着眼于 (~ *at problems all-sidedly* 全面地看问题)．~ ***away*** 把脸转过去，看别的地方．~ ***back*** ①回头看；回顾，追想 (*to; upon*)．②(对事业等)不起劲．***L- before you leap.*** 〔谚〕三思而后行．~ ***beyond the grave*** 考虑身后事．~ ***big*** 洋洋自得，盛气凌人．~ ***black*** 脸色凶恶；形势恶劣．~ ***blue*** (人)无能；灰溜溜的，颓丧．~ ***death*** 杀气腾腾．~ ***death in the face*** 不顾死活．~ ***down*** ①看下面，俯视．②蔑视，看不起 (*on; upon*)．③跌价．~ ***for*** ①寻找．②期待，渴望．~ ***forward to*** 盼望，期待 (~ *forward to a prosperous old age* 盼望一个富裕的晚年．~ *forward to seeing you again* 期望重见你们．) ***L- here!*** 喂，注意！~ ***ill*** ①看上去有病，看来不漂亮．②(事情)很糟．~ ***in*** ①看看，一瞥 (*at sth.*)．②顺便访问 (*on sb.*)．~ ***into*** ①窥视．②调查；过问．~ ***like ...*** 好象；象要 (*The place* ~*s like rabbits.* 这地方好象有兔子)．~ ***off*** 把眼睛转开．~ ***on*** ①看做 (*as*)．②旁观，观看 (~ *on the bright [dark] side* 看光明[黑暗]的一面)．③面向 (*to*) ~ **on with sb.** 和某人同看一本书．~ ***one's age*** 和年龄相称．~ ***oneself*** 和平常一样，不改常态 (~ *quite oneself again* 完全恢复(健康)了)．~ ***out*** ①注意，警惕．②期待 (*for*)．③看外头；展望 (*on; over*)．④找出，挑选，寻找．~ ***over*** ①过目，大致看一看．②检验，调查，查究．③放过，宽待．~ ***round*** ①掉头看，环顾，到处寻找．②仔细考虑，察看．~ ***sharp*** 非常留心(看)；赶快．~ ***through*** ①透过(玻璃等)看．②看穿，看破．③彻底调查；从头看完，通读一遍．~ ***to*** ①注意；照料，照应．②依赖，指望 (~ *to sb. for help* 指望某人帮助)．③〔美〕倾向…，以…为目的，企图．~ ***to be*** 〔美〕象… (*It* ~*ed to be about eight feet tall.* 看上去有八英尺高)．~ ***to it that*** 注意，留心．~ ***toward(s)*** ①〔口〕为…干杯．②〔美〕倾向…，趋向，取…的方向，指向．~ ***up*** ①向上看．②(物价等)上涨；(市面等)兴旺．③(在词典中)查找，查出．④访问，看望．⑤尊敬 (*to*)．~ ***upon***=~on. ~ ***well*** ①象很健康；看上去漂亮．②(事情)顺利．***L- you!*** 注意！***to*** ~ ***at sb. [sth.]*** 〔常用作插入语〕据某人[某事]的外表下判断．— *n.* ①〔常 *pl.*〕容貌，相貌，面貌．*Don't judge a man by his* ~*s.* 不要凭外表判断人．*good* ~*s* 好相貌．*lose one's* ~*s* (女子)容颜衰老．*the* ~ *of his face* 他的面貌．②脸色．③样子，外表．*a kind* ~ 温和的样子．*an amused* ~ *in sb.'s eyes* 某人眼中暗地感到有趣[可笑]的神色．*a serious* ~ 严肃的脸色．*I don't like the* ~ *of him.* 我不欢喜他那个样子．*the* ~ *of the sky* 天色．③一看，一瞥．*give sb. a* ~ 看某人一眼．*give sb. a dirty* ~ 瞪某人一眼．*steal a* ~ 偷看一眼．***cast a*** ~ ***at*** 瞥一眼．***have [take] a (good)*** ~ ***at*** (仔细)看一看．***have a*** ~ ***of*** 象，仿佛．***in good*** ~***s*** 样子很健康．***take on a new*** ~ 具

有新气象. ***take on an ugly*** ～ 情况不佳. ***upon the*** ～ 在寻找中. ***wither sb. with a*** ～〔谑〕看得某人惶恐不安. **～-alike**〔美俚〕面貌很相似的人. ***～-in*** ①一瞥. ②短暂的访问; 走马看花 (*give sb. a ～-in* 顺便访问某人). ③(在比赛中)获胜的希望 (*have a ～-in* 有可能取胜). ④【足球】迅速传球 (给以对角线方向跑向球场中部的球员). **～-over** 粗略的一看. **～-see**〔俚〕走马看花; 调查; 视察旅行. ～ **through** 透视; 监听. **～up** 查找;【自】检查.

look·er [ˈlukə] *n.* ①观看者;〔英〕检查员. ②外貌漂亮的人. *～s on TV* 电视观众. *cloth ～s* 织物检查员. *a good* ～ 美男; 美女. *a handsome* ～ 美男. **～-in** *n.* ***(pl. ～s-in)*** 看电视的人.

look·er-on [ˈlukərˈɔn] *n.* ***(pl. look·ers-on*** [ˈlukəzˈɔn]***)*** 旁观者; 观察者; 观看者. *Lookers-on see most of the game.* 〔谚〕旁观者清.

look·ing-glass [ˈlukiŋglɑːs] *n.* 镜子; 窥镜. —*a.* 完全相反的, 颠倒的, 悖理的. *a* ～ *world* 是非颠倒的世界.

look·ing-in *n.* (在家)观看电视.

look·out [ˈlukˈaut] *n.* ①守望, 看守, 警戒. ②守望者, 看守者. ③了望台, 监视哨. ④远景, 前途. ⑤某人应做的事; 任务, 职守; 警戒. *keep [take] a sharp* ～ *for* 小心提防, 注意戒备. *on the* ～ *for* 注意, 警惕. *an antiaircraft* ～ 对空监视哨. *a* ～ *post [sentry]* 监视哨. *a* ～ *tower* 了望塔. *a bad* ～ *for sb.* 对某人来说并不美妙的前景. *That is his own* ～. 那是他自己的事.

loo·loo [ˈluːluː] *n.* = lulu.

loom[1] [luːm] *n.* ①织布机; 织布法; 织布业. ②桨柄, 橹柄. ③【空】翼肋腹部. *a hand* ～ 手工织机. *a power* ～ 动力织机.

loom[2] [luːm] *vi.* 朦胧出现; (危险、忧虑等)阴森森地逼近. *A ship ～ed (up) through the fog.* 一只船在雾中隐隐出现. *Trifles* ～ *large to an anxious mind.* 顾虑多的人草木皆兵. —*n.* 朦胧出现的形象; 巨大的幻影.

loom[3] [luːm] *n.* ①= loon[2]. ②= guillemot.

loon[1] [luːn] *n.* ①懒人; 废物; 蠢汉. ②疯子, 狂人. ③〔Scot.〕男孩, 小伙子. ④〔Scot.〕情妇; 妓女.

loon[2] [luːn] *n.* ①【动】鹏鹇 *(Gavia immer)*. ②(捕鱼的)潜鸟. *common* ～ 白嘴潜鸟.

loon·ey, loon·y [ˈluːni] *a.* ***(loon·i·er, loon·i·est)*** 〔俚〕笨拙的; 疯狂的. —*n.* ***(pl. loon·ies)*** 疯子; 傻瓜. ～ **bin**〔俚〕精神病院, 疯人院.

loop [luːp] *n.* ①(用线、带等打成的)圈, 环, 匝, 框, 环孔, 线圈;【医】(常 the ～) 宫内避孕环. ②环状物, 搭环, 拎环. ③(铁路上的)让车道, 环道. ④【无】回路, 回线, 波腹, 环形天线. ⑤【数】自变;【计】循环; (程序中)一群指令的重复. ⑥【空】翻圈飞行, 翻筋斗;【溜冰】(单脚)打圈儿. ⑦〔美〕闹市区; 〔the L-〕芝加哥的商业区. *a safety* ～ 保险圈. *a wire* ～ 钢丝套圈. ***knock [throw] for a*** ～〔美俚〕①使神志不清; 打昏, 使醉倒. ②给人极好的印象. ③出色地通过 [做成]. ***on the*** ～〔美〕在匆匆旅行中. —*vt.* ①使(绳等)成圈, 打成圈;【电】把导线连成回路. ②用圈围住; (用环)箍住 *(up; back)*. ③使作环状运动;【空】翻筋斗. —*vi.* ①打环, 成圈. ②【空】翻筋斗. ③(象尺蠖似的)伸屈前进. ～ ***the loop***【空】翻筋斗; (骑自行车等)兜圈子. ～ **aerial [antenna]**【无】环形天线. **～hole** ①(堡垒的)枪眼; 窥孔. ②逃路;〔尤指〕(用来摆脱义务、不遵守法律、不履行合同等的) 遁词, 借口, (契约中的) 漏洞; 欺骗性圈套. ～ **knot** 环结〔绳结的一种〕. ～ **line** 环线, 圈线. ～ **stitch**【纺】连环针脚. **～-the-～** ①(在疾驰或迅速转动中利用离心力使乘坐者在一段路程上头部朝下的娱乐装置) 翻筋斗列车. ②【空】翻筋斗飞行.

looped [luːpt] *a.* ①有圈[环]的; 成圈[环]的. ②〔美〕酩酊大醉的.

loop·er [ˈluːpə] *n.* ①【动】尺蠖. ②【纺】套口机; 缝袜头机; 弯纱轮. ③打环的人; 打环装置. ④(驾飞机)翻筋斗的人.

loop·y [ˈluːpi] *a.* ***(loop·i·er; -i·est)*** ①多环的, 一圈一圈的. ②〔俚〕神经错乱的; 呆头呆脑的.

loose [luːs] *a.* ***(loos·er, loos·est)*** ①松的, 宽的, 松散的. *a cloth of* ～ *texture* 稀松 (不紧实的) 织物. ～ *clothing* 宽大的衣服. *a* ～ *knot* 松的结. ②松开的, 没加束缚的, 自由的. *a* ～ *criminal* 在逃罪犯. *a horse* ～ *of its tether* 没有系住的马. *the* ～ *end of a string* 绳子松开的一端. ③模糊的, 不确切的, 不严谨的. *a* ～ *style* 不简练的文体. *a* ～ *thinker* 思想不严密的人. *a* ～ *translation* 不严密的译文. ④散漫的, 荒淫的, 放荡的. *a* ～ *fish* 浪子. *a* ～ *woman* 放荡的女子. *have a* ～ *tongue* 惯于随口乱讲. *lead a* ～ *life* 过放荡生活. ～ *conduct* 放纵. *lordly, luxurious,* ～ *and idle life* 骄奢淫逸的生活. ⑤松动的. *have* ～ *bowels* 拉肚子. *a* ～ *tooth* 松动的牙齿. ⑥散放的, 散装的. ～ *cash [change, coins]* 零钱. ～ *mushroom* 散装蘑菇. ⑦自由的, 无拘束的. ～ *capital [funds]* 游资. *a* ～ *hour* 闲暇时间. ⑧疏松的. ⑨【化】游离的. ⑩(色、染料等)易退色的. *a* ～ *dye* 容易退色的染料. ⑪【医】咳出痰的. *a* ～ *cough* 咳嗽带痰. ⑫队形散开的. *in* ～ *order*【军】散开的队形. *a* ～ *game [play]*【橄榄球】不互相扭夺的比赛. ***at a*** ～ ***end*** 没有着落; 没有工作[职业]; 未确定解决. ***break*** ～ 逃出, 迸发出. ***cast*** ～ 解开(绳索等); 放出(鹰、犬等). ***come [get]*** ～ 解开, 松开. ***cut*** ～ ①使脱离拘束. ②〔口〕狂欢. ③逃脱, 摆脱 (*cut* ～ *from old habits* 革除旧习惯. *cut* ～ *from old ties* 割断老关系). ***have a screw*** ～ ①螺丝钉松了. ②(精神等)有点失常[不对头]. ***let [turn]*** ～ 放走, 释放. ***let*** ～ ***one's anger*** 发怒, 暴躁起来. ***set*** ～ 放走. ***shake oneself*** ～ 把身体摆脱. ***There is a screw*** ～ ***somewhere.*** 这里面有点不对头 [有点问题]. ***with a*** ～ ***rein*** 放松缰绳; 放任. —*ad.* = loosely. ***hold*** ～ ***to sth.*** 对…漠不关心. —*vt.* ①解(结等); 弄松; 放松; 放掉. ②放(枪、箭) *(off)*. ～ *hold (of)* 松手, 放任. —*vi.* ①变松, 松开, 松弛. ②放射, 开枪. ③〔主英〕放学. ④解缆, 开船. —*n.* 解放, 放任; 发射. ***be on the*** ～〔口〕①无拘束; 散漫; 逍遥法外. ②放荡; 纵情游乐. ***give (a)*** ～ ***to one's feelings [fancy]*** 放纵感情. **～-bodied** *a.* (衣服等)宽大的. **～-box**〔英〕放饲场, 放饲马房. **～-fit·ting** *a.* 配上去稍大的. **～-flow·ing** *a.* 缓缓流着的, 轻轻飘着的. **～-joint·ed** *a.* ①(接头)松动的. ②吊儿郎当的; 随意行动的. **～-leaf** *a.* 活叶(式)的. **～-limbed** *a.* 手脚灵活的 (*a ～-limbed dancer* 舞姿轻盈的舞蹈演员). **～-minded** *a.* 思想散漫的. ～ **pulley [wheel]**【机】游滑轮. ～ **smut**【农】(谷类) 散黑穗病. **～-tongued** *a.* 嘴松的; 言语随便的; 信口开河的; 饶舌的; 唠叨的. **-ly** *ad.* **-ness** *n.*

loos·en [ˈluːsn] *vt.* ①放松. ②使 (纪律) 松弛. ③【医】通大便; 使咳出痰来. —*vi.* 变松, 宽松, 松散. *By degrees her tongue was ～ed.* 她的话渐渐地多起来了. ～ ***up***〔美口〕①宽松, 宽舒. ②信口开河. ③慷慨解囊.

loose·strife [ˈluːsstraif] *n.*【植】排草属; 黄连花; 千屈菜; 纤毛假珍珠菜.

loot[1] [luːt] *n.* ①掠夺物; 战利品. ②(官吏的)赃物, 非法收入. ③抢劫, 掠夺. ④〔俚〕金钱. —*vt., vi.* 劫掠(都市); 洗劫; 抢劫; 强夺; (官吏)贪污.

loot[2] [luːt] *n.*〔美俚〕= lieutenant.

loot·er [ˈluːtə] *n.* 掠夺者, 抢劫者, 强夺者.

lop[1] [lɔp] *vt., vi.* ①伐, 砍; 修剪(树枝) *(off; away)*. ②砍(头), 斩断(手等) *(off, away)*. ③割裂, 删除. —*n.* ①除枝, 修剪. ②剪下的树枝, 小枝.

lop[2] [lɔp] *vt.* (兔子把耳朵)垂下来, 耷拉下来. —*vi.* ①低垂, 垂挂. ②懒洋洋地躺着[靠着]; 懒洋洋地走动[行动]; 吊儿郎当地闲混 *(about)*. ③一跳一跳地走动. *A rabbit ～ped among cabbages.* 一只兔子在白菜之间一跳一跳钻来钻去. —*n.* 垂耳兔. —*a.* 垂下的. ～ *ears* 垂下的耳朵. **～-ear** 垂耳; 垂耳兔. **～-eared** *a.* 垂耳的.

-per 修剪树木的工人；修剪树木的长柄剪刀．**-ping** 修剪；〔常 *pl.*〕修剪下来的树枝．
lop³ [lɔp] *vi.* (水面)起小波．— *n.* 小波．
lope [ləup] *vi.*, *vt.* (使马等)大步跳跃着慢跑，(兔等)跳着飞奔．— *n.* 大步慢跑；飞奔．
lo·pho·branch [ˈləufəˌbræŋk, ˈlɔfə-] *a.*【动】总鳃类的〔包括海龙亚科和海龙科〕．— *n.* 总鳃类的鱼．
lo·pho·phore [ˈləufəˌfɔː, lɔfə-] *n.*【动】触(手)冠，总担；纤毛环．
lop·py [ˈlɔpi] *a.* *(-pi·er, -pi·est)* 散垂的；下垂的．
lop·sid·ed [ˌlɔpˈsaidid] *a.* 倾向一面的；不平衡的，不匀称的，偏重的．*a ~ spill*【美棒球】一面倒的大败．**-ly** *ad.* **-ness** *n.*
loq. = loquitur.
lo·qua·cious [ləuˈkweiʃəs] *a.* ①多嘴的，多话的．②(鸟)啁啾不休的；(水)潺潺不息的．**-ly** *ad.* **-ness** *n.*
lo·quac·i·ty [ləuˈkwæsiti] *n.* 多嘴；喋喋不休；吵闹，喧噪．
lo·quat [ˈləukwɔt] *n.*【植】枇杷树；枇杷．
loq·ui·tur [ˈlɔkwitə] *vi.* 〔L.〕〔略 loq.〕他[她]说．
lor [lɔː] *int.* 〔英俚〕天啊！上帝！(= Lord.)
Lo·ra [ˈlɔurə] *n.* 洛拉〔女子名，Laura 的异体〕．
lor·al [ˈlɔːrəl] *a.* (鸟类，爬虫，鱼类的)眼端的．
lor·an [ˈlɔːrən] *n.* 劳兰〔远航仪〕，长途航海用雷达设备；远距离无线电导航系统〔long-range navigation 的缩略，*cf.* shoran〕．
lor·cha [ˈlɔːtʃə] *n.* 西式中国三桅帆船．
lord [lɔːd] *n.* ①君主．②封建主，领主；贵族；地主．③〔英〕勋爵〔对某些贵族或高级官员的尊称〕．④主〔指上帝，基督〕．⑤主人，所有者．⑥(某一方面的)巨头．⑦〔口〕老爷；丈夫．⑧【占星】首座星．*our sovereign ~ the King* 国王陛下．*the ~ of the manor* 庄园领主．*the ~ of the soil* 地主，领主〔的尊称〕．*the Lords* 英国上议院全体议员．*Civil L-* 海军部文官委员．*First L- of the Admiralty* (英国)海军大臣．*First Sea L-* (英国)海军部第一次官．*the House of Lords* 英国上议院．*the L- mayor of London* 伦敦市长．*L-, how they laughed!* 天哪，他们笑成那个样子了！*a cotton ~* 棉花大王．*the press ~s* 新闻界巨头．*a ~ of few acres* 小地主，小土地所有者．***as drunk as a ~*** 酩酊大醉．***by the L- Harry!*** 见鬼，岂有此理！***be ~ of*** 领有；拥有．***in the year of our L- …*** 在公元…年．***live like a ~*** 过奢华的生活．***~ and master*** ①丈夫，一家之主．②东家，主人．***L- bless me [my soul]! = L- have mercy!*** 老天爷！啊呀！老天保佑！***(the) L- knows!*** 天晓得！谁知道！***L- love you [your heart]***〔俚〕哎呀！真是！***New ~s, new laws.***〔谚〕新官上任三把火．***paper ~***〔Scot.〕由于担任某种职务而得到勋爵称号的人．***swear like a ~*** 乱骂，叱责．***take it as easy as a L- Mayor***〔俚〕满不在乎．***the ~s of creation*** 万物之灵，人类；〔谑〕男人们．***the ~s of the harvest*** ①农场主，收获的所有者．②收割作物的带头人．***treat sb. like a ~*** 对待某人象王公一般，非常阔绰地款待某人．— *vi.* 作威作福．— *vt.* 使成贵族；加贵族封号．***will not be ~ed over*** 不许别人作威作福．***~ it over …*** 称王道霸；作威作福．**L- Bishop** 主教〔正式的称呼〕．**L- Chamberlain** *(of the Household)*〔英〕官务大臣．**L- Chief Justice (of England)** (英国)首席法官．**L- (God)! = Good L-! ~ chancellor** (英国)大法官〔兼任上议院议长〕．**L- High Steward of England** ①英国皇家总管大臣．②贵族法庭审判长．**L- High Treasure** (英国)财务大臣．**L- Justice Clerk** 〔Scot.〕高等法院副院长．**L- Justice General** 高等法院院长．**L- of Host**【宗】耶和华，上帝．**L- of misrule** (中古英国圣诞节饮宴和游戏的)司仪．*(the)* **~ paramount** 君主．**L- President (of the Council)** (英国)枢密大臣．*(the)* **~ Provost** (爱丁堡等都市的市长)．**Lord's day**【宗】主日；星期日．**L- speaker** (英国)上议院议长．**Lord's Prayer**【宗】主祷文．**~s spiritual** 〔英〕上议员主教议员．**Lord's Supper**【宗】①最后的晚餐 (= Last Supper)．②圣餐式；圣餐．**Lord's table**【宗】祭坛；圣餐台．**~s temporal**〔英〕上议院贵族议员．**-less** *a.* 无君主的；无丈夫的．
lord·ing [ˈlɔːdiŋ] *n.* 〔废〕①= lordling．②大人，老爷〔称呼语，通常用复数〕．
lord·ling [ˈlɔːdliŋ] *n.* 〔蔑〕小贵族，小老爷．
lord·ly [ˈlɔːdli] *a.* *(-li·er; -li·est)* ①贵族(似)的；有气派的．②傲慢的．***in ~ way*** 气派十足地．— *ad.* 贵族似地，气派十足地；傲慢地．**-li·ness** *n.*
lor·do·sis [lɔːˈdəusis] *n.*【动】脊柱前凸．**lor·dot·ic** [-ˈdɔːtik] *a.*
Lord's [lɔːdz] *n.* 伦敦大板球场〔即 Marylebone 板球俱乐部总部，= Lord's Cricket Ground〕．
lords-and-la·dies [ˈlɔːdzənˈleidiz] *n.*【植】①斑叶阿若母 *(Arum maculatum)*．②天南星 *(Arisaema triphyllum)*．
lord·ship [ˈlɔːdʃip] *n.* ①贵族〔领主〕的身分．②领主的统治权．③贵族的领地．④〔英〕〔常作 L-〕阁下．*your [his] ~* 爵爷〔对贵族及某些高级官员的尊称，常戏谑地用于常人或动物〕．
lore¹ [lɔː, lɔə] *n.* ①(特殊的)学问，(专门的)知识；博学．②口头传说．③〔古〕传授．*doctors' ~* 祖传医学．*folk ~* 民间文学．*herbal ~* 本草学．*the ~ of the Egyptians* 古代埃及人的知识．
lore² [lɔː] *n.*【动】(鸟的眼与啄之间，爬虫及鱼的眼与鼻之间的)眼端，眼先．
Lor·e·lei [ˈlɔːrəlai] *n.* 罗利勒〔德国传说中一个以美色和歌声迷惑船夫使船遭难的女妖〕．
Lo·ren·zo [lɔˈrenzəu] *n.* 洛伦佐〔男子名〕．
Lo·ret·ta [ləˈretə] *n.* 洛蕾塔〔女子名〕．
lor· gnette [lɔːˈnjet] *n.* 〔F.〕长柄眼镜；(附有长柄的)观剧用望远镜．
lor·gnon [lɔːˈnjɔn] *n.* ①单眼镜或双眼镜〔如夹鼻眼镜〕．②= lorgnette.
lo·ri·ca [ləˈraikə] *n.* *(pl.* ***-cae*** [-siː]*)* ①古罗马胸甲．②【动】兜甲．**-i·cate** [ˈlɔːriˌkeit, lɑːri-], **-i·cat·ed** *a.*
lor·i·keet [ˈlɔːriˌkiːt] *n.*【动】青绿色小鹦鹉．
lo·ris [ˈlɔːris] *n.* *(pl.* ***loris)***【动】懒猴属；懒猴 *(Loris gracilis)*；蜂猴 *(Nycticebus tardigradus)*．
lorn [lɔːn] *a.*〔诗、谑〕被遗弃的，孤单的；荒凉的．**-ness** *n.*
Lor·na [ˈlɔːnə] *n.* 洛娜〔女子名〕．
Lor·raine [lɔˈrein] *n.* 洛林〔法国东北部地名〕．
lor·ry [ˈlɔri] *n.* ①〔英〕运货汽车，卡车(=〔美〕truck)．②平板四轮运货马车．③(矿山、铁路的)手车；矿车；推料车．**~-hop, ~-jump** *vi.* 〔俚〕(不出钱)搭乘卡车旅行．
lo·ry [ˈlɔːri] *n.*【动】猩猩鹦鹉．
LOS = ① line of scrimmage 散兵线．②line of sight 视线，瞄准线．③lunar orbiter spacecraft 月球轨道宇航器．
Los [lɔːs] *n.* 〔美口〕Los Angeles 的简称．
los·a·ble [ˈluːzəbl] *a.* 容易丢失的，能输掉的．**-ness** *n.*
Los Al·a·mos [lɔsˈæləməus] 洛斯阿拉莫斯〔美国城市〕．
Los An·gel·es [lɔsˈændʒiliːz; Am. lɔːs ˈændʒələs] 洛杉矶〔美国城市〕．
lose [luːz] *vt.* *(lost* [lɔst]*)* ①丢失，丧失．*~ one's balance* 失去平衡，跌倒．*~ one's head* 被斩首；被搞糊涂．*~ one's life* 丢了性命．*The doctor ~s his patient.* 医生没有治好病人；病人另找医生了．②迷失，使迷路，使迷惑．*~ oneself [be lost] in the woods* 在森林中迷路．*~ one's way* 迷路．③白费，浪费．*~ no time in beginning work* 立即开始工作．*There is no love lost between the two.* (1)〔废〕他们彼此相爱．(2)他们并不相爱．*There's not a moment to ~.* 一分钟也不能浪费．④错过．*~ an opportunity* 错过机会．*~ one's train* 没赶上火车．⑤看漏，听漏，逸失，放跑．*I did not ~ a word of his speech.* 他的演说我没

有听漏一个字. ~ *the thread of an argument* 抓不住论据的线索. ⑥输掉; 使失败. ~ *a battle* 战败. ~ *a game* 输一局. *The motion was lost by a majority of two.* 动议以两票之差被否决了. ⑦〔主用被动语态〕灭亡,杀死,破坏,湮没. *be lost to all sense of shame* 恬不知耻. *The ship was lost with all hands.* 那艘船和船上所有的人一齐沉没了. ⑧忘记. ~ *one's French* 法语都忘光了. ⑨摆脱,脱离. ~ *one's cold* 伤风好了. ~ *one's fear* 解除忧虑. ⑩使失去. *Reckless driving may ~ you even your life.* 乱开车甚至会送掉你的命. *Such behaviour lost him our trust.* 他这种行为使我们不再信任他了. — *vi.* ①亏本,蚀本; 受损失. *I don't want you to ~ by me.* 我不愿让你为我受损失. ②失败; 输 (*opp.* win). ③(钟、表等) 走慢. *Does your watch gain or ~?* 你的表走得快,还是走得慢? ④衰弱. *The invalid is losing.* 病人在逐渐衰弱. ~ ***in beauty*** (人老)色衰. ~ ***one's labour [pains]*** 白费气力. ~ ***one's temper*** 发怒. ~ ***out*** 〔美口〕失败,输掉. ~ ***the battle [day, field]*** 战败. ~ ***the scent of*** 失去嗅迹,失去猎物的踪迹.

lo·sel [ˈləuzl, ˈluː-] *n.* 〔古、方〕没有价值的人; 无用的人. — *a.* 〔古、方〕没有价值的; 无用的.

los·er [ˈluːzə] *n.* ①损失者; 损失物; 失败者; 输者. ②〔美〕被判过徒刑的罪犯. ③〔英〕= losing hazard. *a good [bad]* ~ 输了不生气[生气]的人, 输了不在乎[反应不好]的人. *a three-time* ~ 服过三次徒刑的罪犯. *Losers are always in the wrong.* 〔谚〕胜者为王,败者为寇. *You shall not be the ~ by it.* 不会让你因此吃亏的. ***come off a*** ~ 损失,亏损; 输; 失败.

los·ing [ˈluːziŋ] *a.* 亏本的; 看来要输的; 失败的. *a ~ game* 无胜利希望的比赛. — *n.* 失败; 〔*pl.*〕(尤指投机等的)损失. ~ **hazard**【台球】击球未能使之落袋,自己的球反而落袋,因此受到罚分.

loss [lɔs] *n.* ①丧失; 丢失,遗失. ②减损,损失,亏损(额); 损耗; 减少,下降. ③失败; 输掉. ④错过; 浪费. ⑤损毁;【军】伤亡; 〔*pl.*〕伤亡及被俘人数. ~ *of sight* 失明. *copper* ~【电】铜耗. *core [iron]* ~【电】铁耗. *a dead* ~ 净亏, 纯损. *an idling* ~ 空转损耗. *a total* ~ 总损失. *His death is a great ~ to the country.* 他的死是国家的大损失. *profit and* ~ 盈亏. *suffer heavy ~es* 遭受重大损失. ~ *of pressure* 压力下降. ~ *in weight* 重量[体重]减少. ~ *of weight* 失重. *the ~ of a war* 战败. ~ *of opportunity* 错过机会. ***at a*** ~ ①无办法, 为难 (*I am at a ~ what to do.* 我就是不知道怎样办才好). ②(猎犬)失去猎物嗅迹. ③亏本地 (*sell sth. at a ~* 赔本卖出某物). ***cut a [the]*** ~ 赶紧脱手以免多受损失. ***for a*** ~ 处于苦恼中(*throw them for a* ~ 使他们苦恼). ***make a*** ~ 亏损. ***without (any) ~ of time*** 即刻,马上. ~ **leader** 为招揽顾客而亏本出售的货物. ~ **list**【军】伤亡名单. ~**maker** 亏本企业. ~-**making** *a.* (显然) 亏本的. ~ **ratio** 损害率〔保险公司在某一时期中支付的赔偿费在收入保险费中所占比率〕.

lost [lɔst] *v.* lose 的过去式及过去分词. — *a.* ①失去了的; 丢失了的; 错过的,放过的. ②输掉的; 失败的; 打败了的. ③浪费了的,白费的. ④不知所措的,为难的. ⑤遭难的; 死去了的. ⑥迷路的; 入迷的,忘我的,忘乎所以的. ⑦被忘却的; 失传的. *a ~ advertisement* 遗失广告. *(the) Lost and Found* 失物招领处. *a ~ battle* 败仗. *cry out ~ and terrible words.* 喊出绝望和可怕的话. ~ *labour* 徒劳. *a ~ opportunity* 错过的机会. *a ~ prize* 没有争取到的奖品. ~ *time* 浪费掉的时间. *A soldier was ~ in him.* 他可惜没有成为战士. *a ~ child* 迷路的孩子. *feel* ~ 不知所措. *a ~ ship* 沉没了的船. *a man ~ in thought* 想得出神的人. *a ~ art* 失传的艺术. *a ~ city* 湮没无闻的城市. ***be ~ on [upon]*** 对…不起作用 (*My kindness is ~ upon him.* 我对他好也没用). ***be ~ to*** 感觉不到…; 不再来,已不可能 (*be ~ to sight* 看不见了. *be ~ to shame* 恬不知耻. *Hope was never ~ to him.* 他从来没有绝望过). ***Get ~!*** 〔美俚〕走开! 别打扰我! ***give sb. up for*** ~ 认为某人已死,认为某人不可救药. ~ ***in astonishment [wonder]*** 惊异万分. ~ ***of wits*** 无能的,老迈昏庸的. ***What's ~ is ~.*** 〔谚〕失者不可复得. ~ **cause** 已告失败[必将失败]的事业[运动]. ~ **generation** 迷惘的一代〔指第一次世界大战前后走投无路的美国青年一代〕. ~ **motion**【机】空动. ~ **river**【地】干河,隐入河. ~ **souls** 永坠地狱的灵魂; 堕落的人们. ~ **tribes** 失去的部落〔组成古代以色列王国的十个部落,公元前722年作为俘虏被带到亚述〕.

lot [lɔt] *n.* ①运气,命运. *His ~ has been a hard one.* 他命运不好. ②(抽)签,(拈)阄. *be chosen by* ~ 通过抽签被选中. *decide by* ~ 抽签决定. *The ~ came to [fell upon] him.* 他中签了. *draw* ~ 抽签. ③(货物等)一堆,一批,一分. *a new ~ of hats* 一批新帽子. *sell by [in] ~s* 分批出售. ④一块地皮. *an open [a vacant]* ~ 空地. *a parking* ~ 停车处. *house and* ~ 房屋与宅地. ⑤〔口〕家伙,人. *a bad* ~ 坏蛋. *a sorry* ~ 一批糟糕的家伙. ⑥〔英〕税. *scot and* ~ (英国从前的)市民税. ⑦〔美〕电影摄影场, 马戏场. ⑧〔口〕大量, 许多; 非常, 相当; 〔the ~〕全部, 一切. *~s [a ~] of people* 许多人. *~s and ~s (of)* 许许多多. *A ~ you care!* 〔讽〕你太费心思啦! *I like him quite a ~.* 我非常喜欢他. *Thanks a ~.* 多谢. *Get away, the whole ~ of you!* 你们统统走开. *That is the (whole) ~.* 整个就是这些了. ***a good [great]*** ~ 大量, 很多. ***a job*** ~ ①整批买卖的杂货. ②杂乱的一伙[一堆]. ***an odd*** ~ 不成整数的一批货色; 不满一百股的零星股票. ***a round*** ~ (热门股票的)一百股或其倍数; (冷门股票的)十股或其倍数. ***cast [throw] in one's ~ with*** 和…同命运. ***cast ~s*** 掷骰子决定. ***It falls to sb.'s ~. = The ~ falls to sb.*** 命该, 命中注定. ***jump across ~s*** 〔美〕从原野中横穿过去; 抄小路走. ~ ***production*** 成批生产. ***the ~ is cast*** 选择已经作出. — *vt.* ①划分(土地等); 分批, 分堆(出售商品) (*out*). ②拈阄分给. — *vi.* 抽签. ~ ***on [upon]*** 〔美俚〕指望,倚赖,期待.

lo·ta(h) [ˈləutə] *n.* 〔Hind.〕铜制小水壶〔常为球形〕.

loth [ləuθ] *a.* = loath.

Lo·tha·ri·o [ləuˈθɑːriəu] *n.* (*pl.* ~*s*) 专事勾引妇女的浪子.

lo·tic [ˈləutik] *a.* 【生态】激流的; 生活于水流〔急湍〕中的.

lo·tion [ˈləuʃən] ①【药】洗液,洗剂. ②洗涤. ③〔英俚〕饮料.

lo·tos [ˈləutəs] *n.* = lotus.

lot·ta [ˈlɔtə] 〔美俚〕= a lot of.

lot·ter·y [ˈlɔtəri] *n.* ①抽彩给奖法, 打彩票. ②不可靠的事. *a ~ ticket* 彩票,奖券. *a great* ~ 虚无飘渺的事.

Lot·tie [ˈlɔti] *n.* ①洛蒂〔女子名〕. ②Charlotte 的别名.

lot·to [ˈlɔtəu] *n.* 落托数卡牌戏〔玩者数人各执一数码卡片,卡上记有数码三行,每行五个数字. 主持人负责从专用的小圆盘中抽摇数码籤. 玩者数码卡的数字与籤码上的数字相同时,可将卡上的数字消去,最先消完者获胜〕.

lo·tus [ˈləutəs] *n.* ①【希神】忘忧树; (吃后就忘记一切、留连忘返的)忘忧果. ②【植】莲属; 荷; 睡莲. ③【建】荷花饰,莲饰. *Indian* ~ 藕莲. ~-**eater**【希神】吃了上述忘忧果而忘记一切、留连忘返的人; 〔喻〕醉生梦死,不负责任、贪图安乐的人. -**eating** ①*n.* 醉生梦死但图安乐的行为. ②*a.* 贪图安乐的. ~ **land** 安乐乡; 安逸. ~ **position** (瑜珈派的)盘腿打坐.

louche [luːʃ] *a.* 品德有问题的; 声名狼藉的.

loud [laud] *a.* ①响亮的, 大声的 (*opp.* quiet, soft). ②高声吵闹的, 喧噪的. ③强调的, 坚持的, 热心的. ④〔口〕怪臭的,难闻的. ⑤〔口〕(衣服、颜色等)过分鲜艳的, 俗气的; (行为等)粗俗的. *a ~ voice* 大声. *a ~ denial* 断然的否认. *be ~ in demands* 啰啰嗦嗦地要求.

be ~ in one's praise 极力称赞. — *ad.* 大声,高声. *laugh ~ and long* 大声笑个不停. *Speak ~er!* 说大声一点. **~-hailer** 手提式电子扩音器; 强力扩声器; 低音大喇叭 (= bullhorn). **~-looking** *a.* 〔美〕过分鲜艳的,花哨俗气的. **~mouth** 吵闹的人,大声说话的人. **~mouthed** *a.* 嘶叫的;吵嚷的. **~-speaker** 扬声器,喇叭. **~-spoken** *a.* 大声说的. **-ish** *a.* 稍响亮的. **-ly** *ad.* ①高声地,大声地. ②扎眼地,花哨地. **-ness** *n.* ①高声,大声. ②喧闹. ③鲜艳夺目,华美;俗气. ④【物】响度,音量.

loud·en [ˈlaudn] *vt., vi.* (使声音)变响亮〔更响亮〕.

Lough [lʌf] *n.* 洛夫〔姓氏〕.

lough [lɔk] *n.* 〔Ir.〕 ①湖泊. ②海湾.

Louie [ˈlu(:)i] *n.* 路易〔男子名, Louis 的异体〕.

Lou·is [ˈlu(:)i, ˈlu(:)is] *n.*路易斯〔男子名〕.

Lou·i·sa [lu(:)ˈi:zə] *n.* 路易莎〔女子名〕.

lou·is d'or [ˈlu:i ˈdɔ:] *n.* 〔F.〕 金路易〔旧时法国金币,值 20 法郎〕.

Lou·ise [lu(:)ˈi:z] *n.* 路易丝〔女子名〕.

Lou·i·si·an·a [lu(:)ˌi:ziˈænə] *n.* 路易斯安那〔美国州名〕.

Lou·i·si·an·an [lu(:)ˌi:ziˈænən], **Lou·i·si·an·i·an** [-niən] *a.* 路易斯安那州的, 路易斯安那州人的. — *n.* 路易斯安那州人.

Lou·is·ville [ˈlu(:)ivil] *n.* 路易斯维尔〔美国城市〕.

lounge [laundʒ] *n.* ①闲荡,闲逛,漫步. ②懒洋洋的步调〔姿势〕. ③(旅馆等的)散步场;休息室,娱乐室. ④(一端有一靠枕,但没有靠背的)长沙发,躺椅. — *vi., vt.* ①闲荡,闲逛 *(about)*. ②懒洋洋地靠〔躺〕*(on a sofa)*. ③吊儿郎当地混日子 *(away)*. ~ **car** 〔美〕沙发〔软席〕车厢. ~ **lizard** 〔美俚〕①常在旅馆休息等处闲混, 追求逸乐的寄生虫. ②爱同妇女厮混的男子; 以陪伴妇女跳舞等为生的男子. ~ **suit** 〔主英〕西装便服〔以别于各种礼服〕. **loung·ing·ly** *ad.*

loung·er [ˈlaundʒə] *n.* 闲逛的人;吊儿郎当的人,懒人.

loup [laup, ləup, lu:p] *vi., vt., n.* 〔Scot.〕跳跃.

loupe [lu:p] *n.* 寸镜〔珠宝店、表店等使用的高倍放大镜〕.

loup-ga·rou [lugaˈru] *n.* *(pl. loups-ga·rous* [lugaˈru]*)* 【神话】变成狼的人, 狼人; 〔泛指〕大而残忍的狼 (= werewolf).

lour [ˈlauə] *vi.* ①皱眉头, 怒目而视 *(at; on; upon)*. ②(天空等)阴起来, 变坏; (云、雪等)就要来似的. — *n.* ①不高兴的面容,愁眉不展的脸色. ②恶劣的天色.

Lou·ren·ço Mar·ques [ləuˈrensəu ˈmɑ:ks] *n.* 洛伦索马贵斯〔莫桑比克城市〕.

lour·ing [ˈlauəriŋ] *a.* ①不高兴的. ②恶劣的; 阴沉的. ~ *looks* 不高兴的面容. ~ *sky* 阴云密布的天空. **-ly** *ad.*

lour·y [ˈlauəri] *a.* = lowery.

louse [laus] *n.* *(pl. lice* [lais]*)* ①虱. ②(附于动、植物上的)小虫; 寄生虫. ③ *(pl. louses)* 〔美俚〕不受欢迎的人,卑鄙的人. — *vt.* 捉虱子,除虱子. ~ ***around*** 〔美俚〕游荡,闲混. ~ ***up*** 〔美俚〕变坏; 弄糟; 毁坏. **~-borne** *a.* 【医】虱传播的. **~-cage, ~-case** *n.* 〔美俚〕①帽子. ②(火车的) 守车. ③(伐木工的) 山中小屋. **~-trap** 〔美俚〕绒线围肚. **~wort** 【植】马先蒿属 *(Pedicularis)*.

lous·y [ˈlauzi] *a.* ***(lous·i·er; -i·est)*** ①尽是虱子的, 多虱的. ②糟糕的; 不清洁的. ③讨厌的, 卑鄙的. ④〔美俚〕富有的,有很多…的. ⑤【纺】(丝)茸毛的. *be ~ with money* 有许多钱. **-i·ly** *ad.* **-i·ness** *n.*

lout[1] [laut] *n.* 蠢人, 丑角般人物. — *vt.* 愚弄,嘲弄,把…当作蠢人.

lout[2] [laut] *vi.* ①鞠躬. ②屈服.

lout·ish [ˈlautiʃ] *a.* 粗野的,不知礼貌的. **-ly** *ad.*

lou·ver, lou·vre [ˈlu:və] *n.* ①【建】固定百叶窗; 〔*pl.*〕百叶窗板 (= ~ board). ②(通风用的)天窗,烟窗. ③(汽车的)散热孔, 放气孔, 放气窗; (有褶缝的)发动机盖. ~ **shutter** 活百叶窗. ~ **window** 固定百叶窗.

Lou·vre [lu:vr] *n.* (巴黎的) 卢佛尔宫〔现为世界著名美术博物馆之一〕.

lov·a·ble [ˈlʌvəbl] *a.* 可爱的. **-a·bil·i·ty** [ˌlʌvəˈbiliti], **-a·ble·ness** *n.* **-a·bly** *ad.*

lov·age [ˈlʌvidʒ] *n.* 【植】拉维纪草(属).

lov·at [ˈlʌvət] *n.* (苏格兰呢常用的) 绿中透蓝灰色的混合色.

love [lʌv] *n.* ①爱,热爱,爱戴. *give [send] one's ~ to sb.* 向某人致意, 问候某人. *mutual ~* 互相爱慕. *show great ~ to [towards] one's comrades* 热爱同志. *~ of one's country* 热爱祖国. ②爱好;所爱的东西. *have a ~ for [of] sports* 爱好体育运动. ③(两性间的)恋爱;爱情. *one-sided ~* 单相思,单恋. ④性关系. ⑤爱人〔尤指女性,意中人〕. ⑥〔L-〕爱的化身, 爱神 (= Cupid). ⑦〔口〕可爱的人; 可爱的东西. *He is an old ~.* 他是个愉快的人. *It's a ~, isn't it?* 真可爱啊,不是么? *What a ~ of a dog!* 这狗多可爱! *What ~s of teacups!* 这些茶杯真好! ⑧爱人,宝贝. *My ~* 〔对爱人、孩子的称呼〕亲爱的; 宝宝. ⑨【体】零分. ~ ***all*** 双方零分,打成零比零. *~ five = five ~* 5 比 0. ***a labour of ~*** 爱做的事,不取报酬而自愿做的事. ***be in ~ with*** 热爱,迷恋. ***be out of ~ with*** 不喜欢,讨厌. ***fall in ~ with*** 爱上. ***fall out of ~ with*** 不再爱, 爱情中断. ***Faults are thick where ~ is thin.*** 爱情淡薄时,样样都不顺眼. ***for ~*** ①由于高兴. ②不要钱,免费. ③(玩牌等)不用钱赌输赢. ***for ~ or money*** 无论出任何代价,无论如何. ***for the ~ of*** 为着,为了. ***for the ~ of Heaven [Mike]*** 千万,看在老天爷面上. ***for (the) ~ of (the) game*** 为了兴趣,不是有所贪图而是为了爱好. ***L- and cough cannot be hid.*** 〔谚〕爱情象咳嗽, 压不住. ***~ at first sight*** 一见钟情. ***L- cannot be forced.*** 〔谚〕爱情不能强求. ***~ in a cottage*** 糟糠夫妻. ***L- is blind.*** 〔谚〕恋爱是盲目的. ***L- is neither bought nor sold.*** 〔谚〕爱情不能买卖. ***L- is the mother of ~.*** 〔谚〕情生情,爱生爱〔爱是互相的〕. ***L- lives in cottages as well as in courts.*** 〔谚〕爱情不分贫富. ***make ~ to sb.*** 向某人调情〔求爱〕. ***No herb will cure ~.*** 〔谚〕相思病无药可治. ***One ~ drives out another.*** 〔谚〕新的爱情来,旧的爱情去. ***play for ~*** (指打牌不是赌钱而只是) 打着玩玩. — *vt.* ①爱,热爱;爱戴. ~ *our motherland* 热爱祖国. ②(两性间)恋慕. ③赞美, 称赞. ④有…的倾向 *(to do)*; 〔口〕欢喜,爱好 *(to do)*. *a plant that ~s shade* 一种喜阴的植物. *Will you come? I should ~ to.* 你打算来么? 我希望能来. — *vi.* 爱. ***L- me, ~ my dog.*** 〔谚〕爱屋及乌. ~ **affair** ①恋爱事件; 风流韵事. ②强烈爱好. ~ **apple** 番茄. ~ **beads** 情爱珠〔六、七十年代西方嬉皮士所带象征情爱的彩色珠串〕. ~ **bird** 相思鸟〔鹦鹉类〕. ~ **child** *(pl. ~-ren)* 私生子 **~-crossed** *a.* 在爱情中不走运的. ~ **feast** ①= agape². ②聚餐会; 恳亲会. ~ **game** (网球等的)败方得零分的比赛, 一方全胜的比赛. **~grass** 【植】画眉草属. **~-in** (嬉皮士等的)友爱大聚会. **~-in-a-mist** = **~-in-a-puzzle** 【植】黑种草. **~-in-idleness** 【植】三色堇. ~ **knot** 相思结, 同心结. ~ **letter** 情书. **~-lies-bleeding** 【植】鸡冠花, (苋科)老枪谷, 千穗谷. ~ **life** 〔口〕(一生中的)恋爱经历. ~ **lock** (女人的)娇发; (伊丽莎白女皇及詹姆斯一世时流行的上层社会中男子在耳边用丝带等结扎下垂的)爱发. ~ **lorn** *a.* 失恋的,害相思病的,苦恋的. **~-making** 调情,谈情说爱,求爱; 性交. ~ **match** 出自爱情的婚姻. **~-nest** 〔美俚〕爱情的窝巢〔新婚家庭,爱人幽会处〕. ~ **philter [philtre, potion]** 媚药〔据信能使人对某人发生爱情〕. ~ **seat** 鸳鸯椅. ~ **set** 【网球】败方得零分的一盘比赛. **~sick** *a.* 害相思病的. **~sickness** 相思病. ~ **song** 情歌, 恋歌. ~ **story** 恋爱小说, 爱情故事. ~ **token** 爱情纪念品. **~struck** *a.* 在爱情中神魂颠倒的.

love·a·ble [ˈlʌvəbl] *a.* = lovable. **-a·bil·i·ty, -ness** *n.*

-a·bly *ad.*

Love·lace [ˈlʌvleis] *n.* 薄情寡义的浪荡子，登徒子〔原为 Richardson 小说 *Clarissa Harlowe* 中人物的名字〕.

love·less [ˈlʌvlis] *a.* 没有爱情的；得不到爱情的. **-ly** *ad.* **-ness** *n.*

Lov·ell [ˈlʌvəl] *n.* 洛弗尔〔姓氏〕.

love·ly [ˈlʌvli] *a.* ***(-li·er; -li·est)*** ①可爱的，美丽的. ②〔口〕快乐的，愉快的. ③高尚的，纯洁的. — *n.*〔口〕①美女. ②漂亮的东西. **-li·ly** *ad.* **-li·ness** *n.*

Lov·er [ˈlʌvə] *n.* 洛弗〔姓氏〕.

lov·er [ˈlʌvə] *n.* ①情人，爱人，情夫. ②〔*pl.*〕相爱的男女. ③嗜好者，爱好者. *a pair of ~s = two ~s* 一对情侣. **-less** *a.* 没有情人的. **-like** *a.* 情人般的. **-ly** *a., ad.*

love·some [ˈlʌvsəm] *a.*〔古、方〕可爱的.

lov·ey-dov·ey [ˈlʌviˈdʌvi] *a.*〔俚〕过分亲爱的；多情的.

lov·ing [ˈlʌviŋ] *a.* 爱的，有爱情的，钟情的，忠实的. *Our ~ subjects*〔英〕我的忠实臣民〔诏敕用语〕. *Your ~ friend* 你的好友〔信尾用语〕. ~ **cup** ①爱盃〔有数个把手以便轮饮的大酒杯〕. ②纪念杯，奖杯. **~-kindness** 慈爱. **-ly** *ad.* 慈爱地，仁慈地，亲切地 (*Yours lovingly = Lovingly yours* 你的亲爱的〔信末用语〕). **-ness** *n.*

low[1] [ləu] ***(-er, -est)***)*opp.* high) *a.* ①低的；浅的，矮的. *~ flight* 低飞. *a ~ temperature* 低温. *~ tide [water]* 低潮. *The glass is ~.* 水银柱降低了. *The water is ~.* 水浅了. ②卑下的；低等的，地位低的. *a ~ fellow* 下流人. *a man of ~ birth [origin]* 出身低微的人. *~ forms of life* 下等动物. ③粗野的，无教养的，下流的. *a ~ style of writing* 粗俗的文体. *~ tastes* 低级趣味. *~ tricks* 卑鄙手段. ④(价值等)低廉的，低下的；(数量)少的. *~ cost* 低成本. *sell at a ~ price* 廉价出售. *a ~ opinion of* 对…评价不高. ⑤消沉的，虚弱的；无精神的. *be ~ in spirits = be in ~ spirits* 无精打采. *feel ~* 情绪低落. *in a ~ state of health* 健康状态不佳. ⑥倒下的，已死的，埋葬了的. *The great man is ~.* 那个伟人已经去世. ⑦(饮食等)粗劣的，没有营养的. *a ~ diet* 简陋的食物. ⑧近年的；时期较近的. *an event of a ~er date* 近期发生的事件. *relics of ~ antiquity* 近古代的遗物. ⑨低调的，低音的，(发音时)舌位放低的. *a ~ vowel* 低元音. *speak in a ~ voice* 低声说话. ⑩〔L-〕【宗】(英国)低教派的，低教会的. ⑪低速的. *a ~ gear*【机】低速档. ⑫〔英〕低年级的. ⑬【气】气压低的. *a ~ area* 低气压区域. *~ cloud ceiling* 低云幕. ⑭不足的，快枯竭的，缺钱的. *be ~ in (one's) pocket* 口袋里无钱. *be ~ on ammunition* 军火供应不足. *~ morale* 士气沮丧. ⑮(衣服)低领的，袒胸露颈的. *a ~ dress* 低领衣，袒胸衣〔妇女夜礼服〕. — *ad.* ①低；低矮；在低处；往下地. *located ~ on the slope of a hill.* 位处山坡低处. *bow ~* 深深地鞠躬. *hit ~* 朝下部打. *The candles are burning ~.* 蜡烛快点完〔已很短〕. *The sands are running ~.* 沙漏里的沙愈来愈低，时间快完；寿命将尽. ②地位低下地，卑下地，卑劣地. *fall ~* 堕落. ③价格〔价值〕低；程度〔能力〕低. *buy sth. ~* 廉价买得某物. ④低声地，以低音调. *I cannot get (down) so ~.* 我不能发那么低的声音. *talk ~* 小声谈话. ⑤收入低；生活水平低. *live ~* 过穷苦日子. ⑥晚近. *I find it as ~ as the 18th century.* 我发现近在十八世纪也有. ***bring ~*** 使减少；使跌落；使恶化. ***lay ~*** 打倒，砍倒(树木)；杀死；埋. ***lie ~*** ①蹲着；倒地不起，死. ②〔口〕隐匿，潜伏. ***play it ~ (down) upon*** 卑鄙地对待，歧视. ***run ~*** 减少. — *n.* ①(汽车等的)低速；低速齿轮. *put it in ~* 放第一档〔低速档〕. ②低气压区. ③〔常 *pl.*〕低地. ④(竞赛的)最低分数；得分最低的人；最小王牌. **~-alloy** *a.*【冶】低合金的. **~-angle** *a.*【军】小俯冲角的 (*~-angle bombing* 小俯冲角轰炸). ~ **beam** 车头短焦距光. ~ **blow** ①【拳击】打击腰部以下部位〔犯规动作〕. ②卑劣的行动；卑劣的进击. **~born** *a.* 出身低微的. **~boy**〔美〕有抽屉的短脚衣橱. **~bred** *a.* ①出身低微的. ②没有教养的，粗鲁的. **~-brow** *a., n.*〔美口〕文化程度低的(人)，教养不高的（人）(*opp.* highbrow). **~-browed** *a.* ①前额低的；(建筑物)入口处低的. ~ **camp** 低级的矫揉做作〔指文艺活动中不自觉地使用夸张陈腐等表现手段，以别于自觉地使用 (high camp)〕. ②阴暗的. ~ **carbon**【冶】低碳的. **L-Church**〔英〕低教派教会. **L--Church** *a.* 低教派教会的. **L--Church·man** *(pl. -men)* 低教派教会教友. ~ **comedy** 滑稽戏，滑稽杂耍. **~-cost** *a.* 低价出售的；低价买得到的. **L- Countries** 低地国〔荷兰、比利时和卢森堡〕. **~-down** ①*a.* 非常低的，下贱的，卑鄙的. ②*n.*〔俚〕真相，内幕 (*get the ~-down on* 得知…的内幕). **~-duty** *a.* 小功率的，轻型的，不重要的. ~ **frequency**【物】低频(率). ~ **gear** 低排档，低速齿轮. **L- German** (在德意志北部和西部使用的)低地德语. **~-grade** *a.* ①低等的，品质低劣的. ②低度的 (*a ~-grade fever* 低烧). **~-key(ed)** *a.* 低强度的；低调的；放低的，有节制的. **L- Latin** 俗拉丁语. ~ **latitude** 低纬度. **~-lev·el** 低水平的，低级别的. **~-life** ①下等社会的人. ②〔美俚〕卑鄙的人. **~-lived** *a.* 生活水平低的；卑劣的. **~-lying** *a.* 低下的；低地的，低洼的；低低的 (*~-lying hills* 低低的群山. *~-lying land* 低洼地). **L-mass** (无烧香、奏乐等的) 小弥撒 (= Private mass). **~-minded** *a.* 低级的；下流的. **~-necked** *a.* 露出胸部的；开领低的；露出颈和胸的〔指妇女衣服等，也叫 ~-neck〕. **~-pitched** *a.* 低调的，低音的；(屋顶)倾斜缓的 (*opp.* high-pitched). **~-pressure** *a.* ①低压的. ②轻松的. ~ **profile** 不引人注目的形象，隐蔽不露的活动；低姿态的活动. **~-priced** *a.* 廉价的，索价不高的. **~-proof** *a.* (酒的)烈度低的，含酒精成分低的. **~-relief** 半浮雕，浅浮雕(=bas-relief). **~-rise** *a.* (房屋，特别是公寓)楼层不多的，不高的. ~ **seam**【矿】薄煤层. **~-spirited** *a.* 没有精神的，意气消沉的. ~ **silhouette** = ~ profile. **L- Sunday** 复活节后第一个星期日. ~ **tea**〔美〕简单的晚餐 *(opp.* high tea*)*. **~-ten·sion** *a.* 低压的；带低压的；低压操作的. **~-test** *a.* (汽油的)高温气化的〔指低级汽油〕. ~ **tide** ①潮水的低潮；低潮时间. ②最低点. ~ **water** 低水位，低潮 (*at ~ water* 处于低潮. *in ~ water* 手头拮据). **~-water mark** ①低潮线；低水位标志. ②最低点. **-ness** *n.*

low[2] [ləu] *vi., vt.* (牛) 哞哞地叫；哞哞地；(牛叫似地)说 *(forth)*. — *n.* 牛叫声，哞.

Low·ell [ˈləuəl] *n.* 洛厄尔〔姓氏，男子名〕.

low·er[1] [ˈləuə] *a.*〔low 的比较级〕①较低的. ②下级的，低级的. *~ animals* 下等动物. ③南部的. *in ~ Manhattan* 在曼哈顿南部. ④早期的. 〔L- 〕【地】早期的. *L- Permain* 二迭纪早期. ⑤下游的. *the ~ Nile Valley.* 尼罗河下游区. ⑥〔英〕低年级的. *a ~ boy*〔英〕低年级男生. *a ~ school* 初级小学. ~ **bound**【数】下界，低界. ~ **case**【印】小写字母盘. **~-case** ①*a.* 小写的. ②*n.* 小写字母. ③*vt.* 用小写字母排印. ~ **class** 下层社会. ~ **classman**〔美〕(大学等的)低级生〔一二年级生〕. ~ **criticism** 对照《圣经》原文的校勘. ~ **deck** ①下甲板. ②〔*pl.*〕〔英〕海军士兵；舰上的低级军官和水手. **L- Empire**【史】东罗马帝国. ~ **fungus**【生】小真菌〔如粘菌〕. **L- House**〔常用 ~ home〕下院，众议院. **~-middle peasant** 下中农. ~ **regions** ①= ~ world. ②〔谑〕地下室，佣人住房，下房. ~ **world** ①【宗】阴间，黄泉 (= nether world). ②尘世；大地，地球. — *vt.* ①放下，放低，降下. *~ a flag* 降旗. *~ the aim of a gun* 把枪瞄得低一些. ②减价. *~ the price* 减低价格. ③减弱；降低. *A cold had ~ed his resistance.* 伤风削弱了他的抵抗力. *~ one's sights* 降低抱负. *~ one's voice* 放低声音. ④〔俚〕吞下，咽下. ⑤贬低. *That remark ~ed him in my opinion.* 那句话降低了他在我观感上的身价. — *vi.* ①降落，降低，减弱. ②放下小艇；降下帆篷. ~ ***oneself*** 降低自己的身份. ~ ***[strike] one's [the] colours [flag]*** 屈服，投降；降低要求，退让，让步.

low·er[2] [ləuə] *vi., n.* = lour.

low·er·ing[1] [ˈləuəriŋ] *a.* ①(天气)阴霾的,昏暗的,恶劣的。②不高兴的,愁眉苦脸的。**-ly** *ad.*

low·er·ing[2] [ˈləuəriŋ] *a.* ①卑劣的。②体力减弱的。— *n.* 低下;减损。

low·er·most [ˈləuəˌməust] *a.* 最下的,最低的。

low·er·y [ˈləuəri] *a.* 阴霾的,昏暗的;阴沉的。

Lowes [ləuz] *n.* 洛斯〔姓氏〕。

low·est [ˈləuist] *a.* 〔low 的最高级〕最下的, 最低的; 最小的; 最便宜的。***at the*** ~ 至少, 至低。~ **common denominator** ①= least common denominator. ②为广大群众接受、理解的事物。~ **common multiple** = least common multiple.

low·ing [ˈləuiŋ] *n.* 牛叫声。

low·ish [ˈləuiʃ] *a.* 有点儿低的;较便宜的;小声的。

low·land [ˈləulənd 名词也读作 -ˈlænd] *n.* 低地。— *a.* 低地的;在低地里的;从低地来的。**the Lowlands** 苏格兰低地。**low·land·er** *n.* 低地人。**Low·land·er** *n.* 苏格兰低地人。

low·ly [ˈləuli] *a.* ***(-li·er; -li·est)*** ①地位低的; 卑下的; 低级的。②普通的,平凡的。③谦恭的。— *ad.* ①卑下地, 低下地。②谦恭地, 客气地。③低声地,不响亮地。**low·li·ness** *n.*

Lowndes [laundz] *n.* 朗兹〔姓氏〕。

lox[1] [lɔks] *n.* 液态氧 (= *l*iquid *ox*ygen).

lox[2] [lɔks] *n.* 熏鲑鱼,熏马哈鱼。

lox·o·drome [ˈlɔksədrəum] *n.* ①【海】斜航; 斜驶线。②【天】恒向线。

lox·o·drom·ic(al) [ˌlɔksəˈdrɔmik(əl)] *a.* 【海】斜航的。**-drom·ics, -od·romy** [lɔkˈsɔdrəmi] *n.* 【海】斜航法。

loy·al [ˈlɔiəl] *a.* 忠诚的;忠实的。*be* ~ *to a cause* 忠于事业。~ *conduct* 正直的行为。— *n.*〔常 *pl.*〕忠实信徒。**-ism** *n.* 效忠,忠诚。**-ist** *n.* ①效忠者〔尤指效忠于旧政权者〕。②〔常用 *pl.*〕(美国革命时期的) 亲英分子。③〔L-〕(西班牙内战时)拥护共和国政府者。**-ly** *ad.* **-ness** *n.*

loy·al·ize [ˈlɔiəlaiz] *vt.* 使忠诚;使效忠。

loy·al·ty [ˈlɔiəlti] *n.* 忠诚;忠心。

loz·enge [ˈlɔzindʒ] *n.* ①菱形。~ ***effect [motive]*** 菱形花纹。②菱形物; 菱形玻璃; (宝石的)菱形面。③【徽】菱形盾〔用于寡妇、未婚女子, 死者的纹章中〕。④【药】锭剂,糖锭。*cough* ~*s* 止咳糖。

LP, L. P., l.p. = ①low pressure 低压;低气压。②long primer【印】十点铅字。③long playing (= ~ record) 密纹的; 密纹唱片。④large paper 大开本。⑤ Labour Party〔英〕工党。⑥large post 大开信纸。

LPM, lpm = lines per minute 每分钟行数。

L'pool = Liverpool.

L.P.S., LPS = ①Lord Privy Seal〔英〕掌玺大臣。② London Press Service 英国新闻处。

L.P.T.B. = London Passenger Transport Board〔英旧〕伦敦客运局。

lq. = liquid.

LR = liquid rocket 液体燃料火箭。

Lr = lawrencium【化】铹。

LRCS = League of Red Cross Societies 红十字会协会。

LRL = lunar receiving laboratory 月球收集物研究室〔密封无菌,用于研究从月球上收集来的样品〕。

LRPA = long-range patrol aircraft 远程巡逻飞机。

LRR = long-range radar 远程雷达。

LRV = lunar roving vehicle 月上爬行车。

L.S. = ①landing ship 登陆舰。②Licentiate in Surgery 有资格开业的外科医生。③〔L.〕*Locus Sigilli* 盖印处。

LSD = lysergic acid diethylamide 麦角酸二乙基酰胺〔一种麻醉药物〕。

L.S.D. = Lightermen, Stevedores and Dockers〔英〕驳船、搬运和码头工人。

l.s.d., £.s.d. = 〔L.〕*librae, solidi, denarii* (= pounds, shillings and pence) 镑, 先令和便士;〔口〕金钱。

LSI = ①large-scale integration 大规模集成(电路)。② launch success indicator 发射成功指示器。

L.S.O. = London Symphony Orchestra.〔英〕伦敦交响乐团。

LSS = landing ship, support 支援登陆舰。

LST = landing ship, tank 坦克登陆舰。

L.S.T. = Local Standard Time【天】地方标准时。

LSU = landing ship, utility 通用登陆舰。

L.S.W.R. = London and South-Western Railway〔英〕伦敦西南铁路。

Lt. = Lieutenant.

L.T.A. = London Teachers' Association〔英〕伦敦教师协会。

Lt. Col. = Lieutenant Colonel〔英〕陆军[海军陆战队]中校;〔美〕陆军[空军、海军陆战队]中校。

Lt. Comdr. = Lieutenant Commander〔英、美〕海军少校。

Ltd. =Limited〔常用于股份有限公司的名称后〕。

Lt. Gen. = Lieutenant General〔英〕陆军 [海军陆战队]中将;〔美〕陆军[空军、海军陆战队]中将。

Lt. Gov. = Lieutenant Governor (省或地区的)代理总督,副总督;〔美〕副州长。

Lt Inf = Light Infantry 轻步兵。

L.T.L. = less-than-truckload 卡车零担的。

l.tn.= long ton 英吨〔重量单位〕。

Lu = ①Louisa. ②Louise. ③【化】lutecium.

Lu·an·da [luːˈɑːndə] *n.* 罗安达〔安哥拉首都〕。

Lu·ang Pra·bang [ˈluɑːŋ prɑːˈbɑːŋ] 琅勃拉邦〔老挝城市〕。

lu·au [luːˈau, ˈluːau] *n.*〔Haw.〕夏威夷宴会〔一般有娱乐节目〕。

Lu·ba [ˈluːbɑː] *n.* ①***(pl. -bas, -ba)*** 卢巴人〔刚果南部农民〕。②卢巴语。

lub·ber [ˈlʌbə] *n.* ①傻大个子, 笨大汉。②无经验的水手。— *a.* 大而笨拙的。~ *grasshopper*【动】钝蝗 *(Romalea microptera)*〔产于美国东南部〕。~**-land** (想象中)极舒适的地方。~**('s) hole**【海】桅楼升降口。~**('s) line [mark, point]**【海】船首基线。~ **world** = ~-land.

lub·ber·ly [ˈlʌbəli] *a.* 粗笨的,笨拙的。— *ad.* 粗笨地,拙劣地。**-li·ness** *n.*

lube [luːb] *n.* ①润滑油 (= ~ oil). ②润滑, 涂油 (= lubrication).

Lub·lin [ˈluːblin] *n.* 卢布林〔波兰城市〕。

lu·bri·ca·ble [ˈluːbrikəbl, ˈljuː-] *a.* 可以涂油的;可弄润滑的。

lu·bri·cant [ˈluːbrikənt] *a.* (使)润滑的。~ *oil* 润滑油。— *n.* ①润滑剂,润滑油。②能减少摩擦的东西。③〔美俚〕奶油,黄油。

lu·bri·cate [ˈluːbrikeit] *vt.* ①【机】涂油,上油;使润滑。②〔俚〕(为了使事情进行顺利些等目的) 劝酒;行贿,收买。—*vi.* ①起润滑作用,充当润滑剂。②〔美俚〕喝一杯。**lubricating oil** 润滑油。**-d**〔美俚〕喝醉了的。

lu·bri·ca·tion [ˌluːbriˈkeiʃən] *n.* 润滑, 油润,上油; 润滑作用。~ *groove* 油槽。*ring* ~ 油环润滑法。

lu·bri·ca·tor [ˈljuːbrikeitə] *n.* ①润滑剂; 注油器。②加润滑剂的人,注油人。

lu·bri·cious [luːˈbriʃəs] *a.* = lu·bri·cous.

lu·bric·i·ty [ljuːˈbrisiti] *n.* ①光滑, 滑润性, 润滑能力。②难捉摸;动摇,不稳定。③狡猾。④淫荡。

lu·bri·cous [ˈluːbrikəs] *a.* ①滑润的, 光滑的。②难捉摸的;动摇的,不稳定的。③淫荡的。

lu·bri·to·rium [luːbriˈtɔːriəm] *n.*〔美〕(汽车)加油站。

Lu·bum·ba·shi [ˌluːbuːmˈbɑːʃiː] *n.* 卢本巴希〔扎伊

尔城市〕.

lu•carne [ˈljuːkɑːn] *n.* 【建】老虎窗,屋顶窗.

Lu•cas [ˈluːkəs] *n.* 卢卡斯〔姓氏〕.

Luce [ljuːs] *n.* 卢斯〔姓氏〕.

luce [lus] *n.* 【动】白斑狗鱼 *(Esox lucius)*.

lu•cen•cy [ˈljuːsnsi] *n.* ①发亮. ②透明.

lu•cent [ˈljuːsnt] *a.* ①发亮的. ②透明的.

Lu•cern(e) [ljuːˈsəːn] *n.* 卢塞恩〔瑞士城市〕.

lu•cern(e) [luːˈsəːn] *n.* 〔主英〕【植】首蓿 (= 〔美〕 alfalfa).

lu•ces [ˈluːsiːz] *n.* lux 的复数异体.

Lu•cia [ˈluːsjə] *n.* 露西娅〔女子名〕.

Lu•cian [ˈluːsjən] *n.* 卢西恩〔男子名〕.

lu•cid [ˈluːsid] *a.* ①清澈的,透明的. ②清楚的;明白的. ③神志清醒的. ④光辉的,明亮的. ⑤【天】肉眼可见的;【植、动】光滑的. ~ *streams* 清澈的河流. *a* ~ *mind* 清楚的头脑. *a* ~ *interval* (精神病患者的)神志清醒时候;(暴风雨,扰乱等的)暂时平静的一段时间. **-ly** *ad.* **-ness** *n.*

lu•cid•i•ty [luːˈsiditi] *n.* ①清澄,透明. ②清楚,明白. ③神志清醒. ④洞察力.

Lu•ci•fer [ˈluːsifə] *n.* ①金星,晓星. ②魔鬼,恶魔〔Satan 的别名〕. *as proud as* ~ 非常傲慢. ③〔l-〕摩擦火柴,安全火柴 (= ~ match).

lu•cif•er•ase [ljuːˈsifəˌreis] *n.* 【生化】荧光(素)酶.

lu•cif•er•in [luˈsifəˌrin] *n.* 【化】荧光素.

lu•cif•er•ous [luːˈsifərəs] *a.* ①发光的,发亮的. ②聪明的;有洞察力的.

Lu•ci•na [luːˈsainə] *n.* 【罗神】司生育的女神.

lu•cite [ˈluːsait] *n.* 【商标】(有机玻璃)留西特,【化】2-甲基丙烯酸,合成荧光树脂.

luck [lʌk] *n.* ①运气,造化. ②幸运,侥幸. ③〔古〕带来幸运的东西. *good* ~ 幸运. *Good* ~ *to you!* 祝你成功;一路平安! *have bad [hard, ill, tough]* ~ 不幸,倒霉. *Bad* ~ *to you!* 你这该死的! *The* ~ *is in favour of me.* 运气来了,走运了. *The* ~ *turns against me.* 运气变坏了,倒霉了. *Just [It is just] my* ~. 唉,又是倒霉! *He has had the* ~ *to succeed.* 他侥幸成功了. ***as good* ~ *would have it*** 幸亏,侥幸. ***as ill* ~ *would have it*** 不幸. ***as* ~ *would have it*** 碰巧;碰得不巧〔意思究竟是幸还是不幸,要根据上下文决定〕. ***be down on one's* ~** 〔口〕倒霉. ***be in* ~** 交好运. ***be in* ~*'s way*** 走运. ***be off one's* ~ = *be out of* ~** 运气不好. ***by (good)* ~** 侥幸,幸亏. ***come to* ~** 走起运来. ***crowd [press, push, stretch] one's* ~** 〔美俚〕过分依靠自己的好运气;碰到好运后指望侥幸再得到好运. ***for* ~** 祝福,祈求好运. ***have no* ~** 运气不好. ***have the* ~ *to*** 幸而,侥幸. ***play in [to] big* ~** 〔美〕走运,得意. ***play (in, to) hard* ~** 〔美〕倒霉,不走运. ***ride one's* ~** 指望运气. ***rough* ~** 倒霉. ***the devil's own* ~** ①〔口〕莫名其妙的好运气. ②〔讽〕非常倒霉. ***try one's* ~** 碰运气. ***wish sb. all the* ~ *in the world*** 祝某人一切顺利. ***worse* ~** 不幸,不巧,偏巧. — *vi.* 侥幸成功,靠运气行事 *(into; on; onto; out; through)*. *Don't expect to* ~ *through without an effort.* 别指望不经过努力就能侥幸成功. ~ **money [penny]** 〔英〕吉利钱〔常指旧时出售牲口的人为求吉利,在成交后还给买主的一小笔钱〕.

luck•less [ˈlʌklis] *a.* 不幸的,运气坏的,倒霉的. **-ly** *ad.* **-ness** *n.*

luck•y [ˈlʌki] *a.* ***(luck•i•er; -i•est)*** ①运气好的,侥幸的. ②兆头好的,吉祥的. ③〔俚〕难得的,碰巧的;顺便的. ④很恰当的. *a* ~ *guess [hit, shot]* 侥幸猜中,碰上. *L- bargee [beggar, devil, dog, rascal]* 幸运儿. *touch* ~ 交好运. *a* ~ *day* 好日子,吉日;很顺利的一天. — *n.* 〔俚〕逃亡. ***cut [make] one's* ~** 逃走. ~ **bag** ①模彩袋. ②(军舰上的)失物箱. ~ **dip** 摸彩袋. ~**strike** 好运气. **luck•i•ly** *ad.* **luck•i•ness** *n.*

lu•cra•tive [ˈluːkrətiv, ljuː-] *a.* 有利的,赚钱的,合算的. ②【军】值得作为目标的. *a* ~ *investment* 有利的投资. *a* ~ *target* 可获战果的攻击目标. **-ly** *ad.* **-ness** *n.*

lu•cre [ˈluːkə] *n.* 利益,赚头;金钱. *filthy* ~ 不义之财,肮脏钱.

Lu•cre•tia [luːˈkriːʃjə] *n.* ①卢克丽霞〔女子名〕. ②罗马传说中的贞妇,贞节的模范.

Lu•cre•ti•us [luːˈkriːʃiəs] *n.* ①卢克莱修〔男子名〕. ② **Carus** ~ 卢克莱修〔99?—55 B.C. 罗马哲学家、诗人〕.

lu•cu•brate [ˈljuːkju(ː)ˌbreit] *vi.* ①(在灯下)刻苦钻研;苦思冥想. ②学究式地写作;详细论述.

lu•cu•bra•tion [ˌljuːkju(ː)ˈbreiʃən] *n.* ①(在灯下)刻苦钻研;苦思冥想. ②苦心孤诣之作. ③〔常作复数〕〔谑〕学究气的作品.

lu•cu•bra•tor [ˈljuːkju(ː)ˌbreitə] *n.* 刻苦钻研者;学究式的写作者.

lu•cu•lent [ˈljuːkjulənt] *a.* ①明亮的,清澈的,透明的. ②明白的,明显的. **-ly** *ad.*

Lu•cul•lus [luːˈkʌləs] 卢库勒斯〔古罗马将军兼执政官,以巨富和举办豪华大宴著名〕. **-cul•lan** [-ən], **-cul•li•an** [-iən], **-cul•le•an** [ˌlukəˈliən] *a.*

Lu•cy [ˈluːsi] *n.* 露西〔姓氏,女子名〕. ~ **stoner** 主张女子结婚后用自己姓名者〔因美国女权主义者露西·斯通 (Lucy Stone, 1818—93) 而得名〕.

Lud [lʌd] *n.* 〔英〕= Lord. *My* ~ = [miˈlʌd] = My Lord.

Ludd•ism [ˈlʌdizm] *n.* = Ludditism.

Ludd•ite [ˈlʌdait] *n.* ①鲁德分子〔英国 1811 年—1816 年以捣毁纺织机械为手段抗议资本家降低工资和解雇工人的团体的成员〕. ②〔l-〕强烈反对提高机械化和自动化者.

Ludd•it•ism [ˈlʌdəˌtizəm] *n.* 强烈反对在任何方面提高机械化和自动化.

lu•dic [ˈluːdik] *a.* 游戏的.

lu•di•crous [ˈluːdikrəs] *a.* 可笑的;荒唐的. **-ly** *ad.* **-ness** *n.*

Lud•wig [ˈlʌdwig] *n.* 路德维格〔男子名, Louis 的异体〕.

lu•es [ˈluːiːz] *n.* 〔L.〕①疫病,传染病. ②梅毒 (= ~ venerea). ~ ***Boswelliana*** [ˌbɔzweliˈɑːnə] 巴斯威尔 (Boswell) 式的夸大〔指过分美化所描述的对象〕.

lu•et•ic [lju(ː)ˈetic] *a.* 梅毒的;疫病的,传染病的. **-al•ly** *ad.*

Luf•be•ry cir•cle [ˈlʌfbəri ˈsəːkl] 【军】(空战中飞机组成圆圈状队形,各机互相掩护的)卢氏圆圈队形.

luff [lʌf] *n.* 【海】①抢风行驶,贴风行驶. ②船首两舷的弯曲部;纵帆的前缘. ③(货物在起重时的)起落摆动. — *vi., vt.* 抢风行驶;(帆船竞赛)驶出(对方)上风. ***L- her* = *L- the helm*** 〔对舵手下达的命令〕转航向风! ~ ***up*** 船侧受风而行.

luf•fa [ˈlʌfə] *n.* ①【植】丝瓜 (= dish-cloth gourd). ②丝瓜筋〔络〕.

luft•mensch [ˈluftˌmenʃ] *n.* ***(pl. -mensch•en*** [-ˌmenʃən]***)*** 〔G.〕空想家,不切实际的人,不脚踏实地的人.

Luft•waf•fe [G.ˈluftvɑfə] *n.* 〔G.〕(第二次世界大战中的)纳粹德国空军.

lug¹ [lʌg] *n.* = lugworm.

lug² [lʌg] *n.* = lugsail.

lug³ [lʌg] *n.* ①用力拉,被拖的东西. ②懒人. ③〔*pl.*〕〔美俚〕摆架子,装腔作势. ④〔美俚〕勒索,敲诈(到的钱财). ***pile [put] on* ~*s*** 〔美俚〕摆架子. ***put the* ~ *on*** 向…敲诈〔勒索〕. — *vt., vi.* ①使劲拉,用力拖 *(about; along; at)*;硬拉走 *(along)*. ②〔口〕引出(无关系的话等) *(in; into)*. ③拖动,沉重地挪动.

lug⁴ [lʌg] *n.* ①〔Scot.〕耳朵. ②耳状物(如柄、把手等). ③【机】突起,凸出部,突缘;【电】焊片,接线片. ④(马具上的)皮环;衔套. ⑤〔俚〕笨家伙.

luge [luːʒ] *n.* (竞赛用单人或双人)平底雪橇. — *vi.* ***(-luged, -luge•ing)*** 雪橇竞赛.

Lu•ger [ˈluːgə] *n.* 〔G.〕鲁格尔〔德国造半自动手枪的商

标名〕. — *n.*〔常用 l-〕鲁格尔手枪.
lug·gage [ˈlʌgidʒ] *n.* ①〔英〕行李,随身行李(=〔美〕baggage). ②〔美〕提包,皮箱. ③红褐色. *check one's* ～ 寄存行李,打行李票. *hand* ～ 手提行李. *excess* ～ 超重行李. *personal* ～ 随身行李,小件行李. *registered* ～ 托运行李. ～**-carrier** *n.* (自行车等的)载物架. ～**-rack** (火车等的) 行李架. ～ **van** 〔英〕行李车(=〔美〕baggage car).
lug·ger [ˈlʌgə] *n.* 斜桁横帆小船.
lug·gie [ˈlʌgi] *n.*〔Scot.〕带耳状拎环的木桶.
lug·sail [ˈlʌgseil, -sl] *n.*【船】斜桁横帆,斜桁四角帆.
lu·gu·bri·ous [lu:ˈgju:briəs] *a.* (象是过分做作而显得可笑的)忧伤的, 悲痛的; 阴郁的, 如丧考妣的. **-ly** *ad.* **-ness** *n.*
lug·worm [ˈlʌgˌwə:m] *n.*【动】沙蠋〔可作钓饵用〕.
Luke [lu:k] *n.* 卢克〔男子名, 基督教《圣经》中译为"路加"〕.
luke·warm [ˈljuːkwɔ:m] *a.* ①微温的. ②不热心的,冷淡的,不起劲的. **-ly** *ad.* **-ness** *n.*
lull [lʌl] *n.* ①间歇, 暂停. ②催眠的东西〔尤指催眠曲〕. *a* ～ *in the storm* 风暴的暂息. *a bombing* ～ 暂时停炸. — *vt.* ①使安静. ②哄骗. ③镇静,缓和. ～ *a baby to sleep* 哄小孩睡觉. ～ *sb. into a false sense of security* 骗某人使产生虚假的安全感. ～ *sb.'s suspicions* 消除某人的猜疑. — *vi.* 变平静. **-ing·ly** *ad.* 催人入睡的.
lull·a·by [ˈlʌləbai] *n.* ①催眠曲,摇篮曲. ②轻柔的声音(如微风吹拂声,潺潺流水声). — *vt.* 唱摇篮曲催眠.
Lulu [ˈlu:lu:] *n.* Louisa, Louise 的爱称.
lu·lu [ˈlu:lu:] *n.*〔美俚〕①突出的人物〔事情〕〔如漂亮的少女; 难学的功课〕. ②特种津贴开支项目. *a* ～ *of a mistake* 明显的错误,大错误. — *a.* 极好的; 第一流的.
lum [lʌm] *n.*〔Scot., 英方〕烟筒.
lum·ba·go [lʌmˈbeigəu] *n.* *(pl.* ～*s)*【医】腰痛, 腰部风湿痛,腰肌痛. **lum·ba·gi·nous** [-dʒinəs] *ad.*
lum·bar [ˈlʌmbə] *a.* 腰(部)的. — *n.*【解】腰动脉; 腰神经; 腰椎.
lum·ber[1] [ˈlʌmbə] *n.*〔美〕①木材,木料,方料;〔英〕原木. ②破烂东西,碎屑,废物. *clear* ～ 上等木材. *the L- State*〔美〕缅因州的别号. — *vt.* ①杂乱地堆积,把烂东西堆满(房屋). ②阻碍 *(up)*. ③采伐(木材). — *vi.* ①阻塞. ②〔美〕采伐木材, 拖运木材. ～**jack** ①伐木工人. ②短茄克衫. ～ **jacket** 伐木者穿的茄克衫. ～**-man** 伐木者;集材者〔尤指监工、经理人等〕; 木材商; 木材运输船. ～**mill** 制材厂, 锯木厂. ～**room** 杂物房. ～**yard** 木材堆置场. **-er** *n.* **-less** *a.* **-ly** *ad.*
lum·ber[2] [ˈlʌmbə] *vi.* 笨重地移动; 隆隆地行进. *a* ～*-ing cart* 隆隆响着走的车. ～ *one's walk* 蹒跚地走. — *n.* 隆隆声.
lum·ber·ing [ˈlʌmbəriŋ] *n.* ①伐木业. — *a.* ①笨重的. ②动作迟缓步子沉重的. ③笨拙的; 表达不流畅的.
lum·ber·some [ˈlʌmbəsəm] *a.* 麻烦的; 笨重的.
lum·bri·ca·lis [ˌlʌmbriˈkeilis] *n.* *(pl.* *-ca·les* [-ˈkei-li:z]*)*【解】蚓(状)肌(= lumbrical).
lum·bri·coid [ˈlʌmbriˌkɔid] *a.* 蚯蚓状的,类似蚯蚓的.
lu·men [ˈljuːmin] *n.* *(pl.* *-mi·na* [-minə]*)* ①【物】流明〔光通量单位〕. ②【解】(管)腔.
lu·mi·naire [ˌljuːmiˈnɛə] *n.*【物】泛光灯〔发光, 照明〕设备; 光源.
lu·min·al [ˈljuminæl] *n.*【药】鲁米那〔一种镇静剂〕.
lu·mi·nance [ˈljuːminəns] *n.* ①发光,光亮. ②亮度,辉度,照度,发光率〔密度〕.
lu·mi·nant [ˈljuːminənt] *a.* 发光的. — *n.* 发光体.
lu·mi·nar flow [ˈljuːminər fləu]【物】片流.
lu·mi·nar·y [ˈljuːminəri] *n.* ①天体. ②发光体. ③(学识等方面的)杰出人物; 名人. *the great* ～ 太阳.
lu·mine [ˈljuːmin] *vt.* = illumine.
lu·mi·nesce [ˌljuːmiˈnes] *vi.* *(-nesc·ed, -nesc·ing)* 发(冷)光; 变明亮.
lu·mi·nes·cence [ˌljuːmiˈnesns] *n.*【物】发光, 发萤〔冷, 磷〕光. **-nes·cent** [-ˈnesnt] *a.*
lu·mi·nif·er·ous [ˌljuːmiˈnifərəs] *a.* 发光的, 发萤〔冷〕光的; 传光的.
lu·mi·nom·e·ter [ˌljuːmiˈnɔmitə] *n.*【物】照度计.
lu·mi·no·phor [ˈljuːminəfɔ:]【物】发光体〔团〕.
lu·mi·nos·i·ty [ˌljuːmiˈnɔsiti] *n.* ①光明, 光辉. ②【物】发光度; (辐射能的)发光效率. ③发光物, 发光体; 辉点.
lu·mi·nous [ˈljuːminəs] *a.* ①发光的; 明亮的; 照耀着的; 辉耀的. ②明白易懂的; 有启发性的. ③明快的, 爽朗的. ④光明的,灿烂的. *a* ～ *body* 发光体. *a* ～ *compass* 夜光罗盘. ～ *paint* 夜光漆. *a square* ～ *with sunlight* 阳光普照的广场. *full of* ～ *ideas* 富有启发性意义的. *His prose is simple and* ～. 他的散文简明易懂. *a* ～ *smile* 爽朗的微笑. *the* ～ *future* 光辉前途. ～ **energy**【物】光能. ～ **flux**【物】光束,光通量. ～ **intensity**【物】发光强度. **-ly** *ad.* **-ness** *n.*
lum·me [ˈlʌmi] *int.*〔英俚〕哎呀! 啊! 噢!〔用以加强语气或表示惊讶、赞同等; = Lord love me!〕
lum·mox [ˈlʌməks] *n.*〔美口〕笨拙的人,笨蛋.
lum·my [ˈlʌmi] *int.*〔英〕= lumme. — *a.*〔英俚〕头等的.
lump[1] [lʌmp] *n.* ①块,团. ②疱,肿瘤,疖子. ③〔俚、方〕一大堆,许多. ④〔口〕笨蛋; 矮胖子. ⑤〔*pl.*〕〔美俚〕责打; 指责; 应得的惩罚. *a* ～ *of sugar* 一块(方)糖. ***all of a*** ～ 结成一团; 肿成一个球似的. ***a*** ～ ***in one's [the] throat*** (由于悲痛要哭)喉咙哽住. ***a*** ～ ***of avarice [selfishness]*** 道地的贪婪鬼〔自私自利者〕. ***a*** ～ ***of clay [earth]*** ①一块泥土. ②【圣】人; 无情的人. ***by [in] the*** ～ ①大批地,成群地. ②总共. ***get [take] one's*** ～ 咎由自取地挨打骂. ***in a [one]*** ～ 一次全部地. ***on a*** ～ ***sum basis*** 按照一次总付的办法. ***take by [in] the*** ～ ①大批地拿. ②总括起来. — *vt.* ①使成块, 使成团; 集总; 总括; 一起处理; 总括起来说 *(together; with; in with; under)*. ②笨重地移动. ③把所有的赌注都下在…上 *(on)*. ～ *the expense* 把开销混在一起计算. ～ *dough* 把面粉揉成团. ～*ed capacity*【无】集总电容. ～*-ed parameter*【物】集总参数. — *vi.* ①成块,成团. ②肿胀成瘤. ③笨重地行走 *(along)*; 一屁股坐下 *(down)*. ～ ***together*** 总计. ～ **sugar** 成块的糖; 糖块, 方糖. ～ **sum** (一次结清的)总额. ～ **work** 总包的工作, 包干工作.
lump[2] [lʌmp] *vt.*〔口〕忍耐,忍受. *If you don't like it, (you may)* ～ *it.* 不高兴也得忍耐.
lump[3] [lʌmp] *n.* = ～fish. ～**fish** *(pl.* ***-fish, -fishes)***【动】圆鳍鱼科 *(Cyclopteridae)*〔尤指圆鳍鱼 *(Cyclopterus lumpus)*〕. ～**sucker** = ～fish.
lump·en [ˈlʌmpən; Am. ˈlumpən] *a.*〔G.〕(从本阶级中)分化出来的; 蜕化出来的. ～**-proletariat** 流氓无产阶级.
lump·er [ˈlʌmpə] *n.* ①码头装卸工人. ②小包工头, 小承包商. ③【生】堆合分类者.
lump·ing [ˈlʌmpiŋ] *a.*〔口〕沉重的,大的; 很多的. *a* ～ *great helping of pudding* 很大的一份布丁. ～ *weight* 很大的重量.
lump·ish [ˈlʌmpiʃ] *a.* ①块状的; 多团块的. ②笨重的; 笨拙的,迟钝的; 矮胖的. ③沉闷的, 学究式的, 令人讨厌的.
lump·y [ˈlʌmpi] *a.* *(lump·i·er, lump·i·est)* ①多团块的; 结成块的. ②满是疙瘩的; 粗糙的. ③波浪起伏的. ④愚钝的; 呆头呆脑的. ⑤〔英俚〕醉醺醺的. ～ **jaw**【医】放线菌病(= actinomycosis). **lump·i·ly** *ad.* **lump·i·ness** *n.*
Lu·na [ˈljuːnə] *n.* ①【罗神】月神; 月亮. ②〔l-〕〔炼金术用语〕银. 〔l-〕～ **moth**【动】天蚕蛾科 *(Tropaealuna)*

的蛾。

lu·na·cy [ˈljuːnəsi] *n.* ①疯颠，精神错乱。②蠢笨的行为，疯狂的行为。

lu·nar [ˈljuːnə] *a.* ①月亮的，太阴的；按月球的运转而测定的。②似月的；新月形的，半月形的。③(光)清冷的，微亮的。④银的，含银的。～ **bone**【解】半月状骨。～ **calendar** 阴历。～ **caustic**【化】硝酸银。～ **distance** 月距〔月与太阳或星之间的角距〕。～ **eclipse** 月蚀。～ **mansions**【天】二十八宿。～ **(excursion) module**【宇】登月舱。～ **month** 太阴月〔约 $29\frac{1}{2}$ 日〕。～ **naut** 登月宇航员。**(the) L- New Year** 阴历新年，春节。～ **observation** 太阴观测。～ **orbit** 绕月轨道。～ **politics** 空论，不切实际的问题。～ **probe** 月球探测。～**rainbow** 月虹，月夜的虹。～ **rover [roving vehicle]** 月上爬行器。～ **scape** 月貌。～ **year** 太阴年〔约 354 日 8 小时〕。

lu·nar·i·an [luːˈnɛəriən] *n.* ①(假想的)月球居民，月球人。②月球研究者。

lu·nate [ˈljuːnit] *a.* 新月形的，半月形的。

lu·na·tic [ˈljuːnətik] *a.* ①疯癫的，精神错乱的。②疯狂的；极端愚蠢的。③为收容精神病人而设的。— *n.* ①精神病人，疯子。②狂人，怪人，愚人。～ asylum 疯人院，精神病院〔现在常称 mental home 或 mental institution〕。～ **fringe** 极端分子，极端主义者。

lu·na·tion [ljuːˈneiʃən] *n.* 太阴月 (= lunar month).

lunch [lʌntʃ] *n.* ①午餐；(两餐之间)便餐，点心。②作午餐[便餐]用的食物；〔美〕便餐。*a ～ party* 午餐会。— *vi., vt.* 吃午餐[便餐]；供给午餐[便餐]。～ **counter** 〔美〕(餐馆的)便餐柜台；便餐馆。～**-hooks**〔美俚〕①手；手指。②牙齿。③非难，恶评。～ **room** 便餐馆，小吃馆。～ **time** 午餐时间。

lunch·eon [ˈlʌntʃən] *n.* ①午餐，午宴，午餐会。②两餐之间吃的一点食物。～ **meat** 午餐肉。

lunch·eon·ette [ˌlʌntʃəˈnet] *n.* 〔美〕小餐馆。

lun·che·te·ri·a [ˌlʌntʃiˈtiəriə] *n.* 简易自助餐馆。

lune[1] [ljuːn] *n.* 半月形，弓形，月牙形；新月形物；月亮。～ *of a sphere*【数】球面二角形。

lune[2] [ljuːn] *n.* 拴鹰隼的皮带。

lunes [ljuːnz] *n. pl.* 精神病的发作。

lu·nette [ljuːˈnet] *n.* ①半月形(物)。②【筑城】眼镜堡〔具有两个正面和两个侧面的突出工事〕；【军】(炮车等上的)牵引环。③【建】弧面窗；弦月窗。④〔*pl.*〕潜水游泳时的护目。⑤玻璃表面。⑥断头台上的断头孔。

lung [lʌŋ] ①肺脏，肺。②(无脊椎动物的)呼吸器官。③【医】辅助呼吸的装置。④〔*pl.*〕〔英〕可供呼吸新鲜空气的地方。*an iron* ～【医】铁肺，人工呼吸器。***at the top of one's ～s*** 用最高嗓子。***have good ～s*** 声音大。***the ～s of London*** 伦敦市内的肺〔指公园等绿化空旷地方〕。***try one's ～s*** 使尽嗓子叫。～**-duster,** ～**-fogger** 〔美俚〕香烟。～**fish** ***(-fish, -fishes)***【动】肺鱼。～ **irritant** 窒息性毒剂。～ **power** 发声力；肺力。～ **sac** 肺囊。～**wort**【植】疗肺草属 *(Pulmonaria)*；肺衣，地衣。

lunge[1] [lʌndʒ] *n.* ①(刀剑的)刺，戳。②突出；突进；猛冲。— *vi.* (用剑等)刺，戳；猛向前冲 *(at; out)*。— *vt.* 刺，推。

lunge[2] [lʌndʒ] *n.* ①练马索。②圆形练马场。—*vt.* 在练马场或用练马索练(马)。

lunged [lʌŋd] *a.* 肺似的，有肺的。*deep-～* 声音洪亮的。*one-～* 单肺的。

lung·er [ˈlʌŋə] *n.* 〔美俚〕肺病病人。

lun·gi [ˈluŋgi] *n.* (印度人用的)腰布；头巾。

lu·ni·form [ˈluːnifɔːm] *a.* 新月形的。

Lu·nik [ˈljuːnik] *n.* 月球卫星。

lu·ni·log·i·cal [ˌljuːnəˈlɔdʒəkəl] *a.* 研究月球的〔尤指研究月球的地质〕。

lu·ni·so·lar [ljuːniˈsəulə] *a.* 月与日的；由于月日的引力的。*the ～ calendar* 阴阳历。～ *cycle [period]* 太阴太阳周期。～ *precession*【天】日月岁差。

lu·ni·tid·al [ˈljuːniˈtaidl] *a.*【天】月潮的。～ **interval**【天】月潮间隔。

lun·ker [ˈlʌŋkə] ①特大物品。②大鱼。

lunk·head [ˈlʌŋkhed] *n.* 〔美俚〕笨人，傻瓜。

Lu·no·khod [ˌljuːnəˈhɔːt] *n.* 〔Rus.〕月上步行者。

lunt [lʌnt, lunt] *n.* 〔Scot.〕①慢燃火柴；火炬。②烟。— *vt., vi.* 〔Scot.〕点燃；冒烟。

lu·nu·la [ˈljuːnjulə] *n.* ***(pl. -lae*** [-liː]***)*** 新月形的东西，新月状表记〔如甲弧影〕(= lunule). **-r** *a.*

lu·nu·late [ˈljuːnjulit, -ˌleit] *a.* ①新月形的。②有新月形标记的 (= lunulated).

lu·nule [ˈljuːnjuːl] *n.* 半月状的东西〔记号〕；甲弧影。

lun·y [ˈluːni] *n.* ***(pl. lun·ies), a. (lun·i·er, lun·i·est)*** = looney, loony.

Lu·per·ca·li·a [ˌljuːpəˈkeiliə, -ˈkæljə] *n. pl.* 古罗马牧神节〔二月十五日〕*(= Lupercal n. sing.)* **Lu·per·ca·li·an** *a.*

lu·pin, lu·pine[1] [ˈljuːpin] *n.*【植】羽扇豆属；白羽扇豆。

lu·pine[2] [ˈljuːpain] *a.* 狼(似)的；凶恶的；贪婪的。

lu·pous [ˈljuːpəs] *a.*【医】狼疮的。

lu·pu·lin [ˈljuːpjulin] *n.*【化】蛇麻腺，忽布素。

lu·pus [ˈljuːpəs] *n.* ①【医】狼疮。②〔L-〕【天】豺狼座。～ **erythematosus** [ˌerəθeməˈtəusəs]【医】红斑狼疮。～ **vulgaris** [ˈvʌlgɛəris]【医】红斑样寻常狼疮。

LUR = London Underground Railway 伦敦地下铁道。

lur [luə] *n.* S 形铜号〔史前期的乐器，尤指北欧地区的〕。

lurch[1] [ləːtʃ] *n.* ①(船忽然发生的)倾侧。②(醉汉的)东歪西倒，蹒跚。③〔美〕倾向，癖好。— *vi.* ①(船)突然倾侧。②东歪西倒，蹒跚。～ *toward* 歪向。～ *against a post* 歪靠在木柱上。

lurch[2] [ləːtʃ] *n.* (某些牌戏中)大败，惨败；〔喻〕极狼狈的处境，困境。***leave sb. in the ～*** 在某人危难时舍弃不顾。

lurch[3] [ləːtʃ] *vi.* 〔英方〕(偷偷摸摸地)徘徊，逡巡；偷偷地躲藏在某处，埋伏。— *vt.* 〔古〕欺骗。— *n.* 〔古〕潜行，徘徊，逡巡；潜伏，埋伏。

lurch·er [ˈləːtʃə] *n.* ①〔古〕小偷。②奸细；间谍。③(偷猎者所用的)杂种猎狗。

lur·dan(e) [ˈləːdn] *n.* 〔古〕懒散无能的人。— *a.* 〔古〕懒散无能的。

lure [ljuə] *n.* ①鹰师系在绳上用以诱回猎鹰的彩色羽毛。②引诱剂，诱惑品，诱饵。③诱惑，魅力。— *vt.* ①用诱物把(鹰)诱回。②引诱，诱惑 *(away; into; on)*。～ *the enemy in deep* 诱敌深入。

Lur·ex [ˈluəreks] 〔一种塑料皮铝线的商标名称〕。— *n.* 〔l-〕塑料皮铝线；铝丝织物。

lu·rid [ˈljuərid] *a.* ①青的，苍白的。②(天空、风景、电光等)可怕的，阴惨的，惊人的。③(夕阳等)血红的，红得象火一样的。④过分渲染的；(画的颜色等)刺目的，俗恶的。*a ～ story [scene]* 悲惨的故事[景象]。***cast [throw] a ～ light on*** 使显得凄惨，说得可怕。**-ly** *ad.* **-ness** *n.*

lurk [ləːk] *vi.* ①潜伏，埋伏 *(about; in; under)*。②潜藏，潜在。③偷偷地行动，鬼鬼祟祟地活动 *(about; along; out)*。～*ing place* 潜伏处，隐藏处。— *n.* ①潜伏，潜在，潜行。②〔英俚〕欺骗，欺诈。***on the ～*** 暗中窥视，偷偷侦察。**-er** *n.* 潜伏者，偷偷侦察的人。**-ing·ly** *ad.* 偷偷地，暗暗地。

Lu·sa·ka [luːˈsɑːkə] *n.* 卢萨卡〔赞比亚首都〕。

Lu·sa·tian [luːˈseiʃən] *n., a.* = Sorbian.

lus·cious [ˈlʌʃəs] *a.* ①甘美的，芬芳的。②过分香甜的，令人腻味的。③形容过甚的，俗恶的。④引起官能欲望的；肉欲的；诱惑性的，色情的。**-ly** *ad.* **-ness** *n.*

lush[1] [lʌʃ] *a.* ①多汁的；味美的，芬芳的。②青葱的；草木茂盛的。③丰富的，豪华的。④繁荣的，有利的。⑤〔口〕(过分)花哨的。**-ly** *ad.* **-ness** *n.*

lush[2] [lʌʃ] 〔俚〕①酒。②醉汉。— *vt., vi.* (使)喝醉。～**-roller,** ～**-worker** 〔美俚〕摸醉汉口袋的扒手。**-ed** *a.*

〔俚〕喝醉了的.
lush·er [ˈlʌʃə] *n.* 〔美俚〕醉汉,酒鬼.
LUSI = lunar surface inspection 月球表面考察.
Lu·si·ta·ni·a [ˌluːsiˈteiniə] ①路西塔尼亚〔古罗马的一个省名,相当于今葡萄牙的大部和西班牙西部的一部分〕. ②"路西塔尼亚号"〔1915年5月7日被德国潜艇在爱尔兰附近海域炸沉的一艘英国轮船〕.
lust [lʌst] *n.* ①欲望;贪欲. ②渴望,热烈追求. ③肉欲,色情. — *vi.* ①渴望,贪求 *(after; for)*. ②好色.
lus·ter[1] [ˈlʌstə] *n.* 好色的人,荒淫的人.
lus·ter[2] [ˈlʌstə] *n.* = lustre[1-2].
lust·ful [ˈlʌstful] *a.* ①多欲的; 贪心的. ②好色的, 淫荡的. ③〔古〕强壮的. **-ly** *ad.* **-ness** *n.*
lust·i·hood [ˈlʌstihud] *n.* 〔古〕精力充沛;强壮.
lust·i·ly [ˈlʌstili] *ad.* 强有力地;活泼地;拼命地,起劲地.
lust·i·ness [ˈlʌstinis] *n.* 活泼;精力充沛.
lus·tra [ˈlʌstrə] lustrum 的复数.
lus·tral [ˈlʌstrəl] *a.* ①除邪的; 去垢的; 净化的. ~ *water* 净水. ②〔古〕每五年的;延续五年的.
lus·trate [ˈlʌstreit] *vt.* *(-trat·ed, -trat·ing)* 祓除. **-tra·tion** [-ˈtreiʃən] *n.*
lus·tre[1] [ˈlʌstə] *n.* ①光泽;光彩;光辉. ②光荣,荣誉. ③〔主英〕光面呢绒[绸缎]. ④釉,光瓷器皿 (= ~ware). ⑤分枝烛台,(吊挂式)分枝灯架. *add ~ to* 给…增光. *shed [throw] ~ on* 使…有光辉. **~ware** 光瓷器皿. **-less** *a.* 无光泽的,无光采的.
lus·tre[2] [ˈlʌstə] *n.* = lustrum.
lus·trine [ˈlʌstrin] *n.* 〔英〕(作衣里用的)光亮绸,羽纱,全丝光亮塔夫绸.
lus·tring [ˈlʌstriŋ] *n.* 【纺】①光亮绸, 羽纱; 加光丝带. ②(纱布等的)加光整理过程.
lus·trous [ˈlʌstrəs] *a.* ①有光泽的; 有光彩的. ②光辉的,灿烂的;显赫的. **-ly** *ad.* **-ness** *n.*
lus·trum [ˈlʌstrəm] *n.* *(pl. ~s, lus·tra* [ˈlʌstrə]*)* ①(古罗马每五年普查人口后举行的) 大祓; (古罗马的)人口普查. ②五年时间.
lust·y [ˈlʌsti] *a.* *(lust·i·er; -i·est)* ①强壮的; 有精神的,活泼的. ②丰盛的,吃得极饱的.
lu·sus na·tu·rae [ˈljuːsəs nəˈtjuəriː] 〔L.〕大自然的玩笑[恶作剧];自然界中的畸形物;天然畸形;畸形的人[动植物];反常现象.
lut·a·nist [ˈluːtənist] *n.* 古琵琶演奏者.
lute[1] [ljuːt] *n.* (14—17世纪时用的)古琵琶. ***play the ~ to a cow*** 对牛弹琴. ***a rift within the ~*** 不和[疯癫]的前兆. — *vi., vt.* 演奏古琵琶.
lute[2] [ljuːt] *n.* ①封泥. ②封闭器. — *vt.* 用封泥封闭.
lu·te·al [ˈluːtiəl] *a.* 【生化】(属于)黄体的.
lu·te·ci·um [luːˈtiːʃiəm, -siəm] *n.* = lutetium.
lu·te·in [ˈluːtiin] *n.* 【生化】①叶黄素. ②黄体制剂.
lu·te·in·ize [ˈluːtiːinaiz] *vt.* *(-iz·ed, -iz·ing)* 【生化】刺激黄体分离. — *vi.* 使成为黄体部分. *luteinizing hormone* 促黄体发生(激)素. **-i·za·tion** *n.*
lu·te·nist [ˈluːtnist] *n.* lutanist 的异体.
lute·o·lin [ˈluːtiəlin] *n.* 【化】毛地黄黄酮.
lu·te·ous [ˈluːtiəs] *a.* 深桔黄色的.
lute·string [ˈluːtistriŋ] *n.* = lustring.
Lu·te·tia [luːˈtiːʃə] *n.* 鲁特西亚〔巴黎的古代名称〕.
Lu·te·tian [ljuːˈtiːʃən] *a.* 巴黎的.
lu·te·ti·um [luːˈtiːʃiəm] *n.* 【化】镥.
Luth. = Lutheran.
Lu·ther [ˈluːθə] *n.* ①卢瑟〔姓氏,男子名〕. ②**Martin ~** 马丁·路德〔1483—1546,德国宗教改革家〕.
Lu·ther·an [ˈljuːθərən] *a.* 马丁·路德的; 路德教(派)的. *the ~ Church* 路德教〔信义会、路德会等的总称〕. — *n.* 路德教教徒;马丁·路德的信徒. **-ism** = **Lu·ther·ism** 路德教(教义).
lu·thern [ˈluːθən] *n.* 老虎天窗,屋顶窗.
lu·thi·er [ˈluːtiə] *n.* 弦乐器工匠.
lut·ing [ˈluːtiŋ] *n.* = lute.
lut·ist [ˈluːtist] *n.* ① = lutanist. ②古琵琶工匠.
Lu·wi·an [ˈluːiən] *n.* 卢威语〔小亚细亚地区的一个语种,已消亡〕. — *a.* 卢威语的 (= Luvian).
lux [lʌks] *n.* *(pl. luxes* [ˈlʌksiz], *luces* [ˈljuːsiːz]*)* 【物】勒克司〔照明单位〕.
Lux. = Luxemburg.
lux·ate [ˈlʌkseit] *vt.* 【医】使脱骱;使脱位;使离线. **lux·a·tion** *n.*
luxe [luks,lʌks] *n.* 〔F.〕上等,华美;奢侈,豪华. *articles de ~* 奢侈品. *édition de ~* 精装本. *train de ~* 特等车.
Lux·em·b(o)urg [ˈluksəmˌbəːg] *n.* ①卢森堡〔欧洲〕. ②卢森堡〔卢森堡首都〕.
lux·me·ter [ˈlʌksˌmitə] *n.* 【物】照度计,勒克司计.
lux·u·ri·ance, -an·cy [lʌgˈzjuəriəns, lʌgˈzjuəriənsi] *n.* ①繁茂;丰富;多产. ②华美;奢华.
lux·u·ri·ant [lʌgˈzjuəriənt] *a.* ①繁茂的; 多产的; 丰富的. ②华美的,绚烂的;奢华的. **-ly** *ad.*
lux·u·ri·ate [lʌgˈzjuərieit] *vi.* ①繁茂. ②生活奢华, 沉迷(在…) *(in;on)*; 享受. *~ in sunshine* 尽情享受日光.
lux·u·ri·ous [lʌgˈzjuəriəs] *a.* ①豪华的,奢侈的. ②非常舒适的. ③精美而昂贵的. ④词藻华丽的. *a ~ table* 奢侈的饭菜[筵席]. **-ly** *ad.* **-ness** *n.*
lux·u·ry [ˈlʌkʃəri] *n.* ①奢侈,豪华. ②奢侈品;美食,美衣. ③乐趣,享受. *the ~ of a good book* 好书的乐趣[享受]; *What a ~ it is to be alone!* 单独一人多舒服. ***be lapped in ~*** 穷奢极欲. ***live in ~*** 生活奢华. — *a.* 奢华的,豪华的. *a ~ hotel* 豪华的旅馆. **~ consumption** 【农】(作物对土壤中的氮或钾碱的)过度吸收.
Lu·zon [luːˈzɔn] *n.* 吕宋(岛)〔菲律宾〕.
LV = ①legal volt 【电】法定伏特. ②low voltage 【电】低压. ③landing vehicle 登陆车辆. ④launch vehicle 活动发射装置;运载火箭.
lv. = leave(s).
LVI = landing vessel, infantry 步兵登陆舰.
Lvov [lvɔf] *n.* 利沃夫〔苏联城市〕.
LVT = landing vessel, tank 坦克登陆舰.
LW = ①left wing 左翼. ②long wave 长波. ③low water 低水位;低潮.
Lw = lawrencium 【化】铹.
LWM = low water mark 低潮标记.
lx = lux.
-ly[1] *suf.* 加在形容词或分词之后,构成副词,表示"方式","状态","时间","地点","程序","程度","方向","方面"等: bold*ly*, great*ly* smiling*ly*, unexpected*ly*; economical*ly*, scientifical*ly*. ★ 以 -le 结尾的词,则应略去 -e 后再加 -ly: feeb*ly* nob*ly*.
-ly[2] *suf.* 加在名词之后,构成形容词,①表示"象…的","有…性质的": king*ly*, man*ly*, scholar*ly*. ②表示"反复发生的","每一特定时期发生一次的","以…为周期的": hour*ly*, dai*ly*, week*ly*, month*ly*, year*ly*.
Ly·all·pur [ˈliːəpur] *n.* 莱亚尔普尔〔巴基斯坦城市〕.
ly·ard, ly·art [ˈlaiəd, ˈlaiət] *a.* 〔Scot.〕带灰白色条纹的,灰白色的.
ly·can·thrope [ˈlaikənθrəup, laiˈkænθrəup] *n.* ①【医】变狼狂患者. ②= werewolf.
ly·can·thro·py [laiˈkænθrəpi] *n.* ①(女巫)化为狼的妖术. ②【医】变狼狂〔自以为已变成狼的精神病〕.
ly·cée [ˈliːsei] *n.* 〔F.〕(法国公立)高级中学,大学预科.
ly·ce·um [laiˈsi(ː)əm] *n.* ①学园,学会;〔美〕文艺团体;文化(教育)宫. ②〔L-〕(亚里斯多德讲学的)莱森学园;亚里斯多德派的哲学. ③〔L-〕(伦敦的) 莱森戏院. ④ = *lycée*.
ly·chee [ˈliːtʃiː] *n.* = litchi.
lych-gate [ˈlitʃgeit] *n.* = lichgate.
lych·nis [ˈliknis] *n.* 【植】剪秋罗属.

ly·co·pod [ˈlaikəpɔd] *n.* 【植】①石松属. ②= lycopodium. ③= club moss.

ly·co·po·di·um [ˌlaikəˈpəudiəm] *n.* ①【植】石松科植物. ②石松粉.

lydd·ite [ˈlidait] *n.* 苦味酸〔立德〕炸药.

Lyd·gate [ˈlidgeit] *n.* 利德盖特〔姓氏〕.

Lyd·i·a [ˈlidiə] *n.* ①莉迪亚〔女子名〕. ②【史】吕底亚〔小亚细亚一古国〕.

Lyd·i·an [ˈlidiən, -djən] *a.* ①吕底亚的; 吕底亚人的; 吕底亚语的. ②柔婉的,柔媚的; 欢乐的; 肉感的. ～ *airs* 哀曲,柔婉的音乐,靡靡之音. 一 *n.* 吕底亚人; 吕底亚语. ～ *stone* 试金石.

lye [lai] *n.* 灰汁; 碱液.

Ly·ell [ˈlaiəl] *n.* ①莱尔〔姓氏〕. ②**Sir Charles** ～ 查尔斯・莱尔〔1797—1875,英国地质学家〕.

ly·gus bug [ˈlaigəs] 【动】 蝽属昆虫〔其中的很多种危害植物〕.

ly·ing[1] [ˈlaiiŋ] lie[2] 的现在分词. 一 *a.* 说谎的,虚妄的,虚伪的. *a* ～ *rumour* 谣传,谎言. 一 *n.* 说谎, 谎话, 虚伪. **-ly** *ad.*

ly·ing[2] [ˈlaiiŋ] lie[1] 的现在分词. 一 *a.* 卧着的,躺着的. 一 *n.* 横卧; 横卧处. ～ ***down*** 躺倒认输; 不作反抗; ～***-in-state*** 著名人物的遗体公开陈列告别仪式 (～*-in-state hall* 遗体告别礼堂).

ly·ing-in [ˈlaiiŋˈin] *n.* 产期; 分娩. 一 *a.* 分娩的; 产科的; 产期的. *a* ～ *hospital* 产院,产科医院. *a* ～ *physician* 产科医生.

lyke-wake [ˈlaikweik] *n.* 〔Scot.〕 夜间守尸.

Lyle [lail] *n.* 莱尔〔姓氏,男子名〕.

Lyl·y [ˈlili] *n.* 利利〔姓氏〕.

Ly·man [ˈlaimən] *n.* 莱曼〔姓氏,男子名〕.

Lym·pa·ny [ˈlimpəni] *n.* 林帕尼〔姓氏〕.

lymph [limf] *n.* ①清泉. ②【解】淋巴(液). ③【医】(淋巴液状)浆,苗. *vaccine* ～ 菌苗, 疫苗. ～ **node**【解】淋巴结〔腺〕.

lym·phad·e·ni·tis [limˌfædiˈnaitis] *n.*【医】 淋巴腺炎.

lym·phan·gi·al [limˈfændʒiəl] *a.*【解】淋巴管的.

lym·phan·gio·gram [limˈfændʒiəgræm] *n.*【医】= lymphogram.

lym·phan·gi·og·ra·phy [limˌfændʒiˈɔgrəfi] *n.*【医】= lymphography. **lymphangiographic** *a.*

lym·phan·gi·tis [ˌlimfənˈdʒaitis] *n.*【医】淋巴管炎.

lym·phat·ic [limˈfætik] *a.* ①【医】淋巴,含淋巴的. ②淋巴质的; 淋巴腺的; 淋巴腺疾病引起的. ③软弱的; 苍白的; 迟钝的. *a* ～ *gland* 淋巴腺. *a* ～ *vessel* 淋巴管. 一 *n.*【解】淋巴腺,淋巴管; 粘液质〔旧时生理学所说人四种气质之一〕. **-i·cal·ly** *ad.*

lym·pho·blast [ˈlimfəblæst] *n.*【医】成淋巴细胞, 淋巴母细胞.

lym·pho·cyte [ˈlimfəsait] *n.*【医】淋巴细胞, 淋巴球. **lym·pho·cyt·ic** [-ˈsitik] *a.*

lym·pho·cy·to·sis [ˌlimfəsaiˈtəusis] *n.*【医】淋巴球增多. **lym·pho·cy·tot·ic** [-ˈtɔtik] *a.*

lym·pho·gram [ˈlimfəˌgræm] *n.*【医】淋巴系造影照片.

lym·pho·gran·u·lo·ma [ˌlimfəˌgrænjuˈləumə] *n.* ***(pl. -mas, -ma·ta*** [-mətə]***)***【医】 淋巴肉芽肿. **-tous** *a.*

lym·phog·ra·phy [limˈfɔgrəfi] *n.*【医】淋巴系造影术. **-pho·graph·ic** *a.*

lymph·oid [ˈlimfɔid] *a.* 淋巴 (腺) 样的; 淋巴腺组织(样)的.

lym·pho·ma [limˈfəumə] *n.* ***(pl.*** ***～s, -ta)***【医】 淋巴(组织)瘤.

lym·pho·poi·e·sis [ˌlimfəupɔiˈiːsis] *n.*【医】淋巴细胞增殖.

lym·pho·sar·co·ma [ˌlimfəusɑːˈkəumə] *n.*【医】淋巴肉瘤. **-lous** *a.*

lym·phous [ˈlimfəs] *a.* 淋巴的,淋巴性的,含淋巴的.

lyn·ce·an [linˈsi(ː)ən] *a.* ①山猫(似)的; 猞猁猕似的. ②山猫眼似的,眼光锐利的.

Lynch [lintʃ] *n.* 林奇〔姓氏〕.

lynch [lintʃ] *n.* 私刑. 一 *vt.* 私刑处死; 〔古〕私刑拷打. ～ **law** *n.* 私刑〔非法杀害〕. **-er** *n.* 施私刑者. **-ing** 私刑.

lynch·pin [ˈlintʃpin] *n.* = linchpin.

Lynd [lind] *n.* 林德〔姓氏〕.

Lynn [lin] *n.* 林恩〔姓氏,男子名,女子名〕.

lynx [liŋks] *n.* ***(pl.*** ***～es,*** 〔集合词〕 ～***)*** ①【动】猞猁狲, 山猫. ②猞猁狲皮, 山猫皮. ③〔L-〕【天】天猫座. ～**-eyed** *a.* 眼光锐利的.

Ly·on [ˈlaiən] *n.* 苏格兰司章的长官〔又叫 ～ King of Arms〕.

ly·on·naise [ˌlaiəˈneiz] *a.*【烹】加洋葱(丝)的.

Ly·on(s) [ˈlaiən(z)] *n.* 莱昂(斯)〔姓氏〕.

Ly·ons [ˈlaiənz; F. ˈliːɔ̃] *n.* 里昂〔法国城市〕.

ly·o·phil·ic [ˌlaiəˈfilik] *a.*【化】亲液的 (= lyophile).

ly·oph·i·lize [laiˈɔfilaiz] *vt.* ***(-liz·ed, -liz·ing)*** 冻干〔尤指生物产品〕. **-r** 冻干机. **-i·li·za·tion** *n.*

ly·o·pho·bic [ˌlaiəˈfəubik] *a.*【化】疏液的.

Ly·ra [ˈlaiərə] *n.*【天】天琴座.

ly·rate [ˈlaiərit] *a.* 竖琴状的.

lyre [ˈlaiə] *n.* ①古希腊七弦竖琴. ②〔the ～〕 抒情诗. ③〔L-〕【天】= Lyra. ④(乐队用的) 乐谱架. ～**bird**【动】琴鸟.

lyr·ic [ˈlirik] *n.* ①抒情诗; 抒情作品. ②〔*pl.*〕民歌中的词句. 一 *a.* ①希腊竖琴的. ②可用希腊竖琴伴奏的. ③抒情的,抒情诗的. ④感情用事的; 感情冲动的. *a* ～ *poet* 抒情诗人. ～ *poetry* 抒情诗. *the* ～ *drama* 歌剧. *explode with* ～ *wrath* 勃然大怒.

lyr·i·cal [ˈlirikəl] *a.* = lyric *(a.)*. *become* ～ 感情冲动起来. **-ly** *ad.* **-ness** *n.*

lyr·i·cism [ˈlirisizəm] *n.* ①抒情诗性质,抒情性; 抒情诗体; 抒情语句. ②感情冲动; 情绪高涨〔激昂〕.

lyr·i·cist [ˈlirisist] *n.* 抒情诗人.

ly·ri·form [ˈlaiərifɔːm] *a.* 竖琴状的.

lyr·ism [ˈlaiərizəm] *n.* ①弹奏竖琴. ②[ˈliərizəm] = lyricism.

lyr·ist [ˈlaiərist, ˈlirist] *n.* ①竖琴演奏者. ②[ˈlirist] 抒情诗人.

lyse [lais] *vt.*, *vi.* ***(lysed, lys·ing)***【生化,医】细胞溶解; 病状渐退.

Ly·sen·ko·ism [laiˈseŋkəuizəm] *n.* (苏联) 李森科学派〔学说〕.

ly·ser·gic acid [laiˈsəːdʒik æsid]【化】麦角酸.

ly·sim·e·ter [laiˈsimitə] *n.*【化】渗水计, 溶度(估定)计. **-met·ric** *a.*

ly·sin [ˈlaisn] *n.*【医】细胞溶素.

ly·sine [ˈlaisiːn] *n.*【医】赖氨酸.

ly·sis [ˈlaisis] *n.* ***(pl.*** **ly·ses** [ˈlaisiːz]***)*** ①【生化】细胞〔菌〕溶解. ②【医】(病的) 渐退,消散; 松解术.

ly·so·cline [ˈlaisəklain] *n.*【海】(海水中的) 分解水层.

ly·so·gen·e·sis [ˌlaisəˈdʒenisis] *n.*【微】溶源性, 溶菌作用的产生.

ly·sol [ˈlaisɔl] *n.*【药】(消毒防腐剂)来沙尔;【化】煤酚皂溶液,杂酚皂液.

ly·so·some [ˈlaisəsəum] *n.*【生】溶 (酶) 体. **-so·mal** *a.*

ly·so·staph·in [ˌlaisəˈstæfən] *n.*【生化】溶葡萄球菌酶.

ly·so·zyme [ˈlaisəzaim] *n.*【生化】溶菌酶.

lyt·ic [ˈlitik] *a.* ①(细胞) 溶素的. ②溶解的; 促使溶解的. ③【医】松解的,渐退的.

lyt·ta [ˈlitə] *n.* ***(pl. -tae*** [-tiː]***)*** (犬等舌下的) 纵行蠕虫状纽带.

Lyt·ton [ˈlitn] *n.* ①利顿〔姓氏〕. ②**Edward George Earle** ～ **Bulwer-1st Baron** 利顿〔1803—1873, 英国小说家,剧作家,政治家〕.

M

M, m [em] *(pl.* **M's, m's**[emz]*)* ①英语字母表第十三字母. ②M 形状的东西;【印】= ϵm. ③M(罗马数字) 1,000. MCML = 1950. M̄ = 1,000,000.

M., m. = ①majesty. ②male. ③mark(s). ④married. ⑤masculine. ⑥medicine. ⑦medium. ⑧〔L.〕*meridies* (= noon): A. M. [a. m.] 午前, 上午. ⑨metre(s). ⑩middle. ⑪mile(s). ⑫minim. ⑬minute(s). ⑭month. ⑮morning. ⑯mountain. ⑰modulus. ⑱【物】mass. ⑲Marshal. ⑳Master. ㉑Medieval. ㉒Monday. ㉓〔F.〕*Monsieur*. ㉔mega-. ㉕mole. ㉖Marquis. ㉗motor. ㉘meridian. ㉙muscle.

M' = Mac, Mc 马克, 米克, 麦克〔苏格兰人和爱尔兰人姓氏附有 Mac 的略称, 如 M'Donald 麦克唐纳〕.

M.A., MA = ①Master of Arts 文学硕士. ②military academy 陆军军官学校; 军事学院.

Ma = ①Minnesota. ②【化】元素钨 (masurium) 的符号.

ma [mɑː] *n.* 〔儿口〕妈〔mamma 之略〕.

ma'am *n.* 〔madam 的缩写〕①[mæm, mɑːm]〔英〕夫人; 女士〔对王族贵夫人的尊称〕. ②[məm, m]〔口〕太太; 小姐〔女仆等对主妇的称呼〕★ 现在仅用于句中或句尾. ～ **school** 乡村或小镇女教师办的小学校 (=dame school).

Maas [mɑːz] *n.* 马斯〔姓氏〕.

Maat [mə'ɑːt] *n.* 【埃神】真理正义之神.

Mab [mæb] *n.* 梅布〔女子名〕.

Ma·bel ['meibəl] *n.* 梅布尔〔女子名〕.

Mac [mæk] *n.* ①麦克〔男子名, *cf.* Mac-〕. ②〔俚〕(称呼用)老兄, 老弟, 伙计.

mac [mæk] *n.* 〔口〕= mackintosh.

Mac- *pref.* 〔后接苏格兰或爱尔兰人名〕= son of〔略 Mc, M^c, M'; 相当于 Welsh 的 Ap-, Irish 的 O', English 的 -son, -s, Norman 的 Fitz-〕: *Mac*donald, *Mac*Donald; *M^c*Donald; *M'*Donald.

ma·ca·bre, ma·ca·ber [mə'kɑːbr, -bə] *a.* 以死亡为主题的; 可怕的, 阴惨的. ***dance*** ～ 死的舞蹈 (= dance of death).

ma·ca·co [mə'keikəu] *n.* *(pl.* *～s)*【动】狐猴.

mac·ad·am [mə'kædəm] *n.* ①碎石(路); 碎石路面. ②〔M-〕麦克亚当〔姓氏〕.

mac·a·dam·i·a nut [ˌmækə'deimiə]【植】澳洲坚果.

mac·ad·am·ize [mə'kædəmaiz] *vt.* 筑(碎石路); 用碎石铺(路). **-zation** [məˌkædəmai'zeiʃən] *n.* 碎石铺路法.

Ma·cao [mə'kau] *n.* 澳门.

ma·caque [mə'kɑːk] *n.* 【动】猕猴; 短尾猴.

mac·a·ro·ni [ˌmækə'rəuni] *n.* *(pl.* *～s, ～es)* ①意大利通心面条, 通心粉. ②(十八世纪伦敦装模作样学欧洲大陆派头的)时髦男子; (泛指)花花公子. ～ **cheese** 干酪烤通心面条. ～ **wheat** 硬质小麦 (= durum wheat).

mac·a·ron·ic [ˌmækə'rɔnik] *a.* 混淆的; (混合现代语和拉丁语尾的)混合体的. — *n.* 〔*pl.*〕两种语言混合写成的诗文.

mac·a·roon [ˌmækə'ruːn] *n.* 蛋白杏仁小甜饼(干).

Mac·Ar·thur [mə'kɑːθə, mk'ɑːθə] *n.* 麦克阿瑟〔姓氏〕.

ma·cas·sar [mə'kæsə] *n.* 望加锡油〔一种植物性发油, 又叫 ～ oil〕.

Ma·cau·lay [mə'kɔːli] *n.* ①麦考利〔姓氏〕. ②**Thomas Babington** ～ 托马斯·巴宾顿·麦考莱〔1800—1859, 英国历史学家、作家、政治家〕.

ma·caw[1] [mə'kɔː] *n.* 【鸟】金刚鹦鹉, 鹦鹉.

ma·caw[2] [mə'kɔː] *n.* 【植】美国棕榈 (= macaw palm, macaw tree).

Mac·beth [mək'beθ] *n.* 麦克佩斯〔莎士比亚所作悲剧之一, 该剧的主人公〕.

Macc. = **Mac·ca·bees** ['mækəbiːz] *n.* 马卡比父子〔曾拯救叙利亚犹太人脱离希腊王暴政 (175—164 B.C.)的犹太人〕; 马卡比家族.

Mac·ca·be·an [ˌmækə'biːən] *a.* 马卡比父子〔家族〕的.

mac·ca·boy, mac·ca·baw ['mækəbɔi, -bɔː] *n.* 马可巴鼻烟.

Mac·Cra·cken [mə'krækən] *n.* 麦克拉肯〔姓氏〕.

Mac·Don·ald [mək'dɔnəld] *n.* 麦克唐纳〔姓氏〕.

Mac·Don·nell [ˌmækdə'nel] *n.* 麦克唐奈〔姓氏〕.

Mac·Dow·ell [mək'dauəl] *n.* 麦克道尔〔姓氏〕.

mace[1] [meis] *n.* ①钉头槌〔中古武器〕. ②(作为市长、大学校长等职权表征的)权标, 权杖; 〔the M-〕(英国下院议长的)职杖; 执权标者 (= macebearer). ③【台球】(从前用来击 bagatelle 球的)平头杆. **～bearer** 执权杖者.

mace[2] [meis] *n.* 豈蔻香料〔肉豈蔻种子的干皮〕; 肉豈蔻(树).

Mace[3] [meis] *n.* 梅斯毒气〔一种暂时伤害性压缩液态毒气〕. — *vt.* 用梅斯毒气向…攻击.

Maced. = Macedonia(n).

mac·é·doine [ˌmæse'dwɑːn] *n.* 〔F.〕①拌蔬菜; 拌水果色拉; 蔬菜水果混合开胃菜. ②混杂物.

Mac·e·do·nia [ˌmæsi'dəunjə] *n.* ①马其顿〔巴尔干半岛中部的古国〕. ②(巴尔干半岛中南部的) 马其顿地区. **-do·ni·an** [ˌmæsi'dəunjən, -niən] *a.*, *n.* 马其顿的; 马其顿人〔语〕〔略 Maced.〕.

Mac·e·don·ic [ˌmæsi'dɔnik] *a.* = Macedonian.

mac·er ['meisə] *n.* ①执权杖者 (= macebearer). ②〔Scot.〕法院官吏.

mac·er·ate ['mæsəreit] *vt.* ①使浸软, 浸渍, 浸解. ②使瘦, 使饿瘦, 折磨, 虐待. — *vi.* 浸软, 饿瘦.

mac·er·a·ter, mac·er·a·tor ['mæsəreitə] *n.* ①浸渍者; 浸解者. ②纸浆制造机.

mac·er·a·tion [ˌmæsə'reiʃən] *n.* ①绝食饿瘦. ②【化】浸软; 浸渍(作用); 离析, 浸解.

Mach [mɑːk; G. max] *n.* 【物】马赫〔超高速单位, 马赫数, = ～ number〕. **～meter** 马赫计. ～ **wave** (原子弹爆炸时的)冲击波.

mach. = machine; machinery; machinist.

mache ['mɑːʃei] *n.* 【化】马谢〔空气或液体中所含氡的浓度单位〕.

ma·che·te [mɑː'tʃeiti] *n.* ①(中、南美人用的)大砍刀. ②葡萄牙四弦小吉他琴.

Mach·i·a·vel [ˌmækiə'vel] *n.* = Machiavellian.

Mach·i·a·vel·li [ˌmækiə'veli] *n.* 尼科洛·马基雅维里〔1469—1527, 意大利政治家及历史学家, 主张为达目的利用权术, 不择手段〕.

Mach·i·a·vel(l)ian [ˌmækiə'veliən] *a.* 马基雅维里式

的；阴谋的；不择手段的．— *n.* 马基雅维里式的政治人物，不择手段的阴谋家．**-vel·l·ism** *n.* 马基雅维里主义；权谋术数，阴谋诡计．**-vel·list** *n.*

ma·chic·o·late [mæ'tʃikəuleit] *vt.* 在…上开堞眼［枪眼］．**-d** *a.* 有堞眼的，有枪眼的．**-la·tion** [mæˌtʃikə'leiʃən].

ma·chi·co·lis [ˌmɑːʃi'kuːli] *n.* 【军】突堞；凸堞枪眼［堞眼］．

machin. = machinery.

ma·chin·a·ble [mə'ʃiːnəbl] *a.* 可用机器制造［加工］的．**-a·bil·i·ty** [məˌʃiːnə'biliti] *n.* (可)切削性；机制性．

mach·i·nate ['mækineit] *vt., vi.* 策划，阴谋．**-na·tion** [ˌmæki'neiʃən] *n.* 策划，阴谋，诡计．**-na·tor** *n.* 阴谋家．

ma·chine [mə'ʃiːn] *n.* ①机(器)，机械；机关，机构．②印刷机器；缝纫机；打字机；汽车；自行车；三轮车；飞机；［美俚］救火机．③机械地工作的人［机构］，机械似的人．④［美］(政党的)领导机关［核心小集团］；干部，党员．⑤【美海】轮机中士．⑥(诗、小说或剧本中所安排的)超自然的力量［人物］．*a mowing* ～ 割草机．*a reaping* ～ 收割机．～ *cotton* 机制线，轴线．～ *oil* 机油［机器润滑油］．～ *printing* 机器印染．— *vt.* 用机器制造；用电动机器缝纫［印刷］；用机械加工．～ **bolt** 机制螺栓．～**-building** 机器制造(工业)．～ **carbine** 冲锋枪，卡宾枪．～ **gun** 机关枪．～**-gun** *vt.* 用机(关)枪扫射．～**-hour** 一台机器在一小时内的工作量．～ **language**【自】机器语言，计算机语言．～**-made** *a.* 机制的 (*opp.* hand-made)．～**-man** 机器工人；(特指)印刷工人．～ **pistol** 自动手枪．～**-readable** *a.* 可直接为计算机使用的．～ **rifle** 自动步枪．～ **screw** 机(器)螺钉．～**-sewed** *a.* 机器缝的．～ **shop** ［美］金工车间；机械工场．～**-smashing** *n.* 捣毁机器．～ **time** ①=～-hour．②计算机时间［完成一个运算项目的时间］．～ **tool** 机床，工作母机．～**-tooled** *a.* 经机床加工而成的；全靠机器的．～ **translation** 机器翻译［由计算机将一种语言译成另一种语言］．～**-wool** 再生毛．～ **work** 机械工作；(用以增强文学作品戏剧效果的)布局，设计．

ma·chin·er·y [mə'ʃiːnəri] *n.* ①［集合词］机器，机械；机件；(机器的)运转部分．②(政府等的)机关，组织，机构．③(小说、戏剧等的)情节，设计［特指为增强效果而安排的超自然的人物或事件］．④工具，手段，方法．*state* ～ 国家机器．

ma·chin·ist [mə'ʃiːnist] *n.* 机械师；机工；钳床［机床］技工；［尤指缝纫车工］；［美］(政党的)干部．～**'s mate**【美海军】轮机军士长．

Mach·ism ['mɑːkizəm] *n.* 马赫主义［即经验批判主义］．**Mach·ist** ['mɑːkist] *n.* 马赫主义者．

ma·chis·mo [mɑː'tʃiːzməu] *n.* ［Sp.］男子(雄武)气概．

ma·cho ['mɑːtʃəu] *n.* ［Sp.］(*pl.* ***-chos*** [tʃəus]) 健壮男子．—*a.* 雄性的；雄武的；有胆量的．

ma·chree [mə'kriː, mə'hriː] *n.* 心肝，宝贝儿［英一爱尔兰亲昵语］．*mother* ～ 我的好妈妈．

Ma·chu Pic·chu ['mɑːtʃuː'piːktʃuː] 玛丘匹克丘［秘鲁中南部古印坎城遗迹］(= Machupicchu)．

mac·in·tosh ['mækintɔʃ] *n.* = mackintosh.

Mac(k) [mæk] *n.* 麦克［男子名］．

Mac·kay(e) [mə'kai] *n.* 麦凯［姓氏］．

mack·er·el ['mækrəl] *n.* (*pl.* ～*s*，［集合词］～)【鱼】鲐鱼［又叫鲭鱼］；马鲛鱼．～ **gale [breeze]** 鲭风［适于捕鲭的较强的风］．～ **sky** 鱼鳞天［有卷积云的天空］．

mack·i·naw ['mækinɔː] *n.* ［美］(双排钮方格纹)厚呢短大衣．**M- blanket** (美国西部人用的)方格厚毛毯．**M- boat** (美国大湖中的)平底船．**M- coat** (= mackinaw).

Mack·in·tosh ['mækintɔʃ] *n.* ①麦金托什［姓氏］．②[m-] 防水胶布；胶布雨衣．

mack·le ['mækl] *n.* 【印】①墨污；污点；污斑．②模糊印张．— *vt., vi.* 【印】印刷模糊；重叠印刷；使模糊．

Ma·claren [mə'klærən] *n.* 麦克拉伦［姓氏］．

ma·cle [mækl] *n.* (钻石的)双晶；短空晶石；(矿物的)黑斑．

Ma·clean(e) [mə'klein] *n.* 麦克莱恩［姓氏］．

Mac·Leish [mək'liːʃ] *n.* 麦克利什［姓氏］．

Mac·Leod [mə'klaud] *n.* ①麦克劳德［姓氏］．②**John James Richard** ～ 约翰·詹姆斯·理查德·麦克劳德［1876—1935，苏格兰生理学家，获 1923 年诺贝尔医药奖］．

Mac·Mil·lan, Mac·mil·lan [mək'milən] *n.* 麦克米伦［姓氏］．

ma·con·o·chie [mə'kɔnɔki] *n.* 军用罐头烩菜肉；罐头食品．

Mac·Pher·son [mək'fəːsn] *n.* 麦克弗森［姓氏］．

macr- *comb. f.* (后接元音) = macro-.

mac·ra·mé [mə'krɑːmi] *n.* (家具装饰用的)流苏，结节，花边 (= ～ lace).

Mac·rea·dy [mə'kriːdi] *n.* 麦克里迪［姓氏］．

mac·ro ['mækrəu] *a.* ①巨大的；极厚的；特别突出的．②大量使用的．— *n.* 【自】宏指令 ［macroinstruction 的缩写］．

macro- *comb. f.* 大，巨，宏，长，粗 (*opp.* micro-).

ma·cro·bi·an [mək'rəubiən] *a.* 长命的，长寿的．—*n.* 长寿者［尤指百岁以上的］．

mac·ro·bi·o·sis [ˌmækrəubai'əusis] *n.* 长命，长寿．

mac·ro·bi·ot·ic [ˌmækrəubai'ɔtik] *a.* 能促进长寿的；长命的，长寿的．

mac·ro·bi·ot·ics [ˌmækrəubai'ɔtiks] *n. pl.* ［动词用单数］长寿术［以特殊饮食延年益寿术］．

mac·ro·ceph·a·l·ous, mac·ro·ce·phal·ic [ˌmækrəu'sefələs, -si'fælik] *a.* 【医】大头的，长头的．

mac·ro·ceph·a·ly [ˌmækrəu'sefəli] *n.* 【医】巨颅，巨头 (*opp.* microcephaly).

mac·ro·chem·is·try [ˌmækrəu'kemistri] *n.* (不用显微镜、不作微量分析的)常量化学．

mac·ro·cli·mate ['mækrəuˌklaimət] *n.* 【气】大气候．**-matic** [-klai'mætik] *a.*

mac·ro·cosm ['mækrəkɔzəm] *n.* ①【物】(大)宇宙，宏观世界．(*opp.* microcosm)．②全域，(大的)整体．**-ic** *a.*

mac·ro·cosmos ['mækrəˌkɔzmɔs] *n.* = macrocosm.

mac·ro·cyst ['mækrəsist] *n.* 【医】大囊肿．

mac·ro·cyte ['mækrəsait] *n.* 【医】(恶性贫血的)大红细胞；巨红血球．**-cyt·ic** [-ˌsitik] *a.*

mac·ro·dont ['mækrədɔnt] *a.* 【医】巨牙的．

mac·ro·eco·nom·ics [ˌmækrəuˌiːkə'nɔmiks] *n.* ［用作 *sing.*］大［宏观］经济学［研究经济体系中起作用的各种因素或经济部门之间的相互关系］．

mac·ro·ev·o·lu·tion [ˌmækrəuˌevə'luːʃən] *n.* 【动】大进化，种外进化［指涉及新品种、新机体的出现的大规模和长时间的进化］．

ma·cro·ga·mete [ˌmækrəu'gæmiːt -gə'miːt] *n.* 【医】大配子．

mac·ro·graph ['mækrəgrɑːf, -græf] *n.* 【物】(实物大小或大于实物的)宏观图 (*opp.* micrograph)；肉眼图．

ma·crog·ra·phy [mə'krɔgrəfi] *n.* 肉眼检查；【医】写字过大症．

mac·ro·in·struc·tion [ˌmækrəuin'strʌkʃən] *n.* 【自】宏指令．

mac·ro·lev·el ['mækrəˌlevl] *a.* 宏观(水平)的．

mac·ro·mere ['mækrəmiə] *n.* 【医】(细胞分裂的)大(分)裂球．

ma·crom·e·ter [mə'krɔmitə] *n.* 测远器．

mac·ro·mol·e·cule [ˌmækrəu'mɔlikjuːl] *n.* 【化】大分子，高分子 (= macromole)．**-lar** *a.*

ma·cron ['mækrɔn] *n.* 长音符(-) ［例：ā, ī, ū］．

mac·ro·nu·cle·us [ˌmækrəu'nuːkliəs] *n.* 【生】(原生动物细胞的)巨核，大核．**-cle·ar** *a.*

M

mac·ro·nu·tri·ent [ˌmækrəuˈnjuːtriənt] *n.* (植物所需的)大量化学养料〔如碳〕.
mac·ro·phage [ˈmækrəfeidʒ] *n.* 【生】巨噬细胞.
mac·ro·phys·ics [ˌmækrəuˈfiziks] *n.* 宏观物理学〔研究可直接地、单独地观察和测量的物体的物理学〕.
mac·rop·ter·ous [mæˈkrɔptərəs] *a.* 【动】有大翅的; 有大鳍的.
mac·ro·scop·ic, -i·cal [ˌmækrəuˈskɔpik, -ikəl] *a.* 【物】肉眼可见的; 宏观的, 粗视的, 粗显的.
mac·ro·spo·ran·gi·um [ˌmækrəuspəˈrændʒiəm] *n.* *(pl.* *-gi·a* [-ə]*)* 【生】大孢子囊 (= megasporangium).
mac·ro·spore [ˈmækrəspɔː] *n.* 【植】大孢子.
mac·ro·struc·ture [ˌmækrəuˈstrʌktʃə] *n.* 【物】宏观结构.
ma·cru·ran [məˈkruərən] *n.* 【动】十足甲壳类〔包括虾、蟹〕. **-cru·rous, -cru·ral, -cru·roid** *a.*
mac·u·la [ˈmækjulə] *n.* *(pl.* *-lae* [-liː]*)* (太阳的)黑点; (矿石的)斑点, 疵瑕; (皮肤上的)痣, (色)斑.
mac·u·lar [ˈmækjulə] *a.* 有斑点的; 有污点的.
mac·u·late [ˈmækjuleit] *vt.* 弄脏, 玷污. — [-lit] *a.* = macular.
mac·u·la·tion [ˌmækjuˈleiʃən] *n.* 斑点, 污点; 【生】斑纹; 玷污.
mac·ule [ˈmækjuːl] *n.* 点; 斑; 疱; (尤指)痣; 太阳的黑点 (= macula).
mac·u·lu·te·a [mækˈluːtiə] *n.* 【解】黄斑.
ma·cum·ba [məˈkumbə] *n.* 马康巴教〔伏都教与基督教的某些教义相结合的巴西的一种宗教〕.
Mad., Madm. = Madam.
mad [mæd] *a.* ***(~der; ~dest)*** ①狂, 发狂的, 疯狂的; (狗等)患狂犬病的. ②凶猛的, 狂暴的; 鲁莽的, 糊涂的. ③狂热的, 入迷的. ④〔口〕愤怒的, 生气的 *(at; about)*. ⑤非常高兴的, 极快活的. *He was very ~.* 〔美〕他非常生气. *a ~ torrent* 激流. ***be ~ about [after; for; on]*** 急切地想, 发狂似地想; 迷于, 迷着…. ***be ~ at*** 对…发怒 (*I was rather ~ at missing my train.* 我没赶上火车, 气极了). ***be ~ with joy*** 狂喜. ***drive [send] sb. ~*** 使(人)发狂. ***go ~*** 发狂. ***have a ~ time*** 欢闹一场. ***hopping ~*** 〔口〕气得直跳; 怒不可遏. ***like ~*** 〔口〕迅速地, 猛烈地. ***~ as a March hare [as a hatter]*** (象春兔一样)疯狂的. ***~ as a wet hen*** 〔美〕非常生气. ***run ~ = go ~. run ~ after something*** 给…迷住, 狂爱…. — *vt., vi.* *(p., p.p.* ***madded)***〔罕〕= madden. **~ apple** 茄子. **~brained** *a.* 莽撞的; 奔放的; 狂热的. **~cap** ① *n.* 狂妄的人, 鲁莽的人. ②*a.* 鲁莽的, 荒唐的 (*~cap pranks* 胡作妄为的恶作剧; 胡闹). **~-doctor** 精神病医生. **~house** 精神病院, 疯人院; 混乱、吵闹的场所; 〔美空俚〕驾驶室. **~man** 疯子; 〔美卡车司机语〕= highjacker. **~ minute** 〔军口〕(一分钟 12—15 发的)猛烈射击. **~ money** 〔美〕女人身边带的钱; 女人藏着以备急需的一点钱, 女人的私财. **~woman** 女狂人, 女疯子. **-ly** *ad.* 疯狂地, 疯狂似地; 莽撞地, 狂热地; 粗野地; 狂怒地; 愚蠢地; 极端地. **-ness** *n.* 癫狂; 狂乱, 狂暴; 疯狂, 热狂.
Mad·a·gas·car [ˌmædəˈgæskə] *n.* ①马达加斯加〔非洲, 马尔加什共和国的简称〕. ②马达加斯加岛〔非洲〕.
mad·am [ˈmædəm] *n.* *(pl.* ***~s,*** 或 ***mes·dames*** [ˈmeidæm]*)* ①夫人, 太太, 女士〔对妇女的尊称, 以前代替 Mrs. 用于姓前称呼长辈的妇女; 在其他字句之后, 口语常略作 ma'am, mam, 俚语略作 marm, mum, m'm 或 m. 例: yes, ma'am; no, ma'am; 〔俚〕 yes, 'm, no, 'm; thank you, ma'am〕. ②(家庭)主妇. ③〔口〕喜欢差使别人的女子. ④妓院鸨母. *This way please, ~.* 这边请, 女士〔接待用语, 复数借用 ladies〕. *(Dear) M-* (亲爱的) 女士〔书信中对不熟识女子的称呼, 可兼指已婚或未婚〕.
mad·ame [ˈmædəm, F. madam] *n.* *(pl.* ***mesdames*** [ˈmeidæm] 或 *~s)* 〔F.〕①太太〔对已婚妇女的法国式称呼〕; 夫人〔用于妇人姓前或称号前的法国式尊称〕; 女歌唱家、艺术家相互间的称号. ②〔美俚〕妓院老板娘, 老鸨. ***M- Tussaud's*** [təˈsəuz, -ˈsɔːdz] (伦敦的)塔梭滋夫人蜡像陈列馆.
mad·a·ro·sis [ˌmædəˈrəusis] *n.* 【医】睫毛脱落; 眉毛脱落.
mad·den [ˈmædn] *vt.* 使发狂; 使大怒. — *vi.* 〔罕〕发狂.
mad·den·ing [ˈmædniŋ] *a.* 使人发狂的; 使人气极的. **-ly** *ad.*
mad·der [ˈmædə] *n.* 【植】茜草属植物茜草根; 【纺】茜草染料; 鲜红色.
mad·ding [ˈmædiŋ] *a.* ①发狂的, 癫狂的, 疯狂的. ②使人狂怒的. *set the world ~* 使举世若狂.
mad·dish [ˈmædiʃ] *a.* 微狂的.
made [meid] *make* 的过去式及过去分词. — *a.* ①…制的, (人工)做成的; 拼成的. ②体格…的. ③保证成功的. ④虚构的. *foreign-~ [ready-~] clothes* 外国做的〔现成的〕衣服. *~ land [ground]* 填筑地. *a ~ story* 编造出来的故事. *He is ~ of money.* 他很有钱. *a ~ dish* 杂烩. *well-~* 体格好的. *a ~ man* 成功者. ***be ~ from*** 由…制成的. ***be ~ of*** …制的, 用…制成的. ***~ up of*** 由…组成. **~-to-order** *a.* 定制的; 合身的. **~-up** *a.* ①制成的; 拼好版的. ②虚构的, 捏造的; 做作的. ③化了妆〔装〕的. ④决定了的; 坚定的 (*a made-up tie* 预制固定式的领结. *made-up lips* 涂了口红的嘴唇).
Ma·dei·ra [məˈdiərə] *n.* ①马德拉(群)岛〔在非洲西北部大西洋中〕. ②〔常 m-〕(马德拉岛产的)白葡萄酒; 马德拉蛋糕(= ~ cake). ③〔*Rio ~*〕马代拉河〔巴西〕.
Ma·de·leine [ˈmædəlin, ˈmædəlein] *n.* ①马德琳〔女子名〕. ②[m-] 重油杯糕.
Ma·de·le·ni·an [ˌmædiˈliːniən] *a.* = Magdalenian.
Mad·e·line [ˈmædəlin, ˈmædəlain] *n.* 马德琳〔女子名〕.
ma·de·moi·selle [ˌmædəməˈzel] *n.* 〔F.〕 *(pl.* ***mes·de·moi·selles*** [ˌmeidmwɑˈzel, ˌmeidəmˈzel]*)* 小姐〔用于未婚女子姓名前的法国式敬称, 与英语 Miss 相当, 单数略为 Mlle., 复数略为 Mlles.〕; 〔英〕法国女(家庭)教师.
Madge [mædʒ] *n.* 玛奇〔女子名, Margaret 的昵称〕.
ma·di·a [ˈmeidiə] *n.* 【植】智利向日葵. **~-oil** 智利葵子油〔橄榄油的代用品, 渣作饲料〕.
Mad·i·son[1] [ˈmædisn] *n.* ①墨迪逊〔姓氏〕. ② **James ~** 詹姆斯·墨迪逊〔1751—1836, 美国第四任总统〕.
Mad·i·son[2] [ˈmædisn] *n.* 麦迪逊〔美国城市〕. **~ Avenue** 麦迪逊大街〔美国纽约市的一条街, 美国广告业中心〕.
Madm. = Madam.
Ma·don·na [məˈdɔnə] *n.* ①【宗】圣母(玛利亚); 圣母画像〔雕像〕. ②〔m-〕〔It.〕= madam. **~ lily** 白百合花.
Ma·dras [məˈdrɑːs] *n.* ①马德拉斯〔印度港市〕. ②〔m-〕马德拉斯狭条衬衫布.
ma·dre [ˈmɑːdre] *n.* 〔Sp.〕母亲.
mad·re·pore [ˌmædriˈpɔː] *n.* 【动】石珊瑚, 石蚕〔珊瑚的一种〕.
mad·re·por·ite [ˈmædriˌpɔːrait] *n.* 【动】(棘皮动物体中, 海水进入脉管系统的)筛板, 穿孔板.
Ma·drid [məˈdrid] *n.* 马德里〔西班牙的首都〕. **-drile·ni·an** [mædriˈliːniən] *a.* 马德里的. — *n.* 马德里人.
mad·ri·gal [ˈmɑdrigəl] *n.* 情歌; 小曲; 【乐】牧歌.
Ma·dri·le·ña [mɑːdriˈlenjɑː] *n.* *(pl.* ***-s)*** 〔Sp.〕马德里(Madrid) 女人.
ma·dri·lène [ˌmædriˈlen; *F.* mɑdriːˈlɛn] *n.* 〔F.〕马德里蕃茄肉汤.
Ma·dri·le·ño [mɑːdriˈleinjəu] *n.* *(pl.* ***-s)*** 〔Sp.〕马德里(男)人.
ma·du·ro [məˈduərəu] *a., n.* 〔Sp.〕浓烈的(雪茄烟).
mad·wort [ˈmædwəːt] *n.* 【植】①庭荠属植物. ②香雪

球 (= alyssum).
mae [mei] *a., n., ad.* 〔Scot.〕 more 的变体.
Mae·ce·nas [mi(:)'si:næs] *n.* 文学、艺术的赞助者〔原为维吉尔 (Virgil) 及霍拉斯 (Horace) 的保护者〕.
Mael·strom ['meilstrəum] *n.* 挪威西海岸的大漩涡; 〔m-〕大旋流;大祸乱,灾害.
mae·nad ['mi:næd] *n.* ①= bacchante. ②激动异常的女人;疯狂的女人. **-ic** [mi'nædik] *a.*
ma·es·to·so [ˌmɑ:es'təuzəu, -səu] *a., ad.* 〔It.〕【乐】庄严的〔地〕,雄伟的〔地〕.
ma·es·tro [mɑ:'estrəu] *n.* *(pl.* ***~s, -tri*** [tri:]; *fem.* ***-tra*** [trə]*)* 〔It.〕 艺术大师〔大作曲家, 名指挥等〕; 〔美俚〕 ['maistrəu] 乐队指挥〔领班〕; (球队等的)领队.
Mae·ter·linck ['meitəliŋk], **Maurice** 梅特林克 〔1862—1947, 比利时剧作家, 诗人. 获 1911 年诺贝尔文学奖〕.
Mae West ['mei'west] 〔军俚〕(飞行员穿的)海上救生衣〔源为美国一电影女明星名〕.
maf·fick ['mæfik] *vi.* 〔英口〕狂欢庆祝,狂喜.
Ma·fi·a, Maf·fi·a ['mɑ:fiə] *n.* 〔It.〕 ①〔m-〕(西西里的)民众对法律和政府的敌视; 反政府秘密组织. ②(美国等)社会黑帮,黑手党.
maf·ic ['mæfik] *a.* 【地】(火成岩的)镁铁质.
Ma·fi·o·si [ˌmɑ:fi'əusi] *n. pl. (sing.* ***-so*** [-ˌsəu]*)* 〔It.〕 ①反政府秘密组织成员; 社会黑帮分子. ②〔m-〕黑手党成员.
MAG =military advisory group 军事顾问团.
mag¹ [mæg] *n.* 〔英俚〕半辨士.
mag² [mæg] *n.* = magneto. *a ~-generator* 永磁发电机; (手摇)磁石发电机.
mag. = ①magazine. ②magnetic; magnetism. ③magneto. ④magnitude.
mag·a·zine [ˌmægə'zi:n] *n.* ①杂志; 期刊〔原义'知识的宝库'〕. ②弹药库,仓库; (连发枪的)弹仓,弹匣, 弹盘. ③(自动加煤炉的)燃料储存仓. ④【摄】底片〔胶卷〕盒. ⑤资源地, 宝库. *an expense ~* 临时弹药库. ~ **gun [rifle]** 连发枪. ~ **stove** 自动加煤炉.
Mag·da·len, Mag·da·le·ne ['mægdəlin, 'mægdəli:n] *n.* ①马格德琳〔女子名〕. ②〔the ~〕【圣】抹大拉的马利亚〔原为妓女, 后改恶向善, 见《路加福音》〕. ③[m-] 从良的妓女; 〔英〕济良所, 妓女收容所 (= ~ home). **Magdalen** ['mɔ:dlin] **College** 英国牛津大学莫德林学院.
Mag·da·le·ni·an [ˌmægdə'li:njen] *a., n.* 【考古】马格德林(期)〔欧洲旧石器时代的最后期〕.
mage [meidʒ] *n.* 〔古〕魔法师; 魔术家; 学者.
Ma·gel·lan [mə'gelən, -'dʒelən], **Ferdinand** 麦哲伦〔1480?—1521, 葡萄牙航海家〕.
Mag·el·lan·ic [mægə'lænik, mædʒə-] *a.* 麦哲伦的; 麦哲伦发现的. ~ **clouds** 【天】麦哲伦云〔南半球所见空中的星云〕.
Ma·gen Da·vid [mɑ:'gein dɑ:'vi:d, 'mɔ:gən 'dɔ:vid] 〔Heb.〕 大卫之星; 六角星〔犹太教和以色列的标志, 由一正一倒的两个等边三角形套在一起组成〕 (= Star of David).
ma·gen·ta [mə'dʒentə] *n.* 红色苯胺染料; (碱性)品红; 洋红. — *a.* 品红色的.
Mag·gie ['mægi] *n.* 玛吉〔女子名〕.
mag·got ['mægət] *n.* ①(尤指干酪蝇的)蛆. ②空想,狂想,奇想. ***have a ~ in one's head [brain]*** 想入非非, 异想天开. ***when the ~ bites*** 有兴致的时候.
mag·got·y ['mægəti] *a.* ①多蛆的. ②胡思乱想的, 想入非非的.
mag·hem·ite [mæg'hemait] *n.* 【矿】磁赤铁矿.
Ma·gi ['meidʒai] *n. pl. (sing.* ***Magus****)* ①【圣】〔the (three) ~〕(由东方来朝拜初生基督的)三贤人. ②古波斯祆教僧侣阶级.
Ma·gi·an ['meidʒiən] *a.* 古波斯祆教僧侣的. — *n.* 古波斯祆教僧侣; 祆教徒; 魔法师,魔术家.
Ma·gi·an·ism ['meidʒiənzəm] *n.* (古波斯的)祆教.
mag·ic ['mædʒik] *a.* 魔术的,巫术的,幻术的; 不可思议的,有奇异魔力的. ~ *words* 咒. *a ~ wand* 魔杖. ~ *beauty* 妖艳无比的美丽. — *n.* 魔法, 巫术, 幻术, 妖术; 魔术,戏法; 不可思议的魔力. *black [white] ~* 驱使恶魔〔天神〕的魔术. *natural ~* (不借助神力的)奇术. ***as (if) by ~*** 象使用魔术般. ***like ~*** 不可思议地快; 立刻,马上. ~ **cube** 魔方〔玩具〕. ~ **hand** (核反应堆等操作时用的)机械手,人造手. ~ **lantern** 幻灯. ~ **nucleus** 【原】幻核. ~ **square** 纵横图,幻方〔一大方框分成井字形的小方框,小方框中的数字纵向相加或横向相加,其和相等〕.
mag·i·cal ['mædʒikəl] *a.* = magic. **-ly** *ad.*
ma·gi·cian [mə'dʒiʃən] *n.* 魔法师,妖道,术士; 魔术家, 变戏法的人.
ma·gilp [mə'gilp] *n.* (油画调色用)溶油 (= megilp).
Maginot Line ['mæʒinəu] 马其诺防线〔第二次世界大战前法国在德法边境所建造〕.
mag·is·te·ri·al [ˌmædʒis'tiərəl] *a.* ①长官(一样)的. ②教师的; 师长作风的; 严正的,有权威的. ③横暴的,傲慢的. ④公平的,公正的(人等). ⑤硕士的.
mag·is·tra·cy ['mædʒistrəsi] *n.* 长官的职务〔职权、职位、任期等〕; 〔集合词〕地方行政官; 地方行政官的管辖区.
ma·gis·tral [mə'dʒistrəl] *a.* 教师的,主人的; 按医师处方的; 〔罕〕有权威的,独断的. *the ~ staff* (学校的)全体教职员.
mag·is·trate ['mædʒistrit, -treit] *n.* (行政兼司法的)长官〔地方长官、市长等〕; 治安法庭法官. *the Chief [First] M-* 君主,元首,总统. *a civil [judicial] ~* 行政〔司法〕官. *a Police M-* 违警罪法庭法官. **-ship** *magistrate* 的职务〔地位、任期〕.
Mag·le·mo·si·an [ˌmægli'məuziən] *a.* (中石器时代中期欧洲北部)马格来莫斯文化的.
mag·ma ['mægmə] *n.* *(pl.* ***~ta*** [-tə], ***~s****)* (矿物,有机物等的)稀糊状混合物; 【地】岩浆; 稠液; 【药】乳浆剂.
magn. = ①magnetism. ②magneto.
Mag·na C(h)ar·ta ['mægnə'kɑ:tə] ①【英史】大宪章. ②(一般)保障公民权利、自由的法令.
mag·na cum lau·de ['mɑ:gnɑ:kum'laude, 'mægnəkʌm'lɔudi:] 〔L.〕 优异成绩 (毕业)〔表彰高等院校毕业生用语〕.
Mag·na est ve·ri·tas, et prae·va·le·bit ['mægnə est 'veritəs et pri:'vælibit] 〔L.〕 真理伟大,终必胜利.
mag·na·li·um [mæg'neiljəm] *n.*、【冶】镁铝合金.
mag·na·nim·i·ty [ˌmægnə'nimiti] *n.* 宽仁, 雅量, 高尚; 宽宏大量的行为; 高尚的行为.
mag·nan·i·mous [mæg'næniməs] *a.* 气量大的, 高尚的. **-ly** *ad.*
mag·nate ['mægneit] *n.* 大资本家,巨头,富豪; 权贵; …大王. *an oil ~* 煤油大王. *a territorial ~* 大地主. *the financial ~s* 金融巨头.
mag·ne·sia [mæg'ni:ʃə] *n.* 【化】氧化镁; 【矿】镁氧; 〔口〕碳酸镁〔泻盐〕. *carbonate of ~* = *~ alba* 碳酸镁. ~ *brick* 镁砖. ~ *cement* 镁氧水泥. ~ *mica* 黑云母. ~ *spar* 菱镁矿. *sulphate of ~* 硫酸镁, 泻盐.
mag·ne·sian [mæg'ni:ʃən] *a.* 镁的; (含)氧化镁的. ~ *limestone* 白云石,含镁石灰岩.
mag·ne·site ['mægnisait] *n.* 【矿】菱镁矿; 【化】碳酸镁.
mag·ne·si·um [mæg'ni:zjəm] *n.* 【化】镁. ~ *alloy* 镁合金. ~ *bomb* 镁燃烧弹. ~ *flare* 镁光照明弹. ~ *light* 【摄】镁光灯.
mag·net ['mægnit] *n.* ①磁体; 磁石; 磁铁. ②有吸引力

M

的东西[人]. *a bar* ~ 条形磁铁[体]. *a horseshoe* ~ 马蹄形磁铁. *a natural* ~ 天然磁.

mag·net·ic [mæg'netik] *a.* ①磁(性)的;(可)磁化的. ②吸引人心的;有魅力的. ③催眠术的. ~ **amplifier**【无】磁放大器. ~ **attraction** 磁吸引. ~ **axis** 磁轴. ~ **bearing** 磁针方位. ~ **bottle**【物】磁瓶. ~ **clutch** 磁力离合器. ~ **compass** 磁罗盘. ~ **core** 磁心. ~ **course** 磁航向, 磁罗盘航向. ~ **declination [deviation]**【物】磁差,磁偏; 偏差; 磁偏角. ~ **detector**【无】磁性检波器. ~ **elements** 地磁要素. ~ **equator**【天】磁赤道. (= aclinic line). ~ **field** 磁场. ~ **flux** 磁通量. ~ **force** 磁力. ~ **hysteresis** 磁滞. ~ **induction**【物】磁感应;磁感应强度 (又作 ~ flux density). ~ **ink** 磁性墨水. ~ **iron** 磁铁. ~ **meridian**【天】磁子午线. ~ **mine** 磁(性水)雷. ~ **moment** 磁矩. ~ **needle** 磁针, 指南针. ~ **north** 磁北. ~ **permeability** 导磁系数,导磁性. ~ **pickup**【无】电磁式拾波[音]器; 变磁阻拾音器. ~ **pole** 磁极. ~ **recorder** 磁录音机;磁记录器; (电视)录像机. ~ **recording**【无】磁录音. ~ **reluctance** 磁阻. ~ **storm** 磁暴. ~ **tape** 磁带. ~ **wire** 磁线,磁导线,磁性钢丝;录音钢丝.

mag·net·ics [mæg'netiks] *n.* 磁学;磁性元件.

mag·net·ism ['mægnitizəm] *n.* ①磁(性),磁力;磁学. ②(人格、道德等的)吸引力,魅力;催眠术. *animal* ~ 动物磁性说. *terrestrial* ~ 地磁;地磁学.

mag·net·ist ['mægnitist] *n.* 磁学家;催眠术家.

mag·ne·tite ['mænitait] *n.*【矿】磁铁矿.

mag·net·i·za·tion [ˌmægnitai'zeiʃən] *n.* 磁化(强度); 起磁.

mag·net·ize ['mægnitaiz] *vt.* ①使磁化,使生磁性;使有磁力. ②吸引, 感动. ③催眠. — *vi.* 受磁. **-r** *n.* 磁化器.

mag·ne·to [mæg'ni:təu] *n.* *(pl.* ~*s)*, 磁电机;永磁发电机〔*magneto-electric machine* 或 *magneto-dynamo* 之略〕; 磁石式,永磁式. ~ *generator* 永磁发电机. ~ *system* 永磁(电话)式.

magneto- *comb. f.* = magnetic.

mag·ne·to·bell [mæg'ni:təubel] *n.* 磁石电铃.

mag·ne·to·elas·tic·i·ty [mæg'ni:təuˌelæs'tisiti] *n.*【物】磁致弹性.

mag·ne·to·e·lec·tric [mæg'ni:təui'lektrik] *a.*【物】磁电的.

mag·ne·to·e·lec·tric·i·ty [mæg'ni:təuiˌlek'trisiti] *n.* 磁电.

mag·ne·to·gas·dy·nam·ics [mæg'ni:təuˌgæsdai'næmiks] *n.* 磁性气体动力学.

mag·ne·to·graph [mæg'ni:təugrɑ:f, -græf] *n.* 地磁强度记录仪.

mag·ne·to·hy·dro·dy·nam·ics [mæg'ni:təuˌhaidrəudai'næmiks] *n. pl.* 〔动词用单数〕磁流体动力学. **-ic** *a.*

mag·ne·tom·e·ter [ˌmægni'tɔmitə] *n.* 磁强计;地磁仪.

mag·ne·to·mo·tive [mægˌni:təu'məutiv] *a.* 起磁的, 生磁流之力的.

mag·ne·ton ['mægnitɔn] *n.* 磁子.

mag·ne·to·phone [mæg'ni:təufəun] *n.* 磁带录音机[器].

mag·ne·tor ['mægnitə] *n.* 磁电机.

mag·ne·to·re·sist·ance [mægˌni:təuri'zistəns] *n.*【物】磁致电阻. **-sistive** *a.*

mag·ne·to·scope [mæg'ni:təuskəup] *n.* 验磁器.

mag·ne·to·sphere [mæg'ni:təusfiə] *n.*【天】磁层. **-sphe·ric** [-'sfiərik, -'sfɛə-] *a.*

mag·ne·to·stric·tion [mægˌni:təu'strikʃən] *n.*【物】磁致伸缩;磁力控制.

mag·ne·to·tel·e·phone [mæg'ni:təu'telifəun] *n.* 永磁电话.

mag·ne·tron ['mænitrɔn] *n.*【无】磁控(电子)管. *rising-sun* ~ 旭日型磁控管.

magni- *comb. f.* 大 (*opp.* micro-).

mag·nif·ic, mag·nif·i·cal [mæg'nifik, -ikəl] *a.*〔古〕庄严的,崇高的,壮丽的,宏伟的,堂皇的;豪言壮语的.

Mag·nif·i·cat [mæg'nifikæt] *n.* (晚祷时唱的)圣母马利亚赞美歌;〔*m*-〕颂歌, 赞美歌. **sing** ~ **at matins** 夏裘冬葛,做事不合时宜〔早祷唱晚祷颂歌〕.

mag·ni·fi·ca·tion [ˌmægnifi'keiʃən] *n.* 放大,扩大;夸张;称赞;【光】放大率[倍数].

mag·nif·i·cence [mæg'nifisns] *n.* 宏大,庄严,壮丽,堂皇,豪华.

mag·nif·i·cent [mæg'nifisnt] *a.* 宏大的,庄严的, 堂皇的; (衣服、装饰等)华丽的; 极其动人的; (体型)优美的, 健壮的;〔口〕顶刮刮的. **-ly** *ad.*

mag·nif·i·co [mæg'nifikəu] *n.* *(pl.* ~*es)* (古时)威尼斯共和国的贵族;要人,权贵.

mag·ni·fi·er ['mægnifaiə] *n.* 放大者;扩大者; 放大镜; 放大器.

mag·ni·fy ['mægnifai] *vt.* ①(凸镜等)扩大, 放大, 映大. ②夸张,夸大;〔古〕推崇,夸奖; 赞美;〔罕〕增大. ~ *oneself* 自大, 自夸. ~ *oneself against* … 尊己抑人. ~**ing glass** 放大镜. ~**ing power** 放大率.

mag·nil·o·quence [mæg'niləkwəns] *n.* (文风、语言等)华而不实;大话;虚夸.

mag·nil·o·quent [mæg'niləkwənt] *a.* 华而不实的, 夸张的,夸大的,吹牛的. **-ly** *ad.*

mag·ni·tude ['mægnitju:d] *n.* 广大,巨大;伟大, 重大, 重要性; 大小; 积; 量;【数】量值;【天】(恒星的)等, 等级, 光度. ~ *equation*【天】星等差. ~ *of eclipse*【天】食分. *of the first* ~ (星的光度)(第)一等的; 最大的; 最重要的(人物等).

mag·no·li·a [mæg'nəuljə] *n.*【植】木兰. **M- State**〔美〕密西西比州的别名.

mag·non ['mægnɔn] *n.*【物】磁振子.

mag·num ['mægnəm] *n.* ①(两夸脱容量的)大酒瓶,一大酒瓶. ②〔M-〕马格南左轮(手枪) (=~ revolver). ~ **bonum** ['bəunəm] 大黄李;大马铃薯.

mag·num o·pus ['mægnəm 'əupəs]〔L.〕个人的重大事业;(文学、艺术上的)大作,杰作,巨著.

Mag·nus effect ['mægnəs i'fekt]【物】马格努斯效应.

mag·nus hitch ['mægnəs hitʃ]【海】三重结〔一种绳结〕.

mag·ot ['mægət, mɑ:'gəu] *n.* ①(中国及日本的瓷制或象牙制的、装在瓶盖等上作捏手的) 奇形偶像. ②【动】北非产无尾猿(=Barbary ape).

mag·pie ['mægpai] *n.* ①【鸟】鹊. ②碎嘴子, 爱说话的人. ③〔俚〕半辨士. ④靶子自外数第二圈, 打中自外数第二圈的一枪〔打中这一圈时, 用黑白旗打信号, 故名〕. ⑤(花边的)黑白花纹.

M. Agr. = Master of Agriculture 农科硕士.

mags·man ['mægzmən] *n.* ①杂志撰稿人. ②〔俚〕骗子.

mag·uey ['mægwei] *n.*【植】龙舌兰; 〔美〕牧童用的索子 (= maguey rope). ~ *hemp* 剑麻.

ma·gus ['meigəs] *n.* *(pl. magi*['meidʒai]*)* ①古波斯僧, 祆教僧. ②(古代的)魔术家,占星家.

Mag·yar ['mægjɑ:] *n.* (匈牙利的)马札尔人;马札尔语, 匈牙利语. — *a.* 马札尔人的, 马札尔[匈牙利]语的. ~ *(blouse)* (袖子和其他部分连成一块的)马札尔衫.

Ma·gyar·or·szág ['mɔdjɑ:ɔ:sɑ:g] "匈牙利"的匈语名称.

ma·ha·ra·ja(h) [ˌmɑ:hə'rɑ:dʒə] *n.* 大君〔印度土邦主〕.

ma·ha·ra·ni, -nee [ˌmɑ:hə'rɑ:ni:] *n.* 大君妃〔印度土邦主的妻〕;女土邦主,女大君.

ma·hat·ma [mə'hætmə] *n.*〔Sans.〕(密教的)大善知识;

大圣,圣雄;圣贤;伟人.

Ma·ha·ya·na [ˌməhɑːˈjɑːnə] *n.* 〔Sans.〕【佛】大乘,摩诃衍.

Mah·di [ˈmɑːdi(ː)] *n. (pl. ~s)* (伊斯兰教)救世主.

Mah·dism [ˈmɑːdizəm] *n.* (伊斯兰教)救世主降临说.

Ma·hi·can [məˈhiːkən] *n.* ①马希坎部落〔美国阿尔衮琴印第安人的一个部落,主要居于哈德逊河上游流域〕. ②马希坎人. ③莫希坎人 (= Mohegan). —*a.* 马希坎人的.

mah-jong(g) [ˈmɑːˈdʒɔŋ] 〔汉〕麻将牌,麻雀牌.

mahl·stick [ˈmɔːlstik] *n.* = maulstick.

ma·hog·a·ny [məˈhɔgəni] *n.*【植】桃花心木; 红木; 赤褐色;〔口〕食桌,餐桌; 蜜味杜松子酒. *the Chinese ~* 香椿. ***be under the ~*** 醉倒在食桌下. ***put [stretch] one's legs under sb.'s ~*** 受人款待; 作某人的食客. ***with one's knees under the ~*** 就席,坐席.

Ma·hom·e·dan, Ma·hom·et·an [məˈhɔmidən, məˈhɔmitən] *a., n.* = Mohammedan.

Ma·hom·et [məˈhɔmit] *n.* = Mohammed.

Ma·hom·et·an·ism [məˈhɔmitənizəm] *n.* = Mohammedanism.

ma·ho·ni·a [məˈhəuniə] *n.*【植】十大功劳属植物.

Ma·hound [məˈhaund -ˈhuːnd] ①〔古〕= Mohammed. ②〔Scot.〕魔鬼.

ma·hout [məˈhaut] *n.* 驭象人,象夫.

Mah·rat·ta [məˈrɑːtə] *n.* (西印度)马哈拉特邦人,马拉他人.

Mah·rat·ti, Mah·ra·ti, Ma·ra·thi [məˈrɑːti] *n.* (印度的)马拉他语.

mah·seer [ˈmɑːsiə] *n.* 马西亚鱼〔印度的一种河鱼〕.

mah·zor [mɑːhˈzɔː, ˈmɑːhzə] *n.* *(pl.* ***-zors*** Heb. ***-zor·im*** [-ˈzɔːrim]) 犹太祷告书〔内有各节日的礼拜仪式〕.

maid [meid] *n.* ①处女,未婚女子,闺女;〔诗〕少女,姑娘. ②婢,侍女,女仆. *an old ~* 老处女. *a lady's ~* 侍女. *a ~ in waiting = a ~ of honour. a ~ of all work* 什么活儿都干的女仆. *a ~ of hono(u)r* ①〔英〕英国女王[王后、公主]的(未婚)女侍从官. ②〔美〕(主要)女傧相. ③杏仁柠檬蛋糊饼.

mai·dan [maiˈdɑːn] *n.* 〔印度英语〕练兵场,操场;(用作市场或散步场的)空地,广场.

maid·en [ˈmeidn] *n.* 〔古〕①处女,未婚女子,闺女;少女. ②【英史】苏格兰的一种断头台. ③= ~ over.— *a.* 〔通常只用作定语〕①处女的,少女的;未婚的. ②纯洁的,清净的. ③初次的,还未用过[经历过等]的;(巡回法庭)无案件的. *a ~ aunt* 独身姑母. *a ~ lady* 未婚女人. *a ~ speech* (议员等的)首次演说. *a ~ voyage* 初次航行. *a ~ battle* 初次战斗. *~ soil* 处女地,未垦地. *a ~ assize* 没有刑事案件的巡回法庭. *a ~ castle [fortress]* 从未陷落过的城寨. *a ~ flight* 初次飞行. *a ~ horse* 从未跑赢过的马. *one's ~ name* 女子的娘家姓氏. *a ~ race* 全由未跑赢过的马参加的赛马. *a ~ sword* 新刀,尚未染过血的剑. **~hair**【植】掌叶铁线蕨;铁线蕨. **~hair tree**【植】银杏树,公孙树,白果树. **~head** ①〔古〕= maidhood, **~hood.** ②【解】处女膜. **~-hood** 处女性,处女时期. **~ over**【板球】未得分的投球.

maid·en·ish [ˈmeidniʃ] *a.* 处女的,处女似的;老处女似的.

maid·en·like [ˈmeidnlaik] *a.* 处女似的;柔和的,羞涩的,羞答答的.

maid·en·li·ness [ˈmeidnlinis] *n.* 处女态;羞涩,柔和,娇羞.

maid·en·ly [ˈmeidnli] *a.* 处女似的,少女似的;谨慎的,柔和的,娇羞的.

maid·ish [ˈmeidiʃ] *a.* 少女(一样)的;老处女的.

maid·ser·vant [ˈmeidsəːvənt] *n.* 女仆.

ma·ieu·tic, -ti·cal [meiˈjuːtik(l)] *a.* (苏格拉底的)启发式问答法的;(思想上的)助产术的.

mai·gre [ˈmeigə] *a.* 素的,吃斋的. *The doctor advised me to live ~ (= on ~ food).* 医生嘱咐我吃素.

mai·hem [ˈmeihem] *n.*【法】①残害人的肢体[器官]的罪. ②蓄意损害;有意识挑起的暴行(=mayhem).

mail[1] [meil] *n.* 锁子甲;铠甲;(动物的)锁子状甲壳. —*vt.* 使穿锁子甲. **~-clad** *a.* 穿着锁子甲的.

mail[2] [meil] *n.* ①邮政;邮袋;〔the ~〕〔美〕(一批)邮件,邮件的一次发送[收集]〔英国限指寄到国外的邮件,一般邮件用 *the post*〕. ②邮件运输工具〔邮船、邮车等〕. ③邮务员,邮递员. ④〔*pl.*〕〔美〕邮递;邮政(制度). ⑤〔古〕袋,旅行包,行囊. *an ordinary [a surface] ~* 平信;陆上(或海上)邮递. *the Indian ~* 〔英〕寄往印度的邮件. *air ~* 航空(邮件). *Is there any ~ for me?* 〔美〕我有信吗? ***by ~*** 〔美〕邮(寄)(=〔英〕by post). —*vt.* 〔美〕把(邮件)投入邮箱;邮寄. *~ a letter* 寄信. **~bag**〔美〕邮袋. **~boat** 邮船. **~box** 邮箱. **~ car** (铁路)邮车. **~ carrier** 邮递员. **~ cart** 邮车;(手推)婴儿车. **~ catcher** 邮包装卸器〔火车行进中将邮包装上或卸下邮车的装置〕. **~ chute** (可使大楼上层邮件自动落入楼下邮箱内的)邮件滑送槽. **~ clerk** 〔美〕邮局办事员;(机关、企业中)邮件管理员. **~coach** 邮件马车. **~ cover**〔美〕邮检制度. **~ day** 邮件截止日. **~ drop** ①邮筒;邮筒槽口. ②秘密通信地址. **~man**〔美〕邮递员. **~ matter** 邮件. **~-order** 函购,邮购 (*a ~-order house* 邮售商行). **~ plane** 邮(政飞)机. **~ train** 邮(政列)车.

mail·a·ble [ˈmeiləbl] *a.* 能邮寄的.

mailed [meild] *a.* 披着锁子甲的,装甲的;【动】被甲的. *the ~ fist* 武力,铁腕.

Mail·er [ˈmeilə] *n.* 梅勒〔姓氏〕.

mail·er [ˈmeilə] *n.* ①邮寄者. ②邮件打戳、分类、称重机. ③邮寄品的容器. ④邮船. ⑤附在信件中的广告印刷品.

mail·ing [ˈmeiliŋ] *n.* 邮寄;邮寄品;邮寄者一次寄发的一批邮件. *a ~ list* 通信[发送]名单. *a ~ machine* = mailer ②. *a ~(-)table* 邮件分理台. *a ~ tube* 邮寄纸筒〔寄印刷品或易碎品用〕.

Mail·lard [ˈmeiləd] *n.* 梅勒德〔姓氏〕.

mail·lot [maiˈjəu] 〔F.〕①(体操运动员)紧身衣. ②整件女游泳衣.

maim [meim] *vt.* 残害;使残废;使负重伤.

maimed [meimd] *a.* 负重伤的,残废的.

main [mein] *a.* ①主要的,主,全,总. ②充分的,尽量的;全力的,有力的. *the ~ clause* 主要分句,主句. *a ~ event* =〔俚〕*a ~ go* 主要比赛. *the ~ fleet* 主力舰队. *~ operations* 主力战. *the ~ pipe* 总管(道). *a ~ squeeze* 〔美俚〕中心人物,首脑,大老板. *the ~ line* 〔英〕(铁路)干线;〔美〕主血管;【电话】中继线. ***by ~ force [strength]*** 全力;全靠武力[力量]. **~ chance** 获利良机 (*have an eye for the ~ chance* 注意抓住谋取私利的良机). ***with ~ strength*** 用全力; —*n.* ①体力,气力,力〔仅用于 *with might and ~* 中〕;主要部分,要点〔仅用于 *for [in] the ~* 中〕; ②〔诗〕大海,大洋;〔古〕本土(= mainland). ③(自来水、煤气等的)总管;干线,干管. ④【海】= mainmast; mainsail. *water from the ~* 自来水. *a water ~* 自来水总管. *a supply ~* 自来水总管;馈电干线. ***for [in] the ~*** 大体上,大致,大抵. ***turn on the ~*** 〔俚〕哭出来. ***with (all one's) might and ~*** 尽全力. —*vt.* 〔美俚〕把(海洛因等)注射进静脉. **~-beam**【海】全船面. **~ body**【军】主力,本队;(文件的)正文. **~ boom**【船】主帆桁. **~ brace**【海】大桅转桁索 (*splice the ~ brace* 〔海俚〕拿酒给船员喝;痛饮). **~ centre** 中枢. **~ course** = mainsail; 主要课程; 主菜. **~ deck**【船】主甲板;(两层甲板时的)上甲板,正甲板;(三层甲板时的)中甲板. **~ drag** 〔美俚〕

(城市、村镇的)主街,大街. ~ **frame** 计算机〔尤指外部辅助装置除外的机器本身〕. ~ **hatch**【船】主舱口;中部舱口. ~ **hold**【船】中部船舱. ~**land** 大陆,本土〔对岛屿、半岛而言〕. ~**line** 主线;(铁路)干线,正线;〔美俚〕主血管;对主血管的海洛英注射. ~**mast**【船】大桅,主桅. ~ **plane**〔英军〕机翼;主翼. ~ **prise**【法】对罪犯按期出庭的保证. ~ **royal**【海】大桅最高第二帆. ~**sail**【船】(横帆船 main yard 上、纵帆船 main gaff 上的)大帆,主帆. ~**sheet** 主帆索. ~**spring** 主发条;主要原因,主要动机. ~**stay**【船】大桅主索;中坚,台柱;靠山,主要的生活来源 (*Agriculture is the ~stay of a country.* 农为国本). ~ **stem** = ~**stream** *n.* 主流;主要倾向;(事物的)极富于生命力的部分. ~**top** *n.*【船】大桅楼 (~*top gallant-mast*【海】大二接桅. ~*top-mast*【海】大一接桅. ~*top-plane*【空】上主翼. ~*topsail*【海】大一接帆). ~ **yard**【船】大桅下桁.

Maine [mein] *n.* ①缅因〔美国州名〕. ②梅恩〔姓氏〕.

main·ly [ˈmeinli] *ad.* 主要;大概,大抵.

mai·no(u)r [ˈmeinə] *n.*【法】赃品.

Main Street [ˈmein striːt] *n.* ①(小城镇的)主街,大街. ②〔美〕乡镇中的实利主义阶层;乡镇典型居民的态度、意见.

main·tain [menˈtein] *vt.* ①保持;维持;继续. ②坚持,维护. ③供养,扶养. ④维修;保养. ⑤(坚决)主张;强调. ~ *discipline* 维持纪律. ~ *peace and order* 维持治安. ~ ***one's ground (against)*** (对…)站稳[坚持]自己立场. ~ ***oneself*** 自立.

main·tain·a·ble [meinˈteinəbl] *a.* 可保持的,可维持的;可供养的;可维修的;可坚持的,可主张的.

main·te·nance [ˈmeintinəns] *n.* ①保持;维持,保养;保管,保存,维护,维修;继续;支持的手段. ②坚持;主张;拥护,支持. ③扶养,供给;生活,生计. ④【法】对诉讼一方的非法援助;依法应负的对他人的赡养义务. *cost of ~* 维持费. *preventive ~* 预防性维修[检修]. *separate ~* (给妻子的)分居津贴. ~ ***of membership***〔美〕工会会员资格保留条款. ~ ***of possession*** 占有,保有,保全. ~ ***of way***【铁道】护路. **M- Command**【英军】保管[维修]总队. ~ **man** 维修工. ~ **work** 维修工作.

Mainz [maints] *n.* 美因茨〔西德城市〕.

mair [mɛə] *a.*〔Scot.〕更多的;更大的;更好的;更高的;另外的;其余的 (= more).

mair·ie [meˈriː] *n.*〔F.〕市府大楼;县区的行政大楼.

Mai·sie [ˈmeizi] *n.* 梅齐〔女子名, Margaret 的昵称〕.

mai·son de cam·pagne [mɛzɔ̃ də kɑ̃pɑɲ]〔F.〕乡下庄宅,田庄.

mai·son de san·té [mɛzɔ̃ də sɑ̃te]〔F.〕私立医院;疗养院.

mai·son·(n)ette [ˌmeizəˈnet] *n.* 小住宅;(二层楼的)公寓房子;〔英〕分别出租的房间.

maist [meist] *a.*〔Scot.〕最多的,最大的,最高的;大概的;大多数的 (= most).

Mait·land [ˈmeitlənd] *n.* 梅特兰〔姓氏〕.

maî·tre [ˈmeitrə] *n.*〔F.〕= master.[1] ~ ***d'hô·tel*** [-dəuˈtel] 旅馆主人;管家,总管;饭店服务员总管;(加)黄油柠檬(调味)酱.

maize [meiz] *n.* ①〔英〕【植】玉蜀黍,玉米. ★ 美国、加拿大叫 corn. ②玉米色. *the ~ country*〔美〕穷乡僻壤. ~ *oil* 玉米油.

mai·ze·na [meiˈziːnə] *n.*〔英〕玉米粉.

Maj. = Major.

ma·jes·tic, ma·jest·i·cal [məˈdʒestik, -tikəl] *a.* 有威严的,庄严的,堂堂的,威风凛凛的. **-i·cal·ly** *ad.*

maj·es·ty [ˈmædʒisti] *n.* ①威严,威风;尊严,庄严. ②主权,统治权;帝位;〔M.〕陛下〔尊称〕. ③光轮中的耶稣[圣母、上帝]圣像. *His Britannic M-* 英国国王陛下〔略 *H. B. M.*〕. *His [Her] Imperial M-* 皇帝[皇后]陛下〔略 *H. I. M.* 或 *H. M.*〕. *Their (Imperial) Majesties* 皇帝皇后两陛下〔略号 *T. (I.) M.*〕. *Your M-* 陛下〔直接对话时的尊称〕. *His Majesty's guests*〔俚〕囚犯. *His Majesty's hotel*〔谑〕监狱. *His Satanic M-*〔谑〕魔王.

Maj. Gen. = Major General〔英〕陆军(或海军陆战队)少将;〔美〕陆军(或空军、海军陆战队)少将.

Maj·lis [mædʒˈlis] *n.* 伊朗(或伊拉克)的议会.

ma·jol·i·ca [məˈjɔlikə, -ˈdʒɔl-] *n.* 马略尔卡陶器〔十六世纪意大利产的装饰用陶器〕;马略尔卡陶器的现代仿制品.

ma·jor[1] [ˈmeidʒə] *a.* (*opp.* minor) ①较大的;较多的;较优的;主要的;第一流的;较大范围的. ②成年的;〔英〕(学校中同姓同学中的)年长的. ③【逻】大(前提);【乐】大调的,大音阶的. *a ~ angle* 优角. *a ~ axis*【数】长轴(线). *the ~ vote* 多数票. *the ~ industries* 主要工业. *Brown ~* 年纪较大的布朗. *a ~ combat* 主力战. *a ~ engagement* 大战,会战. *~ operations* 大规模作战. *a ~ overhaul* 大修. *the ~ part* 过半,大部,多数. — *n.* ①成年人. ②【逻】大名词;大前提. ③【乐】大调;大音阶. ④〔美〕专修科目;专科生. — *vi.*〔美口〕主修,专攻 (*cf.* minor). ~ *in history* 主修历史. ~ **league**〔美〕一级职业棒球队协会 (*cf.* minor league). ~ **mode**【乐】大调调式. ~ **offensive** 主攻,大规模进攻. ~ **order** 高级圣职〔①【天主】司祭;助祭;副助祭. ②(其他一些基督教派的)主教;牧师;助祭〕. ~ **premise**【逻】大前提. ~ **scale**【乐】大音阶. ~ **sceptre**【美体】全国锦标. ~ **seminary**【天主】祭司神学院. ~ **seventh**【乐】大七度. ~ **suit** (桥牌中"黑桃"或"红桃"的)一手高记分值同花. ~ **term**【逻】大名辞;【数】大词,大项. ~ **tone**【乐】大全音. ~ **upset**【美体】大败.

ma·jor[2] [ˈmeidʒə] *n.*〔苏、美等〕陆军[空军]少校;〔英〕陆军少校[空军少校叫 squadron leader];【军俚】= sergeant major;【军】…长. *a drum ~* (军队)鼓手长. ~ **general**〔英〕陆军[海军陆战队]少将;〔美〕陆军[空军、海军陆战队]少将. **-ship** *n.* 陆军少校的职位.

ma·jor-do·mo [ˈmeidʒəˈdəuməu] *n.* ①(意大利,西班牙王室的)管家;〔谑〕大管家. ②〔美〕(南部农牧场的)监管人;(New Mexico 州的)灌溉管理员.

ma·jor·ette [ˌmeidʒəˈret] *n.* 军乐队女领队,军乐队女指挥的简称 (= drum majorette).

ma·jor·i·tar·i·an [məˌdʒɔriˈtɛəriən] *n.* 多数主义者. — *a.* 多数主义的. **-ism** *n.* 多数主义.

ma·jor·i·ty [məˈdʒɔriti] *n.* ①大多数,过半数,大部分. ②(选举)(多于对方全体票数的)多得票数 (*cf.* plurality). ★ 例如: A 得 120 票, B 得 70 票, C 得 30 票时, A 的 majority 是 20 票, A 的 plurality 则是 50 票. ③陆军少校的职位,少校级. ④成年;法定年龄. *The minority is subordinate to the ~.* 少数服从多数. *attain [reach] one's ~* 达到成年. *the ~ opinion* 多数人的意见. ***be in the ~ by***...仅多…票. ***by a ~ of*** 多得…票(当选). ***join [go over to, pass over to] the ~*** 死. ~ **leader** (议会中)多数党领袖. ~ **rule** 多数裁定原则.

Ma·jun·ga [məˈdʒʌŋgə] *n.* 马任加〔马达加斯加港市〕.

ma·jus·cule [ˈmædʒəskjuːl; *Am.* məˈdʒʌskjuːl] *n.* (*pl.* ~*s*, *-culae* [-kjuliː]) 大字体;大写字母. — *a.* 大字体的,大写的.

make [meik] *vt.* (***made*** [meid]) ①(a)做,作,造,制造,做成,造成,建设;创作,著作,拟,起草;制定,设置;征收. *I am not made that way.* 我生性不是那样. ~ *enemies* 树敌. (b)准备,预备,布置,整理;训练,养乖(狗). ~ *a bed* 准备床铺,铺床. ~ *tea* 泡茶,沏茶. ~ *the cards* 洗牌. *M- hay while the sun shines.* 趁晴晒草;〔转义〕勿失良机,利用合适的时机. (c) 构成. *Oxygen and hydrogen ~ water.* 氧和氢构成水. *Cold tea ~s excellent drink in summer.* 凉茶是夏天的好饮料. *The country is made up of meadow and marsh.* 那地区全是草地和沼泽. (d) 行,实行;定,签订,缔结. ~ *a bow* 鞠躬. ~ *a journey* 旅行. ~ *a* *contract* 定契约。(e) 述,说,提出,(赛艇)划得好。～ *a joke* 说笑话;开玩笑。～ *a speech* [〔美〕 *an address*] 演说。(f) 得,获得;挣,赚;【牌】赢;(东西)能卖…;【体】得分。～ *money* 挣钱,赚钱。～ *a reputation* 博得名声。～ *a trick* (玩牌)赢一墩牌。*The picture* ～*s a good price.* 这画卖得好价钱。(g)走,行,进行;【海】开始看见;〔俚〕赶得上…,赶上 (*a train*)。～ *ten miles a day* 一日走十英里。(h)计算,算定,估计;以为,认为,看做;抱有;思想[考虑、推测]…。*What time do you* ～ *it* = *What do you* ～ *the time?* 你看(现在)几点钟了? *He is not such an ass [a goose] as they* ～ *him.* 他并没有象大家想象的那样笨。(i) 成为;等于;总计。*Two and two* ～*s four.* 2 加 2 得[等于] 4。(j) 设计,发明;决定;【商】定(价钱)。(k)【电】开,通(电流) (*opp.* break)。(l) 发生,使发生,成为…的原因。～ *a difference, mark;* ～ *peace, trouble, work,* 等等[见各该名词]。(m)吃。～ *a good dinner [meal]* 吃饱一顿好餐。(n)行动得象…。～ *a fool of oneself.* 丢丑,使自己成为笑柄。(o)翻译,偷。(p)〔美口〕发现,知道,认识;成为…的会员,在…里得到一个地位;使(异性等)着迷。*He made the team.* 他成了队员。②〔make + 宾语 + 补足语〕使…成为(某种人或物);使某人的处境或某事的状况如何。～ *him a soldier* 使他成为军人。～ *China a culturally advanced socialist country* 把我国建设成为一个有高度文明的社会主义国家。～ *her happy* 使她幸福。 ③〔make + 宾语 + 不带 to 的不定式。但在被动语态结构中则用带 to 的不定式〕使(…)…,强迫…(做某事)。～ *him understand [laugh]* 使他了解[笑]。～ *the grass grow* 使草生长。*He was made to go.* 他是被迫去的。④〔make + 宾语 + 过去分词〕使(…)…,使(别人)…。*Too much wine* ～*s men drunk.* 饮酒过多使人醉。～ *oneself understood* 使人了解自己的意思。*What* ～*s him honoured?* 什么使他受人尊敬? ⑤〔make + 间接宾语 + 直接宾语〕做…给…。*I made him a new suit.* 我做了一套新的衣服给他。*She will* ～ *him a good wife.* 她会成为他的好妻子[贤内助]。⑥〔make + 名词常等于与该名词同义的动词〕～ *haste* = hasten。～ *(an) answer* = answer。～ *(an) appointment* = appoint。— *vi.* ①前进,向…去 (*for*);预备去,将去。②开始 (*to do something*);行动得(象…);似乎要。*He* ～*s as if he would escape.* 他装作要逃走的样子。*He made to strike me.* 他要动手打我。③(潮)满,涨;(潮水)开始涨。*The tide is making fast.* 潮水在急涨。*Water was making in the hold.* 舱里的水越来越多。④有效验(*for; against; with*)。⑤指向,趋向,指示;朝某方向前进。*All the evidence* ～*s in the same direction.* 所有的证据都指向同一个方向。⑥在进行中。⑦被制造;被处理。*Bolts are making in this shop.* 这个工厂正在制造螺栓。⑧〔宾语省略,后接形容词,表示某种状态、方式〕: ～ *ready* 作好准备。～ *bold* 冒昧,敢于。⑨进行中,将完成。～ ***a break*** 〔美俚〕做错,出丑,失言;打断谈话;企图越狱;(*with*) 与…断绝关系。～ ***a dead set*** 不屈不挠地干;拚命攻击。～ ***a getaway*** 〔美俚〕逃亡,逃掉。～ ***a go*** 〔美俚〕成功,得到。～ ***a killing*** 〔美俚〕赚大钱,发大财。～ ***a place*** 〔美口〕闯入某处抢东西。～ ***a play for*** 〔美口〕百般勾引,使出浑身解数迷惑,拿出所有本领去求得。～ ***a touch*** 〔美俚〕向人讨钱。～ ***after*** 〔古〕追赶;跟随。～ ***against***和…冲突;不利于…,妨碍(*opp.* ～ for)。～ ***and break*** 接通和切断(电路)。～ ***as if*** =～ ***as though*** 假装,装着。～ ***at*** 向…前进;袭击,攻击;扑向(*The tiger made at the men.* 老虎向人们扑了过来)。～ ***away*** (急急)离去,逃走,逃亡。～ ***away with*** ①带走,拿走,偷;杀死;毁弃,减掉 (～ *away with oneself* 自杀)。②(把钱)花光,用光;浪费;吃掉。～ ***back*** 回来,归。～ ***believe*** 假装。～ ***bold [free]*** ①冒昧,请允许我 (*I* ～ *bold to give you a piece of advice.* 我不揣冒昧,贡献您一点意见)。②对某人放肆无礼,任意[擅自]处理某事 (*with*) (*In his article he* ～*s free with facts.* 他在文章里以随便的态度对待事实)。③随便使用。～ ***colours*** 【海】(早晨八时)升船旗。～ ***contact*** 接通电流;接触。～ ***dead*** 【电】切断。～ *(sth.)* ***do*** = ～ ***do with*** *(sth.)* 用(某物)设法应付。～ ***down*** 清算;改小,准备。～ ***for*** (*opp.* ～ against) ①有利于;对…有益;倾向于。②拥护,支持。③向…前进;袭击。～ *(sth.)* ***from*** 用…做材料[样子]制造 (*Wine is made from grapes.* 葡萄酒是用葡萄酿造的) (*cf.* ～ ***of***)。～ ***harbour*** 入港,到埠。～ ***hey-hey*** [hei-hei] 〔美俚〕胡闹,瞎闹。～ ***him step*** 【美体】使对方尽量奋斗。～ ***in*** 到…去,进入;干涉;参加。～ ***into*** 制成,做成;使转变为。～ ***it*** 赶到;办成功;规定时间;〔美俚〕性交。～ ***it good upon*** *(sb.)* 凭威力使(某人)接受自己的话。～ ***it hot for*** 使受不了,使为难;拚命攻击。～ ***it one's business to do*** 把…当作自己的任务去干。～ ***it pay*** 使合算。～ ***it so*** 【海】命令打钟。～ ***it up*** 和解,讲和 (*with*)。～ ***it up to*** 偿,赎。～ ***of*** ①用(木材等)造(船等)〔制成品保有原材料形状〕(*cf.* ～ ***from***);养成,训练成 (～ *a teacher of one's son* 把孩子培养成教师)。②了解;认为 (*can* ～ *nothing of it* 弄不明白。*I* ～ *nothing of it.* 我认为那没有什么了不起)。～ ***off*** 去,急忙跑掉[离开],逃走,逃亡。～ ***off with*** 拐走,拐跑,偷去,拿走。～ ***one (of the party)*** 加入团体。～ ***one's living*** 谋生;得到生活费。～ ***one's own life*** 决定生活方向。～ ***oneself*** 自学。～ ***oneself strange*** 假装生客;假装吃惊。～ ***oneself understood*** 使了解自己意思。～ ***or mar [break]*** 使(计划等)(完全)成功或(完全)失败。～ ***out*** ①理解,领悟;发现,看出 (*I could not* ～ *out what the police wanted.* 我不明白警察要的是什么。*I* ～ *out a ship in the distance.* 我看见远处有一只船)。②起草,拟,填写,开列 (～ *out a list* 开清单)。③证明;说得象,说成,说是 (*He* ～*s me out a fool.* 他把我说成一个傻瓜)。④成就,完成。⑤消磨(时光)。⑥〔美口〕设法周转,东拼西凑的过日子;扩大,伸张 (*He* ～*s out to keep out of debt.* 他东拼西凑总算是没有背债。*How are things making out?* 事情进展得怎样?) ～ ***out a good case*** 自圆其说。～ ***out of*** ①用…制做… (*cf.* ～ ***of***)。②理解;了解。～ ***over*** 让,转让,移交;改造,改制(特指衣服等) (～ *over a coat* 把一件外套翻新)。～ ***record*** 创造新纪录。～ ***straight shoot*** 〔美口〕走最近的路,采取最直接的方法。～ ***sure*** 尽力做到,保证;深信,有把握。～ ***sure of*** 弄清楚,查明无误(*M- sure of your facts before you write the article.* 先弄明白事实,然后再写文章)。～ ***the air blue*** 〔美〕骂街,满口下流话。～ ***the bull's eye*** (射击)中的;得显著胜利。～ ***the queer*** 〔美俚〕伪造货币。～ ***through with*** 完成。～ ***time*** 急往,急匆匆地去。～ ***towards*** 向…前进。～ ***up*** ①补,弥补,补给,补充,补足 (*for*) (*each making up what the other lacks* 互通有无。～ *up (for) a loss* 弥补损失。～ *up for lost time* 补回损失的时间)。②修理;制作;装配。③(由种种要素)组成,合成;调配成。④作成,起草,编辑,编纂。⑤打扮;【剧】化装。⑥定,决定;签订;调解,排解(争吵、纠纷等) (*shake hands and* ～ *it up* 握手言归于好)。⑦决算,清算。⑧包,收拾。⑨做,缝。⑩捏造。⑪争论。⑫【印】拼版,整版;(印刷品的)编排;【铁道】调配(车辆) (～ *up a train of cars* 调配一列车)。～ ***up to*** 接近;巴结;向女人求爱;补偿,赔还(某人)。～ ***up with*** 和…讲和[和解]。～ ***with*** 做动作;做出;使用;提供。

— *n.* ①构造,组织。②脾性,性格,天性。③体格;形状;样式,样子;种类,品质。④制造;制法;产量。⑤【电】(电路的)接通。*a man of his* ～ 象他那种性格的人。*What* ～ *of car is this?* 这是什么厂出品的汽车? *home [foreign]* ～ 本国[外国]制。*things of Chinese* ～ 中国制品。～ ***and break*** 【电】通断开关。～ ***and mend*** 〔英〕【海】闲暇时候。***on the*** ～ 〔口〕在构成[增长、改进]中;拼命弄钱,拼命吸引异性注意,想尽办法巴结;野心勃勃的,努力向上的;机警的,不落空的。～***bate*** 〔罕〕

挑斗的人，挑唆吵架的人．~**-believe** ①*n.* 假装，假托；假装的人．② *a.* 假装的．~**fast** 系船浮子，拴船柱；系船桩．~**-game** 嘲笑的对象；笑柄．~**-peace** ＝peacemaker. ~**shift** ①*n.* 将就，凑合，一时之计，权宜之计，临时手段(*use an empty box as a ~-shift for a table* 以空箱当饭桌凑合使用)．② *a.* 暂时的，一时的．~**-sport**＝make-game. ~**-up** ①(演员的)装扮，打扮，化装；化装用具；化妆品．②组织，构造，结构．③体格；性格；【印】版面；垫版；拼版 (*elements in one's ~-up* 特征)．④假装，虚构．⑤〔美〕补考，补充，补偿．~**weight**补足重量的东西；填料；(尤指)小蜡烛；没有价值的人〔东西〕；不重要的议论．~**-work** 为使工作者不闲散而分派的工作．

mak·er [ˈmeikə] *n.* ①制造者，制作人，制造商；创造者；出票人．②〔*our, his, the M-*〕造物主，上帝．③〔古〕诗人．④【电】接合器． *the policy ~s* 决定政策的人，决策者．***go to [meet] one's M-*** 死． ~**-up** *(pl. ~s-up)* 【印】拼版工人；〔英〕制品装配工；服装工人．

mak·ing [ˈmeikiŋ] *n.* ①制作(物)，制造(物)，生产；一次制造量；发展〔发达〕过程；成功的原因〔手段〕；组织；〔常 *pl.*〕原料，材料．②〔口〕〔*pl.*〕利益，赚头，所得．③〔*pl.*〕素质，要素．④〔*pl.*〕〔美口〕(自卷自抽的)卷烟材料〔纸和烟〕．⑤(煤矿中挖出来的)粉煤． *the ~s of a good garden* 一个美好的花园的条件．***be the ~ of*** 成为…的基础，保证…的成功 (*His failure has been the ~ of him.* 他的失败成了他成功的原因)．***have the ~s of*** 具有…的素质．***in ~*** 制造中，建设中．***in the ~*** 酝酿中的，在发展过程中的；未完成的．~**-up price** 〔美〕(股票的)核定价格．

-making *suf.* 〔口〕使人…的：*sick-[shy-]~.*

Mak·kah [ˈmækə] *n.* 麦加〔阿拉伯语名称〕．

Ma·ku·a [mɑːˈkuːɑː] *n.* ①*(pl. ~(s))* 马库阿人〔莫桑比克北部和附近的坦噶尼喀人〕．②马库阿语．

ma·ku·ta [mɑːˈkuːtɑː] *n.* likuta (里库塔〔扎伊尔的货币名〕)的复数．

mal [mal] *n.* 〔F.〕＝sickness. ***~ de mer*** [ˈmεə] 晕船．***~ du pays*** [djuˈpei] 怀乡病．

mal- *comb. f.* ①＝bad, badly (*opp.* bene-)：*mal*treat; *mal*development 发育不良．②＝not, un-：*mal*content. ③＝imperfect, deficient：*mal*formation.

Ma·la·bo [ˈmɑːlɑːbəu] *n.* 马拉博〔赤道几内亚首都〕．

Ma·lac·ca [məˈlækə] *n.* ①马六甲〔马来西亚港市〕．②【史】满喇加国． *the Strait of ~* 马六甲海峡〔亚洲〕．~**cane** (用棕榈树干制成的)马六甲手杖．

mal·a·chite [ˈmæləkait] *n.*【矿】孔雀石．

mal·a·co·derm [ˈmæləkədəːm] *n.*【动】软皮动物，(尤指)海葵 (sea anemone).

mal·a·col·o·gy [ˌmæləˈkɔlədʒi] *n.* 软体动物学．

mal·a·cos·tra·can [ˌmæləˈkɔstrəkən] *a.*【动】软甲亚纲 (Malacostraca) 的 (＝malacostracous). **-tra·cous** [-kəs] *n.* 软甲亚纲动物．

mal·ad·dress [ˌmæləˈdres] *n.* 粗鲁，拙笨，笨．

mal·ad·just·ed [ˈmæləˈdʒʌstid] *a.* 精神失调的；【心】不能适应环境的；顺应不良的．

mal·ad·jus·tive [ˈmæləˈdʒʌstiv] *a.* 引起失调的．

mal·ad·just·ment [ˈmæləˈdʒʌstmənt] *n.* ①调节不善，调理不善；失调．②不适应；【心】顺应不良．

mal·ad·min·is·ter [ˈmælədˈministə] *vt.* 胡乱处理，瞎搞，胡搞(公共事务)．**-tration** *n.* 恶政，乱政；(公务、公事的)处理不善，管理不善，紊乱．

mal·a·droit [ˈmæləˈdrɔit] *a.* 笨拙的，拙劣的，愚钝的．**-ly** *ad.* **-ness** *n.*

mal·a·dy [ˈmælədi] *n.* ①毛病，疾病；(社会的)弊端，弊病；歪风．②(葡萄酒的)酸腐．

ma·la fi·de [ˈmeilə ˈfaidi] *ad., a.*〔L.〕不守信义地〔的〕；恶意地〔的〕；不诚实地〔的〕，狡猾地〔的〕*(opp.* bona fide*)*.

ma·la fi·des [ˈmeilə ˈfaidi] *n.* 〔L.〕不诚实，恶意．

Mal·a·ga [ˈmæləgə] *n.* ①马拉加〔西班牙南部省名及其首府名〕．②马拉加白葡萄酒．

Mal·a·gas·y [ˌmæləˈgæsi] *a.* 马尔加什人〔语〕的，马达加斯加岛的．— *n. (pl. ~, -sies)* 马尔加什共和国〔非洲〕；马尔加什人〔语〕；马达加斯加岛人．

mal·a·gue·na [ˈmæləˈgeinjə, -ˈgweinə] *n.* (西班牙)马拉加民歌；马拉加民间曲调；马拉加民间舞蹈．

ma·laise [mæˈleiz] *n.* 〔F.〕不舒服；小病，微恙；精神欠爽．

mal·a·mute [ˈmæləmjuːt] *n.* 阿拉斯加雪橇狗 (＝Alaskan ~).

Ma·lan [ˈmælən] *n.* 马伦〔姓氏〕．

mal·an·ders [ˈmæləndəz] *n. pl.*【兽医】膝皲．

mal·a·pert [ˈmæləpəːt] *a., n.* 〔古〕没礼貌的(人)，脸皮厚的(人)．

mal·a·prop, mal·a·pro·pi·an [ˈmæləprɔp, ˌmæləˈprɔpiən] *a.* 滑稽地错用语词的，文字弄错的，可笑的．

mal·a·prop·ism [ˈmæləprɔpizəm] *n.* 语词的滑稽误用〔如将 loquacity 误为 locality, instinctive 误为 insentive 之类〕；被误用得可笑的词．

mal·ap·ro·pos [ˈmælˈæprəpəu; Am. ˌmælæprəˈpəu] *a.* 〔常用作表语〕不合时宜的；不适当的．— *ad.* 不凑巧．— *n.* 不适当的言行．

ma·lar [ˈmeilə] *n., a.* 颧骨(的)，颊(的)．

ma·lar·i·a [məˈlεəriə] *n.* 〔古〕瘴气；【医】疟疾．**-i·al, -i·an, -i·ous** *a.*

ma·lar·i·al·ist [məˈlεəriəlist] *n.* 疟疾专家．

mal·ate [ˈmæleit, ˈmeileit] *n.*【化】苹果酸，苹果酸盐(或酯)．

mal·a·thi·on [ˌmæləˈθaiən] *n.* 马拉硫磷，马拉息昂，马拉松〔一种有机磷杀虫剂〕．

Ma·la·wi [mɑːˈlɑːwi] *n.* 马拉维〔非洲，旧称尼亚萨兰〕．

Ma·lay [məˈlei] *n.* 马来人〔语〕；【动】马来鸡 (＝~ fowl). — *a.* 马来(半岛)的；马来人〔语〕的．~ **Archipelago [Peninsula]** 马来群岛〔半岛〕．~ **fowl** 马来鸡．

Ma·lay·a [məˈleiə] *n.* 马来亚；马来半岛．

Mal·a·ya·lam [ˌmæliˈɑːləm] *n.* (印度西南海岸 Malabar 的) 德拉维族 (Dravidian) 语．

Ma·lay·an [məˈleiən] *a., n.* ＝Malay.

Ma·lay·o-Pol·y·ne·sian [məˌleiəuˌpɔliˈniːʒən, -ʃən] *a.* 马来-玻里尼西亚语系的；南岛语系的．— *n.* 马来-玻里尼西亚语；南岛语．

Ma·lay·sia [məˈleiʃə] *n.* 马来西亚〔亚洲〕；＝Malay Archipelago 马来群岛．**-n** *a.* 马来西亚的；马来西亚人的．— *n.* 马来西亚人．

Mal·colm [ˈmælkəm] *n.* 马尔科姆〔姓氏，男子名〕．

mal·con·for·ma·tion [ˈmælkɔnfɔːˈmeiʃən] *n.* 难看，丑．

mal·con·tent [ˈmælkɔntent] *a.* (尤指对政府)抱怨的，不满的．— *n.* 不满者；不满．

mal de mer [maldəˈmεə] 〔法〕晕船．

Mal·dive [ˈmɔ(ː)ldiv; Am. ˈmældaiv] *n.* 马尔代夫〔亚洲〕．**-div·i·an** ①*a.* 马尔代夫的．②*n.* 马尔代夫人；马尔代夫语．

Male [ˈmɑːlei] *n.* 马累〔马尔代夫首都〕．

male [meil] *a.* (*opp.* femile) 男、公、雄；男性的；阳性的；【植】雄性的，仅有雄蕊的；全是男人的． *the ~ choir* 男声合唱队． *a ~ flower* 雄花． *a ~ chauwinist pig* (常缩作 MCP) 歧视妇女的人；大男子主义者． *a ~ hormone* 雄性激素．~ *screw* 阳螺旋，柱螺纹． *a ~ tank*(装有轻炮、机枪的)重战车．— *n.* 男，男子，男性；雄性动物；【植】雄性植物；【自】插入式配件．~ **fern**【植】绵马．

male- *comb. f.* (*opp.* bene-) ＝evil, ill.

malease [mæˈliːz] *n.* ＝malaise.

mal·e·dict [ˈmælidikt] *a.* 〔古〕被诅咒的；可恶的，讨厌的．— *vt.* 〔古〕诅咒，咒骂．

mal·e·dic·tion [ˌmæliˈdikʃən] *n.* ①诅咒；诬蔑。②诽谤 (*opp.* benediction). *utter a* ～ 诅咒。
mal·e·fac·tion [ˌmæliˈfækʃən] *n.* 犯罪行为，坏事；罪恶。
mal·e·fac·tor [ˈmælifæktə] *n.* (*opp.* benefactor). 犯罪分子；作恶者；坏人。
ma·lef·ic [məˈlefik] *a.* 有害的，邪恶的。— *n.*【占星】凶星。
ma·lef·i·cence [məˈlefisns] *n.* 邪恶的行径，坏事；毒害；邪恶性。
ma·lef·i·cent [məˈlefisnt] *a.* 犯罪的，做坏事的；有害的 *(to)*；邪恶的。
ma·le·ic [məˈliːik] *a.* ～ **acid**【化】马来酸，顺丁烯二酸。～ **hydrazide**【化】马来酰肼。
mal·e·mute [ˈmælimjuːt] *n.* = malamute.
mal·en·ten·du [malɔːŋˈtɔːŋdy] *a.* 〔F.〕误解的，误会的。— *n.* 误解，误会。
ma·lev·o·lence [məˈlevələns] *n.* 恶意，坏心肠，黑心，恶毒；狠毒的行为。
ma·lev·o·lent [məˈlevələnt] *a.* 有恶意的，心肠坏的，恶毒的，幸灾乐祸的(*opp.* benevolent). **-ly** *ad.*
mal·fea·sance [ˈmælˈfiːzəns] *n.*【法】坏事；(尤指官吏的)非法行为，渎职(罪)。
mal·fea·sant [mælˈfiːzənt] *a.* 胡作非为的，做坏事的。— *n.* 犯罪者。
mal·for·ma·tion [ˌmælfɔːˈmeiʃən] *n.* 畸形(性)；畸形物，畸形体。
mal·formed [ˈmælˈfɔːmd] *a.* 畸形的；残缺的。
mal·func·tion [mælˈfʌŋkʃən] *n.* 失灵；机能失常；故障；事故。*guidance* ～【空】制导设备失灵。
Mal·gache [mælˈgæʃ] Malagasy的法语拼写形式。
mal·gré lui [malˈgreˈlɥi] 〔F.〕非出于本意地，情不自禁地。
Ma·li [ˈmɑːliː] *n.* 马里〔非洲〕。
ma·lic ac·id [ˈmeilik ˈæsid]【化】苹果酸，羟基丁二酸。
mal·ice [ˈmælis] *n.* 恶意，恶感，恶念，毒心；怨恨；【法】预谋。～ *prepense* [*aforethought*] (杀人的)预谋。***bear ～ to* [*towards*]** 对…怀恨。***stand mute of*** ～【法】对被控罪名拒不答辩。
ma·li·cious [məˈliʃəs] *a.* 有恶意的，存心不良的，有敌意的；蓄意的；预谋的。～ *mischief* 蓄意破坏他人财产的行为。***make ～ remarks*** 骂。**-ly** *ad.* **-ness** *n.*
ma·lign [məˈlain] *a.* (*opp.* benign) 有害的，邪恶的；恶性的(疾病等)；〔罕〕有恶意的，恶毒的。*a* ～ *influence* 坏影响。— *vt.* 诬蔑，诽谤；中伤。*His face ～s him.* 他像貌不好人好。**-er** *n.* 诬蔑者。**-ly** *ad.* 有害地；恶意地。
ma·lig·nance, ma·lig·nan·cy [məˈlignəns, -si] *n.* (极端的)恶意；恶毒的行为；不吉，凶；【医】恶性；恶性肿瘤。
ma·lig·nant [məˈlignənt] *a.* ①有恶意的；恶毒的。②恶性的(疾病等) (*opp.* benignant)。③有害的；邪恶的；不吉利的。④【英史】保王党的。— *n.* 怀恶意的人；【英史】保王党党员。～ *cholera* 恶性霍乱症。**-ly** *ad.*
ma·lig·ni·ty [məˈligniti] *n.* 恶意，敌意，毒心；怨恨；【医】(病的)恶性。
ma·li·hi·ni [ˌmæliˈhiːni] *n.* 〔Haw.〕新到夏威夷的人；夏威夷人中的外来者。
ma·lines [məˈliːn; F. maˈlin] *n.* ①梅克林花边 (= Machlin lace) ②马林丝沙罗〔女服或面纱用的一种细丝网〕。
ma·lin·ger [məˈliŋgə] *vi.* (士兵为逃避勤务)装病。**-er** *n.*
ma·lin·ger·y [məˈliŋgəri] *n.* 假病。
Ma·lin·ke [məliŋˈkei] *n.* ①*(pl. -kes, -ke)* (非洲西岸)马林凯人。②马林凯语。
ma·lism [ˈmeilizəm] *n.* 世恶说。
mal·i·son [ˈmælizn, -sn] *n.* 〔古〕诅咒，咒骂；诽谤 (*opp.* benison).
mal·kin [ˈmɔːlkin] *n.* 〔废、英方〕①懒婆娘。②拖布。③稻草人。④野兔。⑤猫。
mall¹ [mɔːl] *n.* = maul.
mall² [mɔːl] *n.* ①林荫路，林荫散步场。②铁圈球(场)；(=pall-mall)。③铁圈球槌。**The M-** [mæl] 伦敦 St. James公园的林荫路。
mal·lard [ˈmæləd] *n.* *(pl. ～(s))* 〔集合词〕【鸟】雄野鸭，绿头鸭，凫；野鸭肉。
mal·le·a·bil·i·ty [ˌmæliəˈbiliti] *n.* (金属的)可锻性，展性；柔顺性，顺从。
mal·le·a·ble [ˈmæliəbl] *a.* 可锻的，可锤薄的，有延展性的，韧性的；柔顺的；顺从的。～ **iron** 韧铁。～ **cast-iron** 韧性铸铁，可锻铸铁。
mal·lee [ˈmæli] *n.* (南澳洲产)小桉树。
mal·lein [ˈmæliin] *n.*【医】(接种诊断用)马鼻疽杆菌。
mal·le·muck [ˈmælimʌk] *n.*【鸟】海洋鸟〔海燕、信天翁等〕。
mal·le·o·lar [məˈliːələ] *a.* 踝的。
mal·le·o·lus [məˈliːələs] *n.*【解】踝；【植】压条。
mal·let [ˈmælit] *n.* 木槌，槌，(打马球等用的)球棍；【解】锤骨；〔*pl.*〕【美体】马球。
mal·le·us [ˈmæliəs] *n.* *(pl. -lei* [-liai]*)*【解】锤骨；〔M-〕【动】撞木贝属；(马)鼻疽。
mal·low [ˈmæləu] *n.*【植】锦葵属。*Indian* ～ 苘麻，青麻。～ **rose**【植】= **rose** ～ 木槿属植物 (尤指草芙蓉)。
malm [mɑːm] *n.* 泥灰岩，柔软的白垩岩；白垩土；钙质砂土；粘土和白垩的混合物；白垩砖。
malm·sey [ˈmɑːmzi] *n.* (希腊)醇香白葡萄酒。
mal·nour·ished [mælˈnʌriʃt] *a.* 营养不良的。
mal·nu·tri·tion [ˈmælnju(ː)ˈtriʃən] *n.* 营养不良。
mal·oc·clu·sion [ˌmæləˈkluːʒən] *n.*【医】(上下牙齿的)错位咬合。
ma·lo·dor·ant [mæˈləudərənt] *a., n.* 恶臭的；恶臭物。
mal·o·dor·ous [mæˈləudərəs] *a.* 有恶臭的。**-ly** *ad.* **-ness** *n.*
mal·o·do(u) [ˌmæˈləudə] *n.* 恶臭，臭气。
Ma·lone [mæˈləun] *n.* 马隆〔姓氏〕。
ma·lon·ic [məˈlɔnik, -ˈləunik] *a.* ～ **acid**【化】丙二酸。
Mal·o·ry [ˈmæləri] *n.* 马洛里〔姓氏〕。
Mal·pigh·i·an [mælˈpigiən] *a.*【解】马尔丕基氏的。～ **bodies [capsules, corpuscles]** 肾小体，马尔丕基氏体。～ **layer**【生】生发层。～ **tubules**【生】马尔丕基氏管。
mal·po·si·tion [ˌmælpəˈziʃən] *n.* 位置不正；【产科】错位；胎位不正。
mal·prac·tice [ˈmælˈpræktis] *n.* ①【医】疗法失当，滥治。②玩忽职守，渎职；歪风，恶癖；【法】违法行为。～*s hindering the construction of key projects* 破坏重点建设的歪风。
malt [mɔːlt] *n.* 麦芽；麦芽酒，啤酒；麦乳精。— *a.* 麦芽的；含麦芽的；麦芽制的。— *vt.* ①使成麦芽。②用麦芽制造〔处理〕。— *vi.* ①(麦粒)发芽。②制麦芽。③〔俚〕喝啤酒。～*ed milk* 麦乳精(奶)。～ **dust** 麦芽糖，麦曲糟。～ **extract** 麦芽膏；麦精。～**horse** 磨麦芽的马；笨人。～**house** 麦芽作坊；麦芽贮藏所。～ **kiln** 麦芽干燥窑。～ **liquor** 啤酒。～**man** 麦芽制造人。～ **sugar** 麦芽糖。～**worm** 〔古〕大酒鬼。
Mal·ta [ˈmɔːltə] *n.* (地中海中的)马耳他〔欧洲〕。～ **fever** 马耳他热〔一种热病〕。
malt·ase [ˈmɔːlteis] *n.*【生化】麦芽糖酶。
Mal·tese [ˈmɔːlˈtiːz] *a.* 马耳他岛(人)的。～ **cat** 马耳他猫〔蓝灰色家猫〕。—*n.* 〔*sing., pl.*〕马耳他岛人〔语〕。～ **cross** ①马耳他十字架。②【植】皱叶剪秋罗。
mal·tha [ˈmælθə] *n.* 软沥青。
Mal·thus [ˈmælθəs] *n.* ①马尔萨斯〔姓氏〕。②**Thomas Robert** ～ 马尔萨斯〔1766—1834，英国经济学家〕。

Mal·thu·si·an [mælˈθju:zjən] *a.* 马尔萨斯的；马尔萨斯人口论的. — *n.* 马尔萨斯人口论者. **-ism** 马尔萨斯人口论；马尔萨斯主义.
malt·ing [ˈmɔ:ltiŋ] *n.* 麦芽制造(法).
malt·ose [ˈmɔ:ltəus] *n.* 【化】麦芽糖.
mal·treat [mælˈtri:t] *vt.* 虐待；乱用. **-ment** *n.*
malt·ster [ˈmɔ:ltstə] *n.* 麦芽制造人.
malt·y [ˈmɔ:lti] *a.* ①麦芽的,含麦芽的,用麦芽做的,象麦芽的. ②〔俚〕喝醉了的. — *n.* 〔美〕啤酒.
Maltz [mɔ:lts] *n.* 莫尔茨〔姓氏〕.
mal·va·ceous [mælˈveiʃəs] *a.* 【植】锦葵属的.
mal·va·si·a [ˌmælvəˈsi:ə] *n.* ①(希腊)莫瓦西亚白葡萄酒. ②酿莫瓦西亚白葡萄酒的葡萄. **-n** *a.*
mal·ver·sa·tion [ˌmælvə:ˈseiʃən] *n.* (公务员的)违法行为；贪污,受贿；盗用公款.
mal·voi·sie [ˈmælvɔizi] *n.* = malmsey.
mam, ma·ma [mæm, məˈmɑ:] *n.* = mamma.
mam·ba [ˈmɑ:mbə] *n.* 树眼镜蛇属的蛇〔尤指非洲树蛇〕.
mam·bo [ˈmɑ:mbəu] *n.* ①曼波乐曲〔源出古巴黑人,4/4拍,第二拍第四拍为强拍〕. ②曼波交际舞. — *vi.* 跳曼波舞.
mam·e·lon [ˈmæmilən] *n.* 圆丘.
Mam·e·luke [ˈmæmilu:k] *n.* ①【史】马穆鲁克〔中世纪埃及的一个军事统治阶层的成员〕. ②〔m-〕奴隶,奴隶兵.
Mamie [ˈmeimi] *n.* 梅米〔女子名, Margaret 的昵称〕.
ma·mil·la [mæˈmilə] = mammilla.
mam·il·late(d) [ˈmæmileit(id)] *a.* = mammillate(d).
Mam·luk [ˈmæmlu:k] *n.* = Mameluke.
mam·ma[1] [məˈmɑ:] *n.* 〔儿〕妈,妈妈. *a ~'s baby* 〔美俚〕漂亮的女学生.
mam·ma[2] [ˈmæmə] *n.* *(pl. -mae* [-mi:]*)* (哺乳动物的)乳房.
mam·mal [ˈmæməl] *n.* 哺乳动物.
Mam·ma·lia [mæˈmeiljə] *n.* 〔*pl.*〕【动】哺乳纲.
mam·ma·li·an [mæˈmeiljən] *n., a.* 哺乳动物(的).
mam·ma·lif·er·ous [ˌmæməˈlifərəs] *a.* 【地】含有哺乳动物遗骸的.
mam·mal·o·gy [mæˈmælədʒi] *n.* 哺乳动物学.
mam·ma·ry [ˈmæməri] *a.* 【解】乳房的；胸的. ~ *cancer* 乳癌. ~ *gland* 乳腺.
mam·mec·to·my [məˈmektəmi] *n.* = mastectomy.
mam·mee, mam·mey [mæˈmi:, meiˈmi:] *n.* 【植】(美洲热带地方的)曼密树；曼密果.
mam·met [ˈmæmit] *n.* ①偶象. ②〔英方〕玩偶；傀儡(= maumet).
mam·mif·er·ous [mæˈmifərəs] *a.* 有乳房的；哺乳动物的.
mam·mi·form [ˈmæmifɔ:m] *a.* 乳房状的.
mam·mil·la [mæˈmilə] *n.* *(pl. -lae* [-li:]*)* 【解】乳头；乳头状突起；疣.
mam·mil·lar·y [ˈmæmiləri] *a.* 乳房的；乳房似的；有乳房状突起的.
mam·mil·late [ˈmæmileit] *a.* ①有乳头的. ②乳头状的. **-la·tion** [-ˈleiʃən] *n.*
mam·mil·li·form [məˈmilifɔ:m] *a.* 乳头状的.
mam·mock [ˈmæmək] *n.* 〔古、方〕碎片,碎屑. — *vt.* 〔古、方〕使成碎片；把…撕成碎片.
mam·mo·gen [ˈmæmədʒən] *n.* 乳腺发育激素.
mam·mo·gen·ic [ˌmæməˈdʒenik] *a.* 促进乳房发育的.
mam·mog·ra·phy [məˈmɔgrəfi] *n.* 【医】早期胸部肿瘤 X 射线透视法.
mam·mon [ˈmæmən] *n.* (作为偶像或罪恶根源看的)财富,金钱；〔M-〕财神.
mam·mon·ism [ˈmæmənizəm] *n.* 拜金主义.
mam·mon·ist [ˈmæmənist], **mam·mon·ite** [ˈmæmənait] *n.* 拜金主义者.
mam·moth [ˈmæməθ] *n.* ①猛犸象〔古生代的巨象〕. ②巨物,庞然大物. — *a.* 巨大的. **M- Cave** (美国 Kentucky 州的)大钟乳洞. ~ **tree** 大树.
mam·my [ˈmæmi] *n.* 〔儿〕妈；〔美南部〕黑人保姆.
man [mæn] *n.(pl. men* [men]*)* ①〔无冠词、单数〕人,人类；【生】人科. ②男人；大人,成年男子；男子汉,大丈夫；要人,名人；〔冠词用 the; my; your 等〕人,对手. ③〔古〕家臣,从者,部下；仆人,〔主 *pl.*〕雇员,工人；〔*pl.*〕水兵；士兵 (*opp.* officers). ④丈夫；〔方〕情人. ⑤(大学的)学生；(某某大学)出身的人. ⑥〔亲爱、轻蔑、焦急意义的称呼〕你,喂. ⑦(象棋)棋子. ⑧〔用作不定代词〕人,谁. ⑨〔the M-〕〔美俚〕警察；〔黑人俚〕白人. *M- is mortal.* 人都是会死的. *a ~ of all work* 多面手,万能先生. *What a piece of work is a ~!* 人呀真是一个杰作! *You don't give a ~ a chance.* 你不给人家一个机会呀. *Be a ~!* 拿出大丈夫气概来. *Let any ~ come, I am his ~.* 谁来都好,我来对付. *I know my ~.* 我知道对手(是怎样一个人). *Come, ~, we've no time to lose.* 喂,来呀,时间不早啦. *officers and men* 官兵. *Hurry up, ~ (alive)!* 赶快,喂! *Nonsense, ~!* 胡说! ★美国商业中对顾客称 gentleman 和 lady, 对自己店员称 man 和 woman. ***a ~ about town*** 出入于娱乐、社交等场所的男子；花天酒地中鬼混的人；〔英〕(伦敦)的高等游民. ***a ~ among men*** 男子汉中的男子汉,特出的人物. ***a ~ and a brother*** 同胞兄弟,亲兄弟. ***a ~ of*** …(某处)生长的人 (*a ~ of Shanghai* 上海人). ***a ~ of the people*** 人民的儿子. ***as a ~*** 一致地；作为一个男子；就人的观点而论. ***as men go*** 就一般人而论. ***as one [a] ~*** 异口同声,团结一致地. ***be one's own ~*** 独立自主,有自己的自由；精力充沛. ***best ~*** 男傧相. ***be the whole ~ at*** 专心…. ***between ~ and ~*** 象男子汉对男子汉；两人中私下讲. ***John Tamson's ~*** 怕老婆的男人. ***like a ~*** 男子汉似的,有丈夫气. ***little ~*** 〔谑、爱〕小鬼,小家伙. ***make (sb.) a ~ =make a ~ of (sb.)*** 使成大人,使能处世成人 (*His father's death has made a ~ of him.* 他父亲死后,他就变得象个大人了). ***M- alive!*** 什么! 这是怎么回事! 〔表示惊讶、抗议〕 ***~ and boy (ad.)*** 从儿童时代以来,从小到大. ***~ and wife*** 夫妇. ***~ for ~*** 以一个人比一个人. ***~ Friday*** 忠仆. ***~ hour*** 工时. ***~ in the moon*** 月中人；空想人物,虚构人物. ***~ in the oak*** 鬼,妖怪. ***~ of God*** 牧师,教士；预言者. ***~ of his hands*** 手巧的人,有手艺的人；武艺家. ***~ of his word*** 守约的人,可靠的人. ***~ of honour*** 有信义的人,君子. ***~ of letters*** 作家,学者,编辑,文人. ***~ of men*** 特出〔优秀〕人物. ***~ of parts*** 才子. ***~ of resources*** 足智多谋的人. ***M- of Sorrows*** 耶稣基督. ***~ of straw*** 稻草人；假想的敌人；场面人物；虚构人物；没钱的人. ***~ of the world*** 通世故的人；上层社交界人物；俗人. ***~ on horseback*** (权势高出政府之上的)军阀,军事领袖；军事独裁者. ***~ on the firing line*** 【美棒球】投手. ***~ to ~ = ~ for ~. mistake one's ~*** 看错对方(是怎样一个人). ***My ~!*** 喂! 〔对下面人的称呼〕. ***new ~*** (新加入某一社会集团的)新人. ***old ~*** ①老前辈,老朋友. ②船长；工头. ③父亲,丈夫. ***play the ~*** 显示男子汉气概. ***the dead ~*** 冗员. ***the forgotten ~*** 被遗忘的人. ***the inner ~*** 精神,灵魂；〔谑〕胃,肚子. ***the ~ in [on] the street*** 〔口〕普通人,一般人 (*opp.* expert). ***(all) to a ~*** 到最后一人,全部；满场一致 (*They were killed to a ~.* 他们全部被杀了). — *vt.* ***(manned; man·ning)*** ①给…配置兵〔人〕员；配置船员(在船上). ②使人就(职位等)；操纵；养乖(鹰等). ③使拿出丈夫气概,使鼓起勇气 *(oneself)*. ~ *the ship* 配置船员；使人上船. ~ *the side* = ~ *the yards* 举行上船礼. ~ *the guns* 就位,准备开炮. ***~ it out*** 硬着骨头干到底,有男子汉气魄. ***~ up*** (给矿业、农业等)补充人力. ***manning table*** 〔美〕战斗

部署表. ~-at-arms *(pl. men-)* (中世纪)兵士; 重骑兵. ~bender【美体】摔跤选手. ~-child *(pl. men-children)* 男孩; 儿子. ~-eater 食人者, 食人虎, 食人鲨鱼, 咬人的马. ~-engine【采】井内载人升降机. ~-god *(pl. men-gods)* 神人. ~handle *vt.* 用人力推动[开动]; [口]虐待, 粗暴地对待. ~handler【美体】摔跤选手. ~-hater 愤世嫉俗的人; 讨厌男人的女人. ~hole 人孔, (阴沟的)检修孔;【铁路】避孔. ~-hour 工时, 一人一小时的工作量. ~ jack 个人 (*every* ~ *jack* 人人, 每人). ~-killer 杀人的人[物]; 〔美〕杀人监〔工作繁重,规则严厉的监狱〕; 不让人接近的烈马. ~-made *a.* 人工的,人造的. ~-midwife *(pl. men midwives)* 〔罕〕产科医生. ~-milliner *(pl. men-milliners)* 女衣帽商〔男性〕; 无事忙(的男子). ~-of-war *(pl. men-of-war)* 军舰 (主指从前木造的兵舰). ~-of-war bird 军舰鸟(=frigate bird). ~ power 人力;【机】人力〔工率单位, = 1/10 马力〕; 有效人员总数. ~-rate *vt.* 对(火箭等)作安全评定〔证实火箭或宇宙飞船能安全进行载人飞行〕. ~rope【海】(作扶手的) 舷梯索. ~servant *(pl. menservants)* 男仆. ~-size(d) *a.* 〔美口〕大人尺寸的; 数目[分量]极大的; 适合[需要]男子(担当)的; 吃力的, 困难的. ~slaughter 杀人, (尤指)【法】过失杀人(罪). ~slayer 杀人的人, 凶手. ~-time *(pl. men-times)* *n.* 人次. ~-to-~ *a.* ①坦率的. ② (球赛中)人钉人的. ~-trap ①*n.(-traps, men-traps)*【英史】(从前捕捉侵入领土内的人用的)捕人机[陷阱]; 危险场所[东西]; 诱惑人的场所[赌场等]. ②*vt. (p., p.p. -pped)* 在…布置捕人机. ~way【矿】人行巷道. ~-year 一人在一年内完成的工作量. -less *a.* 没有人[男人]的; 〔古〕卑鄙的, 残忍的. -let 〔美〕矮小的人; 不足道的人. -like *a.* 象人的; 象男人的, 有大丈夫气概的; 男人似的,(女人)胜过男人的. -wise *ad.* 以男人的本分; 象男子汉那样地.

-man *comb. f.* *(pl. -men)* ①〔职业〕…人: post*man*, dust*man*, clergy*men*. ②〔籍贯〕…国人,…居民: English*man*, country*man*. ③…船: *man*-of-war, merchant*man*, India*man*.

Man. = Manhattan; Manila; Manitoba.

ma·na [ˈmɑːnɑː] *n.* 神力, 超自然力.

man·a·cle [ˈmænəkl] *n.* 〔常 *pl.*〕手铐; 束缚, 拘束. — *vt.* 给…上手铐; 束缚.

man·age¹ [ˈmænidʒ] *vt.* ①办理, 处置, 处理; 支配, 管理; 经营. ②(用手)使用, 驾驭, 操纵, 开动; 训练(马). ③〔主要和 can; be able to 连用〕处理, 办, 做; 〔口〕对付; 吃. ④设法…; 弄得…; 〔反语〕好不容易地把…. ~ *the affairs of a nation* 处理国家事务. ~*cattle* 管理家畜. ~ *a motor-car* 开汽车. *I cannot* ~ *it alone.* 我一个人办不了. *Can you* ~ *another slice?* 能再吃一片吗? *So you* ~*d it after all.* 结果你还是弄成功了. *Did you* ~ *it?* 你们做到了没有? *He* ~*d* (=was foolish enough) *to make a mess of it.* 他真不错, 把事情弄得糟透了. — *vi.* 处理, 办理; 应付, 对付, 敷衍(过去). *I shall* ~ *with the tools I have.* 我要用现有的工具设法对付. ~ ***on one's income*** 按收入过日子. ~ ***to be in time*** 设法及时. ~ ***to make both ends meet*** 设法使收支平衡. ~ ***without*** …在没有…下敷衍过去. ~d currency 管理通货.

man·age² [ˈmænidʒ] *n.* ①〔古〕练马. ②调教过的马的动作和步调. ③骑马学校, 马术练习所 (= manège).

man·age·a·ble [ˈmænidʒəbl] *a.* 易处理的, 易办的; 易管理的; 可以设法的; 易驾驭的, 乖, 温顺的. -bly *ad.* -ness *n.*

man·age·ment [ˈmænidʒmənt] *n.* ①办理, 处理; 管理, 经营; 经营力, 经营手腕. ②安排; 妥善对待. ③〔the ~〕〔集合词〕(工商企业)管理部门; 董事会; 厂方, 资方. *one man* ~ 一长制. *the* ~ *of economy* 经济管理. *land* ~ 土地规划.

man·ag·er [ˈmænidʒə] *n.* ①处理者; 经理(人), 管理人; 经营者. ②干事, 理事;【剧】舞台监督, 导演; 〔*pl.*〕(英议会) 两院协议会委员; 〔英〕【法】财务管理人. ③〔美〕(政党等的)领袖. ④策士, 干才, 干练的人. *a stage* ~ 舞台监督. *a good [bad]* ~ 会[不会]理财的人,(尤指)会[不会]当家的主妇.

man·ag·er·ess [ˈmænidʒəres] *n.* 〔英〕女经理, 女管理人.

man·ag·e·ri·al [ˌmænəˈdʒiəriəl] *a.* 经理的, 管理人的; 处理[管理]上的.

man·ag·er·ship [ˈmænidʒəʃip] *n.* 经理[管理人]身分[职位、任期、权力].

man·ag·ing [ˈmænidʒiŋ] *a.* ①处理的, 管理的; 首脑的. ②善于处理的, 善经营的. ③爱管闲事的, 爱自已操持的(女人等). ④节俭的; 吝啬的. *a* ~ *director* 总经理; 常务董事; 社长. *a* ~ *partner* 执行业务的合伙人. — *n.* 处理, 管理.

Ma·na·gua [məˈnɑːgwə] *n.* 马那瓜〔尼加拉瓜首都〕.

man·a·kin [ˈmænəkin] *n.* ①美洲小艳羽鸟. ②= manikin.

Ma·na·ma [mæˈnæmə] *n.* 麦纳麦〔巴林首都〕.

ma·ña·na [mɑːˈnjɑːnɑː] *n., ad.* 〔Sp.〕明天; (在)不确定的将来.

man·a·tee [mænəˈtiː] *n.*【动】海牛.

Man·ches·ter [ˈmæntʃistə] *n.* 曼彻斯特〔英国城市〕; 纺织工业中心. ~ ***department*** (商店的)棉织品部. ~ ***goods*** 棉布类. ***The*** ~ ***Guardian*** 曼彻斯特卫报. ~ ***terrier*** 曼彻斯特㹴.

Man·ches·ter·ism [ˈmæntʃistərizəm] *n.* 自由贸易主义.

man·chet [ˈmæntʃit] *n.* 〔古、英方〕①精粉面包. ②精粉面包卷; 精粉小面包.

Man·chu [mænˈtʃuː] *a.* 满族的; 满族人的; 满族语的. — *n.* 满族人; 满族的通古斯语.

Man·chu·ria [mænˈtʃuəriə] *n.* 满洲〔东北的旧称〕.

Man·chur·i·an [mænˈtʃuəriən] *a., n.* 满族的; 满族人(的). ~ ash【植】水曲柳. ~ elm 青榆. ~ fir 辽东冷杉.

man·ci·ple [ˈmænsipl] *n.* (大学或修道院等的)伙食承办人.

Man·cu·ni·an [mænˈkuːnjən] *a., n.* (英国)曼彻斯特(Manchester) 的(人); 曼彻斯特公立学校的(人).

-man·cy *comb. f.* 卜, 占: geomancy.

man·da·la [ˈmʌndələ] *n.*【佛、印度教】曼达拿, 曼陀罗, 曼荼罗〔宣传平等周遍十法界的宗教思想〕.

Man·da·lay [ˌmændəˈlei] *n.* 曼德勒〔缅甸城市〕.

man·da·mus [mænˈdeiməs] *n.*【法】(致下级法院的)训令.

Man·dan [ˈmændæn] *n.* ①*(pl.* ~*(s))* 曼丹人〔居于美国北达科他州的平原印第安人〕. ②曼丹语.

man·da·rin¹ [ˈmændərin] *n.* ①(中国清朝的)官吏; 〔M-〕中国官话 (= ~ language) 〔普通话的旧称〕. ②〔谑〕达官, 要人; 守旧的政党领袖. ③穿中国古代官服的玩偶. ~ dialect 中国官话〔中国北京或北方方言的旧称〕. ~ duck【鸟】鸳鸯. ~ fish 桂鱼, 鳜. ~ porcelain 绘有中国古代官吏图像的瓷瓶.

man·da·rin², man·da·rine [ˈmændəriːn, ˈmændərin] *n.* 中国柑桔(树) (= ~ orange); 柑桔酒; 橙黄色(染料).

man·da·tar·y [ˈmændətəri] *n.*【法】受任者, 受托者, 被委托人; 代理人; 受托管理国.

man·date [ˈmændeit] *n.* ①命令, 训令; 指令. ②〔美〕(执行判决的)命令, 指令; 上级法院[官员]对下级法院[官员]的训令. ③(选民对选出的代表, 议会等的)授权. ④【法】财产委托; (国际上的)委托管理. ⑤【商】支付命令; 雇佣契约. — *vt.* 委托管理. *a* ~*d territory* 托管地.

man·da·tor [ˈmændeitə] *n.* 命令者, 委托者.

M

man·da·to·ry [ˈmændətəri] *a.* 命令的，训令的；委任的，委托的 *(upon)*；〔美〕强迫的，义务性质的．～ *administration [rule]* 委托管理．*a ～ power* 受托管理国．— *n.* = mandatary.

Man·de [ˈmɑːndei] *n.* ①*(pl. ～(s))* 曼丁哥人〔西非黑人，包括马林凯人等〕．②曼丁哥语．— *a.* 曼丁哥人的；曼丁哥语的．

Man·de·an [mænˈdiən] *n.* ①曼德恩人〔诺斯替(Gnosti)教派信徒，今伊拉克尚有其后裔〕．②曼德恩语．— *a.* ①曼德恩人的；曼德恩学说的．②曼德恩的．

Man·der [ˈmɑːndə] *n.* 曼德〔姓氏〕．

man·di·ble [ˈmændibl] *n.*【解】下颚骨；颚，(特指)下颚；【鸟】嘴的上部〔下部〕；【虫】上颚；(蝇的)口钩．

man·dib·u·lar [mænˈdibjulə] *a.* 颚的，象颚的．

man·dib·u·late [mænˈdibjuːlit] *a.*【动】具颚的．— *n.* 具颚昆虫．

Man·din·go [mænˈdiŋgəu] *n.* 曼丁哥人〔西非洲黑人民族之一〕；曼丁哥语．

man·do·la, man·do·ra [ˈmændələ, -rə] *n.*〔It.〕【乐】中曼陀林(琴)．

man·do·lin, man·do·line [ˈmændəlin, ˌmændəˈliːn] *n.*【乐】曼陀林(琴)，瓢琴．

man·drag·o·ra, man·drake [mænˈdrægərə, ˈmændreik] *n.* ①【植】曼德拉草〔根可作麻醉剂〕．②*[-drake]*〔美〕(= May apple) 盾叶鬼臼．

man·drel, man·dril [ˈmændril] *n.*【机】轴胎，心轴，紧轴；【冶】(铸造用的)圆形心轴；(采矿用的)鹤嘴锄，铁镐．*built-up ～* 组合心轴．*press ～* 压进心轴．*taper shank ～* 锥柄心轴．

man·drill [ˈmændril] *n.*【动】(西非洲的)狒狒，大猴．

man·du·cate [ˈmændjukeit] *vt.*〔罕〕嚼，咀嚼，吃，狼吞虎咽地吃．

man·du·ca·tion [ˌmændjuˈkeiʃən] *n.* 咀嚼．

man·du·ca·to·ry [mænˈdjuːkətəri] *a.* 咀嚼的，适于咀嚼的．

mane [mein] *n.* (马、狮子等的)鬃毛；(人的)长头发．***make neither ～ nor tail of*** 完全不懂…．

maned [meind] *a.* 有鬃毛的．

ma·nège [mæˈneiʒ] *n.*〔F.〕= manage[2].

ma·nes, M- [ˈmeiniːz] *n.*〔*pl.*〕①〔古罗马〕(祖先等的)灵；灵魂；阴间诸神．②〔M-〕波斯预言家(= Mani).

ma·neu·ver [məˈnuːvə] *n., v.*〔美〕= manoeuvre.

mane·y [ˈmeini] *a.* 鬃毛似的．

Man·fred [ˈmænfred] *n.* 曼弗雷德〔男子名〕．

man·ful [ˈmænful] *a.* 有男子汉气魄的；雄伟的；刚勇的；果断的．**-ly** *ad.* **-ness** *n.*

man·ga·bey [ˈmæŋgəbei] *n.*【动】白眉猴属动物．

man·ga·nate [ˈmæŋgəneit] *n.*【化】锰酸盐．

man·ga·nese [ˌmæŋgəˈniːz, ˈmæŋgəniːz] *n.*【化】锰．*black ～* 氧化锰．～ *ocher* 黑赭石．～ *spar*【矿】菱锰矿．～ *steel* 锰钢．

man·gan·ic [mæŋˈgænik] *a.* (似)锰的；三价锰的；六价锰的．～ *acid* 锰酸．

man·ga·nin [ˈmæŋgənin] *n.* 锰铜；锰镍铜齐．

man·ga·nite [ˈmæŋgənait] *n.*【矿】水锰矿；【化】亚锰酸盐．

man·ga·nous [ˈmæŋgənəs] *a.*【化】亚锰的，二价锰的，锰似的，含锰的．～ *acid* 亚锰酸．

mange [meindʒ] *n.* ①(牛、狗等的)疥癣，癞疮．②皮肤不洁．

man·gel (-wur·zel) [ˈmæŋgl (ˈwəːzl)] *n.*〔英〕【植】饲料甜菜．

man·ger [ˈmeindʒə] *n.* ①秣桶，马〔牛〕槽．②【海】船首挡水板．***dog in the ～*** 占着茅坑不拉屎的人．

man·gi·ly [ˈmeindʒili] *ad.* = mangy.

man·gle[1] [ˈmæŋgl] *vt.* ①乱切，乱砍，割碎；弄伤．②破坏，弄糟，损坏；(因发音拙劣等)使话听不懂．*a ～ corpse* 被砍得血肉模糊的尸体．～ *a piece of music* (因演奏技巧拙劣)糟踏了一个乐曲．**-r** *n.* 乱砍…的人；绞肉机．

man·gle[2] [ˈmæŋgl] *n.* 轧布机；轧板机；砑光机；碾压机；轧液机．— *vt.* 用轧布机砑光．**-r** *n.* (布等的)砑光机；(橡胶的)压延机；绞肉机；榨甘蔗机；轧机操作者．

man·go [ˈmæŋgəu] *n.* *(pl. ～(e)s)* 杧果；杧果树．～ **fish** 印度【动】四指马鲅．～ **trick** (印度魔术)现结杧果．

man·gold (-wur·zel) [ˈmæŋgəld(ˈwəːzl)] *n.* = mangel (-wurzel).

man·go·nel [ˈmæŋgənel] *n.* 古代军用射〔抛〕石机．

man·go·steen [ˈmæŋgəustiːn] *n.* 倒捻子(树)．

man·grove [ˈmæŋgrəuv] *n.*【植】(热带沿海生长的)红树(林)，栲树(林)．～ **cuckoo**【鸟】(西印度群岛的)郭公鸟的一种．

man·gy [ˈmeindʒi] *a.* 生满疥癣的，尽是癞疮的；污秽的，肮脏的；〔口〕卑劣的．

Man·hat·tan [mænˈhætən] *n.* 曼哈顿〔美国纽约市中心〕；曼哈顿商业区；〔m-〕曼哈顿鸡尾酒．～ **District** 第二次世界大战中美国原子弹研究总部．～ **Project** 第二次世界大战中美国原子弹研究计划．

Man·hat·tan·ese [mænˈhætəniːs] *a.* 纽约的．— *n.* 纽约人；纽约话；纽约时髦话．**-tan·ite** *n.*〔美俚〕纽约人．

man·hood [ˈmænhud] *n.* 人的状态；(男性)大人，成人；刚毅，丈夫气；〔集合词〕(成年)男子．*the whole ～ of the country* 全国男子．*a perfect ～* 完人，君子．***arrive at ～*** 成年．***in the prime of ～*** 壮年，盛年．

ma·ni·a [ˈmeinjə, -niə] *n.*【医】狂躁，癫狂；狂热，狂慕，狂爱；…狂，…热，…癖．*a ～ for [the ～ of] dancing* 跳舞狂．*the football ～* 足球狂．

-mania *comb. f.* ①特种习癖：klepto*mania*, megalo*mania*.②狂热的嗜好：biblio*mania*, mono*mania*. ③赞美，醉心：Anglo*mania*.

ma·ni·ac[1] [ˈmeiniæk] *a.* 躁狂的；疯狂的；狂热的．— *n.* 躁狂者；疯子．**-a·cal·ly** *ad.*

ma·ni·ac[2] [ˈmeiniæk] *n.* 一种高速电子数字计算机〔*ma*thematical *a*nalyzer, *n*umerical *i*ntegrator *a*nd *c*omputer 的首字母缩合词〕．

-maniac *comb. f.* ①表示"…狂〔迷、癖〕的"：biblio*maniac*. ②表示"…狂〔迷、癖〕者"：bibliv*maniac*.

ma·ni·a·cal [məˈnaiəkəl] *a.* = maniac. **-ly** *ad.*

ma·nic [ˈmeinik, ˈmeinik] *a.*【医】躁狂的．— *n.* 躁狂者．～**-depressive** *a.* (由两种症候交替发生所致的)躁狂抑郁症的．

Man·i·chae·an, Man·i·che·an [mæniˈki(ː)ən] *n., a.* 摩尼教(的)；摩尼教徒(的)．

Man·i·ch(a)e·ism [ˈmænikiːizəm] *n.* (伊朗的)摩尼教，明暗教；明暗〔善恶〕对立说．

Man·i·chee [ˈmænikiː] *n.* 摩尼教徒．

man·i·cure [ˈmænikjuə] *n.* 修指甲(术)；— *vt.* ①为…修指甲；修…的指甲．②修剪，修平．～ *parlour* 指甲美化室．

man·i·cur·ist [ˈmænikjuərist] *n.* 指甲美化师．

man·i·fest [ˈmænifest] *a.* 明白的，明显的．— *vt.* ①指明，表明；明白表示．②证明；使了解．③把…记在货单上．④〔～ oneself〕(鬼、征候等)出现．— *vi.* ①(鬼等)出现．②表明(政治上的)意见，发表宣言．～ ***itself*** 显出，现出．— *n.*【商】(船长交海关的)船货清单．**M-Destiny** 命定扩张论〔十九世纪为美国向外搞扩张辩解的资产阶级史观〕．**-ly** *ad.*

man·i·fes·ta·tion [ˌmænifesˈteiʃən] *n.* ①表现，表示；显现．②发表政见，政治示威；公开声明．③【心】神秘现象的具体化．

man·i·fes·to [ˌmæniˈfestəu] *n.* *(pl. ～(e)s)* 宣言，声明；告示，布告．— *vi.*〔罕〕发表宣言〔声明〕．

man·i·fold [ˈmænifəuld] *a.* ①许多的；种种的，多样的，多方面的，五花八门．②由许多部分形成的．*maintains*

~ *links with* 和…有千丝万缕的关系. — *n.* ①复写本. ②【机】歧管, 集合管; 复式接头. ③【数】簇, 流形. ~ **paper** 打字纸. ~ **writer** 复写器. — *vt., vi.* (用复写器等)复写,复印.

man·i·hot [ˈmænihɔt] *n.* 木薯 (= cassava).

man·i·kin [ˈmænikin] *n.* ①矮人, 侏儒; (画家等用的)木制模特儿, 人体模型; 人体解剖模型. ②= mannequin. ③= manakin. *a ~ girl* 服装模特儿.

Ma·nil(l)·a [məˈnilə] *n.* 马尼拉〔菲律宾首都〕.

ma·nil·(l)a [məˈnilə] *n.* 吕宋(雪茄)烟; 马尼拉麻; 马尼拉纸. ~ **hemp** 马尼拉麻. ~ **nut** 落花生. ~ **paper** 马尼拉纸. ~ **rope** 吕宋绳,白棕绳.

man·i·oc [ˈmæniɔk] *n.* = cassava.

man·i·ple [ˈmænipl] *n.* ①天主教神父左臂上佩的饰带. ②(古罗马军团的)步兵支队.

ma·nip·u·lar [məˈnipjulə] *a.* ①(古罗马军队的)支队的. ②操作的; 操纵的; 手术的; 应付的. — *n.* 支队的士兵.

ma·nip·u·late [məˈnipjuleit] *vt.* ①(有技巧地)使用,开动(机械等); 巧妙地处理(问题等); 摆布,巧妙地操纵(人等). ②窜改(帐目等). ③操纵(市价、市场), 控制. ~ *a convention* 操纵会议. ~ *voters* 收买投票人. —*vi.* 巧妙地处理,巧妙地使用.

ma·nip·u·la·tion [məˌnipjuˈleiʃən] *n.* ①(熟练的)操作; 操作法; 手法. ②(市场等的)操纵, 控制. ③(外科)手技,手法. *conjoined* ~ 双手操作法. *remote* ~ 远距离操作,遥控. **-tive, -to·ry** *a.*

ma·nip·u·la·tor [məˈnipjuleitə] *n.* ①用手处理[操作]的人; 巧于处理的人. ②操纵者; 控制器. ③窜改者. ④运动器具;【摄】板架,保板器.

man·i·to, man·i·tou, man·i·tu [ˈmænitəu, -tuː] *n.* *(pl. ~s)* (北美 Algonquian 人信奉的)自然神.

man·kind [mænˈkaind] *n.* ①人类,人. ②[ˈmænkaind] 男性,男子 (*opp.* womankind).

man·li·ness [ˈmænlinis] *n.* 男子气, 雄伟, 勇敢, 刚毅, 大胆.

man·ly [ˈmænli] *a.* ①有男子汉气魄的; 雄赳赳的; 大胆的,勇敢的; 果断的, 刚毅的. ②适合男子的. ③男子似的,(女人)胜过男子的.

Mann [mæn] *n.* 曼〔姓氏〕.

man·na [ˈmænə] *n.* ①【圣】吗哪〔《圣经》所说古以色列人漂泊荒野时上帝所赐的食物〕; 神粮; 美味; 不期而获的东西; 振奋精神的东西. ②【医】(作缓泻剂用的)甘露, 木蜜. ~ *in sorts [tears]* 下[上]等木蜜. **~-ash**【植】欧洲白蜡树. **~-croup** 粗小麦粉.

Mann Act [mæn] 麦恩法案〔美国 1910 年 6 月在国会通过的一项法案, 禁止州与州之间贩运妇女作不道德的勾当〕.

man·ned [mænd] *a.* 载人的; 由人操纵的. *a ~ space ship* 载人宇宙飞船.

man·ne·quin [ˈmænikin] *n.* 服装模特儿〔服装店雇佣的以穿时装供展览为职业的妇女〕; (橱窗里的)服装模型.

man·ner [ˈmænə] *n.* ①方法, 做法. ②态度, 样子, 举止; 〔*pl.*〕礼貌, 规矩. ③〔*pl.*〕风俗, 习惯, 惯例, 生活方式. ④(艺术、文学的)风格, 手法, 样式, 体; 癖. ⑤种类. *houses built in the Chinese ~* 中国式住宅. *What ~ of man is he?* 他是怎样一个人? *the grand ~* 高尚的态度. *Where are your ~s?* 规矩呢? 你还有没有礼貌? *good ~s* 有礼貌. *bad ~s* 没礼貌. ***after the ~ of*** 仿效, 学…的样; …式的. ***after this ~*** 照这样, 象这样. ***all ~ of*** 种种,各色各样的(人、东西等等). ***by all ~ of means*** = by all means. ***by no ~ of means*** 决不, 一点也不. ***develop a ~ of one's own*** 独创一派, 自成一家. ***have no ~ of (right)*** 毫无(权利). ***have no ~s*** 不懂礼貌, 没规矩. ***in a ~*** 在某种意义上; 多少, 有点. ***in a ~ of speaking*** 不妨说; 说起来. ***in an all-round ~*** 全面. ***in like ~*** 同样地. ***in the ~*** 在现行中, 当场. ***in the ~ of*** 照…的式样. ***in this ~*** 如此, 照这样. ***in what ~*** 怎么样. ***make [do] one's ~s*** 行礼. ***no ~ of*** 一点没有. ***to the ~ born*** 生来的; 生来适于某种地位[职业]的; 生在那种习惯中的. ***with the ~ = in the ~***.

man·nered [ˈmænəd] *a.* 〔和形容词或副词连用〕举止…的; (文体)墨守旧风格的, 矫揉造作的. *well-~* 有礼貌的. *ill-~* 没礼貌的, 撒野的. *a ~ stye of writing* 矫揉造作的文体.

man·ner·ism [ˈmænərizəm] *n.* ①(尤指文艺上的) 守旧, 作风守旧; 矫揉造作的风格. ②怪癖; (特指演员说话、动作等的)习气.

man·ner·ist [ˈmænərist] *n.* 作风守旧的人; 风格特别的作家[艺术家]; 矫揉造作者; 有怪癖的人.

man·ner·less [ˈmænəlis] *a.* 不懂礼貌的, 没规矩的.

man·ner·ly [ˈmænəli] *a., ad.* 有礼貌的[地], 谦恭的[地], 殷勤的[地]. **-li·ness** *n.*

Mann·heim [ˈmænhaim] *n.* 曼海姆〔西德城市〕.

man·ni·kin [ˈmænikin] *n.* = manikin.

Man·ning [ˈmæniŋ] *n.* 曼宁〔姓氏〕.

man·nish [ˈmæniʃ] *a.* (女人)男子似的; (孩子)大人似的; 适合男子的. *What a ~ way to thread a needle!* 穿针线真象男人一样地笨. **-ly** *ad.* **-ness** *n.*

man·nite [ˈmænait] *n.* 甘露糖醇 (= mannitol). **-nit·ic** [məˈnitik] *a.*

man·ni·tol [ˈmænitəul, -tɔːl] *n.*【化】甘露糖醇.

ma·noeu·ver·a·ble [məˈnuːvrəbl] *a.* ①机动的; 可调动的. ②操纵灵敏的.

ma·noeu·vre [məˈnuːvə] *n.* ①【军】(军队、兵舰的)机动, 调动, 部署; 〔*pl.*〕军事演习. ②策略; 策动; 谋略, 巧计, 诡计, 花招, 伎俩, 手法. *anti-air-raid ~ [drill]* 防空演习. *a political ~* 政治花招. *This ~ of his is a diabolical conspiracy.* 他这一手是个居心叵测的大阴谋. — *vi.* *(-vred, -vered; vring, vering)* 演习; 调动, 部署; 用计, 耍花招. — *vt.* 使演习; 调动; 用策略使…, 用计使…. *a manoeuvering aircraft* 特技飞机. ~ *the enemy into [out of] a position* 用计谋使敌军进入[撤出]某一阵地.

ma·nom·e·ter [məˈnɔmitə] *n.* 【物】流体或气体压力计, 测压器;【医】血压计.

man·o·met·ric [ˌmænəˈmetrik] *a.* 流体压力计的, 用测压器测的. ~ *flames*【物】感压焰. *a ~ thermometer* 压差温度计.

ma non trop·po [mɑːnɔnˈtrɔpəu] 〔It.〕【乐】但不可过度.

man·or [ˈmænə] *n.* ①〔英〕(封建时代由贵族管辖的)采邑, 领地; (现今贵族的、包括贵族邸第在内的)庄园. ②〔美〕永久租借地. *a capital ~* 直属领地. *the lord of the ~* 庄园领主. ~ **house,** ~ **seat** 庄园主的住宅.

ma·no·ri·al [məˈnɔːriəl] *a.* 庄园[采邑]的. *a ~ lord* 领主. *a ~ slave* 农奴. **-ly** *ad.*

man·nose [ˈmænəus] *n.*【化】甘露糖.

man·o·stat [ˈmænəustæt] *n.*【物】稳压器, 恒压器.

man·qué [F. mɑ̃ˈke] *a.* 〔F.〕 *(fem. -quée)* 〔用于名词后〕没有成功的. *a poet ~* 失意落魄的诗人.

man·sard [ˈmænsɑːd] *n.* (法国建筑家 *Mansard* 设计的)复斜屋顶 (*cf.* gambrel roof); (复斜屋顶的)屋顶室, 阁楼.

manse [mæns] *n.* 牧师住宅〔尤指长老教会〕; 〔古〕房主住宅.

Mans·field [ˈmænsfiːld] *n.* 曼斯菲尔德〔姓氏〕.

man·sion [ˈmænʃən] *n.* ①宅第, 公馆. ②〔*pl.*〕〔英〕大楼, 公寓〔美国叫 apartment house〕. ③(大楼中的)一套房间. ④【天】宫, 宿. *lunar ~s*【天】二十八宿 ~ **house** (领主或地主的) 邸宅, 公馆; 〔the M- House〕伦敦市长官邸.

Man·son [ˈmænsn] *n.* 曼森〔姓氏〕.

M

man·sue·tude [ˈmænswitju:d] *n.* 〔古、罕〕柔顺，温和.
man·ta [ˈmæntə; Sp. ˌmɑ:ntɑ:] *n.* ①粗布，粗棉织品；粗布围巾，粗皮披肩. ②马毯，马衣. ③【动】鸢魟；灰色鲸；鮟鱇，琵琶鱼，章鱼，乌贼.
man·teau [ˈmæntəu] *n.* (*pl.* ~*s*, ***man·teaux*** **[-z]**) 〔F.〕斗篷，披风〔尤指女用〕.
man·tel [ˈmæntl] *n.* ①壁炉面饰；炉额. ②壁炉架. ★英国①义说作 ~piece, ②义说作 ~ shelf; 美国①义常说作 ~, ②义常说作 ~piece. ~ **board** 壁炉架. ~**piece** 壁炉面饰，壁炉台. ~**shelf** (*pl.* **-shelves**)壁炉架. ~**tree** 壁炉楣；壁炉面饰.
man·tel·et [ˈmæntəlit] *n.* ①(女用)小斗篷. ②【军】弹盾；移动雉堞；着弹观察所.
man·tel·let·ta [ˌmæntəˈletə] *n.* (红衣主教等穿的)无袖法衣.
man·tic [ˈmæntik] *a.* 占卜的；预言的.
man·til·la [mænˈtilə] *n.* (女用)小披风；(西班牙女人用的)薄头纱；大面纱.
man·tis [ˈmæntis] *n.* (*pl.* ~*es*; ***man·tes*** [ˈmænti:z]) 【虫】螳螂. *a praying* ~ 合掌螳螂. ~ *shrimp* 口脚类动物 (= stomatopod).
man·tis·sa [mænˈtisə] *n.* 【数】假数，(对数的)尾数.
man·tle [ˈmæntl] *n.* ①披风，罩衣. ②一层(被覆)幕，盖罩. ③(煤气灯)纱罩；【解】外表；【动】套膜；(鸟的)翕；【机】(水车的)槽；(高炉的)环梁壳；【地】地幔. ④【徽】徽章背景和周围的彩饰. ⑤继承标帜，衣钵. ⑥= mantel. ***One's ~ falls on [descends to] another.*** 衣钵传给别人，精神影响别人. ***take the ~ (and ring)*** (寡妇)誓不再嫁. — *vt.* 披上斗篷；覆，包；隐蔽. — *vi.* (液体表面)结皮；(酒、汽水等)盖满泡沫；覆；(鸟)展开翅膀；展开，扩展；(脸)涨红. ~ ***with roses*** (两颊)涨满桃红色. ~ **cavity** 套腔. ~ **rock** 风化层，土被，表皮岩.
mant·let [ˈmæntlit] *n.* = mantelet ②.
man·tling [ˈmæntliŋ] *n.* 斗篷料；徽章彩饰；壁炉面饰.
Man·toux test [mænˈtu:, ˈmæntu:] 【医】曼透氏试法〔检查肺结核〕.
man·tra [ˈmʌntrə, ˈmæn-] *n.* 颂歌，圣歌；咒语〔尤指四吠陀经典内作为咒文或祷告唱念者〕.
man·tu·a [ˈmæntjuə] *n.* ①(17—18 世纪流行的)宽松女大衣. ②= mantle.
man(u)- *pref.* 表示"手的，手工的".
man·u·al [ˈmænjuəl] *a.* ①手的，手作的，手工的；用手操作的；便于手头应用的. ②【法】现有的. ~ *labour* 手工劳动. *a* ~ *worker* 体力劳动者. *the* ~ *alphabet* (聋哑人用的) 手语字母. *a* ~ *fire-engine* 手压灭火机. ~ *training* (学校的) 手工学科〔特指木工〕. ~ *exercises* 刀枪操练. *a sign* ~ 签名，亲笔署名. — *n.* ①手册；说明书；便览，指南，宝鉴；教本；(中世纪的)祈祷书. ②【军】刀枪操练. ③【乐】键盘. ④手压灭火机. *a school* ~教科书. *the service* ~ 维修守则，使用细则. **-ly** *ad.* 用手；亲自，实际.
ma·nu·bri·um [məˈnu:bri:əm, -nju:-] *n.* (*pl.* ***-bri·a*** **[-ə]**, ***-bri·ums***) ①柄式结构；柄状突起；柄状体. ②(尤指)【动】(腔肠动物的)垂管；(昆虫的)前腹片；前胸骨；前腹板.
man·u·code [ˈmænjukəud] *n.* 极乐鸟类.
Man·u·el [ˈmænjuel] *n.* 曼纽尔〔男子名，Em(m)anuel 的异体〕.
manuf. = manufactory; manufacture(d); manufacturer.
man·u·fac·to·ry [ˌmænjuˈfæktəri] *n.* 制造厂；工厂.
man·u·fac·ture [ˌmænjuˈfæktʃə] *vt.* ①(成批)生产，制造. ②捏造，虚构；粗制滥造(文学作品等). — *vi.* 从事制造. — *n.* ①(成批的)制造，(特种)工业；工厂. ②制造品，产品；〔蔑〕(文学上的)滥作. *a thing of home [foreign]* ~ 本国〔外国〕制品. *the steel* ~ 制钢工业. *silk* ~*s* 丝织品.
man·u·fac·tur·er [ˌmænjuˈfæktʃərə] *n.* 制造商，厂主；制造厂.
man·u·fac·tur·ing [ˌmænjuˈfæktʃəriŋ] *a.* 制造的；从事工业的. *a* ~ *town* 工业城市. *a* ~ *district* 工业区. *the* ~ *industry* 制造业.
ma·nul [ˈmeinul] *n.* (西藏、蒙古的)小野猫.
man·u·mis·sion [ˌmænjuˈmiʃən] *n.* (农奴、奴隶的)解放；解放证.
man·u·mit [ˌmænjuˈmit] *vt.* 【史】解放(农奴或奴隶).
man·u·mit·ter [ˌmænjuˈmitə] *n.* 解放者.
man·u·mo·tor [ˌmænjuˈməutə] *n.* 手推车.
ma·nure [məˈnjuə] *n.* 肥料. — *vt.* 施肥于…. *artificial* ~ 人造肥料. *nitrogenous* ~ 氮肥. *barn yard [farmyard]* ~ 厩〔堆〕肥. *green* ~ 绿肥. *a* ~ *spreader* 施肥机.
ma·nus [ˈmeinəs] *n.* (*pl.* ***ma·nus***) ①(四肢动物的)手，前掌. ②(罗马法律)夫权.
man·u·script [ˈmænjuskript] *a.* 手写的，手抄的. — *n.* 抄本；(著者的)原稿.〔略：MS.；〔*pl.*〕MSS.〕；手写(*opp.* print). *The work is still in* ~. 那本著作仍旧没有印刷〔原稿未动〕.
man·ward [ˈmænwəd] *ad., a.* 面向人类(的)，关于人(的).
man·wise [ˈmænwaiz] *ad.* 以男人的本分；象男子汉那样.
Manx [mæŋks] *a.* 英国曼 (Man) 岛的；曼岛人〔语〕的. — *n.* 曼岛人〔语〕；〔集合词〕(无尾) 曼岛猫〔又作 ~ cat〕.
Manx·man [ˈmæŋksmən] *n.* (*pl.* ***-men***) 曼(Man)岛人〔男人〕. ~**woman** 曼岛女人.
man·y [ˈmeni] *a.* (***more; most***) (*opp.* few; *cf.* much) 许多的，多数的，很多的，多. ★(1)在口语中，尤其是在英国口语中，除用作肯定句的主语或接用于 too, so, as, how 之后以外，带有否定、疑问、条件意义: M- people think so. Did you see ~ people? (2)在其他肯定句中常作 a lot of, a (large) number of, a great [good] many 等的代用语. (3)文语中通例是以单数用作倒装句法中的表语: Many's the time (=often) I've seen him do it. — *pro.* 许多人〔物〕. *M- of us were tired.* 我们当中的许多人都疲倦了. *I have a few, but not* ~. 我有一点儿，可是不多. — *n.* ①多数人〔东西〕. *There are a good* ~ *of them.* 那样的人很多〔那种东西很多〕. *A great* ~ *stayed away.* 很多人没来. ②〔the ~〕大多数人，一般人，群众. ***a good [great]*** ~ 很多的，非常多的. ***as*** ~ 和…一样多(的)；同数(的) (*He made six mistakes in as* ~ *lines.* 六行里就错了六处) ***as ~ again*** 再同样多的，加倍的. ***as ~ as ...*** ①多少…多少，…的都… (*Take as* ~ *as you want.* 你要多少就拿多少. *They admit as* ~ *as come.* 来多少就可以进去多少). ②整整的〔一般指数目而言〕 (*He has been working at his book as* ~ *as five years.* 他的书已经整整写了五年了). ***as [like] so*** ~ ①象许多人一样 (*He failed like so* ~ *before him.* 象他前面的许多人一样，他失败了). ②同数的，和…一样多的 (= as ~). ***be one too*** ~ 多余的东西，碍手碍脚的东西. ***be (one) too ~ for*** 比某人高明，胜过某人；为某人所不能理解 (*He is (one) too* ~ *for me.* 我弄他不赢，我把他没办法). ***how*** ~ 多少，几何 (*How* ~ *boys are there?* 有多少男孩?) ~ ***a [an]*** 〔诗、古〕许许多多，很多 (~ *a day* 多日〔语气较强于 ~ days〕. ~ ***a*** 〔古〕***an*** ***one*** 许许多多人. ***M- a pickle makes a muckle.*** 积少成多，集腋成裘). ~ ***(and ~)a time*** = ~ ***a time and oft*** 〔诗、古〕= ***on ~ occasions*** = ~ ***times*** 多次，不知多少次. ***not*** ~〔俚〕少许的，些少的. ***not so ~ as*** 没那么多，少于. ***so*** ~ 那么多的，同数的 (*in so* ~ *words* 露骨地(说). *So* ~ *men, so* ~ *minds.* 〔谚〕十人十心. *There are so* ~ *mistakes that I can not count them.* 错误多得数不清). ~**fold** *ad.* 许多倍地. ~**-headed** *a.* 多头的. ~**-minded** *a.* 三心二

意的. ~**plies** 〔*sing.*, *pl.*〕重瓣胃〔反刍类的第三胃(= omasum)〕. ~**-sided** *a.* 【几】多边的;多方面的,多才多艺的,兴趣广博的. ~**-stage** *a.* 多段的,多级的;多串联的. ~**wheres** *ad.* 在许多地方.
many- *comb. f.* = many.
man·za·na [mɑːnˈzɑːnə] *n.* (中南美的)面积单位〔1至2英亩〕.
man·za·ni·ta [ˌmænzəˈniːtə] *n.* 【植】熊果属植物.
Ma·o·ri [ˈmɑːri, ˈmauri] *n.* (*pl.* ~*s*) (新西兰的)毛利人;毛利语. — *a.* 毛利人[语]的.
MAP = Military Aid Program〔美〕军事援助计划.
map [mæp] *n.* ①地图;天体图;图. ②〔美俚〕脸,面孔. ③〔美俚〕(染色体上基因排列的)遗传图. ***off the*** ~〔口〕不重要的;消失的;过时的;陈腐的. ***on the*** ~〔口〕存在的;重要的;有名的,占显著地位的,起主要作用的. ***put oneself on the*** ~ 发生,发现;使自己出名,出人头地. ***put sb. [sth.] on the*** ~ 使某人[某事]出名. ***wipe off the*** ~ 把…消灭掉. — *vt.* 测绘,为…绘制地图;勘测,制订. ②〔美俚〕测定(染色体中基因的)位置. ~ ***out*** 规划,安排. ~ **board** 图板. ~ **measurer** 量图仪,地图里程计算器. ~ **like** *a.* 象地图的. ~**mounter** 裱地图的人. ~ **scale** 地图比例尺.
ma·ple [ˈmeipl] *n.* 【植】槭,枫;枫木;槭糖浆味;淡棕色;〔*pl.*〕【美体】篮球场的地板. *hard* ~ 硬木. *Japanese* ~ 鸡爪枫. ~***s five*** 【美体】篮球队. ~ **sugar** 槭糖. ~ **syrup** 槭糖浆;槭树汁. ~ **leaf** 枫叶〔Canada 的国徽〕.
map·per, map·pist [ˈmæpə, -pist] *n.* 制图者;绘图人.
map·ping [ˈmæpiŋ] *n.* 【数】映像,映射.
Ma·pu·to [mæˈputə] 马普托〔莫桑比克首都〕.
ma·quette [mɑːˈket] *n.* (雕塑、建筑等设计的)小模型.
ma·quil·lage [ˌmækiːˈjɑːʒ] *n.* 〔F.〕化妆品.
Ma·quis [ˈmɑːki] *n.* (*pl.* ***-quis*** [-ˈkiːz]) 马基〔第二次世界大战中抗击纳粹的法国地下组织成员〕.
mar [mɑː] *vt.* 毁损,弄坏,弄糟. ***make [mend] or*** ~ 完全成功或失败到底. — *n.* 损伤,毁损;障碍.
Mar. = March.
mar. = ①married. ②maritime.
Mara [ˈmɑːrə] *n.* 玛拉〔女子名, Mary 的异体〕.
mar·a·bou, mar·a·bout [ˈmærəbuː, -buːt] *n.* 【鸟】(非洲)大鹳;秃鹳;鹳毛;【纺】马拉布生丝;单丝经缎.
Mar·a·bout [ˈmærəbuːt] *n.* 伊斯兰教托钵僧或隐士;伊斯兰教隐士的坟墓或圣祠.
mar·aca [məˈrɑːkə] *n.* (南美等处跳舞乐队用的)响葫芦.
Mar·a·cai·bo [ˌmærəˈkaibəu] *n.* 马拉开波〔委内瑞拉港市〕.
mar·ag·ing steels [ˈmɑːreidʒiŋ] 马氏体钢〔具有极高强度的镍铁合金,从马丁散体钢中以不淬火的方法弭散硬化而成〕.
mar·a·nath·a [ˌmærəˈnɑːθə] *n.* 咒诅话.
mar·a·schi·no [ˌmærəsˈkiːnəu] *n.* (*pl.* ~*s*) 〔It.〕野樱桃酒. ~ *cherries* 野樱桃酒味糖水樱桃.
mar·as·mus [məˈræzməs] *n.* 【医】消瘦,衰弱. **ma·ras·mic** *a.*
Ma·ra·tha [məˈrɑːtə] *n.* (西印度)马拉地族人.
Ma·ra·thi [məˈrɑːtiː] *n.* 马拉地语.
mar·a·thon [ˈmærəθən] *n.* 马拉松长跑〔正式路程是26英里385码(= 42.195公里),又名 ~ *race*〕;长距离赛跑;(各种)持久比赛. — *a.* (比赛等)需要极大持久力的. — *vi.* 参加持久比赛. **-er** 参加持久比赛的人.
mar·a·tho·ni·an [ˌmærəˈθəuniən] *n.* 马拉松赛跑选手. — *a.* 马拉松的.
ma·raud [məˈrɔːd] *vi.*, *vt.* 掠夺,抢劫,劫掠 (*on*; *upon*) — *n.* 〔罕〕劫掠. ~*ing hordes* 盗匪.
ma·raud·er [məˈrɔːdə] *n.* 掠夺者,抢劫者.
mar·a·ve·di [ˌmæreˈveidi] *n.* (*pl.* ~***dis***) 马勒威迪〔西班牙的古铜币〕.
mar·ble [ˈmɑːbl] *n.* ①大理石;〔*pl.*〕大理石雕刻品. ②(小儿游戏用)弹子;〔*pl.*〕弹子戏. ③〔*pl.*〕〔俚〕理智;常识. ***as hard [cold] as*** ~ 大理石一样坚硬[冰冷]的,冷酷无情的. ***Elgin***[ˈelgin] ~***s*** 不列颠博物馆所藏希腊帕特嫩神庙 (*Parthenon*) 的大理石雕刻. ***M- Arch*** (伦敦海德公园东北入口的)大理石拱门. — *a.* ①大理石(似)的;有大理石纹彩的. ②无情的,冷酷的;纯白的. ~ *paper* 云纹纸. ~ *dust* 云石粉. ~ *soap* 斑纹皂. *a* ~ *brow* 白眉毛. ~ *cake* 大理石纹奶油蛋糕. — *vt.* 把(纸、书边、肥皂等)做成大理石花纹形状;〔罕〕把…弄得象大理石一样的白. ~**-edged** *a.* (精装书)云纹边的. ~**-hearted** *a.* 铁石心肠的,无情的,冷酷的;麻木的.
mar·ble·ize [ˈmɑːblaiz] *vt.* 弄成大理石花纹.
mar·bling [ˈmɑːbliŋ] *n.* ①大理石纹著附术,大理石纹加工法. ②大理石纹状.
mar·bly [ˈmɑːbli] *a.* 大理石似的;含大理石的;冒充大理石的;冷酷的,冷淡的.
marc [mɑːk] *n.* (葡萄等的)榨渣,果渣;苹果[葡萄]渣酿制的白兰地酒.
mar·can·do [mɑːˈkɑːndəu] *a.*, *ad.* 〔It.〕【乐】清晰的[地].
mar·ca·site [ˈmɑːkəsait] *n.* 【矿】白铁矿;用作饰品的白铁矿石.
mar·cel [mɑːˈsel] *n.* 波形卷发〔又叫 ~ wave〕. — *vt.* 使(头发)烫成波浪形. **-cel·ler** [-ə] *n.* 烫发师.
mar·cel·la [mɑːˈselə] *n.* 凸纹布.
mar·ces·cent [mɑːˈsesnt] *a.* 【植】凋存的,凋而不落的. **-cence** *n.*
March[1] [mɑːtʃ] *n.* 马奇〔姓氏〕.
March[2] [mɑːtʃ] *n.* 三月〔略作 Mar.〕. *in* ~ 在三月. ~ *comes in like a lion and goes out like a lamb.* 〔谚〕三月天气来如猛狮,去如绵羊. ~ **brown** (钓鱼用的)拟饵;蜉蝣. ~ **hare** 交尾期的野兔 (*mad as a* ~ *hare* 发情若狂).
march[1] [mɑːtʃ] *n.* ①行进;进军,行军;【军】进军行程,推进里程;步调. ②艰苦的长途旅行. ③进展,发展. ④【乐】进行曲. *the Long M-* (中国红军的)长征. *a line of* ~ 行军路线. *a forced* ~ 强行军,兼程行军. *a hunger* ~ (失业者的)饥饿游行. *(a) quick [slow]* ~ 快[慢]步走. *double* ~ 跑步. *the* ~ *of events* 事件的进展. *a dead* ~ 送葬曲. *a* ~ *column* 行军纵队. *a* ~ *formation* 行军队形. ~ *order* 行军次序;行军命令. ~ *table* 行军计划表. ~*es immune from enemy interference* 旅次行军. ~*es subject to hostile interference* 战备行军. ***be on [in] the*** ~ 进行中. ***steal a*** ~ ***(up)on*** 偷袭(敌人);越过;偷偷抢在某人之前. —*vt.* 使前进,使行军,使进军;拖走,拖去. — *vi.* ①进,进行,进军,推进. ②脚步沉重地走. ③(事件等)发展,进展. ~ *against the enemy* 向敌方推进. ~ ***at ease*** 常步前进. ~ ***into*** 长驱直入. ~ ***off*** 出发;使走,带走 (~ *a man off [away] to gaol* 把人带到牢里). ~ ***on*** 继续前进;使前进,逼近,向…推进. ~ ***past*** (检阅时)分列前进. ~**-in** *n.* ①(军队)进入(攻占的城市等). ②(运动员的)进场. ~**ing order** 军装. ~**ing orders** 开拔令. ~**-past** (检阅时的)分列式.
march[2] [mɑːtʃ] *n.* 【史】边界,边境;〔常 *pl.*〕(特指英格兰和苏格兰或威尔斯的)接界地区. *riding the* ~*es* 【史】(都市等的)境界检查. — *vi.* 毗连,邻接 (*upon*; *with*).
March. = Marchioness.
marche funèbre [marʃ fyneːbr] *n.* 〔F.〕送葬曲,哀悼曲.
Mär·chen [ˈmɛːrçən] *n.* 〔G.〕童话,民间传说.
march·er[1] [ˈmɑːtʃə] *n.* 行军者;游行者.
march·er[2] [ˈmɑːtʃə] *n.* ①边疆居民. ②〔英〕边境防务长官.
mar·che·se [mɑːˈkeze] *n.* (*pl.* ***-che·si*** [-ziː]) (意大利

的)侯爵。
mar·che·sa [mɑːˈkezɑː] *n.* (*pl.* **-che·se** [-ze]) (意大利的)女侯爵;(意大利的)侯爵夫人。
mar·chion·ess [ˈmɑːʃənis] *n.* 侯爵夫人, 侯爵未亡人〔也用作称号〕; 女侯爵。
march·pane [ˈmɑːtʃpein] *n.* 杏仁糖霜; 杏仁糖 (= marzipan)。
Mar·cia [ˈmɑːʃə] *n.* 马西娅〔女子名〕。
Mar·cion·ism [ˈmɑːʃənizəm] *n.*【宗史】马西翁教派〔公元 2—3 世纪兴起的一个基督教派, 其教义摈弃《旧约》和《新约》的大部〕. **-cion·ite** [-nait] *n.*
Mar·co·ni [mɑːˈkəuni], **Guglielmo** ~ 马可尼〔1874—1937, 意大利无线电报发明者〕. —〔m-〕*n.* 无线电报. —〔m-〕*vi.*, *vt.* 打无线电报。
mar·co·ni·gram [mɑːˈkəunigræm] *n.* (马可尼式)无线电报. **-co·ni·graph** [-grɑːf] *n.* (马可尼式)无线电报机。
Marconi rig【海】马可尼帆(=Bermuda rig)。
Mar·co Po·lo [ˈmɑːkəu, ˈpəuləu] 马可孛罗〔1254?—1324, 意大利旅行家〕。
Mar·cus [ˈmɑːkəs] *n.* 马库斯〔男子名〕。
Mar·di gras [ˈmɑːdiːˈgrɑː]〔F.〕忏悔火曜日, 食肉火曜日〔=Shrove Tuesday. 四旬节前的狂欢节的最后一日〕。
Mar·duk [ˈmɑːduk] *n.* (巴比伦的)武神。
mare [mɛə] *n.* 牝马, 母马; 母驴. ***go on shanks' ~*** 走着去. ***a grey ~*** 比丈夫能干的女人[妻子]. ***Money makes the ~ (to) go*** 有钱能使鬼推磨. ***The grey ~ is the better horse*** 女人[妻子]当家; 牝鸡司晨. ***Whose ~'s dead?*** 怎么啦? ***win the ~ or lose the halter*** 孤注一掷. **~'s nest** 一场空的发现; 骗人的东西; 一团糟的地方[情况]. **~'s tail**【气】马尾云;【植】杉叶藻。
ma·re [ˈmɛəri] *n.*〔L.〕海;【天】(月亮、火星表面的)海(指阴暗区). ~ ***clau·sum*** [ˈklɔːsəm] 领海 (= closed sea). ~ ***lib·e·rum*** [ˈlaibərəm] 公海 (=open sea). ~ ***nos·trum*** [ˈnɔstrəm] 我们的海〔地中海的罗马名〕; 属于一国或由两国或多国协议共同使用的可通航水域。
Ma·ré·chal Niel [ˈmɑːʃəl niːl] *n.*〔F.〕【植】尼尔元帅黄蔷薇。
ma·rem·ma [məˈremə] *n.* (*pl.* ***-me*** [-miː]) 瘴气多的滨海沼泽低地〔尤指意大利西部的滨海区域〕。
mar·eo·graph [ˈmæriəgrɑːf] *n.* 自记测潮仪。
marg. = margin; marginal.
Mar·ga·ret [ˈmɑːgərit] *n.* 玛格丽特〔女子名, Madge, May 的昵称〕。
mar·gar·ic [mɑːˈgærik] *a.*【化】十七酸的, 真珠酸的. ~ **acid** 十七酸, 真珠酸。
mar·ga·rin(e) [mɑːdʒəˈriːn, ˈmɑːgərin] *n.* 人造黄油, 植物黄油。
mar·ga·rite [ˈmɑːgərait] *n.* ①珍珠云母. ②珠状晶体物质. ③〔废〕珍珠。
mar·gay [ˈmɑːgei] *n.*【动】(南美)虎猫。
marge[1] [mɑːdʒ] *n.*〔诗〕边缘。
marge[2] [mɑːdʒ] *n.*〔英口〕= margarine.
mar·gent [ˈmɑːdʒənt] *n.*〔古〕边缘; (书的)旁注。
Mar·ger·y [ˈmɑːdʒəri] *n.* 玛杰里〔女子名, Margaret 的异体〕。
Mar·gie [ˈmɑːdʒi] *n.* 玛吉〔女子名, Margaret 的昵称〕。
mar·gin [ˈmɑːdʒin] *n.* ①边缘; 边缘部分; 范围, 限界;【军】图廓. ②(版心外)空白; 栏外, 栏外注解. ③【商】原价和卖价之差, 赚头;【股】保证金, 垫头, 储备. ④余裕, 余地; 余额. ⑤差数; 幅度. *the ~ of cultivation* 耕种界限. *the ~ of safety* 安全限度. *the overload ~* 过载定额. *the narrow ~ of profit* 微利. **go near the ~** (道德上)接近危险地步. *safety ~*【物】安全系数. — *vt.* 给…镶边; 在…加旁注;【股】为…付保险金。
mar·gin·al [ˈmɑːdʒinəl] *a.* ①边的, 边缘的; 记在栏外的, 旁注的; 限界的, 边际的. ②收入仅敷支出的. ~ *land* 瘠薄的土地, 不毛之地. *a ~ lake*【地】冰前湖. ~ *notes* 旁注. ~ *profits* 限界利润, 边际利润. ~ *subsistence* 起码的生活. ~ *utility (theory)*【经】边际效用(价值说). **-ize** *vt.* 忽略, 忽视, 排斥。
mar·gi·na·lia [ˌmɑːdʒiˈneiljə] *n.*〔*pl.*〕旁注; 次要的东西。
mar·gin·al·ly [ˈmɑːdʒinəli] *ad.* 在边上; 边沿地。
mar·gin·at·e(d) [ˈmɑːdʒineit(id)] *a.* 有边的, 有边缘的。
Mar·got [ˈmɑːgəu] *n.* 玛戈〔女子名, Margaret 的昵称〕。
mar·gra·vate, mar·gra·vi·ate [ˈmɑːgrəveit, mɑːˈgreiviːeit] *n.* (罗马帝国或德国的)侯爵封地; 边省总督管领地。
mar·grave [ˈmɑːgreiv] *n.*【史】(德国边境省份的)总督; (德国的)侯爵。
mar·gra·vine [ˈmɑːgrəviːn] *n.* margrave 的夫人〔未亡人〕。
Mar·gue·rite [ˌmɑːgəˈriːt] *n.* 玛格丽特〔女子名, Margaret 的异体〕。
mar·gue·rite [ˌmɑːgəˈriːt] *n.*【植】木茼蒿; 雏菊; 延命菊属。
Ma·ri·a [məˈraiə, məˈriə] *n.* 玛丽亚〔女子名, Mary 的异体〕. *a black ~* 囚车。
ma·ri·a·chi [ˈmɑːriːˈɑːtʃi] *n.* (*pl.* ***-chis*** [-z]) ①墨西哥流浪乐队艺人. ②墨西哥流浪乐队. ③墨西哥乐队演奏的乐曲。
ma·ri·age à la mode [ˈmæriɑːʒ ɑː lɑː məud]〔F.〕(基于私利的上流社会)时式结婚。
ma·ri·age de con·science [ˈmæriɑːʒ də kõsjɑ̃s]〔F.〕常婚。
ma·ri·age de con·ve·nance [ˈmæriɑːʒ də ˈkɔ̃ːvənɑ̃ːns]〔F.〕基于利益关系的婚姻; 策略婚姻。
Ma·ri·an[1] [ˈmɛəriən] *a.* 圣母玛利亚的; (英国及苏格兰的)玛利一世女王的. — *n.* 追随(苏格兰女王)玛利一世的保皇派成员。
Mar·i·an[2] [ˈmɛəriən, ˈmæriən] *n.* 玛丽安〔女子名, Mariana 的异体〕。
Ma·ri·an·a [ˌmɛəriˈænə] *n.* 玛丽安娜〔女子名, Mary 的异体〕。
Ma·ri·an·a Islands, Ma·ri·an·as [ˌmɛəriˈænə ˈailəndz, ˌmɛəriˈænəz] 马里亚纳群岛〔西太平洋〕。
Ma·ria·na·o [Sp. ˌmariaˈnao] *n.* 马里亚瑙〔古巴城市〕。
Ma·rie [ˈmɑːri(ː), məˈriːl] *n.* 玛丽〔女子名, Mary 的异体〕。
Mar·i·et·ta [mɛəriˈetə] *n.* 玛丽埃塔〔女子名, Maria 的昵称〕。
mar·i·gold [ˈmærigəuld] *n.*【植】金盏花; 万寿菊. ~ **window**【建】车轮窗, 菊花窗。
ma·ri·jua·na, ma·ri·hua·na [ˌmɑːriˈ*h*wɑːnɑː] *n.* ①野生烟草. ②(印度)大麻; 大麻干叶〔混在香烟里抽, 有麻醉作用〕. *a ~ cigarette* 大麻烟卷。
ma·rim·ba [məˈrimbə] *n.* (中非和南美的) 原始木琴; 现代经过改良的原始木琴。
ma·ri·na [məˈriːnə] *n.* ①小游艇船坞. ②〔M-〕玛丽娜〔女子名〕。
mar·i·nade [ˌmæriˈneid] *n.* (用酒、醋、香料等配合成的)腌泡汁; 在腌泡汁里泡的肉〔鱼〕. — [ˈmærineid] *vt.* = marinate.
mar·i·nate [ˈmærineit] *vt.* 用腌泡汁泡。
ma·rine [məˈriːn] *a.* 海的, 海上的; 海事的, 海运的; 海军的; 生在海中的, 海产的. *a ~ barometer* 船用晴雨计. *a ~ bureau* 航务局. *a ~ cable* 海底电线. *the M- Corps*〔美〕海军陆战队. *the ~ court* 海事法庭. *a ~ store* 旧船具店. ~ *stores*〔英〕船具, 船舶用品; 旧船具类商品. ~ *soap* 船用肥皂, 海水皂. *a ~ engine* 轮机. ~ *insurance* 海上保险. *a ~ policy* 海上保险单. ~ *products* 海产物, 水产物. — *n.* ①海军陆战队士兵〔军官〕; (军舰的)地勤海军. ②海事, 海运业; (欧洲大陆各国的)海军(部); 船舶, 舰队; 海画, 海景. ③〔俚〕空瓶; 新水兵.

blue [red] ~s 海军陆战队炮[步]兵. *the mercantile [commercial] ~* (一国的) 商船 (队). *the ~ belt* 领海. *a (dead) ~* 空瓶. ***Tell that to the ~s [horse-~s]! = That will do for the ~s!*** 〔口〕谁信你那一套! 我才不受你的骗呢!

mar·i·ner [ˈmærinə] *n.* 水手,船员. *a master ~* (商船或渔船的)船长. *~'s card* 海图. *~'s needle [compass]* 罗盘针;航海罗盘.

ma·ri·nism [məˈriːnizəm] *n.* (意大利诗人马利诺(Marino)式的)极讲究技巧的文体.

Mar·i·ol·a·try [ˌmɛəriˈɔlətri] *n.* (迷信式的)圣母玛利亚崇拜〔攻击者用语〕.

Mar·i·ol·o·gy [ˌmɛəriˈɔlədʒi] *n.* 圣母玛利亚论[研究].

Mar·i·on [ˈmɛəriən, ˈmæriən] *n.* ①玛丽恩〔女子名, Mary 的昵称〕. ②马里恩〔姓氏,男子名〕.

mar·i·o·nette [ˌmæriəˈnet] *n.* (木偶戏用的)牵线木偶.

Mar·i·po·sa lily [tulip] [ˌmɑːriˈpəuzə, -sə] 【植】①蝴蝶百合〔产于北美西部,开白、红、黄、紫色的花朵〕. ②蝴蝶百合花.

mar·ish [ˈmæriʃ] *n., a.* 〔诗〕沼泽(的).

Ma·rist [ˈmɛərist] *n.* (天主教的)玛利亚会会员.

ma·ri·tal [ˈmæritl] *a.* 丈夫的; 婚姻的. *~ obligations* 丈夫(对妻子)的义务.

ma·ri·tal·ly [ˈmæritəli] *ad.* 作为丈夫; 婚姻上作为夫妇; 象结了婚似地.

ma·rit·ic·ide [məˈritisaid] *n.* 杀夫[妻]的人[行为].

mar·i·time [ˈmæritaim] *a.* 海的,海上的;海事的, 海运的;沿海的; 生在沿海地带的. *~ association* 海事协会. *~ climate* 海洋性气候. *The M- Customs Administration* (中国的)海关总署. *The M- Exchange* (纽约的)海运交易所. *a ~ power* 海洋国家;海运国. *M- Provinces* (加拿大的)沿海各省.

mar·jo·ram [ˈmɑːdʒərəm] *n.* 【植】茉乔栾那属;牛至属.

Mar·jo·rie, Mar·jo·ry [ˈmɑːdʒəri] *n.* 玛乔里〔女子名, Margery 的异体〕.

Mark,[1] Marc [mɑːk] *n.* 马克〔男子名, Marcus 的异体〕.

Mark[2] [mɑːk] 【宗】(基督教《圣经》中的篇名)《马可福音》; 《马可福音》的作者马可.

mark [mɑːk] *n.* ①印,记号,符号,标记;标志,指标;十字押〔文盲的签名〕. ②靶子;标识;目标. ③迹,痕迹;斑点. ④特征, 特质, 特性. ⑤(考试等的)分数. ⑥显著,高贵,卓越;荣誉,名声. ⑦界限,限度;限界线;〔the ~〕标准. ⑧【海】测标;(船舶)载重线标志;【橄榄球】有踢球权利者用脚在地上画的印,脚跟印(=heel-~);【体】起步线;【拳】心窝. ⑨【史】中世纪日尔曼民族的村落公社. ⑩【美军】(武器的)型号. ⑪〔古〕境界,边境. ⑫〔美〕嗜好;老好人,易受欺骗的人;施钱[食品]给无业游民的场所. *a trade ~* 商标. *a price ~* (商品上的)标价牌. *full ~s* 满分,一百分. *get 80 ~s for English* 英语得80分. *On your ~s!* 【体】各就各位! *a bad ~* 一(项)过(失); 污点. *a good ~* 一(项)功(劳); 优点; 操行良好的标记;良好的声誉或信用. *an easy [a soft] ~* 易受骗的人, 冤大头. ***bear [show] ~s of ...*** 有…的痕迹. ***below the ~*** 在标准以下. ***beside [wide of] the ~*** 不中肯; 不切合, 不恰当. ***beyond the ~*** 过度, 过分. ***Bless the ~! =Save the ~! cut the ~*** (箭)在靶前落下. ***fall [come] short of the ~*** 不到标准, 不合格. ***get off the ~***【体】起步,出发;开始(工作等). ***go wide of the ~*** 没打中, 离目标太远; 离题太远. ***God bless the ~! = Save the ~! have a ~ on*** 喜欢, 爱好. ***hit the ~*** 打中目标,中靶;(发言)中肯;达到目的. ***make one's ~*** 出名. ***~ of mouth*** (表示马龄的)门齿凹〔6 岁左右从下齿起开始无凹〕. ***miss the ~*** 未中的;不成功,失败. ***of ~*** 知名的,杰出的 (*a man of ~* 名人,要人. *a man of no ~* 普通人). ***on the ~***〔美〕作比赛[起步]准备的. ***over [under] the ~*** 估计过高[低]. ***overshoot the ~*** 过度. ***Save the ~!*** ①不要见怪; 不客气地说〔常用作插语〕. ②天哪! 这还了得! 〔表示惊愕、嘲笑、讥讽的话〕. ***shoot [answer] wide of the ~*** 离目标很远; 答非所问. ***short of the ~*** 没有达到标准. ***take one's ~ amiss*** 失算, 失策. ***toe the ~*** (赛跑时)用脚尖踏在起步线上;守规则;负责任. ***up to the ~*** 达到标准, 过得硬;美满;健康;舒适 (*I am not up to the ~.* 我身体不舒服;能力不够). ***within the ~*** 合乎标准; 过得去. — *vt.* ①加记号于,加符号于,作记号于, 记上, 标记上,记录. ②给…记分数;表示…的位置;【猎】记清(禽兽逃匿处);(球赛)钉住. ③指示,使注意. ④〔诗〕注目,注意; 想. ⑤【商】给…标价. ⑥定…的界限,区分,区划. ⑦〔通常用被动式〕使有特色,污点〔伤痕,斑点等〕. ⑧设计,计划;(命运)注定;【军】指定. *M- me [my words].* 注意听. — *vi.* ①注意,想. ②【橄榄球】作脚跟印. ③记分数. ④(马的门齿凹)表示年龄. ~ ***down*** 记下; 减价;【猎】记清(禽兽逃往处). ~ ***off*** (用线条、符号等)划分,区分(*~ off spheres of influence* 划分势力范围). ~ ***out*** 指示,划定,划出;拟订(计划),设计; 注意; 选拔; 消去(*~ out a lawn for tennis* 划定网球场). ~ ***out for*** 选定[决定]给与… (*be ~ed out for promotion* 已选定…给与提升)〔通常 *p.p.*〕. ~ ***papers*** 判卷子, 给考试卷子打分数. ~ ***time***【军】踏步; 踌躇, 犹豫不决. ~ ***up*** 涨价; 记上,加上,赊帐. ~ ***with a white stone*** 当作喜庆[吉利]的事件记下. **~down** 标低售价; 标低的金额. **~ up** 标高售价;标高的金额;(加在商品成本上以决定售价)的金额.

mark[4] [mɑːk] *n.* ①马克〔德国货币〕. ②(英国以前的)马克〔相当于旧制 13 先令 4 辨士〕. ③(中世纪欧洲大陆的)金[银]马克〔通常为 8 盎司〕.

marked [mɑːkt] *a.* ①有记号的,加印记的. ②受监视[注意]的. ③显著的, 著名的, (差别等) 明显的. *a ~ cheque* 【商】保证兑现的支票. *a ~ man* 嫌疑分子;〔美〕累犯;名气不好的人;有异常才能的人. *a ~ difference* 显著的差别. *~ coldness* 故意的冷淡. **-ly** *ad.* **-ness** *n.*

mark·er [ˈmɑːkə] *n.* ①作记号的人;打分数的人; 记分器;划线器;指示器;【无】指点标;(台球等的)记分员. ②【军】标靶兵;标兵;标杆;旗标;书签; 〔美〕纪念标, 纪念碑;里程碑. ③(校中专职)点名先生;经常给学生记分数的先生;监猎人. ④【英军】(轰炸用)照明弹. ⑤〔美〕遗传标记,基因标记. *a ~ light* 标灯. *a ground ~* 地面照明弹. ***not a ~ to [on]*** 〔美〕不能和…相比,远远配不上.

mar·ket [ˈmɑːkit] *n.* ① (尤指牲畜和食品的)集市; 市场;菜市, 菜场. ②需要, 销路; 推销地区. ③市价; 行情, 市面, 市况. ④〔美〕食品店;〔英〕【法】公共市场设置权. *a cotton [stock] ~* 棉花[股票]市场. *There is no ~ for that class of goods here.* 那一类货物这里不需要[无销路]. *The ~ rose [fell]* 行情俏拔[疲落]. *a sick ~* 萧条的市面. *a swimming ~* 兴旺的市面. *The ~ is dull.* 市面呆滞. ***at the ~*** 照市价. ***be on the long side of the ~*** 把持物品或证券以待涨价时出卖; 做多头, 买进期货. ***bring one's eggs [hogs, goods] to the wrong [a bad] ~*** 失策, 失算; 失误. ***bring to ~ = put [place] on the ~*** 出售. ***bull the ~*** (多头)大量抢购,买涨,哄买. ***come into the ~*** 上市. ***corner the ~*** 囤积居奇,大量买进股票[商品]使价格上涨. ***engross [forestall] the ~*** 垄断市场. ***feed to ~*** 为出售而养肥(家畜等). ***find a ~*** 找着销路. ***go badly to ~*** 买[卖]吃亏. ***go to ~*** 上市场买东西; 〔口〕筹办,企图. ***hold the ~*** 垄断市场, 囤积居奇. ***in ~*** 在买卖中. ***in the ~*** 拿去卖; 正要出售. ***in the ~ for*** (某人)想买, 要买. ***lose one's ~*** 放过(买卖)良机. ***make a ~*** 【股】在交易所中故意买卖某企业股票,制造兴旺气象;煽动市面. ***make a [one's] ~ of*** 利用,利用…赚钱,把…当做摇钱树. ***make one's ~*** 出售存货. ***mar another's [one's] ~*** 搞垮别人[自己] 买卖. ***mend one's ~*** 改

进买卖情况. ***overrun one's*** ～ 因不肯脱手失去出售时机. ***overstand one's*** ～ 讨价过高失去出售良机. ***play the*** ～〔美〕做投机买卖. ***raid the*** ～〔口〕使行情发生波动. ***raise the*** ～ ***upon***〔口〕向…要高价. ***rig the*** ～〔口〕操纵市场;捣乱市价. — *vi.* 在市场买卖,作买卖,卖,买.— *vt.* 在市场上出售;把…拿到市场去卖.～ **bell** (报告开市的)市场钟. ～ **cross** (中世纪市场上的)市场十字架. ～ **day** 定期集市日. ～ **garden** 商品菜园(=truck-garden). ～ **gardener** 商品菜园经营者. ～ **letter** (证券交易所等印发的)行情通报. ～ **overt** 公开市场. ～ **place** 市场;商业中心地. ～ **price** 市场价格;时价,市价. ～ **rate** 市价,行情. ～ **research** 市场调研〔研究市场某些具体商品供求关系〕. ～ **town** 特准按期举行集市的小镇. ～**value**(商品的)市场价格,销售价格.

mar·ket·able [ˈmɑːkitəbl] *a.* ①可销售的;适销的;有销路的. ②市场买卖的. ～ *value* 市场价值. **-a·bil·i·ty** *n.*

mar·ket·eer [ˌmɑːkiˈtiə] *n.* 市场商人.

mar·ket·er [ˈmɑːkitə] *n.*〔美〕在市场中买卖的人.

mar·ket·ing [ˈmɑːkitiŋ] *n.* ①商品销售业务. ②商品自生产者转移到消费者手中的一系列有关机能. ③〔集合词〕市场购买的货品;适合市场上销售的货品. ***go [do one's]*** ～ 上市场买〔卖〕东西去. ～ **research** 销售调查. ～ **station** 商业基地.

Mark·ham [ˈmɑːkəm] *n.* 马卡姆〔姓氏〕.

mar·khor [ˈmɑːkɔː] *n.* (阿富汗至印度一带山区的)捻角山羊.

mark·ing [ˈmɑːkiŋ] *n.* ①作记号;记分;记号,印记,点;(尤指鸟兽的皮、羽毛等的)斑纹,条纹. ②【商】(支票的)认付. — *a.* 赋与特征的,使显眼的. ～ **board** (比赛时用的)记分牌;(股票交易所的)行情揭示牌. ～ **gauge** (木工用的)线准;划线规. ～ **ink** (在待洗衣服等上作记号用的)不退色墨水;打印墨水. ～ **iron** 烙印铁.

mark·ka [ˈmɑːkkɑː] *n.* *(pl.* ***-kaa*** [-kɑː]*)* 马克〔芬兰货币单位,等于 100 盆尼 *(penni)*〕.

mark·man [ˈmɑːkmən] *n.*〔废〕= marksman.

marks·man [ˈmɑːksmən] *n.* *(pl.* ***-men****)* 打靶能手;狙击兵;神枪手.【美军】二等射手;轻兵器射手的最低等级. **-ship** *n.* 射击术,枪法,弓术.

Mark Tap·ley [ˈmɑːk ˈtæpli] 极快活的人〔出自 Dickens 所作小说 *Martin Chuzzlewit*〕.

Mark Twain [ˈmɑːk ˈtwein] 马克·吐温〔美国作家 Samuel Langhorne Clemens (1835—1910)的笔名〕.

marl[1] [mɑːl] *n.*【地】泥灰岩灰泥〔肥料用〕;泥灰砖;〔诗〕泥土. ***burning*** ～ 焦热地狱的磨难〔出自英国诗人 Milton 的 *Paradise Lost*〕. — *vt.* 在…撒泥灰土,用泥灰土施肥.

marl[2] [mɑːl] *vt.*【海】用细绳缠(大缆等).

mar·la·ceous [mɑːˈleiʃəs] *a.* 泥灰质的;象泥灰岩的.

Marl·bor·ough [ˈmɔːlbərə, ˈmɑːl-] *n.* 马尔伯勒〔姓氏〕.

Marl·bor·ough House [ˈmɔːlbərə ˈhaus] 英国王储的伦敦宫殿,东宫.

Mar·lene [ˈmɑːliːn, mɑːˈliːn] *n.* 马琳〔女子名〕.

Mar·lin [ˈmɑːlin] *n.* 马林〔男子名〕.

mar·lin [ˈmɑːlin] *n.*【鱼】(sailfish, spearfish 类的)大马林鱼.

mar·line [ˈmɑːlin] *n.*【海】小绳,细索;油麻绳;左捻双股绳. ～**-spike**【船】穿索针;解索针,解缆钻.

marl·ite [ˈmɑːlait] *n.* 抗风化的泥灰岩.

Mar·low(e) [ˈmɑːləu] *n.* ①马洛〔姓氏〕. ②**Christopher** ～ 克里斯托弗·马娄〔1564—1593,英国诗人,剧作家〕.

marl-pit [ˈmɑːlpit] *n.* 泥灰岩采掘场.

marl·stone [ˈmɑːlstəun] *n.*【地】硬质的泥灰岩,泥灰石.

marl·y [ˈmɑːli] *a.* ***(marl·i·er; -i·est)*** 似泥灰土的,泥灰质的;泥灰土多的,土地肥沃的.

marm [mɑːm] *n.*〔俚〕= ma'am.

Mar·ma·duke [ˈmɑːmədjuːk] *n.* 马默杜克〔男子名〕.

mar·ma·lade [ˈmɑːməleid] *n.* (带果皮的)桔子〔柠檬〕果酱. ～ **tree**【植】美国榄 (Calocarpum sapota)〔产于美洲热带地区〕.

Mar·ma·ra [ˈmɑːmərə] *n.* *Sea of* ～ (通黑海的)马尔马拉海.

mar·ma·tite [ˈmɑːmətait] *n.*【矿】铁闪锌矿.

mar·mite [ˈmɑːmait] *n.* ①砂锅. ②〔俚〕壶形炸弹. ③麴精〔专卖品名〕;【化】酸制酵母.

mar·mo·lite [ˈmɑːməlait] *n.*【矿】白蛇纹石〔岩〕.

Mar·mo·ra [ˈmɑːmərə] *n.* =Marmara.

mar·mo·re·an, mar·mo·re·al [mɑːˈmɔːriən, -riəl] *a.*〔诗〕大理石(似)的;似大理石雕像的;滑腻的,白的;大理石制的.

mar·mo·set [ˈmɑːməzet] *n.*【动】(厚毛如绒的南美)狨猴.

mar·mot [ˈmɑːmət] *n.*【动】土拨鼠,旱獭;玛摩游泳帽.

mar·o·cain [ˈmærəkein] *n.*【纺】马罗坎平纹绉.

Mar·o·nite [ˈmærənait] *n.* 马龙教徒〔黎巴嫩的希腊教派〕.

ma·roon[1] [məˈruːn] *n.* ①避居西印度群岛及圭亚那山中的黑人〔原为逃亡黑奴〕. ②被放逐到孤岛的人. — *vt.* 把…放逐到孤岛;(因洪水等)使孤立. ～*ed on roofs* 被(洪水)围困在屋顶上. — *vi.* ①〔美〕带着帐篷旅行〔野营〕. ②闲荡;吊儿郎当地过日子.

ma·roon[2] [məˈruːn] *a.* 酱紫色的,褐红色的. — *n.* 酱紫色,褐红色;纸炮烟火〔玩具〕.

ma·roon·er [məˈruːnə] *n.* 海盗;被流放到孤岛上的人;脱逃的奴隶;〔美〕野营旅行者.

mar·plot [ˈmɑːplɔt] *n.* 好管闲事而破坏了计划〔事业〕的人;害人精.

mar·que [mɑːk] *n.* ①(海上的) 捕拿外国〔敌方〕船只的特许证;有捕拿特许证的船. ②商品(尤指汽车等)的型号〔式样〕. *letters of* ～ *(and reprisal)* (海上)捕拿特许证.

mar·quee [mɑːˈkiː] *n.* 大帐幕;〔美〕(戏院教堂等入口的)门罩;〔英〕马戏团帐幕的正面入口.

Mar·que·san [mɑːˈkeizn, -ˈkeisn] *n.* ①(大洋洲)马克萨斯人. ②马克萨斯语. — *a.* ①马克萨斯群岛的;马克萨斯人的. ②马克萨斯的.

mar·quess [ˈmɑːkwis] *n.*〔英〕= marquis. **M- of Queensbury Rules** 昆斯伯里拳击基本规则〔现代拳术的基本规则,规定所用的手套和分回合等〕.

mar·que·try, mar·que·te·rie [ˈmɑːkitri] *n.* 镶嵌工艺,镶木细工.

mar·quis [ˈmɑːkwis] *(fem.* ***mar·chioness*** [ˈmɑːʃənis]*)* *n.* ①侯爵;公爵长子的尊称. ②〔M-〕马奎斯〔姓氏〕.

mar·quis·ate [ˈmɑːkwizit] *n.* 侯爵的身分〔地位〕;侯爵领地.

mar·quise [mɑːˈkiːz] *n.*〔F.〕①(英国以外的)侯爵夫人. ②拼镶成(切割成)两头尖的椭圆形宝石;镶有这种形状宝石(或数颗这种形座)的戒指. ③〔古〕帐幕,帐篷.

mar·qui·sette [ˌmɑːkiˈzet] *n.* (作窗帘等用的)亮绸;薄纱罗.

mar·quois scale [ˈmɑːkwɔiz ˈskeil]【测】平行线尺.

Mar·ra·kech, Mar·ra·kesh [məˈrækeʃ] *n.* 马拉喀什〔摩洛哥城市〕.

mar·ram [ˈmærəm] *n.*【植】滨草〔生在海边的禾本科植物,又作 ～grass〕.

Mar·ra·no [məˈrɑːnəu] *n.* *(pl.* ***-nos****)* 被迫改信基督教的犹太人〔在西班牙宗教法庭上,为了免被处死或迫害,被迫表示信仰基督教实则仍秘密信犹太教的犹太人〕.

mar·riage [ˈmæridʒ] *n.* ①结婚,婚姻;婚礼;结婚生活,夫妇关系. ②密切结合. ③【牌】同花 king 和 queen 的配合. *a common-law [a Scotch]* ～ 自由结婚,自由同居. *a civil* ～ (不举行宗教仪式的)登记结婚. *a communal [group]* ～ 杂婚;群交共婚制. *his [her] uncle by* ～ 夫系〔妻系〕的叔伯辈姻亲. *the* ～ *of true minds* 真心实意

的结合. ～ *of convenience* 基于利害关系的婚姻, 策略[权宜]婚姻. ***give [sb.] in*** ～ 把某人嫁出. ***take sb. in*** ～ 娶某人. ～ **articles [contract]** (规定财产权等的)结婚契约. ～ **bed** 夫妇关系. ～ **broker** 媒人. ～ **ceremony** 婚礼. ～ **favours** 婚礼花束[缎带花结]. ～ **lines** 〔英〕结婚证明书. ～ **portion** 妆奁,嫁赀. ～ **service** (在教会中举行的)婚礼. ～ **settlement** 夫妇财产契约.

mar•riage•able [ˈmæridʒəbl] *a.* 可以结婚的; 已到结婚年龄的. *a girl of* ～ *age* 已到结婚年龄的姑娘. **-a•bil•i•ty** *n.*

mar•ried [ˈmærid] *a.* 已婚的 (*opp.* single); 夫妇的; 紧密结合着的; 〔美俚〕两手带了手铐的. *a* ～ *man* 已婚男子,有配偶的男人. *a newly* ～ *couple* 一对新婚夫妇. ～ *love* 夫妇的爱. — *n.* (*pl.* ～*s*) 已婚的人.

mar•rier [ˈmæriə] *n.* 结婚者; 为男女双方举行结婚仪式的牧师[官员].

mar•ron•nier [mærɔˈnje] *n.* 〔F.〕【植】七叶树.

mar•rons gla•cés [ˈmærɔn ˈglɑːsei] 〔*pl.*〕〔F.〕蜜饯[糖衣]栗子.

mar•row[1] [ˈmærəu] *n.* ①【解】髓,骨髓. ②精髓,精华; 实质. ③滋养品. ④生气, 活力. ⑤〔英〕食用葫芦. ***the*** ～ ***of the land*** 国力. ***to the*** ～ ***(of one's bones)*** 透骨; 彻底的 (*be frozen to the* ～ 寒冷彻骨. *He is an aristocrat to the very* ～ *of his bones.* 他是一个道道地地的贵族).

mar•row[2] [ˈmærəu] *n.* 〔Scot.〕〔方〕朋友; 配偶; 敌手; 对手; 长得一模一样的人物(*of*).

mar•row•bone [ˈmærəubəun] *n.* 髓骨; (食髓的)胫部牛肉; 〔*pl.*〕〔谑〕膝; 〔*pl.*〕= crossbones. *Bring him to his* ～*s* 揍他; *get [go] down on one's* ～*s* 〔谑〕跪下. *ride in the* ～ *coach [stage]* 骑两脚马去,走着去.

mar•row•fat, mar•row pea [ˈmærəufæt, ˈmærəupiː] *n.* 大(粒品种)豌豆.

mar•row squash [ˈmærəu skwɔʃ]【植】西葫芦〔一种皮硬而光滑的椭圆形瓜〕.

mar•row•y [ˈmærəui] *a.* ①骨髓多的. ②强壮的; 丰富的. ③(文章)简洁有力的.

Mar•rue•cos [mɑːˈwekəus] 摩洛哥的西班牙语名称.

mar•ry[1] [ˈmæri] *vt.* ①结婚; 娶; 嫁. ②使结婚〔用被动语态〕; 把…嫁出; 使娶媳, 使成家. ③(牧师)主持结婚礼; 证婚. ④使结合; 【海】把(绳子的两头)编在一起,捻成一条. *He married his daughter to a farmer.* 他把他的女儿嫁给一个农民. *a ditty married to a beautiful air* 小调配上优美的乐曲. — *vi.* 结婚. ***get married*** 结婚. ～ ***a fortune*** 和有钱人结婚. ～ ***beneath one*** 和身分低的人结婚. ～ ***into the purple*** 与显贵联姻. ～ ***off*** 嫁出. ～ ***over a broomstick*** 同居. ～ ***up*** 使成夫妇[未婚夫妻]. ～ ***with the left hand*** 和身分低微的人结婚.

mar•ry[2] [ˈmæri] *int.* 〔古〕哎呀! 哟! 真! 真是! 〔表示惊愕、轻蔑、愤怒等.〕 *M- come up!* 哎唷! 这怎么啦!

Mars [mɑːz] *n.* ①【天】火星. ②【罗神】玛尔斯,战神,军神; 战争; 骁勇的人.

Mar•sa•la [mɑːˈsɑːlə] *n.* 〔It.〕(西西里岛的)马沙拉白葡萄酒.

Mar•seil•laise [mɑːsəˈleiz] *n.* 马赛曲〔法国国歌〕.

Mar•seilles [mɑːˈseilz] *n.* 马赛〔法国港市〕.

mar•seilles [mɑːˈseilz] *n.* 提花马赛布.

mar•sel•la [mɑːˈselə] *n.* = marcella.

marsh [mɑːʃ] *n.* 沼地,沼泽,湿地. ～ **gas** 沼气,甲烷. ～ **hawk** 鸡鹞 (Circus cyaneus)〔产于美洲,筑窠于地上,捕鼠、蛙、蛇等为食〕. ～ **hen**【动】秧鸡. ～ **mallow**【植】药蜀葵; 果汁软糖. ～ **marigold**【植】立金花; 驴蹄草. ～**-ore** 沼铁矿.

Mar•shal [ˈmɑːʃəl] *n.* 马歇尔〔男子名〕.

mar•shal [ˈmɑːʃəl] *n.* ①(法国等的)陆军元帅〔英国则称 Field-M-〕. ②〔英〕空军元帅 (=M- of the Air). ③宪兵主任[司令官] (=provost-～). ④(英国宫廷的)典礼官; (集会的)司仪. ⑤〔英〕纹章局长 (=Earl M-). ⑥〔英〕(流动法庭的)法官的秘书. ⑦〔英〕大学学监的随员. ⑧〔美〕联邦法院的执行官; 市执法官; 市警察局长. *a field* ～ 〔英〕陆军元帅. *the M- of the Royal Air Force* 〔英〕空军元帅. *an Air Chief M-* 〔英〕空军上将. *an air* ～ 〔英〕空军中将. *the* ～ *of France* 法国陆军元帅. —(〔英〕*-ll-*) *vt.* ①使排列; 〔喻〕安排; 整顿, 整理; 【徽】配列(纹章在盾等上); 【法】(整理破产、分配遗产时)决定分派次序. ②带,领,引导. ～ *a person into his place*). 引某人入坐. — *vi.* 排列,集合. *a marshalling yard* (车站内)货车编组[调车]场.

mar•shal•cy, mar•shal•ship [ˈmɑːʃəlsi, -ʃip] *n.* marshal 的职位[权力].

Mar•shall Islands [ˈmɑːʃəl ˈailəndz] 马绍尔群岛〔西太平洋〕.

Mar•shal•sea [ˈmɑːʃəlˌsiː] ①(在皇室司法官控制下的)英国法庭〔于 1849 年废除〕. ②马夏尔西监狱〔伦敦萨斯瓦克关禁债务人的监狱,已于 1842 年废除〕.

marsh•y [ˈmɑːʃi] *a.* ***(marsh•i•er; -i•est)*** (多)沼地的; 沼泽似的; 生在沼泽的. **-i•ness** *n.*

Mar•so•khod [ˌmɑːsəˈhɔːt] *n.* 〔Russ.〕火星车〔苏联设计的用以对火星作科学考察的飞行车〕.

Mar•ston [ˈmɑːstən] *n.* 马斯顿〔姓氏〕.

mar•su•pi•al [mɑːˈsjuːpjəl] *a.* 【动】有袋(目)的; 袋(状)的. — *n.* 有袋动物. ～ **frog** 背上有卵袋的南美袋蛙.

mar•su•pi•um [mɑːˈsjuːpjəm] *n.* (*pl. marsupia* [-piə]) 【动】袋,育儿袋,卵袋.

mart [mɑːt] *n.* ①〔诗、古〕市场. ②商业中心地. ③拍卖场.

Mart. = Martial.

mar•ta•gon [ˈmɑːtəgən] *n.* 【植】头巾百合 (*Lilium martagon*)〔开白、紫花朵〕.

mar•tel [ˈmɑːtel] *n.* 【史】战槌; 槌.

mar•tel•lo tow•er [mɑːˈteləu ˈtauə]【筑城】(防御海岸的)石造圆形小炮塔.

mar•ten [ˈmɑːtin] *n.* (*pl.* ～**s**, 〔集合词〕～) 【动】貂; 貂皮.

mar•tens•ite [ˈmɑːtnzait] *n.* 马丁体〔显微镜下所见的炼钢的针状组织〕. **-sit•ic** [-tənˈzitik] *a.*

Mar•tha [ˈmɑːθə] *n.* 玛莎〔女子名〕.

mar•tial [ˈmɑːʃəl] *a.* ①战争的, 战时的; 勇武的, 尚武的,好战的; 象军人的; 军事的,陆海军的 (*opp.* civil). ②〔M-〕战神玛尔斯(Mars)的; 【天】火星的. *a court-*～ 军事法庭. ～ *music* 军乐. ～ *spirit* 士气. ～ **art** 技击. ～ **law** 戒严令; 军事管制法; 军法; 军令. **-ly** *ad.* 勇敢地,勇武地,好战地.

mar•tial•ism [ˈmɑːʃəlizəm] *n.* 尚武精神; 士气.

mar•tial•ize [ˈmɑːʃəlaiz] *vt.* 使配合战争; 使军事化; 使整军经武; 激励士气.

Mar•ti•an [ˈmɑːʃjən] *n.* (假想的)火星人. — *a.* 战神的; 火星的; (假想的)火星人的.

Mar•tin [ˈmɑːtin] *n.* 马丁〔姓氏,男子名〕. ***St.*** ～***'s day*** 圣马丁节 (=Martinmas). ***St.*** ～***'s summer*** 〔英〕小阳春〔11 月 11 日圣马丁节前后暖和时期〕. ～ **furnace**【冶】平炉,马丁炉.

mar•tin [ˈmɑːtin] *n.* 岩燕. *a house* ～ 欧洲家燕. *a sand [bank]* ～ 灰沙燕.

Mar•ti•neau [ˈmɑːtinəu] *n.* 马蒂诺〔姓氏〕.

mar•ti•net [ˌmɑːtiˈnet] *n.* 〔主蔑〕(训练上)纪律严肃的人〔尤指陆海军军纪官〕; 严格的人. **-ism** [-izəm] *n.* 严格的训练; 严格.

mar•tin•gal(e) [ˈmɑːtiŋgeil] *n.* 马颔韁,鞅; 【船】第二斜桅的下方支索; 输后加倍下注的赌法.

mar•ti•ni[1] [mɑːˈtiːni] *n.* 马蒂尼枪〔从前英国陆军的步

枪,又名 the Martini Henry rifle].
mar·ti·ni² **(cock·tail)** [mɑːˈtiːni ˈkɔkteil] *n.* 马丁尼鸡尾酒[艾酒、杜松子酒等混合酒].
Mar·ti·nique [ˌmɑːtiˈniːk] *n.* 马提尼克(岛)[拉丁美洲].
Mar·tin·mas [ˈmɑːtinməs] *n.* 圣马丁节[11月11日].
mart·let [ˈmɑːtlit] *n.* ①欧洲燕. ②[诗] = martin. ③【徽】无足鸟[分家后第四子的徽章].
mar·tyr [ˈmɑːtə] *n.* ①殉教者; 殉道者; 烈士, 殉难者, 牺牲者 *(to)*. ②(因病等)长期受痛苦的人 *(to)*. *a* ~ *to a cause* 义士. ***be a ~ to*** 害着…病; 受着…的折磨. ***die a ~ to one's principle*** 为主义而牺牲. ***make a ~ of*** 牺牲, 折磨. ***make a ~ of oneself*** 装出牺牲者[殉教者]姿态博取信誉. — *vt.* (对坚持某种主义或信仰的人进行)杀害; 迫害, 折磨. **-dom** *n.* 殉教; 殉道, 殉难; 殉节; 赴义; 苦恼, 痛苦.
mar·tyr·ize [ˈmɑːtəraiz] *vt.* 使殉难, 把…作牺牲; 折磨.
martyro- *comb.f.* 表示"烈士"; "殉教者": *martyrology*.
mar·tyr·ol·o·gy [ˌmɑːtəˈrɔlədʒi] *n.* 殉教史; 殉教者列传.
mar·tyr·y [ˈmɑːtəri] *n.* 为纪念殉教者而建立的圣祠; 表明殉教者殉难地点或圣骨置放处的建立物.
MARV = manoeuvring reentry vehicle【军】机动重返大气层运载工具.
Mar·va [ˈmɑːvə] *n.* 玛瓦[女子名].
mar·vel [ˈmɑːvəl] *n.* ①惊奇的东西; 可惊叹的人物, (…方面)的非凡人物, 奇才. ②[古] 惊愕, 惊叹. *He is a perfect* ~. [口] 他真是个奇人. *The* ~ *is that* ... 奇异的是…. *The less* ~ *if* ... 如果…便不希奇. *Use lessens* ~, *it is said.* 俗话说, 多见不怪 [少见多怪]. — *vi.* ([Eng.] *-ll-*)[古] ①惊叹, 惊异 *(at; that)*. — *vt.* 对…觉得奇怪, 诧异 *(how; why; if; what)*. ★词义强于 wonder. **~-of-Peru** *n.*【植】紫茉莉, 胭脂花.
Mar·vell [ˈmɑːvəl] *n.* 马维尔[姓氏].
mar·vel·ous, mar·vel·lous [ˈmɑːviləs] *a.* 奇异的, 不可思议的, 奇怪的; [口] 妙极的; 了不起的. — *n.* [the ~] 怪事. **-ly** *ad.* **-ness** *n.*
mar·vie, mar·vy [ˈmɑːvi] *int.* [美俚]妙极了(= marvelous).
Mar·vin [ˈmɑːvin] *n.* 马文[姓氏, 男子名].
Marx·i·an [ˈmɑːksjən] *a., n.* = Marxist.
Marx·ism [ˈmɑːksizəm] *n.* 马克思主义. *~-Leninism* 马克思列宁主义, 马列主义. *~-Leninism-Mao Zedong Thought* 马克思主义、列宁主义、毛泽东思想.
Marx·ist [ˈmɑːksist] *n.* 马克思主义者. — *a.* 马克思的; 马克思主义的.
Ma·ry [ˈmɛəri] *n.* ①玛丽[女子名]. ②[圣]圣母玛利亚[耶稣的母亲]. ~ **Jane** [美俚]大麻 (= marijuana). ~ **Janes** 玛丽·简女用矮跟拖鞋[商标名].
Mar·y·ann [ˌmɛəriˈæn] *n.* 玛丽安[女子名].
Mar·y·land [ˈmɛərilænd] *n.* 马里兰[美国州名].
Mar·y·mass [ˈmɛəriməs] *n.* 圣母玛利亚节; (尤指)报喜节[普通叫 Lady Day]; [Scot.] 圣母升天节.
mar·zi·pan [ˌmɑːziˈpæn] *n.* = march-pane.
MAS = Malaysian Airline System 马来西亚航空公司.
-mas *suf.* 节, 节日: Christ*mas*.
mas., masc. = masculine.
Ma·sai [mɑːˈsai] *n.* ①*(pl.* ~*(s))* 马萨伊人[肯尼亚和坦噶尼喀牧民]. ②马萨伊语.
mas·ca·ra [mæsˈkɑːrə] *n.* (染)睫毛油.
mas·cle [ˈmæskl] *n.* ①(十三世纪铠甲的)菱形钢铠片. ②【徽】中空菱形纹.
mas·con [ˈmæskɔn] *n.* 【地】(月表下的)质量密集, 质量高度密聚.
mas·cot [ˈmæskət] *n.* 福神; 吉人; 吉祥物[物品、动物等].
mas·cu·line [ˈmɑːskjulin] *(opp.* feminine) *a.* ①【语】阳性的. ②男(性)的, 雄的. ③男子气概的; 有力的; 勇敢的; 雄赳赳的. ④(女子)有男子气的. — *n.*【语】阳性; 阳性词; 男性的东西; 男子; 男孩. ~ **ending** [诗](用于行末音节上的)重音行末. ~ **gender**【语】阳性. ~ **rhyme** [诗](仅在行末有重音处才押韵的)阳韵. **-ly** *ad.* **-ness, -linity** [-ˈliniti] *n.* 丈夫气, 刚毅.
mas·cu·lin·ize [ˈmæskjuliˌnaiz] *vt.* ***(-ized; -iz·ing)*** 使男子化; [尤指使(女人)具有男子特征]. **-za·tion** *n.*
mase [meiz] *vi.* 激射; 产生和放大微波.
Mase·field [ˈmeisfiːld] *n.* 梅斯菲尔德[姓氏].
ma·ser [ˈmeizə] *n.* [缩] (*m*icrowave *a*mplification by *s*timulated *e*mission of *r*adiation) 脉泽, 微波激射; 微波激射器, 受激辐射微波放大器.
Ma·se·ru [ˈmæzəruː] *n.* 马塞卢[莱索托首都].
mash¹ [mæʃ] *n.* ①麦芽浆[啤酒原料]; (喂牛马的)面粉[米糠]浆; 捣成糊状的东西; 马铃薯(等捣烂的)泥; 乱糟糟的一团. *sausage and* ~ [俚] 红肠土豆泥. ***all to (a) ~*** …得极烂, 稀烂. — *vt.* 磨碎, 捣烂. ~ **tub** (做)麦芽汁(的)桶.
mash² [mæʃ] [俚] *vt.* 向…调情; 诱惑. — *n.* 使人着迷的人, 情人. ***be ~ed on*** 恋着, 爱着. ***make a ~ on*** [美俚]使爱上, 使看中. ***make one's ~*** 使人神魂颠倒, 使人着迷.
mash·er¹ [ˈmæʃə] *n.* 捣碎机[器]; 捣碎者; 制麦芽浆的工人.
mash·er² [ˈmæʃə] *n.* [俚]调戏女性的人.
Mash·had [mɑːʃˈhɑːd] *n.* 马什哈德 [即 Meshed 迈谢德][伊朗城市].
mash·ie [mæʃi] *n.*【高尔夫球】铁头短球棒.
mash·y [ˈmæʃi] *a.* ***(mash·i·er; -i·est)*** 磨碎的, 稀烂的.
mas·jid [ˈmʌsdʒid] *n.* 伊斯兰教寺院.
mask [mɑːsk, [Am.] -æ-] *n.* ①假面具, 伪装, 掩蔽物; 面罩; 防毒面具(=gas mask);【物】掩模; (劈剑、棒球等用)护面; (用蜡等从死人面部模制成的)蜡模遗容 (= deathmask). ②口实; 掩饰. ③假面跳舞会; 戴假面者; 假面戏. ④(纪念打猎的)狐头, 狐面. ⑤(筑城)遮障, 掩蔽角面堡;【印】蒙片;【摄】蔽光框. ⑥【计】时标, 时间标志. *a flu* ~ 防流感戴的口罩; 卫生口罩. ***assume [put on, wear] the ~*** 戴假面具, 掩盖真面目. ***drop [pull off, throw off] the ~*** 摘下假面具, 现出本来面目. ***under the ~ of*** 假托, 在…假面具下. — *vt.* ①在(脸)上戴假面具; 化装. ②蒙蔽, 遮蔽, 隐, 覆;【军】掩蔽, 隐蔽(兵力、炮位); 掩护; (因逼近敌方)妨碍(友军)炮火射程;【印】(制版时)用蒙片修正(底片色调);【摄】用蔽光框修改(照相的大小、形状等). — *vi.* 戴假面具; 化装; 参加化装舞会. *We could not fire, as we were ~ed by our first line.* 第一线挡住, 我们无法射击.
mas·ka·longe, mas·ka·nonge [ˈmæskəlɔndʒ -ˈnɔndʒ] *n.* = maskinonge.
masked [mɑːskt] *a.* 戴假面具的, 蒙着脸的; 化装的; (感情等)隐蔽着的, 遮蔽着的;【医】潜伏的, 不明的;【植】假面状的. *a* ~ *ball* 化装跳舞会. *a* ~ *battery* 掩蔽炮台. *a* ~ *fever*【医】潜热. *a* ~ *pupa*【动】隐蛹.
Mas·ke·lyne [ˈmæskilain] *n.* ① 马斯基林[人名]. ②**N.** ~ 尼·马斯基林[1732—1811, 英国天文学家, 航海历的发明者.]
mask·er [ˈmɑːskə] *n.* 戴假面具的人; 参加假面舞会的人; 演假面剧者.
mask·ing [ˈmɑːskiŋ] *n.* 伪装; 化装; 掩蔽; 掩模. ~ **tape**【印】不透光胶纸[一般是深红色, 在涂玻璃底版时用来遮盖和保护版边].
mas·ki·nonge [ˈmæskinɔndʒ] *n.* 大梭鱼.
mas·lin [ˈmæzlin] *n.* [英](小麦和裸麦等的)混合粉; 混合粉面包; 谷类和豆类间种的庄稼; 混合物.
mas·och·ism [ˈmæzəkizəm] *n.* ①【心】(色情)受虐狂 (*opp.* sadism). ②自我虐待; 以苦为乐的精神. **-ist** *n.*, **-is·tic** *a.*

Ma•son [ˈmeisn] *n.* ①梅森〔姓氏,男子名〕. ②~ **jar** 梅森食瓶〔一种大口玻璃瓶,有螺旋盖子,供家庭贮藏食品用〕.
ma•son [ˈmeisn] *n.* 石匠;(中世纪的)工匠工会会员;〔M-〕共济会(成员).—*vt.* 用石或砖修建. ~ **bee**【虫】石蜂〔一种孤栖蜜蜂,用粘土、沙子、泥做窠〕.
Ma•son-Dix•on Line [ˈmeisnˈdiksn lain]〔美〕梅逊-狄克逊分界线〔Pennsylvania 和 Maryland 州间的界线,此线延伸为后来区分美国南部和北部的标志〕.
ma•son•ic [məˈsɔnik] *a.* ①(中世纪)石匠工会的. ②〔M-〕共济会(成员)的.
Ma•son•ite [ˈmeisənait] *n.* 梅斯奈纤维板,夹布胶木板〔商标名〕. *m- process* 湿式纤维板制造法.
ma•son•ry [ˈmeisnri] *n.* ①石工技术;石工行业;石造建筑. ②〔M-〕共济会制度〔纲领、仪式〕;〔集合词〕共济会成员.
Ma•so•ra, Ma•so•rah [məˈsɔurə] *n.* 玛索拉〔①犹太人的希伯来文本圣经教义. ②体现此教义的圣经批注.〕
Mas•o•rete, Mas•o•rite [ˈmæsəriːt, -rait] *n.* 玛索拉的编纂者. **-ret•ic** [-ˈretik] *a.*
masque [mɑːsk, mæsk] *n.* (中世纪流行的)假面戏剧;假面戏剧本;化装舞会.
mas•quer [ˈmɑːskə] *n.* = masker.
mas•quer•ade [ˌmæskəˈreid, mɑːs-] *n.* 假面〔化装〕舞会〔聚会〕;假面戏;化装舞会上穿的服装;伪装;假托;掩饰. — *vi.* 参加化装舞会;化装;冒充,假托,假装.
mas•quer•ad•er [ˌmæskəˈreidə] *n.* 化装跳舞者;假装者,冒充者;戴假面具者.
Mass. = Massachusetts.
mass[1] [mæs] *n.* ①块,堆,团. ②群众,集团;〔the ~es〕群众;民众. ③大量;大宗;众多;〔the ~〕大部分,大半;主体;总体. ④【物】质量. ⑤【军】集团纵队,密集队形. ⑥【矿】体. *a ~ of earth* 一大块泥土. *a ~ of letters* 一大堆信件. *The ~es have boundless creative power.* 人民群众有无限的创造力. *a ~ of manoeuvre* 实施机动集团. *proper ~* 静质量. *the ~es* 群众,大众. ***be ~ of*** 一团…,全身…,遍体…(*He is a ~ of bruises.* 他遍体鳞伤). ***from the ~es, to the ~es*** 从群众中来,到群众中去. ***in the ~*** 整个儿地,总体上,合计. ***the (great) ~ of ...*** …的大部分. ***to be at one with the ~es*** 同群众打成一片.—*vt.* 使成一团;集中(力量等);【军】使密集. — *vi.* 集中,聚集. *~ed body*【军】密集部队. *~ed formation*【军】密集队形. ~ **action**【物】质量作用;浓度作用. ~ **attack**【军】集中攻击.~ **balance** 质量平衡. ~ **bargaining** 团体会谈. ~ **breeding** 大量繁殖;大批饲养. ~ **communication** 面向大众的信息传播〔指报刊、广播、电视的宣传〕. ~ **production** 大量〔成批〕生产. ~**cult** 大众文化〔指资本主义社会中通过宣传工具传播的矫揉造作的商业化文化〕. ~ **defect**【物】质量亏损. ~ **flights**【空】大机群飞行,编队飞行. ~ **game** 集体竞赛. ~ **media** 宣传工具〔指报纸、杂志、广播和电视〕. ~ **meeting** (尤指政治性质的)大会,群众大会. ~ **motion**【物】整体运动. ~ **noun**【语】物质名词. ~ **number**【物、化】(原子)质量数. ~ **outbreak**【虫】(瘟疫、虫害等)突然蔓延;大规模流行. ~**-produce** *vt.* 大量〔成批〕生产. ~ **psychology** 群众心理. ~ **society** 群体社会;广大群众. ~ **spectrograph** 质谱仪. ~ **spectrometer** 质谱测定器. ~ **suggestion** 群众煽动. ~ **tactics** 密集战术.
Mass, mass[2] [mæs, mɑːs] *n.* 弥撒;弥撒的仪式〔祷告、音乐〕;弥撒曲. *a high [solemn] ~* (有烧香、奏乐等的)大弥撒. *a low [private] ~* (无烧香、奏乐的)小弥撒. ***by the ~*** 一定,的确. ***say [read] ~*** 作弥撒,念经. ~**-bell** 弥撒钟. ~**-book** (天主教的)弥撒经.
mas•sa [ˈmæsə] *n.*〔美方〕= master.
Mas•sa•chu•setts [ˌmæsəˈtʃuːsits] *n.* 马萨诸塞〔旧译麻省,美国州名〕.

mas•sa•cre [ˈmæsəkə] *n.* 大屠杀,残杀;(牲畜的)成批屠宰. — *vt.* ①屠杀;残杀. ②乱切,乱砍. ③损害,弄糟.
mas•sage [ˈmæsɑːʒ] *n.* 按摩(术),推拿(法). — *vt.* 按摩,推拿;(电子计算机)处理,分理. **-er, -sag•ist** *n.* 按摩师.
Mas•sa•wa, Mas•sa•ua [mɑːˈsɑːwɑː] *n.* 马萨瓦〔埃塞俄比亚港市〕.
mass•cult [ˈmæskʌlt] *a.*〔美口〕大众文化的.
mas•sé [mæˈsei] *n.*〔F.〕【台球】挫杆.
mas•se•ter [mæˈsiːtə] *n.*【解】咬肌. **-ic** *a.*
mas•seur [mæˈsəː] *n.* *(pl. ~s* [-z]*)* 男按摩师.
mas•seuse [mæˈsəːz] *n.* *(pl. ~s* [-iz]*)* 女按摩师.
mas•si•cot [ˈmæsikɔt] *n.*【化】铅黄,黄丹,天然一氧化铅.
mas•sif [ˈmæsiːf] *n.*〔F.〕【地】丛山,山岳;地块,断层块.
Mas•sine [ˈmæˈsiːn] *n.* 马辛〔姓氏〕.
mass•i•ness [ˈmæsinis] *n.*〔古〕大而重,厚重,巨大(= massiveness).
mas•sive [ˈmæsiv] *a.* ①大的,重的. ②魁伟的;结实的;实心的. ③大规模的;大量的. ④(容貌、精神等)有力的,坚定的;【心】宽大的. ⑤【地】块状的,大块的. ⑥【矿】均匀构造的,非晶质的. *a ~ forehead* 宽大的前额. *~ mountains* 块状丛山. *a ~ deposit* 块状矿床.
Mas•son [ˈmæsn] *n.* 马森〔姓氏〕.
mass•y [ˈmæsi] *a.* ***(mass•i•er; -i•est)***〔诗〕= massive【物】有质量的.
mast[1] [mɑːst] *n.* 桅;柱,竿,天线杆,天线塔;(停飞船的)栓柱. ★三桅船从船头起依次为 foremast 前桅,mainmast 大桅,主桅,mizzenmast 后桅. 桅上有接桅时从下而上依次为 lower mast 下桅,top mast 中桅,topgallant mast 上桅,royal mast 顶桅. ***afore [before] the ~*** 作为普通水手. ***at the ~*** 在上甲板大桅下〔水手集合处〕. ***spend a ~*** 桅杆被折断. — *vt.*【船】给…装桅杆;扯(帆). ~**head** ①*n.* 桅顶,〔特指〕下桅桅顶;桅顶瞭望人;〔美〕报头栏;报头;(书刊的)版权页. ②*vt.* 挂(旗等)在桅顶;(罚水手)使爬上桅顶.~**-house** 桅杆制造厂.
mast[2] [mɑːst] *n.* 榉、栎、栗等的果实〔可作猪饲料〕. ~ **cell**【生】肥大细胞.
mas•ta•ba [ˈmæstəbə] *n.*【考古】(古代埃及的)石室坟墓,石椁.
mas•tec•to•my [mæsˈtektəmi] *n.* ***(pl. -mies)***【医】乳房切除术;乳腺摘除术.
-mas•ted [ˈmɑːstid] *a.* 有桅的;…桅的: *a three-~ schooner* 三桅帆船.
mas•ter [ˈmɑːstə] *n.* ①主人;雇主,老板 (*opp.* servant);船长,船主;家长;校长. ②〔常无冠词〕善能〔长于、精通〕…的人;胜者,征服者. ③〔英〕教师,老师,先生(= school-master);师傅. ④〔the M-〕【圣】基督,主. ⑤能手,名家,大师,〔特指〕名画家;名家作品;大家,名人. ⑥〔M-〕〔旧社会中对少年的敬称〕哥儿,少爷〔*M- Tom, M- Smith*〕. ⑦〔M-〕〔Scot.〕子爵〔男爵〕的长子,大少爷〔*the M- of Ballantrae*〕. ⑧〔M-〕硕士〔Doctor 和 Bachelor 间的学位〕. ⑨(Oxford, Cambridge 大学的)学生宿舍主任;【法】助理法官;(英国皇室的)御马长官,宴务局长(等). ⑩原版录音片,主盘〔即唱片的负片〕. ~ *and man* 主人和仆人. *Like ~, like man.* 有其主必有其仆. *the ~ of the house* 户主. *a language ~* 语文老师. *the passed M-* 前任会长〔主任〕. *a passed ~* (世所公认的)名家. *a ~ of oratory* 演说家. *M- of Arts* 文科硕士. *M- of Science* 理工硕士. *a M- in the schools* 硕士初试主考员. *the ~ of ceremonies* (宫廷中的)典礼官;(会场中的)司仪. ***be ~ in one's own house*** 不受别人干涉. ***be ~ of*** 所有;通,精通;能自由处理. ***be ~ of oneself*** 自制. ***be ~ of the situation*** 能够控制局势;善于临机应变. ***be one's own ~*** 能独立自主,不受别人牵制. ***make***

oneself* ~ *of 熟练，精通，能自由控制[掌握]. ***the old ~s*** 画坛大师(的作品). — *a.* 主要的；为首的；优秀的. *a ~ clock* (调整其他电钟的)母钟，标准钟. *a ~ mason* 手艺高超的石匠师傅. *a ~ builder* 建筑承包人；建筑家. *a ~ hand* 能手. *a ~ mind* 伟人，杰出人物. *a ~ station* 【电】主控台. *a ~ stroke* (丰功)伟绩；妙举，大成功. *a ~ switch* 总开关. — *vt.* ①作…的主人，控制，统治. ②制服，征服；压制(情欲)；养乖，养训(动物). ③熟练，精通. ④晾干(染料等). *~ one's temper* 压制着脾气，忍着气. *~ English* 精通英文. *~ a subject thoroughly* 完全掌握某门学问. **~-at-arms** *(pl.* ***mas·ters-at-arms)*** 〔英〕【海】纠察长. **~dom** *n.* 控制(权、力). **~ general** 〔英陆军〕(军需局、军械局的)局长. **~hood**＝mastership. **~ key** (能开一切锁的) 通用[万能]钥匙；难题解决法；关键；【电】总电键. **~ mariner** 船长. **~ mechanic** 熟练技工(尤指工长). **~mind** ① *vt.* 〔英〕策划，暗中指挥. ② *n.* 出谋划策的人；具有极大才智的人. **~piece, ~work** 杰作，名作. **~ plan** 总计划. **~ sergeant** 〔美军〕军士长. **~ship** 硕士学位；校长职位；精通，练达；控制；胜利. **~singer** = meistersinger.

-mas·ter [-ˈmɑːstə] *comb. f.* 有…桅船的: *a four-~* 四桅船.

mas·ter·ful [ˈmɑːstəful] *a.* ①主人派头的；专横的，傲慢的. ②巧妙的；熟练的；名家的.

mas·ter·ly [ˈmɑːstəli] *a.* 巧妙的，熟练的；名家的；〔古〕=masterful. — *ad.* …到家，巧妙地.

mas·ter·y [ˈmɑːstəri] *n.* 控制；控制权，统治力；胜利，制服；首位，优势；精通，熟练. *the ~ of the seas* 制海权. *Gain ~ by striking first.* 先发制人而占上风 〔*cf.* strike〕. ***gain [get, obtain] the ~ of*** 控制；精通，善能. ***strive for ~*** 争雌雄.

mas·tic [ˈmæstik] *n.* (用作亮漆原料、香料等的)乳香(脂)；乳香树；涂料；胶粘剂；乳香酒〔加有乳香的葡萄酒〕；淡黄色.

mas·ti·ca·ble [ˈmæstikəbl] *a.* 可咀嚼的；可撕捏的. **-bil·i·ty** [ˌmæstikəˈbiliti] *n.*

mas·ti·cate [ˈmæstikeit] *vt.* 嚼，咀嚼；撕捏；素炼〔指将橡胶揉成浆状〕.

mas·ti·ca·tion [ˌmæstiˈkeiʃən] *n.* 咀嚼(作用)；【化】撕捏(作用)；捏和(作用)；(橡胶)素炼.

mas·ti·ca·tor [ˈmæstikeitə] *n.* 咀嚼者[器官]；碎肉器；割碎机；撕捏机；素炼机；割碎机等操作者；〔*pl.*〕〔谑〕牙齿.

mas·ti·ca·to·ry [ˈmæstikeitəri] *a.* 咀嚼的，咀嚼器官的；适于咀嚼的；撕捏的. — *n.* (用以促进唾液分泌的)咀嚼物〔橡皮糖、烟草等〕.

mas·tiff [ˈmæstif] *n.* 一种滑皮短腰大看家狗.

mas·ti·goph·o·ran [ˌmæstəˈgɔfərən] *n.* 【动】鞭毛虫 *(Mastigophora)* 动物. — *a.* 鞭毛虫的. **-rous** [-rəs] *a.*

mas·ti·tis [mæsˈtaitis] *n.* 【医】乳房炎，乳腺炎.

mast·less[1] [ˈmɑːstlis] *a.* 无桅的.

mast·less[2] [ˈmɑːstlis] *a.* 不结果实的.

mas·to·car·ci·no·ma [ˌmæstəukɑːsiˈnəumə] *n.* 【医】乳癌.

mas·to·don [ˈmæstədɔn] *n.* 【古生】(第三纪的)柱牙象；庞然大物；〔美拳〕重量级拳击家.

mas·to·don·tic [ˌmæstəˈdɔntik] *a.* 柱牙象的；巨大的.

mas·toid [ˈmæstɔid] *a.* 乳头状的，乳房状的. — *n.* 【解】(耳后的)乳突(骨)；〔俚〕(=mastoiditis).

mas·toid·ec·to·my [ˌmæstɔiˈdektəmi] *n.* *(pl.* ***-mies)*** 【医】乳突切除术.

mas·toid·i·tis [ˌmæstɔiˈdaitis] *n.* 【医】乳突(骨)炎.

mas·tur·bate [ˈmæstəbeit] *vi., vt.* ***(-bat·ed; -bat·ing)*** (对…)行手淫. **-ba·tion** [-ˈbeiʃən] *n.* **-ba·tor** *n.* **-ba·tor·y** [-bətəri] *a.*

ma·su·ri·um [məˈsjuəriəm] *n.* 钨〔元素 technetium 锝的旧名〕.

masut [məˈzuːt] *n.* = mazut.

MAT = Master of Arts in Teaching 教育硕士.

mat[1] [mæt] *n.* ①席子；蹭鞋垫 (=doormat)；(体操等用的)垫子；(花瓶等的)垫子；〔美〕(照片、画等的)垫纸. ②(装糖及咖啡等的)蒲包；一包的量. ③【海】防擦垫. ④ (毛、杂草等的)丛，簇. ⑤【印】铸印版用的纸型. ***leave (a person) on the ~*** 不接待客人. ***on the ~*** 【军俚】被拖到长官面前，被处罚；〔美〕 被责备，受调查. — *vt.* 在…上铺席子，给…盖席子；编织；〔主用 *p.p.*〕使缠结. *matted hair* 乱蓬蓬的头发. —*vi.* 缠结. **~-man** 摔跤手.

mat[2] [mæt] *a.* 无光泽的；闷光的；表面粗糙的. — *n.* (毛玻璃等的)消光(面)；消光器；(绘画等的)衬底纸；(相框的)闷光金边. — *vt.* 使(画面等)不现光泽，使成闷光；给(画)配闷光金边；使(金属玻璃等)褪光.

mat. [mæt] *n.* 〔Am.〕 = matinee.

Ma·ta·be·le [ˌmætəˈbiːli] *n.* *(pl. ~(s))* 马塔比黑人〔1837 年被荷兰殖民者后裔布尔人从德兰士瓦无理驱逐至罗得西亚的祖鲁人〕.

Ma·ta·di [məˈtɑːdi] *n.* 马塔迪〔扎伊尔港市〕.

mat·a·dor [ˈmætədɔː] *n.* ①【斗牛】斗牛士. ②【牌戏】一种王牌.

match[1] [mætʃ] *n.* (一根)火柴；〔古〕(从前大炮发火用的)火绳，导火线. *light [strike] a ~* 擦火柴. *a safety ~* 安全火柴. *a lucifer ~* 黄磷火柴. **~book** 纸夹火柴. **~box** 火柴盒. **~lock** (旧时的)火绳枪. **~maker** 火柴制造人［厂］. **~safe** = ~box. **~stick** 火柴杆. **~wood** ①制火柴杆的木料. ②碎片 (*make ~wood of sth.* = *reduce sth. to ~wood* 把某物弄粉碎).

match[2] [mætʃ] *n.* ①比赛，竞赛. ②对手，敌手；伙伴，(很相配的)一对，一副. ③一对中的一方. ④婚姻；配偶. ⑤【机】假型，配比；【电】匹配. *Have you a ~ for this ribbon?* 有没有和这一样的丝带？ *We shall never see his ~.* 他那样的人恐怕不会有第二个了. *They are right ~es.* 他们正是好配偶. ***be a ~ for*** 可以和…相匹敌；是某人的对手；和…很相配[协调]. ***be more than a ~ for*** 胜过，强过 (*He is more than a ~ for me.* 他比我强). ***be no ~ for*** 敌不过；不是…对手. ***find [meet] one's ~*** 遇到对手，棋逢敌手 (*He never met his ~.* 他从来没有败过). ***make a good ~*** 找到好对象. ***make a ~*** 作媒. ***make a ~ of it*** 结婚. ***play a ~*** 比赛. ***play off a ~*** (平局后)再赛以决胜负. — *vt.* ①使对抗，使较量；敌得过. ②和…相配[相称]. ③使相配，使成对，使相称. ④使结婚. ⑤(掷钱币等) 以作决定. *a ~ed plate method* 双层造型法. *No one can ~ him.* 没有人敌得过他. *~ a colour* 配一种颜色. *Can you ~ me this silk?* 你能替我配一段这样的绸子吗？ *~ strides* 〔美运〕赛跑. —*vi.* 相称，相适合，相配；结合(成为夫妇). *Let beggars ~ with beggars.* 龙配龙，凤配凤，瘸驴配破磨. ***with everything to ~*** 连同一套附属品. **~ ball** = match point. **~ board** 【木工】(一边有槽、另一边有榫、可互相嵌合的) 假型板. **~boarding** 铺假型板. **~joint** 合榫，企口接合. **~maker** 媒人；好作媒的人；运动比赛组织者. **~mark** ①【机】配合记号. ② *vt.* 加配合记号于…. **~play** ①赛球〔如网球比赛等〕. ②【高尔夫】以通盘由球座打入穴中所得的分数计分的比赛. **~ point** 【体】决胜点，争取胜利所必需的最后一分.

match·a·ble [ˈmætʃəbl] *a.* 能匹敌的，敌得过的；对等的，相配的. ***~ to none*** = matchless.

matchet(te) [mæˈtʃet] *n.* =machete.

match·less [ˈmætʃlis] *a.* 无敌的，无比的.

mate[1] [meit] *n.* ①(工人间的)伙伴，同事；老兄，老弟〔工人、水手间的亲密称呼〕. ②配偶〔男女任何一方〕；动物之偶 (尤指鸟类)；(一对中的) 一只；配对物. ③【海】(商船的)大副；驾驶员；【海军】〔美〕二级准尉的助手〔相当于军士级别〕；【医】(军医等的)助手. *the chief [first] ~* (船长之下的)大副. *a boatswain's ~* 水手长的助手. *a surgeon's* ～ 军医助手. ***go*** ～***s with*** 与…合伙, 和…成为伙伴. — *vt., vi.* (使)成伙伴. (使)成配偶 *(with)*, (使)(鸟等)搭配, (使)交配*(with)*; (使)紧密配合.

mate[2] [meit] *n., vt.* 【象棋】逼将; 将军; 将死. ***give*** ～ ***to*** 将军, 将死(对方的王). ***fool's*** ～走动两步棋就出现的败局.

ma·te[3], **ma·té** [ˈmætei] *n.* (用冬青类巴拉圭茶树叶制成的)巴拉圭茶; 巴拉圭茶叶[树]; (用吸管吸的)巴拉圭茶壶.

ma·te·las·sé [ˈmætləˈsei; F. matlɑˈse] *a.* 马特拉斯的; 提花的. —马特拉斯〔一种提花凸纹双层织物, 布面起绗缝垫褥形状〕.

ma·te·lot [ˈmætləu] *n.* 〔F.〕〔俚〕水手.

mat·e·lote [ˈmætələt], ***mat·e·lotte*** [-lɑt] *n.* 〔F.〕①【烹】酒、葱等调料汁燉鱼. ②马塔洛水手舞.

ma·ter [ˈmeitə] *n.* *(pl.* ***ma·tres*** [ˈmeitriz]*)* 〔英〕〔学生俚〕母亲 (=mother).

ma·ter dol·o·ro·sa [ˈmeitəˌdəuləˈrəusə] *n.* 〔L.〕悲伤的母亲; 〔M- D-〕悲伤的圣母玛利亚像.

ma·ter· fa·mil·i·as [ˈmeitəfəˈmiliæs] *n.* 〔L.〕主妇.

ma·te·ri·al [məˈtiəriəl] *a.* ①物质的 (*opp.* spiritual). ②身体上的, 肉体上的; 物欲的, 追求实利的; 卑俗的. ③有形的, 实体的; 物质性的. ④重要的, 实质性的; 必需的. ⑤【逻、哲】实质上的, 实体上的, 内容上的 (*opp.* formal); 【法】本质的. *the* ～ *universe* 物质世界. ～ *civilization* 物质文明. ～ *comforts* 使物质生活舒适的东西〔食品、衣服等〕. ～ *pleasure* 肉体的快乐. ～ *point* 【理】质点. *a* ～ *being* 有形物. ～ *property* 有形财产. *a very* ～ *difference* 重大的差别. *a point* ～ *to one's argument* 论证要点. ～ *element* 要素. ***be*** ～ ***to*** 对于…重要. ***in*** ～ ***form*** 用具体的形式. — *n.* 材料, 原料; (军用)物资; 织物, 料子; 资料; 题材; 素材; 〔*pl.*〕必需品, 用具; 设备; 品质; 人材, 人物. *building* ～*(s)* 建筑材料. *raw* ～*(s)* 原(材)料. *condemned* ～*(s)* 报废器材. ～ *for a novel* 小说素材. *writing* ～*s* 笔墨纸类, 文具. ～ ***noun*** 【语】物质名词.

ma·te·ri·al·ism [məˈtiəriəlizəm] *n.* 【哲】唯物主义, 唯物论; 实利主义; 【美】写实主义. *dialectic(al)* ～ 辩证唯物主义. *historical* ～ 历史唯物主义.

ma·te·ri·al·ist [məˈtiəriəlist] *n.* 唯物主义者; 实利主义者. — *a.* 唯物主义的; 唯物主义者的. ～ *dialectics* 唯物辩证法.

ma·te·ri·a·lis·tic [məˌtiəriəˈlistik] *a.* 唯物主义的; 唯物主义者的; 物质第一主义的; 实物主义(者)的. ～ *interpretation [conception] of history* 唯物史观.

ma·te·ri·a·lis·ti·cal·ly [məˌtiəriəˈlistikəli] *ad.* 在唯物论上, 就唯物主义的观点来看.

ma·te·ri·al·i·ty [məˌtəriˈæliti] *n.* 物质性; 实体性, 有形(物) (*opp.* spirituality); 【法】重要性; 实质性; 〔*pl.*〕物质, 实体.

ma·te·ri·al·ize [məˈtiəriəlaiz] *vt.* 赋与…以形体; 使具体化; 使物质化; 实现; 使(鬼魂等)现形. — *vi.* 具体化, 体现; (希望、计划等)实现, 成为事实. ～ *one's ideas* 实现自己的理想. **-i·za·tion** *n.* 物质化(作用).

ma·te·ri·al·ly [məˈtiəriəli] *ad.* 物质上, 有形地 (*opp.* spiritually); 【哲、逻】实质上; 显著地, 大大地; 相当地.

ma·te·ri·a med·i·ca [məˈtiəriə ˈmedikə] 〔L.〕〔总称〕药物; 药物学; 药物学论著.

ma·té·ri·el [məˌtiriˈel] *n.* 〔F.〕物资; 装备; (军队、团体等的)设备, 设施; 作战物资; 物力; 武器 (*opp.* personel).

ma·ter·nal [məˈtəːnl] *a.* ①母亲的; 象母亲的, 母性的. ②母方的, 母系的; 〔谑〕自己母亲的. ～ *love* 母爱. ～ *impression* 胎教, 母亲印痕. *one's* ～ *grandfather* 外祖父. *one's* ～ *uncle* 舅父. ～ *mortality rate* 产妇死亡率. **-ism** *n.* 纵容, 溺爱. **-ly** *ad.*

ma·ter·ni·ty [məˈtəːniti] *n.* 母性; 母道; 怀孕; 产科医院. — *a.* 产妇用的. ～ **bag** (教区送给贫民的)接生包. ～ **benefit** 产期津贴. ～ **centre** 孕妇顾问处. ～ **clinic** 妇女保健站. ～ **hospital** 产科医院. ～ **leave** 产假. ～ **nurse** 助产士; 产科护士. ～ **ward** (医院里的)产科病房.

mate·y [ˈmeiti] *a.* 〔口〕易接近的, 易为人亲近的.

math [mæθ] *n.* ①〔口〕= mathematics. ②〔英方〕割草.

math. = mathematical; mathematician; mathematics.

math·e·mat·i·cal [ˌmæθiˈmætikəl] *a.* 数学(上)的, 数理的; 严正的, 精确的. ～ *instruments* 制图仪器. ～ *logic* 数理逻辑 (=symbolic logic). ～ **biology** 数理生物学. **-ly** *ad.*

math·e·ma·ti·cian [ˌmæθiməˈtiʃən] *n.* 数学家.

math·e·mat·ics [ˌmæθiˈmætiks] *n.* 数学. ★通常作单数用, 带有"计算能力"意义时, 作复数用, 如: *His* ～ *are not good.* 他不长于计算. *applied [mixed]* ～ 应用数学. *pure* ～ 纯数学.

Math·er [ˈmeiðə, ˈmæðə] *n.* 马瑟〔姓氏〕.

maths [mæθs] *n.* 〔英〕= mathematics.

ma·ti·co [məˈtiːkəu] *n.* 〔Sp.〕【植】狭叶胡椒树; (可作止血剂用的)狭叶胡椒树树叶.

Ma·til·da [məˈtiːldə] *n.* 马蒂尔达〔女子名〕.

mat·in [ˈmætin] *n.* ①〔*pl.*〕【英国国教】早课, 晨祷; 早课时刻; 【天主】(夜半或黎明的)祷告时刻. ②〔*sing., pl.*〕〔诗〕(鸟的)朝鸣, 晨歌. — *a.* 黎明的, 早晨的; 早课的, 晨祷的.

mat·in·al [ˈmætinl] *a.* = matin *a.*

mat·i·née [ˈmætinei] *n.* 〔F.〕(戏剧、音乐会等的)日戏, 日场; 日间的社交集会; (女人早晨穿的)便装. *a* ～ *doll* 穿得漂漂亮亮去看日戏的女人. *the* ～ *hat* 日戏女帽. *a* ～ *idol* 风流小生, (西方影剧界)受到女观众崇拜的男演员.

mat·ing [ˈmeitiŋ] *n.* 【生】交配.

mat·jes herring [ˈmɑːtjəs] 糟青鱼.

mat·lo(w) [ˈmætləu] *n.* 〔英俚〕= matelot.

mat·rass [ˈmætrəs] *n.* 【化】(旧时蒸馏用的)长颈卵形瓶.

matri- *comb. f.* 母: matriarch.

ma·tri·arch [ˈmeitriɑːk] *n.* 女家长, 女族长; 〔通例、谑〕家长[族长]的妻子.

ma·tri·ar·chal, ma·tri·ar·chic [ˌmeitriˈɑːkəl, -kik] *a.* 女家长[族长]的; 母权的, 母系(继承)的.

ma·tri·ar·ch·y [ˈmeitriɑːki] *n.* 女家长[族长]制, 母权制.

ma·tric [məˈtrik] *n.* 〔matriculation 之略〕大学入学考试.

ma·tri·ces [ˈmeitrisiːz] *n.* matrix 的复数.

ma·tri·cid·al [ˌmeitriˈsaidəl] *a.* 杀母的.

ma·tri·cide [ˈmeitrisaid] *n.* 杀母(罪); 杀母者.

ma·tric·u·lant [məˈtrikjulənt] *n.* 大学投考人; 被录取的新生.

ma·tric·u·late [məˈtrikjuleit] *vt.* 准许入(大)学; 录取. — *vi.* 被录取; 注册入学. — [-lit] *n.* 被许入学者.

ma·tric·u·la·tion [məˌtrikjuˈleiʃən] *n.* 录取入学; 入学礼; (大学)入学考试.

ma·tri·lin·e·al [ˌmætriˈliniəl] *a.* 母系的. **-ly** *ad.*

mat·ri·mo·ni·al [ˌmætriˈməunjəl, -niəl] *a.* 婚姻的; 夫妇的. *a* ～ *advertisement* 求婚广告. **-ly** *ad.*

mat·ri·mo·ny [ˈmætriməni] *n.* ①结婚, 婚姻; 婚姻生活; 夫妇关系. ②抽对子〔一种纸牌戏〕. ～ **vine** 【植】宁夏枸杞.

ma·trix [ˈmeitriks] *n.* *(pl.* ***ma·trices*** [ˈmeitrisiːz] 或 ～*es)* ①【解】子宫; 母体; 发源地, 策源地, 摇篮; 【生】衬质细胞; 间质; 基质; 母质. ②【矿】母岩; 脉石; 【冶】基体; 【地】脉石; 填质; 杂矿石. ③ [ˈmætriks] 【印】字模; 型版, 纸型; 铸型, 阴模. ④【数】(矩)阵, 方阵; 母式; 【物】间架; 【无】矩阵变换电路. ⑤【染】原色〔红黄蓝白黑五种〕. *the* ～ *of a nail* 【解】指甲床. ～ **algebra** 【数】矩阵代

数. ～ **sentence**【语法】基句,母句.

ma·tron [ˈmeitrən] *n.* ①(年龄相当大的、有声望的)妇女,主妇;保姆;(学校等的)女主任;女舍监;护士长;(妇女组织等的)女会长;女主席;总干事. ②母种畜. *a police* ～(女监狱的)女管理员;女看守. *a* ～ *of honour*〔美〕(新娘的已婚)主伴娘.

ma·tron·age [ˈmeitrənidʒ] *n.* 主妇等的身分〔职责〕;〔集合词〕主妇们,保姆们.

ma·tron·ize [ˈmeitrəˌnaiz] *vt.* ***(-ized; -izing)*** ①使显出主妇的派头. ②陪伴,伴随.

ma·tron·like, ma·tron·ly [ˈmeitrənlaik -trənli] *a.* 主妇似的,管家婆似的;保姆似的;有威严的,严肃的;安详的;沉着的.

ma·tron·ship [ˈmeitrənʃip] *n.* 主妇等的身分〔地位、任务〕.

mat·ro·nym·ic [ˌmætrəˈnimik] *a.* 取自母名的;母名的.

M.A.T.S. = Military Air Transport Service〔美〕军事空运局.

Matt [mæt] *n.* 马特〔男子名, Matthew 的昵称〕.

Matt. = Matthew, Matthias.

matt, matte [mæt] *a., n., vt.* = mat[2].

mat·ta·more [ˈmætəmɔː] *n.*〔罕〕地下室(仓库).

matte [mæt] *n.*【冶】锍,冰铜. — *vt.* 使(硫化铜矿等)成为冰铜.

mat·ted [ˈmætid] *a.* ①铺着席子的. ②编织的,编织成席的. ③(杂草等)遍地丛生的;乱蓬蓬的. ～ *hair* 乱蓬蓬的头发.

mat·ter [ˈmætə] *n.* ①物质 (*opp.* spirit, mind);物体. ②【逻】命题的本质;【哲】内容 (*opp.* form);(书籍、演说等的)内容、主旨 (*opp.* manner, style). ③材料,要素,成分. ④原因,根据,理由. ⑤物品,物件;邮件. ⑥事,事情,事件;〔*pl.*〕〔代名词性质的用法〕事态,情形,情况. ⑦重大事件,重要事故;麻烦,毛病. ⑧(议论、讨论等的)问题. ⑨【医】脓;【印】原稿;排版. *animal [vegetable, mineral]* ～ 动物〔植物,矿物〕质. *solid [liquid, gaseous]* ～ 固〔液,气〕体. *coloring* ～ 色素. *printed* ～ 印刷品. *postal* ～ 邮件. *M-s are different.* 情形有所不同. *How have* ～*s stood?* 一向情况怎样? *What's the* ～ *with you?* 你怎么啦? 出了甚么事?〔对不平、不幸等说〕*Nothing is the* ～ *(with me).* (我)没甚么. *It won't* ～. 那也不要紧. *It is no laughing* ～. 这可不是开玩笑的事. *a* ～ *of political power* 政权问题. ***a*** ～ ***for [of] complaint*** 令人抱怨的事. ***a*** ～ ***in dispute [question]*** 争执中的问题. ***a*** ～ ***in hand*** 当前的问题,眼前的问题. ***a*** ～ ***of*** ①…的问题(*a* ～ *of life and death* 生死攸关的问题. *a* ～ *of habit* 习惯问题). ②大约;…左右 (*for a* ～ *of 30 years* 约三十年). ***a*** ～ ***of course*** 理所当然的(事情) (*cf.* ～-of-course). ***a*** ～ ***of fact*** ①事实,事实问题 (*cf.* ～-of-fact). ②【法】按证据来判定可靠与否的陈述. ***a*** ～ ***of opinion*** 有争论余地的问题. ***a*** ～ ***of record*** 法院有案可查的案件. ***as a*** ～ ***of fact*** 事实上,其实. ***as*** ～***s stand*** = ***as the*** ～ ***stands*** 照目前状况. ***carry*** ～***s with a high hand*** 处事专横. ***for that*** ～ = ***for the*** ～ ***of that*** 讲到那件事;关于那一点. ***in the*** ～ ***of*** 关于…;就…而论. ***no*** ～ 没事儿,不要紧(*It is no* ～. = *It makes no* ～. 那不算一回事. 那不要紧). ***no*** ～ ***how [what, when, which, who, where …]*** 不管怎样〔什么,什么时候,哪一个,谁,什么地方〕(*No* ～ *what he says, don't go.* 不管他怎么讲都不要去. *It is not true, no* ～ *who may say so.* 不管谁那样讲都不是真的). ***on certain specialized*** ～***s*** 就某些专业方面. ***take*** ～***s easy [seriously]*** 轻视〔重视〕问题. ***take up a*** ～ ***with*** 和…交涉. ***to make*** ～***s worse.*** 尤其糟糕的是. ***What is the*** ～ ***with …?*** 怎么啦? 出了什么事? 出了什么毛病?〔谑〕…有什么不好? ***What's the*** ～***?*** 怎么一回事? 出了什么事? ***What*** ～***?*** = ***No*** ～. 那有什么要紧? 不要紧. — *vi.* ①要紧,重要,有重大关系. ★主要用于否定句、疑问句. ②化脓,出脓. *It does not* ～ *(if …).* (即使…也)不要紧. *What does it* ～*?* 那有什么要紧? ～**-of-course** *a.* 当然的,不用说的. ～**-of-fact** *a.* 事实上的,实际上的,如实的,实事求是的;平凡的,乏味的.

Mat·thew [ˈmæθjuː] *n.* ①马修〔男子名〕. ②【宗】马太〔耶稣十二门徒之一〕;(基督教《圣经》中的)《马太福音》.

Mat·thews [ˈmæθjuːz] *n.* 马修斯〔姓氏〕.

Mat·thi·as [məˈθaiəs] *n.* ①马赛厄斯〔男子名〕. ②【圣】马提亚〔代替 Judas Iscariot 成为基督十二门徒之一〕.

mat·ting [ˈmætiŋ] *n.* = mat[1], mat[2].

mat·tins [ˈmætnz] *n.* = matins.

mat·tock [ˈmætək] *n.* 鹤嘴锄;掘根耙.

mat·toid [ˈmætɔid] *n.* 半疯子;奇人,怪人.

mat·tress [ˈmætris] *n.* ①(床用)垫子. ②【土木】(护岸)木排,枝篱. *a spring [straw]* ～ 弹簧〔草〕垫子.

Mat·ty [ˈmæti] *n.* 马蒂〔Martha, Mathilda 的昵称〕.

mat·u·rate [ˈmætjureit] *vi., vt.*【医】(使)化脓;(使)成熟.

mat·u·ra·tion [ˌmætjuˈreiʃən] *n.*【医】化脓;(果实等的)成熟;(才能等的)圆熟;(化学纤维的)老成.

mat·u·ra·tive [məˈtjuərətiv] *a., n.*【医】促使化脓的;化脓药.

ma·ture [məˈtjuə] *a.* ***(-tur·er; -tur·est)*** ①(有机体)熟的,成熟的;(精神、智力)圆熟的,发达完全的. ②(葡萄酒等)酿成的. ③成年人的;【地】壮年的. ④仔细考虑过的,慎重的;贤明的. ⑤(票据等)已到期的. *the* ～ *age [years]* (能辨是非的)成熟年龄. *a* ～ *plan* 慎重的计划. — *vt.* 使熟;使成熟;完成,慎重拟定(计划等). — *vi.* 熟,成熟;(票据等)到期. *Wine and judgement* ～ *with age.* 酒老味醇,人老识深. **-ly** *ad.*, **-ness** *n.*

Ma·turin [ˈmætjurin] *n.* 马丘林〔姓氏〕.

ma·tu·ri·ty [məˈtjuəriti] *n.* 成熟(度),完成;(票据等的)到期;【医】化脓;【地】壮年;壮年期. ***come to*** ～ 成熟. ***on [at]*** ～ 满期,到期.

ma·tu·ti·nal [ˌmætju(ː)ˈtainl] *a.* 清晨的,拂晓的;早. **-ly** *ad.*

mat·zo [ˈmɑːtsəu] *n.* ***(pl. mat·zot, mat·zoth*** [-tsəut, -tsəuθ]***~s)*** 犹太逾越节薄饼〔逾越节期间犹太人所吃的一种扁而薄的硬面饼〕(= matsah).

mat·y[1] [ˈmæti, ˈmeiti] *n.*〔印〕男仆.

ma·ty[2] [ˈmeiti] *a.* = matey.

maud [mɔːd] *n.* (苏格兰牧羊人穿的)柳条灰呢;柳条灰呢旅行毯.

Maud(e) [mɔːd] *n.* 莫德〔女子名〕.

maud·lin [ˈmɔːdlin] *a.* 易哭的,易感伤的;喝醉了就哭的. — *n.* 脆弱的感情.

Maugham [mɔːm] *n.* 莫姆〔姓氏〕.

mau·gre, mau·ger [ˈmɔːgə] *prep.*〔英古〕不管,不顾,虽.

mau·kin [ˈmɔːkin] *n.* ①懒婆娘. ②拖布. ③稻草人. ④野兔. ⑤猫 (=malkin).

maul [mɔl] *n.* 大木槌. ～ *and wedges*〔美〕樵夫用的各种工具;全部. — *vt.* ①打伤;打破,抓破,刺破;虐待,粗暴地对待,粗笨地处理. ②严厉批评. ③〔美〕用楔和大槌劈开. *badly* ～*ed* 焦头烂额. *Stop* ～*ing the cat.* 别虐待猫.

maul·er [ˈmɔːlə] *n.* 使用木槌的人;粗暴对待别人的人;〔美俚〕拳头;拳击家.

maul·ey, maul·ie [mɔːli] *n.*〔俚〕手,拳头.

maul·stick [ˈmɔːlstik] *n.* (画家描绘细线时支持右手用的)腕杖.

Mau Mau [ˈmauˌmau] ***(pl. Mau Mau, Mau Maus)*** "茅茅"〔肯尼亚 1951 年出现的反对英国殖民统治的爱国武装组织名称〕.

mau-mau [ˈmauˌmau] *vt.*〔美俚〕恐吓.

mau·met [ˈmɔːmit] *n.* ①〔废〕偶像. ②〔英方〕玩偶,傀儡.

maun [mɔːn] *v. aux.* 〔Scot.〕 = must[1] *(v. aux.)*

Mau·na Ke·a [ˈmaunə ˈkeiə] *n.* 莫纳克亚山〔夏威夷岛的死火山，太平洋上最高山，4,183 米〕.

Mau·na Lo·a [ˈmaunə ˈləuə] *n.* 莫纳罗亚山〔夏威夷岛的活火山〕.

maund [mɔːnd] *n.* 印度、土耳其、伊朗等国大小不等的衡量名〔尤指折合 82.28 磅的印度重量单位〕.

maun·der [ˈmɔːndə] *vi.* 〔英方〕唠唠叨叨地讲，咕哝；懒洋洋地动作，颟顸，呆呆地闲荡 *(along; about)*. **-er** *n.*

maun·dy [ˈmɔːndi] *n.* ①【宗】濯足礼. ②〔英〕(在濯足节举办的) 贫民抚恤金的赐与. ～ *money* 〔英〕贫民抚恤金. **M- Thursday** 濯足节〔复活节前的星期日〕.

Maur·a [ˈmɔːrə] *n.* 莫拉〔女子名〕, Ir. = Mary.

Mau·rice [ˈmɔris] *n.* 莫里斯〔姓氏，男子名〕(L. = Moorish, dark-coloured).

Mau·ri·ta·ni·a [ˌmɔ(ː)riˈteinjə] *n.* 毛里塔尼亚〔非洲〕.

Mau·ri·ti·us [məˈriʃəs] *n.* 毛里求斯〔非洲〕.

Mau·ser [ˈmauzə] *n.* 〔商标名〕毛瑟枪〔又作 Mauser rifle〕.

mau·so·le·um [ˌmɔːsəˈliəm] *n. (pl. ～s, -le·a* [-ˈliːə]*)* ①〔M-〕(小亚细亚七大奇迹之一的) 卡里亚 (Caria) 王陵(350 B.C.) ②陵庙，陵. ③大而阴森的房屋〔房间〕. **mau·so·le·an** [ˌmɔːsəˈliən] *a.*

mau·vais quart d'heure [ˈməuveiz kaːˈdəː] 〔F.〕不愉快的一刻工夫.

mau·vais su·jet [ˈməuveiz ˈsuːʒei] 〔F.〕废物，没出息的人，饭桶；无赖.

mau·vaise honte [ˈməuveizˈɔ̃ːnt] 〔F.〕 抱歉；不好意思，羞涩；假谦虚.

mauve [məuv] *n.* 苯胺紫(染料)；红紫色. — *a.* 红紫色的.

ma·var [ˈmævɑː] 〔缩〕 *n.* (*m*ixer *a*mplification by *va*riable *r*eactance 的首字母缩略词) 脉伐〔可变电抗混频放大〕；低噪声微波放大器.

mav·er·ick [ˈmævərik] *n.* 〔美西部〕无畜主烙印的小动物〔多指离开母牛而迷失的小牛〕；〔口〕(团体中) 闹独立性的人；持异见者；无党无派的政治家. — *vi.* 迷路，迷失.

Ma·vis [ˈmeivis] *n.* 梅维斯〔女子名〕.

ma·vis [ˈmeivis] *n.* 〔Scot.〕〔诗〕【鸟】善鸣画眉.

ma·vour·neen, ma·vour·nin [məˈvuəniːn] *n., int.* 〔Ir.〕(对女人说) 我的亲爱的(!).

maw [mɔː] *n.* 动物的胃；反刍动物的第四胃；(动物、鱼类等的)喉咙；食管；口部；〔谑〕人胃，肚子. **～-bound** *a.* (牲畜)便秘的. **～-worm** *n.* 线虫；伪君子.

maw·kin [ˈmɔːkin] *n.* = malkin.

mawk·ish [ˈmɔːkiʃ] *a.* ①叫人作呕的；讨厌的；不好吃的，无味的. ②易流泪的，易感伤的. **-ly** *ad.*, **-ness** *n.*

maw·seed [ˈmɔːsiːd] *n.* 罂粟子.

Maw·son [ˈmɔːsn] *n.* 莫森〔姓氏〕.

Max [mæks] *n.* 马克斯〔男子名，Maximilian 的昵称〕.

max. = maximum.

maxi [ˈmæksi] *n.* ① = maxiskirt. ②长大衣.

maxi- *pref.* 表示"特别长的"，"特大的".

max·il·la [mækˈsilə] *n. (pl. -lae* [-liː]*)* 【解】颌骨；上颌；【动】下颌肢，小颚，下颚. **-ry** *a.* 【解】上颌(骨)的. *n.* 上颌骨.

max·il·li·ped [mækˈsiliˌped] *n.* 【动】(甲壳类的) 颚足；(昆虫的) 颚肢.

Max·im [ˈmæksim] *n.* 马克沁机关枪〔一种老式机枪〕(=～ gun).

max·im [ˈmæksim] *n.* 格言，箴言；谚语；原理，主义；(行为的)准则.

max·i·ma [ˈmæksimə] *n.* maximum 的复数.

max·i·mal [ˈmæksiməl] *a.* 极为可能的；最大的；最高的；最全的. **-ly** *ad.*

max·i·mal·ist [ˈmæksiməlist] *n.* 最高纲领主义者 *(opp.* minimalist*)*.

Max·i·mil·i·an [ˌmæksiˈmiljən] *n.* 马克西米利安〔男子名，其昵称为 Max.〕.

max·im·ite [ˈmæksiˌmait] *n.* 马克沁炸药〔一种用于穿甲弹的高爆力炸药〕.

max·i·mize [ˈmæksmaiz] *vt.* 使…增加(扩大、加强)到最大限度；充分重视；找出…的最高值 *(opp.* minimize*)*. — *vi.* 【神】尽量广义地解释(教义等). **-za·tion** *n.*

max·i·mum [ˈmæksiməm] *n. (pl. ～s, -ma* [-mə]*)* 极点，最大，最高，最高额，最大值；最高点；最大限度；【数】极大(值) *(opp.* minimum*)*. *The excitement was at its ～.* 兴奋到极点. — *a.* 最大的，最高的，顶点的，最多的. ～ *draught [draft]* 【海】最大吃水深度. ～ *obscuration* 【天】蚀甚. *a ～ range* 最大射程. *a ～ thermometer* 最高温度计.

Max·ine [mækˈsiːn] *n.* 马克辛〔女子名〕.

max·i·skirt [ˈmæksiˌskəːt] *n.* 长及脚踝的长裙.

Max·well [ˈmækswəl] *n.* 马克斯韦尔〔姓氏，男子名〕.

max·well [ˈmækswel] *n.* 麦(克斯韦)〔磁通量单位〕. *M- field equations* 麦克斯韦(电磁)场方程(式).

May[1] [mei] *n.* 梅〔姓氏，女子名，Mary 的昵称〕.

May[2] [mei] *n.* ①五月. ②〔英〕五朔节的庆祝活动. ③〔诗〕青春. ④〔m-〕〔英〕山楂属植物. ⑤〔*pl.*〕(*Cambridge* 大学的)五月考试；五月赛艇. *the queen of (the) ～* = May-queen. — *vi.* 庆祝五朔节；采五月花. ～ **apple** 【美植】鬼臼〔五月结黄色卵形果实〕；鬼臼果. ～ **beetle,** ～ **bug** 【虫】鳃角金龟科吃植物叶片的甲虫 (如跳甲). **～-blob** 驴蹄草. ～ **bush** 山楂. ～ **Day** 五一劳动节；五朔节. **～day** 无线电话中呼救信号. ～ **dew** 五月(一日的)朝露. **～fair** 五月墟市，伦敦海德公园东面的贵族住宅区；伦敦上层社交界. **～flower** ①〔m-〕五月开放的花；〔英〕山楂；〔美〕岩梨. ②〔the ～flower〕"五月花号"〔1620 年把清教徒由英国运到美国的船〕. **～fly,** ～ **fly** 【虫】蜉蝣；【虫】飞蝼蛄；(钓鱼用的)人造飞蝼蛄〔蜉蝣〕. ～ **games** 五月节的游戏；嬉戏，闹玩. **～-grass** 复活节钟草. **～pole** (花和彩条装饰的) 五月柱〔少年男女于五朔节围绕跳民间舞〕. ～ **queen** 五月女王〔在五朔节游戏中扮女王的少女〕. **～thorn** = hawthorn. **～tide, ～time** 五月(的季节). ～ **tree** 【植】英国山楂. **～weed** 【植】母菊属；臭甘菊 (= dog fennel). ～ **Week** 〔Cambridge 大学〕五月赛艇周〔五月底到六月初〕. ～ **wine** 五月酒〔一种用车叶草、菠萝和柑桔片调味的白酒制作的混合酒〕.

may[1] [mei] *aux. v. (neg. ～ not, mayn't* [meint]; *p. might* [mait], *neg. might not, mightn't* [ˈmeitnt]*)* ★无不定式、分词、动名词等；第三人称现在时单数也不加 s；常后接不带 to 的不定式. ①(a) 〔表示可能性，否定形用 ～ *not*〕或许，也许，可能，也未可知，也说不定. *He ～ [～ not] go.* 他也许〔不〕去. *Who knows but it ～ be true?* 说不定是真的. *She ～ be idle for aught I know.* 她或许闲着也说不定. (b) *(～＋have done, have been)* 也许…了，也许是…. *He ～ have done so.* 他也许那样做了. ②〔表示许可，或用于请求许可，否定式用 *must not*〕可，可以. *M- I come and see you?* 我可以来看你吗? *M- I smoke here? — Yes, you ～ (smoke). No, you must not.* 可以在这里抽烟吗? —— 可以(抽). 不可以(抽). 〔～ not 语气较弱: You ～ not smoke here. 这儿最好不抽烟.〕 ③〔表示有充分理由，常与 well 连用，否定式用 cannot〕(完全)能，(满)可以，不妨. *You ～ call him a scholar, but you cannot call him a genius.* 你可以说他是学者，但不能说他是天才. *You ～ well say so.* 你完全可以这样说. ④〔用在表示目的的状语从句中〕(使…)可以；为…；(以便)能. *We work hard (so) that we ～ succeed.* 我们为想成功拼命工作. ⑤〔用在表示让步的状语从句中〕不管，无论，尽管. *whoever ～ say so = no matter who ～ say so* 无论谁那么说. *Come what ～, I will try it.* 无论发生什么，我要试它一试. ⑥〔表示祈求、愿望、诅咒〕愿. *Long ～ he live!*

愿他长命百岁! *M- you succeed!* 祝你成功! 〔主语和动词位置常颠倒〕。⑦〔在疑问句中表示不确定〕会; 究竟; 不知道是 (谁, 什么, 为什么…) 〔多和 ask, think, wonder, doubt 等动词连用〕。*Who ~ you be?* 不知道你是那一位啊? ⑧〔= can〕能,可以。*One ~ see that at a glance.* 那是一眼就看得清的。*He who runs ~ read.* 可以边跑边读 (明白简易到极点)。⑨〔用在表示可能的名词性从句中〕*It is possible that he ~ come tomorrow.* 他也许明天会来。⑩〔书〕〔用在表示要求、希望等的名词性从句中〕能够,会。*I hope he ~ succeed.* 希望他会成功 (*cf.* might). ***as best one ~*** 极力设法,尽最大努力。***as the case ~ be*** 依情形,看情况。***be that as it ~*** 虽然; 就算是这样。**~ *as well* ...,** 最好…,还是…好 (*You ~ as well begin at once.* 你最好立刻开始。*You ~ as well go.* 你还是去好〔其后 as not 的意义变得极弱而被省略〕)。***(it) ~ be*** 多半。***that ~ well be*** 这事很可能是有的。

may² [mei] *n.* 〔诗〕少女,姑娘。

Ma·ya [ˈmɑːjə] *n.* 玛雅人〔中美洲的印第安人,在美洲被西方发现前已有高度文化〕; 玛雅语。**Mayan** *a., n.* 玛雅人〔语〕的; 玛雅人〔语〕。

ma·ya [ˈmɑːjə] *n.* 〔Sans.〕幻影; 虚妄。

may·be [ˈmeibi] *ad.* 大概,多半,或许。*And I don't mean ~ (either).* 〔美俚〕我可不是说了不算的〔往往是恐吓话〕。

May·er(s) [ˈmeiə(z), mɛə(z)] *n.*迈耶(斯)〔姓氏〕。

may·est [ˈmeiist, meist] may 的古体〔may 的第二人称单数现在时陈述语气与 *thou* 合用〕。

may·hap [ˈmeihæp] *ad.* 〔古〕= perhaps.

may·hem [ˈmeihem] *n.* 【法】残害人的肢体〔器官〕罪〔泛指故意的损害或暴力行为〕; 〔美〕【拳击】打倒。

May·ing [ˈmeiiŋ] *n.* 五朔节的庆祝(活动); 五朔节采花活动。*go (a-)maying* 举行五朔节; 去采五月花。

May·nard [ˈmeinəd] *n.* 梅纳德〔男子名〕。

mayn't [meint] 〔口〕= may not.

may·on·naise [ˌmeiəˈneiz] *n.* 〔F.〕蛋黄酱,蛋黄汁; 搀〔浇〕蛋黄酱的食物(鱼、肉、菜等)。

may·or [ˈmɛə] *n.* 市长。*a Lord M-* (伦敦及其他大都市的)市长。*The Lord M-'s Day* 伦敦市长就职日。*the M- of the Palace* 【法史】(法兰克王国的) 大宰相。**-al** [ˈmɛərəl]*a.* **-al·ty** [ˈmɛərəlti], **-ship** *n.* 市长的职位〔任期〕。

may·or·ess [ˈmɛəris] *n.* 市长夫人; 女市长。

mayst [meist] *v.* 〔古〕= mayest.

maz·ard [ˈmæzəd] *n.* ①野樱。②〔废〕头; 脸。

maz·a·rine [ˌmæzəˈriːn] *a.* 深蓝色的。— *n.* 深蓝色; 深蓝色衣服〔衣料〕; (穿深蓝色长袍的)伦敦市政会成员。*the ~ robe* (伦敦市政会成员所穿的)深蓝色长袍。

Maz·da [ˈmæzdə] *n.* (拜火教的)创造主; 美国麦芝达牌电灯泡。

Maz·da·ism, Maz·de·ism [ˈmæzdəizəm] *n.* (古波斯的)拜火教 (= Zeroastrianism).

maze [meiz] *n.* 迷津,迷宫,迷魂阵; 困惑,为难。— *vt.* 〔多用 *p.p.*〕使困惑,使为难,迷惑。

maz·el tov maz·el·tov, maz·zel·tov [ˈmɑːzlˌtəuv, -ˌtɔːv] 〔希伯来语〕祝你走运〔祝贺语〕。

ma·zer [ˈmeizə] *n.* (木制或金属的)大杯,大盏。

ma·zu·ma [məˈzuːmə] *n.* 〔美俚〕钱。

ma·zur·ka [məˈzəːkə, -ˈzuəkə] *n.* 玛祖卡舞〔轻快活泼的波兰舞〕; 玛祖卡舞曲。

ma·zut [məˈzuːt] *n.* 重油; 黑油。

ma·zy [ˈmeizi] *a.* *(-zi·er; -zi·est)* (迷津一样)弯曲回绕的; 纠缠不清的, 混乱的; 为难的; 困惑的。**-i·ly** *ad.,* **-i·ness** *n.*

maz·zard [ˈmæzəd] *n.* 欧洲甜樱桃树; 欧洲甜樱桃 (= sweet cherry).

M.B., MB = 〔L.〕①*Medicinae Baccalaureus* 医学士 (= Bachelor of Medicine). ②*Musicae Baccalaureus* 音乐学士 (= Bachelor of Music). ③Memorandum book 备忘录,记事录。

M.B.A. = Master of Business Administration 工商业管理硕士。

Mba·ba·ne [mbɑːˈbɑːn] *n.* 姆巴巴纳〔斯威士兰首都〕。

M.B.E., MBE = Member (of the Order) of the British Empire 〔英〕帝国勋章获得者。

MBS = Mutual Broadcasting System 〔美〕相互广播公司。

Mbun·du [mˈbuːnduː] *n.* ①*(pl. ~(s))* 姆邦杜人〔安哥拉中西部讲班图语的人〕。②姆邦杜语。

M.C., MC = ①master of ceremonies 典礼官; 司仪。②medical corps 医疗队。③Member of Congress 国会议员。④Military Cross 〔英〕军功十字勋章。⑤margin(al) credit 限界信贷,边际信用。

mc = ①machine. ②megacycle. ③millicurie 毫居里(放射单位)。

M.C.C. = Marylebone Cricket Club 〔英〕马里列博恩板球俱乐部。

Mc·Car·thy [məˈkɑːθi] *n.* 麦卡锡〔姓氏〕。

Mc·Car·thy·ism [məˈkɑːθiːizəm] *n.* 麦卡锡主义〔美国反动议员麦卡锡迫害进步人士的行径〕。

Mc·Car·thy·ite [məˈkɑːθiait] *n.* 麦卡锡主义分子。

Mc·Clel·lan [məˈklelən] *n.* 麦克莱伦〔姓氏〕。

Mc·Clure [məˈkluə] *n.* 麦克卢尔〔姓氏〕。

Mc·Cor·mack [məˈkɔːmək] *n.* ①麦考马克〔姓氏〕。

Mc·Cor·mick [məˈkɔːmik] *n.* ①麦考密克〔姓氏〕。②C. H. ~ 麦考密克〔1809—1884, 美国收割机发明者〕。

Mc·Coy [məˈkɔi] *n.* 麦科伊〔姓氏,用于美俚短语〕。*the real ~* 真正的〔出色的〕人〔东西〕。— *a.* 真正的。

Mc·Do·nald [məkˈdɔnəld] *n.* 麦克唐纳〔姓氏〕。

Mc·Dowell [məkˈdauəl] *n.* 麦克道尔〔姓氏〕。

Mc·Fee [məkˈfiː] *n.* 麦克菲〔姓氏〕。

M.Ch. = 〔L.〕*Magister Chirurgiae* (= Master of Surgery) 外科硕士。

Mc·In·tosh [ˈmækinˌtɔʃ] *n.* ①麦金托什苹果〔美国人麦金托什培育的一种晚熟的红苹果〕(= McIntosh Red). ②麦金托什〔姓氏〕。

Mc·In·tyre [ˈmækintaiə] *n.* 麦金太尔〔姓氏〕。

Mc·Ken·na [məˈkenə] *n.* 麦肯纳〔姓氏〕。

Mc·Kin·ley [məˈkinli] *n.* 麦金利〔姓氏〕。

M.C.L. = Master of Civil Law 民法硕士。

Mc·Mil·lan [məkˈmilən] *n.* 麦克米伦〔姓氏〕。

Mc·Na·ma·ra [ˌmæknəˈmɑːrə] *n.* 麦克纳马拉〔姓氏〕。

MCS = ①Master of Commercial Science 商学硕士。②Master of Computer Science 电子计算机科学硕士。③Missile Control System 导弹控制系统。

M.D., MD = ①〔L.〕*Medicine Doctor* 医学博士(=Doctor of Medicine). ②medical department 医务部。③mentally deficient 精神上有缺陷的。④maximum demand 最大负荷; 最大需要(量)。

M/D, m/d = ①memorandum of deposit 存款单,送款单。②month's date [months after date] 发票后…月。

Md = mendelevium.【化】钔。

Md. = Maryland.

MDAP = Mutual Defense Assistance Program 〔美〕共同防御援助计划。

M-Day [ˈemdei] *n.* 【军】= Mobilization day 动员日。*the ~ plan* 动员计划。

Mdlle. = 〔F.〕*Mademoiselle* 小姐。

Mdm. = Madam 夫人,女士。

Mdme. = 〔F.〕*Madame* 夫人,女士。

mdnt = midnight 午夜。

M.D.S. = Master of Dental Surgery 牙(外)科硕士。

mdse; mdse. = merchandise 商品,货物(总称)。

M.E., ME = ①Mechanical Engineer 机械工程师。②

Military Engineer 工程兵；军事工程师．③Mining Engineer 采矿工程师．④Middle English 中古英语．⑤Methodist Episcopal (基督教)卫理公会主教派的．
Me = methyl【化】甲基．
Me. = Maine.
m.e. = most excellent 最杰出的．
me [mi:, mi] *pro.* ①〔I 的宾格〕我〔把我，对我，给我等〕．②〔口〕〔用作表语 = I〕．*It's* ~〔口〕是我(= It is I)．③〔口〕〔用于 than 后面，= I〕．*She's stronger than* ~．她比我坚强．④〔古、诗〕我自己 (= myself)．*I will lay* ~ *down and sleep.* 我要躺下睡了．⑤〔用在感叹句中〕*Ah* ~！哎呀！噫！*Dear* ~！〔诗〕唷！哎哟！哎呀！*Woe is* ~！〔诗〕可怜！哀哉．★此外特别是在伊丽莎白王朝时代只用来加强语调，如：Where goeth ~ this track? 这条小道究竟通到哪里？He ate ~ a pound of beef. 他吃了我一磅牛肉．I built ~ a house〔美俚〕我盖了所房子〔这里的 me 是冗语〕．~ ***and you both***〔美俚〕关于这点我赞成你．***take it from*** ~〔俚〕我的话千真万确．
me•a cul•pa [ˈmi:ə ˈkʌlpə, ˈmeiɑ:ˈkulpɑ:]〔L.〕(这是)我的过失！是我不对！赖我！
mead[1] [mi:d] *n.*〔诗〕= meadow.
mead[2] [mi:d] *n.* 蜂蜜酒．
Mead(e) [mi:d] *n.* 米德〔姓氏〕．
mead•ow [ˈmedəu] *n.* (特指割制干草用的)草地，草原；(河边)低草地．*a floating* ~ 易涝牧场．~ *ore* 冶铁矿．~ *soil* 草甸土．~ **beauty**【植】瑞克希阿属(拟)*(Rhexia)* 植物．~ **bright** 驴蹄草．~ **clover**【植】红苜蓿．~ **fescue**【植】牛尾草．~ **foxtail**【植】草原看麦娘〔狗尾草等〕．~ **lark**【鸟】(美国)野百灵鸟类．~ **lily** = Canada lily (【植】加拿大百合)．~ **mouse** = field mouse 野鼠，田鼠．~ **mushroom** 洋蘑菇．~ **pine**【植】问荆．~ **rue**【植】唐松草属．~ **saffron**【植】秋水仙属．~**sweet**【植】笑靥花；珍珠花；麻叶绣球．
mead•ow•y [ˈmedəui] *a.* 草原(似)的；有草地的；牧场多的．
mea•gre, mea•ger [ˈmi:gə] *a.* (人、动物等)瘦的；(土地)不毛的；粗陋的，贫弱的；思想贫乏的；枯燥的(作品等)．*a* ~ *person* 瘦人．**-ly** *ad.* 瘦；粗陋．**-ness** *n.*
meal[1] [mi:l] *n.* 餐，饭，一餐，一顿(饭)，一客(饭)；进餐(时间)；〔英〕一次挤奶量．*a square [light]* ~ 盛〔便〕餐．***at*** ~***s*** 在吃饭时．***between*** ~***s*** 在两餐之间．***during the*** ~ 在吃饭时候．***have [take] a*** ~ 进餐，吃饭．***make a [hearty]*** ~ ***of*** 饱餐一顿…．~***s on wheels*** 上门福利餐〔每日给老人或病残人送饭上门的服务〕．— *vi.* 进餐，吃饭．~ **ticket** *n.* ①饭票．②〔美俚〕供给吃饭〔生活费〕的人；施舍的人；老好人，易被欺骗的人，傻子．③赖以为生的东西〔指手艺、才能、双手等〕．~ **time** *n.* 吃饭时间．
meal[2] [mi:l] *n.* (小麦以外的谷、豆等没有筛过的)粗粉；(种子、油饼等的)碎粉；〔美〕玉米楂子；〔Scot., Ir.〕燕麦片．~ **worm**【虫】粉虫．— *vt.* 碾碎．
meal•er [ˈmi:lə] *n.*〔美俚〕住在一处而在另一处吃饭的房客．
meal•ie [ˈmi:li] *n.*〔*pl.*〕玉米．
meal•i•ness [ˈmi:linis] *n.* 粉状，粉性；撒粉状；婉转柔和的话；甜言蜜语．
meal•y [ˈmi:li] *a.* ***(meal•i•er; -i•est)*** ①粉状的；粉质的，富含淀粉的；(翅等)有粉的；(脸色等)苍白的；(马)毛色有白花的．②〔口〕说话委婉的；甜言蜜语的．~**-bug**【虫】水蜡虫，粉虫〔葡萄害虫〕．~**-mouthed** *a.* 转弯抹角说的；油嘴滑舌的，会说话的．
mean[1] [mi:n] ***(p.,p.p. meant)*** *vt.* ①意，有…的意思，意思是…．②意指，用…意思说；意味着，就是．③(用语言、绘画等)表示意思，表示．④预定，计划，图谋；〔作被动用〕企图表现．⑤预定 (人或东西) 作某种用途，弄成…；暗指着说．*What does this word* ~? 这个字是什么意思？*I* ~ *what I say.* 我是说的正经话〔不是开玩笑〕；我是说到就要做到的，我讲的话是算数的．*I meant it for [as] a joke.* 我是说着玩的．*You don't* ~ *to say so!* 不会吧！你是开玩笑吧！*I* ~ *that you are a liar.* 我说你是个撒谎的．*What do you* ~ *by that?* 你做的〔说的〕那是什么意思？*What do you* ~ *by 'passion'?* 你所说的 *passion* 是什么意思？*What do you* ~ *to do?* 你打算作什么？*I* ~ *you to go.* 我打算叫〔请〕你去．*I did not* ~ *to deceive you.* 我并没有打算欺骗你．*My father* ~*s me to be a worker.* 我父亲打算叫我成为一个工人．*He was meant for [to be] a soldier.* 他生来是要成为一个军人的；他父母是要把他培养成一个军人的．*This portrait is meant for me.* 这张肖像是要给我的．— *vi.* ①用意．②具有意义．***and to*** ~ ***it*** 说到做到．~ ***a great deal [much]*** 意味深长；重要．~ ***business*** 认真；算数的．~ ***mischief*** 有恶意，有坏心眼儿；有凶兆．~ ***well [ill] by [to, toward]*** 对…有好意〔恶意〕．
mean[2] [mi:n] *a.* ①下贱的，卑劣的；(身分)低微的，卑贱的；卑鄙的；自私的．②下等的，劣等的；普通的，中等的，平庸的．③汗颜的，难看的；吝啬的，小气的．④〔美俚〕害羞的，觉得不好意思的；(马)脾气坏的；讨厌的，麻烦的；没精神的，不大舒服的；〔美俚〕老练的，巧妙的；极好的；可爱的；非常愉快的．*people of* ~ *birth* 出身低微的人．*a* ~ *cottage* 简陋的乡下房子．***be*** ~ ***about [over]*** 在…方面很小气〔吝啬〕．***feel*** ~〔美俚〕觉得不好意思，害臊．***have a*** ~ ***opinion of*** 蔑视，轻视，瞧不起 (*He has a* ~ *opinion of himself.* 他很自卑)．***no*** ~ 相当的，不差的，很好的 (*of no* ~ *ability* 很有才能)．***of*** ~ ***understanding*** 理解力差的，笨的．***the great and the*** ~ 贵贱上下．
mean[3] [mi:n] *a.* 中间的；中庸的；平均的；中等的；中项的．*the* ~ *deviation*【统】平均差．*the* ~ *distance* 平均距离．*a* ~ *proportional*【数】比例中项．*the* ~ *(solar) time [day]*【天】平(太阳)时〔日〕．*the* ~ *sun*【天】平太阳．*the* ~ *temperature* 平均温度．*the* ~ *velocity* 平均速度．***for the*** ~ ***time*** 在此期间，暂时．***in the*** ~ ***time*** = in the meantime. ~ ***line*** 等分线．~ ***sea level*** 平均海平面，海拔〔略 M.S.L.〕．— *n.* ①(两端的)中央，中部，中间；【数】平均(数、值)，中数；【逻】(三段论的)中项；中名辞，媒辞 (= ~ term)；【伦】中庸；【乐】中音部．②〔*pl.*〕〔常作单数看待〕方法，手段，工具；媒介．③〔*pl.*〕〔常作单数看待〕财产，资力，资产，收入．~*s of production* 生产资料；生产手段．*an arithmetic [a geometric]* ~ 等差〔等比〕中项．*the* ~*-square deviation*【统】差方均．*There is a* ~ *in all things.* 凡事都有一定限度．*a* ~*s to an end* 达到目的的手段．*a man of* ~*s* 资本家，财主．***by all (manner of)*** ~***s*** ①必定，务必；千方百计；不惜一切．②〔回答〕好的，当然当然．***by any*** ~***s*** 无论如何；以一切可能的手段．***by fair*** ~***s or foul*** 千方百计地，不择手段地．***by*** ~***s of*** 用，以，依靠．***by no (manner of)*** ~***s*** 决不，无论如何也不，丝毫不，一点也不；并没有(*He is by no* ~*s a pleasant man to deal with.* 他决不是一个好打交道的爽快人)．***by some*** ~***s (or other)*** 设法；用某种办法．***by what*** ~***s*** 怎么；用什么办法．***live beyond [within] one's*** ~***s*** 不按照〔按照〕收入过日子．~***s of living*** 生活手段．~***s test***〔英〕(发放失业救济金前举行的)生活状况调查．***using every possible*** ~***s*** 千方百计．
me•an•der [miˈændə] *n.* ①〔*pl.*〕河曲，蜿曲，弯曲；曲曲折折的路．②漫步，散步；〔常 *pl.*〕迂回旅行．③漫谈；闲聊．④【建】回纹波形饰．— *vi.* ①曲曲折折地流．②没目的地散步 *(along)*；聊天，漫谈．~ **line**【测】折测线．
me•an•der•ing [miˈændəriŋ] *n.* ①曲折的路．②聊天，漫谈．— *a.* 曲折的；弯弯曲曲的；散步的；聊天的．**-ly** *ad.*
me•an•drine [miˈændri(:)n] *a.*〔罕〕弯弯曲曲的；(珊

瑚表面)蟠曲的.

mean·ie, mean·y [ˈmiːni] *n. (pl. mean·ies)* 〔口〕小气的人;自私的人;残暴的人.

mean·ing [ˈmiːniŋ] *n.* ①意思,意义. ②〔古〕主意,企图,目的. ③【逻】内涵;外延. — *a.* 有意思的,意味深长的;有所企图的. *a literal* ~ 字面意义,字义. ***full of*** ~ 意味深长的. ***ill-***~ 恶意. ***well-***~ 善意. ***with*** ~ 有意思的. **-ful** *a.* 意味深长的. **-less** *a.* 无意义的,没意思的. **-ly** *ad.* 有意思地,故意地.

mean·ly [ˈmiːnli] *ad.* 下贱地,卑劣地;卑鄙地;汗颜地;小气地,吝啬地. *think* ~ *of* 藐视,看不起.

mean·ness [ˈmiːnnis] *n.* 下贱,卑劣,卑鄙;粗野;劣等,粗恶;吝啬,小气.

mean-spir·it·ed [ˈmiːnˈspiritid] *a.* 卑劣的.

meant [ment] mean 的过去式及过去分词.

mean·time, mean·while [ˈmiːnˈtaim, ˈmiːnhwail] *ad.* 其间,在那当中,一会儿的工夫;到那个时候以前,一方面,同时. — *n.* 中间,当中时间. ***in the meantime [meanwhile]*** 在这期间,这时.

mea·sled [ˈmiːzld] *a.* 患麻疹的,出着痧子的.

mea·sles [ˈmiːzl] *n. pl.* ①【医】〔作单数用〕麻疹,痧子 (*M- is decidedly infectious.* 麻疹肯定是有传染性的);〔美俚〕梅毒;〔作复数用〕麻疹的红斑点(*The* ~ *begin to turn pale on the face.* 脸上的疹子颜色开始转淡). ②〔作单数用〕【兽医】(牛、猪的)囊虫病. ③〔作复数用〕【摄】斑点. *false [French, German, hybrid]* ~ 风疹.

mea·sly [ˈmiːzli] *a.* ***(-sli·er; -sli·est)***①麻疹(似)的,出着痧子的;有囊虫病的;含绦虫的. ②〔俚〕没用的,没价值的;卑鄙的,下贱的,使人看不起的;微不足道的;少[小]得可怜的.

meas·ur·a·ble [ˈmeʒərəbl] *a.* 可量的,可测量的,相当的,适当的. ***come within a*** ~ ***distance of*** 临,逼近,接近. **-bly** *ad.* 到可以测定的程度,多少;适当;到某种程度. **-bil·i·ty, -ness** *n.*

meas·ure [ˈmeʒə] *n.* ①尺寸,尺度,量,分量;【数】测度;度量法;计量单位. ②量具,量器. ③(衡量)标准,准绳;程度;限度,界限,范围;适度,分寸;本分,份儿. ④【数】约数. ⑤【韵】韵律;【乐】拍子,调子;小节;(慢而庄重的)舞蹈;〔古〕跳舞,舞蹈. ⑥〔常 *pl.*〕手段,措施,策略,步骤,方法,办法. ⑦法案,议案,方案. ⑧【印】行宽;页宽;〔*pl.*〕【地】层组;地层. *angular* ~角度. *circular* ~ 弧度. *apothecaries'* ~ 药衡制(容积单位). *cubic* ~ 体积. *dry [liquid]* ~ 干[液]量. *linear* ~ = *long* ~ 长度. *solid* ~ 容积. ~ *of capacity* 容量. *square [superficial]* ~ 面积. *yard* ~ 码尺. *weights and* ~*s* 权度,度量衡. *a* ~ *or so of grain* 一升半碗粮食. *a common* ~ 公约数. *the greatest common* ~ 最大公约数〔略作 G.C.M.〕. *hygienic* ~ 卫生措施. *coal* ~*s* 煤层. ***adopt*** ~***s*** 采取措施,处置. ***beyond [above, out of]*** ~ 无可估量,过分,极度. ***by*** ~ 按大小;论升;按尺寸. ***drink a*** ~ 喝一点儿. ***give full [good]*** ~ 给足分量. ***give short*** ~ 少给分量. ***give [show] the*** ~ ***of*** 成为…的标准,表示…的程度 (*This book shows the* ~ *of the author's intelligence.* 由这本书可看出作者的智慧水平). ***have sb.'s*** ~ ***to an inch*** 看穿[看透]某人. ***in(a) great [large]*** ~ 很,大半,大部分. ***in a*** ~ = ***in some*** ~ 有几分,多少,稍稍. ***keep [observe]*** ~***(s)*** 守中庸之道. ***keep*** ~***s with*** 宽大对待. ***know no*** ~ 没有边际,没有止境. ~ ***for*** ~ 报复,以牙还牙. ~***s to an end*** 达到目的的手段. ***set*** ~***s to*** 限制. ***take*** ~***s*** = ***adopt*** ~***s. take*** ~ ***of*** 测定. ***take one's*** ~ = ***take the*** ~ ***of*** ... 量某人的尺寸;打量某人. ***take the*** ~ ***of sb.'s foot*** 看穿某人的根底[能力]. ***to fill up the*** ~ ***of*** 使(不幸等)越过能忍受的程度;更糟糕的是. ***to*** ~ 照尺寸;按拍子,合调子. ***tread a*** ~〔古〕跳舞. ***use hard*** ~***s*** 虐待,用残暴手段. ***within*** ~ 适度地,适可地. ***without*** ~ 非常,过度. — *vt.* ①量,计量,测量(大小、容量、尺寸等). ②打量,估量,判断(人物、力量). ③比较,比赛,较量 *(with)*. ④区分 *(off)*; 分派 *(out)*. ⑤使均衡,使相称,调整. ⑥〔诗〕通过,去,走,遍历. ~ *sb. for new clothes* 为某人量尺寸做新衣. ~ *one's strength with another* 和人赛力. ~ *one's desires by [to] one's fortune* 使欲望同财力相适合. —*vi.* ①量尺寸. ②有…长[宽、高等]. *The room* ~*s 20 feet across.* 房间宽 20 英尺. ~ ***an opponent***【美体】打败对方. ~ ***another's corn by one's own bushel*** 照自己标准去判断别人;以己度人. ~ ***back*** 后退. ~ ***off*** 区分,区划. ~ ***oneself with*** 和…比赛. ~ ***one's length*** 卧倒地上. ~ ***out*** 分给(一定分量). ~ ***strides***【美体】赛跑. ~ ***swords with*** (在决斗前)和人比剑的长短;拿剑和…相斗;和…相争. ~ ***thrice and cut once*** 三思而后行. ~ ***up***〔美〕合标准,合格. ~ ***up to [with]***〔美〕符合,达到(希望等). ~ ***(sb.) with one's eye*** 上上下下打量(人).

meas·ured [ˈmeʒəd] *a.* ①量过的,合标准的;适度的. ②慎重的,仔细想[考虑]过的(话等). ③整齐的(步调等). ***speak in*** ~ ***terms*** 考虑着说,谨慎小心地说. **-ly** *ad.*

meas·ure·less [ˈmeʒəlis] *a.* 无可估量的,无限的,非常的.

meas·ure·ment [ˈmeʒəmənt] *n.* ①测量,计量,量度. ②分量,尺寸,大小,宽度,厚度,深度(等). ③测量法. ~ *goods* (按体积、容积计算的)体积货物.

meas·ur·ing[ˈmeʒəriŋ] *n.*, *a.* 测量(的),测量用(的). *remote* ~ 遥测. ~ **chain** 测链. ~ **glass [cup]** 量(液)杯. ~ **line** 测线,测绳. ~ **tape** 卷尺. ~ **worm**【虫】尺蠖.

meat [miːt] *n.* ①(食用)肉. ②〔古〕食物;〔古〕餐. ③(蛋、贝、果子等的)肉;(蟹、虾等的)肉. ④(书的)内容,实质. *butcher's* ~ 家畜的肉. *white [light]* ~ 白肉〔指鸡等禽类胸脯肉〕. *red* ~ 红肉〔指牛肉、羊肉等〕. *dark* ~ 黑肉〔指烧不白的鸡(腿)肉〕. *green* ~ 青菜,蔬菜. *inside* ~ 可吃的内脏. *One man's* ~ *is another man's poison.* 利于甲者未必利于乙. ***after*** ~***, mustard*** 饭后上芥末,〔转义〕雨后送伞. ***as full*** *(of errors)* ***as an egg is of*** ~ (头脑等)充满了(错误);尽是(错误). ***be at*** ~ 正在吃饭. ***be*** ~ ***and drink to*** 对(某人)是无上的乐趣. ***be*** ~ ***for sb.'s master*** 太好. ~ ***and potatoes***〔美俚〕重点,基本. ***sit at*** ~ 就席. ~**-and-potatoes** *a.*〔美俚〕首要的,基本的. ~**ball** (1) 肉丸. (2)〔俚〕笨蛋;令人讨厌的人. ~ **chopper,** ~ **grinder** 绞肉机,碎肉机. ~**-eating** *a.* 吃肉的. ~ **fly**【虫】肉蝇. ~ **head**〔俚〕笨蛋. ~ **hooks**〔*pl.*〕〔美俚〕拳头;手. ~ **maggot** 肉蝇的幼虫,蛆. ~**man** 卖肉佬;屠夫. ~ **market**〔美〕肉店. ~**-packing** 肉类工业〔包括屠宰、加工、包装、批发等〕. ~ **pie** 肉馅饼. ~ **safe** (防猫鼠等的)厨柜,菜柜,金属纱罩. ~ **screen** (烤肉用的)热反射板. ~ **tea** (有肉食冷盘等的下午)正式茶点小餐. ~**works** 屠宰场;肉品加工厂.

me·a·tus [mi(ː)ˈeitəs] *n. (pl.* ~***es,*** ~*)* 〔L.〕【解】道,管. *the urethral* ~ 尿道.

meat·y [ˈmiːti] *a.* ***(meat·i·er; -i·est)*** 肉(似)的;多肉的;滋养的;内容丰富的;有力的. ~ *cotton* (杂质少的)纯净棉.

mec., mech. = mechanic.

Mec·ca [ˈmekə] *n.* ①麦加〔沙特阿拉伯,希贾兹首府〕. ②〔常作 m-〕朝拜的地方,圣地;仰慕的目标;发祥地,发源地. **-n** *n.*, *a.* 麦加人(的).

Mec·ca·no [məˈkɑːnəu] *n.* (儿童)钢件结构玩具〔商标名〕.

mech. = mechanical; mechanics.

me·chan(o)- *comb. f.* 机械: *mechanism.*

me·chan·ic [miˈkænik] *n.* ①机工;技工;机械地工作的人. ②〔*pl.*〕= mechanics. ③〔美俚〕专开保险箱的盗贼;玩牌(等赌具)时专门弄虚做假的人. *a radio* ~ 无线电技工. — *a.*〔古〕= mechanical. ~**'s lien** 技工

留置权〔建筑施工中的工资和费用的扣押权〕.

me·chan·i·cal [miˈkænikəl] *a.* ①机械的; 机械制的. ②机械学的,力学的; 物理上的 (*opp.* chemical). ③机工的,技工的; 自动的; 机械(地工作)的,无意识的; 勉强的. ④【哲】机械论的. ⑤〔古〕粗野的. *a ~ brake* 机力制动器. *a ~ stoker* (自动)加煤机. *~ labour* 体力劳动. *~ equivalent of heat* 【物】热功当量. *~ drawing* 机械制图. *~ energy* 机械能. *~ movement* 机械运动. *~ power* 机械功率. *~ resistance* 【物】力阻. *~ tissue* 【植】机械组织. *the ~ transport* 【英陆军】汽车运输队〔略 M.T.〕. ~ **astronomy** 天体力学. ~ **bank** 玩具储蓄箱. ~ **engineer** 机械工程师. ~ **engineering** 机械工程. **-ly** *ad.* 机械地; 无意识地; 用机械. **-ness** *n.* 机械性,自动.

me·chan·i·cal·ism [miˈkænikəlizəm] *n.* ①【哲】机械论. ②机械行动.

me·chan·i·cal·ist [miˈkænikəlist] *n.* 机械论者.

mech·a·ni·cian [ˌmekəˈniʃən] *n.* 技师; 机械学家; 技工.

me·chan·ics [miˈkæniks] *n. pl.* ①〔作单数用〕力学 (*cf.* statics; kinetics; kinematics); 机械学. ②〔作复数用〕结构; 构成法; 技巧. *quantum ~* 量子力学.

mech·a·nism [ˈmekənizəm] *n.* ①(机械)结构; 机械装置〔作用〕; (故事的)结构. ②【哲】机械论 (*opp.* vitalism). ③【文艺】手法; 技巧; 途径 (*cf.* style, expression). ④(自然现象等的)作用过程; 【化】历程. ⑤【生】机制,机能; 【药】机理; 【心】作用机理; *preset ~* 程序机构. *early development ~* 【遗传】初期发育规律. *migration ~* 【生】迁移机能. *~ of hearing* 听的机能. *~ of action* 【生化】作用动力. *~ of polymerization* 【化纤】聚合历程.

mech·a·nist [ˈmekənist] *n.* ①〔罕〕= mechanician. ②【哲】机械论者.

mech·a·nis·tic [ˌmekəˈnistik] *a.* ①机械论的; 依据机械论的. ②机械学的; 力学的; 机械概念的. **-ti·cal·ly** *ad.*

mech·a·nize [ˈmekənaiz] *vt.* 使机械化; 用机械装备; 使机能化. *a ~d unit = a ~d force* 机械化部队. **-za·tion** [ˌmekənaiˈzeiʃən] *n.* (军队等的)机械化; 机能化.

mech·an·o- *comb. f.* = mechan-.

mech·an·o·ther·a·py [ˌmekənəuˈθerəpi] *n.* 【医】机械〔力学〕疗法.

Mech·lin [ˈmeklin] *n.* 梅克林花边〔比利时 Mechlin 城产,又作 ~ lace〕.

Mechs [meks] *n.* 〔军俚〕= mechanized force 机械化部队.

me·co·nic [miˈkɔnik] *a.* ~ **acid** 【化】袂康酸〔得自鸦片中〕.

me·co·ni·um [miˈkəuniəm] *n.* 【医】胎粪,胎尿; 蛹便; 〔废〕鸦片.

me·cop·ter·an [miˈkɔptərən] *n.* 【动】长翅目 (*Mecoptera*) 昆虫. **-ter·ous** [-əs] *a.*

M.ED.,MED = 〔美〕Master of Education 教育学硕士.

med. = ①medical; medicine. ②medieval. ③medium.

Med [med] *n.* 〔美俚〕地中海.

med·al [ˈmedl] *n.* 奖章; 徽章; 勋章; 纪念章; 证章. *a ~ of honor* 〔美〕荣誉勋章. *a prize ~* 奖章〔牌〕. *a ~ bar* 〔美〕胜利纪念章. *a war ~* 从军纪念章. —*vt.* 授予…奖章. ***M- for Merit*** 〔美〕功绩奖章〔对有特殊功绩的非军事人员所发的军事奖章. ***M- of freedom*** 〔美〕自由勋章〔1963 年前对在战争中有特殊贡献的非军事人员发的军事勋章, 1963 年后,有贡献的军事人员也可获得〕. ***the reverse (side) of the ~*** 问题的另一方面. ~ ***play*** 【高尔夫球】按全盘击数计分的比赛. **~ed, medalled** *a.* 受奖章的; 带徽章的.

med·al·et [ˈmedlet] *n.* 小奖章〔徽章〕.

me·dal·lic [miˈdælik] *a.* ①(象)奖章〔徽章〕的. ②奖章上显示的.

me·dal·lion [miˈdæljən] *n.* ①大奖章,大徽章. ②(肖像等的)圆形浮雕; 团花图样. ③〔美俚〕出租汽车经营牌照,有牌照的出租汽车. *~ carpet* 团花毯.

med·al(l)·ist [ˈmedəlist] *n.* 得奖章者; 奖章雕刻家; 奖章搜集家. *a gold ~* 金质奖章获得者.

Me·dan [meˈdɑːn] *n.* 棉兰〔印度尼西亚城市〕.

med·dle [ˈmedl] *vi.* ①弄,摸弄,用手玩弄; 参与,发生关系 (*with*). ②干涉, 插手, 多事 (*with; in*). *Don't ~ with the clock.* 不要弄钟. ***neither make nor ~*** 〔口〕不干涉.

med·dl·er [ˈmedlə] *n.* 多事者,好管闲事者; 干涉者.

med·dle·some [ˈmedlsəm] *a.* 爱管闲事的. **-ness** *n.*

Mede [miːd] *n.* (伊朗西北部 Media 地方的)米堤亚人. ***the law of the ~s and Persians*** 不可改的制度〔习惯〕.

Me·de·a [miˈdiə] *n.* 【希神】美狄亚〔科尔喀斯国王之女,以巫术著称,曾帮助伊阿宋取得金羊毛〕.

Me·del·lin [ˌmedeˈjiːn] *n.* 麦德林〔哥伦比亚城市〕.

med·e·vac [ˈmedəvæk] *n.* 〔美口〕救伤直升机. — *vt.* 用救伤直升机运送(伤员).

me·di- *comb. f.* 表示"中间的": *medi*eval.

me·di·a[1] [ˈmediə; Am. ˈmiːdiə] *n.* (*pl.* **-di·ae** [-diiː]) ①〔L.〕【语】带声破裂辅音; (带声)不送气破裂音 ([b] [d] [g]). ②【解】血管的中膜; 【虫】中脉. ③〔M-〕伊朗西北部的古王国.

media[2] [ˈmiːdjə] *n.* medium 的复数. ~ **event** 媒介事件〔无新闻价值但仍安排于电视等上播出,旨在加强宣传〕.

me·di·a·cy [ˈmiːdiəsi] *n.* 介在,媒介; 灵媒.

me·di·ad [ˈmiːdiæd] *ad.* 【生】中向,中央向.

me·di·ae·val [ˌmediˈiːvəl] *a.* 中世纪的; 中古(式)的, 中世(风)的. **M- Greek** 中世纪希腊语. **M- Latin** 中世纪拉丁语. **-ly** *ad.* 成中古式,依中古精神.

med·i·ae·val·ism [ˌmediˈiːvəlizəm] *n.* ①中世纪精神, 中世纪信仰; 中世纪风俗. ②热中于中世纪信仰〔习惯、风俗等〕; 欣赏中世纪特征的信仰〔风俗等〕; 中世纪遗风.

med·i·ae·val·ist [ˌmediˈiːvəlist] *n.* 中世纪史〔文艺〕研究家; 中世纪风俗〔信仰〕爱好者.

med·i·ae·val·ize [ˌmediˈiːvəlaiz] *vt.* 使成中古式, 使符合中世纪习惯〔理想等〕.

me·di·al [ˈmiːdjəl] *a.* 中间的,中央的,中部的,平均的, 普通的,中常的. *a ~ consonant* 【语】(在词中的)中间辅音. *~ temperature* 平均温度,中位温度. *the ~ section* 【数】中外比分割,黄金分割. **-ly** *ad.*

me·di·an [ˈmiːdjən] *a.* ①中央的, 中间的. ②【数】中线的; 中(位)数的,中值的. ③【语】(舌)边音的; 舌边中间开放的. *the ~ line* 中线. *the ~ artery (vein)* 中动〔静〕脉. *the ~ section* 正中切面〔切片〕. *the ~ point* 【数】重心. —*n.* 【解】中动脉; 中静脉; 正中神经; 【数】中线; 中(位)数,中值. **-ly** *ad.*

me·di·ant [ˈmiːdjənt] *n.* 【乐】中音〔音阶的第三音〕.

me·di·as·ti·num [ˌmiːdiæsˈtainəm] *n.* (*pl.* **-na** [-nə]) 【解】(胸腔)纵隔.

me·di·ate [ˈmiːdiit, -djət] *a.* ①〔罕〕中间的. ②要靠媒介的; 间接的. *~ inference* 间接推理. — [ˈmiːdieit] *vt.* 调停,调解; 传达(思想等). — *vi.* 调解, 斡旋, 作中人仲裁(*between*); 处在中间, 介于. **-ly** *ad.* 在中间, 居中; 间接.

me·di·a·tion [ˌmiːdiˈeiʃən] *n.* 调解, 调停, 仲裁; 【天】中天.

me·di·a·ti·za·tion [ˌmiːdiətaiˈzeiʃən] *n.* 并吞.

me·di·a·tive [ˈmiːdieitiv] *a.* 调停的,调解的.

me·di·a·tize [ˈmiːdiətaiz] *vt.* ①(大国)并吞(小国); 【史】(保留旧君主名义上的主权而)合并(其国). ②使处于中间〔附属〕地位. — *vi.* 进行调解; 【史】成为神圣罗马帝国的间接属国.

me·di·a·tor [ˈmiːdieitə] *n.* 调解人,斡旋者,中人; 〔the M-〕【宗】耶稣基督; 【化】【生】介体.

me·di·a·to·ri·al, me·di·a·to·ry [ˌmiːdiəˈtɔːriəl,-təri]

a. 调解的.
me·di·a·tress [ˈmiːdieitris] *n.* 女调解人.
me·di·a·trix [ˌmiːdiˈeitriks] *n.* *(pl.* **-tri·ces** [-ˈtraisiːz]*)* = mediatress.
med·ic[1] [ˈmedik] *n.* 〔美俚〕医生;【美军】军医助手;医学生.
med·ic[2] [ˈmedik] *n.* 苜蓿属.
med·i·ca·ble [ˈmedikəbl] *a.* 可医治的,医得好的.
Med·i·caid [ˈmedikeid] *n.* 〔亦 m-〕〔美〕公共医疗补助制.
med·i·cal [ˈmedikəl] *a.* ①医学的,医术的;医疗的;医师的. ②医药的. ③内科的 (*opp.* surgical). ~ *jurisprudence* 法医学. *a* ~ *man [practitioner]* 医生,开业医生〔包括 physician, surgeon 等〕. *a* ~ *officer* 军医,医官. *the* ~ *art* 医术. *a* ~ *certificate* 健康证明书,诊断书. *the* ~ *department* 医务部. ~ *science* 医学. *a* ~ *examination* 体格检查. *a* ~ *examiner* 法医;验尸员;体检医生. *a* ~ *orderly* 看护兵. *free* ~ *care* 公费医疗. ~ *troops* 卫生队. ***under*** ~ ***treatment*** 在治疗中. — *n.* 〔口〕医科学生;医生;体格检查. **-ly** *ad.* 医学上;用医药〔医术、医学〕.
me·dic·a·ment [meˈdikəmənt] *n.* 药物,药剂.
Med·i·aid [ˈmediˌeid] *n.* 〔美〕医疗补贴计划.
Med·i·care [ˈmediˌkεə] *n.* 〔亦 m-〕〔美,加〕国家医疗照顾制〔对老年病人的某些医疗费和住院费由国家负担的制度〕.
med·i·cas·ter [ˈmedikæstə] *n.* 江湖医生;庸医.
med·i·cate [ˈmedikeit] *vt.* 用药治疗;在…中加入药品. *a* ~*d bath* 药浴. ~*d soap* 药皂.
med·i·ca·tion [ˌmediˈkeiʃən] *n.* ①药物疗法;加入药物;药物处理. ②药物,药剂.
med·i·ca·tive [ˈmedikətiv] *a.* 有药效的,可医治的;加有药品的.
Med·i·ce·an [ˌmediˈtʃi(ː)ən] *a.* (中世纪意大利佛罗伦萨)美第奇 (Medici) 家族的.
med·i·chair [ˈmeditʃεə] *n.* 医疗椅〔装有电子传感器,能测知人的生理活动状况〕.
me·dic·i·na·ble [meˈdisinəbl] *a.* = medicinal.
me·dic·i·nal [meˈdisinəl] *a.* 医学的,医药的,药用的;医疗的,治病的. *a* ~ *herb* 药草. ~ *preparations* (内服或外用)药剂,药膏. **-ly** *ad.*
med·i·cine [ˈmedsin, -disin] *n.* ①医药;(尤指)内服药. ②医学,医术;内科(治疗) (*opp.* surgery). ③有功效的东西;良药. ④(北美印第安人的)咒术,魔术. ⑤〔俚〕酒. ⑥〔美俚〕情报. *patent* ~*s* 专卖药;成药. *a good* ~ *for cold* 感冒良药. *practise* ~ 开业行医. ***no*** ~ 〔美俚〕与事无关的情报. ***take*** ~ 吃药. ***take one's*** ~ 吃苦药;受到惩罚;忍气吞声做应做的事;〔俚〕喝酒. ***the virtue of*** ~ 药的功效. — *vt.* 〔古〕使…吃药,下药. ~ **ball** (锻练身体用的)实心软皮球. ~ **chest** 药箱,药柜. ~ **dance** 驱病舞;巫术舞. ~ **man** (原始人的)巫医;〔美俚〕医生. ~ **show** 走江湖卖膏药.
med·i·co [ˈmedikəu] *n.* *(pl.* ~*s)* 〔谑〕医生;医科学生.
med·i·co- *comb. f.* = medical.
med·i·co·bo·tan·i·cal [ˈmedikəuˈtænikəl] *a.* 药用植物学的.
med·i·co·le·gal [ˈmedikəuˈliːgəl] *a.* 法医学的.
me·di·e·val [ˌmediˈiːvəl] *a.* = mediaeval.
Me·di·na [meˈdiːnə] *n.* 麦地那〔伊斯兰教圣地之一,位于沙特阿拉伯西北部〕.
me·di·o [ˈmiːdiəu] *n.* 〔美俚〕五分镍币.
me·di·o·cre [ˈmiːdiəukə] *a.* 普普通通的,中等的,平庸的;〔蔑〕劣等的,无价值的.
me·di·oc·rity [ˌmiːdiˈɔkriti] *n.* 普通,平凡;平庸;平平常常的才能;平凡的人.
Medit. = Mediterranean (Sea).
med·i·tate [ˈmediteit] *vi.* ①深思;沉思,冥想;反省 (*on; upon*). —*vt.* 考虑;企图;策划,计划. ~ *revenge* 企图复仇. ~ *the Muse* 构想诗句. **-ta·tion** *n.* 熟虑;(特指宗教上的)默想;〔*pl.*〕冥想录 (*religious meditation* ~*s* 坐禅). **-ta·tive** *a.* 默想的,冥想的. **-ta·tor** 默想者,冥想家;计划者.
Med·i·ter·ra·nean [ˌmeditəˈreinjən] *n.* ①地中海 (= ~ Sea). ②地中海地区的居民. ③地中海沿岸的高加索人. *the* ~ *race* 地中海沿岸的高加索人种. — *a.* ①地中海 (地区) 的. ②地中海沿岸的高加索人的. ③〔m-〕陆地包围着的;〔军〕离海岸远的. ~ **climate** 地中海气候. ~ **fever**【医】地中海热,波状热. ~ **fruit fly** 地中海果蝇〔一种危害水果的双翅蝇类〕.
me·di·um [ˈmiːdjəm] *n.* *(pl.* ~***dia*** [-diə, -djə]*)* ①媒介物;传导体;媒质,基质,介质,介体;中间物;环境、生活情形. ②手段,方法;媒介;〔*pl.*〕宣传工具〔指报刊、广播、电视等〕. ③中间,中庸;【数】中数,平均;【逻】中名辞;【生】培养基,培养液;颜料溶解液. ④女巫,降神者. ⑤【剧】(射火灯灯前的)隔板. ⑥(纸张的)中号尺寸;〔*pl.*〕中型轰炸机. *mass media* 大众宣传媒介;宣传工具. *the happy* ~ 中庸. *the circulating* ~ = *the* ~ *of circulation* 通货. — *a.* 中等的,中级的,普通的;平均的. ~ *quality* 中级 (物品). *a* ~ *bowler*【板球】(速球与缓球之间的) 中球投球员. ***by [through] the*** ~ ***of*** 通过,以…为媒介. ~ ***of advertisement*** 广告媒介〔指报刊等〕. ~ ***of exchange*** 交换媒介;货币;支票. ~ **frequency**【电】中频. ~ **shot**【摄】中景. ~ **steel** 中硬钢. ~ **wave**【无】中波. ~**-sized** *a.* 中等大的.
me·di·um·is·tic [ˌmiːdjəˈmistik] *a.* 巫术的.
me·di·us [ˈmiːdiəs] *n.* = mediant.
med·lar [ˈmedlə] *n.*【植】欧楂. *the Japan(ese)* ~ 枇杷. *the* ~*-bush* 卵圆叶唐棣.
med·ley [ˈmedli] *n.* ①混合,混杂,乌合之众. ②杂录;集成歌(曲);杂色布;【美体】混合径赛;混合径赛参加者. ③〔古〕混战. *a* ~ *of races* 杂族共聚. — *a.* 混合的,混杂的. ~ **race [relay]** ①混合接力赛跑. ②各段不同游泳式的游泳赛.
Mé·doc [ˈmedɔk] *n.* (法国 Médoc 地方的)红葡萄酒.
Med·res·co [ˈmedreskəu] *n.* 助听器〔商标名〕.
me·dul·la [meˈdʌlə] *n.* *(pl.* ***-lae*** [-liː]*)* 〔L.〕①【解】骨髓;脊髓;延髓;髓(质);(特指心脏的)中心;(神经纤维的)髓鞘. ②【植】木髓. ③【微】菌髓. ~ ***ob·lon·ga·ta*** [ˌɔblɔŋˈgɑtə] 延髓. ~ ***spi·na·lis*** [ˈspainəlis] 脊髓.
me·dul·lar·y [meˈdʌləri] *a.* ~ **ray**【解、植】髓(射)线. ~ **sheath**【解、植】髓鞘.
med·ul·lat·ed [ˈmedəleitid] *a.* ①具髓的;具髓质的. ②有髓的.
me·dul·li·tis [ˌmedəˈlaitis] *n.*【医】骨髓炎.
Me·du·sa [miˈdjuːzə] *n.*【希神】美杜莎,蛇发女怪. **-like** *a.* 象蛇发女怪的,令人恐怖的.
me·du·sa [miˈdjuːzə] *n.* *(pl.* ~***s***, ***-sae*** [-siː, -ziː]*)* 【动】水母(体). *a.* 水母的;水母体的;伞盖体的.
me·du·soid [miˈdjuːsɔid] *a.* 类水母体的. — *n.* 类水母体.
meed [miːd] *n.* 〔诗〕报酬;奖赏,赏与;称赞;足够的份儿,值得接受的东西 (*of*). *one's* ~ *of praise* 应有的称赞.
meek [miːk] *a.* 温顺的,柔和的;虚心的;卑恭屈节的 (*opp.* selfassertive);逆来顺受的;善忍的. ***as*** ~ ***as a lamb [a maid, Moses]*** 非常柔和,非常温顺. ~**-eyed** *a.* 眼光柔和的. **-ly** *ad.* 温顺,柔和;卑恭屈节地. **-ness** *n.* 温顺,柔和;卑恭屈节.
meer·kat [ˈmiəkæt] *n.* ①(南非) 海岛猫鼬,蒙哥. ②〔废〕猴子.
meer·schaum [ˈmiəʃəm] *n.* ①【矿】海泡石. ②海泡石烟斗.
meet[1] [miːt] *vt.* *(**met*** [met]*)* ①遇见,碰上;擦过,相遇. ②迎接,出迎;会见,见面;面谈. ③认识,初次会见. ④面临;抵抗,和…会战;答复,反驳. ⑤满足,迎合. ⑥如期偿付；偿还；践约．⑦(路、河流等)相合，交叉；和…接触．⑧辩明．*I must go to the station to ~ my friend.* 我该到车站去接朋友了．*I'm very glad to ~ you.* 会见你很高兴；久仰久仰．*I have arranged to ~ him at the hotel at six o'clock.* 我已约好六点钟在旅馆同他会见．*More is meant than ~s the ear.* (话中)意义比听到的更多；大有言外之意．*~ the eyes* 被看到．*M- Mr. Brown* 〔美〕这位是布朗先生．*~ the requirements of students and laymen.* 满足学生和一般人的要求．*~ expenses* 偿付开支．*~ a bill* 支付到期的票据．*The buses ~ all trains.* 公共汽车联系着所有(到站)列车．*~ objections* 反驳反对意见．— *vi.* ①相会，相遇；会合．②(线的两端)相合；相交，相连接．③见面；聚会；集会，开会．④(品质)兼备，共存 *(in)*．⑤合意，和解．⑥会战．*Political integrity and ability ~ in her.* 她德才兼备．*This belt won't ~ round my waist.* 这个裤带不够长．*~ in battle* 兵戎相见，战场周旋．***be met by*** 遇着．***make both ends ~*** 使收支相抵；量入为出．*~ (sb.)* ***halfway*** 和人妥协〔相让〕；迁就某人．*~* ***one's end [fate, death]*** 死 (*~ one's fate calmly* 从容死去)．*~* ***one's engagements*** 践约，履行契约；偿债．*~* ***one's liabilities*** 偿还债务．*~* ***sb.'s eye*** 和某人的目光相遇；回看某人．*~* ***the case*** 适合，合用．*~* ***together*** 集合，会合．*~* ***trouble halfway*** 自寻烦恼，杞人忧天．*~* ***up with*** 〔美方〕遇着，碰见．*~* ***with*** 遇见，碰见；遭遇，经验；偶然发见；达到，〔美〕符合．— *n.* ①集合，会；赛会．②集合者；集合地点．③〔英〕(打猎竞赛等)出发前的集合．④【数】(直线或平面的)交点，交线；交(集)．*an athletic ~* 运动会．*an air ~* 〔美〕航空大会．

meet[2] [miːt] *a.* 〔古〕适当的，适合的，相称的 *(for; to do, to be done; that)*. *It's ~ that we should help each other.* 我们应当互助帮助．**-ly** *ad.* **-ness** *n.*

meet·ing [ˈmiːtiŋ] *n.* ①会合，集合；会见；会议，(特殊的)大会，集会，会；会众．②决斗；会战；遭遇．③〔M-〕(Quaker 教徒的)礼拜会．④(河川的)合流点，连接点．*an on-the-spot ~* 现场会议．*an accusation ~* 控诉大会，诉苦大会．*a basket-~* 郊游会．*a farewell [welcome] ~* 欢送〔欢迎〕会．*a general [ordinary] ~* 大〔例〕会．*a social ~* 联欢会，同乐会．*a mass ~* 群众大会．*an indignation ~* 示威大会．***address the ~*** 向到会者致祝词．***break up [dissolve] a ~*** 解散会议，闭会．***call a ~*** 召集大会．***hold a ~*** 开会．*~* ***engagement*** 遭遇战．***speak in ~*** 〔美〕发表意见．*~* ***of minds*** 意见一致．*~***house** 〔美〕〔英蔑〕教堂，礼拜堂；〔英〕非国教徒的礼拜堂．*~* **place** 会场．

M.E.F. =Middle East Forces〔英〕驻中东(武装)部队．

meg(a)r *comb. f.* ①大．②兆，百万．

meg·a·buck [ˈmegəbʌk] *n.* 〔俚〕一百万美元．

meg·a·ce·phal·ic, meg·a·ceph·a·lous [ˌmegəsiˈfælik, -ˈsefələs] *a.* 巨头的．

meg·a·cy·cle [ˈmegəˌsaikl] *n.* 【无】兆周．

meg·a·death [ˈmegəˌdeθ] *n.* 百万人死亡〔搞核讹诈者用以计算核爆炸杀伤力的所谓计算单位〕．

meg·a·dyne [ˈmegədain] *n.* 【物】兆达(因)．

meg·a·erg [ˈmegəˌəːg] *n.* 【物】兆尔格．

meg·a·far·ad [ˌmegəˈfærəd] *n.* 【电】兆法(拉)．

meg·a·fog [ˈmegəfɔg] *n.* 雾信号器．

meg·a·game [ˌmegəˈgeim] *n.* 大赛．

meg·a·ga·mete [ˌmegəˈgæmit, -gæˈmiːt] *n.* 【医】大配子(= macrogamete).

meg·a·hertz [ˈmegəˌhəːts] *n.* *(pl.* ***-hertz)*** 【物】兆赫(兹)．

meg·a·lith [ˈmegəliθ] *n.* (史前建筑遗存的)巨石；巨碑．

meg·a·lith·ic [ˌmegəˈliθik] *a.* 巨石的．

megalo- *comb. f.* 大，巨大．

meg·a·lo·blast [ˈmegələublɑːst] *n.* 【医】巨成红血细胞，巨胚红血球．**-ic** [ˌmegələuˈblæstik] *a.* (*megaloblastic anaemia* 有核巨红血球性贫血)．

meg·a·lo·car·di·a [ˌmegələuˈkɑːdiə] *n.* 【医】心肥大．

meg·a·lo·ceph·a·ly [ˌmegələuˈsefəli] *n.* 异常大的头．**-ce·phal·ic** [-seˈfælik] *a.* 头部异常巨大的．

meg·a·lo·ma·ni·a [ˈmegələuˈmeinjə] *n.* 自大狂；妄自尊大；【医】夸大妄想狂．

meg·a·lo·ma·ni·ac [ˌmegəˈləuˈmeiniæk] *n., a.* 妄自尊大的(人)；患夸大狂的(人)．**-man·ic** [ˈmegələuˈmænik] *a.*

meg·a·lop·o·lis [ˌmegəˈlɔpəlis] *n.* 特大城市．**-pol·i·tan** [-ləˈpɔlitən] *a., n.*

meg·a·lops [ˈmegəˌlɔps] *n.* *(pl.* ***-lops, -lop·ses)*** (蟹)大眼幼体期．**-lop·ic** *a.*

meg·a·lo·sau·rus [ˌmegələˈsɔːrəs] *n.* 【古生】斑龙．

mega·parsec [ˌmegəˈpɑːsek] *n.* 【天】 百万秒差距．

meg·a·phone [ˈmegəfəun] *n.* 扩音器；喇叭筒，喊话筒；传声筒．— *vt., vi.* 用喇叭筒喊话；广泛宣传．

meg·a·pod [ˈmegəˌpɔd] *a.* 大足的．— *n.* = megapode.

meg·a·pode [ˈmegəˌpəud] *n.* 【动】营冢鸟〔产于澳大利亚和东印度群岛〕．

meg·a·scope [ˈmegəskəup] *n.* 【物】(放大不透明物体的)放大幻灯．**-scop·ic** [-ˈskɔpik] *a.* 肉眼可见的，宏观的；粗视的；放大幻灯的；被扩大的．

meg·a·spo·ran·gi·um [ˌmegəspəˈrændʒiəm] *n.* *(pl.* ***-gi·a*** [-ə]*)* 【植】大孢子囊．

meg·a·spore [ˈmegəspɔː] *n.* 【植】大孢子．**-sporic** [-ˈspɔːrik] *a.*

meg·a·spo·ro·phyll [ˌmegəˈspɔːrəfil] *n.* 【植】大孢子叶．

me·gasse [miˈgæs] *n.* (尤指甘蔗的)榨渣．

meg·a·tan·ker [ˌmegəˈtæŋkə] *n.* ①百万吨级油轮，超级油轮．②兆，百万〔量度单位〕．

meg·a·there [ˈmegəθiə] *n.* 【动】大懒兽〔一种古生物〕．

Meg·a·the·ri·um [ˌmegəˈθiəriəm] *n.* 【古生】大懒兽科．

meg·a·ton [ˈmegəˌtʌn] *n.* ①百万吨．②百万吨级〔核爆力计算单位〕．**-ic** [ˌmegəˈtʌnik] *a.*

meg·a·tron [ˈmegətrʌn] *n.* 【无】塔形(电子)管．

meg·a·volt [ˈmegəvəuit] *n.* 【电】兆伏(特)，百万伏特．

meg·a·watt [ˈmegəwɔt] *n.* 【电】兆瓦(特)．

meg·ger [ˈmegə] *n.* 【电】高阻表，兆欧表，摇表，迈格表．

me·gil·lah [məˈgilə] *n.* 【俚】①颇费唇舌的解释；说来话长的故事．②复杂事情．

me·gilp [məˈgilp] *n.* (油画用)溶油剂．

meg·ohm [ˈmegəum] *n.* 【电】兆欧(姆)．

me·grim[1] [ˈmiːgrim] *n.* ①【医】周期性偏头痛．②〔*pl.*〕忧郁．③【兽医】眩晕〔马脑充血〕．④空想，幻想；怪念头．

me·grim[2] [ˈmiːgrim] *n.* (一种)鲽鱼．

Mei·ji [ˈmeidʒiː] 〔Jap.〕明治〔明治天皇年号〕．

mein·ie, mein·y [ˈmeini] *n.* ①〔废〕(封建的)家臣；随从；门客；家族；家户．②〔Scot.〕群众；大众．

Mein Kampf [main ˈkɑːmpf] 〔G.〕《我的奋斗》〔希特勒所写宣扬其法西斯主义的书〕．

mei·o·bar [ˈmaiəbɑː] *n.* 【气】低压区等压线；低压区．

mei·o·sis [maiˈəusis] *n.* *(pl.* ***-ses*** [-siːz]*)* ①【生】减数分裂；成熟分裂．②【修】间接肯定法，曲言法 (= litotes)〔例：not a few regrets〕．

Meis·ter·sing·er [ˈmaistəˌsiŋə] *n.* *(sing., pl.)* 〔G.〕(14—16 世纪德国的)职工歌手；职工诗歌协会会员．

Mek·ka [ˈmekə] = Mecca.

me·kom·e·ter [miːˈkɔmitə] *n.* (枪炮的)测距器．

Me·kong [ˈmeiˈkɔŋ] *n.* 湄公河．

mel [mel] *n.* 蜂蜜〔尤指药用蜜〕．

mel·a·mine [ˈmeləmi(ː)n] *n.* 【化】三聚氰(酰)胺，蜜胺．*~* **resin** 【化】蜜胺树脂；三聚氰酰胺树脂．

mel·an- *comb. f.* ①表示"黑"：*melanian*．②表示"黑素"：*melanotic*.

mel·an·cho·li·a [ˌmelənˈkəuljə] *n.*【医】忧郁病. **-cho·li·ac** *a., n.* 患忧郁病的(人).
mel·an·chol·ic [ˌmelənˈkɔlik] *a.* 忧郁(症)的; 使人抑郁的; 神经质的. — *n.* 忧郁病患者.
mel·an·chol·y [ˈmelənkəli] *n.* ①忧郁; 忧郁症. ②愁思,沉思. —*a.* ①忧郁的; 令人伤感的; 意气消沉的. ②沉思默想的.
Mel·a·ne·sia [ˌmeləˈniːzjə] *n.* 美拉尼西亚〔西南太平洋的岛群〕.
Mel·a·ne·si·an [ˌmeləˈniːzjən, -ziən, -ʒiən] *n., a.* (大洋洲中部)美拉尼西亚人[语](的).
mé·lange [meiˈlɑ̃ːnʒ] *n.* 〔F.〕①混合物, 什锦,杂烩;(文学)杂记,杂集. ②【纺】混色毛纱; 混色效应; 混条机.
me·la·ni·an [miˈleiniən] *a.* ①〔常作 M-〕【人种】黑发黑肤的,黑色人种的. ②黑色素的.
me·lan·ic [məˈlænik] *a.*【动】黑变病的; 有黑变病特征的. ②黑色素过多的.
mel·a·nin [ˈmelənin] *n.*【医】黑(色)素.
mel·a·nism [ˈmelənizəm] *n.*【医】黑色素过多; 黑素沉着症;【生】黑化,暗化.
mel·a·nite [ˈmeləˌnait] *n.*【地】黑榴石.
mel·a·nize [ˈmelənaiz] *vt.* ***(-nized, -niz·ing)*** ①黑化. ②使…变黑,使成黑色.
mel·a·no- *comb. f.* = melan-.
Mel·a·noch·ro·i [ˌmeləˈnɔkrəuai] *n.*【人种】淡黑白色人种〔高加索人种中头发浓黑肤色淡白的种族〕.
mel·a·no·cyte [ˈmelənəuˈsait, məˈlænə-] *n.*【医】黑素细胞.
mel·a·noid [ˈmelənɔid] *a.* ①【生化】染黑的, 暗黑的. ②【医】黑变病的; 黑变病状的.
mel·a·no·ma [ˌmeləˈnəumə] *n.* *(pl.* ***-mas, -ma·ta*** [-mətə]*)*【医】黑瘤.
me·la·no·sis [ˌmeləˈnəusis] *n.*【医】色素浸润,黑变病.
mel·a·no·tic [ˌmeləˈnɔtik] *a.* 以黑色素为特征的; (患)黑变病的.
mel·a·nous [ˈmelənəs] *a.* 黑肤黑发的.
mel·a·phyre [ˈmeləˌfaiə] *n.* 〔废〕【地】暗斑岩.
mel·a·stome [ˈmeləˌstəum] *a.*【植】野牡丹科植物的.
Mel·ba [ˈmelbə] *n.* 梅尔巴〔女子名〕.
melba toast [ˈmelbə təust] (烘烤得很脆的)薄片面包干.
Mel·bourne [ˈmelbən] *n.* 墨尔本〔即新金山, 澳大利亚港市〕.
Mel·chers [ˈmeltʃəz] *n.* 梅尔彻斯〔姓氏〕.
Mel·chior [ˈmelkiɔː] *n.* 梅尔基奥尔〔姓氏〕.
Mel·chite, Mel·kite [ˈmelkait] *n.* (埃及、以色列和叙利亚行拜占廷仪式的)阿拉伯语天主教徒.
meld [meld] *vt., vi.* 〔美〕吞没; 合并.
mê·lée [ˈmelei] *n.* 〔F.〕互殴,乱斗,混战; 激烈的论战; 混乱的人群[一堆].
mel·ic [ˈmelik] *a.* ①歌的; 诗的〔尤指成诗节的希腊诗〕. ②抒情的; 抒情诗的; 拟加以咏唱的.
mel·i·lot [ˈmeliˌlɔt] *n.* 草木犀属植物(= sweet clover).
mel·i·nite [ˈmelinait] *n.* 麦宁炸药〔含有苦味酸的猛烈炸药〕.
mel·io·rate [ˈmiːljəreit] *vt., vi.* = ameliorate. **-ra·tion** *n.* 土壤改良 (= amelioration). **-ra·tive** *a.* = ameliorative. **-rat·or, -rat·er** *n.* = ameliorator. ★英国多通用 ameliorate 等.
mel·io·rism [ˈmiːljərizəm] *n.* 世界向善论; 社会改善论.
mel·ior·i·ty [miːˈljɔriti] *n.* 改善,进步; 卓越,优越性.
me·lis·ma [məˈlizmə] *n.* *(pl.* ***-ma·ta*** [-mətə], ***-mas****)*【乐】装饰音. **-ma·tic** [ˈmelizˈmætik] *a.*
me·lis·sa [miˈlisə] *n.*【植】蜜蜂花〔薄荷属〕.
me·li·te·mi·a [meliˈtiːmiə] *n.*【医】糖血症.
mell [mel] *vt., vi.* 〔英方〕①混合; 加入. ②弄, 摸弄; 参与; 干涉.
mel·lay [ˈmelei] *n.* 〔古〕 = mêlée.
mel·ler [ˈmelə] *n.* 〔美俚〕 = melodrama.
mel·lif·er·ous [meˈlifərəs] *a.* 产蜜的,带蜜的; 甜的.
mel·lif·lu·ence [meˈlifluəns] *n.* (声音、言词的) 甜美; 流畅; 迷人.
mel·lif·lu·ent, mel·lif·lu·ous [meˈlifluənt, -əs] *a.* 〔古〕(话、声音等)甘美的,甜蜜的, 流畅的. *a ~ speech* 甜言蜜语. **-ly** *ad.*
mel·lit·ic [meˈlitik] *a.* ~ *acid*【化】苯六(羧)酸.
Mel·lon [ˈmelən] *n.* 梅隆〔姓氏〕.
mel·lo·phone [ˈmeləfəun] *n.* 一种类似中音萨克号的圆形铜管乐器〔在乐队中常代替法国号〕.
mel·lo·tron [ˈmelətrɔn] *n.* 电子琴.
mel·low [ˈmeləu] *a.* ***(~er; ~est)*** ①甘美多汁的,(瓜、果等)成熟的; (酒)芳醇的. ②(土壤等)肥沃的. ③(人格、思想等)老练的,完美的. ④(音、色、光等)柔美的,圆润的,丰美的. ⑤〔口〕高兴的,愉快的; 温和的; 有点醉的. ~ *age* 成熟的年龄. — *vt.* ①使柔和; 使芳醇. ②使成熟,使丰美. —*vi.*①变柔和; 变芳醇. ②成熟; 变得丰美[柔和]. **-ly** *ad.* **-ness** *n.*
mel·low·y [ˈmeləui] *a.* = mellow.
melo [ˈmeləu] *n.* 〔美俚〕 = melodrama.
me·lo·de·on, me·lo·dion, me·lo·dium [miˈləudiən, -diəm] *n.* 小型脚踏风琴〔一种谐音手风琴〕.
me·lo·di·a [məˈləudiə] *n.*【乐】八尺风琴音栓.
me·lod·ic [meˈlɔdik] *a.* 旋律的; 调子美妙的.
me·lod·i·ca [miˈlɔdikə] *n.* 口风琴.
me·lod·ics [miˈlɔdiks] *n.* 旋律学.
me·lo·di·ous [miˈləudjəs] *a.* (有)旋律的,旋律优美的,音调悦耳的. **-ly** *ad.* **-ness** *n.*
mel·o·dist [ˈmelədist] *n.* 歌唱家; (作曲旋律优美的)作曲家.
mel·o·dize [ˈmelədaiz] *vt.* 使有优美的旋律, 使悦耳动听; 把…谱成乐曲. —*vi.* 作曲, 谱曲; 产生旋律.
mel·o·dra·ma, mel·o·drame [ˈmelədrɑːmə, ˈmelədræm] *n.* 情节剧,传奇剧; 戏剧性的事件〔行为〕;〔古〕乐剧.
mel·o·dra·mat·ic [ˌmeləudrəˈmætik] *a.* 情节剧作风的; 戏剧似的; 感情夸张的; 惊人的,轰动的. **-i·cal·ly** *ad.*
mel·o·dra·mat·ics [ˌmeləudrəˈmætiks] *n.* 〔*pl.*〕感情夸张的[情节剧似的、轰动的]行为.
mel·o·dram·a·tist [ˌmeləuˈdræmətist] *n.* 情节剧作者.
mel·o·dram·a·tize [ˌmeləuˈdræmətaiz] *vt.* 使具有情节剧特点; 把(小说等)改写成情节剧.
mel·o·dy [ˈmelədi] *n.* ①甜蜜的音乐,好听[和谐]的调子; 好听的声音; 歌曲; 适合唱歌的诗. ②【乐】旋律,曲调; 主调. ~ *of one's utterance* 讲话的抑扬顿挫.
mel·o·lon·thid [ˌmeləˈlɔnθid] *n.*【动】鳃角金龟〔一种食植物根的昆虫〕.
mel·o·ma·ni·a [ˌmeləˈmeinjə] *n.* 音乐狂. **-ic** *a.*
mel·on [ˈmelən] *n.* ①【植】甜瓜. ②〔美俚〕额外红利; 横财. *water* ~ 西瓜. *musk* ~ = *oriental* ~ 香瓜,甜瓜. ***cut a*** ~ 〔俚〕分配额外红利; 分红; 分赃. ***cut the*** ~ 〔俚〕瓜分利益. ~ **cutting** 〔美俚〕瓜分; 分赃. ~ **tree**【植】蕃栭树.
Mel·pom·e·ne [melˈpɔmini(ː)] *n.*【希神】掌管悲剧的女神.
melt [melt] *vi.* ***(~ed; ~ed, molten)*** ①融化; 熔化; 液解. ②逐渐消散[消失,变淡]. ③(心等)变软,生怜悯的心情; (决心等)软化. ④溶合,逐渐转化成. ⑤(云等)变成雨. ⑥(音乐、声音等)变得柔润. ⑦〔口〕感到热极. *I am simply ~ing (with heat).* 〔口〕热死了, 热得要命. *Clouds ~ away.* 云变成雨了. — *vt.* ①使融化[熔化、溶解]. ②使软化,使感动. ③使消散[消失]. ④浪费;〔英俚〕(把支票等)兑现. *Heat will ~ iron.* 热度可使铁熔化. ~ ***away*** 融掉; 消失; (钱)渐渐花光; (使)着迷,弄得恍恍惚惚 (*The snow soon ~ed away.* 雪不

久就化了)。~ ***down*** 熔化,销毁(货币等);〔俚、谑〕变卖财产。~ ***into***…熔成…,化为;消散于…;因心软而…,感动得(~ *into air* 化为云烟,消失。~ *into distance* 消失在远方。~ *into tears* 心变软而哭起来)。~ ***like wax*** 象蜡一样融化。~ ***up*** 〔美〕=~ ***down*** — *n.* 熔[溶]解;熔化了的金属,溶化物;熔[溶]解量;熔炉的一次装料。

melt·age [ˈmeltidʒ] *n.* ①熔化。②熔化物;熔化量。

melt·ing [ˈmeltiŋ] *a.* ①融[熔]化的。②心软的,受感动的,易感动的。③使人感动的,使人感伤的,温柔的,动人的。*a* ~ *mood* 感伤的心情。~ **point** 熔点。~ **pot** 坩埚,熔化锅;各种族融合之国〔通常指美国〕(*go into the* ~ *pot* 被改造;(心等)变软,软化。*put* [*cast*] *into the* ~ *pot* 重作,改造)。

mel·ton [ˈmeltən] *n.* (英国)麦尔顿呢〔又作 M-Cloth〕。— *a.* 麦尔顿呢做的。

Mel·va [ˈmelvə] *n.* 梅尔瓦〔女子名〕。

Mel·ville [ˈmelvil] *n.* 梅尔维尔〔姓氏,男子名〕。

Mel·vin, Mel·vyn [ˈmelvin] *n.* 梅尔文〔姓氏,男子名〕。

mem. = ①member. ②memento. ③memoir. ④memorandum. ⑤memorial.

mem·ber [ˈmembə] *n.* ①(团体的)一分子,成员;会员;社员;议员;委员。②政党支部。③手足,肢体;身体各部,(人及动物的)器官。④各部,部分。⑤【语法】分句;成分。⑥【数】元,分子,(方程的)端边;【逻】推论的命题;【机】构件,部件;【化】节,(环中)原子数。*commune* ~ (人民公社)社员。*a League* ~ 团员。*a Party* ~ 党员。~*s of the Party Committee* 党委委员。*a M- of Congress* 〔美〕国会议员〔略作 M.C.〕.*a M- of Parliament* 〔英〕下院议员〔略作 M.P.,〔*pl.*〕M.P.s 或 MM. P.〕。*a* ~ *of a family* 家庭的一分子。*a* ~ *as of right* 当然会员。*a full* [*probationary*] ~ 正式[非正式]会员。*the unruly* ~ 难于控制的器官〔指舌头〕。*a driven* [*driving*] ~ 【机】从动[主动]构件。~ *bank* 〔美〕(联邦准备银行的)会员银行。**-ship** *n.* 会员[委员]的身分[地位、资格];会籍;会员人数;会员全体 (*Party membership* 全体党员;党籍)。

(-)membered [ˈmembəd] *comb. f.* …手足的;有…肢体的;有…会员的: *large-*~ 手足巨大的。

mem·bra·na·ceous [ˌmembrəˈneiʃəs] *a.* = membranous.

mem·brane [ˈmembrein] *n.* ①【解、生】(薄)膜,隔膜。②〔古〕(古文件的)(一页)羊皮纸。*the mucous* ~ 粘膜。~ **bone** 【解】膜[成]骨。~ **labyrinth** 【解】膜迷路。**-bra·neous** [-niəs], **-bra·nous** [-njəs] *a.* 膜(状)的,膜质的;隔膜的。

mem·brum vi·ri·le [ˈmembrəm viˈraili] 〔L.〕阴茎(=penis)。

me·men·to [meˈmentəu] *n.* (*pl.* ~*s*, ~*es*) 纪念品;令人回忆的东西;令人警惕的东西;〔谑〕记忆;做梦似的心境。

me·men·to mo·ri [meˈmentəu ˈmɔːrai] 〔L.〕死的警告,死的象征〔髑髅等〕。

mem·o [ˈmeməu] *n.* 〔口〕= memorandum.

mem·oir [ˈmemwɑː] *n.* ①传记,实录;〔*pl.*〕回忆录,自传。②研究报告,论文;〔*pl.*〕…学会纪要,…学会论文集。③〔罕〕(外交上的)备忘录。

mé·moire [meˈmwɑː] *n.* 〔F.〕(外交上的)备忘录。

mem·o·ra·bil·i·a [ˌmeməraˈbiliə] *n. pl.* (*sing.* ***-rab·i·le*** [-ˈræbiliː]) 〔L.〕值得记忆的事情;应记录下来的地方〔东西〕;(重大事件的)记录;(伟大人物的)言行录。

mem·o·ra·ble [ˈmemərəbl] *a.* 可记忆的,不可忘记的,难忘的;重大的,著名的。**-bly** *ad.*, **-bil·i·ty** [ˌmeməraˈbiliti] *n.*

mem·o·ran·dum [ˌmeməˈrændəm] *n.* (*pl.* ~*s*, ①亦作 ***-da*** [-də]) 〔L.〕①记录。②【外交】照会,备忘录。③【商】便笺[函];(按一定格式印好的)通知书;寄售物品通知书。④【法】(契约等条文的)节略;摘要;会章,(公司)规章。*send a thing on* ~ 拿东西寄售。*the* ~ *of an association* 〔英〕(公司、协会的)成立简章。*the* ~ *of complaint* 【法】抗告状。~ **book** 备忘录。

mem·o·ri·al [miˈmɔːriəl] *a.* 纪念的;记忆的;追悼的。— *n.* ①纪念物,纪念品;纪念日;纪念馆;纪念碑;纪念仪式。②〔常 *pl.*〕记录,备忘录;年代记,编年史。③(提交议会等的)建议书;(外交上的)备忘录。④请愿书;抗议书。*a* ~ *festival* 纪念节。*a* ~ *service* 追悼会;追思礼拜。**M- Day** 〔美〕= Decoration Day.

me·mo·ri·al·ist [miˈmɔːriəlist] *n.* ①建议[请愿]书起草人[署名人];建议[请愿]者。②回忆录[传记]作者。

me·mo·ri·al·ize, me·mo·ri·al·ise [miˈmɔːriəlaiz] *vt.* ①向…请愿 [建议];上条陈。②纪念。**-iz·er** *n.* **-i·za·tion** *n.*

me·mo·ri·a tech·ni·ca [miˈmɔːriə ˈteknikə] 〔L.〕记忆术,记忆加强法。

me·mor·i·ter [miˈmɔritə] *ad.* 〔L.〕凭记忆。— *a.* 暗记的。

mem·o·rize, mem·o·rise [ˈmeməraiz] *vt.* ①记忆,暗记。②〔罕〕记录。③【自】存储。**-riz·er** *n.* **-ri·za·tion** *n.*

mem·o·ry [ˈmeməri] *n.* ①记忆;记忆力;【自】存储器;信息存储方式;存储量。②回忆。③纪念。④死后的名声,遗芳。⑤追想得起的年限[范围]。*artificial* ~ 记忆法。*retentive* ~ 良好的记忆力。*a translation* ~ (电子计算机的)译码存储器。*Keep your* ~ *active.* 好好记住,不要忘记。*It is but a* ~. 那不过是往事而已。***bear*** [***have, keep***] ***in*** ~ 记着,没有忘记。***beyond*** [***within***] ***the*** ~ ***of man*** [***men***] 在有史以前[以来]。***cherish the*** ~ ***of*** (*sb.*) 怀念(某人)。***come to one's*** ~ 想起,忆及,苏醒。***commit to*** ~ 记住。***from*** ~ 凭记忆。***have a good*** [***bad, poor, short***] ~ 记性好[坏]。***have no*** ~ ***of*** 完全忘记。***If my*** ~ ***serves me.*** 如果我的记性不错。***in*** ~ ***of*** 纪念…。***of blessed*** [***famous, happy, glorious***] ~ 故〔加在已死王公名上的颂词〕(*King Charles of blessed* ~ 已故查理王)。***slip sb.'s*** ~ 被某人一时忘记。***to the best of one's*** ~ 就记忆所及。***to the*** ~ ***of*** 献给…〔著者书前纪念性题词〕。***within living*** ~ 现在还被人记着。~ **bank** 【自】存储体,记忆体。~ **drum** 【自】存储磁鼓〔电子计算机存储装置上记录资料的磁带或磁道组〕。~ **switch** 【计】(需由电脉冲关闭的)存储开关。~ **trace** 【生化】记忆痕〔脑部吸收或记忆资料时产生的化学变化〕。

Mem·phis [ˈmemfis] *n.* ①孟菲斯〔古埃及城市〕。②孟菲斯〔美国城市〕。

mem·sa·hib [ˈmemˌsɑːib, -ˈsɑːb] *n.* 〔Ind.〕夫人;太太;女士;小姐〔原称欧洲妇女〕。

men [men] *n.* man 的复数。

men·ace [ˈmenəs] *vt.* 吓,恐吓,胁迫;使有危险(*with*). *My plan is* ~*d with failure.* 我的计划有失败的危险。—*vi.* 进行威胁。— *n.* 胁迫,威吓;威胁,危险。**-r** *n.* 威胁者,恐吓者。**menacing** *a.* 威胁的,险恶的。

men·ac·ing·ly [ˈmenəsiŋli] *ad.* 威胁地,恐吓着;险恶,逼近。

me·nad [ˈmiːnæd] *n.* = maenad.

men·a·di·one [ˌmenəˈdaiəun] *n.*【化、药】甲萘醌,维生素K.

mé·nage [meˈnɑːʒ] *n.* 〔F.〕家庭;家务(管理),家政。

mé·nage à trois [menɑːʒɑ ˈtrwɑ] 〔F.〕三人姘居〔夫妇和其一的姘头共同生活〕。

mé·nag·er·ie [miˈnædʒəri] *n.* 〔F.〕动物园;供展览的一批动物。

men·ar·che [miˈnɑːki] *n.* 月经初期。

Men·cken [ˈmeŋkin, ˈmeŋkən] *n.* 门肯〔姓氏〕。

mend [mend] *vt.* ①修补,修理;织补,缝补。②改正,纠正;改进,改善;订正,改订。③加强;加快;加(火);增加…的引诱力〔魔力、力量〕. ④治愈，使恢复健康. ～ *a road* 修路. ～ *a fire* 加(柴、炭给)火. ～ *one's ways* 改正（不良）行为. ～ *one's pace* 加快脚步. — *vi.*(事态过错、毛病等)变好，好转，改好，改善；痊愈. *It is never too late to* ～. 改过不嫌迟；过则勿惮改. ***Least said, soonest ～ed.*** 话少易正，少说为妙. ***～ matters [the matter]*** 改善情况. ***～ or end*** 要么改进要么停办；不改则废. ***on the ～ing hand = on the ～.*** — *n.* 改进；修理；修理部分；痊愈. ***on the ～*** （病）将好；（情况）在好转. **-a·ble** *a.* 可修补的，可改善的，可改正的.

men·da·cious [menˈdeiʃəs] *a.* 虚假的；捏造的；爱扯谎的. **-ly** *ad.*

men·dac·i·ty [menˈdæsiti] *n.* 虚假，谎话；捏造；撒谎；撒谎癖.

Men·del [ˈmendl],**Gregor Johann** 孟德尔〔1822—1884，奥地利遗传学家〕. ～*'s Law* 孟德尔定律.

Men·de·le·ev [ˌmendeˈleief] D. I. 门捷列夫〔1834—1907，俄国化学家〕. ～*'s Law* 【化】门捷列夫定律，化学元素周期律.

men·de·le·vi·um [ˌmendəˈleiviəm] *n.* 【化】钔.

Men·de·lian [menˈdiːljən] *a., n.* 孟德尔(定律)的；孟德尔学派的人.

Men·del·ism, Men·de·li·an·ism [ˈmendəlizəm, -ˈdiːliənizəm] *n.* 【生】孟德尔遗传学说；孟德尔主义.

Men·dels·sohn [ˈmendlsn] *n.* ①门德尔森〔姓氏〕. ② **～-Bartholdy, Felix** 门德尔森〔1809—1847，德国作曲家〕.

mend·er [ˈmendə] *n.* 修理者，改正者，修正者.

men·di·can·cy [ˈmendikənsi] *n.* 乞讨生活；行乞.

men·di·cant [ˈmendikənt] *a.* 行乞的，乞食的. — *n.* 乞丐；托钵僧. *a* ～ *friar* 托钵僧. ～ *orders* 托钵僧团.

men·dic·i·ty [menˈdisiti] *n.* = mendicancy.

mend·ing [ˈmendiŋ] *n.* ①织补，缝补；修理. ②织补物.

men·folk(s) [ˈmenfəuk] *n.* 〔口〕(家里的)男人们；〔诗〕人.

M. Eng. = Master of Engineering 工程(学)硕士.

men·ha·den [menˈheidn] *n.* 〔*sing., pl.*〕【鱼】(作肥料或炼油用的)鲱鱼，步鱼.

men·hir [ˈmenhiə] *n.* 【考古】巨石，糙石巨柱〔史前遗物〕.

me·ni·al [ˈmiːnjəl] *a.* 奴性的，卑下的；奴仆的，仆人的. — *n.* 奴仆；卑下[奴性]的人. **-ly** *ad.* 奴仆似地，奴颜婢膝地.

Ménière's syndrome [disease] [meiˈnjɛəz] 【医】美尼尔氏症〔内耳功能失调，症状是晕眩、呕吐、耳鸣等〕.

me·nin·ges [miˈnindʒiːz] *n. pl.* (*sing.* ***me·ninx*** [ˈmiːniŋks]) 【解】脑[脊]膜. **-geal** [-dʒiəl] *a.*

men·in·gi·tis [ˌmeninˈdʒaitis] *n.* 【医】脑膜炎. **-git·ic** *a.*

me·nin·go·cele [məˈniŋgəsiːl] *n.* 【医】脑(脊)膜突出.

me·nin·go·coc·cus [məˌniŋgəuˈkɔkəs] *n.* (*pl.* ***-coc·ci*** [-ˈkɔksai]) 脑膜炎双球菌. **-coc·cal** [-ˈkɔkl] **-coc·cic** [-ˈkɔksik] *a.*

me·ninx [ˈmiːniŋks] *n.* meninges 的单数.

me·nis·cus [miˈniskəs] *n.* (*pl.* ***～es, -ci*** [-sai]) 新月形(物)；【物】凹凸透镜；【物】(由毛管现象形成的)管内液面的凹[凸]面〔水呈凹形，水银呈凸形〕；【解】半月板.

me·no [ˈmenəu] *ad.* 〔It.〕【乐】更少，较少.

men-of-war [ˈmenəvˈwɔː] *n.* man-of-war 的复数.

men·ol·o·gy [miˈnɔlədʒi] *n.* ①月志. ②【希腊教】圣徒节日历；诸圣略传.

Me·nom·i·ni [məˈnɔmini] *n.* ①(*pl.* ***-nis, -ni***) 梅诺米尼人〔原居于美国密执安，现居威斯康辛州的一支印第安人〕. ②梅诺米尼语 (= Menominee).

me·no mos·so [ˈmeinəu ˈmɔsəu] 〔It.〕【乐】稍慢.

men·o·pause [ˈmenəpɔːz] *n.* 【医】停经；经绝(期)〔45—50 岁间〕.

men·o·rah [məˈnaurə, -ˈnɔːrə] *n.* 大烛台；分枝烛台〔尤指犹太教七分枝烛台或犹太圣节用九分枝烛台〕.

men·or·rha·gia [ˌmenəˈreidʒiə] *n.* 【医】月经过多.

mens [menz] *n.* 〔L.〕心，精神. ～ ***conscia recti*** [ˈmenz ˈkɔnʃiəˈrektai] 坦然的心，自问无愧的心. ～ ***sana in corpore sano*** [menz ˈseinə in ˈkɔːpəri ˈseinəu] 有健全的身体才有健全的精神；健全的精神寓于健全的身体.

Men·sa [ˈmensə] 【天】山案(星)座.

men·sal¹ [ˈmensəl] *a.* 饭桌上(用)的.

men·sal² [ˈmensəl] *a.* 每月的.

men·ses [ˈmensiːz] *n. pl.* 月经.

Men·she·vik [ˈmenʃəvik] *n.* 〔Russ.〕(*pl.* ***～s, -vi·ki*** [-viːki]) 孟什维克，少数派. — *a.* 孟什维克的.

Men·she·vism [ˈmenʃivizəm] *n.* 孟什维主义.

Men·she·vist [ˈmenʃivist] *n.* 孟什维主义者. — *a.* 孟什维主义的.

men·stru·al [ˈmenstruəl] *a.* ①【天】每月(一回)的. ②月经的. ～ *flow* 月经. ～ *disorder* 月经不调.

men·stru·ate [ˈmenstrueit] *vi.* 来月经，行经.

men·stru·a·tion [ˌmenstruˈeiʃən] *n.* 月经；月经期间. *irregular* ～ 月经不调.

men·stru·ous [ˈmenstruəs] *a.* (有)月经的；行经的.

men·stru·um [ˈmenstruəm] (*pl.* ***～s, -tru·a*** [-struə]) *n.* 溶媒，溶剂.

men·sur·a·ble [ˈmenʃurəbl] *a.*①可度量的，可测量的. ②【乐】定量的；有固定节奏的. **-bil·i·ty** *n.* 可测性.

men·su·ral [ˈmenʃurəl] *a.* ①关于度量的；量的. ②【乐】有定律的.

men·su·ra·tion [ˌmensjuəˈreiʃən] *n.* 测定，测量；【数】测定法，求积法；【物】量法.

mens·wear [ˈmenzˌwɛə] *n.* 男人服装；男子服饰用品 (= men's wear).

-ment *suf.* 前接动词[〔罕〕形容词]以形成表示动作、结果、状态等的名词，例：atone*ment*; employ*ment*; achieve*ment*.

men·tal¹ [ˈmentl] *a.* ①内心的；精神的，思想的；心理的 (*opp.* corporal). ②智慧的，智[脑]力的. ③闷在心里的，暗自思考的. ④〔口〕精神病的；意志薄弱的，愚笨的. — *n.* 精神(的东西)；〔口〕意志薄弱的人；傻子，糊涂虫. *a* ～ *worker* 脑力劳动者. ～ *disorder [derangement]* 精神错乱. ～ *culture* 精神修养. ～ *age* 智力年龄. ～ *deficiency* 智力缺陷. ～ *faculties* 智力，智能. *a* ～ *test* 智力测验. ～ *reservation* 内心保留〔对某事有看法但不说出来〕. ～ *arithmetic* 心算. *a* ～ *home* 精神病院. *a* ～ *case [patient]* 精神病患者. *a* ～ *specialist* 精神病专科医生. —*n.* 〔口〕精神病；精神病患者. ***make a ～ note of*** 记住. ～ **healing** 【医】心理治疗，精神治疗. ～ **retardation** 智力缺陷，精神薄弱，智力迟钝. ～ **telepathy** 心电感应. **-ly** *ad.* 在心里，精神上；智力上.

men·tal² [ˈmentl] *a.* 【解】颚的，颏的.

men·tal·ism [ˈmentlizəm] *n.* 精神第一性论〔资产阶级唯心主义的一种〕. **-tal·is·tic** *a.* **-is·ti·cal·ly** *ad.*

men·tal·ist [ˈmentlist] *n.* ①精神第一性论者. ②自称可洞察思想的人；算命先生.

men·tal·i·ty [menˈtæliti] *n.* 脑力，智力；精神；心理，意识；思想. *a war* ～ 战争心理. *the mountain-stronghold* ～ 山头主义. *the "small group"* ～ 小团体主义. *the peasant* ～ 农民意识.

men·ta·tion [menˈteiʃən] *n.* 精神[心理]作用；心理活动；思想.

Men·tha [ˈmenθə] *n.* 【植】薄荷属.

men·tha·ceous [menˈθeiʃəs] *a.* 【植】薄荷科的，唇形科的.

men·thene [ˈmenθiːn] *n.* 【化】薹烯.

men·thol [ˈmenθɔl] *n.* 【化】薄荷醇，薹醇. *a* ～ *pencil* 薄荷锭.

men·tho·lat·ed [ˈmenθəleitid] *a.* 【化】薄荷醇的；薄荷

醇处理的；薄荷醇浸的。

men·tion [ˈmenʃən] *vt.* ①说起，讲到，谈到，提到，写到；记载。②提述；提名表扬。*Don't* ～ *it.* 不要客气，哪儿的话。**not to** ～…不用说，更不必说。**(not) worth** ～**ing** (不)值得一说［一提］。**without** ～**ing** 更不必说了 — *n.* 说到，提及；提述；提名表扬。*an honourable* ～ 表扬。**at the** ～ **of** 当说到…，一说到…。**make** ～ **of** 说到，写到，提到 (*He made no* ～ *of it.* 他没有提到那件事。*M- was made of it.* 曾提到那件事)。**make no** ～ **of** 不提，不谈；不写。 **-a·ble** *a.* 可以提起的；值得一提的。

(-)men·tioned *comb. f.* 说到的，提到的。*above-*～ 上述。*before-*～ 前述。

men·tor [ˈmentɔː] *n.* ①辅导教师；指导人；(美国足球)教练。②〔M-〕曼托尔〔希腊史诗《奥德赛》中奥德修斯的忠诚朋友，奥德修斯之子的良师〕。

men·u [ˈmenjuː] *n.* (*pl.* ～*s*) ①菜单。②餐，饭菜；菜肴。*We had an admirable* ～. 我们吃了一顿美餐。

Men·u·hin [ˈmenjuin, ˈmenu*h*in] *n.* 梅纽因〔姓氏〕。

me·ow [mjuː, mjau] *vi.* ①(猫)咪咪地叫。②吐恶言毒语；〔美俚〕发牢骚。—*n.*①猫叫声。②怨言。

me·per·i·dine [məˈperidiːn] *n.*【药】哌替啶〔用作镇静剂和止痛药〕。

Me·ph·is·to·phe·le·an, -li·an [ˌmefistəˈfiːliən,-ljən] *a.* 靡菲斯特 (Mephistopheles) (似)的；狡猾刻毒的；恶魔般的。

Meph·is·toph·e·les [ˌmefisˈtɔfiliːz] *n.* 靡菲斯特〔歌德 (Goethe) 所作《浮士德》中的恶魔〕；魔鬼般的人；狡猾刻毒的人。

me·phit·ic, me·phit·i·cal [meˈfitik(əl)] *a.* 有毒的；有恶臭的；毒气的。*mephitic air* 二氧化碳气。

me·phi·tis [meˈfaitis] *n.* 臭气；毒气；恶臭。

me·pro·ba·mate [məˈprəubəmeit] *n.*【药】氨基丙二酯〔商品名称为眠尔通〕。

meq. = milliequivalent.

mer. = meridian; meridional.

mer·bro·min [məˈbrəumin] *n.* 汞溴红〔红汞水〕。

mer·can·tile [ˈməːkəntail] *a.* ①商人的，贸易的，商业的。②【经】重商主义的。*a* ～ *paper* 商业票据。*a* ～ *firm* 商店。*the* ～ *law* 商法。*the* ～ *marine* (全国)商船；(一国的)商船船员。*the* ～ *system [doctrine, theory]* 重商制度［主义］。

mer·can·til·ism [ˈməːkəntailizəm] *n.* ①重商主义。②商人性格；商业本位；商业理论［活动］；商用术语。

mer·can·til·ist [ˈməːkəntailist] *n.* 重商主义者。

mer·cap·tan [məˈkæptæn] *n.*【化】硫醇。

mer·cap·tide [məˈkæptaid] *n.*【化】硫醇盐。

mer·cap·to [məˈkæptəu] *a.*【化】巯基，氢硫基。

Mer·ca·tor [məˈkeitəː], **G.** 麦卡托〔1512—1594，佛兰德(Flanders)的地理学家，(地图)制图学家〕。～**'s chart** 麦卡托地图。～**'s projection** 麦卡托投影图法。

Mer·ce·des [ˈməːsidiːz] *n.* 默西迪丝〔女子名〕。

mer·ce·na·ry [ˈməːsinəri] *a.* 图利的，为了金钱工作的；被雇佣的。～ *attitude* 雇佣观念。— *n.* (外国的)雇佣兵 (= ～ troops).

mer·cer [ˈməːsə] *n.*〔英〕布商，(尤指)绸缎商人。

mer·cer·i·za·tion [ˌməːsəraiˈzeiʃən] *n.* 碱液处理，丝光处理［工艺］；碱化，浸碱作用。

mer·cer·ize [ˈməːsəraiz] *vt.* 对…施行碱液处理［丝光处理］。～*d cotton* 府绸，丝光棉布。

mer·cer·y [ˈməːsəri] *n.*〔英〕①绸布店；绸布业。②绸布类货物。

mer·chan·dise [ˈməːtʃəndaiz] *n.*〔集合词〕商品，货；〔古〕商业。*general* ～ 杂货。*the M- Marks Act*〔英〕商标法。— *vi.*〔美〕做买卖，做生意。—*vt.*〔美〕买卖；推销。**-dis·er** *n.*商人。

mer·chant [ˈməːtʃənt] *n.* ①商人；〔英〕批发商；(尤指)贸易商。②〔美〕零售商〔英国仅用于 *a coal* ～, *a wine* ～〕。③〔蔑〕家伙，人。④…狂。*a speed* ～ 乱用高速开汽车的人。*a* ～ *of death* 死亡商人〔指军火制造商〕。— *a.* 商人的；商业的。*the* ～ *marine [service]* (全国)商船；(一国)商船船员。*a* ～ *ship [vessel]* 商船。*a* ～ *bank*〔英〕证券银行。*a* ～ *captain* (商船的)船长；船主。*a* ～ *prince* 豪商。*the M- Queen* (意大利的)威尼斯市。*a* ～ *seaman* (商船的)船员。*the M- Shipping Act*〔英〕商船条例。*a* ～ *tailor* 兼售衣料的裁缝店。**-able** *a.* 可买卖的，有销路的。**-like** *a.* 象商人的。**-man** (*pl.* **-men**) 货船，商船；〔古〕商人。

Mer·cia [ˈməːʃə] *n.* 莫西亚〔原英格兰中部和南部的一个盎格鲁-撒克逊王国〕。

Mer·cian [ˈməːʃən] *a.* 莫西亚的；莫西亚人的；莫西亚方言的。— *n.* ①莫西亚人。②莫西亚古英语方言。③〔偶指〕(由莫西亚方言演变而来的)中世纪英语方言。

mer·ci·ful [ˈməːsiful] *a.* 仁慈的，温和的；(情形)良好的，顺利的；(处罚)宽大的。**-ly** *ad.* **-ness** *n.*

mer·ci·less [ˈməːsilis] *a.* 冷酷无情的，狠心的，残忍的。～ *blows* 无情打击。**-ly** *ad.* **-ness** *n.*

mer·cu·rate [ˈməːkjureit] *vt.*【化】使汞化，用汞处理。— *n.* 汞化产物。

mer·cu·ri·al [məːˈkjuəriəl] *a.* ①〔M-〕墨丘利 (Mercury) 神的；【天】水星的。②轻松的，活泼的；有机智的；三心二意的。③雄辩的；狡诈的；贼性的。④水银的，含水银的，汞的。～ *gaiety* 活泼开朗。～ *exchange rates* 变动不定的兑换率。*a* ～ *barometer* 水银气压计。*a* ～ *column* 水银柱。*a* ～ *gauge [barometer]* 水银气压计。～ *ointment* 含汞药膏。～ *poisoning* 水银［汞］中毒。～ *treatment* 水银疗法。— *n.* 水银剂，汞制剂。**-ly** *ad.* **-ism** *n.* 水银［汞］中毒。

mer·cu·ri·al·i·ty [ˌməːkjuəriˈæliti] *n.* 敏捷，活泼；易变，三心二意；多机智。

mer·cu·ri·al·ize [məːˈkjuəriəlaiz] *vt.* ①用水银处理；【医】对…施行汞剂疗法。②使活泼［轻松、敏捷、愉快］。

Mer·cu·ri·an [məːˈkjuəriən] *a.* 水星的；墨丘利 (Mercury)神的。

mer·cu·ric [məːˈkjuərik] *a.* 水银的，含水银的；【化】汞的；含二价汞的。～ **chloride** 氯化汞，升汞。～ **oxide**【化】氧化汞；一氧化汞；三仙丹。

mer·cu·rize [ˈməːkjuraiz] *vt.*【化】= mercurate.

mer·cu·ro·chrome [məˈkjuərəkrəum] *n.* ①【药】汞溴红，红汞。②〔M-〕红药水〔商标名〕。

mer·cu·rous [ˈməːkjurəs] *a.*【化】亚汞的；含一价汞的。～ *chloride* 氯化亚汞，甘汞。

mer·cu·ry [ˈməːkjuri] *n.* ①【化】汞，水银。②水银柱；水银剂；温度表；晴雨表。③活气，活泼；精神，元气。④〔M-〕【罗神】墨丘利〔诸神的使神；工匠、盗贼等的保护神〕；【天】水星。⑤〔谑〕使者；〔M-〕信使；报导者〔常用作报纸、杂志名〕。⑥【美体】赛跑家，径赛选手。⑦【植】山靛。*The* ～ *is rising.* 温度正在上升；市况正在好转；情绪好起来，高兴起来。*He has no* ～ *in him.* 他没有精神。～ **air pump** 汞(汽)泵〔排气用〕。～ **arc**【电】汞弧。～**-arc lamp** 水银弧光灯。～ **barometer [therometer]** 水银晴雨［温度］表。～ **chloride** ①氯化汞；升汞。(= mercuric chloride)。②甘汞；氯化亚汞 (=calomel)。～**-vapour lamp** 水银灯。～**-vapour rectifier** 汞汽［水银］整流器。

mer·cy [ˈməːsi] *n.* ①仁慈；怜悯；宽恕；恩惠。②幸运；侥幸；〔美口〕感谢。*the heart of the Goddess of Mercy* 菩萨心肠。*Mercy!* = *Mercy (up) on us!* 啊呀！我的天哪！*That is a* ～. 那真是幸运。**at the** ～ **of** 完全受…支配，任由…摆布，在…掌握中。**for** ～ = **for** ～**'s sake!** 请大发慈悲！请可怜可怜！求求您！**have** ～ **(up)on** = **show** ～ **to** 可怜…，怜悯。**leave to the tender mercies of**〔反〕任由…摆布，使吃…的苦头 (*He was left to the tender mercies of the landlord.* 他大受地主的虐待)。**What a** ～ **that ...!** 幸好，幸亏 (*What a* ～

[It is a ~] that you did not go! 幸亏你没去). ***without ~*** 狠着心肠,毫不容情地,残忍地. ~ **killing** 减少痛苦的处决; 无痛苦致死术 (= euthanasia). ~ **seat**【宗】约柜上的金板;上帝的御座.

mere[1] [miə] *a.* ①单单的,只,不过. ②全然的,纯粹的. *a ~ child* 仅仅是个孩子. *a ~ pretext* 不过(是)托辞[口实]. *That is the merest folly.* 那真糊涂透了. *of ~ motion*【法】自动的.

mere[2] [miə] *n.* 〔诗、方〕池沼.

mere[3] [miə] *n.* 〔英〕边境(线).

Mer·e·dith [ˈmeridiθ] *n.* 梅雷迪思〔男子名〕.

mere·ly [ˈmiəli] *ad.* 单; 只; 纯粹; 全然. ~ *a matter of form* 完全是一个形式问题. ***not ~ … but also*** 不仅…而且 (*She was not ~ beautiful, but (also) talented.* 她不仅长得美,而且有才干).

mer·en·gue [məˈreŋgei] *n.* ①梅伦格舞〔海地和多米尼加的一种交际舞〕. ②梅伦格舞曲.

mer·e·tri·cious [ˌmeriˈtriʃəs] *a.* ①〔古〕娼妓(一样)的. ②(装饰、文体等)耀眼的; 俗不可耐的, 俗气的. ③(论据等)虚夸的. **-ly** *ad.*

mer·e·trix [ˈmeritriks] *n.* (*pl.* ***meretrices*** [-traisiːz]) 娼妓.

mer·gan·ser [məːˈgænsə] *n.* (*pl.* *~s* 〔集合词〕*~*)【鸟】秋沙鸭.

merge [məːdʒ] *vt.* 吞没, 吸收; 使消失(在…中) (*in; into*);【法】合并(公司等)使并入, 使结合, 融合 (*into; with*). *All fear was ~d in curiosity.* 在好奇心驱使下忘了一切恐怖. —*vi.* 被吞没,被吸收, 没入, 消没在; 合并, 并入. *The twilight ~d into darkness.* 薄暮已消失在黑暗之中. ~ *with the masses* 同群众打成一片.

mer·gee [ˈməːdʒiː] *n.* 合并的一方.

mer·ged [məːdʒd] *a.* 〔美俚〕结了婚的.

mer·gence [ˈməːdʒəns] *n.* 没入,消失;合并,结合,融合.

merg·er [ˈməːdʒə] *n.* (企业等的)合并,并吞;结合;合并者(= mergence);【法】托拉斯 (= trust).

me·rid·i·an [məˈridiən] *n.* ①【天】子午圈[线]; 正午. ②顶点,绝顶;全盛期. *the prime [first] ~* 本初子午线, 格林威治子午线. *the ~ of life* 壮年. —*a.* 子午圈的; 正午的; 顶点的,绝顶的;全盛时期的. ***be calculated to [for] the ~ of*** 为了适合…的兴趣[能力、习惯等]. ~ **altitude** 中天高度. ~ **passage [transit]** 中天. ~ **sun** 正午的太阳.

me·rid·io·nal [məˈridiənl] *a.* ①子午圈[线]的; 最高的, 全盛的. ②南欧(人)的, 法国南部人的; 南方的. —*n.* 南欧人,(尤指)法国南部人.

me·ringue [məˈræŋ] *n.* ①(覆盖在糕、饼上烤熟的)蛋白糖霜. ②(盛冰淇淋、水果的)蛋白酥皮筒[卷]; 蛋白甜饼.

me·ri·no [məˈriːnəu] *n.* (*pl.* *~s*) (原产西班牙的)美利奴绵羊;美利奴羊毛;美利奴呢(衣);美利奴绒线.

mer·i·stem [ˈmeristem] *n.*【植】分生组织.

mer·it [ˈmerit] *n.* ①价值;美点,长处,优点. ②〔常 *pl.*〕功劳,功绩,功勋;成就;良好的品质[事实、行为];(学校里的)记功分〔罚分之对〕. ③〔常 *pl.*〕功过,功罪. ④〔*pl.*〕【法】法律意义[根据];是非曲直. *a man of ~* 有长处的人, 有功劳的人. *a certificate of ~* 奖状. *His teacher gave him ten ~s.* 老师给他记了十个功分. *the ~s and demerits of* …的优点和缺点; …的功过[得失]. ***according to one's ~s*** 按价值, 按资质. ***make a ~ of = take ~ to oneself for*** 把…当做自己的功劳宣传, 自夸…是自己的功劳. ***on one's own ~s*** 靠实力, 靠真价. ***on the ~s of the case*** 按事件的是非曲直. ***the order of [for] M-*** 〔英〕殊勋勋章. —*vt.* 有…的价值,值得…; 应受; 因功而得. ~ *reward* 应该受奖. ~ **roll** 成绩表, 赏罚表. ~ **system** (量才录用或提升的)人才制度.

mer·i·toc·ra·cy [ˌmeriˈtɔkrəsi] *n.* ①学术界名流. ②英才教育. ③能人统治. **-crat** *n.* 能人统治集团的一员. **-crat·ic** *a.*

mer·i·to·ri·ous [ˌmeriˈtɔːriəs] *a.* 有功助的,有功劳的;有价值的;可称赞的;值得奖励的. *a ~ service medal* 勋绩奖章. **-ly** *ad.* 可赞美. **-ness** *n.*

merl(e) [məːl] *n.* 〔Scot.〕【鸟】〔古〕= blackbird.

Mer·lin, Mer·lyn [ˈməːlin] *n.* ①默林〔男子名〕. ②亚瑟王 (King Arthur) 传说中的预言家,魔术师. ③〔m-〕【鸟】欧洲鸽鹰,灰背隼.

mer·lon [ˈməːlən] *n.* (筑城)城齿.

mer·maid [ˈməːmeid] *n.* (传说中的)美人鱼;美人鱼徽章;〔美〕女游泳健将.

mer·man [ˈməːmæn] *n.* (传说中的)雄性人鱼;〔美〕男子游泳健将.

mero- *comb. f.* 一部分;部分的.

mer·o·blast [ˈmerəblæst] *n.*【生】不全裂卵.

mer·o·blas·tic [ˌmerəˈblæstik] *a.*【遗传】不全裂卵的. **-al·ly** *ad.*

mer·o·crine [ˈmerəkrin, -krain, -kriːn] *a.* 局泌的,局部分泌腺的.

me·rog·o·ny [məˈrɔgəni] *n.*【生】无核卵发育, 卵片发育.

mer·o·hed·ral [ˌmerəˈhedrəl] *a.* (水晶)缺面体的.

mer·o·mor·phic [ˌmerəˈmɔːfik] *a.*【数】半纯的,有理型的,逊纯的.

mer·o·plank·ton [ˌmerəˈplæŋktən] *n.*【动】季节浮游生物.

-merous *suf.*【植】分成许多部分的: penta*merous* = 5-merous. 五基数的.

mer·o·zo·ite [ˌmerəˈzəuait] *n.*【生】裂殖子,裂体性芽胞.

mer·ri·ly [ˈmerili] *ad.* 快乐地,愉快地,高兴地.

Mer·ri·mac [ˈmeriˌmæk] *n.* ①梅里麦克〔美国南北战争时南部联邦的一艘装甲舰名〕. ②美国梅里麦克河 (= Merrimack).

mer·ri·ment [ˈmerimənt] *n.* 欢乐.

mer·ri·ness [ˈmerinis] *n.* 愉快,快活.

Mer·ritt [ˈmerit] *n.* 梅里特〔姓氏,男子名〕.

Mer·ry [ˈmeri] *n.* 梅丽〔女子名〕.

mer·ry [ˈmeri] *a.* (***-ri·er; -ri·est***) ①愉快的, 快活的; 有趣的,生动的;轻快的;激烈的. ②〔口〕微醉的. ***as ~ as a cricket [a grig, a lark]*** 非常快活. ***make ~*** 作乐,宴乐,逗乐. ***make ~ over*** 嘲弄,挖苦. ~ ***men*** (已往骑士或土匪首领的)随从, 侍从. ~ ***men of May*** 落潮时的危险潮流. ~**-andrew** 丑角,滑稽演员;笨人. ~ **dancers** 北极光. ~**-go-down** 〔口〕强烈的啤酒. ~**-go-round** 旋转木马;走马灯; 使人忙得团团转的事务;〔口〕蛛网式道路;〔美俚〕(对决定事项或接见客人的)故意拖延 (*get the ~-go-round* 〔美俚〕苦等,久等). ~**make** *vi.* 〔古〕快快活活玩,欢乐. ~**making** 欢乐, 喝酒作乐, 狂欢. ~**-run-round** 〔美〕= merry-go-round. ~**thought** (鸟胸的)叉骨 (= wishbone).

Mer·ton [ˈməːtn] *n.* 默顿〔姓氏〕.

Mer·vin [ˈməːvin] *n.* 默文〔男子名, Marvin 的异体〕.

me·sa [ˈmeisə] *n.* ①〔美〕台地, 方山. ②【无】台式晶体管.

mé·sal·liance [meiˈzæliəns] *n.* 〔F.〕和身分低的人缔结的婚姻.

mes·arch [ˈmezɑːk, mes-] *a.* ①【植】中始式的. ②【生态】中生演替的.

mes·cal [mesˈkæl] *n.* ①(墨西哥人爱喝的)龙舌兰酒. ②(其汁能制酒的)龙舌兰. ③【植】球顶仙人鞭〔其球状茎头叫 ~ button〕.

mes·ca·line [ˌmeskəliːn, -lin] *n.*【化】墨斯卡灵〔一种生物碱,用做幻觉剂〕.

mes·dames [meiˈdæm] 〔F.〕*madame* 的复数.

mes·de·moi·selles [ˌmeidəmwɑːˈzel] 〔F.〕*mademoiselle* 的复数.

me·seems [mi(:)ˈsi:mz] *vi.* *(p. -seemed)* 〔古〕据我想,我以为.

mes·em·bri·an·the·mum [miˌzembriˈænθimәm] *n.* 【植】松叶菊;日中花属.

mes·en·ceph·a·lon [ˌmesenˈsefәlɔn] *n.* 【解】中脑.

me·sen·chy·ma [miˈzeŋkimә] *n.* = mesenchyme.

mes·en·chyme [ˈmezәnkaim, ˈmes-] *n.* 【遗传】间(充)质. **-chy·mal** [meˈzeŋkimәl, mes-] *a.*

mes·en·ter·i·tis [ˌmezentiˈraitis, mes-] *n.* 【医】肠系膜炎.

mes·en·ter·on [meˈzentәrɔn, mes-] *n.* *(pl. -ter·a* [-ә]*)* 中肠(= midgut). **-ic** *a.*

mes·en·te·ry [ˈmesәntәri] *n.* 【解】肠系膜;隔膜.

mesh [meʃ] *n.* ①网眼;筛孔;〔*pl.*〕网,网状物;网络;网丝;铜纱;〔*pl.*〕法网. ②【机】(齿轮的)啮合. *a 60 ~ screen* (每英寸有)60孔的筛子. *a net with half-inch ~es* 半英寸孔的网. — *vt.* ①用网捕;使缠住. ②【机】(使)咬合,钩住*(with)*. ③编[织]网;使成网状. *~ a net* 编网. — *vi.* ①被网住,落网. ②紧密配合;【机】互相啮合*(with)*. ***be caught in ~es of the law*** 陷入法网. ***be in ~*** (齿轮)互相咬住. **~ knot** 单索花 (= sheet bend). **~work** 网状物,网.

Mesh·ed [ˈmeʃed; 美 mәˈʃed] *n.* 麦什德(即 Mashhad 马什哈德)〔伊朗城市〕.

me·shu·ga, me·shug·ga, me·shu·gah [mәˈʃugә] *a.* 〔俚〕疯狂的,发狂的,精神病的.

me·si·al [ˈmi:zjәl, ˈmezjәl] *a.* 中央的, 中间的, 中部的(*opp.* lateral). *the ~ plane* (动物体的)正中面.

me·sic [ˈmezik, ˈmes-; ˈmi:zik, -sik] *a.* ①【植】需中湿水分的. ②【生态】中湿的. ③【物】介子的;与介子有关的.

me·sit·y·lene [miˈsitәli:n] *n.* 【化】苿.

mes·jid [ˈmesdʒid] *n.* 伊斯兰教寺院 (= masjid).

mes·mer·ic [mezˈmerik] *a.* 催眠(术)的;使人迷惑的;难以抗拒的. **-i·cal·ly** *ad.*

mes·mer·ism [ˈmezmәrizәm] *n.* 催眠术;催眠状态;催眠力;难以抗拒的魅力. **-mer·ist** *n.* 催眠术师.

mes·mer·i·za·tion [ˌmezmәraiˈzeiʃәn] *n.* 施催眠术;催眠状态.

mes·mer·ize [ˈmezmәraiz] *vt.* 给…施行催眠术;迷惑;感化. **-r** *n.* 催眠者.

mesn·al·ty [ˈmi:nәlti] *n.* ①(英国古代)中层领主的土地. ②中层领主主(身份).

mesne [mi:n] *a.* 【法】中间的. *the ~ process* (诉讼的)中间手续[程序]. *the ~ profits* 中间收益. **~ lord** 中层封建领主.

meso- *comb.f.* 中央,中间,中,适.

mes·o·ben·thos [ˌmesәuˈbenθɔs, ˌmez-] *n.* 深海生物.

mes·o·blast [ˈmesәublɑ:st] *n.* 【生】= mesoderm.

mes·o·carp [ˈmesәkɑ:p] *n.* 【植】中果皮.

mes·o·ce·phal·ic [ˌmesәusiˈfælik, ˌmez-] *a.* 【解】具中等头型的;具颅指数在 76—80.9 之间的头颅的 (= mesocephalous). **-ceph·a·ly** [-ˈsefәli] *n.*

meso·chro·ic [ˌmesәuˈkrәuik, ˌmez-] *a.* 肤色在深浅之间的.

mes·o·cra·ni·al [ˌmesәuˈkreiniәl, ˌmez-] *a.* 具中颅的〔颅指数在 76—80.9 之间〕(= mesocranic). **-cra·ny** [-ˌkreini] *n.*

mes·o·crat·ic [ˌmesәuˈkrætik, ˌmez-] *a.* 【矿】中色的;包含 30—60% 的矿物的.

mes·o·derm [ˈmesәdә:m] *n.* 【生】中胚层.

mes·o·gas·tri·um [ˌmesәuˈgæstriәm, ˌmez-] *n.* *(pl. -tri·a* [-ә]*)* 【解】①胃系膜. ②中腹部. **-gas·tric** *a.*

mes·o·gle·a, mes·o·gloe·a [ˌmesәuˈgliә, ˌmez-] *n.* 【解】中胶层. **-gle·al, -gloe·al** *a.*

mes·o·lim·ni·on [ˌmesәuˈlimniәn, ˌmez-] *n.* 温水层 (= thermocline).

Mes·o·lith·ic [ˌmesәuˈliθik, ˌmez-] *a.* 中石器时代的.

me·som·er·ism [miˈsɔmәrizәm] *n.* ①【化】中介(现象);稳[缓]变异构(现象). ②【无】共振.

mes·on [ˈmesɔn, ˈmi:s-] *n.* ①【物】介子,重电子. ②【动】正中面. **~ factory** 介子工厂〔能产生强烈介子射线以探索原子核的粒子加速器〕. **-ic** *a.*

mes·o·neph·ros [ˌmesәuˈnefrɔs, ˌmez-] *n.* 【解】中肾. **-neph·ric** *a.*

mes·o·ni·um [miˈsәunjәm] *n.* 【物】介子素.

mes·o·pause [ˈmesәˌpɔ:z, ˈmez-] *n.* 【气】中间层顶.

mes·o·pe·lag·ic [ˌmesәupәˈlædʒik] *a.* 海洋中层的〔深约 650—3000 英尺〕.

mes·o·phyll [ˈmesәfil] *n.* 【植】叶肉,含绿组织;中形叶.

mes·o·phyl·lic [ˌmesәuˈfilik, ˌmez-] *a.* 【植】叶肉的(= mesophyllous).

mes·o·phyte [ˈmesәfait, ˈmez-] *n.* 【植】(在中等湿度下生长的)中生植物;中生代植物. **-phyt·ic** [-ˈfitik] *a.*

mes·o·plasm [ˈmesәplæzәm] *n.* 【生】中胚层质.

mes·o·plast [ˈmesәplɑ:st] *n.* 【生】细胞核.

Mes·o·po·ta·mi·a [ˌmesәupәˈteimjә, -miә] *n.* 美索不达米亚〔小亚细亚 Tigris 和 Euphrates 两河流域间的古王国,现今伊拉克所在地〕. **-mian** *a., n.* 美索不达米亚的;美索不达米亚人(的).

mes·o·some [ˈmesәsʌm] *n.* 【生】中间体,细胞膜中层.

mes·o·sphere [ˈmesәsfiә] *n.* 【气】中圈,中层,散逸层.

mes·o·the·li·al [ˌmesәuˈθi:liәl, -ˌmez] *a.* 【解】间皮的.

mes·o·the·li·o·ma [ˌmesәuˌθi:liˈәumә, -ˌmez] *n.* 【医】间皮瘤.

mes·o·the·li·um [ˌmesәuˈθi:liәm, ˌmez-] *n.* *(pl. -li·a* [-ә]*)* 【解】间皮.

mes·o·tho·rac·ic [ˌmesәuθɔ:ˈræsik, ˌmez-] *a.* 【动】(昆虫的)中胸的.

mes·o·tho·rax [ˌmesәuˈθɔ:ræks, -ˌmez] *n.* 【虫】中胸.

mes·o·tho·ri·um [ˌmesәuˈθɔ:riәm, ˌmez-] *n.* ①新钍. ②新钍-I 〔镭同位素 Ra^{228}〕. ③新钍-II 〔锕同位素 Ac^{228}〕.

mes·o·tron [ˈmesәtrɔn] *n.* = meson.

mes·o·tro·phy [ˈmesәˌtrɔfi] *n.* 【微】半自养,中间营养.

Mes·o·zo·a [ˌmesәuˈzәuә, -ˌmez] *n.* 〔*pl.*〕【动】中间动物〔原生动物与腔肠动物中间的一种动物〕.

Mes·o·zo·ic [ˌmesәuˈzәuik, -ˌmez] *n., a.* 【地】中生代(的),中生代岩石(的).

mes·quite, mes·quit [mesˈki:t, ˈmeski:t] *n.* 【植】①牧豆树属植物. ②螺丝豆〔牧豆树属植物的豆荚〕;螺丝豆树 (= screwbean).

mess [mes] *n.* ①(尤指流体的)食品;(给猎狗等吃的)混合饲料. ②混乱,纷乱;大杂烩;肮脏,污秽. ③过失,错误;困境. ④(尤指海陆军的)伙食团;集体用膳人员;〔无冠词〕会餐,聚餐;食堂;(普通的)餐,膳食,伙食. ⑤(鱼的)一网;〔英方、美〕一次挤得的牛奶. ⑥〔美俚〕笨人,邋遢鬼. *a complete ~* 一团糟. *the army's supplies and ~* 军队的给养和伙食. ***be at ~*** 在食堂吃饭. ***get into a ~*** 陷入困境;犯错误. ***go to ~*** 去食堂吃饭. ***in a ~*** ①肮脏,尽是泥. ②混乱,紊乱. ③困难. ***lose the number of one's ~*** 死,被杀死. ***make a ~ of*** 把…弄糟[弄坏]. ***make a ~ of it*** 把事情搞得一团糟. ***a ~ of pottage*** 付出巨大代价得到的物质享受;眼前小利. — *vt.* ①弄脏;搞乱,弄糟. ②〔古〕为…配给食物;给…供膳. ③妨碍;干扰. ④粗暴对待[处理]. — *vi.* ①供膳. ②集体用膳. ③搞乱. ④瞎摆弄;干涉. ***~ about*** 磨洋工;闲荡. ***~ around*** 〔美俚〕浪费时间;混(日子);乱管闲事. ***~ up*** 〔美俚〕陷入困境;弄糟(计划等);粗暴处理. **~ deck** 【海】住舱甲板〔船员吃饭处〕. **~ gear** 〔美〕吃饭用具〔刀、叉和匙子〕. **~ hall** 〔美〕食堂. **~ jacket** 短制服〔紧身短上衣,公共场所服务人员的制服或军便服〕. **~ kit** 【军】野战食具 (= **~ gear**). **~mate** 〔主水手语〕同吃饭的伙伴. **~ rack** 食橱. **~**

table(船内的)共同餐桌. ~**tin** (军用)饭盒. ~**-up**〔口〕混乱.

mes·sage [ˈmesidʒ] *n.* ①通信;口信;问候;祝词;讯,消息,情报,电报,通报;【物】信息;【生】遗传密码单位〔表明氨基酸合成某种蛋白质时的排列顺序〕. ②〔美〕(总统的)咨文. ③启示;教训;(预言者的)神示;要旨;寓言. ④(使者接受的)任务,使命. ⑤广告词句. *an oral [a verbal]* ~ 口信. *a wireless* ~ 无线电报. *a* ~ *to the nation* 告国人书. *a congratulatory* ~ 贺电,贺辞,献词. *a* ~ *centre* 通讯社;收发室. *a New Year* ~ 新年祝贺. ~ *rate* (电话的)计次价目. *State of the Unions M-* 〔美〕国情咨文. ***go on [do] a*** ~ 出外为人办事. ***leave a*** ~ 留一个话. ~ ***of greetings*** 贺电,贺信;祝词. ***send a person on a*** ~ 派人出去. — *vt.* 通知,通告;发信号告知.

mes·sa·line [ˌmesəˈliːn] *n.* 美色林全丝软缎.

mes·sei·gneurs [ˌmeseˈnjəːz] *n.* 〔F.〕 monseigneur 的复数.

mes·sen·ger [ˈmesindʒə] *n.* ①使者,送信人,邮递员,信差;【军】通信兵,传令兵. ②前驱;先驱者. ③顺着风筝线送到天空的纸片. ④【海】大轮索;传递(重索的)细索;引绳. ⑤【生】信使〔一种传递遗传信息的化学物质〕. *a corbie* ~ 一去不回的送信人;回得很晚的使者〔源出基督教《圣经》的《创世纪》〕. *Dawn is the* ~ *of day.* 黎明是白昼的先驱. *a King's [Queen's]* ~〔英〕送公文的差役. ~ **call** 传呼(电话). ~ **RNA**【生】信使核糖核酸. ~ **service**【军】传令勤务.

Mes·si·ah [miˈsaiə] *n.* ①〔the ~〕弥赛亚〔犹太人所期待的救世主〕. ②【基督教】救世主,基督. ③〔m-〕(人民、国家等所期待的)救星,解放者. **mes·si·an·ic** [ˌmæsiˈænik] *a.* 救世主的;以救世主自居的.

Mes·sias [məˈsaiəs] *n.* 〔m-〕(人民、国家等所期待的)救星,解放者 (= Messiah).

mes·sieurs [ˈmesəz] *n.* 〔*pl.*〕〔F.〕 monsieur 的复数〔略作 Messrs.〕.

Mes·si·na [meˈsiːnə] *n.* 墨西拿. ***the Strait of*** ~ (意大利与西西里岛间的)墨西拿海峡.

Messrs. [ˈmesəz] = Messieurs.

mes·suage [ˈmeswidʒ] *n.*【法】宅院.

mess·y [ˈmesi] *a.* ***(mess·i·er; -i·est)*** 污秽的,肮脏的. *a* ~ *job* 脏活;难搞的工作.

mes·ti·zo [mesˈtiːzəu] *n.* 混血人〔尤指印第安人与白人的混血人〕.

MET = Middle Europe Time 中欧时间.

met [met] meet 的过去式及过去分词.

met. = ①metaphor. ②metaphysics. ③meteorological. ④metropolitan.

met(a)-, meth- *pref.* 后;间,中;同;变;亚;元(等). ★元音前用 met-; 辅音前用 meta-; 送气音(aspirate)前用 meth-.

me·tab·a·sis [meˈtæbəsis] *n.* ***(pl. -ses*** [-siːz]***)*** ①【医】变症,转移;病状转变. ②【修】主题[题材]转移.

met·a·bol·ic [ˌmetəˈbɔlik] *a.* ①变化的,变形的. ②【生】新陈代谢的,代谢作用的. ~ **nucleus** 静止核. ~ **stage** 代谢期. ~ **water**【生】同化水.

me·tab·o·lism, me·tab·o·ly [meˈtæbəlizəm, meˈtæbeli] *n.*【生】新陈代谢,代谢作用.

me·tab·o·lite [miˈtæbəlait] *n.*【生化】代谢物.

me·tab·o·lize [məˈtæbəlaiz] *vt., vi.* ***(-lized; -liz·ing)*** (使发生)代谢变化. **-liz·a·ble** *a.*

me·tab·o·lous [ˌməˈtæbələs] *a.*【生】变态的;变质的;变形的.

met·a·car·pus [ˌmetəˈkɑːpəs] *n.* ***(pl. -pi*** [-pai]***)***【解】掌,(尤指)掌骨. **-car·pal** *a.*

met·a·cen·tre, 〔Am.〕 **met·a·cen·ter** [ˈmetəˌsentə] *n.* (浮力的)定倾中心. **-tric** *a.*

met·a·chem·is·try [ˌmetəˈkemistri] *n.* 原子结构化学;超级化学.

met·a·chro·ma·tism [ˌmetəˈkrəumətizəm] *n.*【医】变色(反应).

met·a·chro·sis [ˌmetəˈkrəusis] *n.*【动】变色(机能).

met·a·gal·ax·y [ˈmetəˌgæləksi] *n.*【天】总星系,宇宙. **-lac·tic** [ˌmetəgəˈlæktik] *a.*

met·age [ˈmiːtidʒ] *n.* 容量[重量]的官方检定;(容量、重量)检定费.

met·a·gen·e·sis [ˌmetəˈdʒenisis] *n.*【生】(有性生殖与无性生殖)世代交替. **-gen·et·ic** [ˌmetədʒiˈnetik] *a.*

me·tag·na·thous [məˈtægnəθəs] *a.* ①(交喙鸟等)下颚骨尖交叉的. ②交嘴的. **-na·thism** *n.*

met·al [ˈmetl] *n.* ①金属;金属制品;金属合金. ②【化】金属元素 (*opp.* alloy);金属性. ③【徽】金色;银色. ④【海】(全舰)炮数;(一次发出的)炮火力. ⑤铸铁熔液;熔解玻璃. ⑥(铺路的)碎石料〔通常叫 road ~〕. ⑦〔*pl.*〕〔英〕铁轨. ⑧成色,成分;勇气;气质;根性. ⑨【印】活字金;排好活字的版. ⑩〔英〕〔总称〕【军】坦克,装甲车. *base* ~*s* 贱金属〔铜、铁、铅等〕;基底金属;碱金属. *heavy* ~*s* 重金属;〔总称〕重型坦克[装甲车];重炮;巨弹;强敌. *light* ~*s* 轻金属. *noble [perfect, precious]* ~*s* 贵金属. *He is of true* ~. 他是一个真正有勇气的人. ***run off [leave] the*** ~***s*** (火车)出轨. — *vt.* (〔英〕***-ll-***) 用金属包;用碎石铺(路面). *a* ~*ed road* 碎石路. ~ **ceramic** 金属陶瓷. ~ **lath** 金属网,钢丝网. ~. **master [negative]** 录声主盘. ~ **positive** 第一模盘. ~**ware** 金属器皿〔如厨房用具等〕.

metal(l). = metallurgical; metallurgy.

met·al·de·hyde [miˈtældəhaid] *n.*【化】介乙醛,低聚乙醛.

met·a·lin·guis·tics [ˌmetəliŋˈgwistiks] *n. pl.* 〔动词用单数〕语言文化因素学〔研究语言和文化的其他因素之间的关系〕.

met·al·ize [ˈmetəlaiz] *vt.* = metallize.

me·tal·lic [miˈtælik] *a.* 金属的;金属性的,金属质的;金属制的. ~ *currency* 金属硬币,硬币. ~ *lustre* 金属光泽. ~ *prints* 金属粉印花布. *a* ~ *pile* 伏打电池. ~ *soap*【化】金属皂. *the* ~ *standard*【经】金银本位. **-li·cal·ly** *ad.*

met·al·lide [ˈmetəlaid] *vt.* 电解电镀.

met·al·lid·ing [ˈmetəlaidiŋ] *n.* 电解电镀法.

met·al·lif·er·ous [ˌmetəˈlifərəs] *a.* 产金属的;含金属的. ~ *mines* 金属矿山.

met·al·line [ˈmetlin, ˈmetəˈlain] *a.* ①似金属的;金属质的;含金属的. ②含金属盐的.

met·al·list, met·al·ist [ˈmetlist] *n.* ①金属工. ②主张使用硬币者.

met·al·lize [ˈmetəlaiz] *vt.* ①用金属(或金属化合物)处理;使金属化. ②使(橡皮)硬化. ③喷镀金属(粉)于;使导体化. **-za·tion** [ˌmetəlaiˈzeiʃən] *n.* 敷金属(法),金属喷镀(法).

met·al·lo·graph [miˈtæləgrɑːf, -græf] *n.* ①(装有照相机的)金相显微镜. ②(金属表面的)显微照片;射线[电子]显微照片.

met·al·log·ra·phy [ˌmetəˈlɔgrəfi] *n.* 金相学.

met·al·loid [ˈmetəlɔid] *a.* 似金属的;非金属的. — *n.* 非金属;类金属,准金属.

met·al·lo·scope [miˈtæləuskəup] *n.* 金相显微镜.

met·al·lur·gic, met·al·lur·gi·cal [ˌmetəˈləːdʒik, -dʒikəl] *a.* 冶金(学)的;冶金术的. ~ *coal* 冶金煤,炼焦煤. ~ *coke* 冶金焦炭. ~ *industry* 冶金工业. **-gi·cal·ly** *ad.*

met·al·lur·gist [meˈtælədʒist] *n.* 冶金学家.

met·al·lur·gy [meˈtælədʒi] *n.* 冶金;冶金学;冶金术.

met·al·work [ˈmetlwəːk] *n.* 金属制品[制造]. **-er** 金属制造工. **-ing** 金属制造;金属加工.

met·a·math·e·mat·ics [ˌmetəˌmæθiˈmætiks] *n. pl.* 〔动词用单数〕数理哲学.

met·a·mer [ˈmetəmiə] *n.* 【化】位变异构体；【植】单体；【物】条件等色.
met·a·mere [ˈmetəmiə] *n.* ①= metamer. ②【动】体节,分裂片.
met·a·mer·ic [ˌmetəˈmerik] *a.* ①【化】位变异构的. ②【动】分节的. **-i·cal·ly** *ad.*
me·tam·er·ism [meˈtæmərizəm] *n.* ①【化】位变异构(现象)；同分异构性. ②【动】体节分裂,分节(现象). ③【物】条件配色.
met·a·mor·phic [ˌmetəˈmɔːfik] *a.* ①变化的,变形的；改变结构的. ②【地】变成的,变性的，变质的. ～ *rock* 变质岩.
met·a·mor·phism [ˌmetəˈmɔːfizəm] *n.* ①【地】变质(作用). ②变态,变形,变化.
met·a·mor·phose [ˌmetəˈmɔːfəuz] *vt.* 使变形[质]；使变成 *(to; into)*. *a* ～*d leaf* 变态叶. — *vi.* 变形；变质.
met·a·mor·pho·sis [ˌmetəˈmɔːfəsis] *n.* *(pl.* *-ses* [-siːz]*)* 变形,变状；(一般)变质；【生】变态.
met·a·neph·ros [ˌmetəˈnefrɔs] *n.* *(pl. -roi* [rɔi]*)* 【解】后肾. **-neph·ric** *a.*
met·aph. =metaphor(ical)；metaphysical；metaphysics.
met·a·phase [ˈmetəfeiz] *n.* 【生】中期〔细胞分裂的一个时期〕.
Met·a·phen [ˈmetəfen] *n.* 袂塔酚〔一种防腐剂商标名〕.
met·a·phor [ˈmetəfə] *n.* 【修】隐喻,暗喻〔the curtain of night 之类〕.
met·a·phor·i·cal [ˌmetəˈfɔrikəl] *a.* 隐喻的； **-ly** *ad.* 用隐喻；用比喻.
met·a·phos·phate [ˌmetəˈfɔsfeit] *n.* 偏磷酸盐.
met·a·phos·phor·ic [ˌmetəfɔsˈfɔːrik] *a.* ～ **acid** 偏磷酸,二缩原磷酸.
met·a·phrase [ˈmetəfreiz] *vt.* ① 逐字翻译,直译 (*cf.* paraphrase). ②修改…的词句. ③〔古〕以诗体翻译. — *n.* ①直译,逐字逐句的翻译. ②〔古〕诗体翻译.
met·a·phrast [ˈmetəˌfræst] *n.* 改写者〔如将散文改写为诗的人〕.
met·a·phras·tic [ˌmetəˈfræstik] *a.* 直译的.
met·a·phys·ic [ˌmetəˈfizik] *n.* 形而上学；玄学；玄学体系. — *a.* = metaphysical.
met·a·phys·i·cal [ˌmetəˈfizikəl] *a.* ①形而上学的；玄学的. ②超自然的；先验的，超感觉的. ③玄奥的；抽象的；穿凿入微的，过分细腻的. **-ly** *ad.*
met·a·phy·si·cian, met·a·phys·i·cist [ˌmetəfiˈziʃən, -ˈfizist] *n.* 形而上学家；玄学家.
met·a·phys·i·cize [ˌmetəˈfizisaiz] *vi.* 形而上学地思维[研究、讲、写等].
met·a·phys·ics [ˌmetəˈfiziks] *n. pl.* 〔作单数用〕形而上学,玄学 (*opp.* dialectics)；纯抽象的空论；空谈.
met·a·pla·sia [ˌmetəˈpleiʒə] *n.* ①【生】组织转化. ②组织变形〔如软骨的骨化〕. **-plas·tic** [-ˈplæstik] *a.*
met·a·plasm [ˈmetəplæzəm] *n.* 【语】词形变化；【生】后成质 (*cf.* protoplasm).
met·a·pol·i·ti·cian [ˌmetəˌpɔliˈtiʃən] *n.* 〔常蔑〕形而上学政治学家.
met·a·pol·i·tics [ˌmetəˈpɔlitiks] *n.* 〔常蔑〕形而上学政治学. **-lit·i·cal** *a.*
met·a·po·si·tion [ˌmetəpəˈziʃən] *n.* 【化】间位.
met·a·pro·tein [ˌmetəˈprəutiːn] *n.* 【生化】变性蛋白.
met·a·psy·chol·o·gy [ˌmetəsaiˈkɔlədʒi] *n.* 心理玄学.
met·a·scope [ˈmetəskəup] *n.* 【物】①红外线指示器. ②(借投射红外线能在荧光屏上看见黑暗中物体的一种)红外线望远镜.
met·a·se·quoi·a [ˈmetəsiˈkwɔiə] *n.* 【植】水杉.
met·a·sil·i·cate [ˌmetəˈsilikit] *n.* 【化】硅酸盐.
met·a·so·ma·tism [ˌmetəˈsəumətizm] *n.* 【地】交代(作用),交代变质(作用). **-mat·ic** [-səuˈmætik] *a.*
met·a·so·ma·to·sis [ˌmetəˌsəuməˈtəusis] *n.* = metasomatism.
met·a·some [ˈmetəsəum] *n.* 【地】代替矿物,交代矿物；新成体.
met·a·sta·ble [ˌmetəˈsteibl] *a.* 【化】亚稳的，准稳的. ～ **atom** 亚稳原子. **-bil·i·ty** [-ˈbiliti] *n.* 亚稳度.
me·tas·ta·sis [meˈtæstəsis] *n.* *(pl. -ses* [-siːz]*)* ①【医】(病毒)转移. ②【生】新陈代谢. ③【地】同质蜕变. ④【修】(话题)急转，(主题)急变. ⑤〔罕〕变形，变态. **-stat·ic** *a.*
me·tas·ta·size [məˈtæstəˌsaiz] *vi.* *(-sized; -siz·ing)* 【医】(癌等向身体其他部位)转移.
met·a·tar·sal [ˌmetəˈtɑːsəl] *n., a.* 跖骨(的).
met·a·tar·sus [ˌmetəˈtɑːsəs] *n.* *(pl. -si* [-sai]*)* 【解】跖骨；【虫】跗基节；【鸟】跗跖.
me·tath·e·sis [meˈtæθəsis] *n.* *(pl. -ses* [-siːz]*)* ①【语】换位 (作用)；换位构成的词. ②【医】病变移位法. ③【化】复分解,置换(作用)；易位(作用). **-thet·i·cal** *a.*
met·a·tho·rax [ˌmetəˈθɔːræks] *n.* 【虫】后胸.
me·tat·ro·phy [miˈtætrɔfi] *n.* ①(菌类等的)寄生吸食；后生营养. ②【医】营养障碍,营养异常.
met·a·xy·lem [ˌmetəˈzailem] *n.* 【植】后生木质部.
mé·ta·yage [ˈmeteijɑːʒ] *n.* 〔F.〕分益佃耕制.
mé·ta·yer [miˈteiə] *n.* 〔F.〕分益佃农.
met·a·zo·an [ˌmetəˈzəuən] *n., a.* 【动】后生动物(的).
Met·calfe [ˈmetkɑːf] *n.* 梅特卡夫〔姓氏〕.
Metch·ni·koff [ˈmetʃnikɔf], **Elie.** 梅奇尼可夫〔1845—1916,俄国生物学家、细菌学家〕.
Met Co = meteorological company 〔美〕气象连.
mete[1] [miːt] *vt.* ①〔诗〕量，测量. ②评定(功过)；派定，分给. ～ *out rewards* 给予报酬.
mete[2] [miːt] *n.* 境界；界石. ～*s and bounds* 【法】边界，分界.
met·em·pir·ics [ˌmetemˈpiriks], **met·em·pir·i·cism** [ˌmetemˈpirisizəm] *n.* 【哲】先验主义，先验论. **-pir·i·cal** *a.* (*opp.* empirical).
met·em·pir·i·cist [ˌmetemˈpirisist] *n.* 先验论者.
met·em·psy·cho·sis [ˌmetempsiˈkəusis] *n.* *(pl. -ses* [-siːz]*)* 【宗】(灵魂的)轮回,转生.
met·en·ceph·a·lon [ˌmetenˈsefəˌlɔn] *n.* *(pl. -la* [-lə]*)* 【解】后脑. **-phal·ic** [-səˈfælik] *a.*
me·te·or [ˈmiːtjə] *n.* ①流星. ②(流星的)曳光；昙花一现的东西. ③〔古、罕〕大气现象.
me·te·or. = meteorology.
me·te·or·ic [ˌmiːtiˈɔrik] *a.* ①大气的；气象上的；流星的，陨星的. ②流星似的；使人眼花缭乱的；闪烁的；昙花一现的，迅速的. ～ *iron* 陨铁. *a* ～ *shower* 流星雨. *a* ～ *stone* 陨石. *the* ～ *theory of nebula* 星云流星说. *water* ～ 天落水,大气水. *a* ～ *career* 昙花一现的生涯.
me·te·or·ite, me·te·or·o·lite [ˈmiːtjərait, ˈmiːtjərəlait] *n.* 陨星；陨石,陨铁.
me·te·or·it·ic [ˌmiːtiəˈritik] *a.* 【地】陨石的.
me·te·or·it·ics [ˌmiːtjəˈritiks] *n. pl.* 〔用作 *sing.* 或 *pl.*〕陨星学,流星学.
me·te·or·o·graph [ˌmiːtiˈɔːrəgrɑːf, -græf；ˈmiːtiːərə-] *n.* 气象计. **-graph·ic** *a.*
me·te·or·oid [ˈmiːtjərɔid] *n.* 流星体,陨星体. **-al** *a.*
me·te·or·o·log·ic, -i·cal [ˌmiːtjərəˈlɔdʒik(əl), -tiə-] *a.* 气象的，气象学(上)的. *a* ～ *code* 气象符号. *a* ～ *observatory* 气象台. *the M- Office* 〔英〕气象台. *a* ～ *report* 天气预报. *a* ～ *station* 气象(观测)站. **-ly** *ad.*
me·te·or·ol·o·gist [ˌmiːtjəˈrɔlədʒist, -tiə-] *n.* 气象学家.
me·te·or·ol·o·gy [ˌmiːtjəˈrɔlədʒi] *n.* 气象学；(某一地区的)气象(状态).
me·ter[1] [ˈmiːtə] *n.* ①测量仪表,计量器；计,表. ②计量人；计量官. *a dry [wet]* ～ 干[湿]式煤气表. *an electric* ～ 电表. *a gas* ～ 气量计；煤气表. *a water* ～ (自来)

水表。— *vt.* 用表计算[测量、记录]。~ **maid** 处理违犯交通规则[如停车超时,乱过马路等]的女警察。~**ed mail** 收费邮件[以现金代邮票的邮件,收费数目用戳子盖在信封上]。

me·ter[2] [ˈmiːtə] *n.* [美] = metre.

-meter *suf.* ①…计,…表: bar*ometer*, therm*ometer*; ped*ometer*; gas*ometer*, speed*ometer*. ②[美] 米: kil*ometer*. ③【韵】音步: hex*ameter*.

me·ter·age [ˈmiːtəridʒ] *n.* 量度,测度;用度费用。

met·e·strus [metˈiːstrəs] *n.*【动】动情后期。

mete-wand, mete-yard [ˈmiːtwɔnd, ˈmiːtjɑːd] *n.* [英] 评价的标准。

meth- = met(a)-.

Meth. = Methodist.

meth [meθ] *n.* [美俚]甲安非他明 [一种兴奋剂 = methamphetamine]。

meth·ac·ry·late [meθˈækrəleit] *n.* 异丁烯酸盐[酯],甲基丙烯酸盐[酯]。~ **resin** 异丁烯酸酯树脂,甲基丙烯酸酯树脂。

meth·a·cryl·ic acid [ˌmeθəˈkrilik] 异丁烯酸;甲基丙烯酸。

meth·a·done [ˈmeθədəun] *n.*【药】美沙酮 [一种镇痛药]。

meth·ane [ˈmeθein] *n.*【化】甲烷,沼气。~ **series**【化】甲烷系。

meth·a·nol [ˈmeθənɔl, -nəul] *n.*【化】甲醇,木醇。

Meth·e·drine [ˈmeθidriːn] 脱氧麻黄碱的商标。— *n.* [m-] 脱氧麻黄碱[用做解除忧郁、疲劳的药物]。

me·theg·lin [miˈθeglin] *n.* 蜂蜜酒。

met·he·mo·glo·bin [metˈhiːməˌgləubin, -ˈhemə-] *n.*【生化】正铁血红蛋白。

me·the·na·mine [məˈθiːnəmiːn, -min] *n.* 亚甲四胺,乌洛托品[用于橡胶、药品、炸药的制造]。

me·thinks [miˈθiŋks] *(p. methought) vi.* [无人称动词][古] 我想,据我看来(=it seems to me)。

me·thi·o·nine [meˈθaiəniːn] *n.*【化】蛋氨酸,甲硫(基丁)氨酸[用做药品]。

metho-, meth- *comb. f.* 甲基: *metho*xide.

meth·od [ˈmeθəd] *n.* ①方法,方式;顺序。②(思想、言谈上的)条理,规律,秩序。③【生】分类法。④[M-]【剧】溶入法[指演员完全溶入角色的精湛演技]。*the cut and trial* ~ 试凑法。*the zero [null]* ~ 衡消法。*the oral* ~ 口授法。*a man of* ~ 有条有理的人。*There's* ~ *in his madness.* 他虽似疯狂其实颇有理性。*work with* ~ 照手续[规矩]办事。

me·thod·ic, me·thod·i·cal [miˈθɔdik, -ikəl] *a.* 有次序的,有组织的;有计划的,有条不紊的,有一定方式的。**-i·cal·ly** *ad.*, **-i·cal·ness** *n.*

Meth·od·ism [ˈmeθədizəm] *n.* ①【宗】卫理公会派(教义、仪式)。②[m-] 严守法则;墨守成规。

Meth·od·ist [ˈmeθədist] *n.* ①【宗】卫理公会教徒。②[m-][蔑] 在宗教上极严格的人。③[m-] 方法论者;【生】分类学家。— *a.* = Methodistical.

Meth·o·dis·tic, Meth·o·dis·ti·cal [ˌmeθəˈdistik, -tikəl] *a.* ①卫理公会派的。②[m-] 有次序的,循规蹈矩的,一丝不苟的,严格的。

meth·od·ize [ˈmeθədaiz] *vt.* 为…定次序 [规矩,方式等],使(工作等)有条理,给…分门类。

meth·od·ol·o·gist [ˌmeθəˈdɔlədʒist] *n.* 方法学家。

meth·od·ol·o·gy [ˌmeθəˈdɔlədʒi] *n.* 方法学,方法论;研究法;【生】分类法。**-log·i·cal** [ˌmeθədəˈlɔdʒikəl] *a.*

meth·o·trex·ate [ˌmeθəˈtrekseit] *n.*【药】甲氨蝶呤钠[用以治白血病和肿瘤]。

me·thought [miˈθɔːt] methinks 的过去式。

meth·ox·ide [meˈθɔksaid] *n.* 甲醇盐;甲氧基金属;甲氧化物 (= methylate).

meth·ox·y·chlor [məˈθɔksiklɔː] *n.*【化】甲氧氯;甲氧滴滴涕[杀蚊蝇剂]。

Me·thu·se·lah [miˈθjuːzələ] *n.* ①麦修彻拉 [《圣经》中的长寿者]。②[m-] 大酒瓶[容量为 6.5 夸脱]。

meth·yl [ˈmeθil, ˈmiːθail] *n.*【化】甲基。~ **acetate** 醋酸甲酯。~ **alcohol** 甲醇,木醇。~ **benzene** 甲苯 (= toluene)。~ **blue** 甲基蓝。~ **bromide** 甲基溴,溴代甲烷。~ **chloride** 甲基氯,氯代甲烷。~ **violet** 龙胆紫 (= gentian violet).

meth·yl·al [ˌmeθiˈlæl, ˈmeθilæl] *n.*【化】甲缩醛,甲醛缩二甲醇[用做溶剂、麻醉剂]。

meth·yl·a·mine [ˌmeθiləˈmiːn, -ˈlæmiːn] *n.*【化】甲胺。

meth·yl·ate [ˈmeθileit] *vt.* 使甲基化,向…导入甲基[加入甲醇]。— *n.* 甲基化产物;甲醇金属。~**d spirit(s)** 甲基化酒精,用甲醇变性的酒精。

meth·yl·ene [ˈmeθiliːn] *n.*【化】甲叉,甲撑,亚甲。~ **blue**【化】(碱性)亚甲蓝。

me·thyl·ic [miˈθilik] *a.* 甲基的,得自甲基的,含甲基的。

me·tic·u·lous [miˈtikjuləs] *a.* ①过分注意琐事的,小心翼翼的,胆小的。②细致的,明察秋毫的。~ *cares* 无微不至的关怀。*careful and* ~ *calculation* 精打细算。**-ly** *ad.*

mé·tier [ˈmeitjei] *n.* [F.] 职业,生意,工作;专长(尤指得心应手的工作)。

mé·tis [meiˈtiːs] *n.* [F.] *(fem. mé·tisse* [meiˈtiːs]) (尤指加拿大的) 白种人和印第安人的混血人;[美] 黑白混血人;【动】杂种。

me·tol [ˈmiːtɔl] *n.* 甲氨基酚,密妥耳[显象药]。

me·ton. = metonymy.

Me·ton·ic [meˈtɔnik] *a.* (公元前五世纪雅典天文学家) 梅通 (Meton) 的,梅通发见的。*the* ~ *cycle* 梅通周期。

met·o·nym [ˈmetənim] *n.* 换喻词,转喻词。

me·ton·y·my [miˈtɔnimi] *n.*【修】换喻,转喻 [如用 crown 表 king, 用 sword 表 war]。**-nym·ic, -i·cal** *a.*

me-too [ˈmiːˈtuː] *a.* [美口] 行仿效计策的;持仿效态度的(尤指政客仿效其政敌的策略的态度)。— *vt.* [美口] 模仿,同意(对方的政见等)。**-ism** *n.*

met·ope [ˈmetəup] *n.*【建】排档间饰。

me·top·ic [miˈtɔpik] *a.*【解】额的;前面的。

met·o·pon [ˈmetəpɔn] *n.*【药】米托本,甲基二氢吗啡酮[一种麻醉镇痛剂]。

met·o·pos·copy [ˌmetəˈpɔskəpi] *n.* 相学,观相术,骨相学。

Met. R. = Metropolitan Railway [英] 首都地下铁道。

me·tral·gi·a [miˈtrældʒiə] *n.*【医】子宫痛。

Met·ra·zol [ˈmetrəzɔl] *n.*【药】五甲烯四氮唑[一种中枢神经系刺激剂]。

me·tre[1] [ˈmiːtə] *n.*【韵】韵律;格律;(诗的)音步形式;【乐】拍子。

me·tre[2] [ˈmiːtə] *n.* 米。*a running* ~ 直线米。~ **bridge** 滑线电桥。

me·ter-kil·o·gram (me) -sec·ond [ˈmiːtəˈkiləgræm ˈsekənd] *a.* 米公斤秒制。

met·ric [ˈmetrik] *a.* ①公制的,米制的;十进制的;习惯于用公制的。②度量的。~ *space* 距离空间。*a* ~ *ton* 公吨 (= 1000 公斤)。*the* ~ *system* 米制,公制。~ **count**【纺】公制支数。~ **hundredweight** 公担[等于 50 公斤的一种衡制]。~ **mile**【体】一千五百米。~ **space** 度量空间。

met·ri·cal [ˈmetrikəl] *a.* ①韵律的,格律的;诗的。②测[度]量(用)的。~ *compositions* 韵文,诗。*a* ~ *romance* 韵文小说。~ *geometry* 测量几何。**-ly** *ad.*

me·tri·cian, met·rist [miˈtriʃən, ˈmetrist] *n.* 韵文作者;精于韵律者;韵律学家。

met·rics [ˈmetriks] *n.* 韵律学,诗作法。

met·ri·fy [ˈmetrifai] *vt., vi. (-fied; -fy·ing)* ①(使) 采用十进制。②用韵律写;(把…)写成诗;改(散文)成诗。**-fic·a·tion** [ˌmetrifiˈkeiʃən] *n.* 采用十进制。

me·tri·tis [miˈtraitis] *n.*【医】子宫炎。

Met·ro [ˈmetrəu] *n.* 〔英〕①=the Metropolitan Railway. ②地下铁道. ③〔m-〕大都市地方政府. — *a.* 〔m-〕大都市的.
Met·ro·lin·er [ˈmetrəlainə] *n.* (行驶于华盛顿与纽约之间的)快速火车.
me·tro·log·i·cal [ˌmetrəˈlɔdʒikəl] *a.* 计量学的.
me·trol·o·gist [miˈtrɔlədʒist] *n.* 计量学家; 度量衡工作者.
me·trol·o·gy [miˈtrɔlədʒi] *n.* 计量学〔制〕; 度量衡学〔制〕.
me·tro·ma·ni·a [ˌmetrəˈmeinjə] *n.* 作诗狂.
met·ro·nome [ˈmetrənəum] *n.* 【乐】节拍器. ***repeat like a*** ~ 机械地重复.
met·ro·nom·ic [ˌmetrəˈnɔmik] *a.* 节拍器的; 象节拍器的.
me·tro·nym·ic [ˌmiːtrəˈnimik, ˌme-] *a.* 来自母亲(或女系祖先)的姓名的 (*opp.* patronymic). *a* ~ *family* 母姓家庭. ~ *tribes* 母姓部落.
me·tron·ymy [meˈtrɔnimi] *n.* 【社】母姓制.
me·trop·o·lis [miˈtrɔpəlis] *n.* ①首都. ②【宗】大主教教区. ③(产业、艺术等的)中心; 主要都市,都会. ④【希腊史】殖民地的母国. ⑤【生】种属中心地. *the M-* 〔英〕伦敦. *a* ~ *of commerce* 商业中心.
met·ro·pol·i·tan [ˌmetrəˈpɔlitən] *a.* ①首都的; 主要城市的. ②大主教教区的. ③宗主国的. *the* ~ *district* 首都行政区. *the M- Railway* 〔英〕伦敦地下铁道. *the* ~ *state* 宗主国. *the* ~ *(bishop)* 大主教. — *n.* 大城市人; 有大城市气派的人; 大主教.
met·ro·pol·i·tan·ize [ˌmetrəˈpɔlitənaiz] *vt.* ***(-ized; -iz·ing)*** 使大都会化; 使具有大都会特点. **-tan·ism** *n.* 大都会主义; 大都会生活的特点; 大都会对其居民的影响. **-tani·za·tion** [ˌmetrəˌpɔlitəˈnaizeiʃən] *n.*
me·tror·rha·gi·a [ˌmiːtrəˈreidʒiə] *n.* 【医】子宫出血,血崩症.
-metry *suf.* …测定法〔术〕,…测定学: geo*metry*.
met·tle [ˈmetl] *n.* 气质,脾性,性格; 热情,勇气; 精神,气概. *a man of* ~ 有气概的人. ***be (up) on one's*** ~ 奋发,鼓起勇气. ***put [set] sb. to [on, upon] his*** ~ 激励〔鼓励〕某人.
met·tled, met·tle·some [ˈmetld, ˈmetlsəm] *a.* 有精神的,精神饱满的,勇敢的,威风凛凛的. **-ly** *ad.*
Metz [mets] *n.* 梅斯〔法国城市〕.
me·um [ˈmiːəm] *pro.* 〔L.〕我的东西. ~ ***et tu·um*** [etˈtjuːəm] 〔L.〕我的和你的 (= mine and thine); 人我之别; 各自所有权.
meu·nière [muˈnjeə] *a.* 〔F.〕黄油炸鱼的〔鱼沾上面粉,用黄油炸后撒上柠檬汁和芥末〕.
MEV, Mev, mev, m.e.v. = million electron volts 兆电子伏(特),百万电子伏(特).
MEW = microwave early warning 【军】微波预先警报.
M.E.W. = Ministry of Economic Warfare. 〔英旧〕经济作战部.
mew[1] [mjuː] *n.* 咪咪〔猫叫声〕. — *vi.* (猫、海鸟等)咪咪地叫.
mew[2] [mjuː] *n.* 【鸟】海鸥〔通常叫 sea-mew〕.
mew[3] [mjuː] *n.* ①(换羽时用的)鹰笼. ②(催肥鸡等用的)育肥笼. ③换羽. ④〔*pl.*〕〔英〕〔作单数用〕(设有马车房的)马店. — *vt.* 把(鹰)关在笼里; 关起,藏起 (*up*).
mew[4] [mjuː] *vt., vi.* 〔古〕(使)(鹰等)换羽; (使)(鹿)换角.
mewl [mjuːl] *n.* (婴儿等的)低哭声. — *vi.* 低声哭泣; (猫)咪咪地叫.
Mex. = Mexican; Mexico.
Mex·i·can [ˈmeksikən] *n.* ①墨西哥人. ②〔美方〕有墨西哥人和印第安人血统的人. ③(印第安语系中的)一种阿茨蒂克 (Aztec) 语. — *a.* 墨西哥(人)的. ~ **bean beetle** 【动】墨西哥瓢虫. ~ **hairless (dog)** 墨西哥秃狗〔除头上有一片毛和尾端有毛之外全身无毛〕.
Mex·i·co [ˈmeksikəu] *n.* ①墨西哥〔拉丁美洲〕. ②墨西哥〔墨西哥州名〕. ③墨西哥城〔墨西哥首都〕(=~ City).
Mey·er [ˈmaiə] *n.* 迈耶〔姓氏〕.
Mey·er·hof [ˈmaiəhɔːf], **O.** 梅尔霍夫〔1884—1951,德国生理学家〕.
mez·ca·line [ˈmezkəliːn] *n.* 墨斯卡灵〔一种幻觉剂 = mescaline〕.
me·ze·re·um [məˈziəriəm] *n.* ①【植】欧亚瑞香. ②欧亚瑞香皮. — *a.* 瑞香料的 (= mezereon).
me·zu·za [məˈzuzə, -ˈzuː-] *n.* ***(pl. -zot(h)*** [-zəut], ***-za(h)s)*** 【犹】门柱圣卷〔犹太家庭挂于门柱之上的小羊皮纸圣经卷〕.
mez·za·nine [ˈmezəniːn] *n.* (底楼与二楼之间的)夹层(楼面); (戏院的)楼厅包厢; (舞台下的)底层.
mez·zo [ˈmedzəu] *a., ad.* 〔It.〕【乐】中,适中,半. ~ ***forte*** 【乐】中强,不很响. ~ ***piano*** 【乐】中弱,不很轻. ~***-soprano*** 【乐】女中音; 女中音歌手.
mez·zo-ri·lie·vo [ˈmedzəurilˈjeivəu] *n.* 〔It.〕***(pl. mez-zi-ri·lie·vi)*** 半凸雕.
mez·zo·tint [ˈmedzəutint] *n., vt.* 镂刻凹版(作品); 制成镂刻凹版,印刷法〔印刷品〕. — *vt.* 把…制成镂刻凹版.
MF = ①〔常作 mf〕medium frequency 【无】中频. ②〔It.〕〔常作 mf〕*mezzo forte* 【乐】不很响,中强. ③machine finish〔mill finish〕机械光滑度〔印书纸或封面纸由砑光机砑出的光滑程度〕. ④Middle French 中世纪法语. ⑤middling fair〔美〕一级棉.
mf. = ①microfarad. ②millifarad. ③manufacture.
mfd. = manufactured.
mfg. = manufacturing.
MFN = most favo(u)red nation 最惠国.
MFR = manufacturer.
mfr. = manufacturer.
mfs. = manufactures.
M.F.V. = motor fleet vessel 海军内燃机船.
MG = machine gun 机枪.
Mg = magnesium 【化】镁.
mg. = milligram(me)(s).
M.G.C. = Machine Gun Corps 机枪队.
MGM = Metro-Goldwin-Mayer 美国米高梅影片公司.
Mgr. = ①manager. ②〔F.〕*Monseigneur*. ③〔It.〕*Monsignor(e)*.
M.H.G. = Middle High German 中世纪高地德语.
mho [məu] *n.* 〔Ohm 的倒写〕【电】姆(欧).
M.H.R. = Member of the House of Representatives 〔美〕众议院议员.
MI = ①military intelligence 军事情报; 军事情报工作; 军事情报部门. ②medical inspection 检疫. ③malleable iron 【冶】可展铁,锻铁.
Mi = Mississippi 密西西比.
mi [miː] *n.* 〔It.〕【乐】全音阶第三音.
mi. = mile.
MIA = missing in action 【军】战斗失踪人员.
Mi·am·i [maiˈæmi] ***(pl. ~(s))*** *n.* 迈阿密〔美国港市〕. ②迈阿米人〔美国印第安人的一支〕.
mi·aow, mi·aou [mi(ː)au] *n.* 喵〔猫叫声〕. — *vi.* 喵喵地叫.
mi·as·ma [miˈæzmə] *n.* ***(pl. ~s, ~ta*** [-tə]***)*** (腐败有机物发散的)毒气,(尤指)瘴气; 有害的气氛〔影响〕.
mi·as·mal, mi·as·mat·ic, mi·as·mic [miˈæzməl, miəzˈmætik, miˈæzmik] *a.* 毒气的,瘴气的. *miasmic fever* 疟疾.
mi·au(l) [miˈau, miˈaul] *vi.* = miaow.
mi·ca [ˈmaikə] *n.* 【矿】云母.
mi·ca·ceous [maiˈkeiʃəs] *a.* ①云母(似)的; 含云母的. ②分层的; 有光彩的.
Mi·cah [ˈmaikə] *n.* ①迈卡〔男子名〕. ②弥迦〔公元前八世纪的希伯来先知〕;《圣经·旧约》中的篇名《弥迦书》.

mi·ca·schist, mi·ca·slate [ˈmaikəsist, -sleit] *n.*【地】云母片岩.
Mi·caw·ber·ism [miˈkɔːbərizəm] *n.* 幻想突然走运的乐天主义〔出自 Dickens 所著小说 David Copperfield 中人物 Micawber〕.
M.I.C.E. = Member of the Institute of Civil Engineers 〔英〕土木工程师学会会员.
mice [mais] *n.* mouse 的复数.
mi·cel·la [maiˈselə] *n.* ***(pl. -lae*** [-liː]***)*** = micell(e).
mi·celle [maiˈsel, mi-] *n.* ①【生】分子团. ②【化】胶束;胶态离子;细胞束;胶粒. **-cel·lar** *a.*
Mich. = Michael; Michaelmas; Michigan.
Mi·chael [ˈmaikl] *n.* ①迈克尔〔男子名〕. ②米迦勒〔天使长〕. *the Order of St.* ～ *and St. George* 圣米迦勒与圣乔治勋章〔英国文官勋章之一〕.
Mich·ael·mas [ˈmiklməs] *n.* 米迦勒节〔9月29日, 英国四大结帐日 (Quarter days) 之一〕. ～ **daisy**【植】紫苑. ～ **goose** 米迦勒节吃的鹅.
Mi·chel(le) [miːˈʃel] *n.* 米歇尔〔女子名〕.
Mi·chel·an·ge·lo [ˌmaikəˈlændʒiləu], **Buonarrotti** 米开朗基罗〔1475—1564, 意大利雕刻家、画家、建筑家、诗人〕.
Mi·chel·son [ˈmitʃəlsn, ˈmikəlsn] *n.* 米切尔森〔姓氏〕.
Mich·el·son [ˈmitʃəlsn, ˈmaikəlsən], **Albert Abraham** 米切尔森〔1852—1931, 美国物理学家〕.
Mi·che·ner [ˈmitʃinə] *n.* 米切纳〔姓氏〕.
Mich·i·gan [ˈmiʃigən] *n.* ①密歇根[密执安]〔美国州名〕. ②密歇根[密执安]湖〔美国〕(= Lake ～).
mich·ing [ˈmitʃiŋ] *a.* 〔方〕隐藏着的.
Mick [mik] *n.* 〔美俚, 蔑〕爱尔兰人.
Mick·ey [ˈmiki] *n.* 米基〔男子名, Michael 的昵称〕.
mick·ey[1] [ˈmiki] *n.* 〔加拿大俚〕十三两装的威士忌酒.
mick·ey[2] [ˈmiki] *n.* 〔英俚〕精神;骄傲,傲慢;自夸. ★ 主要用于下述短语中: *take the* ～ 取笑;嘲弄. *take the* ～ *out of* 杀某人的威风.
Mick·ey (Finn), mick·ey (finn) [ˈmiki ˈfin] 〔美俚〕混有麻醉药[泻药]的酒.
Mick·ey Mouse [ˈmiki maus] *n.* ①米老鼠〔美国动画片中的主角〕. ②〔英空口〕分掷炸弹的装置. ③〔美军俚〕多余或无关重要的东西. ④〔美学俚〕简单容易的学院课程. — *a.* ①〔美俚〕幼稚的, 过于简单的; 不重要的, 与实际无关的. ②〔美俚〕(伴舞音乐)陈旧乏味的.
mick·le [ˈmikl] *a.* 〔Scot.〕〔古〕大的;许多的. — *n.* 大量, 多量. *Many a little [pickle] makes a* ～. = *Every little makes a* ～ *[muckle].* 积少成多.
Mick·y [ˈmiki] *n.* 米基〔男子名, Michael 的昵称〕.
Mic·mac [ˈmikmæk] *n.* ①***(pl. -macs, -mac)*** 密克马克人〔纽芬兰和加拿大沿海各省的一支印第安人〕. ②密克马克语.
mi·cra [ˈmaikrə] *n.* micron 的复数.
mi·cri·fy [ˈmaikrifai] *vt.* ***(-fied; -fy·ing)*** 使变小, 使无足轻重.
micr(o)- [maikr(əu)-] *comb. f.* ①小, 微: *micro*cosm. ②扩大: *micro*phone. ③显微镜的: *micro*örganism. ④微(= 100万分之一): *micro*ampere 微安(培). *micro*farad 微法(拉). *micromicro*farad 微微法. *micro*mho 微姆(欧). *micro*volt 微伏(特).
mi·cro [ˈmaikrəu] *n., a.* 〔美口〕特超短裙(的).
mi·cro·al·loy [ˈmaikrəuˈælɔi] *n.* 微合金. ～ *diffused transistor* 微合金型扩散晶体管.
mi·cro·am·pere [ˈmaikrəuˈæmpɛə] *n.*【电】微安(培).
mi·cro·a·nal·y·sis [ˈmaikrəuəˈnælisis] *n.*【化】微量分析. **-an·a·lyst** [-ˈænlist] *n.*
mi·cro·bal·ance [ˈmaikrəuˈbæləns] *n.* 微量天平.
mi·cro·bar [ˈmaikrəubɑː] *n.* 微巴〔压力单位〕.
mi·cro·bar·o·graph [ˈmaikrəuˈbærəgræf] *n.*【气】微(气)压计.
mi·crobe [ˈmaikrəub] *n.* (通例指植物性的)微生物, 细菌.
mi·cro·bi·al, mi·cro·bi·an, mi·cro·bic [maiˈkrəubiəl, -biən, -bik] *a.* 微生物的, 细菌的, 因细菌而起的.
mi·cro·bi·cide [maiˈkrəubisaid] *n.*【化】杀微生物剂. **-cidal** *a.*
mi·cro·bi·ol·o·gy [ˈmaikrəubaiˈɔlədʒi] *n.* 微生物学.
mi·cro·bi·o·ta [ˈmaikrəuˈbaiəutə] *n.* 微生物群.
mi·cro·bi·ot·ic [ˈmaikrəubaiˈɔtik] *a.* 微生物群的.
mi·cro·bus [ˈmaikrəubʌs] *n.* 〔美〕微型公共汽车.
mi·cro·ca·lip·ers [ˈmaikrəuˈkælipəz] *n.*【机】千分尺; 测微器.
mi·cro·card [ˈmaikrəukɑːd] *n.* 缩微卡〔每张可缩印印刷物二百页以上, 供以后放大阅读〕.
mi·cro·ceph·a·lous [ˈmaikrəuˈsefələs] *a.* 头异常小的.
mi·cro·chem·is·try [ˈmaikrəuˈkemistri] *n.* 微量化学.
mi·cro·chip [ˈmaikrəutʃip] *n.* 〔美口〕微型集成电路片; 微晶片.
mi·cro·chro·nom·eter [ˈmaikrəukrəˈnɔmitə] *n.* 分秒表, 瞬时计.
mi·cro·cir·cuit [ˈmaikrəuˈsəːkit] *n.*【无】微型电路. **-cuit·ry** *n.* 微型电路技术.
mi·cro·cli·mate [ˈmaikrəuˈklaimit] *n.* 小气候. **-mat·ic** *a.*
mi·cro·cli·ma·tol·o·gy [ˌmaikrəuˌklaiməˈtɔlədʒi] *n.* (微)小气候学. **-gist** *n.* 小气候学者.
mi·cro·cline [ˈmaikrəuklain] *n.*【地】微斜长石.
mi·cro·coc·cus [ˌmaikrəuˈkɔkəs] *n.* ***(pl. -coc·ci*** [-ˈkɔksai]***)*** 小球菌, 球状细菌.
mi·cro·com·put·er [ˈmaikrəukəmˈpjuːtə] *n.* 微型电子计算机.
mi·cro·co·py [ˈmaikrəuˈkɔpi] *n.* (用缩微胶卷摄制成的)缩微(复制)本, 缩微副本.
mi·cro·cosm [ˈmaikrəukɔzəm] *n.* ①微观世界[宇宙] (*opp.* macrocosm) (为宇宙缩影的)人; 人类社会. ②缩影. *Each day is a* ～ *of all life.* 一天是一生的缩影.
mi·cro·cos·mic, mi·cro·cos·mi·cal [ˈmaikrəuˈkɔzmik, -mikəl] *a.* (象)微观世界的. ～ *salt*【化】小天地盐〔四水合磷酸氢铵钠的别名〕.
mi·cro·crith [ˈmaikrəukriθ] *n.*【化】(作为单位的)氢原子量.
mi·cro·crys·tal·line [ˈmaikrəuˈkristlin] *a.*【化】微晶(质)的.
mi·cro·cyte [ˈmaikrəusait] *n.*【医】小红血球. **-cyt·ic** [-ˈsitik] *a.*
mi·cro·dont [ˈmaikrəudɔnt] *a.* 有小牙的 (= microdontous). **-ism** *n.*
mi·cro·dot [ˈmaikrəudɔt] *n.*【摄】微点拷贝, 微点照片〔进行间谍活动等拍摄文件等用〕.
mi·cro·e·lec·tron·ics [ˈmaikrəuilekˈtrɔniks] *n.* *pl.* 〔动词用单数〕微电子学, 超小型电子工学. **-tronic** *a.*
mi·cro·el·e·ment [ˈmaikrəuˈelimənt] *n.* ①【化】微量元素. ②微型元件, 超 型元件.
mi·cro·en·cap·su·lat [ˌmaikrəuinˈkæpsəleit, -sju-] *vt.* 把 (微粒药物、液滴的)用胶囊封闭. **-su·la·tion** *n.*
mi·cro·en·vi·ron·ment [ˈmaikrəuinˈvaiərəmənt] *n.*【生】(动植物生长的)小环境.
mi·cro·ev·o·lu·tion [ˌmaikrəuˌevəˈljuːʃən] *n.*【生】微进化, 种内进化.
mi·cro·fac·tion [ˈmaikrəuˈfækʃən] *n.* 小宗派, 小集团.
mi·cro·far·ad [ˈmaikrəˈfærəd, -əd] *n.*【电】微法(拉)〔电容单位〕.
mi·cro·fiche [ˈmaikrəufiːʃ] *n.* 缩微胶片.
mi·cro·film [ˈmaikrəufilm] *n.* (印刷品等的)缩微胶卷; 缩微照片. — *vt.* 用缩微法摄制(印刷品等). — *vi.* 摄制缩微胶卷. **-er** 缩微摄影机.
mi·cro·form [ˈmaikrəufɔːm] *n.* (文件等的)缩微过程; 〔集合词〕缩微印刷品. — *vt.* 把…复制在缩微材料上.

mi·cro·ga·mete [ˈmaikrəuˈgæmit] *n.* 【生】小配子.
mi·cro·gram [ˈmaikrəugræm] *n.* ①微克〔重量单位,符号为 μg〕(= microgramme). ②显微照片;微写器.
mi·cro·graph [ˈmaikrəugrɑːf, -græf] *n.* 微写器;【物】微动扩大测定器;显微(镜)制图〔照相、照片〕.
mi·crog·ra·phy [maiˈkrɔgrəfi] *n.* ①显微(镜)照相(检查);显微照相术. ②【医】字体过小症.
mi·cro·groove [ˈmaikrəugruːv] *n.* (唱片的)密纹. ~ *recording* 密纹录声.
mi·crohm [ˈmaikrəum] *n.* 【电】微欧(姆).
mi·cro·lite [ˈmaikrəulait] *n.* ①【物】微晶. ②【矿】细晶石,钽烧绿石.
mi·cro·lith [ˈmaikrəuliθ] *n.* (中石器时代的)细小石器.
mi·cro·li·tre, mi·cro·li·ter [ˈmaikrəuˈliːtə] *n.* 微升(千分之一毫升).
mi·crol·o·gy [maiˈkrɔlədʒi] *n.* ①显微学. ②留心琐事,剖析毫末.
mi·cro·mech·an·ism [ˈmaikrəuˈmekənizəm] *n.* 【物】微观机构.
mi·cro·mere [ˈmaikrəumiə] *n.* 小(分)裂球,小裂细胞.
mi·cro·me·rit·ics [ˈmaikrəuˈmiritiks] *n.* 微晶(粒)学;微尘学.
mi·cro·me·te·or·ite [ˈmaikrəuˈmiːtiərait] *n.* 【地】微陨星,陨石微粒.
mi·cro·me·te·or·oid [ˈmaikrəuˈmiːtiərɔid] *n.* 【天】微流星体.
mi·cro·me·te·or·ol·o·gy [ˌmaikrəuˌmiːtiəˈrɔlədʒi] *n.* 微气象学. **-gist** *n.*
mi·crom·e·ter [maiˈkrɔmitə] *n.* 【机】测微计,千分尺;【天】测距器. ~ **caliper [gauge]** 千分卡尺,螺旋测径器. ~**screw** 【机】测微螺旋. ~ **sight** 察微瞄准器.
mi·crom·e·try [maiˈkrɔmitri] *n.* 测微术,测微法.
mi·cro·mi·cron [ˈmaikrəuˈmaikrɔn] *n.* 微微米〔10^{-12}米〕.
mi·cro·min·i [ˈmaikrəuˈmini] *n.* 超超短裙.
mi·cro·min·i·a·ture [ˈmaikrəuˈminiətʃə, -ˈminitʃə] *a.* (电子元件,线路等)超小型的,微型的;使用超小型电子元件(线路)的;使用微型电子元件(线路)的.
mi·cro·mi·ni·a·tur·i·za·tion [ˈmaikrəuˌminjətʃəraiˈzeiʃən] *n.* 超小型化,微型化生产.
mi·cro·min·i·a·tur·ize [ˈmaikrəuˈminiətʃəraiz] *vt.* *(-ized; -iz·ing)* 使超小型化,使微型化.
mi·cro·mod·ule [ˈmaikrəuˈmɔdjuːl] *n.* 【无】微型组件,超小型器件.
mi·cro·mo·tor [ˈmaikrəuˈməutə] *n.* 【电】微电机.
mi·cron [ˈmaikrɔn] *n.* *(pl. ~s, -cra* [-krə]*)* 微米〔100万分之一米;符号 μ〕.
Mi·cro·ne·sia [ˈmaikrəuˈniːzjə] *n.* 密克罗尼西亚〔西太平洋的岛屿〕.
Mi·cro·ne·sian [ˈmaikrəˈniːzjən, -ʃən] *a., n.* 密克罗尼西亚(人、语)的;密克罗尼西亚人(语).
mi·cron·ize [ˈmaikrənaiz] *vt.* *(-ized; -iz·ing)* 使成为(直径小到几微米的)粒子.
mi·cro·nu·cle·us [ˈmaikrəuˈnjuːkliəs, -ˈnuː-] *n.* 【生】小核. **-clear** *a.*
mi·cro·nu·tri·ent [ˈmaikrəuˈnjuːtriənt, -ˈnuː-] *n.* 微量营养素.
mi·cro·or·gan·ism [ˈmaikrəuˈɔːgənizəm] *n.* 微生物.
mi·cro·par·a·site [ˈmaikrəuˈpærəsait] *n.* 【生】微寄生物. **-sit·ic** [-ˈsitik] *a.*
mi·cro·phone [ˈmaikrəufəun] *n.* 话筒,传声筒,麦克风〔略 mike〕. ~ *capsule* (电话)炭精盒. **-phon·ic** *a.*
mi·cro·phon·ics [ˈmaikrəuˈfɔniks] *n.* *pl.* 〔动词用单数〕【无】颤噪效应,颤噪声.
mi·cro·pho·to·graph [ˈmaikrəuˈfəutəgrɑːf] *n.* 显微照相(片);缩微照片;缩微放大照片.
mi·cro·pho·tog·ra·phy [ˈmaikrəufəˈtɔgrəfi] *n.* 显微〔缩微〕照相术.
mi·cro·phyte [ˈmaikrəufait] *n.* 微小植物,微生物,细菌.
mi·cro·porous [ˈmaikrəuˈpɔːrəs] *a.* 多微孔的,微孔性的.
mi·cro·print [ˈmaikrəuˌprint] *n.* (文件等的)缩微印刷品.
mi·cro·probe [ˈmaikrəuprəub] *n.* 微探针〔一种使用细聚焦电子束的仪器〕.
mi·cro·pyle [ˈmaikrəpail] *n.* ①【植】珠孔;卵孔. ②【动】卵(膜)孔. **-py·lar** [-ˈpailə] *a.*
mi·cro·py·rom·e·ter [ˌmaikrəupaiˈrɔmitə] *n.* 精测高温计.
mi·cro·ra·di·o·graph [ˌmaikrəuˈreidiəugrɑːf, -græf] *n.* X 射线显微相片. **-graph·ic, -i·cal,** *a.* **-gra·phy** [-ˌreidiˈɔgrəfi] *n.*
mi·cro·read·er [ˈmaikrəuˌriːdə] *n.* 显微阅读器.
mi·cros. = microscopy.
mi·cro·scope [ˈmaikrəuskəup] *n.* 显微镜. *a binocular* ~ 双目显微镜. *an electron* ~ 电子显微镜. *a field ion emission* ~ (比电子显微镜效率大5—10倍的)场致离子投影显微镜. *a reading* ~ 读数显微镜. *a solar* ~ 日光显微镜.
mi·cro·scop·ic, mi·cro·scop·i·cal [ˌmaikrəuˈskɔpik, -ikəl] *a.* ①(象)显微镜的. ②用显微镜可见的;微观的;极微的 (*opp.* macroscopic). *a* ~ *examination* 显微镜检查. *a* ~ *organism* 微生物. **-i·cal·ly** *ad.*①用显微镜. ②极微.
mi·cros·co·pist [maiˈkrɔskəpist] *n.* 会用显微镜的人.
mi·cros·co·py [maiˈkrɔskəpi] *n.* 显微镜学;显微镜使用术.
mi·cro·se·cond [ˈmaikrəuˈsekənd] *n.* 微秒〔百万分之一秒〕.
micro-sec·tion [ˈmaikrəuˈsekʃən] *n.* (显微镜检查用的)薄切片,(显微)磨片.
mi·cro·seism [ˈmaikrəsaizəm] *n.* 【地】微震,脉动. **-seis·mic, -seis·mi·cal** *a.*
mi·cro·seis·mo·graph [ˌmaikrəuˈsaizməgrɑːf] *n.* 微震计,微动计.
mi·cro·seis·mol·o·gy [ˈmaikrəusaizˈmɔlədʒi] *n.* 【地】微震学.
mi·cro·seis·mom·e·ter [ˌmaikrəusaizˈmɔmitə] *n.* 微震计.
mi·cro-slide [ˈmaikrəuslaid] *n.* (显微镜的)载玻片.
mi·cro·some [ˈmaikrəusəum] *n.* 【生】微粒体,微体.
mi·cro·sphere [ˈmaikrəusfiə] *n.* 【动】中心球,缩小球体.
mi·cro·spo·ran·gi·um [ˌmaikrəuspəˈrændʒiəm] *n.* *(pl. -gi·a* [-ə]*)* 【植】小孢子囊.
mi·cro·spore [ˈmaikrəuspɔː] *n.* 【植】小孢子;(显花植物的)花粉粒.
mi·cro·spo·ro·phyll [ˈmaikrəuˈspɔːrəfil] *n.* 【植】小芽胞叶.
mi·cro·stom·a·tous [ˈmaikrəuˈstɔmətəs, -ˈstəumə-] *a.* 有小口的 (= microstomous).
mi·cro·struc·ture [ˈmaikrəuˈstrʌktʃə] *n.* 显微结构,微观结构〔如金属或合金放在显微镜下所看到的结构〕.
mi·cro·sur·ger·y [ˈmaikrəuˈsəːdʒəri] *n.* 显微外科手术.
mi·cro·syn [ˈmaikrəusin] *n.* 微动同步器;微动调协器;精密自动同步机.
mi·cro·tome [ˈmaikrəutəum] *n.* (显微)切片机〔刀〕.
mi·crot·o·my [maiˈkrɔtəmi] *n.* 【医】切片法. **-mist** *n.* 制作切片专家.
mi·cro·tone [ˈmaikrəutəun] *n.* 【音】微分音.
mi·cro·tron [ˈmaikrəutrɔn] *n.* 电子回旋加速器.
mi·cro·tron·ics [ˌmaikrəuˈtrɔniks]〔*pl.*〕*n.* 〔用作 *sing.*〕

【无】微(型)电子学.

mi•cro•waves [ˈmaikrəuweivz] *n. pl.* 微波，超短波. ～ **oven** 微波炉〔用以烧烤食品〕.

mi•cro•zyme [ˈmaikrəuzaim] *n.* 酵母菌.

mic•tu•rate [ˈmiktʃureit] *vt., vi.* (使) 排尿 (= urinate).

mic•tu•ri•tion [ˌmiktjuəˈriʃən] *n.*【医】排尿.

mid[1] [mid] *a.* (*superl.* **midmost** [ˈmidməust]) ①中央的，中部的，中间的〔常构成复合词〕. ②【语】央元音的，半开元音的. *from ～ May to ～ September* 从五月中旬到九月中旬. *in ～ air [mid-air]* 在半空中. *in ～ career [course]* 在中途. ～**day** *n., a.* 正午(的)，日中(的) (～*day flower* 松叶菊). ～**heaven** 中空，中天;【天】子午圈. ～**iron**【高尔夫球】(在 cleek 与 mashie 之间的) 中铁头棒. ～**land** *n., a.* 内地(的); 中部地方(的); 被陆地包围着的; 〔M-〕英国中部地方(的方言); 美国中部及东部一些州(的方言) (*the Midlands* 英国中西部诸郡〔伯明翰四周〕). ～**most** *a.* (= middlemost). ～**night** *n., a.* 午夜(的); 漆黑(的) (*the ～night sun* (极圈内盛夏或隆冬出现的) 夜半的[子夜的]太阳. *burn the ～night oil* 用功到深夜，开夜车). ～**noon** 〔罕〕中午，正午. ～**-off**【板球】投球员左侧的外场守场员 (的位置). ～**-on**【板球】在投球员右侧的外场守场员(的位置). ～**point** 中点; 中心点; 近中心点. ～**rib**【植】叶的中脉. ～**-sea** 外海，外洋. ～**section** 中部. ～**ship** 船身中部. ～**shipman** 〔英〕海军军官候补生〔俗称 *middy*, 因值班时常在舰中央〕; 〔美〕海军学校学生. ～**-shipmite** 〔谑〕= midshipman. ～**ships** *ad., n.*【海】(在) 船的中央; (在) 船身中部. ～**-shot**【摄】中景. ～**stream** 中流. ～**summer** 盛夏，仲夏; 夏至〔6月21日〕前后 (*the ～summer daisy* 法国菊. *the Midsummer Day* 施洗约翰节〔6月24日，英国四结帐日之一〕. *the ～summer madness* 大疯狂). ～**week** 一周的当中; (教友派的) 星期. ～**winter** 仲冬，冬至. ～**year** 〔口〕在学年中期举行的考试; 〔*pl.*〕学年中期考试时期.

mid[2], **'mid** [mid] *prep.* 〔诗〕= amid.

mid. = ①middle. ②midnight. ③midshipman.

MIDAS = ①Missile Defense Alarm System (美国空军) 导弹防御警报系统. ②missile defence alarm satellite 导弹防御警报卫星.

Mi•das [ˈmaidəs] *n.* ①【希神】迈达斯〔弗利治亚(Phrygia) 国王. 相传贪财，求神赐给点物成金的法术〕. ②大富豪.

mid•brain [ˈmidˌbrein] *n.* 中脑 (= mesencephalon).

mid•cult [ˈmidˈkʌlt] *n.* 〔美口〕商业化的中产阶级文化.

mid•den [ˈmidn] *n.* 〔方〕粪堆;【考古】贝塚 (= kitchen ～).

mid•dle [ˈmidl] *n.* ①中央，正中; 中间，中部; 中途. ②人体的中部，腰部. ③中间物，媒介物; 中人，中间人，调解人; 中间派. ④【逻】中名词，媒辞;【语】(希腊语动词的) 中间态.【数】中项 (= ～ term). ④〔常 *pl.*〕(报纸等的) 文学性短文，中间读物;【商】中级(货)品. ⑤【板球】防守中柱 (～ stump) 的球棍拿法. ⑥【足球】从左右翼将球传到锋线中央，中央传球. ⑦【美拳】中量级拳击选手. *in the ～ of* 正在…当中; 在…的中途; 在…的中央; 在…的中部. *knock [send] sb. into the ～ of next week* 把(某人)打昏过去. — *a.* ①中央的，正中的，中间的. ②中等的，中级的. ③〔M-〕(英语等) 中古的. ～**age** 中年，壮年〔约35—55岁间或40—60岁间〕. ～**-aged** *a.* 中年的. **M- Ages** 中世纪. **M- America** ①中美洲. ②美国中产阶级社会(有时尤指美国中西部中产阶级). ～ **article** 〔英〕(周刊杂志等的) 文学性随笔，中间读物〔因排在政治论文与新书评介的中间〕. **M- Atlantic States** 美国大西洋中部各州〔即纽约州，新泽西和宾夕法尼亚〕. ～**break•er** *n.* 双壁开沟犁. ～**-brow** ①*n.* 〔口〕中产阶级趣味 (或观点) 的人. ② *a.* 〔口〕中产阶级趣味[观点]的〔常当轻蔑或取笑词用〕. ～ **class** 中产阶级，中间阶层. ～**-class** *a.* 中间阶级的; 〔罕〕品质中等的. ～ **course [way]** 中庸，中道. ～ **distance [ground]**【绘】(前景和背景间的) 中景; 中距离. ～ **dress** 水手服装式运动衣. ～ **ear**【解】中耳. ～ **earth** 〔诗〕地球〔因在天国和地狱之间〕. **M- East** 中东〔地中海东岸至印度地区，通常包括 Near East 在内〕. **M- Empire**【史】埃及中王国. **M- English** 中世纪英语〔略 M.E.〕. ～ **finger** 中指. **M- French** 中世纪法语〔指14—16世纪的法语〕. **M- Greek** 中世纪希腊语 (= Medieval Greek). ～ **ground** 中间立场，中立. ～ **height** 中等身材; 半山腰. **M- High German** 中世纪高地德语. **M- Irish** 中世纪爱尔兰语. ～ **life** ①= middle age. ②中等生活. **M- Low German** 中世纪低地德语. ～**man** 掮客; 中间人. ～**most** *a.* 正中的. ～**-of-the-road** 中间路线. ～**-of-the-roader** 中间派，中间人物[势力]. ～ **piece** 〔美〕马甲. ～ **school** 中学校. ～**-sized** 中等尺寸的，中号的. **M- States** 〔美〕中部诸州. ～ **stick** 中尺〔36英寸半〕. ～ **term**【逻】中名词;【数】中项. ～ **tooth** 主牙. ～ **watch**【海】夜半值班〔午夜零时到四时〕. ～**weight** ① *a.*【拳、摔交】中量级(的). ②*n.* 中量级拳击[摔交等]选手〔147—160磅 (66—72公斤)〕. **M- West** 〔美〕中西部(各州). **M- Western** 中西部(各州)的. **M- Westerner** 中西部(各州)的人.

Mid•dle•ton [ˈmidltən] *n.* 米德尔顿〔姓氏〕.

mid•dling [ˈmidliŋ] *a.* 中等的，普通的; 第二流的; 不好不坏的. *I feel only ～.* 我精神还好. — *ad.* 中等，相当. ～ *good* 相当好的. — *n.* 〔常 *pl.*〕中级品; (小麦的) 粗粉; 〔美〕标准[中等]棉花; 中纱.

mid•dor•sal [ˈmidˈdɔːsəl] *a.*【解】背部中央的.

mid•dy [ˈmidi] *n.* ①〔口〕= midshipman. ②(妇女、小孩穿的) 水手式服装 (= ～ blouse).

Mid•gard [ˈmidgɑːd] *n.*【北欧神】尘世，凡间 (*cf.* Asgard).

midge [midʒ] *n.* ①(蚊、蚋等) 小虫; 蠓; 极小的鱼. ②小个子; 侏儒. *a wheat ～* 小麦吸浆虫.

midg•et [ˈmidʒit] *n.* ①小个子(的人); 侏儒. ②〔加拿大〕蚋. ③小照片(又叫 ～ photograph). ④(同类事物中) 极小者. *a ～ submarine* 小型[袖珍]潜艇. *a ～ tractor* 微型拖拉机.

mid•gut [ˈmidˌgʌt] *n.*【解】中肠.

Mi•di [miˈdi] *n.* 〔F.〕南法，法国南部.

mi•di [ˈmidi] *n.* 〔美〕(一种长及腿肚子的) 半长裙[衣].

mid•i•nette [ˌmiːdiːˈnet] *n.* 〔F.〕〔俚〕(巴黎的) 女店员.

mid•leg [ˈmidleg] *n.* ①中足. ②(昆虫的) 中对足. — *ad.* 向中足.

mid•line [ˈmidlain] *n.* 中线.

mid•rash [ˈmidˌrɑːʃ] *n.* (*pl.* ***mid•rash•im*** [midˈrɑːʃim], ***mid•rash•oth*** [-ʃəut]) (从犹太人被巴比伦俘虏奴役时期开始到公元1,200年间所作的) 犹太法学博士的圣经注释. **the M-** 上述注释的总称. **-ic** *a.*

mid•riff [ˈmidrif] *n.* ①【解】横膈膜. ②〔美俚〕肚子，下腹部. ③(女子的) 露腰上衣. — *a.* 腰线露在外的.

midst[1] [midst] *n.* 中，中间，中央. ★现在只用在如下成语中. *from [out of] the ～ of ...* 从…当中. *in our [your] ～* 在我们[你们]中间. *in the ～ of us* 在我们当中. *in [into] the ～ of* 在[向]…当中. — *ad.* 在中间，在中央. *first, ～, and last* 始终一贯，彻头彻尾.

midst[2], **'midst** [midst, mitst] *prep.* 〔诗〕= amidst.

mid-Vic•to•ri•an [ˌmidvikˈtɔːriən] *a.* 〔英〕①维多利亚王朝中期(1850—1890)的; 维多利亚中期文化〔道德、艺术〕的. ②旧式的，一本正经的; 操行严谨的; 沉闷的. — *n.* ①维多利亚王朝中期时代的人. ②具有维多利亚时代中期思想观点举止的人.

mid•way [ˈmidˈwei] *n.* ①中途，半路. ②〔美〕(展览会等的) 商场，娱乐场. — *a.* 中途的. *a ～ station* 错车站. —[ˈmidwei] *ad.* 在中途，在半路.

Mid•way Islands [ˈmidwei ˈailəndz] *n.* 中途岛.

Mid•west [ˈmidˈwest] *n.* 〔美〕= Middle West. **-ern**

a., **-ern•er** *n.*

mid•wife [ˈmidwaif] *n.* ***(pl. -wives)*** 助产士,接生员〔婆〕. — *vt.* 为…接生;〔喻〕协助…的产生.

mid•wife•ry [ˈmidwifəri] *n.* 助产术,产科学.

M.I.E.E. = Member of Institute of Electrical Engineers 〔英〕电机工程师学会会员.

micn [miːn] *n.* 风采,态度,样子.

miff [mif] *n.* 〔口〕小争执;生气. — *vt., vi.* 〔口〕(使)发脾气,(使)生气. ***be ~ed with [at]*** 生…的气. ***get [have, take] a ~*** 生气. ***in a ~*** 生着气.

miffed [mifd] *a.* 〔美口〕生气的,发怒的;恼火. *I was ~ when they laughed at my new wig.* 每当他们嘲笑我的新假发,我就感到恼火.

MIG [mig] *n.* (苏联的)米格式飞机.

mig•gle [ˈmigl] *n.* 〔方〕①(小孩玩的)玻璃弹子. ②〔*pl.*〕弹珠戏.

might[1] [mait] *v. aux.* may 的过去式. ①〔在陈述句中,为 may 的过去式,表示一般的可能性〕可能,会. *No one but a king or prince ~ build a castle.* 除了国王或公国君主外,那时什么人都不能修建城堡. *I said that it ~ rain.* 我说过可能会下雨. ②〔表示不太确实的可能性〕也许,或许. *I'm afraid it ~ rain tonight.* 我看今晚恐怕要下雨. *Who ~ the man be?* 这个人会是谁呢? *Did you see that car nearly hit me? I ~ have been killed.* 那辆汽车几乎撞着我,你看见了吗? 要是撞上,我也许就完蛋了. ③〔表示许可,在疑问和建议时比 may 更委婉和礼貌〕可以. *I asked him if I ~ leave.* 我问他可不可以离开. "M- I come in?" "Yes, you may." "我可不可以进来?""可以,请." *M- I suggest a stroll after lunch?* 午饭后是不是可以去散步? ④〔表示愿望、祝愿、请求、嘱咐和轻微的责备〕请,愿,…就好了;该;还是…好. *I hoped you ~ succeed.* 我原是希望你成功的. *I wish I ~ help you.* 我能帮助你就好了. *You ~ post this letter for me.* 请代我把这封信寄一下. *O! ~ I see him just once more!* 唉! 我能再见他一次就好了! *You ~ write more frequently.* 你该经常写信才是. *You ~ at least offer to help!* 你至少该帮帮忙. *You ~ as well go.* 你还是去好. *No one will eat this food; it ~ just as well be thrown away.* 这东西没人吃,不如扔掉好. ⑤〔在条件句中,主句或从句的叙述含有推测或虚拟意味〕如能〔从句中〕;便会;说不定会〔主句中〕. *I would go if I ~.* 如我能去我就去. *You ~ believe me if you read it.* 你读一读,便会相信我了. *If you had tried a little harder, you ~ have succeeded.* 当初你如果再努力一下,说不定你会成功的. *We lost the football match, but we ~ well have won if one of our players hadn't been hurt.* 这场足球比赛我们输了,可是如果我们的一位运动员不受伤的话〔事实上受了伤〕,那我们说不定会踢赢的. ⑥〔在 that ...might 结构中,表示目的〕为了. *He studied hard that he ~ serve the country well.* 为了很好地为祖国服务,他曾刻苦钻研. *She turned away so that no one ~ see that her eyes were filled with tears.* 为了不让人看出她泪水盈眶,她把脸背过去了. ⑦〔用于从句中,表示让步〕虽然,尽管,无论. *Whatever ~ happen, he was determined to do it.* 无论发生什么,他决心去干. *You ~ think you're very clever, but that doesn't give you the right to order me about.* 尽管你认为自己非常聪明,但这决不是说你有随意摆弄我的权利. **~-have-been** *n.* 本来或许可以发生的事情; 本来或许可以有所成就的人.

might[2] [mait] *n.* ①(身体或精神的)力,力气. ②权力;势力;兵力. ③智力,才干,能力. ***by ~*** 用武力. ***with ~ and main = with all one's ~*** 尽全力,拼命.

might•i•ly [ˈmaitili] *ad.* ①强烈地,猛烈地,有力地. ②〔口〕非常,极.

might•i•ness [ˈmaitinis] *n.* ①强大,有力;伟大. ②高位,高官. ③〔古〕〔M-〕阁下〔对高官贵人的尊称: His M-〕. *his high ~* 〔反〕尊贵的阁下〔指高傲的人〕.

mightn't [ˈmaitnt] = might not.

might•y [ˈmaiti] *a.* ***(might•i•er; -i•est)*** ①强大的,有力的;伟大的;刚毅的. ②巨大的,非凡的. ③〔口〕大的,非常的. *a ~ hit* 极其轰动的作品〔事物、人物〕. *a ~ wind* 猛烈的风,大风. *~ works* 奇迹. ***high and ~*** 趾高气扬,神气活现. ***make a ~ bother*** 搞出大麻烦. — *ad.* 〔方、美口〕非常,很,大. *a ~ good thing* 非常好的事情. *It is ~ easy.* 容易透顶.

mig•ma•tite [ˈmigmətait] *n.* 【地】混合岩.

mi•gnon [ˈmi(ː)njɔn] *a.* 〔F.〕 娇小玲珑的,可爱的. — *n.* 可爱的孩子.

mi•gnon•ette [ˌminjəˈnet] *n.* 【植】①木犀草. ②灰绿色. ③法国细丝花边. ~ **tree** 【植】散沫花,指甲花. ~ **wood** 【植】菱叶海桐花.

mi•graine [ˈmiːgrein] *n.* 〔F.〕【医】周期性偏头痛.

mi•grant [ˈmaigrənt] *a.* = migratory. — *n.* 候鸟;移栖动物;移居者 (*cf.* emigrant, immigrant).

mi•grate [maiˈgreit, ˈmaigreit] *vi.* 迁移;移居,(尤指)移居海外;(鸟的)定期移栖;(鱼的)回游.【化、物】移动,徙动.

mi•gra•tion [maiˈgreiʃən] *n.* ①移住,迁移;移动;徙动. ②(鸟)移栖,迁徙;(鱼)回游;(植物)侵移. ③移住者群,移栖群. ④【化、物】原子移动;电离子的移动.

mi•gra•tor [maiˈgreitə] *n.* 移居者;候鸟.

mi•gra•to•ry [ˈmaigrətəri] *a.* 移栖的,移居的;移动的;游牧的,漂泊的. *a ~ bird* 候鸟.

mih•rab [ˈmiːrɔb] *n.* (清真寺院面向麦加的那道墙内的)壁龛.

M.I.J. = Member of the Institute of Journalists 〔英〕新闻工作者学会会员.

mi•ka•do [miˈkɑːdəu] *n.* 〔常作 M-〕日本天皇〔西洋人对日本天皇的称呼〕.

Mike [maik] *n.* 迈克〔男子名, Michael 的昵称〕.

mike[1] [maik] *vi., n.* 〔俚〕偷懒,鬼混,怠工. *on the ~* 偷着懒,吊儿郎当地.

mike[2] [maik] *n.* 〔microphone 之略〕〔口〕话筒;送话器,微音器. ~ **fright** 话筒前的胆怯.

mi•kron [ˈmaikrɔn] *n.* 〔G.〕 = micron.

mil [mil] *n.* ①【电】密耳(千分之一英寸). ②【军】密位〔= 1/6400 周角〕. ③= milliliter.

mil. =①mileage. ②military. ③militia. ④million.

mi•la•di, mi•la•dy [miˈleidi] *n.* ***(pl. -dies)*** ①夫人,太太〔欧洲大陆人对英国贵妇的称呼〕; 英国贵妇人. ②非常时髦的女人,上流女人.

mil•age [ˈmailidʒ] *n.* = mileage.

Mi•lan, Mi•la•no [miˈlæn, It. miˈlɑːno] *n.* ①米兰〔意大利城市〕. ②〔m-〕米兰草帽.

Mi•la•nese [ˌmiləˈniːz] *n.* 〔*sing., pl.*〕米兰人. — *a.* 米兰人的. *the M-* 旧米兰公国领地.

milch [miltʃ] *a.* 有奶的,生乳的,挤奶用的. *a ~ cow* 乳牛;〔口〕财源;摇钱树. *treat sb. as a ~ cow* 把某人当作摇钱树.

mild [maild] *a.* ①温和的,温厚的,温良的,柔和的,静淑的. ②(处罚等)宽大的;(病等)轻微的;适当的. ③不苦的,适口的. ④【冶】低碳的,软的. *~ base* 弱碱. *a ~ cigar* 味淡的雪茄烟. *a ~ case* 轻症. *~ steel* 软钢. *~ weather* 温暖的天气. ***as ~ as a lamb [a dove, May, milk]*** 非常温和的. ***be ~ in disposition*** 性格温柔. ***be ~ of manner*** 态度温和. ***draw it ~*** 说〔做〕得适度,不夸张. **~-cured** *a.* 少量盐腌的. **~-spoken** *a.* 说得婉转的.

mild•en [ˈmaildn] *vt., vi.* (使)温和; (使)变暖和; (使)和缓.

mil•dew [ˈmildjuː] *n.* ①霉. ②【植】霉病. *the powdery ~* 白粉菌;白粉病. — *vt., vi.* (使)发霉.

mil•dewed, mil•dew•y [ˈmildjuːd, -i] *a.* ①发了霉的,发霉臭的. ②陈腐的.

mild·ly [ˈmaildli] *ad.* ①温和地,柔和地. ②适度地. ***put it*** ~ 说得婉转些.
mild·ness [ˈmaildnis] *n.* 温和;柔和.
Mil·dred [ˈmildrid] *n.* 米尔德丽德〔女子名〕.
mile [mail] *n.* ①英里,哩(=1609 米). ②一英里赛跑. *He was ~s and ~s my superior.* 他比我强得多. *the international nautical [air]* ~ 国际海[空]里(=1852 米). *a nautical [geographical]* ~ 海里,浬(〔英〕=6,080 英尺〔英国又叫 *admiralty* ~〕,〔美〕=6,080.27 英尺). *the statute* ~ 法定英里〔5280 英尺〕. *the three ~s limit [belt, zone]* 领海三英里. ***be ~s easier*** 容易得多. ***It stands [sticks] a*** ~. 〔俚〕十分明白,显而易见. ***not a hundred ~s from [off]*** 离…不远,差不多. ~**post** 哩程标. ~**-stone** ①里程碑; 哩程标. ②(一生中或历史上的)划时代事件.
mile·age, mil·age [ˈmailidʒ] *n.* ①英里数,里程. ②(按英里计算的)运费. ③〔美〕(公务员出差时)按英里支付的旅费. ④汽车消耗一加仑汽油所行的平均里程. ⑤好处;利润. *traffic* ~【交】周转量.
mil·er [ˈmailə] *n.* 〔口〕作一英里赛跑的运动员[马];一英里赛跑.
Miles, Myles [mailz] *n.* 迈尔斯〔男子名〕.
mi·les glo·ri·o·sus [ˈmailiːz ˌglɔːriˈəusəs, ˈmiːleis-]〔L.〕骄兵〔尤指古典喜剧中爱自吹自擂的士兵角色〕.
Mi·le·sian [maiˈliːziən, -zjən] *n.* 爱尔兰人. —*a.* 爱尔兰的.
mil·foil [ˈmilfɔil] *n.*【植】蓍草[芪草];小二仙草.
Mil·ford [ˈmilfəd] *n.* 米尔福德〔姓氏,男子名〕.
mil·i·a·ri·a [ˌmiliˈɛəriə] *n.* 粟疹,(热)痱子,汗疹.
mil·i·ar·y [ˈmiliəri] *a.* 粟粒状的;【医】粟疹的. ~ *fever* 粟疹(热).
mi·lieu [ˈmiːljəː] *n.* 〔F.〕周围,(社会)环境;背景.
milit. = military.
mil·i·tan·cy [ˈmilitənsi] *n.* ①交战状态;好战. ②战斗精神,战斗性.
mil·i·tant [ˈmilitənt] *a.* ①战斗中的,交战中的. ②斗志昂扬的,富于战斗性的. ③好战的. *a ~ task* 战斗任务. *always ~ in struggle* 斗志昂扬. — *n.* 富有战斗精神的人,斗士. **-ly** *ad.*
mil·i·ta·rism [ˈmilitərizəm] *n.* ①黩武主义,军国主义 (*opp.* pacifism); 黩武政治. ②尚武(精神).
mil·i·ta·rist [ˈmilitərist] *n.* ①军国主义者,军阀. ②军事专家. **-ic** *a.*
mil·i·ta·rize [ˈmilitəraiz] *vt.* ①使军事化; 武装. ②使军国主义化;使好战. **-za·tion** *n.*
mil·i·tar·y [ˈmilitəri] *a.* ①(*opp.* civil) 军人的,军队的. ②陆军的. ③军事的,军用的. ④好战的,战斗性的. ⑤〔军俚〕不好的,讨厌的. *a ~ academy [institute, school]* 陆军军官学校; 军事学院. *a ~ adviser* 军事顾问. *a ~ aeronautical school* 军事航空学校. *a ~ aeroplane* 军用机. ~ *affairs* 军事,军务. ~ *age* 兵役年龄. ~ *arts* 军事艺术. *a ~ band* 军乐队. ~ *circles* 军界. *a ~ commentator* 军事评论家. *a ~ correspondent* 随军记者. ~ *courtesy* 陆军礼节,军礼. ~ *discipline* 军纪. ~ *drill* 军事训练. ~ *expenditures [expenses]* 军费. ~ *fever* 伤寒症. ~ *history* 战史. *a ~ hospital* 陆军医院. ~ *intelligence* 军事情报;军事情报工作[部门]. ~ *law* 军法. *a ~ man* 军人. ~ *operation* 作战;军事行动. ~ *organization* 军制,陆军编制. ~ *pits* 散兵坑. *the ~ police* 宪兵(队). ~ *prestige* 武威. ~ *regulations* 军事法规. *a ~ review* 阅兵式. ~ *science* 军事科学. ~ *secrets* 军事机密. ~ *service* 兵役. ~ *merits* 军功,武功. ~ *stores* 军需品. *the ~ top* (兵舰的)战斗桅楼. ~ *training* 军事训练. — *n.* 〔集合词〕军队;军人;〔the ~〕军方. ***call in the*** ~ 借军队的力量. ~**-industrial complex** 军事—产业部门复合体〔军事权力机构与军事物资工业的联合,被认为是操纵美国经济与对外路线的强大势力集团〕. **-tar·i·ly** *ad.* 在军事上,从军事角度.
mil·i·tate [ˈmiliteit] *vi.* ①发生影响,起作用. ②〔废,罕〕服兵役;战斗,争,冲突 (*against*). *I'll health ~d against his chance of success.* 身体不好误了他成功立业的机会. ~ *in favor of* 便于,有助于,促进.
mi·li·tia [miˈliʃə] *n.* 民兵;〔英〕国民军. ~**man** (男)民兵.
mil·i·um [ˈmiliəm] *n.* (*pl.* ***-i·a*** [-ə])【医】粟粒疹.
milk [milk] *n.* ①乳,奶;牛奶. ②乳状物;乳状液;【药】乳剂. ③〔废〕鱼子. ④【赛马】不正当利益. ⑤〔美俚〕雪. ⑥【物】子同位素. *as white as* ~ 牛奶一样白,纯白. *a ~ diet* 牛奶餐,乳饵. *condensed [Swiss]* ~ 炼乳. *separated ~, skimmed* ~ 脱脂乳. *whole* ~ 全脂乳. *a powder(ed)* ~ 奶粉. *blue* ~ 搀水牛奶 (= watered ~); (因细菌)变青的牛奶. *acidophilus* ~ 酸牛奶. *Bristol* ~ 布里斯托尔酒. ~ *of lime* 石灰乳. ~ *of magnesia* 镁乳(泻药). ~ *of sulphur* 硫黄乳. ***in*** ~ 在授乳期的 (*a cow in ~*乳牛). ~ ***and honey*** 乳和蜜(般的享受); 丰饶,繁荣. ~ ***and roses*** 白中泛红的脸色. ~ ***and water*** 搀水的牛奶;无味的谈话[讲义];过分的感伤 (*cf.* ~-and-water). ~ ***for babes*** (读物、教理等)适合儿童的东西,初步的东西 (*opp.* strong meat). ~ ***of human kindness*** 自然而然的人情;同情心. ***M- Route*** 〔美俚〕奶路〔商人向华盛顿各政府机关做买卖的门道〕; ~ ***route*** 〔美空俚〕短距离航线; 美大陆横断航线给油机. ***spilt*** ~ 不可挽回的事情 (*It's [There's] no good [use] crying over spilt* ~. 无法挽回的事哭也无益). — *vt.* ①挤…的奶;挤(奶). ②〔卑〕榨取,剥削,鱼肉(他人). ③抽取(树液); 拔(蛇毒等的)毒. ④〔俚〕套出消息; (自电线)偷听(电报电话). — *vi.* ①出奶,挤奶. ②(天气)变阴 (*up*). *The cows are ~ing well this season.* 这一季乳牛出奶很旺. ~ ***the audience***【美剧】为想博得喝采过分卖力. ~ ***the bull [ram]*** 缘木求鱼,做没希望的事情. ~ ***the market [street]*** 〔美俚〕操纵股票市场从中渔利. ~ **abscess**【医】乳房脓疮,奶疮. ~**-and-water** *a.* 无味的,无力的;动辄感伤的. ~ **bar** 奶品冷饮点心铺. ~ **crust** (婴儿头上、脸上的)小泡湿疹;乳痂. ~**fish** 遮目鱼. ~ **fever** (产妇的)产乳热. ~ **float** 〔英〕送牛奶的车. ~ **glass** 乳白色玻璃. ~ **leg**【医】产妇股白肿. ~**-livered** *a.* = white-livered. ~**maid** 挤奶女工. ~**man** 卖[送]牛乳的人;挤牛乳的人. ~ **pudding** 牛奶布丁. ~ **punch** 牛奶和酒等的混合甜饮料. ~ **ranch** 〔美〕奶品农场. ~ **run** 〔美空俚〕(清晨执行来回轰炸[侦察]任务的)定期飞行;容易执行的常规飞行任务. ~ **shake** 牛奶和冰淇淋等的混合饮料. ~ **sickness** (乳牛因食毒草而引起的)奶病;(因食奶病牛牛奶或牛肉而引起的)饮乳病,毒乳病. ~ **snake** 〔美〕黑边乳蛇. ~**sop** 懦夫,没骨气的人. ~**sop·ism** 怯懦. ~ **stage** (农作物的)乳熟期;灌浆. ~ **sugar** 乳糖. ~ **toast** 热奶泡烤面包片〔一道名菜〕. ~ **tooth**【解】乳齿. ~ **vetch**【植】黄芪[黄耆]属;紫云英. ~ **walk** 送乳区域. ~**weed**【植】马利筋属. ~**-white** *a.* 乳白的. ~**wood** 〔口〕(热带产)乳树. ~**wort** 〔口〕【植】远志属.
milk·er [ˈmilkə] *n.* ①挤奶人;挤奶器. ②乳牛. ③【物】子同位素发生器.
milk·i·ness [ˈmilkinis] *n.* ①(液体的)乳状(性); 浊白色;乳白色. ②柔弱,温顺.
milk·shed [ˈmilkˌʃed] *n.* 供应城市牛奶的牛奶场区.
milk·y [ˈmilki] *a.* (***milk·i·er; -i·est***) ①(颜色或组织)象牛奶的,乳白色的;浑浊的;柔弱的. ②(食品)加了牛奶的;(植物)分泌乳汁的. ~ ***in the filbert*** 〔美〕神经错乱的;疯狂的;笨的. **M- Way**【天】银河.
Mill [mil] *n.* ①米尔〔姓氏〕. ②**James** ~ 詹姆斯·米尔〔1773—1836,英国经济学家〕. ③**John Stuart** ~ 米尔

〔1800—1873,英国逻辑学、经济学家〕.
mill[1] [mil] *n.* ①风力〔水力、汽力〕磨粉机,风磨,水磨,水碾(等);磨坊,面粉厂.②厂,工场. ③(咖啡、胡椒等的)粉碎器,碾碎器;(水果的)压榨机;铸币机;【冶】轧钢机;(矿石等的)研磨机;裁断机. ④【机】铣床;铣刀. ⑤〔俚〕拳赛;互殴,可随意加入的比赛. ⑥〔美俚〕拷问;监狱. ⑦打字机. ⑧〔美俚〕机车;马达. ⑨缓慢前进的过程. *Much water runs by the ~ that the miller knows not of.* 见远不见近. *No ~, no meal.* 不磨面,没饭吃. *a paper ~* 造纸厂. *a bar ~* 小型轧钢厂. *a coffee ~* 咖啡研磨机. *a stamp ~* 捣碎机. *a wash ~*淘泥机. *Bristol ~* 卡(片)纸板. *gin ~* 小酒店. ***draw water to (one's) ~*** 为自己打算. ***go [put] through the ~*** (使)饱尝辛酸,(使)身经磨炼. — *vt.* ①磨碎,碾碎;锯(木材);【机】磨;铣. ②粉碎. ③碾(铁)成棒状;砑(布)使紧密;轧花边(在纸币上). ④搅拌;使…起泡. ⑤〔俚〕拿拳头打. — *vi.* ①使用水车〔制粉机等〕. ②〔俚〕用拳头殴斗. ③(家畜)成群兜圈子;(鲸鱼)突然兜转方向. ~**board** 书皮纸板. ~ **cake** 亚麻子饼;油饼. ~ **construction**【建】工厂建筑;耐火构造. ~**dam** (水磨用的)水闸〔贮水池〕. ~ **hand** 磨坊工人,制粉工人;(尤指)纺纱工人. ~**-in** *n.* 环行示威〔示威者团团转地游行,造成交通阻塞的示威行动〕. ~ **man** 轧钢工,滚轧工人. ~**-pond,** ~**pool** 水磨用贮水池. ~**race** *n.* ①(推动水车的)水流. ②(水车用)水沟. ~**run** ①= ~race. ②(用碾磨测定矿质的)一定量矿砂. ③锯木厂可售出的木材产量. ④普通产品;〔喻〕平庸普通的人;平凡的东西. ~**-run** *a.* ①刚从机器中生产出来的;未经检验的;未分等级的. ②一般的,普通的. ~**stone** 磨石;粉碎器;重担 *(between the upper and the nether ~stones* 陷在苦境. *hard as the nether ~stone* 残酷. *~stone grit* 【地】磨石硬沙岩. *see [look] through [into, far into] a ~stone* 感觉(尤指眼光)十分锐利. *weep ~stones* 〔口〕决不哭;毫不伤心). ~**stream**=mill race. ~ **tail** (水磨的)排水沟. ~**wheel** 水车(的轮子). ~**work** 水磨(厂)机械;水磨机械的安装〔设计〕;构件加工 (*~work plant* 加工工厂). ~**-wright** 水磨匠,水磨设计人;机械安装工人.
mill[2] [mil] *n.* 〔美〕密尔〔一美元的千分之一〕.
mil·lage [ˈmilidʒ] *n.* 按每美元值抽若干密尔(千分之一美元)的税.
Mil·lais [ˈmilei] *n.* 米莱〔姓氏〕.
Mil·lard [ˈmiləd, ˈmilɑːd] *n.* 米勒德〔姓氏,男子名〕.
Mil·lay [miˈlei] *n.* 米莱〔姓氏〕.
milled [mild] *a.* ①碾碎的,碾磨过的;粉碎的;铣过的. ②(硬币的)边缘弄高并轧花边的.
mille·fleurs [ˌmiːlˈfləː] *a.* (挂毯图案的)万花斑驳的.
mil·le·nar·i·an [ˌmiliˈnɛəriən] *a.* ①一千年的. ②【基督教】一千年至福的. ③(相信)太平盛世(会到来)的. — *n.* 相信一千年至福说的人. **-ism** *n.* 一千年至福说.
mil·le·nar·y [ˈmilineri] *a.* ①一千年的. ②一千年至福的;信奉一千年至福说的. — *n.* ①一千年(期间);千周年纪念. ②信奉一千年至福说的人.
mil·len·ni·al [miˈleniəl] *a.* ①一千年的. ②一千年至福的. **-ism** *n.* = millenarianism.
mil·len·ni·um [miˈleniəm] *n.* ***(pl.** ~s, **-ni·a*** [-niə]***)*** ①一千年(间);千周年纪念. ②一千年至福. ③(幻想中的)黄金时代,太平盛世.
mil·le·ped, mil·le·pede [ˈmiliped, -piːd] *n.* 【动】马陆;千足虫.
mil·le·pore [ˈmilipɔː] *n.* 千窝珊瑚,千孔虫.
Mil·ler [ˈmilə] *n.* 米勒〔姓氏〕.
mill·er [ˈmilə] *n.* ①磨坊主,面粉厂主;工厂经营人. ②铣床;铣工. ③碾磨机工人. ④粉翅蛾. ⑤〔卑〕拳击家. *Too much water drowned the ~.* 过犹不及. ***~'s-thumb*** 杜父鱼;杜父鸟.
mill·er·ite [ˈmilərait] *n.* 【矿】针镍矿.
mil·les·i·mal [miˈlesiməl] *a.* 千分之一的. — *n.* 千分之一.
mil·let [ˈmilit] *n.* ①【植】小米,粟. ②狗尾草属植物. *African ~* 稷,龙爪稗. *German [Hungarian] ~= small foxtail ~* 粟,小米. *hog [bread] ~* 黍,糜. *Indian ~ =great ~* 高粱. *Italian ~* 粟. *~ grass* 粟草属.
milli- *comb. f.* (表示)"毫","千分之一".
mil·li·am·pere [ˌmiliˈæmpɛə] *n.* 毫安(培).
mil·liard [ˈmiljɑːd] *n.* 〔英〕十亿,十万万(=〔美〕billion).
mil·li·ar·y [ˈmiliˌɛəri] *a.* 古罗马里的;千步尺的. —*n.* *(pl.* ***-ar·ies)*** 古罗马里程碑.
mil·li·bar [ˈmilibɑː] *n.* 【气】毫巴〔气压的单位 = $^1/_{1000}$ bar〕.
Mil·li·cent [ˈmilisnt] *n.* 米莉森特〔女子名〕.
mil·li·cron [ˈmilikrɔn] *n.* = millimicron.
mil·li·cu·rie [ˈmiliˌkjuriː] *n.* 【物】毫居(里)〔$^1/_{1000}$ 居里〕.
Mil·lie [ˈmili] *n.* 米莉〔女子名, Mildred 的昵称〕.
mil·lieme [miːˈljem] *n.* 米利姆〔埃及、苏丹和利比亚的货币名称,等于 $^1/_{1000}$ 镑〕.
mil·lier [miˈljei] *n.* 〔F.〕法吨(=1,000 公斤).
mil·li·far·ad [ˈmiliˌfæræd, -əd] *n.* 【电】毫法(拉)〔千分之一法拉;电容单位〕.
mil·li·gal [ˈmiliˌgæl] *n.* 【物】毫伽〔重力加速度单位〕.
mil·li·gram(me) [ˈmiligræm] *n.* 毫克〔千分之一克〕.
mil·li·hen·ry [ˈmiliˌhenri] *n.* 【电】毫亨(利)〔电感单位〕.
Mil·li·kan [ˈmilikən] *n.* 米利肯〔姓氏〕.
mil·li·li·tre, mil·li·li·ter [ˈmililiːtə] *n.* 毫升〔千分之一升〕.
mil·lime [ˈmiliːm, -im] *n.* 米利姆〔突尼斯货币和硬币名称,等于 $^1/_{1000}$ 第纳尔〕.
mil·li·me·tre, mil·li·me·ter [ˈmiliˌmiːtə] *n.* 毫米〔千分之一米〕.
mil·li·mi·cron [ˈmiliˌmaikrɔn] *n.* ***(pl.** **-cra*** [-krə]***)*** 毫微米〔千分之一微米〕.
mil·li·mi·cro·se·cond [ˈmiliˌmaikrəuˈsekənd] *n.* 毫微秒.
mil·line [ˈmilˈlain] *n.* ①百万行〔广告的计算单位,即用 $5^1/_2$ 点字体登一栏(长 $^1/_{14}$ 英寸)印出于百万份的刊物上〕. ②登"百万行"广告的费用.
mil·li·ner [ˈmilinə] *n.* ①女帽头饰商〔通例指女性〕. ②〔废〕杂货商〔卖意大利 Milan 地方产花边、帽子、针、缎带等杂货的商人,通常指男性〕. *a man-~* 为小事忙忙碌碌的人.
mil·li·ner·y [ˈmilinəri] *n.* 女帽类;女帽商.
mill·ing [ˈmiliŋ] *n.* ①磨;制粉;碾碎. ②【机】铣;铣削法;铣出的齿边. ③轧货币的花边,轧出的花边;浆洗. ④〔俚〕拳击;殴打. ⑤考验,磨炼. ⑥〔美〕(家畜)成群兜圆圈. ⑦旋转犁. ⑧【矿】选矿. ⑨【纺】缩绒,缩呢,毡合. ~ **machine** 铣床;缩绒机,缩绒呢. ~ **tool [cutter]** 铣刀.
mil·li·nor·mal [ˈmiliˈnɔːməl] *a.* 【化】毫规度的,毫克当量的.
mil·lion [ˈmiljən] *num.* 百万;百万个(人或物). ★复数形式为 ~(s), 如 five ~(s). —*n.* ①〔*pl.*〕无数,许许多多. ③百万元;百万(镑、美元、法郎). *The force of habit in ~s and tens of ~s is a most formidable force.* 千百万人的习惯势力是最可怕的势力. ***~s upon ~s of the masses*** 千千万万的群众. ***the ~*** 群众.
mil·lion·aire, 〔*fem.*〕 **mil·lion·air·ess** [ˌmiljəˈnɛə, -ris] *n.* 百万富翁,大富翁,富豪.
mil·lion·ette [ˌmiljəˈnet] *n.* 小百万富翁,小富豪.
mil·lion·fold [ˈmiljənfəuld] *a., ad.* 百万倍的〔地〕;成百万倍.
mil·lionth [ˈmiljənθ] *num.* 第一百万(个);百万分之一(的).

mil·li·pede, mil·li·ped [ˈmilipiːd, -ped] *n.* = millepede.
mil·li·rad [ˈmiliˌræd] *n.* 毫拉(德)〔千分之一拉德,辐射剂量单位〕.
mil·li·sec·ond [ˈmiliˌsekənd] *n.* 毫秒.
mil·li·volt [ˈmiliˌvəult] *n.*【电】毫伏(特).
mil·li·watt [ˈmiliwɔt] *n.*【电】毫瓦(特).
Mills bomb [ˈmilzˈbɔm] *n.* 卵形手榴弹.
Milne [mil, miln] *n.* 米尔恩〔姓氏〕.
Milner [ˈmilnə] *n.* 米尔纳〔姓氏〕.
mi·lo [ˈmailəu] *n.* ①白(或黄)穗芦粟. ②〔M-〕迈洛〔男子名〕.
mi·lor(d) [miˈlɔː(d)] *n.* 先生,老板 (= my lord)〔法国人对英国绅士的称呼〕.
milque·toast [ˈmilktəust] *n.*〔美俚〕意志薄弱的人,没勇气的人. **-ish** *a.*
mil·reis [ˈmilreis] *n.* (*sing., pl.*)①(从前的) 葡萄牙金币. ②巴西货币单位 (= 1,000 reis).
MILSAT = military satellite 军事卫星.
milt [milt] *n.* ①【解】脾脏. ②鱼精液. — *a.* 产卵期雄鱼的. — *vt.* 使(鱼卵)受精.
milt·er [ˈmiltə] *n.* ①射精期的雄鱼. ②鱼精液.
Mil·ton [ˈmiltən] *n.* ①米尔顿〔姓氏,男子名〕. ②**John** ～ 约翰·密尔顿〔1608—1674, 英国诗人, *Paradise Lost* 的作者〕.
Mil·to·ni·an, Mil·ton·ic [milˈtəuniən, -tɔnik] *a.* ①(英国诗人) 密尔顿的,密尔顿诗风的. ②雄浑的,(文体等)庄严的.
Mil·wau·kee [milˈwɔːki(ː)] *n.* 密尔沃基〔美国城市〕.
mim [mim] *a.* 〔英方〕故作恬静的;假装羞怯的;假作端庄的.
mime [maim] *n.* ①(古希腊、罗马的) 笑剧; 摹拟表演. ②丑角,小丑; 哑剧演员. — *vi.* 作摹拟表演, 演滑稽角色〔通常为哑剧〕.
M.I. Mech.E. = Member of the Institution of Mechanical Engineers〔英〕机械工程师学会会员.
mim·e·o [ˈmimiə] *n.*〔美口〕油印品. — *vt.* 用油印机油印.
mim·e·o·graph [ˈmimiəgrɑːf] *n.* (商标名)滚筒油印机; 油印品. — *vt.* 用滚筒油印机印刷,油印.
mi·me·sis [maiˈmiːsis, mi-] *n.* ①模仿, 摹拟. ②【生】拟态.
mi·met·ic [miˈmetik, mai-] *a.* ①模仿的, 摹拟的, 巧于模仿的. ②【生】拟态的;【病】拟似的;【矿】类似的. ③【语】拟声的. ～ *gestures* 模仿性的姿态. *a* ～ *crystal*【矿】拟晶,似晶. **-i·cal·ly** *ad.*
mim·e·tism [ˈmimitizəm] *n.*【生】拟态;【心】模仿性.
mim·ic [ˈmimik] *a.* ①模仿的, 摹拟的, 假的. ②【生】拟态的. *a* ～ *battle* 模拟战. *a* ～ *gene*【生】同效基因. ～ *tears* 假哭, 假流泪. — *n.*① 巧于模仿的人; 摹拟笑剧的演员, 丑角. ② 仿造物, 模写物. — *vt.* ***(mimicked; mimicking)*** 学样; 学样取笑; 摹拟; 模写; 活象…. ②【生】拟形, 拟色. **-al** *a.*
mim·ick·er [ˈmimikə] *n.* 学人样的人, 模仿者.
mim·ic·ry [ˈmimikri] *n.* ①模仿; 摹拟; 学样; 模写; 仿造品. ②【生】拟态.
mim·in·y-pim·i·ny [ˈmiminiˈpimini] *a.* = niminy-piminy.
M.I.M.M. = Member of the Institution of Mining and Metallurgy〔英〕采矿及冶金学会会员.
mi·mo·sa [miˈməuzə] *n.*【植】含羞草属.
Min. = ①Minister. ②Ministry.
min. = ①mineralogy. ②minim. ③minimum. ④mining. ⑤minor. ⑥minute.
mi·na[1] [ˈmainə] *n.* ***(pl. -nae*** [-niː], ～*s)* 古希腊等地的货币单位和重量单位〔约等于 100 drachma〕.
mi·na[2] *n.* = myna.
min·a·ble, mine·a·ble [ˈmainəbl] *a.* 可采掘的, 可采矿的.
mi·na·cious, min·a·to·ry [miˈneiʃəs, ˈminətəri] *a.* 威吓的, 威胁性的.
mi·nac·i·ty [miˈnæsiti] *n.* 威吓.
mi·nar [miˈnɑː] *n.* ①灯塔. ②小塔, 望楼.
min·a·ret [ˈminəret] *n.* (伊斯兰教寺院的)尖塔.
mince [mins] *vt.* ①切碎, 剁碎, 斩细, 绞碎(肉等). ②婉曲地说, 半吞半吐地说. — *vi.* ①(用小步子)装腔作势地走. ②装腔作势地讲. ***not ～ matters [one's words]*** 直说, 坦白地说, 不吞吞吐吐. — *n.* 肉末 (= ～d meat). **～meat** (加有葡萄干、苹果、糖、牛板油、香料等的做馅用的)百果馅; 肉末 (*make ～meat of* 把…剁成肉末, 粉碎, 彻底击败; 歼灭). **～-pie** *n.* 百果馅饼; 〔*pl.*〕〔美俚〕眼睛.
minc·er [ˈminsə] *n.* ①绞肉机. ②装腔作势的人. ③走路忸怩作态的人.
minc·ing [ˈminsiŋ] *a.* ①(说话、举动)装腔作势的, 装模作样的. ②剁碎用的. **-ly** *ad.*
mind [maind] *n.* ①心, 精神 (*opp.* body); 心力, 知, 智力, 智慧 (*opp.* heart). ②愿望, 目的; 意向, 意志, 决心; 见解, 意见. ③记忆, 记性, 记忆力; 回想. ④心胸, 头脑; 人. ⑤【宗】追思弥撒;【基督】〔M-〕上帝; 神道. *Nothing in the world is difficult for one who sets his ～ to it.* 世上无难事, 只怕有心人. *a frame [state] of ～* (一种)心境, 心情; 精神状态. *the Greek ～* 希腊精神. *the public ～* 公众意见, 舆论. *Out of sight, out of ～.* 眼不见, 心不想; 离久情疏. *a turn [cast] of ～* 心地, 癖性, 脾气. *It had gone [passed] out of my ～.* 这事我已经记不起了. *I awoke to my full ～.* 我醒过来了[神志清醒了]. *a scientific ～* 科学头脑. *the great ～(s) of the time* 当代有才智的人(们). *the master ～* 卓绝伟才. ***absence of ～*** 心不在焉. ***after one's ～*** 合…的心意. ***a month's ～*** 人死后一月举行的追思弥撒;〔英〕爱好. ***apply [bend] the ～ to*** 专心…, 把精神灌注在…, 一心一意…, ***bear [have, keep] in ～*** 记住, 记在心里 (*Bear what I say in ～.* 别忘记我的话). ***be in two [several] ～s*** 犹豫不决, 三心两意, 心里动摇 *(about)*. ***be of a [one] ～*** 意见一致, 抱同样的看法. ***be of your ～*** 同你意见一致. ***blow one's ～*** 〔美俚〕经历迷幻感, 极度刺激. ***bring [call] to one's ～*** 想起. ***change [alter] one's ～*** 改变想法 [主意], 变卦. ***come to [into] one's ～*** 想起. ***dawn on one's ～*** 开始明白. ***disclose [say, speak, tell] one's ～*** 直率表明意见, 说明心事. ***give (sb.) a bit [piece] of one's ～*** 直率说给(某人)听; 当面责骂. ***give one's (whole) ～ to*** 一心一意地…, 专心…. ***go out of one's ～*** 被忘却; 发狂. ***have a great [good] ～ to*** 非常想…, 极有意…. ***have a ～ of one's own*** 自有定见. ***have a ～ to*** *(do)* 想, 有意. ***have half a ～ to*** *(do)* 有几分想…. ***have in ～*** 记住; 考虑; 想, 打算, 企图. ***have no [little] ～ to*** *(do)* 一点儿也[简直]不想…. ***have*** *(something)* ***(up) on one's ～*** 把…挂在心上, 担心着, 惦念着. ***in [to] my ～*** 我以为…, 我认为…. ***in sound [one's right] ～*** 精神无异状, 神志清醒 (*He cannot be in his right ～.* 他一定是疯了). ***keep an open ～*** 不抱成见; 虚心. ***keep [have, set] one's ～ on*** 注意, 留意; 专心. ***keep one's own ～*** 有决断; 自有主意. ***let*** *(sb.)* ***know one's ～*** 不客气地对人提意见. ***lose one's ～*** 发狂. ***make up one's ～*** 决心 *(to do)*. ***of a [one, the same] ～*** 意见一致; 看法相同. ***of sound ～*** 神志清醒. ***off one's ～*** 丢开不再想, 忘怀, 置诸脑后 (*That is off my ～.* 那我已经忘了). ***one's ～'s eye*** = the ～'s eye. ***open one's ～ to*** 告诉意见[心思]给…. ***out of one's ～*** 在发疯; 忘记. ***pass [go] out of ～*** 被忘却. ***presence of ～*** 沉着, 镇定. ***put [keep] sb. in ～ of*** 使 (某人)想起…; 提醒某人. ***read another's ～*** 看出别人的心

思. ***rush upon one's ~*** 突然想起. ***set one's ~ at rest [ease]*** 安心. ***set one's ~ upon*** 专心于. ***speak one's ~ out*** 把心里话说出来. ***take one's ~ off*** 丢开不再想. ***tell sb. one's ~*** 把心意告诉给某人;坦率对某人提意见. ***the ~'s eye*** 心眼,想象. ***time out of ~*** 太古时代;从太古. ***to one's ~*** 个人认为;合意. ***turn one's ~ to*** 注意. ***weigh on one's ~*** 挂在心上;担心. ***uppermost in one's ~*** 在某人头脑里占第一位,成为某人注意的中心. ***with ... in ~*** 把…搁在心上. — *vt.* ①注意,留心,当心;〔命令〕留心. ②照应,照料. ③〔否定、疑问、条件句〕对…不高兴,反对. ④〔Scot.〕〔古〕记着. ⑤〔罕〕使想起. *M- your own business.* 别管闲事. *M- your head.* 当心你的头. *M- your eye!* 〔俚〕当心! 留神! *M- what you are about.* 当心点;别胡闹呀. *M- you come early.* 记住一定早点来呀. *M- what I tell you.* 记住我的话. *Never ~ (about) the expense!* 花多花少请你别在意. *Never ~ him!* 别管他. *I should not ~ a glass of beer.* 有一杯啤酒喝也好〔真想喝〕. *M- you'll slip!* 当心! 别滑倒啦. *I don't ~ a bit.* 我一点也不在意. — *vi.* ①注意,留心,当心. ②反对,不高兴. ③挂在心上,记住,牵挂,担心. *Never ~!* 不要紧!没什么! ***I don't ~ (doing sth.), but I do ~ (...ing).*** 我不在乎〔不计较〕…,我就怕…. ***if you don't ~ ...*** 要是你不反对,要是你不介意. ***~ one's P's and Q's*** 言行谨慎,谨言慎行. ***~ out!*** 〔俚〕当心! 让开! ***~ that ...*** 留心…,一定…. ***~ you*** 你听着〔表示让步或提出条件的插句〕 (*But I have no objection, ~ you.* 不过,你听着,我并不反对). ***Would [do] you ~ (doing sth.)?*** …可以吗? 你不反对…么? 对不起,请你…. (*Would you ~ shutting the door?* 对不起,请你把门关上好吗?). **~-blow** *vt.* 〔美俚〕使产生幻觉,使经历迷幻感,极度刺激. **~-blower** *n.* ①迷幻剂. ②②吸毒者(尤指吸服迷幻剂者). ③迷幻的感受. ④动人心弦〔引起幻觉〕的东西. **~-blowing** *a.* 动人心弦的;(麻醉品等)引起幻觉的. **~ cure, ~ healing** 精神疗法. **~ reader** 自称能知他人心事的人. **~ reading** 测心术. **~-set** 思想的倾向. **~ stuff** 【哲】精神素材. **~'s eye** 想象.

Min·da·na·o [ˌmindɑːˈnau] *n.* 棉兰老(岛),明达瑙(岛)〔菲律宾〕.

mind·ed [ˈmaindid] *a.* ①有意志的〔用作定语〕. ②想…的〔用作表语,与不定式连用〕. ③有…之心的,有…精神的,热心…的,关心…的〔构成复合词〕. *He is ~ to do so.* 他是想这样干的. *small-~* 气量小的. *low-~* 卑鄙的. *feeble-~* 低能的;意志薄弱的. *air-~* 热心航空的.

mind·er [maində] *n.* (家畜、机器、幼儿等的)看管人.

mind·ful [ˈmaind*f*ul] *a.* 〔通例用作表语〕注意…的,留心…的;不忘…的 *(of)* (*opp.* forgetful). **-ly** *ad.*, **-ness** *n.*

mind·less [ˈmaindlis] *a.* ①不注意的,不留心的;无心的,无意识的. ②愚钝的. **-ly** *ad.*, **-ness** *n.*

Min·do·ro [minˈdɔːrəu] *n.* (菲律宾中部的)民都洛.

mine[1] [main] *pro.* ①〔I 的物主代词〕我的(东西),我的家属,我的亲戚. *The book is ~.* 这本书是我的. *He was kind to me and ~.* 他对我和我的家属都好. *That is no business of ~.* 那不关我的事情. *The game is ~.* (比赛的结果)是我赢了. ②〔古、诗〕我的 (= my): (a) 用在头一个字母是元音或 *h* 的名词前: *~ eye, ~ heart.* (b) 用在名词后: *lady ~.*

mine[2] [main] *n.* ①矿,矿山,矿井;【矿】铁矿. ②资源;(知识、资料等的)源泉,宝库. ③【军】坑道;地雷坑. ④地雷 (= land ~);水雷;火箭炮弹. ⑤【动】(昆虫的)潜道. *a coal ~* 煤矿. *a gold ~* 金矿. *the ~s* 矿业. *a ~ of information* 知识的宝库. *an acoustic [a sonic] ~* 音响引爆水雷,感音水雷. *a floating [drifting, surface-] ~* 漂流水雷. *a magnetic ~* 磁性水雷. *a submarine contact ~* 海中触发水雷. ***charge a ~*** 装填地雷. ***lay a ~*** 布置地雷〔水雷〕;推翻 *(for)*. ***spring a ~ on (sb.)*** 冷不妨袭击(某人). ***strike a ~*** 触雷. ***work a ~*** 办矿,开矿. —*vt.* ①开(矿),采(矿),采掘;打(矿井),挖(矿道). ②在…中〔下〕敷设地雷〔水雷〕;发射(火箭炮弹);(用雷)炸毁,爆破. ③用阴谋暗害,破坏. *~oil shale* 开采油页岩. —*vi.* ①开矿,采矿;挖坑道. ②布雷. **~ barrage** 雷幕. **~ belt** 雷带. **~ captain** 矿工头. **~ chamber** 雷室. **~ clearance** 扫雷,排雷. **~ detector** 探雷器. **~ dragging** 水雷扫除工作. **~ dredger** 扫雷艇. **~ field** 矿区;【军】布雷区〔场〕. **~ layer** 布雷舰艇 (= mine-laying vessel). **a ~-laying squad** 布雷队. **~-laying submarine** 布雷潜水艇. **~ planter** 布雷船;布雷兵. **~-prop** 矿柱,坑木. **~-run** 原矿. **~ sweeper** 扫雷舰〔器〕. **~-sweeping** 海上扫雷(工作). **~ thrower** 掷雷筒. **~ vessel** 水雷舰. **~ warfare** 地雷战;水雷战. **~-water** 【矿】矿水,井下水. **~-worker** 〔主美〕矿工.

Mi·nen (wer·fer) [ˈmiːnən(vɛəfə)] *n.* 〔G.〕德式迫击炮.

min·er [ˈmainə] *n.* ①矿工;地雷工兵;采矿机. ②〔*pl.*〕〔美商〕矿业股. **coal ~** 采煤工人. **~'s disease** 矿工病. **~'s friend** 达维式 (Davy) 式安全灯. **~'s phthisis** 【医】矽肺;矿工痨病;炭末入肺病.

min·er·ag·ra·phy [ˌminəˈrægrəfi] 【矿】矿相学.

min·er·al. = mineralogy.

min·er·al [ˈminərəl] *n.* ①矿物;〔口〕矿石;【化】无机物. ②〔英〕〔*pl.*〕= ~ water. — *a.* 矿物(性)的;含矿物的;无机的. *the ~ kingdom* 矿物界. **~ detector** 【无】矿石〔晶体〕检波器. **~ fertilizer** 无机肥料. **~ jelly** 矿冻,矿物冻. **~ oil** 矿物油. **~ rights** 开矿权. **~ spring** 矿泉. **~ tar** 软沥青 (= maltha). **~ vein** 矿脉. **~ water** 矿泉(水),矿质水. **~ wax** 地蜡,石蜡 (= ozokerite). **~ wool** 矿渣绒.

min·er·al·ize [ˈminərəlaiz] *vt.* 使矿物化,使矿化;使含矿物. — *vi.* 探矿;促进矿化. **-i·za·tion** [ˌminərəlaiˈzeiʃən] *n.* 【地】矿化(作用);成矿作用. **-r** *n.* ①【化】造矿元素;【地】矿化因素. ②探矿者,采矿者.

min·er·a·log·i·cal [ˌminərəˈlɔdʒikəl] *a.* 矿物学(上)的.

min·er·al·o·gist [ˌminəˈrælədʒist] *n.* 矿物学家.

min·er·al·o·gy [ˌminəˈrælədʒi] *n.* 矿物学.

min·er·al·oid [ˈminərəlɔid] *n.* 类矿物,似矿物,准矿物.

Mi·ner·va [miˈnəːvə] *n.* 【罗神】米涅瓦〔司智慧、学问、战争等的女神〕.

mi·ne·stro·ne [ˌmiːneiˈstrəunei] *n.* 〔It.〕意大利浓菜汤.

min·e·ver [ˈminivə] *n.* (中世纪贵族用作里子或装饰用的)白毛皮.

min·gle [ˈmiŋgl] *vt.* 使相混,使混合. *with ~d feelings* 悲喜交集地. — *vi.* ①混合 *(with)*. ②混在一起;参加,加入 *(among; in)*;交际 *(with)*. *~ in [with] the crowd* 混入人群. *They ~ very little in society.* 他们很少交际. **~-mangle** 混合.

min·gy [ˈmindʒi] *a.* 〔英口〕卑鄙的;吝啬的,小气的.

min·i [ˈmini] *n.* ①同类中的极小者. ②超短裙 (= miniskirt). ③微型汽车 (= minicar).

min·i·ate [ˈminieit] *vt.* ①在…上涂朱红在…. ②用彩色文字装饰(抄本).

min·i·a·ture [ˈminjətʃə] *n.* ①(中世纪抄本上的)彩饰画;(象牙等上的)微小画像,纤细画(术);缩图,缩模;小型器件. ②【影】模型布景,模型舞台装置. — *a.* 小型的,缩小的;小规模的. *a ~ camera* 小型照相机. *a ~ car* 微型汽车. *a ~ war* 小规模战争. ***in ~*** 小型的,小规模的,缩图的;用纤细画法画成的. — *vt.* ①使成小型. ②把…画成纤细画,缩写.

min·i·a·tur·ist [ˈminjətʃərist] *n.* 纤画家,微图画家.

min·i·a·tur·ize [ˈminiətʃəraiz] *vt.* 使微型化. **-i·za·tion** [ˌminiətʃəraiˈzeiʃən] *n.*

min·i·boom [ˈminibuːm] *n.* 短暂繁荣.

min·i·bus [ˈminibʌs] *n.* 微型公共汽车.
min·i·cab [ˈminikæb] *n.* 微型出租汽车.
min·i·cam [ˈminikæm] *n.* = miniature camera.
min·i·cri·sis [ˈminikraisis] *n.* 短暂危机.
Min·i·é [ˈmini:, ˈmini:ei] **ball** 锥形来福枪弹.
min·i·fy [ˈminifai] *vt.* 弄小(少),使缩小;削减;轻视.
min·i·kin [ˈminikin] *n.* 微小的东西;小扣针;小人,小动物;【印】最小铅字. — *a.* 微小的,纤小的;矫揉造作的.
min·im [ˈminim] *n.* ①微物,一滴,一点点,一丝丝;〔蔑〕极矮小的人. ②(药剂用)量滴〔液量最小单位,英制 = 0.0592 cc., 美制 = 0.0616 cc.〕. ③一画,一笔(尤指 m, n 等字母中自上至下的一笔). ④【乐】半音符.
min·i·ma [ˈminimə] *n.* minimum 复数的异体.
min·i·mal [ˈminiməl] *a.* ①最小的,极微的,最低(限度)的. ②最简单派艺术的. — *n.* 最简单派艺术作品〔抽象艺术的一种〕. ~ **art** 最简单派艺术.
min·i·mal·ist [ˈminiməlist] *n.* (政治上的)最低纲领派 (*opp.* maximalist); 最简单派艺术家.
min·i·mize [ˈminimaiz] *vt.* ①使减到最少,按最小限度估计. ②轻视. **-za·tion** [ˌminiməlaizeiʃən] *n.*
min·i·miz·er [ˈminimaizə] *n.* 把事情估计得过低的人,轻视(哲学难题等)的人.
min·i·mum [ˈminiməm] *n.* (*pl.* ~*s*, -*ma* [-mə]) 最小,最低,最少限度;【数】极小(值). *the irreducible* ~ 无法减少的最小限度. *The thermometer reached the* ~ *for the the year.* 寒暑表降到当年最低度数. — *a.* 最少的,最小的,最低的. *the* ~ *value*【数】极小值. ~ **range** 最小射程. ~ **thermometer** 最低温度计. ~ **wage** (法定)最低工资.
min·i·mus [ˈminiməs] *a.* 〔英〕(学校里同姓同学)年纪最轻的. ★ 琼斯三弟兄依年龄大小称为 Jones major, Jones minor, Jones ~.
min·ing [ˈmainiŋ] *n.* ①采矿;采矿业,矿业. ②敷设地雷〔水雷〕. — *a.* 开矿的,采矿的. *a* ~ *engineer* 采矿工程师. ~ *engineering* 采矿工程(学). *the* ~ *industry* 采矿工业.
min·ion [ˈminjən] *n.* ①〔贬〕宠儿,宠臣,宠物. ②走狗,奴才. ③〔称呼〕顽皮姑娘. ④(七点大小的)小活字. ⑤僚属. *a* ~ *of fortune* 〔蔑〕幸运的宠儿. *the* ~*s of the law* 〔蔑〕狱吏;警察.
min·is·cule [ˈminiskju:l] *n.* (= minuscule) ①(中世纪古抄本的)小书写体. ②小书写体字母. ③小字. — *a.* ①小书写体的;小书写体字母的;小字的. ②极小的,微小的,细微的.
min·ish [ˈminiʃ] *vt.* 〔古〕减少,缩小.
min·i·skirt [ˈminiˌskə:t] *n.* 超短裙.
min·is·ter [ˈministə] *n.* ①部长;阁员,大臣;〔*pl.*〕政府. ②公使;外交使节. ③【宗】牧师;〔英〕非国教派牧师. ★ 英国国教派牧师叫 vicar, rector, curate. ④【军】代理人. ⑤仆人,侍从,臣下. *the Prime M-* 内阁总理,首相. *the M- for [of] Foreign Affairs* 外交部长. *the M- of Defense* 国防部长. *the Council of Ministers* (苏联等国的)部长会议. *the* ~ *plenipotentiary* 全权公使. — *vi.* ①做牧师;侍奉;伺候,服侍. ②尽力,出力,帮助;对…有帮助,有贡献 (*to*). *a* ~*ing angel* 救星. ~ *to a person's vanity* 满足某人的虚荣心. ~ *to a sick man's wants* 照顾病人需要. — *vt.* 〔古〕①供给. ②举行(祭祀).
min·is·te·ri·al [ˌminisˈtiəriəl] *a.* ①部长〔牧师、公使等〕的. ②代理的;辅助的,附属的(*opp.* directing);有帮助的,有贡献的. ③行政(上)的 (*opp.* judicial). *the* ~ *party* 〔英〕政府党. *the* ~ *benches* (英国议会下院)政府党(席)(*opp.* opposition benches). **-ist** *n.* 〔英〕内阁支持者. **-ly** *ad.* 作为部长〔大臣、牧师〕.
min·is·trant [ˈministrənt] *a.* 服务的,侍奉的,辅佐的. —*n.* 侍奉者,辅助者.
min·is·tra·tion [ˌminisˈtreiʃən] *n.* ①行宗教仪式;(特指牧师的)职务;服务. ②救助,救济.
min·is·tra·tive [ˈministrətiv] *a.* = ministrant.
min·is·try [ˈministri] *n.* ①服务,侍奉. ②牧师的职务;〔集合词〕牧师. ③部长的任务〔职务、任期〕. ④〔常作 M-〕〔英〕内阁;〔英〕(政府的)部(=〔美〕department). ⑤公使团. *The M- has resigned.* 内阁辞职了. *the M- of Foreign Affairs* 外交部.
mini·sub [ˈminisʌb] *n.* 小型潜水艇.
mini·track [ˈminitræk] *n.* 人造卫星〔火箭〕的电子跟踪系统.
min·i·tube [ˈminitju:b] *n.* 小型〔袖珍〕电视机.
mini·type [ˈminitaip] *n.* 微型,小型.
min·i·um [ˈminiəm] *n.* 朱红色;【化】铅丹,红铅,四氧化三铅.
min·i·ver [ˈminivə] *n.* = minever.
mink [miŋk] *n.* ①【动】水貂. ②貂皮.
Minn. = Minnesota.
Min·na [ˈminə] *n.* 明娜〔女子名〕.
Min·ne·ap·o·lis [ˌminiˈæpəlis] *n.* 明尼阿波利斯〔美国城市〕.
min·ne·sing·er [ˈminiˌsiŋə] *n.* 〔G.〕(德国中世纪的)吟游诗人.
Min·ne·so·ta [ˌminiˈsəutə] *n.* 明尼苏达〔美国州名〕.
Min·nie [ˈmini] *n.* 明妮〔女子名, Mary 的昵称〕.
min·nie [ˈmini] *n.* 〔军俚〕= Minenwerfer.
min·now [ˈminəu] *n.* 【鱼】鲦鱼;小鱼,杂鱼. ***a Triton among [of] the* ~*s*** 鸡群一鹤. ***throw out a* ~ *to catch a whale*** 弃小引大.
Mi·no·an [miˈnəuən] *a.* (公元前 2800—1100 年前后以克里特 (Crete) 岛为中心发达起来的) 米诺斯文化的.
Mi·nol [ˈmainɔl] *n.* 【海军】(比 T.N.T. 约强 50%的)猛烈炸药.
mi·nor [ˈmainə] *a.* (*opp.* major) ①较小的,少数的,小…. ②不重要的,二三流的,较次的. ③未成年的;〔英〕(在两个同姓学生中)年纪较小的,小…. ④【乐】小调的,小音阶的. ⑤〔美〕(大学中)次要学科的. *a* ~ *fault* 轻微过失. *a* ~ *injury* 轻伤. *a* ~ *matter* 小事. *a* ~ *arc* 【数】小弧,劣弧. ***in a* ~ *key*** 用小调;用小音阶;小声闷气的(谈话等). — *n.* ①【法】未成年者. ②【数】子式;【逻】小名词,小前提;【乐】小调,小音阶. ③〔*M-*〕【天主】方济各派修道士. ④(美大学)副科,选修科;【橄榄球】在对方球门后将球打落;〔*pl.*〕=~ leagues. — *vi.* (美大学)兼修,把…选作副科 (*in*). **M- Leagues** 〔美〕 Major League 以下的美国职业棒球队. ~ **mode**【乐】小调调式. ~ **order**【天主】四个低级圣职人员之一. ~ **planet**【天】小行星. ~ **premise**【逻】小前提. ~ **scale**【乐】小调,小音阶. ~ **seminary**【天主】初级神学院. ~ **term**【逻】小名词.
Mi·nor·ca [miˈnɔ:kə] *n.* ①米诺卡岛〔西地中海〕. ②〔m-〕米诺卡鸡 (= ~ fowl).
Mi·nor·ite [ˈmainərait] *n.* = Franciscan.
mi·nor·i·ty [maiˈnɔriti, mi-] *n.* (*opp.* majority)①【法】未成年(时期). ②少数;少数党;较少票数;少数民族. *The* ~ *is subordinate to the majority.* 少数服从多数.
Mi·nos [ˈmainɔs] *n.*【希神】迈诺斯〔克里特岛的王,死后做阴间法官〕.
Mi·not [ˈmainət] *n.* 迈诺特〔姓氏〕.
Min·o·taur [ˈmainətɔ:] *n.*【希神】人身牛头怪物.
Min. Plen. = Minister Plenipotentiary 全权公使.
Minsk [minsk] *n.* 明斯克〔苏联城市〕.
min·ster [ˈminstə] *n.* 修道院附属礼拜堂;大教堂.
min·strel [ˈminstrəl] *n.* ①(中世的)吟游诗人. ②〔诗〕诗人,乐人,歌手,音乐家. ③旅行音乐师;〔*pl.*〕(常由白人扮演的)化装黑人乐队 (= negro 〔Christy〕 ~s). ~ *show* 化装黑人乐队的演出.
min·strel·sy [ˈminstrəlsi] *n.* ①吟游诗人的诗(歌);弹琴,吟唱. ②〔集合词〕吟游诗人;诗歌集. ③〔诗〕(鸟的)歌;诗歌.

mint[1] [mint] *n.*【植】薄荷. ***pay tithe of ~ (and anise) and cummin*** 放弃大事守小节〔出自《圣经》马太福音第23章第23节〕. ~ **oil** 薄荷油. ~ **sauce** 薄荷卤汁〔吃烤小羊肉拌用〕;〔英俚〕钱.

mint[2] [mint] *n.* ①造币厂. ②巨额. ③富源. *a ~ of money* 大量金钱,巨额财富. *a ~ of trouble* 千辛万苦. ~ *drops*〔美俚〕钱. — *a.* 崭新的,完美的;新造的. ***in ~ state [condition]*** (书籍、邮票等)崭新的,刚印好的. — *vt.* ①铸造(货币). ②创造(新词、新句等). ~ **mark** (币面)刻印. ~**master** 造币厂长. ~ **weight** (货币的)标准重量. **-er** *n.* 造币厂工人,造币者.

mint[3] [mint]〔主 Scot.〕①打算,准备(做某事)〔与不定式连用〕. ②试图,尝试〔后接名词〕. ③把矛头指向某人[事],打击某人. *They ~ to leave tomorrow.* 他们准备明天走. ~ *another stroke* 试图再次打击. — *vi.* ①装腔做势,磨蹭 *(at)*. ②渴求 *(at)*. ③暗示,表示 *(at)*. *Don't ~ at it, do it.* 别磨蹭,说干就干. *They cannot understand what we ~ at, unless we speak it out.* 我们不讲明,他们不会了解我们的意思. — *n.* 尝试. *Make a ~ at.* 试试看.

mint·age [ˈmintidʒ] *n.* ①铸造钱币;造币权;造币费. ②造币材料. ③(货币等的)刻印. ④〔总称〕硬币.

min·u·end [ˈminjuend] *n.*【数】被减数 (*opp.* subtrahend).

min·u·et [ˌminjuˈet] *n.* (17世纪兴起的三拍子)小步舞(曲).

mi·nus [ˈmainəs] *a.* (*opp.* plus) 负(的),减的;零下的. *a ~ sign* 负号,减号. *a ~ quantity* 负数,负量. ~ *charge*【电】负电荷. ~ *electricity* 阴电,负电. ~ *material* 次品. *The temperature is ~ twenty degrees.* 温度是零下二十度. — *prep.* 没有…的;丢掉,失去;减(去);少掉. *Seven ~ four is three.* 七减四等于三. *a purse ~ its contents* 空钱袋. *He came back ~ an arm.* 他失去了一只胳膊回来了. *He was ~ fifty dollars.* 他花了五十块钱. — *n.* 负数,负量;负号,减号;差少,欠缺,损失.

mi·nus·cule [miˈnʌskjuːl] *n.* = miniscule.

min·ute[1] [ˈminit] *n.* ①分〔一小时或一度的1/60〕. ②一会儿工夫;一瞬间,刹那. ③备忘录,笔记;〔*pl.*〕(会议)记录. *Wait a ~.* 等一下. *five ~s to [past] six* 六点差[过]五分. ***in a few ~s*** 几分钟工夫就,立刻. ***in a ~*** 马上,即刻. ***make a ~ of*** 记录,记下. ***the ~ (that)*** 一…(就)〔作连词用,引出时间状语从句〕(*I knew him the ~ I saw him.* 我一见他就认出了他). ***this ~*** 现在就,即刻. ***to the ~*** 一分不差,正,恰好 (*He appears at five o'clock to the ~.* 他正巧五点钟来到). ***up to the ~*** 最新的. — *vt.* ①精确地测定…的时间. ②记录,记下 *(down)*. ~ **bell** 分钟〔报丧或举行丧礼时每分钟鸣钟一次〕. ~ **book** (会议)记录簿,记事簿. ~ **glass** 计时沙漏. ~ **gun** 分炮〔为高级军官举行葬礼或船舶遇难时每分钟发一次的号炮〕. ~ **hand** (钟表的)分针,长针. ~**man**【美史】(独立战争期间的) 后备民兵. ~ **mark** 分的符号. ~ **steak** 快熟薄肉排. ~**-to-minute broadcasting** 实况广播.

mi·nute[2] [maiˈnjuːt] *a.* ①微小的,细小的;琐碎的;极少的. ②详细的,精密的. ~ *discriptions* 细致的描写[记述,说明]. *a ~ observer* 细心的观察者. **-ly** *ad.* **-ness** *n.*

min·ute·ly [ˈminitli] *ad., a.* ①每分钟(的). ②时常发生(的).

mi·nu·ti·ae [maiˈnjuːʃiiː] *n.*〔*pl.*〕细节,细目;小节,琐事.

minx [miŋks] *n.* 疯姑娘,顽皮姑娘.

min·yan [minˈjɑːn, ˈminjən] *n.* (*pl.* ***min·ya·nim*** [-jɑːˈniːm] ~***s***)〔Heb.〕【犹】祈祷班〔由十名十三岁以上男子组成〕.

Mi·o·cene [ˈmaiəsiːn] *n., a.*【地】第三纪中新统(的),第三纪中新世(的).

mi·o·sis [ˈmaiəusis] *n.*【医】瞳孔缩小.

MIP = ①marine insurance policy 海运保险单. ②〔常作 m.i.p.〕mean indicated pressure 平均指示压力.

Miq·ue·lon Is. [ˌmikəˈlɔn] *n.* 密克隆岛.

mir [miə] *n.*〔Russ.〕【社】米尔〔沙俄农村公社〕,村社.

Mi·ra·bel [ˈmirəbel] *n.* 米拉贝尔〔女子名〕.

mir·a·belle [ˈmiərəˌbel, ˌmiərəˈbel] *n.*【植】①布拉斯李树〔产于欧洲〕. ②布拉斯李子. ③布拉斯白兰地.

mi·ra·bi·le dic·tu [maiˈræbiliː ˈdiktjuː]〔L.〕说也奇怪.

mi·rab·i·le vi·su [miˈræbili ˈvaisju]〔L.〕光怪陆离的.

mi·ra·bi·li·a [ˌmiərəˈbiliə] *n. pl.*〔L.〕奇事;奇迹.

mi·rab·i·lite [miˈræbilait] *n.*【化】芒硝.

mir·a·cle [ˈmirəkl] *n.* ①奇迹;奇事,奇人. ②奇迹剧. ***to a ~*** 奇迹般地;不可思议地. ***work ~s*** 创造奇迹. ~ **fruit** 奇迹果〔一种核浆果,食后可使接着吃的东西带甜味〕. ~ **play** (中世纪基督教)奇迹剧.

mi·rac·u·lous [miˈrækjuləs] *a.* ①奇迹般的,不可思议的,令人惊叹的;非凡的. ②(能够)创造奇迹的. **-ly** *ad.* **-ness** *n.*

mir·a·dor [ˌmirəˈdɔː] *n.*〔Sp.〕(可供眺望的)角塔;窗户;阳台.

mi·rage [ˈmirɑːʒ] *n.* 海市蜃楼,蜃景;幻想,妄想.

Mi·ran·da [miˈrændə] *n.* 米兰达〔女子名〕.

mir·bane [ˈməːbein] *n.*【化】硝基苯;密斑油.

mire [ˈmaiə] *n.* ①泥沼;淤泥;矿泥. ②〔罕〕沾污,污辱;污物. ***drag (sb.) through the ~*** 使丢丑,侮辱,搞臭. ***find [stick] oneself in the ~*** 弄得一筹莫展,束手无策,陷进泥坑里. — *vt.* ①使溅满泥泞;使陷进泥坑里. ②使进退不得;使为难. — *vi.* ①弄得浑身是泥;陷入泥坑. ②进退不得,一筹莫展. *She ~d her car and had to go for help.* 她开的车陷入泥泞中,不得不请人帮助.

Mir·i·am [ˈmiriəm] *n.* 米丽亚姆〔女子名, Mary 的异体〕.

mir·i·ness [ˈmaiərinis] *n.* 泥泞.

mirk [məːk] *n., a.* = murk.

mirk·y [ˈməːki] *a.* = murky.

mir·ror [ˈmirə] *n.* ①镜;反射镜. ②反映;借鉴;榜样. *a concave [convex] ~* 凹[凸]镜. *an electron ~* 电子反射镜. *the ~ of fashion* 流行事物的代表. *a ~ of the times* 时代的反映. ***done with ~s***〔美俚〕用诡计弄成功的;神秘莫测地完成的. ***hold the ~ up to nature*** 反映自然. — *vt.* 映,反射;反映. ~ **image**【物】镜像;镜中人;镜中物. ~ **writing** *n.* 倒写.

mirth [məːθ] *n.* 欢乐;欢笑.

mirth·ful [ˈməːθful] *a.* 欢乐的,高兴的;欢笑的. **-ly** *ad.* 快快乐乐,高高兴兴. **-ness** *n.*

mirth·less [ˈməːθlis] *a.* 不快乐的,悲伤的,郁闷的. **-ly** *ad.* **-ness** *n.*

MIRV = multiple independently targeted reentry vehicle【军】多弹头分导重返大气层运载工具. ~ *missile* 分导式多弹头导弹.

mir·y [ˈmaiəri] *a.* (***mir·i·er; -i·est***) 泥泞的,泥深的;沾满泥的,脏的. **mir·i·ness** *n.*

mir·za [ˈməːzə] *n.*〔波斯〕加在皇族姓名下的尊称;冠于学者、官吏姓名前的敬称.

mis-[1] *pref.* 错,错误的;坏,不利的. ★在动词和形容词前起副词作用,在动名词和名词前具有形容词的意味,在已有坏义的字前时,通常属古语,表示加强意义: *mis*dread, *mis*doubt.

mis-[2] *comb. f.*〔用于元音前〕= miso-.

mis·ad·ven·ture [ˈmisədˈventʃə] *n.* 意外事故,不幸,灾难,横祸. ***by ~*** 因意外事故;因过失. ***homicide [death] by ~***【法】过失杀害,误杀.

mis·ad·vice [ˌmisədˈvais] *n.* 错误的劝告;馊主意.

mis·ad·vise [ˈmisədˈvaiz] *vt.* 给…出馊主意;错误地劝告.

mis·aimed [ˈmisˈeimd] *a.* 看错了的;打错了主意的.

mis·al·li·ance [ˈmisəˈlaiəns] *n.* 不适当的配合;不相称

的结合[婚配]。
mis·al·ly [ˌmisəˈlai] *vt.* *(-lied; -ly·ing)* 不适当地结合[配合]；错配。
mis·an·dry [ˈmisændri] *n.* (女子)嫌恶男子。
mis·an·thrope, mis·an·thro·pist [ˈmizənθrəup, miˈzænθrəpist] *n.* 厌恶人类者，厌世者 (*opp.* philanthropist)。
mis·an·throp·ic, mis·an·throp·i·cal [ˌmizənˈθrɔpik, -ikəl] *a.* 厌恶人类(者)的，厌世(者)的。
mis·an·thro·pize [miˈzænθrəpaiz, miˈsæn-] *vi.* 厌恶人类，厌世。
mis·an·thro·py [miˈzænθrəpi] *n.* 厌恶人类，厌世，愤世嫉俗。
mis·ap·ply [ˈmisəˈplai] *vt.* 误用，错用，滥用。**-plication** *n.*, **-plied** *a.* 被误用了的。
mis·ap·pre·hend [ˈmisˌæpriˈhend] *vt.* 误解，误会。**-hen·sion** *n.*, **-hen·sive** *a.* 易误会的。
mis·ap·pro·pri·ate [misəˈprəuprieit] *vt.* 乱用；挪用(别人的钱)；私吞；【法】侵占，霸占。**-ation** *n.*
mis·ar·range [ˈmisəˈreindʒ] *vt.* ①排错。②安排不当。
mis·ar·range·ment [ˌmisəˈreindʒmənt] *n.* 误排，错列，排错，错乱次序。
mis·be·come [ˈmisbiˈkʌm] *vt.* *(-be·came* [-biˈkeim], *-be·come* [-biˈkʌm]) 不合，不适合，不配。**-coming** *a.*
mis·be·got·ten, mis·be·got [ˈmisbiˌgɔtn, -gɔt] *a.* 私生的；非法产生的；起源不光彩的。
mis·be·have [ˈmisbiˈheiv] *vt.* 使行为不当 (*~ oneself*)。— *vi.* ①做坏事，行为不当，不规矩，作弊。②行为失常。**-d** *a.*
mis·be·ha·v·io(u)r [ˈmisbiˈheivjə] *n.* 不规矩 (行为)，品行不良。
mis·be·lief [ˈmisbiˈliːf] *n.* 误信，谬见；信奉邪教；信仰错误。
mis·be·lieve [ˈmisbiˈliːv] *vi.* 误信，信邪说，信仰邪教。— *vt.* 不信。**-liev·er** 异教徒；误信者，信邪说者。**-liev·ing** *a.* 异端的，信仰邪教的。
mis·be·seem [ˈmisbiˈsiːm] *vt.* = misbecome.
mis·birth [ˈmisˈbəːθ] *n.* = miscarriage②.
mis·brand [ˈmisˈbrænd] *vt.* ①把…打错了标记[烙印]。②把…贴上假标记[商标]。
misc. = miscellaneous; miscellany.
mis·cal·cu·late [ˈmisˈkælkjuleit] *vt.*, *vi.* 算错，估错，错认。**-lation** *n.*
mis·call [ˈmisˈkɔːl] *vt.* 叫错，误称；[英方]谩骂某人。
mis·car·riage [misˈkæridʒ] *n.* ①失策，失败。②流产，早产。③(信件等的)误投，误送。*~ of one's plans* 计划失败。*a ~ of justice* 误判(案)；审判不公(案件)。
mis·car·ry [misˈkæri] *vi.* ①失策，失败。②流产，早产。③(信等)被误投[误送]。
mis·cast [ˈmisˈkɑːst, -ˈkæst] *vt.* *(-cast; -cast·ing)* ①使做不相称的事；使(演员)扮演不相称的角色。②对(戏剧)作不适当的角色分配。
mis·ce·ge·na·tion [ˌmisidʒiˈneiʃən] *n.* 人种混杂；混血。
mis·cel·la·ne·a [ˌmisiˈleiniə] *n.* [*pl.*] 杂集；杂录，杂记。
mis·cel·la·ne·ous [ˌmisiˈleinjəs, -niəs] *a.* 各种各样的，五花八门的，混杂的；多方面的。*~ business* 杂务。*~ goods* 杂货。*a ~ writer* 多面手作家，多才多艺的作家。
mis·cel·la·ny [miˈseləni] *n.* ①[*pl.*] 杂集，杂录，杂记。②混合物，杂物。**-nist** *n.* 杂文[杂记]作家。
mis·chance [misˈtʃɑːns] *n.* 不幸，灾难，横祸；故障。*by ~* 不幸，不巧。
mis·chief [ˈmistʃif] *n.* *(pl. ~s)* ①(物质上的)损害，灾害，灾祸，危害；(身体、机器等的)毛病，故障。②(精神上的)毒害，坏影响。③造成损害的人；祸根。④顽皮，淘气；[口]顽皮孩子，淘气精；[口] = devil. *There is carelessness, but no ~.* 粗心大意是有的，恶意倒没有。*One ~ comes on the neck of another.* 祸不单行。*a regular little ~* 十分淘气的孩子。*What the ~ (= the devil) do you want?* 你究竟要什么？ ***cause ~*** 引起灾祸。***do ~*** 造成损害。***do sb. a ~*** [口]使某人受到损害；打伤某人，使某人受伤；杀死某人。***go [get] into ~*** 玩起鬼把戏来，淘气起来。***keep out of ~*** 不胡闹。***make ~ between*** 使双方不和，离间。***mean ~*** 抱恶意。***out of (pure) ~*** 闹着玩儿。***play the ~ with*** 弄坏…的身体[健康]，加害；弄坏(机器等)，使发生毛病；把…弄得一塌糊涂(*The wind has played the ~ with my papers.* 风把我的文件吹得乱七八糟)。***The ~ (of it) is that ….*** 麻烦的是，伤脑筋的是…。***up to ~*** 要胡闹[捣蛋]，在玩鬼把戏 (*The children are up to ~.* 小孩子们想胡闹)。**~-maker** 离间者。**~-making** *n.*, *a.* 离间(的)；离间手段。**~-monger** 离间者。
mis·chie·vous [ˈmistʃivəs] *a.* ①为害的，有害的；爱玩鬼把戏的。②顽皮的，淘气的；有点带恶意的。*a ~ glance* 恶意的一瞥。**-ly** *ad.* **-ness** *n.*
mis·ci·bil·i·ty [ˌmisiˈbiliti] *n.* ①可混性，混和性；溶混性。②混和法。
mis·ci·ble [ˈmisibl] *a.* 可溶和的，易混合的 *(with)*。*~ oil* 混合油剂。
mis·code [ˈmiskəud] *vt.* 【自】错编〔提供错误的遗传密码〕。
mis·col·our [misˈkʌlə] *vt.* ①把…着错色粉。②对…作歪曲叙述；颠倒黑白。
mis·con·ceive [ˈmiskənˈsiːv] *vt.* 误解。— *vi.* 有错误看法 *(of)*。
mis·con·cep·tion [ˈmiskənˈsepʃən] *n.* 误解，错觉，看法错误。
mis·con·duct [misˈkɔndʌkt] *n.* ①行为不正，不规矩；(尤指官吏等的)胡作非为，渎职。②通奸。③办错，处置失当。*commit ~ with* 和…通奸。— [miskənˈdʌkt] *vt.* ①办错，处理…失当。②〔*~ oneself*〕不规矩；与…通奸 *(with)*。
mis·con·struc·tion [ˈmiskənsˈtrʌkʃən] *n.* 误解，误会；解释错误，曲解；(房屋)盖错。
mis·con·strue [ˈmiskənˈstru] *vt.* 误会，误解；曲解。
mis·count [ˈmisˈkaunt] *vt.*, *vi.*, *n.* 算错；(尤指投票数的)点错，计数误差，计算误差。
mis·cre·ant [ˈmiskriənt] *a.* ①邪恶的，恶劣的。②〔古〕异端的。— *n.* ①恶棍，歹人。②邪教徒；不信教的人。
mis·cre·ate [ˈmiskriˈeit] *vt.*, *vi.* 误造，误创，误作。
mis·cre·at·ed [ˈmiskriˈeitid] *a.* 畸形的，丑怪的。
mis·cue [ˈmisˈkjuː] *n.*, *vi.* 【台球】弹子棒打滑；【剧】错过提示；反应不及时。
mis·date [ˈmisˈdeit] *vt.* 写错[弄错](日期)。— *n.* 错写的日期[年代]。
mis·deal [ˈmisˈdiːl] *n.* 【牌】发错牌。— *(-dealt* [-ˈdelt]) *vi.*, *vt.* 发错(牌)。
mis·deal·er [misˈdiːlə] *n.* 【牌】发错牌者。
mis·deal·ing [ˈmisˈdiːliŋ] *n.* 做错，不正当行为。
mis·deed [ˈmisˈdiːd] *n.* 恶劣行为；罪行。
mis·de·mean [ˌmisdiˈmiːn] *vt.*, *vi.* 〔罕〕 = misbehave.
mis·de·mean·ant [ˌmisdiˈmiːnənt] *n.* 行为不端[不规矩]的人；【法】轻罪犯人。
mis·de·mean·o(u)r [ˌmisdiˈmiːnə] *n.* (一般的)不正当的行为，恶劣的品行；坏事；【法】轻罪。*commit a ~* 犯轻罪。*a high ~* 【法】重罪。
mis·de·scrip·tion [ˈmisdisˈkripʃən] *n.* 不完全的记述，(特指契约中要点项目的)误记。
mis·dial [ˈmisdaiəl] *vt.* 拨错(电话号码)。
mis·di·rect [ˈmisdiˈrekt] *vt.* ①指导[指挥]错误。②写错(信封)。③指错(地点、方向)给…。④(法官对陪审员)指示错误。⑤瞄错，打歪；用错(精力、才能等)。

mis·do [misˈduː] *vt.* (*-did, -done; -do·ing*) 错办. — *vi.* 〔废〕干坏事,作恶.

mis·do·ing [ˈmisˈdu(ː)iŋ] *n.* 坏事,恶行.

mis·doubt [misˈdaut] *vt.* 〔古〕怀疑;挂念,担心 (*that*). — *n.* 〔古〕怀疑;悬念.

mise [miːz, maiz] *n.* ①【史】协定. ②赌注. ③【法】权利令状上的争论点.

mis·ease [misˈiːz] *n.* ①〔古〕不安;苦恼. ②〔废〕贫穷.

mis·ed·u·ca·tion [ˈmisˌedju(ː)ˈkeiʃən] *n.* 错误教育.

mis·em·ploy [ˌmisemˈplɔi] *vt.* 误用;滥用. **-ment** *n.*

mise en scène [ˈmiːzɑ̃ːnˈsein] 〔F.〕 ①舞台演出的调度. ②舞台的布景道具. ③导演. ④自然[社会]环境.

mi·ser[1] [ˈmaizə] *n.* 吝啬的人,小气鬼,守财奴;〔古〕可怜的人.

mi·ser[2] [ˈmaizə] *n.* (矿山、凿井用)钻孔机,凿井机;【矿】管形提泥钻头.

mis·er·a·ble [ˈmizərəbl] *a.* ①不幸的,痛苦的,可怜的,(生活)悲惨的,(消息)使人伤心的;(肉体上)受折磨的. ②卑劣的,不要脸的,可耻的. ③简陋的,(饮食)粗陋的;破烂的,肮脏的;糟糕的;缺乏的,不充足的. *a ~ cold* 重感冒. *~ with hunger and cold* 饥寒交迫. *a ~ scoundrel* 无耻之徒. — *n.* 不幸的人;穷困不堪的人.

mis·er·a·bly [ˈmizərəbli] *ad.* ①不幸地,可怜地,悲惨地;糟糕地;卑劣地. ②非常,极,大大地 (*fail ~*).

Mis·e·re·re [ˌmizəˈriəri] *n.* ①(拉丁语译《圣经》的)第51篇赞美歌. ②〔*m-*〕哀求,乞怜;【建】= misericord(e)①.

mis·er·i·cord(e) [miˈzerikɔːd] *n.* ①(教堂中装在折椅上以便起立时支持身体用的)椅背突板. ②(修道院中的)斋堂. ③短剑.

mi·ser·li·ness [ˈmaizəlinis] *n.* 吝啬.

mi·ser·ly [ˈmaizəli] *a.* 吝啬的,小气的.

mis·er·y [ˈmizəri] *n.* 苦难,不幸;苦痛,疼痛;惨状,悲惨的境遇;贫穷. *M- loves company.* 同病相怜.

mis·es·teem [ˌmisəˈstiːm] *vt.* 对…不能正确评价;误估…的价值. — *n.* 缺乏适当的估价.

mis·es·ti·mate [misˈestiˌmeit] *vt.* 误算, 误估. — *n.* [-mit] 错误的估计. **-ma·tion** *n.*

mis·fea·sance [misˈfiːzəns] *n.* 犯罪,违法;【法】不法行为,滥用职权.

mis·file [ˈmisˈfail] *vt.* 把(文件等)归错档案.

mis·fire [ˈmisˈfaiə] *n.* (枪等的)不发火,射不出;(内燃机的)不着火. — *vi.* 不发火,打不出;不着火,开动不起来;不奏效,不中要害. ***~d points*** 不得要领的[不中肯的]论点.

mis·fit [ˈmisˈfit] *n.* 不适合;不合身的衣着;不容易适应环境的人. — *vt., vi.* ①(对…)不合适;(衣服等)对…不合身. ②【物】错合. *This coat ~s me.* 这件上衣对我不合身.

mis·for·tune [misˈfɔːtʃən] *n.* ①背运,倒霉,不幸;灾难,灾祸. ②私生子;生私生子. *M- might be a blessing in disguise.* 塞翁失马,安知非福. *M-s tell us what fortune is.* 不经灾难不知福. *M-s never come singly [alone] = One ~ rides upon another's back.* 祸不单行. ***by ~*** 不幸. ***have the ~ to*** (*do*) 不幸(而)….

mis·give [misˈgiv] *vt.* (*-gave* [-ˈgeiv]; *-giv·en* [-ˈgivn]) 使疑惑[害怕、焦心、忧虑等]起来. *His heart misgave him.* 他疑惑[害怕、担心]起来了.

mis·giv·ing [misˈgiviŋ] *n.* 〔否定以外通常用 *pl.*〕疑惑,忧虑,担心,不安. *full of ~(s)* 满心疑惑,十分不安.

mis·got·ten [ˈmisˈgɔtn] *a.* ①以不正当手段取得的. ② = misbegotton. ***~ treasure*** 不义之财.

mis·gov·ern [ˈmisˈgʌvən] *vt.* 对(政务等)管理不当. **-ment** *n.* 错误的行政管理.

mis·growth [ˈmisˈgrəuθ] *n.* 异常发育.

mis·guide [ˈmisˈgaid] *vt.* 〔主用 *p.p.*〕指导错误;带错方向;使误入歧途. **-guid·ance** *n.* 错误的指导.

mis·guid·ed [ˈmisˈgaidid] *a.* 被指导错误的,被带错的,搞错的;误入歧途的. **-ly** *ad.* **-ness** *n.*

mis·han·dle [ˈmisˈhændl] *vt.* ①用错;瞎弄,乱弄. ②粗暴对待,虐待. ③办错;胡乱处置.

mi·shan·ter [mĭˈʃæntə] *n.* 〔Scot.〕不幸,灾祸,灾难.

mis·hap [ˈmishæp, misˈhæp] *n.* 不幸的事,灾难. *the haps and ~s of life* 人生祸福. ***without ~*** 平安无事.

mis·hear [ˈmisˈhiə] *vt., vi.* (*-heard* [-ˈhəːd]) 听错.

mis·hit [ˈmisˈhit] *n.* 打歪. — [misˈhit] *vt.* 把…打歪.

mish·mash [ˈmiʃmæʃ] *n.* 混杂物;杂烩.

Mish·na, Mish·nah [miʃˈnɑː, ˈmiʃnə] *n.* (*pl. Mishna·yot* [ˌmiʃnɑːˈjəut]) ①犹太教法典的第一部分. ②犹太教法典的第一部分的注释. ③著名犹太法学博士的教义. **Mish·na·ic** *a.*

mis·in·form [ˈmisinˈfɔːm] *vt.* 误传,传错,报错. **-forma·tion** *n.* 误传,误报,错误的消息.

mis·in·form·ant [ˌmisinˈfɔːmənt] *n.* 误报者,提供不正确消息者,误传者(= misinformer).

mis·in·ter·pret [ˈmisinˈtəːprit] *vt.* 曲解,误释,误译. **-pre·ta·tion** *n.* **-pre·ter** [ˌmisinˈtəːpritə] *n.* 误译者;误解者;误释者.

mis·join·der [ˌmisˈdʒɔində] *n.* 【法】诉讼当事人的不当的联合.

mis·judge [ˈmisˈdʒʌdʒ] *vt., vi.* ①判断错,看错. ②低估,轻视. **-ment, -judg·ment** *n.*

Mis·kolc [ˈmiʃkəults] *n.* 米什科尔茨〔匈牙利城市〕.

mis·la·bel [misˈleibl] *vt., vi.* (*-beled, -belled; -bel·ing, -bel·ling*) (在…上)误贴标签.

mis·land [misˈlænd] *vt.* 【海】弄错(起卸港), 卸错(船货).

mis·lay [misˈlei] (*-laid* [-ˈleid]) *vt.* 把(东西)误放;搁忘;丢失.

mis·lead [misˈliːd] (*-led* [-ˈled]) *vt.* 把…带错路;把…引入歧途;使迷惑[误解];哄骗.

mis·lead·ing [misˈliːdiŋ] *a.* 引入歧途的;使人误解的,晦涩的;骗人的;使人迷惑的. **-ly** *ad.*

mis·like [misˈlaik] *vt.* 〔古、方〕嫌,厌恶.

mis·man·age [ˈmisˈmænidʒ] *vt.* 把…办错, 对…管理不当,对…处理失当. **-ment** *n.*

mis·mar·riage [ˈmisˈmæridʒ] *n.* 不相配的婚姻.

mis·match [ˈmisˈmætʃ] *vt.* 配错,使不适当地配合. — *n.* 错配;不适当的婚姻.

mis·mate [misˈmeit] *vt., vi.* (使)配合不当; (使)配偶[结婚]不当;(使)配合拙劣.

mis·name [ˈmisˈneim] *vt.* 叫错(名字);误称.

mis·no·mer [ˈmisˈnəumə] *n.* 误称; 使用不当的名称;用词不当.

mis·o- *comb. f.* 嫌,厌 (*opp.* philo-): *miso*capnic.

mis·o·cap·nic [misəˈkæpnik] *a.* 厌恶香烟的. **-nist** *n.* 厌恶香烟的人.

mi·soc·y·ny [miˈsɔsini] *n.* 厌犬症. **-nist** *n.* 讨厌狗的人.

mi·sog·a·my [miˈsɔgəmi] *n.* 厌恶结婚;厌婚症. **-mist** *n.* 厌恶结婚的人.

mi·sog·y·nic [ˌmaisəˈdʒinik, ˌmi-] *a.* 厌恶女人的.

mi·sog·y·ny [maiˈsɔdʒini, miˈs-] 厌恶女人; 厌女症[癖]. **-nist** *n.* 厌恶女人的人.

mi·sol·o·gy [miˈsɔlədʒi] 厌恶理论[说理]. **-gist** *n.* 厌恶理论的人.

mis·o·math [miˈsɔmæθ] *n.* 厌恶数学的人.

mis·o·ne·ism [ˌmisəuˈniːizəm] *n.* 厌新(症),守旧主义.

mis·o·pe·dia [ˌmisəuˈpiːdiə] *n.* 嫌子女症. **-dist** *n.* 嫌子女症患者.

mis·o·pho·bia [ˌmisəuˈfəubiə] *n.* 【医】极端的洁癖;不洁恐怖.

mis·o·po·lem·i·cal [ˌmisəupəuˈlemikəl] *a.* 厌恶战争的.

mis·per·ceive [ˌmispəˈsiːv] *vt.* 误解, 错误感觉. **-per-**

ception *n.*
mis·pick·el [ˈmispikəl] *n.* 【矿】毒砂,砷黄铁矿.
mis·place [ˈmisˈpleis] *vt.* ①把…放错地方;〔口〕忘记把…放在什么地方. ②爱[信]错(人)〔多用被动语态〕. **-ment** *n.* 误放.
mis·play [ˈmisˈplei] *n.* 〔美〕(球类运动)动作错误,失误;误演;误奏. — *vt.* (打球时)使(球)失误;打错(牌).
mis·plead [ˌmisˈpliːd] *vt., vi.* ***(-pled; -plead·ing)*** (为…)不正确地辩护.
mis·plead·ing [ˌmisˈpliːdiŋ] *n.* 【法】(辩护时所作的)不正确的申述[疏漏].
mis·print [misˈprint] *n., vt.* 【印】印错,误印.
mis·prise [misˈpraiz] *vt.* = misprize.
mis·pri·sion[1] [misˈpriʒən] *n.* ①(特指公职人员的)玩忽职守,溺职. ②【法】知情不报;隐匿犯人. ③(反对政府、法院等的)煽动行为. ④误解,搞错. ~ *of felony* 隐匿重罪犯人.
mis·pri·sion[2] [misˈpriʒən] *n.* 〔英古〕蔑视,轻视.
mis·prize [misˈpraiz] *vt.* 蔑视,轻视,看不起.
mis·pro·nounce [ˈmisprəˈnauns] *vi., vt.* 读错(发音).
mis·pro·nun·ci·a·tion [ˈmisprəˌnʌnsiˈeiʃən] *n.* 错误的发音.
mis·quote [ˈmisˈkwəut] *vt.* 引错,误引(文字、语句). **-ta·tion** [-kwəuˈteiʃən] *n.*
mis·read [misˈriːd] ***(-read*** [-red]***)*** *vt.* 读错,解释错…的意思.
mis·reck·on [ˌmisˈrekən] *vt.* 误算.
mis·re·mem·ber [ˌmisriˈmembə] *vt., vi.* ①记错. ②〔方〕忘记.
mis·re·port [ˌmisriˈpɔːt] *vt.* 误报;谎报. — *n.* 误报;谎报.
mis·rep·re·sent [ˈmisˌrepriˈzent] *vt.* ①传错,误传;曲解;诬告,把…颠倒黑白. ②不尽职[不正当地]代表. **-er** *n.* 传达错误的人;不尽职[不正当]的代表. **-ta·tion** *n.* ① 错误的传达. ②【法】虚伪的陈述,诈称.
mis·rule [ˈmisˈruːl] *n.* ①不正确的[作风恶劣的]行政管理,虐政,苛政. ② 无秩序,紊乱. — *vt.* 管错;作风恶劣地管理.
miss[1] [mis] *n.* ***(pl. -es)*** ①〔*M-*〕…小姐. ★ ①有两个以上未婚罗滨逊姐妹时,姐姐通常加在姓前叫 M- Robinson, 妹妹加在姓及洗礼名前叫 M- Joan (Robinson); 姐妹一起叫 the M- Robinsons 或〔古〕*the Misses Robinson*. ② *pl.* 的 misses 发音与 Mrs. [ˈmisiz] 相同,也有发音作[ˈmisiːz]的. ②〔谑、蔑〕姑娘,(特指)小女学生. ③〔对女佣人、女店员的称呼〕小姐. ④〔古〕情妇. *a saucy* ~ 莽撞的姑娘.
miss[2] [mis] *vt.* ①把(看准的东西)失去,让…跑掉,没打中;没猜中;没到手,没拿到,没抓到,没达到;没赶上(车子等);没看到,看漏;漏掉;失落;达不到…的标准,够不上,不够. ②不守(约),不尽(义务);缺;发觉没有[不在]. ③因…没有[不在]而感觉寂寞[不方便];惦念. ④缺席,旷工. ⑤逃却,免去,躲避. ~ *one's aim* 没打中. ~ *one's hold* 放掉,放跑(已经抓住了东西的). ~ *an opportunity* 失去机会. ~ *a catch* 【板球】接漏. *He ~ed the bank.* 他跳不过河而落水了. *I ~ed him in a crowd.* 我在人群中把他挤丢了. ~ *the train* 没赶上火车. *It ~es being a great picture.* 这算不了一幅名画. *I shall ~ you very much.* 你不在我就寂寞了. *He barely ~ed being killed.* 他几乎送了命. *He hasen't ~ed a day's work in years.* 他多年来一天也未旷工. — *vi.* ①打不中,打歪;失败. ②不见;得不着,没…着 *(of; in)*. ~ ***fire*** (枪炮)打不响;(俏皮话等)不好笑;得不到预想的效果. ~ ***one's dinner*** 吐饭. ~ ***one's step [footing]*** 失脚,踩滑. ~ ***one's tip*** 出岔子;失败,没达到目的. ~ ***one's way*** 迷路. ~ ***stays*** (船)抢风失败. ~ ***the bus*** 〔口〕失去好机会. ~ ***the [one's] mark*** 没打中目标;认错目标;失败;不恰当. ~ ***the point*** 不懂(俏皮话等的)妙处. — *n.* ①得不着,寻不着;猜错,不中;失败. ②故意逃避;逃脱. ③〔俚〕没有了…的寂寞. *A ~ is as good as a mile.* 小失败也是失败[差之毫厘失之千里]. *It's hit or ~.* 不计成败,好歹一试,孤注一掷. *She feels the ~ of her children.* 她感到没了孩子的寂寞. ***give a*** ~ 【台球】故意打一个空球;避免,避开;不碰动. ***give sb. a*** ~ 假装没有看见某人,故意避开某人. ***give it a*** ~ 〔美俚〕跳过去;略去,省去. ***near*** ~ 虽不命中但近得足够毁坏目标.
Miss. = Mississippi.
mis·sa [ˈmisə] *n.* 【天主】弥撒 (=Mass).
mis·sal [ˈmisəl] *n.* 【天主】弥撒书;祷告书.
mis·say [misˈsei] *vt., vi.* ***(-said*** [-ˈsaid]; ***-say·ing)*** 〔主古〕①误言,失言. ②说(…的)坏话,诬蔑,谩骂,毁谤.
mis·sel (thrush) [ˈmizəl] *n.* 【鸟】大鸫.
mis·send [ˈmisˈsend] *vt.* ***(-sent*** [-ˈsent]***)*** 送错(邮件等).
mis·sense [ˈmisˌsens] *n.* 【生】误义〔包括一个或一个以上密码子转变的遗传突变〕.
mis·shape [misˈʃeip] *vt.* 弄丑,使残废;使破相. **mis·sha·pen** *a.* 残废的,畸形的;破相的,丑陋的.
mis·sile [ˈmisail, Am. ˈmisəl] *n.* 投射器;飞射器[箭、炮弹等],射弹,飞弹;导弹. *an air-to-air (guided)* ~ 空对空导弹,机载导弹. *an atom-tipped* ~ 原子弹头导弹. *a homing* ~自动寻的导弹. *an intercontinental ballistic* ~ 洲际弹道导弹〔略 I.C.B.M.〕. *an infrared homing* ~ 红外线寻的导弹,红外线自动导引导弹. *a staged* ~多级导弹. *a development* ~ 试验导弹. **-man** *n.* 导弹制造者[设计者];火箭发射手,导弹操作手;导弹专家. **-ry** *n.* 导弹技术;导弹〔总称〕.
miss·ing [ˈmisiŋ] *a.* 失去的,不见了的,下落不明的,失踪的. *killed, wounded, or* ~ 死伤或失踪者. *the* ~ *link* (体系中)缺少的一环;【动】类人猿与人类之间的假想过渡动物. *There is a page* ~. 缺少一页.
mis·sion [ˈmiʃən] *n.* ①派遣;国家代表团的派遣;代表团;使团;(伊斯兰教的)朝觐团;特使;〔美〕驻外使节,大[公]使馆. ②使命,任务;天职;【军】战斗任务;飞行任务. ③传道,传教;(特指到国外的)传道团体[本部、根据地];传道区;传道期间;传道权;传道馆;传道会;贫民救济会. *an economic* ~ 经济代表团. *the* ~ *at Moscow* 驻莫斯科大使馆. *a diplomatic* ~ 外交使团. *be sent on a* ~ 是带有使命派出去的. *It seems to be his* ~ *to help others.* 他的天职好象就是帮助别人. — *vt.* ①给…交代任务;派遣;把任务交给. ②向…传教.
mis·sion·ar·y [ˈmiʃənəri] *a.* 传教(士)的. — *n.* 传教士;(某某主义的)宣传者.
mis·sion·er [ˈmiʃənə] *n.* (教区)传教士 (= missionary).
mis·sion·ize [ˈmiʃənaiz] *vt.* 向…传教;对…宣传…主义;使…皈依自己的宗教信仰. — *vi.* 进行传道.
mis·sis [ˈmisiz] *n.* ①〔用于已婚妇女姓前〕…夫人〔普通写作 Mrs.〕. ②〔口、爱称〕太太〔仆人对女主人的称呼〕;(自己或别人的)太太,妻子,夫人. *How's your ~?* 你的夫人好吗?
miss·ish [ˈmisiʃ] *a.* 小姑娘似的,女学生似的;小姐般一本正经的.
Mis·sis·sip·pi [ˌmisiˈsipi] *n.* ①密西西比〔美国州名〕. ②〔the ~〕密西西比河〔美国〕.
mis·sive [ˈmisiv] *a.* 〔古〕已经送出去的,指令的. — *n.* 公文;书信.
Mis·sour·i [miˈzuəri] *n.* ①密苏里〔美国州名〕. ②〔the ~〕密苏里河〔美国〕. ***from*** ~ 〔美俚〕怀疑的,不轻易相信的 (*I'm from* ~. 我要见到确实证据才相信).
mis·speak [misˈspiːk] *vt., vi.* ***(-spoke***[-ˈspəuk]; ***-spoken***[-ˈspəukən]; ***-speak·ing)*** 误言,失言.
mis·spell [ˈmisˈspel] ***(-spelled*** [-ˈspelt], ***-spelt)*** *vt.* 拼错. **-ing** *n.* 拼写错误.
mis·spend [ˈmisˈspend] *vt.* ***(-spent*** [-t]***)*** 浪费;虚度. *a misspent youth* 浪费了的青春.

mis·state [ˈmisˈsteit] *vt.* 错说；虚称；谎报．**-ment** *n.* 误言．
mis·step [ˈmisˈstep] *n.* 失足；失策，错误．
mis·sus [ˈmisəz] *n.*〔口、方〕= missis.
miss·y [ˈmisi] *n.*〔口、爱称〕小姑娘；小姐．
mist [mist] *n.* ①雾．★ mist 较 fog 淡，较 haze 浓．②(眼睛的)迷糊，朦胧．③起蒙蔽作用的东西．*Scotch* ~ (苏格兰山区特多的)浓雾；雾雨．***cast [throw] a ~ before sb.'s eyes*** 蒙蔽[迷糊]某人．***in a ~*** 迷惑着，心里彷徨着．— *vt.* 给雾蒙住；使朦胧，使模糊，使迷糊．— *vi.*〔主语用 it〕下雾．
mis·tak·a·ble [misˈteikəbl] *a.* 易错的；易误会的．
mis·take [misˈteik] *vt., vi.* **(*-took*[-ˈtuk]; *-taken* [-ˈteikən])** 弄错；误会，想错；看错；误解．*He mistook that stick for a snake.* 他把那根棍子错看成蛇了．*She has mistaken me.* 她误会了我的话了．— *n.* 错误，过失；事故；想错，看错；误会，误解．*There is no mistaking.* 没错．*There is no ~ about it.* 那是确实无误的．***and no ~***〔口〕(加强以上所述)确确实实 *(They have come to grief and no ~.* 他们确确实实失败了)．***by ~*** 错，误．***make a ~*** 犯错误，做错，想错．
mis·tak·en [misˈteikən] mistake 的过去分词．— *a.* 错误的；想错了的；看错了的；误解了的，误会了的．*You are ~.* 你(弄)错了．~ ***identity*** 认错人．**-ly** *ad.* 错，误．
mis·taught [ˈmisˈtɔːt] *a.* 被教错的．
mis·ter [ˈmistə] *n.* ①〔通常作 Mr.〕先生〔男子姓名前或职称前：*Mr. Smith, Mr. Henry Smith, Mr. President*〕．②〔口〕先生〔招呼不知姓名的人〕．③老百姓，平民．④丈夫．*Look here, ~!* 喂，先生！*be he prince or mere ~.* 不管他是王子还是平民．*a plain ~* 普通人．— *vt.* 称…先生．*Don't ~ me.* 不要叫我先生．**M-Charley [Charlie]**〔美黑人俚〕白人．
mis·ter·y [ˈmistəri] *n.* = mystery².
mist·flow·er [ˈmistˌflauə] *n.*【植】雾花泽兰〔产于美洲东部〕．
mist·ful [ˈmistful] *a.* = misty.
mis·think [misˈθiŋk] *vi.* **(*-thought*[-ˈθɔːt]; *-think·ing*)**〔古〕想错了．— *vt.*〔古〕对…有坏的看法．
mist·i·ly [ˈmistili] *ad.* 雾深地；朦胧地，迷迷糊糊地．
mis·time [ˈmisˈtaim] *vt.* ①使(言行等)不合时宜．②搞错…的时间．③打错(拍子)．*~d remarks* 不合时宜的话．
mist·i·ness [ˈmistinis] *n.* 薄雾状；朦胧；模糊，不明了．
mis·tle·toe [ˈmisltəu] *n.*【植】槲寄生〔其小枝常用作圣诞节的装饰〕．*giant ~s*【植】桑寄生．**~fig**【植】黄榕．**~honeysuckle**【植】五室忍冬．**~ thrush** 槲鸫 (=mistle thrush).
mis·told [misˈtəuld] *ad.* 被传错，被误报．
mis·took [misˈtuk] mistake 的过去式．
mis·tral [ˈmistrəl] *n.* (法国地中海沿岸一带的)干燥寒冷的北风．
mis·trans·late [ˈmistrænsˈleit] *vt.* 译错．**-la·tion** [-ʃən] *n.* 误译．
mis·treat [misˈtriːt] *vt.* 虐待．**-ment** *n.*
mis·tress [ˈmistris] *n.* ①(*opp.* master) 女主人，主妇；老板娘；女…的名家[能手]．②〔M-〕〔古〕…夫人，…小姐．★现只用缩写 Mrs. [ˈmisiz] 放在夫姓前，如 *Mrs. Jones, Mrs. Henry Jones, Mrs. Henry (Jones)*；法律文件等中写作 *Mrs. Mary Jones.* 17 世纪以前写作 Mistress. ③〔英〕女教师．④情妇；〔诗〕情人，爱人〔指女子〕．*The moon, the ~ of the night.* 月亮，夜的女王．*a French ~* 法语女教师．***be one's own ~*** 自己(女子)作得了主．***be ~ of ...*** 占有着….***be ~ of the situation*** 能控制局面．***be ~ of the world*** 称霸世界．***M- of the Adriatic*** = Venice. ***M- of the Robes***〔英〕女王的女侍长．***M- of the seas*** 海上霸主〔旧指英帝国〕．***M- iof the World*** 世界霸主〔罗马帝国的别称〕．**-ship** *n.* mistress 的身分．
mis·tri·al [ˈmisˈtraiəl] *n.*【法】①(因手续错误形成的)无效审判．②〔口〕(因陪审员意见不一的)未决审判．
mis·trust [ˈmisˈtrʌst] *n., v.* 疑心，疑惑，不相信．**-er** *n.* 疑心者．**-ing·ly** *ad.*
mis·trust·ful [ˈmisˈtrʌstful] *a.* 多疑的，不相信的 *(of)*．**-ly** *ad.*
mist·y [ˈmisti] *a.* **(*mist·i·er; -i·est*)** ①有薄雾的；朦胧的．②(思想等)不清的，模糊的．③(眼睛)泪汪汪的．④无知识的，蒙昧的．**-i·ly** *ad.* **-i·ness** *n.*
mis·un·der·stand [ˈmisʌndəˈstænd] **(*-stood* [-ˈstud])** *vt.* 误会，误解；曲解．**-ing** *n.* 误会，误解；不和，隔阂，争执．
mis·us·age [ˈmisˈjuːzidʒ] *n.* ①(字句等的)误用．②虐待．
mis·use [ˈmisˈjuːz] *vt.* 错用(字句等)；滥用；虐待．— [-ˈjuːs] *n.* 误用，滥用．
mis·us·er [ˈmisˈjuːzə] *n.* 误用者；虐待者；【法】滥用者．
mis·val·ue [ˌmisˈvæljuː] *vt.* 误估，低估．
mis·word [misˈwəːd] *vt.* 措词不当．
mis·write [misˈrait] *vt.* **(*-wrote*[-ˈwrəut]; *-writ·ten* [-ˈritən]; *-writ·ing*)** 误写，错写．
MIT = Massachusetts Institute of Technology〔美〕马萨诸塞理工学院，麻省理工学院．
Mitch·ell [ˈmitʃəl] *n.* 米切尔〔姓氏，男子名〕．
mite¹ [mait] *n.* ①极小的东西．②(从前 *Flanders* 通用的)小铜币；小钱；〔英俚〕= half a farthing. ③小孩子．④〔口〕一点点；少而难得的捐助，一臂之力．***a ~ of a(child etc.)*** 小得可怜的(孩子等)．***contribute one's ~ to*** 为…尽微力．***not a ~*** 一点也不…．***offer a ~ of comfort*** 仅能用心里话安慰．***the widow's ~*** 寡妇的一文钱〔少而可贵的捐助〕．
mite² [mait] 小虫；螨类；干酪蛆．*a red ~* 红蜘蛛．*a ~ on an elephant* 大小悬殊．*~ of grape* 葡萄毛毡病．
mi·ter [ˈmaitə] *n., vt.* = mitre.
Mit·ford [ˈmitfəd] *n.* 米特福德〔姓氏〕．
Mith·ra·i·cism, Mith·ra·ism [miθˈreiisizəm, ˈmiθrəizəm] *n.* (古波斯的)太阳神崇拜．
Mith·ra·ist [ˈmiθrəist] *n.* (古波斯的)崇拜太阳神者．
Mith·ras [ˈmiθrəs] *n.* (波斯的)太阳神．
mith·ri·date [ˈmiθrideit] *n.* 万应解毒药〔一种早先被认为是一切毒药的解毒剂的药剂〕．
mith·rid·a·tize [miθˈridətaiz] *vt.* (常服小量毒药)使有人工耐毒作用．
mit·i·cide [ˈmaitisaid] *n.* 杀螨药．
mit·i·gate [ˈmitigeit] *vt., vi.* 镇静，缓和；减轻．*to mitigate the flood* 分洪．**-tion** *n.* 镇静，缓和；减轻．**-tive** ①*a.* 缓和性的．②*n.* 缓和剂．**-tor** *n.* 缓和者；缓和剂．**-to·ry** *a.* = mitigative.
mi·to·chon·dri·a [ˌmaitəˈkɔndriə] *n. pl.* **(*sing. -drion*** **[-driɔn])**【生】粒线体．
mi·to·sis [miˈtəusis] *n.* **(*pl. -ses*** **[-siːz])**【生】有丝分裂，丝状核分裂．
mi·tot·ic [miˈtɔtik] *a.*【生】有丝分裂的．
mi·trail·leur [ˌmitraiˈəː, F. mitrɑˈjœːr] *n.*〔F.〕机枪手．
mi·trail·leuse [ˌmitraiˈəːz] *n.*〔F.〕机关枪．
mi·tral [ˈmaitrəl] *a.* 僧帽瓣状的，主教冠(状)的．*~ stenosis* 僧帽瓣硬化．*~ valve* 僧帽瓣．— *n.*【解】(心脏的)僧帽瓣，二尖瓣(= ~ valve).
mi·tre [ˈmaitə] *n.* ①主教冠；僧帽；主教等的职位〔职权〕．②【木工】斜接；斜角缝；斜榫；斜角尺．— *vt.* ①给与…以主教冠；升任某人为主教(等)．②使斜接．*a ~ joint* 斜削接头，斜面接合，斜角联接．*a mitring machine*【印】斜切机．**~ box** 辅锯箱，夹背锯箱．**~ gear** 等径伞齿轮．**~ wheels**〔*pl.*〕正角斜齿轮．
m·tred [ˈmaitəd] *a.* ①戴了主教冠的；担任了主教的．

②有斜面接合的.
mitt [mit] *n.* ①= mitten. ②〔俚〕手,掌;拳头;〔美俚〕无手人;〔美俚〕逮捕;〔*pl.*〕手铐;〔美俚〕看手相的(= ~reader). — *vt.* 〔美俚〕和…握手. ***give sb. the frozen*** ~ 极端冷对某人. ***tip sb.'s*** ~ 〔美〕泄露某人的企图.
mit·ten [ˈmitn] *n.* ①(仅拇指分开的)两指手套;(女用)露指长手套. ②〔*pl.*〕〔美俚〕拳击手套,棒球手套;手. ***get the*** ~ (向女人求爱)遭到拒绝;被解雇,被撵走. ***give (sb.) the*** ~ (女人)拒绝求爱,给碰钉子;解雇,撵走. ***handle without ~s*** 不客气地处置,无情对待. ~ **sport** 〔美俚〕拳击.
mit·ti·mus [ˈmitiməs] *n.* 〔口〕解雇通知,免职,解雇;【法】徒刑执行令,下狱状;法院转移案卷的命令. ***get one's*** ~ 被免职,被解雇.
mity [ˈmaiti] *a.* 多螨的.
mitz·vah, mits·vah [mitsˈvɑː, ˈmitsvə] *n.* ***(pl. mitz·voth*** [-ˈvəut] ***mitz·vahs)*** 【犹太教】①诫命. ②奉行神命.
mix [miks] *vt.* ***(-ed,*** 〔古〕***mixt***[mikst]***)***①混,混合,搀合;混合起来做. ②使结合;使结交,使交往. ③使(动物)杂交. ④混淆,混同(无形物) ***(with)***. ⑤(给…)配制;调制. ~ *a salad* 拌凉拌. ~ *wine with water* = ~ *water in wine* 用水搀酒. — *vi.* ①混,相混合,相溶合 ***(in; with)***. ②结合,结交,交往 ***(with)***; 亲密地来往,合得来. ③变成杂种. ④有牵连,参与 ***(in)***. ⑤〔美俚〕参加殴斗〔比赛〕(= ~ *it*). *They do not* ~ *well.* 他们不大合得来. ***be [get] ~ed up in [with]*** 加入(流氓组织等),参与(坏事). ~ ***in society*** 出入社交界. ~ ***it up*** 〔俚〕做骗人的比赛〔假比赛〕;通同作弊. ~ ***up*** 调匀,拌匀;混淆,混同;使结交坏朋友;【拳击】猛烈互击. — *n.* 混合;〔口〕混杂,混乱;〔美俚〕打架;比赛.
mix·a·ble [ˈmiksəbl] *a.* 可混的;可混合的;可混杂的.
mixed [mikst] *a.* ①混成的,混合的. ②混杂的,各式各样的. ③男女混合(成)的;各阶层混合成的. ④〔英〕男女同校的. ⑤〔口〕头脑混乱的;喝醉了的 ***(up)***. ~ *biscuits* 什锦饼干. ~ *motives* 不纯洁的动机. *a* ~ *train*(客、货)混合列车. *a* ~ *number* 【数】带分数. *a* ~ *chorus* 混声合唱(团). *a* ~ *vowel* (中)央元音. ***have ~ feelings*** 悲〔惊〕喜交集. ~ **bag** 混杂;(尤指)杂七杂八混在一起的东西〔人〕等. ~ **bud** 【植】混合芽. ~ **doubles** 【球赛】(每队一男一女的)混合双打. ~ **foursome** 〔美〕由两对男女举行的高尔夫球比赛. ~ **grades** 异级混合物,(石油产品的)不同类混合物. ~ **marriage** 异族〔教〕通婚. ~ **media** ①艺术的混合效应法〔如表演、彩色灯光、录音带等多种手段的混合运用〕. ②混合画法〔如在一幅作品上采用水彩和蜡笔〕. **~-up** *a.* 混乱的;迷惑的. **-ness** *n.* 混合,混成;混杂.
mix·en [ˈmiksn] *n.* 〔古、方〕粪堆.
mix·er [ˈmiksə] *n.* ①混合者. ②混合〔搅拌〕器;【冶】混铁炉;混频器;【无】混频管. ③〔原美、口〕交际家;交谊会;【无】录音师. *a good [bad]* ~ 会〔不会〕交际的人.
mix·ing [ˈmiksiŋ] *n.* 混合;【影】录音;【无】混频.
mix·ol·o·gist [mikˈsɔlədʒist] *n.* 〔美俚〕酒吧侍者,酒吧间配酒者.
mix·o·lyd·i·an [ˌmiksəˈlidiən] *a.* 【乐】①混合里第亚调式. ②中世纪教堂音乐调式〔相当于带小七度的现代大调式〕.
mixt [mikst] mix 的异体过去式和过去分词.
mixt. = mixture.
Mix·tec [ˈmiːstek] *n.* ①***(pl. -tecs, -tec)*** 米斯特克人〔墨西哥瓦哈卡、盖雷罗和普埃布拉州的一支印第安人〕. ②米斯特坎语.
Mix·tec·an [miːsˈtekən] *n.* 米斯特坎语〔墨西哥四个印第安语族之一〕.
mix·ture [ˈmikstʃə] *n.* ①混合,混杂;混合状态. ②混合物;混合体;(内燃机等用的)混合气;【医】混合剂,药水;混合烟草〔又叫 *smoking* ~〕. ③【织】麻花织品;优缺点均有的人. *a* ~ *of grief and comfort* 悲喜交集(的感情). ***the*** ~ ***as before*** 照处方笺配药;〔口〕处理办法如前. ***with a*** ~ ***of*** 夹有,加有,带有. ~ **ratio** 混合比. ~ **strength** 混合浓度.
mix-up [ˈmiksʌp] *n.* 〔口〕混乱;混战;混合物;迷惑.
Mi·zar [ˈmaizɑː] 【天】开阳,北斗六〔大熊(星)座〕.
miz·zen, miz·en [ˈmizn] *n.* 【船】后桅〔又叫 mizzen-mast〕;后帆;最后部的纵帆〔又叫 mizzen sail〕. **~mast** 【船】(三桅船上的)后桅. ~ **rigging** 后桅索具. ~ **sail** 后桅帆. **~top** 【船】后桅楼. **~yard** 【船】后帆桁.
miz·zle[1] [ˈmizl] *vi., n.* 〔英〕(下)毛毛雨,蒙蒙雨,细雨. *It ~s.* 下毛毛雨了.
miz·zle[2] [ˈmizl] *vi.* 〔英俚〕逃亡,逃走;撤走.
miz·zle[3] [ˈmizl] *vt.* 〔方〕使糊涂,使迷惑.
miz·zly [ˈmizli] *a.* 下着毛毛雨的,蒙蒙雨的.
MK, mk. = markka.
MKS = metre-kilogram(me)-second system. 米-千克-秒单位制.
mks. = marks.
mkt. = market.
ML =①Master of Laws 法学硕士. ②minelayer 布雷舰艇. ③motor launch 摩托艇,汽艇. ④muzzle-loading 前装式的,前膛的. ⑤Licentiate in Medicine 有资格开业的医生. ⑥Licentiate in Midwifery 有资格开业的助产士.
ml. = millilitre(s).
M.L.A. = ①Modern Language Association〔英〕现代语言学会. ②Member of the Legislative Assembly. 立法议会议员;立宪(制宪)议会议员.
MLD = median lethal dose【医】半数致死量.
M.L.D. = minimum lethal dose【医】最小致死量.
MLG = Middle Low German 中世纪低地德语.
Mlle. = 〔F.〕*Mademoiselle.*
Mlles. = 〔F.〕*Mesdemoiselles.*
M.L.N.S. = Ministry of Labour and National Service. 〔英旧〕劳工及国民义务兵役部.
MLR = main line of resistance 〔美〕防御主阵地前沿.
M.L.S. = Master of Library Science 图书馆学硕士.
MM. = 〔F.〕*Messieurs.*
M.M. = ① Military Medal〔英〕军功章. ②Ministry of Munitions 军需部. ③Machinist's Mate【美海】机械军士. ④mercantile marine 商船(总称). ⑤〔L.〕mutati mutandis 作相应的变更,作必要的修改.
mm; mm. = ①millimetre. ②〔L.〕*millia.*
Mme. = 〔F.〕*Madame.*
Mmes. = 〔F.〕*Mesdames.*
MMRBM = mobile medium-range ballistic missile 机动中程弹道导弹.
M.Mus., M Mus = Master of music 音乐硕士.
MN = magnetic north 磁北.
Mn = manganese【化】锰.
mne·mon·ic [mni(ː)ˈmɔnik] *a.* 记忆的;记忆术的;增进记忆的. *a* ~ *system* 记忆法. ~ *rhymes* (帮助记忆的)顺口溜(等). **-s** [-s] *n.* 记忆法〔术〕.
Mne·mos·y·ne [mni(ː)ˈmɔzini] *n.* 【希神】记忆女神.
mne·mo·tech·ny [*m*ˌniːməˈtekni] *n.* =mnemonics.
M.O., MO, m.o. =①money order 汇票;邮政汇票. ②mail order 函购,邮购. ③medical officer 军医;军医主任. ④mass observation 民意调查.
Mo = ①Monday. ②molybdenum【化】钼.
Mo. = Missouri 密苏里〔美国州名〕.
mo [məu] *n.* 〔俚、谑〕= moment. *Wait half a* ~. 请等一等.
mo. = month; monthly.
-mo *suf.* (纸张的)开: 16 mo = sixteen*mo* 十六开〔略作 16°〕; 12 mo = duodeci*mo* 十二开〔略作 12°〕.

mo•a [ˈməuə] *n.* 【鸟】恐鸟〔现已绝灭〕.
Mo•ab•ite [ˈməuəbait] *n. (fem.* ***-it•ess*** [-ˌbaitis]*)* ①(死海东部和南部古国)古莫阿布人. ②古莫阿布语〔已消亡〕. —*a.* 古莫阿布的;古莫阿布人的(= Moabitish).
moan [məun] *vi., vt.* 呻吟,哼;〔古、诗〕悲叹,哭. — *n.* 呻吟声;(波浪、风等的)号,啸,萧萧声;悲叹声,呜咽声;〔诗〕悲叹. ***make (one's)*** ~〔古〕悲诉,诉委屈. **-ing•ly** *ad.*
moan•ful [ˈməunful] *a.* 呻吟的,悲叹的;忧伤的. **-ly** *ad.*
moat [məut] *n.* 【筑城】(城)壕;护城河. — *vt.* 挖壕围绕.
mob [mɔb] *n.*〔集合词〕①〔蔑〕暴民,暴徒;群众,民众,乌合之众. ②〔俚〕(盗贼等的)一党,一伙. ③〔美俚〕匪帮,匪党;一群罪犯;观众. *a ~ of rioters* 一伙暴徒. *the swell ~* 穿得很讲究的扒手或骗子. — *vt.* ***(-bb-)*** 群众袭击,成群暴动,聚众滋扰;成群欢呼. *The returning soldiers were mobbed in the streets.* 归来的兵士们在街上受到了群众的欢呼. ~ *it* 聚众滋扰. — *vi.* 乱挤. ~ *forward* 向前乱挤. ~ **law** 暴民的法律;私刑. ~ **psychology** 群众心理. ~ **scene**【影】群众场面.
mob. = mobile.
mob•bish [ˈmɔbiʃ] *a.* 暴徒似的,骚扰的,暴乱的,无纪律的.
mob•cap [ˈmɔbkæp] *n.* (于18 世纪和 19 世纪初流行的室内)头巾式女帽.
mo•bile [ˈməubail, -bil] *a.* ①活动的,运动的;可动的. ②易变的;易感动的;易变通的,灵活的;反复无常的. ③机动的,流动的;装在车上的;用车辆运输的. ④运动物体的,活动装置的. — *n.* ①可动物;可动装置;(现代抽象派艺术)动的雕塑. ②〔美口〕汽车,(特指)蒸汽汽车. ③〔古〕= mob. *a ~ floodlight* 活动探照灯. ~ *warfare*【军】运动战. ~ *features* 富有表情的面貌. *a ~ mind* 多变的心思. ~ *troops [units]* 快速部队. *a ~ drama group* 巡回剧团. ~ **home** 活动住房〔由大型拖车改装而成多少可长期在某处停放的住房〕. ~ **unit** 活动专门设备车〔如广播宣传车、巡回爱克斯光检查车、电视摄像汽车、救护车等〕.
mo•bil•i•ty[1] [məuˈbiliti] *n.* ①可动性,活动性,能动性. ②灵活性,可变动性. ③【物】动性,迁移率;【化】淌度;【军】运动性,机动性. *the ionic ~* 游子迁移率[淌度].
mo•bil•i•ty[2] [məuˈbiliti] *n.* 群众. ~ *and nobility* 〔谑〕老百姓和贵族.
mo•bi•liz•a•ble [ˈməubilaizəbl] *a.* 可动员的.
mo•bi•li•za•tion [ˌməubilaiˈzeiʃən] *n.* ①动员;流通,应用. ②【法】不动产的动产化;【地】活动作用. ~ *orders*【军】动员令. *national ~* 国民总动员. *the ~ of financial resources* 财力的动用.
mo•bi•lize [ˈməubilaiz] *vt.* ①发动,调动;使可动. ②使流通;使(不动产)变成动产. ~ *the masses* 发动群众. — *vi.* 动员(起来).
mob•oc•ra•cy [mɔˈbɔkrəsi] *n.* ①暴徒统治;暴民政治. ②作为统治者的暴民.
mob•o•crat [ˈmɔbəkræt] *n.* 暴民领袖;支持暴民政治的人;惑众取宠的政治家.
MOBS = Multiple Orbit Bombardment System 多弹头轰炸系统.
mobs•man [ˈmɔbzmən] *n.*〔口〕①暴民中的一个成员. ②服装漂亮的扒手.
mob•ster [ˈmɔbstə] *n.*〔俚〕暴徒,匪徒,歹徒.
mo•camp [ˈməukæmp] *n.* 旅馆式营地,旅行营地.
moc•ca•sin [ˈmɔkəsin] *n.* (北美印第安人等穿的)鹿皮靴;硬底软(拖)鞋;(南美)有毒水蛇;噬鱼蛇. ~ **flower**【植】老虎七,鬼督邮,杓兰.
Mo•cha [ˈməukə] *n.* 穆哈〔也门一港口名〕.
mo•cha [ˈməukə] *n.* ①(原指阿拉伯产的)穆哈咖啡〔又叫 Mocha coffee〕;上等咖啡;〔口〕任何咖啡. ②穆哈皮〔阿拉伯山羊的鞣皮,做手套用〕. ③穆哈(调味)香料〔用咖啡(或与巧克力混合)制成的调味浸剂〕. — *a.* ①加有穆哈香料的. ②一种深褐色的. ~ **stone**【矿】苔纹玛瑙.
mock [mɔk] *vt.* ①嘲笑,挖苦. ②学样子嘲弄;模拟. ③骗,引诱,钓. ④使徒劳;使失望. ⑤使无效,挫败;无视. *be ~ed with false hopes* 被空幻的希望欺骗了. *The river ~ed all their efforts to cross.* 他们作了一切努力还是没能渡过这条河. — *vi.* 嘲弄,愚弄 *(at)*. ~ ***up*** 制作大模型. — *n.*〔古〕= mockery. ***make a ~ of*** = make a mockery of. — *a.*〔用作 Attrib.〕假的;虚幻的;模拟的. *a ~ battle* 模拟战,演习. ~ *lead* = ~ *ore* 闪锌矿. *a ~ trial* 模拟裁判. *a ~ moon* 幻月〔月晕的光轮〕. ~ *modesty* 假谦虚,假客气. ~ **auction** ①= Dutch auction. ②(使用囮子的)骗人拍卖. ~ **duck** 充鸭〔做成鸭形的羊肩肉〕. ~**-heroic** *a., n.* 嘲弄[滑稽]地模仿英雄风格的(作品、诗歌). ~**-majesty** 虚张声势,空架子. ~ **orange**【植】山梅花;桑橙;葡萄牙桂樱,象橙子的葫芦. ~ **plane** 假挪威槭. ~ **soup**, ~ **turtle soup** 充海龟汤的小牛头汤. ~ **strawberry** 蛇莓属. ~**-up** ①(教学实验用的)实物大模型(飞机、大炮、机械等). ②【军】伪装工事.
mock•er [ˈmɔkə] *n.* 嘲笑者;学人样嘲弄人的人;【鸟】= mockingbird.
mock•er•y [ˈmɔkəri] *n.* ①愚弄,嘲笑,挖苦. ②笑柄. ③学样,冒牌,(拙劣的)模仿. ④恶劣[可鄙]的事例. ⑤徒劳. *They went through the ~ of a trial.* 他们遭受了不公正的审判. ***hold (sb., sth.) up to ~*** 拿某人[某事]寻开心,玩弄…. ***make a ~ of*** 嘲笑,戏弄,以某人作为笑柄.
mock•ing•bird [ˈmɔkiŋbəːd] *n.*【鸟】模仿鸟〔产北美南部及西印度群岛〕.
mock•ing•ly [ˈmɔkiŋli] *ad.* 嘲笑地,愚弄地.
mock•ing-stock [ˈmɔkiŋsˈtɔk] *n.* 笑柄.
mod [mɔd] *n.*〔亦 M-〕〔英〕现代派分子,时髦派分子〔英国六十年代的嬉皮士〕. — *a.*〔亦 M-〕现代派分子的;有现代派分子的特点的.
mod. = ①moderate. ②modern. ③modulus.
mod•a•cryl•ic [ˌmɔdəˈkrilik] *a.*【化】变性聚丙烯腈的.
mo•dal [ˈməudl] *a.* ①方式上的,形态上的;【哲】(对本质、内容说的)形式(上)的. ②【语法】语气 (mood) 的;表示情态 (manner) 的. ③【逻】程式的;【乐】调式的;【法】规定执行[应用]方式的;【统计】众数的. *a ~ legacy* 指定用途的遗产. ~ *auxiliary* 情态助动词 *(can, may, might, must, should, would* 等*)*. **-ly** *ad.*
mo•dal•i•ty [məuˈdæliti] *n.* 形态,样式,方式;【数】模态;【逻】程式;感觉道〔如视觉道〕;物理疗法.
mode [məud] *n.* ①法,样,方法,方式. ②模,型;样式,体裁,款式;习惯. ③风尚;〔the ~〕流行,时髦. ④【语法】= mood. ⑤【乐】(古希腊的)旋法调,(近代的)调式. ⑥【逻】程式,样式,论式;【统计】众数. ***all the ~*** 非常流行. ***become the ~*** 流行起来. ***in ~*** 正流行,新式. ***out of ~*** 不流行,老式. ~**-locked** *a.* 锁模的(指激光器调整了光相位,能产生极短暂脉冲的).
Mod E, Mod. E. = Modern English. 近代英语.
mod•el [ˈmɔdl] *n.* ①模型,雏型;原型;设计图;模范;(画家、雕刻家的)模特儿;样板. ②典型,模范. ③(女服装店雇用的)时装模特儿. ④样式,型. ⑤〔口〕极相似的人[东西]. — *a.* 模型的,模范的. *a clay ~*【雕】粘土原型. *a working ~* 机器的运转模型. *a ~ shot*【摄】模型镜头. *a ~ aeroplane* 模型飞机. *a ~ test* 典型试验. *The boy is the perfect ~ of his father.* 这孩子活象他父亲. ***after [on] the ~ of*** 仿效…,拿…当做模范. ***stand ~*** 做模特儿. — ***(〔英〕-ll-)*** *vt.* ①作…的模型[雏型]. ②(依照模型)制作,仿造,建造 *(after; on; upon)*. ③设计,仿照,拿…做模范. — *vi.* 做模型;做模特儿. *delicately ~ed features* 清秀的面貌. *~ a garden after the manner of Kew* 仿照(伦敦) Kew 植物园设计

的花园. ~ ***oneself up(on) sb.*** 仿效某人.

mod·el·ler, mod·el·er [ˈmɔdlə] *n.* 模型(尤指塑像)作者;造型者.

mod·el·ling, mod·el·ing [ˈmɔdliŋ] *n.* 制造模型的方法,造型(术);塑像术;【美】立体感(表现法);模特儿职业. *the* ~ *of one's features* 某人脸部的形象.

mo·dem [ˈməudem] *n.*【无】调制解调器.

mod·e·na [ˈmɔdinə] *n.* 深紫色.

mod·er [ˈməudə] *n.*【自】脉冲编码装置.

mod·er·ate [ˈmɔdərit] *a.* 有节制的,温和的,稳健的;中庸的;中等的;适度的;普通的;〔美俚〕(人等)慢吞吞的,迟钝的;【物】慢化的,减速的. *a* ~ *breeze* 和风,四级风. *a* ~ *gale* 疾风,七级风. ~ *prices* 公道的价格. ~ *terms* 适度的条件[代价]. — *n.* 稳健的人,温和主义者. — [ˈmɔdəreit] *vt.* 使和缓,使减轻;节制,节约;调节;【物】慢化,减速. — *vi.* 变和缓;变稳定;做调人,做会场司仪,主持(会议). ***exercise a moderating influence on*** 对…起缓和作用. **-ly** *ad.* 适度,适中,普通. **-ness** *n.*

mod·er·a·tion [ˌmɔdəˈreiʃən] *n.* ①缓和,减轻;节制;温和,缓和;中庸,适度,中等. ②稳定,镇定;【物】慢化,延时,减速(作用). ③〔*pl.*〕(牛津大学)B.A.学位的第一次考试〔略 *mods.*〕. ~ *in eating and drinking* 节制饮食. ***in*** ~ 适中地.

mod·er·a·tism [ˈmɔdərətizəm] *n.* (政治、宗教上的)稳健[温和、中庸]主义. **-list** *n.* 稳健主义者.

mod·e·ra·to [ˌmɔdəˈrɑːtəu] *ad., a.* 〔It.〕【乐】中速地(的),有节制地(的),中板,用中板. *allegro* ~ 中快板.

mod·er·a·tor [ˈmɔdəreitə] *n.* ①仲裁者,调解者. ②(牛津大学 B.A. 学位第一次考试的)主考员;(剑桥大学数学优等考试的)监考员. ③〔美〕主席,议长;审判者;【宗】长老会会议主席. ④【物】(原子堆中的)减速剂,慢化剂;【化】阻滞剂,缓和剂. **-ship** *n.* moderator 的职位[任期].

mod·ern [ˈmɔdən] *a.* 现代的;近代的;现代式[化]的,时新的,新派的,时髦的,摩登的. — *n.* 现代人;近代人;新思想家,现代派人物;【印】近代铅字字体. ~ *history* 近代史. ~ *languages* 近代语言. *a* ~ *army* 现代化部队. ~ *automatic weapons* 现代自动武器. ~ *dance* 现代舞蹈[西方近代舞蹈]. *M- English* 近代英语〔略 Mod. E.〕. *M- Hebrew* 近代希伯来语〔尤指近代以色列语〕. ~ *school [side]* 〔英〕近代学科分部. ~ *times* 现代. *the M- Athens* 现代雅典〔〔英〕爱丁堡,〔美〕波士顿的别名〕. *the M- Babylon* 现代巴比伦〔伦敦市的别名〕. **-ly** *ad.* **-ness** *n.*

mod·ern·ism [ˈmɔdənizəm] *n.* ①现代式;现代语法;现代习惯,现代用法;近代思潮;(19世纪末20世纪初资产阶级文学及造型艺术上的)现代主义,现代派. ②【宗】现代主义.

mod·ern·ist [ˈmɔdə(ː)nist] *n.* 现代主义者.

mod·ern·is·tic [mɔdəˈnistik] *a.* 现代派的,现代作风的;现代主义(者)的.

mo·der·ni·ty [mɔˈdəːniti] *n.* (*opp.* antiquity) 现代性,新式,现代作风;〔*pl.*〕现代事物.

mod·ern·i·za·tion [ˌmɔdənaiˈzeiʃən] *n.* ①现代化,维新. ②现代化的事物[版本等]. *achieve* ~ *of science and technology* 实现科学技术的现代化. *produce* ~*s of Shakespeare's plays* 出版莎士比亚剧作的现代化版本.

mod·ern·ize [ˈmɔdə(ː)naiz] *vt., vi.* 使现代化;近代[现代]化;用现代化方法,维新.

mod·est [ˈmɔdist] *a.* 谨慎的,谦虚的,客气的;羞怯的;(尤指妇女)端庄的;优雅的,淑静的,贞节的;有节制的,适度的,适中的;不大的. ***Be*** ~ 要谦虚. **-ly** *ad.*

mod·es·ty [ˈmɔdisti] *n.* 谨慎,谦虚,虚心;(尤指妇女的)端庄,淑静;节制,中肯;朴实;羞怯. *M- helps one to go forward.* 虚心使人进步.

modi [ˈməudai] *n.* modus 的复数.

mod·i·cum [ˈmɔdikəm] *n.* 〔常用 *sing.*〕一点点,少量. *a* ~ *of sleep* 小睡.

mod·i·fi·a·ble [ˈmɔdifaiəbl] *a.* 能 modify 的. **-bil·i·ty** *n.*

mod·i·fi·ca·tion [ˌmɔdifiˈkeiʃən] *n.* 变更,更改,修正;改良,改进;缓和;修改;减轻;限制;【生】诱发变异,变态,变体,变型;【语法】修饰;(用变音符号的)元音改变.

mod·i·fi·ca·tor [ˈmɔdifikeitə] *n.* ①更改者;修改者. ②【语法】修饰语.

mod·i·fi·ca·to·ry [ˈmɔdifiˈkeitəri] *a.* 修正的;更改的;调整的;缓和的,减轻的;【语法】修饰的.

mod·i·fi·er [ˈmɔdifaiə] *n.* 修改者;更改者;【橡胶】改良剂,调节剂;【语法】修饰语.

mod·i·fy [ˈmɔdifai] *vt.* 变更;修改;减轻,缓和,调节;限制;【哲】规定,限定;【语法】修饰;(用变音符号)改变(元音). ~ *one's demands* 减低要求. ~ *the terms of the contract* 变更契约条款. *modified wool* 变性羊毛.

mo·dil·lion [məuˈdiljən] *n.*【建】托饰.

mo·di·o·lus [məuˈdaiələs] *n.* ***(pl. -o·li*** [-lai]***)*** 【解】蜗轴.

mod·ish [ˈməudiʃ] *a.* 〔古〕流行的,时髦的. **-ly** *ad.* **-ness** *n.*

mod·iste [məuˈdiːst] *n.* 〔F.〕(专做妇女衣、帽的)女裁缝.

MODS = manned orbital development station【宇】载人轨道研究站.

mods 〔英〕= moderations ③.

mod·u·la·bil·i·ty [ˌmɔdjuləˈbiliti] *n.*【无】调制能力,调制本领.

mod·u·lar [ˈmɔdjulə] *a.* ①【数】模的,模数的,系数的. ②组件的,制成标准尺寸的.

mod·u·lar·i·ty [ˌmɔdjuˈlæriti] *n.*【自】积木性,模块性〔指应用模块装组电子计算机等〕.

mod·u·late [ˈmɔdjuleit] *vt.* ①调节,调整(声音等). ②缓和,减轻. ③【无】使改变周波数,调制;【乐】使转调,使变调. —*vi.*【乐】变调,转调;【无】调制.

mod·u·la·tion [ˌmɔdjuˈleiʃən] *n.* 调整,调节;(声调的)抑扬,变化;【乐】转调,变调;【无】调制. *amplitude* ~ 振幅调制,调幅. *frequency* ~ 频率调制,调频. *over* ~ 过(度)调(制).

mod·u·la·tor [ˈmɔdjuleitə] *n.* 调整者,调节者;【无】调制者,调节器.

mod·ule [ˈmɔdjuːl] *n.* ①测量流水等的单位〔1秒100升〕. ②【建】圆柱下部半径度. ③【物】模,系数,模数,模量. ④【无】微型组件;组件;模块. ⑤(宇宙飞船上各个独立的)舱.

mod·u·lo [ˈmɔdjuləu] *prep.*【数】对…模.

mod·u·lus [ˈmɔdjuləs] *n.* ***(pl. -li*** [-lai]***)***【数、物】模数,模量;系数. *a* ~ *of elasticity* 弹性模量.

mo·dus [ˈməudəs] *n.* ***(pl. mo·di*** [-dai], ***~es)*** 〔L.〕法,方法,方式. ~ ***operandi*** [ɔpˈrændai] 运用法,做法,操纵法. ~ ***vivendi*** [viˈvendai] 生活方法,生活态度;(争执双方之间的)暂时协定;权宜之计,妥协.

Moe·so-Goth, Moe·so·goth [ˈmiːsəuˌgɔθ] *a.* 密西哥特人〔公元三世纪古罗马密西亚省的哥特族人〕.

Moe·so-Goth·ic, Moe·so·goth·ic [ˌmiːsəuˈgɔθik] *a.* 密西哥特人的;密西哥特语的.

M of E = Maintenance of equipment 设备维修(保养).

mo·fette, mof·fette [məuˈfet] *n.*【地】炭酸喷气孔.

mo·fus·sil [məuˈfʌsil] *n.* 〔Hind.〕乡下,乡村.

M of W = Maintenance of way【铁路】养路,线路养护.

mog [mɔg] *vi.* ***(mogged; mog·ging)*** 〔方〕①重步稳步前进. ②撤退,撤营;离开,移去.

Mo·ga·di·shu, Mo·ga·di·scio [ˌmɔgəˈdiʃuː, ˌmɔgəˈdiʃiəu] *n.* 摩加迪沙〔索马里首都〕.

mo·gi·la·lia [mɔdʒiˈleiliə] *n.*【医】口吃;发音困难症.

Mo·gul [məuˈgʌl, ˈməugʌl] *n.* ①(十六世纪征服并统治

印度的)莫卧儿人;(尤指历史上的)蒙古人.②〔m-〕〔美〕富豪,权贵,贵族,专制君主;大人物;货车;火车头. *a high* ~〔美〕贵族,大官. *the Great [Grand]* ~ 印度莫卧儿帝国的皇帝.

mo·gul [ˈməugl] *n.*【滑雪】滑雪道拐弯处的雪坡.

MOH, M.O.H. =①medical officer of health 军医官. ②Ministry of Health〔英〕卫生部.

mo·hair [ˈməuhɛə] *n.* 安哥拉山羊毛; 安哥拉山羊毛仿制品.

Moham. = Mohammedan.

Mo·ham·med [məuˈhæmed] *n.* 穆罕默德〔570?—632伊斯兰教祖〕.

Mo·ham·me·dan [məuˈhæmidən] *a.* Mohammed 的; 伊斯兰教的. — *n.* 穆斯林. **-ism** *n.* 伊斯兰教.

Mo·ha·ve [məuˈhɑːviː] *n.* *(pl. -ves, -ve)* ①莫哈维人〔居住在美国亚利桑那地区科罗拉多河两岸的印第安人〕. ②莫哈维语. — *a.* 莫哈维人的.

Mo·hawk [ˈməuhɔːk] *n.* (纽约州中部的)印第安莫霍克族;莫霍克语;【溜冰】莫霍克步〔用一冰鞋的一刀刃前进,再用另一冰鞋的另一刀刃后退〕.

Mo·he·gan, Mo·hi·can [məuˈhiːgən, məuˈhiːkən] *n.* (原住于 Connecticut 州的印第安族)莫希干族〔人〕.

moh·ism [ˈməuˌizəm] *n.* 墨翟〔墨子〕的学说; 墨家学说.

Mo·ho [ˈməuhəu] = Mohorovičić discontinuity.

Mo·hole [ˈməuˌhəul] *n.*【地】超深钻.

Mo·ho·ro·vi·čić discontinuity [ˌməuhəuˈrəuvətʃitʃ]【地】莫霍(洛维奇契)不连续面.

Mohs' scale [məuz]【矿】莫氏硬度标.

mo·hur [ˈməuhə] *n.* 印度旧金币名〔值 15 rupees〕.

M.O.I. = Ministry of Information〔英〕新闻部.

moi·der [ˈmɔidə] *vt.*〔英方〕①使混乱; 迷惑,使摸不着头脑. ②使分心,打扰. — *vi.* ①发呓语. ②闲荡; 瞎走.

moi·dore [ˈmɔidɔː] *n.* 摩伊多〔葡萄牙旧金币名〕.

moi·e·ty [ˈmɔiəti] *n.*【法】(财产等的)一半; 二分之一; 一部分. *only a small* ~ *of* ... 仅仅一小部分.

moil [mɔil] *vi.* 劳动,辛辛苦苦做工. — *n.* 辛苦, 苦工; 混乱; 麻烦. *toil and* ~ 辛辛苦苦做工. **-er** *n.*, **-ingly** *ad.*

Moi·ra [ˈmɔirə] *n.*【希神】命运.

moire [mwɑː] *n.* 云〔波〕纹绸〔又叫 ~ antique〕.

moi·ré [ˈmwɑːrei] *a.* 有波纹的,有云纹的; 波纹的; 云纹绸似的. — *n.* ①波纹,云纹. ②=moire.

moist [mɔist] *a.* ①润湿的,潮湿的. ②多雨的;【医】流出物多的; 湿性的; 有分泌物的. ③(眼睛)泪汪汪的; 易感伤的. ~ *colours* (软膏状)水彩颜料. ~ *season* 雨季. ~ *steam* 湿蒸汽,饱和水蒸汽. *be emotionally* ~ 容易感伤〔激动〕. **-ly** *ad.* **-ness** *n.*

mois·ten [ˈmɔisn] *vt., vi.* 濡湿,弄湿; 变湿. *be* ~*ed by rain* 被雨淋湿. ~ *at the sight of* 一见…就泪眼汪汪. ~ *at one's eyes* 含泪. ~ ***one's clay [lips, throat]*** 喝酒.

mois·ten·er [ˈmɔisnə] *n.* 湿润器.

mois·ture [ˈmɔistʃə] *n.* 湿气,水分,潮湿; 湿度; (空气中的)水蒸气; 泪. ~ **equivalent**【土壤】持水当量. ~ **regain** 回潮. ~**-free, -less** *a.* 没湿气〔水分〕的, 干燥的.

mois·tur·ize [ˈmɔistʃəˌraiz] *vt., vi.* *(-ized; -iz·ing)* 给(皮肤、空气等)增加〔提供、保持〕水分.

Mo·ja·ve, Mo·ha·ve [məuˈhɑːviː] *n.* ①莫哈维人. ②莫哈维语. — *a.* 莫哈维人的.

moke [məuk] *n.*〔英俚〕驴子; 笨人,傻子;〔美俚,蔑〕黑人;〔澳俚〕小马; 驽马.

MOL = manned orbiting laboratory【宇】载人(绕)轨道实验室.

mol [məul] *n.*【化】克分子(量) = mole⁴.

mol. = molecular; molecule.

mo·la [ˈməulə] *n.*【动】翻车鱼.

mo·lal [ˈməuləl] *a.*【化】①(重量)克分子的. ②重模的, (重量)克分子(浓度)的. ~ *solution* 重模溶液. **-i·ty** [məuˈæliti] *n.* 重模; (重量)克分子浓度.

mo·lar¹ [ˈməulə] *a.* 磨的, 适宜于〔用来〕磨的; 臼齿的, 臼齿附近的. — *n.* 臼齿; 〔*pl.*〕〔美俚〕牙齿. *a false* ~ 小臼齿.

mo·lar² [ˈməulə] *a.*【物】质量(上)的;【化】(体积)克分子的; 容模的; (体积)克分子(浓度)的. **-i·ty** [məuˈlæriti] *n.* 体积克分子浓度; 容模.

Mo·lasse [məˈlɑːs] *n.*【地】磨砾层(相).

mo·las·ses [məˈlæsiz] *n. pl.*〔作 *sing.* 用〕〔美〕糖浆, 糖蜜.

mold [məuld] = mould.

Mol·da·vi·a [mɔlˈdeivjə] 摩尔达维亚〔苏联加盟共和国〕. **-n** ①*a.* 摩尔达维亚的. ②*n.* 摩尔达维亚人. **Moldavian Soviet Socialist Republic** 摩尔达维亚苏维埃社会主义共和国.

mold·er [ˈməuldə] = moulder.

mold·ing = moulding.

Mol·do·va [mɔlˈdɔvɑː] *n.* 摩尔多瓦〔罗马尼亚一地区〕.

mold·y = mouldy.

mole¹ [məul] *n.* ①【动】鼹鼠,田鼠. ②地下工作者; 在黑暗中工作的人. ***as blind as a*** ~ 全盲, 全瞎. ~**cast** = molehill. ~ **cricket**【虫】蝼蛄. ~**hill** 鼹鼠窝,鼹鼠丘,丘垤 (*make a mountain out of a* ~ *hill* 小题大做,夸大). ~ **plough** 挖沟犁,鼹鼠犁. ~ **rat** 地鼠. ~**skin** 鼹鼠皮; (鼹鼠皮一样的)厚布; 〔*pl.*〕鼹皮布裤.

mole² [məul] *n.* 黑痣.

mole³ [məul] *n.* 防波堤; 人工港.

mole⁴ [məul] *n.*【化】克分子(量), 克模; 衡分子. ~ **fraction**【化】克分子份数.

mole⁵ [məul] *n.*【医】胎块.

mo·lec·u·lar [məuˈlekjulə] *a.* 分子的, 由分子形成的, 分子内〔间〕的. ~ **attraction** 分子引力. ~ **biology** 分子生物学. ~ **conductivity** 克分子电导〔传导〕率. ~ **film** 分子层,分子膜. ~ **force**【化】分子力. ~ **formula** 分子式. ~ **rays** 分子射线. ~ **sieve**【物】分子筛. ~ **theory** 分子(理)论. ~ **weight** 分子量. **-ly** *ad.*

mo·lec·u·lar·i·ty [məuˌlekjuˈlæriti] *n.* 分子状态; 分子性; 分子作用.

mol·e·cule [ˈmɔlikjuːl, ˈməu-] *n.*【物、化】分子; 克分子;〔口〕微小颗粒. *gram* ~ 克分子. *nonpolar* ~*s* 无极(性)分子. *polar* ~*s* 有极分子.

mo·lest [məuˈlest] *vt.* 使烦恼,折磨,欺负,作弄; 无故向人攀谈,恶意干涉,妨害; (对女性)动手动脚,调戏. **-er** *n.* **-ta·tion** [ˌməulesˈteiʃən] *n.*

mol·et [ˈmɔlit] *n.* = mullet ②.

mo·line [məuˈlain, ˈməulin] *a.* 四臂端分叉后弯的十字架的.

Moll [mɔl] *n.* 莫尔〔女子名, Mary 的昵称〕.

moll [mɔl] *n.*〔俚〕妓女; 〔美俚〕盗贼的姘妇; 女流氓, 女匪.

mol·la(h) [ˈmɔlə] *n.* = mullah.

mol·les·cent [məˈlesnt] *a.* 柔软的; 趋于缓和的. **-cence** *n.*

mol·li·fi·ca·tion [ˌmɔlifiˈkeiʃən] *n.* ①平息, 缓和, 安慰. ②使人安慰的事物; 使缓和的事物. *No* ~ *of her anger appeared likely.* 她的怒气看来无法缓和.

mol·li·fi·er [ˈmɔlifaiə] *n.* ①安慰者. ②【医】缓和剂, 镇静药.

mol·li·fy [ˈmɔlifai] *vt.*〔罕〕使软化; 缓和, 减轻; 使平静,平息,抚慰.

mol·lusc [ˈmɔləsk] *n.*【动】软体动物.

Mol·lus·ca [mɔˈlʌskə] *n.*〔*pl.*〕【动】软体动物(门).

mol·lus·can [mɔˈlʌskən] *a.* 软体动物(门)的. — *n.* 软

体动物.
mol•lus•coid [mɔˈlʌskɔid] *n.*, *a.* 软体动物(似的); 拟软体动物(的).
Mol•lus•coi•da, Mol•lus•coi•de•a [ˌmɔləsˈkɔidə, -diə] *n.* 〔*pl.*〕【动】拟软体动物类.
mol•lus•cous [mɔˈlʌskəs] *a.* = molluscan.
mol•lusk [ˈmɔləsk] *n.* = mollusc.
Moll•wei•de projection [ˈmɔːlvaidə] 【测】摩尔魏特投影.
Mol•ly, Mol•lie [ˈmɔli] *n.* 莫莉〔女子名, Mary 的昵称〕.
mol•ly [ˈmɔli] *n.* 〔口〕娇嫩的男人[男少年].
mol•ly•cod•dle [ˈmɔlikɔdl] *n.* 女人气的[柔弱的、没骨气的]男子; 懦夫; 娇生惯养的人. — *vt.* 溺爱, 娇养.
Mo•loch [ˈməulɔk] *n.* ① 莫洛克神〔古 Phaenicia 人的火神, 以儿童为祭品〕; 〔喻〕要求重大牺牲的可怕力量[势力]. ②〔m-〕【动】(澳大利亚)四脚蛇, 棘蜥.
Mo•lo•kai [ˌməuləuˈkai] *n.* 莫洛凯〔美国夏威夷群岛中的一岛, 是麻风病人的隔离地〕.
mo•los•sus [məˈlɔsəs] *n.* (诗歌中)三个长音节构成的音步.
Mo•lo•tov [ˈmɔlətɔf], **V.M.** 莫洛托夫〔1890—　, 苏联政治家〕. ~ **bread basket** 〔俚〕莫洛托夫面包篮〔一种炸弹, 内装许多小燃烧弹, 空投后分散落下〕. ~ **cocktail** 〔俚〕燃烧瓶〔一种反坦克手榴弹〕.
molt [məult] *vi.*, *vt.*, *n.* = moult.
mol•ten [ˈməultən] melt 的过去分词. — *a.* 熔化了的, 熔融的; 浇铸的. *a* ~ *image* 铸像. ~ *pig* 铁水.
mol•to [ˈmɔltəu] *ad.* 〔It.〕【乐】很, 最. ~ ***adagio*** 极慢.
Mo•luc•cas [məˈlʌkəz] *n.* (印尼的)摩鹿加群岛〔又叫 Spice Islands〕.
mol. wt. = molecular weight 分子量.
mo•ly[1] [ˈməuli] *n.* ①(传说中有魔力的)白花黑根草. ②【植】黄花茖葱.
mol•y[2] [ˈmɔli] 【化】钼 = molybdenum.
mo•lyb•date [məˈlibdeit] *n.* 【化】钼酸盐.
mo•lyb•de•n•ite [mɔˈlibdinait, ˈmɔlibˈdiːnait] *n.* 【矿】辉钼矿.
mo•lyb•de•num [mɔˈlibdinəm] *n.* 【化】钼.
mo•lyb•dic [məˈlibdik] *a.* 【化】钼的〔指含三价钼或六价钼的盐的〕.
mo•lyb•dous [məˈlibdəs] *a.* 【化】二价钼的; 亚钼的.
mom [mɔm] *n.* 〔口〕妈妈 (= mamma). ~ ***and pop store [stand]*** 夫妻店, 家庭经营的小零售店[小摊].
Mom•ba•sa [mɔmˈbæsə] *n.* ①蒙巴萨岛〔肯尼亚〕. ② 蒙巴萨〔肯尼亚港市〕.
mome [məum] *n.* 〔古〕笨蛋, 傻瓜.
mo•ment [ˈməumənt] *n.* ①一转眼功夫, 片刻, 瞬息, 刹那; 时刻. ② 时机, 机会; 场合; 危机; 当前. ③ 重要, 紧要; 【哲】要素, 契机. ④【物】矩, 转矩, 力矩; 势头; 能率; 积率. ⑤【统计】动差. ⑥(历史发展的)阶段. *One* ~. = *Half a* ~. = *Wait a* ~. 等一会儿. *There is not a* ~ *to be lost.* 刻不容缓. *Go this very* ~. 现在马上去吧. *Seize the* ~ 抓住机会. *matter of great* ~ 重大事件. ***at a*** **~*'s notice*** 一经通知; 随时; 立刻, 马上. ***at any*** ~ 随时, 无论什么时候, 不知何时. ***at*** **~*s*** 时时, 常常. ***at odd*** **~*s*** 抽暇, 空闲时. ***at the last critical*** ~ 在最后关头. ***at the*** ~ 此刻[现在]; (正当)那时[过去]. ***at the same*** ~ 同时. ***every*** ~ 时时刻刻, 每一刻. ***for a*** ~ 片刻, 一会儿. ***for [at] the*** ~ 暂时, 现在. *(the man)* ***for this [the]*** ~ 能应付当前危局的(人). ***half a*** ~ 片刻, 一会儿. ***in a*** ~ 立即, 马上, 一会儿工夫. ***in a*** ~ ***of anger*** 趁着气愤, 一时气愤. ***in the*** ~ ***of danger*** 一到危险关头, 一有危险. ~ ***of couple*** 【机】偶矩. ~ ***of force*** 【物】力矩. ~ ***of inertia*** 【机】惯性矩; 【物】转动矩量; ~ ***of stability*** 【机】安定矩. ~ ***of truth*** (1)斗牛士击杀牛的时刻. (2)关键时刻〔检验人的本色, 或使人面对事实的时刻〕. ***of little*** ~ = ***of no*** ~ 不重要的, 无足轻重的. ***of the*** ~ 此刻, 现在. ***one*** ~ = half a ~. ***the man of the*** ~ 当代要人; 时人. ***the (very)*** ~〔用作连词引出时间状语从句〕—…(就) (= as soon as) (*I tell him the* ~ *he comes in.* 他一进来我就告诉他). ***to the (very)*** ~ 准时, 不差片刻, 正好. ***(up)on the*** ~ —…马上就. ~ **coefficient** 【机】矩系数.
mo•men•tal [məuˈmentl] *a.* 【机】动量的; 力矩的. *a* ~ *ellipse* 动量椭圆.
mo•men•ta•ri•ly [ˈməuməntərili] *ad.* 一会儿, 暂时; 时时刻刻地; 每刻.
mo•men•tar•i•ness [ˈməumənˌterinis] *n.* ①倾刻, 瞬息. ②〔现罕〕随时, 经常. ③随时可能发生.
mo•men•ta•ry [ˈməuməntəri] *a.* 瞬息间的, 顷刻的, 暂时的; 时时刻刻的. *in* ~ *expectation* 没有一刻不盼望.
mo•ment•ly [ˈməuməntli] *ad.* = momentarily.
mo•men•to [məˈmentəu] *n.* = memento.
mo•men•tous [məuˈmentəs] *a.* 重大的, 重要的, 声势浩大的(斗争). **-ly** *ad.* **-ness** *n.*
mo•men•tum [məuˈmentəm] *n.* ***(pl.*** **~*s*, -*ta*** [-tə]***)*** 【物】动量; 【火箭】总冲量; 〔口〕惰性; 势头; 要素, 契机. *the* ~ *of attack* 进攻的锐气[劲头].
mom•ism [ˈmɔmizəm] *n.* 唯母是尊, 母亲崇拜.
Momm•sen [ˈmɔmzən], **Theodor** 莫姆森〔1817—1903, 德国历史学家〕.
Mo•mus [ˈməuməs] *n.* 【希神】莫墨斯〔嘲弄之神; 爱挑错儿的人〕. *a disciple [son, daughter] of* 爱挑错儿的人; 滑稽的人.
Mon [məun] *n.* ***(pl.*** **~*(s))*** ①孟族人〔缅甸仰光东部的一个少数民族〕. ②孟族语.
mon [mɔn] *n.* 〔Scot., North Eng.〕man 的变体.
Mon. = ①Monday. ②Monastery. ③〔It.〕*Monsignor(e)*.
mon. = ①monetary. ②monastery.
mon- *comb.f.* = mono.
Mo•na [ˈməunə] *n.* 莫娜〔女子名〕.
mon•a•c(h)al [ˈmɔnəkəl] *a.* 修道士的, 僧侣的; 修道生活的; 修道院的.
mon•a•chism [ˈmɔnəkizəm] *n.* 修道(生活); 修道院制度. **-chist** *a.*, *n.* 修道主义的(者).
mon•a•chize [ˈmɔnəkaiz] *vt.* 使成为僧侣[修道士]. — *vi.* 当修道士, 过修道士生活.
mon•acid [mɔˈnæsid] *a.* 【化】一酸的.
Mon•a•co [ˈmɔnəkəu] *n.* ①摩纳哥〔欧洲〕. ② 摩纳哥〔摩纳哥首都〕.
mo•nad [ˈmɔnæd] *n.* 【哲】单子, 单元〔Leibnitz 哲学中的实在的、非物质的、基本单位〕; 【化】一价物; 一价基; 【物】单轴; 【生】单分体, 单孢体; 个体; 【原】单原子元素. **-ic, -i•cal** *a.*
mon•a•del•phous [ˌmɔnəˈdelfəs] *a.* 【植】单体(雄蕊)的.
mon•ad•ism, mon•ad•ol•o•gy [ˈmɔnædizəm, ˌmɔnəˈdɔlədʒi] *n.* 【哲】单子论〔德国唯心主义哲学家 Leibnitz (莱布尼茨)的学说, 认为宇宙是由单子组成的〕.
mo•nad•nock [məˈnædnɔk] *n.* 【地】残丘.
mon•ak•er *n.* = moniker.
Mo•na Li•sa [ˈməunəˈliːsə, -zə] 蒙娜·丽莎〔意大利画家 *Leonardo da Vinci* (达·芬奇)的名肖像画名〕(= *la Gioconda*).
mo•nan•drous [mɔˈnændrəs] *a.* ①【植】具一雄蕊的. ②一夫制的.
mo•nan•dry [mɔˈnændri] *n.* 一夫制; 【植】单雄蕊式.
mon•arch [ˈmɔnək] *n.* ①王, 帝王, 君主, 元首, 统制者. ②〔喻〕(大)王. ③大花蝶. ④【植】单原型. *an absolute* ~ 专制君主. *the* ~ *of the forest* 森林之王〔树木中的橡树, 动物中的狮子或老虎〕. *the* ~ *of the glen* 溪谷之王〔雄鹿〕.
mo•nar•chal [mɔˈnɑːkəl] *a.* 〔诗〕君主似的; 帝王似的;

君主政治的. **-ly** *ad.*

mo·nar·chi·al [mɔ'nɑːkiəl] *a.* = monarchal.

Mo·nar·chi·an·ism [mə'nɑːkiənizəm] *n.* 唯一神论〔二、三世纪基督教某些教派的教义，认为三位一体的三位乃上帝的化身〕.

mo·nar·chic, mo·nar·chi·cal [mɔ'nɑːkik, -kikəl] *a.* 君主(国)的,君主政体的,帝制的.

mon·arch·ism ['mɔnəkizəm] *n.* 君主主义; 君主政治〔制度〕.

mon·arch·ist ['mɔnəkist] *n.* 君主主义者，拥护君主制度者.

mon·ar·chis·tic [ˌmɔnɑː'kistik] *a.*君主主义的,君主政治的.

mon·ar·chy ['mɔnəki] *n.* 君主政治,君主政体; 君主国; 独裁君主权,大权. *an absolute* ~ 君主专制制度. *a constitutional [limited]* ~ 君主立宪制度. *a despotic* ~ 专制君主政体; 专制君主国.

mo·nar·da [mə'nɑːdə] *n.* 长叶薄荷 (= horsemint).

mon·as·te·ri·al [ˌmɔnəs'tiəriəl] *a.* 寺院的,修道院的.

mon·as·ter·y ['mɔnəstri] *n.* 修道院,寺院,庙宇.

mo·nas·tic [mə'næstik] *a.* ①修道院的; 庙宇的,寺院的. ②僧侣的; 修道士的; 修女的. ③出家的; 禁欲的. — *n.* 修道士; 僧侣; 修女; 尼姑. **-ti·cal** *a.*, **-ti·cal·ly** *ad.*

mo·nas·ti·cism [mə'næstisizəm] *n.* 寺院制度; 修道生活; 出家; 禁欲主义.

mon·a·tom·ic [ˌmɔnə'tɔmik] *a.* 【化】(具)单原子的; 含有一个可代换原子的; 一价的,独价的.

mon·au·ral [mɔn'ɔːrəl] *a.* 单耳的,单耳听觉的. **-ly** *ad.*

mon·ax·i·al [mɔn'æksiəl] *a.* 仅有单轴的; 一轴的.

mon·a·zite ['mɔnəˌzait] *n.* 【地】独居石.

Mond [mɔnd] *n.* 蒙德〔男子名〕.

mon·daine [mɔ̃ːn'dein] 〔F.〕 *n.* 社交界的时髦女人; 俗气的女人. — *a.* 时髦的; 俗气的.

Mon·day ['mʌndi, 'mʌndei] *n.* 星期一，礼拜一. ***a ~ morning quarterback*** 〔口〕放马后炮的人,事后诸葛亮. ***Black*** ~ 〔学俚〕(放假后的) 开学第一天. ***blue*** ~ ①〔口〕烦闷的星期一〔相对于欢乐的周末而言〕; 〔喻〕精神沮丧的时期. ②四旬斋(Lent)前的星期一. ***Mad*** ~ 忙乱的星期一〔指交易所这一天特别忙乱〕. ***St. [Saint]*** ~ 懒懒散散、工作很少的星期一. **-ly** *ad.* 〔美〕每星期一; 在任何星期一.

Mon·days ['mʌndiːz, -deiz] *ad.* 每星期一.

mon·day·ish ['mʌndiiʃ] *a.* 〔口〕(由于星期日过于劳累以致)星期一不想做事的; 疲倦的.

monde [mɔ̃ːnd] *n.* 〔F.〕 ①时髦社会; 社交界上流社会(= *beau* ~). ②个人的生活圈子; 社会.

mon·dial ['mɔndiəl] *a.* 全世界的.

mon Dieu [mɔ̃ːn 'djuː] 〔F.〕上帝呀! 哎呀! (=my God).

mo·ne·cious [mə'niːʃəs] *a.* 雌雄同株的，雌雄同体的(= monoecious).

Mo·nel [məu'nel] **metal** 【冶】莫涅耳合金〔镍、铜、铁、锰的合金,有抗酸性〕.

mo·ne·tar·y ['mʌnitəri] *a.* 货币的; 金钱的; 金融的; 财政(上)的. *the* ~ *system* 货币制度. *a* ~ *unit* 货币单位. ***in ~ difficulties*** 财政困难. **-i·ly** *ad.*

mon·e·tize ['mʌnitaiz] *vt.* ①把…作为法定货币. ②使具有货币性质. ③把…铸成货币. *demonetize gold and* ~ *silver* 停止把黄金作为法定货币，而把白银作为法定货币. **-za·tion** [ˌmɔnitai'zeiʃən] *n.*

mon·ey ['mʌni] *n.* ①货币; 钱，金钱. ②财产，财富，财力. ③〔主 *pl.*〕(特种)货币; 通货; 〔*pl.*〕〔古〕【法】金额〔常用 monies 这一特殊复数写法〕. ④【经】交换媒介物，货物货币. ⑤大富翁; 金融集团. ⑥(优胜)奖金. *fairy* ~ (终要变成树叶的)魔钱; 拾得的钱. *paper* ~ 纸币. *ready* ~ 现金. *soft* ~ 〔美口〕纸币. *hard* ~ 硬币. *small* ~ 零钱. *What's the* ~? 要多少钱? 价钱是多少? *Those with* ~ *should contribute* ~. 有钱出钱. *There is* ~ *in it.* 可以赚钱，有利可图. ***at the*** ~ = for the ~. ***be in the*** ~ 〔俚〕有钱，富裕; (在赛狗、赛马中)得奖，赌胜，赢. ***be made of*** ~ 钱多得不得了. ***cheap at the*** ~ 价钱便宜. ***coin*** ~ 〔口〕大赚其钱,暴发. ***covered*** ~ 〔美〕国库存款. ***everybody's [every man's]*** ~ 〔口〕人人欢迎的东西 (*He's not everybody's* ~ 他不是人人都欢迎的人). ***for love or*** ~ 无论怎样都. ***for*** ~ 为钱; 【商】直接〔现款〕交易. ***for my*** ~ 〔口〕在我看来; 正合我意 (*He is the man for my* ~. 他是合我心意的人). ***for the*** ~ 照所付的代价. ***get one's ~'s worth*** (钱花得)合算，值得; 无损失. ***in the*** ~ = be in the ~. ***keep in*** ~ 借给钱,垫钱. ***lose*** ~ 亏本 *(over)*. ***make*** ~ 赚钱，发财 (*cf.* ~-making). ***make ~(out) of*** 用…赚钱. ~ ***crops*** 专供销售的农作物. ~ ***down*** 现金，现款. ~ ***for jam*** 〔英俚〕容易赚的钱. ***M- makes the mare (to) go.*** 〔谚〕有钱能使鬼推磨; 金钱万能. ~ ***market*** 金融市场. ~ ***of account*** 记帐货币〔如美国的 mill, 英国的 *guinea*〕. ~ ***on [at] call*** = ***call-money*** 随时可以收回的借款. ~ ***on the line*** 【美拳】当天卖票收入. ~ ***out of hand*** = ~ down. ***M- talks.*** 〔美〕 金钱万能. ***on the*** ~ 〔美俚〕 在最适当的时间〔地点〕. ***out of*** ~ 拮据; 吃亏 *(by)*. ***out of the*** ~ 〔美〕赛马输掉. ***raise ~ on*** 以…抵押筹措款项. ***sink*** ~ 浪费金钱. ***throw good ~ after bad*** 吃亏了又吃亏. ~ **bag** *n.* 钱袋，钱包; 〔*pl.*〕〔口、喻〕财富，财产; 〔*pl.*〕〔俚〕富翁,守财奴. ~ **belt** 钱带〔里边有放钱小格子的带子〕. ~ **bill** 财政法案. ~ **box** 钱箱. ~ **broker, ~changer,** ~ **dealer** 货币兑换商. **~-changing** 货币兑换 (尤指外币兑换). **~-grubber** 贪财谋利的人. **~-grubbing** 贪财谋利. **~lender** 放债的人. **~-maker** 会赚钱的人; 赚钱的东西. **~-making** ① *a.* 贪财谋利的，很会赚钱的; (事业等)有利的. ② *n.* 赚钱，积财. **~man** 金融专家. ~ **market** 金融市场,金融界. ~ **matter** (金钱上的)借贷事件; 〔主 *pl.*〕金钱〔财政〕问题. ~ **order** 汇票，邮政汇票. ~ **player** 【美运】职业运动家. ~ **position** 【美运】比赛胜利者(尤指赛马的). ~ **rates** 利息. **~'s worth** 可变钱的东西; 金钱上的价值. **~spinner** (传说爬到身上就会使人走运的)财喜小蜘蛛; 投机〔放债〕发财的人; 很赚钱的东西. **~wort** 【植】铜钱状珍珠菜.

mon·eyed ['mʌnid] *a.* ①富有的，有钱的. ②金钱(上)的. ~ *interest* 金钱关系; 财界，金融界; 金融业者; 财界人物. ~ *assistance* 金钱上的援助.

mon·ey·er ['mʌniə] *n.* 铸币人.

'mong [mʌŋ] *prep.* 〔诗〕= among.

mon·ger ['mʌŋgə] *n.* 〔英〕〔主要构成复合词〕…商，…贩子: fish*monger*, iron*monger*, scandal*monger*, etc.

mon·go ['mɔŋgəu] *n.* *(pl.* ***-gos)*** 蒙戈〔蒙古货币名，等于 1/100 图格里克〕.

Mon·gol ['mɔŋgɔl] *n.*, *a.* 蒙古人[语]; 蒙古人[语]的.

Mon·go·lia [mɔŋ'gəuljə] *n.* ①蒙古〔亚洲〕. ②内蒙古. *Inner* ~ 内蒙. *the Inner* ~ *Autonomous Region* 内蒙古自治区.

Mon·go·li·an [mɔŋ'gəuljən] *n.* ①蒙古人[语]. ②【医】先天愚型病人. — *a.* ①蒙古(人种)的，黄种人的. ②【医】(患)先天愚型病的. ~ **idiocy** = Mongolism. ~ **People's Republic** 蒙古人民共和国. ~ **race** 黄种.

Mon·gol·ic [mɔŋ'gɔlik] *n.*, *a.* 蒙古人[语](的).

Mon·gol·ism ['mɔŋgəlizəm] *n.* 【医】先天性愚型，伸舌样白痴〔一种先天性畸形病症，表现为扁平额、斜眼、小指头短等〕.

Mon·gol·oid ['mɔŋgəlɔid] *a.* (象)蒙古人种的; 蒙古人〔族〕的. — *n.* 蒙古人种，黄种人.

mon·goos(e) ['mɔŋguːs] *n.* ①【动】(印度产)猫鼬，獴. ②马达加斯加(Madagascar)狐猿 (= mongoose lemur).

mon·grel ['mʌŋgrəl] *n.* 杂种(动植物); (特指) 杂种狗; 〔蔑〕杂种，混血儿. — *a.* 杂种的，混血的. **-grel·ize** *vt.*

使成杂种.
mongst [mʌŋst] *prep.* = amongst.
mo·ni·al [ˈməuniəl] *n.* = mullion.
Mon·i·ca [ˈmɔnikə] *n.* 莫妮卡[女子名].
mon·ied [ˈmʌnid] *a.* = moneyed.
mon·ies [ˈmʌnis] *n.* [罕] money③ 的复数.
mon·i·ker, mon·i·cker [ˈmɔnikə] *n.* ①徒步旅行者认路的记号. ②[俚] 名字; 外号, 绰号.
mo·nil·i·form [məuˈniliˌfɔːm] *a.* 念珠状的; (尤指)【生】(如茎和触角的)项圈形的.
mon·ish [ˈmɔniʃ] *vt.* [古] ①告诫; 警告. ②规谏. ③敦促; 劝告. ④(以警告方式)通知, 提醒 (=admonish).
mon·ism [ˈmɔnizəm] *n.*【哲】一元论;【生】一元发生说. *idealistic [materialistic]* ~ 唯心[唯物]一元论.
mon·ist [ˈmɔnist] *n.* 一元论者.
mon·is·tic, mon·is·ti·cal [mɔˈnistik(əl)] *a.* 一元论的.
mo·ni·tion [məuˈniʃən] *n.* ①告诫, 警告; (危险等的)预兆. ②(法院的)传票; (主教、宗教法庭的)告诫书.
mo·ni·tor [ˈmɔnitə] *n.* ①告诫物, 提醒物; [古]忠告者; 劝告[告诫、警告]者. ②班[级]长, 教务助理生, 导生. ③(水利、采矿用的)水枪, 喷射口. ④【海】浅水炮舰. ⑤【无】(对外国广播等的)监听员[器]; 监视器, 监控器; 放射能检验器; (火箭的)追踪器;【火箭】稳定装置;【影】调音员. ⑥【动】大壁虎, 巨蜥. — *vi., vt.*【无】监听(外国广播); 监督, 监视; 监控; 检验, 检查; 调节; 探索, 追踪. *a pilot* ~【空】自动驾驶仪. ~ **roof,** ~ **top** [美](客车等的)采光屋顶, 通风顶. ~ **screen** 检查[选择]播送内容的电视屏.
mon·i·to·ri·al [ˌmɔniˈtɔːriəl] *a.* 劝告者的; 班长的; 教务助理生的; 使用监听器[监视器]的; 劝告的, 警告的. *the* ~ *system* 导生制.
mon·i·tor·ship [ˈmɔnitəˌʃip] *n.* 监听者的身份[职务]; 劝告者的身份[地位]; 警告者的身份[地位]; 班长的身份[职务].
mon·i·to·ry [ˈmɔnitəri] *n.*【宗】告戒状. — *a.* 劝告的, 训戒的, 警告的.
mon·i·tress, mon·i·trix [ˈmɔnitris, -triks] *n.* 女的 monitor.
monk [mʌŋk] *n.* 僧侣, 修道士;【史】隐士. ~**'s cloth** ①[原义]僧侣袈裟呢料. ②[现义] 方平织纹的厚布[作布帘等].
monk·er·y [ˈmʌŋkeri] *n.* ①僧侣生涯. ②[集合词]修道士, 僧侣. ③修道院.
mon·key [ˈmʌŋki] *n.* ①猴子; 猿 (*cf.* ape); 长毛猴的毛皮. ②顽童; 淘气精. ③打桩锤; (制造玻璃等用的)小坩埚. ④[美俚]吸毒瘾. ⑤[英俚]五百英镑; [美俚]五百美元. ***have a ~ (with the long tail) on a house [up the chimney]*** [方] 抵押房屋. ***have a ~ on one's back*** ①毒瘾很深. ②为麻烦的问题等而苦恼. ***have [get] one's ~ up = get a ~ on one's back*** [英俚] 生气, 发脾气. ~ **money** [美俚] 公司的临时股票; 期票; 外国货币. ~ ***with a long tail*** [卑] 抵押. ***put one's ~ up*** [英俚]使人发怒. ***suck [sup] the ~*** [英俚]插管子入酒桶里吸酒; 喝酒; 吸饮装在椰子壳里的酒. — *vi.* 恶戏, 恶作剧; 管闲事, 干涉 (with). — *vt.* 学样, 嘲弄. ~ ***(about) with*** [美俚] 用…逗…玩; 嘲弄; 瞎搞, 插嘴; 打搅. ~ ***with a buzz saw*** [美俚] 孤注一掷, 好歹干一下. ~ **block**【海】附有转环的滑车. ~ **bread**【植】猴面包(树、果). ~ **business**[美俚] 狡猾的恶作剧, 顽皮行为, 嘲弄, 胡闹, 欺骗, 耍花招. ~ **clothes** [美俚]礼服, 军礼服, 燕尾服. ~ **chocolatetree** 窄叶可可. ~ **drill** [俚] 柔软体操. ~ **engine** 打桩机. ~**-face** 猴子(似的)脸. ~ **forecastle**【船】艏楼; 前甲板. ~ **flower** 沟酸浆属 (mimulus) 植物. ~ **jack** 坚硬面包果. ~ **jacket** (水手冷天穿的)紧身短上衣. ~ **meat** [美军俚] 罐头牛肉. ~ **money** [美俚] 公司的临时股票; 期票; 外国货币. ~ **nut** [英]【植】落花生. ~ **puzzle**【植】(叶尖锐, 猴子也难爬上去的) 智利松; 智利南美杉. ~***'s allowance*** 虐待. ~**shines** [美俚] 恶作剧. ~ **suit** [美俚]制服, 礼服, 军装, 航空装. ~**-swill** [美俚]酒. ~ **wrench** 活动扳手[扳钳、扳头]; 引起破坏的东西 (*throw a ~ into* [美俚](把活动扳手丢进机器里使不能转动, 转为)妨碍, 破坏). **-ish** *a.* 猴子似的; 顽皮的.
Mon-Khmer [ˈməunkˈmeə] *a.* 孟-高棉语的 [澳亚语系的一个语支, 包括孟语和高棉语, 主要讲用区是印度支那].
monk·hood [ˈmʌŋkhud] *n.* 修道士 [僧侣] 的身分 [生活]; [集合词]修道士, 僧侣.
monk·ish [ˈmʌŋkiʃ] *a.* [蔑] 修道士[僧侣]似的; 修道院的. **-ly** *ad.* **-ness** *n.*
monk's·hood [ˈmʌŋkshud] *n.*【植】附子, 舟形乌头.
mon(o)- *comb.f.* 独, 单, 一;【化】含一原子 (*opp.* poly-; *cf.* soli-, multi-). ★元音前用 mon-: *mon*arch.
mono [ˈmɔnəu] *a.* [口] 单声道的(= monaural).
mon·o·ac·id [ˌmɔnəuˈæsid] *n.*【化】一元酸.
mon·o·a·cid·ic [ˌmɔnəuəˈsidik] *a.*【化】一(酸)价的, 一元的, 一酸的.
mon·o·a·tom·ic [ˌmɔnəuəˈtɔmik] *a.* ①【化】单原子的; 具单原子的. ②包含一可交换原子 [原子团]的. ③【生】单价的;【化】一价的, 独价的.
mon·o·bas·ic [ˌmɔnəuˈbeisik] *a.*【化】①一(碱)价的, 一元的. ②一代的. **-sic·i·ty** [ˌmɔnəbeiˈsisiti] *n.*
mon·o·car·box·yl·ic [ˈmɔnəuˌkɑːbɔkˈsilik] *a.*【化】一元羧基的.
mon·o·car·pel·lar·y [ˌmɔnəuˈkɑːpələri] *a.*【植】包含单一心皮的, 具一心皮的; 包含单一果爿的, 具一果爿的.
mon·o·car·pic [ˌmɔnəuˈkɑːpik] *a.*【植】结一次果的(= monocarpous).
mono·ceph·a·lous [ˌmɔnəuˈsefələs] *a.*【植】单头花序的.
Mo·noc·er·os [məˈnɔsərəs]【天】麒麟(星)座.
mon·o·cha·si·um [ˌmɔnəuˈkeiʒiəm, -ziəm] *n.* *(pl. -sia [-ə])*【植】单歧聚伞花序, 单歧式.
mon·o·chla·myd·e·ous [ˌmɔnəukləˈmidiəs] *a.*【植】单被的, 有单被花的.
mon·o·chlo·ride [ˌmɔnəuˈklɔːraid] *n.*【化】一氯化物.
mon·o·chord [ˈmɔnəukɔːd] *n.* 一弦琴; 一弦的音程测定器; 和谐; 一致.
mon·o·chro·mat [ˌmɔnəuˈkrəumæt] *n.*【医】全色盲者. **-ism** *n.* 全色盲.
mon·o·chro·mat·ic [ˌmɔnəukrəuˈmætik] *a.* 一色的; 单色光的;【物】由一波长的光形成的;【医】单色觉的, 全色盲的. ~ *lamp* 单色灯.
mon·o·chrome [ˈmɔnəukrəum] *n.* 单色画 [照片]. — *a.* 单色的, 一色的. **-chrom·ist** *n.* 单色画家. **-chro·mic, -mi·cal** *a.*
mon·o·cle [ˈmɔnɔkl] *n.* 单片眼镜.
mon·o·cli·nal [ˈmɔnəuˈklainl] *a.*【地】(地层)单斜的.
mon·o·cline [ˈmɔnəuklain] *n.*【地】单斜褶皱.
mon·o·clin·ic [ˌmɔnəuˈklinik] *a.*【化】单斜(晶)的.
mon·o·cli·nous [ˌmɔnəuˈklainəs] *a.*【植】雌雄(蕊)同花的.
mon·o·coque [ˈmɔnəukəuk] *n.* (飞机的)硬壳式结构; (汽车等的)无大梁结构.
mon·o·cot·y·le·don [ˌmɔnəuˌkɔtiˈliːdən] *n.*【植】单子叶植物. **-ous** *a.*
mo·noc·ra·cy [mɔˈnɔkrəsi] *n.* 独裁政治.
mon·o·crat [ˈmɔnəukræt] *n.* 独裁主义者; 独裁者; [美] (亲英的)联邦党员.
mo·noc·u·lar [mɔˈnɔkjulə] *a.* 单眼的; 单眼用(的) (*opp.* binocular). *a ~ microscope* 单眼显微镜.
mon·o·cul·ture [ˈmɔnəukʌltʃə] *n.* [美]【农】单作, 单一经营, 单种栽培.

mon•o•cy•cle [ˈmɔnəusaikl] *n.* 独轮车.
mon•o•cy•clic [ˌmɔnəuˈsaiklik] *a.* ①单环的,单周期的,单轮的. ②【化】单环的,一环的.
mon•o•cyte [ˈmɔnəuˌsait] *n.*【生】单核细胞,单核白血球. **-cyt•ic** [-ˈsitik] *a.*
mon•o•dist [ˈmɔnəudist] *n.* 单声部旋律作品的作者[歌唱者].
mon•o•dra•ma [ˈmɔnəudrɑːmə] *n.* 独脚戏,单人剧;单人剧剧本.
mon•o•dy [ˈmɔnədi] *n.*【希腊剧】(悲剧的)抒情独唱;(对死者的)悼诗,挽歌;【乐】单音曲;单声部旋律的作品;无伴奏的齐唱作品. **-ic, -i•cal** *a.*, **-i•cal•ly** *ad.*
Mo•noe•cia [məˈniːʃiə] *n.* 雌雄同株植物;【动】雌雄同体. **mo•noe•cious** *a.* 雌雄同株的;雌雄同体的.
mon•o•fil•a•ment [ˌmɔnəuˈfiləmənt] *n.*【纺】单丝,单纤(维)丝 (= monofil).
mon•o•fu•el [ˈmɔnəufuəl] *n.*【宇】单元燃料;单元推进剂.
mo•nog•a•mist [mɔˈnɔgəmist] *n.* 一夫一妻主义者;主张[实行]一生一婚制者.
mo•nog•a•mous [mɔˈnɔgəməs] *a.* 一夫一妻制的;一生一婚制的;【动】一雌一雄的,单配的.
mo•nog•a•my [mɔˈnɔgəmi] *n.* 一夫一妻制;一生一婚制;单配偶,单配性.
mon•o•gen•e•sis [ˌmɔnəuˈdʒenisis] *n.*【生】一元发生说;单性生殖,无性生殖.
mon•o•ge•net•ic [ˌmɔnəudʒiˈnetik] *a.* ①一元发生说的;无性生殖说的;关于一元发生说的;关于无性生殖说的. ③单殖动物的.
mon•o•gen•ic [ˌmɔnəuˈdʒenik] *a.*【动】单基因的. **-nog•e•ny** [məˈnɔdʒini] *n.*
mo•nog•e•nism [məˈnɔdʒinizm] *n.* 人类单一起源说.
mo•nog•e•ny [mɔˈnɔdʒini] *n.* 人类一元发生说;【生】= monogenesis.
mon•o•glot [ˈmɔnəglɔt] *a.*, *n.* 只会说[写]一种语言的(人);只用一种语言写成的.
mon•o•gram [ˈmɔnəugræm] *n.* (姓名、名称等首字母组合成的)组合文字,花押字. **-ma•tic** *a.*
mon•o•graph [ˈmɔnəugrɑːf] *n.* 专题著作[论文],专论. **-er** *n.* 专题文章的作者. **-ic, -i•cal** *a.* 专题性的. **-ist** *n.* = monnographer.
mo•nog•y•nous [mɔˈnɔdʒinəs] *a.* 一夫一妻的;只有一妻的;【植】单雌蕊的;【动】单雌群的.
mo•nog•y•ny [mɔˈnɔdʒini] *n.* 一妻制 (*opp.* polygyny).
mon•o•hy•drate [ˌmɔnəuˈhaidreit] *n.*【化】一水合物,一水化物.
mon•o•hy•dric [ˌmɔnəuˈhaidrik] *a.* ①【化】一羟基的. ②〔罕〕【化】一羟的,一元的 (= monohydroxy).
mon•o•hy•drox•y [ˌmɔnəuhaiˈdrɔksi] *a.*【化】一羟基的.
mon•o•i•de•ism [ˌmɔnəuˈaidiizəm] *n.*【医】孤独意想.
mo•nol•a•try [mɔˈnɔletri] *n.* 一神崇拜.
mon•o•lay•er [ˈmɔnəuˌleiə] *n.*【物】单层,单分子层.
mon•o•lin•gual [ˌmɔnəuˈliŋgwəl] *a.* 用一种语言表达的,只懂一种语言的. — *n.* 只懂一种语言的人.
mon•o•lith [ˈmɔnəuliθ] *n.* 磐石,独石;独石柱[碑、像];整料. **-ic** *a.* (坚如)磐石的;铁板一块的 (*monolithic circuit*【无】单片电路,单块电路. *monolithic unity* 坚如磐石的团结).
mon•o•lith•ism [ˌmɔnəuˈliθizəm] *n.* 磐石一块,铁板一块.
mon•o•log [ˈmɔnəulɔg] *n.* = monologue.
mono•log•ic(al) [ˌmɔnəuˈlɔdʒik(əl)] *a.* ①【戏】独白的. ②独白式的. ③滔滔不绝的.
mo•nol•o•gist [mɔˈnɔlədʒist] *n.* 独白[自言自语]的人;独演者;独自把持着说话的人.
mo•nol•o•gize [mɔˈnɔlədʒaiz] *vi.*【剧】独白;自言自语;独说独讲;滔滔不绝地说.
mon•o•log(ue) [ˈmɔnəlɔg] *n.*【剧】独白;独白场面;独脚戏剧本;(不使别人开口的)独说独讲;独白诗.
mon•o•logu•ist [ˈmɔnəlɔgist] *n.* = monologist.
mon•o•ma•ni•a [ˌmɔnəuˈmeinjə] *n.* 单狂,偏癖,偏执狂[热中于一物或一事]. **-ma•ni•ac** [-ˈmeiniæk] *n.* 单狂者;偏执狂者. **-ma•ni•a•cal** *a.*
mon•o•mark [ˈmɔnəumɑːk] *n.*〔英〕(用表示商品名称、地址的文字、数字作成的)注册标记[符号,代号,略名].
mon•o•mer [ˈmɔnəmə] *n.*【化】单体,单聚物,单量体. **-ic** [-ˈmerik] *a.*
mo•nom•er•ous [məˈnɔmərəs] *a.*【植】一基数的.
mon•o•me•tal•lic [ˌmɔnəumiˈtælik] *a.*【化】一金属的;【经】单本位制的.
mon•o•met•al•lism [ˌmɔnəuˈmetəlizəm] *n.* (货币的)单本位制 (*cf.* bimetallism).
mo•no•mi•al [mɔˈnəumiəl]【数】一项的,单项的;【生】一个词的,单名的. — *n.*【数】单项式;【生】单名.
mon•o•mo•lec•u•lar [ˌmɔnəməuˈlekjulə] *a.*【物】单分子层的;【化】单(个)分子的.
mon•o•mor•phic [ˌmɔnəˈmɔːfik] *a.* ①单型的. ②具有同型(或大体同型)结构的 (= monomorphous).
mon•o•nu•cle•o•sis [ˌmɔnəuˌnjuːkliːˈəusis, -nuː-] *n.* ①传染性单核细胞增多. ②单核细胞增多 (=infectious mononucleosis).
mo•noph•a•gous [məˈnɔfəgəs] *a.*【生】单食性的.
mon•o•pho•bi•a [ˌmɔnəuˈfəubjə] *n.*【医】独居恐怖,单身恐怖(症).
mon•o•phon•ic [ˌmɔnəuˈfɔnik] *a.* ①单音的;单音性的;单音调(乐曲)的;单音调(乐曲)性的. ②单路输音的.
mo•noph•o•ny [məˈnɔfəni] *n.* ①单音调乐曲. ②【希腊剧】(悲剧的)抒情独唱;悼诗,挽歌;(波浪的)单调声响. ③【乐】单旋律曲体;单旋律乐曲 (=monody).
mon•oph•thong [ˈmɔnəufθɔŋ] *n.* 单元音 (*cf.* diphthong). **-al** *a.* **-ize** *vt.* (把双元音)单元音化.
mon•o•phy•let•ic [ˌmɔnəufaiˈletik] *a.* ①单源的,单种的. ②由同一亲型进化的. **-phy•le•tism** [-ˈfailitizm] *n.*
mon•o•phyl•lous [ˌmɔnəuˈfiləs] *a.* ①【植】仅具单叶的;单叶组成的. ②有合萼的;有合瓣的.
mono•phy•odont [ˌmɔnəuˈfiədɔnt] *a.*【动】有不换性牙齿的,单套牙的.
Mo•noph•y•site [məˈnɔfiˌsait] *n.* 单一性灵论者〔科普特教派的论点,认为基督的人性与神性合一〕. **-sit•ic** [-ˈsitik] *a.*
mon•o•pitch [ˈmɔnəupitʃ] *n.* (话声等的)单调.
mon•o•plane [ˈmɔnəuplein] *n.* 单翼(飞)机. **-plan•ist** *n.* 单翼机飞行员.
mon•o•ple•gi•a [ˌmɔnəuˈpliːdʒiə, -ˈpliːdʒə] *n.*【医】单瘫. **-ple•gic** [-ˈpliːdʒik, -ˈpledʒik] *a.*
mon•o•ploid [ˈmɔnəuˌplɔid] *a.*, *n.*【生】单元体的,单倍体的;单倍体 (= haploid).
mon•o•pode [ˈmɔnəuˌpəud] *a.* 仅具一足的. — *n.* ①单足生物;(尤指)(神话中的)独脚人种人. ②【植】单轴 (= monopodium).
mon•o•po•di•um [ˌmɔnəuˈpəudiəm] *n.* (*pl.* **-di•a** [-ə])【植】单轴,单茎. **-po•dial** *a.*
mo•nop•o•lism [məˈnɔpəlizəm] *n.* 垄断主义[制度].
mo•nop•o•list [məˈnɔpəlist], **mo•nop•o•liz•er** [-laizə] *n.* ①独占者,垄断者;专利者. ②[-list] 垄断论者;专利论者.
mo•nop•o•lis•tic [məˌnɔpəˈlistik] *a.* 垄断[专利]的.
mo•nop•o•li•za•tion [məˌnɔpəlaiˈzeiʃən] *n.* 独占,垄断,包办;专利.
mo•nop•o•lize [məˈnɔpəlaiz] *vt.* 独占,垄断,包办;得到…的专利权. ~ *the conversation* 独占谈话. ~ *the conduct of affairs* 包办.
mo•nop•o•ly [məˈnɔpəli] *n.* ①垄断[独占](权),专利

(权)*(of,*〔美〕*on)*. ②垄断[专利]公司; 独占[专利]事业. ③专利品. *a government* ～ 政府专利(品). *make a* ～ *of* 独家经售; 垄断. *a* ～ *capital(ist)* 垄断资本(家). *the* ～ *capitalist class* 垄断资产阶级.

mon·o·pro·pel·lant [ˌmɔnəuprəˈpelənt] *n.* 单元喷气燃料,单一组分的喷气机燃料.

mo·nop·so·ny [məˈnɔpsəni] *n.* *(pl. -nies)*【经】独家主顾.

mon·o·rail [ˈmɔnəureil] *n.* 单轨;单轨铁路.

mon·o·sac·cha·ride [ˌmɔnəuˈsækəraid] *n.*【化】单糖.

mon·o·scope [ˈmɔnəuskəup] *n.*【电视】单象管; 存储管式示波器.

mon·o·sep·al·ous [ˌmɔnəuˈsepələs] *a.*【植】合萼的(= gamosepalous).

mon·o·so·di·um glu·ta·mate [ˌmɔnəuˈsəudiəm-ˈgluːtəˌmeit] 谷氨酸钠〔俗名味精,味素〕.

mon·o·some [ˈmɔnəusəum] *n.*【植】单体〔指染色体〕. **-so·mic** *a.*

mon·o·sper·mous [ˌmɔnəuˈspəːməs] *a.*【植】仅具单子的.

mon·o·sper·my [ˈmɔnəuspəːmi] *n.*【动】单精受精. **-sper·mic** *a.*

mon·o·stable [ˌmɔnəuˈsteibl] *n., a.* 单稳态(的). ～ *multivibrator* 单稳多谐振荡器.

mon·o·ste·le [ˌmɔnəuˈstiːli, ˈmɔnəustiːl] *n.*【植】单体中柱. **-ste·lic** *a.*

mon·o·stich [ˈmɔnəustik] *n.* ①单行诗. ②单行诗句.

mo·nos·ti·chous [məˈnɔstikəs] *a.*【植】单列的.

mon·o·stome [ˈmɔnəustəum] *a.*【动】具单口的,具单吸盘的 (= monostomous).

mo·nos·tro·phe [məˈnɔstrəfi, ˈmɔnəuˌstrəuf] *n.* 单律诗.

mon·o·sty·lous [ˌmɔnəuˈstailəs] *a.*【植】仅具单花柱的.

mon·o·syl·lab·ic [ˈmɔnəusiˈlæbik] *a.* 单音节的; 由单音节构成的. **-i·cal·ly** *ad.*

mon·o·syl·la·bism [ˌmɔnəuˈsiləbizəm] *n.* 单音节语使用(癖); 单音节语倾向.

mon·o·syl·la·ble [ˈmɔnəuˌsiləbl] *n.* 单音节词. *speak [answer] in* ～*s* 只冷淡的说[答] yes 或 no.

mon·o·sym·met·ric(al) [ˌmɔnəusiˈmetrik(əl)] *a.* ①【化】单斜晶系的 (= monoclinic). ②【生】两侧对称的; (生物、器官等的)从中轴可等分的 (= zygomorphic).

mon·o·the·ism [ˈmɔnəuθiːizəm] *n.* 一神教[论]. **-ist** *n.* 一神教信徒; 一神论者. **-is·tic** *a.*

mon·o·the·is·ti·cal [ˌmɔnəuθiːˈiztikl] *a.* 信一神的,一神教的. **-ly** *ad.*

mon·o·tint [ˈmɔnəutint] *n.* = monochrome.

mon·o·tone [ˈmɔnəutəun] *n., a.*【语】单调音(的); (颜色、文体等的)单调(的). — *vt., vi.* 单调地读[说、唱].

mon·o·ton·ic [ˌmɔnəuˈtɔnik] *a.* 单调的.

mo·not·o·ny [məˈnɔtəni] *n.* 单音; 单调; 无变化,千篇一律; 无聊. **-not·on·ous** [-tənəs] *a.*

Mon·o·trem·a·ta [ˌmɔnəuˈtremətə] *n.*【动】单孔目.

mon·o·treme [ˈmɔnəutriːm] *n.*【动】单孔目动物〔包括鸭嘴兽和针鼹〕. **-trem·a·tous** [-ˈtremətəs,-ˈtriːmə-] *a.*

mo·not·ri·chous [məˈnɔtrikəs] *a.*【生】单鞭毛的.

mon·o·type [ˈmɔnəutaip] *n.*【印】①〔M-〕莫诺铸排机〔一种单字自动铸排机〕. ②【生】单型; 独模标本; 单版画(制作法). **-typ·ic** *a.*

mon·o·va·lent [ˌmɔnəuˈveilənt] *a.* ①【菌】单价的. ②【化】单价的, 独价的 (= univalent). **-va·lence, -va·len·cy** *n.*

mon·ovu·lar [mɔˈnəuvjulə] *a.* 单卵的. ～ *twins* 单卵双生.

mon·ox·id, mon·ox·ide [mɔˈnɔksid, mɔˈnɔksaid] *n.*【化】一氧化物.

Mon·roe [mənˈrəu] *n.* ①门罗〔姓氏,男子名〕. ②James ～ 门罗〔1758—1831, 美国第五任总统〕. ～ *Doctrine* 门罗主义.

Mon·roe·ism [mənˈrəuizəm] *n.* 〔美〕门罗主义. **-ist** *n.* 〔Am.〕门罗主义者.

Mon·ro·vi·a [mənˈrəuviə] *n.* 蒙罗维亚〔利比里亚首都〕.

Mons. = *Monsieur.*

Mon·sar·rat [ˌmɔnsəˈræt] *n.* 蒙萨拉特〔姓氏〕.

mon·sei·gneur, M- [ˌmɔnsenˈjəː] *n.* 〔F.〕 *(pl. mes·sei·gneurs, M-* [mesenˈjəːz]*)* 阁下〔对王族、大主教等的敬称〕; 称为阁下的人.

mon·sieur [məˈsjəː] *n.* 〔F.〕 *(pl.* ***messieurs*** [meˈsjəː, ˈmesəz]*)* 先生〔和英语 Mr. 及招呼语 sir 相当,略 ***M., Mons.*** *pl.* ***Messrs., MM.***〕; 绅士;〔蔑〕法国人.

Monsig. = Monseigneur; *Monsignor.*

mon·si·gnor, **Mon·si·gnor** [mɔnˈsiːnjə] *n.* 〔It.〕 *(pl.* ～*s, mon·si·gno·ri, M-)* = *monseigneur.*

mon·soon [mɔnˈsuːn] *n.* ①季(节)风〔在印度洋和亚洲南部 5—9 月自西南、10—12 月自东北吹的风〕. ②(印度的)雨季,夏季季风期. *the Indian* ～ 东亚季候风. *the dry [wet]* ～ 冬[夏]季季风; 干[湿]季风. *a* ～ *forest* 季雨林. *the* ～ *rain* 季风雨.

mon·soon·al [mɔnˈsuːnl] *a.*【气】季风的.

mons pu·bis [ˌmɔnz ˈpjuːbis] 〔L.〕【解】阴阜.

mon·ster [ˈmɔnstə] *n.* ①(想象中的)怪物〔centaur, dragon, sphinx, griffin 等〕. ②(尤指史前的)怪兽,巨兽〔mammoth, ichthyosaurus 等〕; 畸形(生物);【医】畸胎; 巨人; 巨物; 残忍的人,穷凶极恶的人. *a green-eyed* ～ 嫉妒. ～*s of the deep* 大鱼. — *a.* 巨大的. *a* ～ *ship* 巨舰.

mon·strance [ˈmɔnstrəns] *n.*【天主】圣体匣.

mon·stros·i·ty [mɔnsˈtrɔsiti] *n.* 异形,畸形; 怪异; 怪物; 异常大的东西; 穷凶极恶.

mon·strous [ˈmɔnstrəs] *a.* ①异形的,畸形的,巨大的. ②可怕的; 穷凶极恶的. ③〔口〕荒谬的,笑死人的. ～ *crimes* 滔天罪行. — *ad.* 〔美口、英古〕非常,很,极. **-ly** *ad.* **-ness** *n.*

mon·strous·ness [ˈmɔnstrəsnis] *n.* 异形,畸形,怪异.

mons ven·er·is [ˌmɔnz ˈvenəris] (妇女的)阴阜.

Mont. = Montana.

mon·tage [mɔnˈtɑːʒ, ˈmɔntidʒ] *n.* 〔F.〕 ①辑绘; 辑绘图画. ②【影】剪辑画面; 蒙太奇. ③装配.

Mon·ta·gnard [ˌmɔntənˈjɑːd] *n.* ①(越南中部的)山民. ②(美国落矶山北部的)印第安部族山民.

Mon·ta·gu(e) [ˈmɔntəgjuː, ˈmʌntəgjuː] *n.* 蒙塔古〔姓氏,男子名〕.

Mon·tan·a [mɔnˈtænə] *n.* 蒙大拿〔美国州名〕.

mon·tane [ˈmɔntein] *a.* 山多的; 山区的; 住在山区的.

mon·tan·ic [mɔnˈtænik] *a.* ～ **acid**【化】褐煤酸; 廿九烷酸.

mon·tan wax [ˈmɔntæn]【化】褐煤蜡,山蜡.

Mont Blanc [mɔ̃ŋ blɑːŋ] 〔F.〕 勃朗峰〔阿尔卑斯山脉的最高峰〕.

mont·bre·ti·a [mɔnˈbriːʃjə] *n.*【植】蒙布里雪氏观音兰.

mont-de-pié·té [mɔ̃dəpjete] *n.* 〔F.〕 *(pl. monts-)* 官营当铺.

mon·te [ˈmɔnti] *n.* (一种西班牙式)纸牌戏. *three-card* ～ (起源于墨西哥的)三张牌戏.

Mon·te, Mon·ty [ˈmɔnti] *n.* 蒙蒂〔男子名, Montague 的昵称〕.

Monte Carlo [mɔnti ˈkɑːləu] ①蒙特卡洛〔摩纳哥城市〕. ②【自】采用随机抽样法的. *Monte Carlo method* 蒙特卡罗法〔一种随机抽样检验法〕.

Mon·te·ne·grin [ˌmɔntiˈniːgrin] *a.* (南斯拉夫联邦的)门的内哥罗的. — *n.* 门的内哥罗人.

Mon·te·ne·gro [ˌmɔntiˈniːgrəu] *n.* 门的内哥罗 〔旧译

黑山〕〔南斯拉夫一地区〕.

mon·te·ro [mɔn'tɛərəu] *n.* *(pl. -ros)* (有帽沿的)圆猎帽.

Mon·ter·rey [ˌmɔntə'rei] *n.* 蒙特雷〔墨西哥城市〕.

Mon·tes·quieu [ˌmɔntes'kjuː], **Charles** 孟德斯鸠〔1689—1755,法国政治哲学家、法学家〕.

Mon·te·vid·e·o [ˌmɔntivi'deiəu] *n.* 蒙得维的亚〔乌拉圭首都〕.

Mont·fort ['mɔntfət] *n.* 蒙特福特〔姓氏〕.

Mont·gol·fi·er [mɔnt'gɔlfiə] *n.* ①孟高尔费〔姓氏〕. ②**Joseph Michel** ～ 约瑟夫·米海尔 (1740—1810), **Jacques Etienne** ～雅克·艾甸 (1745—1799)〔弟兄二人均为法国轻气球发明者〕. ③〔m-〕热空气气球.

Mont·gom·er·y [mənt'gʌməri] *n.* 蒙哥马利〔姓氏〕.

month [mʌnθ] *n.* (岁月的)月;一个月的时间. *a calendar* ～ 历月. *a lunar* ～ 太阴月. *a solar* ～ 太阳月. *this* ～ 本月. *last* ～ 上月(例: *He came here last* ～. 他是上月来这里的). *the last* ～ = *the past* ～ 到今天为止的一个月(期间)(例: *I have been here the last [past]* ～. 我在这里已有一个月了). *next* ～ 下一个月. *the* ～ *before last* 上上个月. *the* ～ *of July* 七月. *the* ～ *after next* 再下一个月. *for* ～ *of May* 五月份. *four times a* ～ 一月四次. ***a*** ～ ***of Sundays*** 〔口〕很长的时间,许久 (*not once in a* ～ *of Sundays* 很久很久没有…, 决没有…). ***a*** ～***'s mind*** 周月(人死后一个月举行的纪念)弥撒; 渴求. ～ ***after*** ～ = ～ ***by*** ～ 逐月,每月, 一月又一月. ～ ***in,*** ～ ***out*** 月月, 每月. ***this day*** ～ 下[上]一个月的今天.

month·ly ['mʌnθli] *a.* 每月的; 每月一次的; 按月的. ～ *pay* 月薪. *a* ～ *nurse* (照料产妇的)产褥护士. *a* ～ *rose* 【植】月季花. — *ad.* 每月一次,每月. — *n.* 月刊; 〔*pl.*〕月经.

mon·ti·cule ['mɔntikjuːl] *n.* 小山, 冈; 火山丘; 【动】小阜.

mont·mo·ril·lon·ite [ˌmɔntmə'riləˌnait] *n.* 【地】蒙脱石; 蒙脱土.

Mont·re·al [ˌmɔntri'ɔːl] *n.* 蒙特利尔〔加拿大港市〕. **-er** 蒙特利尔市民.

Mont·ser·rat [mɔntse'ræt] *n.* 蒙特塞拉特岛〔美洲〕.

mon·u·ment ['mɔnjumənt] *n.* 纪念碑,石碑;墓碑;纪念物,纪念像,纪念门,纪念馆;遗迹;遗址;遗物;不朽的功业[著作](等); 标石, 界石; 〔古〕纪录; 标记. *ancient [natural]* ～*s* 历史[天然]纪念物[遗迹]. *the M-* 〔英〕(1666 年) 伦敦大火纪念塔. *cultural objects and historic* ～*s* 文物古迹.

mon·u·men·tal [ˌmɔnju'mentl] *a.* 纪念碑的; 纪念的; 巨大的,雄伟的;不朽的,不灭的;〔口〕(恶意的)非常的, 极大的. *a* ～ *work* 不朽的著作[作品]. *a* ～ *inscription* 碑铭. ～ *ignorance* 极端的愚蠢. **-ly** *ad.* 用纪念碑; 为纪念;〔口〕非常,极.

mon·u·men·tal·ize [ˌmɔnju'mentəlaiz] *vt.* 立碑纪念; 永远传下去; 树碑立传.

-mony *suf.* 表示动作、结果、状态: cere*mony*, matri*mony*, testi*mony*.

mon·zo·nite ['mɔnzəˌnait] *n.* 【地】二长岩.

moo [muː] *n.* 哞〔牛叫声〕;〔美俚〕牛肉;牛. — *vi.* (牛)哞哞地叫. ～**-cow** *n.* 〔儿〕哞哞〔母牛〕.

M.O.O. = Money Order Office. 邮汇处,邮汇部.

mooch [muːtʃ] *vi.* 〔俚〕鬼鬼祟祟地走 (along); 打转儿; 荡来荡去, 徘徊 *(around, round)* — *vt.* 〔美俚〕揩油; 招摇撞骗, 讹诈; 偷偷拿走; 偷取; 索取. **-er** *n.* 〔美俚〕靠揩油过日子的人; 招摇撞骗的人; 寄生虫,食客.

mood[1] [muːd] *n.* ①〔古〕怒. ②(一时的)心情, 情绪, 心地. ③〔*pl.*〕不高兴, 闹脾气. ④基调. *a man of* ～*s* 喜怒无常的人. ***be in no*** ～ ***for [to]*** 不想…,无意…. ***be in the melting*** ～ 伤感得要哭,眼泪汪汪. ***change one's*** ～ 转换心情. ***in a laughing*** ～ 快快活活, 高高兴兴, 笑着. ***in an melancholy*** ～ 忧郁地,郁郁不乐地. ***in a melting*** ～ 心肠软化,易受感动. ***in the*** ～ ***for [to]*** 想…,有意….

mood[2] [muːd] *n.* ①【逻、乐】论式, 调式(= mode). ②【语】语气.

Mood·y ['muːdi] *n.* 穆迪〔姓氏〕.

mood·y ['muːdi] *a.* ***(mood·i·er; -i·est)*** 动不动发脾气的,易怒的; 喜怒无常的; 郁郁不乐的, 不高兴的. **-i·ly** *ad.* **-i·ness** *n.*

mool [muːl] *n.* 〔Scot.〕①耕土,腐植土. ②墓土. ③墓.

moo·la(h) ['muːlə] *n.* 〔美俚〕钱.

mool·lah ['muːlə] *n.* = mullah.

mool·vie, -vee ['muːlvi] 伊斯兰教法学家; 先生〔尤用于印度伊斯兰教徒间〕.

moon [muːn] *n.* ①月,月球,月亮. ★ (1) 语法上常作女性处理. (2)形容词是 lunar. ②〔诗〕(一个)月,太阴月; 〔诗〕月光; 月状物,新月形物; (指甲的)甲弧影; 卫星; (尤指)新月旗〔土耳其的国旗〕. ③〔美俚〕酒,私酿的威士忌酒. ④【天】月相. *a full* ～ 满月. *a new* ～ 新月. *a crescent* ～ 蛾眉月. *a blue* ～ 不可能的事物,难得遇见的事物. *There is a [no]* ～. 有[没有]月亮. ***bark at (bay) the*** ～ (狗)咬月亮,(狂犬)吠月; 瞎嚷嚷; 无事自扰. ***below the*** ～ 月下的,尘世的. ***cry for the*** ～ 渴望[要求]做不到的事情[得不到的东西]. ***know no more than the man in the*** ～ 完全不知道. ～***'s phase*** 月相, 月的盈虚. ***once in a blue*** ～ 〔口〕极少, 极难得, 千载难逢. ***shoot the*** ～ 〔英俚〕(避债) 夜逃. ***the man in the*** ～ 月中人〔指月面的黑斑〕; 假想的人. ***the old*** ～ ***in the new*** ～***'s arms*** (因地球反光致黑暗面隐约可见的) 新月,初弦月. — *vi.* 〔口〕懒洋洋地闲荡; 出神; 呆看, 没精打采地东瞧西望 *(about; around)*. — *vt.* 虚度时间; 稀里糊涂度过 (时日) *(away)*. ～ **age** 月球时代 (指人类登上月球的时代). ～**beam** (一线) 月光. ～**blind** *a.* 夜盲的; (马的)月光盲的. ～ **blindness** 【医】夜盲症; 【兽医】月盲症. ～**buggy** 月球车. ～ **cake** (我国的)月饼. ～**calf** ***(pl. -calves)*** 怪物,畸形动物 [植物]; 白痴. ～ **car**=～buggy. ～**craft** 月球探测机. ～ **crawler** =～buggy. ～**down** 〔美〕月落; 月落时. ～**eye**=moon-blindness. ～**-eyed** *a.* = moon-blind; 圆睁着双眼的. ～**face** 圆脸. ～**-faced** *a.* 圆脸的. ～**fall** 月面降落. ～**fish** 【鱼】月鲹, 月鱼. ～**flight** 向月飞行. ～**flower** 〔Am.〕月光花; 〔英〕法国菊. ～ **gate** (中国建筑中的)月洞门. ～**head** 〔美〕笨蛋,傻瓜. ～**light** ① *n.* 月光. ② *a.* 月光的; 月光下的 (～*light flitting* 夜逃, 夜奔. *a* ～*light school* 〔美〕(乡村)夜校). ～**lighter** 月光团员;〔美〕= moonshiner; 参与夜袭的人; 日夜身兼两职的人. ～**lighting** (月光团员的) 夜袭; 月光下的活动; 身兼两个职业的人. ～**lit** *a.* 照着月亮的,有月亮的,月明的. ～**-mad** *a.* 月狂的. ～**-madness** 月狂〔因注视月亮过久发生的神经错乱〕. ～**man** 登月太空人. ～**nik** (苏联的)月球火箭〔卫星〕. ～ **month** 太阴月. ～**port** 月球火箭发射站. ～**quake** 月震. ～**-raker** 〔英俚〕笨蛋, 傻瓜; 走私贩子. ～**rise** 月出(时). ～**scape** 月亮的表面 (景色). ～**scooper** (在月球上挖土的)宇宙车. ～**scope** 卫星观察镜. ～**seed** 【植】防已科 *(Menispermaceae)* 蝙蝠葛属 *(Menispermum)* 植物. ～**set** 月落 (时). ～**shine** ① *n.* 月光; 荒唐的空想〔计划〕, 梦话;〔美俚〕走私酒. ② *a.* 月光的, 月夜的; 空的, 无聊的. ～**shiner** 〔美俚〕非法私酿〔贩卖〕威士忌酒的人. ～**shiny** *a.* 月光照耀的,月色皎皎的; 月光似的; 空想的. ～**ship** 月球飞船. ～**shot** 向月球发射月球探测器. ～**stone** 【矿】月长石. ～**struck** *a.* 发狂的, 神经错乱的. ～**walk** *n.* 月球漫步. ～**wort** 【植】①阴地蕨属 *(Botrychium)* 植物 〔尤指月阴地蕨 *(Botrychium lunarium)*〕. ②= honesty (缎花属 *(Lunaria)* 植物〔尤指一年生缎花 *(Lunaria annua)*〕). **-less** *a.* 无月光的. **-let** 小月亮; 人造卫星; 小卫星.

mooned [mu:nd, 〔诗〕ˈmu:nid] *a.* 〔诗〕月亮般的；(新)月形的；有月形彩饰的.
Moo·ney [ˈmu:ni] *n.* 穆尼〔姓氏〕.
moon·ish [ˈmu:niʃ] *a.* 月亮似的，三心两意的.
moon·shee [ˈmu:nʃi:] *n.* 〔Hind.〕(印度籍的)语言教师；译员；秘书；雇员.
moon·y [ˈmu:ni] *a.* ***(moon·i·er; -i·est)*** 月亮的；月状的；新月形的；月光下的；月光似的；恍惚的；头脑错乱的；笨的；〔美俚〕有点醉的.
moor[1] [muə] *n.* 〔英〕(特指生长石南属植物的)荒野，高原沼地；〔英〕(尤指打松鸡的)猎场. ～ **coal** 沼煤，泥煤. ～**cock** 公赤松鸡. ～**fowl,** ～ **game** 赤松鸡. ～ **hen** 母赤松鸡；鷭，水鸡.
moor[2] [muə] *n.* 停泊，抛锚；系留. — *vt.* (把船)系住，停住，使停泊；(把飞船)拴在系留塔上. — *vi.* 被系住，固定；系泊，系留.
Moor [muə] *n.* 摩尔人〔非洲西北部伊斯兰教民族〕.
moor·age [ˈmuəridʒ] *n.* 系泊；系泊处；系泊费.
Moore [ˈmuə] *n.* 穆尔〔姓氏〕.
moor·ing [ˈmuəriŋ] *n.* 系泊，系留；〔常 *pl.*〕系泊用具；〔*pl.*〕系泊处. 〔*pl.*〕支撑物，依靠物. ～ **buoy** 系泊浮筒. ～ **drag** 活动锚. ～ **guy** 系留索. ～ **loop**【军】沙包索圈. ～ **mast,** ～ **tower** (飞船的)系留塔. ～ **post** 系留柱.
moor·ish [ˈmuəriʃ] *a.* 荒野的，沼地的；住在沼地的；生在沼地的.
Moor·ish [ˈmuəriʃ] *a.* 摩尔人的，摩尔人式的(建筑). ～ **arch** 马蹄拱.
moor·land [ˈmuələnd] *n.* 〔英〕(长满石南属植物的)荒野，高沼地.
moor·stone [ˈmuəstəun] *n.* 松碎花岗岩.
moor·y [ˈmuəri] *a.* 荒野(似)的；沼地的.
moose [mu:s] *n.* 〔*sing., pl.*〕①【动】大角麋；驼鹿. ② = elk. ③〔M-〕= Bull Moose. ～**bird** 〔Canad.〕= Canada jay 加拿大噪鸦. ～**wood** 条纹槭.
moot [mu:t] *vt.* 讨论；提出(问题)；(在假设法庭上)实习辩论. — *n.* 讨论；(法科学生等的)假设案件辩论会；【英史】(聚议公共问题的)讨论会. — *a.* 有讨论余地的，未决的. ～ **court** (法科学生实习的)假设法庭. ～ **hall**【英史】集会所.
mooted [mu:tid] *a.* 〔美〕未决定的，有疑问的.
mop[1] [mɔp] *n.* 墩布，拖把；类似拖把的东西. *a* ～ *of hair* 乱蓬蓬的头发. — *vt.* 拿墩布拖；擦(泪、汗等). ～ ***the floor [the earth] with sb.***〔俚〕把(人)打得一败涂地，痛击，凌辱. ～ ***up*** ①擦去，揩干. ②〔俚〕【军】肃清，扫荡. ③〔俚〕榨取，吸取(利润等). ④打倒，痛击. ⑤〔口〕狼吞虎咽地吃〔喝〕. ⑥〔美剧〕大大成功. ～**board**【建】护壁板 = baseboard. ～**-head** 乱蓬蓬的头. ～**-stick** 拖布把柄.
mop[2] [mɔp] *n.* 愁脸，搭拉脸；扭歪嘴的人. ～***s and mows*** 怪相，鬼脸. — *vi.* 歪嘴，搭拉着脸. ～ ***and mow*** 做怪相，扮鬼脸.
mop[3] [mɔp] *n.* 〔英〕(秋收时的)雇工集市.
mope [məup] *vt., vi.* (使)郁郁不乐；(使)扫兴；闲荡. ～ ***about*** 呆痴痴地走来走去. ～ ***oneself*** 垂头丧气；烦闷. ～ ***one's time away*** 闷闷不乐地度过(日子). — *n.* 郁郁不乐的人，忧郁的人；〔美俚〕讨厌的人；〔*pl.*〕忧郁. ***have (a fit of) the*** ～***s*** 郁闷；闹情绪.
mo·ped [ˈməuˌped] *n.* 摩托自行车，机动脚踏两用车.
mo·per·y [ˈməupəri] *n.* 〔美俚〕①小小的违法行为；莫须有的罪名. ②闲荡，浪费时间.
mop·ish [ˈməupiʃ] *a.* 郁郁不乐的，忧郁的，垂头丧气的. **-ly** *ad.*, **-ness** *n.*
mopoke [ˈməupəuk] *n.* ①【动】枭. ②〔澳〕笨人.
mop·pet [ˈmɔpit] *n.* 〔儿〕(布做的)玩偶；〔口〕小孩，娃儿；巴儿狗.
mop·py [ˈmɔpi] *a.* 拖把似的；乱蓬蓬的.
mop·ping-up [ˈmɔpiŋʌp] *a.* 扫荡性的；扫尾的. *a* ～ *operation* 扫荡.
mop-up [ˈmɔpˌʌp] *n.* 扫荡残敌，肃清残敌；扫尾工作.
mop·us [ˈməupəs] *n.* 〔美俚〕(现)钱.
mo·quette [məuˈket] *n.* 短毛绒织品〔做座垫、地毯等用〕.
mor [mɔ:] *n.* 粗腐殖质〔森林中的浮层土壤〕.
Mor. = Morocco.
MOR = middle of the road 中间道路.
mo·ra [ˈmɔ:rə] *n.* ***(pl. -rae*** [-i:], ***-ras)*** ①【语】音节延长度. ②〔作诗法〕韵律节拍单位，通常用短音符(˘)来表示.
mo·ra [ˈmɔ:rə] *n.* 〔It.〕(意大利)豁拳，划拳.
mo·raine [mɔˈrein] *n.* 【地】冰碛，冰碛层，冰川堆石. **mo·rain·ic** *a.*
mor·al [ˈmɔrəl] *a.* ①道德(上)的，道义(上)的；守德行的；(特指男女关系上)品行端正的 (*opp.* immoral). ②教导道德的. ③精神上的 (*opp.* physical, practical). ④(虽未证明但)无疑的，当然的；【逻】盖然的，可能的 (*opp.* demonstrative). *a* ～ *agent [being]* 道德的行为者，人. *a* ～ *victory* 精神胜利. *a* ～ *blow* 精神上的打击. ～ *authority* 道义. ～ *certainty* (虽不能证明但)确实可靠. ～ *character* 品性. ～ *courage* 信仰坚定不移的勇气，义勇. ～ *culture* 德育. ～ *depreciation*【机】无形损耗 (*opp.* physical depreciation). ～ *education* 思想品德教育；德育. ～ *faculty [sense]* 是非之心，良心. ～ *good* 德行. ～ *inexhaustibility* 百折不挠的精神. ～ *law* 道德律. ～ *obligations* 道义上的责任. ～ *outlook* 人生观. ～ *philosophy* 道德哲学，伦理学；〔古〕心理学. ～ *principles* 道义. ～ *rearmament (Movement)* 〔美〕重振道德运动. ～ *science* 精神科学(=～ *philosophy*). ～ *support* 精神上的支持. ～ *tone* 品格. ～ *virtues* 德，自然道德. — *n.* ①(寓言等的)寓意，教训；寓言剧；〔*pl.* 但通常作单数用〕修身，伦理(学)；〔*pl.*〕(尤指男女间的)品行；〔罕〕= morale. ②〔古〕相对者；逼肖者. *point a* ～ 用实例训导. *The boy is the very* ～ *of his father.* 这孩子活象他父亲. ～ **law**【哲】道德律. ～ **hazard**【保险】道德上的风险〔因被保险人的不道德或轻率而对保险公司所造成的风险〕.
mo·rale [mɔˈrɑ:l], *n.* (军队的)士气；风纪；精神；信心，信念；道义，道德. *the* ～ *of the colony*【蜂】群势. *boost the* ～ *of* 长…的志气，给…打气.
mor·al·ism [ˈmɔrəlizəm] *n.* 道德(主义)；道义；修身训言，格言. **mor·al·ist** *n.* 道德家；道学家，道德主义者；伦理学家. **mor·al·is·tic** *a.* 道学的，教训的；道德主义的.
mo·ral·i·ty [məˈræliti] *n.* ①道德，道义；伦理学；〔*pl.*〕伦理；德性，德义，德行；(尤指男女间的)品行. ②是非善恶；寓意，教训. ③(15—16世纪的)劝善惩恶的宗教剧，寓意剧 (= ～-play). *commercial* ～ 商业道德.
mor·al·ize [ˈmɔrəlaiz] *vt.* ①训导；赋与…德性，启发…的德性；德化，教化. ②说道，讲道，用道德意义解释(寓言等). —*vi.* 说教，讲道；给与道德上的感化. **-i·za·tion** [ˌmɔrəlaiˈzeiʃən] *n.* **-iz·er** *n.* 说教者.
mor·al·ly [ˈmɔrəli] *ad.* ①道德上，德义上；从道德上. ②规规矩矩，正直地. ③的确. *be* ～ *bound to fail* 的的确确会失败.
mo·rass [məˈræs] *n.* 泥淖，沼泽；艰难，困境；堕落. ～ **ore**【矿】沼铁矿.
mo·rass·y [məˈræsi] *a.* 泥淖一样的.
mo·rat [ˈmɔ:ræt] *n.* (中世纪)桑葚调味的酒.
mor·a·to·ri·um [ˌmɔrəˈtɔ:riəm] *n.* ***(pl.*** ～***s, -ri·a*** [-riə]) ①【法】延期偿付权；延缓偿付期. ②(行动、活动等的)暂停，暂禁.
mor·a·to·ry [ˈmɔrətəri] *a.* 延期偿付的.
Mo·ra·vi·a [məˈreivjə] *n.* 摩拉维亚〔捷克斯洛伐克一地区〕.

Mo·ra·vi·an [məˈreivjən] *a.* 摩拉维亚的. — *n.* 摩拉维亚人;〔*pl.*〕【宗】摩拉维亚教徒, 弟兄派教友.
mo·ray [ˈmɔːrei; mɔːˈrei] *n.* 【动】海鳝科鱼, 海鳝 (moray eel).
mor·bid [ˈmɔːbid] *a.* ①(精神上)不健全的, 病态的; 病态过敏性的. ②关于病的; 致病的; 病理学的. ③恶性的; 可怕的; 令人毛骨悚然的. ~ *anatomy* 病理解剖学. *a ~ growth* 肿疡. **-ly** *ad.* **-ness** *n.* (精神的)病态.
mor·bi·dez·za [ˌmɔːbiˈdetsə] *n.* 〔It.〕【美术】(肤色等逼真的)柔美.
mor·bid·i·ty [mɔːˈbiditi] *n.* ①病况, 病状. ②(一地的)发病率, 致病率.
mor·bif·ic(al) [mɔːˈbifik(əl)] *a.* 引起疾病的.
mor·bil·li [mɔːˈbilai] *n.* 〔*pl.*〕【医】麻疹.
mor·ceau [mɔːˈsəu] *n.* 〔F.〕 ***(pl.*** **~x [-z]*)*** ①小片; 片断. ②文艺小品;【乐】作品, 乐曲; 小曲.
mor·da·cious [mɔːˈdeiʃəs] *a.* 挖苦的, 恶毒地讽刺的, 尖酸刻薄的.
mor·dac·i·ty [mɔːˈdæsiti] *n.* 尖酸的讽刺, 挖苦; 刻薄.
mor·dan·cy [ˈmɔːdənsi] *n.* = mordacity.
mor·dant [ˈmɔːdənt] *a.* ①讽刺的, 尖酸的, 尖嘴辣舌的. ②媒染性的; 腐蚀性的; 破坏组织的. — *n.*【染】媒染剂[料];【印】金属腐蚀剂; 金箔粘着剂. **-ly** *ad.*
mor·dent [ˈmɔːdənt] *n.*【乐】波音.
Mo·re [ˈmɔː] *n.* 莫尔〔姓氏〕.
Mo·ré [mɔːˈrei] *n.* ①(苏丹中西部的) 莫西人. ②莫西语 (= Mossi).
more [mɔː, mɔə] *a.* (many, much 的比较级; 最高级是 ***most***) (*opp.* less) ①(数、量、程度等)更多的, 较多的, 更大的, 更好的. ②〔废〕(地位、身份等) 更高的. ③另外附加的, 其余的, 此外, 还(有等). *There was ~ smoke than fire.* 烟多火小. ★ (1) more 后的名词常略而不言: The ~, the merrier. 人愈多愈快活. (2)〔more than one + 单数名词〕: M- than one person has found it so. 这样想的人不只一个. One word ~ 还有一句话. And what ~ do you want? 你还要什么(难道还不够吗)? — *n.* 更多的数量[程度]; 其余的事, 附加, 添加. *I hope to see ~ of you.* 我希望更多看到你们; 我希望再看到你. *M- is meant than meets the ear.* 大有言外之意. — *ad.* ①〔much 的比较级〕更多, 更大. ②〔形成二音节以上的形容词和副词的比较级〕更, 格外〔例: ~ *beautiful(ly)*〕. ③再. ④反而. *He was ~ frightened than hurt.* 他吓得厉害, 伤倒不大. ***a little*** **~** 再…一点. ***all the ~*** 格外, 越发, 更加. ***and no ~*** 不过是…罢了. ***(and) what is ~*** 加之, 而且. ***any ~*** 还; 更;〔带否定语〕已经 (*Have you any ~ money?* 钱还有没有?). **~ *and ~*** 越来越…. **~ *brave than wise*** 有勇无谋. **~ *or less*** ①有几分, 有点儿 (*~ or less beautiful* 颇有姿色). ②约, 左右 (*$100 ~ or less* 一百元左右). ③〔在否定语后〕一点也… (*I could not afford to ride, ~ or less.* 我根本坐不起车子). **~ *than*** 多过, 大过, …以上; 比…更 (*I went ~ than a mile.* 我走了一英里多路. *That is ~ than I can tell.* 那我就不知道了. *~ than ten years ago* 十几年前). **~ *than all*** 尤其. **~ *than enough*** 足够; 太多. **~ *than ever*** 越发(用功等), 更多(的). **~… *than not*** (性能、状态)极其, 相当, 非常; (时间)往往, 屡见不鲜. **~ *than pleased*** 十分高兴. ***much ~*** 更; 何况 (*She knows French, much ~ English.* 她法语也懂, 英语就不必说了). ***neither ~ nor less than*** 恰, 正, 不多不少. ***never ~*** 决不再. ***no ~*** (此后)不再; 死了; …也不[没有] (*He is no ~.* 他死了). ***no ~ than***〔than 后接名词〕只, 仅仅, 不过是 (*no ~ than five* 仅五个. *no ~ than a puppet* 不过是个傀儡). ***no ~… than***〔than 引出从句〕和某甲一样不…, 某甲不[是, 能]…, 某乙也不[是, 能]… (*He is no ~ a god than we are.* 他和我们一样不是神). *He cannot speak French any ~ than I can.* 我不会讲法语, 他也不会讲法语). ***none the ~ = not the ~*** 虽…仍旧[还是]…. ***not any ~ than*** = no ~ than. ***not ~*** 不再…; 不再有, 已经没有. ***not ~ than***〔than 后接名词〕不超过, 至多 (*not ~ than five* 最多五个). ***not ~… than***〔than 引出从句〕不比某乙更… (*This book is not ~ expensive than that one.* 这本书不比那本书更贵). ***once ~*** 再一次[回]. ***one ~*** 还(有)一个, 再(来)一个. ***or ~*** 或许更多一点, 至少 (*a mile or ~* 至少一英里). ***some ~*** 再…些. ***still ~*** = much ~. ***the ~*** 越发, 更. ***the ~ and the less*** 地位高的和地位低的人. ***the ~ … because [as, that]*** 因为…更. ***the ~ … the ~ …*** 愈…愈, 越是…越是 (*The ~ I know him, the ~ I like him.* 越是了解他, 越是喜欢他). ***what is ~*** = and what is ~.
-more *suf.* 更…: further*more*, inner*more*. 但 ever*more*, forever*more*, never*more* 等的 *-more* 仅属加强意义.
Mo·re·a [mɔ(ː)ˈriə] *n.* (希腊南部的) 摩利亚半岛〔旧名 Peloponnesus 伯罗奔尼撒斯〕.
mo·reen [mɔːˈriːn, ˈmɔːriːn] *n.* (做窗帘、帷幕等用的)云纹毛呢, 云纹棉毛混纺呢.
mo·rel [məˈrel] *n.*【植】羊肚菌; 龙葵.
mo·rel·lo [məˈreləu] *n.* ***(pl.*** **~s*)*** 黑樱桃.
mo·re·o·ver [mɔːˈrəuvə] *ad.* 况且, 并且, 加之, 此外, 又.
more·pork [ˈmɔːpɔːk] *n.* = mopoke.
mo·res [ˈmɔːriːz] *n.* 〔L.〕〔*pl.*〕(社会)风俗, 习俗, 惯例; 道德态度.
Mo·resque [məˈresk] *a.* 摩尔 (Moor) 式装饰的.
Mor·gan[1] [ˈmɔːgən] *n.* (美国佛蒙特州的)摩根品种马.
Mor·gan[2] [ˈmɔːgən] *n.* ①摩根〔姓氏, 男子名〕. ②**Thomas Hunt ~** 摩根〔1866—1945, 美国生物学家, 曾获 1933 年诺贝尔医学奖〕.
mor·ga·nat·ic [ˌmɔːgəˈnætik] *a.* 社会身份高的男子和身分低的女子结婚的.
mor·gan·ite [ˈmɔːgəˌnait] *a.*【地】铯绿柱石.
mor·gen [ˈmɔːgən] *n.* ***(pl. -gen, gens)*** 摩肯〔地积单位; 荷兰及其属地以及南非使用, 相当于二英亩. 普鲁士、丹麦和挪威早先的地积单位; 相当于一英亩的三分之二〕.
Mor·gen·thau [ˈmɔːgənθɔː] *n.* 摩根索〔姓氏〕.
morgue [mɔːg] *n.* ①陈尸所, 停尸室. ②〔美〕(报馆等的)资料室, 图书室.
morgue [mɔːg] *n.* 〔F.〕 傲慢. **~ *anglaise*** [-ɑ̃ːŋgleiz] 英国人特有的傲慢态度.
mor·i·bund [ˈmɔ(ː)ribʌnd] *a.* 濒死的, 垂死的, 奄奄一息的; 死气沉沉的. — *n.* 将死的人. **-bun·di·ty** *n.* **-ly** *ad.*
mo·ri·on[1] [ˈmɔriən] *n.* (没有面甲的)高顶盔.
mor·ion[2] [ˈmɔriən] *n.* 墨晶.
Mo·ris·co [məˈriskəu] *a.* Moor 式的. — *n.* ***(pl.*** **~s, ~es*)*** 摩尔人(尤指西班牙的 Moor 人).
Mor·i·son [ˈmɔrisn] *n.* 莫里森〔姓氏〕.
Mor·ley [ˈmɔːli] *n.* 莫利〔姓氏〕.
Mor·mon [ˈmɔːmən] *n.* 摩门(基督复兴教) 教徒;〔*pl.*〕〔美〕 Utah 州人的别名; 一夫多妻主义者. **-ism** *n.* 摩门教.
morn [mɔːn] *n.* 〔诗、古〕黎明, 早晨;〔Scot.〕明天. ***at ~*** = in the morning. ***the ~'s morn*** 〔Scot.〕明早.
morn·ing [ˈmɔːniŋ] *n.* ①早晨. ②上午;〔废、古〕(上层社会晚餐前的) 白天〔例: ~ *performance*〔英〕(午后开演的日戏)〕. ③初期, 早期. ④〔诗〕黎明;〔M-〕黎明的女神. *It is ~.* 天亮了. *Good ~!* 早上好! 早安! *the ~ of life* 青春时代. ***from ~ till [to] night [evening]*** 从早到晚. ***in the ~*** 在早晨, 在午前. ***of a ~*** 往往在早上. **~ after** 〔口〕宿醉; 痛苦的后果. **~-after pill** 后服避孕丸. **~ call** 午后的正式访问. **~ coat** 晨礼服. **~ draft** (早餐前喝的)晨酒. **~ dress** ①女人便服. ②常礼服〔白天集会或结婚时穿的男服〕.

~ **gift** (丈夫婚后第二天早晨送妻子的)晨礼. ~(-) **glory**【植】①牵牛花. ②后劲不足者. ~ **gun**【军】晨炮,早晨升旗礼炮. ~ **land**【诗】东洋. ~ **paper** 晨报. ~ **room** (上午家属公用的)起居室〔有别于 drawing room〕. ~ **sickness**【医】孕妇晨吐. ~ **star** 晓星,金星. ~**tide** 〔诗〕早晨. ~ **watch**【海】早班〔自上午4时至8时〕.

Mo·ro [ˈmɔːrəu] *n., a.* (非律宾伊斯兰教马来族之一的)摩洛族(的);摩洛语(的).

Mo·roc·co [məˈrɔkəu] *n.* ①摩洛哥〔非洲〕. ②〔m-〕〔*pl.* ~*s*〕(摩洛哥山羊鞣制成的)摩洛哥皮. *the Levant m-* 上等摩洛哥皮. **-can** [-kən] ①*a.* 摩洛哥的. ②*a.* 摩洛哥人(的).

mo·ron [ˈmɔːrɔn] *n.* 白痴; 〔口〕低能的人. **mo·ron·ic** [mɔːˈrɔnik] *a.* 〔美〕白痴的, 低能的. **mo·ron·ism** **mo·ron·i·ty** [mɔːˈrɔniti] *n.* 白痴,低能.

Mo·ro·ni [məˈrɔni] *n.* 莫罗尼〔科摩罗首都〕.

mo·rose [məˈrəus] *a.* 愁眉苦脸的; 郁闷的; 不高兴的; 脾气坏的; 乖僻的. **-ly** *ad.* **-ness** *n.*

morph. = morphology.

morph- *comb.f.* = morpho-.

morph [mɔf] *n.* (动植物的)变种,变体.

morph·al·lax·is [ˌmɔfəˈlæksis] *n.* **(***pl.* **-lax·es** [-siːz]**)** 【动】变形再生.

mor·pheme [ˈmɔːfiːm] *n.*【语】词素;语素;形素.

mor·phe·mics [mɔːˈfiːmiks] *n. pl.* 〔动词用单数〕词素学.

Mor·pheus [ˈmɔːfjuːs] *n.*【希神】梦神; 睡神, 睡梦之神. ***in the arms of*** ~ 在睡神怀抱中; 睡着.

mor·phi·a, mor·phine [ˈmɔːfjə, ˈmɔːfiːn] *n.* 【化】吗啡.

mor·phin·ism [ˈmɔːfinizəm] *n.* 【医】吗啡中毒; 吗啡瘾.

mor·phino·ma·ni·a [ˌmɔfinəˈmeinjə] *n.* 吗啡瘾, 吗啡狂.

mor·phi·no·ma·ni·ac [ˌmɔːfinəˈmeiniæk] *n.* 有吗啡瘾的人,吗啡中毒者.

mor·pho- *comb.f.* 表示"形状","形态": *morpho*genesis.

mor·pho·gen·e·sis [ˌmɔːfəˈdʒenisis] *n.* 【动】①形态发生, 形态形成. ②器官发生, 器官形成. **-ge·net·ic** [-dʒiˈnetik] *a.*

mor·phol. = morphological; morphology.

mor·pho·log·ic (al) [ˌmɔːfəˈlɔdʒik(əl)] *a.* 形态学(上)的;【语】词法的,形态的.

mor·phol·o·gy [mɔːˈfɔlədʒi] *n.* 【生、地】形态学;【语法】词法; 词态学;【生】组织, 形态. **-gist** *n.* 形态学家.

mor·pho·pho·ne·mics [ˌmɔːfəufəˈniːmiks] *n. pl.* 〔动词用单数〕①词素音素变异学. ②词素音素分布学. ③(某语言中)词素音素变异的全类. **-pho·ne·mic** *a.*

-mor·pho·sis [mɔːˈfəusis] *n.* **(***pl.* **-ses** [siːz]**)** 【生】形态形成. **-phot·ic** [-ˈfɔtik] *a.*

mor·ris [ˈmɔris] *n.* (打扮成 Robin Hood 等传奇人物跳的)莫利斯舞.

Mor·ris [ˈmɔris] *n.* 莫里斯〔姓氏,男子名, Maurice 的异体〕. ~ **chair** 莫里斯式靠椅 〔靠背斜度可自由调节〕.

Mor·ri·son [ˈmɔrisn] *n.* 莫里森〔姓氏〕. ~ **shelter** 〔英〕屋内钢壁防空室. ~ **tube** 莫利斯式枪筒.

mor·row [ˈmɔrəu] *n.* ①〔古〕早晨. ②〔诗〕翌日,次日,第二天. ③紧接在后的时间. ***on the*** ~ ***of*** 紧接着….

Morse [mɔːs] *n.* ①莫尔斯〔姓氏〕. ②**Samuel Finley Breese** ~ 莫尔斯〔1791—1872,美国电报机发明家〕. ③【电信】莫尔斯电码. — *a.* 莫尔斯电码(的). ~ **alphabet [code]** 莫尔斯电码. ~ **instrument** 莫尔斯机. ~ **receiver** 莫尔斯收报机.

morse¹ [mɔːs] *n.*【动】海象.

morse² [mɔːs] *n.* (镶有宝石的)法衣襻扣.

mor·sel [ˈmɔːsəl] *n.* (食物的)一口; 一小片; 少量; 一点点; 佳肴.

mort [mɔːt] *n.* ①死. ②【猎】报告猎物已死的号角声. ③三岁的鲑鱼. ④〔方〕许多, 大量 *(of)*. ⑤〔俚〕少女, 女人.

mort. = mortuary.

mor·ta·del·la [ˌmɔːtəˈdelə] *n.* 意大利大香肠.

mor·tal [ˈmɔːtl] *a.* ①死的; 有死的, 不能不死的 (*opp.* immortal). ②凡人的; 人的,人类的. ③性命攸关的,致命的; 临终的, 临死的. ④要堕地狱的, 不能宽恕的. (*opp.* venial). ⑤非杀不可的,不共戴天的. ⑥〔口〕冗长的, 烦人的. ⑦〔口〕非常的, 极大的. ⑧〔口〕〔与 all, every, no 等连用〕可能的. *Man is* ~. 人是会死的. ~ *remains* 遗体, 死尸. *a* ~ *wound* 致命伤. *a* ~ *disease* 绝症. ~ *agony* 临死时的痛苦. ~ *weapon* 凶器. *the* ~ *hour* 将死的时候. *a* ~ *combat* 你死我活的战斗; 决斗. *a* ~ *enemy [foe]* 不共戴天的敌人. *two* ~ *hours* 长得要命的两个钟头. ~ *sins* 不可饶恕的大罪. *It is of no* ~ *use.* 全无用处. ***in a*** ~ ***funk*** 〔俚〕吓得要死. ***in a*** ~ ***hurry*** 〔俚〕急急忙忙. ***in*** ~ ***fear*** 极端害怕. ***past all*** ~ ***aid*** 无法援救. — *ad.* 〔俚、方〕极, 非常. — *n.* ①不能不死的生物; 人类; 凡人. ②〔谑〕人. *a jolly* ~ 有趣的人. **-ly** *ad.* 致命地; 人性上; 〔口〕非常, 很. *be mortally afraid* 怕得要命. *be -ly wounded* 受了致命伤.

mor·tal·i·ty [mɔːˈtæliti] *n.* 必死的命运〔性质〕; 致命性; 死亡数; 死亡率; 大量死亡; 失败数; 失败率; 人,人类. *the* ~ *from automobile accidents* 由于汽车事故造成的死亡人数. ~ **table**【保险】死亡率表.

mor·tar¹ [ˈmɔːtə] *n.* 灰泥; 灰浆; 胶泥;【地】碎斑结构. — *vt.* 用灰泥涂抹[接合].

mor·tar² [ˈmɔːtə] *n.* 臼,捣钵,研钵;【军】臼炮,迫击炮;【矿】(试验炸药用的) 臼炮. — *vt.* 用迫击炮轰击. ~-**board** 灰泥板,镘板;〔口〕学士帽;学位帽.

mort·gage [ˈmɔːgidʒ] *n.*【法】抵押; 抵押权; 抵押契据; 受押人对抵押品的权利. ***on*** ~ (拿房屋等)作抵押. ~ **bond** 抵押债券. — *vt.* 抵押; 把…许给. ~ *oneself [one's life] to the revolutionary cause* 献身革命事业.

mort·ga·gee [ˌmɔːgəˈdʒiː] *n.*【法】接受抵押者, 受押人; 抵押权人.

mort·ga·ger, mort·ga·gor [ˈmɔgədʒə, ˌmɔːgəˈdʒɔː] *n.*【法】抵押人.

mor·tice [ˈmɔːtis] *n., vt.* = mortise.

mor·ti·cian [mɔːˈtiʃən] *n.* 〔美〕承办丧葬的人; 殡仪业者 (=〔英〕undertaker).

mor·ti·fi·ca·tion [ˌmɔːtifiˈkeiʃən] *n.* ①【医】脱疽, 坏疽. ②【宗】禁欲, 节食, 苦行. ③耻辱, 屈辱; 悔恨, 遗恨. ④【废】【化】中和. ⑤【植】枯斑, 坏死.

mor·ti·fy [ˈmɔːtifai] *vt., vi.* ①抑制 (情欲等). ②使悔恨,使感耻辱; 伤害(感情). ③【医】(使)患脱疽. ④【植】生枯斑,坏死.

mor·ti·fy·ing [ˈmɔːtifaiiŋ] *a.* ①叫人呕气的,气死人的, 痛心的. ②禁欲修行的. ③坏疽的.

Mor·ti·mer [ˈmɔːtimə] *n.* 莫蒂默〔男子名〕.

mor·tise [ˈmɔːtis] *n.* ①榫眼,榫孔. ②固定,安定. *a* ~ *chisel* 榫凿. *a* ~ *and tenon joint* 镶榫接头. *a* ~ *lock* 插锁. — *vt.* 开榫眼; 用榫眼接合.

mort·main [ˈmɔːtmein] *n.*【法】永久管业权〔永远不能变卖公产〕; 永远保有; 传统势力.

Mor·ton [ˈmɔːtn] *n.* 莫顿〔姓氏,男子名〕.

mor·tu·a·ry [ˈmɔːtjuəri] *n.* ①停尸所. ② = morgue¹. ③【英史】(教区牧师从已故教区居民遗产中获得的) 布施. — *a.* 死亡的,纪念死的; (关于)丧葬的. ~ *rites* 葬仪. *a* ~ *urn* 骨灰瓮.

mor·u·la [ˈmɔːrjulə, ˈmɔr-; -ulə] *n.* **(***pl.* **-lae** [-ˌliː]**)** 【生】桑葚胚; 桑葚体. **mor·u·lar** *a.* **mor·u·la·tion** *n.*

Mo·rus [ˈmɔrəs] *n.*【植】桑属.

mos. = months.

mo·sa·ic [məˈzeiik] *n.* ①马赛克，镶嵌细工，拼花工艺；拼花图样；拼制图画；编写作品；拼制物；【建】镶嵌砖；【军】镶嵌图。②【植病】花叶病。③【生】嵌合体。④【电视】感光镶嵌幕，嵌镶光电阴极。— *a.* 马赛克式的，镶嵌细工的；用拼花方式制成的。~ *gold* 彩色金（颜料）；仿金的铜合金。*a* ~ *pavement* 拼花道路。~ *wool-work* 拼花绒线编织品。— *vt.* ***(mo·sa·icked, mo·sa·ick·ing)*** 用拼花图案装饰。

Mo·sa·ic, -i·cal [məuˈzeiik, -ikəl] *a.* 摩西 (Moses) 的。

mo·sa·i·cism [məuˈzeiːsizəm] *n.* 【生】镶嵌性。

mo·sa·i·cist [məuˈzeiisist] *n.* 拼花工艺者；镶嵌细工师。

Mos·by [ˈmɔzbi] *n.* 莫斯比〔姓氏〕。

mos·chate [ˈmɔskeit, -kit] *a.* 麝香味的，麝香气的。

Mos·cow [ˈmɔskəu] *n.* 莫斯科〔苏联首都〕。

mo·selle [məˈzel] *n.* (法国莫赛尔 Moselle 河流域出产的)莫赛尔白葡萄酒。

Mo·ses [ˈməuziz] *n.* ①摩西〔姓氏，男子名〕。②(基督教《圣经》)率领希伯来人出埃及的领袖。③〔喻〕领袖；立法者。④放债的犹太人。

mo·sey [ˈməuzi] *vi.* 〔美俚〕离开，走开；闲荡，信步。*M- along!* 滚！出去！

mo·shav [məuˈʃɑːv] *n.* *(pl.* ***mo·sha·vim*** [ˌməuʃɑːˈviːm]*)* 私人租地集体耕作制〔以色列的一种定居方式〕。

mos·ke·neer [mɔskiˈniːə] *vt.* 〔英俚〕(当贵东西)使当铺上当。

mos·ker [ˈmɔskə] *n.* 〔英俚〕当贵东西得到便宜的人。

Mos·lem, Mus·lim [ˈmɔzlem, ˈmɔzlim] *n.* *(pl.* ~*s,* ~*in* 〔集合词〕~*)* *a.* 穆斯林(的)；伊斯兰教徒(的)。

Mos·ley [ˈmɔzli, ˈməuzli] *n.* 莫斯利〔姓氏〕。

mosque [mɔsk] *n.* 伊斯兰教寺院，清真寺。

mos·qui·to [məsˈkiːtəu] *n.* *(pl.* ~*es,* ~*s)* 蚊子；〔M-〕〔英〕蚊式轰炸机；(瑞士)蚊式地对空导弹；〔M-〕〔美〕New Jersey 州的别名。~ **boat** 鱼雷快艇。~ **bomb** 灭蚊弹。~**cide** 灭蚊药；灭蚊。~ **craft** 快艇。~ **curtain [bar, net]** 蚊帐。~ **fever** 疟疾。~ **fish** 食蚊鱼。~ **fleet** 鱼雷〔轻快〕艇队。~ **hawk** 蜻蜓。~ **sortie** 【空】蚊式突击。

MOSS = manned orbital space station【宇】载人轨道空间站。

moss [mɔs] *n.* ①【植】苔，藓；地衣。②〔Scot.、北英〕沼，泥淖；泥炭沼。③〔M-〕莫斯〔男子名〕。④〔美俚〕平凡的东西，守旧的人。— *vt.* 拿苔覆盖；使长满苔藓。~ **agate**【矿】藓纹玛瑙。~**back** 〔美俚〕(背上长了水草的)老乌龟；绿毛龟；〔美俚〕极端守旧的人，老顽固；〔美俚〕盲目效忠本党的政治家。~**bunker** 步鱼(= menhaden)。~ **fern**【植】水龙骨。~**-grown** *a.* 生了苔的；旧式的，过时的。~ **hag** 泥炭采后的废坑。~ **pink**【植】丛生福禄考。~ **rose**【植】毛萼洋蔷薇。~**trooper** (沼地)劫掠者；土匪；强盗。

Möss·bau·er effect [ˈmɔːsbauə]【物】穆斯堡尔效应。

Mos·si [ˈmɔsiː] *n.* ①*(pl.* ***Mos·sis, Mos·si****)* 莫西人〔苏丹中西部一部族名〕。②莫西语。

moss·i·ness [ˈmɔsinis] *n.* 长满藓苔。

moss·like [ˈmɔːsˌlaik] *a.* 似苔的。

moss·y [ˈmɔsi] *a.* ***(moss·i·er; -i·est)*** 生了苔的；多苔的；苔状的。

most [məust] *a.* ***(many, much*** 的最高级；比较级是 ***more)*** *(opp.* least). ①〔常作 the ~〕(数、量、程度)最多的，最大的，最高的。②〔通例无冠词〕大概的，大多数的，大部分的。— *n.* *(pron.)* ①〔常作 the ~〕②〔通例无冠词〕最大限度；大部分；〔作复数用〕大多数人。*M- people think so.* 大多数人都这样想。~ *effective range* 最有效射程。*That is the* ~ *I can do.* 我能做的就仅仅这样。*M- of us know it.* 大多数人都知道。***at (the)*** ~ 至多，最多，充其量（不过）。***for the*** ~ ***part*** 基本上。***make the*** ~ ***of*** 充分使用；尽量使好〔不好〕看；极为重视；尽量称赞〔贬损〕；把…形容尽致；尽（欢）。— *ad.* ①(***much*** 的最高级)最，最多。②〔主要用以形成两个音节以上的形容词、副词的最高级〕：*the* ~ *beautiful, cleverly.* ③〔不加 the〕非常，很，极。*a* ~ *beautiful woman;* ~ *certainly.* ④〔方、美〕差不多，几乎 = almost: ~ *any boy.* ⑤〔尊称用语〕：*M- Noble*〔公爵的称号〕。*the M- High* 天老爷。★形容词、副词前若有 the 则是最高级，若没有 the 则仅仅表示加重语气。~ ***and least*** (诗)全体的，统统，都，皆。***the*** ~ ***favoured nation (clause)***【国际法】最惠国〔条款〕。

-most *suf.* 最〔用作表示位置、时间、顺序的形容词、副词、名词的后缀以形成形容词〕：end*most*, top*most*, inner*most*, ut*most*.

most·ly [ˈməustli] *ad.* 大部分，多半；通常，主要地，基本上。*They are* ~ *out on Sunday.* 星期天他们通常不在家。*The work is* ~ *done.* 工作基本上做好了。

mot [məu] *n.* 〔F.〕 *(pl.* ~*s* [-z]*)* 警句，妙语。***bon*** ~ 良言，名言。~ ***à*** ~ [məutɑːˈməu] 逐字(对译)。~ ***d'ordre*** [ˈdɔədr] 命令。~ ***juste*** [ʒust] 适当的语词。

mote[1] [məut] *n.* 尘埃，尘屑；〔喻、古〕污点，瑕疵。~ ***and beam*** 别人的小缺点和自己的大过错。~ ***in another's eye*** 别人眼睛里的灰尘；不看见自己大过错的人所见到的别人的小缺点；不反省自己只责备别人。

mote[2] [məut] *aux.v.* 〔古〕 = may, might. *So* ~ *it be.* 那样也好。

mote[3] [məut] *n.* moot 的别字。

mo·tel [məuˈtel] *n.* 〔美〕(专为)汽车游客(开设的)旅馆〔有停车场〕(= *mo*torist's ho*tel*).

mo·tet [məuˈtet] *n.* 【乐】赞美诗，圣歌；赞歌。

moth [mɔθ] *n.* ①蛾。②〔集合词，*sing.*, *pl.*〕蛀虫，蠹，腐蠹物。③轻快的飞机。④摧毁雷达台的导弹。~**balls** *n.* 〔*pl.*〕卫生球〔樟脑丸等〕。~**ball fleet** 〔美俗〕预备舰队。~**-eaten** *a.* 虫蛀的；陈旧的。~**proof** *a.* 防蛀的。— *vt.* 使…防蛀。

moth·er[1] [ˈmʌðə] *n.* ①母，母亲；〔常无冠词，M-〕(自己的)妈妈。②母，本源，根由。③老伯母，老大娘，老太太〔称呼年长女人时代替 Mrs. 用，如 M- Jones〕。④修女院长（= ~ superior)。⑤人工孵卵器。⑥航空母舰；航空母机；【电讯】第一模盘。⑦〔M-〕大猩猩(品种)苹果。*Necessity is the* ~ *of invention.* 需要是发明之母。*an artificial* ~ 人工孵卵器〔养小鸡用〕。— *a.* 母的，母国的，本国的。*a* ~ *bird* 母鸟。— *vt.* ①当作儿女抚养，象母亲一样照管，保育。②产，生〔通常在修辞上使用〕。③承认是(孩子)的母亲；声明自己是(小说等)的作者。④【军】掩护。**every** ~**'s son** 〔口〕人人= *everyone, everybody.* **M- Carey's chicken [hen]**【鸟】海燕〔海雀〕。~ **cell**【生】母细胞。~**-chrysanthemum** 野菊。**M- Church** 〔拟人语〕教会，所喜欢的教会；镇里最老的教会。~ **country** 本国〔对殖民地说〕，母国〔对私人说〕；父母之邦；发祥地。~ **earth** 大地；〔谑〕地，地面 (*kiss the* ~ *earth* 跌在地上)。**M- Goose** 鹅妈妈〔①查尔斯·裴劳特 (Charles Perraut) 作的故事集中想象的叙述者。②1765 年前后伦敦出版的儿歌集的假想作者〕。~ **hood** 母道，母亲的义务；母性；母权。**M- Hubbard** 鹅妈妈儿歌集中的女主人公；女长大衣。~ **image [figure]** 心目中的母亲。~**-in-law** *(pl.* ~*s)* 姑母，岳母；〔废〕继母。~ **land** 母国，祖国。**-less** *a.* 没有母亲的。~ **lode** 主矿脉，母脉。~**-naked** *a.* 象出娘胎时那样赤条条的。~**-of-pearl** 珍珠母，青贝，螺钿。**M- of Presidents** 〔美〕总统之乡〔指弗吉尼亚州，因出过好几个总统之故〕。**M- of States** 〔美〕各州之母〔弗吉尼亚州的别名〕。~**-of-thyme**【植】欧百里香。~ **oil** (石油)原油。~ **rod** 主联杆。**M-'s Day** (美国和加拿大的)母亲节〔五月第二个星期日〕。~ **ship** 〔英〕母舰，航空母舰。~ **superior** 女修道院院长。~ **tongue** 母语，本国语，本民族语言。~ **wit** 天生的智慧；常识。~**wort**【植】益母草属。

moth·er[2] [ˈmʌðə] *n.* 醋母 (= ~ of vinegar); 渣滓, 糟. — *vt.* 生醋母.

moth·er·ing [ˈmʌðəriŋ] *n.* 〔英〕省亲,探亲.

moth·er·li·ness [ˈmʌðəlinis] *n.* 象母亲,母爱,慈母心.

moth·er·ly, moth·er·like [ˈmʌðəli, -laik] *a.* 母亲(似)的,母爱的,慈爱的.

moth·er·y [ˈmʌðəri] *a.* 醋母性的;含醋母的;象醋母的.

moth·y [ˈmɔθi] *a.* ***(moth·i·er; -i·est)*** 多蛾的;蛀了的,虫蛀的.

mo·tif [məuˈtiːf] *n.* 〔F.〕(艺术作品的)主题,要点,特色; 动机,主旨;衣服的花边;(图案的)基本花纹; 基本色彩; 【物】型主.

mo·tile [ˈməutail, -til] *a.* 【生】有自动力的,能动的. — *n.* 【心】运动型〔指人的想象力是能动的,而不仅仅是凭借视觉和听觉〕. **mo·til·i·ty** [məuˈtiliti] *n.* 【生】运动力,自动力;机动性;【化】游动(现象).

mo·tion [ˈməuʃən] *n.* ①运动,动,移动 (*opp.* rest). ②(天体的)运行;(车、船等的)动摇;(机器的)开动,运转;【机】机械装置,机制. ③动作,举动;手势;眼色;恣态;〔*pl.*〕(个人或团体的)行动,举动,活动. ④(议会中的)提议,动议;动机,意向;刺激;【法】申请,请求. ⑤大便;〔*pl.*〕排泄物. ⑥【乐】(旋律、曲调的)变移. *M- itself is a contradiction.* 运动本身就是矛盾. *All her ~s were graceful.* 她的一举一动都优美. *The ~ to adjourn was carried.* 休会的提议通过了. ***in ~*** 动着,运转着,活动着. ***make a ~ [~s]*** 用手势示意;提议. ~ ***study*** 操作研究. ***of one's own ~*** 自动地,自愿地,出自本意. ***on the ~ of*** 经…的动议. ***put [set] in ~*** 使动,启动,发动. — *vi.* 打手势要求〔指示〕 *(to; towards; away)*. ~ *(to) sb. to take a seat* 用手指椅子请某人坐下. — *vt.* 向某人打手势;向某人点头或摇头示意. ~ *sb. away [out]* 打手势叫某人走开〔出去〕. ~ **picture** *n., a.* 电影(的), 影片(的). ~ **sickness** 【医】运动病〔指晕车、晕船等〕. **-less** *n.* 不动的,静止的.

mo·tion·al [ˈməuʃənl] *a.* 运动的;由运动而生的;起动的.

mo·ti·vate [ˈməutiveit] *vt.* 给与动机,促动,激发,诱导. **-va·tor** *n.*

mo·ti·va·tion [ˌməutiˈveiʃən] *n.* 动机的行成; 动机因素;动力. **-al** *a.* (*motivational research* 动机研究〔用于广告、销售活动〕).

mo·tive [ˈməutiv] *a.* 引起运动的,发动的,运动的; 成为(行动的) 动机的. — *n.* ①动机, 动因; 主旨; 目的. ②(艺术作品的)主题; 题材. ***of [from] one's own ~*** 自动. — *vt.* ①= motivate. ②成为(艺术作品的)主题. ~ **power [force]** 动力〔电、汽力等〕;〔集合词〕机车, 拖拉机.

mo·tive·less [ˈməutivlis] *a.* 没有动机〔目的、理由〕的,妄动的.

mo·tiv·i·ty [məuˈtiviti] *n.* (发)动力,原动力.

Mot·ley [ˈmɔtli] *n.* 莫特利〔姓氏〕.

mot·ley [ˈmɔtli] *a.* 杂色的;穿着杂色衣服的;繁杂的,混杂的;杂凑成的. — *n.* 杂色;(丑角穿的)杂色衣服;穿着杂色衣服的小丑. *wear (the) ~* 扮演丑角;装傻.

mot·mot [ˈmɔtmɔt] *n.* 〔动〕翠鴗〔产于美洲热带和副热带地区〕.

mo·to·neu·ron [ˌməutənjuərən, -nuər-] *n.* 【医】运动神经元.

mo·tor [ˈməutə] *n.* ①原动者;原动力. ②发动机;马达;电动机;【火箭】助推器; 汽车. ③【解】运动肌; 运动神经. *an electric ~* 电动机. *a chemical fuel ~* 火箭发动机. — *a.* 使动的,发动的,原动的;【解】运动的. ~ *gasoline* 动力汽油. *a ~ nerve* 运动神经. *a ~ skinner* 〔美〕汽车司机. — *vt.* 用汽车搬运. — *vi.* 坐汽车,开汽车. ~ *a friend home* 用汽车送朋友回家. **~bicyle [bike]** 摩托(自行)车. **~boat** 汽艇, 汽船. **~boating** 乘汽艇出游;【无】汽船声〔低频寄生振荡〕. **~bus** 公共汽车. **~cab** 出租汽车. **~cade** 〔美〕汽车的长蛇阵〔长列〕. **~car** 汽车. ~ **coach** = ~bus. ~ **court** 〔美〕= motel. **~-cross** 摩托车越野赛. **~cycle** *n., vi.* (骑)摩托车. **~cyclist** 骑摩托车的人;【军】摩托兵. ~ **drawn** *a.* 汽车牵引的. ~ **drive** 电机驱动系统〔装置〕. **~drome** 汽车试车场; 汽车比赛场. ~ **gen,** ~ **generator** 〔美〕电动发动机组. ~ **home** 活动住宅,住房汽车. ~ **hotel [inn]** (市内的) 汽车酒店〔多建有停车房等〕. ~ **launch** 汽艇. **~-lorry** 〔英〕 运货汽车. ~ **maker** 〔美〕汽车制造人〔厂〕. **~man** 〔美、加拿大〕(电车、电气机车的)司机;电机操作者. ~ **meter** 电力测定器;汽车仪表. **~-polo** = auto-polo. ~ **pool** (军政机关)汽车集中调度场. ~ **roller** 机碾. ~ **scooter** 低座小摩托车. ~ **ship** 机船,汽船. ~ **spirit** 汽油. ~ **squadron** 【军】汽车队. ~ **starter** (电动机)起动器. ~ **torpedo boat** 鱼雷快艇. ~ **truck** 〔Am.〕运货汽车. ~ **vehicle** 机动车; 汽车. ~ **wag(g)on** 小卡车. **-less** *a.* 无动力的 (*motorless flying* 滑翔飞行).

mo·tor·a·ma [ˌməutəˈræmə] *n.* 新车展览.

mo·to·rial [məuˈtɔːriəl] *a.* 运动的,原动的; 引起运动的;【解】运动神经的.

mo·tor·ist [ˈməutərist] *n.* 开汽车的人; 乘汽车旅行的人.

mo·tor·ize [ˈməutəraiz] *vt.* 使(车)机动化,汽车化;(废掉马车)改用汽车,摩托化;电化(铁路等). *a ~d infantry division* 【军】摩托化步兵师. *a ~d unit* 【军】摩托化部队.

mo·to·ry [ˈməutəri] *a.* = motorial.

Mo·town [ˈməuˌtaun] *a.* "汽车城"节奏的〔指一种节拍强而慢的节奏和布鲁斯舞曲;"汽车城"为美国底特律的别称〕.

Mott [mɔt] *n.* 莫特〔姓氏〕.

motte [mɔt] *n.* 〔美〕(大草原中的)丛林;小树林子.

mot·tle [ˈmɔtl] *vt.* 使成杂色, 弄斑驳. — *n.* 斑点; 斑纹;【生】斑驳病;杂色绒线〔毛纱〕. *~d iron* 麻口铁.

mot·to [ˈmɔtəu] *n.* ***(pl. ~es, ~s)*** ①(简明的)标语;座右铭, 训言,(特指刻在盾上或徽章上的)箴言. ②(书籍卷首或章头引用的)题词,题句;【乐】主题句. ③附有题句或卦签的糖果袋. ~ **kiss** 附有题句等的糖果.

mou [muː] 〔单复同〕*n.* 〔Chin.〕亩 = *mu.*

mou·choir [muʃwaːr] *n.* 〔F.〕手绢儿,手帕.

moue [muː] *n.* = pout[1].

mouf·(f)lon [ˈmuːflɔn] *n. sing., pl.* 摩弗伦羊〔南欧野羊〕.

mouil·lé [muːˈjei] *a.* 【语音】颚化的.

mou·jik [ˈmuːʒik] *n.* ①(俄国) 农夫. ②女用宽皮披肩(= muzhik).

mou·lage [muːˈlɑːʒ] *n.* ①(刑事侦察中用的)印模术,复制印痕术. ②印模,印痕.

mould[1] [məuld] *n.* ①(阴)模,铸模,模型;外型;铸型; 字模,字型;模制品. ②形状,性格,气质;状况. ③【建】(装饰)线条, 花边, 线脚. *a ~ of pudding* 一个布丁. ***be cast in a ... ~*** 具有…的脾气,生就…的性格. ***be cast in the same ~*** 性格完全相同. ***of gentle ~*** 脾气温和的. — *vt.* ①造形,翻砂,铸,放在模子里做;【建】用线条(或雕刻)装饰. ②捏. ③形成(性格); 陶冶, 训练(人格). ~ ***one's own destiny*** 决定自己的命运. ~ ***(up)on*** 按…的模子作.

mould[2] [məuld] *n.* 肥土,壤土;〔古〕土,土地. — *vt.* 用土覆盖. *leaf ~* 腐殖质土. *a man of ~* (终要入土的)凡人,人类. ~ *up (potatoes)* 拿土覆盖(马铃薯). **~-board** 犁壁;模板,型板. **~-planting** 丘植法.

mould[3] [məuld] *n.* 霉; 霉菌, 霉病. — *vt., vi.* (使)发霉. ~ *rains* 梅雨.

mould·er[1] [ˈməuldə] *vi.* ①朽,朽坏 *(away)*. ②颓废,堕落;消衰,退化;吊儿郎当地度日. — *vt.* 使腐朽.

mould·er[2] [ˈməuldə] *n.* 模塑者, 造型者; 模; 造型物; 【印】(复制用的)电铸板.

mould·ing[1] [ˈməuldiŋ] *n.* 模塑,作模;造型;翻砂,铸造;铸造物,模塑物;(常 *pl.*)【建】花边,线脚,风景线.
mould·ing[2] [ˈməuldiŋ] *n.* 覆土;覆盖的土壤.
mould-loft [ˈməuldlɔft] *n.* (造船厂内的)大制图室.
mould·y[1] [ˈməuldi] *a.* ***(mould·i·er; -i·est)*** 发了霉的;霉烂的;陈腐的;〔俚〕十分无聊的.
mould·y[2] [ˈməuldi] *n.* 〔海俚〕鱼雷,空投鱼雷.
moul·lin [ˈmu:lɛ̃:ŋ] *n.* 〔F.〕【地】冰川锅穴,冰河竖坑.
Moul·mein [maulˈmein] *n.* 毛淡棉〔缅甸港市〕.
moult [məult] *vi.* (羽毛等)脱换,脱落. — *vt.* 使脱换(羽毛等). — *n.* 脱换,脱落,脱皮.
Moul·ton [ˈməultən] *n.* 莫尔顿〔姓氏〕.
moul·vi [ˈmulvi] *n.* = moolvee, maulvi.
mound[1] [maund] *n.* 堤;(尤指城堡的)护堤;土墩,土山;小山,小丘;【棒球】投球员的踏板. *the Indian ~s* 美洲印第安人史前时代在密西西比河东岸所筑的土墩子. *the M- City* 〔美〕St. Louis 市的别名〔因土墩子很多〕. *take the ~*【棒球】作投球员. — *vt.* 筑堤;造土墩子;筑堤防御. ~ **builder** *n.* ①筑墩者. ②〔M- Builder〕*(pl.)* 北美五大湖地区的史前印第安人. ③大足鹑,营冢鸟.
mound[2] [maund] *n.* (象征王权、王位的)宝球,宝珠;帝位的象征.
mount[1] [maunt] *vt.* ①登,上(山、梯、王位等). ②骑,乘(马等). ③使人骑上(马),扶上(马);使做骑兵. ④安装,装配,架(炮等);装置,装备;裱(画、地图等);镶(宝石等);封固,(把检镜物)固定在载(玻)片 *(slide)* 上,剥制(动物). ⑤准备服装、道具,上演(剧本). ⑥穿,戴. ⑦测定,确定;规定. — *vi.* ①登,上;(血)上面孔. ②骑马;乘 *(on)*. ③(数量等)增长;增高;上升. ~ *the stairs* 上楼梯. ~ *a horse* 骑上马. ~ *insects* 制昆虫标本. ***be well [poorly] ~ed*** 骑着好[劣]马. ~ ***(an offensive) against*** 对…发动(攻势). ~ **guard** 站岗. ~ ***guard over*** 守望,守卫. ~ ***(gems) in*** 镶(宝石)在…. ~ ***(a gun) on*** 把(大炮)安在…上. ~ ***the high horse*** 趾高气扬;自大. ~ ***up to*** …(金额)增加到…. — *n.* ①坐骑〔马,骡,自行车等〕;〔俚〕(尤指赛马时的)骑马的机会;登,爬上;骑马. ②(衬托相片等用的)硬板纸,衬托纸,裱画纸;(家具的)边饰;(镶宝石的)宝石托;(显微镜的)载(玻)片;踏脚台;炮架,支架. ③扇把,扇骨. ④(电子管)管脚. ***get down from one's ~*** 下马.
mount[2] [maunt] *n.* ①〔书〕山,丘;〔M-〕…山,…峰〔通常略作 Mt〕. ②【手相】宫〔掌肉隆起处〕.
moun·tain [ˈmauntin] *n.* ①(比 hill 大的)山,山岳;〔*pl.*〕山脉. ②〔the M-〕山嶽党〔法国第一次革命时占据议会最高座位的左派政党〕. ③山一样(巨大)的东西;大量. *the Rocky Mountains* 〔美〕落基山脉. *rolling ~s* 滔天大浪. *a ~ of rubbish* 垃圾堆. ***a ~ of (difficulties, debts)*** 山一般的(困难、债等). ***a ~ of flesh*** 大胖子. ***make a ~ out of a molehill*** 小题大做. ***remove ~s*** 移山倒海;行奇迹,做惊人举动. ***The ~ has brought forth a mouse.=the ~ in labour*** 费力大收效小;雷声大雨点小. ~ **artillery** 山炮;山地炮兵. ~ **ash**【植】花楸,山楸属. ~ **avens**【植】多瓣木,仙女木;三叶水杨梅. ~ **battery** 山炮队. ~ **canary** 〔美口〕小驴子. ~ **cat** = cougar. ~ **chain** 山脉. ~ **cloth [cork, flax, leather]** 石棉. ~ **cranberry** = cowberry 牙疙瘩〔越桔〕. ~ **crystal** 水晶. ~ **deer**【动】羚羊. ~ **dew** 苏格兰威士忌酒(尤指非法私造的);〔美俚〕酒,威士忌酒. ~ **division** 山地作战师. ~ **goat** ①【动】(落基山脉产的)野生白山羊. ②〔俚〕声波定位器,声纳. ~ **green** 孔雀石. ~ **group** 山群. ~ **gun** 山炮. **~-high** *a.* 高如山的(大浪等). ~ **howitzer** 山地榴弹炮. ~ **laurel** ①【植】山月桂. ②加州桂(= California laurel). ~ **lion** = cougar. ~ **railway** 山区铁道. **~range** 山脉. ~ **rice** 野麦. ~ **sheep**【动】野羊. **~side** 山腰. ~ **sickness** 高山病,山岳病. ~ **spinach** 法国菠菜. ~ **spur** 山脊. **M- State** 山地州〔美国落基山脉地区八个州之一〕. **~-stronghold** 山寨 (*~-stronghold mentality* 山头主义). ~ **system** 山系. **M- (Standard) Time** (美国)山地标准时间〔比格林威治时间晚七小时〕. ~ **warfare** 山地战. ~ **white oak** 蓝栎. ~ **wine** 山地白葡萄酒 (= Malaga wine). ~ **wood** 石棉,不灰木.
moun·tained [ˈmauntind] *a.* 山一样的;多山的.
moun·tain·eer [ˌmauntiˈniə] *n.* 山地人;登山家. — *vi.* 登山. **-ing** *n.* 登山(运动).
moun·tain·ous [ˈmauntinəs] *a.* 山多的;山似的;巨大的. *a ~ country* 山国.
moun·tain·y [ˈmauntini] *a.* ①= mountainous. ②〔爱尔兰〕住在山地的. *~men* 山地人.
Mount·bat·ten [mauntˈbætn] *n.* 蒙巴顿〔姓氏〕.
mount·e·bank [ˈmauntibæŋk] *n.* 走江湖的江湖医生;骗子. **-ery** 骗子行为;大话.
mount·ed [ˈmauntid] *a.* ①骑在马[自行车]上的. ②装好在架子上的;贴在衬纸上的,裱上的;镶嵌的. *a ~ bandit* 马贼. *~ infantry* 骑马步兵. *a ~ point* 骑兵尖兵. *~ police* 骑警(队). *~ units* 骑兵部队,乘车部队. *a ~ gun* 装好炮架的大炮. *a silver-~ sword* 镶银宝剑.
Mount·ie, Mount·y [ˈmaunti] *n.* 〔俚〕加拿大皇家骑警.
mount·ing [ˈmauntiŋ] *n.* (大炮等的)架设;装置;座,架,【军】炮架;衬托纸;裱;镶嵌;装饰;攀登;登上;上马;上车;乘骑;(鸟等的)剥制;(镜检物的)装片;封固;〔*pl.*〕马具;附件,配件. *a gimbal ~* 万向接头架. *a ~ block* 骑马台.
mourn [mɔ:n] *vi., vt.* 悲,悲伤,悲叹 *(over; for)*;弔,哀悼;穿丧服,戴孝;【宗】奋兴会上的公开忏悔者.
mourn·er [ˈmɔ:nə] *n.* 悲叹的人,悲伤的人,哀伤的人,哀悼的人;守丧的人,送丧的人;雇用的送丧人;〔美〕忏悔的人;【拳击】眼圈被打得发黑的拳手. ***~'s bench*** 〔美〕(教堂中供人下跪的)凳子;(教堂中的)前排座位. ***the chief ~*** 丧主;死者最近的亲属;遗嘱执行人.
mourn·ful [ˈmɔ:nful] *a.* 悲哀似的,哀痛的;使人伤心[沮丧]的.
mourn·ing [ˈmɔ:niŋ] *n.* ①悲伤,哀悼,哀伤. ②丧,居丧;丧服;丧章;丧帘;半旗,丧旗. *deep ~* (纯黑的)正式丧服. *half ~* (灰色的)半丧服. *a ~ band* (服丧所戴)黑纱. ***be in ~*** 戴着孝;〔俚〕被打得眼圈发黑;(指甲等)肮脏的,污黑的. ***be out of ~*** 服满,除服. ***go into [put on, take to] ~*** 举哀;服丧,戴孝. ***leave off [go out of] ~*** 服满;除服. ***nails in ~*** 〔谑〕塞满污垢的指甲. ***put into ~*** 使服丧,使穿孝. ~ **border** (表示哀悼的)黑边,黑框. ~ **card** (服丧时用的)黑边卡片. ~ **cloak**【动】蛱蝶. ~ **coach** (黑色的)灵柩车;出殡车. ~ **dove** 〔美〕(鸣声有哀感的)斑鸠. ~ **paper** 黑边信纸. ~ **ring** (镶有死者小像的)纪念戒指. ~ **stuff** 丧服料.
MOUSE = minimum orbital unmanned satellite of the earth 不载人的最小人造地球卫星〔仪表载重五十公斤以下〕.
mouse [maus] *n.* *(pl.* mice [mais]*)* ①【动】(比 rat 小的)小鼠,耗子. ②胆小的人. ③〔俚〕女人;姑娘. ④〔俚〕(眼睛周围被打而起的)青肿. ⑤(上下窗户用的)坠子. ⑥【海】缠口结. ⑦〔美俚〕小火箭. — *a.* 鼠灰色的. *a field [wood] ~* 野鼠. *a house ~* 家鼠. ***like a drowned ~*** 象落水鼠一样(狼狈). ***~ and man*** 一切生物,众生 *(the best-laid plans of mice and men* 最妥善的计划). ***play like a cat with a ~*** 象猫捉耗子似地欺负[折磨]. — [mauz, maus] *vi.* ①(猫或枭)捉耗子. ②来回窥探. — *vt.* ①搜捕;搜寻;探出. ②(象猫对耗子一样)欺负,虐待;扯开,撕裂;【海】用鼠装饰;(钩口)用绳子扎紧. **~bird**【动】鼠鸟 (= coly). ~ **colo(u)r** 鼠灰色. ~ **deer**【动】= chevrotain. **~-ear**【植】卷耳

属;山柳菊,勿忘草. ~ **hole** 耗子洞,鼠穴;狭窄的出[入]口;小房间. ~**tail** 鼠尾巴属植物. ~**trap** ①捕鼠器;〔谑〕小屋子. ②〔美、剧〕演出技巧极坏的演员. ③小戏院;下等夜总会. ④防空气球网.

mous·er [ˈmauzə] *n.* 捕鼠动物〔猫或枭〕; 来回窥探的人;〔美俚〕堕落的人;〔俚〕侦探.

mous·ey = mousy.

mous·ie [ˈmausi] *n.* 小小耗子〔爱称〕.

mous·ing [ˈmauziŋ] *n.* 捕鼠;【海】扎钩口的绳子.

mous·que·taire [muskəˈtεə] *n.* 〔F.〕 = musketeer.

mous·sa·ka [muːˈsɑːkə] *n.* 茄片夹肉,茄合〔希腊的一道菜名:盖以白酱汁和干酪然后烤熟〕.

mousse [muːs] *n.* 〔F.〕 奶油冻.

mousse·line [muːsˈliːn] *n.* 〔F.〕 细棉布;木斯林玻璃〔制上等杯子用〕.

mousse·line de laine [muːsˈliːndəˈlein] *n.* 〔F.〕 毛棉混纺薄呢.

mousse·line de soie [muːsˈliːn dəˈswɑː] 〔F.〕 全丝薄纱〔用作婚礼服〕.

mous·tache [məsˈtɑːʃ, mus-] *n.* ①〔常 *pl.*〕(嘴唇上面的)髭;小胡子. ②(猫等的)须. *old* ~ 老兵,富有经验的士兵.

mous·ta·chio, mus·ta·chio [məˈstɑːʃəu] *n.* 浓密的胡子.

Mous·te·ri·an [muːsˈtiəriən] *a.*【地质】(旧石器时代)莫斯特期的.

mous·y [ˈmausi] *a.* ***(mous·i·er; -i·est)*** 耗子似的; 耗子多的;鼠臭的;鼠灰色的;胆小的;(小说等)乏味的.

mouth [mauθ] ***(pl. ~s [mauðz])*** ①口,口腔,嘴. ②〔*pl.*〕口,人;动物. ③口状物,出入口;孔,穴;枪口;河口,港口,喷火口;袋口(等);(乐器的)吹口. ④咧嘴,怪脸,苦相;话,发言;代言人;人言,传闻,传说;〔俚〕傲慢话,厚脸. ⑤(啤酒等的)味儿. *Shut your ~!*〔卑〕住口! *a useless* ~ 没用的人,饭桶. *a big* ~〔美俚〕碎嘴子,说话冒失的人. *hungry ~s* 饥饿的人们. ~ *parts*【虫】口器. ***by word of*** ~ 口头通知,当面告诉,口说. ***down in the*** ~ 沮丧,垂头丧气,气馁. ***from hand to*** ~ 现挣现吃;过一天算一天. ***from*** ~ ***to*** ~ 口口相传;挨次. ***give*** ~ (猎狗)吠起来. ***give*** ~ ***to*** 说出,吐露. ***have a foul*** ~ 嘴不干净,嘴坏. ***have a good [bad, hard]*** ~ (马)驯顺〔不驯顺〕. ***have one's*** ~ ***made up*** *(for sth.)*〔美〕张开嘴准备吃东西;垂涎;期待,渴望得到. ***in everyone's*** ~ 人人都如此说. ***in [with] a French*** ~ 用法国腔调. ***in the*** ~ ***of*** 出于…之口,据…说. ***Keep your ~ shut and your ears open.***〔谚〕多听少讲. ***laugh on the wrong side of one's*** ~ 由得意变失意,转喜为悲. ***make a ~ [make ~s] at*** 对…咧嘴,皱眉头. ***make one's ~ water*** 使垂涎,使羡慕. ***open one's*** ~ 开口,开始说话. ***open one's ~ too wide*** 口气过大,要求过多,要价过高. ***put words into one's*** ~ 说是某人那样讲过;教某人怎样讲. ***shoot off one's*** ~〔俚〕信口开河,滔滔不绝. ***sound strange in one's*** ~ 某人讲就觉得奇怪. ***stop sb.'s*** ~ 堵住某人的嘴;强使人停止讲话. ***take the bread out of sb.'s*** ~ 夺人饭碗,夺人生计. ***take the words out of sb.'s*** ~ 说出某人心里要讲的话. ***with full [open]*** ~ 大声地. ***with one*** ~〔罕〕异口同声地. — [mauð] *vt.* ①说出;用演说腔调讲;附和着说;含糊地说. ②用口衔;放进嘴里嚼;嚼;吃. ③使(马)咬惯马嚼子. ④用嘴接触,吻. — *vi.* ①(特指轻蔑时的)歪嘴. ②大声讲,叫骂;怒骂;装腔做势地讲. ③(河)注入 *(in; into)*. ~**breeder** 非洲鲫鱼. ~**-filling** *a.* (句子)长的; 夸大的. ~ **friend** 口头上的朋友. ~ **organ** ①口琴. ②=Panpipe. ~**part**【动】口器. ~**-to-**~ *a.* 口对口的〔人工呼吸的一种方式〕. ~**wash** 漱口水,洗口药. ~**watering** *a.* 使人流馋涎的;味道好的.

-mouthed [mauðd] *comb. f.* 有口的,嘴…的. *a foul-~ man* 嘴坏的人,说话刻薄的人. *a hard-~ horse* 不驯顺的马.

mouth·er [ˈmauðə] *n.* 吹牛的人,说大话的人.

mouth·ful [ˈmauθˈful] *n.* 满口,一口,少量(的食物);〔俚〕适当[不适当]的批评[暗示]. *You said a ~.*〔美俚〕你说得极对[真妙]. ***at a*** ~ 一口. ***make a ~ of*** *(sth.)* 一口吞下.

mouthing [ˈmauðiŋ] *n.* ①怪脸,苦相. ②说话;夸口话. ③使马咬马嚼子的训练.

mouth·piece [ˈmauθpiːs] *n.* ①烟嘴口;乐器的吹口;马衔铁;口罩. ②【物】接口管;【电话】口承. ③喉舌,发言人;代言人;〔英俚〕刑事律师,代理人.

mouth·y [ˈmauði] *a.* ***(mouth·i·er; -i·est)*** 说大话的,夸口的;嘴碎的,爱说话的. **-i·ly** *ad.*, **-i·ness** *n.*

mou·ton [ˈmuːtɔn] *n.* 染色绵羊毛皮.

mou·ton·née [muːtnˈei] *a.* 圆如羊背的〔指岩层〕— *n.*【地】羊背石 (= roche moutonnée).

mov·a·bil·i·ty [ˌmuːvəˈbiliti] *n.* 可动,易动,可动性.

mov·a·ble [ˈmuːvəbl] *a.* 可动的,可移动的;【法】动产的 (*opp.* real); 变动不定的. ~ *property* 动产. *a* ~ *sleeve* 活动套筒. *a* ~ *feast* 节期因年而异的节日. — *n.* 家具 (*opp.* fixture);【法】〔*pl.*〕动产 (*opp.* immovable). **-ness** *n.*

mov·a·bly [ˈmuːvəbli] *ad.* 可动,易动.

move [muːv] *vt.* ①动,移,移动,搬动 (*opp.* fix); 开动;使运行;摇动. ②感动,鼓动,激动;使感动得…;引起(人)…的兴致,打动,发动;刺激,鼓励 *(to do)*. ③提议,动议. ④通(大便). ⑤卖,推销(货物). — *vi.* ①动;生活,活动;行动;〔口〕出发. ②摇,摇动,动摇;(机器)开动. ③迁移,(民族)移住 *(into)*; (尤指)搬(家) *(in; into)*. ④(事件等)发展;(火车、轮船等)前进;(自然物)生长;出芽. ⑤动议,提议. ⑥【象棋】走(棋子). ⑦通(大便). ⑧卖. *He ~d in his sleep.* 他熟睡时翻来覆去. *It's time to be moving.* 该动身了. ***be ~ed by*** 被…感动. ***feel ~d to*** 觉得想…. ~ ***about*** 到处活动;动来动去;老是改变住处,老在搬家 (*They ~d about in armed groups.* 他们组成武装小队四出活动). ~ ***aside*** 搁在旁边;除去. ~ ***away*** 离开,退出. ~ ***back*** (使)退. ~ ***for*** 动议,提议,要求. ~ ***forward*** 前进. ~ ***heaven and earth to*** *(do)* 想方设法,尽量努力. ~ ***house*** 搬家. ~ ***in*** 搬进. ~ ***in good society*** 在上层社交中活动. ~ ***in on***〔美俚〕(为了捕获而)潜近;企图从某人手中夺取对某物的控制权. ~ ***off*** 离去,走掉;〔俚〕死;(货物)畅销. ~ ***on*** (使)继续前进,不停地向前走;〔交通警察命令〕向前! 不要站着! ~ ***one's blood*** 使人奋发. ~ ***out*** 搬出,搬走;【军】开始行动. ~ ***right down the car!*** 往里走走! ~ ***the bowels*** 通大便. ~ ***sb. to*** *(anger; tears; laughter)* 使感动得(发怒、掉泪、发笑). ~ ***to*** 搬到. ~ ***up*** 提上,上升. ~ ***upon*** 进逼. — *n.* ①动,运动,移动. ②发展,推移. ③搬家. ④【象棋】一着,该走的人;步骤,措施,处置,手段. ***be up to every ~ on the board = be up to [know] a ~ or two = know every*** ~ 不落空,精明;机敏. ***first*** ~ 先着,先走棋者. ***get a ~ on***〔口〕赶紧,赶急;〔命令〕行动起来;快! 赶快! ***lost a ~ to*** 输了一着. ***make a*** ~ 动;(准备)出发;走开;搬家;采取措施;行动;动一着(棋). ***on the*** ~ 一直在动;开始活动;(事件)正在发展.

move·a·ble [ˈmuːvəbl] *a.*, *n.* = movable.

mov·e·list [ˈmuːvəlist] *n.* 电影小说作家.

move·ment [ˈmuːvmənt] *n.* ①运动;活动;进退,行动,动静;动摇;动作,举动;〔*pl.*〕姿势;态度. ②移动,迁移. ③(市面的)活动,活跃;(行市等的)变动. ④(时代、社会等的)动向,倾向;动态;(小说、戏剧的)曲折;变化.【乐】乐章;速度;【语】节奏,韵律;(绘画、雕刻的)动势,生动效果;(诗的)韵律结构. ⑤【机】动程;机械装置,机构,(钟、表的)机件;(机器的)运转(状态). ⑥(政治)运动. *international communist* ~ 国际共产主义运动. *national* *liberation* ～ 民族解放运动. *labour* ～ 工人运动. *the* ～ *for agricultural coorperation* 农业合作化运动. ⑦【军】调动,调迁;输送. ⑧(植物的)发芽,生长. ⑨通便;排泄物. *quick* ～【乐】快速调. *slow* ～【乐】徐缓调. *the temperance* ～ 禁酒运动. *The play lacks* ～. 那出戏缺乏变化. *the first* ～ *of a symphony* 交响曲第一乐章. *a dance* ～ 舞蹈的节奏. ***in the*** ～ 跟着时势前进,不落伍.

mov·er [ˈmuːvə] *n.* ①(使)动的人[东西]; (尤指)搬场工人[服务业];运转者;发动机,动力;主动人;鼓舞者;煽动者. ②提议人. *the first [prime]* ～ 主动者,发起人;发动机;动力.

mov·ie [ˈmuːvi] *n.* 〔常 *pl.*〕〔英俚、美口〕电影(院);影片. *go to the* ～*s.* 去看电影. ～ **actor** 电影男演员. ～ **fan** 影迷. ～ **house** 电影院. ～ **star** (电)影(明)星. ～**dom** 电影界. ～**goer** (常)看电影的人. ～**-land** = moviedom. ～ **maker** 电影制片者. ～**-tone** 有声电影.

mov·ing [ˈmuːviŋ] *n.* ①活动,移动;煽动,感动. ②〔*pl.*〕〔口〕电影. — *a.* ①动的;移动的. ②使人感动的,动人的. ③主动的,原动力的. ～ **day** (房客)迁让日,(雇员)解雇日〔美国若干地方是5月1日和10月1日〕. ～ *force* 动力;感染力. ～ ***of the waters*** 〔喻〕扰嚷;兴奋;刺激;(事件发展中的)变化,阻碍. ～ **picture** 影片,电影. ～ **platform** 自动搬运台. ～ **sidewalk [walk]** 自动人行道. ～ **staircase [stairway]** 自动楼梯. ～ **target** 【军】活动目标. ～ **vane** 【空】动翼.

Mov·i·o·la, mov·ie·o·la [ˌmuːviˈəulə] 一种编辑电影用(检查剪辑)的机器商标名. — *n.* 〔m-〕电影剪辑机.

mow[1] [məu] ***(-ed; mown)*** *vt.* ①刈,割(草、麦等);收割. ②刈倒,扫除;扫射,扫杀;扫平,摧毁 *(down; off)*. — *vi.* 割,刈割.

mow[2] [məu; Am. mau] *n.* 干草堆,麦秆堆;干草堆积处;谷堆.

mow[3] [mau] *n., vi.* 皱眉头,(做)鬼脸 (*cf.* mop².)

M.O.W. = Ministry of Works〔英〕建筑工程部.

mow·er [ˈməuə] *n.* 割草人;割草机.

mow·ing [ˈməuiŋ] *n.* ①割草,割谷. ②一次割下的草量. ③饲料地. ～ **machine** 割草机.

mown [məun] mow¹ 的过去分词. — *a.* 割下的.

mox·a [ˈmɔksə] *n.* 【医】艾绒;灼烙剂;【植】艾.

mox·i·bus·tion [ˌmɔksiˈbʌstʃən] *n.* 艾灸,艾灼. *acupuncture and* ～ 针灸.

mox·ie [ˈmɔksi] *n.* 〔俚〕有胆量,有气魄,坚忍不拔,刚毅.

Mo·zam·bique [ˌməuzəmˈbiːk] *n.* 莫桑比克〔非洲〕.

Moz·ar·ab [məuˈzærəb] *n.* 穆萨拉布〔摩尔人统治时期内被允许有抑制地奉行其宗教的西班牙基督教徒〕. **-ic** *a.*

Mo·zart [ˈməutsɑːt], **Wolfgang Amadeus** 莫扎特〔1756—1791,奥地利作曲家〕.

moz·za·rel·la [ˌmɔtsəˈrelə] *n.* 意大利干酪〔尤指用于烹饪者〕.

moz·zet·ta, mo·zet·ta [məuˈzetə] *n.* (天主教皇等披于法衣上的)有头巾的披肩.

moy·a [ˈmɔiə] *n.* 【地】火山泥;泥熔岩.

moy·en age [mwaˌjẽˈnɑːʒ] 〔F.〕中世纪.

MP, M.P. = ①Member of Parliament〔英〕下院议员. ②military police 宪兵队; military policeman 宪兵. ③metropolitan police 首都警察队. ④〔It.〕*mezzo piano*【乐】不很轻. ⑤milepost 英里程标. ⑥motion picture 电影. ⑦mounted police 骑警队. ⑧municipal police 市警队. ⑨Master of Painting 绘画硕士. ⑩melting point 熔点,融解点.

M.Pd. = Master of Pedagogy 教育学硕士.

M.P.E. = Master of Physical Education 体育硕士.

mpg, m.p.g. = miles per gallon 英里/加仑.

M.Ph. = Master of Philosophy 哲学硕士.

mph, m.p.h. = miles per hour 英里/时.

MPO = military post office 军邮局.

M.R. = machine rifle 自动步枪.

Mr., Mr [ˈmistə] (*pl.* Messrs.) …先生〔Mister 的略语,用于男子名或职衔前: *Mr. Smith, Mr. President.*〕 *the* ～〔美俚〕丈夫. ～ ***Fix-it [Fixit]***〔美俚〕办理〔解决〕一切的人.

MRA, M.R.A. = Moral Rearmament 道德重整运动.

MRBM = medium-range ballistic missile 中程弹道导弹.

M.R.C.P. = Member of the Royal College of Physicians〔英〕皇家内科医师学会会员.

M.R.C.S. = Members of the Royal College of Surgeons〔英〕皇家外科医师学会会员.

M Rep = Motor Repair 汽车修理.

mRNA = messenger RNA【生化】信使核糖核酸.

Mrs., Mrs [ˈmisiz] (= Mistress) 夫人. ～ **Smith** 史密斯太太.

MRV = multiple reentry vehicle【军】多弹头重返大气层运载工具.

MS = ①manuscript. ②Master of Science 理科硕士. ③Mississippi. ④motor ship 内燃机船. ⑤mass spectrometer【物】质谱仪.

M.S. = Master of Surgery 外科硕士.

m.s., M/S = months after sight【商】见票后…月.

Ms. [miz] 女士 (= Miss 或 Mrs.)〔用在婚姻状况不明的女子姓名前〕.

MSc, M.Sc. = Master of Science 理科硕士.

msec. = millisecond.

msg; msg. = message.

msgr; msgr. = messenger.

M.Sgt., M/Sgt., MSgt = Master Sergeant〔美〕陆军[空军、海军陆战队]军士长.

MSI = medium-scale integration【自】中规模集成电路.

m.s.l. = mean sea level 平均海平面.

MSR = missile site radar 导弹发射场雷达.

MSS = manuscripts.

MST = Mountain Standard Time 山区标准时间〔指国际时区西七区的区时〕.

Msth, Ms-Th【化】新钍 (= mesothorium).

MT = ①mean time【天】平时〔平太阳时〕. ②metric ton 公吨. ③mechanical [motor] transport 汽车运输;【英陆军】汽车运输队. ④= MST. ⑤Montana. ⑥megaton.

Mt. = Mount, Mountain.

MTB = motor torpedo boat 鱼雷快艇.

M.T.C. = Mechanized Transport Corps. 机械化运输兵.

MTD = mean temperature difference 平均温差.

Mtd = mounted.

mtg. = ①meeting. ②mortgage.

mtge. = mortgage.

mth, mth. = month.

M Tk = medium tank 中型坦克.

Mtn, mtn. = mountain.

Mt.Rev. = Most Reverend【宗】最尊敬的(对大主教的尊称).

M Trk = Motor Truck.

Mts; mts. = mountains.

MTU = mobile training unit【军】巡回训练队.

mu [mjuː] *n.* 希腊语的第十二字母〔M, μ〕;百万分之一;千分之一毫米.

much[1] [mʌtʃ] (*opp.* little) *a.* ***(more; most)***〔用于修饰不可数名词〕很多的,许多的;大量的;很大程度的;(时间)长的 *(～ water, wine, money, hope, courage, time)*. ★ ①主要在英国口语中,除用作肯定句主语之一或与

how, too, as, so 连用外,多用于代替 a lot of, a great quantity of, a good deal of, a great deal of 等. 如: *I don't drink ~ wine.* 我酒喝不多 (*cf.* He drinks a great deal of wine. 他酒喝得很多). *Does he take ~ interest in it?* 他对此是否很感兴趣? ②常用作反语表示 no 的意思如: M- right he has to interfere with me. 他根本没有干涉我的权利. ***~ cry and little wool*** 雷声大雨点小. — *n.* 大量,许多. *I don't see ~ of him.* 我不常见他. ***be too ~ for one*** 〔口〕非…力所能及; 干不了; 受不了; 搞不赢; 应付不来 (*He is too ~ for me.* 我敌他不过). ***do ~ to [toward]*** 对…很尽责〔有利、有贡献〕. ***make ~ of*** 尊重, 重视; 充分利用; 夸奖, 恭维,谄媚; 悉心照顾; 理解. ***~ of a ...*** 了不起的 (*He is not ~ of a scholar.* 他不是什么了不起的学者). ***M- would have more.*** 人心不足蛇吞象. ***not ~*** 〔口〕哪里的话,当然不 (*Go home? Not ~.* 回家? 哪里的话). ***so ~ for*** …的事不必再往下说〔就这样完了〕; …不过是这样, 如果…就要吃苦头. ***think ~ of*** 重视, 认为了不起. ***this ~ = thus ~*** 到这里为止,这么些(是对的等). ***too ~*** 太不象话,太过分 (*That is too ~ of a good thing.* 那事好过了头. 那个好倒好, 可是受不了). — *ad.* ***(more; most)*** 很,非常,多; 几乎,大致. *This is ~ better of the two.* 两个当中这个好得多. *Thank you very ~.* 多谢多谢. ★修饰动词时用 very ~ 比单用 ~ 普通. ***argued so ~*** 争论够了. ***as ~*** 同样,一样,正是如此 (*I think as ~.* 我也那样想). ***as ~ again as*** …的二倍. ***as ~ (...) as*** 尽,尽…那样多; …跟…到同一程度 (*as ~ (money) as you like* 尽你要多少. *as ~ as possible* 尽可能). ***as ~ as a single sharp rebuff*** 一点点稍为尖锐的驳斥. ***as ~ as to say*** 等于是说 (*He gave a look as ~ as to say "Mind your own business!"* 他摆出一副好象是说"不用你管!"似的面孔). ***half as ~ again (as)*** (…的)一倍半. ***half as ~ (as)*** (…的)一半. ***how ~*** 多少; 什么价钱; 到什么程度. ***however ~*** 不管. ***~ as ...*** 和…几乎一样; 尽管, 虽然. ***~ at one*** 几乎相同, 几乎等价. ***~ good*** 〔主要用于否定句〕擅长, 巧妙 (*I am not ~ good at this sort of work.* 这种工作我不擅长). ***~ less*** 何况〔否定〕(*He cannot speak French, ~ less Russian.* 他连法语都不会讲,俄语就更不必提了). ***~ more*** 何况〔肯定〕. ***~ of an age*** 差不多同年纪. ***~ of a size*** 差不多大小. ***~ of a sort*** 差不多同种类的. ***~ the same*** 差不多相同. ***not so ~ as*** ①甚至于不〔没有〕(*He cannot so ~ as write his own name.* 他甚至于自己的名字都写不来). ②与其说是…不如说是 (*He is not so ~ a scholar as a writer.* 他与其说是学者不如说是作家). ***so ~*** 那么多的 (*I have not so ~ money as you think.* 我并没有你想象那么多钱). ***twice [three times] as ~*** 两倍〔三倍〕. ***without so ~ as*** 甚至于不….

mu·cha·cha [muːˈtʃɑːtʃə] *n.* ***(pl.-chas)*** 〔Sp.〕姑娘; 年青女人. **mu·cha·cho** [-tʃəu] *n.* 男孩,少年男子.

much·ly [ˈmʌtʃli] *ad.* 〔谑〕非常.

much·ness [ˈmʌtʃnis] *n.* 〔口〕很多,许多. ***be much of a ~*** 〔口〕, 大同小异,半斤八两.

muci- *comb.f.* 粘液.

mu·cic [ˈmjuːsik] *a.* (分泌)粘液的. ~ **acid**【化】粘液酸.

mu·cid [ˈmjuːsid] *a.* 发了霉的,有霉味的.

mu·cif·er·ous [mjuːˈsifərəs] *a.* 分泌粘液的,生粘液的.

mu·ci·lage [ˈmjuːsilidʒ] *n.* (植物分泌的)粘液, 粘质; 〔主、美〕胶水 〔=〔英〕gum〕.

mu·ci·lag·i·nous [ˌmjuːsiˈlædʒinəs] *a.* 粘液质的, 粘的; 分泌粘液的.

mu·cin [ˈmjuːsin] *n.*【生化】粘蛋白,粘液素,粘朊. **-oid, -ous** *a.*

mu·cin·o·gen [mjuːˈsinədʒən] *n.*【生化】粘蛋白原.

muck [mʌk] *n.* ①牛马粪; 粪肥; 湿粪; 腐殖土; 垃圾; 污物; 讨厌的东西; 〔口〕肮脏,污秽; 乱七八糟的状态. ②拙劣〔中伤〕的作品; 胡话; 〔美俚〕钱. *a ~ grubber* 〔美俚〕小气鬼, 吝啬鬼. ***all of a ~ of sweat*** 浑身淌着臭汗. ***be in [all of] a ~*** 浑身是泥. ***make a ~ of*** 弄脏; 弄糟. ***throw ~ at sb.*** 中伤某人. — *vt., vi.* ①上粪, 施肥; 除去赃物 ***(= clear of ~)***. ②〔口〕弄脏 ***(up)***; 〔俚〕弄糟; 〔美〕用手采捞矿石. ~ ***about*** 〔英〕混日子; 闲荡; 做笨事. ~ ***up*** 〔美俚〕弄坏; 搞乱; 清除(污物). **~rake** ① *n.* 粪耙; 〔喻〕爱好丑闻 (*the man with the ~* 到处探听丑闻的人). ② *vi.* 〔喻,美〕搜集并揭发名人的丑事〔尤指公务人员的贪污渎职行为〕. **~raker** 专门报道丑事的人〔新闻记者〕. **~-up** 〔英俚〕*n.* 一团糟,一片混乱. **~-worm** 粪蛆; 守财奴; 吝啬鬼; 流浪儿童.

muck·a·muck¹ [ˈmʌkəmʌk] *n.* 〔美方〕食物. — *vt., vi.* 吃.

muck·a·muck² [ˈmʌkəmʌk] *n.* 大人物, 大亨. *a high ~* (骄傲自大的)要人.

muck·er [ˈmʌkə] *n.* ①〔英俚〕沉重地跌落; 摔倒; 灾难. ②〔美俚〕下流的人,无赖. ③清除废矿的矿工; 采矿系大学生; 掘壕机, 掘沟机. ***come a ~*** 〔英俚〕重重跌倒; 失败,遭到不幸. ***go a ~*** 〔英俚〕滥花钱; 买奢侈〔高价〕东西 ***(on; over)***. **-ism** *n.* 〔美俚〕下流行为.

muck·le [ˈmʌkl] *a., n.* ①= mickle. ②〔美方〕杀鱼用的棒子.

muck·luck, muc·luc [ˈmʌklʌk] *n.* = mukluk.

muck·y [ˈmʌki] *a.* ***(muck·i·er; -i·est)*** 湿粪的; 多腐殖土的; 污秽的; 讨厌的; 可耻的; 卑劣的.

muco- *comb. f.* 粘液: *muco*protein.

mu·co·cu·ta·ne·ous [ˌmjuːkəukjuːˈteinjəs] *a.*【医】粘膜与皮肤的.

mu·coid [ˈmjuːkɔid] *n.* 类粘蛋白. — *a.* 类粘蛋白的; 粘液状的.

mu·co·pol·y·sac·cha·ride [ˌmjuːkəuˌpɔliˈsækəˌraid] *n.*【生化】粘多糖.

mu·co·pro·tein [ˌmjuːkəuˈprəutiːn, -ˈprəutiin] *n.*【生化】粘蛋白.

mu·co·pu·ru·lent [ˌmjuːkəuˈpjuərjulənt] *a.*【医】含粘液脓的.

mu·cor [ˈmjuːkə] *n.* 毛霉菌.

mu·co·sa [mjuːˈkəusə] *n.* ***(pl. -sae*** [-siː]***,-sas)*** 粘液膜 (=mucous membrane). **-sal** *a.*

mu·co·se·rous [ˌmjuːkəuˈsiərəs] *a.*【生】产生〔含有〕粘液及浆液的.

mu·cos·i·ty [mjuːˈkɔsiti] *n.* 粘(性); 粘液.

mu·cous [ˈmjuːkəs] *a.* 粘液(似)的; 粘液质的; 分泌粘液的. *a ~ cough*【医】痰咳. *the ~ membrane* 粘膜.

mu·cro [ˈmjuːkrəu] *n.* ***(pl. -cro·nes*** [mjuːˈkrəuniːz]***)***【植,动】短尖头; 端节; 锐突.

mu·cro·nate [ˈmjuːkrənit] *a.*【植、动】具短尖的; 具锐突的 (= mucronated). **-na·tion** *n.*

mu·cus [ˈmjuːkəs] *n.* (动植物的)粘液. *nasal ~* 鼻涕.

mud [mʌd] *n.* 泥,泥浆; 泥淖; 没价值的东西; 污物; 〔美俚〕咖啡,巧克力布丁; 不清楚的电报信号; 诽谤的话; 恶意的攻击. *consider sb. as ~ [the ~ beneath one's feet]* 把某人当做脚下的泥,轻视某人. *His name is ~.* 他名声很坏〔信用扫地〕. ***fling [throw] ~ at*** 拿泥扔…; 毁谤,中伤; 糟蹋,骂. ***stick in the ~.*** 掉在泥坑里; 墨守旧规; 停滞不前. **~-apron** 挡泥板. ~ **bath** 泥浴. ~ **cat**【动】泥鮰. ~ **crack**【地】泥裂. ~ **dauber**【动】泥蜂. ~ **drag,** ~ **dredge** 疏浚机. ~ **eel**【动】鳗螈. **~fish** 泥鱼〔泥鳍等〕. ~ **flat** (退潮时露出的)泥地; 泥滩. **~grass** 莎禾(属). **~guard** (车子的)挡泥板,叶子板. **~heads** 〔*pl.*〕〔美〕Tennessee 州人的绰号. ~ **hen** 秧鸡科动物〔如大鹬等〕. **~hole** (道路等的)泥孔,泥坑. ~ **hooks** 〔*pl.*〕〔美俚〕脚. ~ **lark** 〔俚〕(退潮时)在河泥中拾破烂的人; 街头流浪儿童; 〔俚〕在泥道上跑得很快的马; 〔英〕沼地云雀. **~-opera** 〔美俚〕马戏,野兽展览. **~pack** 面部美容泥敷膏〔以漂土、

收敛剂等制成〕. ~**-puppy**〔Am.〕泥狗〔美洲蝾螈〕；大鲵鱼. ~**-runner** 会跑泥地的马. ~ **sill**（房子的）底基，下槛；〔美南部〕出身低微的人. ~ **skipper**【鱼】弹涂鱼；大弹涂鱼；飞鲨. ~ **slinger**〔美俚〕毁谤者，中伤者，骂人者. ~ **slinging**（政界的）诬蔑，毁谤. ~ **snake**【动】蓝黑泥蛇. ~**stone**【地】泥岩. ~ **turtle**【动】香龟属动物. ~ **volcano**【地】泥火山. ~ **wort** 水芒草属.

mu·dar [mə'dɑː] *n.*【植】（缅甸、印度的）牛角瓜（树）.

mud·der ['mʌdə] *n.*〔美俚〕在泥地上跑得最快的马；善于在泥湿场地上比赛的运动员.

mud·di·ly ['mʌdili] *ad.* 沾满污泥地，浑身是泥，肮脏；污浊；糊涂地.

mud·di·ness ['mʌdinis] *n.* 泥污；泥泞；溷浊；（头脑的）混乱.

mud·dle ['mʌdl] *vt.* ①〔罕〕使多淤泥；使（颜色）混浊. ②使混乱，使慌张；（酒）使（脑子）糊涂. ③混，混淆 *(up; together)*；搅拌. ④弄糟. ⑤糊里糊涂地打发；浪费 *(away)*. — *vi.* ①〔古〕弄得尽是泥. ②瞎搞，胡搞；胡乱对付，鬼混. ③（喝得）糊里糊涂. ~ *a plan* 将计划弄糟. ~ ***about*** 漂游浪荡；瞎搞工作. ~ ***on [along]*** 敷衍过去，胡乱混过去，得过且过；混日子. ~ ***through***（屡次失败后）好容易达到目的. — *n.*〔a ~〕混乱，杂乱；（头脑的）糊涂，昏迷. ***in a*** ~ 杂乱无章，一塌糊涂；糊糊涂涂. ***make a ~ of*** 弄糟. ~**-headed** *a.* 昏头昏脑的；愚蠢的，笨拙的. ~**-head·ed·ness** 糊涂.

mud·dler ['mʌdlə] *n.* ①搅拌饮料的棍子. ②想法〔作法〕糊涂的人.

mud·dy ['mʌdi] *a.* ***(-di·er; -di·est)*** ①泥多的，泥泞的；尽是泥的；脏的；泥色的. ②不透明的，混浊的；模糊的（光、色、声等）. ③〔罕〕不纯粹的；下流的. ④混乱的；糊涂不清的，暧昧的. *a ~ plow*〔美俚〕丑妇. ~ *water*〔美俚〕法国啤酒. — *vt., vi.*（使）给泥弄脏，搅混，弄浊；使头脑混乱［糊涂］. ~ *a candidate's name* 损毁候选人的名声. *The first blow muddied his head.* 头一击就把他打糊涂了. ~ **lark** 街头流浪汉.

mu·dir [mu'diə] *n.*（埃及的）省长；（土耳其的）村长.

Muen·ster ['mʌnstə, 'mun-] *n.* 明斯特干酪〔一种半软、淡黄、味淡的干酪〕.

mu·ez·zin [mu(ː)'ezin] *n.*（伊斯兰教寺院的）祷告时间报告人.

muff[1] [mʌf] *n.* 皮手笼；手筒〔女人插手防寒用〕；【机】保温套，衬套；套筒.

muff[2] [mʌf] *n.* ①笨人，笨蛋；拙劣，笨拙；【球戏】接球失误；〔美俚〕失败，错误. ②〔美俚〕少女；女人. ③〔美俚〕下巴胡子. ④〔英〕白喉雀. ***make a ~ of the business*** 把事情弄糟. ***make a ~ of oneself*** 出丑，自讨人笑. — *vt., vi.*（使）失败，（使）做出笨事，弄糟；错过（机会）；【球戏】漏接（球）.

muf·fe·tee [ˌmʌfi'tiː] *n.*〔英〕（女人用的）绒线腕套.

muf·fin ['mʌfin] *n.* ①松饼，小松糕. ②（陶土制的）小盘子. ③追逐年轻女人的男子. ~**-bell**〔英〕卖松饼小贩摇的铃. ~**-cap**〔英〕（慈善学校男生戴的）松饼形状的呢帽. ~**man**〔英〕卖松饼的小贩. ~**-worry** 茶话会.

muf·fin·eer [ˌmʌfi'niə] *n.*（有盖的）松饼盘；（吃松饼时撒盐和糖用的）调味瓶子.

muf·fle[1] ['mʌfl] *vt.* ①覆；裹住；用围巾围住 *(up)*. ②蒙住（人的）头［眼睛］（不许声张）. ③捂住（铃等）断绝声音. ④〔通常被动〕灭（音），压抑，使钝. — *vi.*〔罕〕咕哝. ~ *oneself (up) well* 把自己裹得紧紧的. *a ~d voice*（嘴被蒙住时的）闷塞的声音. *~d curses*（嘴被蒙住时的）闷声瓮气的骂人话. — *n.* ①拳击用手套；疯子用皮手套〔防止撕衣用〕；围巾；头巾. ②【机】消声罩［套］，减音器；【化】蒙烰；隔焰甑，闭（式烤）炉. ~ **kiln** 隔焰窑，蒙烰窑.

muf·fle[2] ['mʌfl] *n.*（反刍动物等的）上唇露肉部分和鼻子.

muf·fler ['mʌflə] *n.* ①围巾；头巾. ②（无指）厚手套；拳击用手套. ③消声器，减音器.

muf·ti ['mʌfti] *n.* 伊斯兰教法典说明官；（平时穿着制服者所穿的）便衣，便服. ***in*** ~ 穿着便衣.

mug[1] [mʌg] *n.* ①（有柄）大杯；一大杯；〔美运〕优胜杯. ②〔俚、卑〕脸，嘴，皱着眉头的脸. ③〔俚〕笨蛋；傻瓜；生手. ④暴徒；流氓阿飞. — *vt.*〔美俚〕向…装怪脸；给…拍照；对…行凶抢劫（尤指从背后袭击）. *a ~ of murk*〔美俚〕一杯咖啡. *a ~ chaser [hunter]*〔美运〕想得到优胜杯的人. *make a ~* 皱眉头；装怪脸. ~ **shot**【摄】特写镜头；面部照片；（警局存查的）嫌疑犯照片.

mug[2] [mʌg] *n.* ①〔英俚〕用功的人；自充有学问的人；考试. ②〔美俚〕下巴；接吻，亲嘴；（尤指警局存查的）照片. — *vi.* ①〔英俚〕用功 *(at)*. — *vt.* 攻读 *(up)*. ②〔美警察俚〕拍照；亲嘴.

mugg [mʌg] *n.*〔美俚〕没能耐的拳击家；无赖，恶棍.

mug·ger, mug·gar, mug·ur ['mʌgə] *n.* ①【动】（印度）阔鼻鳄鱼，泽鳄. ②装怪脸者. ③行凶抢劫的路贼. ④人像摄影家.

mug·ging ['mʌgiŋ] *n.*〔美剧〕哑剧，默剧.

mug·gins ['mʌginz] *n.* ①蠢人，笨蛋. ②一种骨牌戏；一种纸牌配套游戏. ***talk ~s*** 讲傻话.

mug·gy ['mʌgi] *a.* ***(-gi·er; -gi·est)*** 闷热的，潮湿的；〔美〕喝醉了的. **-gi·ness** *n.*

mu·ghal, mu·ghul ['muːgəl] *n., a.* (= mogul).

mug·man ['mʌgmən] *n.*〔美俚〕照相师.

mug·wort ['mʌgwəːt] *n.*【植】艾蒿.

mug·wump ['mʌgwʌmp] *n.*〔美〕①〔谑〕大人物，大老板，头子. ②1884年大选时脱离共和党的人；标榜独立行动的选举人，独立分子，超然派.

Mu·ham·mad·an [mu'hæmədən] *a., n.* = Mohammedan.

Mu·har·ram [mu'hærəm] *n.* = Moharram.

Muir [mjuə] *n.* 缪尔〔姓氏〕.

mu·jik [muː'ʒik] *n.* = moujik.

muk·lek, muk·luk ['mʌklʌk] *n.*（爱斯基摩人穿的）海豹皮靴.

mu·lat·to [mju(ː)'lætəu] *n.* ***(pl. ~es)*** 黑白混血儿；黑白混血种的后裔. — *a.* 黑白混血儿的；黄褐色的.

mul·berry ['mʌlbəri] *n.* ①【植】桑，桑属；桑葚. ②深紫红色. ③〔M-〕【军】（D Day 数小时内建造成的）装配式补助港〔原为暗号名〕. *paper ~* 楮，构. ~ **bush**（孩子们一面唱着 *Here we go round the ~ bush* 一面玩的）桑木林游戏.

mulch [mʌltʃ] *n.*【林】林地覆盖物；护根物；地面覆盖料. — *vt.* 覆盖树根［地面］. ~**-cover** 落叶层.

mulct [mʌlkt] *n.* 罚金；惩罚. — *vt.* 处以罚金；（用计）骗取（钱财）. ~ *sb. (in) £10* 骗去某人十英镑.

mule[1] [mjuːl] *n.* ①骡子，马骡. ②执拗的人，顽固的人. ③【纺】走锭精纺机. ④杂种. ⑤小型电动机车；轻便牵引机. ⑥〔美俚〕（玉米）威士忌酒，酒. ⑦〔美俚〕（学生用的）注解书. ⑧〔美俚〕运毒者. ~ **deer**【动】大耳黑尾鹿. ~**-driver** 赶骡人. ~ **skinner**〔美〕赶骡人.

mule[2] [mjuːl] *n.* 脚跟周围无帮的女（拖）鞋；无后跟的拖鞋.

mule[3] [mjuːl] *n.* 冻疮.

mule[4] [mjuːl] *v., n.* = mewl.

mu·le·ta [muː'leitə, -'letə] *n.* 斗牛士用的红布.

mu·le·teer [ˌmjuːli'tiə] *n.* 赶骡子的.

mul·ey, mulley ['mju(ː)li] *n.* 无角母牛；牝牛，乳牛. — *a.* 无角的；截角的. ~ **saw** 直锯〔锯木厂用锯的一种〕.

mu·li·eb·ri·ty [ˌmjuːli'ebriti] *n.* 女性；女人性格，温柔；女子的身分［地位］.

mul·ish ['mjuːliʃ] *a.* 骡子似的；执拗的，顽固的；杂种的. **-ly** *ad.* **-ness** *n.*

mull[1] [mʌl] *n.*【纺】细软薄棉布；人造丝薄绸.

mull² [mʌl] *n.* 〔英口〕失败,混乱,乱七八糟. ***make a ~ of*** 弄糟,弄坏. — *vt.* ①〔英口〕弄糟,弄乱,弄坏;粉碎,磨碎. ②〔美口〕仔细考虑〔讨论〕. — *vi.* 〔美口〕深思熟虑 *(over)*.
mull³ [mʌl] *vt.* 〔主用被动语态〕(加糖、香料等)烫热(酒等). *~ed ale* 香甜的热酒.
mull⁴ [mʌl] *n.* 〔Scot.〕鼻烟壶.
mull⁵ [mʌl] *n.* 〔方〕母牛.
mul·lah [ˈmʌlə] *n.* 师, 先生, 毛拉〔伊斯兰教徒间对高僧、学者的敬称〕;伊斯兰教的法律学家.
mull·ark·ey [mʌlˈɑːki] *n.* 〔美俚〕①奉承, 拍马屁. ②不恳切的话;无聊话;胡话,梦话.
mull·ein, mul·len [ˈmʌlin] *n.*【植】毛蕊花属. ~ **pink**【植】毛缕.
Mul·ler [ˈmʌlə] *n.* ①马勒〔姓氏〕. ②**H. J.** ~ 马勒〔1890—1967,美国遗传学家〕.
Mül·ler [G. ˈmylə], **P.** 穆勒〔1899—1965, 瑞士化学家〕.
mull·er¹ [ˈmʌlə] *n.* 研磨器,粉碎机;研杵;搅棒.
mull·er² [ˈmʌlə] *n.* 烫酒的人;烫酒器.
mul·let¹ [ˈmʌlit] *n.* *(pl. ~s,* 〔集合词〕 *~)*【鱼】鲻;鲱鲤科鱼.
mul·let² [ˈmʌlit] *n.*【徽】(中有圆孔的)星形.
mul·ley [ˈmu(ː)li] = muley.
mul·li·gan [ˈmʌligən] *n.* 〔美俚〕蔬菜烩肉.
mul·li·ga·taw·ny [ˌmʌligəˈtɔːni] *n.* (印度的) 咖哩肉汤 (= ~ soup).
mul·li·grubs [ˈmʌligrʌbz] *n.* 〔*pl.*〕〔作单数用〕〔口〕①肚子痛. ②消沉,忧郁.
mul·lion [ˈmʌliən] *n.*【建】(窗门的)直棂, 竖框. **-ed** [-d] *a.* 有直棂的.
mul·lock [ˈmʌlək] *n.* ①〔方〕废料, 垃圾. ②〔澳、方〕金矿废石. ③混乱的状态,一团糟.
mult-, mul·ti- [mʌlt-,ˈmʌlti] *comb. f.* 多,多倍: *multipartite.*
mul·tan·gu·lar [mʌlˈtæŋgjulə] *a.* 多角的.
mul·ti·ac·cess [ˌmʌltiˈækses] *a.*【自】同路存取的.
mul·ti·an·gu·lar [ˌmʌltiˈæŋgjulə] *a.* = multangular.
mul·ti-arch [ˈmʌltiˈɑːtʃ] *a.* 连拱的. *a ~ dam* 连拱坝.
mul·ti·bar·rel [ˌmʌltiˈbærəl] *a.* 多管(式)的. *a ~ rocket* 多管火箭.
mul·ti·buck·et [ˌmʌltiˈbʌkit] *a.* 多斗(式)的. *a ~ trench digger* 多斗式挖沟机.
mul·ti·cel·lu·lar [ˌmʌltiˈseljulə] *a.*【生】多细胞的;多室的.
mul·ti·chan·nel [ˌmʌltiˈtʃænl] *a.*【讯】多通道的, 多路的,多波道的,多频道的.
mul·ti·col·o(u)red [ˌmʌltiˈkʌləd] *a.* 多色的.
mul·ti·di·men·sion·al [ˌmʌltidiˈmenʃənl] *a.* 多面的;【数】多维的.
mul·ti·dis·ci·pli·nar·y [ˌmʌltiˈdisiplinəri] *a.* 多种不同学科的综合训练方式的.
mul·ti·fa·ri·ous [ˈmʌltiˈfɛəriəs] *a.* 形形色色的, 千差万别的,五花八门的. **-ly** *ad.* **-ness** *n.*
mul·ti·fid [ˈmʌltifid] *a.*【生】多裂的. *a ~ leaf*【植】多裂叶.
mul·ti·fil·a·ment [ˌmʌltiˈfiləmənt], **mul·ti·fil** [ˈmʌltifil] *n.*【纺】复丝;多纤(维)丝.
mul·ti·flo·ra rose [ˌmʌltiˈflɔːrə] *n.* 蔷薇 *(Rosa multiflora).*
mul·ti·flo·rous [ˌmʌltiˈflɔːrəs] *a.*【植】多花的.
mul·ti·foil [ˈmʌltifɔil] *n.*【建】繁叶饰,多叶饰.
mul·ti·fold [ˈmʌltiˌfəuld] *a.* ①双倍的或成几倍的. ②许多的; 种种的, 多样的; 多方面的, 五花八门的 (= manifold). — *n.* 复写体,拷贝.
mul·ti·form [ˈmʌltifɔːm] *a.* 多种形式的,多样的.
mul·ti·formi·ty [ˌmʌltiˈfɔːmiti] *n.* 多形性, 多样性 *(opp.* uniformity).
Mul·ti·graph [ˈmʌltigrɑːf] *n.*【商标】轮转印刷机. — *vt., vi.* 〔m-〕用轮转油印机印刷.
mul·ti·head·ed [ˌmʌltiˈhedid] *a.* (核武器)多弹头的.
mul·ti-in·dus·try [ˈmʌltiˈindʌstri] *n.* 多种经营的工业.
mul·ti·lat·er·al [ˌmʌltiˈlætərəl] *a.* 多边的. *a ~ treaty* 多边条约. **-ism** *n.*, **-ly** *ad.*
mul·ti·line pro·duc·tion [ˈmʌltilain prəˈdʌkʃən] (飞机的)分类生产法〔一厂生产一种零件的方法〕.
mul·ti·lin·e·al [ˌmʌltiˈliniəl] *a.* 多线的.
mul·ti·lin·gual [ˌmʌltiˈliŋgwəl] *a.* 多种语言〔文字〕的;懂多种语言〔文字〕的. — *n.* 懂多种语言〔文字〕的人.
mul·til·o·quent [mʌlˈtiləkwənt], **mul·til·o·quous** [-kwəs] *a.* 多嘴的,嘴碎的,爱说话的. **-quence** *n.*
mul·ti·me·di·a [ˌmʌltiˈmiːdjə] *n.* ①混合舞台效果. ②【绘画】混合画法 (= mixed media). — *a.* 使用多种媒介〔手段〕的.
mul·ti·mil·lion [ˌmʌltiˈmiljən] *n.* 〔常 *pl.*〕 数百万.
mul·ti·mil·lion·aire [ˈmʌltiˌmiljəˈnɛə] *n.* 亿万富翁, 大富豪.
mul·ti·na·tion·al [ˈmʌltinæʃənl] *a.* 多民族〔国家〕的;多国公司的;跨国公司的.
mul·ti·no·mi·al [ˌmʌltiˈnəumiəl] *a.*【数】多项的. — *n.* 多项式.
mul·ti·nu·cle·ate [ˌmʌltiˈnjuːkliit, -eit; -ˈnuː-] *a.*【生】多核的 (= multinucleated, multinuclear).
mul·ti·pack [ˌmʌltiˈpæk] *n.* (当作一件商品出售的)多件头商品小包.
mul·tip·a·ra [mʌlˈtipərə] *n.* 经产妇, 再产妇, 非初产妇.
mul·tip·a·rous [mʌlˈtipərəs] *a.* ①一产多胎的. ②经产的. ③【植】多出状的.
mul·ti·par·tism [ˌmʌltiˈpɑːtizəm] *n.* 多党制.
mul·ti·par·tite [ˌmʌltiˈpɑːtait] *a.* 多歧的; 分为多部的;多方的,多国参加的.
mul·ti·par·ty [ˌmʌltiˈpɑːti] *a.* 多党的.
mul·ti·ped, mul·ti·pede [ˈmʌltiped, -piːd] *a., n.* 多足的,多足虫〔动物〕.
mul·ti·phase [ˈmʌltifeiz] *a.* 多方面的;【电】多相的.
mul·ti·plane [ˈmʌltiplein] *a., n.* 多翼的;多翼飞机. *a ~ camera* 动画摄影机.
mul·ti·ple [ˈmʌltipl] *a.* ①多重的; 复合的, 复式的, 多数的,多样的. ②倍数的, 倍. ③【电】并联的; 多路的, 复接的. ④【植】聚花的. *a man of ~ interests* 兴趣广博的人. — *n.* ①【数】倍数. ②【电】并联; 多路系统. ③相联成组. ④成批生产的艺术品〔画、雕塑、工艺品等〕. *common ~* 公倍数. *least common ~* 最小公倍数. ~ **antenna**【无】复合天线. ~ **bank**【无】复接排. **~-choice** *a.* 可以从几个答案中选出正确答案的. ~ **cropping**【农】复种. ~ **earth**【无】多重接地. ~ **factors**【生】多对因子; 多基因. ~ **fruit**【植】复果, 聚花果. ~ **modalation**【无】复调制. **~-nozzle** *a.* 多喷嘴的. **~-party** *a.* 多党的. ~ **sclerosis**【医】多发性硬化. ~ **shop**〔Eng.〕联号 (=〔美〕chain store). ~ **star**【天】聚星. ~ **telegrams** (同时发给各方的)同文电报,通电. ~ **valve**【无】复真空管;【电】复联,并联;多路系统. ~ **voting** 重复投票.
mul·ti·plet [ˈmʌltiplet] *n.*【物】多重(谱)线.
mul·ti·plex [ˈmʌltipleks] *a.* 多部的,复合的,多样的,多重的;【电讯】多路传输的; 多路复用的;【植】多襞的. ~ **telegraphy** 多路通报〔电报〕. ~ **telephony** 多路电话. — *vt., vi.* 多路传输,多路复用.
mul·ti·pli·a·ble, mul·ti·pli·ca·ble [ˈmʌltiplaiəbl, -plikəbl] *a.* 可增加的,可增殖的;可倍增的;可乘的.
mul·ti·pli·cand [ˌmʌltipliˈkænd] *n.*【数】被乘数.
mul·ti·pli·cate [ˈmʌltipliˌkeit] *a.* 〔现罕〕多的, 多重的,多倍的.

mul·ti·pli·ca·tion [ˌmʌltipliˈkeiʃən] *n.* 增加,增殖;倍增;【数】乘法;乘法运算. ~ **factor [constant]**【物】放大系数;倍增常数;核燃料再生常数. ~ **table** 九九表.

mul·ti·plic·a·tive [ˌmʌltiˈplikətiv] *a., n.* 趋于增加的,倍增的,增殖的;乘法的;【语法】倍数词〔double, triple 之类〕.

mul·ti·pli·ca·tor [ˈmʌltiplikeitə] *n.* 【数】乘数;【电】放大器,倍增器.

mul·ti·plic·i·ty [ˌmʌltiˈplisiti] *n.* 多,多样,重复;多样性,重复度,多重性;复杂. ***a [the]*** ~ ***of*** 多重,许许多多.

mul·ti·pli·er [ˈmʌltiplaiə] *n.* ①增加者,增殖者,繁殖者. ②【数】乘数;【电】倍增器,扩程器,增效器,倍率器. ③【经】收益增殖率.

mul·ti·ply[1] [ˈmʌltiplai] *vt., vi.* 增殖;繁殖;(成倍)增加;【数】乘. ~ *5 by 3* 以三乘五. ~**ing gear**【机】增速齿轮;增速装置 *(opp.* reduction gear*)*. ~**-ing glass** 扩大镜,放大镜.

mul·ti·ply[2] [ˈmʌltipli] *ad.* 复合地;多样地;多倍地;多重地;复杂地;【电】并联地,多路地.

mul·ti-ply [ˈmʌltiplai] *a.* 多股的;多层的.

mul·ti·po·lar [ˌmʌltiˈpəulə] *a., n.* 多极的;【电】多极电磁机.

mul·ti·pole [ˈmʌltipəul] *a., n.* 【物】多极(的),复极(的).

mul·ti·pol·y·mer [ˌmʌltiˈpɔlimə] *n.* 【化】共聚物.

mul·ti-pur·pose [ˈmʌltiˈpəːpəs] *a.* 多能的,多效应的;多用的;多方面的.

mul·ti·ra·cial [ˈmʌltiˈreiʃəl] *a.* 多种族的.

mul·ti·ro·ta·tion [ˌmʌltirəuˈteiʃən] *n.* 【物】变异旋光.

mul·ti·seat·er [ˈmʌltiˌsiːtə] *n.* 【空】多座机.

mul·ti·shift [ˈmʌltiʃift] *a.* 多班制的,轮班制的.

mul·ti·stage [ˈmʌltisteidʒ] *a.* ①多级(式)的. ②分阶段进行的. *a* ~ *missile* 多级导弹. *a* ~ *rocket* 多级火箭.

mul·ti·state [ˈmʌltisteit] *a.* 〔美〕在许多州都有分公司的.

mul·ti·sto·r(e)y [ˈmʌltistɔːri] *a.* (楼)有多层的. *a* ~ *building* 多层大楼.

mul·ti·tude [ˈmʌltitjuːd] *n.* ①多,许多,大量. ②大群人,群众. ③【物】集;组. *as the stars in* ~ 多得象星星一样. *a* ~ *of* 许多. *the* ~ 民众,群众,大众. *Fair skin covers the* ~ *of sin.* 金玉其外,败絮其中.

mul·ti·tu·di·nism [ˌmʌltiˈtjuːdinizəm] *n.* 利多主义 *(opp.* individualism*)*.

mul·ti·tu·di·nous [ˌmʌltiˈtjuːdinəs] *a.* 许多的;大群的,人多的;由许多部分形成的. **-ly** *ad.* **-ness** *n.*

mul·ti·va·lent [ˌmʌltiˈveilənt] *a.* 【化】多价的;多义的. **-lence** *n.*

mul·ti·ver·si·ty [ˌmʌltiˈvəːsiti] *n.* *(pl.* **-ties***)* 大型综合性大学〔有很多学院,系科和附设单位〕.

mul·ti·vi·bra·tor [ˈmʌltivaiˈbreitə] *n.* 【无】多谐振荡器.

mul·tiv·o·cal [mʌlˈtivəkəl] *a.* 多义的;暧昧的,含糊的;喧嚣的. — *n.* 多义语.

mul·ti·vol·tine [mʌlˈtivəltin] *a.* 【虫】多化的.

mul·toc·u·lar [mʌlˈtɔkjulə] *a.* 多眼的;(昆虫)复眼的.

mul·tum in par·vo [ˈmʌltəm in ˈpɑːvəu] 〔L.〕小型而内容丰富;小中见大;大寓于小.

mul·ture [ˈmʌltʃə] *n.* 给水力磨坊的报酬〔麦子或面粉的一部分〕;磨谷费.

mum[1] [mʌm] *a.* 无言的,沉默的,不说话的. — *n.* 〔口〕沉默. *as* ~ *as a mouse [an oyster]* 一点也不开口. *keep* ~ *(about it)* (严守秘密)决不开口. *Mum's the word!* 别响! 别声张! — *int.* 别说了! 别响! — *vi.* 闭口,不讲话;演哑剧.

mum[2] [mʌm] *n.* ①〔口〕= madam. ②〔英儿〕妈.

mum[3] [mʌm] *n.* (德国)烈性啤酒.

mum[4] [mʌm] *n.* 〔美俚〕菊花〔chrysanthemum 的略语〕.

mum·ble [ˈmʌmbl] *vi., vt.* (在嘴里)咕噜咕噜地说;闭着嘴用牙根嚼. — *n.* 咕噜,嗫嚅,含糊的话. **-bling-ly** *ad.*

mum·bler [ˈmʌmblə] *n.* 说话含糊不清的人,咕咕哝哝的人.

mum·ble·ty·peg [ˈmʌmbltiˌpeg] *n.* 抛刀游戏〔上抛刀子使之插入地上,(原先)输者须用牙叨出插进地里的木钉〕.

Mum·bo-Jum·bo [ˈmʌmbəuˈdʒʌmbəu] *n.* ①摩包君婆〔西非洲黑人崇拜的守护神〕. ②〔m- j-〕迷信的崇拜物;令人畏惧的东西;迷惑人的做法;莫名其妙的话.

mu-meson [ˈmjuːˌmizɔn] *n.* 【原】μ 介子.

Mum·ford [ˈmʌmfəd] *n.* 芒福德〔姓氏〕.

mum·mer [ˈmʌmə] *n.* (滑稽)哑剧演员;〔蔑〕戏子;爱打扮的人.

mum·mer·y [ˈmʌməri] *n.* 哑剧;假面舞;〔蔑〕虚礼;做作的表演.

mum·mied [ˈmʌmid] *a.* 变成了木乃伊的.

mum·mi·fy [ˈmʌmifai] *vt., vi.* 使成[变成]木乃伊;弄干保存;(使)干瘪;(使)皱缩. **-fi·ca·tion**[ˌmʌmifiˈkeiʃən] *n.* 僵化(现象).

mum·my[1] [ˈmʌmi] *n.* ①木乃伊;(普通)干尸;木乃伊似的人;干瘪的人. ②木乃伊粉(刀伤药). ③【化】(沥青中取出的)褐色颜料;普鲁士红;褐色氧化铁粉. ***beat to a*** ~ 打得半死[稀烂]. ~ **bag** 轻便睡袋. ~ **case** 木乃伊箱. ~ **cloth** 包木乃伊的麻布;〔美〕(棉[丝]毛混纺的)马米布[绉]. ~ **wheat** (由木乃伊箱中所得古代麦粒繁殖成的)埃及小麦.

mum·my[2] [ˈmʌmi] *n.* 〔英、儿〕妈妈.

mump [mʌmp] *vi., vt.* 〔主方〕①闹彆扭;(使)郁郁不乐;装正经. ②(哭诉着)行乞,讨钱;骗. ③咕哝. **-ish** *a.* **-er** *n.* **-ing** *a.*

mumps [mʌmps] *n. pl.* ①〔作单数用〕【医】流行性腮腺炎. ②闹彆扭;愠怒;不开心. *have the* ~ 郁郁不乐.

munch [mʌntʃ] *vi., vi.* 用力[大声]地咀嚼;贪馋地咀嚼.

Mun·chau·sen [mʌnˈtʃɔːzn, -ˈtʃauzn] *n.* 吹牛(的人)〔原为德国 *Rudolph Raspe* 所著冒险故事中的主人公〕. — *a.* (故事)虚夸的.

Mün·chen [G. ˈmynçən] *n.* 明兴〔即 Munich 慕尼黑〕〔德意志联邦共和国城市〕.

Mun·da [ˈmundə] *a.* (奥亚语系)蒙达语的.

mun·dane [ˈmʌndein] *a.* ①世俗的,现世的,尘世间的〔*cf.* spiritual, heavenly〕;庸俗的. ②宇宙的. ~ *affairs* 俗事. *the* ~ *era* 世界的纪元. **-ly** *ad.*

mun·dun·gus [mʌnˈdʌŋgəs] *n.* 〔古〕孟顿古斯烟草〔一种气味恶劣的暗黑色烟草〕.

mung·bean [ˈmɔŋˈbiːn] *n.* 绿豆.

mun·go [ˈmʌŋgəu] *n.* (用旧呢绒做成的)硬再生毛;短弹毛.

mun·goos(e) [mʌŋˈguːs] *n.* = mongoose.

Mu·nich [ˈmjuːnik] *n.* ①慕尼黑〔德意志联邦共和国城市〕. ②= ~ Accord. ③可耻的绥靖事件. ~ **Accord [Agreement, Pact]** 慕尼黑协定〔1938 年英法出卖捷克而和德意签订的协定〕.

mu·nic·i·pal [mju(ː)ˈnisipəl] *a.* ①市的,都市的;市营的;市制的. ②内政的〔仅用于 ~ law 国内法〕. — *n.* 〔*pl.*〕地方债. *a* ~ *council* 市议会. *a* ~ *office* 市政府(办公楼). ~ *government* 市政,市政府. ~ *undertakings* 市营企业. **-ism** *n.* 市自治主义. **-ist** *n.* 市自治主义者;市政当局;市政通. **-ity** [mjuːˌnisiˈpæliti] *n.* 自治市,自治区;市政府;市政当局.

mu·nic·i·pal·ize [mju(ː)ˈnisipəlaiz] *vt.* 把…归市有〔作市营〕. **-i·za·tion** [mjuːˌnisipəlaiˈzeiʃən] *n.*

mu·nic·i·pal·ly [mju(:)ˈnisipəli] *ad.* 市政上；市营地. *be ~ managed* 市营的.
mu·nif·i·cent [mju(:)ˈnifisnt] *a.* 慷慨给予的，毫不吝惜的；宽厚的，宽大的. **-cence** *n.*, **-cently** *ad.*
mu·ni·ment [ˈmju:nimənt] *n.* ①【法】〔*pl.*〕契据，证券，文件. ②防御〔保护〕手段.
mu·ni·tion [mju(:)ˈniʃən] *n.*〔除作定语外用复数〕军需品，军用品(尤指枪、炮、弹药)；军火；(紧急时的)必需品，资金. *~s of war* 军需品. *a ~ plant* 军需工厂. — *vt.* 供给…军需品. **-er** *n.* 军火制造人.
mun·nion, mul·lion [ˈmʌnjən, ˈmʌljən] *n.*〔古〕【建】直棂.
Mun O = Munition Officer〔美〕军械官，弹药补给主任.
Mün·ster [ˈminstə] *n.* 明斯特〔德意志联邦共和国城市〕.
munt·jac, munt·jak [ˈmʌntdʒæk] *n.*【动】鹿属 *(Muntiacus)* 动物.
Muntz met·al [ˈmʌnts ˈmetl] *n.* (锌与铜合成的)孟次黄铜，熟铜.
mu·on [ˈmju:ɔn] *n.*【原】= mu-meson.
mu·ral [ˈmjuərəl] *a.* 墙壁(上)的；墙壁似的，险峭的. — *n.* 墙壁；壁画；〔美〕壁饰. *a ~ painting* 壁画. *~* **circle**【天】墙仪. *~* **crown** 壁形金冠〔古罗马奖给先登上敌垒的人〕. **-ist** *n.* 壁画家；壁饰家.
Mur·cott [ˈmə:kɔt] *n.* 默科特柑桔〔美国柑桔培育家 *Charles Murcott* (默科特)培育的一种柑桔，果肉深黄，易剥皮，易分瓣，据认为是一杂交品种〕(= Murcot orange).
mur·der [ˈmə:də] *n.* ①凶杀，杀害；屠杀；【法】谋杀；谋杀案〔罪〕. ②极艰险的事. *M- will out.* 杀了人〔恶事〕终必败露. *The ~ is out.* 真相大白. *~ in the first [second, third] degree* 谋〔故、误〕杀. *judicial ~* 合法但不公正的死刑判决. ***cry blue ~***〔俚〕大声嚷叫. ***cry '~'*** 喊'杀人啦'! — *vt.* ①杀害；凶杀；谋杀；屠杀. ②扼杀；糟踏；折磨；毁坏，弄坏. *~ a song by poor singing* 拙劣的唱腔糟踏了一只歌曲. — *vi.* 犯杀人罪.
mur·der·er [ˈmə:dərə] *n.* ***(fem. ~ess)*** 杀人犯，凶手.
mur·der·ous [ˈmə:dərəs] *a.* 杀人(用)的，行凶的；凶恶的，残忍的；厉害的，要人命的. *a ~ weapon* 凶器. *~ heat* 要命的炎热.
Mur·doch [ˈmə:dɔk] *n.* ①默多克〔男子名〕. ②〔苏方〕水手，海员〔苏格兰盖尔语〕.
mure [mjuə] *vt.* 用墙壁围绕；幽禁 *(up)*；= immure.
mur·ex [ˈmjuəreks] *n.* ***(pl. -rices*** [-risi:z], ***-es)***【贝】骨螺.
mu·ri·ate [ˈmjuəriit] *n.*〔罕〕【化】氯化物.
mu·ri·at·ic [ˌmjuəriˈætik] *a.*【化】氯化的. *~* **acid** (粗)盐酸.
mu·ri·cate [ˈmjuəriˌkeit] *a.* 由于芒刺而变粗糙的 (= muricated).
mu·rid [ˈmjuərid] *n.* ***(pl. Mu·ri·dae*** [ˈmjuridi]***)*** 鼠科动物〔包括老鼠和鼷鼠〕.
Mu·ri·el [ˈmjuəriəl] *n.* 缪丽尔〔女子名〕.
mu·rine [ˈmjuərain, -in] *a.* 鼠科〔包括鼠和鼷鼠〕的. — *n.* 鼠科动物.
murk [mə:k] *n.*, *a.*〔古、诗〕黑暗(的)，阴暗(的).
murk·y [ˈmə:ki] *a.* ***(murk·i·er; -i·est)*** 暗，阴暗的，(雾等)浓的；阴郁的；含糊的，暧昧的. **-i·ly** *ad* **-i·ness** *n.*
Mur·mansk [muəˈmɑ:nsk] *n.* 摩尔曼斯克〔苏联港市〕.
mur·mur [ˈmə:mə] *n.* ①(浪、树叶等的) 沙沙声，潺潺声，淙淙声；私语声，低语声. ②咕哝，嘟哝，牢骚，怨言. ③【医】(不正常的)心脏杂音. — *vi.* ①小声说，私语；沙沙地响. ②咕哝；发牢骚，诉怨 *(at; against)*. — *vt.* 低声说(秘密等). **-er** *n.*, **-ing·ly** *ad.*
mur·mur·ous [ˈmə:mərəs] *a.* 小声说的；沙沙响的；低声怨语的，嘟嘟喃喃的.
mur·phy [ˈmə:fi] *n.* ①〔俚〕马铃薯，土豆；〔美〕(不用时可以隐藏在墙壁里的)隐壁床，折床 (= M- bed). ②〔M-〕墨菲〔姓氏〕.
mur·rain [ˈmʌrin] *n.* ①炭疽热，鹅口疮，得克萨斯牛瘟(等)家畜传染病. ②〔古〕瘟疫. *A ~ on [to] you!* = *M- take you!*〔古〕该死的！你这遭瘟的！
Mur·ray [ˈmʌri] *n.* 默里〔姓氏〕.
murre [mə:] *n.* ***(pl. ~(s))*** 海鸠 *(Uria columba)*.
murre·let [ˈmə:lit] *n.*【动】海雀〔主要发现于北太平洋岛屿〕.
mur·rey [ˈmə:ri] *n.* 紫红色；桑葚色. — *a.* 紫红色的.
mur·rhine [ˈmʌrin, -rain] *a.* 亚宝石的，萤石的. *~* **glass** 仿古罗马亚宝石器皿；精致萤石器皿.
Mur·ry [ˈmʌri] *n.* 默里〔男子名〕.
mur·ther [ˈmə:ðə] *n.*, *v.*〔方〕= murder.
Mus. = ①museum. ②music; musical.
Mus.B., Mus.Bac. =〔L.〕*Musicae Baccalaureus* (Bachelor of Music) 音乐学士.
Mus·ca [ˈmʌskə] *n.*【天】苍蝇座；【动】蝇属.
mus·ca·del [ˌmʌskəˈdel] *n.* = muscatel.
mus·ca·dine [ˈmʌskədin] *n.* 麝香葡萄(酒).
mus·ca·rine [ˈmʌskərin] *n.*【化】蝇蕈碱，腐鱼毒.
Mus·cat [ˈmʌskət, ˈmʌskæt] *n.* 马斯喀特〔阿曼首都〕.
mus·cat [ˈmʌskət, -kæt] *n.* ①麝香葡萄. ②麝香葡萄酒 (= muscatel).
mus·ca·tel [ˌmʌskəˈtel] *n.* ①麝香葡萄酒. ②麝香葡萄 (= muscat, muscadel).
mus·cid [ˈmʌsid] *a.* 家蝇科 *(Muscidae)* 的〔包括家蝇〕. — *n.* 家蝇科昆虫.
mus·cle[1] [ˈmʌsl] *n.*【解】肌(肉)；体力，膂力，力气. *an involuntary ~* 不随意肌. *a voluntary ~* 随意肌. *a man of ~* 大力士. ***not move a ~*** 毫不动容，神色不变. — *vi.*〔美俚〕发挥膂力；用力挤着前进 *(through)*. *~* ***in*** 硬挤进；干涉，侵入；强夺. *~***-bound** *a.* (因运动过度而)肌肉僵硬的. *~***-flexing** 炫耀武力. *~***man** *n.*〔美俚〕摔角家；体格魁梧的演员；(被雇用的)打手，保镖. **racket**〔美俚〕职业摔角. *~* **sense**【医】肌肉觉. **-less** *a.* 无肌肉的；没力气的.
mus·cle[2] [ˈmʌsl] *n.* = mussel.
mus·col·o·gy [mʌsˈkɔlədʒi] *n.* 苔藓学.
mus·co·va·do, mus·co·va·to [ˌmʌskəˈvɑ:dəu, -təu] *n.* 混糖.
Mus·co·vite [ˈmʌskəvait] *n.*〔古〕莫斯科人；俄国人. — *a.*〔古〕莫斯科(人)的；俄国(人)的.
mus·co·vite [ˈmʌskəvait] *n.*【矿】白云母.
Mus·co·vy [ˈmʌskəvi] *n.*〔古〕俄国. *~* **duck** = musk-duck.
mus·cu·lar [ˈmʌskjulə] *a.* ①肌(肉)的. ②肌肉发达的，有膂力的，壮健的. *the ~ system* 肌肉系统. *~ motion [movement]* 肌肉运动. *a ~ strain* 肌肉过劳. *~ strength* 膂力，力气. *~* **dystrophy**【医】肌肉萎缩症. **-ly** *ad.*
mus·cu·lar·i·ty [ˌmʌskjuˈlæriti] *n.* 肌肉发达，强壮；膂力.
mus·cu·la·ture [ˈmʌskjulətʃə] *n.*【解】肌肉组织；肌序.
Mus. D. =〔L.〕*Musicae Doctor* (Doctor of Music) 音乐博士.
Muse [mju:z] *n.* ①【希神】文艺、美术、音乐等的女神；缪斯. ②〔M- 或 m-〕诗思，诗才；诗，诗歌；〔m-〕〔诗〕诗人. ***the ~s*** 司文艺、美术等的九女神；诗神；诗歌；文艺，美文学.
muse [mju:z] *vi.* ①沉思，默想 *(on; upon)*. ②呆看；细心周到地说. — *n.*〔古〕沉思，默想，冥想. *be lost in a ~* 一味冥想. *~ (up)on a distant scene* 呆看远处风景.
muse·ful [ˈmju:zfəl] *a.*〔古〕沉思的，默想的，冥想的.
mu·sette [mju(:)ˈzet] *n.* ①小风笛；风笛曲；风笛舞. ②【乐】(风琴的)簧管音栓. *~* **bag** (士兵的)野战背包.

mu·se·um [mju(:)ˈziəm] *n.* 博物馆;〔Am.〕美术馆. ～ **piece** *n.* 重要美术品;珍品;〔贬〕老古董〔指过时的人或物〕.

mush[1] [mʌʃ] *n.* ①软块;〔Am.〕玉米面粥. ②多愁善感;痴情;废话,胡话;〔美俚〕罗罗唆唆说情求爱. ③噪声,干扰. ***make a ～ of*** 〔口〕弄糟. ～ ***and molasses*** 〔美〕废话,糊涂话. — *vt.* 〔方〕使成软糊状. —*vi.* (飞机因控制器失灵)半失速飞行;升不高.

mush[2] [mʌʃ] *n., vi.* 〔美西北部〕坐狗拉的雪橇旅行.

mush[3] [mʌʃ] *n.* ①〔英俚〕伞;出租马车车主. ②〔俚〕嘴;脸.

mush[4] [mʌʃ] *vt.* 〔Scot.〕刻痕于.

mush·er [ˈmʌʃə] *n.* ①赶狗拉雪橇的人. ②〔英俚〕〔*pl.*〕阿拉斯加人.

mush·room [ˈmʌʃrum] *n.* ①(主指食用)蕈,蘑菇. ②暴发户. ③蘑菇状物;蘑菇状烟云;〔口〕(女用)蘑菇形草帽 (= ～ hat);〔俚〕伞. — *a.* 蘑菇形的;雨后蘑菇似的;蘑菇一般短命的. ～ *growth* 猛长. *a* ～ *millionaire* 暴发户. *a* ～ *town* 新兴城市. ～ *fame* 短暂的命运. — *vi.* ①迅速增长. ②采集蘑菇. ③子弹打扁成蘑菇形. ④〔美〕(火)猛然的扩大. *go* ～*ing* 去采蘑菇.

mush·y [ˈmʌʃi] *a.* 柔软的;软弱的,易掉眼泪的;感伤的. **-i·ness** *n.*

mu·sic [ˈmju:zik] *n.* ①音乐,乐曲;乐谱. ②佳调,乐音,妙音;音乐赏鉴力;(军)乐队,合唱队. ③【猎】狗叫声. ④〔美口〕激烈的辩论,吵闹;法律制裁,惩处. *vocal [instrumental]* ～ 声[器]乐. *play without* ～ 不用乐谱演奏. *He has no* ～ *in himself.* 他没有音乐鉴赏力. *rough* ～ (故意使人讨厌的)吵闹,喧嚣. ***face the*** ～ 临危不惧. ***jerk chin*** ～ 谈话. ***set*** *(a poem)* ***to*** ～ 为诗谱曲. ～ **book** 乐谱. ～ **box** 八音盒. ～ **case** 乐谱夹子. ～ **drama** 音乐戏剧〔尤指德国作曲家华格纳发展而成的具有主旋律的歌剧〕. ～ **hall** 〔美〕音乐厅;〔英〕杂耍剧场. ～ **paper** 五线谱纸. ～ **school** 音乐学校. ～ **stand** 乐谱架. ～ **stool** (奏)钢琴(用)凳(子).

mu·si·cal [ˈmju:zikəl] *a.* ①音乐的;配乐的. ②音乐似的;好听的. ③爱好音乐的;精通音乐的. *a* ～ *composer* 作曲家. *a* ～ *director* 音乐指挥. *a* ～ *evening* 音乐晚会. *a* ～ *instrument* 乐器. *a* ～ *performance* 演奏. ～ **chairs** 抢座位游戏〔游戏者在音乐伴奏下围着按人数计少一只的椅子转,音乐一停,就抢座位,每次淘汰一人并减少一张椅子〕. ～ **comedy** 音乐(喜)剧. ～ **drama** 音乐剧. ～ **glasses** (装入不同水量形成的一组)乐杯. ～ **play** 音乐剧. ～ **ride** (英国近卫骑兵队)有音乐伴奏的骑马舞. ～ **saw** (演奏用)钢锯. ～ **soirée** 音乐晚会. — *n.* 〔口〕①(社交性的)音乐会. ②【影】歌舞片. ③音乐(喜)剧 = ～ comedy.

mu·si·cale [ˌmju:ziˈkæl] *n.* 〔Am.〕(社交性的)音乐会,演奏会.

mu·si·cal·ly [ˈmju:zikəli] *ad.* 音乐上,象音乐;音调佳妙,和谐. **-cal·ness** *n.*

mu·si·cas·sette [ˈmju:zikəset] *n.* 卡式音乐录音带.

mu·si·ci·an [mju(:)ˈziʃən] *n.* 音乐家;乐师;作曲家. **-ly** *a.* 有音乐家才能的;音乐家似的.

mu·si·col·o·gy [ˌmju:ziˈkɔlədʒi] *n.* 音乐学,音乐研究. **-log·i·cal** *a.* **-gist** *n.*

mu·sique con·crète [mju:zi:k kəunˈkret] 具体音乐〔现代西欧资产阶级的一个乐派作为"抽象"乐派之对,该乐派将自然声响和噪音(如乐器声、雨声等)加以歪曲和改变,直接谱于磁带上〕.

mus·jid, mas·jid [ˈmʌsdʒid] *n.* 清真寺院,伊斯兰教寺院.

mus·ing [ˈmju:ziŋ] *n., a.* 沉思(的),冥想(的). **-ly** *ad.*

musk [mʌsk] *n.* 麝香;【动】麝;【植】香沟酸浆. ～ **cat** 麝香猫;〔废〕花花公子. ～ **deer**【动】麝. ～ **duck** (原产南美的)(澳洲)麝香鸭. ～ **mallow** 麝香锦葵;黄葵. ～ **melon**【植】香瓜,甜瓜. ～ **ox** (北极)麝牛. ～ **plant**【植】香沟酸浆. ～**rat**【动】麝鼠;〔*pl.*〕〔美俚〕*Delaware* 人. ～**root** 五福花(属). ～ **rose**【植】麝香蔷薇. ～ **tree**, ～ **wood** 麝香树.

mus·kal·longe = muskellunge.

mus·keg [ˈmʌskeg] *n.* 青苔沼泽地〔有厚层腐植质,上面长满青苔,尤指加拿大和阿拉斯加的青苔沼泽地〕.

mus·kel·lunge [ˈmʌskiˌlʌndʒ] *n.* ***(pl. -lunge)*** 北美大梭鱼 *(Esox masquinongy)* 〔发展于北美五大湖区和密西西比河上游,是有名的食用鱼〕(= muskie).

mus·ket [ˈmʌskit] *n.* 滑膛枪〔旧式步枪〕. ～ **shot** 步枪子弹;步枪射程.

mus·ke·teer [ˌmʌskiˈtiə] *n.* ①【史】滑膛枪装备的步兵. ②酒友.

mus·ke·toon [ˌmʌskiˈtu:n] *n.*【史】短枪.

mus·ket·ry [ˈmʌskitri] *n.* ①〔集合词〕滑膛枪,旧式步枪;步枪队. ②步枪火力. ③步枪操法[射击法].

Mus·kie [ˈmʌski] **Act** 美国 1970 年"防止大气污染法"的俗称.

musk·i·ness [ˈmʌskinis] *n.* 有麝香气.

Mus·ko·ge·an, Mus·kho·ge·an [mʌsˈkəugiən, -dʒi:] *a.* 摩斯科格语的〔美国东南部印第安语的一种〕.

Mus·ko·gee [mʌsˈkəugi:] *n.* ***(pl. -gees, -gee)*** ①克里克人. ②马斯科吉语 (= Creek).

musk·y [ˈmʌski] *a.* ***(musk·i·er; -i·est)*** 麝香的,有麝香气[质]的.

Mus·lem, Mus·lim [ˈmuzlim] ① *n., a.* = Moslem. ②〔美〕"黑色穆斯林"〔美国一黑人穆斯林组织〕.

mus·lin [ˈmʌzlin] *n.* ①平纹细布;〔美〕棉布. ②〔俚〕女性,妇女. *a bit of* ～ 〔英口〕妇女,少女.

mus·lin delaine [ˈmʌzlin dəˈlein] *n.* = mousseline-de-laine.

mus·quash [ˈmʌs-kwɔʃ] *n.*【动】麝香鼠;麝鼠皮.

muss [mʌs] *vt.* 〔美口〕使混乱,把…弄乱 *(up)*;弄脏,弄皱(衣服) *(up)*. — *n.* 混乱,杂乱;吵闹,骚乱.

mus·sel [ˈmʌsl] *n.*【贝】蛤贝,贻贝;蠔;壳菜,淡菜. ～ **plum** (深紫色的)李子.

mus·suck [ˈmʌsək] *n.* (印度的)皮水袋.

Mus·sul·man [ˈmʌslmən] *n.* ***(pl. ～s)*** 穆斯林. — *a.* 穆斯林的.

mus·sy [ˈmʌsi] *a.* ***(-si·er; -si·est)*** 〔美口〕杂乱的,混乱的;吵闹的;肮脏的.

must[1] 〔强 mʌst; 弱 məst〕〔词形无变化,三人称单数不加 s, 无不定式和分词等形式,后面接不带 to 的动词不定式〕*v. aux.* ①必须,要,应当〔否定用 need not (不必), must not (不可)〕. *I* ～ *work.* 我必须工作. *You* ～ *not do it.* 你不可以做那件事. *He* ～ *be told.* = *We* ～ *tell him.* 必须告诉他. ★过去、未来、完成等式用 have to 的相应形式代替,如: I ～ [have to] go today (tomorrow); I had to go yesterday; I shall have to go there some day. ②〔必然的推断〕一定;谅必,很可能〔否定用 cannot be, could not have + p. p.〕*He* ～ *be honest.* 他谅必是诚实的. *It cannot be true.* 那一定不可靠. *He* ～ *have arrived by this time.* 这时候他总该到了. ③〔主张〕一定要,坚持要. *He* ～ *always has his own way.* 他总是自行其是. ④〔表示不愿意发生或不耐烦〕偏要. *If you* ～, *you* ～. 你说自己一定要怎样,那也就只好怎样了. *Why* ～ *it rain on Sunday?* 偏要在星期天下雨,讨厌! *She said that she* ～ *see the manager.* 她说了她一定要见经理. ⑤〔过去的事,作为历史的现在叙述〕必须,只好. *It was too late now to retreat, he* ～ *make good his word.* 当时退缩已迟,他只好照他自己的话做了. ⑥〔过去或历史的现在〕不巧,偏偏. *Just as I was busiest, he* ～ *come bothering me.* 正在我最忙的时候,他偏要来打搅! ～ ***have been [done]*** ①〔必然〕*(She* ～ *have been a beauty in her day.* 她年轻时一定是个美人. *What a sight it* ～ *have been!* 一定很好看呢. *How you* ～ *have hated me!* 你一定把我恨死了. 〔间接叙述法〕*I said he*

~ *have lost his way*. 我说他一定是迷了路了). ②〔~ = should 或 would surely〕(*You ~ have caught the train if you had hurried*. 你要是快一点就一定赶上火车了). ③〔必须〕(*Applicants ~ have finished the middle school*. 报名者必须中学毕业). — [mʌst] *n.* 〔口〕必须做的事,不可不做的事;必需的东西. *This order is a ~*. 这个命令必须执行. — *a.* 〔口〕绝对需要的,不能缺少的. ~ *legislation* 不可缺少的立法. *a ~ item*. 重要项目. *a ~ book* 必读书. *a ~ subject* 必修科目.

must[2] [mʌst] *n.* (发酵前或发酵中的)葡萄汁;新葡萄酒.

must[3] [mʌst] *n.* (象等在交尾期中的)狂暴状态; 交尾期的象. — *a.* (特指象因性欲冲动而)狂暴的.

must[4] [mʌst] *n.* ①霉臭;霉. ②麝香.

mus·tache [məsˈtɑːʃ] *n.* = moustache.

mus·ta·chio [məsˈtɑːʃəu] *n.* *(pl. ~s)* = mustache.

mus·tang [ˈmʌstæŋ] *n.* (美国西南平原地带的)(半)野马;〔美俚〕海员出身的海军军官. 〔M-〕(美国)野马式战斗机. ~ **grape** 白亮葡萄.

mus·tard [ˈmʌstəd] *n.* 【植】芥;芥子,芥末; 芥末色,深黄色;〔美俚〕热性物品; 热情的人. *English [French] ~* 加水[加醋]芥末. ~ *and cress* 〔英〕拌生菜用小芥叶. ***a grain of ~ seed*** 一粒芥子;〔喻〕前途大有发展的微小事物. ***cut the ~ (be up to the ~)*** 〔美俚〕符合要求. ~ **gas** 芥子气〔一种糜烂性毒气〕. ~ **greens** 〔美〕芥菜叶. ~ **oil** 芥子油. ~ **plaster** 芥末软膏. ~ **pot**, ~ **poultice** 芥末瓶.

mus·tee [mʌsˈtiː, ˈmʌstiː] *n.* ①(有八分之一黑人血统的)黑白混血儿〔白种人与有四分之一黑人血统混血儿所生的人〕(= octoroon). ②混血儿.

mus·te·line [ˈmʌstiˌlain -lin] *a.* 鼬鼠科 *(Mustelidae)* 的〔包括伶鼬、貂、鸡貂、水貂等〕.

mus·ter [ˈmʌstə] *n.* ①(检阅点名时的)召集, 集合; 检阅,集合人员; 群集; 花名册; 清单. ②孔雀群. ③【商】样品. ***pass [cut the] ~*** 及格, 符合要求. — *vt.* 调,召集(兵员),集合,集中;拼凑,振奋,鼓起(勇气等). — *vi.* 集合. ~ ***in*** 〔美〕征召…入伍. ~ ***out*** 使退伍. ~ ***up*** 振起,鼓起. ~ **book**, ~ **roll** (军队,舰队的)名册. ~ **master** 检阅官.

musth [mʌst] = must[3].

must·n't [ˈmʌsnt] 〔口〕= must not.

must've 〔口〕= must have.

must·y [ˈmʌsti] *a.* *(-ti·er; -ti·est)* 发霉的, 霉臭的; 陈腐的;无气力的. **-ti·ly** *ad.* **-ti·ness** *n.*

mut [mʌt] *n.* = mutt.

mut. = mutual.

mu·ta·bil·i·ty [ˌmjuːtəˈbiliti] *n.* 可变性; 易变性. ~ *of human affairs* 人世沧桑.

mu·ta·ble [ˈmjuːtəbl] *a.* 可变的;易变的,不定的,无常的;没准性的,三心二意的. **-ness** *n.* **-bly** *ad.*

mu·ta·fa·cient [ˌmjuːtəˈfeiʃnt] *a.* 【生】突变加强的.

mu·ta·gen [ˈmjuːtədʒən] *n.* 【生】诱变因素. —*a.* **-gen·i·cal·ly** *ad.*

mu·ta·gen·e·sis [ˈmjutəˈdʒenisis] *n.* 突变.

mu·tant [ˈmjuːtənt] *a.* 【生】变异的;变异所引起的; 与突变[变种]有关的, 经过突变[变种]的. — *n.* 突变[变种]型生物;突变.

mu·tate [mjuːˈteit] *vt., vi.* (使)变异;【生】(使)突变.

mu·ta·tion [mju(ː)ˈteiʃən] *n.* ①变化,变异,更换;【生】突变;突变种;【语】元音变化;【乐】(提琴的)变换把位;变声;【法】让受. ②(人世的)浮沉,盛衰. ~ **plural** 元音变化构成的复数〔men < man, geese < goose 等〕.

mu·ta·tis mu·tan·dis [mjuːˈtɑːtis mjuːˈtændis] 〔L.〕已作必要的修正.

mu·ta·tive [ˈmjuːtətiv] *a.* 【生】突变[变种]的; 有突变[变种]趋势的;有突变[变种]特点的.

mutch·kin [ˈmʌtʃkn] *n.* 〔Scot.〕姆尺肯〔苏格兰液衡名,稍少于一品脱〕.

mute[1] [mjuːt] *a.* ①哑的; 缄默无言的; (一时)说不出话的;(猎狗)不叫的;(金属)不响的;【法】拒绝答辩的. ②【语】闭止音的〔b, p, d, t, k, g 等〕; 不发音的, 哑音的〔如 mute 中的 e〕. *a ~ appeal* 无言的恳求. *stand ~ of malice* 【法】对被控罪名拒不答辩. — *n.* ①哑子,哑吧,(尤指)又聋又哑的人; 沉默的人;【法】拒绝答辩的被告人. ②【语】闭止音;不发音的字母. ③雇用的送丧人;(没有台词讲的)无言演员. ④【乐】弱音器. — *vt.* 减弱…的声音;柔和…的色调. **-ly** *ad.* **-ness** *n.*

mute[2] [mjuːt] *vi., vt.* (鸟)拉屎,排泄. — *n.* 鸟粪.

mu·ti·cate [ˈmjuːtiˌkeit] *a.* ①【植】无芒刺的. ②【动】无(齿、爪等)防卫结构的 (= muticious).

mu·ti·late [ˈmjuːtileit] *vt.* 切断(手足等); 使断肢; 残害, 毁伤, 毁坏; (删去作品中的主要部分)使残缺不全. **-la·tion** *n.* (手足等的)切断; 毁伤. **-til·a·tor** *n.* 切断者,毁伤者.

mu·ti·neer [ˌmjuːtiˈniə] *n.* 暴动者,造反者,叛变者,反抗者;反抗长官者. — *vi.* 〔古〕暴动; 造反, 叛变,反抗; 反抗长官.

mu·ti·nous [ˈmjuːtinəs] *a.* 暴动的,叛变的,反抗的;反抗长官的,违抗命令的. **-ly** *ad.*

mu·ti·ny [ˈmjuːtini] *n.* 暴动,造反,叛变; 兵变. — *vi.* 暴动,造反,叛变;反抗.

mut·ism [ˈmjuːtizəm] *n.* 【医】哑;【心】不言症,缄默症.

mu·to·graph [ˈmjuːtəgrɑːf] *n.* (初期的)电影摄影机. — *vt.* (用电影摄影机)拍摄.

mu·to·scope [ˈmjuːtəskəup] *n.* (初期)电影放映机.

mutt [mʌt] *n.* 〔美俚〕傻子,笨蛋,无足轻重的人;杂种狗,野狗,小狗.

mut·ter [ˈmʌtə] *n.* 咕哝,小声低语;抱怨,怨言. — *vt., vi.* 低声说;咕哝,喃咕,抱怨地说 *(at; against)*; 发出低沉轰隆声. ~ ***and mumble*** 吞吞吐吐. ~ ***away to oneself*** 喃喃自语. ~ ***threats at*** 低声恐吓. ~ ***to oneself*** 喃喃自语. **-er** *n.* **-ing·ly** *ad.*

mut·ton [ˈmʌtn] *n.* 羊肉;〔谑〕羊; 〔俚〕娼妓. ***dead as ~*** 真死, 僵死. ***eat [take] one's ~ with*** 和…共餐. ***return to one's ~s*** 〔谑〕言归正传, 回到本题. ~ **bird** 【鸟】细嘴海燕. ~ **chop** 羊排; 羊肉片;〔*pl.*〕上细下圆的络腮胡子. ~ **fist** 〔口〕粗壮的大手;手粗大的人. ~ **ham** 腊羊肉. ~**head** 〔口〕笨人,傻子. ~ **top** 〔美俚〕笨蛋.

mut·ton·y [ˈmʌtəni] *a.* 羊肉味的;羊膻气的.

mu·tu·al [ˈmjuːtjuəl, ˈmjuːtʃuəl] *a.* ①相互的. ②〔口〕共有的,共同的. ~ *affection* 互爱,相爱. ~ *aid* 互相援助. *a ~ aid team* 互助组. *a ~ admiration society* 一批互相吹捧的人们. *our ~ friend* 我们共同的朋友. *by ~ consent* 双方同意. ~ *association* 互助会,共济会. ~ *benefit and collaboration* 互惠合作. ~ *preferential duties* 互惠关税. ~ **capacitance** 【电】互容. ~ **conductance** 【电】互导. ~ **induction** 【电】互感. ~ **characteristic** 屏-栅特性. ~ **coupling factor** 耦合系数. ~ **fund** 合股投资(公司). ~ **savings bank** 互助储蓄会. **-ly** *ad.*

mu·tu·al·ism [ˈmjuːtjuəlizəm, ˈmjuːtʃuəlizəm] *n.* 互助论;【生】互惠共生(现象).

mu·tu·al·ist [ˈmjuːtjuəlist] *n.* ①互助论者. ②【生】依生生物.

mu·tu·al·i·ty [ˌmjuːtjuˈæliti, mjuːtʃuˈæliti] *n.* ①相互关系,相关;(相互)依存. ②同感;亲密.

mu·tu·el [ˈmjuːtjuəl, ˈmjuːtʃuwəl] *n.* ①【赛马】买中赢马者除手续费一成外分得全部赌金的方法 (= pari-mutuel). ②赌金计算机.

mu·tule [ˈmjuːtjuːl] *n.* 【建】Doric 式檐饰.

mux [mʌks] *vt.* 〔美俚〕使弄糟,弄坏.

Mu·zak [ˈmjuːzæk] 音乐广播网〔通过电话线或广播传送配乐录音到饭店、商店、工厂的广播网的商标名称〕. — *n.* 音乐广播网.

mu·zhik, mu·zjik [ˈmuːʒik] *n.* (= moujik).

muzz [mʌz] *vt., vi.* 〔英俚〕使(醉得)发呆;拚命用功.

muz·zle [ˈmʌzl] *n.* ①(动物的)口部,口鼻;(狗、马等的)口套,口络. ②枪口,炮口;喷口,喷嘴. ③压制言论的事物. — *vt.* 上口套;封住…的嘴;使缄默;压制[扭制]…的言论;〔方〕(猪等)用嘴掘;〔方〕大口大口喝;收(帆);〔美俚〕亲嘴. *a ~ cover* 枪口罩. **~-loader** *n.* 前装枪[炮]. **~-loading** *a.* 前装式的,前膛的. **~ velocity** (枪弹的)初速,腔口速度.

muz·zy [ˈmʌzi] *a.* *(-zi·er; -zi·est)* 〔口〕头脑混乱的;迟钝的;迷惑的;(醉得)发呆的. **-zi·ly** *ad.*

MV = ①market value 市面价值. ②mean variation 平均变化. ③medium voltage【电】中压. ④merchant vessel 商船. ⑤motor vessel 内燃机船. ⑥muzzle velocity 初速(射炮离开炮口瞬间的速度). ⑦main verb【语法】主要动词.

mv. = millivolt.

M.V.O. = Member of the Royal Victorian Order 〔英〕维多利亚勋章获得者.

MVP = most valuable player 〔美〕最高身价球员.

MW = military works 军事工程,筑垒.

M.W. = ①molecular weight 分子量. ②Most Worshipful 〔英〕最尊敬的(用于对治安法官、市参议员等的称呼). ③Most Worthy 最尊敬的.

mw. = milliwatt.

M.W.A. = Modern Woodmen of America 美国现代猎人协会.

Mx = Middlesex 〔英〕米德尔塞克斯(郡).

Mx.; mx = maxwell 麦克斯韦〔磁通量单位〕.

my [mai, 弱 mi] *pro.* ①〔I 的所有格〕我的. *~ and her father* 我和她两人的父亲. *~ and her father(s)* 我的父亲和她的父亲. ②〔用于称呼〕*~ dear fellow = ~ good man* 喂,老朋友. *My Lord [m- l-]* [miˈlɔːd] 大人,老爷〔对于贵族、主教、法官等的尊称〕. — *int.* 〔口〕〔表示惊奇〕***My! = Oh, ~! = My goodness!*** 嗳呀!呵唷!天哪 *(My, what a mist!* 哎呀,多大的雾呀)! ***my eye!*** (带有反驳或难于置信的口气)嗬!天晓得!去你[他]的!

my·al·gi·a [maiˈældʒiə] *n.*【医】肌肉风湿痛,肌痛.

my·al·ism [ˈmaiəlizəm] *n.* (西印度群岛的)巫术.

my·all [ˈmaiɔːl] *n.* 澳大利亚洋槐.

my·as·the·ni·a [ˌmaiæsˈθiːniə] *n.*【医】肌无力,肌衰弱. **~ gravis**【医】重症肌无力. **-then·ic** *a.*

myc- *comb. f.* 真菌: *mycosis.*

my·ce·li·um [maiˈsiːliəm] *n.* *(pl. -li·a* [-ə]*)*【生】菌丝(体). **-li·al** *a.*

My·ce·nae·an [ˌmaisiˈniːən] *a.*【考古】(古代希腊都市)迈西尼 (Mycenae) (文化)的.

my·ce·to·ma [ˌmaisiˈtəumə] *n.*【医】足分支菌病.

my·ce·to·zo·an [maiˌsiːtəˈzəuən] *n.*【生】粘菌类生物 (= myxomycete). —*a.* 粘菌类的 (= myxomycetous).

myco- *comb. f.* (用于辅音前) = myc-.

my·co·bac·te·ri·um [ˌmaikəubækˈtiəriəm] *n.* *(pl. -ri·a* [-ə]*)*【生】分支杆菌属.

mycol. = mycology.

my·co·log·ic, my·co·log·i·cal [ˌmaikəuˈlɔdʒik(əl)] *a.* 真菌学的.

my·col·o·gy [maiˈkɔlədʒi] *n.* 真菌学. **-gist** *n.*

my·co(r)·rhi·za [ˌmaikəuˈraizə] *n.*【微】菌根.

my·dri·a·sis [miˈdraiəsis] *n.*【医】瞳孔开大,瞳孔放大. **myd·ri·at·ic** [ˌmidriˈætik] *a., n.* 瞳孔开大的(药).

my·e·len·ceph·a·lon [ˌmaiəlenˈsefəˌlɔn] *n.* *(pl. -la* [-lə]*)*【解】末脑,延髓.

my·e·lin [ˈmaiəli(ː)n] *n.*【解】髓磷脂. **-ic** *a.*

my·e·li·tis [ˌmaiəˈlaitis] *n.*【医】脊髓炎;骨髓炎.

my·e·lo·gen·ic [ˌmaiələuˈdʒenik] *a.* 生于骨髓内的;生于骨髓的 (= myelogenous).

my·e·lo·gram [ˈmaiələuˈgræm] *n.* 脊髓爱克斯线相;脊髓细胞分类计数. **-log·ra·phy** [-ˈlɔgrəfi] *n.*

my·e·loid [ˈmaiəˌlɔid] *a.* ①骨髓的;骨髓状的;由骨髓而来的. ②脊髓的.

my·e·lo·ma [ˌmaiəuˈləumə] *n.* *(pl. ~s, -ma·ta* [-mətə]*)*【医】骨髓瘤. **-tous** [-ˈlɔmətəs, -ˈləumə-] *a.*

myg. = myriagram(me).

my·i·a·sis [maiˈaiəsis] *n.* 蛆病.

myl [mail] 万立升〔法国容量名〕.

My·lar [ˈmailɑː] 迈拉〔一种聚酯类高分子物的商品名〕.

my·lo·nite [ˈmailəuˌnait] *n.*【地】糜棱岩.

mym [maim] 万米〔长度单位〕.

my·na, mi·na(h) [ˈmainə] *n.*【鸟】印度燕八哥;鹩哥;椋鸟.

Myn·heer [mainˈhiə, -ˈheə] *n.* ①〔D.〕= Mr., Sir. ②〔m-〕荷兰人.

my·o·car·di·al [ˌmaiəuˈkɑːdiəl] *a.*【解】心肌的. **~ infarction**【医】心肌梗塞.

my·o·car·di·o·graph [ˌmaiəuˈkɑːdiəˈgrɑːf, -græf] *n.*【医】心肌动(描)记器.

my·o·car·di·tis [ˌmaiəukɑːˈdaitis] *n.*【医】心肌炎.

my·o·car·di·um [ˌmaiəuˈkɑːdiəm] *n.*【解】心肌(层). **-car·di·cal** *a.*

my·oc·lo·nus [maiˈɔklənəs] *n.*【医】肌阵挛. **-clon·ic** [ˌmaiəˈklɔnik] *a.*

my·o·e·lec·tric [ˌmaiəuiˈlektrik] *a.*【医】肌电位的. **-al·ly** *ad.*

my·o·gen [ˈmaiədʒin] *n.*【生化】肌浆蛋白.

my·o·gen·ic [ˌmaiəuˈdʒenik] *a.*【解】肌原性的;肌生的.

my·o·glo·bin [ˈmaiəugləubin, ˌmaiəuˈgləubin] *n.*【医】肌红蛋白.

my·o·graph [ˈmaiəugrɑːf, -ˌgræf] *n.*【医】肌动(描)记器.

my·ol·o·gy [maiˈɔlədʒi] *n.*【医】肌学. **-log·ic, -log·i·cal** *a.*

my·o·ma [maiˈəumə] *n.* *(pl. -mas, -ma·ta* [-mətə]*)*【医】肌瘤. **-tous** [-ˈɔmətəs, -ˈəumə-] *a.*

my·o·neu·ral [ˌmaiəuˈnjuərəl, -ˈnuər-] *a.* 有关肌神经的(尤指有关肌纤维神经末梢的).

my·op·a·thy [maiˈɔpəθi] *n.*【医】肌病.

my·ope [ˈmaiəup] *n.* 患近视者;眼光短浅者.

my·o·pi·a [maiˈəupiə], **my·o·py** [ˈmaiəpi] *n.*【医】近视 *(opp.* hypermetropia*)*. **-opic** [-ˈɔpik] *a.* 近视眼的;缺乏远见的.

my·o·sin [ˈmaiəsin] *n.*【医】肌浆球蛋白.

my·o·sis [maiˈəusis] *n.*【医】瞳孔缩小,缩瞳症.

my·o·si·tis [ˌmaiəuˈsaitis] *n.*【医】肌炎.

my·o·so·tis [ˈmaiəuˈsəutis] *n.* 勿忘草属 *(Myosotis)* 植物〔包括勿忘草〕.

my·ot·ic [maiˈɔtik] *a., n.*【医】缩瞳孔的(药).

my·o·tome [ˈmaiəuˈtəum] *n.*【解】①肌刀. ②生肌节.

my·ot·o·my [maiˈɔtəmi] *n.*【解】肌切开术.

my·o·to·ni·a [ˌmaiəuˈtəuniə] *n.*【医】肌强直. **-ton·ic** [-ˈtɔnik] *a.*

My·ra [ˈmaiərə] *n.* 迈拉〔女子名〕.

myr·i(a)- *comb. f.* 一万〔仅用于米制〕;无数.

myr·i·ad [ˈmiriəd] *n.* 〔诗〕万,一万;无数,极大数量. —*a.* 无数的;众多方面的. *a ~ of stars* 无数的星斗. **~-minded** *a.* 才气纵横的,多才多艺的.

myr·i·a·dyne [ˈmiriədain] *n.*【物】万达因.

myr·i·a·gram(me) [ˈmiriəgræm] *n.* 万克(即十公斤).

myr·i·a·li·tre, myr·i·a·liter [ˈmiriəliːtə] *n.* 万升.

myr·i·a·me·tre, myr·i·a·me·ter [ˈmiriəˌmiːtə] *n.* 万米(即十公里).

myr·i·a·pod [ˈmiriəpɔd] *a., n.* 多足(类)的;多足类动物,节足动物.

myr·i·cin [ˈmirisin] *n.*【化】蜂酯;杨梅脂.

myr·i·o·ra·ma [ˌmiriəuˈrɑːmə] *n.* 万景画〔将许多小

画组成的画〕；万景画会.
my·ris·tate [miˈristeit] *n.* 【化】十四(烷)酸盐[酯]，肉豆蔻酸盐[酯].
my·ris·tic [miˈristik] *a.* ～ **acid** 肉豆蔻酸，十四(烷)酸.
My·ris·ti·ca [miˈristikə] *n.* 【植】肉豆蔻属.
myr·me·co- [ˈməmikəu-] *comb. f.* 蚁.
myr·me·co·log·i·cal [ˌmə:mikəuˈlɔdʒikl] *a.* 蚁学的.
myr·me·col·o·gy [ˌmə:miˈkɔlədʒi] *n.* 蚁类研究，蚁学.
myr·me·coph·a·gous [ˌmə:miˈkɔfəgəs] *a.* 食蚁的.
myr·mi·don [ˈməmidən] *n.* ①盲目执行主子命令的人，顺从的部下；职业暴徒. ②〔M-〕〔希神〕迈密登. *～s of the law* 〔蔑〕法律执行吏，警察(等).
my·rob·a·lan [maiˈrɔbələn, mi-] *n.* ①诃子(诃黎勒，藏青果). ②樱桃李 (= cherry-plum).
My·ron [ˈmaiərən] *n.* 迈伦〔男子名〕.
myrrh [mə:] *n.* 没药〔热带树脂，可作香料、药材〕；没药树；没药树脂. **-rhic** *a.*
myrrh·y [ˈmə:ri] *a.* 有没药香味的.
myr·tle [ˈmə:tl] *n.* ①【植】桃金娘，番樱桃；爱神木；长春花；加州桂；铜钱状珍珠等. ②〔M-〕默特尔〔女子名〕. ③= ～ green. *the wax [candleberry]* ～ 杨梅. **～-berry** 爱神木果实. ～ **green** *n.* 墨绿色.
my·self [maiˈself] *pro.* ***(pl. ourselves)*** (我)自己；(我)亲自. ①〔加重 I 的语气〕*I ～ saw it.* = *I saw it ～.* 我亲自看见的. ②〔me 的反身形〕. *I have hurt ～.* 我受伤了. ***as for ～*** (至于)我自己，讲到我自己. ***(all) by ～*** 我独自地；独力地. ***I am not ～.*** 我身体不舒服；我精神不正常. ***I came to ～.*** 我清醒过来了.
my·sid [ˈmaisid] *n.* 糠虾目 *(Mysidacea)* 动物.
My·sis [ˈmaisis] *n.* 糠虾属；〔m-〕糠虾期，幼体期.
Myst. = Mysteries.
mys·ta·gogue [ˈmistəˈgɔg] *n.* 神秘教义的解释者〔传播者〕；引人入秘教者. **-gog·ic** [-ˈgɔdʒik] *a.*, **-go·gy** [-ˌgəudʒi] *n.*
mys·te·ri·ous [misˈtiəriəs] *a.* 神秘的，不可思议的；暧昧的，可疑的；故弄玄虚的. **-ly** *ad.* **-ness** *n.*
mys·te·ri·um [misˈtiəriəm] *n.* 【天】神秘波源〔被认为是银河系几个区域中发出一种特别的无线电波频的羟基酸报〕.
mys·ter·y[1] [ˈmistəri] *n.* ①神秘的事物，不可思议的事物. ②神秘，秘密；诀窍，秘诀，秘传；玄妙，奥妙. ③〔常 *pl.*〕(古代宗教中的)神秘仪式；玄义；〔*pl.*〕(基督教的)圣餐礼. ④〔美口〕烤什锦. ⑤= ～ play. ⑥疑案小说〔故事，戏剧〕，侦探小说. *the mysteries of nature* 自然界的奥秘〔奇迹〕. *mysteries of a trade* 某一行业的诀窍. *mysteries of woods and rivers* 打猎和捕鱼的秘诀. ***be a ～ to*** (某人)不能理解. ***be wrapped in ～*** 包在秘密中. ***dive into the mysteries of*** 探究…的秘密. ***make a ～ of*** 把…神秘化，把…弄成秘密，卖弄虚玄. ～ **play** 神秘剧〔欧洲中世纪宣传宗教的戏剧〕. ～ **ship [boat]** 伪装猎潜舰(= Q-ship, Q-boat).
mys·ter·y[2] [ˈmistəri] *n.* 〔英、古〕手艺，手工业；行业；行会. *the art and ～ of* …的技术和手艺〔学徒满期证书上用语〕.
mys·tic [ˈmistik] *a.* ①神秘的，不可思议的，奥妙的；引起惊奇[畏惧]的. ②秘诀的，秘法的；秘传仪式的. ③神秘主义(者)的. — *n.* 神秘主义者.
mys·ti·cal [ˈmistikəl] *a.* = mystic. **-ly** *ad.* **-ness** *n.*
mys·ti·cism [ˈmistisizəm] *n.* 神秘，玄妙；暧昧；玄想(的谬说)；神秘主义；神秘教.
mys·ti·fi·ca·tion [ˌmistifiˈkeiʃən] *n.* 使人迷惑的事物；神秘举动〔行动、现象〕；不可思议；迷惑；神秘化.
mys·ti·fy [ˈmistifai] *vt.* 使神秘化，蒙蔽，迷惑. ***be mystified by*** 给…弄得莫名其妙. **-fing·ly** *ad.*
mys·tique [misˈti:k] *n.* 神秘性，神秘气氛；不可言传的性质；(技艺的)秘诀.
myth [miθ] *n.* ①神话；神怪故事. ②奇人，奇事，怪物；虚构的故事；荒诞的说法. —*vt.* 使神化.
myth. = mythological, mythology.
myth·ic, myth·i·cal [ˈmiθik(əl)] *a.* 神话(式)的；神话时代的；虚构的，非现实的，想象〔传说〕上的. **-cal·ly** *ad.*
myth·i·cism [ˈmiθisizəm] *n.* 神话式的解释；神话说，神话主义. **-i·cist** *n.* 神话研究〔解释〕者；相信神话者.
myth·i·cize [ˈmiθisaiz] *vt.* 把…当作神话；使神话化；对…作神话解释. **-ciz·er** *n.* 编神话者；解释神化者.
mytho- *comb. f.* 神话.
myth·o·gra·pher [miˈθɔgrəfə, mai-] *n.* 神话作者.
myth·og·ra·phy [miˈθɔgrəfi] *n.* (绘画、雕刻等的)神话艺术.
mythol. = mythological; mythology.
myth·ol·og·ic, -i·cal [miθəˈlɔdʒik(əl)] *a.* 神话(中)的；神话学(上)的；神话似的，凭空想象的，荒唐无稽的. **-i·cal·ly** *ad.*
myth·ol·o·gist [miˈθɔlədʒist] *n.* 神话学者；神话作者〔搜集者〕.
myth·ol·o·gize [miˈθɔlədʒaiz] *vt.*, *vi.* ①(把…)当作神话. ②(对…)作神话解释. ③讲述(神话). ④给(神话)分类.
myth·ol·o·gy [miˈθɔlədʒi] *n.* ①神话学. ②〔集体词〕神话；神话集，神话志. *Greek ～* 希腊神话.
myth·o·pe·ic, myth·o·poe·ic [ˌmiθəˈpi:ik] *a.* 神话时代的；创作〔产生〕神话的.
myth·os [ˈmaiθɔs] *n.* ***(pl. my·thoi*** [ˈmaiθɔ:i]***)*** (一个)神话；〔集体词〕神话(集)；虚构的故事〔事物〕；代表某一集体的态度、信仰等特征的类型；(文艺作品的)主题.
my·thus [ˈmaiθəs] *n.* 神话 = myth.
myx(o)- *comb. f.* 粘液.
myx·oe·de·ma [miksiˈdi:mə] *n.* 【医】粘液(性)水肿.
myx·o·ma [mikˈsəumə] *n.* ***(pl. ～s, -ma·ta*** [-mətə]***)*** 【医】粘液瘤. **-tous** [-təs] *a.*
myx·o·ma·to·sis [ˌmiksəuməˈtəusis] *n.* ①粘液瘤(菌)的存在. ②多发性粘液瘤，粘液瘤病.
myx·o·my·cete [ˌmiksəumaiˈsi:t] *n.* 粘菌.

N

N, n [en] ***(pl. N's, n's*** [enz]***)*** ①英语字母表第十四字母. ②【印】对开〔em 字母全身的一半 = en〕. ③ N 形物. ④〔n〕【数】任意数，不定数，不定量. ②【遗】单位(染色体)数. *an N girder* N 字桁. ***to the nth (power)*** 【数】到 n 次(幂)；到极度，极端.
N ①【罗马数字】90 〔$\bar{N}$ = 90,000〕. ②【化】= nitrogen. ③= North(ern).
N., n. = ①name. ②navy. ③neuter. ④new. ⑤nominative. ⑥noon. ⑦north; northern. ⑧noun. ⑨【化】normal. ⑩National; Nationalist. ⑪Norse. ⑫Novem-

ber. ⑬nephew. ⑭net. ⑮note. ⑯number.

-n *suf.* = *-en, -an.*

'n¹ =〔美口〕than.

n'²〔口〕= and.

NA =〔美〕National Archives 国家档案馆.

Na =【化】natrium (〔L.〕= sodium).

N.A., NA = ①national academician 国家科学院院士. ②national academy 国家科学院. ③national army 国民军. ④North America北美洲.

NAA = National Aeronautic Association〔美〕全国航空协会.

NAACP = National Association for the Advancement of Colored People〔美〕全国有色人种协进会.

NAAFI, Naafi [ˈnæfi] = Navy, Army and Air Force Institutes〔英〕海陆空军小卖店经营机构.

nab [næb] *vt.*〔口〕逮捕,拘捕;猛然抓住;抢去(东西),攫夺.

Na·bar·ro [nəˈbɑːrəu] *n.* 纳巴罗〔姓氏〕.

Nab·by [ˈnæbi] *n.* Abigail 的爱称.

nabe [neib] *n.*〔美〕邻里电影院.

na·bob, na·wab [ˈneibɔb, nəˈbɔb; nəˈwɔb] *n.* ①对有身分的穆斯林的尊称. ②【史】(印度莫卧儿帝国时代的)太守[总督]. ③〔古〕在印度发了大财的英国人;富翁,大财主. ④〔美俚〕名士. **-ism, -er·y** *n.* 财主气概[行为].

Na·both [ˈneibɔθ] *n.* 拿伯〔《圣经》故事中的葡萄园主,国王欲占其葡萄园而把他杀死〕. **~'s vineyard** 被别人垂涎的东西.

NACA〔Am.〕= National Advisory Committee for Aeronautics〔美旧〕国家航空咨询委员会.

nac·a·rat [ˈnækəræt] *n.* ①胭脂红,洋红. ②胭脂红夏布[绉绸].

na·celle [nəˈsel] *n.* ①【空】机舱,客舱. ②(轻气球的)吊篮;(飞艇的)吊舱.

nach·us, nach·as [ˈnɑːkəs] *n.*〔Heb.〕骄傲而津津乐道的事.

na·cre [ˈneikə], **nack·er** [ˈnækə] *n.* 珍珠蚌;(蚌壳内的)真珠层;真珠光泽.

na·cred [ˈneikəd] *a.* 有珍珠层的.

na·cre·ous [ˈneikriəs], **na·crous** [ˈneikrəs] *a.* 真珠蚌的;珍珠层的;(有)珍珠光泽的.

na·crite [ˈneikrait] *n.* 珍珠陶土.

N.A.D. = National Academy of Design〔美〕全国设计院.

NADGE = NATO Air Defence Ground Environment 北大西洋公约组织防空警备体系.

na·dir [ˈneidiə, -də] *n.* ①天底〔天体观测者脚下正中点〕(*opp.* zenith). ②最下点,最低点. ③最低温度. ***at the ~ of*** 在…的最下层[低点] (*His fortune was at its ~.* 他的运气坏到极点).

nae [nei]〔Scot.〕*a., ad.* = no; not.

nae·vus [ˈniːvəs] *n.* (*pl.* ***nae·vi*** [-vai])【医】痣;(一般的)斑点. *a pigmentary ~* 黑痣,黑痦子.

nag¹ [næg] *n.* ①(骑用)小马;〔口〕(老)马;〔口〕驽马;〔美俚〕劣等赛马用马. ②旧汽车.

nag² [næg] *n.* ①嫌言怨语;唠叨;不停的责骂. ②〔口〕爱唠叨的人(尤指妇女). — *vt., vi.* (***nagged; nag·ging***) ①发牢骚,唠叨;责骂;老是催促;不断地找(…的)岔子. ②困扰;恼人. *She nagged (at) him all day long.* 她对他终日唠叨不已.

Na·ga·sa·ki [ˌnægəˈsɑːki] *n.* 长崎〔日本港市〕.

nag·ger [ˈnægə] *n.* 爱唠叨的人;牢骚多的女人;泼妇.

nag·ging [ˈnægiŋ] *a.* ①责天怨地的,爱唠叨的;尽找岔的. ②恼人的. — *n.* 嫌言怨语. *~ criticism* 嫌言怨语式的批评.

nag·gish¹ [ˈnægiʃ] *a.* 小马的;小的,劣的.

nag·gish² *a.* 有些爱唠叨的.

nag·gy [ˈnægi] *a.* = nagging.

Na·go·ya [nɑːˈgəujɑː] *n.* 名古屋〔日本城市〕.

na·grams [ˈneigrɑmz] *n.*〔美俚〕忧郁,悲观.

nah [nɑː] *a.*〔美俚〕= no.

Na·ha [ˈnɑːhɑː] *n.* 那霸〔日本港市〕.

Na·hal [nɑːˈhɑːl] *n.* ①以色列的"农垦"部队. ②以色列的武装"移民区".

Na·hua [ˈnɑːwə] *n.* (*pl.* ~*s*;〔集合词〕~). =Nahuatl (*a.*).

Na·huat [ˈnɑːwɑːt] *n.* ①(*pl.* ~(*s*)) 那瓦特族人〔墨西哥印第安人的一个部落〕. ②那瓦特语.

Na·hua·tl [ˈnɑːwɑːtl] *n.* ①(*pl.* ~(*s*)) (墨西哥乌托-阿兹特克部落) 那瓦特人. ②那瓦特语. ③(乌托-阿兹特克语系的)那瓦特语支. — *a.* 那瓦特人[语]的.

Na·hua·tlan [ˈnɑːwɑːtlən] *a.* 那瓦特语支的. — *n.* ①那瓦特人. ②那瓦特语. ③(乌托-阿兹特克语系的) 那瓦特语支 (=Nahuatl).

Na·hum [ˈneiəm] *n.* 内厄姆〔姓氏〕.

nai·ad [ˈnaiæd] *n.* (*pl.* ~*s*, ***nai·a·des*** [ˈnaiədiːz]) ①【希、罗神】水精,水仙女. ②女游泳者. ③【虫】稚虫.

naif [nɑːˈiːf] *a.*〔F.〕= naive.

nail [neil] *n.* ①指甲,爪;喙甲. ②钉. ③纳尔〔旧量布尺度名,约合 5.715 cm.〕 ***a ~ in [to] one's coffin*** 促人早死的事物(*drive [put] a ~ in [add a ~ to] sb.'s coffin* 促人早死,催命. *It was a final ~ in the Government's coffin.* 那是对政府的一个致命打击). ***(as) hard as ~s*** 身体强壮;冷酷无情. ***be [go] off at the ~*** 无法控制自己,忘形,神经失常;有点醉. ***drive the ~ [up to] the head [knock the ~ home]*** 把钉子钉到头;坚持到底,贯彻始终. ***He must have iron ~s that [who] scratches a bear.*** 搔熊者必具铁爪;要干危险的事,就得有充分的准备. ***hit the (right) ~ on the head*** 说得对,中肯,一针见血,正中要害. ***~s in mourning*** 有污垢的指甲. ***on the ~***〔口〕①立即;被捕. ②在讨论中的 (*pay on the ~* 立即付与. *the subject on the ~* 当前的问题). ***right as ~s*** (钉子般)直的;没错的. ***to the [a] ~*** 完全,彻底;极其. — *vt.* ①敲钉,钉住 (*on; to*). ②〔口〕捉住,抓住;〔美俚〕逮捕;〔俚〕打. ③〔学生俚〕揭发,看穿,发觉. ④吸引住(注意等),不放松(人家的声明等),使不能逃避. ⑤〔美俚〕偷. ⑥【棒球】使 (跑垒者) 被开出局. *have one's boots ~ed* (请人)在靴底上钉钉子. *~ a notice on [to] the door* 在门上钉一块告白. *be ~ed going off without leave.* 被发觉擅自外出. ***~ a blow***〔美拳击〕打. ***~ a lie to the counter [barn-door]*** 揭发弊端,拆穿西洋镜〔从前商人把伪币钉在帐柜上示众的习惯,故有此说〕. ***~ (sb.) down to*** (用诺言、声明等)约束某人,要求某人履行诺言 (*He was confused when we ~ed him down to his promise.* 当我们坚持要他守诺言时,他狼狈了). ***~ it***〔美俚〕(考试)及格;成功. ***~ one's colours to the mast*** 坚持到底,极有决心;决不屈服〔原义:把舰旗钉死在桅杆上,使不能扯下来投降〕. ***~ up*** ①把…钉在较高处. ②钉牢[关系](门、窗). **~-biting** ①咬指甲. ②焦虑,束手无策. **~brush** 指甲刷. **~clippers** 指甲钳. **~ file** 指甲锉. **~head** 钉头(饰). **~-headed** *a.* 钉头状的 (*~-headed characters* 楔形文字). **~hole** ①钉眼. ②指甲孔〔用指甲开小刀的地方〕. **~-machine** 制钉机. **~-nippers, ~-scissors**〔*pl.*〕指甲剪. **~ polish** 染甲水,指甲油. **~ puller** 起钉钳. **~ set** (木工用的) 钉凿. **~sick** *a.* (板材等)因屡钉而变得不结实;钉眼漏水的. **-less** *a.* 无指甲的;无钉的.

nail·er [ˈneilə] *n.* ①制钉者,制钉工人. ②敲钉人;自动敲钉机. ③〔俚〕热心(工作等)的人 (*on; to*); (竞赛等的)能手,好手. *a ~ on one's work* 热心工作的人. *a ~ at golf* 高尔夫球的能手. ***as busy as a ~*** 忙得很.

nail·er·y [ˈneiləri] *n.* 制钉厂.

nail·ing [ˈneiliŋ] *a.* ①敲钉用的. ②〔俚〕极好的. ***a ~ stroke*** 极好的运气. — *ad.*〔俚〕极好.

nain·sook [ˈneinsuk] *n.* (印度)薄棉布；南苏克布．

Nai·ro·bi [ˌnaiəˈrəubi] *n.* 内罗毕〔肯尼亚首都〕．

na·ïve, na·ive [nɑːˈiːv, naiˈiːv] *a.* 天真的；自然的，朴素的；戆的．★现在以写作 naive 较普通．～ **materialism** 【哲】朴素唯物论．～ **realism** 【哲】朴素实在论．**-ly** *ad.* **-ness** *n.*

na·ïve·té, na·ïve·ty, na·ive·ty [nɑːˈiːvtei] *n.* 质朴，朴素；天真；天真的行为；天真的话．

na·ked [ˈneikid] *a.* ①裸体的；露出的．②无…的 *(of)*；无叶的；【植】(种子等)裸出的；荒瘠的．③【诗】无防备的．④率直的，如实的，赤裸裸的；露骨的；明白的；(引句等)无注释的；【法】无证据的．*a* ～ *dance* 〔美俚〕裸体舞．～ *feet* 赤脚．*a* ～ *sword* (拔出了刀鞘的)明晃晃的刀．～ *fields* 荒地．*a* ～ *flower* 无被花．*the* ～ *eye* 肉眼．*a* ～ *heart* 赤裸裸的心．*the* ～ *truth* 明明白白的事实．*a* ～ *debenture* 〔英〕无担保证券．***as* ～ *as when one was born*** 赤条条，裸体．***stark* ～** 赤身露体，一丝不挂．***strip (sb.)* ～** 剥光．***with* ～ *fists*** 赤手空拳地．～ **ape** 人〔出自英国人类学家 Dr. Morris 所著同名作品〕．**-ly** *ad.* ①光着身子；赤裸裸地．②如实．

na·ked·ness [ˈneikidnis] *n.* ①裸，裸出，露出．②坦白；无掩饰；光秃．③〔古、圣〕阴部 (= privates)．*the* ～ *of the land* (个人、团体、国家等的)无资力〔无防备〕状态．

na·ked·ize [ˈneikidaiz] *vt., vi.* (使)成为裸体．

na·ker [ˈneikə] *n.* 〔古〕鼓 (= kettle drum)．

NAM = National Association of Manufacturers 〔美〕全国制造商协会．

Na·ma [ˈnɑːmɑː] *n.* ①那马部族〔西南非洲霍屯督族中的一主要部落〕．②霍屯督人．③霍屯督语．

nam·a·ble, name·a·ble [ˈneiməbl] *a.* ①说得出名称的，可指名的；可命名的．②值得提起的；有名的．

nam·by-pam·by [ˈnæmbiˈpæmbi] *a., n.* ①多愁善感的(人)；没有决断的(人)；感伤的(谈话)．②柔弱的(文风)浮华的(诗、文)．

name [neim] *n.* ①名，名字，姓名；名称．②名声，名誉；空名，虚名；名义，名目；【逻、语法】概念的名称；名词．③知名之士，名士；一族，一门．④〔pl.〕恶骂．*What is your* ～*?* 你叫什么名字？ *What* ～*, please?* = *What* ～ *shall I say?* 你是怎样称呼的？ *It stands in my* ～. 那是顶我的名．*a pen* ～ 笔名．*a common* ～【语法】普通名词．*an assumed* ～ 假名．*the Christian [first, given]* ～ 名字；教名，洗礼名，(对姓而言的)名．*a family* ～ 姓．*a double-barreled* ～ (以两个姓合成的)双姓．*a* ～ *ship* 同型舰中的代表舰．*an ill* ～ 臭名．*a man of* ～ 知名之士．*a man of no* ～ 无名小卒．*many great* ～*s* 许多名士．*a draw* ～〔美俚〕红演员．*a* ～ *scribber* 〔美俚〕时评作者．***by* ～** ①指名 (*call by* ～ 喊名字)．②名叫 (*John by* ～ = *by* ～ *John* 名叫约翰)．③只…名字 (*know sb. by* ～ (没见过面)只知道某人的名字)．***by the* ～ *of*** 名叫…的．***call sb.* ～*s*** 骂某人．***get a* ～** 得到名声，成名．***get [win] oneself a* ～** 成名．***Give it a* ～.** 〔口〕(请客时)你要什么，讲吧．***give one's* ～** 报名．***go by [under] the* ～ *of*** 名叫…，以…的名字为人所知，以…的名义发表．***have a* ～ *for* (bravery) = *have the* ～ *of* (being brave)** 有(勇敢)之名．***have one's* ～ *up*** 有名起来；成名．***in* ～** 名义上的，有名无实的．***in one's own* ～** 用自己的名义，独立．***in the* ～ *of*** ①凭…的名，对…发誓 (*in the* ～ *of common honesty* 凭诚实之名(决不说谎))．②作…的代表，代替 (*I speak in the* ～ *of her.* 我代表她发言．③为…的缘故，究竟．(*What in the* ～ *of God is it?* 这究竟是什么？ ***keep sb.'s* ～ *off the books.*** 不让某人参加某机构．***keep one's* ～ *on the books*** 保留学籍，保留会籍．***leave a* ～ *behind*** 留名后世．***make a* ～ *for oneself*** 成名．***of* ～** 有名．***of no* ～** 无名的．***of the* ～ *of*** 名叫…的．***put one's* ～ *down for*** 写下某人认捐的款额；把某人的名字列在名单上，替某人报名(参加运动、组织等)；提出某人为候选人．***send in one's* ～** 报名申请(参加竞赛等)．***take a* ～ *in vain*** 滥用名字．***take sb.'s* ～ *off the books*** 从名册上涂去某人的名字，退学，退会．***the* ～ *of the game*** 事情〔问题〕的本质，真正重要的东西．***to one's* ～** 属于自己的东西 (*He has not a penny to his* ～. 他一个铜子儿也没有)．***to the* ～ *of*** 成…的名义．***under one's own* ～** 用自己的名字(发表)．***under the* ～ *of*** = by the ～ of. ***without a* ～** ①= nameless. ②名字说不出来．— *vt.* ①给…命名，给…取名；喊…的名字；正确说出…的名字．②提名；任命；指定，说出．③〔英〕(下院议长)指出…名字谴责．*Mr. A has been* ～*d for the vacancy. A* 氏被指定为继任者．*N-!* (听众要求发言人)请指出名字来！— *a.* ①〔美口〕著名的．②(作品等)据以取名的．*a* ～ *band* 著名乐队．～ ***after*** =〔美〕～ ***for*** 用(别人、别物的名字)命名．～ ***the day*** (女人)择定结婚日期．***not to be* ～*d on [in] the same day*** *(with)* 与…不可同日而语．～**board** 招牌；站名牌；船名牌．～**-calling** 骂人．～**child** 用某人名字命名的孩子 (*his* ～*-child* 照他的名字取名的孩子)．～ **day** 命名日；和本人同名的圣徒纪念日；〔英〕【股】结算日，交割日．～**-dropper** 言谈中常以亲密、随意的口吻提到显要人物以抬高自己身价的人．～ **father** 命名父．～ **part** 【剧】和剧名同名的角色．～ **plate** 姓名牌，名称牌；(报头上的)报刊名．～**sake** 同姓名的人；(特指)沿用某人名字的人．～ **tape** 标名的布条．

name·a·ble [ˈneiməbl] *a.* (= namable).

named [neimd] *a.* 被指名的，指定的．*above* ～ 上述的，上开的．

name·less [ˈneimlis] *a.* ①没有名字〔名称〕的；没有署名的，匿名的．②无名声的，不知名的．③难以名状的；说不出的，难以形容的．*a well-known person who shall be* ～ 暂不说明他的名字的某知名人士．*the* ～ *dead* 无名死者．*a* ～ *horror* 说不出的恐怖．**-ly** *ad.* **-ness** *n.*

name·ly [ˈneimli] *ad.* 即，就是，换句话说〔口语常说 that is to say〕．

nam·er [ˈneimə] *n.* 命名人；指名人．

Na·mib·i·a [nəˈmiːbiə] *n.* 纳米比亚(西南非洲)〔非洲〕．**-i·an** 纳米比亚人．

nam·met [ˈnæmit] *n.* (= nummet).

NAMTC = 〔Am.〕Naval Air Missile Test Center 〔美〕海军航空导弹试验中心．

nan-, nano- *comb. f.* 表示"纤"(毫微，= 10^{-9})：nanosecond.

Na·na [ˈnɑːnɑː] *n.* ①巴比仑神话中的女神．②娜娜〔法国作家左拉著同名小说中的女主人公，为一美貌妓女〕．

NANA = North American Newspaper Alliance 北美报业联盟．

nance, nan·cy [næns, ˈnænsi] *n.* 〔美俚〕女人气的男子，搞同性关系的男人．— *a.* 女人似的，柔弱的；搞同性关系的．

Nan·cy [ˈnænsi] *n.* ①南希〔女子名，Ann 的昵称〕．②南锡〔法国城市〕．

NAND [nænd] *n.* 【自】"与非"电路〔一种电子计算机逻辑电路〕．

na·nism [ˈneinizəm] *n.* 矮小；矮态．

nan·keen, nan·kin [næŋˈkiːn] *n.* ①(耐穿的)本色布〔原产我国南京〕；〔*pl.*〕本色布制裤子．②本色，淡黄色．③(我国制)白底青花瓷器．

nan·no·plank·ton, na·no·plank·ton [ˌnænəuˈplæŋktən] *n.* 微小浮游生物．

nan·ny [ˈnæni] *n.* 〔英〕(儿童的)保姆．～ **goat** 雌山羊．

nano- *comb. f.* = nan-〔用于元音前〕．

nan·o·se·cond [ˈnænəuˌsekənd] *n.* 毫微秒．

na·no·watt [ˈneinəuwɔt, ˈnæ-] *n.* 毫微瓦．

Nan·sen [ˈnænsn], **Fridtjof** 南森〔1861—1930，挪威北

极探险家、博物学家,曾获 1922 年诺贝尔和平奖〕.
Nantes [nænts; F. nɑ̃:t] *n.* 南特〔法国城市〕.
Nantz [nænts] *n.* 〔古〕白兰地酒. *good [right]* ~ 地道的白兰地.
Na·o·mi [ˈneiəmi] *n.* 内奥米〔女子名〕.
na·os [ˈneiɔs, ˈnɑ:-] *n.* ***(pl. na·oi*** [-ɔi]) ①古寺院. ②古寺院的内院;内殿,内堂.
nap[1] [næp] *n.* (尤指白天的)小睡,打盹. *take [have] a* ~ 睡午觉; 打一个瞌睡. — *vi.* 〔除现在分词外罕用〕打瞌睡;疏忽. *take [catch] sb. napping* 发现人在打瞌睡;乘人不备时抓住他的疏忽〔偷懒表现等〕. — *vt.* 在瞌睡中度过 *(away)*.
nap[2] [næp] *n.* (呢绒的)绒; (植物表面的)短茸毛. — *vt.* 使起绒.
nap[3] [næp] *n.* 〔俚〕①一种牌戏 (= napoleon). ②孤注一掷. ***a ~ hand*** 一手可获全胜的牌;肯冒险就可获全胜的地位,机会. ***go ~*** 想在拿破仑牌戏中全赢 5 次;大冒险. ***go ~ on*** 对…孤注一掷;确信(事实等). ***~ or nothing*** 成败在此一举. — *vt.* 预测(某匹马)必赢.
na·palm [ˈneipɑ:m] *n.* ①凝固汽油. ②凝固汽油弹. — *vt.* 用凝固汽油(弹)进攻,用凝固汽油燃烧.
nape [neip] *n.* 颈背,后颈,项部.
na·per·y [ˈneipəri] *n.* 〔Scot.〕餐巾,揩嘴布;桌布.
naph·tha [ˈnæfθə] *n.* 【化】粗挥发油;〔废〕石油;石脑油.
naph·tha·lene, -line [ˈnæfθəli:n], **-lin** [-lin] *n.* 【化】萘. ~ **ball** 萘球,卫生丸.
naph·thene [ˈnæfθi:n] *n.* 【化】①环烷,环烷属烃. ②萘的旧名. **-then·ic** [-ˈθi:nik] *a.*
naph·thol [ˈnæfθɔl] *n.* 【化】萘酚; 含有萘环的羟基衍生物.
naph·thyl [ˈnæfθil] *n.* 【化】萘基,从萘衍生的一价基.
Na·pi·er [ˈneipiə] *n.* ①纳皮尔〔姓氏〕. ②**John** ~ 纳皮尔〔1550—1617,英国数学家,对数发明者〕. ③〔m-〕【物】内庇〔衰耗单位〕(= neper).
Na·pi·er·ian log·arithm [nəˈpiəriən ˈlɔgəriθəm]【数】讷氏对数,自然对数.
na·pi·form [ˈneipifɔ:m] *a.* 【植】芜菁状的.
nap·kin [ˈnæpkin] *n.* (食桌上用的)餐巾,揩嘴布;〔英〕(婴儿的)尿布. 〔英方〕手绢、手帕;头巾. ***lay up [hide, wrap] in a ~*** 藏着不用. ~ **ring** (银制或骨制)揩嘴布套环.
Na·ples [ˈneiplz] *n.* 那不勒斯〔意大利港市〕.
nap·less [ˈnæplis] *a.* (呢绒上)没有绒毛的;磨破了的.
Na·po·le·on [nəˈpəuljən, -liən] *n.* 拿破仑〔全称 *Napoleon Bonaparte,* 1769—1821, 即拿破仑一世 (Napoleon I), 法国皇帝,其侄. 拿破仑三世 (Napoleon III, 1808—1873)为 1852—1870 年在位的法国皇帝〕.
na·po·le·on [nəˈpəuljən] *n.* ①旧法国金币〔值 20 法郎〕. ②(每人发5张牌的)拿破仑牌戏〔通例叫 nap〕. ③(19世纪中叶的)拿破仑式长统靴. ④〔美〕法国式奶油夹心千层酥. ⑤红三叶草. ⑥〔N-〕拿破仑品种甜樱桃.
Na·po·le·on·ic [nəpəuliˈɔnik] *a.* 拿破仑(一世时代)的; 拿破仑(一世)似的; 专制的. *a ~ attitude toward one's employees* 对雇员的专横态度. ~ **Code** 拿破仑法典. ~ **Wars** 拿破仑一世进行的历次重大战争. **-cal·ly** *ad.*
Na·po·le·on·ism [nəˈpəuljənizəm] *n.* 拿破仑主义.
Na·po·le·on·ist [nəˈpəuljənist] *n.* 拿破仑主义者.
Na·po·li [It. ˈnɑ:poli] *n.* 那波利〔即 Naples (那不勒斯),意大利港市〕.
na·poo [nɑ:ˈpu:] *a., int.* ①〔军俚〕完蛋了,没用了. ②〔美俚〕死了〔由法语 *il n'y a plus* = there is no more 变来〕. *He's ~.* 他打死了. ~ *fine* 〔美俚〕完了,去了;看不见了. — *vt., vi.* 结束,(使)完蛋;杀死.
nap·per[1] [ˈnæpə] *n.* 打盹的人;〔英俚〕头.
nap·per[2] [ˈnæpə] *n.* 拉毛工人〔装置、机器〕.
nap·per·kids [ˈnæpəkidz] *n.* 〔*pl.*〕〔美俚〕拐子.
nap·py[1] [ˈnæpi] *n.* 〔英口〕尿布.
nap·py[2] [ˈnæpi] *a.* 起毛的,起绒的;柔软的.
nap·py[3] [ˈnæpi] *n.* 菜盆.
nap·py[4] [ˈnæpi] *a.* 〔Eng.〕(啤酒)起泡沫的;浓烈的. — *n.* 〔Eng.〕啤酒.
na·prap·a·thy [nəpˈræpəθi] *n.* 【医】矫正疗法,推拿疗法,按摩疗法.
na·pu[1] [ˈnɑ:pu:] *n.* 【动】(爪哇)矮麝;马来麈.
na·pu[2] [nəˈpu:] *n.* 〔美俚〕= napoo.
Na·ra [ˈnɑ:rə] *n.* 奈良〔日本城市〕.
Nar·a·ka [ˈnærəkə] *n.* 【印度神话】地狱.
narc [nɑ:k] *n.* 〔美俚〕专捉毒品犯的便衣警察.
nar·ce·ine [ˈnɑ:sii:n] *n.* 【化】副鸦片碱,那斯因碱.
nar·cis·sism [nɑ:ˈsisizəm] *n.* (精神分析学中所说的)自我陶醉〔崇拜〕;自恋.
nar·cis·sist [nɑ:ˈsissist] *n.* 自我陶醉者. **-ic** *a.*
Nar·cis·sus [nɑ:ˈsisəs] *n.* ①***(pl. ~es, -cis·si*** [-ˈsisai]) 【植】水仙属;〔n-〕水仙. ②【希神】纳克素斯〔爱上自己映在水中的美丽影子以致淹死而变为水仙的美少年〕;〔n-〕以美貌自夸的青年.
nar·co- *comb. f.* 表示"麻木","失去知觉".
nar·co·a·nal·y·sis [ˌnɑ:kəuəˈnælisis] *n.* 精神麻醉分析.
nar·co·lep·sy [ˈnɑ:kəlepsi] *n.* 【医】嗜眠病.
nar·co·ma·ni·a [ˌnɑ:kəuˈmeinjə] *n.* 麻醉剂狂; 麻醉药癖.
nar·co·sis [nɑ:ˈkəusis] *n.* = narcotism.
nar·co·syn·the·sis [ˌnɑ:kəuˈsinθisis] *n.* (精神病的)麻醉剂疗法.
nar·co·ther·a·py [ˌnɑ:kəuˈθerəpi] *n.* 【医】麻醉疗法;睡眠疗法.
nar·cot·ic [nɑ:ˈkɔtik] *a.* ①麻醉(性)的,起麻痹作用的;麻醉剂的;安眠用的. ②吸毒成瘾者的;护理〔照料〕吸毒成瘾者的. — *n.* ①麻醉剂,麻药;安眠药;起麻痹作用的东西. ②吸毒成瘾的人.
nar·co·tine [ˈnɑ:kəti:n] *n.* 【化】碱溶鸦片碱,那可汀.
nar·co·tism [ˈnɑ:kətizəm] *n.* 【医】麻醉(状态);麻醉作用;麻醉剂中毒,昏睡,不省人事;麻醉品嗜好.
nar·co·ti·za·tion [ˌnɑ:kəutaiˈzeiʃən] *n.* 麻醉.
nar·co·tize [ˈnɑ:kətaiz] *vt.* (使)麻醉;弄弱.
nard [nɑ:d] *n.* 【植】甘松; 甘松油脂. ~**grass** *n.* 亚香茅.
na·res [ˈneəri:z] *n.* 〔*pl.*〕***(sing. na·ris*** [-ris]) 鼻孔.
nar·g(h)i·le [ˈnɑ:gili] *n.* (印度)水烟袋.
nark [nɑ:k] *n.* 〔英俚〕(警察的)密探; 告密者 (=narc). —*vt.* ①告…的密. ②使…发怒. — *vi.* ①告密. ②发怒. ~ ***it!*** 住口! 肃静!
nark·y [ˈnɑ:ki] *a.* 〔俚〕易生气的.
Nar·ra·gan·sett [ˌnærəˈgænsit] *n.* (旧时美国 Rhode Island 地方的)纳拉干族(人)〔北美印第安人的一支〕.
nar·rate [næˈreit] *vt., vi.* 叙述,讲(故事);写〔编〕(故事). ~ *one's adventures* 讲自己的冒险故事. **nar·rat·er** *n.* 〔Am.〕= narrator 讲述者,叙述者.
nar·ra·tion [næˈreiʃən] *n.* 叙述; 故事; 【语】叙述法. *direct [indirect]* ~【语】直接〔间接〕叙述法.
nar·ra·tive [ˈnærətiv] *a.* 叙述的; 故事体的; 善于叙述的. — *n.* ①叙述,记事;记叙文;记叙体;叙述手法. ②〔Scot.〕【法】(证件等的)事实证明部分. *a writer of great ~ power* 叙述手法高超的作家. ~ *economy* 历史学派经济学. **-ly** *ad.* 用故事体.
nar·ra·tor [næˈreitə] ***(fem. -tress*** [-tris]) *n.* 讲述者,叙述者,讲故事者,解说员.
nar·row [ˈnærəu] *a.* ①狭, 窄, 狭隘的, 狭小的 *(opp.* broad, wide*)*. ②有限的, 受限制的; 有偏见的, 气量小的,心眼儿窄的;眼光短浅的. ③仅仅的,勉强的. ④(资力)薄弱的,贫穷的;〔英方, Scot.〕吝啬的,小气的. ⑤精细的, 严密的. ⑥【语】窄音的. ⑦(空气)缺乏的. *have*

a ~ circle of friends 交游不广. *in a ~ sense* 狭义的. *~ cloth* (52英寸以内的)窄幅布. *a ~ mind* 小心眼儿, 小气量. *a ~ victory* 勉强胜利. *a ~ majority* 勉强的多数. *a ~ examination* 严格的检查. *~ circumstances [means]* 穷困. *~ market* 呆滞的市场. *~ vowels* 窄元音. *within ~ bounds* 在小范围内. ***have a ~ escape [shave, squeak]*** 九死一生. ***the ~ bed [cell, house]*** 坟墓. ***the ~ way*** 正直; 正义. — *n.* ①〔常作 *pl.*〕海峡, 峡谷. ②(场所、物品等的)狭窄部分. ***the Narrows*** ①达达尼尔海峡的最狭窄处. ②美国纽约 Staten Islands 和 Long Islands 之间的海峡. — *vt.* ①使狭, 弄窄, 收缩. ②限制, 缩小. *~ an argument down* 限制争论的范围. — *vi.* 变狭, 变窄;【编织】收小. **~-fisted** *a.* 吝啬的. **~-gauge(d)** *a.*【铁路】狭轨的 *(opp.* broadgauge*)*. **~ minded** *a.* 气量小的, 心眼儿窄的; 极端保守的; 思想僵化的. **-ness** *n.* 狭窄, 狭小; 偏狭; 穷困.

nar·row·ish [ˈnærəuiʃ] *a.* 有些狭窄的.

nar·row·ly [ˈnærəuli] *ad.* ①勉强地, 好容易(才). ②严密地, 仔细地. ③严格地; 过细地. ④猛烈地. *He ~ escaped drowning.* 他险些儿淹死.

nar·w(h)al, nar·whale [ˈnɑːwəl] *n.*【动】一角鲸.

nar·y [ˈnɛəri] *a.*〔方、美〕连…也没有. *~ a cent* 一个铜钱也没有.

NAS = National Academy of Sciences〔美〕全国科学院.

N.A.S. = Nursing Auxiliary Service 护士辅助勤务队.

NASA = National Aeronautics and Space Administration〔美〕国家航空和宇宙航行局.

na·sal [ˈneizəl] *a.* 鼻的;【语】鼻音的. *the ~ opening* 鼻孔. *the ~ organ*〔谑〕鼻子. *a ~ discharge* 鼻涕. *a ~* 鼻音字母. — *n.* ①【语音】鼻音, 鼻音字母〔m, n, ng [ŋ]〕. ②【解】鼻骨. ③(钢盔的)护鼻. **-ly** *ad.*

na·sal·ism [ˈneizəlizəm, -zli-] *n.* 鼻音法.

na·sal·i·ty [neiˈzæliti] *n.* 鼻音性, 鼻音.

na·sal·ize [ˈneizəlaiz] *vi., vt.* 发(鼻音); (使)鼻音化. **-za·tion** [ˌneizəlaiˈzeiʃən] *n.*

nas·cence [ˈnæsns], **nas·cen·cy** [-snsi] *n.* 发生, 起源.

nas·cent [ˈnæsnt] *a.* 发生中的, 初期的,【化】初生的, 新生的. *the ~ literature and art* 萌芽状态的文艺. *~* **oxygen** 原子态氧. *~* **state**【化】初生态, 新生态.

nase·ber·ry [ˈneizberi] *n.* *(pl.* ***-ries****)* 人心果树; 人心果 (= *sapodilla*).

Nash [næʃ] *n.* 纳什〔姓氏〕.

Nas·myth [ˈneizmiθ] *n.* 内史密斯〔姓氏〕.

na·so·fron·tal [neizəuˈfrʌntl] *a.* 鼻额的, 鼻额骨的.

na·so·phar·ynx [ˌneizəuˈfæriŋks] *n.*【解】鼻咽. **-pha·ryn·ge·al** [-fəˈrindʒiəl] *a.*

Nas·sau [ˈnæsɔː] *n.* 纳索(拿骚)〔巴哈马首都〕.

nas·tic [ˈnæstik] *a.*【植】感性运动的.

nas·ti·ly [ˈnɑːstili] *ad.* 污秽, 不清洁, 肮脏; 淫秽〔参见 nasty〕.

nas·tur·tium [nəsˈtəːʃəm] *n.*【植】旱金莲(花).

nas·ty [ˈnɑːsti] *a.* ①脏得怕人的, 非常邋遢的; 使人不愉快的, 卑劣的, 下流的; 淫秽的; 讨厌的. ②(天气)恶劣的; 艰险的; 痛苦的, 厉害的. ③难应付的; 难弄的; 严重的. *a ~ smell* 令人作呕的气味. *~ medicine* 难吃的药. *a ~ job* 不愉快的工作. *a ~ temper* 讨厌的脾气. *a ~ sea* 大风浪. *Don't be ~.* 不要发脾气啦. ***a ~ one*** 责骂; 严重的打击. ***get oneself into a ~ mess*** 陷入困境. ***leave a ~ taste in the mouth*** 留下讨厌的气味[印象]. ***(a) ~ piece of work*** 别扭行为;〔口〕下流坯; 讨厌的家伙. ***turn ~*** 发怒; 闹别扭. **nas·ti·ness** *n.*

nat. = national; native; natural.

nat [næt] *n.*〔美俚〕民族主义者.

na·tal [ˈneitl] *a.* 出生的, 诞生的;〔诗〕故乡的. *one's ~ day [place]* 生日[诞生地].

Nat·a·lie [ˈnætəli] *n.* 纳塔莉〔女子名〕.

na·tal·i·ty [neiˈtæliti] *n.* 出生率, 产生率.

na·tant [ˈneitənt] *a.* 浮在水上的, 浮游的. **-ly** *ad.* 浮在水上.

na·ta·tion [neiˈteiʃən] *n.* 游泳; 游泳(术).

Na·ta·to·res [ˌneitəˈtɔːriːz] *n.*〔*pl.*〕【动】水禽类, 游禽类.

na·ta·to·ri·al [ˌneitəˈtɔːriəl], **na·ta·to·ry** [-təri] *a.* 游泳(用)的. *~ birds* 水鸟.

na·ta·to·ri·um [ˌneitəˈtɔːriəm] *n.* *(pl.* ***~s, -ri·a*** [-riə]*)* 游泳池.

natch [nætʃ] *ad.*〔美俚〕自然地, 当然 (= naturally).

Natch·ez [ˈnætʃiz] *n.* ①*(pl.* ***Natch·ez****)* 纳齐兹部族人〔原是居住在美国密西西比州西南部的印第安人的一个部落, 现已灭绝〕. ②纳齐兹语. **Natchez Trace** 纳齐兹古道遗迹〔十九世纪由印第安人从美国密西西比的纳齐兹到田纳西的纳什维尔走出来的一条古道〕.

na·tes [ˈneitiːz] *n.*〔*pl.*〕【解】臀部.

Na·than [ˈneiθən] *n.* 内森〔姓氏, 男子名〕.

Na·than·i·el [nəˈθənjəl] *n.* 纳撒尼尔〔男子名〕.

nathe·less [ˈneiθlis], **nath·less** [ˈnæθlis] *ad.*〔古、诗〕= nevertheless. — *prep.* = notwithstanding.

na·tion [ˈneiʃən] *n.* ①民族; 国家; 种族;〔美〕印地安人的部落(联盟). ②(中世纪大学或苏格兰大学中的)学生同乡会. *the ~s* 世界各国人民. *the top industrial ~ of the world* 世界最大工业国. *the law of ~s* 国际公法. *the League of Nations* (第一次大战后成立的)国际联盟. *the United Nations* (第二次大战后成立的)联合国. *the most favoured ~ (clause)* 最惠国(条款). ***the ~s***【圣】异教徒〔指非犹太的各民族〕. ~ **state** 民族国, 单一民族国家. **~-wide** *a.* 全国性的. **-hood** 作为一个国家的地位.

na·tion·al [ˈnæʃənəl] *a.* ①民族的; 国民的; 国家的; 国民特有的. ②国家主义的; 爱国的. ③国立的, 国有的, 国定的; 全国性的 *a ~ air [anthem]* 国歌. *the ~ assembly* 国民议会. *the ~ debt* 国债. *a ~ bank* 国家银行;〔美〕(加入联邦准备银行 Federal Reserve System 有发行钞票特权的)国民银行. *a ~ struggle* 民族斗争. *~ salvation* 救国. *~ independence* 民族独立. *a ~ park* 国立公园. *a ~ enterprise* 国营企业. ***go ~***〔美〕把事业扩张到全国. — *n.* ①国民(一分子);〔*pl.*〕(尤指侨居国外的)同国人, 同胞. ②〔美〕有许多支部的大学生联谊会. ③〔常 *pl.*〕全国性体育比赛. ***the Grand National*** (每年三月举行的)全国性大赛马. **N- Archives**〔美〕档案处. ~ **bourgeoisie** 民族资产阶级. **N- Coal Board**〔英〕煤炭部. **N- Convention**〔美〕(决定总统候选人的)全国大会. **N- Day** 国庆日. ~ **defense** 国防. ~ **domicile** 国籍. ~ **economy** 国民经济. ~ **emergency** 全国紧急状态, 国难. ~ **flag [ensign]** 国旗. **N- Guard**〔美〕国民警卫队. ~ **guildman** 基尔特社会主义者. ~ **holiday** 国定假日; 国庆日. ~ **income** 国民收入. ~ **independence movement** 民族独立运动. **N- Insurance** 国民保险〔英国对疾病、失业等的强制保险〕. **N- Militia** 民兵. ~ **mobilization** 全国动员, 总动员. ~ **monument** (美国联邦政府管理的)名胜古迹〔指由美国政府保护供旅游的诸如高山、峡谷、古堡等〕. **N- People's Congress** 全国人民代表大会. ~ **policy** 国策. ~ **purse** 国富, 国库. ~ **revenue** 国家收入. ~ **seashore**〔美〕由联邦政府管理的海边旅行地. ~ **self-determination** 民族自决. **N- Service**〔英〕国民兵役. ~ **socialism** 国家社会主义(即纳粹主义). ~ **united front** 民族统一战线. **N- Weather Service** 国家气象服务站.

na·tion·al·ism [ˈnæʃənəlizəm] *n.* 爱国心; 国风, 民族性, 民族特征; 民族主义, 国家主义 *(opp.* internationalism*)* (尤指爱尔兰的)国家独立主义; 工业国有化政策.

na·tion·al·ist [ˈnæʃənəlist] *n.* 国家主义者; 民族主义者; (爱尔兰的)民族自治论者; 主张工业国有化的人. — *a.* 国家主义的, 民族主义的. *a ~ country* 民族主义国家.

na·tion·al·is·tic [ˌnæʃənəˈlistik] *a.* 国家主义的，民族主义的．**-ti·cal·ly** *ad.*

na·tion·al·i·ty [ˌnæʃəˈnæliti] *n.* 国民性，民族性，国风；国籍，船籍；国民；国家，民族(独立)．*the minority nationalities* 各少数民族．*the question of the dual* ～ 双重国籍问题．*men of all nationalities* 世界各国人民．

na·tion·a·lize [ˈnæʃənəlaiz] *vt.* ①使成一国［独立国家］；使国家化；使民族化．②把…收归国有［国营］，使国有化．③〔罕〕使归化．**-za·tion, -r** *n.*

na·tion·al·ly [ˈnæʃənəli] *ad.* 全国性地；从国民立场；举国一致；从国家立场，以国家为本位．*a* ～ *independent country* 民族独立国家．

na·tive [ˈneitiv] *a.* ①出生地的，本国的，本地的．②土著的，本地人的；土产的，国内的．③生来的，天赋的．④天生的，天然的；纯粹的．⑤天真的，纯朴的．～ *country [land]* 本国，祖国．～ *place* 故乡．*a* ～ *son* 本地人，土生土长的儿子．*a N- Son* 〔美俚〕加利福尼亚人．～ *sons of New York* 纯粹的纽约人．～ *fruit* 当地水果．*fruits* ～ *and foreign* 国内外的水果．～ *copper* 纯铜，自然铜．～ *rubber* 天然橡胶．**go** ～ 采取简单朴素的生活方式；作当地人，过当地生活．—*n.* ①土著，生在…的人 *(of)*．②〔澳〕生在澳大利亚的白种人；〔澳〕象英国种的(动植物)．③〔常贬〕土人，未开化人；当地人；当地动植物．④〔英〕(人工蠔场的)本场蠔［牡蛎］．**～-born** *a.* 本地［本国］生的．**-ly** *ad.* **-ness** *n.*

na·tiv·ism [ˈneitivizəm] *n.* ①【哲】先天论，天性论．②本土主义，排外主义．**-tiv·ist** *n.*

na·tiv·i·ty [nəˈtiviti] *n.* ①出生，诞生．②〔N-〕耶稣诞生(图)；圣诞节；圣母马利亚诞生节．③【占星】算命天宫图．*cast [calculate] one's* ～ 算命．

natl. = national.

NATO [ˈneitəu] (= North Atlantic Treaty Organization) 北大西洋公约组织，北约组织．

na·tri·um [ˈneitriəm] *n.*【化】钠〔sodium 的旧名〕．

nat·ro·lite [ˈnætrəlait, ˈneitrə-] *n.*【地】钠沸石．

na·tron [ˈneitrən] *n.*【矿】泡碱，冰碱；氧化钠；含水苏打．

nat·ter [ˈnætə] *vi.* 〔主英〕①闲谈，瞎扯．②发牢骚．—*n.* 谈话，交谈，闲谈．

nat·ter·jack [ˈnætədʒæk] *n.*【动】黄条贝蟾蜍．

nat·thex [ˈnɑːθeks] *n.* ①教堂西门〔指早期基督教堂的西门，非忏悔者不许进入〕．②教堂前厅．

nat·ti·er [ˈnætiə] *a.* 〔natty 的比较级〕．～ *blue* 淡蓝色．

nat·ti·ly [ˈnætili] *ad.* 整洁，清爽．

nat·ty [ˈnæti] *a.* *(-ti·er; -ti·est)* ①(外貌、衣着)整洁的，干净的；清爽的；潇洒的．②灵巧的，敏捷的．**-ti·ness** *n.*

Na·tu·fi·an [nəˈtuːfiən] *a.* 西南亚中石器时代文化的．

nat·u·ral [ˈnætʃərəl] *a.* ①自然界的；关于自然界的．②天然的；未开垦的；野生的．③固有的，生来的，天赋的 *(opp.* acquired*)*；出乎本性的．④自然的，不加修饰的，不加做作的．⑤本来的；(论理上或人情上)当然的，不勉强的，常态的；普通的，平常的．⑥逼真的．⑦私生的，庶出的．⑧【乐】本位的；标明本位号的．⑨【数】自然数的；真数的．*the* ～ *day* 自然日〔由日出至日没〕．*the* ～ *forces* 自然力．～ *phenomena* 自然现象．*the* ～ *world* 自然界．*the* ～ *year* 自然年，太阳年．～ *gas* 天然气．～ *resources* 天然资源．*It is quite* ～ *that you (should) succeed [for you to succeed].* 你的成功是很自然的．*Speaking comes* ～ *to him.* 他的演说流畅而自然．～ *disposition* 天性，本性．*a* ～ *gift* 天资，天禀．～ *poet* 天生的诗人．～ *vibration* 固有振动．～ *sine* 正弦真数．*one's* ～ *life* 寿命，寿限．～ *wages* 实物工资．*a* ～ *sign* 【乐】本位记号(♮)．—*n.* ①(生来的)白痴．②【乐】(风琴等的)白键；本位音；本位号〔♮〕．③(二十一点牌戏)一分牌就赢的两张牌．④〔美俚〕未曾受过训练而表演得意外出色的人，意外出色的表演；〔口〕对某方面(似乎)有天生特长的人．⑤〔美口〕可望立即成功的事物．**～-born** *a.* 天生的，生来的；本国出生的．～ **childbirth** 自然分娩法．～ **classification**【生】自然分类．～ **frequency**【物】固有频率．～ **guardian** 父母．～ **history** 博物学．～ **law** 自然规律；天理，自然法．～ **man** 蒙昧人．～ **number**【数】自然数．～ **orders** (植物分类上的)目〔普通仅说作 orders〕．～ **person**【法】自然人．～ **philosopher** 自然哲学家．～ **philosophy** 自然哲学〔旧指自然科学，尤指物理学〕；～ **right** 天赋权利，人权．～ **rock** 天然沥青．～ **science** 自然科学．～ **selection** 自然淘汰，自然选择，天演．～ **system**【植】自然分类〔据根形态的类似〕．～ **theology** 自然神学．～ **weapons** 天然武器〔爪、牙、拳等〕．～ **weight** 容积重．

nat·u·ral·ism [ˈnætʃərəlizəm] *n.* ①自然，自然状态．②【哲、文艺】自然主义．③本能行动．

nat·u·ral·ist [ˈnætʃərəlist] *n.* ①博物学家，(现特指)生物学家；自然主义者．②〔主英〕鸟商；剥制师．—*a.* = naturalistic.

nat·u·ral·is·tic [ˌnætʃurəˈlistik] *a.* ①自然的．②自然主义的；写实的．③博物学的．

nat·u·ral·i·za·tion [ˌnætʃərəlaiˈzeiʃən] *n.* ①顺化，归化；入国籍．②驯化，风土化．

nat·u·ral·ize [ˈnætʃərəlaiz] *vt.* ①使归化；使入国籍；采纳(外国语言、风俗等)．②移养，移植(动植物)．③按自然规律说明，使不神秘．—*vi.* ①归化；土著化．②驯化．③研究博物学．*become* ～*d as a Chinese citizen* = *become* ～*d in China* 入中国籍．

nat·u·ral·ly [ˈnætʃərəli] *ad.* ①自然地．②生来；天然地．③自自然然，不做作地．④容易地．⑤当然，不用说．*She is* ～ *musical.* 她生来喜欢音乐．*I* ～ *accepted.* 我当然接受了．**come** ～ **to sb.** (做某事)对某人很容易 *(Driving comes* ～ *to him.* 他开车一点不费劲)．

nat·u·ral·ness [ˈnætʃərəlnis] *n.* ①自然；当然；纯真．②【无】逼真度．

na·ture [ˈneitʃə] *n.* ①自然(现象)，大自然；自然界；自然力；〔拟人化时作 N-，作阴性用〕造化，造物主．②自然状态，原始状态；裸体；野生状态．③(物体的)本质，(人、动物的)天性，本性，性格，脾性；特质，特征，性质；品种，类别；(子弹等的)大小．④生命力；体力，活力，精力；本能的力量，冲动；肉体的要求．⑤天理，道理．⑥自然景色，风景．⑦树脂；树液．⑧【宗】(人)尚未赎罪的状态．*all* ～ 万物．*All* ～ *looks gay.* 万物喜洋洋．*All* ～ *looks bleak.* 满目荒凉．*human* ～ 人性，人情．*the animal* ～ 兽性．*the rational* ～ 理性．*a man of good [ill]* ～ 脾气好［坏］的人．*N- will out.* 本性难隐．*sanguine* ～*s* (性格)快活的人，乐天派的人．*events of this* ～ 这一类事件．*Such a diet will not support* ～. 吃这种东西身体支持不住．*N- is exhausted.* 体力耗尽．***against*** ～ 不自然地；奇迹地；违反自然［人性］．***by*** ～ 生就，生来，本来．***by the*** ～ ***of things*** = in the ～ of things. ***call [necessity] of*** ～ 自然［生理］的要求，要大小便．***contrary to*** ～ = against ～. ***draw from*** ～ 写生．***ease [relieve]*** ～ 解大［小］便．***freak of*** ～ 造化的恶作剧〔天然的畸形〕．***in a [the] state of*** ～ 在自然［野蛮］状态中，尚未开化；裸体．***in*** ～. ①现在存在；事实上．②〔疑问词、否定语的加重语气〕究竟，什么地方也(没有等) *(What in* ～ *do you mean?* 你究竟是什么意思呢?)．***in the course of*** ～ 依自然之势，顺乎自然．***in [of] the*** ～ ***of*** 具有…的性质，象，类似 *(His request is in the* ～ *of a command.* 他的请求简直象命令)．***in [by, from] the*** ～ ***of things [the case]*** 在道理上，照道理说；当然，必然．***like all*** ～〔美口〕完全．***Nature's engineering*** 天工．***one of Nature's gentlemen*** 地位虽低但志行高洁而有同情心的人．***one of Nature's noblemen*** 〔反语〕老粗．***pay one's debt to*** ～, ***pay the debt of*** ～ 死．***true to*** ～ 逼真．～ **cure** 自然疗法．～ **deity,** **～-god** 自然神．～ **myth**

自然神话. ~ **printing** (把原物直接制成印版的)自然印刷法. ~ **study** (学校的)自然课. ~ **worship** 自然崇拜.

-na·tured *comb. f.* "有…性质的","有…脾气的": good-*natured* 脾气好的. ill-*natured* 脾气坏的.

na·tur·ism [ˈneitʃərizəm] *n.* 对自然现象的崇拜;〔婉〕裸体主义. **na·tur·ist** *n.* 自然现象崇拜者;〔婉〕裸体主义者.

na·tur·o·path [ˈneitʃərəpæθ] *n.* 物理治疗家,理疗家.

na·tur·op·a·thy [ˌneitʃəˈrɔpəθi] *n.* 理疗,物理疗法. **-o·path·ic** [ˌneitʃərəˈpæθik] *a.*

naught [nɔːt] *n.* 〔古〕①无;无价值. ②【数】零〔作此义时通常用 nought〕. ③〔古〕邪恶;坏人,恶人. ***all for ~*** 无益,徒然. ***a thing of ~*** 没价值的东西,没有用的东西. ***bring to ~*** 破坏,挫败,使无效,使成泡影. ***care ~ for*** 一点不把…放在心上,丝毫不理会. ***come to ~ [nothing]*** 毫无结果,等于零;失败,枉费心机. ***set at ~*** 轻视,藐视,忽视;一笔抹杀;使成泡影,完全破坏.

naught·y [ˈnɔːti] *a.* ***(-ti·er; -ti·est)*** ①顽皮的,淘气的,任性的,不听话的,撒野的,没规矩的. ②卑劣的;猥亵的,下流的. ③〔古〕邪恶的. *a ~ pack* 淘气鬼;坏蛋. **-ti·ly** *ad.* **-ti·ness** *n.*

nau·ma·chi·a [nɔːˈmeikiə] *n.* ***(pl. ~s, -chi·ae*** [-ˌiː]***)*** ①古罗马海战演习. ②古罗马海战演习场 (= naumachy).

Na·u·ru [nɑːˈuːruː] *n.* ①瑙鲁〔西太平洋〕. ②瑙鲁〔瑙鲁首都〕. **-n** *n.* 瑙鲁人.

nau·se·a [ˈnɔːsjə] *n.* ①恶心,作呕,晕船. ②极度厌恶,引起人极度厌恶的东西. *be seized with ~* 要吐,欲呕.

nau·se·ant [ˈnɔziːənt] *n.* 呕吐剂.

nau·se·ate [ˈnɔːsieit] *vt.* ①使呕吐,使恶心. ②使厌恶;嫌,厌. — *vi.* ①作呕. ②厌恶 *(at)*.

nau·se·at·ing [ˈnɔːsieitiŋ] *a.* 使人呕吐的;使人厌恶的. **-ly** *ad.*

nau·se·a·tion [ˌnɔːsiˈeiʃən] *n.* 恶心,呕.

nau·se·ous [ˈnɔːsjəs] *a.* 令人作呕[恶心]的;讨厌的. **-ly** *ad.*

naut. = nautical.

nautch [nɔːtʃ] *n.* (印度专业舞女的)舞蹈(表演). ~ **girl** (印度的职业性)舞女.

nau·ti·cal [ˈnɔːtikəl] *a.* 海上的,航海的;船舶的;海员的,水手的. *a ~ almanac* 航海天文历. *a ~ mile* = a sea mile〔见 mile 条〕. ~ *terms* 航海用语. **-ly** *ad.*

nau·ti·loid [ˈnɔːtilɔid] *n.* 鹦鹉螺目动物〔包括鹦鹉螺、舡鱼、蛸船〕.

nau·ti·lus [ˈnɔːtiləs] *n.* ***(pl. ~es, -li*** [-lai]***)*** ①【动】鹦鹉螺 (= pearly ~). ②【动】舡鱼 (= paper ~);蛸船.

nav. = ①naval. ②navigable. ③navigation.

Nav·a·ho, Nav·a·jo [ˈnævəhəu] *n.* ***(pl. ~s)*** ①(美国新墨西哥、亚利桑那、犹他等州的)印第安纳瓦霍族人;纳瓦霍语. ②[n-]橙红色. ③〔美〕超音速巡航导弹;远距离无线电领航系统.

nav·aid [ˈnæveid] *n.* 助航装置[系统] (= navigational aid).

na·val [ˈneivəl] *a.* (有)海军的;军舰的;船的. *a ~ action [engagement]* 海战. *N- Academy [College]* 海军学院. *a ~ architect* 造船工程师. *~ architecture* 造船工程. *a ~ base* 海军根据地. *a ~ brigade* 海军陆战队. *a ~ cadet* 海军军官学员. *a ~ captain* 海军上校. *the N- Department*〔美〕海军部. *a ~ engineer* (海军)轮机官. *the N- Engineering College* 海军轮机学校. *~ forces* 海军. *the N- General Board*〔美〕海军将领会议. *the N- Intelligence Division*〔英〕海军参谋部情报处. *a ~ machinist* (海军)修械师. *~ manoeuvres* 海军演习. *~ officer* 海军军官;〔美〕海关人员. *a ~ port* 军港. *the ~ powers* 海军强国. ~ **stores** ①海军补给品. ②松脂(制品). **-ly** *ad.*

na·val·ism [ˈneivəlizəm] *n.* 海军至上主义;海军攻势主义. **-ist** *n.* 海军至上主义者. **-istic** *a.*

nav·ar [ˈnævɑː]【空】指挥飞行的雷达系统.

nav·arch [ˈneivɑːk] *n.* 古希腊舰队指挥官.

nave[1] [neiv] *n.*【建】(教堂的)中殿,听众席;(铁路车站等建筑的)中央广场.

nave[2] [neiv] *n.* (车)毂.

na·vel [ˈneivəl] *n.* 脐;中央,中心. ~ **orange** 脐橙〔一端有脐状凹陷的无核橙子〕. ~ **string [cord]** 脐带.

na·vel·wort [ˈneivəlwəːt] *n.*【植】①琉璃草属植物. ②俯垂脐景天. ③美洲石胡荽.

nav·i·cert [ˈnævisəːt] *n.* (交战国发给的)中立国船只运照,特准运照;(交战国对中立国船只的)运照制度 (= ~ system).

na·vic·u·lar [nəˈvikjulə] *a.* 船形的(尤指骨). *the ~ bone* 舟骨. — *n.*【解】舟骨.

navig. = ①navigation. ②navigator.

nav·i·ga·ble [ˈnævigəbl] *a.* ①(河湖等)可航行的,可通船的. ②(船)适于航行的,耐航行的. ③(气球等)可操纵航向的;适于航空的. — *n.* 〔罕〕飞艇. **-bil·i·ty** [ˌnævigəˈbiliti] *n.* 适航性. **-bly** *ad.*

nav·i·gate [ˈnævigeit] *vt.* ①驾驶(船舶、飞机等);导航. ②(人、船等)航行于;横渡. ③〔美〕(稳定地)笔直走;使通过(议案等). *She has trouble navigating the stair.* 她上下台阶(楼梯)有困难. — *vi.* 航行;航空;横穿;驾驶船舶[飞机]. *a navigating light* 航空灯. *navigating-jack [lieutenant, officer]* (海军)航海长,航海人员.

nav·i·ga·tion [ˌnæviˈgeiʃən] *n.* ①航行;导航;领航;航海[航空]术. ②〔集合词〕船. ③〔古〕航路;海上交通. *aerial ~* 空中航行. *inland ~* 内河航行. *astro ~* 宇宙航行;天文导航. *blind ~* 仪表导航. *the N- Acts*〔英〕航海条例. *There has been an increase in ~ through the canal.* 通过那条运河的船数增多了. ~ **coal** 锅炉煤,蒸汽煤. ~ **light** 飞机夜航时机身上的灯光. **-al** *a.*

nav·i·ga·tor [ˈnævigeitə] *n.* ①航行者,航海者;(船舶、飞机的)驾驶员,领航员;海洋探险家. ②航海书. ③〔英罕〕= navvy. *(the) radar ~* 雷达导航设备.

Nav Torp Sta (= naval torpedo station) 海军鱼雷艇站.

nav·vy [ˈnævi] *n.* ①〔英〕(开挖运河、修筑铁路等的)工人;壮工. ②掘土机;挖泥机. ③〔海俚〕= navigating-officer. *a steam ~* 蒸汽掘土机. *work like a ~* 尽力做(讨厌的工作). *a mere ~s work* (不用脑的)粗活. — *vi.* 做(开河、筑路的)工人. — *vt.* 掘(地).

na·vy [ˈneivi] *n.* ①〔常 N-〕海军. ②〔集合词〕海军官兵. ③〔英〕海军部. ④〔诗〕(商船)船队. ⑤藏青色 = ~ blue. *the PLA N-* 中国人民解放军海军. *the Royal N-* 英国海军. *the N-, Army, and Air Force(s) Institutes*〔英〕海陆空军招待所. *the Department of the N-* = *the N- Department*〔美〕海军部. *the secretary of the N-*〔美〕海军部长. ***bare ~*** 〔美海军俚〕只发罐头食品的配给制度. ***The N- League*** 〔英〕海军协会. ~ **blue** (英国海军制服的)藏青色,深蓝色. ~ **bean** 〔美〕【植】海军豆〔因美国海军中普遍食用而得名,粒小,白色,晒干〕. **N- Cross** 〔美〕海军十字勋章. ~ **cut** 〔英〕切成薄片的块状板烟. ~ **day** 海军节. ~ **"E" gunnery** (海军)优等射手. ~ **list** 海军名簿,海军一览. ~ **yard** 〔美〕海军造船厂.

naw [nɔː] *ad.* 〔美俚〕= no.

nay [nei] *ad.* 〔古〕①否,不 *(opp.* yea*)*. ②不但如是,而且;宁〔发言时表示"好,唔,是的"等语气〕. *N-, then, I will essay it.* 好,那么我来试试看. *It is weighty, ~, conclusive.* 那很重要,不,有决定的作用. ***~ more*** 不仅…甚至…. ~,~〔美俚〕= no. — *n.* 〔古〕否,拒绝,反对;反对投票(者). *Let your yea be yea and your ~ be ~.* 赞成与否请说个明白. *yea and ~* 支支吾吾,磨棱两可. *the yeas and ~s* 赞否(之数). ***say (sb.) ~*** 跟某人说"不行";拒绝请求;禁止. ***will not take ~ [no]*** 不许

人说个“不”字，不接受否定的答案。

nay·say [ˈneisei] *n.* 拒绝，否认。— *vt.* [neiˈsei] ***(nay-said, nay·said*** [ˈneiˈseid]***)*** 拒绝，否认，反对。**-er** [ˈnei-seiə] *n.* 反对者，否认者，拒绝者；老爱唱反调的人。

Naz·a·rene [ˌnæzəˈriːn] *n.* 拿撒勒人；〔the N-〕耶稣；(犹太人及穆斯林所说的)基督教徒。— *a.* 拿撒勒人的。

Naz·a·reth [ˈnæzəriθ] *n.* 拿撒勒〔巴勒斯坦北部古城，相传为耶稣的故乡〕。

Naz·a·rite [ˈnæzərait] *n.* ①拿撒勒人。②(不剪发、不剃须、不喝酒的)古希伯来修行者。~ *hair* 长发。

naze [neiz] *n.* 〔罕〕岬，海角。

Na·zi [ˈnɑːtsiː] *n.* ***(pl. ~s)*** *a.* 德国国家社会党(的)，纳粹党(的)，纳粹党员(的)；纳粹分子(的)，法西斯分子(的)。**-dom** 纳粹党的势力范围。**-fi·ca·tion** [-fi-ˈkeiʃən] *n.* 纳粹化。**-fy** [-fai] *vt.* 使纳粹化，把…置于纳粹控制或影响之下；纳粹化。**-(i)sm** *n.* 纳粹主义。

na·zim [ˈnɑːzim] *n.* 纳济姆〔印度及伊斯兰教各国高级警官〕。

na·zir [ˈnɑːziə] *n.* (印度、穆斯林国家的)法官。

N.B., NB, n.b. = ①〔L.〕*nota bene* 注意，留心(= note well)。②New Brunswick 新不伦瑞克。③North British 苏格兰的。

Nb = 【化】niobium 铌。

NBC = National Broadcasting Company 〔美〕全国广播公司。

NbE, N by E = north by east 北偏东。

N-bomb = nuclear bomb 氢弹。

N.B.R. = North British Railway〔英〕苏格兰铁路。

NBS = National Bureau of Standards〔美〕国家标准局。

NbW, N by W = north by west 北偏西。

N.C., NC = ①North Carolina 北卡罗来纳〔美国州名〕。②= numerica control【自】数字控制。

N.C., n.c.【化】= nitrocellulose 硝化纤维(火药)。

NCNA = New China News Agency 新华通讯社。

N.C.O., NCO = noncommissioned officer 军士。

N.C.U. = National Cyclists' Union 〔英〕全国自行车运动员联合会。

Nd = 【化】neodymium 钕。

N.D., ND = ①North Dakota 北达科他〔美国州名〕。②no date; not dated 无日期。

n.d. = ①no date; not dated 无日期。②nothing doing〔俚〕不行！不干！完了！③no delivery 未交付，未到货；无法投递。

-nd *suf.* ①用于拉丁动形容词之后形成名词及形容词：rever*end*, divid*end*. ②由拉丁动形容词形成的形容词的后缀：jocu*nd*, moribu*nd*. ③用于形成名词：fie*nd*, frie*nd*.

NDAC = National Defense Advisory Committee〔美〕国防顾问委员会。

N.Dak. = North Dakota 北达科他〔美国州名〕。

Ndjamena [nˈdʒɑːmenɑː] *n.* 恩贾梅纳〔旧称 Fort-Lamy 拉密堡〕〔乍得首都〕。

Ndola [nˈdəulɑː] *n.* 恩多拉〔赞比亚城市〕。

N.E., NE, n.e. = ①northeast; northeastern. ②New England 新英格兰(美国东北六州之总称)。③no effects 无存款。

Ne = neon【化】氖。

NEA = Northeast Airlines〔美〕东北航空公司。

N.E.A. = National Education Association 〔美〕全国教育协会。

Ne·an·der·thal [niˈændətɑːl] *a.*【人类】尼安得特尔人的。~ **man**【人类】尼安得特尔人。

neap [niːp] *n., a.* 小潮(的)，最低潮(的)。— *vi.* (潮水)达小潮最低点。— *vt.* (因小潮)使(船)搁浅。***be ~ed*** (船)因小潮搁浅。

Ne·a·pol·i·tan [niəˈpɔlitən] *a.* (意大利)那不勒斯(Naples)(人)的。— *n.* 那不勒斯人。~ **ice (cream)** 三色〔多色〕冰砖。

near [niə] *ad.* ①近，接近，邻接 *(opp.* far*)*。②〔口〕几乎，差不多，将近。③节省地。*He stood ~ to the door.* 他站在门附近〔在比较级和最高级之后亦常用 to. 如：I live ~er to the school than you. 我比你住得离学校近一些〕。*He lives very ~.* 他生活很节俭。***as ~ as*** 和…一样；在…限度内。***come ~*** 接近，赶得上，不亚于。***come [go] ~ to …ing*** 几乎，差点儿，差不多。***draw ~*** 接近，迫近。***far and ~*** 到处，远近。***~ at hand*** 在手边，在近旁；即将到来。***~ by*** 在附近。***~ upon*** 几乎，将近(*The old man is ~ upon eighty.* 那老人将近八十了)。***not ~ so …*** = not nearly so. ***nowhere ~*** = ***not anywhere ~*** 附近都不，远远不(*That's nowhere ~ enough.* 那是远远不够的)。— *prep.* 接近，在…的近旁；快要。*sail ~ the wind* (船)抢风而驶；做危险事情。*The time draws ~ New Year.* 时节将近新年。*She came [went] ~ being drowned.* 她差点儿淹死了。*The sun is ~ setting.* 太阳快落了。*It kept him awake till ~ morning.* 这使他直到快天亮还醒着。***be ~ one's end*** 快要死，接近死期。***lie ~ one's heart*** 为某人所关怀〔关切〕。— *a.* ①近(的)，接近的。②近亲的；亲密的，关系深的。③近似的，和原物难分的。④(马或车的)左侧的 *(opp.* off*)*。⑤近道的；直达的。⑥吝啬的。⑦〔口〕危险的。⑧〔美口〕仿制的，冒充的。~ *sight* 近视。*the ~ distance* (绘画等的)近景。*the ~ future* 不久的将来。*the ~(er) way* 捷径，近路。*a ~ friend* 亲密的朋友。~ *concern* (有)密切利害关系。*a ~ resemblance* 酷似。*a ~ horse* (马车)左侧的马。*a ~ guess* 相差不很多的推测。~ *silk*〔美〕极象真丝的人造丝。*a ~ translation* 直译，接近原文的翻译。***be ~ with one's money*** 吝啬。***~ and dear*** 极亲密的。***on a ~ day*** 日内，三五天内。— *vt., vi.* 近，接近，靠拢；迫近。~ **beer** 淡啤酒。~**by**〔原美〕①*a.* 附近的。②*ad.* (靠)近〔英国分写作 ~ by〕。~ **continent** 近欧〔英国指比利时、荷兰、法国、丹麦等〕。**N- East** 近东。~ **miss**【军】①接近击中(目标)弹。②接近，但不够理想的成功。③(飞机)幸免相撞。~ **point**【医】近点。~ **race** 难分上下的赛跑。~**-sighted** *a.* 近视的。~**-sightedness** 近视眼。~**-sonic** *a.*【空】近音速的。~**-term** *a.* 近期的。~ **thing [escape, touch]** 九死一生，仅以身免。~ **wheel** (马车的)左轮。~ **wheeler** (四马马车的)左后马。~ **work** 精密工作〔因须接近眼睛〕。

near- *pref.* 〔Am.〕= almost: *near*-white 准白种人的；*near*-nude 差不多一丝不挂的。

Ne·arc·tic [niːˈɑːktik] *a.*【动、植】新北区〔包括北美洲寒带及格陵兰〕的。

near·ly [ˈniəli] *ad.* ①近，接近；将近，大约，几乎，差不多。②好容易。③近似，密切，亲；精密。④〔罕〕细心；节俭地，吝啬地。~ *three o'clock* 将近三点钟。*She ~ fell over the cliff.* 她险些儿从崖上掉了下来。*It concerns me ~.* 这事对我有密切关系。*escape ~* 九死一生，仅以身免。***not ~*** 远不及；根本没有；相差很远 (*It is not ~ so pretty as it was before.* 远不及以前漂亮。*It's not ~ enough* 差得远。*There weren't ~ enough people to settle all that land.* 当时来这一地区移居的人根本不多)。

near·ness [ˈniənis] *n.* 近；接近；密切；亲近，亲密；节俭，吝啬。

neat[1] [niːt] *a.* ①干净的，整洁的；匀整的，端正的。②(文字)简洁的，适当的；灵巧的，精巧的。③〔俚〕好的；美妙的。④〔英〕纯的，没搀水的；洁的。*a ~ dress* 整洁的服装。~ *weight* 净重。***as ~ as a pin*** 干干净净，非常整洁。***brandy ~*** 纯白兰地酒。***make a ~ job of it*** 做得干净利落。***~ but not gaudy***〔美〕麻利的，灵巧的。~**-handed** *a.* 手巧的；灵活的，敏捷的。**-ly** *ad.* **-ness** *n.*

neat[2]〔古〕*n.* 〔*sing., pl.*〕〔集合词〕牛；牛类。~ **herd** 牧牛人。~ **house** 牛棚。~**'s foot** 牛脚〔食用〕。~**'s-foot oil** 牛脚油〔鞣革剂〕。~**'s leather** 牛皮。~**'s-**

tongue 牛舌〔食用〕.
neat·en [ˈniːtn] *vt.* 使整洁,使整齐,使干净〔常与 up 连用〕.
'neath [niːθ] *prep.* 〔古、诗〕= beneath.
neb [neb] *n.* 〔Scot.〕(鸟的)嘴;(兽的)鼻子;(人的)口,鼻;尖端,尖头;(笔)尖.
NEB = New English Bible 新英语圣经.
Neb. = Nebraska.
neb·bish [ˈnebiʃ] *n.* 〔美俚〕①无能的人;呆笨的人;胆小害臊的人. ②倒霉的人,十分不幸的人.
NEbE, NE by E = northeast by east 东北偏东.
Ne·bel·trup·pe [ˈneibəltrupə] *n.* 〔G.〕烟幕部队.
NEbN, NE by N = northeast by north 东北偏北.
Nebr. = Nebraska.
Ne·bras·ka [niˈbræskə] *n.* 内布拉斯加〔美国州名〕.
Ne·bras·kan [nibˈræskæn] *n.* 内布拉斯加人.
Neb·u·chad·nez·zar [ˌnebəkədˈnezə] 尼布甲尼撒〔巴比仑王 (605—562 B.C.),曾破坏耶路撒冷,将犹太人幽禁在巴比仑〕.
neb·u·la [ˈnebjulə] *n.* ***(pl. -lae*** [-liː] ***~s)*** ①【天】星云;云状,雾影;【医】角膜翳. ②(小便的)溷浊;喷雾剂. *a ring [spiral] ~* 环状星云. *a planetary ~* 行星状星云. *a stellar ~* 星云群.
neb·u·lar [ˈnebjulə] *a.* 星云(状)的. *the ~ theory [hypothesis]* 星云说〔认为太阳系是由星云状物质形成的假说〕.
neb·u·lium [niˈbjuːliəm] *n.* 【天】氰.
neb·u·lize [ˈnebjuˌlaiz] *vt.* ***(-liz·ed; -liz·ing)*** ①使成水花,使喷水花. ②喷雾;喷药水. **-za·tion** *n.* **-r** *n.*
neb·u·los·i·ty [ˌnebjuˈlɔsiti] *n.* ①星云状态;星云物质;星云状物. ②云雾状态. ③朦胧.
neb·u·lous [ˈnebjuləs] *a.* ①星云(状)的. ②云雾似的. ③形体不明的,朦胧的,模糊的. **-ly** *ad.*
NEC = ①Nippon Electric Company 日本电气公司. ②National Emergency Council〔美〕国家非常时期对策会议.
nec·es·sar·i·an [ˌnesiˈsεəriən] *a.* 必然论[宿命论]的. — *n.* 必然论[宿命论]者.
nec·es·sa·ri·ly [ˈnesisərili; ˌnesiˈseriəli] *ad.* 必定,必然;当然. *It ~ follows that* 必然(得出…的结论). ***not ~*** 不一定,未必 (*You don't ~ have to attend.* 你不一定要出席).
nec·es·sa·ry [ˈnesisəri] *a.* 必要的,不可缺的;必须的,强迫的;必然的,必定的. *a ~ result* 必然的结果. *a ~ evil* 难免的危害[坏事]. *a ~ house* 〔古〕厕所. ***be ~ to [for]*** 为…所必要. ***if ~*** 如果必要的话. ***It is ~ that one should (do). = It is ~ for one to (do).*** 某人必须…. —*n.* ①必需品;〔the ~〕〔口〕必需的金钱[行动〕. ②〔美方〕厕所. *daily necessaries* 日用品. *the necessaries of life* 生活必需品. *provide [find] the ~* 〔俚〕筹款.
ne·ces·si·tar·i·an [niˌsesiˈtεəriən] *n.* 必然论者,宿命论者. **-ism** *n.* 必然论,宿命论.
ne·ces·si·tate [niˈsesiteit] *vt.* ①使成为必需;使需要. ②强迫,迫使. *Language learning usually ~s conscious mimicry.* 一般地说,学习语言就要进行有意识的摹仿. *We were ~d to leave at once.* 我们不得不马上离开.
  ne·ces·si·ta·tion [ˌnisesiˈteiʃən] *n.* 迫使;被迫.
ne·ces·si·tous [niˈsesitəs] *a.* 穷;贫困的;紧迫的;必需的;不可避免的. *~ areas* 贫民区. **-ly** *ad.*
ne·ces·si·tous·ness [niˈsesitəsnis] *n.* ①贫困;贫乏. ②必需,不可缺. ③紧迫.
ne·ces·si·ty [niˈsesiti] *n.* ①需要,必要性. ②〔常 *pl.*〕必需品. ③必然(性). ④〔常 *pl.*〕贫穷;困难;危急. *physical ~* 必然力,命运. *logical ~* 逻辑的必然. *the doctrine of ~* 宿命论. *N- is the mother of invention.* 需要是发明之母. ***as a ~*** 必然地. ***be in dire necessities*** 穷困极了. ***be under the ~ of*** *(doing)* 不得已而…;必须做某事. ***bow to ~*** 服从命运;屈服于需要. ***by absolute ~*** 万不得已. ***from (sheer) ~*** 因(十分)需要. ***in case of ~*** 必要时. ***make a virtue of ~*** 做非做不可的事而装成出于高尚动机. ***of ~*** 必然,必定;不得已;不可避免地 (*That discussion must of ~ be postponed for a while.* 讨论会不得不延期举行).
neck[1] [nek] *n.* ①颈,脖子;(衣)领;颈肉(尤指羊颈肉);(器物的)颈状部;【化】短管. ②海峡;地峡,狭路. ③【建】颈弯饰. ④【地】岩颈. ***a stiff ~*** 固执(的人),顽固. ***bend one's ~*** 俯首听命,屈从. ***break one's ~*** 折断颈骨(致死). ***break the ~ of*** 做完(工作等的)最难部分. ***fall upon sb.'s ~*** 搂住人家的脖子(拥抱). ***escape with one's ~*** 好容易逃脱性命. ***get [catch, take] it in the ~*** 〔俚〕大受攻击[处罚、责骂];〔美俚〕受罚,遭不幸,遭殃. ***harden the ~*** 变顽固,变刚愎. ***~ and crop*** 迅速地,急剧地;立即,马上;完全,彻底,整个地. ***~ and ~*** (赛跑时)并驾齐驱,不分上下;〔美〕平等的. ***~ of the woods*** 〔美〕①森林区新村落. ②近邻,附近地方,周围〔此义和树林等无关〕. ***~ oil*** 〔美俚〕酒. ***~ or nothing [nought]*** 拚命 (*It is ~ or nothing.* 孤注一掷). ***on [over] the ~ of*** 紧紧跟在…的后头. ***risk one's ~*** 拚着性命. ***save one's ~*** 免受绞刑,得免一死;〔和否定连用〕无论如何不…. ***speak [talk] through (the back of) one's ~*** 说糊涂透顶的话;吹牛,说话尖锐. ***tread on the ~ of*** 压服,压制,虐待. ***win by a ~*** (赛马时)以一颈之差得胜;勉强得胜. — *vt.* ①割颈杀死(家禽等). ②缩小…的口径使成颈状. ③〔美俚〕与…互相搂住脖子亲嘴;拥抱. — *vi.* ①〔美俚〕接吻,拥抱. ②缩小. **~band** 领圈,领巾. **~beef** 牛颈肉. **~cloth** 〔古〕领饰. **~ journal** 【机】轴颈. **~lace** (宝饰等做的)项圈,脖链儿;〔俚〕绞索. **~ let** 小项圈;小皮围巾. **~line** 领口. **~-piece** ①装饰性围巾(尤指皮围巾). ②颈甲〔保护脖颈的盔甲〕. **~tie** 领带;〔美俚〕绞索. **~wear** 〔口〕颈部服饰〔如围巾,领带之类〕.
neck[2] [nek] *n.* 〔英〕(地中谷物的)最后一捆.
neck·er·chief [ˈnekətʃif] *n.* 〔古〕围巾,围脖儿.
neck·ing [ˈnekiŋ] *n.* ①【建】柱颈,柱颈部花边装饰. ②〔美俚〕搂颈亲热.
necr(o)- *comb. f.* = corpse (死尸).
nec·ro·bi·o·sis [ˌnekrəubaiˈəusis] *n.* 【医】渐进性(细胞)坏死.
nec·ro·gen·ic [ˌnekrəuˈdʒenik] *a.* 腐尸的;寄生于腐尸的;从腐尸发出的.
ne·crol·a·try [neˈkrɔlətri] *n.* 对死人的崇拜.
nec·rol·o·gy [neˈkrɔlədʒi] *n.* 死亡表,死者名单;死亡通知;讣告. **-log·i·cal** [ˌnekrəˈlɔdʒikəl] *a.* **-o·gist** *n.* 编死亡表的人;写讣告的人.
nec·ro·man·cer [ˈnekrəumænsə] *n.* 巫,巫师,降神者;行妖术的人.
nec·ro·man·cy [ˈnekrəumænsi] *n.* 向亡魂问卜的巫术,妖术;魔术. **-mant·ic** [-ˈmæntik] *a.*
nec·ro·pha·gi·a [ˌnekrəuˈfeidʒiə] *n.* 吃死尸肉,以腐尸为食. **ne·croph·a·gous** [neˈkrɔfəgəs] *a.*
nec·ro·pho·bi·a [ˌnekrəuˈfəubiə] *n.* 尸体恐怖(症).
ne·crop·o·lis [neˈkrɔpəlis] *n.* 大墓地(尤指古代城市或史前遗迹).
nec·rop·sy [ˈnekrɔpsi], **nec·ros·co·py** [neˈkrɔskəpi] *n.* 【医】验尸;尸体剖检.
nec·ro·sis [neˈkrəusis] *n.* ***(pl. -ses*** [-siːz]***)*** 【医】坏死,坏疽;骨疽;【植】枯斑,坏死. **nec·rot·ic** [neˈkrɔtik] *a.*
ne·crot·o·my [neˈkrɔtəmi] *n.* ***(pl. -mies)*** ①尸体解剖. ②尸体切除.
nec·tar [ˈnektə] *n.* ①【希神】神酒,众神饮的酒;甘美的饮料,甘露. ②【植】花蜜. ③一种汽水.
nec·tar·e·an [nekˈtεəriən], **nec·tar·e·ous** [-ˈtεəriəs] *a.* 神酒(似)的;甘美的;【植】花蜜的.
nec·tared [ˈnektəd] *a.* 甘美的;充满神酒[甘露]的.

nec·tar·if·er·ous [ˌnektəˈriferəs] *a.*【植】分泌花蜜的. ～ *glands* (植物的)蜜腺.

nec·tar·ine [ˈnektərin] *n.*【植】油桃. — *a.*〔古〕甘美的.

nec·ta·rous [nekˈtεrəs] *a.* = nektarean.

nec·ta·ry [ˈnektəri] *n.*【植】蜜腺;【虫】蜜管.

Ned [ned] *n.* 内德〔男子名〕.

ned [ned] *n.*〔美俚〕十元金币.

N.E.D., NED = New English Dictionary 牛津大词典(= Oxford English Dictionary).

ned·dy [ˈnedi] *n.* ①〔口〕驴子,马;笨蛋,蠢货. ②〔N-〕〔英谑〕英国国家经济发展委员会(源出 National Economic Development Council of Great Britain 前三字的起首字母).

Nedra [ˈnedrə] *n.* 内德拉〔女子名〕.

née [nei] *a.*〔F.〕(已婚妇女的)娘家姓…. *Mrs. Smith,* ～ *Jones* 娘家姓琼斯氏的史密斯夫人.

need [niːd] *n.* ①必要,需要. ②缺乏,不足. ③需求;需用的东西. ④危急的时候,一旦有事的时候. ⑤贫穷. *There is no* ～ *for [of] hurrying* = *There is no* ～ *to hurry.* 不用着急. *There is a great* ～ *of money.* 急需要钱. *A friend in* ～ *is a friend indeed.* 患难朋友才是真朋友. *He is in great* ～. 他穷得很. ***at (one's)*** ～ 在紧急时 (*be good at* ～ 在急需的时候有用). ***be in*** ～ ***of*** 需要. **do one's** ～**s**〔俚〕解大[小]便,解溲,撒尿. ***had*** ～ ***(to)*** *(do).* 必须… (*I have* ～ *to go to town.* 我必须进城). ***have no*** ～ ***of*** 不需要. ***If*** ～ ***be [were]*** 如果必要的话. ***in case [time] of*** ～ 在紧急的时候,万一有事时. ***stand in*** ～ ***of*** 需要. — *vt.* 要,需要,必须,有…的必要. *This house* ～*s repair.* 这个房子要修理了. *He* ～*s to go.* 他必须去. *Does he* ～ *to know?* 有告诉他的必要吗? — *v.aux.* 不得不,必须 ★(1)在否定句或疑问句中,第三人称现在时单数也不加 s; 过去时用 had to 来代替,将来时用 will (或 shall) have to 来代替. need not (〔口〕 needn't) 相当于 must 的否定形式. 如: He ～ not come. 他不必来. N- she go? 她必须去吗? It ～ hardly be said that … 简直用不着说. (2) She ～ not go. 这句话,口语常说作 She doesn't ～ [have] to go. —*vi.* ①生活贫困. ②〔古〕需要〔主要用于无人称句〕. *It* ～*s not.* 不需要. *more than* ～*s* 超过需要. *There* ～*s no apology.* 用不着辩解. *Give to those that* ～. 救济贫困者.

need·fire [ˈniːdfaiə] *n.*【条顿族神话】净火;〔Scot.〕烽火,狼烟,篝火.

need·ful [ˈniːdfəl] *a.* ①需要的,必要的,不可缺少的 *(to; for).* ②〔古〕穷困的. — *n.*〔*the* ～〕〔俚〕(必需的)钱,现金;必需的事物. ***do the*** ～ 做该做的事. **-ly** *ad.* 必然地,不得已.

Need·ham [ˈniːdəm] *n.* 尼达姆〔姓氏〕.

need·i·ly [ˈniːdili] *ad.* 在贫穷中.

need·i·ness [ˈniːdinis] *n.* 穷困,贫穷.

nee·dle [ˈniːdl] *n.* ①针,缝针;编织针. ②(注射、唱片等的)针;磁针,罗盘针,指针. ③尖岩,尖峰;方尖碑;【化、矿】针状结晶;【植】针叶;【建】横撑木. ④〔the ～〕〔英俚〕神经上的刺激;〔美俚〕麻醉毒品;注射. *a* ～*'s eye* 针鼻,针眼. *the eye of a* ～ 针眼〔指'狭缝'说〕. ***get the*** ～ 急躁;恼怒. ***give (sb.) the*** ～ 使(某人)恼怒[急燥],刺激(某人). ***have the pins and*** ～***s*** (脚等)发麻. ***hit the*** ～ (箭)射中靶心;击中要害. ***look for a*** ～ ***in a bottle [bundle] of hay*** 海底捞针〔徒劳无益〕. ***on the*** ～ 有服用毒品瘾. ***pass through the eye of a*** ～ 穿过针眼. ***(as) sharp as a*** ～ 非常机敏. ***thread a*** ～ 穿针引线;完成一件困难的工作. —*vt., vi.* ①拿针缝;拿针穿;【医】用针治疗. ②穿过 *(through).* ③(使)结晶成针状;【建】用横撑木撑住. ④刺激. ⑤〔美〕加酒精(入啤酒等),加强酒性. ～ **antimony** 粗锑. ～ **bar** (缝纫机等的)针天心;针床;针座. ～ **bath** 喷射淋浴. ～ **beam**【建】簪梁. ～**-beer**〔美俚〕加了酒精的啤酒. ～**-book** 书形针盒. ～ **case** 针盒. ～ **craft** = ～ work. ～ **dam** 横栅活坝. ～ **file** 什锦锉,组锉. ～ **fish**【鱼】颌针鱼;长喙鱼;海龙属鱼. ～ **lace** 针绣花边. ～ **man**〔美〕股票经纪的囮子. ～ **match** 对抗心浓厚而有敌意的比赛. ～**point** 针尖;针绣;针绣花边〔全称 needlepoint lace〕. ～ **time**〔主英〕(电台广播节目中编定的)播放唱片音乐的时间. ～ **valve**【机】针阀. ～ **woman** 针线好的妇女;做针线活的妇女;缝纫女工. ～ **work** 针线活,女红;刺绣,缝纫. ～ **worker** *n.* 刺绣工;缝纫工. **-ful** *n.* 穿在针上的一次用线.

need·less [ˈniːdlis] *a.* 不必要的,不需要的;无用的,多余的. *(it is)* ～ *to say [add]*〔插入句〕不用说. **-ly** *ad.*

need·ments [ˈniːdmənts] *n.*〔*pl.*〕〔英〕(旅行用)必需品.

need·n't [ˈniːdnt]〔口〕= need not.

needs [niːdz] *ad.* 必须,一定;务必〔现与 must 前后并用〕. ***must*** ～ ①偏偏,偏要. ②必须,必然,不得不 (*It must* ～ *be so.* 必然如此). ***must*** ～ ***do*** ① =～ must do. ②坚持说要(*He must* ～ *come.* 他一口咬定要来). ～ ***must do*** 必须,不得不 (*A man* ～ *must lie down when he sleeps.* 人睡时非躺下来不可. *N- must when the devil drives.* 魔鬼从后撵,就得向前跑;情势所迫).

need·y [ˈniːdi] *a.* ***(need·i·er; -i·est)*** 贫穷的,贫困的. *the poor and* ～ 穷苦的人们.

ne'·er [nεə] *ad.*〔诗〕= never.

ne'·er-do-well, ne'er-do-weel [ˈnεəduːwel, -wiːl] *n.* 没用的人,废物,饭桶. — *a.* 不中用的;无价值的.

nef [nef] *n.* (食桌上搁盐、拭嘴布、匙子等用的)船形盆.

ne·far·i·ous [niˈfεəriəs] *a.* 恶毒的;穷凶极恶的;极坏的. **-ly** *ad.* **-ness** *n.*

neg. = negative (by).

ne·gate [niˈgeit] *vt.* 否定,否认;取消,使无效;抹杀;使作废.

ne·ga·tion [niˈgeiʃən] *n.* ①否定,否认 *(opp.* affirmation);拒绝,反对;反对论;消极;无,不存在. ②【逻】否定断定,命题的否定. ～ ***of*** ～ 否定之否定.

ne·ga·tion·al [niˈgeiʃənəl] *a.* ①否定的;否认的;拒绝的. ②对立的. ③虚无的,不存在的.

ne·ga·tion·ist [niˈgeiʃənist] *n.* 否定论者.

neg·a·tive [ˈnegətiv] *a.* ①否定的,否认的;拒绝的 *(opp.* affirmative*)*;反对的,反面的;消极的. ② *(opp.* positive*)*【电】阴的,阴性的;负的;【数】负的;【摄】底片的;【医】阴性的. ③【植】(对日光或地面刺激等)有反作用的;【心理】反抗性的,不妥协的. *a* ～ *vote* 反对票. *the* ～ *side [team]* (讨论会的)反对方面. ～ *criticism* 消极的批评. *a* ～ *plea*【法】抗辩. ～ *capital* 负债. ～ *debt* 资本. *the* ～ *pole*【电】负极,阴极. *a* ～ *charge* 阴(电)荷. *a* ～ *quantity*【数】负量;〔口〕无. *the* ～ *sign*【数】负号(—). *a* ～ *plate*【摄】底片. ***on*** ～ ***lines*** 消极地. — *n.* ①否定词语;否定的观点;否定言论;否定回答;否定命题(等). ②消极性. ③【电】阴电;阴极板;【摄】底片;【数】负数,负量. *The answer is in the* ～. 回答是'不'. *Two* ～*s make an affirmative.* 两个否定等于肯定,负负得正. ***answer in the*** ～ = ***return a*** ～ 回答说'不'. ***decide in the*** ～ 否决. ***eliminate the*** ～〔美俚〕消除自卑观念. ***in the*** ～ 否定地,反对地,否认地. ***prove a*** ～ 举反证. — *vt.* ①否认;否定;驳斥;否决;拒绝;反证;反对. ②使无效;抵销;使中和. ～ **income tax**〔美〕低收入补助. ～ **proton**【物】负质子.

neg·a·tive·ly [ˈnegətivli] *ad.* 否定地;消极地. *answer* ～ 回答说不. *be* ～ *friendly* 交情(虽不好,但)还没有破裂.

neg·a·tive·ness [ˈnegətivnis], **neg·a·tiv·i·ty** [ˌnegəˈtiviti] *n.* 否定[消极]性.

neg·a·tiv·ism [ˈnegətivizəm] *n.* 否定论;否定态度;消极主义;怀疑主义;违拗性;【医】违拗症;抗拒症;【心】抗拒性.

neg·a·tiv·ist [ˈnegətivist] *n.* 否定论者；取否定态度者；消极主义者；怀疑主义者。

neg·a·to·ry [ˈnegətɔːri] *a.* ①否定的；否认的。②反面的；消极的。

neg·a·tron [ˈnegətrɔn] *n.* ①【物】双阳极负阻管。②【物】负电子，阴电子。

neg·lect [niˈglekt] *vt.* 轻忽，玩忽；轻视，忽视，无视，不顾；忽略；漏做；不… *(to do; doing)*. — *n.* 疏忽；忽略；玩忽，轻忽；轻视，忽视 *(of)*. ~ *of duty* 失职，溺职，玩忽职守。*Her children were in a terrible state of* ~. 她的孩子们简直没人管。*treat with* ~ 不理睬，怠慢。**-er, -or** *n.* 疏忽者，忽视者。

neg·lect·able [nigˈlektəbl] *a.* = negligible.

neg·lect·ful [nigˈlektful] *a.* 玩忽的，疏忽的 *(of)*；不留心的，不注意的；不理睬的，不介意的，冷淡的 *(of)*. **-ly** *ad.* **-ness** *n.*

neg·li·gee, né·gli·gé [ˌngliaˈʒei, ˈnegliːʒei] *n.* 〔F.〕（女人）便服，长睡衣。— *a.* （穿得）随便的。

neg·li·ge·able [ˈneglidʒəbl] *a.* 〔罕〕 = negligible.

neg·li·gence [ˈneglidʒəns] *n.* ①玩忽，疏忽；失职；【法】过失；不留心，粗心大意；不介意，冷淡。②懒散，邋遢，不整齐。③【文艺】奔放不羁。*an accident out of* ~ 责任事故。*The accident was due to* ~. 事故是由于疏忽引起的。

neg·li·gent [ˈneglidʒənt] *a.* 对…玩忽〔疏忽〕*(of, in, about)*；不留心的，粗心大意的；不检点的；随便的，懒散的。*be* ~ *of one's duties* 玩忽职务。*a writer* ~ *of punctuation* 不注意标点的作家。*be* ~ *in dress* 不讲究服饰。*One should not be* ~ *in traffic regulations.* 对交通规则不可掉以轻心。**-ly** *ad.*

neg·li·gible [ˈneglidʒəbl] *a.* 可以忽视的；无足轻重的（人）；不足取的；很小的，微不足道的。*a* ~ *quantity* 可忽略的量〔因素〕。**-bil·i·ty** *n.* **-bly** *ad.*

ne·go·ti·a·ble [niˈgəuʃiəbl] *a.* ①可协商的，可谈判的。②（票据、证券等）可转让的，可流通的。③（道路等）可通行的。*a* ~ *bill* 流通票据。~ *credit instruments* 流通证券。**-bil·i·ty** [niˌgəuʃiəˈbiliti] *n.* 流通性，可转移性，流通能力。

ne·go·ti·ant [niˈgəuʃiənt] *n.* 交涉者，协商者；交易人。

ne·go·ti·ate [niˈgəuʃieit] *vt.* ①议定，商定，通过谈判使…。②卖〔让〕与；使（证券、票据等）流通，转让，兑现。③〔口〕处置；处理；克服（困难等）；〔口〕通过，跳过（障碍）。— *vi.* 协议，谈判，交涉 *(with)*.

ne·go·ti·a·tion [niˌgəuʃiˈeiʃən] *n.* 〔常 *pl.*〕①协商，谈判，交涉，协定。②让与，转付，流通；交易。***be in*** **~*s with sb. over sth.*** 与某人协商某事。***break off*** **~*s*** 中断谈判。***carry on*** **~*s*** 继续交涉。***enter into [upon] a*** **~ *with*** 开始和…进行谈判。

ne·go·ti·a·tor [niˈgəuʃieitə] *n.* *(fem.* ***-tress*** [-ʃiətris] ***-trix*** [-triks]*)* ①协商者，谈判者。②让与人；交易人。

ne·go·ti·a·to·ry [niˈgəuʃiətəri] *a.* 协商的，谈判的，交涉的。

Ne·gress [ˈniːgris] *n.* 〔贬〕女黑人。

Ne·gril·lo [niˈgriləu] *n.* *(pl.* *~s)* （中非及南非的）矮小黑人。

Ne·grit·tic [niˈgritik] *a.* （象）（矮小）黑人的。

Ne·gri·to [niˈgriːtəu] *n.* *(pl.* *~s, ~es)* ①(Polynesia 地方的)矮小黑人。②矮小黑人种〔包含 Negrillo〕。

ne·gri·tude [ˈnegritjuːd, ˈniːgri-] *n.* 〔亦作 N-〕对（非洲）黑人（文化）传统的自豪感。

Ne·gro [ˈniːgrəu] *n.* *(pl.* *~es)* 黑人，黑种人〔目前带有贬义，一般改用 black〕。— *a.* ①黑（种）人的；黑人住的；关于黑人的。②黑的。~ **ant**【虫】黑蚁。~ **minstrels** 黑人〔化装黑人〕歌舞团。

ne·gro·head [ˈniːgrəuhed] *n.* （压缩的）烟砖；劣等树胶。

Ne·groid [ˈniːgrɔid] *a.* 黑人（似）的 (= Negroidal). — *n.* 黑人。

ne·gro·land [ˈniːgrəulænd] *n.* （非洲）黑人居住的地方。

Ne·gro·phil(e) [ˈniːgrəfail] *a., n.* 亲〔关心〕黑人的（人）。**-ism** *n.* ①认为黑人应有平等权利的主张。②黑人特有的发音等。

Ne·gro·phobe [ˈniːgrəfəub] *n.* 〔有时作 n-〕畏惧黑人的人，强烈厌恶黑人者。**-pho·bi·a** *n.* 畏惧黑人。

ne·gus [ˈniːgəs] *n.* 尼格斯酒〔由热水、糖、柠檬、香料和酒混合成的饮料〕。

Ne·gus [ˈnigəs] *n.* 埃塞俄比亚皇帝的称号。

Neh·ru [ˈneiruː], **Jawaharlal** [dʒəˈwɑːnbərˈlɑːl] 尼赫鲁〔1889—1964，印度政治家〕。~ **coat [jacket]** 尼赫鲁上装〔一种窄身高领的上装〕。

neigh [nei] *n.* 嘶鸣声。— *vi.* （马）嘶。

neigh·bo(u)r [ˈneibə] *n.* ①邻人，邻居；邻近的人；邻国（人）。②邻座（的人）；邻接的东西。③同胞；世人。④（对任何不知姓名的人的直接称呼）朋友。*a next-door* ~ 紧邻，隔壁邻居。*our* ~*s across the Channel* 海峡对面的邻人〔英国人指法国人〕。*a good [bad]* ~ 和邻居相处得好〔不好〕的人。— *vt.* ②邻近，毗邻。②使接近，使邻近。*The building* ~*s the river.* 大楼邻近河边。— *vi.* ①与…接壤，位于…附近。*on; upon.* ②与…有睦邻关系 *(with)*. *The building* ~*s upon the river.* 大楼与河邻近。

neigh·bo(u)red [ˈneibəd] *a.* 有某种邻居〔环境〕的。*a beautifully* ~ *city* 环境秀丽的城市。

neigh·bo(u)r·hood [ˈneibəhud] *n.* ①邻近，接近；附近；周围。②四邻，街坊；街道，地区；聚居区。③近邻的人们。④邻居关系，邻人的情谊，和睦善邻〔通例 good ~〕。⑤【数】邻域。*The* ~ *of the railway is a drawback.* 靠近铁路是个缺点。***in the*** **~ *of*** ①在…的附近。②〔口〕大约 (*in the* ~ *of* £*100* 约一百镑)。— *a.* 〔美〕附近的，地方的 (=〔英〕local). *a* ~ *newspaper* 地方报纸。~ **unit** 住宅区。

neigh·bo(u)r·ing [ˈneibəriŋ] *a.* 邻近的，附近的；邻接着的，毗邻的，接壤的。

neigh·bo(u)r·less [ˈneibəlis] *a.* 没邻人的；孤独的。

neigh·bo(u)r·li·ness [ˈneibəlinis] *n.* 善邻，睦邻；和睦，亲近。

neigh·bo(u)r·ly [ˈneibəli] *a.* ①象邻人的；亲切的，和睦的，易亲近的。②住在邻近的。*live on* ~ *terms with* 同某人和睦相处。

Neil, Neal [niːl] *n.* 尼尔〔男子名〕。

nei·ther [ˈnaiðə, ˈniːðə] 〔not+either〕*ad.* ①〔和 *nor* 配合使用〕两者都不…，（…不）…也不…。〔动词应与最后一个名词〔代名词〕相一致〕。*N- he nor I know.* 他不知道，我也不知道。*N- you nor I nor anybody else has seen it.* 你我和其他任何人都没看见。②〔古、方〕〔放在句尾加强前面的否定词〕也 (= either). *I don't know that* ~. 那事我也不晓得。③〔用于否定条件句的结尾部分〕…也不。*If you do not go,* ~ *shall I.* 如果你不去，我也不去。— *conj.* 〔古〕也不。*I know not,* ~ *can I guess.* 我不晓得，也猜不出来。— *a.* （两者）都不的，两者都不…。*N- accusation is true.* 两项责难都不对。*He took* ~ *side in the dispute.* 在争论中他任何一方都不参加。— *pro.* 两者中无…，两者都不…。*N- of them knows.* 他们两个都不知道。~ ***flesh nor fish*** 非驴非马，不三不四。~ ***here nor there*** 无关紧要，不相干。~ ***more nor less than*** 和…完全一样；不多不少。~ ***rhyme nor reason*** 不伦不类；莫名其妙；无缘无故。

Nejd [neʒd, neid] *n.* 内志〔阿拉伯中部伊斯兰教国，与 Hejaz 合并称沙特阿拉伯 (Saudi Arabia) 王国〕。

nek [nek] *n.* 〔南非〕山峡〔两峰间的洼处〕。

nek·ton [ˈnektən] *n.*【动】自游生物。**-ic** *a.*

Nel·da [ˈneldə] *n.* 内尔达〔女子名〕。

Nell [nel] *n.* 内尔〔女子名，Helen 的爱称〕。

Nel·lie [ˈneli] *n.* 内莉〔女子名〕。

nel·ly [ˈneli] *n.*【鸟】大海燕。***not on your N-*** 〔英俚〕

绝不会,不可能.

Nel·son [ˈnelsn] *n.* ①纳尔逊〔姓氏,男子名〕. ②**Horatio** ～ 纳尔逊〔1758—1805, 英国海军大将, Trafalgar 海战的胜利者〕.

ne·lum·bo [niˈlʌmbəu] *n.* ***(pl. -bos)*** 【植】莲属植物 (= nelumbium).

ne·ma [ˈniːmə] *n.* nematode (线虫纲动物)的缩略词.

nem·a·cide [ˈneməsaid] *n.* 杀线虫剂.

nem·a·thel·minth [ˌneməˈθelminθ] *n.* 【动】线形动物门动物.

ne·mat·ic [niˈmætik] *a.* 【物】(液晶中细长分子的位置)向列的.

nemat(o)- *comb. f.* 表示"线","线虫类": *nemato*logy.

nem·a·to·cyst [ˈnemətəusist] *n.* 【动】刺丝囊 (刺丝胞). **-ic** *a.*

nem·a·to·cide [ˈnemətəusaid] *n.* = nemacide.

nem·a·tode [ˈnemətəud] *n.* 线虫纲动物〔如钩虫、蛲虫〕.

nem·a·tol·o·gy [ˌneməˈtɔlədʒi] *n.* 线虫学.

Nem·bu·tal [ˈnembjutɔːl, -tæl] 耐波他〔pento-barbital sodium (戊巴比妥钠)的美国商标名〕.

nem. con. [ˈnem ˈkɔn] = 〔L.〕 *nemine contradicente* [ˈniːminiː ˌkɔntrədaiˈsenti] 无异议地; 全体一致地 (= no one contradicting). *The resolution was passed nem. con-* 决议案无异议地通过.

nem. dis(s). [ˈnem ˈdis] = 〔L.〕 *nemine dissentiente* [ˈniːminiː diˌsentiˈenti] 无异议地; 全体一致地 (= no one dissenting).

Nem·e·sis [niˈmisis] *n.* ***(pl. -ses*** **[-siːz]*)*** ①【希神】复仇〔报应〕女神. ②〔n-〕天罚; 报应. ③〔n-〕复仇者; 给以报应者. **Nem·e·sic** [niˈmesik] *a.*

ne·mine con·tra·di·cen·te [ˈniːmin kɔntrədaiˈsenti] 〔L.〕 = nem. con.

ne·mine dis·sen·ti·en·te [lˈniːmindisentiˈent] 〔L.〕 = nem. dis(s).

ne·moph·i·la [niˈmɔfilə] *n.* 喜林草属植物〔产于美洲西部〕.

ne·ne [ˈneiˌnei] *n.* 【动】黄颈黑雁.

N. Eng. = ①New England 新英格兰〔美国东北六州之总称〕. ②North England 北英格兰〔英国〕.

nen·u·phar [ˈnenjufɑː] *n.* 【植】(欧洲)白(黄)睡莲.

neo- *comb. f.* 表示"新","近代(的)";"复活": *neo*-impressionism.

ne·o·an·throp·ic, ne·an·throp·ic [ˌni(ː)əuænˈθrɔpik] *a.* 【人类学】新人的, 类新人的.

ne·o·ars·phen·a·mine [ˈni(ː)əuɑːsˈfenəmiːn] *n.* 【化】新胂凡纳明, 九一四.

Ne·o·Cam·bri·an [ˈni(ː)*əu*ˈkæmbriən] *a.* 【地】晚寒武纪的.

Ne·o·Cath·o·lic [ˈni(ː)*əu*ˈkæθəlik] *n., a.* 新天主教派(的).

Ne·o·cene [ˈni(ː)əsiːn] *n., a.* 【地】晚第三纪(的).

ne·o·class·ic, -si·cal [ˈni(ː)əuklæsik, -sikəl] *a.* 新古典主义的.

ne·o·clas·si·cism [ˈni(ː)*əu*ˈklæsisizəm] *n.* 新古典主义.

ne·o·co·lo·ni·al·ism [ˈni(ː)əukəˈləuniəlizəm] *n.* 新殖民主义. **-al·ist** ① *n.* 新殖民主义者. ② *a.* 新殖民主义的.

ne·o·co·lo·ny [ˈni(ː)*əu*ˈkɔləni] *n.* 新殖民地.

Ne·o·co·mi·an [ˈni(ː)*əu*ˈkəumiən] *a.* 【地】(中世代的)前绿砂期[统]的.

Ne·o·Dar·win·ism [ˈni(ː)*əu*ˈdɑːwinizəm] *n.* 新达尔文主义.

ne·o·dox·y [ˈni(ː)əudɔksi] *n.* 新学说, 新见解.

ne·o·dym·i·um [ˌni(ː)əˈdimiəm] *n.* 【化】钕.

Ne·o·g(a)e·a [ˌni(ː)*əu*ˈdʒiːə] *n.* 新热带区〔南北美热带地区〕; 新界. **-n** *a.*

Ne·o·gene [ˈni(ː)əudʒiːn] *n.* 【地】晚第三纪.

ne·o·gen·e·sis [ˌni(ː)*əu*ˈdʒenisis] *n.* 新生, 再生. **-genet·ic** [-dʒiˈnetik] *a.*

Ne·o-Greek [ˈni(ː)*əu*ˈgriːk] *a.* 【建、美】新希腊派的.

Ne·o·He·bra·ic [ˈni(ː)əuhiˈbreiik] *n., a.* 近代希伯来语(的), 近代以色列语(的).

Ne·o·He·ge·li·an [ˈni(ː)*əu*heiˈgiːljən] *a.* 新黑格尔主义的. — *n.* 新黑格尔主义者.

Ne·o·He·ge·li·an·ism [ˌni(ː)*əu*heiˈgeiliənizəm] *n.* 【哲】新黑格尔主义.

Ne·o·Hel·len·ism [ˈniəuˈhelinizəm] *n.* 【文艺】新希腊主义.

ne·o·im·pres·sion·ism [ˈni(ː)*əu*imˈpreʃənizəm] *n.* 【美】新印象主义.

Ne·o·Kant·i·an [ˈni(ː)*əu*ˈkæntiən] *a.* 新康德主义的. — *n.* 新康德主义者.

Ne·o·Kant·i·an·ism [ˈni(ː)*əu*ˈkæntiənizəm] *n.* 【哲】新康德主义.

Ne·o·La·marck·ism [ˈni(ː)*əu*ləˈmɑːkizəm] 【生】新拉马克主义.

Ne·o·Lat·in [ˈni(ː)*əu*ˈlætin] *n.* 新拉丁语(族).

ne·o·lite [ˈni(ː)*əu*lait] *n.* 【地】新石.

ne·o·lith [ˈni(ː)*əu*liθ] *n.* (新石器时代的)新石器.

ne·o·lith·ic [ˈni(ː)*əu*ˈliθik] *a.* ①〔N-〕新石器时代的. ②过时的.

ne·o·lo·gi·an [ˌni(ː)*əu*ˈləudʒiən] *a.* 【宗】主张[遵守]新教义的. — *n.* 新教义主张者.

ne·o·log·i·cal [ˌni(ː)*əu*ˈlɔdʒikl] *a.* 新词的, 旧词新义的; 新词语的使用的. **-ly** *ad.*

ne·ol·o·gism, ne·ol·o·gy [ni(ː)ˈɔlədʒizəm, -dʒi] *n.* ①新词; 旧词新义[新用法]. ②新词[新义]的使用. ③【宗】新教义的遵守[采用]. **-gist** *n.* ①新词[新义]的创造者[使用者]. ②(= neologian).

ne·ol·o·gis·tic, ne·ol·o·gis·ti·cal [ˌni(ː)ɔlə*u*ˈdʒistik, -tikl] *a.* ①新词的, 旧词新义的. ②使用新词的, 使用(旧词的)新义的.

ne·ol·o·gize [ni(ː)ˈɔlədʒaiz] *vi.* 创造新词[新义]; 使用新词[新义]; 【宗】采用新说.

Ne·o·Mal·thu·si·an·ism [ˈni(ː)əumælˈθjuːzjənizəm] *n.* 新马尔萨斯主义.

ne·o·my·cin [ˌni(ː)*əu*ˈmaisin] *n.* 【生化】新霉素, 新链丝菌素.

ne·on [ˈniːən] *n.* ①【化】氖. ②氖光灯, 霓虹灯. *a* ～ *lamp* 霓虹灯. *a* ～ *sign* 广告霓虹灯.

ne·o·nate [ˈniːəneit] *n.* 出生不满一个月的婴儿; 新生婴儿.

ne·o·orth·o·dox·y [ˌni(ː)əuˈɔːθədɔksi] *n.* 新正教. **neo-orthodox** *a.*

ne·o·phyte [ˈni(ː)*əu*fait] *n.* ①【教会史】新入教者; 【天主】新祭司. ②新来者, 初学者, 生手; 〔美〕大学一年级生. ③【植】新来杂草植物; 新引种植物. *The* ～ *must not despair of mastering the rules and procedures.* 初学的人不必在熟悉规则和程序中感到失望.

ne·o·pla·sia [ˌni(ː)*əu*ˈpleiʒə, -ziə] *n.* 【医】瘤形成.

ne·o·plasm [ˈni(ː)*əu*plæzəm] *n.* 【医】异常新生物, (尤指)赘生物, 瘤. **-plas·tic** *a.* 瘤的, 赘生物的; 新造型主义的.

ne·o·plas·ti·cism [ˈni(ː)*əu*ˈplæstisizəm] *n.* 【美】新造型主义.

ne·o·plas·ty [ˈni(ː)*əu*plæsti] *n.* 【外】造形术, 修补术.

Ne·o·Pla·to·n·ism [ˌni(ː)*əu*ˈpleitənizəm] *n.* 新柏拉图主义.

ne·o·prene [ˈni(ː)*əu*priːn] *n.* 【化】氯丁(二烯)橡胶.

Ne·o·Re·al·ism [ˈni(ː)*əu*ˈriəlizəm] *n.* ①【哲】新实在论. ②【文艺】新现实主义.

ne·o·sal·var·san [ˈni(ː)əuˈsælvəsən] *n.* 【医】九一四; 新洒尔佛散.

Ne·o·Scho·las·ti·cism [ˈni(ː)əuskəˈlæstisizəm] *n.* 新

经院哲学。
ne·ot·e·ny [ni(:)ˈɔtini, ˈniɔtini] *n.*【动】幼态持续,幼期性熟. **-ten·ic** [-ˈti:nik, -ˈtenik] *a.*
ne·o·ter·ic [ˌni(:)əuˈterik] *a.* 现代的;崭新的;新发明的. — *n.* 现代人;现代作家.
ne·o-Tho·mism [ˈni(:)əuˈtəumizm] *n.*【哲】新托马斯主义.
ne·o·trist [ˈni(:)əutrist] *n.* 创造新词者.
ne·o·trop·i·cal [ˈni(:)əuˈtrɔpikəl] *a.* 新热带区的.
ne·o·zo·ic [ˈni(:)əuˈzəuik] *a.*【地】新生代的.
NEP, Nep, nep [nep] (=New Economic Policy)【史】(苏联)新经济政策.
Nep. = Neptune.
Ne·pal [niˈpɔ:l] *n.* 尼泊尔〔亚洲〕.
Ne·pal·i [niˈpɔ:li, -ˈpɔl-] *n.* 尼泊尔语〔尼泊尔的印度语〕.
Nep·a(u)·lese [ˌnepɔ:ˈli:z] *n.* 尼泊尔人. — *a.* 尼泊尔(人)的.
ne·pen·the [neˈpenθi] *n.*〔诗〕(古希腊传说中的)忘忧药.
ne·pen·thes [neˈpenθi:z] *n.* ①【植】猪笼草属. ② = nepenthe.
ne·per [ˈneipə, ˈni:pə] *n.*【无】奈培〔衰耗单位 = 8.686 分贝〕.
neph·al·ism [ˈnefəlizəm] *n.* 完全戒酒.
neph·al·ist [ˈnefəlist] *n.* 完全戒酒论者;〔美〕禁酒主义者.
neph·a·nal·y·sis [ˌnefəˈnælisis] *n.* *(pl.* **-ses** [-si:z]*)*【气】云层分析;云层分析图.
neph·e·line [ˈnefəlin], **neph·e·lite** [-lait] *n.*【矿】霞石.
neph·e·lin·ite [ˈnefilinait] *n.*【地】霞岩.
neph·e·lom·e·ter [ˌnefiˈlɔmitə] *n.*【化】(散射)浊度计,(散射)比浊计,混浊计.
neph·ew [ˈnevju(:), ˈnefju(:)] *n.* ①侄子;外甥. ②〔古〕孙;子孙. ③〔婉〕(教士的)私生子.
neph·o·gram [ˈnefəgræm] *n.*【气】云图.
ne·phol·o·gy [niˈfɔlədʒi] *n.*【气】云学.
neph·o·scope [ˈnefəskəup] *n.*【气】测云器.
ne·phral·gi·a [neˈfrældʒiə] *n.*【医】肾痛.
ne·phrec·to·my [neˈfrektəmi] *n.* *(pl.* **-mies***)*【医】肾切除术.
ne·phrid·i·um [neˈfridiəm] *n.* *(pl.* **-phrid·i·a** [-ə]*)*【解】肾,肾管. **-phrid·i·al** *a.*
neph·rite [ˈnefrait] *n.*【矿】软玉.
ne·phrit·ic [neˈfritik] *a.* 肾的;肾病的,治肾病的. *the ~ stone* 肾结石.
ne·phri·tis [neˈfraitis] *n.*【医】肾炎.
nephro *comb. f.* 表示"肾"的意思: *nephrotomy.*
neph·ro·gen·ic [ˌnefrəuˈdʒenik] *a.* ①肾内产生的. ②形成肾组织的.
neph·roid [ˈnefrɔid] *a.* 肾形的.
neph·ron [ˈnefrɔn] *n.* 肾单位.
ne·phro·sis [neˈfrəusis] *n.*【医】肾变病. — **ne·phrot·ic** [-ˈfrɔtik] *a.*
ne·phrot·o·my [neˈfrɔtəmi] *n.* *(pl.* **-mies***)*【医】肾切开术.
ne plus ul·tra [ˈni: plʌs ˈʌltrə]〔L.〕至上,至高,无上;极致,极点,顶点.
Nep·man [ˈnepmən] *n.* 苏联施行新经济政策 (N.E.P.) 时的资本主义分子,耐泼曼.
ne·pot·ic [niˈpɔtik] *a.* 袒护[重用]亲戚的.
nep·o·tism [ˈnepətizəm] *n.* 袒护[重用]亲戚;任人唯亲作风;裙带关系;族阀主义.
nep·o·tist [ˈnepətist] *n.* 重用亲戚者,族阀主义者.
nep·o·tis·tic [ˌnepəˈtistik] *a.* 袒护亲戚的,重用亲戚的;裙带关系的.
Nep·tune [ˈneptju:n] *n.* ①【罗神】尼普顿〔海神〕. ②【天】海王星. ③海,海洋. ④(美国的)海王式巡逻机. **~'s cup** 杯状大海绵. **~'s revel** 赤道节. **son of ~** 船夫,水手.
Nep·tu·ni·an [ˈneptjuniən, -njən] *a.* ①海神尼普顿的;海王星的. ②〔n-〕【地】水成(论)的. — *n.*〔n-〕水成论者.
nep·tun·ism [ˈneptjunizəm] *n.*【地】岩石水成论.
nep·tun·ist [ˈneptjunist] *n.*【地】岩石水成论者.
nep·tu·ni·um [nepˈtju:niəm] *n.*【化】镎〔旧译錼〕. **~ series**【化】镎系(列).
N.E.R.A. = National Emergency Relief Administration〔美〕国家紧急救济署.
Ner·chinsk [ˈnεətʃinsk] *n.* 涅尔琴斯克〔苏联城市,即尼布楚〕.
Ne·re·id [ˈniəriid] *n.* *(pl.* **~s, ~es***)* ①【希神】海中仙女. ②〔n-〕【动】沙蚕.
ne·re·is [ˈniəri:is] *n.* *(pl.* ***ne·re·i·des*** [niˈriədi:z]*)* 沙蚕属动物.
ne·rit·ic [niˈritik] *a.* 浅海的.
Nernst [G. nεrnst] **Walther Hermann** 内恩斯特〔1864—1941, 德国物理学家、化学家,曾获 1920 年诺贝尔化学奖〕.
Ne·ro [ˈniərəu] *n.* 尼禄〔古罗马暴君,37—68〕.
ner·o·li [ˈniərəli] *n.*【化】橙花油 (= ~ oil).
Ne·ro·ni·an [niˈrəuniən] *a.* 尼禄(似)的;暴虐的;荒淫的.
ner·sy [ˈnə:zi] *a.*〔美俚〕声音大的,嘈杂的.
nerts, nertz [ˈnə:tz] *int.*〔美俚〕我不相信;胡说八道 (= nuts). *N- to you!* 胡说!
nerv·al [ˈnə:vəl] *a.* 神经(组织)的.
nerv·ate [ˈnə:veit] *a.*【植】有叶脉的,具脉的.
ner·va·tion [ˈnə:veiʃən] *n.*【动、植】脉序.
nerve [nə:v] *n.* ①【解】神经. ②〔诗〕筋,腱;精力,气力. ③胆力,勇气;沉着,果断;大胆,胆量;〔口〕厚脸,冒昧. ④〔*pl.*〕神经过敏;胆怯,忧郁. ⑤主要部分,核心,中枢. ⑥【植】脉,叶脉;【昆虫】翅脉. ⑦回缩性,(弹性)复原性. *a war of ~s* 神经战. *You have a ~!*〔口〕无耻! *a fit of ~s* 神经过敏,神经病发作. *She is all ~s.* 她太神经过敏了. *Banks are the ~s of commerce.* 银行是商业的中枢. *It is trying to the ~s.* 精神痛苦不堪. *He does not know what ~s are.* 他不知道什么叫害怕;他从不紧张. ***be all ~s*** 神经紧张,高度不安. ***brace one's ~ for an effort*** 为某项努力鼓起勇气. ***get [jar] on one's ~s*** = ***give one the ~s*** 刺激神经;使人不安[心烦];惹恼人. ***have a fit of ~s*** 发神经病. ***have iron ~s*** = ***have ~s of steel*** 神经坚强,有胆量. ***have no ~s*** (好象没神经一样)泰然自若,满不在乎. ***have the ~ to (do)*** 有…的勇气;〔口〕好意思…,厚着脸皮…. ***lose one's ~s*** 害怕起来;不知所措;变得慌张. ***strain every ~*** 尽心竭力. — *vt.* 鼓励,激励. ***~ oneself*** 鼓勇,提起精神. **~ agent** 神经毒剂. **~ air raid** (扰乱性的)神经空袭. **~ block**【医】神经传导阻滞. **~-bank** 神经库. **~ cell** 神经细胞. **~ centre, ~ center** ①【解】神经中枢. ②中枢,核心;要害. **~ fibre, ~ fiber** 神经纤维. **~ gas** (能透入皮肤、毒性剧烈的)神经错乱性毒气,神经毒气,中毒性毒气. **~ impulse** 神经冲动. **~ knot** 神经节. **~ strain** 神经过劳. **~-racking, ~-wracking** *a.* 使人心烦的;伤脑筋的.
-nerved [nə:vd] *comb. f.*〔用以构成复合词〕①神经…的: strong*nerved.* ②【植】有…叶脉的;【虫】有…翅脉的: five*nerved.*
nerve·less [ˈnə:vlis] *a.* ①无力的,没生气的;(文体等)松懈的. ②沉着的,镇静的. ③【解、动】没有神经的;【植】无叶脉的;【虫】无翅脉的. **-ly** *ad.*
ner·vine [ˈnə:vi:n] *a.* ①神经的. ②镇定神经的. — *n.*【医】神经强健剂.

nerv·ous [ˈnəːvəs] *a.* ①神经(方面)的, 对神经起作用的. ②神经过敏的,神经质的,紧张不安的,胆小的;易激动的,易怒的. ③强健的,有勇气的;有力的,(文体等)简练刚劲的. *the ~ center* 神经中枢. *~ disorder* 神经错乱. ***feel ~ about*** 以…为苦, 担心…, 害怕…. **~ breakdown [debility, depression, exhaustion, prostration]** 神经衰弱[崩溃]. **~ disease** 神经病. **~ Nellie** 〔俚〕胆小鬼;无用的人. **~ system** 神经系统. **-ly** *ad.* ①神经质似地, 胆怯似地. ②强健地; 有力地. **-ness** *n.* 神经过敏,神经质;急躁;胆小.

ner·vure [ˈnəːvjuə] *n.* 【植】叶脉;【虫】翅脉.

nerv·y [ˈnəːvi] *a.* ①〔诗〕肌肉发达的, 强壮的. ②〔美〕有勇气的,大胆的;〔俚〕冷静的; 粗鲁的; 脸厚的;〔俚〕刺激神经的; 使人心烦的. ③〔英口〕神经质的, 神经紧张的; 易激动的.

n.e.s., N.E.S. = not elsewhere specified 不另说明.

nes·ci·ence [ˈnesiəns, -sjəns] *n.* ①无学,无知. ②【哲】不可知论.

nes·ci·ent [ˈnesiənt, -sjənt] *a.* ①无学的,无知的,不知的 *(of)*. ②【哲】不可知论的. — *n.* 不可知论者.

ness [nes] *n.* 海岬,海角; 岬(角).

-ness *suf.* 〔附在形容词、分词、复合形容词后形成抽象名词〕表示'性质'、'状态'、'精神'、'程度': bitter*ness*, tired*ness*, up-to-date*ness*, etc.

Nes·sie [ˈnesi] *n.* (苏格兰的)尼斯湖"怪兽".

Nes·sus [ˈnesəs] *n.* 【希神】(大力神 Hercules 用毒箭射死的)人头马腿怪物.

nest [nest] *n.* ①巢; 窝; 窟,穴. ②安息处,休息处; 住处,家; 避难处, 隐退处. ③(盗贼等)的巢窟; (罪恶等的)发源地,渊薮,温床. ④【集合词】一窝雏; (鸟、虫等的)群; (同种类物的) 集合. ⑤(上下叠放着的碗、碟等的) 一套 *(of)*. ⑥【地】矿巢;【建】蜂窝(混凝土缺陷). ⑦〔美俚〕导弹基地. *a birds ~* 鸟巢. *a ~ of brigands* 一窝匪徒. *a ~ of tables* (大小顺次套放在一起的)一套桌子. ***a mare's ~*** 幻想的 [不存在的] 东西. ***arouse a ~ of hornets*** 捅马蜂窝; 惹麻烦; 树敌招怨; 犯众怒. ***feather one's ~*** 自肥; 营私. ***foul one's own ~*** 说自己家里[党内]的坏话; 家丑外扬. ***take a ~*** 摸巢, 盗巢 [偷鸟巢里的蛋或雏]. — *vi.* ①筑巢; 入巢, 伏窝. ②找鸟窝. ③相互套入. ④〔美俚〕蹲下来. *go ~ing* 去找鸟窝. — *vt.* ①使入窝,使伏窝. ②把(大小箱子)套起来; 安顿,放置(碗碟等). *the ~ed region* 【数】区域套. **~ egg** 留窝蛋;〔喻〕囮子,引诱物; 储备金[物].

n'est-ce pas? [nesˈpɑː] 〔F.〕 不是这样的吗? 对吧?

nes·tle [ˈnesl] *vi.* ①〔罕〕(鸟)造窝, 营巢. ②舒舒服服地安顿下来; 安居, 安身; 安卧 *(down; in; into; among)*. ③偎依,贴靠 *(up to; against)*. ④半隐半现地处于. *The town ~s among the hills.* 这个城市座落在群山之中. *The child ~d against [up to] his mother.* 孩子紧紧贴着妈妈. — *vt.* ①抱; 使(头、脸、肩膀等)紧贴. ②使安顿. *~ a baby in one's arms* 怀抱着孩子.

nest·ling [ˈnestliŋ] *n.* 刚孵出的雏, 还不能离窝的雏; 婴孩.

Nes·tor [ˈnestɔː,-tə] *n.* ①【希神】内斯特〔特洛伊战争中希腊的贤明长老〕. ②〔常作n-〕贤明的老人; 长老; 耆宿 *(of)*.

Nes·to·ri·an [nesˈtɔːriən] *a.* (五世纪君士坦丁大主教 Nestorius 创立的)聂斯托里教派的,景教的. —*n.* 景教徒. **~ism** 聂斯托里的宗教主张; 景教.

net[1] [net] *n.* ①网; 网眼织物; (花边的)织物. ②网状物; 网状组织; 网状系统; 通信网. ③(乒乓、网球的) 球网; 落网球. ④罗网,陷阱. ⑤(蜘)蛛网. *a fish ~* 鱼网. *a mosquito-~* 蚊帐. *a ~ artist* 〔美〕网球选手. ***be caught in a ~*** 陷入罗网,上了圈套. ***cast [throw] a ~*** 撒网. ***draw in a ~*** 拉网. ***spread one's ~ for (sb.)*** 给某人布置好圈套,设法叫某人上钩. ***sweep everything into one's ~*** 把可以到手的一切都攫为己有,一切尽归私囊. —*vt.* ①用网捕; 撒(网); 张(网); 用网覆; 用网制作; 用…编成网状物. ②把…诱入圈套[罗网]. ③〔美俚〕(努力、设法)得到(结果), 捞得. ⑤打(球)落网; 触网. — *vi.* 编网; 编结网状物;〔诗〕成网状. *~ strawberries* 用网覆盖草莓. *~ a river* 在河上撒网. *~ a handsome profit* 捞到一大笔利润. *netted sunbeam* 映在水底上的网形日光. **~-ball** 少女玩的一种篮球; 【乒乓球、网球】触网球. **~-winged** *a.* (昆虫)有翅网脉的.

net[2] [net] *a.* 净的; 纯的 *(opp.* gross); 无虚价的; 基本的; 最后的. *a ~ interest* 纯利,净赚. *a ~ loss* 纯损,净亏. *a ~ profit [gain]* 纯利润. *a ~ price* 实价. *at 5 dollars ~* 实价5美元. *~ ton* 净吨,美吨(2,000磅)〔英吨叫 gross ton (2,240 磅)〕. *~ weight* 净重. *the ~ result* 最后结果. — *n.* 纯利; 净值; 实价; 纯量,净数,净重. — *vt.* 得到; 使得到; 净得,净赚. *~ $10,000 a year* 每年净赚一万元.

neth·er [ˈneðə] *a.* 〔古、诗〕下面的. *a ~ lip* 下唇. *the ~ millstone* 磨石的下一扇. *the ~ regions* 冥府, 地狱, 阴间;〔罕〕下界,人世间. *the ~ man* 〔谑〕腿. *~ garments* 〔谑〕裤子. *the N- House* 下院,众议院. ***as hard as the ~ millstone*** 冷酷的; 铁石心肠. **~ world** 阴间; 来世; 下层社会.

Neth·er·land·er [ˈneðələndə] *n.* 荷兰人.

Neth·er·land·ish [ˈneðləndiʃ] *a.* 荷兰的; 荷兰人的; 荷兰语的. — *n.* 荷兰语.

Neth·er·lands [ˈneðələndz] *n.* 〔*pl.*〕〔the ~〕〔*sing., pl.*〕荷兰[欧洲] (=Holland).

neth·er·most [ˈneðəməust, -məst] *a.* 最下面的, 最低的.

neth·er·ward, neth·er·wards [ˈneðəwəd, -dz] *ad.* 向下,向下方.

net·man [ˈnetmən] *n.* 〔美〕网球选手.

NETR = Nuclear Engineering Test Reactor 核子工程试验反应堆.

nets·man [ˈnetsmən] *n.* 用网(捕鱼等)的人.

nett [net] *a.* (=net[2]).

net·ted [ˈnetid] *a.* 用网捕的,用网包的,网状的.

net·ter [ˈnetə] *n.* 〔Am.〕 = netman.

Net·tie [ˈneti] *n.* 内蒂〔女子名, Janet 的昵称〕.

net·ting [ˈnetiŋ] *n.* 网; 网状(织)物; 网细工; 结网, 撒网, 网鱼; (金属)丝布. *a ~ needle* 结网针. *mosquito ~* 蚊帐纱. *wire ~* 金属网; 铁纱. **~ knot** (= sheet bend) 单索花结[绳结的一种].

net·tle [ˈnetl] *n.* 荨麻;〔喻〕使人烦恼的事, 苦恼. — *vt.* 拿荨麻打,拿荨麻刺; 激,惹,激怒. ***grasp the ~*** 向困难搏斗; 大胆抓起棘手问题. **~-creeper** 白喉蜂雀. **~-grasper** 敢于向困难搏斗的人. **~ rash** 【医】荨麻疹, 风疹块. **-some** [-səm] *a.* 恼火的.

net·ty [ˈneti] *a.* 网状的,网细工的.

net·work [ˈnetwəːk] *n.* ①网眼织物. ②(铁路、河道等的)网状系统; 网状组织; 广播网; 电视网; 广播[电视]联播公司. ③【无】网络,电路. *a ~ of railways* 铁路网. *a ~ of falsehoods* 一大套谎话,谎话连篇. **~ analysis** (用数学或统计学进行的)网络分析.

neuk [njuːk] *n.* 〔Scot.〕凹角处,隐避处; 角落.

neum(e) [njuːm, nuːm] *n.* 中世纪教堂音乐的一种乐谱符号. **neu·mat·ic** [-ˈmætik] *a.*

neur- *comb. f.* 〔用于元音前〕 = neuro-.

neu·ral [ˈnjuərəl] *a.* 【解】神经 (系统) 的; 神经中枢的; 【解】背的, 背侧的. **~ arch** 【动】髓弓. **~ canal** 【解】神经沟. **~ tube** 【解】神经管. **-ly** *ad.*

neu·ral·gia [njuəˈrældʒə] *n.* 【医】神经痛. **-ral·gic** [-dʒik] *a.*

neu·ras·the·ni·a [ˌnjuərəsˈθiːniə,-njə] *n.* 【医】神经衰弱. **-then·ic** [-ˈθenik] *a., n.* 神经衰弱的(人).

neu·ra·tion [njuəˈreiʃən] *n.* = nervation.

neu·rec·to·my [njuəˈrektəmi] *n.* 【医】神经切除 (术).

neu·ri·lem·ma [ˌnjuəriˈlemə,nuə-] *n.* 【解】神经膜，神经鞘.

neu·rine [ˈnjuəri:n, ˈnuər-] *n.* 神经碱.

neu·ri·tis [njuəˈraitis] *n.* 【医】神经炎. **-rit·ic** [-ˈritik] *a.*

neuro- *comb. f.* 〔用于辅音前〕表示"神经": *neuro*fibril.

neu·ro·act·ive [ˌnjuərəuˈæktiv] *a.* 刺激神经的.

neu·ro·bi·ol·o·gy [ˌnjuərəubaiˈɔlədʒi] *n.* 神经生物学.

neu·ro·blast [ˈnjuərəublæst] *n.* 成神经细胞.

neu·ro·coel, neu·ro·coele [ˈnjuərəsi:l] *n.* 【解】神经管腔.

neu·ro·ep·i·the·li·um [ˌnjuərəuepiˈθiliəm] *n.* 【动】神经上皮. **-the·li·al** [-liəl] *a.*

neu·ro·fi·bril [ˌnjuərəuˈfaibril] *n.* 神经原纤维. **-lar·y** [-əri] *a.*

neu·ro·gen·ic [ˌnjuərəuˈdʒenik] *a.* ①起源于神经组织的. ②神经原的，神经性的. ③受神经冲动控制的. **-al·ly** *ad.*

neu·rog·li·a [njuˈrɔgliə, nu-] *n.* 神经胶质. **-li·al** *a.*

neu·ro·hor·mone [njuərəuˈhɔ:məun] *n.* 【医】神经激素.

neu·rohu·mo(u)r [ˌnjuərəuˈhju:mə] *n.* 神经液.

neu·ro·log·i·cal [ˌnjuərəuˈlɔdʒikəl] *a.* 神经病学的.

neu·rol·o·gist [njuəˈrɔlədʒist] *n.* 神经病学家；神经病专科医生.

neu·rol·o·gy [njuəˈrɔlədʒi] *n.* 神经病学.

neu·ro·ma [njuˈrəumə, nu-] *n.* *(pl.* **~s, *-ma·ta*** [-mətə]*)* 【医】神经瘤.

neu·ro·mo·tor [ˌnjuərəuˈməutə] *a.* 传出神经兴奋的.

neu·ro·mus·cu·lar [ˌnjuərəuˈmʌskjulə, nuər-] *a.* 神经肌肉的.

neu·ron(e) [ˈnjuərɔn] *n.* 【解】神经原，神经细胞. **neu·ron·ic** *a.*

neu·ro·path [ˈnjuərəpæθ] *n.* 【医】神经病患者；神经质者. **-ic** *a.*, *n.*

neu·rop·a·thist [njuəˈrɔpəθist] *n.* 神经病学家〔专家、医生〕.

neu·ro·pa·thol·o·gy [ˌnjuərəupəˈθɔlədʒi, ˌnuər-] *n.* 神经病理学. **-thol·o·gist** *n.*

neu·rop·a·thy [njuəˈrɔpəθi] *n.* 神经(系)病.

neu·ro·phys·i·ol·o·gy [ˌnjuərəuˌfiziˈɔlədʒi, ˌnuər-] *n.* 神经(系统)生理学.

neu·ro·psy·chi·a·try [ˌnjuərəusiˈkaiətri] *n.* 神经精神病学. **-at·ric** [-ˈætrik] *a.*

neu·ro-psy·chic [ˌnjuərəuˈsaikik] *a.* 【医】神经与精神的.

neu·rop·ter·an [njuˈrɔptərən, nuə-] *n.* 脉翅目昆虫〔包括沙挼子，蚁狮〕. **-ter·ous** [-tərəs] *a.*

neu·rop·ter·ous [njuˈrɔptərəs] *a.* 【虫】脉翅类的.

neu·ro·sis [njuəˈrəusis] *n.* *(pl.* ***-ses*** [-si:z]*)* 【医】神经(机能)病；精神神经病；【心】神经感动.

neu·ro·sur·ger·y [ˌnjuərəuˈsə:dʒəri, nuə-] *n.* 神经外科学.

neu·rot·ic [njuəˈrɔtik] *a.* 神经的；神经(机能)病的；神经质的；神经过敏的. — *n.* ①神经病人；神经过敏者. ②神经刺激剂.

neu·rot·o·my [njuˈrɔtəmi] *n.* *(pl.* ***-mies****)* 神经切断术；神经解剖学.

neu·ro·tox·ic [ˌnjuərəuˈtɔksik, nuə-] *a.* 毒害神经的.

neu·ro·tox·in [ˌnjuərəuˈtɔksin, nuə-] *n.* 神经毒素.

neu·ro·trop·ic [ˌnjuərəuˈtrɔpik, ˌnuər-] *a.* 嗜神经组织的，亲神经的，趋神经系的.

neus·ton [ˈnju:stɔn, ˈnu:-] *n.* 【动】漂浮生物. **neus·tic** *a.*

neut. = ①neuter. ②neutral.

neut [nju:t] *n.* 〔美口〕中子弹.

neu·ter [ˈnju:tə] *a.* ①【语】(名词等)中性〔无性〕的；(动词)不及物的. ②【植、动】中性的，无性的. ③〔罕〕中立的. *the* ~ *gender* 中性. *a* ~ *noun* 中性名词. *Worker bees are* ~. 工蜂是中性蜂. *stand* ~ 中立. — *n.* ①【语】中性；中性词〔名词、形容词、代名词〕；中性形式；不及物词. ②无性生物〔动物，植物〕；工蜂；去势动物. ③中立者.

neu·tral [ˈnju:trəl] *a.* ①中立的；中立国的. ②不偏不党，公平的；中庸的；中间的；不伦不类的，不明确的；不鲜艳的，暗淡的；非彩色的〔指灰、黑或白色的〕. ③【机】空档的；【化、电】中性的；中和的；不带电的；【植、动】无性的，无雌雄之别的. ④【语】(元音)松弛的，中性的. *a* ~ *state [zone]* 中立国〔地带〕. *a* ~ *sort of person* 无显著特征的人，平常的人. ~ *equilibrium* 随遇平衡. *a* ~ *colour* 无彩色. *a* ~ *tint* 不鲜明的色彩〔如灰色、青灰色〕. — *n.* ①中立者；中立国(国民). ②【机】(汽车等的传动装置)空档. ③非彩色. ~ **vowel**【语】中性元音〔不重读的元音，如 about 中的 a〕. **-ly** *ad.*

neu·tral·ism [ˈnju:trəlizəm] *n.* 中立主义.

neu·tral·ist [ˈnju:trəlist] *a.*, *n.* 中立主义(的)；中立主义者. **-ic** [-ˈlistik] *a.*

neu·tral·i·ty [nju:ˈtræliti] *n.* ①中立；中立地位；不偏不党. ②【化】中性；中和. *armed* ~ 武装中立.

neu·tral·ize [ˈnju:trəlaiz] *vt.* ①使中立化. ②【化、电】使中和；【物】平衡. ③使失效，抵消；【军】压制(火力). ~ *a place* 以某地为中立地. *a* ~*d state* 永久中立国. **-za·tion** [ˌnju:trəlaiˈzeiʃən] *n.* 中立化，中立状态；中和；失效；平衡. **-iz·er** *n.* 【化】中和剂；【电】中和器.

neu·tret·to [nju:ˈtretəu] *n.* 【物】中介子.

neu·tri·no [nju:ˈtri:nəu] *n.* 【物】中微子.

neutro- *comb.f.* 表示"中性"，"中和": *neutro*sphere.

neu·tro·don [ˈnju:trəudən] *n.* 中和电容器.

neu·tro·dyne [ˈnju:trəudain] *n.* 【无】中和式高频调谐放大器；衡消接收法；中和接收法. — *a.* 【无】(接收机)衡消式的. *a* ~ *receiver* 衡消接收机.

neu·tron [ˈnju:trɔn] *n.* 【物】中子. ~ **bomb** 中子弹. ~ **number**【原子】(核内)中子数. ~ **star**【天】中子星. **-ics** *n.* 中子(物理)学.

neu·tro·pe·nia [ˌnju:trəuˈpi:niə] *n.* 【医】嗜中性白血球减少症.

neu·tro·phil, neu·tro·phile [ˈnju:trəufil, -fail] *n.* 【医】嗜中性. — *a.* 嗜中性的.

neu·tro·sphere [ˈnju:trəusfiə] *n.* 【天】中性圈.

Nev. = Nevada.

Ne·va [ˈneivə] *n.* 内瓦〔女子名〕.

Ne·vad·a [neˈvɑ:də] *n.* 内华达〔美国州名〕. **-dan** [-dən] *a.*, *n.* 内华达的(人).

né·vé [ˈnevei] *n.* 〔F.〕(冰河上层的)碎粒冰雪，粒雪；冰原；(由碎粒冰雪形成的)万年雪. ~ **line** 雪线.

nev·er [ˈnevə] *ad.* ①〔ever 的否定形式；加强否定语气；用于句首时，主谓语次序倒装〕决不，永不；从来没有，一点也不. ②〔口〕〔表示怀疑或惊异〕不会…吧；不，没有；不要. *I* ~ *met him before.* 从来没见过他. *He is* ~ *at home on Sunday.* 星期日他从不在家. *He has* ~ *been heard of since.* 此后再也没有听到一点儿他的消息. *N- did he break his promise.* 他从不爽约. *N- fear!* 不要怕！*N- mind!* 不必介意！不要紧！*Better late than* ~. 晚做总比不做好. *Now or* ~. 时不可失，机不再来. *Well, I* ~*!* = *I* ~ *did!* 真想不到，真是没有见过〔听说过〕. *You have* ~ *lost the key!* 不会是丢了钥匙吧！*N- tell me!* 别跟我开玩笑啰！*He* ~ *so much as spoke.* 他连话都没有讲. ***go to the land of*** **~-~** 〔卑〕失去意识，昏过去. **~ *a*** 一个也没有. **~ *a one*** 没有一个(人). ***N- N- (land [country])*** 澳大利亚昆士兰州的北部，人迹稀少的地方. **~ *so*** 〔古〕非常；空前地；〔在条件句中〕即使. **~ *the*** 一点也不〔和比较级连用〕*(I am* ~ *the wiser for it.* 这样我还是一点也不懂). **~ ... *without*** 干什么总是… *(He*

～ *moved a thing without replacing it exactly.* 他挪动过的东西总是要放还原地的). **～-ending** *a.* 不断的,永不完结的,没底的. **～-failing** *a.* 不绝的,不尽的;永远不变的;永不辜负期望的. **～-get-overs** 不治之症. **～-was** *n. (pl. ～-weres)* 〔美俚〕从未取得成功的人. **～-waser** *n.* 〔美俚〕= ～-was.

nev·er·more [ˈnevəˈmɔː] *ad.* 决不再,永不再.

nev·er-nev·er [ˈnevəˈnevə] *n.* ①边远地区,不毛之地. ②理想的地方(=the ～ land). ③〔英俚〕分期付款制. — *a.* 幻想的,理想的,想入非非的. *the ～ land* 幻想中的地方.

nev·er·the·less [ˌnevəðəˈles] *ad.* 仍然(还),不过. *I shall certainly say nothing, but it will come to his ears ～.* 我一定不说什么话,可是这还会传进他的耳朵里的. — *conj.* (尽管如此)还是,然而. *There was no news; ～, she went on hoping.* 尽管杳无音讯,然而她还是盼望着.

Nev·ill(e) [ˈnevil] *n.* 内维尔〔姓氏,男子名〕.

Ne·vin [ˈnevin] *n.* 内文〔姓氏,男子名〕.

Ne·vins [ˈnevinz] *n.* 内文斯〔姓氏〕.

ne·vus [ˈniːvəs] *n. (pl. ne·vi* [-vai]*)* 痣. **ne·void** [-vɔid] *a.*

new [njuː] *a.* ①新的,崭新的;新发现的,新发明的;新开发的. ②初次(听到)的;新奇的. ③新鲜的;新造的;新到的;新就任的. ④改新了的,改变了的;健康恢复了的;重新开始的. ⑤〔the ～〕〔常蔑〕现代的,新式的,摩登的. ⑥生的,不习惯的,未熟悉的. ⑦另加的,附加的. *a ～ invention* 新发明. *a ～ moon* 新月. *the N- Style* 新历. *the N- World* 新世界,美洲大陆. *～ milk* 新鲜牛奶. *the ～ rich* 暴发户. *I am ～ to the work.* = *The work is new to me.* 这个工作我还没有经验. *That information is ～ to me.* 那消息我还是初次听到. *The horse is ～ to harness.* 那匹马还没有养乖. ***make a ～ man of*** 使…改过自新;使…恢复健康. ***N- China News Agency*** 新华通讯社〔略 NCNA〕. ***N- Democracy*** 新民主主义(国家). ***N- Learning*** 十六世纪文艺复兴时输入英国的希腊文艺研究. ***N- Light*** 【宗】新派. ***the N- Deal*** ①(美国 1933 年实施的)新政. ②〔口〕新的领导,新的开始,新的管理. ***the ～ look*** (头发、衣服等的)新式样;〔口〕新式服装. ***turn over a ～ leaf*** 革面洗心. — *ad.* = newly 〔主要与过去分词构成复合词〕. — *n.* 〔the ～〕 新的东西. ～ **blood** 新血液〔指具有新思想又朝气蓬勃的人〕. **～-blown** *a.* (花)刚开的. **～-born** *a.* 新生的,初生的,再生的,复活的. **～-build** *vt.* = rebuild. ～ **candle** 【光】烛光. **～-coined** *a.* (名词等)新造的. ～ **come** *a., n.* 新来的(人),新到的(人). ～ **comer** 新来的人;不认识的人,陌生人. **N- Criticism** 文学新批评〔二十世纪流行的文艺分析方法,着重研究作品的语言、文学手法和结构等〕. **N- England aster** 美国紫菀(红花紫菀)〔产于北美洲东部〕. **N- England boiled dinner** 新英格兰杂烩菜〔由猪肉、腌牛肉、土豆、洋葱、胡罗卜、白菜等烩成〕. **N- English** 新英语〔指 1750 年至今的英语〕. **N- English Bible** 圣经英国新译本〔指 1970 年出版的圣经.《新约》部分已于 1961 年出版〕. **～fangled** *a.* 新花样的,新奇的;爱好新奇的. **～-fashioned** *a.* 新式的,新流行的. **～-found** *a.* 新发现的. **～-laid** *a.* (蛋)才生的. **N- Latin** 新拉丁语〔1500 年以后的拉丁语〕. **～-made** *a.* 才做好的,重新做的. **～-married** *a.* 新婚的. ～ **math** 【数】集论教学体系,基础数学集论教学法. **～-model** *vt.* 改造,改编,改组(军队、政府等). **～-mown** *a.* 新割的. **N- Testament** (基督教《圣经》的)《新约全书》. **N- Thought** 新信念〔西方十九世纪的一种宗教信念,强调精神对健康和幸福的作用〕. ～ **town** 新市镇,卫星城. **-ness** *n.* 新,新奇;未熟,不惯.

New·bolt [ˈnjuːbəult] *n.* 纽博尔特〔姓氏〕.

New·burg [ˈnjuːbəg] *n.* 纽堡酱〔用奶油、蛋黄和酒的浓酱汁调味做的海味〕.

New Cal·e·do·ni·a [ˈnjuː ˌkæliˈdəunjə] 新喀里多尼亚(岛)〔南太平洋〕.

New·cas·tle [njuːˌkɑːsl] *n.* ①纽卡斯尔〔澳大利亚港市〕. ②纽卡斯尔〔英国港市〕.

New Delhi [njuː ˈdeli] 新德里〔印度首都〕.

new·el [ˈnjuːəl] *n.* ①【建】(螺旋梯的)中心柱. ②(楼梯两端支持扶手的)望柱,起柱.

New·ell [ˈnjuːəl] *n.* 纽厄尔〔姓氏,男子名〕.

New Eng·land [ˈnjuː ˈiŋglənd] 新英格兰〔美国东北六州 *Maine, New Hampshire, Vermont, Massachusetts, Connecticut* 和 *Rhode Island* 的总称〕.

New Eng·land·er [ˈnjuː ˈiŋgləndə] *n.* 新英格兰人.

Newf. = Newfoundland.

New·found·land *n.* ① [ˌnjuːfəndˈlænd] 纽芬兰(岛)〔加拿大一地区〕. ② [nju(ː)ˈfaundlənd] 纽芬兰犬(= ～ dog).

New·found·land·er [ˌnjuːˈfaundləndə] *n.* 纽芬兰人.

New·fy [ˈnjuːfi] *n.* 〔美水手语〕纽芬兰人.

New·gate [ˈnjuːgit] *n.* (伦敦旧城的)新兴门监狱〔1902 年废〕. ～ **frill [fringe]** 只留在下巴上的胡子. ～ **knocker** 果菜贩从太阳穴到耳边的 6 字形毛丛. ～ **saint** 死刑犯.

New Guinea [njuː ˈgini] 新几内亚(岛)〔西太平洋〕.

New Hampshire [nju(ː) ˈhæmpʃiə] 新罕布什尔〔美国州名〕.

New Hebrides [njuː ˈhebridiːz] 新赫布里底(群岛)〔南太平洋〕.

new·ie [ˈnjuːiː] *n.* 〔美俚〕新奇的东西,新鲜东西.

new·ish [ˈnjuːiʃ] *a.* 有些新的,相当新的.

New Jersey [nju(ː) ˈdʒəːzi] 新泽西〔美国州名〕.

new·ly [ˈnjuːli] *ad.* ①〔表示时间〕新近,最近. ②〔表示频率〕重新,又,再度. ③〔表示方式、状态〕以新的方式. *a ～ wedded couple* 新婚夫妇. *a ～ built house* 新建住宅. *a ～ developed surburb* 新郊区. *a ～ repeated slander* 旧调重弹的诽谤. *a room ～ decorated* 用新式样装璜的房间. ～ **wed** 新结婚的人.

New·man(n) [ˈnjuːmən] *n.* 纽曼〔姓氏〕.

new·mar·ket [ˈnjuːmɑːkit] *n.* ① 紧身长外套. ②【牌】赶新市〔一种玩法简单的纸牌戏〕.

New Mexico [nju(ː) ˈmeksikəu] 新墨西哥〔美国州名〕.

New Or·le·ans [njuː ˈɔːliənz] 新奥尔良〔美国港市〕.

news [njuːz] *n.* 〔通例作单数用〕①新闻,(新)消息;新闻报道. ②新事件,奇事,奇闻. ③音信. ④〔N-〕〔报纸名〕…新闻报. *foreign [home] ～* 国外[国内]新闻. *Is there any ～?* = *What is the ～?* 有什么新闻? *good [bad] ～* 吉[凶]报. *bad ～* 〔美俚〕帐单. *～ from London* 伦敦通信. *Good ～ goes on crutches.* 好事不出门. *Ill ～ flies apace.* = *Bad ～ travels quickly.* 恶事传千里. *That is no ～.* 那种事并不新奇. *What you say is ～ to me.* 你讲的我还头一次听见. *New York N-* 《纽约新闻报》. ***break the ～ to (sb.)*** (向某人)委婉传达不幸的消息. ～ **agency** 通讯社. **～agent** 报刊经销人. ～ **analyst** 新闻分析[评论]员. **～beat** 新闻记者采访区. **～boy** 报童,送报人. **～break** *n.* 有新闻价值的事件. ～ **cameraman** 〔美〕新闻摄影记者. **～cast** 〔美〕新闻广播. **～caster** 〔美〕新闻广播员. **～casting** 〔美〕新闻广播. ～ **conference** 记者招待会 (=press conference). **～dealer** 〔美〕=newsagent. **～editor** (报刊的)社会新闻编辑. **～film** 【影】新闻片. **～flash** 简明新闻. **～gatherer, ～hawk, ～-hound** 〔美俚〕新闻记者. **～hen** 〔美俚〕女新闻记者. **～letter** 时事通讯;新闻信札;业务通讯. **～magazine** 新闻杂志;时事刊物. ～ **maker** 〔美〕新闻人物;有新闻价值的人物[事件]. **～monger** 爱传播新闻的人;爱聊天的人. **～organ** 〔美〕报纸,新闻杂志;新闻喉舌. ～ **picture** = newsfilm. **～-print** (印报刊用的)新闻纸,白报纸. **～reel** = ～film. **～reeler, reelist** 新闻片摄制人. **～room** 〔英〕 阅报室;〔美〕(报馆、广播台、电视台的)编辑部. **～sheet** ①单张报纸. ② = news-letter. **～stand** 〔美〕报亭,报摊. **～-**

vendor 报纸经销人. ～**worthy** *a.* 有新闻价值的. ～**-writer** 新闻记者. ～**less** *a.* 没有新闻的. ～**man** ①= newsboy. ②新闻记者. ～**woman** 女新闻记者.
news·i·ness [ˈnjuːzinis] *n.* 新闻多；饶舌.
news·paper [ˈnjuːspeipə, Am. ˈnjuːz-] *n.* ①报，报纸. ②新闻纸，白报纸. *a daily [weekly]* ～ 日[周]报. *a* ～ *man* 新闻记者；新闻从业员. *a* ～ *office* 报社. *the* ～ *world* 报界，新闻界. —*vi.* 从事新闻工作. ～**-man** 新闻记者，新闻事业经营者. ～**-woman** 女新闻记者. ～**-dom** *n.* 报界.
news·paper·y [ˈnjuːspepəri] *a.* 报纸式的，浅薄的.
new·speak [ˈnjuːˌspiːk] *n.* (官僚政客等惯常使用的)模棱两可的官腔〔源自 G. Orwell 的一部小说〕.
news·y [ˈnjuːzi] *a.* *(news·i·er; -i·est)* 〔口〕新闻多的，奇闻多的，爱说话的，嘴碎的. —*n.* 〔Am.〕= newsboy.
newt [njuːt] *n.* 【动】蝾螈.
New·ton [ˈnjuːtn] *n.* ①牛顿〔姓氏，男子名〕. ②**Sir Isaac** ～ 牛顿〔1642—1727，英国科学家〕. ③〔n-〕【物】牛顿〔M.K.S. 制的力的单位〕；【化】牛顿〔粘度单位〕.
New·to·ni·an [njuːˈtəunjən, -niən] *a.* 牛顿(学说)的. —*n.* ①信奉牛顿学说的人. ②牛顿式望远镜.
new year [ˈnjuːˈjəː] ①新年. ②〔N- Y-〕=〔美〕New Year's 正月(初旬)；元旦. *(I wish you) a happy New Year!* 恭贺新喜. *New Year's Day* 元旦. *New Year's Eve.* 除夕. *New Year's gifts* 新年礼物. *New Year's greetings [wishes]* 新年的祝贺，贺年.
New York [ˈnjuː ˈjɔːk] ①纽约〔美国州名〕. ②纽约(市)〔美国城市〕(= New York City).
New York·er [ˈnjuːˈjɔːkə] *n.* 纽约市[州]人.
New Zea·land [njuː ˈziːlənd] 新西兰〔大洋洲〕.
New Zea·land·er [ˈnjuːˈziːləndə] *n.* 新西兰人.
next [nekst] *a.* ①其次的；下次的，紧接着来到的. ②隔壁的. ③〔the ～〕任何别的. ～ *Friday* = *on Friday* ～ 在下一个星期五. *Not till* ～ *time.* 下次不再吃了〔无决心戒酒或戒烟时的笑谈〕. *What is the* ～ *article?* 还要什么呢？〔商人对顾客讲的话〕. *the person* ～ *(to) him in rank [age]* 地位[年龄]次于他的人. ★按现在时所说的'来年'等不用 the，按过去时所说的'翌年'等通常都要用 the，但在故事中或当所说语义不致发生误会时，后者也常常不用 the：～ *week [month, year]* 来周[月、年]；*the* ～ *week [month, year]* 翌周[月、年]；*the* ～ *day [morning]* 翌日[晨]. ***as ... as the*** ～ ***fellow*** 跟任何人一样…(*I am as brave as the* ～ *fellow.* 我跟任何人一样勇敢). ***get*** ～ ***to*** 〔美〕知道. ***in the*** ～ ***place*** 其次. ～ ***best*** 其次最好的，次好的. ～ ***but one [two]*** 第二[第三]的. ～ ***door*** 邻家，在隔壁，隔壁的 (*He lives* ～ *door to me.* 他住在我的隔壁. ～ *door but one* 隔壁第二家). ～ ***door to*** 在…隔壁；几乎等于(*He is* ～ *door to a madman.* 他简直是一个疯子). ～***friend*** 【法】(幼儿，无法定能力者的)诉讼代理人. ～ ***man*** 别人，第三者. ～ ***of kin*** 【法】最近亲. ～ ***of skin*** 〔美〕亲戚. ～ ***to impossible [nothing, none]*** 几乎不可能〔等于没有，很少〕. —*n.* 下一个人[东西]. *in my* ～ *(letter)* 在我下一封信中. *To be concluded in our* ～ *(issue).* 下期续完. *He is* ～ *of kin to me.* = *He is the* ～ *of my kin.* 他是我最近的亲戚. *N-, please!* 下一位！〔促人发问或进来时用〕. —*ad.* 其次，然后；下次；贴近. *When I* ～ *saw him, he was lame.* 当我第二次见他的时候，他已经跛了. *the largest city* ～ *to London* 仅次于伦敦的大都市. *He placed his chair* ～ *to me.* 他把椅子搁在我椅子的旁边. ***get [put] (sb.)*** ～ ***to*** 〔美〕给某人知道…，把…告诉某人. ***What*** ～**!** ①有比这更稀奇的(事)吗！？②(店员用语)还要什么？—*prep.* 在…的隔壁，贴近…，在…之次，最近于…. *He sat* ～ *me.* 他紧挨着我坐下. *I always wear flannel* ～ *my skin.* 我常穿法兰绒做贴身衣.
nex·us [ˈneksəs] *n.* 〔*sing., pl.*〕①连系，联络；网络；连杆；关系；连结的一系列，一组. ②【语】主(语)谓(语)关系；二元语核〔丹麦语言学家奥托·叶斯帕森用语，包括一切含有主谓语概念的结构，如主句、分句、不定式短语以及独立分词短语等〕. *the cash* ～ 现金交易关系. *infinitive* ～【语】不定式二元语核〔指 for ... to ... 这种可作主[宾]语、定语、状语的结构〕.
Nez Per·cé [ˈnezpəˈsei, -pəːs] 内珀西人〔北美印第安人的部族之一〕；内珀西语.
N.F. = ①Newfoundland. ②Norman French. ③National Formulary 〔美〕国家处方集.
n/f = no funds. 存款不足.
N.F.S. = National Fire Service 〔英〕全国救火会.
N.F.U., NFU = National Farmers' Union 〔英〕全国农场主联合会.
NG = ①National Guard 〔美〕国民警卫队. ②no good; not good 不行. ③New Granada 〔旧〕新格拉那达〔指原西班牙殖民地，现为委内瑞拉、哥伦比亚、巴拿马和厄瓜多尔〕.
Ng. = Norwegian.
NGr = New Greek 新希腊语.
ngwee [ŋˈgwi] *n.* *(pl. gwee)* 昂格维〔赞比亚货币单位，等于克瓦查的 1/100〕.
N.H., NH = New Hampshire 新罕布什尔〔美国州名〕.
NHA = National Housing Agency 〔美旧〕国家住房管理署.
N.Heb. = New Hebrides.
N.H.I. = National Health Insurance 〔英〕国民健康保险.
N.H.K., NHK = 〔Jap.〕*Nippon Hoso Kyokai* (= Japan Broadcasting Corporation) 日本广播协会.
NHP, n.h.p. = nominal horsepower 额定马力，标称马力.
N.I. = Northern Ireland 北爱尔兰.
Ni 【化】= nickel 镍.
ni·a·cin [ˈnaiəsin] *n.* 【生化】抗癞皮病维生素，烟碱酸(= nicotimic acid).
Ni·ag·a·ra [naiˈægərə] *n.* ①尼亚加拉河〔美国与加拿大交界处的一条大河〕. ②尼亚加拉瀑布 (= ～ Falls)；瀑布；急流；大洪水. ③〔n-〕滔滔不绝的谈话. ***shoot*** ～ 大冒险. ～ **Falls** 〔美〕尼亚加拉瀑布.
ni·ai·se·rie [niˈeizəri] *n.* 〔F.〕无知，单纯，愚笨.
N.I.A.L. = National Institute of Arts and Letters 〔美〕全国文学和艺术学会.
Nia·mey [ˌnjɑːˈmei] *n.* 尼亚美〔尼日尔首都〕.
nib [nib] *n.* ①钢笔尖；鹅管笔的尖端；〔古〕(鸟)嘴. ②(工具的)尖头，尖端. ③〔*pl.*〕可可豆[咖啡]的碎粒. ④(镰刀的)短柄. ⑤〔俚〕要人，重要人物；成功的工作. —*vt.* 在…装尖头；削尖(鹅管笔)；给(笔)插笔尖.
nib·ble [ˈnibl] *vt.* 一点点地咬下；一点点地咬[吃]；啃. —*vi.* ①啃，(鱼等)一点点地咬. ②(对诱惑、交易等)做出有意的样子 *(at)*. ③吹毛求疵，找碴儿 *(at)*. *tactics of nibbling away* 蚕食政策. —*n.* ①一点一点的咬，(鱼)试咬；(兽)(咬)一口. ②咬一口的量；很少量. ③不愿意似的回答. *glorious day for a* ～ 钓鱼的好日子.
Ni·be·lung·en·lied [ˌniːbəˈluŋgənliːt] *n.* 〔the ～〕尼伯龙根之歌〔德国民间史诗〕.
nib·lick [ˈniblik] *n.* 铁头高尔夫球棒〔现在通称为 Iron No. 9〕.
nibs [nibz] *n.* 〔美口〕自以为了不起的要人；头目. *his* ～ 那位大人[先生]. *They were careful not to offend his* ～. 他们小心翼翼，不敢冒犯这位大人.
Nic·a·ra·gua [ˌnikəˈrægjuə] *n.* 尼加拉瓜〔拉丁美洲〕. **-guan** *a., n.* 尼加拉瓜的(人).
nic·co·lite [ˈnikəlait] *n.* 【矿】红砷镍矿.
Nice [niːs] *n.* 尼斯〔法国港市〕.
nice [nais] *a.* ①好的，不错的，美的，漂亮的，有趣的 (*opp.* nasty)；愉快的，吸引人的；亲切的，恳切的，厚道的；有教养的；高尚的. ②爱讲究，爱挑剔的，挑三拣四的。③细致的,精密的;精确的,精巧的,严格的,认真的。④敏锐的,敏感的;微妙的。⑤要慎重的,难决的;要手腕的。⑥〔反语〕困难的,讨厌的。*a ~ dish*好吃的菜。*a ~ day* 好天气。*We had a ~ time yesterday.* 我们昨天玩得很愉快。*He is ~ in his dress.* 他很讲究服装。*a ~ distinction* 细微的区别。*a ~ ear for sound* 听觉敏锐的耳朵。*a ~ point* 微妙之点。*a ~ shade of meaning* 意义的细微区别。*~ taste in art [literature]* 敏锐的艺术[文学]眼光。*Be ~ to the guests.* 对客人要周到。*That isn't ~.* 那不礼貌。*You're a ~ fellow, I must say.*〔反〕你真是个好家伙 [讨厌的家伙]。*Here is a ~ mess.* 这真糟。***in a ~ fix*** 进退为难,非常窘困。*~* ***and***〔同形容词连用〕很(*~ and cool* 很凉快。*The place is ~ and healthy.* 那地方很适合健康)。~ **blackberry**〔美俚〕无聊朋友,讨厌的人。~ **girl**〔美〕好女孩,有礼貌的女孩,(有时指)不活泼的女孩,一本正经的女孩。~ **going**〔美俚〕好〔表示同意〕。~**-looking** *a.* 漂亮的;可爱的。~ **mats**〔美剧〕日场客满。~ **money**〔美俚〕相当多的款子。**-ness** *n.*

nice nel·ly, nice nel·lie, nice Nel·ly, nice Nel·lie [ˈnais ˈneli] *n.* ①委婉语。②装得一本正经的人。

nice-nel·ly, nice-nel·lie, nice-Nel·ly nice-Nel·lie [ˈnaisˈneli] *a.* ①(妇女)装得一本正经的。②委婉语的。

nice-nel·ly·ism [ˈnaisˈneliizəm] *n.* (妇女)装得一本正经;说话委婉。

nice·ly [ˈnaisli] *ad.* ①好好地,漂亮地,精密地;机敏地;愉快地,合适地;规规矩矩地。②非常讲究地。③〔口〕恰恰,恰好。*She's doing ~.*〔口〕她很好;她(身体)渐渐好了。*It suits me ~.* 那正合我意。— *a.*〔口〕健康的,强健的。

Nicene [nɑːˈsiːn] **Council**【宗】奈斯会议〔公元 325 年及 787 年于小亚细亚都会奈斯 (Nice) 开的两次基督教会议,尤指第一次会议,会上谴责阿里安教派,并通过了基督教标准信条〕。

ni·ce·ty [ˈnaisiti] *n.* ①精密,正确;严密。②细微的区别,微妙之处;机敏。③〔常 *pl.*〕细节。④〔常*pl.*〕雅兴,考究。*a point of extreme ~* 极其微妙的一个论点。*the niceties of life* 生活的享受。***to a ~*** ①正确地;恰恰,恰好。②精细入微地 (*judge the distance to a ~* 判断距离很准确)。

niche [nitʃ] *n.* ①壁龛〔搁雕像、花瓶等的墙壁凹处〕;【地】雪凹。②(适合个人性格、能力等的)适当地位,活动范围;【生】小生境。***deserve a ~ in the temple of fame*** 可以流芳百世。***find the right ~ for oneself*** 适得其所;为自己谋得合适的位置[地位]。— *vt.* ①〔常用被动语态〕把…放在壁龛里。②〔常用被动语态或作 ~ oneself〕把自己安顿(在适当场所)。

Nich·o·las [ˈnikələs] *n.* 尼古拉斯〔男子名〕。

Nichol(s) [ˈnikəl(z)] *n.* 尼科尔(斯)〔姓氏〕。

Nichol·son [ˈnikəlsn] *n.* 尼科尔森〔姓氏〕。

nicht wahr? [nihtˈvɑː]〔G.〕对吧?不是这样的吗?

Nick [nik] *n.* ①尼克〔男子名, Nicholas 的昵称〕。②恶魔,魔鬼〔一般作 Old ~〕。

nick[1] [nik] *n.* ①刻口,刻痕;缺口,微凹,裂缝,隙。②骰子掷出所要点以上的大点;〔美俚〕一对骰子的七点〔十一点〕。③【印】(铅字边上的)沟槽。④〔俚〕监狱。⑤恰好的时刻。***in the ~ (of time)*** 在恰好的时候,在紧要关头。— *vt.* ①刻痕于;摘记;弄缺(刀口);切短(马尾)。②说中;恰好赶上。③〔英俚〕逮捕;(掷骰子)掷出(赢点)。④〔俚〕夺;偷;骗。— *vi.* (打猎、赛跑等时)抄近路赶过 (*in*)。*~* ***a hurdle***〔美运〕栏没有跳好。***(be) ~ed on the whiskers***【美拳】下巴挨打。*~* ***it*** 猜中,说中。*~* ***in*** (打猎)抄近路追到。*~* ***the time*** 恰好赶上。

nick[2] [nik] *n.*〔美俚〕五分镍币。

nick·el [ˈnikl] *n.*【化】镍;〔美、加〕五分镍币;(一般)镍币。*a ~ note*〔美〕五元钞票。*a ~ nurser*〔美俚〕小气鬼,守财奴。***don't take any wooden ~s***〔美〕当心,别上当。— *vt.* (〔Eng.〕*-ll-*) 镀镍于。~ **bloom** = annabergite (镍华)。~ **plate** 镀镍层。~**-plated** *a.* 镀镍的。~**-plating** 镀镍。~ **silver** 镍银齐〔一种镍、铜、锌的合金〕。

nick·el·if·er·ous [ˌnikəˈlifərəs] *a.* (矿石等)含镍的。

nick·e·lo·de·on [ˌnikəˈləudiən] *n.*〔美〕①(门票一律五分的)五分戏院[电影院]。②投币式自动点唱机(= jukebox)。

nick·el·ous [ˈnikləs] *a.*【化】亚镍的,二价镍的。

nick·er [ˈnikə] *vi.* ①(马)嘶。②闷笑。— *n.* ①马嘶声。②闷笑。

nick·ey [ˈniki] *n.*〔Am.〕= Nick.

nickle [ˈnikl] *n.* (美国和加拿大的)五分镍币(= nickel)。

nick·nack [ˈniknæk] *n.* = knickknack.

nick·name [ˈnikneim] *n.* ①诨名,绰号。②教名 (*Christian name*) 的略称,爱称〔如称 *Elizabeth* 为 *Bess*, 称 *Robert* 为 *Bob*〕。— *vt.* ①给…加诨名,给…起绰号;用诨名[爱称]称呼。②〔罕〕误称。

Nic·o·bars [ˈnikəubɑːz] *n.*〔*pl.*〕尼科巴群岛〔印度〕(= the Nicobar Islands)。

Nic·ol(l) [ˈnikəl] *n.* 尼科尔〔姓氏〕。

Nic·ol prism [ˈnikəl prizəm]【光】尼科尔偏光镜,棱晶。

Ni·col·son [ˈnikəlsn] *n.* 尼科尔森〔姓氏〕。

Nic·o·si·a [ˌnikəuˈsi(ː)ə] *n.* 尼科西亚〔塞浦路斯首都〕。

ni·co·ti·a [niˈkəuʃiə] *n.* ① = nicotine. ②〔诗〕烟草。

ni·co·ti·an [niˈkəuʃən] *a.* ①烟草的,得自烟草的。②抽烟的。— *n.*〔罕〕抽烟的人。

nic·o·tin·am·ide [ˌnikəˈtinəmaid, -ˈtiːn-] *n.*【化】烟(碱)酰胺。

nic·o·tine [ˈnikətiːn], **nic·o·tin** [-tin] *n.*【化】烟碱,尼古丁,烟草素。

nic·o·tin·ic [ˌnikəˈtinik] *a.*【化】烟碱(酸)的。~ **acid** 烟(碱)酸。

nic·o·tin·ism [ˈnikətiːnizəm] *n.*【医】烟碱中毒,尼古丁中毒。

nic·o·tin·ize [ˈnikətinaiz] *vt.* 使中烟碱毒。

nic·tate [ˈnikteit], **nic·ti·tate** [ˈniktiteit] *vi.* 眨眼睛,眨巴眼儿。**-ating membrane**【动】瞬膜。

nic·ta·tion [nikˈteiʃən], **nic·ti·ta·tion** [ˌniktiˈteiʃən] *n.* 眨眼睛。

ni·cy [ˈnaisi] *n.*〔儿〕糖糖糕糕。

ni·da·men·tal [ˌnaidəˈmentl] *a.* (软体动物) 缠卵的。~ **chamber** 缠卵腔[室]。~ **gland** 缠卵腺,壳腺。

nid·(d)er·ing [ˈnidəriŋ] *a., n.*〔古〕卑鄙的(人),不诚实的(人),怯懦的(人);可怜的(人)。

nid·dle-nod·dle [ˈnidlˈnɔdl] *a.* (打瞌睡时)点着头的。— *vi., vt.* (因打盹等)不断地点(头)。

nide [naid] *n.* 雉窝(中的雏雉)。

ni·dic·o·lous [naiˈdikələs] *a.* ①留在窠里的〔指鸟孵出之后一段时间仍然在窠里〕。②生活在其它禽类窠里的。

nid·i·fi·cate [ˈnidifikeit], **nid·i·fy** [-fai] *vi.* 作巢。**-cation** [ˌnidifiˈkeiʃən] *n.*

ni·dif·u·gous [naiˈdifjugəs] *a.* (象鸡孵出后)立即离窠的。

nid-nod [ˈnidnɔd] *vi., vt.* (使)点着头打盹。

ni·dus [ˈnaidəs] *n.* (*pl.* *-di* [-dai], *~es*) ①【动】胞窝,孵卵所。②病源地,发生地,发源地。③【医】病灶。

niece [niːs] *n.* ①侄女,甥女。②〔婉〕教士的私生女。

ni·el·list [niˈelist] *n.* 黑金镶嵌师。

niel·lo [niˈeləu] *n.* (*pl.* *-li* [-liː], *~es*) 黑金镶嵌术,黑金镶嵌;黑金镶嵌品。

ni·el·lo·ed [niˈeləud] *a.* 镶黑金的。

Nier·stein·er [ˈniəstainə] *n.* (莱茵河畔尼尔斯坦纳产的)白葡萄酒。

Nie·tzsche [ˈniːtʃə], **Friedrich Wilhelm** 尼采〔1844—1900,德国哲学家〕。

Nie·tzsche·an [ˈniːtʃiən] *a.* 尼采哲学的。

Nie·tzsche·an·ism [ˈniːtʃjənizəm], **Nie·tzsche·ism**

[-tʃiizəm] *n.* 尼采哲学.
nieve [niːv] *n.* 〔Scot., 英方〕拳手.
niff [nif] *n.* 〔俚〕难闻的气味. — *vi.* 散发恶臭.
nif·fer ['nifə] *vi., n.* 〔Scot.〕交换;换货;交易.
nif·tic ['niftik] *a.* 〔美俚〕漂亮的;俏皮的.
nif·ty ['nifti] *a.* ***(-ti·er; -ti·est)*** 〔美俚〕俏皮的;漂亮的. — *n.* 俏皮话;漂亮东西,漂亮姑娘. ***It's a ~.*** 这个倒漂亮.
Ni·gel ['naidʒəl] *n.* 奈杰尔〔男子名〕.
Ni·ger ['naidʒə] *n.* ①尼日尔〔非洲〕. ②〔the ~〕尼日尔河. ③〔n-〕皂脚. ~ *(seed) oil* 皂厂杂油.
Ni·ger-Con·go ['naidʒə'kɔŋgəu] *n.* 尼日尔刚果语.
Ni·ger·i·a [nai'dʒiəriə] *n.* 尼日利亚〔非洲〕. **-n** ① *n.* 尼日尼亚人. ② *a.* 尼日尼亚(人)的.
nig·gard ['nigəd] *n.* 小气鬼. — *a.* 〔诗〕吝啬的, 小气的. **-ly** *a., ad.* **-li·ness** *n.*
nig·ger ['nigə] *n.* ①〔口〕〔蔑〕黑人. ②〔蔑〕(东印度、澳洲等处的)肤色黑的本地人. ③化装黑人乐队. ④〔美〕(锯木厂中的) 推木机. ⑤ 非洲生橡胶. ⑥〔口〕(仪器等的) 故障. ⑦(黑色) 皂脚. — *vt.* ①〔美〕耗尽(地力). ②〔英、加〕烧掉(木头). ③〔口〕受黑人影响. ***~ in the woodpile [fence]*** 〔美俚〕隐蔽中的事实、缺点、动机(等);秘密;令人怀疑的情况. ***~s in a snowstorm*** 咖喱饭; 干李子粥. ***work like a ~*** 辛苦工作. ~ **driver** 〔美俚〕凶狠的矿工〔伐木工〕工头. ~ **gin** 〔美俚〕酒. ~ **head** = negro head. ~ **heaven** 〔美俚〕(戏院等的)顶层楼座. ~**-lover** 同情黑人解放运动的人. ~**-melodies** 黑人的歌. **-dom** 黑人身分; 黑人社会. **-ish** *a.* 黑人(似)的.
nig·gle ['nigl] *vi.* 〔英〕为小事花费时间〔操心〕.
nig·gling ['nigliŋ] *a.* ①为小事操心的. ②麻烦的. ③(工作等)难办的;(字等)潦草难认的. — *n.* 麻烦事. *petty ~* 打小算盘.
nigh [nai] *ad.,a.* ***(~er; ~est, next)***, *prep., v.* 〔古、诗、方〕= near.
night [nait] *n.* ①夜, 夜间, 夜晚(*opp.* day). ②黄昏; 黑夜;黑暗. ③蒙昧时代;失意时代. ④盲目,瞎;死. ⑤夜晚的活动〔如晚会等〕. *last ~* 昨晚. *the ~ before last* 前天的晚上. *a dirty ~* 下雨的夜晚, 暴风雨之夜. *N-falls.* 天黑了. *Good ~!* (用于晚上分别时)晚安! 再见! *He closed his eyes in endless ~.* 他的眼睛永远瞎了. *They are wrapped in the ~ of ignorance [barbarism].* 他们完全蒙昧无知. ***all ~ (long)=all the ~ through*** 整夜. ***as black [dark] as ~*** 昏黑,漆黑. ***at [in the] dead of ~*** 在深更半夜. ***at ~*** 在夜里;在黄昏时候;晚上〔下午六时至午夜的时间〕. ***at ~s*** 在夜里经常…. ***by ~*** 在夜间;趁黑夜. ***far into the ~*** 至深夜. ***go forth into the ~*** 走到黑暗处. ***have [pass] a good [bad] ~*** 睡得好〔睡得不好〕. ***have a [the] ~ out [off]*** 在外头玩一晚上;一个晚上不上班. ***in the ~*** 在夜间. ***keep [last] over ~*** 保持〔继续〕到早上. ***late at ~*** 在深夜, 在深更半夜. ***make a ~ of it*** 通宵宴乐;玩到天亮. ***~ about*** 隔夜. ***~ after ~ = ~ by ~*** 每夜, 连夜. ***~ and day*** 日夜,日夜不停地,老是. ***o'~s (= of ~s, on ~s)*** 〔口、方〕= ***by ~***, ***at ~*** *(I cannot sleep o'~s for thinking of that.* 为了担心那件事我晚上总睡不着). ***one's ~ out*** (仆人等) 可以出去玩的一晚, 过节的晚上, 庆祝之夜. ***put up for the ~*** 投宿. ***spend the ~ with*** 在…的家里过夜. ***stay (three) ~s with*** 在…家住了(三)晚上. ***turn ~ into day*** 拿夜晚当白天. ***under cover of ~*** 趁夜,趁黑. ~ **attire** 睡衣. ~ **bell** (医院等)夜间用铃. ~ **bird** ①夜鸟〔枭、夜莺等〕. ②夜间活动者;夜游者;夜盗. ~ **blindness** 【医】夜盲症. ~**-blooming** *a.* 夜间开花的. ~ **boat** 夜(航客)船. ~ **bomber** 【空】夜间轰炸机. ~**breeze** 晚风. ~**cap** 睡帽;〔俚〕夜酒,睡前酒;〔美〕当天最后一场比赛. ~ **cart** 粪车. ~ **cellar** 〔英〕低级地下酒店. ~ **chair** = night-stool. ~ **clothes** 〔*pl.*〕睡衣. ~ **club** 夜总会〔晚上喝酒跳舞的地方〕 ~ **commode** = nightstool. ~ **court** 夜间法庭. ~ **crawler** 〔美〕夜间爬出来的大蚯蚓. ~ **crow** (枭等)夜啼鸟. ~ **dog** 夜猎狗. ~**dress**, ~ **gown** 女睡衣 ~**duty** 夜勤. ~**-eyed** *a.* 黑夜里能看见东西的. ~**fall** 黄昏,傍晚. ~**-flower** 夜开花. ~ **flying** 【空】夜间飞行. ~ **game** 【棒球】夜场比赛. ~**glass** 【海】夜间用望远镜. ~ **hag** 夜间飞行空中的魔女; 梦魇. ~**-haunted** *a.* 晚上出鬼的. ~**hawk** ① *n.* 【鸟】= nightjar;夜间干坏事的人,夜盗;夜间工作的人;夜游的人;夜间出租马车的车夫;夜间出租汽车的司机;〔美〕= nightwrangler. ② *vi.* 在夜间徘徊. ~ **heron** 【鸟】夜鹭. ~**jar** 【鸟】欧夜鹰. ~**-key** 〔Am.〕= latchkey. ~ **landing** 【空】夜间着陆;夜间登陆. ~ **latch** 夜锁〔外用钥匙、内用手开的〕. ~ **letter**, ~ **lettergram** (收费低的)夜间电报,夜信电〔次日送达,略作 NLT〕. ~ **life** 夜生活〔指夜间在剧场、夜总会或类似场所饮酒作乐的活动〕. ~ **light** 夜明灯〔寝室或病室用〕; 通夜蜡烛. ~**line** (夜间垂置水中的)夜钓绳. ~ **liner** 夜间钓鱼的人. ~ **long** *ad., a.* 彻夜(的), 通宵(的). ~**man** 淘粪人,净厕员;守夜人. ~**-mare** ['naitmɛə] ①〔古〕睡魔. ②梦魇,恶梦; 可怕的事情,讨厌的人〔东西〕;恐怖感. ~**-mared** *a.* 梦魇的,做恶梦的. ~**marish** ['naitmɛəriʃ] *a.* 恶梦〔梦魇〕似的. ~**-ops** 〔*pl.*〕〔美〕夜袭, 夜间演习 (= ~ operations). ~ **owl** 【鸟】猫头鹰; 夜猫子, 深夜不睡的人, 夜精. ~ **piece** 夜景画; 夜景文; 夜景诗. ~ **porter** (旅馆、车站等的)夜勤人员. ~ **raid** 【军】夜间空袭, 夜间袭击. ~ **raven** 【诗】夜渡鸟 (尤指夜鹭). ~ **rider** 〔主美〕夜间出现的骑马歹人. ~**school** 夜校. ~**shade** 【植】茄属〔有毒植物〕*(the black ~ shade* 龙葵. *the deadly ~ shade* 颠茄. *the woody ~ shade* 南蛇藤属). ~ **shift** 夜班 (时间); 〔集合词〕夜班工人. ~ **shirt** (男用)睡衣. ~**side** 夜面, 阴面〔月球或行星背向太阳的一面〕; (事物) 黑暗的一面. ~**-sight** 夜间瞄准器. ~ **soil** 大粪. ~ **stand** 床头小桌. ~**-spot** 〔美口〕= night-club. ~**stick** 〔美〕夜勤警棍. ~**stool** (卧室用) 便桶; 尿盆. ~**-stop** *vi.* (飞机)停飞过夜. ~ **stop** (飞机) 夜停. ~ **suit** 睡衣. ~ **sweat** 盗汗. ~ **terror** (小孩的)夜哭. ~**tide** 〔诗〕夜晚; 夜潮. ~**time** 夜间. ~**town** 夜市, 不夜城. ~**-viewer** 夜间观察器, 红外线观察器. ~**walker** 梦游病人;夜间徘徊者;盗贼;夜间徘徊街头的妓女. ~ **walking** 梦中步行,梦游病;夜间徘徊. ~**watch** ①守夜,值更. ②守夜者. ③夜班时间;〔*pl.*〕(夜晚)睡不着的时间 *(in the ~ watches* 在那些忐忑不安的、难于入睡的夜晚). ~ **watcher** 守夜人. ~ **watchman** (工厂等雇用的) 守夜人. ~**wear** 睡衣. ~**work** 夜间工作. ~ **wrangler** 〔美〕牧场的夜间看马人.
night·ie ['naitiː] *n.* 〔口〕小睡衣.
Night·in·gale ['naitiŋgeil] *n.* ①奈廷格尔 (南丁格尔)〔姓氏〕. ②**Florence ~** 南丁格尔〔1820—1910,英国女社会改良家,近代护理制度的创始人,红十字会创办人〕.
night·in·gale ['naitiŋgeil] *n.* ①【鸟】夜莺;夜间鸣叫的鸟. ②歌喉婉转的歌手,声调好听的演说者.
night·ly ['naitli] *a.* ①每夜的,夜夜的. ②〔诗〕夜的, 夜间出来(行动、发生)的. — *ad.* 每夜,夜夜. ~ *dews* 夜露.
nights [naits] *ad.* 〔美〕每夜;大多数夜晚.
night·y ['naiti] *n.* 〔口〕睡衣. — *a.* 夜的.
night·y-night ['naiti'nait] *int.* 〔口〕good night 的变体.
ni·gres·cence [nai'gresəns] *n.* 变黑; (颜色、皮肤、眼睛等的)发黑.
ni·gres·cent [nai'gresənt] *a.* 发黑的, 带黑的; 渐渐变黑的.
nig·ri·fy ['nigrifai] *vt.* ***(-fi·ed; -fy·ing)*** 使变黑,使成黑色. **-fi·ca·tion** [ˌnigrifi'keiʃən] *n.*
nig·ri·tude ['nigritjuːd, 'naig-] *n.* 〔诗〕黑; 漆黑; 黑色

物;〔喻〕邪恶。

ni•gro•sin(e) [ˈnaigrəsi:n]【化】格尼(洛辛),苯胺黑;粒子元。

ni•hil [ˈnaihil]〔L.〕*n.* 无,虚无,空;毫无价值的东西。~ ***ad rem*** [ædˈrem] 不得要领的,牛头不对马嘴的。~ ***obstat*** [ˈɔbstæt] ①【天主】无异议〔经书籍检查官审查认可的证明〕。②官方制裁。

ni•hil•ism [ˈnaiilizəm] *n.* ①【哲】虚无主义;怀疑论。②〔N-〕(俄国)民粹主义;无政府主义。③恐怖手段。**ni-hil•ist** *n.*, **ni•hil•is•tic** [ˌnaiiˈlistik] *a.*

ni•hil•i•ty [naiˈhiliti] *n.*〔罕〕虚无,空,无效,无力;琐事,细事。

-nik *suf.*〔对参加政治运动或支持某种思潮者表示鄙视时在该名词上冠的后缀〕…分子;…迷;以…为特征的人:film*nik*, nogood*nik*.

Ni•ke [ˈnaiki:] *n.* ①【希神】胜利的女神(=(罗马的)Victoria)。②胜利之神。③〔美军〕奈基式地对空导弹。~**-Ajax** 奈基式 I 型地对空导弹。~**-Hercules** 奈基式 II 型地对空导弹。~**-Zeus** 奈基式 III 型地对空导弹。

nik•eth•a•mide [ˈnikeθəmaid, -mid] *n.*【化】尼可刹米,二乙菸酰胺,可拉明。

nil [nil] *n.* 无,零。*three goals to* ~【运】三比零。*the* ~ *method*【算术】零位法。

nil ad•mi•ra•ri [ˈnil ˌædmiˈrɛərai]〔L.〕对任何事都不惊奇的态度,漫不经心,冷淡,漠视。

nil de•sp•ran•dum [ˈnil ˌdespˈrændəm]〔L.〕决不绝望。

nil•gai [ˈnilgai] *n.* = nylghau.

Nile [nail] *n.*〔the ~〕尼罗河〔非洲〕。

Niles [nailz] *n.* 奈尔斯〔姓氏,男子名〕。

nill [nil] *vi.* 不愿〔只在以下句型中应用〕。*Will he* ~ *he*,… 不管他愿意不愿意…。*Will you* ~ *you*,… 不管你愿意不愿意…。— *vt.* 拒绝。

nill ni•si bo•num [ˈnil ˈnaisaiˈbəunəm]〔L.〕*de mortuis nil nisi bonum*(“人死莫言过”)的缩略表示形式。

Nilo-Hamitic [ˈnailəuhæˈmitik] *a.* 尼罗哈米特语〔包括马萨伊语〕。

ni•lom•e•ter [naiˈlɔmitə] *n.*【工】水位计。

Ni•lo-Sa•ha•ran [ˈnailəusəˈherən] *a.* 尼罗-撒哈拉语系的〔指包括沙里-尼罗语族的非洲语系〕。

Ni•lot•ic [naiˈlɔtik] *a.* 尼罗河 (Nile) (流域)的。

nim [nim] *vt.*, *vi.* (***nam*** [nɔm], ***nimmed***; ***no•men*** [ˈnəumən]; ***nome*** [ˈnəum]; ***nim•ming***)〔古〕偷,偷窃。

nim•bi [ˈnimbai] nimbus 的复数。

nim•ble [ˈnimbl] *a.* (***-bler***; ***-blest***) ①敏捷的,灵活的,灵敏的。②聪敏的,头脑敏捷的;机警的;多才的。③流通快的,完成迅速的。***(as)*** ~ ***as a squirrel*** 身手灵活,行动敏捷。***the*** ~ ***sixpence [ninepence, shilling]*** 流通快的银钱;薄利多销。~**-fingered** *a.* 手指敏捷的,善偷窃的。~**-footed** *a.* 脚快的。~**-witted** *a.* 聪敏的,机智的。**-bly** *ad.* **-ness** *n.*

nim•bo•stra•tus [ˈnimbəuˈstreitəs, -ˈstrætəs] *n.*【气】雨层云。

nim•bus [ˈnimbəs] *n.* (*pl.* ~*es*, ***-bi*** [-bai]) ①【气象】雨云。②(神像头上)光轮。③(环境或人的)光彩,气氛。④【美术】后光。*The candidate was encompassed with a* ~ *of fame.* 候选人当时处于蜚声四起的气氛中。

ni•mi•e•ty [niˈmaiəti] *n.*〔罕〕过多,过剩。

nim•i•ny-pim•i•ny [ˈnimiˈniˈpimini] *a.* 做作的,装腔作势的;扭扭捏捏的。*A* ~ *shyness makes frankness impossible.* 装模作样不会是真正的直爽。

Nim•itz [ˈnimits] *n.* 尼米兹〔姓氏〕。

Nim•rod [ˈnimrɔd] *n.* 爱打猎的人,猎迷,有名的猎人。

Ni•na [ˈni:nə] *n.* 尼娜〔女子名〕。

nin•com•poop [ˈninkəmpu:p] *n.* 笨人;傻瓜。

nine [nain] *num.* 九,九个;第九〔用于章节页行等词之后〕。~ *tenths* 十分之九。***a*** ~ ***days' wonder*** 一时新奇,过后即忘的事物。***in the*** ~***-holes***〔美〕为难,窘困。~ ***cases [times] out of ten*** 十之八九,大抵。~***'s complement representation***(十进制)反码。— *n.* ①九个一组的人或物。②九岁。③九点钟。④棒球队。⑤九点(的牌)。***the N- (Muses)***(司文艺、美术的)缪司九女神。***(up) to the*** ~***s*** 完全,完美;(衣饰)华丽。

nine•fold [ˈnainfəuld] *a.* 九倍的,九重的。— *ad.* 九倍,九重。

nine•pins [ˈnainpinz] *n.*〔*pl.*〕〔作单数用〕九柱戏。***fall [be knocked] over like (a lot of)*** ~ 一齐倒下;东倒西歪。

nine•teen [ˈnainˈti:n] *num.*(基数)十九;十九个人[物];第十九(章,页等)。—*n.* 十九岁;十九点钟。***talk [go, run, wag]*** ~ ***to the dozen*** 说个不停。

nine•teenth [ˈnainˈti:nθ] *n.*, *a.* 第十九(的),十九分之一(的);(月的)十九号(的)。~ **amendment** 美国宪法赋予妇女投票权的修正案。~ **hole**〔谑〕高尔夫球场里的酒吧间。

nine•ti•eth [ˈnaintiiθ] *num.*, *n.* 第九十,九十分之一。

nine•ty [ˈnainti] *num.* 九十。—*n.* 九十岁[个]。*the nineties* 九十年代〔略作 '90s〕;九十多岁(九十至九十九岁);(温度表的)九十多度(九十至九十九度)~***-nine times out of a hundred*** 十有九成九,百分之九十九,几乎总是。

Nin•e•reh [ˈninivi] *n.* 尼尼微〔古代亚述首都〕。

Nin•e•vite [ˈninivait] *n.* 古代亚述首都尼尼微人。

nin•ny [ˈnini], **nin•ny•ham•mer** [ˈninihæmə] *n.* 笨人,傻子。

ni•non [ninɔ̃] *n.*〔F.〕尼农绸;薄绸。

ninth [nainθ] *num.* 第九(的);九分之一(的)。— *n.*(月的)第九日;【乐】第九度音程。~ *nerve* 舌咽喉神经。~ *part of a man*〔谑〕裁缝〔从俗话 *Nine tailors make a man* 而来〕。~ **chord**【乐】第九和弦。**-ly** *ad.*

Ni•o•be [ˈnaiəbi] *n.* ①【希神】尼俄伯〔她有十四个儿子,因自夸而全被杀死,悲伤无已,后化为石头〕。②〔诗〕因丧失孩子而终身悲叹的妇女。③【植】中国百合。

ni•o•bic [naiˈəubik] *a.*【化】铌的。

ni•o•bite [ˈnaiəbait] *n.*【矿】铌铁矿。

ni•o•bi•um [naiˈəubiəm] *n.*【化】铌〔旧名columbium〕~ **ore** 铌矿。

ni•o•bous [naiˈəubəs] *a.*【化】亚铌的,三价铌的。

Nip [nip] *n.*〔美口〕= Niponese.

nip[1] [nip] *vt.* ①夹,捏,掐;(马、狗等)咬。②摘取,剪断 *(off)*。③冻伤(手指等),冻死(植株);阻止,阻碍(生长等);使挫折。④〔俚〕抢去;偷;逮捕。*The crab nipped my toe.* 螃蟹夹了我的脚趾。~ ***in the bud*** 在萌芽时摘取,防患于未然,消灭于萌芽状态。— *vi.* ①夹,捏,掐,咬。②(寒风等)刺骨。③〔俚〕跑,赶 *(along; in; off; on)*。~ ***in [out]*** 忽然跳进[出];插嘴(~ *in with a smart question* 乘机提出尖锐的质问)。— *n.* ①一夹,一捏,一掐,使劲的一咬;一小片。②霜害;阻碍;寒气,严寒。③讽刺,痛骂。④【海】(冰对船两边的)强压。⑤【地】狭缩。~ ***and tuck***〔美口〕竞走时不相上下。

nip[2] [nip] *n.*(酒等的)一口,少量。***freshen the*** ~〔口〕以酒解酒〔醉醒后再喝点酒〕。— ***vi.*** 一点儿一点儿地喝,呷。

ni•pa [ˈni:pə, ˈnai-] *n.*【植】①聂帕榈。②聂帕榈茅屋顶或聂帕果。③聂帕果汁。

nip•per [ˈnipə] *n.* ①夹[捏,掐,摘,咬]的人[东西]。②(马的)前齿,(蟹等的)螯。③〔英口〕(无赖)少年;年轻的叫卖小贩;吝啬鬼,小气鬼;(行商、土工等的)帮手。④〔*pl.*〕钳子,镊子。⑤〔*pl.*〕〔俚〕夹鼻眼镜。⑥〔*pl.*〕〔俚〕手铐;脚镣。

nip•ping [ˈnipiŋ] *a.*(风等)刺骨的,砭人肌肤的;讽刺的,尖刻的。

nip•ple [ˈnipl] *n.* ①奶头,奶咂咂;(奶瓶的)橡皮奶头。②(皮肤、山顶、金属面、玻璃面等的)乳头状突起;(枪炮的)火门;【机】喷灯喷嘴,螺纹接套。~ **shield** 乳头罩(保护疼痛的乳头)。~**wort**【植】稻槎菜属。

Nip•po [ˈnipəu] *n.*〔美军俚〕日本人。

Nip·pon [niˈpɔn, ˈnip-] *n.* = Japan.
Nip·pon·ese [ˌnipəˈniːz] *n., a.* = Japanese.
Nip·poni·an [niˈpəuniən] *a.* 日本(人)的。
nip·py [ˈnipi] *a.* *(-pi·er; -pi·est)*〔俚〕①敏捷的,伶俐的,快的。②(天气等)寒冷的,刺骨的。— *n.*〔英口〕法国里昂咖啡馆的女服务员。
nip-up [ˈnipˌʌp] *n.* 叠肋〔杂技的一种起跳动, 由仰卧一跃而起〕。
Nir·va·na [niəˈvɑːnə, nəːˈv-] *n.*〔Sans.〕①【佛教】涅槃;【印度教】生命火焰的熄灭;极乐世界。②〔n-〕(自痛苦、烦恼中的)解脱。*the ~ sutra* 涅槃经。
ni·si [ˈnaisai] *conj.*〔L.〕【法】要不然就,否则。— *a.*【法】非最后的,非绝对的。***decree [order, rule]*** ~ 在一定时日前不提出反对理由时即作确定的判决〔命令、条律〕。
nisi pri·us [ˈnaisaiˈpraiəs]〔L.〕(初审) 在备案法庭中由一个法官与陪审团审理的民事诉讼;〔英〕由巡回审判法官审理的民事诉讼。
Nis·sen [ˈnisən] *n.* 尼森〔姓氏〕。~ **hut** 【军】(加拿大 P.N.Nissen 设计的)尼森式桶形掩体。
ni·sus [ˈnaisəs] *n.*〔L.〕努力,奋力,企图。
nit[1] [nit] *n.* ①虮,虱卵。②〔美〕没用的人,饭桶。
nit[2] [nit] *ad.*〔美俚〕= no.
nit[3] [nit] *n.*【物】尼特〔光度单位〕。
nite [nait] *n.*〔美〕= night. ~ **spot** = nitery.
ni·ter[1] [ˈnaitə] *n.*〔美〕= nitre.
ni·ter[2] *n.* = nighter.
ni·ter·y [ˈnaitəri] *n.*〔美俚〕= night club.
ni·ton [ˈnaitɔn] *n.*【化】radon (氡)的旧名。
nit-pick [ˈnitpik] *vi.* 找碴儿,挑剔。**-er** *n.* 爱挑剔的人。
nit-pick·ing [ˈnitˌpikiŋ] *a., n.* 过于精细(的),挑剔(的),找碴儿(的)。
ni·trate [ˈnaitreit] *n.*【化】硝酸盐;硝酸根;硝酸钾(= potassium ~),硝酸钠(= sodium ~)。*ammonium* ~ 硝酸铵。*Chile* ~ 智利硝(石)。*hydrocellulose* ~ 水化纤维素硝酸酯。~ *bed* 硝石矿床。~ *nitrogen* 硝态氮。~ *of soda* 硝酸钠。~ *of silver* = *silver* ~ 硝酸银。— *vt.* 用硝酸处理,使硝化。
ni·tra·tion [naiˈtreiʃən] *n.*【化】硝化(作用)。*counter-current* ~ 对流硝化。
ni·tre [ˈnaitə] *n.* ①【化】硝石;硝酸钠(制火药用)。②智利硝石,钠硝石〔作肥料用〕。
ni·tric [ˈnaitrik] *a.*【化】氮的,含氮的;〔古〕硝石的。~ *acid* 硝酸。~ *bacteria* 硝酸细菌。~ *oxide* 氧化一氮。
ni·tride [ˈnaitraid] *n.*【化】氮化物。
ni·tri·fy [ˈnaitrifai] *vt., vi.*【化】硝化;(使)变成硝石。**-fi·er** *n.* 硝化(细)菌。**-ca·tion** [ˌnaitrifiˈkeiʃən] *n.* 硝化(作用)。
ni·tril(e) [ˈnaitriːl] *n.*【化】腈 (RCN)。
ni·trite [ˈnaitrait] *n.*【化】亚硝酸盐〔根、酯〕。
ni·tro [ˈnaitrəu] *a.*【化】含硝基的。— *n.* 硝化甘油。
nitro- *comb.f.* 表示"硝基","硝化": *nitro*acid 硝基酸。*nitro*alkane 硝基烷。*nitro*amine 硝胺。
ni·tro·an·il·ine [ˈnaitrəuˈænilain] *n.*【化】硝基苯胺。
ni·tro·bac·te·ri·a [ˈnaitrəubækˈtiərə] *n.* 硝化细菌。
ni·tro·ben·zene [ˈnaitrəuˈbenziːn] *n.*【化】硝基苯。
ni·tro·cel·lu·lose [naitrəuˈseljuləus] *n.*【化】硝化纤维素,棉花火药。~ *powder* 硝化纤维素(炸药)。
ni·tro·chalk [ˌnaitrəuˈtʃɔːk] *n.*【化】钾铵硝石;白垩硝肥。
ni·tro·ex·plo·sive [ˌnaitrəuiksˈpləusiv] *n.* 硝化火药。
ni·tro·fu·ran [ˌnaitrəuˈfjuərən, -fjuˈrɔn] *n.* 硝基呋喃。
ni·tro·gen [ˈnaitrədʒən] *n.*【化】氮,氮气。~ *chloride* 三氯化氮。~ *cycle* 氮循环。~ *dioxide* 二氧化一氮。~ *fixation* 固氮(作用)~*-free extract* 无氮浸出物。~ *monoxide* 一氧化二氮,氧化亚氮。~ *mustard* 氮芥(类);含氮芥子。~ *narcosis* 氮麻醉。~ *oxide* 氧化氮。
ni·trog·e·nize [naiˈtrɔdʒənaiz, ˈnaitrədʒənaiz] *vt.* *(-niz·ed; -niz·ing)* 氮化〔与氮或其化合物相化合或浸渍〕。
ni·trog·e·nous [naiˈtrɔdʒinəs] *a.* 含氮的,氮的。~ *fertilizer* 氮肥。
ni·tro·glyc·er·in(e) [ˈnaitrəuˈglisəriːn] *n.*【化】硝化甘油,炸油,甘油三硝酸脂。
ni·tro·hy·dro·chlo·ric acid [ˌnaitrəuˌhaidrəuˈklɔːrik] 王水,硝基盐酸(= aqua regia)。
ni·trol·ic [naiˈtrɔlik] **acid**【化】硝肟酸。
ni·trom·e·ter [naiˈtrɔmitə] *n.* 测氮管。
ni·tron [ˈnaitrɔn] *n.*【化】硝酸灵〔制造塑胶的原料〕。
ni·tro·par·af·fin [ˌnaitrəuˈpærəfin] *n.*【化】硝基烷。
ni·tro·pow·der [ˈnaitrəuˈpaudə] *n.*【化】硝化火药。
ni·tros·a·mine [ˌnaitrəusəˈmiːn, -ˈæmin] *n.*【化】(某)亚硝胺。
ni·tro·so [naiˈtrəusəu] *a.*【化】亚硝基的。
ni·tro·syl·sul·phu·ric, ni·tro·syl·sul·fu·ric [ˌnaitrəusilsʌlˈfjuːrik] *a.* 硝酸和硫酸混合而成的。~ *acid*【化】混酸。
ni·tro·syl [ˈnaitrəusil] *a.*【化】亚硝酰(基)的。
ni·tro·tol·u·ene [ˈnaitrəuˈtɔljuiːn] *n.*【化】硝基甲苯〔猛烈炸药〕。
ni·trous [ˈnaitrəs] *a.* 亚硝(酸)的;含有三价氮的。~ *acid*【化】亚硝酸。~ *bacteria* 亚硝酸细菌。~ *oxide*【化】一氧化二氮,笑气。
ni·tro·xyl [naiˈtrɔksil] *n.*【化】硝酰〔基〕。
nitsky [ˈnitski] *ad.*〔美俚〕= no.
nit·ty [ˈniti] *a.* *(-ti·er; -ti·est)* 多虱卵的,多小虫卵的。
nit·ty-grit·ty [ˈnitiˈgriti] *n.*〔俚〕基本事实,本质;事实。
nit·wit [ˈnitwit] *n.*〔美俚〕笨蛋,傻子。**nit·witted** [nitˈwitid] *a.*
Ni·u·e [niˈuːei] **Island** *n.* 纽埃岛(新)〔南太平洋〕。
ni·val [ˈnaivl] *a.* 雪的,生于雪中的。
niv·e·ous [ˈniviəs] *a.* 似雪的,雪白的,纯白的。
nix[1] [niks] *(fem.* ***nix·ie*** [ˈniksi]*)* *n.* 水中精灵, **-ie** *n.* 女水精。
nix[2] [niks] *n.*〔美俚〕①没有,无。②〔*pl.*〕没有邮政局的地方;无法投递的邮件,死信。③拒绝。*It must be you or ~.* 不是你才怪呢! ~ **on** 好了,够了 *(N- on your nonsense!* 你别再胡说八道了。*N- on that tune of talk!* 再少说那样的话!)。— *ad.* 不;不行,我不同意(= no)。*say ~ on a plan* 不同意计划。— *vt.* 拒绝;禁止;否决。*The police ~ed the procession.* 警察禁止游行。
nix[3] [niks] *int.*〔英学俚〕当心;(老师、班长等)来了!〔叫其他同伴当心的话〕。*keep* ~ 把风。
nix·ed [nikst] *a.*〔美俚〕被禁止的。*a ~ pic* 被禁映的影片。
nix·ey [ˈniksi] *ad.*〔美俚〕= no; not at all.
Nix·on [ˈniksn] *n.* 尼克松〔姓氏〕。
Ni·zam [naiˈzæm] *n.* ①尼萨〔旧时印度海得拉巴(Hyderabad) 土邦君主的称号〕。②〔n-〕土耳其士兵。
N.J., NJ = New Jersey 新泽西〔美国州名〕。
NKVD, N.K.V.D. (苏联)内务人民委员会。
N.L., NL = ①north latitude 北纬度。②New Latin 新拉丁语。
n.l. = ①〔L.〕*non licet* (not permitted) 不允许。②〔L.〕*non liquet* (not clear) 不清楚。
N. lat. = north latitude 北纬。
NLRB = National Labor Relations Board〔美〕全国劳工关系局。
N.L.T.〔美〕= night letter telegram 夜间书信电报。
NM = night message 夜间电报。
N.M., NM = ① New Mexico 新墨西哥〔美国州名〕。② nautical mile(s) 海里。
n.m. = nuclear moment 核矩。
NMB = National Mediation Board〔英〕全国调解局〔相当于美国的 NLRB〕。

N. Mex. = New Mexico 新墨西哥〔美国州名〕.

NMR = nuclear magnetic resonance 核磁共振.

NMU = National Maritime Union of America 〔美〕全国海员工会.

N.N.E., NNE, n.n.e. = north-northeast.

N.N.W., NNW, n.n.w. = north-northwest.

no[1] [nəu] *a.* ①〔加在单数名词前, 相当于冠词 a, an 的否定形式〕(一个也)没有. *Is there a book on the table?* 桌子上有一本书吗? — *No, there is ~ book there.* 没有, 桌上一本书也没有. *She has ~ mother while he has ~ father.* 她没有母亲, 他没有父亲. ②〔加在复数普通名词及不可数名词前〕一点儿也没有. *There are ~ clouds in the sky.* 天上一点儿云也没有. *She has ~ children.* 她一个孩子也没有. *There is [He has] ~ water [hope, etc.].* 一点儿水[希望等]也没有. ★ No seats are left. 这类句子的强调说法是 Not a seat is left. 一个座位也没有. ③〔加在不表示数量观念的普通名词、抽象名词、动名词之前〕什么也[谁也]没有. *No man is without his fault.* 谁也不会没有缺点. *No one knows.* 谁也不知道. ★ no one 的两个区别. 如: No one can do it. 谁也不能做. No one man can do it. 无论谁,一个人是做不到的. ④〔加在 be 与表语名词或其他形容词之间〕决不是…. *He is ~ scholar.* 他根本不是一个学者〔比较: *He is not a scholar.* 不是学者 (而是…等)〕. *It is ~ joke.* 这决不是开玩笑. *I am ~ match for him.* 我决不是他的对手. *He showed ~ small skill.* 他显出了相当大的本事. ⑤〔在省略句中〕不许,不可,反对,禁止. *No compromise!* 反对妥协! *No surrender!* 不要投降! *No admittance except on business.* 非公莫入. *No scribbing on the walls!* 墙上请勿涂写. *No smoking!* 请勿吸烟. *No thoroughfare.* 禁止通行. *No credit.* 不赊帐. *No cards [flowers].* (报丧广告)谨此报闻,恕不另讣[敬辞赠花]. ⑥〔There is ~ + 动名词〕丝毫不可能, 简直没办法. *There is ~ denying his tale.* 他说的话是无可否认的. *There is ~ saying what may happen.* 简直不晓得今后情况将会怎么样. ~ ***bargain***〔美运〕平凡的. ~ ***bon***〔军俚〕不好,不行. ~ ***bull fighter***〔美俚〕柔弱的男子. ~ ***can do***〔美俚〕= I can't do it. ~ ***confidence vote*** 不信任投票. ~ ***date*** (藏书签等上)无日期〔略 *n.d.*〕. ~ ***end of***〔口〕许多的; 非常的. ~ ***fear!*** 没有那种事; 别怕; 〔拒绝请求时〕不行不行. ~ ***flies on***〔美俚〕活泼, 有精神, 机灵, 聪敏 (*There are ~ flies on him.* 那家伙机灵[聪明]得很). ~ ***go***〔俚〕不行, 没希望, 失败; 〔美俚〕意见不一致 (*= ~ agreement*). ~ ***got***〔美俚〕我没有. ~ ***great shakes***〔美俚〕普通的, 平凡的, 比较上不大重要的. ~ ***likes***〔美俚〕不欢喜; 〔美剧〕收入少的; 不叫座的, 不成功的. ~ ***man's land*** 没有主人的土地; 【军】无人〔真空〕地带〔两对峙阵地间的地带〕; 难于确定性质的领域. ~ ***two ways about it***〔美〕确实的, 显著的. — *ad.* ①〔用于 or 之后〕= not. *Pleasant or ~, it is true.* 无论愉快与否, 事实不假. ②〔用于比较级之前〕一点也没有. *Things are ~ better (than before).* 情况一点也没有(比从前)更好一些. *I can walk ~ further [longer].* 我一点也不能再走了. ~ ***sooner ... than*** 刚一…(就)…, 才…(就). ***whether or ~*** ①是不是 (*Tell me whether or ~ it is true.* 请告诉我那是真是假). ②不管怎样 (*Whether or ~, I will go.* 不管怎样, 我都要去). — *n.* (*pl.* ~(*e*)*s*) ①否定, 否认, 拒绝. ②〔*pl.*〕(投)反对票(者). *I will not take ~ (for an answer).* 不许说不. *Two noes make a yes.* 否定的否定就是肯定. ***The noes have it.*** 投反对票者占多数. **~-account** *a., n.*〔美、方〕没用的(人), 不足道的(人). **~-ball** *n., vt.*【板球】(把…裁判为)犯规投球(应输一分). **~-being** 不存在; 非实在(的东西). **~-cost** *a.*〔美俚〕免费的. **~-count** *a.*〔美方〕= no-account. **~-go area** 禁区. **~-good(-er)**〔美俚〕没用的人, 饭桶. **~-hitter**【棒】无安打赛局. **~-knock** ① *a.* (逮捕、搜查等)强行闯入进行的, 破门而入的. ② *n.* 破门而入的强行搜捕. **~-load** *a.* (出售股票时)免付佣金的. **~-man** ① = nobody. ②〔美俚〕不肯妥协的人, 顽梗的人. **~-nonsense** *a.* 严肃的. **~-show** *n.* 预订了座位而未到的人.

no[2] [nəu] (*opp.* yes) *ad.* ①〔否定的回答〕不, 否. *Will you come?* — *No.* 你来吗? — 不来. ★(1)对否定问话给与否定回答时用. 如: You haven't finished yet? — No, sir. 还没有完吗? — 还没有. (2)有惊奇表现. 如: He even threatened to kill me. — No! — Yes, he did. 他甚至说要杀我. ——不会吧! ——是真的. ②〔和 not 或 nor 同用, 加强否定语气〕不. *A man could not lift it, ~, nor half a dozen.* 一个人是举不起的, 不, 六个人也举不起.

No【化】= nobelium 锘.

No., No, no. = number.

n.o. = natural order【生】自然分类的目(介于纲与科之间).

No. 1 [ˈnʌmbəˈwʌn] = number one. 第一; 第一等, 第一流; 自己; 自己的利益.

No·a·chi·an [nəuˈeikiən], **No·a·chic** [nəuˈeikik] *a.* 诺亚 (时代)的.

No·ah[1] [ˈnəuə] *n.* 诺亚〔男子名〕.

No·ah[2] [ˈnəuə] *n.*【圣】诺亚〔希伯来人的族长〕. ***~'s ark*** 见 *ark* 条. ***~'s ark phrases***〔美〕陈辞滥调. ***~'s nightcap***【植】花菱草.

no·ah·ar·cha·ic [ˌnəuəˈkeiik] *a.*〔美〕非常陈旧[落伍]的, 〔谑〕早已过时的.

nob[1] [nɔb] *n.* ①〔俚〕头; 头上的一击. ②球形门柄. ③【建】雕球饰. *a ~ in the fur trade* 法官. *a ~ of the first water* 第一流人物. — *vi., vt.*【拳击】打(…的)头.

nob[2] [nɔb] *n.*〔俚〕富豪; 贵族; 上流人物.

nob·ble [ˈnɔbl] *vt.*〔英俚〕①【赛马】(为要使马不能取胜)给(马)吃毒药, 使(马)成残废. ②(行贿)收买; 诈骗; 骗取(钱等). ③逮捕(犯人). **-bler** *n.* 诈骗者; 毒马者.

nob·bler [ˈnɔblə] *n.* ①当头一击, 击昏. ②〔澳俚〕一杯烈酒.

nob·but [ˈnɔbət] *ad.*〔口〕只是, 不过是.

nob·by [ˈnɔbi] *a.* (***-bi·er; -bi·est***)〔俚〕贵族的; 头面人物的; 时髦的, 最好的. **nob·bi·ly** *ad.*

No·bel [nəuˈbel] *n.* ①诺贝尔〔姓氏〕. ②**Alfred Bernhard** [ˈɑːlfred beənɑːd] ~ 诺贝尔〔1833—1896, 瑞典化学家, 炸药创制经营者, 诺贝尔奖金的创设者〕. **~-man, ~ Laureate** 诺贝尔奖金获得者. ~ **prizes** 诺贝尔奖金.

No·bel·ist [nəuˈbelist] *n.* 诺贝尔奖金获得者.

no·bel·i·um [nəuˈbeliəm] *n.*【化】锘〔102 号元素〕.

no·bil·i·a·ry [nəuˈbiliəri] *a.* 贵族的. ***the ~ particle [prefix]*** 贵族前缀〔用于姓名前表示某人系贵族〕.

no·bil·i·ty [nəuˈbiliti] *n.* ①高贵的身分[出身]. ②〔the ~〕〔集合词〕贵族(阶层); 〔英〕上院议员及家族. ③崇高, 高贵, 高尚. ④庄严, 雄伟. *a man of true ~* 一个真正高尚的人.

no·ble [ˈnəubl] *a.* (***-bler; -blest***) ①清高的, 崇高的, 高尚的. ②高贵的, 贵族的. ③宏伟的, 堂皇的; 华美的, 壮丽的; 卓越的; 著名的, 有名的. ④贵重的 (*opp.* base). *my ~ friend* 阁下〔演说中对贵族或有 Lord 称号的人的称呼〕. *the ~ lady* 尊夫人〔指贵族的夫人〕. *the ~ Lord* 阁下〔上院议员彼此间或对有 Lord 称号的下院议员的称呼〕. *It was planned on a ~ scale.* 计划规模宏大. *the ~ art (of self defense)* 拳击. *the ~ metals* 贵金属. — *n.* ①贵族. ②【史】诺布尔金币〔英国古金币, 相当于旧制 6 先令 8 便士〕; 〔美工会俚〕工贼, (破坏罢工的)工头. ~ **fir**【植】壮丽冷杉〔产于美国西部〕. ~ **gas** 稀有气体, 惰性气体. **~-minded** *a.* 心地高尚的, 崇高的; 气量大的, 豪爽的. **~man** 贵族. **~woman** 贵妇. **-ness** *n.* 高贵; 崇高, 高尚; 宏大, 庄严.

no·blesse [nəuˈbles] *n.*〔F.〕①(法国)贵族(阶层). ②贵

族身分,高贵的出身. ~ ***oblige*** [ɔbˈliːʒ] 位高则任重.

no·bly [ˈnəubli] *ad.* ①崇高,高贵,出身于贵族. ②华美,宏伟,壮丽. ③豁达,豪爽. *a deed ~ done* 宏伟业绩. *be ~ born* 出身高贵. *~-clad attendants* 服饰豪华的侍者. *The ~ born must ~ do.*出身高尚者行为也应高尚.

no·body [ˈnəubədi, -bɔdi] *pro.* 谁也不, 没人; 无人. *There was ~ present.* 没人出席. *Everybody's business is ~'s business.* 人人负责便是没人负责. *N- will be the wiser.* 没人会知道的. ~ *else* 此外无别人. — *n.* *(pl.* ***no·bod·ies)*** 不足取的人;无名小卒,小人物. *(opp.* somebody). *She has married a ~.* 她嫁了一个无名的人. *He is ~.* 他是一个没出息的人.

no·cake [ˈnəukeik] *n.* 〔美〕炒玉米粉.

no·cent [ˈnəusnt] *a.* 〔废或罕〕①有害的, 伤害的. ②有罪的,犯罪的.

no·ci·cep·tive [ˌnəusiˈseptiv] *a.* 疼痛的, 致痛的;有疼痛反映的.

nock [nɔk] *n.* ①(弓的)弧口;箭的尾端[扣弦处]. ②【海】帆的前部上端. — *vt.* ①给(弓)装弧口. ②搭箭于 (弓上).

noct- *comb. f.* 〔用于元音前〕= nocti-.

noc·tam·bu·lant [nɔkˈtæmbjulənt] *a.* 梦中步行的,梦游的. **-bu·la·tion** [nɔkˌtæmbjuˈleiʃən] *n.* 【医】梦行(症). **-list** *n.* 梦行者.

noc·tam·bule [nɔkˈtæmbjuːl] *n.* 梦中步行者, 梦游病者.

noc·tam·bu·lism [nɔkˈtæmbjulizəm] *n.* 【医】梦行.

nocti- *comb. f.* "夜": *nocti*luca.

noc·ti·flo·rous [ˌnɔktiˈflɔːrəs] *a.* 夜间开花的.

noc·ti·lu·ca [ˌnɔktiˈljuːkə] *n.* 【动】夜光虫; 〔N-〕夜光虫属.

noc·ti·lu·cence [ˌnɔktiˈljuːsns] *n.* 生物 (性) 发光; 磷花.

noc·ti·lu·cent [ˌnɔktiˈljuːsnt] *a.* 夜间发光的.

noc·tiv·a·gant, -gous [nɔkˈtivəgənt, -gəs] *a.* 夜间出游的,夜间徘徊的.

nocto- *comb. f.* = nocti-.

noc·to·vi·sor [ˈnɔktəvisə] *n.* 红外线摄象机 [望远机].

noc·tu·id [ˈnɔktʃuwid] *n.* 夜蛾科昆虫 [如夜盗蛾等].

noc·tule [ˈnɔktjuːl] *n.* (英国产)褐色大蝙蝠.

noc·turn [ˈnɔktəːn] *n.* = nocturne.

noc·tur·nal [nɔkˈtəːnl] *a.* 夜的 (*opp.* diurnal); 夜间(发生)的;夜出的,(花)夜开的;【乐】夜曲的. *a ~ sight* 夜景. *a ~ bird* 夜间活动的鸟. *a ~ journey* 夜间旅行. — *n.* 【天】夜间时刻测定器. **-ly** *ad.* 在夜里; 每夜.

noc·turne [ˈnɔktəːn] *n.* 夜景画;【乐】夜曲,梦幻曲;【宗】夜间礼拜;夜祷.

noc·u·ous [ˈnɔkjuəs] *a.* 有害的;有毒的.

nod [nɔd] *vt.* ①点(头);点头表示 (同意、了解); 点头叫…过来[过去]. ②使弯曲;使屈服. ~ *the head* 点头. ~ *assent [one's farewell]* 点头答应[告别]. — *vi.* ①点头,低头;点头答应[招呼、同意、承诺、命令]. ②打瞌睡;不当心弄错;(花、树等点头似地)摇摆; (房屋)倾斜. ~ *to a person* 点头打招呼. ***(Even) Homer sometimes ~s.*** 〔谚〕智者千虑必有一失. ~ ***to its fall*** 摇摇欲坠. ~ ***and shake the spheres*** 睥睨一世. ***have a nodding acquaintanceship with*** 和…只是点头之交;在…上略知一二. — *n.* ①点头; 点头礼; 打瞌睡. ② (点头)同意. ***be at [dependent (up)on] sb.'s*** ~ 在某人支配下,得由某人点头而定. ***Land of N-*** 睡乡;【圣】睡眠. ***on the*** ~ ①赊购. ②未经正式手续的;有默契的,默认的.

N.O.D. = Naval Ordnance Department 〔英〕海军军械司.

nod·al [ˈnəudəl] *a.* ①节的, 结的. ②【物】波节的. ~ **circle** 【物】波节圆.

nod·die [ˈnɔdi] *n.* 〔美〕糊涂虫,笨货.

nod·dle[1] [ˈnɔdl] *n.* 〔口〕头, 脑袋瓜. *Dressing up doesn't fill an empty ~.* 打扮得整齐弥补不了头脑的空虚.

nod·dle[2] [ˈnɔdl] *vt., vi.* 点(头).

nod·dy [ˈnɔdi] *n.* ①笨人,呆子,傻瓜. ②【鸟】(美国东南海岸常见的)黑燕鸥.

node [nəud] *n.* ①节,结;瘤;【虫】结脉. ②【植】茎节;【医】硬结肿;结,节结;【天】交点. ③【数】结点,交轨点;叉点;【物】节; 波节[振动体的静止点]; 中心点. ④ (情节的)曲折,错综复杂. *a current ~* 电流波节.

no·di [ˈnəudai] nodus 的复数.

nod·i·cal [ˈnəudikl] *a.* 【天】交点的. ~ *month* 交点月.

no·dose [ˈnəudəus] *a.* 有节的;(木材)疖疤多的.

no·dos·i·ty [nəuˈdɔsiti] *n.* 节; 多节; 痛风结.

nod·u·lar [ˈnɔdjulə], **nod·u·lat·ed** [ˈnɔdjuleitid] *a.* ①有节[结、瘤等]的. ②【矿】结核状的;【冶】榴状的. *limestone of ~ structure* 榴状结构石灰石. ~ *(graphite) cast iron* 【冶】球墨铸铁.

nod·u·la·tion [ˌnɔdjuˈleiʃən] *n.* 生节(块); 有节.

nod·ule [ˈnɔdjuːl] *n.* 小结; 小瘤; 【生】小结节;【医】结核,瘤;【地】岩球,矿瘤. ~ **bacteria** 根瘤(细)菌.

nod·u·lose, nod·u·lous [ˈnɔdjuləus, -ləs] *a.* = nodular ①.

no·dus [ˈnəudəs] *n.* *(pl.* ***-di*** [-dai]*)* ①节; 结; 瘤; 【虫】结脉,腹隆节. ②难点;(情节的)曲折,错综复杂.

No·el [ˈnouəl] *n.* 诺埃尔 〔姓氏,男子名,女子名〕.

No·el, Now·el [nəuˈel, ˈnəuəl] *n.* 圣诞节;〔n-〕圣诞颂歌.

no·e·sis [nəuˈiːsis] *n.* 【哲】纯理性的认识作用.

no·et·ic [nəuˈetik] *a.* 【哲】智力的; 纯理智的,理性的. — *n.* 有智力者. *~s* 纯理性论,智能论.

nog[1] [nɔg] *n.* 木钉,木栓;木砖. 【矿】木垛;垛式支架; 支柱垫楔. — *vt.* 用木钉支住; 用木钉钉牢; 在…上砌木砖.

nog[2] [nɔg] *n.* 〔英方〕 ①一种浓烈啤酒. ②〔美〕蛋酒,酒、蛋、奶等混合成的饮料 (= eggnog).

nog·gin [ˈnɔgin] *n.* ①〔古、方〕小杯; 一小杯 (= 1/4 pint). ②〔美方〕铅桶. ③〔美俚〕头;智力,脑筋.

nog·ging [ˈnɔgiŋ] *n.* 木架砖壁; 砌在木架间的砖; 壁砖.

no·how [ˈnəuhau] *ad.* 毫不, 决不, 无论如何不〔通常与 *can* 同用〕. *I can't do it ~.* 我决不能做. — *a.* 不舒服; 心烦意乱. *feel ~* 感到不舒服. *look ~* 显得心烦意乱.

N.O.I.C. = Naval Officer-in-Charge 海军主管军官.

noil [nɔil] *n.* 〔*sing., pl.*〕【纺】精梳短毛; 精梳落棉; 针板落棉;(羊毛、丝等的)刷屑;(头发的)梳屑.

noise [nɔiz] *n.* ①声音,声响. ②叫喊; 嘈杂声, 噪音; 喧闹声;吵闹, 骚动, 骚扰. ③〔古〕谣言, 风声. ④〔美〕东西〔常代替 *stuff* 用〕. *I don't like ~(s).* 我不喜欢吵闹声. ~ *in the ear* 耳鸣. *Hold your ~!* 别作声; 别响. ***make a ~*** 喧嚷, 吵闹; 扬名, 轰动一时 *(about)*. ***make a ~ in the world*** 惹世人评论, 名噪一时. ***make loud ~s about*** 鼓吹. ***make much ~ about*** 叫嚣. ***the [a] big*** ~ 〔口〕主人,东家,要人,名士;最得好评的影片[戏剧];主要事件;耸人听闻的声明;重要歌曲节目;重磅炸弹. ***The ~ goes that …*** 〔古〕据说,据传,谣传. — *vt.* 哄传;谣传,传说. *It is ~d abroad that …* 谣传…. — *vi.* 〔罕〕大声谈论; 吵, 闹. ~ **limiter** 【无】杂音抑制器. ~**maker** 发出嘈杂声的人群;(狂欢时)发噪音的器物. ~ **pollution** 噪音污染. ~**proof** *a.* 防杂音的,隔音的. ~ **suppressor** = ~ limiter.

noise·ful [ˈnɔizful] *a.* 吵闹的.

noise·less [ˈnɔizlis] *a.* 没有声音的;声音很轻的;非常安静的. **-ly** *ad.* 静静地,轻轻地. **-ness** *n.*

noi·sette[1] [nwaːˈzet] *n.* (法国)诺瓦氏 (Noisette) 品种蔷薇.

noi·sette[2] *n.* 〔F.〕〔常作复数用〕【烹】①小块[片]瘦肉. ②在黄油中煎黄的小马铃薯片.

nois·ies [ˈnɔiziz] *n.* 〔美俚〕有声电影.

nois·i·ly [ˈnɔizili] *ad.* 大声,吵闹地,骚然. **nois·i·ness**

n. 吵闹,骚扰.

noi·some [ˈnɔisəm] *a.* 有害的,有毒的; 有恶臭的; 可厌的. **-ly** *ad.* **-ness** *n.*

nois·y [ˈnɔizi] *a.* ***(nois·i·er; -i·est)*** ①(人、地方等) 嘈杂的,喧闹的; (街道)熙熙攘攘的. ②(颜色、服装) 过分鲜艳的; (文体)过分华丽[渲染]的.

No·la [ˈnəulə] *n.* 诺拉〔女子名〕.

No·lan [ˈnəulən] *n.* 诺兰〔男子名〕.

no·lens vo·lens [ˈnəulenz ˈvəulenz]〔L.〕无论愿意不愿意(=willy-nilly).

no·li me tan·ge·re [ˈnəulai miː ˈtændʒiri]〔L.〕① = touch-me-not 【植】凤仙花属. ②复活的耶稣和 Mary Magdalen 相会的图画. ③【医】侵蚀性溃疡,狼疮. ④不许接触[插手](的警告). ⑤不可接触的人[物]. *a ~ manner* 拒绝人接近的态度. *carry a ~ in one's face* 摆出一副铁板面孔.

nol·le pros·e·qui [ˈnɔli ˈprɔsikwai]〔L.〕【法】诉讼中止; 原告[检察官]给法庭部分[全部]撤回起诉的通知.

no·lo con·ten·de·re [ˈnəuləu kənˈtendəri]〔L.〕*n.*【法】无罪申诉〔刑事诉讼中,被告表示不愿进行辩护,但又不承认自己有罪的申诉〕.

no·lo e·pis·co·par·i [ˈnəuləu episkəˈpɛərai]〔L.〕【宗】拒绝担任主教; 拒任负责职位.

nol-pros [nɔlˈprɔs] *vt.* 〔美〕撤回(起诉的通知),中止诉讼.

nol. pros. 〔Am.〕= *nolle prosequi.*

nom [nɔ̃ːm] *n.*〔F.〕名. ~ ***de guerre*** [ˈnɔ̃ːmdəˈgɛə] 假名,化名. ~ ***de plume*** [-pluːm] 笔名.

nom. = ①nomenclature. ②nominal. ③nominative.

no·ma [ˈnəumə] *n.* 【医】水癌,走马疳,坏疽性口炎.

nom·ad [ˈnɔməd, ˈnəumæd] *n.* 游牧民的一员; 流浪者. — *a.*游牧的; 流浪的.

no·mad·ic [nəuˈmædik] *a.* 游牧的; 流浪的. *a ~ way of life* 牧民生活方式. *~ children* 流浪儿童. **-al·ly** *ad.*

nom·ad·ism [ˈnɔmədizəm, ˈnəumædizəm] *n.* 游牧[流浪]生活;【生】漫游(现象).

nom·ad·ize [ˈnɔmədaiz] *vi.,vt.* (使)过游牧生活; (使)流浪.

nom·ad·y [ˈnɔmədi] *n.* 游牧生活(状态).

nom·arch [ˈnɔmɑːk] *n.* (古代埃及或现代希腊的) 省[州]长. **-y** *n.* 省[州]长管区.

nom·bles, num·bles [ˈnʌmblz] *n.*〔*pl.*〕〔古〕鹿内脏.

nom·bril [ˈnɔmbril] *n.* 【解】脐眼.

nome [nəum] *n.* (古代埃及或现代希腊的)省[州].

no·men [ˈnəumən] *n.* *(pl.* ***nom·i·na*** [ˈnɔminə]*)* 中间名字〔古罗马姓名中第一名字与第三名字(姓)之间的名字〕.

no·men·cla·tive [ˈnəumənkleitiv] *a.* 命名的,名称的,术语的.

no·men·cla·tor [ˈnəumənkleitə] *n.* ①(科学术语等的)命名者. ②〔古罗马〕通报来客姓名的侍从. ③宴会中安顿座位的招待员. ④专业词汇集[手册].

no·men·cla·ture [nəuˈmenklətʃə] *n.* ①(科学、文艺等的)(系统)命名法,记名法; 命名原则; 专门用语; 名称,术语(集、表). ②【军】编类名称,型别名称;〔罕〕名称; 目录. *the ~ of music* 音乐术语.

no·mic [ˈnəumik] *a.* 惯用的,普通的. *~ spelling* 普通拚法.

nomin. = nominative.

nom·i·nal [ˈnɔminl] *a.* ①名字的,列名的. ②名义上的,空有其名的; 有名无实的. ③微不足道的,轻微的. ④名称上的; 票面上的. ⑤【语法】名词性的. ⑥按计划进行的; 令人满意的. *~ capital* 名义资本. *a ~ par* 票面价格. *a ~ price* 虚价. *a ~ partner* 名义合伙人. *~ quotation*【商】牌价. *~ wages* 名义工资. *~ horse-power*【物】标称马力. *~ value* 票面价值. *a ~ list of officers* 职员名册. *a ~ register* 名册. — *n.* 名词性的词. **-ism** *n.*【哲】唯名论 (*opp.* realism). **-ist** *n.*【哲】唯名论者. **-lis·tic** *a.*【哲】唯名论的.

nom·i·nal·ly [ˈnɔminəli] *ad.* 名义上,有名无实,空有其名 (*opp.* really). *He was, ~, the leader, but others actually wielded the power.* 名义上他是领导者,但实际上是别人掌握实权.

nom·i·nate [ˈnɔmineit] *vt.* ①任命,指定; 提名,推荐 *(for)*. ②命名. ③【赛马】登记(马名)参加比赛. *He was ~d for President.* 他被提名为总统候选人.

nom·i·na·tion [ˌnɔmiˈneiʃən] *n.* ①任命(权),指定(权); 提名(权),推荐(权). ②【赛马】出场马名登记. *I have a ~ at your service.* 我可以推荐你. *the ~ day* 候选人提名日.

nom·i·na·ti·val [ˌnɔminəˈtaivəl] *a.* 主格的.

nom·i·na·tive [ˈnɔminətiv] *a.* ①【语法】主格的. ②[-neitiv] 被提名[指定]的. — *n.*【语法】主格; 主格语. *Is it ~ or elective?* 提名呢还是选举? *the ~ absolute*【语法】(分词的)独立主格〔如 *This being so, I did nothing.* (情况既然如此,我什么也没做)中的 this〕.

nom·i·na·tor [ˈnɔmineitə] *n.* 提名[指定、任命、推荐]者.

nom·i·nee [nɔmiˈniː] *n.* 被提名[指定、任命、推荐]者.

no·mo·graph [ˈnɔməgrɑːf], **no·mo·gram** [ˈnɔməgræm] *n.* 列线图(解),(计)标图(表),诺谟图.

no·mog·ra·phy [nəuˈmɔgrəfi] *n.* ①法律编撰术,法律编撰论. ② 图解构成术. ③ 列线图解法; 图算学. **-graph·ic** *a.* **-graph·i·cal·ly** *ad.*

no·mol·o·gy [nəuˈmɔlədʒi] *n.* ①法理学. ②(各种科学的)理论部分,法则论. **-log·i·cal** *a.*

nom·o·thet·ic, nom·o·thet·i·cal [ˈnɔməˈθetik, -əl] *a.* ①制定法律的. ② 以法律为根据的. ③ 研究普遍性规律的科学的.

-nomy *suf.* 表示"法","学": econ*omy*, astro*nomy*.

non [nɔn] *ad.*〔L.〕非,不是 (= not). ~ ***assumpsit*** [əˈsʌmpsit]【法】被告否认契约的答辩. ~ ***compos mentis*** [ˈkɔmpɔs ˈmentis]【法】精神错乱的,发狂的. ~ ***esse*** [ˈesi(ː)] = nonexistence. ~ ***est (inventus)*** [ˈest (inˈventəs)] 住址不明 (*He is ~ est.* 他地址不明). ~***-licet*** [ˈlaiset] *a.*〔L.〕不法的. ~ ***liquet*** [ˈlaikwet]【法】(诉讼有疑问时陪审员所作的) 延期审判的评决. ~ ***nobis*** [ˈnəubis] (荣耀)不要归与我们. ~ ***obstante*** [ɔbsˈtæntiː] 违背法律的规定. ~ ***placet*** [ˈpleiset] 不赞成; 投反对票〔教会或大学集会中的〕. ~ ***plus ultra*** [plʌsˈʌltrə] 不可越境; 极点,绝顶,极致 *(=ne plus ultra)*. ~ ***possumus*** [ˈpɔsjuməs] 声明不可能,拒绝行动 (= we cannot). ~ ***prosequitur*** [prəuˈsekwitə]【法】使未按时出席的原告败诉的缺席判决. ~ ***sequitur*** [ˈsekwitə] 不合理的推论,不根据前提而下的论断.

non- [ˈnɔn-] *pref.* 无,非,不〔non- 多表示简单"否定",而 in- [im-, il-, ir-], un- 等则带有积极"反对"之意: *non*human, *in*human; *non*logical, *il*logical; *non*moral, *im*moral; *non*religious, *ir*religious〕.

Nona [ˈnəunə] *n.* 诺娜〔女子名〕.

nona [ˈnəunə] *n.*【医】昏睡病.

non·a·bil·i·ty [ˈnɔnəˈbiliti] *n.* 无能,没本事.

non·ab·stain·er [ˈnɔnəbˈsteinə] *n.* 不戒酒的人; 不节制的人.

non·ac·cept·ance [ˈnɔnəkˈseptəns] *n.* 不答应;【商】不(接受)承兑.

non·ac·cess [ˈnɔnəkˈses] *n.*【法】(夫妇的)不能发生性行为.

non·ac·quaint·ance [ˈnɔnəˈkweintəns] *n.* 不相识.

non·ad·mis·sion [ˈnɔnədˈmiʃən] *n.* 拒绝入场[会,党].

non·age [ˈnɔnidʒ, ˈnəunidʒ] *n.* ①青年时期; 未成熟; 早期. ②【法】未成熟.

no·na·ge·na·r·i·an [ˌnəunədʒiˈnɛəriən] *a., n.* 九十或九十多岁的(人).

non·ag·gres·sion [ˈnɔnəˈgreʃən] *n.* 不侵略,不侵犯.

a ~ *pact* 互不侵犯条约.
non·a·gon [ˈnɔnəgən] *n.* 【几】九边形.
no·na·ry [ˈnəunəri] *a.* 【数】九进的. — *n.* 九个一组的东西.
non·a·ligned [ˈnɔnəˈlaind] *a.* 不结盟的. ~ *nations* 不结盟国家.
non·a·lign·ment [ˈnɔnəˈlainmənt] *n.* 不结盟. *the* ~ *policy* 不结盟政策.
non·an·tag·o·nis·tic [ˈnɔnænˌtægəˈnistik] *a.* 非对抗性的.
non·ap·pear·ance [ˈnɔnəˈpiərəns] *n.* (当事人或证人)不到法庭.
non·a·que·ous [ˈnɔnˈeikwiəs] *a.* 【化】非水的.
non·at·tend·ance [ˈnɔnəˈtendəns] *n.* 不出席,不到.
non·be·ing [ˈnɔnˈbiːiŋ] *n.* 不存在, 不存在的东西 (=nonexistence).
non·bel·lig·er·en·cy [ˈnɔnbiˈlidʒərənsi] *n.* 非交战状态,非交战立场.
non·bel·lig·er·ent [ˈnɔnbiˈlidʒərənt] *a.* 非交战的. *the* ~ *countries* 非交战国. — *n.* 非交战国.
non-book [ˈnɔnˈbuk] *n.* 内容无价值的书,为满足市场需要而滥竽充数的书.
non·can·di·date [ˈnɔnˈkændideit] *n.* 沉默候选人〔尚未宣布或不愿宣布其候选人资格的人〕.
nonce [nɔns] *n.* 现时,目前〔本词只用于下列短语〕: ***for the*** ~ 目前,暂且. — *a.* 临时的,只以当时为限的. *a* ~ *word [noun, verb etc.]* (为某一场合或特殊需要)临时造的词[名词,动词].
non·cha·lance [ˈnɔnʃələns] *n.* 不关心;冷淡,不激动. *with* ~ 冷淡地,漫不经心地,无动于衷地.
non·cha·lant [ˈnɔnʃələnt] *a.* 不关心的,漫不经心的;若无其事的;不激动的,冷淡的. *assume a* ~ *air* 装作不关心的样子. **-ly** *ad.*
non·claim [ˈnɔnˈkleim, ˈnɔnkleim] *n.* 【法】(在规定期间内)不提出要求.
Non·Coll., non·coll [ˈnɔnkəl] *a.,n.* 〔口〕=noncollegiate.
non·col·le·gi·ate [ˈnɔnkəˈliːdʒiit] *a.* 不属于学院的,(大学中)不属于任何学院的; (大学)不设学院的. — *n.* 不属于任何学院的大学生.
non·com [ˈnɔnkəm] *n.* 〔口〕军士 〔noncommissioned officer 的缩略〕.
non·com·ba·tant [ˈnɔnˈkɔmbətənt] *n.,a.* 非战斗人员〔军医、随军牧师等〕(的);(战时)一般市民(的).
non·com·bus·ti·ble [ˈnɔnkəmˈbʌstəbl] *a.* 不燃的. — *n.* 不燃物.
non·com·mis·sioned [ˈnɔnˈkɔmiʃənd] *a.* 无委任状的,未受任命的,无军官衔的. ~ *officer* 军士.
non·com·mit·tal [ˈnɔnˈkɔmitəl] *a.* (态度、观点等)不明朗的,不表明意见的;不承担义务的. *a* ~ *answer* 不明确的回答. *nod a vague and* ~ *assent* 模棱两可含糊其词地点头同意.
non·com·mu·ni·cant [ˈnɔnkəˈmjuːnikənt] *a., n.* 不受圣餐的(人);不做礼拜的(人).
non·com·mu·nist [ˈnɔnˈkɔmjunist] *a.* ①非共产主义的;非共产党员的. ②声明不是共产党员的.
non·com·pli·ance [ˈnɔnkəmˈplaiəns] *n.* 不顺从,不同意;固执.
non·com·pli·ant [ˈnɔnkəmˈplaiənt] *n.* 不顺从的人,固执的人.
non compos mentis [nɔnˈkɔmpəsˈmentis] 〔L.〕【法】精神失常的;精神上不适宜于处理事务的.
non·con·dens·ing [ˈnɔnkənˈdensiŋ] *a.* 不凝的,不能冷凝的. *a* ~ *engine* 排汽蒸汽机.
non·con·duc·ting [ˈnɔnkənˈdʌktiŋ] *a.* 【物】不传导的;绝缘的. ~ *material* 绝缘材料.
non·con·duc·tive [ˈnɔnkənˈdʌktive] *a.* 不传导的;绝缘的.
non·con·duc·tor [ˈnɔnkənˈdʌktə] *n.* 【物】非导体;绝缘体.
non·con·fi·dence [ˈnɔnˈkɔnfidəns] *n.* 不信任. *a vote of* ~ 不信任投票.
non·con·form·ance [ˈnɔnkənˈfɔːməns] *n.* 不服从. ~ *to the tradition of conformity* 【英史】不服从遵奉国教的传统.
non·con·forming [ˈnɔnkənˈfɔːmiŋ] *a.* 不服从国教的;非国教教徒的,新教徒的.
non·con·form·ism [ˈnɔnkənˈfɔːmizəm] *n.* 不遵从传统成规的作风;〔英〕不信奉国教.
non·con·form·ist [ˈnɔnkənˈfɔːmist] *n.* ①〔常 N-〕〔英〕非国教徒, 不信奉国教的人. ②不符合传统规范的人. — *a.* 不信奉国教的;不墨守成规的.
non·con·form·i·ty [ˈnɔnkənˈfɔːmity] *n.* ①不墨守成规. ②不一致,不符合. ③【地】非整合. ④〔常 N-〕不信奉国教;〔集合词〕新教教徒;新教教义.
non·con·tent [ˈnɔnkənˈtent] *n.* (英国上议院中)投反对票的活动;投反对票的议员.
non·con·ten·tious [ˈnɔnkənˈtenʃəs] *a.* 非争论性的,不大会引起争论的.
non·con·tin·u·ous [ˈnɔnkənˈtinjuəs] *a.* 不继续的;间断的.
non·co·op·er·a·tion [ˈnɔnkəuˌɔpəˈreiʃən] *n.* 不合作;(印度甘地的)不合作主义. **-ist** *n.* 采取不合作态度者,不合作主义者.
non·coun·try [ˈnɔnˈkʌntri] *n.* 不存在的国家〔不被承认是国家的地理区域〕.
non·de·liv·er·y [ˈnɔndiˈlivəri] *n.* *(pl. -er·ies)* 无法投递;无法投递的邮件[货物];不能送达.
non·des·cript [ˈnɔnˈdiskript] *a.* 形容不出的; 难区别的,难以归类的;不三不四的,莫明其妙的. — *n.* 不三不四的,莫名其妙的人[东西].
non·dis·junc·tion [ˈnɔndisˈdʒʌŋkʃən] *n.* 【生】不分离,不分裂.
non·du·ra·ble [ˈnɔnˈdjuərəbl] *a.* 不耐用的,不耐久的. — *n.* 〔*pl.*〕不耐用物品,不耐久物品. **-a·bil·i·ty** [nɔnˌdjuərəˈbiliti] *n.*
none[1] [nʌn] *pro.* ①〔指代人、事物或东西的一部分;可以独立使用,也可以同 of 结合;有无前行词均可,动词使用单复数形式均可〕没谁,没人;没有任何事物;没有任何一点. *There were* ~ *present.* 当时没人在场. *N- knows the weight of another's burden.* 彼此谁也不知道对方的难处. *There are faults from which* ~ *of us is (are) free.* 有些错误我们任何人都不能避免. *We should not call one a hero that is* ~. 本来不是英雄的,就不应当说成是英雄. *The children were playing, and she took care that* ~ *were hurt.* 孩子们正在游戏,她小心翼翼,哪一个都不叫他们受伤. *N- were left when I came.* 我来时谁都不在. *They choose* ~ *but the best.* 他们只选最好的. ②〔同 of 结合时带有较强烈的否定意味〕…当中无论哪个都〔谁都,什么都,一点也〕不[没有]. *N- of us are infallible.* 我们当中无论谁都会犯错误的. *N- of them came.* 他们当中谁都没来. *N- of this money is mine.* 这笔钱没有一点是我的. *It is* ~ *of your business.* 这(毫)不干你的事. *N- of your impudence [cheeks]!* 不要无礼! 别厚颜无耻! *N- of this concerns me.* 这事跟我一点也没关系. *We've heard* ~ *of him since.* 从此以后他杳无音信. *N- of his work has been done.* 他的活儿一点也没干. *She tried on five hats, but* ~ *of them were attractive.* 他试戴了五顶帽子,一顶也不合适. ~ ***but*** 只有;除…以外谁都不 *(N- but fools have believed.* 除傻瓜外从来没人相信). ~ ***other than*** 不是别的,而是;恰恰是. — *a.* 〔古〕没有. 〔=no, not any; 通常用在以元音或 h 开头的单词前〕没有. *There is* ~ *available.* 再无别的可弄到的东西了. *They gave me* ~ *other answer.* 他们对我无别的事可以奉告. *make of* ~ *effect* 〔古〕使无效. — *ad.* 〔用于 'the+比较

级'或 too, so 之前〕一点也不…，决没有. *I am ~ the better for it.* 我决未因此而好一点. *He is ~ so wise.* 他不怎样聪明. *You got home ~ too soon.* 你回来得很不早了. **~ the less** 虽然那样还是,仍然.

none² [nəun] *n.* nones ②的单数.

non·ef·fec·tive [ˌnɔniˈfektiv] *a.* ①没效力的; 不起作用的. ②【军】无战斗力的. — *n.*【军】无战斗力的兵员.

non·e·go [ˈnɔnˈegəu, nɔnˈiːgəu] *n.*【哲】非我; 客观, 外界.

non·e·las·tic [ˈnɔniˈlæstik] *a.* 无弹性的,无伸缩性的. **-ity** [ˌnɔnilæˈtisiti] *n.*

non·e·lec·tive [ˈnɔniˈlektiv] *a.* 不依选举(产生)的.

non·e·lec·tro·lyte [ˈnɔniˈlektrəulait] *n.*【化】非电解质; 不电离质.

non·e·lim·i·na·tion [ˈnɔniˌlimiˈneiʃən] *n.* 不排除,不消灭,不消除. *mutual* ~ 互不并吞.

non·en·ti·ty [nɔˈnentiti] *n.* ①不存在,非实在. ②不存在的东西,非实在物,虚构;【哲】不存在的实质. ③[nəˈn-] 不足取[无足轻重]的人[东西].

nones [nəunz] *n.* 〔*pl.*〕①(古罗马历) 3、5、7、10 月的第 7 日,其他各月的第 5 日. ②【宗】9 时课[日出后第 9 时的祈祷]; (一日 7 次的)第 5 次(祈祷).

non·es·sen·tial [ˈnɔniˈsenʃəl] *a.,n.* 非本质的 (东西), 不重要的(人).

none·such, nonsuch [ˈnʌnsʌtʃ] *n.* ①无比的事物, 无以匹敌的人[东西],无双的人,典型. ②〔俚〕狂妄自大的人. ③【植】红色剪秋罗. — *a.* 〔古〕无双的,无比的.

no·net [nəuˈnet] *n.* ①【乐】九重奏[唱](乐曲). ②【物】九重线.

none·the·less [ˌnʌnðəˈles] *ad.* = nevertheless.

non·Eu·clid·e·an [ˈnɔnjuːkˈlidiən] *a.*【数】非欧几里得的. ~ *geometry* 非欧几里得几何(学).

non·e·vent [ˈnɔniˈvent] *n.* 大肆宣扬即将来临而并未发生的事.

non·ex·ist·ence [ˈnɔnigˈzistəns] *n.* 不存在(物); 非实在(物).

non·fea·sance [ˈnɔnˈfizəns] *n.*【法】不履行义务; 懈怠.

non·fer·rous [ˈnɔnˈferəs] *a.* 非铁的. ~ *metals* 有色金属.

non·fic·tion [ˈnɔnˈfikʃən] *n.* 非小说类文学作品〔如随笔,传记等〕.

non·fi·nite [ˈnɔnˈfainait] *a.*【语法】非谓语形式的,非限定的. *the ~ forms of the verb* 动词的非谓语[非限定]形式〔不定式、分词和动名词〕.

non·flam·ma·ble [ˈnɔnˈflæməbl] *a.* 不易燃的.

non·ful·fil(l)ment [ˈnɔnfulˈfilmənt] *n.* 不履行,不完成.

non·grad·ed [ˈnɔnˈgreidid] *a.* ①无(熟练程度)等级的. ②〔美〕(教育)不分班级的.

non·he·ro [ˈnɔnhiərəu, nɔnˈhiərəu] *n.* = anti-hero.

non-ho·ming [ˈnɔnˈhəumiŋ]【无】不归位的.

non·hu·man [ˈnɔnˈhjumən] *a.* 非人类的; 不属于人类的.

non·hy·gro·scop·ic [ˈnɔnˌhaigrəˈskɔpik] *a.* 不收湿的.

non·i·de·al [ˈnɔnaidiəl] *a.*【物】非理想的.

non·i·den·ti·ty [ˈnɔnaiˈdentiti] *n.*【哲】不同一性.

no·nil·lion [nəuˈniljən] *n.* 〔英〕100 万的九次幂[乘方]〔1 后加五十四个 0 之数〕; 〔美, F.〕1,000 的 10 次幂[乘方]〔1 后加三十个 0 之数〕.

non·in·duc·tive [ˈnɔninˈdʌktiv] *a.*【电】无感的. *a ~ resistance* 一个无感电阻.

non·in·ter·fer·ence [ˈnɔnintəˈfiərəns] *n.* 不干涉;【电】不相互干扰. ~ *in each other's internal affairs* 互不干涉内政.

non·in·ter·ven·tion [ˈnɔnintəˈvenʃən] *n.* 不干涉(内政等); 不干涉主义. **-ist** *n.*

non·i·us [ˈnɔnjəs] *n.*【机】游标,游尺.

non·join·der [ˈnɔnˈdʒɔində] *n.*【法】(当事人的)不参预诉讼.

non·ju·ror [ˈnɔnˈdʒuə] *n.*【英史】拒绝立誓臣从者.

non·le·gal [ˈnɔnˈliːgəl] *a.* 非法律的,与法律无关的.

non·le·thal [ˈnɔnˈliːθəl] *a.* 不致命的,非杀伤性的. *a ~ agent* 非杀伤性化学成剂.

non·log·i·cal [ˈnɔnˈlɔdʒikəl] *a.* 不从逻辑得出的,不根据逻辑的.

non·lu·mi·nous [ˈnɔnˈluːminəs] *a.* 无光的,不发光的.

non·mem·ber [ˈnɔnˈmembə] *n.* 非会员,非党人士. **-ship** *n.* 非会员的地位[身分].

non·met·al [ˈnɔnˈmetl] *n.* 非金属. **-tal·lic** [ˈnɔnmiˈtælik] *a.*

non·mor·al [ˈnɔnˈmɔrəl] *n.* 与道德无关的.

non·ne·go·ti·a·ble [ˈnɔnniˈgəuʃjəbl] *a.* 不可谈判的,无商议余地的; 禁止转让的.

non·ni·trog·e·nous [ˈnɔnnaiˈtrɔdʒənəs] *a.* 不含氮的.

non·nu·cle·ar [ˈnɔnnuːkliə, nɔnˈnjuːkljə] *a.* 非核的. — *n.* 非核国家,只拥有常规武器的国家. ~ *warfare* 常规战争.

no-no [ˈnəuˌnəu] *n.* 〔美口〕禁忌,禁例.

non·ob·jec·tive [ˈnɔnəbˈdʒektiv] *a.* 〔美〕非写实派的; 不模仿自然事物的,抽象的.

non·ob·serv·ance [ˈnɔnəbˈzəːvəns] *n.* 不遵从,违反.

non obs., non obst. = *non obstante.*

non·of·fice·hold·ing [ˈnɔnˈɔfishəuldiŋ] *a.* 没有官职的; 下台的,在野的.

non·par·tic·i·pat·ing [ˈnɔnpɑːˈtisipeitiŋ] *a.* 不参加的; 无分红权的.

non·pa·reil [ˈnɔnpərəl] *a.* 无比的,无双的,无上的. — *n.* ①无比的人〔东西〕. ②【印】六点 *(point)* 活字. ③粘有小白糖珠的巧克力糖; (装饰糖果、糕点等的)各色小糖珠. ④(用 nonpareil 命名的) 一种苹果〔鸟、小麦(等)〕.

non·par·ti·san, non·par·ti·zan [ˈnɔnˈpɑːtizən, -zæn] *a.* 超党派的,不受任何党派控制的,非党人的.

non·par·ty [ˈnɔnˈpɑːti] *a.* 无党派的; 非党的; 党外的.

non·pay·ment [ˈnɔnˈpeimənt] *n.* 不支付,无支付能力. *His property was confiscated for ~ of taxes.* 他的财产因不支付税款而被没收了.

non·per·form·ance [ˌnɔnpəːˈfɔːməns] *n.* 不履行, 不实行,不完成.

non·pe·ri·od·ic [ˈnɔnˌpiəriˈɔdik] *a.* 非周期性的.

non·plus [ˈnɔnˈplʌs] *vt.* (〔Eng.〕*-ss-*) 使为难,使狼狈; 使迷惑. — *n.* 狼狈,为难; 迷惑; 难关,窘境. ***at a ~*** 进退两难,左右为难. ***put [reduce] sb. to a ~*** 使某人为难,使窘困.

non·prin·ci·pled [ˈnɔnˈprinsəpld] *a.* 与原则无关的,非原则的.

non·pro·duc·tive [ˈnɔnprəˈdʌktiv] *a.* 不能生产的, 无生产力的; 非生产性的.

non·pro·fes·sion·al [ˈnɔnprəˈfeʃənl] *a.* ①无职业的; 无专行的. ②非科班出身的; 和专门工作无关系的. ③离开了职业的. *The doctor paid me a ~ visit.* 医生以普通朋友的关系来看了我.

non·pro·fit [ˈnɔnˈprɔfit] *a.* 非营利的. *a ~ association* 非营利团体.

non·pro·lif·er·a·tion [ˈnɔnprɔˌlifəˈreiʃən] *n.* 不增生, 不增殖; 不扩散,防扩散(特指防核扩散). ~ **treaty** 防止核扩散条约〔略作 NPT〕.

non pros. = *non prosequitur.*

non-pros [ˌnɔnˈprɔs] *vt.* ***(-pros·sed; -pros·sing)***【法】对(原告)作缺席判决.

non-pro·vid·ed [ˈnɔnprəˈvaidid] *a.* (英国小学)不靠地方当局供给经费的.

non·rat·ed [ˈnɔnˈreitid] *a.* 没有等级的,没有军衔的〔尤指(美国海军)征募来的水兵〕.

non·read·er [ˈnɔnˈriːdə] *n.* 不能阅读的人；阅读能力很差的孩子.

non·rep·re·sen·ta·tion·al [ˈnɔnreprizenˈteiʃənəl] *a.* (艺术)非写实的，抽象的. **-ism** *n.* 非写实主义.

non·res·i·dent [ˈnɔnˈrezidənt] *a.* 不住在工作地点的；通勤的；不寄宿的. *a ~ student* 走读生. — *n.* (不住在工作地点的)通勤员工；暂居的人；走读生. **-tial** [-ʃəl] *a.*

non·re·sis·tance [ˈnɔnriˈzistəns] *n.* 不抵抗(主义)；(对权力、法律等的)屈服；【电】无耗阻.

non·re·sis·tant [ˈnɔnriˈzistənt] *a.* 不抵抗(主义)的. — *n.* 不抵抗主义者；不主张武力抗暴者.

non·re·straint [ˈnɔnriˈstreint] *n.* 无约束，无制止，无禁止〔尤指精神病学方面不用约束衣或其他监禁办法的治疗法〕.

non·re·stric·tive [ˈnɔnrisˈtriktiv, ˈnɔnrisˈtriktiv] *a.* 【语法】非限制性的.

non·rig·id [ˈnɔnˈridʒid] *a.* 【空】软式的；【物】非刚性的. *~ sheeting* 软质片材. *~ plastics* 非刚性塑料.

non·sched·uled [ˈnɔnˈʃedʒuːld, nɔnˈskedʒuːld] *a.* 未作安排的，未排定的；(客机)不定期的. *a ~ airline* 不定期航空公司.

non·sec·tar·i·an [ˈnɔnsekˈtɛəriən] *a.* 非宗派的；不属于任何宗教派别的.

non·sense [ˈnɔnsəns] *n.* ①无意义的话，荒谬[荒唐]话，胡说；废话. ②荒谬[荒唐]的念头[事情]. ③胡闹. — *int.* 荒唐! 无聊! 胡扯! *None of your ~!* 别胡闹! *N-!* = *Stuff and ~!* 胡说八道! ~ **book** 荒谬的书. ~ **verses [rhymes]** 打油诗.

non·sen·si·cal [nɔnˈsensikəl] *a.* 没有意义[条理的].

non se·qui·tur [nɔnˈsekwitə] 〔L.〕【逻】不根据前提的推理 (= it does not follow).

non·sex·ual [ˈnɔnˈseksjuəl] *a.* 无性的，不论性别的.

non-sked [ˌnɔnˈsked] *a.* 〔美口〕(客机)不定期的. — *n.* 〔口〕不定期客机；不定期运输机；不定期航空运输公司. *He got his training with the ~s.* 他在不定期航空公司那里受过训练.

non·skid [ˈnɔnskid] *a.* 防滑的，不滑的. *a ~ tread* (轮胎的)防滑轮距.

non·smok·er [ˈnɔnˈsməukə] *n.* 不抽烟的人.

non·so·cial [ˈnɔnˈsəuʃəl] *a.* 非社交的，不爱交际的.

non·so·ci·e·ty [ˈnɔnsəuˈsaiəti] *a.,n.* 无工会等组织关系的(人、团体).

non·stand·ard [ˈnɔnˈstændəd] *a.* 不标准的，不规范的.

non·sta·ple [ˈnɔnˈsteipl] *n.* 副产品. — *a.* 非主要的，副的. *~ food [foodstuff]* 副食品.

non·stat·ic [ˈnɔnˈstætik] *a.* ①非静止的. ②【电】无静电荷的，静电荷不积聚的. ③【无】不产生无线电干扰的.

non·stop [ˈnɔnˈstɔp] *a.* 不停的，不断的；(列车、飞机等)直达的. *a ~ flight* 直达飞行. — *n.* 直达列车[公共汽车]. — *ad.* 不停地，直达地. *fly ~ from Beijing to Paris* 由北京起飞直达巴黎.

non·stri·at·ed [ˈnɔnstraiˈeitid, nɔnˈstraieitid] *a.* 【解】(肌肉)无横纹的. ~ **muscle** (=smooth muscle) 平滑肌.

non·strik·er [ˈnɔnˈstraikə] *n.* ①不参加罢工的人. ②【板球】没有接着对方来球的击球员.

non·such [ˈnɔnsʌtʃ, ˈnʌnsʌtʃ] *n.* (= nonesuch).

non·suit [ˈnɔnˈsjuːt, -ˈsuːt] *n.* 【法】(因原告证据不足)诉讼驳回. — *vt.* 驳回(原告或诉案).

non·sup·port [ˈnɔnsəˈpɔːt] *n.* 【法】不履行抚养，不负担抚养费.

non·tox·ic [ˈnɔnˈtɔksik] *a.* 无毒的. *~ plasticizer* 无毒增塑剂.

non trop·po [ˈnɔn ˈtrɔpəu] 〔It.〕【音】不太过，适度.

non-U [ˈnɔnjuː] *a.* 与上层阶级[上流社会]不相称[适应]的；(举止、谈吐、趣味等)非富有阶级的.

non·u·ni·form [ˈnɔnˈjuːnifɔːm] *a.* 不一致的，不统一的；不均匀的. **-i·ty** [ˈnɔnˌjuːniˈfɔːmiti] *n.*

non·un·ion [ˈnɔnˈjuːnjən] *a.* 不属于[不加入]工会的；不承认工会的；不遵守工会规章的. — *n.*【医】(骨折等)不愈合. **-ist** *n.* 非工会会员；非工会主义者.

non·u·ple [ˈnɔnjupl] *a.* 九倍的，九重的；九个一组[一套]的.

non·u·plet [ˈnɔnjuplit] *n.* 一胎九婴.

non·use [ˈnɔnˈjuːs] *n.* 不使用，放弃；不形成习惯.

non·us·er [nɔnˈjuːzə] *n.* ①不使用. ②【法】弃权. ③不使用者；无毒瘾者.

non·vi·a·ble [ˈnɔnˈvaiəbl] *a.* 不能生存和成长的；不能发展和活动的.

non·vi·o·lence [ˈnɔnˈvaiələns] *n.* 非暴力主义. *He is too well aware of the doubts about the efficacy of ~.* 对非暴力主义的实效的怀疑，他是深有体会和感触的.

non·vot·er [ˈnɔnˈvəutə] *n.* ①不投票者. ②无表决权的人；无投票权的人.

non·vot·ing [ˈnɔnˈvəutiŋ] *a.* ①不投票的，弃权的. ②无投票权的，无表决权的.

non-white [ˈnɔnˈhwait] *n.,a.* 非白种人(的). *the growth of ~ communities.* 非白种人居民的增长.

non·wo·ven [ˈnɔnˈwəuvən] *a.* 非纺织的. *~ fabric* 非纺织布.

non·yl [ˈnɔnil, ˈnəu-] *n.* 【化】壬(烷)基.

non·ze·ro [ˈnɔnziərəu] *a.* 非零的，非零形态的.

noo·dle[1] [ˈnuːdl] *n.* 笨人，傻子；〔俚〕脑袋瓜，头. — *vt.* 愚弄. **-ness** *n.*

noo·dle[2] [ˈnuːdl] *n.* 面条，鸡蛋面；粉条.

noo·dle[3] [ˈnuːdl] *vi.* 〔口〕①随随便便即兴演奏乐器. ②探索[钻研]某一主意；想出一个主意；思考出一个结论.

noo·dle·head [ˈnuːdlˌhed] *n.* 笨蛋，傻瓜 (= fool, simpleton, blockhead).

nook [nuk] *n.* 凹角；角落；隐匿处，避难处；偏避地方. *look in every ~ and corner* 到处找；查看每一个角落. — *vt.* 把…藏[放]在角落里.

noon [nuːn] *n.* ①正午，中午〔此义一般不加定冠词. 如：at (high) ~ 在中午〕. ②〔诗〕夜半，午夜. ③全盛期，顶点. *a ~ basket* 〔美〕饭篮子 (= lunch-basket). *the ~ of night* 〔诗〕午夜. *the ~ of life* 壮年期. ***as clear as ~*** 明明白白，一清二楚. —*vi.* 〔美〕午时休息，吃午饭. **~-mark** *n.* 【天】(正)午标，(正)午线.

noon·day [ˈnuːndei] *n.* 正午，中午；全盛. — *a.* 中午的. *the ~ meal* 午餐. ***as clear [plain] as ~ [the sun of ~]*** 极明白；一清二楚.

noon·flow·er [ˈnuːnflauə] *n.* 【植】松叶菊.

noon·ing [ˈnuːniŋ] *n.* 〔美〕中午，正午；午餐；午休(时间). *take one's ~* 午休，吃午餐.

noon·tide [ˈnuːntaid] *n.* ①中午 (= noon, noonday). ②〔the ~〕最高点，全盛期. ③〔主诗〕午夜 (= midnight).

noon·time [ˈnuːntaim] *n.* ①中午 (= noon, noonday, noontide). *Will he be home at ~?* 他中午在家里吗?

noose [nuːs, nuːz] *n.* 套索；绞索；〔the〕绞刑；〔喻〕(夫妻等的)羁绊，束缚；圈套. *put one's neck into the ~* 自投罗网. *~s tied round the necks of* 套在…脖子上的绞索. ***The ~ is hanging*** 〔美俚〕万事俱备. — *vt.* 用套索捕捉；处绞刑，绞死；安圈套，诱入圈套.

N.O.P., n.o.p. = not otherwise provided (for) 非供它用.

NOP, N.O.P. = not our publication 非我社出版物.

no·pal [ˈnəupəl, ˌnəuˈpɔl] *n.* 胭脂仙人掌属植物(尤指胭脂仙人掌).

no-par [ˈnəuˈpɑː] *a.* 无票面价值的. *a ~ certificate of stock* 无票面价值的公债券.

nope [nəup] *ad.* 〔美俚〕不[否定的答复] (=no[2]).

no-peck [ˈnəupek] *a.* 〔美俚〕防窥视的.

nor [nɔː; 弱no] *conj.* (既不)…也不，(…没有)…也没有. ①〔和 neither 或 not 连用〕*He can neither read ~ write.*

他不会读也不会写. *Not a man, ~ a child, is to be seen* 大人小孩都不见[没有]. *He can't do it, ~ can I, ~ can anybody.* 他做不来,我也做不来,任何人也做不来. ②〔古、诗〕〔省去 neither〕 *Thou ~ I have made the world.* 创造这个世界的既不是你也不是我. *I cannot go, ~ do I want.* 我不能去,也不想去. *I have never seen her, ~ even heard of her.* 我从来没有看到她,也没有听说过. *He borrows not, ~ lends.* 他不向人借钱,也不借钱给人. *He has no mother ~ father.* 他没有母亲也没有父亲. ③〔诗〕〔nor ... nor = neither ... nor〕 *N- silver ~ gold can buy it.* 黄金白银都买不到它. ④〔同主句中的否定词 not, no, never 配合,表示否定的继续,助动词与主语的排列采用倒装语序〕(不…)也不. *I said I had not seen it, ~ had I.* 我说我没看见那个东西,实际上我也没有看见. ⑤〔在肯定句之后,意义内容与主句一致并有所加强,也用倒装语序〕(=and ... not) 但未,但不. *The tale is long, ~ have I heard it out.* 故事冗长,但我也没有听到底. *I am going, ~ can anybody prevent it.* 我是要去的,这是任何人也阻止不了的. *They are happy, ~ need we worry.* 他们很幸福,我们实际上也不必耽心. ⑥〔用在独立句子的句首,但与上文有衔接关系〕(因此)也不. *N- am I ashamed to confess my ignorance of what I do not know.* (因此)我是不知道的事就承认说不知道,并不害羞. ⑦〔方〕比 (= than.) *Have you ever seen a nicer place ~ this place?* 您曾看见过比这个地方还要美好的地方吗? *I know better ~ you.* 我比你知道得多.

nor' [nɔː] *a.* 【海】= north: *~east, ~west.*

NOR [nɔː] *n.* 【自】"或非"〔一种电子计算机逻辑电路〕.

Nor. = ①North. ②Norway; Norwegian. ③Norman.

No·ra(h) [ˈnɔːrə] *n.* 诺拉〔女子名〕.

NORAD = North American Air Defense 北美空防联合司令部.

Nor·bert [ˈnɔːbət] *n.* 诺伯特〔男子名〕.

Nor·dic [ˈnɔːdik] *a.* 北欧人的; 北欧滑雪赛的. — *n.* ①北欧人. ②〔俚〕亚利安人 (Aryan).

nor·ep·i·neph·rine [ˈnɔˌrepiˈnefrin, -riːn] *n.* 新肾上腺素,去甲肾上腺(激)素.

Nor·folk [ˈnɔːfək] *n.* ①诺福克〔英国东岸一郡名〕. ②美国东岸弗吉尼亚州一港市. ~ **capon** 赤鲱. ~ **dumpling [turkey]** 〔蔑〕英国诺福克人的诨名. ~ **Howard** 〔英俚〕臭虫,床虱. **N- Island pine**【植】南美杉 (Araucaria excelsa). ~ **jacket** 腰部有带的男用宽上衣.

no·ri·a [ˈnɔːriə] *n.* 戽水车.

nor·land [ˈnɔːlənd] *n.* 〔英、诗〕北国, 北部地方. **-er** *n.* 北方人.

norm [nɔːm] *n.* ①规范,模范; 准则; (教育)标准. ②(劳动)定额;【数】模方; 范数. ***above-~*** 定额以上的. ***below-~*** 定额以下的.

Nor·ma [ˈnɔːmə] *n.* 诺玛〔女子名〕.

nor·mal [ˈnɔːməl] *a.* ①正常的,平常的,普通的; 平均的. ②正规的,标准的,额定的,规定的. ③智力正常的; 精神健全的. ④【化】正(链)的; 中性的; 规度的; 当量的;【物】简正的;【几】垂直的; 正交的; 法线的; 中性的. ⑤【生】不受感染的. ⑥【经】按成品最高成本定价的. — *n.* ①常态,正常; (人体的)正常温度; 平温; 平均; 标准. ②【几】法线,垂直(线). ③【物】平均量;【化】当量. ***off*** ~ 离位,不正常. ~ **acceleration** 法向[正交]加速度. ~ **axis** 法线轴,垂直轴. ~ **bud** 定芽. ~ **content [solution]**【化】当量含量[溶液]. ~ **deviate** 正态偏差. ~ **distribution**【统】正态分布. ~ **force** 法向力,正交力,垂直力; 正常武力. ~ **forest** 法正林. ~ **(frequency) curve** (= gaussian curve【物】高斯曲线). ~ *horse power* 正常马力. ~ **infantry division** 普通步兵师. ~ **line**【机】法线. ~ **mode**【物】简正方式. ~ **plane**【机、数】法(线)面. ~ **region** 适生区. ~ **school** 师范学校. ~ **section**【数】正截面,正截口;【机】正断面. ~ **spectrum** 匀排光谱. ~ **state** (= ground state【物】基态). ~ **temperature** 标准温度,正常温度. ~ **vibration** 简正振动.

nor·mal·i·ty [nɔːˈmæliti], **nor·mal·cy** [-məlsi] *n.* 正常状态,标准;【化】规度,当量度.

nor·mal·ize [ˈnɔːməlaiz] *vt.* 使正常化,使标准化,使规格化. **-i·za·tion** [ˌnɔːməlaiˈzeiʃən] *n.* ①正常化,标准化;【化】规定化(作用). ②【冶】正火作用.

nor·mal·iz·er [ˈnɔːməlaizə] *n.* 标准化者,归一化者,规格化者.

nor·mal·ly [ˈnɔːməli] *ad.* 正常情况下,通常,一般说来 (= as a rule).

Nor·man[1] [ˈnɔːmən] *a.* (法国西北部)诺曼底(人、民族)的. — *n.* 诺曼底人 (= Northman); 诺曼底法兰西人; 诺曼底法兰西语 (= Norman-French). ~ **English** 诺曼底英语. ~ **French** 诺曼底法语. ~ **Style**【建】诺曼底式〔以简朴、坚牢、圆拱为特征〕.

Nor·man[2] [ˈnɔːmən] *n.* 诺曼〔男子名〕.

Nor·man·dy, Nor·man·die [ˈnɔːməndi, ˌnɔːmɑ̃ːnˈdiː] *n.* 诺曼底〔法国一地区〕.

Nor·man·esque [ˌnɔməˈnesk] *a.*【建】诺曼底式的.

Nor·man·ism [ˈnɔːmənizm] *n.* 诺曼底式(主义); 对诺曼底文化的袒护.

Nor·man·ize [ˈnɔːmənaiz] *vt., vi.* (使)诺曼化. **-i·za·tion** [ˌnɔːmənaiˈzeiʃən] *n.*

norm·a·tive [ˈnɔːmətiv] *a.* ①标准的,规范的. ②惯用法规律的. ~ **grammar** 规范语法. **-ly** *ad.*

nor·mo·ten·sive [ˌnɔːməuˈtensiv] *a.*【医】正常血压的.

Norn [nɔːn] *n.*【北欧神】诺恩〔命运的三女神之一〕.

nor·nic·o·tine [nɔːˈnikətiːn] *n.*【化】降烟碱; 去甲烟碱.

Nor·ris [ˈnɔris] *n.* 诺里斯〔姓氏,男子名〕.

Norse [nɔːs] *a.* 斯堪的纳维亚的; 挪威的,挪威人[语]的. — *n.* 〔the ~〕〔作复数用〕古代斯堪的纳维亚人[语]; 西斯堪的纳维亚人[语]; 北欧人[语]; 挪威人[语]. *N- mythology* 北欧神话.

Norse·land [ˈnɔːslənd] *n.* 挪威的别称; 北欧国家; 斯堪的纳维亚.

Norse·man [ˈnɔːsmən] *n.* 古代挪威人; 古代斯堪的纳维亚人.

Norsk [nɔːsk] *a., n.* = Norse.

North [nɔːθ] *n.* 诺斯〔姓氏〕.

north [nɔːθ] *n.* ①〔通常作 the ~〕北,北方,北部. ②〔N-〕英国北部;〔N-〕美国北部各州. ③北半球; 北极地方;〔诗〕北风. ~ *by east [west]* 北偏东[西]〔自正北偏东[西] 11°15′〕. *in the ~ of* 在…的北部. *on [to] the ~ of ...* 在…的北面. — *a.* 北的,北方的,北部的; 朝北的; 在北方的; 从北方来的,位于北方的. ***be too far ~*** 〔俚〕太伶俐,过于狡猾. — *ad.* 在北方,向北方,自北方. *due ~* 在正北. *lie ~ and south* 横亘南北. ~ *of* 在…北方. *a room facing ~* 朝北方的房间. **N- Atlantic Treaty Organization** 北大西洋公约组织〔略作 NATO〕. **N- Britain** = Scotland〔略 *N. B.*〕. **N- Country** 英国(或英格兰的)北部; 北美北部〔包括 Alaska 和加拿大的 Yukon 地区〕. **N- Island** 北岛〔新西兰两主岛之一〕. ~ **land**〔诗〕北国,北方. ~ **light** 从北面来的光线 (= north-light); (画室的) 北窗; 北极光. ~ **pole** 北极. **N- Sea** 北海〔英国与西欧之间的海〕. ~ **star** 北极星.

North·amp·ton·shire [nɔːˈθæmptənʃiə] *n.* 北安普敦郡〔英国〕.

North·ants = Northampton(shire).

north·bound [ˈnɔːθˌbaund] *a.* 向北方的,北行的.

North Carolina [ˈnɔːθ ˌkærəˈlainə] 北卡罗来纳〔美国州名〕. **~-lin·i·an** *a., n.* 北卡罗来纳州的(人).

North·cliffe [ˈnɔːθklif] *n.* 诺斯克利夫〔姓氏〕.

North Dakota [ˈnɔːθ dəˈkəutə] 北达科他〔美国州名〕.

North Da·ko·tan [ˈnɔːθ dəˈkəutən] *a., n.* 北达科他州的(人).

north•east [ˈnɔːθˈiːst, 〔海〕ˈnɔːrˈiːst] *n.* 东北；东北地方；〔诗〕东北风. — *a.* 东北的,在东北的,自东北的. — *ad.* 在东北,向东北,从东北. ～ *by east [north]* 东北偏东[北]〔自东北偏东[北] 11°15′〕. **-er** *n.* ①(猛烈的)东北风. ②雨帽. **-er•ly** *a., ad.* 向东北(的)；从东北(吹来)的. **-ern** *a.* = north-easterly. **-ward** ① *ad., a.* 在东北方(的),朝东北(的). ② *n.* 东北地区；东北方. **-ward(s)** *ad.* 在〔向〕东北. **-ward•ly** *ad., a.* 向东北方(的)；来自东北(的).

north•er [ˈnɔːðə] *n.* 〔美〕(冬季吹向墨西哥湾的)寒冷的北风；南下寒潮；剧烈的北风. 北来风. **-ly** *ad., a.* 向北(的)；自北(的).

north•ern [ˈnɔːðən] *a.* *(superl. ～most)* 北的,北方的,住在北部的；北方特有的；〔N-〕美国北部的. — *n.* ①北方人 (= northerner). ②〔美〕北风；(自北而来的)暴风雨. *the N- States* 美国北部各州. *the ～ lights* 北极光. **N- Cross**【天】北十字(天鹅座). **N- Crown**【天】北冕(星)座 (= Corona Borealis). **N- Hemisphere** 北半球. **N- Ireland** 北爱尔兰.

north•ern•er [ˈnɔːðənə] *n.* 北方人；〔N-〕〔美〕美国北方人.

north•ern•most [ˈnɔːðənməust] *a.* 最北端的,极北的.

north•ing [ˈnɔːθiŋ, -ðiŋ] *n.*【海】北进,北驶,北航；【天】(天体的)北偏,北向纬度差；北中天,北中；北赤纬. *make a very little ～* (航行中的船)北进少许.

north•land [ˈnɔːθˈlənd] *n.* 〔诗〕北方,北方地方；〔N-〕(地球的)北部；〔N-〕斯堪的纳维亚半岛.

north-light [ˈnɔːθˈlait] *n.* 〔常 *pl.*〕北极光.

North•man [ˈnɔːθmən] *n.* 古代斯堪的纳维亚人,北欧人；加拿大北方人；北欧海盗.

north-north•east [ˈnɔːθˌnɔːθˈiːst; ˈnɔːnɔː-] *n.* 北东北〔正北偏东 22°30′〕. — *ad., a.* ①北东北(的),向北东北. ②来自北东北(的),吹北东北风(的).

north-north•west [ˈnɔːθˌnɔːθˈwest] *n.* 北西北〔正北偏西 22°30′〕, —*ad., a.* ①北西北(的),向北西北. ②来自北西北(的),吹北西北风(的).

north-po•lar [ˈnɔːθˈpəulə] *a.* 北极的.

North•umb = Northumberland 诺森伯兰郡〔英国〕.

North•um•bri•an [nɔːˈθʌmbriən] *a., n.* (英国)诺森伯兰 (Northumbria) 的(人、方言)；诺森伯兰郡的(人、方言).

north•ward [ˈnɔːθwəd] *a.* 向北的；来自北方的. — *ad.* 向北,向北方；来自北方. — *n.* 向北的方向；北方的地区.

north•ward•ly [ˈnɔːθwədli] *ad., a.* 向北方(的).

north•wards [ˈnɔːθwədz] *ad.* = northward *(ad.)*.

north•west [ˈnɔːθˈwest, 〔海〕ˈnɔːˈwest] *n.* 西北；西北部；西北地方；〔the N-〕美国西北部；加拿大西北部. ～ *by north* 西北偏北〔西北偏北 11°15′〕. ～ *by west* 西北偏西〔西北偏西 11°15′〕.— *a.* 西北的；向西北的；自西北的. — *ad.* 向西北,在西北. **N- Mounted Police** 加拿大西北部骑警队. **N- Passage** 西北航道〔从大西洋经欧亚两洲北部诸海到达太平洋的航道〕. **N- Territories** 西北地区〔加拿大北部一地区,首府为渥太华〕. **-er** 强烈的西北风. **-erly** *ad., a.* 向西北(的),从西北(吹来的). **-ern** *a.* 西北的,在西北的；自西北的. **-ward** *ad., a., n.* = northwest. **-wardly** *ad., a.* = northwestward. **-ward(s)** *ad.* = northwest.

Nor•ton [ˈnɔːtn] *n.* 诺顿〔姓氏,男子名〕.

Norw. = ①Norway. ②Norwegian.

nor•ward(s) [ˈnɔːwəd(z)] *ad., a., n.* = northward(s).

Nor•way [ˈnɔːwei] *n.* 挪威〔欧洲〕. **N- maple**【植】挪威槭 (Acer platanoides)〔美国常种此树以遮荫〕. **N- pine** (= red pine 挪威松). **N- rat**【动】褐家鼠 *(Rattus norvegicus)*. **N- spruce**【植】挪威云杉 *(Picea abies)*.

Nor•we•gian [nɔːˈwiːdʒən] *a.* 挪威(人、语)的. — *n.* 挪威人〔语〕. ～ **elkhound**【动】挪威猎麋犬〔挪威产中等高矮,粗短身材的猎犬,毛灰厚,尾后卷至背部〕.

nor'-west•er [ˈnɔːˈwestə] *n.* ①=northwester. ②一杯烧酒. ③油布帽；〔美〕(水手穿的)油布外套.

Nor•wic. = Norwich.

Nos., Nos, nos, nos. = numbers.

nose [nəuz] *n.* ①鼻；(动物)鼻口部；吻；嗅觉. ②香气,气味 *(of)*. ③管口,筒口,枪口,喷嘴；前缘,头部；船头；【空】机首；【高尔夫球】球棒头；水雷(等)头. ④地角,突出部. ⑤〔英俚〕(警察的)暗探,探员. *the bridge of the ～* 鼻梁. *a vegetable ～* 蒜头鼻子. *an aquiline ～* 鹰鼻,钩鼻. ***as plain as the ～ in [on] one's face*** 非常明白,一清二楚. ***bite sb.'s ～ off*** 气势汹汹地回答某人. ***bloody sb.'s ～*** 伤害某人自尊心,挫伤某人. ***blow one's ～*** 擤鼻子. ***by a ～*** 〔美〕以少许之差(输赢). ***cannot see beyond one's nose*** 鼠目寸光. ***count ～s*** 数赞成人数；单依人数来决定事情. ***cut [bite] off one's ～ to spite one's face*** 拿自己出气；跟自己过不去；为了跟别人怄气而伤害自己. ***follow one's ～*** 笔直走；依本能行动,任性而行. ***have a good ～*** 鼻子灵,嗅觉敏锐. ***have a ～ for news*** 善于采访新闻. ***hold one's ～*** 捏鼻子. ***in spite of sb.'s ～*** 不顾某人反对. ***keep one's ～ clean***〔美〕不喝酒. ***keep [put, hold] one's [sb.'s] ～ to the grindstone*** 使自己[某人]埋头苦干. ***lead sb. by the ～*** 牵着某人鼻子走. ***look down one's ～ at***〔口〕藐视. ***make a long ～ at*** (把拇指搁在鼻端,其余四指张开)对某人表示轻蔑,嘲弄某人. ***make one's ～ swell*** 令人羡慕,使人忌妒. ***measure ～s*** 遇见. ***～ of wax*** 随人摆布的人[东西]. ***not to be able to see beyond one's ～ [see no further than one's ～].*** 眼光短浅；〔转〕鼠目寸光. ***～ to*** 面对面. ***on the ～***〔俚〕①(赛马)跑第一. ②准确,恰,正. ***parson's ～*** 〔喻〕(煮熟的)鸡鸭等禽类的屁股. ***pay through the ～*** 付出惊人巨款,花很多钱；付出很大代价. ***poke [put, thrust] one's ～ into*** *(another's business)* 干涉,插手别人的事情,管闲事. ***put sb.'s ～ out of joint*** 撵走某人；夺走某人的爱；破坏某人的计划；排挤某人(的职位等). ***rub sb.'s ～ in it*** 粗暴地提醒某人别忘记他所犯的错误. ***snap one's ～ off*** = bite one's ～ off. ***speak through one's ～*** 用鼻音说话. ***tell ～s*** = count ～s. ***turn up one's ～ at*** 瞧不起,不理会. ***under one's (very) ～*** 就在某人面前；不顾某人不高兴. ***with one's ～ at the grindstone*** 费力地,辛辛苦苦做活[过日子等]. ***with one's ～ in the air*** 神气活现,自高自大. — *vt.* ①闻,闻着,闻出；探出,侦探出,看出 *(out)*. ②(船等)以头部探(路)小心前进. ③用鼻子触[擦、塞入]. ④〔古〕反对. ⑤用鼻音说[唱]. ～ *a job in everything* 事事都想捞一手. *The ship ～d her way through the winding channel.* 船在蜿蜒的海峡中小心驶过. — *vi.* ①闻、嗅 *(at; about)*. ②探索,打听 *(after; for)*；干涉 *(into a matter)*. ③(船等)小心探索着前进. ④【地】倾斜 *(in)*；露出 *(out)*. ⑤〔英〕送报告,出告. ～ *ahead*〔美运〕以少许之差领前. ～ *down [up]*【空】机首朝下降落[朝上上升]. ～ *out* 嗅出,闻出；察觉出；〔美〕【体】以少量之差打败对方. ～**ape**【动】长鼻猿. ～**bag** 秣囊,马粮袋；〔口〕(旅行等用的)饭盒子；防毒面具. ～ **band** (马的)鼻羁. ～**bleed** 鼻出血,衄血. ～ **candy**〔美俚〕嗅用麻醉品. ～ **cone** (火箭的)头部,前锥体. ～**dive**【空】俯冲,急降；〔喻〕(价格等的)猛跌,暴落；(事业等的)骤衰. ～**-dive** *vi.* 俯冲,急降；暴落. ～**-down** ① *a.*【空】机首朝下的. ② *vi.* 把机头朝下. ～ **drops** 滴鼻药水. ～ **gas** 喷嚏性毒气. ～**gay** (芳香的)花束. ～**-led** *a.* 任人拖着鼻子走的. ～**monkey** *n.* = nose-ape. ～ **ornament** 鼻饰,鼻环. ～ **paint**〔美俚〕酒. ～**piece** 鼻羁；接(线)头；(显微镜按对物镜处的)换镜旋座[盘]；(水管、风箱等的)口,嘴. ～ **rag**〔俚〕手帕. ～ **ring** (牛、猪等的)鼻环,鼻圈. ～**-spike** 顶针. ～ **warmer**〔俚〕短烟嘴. ～**wheel** (飞机机头的)降落轮. ～**wing**【解】鼻翼. **-～less** *a.*, **-～like** *a.*

-nosed [ˈnəuzd] *comb. f.* 〔构成复合词〕 *a.* …(形)鼻子的: bottle-*nosed* 酒壶鼻子的.

nos·er [ˈnəuzə] *n.* 〔俚〕①强逆风,顶头风. ②爱管闲事的人;被雇用的密探. *a dead* ~ 猛烈的顶头风.

nose·y [ˈnəuzi] *a.* ***(nos·i·er; -i·est)*** = nosy.

nosh [nɔʃ] *vt., vi.* 〔俚〕吃(快餐), 吃(小吃). — *n.* 〔俚〕快餐,小吃. ~ **up** 〔主英〕盛筵. **-er** *n.* 吃快餐[小吃]的人.

nos·i·ly [ˈnəuzili] *ad.* 好打听地;爱管闲事地.

nos·i·ness [ˈnəuzinis] *n.* 好打听;爱管闲事.

nos·ing [ˈnəuziŋ] *n.* 【建】突缘饰;梯级突边;突边上的金属包覆物.

noso- *comb. f.* 病: nosography.

no·sog·ra·phy [nəuˈsɔgrəfi] *n.* 疾病记述学,病情学.

nos·o·log·ic, nos·o·log·i·cal [ˌnɔsəˈlɔdʒik, -əl] *a.* 疾病分类学的. **-log·i·cal·ly** *ad.*

no·sol·o·gy [nəuˈsɔlədʒi] *n.* 疾病分类学[表].

nos·tal·gi·a [nɔsˈtældʒiə, -dʒjə] *n.* 怀乡病,乡愁;怀旧,留恋过去. **nos·tal·gic** [nəsˈtældʒik] *a.*

nos·toc [ˈnɔstɔk] *n.* 念珠藻属植物.

nos·to·log·ic [ˌnɔstəˈlɔdʒik] *a.* 老年医学的,老年学的.

nos·tol·o·gy [nɔsˈtɔlədʒi] *n.* 老年病学.

nos·to·ma·ni·a [ˌnɔstəˈmeiniə] *n.* 【心】怀乡病; 留恋过去,怀旧.

Nos·tra·da·mus [ˌnɔstrəˈdeiməs] *n.* ①法国占星术士 *Michel de Nostredame* (1503—1566)的拉丁语形. ②〔n-〕自称能卜未来吉凶的预言者.

nos·tril [ˈnɔstril] *n.* 鼻孔;鼻孔内壁. ***the breath of one's ~s*** (生命中)不可缺少的东西. ***stink in sb.'s ~s*** 被某人厌恶.

nos·tril·(l)ed [ˈnɔstrild] *a.* 有鼻孔的.

nos·trum [ˈnɔstrəm] *n.* ①注册成药;秘方. ②骗人疗法;骗人特效药. ③〔蔑〕(解决政治、社会问题等的)妙策,万应灵药.

nos·y [ˈnəuzi] *a.* ***(nos·i·er; -i·est)*** 〔口〕①大鼻子的;好管闲事的. ②(谷草)发恶臭的; (红茶)有香味的. ③对恶臭很敏感的. — *n.* 〔俚〕大鼻子〔绰号〕 ***N- Parker*** 〔英俚〕爱管闲事的人.

not [nɔt; 助动词后的弱读 nt] *ad.* 不. ①〔谓语、句子的否定语〕ⓐ用作助动词的否定式时,常略作 n't: is*n't*, are*n't*, was*n't*, were*n't*, have*n't*, has*n't*, had*n't*, do*n't*[dəunt], does*n't*, did*n't*, wo*n't*[wəunt], would*n't*, sha*n't*[ʃɑːnt], should*n't*, ca*n't*[kɑːnt], 〔Am.〕 [kænt], may*n't*, might*n't*, must*n't*[mʌsnt], ought*n't*, need*n't*, dare*n't*, used*n't* [juːsnt], ⓑ和其他动词连用时,古语通常放在动词之后,现代语则与 do, does 连用以示否定; 〔古〕 *I know* ~ = 〔书〕 *I do* ~ [duːnɔt] *know* = 〔口〕 *I don't know;* 〔疑问形式〕 *Is it ~?, Will you ~?, Do you ~ (go)?* = 〔口〕 *Isn't it? Won't you? Don't you (go)?* ②〔谓语以外的词、短语、子句的否定〕ⓐ〔在 *Litotes* (婉转反语法) 及 *Periphrasis* (委婉语)中〕 ~ *a few* 不少. ~ *a little* 不少. ~ *once or [nor] twice* 不只一二次,好几次,屡次. ~ *reluctant* 非常高兴,极乐意. ~ *seldom* 常常. ~ *without some doubt* 带着几分怀疑. ⓑ用于分词、不定式之前以示否定〕 *I begged him not to go out.* 我要求他不要出去. *N- knowing, I cannot say.* 我不知道,所以说不出来. ③〔以单词用作全句的否定〕 ~ *any* = no, none. ~ *anybody* = nobody. ~ *anyone* = no one. ~ *anything* =nothing. ~ *anywhere* = nowhere. ~ *either* = neither. ~ *ever* = never. ~ *nearly* = by no means. *Will he come? — N- he* (= No, he won't)! 他会来吗? ——他不会(来). *The French will ~ fight, ~ they.* 法国人恐怕不会打, 他们不会打. ④〔与 all, both 和 every 等连用,表示部分否定〕 *N- everyone can succeed.* 不是人人都会成功的. *All is ~ gold that glitters.* 发亮的东西不一定都是黄金. *I don't know both.* 我并非两方面都知道〔只知道一方面〕. ⑤〔否定的句子、动词、从句等的省略代用语〕 *Is he ill? — N- at all* 他病了吗? ——一点也没病. *Right or ~, it is a fact.* 不管对不对,那是事实. *Is he ill? — I think ~.* 他是病了吗? ——我想不是病. *Will it rain tomorrow? — I hope ~.* 明天会下雨吗? ——希望不会. ⑥〔在动词 believe, expect, fancy, fear, hope, imagine, suppose, think, trust, 副词 perhaps, probably, absolutely 等,和词组 be afraid 等后面以代表其后所否定的从句〕 *I don't think it is now five o'clock yet.* 我认为现在还不到五点钟. ***if*** ~ 不然的话. ~ ***a*** 一个也不… *(N- a man answered.* 一个人也没有回答. ~ *a breath of air* 一丝丝风也没有). ***N- at all*** 〔Eng.〕 (= 〔Am.〕 *You are welcome*). 哪里的话,别客气. ~ ***… but*** 不是…而是… *(He is ~ my son, but my nephew.* 他不是我的儿子,而是我的侄儿). ~ ***but that [what …]*** =〔古〕 ~ ***but*** 然而还是,虽然,但不是不… *(I cannot do it, ~ but that a stronger man might.* 我不能做,但并不是说比我强的人也不能做). ~ ***dry behind the ears*** 〔美俚〕无经验的;乳臭未干的;不成熟的;未学坏的. ~ ***having [taking] any*** 〔美俚〕无意于, 不打算干 *(Risk my life jaywalking? — No! I'm ~ having any.* 要我冒生命危险违章穿过马路吗? ——对不起! 我不干). ~ ***my funeral*** 〔美俚〕不关我事,不是我的责任. ~ ***only … but (also)*** 不仅…而且…. ~ ***so*** 不是那样. ~ ***so hot*** 〔美俚〕并不怎样好[聪明、漂亮、有趣、成功]; 普普通通. ~ ***sufficient*** 〔银行退票用语〕 (存数) 不足〔略 *N.S.*〕. ~ ***that … 并不是*** *((It is) ~ that I dislike you.* 并非是我讨厌你. *If he said so — ~ that he ever did — he lied.* 他要是那样说——并不是说他那样说过——他便撒谎了). ~ ***that … but that…*** 不是(因为)…而是(因为)…. ***N- that I know of.*** 据我所知并不是这样. ~ ***with it*** 〔美俚〕局外人.

no·ta [ˈnəutə] notum 的复数.

no·ta be·ne [ˈnəutə ˈbiːni] 〔L.〕〔略 N.B. 或 n.b.〕注意.

no·ta·bil·i·a [ˌnəutəˈbilie] *n.* 〔*pl.*〕 值得注意的事物.

no·ta·bil·i·ty [ˌnəutəˈbiliti] *n.* ①值得注意的[显著的]性质;显要人物;名人;〔罕〕值得一看的事物. ②〔英、古〕(主妇的) 当家手腕. *notabilities in political and economic circles* 政界和经济界的知名人士.

no·ta·ble [ˈnəutəbl] *a.* ①值得注意的,显著的;著名的,显要的;【化】可知觉的. ②〔英常 ˈnɔtəbl〕(主妇)会当家的. — *n.* ①著名人士,要人. ②〔N-〕【法国史】法王召集参加紧急会议的知名人士. ③〔罕〕著名事物. **-ness** *n.* **-bly** *ad.* 显著地,著名地;格外地,特别地.

no·tal·gi·a [nəuˈtældʒiə] *n.* 【医】背痛.

NOT-AND gate [ˈnɔt-ˈænd geit] *n.* 【自】"与非"门.

no·tan·dum [nəuˈtændəm] *n.* *(pl.* ***-s, -da*** **[-də]***)* 〔L.〕值得注意的事项或其记录;备忘录.

no·tar·i·al [nəuˈtɛəriəl] *a.* 公证人的;公证的. ~ *acts* 公证手续. *a ~ deed* 公证证书. **-ly** *ad.* 由公证人.

no·ta·rize [ˈnəutəraiz] *vt.* ***(-riz·ed; -riz·ing)*** 以公证人资格证实. **-ri·za·tion** [ˌnəutəraiˈzeiʃən] *n.*

no·ta·ry [ˈnəutəri] *n.* 公证人〔又称 ~ public 或 public ~〕. 〔古〕书记,秘书.

no·ta·tion [nəuˈteiʃən] *n.* ①记号,用号,符号,标志(法),表示法. ②【数】记数法. ③【乐】乐谱,记谱法. ④〔罕〕记录;注释. *broad [narrow]* ~ 【语】简略[精密]标音法. *chemical* ~ 化学符号法. *the common scale of* ~ 【数】十进记数法. *decimal* ~ 十进法. *binary* ~ 二进位记数法. *binary-coded decimal* ~ 用二进位编码表示的十进位计数法. **-al** *a.*

notch [nɔtʃ] *n.* ①(v 字形的)槽口,缺口;切口;凹口;箭鞘缺口. ②〔美〕山峡, 峡谷;【地】水浪冲成的洞穴. ③(刻在棍子等上的) 计数刻痕; 选择器标记. ④〔口〕等;级;〔古〕(板球等的)分数. *He is a ~ above the others.* 他比别人高一等. — *vt.* ①在…上开槽口[作凹口,作缺口 *(into)*]; 作刻痕计算(比赛分数等). ②〔古〕(板球等)得(分). ③搭(箭) *(up; down)*. ④砍,切;【林】劈植.

～**back**〔美〕客货两用汽车. ～**-board** 梯级搁板;【机】凹板.

notched, notchy [nɔtʃt, ˈnɔtʃi] *a.* 有凹口的;【植】粗锯齿状的;【动】尖端有缺口的;具缺刻的.

note [nəut] *n.* ①备忘录,笔记,记录,略记;回想,意见. ②注,注解,注释;按语,评论. ③短简,便条,柬帖;(外交上的)照会,通牒;(学术上的)短文. ④(乐器的)调子,音色;样子;口气;特征. ⑤(人)声,(鸟)叫[鸣]声. ⑥印,记号,标记,符号. ⑦注意,注目. ⑧暗示,提示. ⑨名望,显要;〔古〕污名. ⑩〔常 *pl.*〕原稿,草稿. ⑪【乐】律音;音符,音调;(钢琴等的)键;〔诗〕调,曲调,旋律. ⑫【商】纸币,票据,借据. *a ～ of invitation* 请帖. *speak with a ～ of censure* 用责备的口气说. *Frankness is the chief ～ in his character.* 坦白是他性格中的主要特色. *There is the ～ of pessimism in his writings.* 他的著作带有悲观色彩. *a ～ of assurance (in his voice)* 自信的口气. *a bird's merry ～* 愉快的鸟声. *a ～ of exclamation* 惊叹符号. *a man of ～* 知名之士. *a bank-～* 银行钞票. *a ～ of hand* 期票. *£10 in ～s* 钞票十镑. ***change one's ～*** 改变态度[口气]. ***compare ～s*** 交换意见;对笔记. ***make [take] ～s [a ～] of*** 记录,记下,笔记. ***make ～s of*** 作(演说等的)草稿;作札记. ***sound a false ～*** = strike a false ～. ***sound a ～ of warning*** 给与警告. ***sound the ～ of war*** 作主战论调. ***speak from [without] ～s*** 用[不用]草稿演说[发言]. ***strike a false ～*** 做错事,说错话. ***strike the right ～*** 说[做]得恰当. ***take ～ of*** 注意(到),注目. ***worthy of ～*** 值得注意的,显著的. — *vt.* ①笔录;记[摘]下 *(down)*. ②注目,注意(到). ③对…加注释;【乐】用音符记出. ④特别提到;指明,表明. ～**book** 笔记本;期票簿. ～**case**〔英〕钱夹;钱包. ～**head**〔美〕印有住址的信纸;笺头. ～**less** *a.* ①不引人注意的;不著名的. ②音调不和谐的. ～**let** 短简,短信. ～**paper** 信纸;便条纸. ～ **shaver** 高利贷者. ～**s payable** 给债权人的期票. ～**s receivable** 债务人签署的期票.

not·ed [nəutid] *a.* ①著名的,知名的 *(for)*. ②【乐】附有乐谱的. **-ly** *ad.* 显著地 **-ness** *n.*

note·wor·thy [ˈnəutwəːði] *a.* 值得注意的,显著的. *Science has recently made ～ progress especially in this field.* 特别在这一领域内,科学今天已有了显著的进步. **-thi·ly** *ad.*, **-thi·ness** *n.*

noth·ing [ˈnʌθiŋ] *n.* (什么也)没有,没有什么东西[什么事],什么东西[什么事]也不…. *N- venture, ～ have.* 不入虎穴,焉得虎子. *He is ～ of a poet.* 他一点也算不上是个诗人. *N- pleases him.* 什么都不合他的意. ★修饰 nothing 的形容词放在后面. 如: N- great is easy. 大事业是不容易的. ②无,空;不存在(的东西);【数】零;无价值,无意义. *Of ～ comes ～.* 无中不能生有. *There is ～ in it.* 那是空话,毫无意义. *He has ～ in him.* 他一无可取之处. *He is five feet ～.* 他身长刚刚五英尺. ③没价值的人[事、物],微不足道的事,琐事. *My trouble is ～ to theirs.* 我的困难比起他们来算不了什么. ★作名词用时常说作 a ～, ～s. 如: He is a (mere) ～. 他完全是一个废物. the little ～s of life. 人生的琐事. whisper soft ～s. 低声絮絮诉爱. ④【宗】不属任何教派的人;不信教的人,无神论者. *He is ～.* 他不属任何教派. ★作此义解时仅用作表语,前面也不加冠词. — *ad.* 毫不,决不;〔美口〕决不是. *This will help you ～.* 这对你毫无帮助. *This is ～ like as [so] good as that.* = *This is ～ near so good as that.* 这个远不及那个. *She's ～ wiser than before.* 她丝毫也不比以前聪敏. ～ *daunted* 毫不畏缩. ***all to ～*** 十二分,充分地. ***be for ～ in*** 对…没有影响[不起作用]. ***be ～ if not*** 首先;极其;是主要特征 *(He is ～, if not kind.* 亲切是他主要的优点). ***be ～ to*** 对…一点关系也没有;丝毫不能和…相比 *(She is ～ to me.* 我对她无所谓;我根本没有爱她). ***can make ～ of*** 不能了解,弄不懂…;看不清楚;听不清楚;对付不了,不能解决;不能利用. ***come to ～*** 毫无结果,终成泡影,失败. ***dance up(on) ～*** 被绞死. ***do ～ but*** 除了…以外什么也不干;只是…. ***for ～*** ①徒然,白白;没有结果 *(He did not go to Oxford for ～.* 他没有白进牛津大学). ②免费,不要钱 *(I got it for ～* 免费得来). ③没理由地,无缘无故 *(They quarrelled for ～.* 他们无端吵了一架). ***have ～ of*** 不理睬. ***have ～ on sb.***〔美〕没有胜过某人的地方;没有关于某人的罪证,没有抓到某人的小辫子. ***have ～ to do with*** 跟…毫无关系,不跟…来往. ***in ～ flat*** 马上,立刻. ***like ～ on earth*** ①了不起的,再好没有的. ②非常奇怪的. ③最坏的;最讨厌的. ***make ～ of*** 不把…放在眼中,轻视;满不在乎;认为不在话下〔通常与 can 连用,见 can make ～ of〕. ***next to ～*** 差不多没有. ***no ～***〔用在几个否定语后〕什么都没有 *(There is no bread, no butter, no cheese, no ～.* 面包也没有,奶油也没有,干酪也没有,什么都没有). ***～ but = ～ else but [than]*** 只有,不过,不外,简直;〔美〕〔加强语气〕的确 *(I have been working hard, ～ but.* 我拼命工作了,真的呀). ***N- doing***〔俚〕事情行不通,糟了! 完蛋了! 毫无办法,不行,不干〔失败或拒绝要求时说〕. ***～ flat***【美运】零败,吃鸭蛋. ***～ less than = ～ short of*** 完全是,不外. ***～ may come of it*** 落空. ***～ near so*** 远不及,差得远 *(This building is not inferior to that one but ～ near so large.* 这建筑物并不比那一座差,只是远不及那座大). ***～ much*** 非常少. ***～ of that kind*** 决不是那样. ***N- off! = N- to lose!***【海】别让船头掉向下风! ***～ to sneeze at***〔美俚〕不能忽视[轻视]. ***～ to write home about***〔美俚〕不重要,平淡无奇. ***～ very much***〔口〕没有什么特别的,将就过得去,平平常常. ***stop [stick] at ～*** 毫无顾忌;什么都做得出;不择手段. ***Thank you for ～.***〔口、讽〕不劳费心,敬谢不敏. ***There is ～ for it but to (do)*** 除…之外别无方法. ***There is ～ in it.*** ①全是假话,不符事实;不重要,不相干,没有多少道理,没有什么意义. ②(两个竞争者之间)机会相等. ***There is ～ like*** …什么也比不上…,没有比…更好的;远远没有,差得远. ***think ～ of*** 不把…放在心里;看成平常. ***to ～*** (消失得)无影无踪,(消)去. ***to say ～ of ...*** 更不必说,那就根本谈不到.

noth·ing·ar·i·an [ˌnʌθiŋˈɛəriən] *n.* 没有信仰的人.

noth·ing·ness [ˈnʌθiŋnis] *n.* ①无,空;不存在. ②无价值,无聊,空虚;无关紧要;琐细东西;不存在[无价值]的事物. ③人事不省;死.

no·tice [ˈnəutis] *n.* ①注意;认识. ②情报,消息;通知,预告,警告;(正式)通告;呈报. ③(辞退、解雇等的)预先通知. ④公告,告示,布告,招贴. ⑤(报刊等上对戏剧、图书等的)介绍,评介,批评,短评. ⑥客气;有礼的招呼. *I commend her to your ～.* 请多关照关照她. *a ～ of a call* 催缴股款通知书. *a ～ of dishonour* 退票通知书. *The new play got a favorable ～.* 那出新戏得到了好评. *He is sitting up and taking ～.* 〔口〕他忽然感到兴趣;〔谑〕他身体渐渐好了. ***at a moment's ～*** 一经通知;立即,马上,随时. ***at short ～*** 在短时间内,顷刻之间;(军队)得到命令后马上…;接令后立刻…. ***beneath one's ～*** 被某人认为不值得注意,不值一顾. ***be under ～*** 接到(解雇、辞退等的)通知. ***bring to [under] one's ～*** 使某人注意到,使某人看见. ***come into [under] one's ～*** 引起某人注意,给某人看见. ***escape one's ～*** 逃过某人的注意,被某人疏忽,被某人看漏. ***get ～***〔美口〕被解雇,失业. ***get ～ of*** 接到…的通知. ***give ～*** 通知,通告;预先通知(解雇、辞退等) *(give a week's ～* 在一星期前通知). ***give ～ of [that]*** 通知…. ***give ～ to*** 报告. ***have ～ of*** 接到...的通知. ***on short ～*** 忽然;急忙. ***post [put up] a ～*** 贴出布告 *(There is a ～ posted up saying that ...* 一个布告贴了出来说…). ***public ～*** 公告,布告. ***put a ～ in the papers*** 在报上登通告. ***serve (a) ～ to*** 通知;警告. ***take no ～ of*** 不注意,不理会,不管,不采取应有的措施. ***take ～*** 注意;(幼儿)

开始了解事物. ***take ~ of sb.*** 款待某人. ***Take ~ that*** (我)警告你…. ***take sb.'s ~*** 接到某人通知. ***till [until] further ~*** 在另行通知以前…. ***without ~*** 不预先通知; 擅自. — *vt.* ①注意到,看到;留心,注意. ②表示与(某人)认识. ③提及,说到;(在报刊等上)介绍,评介(新书). ④通知…. ⑤优待(儿童等);客气对待;有礼地招呼. *I didn't ~ how he was dressed.* 我没留心他穿什么衣服. *He refused to ~ me.* 他假装没看见我. *~ sb.'s services in a speech* 在报告中提到某人的功劳. *He was ~d to quit.* 他得到了离职的通知. — *vi.* 注意. *I wasn't noticing.* 我没留神. ~ **board** 布告牌. **-a·ble** *a.* 引人注意的,显著的. **-a·bly** *ad.* 显著,显然.

no·ti·fi·a·ble [ˈnəutifaiəbl] *a.* 应通知的;应具报的(传染病等).

no·ti·fi·ca·tion [ˌnəutifiˈkeiʃən] *n.* 通知,通告,布告;通告书,通知单;报告书.

no·ti·fi·er [ˈnəutifaiə] *n.* 通知人,通告人.

no·ti·fy [ˈnəutifai] *vt.* ①通告,宣告,布告;通知. ②申报,报告. *I have been notified that ....* 我接到通知说…. *~ one's intention to the party concerned* 把某人意图通知有关方面.

no·tion [ˈnəuʃən] *n.* ①意见,见解,想法,看法,观点;学说(= theory);打算,意图,意向,意志. ②(空泛的)理解;(空)想,奇想. ③概念;观念. ④〔*pl.*〕〔美〕杂货〔针线等〕;新出精巧实用小物品. ⑤〔*pl.*〕英国温彻斯特(Winchester)学院特有的词汇. *Such is the common ~.* 这就是一般的见解. *I have no ~ of resigning.* 我没有辞职的意思. *I have not the haziest ~ of what he means.* 我完全不懂他究竟是什么意思. *He has a good [has no] ~ of economy.* 他很懂得[完全不懂]节约(的意义). *the first ~*【哲】初概念. ~ **counter**〔美〕杂货柜. ~ **department**〔美〕(商店内的)杂货部. ~ **store**〔美〕杂货店.

no·tion·al [ˈnəuʃənəl] *a.* ①观念上的,概念上的;抽象的,纯理论的;想像中的,非现实的. ②〔美〕空想的,幻想的;一脑门子怪念头[荒唐思想]的. ③名义上的;象征性的. ④【语法】表意的. **-ist** *n.* 理论家. **-ly** *ad.*

no·to·chord [ˈnəutəkɔːd] *n.* ①【动】脊索. ②高级脊椎动物怀胎期的脊索. **-al** *a.*

No·to·gae·a [ˌnəutəˈdʒiːə] *n.* (动物地理分区的)南界,南域〔包括新西兰、澳大利亚地区以及西南太平洋的各岛屿〕. **-an** *a.*

no·to·ri·e·ty [ˌnəutəˈraiəti] *n.* ①有名(多指坏的方面),臭名昭著;丑名. ②声名狼藉的人物.

no·to·ri·ous [nəuˈtɔːriəs, nə-] *a.* (坏的方面)有名的,臭名远扬的,臭名昭彰的,声名狼藉的. *a ~ crybaby* 有名的好哭的孩子. *a ship ~ for ill luck* 有名多灾多难的一条船. ***be ~ for*** 以…出名. ***It is ~ that ..., ...*** 是众所周知的(事实). **-ly** *ad.* **-ness** *n.*

no·tor·nis [nəuˈtɔːnis] *n.*【动】南秧鸟〔新西兰的一种不能飞行的鸟〕.

no·to·un·gu·late [ˌnəutəuˈʌŋgjulit], **no·tun·gu·late** [-leit] *n.* 南美有蹄类动物.

No·tre-Dame [ˌnəutrəˈdɑːm] *n.*〔F.〕①圣母马利亚. ②(巴黎)圣母院.

not-self [ˈnɔtself] *n.*【哲】非我,客观,外界(= non-ego).

no-trump [ˈnəuˈtrʌmp] *a.* ①无将牌的. ②【桥牌】叫无将牌的. — *n.* ①叫无将牌. ②打无将的牌.

Not·ting·ham [ˈnɔtiŋəm] *n.* ①诺丁汉〔英国城市〕. ②诺丁汉郡〔英国郡名〕(= ~shire).

Notts. = Nottingham(shire).

no·tum [ˈnəutəm] *n.* (*pl.* **-ta** [-ə])【动】(昆虫的)背板,(动物的)背部.

not·with·stand·ing [ˌnɔtwiθˈstændiŋ, -wið-] *prep.* 虽然,尽管…仍…. *I shall still go, ~ the rain.* 尽管下雨,我仍然要去. *this ~* 〔古〕尽管如此. — *ad.* 〔古〕虽然,尽管,还是. *There were remonstrances, but he persisted ~.* 虽遭抗议,他仍旧坚持了下去. — *conj.*〔古〕虽然,尽管. *He went ~ (that) he was ordered not to.* 他虽被命令不许去,但他仍旧去了.

Nouak·chott [nuˈɑːkʃɔt] *n.* 努瓦克肖特〔毛里塔尼亚首都〕.

nou·gat [ˈnuːgɑː] *n.* 努加糖,果仁〔杏仁、核桃、花生或各种干果〕(蛋白)糖.

nought, naught [nɔːt] *n.* ①【数】零(0). ②〔古、诗〕无. ③没有价值的人〔东西〕. ~ *decimal two* 零点二(0.2). ***bring to ~*** 使(计划等)落空. ***come to ~*** 失败. ***set at ~*** 蔑视,轻视;嘲笑,揶揄. — *a.*〔古〕无价值的. — *ad.*〔古〕毫无,决无.

Nou·mea [nuːˈmeiə] *n.* 努美阿〔新喀里多尼亚岛首都〕.

nou·me·nal·ism [ˈnjuːmənəlizm, ˈnau-] *n.* 实体主义,本体主义. **-nal·ist** *n.*

nou·me·non [ˈnauminɔn, ˈnuː-] *n.* (*pl.* **-na** [-nə])【哲】实体,实在,本体. **nou·me·nal** *a.*

noun [naun] *n.* ①【语】名词. *abstract [material, common, proper, collective, individual] ~s* 抽象[物质、普通、专有、集合、个体]名词. *countable [uncountable]* 可数[不可数]名词. *a ~ of multitude* 群体名词〔例: Are your *family* all well?〕. *a ~ of action* 动作名词〔arrival, confession〕. ②名词代用语. ③〔古语法〕(有屈折变化的)实词. *a ~ adjective* 形容词(= adjective). *a ~ substantive* 名词(= noun).

nour·ish [ˈnʌriʃ] *vt.* ①滋养;施肥于. ②抚养;教养,助长. ③怀抱(希望、怨恨等). **-er** *n.* **-ing** *a.* 滋养的,滋补的. **-ment** *n.* 食物;营养,滋养,助长,培养.

nous [naus] *n.*【哲】精神;理智;理性;智力;〔口〕常识.

nou·veau riche [ˈnuːvəu ˈriːʃ] (*pl.* ***nou·veaux riches***) 〔F.〕暴发户.

nou·veau ro·man [nuvəu rəuˈmɑːn] (*pl.* ***nou·veaux ro·mans***) 新体小说,新小说〔指 1950 年以来法国流行的反传统格式小说,以描写人物的精神状态为主〕.

nou·veau·té [nuːvəuˈtei] *n.*〔F.〕新奇事,新事物.

nou·velle [nuːˈvel] *n.*〔F.〕中篇小说.

nou·velle vague [nuːˈvel ˈvæg]〔F.〕(现代电影的)新潮(派).

Nov. = November.

nov. = novelist.

no·va [ˈnəuvə, ˈnɔvə] *n.* (*pl.* **~s, -vae** [-viː])【天】新星. *N- Cygni* [ˈsigniː] 天鹅新星.

no·vac·u·lite [nəuˈvækjulait] *n.*【地】均密石英岩.

No·va Sco·tia [ˈnəuvə ˈskəuʃə] 新斯科舍〔加拿大省名〕.

no·va·tion [nəuˈveiʃən] *n.*【法】(契约,义务的)更新,代替.

no·vel[1] [ˈnɔvəl] *a.* 新的,新颖的;新奇的,珍奇的,异常的. *a ~ experience* 新的经验.

nov·el[2] [ˈnɔvəl] *n.* ①(长篇)小说. ②〔N-〕〔常 *pl.*〕【罗马法】新法,附律. *a love ~* 爱情小说.

nov·el·ese [ˌnɔvəˈliːz] *n.* (低级的)小说家的陈词滥调.

nov·el·ette [ˌnɔvəˈlet] *n.* ①中篇小说. ②【乐】新事曲〔幻想曲式的小品曲〕.

nov·el·ist [ˈnɔvəlist] *n.* 小说家.

nov·el·is·tic [ˌnɔvəˈlistik] *a.* 小说的.

nov·el·ize [ˈnɔvəlaiz] *vt.* 将(剧本、事实等)编成小说;使小说化. **-i·za·tion** [ˌnɔvəlaiˈzeiʃən] *n.*

no·vel·la [nəuˈvelə] *n.* (*pl.* **-s, -le** [-le]) 中篇故事.

nov·el·ty [ˈnɔvəlti] *n.* 新奇,珍奇,奇异;新奇的东西〔事情〕;【商】新颖小巧物品〔玩具、服饰等〕.

nov·el·wright [ˈnɔvəlrait] *n.*〔蔑〕小说家.

No·vem·ber [nəuˈvembə] *n.* ①十一月〔略作 Nov.〕. ②通讯中用以代替字母 n 的词.

no·ve·na [nəuˈviːnə] *n.* (*pl.* **-s, -nae** [-niː])【天主】连续九天的祷告.

no·ven·ni·al [nəuˈveniəl] *a.* 每九年的.

no·ver·cal [nəuˈvəːkəl] *a.* 继母(般)的.

Nov·go·rod [ˈnɔvgərɔd] *n.* 诺夫哥罗德〔苏联城市〕.

nov·ice [ˈnɔvis] *n.* ①初学者,新手,生手;初次出场(赛

跑)的马[狗]等. ②【宗】新信徒,见习修道士[修女].
no·vi·ci·ate, no·vi·ti·ate [nəu'viʃiit] *n.* ①修道士[修女]的见习期;见习中的修道士[修女]. ②(新手的)见习(期);初学者,生手.
no·vo·bi·o·cin [ˌnəuvə'baiəsin] *n.*【药】新生霉素.
no·vo·ca·in(e) ['nəuvəkein] *n.*【药】奴佛卡因.
No·vo·si·birsk [ˌnəuvəsi'biəsk] *n.* 诺沃西比尔斯克(新西伯利亚)〔苏联城市〕.
no·vus or·do se·clo·rum ['nəuvəs 'ɔːdəu si'klɔːrəm] 〔L.〕= a new order of the ages.
now [nau] *ad.* ①〔现在〕(a)现在,此刻,目前. *The bell is ~ ringing.* 钟现在正在响. (b)现在(已经),按此刻情形. *It is ~ over.* 已经完了. ②〔未来〕立刻,即刻,马上. *Do it ~.* 马上做吧. *I can come ~.* 我马上可以来. ③〔过去〕(a)刚才,方才. ★现在只用 just ~ 和〔诗〕even ~. (b)(叙述中的)现在,那时,当时;接着,于是,然后;那时已经. *Hannibal was ~ crossing the Alps.* 汉尼拔那时正在翻越阿尔卑斯山. ④〔无时间观念,表示说话者的语气,用于命令、请求、说明、警告、责骂、安慰等句中〕原来,那么;喂;嗳呀,哟. *N- what do you mean by it?* 你这究竟是什么意思呢? *N- tell me.* 那么告诉我吧. *N- Barabbas was a robber.* 却说巴拉巴斯原是个贼. *You don't mean it, ~.* 你这话不会是当真的吧. ★本义的 now 多用于句首,且多用逗号. ***but [even] ~*** 〔古〕= just now. ***(every) ~ and then [again]*** 时常,时而,不时. ***just ~*** 方才,刚才;现在,眼下. ***~ ... ~ [then] = ~ ... and again*** 时而…时而… *(~ hot, ~ cold* 忽热忽冷). ***~ ~ = ~ then*** ①〔口〕好啦! 行啦! 就这么样! ②赶快,来吧! ③喂喂,得啦〔有时是友好的抗议或是警告〕*(N- ~, a little less noise, please!* 喂喂,请安静一点. *N- then, none of your nonsense!* 得啦,别说废话吧!) ***N- or never!*** 机不可失,时不再来;此时不干,更待何时? ***Oh, come ~!*** 嗨,得啦! ***Really ~! = N- Really!*** 嗳呀! 真的吗! 不会吧! 这倒吓了一跳! —*conj.* 既,既然,由于. *N- you mention it, I do remember.* 经你这样一提,我就记起来了. *N- (that) the weather is warmer, we can go outdoors.* 天气既然暖和得多,我们可以到户外去了. ***Well, ~!*** 〔口〕唷! 喂! 呵! 哟,好吧! —*n.* 〔主要用于前置词后〕此刻,目前,现在. ***by ~*** 此刻已经. ***from ~ (on, forward,*** 等) 从现在起,今后. ***till [up to] ~*** 迄今,到现在为止. —*a.* 现在的,当今的;现任的;十分时髦的,领先于潮流的,属于新一代的. **~cast** 即时预报天气〔测得天气情况后即刻预报〕. **N- Generation** "新一代"人. **-ness** 现在性.
now·a·day ['nauədei] *a.* 现今的,当今的.
now·a·days ['nauədeiz] *ad.* 现今,现时,现在. —*n.* 〔古〕当今,现在.
now·a·nights ['nauənaitz] *ad.* 〔美〕在当今的夜晚.
no·way(s), no·wise ['nəuwei(z), 'nəuwaiz] *ad.* 一点也不,决不.
Now·el, now·el ['nəuel] *n.* 〔古〕= Noel.
no·where ['nəuhwεə] *ad.* 什么地方都不到[没有]. *This book is ~ to be had.* 这本书什么地方都没有. *This telles us ~.* 这对我们毫无用处. —*n.* 无人知道的地方;没有…的地方. *He came from ~.* 他不晓得是从哪里来的. *He has ~ to go.* 他没有可去的地方. ***be [come in] ~*** 没有取胜的机会;〔俚〕差得远,大失败 *(His new novel is ~.* 他新写的小说是个大失败). ***can lead ~*** 不可能有什么前途,不可能得到什么结果. ***get us ~*** (使)我们不能有所进展[不能解决问题]. ***~ near*** 离…很远,远远没有,远不及,总不如(那么好等).
no·whith·er ['nəuhwiðə] *ad.* 〔古〕无论向何处都不.
no-win ['nəuwin] *a.* 无法取胜的.
no·wise ['nəuwaiz] *ad.* 〔古〕= noway.
nowt [naut] *n.* *(pl. sing. nowt)* 〔主苏〕牛,公牛.
Nox [nɔks] *n.*【罗神】夜之女神.
nox·ious ['nɔkʃəs] *a.* 有害的,不卫生的,有毒的;对精神上有坏影响的,使道德败坏的;引起反感的,讨厌的. *the ~ influences* 邪气,坏影响. **-ly** *ad.* **-ness** *n.*
no·yade [nwɑː'jɑːd] *n.* 溺刑,溺死刑〔如1794年法国南特(Nantes)地区把大批人淹死的处决〕.
no·yau ['nwaiəu, 'nɔiəu] *n.* 〔F.〕(白兰地加果仁精油制成的)白兰地果仁酒.
Noyes [nɔiz] *n.* 诺伊斯〔姓氏〕.
noz·zle ['nɔzl] *n.* 管嘴;喷嘴;〔俚〕鼻子. *a jet [propelling] ~*【火箭】尾喷管.
NP = ① no protest【商】未拒付(票据等). ② = noun phrase 名词短语.
N.P. = Notary Public 公证人.
Np【化】neptunium. 镎.
n.p. = ①net personalty 纯动产. ②new paragraph 新段落.
N.P.C. = National People's Congress (中国的)全国人民代表大会.
NPD = Nuclear Power Demonstration Reactor〔加拿大〕核动力示范反应堆.
NPL = National Physical Laboratory〔英〕国家物理实验所.
n.p. or d. = no place or date 出版地点或日期不详.
n-pros 〔Am.〕= nervous prostration 神经衰弱.
n.p.t. = normal pressure and temperature 常温常压.
NPT = Nonproliferation Treaty 防止核扩散条约.
N.R. = North Riding〔英〕约克郡北赖丁.
Nr. = near.
N.R.A. = ①National Rifle Association〔英〕全国步枪射击运动会. ②National Recovery Administration〔美旧〕全国(工业)复兴总署.
NRC = National Research Council〔美〕全国科学研究委员会. ②National Resources Committee〔美〕国家资源委员会.
NROTC = Naval Reserve Officers' Training Corps〔美〕海军后备军官训练队.
NRPB = National Resources Planning Board〔美〕全国资源计划委员会.
NRS = National Reemployment Service〔美〕全国再就业事务局.
NRTS = National Reactor Testing Station〔美〕国家反应堆试验站.
NS = ①nuclear ship 核动力船. ②not sufficient〔银行用语〕存款不足.
N.S.A. = National Skating Association of Great Britain 英国全国滑冰协会.
NSB = Nuclear Standards Board 核子标准委员会.
NSC = National Security Council〔美〕国家安全委员会.
NSF = National Science Foundation〔美〕国家科学基金会.
NSW = New South Wales 新南威尔士〔澳大利亚州名〕.
NT = ①*New Testament* (基督教《圣经》的)《新约全书》. ②Northern Territory 北部地区,澳北区〔澳大利亚一地区〕.
Nt【化】= niton 氡〔radon 旧称〕.
-nt *suf.* 〔拉丁语系动词 + -nt →(作形容词用的)现在分词〕: domina*nt*, pleasa*nt*, prevale*nt*.
n't [nt] *ad.* not 之略: could*n't*, did*n't*.
nth [enθ] *a.* ①第n号的,n倍的;n次的,n阶的. ②〔口〕(事物发生、使用的次数、频度)最新的,最近的. ③极度的,极大的. *This is the ~ time I've told you to eat slowly.* 吃饭要慢,至今我也不知告诉你多少回了. ***to the ~ degree [power]*** ①【数】至n次. ②高效能;最大限度,到极点,极度.
NTP = normal temperature and pressure 正常温度〔指摄氏0°〕和压力〔指760毫米水银柱〕.
NTR = Nuclear Test Reactor 核试验反应堆.

NTSC = National Television System Committee〔美〕国家电视制式委员会.

nt. wt. = net weight 净重.

nu [nju:] *n.* 希腊语的第十三字母〔N, ν; 相当于英语的 n〕.

nu·ance [nju:ˈɑ̃:ns, -ˈɔ̃:ns] *n.* *(pl.* **-s** [-iz]*)* (色彩、音调、意义、感情等的)细微差别,微差;细微的表情,神韵.

nu·anced [ˈnju:ɔnst, ˈnu:-; nju:ˈɔnst] *a.* (音调、颜色、意义等)有细微差别的.

nub [nʌb] *n.* ①(煤等的)小块;瘤子,节子. ②〔美口〕(故事的)要点;(事、问题的)核心. *That's the ~ of it.* 要点就在这里.

Nu·ba [ˈnu:bə] *n.* ①*(pl. ~(s))* 努巴人〔住在苏丹中部的黑人〕. ②努巴语.

nub·bin [ˈnʌbin] *n.* ①小块,小片. ②〔美〕玉蜀黍的小穗[发育不全的穗];发育不全的东西.

nub·ble [ˈnʌbl] *n.* 小(煤)块;瘤子,节子. **nub·bly** *a.* 多瘤的,多节的;块状的.

nub·by [ˈnʌbi] *a.* *(-bi·er; -bi·est)* 块状的;瘤多的;节多的;(表面)有结子花的. *a ~ fabric* 结子花织品. **-bi·ness** *n.*

Nu·bi·a [ˈnju:bjə] *n.* 努比亚〔非洲东北部一地区;指苏丹北部和埃及南部的沿尼罗河地带〕.

nu·bi·a [ˈnju:biə] *n.* (女用织造的)披巾.

nu·bi·form [ˈnju:bifɔ:m] *a.* 云形的.

nu·bile [ˈnju:bil, -bail] *a.* (女子)已到结婚年龄的.

nu·bil·i·ty [njuˈbiliti] *n.* (女子的)适婚性.

nu·bi·lous [ˈnju:biləs, ˈnu:-] *a.* ①多云的,多雾的. ②不明确的,模糊的.

nu·cel·lus [nju:ˈseləs, nu:-] *n.* *(pl.* **-cel·li** [-ai]*)*【植】珠心. **nu·cel·lar** *a.*

nu·cha [ˈnju:kə, ˈnu:-] *n.* *(pl.* **-chae** [-ki:]*)*【动】①项. ②(昆虫的)颈背面. **nu·chal** *a.*

nucle- *comb. f.* (= nucleo-).

nu·cle·al [ˈnju:kliəl] *a.* = nuclear.

nu·cle·ar [ˈnju:kliə] *a.* ①核的,成核的;有核的. ②【物】原子核的;原子能的;原子弹的;核动力的. ③〔喻〕核心的,中心的,主要的. ~ **bomb** 核弹. ~**-capable** *a.* 可携带核武器的. ~ **club** 核俱乐部〔有核武器国家的集团〕. ~ **deterrent** 核威慑力量. ~ **division**【生】核分裂. ~ **emulsion** 记录核轨道用的照相乳胶. ~ **energy** 核能 (= atomic energy). ~ **family** 核心家庭〔由父母与子女组成〕. ~ **fission**【物】(原子)核分裂(作用),核裂变. ~ **forces** 核力,强相互作用. ~**-free zone** 无核区. ~ **fuel** (促进原子核连锁反应的)核燃料. ~ **fusion** 核聚变;核合成. ~ **magnetic resonance** 原子核(偶)磁共振. ~ **physics** 原子核物理学. ~ **power** 核大国. ~**-powered** *a.* 核动力的. ~ **reactor** (原子)核反应堆. ~ **sap**【生】核液 (= karyolymph). ~**-tipped** *a.* 有核弹头的. ~ **warhead** 核弹头. **-ism** 核武器主义. **-ist** *n.* 核武器主义者.

nu·cle·ase [ˈnju:klieis] *n.*【生化】核酸酶.

nu·cle·ate [ˈnju:klieit] *vt., vi.* (使)成核. — [ˈnju:kliit] *a.* 具核的. **nu·cle·at·ed** *a.* 有核的,核形的. **nu·cle·a·tion** [ˌnju:kliˈeiʃən] *n.*【物、化】成核(现象);晶核过程,核子作用;集结;人工降雨作用.

nu·cle·i [ˈnju:kliai] *n.* nucleus 的复数.

nu·cle·ic [ˈnju:kli:ik] *a.* 核的. ~ *acid* 核酸.

nu·cle·in [ˈnju:klin] *n.* 核素,核蛋白质.

nucleo- *comb.f.* 〔nucleus, nuclear 以及 nucleic acid 三词有关的构词成分〕核的: *nucleo*protein.

nu·cle·o·gen·i·sis [ˌnju:kliəuˈdʒenisis] *n.* 核起源.

nu·cle·o·lar [nju:kˈli:ələ] *a.*【生】核仁的.

nu·cle·o·lat·ed, nu·cle·o·late [nju:ˈkli:əˌleitid] *a.* 有细胞核的.

nu·cle·o·lus [nju:ˈkli:ələs] *n.* *(pl.* **-li** [-lai]*)*【生】(细胞核内的)核仁.

nu·cle·o·met·er [ˌnju:kliˈɔmitə] *n.*【原】核子计.

nu·cle·on [ˈnju:kliɔn] *n.*【物、化】核子,单子.

nu·cle·on·ic [ˌnju:kliˈɔnik] *a.* 核子的.

nu·cle·on·ics [ˌnju:kliˈɔniks] *n.* 原子核物理学,核子学.

nu·cle·o·phile [ˈnju:kliəfail] *n.* 亲核试剂. **-phil·ic** [-ˈfilik] *a.* 亲核的,亲质子的.

nu·cle·o·plasm [ˈnju:kliəplæzm] *n.*【生】核原生质. **-ic** *a.*

nu·cle·o·pro·te·in [ˌnju:kli:əuˈprəuti:n; -ˈprəuti:in] *n.*【生化】核蛋白.

nu·cle·o·side [ˈnju:kliəsaid] *n.*【生化】核苷.

nu·cle·o·tide [ˈnju:kliətaid] *n.*【生化】核苷酸.

nu·cle·us [ˈnju:kliəs] *n.* *(pl.* **-es, nu·cle·i** [ˈnju:kliai]*)* 核;核心;【生】细胞核;核;【物】原子核;【化】有机化合物的原子团,环;(晶)核;【天】慧核. ~ *electron* 核电子. ~ *formation* (原子)(晶)核生成(作用).

nu·clide [ˈnju:klaid] *n.*【物】核素. **-ic** [nju:ˈklaidik] *a.*

nude [nju:d] *a.* ①裸的,裸体的;裸出的,赤裸裸的. ②(房间等)没有装饰的;光秃的;(袜子等)肉色的;没有草木的;【动、植】无鳞的,无羽毛的,无叶的. ③【法】无效的,无偿的. *a ~ contract*【法】有条件的无效契约. *a ~ matter*【法】直率的陈述. — *n.*【美】裸体画[雕像];裸体者; *the ~* 裸体(状态). ***in the ~*** 裸体的;露骨的,赤裸裸的. — *vt.* 〔罕〕使裸. ~ *it* 〔美俚〕脱光身体;实行裸体主义;加入裸体主义团体. **-ly** *ad.* **-ness** *n.*

nudge [nʌdʒ] *vt., n.* (用胳肘)轻推(促其注意);〔喻〕促…注意;接近.

nudi- [ˈnju:di] *comb. f.* 裸: *nudi*caul.

nu·di·branch [ˈnju:dibræŋk] *n.* 裸鳃亚目动物. **-bran·chi·ate** [-ˈbræŋkiit] *a., n.*

nu·di·caul [ˈnju:dikɔ:l], **nu·di·cau·lous** [ˌnjudiˈkauləs] *a.*【植】茎上无叶的,裸茎的.

nud·ie [ˈnju:di:] *n.* 〔美俚〕廉价的黄色影片[戏剧、报刊等];卖弄色相的女演员[舞女等].

nud·ism [ˈnju:dizəm] *n.* 裸体主义;裸体主义的实行.

nud·ist [ˈnju:dist] *n., a.* 裸体主义者(的).

nu·di·ty [ˈnju:diti] *n.* 裸露;裸体;〔常 *pl.*〕裸出部;【美】裸体画[像].

nud·nik [ˈnudnik] *n.* 〔美俚〕无聊的人;惹人讨厌的人.

Nu·er [ˈnu:ə] *n.* *(pl.* **Nu·ers, Nu·er***)* ①努尔人〔苏丹境内和埃塞俄比亚边界上的尼罗特人牧民〕. ②努尔语〔属东苏丹语〕.

nuf(f), 'nuf(f) [nʌf] *a., n., ad., int.* 足够 (= enough). ***nuf ced [sed]*** 〔美口〕够了! 别再说了! 说得已经够多的了! 话明白了.

nu·gae [ˈnju:gi, -dʒi] *n.* 〔*pl.*〕〔L.〕无聊的笑话;无聊事儿,琐事.

nu·ga·to·ry [ˈnju:gətəri] *a.* 琐碎的;没价值的,没用的;无效的;不起作用的.

nug·gar [ˈnʌgə] *n.* (尼罗河上游用的)大驳船.

nug·get [ˈnʌgit] *n.* ①(天然)块金;矿块;贵重的东西. ②〔美俚〕棒球. ③〔*pl.*〕〔美口〕金钱. *~s of wisdom* 至理名言;金言(集).

nui·sance [ˈnju:sns] *n.* ①使人为难的行为,讨厌[有害]的东西[行为],麻烦事情. ②讨厌[麻烦]的人. ③〔罕〕(非法)妨害,损害. *the Inspector of ~* 〔英〕取缔有碍公益的巡官. *Commit no ~.* 禁止小便! *What a ~!* 真讨厌! ***indict sb. for ~*** 控告某人非法妨害. ***make a ~ of oneself = make oneself a ~*** 被人讨厌;捣蛋. ~ **ground** 〔Can., 方〕垃圾场. ~ **parameters**【统】多余参量. ~ **raid** 扰乱性空袭;扰乱性袭击. ~ **tax** 〔美〕小额消费品税.

nuke [nju:k] *n.* 〔美俚〕①〔*pl.*〕核武器. ②核电站. — *vt.* 用核武器攻击.

Nu·kua·lo·fa [ˌnu:kuəˈlɔ:fə] *n.* 努库阿洛法〔汤加首都〕.

N.U.J. = National Union of Journalists〔英,马来西亚〕全国记者联合会.
null [nʌl] *a.* ①无效力的,无束缚力的. ②无效的,无用的,无益的;无价值的. ③没特征[个性]的,没表情的. ④〔罕〕不存在的,没有的;零(位)的;空的. — *n.*【数】零,零位;空;【无】零讯号,微弱讯号. *a* ~ *indicator* 零示器;零位指示器. *the* ~ *method* 衡消法. ~ ***and void***【律】无效;失效 (*This check is* ~ *and void.* 本支票无效). — *vt.* 使无效.
nul·lah [ˈnʌlə] *n.* (印度等地的)水道;河床;干涸的河床;山峡,峡谷.
nul·li·fi·ca·tion [ˌnʌlifiˈkeiʃən] *n.* ①无效;废弃,取消,作废. ②【美史】州对联邦法令的拒绝执行[承认].
nul·li·fid·i·an [ˌnʌliˈfidiən] *n.* 无宗教信仰的人.
nul·li·fi·er [ˈnʌlifaiə] *n.* 使…无效者,废弃者,取消者;无效论者.
nul·li·fy [ˈnʌlifai] *vt.* 使无效,废弃,毁弃;取消;使无价值;抹杀.
nul·lip·a·ra [nʌˈlipərə] *n.* (*pl.* ~*s*, ***-lip·a·rae*** [-ˈlipəriː]) 未产妇 (= nulliparity). **-lip·a·rous** [-ˈlipərəs] *a.*
nul·li·pore [ˈnʌlipɔː] *n.* 红藻科植物;珊瑚藻.
nul·li·ty [ˈnʌliti] *n.* ①无效,无效行为[证件等]. ②无,全无. ③无用的东西;废物[指人或物]. *an action of* ~【法】要求宣判契约无效的诉讼. *a* ~ *suit* 要求宣判结婚无效的诉讼.
nul·lo [ˈnʌləu] *n.*【牌戏】不拿墩〔五百分牌戏中的一种叫牌法. 叫这副牌的人没有对家. 不拿墩,只要拿墩,就要扣掉 250 分,其他对手则每墩各加 10 分〕.
Num., Numb. = Numbers.
num. = numeral(s).
numb [nʌm] *a.* 麻木的,冻僵了的 (*with*);没有[失去]感觉的,钝的. ~ *with cold* 冻僵. *a* ~ *hand*〔俚〕蠢物. — *vt.* 使失去感觉,使麻木;使冻僵. ~ **skull** = numskull. **-ly** *ad.* **-ness** *n.*
num·ber [ˈnʌmbə] *n.* ①数;数字;〔*pl.*〕算术. ②(汽车等的)号码;第…号,第…卷,第…期〔通常略作 No. (复数 Nos.),用于数字之前〕. ③伙伴;号子,囚犯. ④数目;〔*pl.*〕大批,数量上的优势,许多,若干. ⑤【乐、韵】音律,韵律;〔*pl.*〕【乐】乐谱,调子,节奏,拍子;〔*pl.*〕【诗】诗,韵文;【语法】数. ⑥〔口〕(从多数当中挑选出来的)人,物. ⑦一群人,一帮人. *cardinal* [*ordinal*] ~*s* 基[序]数. *an even* [*odd*] ~ 偶[奇]数. *a whole* [*an integral*] ~ 整数. *the acid* ~【化】酸值. *the atomic* ~ 原子序数. *a high* [*low*] ~ 大[小]数. *the science of* ~*s* 算术. *a telephone* ~ 电话号码. *the* ~ *of a car* 车号. *a dead* ~ 空号. *the April* ~ (杂志的)四月号. *Nos. 1—5* 第一号到第五号. *No. 9 (pill)*〔美军〕百宝丹,清导丸,通便丸. *He is not of our* ~. 他可不是我们中的一分子. *He is among the* ~ *of the dead.* 他也在死亡之列. *a* ~ *of books* 许多书. *a great* [*large*] ~ *of people* 很多很多的人. *the singular* [*plural*] ~ 单[复]数. ***a*** ~ ***of*** 若干;〔口〕= ~***s of*** 许多的. ***back*** ~ 过了期的一期报刊杂志;过时的人或事物;落后、顽固、反动的人物. ***by*** ~ = in ~. ***get*** [***have***] ***sb.'s***〔美俚〕对某人的性格,动机等作确实的估价. ***have sb.'s*** ~ ***on it***〔美俚〕注定是某人死亡的原因. ***in*** ~ 总共;用数字表示,在数字上. ***in*** ~***s*** (杂志等)分为数册,分数次 (*The story is issued in* ~*s.* 那部小说是分册出版的). ***in round*** ~***s*** 以整数[约数]表示;约莫,大概;总而言之. ***lose the*** ~ ***of one's mess***〔英海军行话〕死,"报销". ***make up by*** ~***s*** 以多为胜. ~ ***one*** ①头号(的),第一流(的). ②〔口〕自已;自已的利益 (*take care of* [*look after*] ~ *one* 替自已打算). ③〔口〕小便. ~***s pool*** 猜数字小赌博. ***One's*** ~ ***is up.***〔俚〕某人劫数[死期]已到. ***one's*** ~ ***two*** 副手,副职,接班人. ***one's opposite*** ~ 对等的人[物]. ***out of*** [***without***] ~***(s)*** 无数的. ***the*** ~***s*** = ~s pool. ***There are*** ~***s who ...,*** …的人很多. ***to the*** ~ ***of ...*** 多到. ***win by (force of)*** ~***s*** 靠人多得胜. ***without*** [***beyond***] ~ = out of ~. — *vt.* ①给…编号[记号数,加号码]. ②达…之数,共计…,(人口)有…. ③算入…(数)内;认为 (*among; in; with*). ④〔主用被动形〕已有限定,有限;〔古,雅〕数,计算. ⑤活了…岁,足…岁. *The guests* ~ *20.* 客人有二十位. *His days are* ~*ed.* 他(在世)的日子不多了. — *vi.* 算在…数内;计;报数. ~ ***off***〔上操〕报数;〔口令〕号码! ~ **dummy**〔美俚〕①(旅馆)服务员. ②(铁路)调度员. ~**ing machine** 号码机,编码机. ~ **plate** 号码牌. ***N- Ten*** 唐宁街 10 号〔英国首相官邸,用以指英国政府〕. **-er** *n.* 编号人;计数员.
num·ber·less [ˈnʌmbəlis] *a.* ①数不清的,无数的. ②无号码的.
Num·bers [ˈnʌmbəz] *n.*【圣】民数纪〔= *the book of* ~,略 *Num.* 或 *Numb.*〕.
numb·fish [ˈnʌmfiʃ] *n.*【鱼】电鳗,电鳐.
num·bles [ˈnʌmblz] *n. pl.*〔古〕鹿内脏.
num·dah [ˈnʌmdɑː] *n.* 毡子鞍垫.
nu·men [ˈnjuːmən, ˈnuː-] *n.* (*pl.* ***-mi·na*** [-minə]) ①【罗神】守护神. ②引导力量[精神].
nu·mer·a·ble [ˈnjuːmərəbl] *a.* 可(计)数的.
nu·mer·al [ˈnjuːmərəl] *a.* 数的;表示数的. — *n.* ①数字;【语法】数词〔*pl.*〕. ②〔美〕(因体育运动成绩优异奖给学校中班级的)荣誉年号. *Roman* ~*s* 罗马数字. *the cardinal* [*ordinal*] ~*s* 基数[序数]词.
nu·mer·a·ry [ˈnjuːmərəri] *a.* 数的,与数有关的.
nu·mer·ate [ˈnjuːməreit] *vt.* ①数点;计算. ②(按照命数法)读数. — *a.*〔美〕有丰富思维能力的.
nu·mer·a·tion [ˌnjuːməˈreiʃən] *n.* 计算;读数;【数】命数法;读数法. *the* ~ *table* 数字表.
nu·mer·a·tor [ˈnjuːməreitə] *n.* ①【数】(分数的)分子. ②计算者. ③计数器[管];示号器,回转号码机.
nu·mer·ic [njuːˈmerik] *n.*【数】数,数字;分数;不可通约的比例. — *a.* = numerical.
nu·mer·i·cal [nju(ː)ˈmerikəl] *a.* 数字的;数值的;用数字表示的. *(a)* ~ *order* 号数. *a* ~ *statement* 统计. *the* ~ *strength* 人数,兵数. ~ **control**【计】(利用穿孔带对机械操作进行的)数字控制,数控. ~ **notation**【乐】数字记谱法;简谱. **-ly** *ad.* 用数字,在数字上.
nu·mer·ol·o·gy [ˌnjuːməˈrɔlədʒi, ˌnuː-] *n.* 算八字术,占八卦.
nu·mer·o·scope [ˈnjuːmərəskəup] *n.* 示数器;数字记录器.
nu·mer·ous [ˈnjuːmərəs] *a.* ①〔修饰单数集合名词〕由多数人形成的,人数多的. *a* ~ *army* 一支庞大的军队. *a* ~ *class* 学生人数多的一个班. ②〔修饰复数名词〕许多的,大群的,大批的. ~ *errors* 许许多多错误. ③〔罕〕多数人们的. ④〔古、诗〕和谐的,有节奏的. **-ly** *ad.* **-ness** *n.*
num·head [ˈnʌmhed] *n.*〔美〕= numskull.
Nu·mid·i·a [njuːˈmidiə] *n.* 努米底亚〔北非一古国,其位置相当于现代的阿尔及利亚〕.
Nu·mid·i·an [njuːˈmidiən] *a.* 努米底亚人的,努米底亚语的. — *n.* ①努米底亚人. ②努米底亚语. ~ **crane** 蓑羽鹤 (= demoiselle).
nu·min·ous [ˈnjuːminəs] *a.* ①超自然的;神秘的;神圣的,精神上的. ②使人深受精神影响的.
numis. = numismatics.
nu·mis·mat·ic, nu·mis·mat·i·cal [ˌnjuːmizˈmætik, -ikəl] *a.* 货币的;古钱的;金属徽章的;钱币学的.
nu·mis·mat·ics [ˌnjuːmisˈmætiks] *n. pl.*〔作单数用〕钱币学,古钱学;徽章学.
nu·mis·ma·tist [njuːˈmizmətist] *n.* 古钱学家;钱币研究家.
nu·mis·ma·tol·o·gy [njuːˌmizməˈtɔlədʒi] *n.* = numismatics.

num·mary [ˈnʌməri] *a.* 关于钱币的；有关货币的．
num·met [ˈnʌmit] *n.* 〔英方〕午餐 (lunch)．
num·mu·lar [ˈnʌmjulə] *a.* ①硬通货形的．②有关货币的 (= nummary)．
num·mu·lite [ˈnʌmjulait] *n.* 【古生】货币化石贝．
num·mu·lit·ic [ˌnʌmjuˈlitik] *a.* 【古生】货币虫的；钱币虫属的．
num·nah [ˈnʌmnɑː] *n.* = numdah.
num·skull [ˈnʌmskʌl] *n.* 〔口〕笨蛋；笨脑瓜．
nun [nʌn] *n.* ①修女，尼姑．②【鸟】修女(品种)家鸽；【虫】毛松虫白蛾．～*'s cloth* 【纺】修女黑色薄呢．～*'s thread* 【纺】细白线．～*'s veiling* 【纺】修女薄纱．～ **buoy** 【海】纺锤形浮标．**-hood** *n.* 修女的身分．**-like, -nish** *a.* 修女似的；温和的；贞洁的；规矩的．
Nunc Dim·it·tis [ˈnʌŋk diˈmitis] 〔L.〕 ①【圣】用"西面祷词" (Simeon) 开头的颂歌〔路加福音 2 章 29—32 节，俱以"安然去世"等语开头〕；辞别．②〔n- d-〕告别，离去；去世．*sing one's nunc dimittis* 含笑辞别〔安然去世〕．
nun·ci·a·ture [ˈnʌnʃiətʃə] *n.* ①罗马教皇使节的职位〔任期〕．②罗马教皇使团．
nun·ci·o [ˈnʌnʃiəu] *n.* *(pl. ～s)* ①罗马教皇的大使．②使者．
nun·cle [ˈnʌŋkl] *n.* 〔古、方〕 = uncle.
nun·cu·pate [ˈnʌŋkjupeit] *vt.* 口述(遗嘱、证词等)．**-pation** [ˌnʌŋkjuˈpeiʃən] *n.* 口述．**-pa·tive, -pa·to·ry** *a.* 【法】口头的，口述的．
nun·na·tion, nun·a·tion [nʌˈneiʃən] *n.* 名词后缀上加 "n" 的变化〔如阿拉伯语的名词变化〕．
nun·ner·y [ˈnʌnəri] *n.* 女修道院；尼庵．
nu·per·ca·ine [ˈnjuːpəkein] *n.* 【药】奴白卡因．
nu·phar [ˈnjuːfə] *n.* 【植】黄睡莲．
nu·plex [ˈnjuːpleks] *n.* 核动力综合企业．
nup·tial [ˈnʌpʃəl] *a.* ①结婚的，婚姻的；婚礼的．②【动】交配期所特有的．*a ～ ceremony* 婚礼．*a ～ flight* (蜂等)的婚飞．— *n.* 〔*pl.*〕婚礼．～ **plumage** (某些鸟)在交配期所长的羽毛．
N.U.R. = National Union of Railwaymen〔英〕全国铁路工人联合会．
Nu·rem·berg [ˈnjuərəmbəːg] **Nürn·berg** [德 ˈnyrnbəːk] *n.* 纽伦堡〔西德城市〕．
nurse[1] [nəːs] *n.* ①奶妈〔通常叫 wet ～〕；保姆〔通常叫 dry ～〕；阿妈 (= ～-maid)；保育员．②护士，看护．③保护人；培养者；养成所，发祥地 *(of)*．④【植】保护树；【虫】保护虫，保育虫；【动】世代交替的无性期的个体．*at* ～ 交奶妈〔保姆〕领养中．***put out to*** ～ 托人喂养，寄养．***under a ～'s charge*** 交给奶妈领着．— *vt.* ①喂奶，带养(婴儿、幼兽)．②看护，照料(病人)．③小心管理；爱惜，小心使用；养；培养；养成，助成．④抱(希望等)．⑤〔英〕讨好(选举区民等)；爱抚；抱，搂抱．⑥【台球】将(球)凑拢．～ *a baby* 喂孩子奶．～ *a horse* (不使过劳地)爱惜用马．～ *a cat* 怀抱着猫．～ *one's knees* 抱着膝盖．*be ～d in luxury*受娇养．～ *a plant* 培养植物．～ *a hatred* 怀恨．～ *the fire* 靠着火不离开．— *vi.* 看护，照料；喂奶；(小孩)吃奶．～ **balloon** 【空】补助气囊．～ **cell** 营养细胞；滋卵细胞．～ **child** 养子．～ **crops** 保护作物．～ **frog** 【动】产婆蛙．～**girl,** ～**maid** 照看孩子的年轻保姆．～**-keeper** 看护．～ **ship** (英国海军保护鱼雷艇，潜水艇等的)母舰．
nurse[2] [nəːs] *n.* 【动】角鲨．
nurse·ling [ˈnəːsliŋ] *n.* ①(特指奶妈领养的)婴儿．②爱儿，珍爱的东西；【植】苗木．
nurs·er [ˈnəːsə] *n.* ①奶妈，抚养人．②培育者，赞助者．③奶瓶．
nurs·er·y [ˈnəːsəri] *n.* ①托儿所，育儿室．②苗床，苗圃；养鱼场；动物养殖场．③养成所．④【台球】集拢一起的球．*a day* ～ 日间托儿所．*a bush* ～ 临时苗圃．～ **garden** 苗圃．～ **governess** 兼做保姆的家庭教师，保育员．～**maid** = nursemaid. ～**man** 园丁，花圃工、苗木培养工．～ **noodle** 〔美俚〕一本正经的批评家．～ **rhyme [song]** 童谣，儿歌．～ **room** 育婴室．～ **school** 幼儿园．～ **tale** 童话．
nurs·ey, nurs·ie [ˈnəːsi] *n.* 〔儿〕阿妈．
nurs·ing [ˈnəːsiŋ] *a.* 领养(孩子)的；被领养的．— *n.* (职业性的)保育；护理．*the ～ father [mother]* 养父〔母〕．～ *profession* 护士业．*take up ～ as a career* 就任护士工作．～ **bottle** 奶瓶．～ **home** 私人疗养所；〔英〕小型私人医院．
nurs·ling [ˈnəːsliŋ] *n.* = nurseling.
nur·ture [ˈnəːtʃə] *n.* ①养育；培育，训练，教养．②营养物，食物．③环境因素．*nature and ～* 本性和教养，遗传和环境．— *vt.* 养育，培育；教养；给…营养．**-r** *n.* 养育者；营养物．
N.U.S. = National Union of Students. 全国学生联合会．
N.U.T. = National Union of Teachers. 〔英〕全国教师联合会．
nut [nʌt] *n.* ①坚果〔核桃、榛、栗等的果实〕；坚果果仁．②难事，难题；难对付的人．③【机】螺帽，螺母；【乐】弓根〔收紧弓弦的装置〕．④〔美俚〕脑袋；笨蛋，傻瓜；疯子，怪人；觉得好〔有趣〕的东西．⑤〔罕〕花花公子，纨袴子．⑥〔*pl.*〕小煤块 (*cf.* nuts)．*grass [ground, earth]* ～ (落)花生．⑦【乐】(弦乐器的)琴马；⑧【印】对开．*I have a ～ to crack with you.* 我有事要和你讨论．*It's the ～s.* 〔美俚〕这倒不错．***a hard ～ (to crack)*** 难事，难题；难对付的人．***a tough*** ～ 〔俚〕有胆量的人；横蛮的家伙．***be (dead) ～s on*** 〔俚〕极喜欢，极爱，是…迷；是…的能手，精通．***be ～s to [for]*** 〔俚〕是…极喜欢的东西．***do one's ～(s)*** 〔英俚〕象疯子般行动．***don't care a (rotten)*** ～ 毫不在乎．***for ～s*** 〔俚〕〔和否定语同用〕一点(不)，怎么也(不) (*I can't play golf for ～s.* 我怎么也打不来高尔夫球)．***off one's*** ～ 神经有点不正常，有点疯狂；酩酊大醉 (*go off one's ～* 失去理智；发狂)．***on the*** ～ 〔美〕分文没有的．— *vi.* 采坚果，拾核果．*go nutting* 去拾核果．～**burger** 〔美〕碎果肉饼〔排〕．～**-brown** *a.* 深栗色的 (尤指少女、啤酒的颜色等)．～ **butter** (坚)果仁酱〔黄油的代用品〕．～**cake** 〔美〕①油煎圈饼 (=doughunt)．②果仁蛋糕．～ ***college [factory, foundry]*** 〔美俚〕疯人院，精神病院．～ **cracker** 〔常 *pl.*〕 ①轧碎坚果的钳子；核桃夹子．②【鸟】星鸟．③(因牙齿脱落等) 下巴和鼻子挤在一块的脸，瘪嘴脸 (*a ～cracker face*)．④〔美俚〕不受欢迎的人(尤指女人)．～**gall** 五倍子，没食子．～ **hatch** 【鸟】鸸，五十雀．～ **house** = ～ college. ～ **meat** 坚果仁，核仁．～ **oil** 坚果油；核桃油；桐油．～**pick** *n.* ①剔取坚果仁的扦子．②〔美俚〕精神病医生．～**s and bolts** 主要特点；基本组成部分．～ **tree** 坚果树，(尤指)榛．
nu·tant [ˈnjuːtənt] *a.* 【植】俯垂的，点垂的．
nu·tate [njuːˈteit] *vi.* 【植】(茎等)俯垂，下垂．
nu·ta·tion [njuːˈteiʃən] *n.* ①垂头，下垂，下俯；点头．②【植】转头(运动)，旋转性．③【机、天】章动〔轴的微动〕．④【医】点头病．～ **angle** 【无】(雷达的)盘旋角．
nut·let [ˈnʌtlit] *n.* ①小坚果．②樱桃核，桃核；李属核．③子房，细裂片．
nut·meg [ˈnʌtmeg] *n.* ①【植】肉豆蔻(树)．②〔美〕自负不凡的蠢货〔又叫 gilded ～〕．③〔N-〕〔美〕康涅狄格 (Connecticut) 州的别名 (= N- State)．～ **apple** 肉豆蔻的果实．～ **liver** 【医】豆蔻肝．～ **tree** 肉豆蔻树．
nut·meg·gers [ˈnʌtmegəz] *n.* 〔*pl.*〕〔美〕康涅狄格州人的别名．
nu·tri·a [ˈnjuːtriə] *n.* (南美)海狸鼠；海狸鼠毛皮．
nu·tri·ent [ˈnjuːtriənt] *a.* 营养的，滋养的 —*n.* 营养物，营养品，养分，养料；营养剂．～ *broth* 肉汁．～ *medium* 培养基．
nu·tri·ment [ˈnjuːtrimənt] *n.* 营养物，食物．**-al** *a.* =

nutrient.
nu·tri·tion [nju:ˈtriʃən] *n.* ①营养(作用),滋养. ②营养物,食物;【农】追肥. **-al** *a.* 营养的;营养物的;食物的. **-ally** *ad.* 在营养上. **-ist** *n.* 营养学[专]家.
nu·tri·tious [nju:ˈtriʃəs] *a.* 有营养的,滋养的. **-ly** *ad.* **-ness** *n.*
nu·tri·tive [ˈnju:tritiv] *a.* (关于)营养的. — *n.* 富于营养的食物. **-ness** *n.*
nuts [nʌts] *a.* 〔美俚〕笨的,蠢的;发疯的;狂热的;忙乱的. — *int.* 呸! 不见得! 废话! 胡扯! 混蛋! 〔表示讨厌、失望、拒绝、不赞成、藐视、不相信〕. ***be (dead) ~ on, be ~ over [about]*** ①热爱着;狂热于. ②精通…的.
nut·shell [ˈnʌt-ʃel] *n.* ①坚果的外壳. ②极小的容器;窄小的房屋. ③没有价值的东西,无聊的东西;小数量的东西. ④最简单扼要的表现法,大要. ***in a ~*** 用一句话概括起来,极简单地,在极小范围内 (*I can give it you in a ~*. 我可以用几句话加以说明). ***lie in a ~*** 简单明了,容易理解;一言可尽,容易解决 (*The whole thing lay in a ~*. 一切都非常简单明了). — *a.* 〔美〕简洁的,扼要的.
nut·ted [ˈnʌtid] *a.* 安上螺帽的,用螺帽固定的;〔美〕没考取的.
nut·ter [ˈnʌtə] *n.* 拾坚果的人;〔英俚〕古怪的人.
nut·ting [ˈnʌtiŋ] *n.* 采拾坚果.
nut·ty [ˈnʌti] *a.* ①有许多坚果的,生坚果的. ②有坚果味的;美味的;愉快的;内容充实的. ③〔俚〕古怪的;傻的;发疯的;有神经病的;可笑的;愚蠢的. ④〔俚〕潇洒的,漂亮的. ⑤〔俚〕狂热于…的,迷恋着…的 *(on; upon)*. **-ti·ness.**
nux [nʌks] *n.* 〔美俚〕茶.
nux vom·i·ca [ˈnʌks ˈvɔmikə] 【植】马钱子,番木鳖〔产于东印度〕;马钱子的种子.
nuz·zle [ˈnʌzl] *vt.* ①将鼻突入;用鼻子掘;用鼻子擦[触]. ②紧挨,抱抚(示爱). — *vi.* ①用鼻子掘洞;用鼻子擦[触] *(into; against)*;用鼻子闻. ②舒舒服服地蜷卧,挨紧着躺. ***~ oneself*** 使紧挨着…[舒服地]躺着.
N.W., NW, n.w. = northwest; northwestern.
NWA = Northwest Airlines 〔美〕西北航空公司.
N-War = nuclear war 核战争.
NWbN, NW by N = northwest by north 西北偏北.
NWbW, NW by W = northwest by west 西北偏西.
N.W.T. = North-West Territories 〔加拿大〕西北地区.
n. wt. = net weight 净重.
N.Y., NY = New York 纽约〔美国州名〕;纽约(市)〔美国城市〕.
nya·la [ˈnjɑːlə] *n. (pl. -la, ~s)* 捻角羚属动物〔东非所产的一种羚〕.
N.Y.C., NYC = New York City 纽约(市)〔美国城市〕.
nyc·ta·lo·pi·a [ˌniktəˈləupiə] *n.* 【医】夜盲(症) *(opp.* hemeralopia*)*. **-lop·ic** *a.*
nyc·tan·thous [nikˈtænθəs] *a.* (花)夜开的.
nyc·ti·nas·ty [ˌniktiˈnæsti] *n.* 【植】感夜性.
nyc·ti·trop·ic [ˌniktiˈtrɔpik] *a.* 【植】(树叶)感夜的,夜间变更方向的.
nyc·to·pho·bi·a [ˌniktəˈfəubiə] *n.* 【医】黑夜恐怖.
Nye [nai] *n.* 奈〔姓氏〕.
nyet [njet] *ad.* 〔Russ.〕不. **~ diplomacy** 否决外交(指苏联常在联合国安理会运用否决权的做法).
nyl·ghau, nyl·ghai [ˈnilgau, -gɔː, -gai] *n.* 【动】印度大羚羊.
ny·lon [ˈnailən] *n.* ①【纺】尼龙,耐纶. ②〔*pl.*〕〔口〕尼龙长袜. *~ hose* 尼龙长袜.
nymph [nimf] *n.* ①【希神】宁芙〔半神半人的少女〕;〔诗〕美少女. ②【虫】若虫. **-al** *a.* **-like** *a.*
nym·pha [ˈnimfə] *n. (pl. -phæ* [-fiː]*)* ①【虫】若虫. ②〔*pl.*〕【解】小阴唇.
nym·pha·lid [ˈnimfəlid] *n.* 蛱蝶科动物. — *a.* 蛱蝶科的.
nym·phe·an [nimˈfiːən], **nymph·ish** [-fiʃ] *a.* 宁芙女神(似)的.
nymph·et [ˈnimfət, nimˈfet] *n.* 进入青春期的姑娘. **-ic** *a.*
nym·pho·lep·sy [ˈnimfəlepsi] *n.* ①(想得到不可得到之物的)狂乱;入迷;妄想狂;【医】情欲增盛. ②【医】小阴唇切除术. **-pho·lept** *n.* 狂乱者;狂热者. **-pho·lep·tic** [ˌnimfəˈleptik] *a.* 狂乱的;热狂的;妄想的.
nym·pho·ma·ni·a [ˌnimfəˈmeiniə] *n.* 【医】女子色狂,慕男狂,花癫,花痴. **-ni·ac** *a., n.* 慕男狂患者(的).
nys·tag·mic [nisˈtægmik] *a.* 【医】眼球震颤(症)的.
nys·tag·mus [nisˈtægməs] *n.* 【医】眼球震颤(症).
nys·ta·tin [ˈnistətin] *n.* 【药】制霉菌素.
NYT = *New York Times* 〔美〕《纽约时报》.
Nyx [niks] *n.* 【希神】夜之女神.
NZ = ①New Zealand 新西兰. ②New Zealand National Airways Corporation 新西兰国家航空公司.

O

O[1], o [əu] *(pl.* **O's, o's**[əuz]*)* ①英语字母表第十五字母. ②一系列中之第十五. ③ O 字形物;圆. ④【数】零. *a round O,* 圆.
O[2] [əu] *int.* 〔常用大写字母〕哦! 哟! …啊! 唉! 哎呀〔表示惊讶、恐怖、赞叹、愿望等〕. *O for a rest!* 唉! 休息休息才好! *O Life!* 啊,生活! *O! Mr. John!* 唷,原来是约翰先生. ***O dear (me)!*** 哎呀! 哎唷! ***O that*** …〔诗〕但愿…!
O., o. = ①old. ②Observer. ③Ocean. ④October. ⑤Ohio. ⑥Oregon. ⑦off. ⑧only. ⑨order. ⑩officer. ⑪*octarius* 〔L.〕品脱(容量单位). ⑫ohm 【物】欧姆(电阻单位).
o' = ①= of: seven o'clock 七点钟. man-o'-war 军舰. ②〔方〕= on: o'nights 晚上.
O' [ə, o] *pref.* 用于爱尔兰人姓前,表示"某人之后裔"(son *of*)之意: O'Conner.
O- *pref.* 〔用于m之前〕= ob-: omit.
-o- *comb. f.* 〔构成复合词〕本来只用于来自希腊语复合词,现在广泛用于科学术语(等)上;用法: ①第一要素修饰第二要素: Franc*o*-British. ②第一第二要素为同位: Russ*o*-Janpanese war. ③构成带有 *-cracy, -logy, -meter* 等希腊系词尾的派生词: techn*o*cracy, techn*o*logy, speed*o*meter.
o/a = on account 作为部分付款.
OA = Omni-Antenna 全向天线.
OAAPS = Organization for Afro-Asian People's Solidarity 亚非人民团结组织.
o.a.d. = overall dimension 全尺寸,外廓尺寸.

oaf [əuf] *n.* *(pl. ~s; oaves* [əuvz]*)* ①〔古〕换孩〔妖魔换置的丑小孩〕. ②畸形儿; 痴儿. ③白痴; 半傻子, 呆子.

oaf·ish [ˈəufiʃ] *a.* 畸形儿 (oaf) 似的; 痴呆的; 丑陋的.

O·a·hu [əuˈɑːhuː] *n.* 瓦胡岛〔美国夏威夷群岛中的重要岛屿〕.

Oak [əuk] *n., int., vt.* = O.K.

oak [əuk] *n.* ①栎树, 橡, 柽, 槲; 栎木, 栎叶; 栎树嫩叶色. ②〔英大学〕坚牢的(栎木)大门. ③栎木家具[木器]. ④〔诗〕木船. — *a.* 栎(木制的). *an ~ table* 栎木桌子. ***a heart of ~*** 坚忍不拔的人, 勇士. ***~ may fall when reeds stand the storm.*** 〔谚〕树大招风. ***sports one's ~*** 〔英、大学生俚〕闭门谢客. ***the hearts of Oak***【英海军】军舰和水兵. **~ apple, ~ gall** 栎五倍子. **~-leaf cluster** 橡叶簇铜质奖章〔美空军或陆军的一种奖章, 银质者等于五个铜质者〕. **~ leather** 栎树皮鞣革. **O-Ridge** 橡树岭〔美国市镇, 为原子能研究中心〕. **~ wilt**【植病】橡萎蔫病.

oak·en [ˈəukən] *a.* 〔古、诗〕栎(木制)的.

Oak·land [ˈəuk-lənd] *n.* 奥克兰〔美国港市〕.

oak·let, oak·ling [ˈəuklit, -liŋ] *n.* 栎树苗; 小栎树.

Oak·ley [ˈəukli] *n.* 〔美俚〕 = Annie ~.

oa·kum [ˈəukəm] *n.*【海】填絮, 麻絮. *pick ~* (从前让囚犯、穷人从事的)拆麻絮.

o.a.o. = off and on 断断续续.

OAO = orbiting astronomical observatory 天体观测卫星.

OAPEC = Organization of the Arab Petroleum Exporting Countries 阿拉伯石油输出国组织.

oar [ɔː, ɔə] *n.* ①桨; 橹. ②桨手, 划手. ③划子, 船. ④桨状物, 桨状器官〔翼、鳍、腕等〕. *This boat pulls [rows] six ~s* 这只船用六把桨划. *a pair [an eight] ~* 双桨[八桨]船. *a good [bad] ~* 好[笨]桨手. ***be chained to the ~*** 被强迫做苦工. ***bend to the ~s*** 用力划桨. ***boat the ~s*** 停划收桨. ***have an ~ in every man's boat*** 任何人的事情都要插手干涉, 爱管闲事. ***have the labouring ~*** 担任苦活, 负担工作中最繁重或最艰苦的部分. ***peak the ~s*** 高举桨尾(出水中). ***pull a good ~*** 划得一手好桨. ***pull a lone ~*** 独自干. ***put [thrust] one's ~ in*** 干预; 多管闲事. ***rest [lie] on one's ~s*** 搁桨停划; (暂时)歇一歇; 吃老本. ***ship [unship] an ~*** 上[下]桨. ***take [have, pull] the labouring ~*** 担任苦活. ***toss the ~s*** 举桨(敬礼). ***trail the ~s*** 任桨随水漂流. — *vi., vt.* 〔诗〕划, 荡(桨); 象桨一样摆动(手等). *~ one's way* 划桨前进.

oar·age [ˈɔːridʒ] *n.* 〔诗〕划桨, 划艇; 划具.

oared [ɔːd] *a.* 有(…)桨的. *two-~* 双桨的.

oar·fish [ˈɔːfiʃ] *n.* *(pl. ~(es))* 皇带鱼属 *(Regalecus)* 动物.

oar·lock [ˈɔːlɔk] *n.* U 形桨架.

oars·man [ˈɔːzmən] *n.* (划船比赛中的)划手; 划桨能手. **~ship** *n.* 划船法; 划船本领.

oars·wom·an [ˈɔːzwumən] *n.* 女划手.

oar·y [ˈɔːri] *a.* 〔诗〕有桨的, 桨状的.

OAS = Organization of American States 美洲国家组织.

O.A.S. = on active service 服现役.

oa·sis [əuˈeisis] *n.* *(pl. oa·ses* [-siːz]*)* ①(沙漠中的)绿洲; (不毛之地中的)沃洲; 宜人的地方. ②慰藉物. *He worked hard six days a week and looked forward to his day off as an ~ of rest and relaxation.* 他一星期艰苦工作六天, 盼望有个假日, 作为憩歇和轻松的慰藉.

oast [əust] *n.* (烘麦芽等的)烘炉, 烤房, 干燥室.

oat [əut] *n.* ①〔常 *pl.*〕【植】燕麦, 雀麦. ★ oats 是马的饲料, 人吃的叫 oatmeal. ②〔常作 *pl.*, 用作单或复〕燕麦田; 燕麦种子. ③〔常作 *pl.*, 用作单〕= ~meal. ④〔诗〕麦笛, 牧笛; 牧歌. — *a.* 燕麦做的; (燕麦)麦秆做的. ***be off one's ~s*** 没有胃口. ***feel one's [its] ~s*** (吃了燕麦的马)活泼地跳来跳去; 〔美俚〕(人)自负, 得意起来; 〔美俚〕精神饱满, 热情洋溢. ***smell one's ~s*** (马)快起来; (人)振奋起来. ***sow one's wild ~s*** 干年轻人的荒唐事; (年轻时)放荡; 浪费青春. **~-cake** 燕麦饼. **~ grass**【植】燕麦草属植物. **~meal** 燕麦粉; 燕麦片; 燕麦粥. **~ opera** = oater.

oat·en [ˈəutn] *a.* 〔诗〕= oat *(a.)*. *~ cakes* 燕麦饼. *an ~ pipe* 麦笛, 牧笛.

oat·er [ˈəutə] *n.* 〔美俚〕西部电影[电视节目].

Oates [əuts] *n.* 奥茨〔姓氏〕.

oath [əuθ] *n.* *(pl. oaths* [əuðz]*)* ①誓言, 誓约;【法】宣誓. ②(咒骂、强调、发怒等时的)妄用神名; 渎神的言词; 诅咒; 咒骂语〔God damn you! 之类〕. *an ~ of allegiance* 效忠宣誓. *an ~ of office = an official ~* 就职宣誓. *a false ~* 伪誓. ***grind out an ~*** 切齿诅咒. ***make an ~*** 立誓, 宣誓. ***on [upon, under] ~ = (up)on my ~*** 发誓, 必定. ***put*** *(sb.)* ***on*** *(his)* ***~*** 使(某人)立誓. ***take [swear] an ~*** = make ~. ***take one's ~ that ...*** 立誓说…是千真万确的.

-oate *comb. f.* 表示有 ester (酯)存在的化学合物: benz*oate.*

OAU = Organization of African Unity 非洲统一组织.

Ob [əub, ɔːb] *n.* (西伯利亚的)鄂毕河.

ob- *pref.* 表示下列诸义. ①对面, 颠倒(方向): *ob*lique, *of*fer. ②阻碍: *ob*stacle. ③反对, 抵抗: *ob*stinate, *op*pose· ④抑压: *op*press. ⑤隐蔽; *ob*fuscate, *ob*scure. ★ 在 m, c, f, g, p, t 前分别变为 o-, oc-, of-, og-, op-, os-.

O.B. 〔Am.〕 = obie.

ob. = ①〔L.〕*obiit.* ②〔L.〕*obiter.* ③oboe.

O·ba·di·ah [ˌəubəˈdaiə] *n.* ①奥巴代亚〔男子名〕. ②《俄巴底亚书》〔基督教《圣经》中旧约的一卷〕.

ob·bli·ga·to [ˌɔbliˈgɑːtəu] *a.* 〔It.〕【乐】(伴奏)不可缺少的, 必要的〔但现在通常指可以省略的伴奏〕. — *n.* *(pl. ~s, -ga·ti* [-ˈgɑːtiː]*)* 伴奏.

ob·bo [ˈɔbəu] *n.* 〔美〕观测气球.

ob·con·ic, ob·con·i·cal [ɔbˈkɔnik, -əl] *a.*【植】倒圆锥状的.

ob·cor·date [ɔbˈkɔːdeit] *a.*【植】(叶子)倒心形的.

obdt. = obedient.

ob·du·ra·cy [ˈɔbdjurəsi, ɔbˈdjuː-] *n.* 顽固, 执拗; 冷酷.

ob·du·rate [ˈɔbdjurit] *a.* 顽固的, 执拗的; 冷酷的. **-ly** *ad.* **-ness** *n.*

O.B.E., OBE = ①Officer (of the Order) of the British Empire (获得帝国勋章的)英国军官. ②Office of Business Economics (美国商业部)商业经济管理局.

o·beah [ˈəubiə] *n.* (非洲、西印度群岛等地某些黑人中曾行使的)一种巫术; (作这种巫术时使用的)神物.

o·be·di·ence [əˈbiːdjəns, -diəns] *n.* ①服从; 遵守; 忠顺; 〔古〕(国王等的)属下. ②【天主】归依; 〔集合词〕管区的信徒; (教会的)权威, 管辖; 管区. *filial ~* 孝顺. *humble ~* 恭顺. *blind ~* 盲从. *the Roman ~* 天主教信徒. ***hold sb. in ~*** 使某人服从. ***in ~ to*** 遵从, 服从. ***reduce to ~*** 使服从.

o·be·di·ent [əˈbiːdjənt, -diənt] *a.* 服从的, 顺从的, 忠顺的, 孝顺的, 驯良的. ***be ~ to*** 顺从, 遵奉. ***Your (most) ~ servant*** 您的恭顺的仆人; 谨启(等)〔信尾用语〕. **-ly** *ad.* *(Yours obediently [Obediently yours] = Yours ~ servant).*

o·bei·sance [əuˈbeisns] *n.* 〔古〕①敬礼〔如鞠躬、屈膝礼等〕. ②尊敬, 服从. ***do [make, pay] ~ to*** 向…表示敬意. ***make an ~ to*** 向…致敬礼.

ob·e·lisk [ˈɔbilisk] *n.* ①(埃及的)方尖塔[碑], 方尖碑形物〔山峰、树木等〕; 火山柱. ②【印】剑号 (†); (古代写本中的)疑问记号〔— 或 ÷〕. *a double ~*【印】双剑号 (‡).

ob·e·lize [ˈɔbilaiz] *vt.* 在…上加剑号[问号].

ob·e·lus [ˈɔbiləs] *n.* *(pl.* **-li** [-lai]*)* = obelisk.

O·ber·on [ˈəubərən] *n.* ①【中世神话】奥白龙〔Titania 的丈夫,小仙女的王〕. ②【天】天王卫四(星). ③〔o-〕〔俚〕控制炸弹的雷达系统.

o·bese [əuˈbiːs] *a.* 肥胖的,肥大的.

o·bese·ness, o·be·si·ty [əuˈbiːsnis, əuˈbisiti] *n.* 肥胖,肥大;【医】肥胖症;多脂.

o·bey [əˈbei] *vt.* ①服从,听(人家的)话;遵守(命令等);照(命令). ②听由,随(理性等)行动;任(冲动等)摆布. ~ *one's parents* 听父母的话. *A ship ~s her helm.* 船随舵行动. — *vi.* 服从;听话.

ob·fus·cate [ˈɔbfʌskeit] *vt.* ①使暗淡;使模糊. ②使糊涂,使迷,使困惑. **-ca·tion** [ˌɔbfʌsˈkeiʃən] *n.*

ob·fus·ti·cate [əbˈfʌstikeit] *vt.* 〔美〕使困惑,使为难.

o·bi [ˈəubi] *n.* ① = obeah. ②(日本妇女系和服用的)宽腰带.

o·bie [ˈəubiː] *n.* 〔美口〕邮局.

ob·i·it [ˈɔbiit] *vi.* 〔L.〕卒,逝世. 〔第三人称单数过去,略为 ob.,用于死亡年月前〕. ob. 1920 卒于一九二〇年.

o·bit [ˈɔbit, ˈəubit] *n.* 〔古〕葬礼;〔古〕(周年)祭奠;〔美〕 = obituary.

ob·i·ter [ˈɔbitə] *ad.* 〔L.〕顺便,便中,附带. ***~ dictum** (pl. **ob·i·ter dic·ta**)* 【法】附论〔法官的附带意见〕;附言,余论,附带讲的话.

o·bit·u·a·r·ist [əˈbitjuərist] *n.* 写死亡新闻者;死者略传的作者;讣告执笔者.

o·bit·u·a·ry [əˈbitjuəri] *a.* 有关死亡[死者]的. *an ~ notice* (报上的)讣告,死亡新闻,死者略传. — *n.* 讣告;死者传略;【天主】死名簿,死者周年祭日的登记簿.

obj. = ①object. ②objection. ③objective.

ob·ject [ˈɔbdʒikt] *n.* ①物,物体,物件. ②目标 *(of; for)*;目的,宗旨. ③【哲】对象,客体,客观 *(opp.* subject*)*;【语法】宾语. ④〔口〕(可笑或可怜的)人[物]. *a small [strange] ~* 小[奇怪]东西. *the ~ of study* 研究的对象. *the direct [indirect] ~* 直接[间接]宾语. *What an ~ you have made (of) yourself!* 〔口〕你这家伙把自己搞得真不象样子! ***attain [achieve, gain, secure] one's ~*** 达到目的. ***fail [succeed] in one's ~*** 没有达到[达到]目的. ***for that ~*** 为了那个目的. ***no ~*** 〔广告用语〕怎样都好,不成问题;没有困难 *(Distance is no ~* (待聘者)上班距离(远、近)不成问题). ***propose an ~ to oneself = set an ~ before one*** 立志,立下目标. ***with that ~ in view*** 怀着那个目的. — [əbˈdʒekt] *vi.* ①反对,抗议,表示异议 *(against, to)*. ②抱反感,不服气,有意见. — *vt.* 提出…作反对的理由 *(that)*. *If you don't ~.* 假使你不反对. *I ~.* 〔英下院〕我反对. *I ~ against him that he is a hypocrite.* 我反对他,因为他是个伪君子. ~ **to** ①反对 *(I ~ to your doing that.* 我反对你做那件事). ②讨厌 *(I ~ very much to a wet weather.* 我非常讨厌潮湿的天气). ~ **ball** 【台球】目的球. ~ **glass** (显微镜等的)物镜. ~ **language** 对象语言,目的语. ~ **lens** = object-glass. ~ **lesson** 实物教授课;(某原理的)具体实例;可作教训的实例. ~**line** 轮廓线. ~**plate** 检镜片〔显微镜的载物玻璃片〕. ~ **staff** (测量用)函尺,准尺. ~ **teaching** 实物[直观]教授(法). ~ **writing** 物体文字(如结绳纪事等). **-less** *a.* 没有目的[宗旨]的,没有物象的.

ob·jec·ti·fy [ɔbˈdʒektifai] *vt.* 使客观化,使具体化,体现. **-fi·ca·tion** [-ˈkeiʃən] *n.*

ob·jec·tion [əbˈdʒekʃən] *n.* ①反对;异议;不承认;不情愿,嫌恶. ②缺点;缺陷. ③障碍,妨碍. ④反对的理由. *The chief ~ to this book is its great length.* 这本书的主要缺点是太长. *There is no ~ to your leaving at once.* 你现在即刻走也不碍事. ***feel an ~ to*** *(doing)* 不愿意…. ***have no ~ to*** *(doing)* 不反对…. ***make an [take] ~ to [against]*** 对…表示异议,反对…. ***open to ~*** 有可议之处,有不合理之处 *(The plan is open to ~.* 该计划大有可商榷之处). ***raise an ~*** 提出抗议[异议].

ob·jec·tion·a·ble [əbˈdʒekʃənəbl] *a.* ①引起反对的,要不得的. ②令人讨厌的,令人不愉快的;有伤风化的. **-bly** *ad.*

ob·jec·tive [ɔbˈdʒektiv] *a.* ①【哲】客观的;真实的,实在的 *(opp.* subjective*)*;外界的;如实的;无偏见的. ②目的的;目标的. ③【语】宾格的. ④【医】病状除本人外也为他人感觉到的. — *n.* ①目的,目标,任务;【军】出击目标. ②【语】宾格. ③【物】物镜. ④客观事物,实在事物. *military ~s* 军事目标. ~ **case** 【语法】宾格. ~ **complement** 【语法】宾语补语. ~ **lens** = object glass. ~ **sympton** 【医】他觉症状. **-ly** *ad.* 在客观上. **-ness** *n.* 客观(性).

ob·jec·tiv·ism [ɔbˈdʒektivizəm] *n.* 客观主义;客观性 *(opp.* subjectivism*)*.

ob·jec·tiv·i·ty [ˌɔbdʒekˈtiviti] *n.* 客观(性);客观现实.

ob·jec·tor [əbˈdʒektə] *n.* 反对者.

ob·'jet d'art [F. ˌɔbʒɛ ˈdɑː] *(pl.* ***ob'jets d'art*** [ɔbʒɛ]*)* 小美术(工艺)品;古玩.

ob·jur·gate [ˈɔbdʒəːgeit] *vt.* 骂,斥责,谴责. **-tion** [ˌɔbdʒəːˈgeiʃən] *n.* **-tor** 斥责者. *n.* **-tory** *a.*

obl. = ①oblique. ②oblong.

ob·lan·ce·o·late [ɔbˈlɑːnsiəlit, -ˌleit] *a.* 【植】(叶子)倒披针形的.

ob·last [ˈɔblɑːst] *n.* 〔Russ.〕州,地方,区域,地区;省;外省;省会.

ob·late[1] [ˈɔbleit] *n.* ①献身教会工作的人;被父母许愿献身教会的儿童. ②在修道院生活而不遵守修道士戒规的人. ③〔O-〕某些天主教团体的信徒. — *a.* 献身教会工作的.

ob·late[2] [ˈɔbleit, əuˈbleit] *a.* 【数】扁圆形的;扁球形的 *(opp.* prolate*)*. **-ness** *n.*

ob·la·tion [əuˈbleiʃən] *n.* 供奉;供献(物),祭品;圣体〔面包和葡萄酒〕供献(礼);(对教会等的)捐献. **-al, -la·tory** *a.*

ob·li·gate [ˈɔbləgit] *vt.* ①使负(法律上或道义上的)义务. ②强迫,强制. ③使感激. ④规定(某款)作还债专用. *I am ~d to do it.* 我有责任去做它. — *a.* 强制性的;有责任的;必需的;【生】专性的. *~ parasites* 专性寄生物.

ob·li·ga·tion [ˌɔbliˈgeiʃən] *n.* ①义务;职责,责任;负担. ②契约,合约;证券;债务. ③恩惠,恩义. ④债务,欠下的人情. *the ~ of tax* 纳税的义务. ***be [lie] under an ~ to*** 对…有义务;受过…的恩. ***lay an ~ upon*** 使负债务. ***of ~*** 义务上的;义务性的. ***meet one's ~s*** 偿还债务. ***put [lay] sb. under an ~*** 施恩惠给某人;使某人欠人情,使某人承担义务. ***repay an ~*** 报恩.

ob·li·ga·to [ˌɔbliˈgɑːtəu] *a.*, *n.* 〔It.〕 = obbligato.

ob·lig·a·to·ry [ɔˈbligətəri] *a.* ①义务的;应尽的;强制性的. ②【生】专性的. *~ military service* 义务兵役. *an ~ right* 债权. *the ~ term* 义务年限. ~ **parasilism** 【生】专性寄生. **-ri·ly** *ad.*

o·blige [əˈblaidʒ] *vt.* ①迫使;责成,使负义务. ②施恩于,施惠于;答应…的请求;使满足 *(by, with)*;使感激;给,借 *(with)*. *Your recalcitrance ~s firmness on me.* 你们不听话,那我就得采用果断措施. *We are much ~d to you for your help.* 非常感谢您对我们的帮助. *I won't ~ you to stay here any longer.* 你不必再呆在这儿啦. *Circumstances ~ me to do that.* 情况使我不得不那样做. *I am sorry I cannot ~ you.* 很抱歉,我不能答应你的请求. *Excuse me, but could you ~ me with a match?* 对不起,请给我一根火柴好吗? *Will any gentleman ~ a lady?* 请哪位先生把位子让给一位女士好吗? — *vi.* 做好事,效劳. *I'll do anything within reason to ~.* 能办到的,我

都愿尽力[效劳]. **be ~d to** ①感谢 ((*I am*) *much ~d* (*to you*). 多谢多谢). ②不得已而…(*I was ~d to go.* 我不得不去). **~ (one) by ...ing** 替人… (*Will you ~ me by closing the door?* 请替我关上门好吗?). **~ (one) with** 给… (*O- us with your presence [an answer]* 务请出席[赐复]. *Could you ~ me with ten dollars?* 借十块钱给我好吗?).

ob·li·gee [ˌɔbliˈdʒiː] *n.* ①【法】权利人, 债权人, 债主 (*opp.* obligor). ②受惠者 (*opp.* obliger).

o·blig·ing [əˈblaidʒiŋ] *a.* 恳切的; 乐于助人的; (女仆等)勤快的; 〔古〕(言行等)谦和的, 有礼貌的. **-ly** *ad.* **-ness** *n.*

ob·li·gor [ˌɔbliˈgɔː] *n.* 【法】义务人, 债务人, 负债人 (*opp.* obligee).

ob·lique [əˈbliːk] *a.* ①斜, 倾斜的. ②(道德上)不正当的, 邪恶的. ③间接的; 暗中的; 不坦率的, 转弯抹角的. ④【植】歪叶的〔两侧不对称的〕. ⑤【语法】间接格的. ⑥【数】非直角的; 非垂直的; 斜线的, 斜角的, 斜面的. ⑦【军】(照片)从空中倾斜摄制的. **~** *dealings* 不正当交易. *the ~ case* 【语法】间接格〔主格、呼格以外各格的总称〕. *the ~ narration* 间接叙述(法). *an ~ plane* 斜面. **make an ~ reference to** 转弯抹角地说到. — *vi.* ①倾斜, 歪. ②【军】(成 45 度)斜进; 斜行进. — *n.* ①倾斜物. ②【解】斜肌(尤指腹部的肌肉). ③【军】倾斜航空照片. — *ad.* 【军】以 45 度角. *To the left ~, march!* 【军】向左成 45 度角, 正步走! **~ angle** 【数】斜角. **~ sailing** 【海】斜航. **-ly** *ad.* **-ness** *n.*

ob·liq·ui·ty [əˈblikwiti] *n.* ①斜, 倾斜, 歪斜; 倾度, 倾角. ②【天】斜交. ③(说话、行为的)不明, 暧昧, 转弯抹角. ④(行为等的)不正, 邪; 精神变态.

ob·li·ter·ate [əˈblitəreit] *vt.* ①涂去, 擦去, 删去 (文字等); 消灭…的痕迹. ②使消失; 除去; 抹煞; 使湮没; 使被忘却. **-ative** *a.* **-a·tor** *n.*

ob·lit·er·a·tion *n.* ①涂去, 删除; 清除; 灭迹, 消灭, 湮没. ②【医】管腔闭合.

ob·liv·i·on [əˈbliviən] *n.* ①忘却; 易忘, 健忘; 被忘却; 埋没, 湮没; 漠视. ②大赦. *the Act [Bill] of O-* 大赦令. **be buried in ~** 全被人们忘记. **fall [sink, pass] into ~** 渐为(世人)忘却; 湮没无闻.

ob·liv·i·ous [əˈbliviəs] *a.* ①易忘的, 健忘的. ②忘却, 忘记 (*of*). ②不在意的, 呆呆的, 茫然的. ③〔诗〕使忘却的〔通过睡眠等〕. **-ly** *ad.* **-ness** *n.*

Ob·lo·mov [ɔbˈləuməf] *n.* 奥勃洛摩夫〔俄国作家冈察洛夫所作同名小说中的主人公, 善良而怠惰〕. **-ism** 沉溺于空想而一味怠惰懒散的作风.

ob·long [ˈɔblɔŋ] *n., a.* 长方形(的), 椭圆形(的).

ob·lo·quy [ˈɔbləkwi] *n.* ①大骂, 斥责. ②(由于受到强烈指责而造成的)污名, 丑名, 耻辱.

ob·mu·tes·cence [ˌɔbmjuːˈtesns] *n.* 死不吭声.

ob·nox·ious [əbˈnɔkʃəs] *a.* ①可憎的, 讨厌的. ②〔古〕易受…的. ③【法】有责任的. ④应受谴责的. **-ly** *ad.* **-ness** *n.*

o·boe [ˈəubəu, ˈəubɔi] *n.* ①【乐】双簧管, 欧巴. ②(风琴的)欧巴音程.

obo·ist [ˈəbəuist] *n.* 吹双簧管者.

ob·o·lus [ˈɔbləs] *n.* (*pl.* **-li**[-lai]) 〔L.〕欧布鲁斯〔古希腊价值 1/6 德拉克马的硬币; 相当于 $11^1/_4$ 谷(喱)的重量单位; 以前欧洲通用的小硬币〕.

ob·o·vate [ɔbˈəuveit] *a.* 【植】倒卵形的〔如某些叶〕.

ob·o·void [ɔbˈəuvɔid] *a.* 【植】倒卵球形的〔指某些果〕.

O'Bri·en [əuˈbraiən] *n.* 奥布赖恩〔姓氏〕.

obs. = ①observation. ②observatory. ③obsolete.

ob·scene [ɔbˈsiːn] *a.* ①猥亵的, 淫猥的; 淫荡的. ②〔古、诗〕污秽的, 丑恶的, 讨厌的. **~** *pictures* 淫画. *an ~ publication* 【法】伤风败俗的刊物, 淫书. *a ~ bird* 乌鸦. **-ly** *ad.*

ob·scen·i·ty [ɔbˈsiːniti] *n.* 猥亵, 诲淫; 淫行、淫话.

ob·scur·ant [ɔbˈskjuərənt] *n.* 蒙昧主义者 —*a.* 蒙昧主义的, 使愚昧的. **-ism** *n.* 愚民政策, 蒙昧主义. **-ist** *n., a.* 蒙昧主义者 (的); (似) 蒙昧主义的 (*an obscurantist policy* 愚民政策).

ob·scur·an·tic [ˌɔbskjuˈræntik] *a.* 蒙昧主义的, 愚民政策的.

ob·scur·a·tion [ˌɔbskjuəˈreiʃən] *n.* ①黑暗化, 阴暗, 朦胧; 遮蔽; (知识等的)蒙昧化, (真理、语意的)暧昧化. ②【天】掩星, 食.

ob·scure [əbˈskjuə] *a.* ①暗(夜), 黑暗的; 黑夜里的; 阴(天), 朦胧的. ②不清楚的, 不鲜明的, 不明了的, 含糊的, 暧昧的; 难解的, 晦涩的. ③隐蔽的, 偏僻的; 不出名的, 无名的, 低微的. *an ~ day* 阴天. *~ yellow* 闷黄色. *an ~ meaning* 晦涩不明的意义. *an ~ retreat* 隐居处. *an ~ village* 穷乡僻壤. *a host of ~ writers* 一大群无名作家. **be of ~ origin [birth]** 出身微贱. — *n.* 〔诗〕阴暗, 朦胧; 黑夜. — *vt.* ①使(黑)暗. ②遮蔽, 隐藏. ③使(发音等)暧昧[含糊、不明]. ④使难理解; 搞混. ⑤掩蔽(名声等), (比较的结果, 使别人)相形见绌[暗然无光]. *The sun was ~d by clouds.* 太阳被云遮了. *~d glass* 闷光玻璃. — *vi.* 变模糊; 隐藏起来. *This language serves to disguise and ~.* 这种话是用来文过饰非的. **-ly** *ad.* 暗, 朦胧, 暧昧; 暗暗. **-ness** *n.* = obscurity. **-r** *n.*

ob·scu·ri·ty [əbˈskjuəriti] *n.* ①暗(淡); 朦胧. ②含糊, 暧昧, 不明; 难解处, 不明处, 费解的话. ③无名的人[地方]; 低微的人[处境]. **retire into ~** 隐退. **rise from ~** 出身微贱. **sink into ~** 被世人忘掉, 湮没无闻.

ob·se·crate [ˈɔbsikreit] *vt.* (**-crat·ed; -crat·ing**) 〔罕〕恳求, 恳请, 请愿. **-cra·tion** [ˌɔbsiˈkreiʃən] *n.*

ob·se·cra·tion [ˌɔbsiˈkreiʃən] *n.* 恳求, 恳请; 【宗】以 by 开始的恳求祈祷句.

ob·se·qui·al [ɔbˈsiːkwiəl] *a.* 葬[丧]礼的.

ob·se·quies [ˈɔbsikwiz] *n. pl.* 葬[丧]礼.

ob·se·qui·ous [əbˈsiːkwiəs] *a.* 谄媚的, 奉承的; 〔古〕顺从的, 死心塌地的. *be ~ to the great* 巴结权贵. **-ly** *ad.* **-ness** *n.*

ob·serv·a·ble [əbˈzəːvəbl] *a.* ①看得见的, 观察得出的; 常见的. ②值得注意的, 显著的. ③可[应]庆祝的. ④可[应]遵守的. — *n.* ①值得注意的东西; 感觉到[看得见]的事物. ②【物】可观察量; 观察算符. **-bly** *ad.*

ob·serv·ance [əbˈzəːvəns] *n.* ①(法律、义务、仪式等的)遵守 (*of*). ②仪式; (宗教)典礼; 纪念, 庆祝. ③习惯, 惯例. ④〔古〕恭顺. ⑤教规, 戒律. ⑥〔罕〕注意, 观察. *the ~ of the emperor's birthday* 皇帝祝寿大典. *the ~ of the Sabbath* 守安息日〔宗教信徒在主日停止工作, 基督教徒为星期日, 犹太教徒为星期六〕. *~ of national sovereignty* 尊重国家主权. *~ of territorial integrity* 尊重领土完整.

ob·serv·ant [əbˈzəːvənt] *a.* ①注意, 留心; 盯着, 看牢 (*of*). ②观察力敏锐的, 机警的. ③严格遵守…的 (*of*). *an ~ boy* 机警的男孩子. *be ~ of the traffic rules* 严格遵守交通规则. *be ~ of one's duties* 克尽责守. *be ~ to avoid danger* 注意避免危险. — *n.* 〔古〕遵守者, 严守者; 〔O-〕【天主】(方济各会)严守教规的修道士. **-ly** *ad.*

ob·ser·va·tion [ˌɔbzə(ː)ˈveiʃən] *n.* ①观察, 注意; 观察力; 瞭望. ②观测, 实测; 【海】测天; 【军】观测, 监视, 侦察. ③(观察得的)知识, 经验; 〔*pl.*〕观察[观测]报告[资料]. ④经验谈, 讲话, 谈话; 评述, 按语, 短评, 意见. (*on*). ⑤〔口〕发言, 言论. *a man of no ~* 没有观察力的人. *an expedition of ~* 观测队. *sampling ~* 抽查. *service ~* 业务检查. *a witty [foolish] ~* 聪明[糊涂]话. **come [fall] under one's ~** 看见, 瞧见. **keep a suspect [patient] under ~** 监视[观察]一个可疑的人[病人]. **make a few ~s on** 简单谈谈对…的几点看法. **take an ~** 【海】测天. **~ balloon** 【军】观测气

球. ~ **car** (火车的)游览车厢. ~ **check** 外部检验. ~ **plane**【空】侦察机. ~ **post**【军】监视哨, 瞭望哨〔略为 O Pip〕. ~ **station** 观察所,观察站; 气象台, 观象台.

ob·ser·va·tion·al [ˌɔbzə(:)ˈveiʃənəl] *a.* 观察[观测]的,监视的; 根据观测[观察]的. **-ly** *ad.*

ob·serv·a·to·ry [əbˈzə:vətəri] *n.* ①观测所; 观象台,气象台,天文台. ②观察台,瞭望台,望楼;【军】(炮台的)监视郭.

ob·serve [əbˈzə:v] *vt.* ①遵守(时间,法律、习惯等); 举行(仪式等); 纪念,庆祝(节日、生日等). ②观察,观测(天体、气象等); 监视(敌人行动等). ③通过观察认识到,注意到,看到,知道. ④说,讲; 陈述(所见); 评述,评论. ~ *silence* 保持沉默. ~ *a rule* 遵守规则. ~ *a suspected person* 监视有嫌疑的人. *Allow me to* ~ *that ....* 请允许我这样批评. *I didn't* ~ *the colours of her eyes.* 我没有注意到她眼睛的颜色. — *vi.* ①观察; 注意. ②陈述意见,评述,简评 *(on; upon)*. *I have very little to* ~ *on what has been said.* 关于刚才所听到的我没什么话好讲. *as I was going to* ~ 象我本来想讲的. *strange to* ~ 讲起来虽奇怪. ***the ~d of all observers*** 众矢之的, 被大家注视的人.

ob·serv·er [əbˈzə:və] *n.* ①注视者; 观察者; 观测员; 测候员. ②遵守者, 奉行者; (仪式等的)举行者. ③观察家,评论者. ④【军】观察员,观测员; 机上侦察员. ⑤监视人,见证人,目击者,旁观者; 旁听人. *a plot* ~ 测绘员. *an automatic* ~【火箭】自动记录仪.

ob·serv·ing [əbˈsə:viŋ] *a.* 注意周到的; 观察力敏锐的. **-ly** *ad.*

ob·sess [əbˈses] *vt.* (魔鬼、妄想等)缠住,迷住; 使着迷; 使窘困,使烦扰〔常用被动结构〕. ***be ~d by [with]*** 被…附上[缠住,迷住心窍]. **-ive** *a.* 成见(性)的; 引起成见的.

ob·ses·sion [əbˈseʃən] *n.* 着魔; 执意,积念,迷念,摆脱不了的思想[情感等]. ***be under an ~ of*** 在思想[情感]上被…缠住. ***suffer from an*** ~ 耿耿于怀.

ob·ses·sion·al [əbˈseʃənəl] *a.* 摆脱不了的. *an* ~ *neurosis* 强迫观念性神经病.

ob·sid·i·an [əbˈsidiən] *n.*【矿】黑曜岩.

Obsn. = observation.

ob·so·les·cent [ˌɔbsəˈlesnt] *a.* (词语、习惯等)逐渐被废弃的; 快要不用的;【生】废退的, 萎缩的. **-les·cence** *n.* 渐,逐渐过时;【生】(器官的)废退, 萎缩.

ob·so·lete [ˈɔbsəli:t] *a.* ①已废弃的,已不用的,已失时效的. ②陈旧的, 已过时的. ③【生】已废退的, 萎缩了的,不发育的; 不明显的. *an* ~ *vessel* 废舰. *an* ~ *word* 已废的词. —*n.* 废词; 被废弃的事物. **-ly** *ad.* **-ness** *n.*

ob·so·le·tism [ˈɔbsəli:tizəm] *n.* 废弃, 陈腐; 废词语, 废弃了的习惯[用法].

Obsr. = observer.

ob·sta·cle [ˈɔbstəkl] *n.* 障碍(物), 妨害, 阻碍, 干扰. ***an ~ to (progress)*** (进步)的障碍. ***throw ~s in sb.'s way*** 妨害, 阻碍某人. ~ **course** 障碍赛跑训练场. ~ **race** 障碍赛.

obstet. = ①obstetric(al). ②obstetrics.

ob·stet·ric, ob·stet·ri·cal [ɔbsˈtetrik, -kəl] *a.* 产科(学)的, 助产的. *an* ~ *nurse* 助产护士.

ob·ste·tri·cian [ˌɔbsteˈtriʃən] *n.* 产科医生.

ob·stet·rics [ɔbˈstetriks] *n.* 产科学, 助产术.

ob·sti·na·cy [ˈɔbstinəsi] *n.* ①顽固, 顽强, 固执, 顽梗; 不易克服性. ②〔an ~〕顽固的言行 *(against)*. ③(病痛等)难治, 难解除, 难抑制. ***with*** ~ 顽强地, 顽固地.

ob·sti·nate [ˈɔbstinit] *a.* 顽固的; 顽强的; 不易克服的; 难治的. ~ *resistance* 顽强的抵抗. **-ly** *ad.*

ob·sti·nate·ness [ˈɔbstinitnis] *n.* ①固执, 顽固, 执拗; 顽强. ②抵药物性, 抗治疗性. ③不屈, 坚持.

ob·sti·pa·tion [ˌɔbstiˈpeiʃən] *n.* 〔罕〕【医】便秘.

ob·strep·er·ous [əbˈstrepərəs] *a.* ①吵闹的, 喧嚣的. ②任性的, 暴躁的; 顽固对抗的; 难驾驭的. **-ly** *ad.* **-ness** *n.*

ob·struct [əbˈstrʌkt] *vt., vi.* 堵[阻]塞; 遮住; 妨碍, 阻挠; (给…)设置障碍. ~ *a passage* 堵塞通路. ~ *the traffic* 阻塞交通. ~ *the view* 挡住视线. ~ *sb. [from] doing something* 阻挠某人做某事. **-er, -or,** *n.*

ob·struc·tion [əbˈstrʌkʃən] *n.* ①堵塞, 遮断, 妨碍, 阻碍, 障碍;【议会】妨碍议事进程. ②遮断物, 障碍物. ~ **guard** (火车头前的)护栏, 排障器. **-ism** *n.* 故意妨碍议案通过. **-ist** *n.* 妨碍议事者.

ob·struc·tive [əbˈstrʌktiv] *a.* 引起阻塞的; 妨害的, 阻碍的; 妨碍议事的. ***be ~ to*** 成为…的障碍. — *n.* 妨碍物, 障碍; 妨碍(议事)者. **-ly** *ad.* **-ness** *n.*

ob·stru·ent [ˈɔbstruwənt] *a.* 〔罕〕闭塞的, 阻碍的. — *n.* 〔罕〕【解】(体内通道的)堵塞物〔例如肾石〕.

ob·tain [əbˈtein] *vt.* 得到, 获得, 买到; 达到(目的). ~ *a reward* 得到报酬. ~ *a prize* 得奖. ~ *a hearing* 得到发言机会. ~ *a high price* 卖得好价钱. — *vi.* (习惯等)通行, 流行; 投合一般人心理, 得到(众人)承认. *These ideas no longer* ~. 这些见解已经行不通了. *This ~s with most people.* 这是多数人公认的. **-able** *a.* 能得到的; 能达到的. **-er** *n.* 获得者. **-ment** *n.* 〔古〕获得; 达成.

ob·tect [ɔbˈtekt] *a.*【虫】被甲的, 具被的 (= obtected).

ob·test [ɔbˈtest] *vt.* 〔古〕乞, 央求, 恳求; 请求(某人作证). — *vi.* ①〔罕〕抗议. ②恳求.

ob·tes·ta·tion [ˌɔbtesˈteiʃən] *n.* ①祈求. ②〔罕〕抗议.

ob·trude [əbˈtru:d] *vt.* ①逼人接受; 强行; 强迫. ②挤出, 冲出; (乌龟)伸出(头来). ~ *one's opinions (up)on others* 把自己意见强加于人. ~ *oneself* 硬管闲事, 硬插手 *(upon; into)*. — *vi.* 闯入; 打扰 *(upon)*.

ob·tru·sion [əbˈtru:ʒən] *n.* ①(意见等的)强迫(别人)接受 *(on others)*; 强挤; 强加, 强求. ②管闲事, 多嘴; 闯入; 莽撞.

ob·tru·sive [əbˈtru:siv] *a.* ①强迫人的. ②爱管闲事的, 爱多嘴的. ③伸出的, 突出的; 炫耀的. **-ly** *ad.* **-ness** *n.*

ob·tund [əbˈtʌnd] *vt.* 使迟钝, 使失去感觉;【医】缓和, 抑制(疼痛等).

ob·tund·ent [əbˈtʌndənt] *a.* 使感觉迟钝的; 止痛的; 减少疼痛的, 减少刺激的. —*n.* 止痛药, 缓和剂.

ob·tu·rate [ˈɔbtjuəreit] *vt.* 塞, 闭塞; 封闭, 紧塞; (开炮时)密闭(炮尾). **-ra·tion** *n.* 封闭, 闭塞, 紧塞. **-ra·tor** *n.* 口盖, 管塞;【军】气密装置, 封闭器〔炮的尾塞〕;【植】珠孔塞.

ob·tuse [əbˈtju:s] *a.* ①钝的, 不尖的, 不锐利的;【数】(角)钝的 *(opp.* acute);【植】(叶子尖)钝形的, 圆头的. ②(感觉)迟钝的, 愚钝的; (印象)不鲜明的; (疼痛)不剧烈的. *an* ~ *angle*【数】钝角. *an* ~ *pain* 闷痛. *be* ~ *in understanding* 头脑迟钝. **-ly** *ad.*

ob·tuse·ness [əbˈtju:snis] *n.* ①不尖, 不锐利; 钝. ②钝角. ③愚钝. ④不鲜明, (疼痛)不剧烈 (= obtusity).

ob·verse [ˈɔbvə:s] *n.* ①(货币、奖章等的)表面, 正面 *(opp.* reverse*)*; (事物两面的)较显著面; 相互对应面. ②【逻】换质说明法. — *a.* ①表面的, 正面的; 显著面的; 对应面的. ②【植】(叶形)钝头形的, 倒置的. *We must learn to look at problems all-sidedly, seeing the reverse as well as the* ~ *side of things.* 我们必须学会全面地看问题, 不但要看到事物的正面, 也要看到它的反面. **-ly** *ad.*

ob·ver·sion [ɔbˈvə:ʃən] *n.* ①将表面反过来的动作. ②【逻】换质法〔将 All men are mortal 改成 No men are immortal〕.

ob·vert [əbˈvə:t] *vt.* ①将(表面)反过来. ②【逻】(用换质法)使(命题)换质.

ob·vi·ate [ˈɔbvieit, -vjeit] *vt.* 除去, 排除(障碍、危险等), (事前)防止, 避免. **-a·tion** [ˌɔbviˈeiʃən] *n.* **-a·tor** *n.*

ob·vi·o·sit·y [ˌɔbviˈɔsiti] *n.* 不言而喻的东西.

ob·vi·ous [ˈɔbviəs, -vjəs] *a.* ①明显的,明白的. ②(感情、戏谑等)明明白白的, 显而易见的; 显著的. *an ~ advantage* 显著的优势. *It is ~ that you are wrong.* 显然你错了. **-ly** *ad.* **-ness** *n.*

ob·vo·lute [ˈɔbvəljuːt] *a.* 【植】跨褶的〔指叶或花瓣〕(= obvolutive). **-lu·tion** [ˌɔbvəˈljuːʃən] *n.*

O.C., OC = ① officer commanding 指挥官. ② oral contraceptive 口服避孕药.

o.c. = 〔L.〕*opere citato* 见前引书 (= in the work cited).

oc. = ocean.

o/c = outward collection 出口托收.

oc- *pref.* 〔用于字母C 前〕= ob-.

oc·a·ri·na [ˌɔkəˈriːnə] *n.* 【乐器】奥卡利那笛; 洋埙〔陶制的蛋形笛〕.

OCAS = Organization of Central American States 中美洲国家组织.

o.c.b. = oil circuit breaker. 油开关,油断路器.

Oc·cam [ˈɔkəm] *n.* 奥克姆〔姓氏〕.

occas. = occassional(ly).

O'Ca·sey [əuˈkeisi] *n.* ①奥凯西〔姓氏〕. ②**Sean ~** 希安·奥凯西〔1884—1964,爱尔兰剧作家〕.

oc·ca·sion [əˈkeiʒən] *n.* ①(庆祝等的特殊)场合; (重大)时节,时刻. ②机会,(适当的)时机; 〔O-〕〔拟人语〕好机会. ③原因, 诱因, 近因. ④(怒、笑等的)根据, 理由,必要. ⑤〔*pl.*〕〔古〕事,事务, 工作, 职业. *She was the ~ of the trouble.* 她是纠纷的根源. *There is no ~ to be angry.* 没有生气的理由. *one's lawful ~s* 〔古〕本职. *The national-day celebration was a great ~.* 国庆节庆祝仪式很盛大. ***as ~ demands*** 遇必要时; 及时. ***for one's ~*** 为某人. ***for the ~*** 临时. ***give ~ to*** 引起,使发生. ***have no ~ for*** 没有的根据. ***have no ~ to (do)*** 没有…的理由〔必要〕(*I had no ~ to see him.* 我没有会见他的必要). ***have ~ for*** 需要. ***if the ~ arises [should arise] = should ~ arise*** 必要的时候. ***improve the ~*** 抓紧时机,乘机说教. ***in honour of the ~*** 为表示庆贺,为道贺. ***on great ~s*** 在大庆〔盛典〕时期. ***on [upon] ~*** 有时,间或; 遇必要时. ***on one ~*** 曾经,有一个时候. ***on several ~s*** 屡次,好几次. ***on the first ~*** 一有机会. ***on the ~ of*** 在…的时候,在…时. ***on the present ~*** 当时. ***on this ~*** 这一次. ***rise to the ~*** 起来对付; 善处难局. ***take [seize the] ~ to (do)*** 抓住…的好机会, 乘机…. — *vt.* 惹起, 引起. *His conduct ~s me great anxiety.* 他的行动使我非常担心.

oc·ca·sion·al [əˈkeiʒnəl] *a.* 非经常的; 偶尔的; 必要时的; 不定期的,临时的; 特殊场合的. *That sort of thing is quite ~.* 那种事是很偶然的. *an ~ writer* 应时作家. *an ~ workman* 临时雇工. **-ly** *ad.* 非经常地; 偶然. **-ism** *n.* 【哲】偶因论.

Oc·ci·dent [ˈɔksidənt] *n.* 〔诗、古〕①〔the ~〕(包括欧洲和美国在内的)西洋 *(opp.* the Orient*)*; 西方(文明); ②〔the o-〕西方.

Oc·ci·den·tal [ˌɔksiˈdentl] *a.* ①西洋的 *(opp.* Oriental*)*. ②〔o-〕西方人〔文化〕的;【天】西天的. — *n.* 西方人; 欧美人. **-ism** *n.* 西式; 西方文化; 西洋风味. **-ist** *n.* 西方文化研究者. **-ize** *vt.* 使西方化,欧化. **-ly** *ad.* 照西式.

oc·cip·i·tal [ɔkˈsipitl] *a.* 【解】枕骨的;【虫】后头部的. *~ bone* 后头骨. — *n.* 后头骨.

oc·ciput [ˈɔksipʌt] *n.* 【解】枕骨部 *(opp.* sinciput*)*; 【虫】后头.

oc·clude [ɔˈkluːd] *vt.* 使闭塞; 使堵塞; 封锁; 遮蔽; 使不发生作用;【化】吸藏,吸留;【气】使(气旋等)锢囚. — *vi.* 【医】(上齿与下齿)咬合;【气】(气旋)锢囚. *~d front* 【气】锢囚锋. **oc·clu·sive** *a.*

oc·clu·sion [əˈkluːʒən, ɔ-] *n.* ①闭塞. ②【牙】咬合; 闭塞,闭合. ③【气】锢囚锋(= occluded front). ④【语】全闭合音.

oc·cult [ɔˈkʌlt] *a.* ①神秘的; 玄妙的; 超自然的. ②秘密的; 秘传的; 不公开的; 隐伏的; 看不见的. — *n.* 〔the ~〕秘学. *~ arts* (炼金术、占星术等的)秘术. *~ blood* 【医】潜血. — *vt., vi.* 【天】(使)掩(星); 掩蔽; 隐藏,(使)变暗. **~ing light** 连闭灯,明暗灯,隐显灯.

oc·cul·ta·tion [ˌɔkəlˈteiʃən] *n.* ①【天】掩星,星蚀. ②荫蔽,掩蔽,隐伏,不见; 消失.

oc·cult·ism [ɔˈkəltizəm] *n.* 神秘学; 神秘论; 神秘主义. **-ist** *n.* 神秘学者; 神秘主义者.

oc·cu·pan·cy [ˈɔkjupənsi] *n.* ①占有; 占领; 占用; 居住. ②占有期间,居住期间. ③【法】据有,先占,占据.【物】占有率. *during the ~ of his post* 当他在职期间.

oc·cu·pant [ˈɔkjuːpənt] *n.* (土地、房屋、地位等的)占有人; 居住者;【法】占据者.

oc·cu·pa·tion [ˌɔkjuˈpeiʃən] *n.* ①占有,领有; 占领(状态); 占据; 占领军(当局); 占有〔占据〕期间 *(of)*; 占有权; 占领地; 居住. ②职业; 工作, 事情, 业务; 消遣. *an ~ bridge [road]* 专用〔占用〕桥梁〔道路〕. *an army of ~* 占领军. *an ~ census* 职业统计调查. *domestic side-line ~s* 家庭副业. *rural subsidiary ~s* 农村副业. *men out of ~* 失业者.

oc·cu·pa·tion·al [ˌɔkjuˈpeiʃənəl] *a.* ①职业的; 职业引起的. ②军事占领的. *an ~ desease* 【医】职业病. **~ therapy** 工作疗法〔使患者从事一种工作 (如艺术或工艺)以转移心思或矫正某种身体缺陷〕.

oc·cu·pi·er [ˈɔkjupaiə] *n.* = occupant.

oc·cu·py [ˈɔkjupai] *vt.* ①占领,占据; 占有,领有; 占用. ②住在…; 使用(房间、办事处等); 租用(房子等). ③占(地位、职务、空间); 充满; 花费, 需要(时间). ④〔常用被动或反身结构〕使从事; 使忙碌. ⑤处于(某种地位); 担任(职务). *~ a fort* 占领要塞. *~ an important position* 占重要地位. *The house is occupied.* 那房子有人住着. *Anxieties occupied his mind.* 他心里充满了焦虑. *I am occupied.* 我没有空. ***be occupied*** *(in doing sth., with affairs)* 在做…, 在忙…. ***~ oneself about [in, with]*** … (正)从事…. **occupied fallow**【农】半休闲.

oc·cur [əˈkəː] *vi.* ①(事件等)发生. ②被想到,想起. ③出来,出现; 存在; 被发现. *An accident ~red.* 发生了一件事故. *if anything should ~* 如果发生什么事的话. *A happy idea ~red to me.* 我想起了一个好办法. *It ~red to me that …* 我想到….

oc·cur·rence [əˈkʌrəns] *n.* ①(事件的)发生,出现,有; 【矿】存象,(矿床等的)埋藏; 产地. ②遭遇,事件,事故. *daily ~s* 日常发生的事. *oscillatory ~* 振荡现象. *be of frequent [rare] ~* 是常〔少〕有的. ***make allowance for unfavourable ~s*** 留有余地.

oc·cur·rent [əˈkʌrənt] *a.* 目前正在发生的; 偶然发生的.

oc·cur·ring [əˈkəːriŋ] *n.* 〔美口〕事变,事件,事故.

OCD = Office of Civil Defense 民防局.

OCDM = Office of Civil and Defense Mobilization 〔美〕民防国防动员署.

o·cean [ˈəuʃən] *n.* ①洋,大海; (有别于内海的)外洋. ★英国用 sea 的地方,美国常用 ocean. 如: spend some weeks by the ocean 在海边住几个星期. ②(五大洋的)…洋. ③一望无垠(的),茫茫(的) *(of)*; 无限,无量; 〔常 *pl.*〕〔口〕极多(的),许许多多(的) *(of)*. *the Atlantic [Pacific, Indian, Arctic, Antarctic] O-* 大西〔太平、印度、北冰、南冰〕洋. ★ Ocean 常可省去. 如: the Atlantic [Pacific]. *a vast ~ of foliage* 树海. *~s of money* 大量的钱. ***be tossed on an ~ of doubts*** 堕入五里雾中. **~-going** *a.* 行驶外洋的,远洋的 (*~-going commerce* 海外贸易). ***sweep back the ~*** 做显然不可能做到的事. *~* **greyhound** 外洋快船 (尤指定期客船). *~* **lane [route]** 外洋航线. *~* **liner** 远洋定期客轮. *~* **sunfish** 【动】翻车鲀. (Mola mola). *~* **tramp** 无一定航线的远洋货轮.

o·cean·ar·ium [ˌəuʃəˈnɛəriəm] *n.* 〔美〕大型海水水族馆.
o·cean·front [ˈəuʃənfrʌnt] *n.* 海洋地带.
o·cean-gray [ˈəuʃənˈgrei] *n, a.* 浅灰色(的).
O·ce·an·i·a [ˌəuʃiˈeinjə] *n.* 大洋洲.
O·ce·a·ni·an [ˌəuʃiˈeiniən] *a., n.* 大洋洲的(人).
o·ce·an·ic [ˌəuʃiˈænik] *a.* ①大洋的,大海的;大洋产的,(生活)在大洋中的;大洋一样的,广阔无边的. ②〔O-〕大洋洲的.
O·ce·an·i·ca [ˌəuʃiˈænikə] *n.* = Oceania.
O·ce·a·nid [əuˈsi:ənid] *n.* ***(pl.*** ***~s; -ni·des*** [ˌəusiˈænidi:z]***)*** ①【希神】大洋的女神. ②〔o-〕海贝.
o·ce·a·nog·ra·phy [ˌəuʃiəˈnɔgrəfi] *n.* 海洋地理学. **-graph·ic** [ˌəuʃiənəuˈgræfik], **-i·cal** *a.* **-nog·ra·pher** *n.* 海洋地理学家.
o·ce·an·ol·o·gy [ˌəuʃəˈnɔlədʒi] *n.* ①海洋学. ②海洋地理学 (= oceanography). **-ol·o·gist** *n.* 海洋(地理)学家.
o·ce·an·aut [ˈəuʃənɔ:t] *n.* 潜航员,海中作业员.
oc·el·late [ˈɔsiˌleit, əuˈselit] *a.* ①似脑眼的;似单眼的;似具瞳点的. ②具单眼的;具瞳点的. ③有斑点的.
oc·el·la·tion [ˌɔsiˈleiʃən] *n.* 眼状斑点.
o·cel·lus [əuˈseləs] *n.* ***(pl.*** ***o·cel·li*** [-ai]***)*** 〔L.〕 ①(昆虫的)单眼;具瞳点. ②脑眼. ③(孔雀尾上的)眼形花斑.
o·ce·lot [ˈəusilɔt] *n.* 豹猫〔南美、中美产〕.
och [ɔx] *int.* 〔Ir., Scot.〕啊! 呀! 唷!
o·cher [ˈəukə] *n.* = ochre.
o·cher·ous [ˈəukərəs] = ochreous.
och·loc·ra·cy [ɔkˈlɔkrəsi] *n.* 暴民政治,暴民的统治. **-cra·tic** [ˌɔkləˈkrætik], **-i·cal** *a.*
och·one [əˈhəun] *int.* 〔Scot., Ir.〕哎呀! 哎哟! 惨哉!
o·chre [ˈəukə] *n.* ①【矿】赭石〔可作颜料用〕. ②赭色,黄褐色. ③〔美俚〕金钱.
o·chre·ous [ˈəukriəs], **o·chrous** [-kərəs] *a.* 赭石质的;赭石色的.
o·chroid [ˈəukrɔid] *a.* 似赭土的,深黄赭色的.
-ock *suf.* 小: hill*ock* 小山.
o'clock [əˈklɔk] 〔of the clock 的缩写〕…点钟. *What ~ is it now?* 现在几点钟? *It's just seven (~).* 刚好七点. ***know what ~ it is*** 样样都晓得;熟悉情况. ***like one ~*** ①非常迅速地,马上. ②非常乐意地,津津有味地;很有力地;很带劲地.
O'Con·nell [əuˈkɔnl] *n.* ①奥康内尔〔姓氏〕. ②**Daniel ~** 达尼尔·奥康纳尔〔1775—1847, 爱尔兰民族主义运动领导者〕.
O'Con·nor [əuˈkɔnə] *n.* ①奥康纳〔姓氏〕. ②**Arthur ~** 阿塞·奥康纳〔1763—1852 爱尔兰革命家〕. ③**Thomas Power ~** 托马斯·波厄·奥康纳〔1848—1929爱尔兰作家,政治家〕.
OCR = optical character recognition【计】光符号识别.
oc·re·a [ˈɔkriə, ˈəukriə] *n.* ***(pl.*** ***-re·ae*** [-i:]***)***【植】托叶鞘. **o·cre·ate** [-ˌeit, -it] *a.*
Oct. = October.
oct. = octave.
oct-, octa- *comb. f.* 八: *Octa*chord.
oc·ta·chord [ˈɔktəkɔ:d] *n.* 八弦琴.
oc·tad [ˈɔktæd] *n.* 八个一组;【化】八价物;八价原素;八进制.
oc·tad·ic [ɔkˈtædik] *n., a.* 八个一组(的);【化】八价(的);【数】八进位(的).
oc·ta·gon [ˈɔktəgən] *n.*【几】八边形;八角形物;八角建筑物. — *a.* 八边形的.
oc·tag·o·nal [ɔkˈtægənl] *a.* 八边形的.
oc·ta·he·dral [ˌɔktəˈhedrəl] *a.* (有)八面的;八面体的.
oc·ta·he·drite [ˌɔktəˈhi:drait] *n.*【地】八面石〔锐钛矿〕.
oc·ta·hed·ron [ˌɔktəˈhedrən] *n.* ***(pl.*** ***~s, -he·dra*** [-drə]***)*** 八面体. *a regular ~* 正八面体.
oc·tal [ˈɔktl] *a.* ①八的,第八的. ②【无】八面的,八边的;八管脚的,八进制的.
oc·tam·er·ous [ɔkˈtæmərəs] *a.* (花的)八基数的.
oc·tam·e·ter [ɔkˈtæmitə] *n.* 八音步诗〔由八音步组成的诗行〕. — *a.* 有八音步的.
oc·tan [ˈɔktən] *a.* 在每第八日发生的,有一周的间隔的,隔周的. — *n.*【医】八日热.
oc·tane [ˈɔktein] *n.*【化】辛烷. **~ number [rating, value]** 辛烷值.
oc·tan·gle [ˈɔktæŋgl] *n.* 八边形;八角形 (= octagon).
oc·tan·gu·lar [ɔkˈtæŋgjulə] *a.* 有八角的.
oc·ta·nol [ˈɔktənɔ:l] *n.*【化】辛醇.
Oc·tans [ˈɔktænz] *n.*【天】南极(星)座.
oc·tant [ˈɔktənt] *n.* ①八分圆;八分区;卦限;八分仪;【植】八分体. ②【天】相对两天体成四十五度的位置.
oc·tarch·y [ˈɔktɑ:ki] *n.* ***(pl.*** ***-tarch·ies)*** ①八人执政. ②八政府〔王国〕集团〔有时指盎格鲁-撒克逊时代英格兰的七国〕.
oc·ta·style [ˈɔktəstail] *n.*【建】八柱式.
oc·ta·teuch [ˈɔktətju:k] *n.* 旧约圣经的前八卷.
oc·tave [ˈɔkteiv, -tiv] *n.* ①【宗】节日开始(第)八天. ②[ˈɔktiv]【乐】八音度;一音阶;高〔低〕八度音;低频程;【物】倍频程. ③【韵】十四行诗 *(sonnet)* 的起首八行;八行(体)诗. ④八个一组的事物. ⑤【剑术】八种防守姿势中的第八式. ⑥〔英〕装 $13\frac{1}{2}$ 加仑的酒桶. — *a.* ①八个一组的;八行的. ②【乐】高八度音的.
Oc·ta·vi·a [ɔkˈteivjə] *n.* 奥克塔维亚〔女子名〕.
Oc·ta·vi·us [ɔkˈteivjəs] *n.* 奥克塔维厄斯〔男子名〕.
oc·ta·vo [ɔkˈteivəu] *n.* ***(pl.*** ***-s)*** 八开;八开本〔略为 8*vo* 或 8° 或 oct.〕;八开纸;八开页. *a cap ~* $4\frac{1}{4}\times7$ 英寸版本. *a crown ~* $5\times7\frac{1}{2}$ 英寸版本. *an imperial ~* $8\frac{1}{4}\times11\frac{1}{2}$ 英寸版本. *a medium ~* $6\times9\frac{1}{2}$ 英寸版本. *a royal ~* $6\frac{1}{2}\times10$ 英寸版本.
oc·ten·ni·al [ɔkˈtenjəl, -niəl] *a.* 每八年的,八年一回的;第八年的;八年间的.
oc·tet(te) [ɔkˈtet] *n.* 八个一组的东西;【乐】八重唱(曲). 八重奏(曲);八重唱〔八重奏〕演出小组;【韵】十四行诗 (sonnet) 的起首八行;【物】八偶;八重线,八角(体).
oc·til·lion [ɔkˈtiljən] *num.* 〔英〕百万的八次幂〔乘方〕〔一后加四十八个零之数〕;〔法、美〕千的九次幂〔乘方〕〔一后加二十七个零之数〕.
oc·tin·gen·te·na·ry [ˌɔktindʒenˈti:neri] *n.* = octocentenary.
octo- = oct-.
Oc·to·ber [ɔkˈtəubə] *n.* 十月. *the ~ Revolution* (苏联)十月革命.
Oc·to·brist [ɔkˈtəubrist] *n.*【俄史】十月党人.
oc·to·cen·te·na·ry [ˌɔktəusenˈti:nəri], **oc·to·cen·te·ni·al** [ˌɔktəusenˈtenjəl] *n.* 八百周年纪念日.
oc·to·dec·i·mo [ˈɔktəuˈdesiməu] *n.* ***(pl.*** ***~s)*** 十八开 十八开本〔略 18 mo.〕. — *a.* 十八开的.
oc·to·ge·na·r·i·an [ˌɔktəudʒiˈnɛəriən] *a., n.* 八十岁的(人),八十多岁的(人).
oc·to·nal [ˈɔktənl] *a.* 八进位的;【韵】八音步的.
oc·to·na·r·i·an [ˌɔktəuˈnɛəriən] *a., n.*【韵】八音步的(诗句).
oc·to·nar·y [ˈɔktənəri] *a.* 八数的,八之数组成的,八进的,用八进法的. — *n.* ***(pl.*** ***-nar·ies)*** ①用八数所成的一组. ②八行诗节;八行诗.
oc·to·pod [ˈɔktəpɔd] *n.* 八腕亚目 *(Octopoda)* 动物〔包括章鱼和魟鱼〕. **-an** *a., n.* **-ous** *a.*
oc·to·pus [ˈɔktəpəs] *n.* ***(pl.*** ***~es, -pi*** [-pai]***)*** ①【动】章鱼;蛸;〔O-〕章鱼属. ②周围爪牙众多的人〔团体〕.
oc·to·push [ˈɔktəpuʃ] *n.* 水中曲棍球.
oc·to·roon [ˌɔktəuˈru:n] *n.* (有黑人血统八分之一的)黑白混血儿.

oc·tose [ˈɔktəus] *n.* 【化】辛糖

oc·to·syl·lab·ic [ˈɔktəusiˈlæbik] *a., n.* 八音节的(词、诗句)。

oc·to·syl·la·ble [ˈɔktəuˌsiləbl] *n.* 八音节词;八音节诗句. —*a.* 八音节的.

oc·troi [ˈɔktrwɑː] *n.* 〔F.〕(法国或印度的)入市税;入市税征收区;入市税征收所[征收员].

O.C.T.U. = Officer Cadet Training Unit 〔英〕军官学校学员训练队.

oc·tu·ple [ˈɔktju(ː)pl] *a.* 八倍的,八重的;八部分组成的. —*n.* 八倍之物. —*vt., vi.* 增加成八倍.

oc·tyl [ˈɔktəl] *n.* 【化】辛基.

oc·u·lar [ˈɔkjulə] *a.* 眼睛的,视觉上的,用眼的;眼状的. ~ *demonstration* 直观演示. *an* ~ *witness* 目击者,见证人. —*n.* 目镜;〔谑〕眼睛. **~-net** 网格目镜. **-ly** *ad.*

oc·u·lar·ist [ˈɔkjulərist] *n.* 制造假眼的人.

oc·u·list [ˈɔkjuːlist] *n.* 眼科医生[专家].

oc·u·lo·mo·tor [ˌɔkjuləuˈməutə] *a.* ①眼球运动的;动眼的. ②【解】动眼神经的. —*n.* 【解】动眼神经.

O.D., OD = ①officer of the day 值日军官. ②overdraft, overdrawn 透支. ③outside diameter 外径. ④an overdose of drugs 过度剂量的毒品. ⑤olive drab 橄榄色.

od[1] [ɔd] *n.* 假想的自然力. 〔德国化学家 Reichenbach 等为说明磁力、化学作用等而假定自然界存在的一种力〕.

od[2], **'od, Od** [ɔd] *n.* 〔卑〕= God. *Od's wounds!* 〔古〕他妈的! 哎呀! (= zounds).

o·da·lisk, o·da·lisque [ˈəudəlisk] *n.* (伊斯兰教国家后宫里的)女奴,婢妾.

o·day [ˈəudei] *n.* 〔美俚〕钱.

odd [ɔd] *a.* ①奇妙的,奇特的,古怪的,可笑的. ②临时的,不固定的;额外的. ③余的,残余的;有零数的,带零头的;零星的. ④(一双、一对中的)吊单的,不全的,无配对的;零散的. ⑤奇数的,二除不尽的;单(数)的,奇数号的. ⑥偏僻的. *an* ~ *fellow* 奇人. ~ *customs* 奇怪的风俗. ~ *jobs* 临时工作,零活. *an* ~ *hand [man]* 临时雇工,打杂短工. *do it at* ~ *moments* 在有空的时间做. *sixty* ~ *thousand* 六万几千. *sixty thousand* ~ 六万多,六万挂零. ~ *money* (剩下的)零钱. *There is no contending against* ~. 众寡不敌. *an* ~ *glove* 单只手套. ~ *numbers of a magazine* 零星本的杂志. ~ *numbers* 奇数. ~ *months* 大月. ~ *volumes* 零本,散册. ~ *moments* 余暇. ***ask [beg] no*** **~s** 〔美〕不要求照顾;(比赛)不要求让步. ***at*** **~** ***times [hours]*** 在闲暇的时候,抓工夫,忙里偷闲地,用零碎的时间. ***in some*** **~** ***corner*** 在某个角落里. **~** ***and [or] even*** 猜单双. —*n.* 【高尔夫球】让较弱的对手从打球进一个洞的击球次数中减去一次击球;〔the ~〕多于对方的一次击球 (*cf.* odds). **~ball** *a., n.* 古怪的(人). **~-come-short** (布的)零头;〔*pl.*〕碎屑,零碎物件. **~-come-shortly** 〔口〕不日 (*one of these odd-come-shortlies* 过几天,过些时,不久). ~ **job** *vi.* 干零活,打散工. **~-looking** *a.* 怪,古怪的. ~ **lot** 零星货物,不成套的东西;【交易所】零星股. ~ **man** (赞否各半时)余外握有表决权的一个人. **~-man-out** ①(三人投钱)吊单者中选(法). ②和环境合不来的人. ③局外人. ~ **trick** 【牌戏】决胜负的最后一墩牌. **-ness** *n.*

Odd-fel·low, Odd·fel·low [ˈɔdfeləu] *n.* (18 世纪英国一种近似 Free mason 的)秘密共济会的会员.

odd·ish [ˈɔdiʃ] *a.* 有点古怪的.

odd·i·ty [ˈɔditi] *n.* ①古怪,奇特;怪癖,怪脾气. ②怪人;奇妙的东西.

odd·ly [ˈɔdli] *ad.* ①奇妙地,奇怪地. ②零碎地,成奇数. ③额外地,附加地. ~ ***enough*** 说也奇怪. ~ **even** 奇数和偶数的积. ~ **odd** 奇数和奇数的积.

odd·ment [ˈɔdmənt] *n.* 零头,碎屑;〔*pl.*〕零碎物件,残余,残品;〔*pl.*〕【印】书的本文以外的部分.

odd-pin·nate [ˈɔdˈpineit] *a.* 【植】奇数羽状的〔指复叶〕.

odds [ɔdz] *n. pl.* 〔常用作单数〕①不平等(的东西);差额. ②胜算,差异;差距,优劣之差;(优者给对方的)让步;〔美〕恩惠. ③不和,相争. ④希望,可能性. ⑤赛过. ⑥遭遇. *What's the ~?* 那有什么要紧? *The ~ are in our favour.* 我们胜利的希望多. *The ~ are against you.* 形势对你不利. *It is ~ that* [〔古〕*but*] ... = *The ~ are that ...* 多半,想必. *It sounds a bit over the ~.* 不会有的. *It is within the ~.* 可能有的. ***ask no*** ~ 〔美〕不要求照顾;(比赛中)不要求先让步. ***be at*** ~ ***with*** 和…闹别扭,和…不和,和…有矛盾;处于不利的条件下 (*be at ~ with fate* 遭遇不好). ***by long [all]*** ~ 大大超过地,远远地;肯定地,无疑地. ***fight against longer*** ~ 以寡敌众,以弱敌强. ***lay [give]*** ~ ***of (three) to (one)*** 以对方(一)自己(三)之比和人打赌〔赢则取三,输则赔一〕. ***lay [give] the*** ~ 给与有利条件,给与让步. ***make no*** ~ 没有不相称,平均 (*It makes (or is) no ~.* (两者)没有多大区别,怎么都好). ***make*** ~ ***even*** 除去优劣之差,拉平. ~ ***and ends*** 残余,零碎物件〔事情〕,零星杂品. ***set at*** ~ 使相争. ***shout the*** ~ 说大话. ***take [receive] the*** ~ (打赌时)接受有利的条件,得到让步.

odds-on [ˈɔdzˈɔn] *a.* 大半有希望赢的. *an ~ bet* 大半有希望赢的打赌. *an ~* 得人望的人.

ode [əud] *n.* 颂歌,颂诗,赋〔对意中人、物等所作的抒情诗〕;(古希腊戏剧中合唱队配合音乐舞蹈歌唱的)合唱歌. *Ode to (a) Skylark* 云雀赋. *the book of Odes* (中国的)诗经.

O·dels·thing [ˈəudelstiŋ] *n.* 挪威的众议院.

O·den·se [ˈəuðənsei] *n.* 欧登塞〔丹麦港市〕.

o·de·on [əuˈdiːən], **o·de·um** [əuˈdiːəm] *n.* ***(pl.*** ~***s, o·de·a*** [-ə]***)*** ①〔古希腊、罗马〕(有屋顶的)奏乐堂〔常被用作法庭〕. ②音乐堂,戏院.

O·des·sa [əuˈdesə] *n.* 敖德萨〔苏联港市〕.

O·dets [əuˈdets] *n.* 奥德茨〔姓氏〕.

O·dette [əuˈdet] *n.* 奥德特〔女子名, Ottilia 的爱称〕.

o·de·um [əuˈdiəm] *n.* ***(pl. o·de·a*** [əuˈdiːə]***)*** ①音乐厅,剧场. ②(古希腊、罗马)奏乐厅,音乐堂.

od·i·c [ˈəudik] *a.* 颂诗的,颂歌的.

O·din [ˈəudin] *n.* 【北欧神话】奥丁神〔司智慧、艺术、诗词、战争的神〕.

o·di·ous [ˈəudjəs, -diəs] *a.* 讨厌的;可憎的;丑恶的. **-ly** *ad.* **-ness** *n.*

o·di·um [ˈəudiəm, -djəm] *n.* ①憎恨,厌恶,反感;公愤;臭名;耻辱. ②被憎恨的对象. *expose (sb.) to* ~ 使某人招致公愤.

o·do·graph [ˈəudəgrɑːf, -græf] *n.* 里程表;自动记程仪,航线记录器,计步器.

o·dom·e·ter [ɔˈdɔmitə] *n.* 里程表,路程计.

od·on·tal·gi·a [ˌɔdɔnˈtældʒiə, 〔Am.〕əud-] *n.* 【医】牙痛.

-odont *suf.* 齿.

od·on·t(o)- *comb. f.* 牙齿: *odontology.*

od·on·to·blast [ɔˈdɔntəblæst] *n.* 【解】成牙质细胞. **-ic** *a.*

od·on·to·clast [ɔˈdɔntəklæst] *n.* 【解】破牙质细胞.

O·don·to·glos·sum [ɔˌdɔntəuˈglɔsəm] *n.* 【植】(中南美野生的)兰属;〔o-〕兰;具有舌形唇瓣的兰花.

o·don·to·graph [əuˈdɔntəgrɑːf, -græf] *n.* ①【仪】画齿规. ②【医】牙面描记器.

od·on·toid [ɔˈdɔntɔid] *a.* 齿状的,牙样的.

o·don·tol·o·gist [ˌəudɔnˈtɔlədʒist] *n.* 牙医师.

od·on·tol·o·gy [ˌɔdɔnˈtɔlədʒi] *n.* 齿科学.

o·don·to·phore [əuˈdɔntəfɔː] *n.* 【解】牙嵴板. **-toph·o·ral** *a.*

o·dor [ˈəudə] *n.* 〔Am.〕= odour.

o·dor·ant [ˈəudərənt] *n.* 有气味的物质〔东西〕.

o·dor·if·er·ous [ˌəudəˈrifərəs] *a.* 有香气的,香;〔口〕

有气味[臭味]的. **-ly** *ad.*

o·dor·ous [ˈəudərəs] *a.* 〔诗〕= odoriferous. **-ly** *ad.* **-ness** *n.*

o·dour [ˈəudə] *n.* ①(臭或香的)气味;香,香气;臭气. ②味道;迹象. ③声望,名誉;名气. ④香水;香料. *the ~ of roses* 玫瑰香. *an ~ of sanctity* 崇高的声誉. ***be in [fall into] bad [ill] ~*** 名誉不好[变坏]. ***be in good ~ with*** 对…有威望;受…欢迎. **-less** *a.* 没有香气[气味]的.

ODT = Office of Defense Transportation 〔美旧〕国防运输局.

od·yl [ˈɔdil] *n.* = od[1]

O·dys·se·us [əˈdisjuːs] *n.* 【希神】奥德修斯〔荷马史诗《奥德赛》中的主人公. 曾指挥特洛伊战争,献木马计,使希腊获胜〕.

Od·ys·sey [ˈɔdisi] *n.* ①《奥德赛》〔荷马所著史诗〕. ②〔o-〕长期的漂泊[冒险旅行]. *His odyssey of passion, friendship, love, and revenge was now finished.* 他的热情、友谊、爱情和复仇的漫长历程,到此结束了.

Oe- 为希腊语和拉丁语 'e-' 字母的变体,旧时在词书中写为 œ, 今多拼为 oe, 有时亦作 e, 如 oecology 亦作 ecology.

O.E., OE = ①Old English 古代英语. ②omissions excepted 遗漏不在此限〔常印在帐单上;也作 o.e.〕.

OECD = Organization for Economic Cooperation and Development 经济合作与发展组织.

oe·cist [ˈiːsist] *n.* (古希腊)殖民地开拓者.

oe·col·o·gy [iːˈkɔlədʒi] *n.* = ecology.

oec·u·men·i·cal [ˌiːkjuːˈmenikəl] *a.* = ecumenical.

OED = Oxyethylene Docosanol 羟乙基 22 碳烷醇〔水温上升剂〕.

O.E.D., OED = *Oxford English Dictionary* 《牛津大词典》.

oe·de·ma [iːˈdiːmə] *n.* 【医】浮肿,水肿.

oed·i·pal [ˈiːdipəl, ˈedi-] *a.* 【心】恋母情结的.

Oe·di·pus [ˈiːdipəs, 〔Am.〕 ˈedipəs] *n.* 【希神】俄狄浦斯〔底比斯王子,曾破解怪物斯芬克斯 (Sphinx) 的谜语,后误杀其父并娶母为妻,发觉后自刺双目,死于流浪中〕;〔喻〕解迷的人. ~ **complex** 【心】恋母情结.

O.E.E.C. = Organization for European Economic Cooperation 欧洲经济合作组织.

oeil-de-boeuf [əːidəˈbəːf] *n.* 〔F.〕【建】圆窗.

oeil·lade [œˈjad] *n.* 〔F.〕媚眼,秋波.

oe·nol·o·gy [iːˈnɔlədʒi] *n.* 酿酒学,酒类研究. **-log·i·cal** *a.* **-ogist** *n.* 酒类学家.

oe·no·mel [ˈiːnəmel] *n.* ①(古希腊) 蜜酒. ②【诗】甜言蜜语,花言巧语.

o'er [əuə, ɔə] *ad., prep.* 〔诗〕= over.

Oer·li·kon [ˈəːlikən, -kɔn] *n.* 厄利肯式自动高射炮.

oer·sted [ˈəːsted] *n.* 【电】奥斯忒〔磁场强度单位〕. **~-meter** 磁场强度计.

oe·so·ph·ag·e·al [iːˌsɔfəˈdʒi(ː)əl] *a.* 食道的.

oe·soph·a·gus [iːˈsɔfəgəs] *n.* *(pl.* *~es, -gi* [-gai]*)* 【解】食道.

oes·tri·ol [ˈiːstriɔl] *n.* 【生化】雌三醇 (= estriol).

oes·tro·gen [ˈiːstrədʒən] *n.* 【生化】雌激素.

oes·trum [ˈiːstrəm], **oes·trus** [ˈiːstrəs] *n.* ①机能亢进,激烈的冲动;狂热;【动】动情(期),发情(期) *(opp.* anoestrum*)*. ②牛虻.

oeuvre [ˈəːvr] *n.* 〔F.〕(文艺)作品.

OF = Old French 古法语.

O.F. = Odd Fellows 〔英〕一种秘密共济会的会员.

of [强 ɔv; 弱 əv, v, f] *prep.* ①〔表示所属关系〕…的,属于…的. *the house ~ my elder brother* 我哥哥的家. *men ~ that time* 当时的人们. *the secret ~ success* 成功的秘密. ②〔部分〕…之中的;在…中. *a friend of mine* 我的一位朋友. *one ~ them* 他们中间的一个. *the most dangerous ~ enemies* 敌人当中最危险的. *five ~ us* 我们当中的五个. ③〔数量、程度〕…的,…数量的. *three pieces ~ meat* 三块肉. *a cup ~ tea* 一杯茶. *a ton ~ coal* 一吨煤. ④〔材料〕…做的,用…制的. *a box ~ wood* 木头(制的)箱子. *a house ~ stone* 石头砌的房子. *made ~ gold* 金子做的. *make a fool ~ him* 拿他当傻子. *make a teacher ~ one's son* 把儿子训练成教师. ⑤〔表示范围、方面〕关于…,对…如何,在…方面怎样. *a story ~ adventures* 冒险故事. *think well ~ sb.* 觉得某人好. *think ~* 想起…. *blind ~ one eye* 瞎一只眼. *afraid ~ a dog* 怕狗. *swift ~ foot* 脚快. *quick ~ eye* 眼快. *ten years ~ age* 年纪十岁. *inform sb. ~* 控诉某人(什么罪). *It is true ~ every case.* 在任何情形下都是真的. *What ~ the danger?* 危险算什么. ⑥〔同格关系〕…这个. *the city ~ Rome* 罗马城. *the name of James* 詹姆士这个名子. *the action ~ running* 跑这个动作. *the fact ~ my having seen him* 我见过他这个事实. *that fool ~ a man* 那个蠢汉. *an angel ~ a woman* 一个天使般的女人. *the five ~ us* 我们五个人. *this only son ~ mine* 我的这个独生子. ⑦〔距离、位置、分离、除去、摆脱〕…的,距离…. *within ten miles ~ Beijing* 距北京十里以内. *loss ~ energy* 精力的消耗. *free ~ charge* 免费. *independent ~* 不受…支配的. *to the north ~ Paris* 在巴黎的北方. *cure [heal] sb. ~ a disease* 医好某人的病. *steal sb. ~ his watch* 偷去某人的手表. ⑧〔起源、根源、原因〕…的,从,向;因…,害…. *He comes ~ a good stock.* 他出身好. *borrow [buy, learn] a thing ~ sb.* 向某人借[买、学习]东西. *sick ~ measles* 出疹子. *die ~ consumption* 死于肺病. *be sick ~ inaction* 懒散得发腻. *be weary ~ life* 厌世. ⑨〔同表示性质、状态的名词搭配构成定语、表语〕…的,有…的. *a ship ~ 800 tons* 八百吨位的船. *a girl ~ ten (years old)* 十岁的姑娘. *a matter ~ importance* 重要事件. *a man ~ ability* 有能力的人. *be ~ the opinion that* 认为. ⑩〔动宾关系〕 *the telling ~ lies* 说谎. *the betrayal ~ a secret* 泄露秘密. *the creation ~ man* 创造人类. *in search ~ knowledge* 探求知识. *take care ~ one's health* 注意健康. *be glad ~* 喜欢. ⑪〔著作或行为的主体〕 *the works of Shakespeare* 莎士比亚的作品. *He is beloved ~ all.* 他为众人所爱戴. *It is clever ~ you to do so.* 你那样做真聪明. ⑫〔构成时间状语〕. *He comes ~ an evening.* 他常在傍晚时候来. *all ~ a sudden* 突然. *~ course* 当然. *~ late* 近来. *~ late years* 近年来. *~ this date* 〔美〕从即日起 (=〔英〕 as from this date). ⑬〔时间〕〔美口〕…点差几分〔= to …〕 *(opp.* 〔美〕 after; 〔英〕 past*)*. *five minutes ~ four* 差五分四点. *a quarter ~ ten* 十点差一刻.

of- *pref.* 〔用于f之前〕= ob-.

O.F.C. = Overseas Food Corporation 海外粮食公司.

Ofc = ①office. ②official.

off [ɔːf, ɔf] *ad.* ①〔运动〕向那边,隔开. *be ~* 走,去,逃. *I must be ~.* 我得走了. *Where are you ~ to?* 你去哪里? *fly ~* 飞去. *go ~* 走掉〔*cf.* O- you go! 滚!〕. *run ~* 跑掉. ②〔移动〕离开,脱掉 *(opp.* on*)*. *beat ~* 打退(敌人). *put ~* 延期. *ward ~ an attack* 挡开攻击. *come ~* 脱落,(柄)脱掉. *get ~* 脱(衣);下(马). *fall ~* (从马上)掉下来. *look ~* 掉转视线,朝别处看. *take ~* 脱(衣服、帽子、鞋子等). ③〔断、断绝、脱落、消失〕 *bite ~* 咬下来,咬断. *clip ~* 剪下来,剪断. *cut ~* 割下来,切断,割掉. *cut ~ the gas [water]* 关掉煤气[自来水]. *cut ~ from the telephone* 挂断电话. *tear ~* 扯下来. *The flowers were all ~.* 花全落了. *The gilt is ~.* 镀金脱落. ②〔静止位置、距离、时间〕离开,隔着,在那边,有(几里)远. *a mile ~* 有一英里路. *a little way ~* 有一小段路. *far ~* 远,远在. *How far ~ is it? — A great way ~.* 有多远? ——很远. *only three months ~* 只要再过三个月;只在三个月

前。③〔动作的完了、中止等〕…完，…光。*drink* ~ 喝完。*pay* ~ 付清。*finish* ~ 做完。*leave* ~ *work* 停止工作。*break* ~ 忽然中止，中断。*be* ~ *with* 和…断绝关系。*The game was called* ~. 比赛取消了。④〔折扣〕. *10 per cent* ~ *on all cash purchases* 现款购货一律九折。⑤〔渐渐〕减少，…下来[起来]. *fall* ~ 扫兴颓丧；(利益等)减少。*cool* ~ 冷起来，(热情)低落；平静下来。*wear* ~ (精力)衰退；(衣服等)渐破。⑥〔休息〕. *I had an afternoon* ~. 我下午休息了半天。***be badly*** ~ 生活困难；贫穷；运气不佳。***be better*** ~ 处境较好，生活条件比较好，比较宽裕。***be comfortably*** ~ 收入很多，生活有保障。***be well*** ~ 生活好过，处境良好。***be worse*** ~ 情况恶化，情况更差；更加贫困。***either*** ~ ***or on*** 总之，不管怎么样。~ ***and on*** = *on and* ~ 断断续续，不规则地；偶尔；(航海)时而离开陆地，时而转向陆地 (*It rains* ~ *and on.* 雨忽下忽停)。***take oneself*** ~ 走，去，逃。— *int.* 走开！ 躲开！ ***Off!*** = ***Be*** ~***!*** = ***Stand*** ~***!*** 滚开！ ***Off with*** 〔祈使语气〕去；去掉 (*Off with you!* 去你的！ *Off with your cap!* 脱帽！)去！ 滚！ — *a.* ①远的，那一边的。*the* ~ *side of the wall.* 墙那边[后面]。②(特指车、马的)右侧的，右边的 (*opp.* near). *an* ~ *horse* 右边的一匹马。*the* ~ *front [hind] wheel* (马车)右边的前[后]轮。*the* ~ *side of the road* 路的右手边；【板球】打球员右前方[投球员左方]的 (*opp.* on). ③离开大路的，横的；枝节的；〔仅用作表语〕掉，落 *an* ~ *road* 横街。*an* ~ *issue* 枝节问题。*the wheel is* ~ 车轮脱了。④没事的，休息的。*an* ~ *day* 休息日。*during* ~ *hours* 在闲空时。*an* ~ *season* 闲季，非生产季节。⑤腐坏的(鱼、肉等)。*The fish is a bit* ~. 这条鱼有点坏了。⑥〔口〕有毛病，不对；〔美俚〕有点失常；怪的，疯的。*I was* ~ *by a week.* 我算差了一个星期。*I am feeling rather* ~ *to-day.* 今天总觉得不大舒服。*That old man is a bit* ~. 那个老头子有点儿怪。⑦偶尔，万一。*I came on the* ~ *chance of finding [that I would find] you.* 我是碰巧来的。~ *flavour* 臭气，臭味。~ *gas* 废气。~ *products* 副产物。~ *side* = offside. ~ *year* (水果等的)小年；(生产的)不景气年；〔美〕非大选年。*an* ~ *year election* 中期选举。— *n.* 【板球】(打球员的)右前方 (= ~ side). — *vt.* 〔口〕通知中止(交涉、契约、计划等)，中止(和人)交涉，停约；除去；杀掉。—*vi.* 走开，离开。*He* ~*ed with his coat.* 他脱去了上衣。— *prep.* ①离开，脱离，从，由。②【海】在…海面。~ *the track* 出轨。*fall* ~ *a ladder* 从梯子上掉下。~ *the stage* 离开舞台。*Keep* ~ *the grass!* 禁入草地！ *be thrown* ~ *the horse* 从马上摔下来。*cut a slice* ~ *the joint* 从肉块上切一片下来。*three years* ~ *forty* 四十不足三岁。*He played* ~ *5.* 〔比赛〕他让了5分。*5 miles* ~ *the coast of Wenchow* 在离温州海岸5英里的海面上。*dine* ~ *bread and butter* 吃涂有黄油的面包。~ ***one's base*** 〔美口〕有病的，不舒服的。~ ***one's eggs*** 〔美俚〕误解。~ ***one's feed*** 〔美俚〕无食欲。~ ***the beam*** 〔美俚〕不对，错误。~ ***the reel*** 〔美〕立即，马上。~**-camara** *a.* ①在电影[电视]镜头之外的。②私生活中的。~**cast** [ˈɔːfˌkɑːst, -ˌkæst] ①*a.* 被抛弃的，被遗弃的；放荡的。②无用的人[物] (= castoff). **off-chance** [ˈɔːftʃɑːns] *n.* 不大会有的机会，万一的希望，侥幸。~**-colour** [ˈɔːfˌkʌlə] *a.* ①不对头的。②不十分合适的；低级趣味的；有伤风化的，猥亵的。*an* ~ *joke* 下流的玩笑。~**-design** *a.* 未预计的。~**-grade** *a.* 等外，级外的，低级的。~**-duty** *a.* 下班后的；业余的。~**-guage** *a.* 非标准的。~**-hour** *n.* ①不在值勤的时间。②(交通等)不拥挤的时间。~**-island** (与海岸完全脱离的)离岛。~**-key** [ˈɔːfˈkiː] *a.* ①走音的，走调的。②不正常的，不适合的，不协调的。~**-limits** [ˈɔːfˈlimits] *a.* 禁止入内的〔指某种场所奉令不让某类人进入〕，不许参观的，谢绝惠顾的。~**-line** [ˈɔːfˈlain] *a.* ①【自】离线的。②不在铁路沿线的。~**load** [ˈɔːfˈləud] *vt., vi.* ①卸货，退载；从…卸下货物。②发泄(忧伤、苦闷等)，抒发；解除(苦闷、负担等)。③(从枪膛中)退出子弹。④处理。⑤卸(货)。~**mike** [ˈɔːfmaik] *ad.* 在离开扩音话筒较远处；不用扩音话筒(时)。~**-off-Broadway** [ˈɔːfˈɔːfˈbrɔːdˌwei] ①*a.* (在纽约市的小礼堂、教堂、咖啡馆等所作的)试验性、非商业性演出的；与此种演出有关的。② *ad.* 在此种演出中；在这种方式上演的场所中。③*n.* 此种演出。~**-pollination**【生】混杂授粉。~**-put** *vt.* 〔英俚〕使困窘，使为难。~**-putting** [ˈɔːfˌputiŋ] *a.* 〔主英〕老是推脱的；使人懊恼的，讨厌的。~**take** 出口；泄水处；排水渠；支管；【电】分接头。~**-the-bench** *a.* 法庭以外的。~**-the-peg,** ~**-the-rack** *a.* 非定做的，现成的。~**-the-shelf** [ˈɔːfðəˈʃelf] *a.* 买来就可用的〔商品，尤指军用品无需改装〕。~ **track** 恶劣的跑道。~**-white** [ˈɔːfˈwait] *a.* 米色的，灰白色的，黄白色的。

off. = ①offered. ②office; officer; official.

of·fal [ˈɔfəl] *n.* 碎屑，垃圾；食品下脚料〔碎肉等〕；内脏，下水；杂鱼，低级鱼；糠，麸(等)；废料；次品。

off·beat [ˈɔːfbiːt] *a.* 次要的；不规则的；不落俗套的。— *n.* 【乐】弱拍。

Of·fen·bach [ˈɔːfənbɑːk], **Jacques** 奥芬巴克(1819—1880)法国歌剧作曲家。

of·fence [əˈfens] *n.* ①罪，罪过；【法】犯罪；违犯，违反 (*against*). ②无礼，侮辱；冒犯，触怒。③引起反感的事物。④【军】攻击 (*opp.* defense)；〔集合词〕攻击部队。⑤【圣】罪源，绊脚石。*a first* ~ 初犯。*an* ~ *against decency [good manners]* 无礼，没规矩。*No* ~ *was meant.* 并没有触犯的意思；不是恶意讲(做)的。*O- is the best defense.* 攻击是最好的防御。***commit an*** ~ ***against*** 犯(法)，违背[破坏](法律、风俗)，侵犯(权利)。***give [cause]*** ~ ***to*** 触怒…，使…生气，得罪。***take*** ~ 见怪，生气，感到自己受委屈或侮辱。***without*** ~ 不使人见怪，不触犯人；没有生气。**-less** *a.* 不得罪人的，老实的，温和的；无力进攻的。

offend [əˈfend] *vt.* ①冒犯，触犯，得罪；激怒；侮辱；伤害(…的感情)。②使不舒服。③使绊倒，使犯罪。~ *sb. unintentionally* 无意中得罪人。~ *the ear [eye]* 刺耳[眼]，逆耳[难看]。***be*** ~***ed with (sb.) for (his act) [at (his words)]*** (因某人的行为，言语而)发怒，生气。— *vi.* ①犯罪，犯过错。②违犯，违背(礼仪等) (*against*). ③引起不舒服；得罪人。~ ***against*** *(the law)* 违犯(法律)。

of·fend·er [əˈfendə] *n.* 罪犯，犯人；得罪人的人，冒犯者。*a first* ~ 初犯。*a juvenile* ~ 少年犯。*an old [a repeated]* ~ 惯犯，积犯。

of·fense [əˈfens] *n.* 〔Am.〕= offence.

of·fen·sive [əˈfensiv] *a.* ①讨厌的，令人不快的。②无礼的；冒犯的；唐突的。③进攻(性)的，攻击的，攻势的 (*opp.* defensive). *an* ~ *sight [smell, sound]* 令人不快的景象[气味，声音]。*an* ~ *person* 无礼的人，讨厌的人。~ *weapons* 进攻性武器。*an* ~ *defence* 进攻性的防御。*an* ~ *and defensive alliance* 攻守同盟。— *n.* 进攻，攻势。*a peace* ~ 和平攻势。*a* ~ *on a large scale* 大举进攻。***act on [take, assume] the*** ~ 采取攻势。**-ly** *ad.*

of·fer [ˈɔfə] *vt.* ①提供；提出；提议；伸出(手等)。②【商】出价，开价；出售，出卖。③贡献，供奉。④企图，想要。⑤表示愿意。⑥使出现；呈现出；演出。*He* ~*ed me his seat.* 他把他的座位让给了我。~ *a few ideas* 提几点意见。~ *the house for £1,000* 出售房屋要价千镑。~ *£1,000 for the house* 对该屋出价千镑。~ *without engagement* 【商】虚盘。~ *resistance* 进行抵抗。~ *battle to the enemy* 向敌人挑战。— *vi.* ①出现，呈现，自告奋勇。②提议；求婚。③献祭。④〔古〕企图，尝试 (*at*). ***as opportunity*** ~***s*** 有机会的时候。~ ***itself*** 呈现，出现。~ ***one's hand*** ①伸手(给人握手)。②向女人求婚。~ ***up oneself*** 牺牲自己。***take the first opportunity that*** ~***s*** 一有机会就利

用. — *n.* ①提议;提供,提出. ②【商】出价,作价;报价;发价. ③贡献. ④〔古〕求婚〔~ of marriage 之略〕. ⑤〔古〕企图. ***accept [decline] an ~*** 接受[不接受]提议. ***make an ~ (of)*** ①提议;提供. ②出价. ***on ~*** 出卖. ***receive an ~*** 接受提议. **-er, -or** *n.*

of·fer·ing [ˈɔfəriŋ] *n.* ①提议;提供. ②贡献;供品,祭品,(给教会的)捐款. ③礼物. ④(上市的)股票,公债;出售物. ⑤课程. *a free-will ~* 自由捐献. *a peace ~* (要求和解[赔不是]的)友好赠品.

of·fer·to·ry [ˈɔfətəri] *n.* ①【天主】奉献仪式;奉献歌;(英国教会收集施舍金时念的)圣语;收集施舍金. ②献纳;捐献品;献金,捐款.

off·hand [ˈɔːfˈhænd, ˈɔf-] *a.* ①临时的;即席的,无准备的;随便的. ②唐突的,简慢的. ③自动的,无人管理的. ④(射击)无依托立射的. *an ~ manner* 随随便便. *~ remarks* 随便说出的话. ***act in an ~ way*** 举止不检点. ***be ~ with sb.*** 对人简慢. — *ad.* ①立即;即席. ②随便;唐突. *I can't tell ~ how much it will cost.* 我不能立刻告诉你它值多少钱.

off·hand·ed [ˈɔːfˈhændid, ˈɔf-] *a.* 〔口〕 = offhand. **-ly** *ad.* **-ness** *n.*

of·fice [ˈɔfis] *n.* ①职务,任务. ②公职,官职;职责,任务. ③政府机关,公署,部,司,处,局,科. ④〔常 *pl.*〕办公室;办事处,事务处;营业处,…处;〔美〕诊室,诊所. ⑤号,店,公司,〔英〕保险公司. ⑥职员,全体职工. ⑦〔常 *pl.*〕帮助,斡旋. ⑧【宗】礼拜式,仪式,祷告;祭礼;圣餐. ⑨〔*pl.*〕〔口〕厨房;〔口〕厕所;〔美俚〕学生偷懒玩要的地方;〔英空俚〕驾驶员座位. ⑩〔英俚〕暗示. *the ~ of host* 主人的任务. *the Home O-* 〔英〕内务部. *the War O-* 〔英〕陆军部. *the Post O-* 邮政局. *the O- of Works* 工务科. *a lawyer's ~* 律师事务所. *a box ~* (戏院的)售票处. *a ticket* (〔英〕*booking*) *~* (车、船等的)售票处. *an inquiry ~* 询问处. *a dentist's ~* 〔美〕牙科诊所. *a printing ~* 印刷所. *a fire [fire-insurance] ~* 火灾保险公司. *say O- = say one's O-* 做祷告. ***be in an ~*** 在办事处工作. ***be in ~*** 在职;(内阁)当政,执政. ***be out of ~*** 离职;下台. ***by [through] the good ~s of*** 由…的斡旋,由…的尽力. ***do sb. kind ~s*** 帮某人忙. ***do the ~ of*** 担任…职务. ***enter upon ~*** 就职. ***fat ~*** 肥缺. ***give the ~*** 〔俚〕暗示. ***go out of ~*** 下野,放弃政权. ***hold an ~ = hold ~*** 任职,有职,在职. ***leave [resign] ~*** 辞职. ***~ procedure*** 【计算机】管理方法. ***~s of profit*** 收入好的职务,好差事. ***perform the last ~s*** 举行葬礼. ***take ~*** 就职,上台,掌权. ***take the ~*** 接受暗示. ***the Holy O-*** (天主教的)宗教法庭. ***the party in ~ [out of ~]*** 执政党[在野党]. — *vt.* 〔美俚〕警告,告诉内幕. **~-bearer** 〔英〕官员,公务员,职员. **~-block** 办事处集中的街段. ~ **boy** (办公室的)勤杂员. ~ **building [block]** 办公大楼. **~clerk** 职员,办事员. ~ **copy** 公文正本;正式抄本. ~ **girl** 女职员,女办事员. **~holder** 〔美〕官员 = office-bearer. ~ **hours** 〔*pl.*〕办公时间,营业时间;〔美〕(医生的)门诊时间. ~ **hunter [seeker]** 〔美〕谋求官职的人,猎官者. ~ **procedure** (计算机的)管理方法. ~ **tickler** 【商】(放备忘录用的)备忘箱. ~ **work** 办公室工作,事务,公务.

of·ficer [ˈɔfisə] *n.* ①官员,办事员,(高级)职员. ②【军】军官,武官;警官;法警;【海】(商船的)船长,高级船员. ③干事,理事. *a police ~* 警官. *a public ~* 官员. *an ~ of state* 〔英〕大臣. *a commanding ~* 司令官. *a general ~* 将级军官. *a flag ~* (海军)将官. *a chief petty ~* 【海军】〔英〕上士,〔美〕军士长. *a petty ~ 1st [2nd] class* 【海军】〔英〕中士[下士],〔美〕上士[中士]. *a military [naval] ~* 陆[海]军军官. *an ~ of the day* 【军】值日军官. *an ~ of the watch* 舰上值班军官. *~s and men* 官兵. *a first ~* 【海】一级驾驶员,大副. *~ of the day [week]* 值日[星]官. *~'s morale* 〔军俚〕威士忌. — *vt.* 〔常用被动式〕①给…配置军官[高级船员]. ②(做军官)指挥,统率. ③管理. *~ an army* 给军队配备军官.

of·fi·cial [əˈfiʃəl] *a.* ①职务上的,公务上的,官员的,公的;担任官[公]职的. ②(出自)官方的,法定的,公认的,正式的. ③官气十足的;讲究形式的. ④依据药典(配制)的;收入药典的. *~ duties* 公务. *~ responsibilities* 职责. *an ~ residence* 官邸. *an ~ gazette* 〔Eng.〕官方通报. *an ~ letter [note]* 公函;公文. *an ~ report* 公报. *an ~ record* 正式记录. *an ~ list (of quotation)* 【商】公定行市表. *~ sanction* 批准,核准. *~ circumlocution [red-tape]* 官僚主义,文牍主义. *with ~ solemnity* 要官腔,摆官僚架子. — *n.* ①官员,行政人员,高级职员. ②宗教法庭法官. ③【运】裁判. *governmental ~s* 政府官员. *public ~s* 官员. *bank ~s* 银行职员. **~dom** *n.* 〔集合词〕官员;官场;官派,官僚作风. ~ **family** 内阁,部长们. **-ism** *n.* 官制;官派,拖拉作风等;文牍主义,官僚主义,官僚脾性. **-ize** *vt.* 使成为正式的;使经过例行手续;把…置于官方控制下. **-ly** *ad.* 以职员身分;用职权;职务上;正式.

of·fi·cial·ese [əfiʃəˈliːz] *n.* 〔美〕公文英语;官场公文体.

of·fi·ci·ant [əˈfiʃiənt] *n.* 司仪牧师,主祭.

of·fi·ci·ar·y [əˈfiʃiəri] *n.* (*pl.*-**ar·ies**) 官员团. — *a.* 与职务有关的,由任职而得来的.

of·fi·ci·ate [əˈfiʃieit] *vi.*, *vt.* ①执行(职务),主持(会议);做(*as*). ②【宗】(为…充当)司祭;(主持仪式). ③充当(比赛等的)裁判. ***~ as best man*** 做男傧相. ***~ as host*** 作东道主,当东. ***~ at a marriage*** 主持婚礼.

of·fi·ci·nal [ˌɔfiˈsainl, ɔˈfisinl] *a.* ①(植物等)药用的;成药的. ②依据药方的. — *n.* (一般)成药.

of·fi·cious [əˈfiʃəs] *a.* ①爱管闲事的. ②【外交】非官方的,非正式的 (*opp.* official). ③〔古〕亲切的,好意的;殷勤的. *an ~ statement* 非正式声明. **-ly** *ad.* **-ness** *n.*

off·ing [ˈɔfiŋ, ˈɔːf-] *n.* (岸上能见的远处)海上,海面,洋面;〔喻〕不远的将来. ***gain [keep] an ~*** 驶出海面;航行在海面上. ***in the ~*** 在海面;在附近;好象就要来似的. ***take an ~*** 驶出海面;〔口〕逃走.

off·ish [ˈɔfiʃ, ˈɔːf-] *a.* 〔口〕不亲热的,冷淡的,疏远的;刚愎的.

off-li·cence [ˈɔ(ː)f-laisəns] *n.* 〔英〕(不许堂饮只许外卖的)卖酒执照 (*opp.* on-license).

off-lim·its [ˈɔ(ː)fˈlimits] *n. pl.* 禁止入内(地区).

off·print [ˈɔːfprint, ˈɔf-] *n.*, *vt.* 翻印,抽印,选刊.

off·scour·ings [ˈɔːfskauəriŋz, ˈɔf-] *n. pl.* 污物;垃圾;破烂东西,废料;(人类的)渣滓.

off·set [ˈɔːfset, ˈɔf-] *n.* ①抵销,抵销物,(优点对缺点等的)弥补,补偿 (*to; against*). ②分支;支脉;【植】短匐茎,侧枝,萌蘖枝. ③【机】偏置(管);迂回管;支管;【测】支矩;【印】胶印;背面蹭脏;【建】壁阶;【地】水平断错;【船】型值;船体尺码表. ④〔罕〕出发. ⑤出发,开始. ⑥【矿】纵坑道. *~ construction* 支距画图法. *an ~ cylinder* 偏置汽缸. *an ~ pipe* 偏置管,迂回管. *~ tool* 偏刀,鹅颈刀. —*vt.* [ɔːfˈset, ɔf-] (***off·set***) ①抵销;(拿优点)弥补(缺点). ②【印】用胶印法印刷;蹭脏(纸的)背面;【建】为…建壁阶;【机】在…作迂回管;偏置. *~ the loss* 弥补损失. *~ debits against credits* 进行借方贷方的冲帐结算. — *vi.* ①形成分支. ②【印】蹭脏背面. ~ **printing** 胶印.

off·shoot [ˈɔːfʃuːt, ˈɔf-] *n.* ①分枝,侧枝,萌蘖枝. ②支脉;支流;横路. ③衍生物 (*from*). ④旁系子孙;分支.

off·shore [ˈɔːfʃɔː, ˈɔf-] *a.* (风等)(从海岸)向海面吹的;离岸的;海面上的. *an ~ bar* 滨外沙洲. — [ˈɔːfˈʃɔː, ˈɔf-] *ad.* 向海面;离岸;近海岸. ~ **fund** 〔美〕海外投资.

off·side [ˈɔːfˈsaid, ˈɔf-] *a.* ①在对方界内. ②【足球、曲棍球等】越位(犯规) (*opp.* onside);【橄榄球】己方带球球员的前方. ③〔主英〕(车马等的)右边.

off·spring [ˈɔːfspriŋ, ˈɔf-] *n.* 子女;子孙,后代;产物,结果;幼苗;(动物的)仔.
off-stage [ˈɔ(ː)fˈsteidʒ] *n., ad., a.* 舞台后面(的);后台(的);幕后(的).
off·take [ˈɔfteik] *n.* ①排出,排出管道出口;泄水处. ②支管.
off-the-re·cord [ˌɔfðəˈrekɔːd] *a.* 不留记录的;不许发表〔引用〕的,非正式的.
O'Fla·her·ty [əuˈflεəti] *n.* 奥弗莱厄蒂〔姓氏〕.
oft [ɔːft, ɔft] *ad.* 〔古、诗〕经常,常常=often. ***many a time and*** ~ 屡次,再三. ~ ***repeated*** 常常重复的. ~ ***told*** 常常谈起的.
of·ten [ˈɔ(ː)fn, ˈɔːftən] *ad.* 常常,往往,屡次,再三. *How ~ does the tram run?* 这电车多久一班? ***as ~ as*** … 每当. ***as ~ as not*** 屡次,往往. ~ ***and*** ~ 屡次三番,经常. ***more ~ than not*** 往往,多半,大概. ★ ①often 一般用于动词之前,be 及助动词之后;有时也用于句末以加强语气. 如: He ~ goes there. I've ~ been there. I haven't been there very ~. ②〔-t-〕主要是方言发音;在唱歌里需要唱出两个音节的地方也作〔-t-〕.
of·ten·times, oft·times [ˈɔ(ː)fəntaimz] *ad.* 〔古〕屡次,常常.
OG = ①Olympic Games 奥林匹克运动会,奥运会. ②Officer of the guard 卫兵长.
o·gee [ˈəudʒiː, əuˈdʒiː] *n.* 【建】S 形(曲)线;葱形饰;葱形拱. ~ **arch** 葱形拱. ~ **curve** 双弯曲线,S 形曲线.
og·am [ˈɔgəm] *n.* = ogham.
Og·den [ˈɔːgdən] *n.* ①奥格登〔姓氏〕. ②**Charles Kay** ~ 查尔士·开伊·欧格登〔1889—1957,英国心理学家,Basic English 的创议者〕.
og·do·ad [ˈɔgdəuˌæd] *n.* ①数目字八. ②八数所成的群或组.
og·ham [ˈɔgəm] *n.* (古代英国及爱尔兰人的)欧甘文字;欧甘碑铭. — *a.* 欧甘文字的.
o·give [ˈəudʒaiv, əuˈdʒ-] *n.* 【建】交错骨;尖顶穹窿;葱形饰;尖顶部;(炮弹的)蛋形部分. *false* ~ 【物】整流罩. **o·giv·al** *a.*
o·gle [ˈəugl] *n.* 秋波,媚眼. ***an ~ list*** 〔美俚〕病假表. — *vi., vi.* (对…)送秋波,(向…)施媚眼.
O·gle·thorpe [ˈəuglθɔːp] *n.* 奥格尔索普〔姓氏〕.
O gosh [əu gɔʃ] 〔美俚〕向左〔从法语 à gauche 变来〕.
o·gre [ˈəugə] *(fem. o'gress* [ˈəugris]*) n.* (童话等中的)吃人魔鬼;残暴的人;丑怪的人.
o·gr(e)ish [ˈəug(ə)riʃ] *a.* 吃人魔鬼似的.
Og·y·gian [əuˈdʒidʒiən] *a.* 史前的,太古时代的.
oh, Oh [əu] *int.* 哦!啊!呀! ①〔冠于人名前,起呼语作用〕*Oh Jack!* 哦,杰克! *Oh Mary, look!* 玛丽啊,看呀! ②〔表示惊讶、恐惧、痛苦、快乐、悲伤等〕呀,啊. *Oh, what a surprise!* 啊! 真是想不到的事! *Oh, dear!* 啊呀! *Oh, my!* 啊呀! *Oh, yes.* 啊,是的. *Oh, no.* 啊,不. ★同 O,但 Oh 后一般均加用惊叹号!
O'Hare [əuˈhεə] *n.* 奥黑尔〔姓氏〕.
oh-dee [ˈəuˈdiː] *vi.* 〔美俚〕因为〔象是〕服用过量药物致死.
OHG, O.H.G. = Old High German 古代高地德语.
O·hi·o [əuˈhaiəu] *n.* 俄亥俄〔美国州名〕.
ohm [əum] *n.* 欧姆〔电阻单位〕. ~**-ammeter** 欧安计. ~**meter** 欧姆计〔表〕. **Ohm's law** 欧姆定律.
ohm·ic [ˈəumik] *a.* ①欧姆的. ②以欧姆计算的. ③使用欧姆定律的原理装置的.
O.H.M.S. = On His (Her) Magesty's Service 为英王(女王)陛下效劳〔英国公函免付邮费的戳记〕.
o·ho [əuˈhəu] *int.* 嗳哟! 哦嗬! 哦! 〔惊喜、惊异声〕.
o·ho yes [əu jes] = oyes, oyez.
-oid *suf.* …状的(东西),象…的(东西),…质的: **alkaloid, negroid.**

oil [ɔil] *n.* ①油;油类;油状物〔一般是不可数名词,表示种类时则用 *pl.* 如: vegetable and animal ~s 植物油和动物油〕. ②〔*pl.*〕油画颜料;〔口〕油画作品. ③〔*pl.*〕油布;油布雨衣〔衣裤〕. ④〔美俚〕恭维话,奉承话;鬼话,油滑的话. *vegetable [animal, mineral]* ~ 植物〔动物、矿物〕油. *fixed [volatile]* ~ 固定〔挥发〕油. *crude* ~ 原油. *heavy [light]* ~ 重〔轻〕油. *machine* ~ 机器油. ~ *feed* 加油. ~ *feeder* 加油器. ***burn [consume] the midnight*** ~ 焚膏继晷;用功到深夜,开夜车. ***have the*** ~ 〔美俚〕具有讨人喜欢的态度. ***paint in ~s*** 画油画. ***pour [add, put]*** ~ ***on the flame*** 火上加油;使怒气更盛;使争吵更激烈. ***pour [throw]*** ~ ***on the (troubled) waters*** 劝人息怒;调停争端,平息风波. ***smell of*** ~ (作品等)有煞费苦心作成的迹象. ***strike*** ~ 钻探到油脉,发现油矿;〔美〕大获成功,发横财,暴富. — *vt.* ①在…上涂油;给(机器等)上油,加油;把…浸在油中;弄滑. ②使融化. ③收买,行贿. —*vi.* ①(脂肪等)融化,熔化. ②(轮船等)加燃料油. ***have a well-oiled tongue*** 油嘴滑舌,会说话. ~ ***sb.'s hand [palm]*** 贿赂某人. ~ ***one's tongue*** 油嘴滑舌地恭维. ~ ***the wheels*** 加油在轮上;用圆滑手段〔贿赂〕使事情进行顺利. ~ ***the whistle*** 〔美口〕喝一杯. ~**-bearing** *a.* 产油的 (*~-bearing crops* 油料作物). ~ **beetle** 【动】泌油甲〔一种甲虫,受碰扰时,足肢的腺体产生一种油性分泌〕. ~**bird** ①【动】油鸱. ②〔美俚〕老手;老世故. ~ **box** 油箱,润滑油盒. ~ **bunker** 油槽;油库;燃油舱. ~**burg** (二十万吨或更大的)超级油轮. ~ **burner**(暖房用的)油炉;柴油舰〔船〕;〔美俚〕耗油的旧车辆〔船只〕;〔美俚〕常吃嚼烟的人. ~ **cake** 油渣饼. ~**can** 加油器,油壶;〔美俚〕无赖;运油车. ~**-carrier** 油船. ~**cloth** 油布,漆布. ~ **colo(u)r** 〔常 *pl.*〕油画颜料;油画;油漆;油溶性染料. ~ **crop** 油料作物. ~ **cup** 油杯. ~ **dorado** [dəˈrɑːdəu]〔美〕产油丰富的地方;油乡. ~ **engine** 柴油机. ~ **fever** 〔美〕石油采掘热. ~ **field** 油田. ~ **meal** 油渣粉. ~ **and vinegar** 油和醋〔互不相容之物〕. ~ **creek humbug** 〔美俚〕不出油的油井;白费力,徒劳. ~ **of joy** 〔美〕酒类. ~ **of vitriol** 硫酸. ~ **paint** 油画颜料;油漆. ~ **painting** 画油画,油画法. ~ **palm** 油椰 (Elaeis guineensis)〔非洲热带地区产,其籽含椰子油〕. ~**paper** 油纸. ~ **plant** 油料作物. ~ **press** 榨油器. ~ **shale** 【地】油页岩. ~ **share** 石油股票. ~ **sheet** 薄油层. ~**skin** ①油布,防水布. ②〔*pl.*〕油布工装. ~ **slick** (水面上的一层)浮油. ~ **spring** 石油泉〔井〕. ~ **stick** 水面浮油. ~**stone** 油磨石. ~**stove** 煤油炉. ~ **tank steamer,** ~ **tanker** 油船,油轮. ~ **well** 油井. ~ **witch** 〔美〕自称能发现油矿的人. ~ **tight** *a.* 防油的,油渗不进的. **-man** 制油工;石油巨头;油商;油画颜料商.
oil·a·teer [ɔiləˈtiːə] *n.* 〔美〕汽车加油站的职员.
oiled [ɔild] *a.* ①涂了油的;油浸的;化成油状的. ②〔俚〕喝了酒的,有点醉的.
oil·er [ˈɔilə] *n.* ①油商;涂油者;注油器,注油人,注油机;油船,油轮. ②〔口〕油布衣. ③〔口〕马屁精. ④〔O-〕〔美〕墨西哥人的绰号.
oil·i·ly [ˈɔilili] *ad.* ①油一样地;滑溜溜地. ②油嘴滑舌地;会奉承地.
oil·i·ness [ˈɔilinis] *n.* ①油质,油气;含油,油腻. ②会拍马屁,奉承.
oil·y [ˈɔili] *a.* ***(oil·i·er; -i·est)*** ①油的,油质的;含油的,油多的;油腻的;油垢不堪的. ②油滑的,会奉承的.
oink [ɔink] *n.* 猪哼声;仿猪哼声. —*vi.* 学猪哼;效猪哼.
oint·ment [ˈɔintmənt] *n.* 软膏;药膏;油膏. *a fly in the* ~ 白璧之瑕;美中不足.
Oir·each·tas [ˈiərəxθæs] *n.* 〔Ir.〕爱尔兰自由邦议会.
OIRT = 〔F.〕*Organisation Internationale de Radiodiffusion et Télévision* 国际广播电视组织 (= International Radio and Television Organization).

O·jib·way, O·jib·wa [əuˈdʒibwei] *n. (pl. Ojibway, Ojibwa; ~s)* (北美)奥吉韦印第安人.
OK, O.K. [ˈəuˈkei] *a.* 〔口〕好;对,不错;可以;行;阅.— *n. (pl. OK's, O.K.'s)* 同意,许可,签认;阅讫,查讫(等). *He put his OK on the shipment.* 他在装运的货物上写上'查讫'二字. — *vt.* ***(O.K.'d)*** 签上 O.K.〔表示校好等〕;(签上 O.K.)承认,同意;批准;核准.
o·ka·pi [əuˈkɑːpi] *n.* 【动】(似长颈鹿但颈不长的)俄卡皮鹿.
o·kay, o·keh, o·key [ˈəuˈkei] *a., n., vt.* = O.K.
oke [əuk], **o·key do·ke(y)** [ˈəuki ˈdəuk(i)] *a., int.* 〔美俚〕= O.K.
O'keef(f)e [əuˈkiːf] *n.* 奥基夫〔姓氏〕.
O'Kel·ly [əuˈkeli] *n.* 奥凯利〔姓氏〕.
Ok·hotsk [əuˈkɔtsk], ***the sea of ~*** 鄂霍次克海.
O·kie [ˈəuki] *n.* 〔美口〕(俄克拉何马州的)流动雇农.
O·ki·na·wa [ˌəukiˈnɑːwə] *n.* 冲绳(群岛); 冲绳(岛)〔日本〕.
ok·ka [ˈɔkə] *n.* 沃克〔土耳其、约旦的一种重量单位,约等于 $2^3/_4$ 磅〕.
Okla. = Oklahoma. **-n** *n.* 冲绳人.
O·kla·ho·ma [ˌəukləˈhəumə] *n.* 俄克拉何马〔美国南部州名. **-n** *a., n.* (美国)俄克拉何马州的(人). ~ **plum** 【植】细弱李. ~ **rain** 〔美〕夹沙暴风.
o'kra [ˈəukrə] *n.* 【植】黄秋葵;秋葵纤维.
Ol. = Olympiad.
-ol *suf.* 【化】(表示)醇;酚;油: naphth*ol*, phen*ol*.
O·laf [ˈəuləf, ˈɔl-] *n.* 奥拉夫〔男子名〕〔Scand. 语中意为 ancestor-relics〕.
old [əuld] *a.* ***(-er; -est;*** 表示兄弟姊妹关系时用 ***eld·er; eld·est).*** ①老,上了年纪的,年老的 *(opp.* young*)*; 衰老的,老迈的;老成的;老练的;熟练的. ②…岁的;…久的. ③古时的,古代的 *(opp.* modern*)*;古老的,积年的,陈年的,多年来的,旧交的;熟悉的. ④*(opp.* new*)* 过去的,过时的;旧的;破旧的;用旧了的;旧式的,陈腐的. ⑤〔口〕亲爱的,亲密的. ⑥〔口〕极好的〔通常用以加强其他形容词语气〕. *grow [get] ~* 老起来,上年纪. *How ~ is he?* 他多大岁数? *He is eighteen years ~.* 他十八岁. *~ in diplomacy* 擅长外交. *an ~ bachelor* 老独身汉. *~ gaolbird* 老囚犯;惯犯. *an ~ offender* 惯犯. *an ~ friend* 老朋友. *an ~ Oxonian* 牛津大学的老校友. *~ fashions* 旧式. *~ iron* 废铁. *~ jokes* 陈腐的俏皮话. *~ wine* 陈年老酒. *the ~ country [home]* 故乡. *the ~ thing* (老)家伙. *I had a fine ~ time* 〔口〕过得非常愉快. ***an ~ head on young shoulders*** 少年老成. ***any ~ thing*** 〔俚〕随便什么(东西). ***for an ~ song*** 非常便宜地. ***for ~ sake's sake*** 因老交情. ***in ~ time*** 在从前. ***never too ~ to learn*** 活到老学到老;学无止境. ***of ~ standing*** 多年的,由来已久的. ***as ~ as the hill*** 很老. ***~ familiar faces*** 老相识(的人们). ***O- Lady of Threadneedle Street*** 〔英〕Bank of England 的别名. ~ **man of the sea** 死缠着不走的人. ***~ ten in the hundred*** 高利贷. ***the good ~ times*** (老人们所怀念的)过去. ***the ~ gentleman = the ~ one*** 〔口〕老头儿,父亲. ***the ~ year*** 去年,就要过去的一年. — *n.* ①古时,往时. ②…岁的人〔动物〕. ③〔集合词〕老年的人们;〔the ~〕古物;令人怀念的往事〔风俗(等)〕. *the men of ~* 古代的人们. *four-year-olds* 四岁的马. ***as of ~*** 仍旧,照旧. ***from of ~*** 自昔,早就. ***in days of ~*** 从前,以前. ***of ~*** 从前的,往时的;从前是,(老早)以前是;自古,从老早以前. ***~ and young = young and ~*** 无论老少. **O- Abe** [eib] 〔美〕Abraham Lincoln 的爱称. ~ **age** 老年,晚年. **O- Bailey** (伦敦老贝利街的)中央刑事法院. ~ **bean [boy, cock, chap, egg, fellow, fruit, man, thing, top]** 〔俚〕(招呼)喂,老兄! 老弟! 老朋友! ~ **bird** 老手,老经验,老世故. ~ **bloke [buffer, card, codger]** 〔蔑〕不中用的老家伙,老古板,老派的人. ~ **boy** 校友,老同学;(英国公学的)毕业生;〔the O- B-〕〔谑〕魔鬼. **O- Catholic** 老罗马天主教徒〔1870 年罗马天主教徒所组成的教派,不接受教皇圣明论〕. **O- Church Slavic** 古教堂斯拉夫语 (= Old Church Slavonic, Old Bulgarian). **~-clothes man** 旧衣商. **O- Colonials** 〔美〕Massachusetts 人的别名. ~ **country** 故国(移居外国的人对本国的称呼;特指对欧洲). **O- Dealer** 反对罗斯福新政的人. **O- Dirigo** [diˈriːgəu] 〔美〕Maine 州的别名. ~ **doc** 【军】军医长. **O- Dominion** 〔美〕Virginia 州的别名. **O- Dutch** 古荷兰语. **O- English** 古代英语;【英】哥特体(铅字). **O- English sheep-dog** 英国牧羊狗. **~fangled** *a.* 老式的;守旧的. **~-fashioned** *a.* 旧式的,老式的,过时的;不爱时髦的. ~ **floppy** 〔英空俚〕阻隔气球. ~ **fogy,** ~ **fogey** 守旧者,老家伙. **~-fogyish, ~-fogeyish** *a.* 老派的,守旧的. ~ **folks** 〔美马戏团〕猴子. **O- French** 古法语. **O- Glory** 美国国旗的俗称. ~ **goat** 〔美俚〕讨厌的老家伙;老色迷. ~ **gold** 浅黄色. **O- Guard** 拿破仑一世的近卫队;〔美〕共和党的极端保守派;〔o- guard〕保守派,保守分子. ~ **hand** 熟练工人;老手 (at);惯犯,老犯 (*an ~ hand at the game* 此道老手). **O- Harry** 魔鬼. ~ **hat** 〔俚〕①旧式的;过时的. ②老套的,陈腐的. **O- High German** 古高地德语〔标准德语〕. **O- Home Week** ①一个居民点的居民邀请过去旧居民的联欢周. ②旧同事〔同学〕的重聚联欢周. ~ **horse** 咸牛肉干. **O- Icelandic** 古冰岛语. **O- Indic** ①古印度语. ②梵语的吠陀梵语. **O- Ionic** 古爱奥尼亚语. **O- Irish** 古爱尔兰语. **O- Ironsides** 美国快速炮舰〔于 1812 年战争中服现役〕. **O- Jamica** 【海】太阳. ~ **Lady** 妻子; 母亲; 老处女式的人. ~ **lag** 惯犯. **O- Latin** 古拉丁语〔指公元前 75 年以前的拉丁语〕. **O- Line** 〔美〕马里兰州的别名. **~line** *a.* 保守的;厂史性的,传统的;老资格的;老牌的. ~ **liner** 守旧者,保守派的人;〔英〕〔O- L-〕保守党党员. **O- Low Franconian** 古代低地法兰克语〔莱茵河下游的法兰克人在公元 1100 年以前讲的西日耳曼语〕. **O- Low German** 古低地德语. ~ **maid** ①老处女. ②怯懦而又斤斤计较的歇斯底性的男子. ③【牌】找寡妇〔一种简单的抽对子牌戏〕. **~-maidish** *a.* 带一点老处女脾气的;象老处女的. ~ **man** ①〔an〕老头子. ②〔one's〕〔口〕丈夫;父亲. ③〔the〕〔口〕老板;船长;长官;【剧】老先生. ④〔招呼话〕=~ chap. ⑤老前辈. ⑥【宗】(皈依基督教前的)旧我(*So's your ~ man.* 〔美俚〕去你的! 胡说!). **O- Man River** "老人河"〔密西西比河的绰号〕. ~ **master** 古代画家,(特指)18 世纪前的大画家(或其作品). **O- Masters** 英国美术院冬季展览. ~ **moon** 下弦月. **O- Nick** 魔鬼,恶魔,撒旦,魔王. **O- Norman French** 诺曼(底)语〔中世纪诺曼人或诺曼底人讲的法语〕. **O- Norse** ①古诺斯语〔14 世纪前斯堪的纳维亚人所讲的北日耳曼语〕. ②古冰岛语(= O- Icelandic). **O- North** 〔美〕北卡罗来纳州的别名. **O- North French** 古北方法语〔法国北部,尤指皮卡地和诺曼地所讲的古法语的方言〕. **O- Persian** 古波斯语. **O- Prussian** 古普鲁士语〔属波罗的语族,17 世纪时已消亡〕. ~ **rose** 略带紫的〔略带灰的〕玫瑰色. ~ **saw** 老话,民间格言. **O- Saxon** 古撒克逊语. **~-school** *a.* 老派的, 老式的. ~ **school** 守旧派. **O- Scratch** 魔鬼. **O- Shake** 〔美口〕莎翁,老莎士比亚(= Shakespeare). ~ **shell** 【海】水手. **O- Siwash** [saiwɔʃ] 〔美俚〕大学. **O- Slavic** (= O- Church Slavic 古教堂斯拉夫语). ~ **sledge** (= seven-up 七点儿〔牌戏,二、三、四人玩,七点就成局〕). ~ **smoky** 〔美俚〕(死刑用的)电椅. **O- Socks** 〔美俚〕老兄〔爱称〕. **O- Sol** 〔谑〕太阳. **O- South** 旧南方〔指美国内战以前的南方〕. **O- Spanish** 古西班牙语. ~ **squaw** 冰凫 (Clangula hyemalis). ~ **stager** 〔美 ~ **coon**〕 经验丰富的人,识途老马,老手,过来人. ~ **standers** 随舰长调动的老练水兵.

~ **stuff** 〔美〕陈话，听腻了的话．~ **style** *n.* 旧式的东西；【印】旧体铅字；〔O- Style〕西洋旧历．**O- Testament** (基督教《圣经》的)《旧约全书》．~**-time** *a.* 古时的，旧时的，老资格的．~**-timer** 〔口〕老前辈；老手，老资格的人；守旧的人；上了年纪的人；〔美俚〕老朋友；可靠的朋友；可靠而有经验的人．~ **tim(e)y** *a.* 〔口〕旧时的；早期的．**O- Tom** 一种杜松子酒．~ **top** 〔美口〕好朋友，伙伴儿，老搭档．**O- Welsh** 古威尔斯语．~ **wife** 唠唠叨叨的老太婆．~ **wives' tale** 无稽之谈．~ **woman** (an) 老太婆；〔one's〕〔口〕妻，老婆；〔one's〕〔美口〕老母；〔an〕婆婆妈妈似的男人．~ **womanish** *a.* 有老婆子性格的；适宜于老婆子的；婆婆妈妈的．~**-world** *a.* 旧世界的，太古的；老式的；古色古香的(*~-world arrowhead* 慈菇)．**O- World** 旧世界〔欧洲、亚洲、非洲，尤专指欧洲〕；东半球．~ **year's day** 除夕．

Old·cas·tle [ˈəuldˌkɑːsl] *n.* 奥尔德卡斯尔〔姓氏〕．

old·en [ˈəuldən] *a.* 〔古〕古昔的．*in (the) ~ days* (= *in ~ times* 古昔，从前)．— *vt.* 〔罕〕使老，使旧．— *vi.* 变老，变陈旧．*In three months she ~ed more than she had done or 10 years before.* 她在三个月中比在以前十年还要老得快些．

old·ie, old·y [ˈəuldi] *n.* *(pl. old·ies)* 〔口〕老笑话；老话；传说；老歌子；老影片．

old·ish [ˈəuldiʃ] *a.* 有点老的，稍旧的．

Ol·do·wan [ˈɔldəwən] *a.* 奥尔杜韦文化的〔奥尔杜韦是坦桑尼亚地名，于该地发掘的文物属于石器时代最早期文化产物〕．

old·ster [ˈəuldstə] *n.* 〔口〕上了年纪的人．

Old Test. = Old Testament.

-ole *suf.* 油．

o·lé [ɔˈlei] *int., n.* 〔Sp.〕好！好极了！〔看斗牛或吉普赛舞时的喝采〕．

o·le·a [ˈəuliə] *n.* oleum 的复数．

o·le·ag·i·nous [ˌəuliˈædʒinəs] *a.* ①含油的，油质的；油腻的；产油的；有油气的．②油嘴滑舌的，会拍马屁的．**-ness** *n.* 含油性质．

o·le·as·ter [ˌəuliˈæstə] *n.* 【植】胡颓子属植物．

o·le·ate [ˈəulieit] *n.* 【化】油酸盐；油酸酯．

o·lec·ra·non [əuˈlekrənɔn, ˌəuliˈkreinɔn] *n.* 【动】鹰嘴，肘突．

o·le·fin, o·le·fine [ˈəulifin] *n.* 【化】烯(属)烃．**-ic** *a.*

o·le·ic [əuˈliːik] *a.* 油的；油酸的．~ **acid** 【化】油酸．

o·le·in [ˈəuliːin] *n.* 【化】油精；三油精；甘油三油酸酯．

o·len·an·der [ˌəuliˈændə] *n.* 【植】(欧洲)夹竹桃．

o·le·o [ˈəuliəu] *n.* 〔美〕= oleomargarine．~ **oil** 【化】油，(从动物脂肪炼成的)黄油状油．

o·le·o·graph [ˈəuliəugrɑːf] *n.* 油画式的石版画．

o·le·o·mar·ga·rin(e) [ˈəuliəuˌmɑːdʒəˈriːn] *n.* 人造黄油，代黄油．

o·le·om·e·ter [ˌəuliˈɔmitə] *n.* 油比重计；量油计．

o·le·o·res·in [ˌəuliəuˈrezin] *n.* 【化】含油树脂．

o·le·o strut [ˈəuliəˈstrʌt] *n.* 【空】油液空气减震器[柱]．

ol·er·i·cul·ture [ˈɔləriˌkʌltʃə] *n.* 蔬菜学．

o·le·um [ˈəuliəm] *(pl. o·le·a* [ˈəuliə]*)* ①油．②*(pl. ~s)*【化】发烟硫酸．

ol·fac·tion [ɔlˈfækʃən] *n.* 嗅觉作用；嗅觉．

ol·fac·tom·e·ter [ˌɔlfækˈtɔmitə] *n.* 气味测量计．**-metric** [-ˈmetrik] *a.* **-e·try** *n.*

ol·fac·to·ry [ɔlˈfæktəri] *n.* 〔常 *pl.*〕嗅觉；嗅觉器官，鼻．—*a.* 嗅觉器官的，嗅觉的．~ **nerves** 嗅神经．~ **organ** 嗅觉器官；〔谑〕鼻子．

ol·fac·tron·ics [ˌɔlfækˈtrɔniks, ˌəul-] *n. pl.* 〔动词用单数〕气味测定学．

Ol·ga [ˈɔlgə] *n.* 奥尔加〔女子名〕．

ol·ib·a·num [ɔˈlibənəm, əu-] *n.* 乳香．

ol·id [ˈɔlid] *a.* 臭的；发恶臭的．

olig(o)- *comb. f.* 稀，微，减，寡，少．

ol·i·garch [ˈɔligɑːk] *n.* 寡头政治的执政者[支持者]．*a financial ~* 金融寡头．**-gar·chy** [-i] *n.* 寡头政治；寡头统治的国家[政权]；寡头政治集团．**-chic, -chi·cal** *a.*

ol·i·ge·mi·a [ˌɔliˈdʒiːmiə] *n.* 【医】血量减少．

O·li·go·cene [ɔˈligəusiːn] *n., a.* 【地】渐新世(的)；渐新统(的)．

ol·i·go·chaete [ˈɔligəuˌkiːt] *n.* 【动】寡毛纲 *(Oligochaeta)* 动物．**-chae·tous** [-ˌkiːtəs] *a.*

ol·i·go·clase [ˈɔligəuˌkleis] *n.* 【地】奥长石．

ol·i·goph·a·gous [ˌɔliˈgɔfəgəs] *a.* 【动】寡食性的．

ol·i·gop·o·ly [ˌɔliˈgɔpəli] *n.* *(pl. -lies)* 商品供应垄断〔资本主义市场少数公司或供货人搞的控制〕．**-gop·o·list** *n.* 市场供应垄断者．**-lis·tic** [-ˈlistik] *a.*

ol·i·gop·so·ny [ˌɔliːˈgɔpsəni] *n.* *(pl. -nies)* 商品采购垄断〔资本主义市场少数买主对市场商品采购搞的控制〕．**-so·nist** *n.* 商品采购垄断者．**-so·nis·tic** [-ˈnistik] *a.*

ol·i·go·sac·cha·ride [ˌɔligəuˈsækəraid] *n.* 【化】低聚糖，寡糖．

ol·i·go·tro·phic [ˌɔligəuˈtrɔfik, -ˈtrəufik] *a.* 寡营养的(指湖沼地)．**-ro·phy** [ˌɔliˈgɔtrəfi] *n.*

ol·i·gu·ri·a [ˌɔliˈgjuəriə] *n.* 【医】尿少．

o·lim [əuˈliːm] *n.* 〔Heb.〕迁进以色列的犹太移民．

o·li·o [ˈəuliəu] *n.* *(pl. ~s)* 〔Sp.〕①【烹】杂烩．②混杂物，杂凑，杂拌．③杂曲集；杂录．

ol·iva·ceous [ˌɔliˈveiʃəs] *a.* 橄榄的；象橄榄的(尤指颜色)；橄榄绿的．

ol·i·va·ry [ˈɔlivəri] *a.* 【解】橄榄形的；延髓侧突出的两橄榄个体之一的．

ol·ive [ˈɔliv] *n.* ①【植】齐墩果，油橄榄；橄榄树；橄榄树枝；(橄榄枝叶做的)橄榄冠 (= ~-crown)；橄榄木．②橄榄色，茶青色．③橄榄形钮扣．④〔*pl.*〕【烹】小肉片菜卷．— *a.* 橄榄的；橄榄色的．~ **branch** ①橄榄枝〔和平[和解]的象征〕(*hold out the [an] ~ branch* 伸出橄榄枝；要求和解)．②〔常 *pl.*〕〔谑〕小孩，儿童．~ **crown** (古时希腊胜利者戴的)橄榄冠．~ **drab** 草绿色；草黄色；〔美陆军〕草绿色呢制服．~ **green** 橄榄绿，茶青色．~ **oil** 橄榄油；〔美俚〕再会；〔从法语 *au revoir* 变来〕．~ **tree** 橄榄树．~ **wood** 橄榄木．

Ol·ive [ˈɔliv] *n.* 奥莉夫〔女子名〕．

o·liv·en·ite [əuˈlivəˌnait, ˈɔlivə-] *n.* 【矿】橄榄铜矿．

Ol·i·ver [ˈɔlivə] *n.* 奥利弗〔姓氏，男子名〕．

ol·i·ver [ˈɔlivə] *n.* 脚踏铁锤．

ol·i·vet [ˈɔlivet] *n.* 人造珍珠．

ol·i·vet(te) [ˈɔlivet] *n.* 剧场用强力泛光灯．

O·liv·i·a [ɔˈliviə] *n.* 奥莉维亚〔女子名〕．

ol·i·vin(e) [ˌɔliˈviːn] *n.* 【矿】橄榄石．

ol·la [ˈɔlə; Sp. ˈəuljɑː] *n.* ①土缸，土锅．②放入很多调料做成的肉与蔬菜的燉菜．

ol·la po·dri·da [ˈɔlə pɔˈdriːdə] 〔Sp.〕= olio ①．

Ol·lie [ˈɔli] *n.* 奥利〔男子名，Oliver 的昵称〕．

Ol·mec [ˈɔlmek] *n.* *(pl. ~(s))* 奥尔麦克人〔墨西哥的古印第安人〕．— *a.* 奥尔麦克文化的〔特点是高度发展的农业，巨大的雕塑头像和雕刻玉器〕．

ol·o·gy [ˈɔlədʒi] *n.* 〔常 *pl.*〕〔谑〕学问，科学；空论．

-ol·o·gy *suf.* = -logy．

O·lym·pi·a [əuˈlimpiə] *n.* ①奥林匹亚〔希腊一地区〕．②奥林匹亚〔美国城市〕．

O·lym·pi·ad [əuˈlimpiæd] *n.* 〔常用 o-〕①(古希腊)四年周期〔两次奥林匹克运动会之间的四年周期．古希腊用以计算时间〕．②奥林匹克运动会．

O·lym·pi·an [əuˈlimpiən, -pjən] *a.* ①奥林匹斯 (Olympus) 山的；奥林匹斯山诸神的；奥林匹斯山上似的，天上的；神仙一样的．②威仪堂堂的，气派十足的．③奥林匹克运动大会的．— *n.* ①【希神】奥林匹斯山十二神之一．②奥林匹亚人．③奥林匹克运动会选手．

O·lym·pic [əuˈlimpik] *a.* 奥林匹亚的；奥林匹斯山的. *the ~ games* ①(古希腊祭祀宙斯神每四年举行一次的)体育和文艺竞赛大会. ②奥林匹克世界运动大会〔1896年在雅典首次举行，以后每四年举行一次〕.
O·lym·pics [əuˈlimpiks] *n.* 〔*pl.*〕= Olympic games.
O·lym·pus [əuˈlimpəs] *n.* ①(希腊)奥林匹斯山. ②【希神】奥林匹斯山(诸神的住所). ③天.
O.M. = ①old measurement 旧度量制. ②Order of Merit〔英〕功绩勋章.
-oma *suf.* 肿，瘤：fibr*oma*.
om·a·dhaun [ˈɔmədɔːn] *n.* 〔Ir.〕傻子，笨蛋.
O·ma·ha [ˈəuməhɑː] *n.* ①*(pl. ~(s))* 奥马哈人〔内布拉斯加东北部的印第安人〕. ②奥马哈语. ③奥马哈〔美国城市〕.
O·man [əuˈmɑːn] *n.* 阿曼〔亚洲〕.
O·mar Khay·yam [ˈəumɑː kaiˈjɑːm] 奥玛开阳〔1025?—1133，波斯诗人及天文学家〕.
o·ma·sum [əuˈmeisəm] *n.* *(pl. -sa* [-sə]*)* 【解】(反刍动物的)重瓣胃.
om·ber, om·bre [ˈɔmbə] *n.* ①翁博牌戏〔西班牙三人玩的四十张牌的牌戏〕. ②翁博牌戏的赌牌者.
om·bré [ˈɔmbrei] *a.* (颜色)渐变的.
om·brol·o·gy [ɔmˈbrɔlədʒi] *n.* 雨学.
om·brom·e·ter [ɔmˈbrɔmitə] *n.* 雨量器.
om·buds·man [ˈɔmbədzmən] *n.* *(pl. -men* [-men]*)* 巡视官〔被委派去调查市民对官员侵犯个人权利案件的控告的政府官员〕.
Om·dur·man [ˌɔmdəːˈmɑːn] *n.* 恩图曼〔苏丹城市〕.
o·me·ga [ˈəumigə] *n.* 希腊字母末字 [Ω,ω]；终，末尾；结论，死；【数】自然数有序序列的序数（常用 ω 表示）. *alpha and ~* 始与终，首尾，始末，全部.
om·e·let(te) [ˈɔmlit, -let] *n.* 煎蛋饼，摊鸡蛋〔常对折成半月形〕. *plain ~* 清摊鸡蛋. *savoury [sweet] ~* 咸味馅[果酱馅]摊鸡蛋. ***You can't make an ~ without breaking eggs.*** 不打碎鸡蛋做不出摊鸡蛋；做事不可畏首畏尾.
o·men [ˈəumen] *n.* 前兆，预兆，兆头. *an evil [ill] ~* 凶兆. *a good ~* 吉兆. *be of good [bad] ~* 兆头好[不好]. — *vt., vi.* 〔诗、修辞〕预示，预告.
o·men·tal [ˈəumentəl] *a.* 【解】网膜的.
o·men·tum [əuˈmentəm] *n.* *(pl. -ta* [-tə]*)* 【解】(肠的)网膜.
o·mer [ˈəumə] *n.* ①欧麦〔古希伯来的干量，等于十分之一的依法〕. ②〔常用 O-〕〔犹太教〕从逾越节的第二天到五旬节前一天的四十九天期间.
o·mi·cron [əuˈmaikrən] *n.* 希腊字母表第十五字母〔O, o〕.
om·i·nous [ˈɔminəs] *a.* ①预兆的，预示的 *(of)*. ②不吉的，不祥的，兆头坏的. *an ~ silence* 可怕的沉默. **-ly** *ad.* **-ness** *n.*
o·mis·sible [əuˈmisibl, -səbl] *a.* 可以省去的.
o·mis·sion [əuˈmiʃən] *n.* ①省略；删节；遗漏. ②疏忽；失职. ③【法】不作为；懈怠；不履行法律责任 *(opp.* commission*)*. *sins of ~* 因未做该做的事而引起的罪责，不作为罪.
o·mis·sive [əuˈmisiv] *a.* ①略去的，遗漏的. ②忽视的，失职的，怠慢的. **-ly** *ad.*
o·mit [əuˈmit] *vt.* ①(有意)省去，删去，略去. ②(无意中)遗漏，忽略，忘记 *(to do)*；怠慢，疏忽，不留神. *~ an item from a list* 自目录中略去一项. *~ to lock the door* 忘记锁门. *He ~ted making his bed.* 他忘记了铺床. **-ter** *n.*
o·mit·tance [əuˈmitəns] *n.* 〔古〕遗漏.
om·ma·tid·i·um [ˌɔməˈtidiəm] *n.* *(pl. -i·a* [-ə]*)* 【解】小眼. **-tid·i·al** *a.*
om·mat·o·phore [əˈmætəfɔ] *n.* 【动】承眼肉茎，眼柄 (=eyestalk).

Om·mi·ad, O·may·yad [əuˈmaiæd] *n.* *(pl. ~s, -a·des* [-əˈdiːz]*)* 【阿拉伯史】倭马亚朝
om·ni- *comb. f.* 全，总，遍：*omni*bus, *omni*potent.
om·ni·bus [ˈɔmnibəs] *n.* ①公共汽车；公共马车〔略 bus〕. ②(接送客人用的)旅馆汽车，旅馆马车 (= hotel ~). ③= ~ book. ④〔口〕(旅馆等的)助理服务员. *a family [private] ~*(铁路公司供应旅客的)包车[专车]. — *a.* 总括的；多项的；混合的. *an ~ bill* 混合议案. **~ book** (廉价普及版本的)选集[文集]. **~ box** (戏院的)合用大包厢. **~ film** 短片集锦. **~ train** 〔美〕逢站必停的慢车 (= accommodation train).
om·ni·comp·e·tent [ˌɔːmniˈkɔmpitənt] *a.* 【法】有全权的.
om·ni·di·rec·tion·al [ˌɔmnidiˈrekʃənl] *a.* 【无】全向的，无定向的.
om·ni·far·i·ous [ˌɔmniˈfɛəriəs] *a.* 各种各样的，五花八门的(知识等).
om·nif·ic, om·nif·i·cent [ɔmˈnifik, -fisnt] *a.* 创造万物的.
om·ni·par·i·ty [ˌɔmniˈpæriti] *n.* 一切平等.
om·ni·phib·i·ous [ˌɔmniˈfibiəs] *a.* 【空】能在任何面上(水上、雪上、冰上、地面上)降落的.
om·nip·o·tence [ɔmˈnipətəns] *n.* 全能，万能；无限权力；无限权威；〔O-〕(全能的)上帝.
om·nip·o·tent [ɔmˈnipətənt] *a.* 全能的；有无限权力[威力]的；〔谑〕万能的，样样都能的；真正的，彻底的. — *n.* 万能者；〔the O-〕上帝，神. **-ly** *ad.*
om·ni·pres·ence [ˈɔmniˈprezəns] *n.* 无所不在，普遍.
om·ni·pres·ent [ˈɔmniˈprezənt] *a.* 无所不在的.
om·ni·range [ˈɔmniˌreindʒ] *n.* 【空】全向导航台.
om·nis·ci·ence [ɔmˈnisiəns] *n.* ①无所不知，全知. ②〔O-〕【宗】无所不知者，上帝.
om·nis·ci·ent [ɔmˈnisiənt] *a.* 无所不知的，博识的. — *n.* 〔the O-〕上帝，神. **-ly** *ad.*
om·ni·tron [ˈɔmnitrɔn] *n.* 【原】全能加速器.
om·ni·um [ˈɔmniəm] *n.* 【商】担保证券的总值；〔口〕总额；全部. **~-gatherum** [-ˌgæðərəm] *n.* 杂凑；拼凑的一群人[一批东西].
om·ni·vor·a [ɔmˈnivərə] *n.* 〔*pl.*〕〔集合词〕杂食动物.
om·ni·vore [ˈɔmniˌvɔː] *a.* 杂食动物的.
om·niv·o·rous [ɔmˈnivərəs] *a.* ①【动】杂食性的 *(cf.* carnivorous, herbivorous*)*. ②随手采取的；滥读的. *an ~ reader* 无书不读的人. **-ly** *ad.* **-ness** *n.*
o·mo·pha·gi·a [ˌəuməˈfeidʒiə, -ˈfeidʒə] *n.* 食生肉. **-moph·a·gist** [-ˈmɔfədʒist] *n.* 食生肉者. **-moph·agous** [-gəs], **-mo·phag·ic** [-ˈfædʒik] *a.*
o·mo·plate [ˈəuməpleit] *n.* 【解】肩胛骨.
omphalo- *comb. f.* 脐：*omphalos*.
om·pha·los [ˈɔmfəlɔs] *n.* ①〔古希腊〕盾中央的浮凸饰；(Apollo 神殿的)半圆石祭坛. ②中心点，中枢. ③【解】脐.
om·pha·lo·skep·sis [ˌɔmfələuˈskepsis] *n.* 意守丹田〔搞玄术者的一种功夫〕.
on [ɔn] *prep.* ①〔支持、接触、附属〕在…上；盖着；属于，为…的成员. *~ foot* 徒步. *go ~ all fours* 爬着走. *a book to be read ~ a railroad train* 〔美〕在火车上看的书 (=〔英〕in a railway train). *~ the table* 在桌子上. *with his hat ~ his head* (头上)戴着帽子. *turn ~ a pivot* 在轴上旋转. *Have you a match ~ you?* 你身边有火柴吗？ *The dog is ~ the chain.* 狗拴着链子. *He is ~ the committee.* 他是委员之一. *Will you be ~ any team?* 你想参加一个队吗？ ②〔基础、理由、原因〕依据；靠；因…；从…得来的；(费用等)由…承担[支付]. *act ~ principle* 照原则办事. *~ one's honour* 以名誉担保. *On what ground?* 凭甚么理由？ *live [feed] ~* 靠[吃]…生活. *~ suspicion* 因嫌疑. *borrow money ~ jewels* 拿宝石做抵押借钱. *a profit ~ sales* 销售所得的利润. *This*

dinner is ~ him. 这顿饭由他请客. ③〔动作的方向、对象〕(a) 向…,朝…. *throw it ~ the floor* 摔在地板上. *hit him ~ the head* 打他的头. *make an attack ~ the enemy* 向敌人进攻. *steal ~ sb.* 偷偷逼近某人. *march ~ London* 向伦敦前进. *turn one's back ~* 把背掉向…,背弃,遗弃. *lay hold [seize] ~* …,抓住,捉住. *leave a card ~ a person* 留名片给某人. *The window looks ~ the street.* 窗户朝街. (b)〔美〕针对…. *begin a legal fight ~ his opponents* 跟对方打起官司来. *confer a degree ~ sb.* 授予某人学位. ④〔接近〕接近…, 沿…. *the inn ~ the road* 路旁的旅店. *It borders ~ absurdity.* 那是近乎荒谬的. ⑤〔日、时〕在(某日);在(某日的晨、午、夜);和…同时,刚一…. *~ Sunday* 在星期日. *~ the morning of May 5th* 在五月五日的早晨. *~ the instant* 即刻. *~ arriving home* 一到家(就). *~ yesterday*〔美〕昨天. ⑥〔后接定冠词加某些形容词的形式表示方式、状态等〕*travel ~ the cheap* 花很少用费旅行. *~ the quiet* 偷偷. ⑦〔方法、状态、动作〕*hear music ~ the radio* 用收音机听音乐. *~ guard [the watch]* 看守. *~ duty* 值班. *~ sale* 出售的;上市的. *be ~ strike* 正在罢工. *come ~ horseback* 骑马来. *a house ~ fire* 失火的房子. *go ~ an errand* 办差事. *go to Beijing ~ business* 到北京出差. *~ the move* 动着. *~ the run* 跑着. *a bird ~ the wing* 飞着的鸟. *~ an official visit to a country* 对某国进行正式访问. ⑧〔关系、影响〕关于…,论述…,影响到…. *speak ~ finance* 讲财政问题. *take notes ~ (=of) the lectures*〔美〕听讲记笔记. *a book ~ grammar* 语法书. *works ~ philosophy* 哲学论著. *The heat told ~ him.* 他中了暑. *It is binding ~ all.* 此事人人有责. ⑨〔累加〕加. *ruin ~ ruin* 垮台加垮台. *loss ~ loss* 一再损失. *heaps ~ heaps* 许许多多. ⑩冒…之险. *~ pain of death* 冒生命危险. **~ a bender**〔美俚〕喝醉;痛饮. **~ a bust [jag]**〔美俚〕酩酊大醉. **~ and after** …以后. (*~ and after April 1* 四月一日以后). **~ ice** ①准成功的;准赢的. ②在狱中. **~ one's high horse**〔美俚〕傲慢的,架子十足的;生气的,愤慨的;冷淡的. **~ schedule** 按时,准时. **~ the air** ①(正在)广播. ②〔美俚〕瞎谈着;哭着;闹着 (*cf.* air). **~ the beach**〔美俚〕失业的 (*cf.* beach). **~ the beam** 航行正确的;运行正常的;〔美俚〕对,不错. **~ the big green carpet**〔美俚〕(囚犯)被狱官传问. **~ the blink**〔美俚〕①破了,坏了,有毛病,情况不好的. ②喝醉的. **~ the bones of his back** 穷到分文没有. **~ the book**〔美〕预定好的,预约好的. **~ the boost**〔美俚〕冒充顾客行窃. **~ the button**〔美俚〕①准确,确切;准时,按时. ②击中下颌. **~ the crack**〔美俚〕干强盗勾当. **~ the cuff**〔美俚〕赊欠. **~ the cushions**〔美俚〕生活舒服,养尊处优. **~ the dodge**〔美〕逃过法网,逃亡. **~ the dogs**〔军俚〕在休假. **~ the Erie**〔美俚〕耸着耳朵;警惕着. **~ the fence**〔美俚〕骑墙派的;迟迟不决的;守中立的. **~ the fire**〔美〕准备[计划]中 (=〔英〕~ the stocks);变更中. **~ the floor**〔美议会〕在发言中. **~ the fly**〔美俚〕逃亡中. **~ the I. C.**〔美〕警惕着;当心. **~ the in**〔美〕受欢迎,名气好. **~-the-spot meetings** 现场会议. **~ time**〔美〕按时,及时 (*arrive at a meeting ~ time* 及时到会). **~ top of the heap [world]**〔美〕大大成功;名声赫赫的;一切顺利的. — *ad.* ①〔接触、覆盖〕上去;开. (*opp.* off). *turn ~ the light [radio, water, gas]* 开电灯[收音机、自来水、煤气]. *put [have] one's coat ~* 穿[穿着]上衣. *On with your hat!* 把帽子戴上! ②〔动作的方向、时间的持续〕向前;向着;进行着,继续着. *move ~* 继续前进. *farther ~* 再向前. *later ~* 后来. *It is getting ~ for 3 o'clock.* 快三点钟,将近三点钟. — *a.*〔多用作表语〕①在进行;在发生;在活动. *The debate is ~.* 辩论正在进行. *The new play is ~.* 新戏正在上演. *The radio is ~ (the air).* 无线电正在广播. *He is ~ as Hamlet.* 他扮演哈姆雷特. *It was well ~ in the night.* 已经夜深了. *Breakfast is ~ from 8 to 10.* 早餐是 8 点到 10 点. *There's nothing ~* 没有甚么事. *What's ~?* (发生)什么事? 上演什么节目? ②〔流通〕通着,点着 (*opp.* off). *Is the water ~ or off?* 水开着还是关着? *Gas is ~.* 煤气开着. ③〔美俚〕熟悉;深知 *(to). I am ~ to your little game.* 我知道你搞的什么鬼. ④有点醉意. *I am a bit ~.* 我有点醉意了. **and so ~** 等等. **be ~ it**〔美口〕准备就绪;决定动手. **be well ~** 进行得宜, 进行顺利;有赌赢希望. **just ~** 差不多. **neither off nor ~** 优柔寡断的,没有决断力的;未决定的;三心两意的;没有关系的 *(to).* **off and ~ = ~ and off** 断断续续,不规则地. **~ and ~** 继续,不停地,不断地. **~ with** 穿上;戴上;开始;继续. — *n.*【板球】(打球人的)左边 (*opp.* off). **~-again-off-again** *a.* 时有时无的,断断续续的;犹豫不决的;无结论的. **~-glide** 滑移〔发音时发声器官从静止状态或一个音的发音部位滑向该音所要求的部位〕. **~-line** *a.*【自】在线的〔指仪器、设备直接受电子计算机的操纵〕. **~stage** *ad., a.* 在前台(的). **~-stream** *ad., a.* 在生产中(的).

ON, O.N. = Old Norse 古斯堪的纳维亚语,古挪威语.

on- *comb.*〔与动词或动名词组成名词或形容词, 重音常在第一音节〕: *oncoming, onfall, onlooker.*

on•a•ger [ˈɔnədʒə] *n.* (*pl.* ~*s*, *-gri* [-grai]) ①【动】(中亚细亚产)野驴. ②石弩,投石器〔中世纪用〕.

o•nan•ism [ˈəunənizəm] *n.*【医】①交媾中断. ②手淫.

once [wʌns] *ad.* ①一次,一趟,一回,一遍;一倍. *I should like to see him ~ before I go.* 在我走以前我想看他一次. *~ a year* 每年一次. *We die but ~.* 我们不过死一次罢了. *O- bit, twice shy.* 一度被咬,再见胆小. *O-nought is nought.* 零零得零. ②从前,曾经. *O- I lived in London* 我从前在伦敦住过. *I ~ saw him playing Hamlete* 我曾经看过他演汉姆雷特. *a ~ powerful nation* 曾经强盛过的国家. ③一旦…; *when ~ he understands* 他一旦了解时. ④一次也(不), 无论何时也(不)〔用于否定结构〕. *I have not seen him ~.* 我一次也没见过他. **every ~ in a while**〔美〕偶尔. **if ~ = when ~** 一旦… (*If we ~ lose sight of him, we shall never set eyes on him again.* 倘若我们一旦丢了他,就再也找不着他了). **more than ~** 不只一次,好多次. **not ~** 一次也不…. **~ again = ~ more. ~ and again**〔书〕一再, 再三. **~ and away = ~ for all. ~ (and) for all [always]** 一劳永逸,限此一次;断然, 爽爽快快 (*I shall explain it fully ~ for all.* 我详细解说一次以后就不再解说了. *Tell him so ~ for all.* 干脆就此一次把话对他说了吧). **~ in a way [while]** 有时, 间或, 偶尔. **~ more** 再一次, 再来一次. **~ or twice** 一两次 (*not ~ or twice* 一再, 再三, 好几次). **~ over = ~ more. ~ upon a time** 从前. — *conj.* 一…(便)…, 一经, 一旦. *O- you begin you must continue.* 一旦开始你就不可以中断了. —*a.* 从前的. *my ~ master* 我从前的主人. — *n.* 一次,一回. *O- is enough for me.* 我一次就够了. **all at ~** 忽然,突然. **and ... at ~** 也;同时 (*interesting and instructive at ~* 既有趣又有益). **at ~** 立刻, 马上;同时 (*Come at ~.* 马上来. *at ~ interesting and instructive* 既有趣又有益). **for that ~** 只那一次, 就是那回. **for (this) ~** 这一次(特别要), 就这一回 (*Do it for this ~.* 就干这一次吧).

once-over [ˈwʌnsəuvə] *n.*〔美俚〕随随便便的看一看,草草率率的检查. *give sb. the ~* 略为看望一下(某人).

onc•er [ˈwʌnsə] *n.*〔英口〕(为义务关系)只做一次的人;一年只到一次的人;从一而终的女子.

on•co•gene [ˈɔnkədʒiːn] *n.* 致癌基因.

on•col•o•gy [ɔŋˈkɔlədʒi, ɔn-] *n.*【医】肿瘤学. **-log•ic** [-ˈlɔdʒik] *a.* **-col•o•gist** *n.* 肿瘤学家.

on•com•ing [ˈɔnkʌmiŋ] *n., a.* 迎面而来(的);接近(的). *the ~ of winter* 寒冬逼临. *the ~ tide* 汹涌而来的潮水.

on-dit [ɔ̃:nˈdi:] *n.* 〔F.〕 *(pl. ~s* [-ˈdi:]*)* 风闻，传说；谣传.

on·do·graph [ˈɔndəgrɑ:f] *n.*【电】高频示波器.

on·dom·e·ter [ɔnˈdɔmitə] *n.*【讯】波形测量器.

one [wʌn] *num.* ①(基数)一；第一〔用于表示章节、行页等名词之后，起前置的序数的作用〕. ②一个(人)，一个(事物)〔用于名词前，只起数量限定作用〕. *Once ~ is ~*. 一乘一等于一. *Line ~* 第一行. *~ half* 一半. *~ or two people* 一两个人. —*a.* ①独一个的，单一的. *~ hand* 一只手. *~ shot* 只出一期的杂志. *O- swallow doesn't make a summer.* 孤燕不成夏. *O- man ~ vote.* 一人一票. *No ~ man can do it.* 一个人来干，是谁也干不了的. ②某（一个人）. *~ Smith* 一个叫史密斯的人. *Some ~ man must direct.* 总得有一个人指挥才行. *~ day [morning, afternoon, evening, night]* 有一天，改天，他日，有一个[早晨，下午，傍晚，晚上]. ③一方的，一头的. *from ~ side of the room to the other* 从房间一头到另一头. ④〔the ~〕唯一的. *the ~ thing needful* 唯一需要的东西. *my ~ and only hope* 我的唯一希望. ⑤一体的，一致的；同一的；不变的. *be ~ and undivided* 是不可分的一个整体；是联合一致牢不可破的. *of ~ age* 同时代的. *I am ~ [of ~ mind] with you on this.* 在这点上我和你是一致的. *It is all ~ to me.* 对我都一样［怎么都行］. *remain for ever ~* 永久不变. ⑥〔与 one, another, the other 对比〕*~ foot in sea, and ~ on shore* 一只脚在海里，一只在岸上. *If he said ~ thing, she was sure to say another.* 他无论说什么，她总是反对. *from ~ side to the other* 从一边到另一边. **become ~** 结合一体；成夫妇 (*become ~ with the people* 和人民打成一片). **be made ~** 一体化；结成夫妇. **For ~ thing (he drinks).** 一则（举一个例来说）(他喝酒). **in ~ word** 一句话，一言以蔽之，总之. **on the ~ hand** 一方面〔常与 *on the other hand* 连用〕. **~ and the same thing** 同一个东西（一件事情）. **with [in] ~ voice** 异口同声. — *n.* ①一岁；一点钟；一个人，独一；单位；一体. *at ~ and thirty* 三十一岁时. *at ~ (o'clock)* 在一点钟. *by ~s* 一个一个. *~-and-twenty (= twenty-~)* 二十一〔同样可说 *~-and-ninety,* 但在实际上大数目是很少这样说的〕. ②一击. ③(食物)一客. ④〔口〕怪人；蠢人；胆大妄为的人. *Oh! You are a ~, telling that joke in front of the priest.* 你敢在牧师前这样开玩笑，真了不起. *You're a right ~, losing the tickets again!* 又把票丢了，真没出息. ⑤1 (号)；1(的记号). *(live) at No. 1 in Black Street* (住)布莱克街 1 号. *Your 1's* [ˈwʌnz] *are like 7's.* 你写的 1 总是象 7. **all in ~** 一致；一人全备 (*a knife, a screwdriver, and a corkscrew all in ~* 兼备旋凿［螺丝起子］和塞拔［螺旋锥］的小刀). **at ~** 一致，合力，协力. **by ~s and twos** 三三两两地. **for ~** 至少，举个例说 (*I, for ~, will not go.* 拿我来说，我就不会去). **in ~** 结合起来，团结一致. **in ~s** 一个一个地. **in the year ~** 很久很久以前. **like ~-o'clock** 〔俚〕好得很. **make ~** 参加；使成为一体. **~ after another** 一个又一个地，接连地. **~ and all** 每个人，谁都，全都. **~ another** 互相. **~ by ~** 一个一个，挨次. **~ of these days** 过几天，这几天里头；总有一天. **~ too many** 多余的一个；〔美口〕过量的酒. **taken ~ with another** 总的看来. **ten to ~** 〔多用在否定句中〕一定，必定；十之八九，多半. **(the) ~... the other** 一个是…(另)一个是… (*O- is immoral, the other is non-moral.* 一个是不道德，另一个是无道德). **the ~... the other** 前者是…后者是〔有时相反〕. — *pro.* 〔宾格 one. 所有格 one's. 反身形 oneself〕. ①人；〔古〕有人. *O- who writes is called a writer.* 写作的人就叫做作家. ②〔不定代名词〕我们，任何人. *O- must observe the rules.* 我们（任何人）必须守规则. ★ ① 这一用法的 one，尤其是在同一句中再用时，是形式说法，一般口语常说 you: 如 One [You] can't be too careful, can ~ [〔口〕 you]? 不怕过分小心，只怕力不从心. ②在同一句中重说 one 时，英国正规语法仍说 one [one's, oneself]，美国习惯上则改说 he [his, him, himself] 或 she [her, herself]: 如 If ~ cuts off ~'s [〔美〕 his] nose, ~ [〔美〕 he] hurts only oneself [〔美〕 himself]. ④〔装腔作势的说法〕本人，人家，我. *O- is rather busy just now.* 人家现在很忙. ⑤〔*pl.* **ones**〕东西. *Which ~ [~s] do you like? — This [That] ~ will do.* 你喜欢那个？——这个［那个］好. *Give me a good ~.* 给我一个好的. *He is the ~ I mean.* 他就是我说的那个人. *Among these factors, the three main ~s are ....* 这些因素中的三个主要因素是…. 〔代替前面曾经说及的普通名词〕 *I have lost my umbrella, I think I must buy ~.* 我丢了伞，非另买一把不可了. ★①这一用法的 one, 其复数为 some. ②one 系泛指同种物，it 则是特指同一物. *I don't like this hat. Can you show me a better ~?* 我不喜欢这顶帽子，请给我一顶更好一些的看看. *I want large ~s, not small ~s.* 我要大的，不要小的. ★①单数的 one，其形容词前附用冠词 a(n). ②代替不可数名词时，one 可略去，仅用形容词即可. 如: I like red wine better than white. 我比较喜欢红葡萄酒不喜欢白的. ⑥〔与 another, the other 对比〕一，一个；前者. *O- succeeds where another fails.* 一个成功，一个失败. *O- is black and the other is white.* 一黑一白. *the ~ ... the other* 前者…后者. **any ~** 无论谁. **dear [little, loved] ~s** 可爱的孩子们. **every ~** 每个人，谁都. **many a ~** 好些人. **no ~** 没人…. **some ~** 有人，某人. **such a ~** 那样的人，那种人，那种家伙. **the Evil [Old] O-** 魔鬼. **the Holy O- = O- above** 上帝. **~-armed bandit** 〔俚〕吃角子老虎〔一种赌具〕. **~-base hit** 〔棒〕安全进一垒＝〔俚〕**~bagger.** **~-crop system**【农】连作制. **~-eyed** *a.* 独眼的；眼光狭窄的. **~ fold** *a.* 〔罕〕= single. **~-horse** *a.* 单马拉的；仅有一匹马的；〔美口〕极小的；有限的；简陋的；次要的. **~-hundred-percenter** 〔美俚〕= hundred-percenter. **~-ide·ad, ~-ide·a·ed** *a.* 固持一种思想的，偏狭的. **~-liner** *n.* 简短、机警的诙谐语. **~-man** *a.* 只要一个人的；只关于一人的；个人的 (*an ~-man show* 个人展览会；独角戏). **~-night stand** 一夜的停留演出〔巡回演出，演讲者等〕. **~-off** *a.* 只供使用一次的；只供一人使用的；只供在一种场合使用的. **~-pair** *a.* 〔英〕二楼的. **~-seater** 单座的飞机［汽车］. **~-shot** *a.* 〔俚〕①只发生一次的，只出现一次的. ②只此一个的；不是一连串之中的. **~-sid·ed** *a.* 单方的，一边的，只一方发达的；倾向一边的；偏于一方的，片面的，不公道的；【法】片务的，单边的 (*an ~-sided street* 一边有房子的街. *an ~-sided view* 片面的看法，偏见. *It is ~-sided to regard everything either as all positive or as all negative.* 肯定一切或者否定一切，都是片面性的). **~-time** *a.* 过去的，一度的；只发生一次的. **~-time pad** 只使用一次的密码. **~-to-~** *a.* 一对一的. **~-track** *a.* ①单轨的. ②(= one-idea'd) (*an ~-track mind* 偏狭的头脑). **~-up** ① *a.* 〔口〕胜人一筹的〔常用于短语 *be ~ on ...* 胜某人一筹〕. ② *vt.* **(-upped, -up·ping)** 〔口〕胜人一筹，优于. **~-upmanship** *n.* 〔口〕胜人一筹. **~(-)way** *a.* ①单向的，单行的 (*an ~ way street* 单行路)，〔美〕单程的(车票). ② *n.* 〔美〕单程车票. **~-way** *a.* ①单程的，单行的. *~-way street* 单行道. ②片面的，单方面的. **~-worlder** 国际主义者.

-one *suf.*【化】= ketone.

O·nei·da [əuˈnaidə] *n.* ①*(pl. ~(s))* 奥奈达人〔美国纽约州、威斯康辛州、安大略州的印第安人〕. ②奥奈达语.

O'Neil(l) [əuˈni:l] *n.* ①奥尼尔〔姓氏〕. ② **Eugene Gladstone** ~尤·奥尼尔〔1888—1953，美国剧作家〕.

o·nei·ric [əuˈnairik] *a.* 做梦的，与做梦有关的.

o·nei·ro·crit·ic [əuˌnairəˈkritik] *n.* 圆梦者，解梦者. **-al** *a.*

o·nei·ro·man·cy [əuˈnaiərəumænsi] *n.* 梦卜，占梦，圆梦.

one·ness [ˈwʌnnis] *n.* ①独一,唯一无二,独特. ②完整,一体;统一,一致;同一.

on·er [ˈwʌnə] *n.* ①〔俚〕无比的人〔物〕. ②〔俚〕猛烈的一击. ③〔英俚〕大谎. ④【板球】〔口〕一分.

on·er·ous [ˈɔnərəs] *a.* 繁重的，麻烦的；【法】负有法律义务的. **-ly** *ad.*, **-ness** *n.*

one·self [wʌnˈself] *pro.* ①〔返身用法〕自己,自身. *To starve ~ is suiside.* 饿自己等于自杀. ②〔加强语气〕自己,自行,亲自. *To do right ~ is the great thing.* 自己行为端正才是最重要的. ***absent ~*** 缺席. ***be pleased with ~*** 自满. ***by ~*** 独自,独力. ***exert ~*** 努力. ***for ~*** 为自己;亲自,独自(*There are somethings one can't do for ~* 有些事情是不能独自一人做的). ***in spite of ~*** 不知不觉地. ***of ~*** 独自,自发地. ***read ~ to sleep*** 看书看睡着了. ***speak to ~*** 自言自语. ***teach ~*** 自修.

on·fall [ˈɔnfɔːl] *n.* 攻击,袭击.

on·flow [ˈɔnfləu] *n.* 奔流,洪流.

on·go·ing [ˈɔngəuiŋ] *a.* 前进的，进行的. — *n.* 前进，发展;〔*pl.*〕(奇怪的或不适当的)处置，行动;行为,工作,事务.

on·ion [ˈʌnjən] *n.* ①【植】洋葱; 葱头;【植】葱属. ②〔俚〕(西大西洋)百慕大(Bermuda)岛本地. ③〔美俚〕头,脑袋;脸;棒球. *a good ~* 〔美俚〕讨人欢喜的人;不讨人嫌的朋友. *spring ~* 小葱. *Welsh ~* 大葱. — *vt.* 用洋葱擦(眼睛)使流泪. ~ **dome**〔美〕(教堂等的)洋葱性圆顶. ~**skin** 葱皮;葱皮纸.

On·ions [ˈʌnjənz] ①阿尼恩斯〔姓氏〕. ②**Charles Talbut** ~阿尼恩斯〔1873—1965,英国语言学家、词典编纂家〕.

on·ion·y [ˈʌnjəni] *a.* 洋葱似的;有洋葱气味的.

on-li·cence [ˈɔnlaisəns] *n.* (店内可供堂饮的) 酒吧营业执照 (*opp.* off-licence).

on·look·er [ˈɔnlukə] *n.* 目击者;(袖手)旁观者;观看者.

on·look·ing [ˈɔnlukiŋ] *n.*, *a.* 旁观(的).

on·ly [ˈəunli] *a.* ①唯一的. ②无比的,独一无二的;最适当的. *an ~ child* 独生子. *This is the ~ example [These are the ~ examples] I know.* 我知道的例子只有这一个〔这些〕. *one's ~ hope* 某人的唯一希望. *the ~ man present* 唯一的出席者〔在场的人〕. *He's the ~ man for the position.* 他是最适宜那个职位的人. — *ad.* ①仅仅;只,单,才;不过. ②结果却;不料. *I can ~ guess [guess ~].* 我只能推测罢了. *O- I [I ~] can guess.* 只有我能够猜得出. *O- fancy!* 想想看罢! *He came ~ yesterday.* 他是昨天才来的. *He went to the seaside ~ to be drowned* 他去海边游泳结果却淹死了. ***if ~*** 只要…;只要…就好了 (*If ~ he would stop talking!* 只要他不讲话就好了). ***not ~ ... but (also)*** 不但…而且…. ***~ by ... can ...*** 只有…才能…. ***~ just*** 好容易;刚刚才;恰好 (*I have ~ just received it.* 我才收到. *I was ~ just in time.* 刚好赶上). ***~ not*** 简直是;跟…差不多. ***~ too*** 极,太,非常;实在;可惜 (*~ too glad* 实在感谢，极乐意 *(to do)*. *~ too true* 千真万确). — *conj.* ①但是,可是. ②〔与 that 同用〕除了…，要不是…. *He makes good resolutions, ~ he never keeps them.* 他决心虽好，但不能持久. *I should like to go, ~ that I am ill.* 我倒很想去，可是我有病. ***~ for*** 要是没有 (*O- for my tea, I should have had the headache.* 要是不喝茶,我又会犯头痛病了).

O. No.; O/No = order number 订单号数.

on·o·man·cy [ˈɔnəumænsi] *n.* 依姓名算命.

on·o·mas·tic [ˌɔnəuˈmæstik] *a.* ①姓名的,名称的. ②【法】亲笔签名的.

on·o·mas·tics [ˌɔnəuˈmæstiks] *n. pl.* 〔动词用单数〕①专门词汇词源学. ②人名地名研究.

on·o·mat. = onomatopoeia.

on·o·mat·o·poe·ia [ˌɔnəumˌætəuˈpi(ː)ə] *n.* 【语】拟声,拟声(法)构词〔cuckoo 等〕;象声词;【修】拟声法. **-poe·ic, -po·et·ic** *a.* **-po·et·i·cal·ly** *ad.*

On·on·da·ga [ˌɔnənˈdɔːgə, -ˈəun-; -ˈdɑː-] *n.* ①*(pl. ~(s))* 奥内达加族人〔北美印第安人〕,奥内达加人. ②奥内达加语. **-gan** *a.*

ONR = Office of Naval Research〔美〕海军研究局.

on·rush [ˈɔnrʌʃ] *n.* 突击;冲锋;(水的)奔流.

on·set [ˈɔnset] *n.* 攻击，突击;开始，动手;【医】发作;【印】静电印刷法〔通过印版和滚筒间的空隙,利用静电作用使油墨涂在纸上〕. ***at the very ~*** 刚一开始.

on·shore [ˈɔnˈʃɔː] *a.* 向着海岸方面的;陆上的. — *ad.* 向着海岸;在陆上.

on·side [ˈɔnˈsaid] *a.*, *ad.* 【足球,曲棍球】在(不犯规的)正规位置上(的).

on·site [ˈɔnˈsait] *a.* 当地的.

on·slaught [ˈɔnslɔːt] *n.* 突击,猛袭,猛攻.

Ont. = Ontario 安大略〔加拿大州名〕.

On·tar·i·an [ɔnˈteəriən] *a.*, *n.* 安大略省的(人).

On·tar·i·o [ɔnˈteəriəu] *n.* ①安大略湖〔北美洲〕(= Lake ~). ②安大略〔加拿大省名〕.

on·tic [ˈɔntik] *a.* 实体的.

on·to [强 ˈɔntuː, 弱(元音前) -tu, (辅音前) -tə] *prep.* 到…上. *get ~ a horse* 骑到马上. ★①美国一般与前置词 into 一样,作一个词处理,英国则以分写作 on to 为普遍; 美国口语中可作为 on 或 to 的代用语. 如: They finally got ~ (= on) the bus. The crowd got ~ (= to) the street. ②须注意勿与各有独立意义的 on 和 to 相混淆,如: They drove on to the town.

on·to·gen·e·sis [ˌɔntəuˈdʒenisis] *n.* = ontogeny ①.

on·tog·e·ny [ɔnˈtɔdʒəni] *n.* ①【生】个体发生〔发育〕. ②个体发生学,胎生学.

on·tol·o·gy [ɔnˈtɔlədʒi] *n.* 【哲】本体论,实体论. **-log·ic, -log·i·cal** *a.*,**-o·gist** *n.* 本体论者.

o·nus [ˈəunəs] *n.* 〔L.〕义务;责任;负担;重担. ~ ***probandi*** 作证的义务.

on·ward [ˈɔnwəd] *a.* 前进的，向前的，向上的. — *ad.* = onwards.

on·wards [ˈɔnwəːdz] *ad.* 向前，前进;在前面. ***from this day ~*** 从今天起.

o·ny·mous [ˈɔniməs] *a.* 有名字的;署名的.

on·yx [ˈɔniks] *n.*【矿】缟玛瑙;石华. ~ **marble** 条纹大理石.

O/o = 【商】order of.

oö- *comb. f.* 卵,蛋: oocyte.

OO, O.O. = Ordnance Officer 军械军官.

O.O. [ˈdʌbl ˈəu] 〔Am.〕重做,检查〔又写作 double O〕(= once over). *give the O.O.* 〔美俚〕看一下;检查一下.

OOB = off-off-Broadway 纽约第三戏剧界.

o·o·cyte [ˈəuəsait] *n.*【胎】卵母细胞.

OOD, O.O.D. = Officer of the Deck 舰上值班军官.

oo·dles [ˈuːdls] *n.* 〔美口〕大量,巨额 *(of money)*.

oof [uːf] *n.* 〔英俚〕金钱,财富;精力,力量. **~-bird** 财主,有钱人;财源.

oof·y [ˈuːfi] *a.* 〔英俚〕富有的,有钱的.

o·og·a·mous [əuˈɔgəməs] *a.*【生】异配生殖的,异配的. **-a·my** [-mi] *n.*

o·o·gen·e·sis [ˌəuəˈdʒenisis] *n.* 【生】卵子发生. **-ge·net·ic** [-dʒiˈnetik] *a.*

o·o·go·ni·um [ˌəuəˈgəuniəm] *n.* *(pl.* ***-ni·a*** [-ə], ***-ums)*** ①卵囊. ②【胎】卵原细胞.

oo-la-la [uːlɑːlɑː] *a.* 〔美俚〕舒服的,舒适的;有趣的,可爱的,吸引人的.

o·o·lite [ˈəuəlait] *n.* ①【地】鲕石,鲕状岩. ②〔O-〕英国侏罗系的上部.

o·öl·o·gy [əuˈɔlədʒi] *n.* 鸟卵学;蛋学. **-gist** *n.* 鸟卵学家.

oo·long [ˈuːlɔŋ] (中国)乌龙茶.
oom [uːm] *n.* 〔南非〕= uncle.
oo·mi·ak [ˈuːmiæk] *n.* (爱斯基摩人用的)木框皮舟(= umiak).
oom·pah, oom-pah [ˈuːmˌpɑː] *n.* 〔拟声〕翁巴〔行进中乐队的大号所发出的低沉的节奏声〕. — *a.* 作翁巴声的 (= oom-pah-pah).
oomph [uːmf] *n.* 〔美俚〕魅力;性感;精力. *a girl with* ~ 极迷人[性感]的女子. *The book has* ~. 这本书动人极了. — *a.* 极有魅力的. *an* ~ *girl* 性感女子,极迷人的女子.
oont [uːnt] *n.* 〔Hind.〕骆驼.
o·o·pho·rec·to·my [ˌəuəfəˈrektəmi] *n.* *(pl. -mies)* 【医】卵巢切除术.
o·o·pho·ri·tis [ˌəuəfəˈraitis] *n.* 【医】卵巢炎.
o·o·phyte [ˈəuəˌfait] *n.* 有藏卵器的植物的生殖器发育期. **-phyt·ic** [-ˈfitik] *a.*
oops [uːps, ups] *int.* 喔! 〔绊足后恢复平衡时或失言后脸色恢复自然时所发出惊叹声〕(=whoops).
o·o·sperm [ˈəuəspəːm] *n.* 〔废〕= oöspore.
o·o·sphere [ˈəuəˌsfiə] *n.* 【植】卵球.
o·ö·spore [ˈəuəspɔː] *n.* 【植】卵胞子;受精卵;被囊合子.
o·o·the·ca [ˌəuəˈθiːkə] *n.* *(pl. -cae* [-siː]*)* 【生】卵鞘;卵囊. **-cal** *a.*
o·o·tid [ˈəuətid] *n.* 【生】卵子细胞.
O.O.W. 【军】= Officer of the Watch 舰上机电部门值班军官.
ooze[1] [uːz] *vi.* ①渗出,徐徐流出,滴出,分泌. ②(秘密等)泄漏 *(out)*; (勇气等)渐渐消失 *(away)*. ③溜走. — *vt.* ①渗出. ②泄漏(秘密等). ~ ***out*** 〔美俚〕偷偷溜出. ~ ***with (water)*** 漏(水). — *n.* ①渗漏,分泌;分泌物. ②鞣皮用的浸液.
ooze[2] [ˈuːz] *n.* (海底、河底的)淤泥;沼地.
oo·zy [ˈuːzi] *a.* *(-zi·er; -zi·est)* (有)淤泥的;渗出的,滴出的,漏出的. **ooz·i·ly** *ad.*
OP, O.P. = observation post 【军】观测所.
Op = operator.
op = out of print (书刊等)已售完;已绝版.
op. = ①opera. ②operation. ③opposite. ④opus. ⑤ opposite.
op- *pref.* 〔用于p前〕= ob-.
op, Op [ɔp] *n.* 〔口〕光效应画派〔利用几何图形等以产生各种视错觉及光效应的抽象派绘画风格〕(=op art, optical art).
OPA 〔美〕= Office of Price Administration 〔美旧〕物价管理局.
o·pac·i·ty [əuˈpæsiti] *n.* ①不透明(体),不透明部. ②意义模糊;暧昧. ③愚钝. ④【物】不透明性[度]; 不反光;混浊度;暗度. ⑤愚钝的人.
o·pah [ˈəupə] *n.* 【动】月鱼 *(Lampris regius)* 〔产于太平洋和大西洋〕.
O·pal [ˈəupəl] *n.* 奥珀尔〔女子名〕.
o·pal [ˈəupəl] *n.* 【矿】蛋白石; (半透明的) 乳色玻璃; 〔*pl.*〕〔英〕轧光细棉布. — *a.* 乳白的.
o·pal·esce [ˌəupəˈles] *vi.* 发乳光. **-escence** *n.* 乳光. **-es·cent, -esque** *a.* 乳色的.
o·pa·line [ˈəupəlain] *a.* 蛋白石(似)的,发乳光的. — [-liːn] *n.* 乳色玻璃;细软白布.
o·pa·lize [ˈəupəlaiz] *vt.* 使成乳色.
o·paque [əuˈpeik] *a.* ①不透明的. ②(对电、热等)不传导性的. ③无光泽的, (颜色)晦暗的. ④含糊的; 迟钝的. — *n.* 〔the ~〕不透明,晦暗;【建】遮檐;【摄】遮光涂料. ~ **projector** 【无】反射型(电视)放映机. **-ly** *ad.* **-ness** *n.*
op·art [ˈɔpɑːt] = op.
op·cit. [ˈɔpsit] = *opere citato* (〔*L.*〕= in the work cited) 见前引书.

OPDAR = optical detection (direction) and ranging 光学定向和测距,光雷达.
ope[1] [əup] *vt., vi.* 〔诗〕= open.
ope[2] [əup] *n.* 〔美俚〕= opium.
OPEC = Organization of Petroleum Exporting Countries 石油输出国组织.
o·pen [ˈəupən] *a.* ①开着的,开放的;可进入的,可分享的 *(to)*; 无盖的,敞口的;敞开的,展开的;开的;开阔的,开旷的,广漠的. ②公开的,公共的,出入自由的;自由的,无限制的. ③宽大的,豪爽的,豁达的;易受…的*(to)*;议论自由的,有议论余地的; 未决定的; 未决算的; 取舍自由的,选择自由的;【军】不设防的. ④坦白的,直率的; 公然的,非秘密的. ⑤(商店、展览会等)开着的;(戏院)开演着的; 活动着的. ⑥【语音】开口音的;末尾为元音的音节;【乐】不用指按的,开键的, 空弦的. ⑦有空的,有空隙的;粗疏的(针织品);【印】版面疏松的. ⑧没有冰冻的(河等);冰雪不厉害的, 温和的(天气). ⑨〔美〕无法律限制的,公许的, (赌场等)不受禁止的; 不征收关税[通行税等]的, (港) 自由的. ⑩【医】(大便) 畅通的. *an* ~ *window* 开着的窗子. *an* ~ *boat* 无甲板的船. *an* ~ *car* 敞篷车. *an* ~ *field* 空旷的田野. *an* ~ *road* 畅通无阻的道路. *the* ~ *sea* 公海. *an* ~ *port* 不冻港;自由港,通商口岸. *an* ~ *shop* 〔美〕自由雇用企业〔指可自由雇用非工会会员的工厂[商店]〕. *an* ~ *system* 外通系统. *an* ~ *winter* 无冰冻的冬天. *the* ~ *water in arctic regions* 北极地区的不冰封海面. *leave the matter* ~ 把事情搁着暂不解决. *There are three courses* ~ *to us.* 我们有三条路可以走. *an* ~ *account* 往来账户. *an* ~ *season [time]* 渔猎解禁期. *The bowels are* ~. 【医】大便畅通. ***be*** ~ ***to*** ①易接受(*He is* ~ *to advice.* 他容易接受忠告). ②易受 (*The city is* ~ *to attack.* 该市易受攻击). ③对…开着门. ***be*** ~ ***with sb. about sth.*** 关于某事对某人毫无隐瞒. ***in the*** ~ ***air*** 在户外[野外]. ***keep an*** ~ ***door [house, table]*** 欢迎来客,好客. ***keep one's eyes [ears]*** ~ 留心地看着[听着]; 保持警惕. ~ ***as the day*** 光明磊落,开诚布公. ***throw*** ~ ***the door to*** 送机会给…, 迎接…. ***with an*** ~ ***hand*** 大方,慷慨. ***with*** ~ ***arms*** 张着手臂,热烈(欢迎). ***with eyes*** ~ = ***with open eyes*** 睁着眼睛; 留神;吃惊地. ***with*** ~ ***hands*** = with an ~ hand. ***with*** ~ ***mouth*** ①张着口,想说. ②天真地. ③哑然;伸长脖子(等). — *n.* 〔the ~〕空地,旷场,旷野;汪洋大海;露天,户外. ***be in the*** ~ 是公开的. ***come (out) into the*** ~ 公开;表明心意. ***in*** ~ 公然. ***in the*** ~ 露天,在户外. — *vt.* ①开;打开;【医】切开,割开(腹部等);开垦,开发,开辟;启发. ②公开,开放;张开(翅膀),伸开,展开;【军】疏开(队列);开始;开立;开设. ③泄露; 揭开; 表明 *(to)*. ④解释,说明,论. ⑤【海】(改变船位)来到看得见…的地方. ⑥【电】断(电路). ⑦通 (便). ~ *a door* 开门. ~ *a park* 开放公园. ~ *a debate* 开始辩论. *We* ~*ed a white pagoda to the port.* 【海】左舷方面看出一座白塔来了. — *vi.* ①开;张开;裂开; (花)开; (疮等)开口;变广(大);(知识等)发达; 广阔地展开; (门、窗等)通向 *(to; into)*; 朝, 向 *(on)*. ②开始 *(with)*; (猎狗嗅出鸟兽)吠起来;〔蔑〕(人)开口,说起话来. ③【海】(方向变化的结果)看得见; 现出; 展现. ④散开; 翻开; 开炮. *Parliament* ~*s today.* 议会今天开会. *The ranks* ~*ed.* 队伍散开了. *O- at page 12.* 请翻开第12页. ~ ***fire*** *(on, at)* (向…)开炮. ~ ***into*** *[on, onto]* …通到, 通向. ~ ***one's eyes*** 睁眼;吃惊;使觉悟,启发. ~ ***out*** 开,张开,膨胀,展开;发展,发育;展现,出现;开诚布公,倾吐衷怀;【物】加速 (~ *out to each other* 互相融洽起来). ~ ***the door to*** 给…大开方便之门, 给…造机会. ~ ***up*** (打)开;割开;开发(资源); 揭示;展现;开辟(可能性);开始;开火;开口(说话);滔滔不绝地谈;透露. ~ ***upon*** 朝向,俯瞰;展望. **~-air** *a.* 户外的,野外的,露天的;爱野外的. **~-and-shut** *a.* 容易决定的;很简单的,很明显

的．(*an ~-and-shut case* 一目了然的事情．)~**-armed** *a.* 衷心的,热诚的．~ **ballot** 无记名投票．~ **bar**（婚宴等场合)免费供应饮食的酒吧．~ **bundle** 无限维管束．~**cast coal** 露天开采的煤．~ **chain**【化】开链．~ **champion** 自由比赛的优胜者．~ **channel** 明渠．~ **cheque** 普通支票 (*opp.* crossed cheque 划线支票)．~ **circuit**【电】开路．~**-circuit** *a.*【电】开路的(尤指公开广播的电视)．~ **city.** 不设防城市．~ **competition**【运】公开比赛．~ **country** 旷野．~ **credit** 信用贷款；信用往来．~**cut tunnel** 露天开掘的隧道．~ **day**〔美〕没有应酬的日子．~ **door**【外交】门户开放．~**-eared** *a.* 倾耳静听的．~**-end** *a.* ①开发的〔指发行不限量的随时可兑换现金的股票等〕．②(借款) 不受限制的．③=open-ended. ~**-ended** *a.* ①(时间、方向、数量、数学等) 没有固定限度的；广泛的,无限度的,无约束的 (*an ~-ended discussion* 漫谈)．②可以变更的．③随意回答的〔选择答案的问题之对〕．~**-eyed** *a.* 睁着眼睛的, 吃惊的 (*~-eyed astonishment* 大惊)．~ **face** ①老老实实的面孔, 和蔼的面孔．②(钟表) 没有盖子的一面．~**-faced** *a.* ①不掩盖的．②坦率的．~**-face pie**〔美〕无上皮馅饼, 无盖排．~ **fire** 明火, 活火．~**-handed** *a.* 慷慨的,豪爽的．~ **heart** 坦率的胸怀．~**-hearted** *a.* 坦白的, 直率的．~**-heart surgery** 体外循环心脏手术．~**-hearth** *a.* ①平炉的．②使用平炉的．~ **house** ①家庭招待会〔宾客可随意来去〕．②(学校、机关等) 开放参观．~ **letter** 公开信．~ **list** 船员名册．~ **market policy**【经】市场开放政策．~ **mind** 开通的头脑；谦虚．~**-minded** *a.* 虚心的,没有偏见的．~ **mouthed** *a.* 张大着嘴合不拢的；歔歔的,吃惊的；吵闹的；贪馋的．~**-pit** *a.* (矿) 露天采掘的．~**-pollination** *n.* 自然传粉〔指由风媒、虫媒等传粉〕．~ **primary** 公开预选会〔选举人不需要宣布党派关系的预选会〕．~**-punctuation** (文章的) 少用标点符号．~ **question** 未决问题．~ **secret** 公开的秘密．~ **sentence**【数】开句〔包含着一个或一个以上未知量的数学方程式〕．~ **sesame** 开门咒；过关咒；〔喻〕敲门砖；护照．~ **sore**〔喻〕永远的耻辱．~ **stock** 可以拆散零售的成套商品〔如盘碟〕．~ **warfare**【军】野战．~**work** *n.* (薄纱、雕刻等的)透雕细工,透孔制品〔织物〕(*~ work hose* 网眼袜)．**-ness** *n.* 开放；公开；坦白；无私；宽大．

o·pen·a·ble [ˈəupənəbl] *a.* 能开的．

o·pen·er [ˈəupənə] *n.* ①开的人；开始者；开具；〔美〕剥蠓刀．②〔*pl.*〕〔美〕泻药．*a tin ~* 开听刀．

o·pen·ing [ˈəupniŋ] *n.* ①开,开放；开始,着手；开端,开头；开场,开幕．②口,孔,缝,洞；空隙；通路．③空地,空场；〔美〕林间空地．④(职位的)空缺；好机会 (*for*)．⑤【象棋】开局,头几着．⑥【律】辩护人的申辩书．⑦【商】开盘,交易开始时间．— *a.* 开始的．*an ~ address [speech]* 开会辞．*an ~ ceremony* 开会〔开学、开幕、通车〕典礼．*look out for an ~* 谋事,找就职机会．~ **stock** 期初存货．~ **sales** 开张大廉价．

o·pen·ly [ˈəupənli] *ad.* 公开地；老老实实地；坦白；直率．

oper. = ①operation. ②operator.

op·er·a¹ [ˈɔpərə] *n.* 歌剧；〔口〕歌剧院．*a comic ~* 喜歌剧．*a grand ~* 大歌剧．*a light ~* 轻歌剧．★艺术部门之一的歌剧或上演时的歌剧都是 uncountable. 如: the history of ~ 歌剧史. Are you fond of ~? 你喜欢看歌剧吗? ~ **cloak** 赴剧院〔夜会〕穿的女大衣．~ **glass(es)** 看戏用的小望远镜．~ **hat** 歌剧帽〔可折叠的高帽〕．~ **hood** 看戏〔夜会〕用的女头巾．~ **house** 歌剧院．~ **window** 汽车尾座门上的小窗．

op·e·ra² [ˈɔpərə] *n.*〔L.〕opus 的复数．

op·er·able [ˈɔpərəbl] *a.* ①可实行的,行得通的．②可施手术的,可开刀的．**-a·bil·i·ty** [ˌɔpərəˈbiliti] *n.* **-a·bly** *ad.*

op·er·and [ˈɔpəˌrænd] *n.*【数】运算域．

o·pe·ra se·ri·a [ˈɔpərə ˈsiəriə; It. ˈaupera: ˈseri:a:]〔It.〕悲歌剧,正歌剧．

op·er·ate [ˈɔpəreit] *vi.* ①操作,工作；(机械等)动作,运转．②起作用,生影响 (*on; upon*)；见效果,(药)见效．③【医】动手术,开刀；用泻药．④【军】作战,采取军事行动．⑤【商】操纵市场；从事投机．— *vt.* ①开动,操纵(机器等)．②〔美〕经营, 管理．③完成；引起(变化等)．④导致, 决定．⑤对…动手术, 对…动刀．

op·er·at·ic [ˌɔpəˈrætik] *a.* 歌剧的；歌剧式的, 歌剧体的．**-i·cal·ly** *ad.*

op·er·at·ing [ˈɔpəreitiŋ] *a.* ①运行的；操作的；工作的．②关于业务的；营业上的；关于收支的．③外科手术的．~ *costs* 营业费,事业费；经营成本；生产费用．~ *expenses* 业务开支；营业费．~ *funds* 流动资金．~ *personnels* 管理人员．~ **income** 营业收入．~ **lever** (大炮的) 尾栓开闭杆,【机】司动杆．~ **line** 工作线,操作线．~ **room** *[table]* 手术室〔台〕．~ **speed [time]** 操作速度〔时间〕．~ **statement** 收支报告．~ **theatre** 手术示教室．~ **wave**【物】工作波．

op·er·a·tion [ˌɔpəˈreiʃən] *n.* ①动作,行动,活动；业务,工作；作用．②效果,效力；有效范围,有效期间．③【工】工序；开动,运转；操作,运用；施行,实施．④【数】运算；【医】手术；【军】〔常 *pl.*〕军事行动, 作战；〔*pl.*〕【空】地面指挥所；【商】(资金的)运用；交易；投机买卖；〔美〕经营．~ *of breathing* 呼吸作用．*regulations for technical ~s* 技术操作规程．*directing ~*【火箭】控制程序．*the ~ of a machine* 机器的运转．*a capital ~* 大手术．*four ~s* (算术的)四则, 加减乘除．*a base of ~s* 作战根据地, 作战基地；策源地．*a plan of ~s* 作战计划．*main ~s* 主力战．*~s on exterior [interior] lines* 外线〔内线〕作战．***come [go] into ~*** 开始工作,开始运转；生效．***in ~*** 活动着；运转着；施行着．***perform an ~ (on sb. for a disease)*** (给某人)动(外科)手术．***put into ~*** 实施, 施行．***undergo an ~*** 受手术．~ **sheet** (机床等的)工作说明书．~**s research**〔美〕运筹学．

op·er·a·tion·al [ˌɔpəˈreiʃənl] *a.* ①(装置、系统、工艺等)工作的, 运转的．② 可以使用的, 可以工作的, 可以运转的．③ 正在使用的, 正在工作的, 正在运转的．④军事行动的,准备在军事行动中使用的．~ *research* 运筹学．**-ly** *ad.*

op·er·a·tion·al·ism [ˌɔpəˈreiʃənlizm] *n.*【哲】操作主义(= operationism). 亦 **op·era·tion·ism, -al·ist** *n.* 操作主义者．**-al·is·tic** *a.*

op·er·a·tion·al·ize [ˌɔpəˈreiʃənlaiz] *vt.* ***(-ized; -izing)*** 使工作,使运转；投入生产．**-i·za·tion** [-laiˈzeiʃən] *n.*

op·er·a·tive [ˈɔpərətiv,ˈɔpəreitiv] *a.* ①工作着的,操作的,运转的．②起作用的；有效验的, 有效力的．③【医】手术的．④实施的；实地的．***become ~*** 实施, 起作用 (*External causes become ~ through internal causes.* 外因通过内因而起作用)．— [ˈɔpərətiv] *n.* ①职工, 工人．②〔美〕私人侦探．

op·er·a·tize, op·er·a·tise [ˈɔpərətaiz] *vt.* 把…编成歌剧．

op·er·a·tor [ˈɔpəreitə] *n.* ①操作者,机务员；司机,驾驶员；【军】电话兵；【电话】接线员, 话务员 (= telephone ~)；【电报】报务员．②(外科)施行手术者．③掮客,经纪人．④【语法】功能词．⑤【数】算子,算符．⑥经营者；〔美〕工厂主, 资方．⑦投机商人；骗子；精明圆滑的人．⑧【剧】灯光助理员．*an ~'s set* 话务员的电话机．*a telegraph ~* 电报报务员．*an unitary ~* 公正算符．*a mine ~* 矿山经营者,矿主．

o·per·cu·lar [əuˈpə:kjulə] *a.* ①【植】有盖的；有蒴盖的；有囊盖的；有孔盖的．②【动】有鳃盖骨的〔指鱼类〕；有壁的〔指软体动物〕；有盖的〔指昆虫〕．

o·per·cu·late [əuˈpə:kjulit, -leit], **-cu·lat·ed** *a.* 有盖的；有蒴盖的；有囊盖的；有孔盖的．

o·per·cu·lum [əu'pəːkjuləm] *n.* *(pl.* **-la** [-lə]*)*【植】果盖,藓盖;【动】螺的厣;(鱼的)鳃盖骨;【昆】盖.

op·e·re ci·ta·to ['ɔpəriː saiteitəu] = op. cit.

op·er·et·ta [ˌɔpə'retə] *n.* 小歌剧,轻歌剧.

o·per·on ['ɔpəˌrɔn] *n.*【生】操纵子.

op·er·ose ['ɔpərəus] *a.* 费了力气的,下了工夫的;费力的;繁忙的;勤快的,用功的.

O·phel·ia [əu'fiːljə] *n.* ①我菲丽亚〔女子名〕.②莎士比亚剧作《汉姆雷特》中女主人公.

oph·i·cleide ['ɔfiklaid] *n.* 类似大号的旧式铜管乐器.

o·phid·i·an [ɔ'fidiən] *n., a.* 蛇(似的).

ophio- *comb. f.* 蛇: *ophio*logy.

oph·i·ol·a·ter [ˌɔfi'ɔlətə] *n.* 崇拜蛇的人.

oph·i·ol·a·try [ˌɔfi'ɔlətri] *n.* 蛇崇拜.

oph·i·ol·o·gy [ˌɔfi'ɔlədʒi] *n.* 蛇类学,蛇学.

O·phir ['əufə] *n.*【圣】俄斐〔产金地,见旧约《列王纪》〕.

o·ph·ite ['ɔfait] *n.*【地】纤闪辉绿岩.

o·phit·ic [əu'fitik] *a.*【地】辉绿岩的.

Oph·i·u·chus ['ɔfjuːkəs, 'əufi-]【天】蛇夫(星)座.

oph·thal·mia [ɔf'θælmiə], **oph·thal·mi·tis** [-'maitis] *n.*【医】眼炎;结膜炎.

oph·thal·mic [ɔf'θælmik] *a.* 眼的;眼科的;眼炎的;治眼病的.— *n.* 眼药. *an ~ hospital* 眼科医院.

oph·thal·mol·o·gist [ˌɔfθæl'mɔlədʒist] *n.* 眼科医师.

oph·thal·mol·o·gy [ˌɔfθæl'mɔlədʒi] *n.* 眼科学,眼科医学. **-log·i·cal** *a.*

oph·thal·mo·scope [ɔf'θælməskəup] *n.*【医】眼膜曲率镜. **-scop·ic** [-'skɔpik] *a.* **-mos·co·py** *n.*

oph·thal·mot·o·my [ˌɔfθæl'mɔtəmi] *n.*【医】眼球切开术.

o·pi·ate ['əupiit] *n.* 鸦片剂,麻醉剂 — *a.*〔古〕加有鸦片的,用鸦片制的;麻醉性的,催眠性的,有镇静作用的.— ['əupieit] *vt.* 加鸦片麻醉;使(感觉)迟钝;使缓和. **-pi·at·ic** [-'ætik] *a.* 鸦片剂(一样)的.

o·pine [əu'pain] *vt.,vi.*〔谑〕想,认为,以为〔常用 ~ that ...〕;发表意见. *I ~ that it will rain before night.* 我想天黑以前要下雨的.

o·pin·ion [ə'pinjən] *n.* ①意见;看法;见解;〔常 *pl.*〕主张.②舆论(= public ~);(善恶的)判断,评价.③(专家的)鉴定;判定. *one's political ~s* 政(治)见(解). *a medical ~* 医生的意见. *a counsel's ~* 律师的意见. ***act up to one's ~s*** 遵循自己的信念而行动;照自己主张行事. ***a matter of ~*** 看法不同的问题. ***be of the ~ that ...*** 相信,以为,认为. ***get another ~*** 征求别人意见. ***have [form] a bad [low, mean, poor, unfavourable] ~ of*** (对某人或某事)评价甚低,轻视,瞧不起. ***have [form] a good [high, favourable] ~ of*** (对某人或某事)有很高的评价,重视,佩服. ***have another ~*** 请别人鉴定一下. ***have no ~ of*** 不大理会,不大佩服. ***have the best ~*** 请教高明的专家. ***have the courage of one's ~s*** 勇敢的陈述[实行]主张. ***in one's ~*** 据某人意见. ***in the ~ of*** 据…的见解. ***of the same ~*** 抱同一意见. ***pass on ~*** 下结论. ***win (the) golden ~s*** 受众人尊敬. ~ **book**【商】信用调查录. ~ **poll** 民意测验.

o·pin·ion·at·ed [ə'pinjəneitid] *a.* 坚持己见的,不易说服的;极自负的;教条式的. *become ~* 自以为是.

o·pin·ion·ist [ə'pinjənist] *n.* 持有特定见解的人;持有非寻常见解[异端信仰]的人.

O Pip, o·pip. ['əu'pip]〔信号用文字〕〔军口〕= observation post.

op·is·o·me·ter [ˌɔpi'sɔmitə] *n.* (测量地图等曲线距离用的)计图器.

op·is·thog·na·thous [ˌɔpis'θɔgnəθəs] *a.*【动】后口的.

o·pis·tho·graph [ə'pisθəgrɑːf] *n.* 两面书写的原稿〔羊皮纸,羊皮书〕.

o·pi·um ['əupjəm, -piəm] *n.* 鸦片;麻醉剂;起鸦片作用的事物;【动】寄生群落. ~ *den* 鸦片窟,鸦片烟馆. ~ *eating [smoking]* 吸鸦片. ~ *habit* 鸦片烟瘾.— *vt.* 用鸦片处理. ~**-pop·py** 罂粟. **O- War** 鸦片战争(1839—1842).

o·pi·um·ism ['əupjəmizəm] *n.* 鸦片烟瘾,鸦片中毒.

o·pi·um·ize ['əupjəmaiz] *vt.* 用鸦片渗透;使麻醉.

OPL outpost line〔美〕警戒线.

OPLR = outpost line of resistance〔美〕警戒防御线.

OPM = ①other people's money 别人的钱.②output per man 每人产量.

Opn = operation.

op·o·del·doc [ˌɔpəu'deldɔk] *n.* 肥皂樟脑涂擦剂.

o·pop·a·nax [əu'pɔpənæks] *n.* 苦树脂;卡他夫没药.

O·por·to [əu'pɔːtuː] *n.* 波尔图〔葡萄牙港市〕(=Porto).

o·pos·sum [ə'pɔsəm] *n.*【动】鼬〔又名负鼠〕. ***play [act] ~*** 〔美俚〕装死;装蒜. ~ **shrimp**【动】糠虾.

opp. = ①opposed.②opposite.

Op·pen·heim ['ɔpənhaim] *n.* 奥本海姆〔姓氏〕.

Op·pen·hei·m·er ['ɔpənhaimər] ①奥本海默〔姓氏〕.②**J.R.** ~ 奥本海默〔1904—1967,美国原子物理学家,原子弹计划主持人〕.

op·pi·dan ['ɔpidən] *a.*〔罕〕城市的;城里的.— *n.*〔罕〕城里人,市民;(英国伊顿公学的)校外寄宿生(*opp.* colleger).

op·pi·late ['ɔpileit] *vt.* 使(毛孔等)阻塞;使便秘. **-la·tion** [-'leiʃən] *n.*

op·po·nen·cy [ə'pəunənsi] *n.* 反对,对抗.

op·po·nent [ə'pəunənt] *a.* 对立的,对抗的,反对的.— *n.* ①反对者,对手,敌手.②【解】对抗肌.

op·por·tune ['ɔpətjuːn, ˌɔpə't-] *a.* 凑巧的,恰好的,时机好的;及时的,合时宜的,适切的 *at ~ moments* 相机. **-ly** *ad.* **-ness** *n.*

op·por·tun·ism ['ɔpətjuːnizəm] *n.* 机会主义. **-ist** *n.* 机会主义者. **-is·tic** *a.*

op·por·tu·ni·ty [ˌɔpə'tjuːniti] *n.* 机会,好机会;〔罕〕凑巧,方便. *a good [favourable] ~* 好机会,良机. ***afford [find, get, give, make, miss, seize, take] an [the] ~*** 给[找着,得着,给,造,失去,抓住,利用]机会(*I take every ~ of speaking English.* 我利用一切机会讲英语). ***at the earliest [at the first, on the first] ~*** 一有机会. ***equality of ~*** 机会均等. ***have an [no, little] ~ for doing [to do] sth.*** 有[没有]做某事的机会. ***make the most of an ~*** 尽力利用机会.

op·pos·a·ble [ə'pəuzəbl] *a.* 可反对的,可反抗的;可相对的;可使对立[面对面、头对头]的. **-bil·i·ty** [əˌpəuzə'biliti] *n.*

op·pose [ə'pəuz] *vt.* ①反对,反抗,对抗,抗议;妨碍.②使对立,使对抗;使对照,使对比;使相对,使面对面,使头对头. ~ *a scheme* 反对一个计划. *He ~d his arms to the blow.* 他用胳臂挡住了打击. ~ *violence with violence* 用暴力对付暴力. *A swamp ~d the advance of the army.* 沼地阻碍了军队的前进. **-r** *n.* 反对者,反抗者,对立者.

op·posed [ə'pəuzd] *a.* 反对的,敌对的,对抗的;对面的,对立的;相反的. *words ~ in meaning* 意义相反的词儿,反语. *Black is ~ to white* 黑是白之对. ~ **engine**【机】对置气缸发动机. ~ **pistons**【机】对动活塞. ~ **landing**【军】敌前登陆.

op·pose·less [ə'pəuzlis] *a.*〔诗〕反对不来的;不可抵抗的;无敌的;无可反驳的.

op·po·site ['ɔpəzit] *a.* ①相对的,对面的,对立的.②背对背的,面对面的 *(with)*;正相反的,敌对的,不相容的 *(to; from)*.③【植】对生的;(花部)重迭的. *the tree ~ (to) the house* 房子对面的树木. ~ *angles*【数】对角. *the ~ sex* 异性. ~ *number* 职务对等的人. ***in the ~ direction [way]*** 朝相反的方向. ***on the ~ side*** 在反对方面;在敌方.— *n.* 相反的事物[人];反语;对立面;〔口〕对面的人. *The most extreme ~s have some qualities* *in common.* 极端相反的事物间是多少有些共性的. *I thought quite the ~.* 我想的刚刚相反. — *ad.* 在相反的位置,在对面. *sit ~ to* 坐在…的对面. *play ~ (to)* 作对手 — *prep.* 在…的对过, 在…的反对地位[场所、方向]. *sit ~ each other* 面对面[背对背]地坐. ~ **prompter** 【剧】在提词人反对方面,在演员的左首[略 o.p.].

op·po·si·tion [ˌɔpəˈziʃən] *n.* ①反对,敌对;对抗,抵抗;对照,对立;面对,相对;反对物;妨害. ②[the ~][常 O-](政府的)反对党,在野党. ③【逻】对当;对偶. ④【天】冲,(月的)望. *the O- = His Majesty's O-*[英]在野党. *the O- benches*[英](下院)在野党席位. ***break down ~*** 打破障碍. ***in ~*** 在野 (*opp.* in office). ***in ~ to*** 反对[反抗]着. ***meet with ~*** 遇到抵抗. ***offer ~ to*** 反对. **-al** *a.*

op·press [əˈpres] *vt.* ①压迫;压制;虐待,欺侮. ②给与沉重的感觉;使意气消沉,使气馁;使无精神. ③[古]压倒. ~ *the poor* 压迫穷人. *feel ~ed with the heat* 热得难受. *the ~ed class* 被压迫阶级.

op·pres·sion [əˈpreʃən] *n.* ①压迫;镇压;压制;抑制;压制物;虐待. ②沉闷,忧郁;苦恼,苦闷. *relieve the ~ of the heart* 消除心头的沉闷. *Wherever there is ~, there is resistance.* 哪里有压迫,那里就有反抗.

op·pres·sive [əˈpresiv] *a.* ①压制的,压迫的;暴虐的. ②沉重的;闷热的;忧郁的. *an ~ ruler* 暴虐的统治者. *The air is ~.* 空气闷热. ~ *heat* 闷热. **-ly** *ad.* **-ness** *n.*

op·pres·sor [əˈpresə] *n.* 压迫者,暴君.

op·pro·bri·ous [əˈprəubriəs] *a.* 无礼的;鄙俗的,下流的;(话等)骂人的;该骂的;可耻的. **-ly** *ad.*

op·pro·bri·um [əˈprəubriəm] *n.* ①臭名,耻辱. ②骂詈,责骂;轻蔑.

op·pugn [ɔˈpjuːn] *vt.* [罕]反驳;质问;反对;抗辩;攻击;抗击. **-er** *n.* 反驳者,质问者,抗击者.

op·pug·nant [əˈpʌgnənt] *a.* [罕]敌对的,对抗性的. **-nan·cy** *n.*

O.P.S., OPS = Office of Price Stabilization [美旧](经济稳定署)物价稳定局.

op·si·math [ˈɔpsimæθ] *n.* 年老开始学习的人.

op·sim·a·thy [ɔpˈsiməθi] *n.* ①晚学;接受教育晚. ②年长后学得的东西.

op·sin [ˈɔpsiŋ] *n.*【生化】视蛋白.

op·son·ic [ɔpˈsɔnik] *a.*【细菌】调理素的. ~ *action* 调理(素)作用. ~ *reaction* 调理素反应.

op·son·i·fy [ɔpˈsɔnifai] *vt.* ***(-fied; -fy·ing)*** (= opsonize). **-fi·ca·tion** *n.*

op·so·nin [ˈɔpsənin] *n.*【细菌】调理素;助蚀菌素.

op·so·nize [ˈɔpsənaiz] *vt.* ***(-nized; -niz·ing)***【生化】使(细菌)易受调理素的作用. **-za·tion** *n.*

opt. = ①optative. ②optics. ③optician. ④optional.

opt [ɔpt] *vi.* 选择. ~ *for* 选取;赞成. ~ *out* 撤退;退出;辞职.

op·ta·tive [ˈɔptətiv] *a.* 表祈愿的,希求的. *the ~ mood*【语法】祈愿语气. — *n.*【语法】祈愿语气;表示祈愿语气的动词. **-ly** *ad.*

op·tic [ˈɔptik] *a.*【解】眼的;视力的;视觉的;【物】光学(上)的. — *n.* ①[谑]眼睛. ②(光学仪器)镜片. ③[英](酒馆中罩在酒瓶上的)量酒玻璃杯. *an ~ angle* 视角. *the ~ nerve*【解】视神经. ~ **axis**【理】光轴. ~ **disk** 盲点.

op·ti·cal [ˈɔptikəl] *a.* 眼的;视觉的;视力的;帮助视力的;光学(上)的. ~ *activity*【物】旋光性. *an ~ axis* 光轴[线]. *an ~ center* 光心. *an ~ square* 直角转光器. *an ~ illusion* 光幻视. *an ~ radar* 光雷达. ~ **art** = op. ~ **double (star)** (= double star)【天】双星. ~ **fibre** 光学纤维. ~ **isomerism** 旋光异构(现象). **-ly** *ad.* 光学上,用视力.

op·ti·cian [ˈɔptiʃən] *n.* 光学仪器商,眼镜商.

op·ti·cist [ˈɔptisist] *n.* 光学家.

op·tics [ˈɔptiks] *n. pl.* [作单数用]光学.

op·ti·mal [ˈɔptiməl] *a.* 最适宜的;最理想的;最好的 (*opp.* pessimal).

op·time [ˈɔptimi] *n.* 剑桥(Cambridge) 大学数学学位考试考中第二名或第三名的学生[前者叫 senior ~ 后者叫 junior ~].

op·tim·ism [ˈɔptimizəm] *n.* 乐观主义. *revolutionary ~* 革命乐观主义,乐观 (*opp.* pessimism). **-ist** *n.*

op·ti·mis·tic, -ti·cal [ˌɔptiˈmistik, -tikəl] *a.* 乐天主义的;乐观的. **-ti·cal·ly** *n.*

op·ti·mi·za·tion [ˌɔptimaiˈzeiʃən] *n.* 最佳化,最优化.

op·ti·mize [ˈɔptimaiz] *vi.* ~ *about the future* 对未来持乐观看法,表示乐观. — *vt.* 乐观地对待[考虑];使尽可能完善;使(劳动安排,机器运转等)发挥最大的效益;使最优化,使最佳化.

op·ti·mum [ˈɔptiməm] *n.* ***(pl. ~s, -ma*** [-mə]***)***【主、生】(成长繁殖等的)最适条件,最适度. — *a.* 最适宜的. *the ~ temperature* 最适温度.

op·tion [ˈɔpʃən] *n.* 选择,取舍;选择权,选择自由;可选择的东西;【商】(在契约有效期可附加一定贴水的)选择买卖的特权. *imprisonment without the ~ of a fine* 不能用罚款代替的禁锢刑. *There are three ~s in our college.* 我们大学里有三种选科. ***at one's ~*** 任意,随意. ***have no ~ but to (do)*** …除…外别无办法,只好. ***leave to one's ~*** 随人选择. ***make one's ~*** 选择. ~ **market** 期货市场.

op·tion·al [ˈɔpʃnəl] *a.* 可自由选择的;随意的,任意的;非强制的 (*opp.* compulsory). — *n.*[美]选修科. *It is ~ with you.* 那是你的自由. **-ly** *ad.* 随意,任意,自由.

optns. = operations.

op·to·e·lec·tron·ic [ˌɔptəuilekˈtrɔnik] *a.* 光电子的. **-s** *n.* 光电子学.

op·tom·e·ter [ɔpˈtɔmitə] *n.* 视力计.

op·tom·e·trist [ɔpˈtɔmitrist] *n.* 验光配镜师.

op·tom·e·try [ɔpˈtɔmitri] *n.* ①视力测定(法). ②验光配镜业,验光配镜术. **-met·ric, -met·ri·cal** *a.*

op·to·phone [ˈɔptəufəun] *n.* 听音辨光器[可变光为音,以便盲人分辨].

op·to·type [ˈɔptəutaip] *n.*【医】试验视力字标型.

op·tron [ˈɔptrɔn] *n.* 光导发光元件.

op·u·lence [ˈɔpjuləns] *n.* 富裕;丰富,丰饶.

op·u·lent [ˈɔpjulənt] *a.* 富裕的;丰富的,丰饶的;(文章等)华丽的. *an ~ feast* 丰盛的酒席. ~ *foliage* 茂盛的树叶.

o·pun·ti·a [əuˈpʌnʃiə, -ʃə] *n.* 仙人掌属 (*Opuntia*) 植物[包括霸王树、仙人掌].

o·pus [ˈəupəs, ˈɔpəs] *n.* ***(pl. o·pus·es; op·e·ra*** [ˈɔpərə]***)*** [L.] ①(艺术)作品. ②乐曲[按乐曲发表次序编号时用,略作 op.]. ③[美口]广播剧,电视剧;(一部)电影. ~ *magnum = magnum ~* 杰作. *Beethoven op. 47,* 贝多芬作曲第 47 号.

o·pus·cule [ɔˈpʌskjuːl] *n.* ***(pl. ~s)*** [F.]小作品;小曲.

o·pus·cu·lum [ɔˈpʌskjuləm] *n.* ***(pl. -la*** [-lə]***)*** [L.] = opuscule.

o·quas·sa [əuˈkwæsə] *n.*【动】缅因红点鲑 (*Salvelinus Oquassa*)[产于美国缅因州西部湖里].

or[1] [ɔː; 弱 ə] *conj.* [表示对前后二语词或结构的选择、区别关系]①或,或者,还是,抑或是. *white ~ black* 是白呢还是黑. *white ~ grey ~ black* 白的、灰的、还是黑的. *white, grey, ~ black* 白,灰或黑. *white ~ black, red ~ yellow, blue ~ green* 白或黑,红或黄,蓝或绿. *Shall you be there ~ not?* 你是否会到那里? *any Tom, Dick, ~ Harry* 随便哪个汤姆、狄克、或哈利;不论哪个张三李四. ★ ①有 or 联系着的几个主语全为单数时,动词用单数. 如: John or Tom is wanted. ②主语单复不一,人称不一时,动词须与其紧接之主语相一致. 如: John or I am to blame. ③通常不宜说 Is he or we wrong? 宜说 Is he wrong, or are we? ④弱音的 or [ə], 选择意义很微弱,一般常用以表示不定意义. 如: two ~ [ɔː] three miles 两英里或三英里. *two* ~ [ə] *three miles* 两三英里. ②〔表示后一词语或结构同前面的词语有同义关系; 对前面的词语作进一步阐释〕即; 或者说; 换句话说就是. *the culinary art ~ art of cookery* 烹调术即烧菜法. ~ *more correctly* 说得更正确一些. ~ *rather* (或者)说得更正确点. ③〔在否定结构中,否定的是前后二者〕甲也不,乙也不; 甲和乙都不[没有]. *He cannot read ~ write.* 他不会读,也不会写. *Wolves ~ bears are never seen in that part of the country.* 在国内的那部分地区, 从来没有看到过狼和熊. ④〔古〕〔用于句首,起转折作用〕可是; 会…吗? 再说. *Or what man of you, if his son asks him for a loaf, will give him a stone?* 你们中间, 谁有儿子求饼, 能给他石头吗? ⑤〔构成让步结构〕不管…还是; …也好…也好. *Rain ~ shine, I'll go.* 不管下雨还是晴天,我一定去. ⑥〔表示不明确的情况或约数〕左右,大概; 某(地等). *more ~ less* 或多或少,总有一点. *two ~ three pounds* 两三镑. *He's ill ~ something* 他大概是病了,还是怎么的. ⑦〔在祈使语气结构后, 常与 else 连用,引出相反情况〕否则,要不然 *Make haste, or (else) you will be too late.* 赶快,不然就太晚啦. *Do it at once, or else!* 不立刻动手可不行呀; ***either ... or*** 或, 不是…就是 *(Can he speak either English or French?* 他能说英语或法语吗? *It must be either black or white.* 那不是黑就是白). ***or else*** 不然, 否则. ***or ... or***〔诗〕= either ... or, whether ... or. ***or so*** 上下,左右,大约; 或许 (*two miles or so* 两英里上下). ***whether ... or*** 是…还是…,是不是; 不管 (*I don't know whether it is true or not.* 我不知道它真不真. *Ask him whether he will come or not.* 问他来(还是)不来).

or² [ɔː] *prep., conj.* 〔古、诗〕在…之前, 比…更早〔普通用 ~ ever, ~ e'er〕.

or³ [ɔː] *n.*【徽】黄金色,黄色.

-or¹ *suf.* 表示动作、状态、性质的拉丁名词词尾 (英国拼作 our): favor [favour], labor [labour]. ★美国对释义为基督的 Saviour 普通仍作 -our, 对 glamour 虽也原字不变,但也逐渐有略去u的倾向.

-or² *suf.* 加在拉丁语系动词(尤其是词尾 -ate 的动词)后, 造成'…人[物]'之意的名词, 代替英语原有的 -er 或两者并用; 并用时有时 -or 比较具有专门性的意义; audit*or*, elevat*or*, tail*or*, sail*or*.

Or. = Oriental.

O.R., o.r. = owner's risk 风险所有主承担.

O·ra ['ɔurə] *n.* 奥拉〔男子名〕.

o·ra ['ɔːrə] *n.* os² 〔L.〕(口,口腔; 孔穴,通路)的复数.

or·ach, or·ache ['ɔrətʃ] *n.* 滨藜属 *(Atriplex)* 植物(尤指法国菠菜 *(A. hortensis)*).

or·a·cle ['ɔrəkl] *n.* ①天启, 神谕; (古希腊的)神谕宣示所. ②【宗】神殿; (古犹太神神殿的) 至圣所. ③神使, 先知,预言者; 大智者;〔常谑〕圣人, 哲人. ④预言; 圣言, 名言; 善断, 聪明的判断. ⑤〔*pl.*〕基督教《圣经》. *a great ~ on* …方面的绝对权威. ~ *bone (inscriptions)* 甲骨(文). ***Sir O-*** 独断的人. ***work the ~*** (贿赠僧侣而)得到自己希望的天启; (用贿赂)达到自己的目的; 用手段诱人赞助使计划实现.

o·rac·u·lar [ɔ'rækjulə] *a.* ①天启的, 神谕的. ②天启似的,象神谕的; 暧昧的; 谜似的. ③严肃的; 明智的; 预言的; 圣言的; 装做预言者的; 宣示天启的. **-ly** *ad.* **-i·ty** [ɔˌrækju'læriti] *n.*

o·rad ['ɔːræd] *ad.*【动】口向.

o·ral ['ɔːrəl] *a.* 口头的,口述的;【解】口的; 口部的;【语】口腔发声的;【动】口的; 前的, 前面的. ~ *calisthenics* 〔美〕得意话,用来自夸的故事. *an ~ examination* 口试. ~ *instruction* 口授. *the ~ method* 口(头教)授法. *an ~ offence* 〔英口〕口臭. ~ *traditions* 口碑. *an ~ contract* 口约. *the ~ cavity [opening]* 口腔. ~ *administration* (药品的)口服. — *n.* 〔美〕口试; 口服避孕药. **-ly** *ad.* 口头上.

O·ran [ɔː'rɑːn] *n.* 奥兰〔阿尔及利亚一省或该省省会〕.

o·rang ['ɔːrəŋ] *n.* = orang-utan.

o·rang [ɔː'ræŋ, ə-] *n.* 猩猩 (= orangutan).

Or·ange ['ɔrindʒ] *a.*【史】奥林奇派的. **-ism** *n.* 奥林奇派的主张和作法. **-man** *n.* 奥林奇派分子〔1795 年北爱尔兰的一个秘密团体的成员,支持新教〕.

or·ange ['ɔrindʒ] *n.* ①【植】橘,香橙; 橙; 柑橘类. ②橙色. ③〔美俚〕棒球. *the bitter [sour, Seville] ~* 臭橙. *the horned ~* 佛手柑. *the king ~* 柑. *the loose skinned ~* 橘. *the mandarin(e) [tangerine] ~* 中国柑橘. *the mock ~* 山梅花. *the ~ pekoe* (印度、锡兰产)橙香红茶. ***squeeze the ~*** 榨干, 尽取其利, 点滴不留. ***the squeezed ~*** 已被充分利用过的东西, 无用的糟粕; 用处不大的人物. — *a.* 橘子(一样)的; 橙色的. ~ **blossom** 香橙花〔新娘子戴着表示纯洁〕. ~**-colo(u)red** *a.* 橙色的. ~ **hawkweed** (= devil's paintbrush 枯黄山柳菊). ~ **stick** 指甲签. ~**wood** 橙木.

or·ange·ade ['ɔrindʒ'eid] *n.* 橘子水; 橘子汽水.

or·ange·ry ['ɔrindʒəri] *n.* 橙园; 养橙温室.

o·rang-ou·tang [ə'ræŋu'tæŋ], **o·rang-u·tan** [-'tæn] *n.*【动】猩猩.

o·rate [ɔː'reit, ɔ'r-] *vi.* 〔谑〕演说, 演讲, 用演说腔调说话.

o·ra·ti·o di·rec·ta [ə'rɑːtiəu di'rektə] 〔L.〕= direct narration.

o·ra·tion [ə'reiʃən] *n.* ①演说, 演讲. ②【语】引语. ***make [deliver] an ~*** 演说.

or·a·ti·o ob·li·qua [ə'bliːkwə] 〔L.〕= indirect narration.

or·a·tor ['ɔrətə] *(fem. -tress [-tris]) n.* ①演说者,演讲者; 雄辩家, 擅长演说的人; 辩护人, 拥护者. ②【法】原告, 请愿人. ***the Public O-*** 〔英〕(Cambridge 或 Oxford 大学的)校方发言人.

or·a·to·ri·al [ˌɔrə'tɔːriəl] *a.* = oratorical.

or·a·tor·i·cal [ˌɔrə'tɔrikəl] *a.* 演说(家)的; 雄辩家似的; 演说[雄辩]术的; 修辞上的. *an ~ contest* 演讲比赛. **-ly** *ad.* 演说似地; 修辞学上.

or·a·to·ri·o [ˌɔrə'tɔriəu] *n.* *(pl. ~s)*【乐】圣乐(歌曲); (以基督教《圣经》故事为主题的)清唱剧.

or·a·to·rize, or·a·to·rise ['ɔrətəraiz] *vi.* (= orate).

or·a·to·ry¹ ['ɔrətəri] *n.* 雄辩(术),演讲(术); 修辞; 夸张的文体.

or·a·to·ry² ['ɔrətəri] *n.* ①祈祷室, 小礼拜堂. ②〔O-〕【宗史】奥拉托利会.

orb [ɔːb] *n.* ①球; 天体, 地球; 〔罕〕世界. ②(象征王权的)宝珠. ③浑一体. ④〔诗〕眼球, 眼睛; 〔罕〕圈; 环; 圆; 圆面. ⑤轨道; (星体等的) 影响范围. — *vt.* ①把…作成球体,把…弄圆. ②卷,围,包围.

orb·ed [ɔːbd, 〔诗〕'ɔːbid] *a.* ①球状的, 圆的. ②有眼的. ③十全的; 圆满的. ④被包围着的.

or·bic·u·lar [ɔː'bikjulə] *a.* 球状的, 扁圆(形)的; 浑然一体的, 完整的, 圆满的;【植】(叶子)正圆形的. *the ~ bone*【解】环骨. *the ~ muscle*【解】括约肌. **-i·ty** [ɔːˌbikju'læriti] *n.* **-ly** *ad.*

or·bic·u·late [ɔː'bikjulit] *a.* = orbicular.

or·bit ['ɔːbit] *n.* ①【天】轨道;【解】眼窝, 眶; (鸟或昆虫的)复眼缘的颊部. ②(人生的)旅程, 生活过程; 势力范围. — *vt.* 使 (人造卫星、宇宙飞船等) 进入空间轨道运行; 环绕(天体等)作轨道运行. — *vi.* 环行; (人造装置等) 沿轨道运行; 达到轨道飞行所需的速度. ~ **trajectory**【军】轨道弹道. **-er** *n.* (绕)轨道飞行器.

or·bit·al ['ɔːbitl] *a.* ①【解】眼窝的. ②【天】轨道的. ~ **angular momentum**【物】轨角动量. ~ **velocity** (人造卫星等)沿轨道飞行所需的速度.

orc [ɔːk] *n.* 逆戟鲸.

Or·ca·di·an [ɔːˈkeidiən, -djən] *a., n.* (苏格兰)奥克内群岛 (Orkney Islands) 的(人).
or·ce·in [ˈɔːsiːin] *n.*【化】苔红素,地衣红.
orch. = orchestra.
or·chard [ˈɔːtʃəd] *n.* 果园; 果园里的全部果树;〔美俚〕棒球场. ～ **grass** 鸭茅,鸡足草. **-ist, -man** 果树栽培家;果园经营人.
or·ches·tic [ɔːˈkestik] *a.* 舞蹈的.
or·ches·tics [ɔːˈkestiks] *n.* 舞蹈术.
or·ches·tra [ˈɔːkistrə, -kes-] *n.* ①管弦乐; 管弦乐队; (舞台前的) 乐队席; 管弦乐队的全部乐器. ②〔美〕(舞台前的)正厅前排〔又叫～ chairs〕;(古希腊剧场中的)合唱队席; (古代罗马剧场中舞台前面的半圆形) 贵人席. ～ **stalls** 〔英〕正厅前排.
or·ches·tral [ɔːˈkestrəl] *a.* 管弦乐(队)的; 供管弦乐队演奏的. ～ *instruments* 管弦乐器. *an* ～ *performance* 管弦乐队的演出. **-ly** *ad.*
or·ches·trate [ˈɔːkistreit, -kes-] *vt., vi.* 为(管弦乐队)谱写音乐; 给…配管弦乐;使和谐地结合起来. **or·ches·tra·tion** [-ˈtreiʃən] *n.* 为管弦乐配器; 和谐的安排 [组织、结合].
or·ches·tri·na [ˌɔːkisˈtriːnə], **or·chestri·on** [ɔːˈkestriən] *n.* (发音似的管弦乐的) 桶形手摇风琴.
orchi-,orchido- *comb. f.* 表示"睾丸" (testicle): *orchitis.*
or·chid [ˈɔːkid] *n.* ①【植】(温室栽培种)兰,兰花. ②淡紫色. ③〔*pl.*〕〔美俚〕感谢,祝贺,恭维话,贺词. *Orchids to you for your fine performance!* 恭喜你表演得出色.
or·chi·da·ceous [ˌɔːkiˈdeiʃəs] *a.* 兰(科)的;兰花般的.
or·chi·dec·to·my [ˌɔːkiˈdektəmi] *n.*【医】睾丸切除(术).
or·chid·ol·o·gy [ˌɔkiˈdɔlədʒi] *n.*【植】兰花栽培学.
or·chid·o·ma·ni·a [ˌɔːkidəˈmeiniə] *n.* 爱兰癖.
or·chid·o·ma·ni·ac [ˌɔːkidəˈmeiniæk] *n.* 兰迷.
or·chid·ot·o·my [ˌɔkiˈdɔtəmi] *n.* *(pl.* **-mies***)*【医】睾丸切开术.
or·chi·ec·to·my [ˌɔːkiˈektəmi] *(pl.* **-mies***)* *n.*【医】睾丸切除(术).
or·chil [ˈɔːtʃil] *n.* = archil.
Or·chis [ˈɔːkis] *n.*【植】红门兰属; 〔O-〕(野生)兰; 红门兰.
or·chi·tis [ɔːˈkaitis] *n.*【医】睾丸炎.
or·cin [ˈɔːsin] *n.*【化】苔黑素,苔黑粉.
or·cin·ol [ˈɔːsinəul, -nɔːl] *n.*【化】地衣酚, 5-甲基间苯二酚 (= orcin).
ord. = ①ordained. ②order. ③ordinance. ④ordinary. ⑤ordnance.
or·dain [ɔːˈdein] *vt.* ①(命运)注定; (法律等)规定, 制定,命令. ②任命(牧师、圣职). *Nature has* ～*ed us mortal [to die].* 自然注定我们会死. *It seemed that fate had* ～*ed the meeting.* 这次相会好象是命中注定的. *He* ～*ed that the restrictions were to be lifted.* 他下令撤销各种限制. ～ *a new type of government* 制订新政府体制. *be* ～*ed for the priesthood* 获得牧师的职位. — *vi.* 任命,命令. **-er** *n.* **-ment** *n.*
or·deal [ɔːˈdiːl, -ˈdiːəl] *n.* (古代条顿民族间所行的)神裁法;试罪法; (人格、忍耐力等的)严峻考验; 苦难的经验;折磨. *pass through a terrible* ～ 渡过可怕的考验.
or·der [ˈɔːdə] *n.* ①次序,顺序,整齐; (社会)秩序,治安; 状况,常态;健康状态;条理; 会场次序; 议事程序, 日程; 组织,体系. ②〔常 *pl.*〕 命令, 训令; 指挥, 号令;【计】指令. ③席次;阶级, 地位; 等级, 品级. ④牧师的地位; 〔*pl.*〕 牧师职. ⑤教团,修道会; (中世纪)骑士团; 结社, 公会. ⑥【商】定货,定单;汇兑,汇票,汇单. ⑦勋位, 勋章. ⑧种类;种;【生】目(介于纲和科之间). ⑨规则; 规定;制度, 礼法;【宗】仪式, 祭礼. ⑩【建】柱式, 式样;【军】整队,排队;序列,队形;【数】阶,级,次,度;序模;【修】布置;调配,处理. ⑪【剧】(免费)入场券,优待卷. ⑫【法】(法院等的) 决议 (指非最后的判决). ⑬(转让产业的) 许可证, 授权证明书. *a revolution of a world* ～ 世界性的革命. *in alphabetical [chronological, numerical]* ～ 按 ABC [年代、号码] 顺序. *the old* ～ 旧制度, 旧理想. *the* ～ *of nature [things]* 自然 [事物]的条理. *a high* ～ *of culture* 高度文化. *give* ～*s [an* ～*] for sth. to be done [that sth. should be done]* 下命令做某事. *the military* ～ 军界. *all* ～*s and degrees of men* 一切阶级的人们. *the higher [lower]* ～*s* 上层[下层]阶级. *a large [tall, strong]* ～ 大批定货; 〔俚〕艰巨的工作; 不当要求. *a postal [money,* 〔英口〕 *postoffice]* ～ 邮汇. *the O- of the Garter* 嘉德勋位, 嘉德勋章. *the standing* ～*s* 议事规程;【军】标准作战规定. *talents of a high* ～ 优秀的才能,天才. *a battle [close]* ～ 战斗[密集]队形. ***be on*** ～ 已在定购. ***by*** ～ 奉命令 (*by* ～ *of the authorities* 奉当局命令). ***call a meeting to*** ～ 宣布开会. ***call for*** ～***s*** 做推销员. ***call to*** ～ (主席)请发言人遵守会场规则; 〔美〕 宣布开会. ***draw (up) in*** ～ 使排整齐. ***fill an*** ～ 供应定货. ***get out of*** ～ 损坏,发生故障. ***give an*** ～ ***for*** 定 (货). ***in*** ～ ***of age [merit]*** 按年龄 [成绩] 次序. ***in*** ～ 整整齐齐; 合规则;情况正常;健康 (*The goods arrived in good* ～. 货物安全到达). ***in*** ～ ***that*** 以便, 为了…起见. ***in*** ～ ***to*** 为要…起见,…才能. ***in short*** ～〔美〕迅速地;在短期内;〔美〕 立即, 马上, 毫不拖延. ***keep in*** ～ 整理好;保持井然有序. ***keep*** ～ 维持秩序. ***made to*** ～ 定做的. ***on the*** ～ ***of*** 跟…相似的; 属于…同类的. ～ ***of group***【数】群阶. ～ ***of march*** 行进序列; 行军命令. ***O- of Merit*** 勋章〔略 O. M.〕. ～ ***of the day*** (议会等的)议事日程, 工作日程;日常的事,习俗,风气, 惯例. ～ ***on*** ～ ***of*** *(sculptured figures)* 一排一排的 (雕像). ***O-! O-!*** 违章! 违章! 〔议会等中有人违反规则时向主席提出的抗议〕; 秩序! 秩序! 〔主席等要搅乱秩序者守秩序〕. ***out of*** ～ 乱, 混乱,杂乱无章;不合规则; 情况反常;有故障;有病,不舒服. ***place an*** ～ ***with*** *(a company)* ***for*** *(sth.)* 向 (某公司) 定(某货). ***put [set, take] in*** ～ 整顿, 整理,修整. ***rise to (a point of)*** ～ (议员)起立对议会是否遵守议事规程提出质问 (通常是打断他人的发言). ***take (holy)*** ～***s*** 接受圣职,做牧师. ***take*** ～***s from sb.*** = ***take sb.'s*** ～***s*** 受某人的指挥. ***take*** ～ ***to (do)*** 采取适当手段去(做…). ***take*** ～ ***with*** 安排, 处理. ***take things in*** ～ 依次做事. ***to*** ～ 定做的, 照规格 [计划]做的. ***under the*** ～***s of*** 在…的命令下, 带着…的命令. — *vt.* ①命令,指令; 命令去…. ②购; 要求供应. ③整理;整顿, 调整;安排,处理;建立(秩序). ④(命运等)注定. ⑤任命(某人)为牧师;授给…圣职. ～ *a retreat* 下令退却. ～ *a taxi to take sb. to the airport* 安排出租汽车送人到机场. ～ *sth. (to be) done [sb. to do ..., that sb. (should) do ....]* 吩咐某人做某事. ★可略去过去分词前的 to be 的主要是〔美〕; that 后的虚拟式现在时用法为〔美〕,近来〔英〕也这样说了. *He was* ～*ed to Egypt.* 他被派到埃及去了. *O- arms!* 〔口令〕枪放下(立正); ～ *dinner* 叫饭,定菜. ～ *one's affairs* 料理私事. ～*ed alloy* 有序合金. ～ ***about [around]*** 东派西使, 驱使, 摆布, 发号施令. ～ ***away [back]*** 命令离去[返回]. ～ ***from*** 向…定购 (～ *some new books from England* 向英国定购几本新书). — *vi.* ①发命令;吩咐. ②定货. *Please* ～ *for me.* 请替我点菜. ～ **book** 定货簿; (英国下院的)提议通告簿;【军】命令簿. ～ **cheque**【商】记名支票. ～ **form [blank]** 定单. ～ **number**【物】原子序(数). ～ **port** 商船停泊以装卸货物的港口.
or·der·li·ness [ˈɔːdəlinis] *n.* 整洁;整齐;有秩序, 秩序井然;守纪律.
or·der·ly [ˈɔːdəli] *a.* ①整洁的. ②有秩序的, 整齐的. ③有组织的, 有规则的; 有纪律的; 守法的;安静的. ④【军】有关命令的,传达的,值班的. — *n.* ①【军】传令下士,传令兵;勤务兵;通讯员; (尤指陆军医院的) 卫生员,护理员. ②〔英〕街道清洁工，清道夫. — *ad.* 依次地，顺序地；有规则地；有条理地. ~ **bin**〔英〕(路旁的)废物箱. ~ **book** 命令簿. ~ **man**【军】传令兵. ~ **officer**【军】值班军官. ~ **room** (兵营内的) 文书室.

or·di·nal [ˈɔːdinl] *n.* ①序数 (词) 〔*oppo.* cardinal〕. ②〔O-〕【英国国教】授任仪式书；【天主】弥撒规则书. — *a.* 依次的，顺序的；【生】目 (order) 的. ~ **number** 序数.

or·di·nance [ˈɔːdinəns] *n.* ①法令；训令；条令，条例. ②布告；传统的风俗习惯. ③【宗】仪式，(尤指)圣餐式；(神或命运)注定的事. *an Imperial* ~ 〔英〕敕令.

or·di·nand [ˌɔːdiˈnænd] *n.*【宗】圣职候选人.

or·di·na·ri·ly [ˈɔːdnərili, ˈɔːdnrili] *ad.* 通常，普通；大概，大抵；平凡，一般. *O- he sleeps until the last possible minute.* 他通常要尽可能睡到最后一分钟才起床. *expect sb. to be* ~ *honest.* 期望某人达到一般的诚实水平.

or·di·na·ry [ˈɔːdinəri, ˈɔːdnri] *a.* ①普通的，平常的，正常的. ②规定的，照常的；平凡的；拙劣的. ③〔卑〕不标致的. ④【法】直辖的. ***in an* ~ *way*** 普通，按常例. — *n.* ①普通事，常事，常例. ②〔英〕小客店的客饭；备有客饭的小客店；便饭馆；〔美〕客店 (食堂)；吃客饭的人. ③【宗】礼拜仪式次序书，仪式次序；【徽】普通徽〔又叫 *honourable* ~, 指 *bar, bend, chevron, cross, fess, pale* 或 *saltire*〕. ④法官；宗教法官. ⑤【宗】罪犯的忏悔牧师；〔*the O-*〕大主教；教区主教. ⑥〔英〕【商】普通股. ⑦(前轮特大后轮特小的早期) 大小轮自行车. ***in* ~** ①常任的，直属的 (*a physician in* ~ *to the king* (国王的)侍医). ②【海】后备的. ***out of the* ~** 不寻常的，非凡的，例外的. ~ **point**【数】寻常点. ~ **seaman** 新水兵，见习水兵〔略 O.S.〕. ~ **signalman**〔英〕三等信号兵. ~ **wave**【无】正常波.

or·di·nate [ˈɔːdiənit] *n.*【几】纵标，纵坐标.

or·di·na·tion [ˌɔːdiˈneiʃən] *n.* ①整理；排列；分类. ②颁布法令. ③委任；受委任. ④【宗】圣职授任，按手礼.

or·di·nee [ˌɔːdiˈniː] *n.* 新任教会执事.

ord·nance [ˈɔːdnəns] *n.*〔集合词〕①大炮；军械，武器. ②军用品，军需品；〔英〕军械部门；军械署. *the Royal Army O- Corps* 英国陆军军械厂. **O- Department**〔美〕兵工署，军械处. ~ **factory** (炮)兵工厂. ~ **map**〔英〕陆地测量部地图. ~ **officer**〔美、海军〕炮术长；军械官. ~ **store** 军械库. **O- Survey**〔英〕陆地测量部.

or·do [ˈɔːdəu] *n.* (*pl.* ~*s*, *-di·nes* [-dəˌniːz])【天主】弥撒祷告历〔罗马天主教对每天做弥撒和祷告作出指示的日历〕.

or·don·nance [ˈɔːdənəns] *n.* ①配置，安排〔指绘画、建筑物等说〕. ②【法】命令，法令.

Or·do·vi·cian [ˌɔːdəˈviʃən] *n.*【地】奥陶纪；奥陶系；〔the O-〕奥陶时期；奥陶纪层. — *a.*【地】奥陶纪〔系〕的.

or·dure [ˈɔːdjuə] *n.* ①粪便；肥料；脏东西；排泄物. ②猥亵；粗卑话，下流话.

Ore. = Oregon.

ore [ɔː, ɔə] *n.* 矿；矿砂，矿石；〔诗〕金属(尤指贵金属). ***be in* ~** 含有矿物. ~ **body** 矿体. ~ **carrier** 矿砂运输货船. ~ **deposit** 矿床. ~ **dressing** 选矿.

ö·re [ˈəurə] *n.* (*pl.* ***öre***) ①欧尔〔瑞典货币单位，等于 1/100 克朗〕. ②欧尔硬币.

ø·re [ˈəurə] *n.* (*pl.* ***ø·re***) ①欧尔〔丹麦或挪威货币名，等于 1/100 克朗〕. ②欧尔硬币.

o·re·ad, O- [ˈɔːriæd] *n.*【希神】山精，山的女神.

o·rec·tic [ɔˈrektik] *a.*【哲】欲望的，愿望的；【医】食欲的，增加胃口的.

Oreg. = Oregon.

o·reg·a·no [ɔːˈregənəu, ə-] *n.*【植】牛至 (*Origanum vulgare*)〔叶子芳香，可做调料〕.

Or·e·gon [ˈɔrigən] *n.* 俄勒冈〔美国州名〕. ~ **boot**〔美俚〕脚镣，附有铁球的链子. ~ **fir**, ~ **pine**【植】花旗松，洋松 (=Douglas fir). **-ian** *a.* 俄勒冈州(人)的. *n.* 俄勒冈州人.

o·reide [ˈɔːrid] *n.* = oroide.

O·res·tes [ɔˈrestiːz] *n.*【希神】奥列斯特〔迈锡尼亚亚加农之子，曾杀母为父报仇〕. ~ **complex**【心】弑母情结〔儿子思杀其母的欲念〕.

o·rex·is [ɔˈreksis] *n.* ①欲望，愿望. ②【医】食欲 (= appetite).

orf(e) [ɔːf] *n.*【鱼】黄色金鱼.

org. = ①organ. ②organic. ③organism. ④organization.

or·gan [ˈɔːgən] *n.* ①【乐】(教堂用的)管风琴 (=〔美〕pipe ~)；(足踏)风琴；手摇风琴；口琴. ②(生物的)器官；人类的发音器官. ③嗓音(尤指音量、音质说). ④机构；机关；机关报〔杂志〕；喉舌；报刊. ⑤【机】元件，机件，工具. ⑥〔美军〕编制 (= organization). *a government* ~ 政府机关报. *state* ~*s* 国家机构. ~*s of public security* 公安机关. *internal* ~*s* 内脏. *essential* ~*s* 花的雌雄蕊. *have a fine [splendid]* ~ 嗓子好. ~*s of generation [reproduction]* 生殖器. ~*s of hearing* 听觉器官. ~*s of smell* 嗅觉器官. ~ *of speech* 发音器官. ~ **grinder** (街头的) 手摇风琴师. ~ **loft** 教会放置管风琴的二楼；〔美〕剧场中放背景的地方. ~ **pipe** 风琴管. ~ **transplant** 器官移植.

or·ga·na [ˈɔːgənə] *n.* organon 和 organum 的复数形式.

or·gan·die, -dy [ˈɔːgændi] *n.*【纺】蝉翼纱；玻璃纱；薄棉布. — *a.* 蝉翼纱〔玻璃纱〕制的.

or·gan·elle [ˌɔːgəˈnel] *n.*【生】细胞器.

or·gan·ic [ɔːˈgænik] *a.* ①【医】器官的；器质性的；有机体的；【化】有机的 (*opp.* inorganic). ②有组织的，有系统的；有机的；结构的；建制的；根本的；生来的，固有的. *an* ~ *disease* 器官病. ~ *matter* 有机物. ~ *chemistry* 有机化学. *an* ~ *whole* 有机统一体. — *n.* 分子有机体. ~ **act** [**law**]〔美〕【法】建制法；基本法. ~ **artillery**【军】建制炮兵. ~**-cooled** *a.* (核反应堆) 用有机化合物冷却的. ~ **reserves**【军】后备队. **-i·cal·ly** *ad.*

or·gan·i·cism [ɔːˈgænisizm] *n.*【生】机体说. **-cist** *n.*, 机体论者. *a.*

or·gan·ise *v.* = organize.

or·gan·ism [ˈɔːgənizəm] *n.* ①有机体；生物体；微生物. ②有机组织〔社会等〕；组织，结构，构造. *the social* ~ 社会.

or·gan·ist [ˈɔːgənist] *n.* 风琴演奏者；风琴手.

or·gan·iz·a·ble [ˈɔːgənaizəbl] *a.* 可变为有机体的；可以组织起来的.

or·gan·i·za·tion [ˌɔːgənaiˈzeiʃən] *n.* ①组织，构成，编制. ②体制，机构；【生】有机体. ③团体，公会，协会. ④〔美〕(政党的)委员会. *peace [war]* ~ 平时〔战时〕编制. *the* ~ *of the human body* 人体的结构. ***O- of American States*** 美洲国家组织. ~ **man** (组织机构内)驯顺的成员；(大公司内)听话的职员. **-al** *a.*

or·gan·ize [ˈɔːgənaiz] *vt.* ①组织；编组；创立，创办，发起. ②〔通常用被动语态〕使有器官；给与…生机，使有机化. ③使组成工会；使加入工会. ④〔口〕使 (自己思想)有条理. ~ *an army* 编组军队. ~ *a factory* 创办工厂. *an* ~*d body* 有机体. *the* ~*d labour*〔美〕(集合词)在编工会会员. — *vi.* 组织起来，成立组织；〔美〕参加共同事业；成立工会. *the organizing committee* 创立委员会.

or·gan·iz·er [ˈɔːgənaizə] *n.* 组织者；编制者；创立人，发起人；工会组织人；【生】形成体.

organo- *comb. f.* 表示器官、有机等义: *organology.*

or·ga·no·gen·e·sis [ˌɔːgənəuˈdʒenisis] *n.*【生】器官发生，器官形成. **-ge·net·ic** *a.*

or·ga·no·graph·i·cal [ˈɔːgənəuˈgræfikəl] *a.* 器官学的；器官学有关的.

or·ga·nog·ra·phy [ˌɔːgəˈnɔgrəfi] *n.*【生】器官学.

or·ga·no·lep·tic [ˈɔːgənəuˈleptik] *a.* ①影响(或涉及)器官(尤指味觉、嗅觉或视觉器官)的. ②对感官刺激敏感的.

or·ga·nol·o·gy [ˌɔːgəˈnɔlədʒi] *n.*【医】器官学. **-log·ic, -log·i·cal** *a.* **-gist** *n.* 器官学家,器官研究者.

or·ga·no·me·tal·lic [ˌɔːgənəumiˈtælik] *a.*【化】有机金属的,碳金属链合的.

or·ga·non [ˈɔːgənɔn] *n.* *(pl.* ***or·ga·na*** [-nə], *~s)* ①(科学研究的)原则, 研究法; 方法论上的原则. ②〔O-〕《工具论》〔希腊古代哲学家亚里士多德所著〕.

or·ga·no·sil·i·con [ˌɔːgənəuˈsilikən] *n.*【化】有机硅(化合物).

or·ga·no·sol [ɔːˈgænəsɔl] *n.*【化】有机溶胶.

or·ga·no·ther·a·py, -ther·a·peu·tics [ˌɔgənəuˈθerəpi, -ˈpjutiks] *n.*【医】器官疗法; 内脏制剂疗法.

or·ga·no·tro·pic [ˌɔːgənəuˈtrɔpik] *a.*【医】①向器官的. ②亲器官的.

or·ga·num [ˈɔːgənəm] *n.* *(pl.* *~s,* ***or·ga·na*** [-nə]) ①= organon. ②【乐】(相差四度或五度音程的)=重场. ***Novum O-*** 《新工具》〔英国哲学家培根的主要著作〕.

or·gan·za [ɔːˈgænzə] *n.*【纺】透明硬纱.

or·gan·zine [ˈɔːgənziːn] *n.*【纺】经丝.

or·gasm [ˈɔːgæzəm] *n.* ①(感情的) 极端的兴奋. ②【医】情欲亢进;【生】性交高潮.

or·gas·tic [ˈɔːgæstik] *a.* 极度兴奋的; 情欲亢进的.

or·geat [ˈɔːʒæt] *n.* 杏仁糖浆〔作为鸡尾酒的一种配料或食品的香料,不含酒精〕; 杏仁橘花香茶〔一种不含酒精的清凉甜饮料〕.

or·gi·as·ti·c [ˌɔːdʒiˈæstik] *a.* 有酒神节气氛的; 狂饮的; 狂欢的; 狂乱的.

or·gie, or·gy [ˈɔːdʒi] *n.* ①〔常 *pl.*〕 喧闹的宴会; 纵酒宴乐. ②〔口〕狂欢; 乱舞; 无节制; 放荡. ③〔*pl.*〕【古希腊,罗马】(秘密举行的) 酒神节. *an ~ of bloodshed* 流血大惨剧.

org-man [ˈɔːgmən] *n.* 〔美口〕 = organization man.

-orial *suf.*〔构成形容词〕表示"…的","属于…的": profess*orial*, purgat*orial*.

Ori·ana [ɔriˈɑːnə] *n.* 奥里阿娜〔女子名〕.

or·i·bi [ˈɔːribi] *n.*【动】侏羚 *(Ourebia ourebia)*〔产于非洲〕.

o·rie-eyed [ˈɔːriaid] *a.* 〔美〕醉眼朦胧的.

o·riel (window) [ˈɔːriəl] *n.*【建】凸肚窗.

o·ri·ent [ˈɔːriənt] *a.* ①〔诗〕东方的; 东洋的. ②(太阳等)上升的; 新生的. ③光辉灿烂的; (珍珠等)光耀的. —*n.* ①〔the O-〕东方 *(opp.* occident*)*; 亚洲; 东亚; 东洋; 远东. ②〔诗〕东方, 东天. ③(东方产的)优质珍珠; 珍珠的光泽. — [ˈɔːrient] *vt.* ①使(建筑物等)向东方; 以东方做标准定…的位置; 定…的方位;【化】使定向. ②把(脚)向东摆,朝西摆(尸体); 坐东朝西盖(教堂). ③摆正(地图、磁石等的)方向; 〔喻〕究明(事物)的真相, 正确地判断; (按照已知的事实或原则)修正; 使适应(新环境). *~ oneself* 决定自己的方针, 表明态度. — *vi.* 面向东; 适应形势. *~* **circle** 有向圆.

o·ri·en·tal [ɔ(ː)riˈentl] *a.* ①〔O-〕东, 东方的, (尤指)远东的; 从东方来的, 东方国家的; 东方人特有的; 东方式的. *(opp.* occidental*)*. ②(珠宝等)最优质的; 贵重的; 有特殊光泽的; 华美的. — *n.* 〔O-〕 东亚人, 东方人〔尤指中国人、日本人〕. **O- emerald**绿玉. **O- poppy**【植】近东罂粟 (Papaver orientale). **O- rug [carpet]** 东方地毯, **O- shagreen** 人造鲨鱼皮. **-ly** *ad.*

O·ri·en·tal·ism [ɔ(ː)riˈentəlizəm] *n.* ①东方风格; 东方风俗〔习惯〕. ②东方知识, 东方学; 东方文化研究. **-ist** *n.* ①东方人. ②东方通,东方学专家,东方文化研究者.

O·ri·en·tal·ize [ˌɔriˈentəlaiz] *vt., vi.* (使)东方化, (使)具有东方特征.

o·ri·en·tate [ˈɔːrienteit] *vt.* = orient.

o·ri·en·ta·tion [ˌɔ(ː)rienˈteiʃən] *n.* ①向东; (礼拜时)东向; 置于东端. ②(房屋等的)方向; 找出东方; 定位, 定向; 取向, 排列方向. ③(外交等的)方针〔态度〕的确定; (对周围环境等的) 倾向性. ④【动】(鸽等的) 回家本能; (对新环境的)适应. *a firm and correct political ~* 坚定正确的政治方向. *radio range ~* 无线电定向.

o·ri·en·teer·ing [ˌɔːrienˈtiəriŋ] *n.* 越野识图比赛.

or·i·fice [ˈɔrifis] *n.* (管子等的)口,孔, 锐孔,【化纤】喷丝孔.

or·i·flamme [ˈɔriflæm] *n.* (古时法国的)红色王旗; (王室等的)军旗; 勇气和忠诚的表征; 党的标记.

orig. = ①origin. ②original. ③originally.

o·ri·ga·mi [ˌɔːriˈgɑːmi] *n.* 〔Jap.〕①(日本传统艺术)折纸手工〔用纸折成花、动物等〕. ②折纸手工品.

or·i·gan [ˈɔrigən], **o·rig·a·num** [ɔˈrigənəm] *n.*【植】牛至属植物.

or·i·gin [ˈɔridʒin] *n.* ①开始,发端; 根源,起源; 起因,由来. ②出身,来历; 血统. ③【数】原点; 起点;【解】(筋、神经的)起端. *He is a Dane by ~.* 他原籍丹麦. *He comes of Scottish ~.* 他的祖先是苏格兰人. *country of ~* 原产地. *of worker and peasant ~* 工农出身的.

o·rig·i·nal [əˈridʒənəl] *a.* ①原始的, 固有的, 本来的; 最初的, 初期的. ②原物的,原本的,原文的,原图的. ③独创的,创造性的,别出心裁的; 新颖的, 崭新的, 新奇的; 古怪的. *an ~ bill* 原案. *an ~ edition* 原版. *one's ~ domicile* 原籍. *What does the ~ Greek say?* 希腊原文是怎么讲的? *Few plots of plays are entirely ~.* 完全独出心裁的戏剧结构很少见. — *n.* ①原物, 原型, 雏型, 模型; 原文, 原作; 〔罕〕起源. ②有独创性的人. ③怪人. ***in the ~*** 用原文〔原书〕. *~* **gum** 邮票背面原有的胶质. *~* **house**【法】(女子的)娘家. *~* **sin**【宗】原罪.

o·rig·i·nal·i·ty [ˌəridʒiˈnæliti] *n.* ①独创性, 创造力; 创见; 创举; 独出心裁; 新颖. ②怪人; 珍品. ③原物, 本物.

o·rig·i·nal·ly [əˈridʒənəli] *ad.* ①本来,原来; 第一, 最初. ②独创地, 独出心裁地. *a plant ~ African* 原产非洲的植物. *a house ~ small* 原来就小的房子.

o·rig·i·nate [əˈridʒineit] *vt.* ①发起; 引起. ②创办, 创设; 创作; 创始; 发明. — *vi.* 开始, 发生〔起始于某事或某地多用 *from* 或 *in*; 起始于某人多用 *from* 或 *with*〕. *What ~d the Great War?* 大战的原因是什么? 大战是怎样引起的? *All genuine knowledge ~s in direct experience.* 一切真知都是从直接经验发源的. **-na·tion** [-ˈneiʃən] *n.* 开始,草创; 创作; 发明; 起点, 起因. **-na·tive** *a.* 独创的; 有创作力的; 新奇的. **-na·tor** *n.* 创作者,创设者,创办人,发起人.

Or(r)in [ˈɔrin] *n.* 奥林〔姓氏,男子名〕.

o·ri·na·sal [ˌɔːriˈneizl] *a.*【语】鼻化元音的. — *n.* 鼻化元音.

ORINS = Oak Ridge Institute of Nuclear Studies 〔美〕橡树岭原子核研究所.

o·ri·ole [ˈɔːriəul] *n.*【鸟】(欧洲)金莺; 黄鹂.

O·ri·on [əˈraiən] *n.*【天】猎户座;【希、罗神】奥利安〔健美的猎人〕. *~'s Belt* 猎户座的带纹三明星. *~'s Hound* 天狼星.

or·ison [ˈɔrizən] *n.* 〔古、诗〕〔常 *pl.*〕 祈祷.

ork [ɔːk] *n.* 〔美口〕 = orchestra.

Or·lan·do [ɔːˈlændəu] *n.* 奥兰多〔男子名 Rol(l)and 的异体〕.

orle [ɔːl] *n.*【徽】盾的内边,沿着盾章的外缘.

Or·le·ans [ɔːˈliənz, ˈɔːl-] *n.* ①奥尔良〔法国中部城市〕. ②(法国)奥尔良李子. ③奥尔良棉毛混纺衣料.

Or·lon [ˈɔːlɔn] *n.* 奥纶〔聚丙烯腈短纤维的商标名称〕. —*n.* 〔o-〕 奥纶纤维.

or·lop [ˈɔːlɔp] *n.* 最下层甲板.

Or·mazd [ˈɔːməzd] *n.*【祆教】最高的神,创世主,善灵.

or·mer [ˈɔːmə] *n.* 〔英方〕鲍鱼 (= abalone).
or·mo·lu [ˈɔːməluː] *n.* ①镀金用金箔〔铜、锌、锡的合金〕,金色黄铜;金箔颜料. ②镀金物.
Ormsby [ˈɔːmzbi] *n.* 奥姆斯比〔姓氏〕.
Orn =【化】ornithin(e).
orn.; ornith.; ornithol. = ①ornithology. ②ornithologic(al). ③ornithologist.
or·na·ment [ˈɔːnəmənt] *n.* ①装饰,修饰;装饰物[品]. ②增添光彩的人[物、行为];勋章;风致. ③〔常 *pl.*〕礼拜用品. ④装饰用家具. ⑤【乐】装饰音. *a tower rich in* ~ 富于装饰的塔. *by way of* ~ 当作装饰. *personal* ~ (珠宝等)装饰品. *He was an* ~ *to his country.* 他是为国增光的人物. — [ˈɔːnəment] *vt.* 装饰;美化.
or·na·men·tal [ˌɔːnəˈmentl] *a.* 装饰的;作装饰用的;增加风致[光彩]的. *an* ~ *plantation* 风致林. ~ *writing* 装饰性的书写文字. — *n.* ①〔*pl.*〕装饰物. ②观赏植物. **-ist** *n.* 装饰家,设计家. **-ize** *vt.* 装饰. **-ly** *ad.* 装饰着,作为装饰.
or·na·men·ta·tion [ˌɔːnəmenˈteiʃən] *n.* 装饰,修饰;装饰术;〔集合词〕装饰品.
or·nate [ɔːˈneit, ˈɔːneit] *a.* 装饰的,华美的;修辞上极考究的;(文体)华丽的;矫揉造作的. **-ly** *ad.* **-ness** *n.*
or·ner·y [ˈɔːnəri] *a.* 〔美口〕①低劣的;卑劣的,品行坏的. ②脾气坏的;爱争吵的. ③平凡的;一般的. **-i·ness** *n.*
or·nis [ˈɔːnis] *n.* 地方鸟类;地方鸟类志 (= avifauna).
ornith- 〔元音前〕, **ornitho-** *comb. f.* 鸟: *ornith*oid.
or·nith·ic [ɔˈniθik] *a.* 鸟的,有鸟的特征的.
or·ni·thin(e) [ˈɔːniθiːn] *n.*【生、化】鸟氨酸.
or·ni·thoid [ˈɔːniθɔid] *a.* 外形似鸟的,结构似鸟的.
or·ni·tho·log·ic, or·ni·tho·log·i·cal [ˌɔːniθəˈlɔdʒik, -ikəl] *a.* 鸟(类)学的,禽学的.
or·ni·thol·o·gist [ˌɔːniˈθɔlədʒist] *n.* 鸟(类)学家,禽学家.
or·ni·thol·o·gy [ˌɔːniˈθɔlədʒi, -nai-] *n.* 鸟(类)学,禽学;鸟学论文[著作].
or·ni·tho·pod [ˈɔːniθəpɔd, ɔːˈniθə-] *n.* 鸟脚亚目 *(Ornithopoda)* 动物.
or·ni·thop·ter [ˌɔːniˈθɔptə] *n.* 扑翼(飞)机 (= orthopter).
Or·ni·tho·rhyn·chus [ˌɔːniθəˈriŋkəs] *n.*【动】鸭獭属(动物),〔o-〕鸭嘴兽 (= duckbill).
or·ni·tho·sis [ˌɔːniˈθəusis] *n.* 鸟传病毒病〔如鹦鹉热〕.
ORNL = Oak Ridge National Laboratory〔美〕橡树岭国立实验室.
oro¹- *comb. f.* 表示"山": *oro*geny.
oro²- *comb. f.* 表示"口": *oro*pharynx.
o·rog·e·ny [ɔˈrɔdʒini] *n.*【地】造山运动,造山作用. 亦 **-gen·e·sis** [-ˈdʒenisis]. **-gen·ic, -net·ic** *a.*
or·o·graph·ic, -i·cal [ˌɔrəˈgræfik(-ikəl)] *a.* 山志的,山形的. *a* ~ *factor* 地形因素.
o·rog·ra·phy [ɔˈrɔgrəfi] *n.* 山志学,山岳形态学.
o·ro·ide [ˈɔːrəuid] *n.* 铜、锡、锌等的金色合金.
o·rol·o·gy [ɔˈrɔlədʒi] *n.* 山理学;山岳成因学.
o·rom·e·ter [ɔˈrɔmitə] *n.* 山岳气压计,山岳高度计.
o·ro·tund [ˈɔ(ː)rəutʌnd] *a.* (声音)朗朗的;(说话、文章等)浮夸的,做作的.
or·phan [ˈɔːfən] *n.,a.* 孤儿(的),没有父母(或其中之一)的(孩子). — *vt.* 〔常用被动语态〕使成孤儿. *an* ~ *asylum*孤儿院. *an* ~ *child* 孤儿. *children* ~*ed by the war* 战争造成的孤儿. **-age** *n.* 孤儿院;孤儿身分[状态];〔集合词〕孤儿. **-hood** *n.* 孤儿的身分[状态];(集体的)孤儿.
or·phan·ize [ˈɔːfənaiz] *vt.* 使成孤儿.
Or·phe·an [ɔːˈfi(ː)ən] *a.* 〔诗〕(希腊神话中竖琴名家)俄耳甫斯的;美妙的;好听的,令人神往的,迷人的.
Or·phe·us [ˈɔːfjuːs] *n.*【希神】俄耳甫斯〔竖琴名家〕.
Or·phic [ˈɔːfik] *a.* ①= Orphean. ②崇拜酒神的神秘教的. ③〔或 o-〕神秘的.
Or·phism [ˈɔːfizm] *n.* 俄耳甫斯教义〔据说是由希腊神话中的歌手俄耳甫斯创立的一种宗教和礼仪〕.
or·phrey [ˈɔːfriː] *n.* ①法衣上的绣带. ②精致的刺绣,精致的刺绣品.
or·pi·ment [ˈɔːpimənt] *n.*【矿】雌黄,三硫化二砷.
or·pin(e) [ˈɔːpin] *n.*【植】紫花景天.
Or·ping·ton [ˈɔːpiŋtən] *n.* (英国)奥尔平顿种大鸡.
or·rer·y [ˈɔrəri] *n.* 太阳系仪.
or·ris¹ [ˈɔris] *n.* 金[银]花边;金[银]刺绣.
or·ris² [ˈɔris] *n.*【植】①白花鸢尾,香鸢尾,菖蒲. ②菖蒲根,香根鸢尾 (=orrisroot).
ort [ɔːt] *n.* ①〔方、古〕〔常 *pl.*〕残羹剩饭. ②废品.
or·thi·con [ˈɔːθikɔn], **or·thi·con·o·scope** [ɔːθiˈkɔnɔskəup] *n.*【电视】正析(摄)像管.
orth(o)- *comb. f.* 正,直;原,邻(位);正形: *ortho*chromatic; *ortho*hombic; *ortho*diazine; *ortho*paedics.
or·tho·ax·is [ˌɔːθəuˈæksis] *n.*【数】正轴.
or·tho·caine [ˈɔːθəukein] *n.*【药】原卡因.
or·tho·ce·phal·ic [ˌɔːθəusiˈfælik] *a.* 有着高度为长度的70.1—75%的头颅的 (= orthocephalous). **-ceph·a·ly** *n.*
or·tho·chro·ma·tic [ˌɔːθəukrəuˈmætik] *a.*【像】正色的,现天然色的浓淡的. ~ *film* 正色胶片.
or·tho·clase [ˈɔːθəukleis] *n.*【矿】正长石.
or·tho·di·a·zine [ˌɔːθəuˈdaiəziːn] *n.*【化】哒嗪;邻二氮苯.
or·tho·dome [ˈɔːθəudəum] *n.*【物】正轴坡面.
or·tho·don·tia [ˈɔːθəuˈdɔnʃiə] *n.*【医】正牙学;畸齿校整术.
or·tho·don·tics [ˌɔːθəuˈdɔntiks] *n. pl.* 〔动词用单数〕【医】正牙学(= orthodontia). **-don·tic** *a.*, **-don·tist** *n.* 正牙医师.
or·tho·dox [ˈɔːθədɔks] *a.* ①奉正教的;正统派的;〔O-〕正教会的,希腊教会的. ②(尤指神学上)一般认为正当的,正统的;传统的,习俗的;惯例上的;保守的;常有的,平常的. *the O- Church* 希腊教会、东正教会. *an* ~ *pair of lovers* 通常的一对爱人. ~ *party* 正统派. ***in the*** ~ ***manner*** 正式. ~ **scanning**【电】正则扫描. ~ **sleep**【医】无梦睡眠. **-ly** *ad.*
or·tho·dox·y [ˌɔːθəˈdɔksi] *n.* 正教,信奉正教;正统性;正统派的观念[学说、做法等];服从一般说法. *to discard the classics and rebel against* ~ 离经叛道.
or·tho·e·py [ˈɔːθəuepi] *n.* 正音学;正音法;标准发音. **-ëp·ic, -i·cal** *a.* **-ëp·ist** *n.* 正音学者.
or·tho·gen·e·sis [ˌɔːθəuˈdʒenisis] *n.*【生】直(向)演(化);直生现象;直生论.
or·thog·na·thous [ɔːˈθɔgnəθəs] *a.* 正颌的. **-na·thism** *n.*【解】正颌〔面部侧影近于垂直〕.
or·thog·o·nal [ɔːˈθɔgənl] *a.* ①直角的,互相垂直的;正交的;直交的. ②(统计数字)互不相关的. *an* ~ *section* 正(交)剖面.
or·tho·grade [ˈɔːθəgreid] *a.*【动】直立行走的.
or·tho·graph [ˈɔθəgrɑːf] *n.* 正投影图;正视图.
or·thog·ra·pher, or·thog·ra·ph·ist [ɔːˈθɔgrəfə, -fist] *n.* 正字学家.
or·tho·graph·ic, -i·cal [ˌɔːθəˈgræfik, -ikəl] *a.* 正字法的;缀字正确的;【几】直线的,直角的;用直线投射的,用直线画的. *an* ~ *projection*【几】正投影. **-i·cal·ly** *ad.*
or·thog·ra·phy [ɔːˈθɔgrəfi] *n.* 正字法;缀字法;表音法;【建】面图投影;【数】正交射影.
or·tho·pae·dic, -pe·dic [ˌɔːθəuˈpiːdik] *a.*【医】矫形的. *an* ~ *hospital [surgeon]* 矫形医院[医师]. ~ *treatment* 矫形手术.
or·tho·pae·dics [ˌɔːθəuˈpiːdiks] *n.* 矫形学.
or·tho·pae·dy, or·tho·pe·dy [ˈɔːθəupiːdi] *n.*【医】

矫正术,矫形术;矫形学.

or•tho•phos•phate [ˌɔːθəuˈfɔsfeit] *n.* 【化】正磷酸盐.

or•tho•phos•phor•ic [ˌɔːθəufɔsˈfɔːrik] 【化】正磷酸的. ~ *acid* 正磷酸.

or•tho•psy•chi•a•try [ˌɔːθəusaiˈkaiətri] *n.* 精神卫生学,行为精神病学. **-at•ric** *a.*, **-a•trist** *n.* 精神卫生学家.

or•thop•ter [ɔːˈθɔptə] *n.* 扑翼(飞)机.

Or•thop•ter•a [ɔːˈθɔptərə] *n.* 〔*pl.*〕【动】直翅目.

or•thop•ter•an [ɔːˈθɔptərən] *n.* 【动】直翅目 *(Orthoptera)* 动物〔包括蟋蟀、蚱蜢、蝗虫、蝉等〕.

or•thop•ter•ous [ɔːˈθɔptərəs] *a.* 【动】直翅类的.

or•thop•tic [ɔːˈθɔptik] *a.* 【医】矫正视轴的, 矫正斜眼的〔尤指通过强化眼肌的活动〕.

or•tho•rhom•bic [ˌɔːθəuˈrɔmbik] *a.* 【物】斜方(晶)的, 正交(晶)的.

or•tho•scope [ˈɔːθəuˌskəup] *n.* 【医】水层检眼镜.

or•tho•scop•ic [ˌɔːθəuˈskɔpik] *a.* 准确显像的.

or•tho•stat•ic [ˌɔːθəuˈstætik] *a.* 正立位置的,由正立位置引起的. ~ *hypotension* 正立位血压过低.

or•thos•ti•chy [ɔːˈθɔstiki] *n.* *(pl.* **-chies)** 【植】直列线. **-ti•chous** *a.*

or•tho•tro•pic [ˌɔːθəuˈtrɔpik] *a.* ①【道】支架桥面合一的〔指一种桥设计,支架结构同时也是桥面或路面〕. ②【植】直生的.

or•thot•ro•pism [ɔːˈθɔtrəpizm] *n.* 【植】直生性.

or•thot•ro•pous [ɔːˈθɔtrəpəs] *a.* 【植】直生的〔指胚珠及其种脐、珠孔在一直线上〕.

or•to•lan [ˈɔːtələn] *n.* 【鸟】蒿雀类;〔美〕食米鸟;圃鹀.

O•ru•ro 〔Sp. əuˈrurəu〕 *n.* 奥鲁罗〔玻利维亚省,省会〕.

Or•ville [ˈɔːvil] *n.* 奥维尔〔姓氏,男子名〕.

-ory[1] *suf.* 〔缀于名词、动词后构成形容词〕…性质的,像…的: declamat*ory*, preparat*ory*, prefat*ory*.

-ory[2] *suf.* …所,…的地方: dormit*ory*, fact*ory*, laborat*ory*.

or•yx [ˈɔriks] *n.* *(pl.* ~*es*, 〔集合词〕~*)* 【动】(非洲)大羚羊.

O.S., OS = ①old school〔总称〕守旧派. ②Old Style 西洋旧历. ③ordinary seaman (英国海军)新水兵. ④Old Saxon 古撒克逊语. ⑤old series (刊物等的)旧期(号、卷) ⑥outsize 超过普通尺寸的,特大的.

Os 【化】osmium.

o/s = out of stock 已脱销.

os[1] [ɔs] *n.* 〔L.〕*(pl.* **os•sa** [-ə]*)* 【解、动】骨.

os[2] *n.* 〔L.〕*(pl.* **o•ra** [ˈɔːrə]*)* 【解】口,口腔;孔穴;通路.

os- *pref.* 〔用于 c, t 之前〕= ob-.

O•sage [əuˈseidʒ, ˈəuseidʒ] *n.* ① *pl.(O•sag•es, O•sage)* 奥赛治人〔曾一度移居米苏里州奥赛治河岸,现居于俄克拉荷马州的美国印第安人〕. ②奥赛治语. **O- orange** 【植】①桑橙树 (Maclura pomifera)〔原生长于美国中部,常种作篱障等〕. ②桑橙.

O•sa•ka [ˈɔːsəkə, əuˈsɑːkə] *n.* 大坂〔日本港市〕.

Os•bert [ˈɔzbəːt] *n.* 奥斯伯特〔男子名〕.

Os•born(e) [ˈɔzbən] *n.* 奥斯本〔姓氏〕.

Os•can [ˈɔskən] *n.* ①奥斯肯族〔古代居于意大利康帕尼亚的人〕. ②奥斯肯语. — *a.* 奥斯肯族的;奥斯肯语的.

Os•car[1] [ˈɔskə] *n.* 奥斯卡〔男子名〕.

Os•car[2] [ˈɔskə] *n.* ①〔美〕【影】奥斯卡金像奖;〔喻〕奖(章). ②〔o-〕〔美俚〕手枪,左轮. ③〔Aust.〕钱, 现款.

os•cil•late [ˈɔsileit] *vi.* ①(摆似地)摆动; 振动;【物】振荡. ②(意见等)动摇, 犹豫, 彷徨. ③蹒跚. ④【无】发杂音. — *vt.* 使摆动〔振动〕; 使动摇. *an oscillating charge [current]* 振荡电荷〔电流〕.

os•cil•la•tion [ˌɔsiˈleiʃən] *n.* ①【物】振荡,摆动,振动;振幅. ②动摇,犹豫,彷徨. ③蹒跚. ④【无】发杂音. *the duration of* ~ 振荡期间. *local* ~ 本身振荡.

os•cil•la•tor [ˈɔsileitə] *n.* ①摇摆者. ②【电】振荡器,振动器,振动子;振动部. *a driving* ~ 主控振荡器. *a pulsed* ~ 脉冲发生器.

os•cil•la•to•ry [ˈɔsileitəri, -lətəri] *a.* ①振动的, 振荡的,摆动的. ②动摇不定的. *an* ~ *circuit* 振荡电路. *an* ~ *discharge* 振荡放电.

os•cil•lo•gram [ɔˈsiləˌgræm, ə-] *n.* 【电】示波图; 波形图.

os•cil•lo•graph [ɔˈsiləgrɑːf] *n.* 【电】示波器;录波器.

os•cil•lo•scope [ɔˈsiləskəup] *n.* 【物】示波器. **-scop•ic** [-ˈskɔpik] *a.*

os•cil•lo•tron [ˈɔsilətrɔn] *n.* 电子射线(示波)管;(阴极射线)示波管.

os•cine [ˈɔsin, -ain] *a.* 鸣禽类的〔如百舌鸟、云雀、颊白鸟〕. — *n.* 鸣禽类 *(Oscines)* 动物.

os•ci•tan•cy [ˈɔsitənsi] *n.* 想睡,困倦;不活跃;冷淡,漠不关心.

Os•co-Um•bri•an [ˈɔskəuˈʌmbriən] *n.* 奥斯肯-翁布里亚语〔意大利语族的一个语支,由奥斯肯语和翁布里亚语组成〕.

os•cu•lant [ˈɔskjulənt] *a.* ①〔谑〕接吻的. ②【动】固着的;连结的;【生】中间型的.

os•cu•lar [ˈɔskjulə] *a.* ①〔谑〕嘴的; 接吻的. ②【动】孔的,吸盘的.【数】密切的.

os•cu•late [ˈɔskjuleit] *vi.* 〔谑、罕〕接吻;【生】有共通性,与…接触*(with)*. —*vt.* ①【生】(通过中间物种)接触;【数】密切. ②(知识的范围等)与…有共同点.

os•cu•la•tion [ˌɔskjuˈleiʃən] *n.* 接吻;【几】密切.

os•cu•la•to•ry[1] [ˈɔskjuleitəri, -lətəri] *a.* 〔谑〕接吻的;【几】密切的.

os•cu•la•to•ry[2] [ˈɔskjulətəri] *n.* = pax.

os•cu•lum [ˈɔskjuləm] *n.* *(pl.* **-la** [-lə]*)* 【动】(海绵等的)排水孔;(条虫等的)吸盘.

-ose[1] *suf.* = ous ①…多的: verb*ose*. ②爱…的: joc*ose*. ③…性的: schist*ose*.

-ose[2] *suf.* 【化】①碳水化合物名称的后缀: cellul*ose*, fruct*ose*. ②蛋白质诱导体名称后缀: prote*ose*.

o•sier [ˈəuʒə] *n.* 【植】①〔英〕杞柳;柳条,柳枝. ②(美国)梾木. — *a.* 柳条的;柳条做的. **~-bed** 柳园;柳林.

os•i•fer [ˈɔsifə] *n.* 〔美俚〕军官;官吏.

O•si•ris [əuˈsaiəris] *n.* (古埃及神话中的)地狱判官.

-osis *suf.* 表示'过程''状态'等意义的病名: metamorph*osis*, neur*osis*.

-osity *suf.* 用于词尾为 -ose, -ous 的形容词后构成名词; 例: joc*osity*, curi*osity*.

Os•lo [ˈɔzləu] *n.* 奥斯陆〔挪威首都〕.

Os•man [ɔzˈmɑːn, ɔs-] *n.* ①奥斯曼〔1259-1326,奥托曼(Ottoman) 帝国的创建者〕. ②= Osmanli.

Os•man•li [ɔzˈmænli, -ɔs-] *n.*, *a.* 西支土耳其人〔语〕(的).

os•man•thus [ɔsˈmænθəs] *n.* 【植】①〔O-〕木犀属. ②木犀属植物. *sweet* ~ 桂花,木犀. *orange* ~ 丹桂,金桂.

os•mic [ˈɔzmik] *a.* 【化】锇的.

os•mics [ˈɔzmiks] *n.* 臭味学;臭的研究.

os•mir•i•di•um [ˌɔzmiˈridiəm] *n.* 铱锇矿 (= iridosmine).

os•mi•um [ˈɔzmiəm, -mjəm] *n.* 【化】锇.

os•mom•e•ter [ɔzˈmɔmitə] *n.* 渗透压力计.

os•mose [ˈɔzməus] *vt.*, *vi.* (使)渗透.

os•mo•sis [ɔzˈməusis] *n.* 【生理】渗透(作用), 渗透性.

os•mot•ic [ɔzˈmɔtic] *a.* 渗透的. ~ **pressure** 渗透压(力),浓差压. **-mot•i•cal•ly** *ad.*

os•mous [ˈɔzməs] *a.* 【化】三价锇的.

os•mund(a) [ˈɔzmənd(ə)] *n.* 【植】薇.

os•na•burg [ˈɔznəbəːg] *n.* 低支纱柳条或方格棉布; 粗(口)袋布.

OSO = orbiting solar observatory 太阳观测卫星.

OSP, osp = 〔L.〕obiit sine prole 死时无子嗣 (= he died without issue).

os•pray, os•prey [ˈɔspri] *n.* ①【鸟】鹗，鱼鹰．②白鹭的羽毛〔女帽业用语〕．
OSRD; O.S.R.D. = Office for Scientific Research and Development〔美旧〕科学研究与发展局．
OSS = Office of Strategic Services〔美〕战略情报局．
Os•sa [ˈɔsə] *n.*【希神】奥萨山〔希腊神话中巨人们妄图登天进攻天上诸神，将 Pelion 山叠于 Ossa 山之上，借以攀登 Olimpus 山〕．***heap [pile] Pelion upon ～*** 难上加难，作办不到的事．
os•sa [ˈɔsə] *n.* **os**[1]（骨）的复数．
os•se•in [ˈɔsiːin] *n.*【生化】骨胶原．
os•se•ous [ˈɔsiəs] *a.* 骨的，有骨的；骨质的，骨似的．**-ly** *ad.*
Os•set [ˈɔset], **Os•sete** [ˈɔsiːt] *n.* 奥塞特人．
Os•set•i•a [ɔˈsetiə] *n.* 奥塞特〔苏联北高加索一地区〕．
Os•set•ic [ɔˈsetik] *a.* 奥塞特人的，奥塞特区的．— *n.* 奥塞特语．
Os•si•an [ˈɔsiən] *n.* 欧希安〔传说中三世纪苏格兰高地的英雄诗人〕．
Os•si•an•ic [ɔʃiˈænik] *a.* 欧希安 (Ossian) 式的；夸张的．
os•si•cle [ˈɔsikl] *n.*【解、动】小骨；小骨片．
os•si•fer [ˈɔsifə] *n.* = osifer.
os•sif•er•ous [ɔˈsifərəs] *a.*（矿藏中）有骨的．
os•si•fi•ca•tion [ˌɔsifiˈkeiʃən] *n.* ①【生】成骨，骨化．②（思想等的）僵化．
os•si•frage [ˈɔsifridʒ] *n.*〔诗、古〕①鹗，鱼鹰．②（南美、欧洲产）髭秃鹰．
os•sify [ˈɔsifai] *vt.* ①骨化；使（象骨头一样）硬化．②使僵化；使无情，使冷酷；使顽固；使不进展．— *vi.* ①变成骨头，骨化；硬化．②变成铁石心肠；变顽固，僵化．
os•so bu•co [ˈəusəuˈbuːkəu]〔It.〕燉小牛胫〔一种意大利菜〕．
os•su•ar•i•um [ˌɔʃuːˈɛəriəm] *n.* ***(pl. -ar•i•a*** [-ˈɛəriə]***)*** = ossuary.
os•su•a•ry [ˈɔsjuəri] *n.* ①骨罐，骨瓮．②藏有古代遗骨的洞穴．③藏骨堂．
os•te•al [ˈɔstiəl] *a.* 骨的，骨（状）的．
os•te•i•tis [ˌɔstiːˈaitis] *n.*【医】骨炎．
os•ten•si•ble [ɔsˈtensəbl, -sibl] *a.* ①外表的，表面上的．②假装的；诡称的．③可公开的；显然的．*an ～ partner* 名义合伙人．*His ～ object was to ....* 他的表面目的是⋯．**-bly** *ad.*
os•ten•sive [ɔsˈtensiv] *a.* ①用实物〔动作〕表示的；外表的．②诡称的．③【逻】直接证明的．*an oral-～ method* 口示法，口授法．
os•ten•so•ry [ɔsˈtensəri] *n.*【天主】盛圣餐面包的容器．
os•ten•ta•tion [ˌɔstenˈteiʃən] *n.* 夸示；卖弄；风头主义，讲排场，虚饰．*do sth. out of ～* 为外表好看而做某事．
os•ten•ta•tious [ˌɔstenˈteiʃəs] *a.* 夸示的，得意扬扬地给人看的；（态度）自负的；讲排场的，虚饰的；外观美丽的，浮华的．**-ly** *ad.*
osteo- *comb. f.* 骨：*osteo*arthritis.
os•te•o•ar•thri•tis [ˌɔstiːəuɑːˈθraitis] *n.*【医】骨关节炎．
os•te•o•blast [ˈɔstiəˌblæst] *n.*【生】成骨细胞．**-ic** [-ˈblæstik] *a.*
os•te•oc•la•sis [ˌɔstiˈɔkləsis] *n.* ①骨破折．②折骨术．
os•te•o•clast [ˈɔstiəklæst] *n.* ①破骨细胞．②折骨器．
os•te•o•cran•i•um [ˌɔstiəˈkreinjəm]【医】骨颅．
os•te•o•gen•e•sis [ˌɔstiəˈdʒenisis] *n.*【医】骨生成，骨发生；成骨．
os•te•o•gra•phy [ˌɔstiˈɔgrəfi] *n.* 骨论．
os•te•oid [ˈɔstiɔid] *a.* 骨状的．
os•te•o•lite [ˈɔstiəlait] *n.*【矿】土磷灰石．
os•te•o•log•i•cal [ˌɔstiəˈlɔdʒikəl] *a.* 骨学（上）的．
os•te•ol•o•gist [ˌɔstiˈɔlədʒist] *n.* 骨学家．
os•te•ol•o•gy [ˌɔstiˈɔlədʒi] *n.* 骨学．
os•te•o•ma [ˌɔstiˈəumə] *n.*【医】骨瘤．
os•te•o•ma•la•ci•a [ˌɔstiəuməˈleiʃə, -ʃiə] *n.*【医】骨软化，软骨病．
os•te•o•my•e•li•tis [ˌɔstiəuˌmaiəˈlaitis] *n.* 骨髓炎．
os•te•o•path [ˈɔstiəupæθ] *n.* 正骨科大夫，按摩医生．
os•te•op•a•thy [ˌɔstiˈɔpəθi] *n.* 疗骨术，整骨术；骨病．
os•te•o•phyte [ˈɔstiəufait] *n.*【医】骨赘．**-phyt•ic** [-ˈfitik] *a.*
os•te•o•plas•tic [ˌɔstiəuˈplæstik] *a.* ①【解】成骨的．②（外科）装骨的，造骨的．**-plas•ty** *n.*
os•te•o•po•ro•sis [ˌɔstiəupɔːˈrəusis] *n.*【医】骨质疏松．
os•te•o•sis [ˌɔstiˈəusis] *n.* 骨质生成．
os•te•o•tome [ˈɔstiəutəum] *n.*【医】骨凿．
os•te•ot•o•my [ˌɔstiˈɔtəmi] *n.* ***(pl. -mies)*** 骨切开术，切骨术．
os•ter•moors [ˈɔstəmuːəz] *n.*〔*pl.*〕〔美俚〕胡须．
os•ti•ak [ˈɔstiæk] *n.* = ostyak.
os•ti•ary [ˈɔstiˌɛəri] *n.* ***(pl. -ar•ies)*** ①看门人，门房．②（天主教）地位最低的神职人员．
os•ti•na•to [ˌɔstiˈnɑːtəu; It. əustiːˈnɑːtəu] *n.* ***(pl. -tos*** [-əuz; It. -təus]***)***【乐】固定音型〔不断地重复出现的节奏型或旋律型〕．
os•ti•ole [ˈɔstiəul] *n.* 小孔，孔口．**-o•lar** *a.*
os•ti•um [ˈɔstiəm] *n.* ***(pl. -ti•a*** [-ə]***)***【解】口，门，孔，心门．
ost•ler [ˈɔslə] *n.*（旅馆的）马夫．
ost•mark [ɔstˈmɑːk] *n.* 东德马克．
os•to•sis [ɔsˈtəusis] *n.* 骨质生成 (= osteosis).
os•tra•cean [ɔsˈtreiʃiən] *a.* 牡蛎的．— *n.* 牡蛎．
os•tra•cism [ˈɔstrəsizəm] *n.* ①（古希腊用投票办法将异己分子逐出国外 5 年或 10 年，并将票数记在贝壳上的）贝壳流放．②流放，放逐．③排斥．*suffer political [social] ～* 被政界〔社会〕排斥．
os•tra•cize [ˈɔstrəsaiz] *vt.*（依贝壳流放法）流放；放逐；与…绝交，排斥．
os•tra•cod [ˈɔstrəˌkɔd] *n.* 介形亚纲 *(Ostracoda)* 动物．
Os•tra•va [ˈɔːstrəvə] *n.* 俄斯特拉发〔捷克斯洛伐克城市〕．
Os•trea [ˈɔstriə] *n.*【动】牡蛎（蠔）属．
os•trea•cul•ture [ˈɔstriəkʌltʃə], **os•trei•cul•ture** [ˈɔstriikʌltʃə] *n.* 养蠔（法）．
os•trich [ˈɔstritʃ] *n.*【鸟】鸵鸟．***have the digestion of an ～*** 食量大；胃口好．～ **belief** 掩耳盗铃的想法．～**-farm** 鸵鸟饲养场．～ **policy** 鸵鸟政策．
Os•tro•goth [ˈɔstrəˌgɔθ] *n.* 东哥特人〔尤指公元前五世纪征服意大利的东哥特部族人〕．**-ic** [-ˈgɔθik] *a.*
Ost•wald [ˈɔstvalt], **W.** 奥斯特瓦尔德〔1853—1932，德国物理化学家，曾获 1909 年诺贝尔化学奖〕．
Os•ty•ak [ˈɔstiˌæk] *n.* ①奥斯蒂亚克人〔居于西西伯利亚的一支芬兰乌戈尔族人〕．②奥斯蒂亚克语．
Os•wald [ˈɔzwəld] *n.* 奥斯瓦尔德〔男子名〕．
Os•we•go tea [ɔsˈwiːgəu] ①大红香蜂草 *(Monarda didyma)*〔产于北美〕．②大红香蜂草茶．
Oś•wie•cim [ɔːʃˈvjentsiːm] *n.* ①奥斯威辛〔波兰市镇〕．②奥斯威辛集中营〔第二次世界大战时希特勒匪帮建立的〕．
O.T., OT, OT. = *Old Testament*（基督教《圣经》的）《旧约全书》．
ot- *comb. f.* = oto.
o•tal•gi•a [əuˈtældʒiə] *n.*【医】耳痛．
OTC = oxytetracyclin.【药】土霉素．
O.T.C. = Officers' Training Corps.〔英〕军官训练团．
oth•er [ˈʌðə] *a.* ①别的，另外的，其他的；不同的 *(than; from)*；其余的；另一个．②对方的，对面的，相反的．③其次的，第二．④隔一个．⑤不久前的；以前的．*O-people think otherwise.* 别人又是另一种想法．*He has no*

~ *place to go to.* 他别无去处. *on the ~ side of the road* 在路对面. *the ~ thing* 相反. *the ~ way* 相反地. *the ~ day* 上回,那天,前几天. *It must be one or the ~.* 二者必居其一. *the ~ day* 几天前. *in ~ times* 从前. — *ad.* 用其他方法, 另样地. *I can't do ~ than to go.* 我不去不行. ***every ~*** ①每隔一 (*every ~ day* 每隔一日). ②其他的…都 (*every ~ boy* 其他的孩子都). ***none ~ than*** 不是别人, 正是 (*It was none ~ than Jones.* 不是别人正是琼斯). ***on the ~ hand*** 在另一方面, 但是又. ***~ than*** ①与…不同, 而不是. ②除了 (*any ~ person than yourself* 除你以外的任何人. *I do not wish him ~ than he is.* 他就那样好了. *a world far ~ from ours* 和我们世界远不相同的世界). ***~ things being equal*** 如果其他情形都一样. ***the ~ side*** 〔美〕欧洲. ***the ~ party***【法】对方. ***the ~ world*** 来世. — *pro.* ***(pl. ~s)*** (*cf.* ***another***) ①另外一个; 〔*pl.*〕别的东西,别的人; 其他的东西. ②〔the ~(s)〕其余的一个,其他各人〔各物〕. *one or ~ of us* 我们当中的任何一个. *Do good to ~s* 对他人做好事. *I must consult the ~s.* 我必须和其余的人商量. ***among ~s*** 此外还有; 其中也 (*Smith, among ~s, was there.* 除此之外, 史密斯也在那里). ***each ~*** 互相. ***know one from the ~*** 把二者分别清楚. ***of all ~s*** 所有…当中的 (*on that day of all ~s* 偏偏在那天). ***one ... the ~*** 一方面是…,另一方面是…. ***one after the ~*** 一个接一个地; (二者) 相继. ***some ... or ~*** 某一… (*some man or ~* 某一个人 (非做不可等). *Some one of us or ~ will be there.* 我们当中总会有一个人在那里的. *some time or ~* 总有一天,迟早. *Some idiots or ~ have done it* 总是甚么傻瓜们干的那事). ***some ~s*** 另外什么人〔什么东西〕(*Give me some ~s.* 给我另外的吧). ***the one ... the ~*** 前者是…后者是〔但有时相反〕. — *ad.* 不是那样,用别的方法. *I can do no ~ than accept.* 我只好接受.〔除接受外别无办法〕. *If you think ~ than logically.* 你如果不合乎逻辑地推理. **~ half** ①另一部分民众 (*See how ~ half lives.* 看看另一部分民众怎样生活吧!). ②配偶.

oth·er-di·rect·ed [ˈʌðədiˈrektid] *a., n.* 由他人牵着鼻子走的(人),听命于他人的(人); 顺从的(人),随俗的(人).

oth·er·guess [ˈʌðəges] *a.* 〔古、口〕别种的; 不同的.

oth·er·ness [ˈʌðənis] *n.* 〔罕〕不同,相异; 另一物, 不同物;【哲】他,他性.

oth·er·whence [ʌðəhwens] *ad.* 〔古〕从别处.

oth·er·where(s) [ˈʌðə*h*weə(z)] *ad.* 〔诗〕在别处〔某处〕; 向别处〔某处〕.

oth·er·while(s) [ˈʌðə*h*wail(z)] *ad.* 〔古〕在别的时候; 有时候.

oth·er·wise [ˈʌðəwaiz] *ad.* ①不那样, 用别的方法. ②在其他方面. ③在其他状态〔情况〕下. *I think ~.* 我是另外一种想法. *This must be done quite ~.* 这要完全改变做法才行. *be quite ~ engaged* 完全忙别的事. *He never teaches them any ~ than by example.* 他除了示范〔举例〕以外从来不用别的方法教他们. *I could do no ~ than laugh.* 我只好笑了. *He has a squint, but is ~ a handsome fellow.* 除斜视外, 在其他各点上他是一个漂亮的人. *I know him ~ than in business* 在生意以外我也认识他的. *Judas, ~ (called) Iscariot* 犹大, 一名伊斯卡洛. — *conj.* 否则,不然. *Seize the chance, ~ you will regret it.* 抓住机会,否则你要后悔的. — *a.* ①〔用作表语〕别的,另外一种的. *How can it be ~ than fatal?* 怎么能不是致命的呢? *Some are wise, some are ~.* 有聪明的,也有不是这样的. ②〔用作定语〕在其他各方面…的; 在其他不同情况下的. *his ~ equals* 在其他各方面和他不相上下的人们. ***act ~ than one says*** 行不顾言; 言行不一. ***and ~*** 其他, 等 (*He helped me with advice and ~.* 他用忠告等帮助了我). ***or ~*** 或相反 (*his merits or ~ (= or demerits)* 他的优点或缺点). *I am not concerned with its accuracy or ~.* 我倒不管它准确不准确). **~-minded** *a.* 性格两样的, 兴趣〔嗜好〕不同的; 意见不同的; 与舆论相反的; 思想逆潮流的.

oth·er·world·(ly) [ˈʌðəwəːld(li)] *a.* 来世的; 冥界的; 修来世的; 空想中的; 精神上的, 超俗的.

Oth·man [ɔθˈmɑːn, ˈɔθmən] *a., n.* = Ottman.

o·ti·at·rics [ˌəuʃiˈætriks] *n.*【医】耳病学.

o·tic [ˈəutik] *a.*【解】耳的, 耳部的. ~ **bit** 听窝. ~ **capsule** 耳壳. ~ **ganglion**【解】耳神经节.

-otic *suf.* ①患(病)的, 生…的: hypn*otic*, narc*otic* 〔对应名词后缀是 -osis〕. ②似…的: Quix*otic* (<Quixote).

o·ti·ose [ˈəuʃiəus] *a.* ①不必要的,没有用的,多余的; 无效的. ②〔罕〕闲着的, 没事做的; 懒惰的. **-ly** *ad.* **-ness** *n.* **o·ti·os·i·ty** [ˌəuʃiˈɔsiti] *n.*

O·tis [ˈəutis] *n.* 奥蒂斯〔姓氏, 男子名〕.

o·ti·tis [əuˈtaitis] *n.*【医】耳炎. ~ ***externa [interna, media]*** 外〔内、中〕耳炎.

o·ti·um cum dig·ni·ta·te [ˈəuʃiəm kʌmˌdigniˈteiti] *n.* 〔L.〕(= leisure with dignity) 悠然自适.

OTL = output-transformerless【无】无输出变压器的.

o·to·cyst [ˈəutəsist] *n.* ①【动】听泡, 听囊. ②【动】平衡器; (昆虫的)平衡胞.

o·to·lar·yn·gol·o·gy [ˌəutə*u*ˌlæriŋˈgɔlədʒi] *n.*【医】耳鼻喉科. **-gist** *n.* 耳鼻喉科医师.

o·to·lith [ˈəutəliθ] *n.*【解】①耳石. ②(无脊椎动物的)听石. **-ic** *a.*

o·tol·o·gy [əuˈtɔlədʒi] *n.* 耳科学. **-gist** *n.* 耳科医生.

o·to·phone [ˈəutəfəun] *n.* 助听器.

o·to·rhi·no·lar·yn·gol·o·gy [ˈəutə*u*ˌrainə*u*ˌlæriŋˈgɔlədʒi] *n.* 耳鼻喉科学.

o·to·scle·ro·sis [ˌəutə*u*skliˈrəusis] *n.*【医】耳硬化. **-rot·ic** [-ˈrɔtik] *a.*

o·to·scope [ˈəutəskəup] *n.*【医】耳镜; 耳科听诊器.

O·tran·to [ɔˈtræntəu] **Strait of** (意大利与阿尔巴尼亚间的)奥特朗托海峡.

ot·ta·va [əˈtɑːvə] 〔It.〕*a., ad.*【音】以高〔低〕八度.

ot·ta·va ri·ma [ˈɔtəvəˈriːmə] 〔It.〕【诗】八行体(的诗).

Ot·ta·wa [ˈɔtəwə] *n.* 渥太华〔加拿大首都〕.

ot·ter [ˈɔtə] *n.* ***(pl. ~s,*** 〔集合词〕***~)*** ①【动】水獭; 水獭皮. ②一种钓具〔淡水用〕. *a common ~* 獭. *a sea ~* 海獭. **~-dog** = **~-hound** 猎水獭用的猎狗. **~-spear** 刺水獭用的枪.

Ot·to [ˈɔtəu] *n.* 奥托〔男子名〕. ~ **cycle**【物】四冲程循环, 奥托循环. ~ **engine**【机】四冲程发动机, 奥托发动机.

ot·to [ˈɔtəu] *n.* 玫瑰油, 玫瑰精.

Ot·to·man [ˈɔtəmən] *a.* 旧土耳其帝国的; 土耳其人的; 土耳其民族的. — *n.* ***(pl. ~s)*** ①土耳其 (族) 人. ②〔o-〕椅子; (无靠背的)矮脚条椅, 绒垫睡椅. ③楞条绸; 绒脚垫;【纺】粗横棱纹织物. ~ **Empire**【史】奥斯曼帝国, 奥托曼帝国.

Ot·way [ˈɔtwei] *n.* ①奥特韦〔姓氏〕. ②**Thomas** ~ 托马斯·奥特韦〔1652–1685, 英国剧作家〕.

O.U. = Oxford University.

oua·ba·in [wɑːˈbeiin] *n.*【化】乌本(箭毒)苷.

Oua·ga·dou·gou [ˌwɑːgəˈduːguː] *n.* 瓦加杜古〔上沃尔特首都〕.

O.U.A.M. = Order of United American Mechanics 美国机械工人联合会.

ou·bli·ette [ˌuːbliˈet] *n.* (仅头顶有孔可以出入的) 土牢, 密狱.

ouch[1] [autʃ] *n.* 〔英古〕(戒指等上的)珠座, 宝石座; 玉饰, 金饰; 扣子.

ouch[2] [autʃ] *int.* 〔美〕哎唷! 痛呀!

ouch·y [ˈautʃi] *a.* 〔美俚〕神经过敏的; 急躁的; 脾气暴躁的.

oud [uːd] *n.*【乐】乌得〔中东和北非弦乐器名, 似琵琶〕.

ought[1] [ɔːt] *v. aux.* 〔oughtest 或 oughtst 是古体, 现代

英语中过去和现在都用 ought, 常加带 to 的不定式,表示过去时用完成式不定式〕应该,应当;总应该;本应,本当;早应该. *We ~ to love labour.* 我们应当爱劳动. *You ~ to know better.* 你应当更明白些. *It ~ to have been done long ago.* 这事早应该做完的. *You ~ not to do that.* 你不应当做那种事. *It ~ not to be allowed.* 那是不应该允许的. *He ~ to have arrived by this.* 他此刻应该到了.

ought² [ɔːt] *n.* 〔口〕零,全无 (= nought).

ought³ [ɔːt] *n., ad.* 〔古〕 = aught¹.

ought·a [ˈɔːtə] 〔口〕 = ought to.

oughtn't [ˈɔtnt] ought not 的缩合形式.

ou·gui·ya [uːˈkwjə] *n.* 乌吉亚〔毛里塔尼亚货币单位〕.

oui [wiː] *ad.* 〔F.〕是,对.

ounce¹ [auns] *n.* ①盎司, 英两, 唡〔常衡 = $^1/_{16}$ 磅 = 28.4 克; 金衡 = $^1/_{12}$ 磅 = 31.104 克; 略作 oz.〕. ②液唡, 流量唡 (= $^1/_{12}$ pint)(= fluid ~). ③少量. *an ~ of courage* 一点点勇气. *An ~ of practice is worth a pound of theory.* 一分实践当得十分理论. *That will call for every ~ of energy we have.* 这就需要我们全力以赴.

ounce² [auns] *n.* 【动】雪豹;〔诗〕山猫.

O.U.P. = Oxford University Press 〔英〕牛津大学出版社.

ouphe, ouph [auf, uːf] *n.* 淘气的小精灵;丑妖怪;顽皮的小孩儿(=elf).

our [ˈauə] *pro.* 〔we 的所有格〕①我们的. ②〔元首或英国教会主教用来代替 my〕我的. *~ loyal subjects* 我的忠实臣民. ③〔报纸等发表意见时用〕我们的. *in ~ opinion* 我们的看法是. ④正在谈的,(我们)那个. *Well, that isn't ~ business [affair].* 可是, 那事跟我们不相干. *~ gentleman in a black hat* (我们)那个戴黑帽子的绅士. **O- Father** 【宗】天父, 上帝; 主祷文. **O- Lady** 【宗】圣母玛利亚. **O- Saviour** 耶稣.

-our *suf.* = or¹.

ours [ˈauəz] *pro.* 〔we 的所有代名词〕我们的(东西). *O- is a great Party.* 我们的党是一个伟大的党. *Jones of ~* 我们的〔队的或学校的〕琼斯. *This orchard became ~ by purchase.* 这个果树园买成我们的了. *O- is better than yours.* 我方比你方强. ★①O- is a large family. 是文语,口语说作 Our family is a large one. ② this our ... 是古语, 现在说作富有感情意义的 this ... of ours. 如: an old friend of ~ 我们的一个老朋友.

our·self [ˌauəˈself] *pro.* 〔帝王、法官、著者等以及报刊社论中应用时〕 = myself.

our·selves [ˌauəˈselvz] *pro. pl.* ①〔强势用法〕我们自己. ②〔反身用语〕(把)我们自己. *We will do it ~.* 我们自己会做的. *We must not deceive ~.* 我们不可自欺. *We shall give ~ the pleasure of calling (on you).* 我们将高兴地去拜访(你). *We were not ~ for sometime.* 我们有半天不能恢复常态. ***(all) by ~*** 我们独自地; 全靠自己地. ***for ~*** 自己,亲自 (*We do everything (for) ~.* 我们甚么事都亲自做).

-ous *suf.* ①多…的; …性的; 有…癖的; 有特质的; …似的; 盛行…的: perilous, rigorous, gracious, pompous. ②【化】表示"亚…的": nitrous acid 亚硝酸.

ou·sel [ˈuːzl] *n.* = ouzel.

oust [aust] *vt.* ①逐出, 撵走, 驱逐 *(from; of)*. ②【法】(非法)剥夺,夺取,夺去. ③代替,取代. *~ sb. from his post* 把某人撤职. *~ sb. of his inheritance.* 剥夺某人的继承权. *Television has not ~ed radios.* 电视机还未能取代收音机.

oust·er [ˈaustə] *n.* ①驱逐,逐出. ②【法】(尤指非法的)剥夺. ③驱逐〔剥夺〕者.

out [aut] *ad.* ①〔位置及运动的方向〕向外,向外部; 在外, 在外部; 出去,出外,离开; 离岸, 向海面; (船等)开往外国. *go ~* 出去. *run ~* 跑出. *come ~* 出来. *stay ~* (在外头)不回家. *bring [take] sth. ~* 拿走东西. *leave sth. ~* 省去〔遗漏〕(某物). ②〔同各种及物动词和不及物动词连用表示动作的极度〕完,尽; 完全,彻底; 到最后; 显著; 突出. *sell ~* 卖完. *blow ~ a candle* 吹灭蜡烛. ③〔以下各解用作表语, 亦可视为形容词〕出外,在外. *Her son is ~ in Canada.* 她的儿子出门在加拿大. *He is ~.* 他不在〔出去了〕. *anchor a mile ~* 停泊在离岸一英里处. *row ~* 划出(海面). *be ~ at sea* 在海上航行中. ④罢工; 失和. *The workmen are ~.* 工人在罢工. *I am ~ with Jones.* = *Jones and I are ~.* 我跟琼斯闹翻了. ⑤除外; 离开…,被逐出,被排斥;【政】下台, 下野, 退位,退职;【运】退场; 除去(阻碍等). *The Tories are ~.* 托利党下台了. *The batter is ~.* 【棒球】打球员退场了. ⑥不足, 缺乏, 损失. *The wine has run ~.* 酒没有了. *I am ~ fifty pounds through him.* 我为他损失了五十英镑. ⑦消灭; 熄,完,尽,到期,满期. *The fire is ~.* 火熄了. *be tired out* 筋疲力尽, 累极. *before the week is ~* 在本星期内. ⑧失常; 混乱; 脱出, 有毛病. *The arm is ~.* 胳臂脱臼了. *My eye is a bit ~ today.* 今天眼睛有点不好. *My watch is five minutes ~.* 我的表快五分钟. *be ~ in one's calculation* 计算错误. ⑨出世,发表; 出版; 出现在交际场中; 现出; (花)开; (小鸡等)孵出; (秘密)暴露. *The book is ~.* 那本书出版了. *The rose is ~.* 蔷薇开了. ⑩彻底,完全,直率, 坦白; 到最后, 到完. *Tell him right ~.* 爽爽快快的告诉他. *hear one ~* 听完某人的话. ⑪过时, 不流行; 闲着. *The frock-coats have gone ~.* 大礼服已经不流行了. *My hands are ~.* 手闲着. ★美国在 help, lose, start, try, win 等动词之后常加无意义的 out. ***be ~ at (the knees)*** (裤子)(膝部)破了. ***be ~ for [to (do)]*** 〔俚〕努力想得到; 力图要; 总想(做)… (*be ~ for a row* 准备去争吵一番. *be ~ for blood* 要打人;〔美〕期望比赛必胜, 期望雪洗前耻). ***down and ~*** 落魄,败落. ***have one's cry ~*** 哭个够. ***have one's Sundays ~*** 星期日休息. ***~ and about*** (病后)能起床走动. ***~ and away*** 在远方,遥远; 远远,大大; 无比,无疑. ***~ and home*** 来回. ***~ and ~*** 毫无问题地, 彻头彻尾地; 彻底的, 确实无疑的; 绝对的, 顽固不化的, 坏透了的 (*a scoundrel ~ and ~* 十足的无赖). ***~ at the back*** = 〔美〕 ***~ back*** 在房子后面. ***~ from under*** 〔美口〕脱离危境〔困境〕. ***~ here*** (老远)到这里. ***~ like a light*** 〔美俚〕喝醉. ***~ of*** 〔复合前置词〕 *(opp.* in, into, within*)* ①从…里头, 从…当中; 从…, 出自 (*come ~ of the house* 从屋子里出来. *~ of doors* 室外的, 露天的; 向门外, 在门外. *Choose ~ of these.* 从这些当中选择罢. *one ~ of many* 许多当中的一个例子. *nine cases ~ of ten* 十有八九. *~ of Shakespeare* 出自莎士比亚). ②在…的范围外; 向…达不到的地方; 脱出…, 变自由 (*~ of date* 过时的. *~ of hearing* 在听不见的地方. *~ of sight* 看不见). ③失去…,没有… (*swindled ~ of one's money* 被骗去金钱. *~ of breath* 上气不接下气. *~ of repair* 失修的. *~ of work* 失业的; 失效的,不能工作的. *~ of mind* 被忘却). ④因,为了 (*ask ~ of curiosity* 因好奇心而问问看). ⑤用…; 用…做材料 (*~ of one's own head* 自己想出来的. *What did you make it ~ of?* 那个你是用什么做的?). ⑥超出, 离开 (*~ of doubt* 无疑, 确实. *times ~ of number* 无数次, 再三再四. *born ~ of wedlock* 私生的). ⑦违犯,弄错 (*~ of drawing* 不合画法). ***~ of commission*** 退役的;〔美俚〕坏了的; 受了伤的; 有病的; 没有用的,不中用的. ***~ of it*** 不加入; 孤立, 孤独, 寂寞; 窘困,不知怎样才好; 脱节; 弄错, 搞错. ***~ of keeping*** (和周围)不调和. ***~ of line*** 不一致; 不协调; 不符; 〔美俚〕控制不来. ***~ of the glare*** 〔美俚〕不出名; 不显著. ***~ of the lot*** 〔美棒〕惨败的; 打出场外的飞球. ***~ of touch with*** 与…失去联系. ***~ there*** 向那边; 〔口〕到战地. ***~ with*** 〔口〕拿出; 说出; 把…赶出去 (*Out with him!* 赶他出去!). — *prep.* ①〔美〕通过(门、窗等)

而出. *go* ~ *the door* 从门里出去. ②〔美口〕沿着…而去. *Drive* ~ *High Street.* 顺着大街开去. ★英国目前除文语的 from out 外仅用 out of. 如: From the dungeon, came a groan. 从牢中漏出呻吟的声音. — *n.* ①失去了地位[权势]的人; 〔the ~s〕在野党. ②外部,外头; 外出; 外观; 体面. ③【运】守方. ④【印】漏排. ⑤〔美〕缺点,弱点;〔美俚〕(拳击中的)打倒; 辩解,借口,离去的口实,逃脱的手段. ***at the ~s (with)*** 〔美〕跟…不和[闹翻]. ***from ~ to ~*** 从一头到另一头,全长; 外径. ***make a poor ~*** 不成功,搞不很好. ***on the ~s*** 〔美俚〕闹翻了脸,感情不好. ***the ins and ~s*** 朝野两党; 角角落落; 里里外外; 细节,细情,一五一十. — *a.* ①外面的,外头的; 外围的; 远的; 向外去的. ②〔口〕不平常的; 特大的. ③在野的,下台的. ④〔口〕过了时的. ⑤〔美俚〕时新的. ⑥〔美俚〕不省人事的,喝得烂醉的. *an* ~ *match* 外出访问比赛. *the* ~ *side*【运】守方. *an* ~ *size* (西装等)特大型. — *vt.* 〔口〕逐出,赶出;【拳击】打倒,击昏(= *knock* ~);【运】使退场; 使出局; 把(火)弄熄[弄灭]. *Out that man!* 把那个人赶出去! *Murder will* ~. 恶事总必败露. — *vi.* 外出; 败露,破露,显露. — *int.* 〔古〕表示"愤慨""谴责"等. *O- upon you!* 滚! 混蛋!

out- *pref.* ①加在动词、分词或动名词前表示"出","向外","在外","超过","胜过"等意,如 *out* go, *out* play. ②若为名词、形容词及分词,重音通常在 out 上,如: ˈ*out*break, ˈ*out*bound, ˈ*out*going; 若为动词,重音通常在第二音节以后,如: *out*ˈdo.

out·act [autˈækt] *vt.* 行动上胜过.

out·age [ˈautidʒ] *n.* ①出口. ②【商】损耗. ③(检修时船、机器等的)停航,停车;【电】停电. ④(蓄水池的)预留容量;【机】(发动机关闭后的)液体燃料剩余.

out-and-out [ˈautəndaut] *a.* ①完全的,不折不扣的,彻底的. ②公开的,明目张胆的. — *ad.* 完全,彻头彻尾.

out-and-outer *n.* 〔俚〕①十全十美的人; 最好的样品. ②极端派,过激分子. ③大坏蛋; 大谎.

out·ate [autˈet] outeat 的过去式.

out-at-el·bows [ˈautətelbəuz] *a.* 穿旧,磨破,破烂.

out·back [ˈautbæk] *a.* 〔澳〕内地的. — *ad.* 向内地. — *n.* 内地.

out·bade [autˈbeid] outbide 的过去式.

out·bal·ance [autˈbæləns] *vt.* 在重量上胜过; 优于,胜过; 在效果上超过. *The bad in his character is ~d by the good.* 他性格中的优点胜过缺点.

out·bid [autˈbid] *vt.* ***(-bid, -bade*** [-ˈbeid, -ˈbæd]; ***-bid, -bid·den*** [-ˈbidn]***)*** 出价高过(别人); 抢先. ***~ each other*** 互相抬高价钱.

out·board [ˈautbɔːd] *a.* 【海】船外的,舷外的; (汽艇)外部装有推进机的;【空】(飞机)外侧的. — *ad.* 向船外,向舷外; (在飞机)紧靠翼尖处. *an* ~ *motor* 艇外推进机.

out·bound[1] [ˈautbaund] *a.* 开往外国[外地]的,外出的,出差的.

out·bound[2] [ˈautˈbaund] *vt.* 跳过.

out·bounds [ˈautbaundz] *n.* 〔*pl.*〕〔废〕边境.

out·brave [autˈbreiv] *vt.* 用勇气压倒[战胜]; 在勇气上超过; 轻视,不把…放在心上.

out·break [ˈautbreik] *n.* ①(战争、怒气等的)爆发;【虫】(虫害等)突然蔓延. ②暴动,骚扰; 反抗. ③= outcrop. — [autˈbreik] *vi.* 〔诗〕突然发生; 爆发; 花开.

out·breed [ˈautbriːd] *vt.* ***(-bred***[-brəd]***; -breed·ing)*** ①使进行远系繁殖. ②比…繁殖得快.

out·breed·ing [ˈautbriːdiŋ] *n.* ①【动】远系繁殖. ②【社】族外婚.

out·build·ing [ˈautbildiŋ] *n.* 外屋,副屋; 〔*pl.*〕〔美〕农场办事处.

out·burst [ˈautbəːst] *n.* (火山、情感等的)爆发,迸发; 爆炸;【化】爆燃; 溃决; 激增.

out·by(e) [ˈautbai] *ad.* 〔*Scot.*〕在不远的地方; 在户外.

out·cast [ˈautkɑːst] *a.* 被逐出(家庭、国家)的,被排斥的; 被遗弃的; 无家可归的. — *n.* 被驱逐的人; 无家可归的人,流浪者; 流氓,无赖.

out·caste [ˈautkɑːst] *n.* (印度)被剥夺种姓者; 无种姓者; 贱民.

out·class [autˈklɑːs] *vt.* 比…高一等; 大大超过. *He far ~es the other runners in the race.* 他在比赛时远远超过其他的赛跑者.

out·clear·ing [ˈautkliəriŋ] *n.* 【商】应付票据交换额 *(opp.* inclearing*)*.

out-college [ˈautkɔlidʒ] *a.* 〔英〕住在大学校外的; 不属于大学宿舍的.

out·come [ˈautkʌm] *n.* ①结果; 成果; 后果. ②【理】输出口; 〔喻〕出路. *The* ~ *of a war is decided by the people.* 决定战争胜败的是人民.

out·com·er [ˈautˌkʌmə] *n.* 外来者,外国人,陌生人.

out·cor·ner [ˈautkɔːnə] *n.* 【棒球】外角.

out·crop [ˈautkrɔp] *n.* 【地】(岩层等的)露头; 露出地面的岩层.

out·cross [autˈkrɔs] *vt.* 使进行异型杂交. — [ˈautkrɔs] *n.* 【生】异型杂交后代.

out·cross·ing [ˈautkrɔːsiŋ] *n.* 【生】异型杂交.

out·cry [ˈautkrai] *n.* ①喊叫,喧嚷,吆喝,怒号. ②叫卖; 拍卖; 喊价. *raise an* ~ *against* 强烈反对[抗议].

out·curve [ˈautkəːv] *n.* 外曲; 外曲物;【棒球】外曲球. — [autˈkəːv] *vt., vi.* (使)外曲.

out·cut [ˈautkʌt] *n.* 被剪去的影片.

out·dare [autˈdeə] *vt.* ①胆量胜过. ②不怕,蔑视(=defy).

out·date [autˈdeit] *vt.* 使过时.

out·dat·ed [autˈdeitid] *a.* 已经不流行的; 过时的; 陈旧的,古风的.

out·did [autˈdid] outdo 的过去式.

out·dis·tance [autˈdistəns] *vt.* 把(其他赛跑者)远远抛在后头,远远超过; 胜过.

out·do [autˈdu] *vt.* ***(-did*** [-ˈdid]; ***-done*** [-ˈdʌn]***)*** 优于,凌驾,胜过; 打败; 制服; 超越. ***~ oneself*** 得到空前成绩,打破自己以往记录; 尽自己最大的努力.

out·done [autˈdʌn] ①outdo 的过去式. ②*a.* 〔美方〕激怒的,烦恼的.

out·door [ˈautdɔː] *a.* ①户外的,屋外的,露天的; 野外的. ②(医院等)院外的; 〔英〕议院外的. ~ *excercises* 户外运动. *an* ~ *life* 野外生活. *the* ~ *activities* 〔英议院〕院外活动.

out·doors [autˈdɔːz] *ad.* 在户外[屋外、野外]; 向户外[屋外、野外] *(opp.* indoors*)*. — *n.* 〔口〕户外; 露天; 野外; 世间.

out·eat [autˈiːt] *vt.* ***(out·ate*** [autˈet]; ***out·eat·en*** [autˈiːtn]***)*** 吃得比…多.

out·er [ˈautə] *(opp.* inner*)* *a.* ***(superl.*** ***~most, outmost)*** ①外的,外部的,外面的; 外侧的. ②【哲】客观外界的; 物质的. ③远离中心的. *one's* ~ *garment* 外衣. *the O- Bar* 〔英〕〔集合词〕(不属于王室律师的)普通律师. *the* ~ *man* 〔谑〕(人的)外貌,风度; 装束. *the* ~ *world* 外部世界,外界; 世间. — *n.* 靶子环外的部分; 环外命中. ~ **city** 〔美〕市郊,郊区. ~**coat** 轻便大衣; 外套,外衣. ~ **space** ①宇宙空间. ②外层空间,星际空间. ~**wear** 外衣,外套[大衣、雨衣等]; 户外穿的服装. ~**most** *ad., a.* 最外面(的),最远(的),远离中心(的),最后面(的),顶上(的); 在最远处,在最后面,在顶上.

out·face [autˈfeis] *vt.* ①逼视…使其将目光移开; 恐吓. ②厚着脸皮干下去,满不在乎地应付; 反抗; 挑(战),冒(雨).

out·fall [ˈautfɔːl] *n.* ①河口,流口,吐出口,落水口. ②吵架,拌嘴; 不和. ③冲锋,突击; 袭击.

out·field [ˈautfiːld] *n.* ①(远离宅地的)远田,边地; (围

篱以外的)外田；郊外；〔Scot.〕草地. ②边境；未知世界. ③〔通例 the ～〕【棒球】外场,〔集合词〕外野手 *(opp.* infield). **-er** *n.*【棒球】外野手.

out·fight [aut'fait] *vt.* *(**out·fought** [aut'fɔːt])* 战胜,击败.

out·fight·ing ['autfaitiŋ] *n.* 远距离作战.

out·fit ['autfit] *n.* ①(旅行等的)准备；旅费；旅行用品,装置；(一定场合下穿的)全套衣装；(军事)装备；航海用具；商业用具,生财；(一般)设备,用品,工具. ②精神准备,素养. ③〔口〕(一般)团体；有组织的单位；旅行团；探险队；棒球队(等)；采矿[筑路(等)]队；(某人手下的)全班人马；〔美军俚〕(准备出动的)部队. ④牧场；庄园. — *vt.* 〔主用被动语态〕装备；供给；准备；配备 *(with)*.

out·fit·ter ['autfitə] *n.* 服饰用品商店；旅行用品商店；运动用品店；【船】安装机器的机工.

out·fit·ting ['autfitiŋ] *n.* (旅行等的)准备,装束.

out·flank [aut'flæŋk] *vt.* 【军】包抄,迂回敌侧(包围)；突然胜过. *encirclement and ～ing* 包围和迂回.

out·flow ['autfləu] *n.* 流出；流出物；流出口,泛滥. (语言、感情的)爆发. *stem the river's ～* 防止河水泛滥.

out·fly [aut'flai] *vt.* *(**out·flew** [aut'fluː]; **out·flown** [aut'fləun])* 在飞行速度上超过. *～ the speed of sound* 超音速.

out·foot [aut'fut] *vt.* 追过,赶过；〔美〕赛船划胜. *She ～ed me in a climb up a hill.* 在一次爬山中她比我走得快.

out·fought [aut'fɔːt] outfight 的过去式和过去分词.

out·fox [aut'fɔks] *vt.* 瞒过,机智上胜过,比…更狡猾.

out·game [aut'geim] *vt.* 〔美〕比赛领先[赢].

out·gas [ˌaut'gæs] *vt.* *(**-gassed; -gas·sing**)* ①从(行星内部向大气)放出气态物质. ②除去…的气.

out·gen·er·al [aut'dʒenərəl] *vt.* (〔英〕**-ll-**) 战术[谋略]胜过；使堕入术中；在领导[管理]才能上胜过.

out·giv·ing ['autgiviŋ] *n.* 〔美〕公开声明[发言]. — *a.* (态度)自然的,无拘束的.

out·go [aut'gəu] *vt.* *(**-went** [-'went]; **-gone** [-'gɔn])* 比…走得快,超过；优于,胜过. — ['autgəu] *n.* *(pl. ～es)* ①支出,开销 *(opp.* income)；消耗. ②出发,出走,退出；出口；流出. ③结果,产品.

out·go·ing ['autgəuiŋ] *a.* ①出发的；往外去的；退去的；即将离职的. ②对人友好的；开朗的. *an ～ ship* 出航的船,离港船. *the ～ tide* 退去的潮水. *～ ministers* 前任部长. — *n.* ①〔常 *pl.* 作单数用〕支出,开支. ②出去；外出；出发；终. ③〔美〕声明.

out·gone [aut'gɔn] outgo 的过去分词.

out-group ['autgruːp] *n.* 外集团,外人集团.

out·grow [aut'grəu] *vt.* *(**-grew** [-'gruː]; **-grown** [-'grəun])* ①长得比…快[大]. ②因年龄增加而失[脱]去；脱离…的苦痛；发展得不再需要(某事物). *My family has outgrown our house.* 我家人口增加得房屋不够住了. *The children have outgrown their garments.* 孩子们长得衣服穿不上了. *～ a bad habit* 随着年龄增长而戒掉了一个坏习惯. *～ early friends* 长大了幼小时候的朋友也不往来了. *～ one's strength* 年龄小个子长得太大,人小个子大. — *vi.* 生物长出.

out·growth ['autgrəuθ] *n.* ①【植】枝条；瘤. ②(自然的)结果；派生物；副产物. ③(树叶等)长出,长大. *Revolution is a frequent ～ of tyranny.* 革命是暴政促成的常有结果.

out·guard ['autgɑːd] *n.* 【军】警戒哨.

out·guess [aut'ges] *vt.* 猜透；智胜.

out·gun [aut'gʌn] *vt.* 在武器上超过,胜过,超越.

out·haul ['authɔːl] *n.* 【海】把帆扯向帆杠尾端之索.

out-her·od, out-Her·od [aut'herəd] *vt.* *～ Herod* 暴虐胜过希律王；比希律王更希律王. ★可同样类推说 out-Zola Zola 在某人[左拉]特征方面胜过某人[左拉].

out·house ['authaus] *n.* ① =outbuilding. ②〔美〕屋外厕所.

out·ing ['autiŋ] *n.* 外出；出游,游览,旅行；散步. *～* **flannel** 软绒布.

out·island ['autailənd] *n.* 群岛中的非主要岛屿.

out·jock·ey [aut'dʒɔki] *vt.* 骗,哄人上当；用诡计胜过.

out·land ['autlænd] *n.* ①〔常 *pl.*〕〔废〕边远地区,偏僻地区；内地. ②〔古〕外国. — ['autlənd] *a.* ①遥远的,边远的,远离中心的. ②〔古〕外国的.

out·land·er ['autlændə] *n.* 外国人；外地人；外来者；陌生人；〔口〕局外人.

out·land·ish [aut'lændiʃ] *a.* 外国气派的,异国风味的；奇异的；粗鲁笨拙的；〔古〕外国的；偏僻的；边远的.

out·last [aut'lɑːst] *vt.* 较…经久,比…持久；比…命长.

out·law ['autlɔː] *n.* ①丧失公权者,被剥夺法律保护的人；歹徒；惯犯；逃犯；亡命徒. ②难驯服的动物；烈马. — *vt.* ①取缔；剥夺…的法律保护. ②使失法律效力. *an ～ed debt* 〔美〕失时效的债务.

out·law·ry ['autlɔːri] *n.* ①法益剥夺；失时效. ②宣布非法,非法化. ③驱逐令,放逐. ④逍遥法外.

out·lay ['autlei] *n.* 费用,花费；支出.

out·let ['autlet, -lit] *n.* ①出口,出路；排水口；通风口. ②【商】销路. ③批发商店. ④发泄(情感)的方法；排遣. *an ～ for water* 排水孔. *～ water* 废水. *He wants an ～ for his energy.* 他需要一个发挥他的精力的去处.

out·li·er ['autlaiə] *n.* ①不住在工作地点的人,在工作地点外另有住宅的人. ②离开本体的东西,分离物；【地】老围层；外露层 *(opp.* inlier). ③门外汉；局外人.

out·line ['autlain] *n.* ①外形,轮廓；轮廓线；轮廓画法,略图(画法). ②〔常 *pl.*〕梗概,大纲,提纲；草稿；要点；主要原则. *an ～ map* 略图. ***give an ～ of*** 概要说明…. ***in ～*** 只画轮廓(的)；概略(的) *(a horse drawn in ～* 潦潦草草画成的马,马的草图). ***make an ～ of a (composition)*** 为(作文)拟提纲. — *vt.* ①画轮廓；打草图,描略图. ②概括地论述,略述.

out·live [aut'liv] *vt.* ①比…长寿；比…经久；度过…而健在. ②老到超过…的程度；久活而失去. *～ one's contemporaries* 比同时代的人长寿. *～ one's usefulness* 衰老无用. *～ one's health* 年老多病.

out·look ['autluk] *n.* ①景色,风光,景致. ②前景；展望；前途 *(for)*；形势. ③见地,见解；眼界；先见；…观；观点. ④看守,了望；看守人；了望台,望楼. *a room with an ～ on the sea* 望见海景的房间. *the bourgeoisie world ～* 资产阶级世界观. *the proletarian world ～* 无产阶级世界观. *one's ～ on life* 某人的人生观. *the ideological ～* 精神面貌. *the political ～* 政治前景. ***be on the ～ (for)*** 监视着；提防着. — [aut'luk] *vt.* ①盯着看；瞧；以目光压倒(对方). ②比…好看.

out·ly·ing ['autlaiiŋ] *a.* ①在境界[围篱]外的；远离中心[主体]的,边远的. ②无关的；题外的.

out·ma·chine [ˌautmə'ʃiːn] *vt.* 【军】机械化程度超过(敌人).

out·man [ˌaut'mæn] *vt.* *(**-manned; -man·ning**)* 人数胜过,在数量上超过.

out·ma·noeu·vre, 〔美〕 **-neu·ver** [ˌautmə'nuːvə] *vt.* 对…机动制胜；用谋略制胜,计谋胜过…；挫败(敌人的)阴谋.

out·march [aut'mɑːtʃ] *vt.* 进行得比…快[远]；赶过.

out·mar·ry ['autmæri] *vt.* (在婚姻上)高攀〔多与反身代名词连用〕. — *vi.* 与异族结婚.

out·match [aut'mætʃ] *vt.* 胜过,优于,强过. *be ～ed in skill* 技巧方面不及别人.

out-mi·grant ['aut'maigrənt] *a.* 迁徙的,迁走的,他迁的. — *n.* 迁徙者,他迁者,他迁动物. **out·mi·grate** ['aut'maigreit] *vi.* 迁徙,迁走,他迁. **-gra·tion** *n.*

out·mod·ed [aut'məudid] *a.* 过时的.

out·most ['autməust] *a.* = outermost.

out·ness ['autnis] *n.* 【哲】外在性；客观存在性.

out•num•ber [aut'nʌmbə] *vt.* 数量上胜过，比…多. *They ~ed us three to one.* 他们以三与一之比在数量上超过了我们.

out-of-bounds ['autəv'baundz] *adv.* 到界外. *kick a ball ~* 把球踢到界外. — *a.* ①禁止入内的；不可超越的. ②出乎意料的. ③【运】界外的.

out-of-date ['autəv'deit] *a.* 落后的，过时的；不适用的；不使用的，已作废的.

out-of-door(s) [ˌautəv'dɔːz] *a.* = outdoor. — *ad., n.* = outdoors.

out-of-pock•et ['autəv'pɔkit] *a.* ①现款支付的. ②无钱的. ③非预算项下开支的，预算外开支的.

out-of-the-way [autəvðə'wei] *a.* ①边远的，偏僻的. ②奇特的，异常的.

out-of-town•er ['autəv'taunə] *n.* 从其他城市来的参观者，他市来客.

out•pace [aut'peis] *vt.* 跑得比…快，追过；发展快过；胜过.

out•pa•tient [aut'peiʃənt] *n.* 门诊病人.

out•pen•sion•er ['autˌpenʃənə] *n.* (教济院机关等的)院外领取年金的人.

out•per•form [autpə'fɔːm] *vt.* (机器等)性能比…好.

out•play [aut'plei] *vt.* (在球赛中)打得比…好；(比赛中)击败，胜过.

out•point [aut'pɔint] *vt.* (比赛)得分超过；(赛船)比…更迎风航行.

out•poll [aut'pəul] *vt.* 得到的选票超过(他人).

out•port ['autpɔːt] *n.* 外港〔远离海滨或商业中心的海港〕；输出港.

out•post ['autpəust] *n.* 前哨；前哨基地；警戒部队.

out•pour [aut'pɔː] *vt., vi.* 〔诗〕(使)泻出，(使)流出. — ['autpɔː] *n.* 泻出，流出(物).

out•pour•ing ['autpɔːriŋ] *n.* 泻出，流出；(感情等的)流露，洋溢；迸发；〔主 *pl.*〕激动的言语. *the ~s of a sentimental mind* 感伤的话.

out•put ['autput] *n.* ①产量；生产，出产，产品. ②【医】(粪便以外的)排泄物；排泄量. ③【电】发电力，输出功率；供给量. ④输出信号. *monthly ~* 月产量. *the ~ of a factory* 工厂产品. *the literary ~ of the year* 当年文艺作品. *a sudden ~ of effort* 奋发. *~* **data** 输出数据.

out•rage ['autreidʒ] *n.* ①暴举，暴行. ②强奸，凌辱. ③严重违法. ④义愤，痛恨. *~s against the peasants* 鱼肉农民. *commit ~s [an ~] on [upon]* 对…[在…方面]倒行逆施；侮辱. — *vt.* ①伤害；虐待，迫害. ②凌辱，强奸. ③违反；犯(法)；引起…的义愤.

out•ra•geous [aut'reidʒəs] *a.* 粗暴的，残暴的；蛮横的，猖狂的，无法无天的；无耻的，令人不能容忍的；荒谬绝伦的. *commit ~ actions on* 对…[在…方面]倒行逆施；侮辱. **-ly** *ad.* **-ness** *n.*

out•ran [ˌaut'ræn] outrun 的过去式.

ou•trance [uː'trɑ̃ːns] *n.* 〔F.〕极端，最后. ***à ~*** 到底. (*fight à ~* 打到底，死战).

out•range [aut'reindʒ] *vt.* ①在射程上胜过，打得比…远. ②比…看得远.

out•rank [aut'ræŋk] *vt.* 〔美〕等级高于.

ou•tré ['uːtrei] *a.* 〔F.〕逸出常轨的；失当的；过激的；奇怪的，荒诞的；夸大的.

out•reach [aut'riːtʃ] *vt.* 超出…的范围；超过；胜过；伸长. — ['autriːtʃ] *n.* 伸出；展开；达到的范围.

out•re•lief ['autriliːf] *n.* 对不住在济贫院内的贫民的施舍(=〔美〕outdoor relief).

out•ride [aut'raid] *vt.* (*-rode* [-'rəud]; *-rid•den* [-'ridn]) *vt.* 骑得比…快[好、远]；骑胜；(船)冲过(风雨). — *vi.* 在车外骑着马(跟着).

out•rid•er ['autraidə] *n.* (车辆前后、左右的)骑马侍从，驾摩托车的警卫；前驱，前导.

out•rig•ger ['autrigə] *n.* 【海】(伸出船两边支桨用的)叉架；装有舷外铁架的划子[小艇]；(拴绳子等用的)舷外斜木；(防止划子翻倒的)舷外浮材；【空】(支撑机翼用的)外架；承力支架，悬臂支架.

out•right ['aut'rait] *ad.* ①完全，彻底；公然，公开；直率地，痛快地；坦白，不客气地，露骨地. ②即刻，马上，当场. *laugh ~* 放声大笑. *be killed ~* 被当场杀死. *buy ~* 用现金购买. — ['autrait] *a.* 直率的，明白的；十足的，彻底的. *give an ~ denial* 断然否认. *an ~ rogue* 彻头彻尾的恶棍.

out•ri•val [aut'raivəl] *vt.* (*-ll-*) 在竞争中胜过(对手).

out•rode [aut'rəud] outride 的过去式.

out•root [ˌaut'rut] *vt.* ①连根拔起；根绝，绝灭；赶出(住宅等). ②消灭；毁灭(= uproot).

out•run [aut'rʌn] *vt.* (*-ran* [-'ræn]; *-run*) 跑胜，追过；逃走；脱离，超过；超出…界限；比…得更多选票. *let one's zeal ~ discretion* 过分热心实欠谨慎. *His imagination ~s the facts.* 他的想象脱离事实，想入非非.

out•run•ner ['autrʌnə] *n.* 跑得更快[远、好]的人；(跟着马车跑的)侍从；辕外副马；(拉雪橇的)领头狗；先驱者.

out•rush ['autrʌʃ] *n.* 冲出，流出. — *vt.* 比…冲得更前.

out•sail [aut'seil] *vt.* (船)航行航得比…快，追过.

out•sat [aut'sæt] outsit 的过去式和过去分词.

out•scrib•er [aut'skraibə] *n.* 【无】输出记录机.

out•seg [aut'seg] *vt.* 〔美俚〕比…实行更激烈的种族主义.

out•sell [aut'sel] *vt.* (*-sold* [-'səuld]) 卖得比…多[快、贵]；比…更能推销.

out•set ['autset] *n.* 开头，开端，开始. ***at [in] the ~*** 在开头时. ***from the ~*** 从一开始.

out•shine [aut'ʃain] *vt.* (*-shone* [-'ʃɔn]) 比…亮；比…聪明[优秀、漂亮]；胜过，优于；使相形见绌.

out•shoot [aut'ʃuːt] *vt.* (*-shot* [-'ʃɔt]; *-shoot•ing*) ①比…更有效地射击. ②射出. — *vi.* 突出，伸出. — ['autʃut] *n.* ①射击；突然或迅速的突出或伸出. ②突出物，伸出物. ③【棒球】曲线球〔早期用语〕.

out•side ['aut'said] (*opp.* inside) *n.* ①外头，外部，外面，外侧；外观，外表；外界；【电话】外线；【体】出界. ②极端. ③〔英〕(公共马车等的)车顶座位；车顶乘客. ④〔*pl.*〕一束纸最外层上下两张. ⑤〔美俚〕被认为跑赢机会很少的马，冷门马. *He has a rough ~, but a good heart.* 他外貌粗暴心地善良. *impressions from the ~* 表面印象. *open the door from ~* 从外头开门. *those on the ~* 局外人；外界人士. ***at the (very) ~*** 至多，充其量. ***~ in*** 里面翻到外面；彻底地. — ['autsaid] *a.* 〔仅用作表语〕①外面的，外侧的，外部的；外观上的，肤浅的；〔英〕车顶座的. ②极端的，极度的；最大程度的；〔口〕最高的. ③局外的，门外的，没有加入工会[协会等]的. ④〔美俚〕已经出狱的，恢复了自由的. *an ~ broker* (交易所)场外经纪人. *an ~ porter* 〔英〕可以把行李送出站外的服务员. *the ~ edge* 用冰鞋外棱滑；极端的侮辱. *an ~ man* 〔美〕(替盗贼)望风的人. *~ work* (不在工作场所的)外活. *an ~ chance* 几乎没有希望的机会，〔美〕赛赢的机会很少. *~ help* 外来的援助，外援. *~ opinion* 外部意见；【议院】院外意见. *the ~ price* 最高价格. — [aut'said] *ad.* 在外面，在外头，在外部；向户外，在户外；向海上，在海上；【体】出线，出界. *go ~* 到户外. *Come ~!* (挑战)出来！ *Outside!* (放)到外头来！ *ride ~* 〔英〕乘顶座. ***get ~ of*** 〔俚〕喝；吞；吃. ***~ of a horse*** 〔俚〕骑着马. —['aut'said] *prep.* 在[向]…的外边，…外边的；超过…的范围，在…之上，在…以上；从…；〔口〕除…外. *go ~ the house* 走到屋外. *go ~ the evidence* 牵涉到证据以外. *things ~ one's sphere* 本分以外的事情. *No one knows ~ two or three persons.* 除两三人外谁也不知道.

out•sid•er ['aut'saidə, aut's-] *n.* ①外来者，外头人，局外人，没有关系的人；会外的人，党外[院外]人. ②门外汉，外行，没有专门知识的人. ③【赛马】没有胜利希望的马[骑师]. *The ~ sees the best [most] of the game.*

旁观者清.

out·sight [ˈaut-sait] *n.* 对外界事物的观察 *(opp.* insight*)*.

out·sit [autˈsit] *vt.* *(outsat* [-ˈsæt]*)* = outstay.

out·size [ˈautsaiz] *a.* 超过标准尺寸的; 特别大的(衣服鞋帽等). — *n.* 特大型; 特大品. **-d** *a.* (= outsize).

out·skirt [ˈaut-skəːt] *n.*〔常 *pl.*〕郊外; 外边. ***on the ~s of*** 在…的外边; …郊区.

out·smart [autˈsmɑːt] *vt.*〔美〕= outwit.

out·soar [autˈsɔː] *vt.* 飞过, 飞越, 翱翔于…之上.

out·sold [autˈsəuld] outsell 的过去式和过去分词.

out·sole [ˈaut-səul] *n.* 皮鞋[靴]的鞋跟.

out·span [autˈspæn] *vt., vi.*〔南非〕(由车上)解开(牛); 卸(马具). — *n.* ①去轭; 卸马具. ②牲口休息地.

out·speak [autˈspiːk] *vt.* *(-spoke* [-ˈspəuk]; *-spo·ken* [-ˈspəukən]*)* ①在讲话上胜过. ②大胆地说, 坦率地说. — *vi.* 大胆、直率地说.

out·spo·ken [autˈspəukən] *a.* 直言不讳的, 坦率的; 毫无保留的. ~ *criticism* 坦率的批评. *an ~ person* 直率的人. **-ly** *ad.* **-ness** *n.*

out·spread [autˈspred] *vt., vi.* *(-spread)* (使)扩张; (使)展开; (使)伸开; 传播, 散布. — *a.* 伸开的; 扩张的; 展开的.

out·stand [autˈstænd] *vi.* *(-stood* [-ˈstud]*)* ①凸出, 突出. ②【海】离港; 向海上. — *vt.* ①〔古〕忍耐, 停留. ②〔方〕抵抗, 反抗; 经受得起.

out·stand·ing [autˈstændiŋ] *a.* ①显著的; 凸出的, 杰出的. ②未付的, 未清的; 未解决的; 未完成的. ③(股票等)已发行和出售的. *an ~ fact* 显著的事实. *an ~ figure* 杰出人物. *an ~ debt* 未偿债务. *~ accounts* 未清帐款. ~ *check* 未兑现支票. ***leave ~*** ①搁着不理 (*leave a good deal of work ~* 搁着许多工作不做). ②搁置不付[不偿还]. **-ly** *ad.*

out·stare [autˈstɛə] *vt.* ①以目光镇住(对方); 盯得(某人)局促不安; 盯着看. ②面对…而无惧色, 挑战, 对抗.

out·sta·tion [ˈautsteiʃən] *n.* 设在边远地区的分站, 边远哨所.

out·stay [autˈstei] *vt.* ①比(别人)住得[逗留得]久. ②久住而失去. ③在持久力上超过. ***~ one's welcome*** 因住得[逗留]太久而讨人厌恶.

out·step [autˈstep] *vt.* 走过; 超过; 逾越; 过火; 犯. ~ *decency* 越出礼貌以外. ~ *the truth* 夸大事实.

out·stretch [autˈstretʃ] *vt.* ①扩张, 张开, 展开. ②伸展超过….

out·stretched [autˈstretʃt] *a.* 扩张的; 伸长的. *lie ~ on the ground* 直挺挺躺在地上.

out·strip [autˈstrip] *vt.* 超过; 越过; 追过; 优于, 胜过; 逃脱. *overtake and ~* 赶上并超过.

out·talk [autˈtɔːk] *vt.* 比…说得有力[响亮、有技巧]; 说败, 说服.

out·think [autˈθiŋk] *vt.* *(-thought* [-ˈθɔːt]*)* ①思考得比…来得深入、迅速或老练. ②深谋远虑地制胜….

out·throw [autˈθrəu] *vt.* *(out·threw* [autˈθruː]; *out·thrown* [autˈθrəun]*)* ①扔出, 抛出. ②比…扔出得更远, 更准. — [ˈautθrəu] *n.* ①扔出, 迸发. ②中耕翻土, 翻土量. ③碎料, 废料.

out·thrust [autˈθrʌst] *vt., vi.* *(out·thrust* [autˈθrʌst]*)* (使)突出, (使)冲出. — *a.* 突出的, 冲出的. — [ˈaut-θrʌst] *n.* 突出, 冲出; 突出物.

out·trade [autˈtreid] *vt.* 买卖中占…的上风, 占…的便宜.

out·turn [ˈauttəːn] *n.* 产量;【林】出材率; 结果.

out·val·ue [autˈvæljuː] *vt.* 比…有价值; 比…更可贵.

out·vie [autˈvai] *vt.* 比胜, 胜过, 打败. ~ *each other in study* 在学习上一个胜过一个.

out·voice [autˈvɔis] *vt.* 用大声压倒.

out·vote [autˈvəut] *vt.* 投票数胜过…, 得票多于…; 通过投票压倒(对方).

out·vot·er [autˈvəutə] *n.*〔英〕(居住)区外(的)选举人.

out·walk [autˈwɔːk] *vt.* 比…走得远[快]; 走过; 越过.

out·ward [ˈautwəd] *(opp.* inward*)* *a.* ①外头的, 外部的; 外形的, 表面的; 皮毛的; 明显的; 可见的; 公开的. ②向外的, 向外去的, 外出的; 自外得来的; 外来的. ③【宗】物质上的; 肉体上的. *an ~ form* 外表, 外貌. ~ *reformation* 表面改革. *an ~ passage [voyage]* 出航 *(cf.* homeward*)*. ~ *things* 周围的事物, 外界. ~ *eye* 肉眼 *(opp.* mind's eye*)*. ~ ***man***【宗】肉体;〔谑〕衣服, 丰采(等). ***to ~ seeming*** 从外表上看来. — *n.*〔罕〕外部; 外观, 外形, 外表;〔*pl.*〕外在事物; 周围世界. — *ad.* = outwards. ~ ***and homeward*** 来回. **~-bound** *a.* 开往国外的, 出航的(船). **-ly** *ad.* 在外, 在外面; 向外面; 从外面来; 在物质上; 外表上. **-ness** *n.* 客观存在; 客观性.

out·wards [ˈautwədz] *ad.* 在外, 向外; 在外部; 外表上; 表面上; 向国外. *a ship bound ~* 开往国外的船.

out·wash [ˈautwɔːʃ, -wɔʃ] *n.*【地】冰水沉积.

out·watch [autˈwɔtʃ] *vt.* 看到看不见, 看到最后; 比…看得久. ~ *the night* 通宵看守.

out·wear [autˈwɛə] *vt.* *(out·wore* [-ˈwɔː]; *-worn* [-ˈwɔːn]*)* ①比…经久[耐用]. ②穿旧, 穿破; 用旧; 用完, 耗尽; 使(人)疲倦. ③耐心度过.

out·weigh [autˈwei] *vt.* 比…重; 比…重要; 胜过, 强过. *The advantages ~ the drawbacks.* 得多于失, 优点胜过缺点.

out·went [autˈwent] outgo 的过去式.

out·wit [autˈwit] *vt.* ①哄骗; 瞒住; 给…上当; 机智上胜过. ②〔古〕比…更有智慧.

out·work [ˈautwəːk] *n.* ①〔常用 *pl.*〕【军】简易外围工事. ②户外工作, (在单位等)外部进行的工作; 外勤工作. — [autˈwəːk] *vt.* *(-worked, wrought* [rɔːt]*)* 在工作上胜过, 比…做得快[巧].

out·work·er [ˈautwəːkə] *n.* 外出工作的工作人员; 接工作回家做的雇员.

out·wore [autˈwɔː] outwear 的过去式.

out·worn [autˈwɔːn] *a.* ①〔诗〕磨坏了的, 破损的. ②已废的; 过时的, 陈腐的.

ou·zel, ou·sel [ˈuːzl] *n.*【鸟】黑鸫. *a brook ~* 秧鸡.

ou·zo [ˈuːzəu] *n.* 希腊茴香烈酒, 甘露酒.

ov- *comb. f.* 蛋, 卵: oval.

o·va [ˈəuvə] ovum 的复数.

o·val [ˈəuvəl] *a.* 卵形的; 椭圆的;【植】阔椭圆形的. — *n.* 卵形(物); 椭圆运动场(等);【物】卵形度;【数】卵形弧, 卵形线; 椭圆; 美式足球用球. ***the O-*** 伦敦 Kennington 区的板球场. **-ly** *ad.* **-ness** *n.*

o·var·i·an [əuˈvɛəriən] *a.*【解】卵巢的;【植】子房的.

o·var·i·ec·to·my [əuˌvɛəriˈektəmi] *n.* *(pl. -mies)*【医】卵巢切除术.

ovario- *comb. f.* 卵巢: *ovario*tomy.

o·var·i·ot·o·my [əuˌvɛəriˈɔtəmi] *n.* *(pl. -mies)*【医】①卵巢切开术. ②= ovariectomy.

o·va·ri·tis [ˌəuvəˈraitis] *n.*【医】卵巢炎.

o·va·ry [ˈəuvəri] *n.*【植】子房;【解】卵巢.

ovate [ˈəuveit] *a.* 卵圆形的(树叶); 卵(体)形的.

o·va·tion [əuˈveiʃən] *n.* 热烈的欢迎, 热烈的鼓掌, 欢呼; (古罗马) 小凯旋式.

ov·en [ˈʌvən] *n.* 灶, 炉; 炭窑; 干燥炉; 烘箱. *a coke ~ plant* 炼焦厂. ***hot from the ~*** 刚出炉的. ***in the same ~***〔俚〕处于相同的困境. ~ ***dry*** 烘干, 烤干.

ov·en·bird [ˈʌvənbəːd] *n.*【动】灶鸟.

o·ver [ˈəuvə],〔诗〕**o'er** [ə, ɔə, ɔː] *prep.* ①越过…; 越过…向外[向下]; …对过的. *jump ~ it* 跳过它. *fall ~ a precipice* 从崖上掉下. *This fruit will not keep ~ the winter.* 这水果怕保存不到春天. *the tree ~ the river* 河对过的树. ②在…的上面, …上的; 蒙在…上, 悬挂在

…;支配，统治；管制；(职位)在…之上. *an umbrella ~ one's head* 撑在头上的伞. *She put her hands ~ her face.* 她用手蒙住脸. *hang ~ …* 挂在…的上面. *have no command ~ oneself* 不能自制. *set him ~ the rest* 把他安排在其余各人之上. ③全面，遍，到处. *all ~ the body* 浑身. *The mud splashed ~ the garment.* 泥溅满了衣服; *all ~ the world* = all the world ~ 世界到处〔在后一结构中，over 为副词〕. ④关于，对于. *laugh ~ the absurdity of it* 笑它荒谬. *cry ~ split milk* 后悔无及. ⑤一面…一面…. *talk ~ a cup of tea* 一面喝茶一面谈话. *go to sleep ~ one's work* 做着事打瞌睡. ⑥以上. *This hat cost ~ £5.* 这顶帽子化了五镑多. ~ ***all*** 从这头到那头;〔废〕到处，处处. ~ ***and above*** 远远超过…以上; 加之. ~ ***my dead body***〔美俚〕只要我不死就不会同意. ~ ***the air*** 通过无线电. ~ ***the bay***〔美俚〕喝醉的. ~ ***the hill***【海】在大西洋的那一边，越过水平线. ~ ***the hump***〔美俚〕大半已完; 已过难关. — *ad.* ①在上，在高处; 从上向下; 突出，倚靠; 越过. *jump ~* 跳过. *climb ~* 爬过. ②在那边，向那边，(越过马路、河、海等)到那边，从一处到另一处. *Take this ~ to the station.* 把这个拿到那边车站去. *He is ~ in Cuba.* 他已在古巴. *Our friends were ~ yesterday.* 我们的朋友们昨天来过了. *I asked him ~.* 我请过他来的. *When are you coming ~ to see us again?* 你什么时候再请来呢? ③遍，多次. *brush it ~* 刷干净. *paint it ~* 涂遍. ④倒，颠倒; 翻，翻转; 倒过来;〔美〕请看反面 (= P.T.O.). *fall ~* 向前摔倒. *knock a vase ~* 碰倒花瓶. *roll ~* 滚动. *The milk boiled ~.* 牛奶煮得溢出来了. ⑤太，过度，过于; 而且; 更，另外，剩余; …多，…余. *He is ~ anxious.* 他太焦急了. *I do not feel ~ well.* 我感到身体不太舒服. *a yard and ~* 一码多. *give sb. something ~* 另外多给某人一些东西. *I paid my bill and have several pounds ~.* 我付了帐还剩了好几镑. *Five goes into seven once with two ~.* 5 除 7 得 1 剩 2. ⑥〔用作表语〕完了，结束了; 过去了; 关系断绝. *The war will soon be ~.* 战争不久就要结束了. *The good old times are ~.* 好日子已经过去了. ⑦再，重行，重复地. *Try it ~ (again).* 再试试看. ★ over 后加用 again 时主为〔英〕. *count [read] ~* 再数[读]. *Do that three times ~.* 把那重复做三遍. ⑧未解决，未了结. *The matter is left ~.* 那件事还没有解决. *That can stand ~.* 那件事可以暂时搁着不管. ⑨【板球】改变掷球方向〔裁判员的命令〕. ***(be) all ~ (with)*** (某人)完全完了 (*It's all ~ with me.* 我全完啦). ~ ***again*** 再来一次，再做一遍，反复. ~ ***against*** 对着，面对着，对照着. ~ ***and above*** 除…以外，外加. ~ ***and*** ~ 转来转去;〔主美〕反反复复，再三再四. ~***-and-~ addition*** 逐次加法. ~ ***and ~ again***〔英〕三番五次，再三再四. ~ ***here*** 在这边，在这里. ~ ***there*** 在那边，在那里;〔美〕在欧洲;〔大战用语〕在战地. ~ ***with***〔美口〕(做)完 (*get something ~ with* 做完某事;〔英〕*get something ~ (and done with)*). — *n.* ①【板球】彼此由三柱门交互连续所投之球〔通常是 6 球〕; 连续投球比赛. ②剩余，余额. ③【军】远弹〔超过目标落下或爆炸的射弹〕. — *a.* ①在上的，表层的人. ②完了的. ③剩余的. — *vt.* 跳过 (= leap ~)，走过(= go ~).

over- *pref.* ①太、超，过度，过度的: *over*full, *over*eat, *over*do, *over*work. ②在上面(的)，在外部(的)，在外(的): *over*coat, *over*time, *over*all, *over*board, *over*flow ③自上，向下，到，越过，加: *over*balance, *over*haul, *over*throw, *over*whelm. ④完全，全: *over*-persuade.

o·ver·a·bun·dance [ˈəuvərəˈbʌndəns] *n.* 太多，过于丰富; 多余物，奢侈品，不必要的东西. **-dant** *a.*

o·ver·act [ˈəuvərˈækt] *vt., vi.* 过度…，过分…; (把剧中角色等)演得过火.

o·ver·age[1] [ˈəuvəˈridʒ] *n.* (商品等)过剩; 过多; 超额.

o·ver·age[2] [ˈəuvəˈridʒ] *a.* 超龄的，旧式的，老朽的.

o·ver·all [ˈəuvərɔːl] *n.* (套头)工作服，罩衫，(妇女、小儿等的)罩衣;〔*pl.*〕〔美〕工装裤;〔*pl.*〕〔英〕【军】(军官的)紧身军裤. — *a.* 全部的，所有的，全体的，全面的，总的，综合的. *the ~ diameter* 全径. *the ~ length* 全长. *by ~ planning* 统筹兼顾; 全面规划. *~ situation* 总的形势; 全局. *~ utilization* 综合利用. — [ˌəuvərˈrɔːl] *ad.* 全面地，总地.

o·ver·anx·i·e·ty [ˈəuvəræŋˈzaiəti] *n.* 过虑，杞忧.

o·ver·arch [ˈəuvərˈɑːtʃ] *vt., vi.* 在…上架成圆拱形.

o·ver·arm [ˈəuvərɑːm] *a.*【棒球、板球】举手过肩的，由上朝下的;【泳】(划水时)手臂伸出水面的. — *n.*【机】横杆.

over·ate [ˈəuvəˈet] overeat 的过去式.

o·ver·awe [ˌəuvərˈɔː] *vt.* 使畏缩，吓住，威压.

o·ver·bal·ance [ˌəuvəˈbæləns] *vt.* 重过; 重于; 价值超过; 压到; 使失去平均〔平衡〕; 优于. *The gains ~ the losses.* 得多于失. — *vi.* 失去平衡，歪倒下来. — [ˈəuvəbæləns] *n.* (重量、价值的)超额; 不平衡，失均衡. *the ~ of exports* 出超.

o·ver·bear [ˌəuvəˈbɛə] *vt.* ***(-bore*** [-ˈbɔː, -ˈbɔə]; ***-borne*** [-ˈbɔːn]***)*** 压服，制服，威压; 抑压; 超过，压倒; 压碎;【海】比他船挂更多风帆. — *vi.* 结果实过多; 繁殖过度.

o·ver·bear·ing [ˌəuvəˈbɛəriŋ] *a.* 架子十足的，傲慢的，自大的; 专横的; 压倒的; 支配的; 厉害的. *~ heat* 酷热. **-ly** *ad.*

o·ver·bid [ˌəuvəˈbid] *vt., vi.* ***(-bid; -bid·ding)*** ①【桥牌】叫牌超过(上家). ②出价高于(别人)，出价高于(物品价值). — [ˈəuvəbid] *n.* 超过上家的叫牌，过高的叫牌.

o·ver·bite [ˈəuvəbait] *n.* 深复牙〔即上门牙和犬牙过分突出于下牙〕.

o·ver·blouse [ˈəuvəblaus] *n.* 女式长罩衫.

o·ver·blow [ˈəuvəˈbləu] *vt.* ***(-blew*** [-ˈbluː]; ***-blown*** [-ˈbləun]***)*** ①(风等)吹散; 吹落; 吹过; 吹起沙〔雪〕盖住. ②吹(管乐器)过响以至基调失真. ③对(转炉内)吹气时间过长. ④夸张; 过分渲染. — *vi.* 狂吹; (管乐器)吹得过响.

o·ver·blown [ˈəuvəˈbləun] *a.* ①被吹散〔吹落〕了的; 被(吹起的雪)盖住了的，停了的. ②被忘记的; 完了的; (花)开得过盛的，已过盛期的. ③夸张的; 渲染过分的. ④腰围过大的.

o·ver·board [ˈəuvəbɔːd] *ad.* 向船外; (自船上)到水中. ***fall*** ~ 从船上掉在(水里);〔美〕从火车上掉下来. ***go*** ~〔美〕过分爱好; 狂热追求. ***throw*** ~ 丢在船外，丢在水中; 排斥，放弃.

o·ver·bold [ˈəuvəˈbəuld] *a.* 过于胆大的，鲁莽的.

o·ver·book [ˈəuvəˈbuk] *vt.* 预订(机票等)超出所需要的数量，超量预定.

o·ver·bore [ˌəuvəˈbɔː] overbear 的过去式.

o·ver·borne [ˌəuvəˈbɔːn] overbear 的过去分词.

o·ver·bought [ˈəuvəˈbɔːt] overbuy 的过去式和过去分词.

o·ver·bridge [ˈəuvəbridʒ] *n.*【建】天桥，旱桥，跨线桥.

o·ver·brim [ˈəuvəˈbrim] *vt., vi.* (使)满出，溢出. *fill to overbrimming* 倒的满满的.

o·ver·build [ˈəuvəˈbild] *vt.* ***(-built*** [-ˈbilt]***)*** ①建造过多. ②过分讲究地建筑. ③建造在…上面. ④指望过度. ~ ***oneself*** 屋子盖得超过自己的需要; 屋子盖得多到不能卖〔租〕完.

o·ver·bur·den [ˌəuvəˈbəːdn] *vt.* 装载过多; 使负担过度，使过劳; 压垂. *trees ~ed with fruit* 果子结得过多的树. — [ˈəuvəbəːdn] *n.* ①过重的货物，重担，过度的负担. ②【地】浮盖层; 覆盖层; 表土.

o·ver·bus·y [ˈəuvəˈbizi] *a.* 太忙的; 过分爱管闲事的.

o·ver·buy [ˈəuvəˈbai] *vt.* ***(o·ver·bought*** [ˈəuvəˈbɔːt]***)*** 买得过多〔贵〕.

o·ver·call [ˈəuvəˈkɔːl] *vt.*【桥牌】叫牌叫得比…高.

— [ˈəuvəkɔːl] *n.* 过高的叫牌.
o•ver•came [ˌəuvəˈkeim] overcome 的过去式.
o•ver•can•o•py [ˌəuvəˈkænəpi] *vt.* 用帐篷遮盖.
o•ver•ca•pit•al•ize [ˈəuvəkəˈpitəlaiz, ˌəuvəˈkæpitəlaiz] *vt.* 定[估计](资本)过大;对(事业)投资过多.
o•ver•care [ˈəuvəˈkɛə] *n.* 杞人忧天,过虑.
o•ver•care•ful [ˈəuvəˈkɛəful] *a.* 太谨慎的,太小心的.
o•ver•cast [ˈəuvə-kɑːst] *v.* ***(o•ver•cast)*** *vt.* ①云遮掉,使阴,使暗. ②包边缝拢. ③过远地撒(鱼网等). — *vi.* 阴起来,暗起来. — *a.* 多云的,阴的; 阴郁的, 愁闷的. *The sky is ~ with black clouds.* 天空乌云密布. *a ~ day* 阴天. — *n.* ①覆盖; 阴暗的天空. ②【矿】风桥. ③(网等)过远的一撒.
o•ver•cau•tion [ˈəuvəkɔːʃən] *n.* 过分小心, 过分谨慎. **-cau•tious** *a.*
o•ver•charge [ˈəuvəˈtʃɑːdʒ] *vt., vi.* ①(向…) 乱讨价; 向…索费太多; 滥开(帐目). ②装弹(药)过多; 充(电)过度; 装载过多,过重. ③压倒; 夸张(叙述等). *~ a lecture with facts* 讲演中事实摆得过多.
o•ver•clothes [ˈəuvəkləuz,-kləuðz] *n. pl.* 外衣〔大衣、雨衣等〕(= outerwear).
o•ver•cloud [ˌəuvəˈklaud] *vt., vi.* ①(使)给云盖满; (使)变阴. ②(使)忧郁,(使)悲伤; 使生气. ③把(理解等)弄模糊.
o•ver•coat [ˈəuvəkəut] *n.* 大衣; 〔美空俚〕降落伞. **-ing** *n.* 大衣料子.
o•ver•col•o(u)r [ˈəuvəˈkʌlə, ˌəuvəˈkʌlə] *vt.* 〔英〕给…着色过浓; 润饰过度; 夸张(描写等).
o•ver•come [ˌəuvəˈkʌm] *vt.* ***(o•ver•came*** [ˌəuvəˈkeim]; ***-come)*** ①打败,战胜,征服; 克服(困难). ②〔多用被动语态〕压倒,制服,…不堪 *(with; by)*. *He was ~ by their entreaties.* 他屈从了他们的请求. *be ~ by weariness* 累倒. *be ~ with liquor* 喝醉.
o•ver•com•pen•sate [ˌəuvəˈkɔmpənseit] *vt.* 对…给予过多的补偿. — *vi.* 【心】过度补偿〔指为补偿某种生理或心理的缺陷而过分的努力〕. **-sa•tion** *n.* **-sa•tory** *a.*
o•ver•con•fi•dence [ˈəuvəˈkɔnfidəns] *n.* 过分相信; 自信过强; 自负; 厚脸.
o•ver•con•fi•dent [ˈəuvəˈkɔnfidənt] *a.* 过分相信的; 自信过强的; 自负的; 厚脸的.
o•ver-coun•ter [ˈəuvəˈkauntə] *a.* (银行等)不经过交易所而卖出的(指证券等).
o•ver•cred•u•lous [ˈəuvəˈkredjuləs] *a.* 过于轻信的. **-du•li•ty** [ˈəuvəkriˈdjuːliti] *n.* (过度的)轻信.
o•ver•crit•i•cal [ˈəuvəˈkritikəl] *a.* 批评过多的,过分指摘的.
o•ver•crop [ˈəuvəˈkrɔp] *vt.* ***(-cropped; -crop•ping)*** 耕种过度而弄瘦(地力). — [ˈəuvəkrɔp] *n.* 耕种过度.
o•ver•crow [ˈəuvəˈkrəu] *vt.* 对…自鸣得意,夸耀,压倒; 胜过; 打垮,打败….
o•ver•crowd [ˌəuvəˈkraud] *vt.* 使(过分)拥挤,使杂沓. *an ~ed profession* 人浮于事的职业.
o•ver•crust [ˈəuvəˈkrʌst] *vt.* 用外皮[外壳]包[覆盖].
o•ver•cun•ning [ˈəuvəˈkʌniŋ] *n., a.* 过分狡猾(的).
o•ver•cu•ri•ous [ˈəuvəˈkjuəriəs] *a.* 过分好奇多问的.
o•ver•del•i•cate [ˈəuvəˈdelikit] *a.* 过于微妙的,过于纤弱[细巧]的.
o•ver•de•vel•op [ˈəuvədiˈveləp] *vt.* ①【摄】使显影过度. ②使过度发展.
o•ver•do [ˌəuvəˈduː] *vt.* ***(-did*** [-ˈdid]; ***-done*** [-ˈdʌn]***)*** ①过于…, …过度; 夸张. ②〔通常用被动语态或 ~ oneself〕过度使用 (体力等),使过劳; 耗尽. ③〔通常用过去分词形式〕煮过度,烧过度. *~ exercise* 运动过度. *His politeness is overdone.* 他殷勤过度了. *The joke is overdone.* 这个玩笑开得过火了. *~ meat* 把肉煮得过老. ***~ it*** 做得过火; 过劳; 夸张; 演得过火. ***~ oneself [one's strength]*** 勉强,努力过度; 使尽力量.
o•ver•door [ˈəuvədɔː] *n.* 【建】门头饰板.
o•ver•dose [ˈəuvədəus] *n.* 过量用药. — [ˈəuvəˈdəus] *vt.* 使…服药过量,使…用药过量.
o•ver•draft, o•ver•draught [ˈəuvədrɑːft] *n.* ①【商】透支; 透支额. ②【冶】过度通风.
o•ver•draw [ˈəuvəˈdrɔː] *v.* ***(o•ver•drew*** [əuvəˈdruː]; ***-drawn*** [-ˈdrɔːn]***)*** *vt.* ①拉(弓)过度; 把…描绘过分, 夸大, 夸张. ②【商】透支(存款); 过多地开(支票等). — *vi.* 透支.
o•ver•dress [ˈəuvəˈdres] *vt.* 使穿得太考究,使过度装束. — [ˈəuvədres] *n.* (薄)外衣.
o•ver•drink [ˈəuvəˈdriŋk] *vt., vi.* ***(o•ver•drank*** [ˈəuvəˈdræŋk]; ***-drunk*** [-ˈdrʌŋk]***)*** (使) 喝得过度, 暴饮. ***~ oneself*** 喝酒过多把身体喝坏.
o•ver•drive [ˈəuvəˈdraiv] *vt.* ***(o•ver•drove*** [ˈəuvəˈdrəuv]; ***-driven*** [-ˈdrivən]***)*** 驱使过度; 使负担过度; 使(人)操劳过度; 【无】使激励过度. — [ˈəuvədraiv] *n.* 【机】超速传动. *~ clutch* 超速离合器.
o•ver•due [ˈəuvəˈdjuː] *a.* 过期(未付)的; 迟到的, 延误的; 过度的; 早就该实现的. *an ~ check* 过期支票. *The train is ~.* 火车误点了.
o•ver•dye [ˈəuvəˈdai] *vt.* 把…染得过久[过深]; 复染.
o•ver•eat [ˈəuvərˈiːt] *vt., vi.* ***(o•ver•ate*** [ˈəuvəˈet]; ***-eat•en*** [-ˈiːtn]***)***(使)吃得过多,暴食. ***~ oneself*** 吃得过多把身体吃坏.
o•ver•e•lab•o•rate [ˈəuvəriˈlæbəreit] *vt.* 对…过分推敲; 对…阐述过详.
o•ver•em•pha•size [ˈəuvəˈemfəsaiz] *vt., vi.* (使) 过分强调.
o•ver•es•ti•mate [ˈəuvərˈestimeit] *vt.* 估计过高; 过分评价. — [ˈəuvərˈestimit] *n.* 过高的估计; 过分的评价. **-ma•tion** [-ˈmeiʃən] 同上.
o•ver•ex•pose [ˈəuvəriksˈpəuz] *vt.* 【摄】使过度感光; 使过度受光[受辐射].
o•ver•ex•po•sure [ˈəuvəriksˈpəuʒə] *n.* 【摄】感光过度.
o•ver•ex•tend [ˈəuvəiksˈtend] *vt.* 使伸延过长,使超过合理的限度; 使承担超过能力的义务或诺言. **-ten•sion** *n.*
o•ver•fa•tigue [ˈəuvəfəˈtiːg] *vt.* 使疲劳过度,使筋疲力尽. — *n.* 过劳.
o•ver•feed [ˈəuvəˈfiːd] *vt., vi.* ***(o•ver•fed*** [əuvəˈfed]***)*** (给)…吃得太多; 给…进料过多. ***~ oneself*** 吃得过多.
o•ver•fill [ˈəuvəfil] *vt.* 把…装得太满 (= ~ too full). — *vi.* 满得溢出.
o•ver•film [ˈəuvəˈfilm] *vt.* 把薄膜盖在…上.
o•ver•fish [ˈəuvəfiʃ] *vt.* 对鱼类[鱼场]进行过分捕捞.
o•ver•flew [ˌəuvəˈfluː] overfly 的过去式.
o•ver•flight [ˈəuvəflait] *n.* 飞越上空.
o•ver•flow [ˌəuvəˈfləu] *vt.* ***(-flowed, -flew*** [-ˈfluː]; ***-flown*** [-ˈfluːn]; ***flowing)*** 使溢出, 使泛滥; 使涨满; 淹没; 人满得走不进(房间等). *The river overflew its banks.* 河水漫出堤岸. *The river ~ed several farms.* 河水淹没了几个农场. *The goods ~ed the warehouse.* 货物多得仓库堆不下了. — *vi.* 溢流,泛滥,漫出; 满,充满; 洋溢; (资源等)过剩. *a man ~ing with sympathy* 充满同情心的人. *a land ~ing with resources of every kind* 各种资源都很丰富的国家. ***~ with*** 充溢,充满. — [ˈəuvəfləu] *n.* ①泛滥,溢流. ②外溢,充溢,过多,过剩; 超出额; 溢出物. ③溢洪道,排水口. *an ~ gate* 溢水口. *an ~ of population* 人口过剩. — *a.* 溢出的; 充满的 (= overflowing). ***~ meeting*** (由于太挤而) 增设的分会场. ***~ weir*** 越水堰,漫坝.
o•ver•flow•ing [ˌəuvəˈfləuiŋ] *a.* 溢出的, 过剩的; 充满的. *a heart ~ with gratitude* 充满感激的心情. — *n.* ①溢出,过剩; 溢出物. ②〔常 *pl.*〕洋溢,充沛.
o•ver•fly [ˌəuvəˈflai] *vt.* ***(-flew*** [-ˈfluː]; ***-flown*** [-ˈfluːn]; ***fly•ing)*** 飞行在…上空; 飞越; (尤指)飞越(他国领土)作侦察.
o•ver•flight [ˈəuvəflait] *n.* (飞机等的)飞越上空.

o·ver·freight [ˈəuvəˈfreit] *vt.* 载货过多. — [ˈəuvəfreit] *n.* 超载;【船】超过租船合同货量的运费.

o·ver·ful·fill [ˈəuvəfulˈfil] *vt.* 超额生产;超额完成.

o·ver·full [ˈəuvəˈful] *a.* 太满的,充满的;过多的;太用心…的.

o·ver·gar·ment [ˈəuvəgɑːmənt] *n.* 大衣,外衣.

o·ver·gild [ˈəuvəˈgild] *vt.* (*-gild·ed, -gilt* [-ˈgilt]) 镀金在…上;〔喻〕把…染成黄金色.

o·ver·glaze [ˈəuvəgleiz] *n.* (制陶)①第二层釉. ②面釉. — [ˈəuvəˈgleiz] *vt.* 涂釉;涂面釉.

o·ver·gov·ern [ˌəuvəˈgʌvən] *vt.* 统治;(政府等对人民)干涉过度,管制过度.

o·ver·grew [ˈəuvəˈgruː] overgrow 的过去式.

o·ver·ground [ˈəuvəgraund] *a.* ①在地面上的 (*opp.* underground). ②符合现存体制下各种标准的,正统的,官方的. *an ~ route* 陆路. *be still ~* 还活着.

o·ver·grow [ˈəuvəˈgrəu] *vt.* (*-grew* [-ˈgruː]; *-grown* [-ˈgrəun]) *vt.* ①〔主用被动语态〕(杂草等)在…上蔓生,丛生,长满. ②〔~ oneself〕长得过度[过大、过高]. — *vi.* 蔓延过度;长得过大[过快]. *an ~ing city* 正在急速发展中的城市.

o·ver·grown [ˈəuvəˈgrəun] ①overgrow 的过去分词. ② *a.* (人)长得太大的,个子长得过高的;畸形发展的;(因肥大而)难看的,笨拙的;(植物)生长过度的,太繁茂的,没修剪的;(杂草等)生满的. *a garden ~ with weeds* 生满杂草的花园.

o·ver·growth [ˈəuvəgrəuθ] *n.* 繁茂,蔓延;生长过度;生长太快;【医】增生;肥大;生满某场所[建筑物上]的东西;【化】附(晶生)长.

o·ver·hand [ˈəuvəhænd] *a.* ①从上面下手[放手]的. ②(打球等时)举手过肩的,向下打的;(游泳)手臂露出水面的. ③【裁缝】锁缝的. *an ~ knot* 反手结〔一种绳结〕. *an ~ stroke* 两手交拍水面的游泳. — *ad.* ①【球戏】举手过肩地. ②【泳】拍水. ③从上按住. ④锁缝. — *n.* ①上风,优势;胜利. ②手举过肩的运动姿势. — *vt.*〔美〕锁缝.

o·ver·hang [ˈəuvəˈhæŋ] *vt., vi.* (*-hung* [-ˈhʌŋ]) ①倒悬;悬垂;吊在…上;(向…)突出[伸出]. ②(危险等)逼近,威胁. ③(用布幔等)过度装饰. *an overhung door* 吊门. *an ~ing danger* 迫近眼前的危险. — [ˈəuvəhæŋ] *n.* 突出,撑出,【建】悬垂;挑出屋顶;挑出楼房;延伸量,伸出量;【空】多翼机的上翼伸出下翼的长度;(无法兑换黄金的)美元过剩额. *the ~ of a ship's stern* 船尾突出部分.

o·ver·hast·y [ˈəuvəˈheisti] *a.* 过于性急的,草率的.

o·ver·haul [ˌəuvəˈhɔːl] *vt.* ①翻查;仔细检查;检修,翻修,拆修. ②追上(他船);解松(船的)绳索. *be ~ed by a doctor* 受医生仔细检查. — [ˈəuvəhɔːl] *n.* 检查,大修. *a complete ~* 全部检查. *a general ~* 普查,大修. *a top ~* 初步检修. *undergo a thorough ~* 受彻底检查.

o·ver·head [ˈəuvəˈhed] *ad.* ①在上,在头顶上,高高地;在楼上;在空中. ②到头部没入. *O- the stars were out.* 天上星星出来了. *plunge ~ into water* 扑咚地跳入水中. — [ˈəuvəhed] *a.* ①头顶上的;架空的,架设的. ②所有的,总. ③平均的. ④通常开支的. *an ~ railway* 〔英〕高架铁路. *~ seam* 搭缝. *~ wires* 架空线. *~ irrigation* 人工降雨. *the ~ charges [expenses]*【商】经常费,总开销. — [ˈəuvəhed] *n.* ①企业一般管理费用. ②天花板;【船】船舱的顶板. ③【化】塔顶馏出物. ④【体】(网球等的)扣杀.

o·ver·hear [ˌəuvəˈhiə] *vt., vi.* (*-heard* [-ˈhəːd]) 无意中听到;偷听. **-er** *n.* 偷听者;无意中听到的人.

o·ver·heat [ˌəuvəˈhiːt] *vt., vi.* 过度加热,(使)过分激动,(使)变得过热.

o·ver·hours [ˈəuvərauəz] *n. pl.* = overtime.

o·ver·housed [ˈəuvəˈhauzd] *a.* 房子太大的,住在太大的屋子里的.

o·ver·hung [ˌəuvəˈhʌŋ] overhang 的过去式和过去分词.

o·ver·in·dulge [ˈəuvərinˈdʌldʒ] *vt.* 惯适,放纵,姑息. **-dul·gent** [-ˈdʌldʒənt] *a.* 过分放任的. **-gence** [-dʒəns] *n.* 过度放任,放纵,姑息.

o·ver·is·sue [ˈəuvərˈisjuː] *vt.* 滥发(钞票、公债等). — *n.* 滥发.

o·ver·joy [ˌəuvəˈdʒɔi] *vt.* 〔多用被动语态〕使大喜,使狂喜. *be ~ed at (with)* 听见[看见]…开心得要发狂似的. — [ˈəuvədʒɔi] *n.* 大喜,狂喜.

o·ver·kill [ˌəuvəˈkil] *vt.* ①用过多的核力量摧毁(目标). ②重复命中. ③杀尽杀绝. — [ˈəuvəkil] *n.* ①过多的核武器摧毁力. ②杀害过多. ③过多;不必要的过度行动;矫枉过正.

o·ver·knee [ˈəuvəniː] *a.* 过膝的.

o·ver·la·bo(u)r [ˈəuvəˌleibə] *vt.* 使操劳过度,使工作过累;对…作过度用心的刻画.

o·ver·lade [ˈəuvəˈleid] *vt.* (*-lad·ed; -la·den, lad·ed; -lad·ing*) 使过载,使负载过重. *an overladen horse.* 负载过重的马.

o·ver·la·den [əuvəˈleidn] *a.* 装货过多的;(房间)装饰[摆设]过多的.

o·ver·laid [ˌəuvəˈleid] overlay[1] 的过去式和过去分词.

o·ver·lain [ˌəuvəˈlein] overlie 的过去分词.

o·ver·land [ˈəuvəlænd] *a.* 陆上的,陆路的. *an ~ journey* 陆地旅行. *the ~ route* 陆路;〔英〕(从英国经地中海国家不绕好望角到印度的)陆上通路;〔美〕从大西洋岸横贯大陆到太平洋岸的道路. — [ˌəuvəˈlænd] *ad.* 由陆路.

o·ver·lap [ˌəuvəˈlæp] *vt., vi.* ①(与…)交搭;迭盖. ②(与…)部分一致[巧合],(时间等)重复,一致(*in*). — [ˈəuvəlæp] *n.* ①重复,部分一致;交搭;重迭;复合. ②覆盖物,涂盖层;【植】盖覆.【摄】重叠摄影. ③【数】交迭,相交;复合. ④【军】航空照片的重迭部分;【地】超复;累叠地层.

o·ver·lay[1] [ˌəuvəˈlei] *vt.* (*-laid* [-ˈleid]) ①覆,盖;铺;敷,涂;包,镀金. ②盖暗,弄阴. ③压制,压倒. ④【印】加上衬于. — [ˈəuvəlei] *n.* ①【印】轮廓纸;上衬. ②盖在上面的东西;被单;小台布;镀金(等). ③【军】透明图.

o·ver·lay[2] [ˌəuvəˈlei] overlie 的过去式.

o·ver·leaf [ˈəuvəˈliːf] *ad.* (纸的)反面;在次页. — [ˈəuvəliːf] *n.* 反面,次页.

o·ver·leap [ˌəuvəˈliːp] *vt.* (*-leaped* [-ˈlept, -ˈliːpt], *-leapt* [-ˈlept]) ①跳过,越过;[ˈəuvəˈliːp] 跳过头,跳出 (one's mark). ②漏看,忽略,省去. *Ambition often ~s itself.* 野心常因过大而失败,抱负常因过高而不能实现.

o·ver·lie [ˌəuvəˈlai] *vt.* (*-lay* [-ˈlei]; *-lain* [-ˈlein]; *o-ver·ly·ing* [-ˈlaiiŋ]) ①躺[伏]在…上面. ②压在上面闷死(婴儿等).

o·ver·live [ˈəuvəˈliv] *vt.* (比别人或平常寿数)活得长;比…经久. — *vi.* 还活着,残存.

o·ver·load [ˈəuvəˈləud] *vt.* 使装载过重货物,使装载[负担]过重,超载;把(弹药等)装填过度;【电】给…过量充电. *an ~ed style* 过分夸张的文体. — [ˈəuvələud] *n.* 过重装载,过重负担;超负荷;【电】过载.

o·ver·long [ˈəuvəˈlɔŋ] *a., ad.* 太长,过分长.

o·ver·look [ˌəuvəˈluk] *vt.* ①俯视;眺望,了望;(房屋等)耸出,高过…. ②漏看;忽略;假装不见;宽容;放任. ③监督,监视;检查;视察;照顾;检阅;读;〔罕〕随便看一遍. ④(蛇把蛙等)用目光震慑住,使心慌意乱. *~ a valley from a hill* 从小山上俯视山谷. *~ a fault* 宽容过失. *~ ... at work* 监督…工作[劳动]. *His services have been ~ed for years.* 他的功绩好几年来都没有人注意到.

o·ver·lord [ˈəuvəlɔːd] *n.* 霸王;太上皇;大君主;封建领主[君主].

o·ver·ly [ˈəuvəli] *ad.* 〔Scot.〕过度地.
o·ver·ly·ing [ˌəuvəˈlaiiŋ] overlie 的现在分词.
o·ver·man [ˈəuvəmæn] *n.* ①工头;(煤矿的)井内监工;头头. ②调解人,公断人. ③【哲】超人. — *vt.* 给…配备人员过多.
o·ver·man·tel [ˈəuvəmæntl] *n.* 壁炉额上的饰架.
o·ver·man·y [ˈəuvəˈmeni] *a.* 过多的.
o·ver·mast·ed [ˈəuvəˈmɑːstid] *a.* 【海】桅杆太长的,桅杆过重的.
o·ver·mas·ter [ˌəuvəˈmɑːstə] *vt.* 压服;克服;征服;压倒. *an ~ing passion* 压抑不住的强烈情感.
o·ver·match [ˌəuvəˈmætʃ] *vt.* ①优于,胜过;压倒. ②和(门户等)不相称的人结婚. — [ˈəuvəmætʃ] *n.* ①劲敌,强敌. ②优劣悬殊者之间的比赛.
o·ver·mat·ter [ˈəuvəmætə] *n.* (杂志等的)存稿;多余的排版.
o·ver·meas·ure [ˌəuvəˈmeʒə] *vt.* 高估,估量过大. — [ˈəuvəˈmeʒə] *n.* 过量;剩余.
o·ver·mod·est [ˈəuvəˈmɔdist] *a.* 过分谦虚的,太怕羞的.
o·ver·much [ˈəuvəˈmʌtʃ, ˈəuvəm-] *a.* 过多的. — *n.* 过量;剩余. — *ad.* 过度地;过多地.
o·ver·nice [ˈəuvəˈnais] *a.* 过分讲究的;过分吹毛求疵的;过分严格的;过于仔细[谨慎]的.
o·ver·night [ˈəuvəˈnait] *ad.* ①昨晚,昨夜一晚上. ②通宵,从夜晚到天亮;一夜工夫. *stay ~* 住一晚,过夜. — *a.* ①昨晚的,昨夜的. ②通夜的. ③旅行时过夜用的. ④忽然的. *an ~ conversation* 通夜会谈. *an ~ millionaire* 暴发户. — *n.* 〔美〕前一天的晚上.
o·ver·night·er [ˈəuvəˈnaitə] *n.* 短途旅行用的小件行李.
o·ver·paid [ˈəuvəˈpeid] overpay 的过去分词.
o·ver·pass [ˌəuvəˈpɑːs] *vt.* (*~ed, -past* [-ˈpɑːst]) ①渡,过(河);通过;翻过,越过;超出(范围);违背;侵犯. ②忽视;漏看. ③优于,超过. *It ~es endurance.* 那个没法忍受得了. — [ˈəuvəpɑːs] *n.* 〔美〕【交】高架道路;立体交叉;上跨桥;上跨路.
o·ver·pass·ed, o·ver·past [ˌəuvəˈpɑːst] *a.* 过去了的,结束了的.
o·ver·pay [ˌəuvəˈpei] *vt.* (*-paid* [-ˈpeid]) 多付,多给…报酬. *The joy ~s the toil.* 所得的快乐超过付出的辛劳.
o·ver·peo·pled [ˈəuvəˈpiːpld] *a.* 居民过多的,人口过密的.
o·ver·per·suade [ˈəuvəpəˈsweid] *vt.* 硬要说服(不愿听的人等).
o·ver·pitch [ˌəuvəˈpitʃ] *vt.* ①【板球】扔(球)过分接近三柱门;扔(球)过度. ②夸大.
o·ver·play [ˌəuvəˈplei] *vt.* ①把…做得过分;把…演得过火. ②(比赛)胜过(对方). ③【高尔夫球】打球过远. ④过分依赖…的力量.
o·ver·plus [ˈəuvəplʌs] *n.* 剩余,超出的数量;过剩,过多.
o·ver·pop·u·late [ˌəuvəˈpɔpjuˌleit] *vt.* 使(某一地区)人口过剩. **-lation** [-ˈleiʃən] *n.*
o·ver·pow·er [ˌəuvəˈpauə] *vt.* ①打败;制服,压服;(精神上、肉体上)压倒. ②使深深感动. ③供给…过强的力量. *Human will can ~ natural forces.* 人定胜天. *The heat ~ed me.* 热得受不了啦. *Your kindness ~s me.* 深情厚谊衷心铭感.
o·ver·pow·er·ing [ˌəuvəˈpauəriŋ] *a.* 压倒(优势)的;极强大的;难抗拒的;制止不了的. *an ~ smell* 难闻的气味. **-ly** *ad.*
o·ver·praise [ˈəuvəˈpreiz] *vt.* 过度称赞,过奖. — [ˈəuvəpreiz] *n.* 过奖;过分的称赞.
o·ver·pres·sure [ˈəuvəˈpreʃə] *n.* ①过度的重压,过度的压迫;过劳;过压,超压力. ②剩余压力.
o·ver·price [ˈəuvəˈprais] *vt.* 对…定价过高.
o·ver·print [ˈəuvəˈprint] *vt.* ①【印】套印,添印,复印. ②过量印刷;【摄】曝光过度. ③在一个形象上覆印另一形象;在(邮票等)上盖印戳. — [ˈəuvəprint] *n.* ①加印量. ②印戳;盖过印的邮票.
o·ver·pro·duce [ˈəuvəprəˈdjuːs] *vt., vi.* (使)生产过剩. **-duc·tion** [ˈəuvəprəˈdʌkʃən] *n.* 生产过剩.
o·ver·proof [ˈəuvəˈpruːf] *a.* 酒精含量超过标准以上的.
o·ver·pro·tect [ˌəuvəprəˈtekt] *vt.* 过分地保护,过分地爱护(尤指对子女的溺爱). **-ive** *a.*
o·ver·quick [ˈəuvəˈkwik] *a.* 过于快的.
o·ver·ran [ˌəuvəˈræn] overrun 的过去式.
o·ver·rate [ˈəuvəˈreit] *vt.* 估计[估价]过高,高估.
o·ver·reach [ˌəuvəˈriːtʃ] *vt.* ①把(手、脚等)伸得过长;走过头,越过;赶上,追上;非分妄为致使…失败. ②(依靠奸诈)取胜. ③(马)用后脚的前端踢(前脚后跟). *His influence ~ed his audience.* 他的话使听众无限感动. *~ oneself* 伸腰;做过火;弄巧成拙. — *vi.* ①(手、脚等)伸得过长;延伸过远. ②过火,夸张. ③(马等)后蹄踢前蹄.
o·ver·re·act [ˌəuvəriˈækt] *vi.* 反应过度〔情绪过分强烈〕.
o·ver·read [ˈəuvəˈriːd] *vt.* (*-read* [-ˈred]) ①从头读完,通读. ②使读书过度而弄坏身体.
o·ver·re·fine [ˈəuvəriˈfain] *vi.* 加工过度;区分过细.
o·ver·rent [ˈəuvəˈrent] *vt.* 地租[房租等]收得过高.
o·ver·ride [ˌəuvəˈraid] *vt.* (*-rode* [-ˈrəud]; *-rid·den* [-ˈridn]) ①蹂躏(别国等). ②蔑视,藐视(法规);制服,压倒;废弃,推翻(决议). ③奔越过;践踏过;骑着马跳过;把(马)骑累. ④【外】将(断骨)重叠起来. *~ another's authority* 藐视别人职权. *~ one's commission* 滥用职权,作越权处置.
o·ver·ripe [ˈəuvəˈraip] *a.* 过分成熟的;腐朽的,颓废的.
o·ver·rule [ˌəuvəˈruːl] *vt.* ①统治;压制;克服,压倒. ②用权力取消(决定、方针等),废弃;推翻;驳回,批斥;否决;宣布…无效. *The claims were ~d.* 要求被驳回了. *Conscience may be ~d by passion.* 良心可能为感情所支配.
o·ver·run [ˌəuvəˈrʌn] *vt., vi.* (*-ran* [-ˈræn]; *-run*) ①(杂草等)(在…)蔓延;(害虫等)(在…)猖獗,群集(于);(使…)泛滥. ②侵略,蚕食,蹂躏(别国等). ③超出,越过(范围);【机】(使)超限运转. ④〔~ oneself〕跑累. 【印】因移行重排(行、栏、版面). *be ~ with ivy* 茑萝蔓生. *be ~ with mice* 老鼠猖獗. *His speech overran the time allotted.* 他的演说超过了规定时间. *~ **the constable*** 〔口〕①乱花乱用;负债. ②瞎谈不知道的事情. — [ˈəuvərʌn] *n.* ①蔓延;猖獗,跋扈;横行为害;泛滥成灾;超越限度. ②超出量;余额. ③【空】清除区〔机场跑道两端的备用地区〕.
o·ver·sail [ˈəuvəˈseil] *vt., vi.* 【建】(使)连续突腰.
o·ver·saw [ˈəuvəˈsɔː] oversee 的过去式.
o·ver·score [ˌəuvəˈskɔː] *vt.* 在(字、句等上或中间)划一条线. — [ˈəuvəskɔː] *n.* 字、句等上或中间的线.
o·ver·sea(s) [ˈəuvəˈsiː(z)] *a.* ①来自海外的,海外的,外国的. ②往海外的. *an ~ edition* (期刊的)海外版. *the ~ trade* 对外贸易. *an ~ broadcast program* 对(国)外(的)广播节目. *the overseas Chinese* 华侨. *~ remittance.* 侨汇. — *ad.* 向海外,向国外;在海外. *~* **cap** 〔美军〕军便帽,船形帽.
o·ver·see [ˈəuvəˈsiː] *vt.* (*-saw* [-ˈsɔː]; *-seen* [ˈsiːn]) ①俯瞰;了望;监督,监视;检查;视察;管理,照料. ②看漏,错过;宽恕;省略.
o·ver·se·er [ˈəuvəsi(ː)ə] *n.* ①管理员,监工,工头. ②〔英〕(做贫民救济工作的)教区低级职员. *an ~ of schools* 督学.
o·ver·sell [ˈəuvəˈsel] *vt.* (*-sold* [-ˈsəuld]) 过多地卖出(商品等);卖空(股票等);过分吹嘘.
o·ver·sen·si·tive [ˈəuvəˈsensitiv] *a.* 过分敏感的.
o·ver·set [ˈəuvəˈset] *vt.* (*-set; -set·ting*) ①翻转;推翻,颠覆. ②【印】排(版)过密. ③镶嵌(宝石等). —[ˈəuvə-

set] n. ①推翻,破坏,打倒. ②〔美新闻语〕过剩稿件.

o•ver•sew ['əuvəsəu, ˌəuvə'səu] vt. *(-sewed* [-d]; *-sewed, -sewn* [-səun]) 锁(缝);管(边).

o•ver•sexed [ˌəuvə'sekst] a. 纵欲的,耽于色欲的.

o•ver•shad•ow [ˌəuvə'ʃædəu] vt. ①遮阴,遮蔽;使阴 ②使失色,夺去…的光辉,扫…的面子. ③保护,庇护.

o•ver•shoe ['əuvəʃuː] n. 〔美〕〔常pl.〕套鞋.

o•ver•shoot ['əuvə'ʃuːt] v. *(-shot* [-'ʃɔt]) vt. ①把(子弹)打得过高(而未打中),打得过远;在射击上胜过;【军】弹着超越(目标);超过(界限);【空】(飞机在准备着陆时)飞过(指定地点). ②走过头,越过;超出(规定),逸出. ③从高处射下. — vi. ①射击越标. ②做得过分. ~ ***oneself [the mark]*** 做得过分;夸张. ~ ***the field*** 打猎过多致使野兽绝迹. — n.【自】过调量,超越度.

o•ver•shot ['əuvə'ʃɔt] a. ①(水车)上射的. ②上颚突出的. ③〔口〕喝醉的. ④夸大的. — n.【纺】跳花〔一种织疵〕;浮纬花纹.

o•ver•shoul•der ['əuvə'ʃəuldə] adv. 回头;转过头来.

o•ver•side ['əuvəsaid] a. ①从船边的〔指货物的装卸说〕. ②在唱片反面的. —['əuvə'said] ad. ①从船边. ***free*** ~【商】输入港船上交货价格,到港价格〔略 f. o. s.〕.

o•ver•sight ['əuvəsait] n. ①监督,监视;看管. ②疏忽,漏失,失察,失错. ***by (an)*** ~ 不当心,不小心;出于疏忽. ***have the*** ~ ***of*** *(children)* 看管(小孩).

o•ver•sim•pli•fy ['əuvə'simplifai] vt., vi. *(-fied; -fying)* 过分简单化〔以致歪曲、忽略了要点〕. **-pli•fi•ca•tion** [ˌəuvəˌsimplifi'keiʃən] n.

o•ver•size ['əuvə'saiz] a. ①太大的. ②大于一般的;特别大的 (= oversized). — ['əuvəsaiz] n. 大号(物),特大号(物).

o•ver•skirt ['əuvəskəːt] n. 罩裙.

o•ver•slaugh ['əuvəslɔː] n. ①〔英〕【军】(因另有更重要的任务而)免予执行现有任务. ②〔美〕(河川中不利于航行的)浅滩.— vt. ①【军】把(某人)免除现职. ②〔美〕妨碍;阻止. ③〔美〕忽略(某人)不予任用而另用别人.

o•ver•sleep ['əuvə'sliːp] vt., vi. *(-slept* [-'slept]) (使)睡过头;(使)睡得过久.

o•ver•sleeve ['əuvəsliːv] n. 袖套.

o•ver•slip ['əuvə'slip] vt. 滑过;看落,错过(机会等).

o•ver•smoke ['əuvə'sməuk] vt., vi. (把…)弄得满是烟;(使)抽烟过度.

o•ver•sold ['əuvə'səuld] oversell 的过去式和过去分词.

o•ver•soul ['əuvəsəul] n.【哲】(先验论的所谓)超灵,上帝.

o•ver•speed ['əuvə'spiːd] vt., vi. ***(o•ver•sped*** ['əuvə'sped]; ***o•ver•sped•ed*** [-'spiːdid]) (使)超速运行. — ['əuvəspiːd] n. 超速. — a. 超速运行的.

o•ver•spend [əuvə'spend] vt., vi. *(-spent* [-'spent]) 用尽,耗尽;花费过多,开销太大;超支;支出超过(自己的财力). ~ *one's allowance* 不量力地乱花销;入不敷出.

o•ver•spill ['əuvəspil] n. 溢出物;过剩物资;过剩人口.

o•ver•spread ['əuvə'spred] vt., vi. *(-spread)* 铺盖;覆盖;布满;蔓延. *The sky was* ~ *with clouds.* 天空布满了云. *A smile* ~ *his face.* 他笑容满面.

o•ver•state ['əuvə'steit] vt. 把…讲得过分;夸大,夸张. ~ *one's case* 夸大自己的情况. **-ment** n. 言过其实;大话,夸张.

o•ver•stay ['əuvə'stei] vt., vi. (使)逗留过久,(使)坐得过久;【商】勒价观望过久而坐失(良机). ~ ***one's welcome*** 逗留[坐得]过久而使人生厌.

o•ver•steer ['əuvəstiə] n. (汽车)对驾驶盘反应过敏.

o•ver•step ['əuvə'step] vt. 走过头,越过(界限);犯. ~ *one's authority* 越权.

o•ver•stock ['əuvə'stɔk] vt. 使存货过多;进(货)过多;(家畜)饲养过多,(鱼)放养过密. *The market is* ~*ed.* 市场存货过剩. — ['əuvəstɔk] n. 进货过多;存货过剩.

o•ver•strain ['əuvə'strein] vt. 伸张过度;使过度紧张;使工作过度,役使过度. ~ *one's nerves* 用脑过度. — vi. 过度紧张,过度努力. ~ *oneself* 过劳,努力过度. — ['əuvəstrein] n. 过度紧张;过劳;伤力.

o•ver•strength ['əuvəstreŋθ] n. 力量过剩;人员超编. — ['əuvə'strenθ] a. 人员超编制的.

o•ver•stride [ˌəuvə'straid] vt. *(-strode* [-'strəud]; *-strid•den* [-'strədn]; *-strid•ing)* ①跨过. ②优于,超过,越过. ③骑,跨;〔古〕跨过,越过 (= bestride).

o•ver•strung ['əuvə'strʌŋ] a. 紧张过度的,神经过敏的; ['əuvəstrʌŋ] (钢琴)把弦斜向交叉着装的.

o•ver•stud•y ['əuvə'stʌdi] vt., vi. (使)用功过度. — ['əuvəstʌdi] n. 用功过度.

o•ver•stuff ['əuvə'stʌf] vt. 装填…过度. *an* ~*ed chair* 装填得厚厚的椅子.

o•ver•sub•scribe ['əuvəsəb'skraib] vt. 过多定购;超额认购(公债等).

o•ver•sup•ply ['əuvəsə'plai] vt. 过度供给. — ['əuvəsəplai] n. 供应过多.

o•vert ['əuvəːt, əu'vəːt] a. ①(证据等)明显的;公开的,公然的 *(opp.* covert). ②(钱包等)开着的;(翅膀等)展开的. *an* ~ *act*【法】公然的犯罪行为. *a market* ~ 公开市场. **-ly** ad.

o•ver•take [ˌəuvə'teik] vt. *(-took* [-'tuk]; *-tak•en* [-'teikən]) ①追上;赶上;超过;赶补(欠工),赶做(限期快到的工程). ②(暴风雨、灾难等)突然袭击. ③打垮,压倒. *be overtaken by a storm* 遇到暴风雨袭击. *The murderer was overtaken in his crime.* 杀人犯当场被捕. ~*ing of waves* 波浪追推. ***be overtaken in [with] drink*** 喝醉. ***be overtaken with terror*** 被吓倒,被吓垮.

o•ver•task ['əuvə'tɑːsk] vt. 加重…负担,使做过重的工作;使过分辛劳.

o•ver•tax ['əuvə'tæks] vt. ①对…抽税过重,过度征收. ②使负担过重,使过度劳动,过度役使.

o•ver-the-count•er ['əuvəðə'kauntə] a. ①买卖双方直接交易的;(证券等)不通过交易所而直接卖给买方的. ②(药物)不需处方可出售的 (= over-counter).

o•ver•throw [ˌəuvə'θrəu] vt. *(-threw* [-'θruː]; *-thrown* [-'θrəun]) ①推翻,打倒,颠覆;破坏,使瓦解;废除(制度等). ②【板球】投回(守门员投回之球);【棒球】过高投(球);投(球)过远. — ['əuvəθrəu] n. ①倾覆;灭亡,瓦解,垮台,失败;征服. ②【板球】暴投;【棒球】投得过高[过远]的球. ***give the*** ~ 推翻,灭亡. ***have the*** ~ 垮台,灭亡.

o•ver•throw•al [ˌəuvə'θrəuəl] n. 推翻,打倒.

o•ver•thrust ['əuvəθrʌst] n.【地】掩冲断层,上冲断层.

o•ver•time ['əuvətaim] n. ①超时;加班,额外工作时间;额外劳动. ②加班费. ③【体】(为决定胜负的)比赛延长时间. ***be on*** ~ 在加班. — [əuvə'taim] ad. 在规定(工作)时间之外. — ['əuvə'taim] vt. 使历时过久;【摄】使(曝光等)超过时间.

o•ver•tire ['əuvə'taiə] vt., vi. (使)过度疲劳.

o•ver•t•ly ['əuvəːtli] ad. 明显地;公开,公然.

o•ver•toil ['əuvə'tɔil] vt., vi. = overwork. *(v.)* — ['əuvətɔil] n. = overwork *(n.)*

o•ver•tone ['əuvətəun] n. ①【乐】陪音,泛音. ②〔常 pl.〕次要的意义;联想;暗示;言外之意. ③【无】谐波. — ['əuvə'təun] vt.【摄】使曝光过度.

o•ver•took [ˌəuvə'tuk] overtake 的过去式.

o•ver•top ['əuvə'tɔp] vt. 高出,高耸…之上;超出,胜过.

o•ver•trade ['əuvə'treid] vi. 过额贸易〔贸易量大于个人财力或市场需要〕.

o•ver•train ['əuvə'trein] vt., vi. (使)训练过度;(使)练习时间过长.

o•ver•trick ['əuvəˌtrik] n.【牌戏】比所叫的牌数多得一墩.

o•ver•trump ['əuvə'trʌmp] vt., vi.【牌戏】用较高王牌

取胜.

o•ver•ture [ˈəuvətjuə] *n.* ①〔常 *pl.*〕提议,建议,提案. ②开端,序幕;【乐】序曲;前奏曲;序诗. *an ~ of marriage* 求婚. *an ~ of peace* 讲和的表示. ***make ~s*** 提出建议.

o•ver•turn [ˌəuvəˈtəːn] *vt., vi.* ①打翻,(使)翻过来,(使)倒转. ②颠覆;推翻;毁灭;打倒. — [ˈəuvətəːn] *n.* 推翻;垮台,瓦解;灭亡,毁灭. *the ~ of the government* 政府的垮台.

o•ver-un•der [ˈəuvəˈʌndə] *a.* (叠筒枪)双筒上下重叠(而非并列)的. — [ˈəuvəʌndə] *n.* 叠筒双筒枪.

o•ver•use [ˈəuvəˈjuːz] *vt.* 把…使用过度[过久];把…用过头,滥用. — [ˈəuvəjuːs] *n.* 过度[过久]的使用,滥用.

o•ver•val•ue [ˈəuvəˈvæljuː] *vt.* 过于重视;估计过高,高估.

o•ver•view [ˈəuvəvjuː] *n.* 一般观察,总的看法.

o•ver•walk [ˌəuvəˈwɔːk] *vt., vi.* (使)行走过度,(使)走累. ~ ***oneself*** 走累.

o•ver•watch [ˈəuvəˈwɔtʃ] *vt.* ①监视,守候. ②〔多用被动语态〕熬夜熬累.

o•ver•wear [ˌəuvəˈweə] *vt.* ***(-wore*** [-ˈwɔː]; ***-worn*** [-ˈwɔːn]; ***wear•ing)*** 穿破,用旧,用坏,使耗尽.

o•ver•wea•ry [ˌəuvəˈwiəri] *a.* 过度疲劳的. — [ˈəuvəˈwiəri] *vt.* ***(-ried; -ry•ing)*** 使疲劳过度.

o•ver•ween•ing [ˌəuvəˈwiːiŋ] *a.* 自以为了不起的,自负的;傲慢的;夸大了的. **-ly** *ad.*

o•ver•weigh [ˌəuvəˈwei] *vt.* ①重过;比…重要;胜过,强过. ②给…加负担,压迫,压倒,压垮(= outweigh).

o•ver•weight [ˈəuvəweit] *n.* 超重;偏重;优势. — [ˌəuvəˈweit] *a.* 超过规定重量的,超重的. *an ~ luggage* 过重行李. — [ˈəuvəˈwei *t.* 使…装载过重;使…负担过重;在重量上超过.

o•ver•whelm [ˌəuvəˈhwelm] *vt.* ①压倒;压服;推翻;倾覆;淹没;覆盖. ②(用感情等)制服;使十分感动;使不好意思;使不知所措. *be ~ed by superior forces* 被优势兵力打垮. *be ~ed by grief* 伤心已极. *Your kindness quite ~s me.* 你的好意使我感激难言. *The boat was ~ed by the waves.* 小船给浪打翻了.

o•ver•whelm•ing [ˌəuvəˈhwelmiŋ] *a.* 压倒的,势不可挡的. ***by an ~ majority [superior]*** 以压倒的多数[优势]. **-ly** *ad.*

o•ver•wind [ˈəuvəˈwaind] *vt.* ***(-wound*** [-ˈwaund]***)*** 把(发条等)卷得太紧.

o•ver•win•ter [ˈəuvəˈwintə] *vi., vt.* (使)活过冬天;(把…)保存过冬. — *a.* 整个冬季的.

o•ver•word [ˈəuvəwəːd] *n.* 老重复的词句,口头禅;诗歌或乐曲的叠句,副歌.

o•ver•work [ˈəuvəˈwəːk] *vt.* ①使工作过度,使过劳;把…役使过度. ②绣满,饰满〔只用被动语态〕. — *vi.* 工作过度,过劳. ~ *a horse* 把马役使过度. ~ ***oneself*** 过劳,劳累过度. — *n.* ①[ˈəuvəˈwəːk] 过度的劳动;过劳. ②[ˈəuvəwəːk] 加班,额外工作.

o•ver•write [ˈəuvəˈrait] *vt.* ***(-wrote*** [-ˈrəut]; ***-writ•ten*** [-ˈritn]***)*** 写在…上面;写满;过度多写;用夸张、冗长的文体写…. ~ ***oneself*** 因写作过多而写坏身体[名誉等]. — *vi.* 写作过多.

o•ver•wrought [ˈəuvəˈrɔːt] *a.* ①紧张过度的;兴奋过度的;神经质的. ②(作品)写作过分推敲的;不自然的;装饰[刻画等]过多的;太过考究的. ③过劳的.

o•ver•year•ing [ˈəuvəˈjiəiŋ] *n.* 越冬.

o•ver•zeal [ˈəuvəˈziːl] *n.* 过度的热心.

ovi- *comb. f.* 卵: ovicidal.

o•vi•cid•al [ˌəuviˈsaidəl] *a.* 能杀卵的.

Ov•id[1] [ˈəuvid] *n.* 奥维德〔姓氏〕.

O•vid[2] [ˈɔvid] *n.* 奥维德〔公元前48—公元17?,罗马诗人,拉丁全名为 Publius Ovidius Naso〕.

O•vid•i•an [ɔˈvidiən, -djən] *a.* (古罗马诗人)奥维德(Ovid)的,奥维德风格的.

o•vi•duct [ˈəuvidʌkt] *n.*【解】输卵管.

o•vif•er•ous [əuˈvifərəs] *a.*【生】有卵的,携卵的.

o•vi•form [ˈəuvifɔːm] *a.* 卵形的.

o•vig•er•ous [əuˈvidʒərəs] *a.* = oviferous.

o•vine [ˈəuvain] *a.* 羊(似)的;羊科的;绵羊的.

o•vip•a•rous [əuˈvipərəs] *a.*【动】卵生的 (*opp.* viviparous).

o•vi•pos•it [ˌəuviˈpɔzit] *vi.*【昆】产卵,下子. **-sition** *n.*

o•vi•pos•i•tor [ˌəuviˈpɔzitə] *n.*【动】产卵器.

o•vi•sac [ˈəuvisæk] *n.* ①卵鞘;卵囊. ②受卵器(= ootheca).

ovo- *comb. f.* 卵(= ov-).

o•vo•fla•vin [ˌəuvəuˈfleivin] *n.*【化】核黄素.

o•void, o•voi•dal [ˈəuvɔid, əuˈvɔidl] *a.* 卵圆形的. — *n.* 卵形物.

o•vo•lo [ˈəuvələu] *n.* ***(pl. -li*** [-ˌli]***)***【建】馒形饰.

O•von•ic [əuˈvɔnik] *a.*【无】奥夫辛斯基 (Ovshinsky) 作用的,用玻璃作半导体的. — *n.* 双向开关半导体元件. **-s** *n. pl.* 〔作单数用〕交流半导体电子学.

o•vo•tes•tis [ˌəuvəuˈtestis] *n.* 卵精巢.

o•vo•vi•vip•a•rous [ˌəuvəuviˈvipərəs] *a.* 卵胎生的. **-par•i•ty, -ness** *n.* **-ly** *ad.*

o•vu•lar [ˈəuvjulə] *a.* 胚珠的〔指植物〕;卵子的〔指动物〕.

o•vu•late [ˈəuvjuleit] *vi.* 排卵.

o•vu•la•tion [ˌəuvjuˈleiʃən] *n.* 排卵. **-la•to•ry** [-lətəri] *a.*

o•vule [ˈəuvjuːl] *n.*【生】卵细胞;小卵;【植】胚珠.

o•vum [ˈəuvəm] *n.* ***(pl. ova*** [ˈəuvə]***)***【生】卵;卵细胞.

ow. = one way (fare).

o/w = oil in water 油水相.

ow [au] *int.* 喔唷! 喔哟! 〔表示疼痛〕.

owe [əu] *vt.* ①对…负有(义务、债务等),受有…的恩惠,欠. ②(把名誉等)归给…,归功于…,认为是靠…的力量,要感谢(某人). *I ~ him $10 [$10 to him].* 我欠他十元. *I ~ you thanks.* 我得感谢你. *I ~ you my life.* 我受你再生之恩. *I ~ you an apology.* 我当向你道歉. *I ~ them a grudge.* 我对他们怀有怨恨. *We ~ to Newton the principle of gravitation.* 我们全靠牛顿才知道引力的原理. *I ~ it to you that I am still alive.* 亏有你我现在才仍然活着. *She ~s her beauty to artificial assistance.* 她的美全靠打扮. *You ~ it to yourself to say it.* 这话亏你说得出口. — *vi.* 有支付[偿还]义务 (*for*). *Who ~s for the antipasto?* 哪一位的拼盘还没有付款呢?

Ow•en [ˈəuin] *n.* ①欧文〔姓氏,男子名〕. ②**Robert ~** 欧文〔1771—1858,英国空想社会主义者〕.

Ow•en•ism [ˈəuinizəm] *n.* 欧文主义〔Robert Owen 的空想社会主义〕.

ow•ing [ˈəuiŋ] *a.* ①该付的,未付的,欠着的. ②有负于,受恩于,应归功于 (*to*). *I paid what was ~.* 该付的都付了. *the ~ £10* 欠款10镑. ***~ to*** ①由于 (*All this was ~ to ill health.* 这全是由于健康不好的关系所致). ★此义用 due to 较好. ②〔作 *prep.* 用〕因为 (*O- to the drought, crops are short.* 因为天旱收成不好).

owl [aul] *n.* ①【鸟】猫头鹰,鸱鸺,枭. ②做夜工的人,熬夜的人;夜游子,夜生活者. ③一本正经的呆子. ④【美】深夜行驶的电车[火车等]. *Don't be such a silly ~.* 别做那种傻事. ***as blind [stupid] as an ~*** 瞎[笨]透. ***as drunk as a boiled ~*** 〔美俚〕喝得烂醉. ***bring [carry, send] ~s to Athens*** 运枭至产枭极多的雅典;作徒劳无益的事,多此一举〔雅典盛产枭,枭为雅典守护神 Pallas 的标志〕. ***fly with the~s*** 夜游. ***hotter than a boiled ~*** 〔美俚〕醉得兴奋起来的. ***take ~*** 发怒,生气. — *vi.* ①〔方〕象猫头鹰般地叫[凝视]. ②(夜间)走私. **~-eyed** *a.* 〔美俚〕喝醉了的. **~light** 微明,

薄暮. ~ **parrot** 鸮鹦 (= kakapo). ~ **train** 〔美〕夜(行列)车.

owl·ed [auld] *a.* 〔美〕喝醉了的.

owl·er [ˈaulə] *n.* (特指夜间)走私者.

owl·et [ˈaulit] *n.* 小猫头鹰;〔古〕猫头鹰.

owl·ish [ˈauliʃ] *a.* ①象猫头鹰的. ②面孔严肃的;笨的(= owllike). **-ly** *ad.*

own[1] [əun] *a.* ①〔用在所有格之后以加强语气〕自己的;特有的. ②珍贵的,心爱的. ③〔罕〕(不与所有格连用)嫡亲的;同胞的. *He is his ~ man [master]; She is her ~ woman [mistress].* 他[她]是独立自主的人[自己命运的主人]. *Every man has his ~ habit.* 每个人都有他特有的习惯. *The orange has a scent all its ~.* 橘子有一种独特的香味. *She is ~ sister to me.* 她是我的同胞姊妹. — *pron.* 〔起名词作用〕自己的东西[家属、责任、立场(等)];心爱的人. *May I not do what I will with my ~?* 我自己的东西难道不能随意处理吗? *May I have it for my (very) ~?* 我可以拿它当做我自己专有的东西吗? *My ~ did not believe it.* 连我家里的人也不相信. *And his ~ received him not.* 他的家属也不容他. *my ~* (我的)乖乖〔爱称〕. ***come into one's ~*** 取得属于自己的财产[东西];获得应有的名誉[信用等]. ***do it on one's ~*** 照自己的意思[由自己负责]做事. ***get (a bit of) one's ~ back*** 〔口〕雪耻,报仇. ***hold one's ~*** 坚持自己立场,固守立场,不屈服(*The patient is holding his ~.* 病人还照常支持). ***love (truth) for its ~ sake*** 为(真理)而爱(真理). ***of one's ~*** 自己的,自己所有的(*She had never had a room of her ~.* 她从来没有自己的住房). ***on one's ~ (account)*** 〔俚〕独自地;独立地;凭自己力量;主动地;自愿地. ***with one's ~ eye*** 亲眼(看见).

own[2] [əun] *vt.* ①有;拥有;持有. ②承认(是…的作者、父亲、所有人,…的价值、真实等). ③顺受;服从. *a hat that nobody will ~.* 一顶无人认领的帽子. *He ~s that he has done wrong. = He ~s himself in the wrong. = He ~s his own fault.* 他承认他错了. *He ~s himself beaten.* 他认输了. — *vi.* 承认,自白. ~ **to** 承认,自白(*He ~s to the theft.* 他承认偷东西了). ~ ***up*** 〔口〕爽爽快快承认;坦白(*You'd better ~ up.* 你还是爽爽快快地承认为好. ~ *up to a fault* 痛痛快快地承认过失).

own·er [ˈəunə] *n.* 物主,所有人;【商】货主;〔海军俚〕舰长. *a house-~* 房主. *an ~ of lost property* 失主. *an ~-driver* 驾驶自备汽车的人. ***at ~s risk*** 风险由物主负责. ***the ~*** 〔海俚〕船主. **~-occupier** *n.* 〔主英〕住用自己房屋的人,业主. **~ship** *n.* 物主身分,所有;所有权;所有制(*individual ~ship* 个体所有制. *socialist ~ship by the whole people and collective ~ship* 社会主义的全民所有制和集体所有制).

ox [ɔks] *n.* (*pl.* ***ox·en*** [ˈɔksən]) 公牛,阉公牛;(一般的)牛〔不分性别的通称〕;牛属动物. ★ *cf.* bull, cow, steer; 〔其他的牛〕bullock, calf, heifer.

ox·ac·il·lin [ɔkˈsæsilin] *n.* 【药】青霉素P-12,新青霉素.

ox·a·late [ˈɔksəleit] *n.* 【化】草酸盐[酯],乙二酸盐.

ox·al·ic [ɔkˈsælik] *a.* 酢浆草的,采白浆草的. ~ **acid** 【化】草酸,乙二酸.

ox·a·lis [ˈɔksəlis] *n.* 【植】酢浆草.

ox·a·zine [ˈɔksəziːn, -zin] *n.* 【化】嗯嗪;氧氮杂芑.

ox·blood [ˈɔksblʌd] *n.* 深红色.

ox·bow [ˈɔksbəu] *n.* 〔美〕U 字形牛颈弯;(河流的)U 字形弯曲,河套(地区).

Ox·bridge [ˈɔksbridʒ] *n.*, *a.* 牛津及剑桥大学(的).

ox·en [ˈɔksən] ox 的复数.

ox·eye [ˈɔksai] *n.* ①(人的)大眼睛. ②【植】牛眼菊;春白菊. ~ **daisy** 【植】春白菊,滨菊,法兰西菊. **ox-eyed** *a.* 眼睛大的.

Oxf. = Oxford.

ox·fence [ˈɔksfens] *n.* (外围常有壕沟的坚固的)牛栏.

Ox·ford [ˈɔksfəd] *n.* ①牛津〔英国城市,牛津大学所在地〕. ②(英国)牛津(大学). ③〔*pl.* 通例 o-〕〔美〕= ~ shoes. ④〔通例 o-〕= ~ gray. ~ **accent** 装腔作势的口音. ~ **bags [trousers]** 〔英〕宽大的裤子. ~ **blue** 紫蓝色. ~**don** 牛津大学教授. ~**frame** 〔英〕井字形画框. ~ **gray** 深灰色. ~**man** 牛津大学受教育[出身]的人. ~ **movement** 牛津运动〔在英国教会中复活天主教教义与仪式的运动,约在 1833 年发生于牛津大学,亦作 Tractarianism〕. ~ **shirt [shirting]** 细条纹衬衫[料]. ~ **shoes** (系带浅口)牛津式便鞋.

Ox·ford·shire [ˈɔksfədʃiə] *n.* 牛津郡〔英格兰中南部的一郡,首府为 Oxford〕.

ox·head [ˈɔkshed] *n.* 〔俚〕笨人,傻子.

ox·heart [ˈɔkshɑːt] *n.* 牛心樱桃〔一种心形大樱桃〕.

ox·herd [ˈɔkshəːd] *n.* 牧牛人.

ox·hide [ˈɔkshaid] *n.* 牛皮.

ox·id [ˈɔksid] *n.* 〔罕〕= oxide.

ox·i·dant [ˈɔksidənt] *n.* 氧化剂.

ox·i·dase [ˈɔksideis, -deiz] *n.* 氧化酶. **-da·sic** [-ˈdeisik, -zik] *a.*

ox·i·date [ˈɔksideit] *vt.* 使氧化.

ox·i·da·tion [ˌɔksiˈdeiʃən] *n.* 【化】氧化(作用),正化. ~ **reduction** *n.* 氧化还原作用.

ox·ide [ˈɔksaid] *n.* 【化】氧化物. *antimony ~* 锑白,氧化锑. *deuterium ~* 重水,氧化氘. *mercuric ~* 氧化汞. *nitric ~* 一氧化一氮.

ox·i·dize [ˈɔksidaiz] *vt.* 【化】①使氧化;使生锈. ②使脱氢(尤指由于氧的作用). ③使增加原子价;使(原子、离子)除去电子. — *vi.* 氧化;生锈. ~*d silver* 氧化银. *an oxidizing agent* 氧化剂. **-diz·a·ble** *a.* **-diz·a·tion** [ˌɔksidaiˈzeiʃən] *n.*

ox·i·di·zer [ˈɔksidaizə] *n.* 【化】氧化剂.

ox·ime [ˈɔksiːm, -sim] *n.* 【化】肟.

ox·im·e·ter [ɔkˈsimitə] *n.* 【医】血氧定量计.

ox·lip [ˈɔkslip] *n.* 【植】高报春.

Oxon. = ①Oxfordshire. ②Oxonian.

Ox·o·ni·an [ɔkˈsəunjən] *a.* 牛津 (Oxford) (大学)的. — *n.* ①(英国)牛津人,牛津居民. ②牛津大学的学生[毕业生]. ③= Oxford shoes.

ox·o·ni·um [ɔkˈsəunjəm] *n.* 【化】鎓.

ox·peck·er [ˈɔkspekə] *n.* 非洲啄牛鸦.

ox·tail [ˈɔksteil] *n.* 牛尾 (尤指做牛尾汤等用的牛尾).

ox·ter [ˈɔkstə] *n.* 〔*Scot.* 英方〕胳肢窝.

ox·tongue [ˈɔkstʌŋ] *n.* 〔废〕牛舌草属 *(Anchusa)* 植物.

oxy- *comb. f.* ①表示"敏锐,尖锐": *oxy*cephalic. ②表示"氧化": *oxy*chloride.

ox·y·a·cet·y·lene [ˈɔksiəˈsetiliːn] *a.* 【化】氧乙炔的. ~ ***blowpipe*** 氧乙炔吹管.

ox·y·ac·id [ˌɔksiˈæsid] *n.* 【化】含氧酸,羟基酸.

ox·y·carp·ous [ˌɔksiˈkɑːpəs] *a.* 【植】尖刺果的.

ox·y·ceph·a·ly [ˌɔksiˈsefəli] *n.* 【解】尖头. **-phal·ic** [-ˈfælik] **-ceph·a·lous** [-ˈsefələs] *a.*

ox·y·chlo·ride [ˌɔksiˈklɔːraid] *n.* 【化】氯氧化物.

ox·y·gen [ˈɔksidʒən] *n.* 【化】氧,氧气. ~ **acid** = oxyacid 含氧酸. ~ **helmet** (潜水、防火等用的)氧(气)帽. ~ **mask** 氧(气)面罩. ~ **tent** 氧气帐〔罩住病床的透明帐罩,往里输氧,以助病人呼吸〕.

ox·y·gen·ate [ɔkˈsidʒineit] *vt.* 【化】用氧处理,使和氧化合,充氧于. ~*d water* 充氧水,过氧化氢水. **-a·tion** [ɔkˌsidʒiˈneiʃən] *n.* 【化】用氧处理,氧化,充氧(作用).

ox·y·gen·ic [ˌɔksiˈdʒenik], **ox·yg·e·nous** [ɔkˈsidʒənəs] *a.* 氧的;含氧的;似氧的;生氧的.

ox·y·gen·ize [ˈɔksidʒinaiz] *vt.* 【化】= oxygenate.

ox·y·hem·o·glo·bin [ˌɔksiˈhiːməˌgləubin] *n.* 【生化】氧合血红蛋白.

ox·y-house-gas [ˈɔksiˈhausˈgæs] *a.* = oxy-paraffin.

ox·y·hy·dro·gen [ˈɔksiˈhaidrədʒən] *a.* 【化】氢氧的. — *n.* 氢氧,氧氢. ~ **blowpipe** 氢氧吹管. ~ **flame** 氢氧焰.
ox·y·mo·ron [ˌɔksiˈmɔːrɔn] *n.* 【修】矛盾修饰法(例: *a wise fool, cruel kindness*).
ox·y·o·pi·a [ˌɔksiˈəupiə] *n.* 【医】视觉锐敏.
ox·y·par·af·fin [ˈɔksiˈpærəfin] *a.* (火焰)燃气与氧混合产生的.
ox·y·path·or [ˈɔksipæθə] *n.* 氧治疗器.
ox·y·phil [ˈɔksifil] *n.* ①易受酸性感染〔如嗜酸细胞,嗜酸物等〕. (= acidophil) ②嗜酸 (= acidophil, oxyphile). **-ic** *a.*
ox·y·salt [ˈɔksisɔːlt] *n.* 【化】含氧盐.
ox·y·sul·fide [ˈɔksiˈsʌlfaid] *n.* 氧硫化物,氧代硫化物.
ox·y·tet·ra·cy·cline [ˈɔksiˌtetrəˈsaiklin, -klain] *n.* 【药】氧四环素;土霉素.
ox·y·to·cic [ˌɔksiˈtəusik, ˈtɔsik] *a.* 催产的〔如催产素剂〕. — *n.* 催产素.
ox·y·to·cin [ˌɔksiˈtəusin, -ˈtɔsin] *n.* 【生化】后叶催产素.
ox·y·tone [ˈɔksitəun] *a., n.* 【希腊语法】末一音节上有重读的(词).
oy·er [ˈɔiə] *n.* 【法】(刑事案件的)听审,审判;要求听审. ~ ***and terminer*** ①听讼裁判庭令状〔本义为"听讼并裁判",系英国发给巡回法官等的令状中的用语〕;听讼裁判庭. ②从前美国若干州的高等刑事法庭.
o·yes, o·yez [əuˈjes, -z] *int.* 听! 静听! 肃静! 〔促人注意,普通喊三次〕.
oys·ter [ˈɔistə] *n.* ①蠔,牡蛎. ②鸡背肉. ③〔俚〕极少开口的人. ④可以从中取得个人好处的东西. ***an ~ of a man*** 极少开口的人. ***as close as an ~*** 嘴紧得很,不会漏话. ***as dumb as an ~*** 极少说话. ***The world is sb's ~.*** 人生最得意〔最有前途〕的时刻. ~ **bank [bed, farm, field]** 牡蛎塘,养牡蛎场. ~ **bar** 蠔肉菜馆. ~**bird**, ~ **catcher** 蛎鹬. ~ **crab** 豆蟹科 (Pinnotheridae) 动物. ~ **cracker** 牡蛎饼干〔小圆咸梳打饼干与燉牡蛎汤一起吃〕. ~**-diver** 〔美俚〕洗盘子的人. ~ **knife** 撬蠔刀. ~**man** 〔主美〕采牡蛎人,卖牡蛎人;采牡蛎船. ~ **patty** 蠔肉点心. ~ **plant** 〔美〕【植】婆罗门参. ~ **rake** 牡蛎耙子〔一种用于浅水中捞取牡蛎的长把弯齿耙子〕. ~ **saloon** 〔美〕蠔肉菜馆. ~**shell** ① *n.* 牡蛎壳碎粉. ② *vt.* 使(自己)关起门过日子. ~ **stew** 牡蛎燉菜. ~ **tongs** 采牡蛎用的挖具. ~ **white** 灰乳色,牡蛎色.
oz., oz = ounce(s).
Oz·a·lid [ˈɔzəlid] "奥萨里德"晒图机〔直接从原图或印刷品进行正面晒图的机器商标名〕. — *n.* 奥萨里德晒图.
O·zark [ˈəuzɑːk] *n.* 〔美〕密苏里 (Missouri) 州奥扎克族印第安人〔以弓术出名〕;密苏里州的别名;〔*pl.*〕密苏里州西南、阿肯色 (Arkansas) 州西北和俄克拉何马 (Oklahoma) 州东北部的高地.
o·zo·ce·rite, o·zok·e·rite [əuˈzəukərit] *n.* 【矿】地蜡,石蜡.
o·zone [ˈəuzəun, əuˈz-] *n.* ①【化】臭氧. ②〔喻〕爽心怡神的力量;〔口〕新鲜空气. ~ **layer** 臭氧层〔距地球表面20—40英里的高温层〕. ~ **paper** 臭氧纸.
o·zon·ic [əuˈzɔnik], **o·zo·nous** [ˈəuzəunəs] *a.* 臭氧的;似臭氧的;含臭氧的.
o·zon·ide [ˈəuzəunaid] *n.* 【化】臭氧化物.
o·zon·ize [ˈəuzənaiz] *vt.* 对…作臭氧处理,使含臭氧,使(氧)臭氧化. **-r** *n.* 臭氧化器.
o·zo·nom·e·ter [ˌəuzəˈnɔmitə] *n.* 【化】臭氧计.
o·zo·no·sphere [əuˈzəunəsfiə] *n.* 【气】臭氧层 (= ozone layer).
ozs., ozs = ounces.
o·zos·to·mi·a [ˌəuzɔsˈtəumiə] *n.* 口臭.
Oz·zie [ˈɔziː] *n.* 〔美〕澳大利亚兵.

P

P,p [piː] ***(pl. P's, p's*** [piːz]***)*** ①英语字母表的第十六个字母. ②P字形(物). ③〔P〕【象棋】pawn 的符号. ④〔P〕【植】亲本,【动】亲代 (parental generation) 的符号. ⑤〔P〕【化】phosphorus 的符号. ⑥〔P〕【物】压力,压强 (pressure) 的符号. ⑦〔p〕【物】质子,氕核 (proton) 的符号. ***be p and q*** 上等. ***mind [be on] one's P's and Q's*** 谨言慎行,循规蹈矩.
P., p. = ①pastor. ②post. ③power. ④president. ⑤pressure. ⑥priest. ⑦prince. ⑧page. ⑨part. ⑩participle. ⑪past. ⑫penny. ⑬per. ⑭pint. ⑮pole. ⑯population. ⑰pro. ⑱〔It.〕【乐】*piano.* ⑲park. ⑳progressive. ㉑pipe.
PA 〔美〕= Petroleum Administration 石油管理局.
P.A. = ①Press Association; Prosecuting Attorney〔美〕检查官. ②particular average【保险】单独海损. ③press agent 新闻业经理人,新闻广告员. ④power of attorney 委托书,代理权. Press Association, Limited〔英〕报纸联合社. ⑤Purchasing Agent 采购员.
Pa = protactinium【化】镤.
pa [pɑː] *n.* 〔口、儿〕爸〔papa 之略〕.
Pa. = Pennsylvania.
p.a. = ①participial adjective【语法】分词形容词. ②〔L.〕*per annum* 每年.
PAA = Pan American World Airways〔美〕泛美航空公司.
pa·'an·ga [pəˈɑːŋgɑː] *n.* 邦加〔汤加货币单位〕.
PAB; Pab 〔美〕= Petroleum Administration Board〔美〕石油管理委员会.
PAB·A, pab·a [ˈpæbə] = para-aminobenzoic acid 对氨基苯(甲)酸〔解毒药〕.
pab·u·lum [ˈpæbjuləm] *n.* ①食品,养料,食粮;精神食粮. ②柴;燃料. ③单调乏味的文章. *mental ~* 精神食粮〔书籍等〕.
pac [pæk] *n.* ①一种高统鹿皮靴;油皮鞋. ②派克靴〔一种保温防水系带高统靴〕.
P.A.C. = Political Action Committee〔美〕政治行动委员会.
Pac., Pacif. = Pacific.
pac·a [ˈpækə, ˈpɑːkə] *n.* 【动】(中美、南美产)天竺鼠.
pace [peis] *n.* ①步,一步;步子;步幅〔2.5—3英尺〕. ②步态;步调;步速;速度;进度;【棒球】(投手的)球速. ③(文章等笔法的)流畅. ④溜蹄〔马把同一边的两蹄同时并举的步法〕. ⑤【建】梯台,楼梯平台. ⑥〔*pl.*〕(才能等的)显示. *the geometrical [great] ~* 50—60 英寸的步子. *the military [regulation] ~*【军】标准步幅,25—30英寸的步子. *the Roman ~* 约58英寸的步子. *a double-*

time ～ 跑步. *a quick [great]* ～ 快步. *a rattling* ～ (走得格格响的)快步. *an olderman's* ～ 大大方方的步子. *the* ～ *of the table* 【台球】球台的弹性. ***at a foot's*** ～ 用平常步速. ***at a good*** ～ 相当快地; 活泼地. ***at a snail's*** ～ 爬行, 慢吞吞地走. ***do not keep*** ～ ***with*** 跟不上; 和…不相称[适应]. ***go [hit] the*** ～ ①飞快前进, 急驶. ②〔喻〕过享乐生活; 挥霍. ***go through one's*** ～***s*** 显示才能, 显身手. ***hold [keep]*** ～ ***with*** 跟…齐步前进[并驾齐驱]; 向…看齐; 适应. ***mend one's*** ～ 加快步子, 赶. ***off the*** ～ 跑在为首者之后. ***put a horse [sb.] through his*** ～***s*** 试马的步子; 考察人的能力, 使人经受考验, 试验某人是否合用. ***set [make] the*** ～ *(for)* ①(给…)作步调示范; 定出速率; 树立榜样. ②领先, 带头. ③调整速率. ***show one's*** ～***s*** (马)显示步法[速度]; (人)显示本领. ***try sb.'s*** ～***s*** 试某人本领. — *vi.* ①慢慢地走, 踱; (马)溜蹄走. ②〔美〕(在比赛中)继续领先. — *vt.* ①踱步于. ②步测(距离) *(off* 或 *out)*. ③为…定步速; 为…的标兵; 和…并速前进. ④使(马)练步法. ～ *up and down the corridor* 在走廊里踱来踱去. ～ *it* 走, 踱. ～ *a room* 在室内踱步. ～**making** *n., a.* 定步速(的); 当标兵(的).

pa·ce [ˈpeisi] *prep.* 〔L.〕 对不起[陈述反对意见前的客套语]. ～ *Mr. Smith* 对不起史密斯先生(可是…). ～ *tua* [ˈtjuːei] 对不起(你)[请原谅, 冒昧得很](可是…).

-paced [peist] *a.* ①…步的, 步子…的〔用以构成复合词〕. ②步测的. ③(赛马中)定了步速的. ④节奏均匀的. *slow-*～ 慢步的.

pace·mak·er [ˈpeismeikə] *n.* ①(赛跑等的)领跑人, 带步人; 定步速者, 标兵; 样板; 引导者. ②【军】整速舰; 【医】电子起搏器; 【解】起搏点[网].

pac·er [ˈpeisə] *n.* ①慢行者; 步测者; 溜蹄的马. ②= pacemaker.

pace·set·ter [ˈpeisˌsetə] *n.* = pacemaker ①.

pa·cha [ˈpɑːʃə, pəˈʃɑː] *n.* = pasha.

pa·cha·lic [ˈpɑːʃəlik] *a.* = pashalic.

pa·chin·ko [pəˈtʃiŋkəu] *n.* 〔Jap.〕弹球盘〔日本赌具〕.

pa·chu·co [pəˈtʃuːkəu] *n. (pl. -cos)* 〔Mex. Sp.〕花衣墨西哥人〔社会地位低下的墨西哥裔美国人, 以好穿花衣和文身为特殊标记〕.

pachy- *comb.f.* 厚, 厚度; 浓厚: *pachy*derm.

pach·y·derm [ˈpækidəːm] *n.* ①厚皮动物〔象、犀、河马等〕. ②〔喻〕厚脸皮的人; 精神麻木的人. **-der·ma·tous** [ˌpækiˈdəːmətəs] **-der·mous** [ˌpækiˈdəːməs] *a.* 皮厚的; 感觉迟钝的.

pach·y·rhi·zus [ˌpækiˈraizəs] *n.* 【植】豆薯, 凉薯, 地瓜.

pach·y·san·dra [ˌpækiˈsændrə] *n.* 【植】富贵草属*(Pachysandra)* 植物.

Pacif. = Pacific.

pa·cif·ic [pəˈsifik] *a.* ①和平的, 太平的; 平时的. ②爱好和平的, (性质)温和的. ③〔P-〕太平洋的. *mild* ～ *breezes* 温和的微风. ***the P- (Ocean)*** 太平洋. ***the P-slope*** 〔美〕太平洋沿岸各州〔*Sierra Nevada* 及 *Sierra Madre* 以西〕. ～ **blockade** 【国际法】平时封锁. **P-(Standard) Time** 太平洋标准时间〔比格林威治时间晚八小时〕. **-i·cal·ly** *ad.*

pa·cif·i·cate [pəˈsifikeit] *vt.* ①平定; 绥靖. ②抚慰.

pac·i·fi·ca·tion [ˌpæsifiˈkeiʃən] *n.* ①平定; 绥靖. ②媾和(条约), 和约. *ihe P- Guards* 靖卫团.

pa·cif·i·ca·tor [pəˈsifikeitə] *n.* ①调解人. ②平定者.

pa·cif·i·ca·to·ry [pəˈsifikətəri, pəˈsifikeitəri] *a.* ①和解的, 媾和的. ②平定的. ③安抚的.

pac·i·fic·ism [pəˈsifisizəm] *n.* = pacifism.

pac·i·fic·ist [pəˈsifisist] *n.* = pacifist *(n.)*.

pac·i·fi·er [ˈpæsifaiə] *n.* ①平定者. ②使和解人. ③抚慰者. ④(哄小孩的)橡皮奶头.

pac·i·fism [ˈpæsifizəm] *n.* ①和平主义; 绥靖主义. ②消极态度.

pac·i·fist [ˈpæsifist] ① *n.* 和平主义者; 绥靖主义者. ②持消极态度者. ③ *a.* = pacifistic.

pac·i·fis·tic [ˌpæsiˈfistic] *a.* 和平主义的; 绥靖主义的; 持消极态度的.

pac·i·fy [ˈpæsifai] *vt., vi.* ①抚慰; 使镇静. ②平定, 平息; 绥靖; 使安定. ～ *a crying child* 安慰哭闹的孩子. ～ *a commotion* 平定骚乱.

pack[1] [pæk] *vt.* 安插[挑选]自己人充任(委员等); 拉拢, 收买. ～ *a committee* 纠集自己人充实委员会. ～ ***cards with*** 共谋, 串通. — *vi.* 共谋; 串通作弊.

pack[2] [pæk] *n.* ①包, 捆; 行李; 驮子. ②巴克〔一包货物的标准包装量, 如羊毛为 240 磅, 亚麻纱为 60,000 码〕; (一季或一年中鱼、水果等的)包装量[装罐量]. ③一堆; 集合; 大量, 大堆. ④(纸牌等)一组, 一副; (狼等的)一群, (歹人等的)一伙. ⑤积冰, 浮冰 (= pack-ice). ⑥【橄榄球】全体前锋. ⑦【医】(水疗法的)湿布(等); (包裹疗法用的)裹布; 冰袋; 包扎. ⑧【军】背包; 驮包; 驮载; 降落伞包. ⑨〔美〕罐头食品. ⑩【商】包装; 容器. ⑪【电】单元; 部件, 组合件. ⑫【摄】一叠装到照相机内的散页软片, 软片包; 一组同时曝光的彩色软片[硬片]. *a* ～ *of cigarettes* 一包[一箱]香烟. *Wolves hunt in large* ～*s.* 狼成群觅食. *It is all a* ～ *of troubles.* 尽是疙瘩事情. *a* ～ *of lies* 一片谎言. *a* ～ *of radium* 镭源. *a power* ～ 动力装置; 电源组; 供电部分. ***spend [eat] the*** ～〔俚〕耗尽所有. — *vt.* ①包, 把…打包, 包装; 把…包成一捆; 〔美〕把…装罐头. ②装填, 填塞, 填满(空隙) *(with)*. ③压紧; 集中, 收集; 使成一群[一组、一副]. ④把…打发走; 解雇 *(off)*. ⑤【医】(用裹布)包裹. ⑥使(牲口)驮. ⑦〔美西部〕把…(打成包)运输. ⑧〔美〕备有; 配有. ⑨〔俚〕(拳击时)猛击(一拳). *The car was* ～*ed with passengers.* 车里挤满了乘客. ～ *clothes into a trunk [*～ *a trunk with clothes]* 把衣服装箱. ～ *a donkey* 让驴子驮货. ～ *a gun* 带着枪. *Meat* ～*ed in cans.* 罐头肉. — *vi.* ①包装, 打包. ②(牲口)驮货; 停止活动[工作]. ③变结实. ④能(被)包装; 做包装(运输)生意. ⑤(被解雇后)匆匆忙忙走掉 *(off, away)*. ⑥聚集; 成群; 挤. *We must* ～ *up and get ready to start.* 我们得打好行李准备动身了. *Ground* ～*s after a rain.* 雨后地面板结. ～ ***a punch*** 【美棒球】有打击力. ～ ***a real wallop*** = ～ ***a terrific punch*** 〔美拳〕猛打; 有厉害的拳头. ～ ***away [off]*** ①辞退, 解雇. ②慌慌张张走掉. ～ ***'em in*** 〔美〕(戏院)超额满座. ～ ***in*** 停止. ～ ***it in*** 〔俚〕①结束; 承认失败. ②充分利用有利条件. ～ ***it up*** 〔口〕结束, 停止; 别讲下去了! ～ ***mustard*** 〔美俚〕砖头、灰泥等的搬运. ～ ***(on) all sail*** 扯满全部风帆. ～ ***oneself off*** (被解雇的人等)包好自己的东西匆匆走掉. ～ ***up*** ①把…打成包; 打包. ②捆好东西, 收拾行李. ③解雇; 〔俚〕(机器)出故障; 停止运转. ④〔口〕收拾工具, 下班. ⑤〔俚〕死. ***send*** *(sb.)* ～***ing*** 〔美俚〕解雇, 辞退, 撵走, 叫某人立即卷铺盖. — *a.* ①搬运用的; 由驮运牲畜组成的. ②装满了的, 填满了的. ③包装用的. ④〔主 Scot.〕驯良的, 亲切的. *a* ～ *train* 一队驮运东西的牲口. ～ **animal** 驮子, 驮畜. ～ **cloth** 包装布. ～**-drill** 【军】驮载教练; 带着全副武装往返行走〔旧军队中一种处罚〕. ～**-horse** 驮马. 〔喻〕做苦工的人. ～**house** 仓库, 堆栈; 食品加工包装厂. ～ **ice** 积冰; 浮冰. ～**-jammed** *a.* 〔美〕挤满的, 客满的. ～ **load** 驮载量. ～**man** 小贩, 负贩. ～ **needle** 打包针. ～**plane** 主货舱可以拆卸的飞机. ～ **rat** 〔美〕①狐尾大林鼠. ②旅馆的搬行李工人, 侍应生. ③小偷; 陌生人; 不可靠的人. ～ **rope** 打包绳. ～**sack** 旅行背包. ～**saddle** 驮鞍. ～**-staff** 搬货工人用的支杖 *(as plain as a* ～*staff* 极明显的). ～**thread** (包扎用的)粗线; 双股线, 缝线. ～ **twine** (包扎用的)麻线. **-ed** ① *a.* 充满[塞满]…的〔常用以构成复合词〕. ②压结实的. ③挤得满满的, 满座的.

pack·age [ˈpækidʒ] *n.* ①包装, 包扎. ②〔主美〕包, 包裹, 捆, 束, 组; (产品等的)(一)件, 件头. ③包装用物; (包装用的)管壳, 外壳. ④(标准)部件, 组件; 机组; 综合

P

设备;【自】插件;【无】晶体管外壳. ⑤包装费,打包费. ⑥整套的广播[电视]节目. ⑦[俚](罪犯的)前科. ⑧(工会争取到的)合同上的利益〔如退休金、劳保福利等〕. *a guidance* ~【火箭】导引装置部件. — *a.* 一揽子的. *a* ~ *deal* 一揽子交易. *a* ~ *plan* 一揽子计划. — *vt.* ①〔美〕把…打包[装箱]. ②给(商品)加漂亮包装(以吸引顾客). ③把…作为整体提出[推销]. ~ **holiday [tour]** 由旅行社代办的旅行. ~ **store** 瓶装酒小卖店〔所售酒仅供顾客带走外饮〕. **packaging** *n.* (效率高而美观的)包装法;打包.

pack·er [ˈpækə] *n.* ①包装者;打包工;打包商;〔主美〕罐头食品批发商,罐头食品工人. ②〔美方〕赶牲口运货的人;〔澳〕驮子,驮畜. ③打包机. ④(打牌等)作弊的人. ⑤〔美〕(车站等处)搬行李工. **-y** 包装工厂.

pack·et [ˈpækit] *n.* ①包裹;小件行李;(邮件等的)一捆;小批;袋. ②(定期)邮船,班轮. ③〔英俚〕(打赌等中输赢的)大笔钱. ④〔英俚〕倒霉的事. *a* ~ *of letters* 一捆信. *a postal* ~ 邮包. ***a surprise*** ~ 内容出人意料的小包;〔喻〕意想不到的事. ***buy a*** ~ 〔英俚〕被杀. ***catch [cop, stop] a*** ~ 被子弹打死,负重伤,负伤. ***get a*** ~ 受大损失. ***sell sb. a*** ~ 〔俚〕向人扯谎. — *vt.* ①把…作成包裹. ②用邮船运送. ~**boat [~ship, ~-vessel]** 邮船;班船. ~ **day** 邮船开船日;邮件截止日.

pack·ing [ˈpækiŋ] *n.* ①包装,打包,打行李,包扎;包装材料,包装用品;包装法. ②(缝隙)填料〔旧棉絮等〕. ③〔美〕食品加工业;罐头业. ④【机】衬垫;【建】灌筑. ⑤(电视)图象压缩. ⑥〔美〕兵士的口粮;食物. ⑦【医】包扎法;塞法. ⑧集合. *a* ~ *mat* 草包. *the* ~ *industry* 〔美〕食品加工业;罐头工业. ~**box**, ~**case** 货箱;【机】垫料箱. ~ **charges** 打包费. ~ **fraction** ①【化】紧束分数. ②【物】敛集率. ~ **house** 〔美〕牲畜屠宰加工厂;食品加工厂. ~ **needle** 打包针. ~ **paper** 包装纸;【机】垫纸,纸垫. ~ **piece** 垫片. ~ **plant** = ~ **house**. ~ **press** 打包机,压缩机. ~ **sheet** 包装布,包装纸;【医】(水疗法用的)湿布;填齿片.

pack·tong [ˈpækˈtɔn] *n.* = paktong.

pact [pækt] *n.* ①合同,契约. ②盟约;公约;条约. *a peace* ~ 和平条约.

pac·tion [ˈpækʃən] *n.* 〔Scot.〕= pact.

pad[1] [pæd] *n.* ①(防摩擦用的)衬垫,垫料,填料,缓冲物;鞍褥. ②束,捆;小块. ③(能一张一张扯用的)便条本子[吸墨纸本等]. ④(动物的)肉趾;(狐、兔、狼等的)脚;〔美〕(水生植物的)大浮叶. ⑤【海】甲板垫木,(船头的)护船木. ⑥(打球时戴的)护胫[护胸等]. ⑦(钟表的)鳌尖;【机】缓冲器;把手,柄;【电讯】衰减器;(火箭等的)发射台. ⑧绣花线. ⑨〔美俚〕床;房间;公寓. ⑩打印台,印色盒(= stamp ~);墨滚. ⑪(简易机场的)起落地带. ⑫〔美俚〕吸毒窝[娼妓窝等]. *a blotting* ~ 吸墨纸本. *a writing* ~ 信纸簿. *a drawing* ~ 图画纸簿. *a launch(ing)* ~ 【火箭】发射台. ~ *money* 〔美卑〕宿费. ~ *duty* 〔谑〕睡觉. ***hit [knock] the*** ~ 〔美军俚〕上床睡觉. — *vt.* ①填,装填,填塞;在(衣内)装棉花;在(疯人室墙上)装软垫;在(鞍上)铺垫褥,衬塞;(用不必要的材料)拉长,铺张(文章),给…加补白. ②粘连(纸边)(以便一张一张撕下). ③用定色机染,浸染,轧染. ④浮报(名额);虚报(帐目). ⑤减弱…的声音,使(声音)变沉闷. *a cotton-padded coat* 棉袄. ~ *one's age* 虚报年龄.

pad[2] [pæd] *n.* ①〔英方〕路. ②〔罕〕拦路贼,路劫盗. ③慢步而行的马(=~-nag). ④(脚步等的)叭嗒叭嗒声. ***a gentleman [knight, squire] of the*** ~ 拦路强盗. — *vt.* 走(路). —*vi.* 步行;轻步慢行[跑]. ~ ***it*** =~ ***the hoof*** 〔俚〕步行;跋涉;徒步走去.

pad[3] [pæd] *n.* (量水果、鱼等用的)篮子,篓子.

pa·dauk [pəˈdauk] *n.* 紫檀木〔产于亚洲和非洲〕.

pad·ding [ˈpædiŋ] *n.* ①填充,填塞,装填. ②填料,芯. ③(报纸杂志等的)补白. ④定色药[法]. ⑤(文章等的)铺张.

pad·dle[1] [ˈpædl] *n.* ①(短而阔的)桨;桨状物;(轮船等的)蹼轮;桨板;搅棒;捣衣棒;(施杖刑的)板子;(击球用的)球板,球拍. ②【动】(鲸等的)鳍状肢;(蚊蛹的)尾鳍. ③小闸门. ④〔美口〕叭嗒叭嗒的打. — *vi.* ①荡桨. ②(轮船等)用明轮行进. — *vt.* ①用桨划(小船). ②(用划桨的船)运送. ③(用桨状物)搅打;〔美口〕叭嗒叭嗒地打. ~ ***one's own canoe*** 靠自己;管自己的事. ~**-board** 浮板. ~**-fish** 【动】匙吻鲟;白鲟. ~ **steamer** 明轮船. ~**-wheel** 蹼轮;(轮船的)明轮.

pad·dle[2] [ˈpædl] *vi.* ①涉水;用脚玩水;用手划水. ②〔古〕摆弄,抚弄 *(in; on; about)*. ③(小孩)趔趔趄趄地走.

pad·dle foot [ˈpædlfut] *(pl.* ***pad·dle feet*** [ˈpædlfiːt]*)* 〔美俚〕①步兵. ②空军地勤人员.

pad·dock[1] [ˈpædək] *n.* ①(练马用的)围场;(马房附近的)牧场. ②【矿】(井口附近的)矿石临时堆放场地. ③〔澳〕围起来的土地. — *vt.* ①把…关入围场. ②临时堆集(矿石).

pad·dock[2] [ˈpædək] *n.* 〔古、方〕蟾蜍;蛙.

Pad·dy [ˈpædi] *n.* ①Patrick〔男子名〕和 Patricia〔女子名〕的昵称;〔口〕爱尔兰人的绰号. ②〔p-〕〔英口〕= paddywhack. ③〔俚〕警察. ~ **wag(g)on** 〔美俚〕巡逻车;囚车. ~**'s hurricane** 绝对无风. ~**'s land** 爱尔兰. ~**'s lantern** 月亮.

pad·dy [ˈpædi] *n.* 水稻;谷;水稻田. ~**bird** 【鸟】文鸟. ~**field** 水稻田,水田. ~**-rice** 水稻.

pad·dy·whack [ˈpædi*h*wæk] *n.* 〔口〕①〔英〕大怒. ②〔美〕痛打,揍;打屁股. ③〔P-〕〔俚〕爱尔兰人.

Pa·di·sha(h) [ˈpædiʃɑː] *n.* ①君主,大帝〔伊朗的 Shah, 土耳其的 Sultan, (旧印度所称的)英国国王〕. ②〔p-〕〔口〕有权势的人物.

pad·lock [ˈpædlɔk] *n.* 挂锁,扣锁. — *vt.* ①用挂锁锁;把…上锁. ②正式关闭(公共场所等). **-ed** *a.* 〔美〕(剧院等)奉当局命令关掉的.

pa·dre [ˈpɑːdri] *n.* 〔*Sp., Pg.*〕①(意、西、葡和拉美等国的)神父,教士. ②〔俚〕随军牧师.

pa·dro·ne [pəˈdrəuni] *n.* *(pl.* ***-dro·ni*** [-niː], ~***s)*** 〔It.〕①主人;(地中海贸易船的)船主. ②*(pl.* ~*s)*〔美〕意大利搬运工人的工头;过去在美国承包意大利移民工人的包工头. ③意大利旅馆老板. ④意大利童丐头.

pad·u·l(a)·soy [ˈpædju(ə)sɔi] *n.* (十八世纪流行的)棱纹花绸(衣服、帘维等). — *a.* 用棱纹花绸制作的.

pae·an [ˈpiːən] *n.* ①(古希腊)对太阳神的赞歌. ②凯歌;欢乐歌,赞美歌. *a* ~ *of victory* 胜利的凯歌.

pae·deu·tics [piːˈdjuːtiks] *n.* 儿童教育学.

pae·di·a·tric [ˌpiːdiˈætrik] *a.* 儿科学的,小儿科的.

pae·di·a·tri·ci·an [ˌpiːdiəˈtriʃən] *n.* 儿科医生[专家].

pae·di·at·rics [ˌpiːdiˈætriks] *n.* 【医】儿科学;小儿科.

pae·di·at·rist [ˌpiːdiˈætrist] *n.* = paediatrician.

pae·d(o)- *comb.f.* 儿童(=child).

pae·do·bap·tism [ˌpiːdəuˈbæptizəm] *n.* 幼儿洗礼.

pae·do·bap·tist [ˌpiːdəuˈbæptist] *n.* 幼儿洗礼论者.

pae·do·gen·e·sis [ˌpiːdəuˈdʒenisis] *n.* 【动】幼体生殖. **-gen·ic** [-ˈdʒenik], **-ge·net·ic** [-dʒiˈnetik] *a.*

pa·el·la [pɑːˈelə; Sp. pɑːˈelja] *n.* 肉菜饭〔一种西班牙菜饭,用大米与鸡、海味等同煮,用番红花调味〕.

pae·on [ˈpiːən] *n.* 〔诗〕(由一个长[重读]音节与三个短[非重读]音节构成的)四音节的韵脚.

pae·o·ny [ˈpiəni] *n.* = peony.

pae·sa·no [paiˈsɑːnəu, -ˈzɑː-] *n.* *(pl.* ***-ni*** [-niː], ~***s)*** 同国人,同胞〔尤指意大利的同国人〕(=paesan).

pa·gan [ˈpeigən] *n.* ①异教徒,邪教徒;偶像信徒;非基督教徒. ②没有宗教信仰的人. — *a.* 异教的,邪教的,异教徒的;非基督教的;无宗教信仰的. **-dom** 〔集合词〕异教徒. **-ish** *a.* 异教徒的;信奉异教的. **-ism** 异教;信奉异教,偶像崇拜. **-ize** *vt., vi.* (使)变成异教徒.

Page [peidʒ] *n.* 佩奇〔姓氏〕.

page[1] [peidʒ] *n.* ①页(略作 p.); 【印】一页版面. ②(报刊的)专页,专栏. ③〔诗〕〔修〕〔常 *pl.*〕纪录,书,年史. ④(值得记的)插话; 事件. *these ~s* 本书. *a ~ of history* 历史的纪录. *a fat ~* 【印】空白多的版面. *a full ~* 【印】没有空白的版面. *the "Literary Legacy" ~* 《文学遗产》栏. — *vt.* 给…标页数,标记…的页码. — *vi.* 翻书页.

page[2] [peidʒ] *n.* ①小听差,小侍从,侍童;〔美〕(侍候国会议员的)服务员. ②王室侍从官员. ③【史】见习骑士. — *vi.* 当听差. — *vt.* ①侍候,给…当听差. ②〔美〕(在旅馆、俱乐部等处)侍者叫名找(人). **~boy** ①做小听差的男孩. ②童花头〔向下卷的齐肩女孩发型〕. **~hood, ~ship** 侍从[听差]的身分[地位].

pag·eant [ˈpædʒənt] *n.* ①赛会,露天表演. ②盛观; (穿着古装等的)壮丽的游行队伍. ③虚饰; 炫耀. ④(有山水、花鸟、人物等的)挂帐,挂布.

pag·eant·ry [ˈpædʒəntri] *n.* ①壮观,盛观. ②赛会,壮丽的游行队伍. ③(暂时性的)彩饰; 夸耀,虚饰.

pag·i·nal, pag·i·nar·y [ˈpædʒinl, -nəri] *a.* (每)页的,逐页对照的. *a ~ translation* 逐页对照的翻译.

pag·i·nate [ˈpædʒineit] *vt.* 给…记页数, 标…的页码.

pag·i·na·tion [ˌpædʒiˈneiʃən] *n.* 页码标记; 页数(号码).

Pa·go Pa·go [ˈpɑːŋəu, ˈpɑːŋəu] 帕果-帕果〔东萨摩亚首府〕.

pa·go·da [pəˈgəudə] *n.* ①塔,宝塔; (卖报纸等的)宝塔式摊子. ②(印度从前使用的)一种金币. **~-tree** ①【植】长成塔状的东方树木; 槐; 榕树 (*a Japanese ~-tree* 槐). ②(白)鸡蛋花. ③〔喻〕(传说中能产金币的)摇钱树 (*shake the ~-tree* 〔谑〕(在印度等地)发了大财).

pa·gu·rid [pəˈgjuərid, ˈpægjurid] *n.* 寄居虫科 (*Paguridae*) 动物; 寄居虫. — *a.* 寄居虫的 (=pagurian).

pah[1] [pɑː] *int.* 哼! 〔表示轻蔑、憎恶等〕.

pah[2] [pɑː] (新西兰的)毛利人 (Maori) 村寨[村庄].

Pah·la·vi [ˈpɑːləviː] *n.* 巴拉维语〔约在公元第三世纪至第八世纪的伊朗语〕(=Pehlevi).

pa·ho·e·ho·e [pɑːˈhəuiˌhəui] *n.* 〔Haw.〕绳状熔岩.

paid [peid] pay 的过去式及过去分词. — *a.* ①有薪金的; 受雇用的. ②已付的,付清的. *all expenses ~.* 一切费用均可报销. *a ~ cash book* 现金支出帐. ***put "~" to*** 〔口〕结束…,了结…. 付清的.

paid-in [ˈpeidin] *a.* (会费等)已缴讫的.

pai·dol·o·gy [peiˈdɔlədʒi] *n.* 儿童学,儿童研究.

paid-up [ˈpeidʌp] *a.* 已付的; 付清的; (股份)已全额结清的.

pail [peil] *n.* 桶,提桶; 一桶的量; 〔美口〕容器. *a ~ of milk* 一桶牛奶. *a dinner-~* 〔美〕饭盒子. **~ful** *n.* 满桶,一桶之量.

pail·lasse [pælˈjæs, ˈpæljæs] *n.* 草荐 (=palliasse).

pail·lette [pælˈjet] *n.* (用于涂珐琅或装饰妇女服装的)闪闪发光的金属片.

pain [pein] *n.* ①痛,疼痛; (精神上的)痛苦,忧虑,烦闷,悲痛 (*opp.* pleasure). ②〔古〕罚,刑罚. ③〔*pl.*〕费心,苦心; 刻苦; 努力; 辛苦. ④〔*pl.*〕产痛,阵痛. ⑤〔美俚〕嫌恶; 讨厌的人[事物]. *I have ~s all over.* 全身疼痛. *a ~ in the head.* 头痛. *It gives me ~ to do so.* 这样做使我痛苦. *No ~s, no gains [profit].* 不劳无获. *~s and penalties* 刑罚. *You may save your ~s.* 你不必费心. ***a ~ in the neck*** 〔美〕讨厌或惹人生气的家伙〔责任、义务〕. ***be an ass for one's ~s*** 徒劳无功. ***be at the ~s of [be at ~s of*** 或 ***take ~s]*** 努力,尽力设法 (*She is at (the) ~s of finding the answers.* 她在努力寻求答案). ***be in*** ~疼痛; 在苦恼中. ***cause [give] (sb.) ~*** 使痛苦. ***feel no ~*** ①不觉得痛. ②【俚】醉倒; 枉费心机. ***for (all) one's ~s*** 作为劳苦的报酬; 〔反〕尽管费尽力气; 费力反而 (*He got little reward for his ~s.* 他白辛苦了. *I got a thrashing for my ~s.* 我费力反而挨了打). ***on [upon, under] ~ of death*** 违则处死. ***spare no ~s*** 全力以赴,不辞劳苦地. ***take (much) ~s*** 费苦心; 尽力 (*He has taken ~s to study the problem.* 他下功夫研究那个问题). ***with great ~s*** 煞费苦心. — *vt.* 使疼痛,使痛苦,使心痛. *Does your tooth ~ you?* 你牙痛吗? — *vi.* 〔口〕痛. *My arm is ~ing.* 我胳膊痛. **-ed** *a.* ①疼痛的. ②苦恼的,伤了感情的 (*a ~ expression* 痛苦的表情). **~-killer** 〔口〕止疼药.

Pain(e) [pein] *n.* 佩恩〔姓氏〕.

pain·ful [ˈpeinful] *a.* ①疼痛的,使痛苦的. ②讨厌的,使人厌烦的. ③费力的,(工作)困难的. 〔古〕细心的,勤勉的. *the ~ labours of lexicographers.* 编词典人的辛苦. *with ~ care* 煞费苦心地. **-ly** *ad.* **-ness** *n.*

pain·less [ˈpeinlis] *a.* 无痛的,没有痛苦的. *~ death* 没有痛苦的死; 善终. **-ly** *ad.* **-ness** *n.*

pains·tak·er [ˈpeinzteikə] *n.* 不辞劳苦的人,苦干的人,勤勉的人.

pains·tak·ing [ˈpeinzteikiŋ] *a.* ①(不辞)劳苦的, 苦干的,辛勤的; 费力的. ②煞费苦心的. *be ~ with one's work* 苦干. — *n.* 苦干,刻苦,煞费苦心. **-ly** *ad.*

paint [peint] *n.* ①颜料; 涂料; 油漆. ②化妆品; 香粉; 口红; 胭脂; (化装用的)油彩. ③彩色; 装饰,虚饰. *powder and ~* 粉和胭脂. *a luminous [phosphorescent] ~* 发光涂料. ***as fresh as ~*** 精神焕发; 强壮的. ***as smart as ~*** 非常漂亮. ***Fresh P-*** 〔美〕= ***Wet ~*** 〔英〕油漆未干! — *vt.* ①(用颜料)画; 描绘; 给…着色. ②给…上油漆,把…涂成(某种颜色). ③涂(化妆品),搽(脂粉). ④(用文字)描写,叙述(事件等); 想象; 装饰. ⑤(用油漆等)涂掉; 覆盖; 〔喻〕粉饰. *She ~s herself thick.* 她脸上的粉搽得厚. *~ a gate green* 把门漆成绿色. *~ defects* 掩饰缺点. — *vi.* ①(用颜料等)绘画; 成画题. ②搽粉[胭脂],化妆. ③〔古〕脸红. *~ in oils [Indian ink, water colours]* 画油画[墨画、水彩画]. ***as ~ed as a picture*** 搽着很厚的粉. ***~ a black [rosy] picture of*** 非常悲观[乐观]地叙述…. ***~ in*** 用颜色突出. ***~ it red*** 〔美俚〕把事物弄得引人注目,描写得天花乱坠. ***~ out*** (用油漆等)涂掉. ***~ sb. black*** 把某人描写成坏蛋; 给某人抹黑 (*He is not so black as he is ~ed.* 他并不象所说的那样坏). ***~ the lily*** 做多余[无益]的事情; 锦上添花. ***~ the town [city] red*** 〔俚〕(多指夜生活中的)狂欢作乐; 闹酒. **~box** 颜料盒. **~brush** ①画笔,画刷; 漆刷,漆帚. ②【植】桔黄山柳菊; 扁萼花. **~ cards** 〔美俚〕有画的扑克牌〔指 K, Q, J 等牌〕. **-less** *a.* 未油漆的.

paint. = painting.

paint·ed [ˈpeintid] *a.* ①画的; 着了色的. ②油漆了的. ③色彩鲜明的. ④搽了脂粉的. ⑤假的,虚饰的. *~ china* 彩釉瓷器. *the P- Desert* 美国亚利桑那州的红土荒地. *a ~ sepulchre* 伪君子. *a ~ woman* 〔美〕妓女. **~ glass** 彩色玻璃. **~ lady** 【动】苎胥〔蝶的一种〕; 【植】红花除虫菊; 波状延龄草.

paint·er[1] [ˈpeintə] *n.* ①画家; 着色者. ②油漆匠. *a lady ~* 女画家. *a ~'s canvas* 画布. *a ~ and decorator* 油漆装饰工. *a ~'s brush* = paintbrush. **~'s colic** 【医】铅中毒绞痛. **-ly** *a.* ①画家(似)的; 油漆匠的. ②美术的,绘画的.

paint·er[2] [ˈpeintə] *n.* 【海】(小船的)缆索; 系船索. *a large [lazy, small] ~* 大[小]缆索. ***cut [slip] the [one's] ~*** ①解开缆索,使漂流. ②〔喻〕使分离; (殖民地等)和宗主国断绝关系,独立. ③破诡计.

paint·er[3] [ˈpeintə] *n.* 【动】美洲狮 (= cougar).

paint·ing [ˈpeitiŋ] *n.* ①绘画; (一张)油画,水彩画. ②画法; 绘画艺术. ③上色,着色; 搽胭脂; 涂漆. ④颜料,油漆,涂料. *traditional Chinese ~* 中国画. **~-room** 画室.

paint·ress [ˈpeintris] *n.* 女画家.

paint·y [ˈpeinti] *a.* ①(画等)着色过度的. ②被颜料[油漆]弄脏的.

pair [pɛə] *n.* (*pl.* ~(*s*)) ①一对,一双,一套,(眼镜等的)

P

一副;(剪子等的)一把,(裤子等的)一条. ②一对男女,未婚夫妇;(动物的)偶. ③系在一起的两匹马. ④【机】对偶,副. ⑤(成对物的)另一方. ⑥(议会)约好互相弃权的对立两派的两个议员;(比赛等中的)两人合伙关系. ⑦(纸牌等)同点子的一对. ⑧〔英方〕(楼梯等的)一段. *a ~ of shoes* 一双鞋. *two ~(s) of trousers* 两条裤子. *the happy ~* 新郎新娘. *They are a pretty ~.* 他们真是好一对. *a carriage and ~* 双马马车. *the ~ to this sock* 这双袜子的另一只. ***a pigeon ~*** 一男一女的双胞胎;(只有)一个儿子和一个女儿. ***in a ~ = in ~s*** 成双,成对. ***~ of colours*** 〔英军〕国旗和团旗. ***~ of pipes*** 【美】(唱歌或说话的)声音. ***~ of stairs [steps]*** 梯子,楼梯 (*I live up two ~ of stairs front.* 我住在三楼前室). ***~ royal*** 【牌】三张同样的牌;三颗同点的骰子. ***(quite) another [a different] ~ of shoes [boots]*** (完全是)另外一个问题. ***take [show] a clean ~ of heels*** 一溜烟逃走;逃之夭夭. — *vi.* ①成对,配合;交尾;〔俚〕成夫妇 (*with*). ②(议会)相约弃权. — *vt.* ①使成对. ②使成配偶;使交配. ***~ off*** ①使分成[摆成]一对一对. ②两个成一组,成对而去. ***~ off with*** 〔口〕和…结婚. **~-horse** *a.* 双马的. **~-oar** *n., a.* 双桨艇(的). **~ production** 【原】偶产生,对产生.

pair·ing-sea·son [ˈpɛəriŋ-ˈsi:zn] *n.* (鸟等的)交配期.

pai·sa [ˈpaisæ] *n.* (*pl.* ***pa·ise*** [-se]) 派萨〔印度、巴基斯坦、卡塔尔、马斯喀特和阿曼的货币单位,等于百分之一卢比〕.

pai·sa·na [paiˈsɑ:nɑ:] *n.* 〔Sp.〕①女同胞. ②〔俚〕女伙伴.

pai·sa·no, pai·san [paiˈsɑ:nəu, paiˈsɑ:n] *n.* 〔Sp.〕①同胞. ②〔俚〕同志;伙伴. ③乡下人.

Pais·ley [ˈpeizli] *n., a.* 【纺】①(苏格兰)佩斯利(市出产的)涡旋纹花呢(的). ②佩斯利细毛披巾[围巾](的). **~ shawl** 佩斯利细毛围巾.

Pai·ute [ˈpaiju:t, paiˈju:t] *n.* (*pl.* ***~(s)***) ①派尤特人〔美洲的一支印第安人,居住在内华达、加利福尼亚东部、犹他南部和亚利桑那西北部的北美洲等地〕. ②派尤特语.

pa·ja·mas [pəˈdʒɑ:məz] *n.* 〔*pl.*〕宽大的睡衣裤 (= pyjamas). ***the cat's ~*** 〔美俚〕卓越的[出色的、极好的]人[事、物].

pa·ke·ha [ˈpɑ:kihə] *n.* (*pl.* ***~(s)***) 〔新西兰〕白种人.

Pa·ki·stan [ˌpɑ:kisˈtɑ:n] *n.* 巴基斯坦〔亚洲〕.

Pa·ki·stan·i [ˌpɑ:kiˈstɑ:ni] *n.* (*pl.* ***~(s)***) 巴基斯坦人. — *a.* 巴基斯坦的.

PAL = Philippine Air Lines 菲律宾航空公司.

Pal. = Palestine.

pal [pæl] *n.* 〔口〕伙伴,好朋友;同伙,同谋,同犯. — *vi.* 成伙伴,结成好友 (*with*). ***~ up with*** 和…结成好友;和…结伙.

pal·ace [ˈpælis] *n.* ①宫,宫殿. ②(主教)邸宅;宏伟大厦. ③华丽的娱乐场所. *a ~ car* 〔美〕花车,豪华(火车)车厢. *a ~ hotel* 豪华的旅馆. *a movie ~* 电影院. *the (Crystal) P-* 〔英口〕水晶宫. *the ~* 宫庭显贵. **~ revolution** 宫庭政变.

pal·a·din [ˈpælədin] *n.* ①【法史】帕拉丁〔查理曼 (Charlemagne) 大帝部下十二武士之一〕. ②干将;勇士;骑士,武士,游侠.

Pa·l(a)e·arc·tic [ˌpeiliˈɑ:ktik] *a.* 旧北极的,古北区的〔包括欧洲、非洲、北回归线以北的阿拉伯以及喜马拉雅山脉以北的亚洲部分〕.

pa·l(a)e·eth·nol·o·gy [ˌpælieθˈnɔlədʒi] *n.* 古〔史前〕人种学.

palae(o)-, pale(o)- 〔Gr.〕 *comb. f.* 古,旧,原始.

pa·lae·o·an·thro·pol·o·gy [ˈpæliəuˌæθrəˈpɔlədʒi] *n.* 古人类学. **-g·i·cal** *a.*

pa·l(a)e·o·an·throp·ic(al) [ˌpeiliəuænˈθrɔpik(əl), ˌpæli-] *a.* 化石人早期形状的;与化石人早期形状有关的.

pa·l(a)e·o·bot·a·ny [ˈpæliəuˈbɔtəni] *n.* 古植物学,化石植物学.

Pa·l(a)e·o·cene [ˈpeiliəˌsi:n, ˈpæli-] *a.* 【地】古新的〔新生代第三纪的初期或早期的〕. *the ~* 古新纪或该时代的岩石.

pa·l(a)e·o·crys·tic [ˌpæliəuˈkristik] *a.* (冰、海等)长期冻结的.

pa·l(a)e·og. = palaeography.

pa·l(a)e·og·raph [ˈpæliɔgrəf] *n.* ①古代手写本;古抄本. ② = paleographer.

pa·l(a)e·og·ra·pher [ˌpæliˈɔgrəfə] *n.* 古文书学家;抄本研究者;古字体研究者.

pa·l(a)e·o·graph·ic [ˌpæliəuˈgræfik] *a.* 古文(书)学的;古字体的.

pa·l(a)e·og·ra·phy [ˌpæliˈɔgrəfi] 古文书(学);古字体.

pa·l(a)e·o·lith [ˈpæliəuliθ] *n.* 【考古】旧石器.

pa·l(a)e·o·lith·ic [ˌpæliəuˈliθik] *a.* 旧石器时代的. *the P- era* 旧石器时代. *the ~ man* 旧石器时代的人(类).

pal(a)e·on·tol. = pal(a)eontology.

pa·l(a)e·on·tol·o·gy [ˌpælionˈtɔlədʒi] *n.* 【地】古生物学,化石学. **-to·log·ic(al)** [ˈpæliˌɔntəˈlɔdʒik(əl)] *a.* **-tol·o·gist** *n.* 古生物学家.

Pa·l(a)e·o·zo·ic [ˌpæliəuˈzəuik] *a.* 【地】古生代的. — *n.* 〔the ~〕古生代.

pa·l(a)e·o·zo·ol·o·gy [ˌpæliəuzəuˈɔlədʒi] *n.* 古动物学.

pa·l(a)e·phyte [ˈpæliəufait] *n.* 古生代植物.

pa·laes·tra, pa·les·tra [pəˈli:strə, -ˈles-] *n.* (*pl.* ***~s, -trae*** [-tri:]) ①(古希腊、罗马的)角力学校. ②体育场.

pa·lais de danse [pæˈlei də ˈdɑ:ns, F. pale də ˈdɑ:ŋs] *n.* (特别豪华的)舞厅.

pal·an·keen, pal·an·quin [ˌpælənˈki:n] *n.* (东方国家旧时用人抬的)四[六]人大轿.

pal·at·a·ble [ˈpælətəbl] *a.* ①好吃的,可口的;合口味的. ②愉快的,惬意的. **-bly** *ad.* **-bil·i·ty** *n.*

pal·a·tal [ˈpælətl] *a.* 腭的;【语音】腭音的. — *n.* 【语音】腭音.

pal·a·tal·ize [ˈpælətəlaiz] *vt.* 【语音】用腭音发(音),使腭音化. **-ization** [ˌpælətəlaiˈzeiʃən] *n.*

pal·ate [ˈpælit, -ət] *n.* ①【解】腭. ②【植】下唇瓣. ③味觉;嗜好;〔喻〕审美眼光,鉴赏力,判断. *a cleft ~* 豁嘴,缺唇. *a false ~* (实验语音学中用以调整舌腭接触部分的)人工腭. ***have a delicate ~*** 爱考究,挑剔. ***nice to ~*** 好吃. ***suit sb.'s ~*** 合口味. ***top of the ~*** 【解】悬壅垂 (= uvula). **~ bone** 【解】腭骨.

pa·la·tial [pəˈleiʃəl] *a.* 宫殿(似)的;宏伟的;壮丽的. **-ly** *ad.*

pal·a·tine[1] [ˈpælətain] *a.* ①宫殿的. ②宫廷官吏的;有王室特权的. ③〔P-〕(享有王权的)封建领主的. — *n.* ①〔P-〕古罗马的宫廷官吏;古代德国、法国的最高法官;享有王权的封建领主. ②女用皮围巾[披肩]. ***the P- (Hill)*** (罗马市建于其上的)帕拉坦(丘).

pal·a·tine[2] [ˈpælətain] *a.* 腭的. — *n.* 〔*pl.*〕【解】腭骨.

pal·a·to- *comb.f.* 腭: *palato*-dental 前舌齿音的.

pal·a·to·gram [ˈpælətəgræm, pəˈlætəg-] *n.* 【语音】腭位图.

pa·la·ver [pəˈlɑ:və] *n.* ①废话,空谈. ②奉承,拍马屁;笼络;诱骗. ③(尤指非洲人和外来商人间的)交涉,谈判;〔俚〕事务. — *vi.* 闲谈;空谈. — *vt.* 哄骗;笼络.

Pa·laz·zo [pɑ:ˈlɑ:tsəu] *n.* (*pl.* ***-laz·zi*** [-ˈlɑ:tsi]) 〔It.〕豪华的宫殿,邸宅.

pale[1] [peil] *a.* ①灰白的,(脸色等)苍白的. ②(颜色等)淡的;微暗的,(光等)弱;柔弱无力的. *a ~ moon* 朦胧的月光. *be ~ with fear* 吓得面无人色. *look ~* 脸色不好. *~ (ale)* 〔美〕淡啤酒. *~ wine* 白葡萄酒. ***turn ~*** 变苍白;变淡. ***as ~ as death [sheet]*** 面孔象死人一样苍白. ***be***

~ *before [beside, by the side of]* 在…前相形见绌. 失色; 变苍白; (色)变淡; 变暗. — *vi.* 使变苍白, 使发暗. ~**eyed** *a.* 眼睛无神的. ~**-hearted** *a.* 怯懦的, 胆小的. **-ly** *ad.* **-ness** *n.*

pale[2] [peil] *n.* ①桩, (栅栏)尖板条; 围篱, 栅栏. ②境界, 范围; 境内, 栅内; 【徽】竖贯徽章中部的线条. ③〔the P-〕【史】12 世纪后并入英国的爱尔兰东部地区 (= the English [Irish] Pale). *in* ~ 纵向排列. *leap the* ~ 越界, 过分. *within [out of, outside, beyond] the* ~ *of* 在…的范围内〔外〕. — *vt.* 用桩〔栅〕围住, 在…设围篱.

Pa·le(o)- *com. f.* = Palae(o).

pa·le·a [ˈpeiliə] *n.* *(pl. -le·ae* [-lii:]*)* 【植】(禾本科的)内稃; (菊科的)托苞.

pale-buck [ˈpeil-bʌk] *n.* 【动】羚羊.

pale·face [ˈpeilfeis] *n.* 白种人〔据说是北美印第安人用语〕.

Pa·lem·bang [ˌpɑ:lemˈbɑ:ŋ] *n.* 巴邻旁〔印度尼西亚港市〕.

Pa·ler·mo [pəˈlə:məu] *n.* 巴勒莫〔意大利港市〕.

Pal·es·tine [ˈpælistain] *n.* ①巴勒斯坦. ②【圣】圣地 (= Holy Land).

Pal·es·tin·i·an [ˌpælisˈtiniən] *a.* 巴勒斯坦(人)的. — *n.* 巴勒斯坦人.

pa·les·tra [pəˈlestrə] *n.* *(pl.* ~*s,* ~*e* [-tri:]*)* = palaestra.

pal·ette [ˈpælit] *n.* ①调色板; (调色板上的或某画家用的)一套颜料. ②(中世纪铠甲的)关节板. *set the* ~ 把颜料安排在调色板上. ~**-knife** 调色刀.

Pa·ley [ˈpeili] *n.* 佩利〔姓氏〕.

pal·frey [ˈpɔ:lfri] *n.* ①〔古〕(普通)供乘骑的马. ②(供妇女骑的脚步轻快的)小马.

Pal·grave [ˈpɔ:lgreiv, ˈpælgreiv] *n.* 帕尔格雷夫〔姓氏〕.

Pa·li [ˈpɑ:li] *n.* (印度东南部古代的)巴利语〔现已成为佛教的宗教语言〕.

pal·i·kar [ˈpælikə] *n.* (1821—28 年独立战争时的)希腊民兵.

pal·imp·sest [ˈpælimpsest] *n.* ①(可以消去旧字另写新字的)羊皮纸〔石板等〕. ②把背面翻过来另刻的旧黄铜纪念牌.

pal·in·drome [ˈpælindrəum] *n.* 回文〔正读反读都可的语句, 例如: *Madam; Hannah; Able was I ere I saw Elba* 等〕.

pal·ing [ˈpeiliŋ] *n.* ①打桩做栅栏. ②〔集合词〕桩; (栅栏的)尖板条; 栅, 围篱; 围.

pal·in·gen·e·sis [ˌpælinˈdʒenisis] *n.* ①【哲】【宗】新生, 再生; 洗礼; 轮回; 历史循环论. ②【生】重演(性)发生; 【虫】重演(性)变态.

pal·in·ge·net·ic [ˌpælindʒiˈnetik] *a.* 【哲、宗】新生〔再生〕的; 【生】重演性发生的; 【虫】重演性变态的. **-i·cal·ly** *ad.*

pal·i·node [ˈpælinəud] *n.* ①(否定本人旧作内容的)翻案诗. ②正式打消前言.

pal·i·sade [ˌpæliˈseid] *n.* ①桩, 木栅, 栅栏. ②〔*pl.*〕(河边的)断崖. — *vt.* 用栅围绕.

pal·ish [ˈpeiliʃ] *a.* 稍带苍白的.

pal·i·(s)san·der [ˌpæliˈsændə] *n.* (巴西)红木.

pall[1] [pɔ:l] *n.* ①棺衣; 墓布; (内装尸体的)棺材; 【宗】圣杯〔祭台〕罩布; 祭服. ②阴惨的东西; 悲哀. ③〔古〕外套, 披肩. ④Y 字形徽章; = pallium. ⑤遮盖物; 〔喻〕幕. *a* ~ *of darkness* 夜幕. — *vt.* 给…盖棺衣; 覆盖, 包. ~**bearer**, ~**holder**, ~**supporter** (丧礼中的)抬棺人; 执绋人; 〔美俚〕饭馆里撤盘子的人.

pall[2] [pɔ:l] *vi.* ①(酒等)走味, 失味. ②扫兴; 丧失吸引力; 令人感到腻烦; 使人生厌 *(on; upon)*. — *vt.* 使扫兴; 使生厌.

Pal·la·di·an[1] [pəˈleidiən] *a.* ①【希神】智慧女神帕拉斯 (Pallas) 的. ②智慧的, 学问的, 知识的.

Pal·la·di·an[2] [pəˈleidjən] *a.* (十六世纪意大利建筑家)帕拉第奥 (A. Palladio) 的; 帕拉第奥建筑型式的.

pal·lad·ic [pəˈlædik, -ˈleidik] *a.* 【化】钯的; 四价钯的.

Pal·la·di·um [pəˈleidiəm] *n.* ①希腊智慧女神帕拉斯 (Pallas) 的神像. ②〔p-〕*(pl. -dia* [-diə]*)* 守护神; 保障, 保护.

pal·la·dium [pəˈleidiəm] *n.* 【化】钯.

pal·la·dous [pəˈleidəs, ˈpælədəs] *a.* 【化】亚钯的, 二价钯的.

Pal·las [ˈpælæs] *n.* ①【希神】智慧女神帕拉斯〔常作帕拉斯·雅典娜 (~ Athena)〕. ②【天】小惑星.

pal·let[1] [ˈpælit] *n.* ①草荐; 〔主美南部〕铺在地板卧铺上的毛毯. ②小床; 地铺.

pal·let[2] [ˈpælit] *n.* ①(陶工等用的)木抹子. ②【机】棘爪; 鏟垫; (电话机的)衔铁; (棘齿轮的)掣子. ③【建】制模板; 【乐】(风琴等的)调节瓣. ④(画家的)调色板; (供铲车、装卸、搬运用的)货盘.

pal·let·ize [ˈpæliˌtaiz] *vt.* 把…放在货盘上; 用货盘装运. **-i·za·tion** *n.* 货盘化.

pal·li·a [ˈpæliə] pallium 的复数.

pal·li·al [ˈpæliəl] *a.* 【动】(外)套膜的; 【解】外皮的; 大脑皮层的, 大脑皮质的.

pal·liasse [pælˈjæs, ˈpæljæs] *n.* = paillasse.

pal·li·ate [ˈpælieit] *vt.* ①(暂时)减轻(疾病等), 缓和(痛苦等). ②掩饰(罪过等). **-a·tion** *n.* ①减轻, 缓和; 掩饰(罪过等). ②起减轻〔缓和〕作用的东西; 辩解; 掩饰之词. **pal·li·a·tor** [-tə] *n.* ①减轻(疾病等)的人. ②掩饰(罪过等)的人.

pal·li·a·tive [ˈpæliətiv] *a.* ①减轻(疼痛等)的; 缓和的. ②辩解的. ③【医】姑息的; 治标的. — *n.* ①【医】(暂时的)减轻(剂); 姑息剂; 治标剂. ②辩解; 可斟酌的情况; 用以作掩饰的东西. ③姑息手段. **-ly** *ad.*

pal·lid [ˈpælid] *a.* ①苍白的, 没血色的. ②病态的; 无生气的. *make ... seem* ~ *by comparison* 使…相形见绌. **-ly** *ad.* **-ness** *n.*

pal·li·um [ˈpæliəm] *n.* *(pl.* ~*s, pal·li·a* [-liə]*)* ①(古罗马哲学家等的)大披肩; (大主教的)披肩式祭服. ②【解】大脑皮层; 大脑皮质; 【动】外套膜; 【虫】隔膜; 【气】层雨云.

Pall-Mall [ˈpelˈmel, ˈpælˈmæl] *n.* ①蓓尔美尔街〔伦敦一街名, 街上多俱乐部〕. ②英国陆军部〔原在蓓尔美尔街〕.

pall-mall [ˈpelˈmel, ˈpælˈmæl] *n.* 铁圈球; 铁圈球场.

pal·lor [ˈpælə] *n.* (脸色等的)苍白, 灰白.

pal·ly [ˈpæli] *a.* 〔俚, 口〕亲密的. *get* ~ *with sb.* 和某人要好.

palm[1] [pɑ:m] *n.* ①手掌, 手心; 掌尺〔以手掌的长度和宽度为尺, 宽 7.6—10 cm, 长 18—25 cm〕; (手套等的)掌部. ②掌状物; (桨等的)扁平部; 【海】掌皮, 掌盘〔缝帆布时顶针用〕; 锚爪. ③(赌博、变戏法时)藏牌于掌中. *sailmaker's* ~ 帆工掌皮. *cross sb.'s* ~ (用钱币)在某人手心上划一个十字(把钱付给算命者); 〔喻〕贿赂某人. *grease [gild, tickle] sb.'s* ~ 向…行贿. *have an itching* ~ 〔口〕贪贿; 贪财. *know sth. like the* ~ *of one's hand* 对某事了如指掌. — *vt.* ①用手掌抚摩; 用手抚弄; 〔美〕与…握手. ②(变戏法等时)把(东西)藏在手心里; 哄骗, 欺骗. ③(用欺骗手段)把…硬塞给〔卖给〕. ~ *off (sth.) on [upon] (sb.)* 拿假东西硬塞〔硬卖〕给(人). ~ **grease [oil]** 〔美俚〕贿赂〔财物等〕; 小费. **-ful** *n.* 一手心(的量).

palm[2] [pɑ:m] *n.* ①棕榈(树). ②棕榈枝〔叶〕〔胜利的标记〕; 胜利. ③优越; 光荣, 荣誉; 奖赏; 【军】荣誉勋章. *a cocoanut* ~ 椰子. *a date* ~ 枣椰子. *bear [carry] off the* ~ 得胜; 获奖, 博得无上的荣誉. *get the* ~ 【美体】打败竞争者. *yield [give] the* ~ *to* 输给…一着; 认输. ~ **butter** 棕榈油. ~ **civet** (马来群岛产)长尾麝香猫. ~ **crab** 【动】椰子蟹, 桓螯, 尾蟹. ~ **fat** 椰子

油. ~ **house** 温室〔栽培棕榈等用〕. ~ **leaf** 棕榈叶, 棕叶. ~**-lily**【植】朱蕉. ~ **oil** 棕榈油. ~ **sugar** 印度赤砂糖,粗糖〔尤指椰子糖〕, = jaggery. **P- Sunday**【宗】复活节前的星期日.

pal·ma·ceous [pælˈmeiʃəs] *a.*【植】棕榈科的; 棕榈状的.

Pal·ma-Chris·ti [ˈpælməˈkristi] *n.*【植】蓖麻.

pal·mar [ˈpælmə] *a.* (有关)手掌的; 掌中的.

pal·ma·ry [ˈpælməri] *a.* ①最优秀的,杰出的; 胜利者的. ②最重要的,最有价值的.

pal·mate [ˈpælmit] *a.* 掌状的;【动】有蹼的. **-ly** *ad.*

pal·mat·ed [ˈpɑlmeitid] *a.* = palmate.

pal·mat·i·fid [pælˈmætifid] *a.*【植】掌状半裂的.

pal·ma·tine [ˈpælmətiːn] *n.*【药】巴马亭,非洲防已碱.

pal·ma·tion [pælˈmeiʃən] *n.* 掌状分裂; 掌状部分.

Palm·er [ˈpɑːmə] *n.* 帕默〔姓氏,男子名〕.

palm·er¹ [ˈpɑːmə] *n.* ①【宗】(旧时带着棕榈叶做的十字架从圣地回来的)朝圣者; 游方僧. ②假饵钩. ③=~-worm. *a ~'s staff* 锡杖. ~ **worm** 草毛虫,〔美〕果树毛虫.

palm·er² [ˈpɑːmə] *n.* (玩牌等时)作弊的人; 变戏法的人.

Palm·er·ston [ˈpɑːməstən] *n.* ①帕默斯顿〔姓氏〕. ② **Henry J.T.** ~ 亨利·帕默斯顿〔1784—1865, 英国政治家,曾两度任首相〕.

Pam·e·la [ˈpæmilə] *n.* 帕米拉〔女子名〕.

pal·mette [pælˈmet] *n.*【建】棕叶饰.

pal·met·to [pælˈmetəu] *n.* *(pl.* ~*(e)s)* ①【植】美国矮棕榈; 扇状叶的棕榈. ②棕叶帽. **P- State**〔美〕矫棕榈州〔南卡罗来州的别名〕.

pal·mi·ped, pal·mi·pede [ˈpælmiped,-piːd] *a.* 蹼足的. — *n.* 蹼足鸟,游禽类,水鸟.

palm·ist(er) [ˈpɑːmist(ə)] *n.* 看手相者.

palm·is·try [ˈpɑːmistri] *n.* ①手相术. ②〔谑〕(扒手等的)手指灵巧; 手上功夫的变戏法.

pal·mi·tate [ˈpɑːlmiteit, pæ-] *n.*【化】十六碳酸盐,棕榈酸盐,软脂酸盐.

pal·mit·ic [pælˈmitik] *a.* 从棕榈(油)得来的. ~ **acid**【化】棕榈酸,十六酸,软脂酸.

pal·mi·tin [ˈpælmitin] *n.*【化】①棕榈精,三棕榈精,软脂. ②甘油棕榈酸脂,甘油软脂酸酯.

palm·y [ˈpɑːmi] *a.* ①棕榈(似)的; 棕榈多的;〔诗〕棕榈荫遮的; 产棕榈的. ②兴盛的; 得胜的,得意扬扬的. *one's ~ days* (已往的)得意时代,全盛时代.

pal·my·ra [pælˈmaiərə] *n.*【植】扇叶树头榈 *(Borassus flabellifer)*〔生长于印度、锡兰和热带非洲〕.

pal·o·mi·no [ˌpæləˈmiːnəu] *n.* *(pl.* ~*s)* ①〔美西南部〕巴洛米诺马〔脚细,毛淡黄褐色或奶油色〕. ②淡黄褐色.

pa·loo·ka [pəˈluːkə] *n.* ①〔美俚〕平凡的〔蹩脚的〕运动员〔拳师〕. ②傻子,呆子;〔蔑〕人.

pa·lo·ver·de [ˌpæləuˈvəːd] *n.*【植】多花假紫荆 *(Cercidium macrum)*, 兰花假紫荆 *(C. torreyenum)*, 小叶假紫荆 *(C. microphyllum)*〔产于美国西南部和墨西哥〕.

palp [pælp] *n.* (节足动物的)触须 (= palpus).

pal·pa·ble [ˈpælpəbl] *a.* ①摸得出的,可触知的;【医】可以触诊的. ②明白的,明显的. ~ *lies* 露骨的谎话. **-bly** *ad.* **-bil·i·ty** [-ˈbiliti] *n.*

pal·pate¹ [ˈpælpeit] *vt.* 摸认;【医】触诊. **-pa·tion** [-ˈpeiʃən] *n.*【医】触诊,扪诊.

pal·pate² [ˈpælpeit] *a.*【动】有触须的.

pal·pe·bral [ˈpælpibrəl] *a.* 眼睑的; 眼睑上的.

pal·pi [ˈpælpai] *n.* palpus 的复数.

pal·pi·tant [ˈpælpitənt] *a.* 颤抖的,悸动的.

pal·pi·tate [ˈpælpiteit] *vi.* ①(心)跳动, 悸动. ②发抖 *(with)*. ~ *with pleasure* 快乐得浑身颤抖.

pal·pi·ta·tion [ˌpælpiˈteiʃən] *n.* ①颤动,跳动. ②心跳;【医】心悸.

pal·pus [ˈpælpəs] *n.* *(pl.* **pal·pi** [ˈpælpai]*)* = palp.

pals·grave [ˈpælzgreiv, ˈpɔːlz-] *n.*【德史】(在领地内享有部分王权的)独立伯爵.

pal·sied [ˈpɔːlzid] *a.* ①中风的, 瘫痪的; 麻痹的. ②颤抖的.

pal·stave [ˈpɔːlsteiv] *n.* 青铜凿.

pal·sy [ˈpɔːlzi] *n.* ①中风, 瘫痪; 麻痹. ②颤抖; 痉挛. ③无能,无力. ~ *of one side* 半身不遂. ***Bell's*** ~【医】面部神经麻痹,面瘫. — *vt.* 使瘫痪; 使陷入无能境地.

pal·sy-wal·sy [ˈpɔːlziˈwɔːlzi] *n.*〔美俚〕①伙伴. ②好朋友. — *a.* 非常要好的,亲密的.

pal·ter [ˈpɔːltə] *vi.* ①骗,说模棱两可的话,搪塞过去; 玩弄; 敷衍了事; 马马虎虎地处理. ②讨价还价,争论不休. ③瞎谈一通. ~ *with sb.* 把某人搪塞过去. ~ *with sth.* 马马虎虎地处理某事.

pal·try [ˈpɔːltri] *a.* ①不足取的,没有价值的; 微不足道的; 渺小的. ②吝啬的; 可鄙的. **-tri·ly** *ad.* **-tri·ness** *n.*

pa·l·u·dal, pal·u·dine [ˈpæljudl, pəˈljuːdl; ˈpæljudin, -dain] *a.* ①沼泽(多)的; 沼地的; 沼地上发生的. ②疟疾的. ~ *fever* 疟疾.

pal·u·dism [ˈpæludizəm] *n.*【医】疟疾,瘴病.

pal·y [ˈpeili] *a.*〔诗〕有些苍白的.

pal·y·nol·o·gy [ˌpæliˈnɔlədʒi] *n.* 孢粉学. **-no·log·i·cal** [-ˈlɔdʒikəl] *a.* **-nol·o·gist** *n.*

pam. = pamphlet.

pam·a·quin(e) [ˈpæməkwin] *n.*【药】扑疟喹啉.

Pam·e·la [ˈpæmilə, ˈpæmələ] *n.* 帕梅拉〔女子名〕.

Pa·mir·i [pɑːˈmiəriː] *n.* *(pl.* ~*)* 帕米尔高原游牧民族.

Pa·mirs [pəˈmiəz] *n.*〔the ~〕帕米尔高原.

pam·pas [ˈpæmpəz] *n.*〔*pl.*〕①南美大草原〔南美亚马孙河以南的大草原〕. ②〔P-〕南美大草原上的印第安居民. ~ [ˈpæmpəs] **grass**【植】(南美产)蒲苇(属).

pam·pe·an [pæmˈpiːən, ˈpæmpiən] *a., n.* ①南美大草原(的). ②〔P-〕南美大草原印第安人(的).

pam·per [ˈpæmpə] *vt.* ①纵容; 娇养. ②使满足. ③〔古〕给…吃得过饱. ~ *a child* 对孩子娇生惯养. ~ *one's appetite* 拼命吃个痛快.

pam·pe·ro [pɑːmˈpεərəu] *n.* *(pl.* ~*s)* 潘沛罗冷风〔自安第斯山脉横扫南美大草原的强劲冷风〕.

pam·phlet [ˈpæmflit] *n.* 小册子; (时事问题等的)小册子刊物. *a single-article* ~ 单行本. **-ar·y** *a.*

pam·phlet·eer [ˌpæmfliˈtiə] *n.*〔常蔑〕小册子作者. — *vi.* 出版〔编写〕小册子.

pan¹ [pæn] *n.* ①平底锅,盘子,盆子,蒸发皿; 一满盘; 一满锅; 盆状器皿〔灰盆、秤盘等〕;【矿】淘盘; (火枪的)药池; 铰链孔. ②头盖. ③(表面有一层薄土的)硬质地层. ④(积水干涸后常现盐碱的)盘状凹地. ⑤【海】小浮冰. ⑥〔美俚〕面盘,脸. *the ~ of the knee* 膝盖骨. *a salt ~* 晒盐田. ***flash in the ~*** 昙花一现. ***leap [fall] out of the frying ~ into the fire*** 跳出锅里落进火里; 才脱身小困难,又落入大灾难. ***pots and ~s*** 锅盘等炊事用具. ***savour of the ~*** 露出本来面目; 露底. ***shut one's ~***〔俚〕闭嘴不说话; 沉着,不动声色. — *vt.* ①用盘子淘洗(砂金) *(off; out)*. ②用平底锅烧(菜). ③〔美俚〕得到. ④〔美俚〕严厉批评; 骂; 糟蹋(名誉),向…找碴儿. — *vi.* ①淘金; 产金. ②〔口〕结果成为… *(out)*. ~ *out ill [well]* 结果不好[好]. *How did it ~ out?*〔口〕结果怎么样? ***be panned out***〔美俚〕力尽; 破产. ~ ***out [off]*** 选出(沙金);〔俚〕赚钱;〔美〕结果是…. ~**-fish** 煎吃的小鱼. ~**-fry** *vt.* 用平底锅煎炸. **-ful** *n.* 一满锅[盘].

pan² [pæn] *vt., vi.* (电影)摇(镜头); (使)拍摄全景. — *n.* 摇镜头; 摄全景. ~ ***down*** 降下〔镜头垂直下移拍摄全景〕.

pan³ [pæn] *n.* ①(东印度产)蒌叶〔一种胡椒〕. ②用蒌叶制成的咀嚼物.

Pan [pæn] *n.* ①【希神】潘〔牧人之神, 人身、羊脚、头上有角〕. ②自然界之精灵; 基督教以前的世界. **~'s**

pipes 排箫.

pan- *comb.f.* 全，总，万，泛. ①和表示国籍、宗派等的字结合：*pan*-American. ②和后缀 -ism, -ish, -ic 等的派生词结合：*pan*cosmism, *pan*-Hellenist.

Pan. = Panama.

pan·a·ce·a [ˌpænəˈsiə] *n.* ①万应药；秘药. ②(社会弊病等的)补救方法. **-n** *a.*

pa·nache [pəˈnæʃ] *n.* 〔F.〕①(盔等的)羽饰. ②〔喻〕夸示，炫耀；摆架子，耍派头.

pa·na·da [pəˈnɑːdə] *n.* 面包粥〔以面包加糖、牛奶、调味等煮成〕；面糊〔煮汤等用〕.

Pan-Af·ri·can·ism [ˈpænˈæfrikənizəm] *n.* 泛非主义. **Pan-Af·ri·can·ist** [-nist] *n., a.* 泛非主义者(的).

pan·age [ˈpænidʒ] *n.* = pannage.

PAN AM = Pan American World Airways〔美〕泛美航空公司.

Pan·a·ma [ˌpænəˈmɑː] *n.* ①(中美洲)巴拿马；巴拿马运河. ②〔p-〕巴拿马草帽 (= Panama hat). *the ~ Canal* 巴拿马运河. **-ni·an** ① *n.* 巴拿马人. ② *a.* 巴拿马(人)的.

Pan·a·ma Cit·y [ˌpænəˈmɑː ˈsiti] *n.* 巴拿马城〔巴拿马首都〕.

Pan-A·mer·i·can [ˈpænəˈmerikən] *a.* 泛美的，全美洲(各国)的. *the ~ Airways* 泛美航空公司. *the ~ Congress* 泛美会议. *the ~ Day* 泛美联盟成立纪念日〔4月14日〕. *the ~ Union* 泛美联盟〔包括二十三个美洲国家，建于 1890 年〕. **-ism** *n.* 泛美主义，大美洲主义.

Pan-An·gli·can [ˈpænˈæŋglikən] *a.* 泛英国国教主义的.

pan·a·tel·(l)a [ˌpænəˈtələ] *n.* 外形细长的雪茄烟.

pan·a·vi·sion [ˌpænəˈviʒən] *n.* 宽屏幕电视；宽银幕电影.

Pa·nax [ˈpeinæks] *n.* 【植】人参属. *~* **ginseng** 人参.

pan·broil [ˈpænˌbrɔil] *vt.* (在平锅中少放油或不放油)煎烤.

pan·cake [ˈpænkeik, ˈpæŋ-] *n.* ①薄煎饼，烙饼. ②【空】平降，平坠(着陆). ③(极地洋面上的)圆形薄冰 (=~ ice). ***flat as a ~*** 扁平的. — *vt., vi.* 【空】(使)(飞机)平降. *~* **coil**【电】扁平线圈. **P- Day [Tuesday]**〔口〕(照例要吃薄煎饼的)圣灰节〔Ash Wednesday，四旬节的第一天〕的前一天. *~* **engine** 水平对置式发动机. *~* **turner** 广播电台〔电视台〕的唱片放送员.

pan·chax [ˈpænkæks] *n.* 【动】艳鱼类.

pan·chay·at [pʌnˈtʃaiət] *n.* (印度)乡村行政委员会；(由大约五人组成的)乡村自治委员会.

pan·chro·mat·ic [ˌpænkrəuˈmætik] *a.* 【摄】全〔泛〕色的. *~* **film** 全色胶片〔软片〕. *~* **plate** 全色干片.

pan·chro·ma·tise [pænˈkrəumətaiz] *vt.* 【摄】使成全〔泛〕色.

pan·cos·mism [pænˈkɔzmizəm] *n.* 【哲】物质〔泛〕宇宙论.

pan·crat·ic [pænˈkrætik] *a.* ①【光】视界大的；(透镜)可随意调节的. ②(古希腊、罗马)拳击和摔交比赛的.

pan·cra·ti·um [pænˈkreiʃiəm] *n.* (*pl.* ***-ti·a*** [-ə]) (古希腊和罗马)拳击和摔交比赛.

pan·cre·as [ˈpæŋkriəs] *n.* 【解】胰(腺).

pan·cre·at·ic [ˌpæŋkriˈætik] *a.* 胰(腺)的. *~* **juice [secretion]** 胰液.

pan·cre·a·tin [ˈpæŋkriətin] *n.* 【生化】胰酶(制剂).

pan·cre·a·ti·tis [ˌpænkriəˈtaitis, ˈpæŋ-] *n.* 【医】胰腺炎.

pan·da [ˈpændə] *n.* 【动】猫熊，熊猫. *lesser ~* 小熊猫. *giant ~* 大熊猫.

pan·da·nus [pænˈdeinəs] *n.* 【植】露兜树属植物 (= screw pine).

Pan·de·an [pænˈdiːən] *a.* 牧神潘 (Pan) 的. *a ~ pipe* = Panpipe.

pan·dect [ˈpændekt] *n.* ①(某学科的)全论，全书；汇编. 〔*pl.*〕法令全书. ②〔Pandects〕《学说汇纂》〔六世纪东罗马帝国皇帝查士丁尼 (Justinian) 下令编纂的 50 卷本罗马法学家学说摘录全书〕.

pan·dem·ic [pænˈdemik] *a.* ①(疾病)流行全国〔全世界〕的；传染性的，流行性的. ②一般的，普遍的. — *n.* (流行全国〔全世界〕的)传染病.

pan·de·mo·ni·um [ˌpændiˈməunjəm,-niəm] *n.* ①〔常 P-〕群魔殿，魔窟；地狱. ②混乱(场所)；大吵大闹，无法无天.

pan·der [ˈpændə] *n.* 拉皮条者；为妓女拉客者；妓院老板；帮人做坏事的人. — *vt., vi.* 勾引，(为…)拉皮条；怂恿，帮助(…)做(坏事)；煽动；迎合 *(to)*.

pan·dit [ˈpʌndit] *n.* (印度的)博学家；梵学家；〔P-〕学者〔在印度用作尊称〕(= pundit).

P. and L., P. & L., p. and l. = profit and loss account 盈亏帐.

P. and O., P. & O. = Peninsular and Oriental Steam Navigation Company〔英〕半岛和东方航运公司.

Pan·do·ra [pænˈdɔːrə] *n.* 【希神】潘朵拉〔主神宙斯 (Zeus) 命火神用黏土制成的地上的第一个女人〕. **~'s Box** 潘朵拉之盒〔潘朵拉下凡时宙斯神送给她的盒子，她违禁开看，使一切灾害和罪恶跑散世上，只有希望还留在里面〕；〔喻〕灾难〔麻烦、祸害等〕的根源.

pan·do·ra, pan·dore [pænˈdɔːrə, -ˈdɔː] *n.* (古代)三弦琴.

pan·dow·dy [pænˈdaudi] *n.* 〔美〕(上覆酥皮的)厚苹果糕〔布丁〕.

pan·du·rate [ˈpændjureit, -duər-] *a.* 【植】(叶子)提琴形的 (= panduriform).

pan·dy [ˈpændi] *n., vi.* 〔Scot.〕打手心. — *vt.* 打…的手心. *~* **bat** (打学生手心用的)藤鞭.

pane [pein] *n.* ①(一块)窗格玻璃；(棋盘等式的)长方格，长方框. ②(门、墙等上的)嵌板. ③(螺帽、钻石等的)面，边. ④成为一块而互相连接的若干张邮票. — *vt.* ①嵌玻璃于. ②用杂色小布片拼做(衣服). **-d** *a.* ①用布片拼做的. ②嵌有…玻璃的；具有…边〔面〕的 (*a six paned window* 六片玻璃的窗子). **-less** *a.* 无窗格玻璃的.

pan·e·gyr·ic [ˌpæniˈdʒirik] *n., a.* 颂词(的)，赞辞(的)；称赞(的)；推崇(的). *a ~ on [upon] sb. [sth.]* 对某人〔某事〕的颂扬. **-i·cal** *a.* **-i·cal·ly** *ad.*

pan·e·gyr·ist [ˌpæniˈdʒirist, ˈpænidʒirist] *n.* 颂词作者；称赞者.

pan·e·gy·rize [ˈpænidʒiraiz] *vt., vi.* 称赞；作(颂词)；致(颂词).

pan·el [ˈpænl] *n.* ①面，板；【建】四分板，门窗材，幅板，板条；嵌板，镶板；方格；(木工)线板；【绘】(代替画布的)画板上画的画. ②【法】陪审员名单；全体陪审员；(合保险法规定的)地方健康保险医生名单. ③(广播或电视中)进行公开讨论会的小组；〔美〕(大会中的)小组委员会；一组调查对象；(对一组对象进行的)典型调查. ④(女衣上的)直条饰缝. ⑤鞍褥，鞍垫；木架鞍. ⑥(一张)羊皮纸；登记簿. ⑦【摄】长方形大相片. ⑧【空】翼段，翼片. ⑨【电】配电盘，控制板；仪表盘；【军】信号布板. *a ~ board* 镜板. *a meter ~* 仪表面盘. ⑩〔Scot.〕【法】刑事被告. *a power ~* 配电盘. *a control ~* 【火箭】操纵台. *a ~-work* 格子细工；铁工建筑；构架工程. *a ~ doctor* 健康保险医生. ***be in the ~*** 〔Scot.〕【法】在受审中. ***go on the ~*** ①受健康保险医生检查. ②= be in the ~. ***on the ~*** 登记在健康保险医生名单上的. — *vt.* ①在…上嵌板子；在(衣服等上)嵌杂色条纹；在…上置鞍垫. ②选定(陪审员). ③〔Scot.〕【法】对…起诉. *a ~ed door* 格子门. *~* **discussion**〔美〕小组讨论；在(电视或广播)听众面前开的专题讨论会. *~* **heating** 壁板供暖. *~* **house** 设有暗门密室的妓院. *~* **show** 有一组名流参加的电视讨论会〔游艺会等〕. *~* **truck** 小型运货汽车. **-ist** *n.* 专门小组成员〔如评论比赛、公开讨论、参加广播(或电视)演出等的小组成员〕. **-(l)ing** *n.* ①〔集合词〕镜板,镶木. ②嵌板细工.
pan·en·the·ism [pænˈenθiizəm] *n.* 万有在神论〔认为神包括世界而又超越世界〕.
pan·e·tel·(l)a [ˌpæniˈtelə] *n.* (= panatela).
pang [pæŋ] *n.* ①(肉体上的一阵)苦痛, 剧痛. ②(精神上的一阵)极度痛苦. *the ~s of death* 临死的痛苦. *the ~s of conscience* 良心的苦责. — *vt.* 使剧痛;使极度痛苦,折磨.
pan·ga [ˈpɑːŋgə] *n.* (非洲)带钩大切刀.
pan·gen [ˈpændʒin] *n.*【生】胚芽;泛生子.
pan·gen·e·sis [pænˈdʒenisis] *n.*【生】机体再生说, 泛生(子)论.
Pan-Ger·man [ˈpænˈdʒəːmən] *a.* 全德意志的; 大德意志〔日耳曼〕主义的. — *n.* 大德国主义者. **-ism** *n.* 大德意志主义,大德意志运动.
pan·go·lin [pæŋˈgəulin] *n.*【动】鲮鲤,穿山甲.
pan·gram [ˈpæŋgræm] *n.* 字母表所有的字母都出现(最好只出现一次)的句子〔一种文字游戏〕.
Pang·we [ˈpɑːŋwe] *n.* *(pl. ~(s))* (几内亚湾东海岸一带的)潘威人.
pan·han·dle[1] [ˈpænˌhændl] *n.* 平底锅柄;〔原美〕突出的狭长行政区域. *the P- State* 〔美〕西弗吉尼亚 (West Virginia) 州的别名. *the Gansu ~* 甘肃走廊, 河西走廊. **-rs** 〔*pl.*〕〔美〕西弗吉尼亚、得克萨斯、爱达荷 (West Virginia, Texas, Idaho) 各州人的别名.
pan·han·dle[2] [ˈpænˌhændl] *vt., vi.* 〔俚〕(在路上)(向…)讨钱. **-r** 〔俚〕乞丐,叫化子.
pan·head [ˈpænhed] *n.*【机】截锥头,盘(形)头. ~ **bolt** 截锥头螺栓. ~ **rivet** 截锥头铆钉. **-ed** [-ˌhedid] *a.*
Pan·hel·len·ic [ˈpænheˈliːnik] *a.* 大希腊的, 大希腊主义的.
Pan·hel·len·ism [ˈpænˈhelinizəm] *n.* 泛希腊主义.
pan·ic[1] [ˈpænik] *n.* ①恐慌,惊慌;【商】(金融方面的)大恐慌. ②〔美剧俚〕成功; 热狂. ③〔俚〕非常滑稽的人〔事、物〕. ***be seized with a ~*** 恐慌起来. ***get up a ~*** 起恐慌. ***no ~*** 〔美剧俚〕不大高明,平凡. — *a.* ①恐慌的,惊慌的. ②(恐慌心理)没来由的,无谓的;过度的. *a ~ price* 恐慌价格,跌落不已的价格. *a ~ fear [fright]* 无谓的恐惧. — *vt.* ①使起恐慌. ②〔美剧俚〕使狂热,使喝采. — *vi.* 极其惊慌 *(over)*. ~ **button** (飞机上的)紧急按纽 *(hit the ~ button* 在紧急情况下惊惶失措). **~-monger** 制造恐慌的人. **~-stricken, ~-struck** *a.* 恐慌的,受惊恐的,狼狈的.
pan·ic[2] [ˈpænik] *n.*【植】稗;黍,稷,糜子 (=~ grass).
Pan·ic [ˈpænik] *a.* 潘神的,牧人之神的.
pan·ick·y [ˈpæniki] *a.* 〔口〕①恐慌的; 吓慌了的. ②易引起恐慌的. *extremely ~* 恐慌万状.
pan·i·cle [ˈpænikl] *n.*【植】圆锥花序; 散穗花序; 复总状花序.
pa·nic·u·late, pa·nic·u·lat·ed [pəˈnikjuleit, -leitid] *a.* 具圆锥花序的.
pan·ier [ˈpæniə] *n.* = pannier.
pan·i·fi·ca·tion [ˌpænifiˈkeiʃən] *n.* 面包制作.
Pan·ja·bi [pənˈdʒæbi] *n.* 旁遮普人,旁遮普语 (=Punjabi).
pan·jan·drum [pənˈdʒændrəm] *n.* 大亨,大老爷〔讥讽自命不凡者的称呼〕;摆架子的官吏,架子十足的人.
Pank·hurst [ˈpæŋkhəːst] *n.* 潘克赫斯特〔姓氏〕.
pan·log·ism [ˈpænlədʒizəm] *n.*【哲】泛理论, 泛逻辑主义. **pan·lo·gis·tic** [ˌpænləˈdʒistik] *a.*
pan·mix·i·a [pænˈmiksiə] *n.*【生】随机交配;随机交配群体.
Pan·mun·jom [ˌpɑːnˌmunˈdʒʌm] *n.* 板门店〔朝鲜民主主义人民共和国村庄〕.
pan·nage [ˈpænidʒ] *n.* ①【英法】(林内)放猪(权);放猪费. ②(猪采食的)林中饲料〔橡子等〕.
panne [pæn] *n.*【纺】平滑轻柔的天鹅绒, 平绒 (= ~ velvet).
pan·ni·er [ˈpæniə] *n.* ①(挂在驮兽两旁的)驮篮;背篮. ②(从前用来张开女服裙部的)鲸骨框, 裙撑. ③野战用外科器械药品搬运篮.
pan·ni·kin [ˈpænikin] *n.* ①小盘子,小锅. ②(金属制)杯子;杯子里的东西.
pa·no·cha, pa·no·che [pəˈnəutʃə, -tʃi] *n.* (墨西哥)粗糖,红糖;红糖奶油核桃糖.
pan·oply [ˈpænəpli] *n.* ①全副甲胄;防护性覆盖物. ②盛装,礼服. ③壮丽的陈列〔装饰〕. **pan·o·plied** [ˈpænəplid] *a.* ①披戴全副甲胄的. ②盛装的.
pan·op·tic [pænˈɔptik] *a.* 一眼可见全貌的; 一目了然的;显示全貌的.
pan·op·ti·con [pænˈɔptikən] *n.* ①圆形监狱. ②珍品展览室〔会〕. ③望远显微镜.
pan·o·ra·ma [ˌpænəˈrɑːmə] *n.* ①(转现)全景(画); 全景照片; 全景装置. ②概观; 概论. ③一连串的景象〔事件〕.
pan·o·ram·ic [ˌpænəˈræmik] *a.* 全景的,全貌的. *a ~ view* 全景. *a ~ camera* 全景照相机. *a ~ sight*【军】全景瞄准镜. *a ~ sketch* 远景描绘图.
pan·o·ti·tis [ˈpænəˈtaitis] *n.*【医】全耳炎.
Pan-Pa·cif·ic [ˈpænpəˈsifik] *a.* 泛太平洋的, 全太平洋的.
Pan·pipe [ˈpæn-paip] *n.* 潘神笙;(芦杆制)排萧 (=~'s pipes).
pan·psy·chism [pænˈsaikizəm] *n.*【哲】泛心论, 万有精神论.
Pan-Slav·ism [ˈpænˈslɑːvizəm] *n.* 泛斯拉夫主义.
pan·so·phism [ˈpænsəfizəm] *n.* 万事通. **-phist** *n.* 万事通的人.
pan·so·phy [ˈpænsəfi] *n.* ①汎知,博识,万事皆知,无所不知. ②〔*pl.*〕包括各种知识的体系. **-soph·ic, -soph·i·cal** *a.*
pan·sper·mat·ism, pan·sper·my [pænˈspəːmətizəm, pænˈspəːmi] *n.*【生】胚种广布论.
Pan·sy [ˈpænzi] *n.* 潘西〔女子名〕.
pan·sy [ˈpænzi] *n.* ①【植】三色堇,三色紫罗兰. ②〔美俚〕脂粉气的男子; 搞同性恋的男子 (= ~ boy). — *a.* 〔美俚〕(男人)女性化的, 爱打扮的, 脂粉气的. — *vt., vi.* 〔美俚〕打扮 *(up)*.
pant[1] [pænt] *vt.* 气喘吁吁地讲 *(out, forth)*. — *vi.* ①喘气. ②心跳. ③热望,渴想,想 *(for; after)*. ④(机车等)喷气. — *n.* ①气喘. ②心跳. ③喷气声.
pant[2] [pænt] *n., a.* 裤子. ~ **dress** 工装裤. ~ **legs** 裤管.
pant- *comb. f.* 〔用于元音前〕= panto-.
pan·ta- = panto-.
pan·ta·graph [ˈpæntəgrɑːf] *n.* = pantograph.
Pan·tag·ru·el [ˌpæntəˈgru(ː)əl] *n.* 〔F.〕庞大古埃〔法国16世纪作家拉伯雷 (Rabelais) 所作《巨人传》中人物,粗野而喜欢嬉笑谑浪〕. **-i·an** [ˌpæntəˈgrueliən] *a.* 庞大古埃式的;粗野的;嬉笑谑浪的. **-ism** *n.* 粗野和嬉笑谑浪的作用. **-ist** *n.* 粗野和嬉笑谑浪的人.
pan·ta·let(te)s [ˌpæntəˈlets] *n.* ①(19世纪女人的)宽松长裤. ②〔美〕女裤;(骑自行车穿的)短裤.
pan·ta·loon [ˌpæntəˈluːn] *n.* ①〔P-〕(从前意大利喜剧中戴眼镜穿窄裤的)老角; (现代哑剧中为丑角取笑对象的) 傻瓜;傻老头. ②〔*pl.*〕【军】(军官的)马裤;〔*pl.*〕〔美〕裤子.
pan·ta·ta [pænˈteitə] *n.* 〔俚〕要人;老板,头子.
pan·tech·ni·con [pænˈteknikən] *n.* 〔英〕①家具仓库; 家具陈列〔出卖〕所. ②家具搬运车 (= ~ van).
pan·tel·e·graph [pænˈteligrɑːf] *n.* (早期的)有线传真电报.
pan·tel·e·gra·phy [pænˈteligrəfi] *n.* 有线传真电报(术).

pan·the·ism [ˈpænθi(ː)izəm] *n.*【哲】泛神论；对一切神道的崇拜，多神教；自然崇拜．**-the·ist** *n.* 泛神论者．**-the·is·tic, -is·ti·cal** [-ˈistik(əl)] *a.*

pan·the·lism [ˈpænθilizəm] *n.*【哲】唯意志论，意志主义．

pan·the·on [pænˈθi(ː)ən] *n.* ①【史】(古希腊，罗马供奉众神的)万神殿．②〔the P-〕伟人[先哲]祠．③(一个民族信奉的)众神．④(集团、个人、运动、党派等推崇的)英雄人物．*the British P-* 威斯敏斯特大教堂．

pan·ther [ˈpænθə] *n.* (*pl.* ~*s*〔集合词〕~)【动】豹；黑豹；美洲豹．*a Black P-* 黑豹党人．*the Black P- Party* 黑豹党〔美国一黑人组织〕．~ **sweat**〔美俚〕劣等酒．

pan·ther·ess [ˈpænθəris] *n.*【动】母(黑)豹．

pan·ties [pæntiz] *n.*〔*pl.*〕= panty.

pan·tile [ˈpæntail] *n.*【建】波形瓦．

pan·ti·soc·ra·cy [ˌpæntiˈsɔkrəsi] *n.* 理想的平等社会，大同世界．

pan·to [ˈpæntəu] *n.*〔口〕= pantomime.

panto- *comb. f.* 全部，所有，每 = pantology.

pan·to(f)·fle [ˈpæntəfəl] *n.* 拖鞋．

pan·to·graph [ˈpæntəgrɑːf] *n.* ①比例画图仪器，缩放仪．②(类似缩放仪的)动臂装置．③【电】(电车顶上的)导电弓架．**-ic** [ˌpæntəˈgræfik] *a.*

pan·tol·o·gy [pænˈtɔlədʒi] *n.* 百科全论，人类知识综合体系．

pan·to·mime [ˈpæntəmaim] *n.* ①哑剧．②〔英〕(圣诞节上演的)童话剧．③(古罗马的)哑剧演员．④姿势；手势；表意动作．— *vt.* 用手势传(意)．— *vi.* 演哑剧．**-to·mim·ic** [ˌpæntəˈmimik] *a.* **-to·mim·ist** *n.* ①哑剧作者[演员]．②打手势的人．

pan·to·mor·phic [ˌpæntəˈmɔːfik] *a.* 变幻自若的；形态万千的．

pan·to·night [ˈpæntənait] *n.* 有圣诞节童话剧上演的节日[纪念日]．

pan·to·prag·mat·ic [ˌpæntəprægˈmætik] *a.*, *n.*〔谑〕爱管闲事的(人)．

pan·to·scope [ˈpæntəskəup] *n.* 大角度照相机[凸镜]．

pan·to·scop·ic [ˌpæntəˈskɔpik] *a.* ①(照相机、凸镜等)大角度的．②眼界宽广的．*a ~ camera* 全景摄影机 = panoramic camera. ~ *spectacles* 全视眼镜，复眼镜．

pan·to·then·ate [ˌpæntəˈθeneit, pænˈtɔθineit] *n.*【化】泛酸盐[酯]，本多生酸盐[酯]．

pan·to·then·ic [ˌpæntəˈθenik] *a.*【化】泛酸的．~ **acid**【化】泛酸，本多生酸．

pan·toum [pænˈtuːm] *n.*〔Ma.〕盘头诗〔一种马来诗体〕．

pan·trop·ic(al) [pænˈtrɔpik(əl)] *a.* 遍布于热带的．

pan·try [ˈpæntri] *n.* ①餐具室；食品储存室；配膳室．②〔美俚〕胃．~**man** 饭厅管理员．

pants [pænts] *n.*〔*pl.*〕〔pantaloons 之略〕①〔美口〕裤子．②【英商】紧身长衬裤；(男用)短衬裤．③〔美〕(儿童或妇女用)紧身短衬裤．④【空】机轮减阻罩．*a ~ [landing] gear*【空】裤形起落架．*wheel ~* 机轮减阻罩．***be caught with one's ~ down***〔美俚〕措手不及地陷入窘况．***have ants in the ~***〔美口〕烦恼，不安．***keep your ~ [shirt] on***〔美口〕沉住气，别慌；别着急；等一等．***kick in the ~*** 受阻碍；受挫折．***wear the ~*** (妇女)掌权当家．***with one's ~ down*** 处于尴尬境地．~' **leg**〔美俚〕(飞机场的)风向标．~ **suit** = pantsuit.

pant·suit [ˈpæntsjuːt] *n.* (上衣与裤子相配的一种)妇女旅行服．

pan·tun [pænˈtuːn] *n.*〔Ma.〕= pantoum.

pant·y [ˈpænti] *n.*〔常 *pl.*〕①童裤；女裤(= panties)．②= ~ girdle. ~ **girdle** 叉式腰带．~ **hose** 女用连袜裤．

pant·y·waist [ˈpæntiweist] *n.* ①连衫裤童装．②〔美俚〕苗条柔弱的男子，女人气概的男子．

pan·zer [ˈpɑːntsə] *a.*〔G.〕装甲的，机械化的．— *n.* 装甲车，战车，坦克．*a ~ division* 装甲师．~ *troops* 装甲部队，机械化部队．

pap[1] [pæp] *n.* ①〔古、方〕奶头．②〔*pl.*〕奶头状双峰．

pap[2] [pæp] *n.* ①面包粥，奶面糊；果肉．②〔俚〕(官方给与的)援助，津贴；政治上的恩惠．③幼稚的话；纯消遣作品．*His mouth is full of ~.* 他还是个小孩子〔乳臭未干〕．***as easy [soft] as ~*** 易如儿戏．***give ~ with a hatchet*** ①假装不仁慈实际做好事．②假装让人尝甜头实则给人吃苦头．

pap[3] [pæp] *n.*〔美方〕= papa.

Pa·pa [pəˈpɑː] 通讯中用以代表字母P的词．

pa·pa [pəˈpɑː] *n.* ①〔儿〕爸爸．②〔美俚〕丈夫；爱人．

pa·pa·ble [ˈpeipəbl] *a.* 可选做教皇的．

pa·pa·cy [ˈpeipəsi] *n.* ①罗马教皇的职位[任期、权限]．②〔the P-〕教皇制度[统治]．③教皇的继承[系谱]．

Pa·pa·go [ˌpæpəˈgəu] *n.* ①(*pl.* ~*(s)*) 巴巴哥人〔主要居住在亚利桑那州塔克森南部的北美印第安人〕．②巴巴哥人的乌托阿芝特克语．

pa·pa·in [pəˈpeiin, -ˈpaiin] *n.*【医】木瓜蛋白酶．

pa·pal [ˈpeipəl] *a.* 罗马教皇的；天主教的．**P- States** 教皇辖地〔八世纪至1870年意大利的中部和中北部〕．**-ism** *n.* 教皇中心主义，教皇制度[统治]．**-ist** *n.*, *a.* 天主教徒(的)；教皇中心主义者(的)．**-ize** *vt.*, *vi.* ①(使)改信天主教；(使)变成天主教徒．②(使)建立教皇统治．**-ly** *ad.* 由罗马教皇；按天主教方式．

Pa·pan·ic·o·la·ou [ˈpɑːpəˈniːkəlau] *n.* ~ **test** 脱落细胞巴氏染色法〔用以检查早期癌症〕．

Pa·pa·raz·zi [ˌpɑːpɑːˈrɑːtsi] [It.] *n.*〔*pl.*〕(*sing.* **-raz·zo** [-tsəu]) 无固定职业的摄影师．

Pa·pa·ver [pəˈpeivə] *n.* 罂粟属〔俗名 poppy〕．

pa·pa·ver·a·ceous [pəˈpeivəˈreiʃəs] *a.* 罂粟科的．

pa·pav·er·ine [pəˈpævəˌriːn] *n.*【化】罂粟碱．

pa·pa·ver·ous [pəˈpeivərəs] *a.* 罂粟(似)的；催眠的．

pa·paw [ˈpɑːpɔː] *n.* ①【植】巴婆树；巴婆果．②[pəˈpɔː] = papaya.

pa·pa·ya [pəˈpaiə] *n.* 番木瓜(树)．

Pa·pe·e·te [ˌpɑːpiˈeitei] *n.* 帕皮提〔法属波利尼西亚首府〕．

pa·per [ˈpeipə] *n.* ①纸；裱墙纸．②报纸，报．③收据；债券；证券；票据；汇票，钞票(= ~ money)．④〔*pl.*〕身分证．⑤〔*pl.*〕文件，记录；辞呈．⑥论文，论说；考题；答案．⑦〔俚〕招待券，免费入场券；〔集合词〕免费入场者．⑧〔美俚〕火车票；纸牌．⑨(装有东西的)一纸包，一纸袋，一盒．⑩涂有药的纸．*a sheet of ~* 一张纸．*art ~* 铜版纸．*blotting ~* 吸墨纸．*brown ~* 牛皮纸．*carbon ~* 复写纸．*craft ~* 牛皮纸．*crape ~* 绉纸．*glass ~* 砂纸．*manifold ~* (打字、复写用)薄纸．*plotting ~* 方格纸．*sensitive ~* 感光纸．*tracing ~* (半透明)描图纸．*a daily ~* 日报．*a morning [evening] ~* 早[晚]报．*What do the ~s say?* 报纸怎么说？*good ~* 可靠的支票．*state ~s* 公文．*value ~* 有价证券．*a negotiable ~* 流通票据．*collected ~s* 论文集；书信文件集．*The house was largely filled with ~.* 场内免费来宾拥挤不堪．*a ~ of pins* 一包针．***commit sth. to ~*** 把某事记录下来，写下来．***lay ~*** 使用空头支票[假钞票]．***on ~*** 纸上；统计上；理论上，名义上．***put pen to ~*** 开始写，下笔．***send in one's ~s*** (特指陆海军军官)提出辞呈．***set a ~*** 出考试题目．***walking ~s***〔美俚〕解雇通知；(朋友等的)拒绝；要人走开．— *a.* ①纸(做)的．②纸上的，假定的．*a ~ lantern* 灯笼．*a ~ war* (= ~ warfare) 笔战，纸上论战．*a ~ blockade* (只有宣言而无实力的)纸上封锁．*a ~ farmer* (不懂实际操作的)理论农业家．*a ~ army* 有名无实的军队．— *vt.* ①用纸裱(贴)，用纸覆盖，用纸包；(装钉)用纸衬里．②为…供给纸张．③用砂纸擦．④〔俚〕免费观众充塞(剧场)．~ *a room* 用纸裱糊

房间. ~ *a butterfly* 把蝴蝶标本贴到纸上. — *vi.* 贴糊墙纸. ~**back** 纸面本,平装本. ~**backed** *a.* 纸面装的,平装的. ~ **baron** (只限于一代的)挂名男爵. ~ **board** 卡纸板. ~**bound** *a.* (书)纸面的. ~ **boy** 报童, 送报人. ~ **bush**【植】(= ~-tree). ~ **chase** (一些人假扮兔子撒纸屑、另一些人假扮猎犬追赶的) 撒纸屑追踪游戏. ~ **clip** 纸夹; 回形针. ~ **currency** 纸币. ~**-cut** 剪纸. ~ **cutter** 裁纸刀,切纸机. ~ **file** 文件夹. ~ **gold**【经】纸黄金〔即特别提款权〕. ~**hanger** ①裱糊工人,裱褙匠. ②〔美俚〕使用假纸币〔假支票〕的人, 伪造钞票的人. ~**hanging** ①裱糊裱墙纸; 〔*pl.*〕裱糊纸. ②〔美俚〕伪造支票. ~ **house** 〔美俚〕有许多免费招待观众的戏剧〔马戏等〕. ~ **knife** ①(用象牙、木头等做的)裁纸刀. ②(切纸机的)切刀. ~ **machine** 造纸机. ~**maker** 造纸工,造纸者 (~ *maker's alum*【化】造纸明矾). ~**-making** 造纸. ~ **man** 〔美俚〕不看乐谱就不会弹奏的乐师. ~ **match** 纸梗火柴. ~ **mill** 造纸厂. ~ **money** 纸币, 钞票. ~**mulberry** 【植】楮,构树. ~ **muslin** 光滑棉布. ~ **nautilus**【贝】贝葵. ~ **pulp** 纸浆. ~**-reed**, ~**rush** (= papyrus). ~ **stainer** 墙纸制造人〔着色人〕. ~**-thin** *a.* 薄如纸的;极薄弱的. ~ **tiger** 纸老虎,外强中干者. ~**tree**【植】结香属. ~ **twine** 纸绳. ~**-weight** 压纸器,文镇,镇纸. ~ **white** *n.* 多花水仙. ~ **work** 文书档案工作;写作. ~ **worker** = ~ **maker**.

pa·per·y [ˈpeipəri] *a.* 纸状的,纸质的.

pap·e·terie [ˈpæpitriː] *n.* 文具盒.

Pa·phi·an [ˈpeifiən] *a.* ①(塞浦路斯西南部古城)帕福斯(Paphos)(人)的. ②〔p-〕性爱的; 情欲的.

Pa·pia·men·to [ˌpɑːpjɑːˈmentəu] *n.* 巴皮阿孟特语〔一种西班牙土语,其中夹杂着荷兰语和葡萄牙语〕.

pap·ier collé [ˈpæpjei-kɔˈlei] *n.* 〔F.〕拼贴画.

pap·ier-mâ·ché [ˈpæpjeiˈmɑːʃei] *n.* 〔F.〕①【印】纸型. ②制型纸〔纸浆中混入树胶等制成, 具有高度韧性〕. *a ~ mould*【印】纸型,纸版. — *a.* ①制型纸做的. ②人造的,假的. *a ~ facade* 虚饰的门面.

pa·pil·i·o·na·ceous [pəˌpiliəˈneiʃəs] *a.*【植】蝶形的,有蝶形花的.

pa·pil·la [pəˈpilə] *n.* (*pl.* **-lae** [-liː])【解、植】乳头; 乳头状小突起; 味蕾; 吐丝突; 棘.

pa·pil·lar, pa·pil·la·ry, pap·il·late(d) [pəˈpilə,-ləri, ˈpæpileit(id)] *a.* 乳头的; 乳头状突起的; 乳突的.

pap·il·lo·ma [ˌpæpiˈləumə] *n.* (*pl.* **-ma·ta** [-mətə], ~**s**)【医】乳头(状)瘤. **-tous** [-təs] *a.*

pap·il·lose [ˈpæpiləus] *a.* 多乳头状小突起的; 多疣的; 疹状的.

pa·pism [ˈpeipizəm] *n.* 〔蔑〕教皇制度; 罗马天主教.

pa·pist [ˈpeipist] *n.* 歌颂教皇政治者; 〔蔑〕罗马天主教徒. — *a.* 罗马天主教(徒)的.

pa·pis·tic, pa·pis·ti·cal [pəˈpistik, -tikəl] *a.* 〔蔑〕罗马天主教的. **-ti·cal·ly** *ad.*

pa·pist·ry [ˈpeipistri] *n.* 〔蔑〕教皇制度; 罗马天主教(教义).

pa·poose [pəˈpuːs] *n.* ①北美印第安人的婴儿〔幼儿〕. ②〔美俚〕和工会会员一起工作的非会员工人.

pap·pose, pap·pous [ˈpæpəus, ˈpæpəs] *a.*【植】有冠毛的,冠毛的 (=pappous).

pap·pus [ˈpæpəs] *n.* (*pl.* ***pap·pi*** [ˈpæpai])【植】冠毛; 柔毛.

pap·py[1] [ˈpæpi] *a.* 面包粥似的,半流质的; 乳状的; 黏糊糊的.

pap·py[2] [ˈpæpi] *n.* 〔美俚〕爸爸. ~ **guy** 〔美俚〕(一个团体中的)长者.

pa·preg [ˈpeipreg] *n.* 层压纸板.

pap·ri·ka, pap·ri·ca [ˈpæprikə, pæˈpriːkə] *n.* (匈牙利)红辣椒; 辣椒粉.

Pap test [pæp test] *n.* 〔口〕早期子宫颈癌涂片检验 (= Papanicolaou test).

Pap·u·a [ˈpæpjuə, ˈpɑːpuɑː] *n.* 巴布亚〔新几内亚(New Guinea) 岛的旧名〕; 巴布亚人. **Pap·uan** [ˈpæpjuən] ① *n.* 巴布亚语; 巴布亚人. ② *a.* 巴布亚(人,语)的.

Pa·pu·a New Guin·ea [ˈpæpjuə njuː ˈgini] 巴布亚新几内亚〔西太平洋〕.

pap·u·la [ˈpæpjulə] *n.* (*pl.* **-lae** [-liː]) ①【医】丘疹. ②【动】鳃突; 皮鳃;【植】小突起.

pap·ule [ˈpæpjuːl] *n.* = papula.

pap·y·ra·ceous [ˌpæpiˈreiʃəs] *a.* 似纸的,薄的 (= papery).

pa·py·ro·graph [pəˈpaiərəgrɑːf] *n.* 一种复写器.

pa·py·ro·type [pəˈpaiərətaip] *n.* (图片等的)锌版复制.

pa·py·rus [pəˈpaiərəs] *n.* (*pl.* **-ri** [-rai]) ①【植】纸莎草, 大伞莎草. ②(古埃及人等用纸纱草造的)莎草纸. ③〔*pl.*〕(莎草纸的)古写本〔文稿〕.

PAR = ①precision approach radar【空】精确进场雷达. ②pulse acquisition radar【军】脉冲搜索雷达.

par[1] [pɑː] *n.* ①同等, 同位, 同价. ②(两种货币间对比的)制定等价,平价. ③【商】牌价; 票面金额. ④定额,标准; (健康或精神的)常态;【高尔夫球】标准打数. *an issue ~* 发行价格. *a nominal [face] ~* 票面价值. *~ of exchange* (汇兑的)法定牌价; 外汇平价. ***above ~*** 在票面价值以上; 在标准〔一般水平〕以上. ***at ~*** 照票面价值, 与票面价值相等. ***below ~*** ①在票面价值以下; 在标准〔一般水平〕以下. ②身体不舒服. ***on a ~ with*** 和…相等〔同价〕; 和…一样. ***up to ~*** 达到标准〔一般水平、正常状况〕. — *a.* ①与票面价值相等的,平价的. ②常态的,平均的,一般标准〔水平〕的. ~ **value** 票面价值.

par[2] [pɑː] *n.* 〔口〕= paragraph (*n.*).

par[3] [pɑː] *n.* = parr.

par. = ①paragraph. ②parallel. ③parenthesis. ④parish.

par- *pref.* 〔用于元音前〕= para-[1].

pa·ra [ˈpɑːrɑː] *n.* 〔口〕= parachutist; paragraph.

Para. = Paraguay.

para-[1] *pref.* ①侧, 副, 外, 超, 对, 反, 误: *para*llel; *para*logism. ②【化】对(位),聚,仲,副: *para*diazine. ③【医】对,副,衍: *para*typhoid.

para-[2] *pref.* 保护, 庇护, 避难: *para*dos.

para-[3] *pref.* 降落伞、伞兵: *para*operation 伞兵战.

par·a·am·i·no·sal·i·cyl·ic [ˈpæræəˌminəuˌsæliˈsilik] *a.* ~ **acid**【药】对氨基水杨酸(略作 PAS).

par·a·bi·o·sis [ˌpærəbaiˈəusis] *n.* 【生】①异种共生. ②并生. ③间生态. **-bi·otic** [-ˈɔtik] *a.*

par·a·blast [ˈpærəˌblæst] *n.*【胚】副胚层. **-ic** *a.*

par·a·ble [ˈpærəbl] *n.* ①(道德说教性的)寓言; 比喻. ②〔古〕格言. ③〔美俚〕大话.

pa·rab·o·la [pəˈræbələ] *n.* ①【数】抛物线. ②碗状物〔如话筒等〕.

par·a·bol·ic, -i·c(al) [ˌpærəˈbɔlik(əl)] *a.* ①比喻的; 寓言似的. ②抛物线(状)的.

pa·rab·o·lize [pəˈræbəlaiz] *vt.* ①以寓言表示,用比喻说明. ②使成抛物线. **-r** *n.*

pa·rab·o·loid [pəˈræbəlɔid] *n.*【数】抛物面; 抛物体.

para·bomb [ˈpærəbɔm] *n.* 伞投炸弹.

par·a·chor [ˈpærəkɔː] *n.*【物】等张比容.

par·ach·ro·mat·ism [ˈpærəˈkrəumətizəm] *n.*【医】色觉倒错.

par·ach·ro·nism [pəˈrækrənizəm] *n.* (把正确日期错误地记迟的)记迟时误 (*opp.* anachronism).

par·a·chute [ˈpærəʃuːt] *n.* ①降落伞; 降落伞状物. ②【植】风散种子. ③【动】(蝙蝠等的)翅膜; (鳞翅目的)领片. *a heavy-duty ~* 快速降落伞. *a free-fall ~* 手开降落伞. *a cargo ~* 投物伞. *~ troops* 伞兵, 伞兵部队. — *vt.* 用降落伞投送, 伞投. — *vi.* ①用降落伞降落. ②〔美俚〕突然倾斜,突然跌下. **-r, -chut·ist** *n.*【空】跳伞者,伞兵. **-chut·ic** [ˌpærəˈʃuːtik] *a.*

par·a·clete [ˈpærəkliːt] *n.* ①辩护人,调解人; 安慰者.

②〔P-〕【宗】圣灵.
pa·rade [pəˈreid] *n.* ①游行,示威游行;(检阅时的)行进式;盛况,壮观. ②陈列,展览;炫示;虚饰. ③【军】阅兵,检阅,阅兵式;练兵场,操场,校场. ④【英】(尤指海岸等的)散步场,运动场,广场;散步的人群. ⑤【剑】挡开;防御,守势. ⑥(城中的)院子. ⑦〔美俚〕拳赛节目. *dress* ~ 阅兵典礼. *program(me)* ~ 广播〔电视〕节目预告. ***in front of the*** ~ 【美俗】得冠军. ***join the*** ~〔美〕学时髦,跟着大众行动. ***make a*** ~ ***of*** 夸耀,炫示. ***on*** ~ (演员等)全体出场. — *vt.* ①使列队行进;在…游行. ②夸耀(才能等);标榜. — *vi.* ①整步行进,列队游行. ②散步. ③夸耀,自吹. ~ *as an advocate of* 标榜为…的拥护者. **~-ground** 练兵场,校场. ~ **rest** 士兵在校阅时的稍息姿势;发出稍息令. **~r** *n.* 游行者.
par·a·di·chlo·ro·ben·zene [ˌpærədaiˌklɔːrəˈbenziːn, -benˈziːn] *n.* 【化】对二氯苯.
par·a·did·dle [ˈpærədidl] *n.* 〔拟声〕咚咚哒哒声,撕边〔左右两鼓槌交替连续敲鼓声〕.
par·a·digm [ˈpærədaim, -dim] *n.* ①【修】范例;示例. ②【语法】(名词、动词等的)词形变化表.
par·a·dig·mat·ic [ˈpærədigˈmætik] *a.* 作为示范的;例证的. **-al·ly** *ad.*
par·a·di·sa·ic, par·a·di·sa·i·cal [ˌpærədiˈseik(əl)] *a.* = paradisiac.
par·a·dise [ˈpærədais] *n.* ①天堂,乐园;〔P-〕【宗】伊甸乐园(= Garden of Eden). ②地上乐园,乐土,极乐;至福. ③(养有鸟兽的)公园. ④【建】(教堂的)前院;门廊二楼;〔俚〕(戏院的)顶层座位. *a bird of* ~ 极乐鸟,风鸟. *fool's* ~ 虚幻的乐境;幻想的世界. ~ **bird** 极乐鸟,风鸟. ~ **fish** 极乐鱼〔一种供观赏用的热带鱼〕. **P- valley** 〔美〕(美国西部的)世外桃源.
par·a·dis·e·an [ˌpærəˈdisiən, -ˈdizien] *a.* 天堂(似)的,乐园(似)的;极乐的.
par·a·dis·i·ac, par·a·di·si·a·cal [ˌpærəˈdisiæk, ˌpærədiˈsaiəkəl] *a.* = paradisean.
par·a·dis·i·al [ˌpærəˈdiziəl] *a.* = paradisean.
par·a·dos [ˈpærədɔs] *n.* 【军】背墙〔在堑壕或掩体后构筑的防护土垛〕.
par·a·dox [ˈpærədɔks] *n.* ①似非而可能是的论点. ②反面议论,反论,悖论;疑题. ③自相矛盾的话;奇谈,怪论;前后矛盾的事物. ④【物】佯谬. **-er, -ist** *n.* 反论家.
par·a·dox·i·cal [ˌpærəˈdɔksikəl] *a.* ①反论的,反面议论的. ②似非而可能是的. ③悖论的;反常的,荒谬的;自相矛盾的. ④爱诡辩的. **-i·ty** [-ˈkæliti] *n.* 似非而是性. **-ly** *ad.*
par·a·dox·ure [ˌpærəˈdɔksjuə] *n.* 【动】(亚洲南部产)长尾麝香猫.
par·a·dox·y [ˈpærədɔksi] *n.* = paradoxicality.
par·a·drop [ˈpærədrɔp] *vt., n.* 【空】空投,伞投.
par·aes·the·si·a [ˌpæresˈθiːʒə, -ʒiə] *n.* 【医】感觉异常(= paresthesia).
par·af·fin, par·af·fine [ˈpærəfin, ˈpærəfiːn] *n.* ①〔美〕(硬)石蜡. ②【化】链烷(属)烃. ③〔英〕煤油. — *vt.* 用石蜡涂〔浸透〕. **~-oil** 石蜡油;〔英〕煤油. ~ **scale (wax)** 粗石蜡.
par·a·frag [ˈpærəfræg] *n.* 【军】伞投杀伤炸弹.
par·a·gen·e·sis [ˌpærəˈdʒenisis] *n.* 【地】共生,共生次序. **-net·ic** [-dʒiˈnetik] *a.*
par·a·go·ge [ˌpærəˈgəudʒiː] *n.* 【语音】词末附加音〔在词尾附加无意义之音: amid*st*〕.
par·a·gon [ˈpærəgən] *n.* ①(尽善尽美的)模范〔典型〕. ②优秀的人〔物〕;逸品,殊品;完人. ③(100 克拉以上的)大钻石;特大珍珠. ④【印】20点铅字. *Man is the* ~ *of animals.* 人为万物之灵. *a* ~ *of beauty* 美的典型. — *vt.* ①〔诗〕比较 *(with)*. ②〔古〕与…竞争 *(with)*. ③〔古〕胜过,强过.
pa·rag·o·nite [pəˈrægəˌnait] *n.* 【化】钠云母. **-nit·ic** [-ˈnitik] *a.*
par·a·graph [ˈpærəgrɑːf] *n.* ①(文章的)节,段. ②分段符号〔¶〕. ③(报纸的)短文,短评. *an editorial* ~ 短评. *miscellaneous* ~*s* 杂评. ~ *advertisement* 新闻式广告. — *vt.* ①把…分段. ②写短文报导. — *vi.* (为报刊)写短评〔杂评〕.
par·a·graph·er, par·a·graph·ist [ˈpærəgrɑːfə,-fist] *n.* 杂评〔短评〕作者. ★美国多用 paragrapher.
par·a·graph·i·a [ˌpærəˈgræfiə] *n.* 【医】书写倒错.
par·a·graph·ic(al) [ˌpærəˈgræfik(əl)] *a.* ①分段的. ②杂评的. **-cal·ly** *ad.*
Par·a·guay [ˈpærəgwai] *n.* 巴拉圭〔拉丁美洲〕.
Par·a·guay·an [ˌpærəˈgwaiən, -ˈgwei-] *n., a.* 巴拉圭人(的).
par·a·he·li·ot·ro·pism [ˌpærəˌhiːliˈɔtrəpizəm] *n.* 【植】(叶子的)偏日性.
par·a·keet [ˈpærəkiːt] *n.* 【鸟】长尾小鹦鹉.
par·a·kite [ˈpærəkait] *n.* ①(可作降落伞用的)降落风筝. ②(观测气象等用的)无尾风筝.
par·al·de·hyde [pəˈrældihaid] *n.* 【化】(三)聚乙醛〔作安眠药用〕.
par·a·leip·sis, par·a·lip·sis [ˌpærəˈlaipsis, -ˈlip-] *n.* *(pl. -ses* [-siːz]*)* 【修】假省笔法〔省略重要部分反而起强调作用的方法〕.
par·al·lac·tic [ˌpærəˈlæktik] *a.* 【物、天】视差的.
par·al·lax [ˈpærəlæks] *n.* 【物、天】视差. *the equatorial horizonal* ~ 赤道地平视差.
par·al·lel [ˈpærəlel] *a.* ①平行的;并行的 *(to; with)*; 【电】并联的. ②同一方向的,同一目的的. ③相同的,同样的,相似的,对应的. *a* ~ *instance [case]* 同样的例子〔情况〕. *His prudence is* ~ *to his zeal.* 他固然谨慎,也同样热心. ***run*** ~ ***with*** 和…平行. — *n.* ①平行线〔面〕. ②相似,类似;相似物,相当的人〔物〕. ③比较,对比. ④纬度圈,纬线. ⑤【军】平行堑壕. ⑥【印】平行号〔‖〕. ⑦【电】并联. *the* ~ *of altitude [declination, latitude]* 平纬〔赤纬,黄纬〕圈. ***draw a*** ~ ***between*** ... 在…之间作对比. ***in*** ~ ***with*** 和…并行;和…对应. ***without (a)*** ~ 无与匹敌的. — *vt.* ①使成平行;与…平行. ②与…相匹〔配得上,相应〕. ③对比,比较… *(with)*. ~ **bars** 【体】双杠;【机】平行杆. ~ **circuit** 【电】并联电路. ~ **feed** 【电】并联馈电. ~ **feeder** 【电】平行馈(电)线. ~ **resonance** 【电】并联谐振. ~ **ruler** 平行线规.
par·al·le·le·p·i·ped, par·al·lel·e·pip·e·don [ˌpærəleˈlepiped, ˌpærəˌleliˈpipidən] *n.* 【几】平行六面体〔常误拼作 parallelopiped, parallelopipedon〕.
par·al·lel·ism [ˌpærəˈlelizəm] *n.* ①平行. ②相同,类似;比较;对应. ③【哲】心身平行论. ④【生、数】平行现象,平行性. ⑤【修】对句法,对联.
par·al·lel·o·gram [ˌpærəˈleləgræm] *n.* 【数】平行四边形. *a period* ~ 周期格子,周期网. ~ *of forces* 【物】力的平行四边形. **-ic** *a.*
pa·ral·o·gism [pəˈrælədʒizəm] *n.* 【逻】谬误推理,谬论;背理,反理.
pa·ral·o·gize [pəˈrælədʒaiz] *vi.* 作谬误推论.
par·a·ly·sa·tion [ˌpærəlaiˈzeiʃən] *n.* ①麻痹,瘫痪. ②无能为力;气馁;惊呆.
par·a·lyse, par·a·lyze [ˈpærəlaiz] *vt.* ①使麻痹,使瘫痪. ②使无力,使无效;使气馁;使惊呆. ③【电】关闭. *be* ~*d with fear by* 被…吓瘫了,被…所吓倒. ~ *one's efforts* 使努力尽成泡影. **-d** *a.* ①麻痹的;瘫痪的;惊呆的. ②〔美俚〕喝得烂醉的.
pa·ral·y·sis [pəˈrælisis] *n.* *(pl. -ses* [-siːz]*)* ①【医】麻痹,瘫痪;中风. ②无能,无气力. *infantile* ~ 小儿麻痹症. *general* ~ 全身瘫痪. *moral* ~ 道德败坏. ~ **agitans** [ˈædʒitænz] 【医】震颤(性)麻痹.
par·a·lyt·ic [ˌpærəˈlitik] *a.* ①麻痹的,患中风的. ②无

P

能力的. — *n.* 麻痹[中风]病人.

par·a·mag·net·ic [ˌpærəmæg'netik] *a.*【物】顺磁(的). ～ *substance* 顺磁质. **-net·ism** [-'mægnitizəm] *n.*【物】顺磁性.

Par·a·mar·i·bo [ˌpærə'mæribəu] *n.* 帕拉马里博〔苏里南首府〕.

par·a·mat·ta [ˌpærə'mætə] *n.*【纺】棉毛呢;毛葛.

par·a·me·cin [ˌpærə'mi:sin] *n.*【生化】草履(虫)素.

par·a·me·ci·um [ˌpærə'mi:siəm] *n.* *(pl.* ***-ci·a*** [-siə, -ʃiə]*)*【动】草履虫.

par·a·med·ic[1] ['pærəˌmedik] *n.* 伞兵军医; 伞降医师.

par·a·med·ic[2] ['pærəˌmedik] *n.* 护理人员, 医务辅助人员.

par·a·med·i·cal [ˌpærə'medikl] *a.* 医务助理人员的.

par·a·ment ['pærəˌment] *n.* *(pl.* *～s, ～ta* [-tə]*)* (基督教的)祭衣; 装饰品.

pa·ram·e·ter [pə'ræmitə] *n.* ①【数】参数,变数; 参词; 参项. ②【物】参量; (结晶体的)标轴. ③〔废〕【天】通径.

par·a·met·ric [ˌpærə'metrik] *a.* 参(变)数的; 参量的.

par·am·e·tron [pæ'ræmitrɔn] *n.*【无】参变元件,变感元件.

par·a·mil·i·tar·y [ˌpærə'militəri] *a.* ①起军事辅助作用的; 副军事性的; 准军事性的. ②半军事性秘密私人组织的.

par·am·ne·si·a [ˌpæræm'ni:ziə] *n.*【心】记忆错误; 旧事幻现.

pa·ra·mo ['pærəməu] *n.* *(pl.* *～s)* (南美洲热带地方的,尤指安第斯山脉的)荒野高原.

par·a·morph ['pærəmɔ:f] *n.*【矿】副象,同质异晶体. **-ic** [ˌpærə'mɔ:fik] *a.*

par·a·mor·phism [ˌpærə'mɔ:fizm] *n.*【矿】同质异晶现象.

par·a·mount ['pærəmaunt] *a.* ①最高的,至上的,首要的. ②有最高权力的. ③卓越的; 胜过…的 *(to)*. *a* ～ *chief* 帝王. ***of*** ～ ***importance*** 最重要的. — *n.* ①有最高权力的人; 元首; 首长. ②最高, 至上, 主要. *the lady* ～ 女王; 射击赛女冠军. *the lord* ～ 国王. **-ly** *ad.*

par·a·mount·cy ['pærəmaun*t*si] *n.* ①最高权力,主权. ②至上,最上,首要.

par·a·mour ['pærəmuə] *n.* ①奸夫; 情妇. ②〔古、诗〕情人.

par·am·y·lum [pæ'ræmiləm] *n.*【生】副淀粉; 裸藻淀粉.

pa·rang [pɑ:'rɑ:ŋ] *n.* 〔Ma.〕大而重的短刀.

par·a·noi·a, par·a·noe·a [ˌpærə'nɔiə, ˌpærə'ni:ə] *n.*【医】偏执狂,妄想狂.

par·a·noid ['pærənɔid] *a.* ①患妄想狂的,似妄想狂的. ②过分猜疑的; 幻想狂的; 被迫害妄想狂的 (= paranoidal). — *n.* 患妄想狂者 (= paranoiac).

par·a·nor·mal [ˌpærə'nɔ:məl] *a.* 超出科学可了解范围的,超自然的,不平常的.

par·a·nymph ['pærənimf] *n.* 男(女)傧相.

par·a·pack ['pærəpæk] *n.*【军】空投包.

par·a·pet ['pærəpit] *n.* ①(阳台、桥等的)栏杆; 女儿墙. ②【军】(构筑在堑壕和掩体前方的)胸墙, 胸壁. ③〔英方〕人行道. **-ed** [-tid] *a.* 筑有胸墙[栏杆等]的.

par·aph ['pæræf] *n.* (从前防止冒充的)花押,签名后的花押. — *vt.* 在…上画花押.

par·a·pha·si·a [ˌpærə'feiziə] *n.*【医】语言无序, 语言错乱.

par·a·pher·na·li·a [ˌpærəfə'neiljə, -liə] *n.* 〔*pl.*〕①随身用具, 行头; 装饰品. ②各种器具; 机械附件. ③【法】妻子特有的动产[衣服、首饰等]. *camp* ～ 露营行装.

par·a·phrase ['pærəfreiz] *n.* ①释义; 意译. ② 〔Scot.〕圣经章句的诗译. — *vt., vi.* (将…)释义; 意译. ～ *an obscure passage* 将一段晦涩的文字加以意译.

par·a·phrast ['pærəfræst] *n.* 释义〔意译〕者. **-a-phras·tic** [ˌpærə'fræstik] *a.* 意译的; 释义的.

pa·raph·y·sis [pə'ræfisis] *n.* *(pl.* ***-ses*** [-ˌsi:z]*)*【植】隔丝,侧丝(菌).

par·a·ple·gi·a [ˌpærə'pli:dʒiə] *n.*【医】截瘫,下身麻痹.

par·a·ple·gic [-dʒik] *a.*

par·a·prax·is [ˌpærə'præksis] *n.* *(pl.* ***-xes*** [-si:z]*)*【心】动作倒错.

par·a·prax·ia [ˌpærə'præksiə] *n.* = parapraxis.

par·a·pro·fes·sion·al [ˌpærəprə'feʃənl] *a., n.* 辅助专职人员[医师]的(人).

par·a·psy·chol·o·gy ['pærəsai'kɔlədʒi] *n.*【心】灵学.

par·a·res·cue ['pærəˌreskju:] *n.* 伞兵(对遇险者的)营救,伞投人员进行的救援.

par·a·ros·an·i·line [ˌpærərəu'zænlin] *n.*【纺】副蔷薇苯胺,副玫瑰红.

par·a-sail, par·a·sail [ˌpærəˌseil] *n.* 滑翔跳伞. — *vi.* 作滑翔跳伞运动.

par·a·sang ['pærəsæŋ] *n.* 帕拉桑〔古波斯的长度名,〔约合 5.5 公里或 $3\frac{1}{4}$ 英里〕.

par·a·se·le·ne [ˌpærəsi'li:ni] *n.* *(pl.* ***-nae*** [-ni:]*)*【气】幻月〔月晕时的光轮〕.

par·a·shah ['pɑ:rəˌʃɑ:] *n.* *(pl.* ***par·a·shoth*** [-ˌʃəut]*)* (犹太教堂所诵的)摩西五经中五十四段的一段(每周大安息日诵一段,一年诵完); 摩西五经中的选段〔专供节日诵读〕.

par·a·shoot ['pærəʃu:t] *vi.* *(****par·a·shot*** ['pærəʃɔt]*)* 射击敌人伞兵. **-er, par·a·shot** ['pærəʃɔt] *n.* 专打伞兵的射手.

par·a·site ['pærəsait] *n.* ①寄生物; 寄生虫; 寄生菌; 寄生植物; 寄生矿物. ②食客; 清客, 谄媚者. ③反射器. ～ **aeroplane [plane]** (飞行中由母机携带或发射的)子机. ～ **drag**【空】寄生阻力.

par·a·sit·ic(al) [ˌpærə'sitik(əl)] *a.* ①寄生的, 寄生动[植]物的; 寄生体的,寄生质的; (疾病)由寄生虫引起的. ②寄食的; 奉承的. *a* ～ *wasp* 寄生蜂. **-cal·ly** *ad.*

par·a·sit·i·cide [ˌpærə'sitisaid] *a.* 杀寄生虫的. — *n.* 杀寄生虫药.

par·a·sit·i·cin [ˌpærə'sitisin] *n.*【医】苄青霉素.

par·a·sit·ism ['pærəsaitizəm] *n.* ①寄生(现象,状态). ②阿谀, 奉承. ③【医】寄生物传染; (寄生虫引起的)皮肤病.

par·a·sit·ize ['pærəsaitaiz] *vt.* 〔主用 *p.p.*〕寄生于; 侵害; 为寄生虫[食客]…所烦扰.

par·a·sit·oid ['pærəˌsaitɔid] *n.*【动】拟寄生.

par·a·si·tol·o·gy [ˌpærəsai'tɔlədʒi] *n.* 寄生物[虫]学; 寄生分子行为及心理研究.

par·a·sit·o·sis [ˌpærəsai'təusis] *n.* *(pl.* ***-ses*** [-si:z]*)* 寄生物病,寄生虫病.

par·a·sol [ˌpærə'sɔl, 'pærəsɔ:l] *n.* ①(女用)阳伞. ②【空】伞式单翼机. ***the Chinese [sultan's]*** ～ ***(trees)*** 梧桐. ～ **ant** 樵蚁〔产于南美热带地区〕.

par·a·spot·ter [ˌpærə'spɔtə] *n.* 守望伞兵者.

par·a·sym·pa·thet·ic [ˌpærəˌsimpə'θetik] *a.*【解、生】副交感(神经)的.

par·a·sym·pa·tho·mi·metic [ˌpærəˌsimpəˌθəumi'metik] *a.* 副交感神经性的〔指药物、化学药品等而言〕.

par·a·syn·ap·sis [ˌpærəsi'næpsis] *n.*【生】(染色体的)平行配合.

par·a·syn·the·sis [ˌpærə'sinθisis] *n.*【语】双重构词〔从复合词又造派生词, 如 denationalize, tender-hearted 等〕. **-thet·ic** [-'θetik] *a.*

par·a·tax·is [ˌpærə'tæksis] *n.*【语】(不用连接词的)并列结构[关系]; 并列排比; 意合法〔使几个分句不用连接词而排列起来,例如: I came, I saw, I conquered. 或使主句与从句间不用连接词而排列起来,如 Tell me, how are you, 等〕 *(opp.* hypotaxis*)*. **-tac·tic** [ˌpærə'tæktik] *a.*

Par·a·tet·ran·y·chus [ˌpærətetˈrænikəs] *n.*【动】(伤害橘树和胡桃树的)红蜘蛛.

pa·rath·e·sis [pəˈræθisis] *n.* (*pl.* **-ses** [-siːz]) = parenthesis.

par·a·thi·on [ˌpærəˈθaiən] *n.*【化】对硫磷, 硝苯硫磷, 柏拉息昂〔用作农业杀虫剂〕.

par·a·thy·roid [ˌpærəˈθairɔid] *a.* ①甲状旁腺附近的. ②甲状旁腺上或附近的四个小卵圆腺的. — *n.* 甲状旁腺.

par·a·troop [ˈpærətruːp] *n.* 〔*pl.*〕【军】伞兵部队. — *a.* 伞兵的. **-er** *n.* 伞兵.

par·a·tu·nic [ˌpærəˈtjuːnik] *n.* 伞兵上衣.

par·a·ty·phoid [ˌpærəˈtaifɔid] *n., a.*【医】副伤寒(的).

par·a·vane [ˈpærəvein] *n.*【军】破雷卫, 防水雷器〔军舰上切断水雷的一种装置〕; 防潜艇器. ~ **chain** 防雷器链. ~ **davits** 扫雷器吊架.

par a·vi·on [ˌpɑːræˈvjɔ̃ːŋ]〔F.〕由航空邮寄〔邮件标签〕.

par·a·wing [ˈpærəwiŋ] *n.* (可定点降落的)翼状降落伞.

par·bald [ˈpɑːbɔld] *a.* 秃掉一部分的.

par·bleu [pɑːˈbləː] *int.* 〔F.〕嗳呀! 唷!

par·boil [ˈpɑːbɔil] *vt.* ①把…煮成半熟. ②使过热, 晒焦(皮肤等); 使热得难受.

par·buck·le [ˈpɑːbʌkl] *n.* (拉上或放下大桶等用的)套拉绳. — *vt.* 用套拉绳拉上 (*up*); 用套拉绳放下 (*down*).

Par·cae [ˈpɑːsiː] *n. pl.* (*sing.* **-ca** [-kə])〔L.〕【罗神】命运三女神 (= the Three Fates).

par·cel [ˈpɑːsl] *n.* ①包, 小包, 包裹. ②【商】(货物的)一宗. ③【法】(土地的)一块. ④〔蔑〕(人、兽、物的)一群, 一批, 一组; 〔古〕一部分. ⑤〔口〕赢来的〔输掉的〕钱. *a ~ of rubbish* 无聊的事. *by ~ post* 当包裹寄. *by ~s* 一点一点的. *part and ~ (of)* (…的)重要部分. *the ~s room* 〔美〕衣帽间. — *vt.* (〔英〕**-ll-**) ①分, 区分; 把…划成部分后分配 (*out*). ②把…作成包裹, 打包, 捆扎(*up*); 把…拼〔连〕在一起. ③【海】用帆布条包(绳索等); 用帆布条和沥青堵(缝). ~ ***out [into]*** 分配, 分派. — *a.* 部分(时间)的. — *ad.* 〔古〕一部分, 局部地(= partly). ~ *blind* 半盲的. ~ *drunk* 微醉的. ~ *gilt* 部分镀金的. ~ **office** 包裹房. ~ **paper** 包装纸. ~ **post** 包裹邮件; 邮包; 包裹邮递.

par·cel·ling 〔美〕[ˈpɑːsəliŋ] *n.* ①【海】(涂了沥青油包裹绳索用的)帆布条. ②打包. ③划分并分配.

par·ce·na·ry [ˈpɑːsinəri] *n.*【法】共同继承.

par·ce·ner [ˈpɑːsinə] *n.*【法】共同继承人.

parch [pɑːtʃ] *vt.* ①烤, 烘; 使焦. ②使干透; 使极度口渴. ③使冷干皱缩. *be ~ed with thirst* 渴得口干舌燥. — *vi.* ①干透; 烤干; 焦. ②口渴, 心烧.

parched [pɑːtʃt] *a.* 烤干的; 焦的; 干透的. ~ *peas* 干豌豆. ~ *soil* 干透了的土地.

parch·ing [ˈpɑːtʃiŋ] *a.* 烘烤似的, 燃烧般的, 干燥的. ~ *heat* 炎热.

parch·ment [ˈpɑːtʃmənt] *n.* ①羊皮纸; 羊皮纸文件; (羊皮纸般的)上等纸. ②羊皮纸文稿; 大学毕业文凭. ③咖啡子的皮. *vegetable ~* (= ~ paper) 假羊皮纸, 硫酸纸. *virgin ~* (用小羊皮做的)上等羊皮纸.

pard[1] [pɑːd] *n.* 〔英古〕豹 (= leopard).

pard[2] [pɑːd] *n.* 〔美俚〕伙伴, 同伴; 搭档.

par·die, par·di [pɑːˈdiː] *ad., int.* 〔古〕理所当然, 确定不疑〔原为一种誓言〕(= pardy).

pard·ner [ˈpɑːdnə] *n.* 〔美方〕= partner.

par·don [ˈpɑːdn] *n.* ①原谅, 饶恕, 宽恕. ②【法】赦免; 大赦 (= general ~), 特赦 (= free ~). ③【宗】赦罪; 免罪符; 免罪节. ***a thousand ~s for*** *(doing sth.)* 千万请原谅. ***(I) beg your ~.*** 请原谅, 对不起. 〔表示: ①道歉; ②申述自己不同意见; ③重音在句后时意为'对不起, 请再说一遍', 也可只用"Beg ~"或"Pardon", 说时用升调〕. — *vt.* 原谅, 饶恕, 宽恕; 【法】赦免. *P- me for interrupting (you).* 对不起打搅(你)了. *There is nothing to ~.* 好说好说, 哪里哪里.

par·don·a·ble [ˈpɑːdnəbl] *a.* 可以原谅的, 可以饶恕的. **-bly** *ad.*, **-ness** *n.*

par·don·er [ˈpɑːdnə] *n.* ①宽恕者. ②【宗史】获准售卖天主教免罪符的人.

pare [pɛə] *vt.* ①剥, 削(果皮等); 修(指甲等); 削去(角、边等) (*off; away*). ②(逐渐)削减, 缩减, 撙节 (*away, down*). ~ *nails to the quick* 把指甲剪到肉根. ~ *down expenses* 削减费用. ~ *an apple* 削苹果皮. ~ *a layer from a corn* 剥掉玉米的壳.

Pa·ree [pæriː] *n.* 〔美口〕= Paris.

Pare(s) [pɛə(z)] *n.* 佩尔(斯)〔姓氏〕.

par·e·gor·ic [ˌpærəˈgɔrik] *a.*【药】止痛的. — *n.*【药】止痛药; 樟脑阿片酊〔小儿用止痢药〕.

paren. = parenthesis.

pa·ren·chy·ma [pəˈreŋkimə] *n.*【解】腺细胞组织, 实质, 主质; 【植】柔细组织, 薄壁组织. ~ **cells** 薄壁细胞. **-l, -tous** [ˌpæreŋˈkimətəs] *a.*

parens. = parentheses.

par·ent [ˈpɛərənt] *n.* ①父亲; 母亲. ②〔*pl.*〕双亲; 祖先. ③(动、植物的)母体, 亲本. ④根源, 本源. ⑤保护者. *one's ~s* 双亲. *~-teacher association*【教】家长会. *a ~ bird* 老鸟. *a ~ company* 母公司. *~ substance* 母体, 母物. *a ~ stem* 原种. *Ignorance is the ~ of many evils.* 无知是许多罪恶的根源. ~**hood** *n.* 父母的身分.

par·ent·age [ˈpɛərəntidʒ] *n.* ①亲子关系; 父母身分. ②出身; 血统; 家系, 门第. ③来源. ***of good ~*** 出身高贵〔门第高〕. ***of mean ~*** 出身微贱.

pa·ren·tal [pəˈrentl] *a.* ①亲的; 父的; 母的; 父母(一样)的; 【生】(杂种)亲本的. ②作为来源〔渊源〕的. ~ *love* 父母之爱: ~ **home,** ~ **school** 失足儿童教养院. **-ly** *ad.* 象父母.

par·en·ter·al [pæˈrentərəl] *a.* ①非肠道的, 不经肠道的. ②不经消化道带进体内的〔如经过皮下或静脉注射〕. — *n.* 一种肠道外注射物. **-ly** *ad.*

pa·ren·the·sis [pəˈrenθisis] *n.* (*pl.* **-ses** [-siːz]) ①【语法】插入成分; 插入语, 插句. ②〔常 *pl.*〕圆括号〔()〕. ③插曲; 插剧; 插话. ***by way of ~*** 附带地, 顺便. ***in parentheses*** 在圆括号内, 附加上; 附带.

pa·ren·the·size, pa·ren·the·sise [pəˈrenθisaiz] *vt.* ①把…插入圆括号, 用圆括号括起. ②在…插入插句〔插话〕; 把…作为插入语.

par·en·thet·ic, par·en·thet·i·cal [ˌpærənˈθetik, -ikəl] *a.* ①作为插入语〔插句〕的; 作为附带说明(性质)的. ②圆括号〔弧形〕的, 弓形的; 放在括号内的. ③〔喻〕插曲的, 插话的. **-thet·i·cal·ly** *ad.* 作插句; 插话似地.

par·er [ˈpɛərə] *n.* ①削皮的人. ②削皮器, 削皮刀.

par·er·gon [pæˈrəːgɔn] *n.* (*pl.* **-ga** [-gə]) ①副业. ②【建】附属装饰; 辅助装饰. ③补遗, 附录.

par·e·sis [ˈpærisis] *n.* (*pl.* **-ses** [-siːz])【医】①局部麻痹; 轻瘫. ②麻痹性痴呆 (= general paresis).

par·es·the·si·a [ˌpærisˈθiːʒiə] *n.*【医】感觉异常. **-thet·ic** [-ˈθetik] *a.*

pa·ret·ic [pəˈretik] *a.*【医】①局部麻痹的, 轻瘫的. ②麻痹性痴呆的. — *n.* 局部麻痹病患者.

pa·re·u [ˈpɑːreiuː] *n.* 〔Tahitain〕(波利尼西亚男女穿的)彩色长裙.

par·e·ve [ˈpɑːrivə, -ve] *a.*【犹】素馨菜的〔无肉类或乳制品的〕.

par ex·cel·lence [ˌpɑːr ˈeksəlɑ̃ːns]〔F.〕最卓越的〔地〕; 典型的〔地〕.

par ex·em·ple [ˌpɑːr egˈzɑ̃ːmpl]〔F.〕例如 (= for instance).

par·fait [pɑːˈfei] *n.* 〔F.〕冻糕.

par·fect [ˈpɑːfikt] *a.* 〔美俚〕= perfect.

par·fleche [ˈpɑːˌfleʃ, pɑːˈfleʃ] *n.* ①生皮革. ②生皮革制品.

parge [pɑːdʒ] *vt.* 为(密封砖、石制品的表面)涂上灰泥. **parg•ing** *n.*

par•get [ˈpɑːdʒit] *n.*【建】①石膏;灰泥;粗涂灰泥;白色涂料. ②墁饰花纹. — *vt.* ***(parget(t)ed; parget(t)ing)*** 在…上粗涂灰泥;涂饰. **~-work** (尤指16、17世纪的)灰泥[石膏]制品.

par•he•lic, par•he•li•a•cal [pɑːˈhiːlik, ˌpɑːhiˈlaiəkəl] *a.*【气】(似)幻日的. ~ **circle [ring]**【气】幻日环.

par•he•li•on [pɑːˈhiːljən, -liən] *n.* *(pl.* ***par•he•li•a*** [-lje, -liə])【气】幻日,假日[日晕上的光轮].

Par•i•ah [ˈpæriə, ˈpɑːriə] *n.* 贱民[南部印度最下层的民众,社会地位最低]; [p-] 为社会所遗弃者;流浪者.

Pa•ri•an [ˈpɛəriən] *a.* ①(爱琴海中盛产大理石的)帕罗斯 (Paros) 岛的. ②[p-] 白色细瓷器[瓷土]的. — *n.* ①帕罗斯岛人. ②[p-] 帕罗斯白色细瓷器[瓷土].

pa•ri•es [ˈpɛəriˌiːz, ˈpær-] *n.* *(pl.* **pa•ri•e•tes** [pəˈraiəˌtiz])【生】体壁.

pa•ri•e•tal [pəˈraiitl] *a.* ①【解】腔壁的;体壁的;颅顶部的. ②【植】周壁的,周缘的;侧膜的. ③[美学俚]住在校内的;大学校内的生活的. — *n.*【解】(颅)顶骨.

par•i-mu•tu•el [ˈpæriˈmjuːtʃuəl] *n.* [F.]①派利分成法[赛马中扣除手续费和所得税后]赢家分配全部赌金的方法. ②(按上述分享法)计算赌金的机器(= ~ machine).

par•ing [ˈpɛəriŋ] *n.* ①削皮. ②削下来的皮;刨花. ③微少的贮蓄. *potato ~s* (削下的)土豆皮. **~-iron** (兽医、蹄匠等用的)削蹄刀. **~-knife** 削皮刀;指甲刀.

par•i-pas•su [ˈpɛərai ˈpæsjuː] [L.] ①以同一步速[速度]. ②以相同的比例. ③同时. ④【法】无先决权[特权],平等地. *make a ~ advance* 以同一步速前进.

par•i•pin•nate [ˌpæriˈpineit] *a.*【植】偶数羽状的[指复叶].

Par•is[1] [ˈpæris] ①帕里斯[姓氏]. ②【希神】帕里斯[特洛伊王子,因诱走斯巴达王后海伦而引起特洛依战争].

Par•is[2] [ˈpæris] *n.* 巴黎[法国首都]. *~ of America* 美国的巴黎[辛辛那提 (Cincinnati) 市的别名]. ~ **blue** 巴黎蓝. ~ **Bourse** [buəs]【商】巴黎证券交易所. ~ **Commune**【史】巴黎公社. ~ **doll** 女服裁缝用的模型人. ~ **green** 巴黎绿[颜料、杀虫药]. ~ **plaster** 塑模石膏. ~ **white** 亮粉. ~ **yellow** 铬黄.

par•ish [ˈpæriʃ] *n.* ①教区[郡下的分区,每区设一教堂]. ②济贫区. ③教区的全体居民;[美]一教会的全体信徒;[美] (Louisiana 州的)县. ***go on the ~*** 靠教区救济. ~ **child** 教区抚育的孤儿. ~ **church** [英]教区教堂. ~ **clerk** 教区执事. ~ **council** [英]农村教区会. ~ **lantern** [英方]月亮. **~-pump** *a.* 教区范围的;目光偏狭的. ~ **register** (教区教堂登记洗礼、命名、结婚、死亡等的)教区记事录.

pa•rish•ion•er [pəˈriʃənə] *n.* 教区居民.

Pa•ri•sian [pəˈrizjən, -ziən] *a.* 巴黎的,巴黎式的;巴黎人的. — *n.* 巴黎人.

Pa•ri•sienne [pəriziˈen] *n.* [F.] 巴黎女人.

par•i•syl•lab•ic, par•i•syl•lab•i•cal [ˈpærisiˈlæbik, -ikəl] *a.* (希腊语、拉丁语名词在一切词尾变化中)有同数音节的.

par•i•ty [ˈpæriti] *n.* ①同等,平等. ②同格,同位. ③同样;类似,一致. ④等量,等价. ⑤【物】宇称(性),奇偶性. ⑥【商】平价;价值对等; *nuclear ~* 核武器均势. *the law of ~ conservation*【物】宇称守恒定律. *~ non-conservation*【物】宇称不守恒. *~ of treatment* 同等待遇. ***be on a ~ with*** 和…平等. ***by ~ of reasoning*** 由此类推. ***stand at ~*** 居于同等地位. ~ **check**【自】奇偶校验.

Park [pɑːk] *n.* 帕克[姓氏].

park [pɑːk] *n.* ①公园,…场. ②圃囿;【英法】(国王特许的)猎园. ③[美]街头广场;[美]运动场. ④停车场;【军】(露营中放大炮、辎重等的)放置场. ⑤(放置场上所放置的)全部东西;炮兵辎重;材料厂. ⑥养蠔所. ⑦[美]科罗拉多,怀俄明等州的)平原. ⑧[Scot.]牧地,耕地. *a national ~* 国立公园. *a base-ball ~* 棒球场. *an artillery ~* 停炮场. *the P-* [英]海德公园 (= Hyde P-). — *vt.* ①把(某地)圈为公园[游憩场]. ②把(炮车等)摆[排列]在放置场. ③把(车)停在(某处);[美俚]把(东西)寄放在(某地),把(孩子等)交给人看管. *You may ~ your car here.* 你可以把车停在这里. *He ~ed his bag at the club.* 他把皮包摆在俱乐部里. — *vi.* ①停车;停放车辆. ②[美俚]坐下来,安顿下来. *No ~ing here.* 此处禁止停车. ***~ oneself*** [俚]坐下. ***~ one's frame*** [美俚]休息. ~ **land** 疏树草原. **-er** *n.* 停放车辆的人.

par•ka [ˈpɑːkə] *n.* 带兜帽的风雪衣,派克大衣.

Park Avenue [ˈpɑːk ˈævinjuː] 派克大街[美国纽约市街名,街上多大公寓,常为奢华时髦阶层的同义语].

Par•ker•iz•ing [ˈpɑːkəraiziŋ] *a.* ~ **process**【冶】磷酸盐处理[俗称磷化,钢铁防蚀法的一种].

Par•ker [ˈpɑːkə] *n.* 帕克[姓氏,男子名].

par•kin [ˈpɑːkin] *n.* [英方]麦片糖饼.

park•ing [ˈpɑːkiŋ] *n.* [美]停车. ~ **brake** (汽车的)手刹车. ~ **light** 停车指示灯. ~ **lot** 露天停车场. ~ **meter** 停车计时器. ~ **orbit**【宇】驻留轨道. ~ **ticket** (违反停车规则的)罚款传票.

Par•kin•son [ˈpɑːkinsən] *n.* **~'s disease** 震颤(性)麻痹症.

par•kin•son•ism [ˈpɑːkinsənizəm] *n.* ①震颤(性)麻痹. ②震颤(性)麻痹症 (= Parkinson's disease).

park•ish [ˈpɑːkiʃ] *a.* 公园(似)的.

Park•man [ˈpɑːkmən] *n.* 帕克曼[姓氏].

park•way [ˈpɑːkwei] *n.* [美] (两旁有草地和树木的)林园式大路.

park•y [ˈpɑːki] *a.* [英俚]寒冷的.

Parl. = Parliament; Parliamentary.

par•lance [ˈpɑːləns] *n.* ①口调,腔调;(特有的)用语;说法. ②[古]谈判,辩论. ***in common ~*** 照一般的说法. ***in legal ~*** 用法律上的话来说.

par•lan•do [pɑːˈlɑːndəu] *n., a.* [It.]【乐】朗诵调(的).

par•lay [ˈpɑːli, pɑːˈlei] *vt.* [美] ①把(本和利)都押作赌注. ②[口]成功地利用;使增值. — *n.* 连本带利的赌(注).

Par•le•men•taire [ˈpɑːləmɑ̃ːnˈtɛə] *n.* [F.]军事谈判代表.

Par•ley [ˈpɑːli] *n.* 帕利[姓氏].

par•ley [ˈpɑːli] *n.* 会谈;(尤指与敌方的)谈判. ***beat [sound] a ~*** (打鼓或吹号)向对方表示愿意谈判. ***hold a ~ with (the enemy)*** 和(敌人)谈判. — *vi.* 会谈,谈判 *(with)*. — *vt.* [口]讲(外国话等).

par•ley•voo [ˌpɑːliˈvuː] *n.* *(pl.* ***~s)*** [英谑]①法国话. ②[P-]法国人. — *vi.* 说法国话.

par•lez-vous [ˈpɑːleivuː] *vi.* [美俚]讲法语[来自法语 *Parlez-vous français?* 你会讲法国话吗?]. *Can you ~?* 你会讲法语吗?

par•lia•ment [ˈpɑːləmənt] *n.* ①议会,国会;立法机构. ②[P-]英国[加拿大]议会;[P-](1789年法国大革命前的)最高法院. ③中古世纪弗罗伦萨 (Florence) 的武人集会. ④薄姜饼. *a member of P-* [英]下院议员[略作 M.P.] ***convene [summon] ~*** 召开议会. ***dissolve P-*** 解散议会. ***enter (or go into) P-*** 成为下院议员. ***open P-*** 宣布议会开会. ***P- sits [rises].*** 议会开会[休会]. **P- Act** [英] (1911 年限制上院否决权的) 议会法案. ~ **cake** 薄姜饼. ~ **hinge** 长羽铰链.

par•lia•men•tal [ˌpɑːləˈmentəl] *a.* = parliamentary.

par•lia•men•ta•ri•an [ˌpɑːləmenˈtɛəriən] *n.* ①议院法规专家. ②议会雄辩家. ③[英]国会议员;[P-]【英史】十七世纪内战时期反抗查理一世的议会党人. — *a.* 议会(派)的.

par•lia•men•ta•rism [ˌpɑːləˈmentərizəm] *n.* ①议会

主义. ②议会制度.

par·lia·men·ta·ry [ˌpɑːləˈmentəri] *a.* ①议会的;国会的;议会制定的;根据议会法的. ②议员的. ③(言语等)适合议会的;〔口〕(语气)慎重有礼的. *an old* ~ *hand* 精通议院法等的人. ~ **agent** 〔英〕政党的法律顾问. ~ **borough** 〔英〕议员选举区. ~ **company**【商】公益事业公司. ~ **language** (象议会里用的)慎重有礼的言语. ~ **procedure** 议院法. ~ **train** 〔英〕工人减价列车,廉价列车.

par·lo(u)r [ˈpɑːlə] *n.* ①〔古、方〕起居室. ②客厅,会客室,接待室. ③〔美〕营业室;办公室;摄影室;诊室,手术室;停尸场. ④(旅馆等的)休息室. *a billiard* ~ 弹子房. *a dental* ~ 牙科诊室. *a beauty* ~ 美容室. *an icecream* ~ 冷饮店. — *a.* ①客厅的,适于客厅使用的. ②只会空谈的. ~ **boarder** (出高价住在校长家里的)特别寄宿生. ~ **car** 特等豪华客车车箱. ~ **end** 〔美〕公事车的后部. ~ **girl** = ~ maid. ~ **guest** 〔美〕受欢迎的包饭人. ~ **jumping** 〔美〕盗窃. ~**maid** (负责开门、侍候餐桌的)客厅女仆. ~ **match** 〔美〕(不含硫磺的)安全火柴. ~ **pink** 只会空谈的温和激进派. ~ **[armchair] socialist** 空谈的社会主义者. ~ **tricks** 〔贬〕社交上的成就;为了引人注目而采取的举动.

par·lous [ˈpɑːləs] 〔古,谑〕 *a.* ①危险的;靠不住的. ②麻烦的;难对付的. ③厉害的,精明的. — *ad.* 非常地,极;…得吓人. *She is* ~ *handsome.* 她潇洒极了.

par·ly [ˈpɑːli] *n.* 〔俚〕 = parliamentary train.

Par·me·san [ˌpɑːmiˈzæn] *a.* (意大利北部城市)巴马(Parma)的. — *n.* 巴马干酪 (= ~ cheese).

Par·nas·si·an [pɑːˈnæsiən, -sjən] *a.* ①(希腊)帕纳萨斯(Parnassus)山的. ②高蹈派诗人的. *the* ~ *school* 高蹈派〔19世纪下半叶法国诗坛的一派,鼓吹艺术至上,强调形式的谨严〕. — *n.* 高蹈派诗人.

Par·nas·sus [pɑːˈnæsəs] *n.* ①帕纳萨斯〔希腊中部山峰名,传说为太阳神阿波罗及诗神缪斯的灵地〕. ②〔总称〕文学界,诗坛,文坛. ③诗,文学;诗文集. ***climb*** ~ 学作诗.

Par·nell [pɑːˈnel] *n.* 帕内尔〔姓氏〕.

pa·ro·chi·al [pəˈrəukjəl, -kiəl] *a.* ①教区的. ②镇村的;地方性的;狭隘的,偏狭的. *a* ~ *board* 〔Scot.〕教区(贫民救济)委员会. *a* ~ *school* 教区附属学校.

pa·ro·chi·al·ism, pa·ro·chial·i·ty [pəˈrəukjəlizm, pəˌrəukiˈæliti] *n.* ①教区〔镇村〕制度. ②地方观念;眼界狭小,偏狭.

pa·ro·chi·al·ize [pəˈrəukiəlaiz] *vt.* ①使施行教区制. ②使地方化;使眼界狭小.

par·o·dist [ˈpærədist] *n.* 嘲弄性模仿作品〔诗文〕的作者.

par·o·dos [ˈpærədɔs] *n.* ①(通到乐队席的)后台过道. ②(古希腊戏剧中)歌唱队的上场.

par·o·dy [ˈpærədi] *n.* ①(为嘲弄某作者或其诗文而改作的)滑稽性模仿诗文〔作品〕. ②拙劣的模仿. — *vt.* ①把(他人诗文)模仿成滑稽体裁. ②拙劣地模仿.

pa·rol [pəˈrəul] *n.*【法】口头答辩;口头言词. ***prove by*** ~ 口头证明. — *a.*【法】口头的;没有盖章的.

pa·role [pəˈrəul] *n.* ①誓言 (= ~ of honour);【军】(俘虏的)释放宣誓. ②【军】(卫队军官所用的)特别口令,特别暗号. ③〔美〕假释许可;假释出狱;临时入境许可. ④【法】 = parol. — *a.* ①假释的. ② = parol. ***break one's*** ~ 违誓,企图违誓脱逃. ***on*** ~ ①(俘虏)得宣誓释放. ②〔美〕暂许出狱,准许假释(出狱仍在警察管制之下);临时入境许可. ***out on*** ~ 〔美俚〕(女子)离了婚的. — *vt.* ①使(俘虏)宣誓后释放. ②〔美〕准许(犯人)假释出狱;许可(外国人)临时入境. **pa·rol·a·ble** *a.* 可凭宣誓释放的;可假释的.

pa·rol·ee [pəˌrəuˈliː] *n.* 〔美〕得假释出狱的人,假释犯.

par·o·no·ma·si·a [ˌpærənəuˈmeiziə] *n.* ①【修】(尤指同音异义的)双关语〔如 sole 和 soul〕. ②文字游戏.

par·o·nym [ˈpærənim] *n.* ①同源词〔如 wise, wisely, wisdom 等〕. ②(同音而拼法、语源、意义均不同的)形似词〔如 hair 和 hare〕.

pa·ron·y·mous [pəˈrɔniməs] *a.* 同词源的,同词根的.

par·o·quet [ˈpærəket] *n.*【动】长尾小鹦鹉(=parakeet).

pa·rot·ic [pəˈrɔtik, -ˈrəut-] *a.*【解】近耳的.

pa·rot·id [pəˈrɔtid] *n.* ①【解】腮腺,耳下腺 (= ~ gland). ②(武士头盔上的)护耳. — *a.* 耳边的,耳下的,腮腺的.

par·o·ti·tis [ˌpærəˈtaitis] *n.*【医】腮腺炎.

Par·ou·si·a [ˌpɑːruːˈsiə, pəˈruːziə] *n.*【宗】基督再临 (= second coming).

par·ox·ysm [ˈpærəksizəm] *n.* ①(病等的)突然发作;阵发;(感情等的)激发. ②(突然而来的)活动,努力. *in a* ~ *of rage* 突然发起怒来. *a* ~ *of coughing* 一阵咳嗽.

par·ox·ys·mal [ˌpærəkˈsizməl] *a.* 发作性的;爆发性的. **-ly** *ad.*

par·ox·y·tone [pæˈrɔksitəun] *a., n.* 希腊语词尾倒数第二音节有重音的(词).

par·quet [ˈpɑːkei, ˈpɑːkit] *n.* ①木条镶花地板;席纹地面. ②〔美〕(戏院的)前厅,正厅前排. — *vt.* ①在…铺镶花地板. ②用镶木制. ~ **circle** 〔美〕(戏院的)正厅后排,后厅〔在楼厅下〕. ~ **strip** 小板条.

par·quet·ry [ˈpɑːkitri] *n.* 木条镶花;镶木细工;镶花地板.

Parr [pɑː] *n.* 帕尔〔姓氏〕.

parr [pɑː] *n.* ***(pl.*** ~***s*** 〔集合词〕 ~***)***【动】幼鲑.

par·ra·keet [ˈpærəkiːt] *n.* = parakeet.

par·ra·mat·ta [ˌpærəˈmætə] *n.* 毛葛;棉毛呢 (= paramatta).

par·rel, par·ral [ˈpærəl] *n.*【海】装于帆桁中央部两侧的索具.

par·ri·cide [ˈpærisaid] *n.* ①杀父母(的人);杀长上(的人);杀主人(的人),叛国(者). ②叛逆罪;忤逆罪. **par·ri·cid·al** [ˌpæriˈsaidl] *a.*

Par·rish [ˈpæriʃ] *n.* 帕里什〔姓氏〕.

par·rot [ˈpærət] *n.* ①【动】鹦鹉. ②学舌者,应声虫;学人行为的人. — *vt.* ①鹦鹉学舌般复述;做…的应声虫,随声附和;机械地模仿(别人的行为). ②训练(某人)使机械地复述. ~ *the textbook* 死背教科书. — *vi.* 机械地复述,死背;机械地模仿. ~**-cry** 人云亦云的叫喊,学舌. ~ **disease,** ~ **fever**【医】鹦鹉病 (= psittacosis). ~ **fish**【动】隆头鱼;鹦嘴鱼. ~**let** (南美)小鹦鹉. **-like** *a.* 鹦鹉般的.

par·rot·ry [ˈpærətri] *n.* 学舌;机械模仿.

Par·ry [ˈpæri] *n.* 帕里〔姓氏〕.

par·ry [ˈpæri] *vt.* ①挡开;避开,闪开(枪锋等). ②回避(别人的质问). ~ *a question* 避而不答,回避问题;搪塞. — *vi.* ①挡开打击. ②避不作答. — *n.* ①挡开,闪避. ②遁辞.

parse [pɑːz] *vt.*【语】从语法上分析;解析(词句等).

par·sec [pɑːˈsek] *n.*【天】秒差距(天体距离单位,=3.26光年).

Par·see [pɑːˈsiː, ˈpɑːˈsiː] *n.* ①印度祆教徒〔公元7—8世纪逃到印度的波斯祆教教徒的后裔〕. ②祆教经典上的波斯语〔萨珊 (Sassan) 王朝时代的波斯语〕. **-ism** *n.* 印度祆教.

Par·si [ˈpɑːsiː] *n.* = Parsee.

par·si·mo·ni·ous [ˌpɑːsiˈməunjəs, -niəs] *a.* 吝啬的;过度俭省的.

par·si·mo·ny [ˈpɑːsiməni] *n.* 吝啬,小气;过度节俭.

pars·ley [ˈpɑːsli] *n.*【植】欧芹,洋芫荽.

pars·nip [ˈpɑːsnip] *n.*【植】欧洲防风;欧洲防风根.

Par·son [ˈpɑːsn] *n.* 帕森〔姓氏〕.

par·son [ˈpɑːsn] *n.* ①教区牧师. ②〔口〕牧师. ~ *mortal*【法】终身牧师. *the* ~*'s nose* 〔口〕(煮熟供食用的)鸡〔家禽〕屁股. *the* ~*'s week* 从本星期一到下星期六〔13天〕. ~**-bird** (新西兰的)食蜜鸟. **-age** 牧师

住宅；牧师地产；牧师圣俸．**-son·ic, -son·i·cal** [-ˈsɔnik(əl)] *a.* (象)牧师的．

part [pɑːt] *n.* ①部分，一部分；局部 *(opp.* whole*)*．★此义常省去不定冠词．如：a great ~ of one's money. I lost ~ of my money. ②(某特殊的) 部分，部 (*the middle ~ of 19th century* 19世纪中期．*the upper ~ of his face* 脸的上部)；〔*pl.*〕 身体的一部分 (*the inner ~s* 内脏．*the ~s = the private ~s* 阴部，私处)；配件，零件 (*aeroplane ~s* 飞机零件．*repair ~s* 备用零件)．③【数】〔前接序数词〕…分之一 (*a third ~* 三分之一．*two third ~s* 三分之二．简称 *a third, two thirds*)；〔前接基数词〕…分之… (*three ~s* 四分之三)；〔配合比〕分 (*four ~s of vinegar to one of oil* 四分醋一分油)．④【数】整除部分；部分分数；部分分式．⑤(书籍、戏剧、诗等的)部，篇，卷．⑥重要部分，要素，成分；(好、坏等的)方面．⑦〔*pl.*〕地方，领域，附近．⑧关系，关心的事，任务，职责，本分；作用 (*It's not my part to interfere.* 我不便干涉)．⑨(演员的)角色；台词．⑩(交战、争议、贸易等的)一方，…方面 (*No word was spoken by either ~.* 双方都没有讲话)．⑪〔*pl.*〕资质，才能 (*a man of ~s* 有才能的人)．⑫【乐】声部，乐曲的一部．⑬【语】词类 (*~s of speech* 词类)．⑭〔美〕分发缝．***bear a ~ in*** 在…中有一份，参与…．***do one's ~*** 尽职责，尽自己本分．***for one's ~*** 至于某人，讲到某人，对某人来说．***for the greater ~*** 大部分，大半；在很大程度上．***for the most ~*** 在极大程度上；就绝大部分而言；多半．***have neither ~ nor lot in = have no ~ in*** 和…一点关系也没有．***in bad [ill evil] ~*** 心怀怨怒地；生气地；没有好感地．***in good ~*** 欣然；不生气地；毫无恶感地．***in ~*** 一部分地；有几成；在某种程度上，多少．***in ~s*** 分开，分次；分册；处处，到处．***in these ~s*** 在这一带，在这些地方．***on one's ~ = on the ~ of sb.*** ①就某人方面；就…而言；代表…．②由…表现出来的；由…所作出的 (*It was a very queer conduct on the ~ of Smith.* 那是史密斯的一个怪举动．*He apologized on the ~ of his friend.* 他替他的朋友道了歉)．***on the one ~ ... on the other ~*** 一方面…，另一方面；第一点…，第二点…．***~ and parcel*** 重要[基本]部分 *(of)*．***play [take, act] a ~*** 扮演…角色；假装 (*play the ~ of Hamlet* 扮演哈姆雷特)．***play one's ~*** 尽本分．***take a noble [active] ~*** 采取豪爽[积极]行动．***take (sb.'s words) in bad [good] ~*** 恶[善]意解释(某人的话等)．***take ~ in*** 参加；贡献．***take ~ with, take sb.'s ~, take the ~ of sb.*** 袒护；支持．***the best ~*** 最大[最多]的部分．***the better ~*** 较大[较多]的部分；较好的办法[计策]．***the ninth ~ of a man*** 〔贬〕裁缝．— *vt.* ①分，使分开，分割；切断，断绝(关系等)．②【海】斩断(缆索、锚链等)；使(缆索、锚链等)断裂．③拉开；离间．④把…分成若干份；分配．⑤(用化学方法)分解(出)．⑥区别[辨别](学说、理论)．⑦〔英方〕放弃(财产等)．~ *one's hair* 把头发分开．*A smile ~ed her lips.* 笑得她嘴唇儿绽开了．— *vi.* ①分，分开，分离；断裂；(河流等)分叉，分道．②跟…分手 *(from; with)* 断绝关系．③【海】(缆索等)脱了．④放弃．⑤死．⑥〔口〕付钱．*The clouds ~ed.* 云散开了．***~ brass rags with*** 〔俚〕跟…绝交〔水手语〕．***~ company with*** 跟…分手[绝交]；跟…意见不合．***~ friends*** 友好地分手．***~ from*** 和…分手，〔罕〕放掉．***~ with*** 跟…分别；解雇，辞退；卖掉(东西)．— *ad.* 部分地；有几分，多少．*It is made ~ of iron and ~ of wood.* 它部分由铁部分由木而制成．— *a.* 部分的，局部的．*a part truth* 部分真理．~ **exchange** 部分交货贸易．~ **music** 合唱[合奏]乐曲．~ **owner** 【法】(尤指船舶的) 共有人．~**singing** 重唱(法)．~**song** 合唱歌曲〔尤指无伴奏的〕．~**-time** ① *n.* 业余时间．② *a.* 非全日工作的，兼任的，兼职的 *(opp. full-time)*；定时的 (*a ~-time job.* 零活，非全日工作．*a ~-time high school* 定时制高等学校)．③*ad.* 花部分时间；兼任地；兼职地．~**-timer** *n.* 兼职者；定时制学校的学生；〔口〕零工．~**way** *ad.* 到某种程度；部分地．~**work** 分册出版的作品．**-ly** *ad.* ①部分地，不完全地．②几分，多少，在一定程度上．

part. = participle; particular.

part. adj. = participial adjective 分词形容词．

par·take [pɑːˈteik] *vi.* (***par·took*** [-ˈtuk]; ***par·tak·en*** [-ˈteikən]) ①参与，参加 *(of; in)*．②分享，分担；陪同(吃饭) *(of)*；吃[喝]一点儿 *(of)*．③〔口〕吃光，喝光 *(of)*．④有点…，带有某种性质[特征等] *(of)*．*Will you ~ of our breakfast with us?* 和我们一道吃早饭好吗？*His manner ~s of insolence.* 他的态度有点傲慢．— *vt.* ①参加；分担；分得，分享，共享．②同吃[喝等]；单独吃[喝]．~ *a meal with sb.* 同某人一道吃饭．~ *one's meal* (自己)吃饭．

par·tak·er [pɑːˈteikə] *n.* 有关系的人，参与者；陪伴者；共享者；分担者 *(of; in)*．

par·tan [ˈpɑːtən] *n.* 〔Scot.〕 蟹．

parted [ˈpɑːtid] *a.* ①分开的；分成部分的；分散的．②【植】深裂的〔常用以构成复合词〕．③〔古〕已死去的．

par·terre [pɑːˈtɛə] *n.* ①花坛，花圃．②(法国剧场的)正厅；(美国剧场的) 池子〔在 gallery 下〕．③(包括房址的)一块平地．

par·the·no·car·py [ˈpɑːθinəuˌkɑːpi] *n.* 【植】单性结实．**-no·car·pic** [ˌpɑːθinəuˈkɑːpik] *a.* **-no·car·pi·cal·ly** *ad.*

par·the·no·gen·e·sis [ˈpɑːθinəuˈdʒenisis] *n.* 【生】单性生殖，孤雌生殖．**-no·ge·net·ic** [-dʒiˈnetik] *a.*

par·the·nog·e·ny [ˌpɑːθiˈnɔdʒini] *n.* = parthenogenesis.

par·the·no·go·nid·i·um [ˈpɑːθinəugəˈnidiəm] *n.* 【生】无性生殖细胞．

Par·the·non [ˈpɑːθinən] *n.* (希腊雅典祭祀雅典娜女神的)巴台农神殿．

Par·thi·an [ˈpɑːθiən, -θjən] *a.* 【史】(伊朗北部古国)帕提亚 (Parthia) 人的，安息人的；〔转喻〕最后的．— *n.* 帕提亚人〔即安息人〕．~ **glance** 临别的一瞥．~ **shaft [arrow, shot]** 临退时发出的最后的一箭，回马箭；临走时所说的话[做的事]；临退场时的台词．

par·ti [pɑːˈti] *n.* 〔F.〕(结婚的)理想的对象，佳偶．*a good [an eligible] ~* 好配偶．~ ***pris*** [ˈpriː] 成见，偏见．

par·tial [ˈpɑːʃəl] *a.* ①一部分的，局部的，不完全的．②不公平的；偏袒的．③偏爱的，特别欢喜的 *(to)*．④【植】后生的，再生的．~ *drought* 小旱．~ *in one's judgement* 判断不公平的．***be ~ to*** 偏爱 (*He is too ~ to tobacco.* 他太欢喜抽烟了)．~ **fractions**【数】部分分数[式]．~ **pressure**【物】分压力．~ **eclipse**【天】偏蚀．~**vacuum**【物】未尽真空．~ **tone**【音】陪音，泛音；【物】谐音．**-ly** *ad.* **-ness** *n.* = partiality.

par·ti·al·i·ty [ˌpɑːʃiˈæliti] *n.* ①偏心，不公平．②偏爱；特殊爱好；癖好 *(for, to)*．③局部性．

par·ti·ble [ˈpɑːtibl] *a.* 可分的，可剖分的．

par·ti·ceps cri·mi·nis [ˈpɑːtiˌseps ˈkriminis] 〔L.〕同犯，同谋．

par·tic·i·pance, -pancy [pɑːˈtisipəns, -si] *n.* 参与，共享．

par·tic·i·pant [pɑːˈtisipənt] *a.* 参加的，有关系的 *(of)*．— *n.* 参加者，与会代表；参与国．*an active ~ in* 积极参加…的人．*treaty ~s* 条约参加国．~ **observation** (社会学家等通过参加研究对象的活动进行的)现场观察研究．

par·tic·i·pate [pɑːˈtisipeit] *vi.* ①参与，参加，有关系；分担；共享．②有几分 (…的性质等) *(of)*．~ *in a discussion* 参加讨论．— *vt.* 分享；分担．*I ~ your suffering and joy.* 我和你同甘共苦．**-i·pat·ing** *a.* ①由多人[多方]参加的．②(股票等)使持有人有权分享利益的．

par·tic·i·pa·tion [pɑːˌtisiˈpeiʃən] *n.* 关系，参与，参加，

加入;合作;分享. *full* ~ *in the benefit* 分享全部权益.

par·tic·i·pa·tor [pɑːˈtisipeitə] *n.* = participant *(n.)*.

par·tic·i·pa·to·ry [pɑːˈtisipətəri] *a.* 提供参加机会的,供人分享的. ~ **drama** 由观众参与演出的戏剧. ~ **democracy** 分享民主制.

par·ti·cip·i·al [ˌpɑːtiˈsipiəl] *a.* 【语法】分词(状)的. ~ **adjective** 【语法】分词形容词. **-ly** *ad.*

par·ti·ci·ple [ˈpɑːtisipl] *n.* 【语法】分词. *a present* [*past*] ~ 现在[过去]分词.

par·ti·ci·pled [ˈpɑːtisipld] *ad.* 〔俚〕真,极,怪〔分词形咒骂语 damned 等的委婉代用语〕. *They are so* ~ *sensitive.* 他们真是太敏感了.

par·ti·cle [ˈpɑːtikl] *n.* ①颗粒,微粒;微量,极少量. ②【物、数】粒子,质点. ③【语法】虚词,不变词〔冠词、副词、介词、连接词、感叹词等〕;小品词〔*yes, no*等〕,词缀. ④〔古〕(文件中的)条,项. ⑤【天主】一小片圣饼. *He has not a* ~ *of sense.* 他一点脑子也没有. *fundamental* [*elementary*] ~*s* 【物】基本质点,基本粒子. ~**board** 刨花胶合板.

par·ti·col·o(u)red [ˈpɑːtikʌləd] *a.* ①杂色的,斑驳的. ②多样化的;(故事等)变化多的.

par·ti·cu·lar [pəˈtikjulə] *a.* ①特殊的,特别的;特有的,独特的;异常的;显著的. ②特定的;个别的;各个的,各自的;独自的,个人的. ③分项的,列举的. ④详细的,精密的. ⑤严格的;讲究的;苛求的;爱挑剔的. ⑥【逻】特称的. *this* ~ *question* (特别是)这一个问题. *Why do people dislike this* ~ *tax?* 人们为什么单单讨厌这一种税呢? *my* ~ *interests* 个人利益. *Mr. P-* 〔谑〕挑三剔四的人物. *a* ~ *proposition* 【逻】特称命题. *the London* ~ 伦敦的特点〔指雾〕. *be* ~ *about what one eats* 讲究吃喝. *be* ~ *over one's clothes* 讲究穿戴. *exact in every* ~ 正确到毫厘不差. *for no* ~ *reason* 并没有特殊理由. *from the general to the* ~ 从一般到个别. *give a full and* ~ *account* 完整而精确地说明. — *n.* ①(可分类、列举的)项目;(消息等的)一条,一项,一点;某一事项. ②〔*pl.*〕详细情节,细情,细目. ③特色,特点;【逻】特称. ***give*** ~***s*** 详述,细讲. ***go* [*enter*] *into*** ~***s*** 详细列出;详细叙述. ***in every*** ~ 在一切方面. ***in*** ~ 特别,尤其;一一,详细.

par·tic·u·lar·ism [pəˈtikjulərizəm] *n.* ①完全忠于一党〔一种制度,一种理论,一种利益〕. ②【宗】特殊神宠论. ③允许各州[各邦]政治上独立的政策. ④以单一因素阐明复杂的社会现象的倾向.

par·tic·u·lar·i·ty [pəˌtikjuˈlæriti] *n.* ①特别,特殊;特殊性;特性,特征;个性;癖性. ②精确;细致;详细. ③过分讲究;挑剔. ④〔常 *pl.*〕细目;私事.

par·tic·u·lar·ize [pəˈtikjuləraiz] *vt., vi.* ①(使)特殊化. ②详述,细论;缕述. ③列举,分列;特别举出;大书特书. **-lar·i·za·tion** [-ˈzeiʃən] *n.*

par·tic·u·lar·ly [pəˈtikjuləli] *ad.* ①分别,个别;特别,尤其,格外. ②详细地,细致地. *I cannot go into it* ~ *now.* 我现在不能详细讲它. *a* ~ *fine day* 天气特别好.

par·tic·u·late [pəˈtikjulit, -ˌleit] *a.* 粒子状的,微粒的,颗粒的. — *n.* 粒子,微粒. ~ **inheritance** 【遗】单独遗传,颗粒遗传说.

part·ing [ˈpɑːtiŋ] *a.* ①临别的,临别纪念的;最后的;离去的;将要过去的;临终的,临死的. ②分离的,分隔的,分开的. *a* ~ *gift* 临别纪念品. *a* ~ *reception* 欢送会. ~ *words* 临别的话,临别赠言. *a* ~ *line* 分隔线. — *n.* ①分别,离别;死亡. ②分离,分裂,裂开. ③(道路的)岔口;(头发的)分缝;分界;分界处;分界线;分界点. ④分开物,分离物;【冶】分金〔指有色金属如金银的分离〕;【机】(铸工)分离砂,分离材料. *the* ~ *of the ways* 岔口,道路分歧点;十字路口. ***at the*** ~ ***of the ways*** 处在十字路口.

par·ti·san[1], **par·ti·zan**[1] [ˌpɑːtiˈzæn] *n.* ①党羽,党人;同类;党派观念强的人;坚决支持者. ②【军】游击队(队员). — *a.* ①党派性的;有偏袒的. ②由一个党派组成[控制]的. ③游击队的. ~ **spirit** 党派性. ~ **warfare** 游击战. **-ship** ①党派性,对党派的效忠;党派偏见. ②同类,同党.

par·ti·san[2], **par·ti·zan**[2] [ˈpɑːtizn] *n.* 【史】(16—17 世纪)戟的一种;戟兵.

-partism *comb. f.* 党派制: multi-*partism*.

par·ti·ta [pɑːˈtiːtə] *n.* ①一种组曲〔尤指十八世纪的〕. ②一种变奏曲.

par·tite [ˈpɑːtait] *a.* ①分裂的;分成若干部分的〔常组成复合词,如 bi~ 分成二分的,tri~ 分成三分的等〕. ②【植】深裂的. ~ **leaf** 深裂叶.

par·ti·tion [pɑːˈtiʃən] *n.* ①分割;分开;被分开;区分,划分,配分. ②区分线;区分物,隔开物;隔板,隔墙. ③部分;隔开部分;隔开的房间. ④【植】隔膜;【法】分财产;【逻】(把一个类别)分成部分. *a* ~ *line* 缝合线. *a* ~ *wall* 公墙,共有壁. — *vt.* ①把…分成部分,分割,区分,瓜分(土地等). ②(用隔板等)隔开 *(off)*. ~ *a house into rooms* 把房屋隔成若干房间. ~ *off part of a room* 隔出房间的一部分.

par·ti·tive [ˈpɑːtitiv] *a.* ①区分的;分隔的. ②【语法】部分的;表示部分的. *a* ~ *adjective* 部分形容词. — *n.* 【语法】表示部分的词〔如: some, few, any 等〕. **-ly** *ad.*

Part·let [ˈpɑːtlit] *n.* 〔古〕①〔拟人称语〕母鸡〔常作 Dame ~〕. ②老太婆.

part·let [ˈpɑːtlit] *n.* (16 世纪妇女穿的)打褶绣花紧身衫.

part·ner [ˈpɑːtnə] *n.* ①合伙人;合作者,伙伴;配手,搭档 *(with, in)*. ②配偶〔夫或妻〕. ③(跳舞等的)舞伴;同组伙伴. ④【法】(合营事业的)合股人. ⑤〔*pl.*〕【海】桅孔加固板,(护持)木框. *a* ~ *in crime* 共犯. *an acting* [*an active, a working*] ~ 担任经营业务的合股人. *a dormant* [*secret, sleeping, silent*] ~ 隐名合伙人. ~ ***for life*** 终身配偶[伴侣]. — *vt.* ①同…合作[合伙];做…的伙伴. ②使有搭档[配手]. —*vi.* 做搭档,当配手 *(with)*. **-less** *a.* 无伙伴[配手]的.

part·ner·ship [ˈpɑːtnəʃip] *n.* ①合伙[合作]关系;伙伴关系. ②全体合伙[合股]人. ③合伙契约. ④合营公司. *a general* [*an unlimited*] ~ 普通[无限]公司. *a special* [*limited*] ~ 有限公司. ***in*** ~ ***with*** 和…合伙[合作].

par·took [pɑːˈtuk] partake 的过去式.

Par·tridge [ˈpɑːtridʒ] *n.* 帕特里奇〔姓氏〕.

par·tridge [ˈpɑːtridʒ] *n.* *(pl.* ~*s* 〔集合词〕~*)* 【动】鹧鸪;〔美〕松鸡. ~**berry** 【植】蔓虎刺(果). ~**-wood** 一种红色硬木.

par·tu·ri·ent [pɑːˈtjuəriənt] *a.* ①产子的,生产的;临产的;多产的. ②〔喻〕即将形成的. *a* ~ *heifer* 临产的小母牛.

par·tu·ri·fa·cient [pɑːˌtjuəriˈfeiʃənt, -ˌtuər-] *a.* 催产的. — *n.* 催产剂.

par·tu·ri·tion [ˌpɑːtjuəˈriʃən] *n.* 分娩;生产.

par·ty [ˈpɑːti] *n.* ①党,党派;政党;结党,党派活动. ②【军】特遣队,分遣队,部队. ③(交际性质的)聚会,集会,宴会. ④同行者,随行人员;同类,伙伴. ⑤【法】诉讼关系人[原告或被告],当事人,一方;(证件上的)署名人;共犯者. ⑥〔俚、谑〕(一个)人. *a political* ~ 政党. *the Communist P-* 共产党. *the Communist P- of China* 中国共产党. *the Socialists P-* 社会党. *the Socialist-Democratic P-* 社会民主党. *the Workers' P-* 工人党. *a reading* ~ 读书会. *a tea* ~ 茶会. *a dinner* ~ 宴会. *Dr. Johnson and his* ~ 约翰逊博士及其一行. *the parties (concerned)* 有关各方. *a* ~ *interested* = *an interested* ~ 关系人. *a disinterested* [*third*] ~ 非关系人,第三者. *a landing* ~ 登陆特遣队. *an old* ~ 〔俚〕老头儿. *the* ~ *in the white hat* 〔俚〕戴着白帽子的那家伙. ***be* [*become*] *a*** ~ ***to*** 和…发生关系,参加 (*I will never be a* ~ *to such a scheme.* 我决不参加这种计划). ***enter the*** ~ 入党. ***give* [*hold*] *a*** ~ 举办[举行]…会;请客. ***make one's***

P

~ *good* 站稳立场；贯彻〔坚持〕自己主张．— *vt.*〔美〕为…举行社交聚会；为…请客．*The visiting professor was cocktailed, partied and dined.* 为来访的教授举行了鸡尾酒会、晚会和晚宴．— *vi.* 举行〔参加〕社交宴会．— *a.* ①政党的，党派的．②社交的．③【徽】分隔开的，杂色的．*a* ~ *man*党员．*a* ~ *platform* 政纲．~ *spirit* 党性．~ *standing* 党龄．~ **per pale** （盾徽中央）垂直分隔开的．~**-and-party** *a.* 当事人间的．~**-colo(u)red** *a.* (= parti-colo(u)red)．~ **dress** 参加社交活动穿的衣服．~ **girl** ①社交聚会的女招待；妓女．②一心想参加社交活动的女子．~ **line** ①（电话的）合用线；分界线；宅界．②〔美〕政党路线．~ **politics** 党派政治．~ **pooper**〔美俚〕（社交场合）令人扫兴的人．~**-spirited** *a.* 党性强的，有党性的，对党热心的．~ **vote**〔美〕根据本党路线所投的票．~ **wall**【法】（邻接建筑物的）界墙，通墙，公共墙．~ **whip** 在议会中督促本党党员的人．~ **wire**【讯】合用线．

P

par·ty·ism [ˈpɑːtiizəm] *n.* ①党派性．②政党制度．*one [two]-*~ 一〔两〕党制．**-ty·ist** *n.* 党派性强的人．

pa·rure [pəˈruə] *n.* 一副首饰．

par·ve·nu [ˈpɑːvənjuː] *n.*〔F.〕暴发户；新贵．— *a.*（象）暴发户的．

par·vis [ˈpɑːvis] *n.* ①教堂正门的柱廊．②（建筑物，尤其是教堂前面的）天井，前庭．

par·vo·line [ˈpɑːvəliːn, -lin] *n.*【化】杷沃啉，二乙基吡啶．

pas [pɑː, F. pɑ] *n.* (*pl.* ~ [pɑːz, F. pɑ])〔F.〕①先行权；上席；优先权．②舞步；跳舞，舞．***dispute the*** ~ 争优先权．***give [yield] the*** ~ ***to*** 使…坐上席；让…居先；把优先权给….~ ***de deux*** [də ˈdəː]〔F.〕双人舞．~ ***de trois*** [dəˈtrwɑ] 三人舞．~ ***redouble*** [rəˈduːbl]〔F.〕速步舞．~ ***seul*** [-səːl]〔F.〕单人舞．***take [have] the*** ~ ***of*** 坐在…的上席；比…占先；得优先权．

P.A.S., PAS, p.a.s. = para-aminosalicylic acid 对氨基水杨酸〔抗结核药〕．

Pas·cal [ˈpæskəl], **B.** 帕斯卡〔1623—1662，法国数学家、物理学家、哲学家〕．~**'s triangle**【数】帕斯卡三角形．

Pasch [pæsk] *n.*【宗】（犹太人的）逾越节〔见圣经《出埃及记》12 章 27 节〕；逾越节用来祭神的羔羊．②复活节．

pas·chal [ˈpɑːskəl, ˈpæs-] *a.* ①逾越节的．②复活节 (Easter)的．— *n.*（点复活节蜡烛用的）大烛台．~ **lamb** ①逾越节（宰杀吃）的小羊．②〔P- Lamb〕基督；带有灵光圈的羊的图象〔象征基督〕．~ **solemnity** 复活节（前后的）周．

pas de chat [ˌpɑːdəˈʃɑː; F. pɑdəʃɑ]【芭蕾】雀跃步．

pa·se·o [pɑːˈseiəu] *n.* (*pl.* ~*s*)〔Spa.〕①散步〔尤指黄昏时散步〕；闲逛．②公共大道．③斗牛士的入场式．

pash¹ [pæʃ] *n.*〔英方〕头．

pash² [pæʃ] *vt.*〔英方〕打碎，粉碎．

pash³ [pæʃ] *n.*〔美俚〕热恋〔缩略自 passion〕；（女学生的）迷恋．— *vi.*〔美俚〕扮演情感激动的角色．~ **flops**〔美〕热情女郎．

pa·sha, pa·cha [ˈpɑːʃə, pəˈʃɑː] *n.*〔土耳其〕帕夏〔本义为首脑，转指伊斯兰教国家的高级官衔〕．~ ***of three tails [two tails, one tail]*** 最高〔第二级、第三级〕帕夏〔依军旗所加马尾数而言〕．**-dom** 帕夏的身分〔官衔〕．

pa·sha·lik, -lic [pəˈʃɑːlik] *n.* 帕夏管区〔管辖权〕．

pashm [ˈpæʃəm] *n.*（西藏高原等地产的）山羊绒．

Pash·to [ˈpʌʃtəu, ˈpɑːʃ-] *n.* 普什图语〔阿富汗和巴基斯坦用的印欧语系伊朗语支的语言，阿富汗的官方语言之一〕(= Pushto(o))．

pa·so do·ble [ˈpɑːsəu ˈdəubl] *n.* (*pl.* ***pa·so do·bles***) ①斗牛士进行曲〔斗牛士入场时或刺杀牛前的音乐〕．②斗牛士进行曲舞．

pasque·flow·er [ˈpæskflauə] *n.*【植】白头翁；铁线海棠．

pas·quin·ade [ˌpækwiˈneid] *n.*（贴在公共场所的）讽刺诗〔文〕；讽刺．— *vt.* 讽刺．

pass¹ [pɑːs] *v.* (~***ed*** [pɑːst]; ~***ed, past*** [pɑːst]) *vi.* ①经过，通过；穿过；越过；超过；掠过；前进．②（时间）流逝，推移；转化，变化 (*to; into*)．③及格，合格；（议案等）获得通过；被批准；得马虎过去，被宽大放过；被忽略过去．④消失，消灭；平息；停止，完；死；〔美口〕断气 (*out*)．⑤（事件）发生，起；实行，实施．⑥通用，流通；以某种身分出现；被看做…，被认为是 (*for*)；〔美〕（黑人后裔）自称白人；⑦【法】做（陪审员）(*on*)；宣判；下判决；讲 (*on; upon*)．⑧（财产、权利等）转让（别人）；（杯子等）传给（别人）．⑨（球戏）递球，传球；练习传球；【牌】不叫牌，弃权；【剑】刺 (*on; upon*)．⑩〔英〕敲丧钟．⑪【医】（肠里的东西）排泄出来．*The days* ~*ed quickly.* 日子过得快．*I saw what was* ~*ing.* 我从头看到了尾．*It will* ~. 合格；可以．*That won't* ~. 那个不能答应．*Hot words* ~. 互相争论．*I* ~.【牌】我不要，我弃权．— *vt.* ①经过；穿过；通过；超过，横过；渡过．②使移过；使行进；过（时间）；度（日）．③通；穿（针等）；刺穿．④（议案）通过（议会等）；议决（议案等）；使及格．⑤交，让与；传递；使传播；使通用；使流通；使用（伪币）．⑥宽大放过，使马虎过去；随便看一看．⑦【法】宣告（判决）；下（判断）；发（誓）；讲（意见、话）．⑧超过，胜过．⑨〔美〕跳过；把…略过不提；忽略；省去．⑩不支付．⑪拒绝．⑫（球戏）递（球），传（球）．⑬【医】通（便）．*I* ~*ed my time in idleness.* 我把我的时间闲混过去了．*Please* ~ *the butter.* 请把黄油递给我．~ *a rope round a cask* 拿绳子套在桶上．*Please* ~ *your eye over this letter.* 请你看一看这封信．***bring to*** ~ 使发生，使实现；完成，实行．***come to*** ~（事情）发生，实现．~ ***a dividend***〔美〕决定不付红利．~ ***a remark*** 开口，说话．~ ***as*** = ~ ***for***. ~ ***along*** 经过；再往前些．~ ***away*** ①*vi.* 经过；去；终止，完；废；过时；消灭；消失；死．②*vt.* 空费（时间等）；让与（权利等）．~ ***a wet sponge over sth.*** 忘记；删去．~ ***belief*** 使人不能相信．~ ***between***（两人当中）有（磋商等）(*Nothing* ~*ed between us.* 我们当中没有什么事)．~ ***beyond*** 超过．~ ***by*** ①〔by 作副词〕疏忽，忽略，不过问．②〔by 介词〕打…旁边过去；通用（…这个名字）(*I cannot* ~ *by the remark in silence.* 对这句话我不能不过问)．~ ***by on the other side*** 不帮助，不同情．~ ***current***（货币）通用；（谣言）流行．~ ***degree***（英大学）毕业．~ ***for*** 被看做，被认为 (*He* ~*es for a great scholar.* 他被看做大学者)．~ ***from among us***（丢下我们）死掉．~ ***hence***（人）死．~ ***in*** 交，付（支票等）．~ ***in one's checks***〔俚〕死．~ ***in review*** ①检阅，阅兵；使（军队）分列前进．②（顺次）回想．~ ***into*** 变成 (*It has* ~*ed into a proverb.* 那已成了格言．~ *into disuse* 废而不用．~ *into oblivion* 湮没无闻．~ *into the shade* 名声渐渐衰落)．~ ***it***〔美〕搁着不管，不放在心上．~ ***muster*** 及格，合乎要求．~ ***off*** ①拿（假货）卖给 (*on sb.*)．②搪塞过去，敷衍过去，应付过去，混过去．③结束；顺利完成．④把…不放在心上，认为…无关紧要 (*She hated his familiarity, but* ~*ed it off as a joke.* 她讨厌他那种亲昵的态度，但一笑置之)．~(*sth.* [*sb.*]) ***off as [for]*** 把某物〔某人〕冒充为．~ ***on [upon]*** ①前进，通过．②递，传递；传达．③重复．④欺骗，趁．⑤死，逝世．⑥【剑】戳，刺．~ ***one's word*** 发誓，担保 (*to do; that; for*)．~ ***out*** ①出去．②〔美俚〕（被打）昏过去；喝得烂醉；死，不复（存在）；不再（出版）；不能（看见，听到…）．~ ***over*** ①〔over 作介词〕横过，经过，越过，渡过；通入；弹，拉（琴）；过（日子），消磨（时光）；省去．②〔over 作副词〕交，传给，让给；忽略；免除；饶恕，放过，宽容．~ ***(round) the hat*** 募捐．~ ***sb. [sth.] off as [for]*** ... 把某物〔某人〕充作….~ ***sentence [judgement]*** 下判决〔判断〕．~ ***the baby***〔口〕推委．~ ***the bottle*** 递酒．~ ***the buck***〔美俚〕把责任推给别人．~ ***the time of day*** (*with sb.*) 向（某人）早晚请安，同（某人）寒暄．~ ***the word*** 传达命令 (*to do*)．~ ***through*** ①经过，通过，穿过；经历，经验；遭受．②刺穿．~ ***up*** ①〔美俚〕拒绝，绝交；放过；忽略，不理．②上，

登. ~ ***upon the merits of*** ... 评论…的是非. ~ ***water*** 小便,撒尿. ~***ed ball***【棒球】失误球. ***try to ~ it off*** 力图搪塞(过去). — *n.* ①免票;通行证;护照;通行[入场]许可*(to)*. ②及格;合格证书;(英国大学考试的)普通及格. ③情况,形势;遭遇;危机. ④穿过;经过;推移,变迁. ⑤(机器的)一次操作;(飞机、人造卫星的)一次飞过;【牌】(一次)放弃叫[补]牌;【剑】(一次)戳刺. ⑦攻击,讽刺,暗讽;笑话. ⑧(变戏法者、催眠者的)挥手动作;欺骗;勾引手段. ⑨(球戏)传球动作. *No admittance without a pass.* 凭证件[票]方许入内. ***come to a pretty [nice, fine]*** ~ 陷入很困难的处境;变得很尴尬[很糟]. ***make a ~ at*** 〔俚〕对…吊膀子;对…作勾引的表示〔尤指男对女〕;向…调情. ***make ~es*** 施催眠术. ***take a ~*** 接球. ~**book** 〔英〕(银行)存折;顾客赊欠帐簿,提货折,折子. ~**-check** 门票,入场券,通行证. ~ **degree** (英国大学中的)学士学位. ~ **law** (南非迫害有色人种的)通行记法. ~**man** (英国大学的)普通及格生. ~**-word**【军】口令.

pass² [pɑːs] *n.* ①狭路;横路,小路;山路;关口;要隘. ②河口,水口,渡口;蹚水过渡处;(鱼簖上的)过道. ***hold the ~*** 把关;维护利益;捍卫主义[事业]. ***sell the ~*** 让出地位;背叛主义. **-less** *a.* 没有路的,走不通的.

pass. ①= passenger. ②= passive.

pass·a·ble [ˈpɑːsəbl] *a.* ①能通行的. ②通用的;过得去的,还可以的,还好的;合格的,可用的. ③(钱币等)可流通的,真的. **-ness** *n.*

pass·a·bly [ˈpɑːsəbli] *ad.* ①可通行地. ②还好,过得去. *a ~ good novel* 一本还算好的小说.

pass·a·ca·glia [ˌpɑːsəˈkɑːljə, ˌpæs-] *n.* ①帕萨卡里亚舞〔一种慢速庄严的古代意大利舞蹈〕. ②帕萨卡里亚舞曲. ③以此种舞蹈为基础的曲式〔3/4 拍的固定复调形式〕.

pas·sade [pəˈseid] *n.*【马术】回转步.

pas·sa·do [pəˈsɑːdəu] *n.* ***(pl. ~(e)s)***【剑】一脚伸出在前的一刺.

pas·sage¹ [ˈpæsidʒ] *n.* ①通行,通过;经过;转变,演变,变迁,推移;迁移,移住,(鸟的)移栖. ②旅行;(海上、空中)航行;航行权,通行权;通行费,船费,车费. ③通路,走廊;出入口;道路;航线,水路;行程. ④(文章等的)一节;一段;(艺术作品的)细部. ⑤〔美〕(议案的)通过. ⑥〔古〕(已发生的)事件. ⑦对打;争论,讨论;〔*pl.*〕商量,密商;交流;交换. ⑧【医】通便. ⑨〔古〕逝世,死亡. ⑩【乐】经过句. ⑪【生】病原体(如病毒)的培育. ***a bird of ~*** 候鸟;暂时居住的人. *a ~ from that book* 那本书的一节. ***a ~ at [of] arms*** 打架. ***book [engage] one's ~*** 定购船票. ***cut a ~*** 开路. ***force a ~ through (a crowd)*** (在人群中)挤过去. ***have a smooth [rough] ~*** 航程平稳[艰险]. ***have stormy ~s with*** 和…猛烈争论. ***make a ~*** ①航海. ②(鲸鱼)移栖. ***take one's ~*** 定购船票. ***take ~ in*** 搭乘. ***work one's ~*** 以做工抵作船费. — *vi.* ①前进;通过,穿过. ②航海. ③争论. ~ **bird** 候鸟. ~**-money** 船钱,车钱. ~**way** 通路;〔美〕走廊.

pass·age² [ˈpæsidʒ] *vt.*【马术】使(马)用斜横步前进. — *vi.* (马或骑手)以斜横步前进. — *n.* 斜横步.

pas·sa·me·ter [pæˈsɑːmitə] *n.*【机】外径指示规.

pas·sant [ˈpæsənt] *a.*【徽】(举左前足)向右方前行之步态的. ~ *gardant [regardant]* 用正向[左向]步态走.

pas·sa·vant [ˈpɑːsəˈvɑ̃ːŋ] *n.* 〔F.〕通行证.

pas·sé(e) [ˈpæsei] *a.* 〔F.〕①(女子等)已过盛年的;凋残的. ②过时的,陈旧的. *a ~ belle* 老美女.

Pas·se [pæs] *n.* 帕斯〔姓氏〕.

pas·sel [ˈpæsl] *n.* 〔口、方〕一批,一群〔尤指数量相当大者〕.

passe·men·terie [pasˈmɑ̃triː] *n.* 〔F.〕(衣服的)金[银]线花边;珠饰.

pas·sen·ger [ˈpæsindʒə] *n.* ①乘客,(尤指)船客;旅客. ②行人,过路人. ③〔俚〕无能船员[队员];碍手绊脚的人. ***wake up the wrong ~*** 〔美口〕错怪了人. ~ **boat** 客船. ~ **car** 〔指汽车〕轿车;〔指火车〕客车. ~ **liner** 邮船,班轮;班机. ~ **list** 旅客名单. ~ **liner** 班轮,邮船;班机. ~ **plane**【空】客机. ~**-pigeon** (能飞长距离的)北美候鸽〔已绝种〕. ~ **train** (铁路)客车.

passe-partout [pɑːspɑːˈtuː, ˈpæs-] *n.* 〔F.〕①无处不可通行者,通行无阻者. ②万能钥匙. ③嵌画片或照片的框边. ④裱画镶框法. ⑤镶画用的胶纸板.

passe·pied [pɑːsˈpjei] *n.* 〔F.〕①快步舞〔法国十七世纪的一种舞蹈〕. ②快步舞曲.

Pass·er [ˈpæsə] *n.*【动】麻雀属.

pass·er [ˈpɑːsə] *n.* ①过路人,过客;旅客;使通行(通过)的人. ②考试及格者. ③检验工. ④〔美俚〕使用伪币的人.

pass·er-by [ˈpɑːsəˈbai] *n.* ***(pl. passers-by)*** 过路人,经过者.

pas·ser·ine [ˈpæsərain] *a.*【动】雀形目的;雀似的. — *n.* 雀形目的鸟.

pas·si·ble [ˈpæsibl] *a.* 易受感动的,感受力强的〔神学用语〕. **-si·bil·i·ty** [ˌpæsiˈbiliti] *n.*

pas·sim [ˈpæsim] *ad.* 〔L.〕到处,处处,各处〔指在书中到处可见〕. *This occurs in Chaucer ~.* 这在乔叟的作品中处处可见.

pas·sim·e·ter [pæˈsimitə] *n.* ①【机】内径指示规. ②步测计. ③(车站的)自动售票器.

pass·ing [ˈpɑːsiŋ] *a.* ①通行的,通过的;越过的;经过的;过往的;供通行的. ②正在发生的;目前的,现在的. ③一时的,短暂的,刹那间的. ④仓促的,随便的,草率的. ⑤偶然的,附带的. ⑥合乎标准的;及格的. *the ~ time* 现在,现代. ~ *events* 时事. ~ *history* 现代史. *a ~ mark* 及格的分数. — *n.* ①通过,经过. ②消逝,死去. ③(议案的)议决;实施;(考试)及格. ④遗漏,忽略. ⑤通过的手段;穿过的地方. ⑥摆渡,渡口. ***in ~*** 顺便(涉及),附带地(提及). — *ad.* 〔古〕非常,极其. ~ **bell** 丧钟. ~ **light**【空】通过灯. ~ **note**, ~ **tone**【乐】经过音;补足音. ~ **zone** (接力赛的)接棒区. **-ly** *ad.* ①暂时地. ②顺便. ③仓促地. ④〔古〕很.

pas·sion [ˈpæʃən] *n.* ①激情,热情;〔the ~s〕感情〔与理智相对而言〕. ②激怒,忿怒,奋激. ③热恋;〔常 *pl.*〕情欲. ④热心,爱好,热爱,热望*(for)*. ⑤痛苦,悲哀. ⑥〔the P-〕【宗】(十字架上的)耶稣的受难;〔古〕殉教. ⑦〔废〕病痛. *Fishing is a ~ with him.* 他极爱钓鱼. *sexual ~* 色情,性欲. *tender ~* 爱情,恋爱. *one's ruling ~* 对某人起主要作用的感情. ***be in a ~*** 忿怒,在发脾气. ***be subject to fits of ~*** 动不动就发怒. ***break [burst] into a ~ of (tears)*** 突然大(哭)起来. ***fall [get] into a ~*** 发怒,发脾气. ***fly into a ~*** 勃然大怒. ***have a ~ for*** 对…有强烈的爱好. ***up into a ~ = fly into a ~***. — *vi.* 〔诗〕感觉[表现]热情.

pas·sion·al [ˈpæʃənəl] *a.* ①热情的;感情的. ②恋爱的,情欲的. ③爱发脾气的,易怒的. ④渴望的. — *n.* (基督教的)圣徒[殉教者]受难记.

pas·sion·ate [ˈpæʃənit] *a.* ①易动情的,多情的. ②易怒的,急躁的. ③热烈的;激昂的. ④易被情欲所支配的. **-ly** *ad.* **-ness** *n.*

Pas·sion·ist [ˈpæʃənist] *n.* ①(天主教的)受难会修道士. ②〔p-〕热情的人.

pas·sion·flow·er [ˈpæʃənflauə] *n.*【植】西番莲.

pas·sion·less [ˈpæʃənlis] *a.* 没有热情的;不动情的;冷淡的;冷静的.

Pas·sion-music [ˈpæʃən-ˈmjuzik] *n.*【宗】耶稣受难乐.

Pas·sion-play [ˈpæʃən-ˈplei] *n.*【宗】耶稣受难剧.

Pas·sion Sunday [ˈpæʃən ˈsʌndi]【宗】耶稣受难日〔四旬斋 (Lent) 的第五个星期日〕.

Pas·sion·tide [ˈpæʃəntaid] *n.* 复活节前的两星期.

Pas·sion Week [ˈpæʃən ˈwiːk]【宗】耶稣受难周〔复活节前的一周〕.

pas·si·vate [ˈpæsiveit] *vt.*【冶】使钝化. **-va·tion** *n.* **-va·tor** *n.*

pas·sive [ˈpæsiv] *a.* (*opp.* active) ①被动的;守势的. ②不抵抗的;默从的;消极的. ③【语法】被动语态的;被动式的(*opp.* active);【物、化】钝性的;钝态的;无源的;【医】虚性的;【空】不用发动机的;【法】(公债等)无利息的. *the* ~ *voice* 被动语态. ~ *operations* 守势作战. ~ *commerce*【商】倚赖外国船的进出口贸易. *a* ~ *net* (*work*)【电】无源(电)网络. *the* ~ *state*【化】钝态. ~ *congestion*【医】虚性充血. *a* ~ *flight* 滑翔飞行. ~ *bonds* 无利息公债. ~ *immunity*【医】被动免疫性. ~ *resistance* 消极抵抗. — *n.* ①〔*pl.*〕被动消极的东西;被动性. ②【语法】被动语态;被动式. **-ly** *ad.* **-ness** *n.*

pas·siv·ism [ˈpæsivizəm] *n.* ①被动的行为,被动性. ②消极主义. **-ist** *n.* 消极主义者.

pas·siv·i·ty [pæˈsiviti] *n.* ①被动;被动性;消极情绪〔状态〕;消极怠工. ②不抵抗,默从;忍受. ③【物、化】钝性;钝态;无源性. ④【语法】被动语态的结构.

pass·key [ˈpɑːski] *n.* 万能钥匙;专用钥匙;〔美〕盗贼用的钥匙;弹簧锁钥匙. *a* ~ *man*〔美〕贼.

pas·som·e·ter [pæˈsɔmitə] *n.* 计步器.

Pass·o·ver [ˈpɑːsəuvə] *n.* ①【宗】(犹太人的)逾越节. ②〔p-〕逾越节祭神的羔羊. ③耶稣.

pass·port [ˈpɑːspɔːt] *n.* ①护照;通航护照;通行证;入场券〔权〕;执照. ②(达到目的或获得某物的)手段,保障. ***go without a*** ~〔美俚〕自杀. ~ ***to one's favour*** 得宠〔得到照顾〕的手段.

pass-through [ˈpɑːsˌθruː] *n.* ①(厨房与食堂隔墙上的)递菜饭的小窗口. ②(原料成本等的)转嫁价格.

pas·sus [ˈpæsəs] *n.* (*pl.* ~*(e)s*)〔L.〕诗或故事的一段〔一节〕.

past [pɑːst] *a.* ①过去的;完了的. ②刚过去的,上(月、星期等),前(…年). ③前任的;曾任的;老练的. ④【语法】过去(时)的. *the* ~ *month* 上月. *a* ~ *master* 能手,老手;(协会等的)旧会长. *the* ~ *participle*【语法】过去分词. — *n.* ①〔常 the ~〕过去,过去的事,往事. ②(不可告人的)过去的生活经历;可疑的经历. ③【语法】过去时;(动词的)过去式. *We cannot undo the* ~ 往事不能挽回. *a man with a long* ~ 历史复杂的人. ***for some time*** ~ 前些时候;最近以来. ***in the*** ~ 在过去,从前. ***not put it*** ~ ***(sb.)*** 相信(某人)可能会做(某事). ***with a*** ~ 有不可告人的经历. — *prep.* ①(时间)过…,(几点)多,(几岁)以上;通过,走过(某处). ②(和人)错过去;(能力等的)超过. ③(行动等的)越过. ~ *three o'clock* 三点多. *half* ~ *six* 六点半〔美语用 after〕. *an old man* ~ *seventy* 七十多岁的老人. *walk* ~ *the house* 走过那所房子. ~ *endurance* 不能再忍受. ~ *all belief* 简直不可思议. ~ *comprehension* 费解的,无法理解的. ***be*** ~ ***praying for.*** (人)无可救药了. — *ad.* 过. *go* [*come, run*] ~ 打旁边走过〔过来,跑过〕. ***be*** ~ ***due*** (火车等)误点;(支付等)误期.

pas·ta [ˈpɑːstə] *n.* ①(做细条实心面、通心粉、包子、饺子所用的)面团. ②此种面团做的食品.

paste[1] [peist] *n.* ①糊,浆糊;面团;软糖;浓羹,酱. ②糊状物;玻璃质混合物〔制人造宝石的原料〕;铅质玻璃;制陶粘土;软膏. *a bottle of* ~ 一瓶浆糊. *bean* ~ 豆(瓣)酱. *tooth* ~ 牙膏. *a man of a different* ~ 气质不同凡响的人. — *a.* 人造的;假的. — *vt.* ①用浆糊粘贴(*up; on; together*);把(纸等)贴在…上. ②使成面糊状. ~ ***in*** 贴在(书里). ~ ***up*** 贴在…上;封上.

paste[2] [peist] *vt.*〔俚〕狠狠地打;(体育比赛中)把(对方)决定性地击败. — *n.* (用拳头等)狠狠的一击.

paste·board [ˈpeistbɔːd] *n.* ①纸板;擀面板. ②〔俚〕纸牌;名片. ③火车票;〔美俚〕入场券,门票. ~ *and rolling pin* 擀面板和擀面杖. — *a.* ①用纸板制成的. ②薄弱的,不坚实的,虚有其表的;假的. *a* ~ *pearl* 人造珍珠.

pas·tel[1] [pæsˈtel, ˈpæstel] *n.* ①彩色粉笔〔蜡笔〕;彩色粉笔〔蜡笔〕画(画法);粉画(法). ②小品文,散文诗. ③淡而柔和的色调. — [ˈpæstl] *a.* ①彩色粉笔〔蜡笔〕的;彩色粉笔〔蜡笔〕画的;粉画的. ②(色彩)柔和的,淡的. ③虚弱的. **-list,**〔Am.〕**-ist** *n.* 粉画家.

pas·tel[2] [pæsˈtel, ˈpæstel] *n.* ①【植】菘蓝. ②菘蓝染料.

past·er [ˈpeistə] *n.* ①贴浆糊的人或物. ②胶纸.

pas·tern [ˈpæstəːn] *n.* (马足的)骹.

paste-up [ˈpeistˌʌp] *a., n.* 东拼西凑的文章;杂凑成的东西.

Pas·teur [pæsˈtəː] 巴斯德〔1822—1895, 法国化学家、细菌学家〕. ~ **treatment**【医】巴斯德狂犬病预防接种法.

pas·teur·ism [ˈpæstərizəm] *n.*【医】巴斯德狂犬病预防接种法;巴斯德灭菌法.

pas·teur·ize [ˈpæstəraiz] *vt.*【医】对…用巴斯德杀菌法消毒;给…打狂犬病预防针. **pas·teu·ri·za·tion** [-ˈzeiʃən] *n.* 巴氏灭菌法,低热灭菌.

pas·tic·cio [pæsˈtitʃəu] *n.* (*pl.* ~*s*, ***pas·tic·ci*** [-ˈtitʃiː])〔It.〕混成曲〔歌〕;(文学、美术等的)模仿作品;东拼西凑的杂烩.

pas·tiche [pæsˈtiːʃ] *n.*〔F.〕= pasticcio.

pas·til, pas·tille [ˈpæstil, pæsˈtiːl] *n.* 锭剂;香锭;线香.

pas·time [ˈpɑːs-taim] *n.* 消遣,游戏,娱乐. ***by way of*** ~ = ***for a*** ~ 作消遣.

past·i·ness [ˈpeistinis] *n.* 浆糊〔面团、软膏等〕状态〔性质〕.

pas·tis [pɑːsˈtiːs] *n.* (有甘草和八角子味道的)法国无色露酒.

pas·tor [ˈpɑːstə] *n.* ①(基督教的)牧师;(天主教的)大司祭;精神生活方面的指导人. ②〔罕〕牧人,牧羊者. ③【动】粉红椋鸟. **-ship** *n.* 牧师的职务〔地位、任期〕.

pas·to·ral [ˈpɑːstərəl] *n.* ①牧歌,田园诗〔曲、剧、画、雕刻〕. ②牧师写给教区居民的公开信〔又作 ~ letter〕. ③田园景色. — *a.* ①牧人的. ②(土地)适于牧畜的;(诗等)描写田园生活的;牧歌似的;乡村的. ③牧师的,主教的. ~ *age* 牧畜时代. ~ *area* 牧区. ~ *farming* 畜牧. ~ *poetry* [*poem*] 田园诗. ~ *staff*【宗】(主教的)牧杖. **-ist** *n.* ①田园诗〔曲、剧、画等〕的作者. ②放牧者,牧畜者. ③〔澳〕畜牧场主. **-ly** *ad.*

pas·to·ra·le [ˌpæstəˈrɑːli] *n.* (*pl.* ~*s*, ***-li*** [-liː]) ①(欧洲旧时)描写田园生活的歌剧. ②【乐】田园曲.

pas·to·ral·ism [ˈpɑːstərəlizəm] *n.*〔诗〕①田园风味. ②牧畜主义. ③牧歌体.

pas·tor·ate [ˈpɑːstərit] *n.* ①牧师的职务〔任期、身分〕. ②牧师团.

pas·to·ri·um [pæsˈtɔːriəm] *n.*〔美南部〕牧师住宅.

pas·tra·mi [pəsˈtrɑːmi] *n.* 五香熏牛(肩)肉.

pas·try [ˈpeistri] *n.* ①油酥面,油酥面皮;油酥面馅饼〔点心〕. ②精制糕点. **~-cook** 糕饼师傅.

pas·tur·a·ble [ˈpɑːstʃərəbl] *a.* (土地)适于作牧场的.

pas·tur·age [ˈpɑːstjuridʒ] *n.* ①畜牧(业). ②牧场;牧草. ③〔Scot.〕放牧权.

pas·ture [ˈpɑːstʃə] *n.* ①牧场. ②牧草. ③牲畜饲养,放牧. — *vt.* ①放牧;放(牛羊)吃草;(家畜)吃(牧草). ②把(土地)作牧场用. — *vi.* (牛羊)吃草. **~-ground, ~-land** 牧场.

past·y[1] [ˈpeisti] *a.* ①面糊〔面团〕似的. ②(肌肉)松软的. ③(脸色)苍白的 (= ~-faced).

past·y[2] [ˈpæsti, ˈpɑːsti] *n.* 馅饼(尤指肉馅饼).

PA system = public-address system 扩音装备;扩音系统,有线广播.

Pat [pæt] *n.* ①帕特〔男子名, Patrick 的昵称〕. ②〔俚〕爱尔兰人.

pat[1] [pæt] *n.* ①轻拍;轻打;抚;拍;抚摩. ②(有节奏的)轻拍声. ③(黄油等的)小块. ***a*** ~ ***on the back***〔口〕鼓励. — *vt.* ①轻拍,轻拍…使平滑〔成形〕. ②轻拍…以示抚慰〔赞同等〕. — *vi.* ①轻拍,摩,爱抚,抚 (*on;*

upon). ②(跑时等)发出轻拍声. ~ ***oneself on the back*** (自我)满足. ~ ***(sb.) on the back*** 拍背(表示称赞、祝贺、鼓励). ~**-ball** *n.* ①拍球〔类似棒球的英国球戏(= rounders)〕. ②拙劣无力的网球戏.

pat² *a.* ①适当的,恰好的,合式的 (*to*). ②过于巧合的,人为的, ③记得滚瓜烂熟的; 准备好的. ④〔英、方〕快活的,活泼的,神气的. ⑤〔美〕可靠的; 固定不变的. — *ad.* ①适当,恰好,合式; 及时地. ②立即地; 流利地, 顺顺溜溜地. ***come*** ~ *(to)* 来得正好,正适合 (*The story came ~ to the occassion.* 故事恰好适合当时的场合). ***know a lesson off*** ~ 功课记得一点不差. ***have [know]*** ~ 〔口〕①背熟, 熟记. ②准备好. ***stand*** ~ ①【牌】用发到手的牌打〔不再补索新牌〕. ②〔口〕坚持(原样)不变; 固守 (*on*).

pat. = ①patent; patented. ②pattern. ③patrol.

pat·a·cake [ˈpætəkeik] *n.* ①儿歌〔童谣〕的引头词. ②手帮腔〔按儿歌韵律拍手的一种游戏〕.

pa·ta·gi·um [ˌpætəˈdʒaiəm, pəˈteidʒiəm] *n.* (*pl.* ***-gia*** [-ˈdʒiə]) 【动】①(蝙蝠类的) 翅膜. ②(鳞翅目昆虫的) 领片.

Pa·ta·go·ni·an [ˌpætəˈgəunjən, -niən] *a.* (阿根廷南部)巴塔哥尼亚(人)的. — *n.* 巴塔哥尼亚 (Patagonia) 的印第安人〔全世界身量最高的种族〕.

Pa·tan [ˈpɑːtən] *n.* 帕坦〔尼泊尔城市〕.

Pat·a·vin·i·ty [ˌpætəˈviniti] *n.* ①巴塔维尼亚方言的特色〔Patavium 系意大利帕多瓦 (Padua) 市的古名〕. ②〔p-〕(一般的)方言〔土话〕的使用.

patch¹ [pætʃ] *n.* ①补丁, 补片; 金属补片. ②(军服上表示所属部队的布制)臂章. ③饰颜片, 美人斑〔17、18世纪时女人贴在脸上增加美观或掩饰疤痕等的小绸片等〕; (害眼病时用的)眼罩; (伤口上的)敷裹, 膏药. ④碎片, 碎屑; (文章的)一段. ⑤斑点, 斑纹; 【医】斑. ⑥小块地(上的庄稼). ⑦不中用的人, 无聊的人, 帮闲. ⑧〔主英〕时期, 季节. *a ~ of potatoes* 一块马铃薯地; 一块地的马铃薯. ***Don't put a ~ upon it.*** 〔口〕别再表白啦; 别掩饰啦. ***make a ~ against*** 可与…相比. ***not a ~ on*** 〔口〕比…差得远, 远不及…. ***strike a bad ~*** 〔口〕倒霉. — *vt.* ①修补, 补缀; 拼凑 (*up*). ②暂时遮掩一下 (*together; up*); 修理; 平息(吵架等). ③用美人斑装饰(脸). ~ ***up*** ①结束, 解决; 制止. ②匆忙处理. ③拼凑. ~**ing board**【物】接线板. ~ **pocket** 贴袋, 明袋. ~ **reef** 小而孤立的珊瑚礁. ~ **test**【医】(检验过敏症的)皮肤接触测验. ~**work** 补缀品; 拼凑成的东西, 凑合物; 编辑物.

patch² [pætʃ] *n.* 傻瓜.

patch·er·y [ˈpætʃəri] *n.* 补缀; 补片; 弥缝; 拙劣的修补; 拼凑物.

patch·ou·li [ˈpætʃuli(ː)] *n.*【植】广藿香.

patch·y [ˈpætʃi] *a.* ①补缀(而成)的; 尽是补丁的. ②凑成的; 不调和的. ③脾气别扭的.

patd. = patented.

pate [peit] *n.* 〔口〕头, 脑袋; 家伙, 人. *a bald ~* 秃头. *an empty ~* 傻子. *a shallow ~* 没头脑〔浅薄〕的家伙.

pâte [pɑt] *n.* 〔F.〕浆状物〔尤指制陶瓷器的粘土〕.

pâté [ˈpætei; F. pɑte] *n.* 〔F.〕肉末饼 ~ ***de foie gras*** [pɑte də fwaˈgrɑː] 肥鹅肝酱; 鹅肝酱馅饼.

pa·tel·la [pəˈtelə] *n.* (*pl.* ***~s, -lae*** [-liː]) ①【解】髌, 膝盖(骨); 膝节; 【动】杯状部; (龙虱科昆虫的)吸附节; 【植】球状裸子器, 小盘. ②(古代罗马的)小盘子.

pa·tel·lar [pəˈtelə] *a.*【解】膝盖(骨)的. ~ **reflex**【医】膝反射.

pa·tel·late [pəˈtelit] *a.* 膝盖状的; 【植】小盘状的; 【动】荷叶状的.

pa·tel·li·form [pəˈtelifɔːm] *a.*【植】小盘状的.

pat·en [ˈpætən] *n.* ①【宗】圣餐盘, 圣饼碟, 祭碟. ②薄的金属盘; 扁盘.

pa·ten·cy [ˈpeitənsi] *n.* ①明白, 显著. ②【医】开放(性), 不闭合. ③【语音】开音(性).

pa·tent [ˈpeitənt, ˈpæt-] *n.* ①专利(权); 专利品; 专利证书; 专利标记; 〔美〕公产让渡证. ②独享的权利, 特权. ***get [take out] a ~ for [on]*** *(an invention)* 得到(某项发明)的专利权〔证〕. — *a.* ①专利的; 获得专利权〔证〕保护的. ②〔口〕独出心裁的, 巧妙的. ③(门等)开着的; 明白的, 显然的; 公然的; 公开的. ④开展的, 扩张的; 【植】张开的, 伸展的. ⑤〔美〕(面粉) 高级的. *letters ~* 专利证. ~ *right* 专利权. *a ~ agent* 专利代理人. *a ~ fact* 明白的事实. — *vt.* ①批准给予…专利. ②取得…的专利. ~**ambiguity**【法】(文件、证书的)语意暧昧不明. ~ **anchor**【海】无档锚. ~ **digest** 白兰地酒. ~ **flour** 上等面粉. ~ **leather** 漆皮. ~ **log**【海】拖曳式计程仪. ~ **medicine** (专利)成药 **P- Office** 专利局. ~ **pool** 共享专利权的一组企业. ~ **roll** 〔英〕专利特许登记簿.

pa·tent·a·ble [ˈpætəntəble] *a.* 可以取得专利的, 准许专利的.

pa·ten·tee [ˌpætənˈtiː, ˌpei-] *n.* 专利权获得者.

pa·tent·ly [ˈpeitəntli] *ad.* 显然, 公然, 一清二楚地.

pat·en·tor [ˈpeitəntə, ˈpæ-] *n.* ①专利权的授予. ②〔误用〕= patentee.

pa·ter [ˈpeitə] *n.* 〔英俚〕父亲〔学童语〕.

Pa·ter [peitə] *n.* 佩特〔姓氏〕.

pa·ter·fa·mil·i·as [ˈpeitəfəˈmiliæs] *n.* (*pl.* ***pa·ters-fa·mil·i·as*** [peitriːz-]) 【罗马法】一家之父, 男性家长〔今用作诙谐语〕.

pa·ter·nal [pəˈtəːnl] *a.* ①父亲的; 象父亲的. ②父方的; 父系的; 得自父亲的, 世袭的. *be related on the ~ side* 是父方的亲戚. ~ *ancestor* 〔美俚〕父亲. ~ *care* 父亲(般)的关怀, 父心. ~ *government* 温情主义政治. ***bid adieu to one's ~ roof*** 拜别父亲独立生活. **-ly** *ad.* 父亲似地.

pa·ter·nal·ism [pəˈtəːnəlizəm] *n.* 家长主义; (政治上的)温情主义; 家长式统治; 家长作风. **-nal·ist** [-ist] *a., n.* 搞家长式统治的(人).

pa·ter·nal·is·tic [pəˌtəːnəˈlistik] *a.* 家长式统治的; 家长作风的, 家长式的. **-ti·cal·ly** *ad.*

pa·ter·ni·ty [pəˈtəːniti] *n.* ①父亲的身分; 父道; 父性; 父权; 父子关系; 父系. ②〔喻〕渊源; 来源, 出处, 作者.

pa·ter·nos·ter [ˈpætəˈnɔstə] *n.* ①〔常作 Pater Noster〕【基督】主祷文, 念主祷文的祷告〔尤指用拉丁文〕. ②咒文, 符咒. ③(祷告时用的)念珠. ④念珠式钓钩〔每隔一定间隔有钩, 又作 ~ line〕. ***black ~*** 咒诅. ***say the devil's ~*** 叽叽咕咕骂人, 发牢骚.

path(ol). = pathological; pathology.

path [pɑːθ] *n.* (*pl.* ~***s*** [pɑːðz]) ①(自然踏成的)路; 路径; (马路边上的)人行道; (车子走不过的)小路; (竞走或自行车比赛的)跑道. ②路线; 路程; 〔喻〕(人生的)道路; (思想、行为、生活的)途径, 方式. ③【天】道, 带. *approach ~*【空】进场航线. *moon's ~*【天】白道. *~ of a total eclipse*【天】全食带. *a ~ strewn with roses* 撒满玫瑰的道路, 安乐的一生. ***a beaten ~*** 踏出来的〔走惯的〕路; 常规, 普通方法. ***break [blaze] a (new) ~*** 开辟一条(新)路. ***cross sb.'s ~*** 碰见某人; 挡住某人去路, 阻碍某人. ***set sb. on the right ~*** 使某人走上正路. ~**-breaker** 开路人; 闯将. ~ **finder** ①探路人; 开拓者; 探索者. ②导航人; 导航飞机; 导航雷达; 【空】投照明弹的飞机. ③〔美卑〕警察的密探. ~**finding** ①领航, 导航; 寻找目标, ~**way** 小路, 小径. **-less** *a.* 无路的, 人迹未到的.

Pa·than [pəˈtɑːn] *n.* 帕坦人〔住在印度或印度西北边境的阿富汗族人〕.

pa·thet·ic, 〔罕〕**pa·thet·i·cal** [pəˈθetik, -kl] *a.* ①可怜的, 悲惨的, 使人感动的. ②感伤的; 感情(上)的, 情绪(上)的. *a ~ scene* (戏剧等的) 悲惨场面. — *n.* ①〔the ~〕感伤性的东西. ②〔*pl.*〕可怜的表现〔动作〕,

感伤的情绪. ~ **fallacy** 感情的误置〔指对自然界现象或无生命事物的拟人化〕. **-thet·i·cal·ly** *ad.*

patho- *comb. f.* ①病;苦;受难. ②热情,感情: *patho*gen, *patho*logy.

path·o·gen, path·o·gene [ˈpæθədʒin, ˈpæθədʒiːn] *n.*【生、医】病原体.

path·o·gen·e·sis [ˌpæθəˈdʒenisis] *n.* 致病;发病.

path·o·ge·net·ic, path·o·gen·ic [ˌpæθədʒiˈnetik, -ˈdʒenik] *a.* 病原的;致病的. **-o·gen·i·cal·ly** *ad.*

path·o·ge·nic·i·ty [ˌpæθədʒiˈnisiti] *n.*【医】致病力,致病原因.

pa·thog·e·nous [pəˈθɔdʒinəs] *a.* = pathogenetic.

pa·thog·e·ny [pəˈθɔdʒini] *n.* 致病原因;发病.

pa·thog·no·mon·ic [pəˌθɔgnəˈmɔnik] *a.* 特殊病症的.

pa·thog·no·my [pəˈθɔgnəmi] *n.*【医、心】病征学.

pathol. = pathological; pathology.

path·o·log·ic, path·o·log·i·cal [ˌpæθəˈlɔdʒik, -ikəl] *a.* 病理学(上)的;病态的;由疾病引起的. ~ *anatomy* 病理解剖. ~ *physiology* 病理生理学. **-log·ical·ly** *ad.*

pa·thol·o·gist [pəˈθɔlədʒist] *n.* 病理学家.

pa·thol·o·gy [pəˈθɔlədʒi] *n.* ①病理学. ②病理;病状. ③〔喻〕反常,变态. *vegetable* ~ 植物病理学. *general [special]* ~ 病理总论[各论].

pa·thom·e·ter [pəˈθɔmitə] *n.* 体内电导率变化探测器.

pa·thos [ˈpeiθɔs] *n.* ①(言词、作品、事件中)引起怜悯[同情]的因素;怜悯,同情,感伤力. ②悲怆,哀婉,凄楚;【心】精神病苦. ③偶然[暂时]因素.

path·way [ˈpɑːθwei] *n.* = path.

-pathy *comb. f.* ①疾病. ②疗法. ③痛苦. ④感情: anti*pathy*, eletro*pathy*, osteo*pathy*.

Pa·tience [ˈpeiʃəns] *n.* 佩欣丝〔女子名〕.

pa·tience [ˈpeiʃəns] *n.* ①忍耐,容忍,忍受;忍耐力,坚韧;耐心,耐性; ②〔主英〕多种单人牌戏之一〔又名 solitaire〕. *Have ~!* 忍耐忍耐! 再等一等! *My ~!* 〔俚〕嗳哟! 啊! *P- is a plaster for all sores.* 忍耐可以减轻一切痛苦. ***be out of [have no] ~ with*** 对…不能忍耐;受不了…. ***lose all (one's) ~ with*** 对…发脾气. ***the ~ of Job*** 极度的忍耐. ***with ~*** 耐心地.

pa·tient [ˈpeiʃənt] *a.* ①能忍耐的,有耐性的;容忍的. ②勤快的,孜孜不倦的;坚韧的;受得了(饥饿、劳累等)的. ③容许的,有…余地的. ④被动性的. ~ ***of*** 能忍受…的;不生气的;容许…意义的 (*be ~ of two interpretations* 可作两种解释). —*n.* (接受治疗的)病人,患者;被动者;(美容院等的)顾客;〔美〕殡仪馆的尸体. *in-~* 住院病人. *out-~* 门诊病人. **-ly** *ad.* 忍耐地,容忍地,耐心地.

pat·i·na[1] [ˈpætinə] *n.* (*pl.* ~*s*) ①(青铜器上的)绿锈,古翠;【美】古色;(木器、墙壁等由年久而产生的)光泽面. ②(长久的经验[习惯]形成的)神情,外貌.

pat·i·na[2] [ˈpætinə] *n.* (*pl.* **-nae** [-niː]) (古罗马的)盘子;(盛圣餐面包的)金属盘.

pat·i·nate [ˈpætineit] *vt., vi.* ①(使)生绿锈. ②(使)产生光泽. (= patinize).

pat·i·nat·ed [ˈpætineitid] *a.* 生了铜绿的;古色古香的. **-i·na·tion** [-ˈneiʃən] *n.*

pat·ine [ˈpætn] *n.* ①祭碟 (= paten). ②古翠;绿锈 (= patina). —[peˈtiːn] *vt.* 使生绿锈.

pat·i·nous [ˈpætinəs] *a.* 生铜绿的;有古色的.

pa·ti·o [ˈpɑːtiəu] *n.* (*pl.* ~*s*) 〔Sp.〕天井,院子;(连接房屋和铺有地面的)室外闲坐[就餐]处.

pa·tis·se·rie [pəˈtisəri] *n.* 〔F.〕 = pastry.

Pat. Off. = Patent Office〔美〕专利局.

pat·ois [ˈpætwɑː] *n.* (*pl.* ***pat·ois*** [ˈpætwɑːz]) 〔*sing., pl.*〕〔F.〕方言,土语;隐语;行话,同行语 (= jargon).

patri- *comb. f.* 父: *patri*cide.

pa·tri·arch [ˈpeitrɑːk] *n.* ①家长;族长;(特指)犹太民族的祖先;(团体的)元老. ②(基督教的)早期主教〔尤指君士坦丁、亚历山大里亚、安提克、耶路撒冷等地的主教〕;【天主】罗马教皇;东正教的最高一级主教. ③(科学、学派、宗教等的)鼻祖,创始人. ④〔*pl.*〕【圣】雅各 (Jacob) 的十二个儿子;亚伯拉罕 (Abraham)、以赛 (Isaac)、雅各 (Jacob) 和他们的祖先.

pa·tri·ar·chal [ˌpeitriˈɑːkəl] *a.* ①家[族]长的;(大)主教的;家长[族长、主教]管辖的;家[族]似的. ②元老的,元老派头的;可尊敬的. *the ~ ideology* 宗法思想. ~**-feudual** 宗法封建性的.

pa·tri·arch·ate [ˈpeitriɑːkit] *n.* ①主教[家长、族长等的]的职位[职务、任期、管区、住宅]. ②= patriarchy.

pa·tri·arch·ism [ˌpeitriˈɑːkizəm] *n.* 家长制度;族长政治.

pa·tri·arch·y [ˈpeitriɑːki] *n.* ①家长制;族长政治;族长制社会;族长管区. ②父权制(社会).

Pa·tri·cia [pəˈtriʃə] *n.* 帕特丽夏〔女子名,昵称为 Pat 或 Patty〕.

pa·tri·cian [pəˈtriʃən] *n.* ①(古罗马的)贵族 (*opp.* plebeian); (一般的)贵族. ②罗马帝国的地方官;中世纪意大利的显贵. ③有教养的人. — *a.* (古罗马帝国的)贵族的;(相貌等)贵族似的.

pa·tri·ci·ate [pəˈtriʃiit] *n.* 贵族阶级[地位,等级].

pat·ri·cide [ˈpætrisaid] *n.* 杀父(行为);杀父者. **-cid·al** [ˌpætriˈsaidl] *a.*

pat·rick [ˈpætrik] *n.* ①帕特里克〔男子名〕. ②**St.** ~ 爱尔兰的守护神.

pat·ri·co [ˈpætrikəu] *n.* 〔吉卜赛俚〕牧师.

pat·ri·lin·e·al [ˌpætrəˈliniəl, ˌpeitrə-] *a.* 父系的. **-ly** *ad.*

pat·ri·mo·ni·al [ˌpætriˈməunjəl, -niəl] *a.* ①父子相传的,世袭的. ②世袭财产的;教会生产的. ~ **sea** 承袭海.

pat·ri·mo·ny [ˈpætriməni] *n.* ①世袭财产,遗产. ②家传;传统;继承物. ③教堂财产[基金].

pa·tri·ot [ˈpeitriət, ˈpæt-] *n.* 爱国者;爱国主义者. — *a.* 爱国的;有爱国心的.

pa·tri·ot·eer [ˌpeitriəˈtiə] *n.* 〔美〕(以爱国为幌子而谋私利的)"爱国"市侩.

pa·tri·ot·ic [ˌpætriˈɔtik, ˌpei-] *a.* 爱国的,有爱国热忱的,爱国主义的. **-ti·cal·ly** *ad.*

pa·tri·ot·ics [ˌpætriˈɔtiks] *n. pl.* ①〔用作 *sing.*〕爱国的作品[演说、活动]. ②爱国精神的表现.

pa·tri·ot·ism [ˈpætriətizəm, ˌˈpei-] *n.* 爱国心,爱国主义.

pa·tris·tic, pa·trist·i·cal [pəˈtristik(əl)] *a.* ①早期基督教会领袖[教父]的. ②关于早期基督教会领袖[教父]著作的,研究教父著作的.

pa·tris·tics [pəˈtristiks] *n. pl.* 〔用作 *sing.*〕早期基督教领袖[教父]著作[教义、传记]的研究;教父学.

Pa·tro·clus [pəˈtrɔkləs] 普特洛克勒斯〔荷马史诗《伊利亚特》中的一个英雄,特洛伊战争中为赫克托所杀〕.

pa·trol [pəˈtrəul] *n.* ①巡逻,巡视,侦察. ②巡逻兵;警察. ③侦察队;哨舰;巡逻机队. ④〔美〕童子军小队. ⑤〔美〕囚车. ***on ~*** 在巡逻,侦察中. — *vt., vi.* 巡视,巡逻,侦察;(在街上)巡游. ~ *the pasture*【美棒球】守外场. ~ **aviation**【空】巡逻飞行. ~ **boat** 哨艇,巡逻艇. ~ **dog** 警犬. ~ **leader**【军】侦察班长. ~**man** ①巡视者,巡逻者. ②(电线等的)保线员. ③〔美〕外勤警察;巡警. ~ **wagon**〔美〕囚车.

pa·tron [ˈpeitrən, ˈpæ-] *n.* ①奖励者,赞助人,支持者;庇护人;恩主;【史】(艺术家等的)保护者. ②(商店的)顾客,主顾;(慈善协会等的)主席. ③【宗】保护圣徒;守护神 (= ~ saint);(英国教会中)有授与牧师职权的人. ④〔古罗马〕释放奴隶后的旧奴隶主;保护平民的贵族. ~ **saint** ①保护圣徒,守护神. ②(团体等的)最初领导人;最高典范.

pat·ron·age [ˈpætrənidʒ] *n.* ①保护人[庇护人、赞助人等]的身分[影响、作用];支援,保护;赞助,奖励. ②(顾客的)光顾,惠顾. ③以恩赐的态度施予的恩惠;沽恩,自命恩人,恩人气派. ④圣职授与权,牧师推荐权;官职任命权. *He has a great deal of ~ in his hands.* 他有很大的任命权. *the P- Secretary* 〔英〕公务员铨衡长官. ***take sb. under one's ~*** 使某人受自己的庇护,使某人听自己的领导. ***under the ~ of*** 在…保护下;承…栽培.

pa·tron·al [pəˈtrəunl, pæˈt-] *a.* 保护的;守护神的;赞助的.

pa·tron·ess [ˈpeitrənis, ˈpæ-] *n.* 女保护人[庇护人、赞助人等].

pat·ron·ize [ˈpætrənaiz] *vt.* ①支援,保护,赞助. ②光顾,惠顾. ③对…以恩人自居;对…摆出屈尊俯就的样子.

pat·ron·iz·ing [ˈpætrənaiziŋ] *a.* 恩人气派的,自命为恩人的;屈尊俯就的;神气十足的;傲慢的. **-ly** *ad.*

pat·ro·nym·ic [ˌpætrəˈnimik] *n.* ①源于父名[祖名]的姓[例: Johnson (= son of John), Macdonald (= son of Donald) 等]. ②姓. — *a.* ①(前缀、后缀)表示父[祖]名的. ②(姓)源于父名[祖名]的.

pa·troon [pəˈtruːn] *n.* ①【美史】(荷兰统治下纽约州及新泽西州享有特权的)大庄园主. ②〔古〕船长.

Pat's = patents.

pa·tsy [ˈpætsi] *n.* 〔美俚〕①容易受骗的人. ②替罪羊. ③懦夫.

pat·(t)a·mar [ˈpætəmɑː] *n.* 【海】(在印度沿海从事贸易的)三角帆船.

pat·ten [ˈpætn] *n.* ①木套鞋,木底靴. ②【建】柱脚,壁脚.

pat·ter[1] [ˈpætə] *vi.* ①啪嗒啪嗒地响;(雨点)嗒嗒地下. ②嗒嗒地跑. — *vt.* 使发出嗒嗒声;使(水等)劈里啪啦地响. — *n.* (急促的)滴嗒声,滴沥声;啪嗒声,劈里啪啦声. *the ~ of little feet* 嗒嗒的小脚步声.

pat·ter[2] [ˈpætə] *n.* ①(摊贩、魔术师等的)顺口溜,快嘴话;喊喊喳喳的谈话;饶舌. ②行话;切口,黑话,隐语. ③(歌剧中的)滑稽顺口溜;〔美电台〕合唱后的间奏曲. ④〔俚〕歌词;(喜剧等的)台词,说白. ⑤(魔术师等的)咒文[通常作 conjuror's ~]. — *vt.* 喊喊喳喳地念[讲];祷告似地说. — *vi.* ①喋喋不休. ②祷告,念经. ③念顺口溜;唱滑稽顺口溜歌曲. ~ **song** (音乐喜剧中的)滑稽顺口溜歌曲.

pat·tern [ˈpætən] *n.* ①模范,榜样;典范. ②型,模型;模式;雏型;【冶】原型. ③花样;式样;(服装裁剪的)纸样;图案,图谱,图表;机构,结构;特性曲线;晶体点阵;(电视的)帧面图象. ④方式;形式;格局;格调. ⑤(衣料等的)样品,样本,样板. ⑥〔美〕一件衣料. ⑦(炮弹等的)散布面;靶子上的弹痕. ⑧(飞机的)着陆航线. *a ~ wife* 模范妻子. *a paper ~ for a dress* 女服纸样. *a machine of a new [an old] ~* 新[旧]型机器. *a cropping ~* 农作制. ***after the ~ of*** 仿…. — *vt.* ①照图样做;仿造,摹制 *(after; upon)*. ②给…加花样,用图案装饰. ③〔英方〕与…相比 *(to, with)*. — *vi.* 形成图案. ***~ oneself after*** 模仿,学…的榜样. ~ **bargaining** 工会按理想的合同方案之一同资方进行的谈判. ~ **bombing** 【军】定型轰炸. ~**maker** 制模工;服装设计师. ~ **mechanism** 【纺】提花装置. ~**-room**, ~**-shop** (翻砂厂等的)制模车间. **-ed** *a.* 被组成图案的. **-ing** *n.* 图案结构,图形;(行为等的)特有型式. **-less** *a.* 无图案的.

pat·tern·ize [ˈpætənaiz] *vt.* ①使符合型式. ②把…构成图案.

pat·tie [ˈpæti] *n.* = patty.

Pat·ti·son [ˈpætisn] *n.* 帕蒂森[姓氏].

Pat·ty, Pat·ti, Pat·tie [ˈpæti] *n.* 帕蒂〔女子名, Patricia 的昵称〕.

pat·ty [ˈpæti] *n.* ①小馅饼 (= pâté). ②小片糖. ~**pan** 烘焙饼锅. ~ **shell** 小馅饼皮.

pat·ty-cake [ˈpætiˌkeik] *n.* ①儿歌[童谣]的引头词. ②手帮腔[按儿歌韵律拍手的一种游戏 (= patacake)].

pat·u·lin [ˈpætjulin] *n.* 【生化】棒曲霉素.

pat·u·lous [ˈpætjuləs] *a.* ①【植】(树枝等)平展的. ②张开的,展开的. **-ly** *ad.* **-ness** *n.*

PAU = Pan American Union 泛美联盟.

pau·ci·ty [ˈpɔːsiti] *n.* ①少许,少量. ②缺乏,贫乏. *a country marked by a ~ of resources* 一个缺乏自然资源的国家.

Paul [pɔːl] *n.* ①保罗[姓氏,男子名]. ②【基督】使徒保罗. ***rob Peter to pay ~*** 劫甲给乙,借东还西. ~ **Bunyan** [ˈbʌŋjən] ①(美国传说中的)伐木巨人. ②〔喻〕大力士. ~ **Pry** ①爱刨根问底的人. ②〔英空俚〕探照灯.

Paul·a [ˈpɔːlə] *n.* 保拉[女子名].

paul·dron [ˈpɔːldrən] *n.* 肩甲,甲的护肩部分.

Pau·li [ˈpauli] 沃夫根·泡利〔1900—58, 德国物理学家〕. ~ **exclusion principle** 【物】泡利不相容原理.

paul·in [ˈpɔːlin] *n.* 防水帆布;船舱盖布.

Paul·ine[1] [pɔːˈliːn] *n.* 保琳[女子名].

Paul·ine[2] [ˈpɔːlain] *a.* ①使徒保罗 (Paul) 的. ②保罗著作[教义]的. ③伦敦圣保罗学校 (St. Paul's School) 的. — *n.* 伦敦圣保罗学校的学生.

Paul·ing [ˈpɔːliŋ] *n.* 保林[姓氏].

Paul·ist [ˈpɔːlist] *n.* ①【天主】(纽约)使徒保罗传道会的神父. ②(印度)耶稣会教士.

pau·lo-post-fu·ture [ˈpɔːləupəustˈfjuːtʃə] *n.* 【希腊语法】未来完成时;〔谑〕最近的将来.

Pau·low·ni·a [pɔːˈləuniə] *n.* ①【植】泡桐属. ②[p-] 泡桐树. ~ **imperialis** 白桐.

paunch [pɔːntʃ] *n.* ①肚子,腹;大肚子. ②瘤胃[反刍动物的第一胃]. ③(昆虫的)囊状附器. ④【海】防摩席. *Fat ~es have lean pates.* 大腹便便,头脑空空. — *vt.* 把…破肚子;破腹摘出…的脏腑.

paunch·y [ˈpɔːntʃi] *a.* 罗汉肚的,大腹便便的.

pau·per [ˈpɔːpə] *n.* ①照救贫法得到救济的人;贫民,穷人. ②【法】(得免除诉讼费用的)贫苦起诉人;〔嘲笑语〕叫化子. *~ children* 贫穷儿童. *a ~ school* 贫民学校. **-dom, -ism** *n.* ①贫穷. ②〔集合词〕穷人,贫民.

pau·per·is [ˈpɔːpəris] *n.* 〔L.〕= pauper. ***sue in forma ~*** 【法】作为贫民上诉.

pau·per·ize [ˈpɔːpəraiz] *vt.* 把…弄穷;使成为贫民. **-i·za·tion** [ˌpɔːpəraiˈzeiʃən] *n.* 贫困化.

Pau·ro·me·tab·a·la [ˌpɔːrəuməˈtæbələ] *n. pl.* 【动】(昆虫的)渐近变态.

pau·ro·me·tab·o·lous, pau·ro·me·ta·bol·ic [ˌpɔːrəumiˈtæbələs, -ˈbɔlik] *a.* 【动】渐变态的. **-o·lism** *n.*

paus·al [ˈpɔːzəl] *a.* 【语法】①(句子结尾等时)停顿的. ②停顿前的词形[元音形式]的.

pause [pɔːz] *n.* ①中止;暂停;踌躇. ②断句;句读,段落;停读;停顿符号[句号,逗号等]. ③【乐】延长;延长号[⌒或⌣]. ***at [in] ~*** 停止着;踌躇着. ***give ~ to*** 使踌躇. ***make a ~*** 中止;歇一下气. — *vi.* ①停止,中止,歇气. ②等 *(for)*;踌躇. ③【乐】延长. ~ ***and ponder*** 停下仔细考虑;踌躇. ~ ***upon*** 在…歇一下气[停一停,想一想].

pav [pæv] *n.* 〔口〕= pavilion.

pav·age [ˈpeividʒ] *n.* ①铺路,铺地. ②铺路税.

pav·an, pav·ane [ˈpævən] *n.* (16、17 世纪流行西班牙的)孔雀舞(曲).

pave [peiv] *vt.* ①铺(路) *(with)*. 作铺设…之用. ②铺设,密布. ~ ***the way for [to]*** 为…铺平道路;使…容易到来.

pa·vé [ˈpævei] *n.* 〔F.〕①铺石路;铺筑过的地面[路面]. ②密镶宝石.

pave·ment [ˈpeivmənt] *n.* ①铺石路,〔英〕人行道 (=〔美〕sidewalk);〔美〕车道 (=〔英〕roadway). ②铺地,铺石;铺路材料. ③【动】铺石状构造[密生的齿列等]. *a desert ~* 沙漠覆盖层. ***on the ~*** 无住处;被抛弃. ***pound the ~(s)*** 〔美俚〕①徘徊街头找工作. ②(警察)巡行街道. ~ **artist** 马路画家;街头展画出售

者. ~-**light**【建】(地窖等的)顶窗.

pav·er [ˈpeivə] *n.* 铺石人;铺路材料;铺路机.

pav·id [ˈpævid] *a.* 〔罕〕害怕的,胆怯的.

pa·vil·ion [pəˈviljən] *n.* ①(尖顶)大帐篷;帐篷形物;穹形物. ②【建】亭子,(装饰性的)楼阁. ③(运动场内搭有帐篷的)选手席;看台;(公园等的)休息处;(医院的)隔离式病楼;(展览馆的)分馆. ④〔古〕天盖,天空. ⑤【解】耳郭;外耳. ⑥多角形钻石的下部(斜面). *a water* ~ 水榭. ~ **hospital** 隔组式医院. ~ **roof** 四角屋顶. — *vt.* 给…搭帐篷(盖住);笼罩.

pav·in [ˈpævin] *n.* 孔雀舞 (= pavane).

pav·ing [ˈpeiviŋ] *n.* ①铺筑过的路面[地面]. ②铺地(工程). ③铺路材料. ~ *in setts [in stone blocks]* 石块铺面. ~ *with pebbles* 卵石铺面. ~ **stone** 铺路石.

pav·io(u)r [ˈpeivjə] *n.* ①铺路工人. ②铺路机. ③铺路材料.

pav·is [ˈpævis] *n.* (中古时期的防护全身的)大盾.

Pav·lov [ˈpɑːvlɔf], **Ivan Pe·tro·vitch** 巴甫洛夫〔1849—1936, 苏联生理学家〕. **-lov·i·an** [pævˈlɔviən] *a.* 巴甫洛夫(学说)的.

Pa·vo [ˈpeivəu] *n.*【天】孔雀座 (= the Peacock).

pav·o·nine, pa·vo·ni·an [ˈpævənain, pəˈvəuniən] *a.* 孔雀(似)的;绚烂多彩的.

paw[1] [pɔː] *n.* ①(狗、猫等的)脚爪, 爪子〔*cf.* hoof〕. ②〔谑〕(人的)手;〔俚〕笔迹. ***a velvet*** ~① (猫的)肉爪. ②笑面虎;笑里藏刀. ***make somebody a cat's*** ~, ***make a cat's*** ~ ***of somebody*** 利用人做爪牙. — *vi., vt.* ①(用脚爪等)搔,抓,扒. ②〔口〕笨拙地使用;盘弄 *(over)*;〔美俚〕爱抚. ③艰苦地行走. ~ **foot** 家具的兽爪撑脚.

paw[2] [pɔː] *n.*〔美口〕= papa.

PAWA = Pan American World Airways〔美〕泛美航空公司.

pa·waw [pəˈwɔː] *n., v.* = powwow.

pawk·y [ˈpɔːki] *a.* ①〔Scot.〕狡猾的; 机警的. ②〔美方〕狂妄的. **-i·ly** [-li] *ad.* 狡猾地. **-i·ness** *n.*

pawl [pɔːl] *n.*【机】(防齿轮倒转的)爪,制转杆;卡子,掣子; 棘爪. — *vt.* 用卡子制住(绞盘). *a feeder* ~【军】拨弹钩. ~ **spring** 制动簧片.

pawn[1] [pɔːn] *n.* (国际象棋中的)兵,卒;〔喻〕爪牙,走卒.

pawn[2] [pɔːn] *n.* ①典,当,押. ②典当物,抵押品;人质. ***be at [in, to]*** ~ 典当着,抵押出去. ***give [put] sth. in*** ~ 典当掉, 抵押掉.— *vt.* ①当掉,把…抵押出去. ②〔喻〕拿(生命、名誉等)作保证. ~ ***one's word*** 许诺,答应,保证. ~ ***sth. off as*** 把某物冒充为…押[拿]出去. ~**broker** 当铺主, 典当商. ~**broking** 典当业. ~-**shop** 当铺. ~ **ticket** 当票;抵押凭据.

Paw·nee [pɔːˈniː] *n.* *(pl.* ~*(s))* ①波尼族印第安人〔住美国普拉特 (Platte) 河沿岸一带, 属喀多语族〕. ②(印第安人的)波尼语.

pawn·ee [pɔːˈniː] *n.* 收当人;接受抵押品的人.

pawn·er, pawn·or [ˈpɔːnə] *n.* 当出人,典出人.

pawn·y [ˈpɔːni] *n.*〔军俚〕= water.

paw·paw [ˈpɔːpɔː] *n.*【植】①木瓜. ②(美国中部和南部的)巴婆树;巴婆果 (= papaw).

PAX, P.A.X. = private automatic exchange (电话)自动小交换机.

pax [pæks] *n.* ①【天主】(耶稣或圣母马利亚的)圣像牌;【宗】(弥撒中的)接吻礼. ②〔英俚〕朋友; 友谊. ③〔P-〕【罗神】和平的女神; 和平. — *int.*〔英学俚〕算了吧!别吵啦,别打啦! ***be [make]*** ~ ***with*** 和…亲热起来. ***cry*** ~ 求和. ***P- Britannica*** 英国统治下的和平. ~ ***Romana*** 〔L.〕①罗马帝国统治下的和平. ② 强加于被征服民族的和平. ~ ***vobis*** [ˈvəubis], ~ ***vobiscum*** [vəuˈbiskəm]〔L.〕祝你们平安.

pax·wax [ˈpækswæks] *n.*〔英方〕(哺乳动物的) 颈部韧带.

pay[1] [pei] *vt.* (~***ed*** [peid],〔罕〕***paid*** [peid]) 在(船底等)上涂柏油[其他防水剂等].

pay[2] [pei] *vt.* (***paid*** [peid]) ①付(款),支付; 付(代价),发(薪水). ②付清,偿清,缴纳. ③给…以报酬;出钱雇;酬答,报答; 报偿; 补偿; 尽(义务等). ④〔口〕报复, 报(仇). ⑤进行(访问等),表示(敬意等), 致(问候), 给予(注意等). ⑥对…有利,合算. ⑦有…收益;(职位等)有…报酬. ⑧〔~***ed***〕【海】放出(缆索等) *(away; out)*. ~ *a doctor* 酬劳医生. ~ *a visit* 访问. *The enterprise will not* ~ *you.* 这项事业怕不合算. *Submission will* ~ *you better.* 你还是服从为好(否则不利). ~ *a compliment to* 称赞,夸奖,恭维. — *vi.* ①支付, 偿清. ②偿还,付出代价;受惩处,得到报应 *(for)*. ③合算,有利,值得. ~ *for the book* 付清书款. *It* ~*s to be polite.* 以礼待人不会吃亏. ~ ***as you go*** ①量入为出. ②帐单到期即付. ③领到薪金即付所得税. ~ ***attention to*** 关心, 注意. ~ ***attentions [addresses] to (a lady)*** 巴结(女人), 向(女子)献殷勤. ~ ***away*** ①付掉. ②【海】放出(缆索等).~ ***back*** 偿还;报答;向…报复(~ *sb. back in his own coin* 以其人之道还治其人之身). ~ ***by instalments*** 分期付款.~ ***court to*** 追求(女人).~ ***down*** ①即时支付. ②(分期付款购货时)先支付部分货款. ~ ***for*** 付开销; 赔偿(损失);(为某种过失)付出代价, 吃亏, 受到惩罚. ~ ***home*** 充分报复, 全力反击. ~ ***in [into]*** 缴款;解款(入银行); 捐款. ~ ***in advance*** 预付. ~ ***in kind*** 以实物 (不拿钱)支付;〔喻〕以同物偿还,报复. ~ ***off*** ①偿清(债务等). ②发清(工钱); 发清工钱解雇. ③报复,惩罚. ④使人得益,使有报偿. ⑤【海】使(船首)转向下风,(船)转向下风. ⑥【海】松出(绳索等). ~ ***it's way*** 有利可图. ~ ***on delivery*** 货到付款. ~ ***one's college*** 靠做工读完大学. ~ ***one's way*** 作到不负债. ~ ***out*** ①支付,还(债). ②拿…出气,痛加责罚. ③【海】放松, 放出(绳子). ④〔美〕赚到钱. ~ ***the debt of nature*** 归天,死. ~ ***the fiddler***〔美〕负担费用; 自作自受. ~ ***the penalty*** 得报应, 受罚. ~ ***through the nose*** 付出过高代价. ~ ***too dear for one's whistle*** 做得不偿失的事. ~ ***up*** (全部或按时) 付清; 缴清(股款等). ***Something is to*** ~. 〔美口〕情况不妙. ***What is to*** ~*?* 出了什么事? — *n.* ①付, 支付; 受雇用. ②薪水, 工资, 津贴; 报酬. ③偿还, 报答; 罚, 报应. ④有支付能力的人; 按期付款的人. ⑤含有富矿藏的土[岩、砂]; 可采矿石; 产(石)油地带[层]. *full [half]* ~ 全[半]薪. ***be good [bad]*** ~. 〔口〕(人)还债可靠[不可靠]. ***hit the*** ~〔美〕掘得石油层. ***in the*** ~ ***of*** … 豢养下的,…御用下的; 被…收买. ***without*** ~ 无酬的, 名誉的. —*a.* ①含有贵重矿物的; 矿藏丰富的. ②〔美〕(自动)收费的, 需付费的. ③有关支付的. ~ *ore* 富矿石. ~ *rock* 含矿岩. *a* ~ *liberary* 收费图书馆. *a* ~ *clerk* 出纳员. ~-**as-you-earn** *n.*〔英〕付工资时预扣所得税法〔略作 PAYE〕. ~-**as-you-see** *a.* 付款收看选定的电视节目. ~**bill** 工资单. ~**check,** ~**cheque** ①工资支票; 薪金; 工资. ②〔美〕播音演出的主办人. ~**day** ①发薪日,支付日. ②【商】(证券市场等的)过户结帐日,交割日. ~ **dirt**〔美俚〕有利可图的含金矿石[矿砂];〔喻〕有利可图的发现. ~ **envelope** 工资[薪水]袋. ~ **grade** (军人)薪金等级. ~ **list** 薪水帐. ~**load** 酬载, 有用负载; 有效负载. ~ **master** (发放薪饷的)出纳员; 军需官. **P- master General**〔英〕财政部主计长;〔美〕军需部长. ~**off** ①发薪(日). ②结清薪水解雇. ③〔口〕结清,算清; 了结, 结束. ④【棒球】第 9 场. ⑤〔美俚〕分赃; 报仇, 报复. ⑥(事件等的)高潮. ⑦决定性的事[因素]. ⑧出乎意料的事情 (*That was the* ~*-off* 那真是意外). ~ **office** (尤指公债利息的) 偿付局. ~-**officer**【军】军需官. ~**out** 花费, 支出. ~-**packet** 工资袋; 薪金袋. ~ **phone [station]** 公用自动收费电话亭. ~**roll**〔美〕①职工名册; 发薪簿. ②应付薪金额 (*on the* ~*roll* 被雇用. *off the* ~*roll* 被解职). ③

(计算机的)计算报表. ~**-roller**〔美〕受薪者,领津贴者〔尤指政府雇员〕. ~ **sheet** 发薪簿. ~ **telephone** 自动收费公用电话. ~**-TV** 收费电视.

pay·a·ble [ˈpeiəbl] *a.* ①可付的; (到期)应支付的. ②(矿山等)有利的,有开采价值的. *bills* ~ 应付票据. ~ *three days after sight* 见票后三日照付. ~ ***at sight*** 见票即付. ~ ***on demand*** 随到随付. **-a·bly** *ad.* 可获利地.

PAYE, P.A.Y.E. = pay-as-you-earn (从薪金中扣除所得税的)所得税预扣法.

pay·ee [peiˈiː] *n.* 收款人,受款人.

pay·er, pay·or [ˈpeiə] *n.* 付款人.

pay·ing [ˈpeiiŋ] *a.* ①支付的. ②有利的, 有益的, 合算的. *a* ~ *teller* (银行)出纳员. *a* ~ *concern* 有利的事业. *a* ~ *guest* 〔英〕在私人家中付费膳宿的人. *a* ~ *in slip* 缴款通知单.

pay·ment [ˈpeimənt] *n.* ①支付; 缴纳; 付款额,报酬; 支付物. ②报偿; 补偿; 赔偿. ③报复, 报仇; 惩罚. ~ ***at full*** =~ in full. ~ ***by instalments*** 分期摊付. ~ ***in advance [part]*** 先付[付一部分]. ~ ***in full*** 全付, 付清. ~ ***in kind*** 实物支付. ~ ***on account*** 分期偿还. ~ ***on terms*** 定期付款. ***received*** ~ 货款收讫. ***suspend*** ~ 无力支付,宣布破产.

Pay·ne [pein] *n.* ①佩恩〔姓氏〕. ②**John Howard** ~ 约翰·H·潘恩〔1791—1852,美国演员,剧作家〕.

pay·nim [ˈpeinim] *n.* 〔古、诗〕异教; 异教徒〔尤指穆斯林〕; 异教国.

payn·ize [ˈpeinaiz] *vt.* 给(木材)灌注药液(以提高防腐效能).

pay·o·la [peiˈəulə] *n.* 〔美俚〕暗中给的贿赂,暗中行贿.

pay·sage [peiˈzɑːʒ, ˈpeizɑːʒ] *n.* 〔F.〕 ①(乡间)风景. ②山水画,风景画.

payt. = payment.

pa·za·za [pəˈzɑːzə] *n.* 〔美俚〕 = money.

PB, P.B. = ①〔L.〕*Pharmacopoeia Britannica* 《英国药典》(= British Pharmacopoeia). ②Prayer Book【宗】《祈祷书》.

Pb = plumbum【化】铅.

p.b.i. = poor bloody infantry 〔英俚〕步兵佬.

PBX, P.B.X. = private branch exchange (电话) 专用小交换机.

PC = ①patrol craft 巡逻舰. ②Post Commander 驻地司令官.

P.C.,PC = ①police constable 〔英〕普通警员. ②Privy Council〔英〕枢密院. ③Privy Councillor 〔英〕枢密院官员; 枢密顾问官. ④Peace Corps 〔美〕和平队.

P/C, p/c = ①petty cash 小额现金收入 (或支出); 零用现金. ②price(s) current 市价表.

pc. = ①piece. ②price(s).

p.c. = ①percent. ②postcard; postal card.

PCB = ①polychlorinated biphenyls【化】聚氯联苯. ②petty cash book【会计】零用现金簿.

P.C.C. = ①Price Control Commission 〔美〕 物价管理委员会. ②Political Consultative Council 〔中〕政治协商会议.

pcl = parcel.

pct. = percent.

P.D. = ①〔L.〕*per diem* 每日, 按日. ②Police Department 警察局. ③Postal District 邮(政)区. ④potential difference (电)位差,势差.

Pd. = palladium【化】钯.

pd. = paid 付讫.

Pd.B = Bachelor of Pedagogy 教育学学士.

Pd D, Pd.D. = Doctor of Pedagogy 教育学博士.

P.D.I. = pilot direction indicator 飞机驾驶员航向指示器.

Pdl. = poundal【物】磅达〔力的单位〕.

Pd.M. = Master of Pedagogy 教育学硕士.

PDQ, pdq = pretty damn quick 〔美俚〕马上, 立刻, 很快.

pdr = pounder.

PDT = Pacific Daylight Time 太平洋夏季时间.

p.e. = personal estate 动产,私人财产.

pea [piː] *n.* ***(pl.*** ***~s,*** 〔古、英方〕 ***~se*** **[piːz]*)*** ①豌豆; 豌豆类. ②豌豆状物; 〔美俚〕棒球. *garden* ~*s* 豌豆. *green* ~*s* 青豌豆〔做菜用〕. *split* ~*s* 去皮干豌豆〔做汤用〕. *sweet* ~ 香豌豆. *Oregon* ~ 绿豆. ~ *coal* 小块煤. ***as like as two ~s*** 一模一样,活象. ~ **bean** 豌豆. ~**coat** = ~ jacket. ~ **flour** 豌豆粉. ~ **green** 青豆色, 黄绿色. ~ **jacket** (水手、水兵、男孩等穿的)粗呢上装. ~**shooter** ①豆子枪, 玩具枪. ②〔俚〕驱逐机. ~ **soup** ①豌豆汤. ②〔美俚〕不中用的人. ③ = ~ souper. ~ **souper** 〔英口〕(尤指伦敦的)黄色浓雾. ~ **soupy** *a.* 〔英口〕(雾)黄而浓的; 黄色浓雾似的.

Pea·bod·y [ˈpiːˌbɔdi] *n.* 皮博迪〔姓氏〕.

peace [piːs] *n.* ①和平; 太平; 平静; 宁静根源; 寂静. ②和好, 和睦; 〔常 P-〕媾和, 讲和; 媾和条约, 和约 (= treaty of ~). ③〔the ~〕治安, 社会秩序. ④安心, 安静; 悠闲; 沉默. *P- cannot be got by begging, it must be fought for.* 和平不能乞求, 和平必须争取. *the pipe of* ~ (北美印第安人)互相传吸表示讲和的烟斗. *the piping times of* ~ 太平时代. *Do let me have a little* ~. 让我安静一下. *P-!* 安静! 别吵! *P- there!* 喂,别闹! *P- be with you!* 祝你平安! *P- to his ashes [memory, soul]!* 愿他安眠地下! ***at*** ~ 和平; 和好, 和睦; 安心; 安静. ***be sworn of the*** ~ 被任命为治安官. ***breach of the*** ~ 妨害治安. ***hold [keep] one's*** ~ 不声不响, 保持缄默. ***in*** ~ 平平安安; 安心 (*live in* ~ 平平安安过日子). ***keep the (king's [queen's])*** ~ 维持治安. ***leave sb. in*** ~ 不打搅某人. ***let sb. go in*** ~ 放过某人,不为难某人. ***make one's*** ~ ***with*** 跟…讲和[重新和好]. ***make*** ~ 和好, 讲和 *(with)*. ~ ***at any price*** 绝对和平(主义). ~ ***of conscience*** 问心无愧. ~ ***with honour*** 体面 [光荣] 的和平. ***swear the*** ~ ***against*** *(sb.)* 揭发某人图谋行凶. ~ **blocade** 平时封锁. ~**-breaker** 破坏和平的人; 扰乱治安者. **P- Corps** 〔美〕和平队. ~**establishment** 【军】平时编制. ~**-loving** *a.* 爱好和平的. ~**maker** 调解人,和事老; 〔谑〕维持和平的工具[手枪、军舰等]. ~**making** 调解,调停. ~**-monger** 〔美〕和平贩子,一味乞求和平的人. ~ **offering** ①和平建议; 和平仪式. ②和解礼物. ③【宗】谢恩[赎罪]供物. ~ **officer** 治安官; 警官. ~ **pipe** = *the pipe of peace.* ~**time** *n., a.* 和平时期 (的); 平时 (的) *(opp.* wartime*)*.

peace·a·ble [ˈpiːsəbl] *a.* ①平和的, 爱好和平的, 息事宁人的, 温和的, 温顺的. ②和平的, 太平的 *in the* ~ *times* 平时. **-ness** *n.* **-a·bly** *ad.*

peace·ful [ˈpiːsful] *a.* ①和平的, 太平的; 平时的. ②宁静的, 安静的. ③爱好和平的, 温和的. ~ *coexistence* 和平共处. ~ *uses of atomic energy* 原子能的和平应用. ~ *penetration* 和平渗透. ~ *picketing* 监视破坏罢工的纠察线. ~ *times* 太平时期. **-ly** *ad.* **-ness** *n.*

peace·nik [ˈpiːsnik] *n.*〔俚〕示威反战者,反战运动分子.

peach[1] [piːtʃ] *vt.* 〔俚〕告发; 出卖(同伙) *(against; on; upon)*. — *vi.* 告密.

peach[2] [piːtʃ] *n.* ①桃子; 桃树. ②桃色,桃红色. ③〔美〕桃酒. ④〔俚〕受人喜欢的人[物]; 漂亮姑娘; 好人; 好东西; 有功劳的人〔常用作挖苦话〕. *flat* ~ 蟠桃. *a* ~ *of a car* 一辆漂亮的车. *a* ~ *of a cook* 一位顶刮刮的厨师. — *a.* 桃色的. ~ ***and cream*** (人)乳白色皮肤而双颊桃红. ~ **blossom** 桃花. ~ **blossom** 桃红色. ~**-blow** ①(中国瓷器的)紫红色釉药,桃色釉. ②紫红马铃薯. ~ **brandy** 桃子酒. ~**-colour(ed)** *a.* 桃色(的). ~**-tree** 桃树.

peach·er·in·o [ˌpiːtʃəˈriːnəu] *n.* 〔美俚〕漂亮女人；了不起的人〔东西〕.
pea·chick [ˈpiːtʃik] *n.* 小孔雀.
peach·y [ˈpiːtʃi] *a.* ①桃子(似)的；桃色的. ②〔美俚〕漂亮的,极好的. **-i·ness** *n.*
Pea·cock [ˈpiːkɔk] *n.* 皮科克〔姓氏〕.
pea·cock [ˈpiːkɔk] *n.* *(pl.* ～*s,* 〔集合词〕～*)* ①(雄)孔雀 *(opp.* peahen*)*. ②爱虚荣的人；爱炫弄自己的人. ③〔the P-〕【天】孔雀座(= Pavo). ***a ～ in (his) pride*** 开屏孔雀；炫耀一时的人. ***as proud as a ～*** 孔雀般高傲. ***play the ～*** 炫耀自己，沾沾自喜，安自尊大. — *vt.* 〔～ oneself〕炫耀. — *vi.* 炫耀,招摇过市,趾高气扬地走. ～ **blue** 孔雀蓝(染料). ～ **ore** 黄铜矿，斑铜矿. ～ **stone** 孔雀石. **-cock·y** *a.*
pea·cock·er·y [ˈpiːkɔkəri] *n.* 炫耀,招摇；虚荣,虚饰.
pea·cock·ish, pea·cock·like [ˈpiːkɔkiʃ, ˈpiːkɔklaik] *a.* 孔雀似的；虚荣心强的；炫耀的.
pea·fowl [ˈpiːfaul] *n.* 孔雀〔雌或雄〕.
pea·hen [ˈpiːˈhen] *n.* 雌孔雀.
peak[1] [piːk] *vi.* ①瘦弱；消瘦,憔悴. ②减少,缩小 *(out)*. ～ ***and pine*** 消瘦；憔悴.
peak[2] [piːk] *n.* ①山峰,山顶；孤山. ②(胡须等的)尖儿；尖端. ③最高点,绝顶；最大量；巅值,峰值；【物】波峰. ④(衣着等的)尖形突出部；(帽子等的)鸭舌,遮蓬. ⑤〔方〕岬,海角. ⑥【海】斜衍尖头；船头〔船尾〕尖舱；锚爪. *a flood* ～ 洪峰. *the* ～ *performance* 最高生产率. *the after* ～ (船的)尾舱. ～ *position* 〔美〕棒球联赛的最高名次. ～ *year* 【统】最高记录年. — *vt.* ①竖起，使成峰状，使高耸. ②使达到最高峰. ③(划船休息时)直竖(桨等)；(鲸鱼)竖起(尾巴). *She pursed her pretty lips and* ～*ed her eyebrows.* 她紧闭美丽的双唇,竖起眉毛. — *vi.* ①高耸,尖起；(桨等不划时)竖起；(鲸鱼等)翘起尾巴. ②达到最高峰. ～**-hour** *a.* 高峰时刻的. ～**-load** ①【电】最大负载,高峰负荷. ②一定时间内的最高运输〔交易〕量. ～**-peak** 峰值中的最大值.
peak·ed[1] [piːkt, 美 ˈpiːkid] *a.* ①憔悴的，瘦削的. ②减少的,缩小的.
peak·ed[2] [pikt] *a.* ①(帽子等)有遮蓬的；有(胡须)尖的. ②有峰的. ③竖起的,高耸的.
peak·y[1] [ˈpiːki] *a.* 〔俚〕消瘦了的；〔美俚〕快腐烂的.
peak·y[2] [ˈpiːki] *a.* 有峰的,多峰的；尖的.
Peal [piːl] *n.* 皮尔〔姓氏〕.
peal [piːl] *n.* ①(雷、大炮、笑声、鼓掌声等的)响声，隆隆声. ②钟声；钟乐；(用作乐器的)一组钟，编钟. *a* ～ *of artillery* 隆隆的炮声. *a* ～ *of thunder* 雷声隆隆. *a* ～ *of applause* [*laughter*] 一阵响亮的喝采〔哄笑〕声. ***ring a ～*** 奏钟乐. — *vt.* ①使鸣响；大声说；夸奖；散布(谣言等). ②〔罕〕使耳朵变聋. — *vi.* (钟、雷等)鸣响，轰响 *(out)*.
pe·an [ˈpiːən] *n.* = paean.
pea·nut [ˈpiːnʌt] *n.* ①落花生；花生果，花生米. ②〔美俚〕小人物,无聊人物；长着狮子鼻的人. ③〔*pl.*〕(总数中的一笔)小数目；小利,小收入；小企业. — *a.* 微不足道的,渺小的. *a* ～ *politician* 〔美俚〕无聊政治家,小政客. ～ **butter** 花生酱. ～ **gallery** 〔美俚〕(戏院的)顶层楼座〔票价最低〕. ～ **oil** 花生油.
pea·pod [ˈpiːpɔd] *n.* (豌豆的)豆荚.
pear [pɛə] *n.* 梨；梨树；梨形物. *balsam* ～ 苦瓜. ～**-shaped** *a.* ①梨形的. ②(声调)圆润的，无鼻音的，清亮的. ～**-tree** 梨树.
Pearl [pəːl] *n.* 珀尔〔女子名〕.
pearl[1] [pəːl] *n.* ①珍珠；珍品；优秀典型，精华；〔*pl.*〕珍珠项练. ②珍珠状物〔露、泪；雪白的牙齿等〕；(铁、煤等的)小片，微粒. ③珍珠色. ④【印】珍珠型铅字〔5 点小型活字〕；〔方〕【医】白内障,星眼. *an artificial* [*a false, an imitation*] ～ 人造珍珠，赝珍珠. *culture(d)* ～ 养殖的珍珠. *a mother of* ～ 珍珠母，珍珠贝. *the* ～ *of his country* 国家的精华〔杰出人物〕. ***cast ～s before swine*** 明珠暗投；把珍贵物送给不识货的人. — *a.* 珍珠(制)的；珍珠似的. — *vt.* ①使呈珠状,使成小圆粒,使象珍珠；把(米、麦等)制成小粒. ②用珍珠装饰,用珍珠镶嵌. ③使成珍珠色，使发珍珠光泽. ④珠子似地散布于. — *vi.* ①采珍珠. ②珠子般地滴下；变成珍珠形〔色〕. *go* ～*-ing* 去采珍珠. ～ **ash** 【化】珍珠灰，粗碳酸钾. ～ **barley** 大麦搓成的圆珠形小颗粒,珍珠麦. ～ **button** 贝壳钮扣. ～ **diver** ①潜水采珠人. ②〔美俚〕洗盆子的人. ～ **eye** ①鸟的眼睛. ②【医】白内障. ～ **fisher** 采珠人,采珠业者. ～**-fishery** 采珠业；采珠场. ～**-fishing** 采珠业. ～ **grain** 珍珠克拉〔珍珠重量单位 =$\frac{1}{4}$carat). ～ **gray** 淡灰色，珍珠色. **P- Harbor** ①珍珠港〔美国军港〕. ②(珍珠港事件式的)偷袭. ～ **oyster** 【贝】珍珠贝. ～**-plant** 【植】紫草；麦家公. ～ **powder** (化粧用)珍珠粉. ～**-sago** 珠粒西米. ～ **shell** 珍珠母,夜光贝，珍珠贝. ～ **white** ①*a.* 珍珠般白的. ②*n.* 鱼鳞粉〔人造珍珠的原料〕；锌钡白〔一种白色颜料〕.
pearl[2] [pəːl] *n., v.* = purl[2].
pearl·ed [pəːld] *a.* ①〔诗〕用珍珠装饰的,镶着珍珠的. ②变成珍珠状小粒的；珍珠似的,有珍珠色泽的.
pearl·es·cent [pəːˈlesnt] *a.* 珠母般的.
pearl·ies [ˈpəːliz] *n.* 〔*pl.*〕①大贝壳扣. ②(水果贩等穿的)钉有许多贝壳扣的衣服〔伦敦小贩的节日服装〕.
pearl·ite [ˈpəːlait] *n.* ①【冶】珠泽铁；珠光体；珠层体. ②【地】珍珠岩. **pearl·it·ic** [pəːˈlitik] *a.*
pearl·ized [ˈpəːlaizd] *a.* 珠母般的.
pearl·y [ˈpəːli] *a.* ①珍珠似的；珍珠色的. ②产珍珠的. ③用珍珠装饰的；珍贵的. ④【乐】响亮的. ～**-nautilus** 鹦鹉螺.
pear·main [ˈpɛəmein] *n.* 苹果品种名. *the American Summer* ～ 祝光苹果. *the White Winter* ～ 青香蕉苹果.
Pear·son [ˈpiəsn] *n.* 皮尔逊〔姓氏〕.
peart [piət] *a.* 〔美方〕愉快的，快活的；活泼的，有生气的. **-ly** *ad.*
peas·ant [ˈpezənt] *n.* ①农民 ★多指非英语国家的自耕农或雇农,英语国家的农民多用 farmer. ②庄稼人，乡下人. *a* ～ *folk* 农民. *a* ～ *farmer* 小自耕农. *landless* ～ 雇农. *poor* ～ 贫农. *middle* ～ 中农. *lower-middle* ～下中农. *poor and lower-middle* ～*s* 贫下中农. *upper-middle* ～ *or well-to-do (better-off, well-off) middle* ～ 富裕中农. *rich* ～ 富农. *a veteran* ～ 老农. *a* ～ *girl* 乡下姑娘. ～ **proprietor (-ship)** 自耕农(制).
peas·ant·ry [ˈpezəntri] *n.* ①〔集合词〕农民. ②农民身分；农民特点,农村习气.
pease [piːz] pea 的复数. ～**-pudding** 豌豆布丁.
peas(e)·cod [ˈpiːzkɔd] *n.* 〔古〕= peapod.
peat[1] [piːt] *n.* 泥炭,草炭，泥炭土. ～**bed,** ～ **bog,** ～**-moor,** ～ **moss** *n.* 泥炭沼. ～**-reek** 泥炭烟.
peat[2] [piːt] *n.* 〔古、贬〕人〔尤指女人〕.
peat·er·y [ˈpiːtəri] *n.* 泥炭产地；泥炭沼.
peat·y [ˈpiːti] *a.* ①泥炭似的. ②多泥炭的.
peau de soie [ˌpəu dəˈswɑː] 〔F.〕双面横棱缎〔法国制〕.
pea·v(e)y [ˈpiːvi] *n.* *(pl.* ～*s)* (翻动木头用的)钩棍，钩梃.
peb·ble [ˈpebl] *n.* ①细砾，砾,卵石,石子. ②水晶；水晶(做的)透镜. ③粒状火药 (= ～-powder). ④粗鞣皮(=～d leather). ⑤(皮革、纸张等表面仿印的)卵石花纹. ***not the only ～ on the beach*** 并非独一无二的(人). — *vt.* ①用石子扔. ②用卵石铺盖. ③使纹理粗糙，使有皱纹〔卵石纹〕. *Scotch* ～*s* 玛瑙. ～ **cultur** 石器文化. ～ **leather** 粗纹皮革. ～ **powder** 粒状火药. ～ **stone** 小卵石. ～**-ware** 一种杂色斑纹陶器.
peb·bly [ˈpebli] *a.* ①卵石多的. ②有卵石花纹的.
peb·rine [pebˈrin] *n.*〔F.〕蚕胞子虫病.
p.e.c. = photoelectric cell 光电管,光电池.
pe·can [piˈkæn] *n.* 【植】(美洲)薄壳山核桃(树).

pec·ca·ble [ˈpekəbl] *a.* 易犯罪的；易有过失的. **-ca·bil·i·ty** [ˌpekəˈbiliti] *n.*
pec·ca·dil·lo [ˌpekəˈdiləu] *n. (pl. ~(e)s)* 轻罪；小过.
pec·can·cy [ˈpekənsi] *n.* ①有罪，犯罪；罪行. ②违章，犯规. ③【医】病态.
pec·cant [ˈpekənt] *a.* ①有罪的，犯罪的；邪恶的. ②违章的；错误的；犯规的. ③【医】病态的，致病的. **-ly** *ad.*
pec·ca·ry [ˈpekəri] *n. (pl. -ries,* 〔集合词〕 *~)* 【动】西貒〔美国一种野猪〕.
pec·ca·vi [peˈkɑːviː] *int.* 〔L.〕 我犯罪了；我忏悔. — *n. (pl. ~s)* 忏悔，认罪. *cry ~* 忏悔；认错.
peck[1] [pek] *n.* ①配克〔英美干量单位，等于八夸脱〕. ②多量，很多. *a ~ of troubles* 很多麻烦.
peck[2] [pek] *vt.* ①啄；啄起，啄穿；啄成；啄掘；啄坏. ②(用尖头工具)凿，琢. ③〔口〕匆匆忙忙地〔一点一点地〕吃；〔谑〕急吻一下. — *vi.* ①啄；凿，琢. ②一点一点地吃. ③找岔子 *(at)*. ④〔俚〕扔(石头等) *(at)*. *~ at* ①啄. ②说…闲话，找…的岔子. *~ out* ①啄出. ②用食指按打字机的键打字〔多为美国记者的工作方式〕. — *n.* ①啄. ②啄痕；啄出的洞. ③〔俚〕食物；〔谑〕轻吻. ④〔俚〕扔石头；找岔子. ⑤〔美俚〕匆忙吃(点东西). ***off one's ~*** 失去胃口. ***~ and perch*** 〔俚〕吃和住. **~(ing) order** 【生】禽鸟强弱次序；社会等级.
peck·er [ˈpekə] *n.* ①会啄的鸟；啄木鸟；啄的人. ②鹤嘴锄，铁镐. ③〔俚〕鸟嘴，啄；穿孔器〔针〕. ④〔俚〕(人的)鼻子. ⑤〔俚〕勇气，精神. ⑥【电】替续板，簧片. ***Keep your ~ up!*** 〔俚〕拿出精神来！打起精神来！ ***put up sb's ~*** 气人，使人不痛快，得罪人.
peck·er·wood [ˈpekəwud] *n.* ①啄木鸟(=woodpecker). ②〔美南部俚〕山里人，山林居民；〔黑人用语，贬〕南方穷苦白人.
peck·ish [ˈpekiʃ] *a.* 〔口〕①饿的，肚子空的. ②生气的，找岔子的. *feel ~* 有点饿.
Peck·sniff [ˈpeksnif] *n.* 伪君子〔英国作家狄更斯的小说 *Martin Chuzzlewit* 中的人物〕.
Peck·sniff·i·an [pekˈsnifiən] *a.* 伪善的；伪装神圣的.
peck·y [ˈpeki] *a.* 有霉斑的，有蛀孔的.
Pé·cos Bill [ˈpekəus bil] 配科斯·比尔〔美国西部、阿根廷传说中的放牛英雄〕.
pec·tase [ˈpekteis] *n.* 【生化】果胶酶.
pec·tate [ˈpekteit] *n.* 【化】果胶酸盐；果胶酸的盐类.
pec·ten [ˈpektən] *n. (pl. ~s, **pec·ti·nes*** [-tiniːz]*)* ①【动】(鸟眼的)梳膜；(昆虫的)栉. ②【解】耻骨. ③【贝】海扇，扇贝.
pec·tic [ˈpektik] *a.* 果胶的，含果胶的，从果胶中得到的. *~* **acid** 【化】果胶酸.
pec·tin [ˈpektin] *n.* 【化】果胶.
pec·ti·nate, pec·ti·nated [ˈpektinit, -neitid] *a.* 梳状的，齿形的.
pec·ti·na·tion [ˌpektiˈneiʃən] *n.* 梳状；梳状物；梳状结构.
pec·to·ral [ˈpektərəl] *a.* ①胸部的；戴在胸部的. ②【医】胸腔病的，肺病的；治肺病有效的；止咳的. ③个人感情引起的；主观的. ④(声音)宏亮的. *a ~ remedy* 肺病药. *~ species* 止咳茶. — *n.* ①(尤指犹太祭司长的)胸饰；遮胸. ②【医】肺病药；止咳药. ③【动】胸鳍 (= ~ fin)；胸肌. *~* **cross** (教长、主教等)带在胸前的十字架. *~* **fin** 【鱼】胸鳍. *~* **girdle [arch]** 【动、解】肩带. *~* **sandpiper** 【动】纹胸滨鹬.
pec·tose [ˈpektəus] *n.* 【化】果胶糖.
pec·ul [ˈpikʌl] *n.* = picul.
pec·u·late [ˈpekjuleit] *vi., vt.* 挪用，盗用，侵吞(公款等). **-u·la·tion** *n.* **-u·la·tor** *n.* 挪用〔盗用、侵吞〕公款者.
pe·cul·iar [piˈkjuːljə, -liə] *a.* ①独特的，特有的*(to)*；特别的，(兴趣等)特殊的. ②特异的，罕见的，奇怪的；异常的. ③个人的，(财产等)私人的. *Language is ~ to mankind.* 语言是人类所特有的. *expressions ~ to English* 英语的特殊表达方式. *~ institution* 〔美隐语〕奴隶制度. *~ motion* 【天】本动. *~ people* 〔总称〕①【基督】上帝的特选子民〔指基督徒〕. ②犹太人. ③〔P- People〕基督教祈祷治病派〔反对医药并相信向神祈祷即能治病〕. — *n.* ①特有财产；特权. ②【宗】特殊教区. ③〔P-〕【基督】上帝的特选子民〔指基督徒〕；犹太人. **-ly** *ad.*
pe·cu·li·ar·i·ty [piˌkjuːliˈæriti] *n.* ①特性，特色，特质. ②癖；怪癖. ③奇形怪状；特殊的东西.
pe·cu·li·um [piˈkjuːliəm] *n.* ①(罗马法)给与奴隶、妻子或孩子的私产. ②私产.
pe·cu·ni·a·ri·ly [piˈkjuːnjərili, -niə-] *ad.* 金钱上，关于金钱.
pe·cu·ni·a·ry [piˈkjuːnjəri] *a.* ①金钱(上)的. ②应付罚金的，应罚款的. *~ aid* 资助. *~ considerations [reward]* 金钱报酬. *~ embarrassment* 财政困难. *~ condition* 财政，经济状况. *~ penalties* 罚金. *~ resources* 财力. ***from [in] a ~ point of view*** 从金钱〔财政〕上来看.
ped *n.* 〔美口〕步行者 (= pedestrian).
ped. = ①pedal. ②pedestal. ③pedestrian.
ped- *pref.* 〔用于元音前〕①= pedi-. ②=pedo-.
-ped *suf.* 足: quadru*ped*.
ped·a·gog [ˈpedəgɔg] *n.* 〔美〕 = pedagogue.
ped·a·gog·ic, ped·a·gog·i·cal [ˌpedəˈgɔdʒik, -kəl] *a.* 教育学的，教授法的；教师的. *~ research group* 教研组. **-gog·i·cal·ly** *ad.*
ped·a·gog·ics [ˌpedəˈgɔdʒiks] *n.* ①教育学，教授法. ②教师职业.
ped·a·gogue [ˈpedəgɔg] *n.* ①(中、小学的)老师，教员；(儿童)教育者. ②= pedant.
ped·a·gog(u)·ism [ˈpedəˌgɔgizəm] *n.* 〔常蔑〕①儿童教授(法). ②老师派头，好为人师的教书匠习气.
ped·a·go·gy [ˈpedəgɔgi] *n.* ①教育学，教授法. ②儿童教育. ③教师职业.
ped·al [ˈpedl, ˈpiːdl] *a.* 〔L.〕 ①[ˈpedl] 【动】足的，脚的；踏板的. ②[piːdl] 【数】垂足(线)的. *~* **brake** 脚刹车. *~ curve [face]* 垂足曲线〔面〕. — *n.* [ˈpedl] ①(缝纫机等的)踏板；【乐】持续音. ②[piːdl] 【数】垂足线，垂足面. — *vi.* ***(pedal(l)ed; pedal(l)ing)*** 踏…的踏板；踩踏板转动. *~ a bicycle* 骑自行车. — *vi.* 踩踏板；骑自行车. *~ along a road* 在路上骑自行车. *~* **point** 【乐】持续音(部). *~* **pusher** 〔美〕①骑自行车的人，自行车比赛选手. ②〔~ pushers〕长及小腿的女式运动裤.
pe·dal·fer [piˈdælfə] *n.* 【地】①淋余土. ②铁铝土. **-fer·ic** [ˌpedəlˈfeərik] *a.*
ped·al·o, ped·all·o [ˈpedələu] *n. (pl. ~s)* 脚踏船〔单人或双人乘坐的用脚踏板带动桨轮的小船〕(= pedal boat).
ped·ant [ˈpedənt] *n.* 卖弄学问的人，书呆子，空谈家；腐儒，学究.
pe·dan·tic [piˈdæntik] *a.* 卖弄学问的；学究式的，迂腐的. **-ti·cism** *n.* 迂腐作风.
ped·an·toc·ra·cy [ˌpedənˈtɔkrəsi] *n.* 腐儒政治(集团).
ped·ant·ry [ˈpedəntri] *n.* ①卖弄学问；学究式想法. ②死守陈规旧套；迂腐.
ped·ate [ˈpedit] *a.* ①【动】具足的；具管足的. ②足状的；用足的. ③【植】(叶子)鸟足状的.
pe·dat·i·fid [piˈdætifid, -ˈdeit-] *a.* 【植】(叶子)鸟足状裂开的.
ped·der [ˈpedə] *n.* 〔Scot.〕 = pedlar.
ped·dle [ˈpedl] *vt.* ①贩卖，零卖，走卖，挑卖，叫卖. ②传播(谣言等)；兜售(理论等). — *vi.* ①做小贩，沿街叫卖. ②忙于做琐事. *~* ***alibis*** [ˈælibaiz] 〔美俚〕托词逃避. *~ **fish stories*** 〔美〕大吹自己的运动本领. ***P- one's papers [fish]*** 不管闲事.
ped·dler [ˈpedlə] *n.* = pedlar.

ped·dler·y [ˈpedləri] *n.* ①小贩生意. ②小贩的货物.
ped·dling [ˈpedliŋ] *a.* ①商贩的，叫卖的. ②琐碎的，不重要的. ③小心眼儿的. ～ *details* 无关宏旨的细节. — *n.* 商贩, **-ly** *ad.*
-ped(e) *comb. f.* 足: centi*pede*.
ped·er·ast [ˈpedəræst, ˈpiːdə-] *n.* 男色者，鸡奸者. —**ped·er·as·tic** *a.* **-as·ti·cal·ly** *ad.*
ped·er·as·ty [ˈpedəræsti, ˈpiːdə-] *n.* 鸡奸.
ped·es·tal [ˈpedistl] *n.* ①基座，底座，台，座子，架；柱脚. ②根底，基础；受人尊敬的地位. ③【机】托轴架，支座. *the* ～ *of the bronze statue* 青铜塑像的底座. *a camera* ～ 照像机三角架. ***put [set] sb. (up)on a*** ～ 非常尊敬(某人)，把某人当偶像崇拜. —*vt.* ①把…搁在架上. ②给…加台脚；支持.
pe·des·tri·an [piˈdestriən] *a.* ①徒步的，步行的. ②(文章等)粗俗的，枯燥的；平凡的；单调的，陈腐的. —*n.* 步行者，徒步旅行者；徒步竞走者；很能走路的人，步行主义者. ～ **crossing** 人行横道. **-ism** *n.* ①步行术，徒步旅行；徒步竞走；徒步主义. ②(文章的)平凡，单调. **-ize** *vi.* 徒步旅行，步行.
pedi-[1] *comb. f.* 足: *pedi*cab.
pedi-[2] *comb. f.* 儿童: *pedi*atrician.
pe·di·at·ric [ˌpiːdiˈætrik] *a.* = paediatric.
pe·di·a·tri·cian [ˌpiːdiəˈtriʃən, pe-] *n.*=paediatrician.
pe·di·at·rics [ˌpiːdiˈætriks] *n.* = paediatrics.
pe·di·at·rist [ˌpiːdiˈætrist] *n.* = paediatrist.
ped·i·cab [ˈpedikæb] *n.* (人力)三轮车.
ped·i·cel, ped·i·cle [ˈpedisəl, ˈpedikl] *n.* 【植】花梗；【动】肉茎，(触角的)梗节.
ped·i·cel·late, pe·dic·u·late [ˈpedisəleit, piˈdikjulit] *a.* 【植】有花梗的；【动】有肉茎的，有(触角)梗节的.
pe·dic·u·lar, pe·dic·u·lous [piˈdikjulə, -ləs] *a.* 满是虱子的.
pe·dic·ul·o·sis [piˌdikjuˈləusis] *n.* 【医】虱病；生虱子.
ped·i·cure [ˈpedikjuə] *n.* ①脚病治疗；足病医师，足医. ②修脚. — *vt.* 修(脚)，医(脚).
ped·i·gree [ˈpedigriː] *n.* ①血统；【生】谱系；(纯种家畜的)血统表；(家畜的)种，纯种；品种形成. ②血统，家谱，家系；身家，出身，门第. ③(语言的)起源；词源. ④〔美俚〕(警察局的)犯罪档案. *a* ～ *seed* 原种；种子. *a* ～ *cattle* 纯种牛. — *a.* = pedigreed. ～**-man** 〔美俚〕有案可查的惯犯.
ped·i·greed [ˈpedigriːd] *a.* (家世)有来历的；(马等)血统明显的.
ped·i·ment [ˈpedimənt] *n.* ①【建】山头，人字墙；(门顶、壁炉顶等的)三角饰. ②【地】碛原. **-al, -ed** *a.* 有人字墙的，人字形的.
pe·dim·e·ter [piˈdimitə] *n.* = pedometer.
ped·i·palp [ˈpediˌpælp] *n.* 【动】须肢.
ped·lar [ˈpedlə] *n.* ①小贩，商贩；传播(谣言等)的人. ②〔美俚〕(各站都停的)慢车. **pedlar's French** (盗贼等的)隐语，暗话.
ped·lar·y [ˈpedləri] *n.* (= peddlery).
ped·ler [ˈpedlə] *n.* = pedlar.
pedo- *comb. f.* = paed(o)-.
pe·do·bap·tism [ˌpiːdəuˈbæptizəm] *n.* = paedobaptism.
ped·o·cal [ˈpedəˌkæl] *n.* 【地】钙层土. **-cal·ic** *a.*
pe·do·don·tics [ˌpiːdəuˈdɔntiks] *n.* 儿童牙科学. **-don·tist** *n.* 儿童牙医.
ped·o·gen·e·sis [ˌpiːdəuˈdʒenisis] *n.* 【地】成土作用. **-gen·ic, -ge·net·ic** *a.*
pe·dol·o·gy[1] [piˈdɔlədʒi] *n.* 〔美〕儿科学；小儿科. **pe·do·log·ic** [ˌpiːdəuˈlɔdʒik], **pe·do·log·i·cal** *a.* **pe·do·log·i·cal·ly** *ad.* **pe·do·lo·gist** *n.* 小儿科医师，儿科专家.
pe·dol·o·gy[2] [piˈdɔlədʒi] *n.* 土壤学. **ped·o·log·ic, ped·o·log·i·cal** *a.* **ped·o·log·i·cal·ly** *ad.* **pe·dol·o·gist** *n.* 土壤学家.
pe·dom·e·ter [piˈdɔmitə] *n.* 【测】计步器，步程计.
ped·o·sphere [ˈpedəsfiə] *n.* (地球的)表土层.
ped·rail [ˈpedreil] *n.* ①(拖拉机等的)履带，链轨. ②履带式拖拉机；履带车.
pe·dro [ˈpiːdrəu, ˈpei-] *n.* ***(pl.*** ～***s)*** 彼得牌戏〔一种纸牌戏〕.
pe·dun·cle [piˈdʌŋkl] *n.* ①【植】总花梗；花梗. ②【解】(肿瘤或息肉的)肉茎，肉柄. **-dun·cu·lar** *a.*
pe·dun·cu·late, pe·dun·cu·lat·ed [piˈdʌŋkjulit, -leitid] *a.* 【植】有(总)花梗的；【解】有肉柄的.
pee [piː] *vi.* 〔口〕撒尿. — *n.* 〔口〕尿，小便.
peek [piːk] *vi.* (从缝隙或隐蔽处)偷看，眯着眼睛看. ～ *in [out] through a hole* 从小孔里向内[向外]偷看. — *n.* 偷偷的一看；一瞥. ***get [take] a*** ～ ***at*** 偷看一下.
peek·a·boo [ˈpiːkəbuː] *n.* (逗小孩玩的)躲猫猫 (=〔美〕bo-peep). — *a.* [ˈpiːkəˈbuː] ①(衣服)用透明[网眼]薄织物做的. ②用网眼刺绣镶边的.
peel[1] [piːl] *n.* ①果皮；(蔬菜、幼苗等的)皮，嫩芽. ②【地】揭片. *candied* ～ 蜜饯果皮. *banana* ～ 香蕉皮. — *vt.* 剥(果实等的)皮，削(皮)，(去)皮；剥(树皮等)(*off*). — *vi.* (蛇等)脱皮；(油漆、壁纸等)剥落；〔俚〕(选手)脱衣服. ***keep one's eyes*** ～***ed*** 〔美俚〕留神监视，睁大眼睛注视. ～ ***it*** 〔美俚〕用足气力跑. ～ ***off*** 离队，离群；【空】开始离队急降[俯冲]；【海军】(护航舰)离队(攻击潜水艇)；〔俚〕解散. ～ ***off a record*** 〔美〕造新纪录. ～ ***out*** 〔美俚〕离开，不辞而别. ***scattered and*** ～***ed*** 〔古〕被劫掠.
peel[2] [piːl] *n.* 长柄木铲〔烤面包时用的器具〕.
peel[3] [piːl] *n.* 【英史】(16世纪英格兰和苏格兰交界处的)堡寨，堡宅，堡塔.
Peel(e) [piːl] *n.* 皮尔〔姓氏〕.
peel·er[1] [ˈpiːlə] *n.* ①剥皮的人，去皮机. ②〔美俚〕蜕皮期间的蛇〔其他动物等〕. ③〔美俚〕跳脱衣舞的演员.
peel·er[2] [ˈpiːlə] *n.* 〔英俚〕警察；【史】爱尔兰的警官队员.
peel·ing [ˈpiːliŋ] *n.* ①剥皮，去皮；蜕皮. ②〔*pl.*〕(马铃薯等)剥下的皮.
peen [piːn] *n.* 锤尖，锤顶. — *vt.* 用锤尖敲打〔弯、拔、打平〕.
peep[1] [piːp] *n.* ①(小鸟、老鼠等的)唧唧声，啾啾声. ②(表示不满的)嘀咕. — *vi.* ①(小鸟等)唧唧地叫. ②小声说；嘀咕.
peep[2] *n.* ①偷看；(通过小孔等)的窥视；一瞥. ②窥视孔. ③出现，隐约显现，露出；〔喻〕露马脚. ***at the*** ～ ***of day*** 黎明时，破晓时. ***have [get, take] a*** ～ ***at*** 偷看一下. — *vi.* ①(从缝隙等中)偷看，窥，窥视. ②(从隐蔽处)出现；(花草、太阳、月亮等)开始显出(*out*). ③〔喻〕露出原形. — *vt.* 微微探出 (头等). *Peeping Tom* (尤指下流的)偷视者；爱偷看的人；爱刨根问底的人. ～**-bo** *n.* = peek-a-boo. ～**hole** 窥孔，透视孔；【军】瞄准孔；(坦克的)展望孔. ～ **show** ①西洋景. ②透过小孔看的下流表演. ～**-sight** (枪炮等的)觇视孔，准门，照门.
pee·pee [ˈpiːpiː] *n.* 〔儿〕小鸡.
peep·er[1] [ˈpiːpə] *n.* ①唧唧叫的鸟[鼠等]；小鸡，小蛙. ②嘀咕的人.
peep·er[2] *n.* ①偷看的人，窥视者；爱刨根问底的人；〔美俚〕私人侦探. ②〔*pl.*〕眼睛；〔*pl.*〕眼镜；镜子；望远镜.
pee·pul [ˈpiːpʌl] *n.* (印度)菩提树 (= pipal).
peer[1] [piə] *n.* ①〔英〕贵族〔*duke, marquis, earl, viscount, baron* 之一〕. ②同辈，同事，伙伴；同等的人；同等地位的公民. *You will not easily find his* ～*s.* 他是一个无与伦比的人物. ～*s of Scotland [Ireland]* 苏格兰[爱尔兰]贵族. *a* ～ *of the blood royal* 〔英〕皇族上院议员. ～*s of the realm [the United Kingdom]* 〔英〕可以入上院的贵族. *the House of Peers* 〔英〕贵族院，上议院. ***without*** ～ 无比的，无匹的. — *vt.* ①可与…相比，和

…同等. ②把…封为贵族. — *vi.* 同等,比得上 *(with)*.

peer² [piə] *vi.* ①盯着看,凝视 *(into, at)*. ②朦胧出现,隐约可见;出现. ~ *at the tag to read the price* 细看标签辨读出价目. *The sun* ~*ed through the clouds.* 太阳从云中朦胧出现了.

peer·age [ˈpiəridʒ] *n.* ①〔集合词〕贵族;贵族阶级. ②贵族的爵位〔地位、身分〕. ③贵族姓名录. *be raised on [to] the* ~ 被封为贵族.

peer·ess [ˈpiəris] *n.* ①贵族夫人,贵族遗孀,贵妇;有爵位的妇女,命妇. ②上议院议员夫人. *a* ~ *in her own right* (凭本身资格的)有爵妇女,女贵族.

peer·less [ˈpiəlis] *a.* 无比的,无双的,绝世的. **-ly** *ad.* **-ness** *n.*

peet·weet [ˈpiːtˌwiːt] *n.* 【动】斑点矶鹞 (= spotted sandpiper).

peeve [piːv] *n.* 〔美口〕①气恼,生气,怨恨. ②讨厌的对象,惹人恨的东西. ***have a*** ~ ***at sb.*** 生某人的气,讨厌某人. — *vt.* 〔口〕使恼怒,使气恼. ***be*** ~***d at sb.*** 讨厌某人,对某人生气.

peeved [piːvd] *a.* 〔美口〕恼怒的,不高兴的. **peev·ed·ly** [ˈpiːvidli] *ad.* **-ness** *n.*

pee·vish [ˈpiːviʃ] *a.* ①发怒的,恼怒的. ②脾气暴躁的. ③倔强的,喜欢闹别扭的. **-ly** *ad.* **-ness** *n.*

pee·vit, pee·wit [ˈpiːvit,ˈpiːwit] *n.* = pewit.

peevy [ˈpiːvi] *n.* 【美林】(翻动木材用的)挺钩 (= pea-v(e)y).

pee·wee [ˈpiːwiː] *n.* ①〔美俚〕矮子;小东西. ②矮小的动〔植〕物. ③= pewee. ④〔儿〕男女的性器官. — *vi.* 〔儿语〕小便.

pee·wit [ˈpiːwit] *n.* = pewit.

Peg [peg] *n.* 佩格〔女子名〕.

peg [peg] *n.* ①木钉,竹钉,钉;桩,支柱;(提琴等的)弦钮,琴栓;【植】胚栓;【建】测标. ②尖头物,爪;(晒衣用的)衣夹;(帽)挂. ③借口,遁词,口实. ④〔英俚〕白兰地〔威士忌〕苏打水. ⑤〔*pl.*〕〔口〕腿;裤子. ⑥〔口〕木制假腿;〔美俚〕装假腿的人. ⑦〔口〕牙齿. ⑧栓与栓的间隔;〔口〕(评选时的)等级;(物价等的)限定标准. *a hat* ~ 帽挂. *a clothes* ~ 晒衣夹. *a tent* ~ 帐篷桩. ***a*** ~ ***to hang (a claim etc.) on*** 提出(要求等)的借口. ***a round [square]*** ~ ***in a square [round] hole*** 工作安排不适当的人,不得其所的人. ***be on the*** ~ 〔口〕被拘留. ***come down a*** ~ 丢脸,受屈辱,降低身分. ***off the*** ~ 〔口〕(服装)现成的. ***put the man on the*** ~ 〔军俚〕把人拖到上司面前(使受处罚). ***take [bring, let] sb. down a*** ~ ***or two [a*** ~ ***lower]*** 打下某人的架子,打掉某人的傲气;杀某人的威风. — *vt.* ①在…上钉木钉,用木钉〔短桩〕钉住*(down; in; out)*. ②固定,限制;限定(工资等);【股】稳住(市价);【财政】(用法令)稳住(货币价值). ③〔口〕扔(石头等). ④用木桩标出(土地等). ⑤【猎】(向狗)指示野物落下的场所. ⑥【牌戏】用竹签记(分数). ⑦〔美俚〕暗中监视. ⑧〔口〕鉴定,识别(某人的价值). — *vi.* ①勤快地工作 *(away)*. ②【牌戏】用竹签计分数. ③扔石头 *(at)*. ④匆忙地走. ~ ***along [away]*** 勤快地工作,努力工作. ~ ***at*** 用木桩打. ~ ***down*** 用木钉把…钉在地上;用(规则等)拘束 *(to rules etc.)*. ~ ***out*** 〔美俚〕①大失败;气力用完,完. ②死,毁灭. ③【牌戏】赢得满分. ④(槌球戏中)在一盘打完时用球打中标桩. ⑤用木桩标明(房屋、庭园等的)界线. ~**board** 木栓板;构图板. ~ **leg** (木制)假腿;〔口〕装假腿的人. ~ **top** ①陀螺. ②〔*pl.*〕(臀宽腿狭的)陀螺形裤子. ~**-top** *a.* (裤子)陀螺形的.

peg·a·moid [ˈpegəmɔid] *n.* 人造革;防水布.

Peg·a·sus [ˈpegəsəs] *n.* ①【希神】(诗神 Muse 的)飞马〔其足踏过之处有泉涌出,诗人饮之可获灵感〕. ②诗兴,诗才. ③〔the ~〕【天】飞马座. ④【动】海蛾属.

Peg·gy [ˈpegi] *n.* 佩吉〔女子名, Margaret 的昵称〕.

peg·gy [ˈpegi] *n.* 〔口〕装假腿的人,独腿人.

peg·ma·tite [ˈpegmətait] *n.* 【矿】伟晶岩.

Pe·gram [ˈpiːgrəm] *n.* 皮格勒姆〔姓氏〕.

peh [pei] *n.* 希伯来语的第十七个字母.

Peh·le·vi [ˈpeilivi:] *n.* 约在公元第三世纪至第八世纪的伊朗语(= Pahlavi).

P.E.I. = Prince Edward Island 爱德华太子岛〔加拿大〕.

pei·gn·oir [ˈpeinwɑː] *n.* 〔F.〕(女用)宽大轻便晨衣;理发披布;浴衣.

peine [pein, F. pɛn] *n.* 〔F.〕痛苦;刑罚,处罚. ***peine forte et dure*** [ˈpɛnˈfɔːt eˈdyːə] 〔F.〕(把叛国罪犯活活压死的)酷刑.

Pei·rae·us [paiˈri(ː)əs] *n.* = Piraeus.

pe·jo·ra·tion [ˌpiːdʒəˈreiʃən] *n.* ①恶化,贬值,变劣 (*opp.* amelioration). ②【语法】(加词尾或词形变化后产生的)词义转贬〔例如在 poet 一词之后加上后缀 -aster 成为 poetaster, 即作"蹩脚诗人"解〕.

pe·jo·ra·tive [ˈpiːdʒərətiv] *a.* 恶化的,变坏的;使带有轻蔑〔贬低〕意义的. *the* ~ *suffix -aster* 带贬意的词尾 "-aster". — *n.* 【语法】轻蔑语. **-ly** *ad.*

pek·an [ˈpekən] *n.* 【动】(北美产)食鱼貂;食鱼貂皮.

peke [piːk] *n.* (原中国产)小狮子狗〔pekingese 的简称〕.

pe·kin [piːˈkin] *n.* ①【纺】宽条绸. ②〔俚〕平民,老百姓〔拿破仑一世部下士兵等的用语〕.

Pe·kin·ese [ˌpiːkiˈniːz] *a., n.* = Pekingese.

Pe·king [piːˈkiŋ,ˈpiːˈkiŋ] *n.* 北京(市)〔中华人民共和国首都〕(=Beijing). ~ **duck** 北京鸭. ~ **Man**【考古】中国猿人,北京人.

Pe·king·ese [ˌpiːkiŋˈiːz] *a.* 北京(人)的. — *n.* 〔*sing., pl.*〕北京人;北京话.

pe·king·ese [ˈpiːkiŋˈiːz] *n.* (原中国产)小狮子狗〔叭儿狗〕.

pe·koe [ˈpiːkəu, ˈpekəu] *n.* (中国的)白毫〔一种高级红茶〕.

pel·age [ˈpelidʒ] *n.* (哺乳动物的)毛皮.

pe·la·gi·an [piˈleidʒiən] *a.* 远洋的 (= pelagic). — *n.* 远洋动物,深海动物. *a* ~ *fish* 远洋鱼,深海鱼. ~ *fishery* 远洋渔业.

pe·lag·ic [piˈlædʒik] *a.* ①大洋的;远洋的,深海的. ②海面的;浮游的. ~ *fishery* 远洋渔业. ~ **larva** 海面幼虫. ~ **zone** 远洋带;【动】浮游带.

pel·ar·gon·ic [ˌpelɑːˈgɔnik] *a.* ~ **acid**【化】壬酸.

pel·ar·go·ni·um [ˌpelɑːˈgəunjəm,-niəm] *n.* ①〔P-〕【植】天竺葵属. ②天竺葵属植物.

Pel·as·gi [peˈlæzgai] *n.* 〔*pl.*〕皮拉斯基人〔曾经生活在地中海东部诸岛上的史前人〕. **-an** *n., a.* 皮拉斯基人(的).

Pe·las·gic [peˈlæzgik,-dʒik] *a.* = Pelasgian *(a.)*.

pe·lec·y·pod [piˈlesiˌpɔd] *n., a.* 瓣鳃纲斧足类动物〔包括蛤、蠓等〕(的).

pel·er·ine [ˈpeləriːn] *n.* (女用)狭长披肩.

pelf [pelf] *n.* ①〔蔑〕钱. ②〔英方〕不义之财,赃物. ③〔俚〕废物,破烂东西.

pel·i·can [ˈpelikən] *n.* ①【鸟】鹈鹕,塘鹅. ②(古代炼金术士用的)鹈鹕形蒸馏器;【徽】鹈鹕印;(牙医用的)拔牙钳子. ③〔P-〕〔美俚〕路易斯安那 (Louisiana) 州人的别名. ④〔美俚〕大肚汉,贪吃的人. *a* ~ *in her piety*【徽】鹈鹕哺雏图〔啄伤胸部以血哺养其雏的鹈鹕图〕. ~ **hook** 塘鹅钩. **P- State** 鹈鹕之州〔美国路易斯安那州的别名〕.

Pe·li·on [ˈpiliən] *n.* 皮立翁山〔希腊〕. ***Pile P- upon Ossa*** 做办不到的事.

pe·lisse [peˈliːs] *n.* ①轻便女大衣. ②(龙骑兵穿的)皮里上衣. ③小儿大衣.

pel·la·gra [pəˈleigrə] *n.* 【医】蜀黍红斑,糙皮病. **-grous** [pəˈleigrəs] *a.* 【医】(患)蜀黍红斑的,(患)糙皮病的.

pel·la·grin [piˈlægrin] *n.* 【医】蜀黍红斑患者.

pel·let [ˈpelit] *n.* ①(纸、面包等团成的)小球;小子弹;石弹;炮弹;小丸药;〔美俚〕(棒球用)球. ②(货币等的)圆浮雕. ③【动】肉食鸟吐出的不消化物;(啮齿动物等的)屎粒. — *vt.* ①用小球扔; 用子弹射击. ②把…弄成小球形. ~ **bomb** 珠形炸弹. ~ **mo(u)lding**【建】丸子饰.

pel·let·ize [ˈpeliˌtaiz] *vt.* 使成小球形; 使成小弹丸形. **-za·tion** [-ˈzeiʃən] *n.*

pel·li·cle [ˈpelikl] *n.* 薄皮,表膜;(感光乳剂上的)薄膜.

pel·li·to·ry [ˈpelitəri] *n.*【植】(药用)墙草属植物(*Parietaria officinalis*) (= wall pellitory).

pell-mell [ˈpelˈmel] *ad., a.* ①乱七八糟(的),混乱(的). ②不顾前后(的),鲁莽(的),匆促(的). *The enemy fled ~ before us.* 敌人仓皇逃窜. — *n.* 纷乱,混乱,杂乱;混战. — *vt.* 使混杂. — *vi.* 仓皇行走.

pel·lu·cid [pəˈljuːsid] *a.* ①透明的,清澄的. ②明瞭的,明白的;易懂的;明晰的. ③头脑清楚的. **-ly** *ad.*

pel·lu·cid·i·ty [ˌpelj*u*ːˈsiditi] *n.* ①透明度,明晰度. ②易懂的程度.

Pel·man·ism [ˈpelmənizəm] *n.* ①配尔曼式记忆训练法〔由配尔曼学院发明〕. ②配尔曼牌戏〔一种训练记忆力的牌戏〕. **-man·ize** [ˈpelmənaiz] *vt.* 用配尔曼式记忆法记忆.

pel·met [ˈpelmət] *n.* (窗或门上遮帷幔挂杆的)狭长木罩〔金属罩〕.

Pel·o·pon·ne·sian [ˌpeləpəˈniːʃən,-ʃiən] *a.* (希腊)伯罗奔尼撒(Peloponnesus)半岛的. — *n.* 伯罗奔尼撒人.

pe·lo·ri·a [piˈlɔːriə] *n.*【植】反常整齐花. **-ric** [piˈlɔːrik] *a.*

pe·lo·rus [piˈlɔːrəs] *n.*【海】方位盘,哑罗经.

pe·lo·ta [piˈləutə; Sp. peˈləutɑː] *n.* 回力球〔源自西班牙的一种使用柳条球拍、类似网球的球戏〕.

pelt[1] [pelt] *n.* ①(牛、羊等的)生皮,毛皮〔尤指羊皮〕. ②皮衣,裘. ③〔谑〕(人的)皮肤. — *vt.* 剥…的皮. ~ **monger** 毛皮商.

pelt[2] [pelt] *n.* ①投掷,打击. ②(雨、雪等的)猛降. ③抨击,责问. ④速度. ⑤〔英方〕大怒. ***go (at) full ~*** 拼命,开足马力(*He went full ~ at it, and had it finished in under an hour.* 他拼命地快做,不到一小时就做好了). — *vt.* ①(连续地)向…投击;连续打击. ②投,扔. ③痛加(质问、责骂等);连续抨击. — *vi.* ①(连续地)投,扔. ②(雨等)猛降. ③〔口〕一股劲儿向前跑,开足马力前进.

pel·tast [ˈpeltæst] *n.* (古希腊)有轻盾武装的兵士.

pel·tate [ˈpelteit] *a.*【植】(叶)盾状的. **-ly** *ad.*

pelt·er[1] [ˈpeltə] *n.* ①〔美〕皮商;剥兽皮者. ②(为取毛皮而饲养的)兽.

pelt·er[2] [ˈpeltə] *n.* ①投掷者;投掷器;〔谑〕手枪. ②〔口〕(雨等的)猛下;骤雨. ③〔英方〕大怒. ④〔美〕跑得快的马. ⑤老驽马. ***in a ~*** 大发脾气,大怒.

pelt·ing[1] [ˈpeltiŋ] *a.* ①〔英方〕盛怒的. ②(雨等)大下特下的. *a ~ rain* 倾盆大雨.

pelt·ing[2] [ˈpeltiŋ] *a.* 〔古〕无价值的,微不足道的.

pelt·ry [ˈpeltri] *n.* ①(一捆或一张)生皮,毛皮. ②皮囊;皮货. ③风箱. ~ **monger** 毛皮商.

pel·vic [ˈpelvik] *a.*【解】骨盆的. — *n.* 骨盆部. ~ **fin**【鱼】腹鳍. ~ **girdle**【动】腰带.

pel·vis [ˈpelvis] *n.* (*pl.* ***~es, pel·ves*** [ˈpelviːz])【解】骨盆. *the ~ major = the false ~* 大骨盆,假骨盆. *the ~ minor = the true ~* 小骨盆,真骨盆.

Pem·broke [ˈpembruk] *n.* ①彭布罗克郡〔英国郡名〕(= ~shire). ②(一种尖耳、直腿、短尾的)威尔士小狗. ③〔p-〕折面桌(= ~ table).

pem·(m)i·can [ˈpemikən] *n.* ①〔美〕干(牛)肉饼. ②(报告等的)摘要,提要.

pem·phi·gus [ˈpemfigəs,pemˈfai-] *n.*【医】天疱疮.

pen[1] [pen] *n.* ①笔尖;笔〔笔尖和笔杆〕;〔古〕鹅毛(管)笔. ②笔力,文体,笔法;文笔;文章. ③书法家;作家. ④【动】雌鹄(*opp.* cob);(乌贼的)羽状壳. ⑤羽茎,翮. ⑥〔美俚〕伪造者(= ~ man). *a fountain ~* 自来水笔. *a quill ~* 鹅毛(管)笔. *The ~ catches [scratches].* 这支笔刮纸. *a fluent ~* 流畅的文体. *the best ~s of the day* 当代第一流作家们. *The ~ is mightier than the sword.* 笔胜于刀,文比武强. ~ *juice* 〔美俚〕墨水. ~ *portraits* 人物描写. ***draw one's ~ [quill] against*** 笔伐…,用笔攻击. ***drive a ~ [quill]*** 写. ***live by one's ~*** 靠写作为生,吃笔墨饭. ***~ and ink*** 笔墨;写作. ***put ~ to paper*** 拿笔写,下笔. ***wield one's ~*** 从事写作. — *vt.* 写,作(文),著(书). **~-and-ink** *a.* ①用钢笔写〔画〕的(*a ~-and-ink drawing [sketch]* 钢笔画〔素描〕). ②从事文书工作的. ③〔罕〕从事文学工作的. **~-driver** 用笔工作的人〔抄写员;记者,作家等〕. **~-friend** 笔友. **~holder** 笔杆;笔架. **~knife** 削铅笔〔鹅毛笔〕刀;袖珍小刀. **~light [lite]** 自来水笔形手电筒. ~ **name** 笔名;〔美俚〕囚犯的号码. ~ **pal** = ~-friend. ~ **point** 〔美〕(钢)笔尖. **~pusher** 〔口〕= pendriver. ~ **rack** 笔架. **~tray** 笔盘. **~wiper** 擦笔尖布. **-ful** *n.* (自来水笔的)一满管(墨水). **-ner** (文件等的)执笔人,写作人.

pen[2] [pen] *n.* ①(家畜等的)围栏,槛. ②一栏〔一圈〕家畜. ③〔美口〕监狱〔penitentiary 之略〕. ④(西印度群岛的)开垦地,农庄,种植. ⑤冰箱,冰房,贮藏室. ⑥潜艇修藏坞(= submarine ~). — ***(penned, pent*** [pent]***)*** *vt.* ①把…关进栏里. ②监禁(*up; in*).

pen[3] [pen] *n.* 雌天鹅.

P.E.N., PEN = (International Association of) Poets, Playwrights, Editors, Essayists and Novelists 国际笔会.

Pen., pen. = peninsula.

pe·nal [ˈpiːnl] *a.* ①刑的,刑事的;刑法上的. ②受刑罚的;该受罚的,当受刑的. ③作为刑罚场所的. *the ~ code [law]* 刑法. ~ *servitude* 惩役;徒刑. *a ~ offense* 刑事罪. *a ~ sum* 罚款. *a ~ colony [settlement]* (流犯的)充军地. *a ~ farm* 劳役农场. — *n.* = ~servitude. ***do ~*** 服徒刑. **-i·ty** [piˈnæliti] *n.* **-ly** *ad.* 用刑罚;刑事上.

pe·nal·ize [ˈpiːnəlaiz] *vt.*【法】宣告…有罪;对…处以刑罚. ②使处于不利地位;【体】处罚(犯规者). **-i·za·tion** [-ˈzeiʃən] *n.*

pen·al·ty [ˈpenlti] *n.* ①刑罚,惩罚. ②罚款;违约罚金. ③报应. ④【牌】罚点;【体】(犯规)处罚. ⑤(行为等造成的)困难、障碍、不利后果(= handicap). *a monetary ~* 罚款处分. *the ~ area*【足球】罚球区域. *a ~ box*【冰球】被罚暂时下场的球员座席. *a ~ kick*【足球】罚球. ***on [under] ~ of*** 违者受…处罚. ~ **clause** 〔美〕"私人冒用者必罚"〔印在政府免费邮件上的字样〕. ~ **envelope** 〔美〕(其上印有'私人不得擅用,违者必罚'等字样的)免费公文信袋. ~ **goal** 罚球踢中球门.

pen·ance [ˈpenəns] *n.* ①忏悔;悔过;(赎罪的)苦行. ②【天主】补赎;忏悔式. — *vt.* 使苦行赎罪;处罚.

Pe·nan·ces [piˈnænsiːz] *n.* Pennsylvannia 州人的别名.

Pe·nang [piˈnæŋ] *n.* ①槟榔屿〔马来西亚州名〕. ②槟城〔即George Town 乔治市〕〔马来西亚港市〕.

pe·nang [piˈnæŋ] *n.* = pinang.

pen·an·nu·lar [piˈnænjulə] *a.* 近于环状的.

Pe·na·tes [peˈnɑːteis,peˈneitiːz] *n.* ①【罗神】家神. ②〔p-〕家财.

Pen-can·cel [ˈpenˈkænsəl] 用笔使印花税票等作废.

pence [pens] penny 的复数.

pen·cel [ˈpensl] *n.* 〔古〕小三角旗;小燕尾旗;狭旗.

pen·chant [ˈpɑ̃ːŋʃɑ̃ːŋ] *n.* 〔F.〕(强烈的)倾向,嗜好,爱好(*for*).

pen·cil [ˈpensl] *n.* ①铅笔;石笔;〔古〕画笔. ②画风,画法. ③【数】束;【物】光线锥. ④毛撮;铅笔形物. ⑤〔美俚〕左轮手枪. *a hair [metallic] ~* 毛〔铁〕笔. *Neither pen nor ~ can express.* 非笔墨所能形容. *a ~ sharpener* 卷笔刀. *a ~ pusher* 〔美俚〕书记,办事员;〔美空俚〕轰炸机领航员. *a diamond ~* 钻石刀〔切玻璃用〕. *a beam ~* 电子束. *a ~ of rays* 射线束. — *vt.* ①用铅笔写. ②用画笔画. ~ *the eyebrows* 画眉毛. ~ **case** 铅笔盒.

～ **ore**【矿】笔铁矿. ～ **sketch** 铅笔画;草图. ～ **stone** 石笔石,滑石 ～ **vase** 笔筒.

pen·cil(l)ed [ˈpensld] *a.* ①画过细线的. ②用铅笔写的;写得好看的. ③【物】成锥状的;【数】成束的. ④(禽类羽毛等)有彩色细纹的. ～ *eyebrows* 用画眉笔描过的眉毛.

pen·cil·(l)er [ˈpenslə] *n.* ①用铅笔写〔画〕的人. ②〔英俚〕(赛马等的)登记赌注者.

pen·cil·(l)ing [ˈpensəliŋ] *n.* ①铅笔〔毛笔〕画. ②铅笔痕;细线;铅笔线花样. ③(墙上沿砖缝画的)白色线条. ④(禽羽的)彩色细纹.

pen·craft [ˈpenkrɑːft] *n.* ①书法;笔迹. ②措辞,文笔. ③著作业.

pend [pend] *vi.* 吊着;悬而未决,待决.

pend·ant [ˈpendənt] *n.* ①下垂物,垂饰,耳环;挂表壳上系表链的环;【建】悬饰;吊灯架. ②附录,附属物;(书的)姐妹篇;(成对物中的)一个;对手 *(to)*. ③【海】短索;旒旗;三角旗,尖旗. *a broad* ～【海】(旗舰的)小燕尾旒. — *a.* = pendent *(a.)*.

pend·en·cy [ˈpendənsi] *n.* ①垂下,悬垂. ②未决,未定. ***during the ～ of*** 在…未定时.

pen·dent [ˈpendənt] *n.* = pendant. — *a.* ①吊着的,下垂的,悬垂的;突出的,(崖石等)悬空的. ②未决的,未定的. ③【语法】不完全的. ④【植】垂头的. *a ～ lamp* 吊灯. *a ～ switch* 拉线开关. *a ～ rock* 悬崖. **-ly** *ad.*

pen·den·te li·te [penˈdenti ˈlaiti] 〔L.〕诉讼中.

pen·den·tive [penˈdentiv] *n.* 【建】穹隅. *a ～ dome* 三角穹圆顶.

pend·ing [ˈpendiŋ] *a.* ①悬垂的. ②迫近的;紧急的. ③未定的,未决的. ④审理中的. ～ *cases* 未决案件. *a ～ question* 悬案,未决问题. ～ *business* 当前急务. — *prep.* ①当…的时候,在…中. ②在…以前. ～ *the negotiations* 在谈判中. ～ *his return* 在他回来以前.

pen·drag·on [penˈdrægən] *n.* 王侯〔古时不列颠〔威尔士〕的首领〕.

pen·du·lar [ˈpendjulə] *a.* 钟摆运动的;摆动的.

pen·du·late [ˈpendjuleit] *vi.* 摆动;摇摆不定,犹豫.

pen·du·line [ˈpendjulin] *a.* ①(鸟巢)下垂的,吊下的. ②(鸟)作吊巢的. — *n.* 作吊巢的鸟 (= ～ bird).

pen·du·lous [ˈpendjuləs] *a.* ①吊着的,下垂的,悬垂的. ②摇摆不定的,未决的. **-ly** *ad.* **-ness** *n.*

pen·du·lum [ˈpendjuləm] *n.* ①(钟等的)摆. ②动摇的人〔物〕;犹豫不决的人. ③吊烛架. *a simple [compound]* ～ 单〔复〕摆. *a centrifugal* ～ 离心力调速器. *a ～ orbit* 【物】穿核轨道. ***play*** ～处于不稳定的状态,左右摇摆. ***the swing of the ～*** ①摆的运动. ②(人心的)向背. ③(政党等的)一盛一衰,形势改变.

Pe·nel·o·pe [piˈneləpi, pəˈneləpi] *n.* ①佩内洛普〔女子名〕. ②【希神】彭妮洛佩〔奥德修斯 (Odysseus) 忠实的妻子〕;贞妇. ***a ～'s web*** 彭妮洛佩之网;永远完不成的工作.

pe·ne·plain, pe·ne·plane [ˈpiːniplein] *n.*【地】(因地面受侵蚀而形成的)准平原. — *vt.* 使成准平原.

pe·nes [ˈpiːniːz] penis 的复数.

pen·e·tra·ble [ˈpenitrəbl] *a.* ①可渗透的;穿得过的,能贯穿的 *(by)*. ②可识破的 *(to)*; 看得穿的. **-tra·bil·i·ty** [ˌpenitrəˈbiliti] *n.* ①渗透性,可穿透性. ②【物】透明性,透明度. ③可识破性. **-tra·bly** *ad.*

pen·e·tra·li·a [ˌpeniˈtreiliə, -ljə] *n.*〔*pl.*〕①内部,最深处. ②内殿,内院. ③秘密;私事.

pen·e·tram·e·ter [ˌpeniˈtræmitə] *n.* = penetrometer.

pen·e·trance [ˈpenitrəns] *n.*【生】外显率.

pen·e·trant [ˈpenitrənt] *a.* ①透入的;透彻的. ②尖锐的. — *n.* 渗透剂.

pen·e·trate [ˈpenitreit] *vt.* ①进入,渗入,突入,透过,贯穿. ②渗透入;弥漫〔扩散〕于;(思想、感情等)深入于,打动. ③看透,看穿,识破,洞察. *～d with discontent* 深为不满. *～sb.'s meaning* 看穿某人的意思. *～ sb.'s design* 看破某人的计划. — *vi.* ①穿入,刺入,渗入,透入,侵入,透过 *(into; through; to)*. ②看穿,看透,识破. ③渗透,弥漫,扩散. ④深入人心,打动人心.

pen·e·trat·ing [ˈpenitreitiŋ] *a.* ①透过的,贯穿的;渗透的. ②(目光)锐利的;有眼光的,聪明的. ③(声音等)尖刺的. ④(伤口等)深的. *a ～ orbit*【物】贯穿轨道. **-ly** *ad.* 深入地;尖锐地.

pen·e·tra·tion [ˌpeniˈtreiʃən] *n.* ①浸透;透过;渗透力. ②侵入,【军】突破;(空战中)深入敌方的飞行. ③贯穿;(炮的)贯穿力;(光学机械的)透视力. ④看破,洞察(力),眼光.

pen·e·tra·tive [ˈpenitreitiv] *a.* ①渗入的;贯穿的;有透入力的. ②(冷风等)彻骨的. ③(思想等)深刻的;深入人心的. ④敏锐的;眼光锐利的. **-ly** *ad.* **-ness** *n.*

pen·e·tra·tor [ˈpenitrətə] *n.* ①穿入者;侵入者;渗透者. ②【军】侵入式飞机.

pen·e·trom·e·ter [ˌpeniˈtrɔmitə] *n.* ①【物】(测量X射线穿透力的)透度计. ②【建】贯入度仪,针入度仪.

pen·e·tron [ˈpenətrɔn] *n.* ①【物】介子〔现名 meson〕. ②〔P-〕(射线)透射密度测量仪.

pen·feath·er [ˈpenfeðə] *n.* 翮.

pen·go [ˈpengəu] *n.* *(pl. -gö,-gös)* 〔Hung.〕辨戈〔匈牙利从前的货币单位, 1964年为福林所代替〕.

pen·guin [ˈpeŋgwin] *n.* ①【动】企鹅. ②【空】(不能飞的)滑走教练机;〔美俚〕非飞行航空人员. ③(第一次大战时的)英国妇女航空会会员.

pe·ni·al [ˈpiːniəl] *a.*【解】阴茎的.

pen·i·cil·late [ˌpeniˈsileit] *a.*【植、动】①具毛撮的,流苏状的. ②有美丽花纹的.

pen·i·cil·li·a [ˌpeniˈsiliə] penicillum 的复数.

pen·i·cil·lin [[ˌpeniˈsilin, pəˈni-] *n.*【药】青霉素,盘尼西林.

pen·i·cil·lin·ase [ˌpeniˈsilineis] *n.*【生化】青霉素酶.

pen·i·cil·li·um [ˌpeniˈsiliəm] *n.* *(pl. ～s, -li·a [-liə])*【微】青霉菌;毛丛.

pen·in·su·la [piˈninsjulə] *n.* ①半岛. ②〔the P-〕【史】(1808—1814年西葡"半岛战争"中指)伊比里亚 (Iberia) 半岛;(第一次世界大战中指)加利波利 (Gallipoli) 半岛.

pen·in·su·lar [piˈninsjulə] *a.* ①半岛(状)的. ②〔P-〕伊比利亚半岛(战争)的. — *n.* ①半岛居民. ②〔P-〕参加伊比利亚半岛战争的兵士. *the P- State* 〔美〕佛罗里达州 (Florida) 的别名.

pe·nis [ˈpiːnis] *n.* *(pl. **pe·nes** [ˈpiːniːz], ～es)*【解】阴茎.

Penit. = penitentiary.

pen·i·tence [ˈpenitəns] *n.*后悔,忏悔,悔悟;悔罪 *(for)*.

pen·i·tent [ˈpenitənt] *a.* 后悔〔悔悟、忏悔、悔罪〕的. — *n.* ①悔过者,忏悔者. ②【天主】苦行会会员. **-ly** *ad.*

pen·i·ten·tial [ˌpeniˈtenʃəl] *a.* ①后悔的,忏悔的. ②苦行赎罪的. — *n.* ①= penitent. ②【天主】苦行赎罪规则(书). **-ly** *ad.*

pen·i·ten·tia·ry [ˌpeniˈtenʃəri] *n.* ①【天主】(听教徒忏悔的)听悔僧;(罗马教廷的)反省院;悔罪所. ②感化院;〔美〕监狱;娼妓收容所. — *a.* ①悔改的. ②苦行赎罪的. ③〔美〕应监禁的. *the Grand P-* (罗马教廷的)反省院院长.

pen·man [ˈpenmən] *n.* ***(pl. penmen** [-men]**)*** ①笔记者,笔者. ②书法家;习字教员. ③作家,文人. ④〔美俚〕伪造者. **-ship** ①书法,笔法;习字;书体;笔迹;工于书法. ②写作,文体.

pen·mate [ˈpenmeit] *n.*〔美口〕狱伴,牢友.

Penn [pen] *n.* 佩恩〔姓氏〕.

Penn., Penna.= Pennsylvania.

pen·na [ˈpenə] *n.* *(pl. -nae [-iː])* 羽毛;翼或鸟尾的羽翮. **-na·ceous** [peˈneiʃəs] *a.*

pen·nant [ˈpenənt] *n.* ①细长三角旗,小燕尾旗;【海】(勤务舰的)旒旗. ②【海】(从帆桁末端垂下的)短索. ③〔美〕(运动比赛中三角形的)优胜锦旗;【乐】钩符(= hook). *a broad* ~ = a broad pendant. *a homeward-bound* ~ 归航旗. *the* ~ *chasers* 〔美〕职业棒球队. ***win the*** ~ 夺得锦标.

pen·nate, pen·nat·ed [ˈpeneit,ˈpeneitid] *a.* ①有羽毛的,有翼的. ②羽状的 (= pinnate).

Pen·nell [ˈpenəl] *n.* 彭内尔〔姓氏〕.

pen·ni [ˈpeni] *n.* ***(pl. -ni·a*** [-ə], ***~(s))*** 盆尼〔铜制芬兰硬币,等于 1/100 马克〕.

pen·nif·er·ous [piˈnifərəs] *a.* 有羽毛的;生羽的.

pen·ni·form [ˈpenifɔːm] *a.* 羽状的.

pen·ni·less [ˈpenilis] *a.* 一文没有的;穷的.

pen·nill [ˈpenil] *n.* ***(pl. ~ion*** [peˈniljən]***)*** (威尔士诗人会上)合竖琴调子唱的即兴诗(的一节).

pen·non [ˈpenən] *n.* ①细长三角旗,小燕尾旗;枪旗;〔美〕三角校旗. ②(一般的)旗帜. ③〔诗〕(鸟类的)翼. **-ed** *a.* 有三角旗的.

pen·non·cel [ˈpenənsel] *n.* 〔古〕小三角旗,小燕尾旗,狭旗 (= pencel).

penn'orth [ˈpennəθ] *n.* 〔俚〕= pennyworth.

Penn·syl·va·ni·a [pensilˈveinjə,-niə] *n.* 宾夕法尼亚〔美国州名〕. ~ **Dutch [German]** 17、18 世纪时移入美国宾州的德国南部人和瑞士人;他们的子孙;他们的语言〔高地德语和英语的混合语〕;他们的民间艺术. ~ **hurricane** 〔美俚〕大谎.

Penn·syl·va·ni·an [ˌpenslˈveinjən, -ˈveiniən] *a.* ①宾夕法尼亚州的. ②宾夕法尼纪〔在密西西比纪后三叠纪前的北美古生代第六时期〕的. — *n.* ①宾夕法尼亚居民. ②〔the ~〕宾夕法尼亚纪;宾夕法尼亚纪岩石.

Pen·ny [ˈpeni] *n.* 彭妮〔女子名,Penelope 的昵称〕.

pen·ny [ˈpeni] *n.* ***(pl. pence*** [pens], ***pen·nies*** [ˈpeniz]***)*** ①便士〔英国辅币单位,硬币= 1/100 英镑;1971年前旧币制 =1/12 先令〕.★(1)表示价格的复数用 pense;表示辅币个数的复数用 pennies.(2)从 twopence 到 elevenpence 以及 twentypence 的 pence 须和前字连写,读 [-pəns],此外须分写成两字,读 [-ˈpens].(3)新制在数字后时通常略作 **p** (如: 10*p* = 10 pence);旧制略作 **d.** (如: 5*d.* = fivepence). ②〔美、加拿大〕***(pl.pennies)*** = cent. ③小钱;钱. ④【圣】一种古罗马银币〔拉丁文作 denarius. 其首字母曾作为英国旧便士的缩略号〕. ~ *arcade* 〔美〕(备有娱乐机器和自动售货机的)便宜游乐场. *a* ~ *blood* 〔口〕廉价的惊险小说. *a* ~ *whistle* 便宜哨子〔玩具〕. *six-~ series* 六便士丛书. ***a bad*** ~ 不受欢迎的人〔物〕. ***a pretty*** ~ 〔口〕一大笔钱. ***a*** ~ ***for your thoughts*** = 〔俚〕***a*** ~ ***for 'em***呆呆地想什么呢. ***A*** ~ ***saved is a*** ~ ***gained.*** 省一文就得一文. ***A*** ~ ***soul never come to twopence.*** 志小者不能成大事. ***have not a*** ~ ***(to bless oneself with)*** 很穷,不名一文. ***In for a*** ~, ***in for a pound.*** 一不做,二不休. ***in*** ~ ***numbers*** 一点一点地. ***not a*** ~ ***the worse*** 比以前一点不坏,一点不吃亏. ~ ***number*** (一便士一本的定期出版的)侦探小说的一分册. ***P- wise, pound foolish*** 小事精明,大事糊涂. ***spend a*** ~ 〔口〕上(公共)厕所. ***Take care of the pence, and the pounds will take care of themselves.*** 小事留意,大事顺利. ***The*** ~ ***dropped.*** 目的已达到;话已听明白. ***think one's*** ~ ***silver*** 〔口〕自负. ***turn an honest*** ~ 挣一点正当的钱〔如干零活等〕. **~-a-line** *a.* 每行一便士的,稿费便宜的;(文章等)拙劣的. **~-a-liner** *n.* 穷文人. **~-a-lining**〔英〕便宜稿子,无聊作品. ~ **ante** 赌注小的赌博(如打扑克等),锁碎小事. ~**dreadful [blood]** 〔英〕廉价惊险小说. **~-farthing** 前轮大后轮小的自行车. ~ **gaff** 〔英口〕便宜小戏院〔杂耍场〕. **~-in-the-slot** 〔英〕一便士自动售货机. **~-pinch** *vt.* 〔美俚〕对…吝啬. **~-pinching** *a.* 〔美俚〕小气的,吝啬的. ~ **post** 〔英〕一便士邮政制. ~**royal** 【植】薄荷属的一种植物 ***(~ royal mint*** 【植】除蚤薄荷). ~ **wedding** 〔Scot.〕贺份结婚. ~**weight** 英钱〔音译"本尼威特",英国金衡,= 1.555 克〕***(略 dwt.) (a ~weight job*** 〔美俚〕偷宝石***)***. **~-wisdom** 省小钱. **~-wise** *a.* 省小钱的 ***(~-wise and pound-foolish*** 贪小失大). ~**wort** 【植】破铜钱属植物. ~**worth** [ˈpenəθ, ˈpeniwəːθ] *n.* ①一便士的价值;一便士的东西,少量. ②交易,买卖 ***(a good [bad] ~worth*** 有利〔不利〕的买卖,便宜〔上当〕货. ***get one's ~worth*** 对过去的牺牲得到报酬;被痛打;大受剥削. ***not a ~worth*** 一点也不…).

pe·nol·o·gist [piːˈnɔlədʒist] *n.* ①刑罚学家,罪犯教育学家. ②监狱学家.

pe·nol·o·gy [piːˈnɔlədʒi] *n.* 刑罚学;监狱学. **pe·no·log·i·cal** [ˌpiːnəˈlɔdʒikəl] *a.*

Pen·rose [ˈpenrəuz] *n.* 彭罗斯〔姓氏〕.

pen·sée [pɑ̃ːnˈsei] *n.* ***(pl. ~s*** [-sei]***)*** 〔F.〕①(用文字表达出的)思想;思索,沉思,默想. ②感想录;格言,箴言.

pen·sile [ˈpensail, -sil] *a.* = penduline.

pen·sion [ˈpenʃən] *n.* ①退休金,恤金,养老金,生活津贴;补助费. ②(给学者、艺术家等的)补助金;【英国教】(缴纳教堂的)牧师酬金;临时津贴. *old-age* ~ 养老金,退休金. *retire on a* ~ 领养老金退休. — *vt.* 给…养老金〔恤金、津贴等〕. ~ ***off*** 发给养老金〔津贴等〕使退职〔休〕.

pen·sion [ˈpɑ̃ːŋsiɔ̃ːŋ] *n.* 〔F.〕①(法国、比利时等的)公寓;寄宿学校. ②膳宿费. ***live en*** [ɑ̃ːn] ~ 过公寓生活.

pen·sion·a·ble [ˈpenʃənəbl] *a.* 有领养老金〔津贴等〕资格〔权利〕的.

pen·sion·a·ry [ˈpenʃənəri] *a.* 领养老金〔津贴等〕的;靠养老金〔津贴等〕过活的;(关于)养老金〔津贴等〕的. — *n.* ①= pensioner. ②被金钱收买的人;帮佣. ③(从前荷兰的)州长 (= Grand P-).

pen·sio·ne [penˈsjəune] *n.* ***(pl.-ni*** [-ni]***)*** 〔It.〕①寄宿学校. ②公寓 (= pension).

pen·sion·er [ˈpenʃənə] *n.* ①领养老金〔津贴等〕的人,退休的人. ②随从,随员,跟班;〔罕〕雇员. ③〔英〕剑桥大学的自费生.

pen·sion·less [ˈpenʃənlis] *a.* 没有养老金〔抚恤金等〕的.

pen·sive [ˈpensiv] *a.* ①沉思的. ②郁郁不乐的;忧愁的,凄凉的. **-ly** *ad.*

pen·ste·mon [penˈstiːmən, ˈpensti-] *n.* 【植】钓钟柳属 *(Penstemon)* 植物〔草本象牙红属植物〕.

pen·ster [ˈpenstə] *n.* 雇佣文人.

pen·stock [ˈpenstɔk] *n.* ①节制闸门,潮门,水门. ②〔美〕(引水的)水渠,水槽;(水电站的)导水管. ③给水栓;〔美〕救火龙头. ④【化】压头管线. ⑤笔杆.

pen·sum [ˈpensəm] *n.* 罚学生做的工作.

pent[1] [pent] *pen*[2] 的过去式及过去分词. — *a.* 被幽闭的;被关闭的;郁积的. **~-up** 被抑制的,被关住的 ***(~-up fury*** 心中郁愤).

pent[2] [pent] *n.* 单斜顶棚;庇檐. ~ **roof** 单坡屋顶.

pent-, penta- *comb.f.* 五.

Penta [ˈpentə] *n.* 〔美口〕五角大楼,美国国防部.

pen·ta·chlo·ro·ni·tro·ben·zene [ˈpentəˌklɔːrəˌnaitrəuˈbenziːn] *n.* 【化】五氯硝基苯.

pen·ta·chlo·ro·phe·nol [ˌpentəˌklɔːrəˈfiːnəul,-nɔːl] *n.* 【化】五氯苯酚.

pen·ta·chord [ˈpentəkɔːd] *n.* 五弦琴;五声音阶.

pen·ta·cle [ˈpentəkl] *n.* = pentagram.

pen·tad [ˈpentæd] *n.* ①五;五个一组. ②五年,五天. ③【化】五价元素,五价物. — *a.* 五价元素的.

pen·ta·dac·tyl, pen·ta·dac·tyl·ate [ˌpentəˈdæktil, -dækˈtilit] *a.* 有五指〔五趾〕的. **-dac·tyl·ism** *n.*

pen·ta·e·ryth·rite, pen·ta·e·ryth·ri·tol [ˌpentəiˈriθrait, -rətəul] *n.* 【化】季戊四醇,支戊四醇.

pen·ta·gon [ˈpentəgən] *n.* ①五角形,五边形. ②(筑城)

五棱堡. *a regular* ~ 正五边形. *the P- (Building)*〔美〕五角大楼; 美国国防部. **pen·tag·o·nal** [penˈtæɡənl] *a.*

pen·ta·gram [ˈpentəɡræm] *n.* 五角星形(☆).

pen·ta·graph [ˈpentəɡrɑːf, -ɡræf] *n.* 连续的五个字母(= pantograph).

pen·ta·grid [ˈpentəɡrid] *n.*【无】五栅管, 七极管.

Pen·tag·y·nia [ˌpentəˈdʒiniə] *n.*〔*pl.*〕【植】五雌蕊纲.

pen·tag·y·nous [penˈtædʒinəs] *a.*【植】(有)五雌蕊的.

pen·ta·hed·ron [ˌpentəˈhedrən] *n.* *(pl.* **~s, -dra** [-drə]*)*【数】五面体. **-ta·he·dral** [ˌpentəˈhedrəl] *a.*

pen·ta·hy·drate [ˌpentəˈhaidreit] *n.*【化】五水化物.

pen·tam·er·ous [penˈtæmərəs] *a.*【生】五跗节的;【植】五基数的 (= 5-merous). **-er·ism** [-rizəm] *n.*

pen·tam·e·ter [penˈtæmitə] *n.*【韵】五音步诗行. — *a.* 五音步的.

Pen·tan·dri·a [penˈtændriə] *n.*〔*pl.*〕【植】五雄蕊纲. **pen·tan·drous** [-drəs] *a.* 五雄蕊的.

pen·tane [ˈpentein] *n.*【化】戊烷.

pen·tan·gle [ˈpenˌtæŋɡl] *n.* = pentagram.

pen·tan·gu·lar [penˈtæŋɡjulə] *a.* (有)五角的.

pen·ta·nol [ˈpentəˌnɔːl] *n.*【化】戊醇 (=amyl alcohol).

pen·ta·ploid [ˈpentəˌplɔid] *a.*【生】有五倍体的. — *n.* 五倍体. **-y** *n.*

pen·ta·quine [ˈpentəkwi(ː)n, -kwin] *n.*【药】戊奎宁.

pen·tarch·y [ˈpentɑːki] *n.* ①五头政治. ②五国联盟.

pen·ta·stich [ˈpentəstik] *n.* 五行诗, 有五行一节的诗.

pen·ta·style [ˈpentəstail] *a.*【建】五柱式的.

pen·ta·syl·la·ble [ˈpentəsiləbl] *n.* 五音节.

Pen·ta·teuch [ˈpentətjuːk] *n.*【基督】《旧约全书》的首五卷.

pen·tath·lete [penˈtæθliːt] *n.* 参加五项运动的运动员.

pen·tath·lon [penˈtæθlɔn] *n.* 五项运动〔田径比赛全能运动之一〕.

pen·ta·tom·ic [ˌpentəˈtɔmik] *a.*【化】五元的.

pen·ta·ton·ic [ˌpentəˈtɔnik] *a.*【乐】五声音阶的.

pen·ta·va·lent [ˌpentəˈveilənt] *a.* ①【化】五价的. ②具有五种不同的价的 (= quinquevalent).

Pen·te·cost [ˈpentikɔst] *n.* ①(犹太人的)五旬节. ②(基督教的)圣灵降临节. **-al** [ˌpentiˈkɔstl] *a.*

pent·house [ˈpenthaus] *n.* ①(大楼平顶上的)楼顶房间; 小棚屋. ②雨篷, 遮篷; (靠墙的)单斜顶棚; 庇檐; 庇檐形物. *a* ~ *roof* 单坡屋顶; 庇檐. *the* ~ *of the eye* 眉. ***make a ~ of the eyebrows*** 皱眉头.

pen·thrit(e) [ˈpenθrait] *n.*【化】季戊炸药.

pent·land·ite [ˈpentləndait] *n.*【矿】镍黄铁矿, 硫镍铁矿.

pen·tode [ˈpentəud] *a.*【无】五极的. — *n.*【无】五极管. *a radio-frequency* ~ 高频五极管. ***a beam*** ~ 电子注管.

pen·tom·ic [penˈtɔmik] *a.*【军】五群制的.

Pen·ton·ville [ˈpentənvil] *n.* (英国伦敦的) 本顿维尔(单人)监狱.

pen·to·san, pen·to·sane [ˈpentəsæn, ˈpentəsein] *n.*【化】戊聚糖, 多缩戊糖.

pen·tose [ˈpentəus] *n.*【化】戊糖.

pen·to·thal [ˈpentəθæl] *n.*【药】喷妥撒.

pen(t)·ste·mon [pen(t)sˈtemən] *n.*【植】钓种柳属植物; 草本象牙红.

pen·tyl [ˈpentil] *n.*【化】戊(烷)基. ~ **alcohol** 戊醇.

pe·nu·che, pe·nu·chi [pəˈnuːtʃi] *n.* = panocha[2].

pe·nult [piˈnʌlt] *n., a.* 词尾倒数第二音节(的); 倒数第二个(的).

pe·nul·ti·mate [piˈnʌltimit] *a., n.* = penult.

pe·num·bra [piˈnʌmbrə] *n.* *(pl.* **-brae** [-briː], **~s***)* ①【物】半影, 黑影周围的半阴影. ②(绘画中)画面浓淡相交处. ③【天】太阳黑子周围的半暗部; (星面部的) 阴影. **-bral** *a.*

pe·nu·ri·ous [piˈnjuəriəs] *a.* ①〔古〕贫穷的; 贫瘠的. ②吝啬的. **-ly** *ad.* **-ness** *n.*

pen·u·ry [ˈpenjuri, -juəri] *n.* ①贫穷; 缺乏 *(of)*. ②吝啬.

pe·on [ˈpiːən] *n.* ①(南美的) 散工, 日工; (墨西哥、美国西南部) 以劳力抵债的奴隶式工人. ②[ˌpjuːn, ˈpiːən]〔印〕步兵; 巡警; 跟班; 侍役. ③(象棋)卒.

pe·on·age [ˈpiːənidʒ] *n.* ①雇用日工; 做日工. ②(美国东南部的)劳力偿债制. ~ **labour** 偿债劳动.

pe·o·ny [ˈpiəni] *n.*【植】芍药属植物. *the herbaceous* ~ 芍药. *the tree* ~牡丹. *blush like a* ~ 脸红.

peo·ple [ˈpiːpl] *n.* *(pl.* ①为 **~s,** 其他为~*)* ①种族; 民族. ②人民. ③居民; (团体、行业等中的)人们. ④〔常与所有格连用〕(对君主而言的) 臣民; 教区教徒; 随从; 家, 家属, 亲属; 〔学〕亲戚; 祖先. ⑤〔the ~〕平民, 老百姓. ⑥(一般的)人, 人们; 人类 (*opp.* animals). ⑦〔作不定代名词用〕人家, 有的人. ⑧〔主诗〕生物. *a warlike* ~ 一个好战的民族. *the English* ~ 英国人民. *the ~s of Europe* 欧洲诸民族. *the ~'s front* 人民阵线. *the village* ~ 村民. *the* ~ *here* 这里的居民. *literary* ~ 文人们. *He has gone to his wife's* ~. 他到他丈母家去了. *My* ~ *have lived here for generations.* 我家世世代代都是住在这里. *a man of the* ~ 一个老百姓. *Few* ~ *know the truth.* 很少人知道实情. ***the National People's Congress*** 全国人民代表大会. ***the People's Courts*** 人民法院. ***the People's Democratic Republic*** 人民民主共和国. ***the ~'s democratic state*** 人民民主国家. ***the People's Liberation Army*** 人民解放军. ***the People's Republic of China*** 中华人民共和国. ***the ~'s war of liberation*** 人民解放战争. ***as ~ go*** 照一般人讲. ***of all*** ~ 在许多〔所有〕人中(偏偏…). ***P- say that*** … 人们说, 据说…. ***the best*** ~〔口〕上流社会人士. ***the Chosen P-***【宗】上帝的选民〔指基督徒〕; 犹太人. — *vt.* ①使人到…去住, 使住满人, 在…殖民. ②把(动物)放养在 *(with)*. ③〔用 *p.p.*〕住在, 栖息在; 布满, 占据. *a thickly [sparsely]* ~*d country* 人口稠密(稀少)的国家. **~-to-~** *a.* 人民之间的.

pep [pep] *n.*〔美俚〕劲头, 锐气, 活力. *a* ~ *talk* (教练等对队员等的)精神讲话, 鼓励士气的讲话. — *vt.* 给…打气, 刺激, 鼓励 *(up)*. ~ **pill**〔美俚〕兴奋药片〔尤指安非他明〕. ~ **rally** 鼓舞士气的集会.

P.E.P. = Political and Economic Planning 政治经济计划.

pep·er·i·no, pep·er·ine [ˌpepəˈriːnəu, ˈpepəriːn] *n.*【地】白榴拟灰岩.

pep·per [ˈpepə] *n.* ①胡椒; 胡椒粉; 〔P-〕【植】胡椒属. ②刺激性; 尖锐的批评. ③暴躁, 急性子. ④〔美俚〕活力, 精力; 劲头; 勇气. *white* ~ 白胡椒. *beaten [ground]* ~ 胡椒粉. *the Chinese [Japanese]* ~ 秦椒. *the water* ~ 蓼. ***take ~ in the nose = grow ~*** 发怒, 动气. — *vt.* ①加胡椒粉于; 撒(胡椒), 用胡椒调(味). ②乱发(质问、子弹); 【美拳】接连速击. ③〔罕〕嘲笑; 痛骂; 重罚. **~-and-salt** *n., a.* 椒盐(的); (衣料)黑白点相间(的). **~box** ①胡椒盒〔瓶〕. ②急性人. **~caster, ~ castor** 胡椒瓶〔盒〕. **~corn** ①干胡椒, 胡椒子. ②无聊的东西; 空有其名的地租〔房租〕(=~ rent); 微不足道的东西. **~-grass**【植】独行菜. **~-mill** 磨胡椒子的小罐. **~mint** ①【植】胡椒薄荷; 薄荷. ②薄荷油. ③薄荷糖. **~pot** ①胡椒瓶〔盒〕. ②〔俚〕急性人. ③(西印度群岛的) 红辣椒燉肉; 红辣椒肉菜汤. ④〔俚〕牙买加岛人. ~ **tree**【植】木兰科植物; 秘鲁乳香. **~wort**【植】胡椒草.

pep·per·y [ˈpepəri] *a.* ①胡椒(似)的. ②(话) 辛辣的. ③易怒的, 暴躁的.

pep·py [ˈpepi] *a.* ①〔美俚〕精神饱满的; 劲头十足的. ②(汽车、飞机)起动快的; 高速运行性能好的.

-pepsia *comb. f.* 消化: brady*pepsia*.

Pep·si·co·la [ˈpepsiˌkəulə] *n.*【美商标】百事可乐〔一种

饮料〕.

pep·sin(e) [ˈpepsin] *n.*【生化】胃朊酶,胃蛋白酶.

pep·sin·ate [ˈpepsineit] *vt.*【生化】用胃蛋白酶处理,用胃蛋白酶混合;向…注入胃蛋白酶.

pep·sin·o·gen [pepˈsinədʒən] *n.*【生化】胃蛋白酶原.

pep·ster [ˈpepstə] *n.*〔美〕激起别人热情的人.

pep·tic [ˈpeptik] *a.* ①胃的,(帮助)消化的. ②(产生)胃(朊)酶的. ③消化液的. —*n.* ①消化剂,健胃剂. ②〔*pl.*〕〔谑〕消化器官. ~ *glands* 胃酶腺.

pep·ti·dase [ˈpeptideis] *n.*【生化】肽酶.

pep·tide, pep·tid [ˈpeptaid, -tid] *n.*【生化】肽;缩氨酸.

pep·ti·mist [ˈpeptimist] *n.*〔美〕精神饱满的人.

pep·tize [ˈpeptaiz] *vt., vi.*【化】使胶溶.

pep·tone [ˈpeptəun] *n.*【生化】胨,蛋白胨.

pep·to·nize [ˈpeptənaiz] *vt.* 使胨化,使蛋白胨化. **-to·ni·za·tion** [-ˈzeiʃən] *n.*

Pepys [ˈpepis] *n.* 佩皮斯〔姓氏〕.

Pe·quot, Pe·quod [ˈpiːkwɔt, -kwɔd] *n.*【美史】佩科特人〔17世纪住在新英格兰南部的 Algonquian 族印第安人的一支〕.

per, *per* [强 pəː; 弱 pə] *prep.*〔L.〕①由,经;以,靠. ②每,一. ③按照,根据. *$2 ~ man* 每人两元. ~ *day [month, year]* 每天[月、年]. ***as ~*** = according to. ***as ~ usual*** 〔谑〕照常. ~ ***annum*** [pəˈrænəm] 每年. ~ ***bearer*** 由来人. ~ ***capita*** [ˈkæpitə] 每人,按人(分配). ~ ***caput*** [ˈkæpət] =~ capita〔误用〕. ~ ***cent(um)*** [ˈsent(əm)] 每百分之(几). ~ ***contra*** [pəːˈkɔntrə] ①反而,相反的. ②在另一方面;在对方. ~ ***diem*** [pəːˈdaiem, -ˈdaiəm] 每日,按日. ~ ***fas et nefas*** [ˈfæs et ˈneifæs] 无论如何. ~ ***mensem*** [ˈmensem] 每月,按月. ~ ***mille*** [ˈmili] 每千. ~ ***post*** 由邮局. ~ ***procurationem*** [prɔkjuəreiʃiˈəunem]〔略 *p. proc., p. pro., p.p.*〕由…所代表;由…代理. ~ ***rail [steamer]*** 由铁路[轮船]. ~ ***saltum*** [ˈsæltəm] 一跃. ~ ***se*** [ˈsei,ˈsiː] 自,自身;本来,性质上.

per. = period, person.

per- *pref.* ①通,总,遍: *per*fect, *per*vade. ②极,甚: *per*fervid. ③【化】过,高: *per*oxide.

per·ac·id [ˈpəːæsid] *n.*【化】①高(某)酸. ②过(某)酸. ③过某(羧)酸.

per·ad·ven·ture [pərədˈventʃə] *ad.*〔古〕①恐怕,或者,可能. ②偶然,万一. ***if ~*** 如果…,要是…,万一…. ***lest ~*** 为恐万一,以防万一. —*n.* ①疑惑,疑问. ②偶然,不确实. ***beyond ~*** = ***without ~*** 无疑地,的确,必定.

per·am·bu·late [pəˈræmbjuleit] *vt.* ①巡行,巡视;勘查. ②走过,穿过;徘徊于. —*vi.* 闲逛,闲荡;徘徊.

per·am·bu·la·tion [pəˌræmbjuˈleiʃən] *n.* ①漫步,闲荡;徘徊. ②巡视;巡行(勘查、测量)区. ③巡视[勘查]报告.

per·am·bu·la·tor [ˈpræmbjuleitə, pəˈræm-] *n.* ①〔主英〕婴儿车〔俗称 pram〕. ②【测】路程计;测程器. ③巡视者;漫步者;徘徊者;勘查者.

per·am·bu·la·to·ry [pəˈræmbjulətəri] *a.* ①漫步的;闲荡的. ②巡行的;巡视的,勘查的.

per an(n). =〔L.〕*per annum* 每年.

per·bo·rate [pəˈbɔːreit] *n.*【化】过硼酸盐.

per·bu·nan [ˈpəːb(j)unən] *n.*【商标】别布橡胶,丁腈橡胶.

per·cale [pəˈkeil] *n.*【纺】高级密织薄纱.

per·ca·line [ˌpəːkəˈliːn, ˈpəːkəliːn] *n.*【纺】波盖勒细棉织品.

per·ceiv·a·ble [pəˈsiːvəbl] *a.* 可察觉的,可看到的,可理解的,可领会的. **-a·bil·i·ty, -ness** *n.* **-a·bly** *ad.*

per·ceive [pəˈsiːv] *vt.* ①察觉,发觉. ②看见,听见. ③理会,领悟,了解;看出,抓住(意义、真相等). *Yes, I ~ (what you say).* 是,不错.

per cent, per·cent [pəˈsent] *n.*〔拉丁语 *per centum* 的缩略,符号为%〕①每百,百分之一…. ②〔*pl.*〕(…厘息)公债[投资等]. ③〔口〕百分率. *7 ~* 百分之七(7%). *get 2 ~ interest* 获三分利. *invest money in 2.5 ~s* 投资于二分五利息的公债.

per·cent·age [pəˈsentidʒ] *n.* ①【数】百分法;百分数;百分比,百分率. ②比例,部分. ③【商】手续费,佣金. ④〔俚〕赚头,不正当的利益;好处;用处. ⑤(根据统计得出的)可能性. ***no ~ in*** 〔美〕没利益,没好处. ~ ***of hits*** 【军】命中率. ~ **table** 百分数表. **-wise** *ad.* 从百分比来看,在百分比上.

per·cen·tile [pəˈsentail] *a.* 百分比的. —*n.* 百分位数(值);百分之一;百分比下降点.

per·cept [ˈpəːsept] *n.* ①【哲】知觉的对象. ②感觉;感受;印象.

per·cep·ti·ble [pəˈseptəbl] *a.* ①可以感觉[感受]到的. ②可理解的,认得出的;看得出的. ③相当的. *quite a ~ time* 很长时间. **-ti·bil·i·ty** [pəˌseptəˈbiliti] *n.* 感觉力,察觉力;领悟[认识]能力.

per·cep·ti·bly [pəˈseptəbli] *ad.* 感觉得出地,认得出地;显然.

per·cep·tion [pəˈsepʃən] *n.* ①【哲】感觉(作用);感受;知觉. ②知觉作用;感性认识;观念,概念;直觉. ③洞察力;理解力. ④【法】(地租等的)征收;(农作物的)收获. *a man of the keenest ~* 感觉敏锐的人. *visual ~* 视觉. **-al** *a.*

per·cep·tive [pəˈseptiv] *a.* ①知觉的. ②感觉(敏锐)的;有理解力的.

per·cep·tiv·i·ty [ˌpəːsepˈtiviti] *n.* ①感觉力;理解力. ②认识能力.

per·cep·tron [pəˈseptrɔn] *n.*【无】视感控器〔类似视神经的电子仪器〕.

per·cep·tu·al [pəˈseptjuəl] *a.* 知觉的,知觉力的,感性的. ~ *knowledge* 感性认识 (*opp.* conceptual knowledge). *the ~ stage of cognition* 认识的感性阶段. **-ly** *ad.*

perch[1] [pəːtʃ] *n.* ①(鸟的)栖木;挂东西的横条. ②(尤指高处的)休息处;高位;有利地位. ③【机】(联系前后车轴的)连杆,主轴;架;驭者座;(弹药车的)车尾;棒,竿. ④杆〔英国长度名(=5码)〕;英国面积单位(=$30\frac{1}{4}$平方码);(石头等的)体积单位(通常为 $16\frac{1}{2}$ ft. × $\frac{1}{2}$ ft. × 1 ft.). ⑤〔美〕虚荣心,自负;棒球场的座位. ⑥皮革的鞣制,皮革破绽的弥补. ⑦【纺】验布架. ⑧【海】浮筒顶标. ***come off one's ~*** 〔口〕失势,没落. ***hop [drop off, tip over] the ~*** 〔口〕败落,死. ***knock sb. off his ~*** 〔俚〕挫败某人;把某人毁掉. —*vi.* ①(鸟)落,歇. ②坐,休息 (*on; upon*). —*vt.* ①使(鸟)歇在栖木上;把(人)放置高处[危险处]〔通常用过去分词形〕. ③验(布). *a town ~ed on a hill* 位于山上的镇市.

perch[2] [pəːtʃ] *n.* (*pl.* ~*es,*〔集合词〕~)【鱼】河鲈.

per·chance [pə(ː)ˈtʃɑːns, -ˈtʃæns] *ad.*〔古〕①偶然. ②或许,可能.

perch·er [ˈpəːtʃə] *n.* ①栖木类的鸟;在高处的人. ②织品检查人,验布工. ③〔口〕将死的人.

Per·che·ron [ˈpɛəːʃərɔ̃ːŋ] *n.*〔F.〕(法国北部 Perche 产的)灰毛马.

per·chlo·rate [pəˈklɔːreit] *n.*【化】高氯酸盐. ~ *explosive* 高氯酸盐炸药.

per·chlo·ric [pəˈklɔːrik] *a.* ~ **acid**【化】高氯酸.

per·chlo·ride [pəˈklɔːraid] *n.*【化】高氯化物.

per·cip·i·ence, per·cip·i·en·cy [pəːˈsipiəns, -ənsi] *n.* ①感觉;知觉. ②洞察力.

per·cip·i·ent [pəːˈsipiənt] *a.* ①感觉的;有知觉的. ②洞察的. —*n.* ①感觉灵敏的人;洞察. ②感觉者.

Per·ci·val [ˈpəːsivəl] 珀西瓦尔〔男子名〕.

per·coid [ˈpəːkɔid] *a.*(鱼)鲈形类 (*Percomorphi*) 的〔包括鲈,翻车鲀等〕. —*n.* 鲈形类的鱼.

per·co·late [ˈpəːkəleit] *vt.* ①滤,使渗滤,使渗透. ②

(用渗滤壶)煮(咖啡). ③刺穿,穿过. — *vi.* 渗开,滤过. — *n.* 渗出液,滤过液.

per·co·la·tion [ˌpəːkəˈleiʃən] *n.* ①渗滤; 渗透(作用); 渗漏. ②【化】穿流(法). *underground* ~ 地下渗流.

per·co·la·tor [ˈpəːkəleitə] *n.* ①渗滤器,(尤指)咖啡渗滤壶. ②进行渗滤的人.

per ct. =〔L.〕*per centum*. 百分之….

per cu·ri·am [pəˈkjuəriˌæm] *a.* 〔L.〕【法】法院的〔指的是整个法庭的判决意见,而不是其中某一法官的意见〕.

per·cuss [pəːˈkʌs] *vt.* ①敲,叩,击. ②【医】扣诊.

per·cus·sion [pəːˈkʌʃən] *n.* ①敲打,叩击; 撞击; 碰撞. ②(由敲打产生的)震动. ③【乐】打击; (乐队的)打击乐器组. ④【军】击发(装置). ⑤【医】扣诊(法). ~ **bullet**【军】爆破炸弹. ~ **cap** 雷管,发火帽. ~ **fuse**【军】着发引信. ~ **gun** 雷管枪. ~ **instrument**【乐】打击乐器. ~ **lock**【军】击发装置. ~ **powder** 起爆药. ~ **primer**【军】引爆药.~ **shrapnel** 着发榴霰弹.

per·cus·sion·ist [pəˈkʌʃənist] *n.* 打击乐乐师.

per·cus·sive [pəːˈkʌsiv] *a.* ①(乐器等)敲击的. ②【医】扣诊的. ③有强大震动力的; 令人震惊的.

per·cu·ta·ne·ous [ˌpəːkju(ː)ˈteiniəs, -njəs] *a.*【医】经皮的,由皮的.

per cwt. = per hundredweight 每英担.

Per·cy [ˈpəːsi] *n.* 珀西〔姓氏,男子名〕.

per·die [pəˈdiː] *ad., int.* 〔古〕必然,一定,确实〔原为一种誓言〕(=pardie).

per·di·tion [pəːˈdiʃən] *n.* ①灭亡, 毁灭. ②【宗】堕地狱,沉沦,永远的死; 永灭; 地狱. ***Go to ~!*** 见鬼去!该死的!

per·du(e) [pəːˈdjuː] *a.* ①看不见的; 隐藏的,潜伏的,埋伏的. ②〔古〕敢死的. *lie* ~ 潜伏,埋伏. — *n.* ①伏兵; 敢死队员. ②很难成功的事[举动].

per·dur·a·ble [pə(ː)ˈdjuərəbl] *a.* 持久的,耐久的; 永久的,不朽的. **-a·bil·i·ty** *n.* **-a·bly** *ad.*

per·dure [pə(ː)ˈdjuə] *vi.* 持久,持续.

père [pɛə] *n.* 〔F.〕①父. ★同名父子,名后加 *père* 时为父,加 *fils* 时为子. ②〔P-〕…神父〔尊称〕.*Alexander Dumas* ~ 大仲马.

per·e·gri·nate [ˈperigrineit] *vi.* 〔古、谑〕流浪; 游历,(徒步)旅行.**-gri·na·tion** [-ˈneiʃən] *n.* 游历, (徒步) 旅行; 旅程; 流浪. **-gri·na·tor** *n.* (徒步)旅行者; 流浪者.

per·e·grin(e) [ˈperigrin] *a.* ①外国的, 外来的, 舶来的; 异国(风味)的.②(鸟)移居的; (人)流浪的,漫游的.— *n.* ①【鸟】(放鹰打猎用的)游隼 (= falcon). ②外侨,居留外国的人; 游历者.

per·emp·to·ry [pəˈremptəri] *a.* ①断然的, 毅然的; 命令式的. ②独断的,专横的; 强制的. ③【法】绝对的,最后决定的. ~ **mandamus** 强制执行命令书. **-to·ri·ly** [-ˈtɔ-] *ad.* **-to·ri·ness** *n.*

per·en·nate [ˈpeərəneit] *vi.* (植物) 多年生长; 持续不断地存在. **-en·na·tion** *n.*

per·en·ni·al [pəˈrenjəl] *a.* ①四季不断的,终年的; 继续多年的; (青春) 永驻的. ②【动】(牙齿等) 不断生长的; (昆虫)活一年以上的. ③【植】多年生的. — *n.* 多年生植物. ~ *river* 常流河. **-ly** *ad.* **-ni·al·i·ty** *n.*

perf. =①perfect. ②perforate. ③performer.

per·fect [ˈpəːfikt] *a.* ①完全的,完美的; 圆满的,理想的; 纯粹的. ②熟练的, 精通的 *(in)*. ③绝对的, 毋容置疑的; 分毫不差的,正确的. ④〔口〕十足的; 厉害的, 过分的. ⑤【植】雌雄(蕊) 同花的; 具备的. ⑥【语法】完成的. ⑦【印】两面印的. *a* ~ *actor to play the role* 扮演这个角色的理想演员. *a* ~ *day* 一个美满快活的日子. *make a* ~ *fool of oneself* 使自己成为一个不折不扣的傻瓜. *a* ~ *tennis player* 熟练的网球家. *a* ~ *storm* 猛烈的暴风雨. ***make*** ~【印】两面印刷. ***the*** ~ ***year*** 犹太历. — *n.*【语法】完成时,完成式. *the present [future, past]* ~ 现在[未来,过去]完成式. — [pə(ː)ˈfekt, ˈpəːfikt] *vt.* ①完成, 贯彻. ②使完全; 使完美; 改善, 改良. ③使熟练, 使精通. ~ *an invention* 完成一项声明. *be constantly* ~*ing one's skill* 对技术精益求精. ~ ***oneself in*** 弄熟,精通. ~ **binding**【印】无线胶粘装订. ~ **gas** 理想气体. ~ **press** 两面印刷轮转机. ~ **square**【数】整方, 完全平方. ~ **stage**【生】有性阶段. ~ **tense**【语法】完成时. **-or** [pə(ː)ˈfektə] *n.*【印】两面印刷机.

per·fect·i·ble [pə(ː)ˈfektəbl] *a.* ①可以完成的. ②可变完善的; 可改善的. **-bil·i·ty** [-ˈbiliti] *n.*

per·fec·tion [pəˈfekʃən] *n.* ①完全, 圆满, 完备; 完成; 成熟; 无缺; 极度, 极致. ②熟习, 熟练. ③优秀人物,典型; 标本. ④〔*pl.*〕才艺,美点. *Beauty is the least* ~ 美貌是她优点中最微不足道的一点. ***be at*** ~ (果子) 正熟; (菜) 做得恰好. ***be the*** ~ ***of (folly)*** (蠢) 到极点,(愚蠢) 之极. ***come [attain] to*** ~ 圆熟,成熟. ***to*** ~ 完全地; 好极.

per·fec·tion·ism [pə(ː)ˈfekʃənizəm] *n.* ①至善论,圆满论; 完全论〔认为人世间可达至善境界〕. ②过度追求尽善尽美. **-tion·ist** *n.* ①至善论者,圆满论者. ②追求尽善尽美者,过分挑剔者.

per·fect·ive [pə(ː)ˈfektiv] *a.* ①使完美〔圆满〕的. ②【语法】(动词体)完成的. — *n.* 完成体(的动词).

per·fec·to [pəˈfektəu] *n.* 〔美〕两头尖的雪茄烟.

per·fer·vid [pəːˈfəːvid] *a.* 非常热心的; 热烈的; 热情的. **-ly** *ad.* **-ness** *n.*

per·fid·i·ous [pəːˈfidiəs, -djəs] *a.* 不忠实的, 叛卖的; 背信弃义的. **-ly** *ad.* **-ness** *n.*

per·fi·dy [ˈpəːfidi] *n.* *(pl. -dies)* ①背信弃义; 不忠. ②叛变,出卖.

per·fo·li·ate [pə(ː)ˈfəuliit] *a.* ①【植】(叶)抱茎的,(茎)穿叶的. ②【动】(昆虫)具叶片的,抱茎状的. *a* ~ *leaf* 贯穿叶. **-li·a·tion** *n.*

Per·fo·ra·ta [ˌpəːfəˈrɑːtə] *n.* 〔*pl.*〕【动】有孔虫目.

per·fo·rate [ˈpəːfəreit] *vt.* ①穿孔于, 凿孔于, 冲孔于, 穿. ②在(纸)上打眼; 打透(花字); 打一排孔于(邮票等). ~*d paper* 穿孔纸带. *a* ~*d electrode*【电】多孔电极. ~*d bricks* 多孔砖. —*vi.* ①穿孔. ②穿过; 贯穿; 刺穿 *(into, through)*. — [ˈpəːfərit] *a.* (邮票等) 有孔的, 穿孔的,有一排孔的. **-ra·tion** [ˌpəːfəˈreiʃən] *n.* ①穿孔, 贯通; 打孔,打眼. ②孔眼,(邮票等的)孔状接缝.

per·fo·ra·tive [ˈpəːfərətiv] *a.* 穿孔的, 穿得过的,有穿孔力的.

per·fo·ra·tor [ˈpəːfəreitə] *n.* ①穿孔器, 凿孔机; 剪票铗;【医】穿头器〔产科用〕. ②穿孔[打眼]的人.

per·force [pəˈfɔːs] *ad.* 〔书〕必然,必要地; 不可避免地. *The story is* ~ *true.* 情况属实. — *n.* 〔罕〕强制, 不得已. ***by*** ~ 用力,强迫. ***of*** ~ 不得已.

per·form [pəˈfɔːm] *vt.* ①履行,实行,干,执行(命令、任务等); 完成(事业). ②演出; 表演; 扮(角色); 演奏. ~ *one's duties* 尽责任.~ *a play* 上演一出戏.~ *a part* 演一个角色. — *vi.* ①进行,履行,实行,执行. ②表演,演奏; (驯兽)玩把戏. ~ *in the role of* 扮演…角色. **-form·a·ble** *a.* 可执行的; 可完成的; 可演出的.

per·form·ance [pəˈfɔːməns] *n.* ①执行, 实行,履行; 完成; 实现; 偿还. ②行为,动作, 行动; 工作. ③性能; 特性. ④功绩; 成绩. ⑤演奏, 弹奏; 演出; (驯兽等的) 表演; 把戏. ⑥【物】演绩. *a* ~ *test*【机】性能试验. *high* ~ 高度准确,性能优良. *an afternoon* ~ 午后的演出,日戏. *two* ~*s a day* 一天演两场. *a fine [wretched]* ~ 成绩好[坏]. *put a monkey through its* ~*s* 使猴子玩种种把戏. ~ *in [of] horse-manship* 马戏; 马术表演. ~ **index** 性能指数,演绩指数.

per·form·er [pəˈfɔːmə] *n.* ①执行者,实行者, 履行者; 完成者. ②演奏者,乐师; 演员, 歌手, 卖艺人. ③能手; 选手. *a good promiser, but a bad* ~ 口惠而实不至的人.

per·form·ing [pəˈfɔːmiŋ] *a.* ①实行的, 完成的. ②表

演的；演奏的。③(狗等)会玩把戏的。

per·fume [ˈpəːfjuːm] *n.* ①香，芳香；香味。②香水；香料。— [pə(ː)ˈfjuːm] *vt.* 使散发香味，把…弄香；洒香水于。～ *one's hair* 给头发洒香水。***a* ～*d talk*** 〔美讽〕坏话，骂人话。

per·fum·er [pə(ː)ˈfjuːmə] *n.* ①香料制造人；香料商。②洒香水的人[器具]。

per·fum·er·y [pə(ː)ˈfjuːməri] *n.* ①〔集合词〕香水类，香料。②〔美〕香水。③香料制造法。④香料厂；香料商；香料店。

per·func·to·ry [pəˈfʌŋktəri] *a.* ①敷衍塞责的，马马虎虎的。②例行公事的；不彻底的，表面的。**-to·ri·ly** *ad.* **-to·ri·ness** *n.*

per·fuse [pə(ː)ˈfjuːz] *vt.* 灌，使充满；铺满，洒遍，撒满。～ *a room with radiance* 使房间光线充足。

per·fu·sion [pə(ː)ˈfjuːʒən] *n.* ①灌注，洒。②【医】灌注法。

per·fu·sive [pə(ː)ˈfjuːsiv] *a.* ①洒的，洒水用的。②易散发的；能渗透的。

per·ga·me·ne·ous [ˌpəgəˈmiːniəs] *a.* 羊皮纸的；羊皮纸似的；羊皮纸做的。

per·ga·ment [ˈpəːgəmənt] *n.* (假)羊皮纸，革纸 (＝～ paper)。

per·go·la [ˈpəːgələ] *n.* ①(用藤架等做顶的)凉亭。②(藤架等底下的)小径，荫廊。③蔓棚，藤架。

perh. ＝perhaps.

per·haps [pəˈhæps, pəˈræps] *ad.* 大概，多半，大半；可能；或许，或者。*I'll come,* ～ *I won't.* 我也许来，也许不来。— *n.* 〔常 *pl.*〕偶然事件；假定，设想。*These are all* ～*es.* 这全是假定。

pe·ri [ˈpiəri] *n.* ***(pl.* ～*s)*** ①【波斯神话】妖精，仙女。②美人。

peri- *pref.* ①周围：*peri*phery. ②近，迫：*peri*helion. ③围绕，围入；包围：*peri*cardiac.

per·i·anth [ˈperiænθ] *n.*【植】花被；萼苞；总苞。

per·i·apt [ˈperiæpt] *n.* 护符，符箓。

per·i·blem [ˈperiˌblem] *n.*【植】皮层原。

per·i·car·di·ac, per·i·car·di·al[ˌperiˈkɑːdiæk, -diəl] *a.*【解】心包的；位于心脏周围的。

per·i·car·di·tis [ˌperikɑːˈdaitis] *n.*【医】心包炎。

per·i·car·di·um [ˌperiˈkɑːdjəm] *n.* ***(pl. -dia*** [-djə]***)***【解】心包；心包膜，围心膜。

per·i·carp [ˈperikɑːp] *n.*【植】果皮；囊果皮。

per·i·chon·dri·um [ˌperiˈkɔndriəm] *n.* ***(pl. -dri·a*** [-ə]***)***【解】软骨膜。**-ri·al, -dral** *a.*

per·i·clase [ˈperikleis] *n.*【矿】方镁石。

Per·i·cle·an [ˌperiˈkliːən] *a.* ①(雅典政治家)培里克里斯 (Pericles) 的。②培里克里斯时代(约自公元前 495 年至 429 年)的，古雅典文化鼎盛时期的。

per·i·cli·nal [ˌperiˈklainl] *a.*【植】①平周的。②【地】穹状的。

per·i·cline [ˈperiˌklain] *n.*【矿】肖纳长石。

pe·ric·o·pe [pəˈrikəpiː] *n.* ***(pl.* ～*s, -pae*** [-piː]***)*** ①(从书中选出的)选段，章节。②(基督教)《圣经》选读。

per·i·cra·ni·um [ˌperiˈkreiniəm] *n.* ***(pl. -ni·a*** [-niə]***)*** ①【解】颅骨膜。②〔谑〕头盖骨；头颅；机智。

per·i·cy·cle [ˈperisaikl] *n.*【植】中柱鞘。**-cy·clic** [-ˈsaiklik, -ˈsiklik] *a.*

per·i·derm [ˈperidəːm] *n.*【植】周皮。**-al, -ic** *a.*

pe·rid·i·um [pəˈridiəm] *n.* ***(pl. -rid·e·a*** [-ˈridiə]***)***【植】包被。**-rid·i·al** *a.*

per·i·dot [ˈperidɔt] *n.*【矿】(浓绿色)橄榄石。

per·i·do·tite [ˌperiˈdautait] *n.*【矿】橄榄岩。

per·i·gee [ˈperidʒiː] *n.*【天、宇】(月球、人造卫星等运行轨道最接近地球的)近地点 *(opp.* apogee*)*. **-ge·al** [ˌperiˈdʒiːəl], **-i·ge·an** [ˌperiˈdiːən] *a.*【天、宇】近地点的，在近地点时间的。

per·i·gla·cial [ˌperiˈgleisjəl] *n.*【地】冰川周缘的。

per·i·gon [ˈperigɔn] *n.*【数】周角，三百六十度角。

per·i·gone [ˈperigəun] *n.*【植】①花盖。②＝perianth. ③(苔藓植物的)雄器苞。

pe·rig·y·nous [pəˈridʒinəs] *a.*【植】子房周位的。**-y·ny** [-ni] *n.*

per·i·he·li·on [ˌperiˈhiːljən, -liən] *n.* ***(pl. -he·lia*** [-hiː-liə]***)***【天、宇】(行星或彗星运行轨道最接近太阳的)近日点 *(opp.* aphelion*)*；最高点，极点。

per·il [ˈperil] *n.* (严重的)危险；冒险。***at one's* ～** (若有…)咎由自取，(…，否则)自找危险 *(Resist at your* ～*!* 若有抵抗，咎由自取。*Keep off at your* ～*!* 注意站开，免遭危险。*Do it at your* ～ 要干尽管干，危险自承当)。***at the* ～ *of*** 冒…的危险。***in* ～** 危急；冒着危险。***in* ～ *of*** 使…发生危险；有…的危险。***in the hour [time] of* ～** 在危险的时刻。— *vt.* 冒危险，拼，置…于危险中。

Pe·ril·la [pəˈrilə] *n.*【植】紫苏属。**～seed** *n.* 苏籽。

per·il·ous [ˈperiləs] *a.* ①危险的；冒险的。②〔古〕可怕的。**-ly** *ad.* **-ness** *n.*

per·i·lune [ˈperiluːn] *n.*【宇】(人造月球卫星在轨道上最接近月球的)近月点。

per·im·e·ter [pəˈrimitə] *n.* ①【数】周，周长；周边。②周围，周界线。③【光】视野计。④【军】(军营、工事、机场等的)环形防线[防御带]。

per·i·met·ric [ˌperiˈmetrik] *a.* ①周的，周长的。②视野计的，视野测定器的 (＝perimetrical). **-cal·ly** *ad.*

pe·rim·e·try [pəˈrimitri] *n.* 视野测定。

per·i·morph [ˈperiˌmɔːf] *n.*【矿】被壳矿物，包被矿物。

per·i·my·si·um [ˌperiˈmiziəm] *n.* ***(pl. -si·a*** [-ə]***)***【解】外肌束膜。

per·i·na·tal [ˌperiˈneitl] *a.* 接近出生时期的，出生前后发生的。

per·i·ne·al [ˌperiˈniːəl] *a.*【解】会阴的。

per·i·neph·ri·um [ˌperiˈnefriəm] *n.* ***(pl. -ri·a*** [-riə]***)***【解】肾包。

per·i·ne·um, per·i·nae·um [ˌperiˈniːəm] *n.* ***(pl.-ne·a*** [-ˈniːə]***)***【解】会阴。**-n(a)e·al** *a.*

per·i·neu·ri·um [ˌperiˈnjuəriːəm] *n.* ***(pl. -ri·a*** [-ə]***)***【解】神经束膜。**-neu·ri·al** *a.*

pe·ri·od [ˈpiəriəd] *n.* ①时代；期；时期；期间；阶段。②〔the ～〕现代，当代。③周期；【地】纪。④终结；句号。⑤【语法】长复合句，圆周句；【修】掉尾句。⑥〔*pl.*〕美词丽句；华丽的词藻。⑦学时，课时，一节课；(比赛的)一节时间。⑧【医】过程，周期。⑨〔*pl.*〕月经(期)。⑩【数】(循环小数的)循环节。⑪【乐】乐段。*the transitional* ～ 过渡时期。*the warm-up* ～【火箭】备射阶段。*the catch-words of the* ～ 现代流行话。*a turned* ～ (字母上面的)上点。*the incubation* ～ (病的)潜伏期。*monthly* ～ 月经。***at fixed* ～*s*** 定期。***at stated* ～*s*** 相隔一定时期；在一定时期。***come to a* ～** 完结。***for a* ～ *of time*** 一个时期，一些时候。***put a* ～ *to sth.*** 使某事终止；取缔某事。***round a* ～** 练句。— *a.* ①(家具、服装、建筑等)某一时代的。②(小说、戏剧等) 逼真地描写某一特定历史时代的。～ *furniture* 仿古家具。*a* ～ *novel* 描写特定历史时代的小说。— *int.*〔口〕就这样〔强调话已经讲完了 ＝That's it! That's final!〕。

per·i·o·date [peˈraiədeit] *n.*【化】高碘酸盐。

pe·ri·od·ic[1] [ˌpiəriˈɔdik] *a.* ①周期的，回归的，定期的，定时的；间歇的，时时的。②某一时期的。③【修】掉尾句的，圆周句的；美词丽句的。～ **function**【数】周期函数。～ **law**【化】周期律。～ **sentence** (主要文意最后出现的)掉尾句，圆周句〔通常指主句在最后出现的一种复合句〕。～ **structure** 循环结构。～ **table**【化】元素周期表。～ **yield(s)** 隔年收获。

per·i·od·ic[2] [ˌpəːraiˈɔdik] *a.*【化】高碘的。

pe·ri·od·i·cal [ˌpiəriˈɔdikəl] *a.* ①周期的，定期的；时常发生的，间歇的。②定期发行的，期刊的。— *n.* (日报以

外的)定期刊物,杂志. *a weekly [monthly]* 周[月]刊. **-ly** *ad.* 周期地;定期,按时.

pe·ri·o·dic·i·ty [ˌpiəriəˈdisiti] *n.* ①定期[周期]性;间发性;周期数. ②周率,频率;【电】周波;【医】定期发作;【天】定期出现;【化】周期表中的位置.

per·i·o·don·tal [ˌperiəuˈdɔntl] *a.* 【解】①牙周的. ②影响牙周齿龈、结缔组织等的.

per·i·o·don·tics [ˌperiəuˈdɔntiks] *n. pl.* 〔动词用单数〕牙周病学 (= periodontia). **-don·tic** *a.* **-don·tist** *n.* 牙周病学家,牙周病医师.

per·i·o·nych·i·um [ˌperiəuˈnikiəm] *n.* *(pl. -i·a* [-ə]*)* 指甲周边的表皮.

per·i·os·te·um [ˌperiˈɔstium] *n.* *(pl. ~s, -tea* [-tiə]*)* 【解】骨膜.

per·i·os·ti·tis [ˌperiɔˈstaitis] *n.* 【医】骨膜炎.

per·i·os·tra·cum [ˌperiˈɔstrəkəm] *n.* *(pl. -tra·ca* [-kə]*)* 【解】角质层.

per·i·o·tic [ˌperiˈəutik, -ˈɔtik] *a.* 【解,动】(内)耳周围的.

per·i·pa·tet·ic [ˌperipəˈtetik] *a.* ①走来走去的,徒步游历的,巡游的,逍遥的. ②〔P-〕亚里士多德学派的,逍遥学派的〔由古希腊哲学家亚里士多德在学园内漫步讲学而得名〕. —*n.* ①徒步游历者;跑来跑去的人;〔谑〕行商,小贩. ②〔P-〕逍遥学派的人. ③〔*pl.*〕到处走动;游历. **-i·cal·ly** *ad.*

Per·i·pa·tet·i·cism [ˌperipəˈtetisizəm] *n.* ①逍遥学派〔亚里士多德学派〕. ②〔p-〕逍遥,走动;游历习惯.

per·i·pe·tei·a, per·i·pe·ti·a [ˌperipiˈtiːə, -ˈtaiə] *n.* 剧情或命运(境遇)的巨变,突变.

pe·riph·er·al [pəˈrifərəl] *a.* ①周围的,外围的;外面的;边缘的. ②【解】(神经)末梢区域的. **-ly** *ad.*

pe·riph·er·y [pəˈrifəri] *n.* ①周围,圆周;外面,外部,外围;边缘. ②【解】(神经)末梢区域.

per·i·phrase [ˈperifreiz] *vi.,vt.* 转弯抹角地说. —*n.* = periphrasis.

pe·riph·ra·sis [pəˈrifrəsis] *n.* *(pl. -ses* [-siːz]*)* ①【修】迂说法,转弯抹角的说法. ②纡回曲折的词句.

per·i·phras·tic [ˌperiˈfræstik] *a.* ①转弯抹角的,迂回的;冗长的,啰嗦的. ②【修】迂说法的. *the ~ conjugation* 【语法】迂说法动词变化〔如不用 *went* 而用 *did go*〕. *the ~ genitive* 迂说法所有格〔如不说 Caesar's, 而说 of Caesar〕. **-ti·cal·ly** *ad.*

pe·rip·ter·al [pəˈriptərəl] *a.* ①【建】围柱式的. ②(飞机等运动物体的)周围气流区的.

pe·rip·ter·os [pəˈriptərɔs] *n.* *(pl. -oi* [-rɔi]*)* 【建】围柱殿,围柱式寺院[建筑物].

pe·rip·ter·y [pəˈriptəri] *n.* ①= peripteros. ②(飞机等运动物体的)周围气流区.

pe·rique [piˈriːk] *n.* 上等黑色烟草〔产于美国路易斯安那州〕.

per·i·sarc [ˈperisɑːk] *n.* 【动】围鞘.

per·i·scope [ˈperiskəup] *n.* 潜望镜〔潜水艇用〕;潜望镜镜头.

per·i·scop·ic, per·i·scop·i·cal [ˌperisˈkɔpik,-ikəl] *a.* ①潜望镜(用)的. ②(照相机等)大角度的,适于瞭望周围的;概观的. *a ~ drift angle sight* 潜望镜式偏航测角器. *a ~ lens* 大角度的镜头. *a ~ wind gauge* 潜望镜式风速计.

per·ish [ˈperiʃ] *vi.* ①灭亡;消灭,死去;暴卒. ②枯萎;腐烂. ③腐败,堕落. *~ in battle* 阵亡. *~ in hunger* 饿死. *~ by the sword* 〔古〕死于刀剑. —*vt.* ①毁坏;消灭;杀死;使死去. ②〔常用被动式〕使非常困苦;使麻木. *We were ~ed with cold.* 我们冻得要死. *P- the thought!* 不要说啦!得了得了! 死了心吧! 〔表示极度厌恶或反对〕. **-less** *a.* 不易死亡[消灭、枯萎、腐败]的. **-ment** *n.*

per·ish·a·ble [ˈperiʃəbl] *a.* 易腐败的;不经久的;脆弱的;会枯的;会死的. —*n.* 〔*pl.*〕易腐败的东西〔尤指食物〕. **-a·bil·i·ty** [-ˈbiliti] *n.* **-a·bly** *n.*

per·ish·er [ˈperiʃə] *n.* 〔俚〕讨厌的家伙,混蛋.

per·ish·ing [ˈperiʃiŋ] *a.* ①死的,灭亡的,枯死的. ②〔俚〕(饥饿、寒冷等)要命的,厉害的;悲惨的. ③讨人厌的,要不得的. *in ~ cold* 在极度寒冷中. —*ad.* …得要命;非常,极. *It is ~ cold today.* 今天冷得要命. **-ly** *ad.*

per·i·sperm [ˈperispəːm] *n.* 【植】外胚乳.

per·i·sphere [ˈperisfiə] *n.* ①〔美〕正圆球. ②中心周球. ③势力范围.

per·i·spo·me·non, per·i·spome [ˌperiˈspəuminən, ˈperispəum] *a.* (希腊文语法中)词尾有扬抑音符的. —*n.* *(pl. -me·na* [-nə]*)* 词尾有扬抑音符的词.

perisso- *comb. f.* 奇,奇数的,多余的: *perisso*dactyl(e).

pe·ris·so·dac·tyl·ate [pəˌrisəuˈdæktilit] *a.* 【动】奇蹄的.

pe·ris·so·dac·tyl(e) [pəˌrisəuˈdæktil] *a.* 【动】奇蹄的. —*n.* 奇蹄类动物. **-ous** *a.*

per·i·stal·sis [ˌperiˈstælsis] *n.* *(pl. -ses* [-siːz]*)* 【生理】(肠壁的)蠕动.

per·i·stal·tic [ˌperiˈstæltik] *a.* ①【生理】(肠壁)蠕动的. ②【电】在两传导体间发生的. **-ti·cal·ly** *ad.*

pe·ris·to·ma, per·i·stome [pəˈristəumə, ˈperistəum] *n.* ①【植】(藓类的)蒴齿. ②【动】螺壳孔边;口缘,唇,口围.

pe·ris·ton [pəˈristən] *n.* 人造血浆.

per·i·style [ˈperistail] *n.* 【建】周柱式;列柱廊;列柱中庭.

per·i·tec·tic [ˌperiˈtektik] *a.* 【物】包晶(体)的.

per·i·tec·toid [ˌperiˈtektɔid] *n., a.* 【物】包析(的);包析体(的).

per·i·the·ci·um [ˌperiˈθiʃiəm] *n.* *(pl. -ci·a* [-ə]*)* 【解】子囊壳. **-ci·al** *a.*

per·i·to·ne·um, per·i·to·nae·um [ˌperitəuˈniːəm] *n.* *(pl. -n(a)e·al* [-ˈniəl]*)* 【解】腹膜. **-n(a)eal** *a.*

per·i·to·ni·tis [ˌperitəˈnaitis] *n.* 【医】腹膜炎.

pe·rit·ri·chous [pəˈritrikəs] *a.* ①【植】周毛的〔指菌〕. ②【动】周生鞭毛的〔指原生动物〕. **-ly** *ad.*

pe·ri·tus [pəˈriːtəs] *n.* *(pl. -ti* [-iː]*)* 〔L.〕专家〔尤指作为顾问的神学家〕.

per·i·wig [ˈperiwig] *n.* 假发.

per·i·wig·ged [ˈperiwigd] *a.* 带假发的.

per·i·win·kle¹ [ˈperiwiŋkl] *n.* 【贝】荔枝螺,海螺,滨螺.

per·i·win·kle² [ˈperiwiŋkl] *n.* 【植】长春花.

per·jure [ˈpəːdʒə] *vt.* ①〔~ oneself〕使发假誓. ②〔用被动语态〕犯伪誓[伪证]罪. *The witness ~d himself.* 证人作假证. **-d** *a.* 发假誓的,作伪证的. **-r** *n.* 发假誓的人,作伪证者.

per·ju·ry [ˈpəːdʒəri] *n.* 【法】伪誓;伪证(罪);大谎. ***commit*** ~犯伪证罪,发假誓.

perk¹ [pəːk] *vi.* ①抬头,昂首,伸腰,突出,翘尾巴;装腔作势 *(up)*;摆架子,逞能 *(up)*. ②振作;(病后)复元 *(up)*. —*vt.* ①抬(头),伸(腰),翘(尾巴);竖(耳朵). ②打扮. ***~ it*** 傲慢,摆架子,逞能. ***~ oneself up*** 打扮;装腔作势;扬扬自得. —*a.* 〔罕〕= perky.

perk² [pəːk] *vt., vi.* 〔口〕过滤,渗透〔percolate 的缩略形式〕.

perk³ [pəːk] *n.* 〔主英口〕津贴,赏钱〔perquisite 的缩略形式〕.

Per·kin(s) [ˈpəːkin(z)] *n.* 珀金(斯)〔姓氏〕.

perk·y [ˈpəːki] *a.* ①得意扬扬的. ②装腔作势的,傲慢的,逞能的. ③鲁莽的,莽撞的. ④打扮得漂漂亮亮的.

per·lite [ˈpəːlait] *n.* ①【地】珍珠岩. ②珠光体;(=pearlite). **per·lit·ic** [pəˈlitik] *a.*

perm [pəːm] *n.* 〔口〕电烫头发 (= permanent wave). *Even a ~ has its term.* 电烫的头发也有变直的时候. —*vt.* 〔口〕给…电烫头发.

per·ma·frost [ˈpə:məfrɔ(:)st] *n.*【地】永久冻土.
per·mal·loy [ˈpə:məlɔi] *n.*【冶】透磁合金.
per·ma·nence [ˈpə:mənəns] *n.* 持久,永久,不变; 永久性,耐久性.
per·ma·nen·cy [ˈpə:mənənsi] *n.* ①= permanence. ②不变的东西; 永久的地位〔终身官职等〕, 终身事业. *I should not like it for a* ～. 我不打算干它一辈子.
per·ma·nent [ˈpə:mənənt] *a.* ①永久的,不变的,耐久的; 持久的,经久的. ②常务的,常设的 (*opp.*temporary). — *n.* 电烫发 (=～ wave). ～ **basis** 〔美〕平时定额. ～ **committee** 常务委员会. **P- Court (of International Justice)** 常设国际法庭. ～ **fortification** 永久工事. ～ **gas** 永久气体. ～ **magnet** 永久磁铁. ～ **output** 长期生产率. ～ **quadrat** 定位样方. ～ **rest camp** 〔美〕墓地. ～ **revolution** 不断革命. ～ **set** 永久变定(物); 固定伸张; 永久应变; 最后凝结. ～ **tooth** 成人齿,恒齿. ～ **wave** 电烫发. ～ **way**【铁路】轨道. **-ly** *ad.*
per·man·ga·nate [pə:ˈmæŋgənit, -neit] *n.*【化】高锰酸盐. ～ *of potassium*【化】高锰酸钾.
per·man·gan·ic [ˌpə:mænˈgænik] *a.* ～**acid**【化】高锰酸.
per·me·a·bil·i·ty [ˌpə:miəˈbiliti] *n.* ①透过性, 可透性,渗透性; 渗蚀度;【空】(气球气体的)透出量. ②【物】磁导率,磁导系数 (= magnetic ～).
per·me·a·ble [ˈpə:miəbl] *a.* 能渗透〔透过、穿过〕的 *(to)*. ～ *plastics* 可透塑料. **-a·bly** *ad.* **-ness** *n.*
per·me·am·e·ter [pə:miˈæmitə] *n.*【物】磁导计.
per·me·ance [ˈpə:miəns] *n.* ①渗入, 渗透, 充满. ②【物】磁导.
per·me·ant [ˈpə:miənt] *a.* 渗入的,渗透的,充满的.
per·me·ate [ˈpə:mieit] *vt.* ①渗入, 透过; 穿过. ②弥漫,充满; 普及. — *vi.* 渗透,渗过; 普及*(in; through; among)*. **-me·a·tion** [-ˈeiʃən] *n.*
Per·mi·an [ˈpə:miən] *a.*【地】二叠纪的; 二叠系的. — *n.* 〔the ～〕二叠纪〔系〕. *the* ～ *period* 二叠纪. *the* ～ *system*【地】二叠系.
per·mil·lage [pəˈmilidʒ] *n.* 千分率; 千分比.
per·mis·si·ble [pə(:)ˈmisəbl] *a.* ①可以允许〔许可〕的; 不碍事的. ②得到准许的. ～ *explosives*〔美〕安全炸药. ～ *load* 容许负荷. **-si·bil·i·ty** [-ˈbiliti] *n.* **-si·bly** *ad.*
per·mis·sion [pə(:)ˈmiʃən] *n.* 许,允许,答应,同意,许可,准许 *(to do)*. *Ask* ～ *of your father.* 请你父亲允许吧. ***ask for*** ～ 请求许可. ***grant*** ～ 准许. ***with*** *(your)* ～ 如果(你)允许的话. ***without*** ～ 未经许可,擅自.
per·mis·sive [pə(:)ˈmisiv] *a.* ①许可的, 准许的; 宽容的. ②自由的; 随意的. ③纵容的. *a* ～ *nod* 表示许可的点头. *a* ～ *mother* 娇惯子女的母亲. **-ly** *ad.*
per·mit [pə(:)ˈmit] *vt.* 许可, 准许,允许,答应; 默许,放任; 使可能. *P- me to explain.* 请容许我解释. *No infringement will be* ～*ed.* 不许有违. ～ *the escape of gases* 使得以漏气. — *vi.* 允许,容许 *(of)*. ～ ***of no delay*** 不可拖延〔耽搁〕. ～ ***of no excuse*** 不许推委. ***weather permitting*** 如果天气好的话. — [ˈpə:mit] *n.* ①准许证, 许可证,执照. ②许可,准许.
per·mit·tiv·i·ty [ˌpə:miˈtiviti] *n.*【电】电容率, 介电常数.
per·mut·a·ble [pə(:)ˈmju:təbl] *a.* ①能交换的; 可置换的; 可变更的. ②【数】可排列的.
per·mute [pə(:)ˈmju:t] *vt.* ①交换; 取代, 变更; 置换. ②【数】排列. ③(用滤沙)软化(水). **-ta·tion** *n.* ①交换,互换; 置换. ②【数】排列 *(permutation and combination*【数】排列组合*)*.
per·mu·tite [ˈpə:mju(:)tait] *n.* 滤(水)沙,软水沙,人造沸石.
per·mu·toid [ˈpə:mju(:)tɔid] *n.*【化】交换体.
per·ni·cious [pə:ˈniʃəs] *a.* 有害的,有毒的; 恶性的,致命的. *a climate* ～ *to health* 有害健康的气候. *a* ～ *scheme* 恶毒的阴谋. ～ **anaemia**【医】恶性贫血. **-ly** *ad.* **-ness** *n.*
per·nick·e·ty [pəˈnikəti] *a.* 〔口〕①爱挑剔的,吹毛求疵的. ②麻烦的,难应付的; 需要小心对待的.
per·noc·ta·tion [ˌpə:nɔkˈteiʃən] *n.* ①守夜, 熬夜; 彻夜不眠; 整夜不归. ②通宵祷告.
Per·nod [pεəˈnəu] 〔F.〕 法国绿茴香酒商标. — *n.*〔p-〕法国绿茴香酒.
per·o·ne·al [ˌperəˈniəl] *a.*【解】①腓骨的. ②腓骨侧的.
Per·o·no·spo·ra·cea·e [ˌperənəuspəˈreisiˌi:] *n. pl.*【植】霜霉科.
per·o·ral [pəˈɔ:rəl] *a.*【医】由口的; 口边的.
per·o·rate [ˈperəreit] *vi.* ①结束演说, 下结论. ②作长篇演说,罗唆地讲. **-ra·tion** [-ˈreiʃən] *n.* ①(演说等的)结论,结尾话. ②夸夸其谈的演说. **-ra·tor** *n.* 作长篇演说的人,罗罗唆唆讲的人.
pe·ro·sis [piˈrəusis] *n.* *(pl. -ses* [-si:z]*)* (小鸡的)骨短粗病. **pe·rot·ic** [-ˈrɔtik] *a.*
per·ox·i·dase [pəˈrɔksideis,-deiz] *n.*【化】过氧化物酶.
per·ox·i·da·tion [pəˌrɔksiˈdeiʃən] *n.*【化】过氧化反应.
per·ox·ide [pəˈrɔksaid] *n.* ①【化】过氧化物. ②〔口〕过氧化氢. — *vt.* 〔口〕用过氧化氢漂白(头发等). ～ *blonde* 〔美俚〕漂白出一头金发的女人. ～ *of hydrogen* 过氧化氢〔漂白、消毒剂〕.
peroxy- *comb. f.* 过氧: *peroxy*sulfate.
per·ox·y·sul·phate [pəˈrɔksiˈsʌlfeit] *n.*【化】过(氧)硫酸盐.
per·pend[1] [ˈpə:pənd] *n.* 【建】贯石(突出墙两面的长石); 穿墙石,控石; 繋石. *a* ～ *wall* 单石薄墙.
per·pend[2] [pə:ˈpend] *vt., vi.* 〔古〕细细考虑; 审议.
per·pen·dic·u·lar [ˌpə:pənˈdikjulə] *a.* ①垂直的; 直立的;【数】成直角的,正交的. ②矗立的; 险陡的,险峻的. ③〔P-〕【建】垂直式的. ④〔谑〕直站着的. *a* ～ *cliff* 绝壁. *a* ～ *line* 垂(直)线. *a* ～ *plate* 水平板. — *n.* ①垂(直)线; 垂直面. ②垂直测器, 锤规. ③直立,直立姿势; 廉直. ④〔P-〕【建】垂直式建筑. ⑤绝壁. ⑥〔俚〕站着的进餐. ***be out of (the)*** ～ 倾斜. **the** ～【数】垂直,正交. **-ly** *ad.* **-u·lar·i·ty** [-ˈlæriti] *n.*
per·pe·trate [ˈpə:pitreit] *vt.* ①施(恶行),做(坏事),犯(过失等); 犯(罪). ②胡说. ～ *a pun [joke]* 〔口〕(不考虑环境情况)瞎讲俏皮话,乱开玩笑,瞎打哈哈. **per·pe·tra·ble** [ˈpə:pitrəbl] *a.* 能做坏事(等)的. **-pe·tra·tion** [-ˈtreiʃən] *n.* 为非作歹, 行凶, 犯罪. **-pe·tra·tor** *n.* 犯人,凶手; 作恶者.
per·pet·u·al [pəˈpetjuəl] *a.* ①永久的, 永恒的, 无穷的; 不断的,不绝的; (官职等)终身的. ②【园艺】四季开花的. ③〔口〕不停的. *a* ～ *calender* 万年历. *a* ～ *lease* 永久租地权. — *n.*【园艺】四季开花的植物; 多年生草. ～ **motion**【物】永恒运动. ～ **rose** 四季蔷薇. **-ly** *ad.*
per·pet·u·ate [pə(:)ˈpetjueit] *vt.* 使永久存在〔继续〕; 使不朽,使不灭.
per·pet·u·a·tion, per·pet·u·ance [pəˌpetjuˈeiʃən, pəˈpetjuəns] *n.* 永存; 不朽, 不灭. ～ *of testimony*【法】证据的保存.
per·pet·u·a·tor [pəˈpetjueitə] *n.* 使永存者, 使不朽的人.
per·pet·u·i·ty [ˌpə:piˈtju(:)iti] *n.* ①永存; 不灭; 不朽; 永恒, 永远. ②永存物. ③终身养老金〔退休金〕. ④【法】永久所有权; (产业的)永久〔长期〕不得转让; 永久〔长期〕不得转让的产业. ⑤单利累计到等于本金的时期. *lease in* ～ 永久租地权. ***in [to, for]*** ～ 永远,不朽.
per·plex [pəˈpleks] *vt.* 〔多用被动结构〕①使窘困,使为难,使狼狈. ②使纠缠,弄复杂化,使混乱,使纠缠不清. ～ *an issue* 使问题复杂化. *be* ～*ed with the question* 被问题纠缠住.

per·plexed [pə'plekst] *a.* ①为难的，困惑的，不知道怎样才好的。②混乱的，纠缠不清的，疙疙瘩瘩的，复杂化的。*a* ～ *air* 为难的样子。*a* ～ *question* 错综复杂的问题。**-ly** *ad.* **-ness** [pə'pleksidnis] *n.*

per·plex·ing [pə'pleksiŋ] *a.* ①使人困惑的；使人为难的。②麻烦的，复杂的。**-ly** *ad.*

per·plex·i·ty [pə'pleksiti] *n.* ①窘困，困惑，为难；窘态，难局。②使人困惑的事物。③纠纷，混乱。

per pro(c). =〔L.〕*per procurationem* (= by proxy) 代表，代理经由。

per·qui·site ['pə:kwizit] *n.* ①临时津贴，临时收入；〔英〕(给仆役等的)赏钱，酒钱。②【法】(庄园领主的)不定期收入；特权享有的东西。

per·qui·si·tion [ˌpə:kwi'ziʃən] *n.* (根据搜查证进行的)彻底搜查。

per·ron ['perən] *n.* 〔F.〕【建】(大建筑物门前的)露天台阶〔石阶，露天梯级〕。

per·ru·qui·er [pe'ru:kiə] *n.* 〔F.〕假发师；理发师。

Per·ry ['peri] *n.* 佩里〔姓氏，男子名〕。

per·ry ['peri] *n.* 〔英〕梨酒。

Pers. = ①Persia. ②Persian.

pers. = ①person. ②personal. ③personnel.

per·salt ['pə:ˌsɔ:lt] *n.* 【化】过盐。

perse [pə:s] *n.*, *a.* 深灰色(的)，深紫色(的)。

per·se·cute ['pə:sikju:t] *vt.* ①(因政治、宗教上意见不同而进行)迫害，摧残。②强求，死缠着要；使为难，困扰。*Corpenicus was terribly* ～*d for his scientific theory.* 哥白尼由于其科学理论而遭到严酷的迫害。～ *sb. with questions* 给某人出难题。

per·se·cu·tion [ˌpə:si'kju:ʃən] *n.* ①迫害；残害；【宗】迫害时期。②苛求；困扰。*be fearless in face of overt or covert* ～ 在明枪暗箭的迫害面前勇敢无畏。***indulge in*** ～ ***of*** 对…大肆进行迫害。

per·se·cu·tor ['pə:sikju:tə] *n.* 迫害者，虐待者。

Per·se·ids ['pə:si:idz] *n. pl.* 【天】英仙(座)流星群，八月流星群。

Per·seph·o·ne [pə:'sefəni] *n.* 【希神】普西芬尼〔阴间女王，冥后〕。

Per·sep·o·lis [pə:'sepəlis] *n.* 珀塞波利斯〔波斯古都〕。

Per·seus ['pə:sju:s,-sjəs] *n.* ①【希神】柏修斯〔宙斯和达那厄 (Danae) 之子，杀死女怪美杜莎 (Medusa) 的神〕。②【天】〔the ～〕英仙座。

per·se·ver·ance [ˌpə:si'viərəns] *n.* ①坚定，不屈不挠；坚持。②【宗】持续蒙受天恩。

per·se·ver·ant [ˌpə:si'viərənt] *a.* 能坚持的；愿意坚持的。

per·sev·er·ate [pə(:)'sevəreit] *vi.* 【医】患持续言语症。

per·sev·er·a·tion [pə(:)ˌsevə'reiʃən] *n.* ①【医】持续言语〔指言语反复不止的病态〕。②【医】(无法停止的)专想某事。**-a·tive** [-reitiv] *a.*

per·se·vere [ˌpə:si'viə] *vi.* 忍耐，熬住；百折不回，不屈不挠，坚持 *(in; with)*.～ *with a task* 对工作坚持不懈。～ *in one's efforts* 坚持努力。— *vt.* 支持，支撑；鼓舞。*unflagging faith that had* ～*d him* 曾经支撑过他的不可动摇的信念。

per·se·ver·ing [ˌpə:si'viəriŋ] *a.* 坚定的，不屈不挠的，百折不回的。**-ly** *ad.* 坚定地。

Per·shing ['pə:ʃiŋ] *n.* 珀欣〔姓氏〕。

Per·sia ['pə:ʃə] *n.* 波斯〔现称 Iran 伊朗，亚洲〕。

Per·sian ['pə:ʃən] *a.* 波斯的；波斯人的，波斯语的。— *n.* ①波斯人；波斯语。②波斯绸。③〔*pl.*〕百叶窗 (=～ blinds). ***the*** ～ ***Gulf*** 波斯湾。～ **blinds** 百叶窗。～ **carpet [rug]** 波斯地毯。～ **cat** 波斯猫。～ **lamb** 波斯羔；波斯羔皮。～ **lilac** 波斯丁香，花叶丁香。～ **powder** 杀虫粉。～ **walnut** 胡桃。～ **yellow (rose)** 波斯臭蔷薇。

per·si·ennes [ˌpə:si'enz] *n.* 〔*pl.*〕百叶窗。

per·si·flage [ˌpɛəsi'flɑ:ʒ] *n.* 挖苦，戏弄，嘲弄，揶揄。

per·si·fleur [ˌpɛəsi'flə:] *n.* 爱挖苦人的人。

per·sim·mon [pə(:)'simən] *n.* 柿子；柿树；美洲柿。***be not a huckleberry to one's*** ～〔美〕不能和…相比。***bring down the*** ～〔美〕得奖，拿锦旗。***rake up [walk off with] the*** ～〔美〕把赢的钱带走；得奖。***That's (all)*** ～***s!***〔美〕那好极了！***The longest pole knocks the most*** ～***s.***〔美〕竿子最长打的柿子最多，强者常胜。

per·sist [pə(:)'sist] *vi.* ①坚持，固执 *(in)*. ②继续存在，存留。～ *in working when ill* 病中坚持工作。*He* ～*s in his bad habit.* 他坚决不改他的坏习惯。

per·sist·ence, per·sist·en·cy [pə'sistəns,-si] *n.* ①坚持；固执；顽固。②持续性；持久；存留。③【无】持久性；(荧光屏上余辉的)保留时间。～ *of energy* 能量守恒。～ *of vision* 视觉暂留。

per·sist·ent [pə'sistənt] *a.* ①坚持的，百折不挠的；顽固的；持久不变的。②持续性的；【植】宿存的 (*opp.* deciduous)；【动】持续生存的。**-ly** *ad.*

per·snick·e·ty [pə(:)'snikiti] *a.* 〔口〕①过于讲究的；挑肥拣瘦的；爱小题大作的。②认真对待的，要求非常仔细处理的 (= pernickety).

per·son ['pə:sn] *n.* ①人；个人。②〔蔑〕家伙。③容貌；身体，人身；人格；本人，自身。④(戏剧、小说的)人物；〔常带有修饰语〕重要人物。⑤【动】个体；【语法】人称；【法】自然人；法人；【神】(三位一体的)位。★表示概称的人时，女性不用 man 而用 person. *She is an attractive* ～. 她是一个吸引人的人。*a young* ～ 年轻人，〔常指〕年轻女人。*He has a fine* ～. 他风度很好。*offenses against the* ～ 暴行。*the natural* ～【法】自然人。*the artificial [legal, juridical]* ～【法】法人。～*s of the play* 出场人物。*chief* ～*s of the state* 国家的重要人物。***accept the*** ～ ***of*** 偏袒…，偏爱…。***in one's own [proper]*** ～ 亲自。***in*** ～ ①亲自。②身体上；外貌上。***in the*** ～ ***of*** ①叫做…的人。②体现于…。③以…的资格；代表…。***no less a*** ～ ***than*** 身分不低于。***respect of*** ～***s*** 偏袒；区别对待；徇私。～ **to-**～ ① *a.* 私人间的；(长途电话)指名受话人受话后才索费的。② *ad.* 个人间地；面对面地。

per·so·na [pə:'səunə] *n.* (*pl.* ***-nae*** [-ni:])〔L.〕①人。②(小说、戏剧中的)人物，角色。③〔*pl.* ～***s***〕(在社交场合的)伪装外表。***dramatis*** ～ 剧中人。***in propria*** [in'prəupriə] ～ 亲自。～ ***(non) grata*** ['greitə] (不)受人欢迎的人〔指外交官而言〕。

per·son·a·ble ['pə:sənəbl] *a.* 容貌漂亮的；风度好的。**-ness** *n.*

per·son·age ['pə:sənidʒ] *n.* ①人，个人。②名士；显贵。③(历史、小说、戏剧中的)人物，角色。④〔谑〕风度。*a very singular* ～ 特号怪人。*public* ～*s* 社会贤达。

per·son·al ['pə:sənl] *a.* ①个人的，私人的；一身的，自身的。②本人的，亲自的。③身体的，容貌的。④人身的；涉及个人的；人物批评的；攻击个人的。⑤【语法】人称的。⑥【法】属于个人的，可动的 (*opp.* real). ⑦(信件)亲启的。～ *matters [affairs]* 私事。*(a)* ～ *acquaintance* 个人的相识。*a* ～ *interview* 亲自接见。～ *appearance* 容貌，风度。～ *abuse* = *a* ～ *affront [attack]* 人身攻击。***become*** ～ ***in a dispute*** 在争论中开始攻击〔批评〕个人。— *n.* ①个人，人员。②【语法】人称代名词。③〔*pl.*〕对人批评，人身攻击。④〔*pl.*〕(报刊上的)人事栏；分类人事广告版。⑤〔*pl.*〕【法】动产。⑥〔*pl.*〕【影】(演员的)初次表演。～ **action**【法】对人诉讼，要求赔偿损失的诉讼 (*opp.* real action). ～ **column** (报纸的)人事消息栏。～**effects**【法】个人财产，个人所有物。～ **equation [error]** ①【天】(观测上的)(个)人(误)差。②(一般的)个人倾向，个性。～ **foul**【体】撞人犯规。～ **pronoun**【语法】人称代名词。～ **property [estate]**【法】动产。～ **rights** 人权。～ **service**【法】直接送达。～ **shopper** (商店等处)代客挑选货物的人。

per·son·al·ism ['pə:snəlizm] *n.* 个人至上论。**-al·ist**

①*n.* 个人至上论者. ②*a.* 个人至上论的. **-al·is·tic** *a.*

per·son·al·i·ty [ˌpəːsəˈnæliti] *n.* ①人的存在; 个性,【心】性格; 人格,品格,做人,为人; 容貌. ②(有名)人物. ③〔常 *pl.*〕人物批评; 攻击个人(的材料). ④【地】地势,地相. ⑤〔罕〕动产. *a man with little* ~ 个性不强的人. *a man of strong* ~个性强的人. *double [dual]* ~【心】双重人格. ~ **cult** 个人崇拜.

per·son·al·ize [ˈpəːsnəlaiz] *vt.* ①使个人化. ②使成个人所有物. ③在(物品)上标出姓名〔记号〕. ④使人格化;【修】拟(某物)为人,使…拟人化. **-al·i·za·tion** *n.*

per·son·al·ly [ˈpəːsənəli] *ad.* ①亲自地. ②作为个人,我个人,就自己而言. ③作为一个人.

per·son·al·ty [ˈpəːsənəlti] *n.*【法】动产 (*opp.* realty).

per·son·ate [ˈpəːsəneit] *vt.* ①扮演,饰(剧中某角). ②假装;〔英〕冒充,冒…的名. ③使(艺术品等)带有个性. ④使人格化. — *a.*【植】假面状的.

per·son·a·tion [ˌpəːsənˈeiʃən] *n.* ①扮装,假装; 扮演. ②假冒身份,冒名; 化身.

per·son·a·tor [ˈpəːsəneitə] *n.* ①假装者; 演员. ②冒名者.

per·son·i·fi·ca·tion [pə(ː)ˌsɔnifiˈkeiʃən] *n.* ①拟人,人格化;【修】拟人法. ②化身,典型; 活例. ③体现;〔*pl.*〕表演. *the* ~ *of patriotism* 爱国典型. *an artistic* ~ *of beauty* 美在艺术(作品)上的具体表现.

per·son·i·fy [pə(ː)ˈsɔnifai] *vt.* ①把(某物)看做人,拟(某物)为人; 赋与…以人性,使人格化. ②是…的化身,象征; 体现. ③= personate.

per·son·nel [ˌpəːsəˈnel] *n.* ①全体人员,职员,班底 (*opp.* materiel). ②人事(部门). *the* ~ *of the new cabinet* 现内阁的班底. *the bureau of* ~ 人事局. ~ *department* 人事处〔科〕.

per·sorp·tion [pə(ː)ˈsɔpʃən] *n.*【化】吸混(作用).

per·spec·tive[1] [pə(ː)ˈspektiv] *a.* (按照)透视画法的; 透视的. *a* ~ *drawing* 透视画. *a* ~ *glass* 望远镜. — *n.* ①透视画法; 透视画; 配景, 远近配置. ②远景,景色,眼界. ③配合, 适当比例. ④洞察力, 眼力. ⑤观点,看法. ⑥希望, 前途. *aerial* ~ (用色调浓淡表现的)空中透视画法. *angular [linear]* ~ 斜线〔直线〕透视画法. ***in*** ~按照透视画法的〔地〕; 展望中的〔地〕; 正确的〔地〕;【数】连成一行(*see things in* ~ 正确地看待事物). ***out of*** ~ 不合透视画法; 不正确地. **-ly** *ad.* 按照透视法; 远近分明地.

per·spec·tive[2] [pə(ː)ˈspektiv] *n.* 透镜; 望远镜.

per·spex [ˈpəːspeks] *n.* 塑胶玻璃,透明塑胶,【化】〔聚合的 2—甲基丙烯酸甲酯〕.

per·spi·ca·cious [ˌpəːspiˈkeiʃəs] *a.* ①颖悟的; 敏锐的; 聪明的. ②〔古〕眼光锐利的. **-ly** *ad.* **-ness** *n.*

per·spi·cac·i·ty [ˌpəːspiˈkæsiti] *n.* 颖悟,聪明; 敏锐,慧眼.

per·spi·cu·i·ty [ˌpəːspiˈkju(ː)iti] *n.* ①(语言、文章等的)明晰,清楚. ②〔口〕= perspicacity.

per·spic·u·ous [pə(ː)ˈspikjuəs] *a.* ①明白易懂的,清楚的; 说话清楚的. ②〔罕〕聪明的. **-ly** *ad.* **-ness** *n.*

per·spi·ra·tion [ˌpəːspəˈreiʃən] *n.* ①出汗; 发汗(作用). ②汗(水).

per·spir·a·to·ry [pəsˈpaiərətəri] *a.* (引起)排汗的.

per·spire [pəsˈpaiə] *vi., vt.* 排(汗); 出(汗); 发(汗).

per·suad·a·ble [pə(ː)ˈsweidəbl] *a.* 能说服的; 可使相信的. **-a·bly** *ad.*

per·suade [pə(ː)ˈsweid] *vt.* 说服,劝服; 使相信. ~ *sb. to do [into doing]* 劝某人作某事. ~ *sb. of [that]* 使某人相信…. ~ *oneself* 信,确信. *I am* ~*d of his innocence.* 我相信他是无罪的. — *vi.* 被说服. *The boy* ~*s easily.* 这孩子听劝.

per·suad·er [pə(ː)ˈsweidə] *n.* ①劝说者,说服的人. ②〔*pl.*〕〔俚〕踢马刺;〔美俚〕威慑物; 手枪. ***clap in the*** ~***s*** 用踢马刺踢马.

per·sua·si·ble [pəˈsweisibl] *a.* = persuadable. **-si·bil·i·ty** [-ˈbiliti] *n.*

per·sua·sion [pə(ː)ˈsweiʒən] *n.* ①说服,劝导. ②说服力; 劝说的话〔论点〕. ③确信,信念; 信仰,信条. ④(持某种信仰的)教派. ⑤〔口、谑〕人种, 种类; 性别; 阶级;〔美〕国籍. *It is my private* ~ *that he is mad.* 我个人认为他是个疯子. *a man of the Christian* ~ 基督教徒. *a man of the artist* ~〔谑〕艺术家. *the male* ~〔谑〕男性.

per·sua·sive, per·sua·so·ry [pə(ː)ˈsweisiv, -səri] *a.* ①有说服本领的, 嘴巧的. ②劝导性的; 劝诱的. — *n.* 动机,诱因; 劝告. **-ly** *ad.* **-ness** *n.*

per·sul·fate, per·sul·phate [pə(ː)ˈsʌlfeit] *n.*【化】过(二)硫酸盐.

per·sul·fu·ric, per·sul·phu·ric [ˌpəːsʌlˈfjuərik] *a.* ~ **acid**【化】过硫酸.

PERT [pəːt] 〔 *P(rogram) E(valuation and) R(eview) T(echnique)*〕 程序计算检查系统〔将一系列互相依赖的事情按照适当的程序安排, 以便最迅速最节约地完成一个(工程)项目〕.

pert [pəːt] *a.* ①冒失的,没规矩的. ②〔美口〕活泼的; 敏捷的. ③(言语等)辛辣的,唐突的. ④(衣饰等)整齐时髦的. **-ly** *ad.* **-ness** *n.*

pert. = pertaining.

per·tain [pə(ː)ˈtein] *vi.* ①附属,属于 *(to)*. ②关于,有关 *(to)*. ③适合,相配 *(to)*. *It does not* ~ *to you to instruct him.* 你不适合教训他.

per·tain·ing [pə(ː)ˈteiniŋ] *a.* 与…有关系的,附属的…, …固有的 *(to)*. *the informations* ~*ing to the case* 有关这一事件的情报. *the infirmities* ~ *to old age* 老年常有的毛病. — *n.* 〔常 *pl.*〕附属(物).

Perth [pəːθ] *n.* 珀斯〔澳大利亚城市〕.

per·ti·na·cious [ˌpəːtiˈneiʃəs] *a.* ①坚持的,顽强的,不屈不挠的; 孜孜不倦的. ②顽固的; 难消除的. **per·ti·nac·i·ty** [-ˈnæsiti] *n.* 执拗,顽固,顽强.

per·ti·nence, per·ti·nen·cy [ˈpəːtinəns, -si] *n.* 恰当,适当; 相关. *a speech without* ~ 文不对题的演讲.

per·ti·nent [ˈpəːtinənt] *a.* ①恰当的,贴切的,中肯的. ②所论的,所指的; 相干的; 和…有关系的,关于…的 *(to)*. ~ *details* 有关的细节. ~ *reply* 得当的回答. *evidences* ~ *to the case* 与案件有关的证据. — *n.* 〔常 *pl.*〕附属物; 参考. **-ly** *ad.*

per·turb [pə(ː)ˈtəːb] *vt.* ①扰乱, 搅乱; 使混乱〔慌张〕,使不安. ②【天】使摄动. **-a·tive** *a.*

per·turb·ance [pəˈtəːbəns] *n.* = perturbation.

per·tur·ba·tion [ˌpəːtəːˈbeiʃən] *n.* ①慌张, 动摇; 混乱. ②狼狈,不安, 焦虑. ③引起不安〔混乱〕的事物; 引起动摇的原因. ④【天】摄动;【物】微扰. **-al** *a.*

per·tus·sis [pə(ː)ˈtʌsis] *n.* 【医】百日咳. **-tus·sal** [-ˈtʌsəl] *a.*

per·ty [ˈpəːti] *a.*〔美卑〕= pretty.

Pe·ru [pəˈruː,piˈruː] *n.* 秘鲁〔拉丁美洲〕.

Peru., Peruv. =Peruvian.

pe·ruke [pəˈruːk] *n.* 长假发. — *vt.* 装(假发).

pe·rus·al [pəˈruːzəl] *n.* ①熟读,精读,细读. ②〔古〕研讨; 仔细察看. *the* ~ *of a letter* 读信.

pe·ruse [pəˈruːz] *vt.* ①熟读,精读; 细读; 读. ②〔古〕研讨; 仔细察看. **-r** *n.* 细读者; 阅读者.

Pe·ru·vi·an [pəˈruːvjən] *a.* 秘鲁(人)的; 秘鲁文化的. — *n.* 秘鲁人. ~ **bark**【植】金鸡纳(树)皮.

per·vade [pə(ː)ˈveid] *vt.* 扩大,蔓延,普及,弥漫,充满; 渗透; 发生影响; 在…当中盛行. *Weariness* ~*d his whole body.* 他全身疲倦. **-va·sion** [pə(ː)ˈveiʒən] *n.*

per·va·sive [pəːˈveisiv] *a.* 扩大的; 普及的, 遍布的; 贯彻的,渗透的; 弥漫的. **-ly** *ad.* **-ness** *n.*

per·verse [pə(ː)ˈvəːs] *a.* ①乖张的, 脾气警扭的; 倔强的,刚愎易怒的; (东西)麻烦的. ②邪恶的; 不正当的,堕落的. ③违背意愿的. ④【法】(判决等)不合法的,不当的. —*n.*【数、医】倒错. ~ *action* 倒行逆施. ~ **verdict**【法】不当判决 **-ly** *ad.* 丧心病狂地. **-ness** *n.*

per·ver·sion [pə(ː)ˈvəːʃən] *n.* ①曲解; 误用, 滥用; 逆用. ②恶化; 败坏, 堕落. ③【数、医】倒错, 颠倒;【心】性反常行为. *sexual* ~ 性变态.

per·ver·si·ty [pə(ː)ˈvəːsiti] *n.* ①邪恶; 堕落; 反常. ②倔强; 乖僻, 刚愎.

per·ver·sive [pə(ː)ˈvəːsiv] *a.* ①弄颠倒的, 反常的. ②曲解的 *(of)*. ③误人的, 把人带坏的.

per·vert [pə(ː)ˈvəːt] *vt.* ①使反常; 颠倒. ②误用, 滥用; 逆用; 曲解; 误解. ③使堕落, 带坏, 诱惑. — *vi.* 变坏, 走邪路, 堕落; 变成背教者 *(to)*. —[ˈpəːvəːt] *n.* ①走入邪路者, 堕落者. ②背教者; 变质者; 反常者; 【心】(特指)性反常者. **-er** *n.* = pervert *(n.)*.

per·vert·ed [pəˈvəːtid] *a.* ①不正当的, 堕落的, 邪恶的. ②性欲反常的. ③误解的, 曲解的, 歪曲的. **-ly** *ad.* **-ness** *n.*

per·vert·i·ble [pəˈvəːtibl] *a.* ①能曲解的, 易被误解的. ②能滥用的. ③能被带上邪路的; 易反常的. **-i·bil·i·ty** [-ˈbiliti] *n.* **-i·bly** *ad.*

per·vi·ous [ˈpəːviəs, -vjəs] *a.* ①能通过的; (光等)能透过的 *(to)*; 可渗透的. ②能了解的, (对道理等)能懂的; (对影响等) 能接受的; 服从的 *(to)*. ③【动】开着的, 有孔的; 【植】开通的. *Glass is* ~ *to light.* 玻璃能透光. ~ **bed** 透水层. **-ness** *n.* 浸透〔通透〕性.

pes [piːz, peis] *n.* *(pl.* ***pe·des*** [ˈpiːdiːz, ˈpediːz]*)*【动】足, 脚.

Pe·sach [ˈpeisɑːh] *n.* (犹太人的)逾越节 (=Passover).

pe·sade [pəˈseid, -zɑːd] *n.* 【马术】腾空〔马前足跃起后足直立的姿势〕.

Pes·ca·do·res [ˌpeskəˈdɔːriz] *n.* 〔*pl.*〕"佩斯卡多尔列岛"〔某些外国人沿用的殖民主义者对我国澎湖列岛的称呼〕.

pe·se·ta [pəˈsetə] *n.* 比塞塔〔西班牙货币单位〕.

pes·e·wa [ˈpesiwɑː] *n.* *(pl. ~(s))* 比塞瓦〔加纳的货币单位, 等于 1/100 塞地〕.

Pe·sha·war [pəˈʃɔːə] *n.* 白沙瓦〔巴基斯坦城市〕.

pes·ky [ˈpeski] *a.* 〔美口〕麻烦的, 讨厌的.

pe·so [ˈpeisəu] *n.* *(pl. ~s)* 比索〔拉丁美洲一些国家和菲律宾的货币单位〕.

pes·sa·ry [ˈpesəri] *n.* 【医】子宫托; 子宫帽; 阴道药栓. *an uterine* ~【医】子宫环.

pes·si·mal [ˈpesiməl] *a.* 最坏的 (*opp.* optimal).

pes·si·mism [ˈpesimizəm] *n.* 悲观, 悲观主义, 厌世主义 (*opp.* optimism).

pes·si·mist [ˈpesimist] *n.* 悲观者, 悲观主义者; 厌世者.

pes·si·mis·tic [ˌpesiˈmistik] *a.* 悲观的, 厌世的; 悲观主义的. *take a* ~ *view of* …对…抱悲观见解. **-cal·ly** *ad.* 悲观地.

pes·si·mize [ˈpesimaiz] *vi.* 悲观; 抱悲观主义.

pest [pest] *n.* ①〔古〕疫病; 鼠疫, 黑死病. ②有害动〔植〕物, 害虫. ③讨厌的人, 害人虫. *a garden* ~ 植物寄生虫. *insect* ~*s* 害虫. *He's a regular* ~. 他是一个十足的坏蛋. ***P- (up)on him!*** 〔诅咒语〕瘟死他! ~**hole** 传染病地区; 瘟疫区. ~**-house**【史】(尤指鼠疫病人的) 隔离医院; (一般传染病人的)隔离医院, 传染病医院.

Pes·ta·loz·zi [ˌpestəˈlɔtsi] 海因利希·倍斯特洛齐〔1746—1827, 提倡实物教学法的瑞士教育学家〕. **-zi·an** [-ən] *a.*, *n.* 主张实物教授法的(人).

pes·ter [ˈpestə] *vt.* 使烦恼, 使为难, 折磨; 纠缠. *be* ~*ed with midges* 给小蚊子烦死.

pes·ti·cide [ˈpestisaid] *n.* 杀虫剂, 农药. **-ti·cid·al** *a.*

pes·tif·er·ous [pesˈtifərəs] *a.* ①传染性的; 得了疫病的. ②有毒的, 有害的; 危险的; 邪恶的, 危害社会的. ③〔美口〕讨厌的, 烦死人的, 纠缠不休的. **-ly** *ad.* **-ness** *n.*

pes·ti·lence [ˈpestiləns] *n.* ①鼠疫; 恶疫, 时疫, 流行病. ②祸害, 洪水猛兽〔指学说等〕. ③伤风败德之事.

pes·ti·lent [ˈpestilənt] *a.* ①(对社会等)有害的, 破坏性的; 弊病多的. ②〔口〕讨厌的, 烦死人的. ③引起传染病的; 危险的, 致疫的. **-ly** *ad.*

pes·ti·len·tial [ˌpestiˈlenʃəl] *a.* ①传染病(性质)的, 发生〔传布〕瘟疫的. ②(对道德等)有害的, 弊端多的. ③〔口〕讨厌的; 无法无天的. **-ly** *ad.*

pes·tle [ˈpestl, ˈpesl] *n.* 乳钵槌, 碾槌, 杵. ***mortar and*** ~ 杵和臼, 乳钵和乳钵槌. — *vt.*, *vi.* (用槌)擂, (用杵)捣; 研碎.

pes·tol·o·gy [pesˈtɔlədʒi] *n.* 害虫学; 鼠疫学.

pet[1] [pet] *n.* ①供玩赏的动物; 爱兽, 爱畜. ②爱物; 爱子; 受宠爱的人; 宝贝儿. — *a.* ①心爱的. ②表示亲昵的. ③得意的, 拿手的. ④〔谑〕第一号的, 特别的. *a* ~ *name* 爱称, 昵称〔如称 Robert 为 Bob 或Rob 之类〕. *my* ~ *theory [plan]* 我的一贯主张〔得意计划〕. *a* ~ *and darling work* 得意之作. ***make a*** ~ ***of*** 把…当作宠儿; 宠爱, 爱. ***one's*** ~ ***aversion*** 最讨厌的东西. — *vt.* 爱, 宠爱, 钟爱; 娇养; 爱抚. — *vi.* 〔美俚〕拥抱, 亲嘴, 爱抚.

pet[2] [pet] *n.* 不高兴; 烦恼; 生气. ***in a*** ~ 不高兴, 烦恼. ~ ***peeve*** 〔美谑〕痛处; 患处; 心病, 弱点. ***take the*** ~ 平白无故地发脾气, 烦恼. — *vi.* 生气, 不开心.

pet. = petroleum.

Pet = Peter.

pet·al [ˈpetl] *n.* 【植】花瓣.

pet·al·ine [ˈpetəlain] *a.* 花瓣(状)的.

pet·al·ite [ˈpetəlait] *n.* 【矿】透锂长石.

pet·al(l)ed [ˈpetld] *a.* 有花瓣的, …瓣的. *five-*~ (花)五瓣的.

pet·al·o·dy [ˈpetəlˌəudi] *n.* 【植】花瓣状的.

pet·al·oid [ˈpetəlɔid] *a.* 花瓣似的, 花瓣状的; 由花瓣形成的.

pet·al·ous [ˈpetələs] *a.* 有花瓣的.

pe·tard [peˈtɑːd] *n.* ① (古代攻城等用的) 炸药包. ②大花炮. ***be hoist with [by] one's own*** ~ 害人反害己, 作法自毙, 搬起石头砸自己的脚.

pet·a·sos, pet·a·sus [ˈpetəsəs] *n.* ①(古希腊、罗马人戴的)阔边帽. ②【希神】天神赫耳墨斯 (Hermes) 的有翼帽.

pet-cock [ˈpetˈkɔk] *n.* 【机】小型旋塞; 油门, 汽门; 手压开关; 龙头.

Pete [piːt] *n.* 皮特〔男子名 Peter 的昵称〕.

pe·te·chi·a [piˈtiːkiə] *n.* *(pl.* ***-chi·ae*** [-iː]*)*【医】瘀斑, 瘀点. **-te·chi·al** *a.*

pete·man [ˈpiːtmən] *n.* *(pl.* ***-men****)* 〔美俚〕强盗; 撬保险箱的强盗.

Pe·ter [piːtə] *n.* ①彼得〔男子名〕. ②【圣】彼得〔耶稣十二门徒之一〕; (基督教《圣经》中的)《彼得书》. ***Blue*** ~【海】开船旗. ~ ***Funk*** 〔美〕(拍卖者等的)囮子. ~ ***Pan*** 彼得·潘〔苏格兰剧作家Barrie剧作中永远不会长大成人的主角〕; 天真而不懂事的成年人; (儿童或妇女衣服上的)小圆领. ~***'s fish*** 胸鳍两旁有黑斑的鱼. ~***'s pence***【英史】每户每年呈交罗马教皇的税金; 天主教徒自愿献给教皇的年金. ***rob*** ~ ***to pay Paul*** 借债还债; 抢甲济乙; 移东补西.

pe·ter[1] [ˈpiːtə] *vi.* 〔口〕①(水流、矿脉等)逐渐枯竭; 消耗掉 *(out)*. ②(渐渐)消失 *(out)*; 终止.

pe·ter[2] [ˈpiːtə] *n.* 〔美俚〕①保险箱. ②单人牢房. ③麻醉品.

pe·ter·man [ˈpiːtəmən] *n.* ①渔夫. ②〔俚〕撬保险箱的强盗; 窃贼; 撬保险箱器具.

Pe·ters [ˈpiːtəz] *n.* 彼得斯〔姓氏, 男子名〕.

Pe·ters·burg [ˈpiːtəzbəːg] *n.* 彼得堡〔苏联城市列宁格勒的旧称〕.

pe·ter·sham [ˈpiːtəʃəm] *n.* ①靛青珠皮大衣呢; 靛青珠皮呢大衣. ②楞条丝带〔棉带〕.

pet·i·o·lar [ˈpetiələ] *a.* 【植】叶柄的; 生在叶柄上的; 从

叶柄上伸出的. ②【动】(昆虫)柄的.

pet·i·o·late(d) [ˈpetiəleitid] *a.* ①有叶柄的. ②(昆虫)具柄的.

pet·i·ole [ˈpetiəul] *n.* ①【植】叶柄. ②【动】(昆虫的)柄,腹柄.

pet·i·o·lule [ˈpetiəljuːl, -əluːl] *n.* ①【植】小叶柄. ②(昆虫的)小柄.

pe·tit, pe·tit [pəˈtiː,ˈpeti] *a.* 〔F.〕小的;次要的;没有价值的,琐碎的. ~ ***bourgeois*** [ˈbuəʒwɑː] 小资产阶级. ~ ***four*** [fɔː] 糖霜小块蛋糕. ~ ***maître*** [ˈmeitr] 花花公子,纨袴子. ~ ***mal*** [ˈmæl] 轻癫痫. ~ ***point*** ①小花边编织法. ②织景画. ~ ***souper*** [ˈsuːpei] 二三知己朋友的小宴. ~***s soins*** [ˈswɛ̃iŋ] 小殷勤. ~ ***verre*** [ˈvɛə] 小杯.

pe·tite, pe·tite [pəˈtiːt] *a.* 〔F.〕①(女人)个子小的,娇小的. ②小的,次要的. ~ ***bourgeoisie*** [ˌbuəʒwɑˈziː] 小资产阶级.

pe·ti·tion [piˈtiʃən] *n.* ①请愿,请求;申请;祈求. ②请愿书;诉状. *the right of* ~ 请愿权. *a* ~ *of appeal*【法】起诉状. *a* ~ *of revision*【法】上诉状. ***file a ~ against ...*** 申请取消[停止]…. ***file a ~ for ...*** 申请获得[实行]…. ***hand in [send in] one's ~ to = lodge one's ~ to*** 向…申请. ***present a ~ to*** 向…提出请愿书. ***put up a ~ to*** *(heaven)* 向(天)祈祷. —*vt.* 向…请愿[祈求]. —*vi.* 请愿,请求 *(for a thing; to do)*;祈求.

pe·ti·tion·a·ry [piˈtiʃənəri] *a.* ①请愿的,请求的;祈求的. ②〔诗〕可怜的.

pe·ti·tion·er [piˈtiʃənə] *n.* ①请愿人,祈求人. ②(离婚诉讼的)原告.

pe·ti·ti·o prin·ci·pi·i [piˈtiʃiəu prinˈsipiai]〔L.〕【逻】预期理由〔一种逻辑错误,以本身尚待证明的判断作为证明论题的论据〕.

pet·i·to·ry [ˈpetitəri] *a.* 提出所有权要求的. *a* ~ *action [suit]* 要求所有权的诉讼.

pet·nap·ping, pet·nap·ing [ˈpetˌnæpiŋ] *n.* 偷窃猫狗〔卖供实验用〕.

Pe·tö·fi [ˈpetəːfi] **San·dor** 裴多菲〔1823—1849, 匈牙利诗人〕.

petr- *comb. f.* (用于元音前),= petro-[1].

Pe·trar·chan [piˈtrɑːkən] *a.* (十四行诗)彼特拉克文体的〔其韵脚为 abba, abba, cdc dcd 或 cde cde〕.

pet·rel [ˈpetrəl] *n.* ①【动】海燕〔相传这种燕子一来就有暴风雨,因此又名 storm(y). ~〕. ②〔喻〕一来就会发生事故的人.

petri- *comb. f.* = petro-[1].

Pe·tri dish [ˈpiːtri ˈdiʃ]【生】(陪替氏)培养皿.

Pe·trie [ˈpiːtri] *n.* 皮特里〔姓氏〕.

pet·ri·fac·tion [ˌpetriˈfækʃən] *n.* ①【地】石化(作用);化石. ②发呆,茫然自失. ③顽固,僵化.

pet·ri·fac·tive [ˌpetriˈfæktiv] *a.* 能使有机物石化的,有石化能力的.

pe·trif·ic [piˈtrifik] *a.* = petrifactive.

pet·ri·fi·ca·tion [ˌpetrifiˈkeiʃən] *n.* = petrifaction.

pet·ri·fy [ˈpetrifai] *vt.* ①【地】使(动植物)石化,石化(动、植物等). ②使变硬;使失去活力;使僵化;使顽固. ③使迟钝;使发呆. *stand petrified* (吓得)呆呆地站着. *be petrified with terror* 吓呆. —*vi.*【地】石化;变僵硬. ②吓呆.

Pe·trine [ˈpiːtrain, -rin] *a.* 圣彼得 (Peter) 的.

petro-[1] *comb. f.* 石,岩.

petro-[2] *comb. f.* 石油.

pet·ro·chem·i·cal [ˌpetrəuˈkemikl] *a.* 石油化学的;岩石化学的. —*n.* 石油化学产品.

pet·ro·che·mis·try [ˌpetrəuˈkemistri] *n.* 石油化学;岩石化学.

pe·trog·e·ny [piˈtrɔdʒini] *n.*【地】岩石发生学.

pet·ro·glyph [ˈpetrəglif] *n.* 原始人石刻〔原始人刻在岩石上的物像[文字]〕.

pet·ro·graph [ˈpetrəgrɑːf] *n.* = petroglyph.

pe·trog·ra·phy [piˈtrɔgrəfi] *n.* 岩相学;岩类学. **pe·tro·graph·i·cal** [-ˈgræfikəl] *a.*

pet·rol [ˈpetrəl] *n.* ①〔英〕汽油〔美国称 gasoline〕. ②〔废〕石油. —*vt.*〔英〕①给…加汽油. ②用汽油消除. **~-engine** 汽油发动机. **~ station** 加油站.

pet·ro·la·tum [ˌpetrəuˈleitəm] *n.*【化】矿脂;凡士林,石油冻.

Pet·rol·ene [ˈpetrəliːn] *n.*【化】沥青脂.

pe·tro·le·um [piˈtrəuliəm] *n.* 石油. *crude [raw]* ~ 原油,重油. ~ **coal** 固体石油. ~ **engine** 石油发动机. ~ **ether** 石油醚. ~ **jelly** 凡士林(= vaseline).

pe·tro·le·ur [F.petrɔlœːr] *n.* 〔F.〕用石油放火者.

pe·trol·ic [piˈtrɔlik] *a.* ①汽油的;石油的. ②从石油中提炼的.

pet·ro·lif·er·ous [ˌpetrəˈlifərəs] *a.* 含石油的;产石油的.

pe·tro·lin(e) [ˈpetrəlin] *n.*【化】石油淋〔一种碳化氢〕.

pet·ro·lize [ˈpetrəlaiz] *vt.* ①用石油点燃. ②用石油处理. ③用石油覆盖(水面). ④用柏油铺(路).

pe·trol·o·gy [piˈtrɔlədʒi] *n.* 岩石学,岩理学. **pet·ro·log·i·cal** [-ˈlɔdʒikəl] *a.* **pe·trol·o·gist** [-ˈlɔdʒist] *n.* 岩石学家.

pet·ro·nel [ˈpetrənəl] *n.* (十五至十七世纪的)手枪,火枪〔一种枪筒粗的,卡宾枪似的武器〕.

pet·ro·phone [ˈpetrəufəun] *n.*【乐】石琴. **pet·roph·on·ist** [-ˈfəunist] *n.* 石琴家.

pet·ro·pol·i·tics [petrəuˈpɔlitiks] *n.* 石油政治.

pe·tro·sal [piˈtrəusəl] *a.* ①硬的,石头似的. ②【解】位于颞骨岩部的.

pet·rous [ˈpetrəs] *a.* ①岩石(似)的,硬的. ②【解】颞骨岩部的.

pet·ti·coat [ˈpetikəut] *n.* ①裙子;衬裙;〔*pl.*〕童装,女装. ②〔俚〕女人,少女;〔*pl.*〕女性;〔俚〕(纸牌的)女王. ③裙状物. ***a ~ affair*** 与女人有关的事件;(尤指)桃色事件. ***in ~s*** ①穿裙子的;女性的. ②幼年时. ~ ***slave*** 〔俚〕怕老婆的人. ***under ~ government*** 在妻子管辖之下. **-ed** *a.* ①穿着裙子的. ②象女人的. **-ism** *n.* 老婆的管辖,女人的统治. **-less** *a.* ①不穿(衬)裙的. ②不象女人的.

pet·ti·fog [ˈpetifɔg] *vi.* ①做讼棍,经办小件法律事务. ②讲歪理;诡辩;挑剔. **-fog·ger** [-ə] *n.* ①小律师,讼棍. ②骗子;诡辩者. **-fog·ger·y** [-gəri] *n.* = pettifogging. **-fog·ging** ① *a.* 小律师(式)的,狡诈的;卑劣的;低贱的;为小事细节而烦恼的. ② *n.* 讼棍行为[手段];狡辩;狡诈.

pet·ti·ly [ˈpetili] *ad.* 卑鄙地;偏狭地;器量小地.

pet·ti·ness [ˈpetinis] *n.* ①微小,琐碎;狭小. ②偏狭;卑劣,器量小.

pet·ting [ˈpetiŋ] *n.* 〔美俚〕拥抱,爱抚,嬉戏. **~-skirt** 〔美〕姑娘,女孩.

pet·ti·pants [ˈpetipænts] *n. pl.* 妇女半长内裤.

pet·tish [ˈpetiʃ] *a.* ①不高兴的,动不动闹脾气的. ②发脾气时说[做]的.

pet·ti·toes [ˈpetitəuz] *n.* 〔*pl.*〕①(食用的)猪脚. ②〔谑〕人的脚〔尤指小孩的脚〕.

pet·to [ˈpetəu] *n.* *(pl. -ti [-iː])* 〔It.〕胸. ***in ~*** 在胸中,秘密.

Pet·ty [ˈpeti] *n.* 佩蒂〔姓氏〕.

pet·ty [ˈpeti] *a.* ①小的,一点点. ②琐碎的;渺小的;不足道的,无聊的. ③器量小的,心眼儿小的,卑劣的. ④小规模的;次要的;下级的. *a* ~ *current deposit* 零星活期存款. *a* ~ *dealer* 小贩. ~ *expenses* 零星杂费. —*n.* ①【簿记】小额. ②〔*pl.*〕厕所. ~ **bourgeois** 小资产阶级分子;小资产者;小资产阶级的. ~ **bourgeoisie** 小资产阶级. ~ **cash** 零用钱,零星收支. ~ **jury** 小陪审团

〔由十二人组成〕. ~ **larceny**【法】轻窃盗罪. ~ **officer** ①小公务员. ②(海军的)下级官佐,军士,下士. ~ **officer stoker** (海军的)锅炉下士. ~ **session**〔英〕即决法庭.

pet·u·lance, pet·u·lan·cy [ˈpetjuləns, -si] *n.* ①易怒;暴躁,坏脾气;警扭,闹气;急躁言行. ②〔古〕无礼,狂妄.

pet·u·lant [ˈpetjulənt] *a.* ①急躁的,易怒的,爱闹气的,脾气坏的. ②〔古〕狂妄的,无礼的.

pe·tu·ni·a [piˈtjuːnjə, -niə] *n.* ①【植】(南美产)矮牵牛花属植物. ②暗紫色.

pe·tun·se [peˈtunsi], **pe·tun·tse, pe·tun·tze** [peˈtuntsi] *n.* (中国的)瓷泥〔制造瓷器用〕.

peu a peu [pəːəˈpəː; pø ɑ pø] 〔F.〕一点一点地,逐渐.

pew [pjuː] *n.* ①(教堂的)条凳式座位;一家人专用包厢式座位. ②〔*pl.*〕坐在教堂椅子上的人们;会众. ③〔古〕(讲道者或司仪用的)讲台. ④〔口〕椅子,座位. *Take a* ~. 请坐〔对客人讲〕. —*vt.* ①为(教堂)安座位;②把…围成包厢式座位. ③使在教堂座位中就座. ~ **chair** 折叠式添座椅子. ~ **opener** 教堂的领坐人. ~ **rent** 教堂座位费.

pew·age [ˈpjuːidʒ] *n.* ①教堂条凳. ②教堂座位费.

pe·wee [ˈpiːwiː] *n.*【鸟】①京燕类. ②〔美〕山鹬.

pe·wit [ˈpiːwit] *n.*【鸟】①= pewee. ②田凫. ③红嘴鸥.

Pewks [pjuːks] *n.* 〔美〕密苏里 (Missouri) 州人的绰号.

pew·ter [ˈpjuːtə] *n.* ①【冶】白镴〔锡和铅的合金〕. ②锡镴制器皿,白镴锅,白镴酒杯. ③〔俚〕悬赏杯,奖金;〔美俚〕钱. — *a.* 白镴(制)的. ~**-wort**【植】木贼.

PF = pulse frequency【无】脉冲频率.

pf. = ①perfect. ②preferred.

p.f. = 〔It.〕***più forte*** 〔It.〕(=louder).【乐】更大声些.

PFC, Pfc. = Private First Class〔美〕陆军〔海军陆战队〕一等兵.

pfd; pfd. =preferred.

pfen·nig [ˈpfenig] *n.* (*pl.* ~*s* ***pfen·ni·ge*** [ˈpfɛnigə]) 芬尼〔德国铜币 = 1/100 mark〕.

PG = parental guidance (指电影)适合一般观众观看但建议父母(对儿童观众)加以指导.

P.G. = ① paying guest 搭伙房客. ② postgraduate (大学的)研究生.

Pg. = ① Portugal. ② Portuguese.

Pgn., pgn = pigeon 军用鸽,通信鸽.

PH = public health 公共卫生.

P.H. = pinch-hitter (棒球赛关键时上场的)替补击球员.

Ph. =① phenyl【化】苯基. ② phase.

p.h. = per hour 每小时.

pH =【化】表示氢离子浓度的倒数的对数的符号.

PHA = Public Housing Administration〔美〕公众房产管理局.

Pha·ë·thon [ˈfeiəθən] *n.*【希神】法厄同〔太阳神赫利俄斯的儿子〕.

phae·ton [ˈfeitn] *n.* ①二马四轮轻便马车. ②活顶游览汽车. ~ **butterfly**〔美〕火焰斑纹黑蝴蝶.

-phag, -phage *comb. f.* 食,噬: bacterio*phage*.

phage [feidʒ] *n.*【医】噬菌体 (= bacte riophage).

phag·e·de·na, phag·e·dae·na [ˌfædʒiˈdiːnə] *n.*【医】崩蚀性溃疡. **-e·den·ic** [-ˈdenik] *a.*

phago- *comb. f.* 食,噬: *phago*cyte.

phag·o·cyte [ˈfægəsait] *n.*【生理】吞噬细胞,白血球. **-o·cyt·ic** [ˌfægəˈsitik] *a.* **-o·cy·to·sis** [ˌfægəsaiˈtəusis] *n.* 噬菌(作用).

-phagous *suf.* 噬…的: creo*phagous*.

-phagy *comb. f.* 常食…者: alotrio*phagy*.

phal·ange [ˈfælənd̥ʒ] *n.*【解】指骨;趾骨(= phalanx④).

phal·an·ge·al [fəˈlændʒiəl] *a.*【解】指骨的;趾骨的. ~ **joint**【解】指〔趾〕关节.

pha·lan·ger [fəˈlændʒə] *n.* (澳大利亚的)袋貂科 (*phalangeridae*) 动物.

pha·lan·ges [fæˈlændʒiːz] phalanx 的复数.

phal·an·ster·y [ˈfælənstəri] *n.* ①法伦斯泰尔〔法国空想社会主义者傅立叶幻想的社会主义基层组织〕. ②法伦斯泰尔成员的公共住所. ③类似法伦斯泰尔的组织.

phal·anx[ˈfælæŋks] *n.* (*pl.* ~*es, phalanges*[fæˈlændʒiːz]) ①(古希腊重武装步兵的)方阵. ②密集队伍;集结;集团,结社. ③法郎吉〔傅立叶空想社会主义的社会组织,即 phalanstery〕. ④(*pl.* ***pha·langes***)【解】指〔趾〕骨;【虫】跗亚节. ⑤(*pl.* ***phalanges***)【植】雄蕊束.

phal·a·rope [ˈfælərəup] *n.*【动】瓣蹼鹬.

phal·lic, phal·li·cal [ˈfælik, -likəl] *a.* ①阴茎的. ②崇拜男性生殖器的.

phal·li·cism, phal·lism [ˈfælisizəm, -lizəm] *a.* 生殖器崇拜;阴茎崇拜.

phal·lus [ˈfæləs] *n.* (*pl.* ***phal·li*** [-lai]) ①(作为崇拜对象的)男性生殖器形象. ②【解】阴茎;阴核.

phan·er·o·gam [ˈfænərəugæm] *n.*【植】显花植物 (*opp.* cryptogam).

Phan·er·o·gam·i·a [ˌfænərəuˈgeimiə] *n.*【植】显花植物门.

phan·er·o·gam·ic, phan·er·og·a·mous [ˌfænərəuˈgæmik, -ˈrɔgəməs] *a.* 显花的,开花的.

phan·er·o·phyte [ˈfænərəufait] *n.*【植】显花植物.

phan·si·gar [ˈfænsigɑː] *n.* 〔Hind.〕谋财害命的暴徒 (= thug.).

phan·tasm [ˈfæntæzəm] ①幻象,幻影. ②幽灵. ③幻想,空想. ④〔古〕幻觉,错觉.

phan·tas·ma [fænˈtæzmə] *n.* (*pl.* ~*ta* [-tə]) = phantasm.

Phan·tas·ma·go·ri·a [ˌfæntæzməˈgɔːriə] *n.* ①幻觉效应〔尤指屏幕上形象向后缩小或骤然增大如向观众扑来的光学效应〕. ②变幻不定的情景. ③(1802 年伦敦举行的)大幻灯会. **-ma·gor·i·al** [-ˈgɔriəl], **-ma·gor·ic** [-ˈgɔrik] *a.* 幻影(似)的,变幻不定的.

phan·tas·mal, phan·tas·mic [fænˈtæzməl, -mik] *a.* ①幻影(一样)的;幽灵(一样)的. ②幻想的,空想的. **-ly** *ad.*

phan·ta·sy [ˈfæntəsi] *n.* = fantasy.

phan·tom [ˈfæntəm] *n.* ①鬼怪,妖怪;幽灵;使人害怕的东西. ②错觉,妄想. ③幻影,幻象;影象,印像 (*of*);实际上不存在的人〔物〕;〔美俚〕工资单上挂假名的人. ④【解】(人体)模型. ⑤〔P-〕鬼怪式飞机. —*a.* ①空的,幻想的,幻影的. ②幽灵似的,鬼怪的. ~ **antenna**【无】幻天线. ~ **circuit**【电】幻象电路. ~ **crystal** 先成晶体. ~ **limb** (截肢后依然感到肢体存在的)幻肢(感). ~ **order**〔美〕(武器等的)虚幻订单〔须官方批准后才有效〕. ~ **tumour** (歇斯的里症患者腹部的)一时肿胀,虚瘤. ~ **wire**【电】假想线路.

phar., pharm. =①pharmaceutical. ②pharmacopoeia. ③pharmacy.

Phar·aoh [ˈfɛərəu] *n.* 法老〔古埃及王称号〕. ~**'s chicken [hen]**【动】王鸡〔产于埃及等地的一种兀鹰〕. ~**'s rat [mouse]**【动】埃及獴. ~**'s serpent** 法老蛇〔一点火就呈现蛇形的化学玩具〕. **Phar·a·on·ic** [ˌfɛəreiˈɔnik] *a.*

Phar. B. =Bachelor of Pharmacy 药学士.

Phar. D. =Doctor of Pharmacy 药学博士.

Phar·i·sa·ic, Phar·i·sa·i·cal [ˌfæriˈseiik, -ikəl] *a.* ①法利赛人的. ②〔p-〕【圣】遵守表面教义的;拘泥(宗教)形式的;表面虔诚的,伪善的. **-i·cal·ly** *ad.*

Phar·i·sa·ism [ˈfæriseiizəm] *n.* ①法利赛人的教规〔信仰,习惯〕;法利赛派. ②〔p-〕拘泥形式;伪善.

Phar·i·see [ˈfærisiː] *n.* ①法利赛(派)的人〔古代犹太教一个派别的成员,宣称墨守传统礼仪,《圣经》中称他们为言行不一的伪善者〕. ②〔p-〕(宗教上的)拘泥形式者;伪君子;伪善者.

phar·ma·ceu·ti·cal [ˌfɑːməˈsjuːtikəl] *a.* ①制药(学)上的. ②药剂师的. ③应用药物的. ~ *botany* 药用植物

学. ~ *chemistry* 制药化学,药物化学. *a* ~ *worker* 制药工人. —*n.* 药物. **-ly** *ad.*

phar·ma·ceu·tics [ˌfɑːməˈsjuːtiks] *n. pl.* 〔用作 *sing.*〕制药学.

phar·ma·ceu·tist, phar·ma·cist [ˌfɑːməˈsjutist, ˈfɑːməsist] *n.* 制药者,药剂师,药学家.

phar·ma·co·dy·nam·ics [fɑːməˌkəudaiˈnæmiks] *n. pl.* 〔用作 *sing.*〕药效学. **-na·mic** *a.*

phar·ma·cog·no·sy [ˌfɑːməˈkɔgnəsi] *n.* 生药学.

phar·ma·col·o·gy [ˌfɑːməˈkɔlədʒi] *n.* 药理学;药物学. **-col·o·gist** *n.* 药理〔药物〕学家. **-ma·co·log·i·cal** *a.*

phar·ma·co·poe·ia [ˌfɑːməkˈpiːə] *n.* ①处方书,药典. ②(一批)库存药品,(一批)备用药物. **-poe·ial** *a.*

phar·ma·cy [ˈfɑːməsi] *n.* ①配药学,药学. ②制药业. ③药房. ④(一批)备用药品. ~ **jar** 药瓶.

phar·mic [ˈfɑːmik] *a.* 〔美俚〕有关药物的;关于药学的. —*n.* ①药学讲座. ②药学学生.

Pharm. D. = Phar. D.

Pharm. M. = Master of Pharmacy 药学硕士.

Pharmt. = Pharmacist.

pha·ros [ˈfɛərɔs] *n.* ①〔诗〕灯塔;航线标记;标灯;望楼;炬火. ②〔P-〕(从前亚历山大湾内)法罗斯(Pharos)岛上的灯塔.

pha·ryn·gal, pha·ryn·ge·al [fəˈriŋgəl, ˌfærinˈdʒiːəl] *a.*【解】咽的. ~ **artery** 咽动脉. ~ **tonsil** 咽扁桃体. ~ **tube**【解】食管.

phar·yn·ges [fəˈrindʒiːz] pharynx 的复数.

phar·yn·gi·tis [ˌfærinˈdʒaitis] *n.*【医】咽炎.

pharyng(o)- *comb. f.* 咽: *pharyngology.*

phar·yn·gol·o·gy [ˌfæriŋˈgɔlədʒi] *n.* 咽科学.

pha·ryn·go·scope [fəˈriŋgəskəup] *n.*【医】咽窥器,咽镜.

phar·ynx [ˈfæriŋks] *n.* *(pl. phar·yn·ges* [fəˈrindʒiːz], *~es)*【解】咽.

phase [feiz] *n.* ①形势,局面,状态;阶段. ②方面,侧面. ③【天】(月等的)变相,盈亏;【物、天】相,周相,相位. ④【动】型,期. *a youthful* ~ 青年时期. *The problem has many ~s.* 这问题是多方面的. ~ *distortion*【物】相畸变,周相畸变. ***enter (up)on a new*** ~ 进入一新的阶段. ***from ~ to ~ during this stage*** 这一阶段中的各个时期. ***in*** ~【物】同相的〔地〕;同时协调的〔地〕. ***out of*** ~【物】异相的〔地〕,不同相;非同时协调的〔地〕. —*vt.* ①使调整相位,使定相. ②使分阶段〔按计划〕进行. ~ ***in*** 分阶段引入,逐步采用. ~ ***out*** ①使逐步结束;使逐步撤出;逐步淘汰;逐部停止(活动等). ②(动行等的)逐步停止;逐步撤出. ③逐步转入 *(into).* **~-contrast** *a.* 用相衬显微镜的. ~ **contrast microscope**【物】相衬显微镜. ~ **indicator** 示相器. ~ **meter** 相差计. ~ **modulation**【无】调相,相位调制. ~ **rule** 相律. ~ **splitter** 分相器.

pha·sic [ˈfeizik] *a.* ①阶段的;局面的. ②【天,物】相(位)的. *the* ~ *development*【生】阶段发育.

phas·mid [ˈfeizmid] *n.*【动】竹节虫目 *(Phasmida)* 昆虫〔包括条形虫、枝状虫 *(Diapheromera femorata)*〕.

phat·ic [ˈfætik] *a.* (谈话)落入俗套的,无意义的,交际应酬的. **-i·cal·ly** *ad.*

Ph. B., Ph B = 〔L.〕 *Philosophiae Baccalaureus* 哲学学士(= Bachelor of Philosophy).

Ph.C. = Pharmaceutical Chemist 药物化学家.

Ph.D., Ph D = 〔L.〕 *Philosophiae Doctor* 哲学博士(= Doctor of Philosophy).

pheas·ant [ˈfeznt] *n.* *(pl. ~(s))*【鸟】雉,野鸡. ***shoot the*** ~ 加害无力自卫的人的生命〔名誉〕;欺侮善良无辜者. **~-eyed** *a.* (花等)有雉羽状斑点的. **~'s-eye** *n.*【植】红口水仙.

pheas·ant·ry [ˈfezntri] *n.* 养雉场;【建】雉舍.

Phe·be [ˈfiːbi] *n.* = phoebe.

phel·lem [ˈfeləm] *n.*【植】木栓.

phel·lo·derm [ˈfelədəːm] *n.*【植】栓内层. **-al** *a.*

phel·lo·gen [ˈfelədʒən] *n.*【植】木栓形成层(= cork cambium). **-ge·net·ic** [-dʒiˈnetik], **-gen·ic** [-ˈdʒenik] *a.*

phen- *comb. f.* 〔用于元音前〕= pheno; *phen*azine.

phe·na·caine [ˈfiːnəkein, ˈfenə-] *n.*【化】芬那卡因〔即哈洛卡因,一种局部麻醉药〕.

phe·nac·e·tin(e) [fiˈnæsitin] *n.*【药】非那西汀,乙酰非那替汀〔一种解热镇痛药〕.

phen·a·kis·to·scope [ˌfiːnəˈkistəskəup] *n.* 诡盘〔一种玩具〕.

phen·a·kite [ˈfenəkait] *n.*【化】硅铍石(=phenacite).

phe·nan·threne [fəˈnænθriːn] *n.*【化】菲.

phe·nate [ˈfiːneit] *n.*【化】(苯)酚盐,石炭酸盐.

phen·a·zine [ˈfenəˌziːn, -zin] *n.*【化】吩嗪,(夹)二氮杂蒽.

phene [fiːn] *n.*【化】= benzene.

phe·net·i·dine [fiˈnetidiːn, -din] *n.*【化】氨基苯乙醚,乙氧苯胺.

phen·e·tol(e) [ˈfenitəul, -tɔl] *n.*【化】苯乙醚,乙氧基苯.

Phe·ni·ci·a [fiˈniʃiə] = Phoenicia.

phe·ni·ci·an [fiˈniʃiən, -ʃən] = Phoenician.

phe·nix [ˈfiːniks] *n.* = phoenix.

pheno- *comb. f.* ①【化】〔用于辅音前〕苯,苯基: *pheno*barbital. ②闪光,闪耀: *pheno*cryst.

phe·no·bar·bi·tal [ˌfiːnəuˈbɑːbitæl] *n.*【药】苯巴比妥〔一种安眠药和镇静剂〕.

phe·no·cain [ˈfiːnəkein] *n.* = phenacaine.

phe·no·cop·y [ˈfiːnəˌkɔpi] *n.*【遗传】拟表型.

phe·no·cryst [ˈfiːnəkrist, ˈfenə-] *n.*【地】斑晶.

phe·nol [ˈfiːnɔl] *n.*【化】①(苯)酚,石炭酸(= carbolic acid). ②〔类名词〕酚.

phe·no·lase [ˈfiːnəleis] *n.*【生化】酚酶.

phe·no·late [ˈfiːnəˌleit] *n.*【化】(苯)酚盐,石炭酸盐(= phenate). **-d** *a.* 含碳酸的.

phe·nol·ic [fiˈnɔlik] *n.*【化】(苯)酚的. **-s** *n.* 酚醛塑料.

phe·nol·o·gy [fiˈnɔlədʒi] *n.* 物候学;物候现象. **phe·no·log·i·cal** [ˌfiːnəˈlɔdʒikəl] *a.*

phe·nol·phthal·e·in [ˌfinɔlˈfθæliːn] *n.*【化】(苯)酚酞.

phe·nom [fiˈnɔm] 〔美俚〕 *n.* ①好事;好东西. ②杰出人材,红人〔尤指优秀运动员〕.

phe·nom·e·na [fiˈnɔminə] phenomenon 的复数.

phe·nom·e·nal [fiˈnɔminl] *a.* ①现象的;可以感觉〔认识〕到的;来自自然现象中的;显著的. ②非凡的,少有的,惊人的. ~ **memory** 超人的记忆力. **-ism** *n.*【哲】(唯)现象论. **-ist** *n.* (唯)现象论者.

phe·nom·e·nal·is·tic [fiˌnɔminəˈlistik] *a.* (有关)现象论的. **-ti·cal·ly** *ad.*

phe·nom·e·nal·ize [fiˈnɔminəlaiz] *vt.* ①把…当作现象看待,把…认作现象. ②用现象论解释.

phe·nom·e·nism [fiˈnɔnminizəm] *n.* = phenomenalism. **-nist·ic** *a.*

phe·nom·e·nol·o·gy [fiˌnɔmiˈnɔlədʒi] *n.* 现象学. **-log·i·cal** *a.* **-log·i·cal·ly** *ad.*

phe·nom·e·non [fiˈnɔminən] *n.* ①*(pl. -na* [-nə]*)*【哲】现象 *(opp.* noumenon*)*;事件. ②*(pl. ~s)* 稀有现象;奇迹;珍奇;珍品;非凡的人. ③【医】症候. *the* ~ *of nature* 自然现象. *social* ~ 社会现象. *an infant* ~ 神童.

phe·no·thi·a·zine [ˌfiːnəuˈθaiəziːn] *n.*【化】吩塞嗪,夹硫氮杂蒽.

phe·no·type [ˈfiːnətaip] *n.*【生】①表现型,表型. ②具有共同表型的一类有机物.

phe·nox·ide [fiˈnɔksaid] *n.*【化】(苯)酚盐,苯氧化物;石炭酸盐(= phenate).

phe·nox·y [fiˈnɔksi] *a.*【化】(含)苯氧基的.

phe·n·yl(e) [ˈfenəl, fiːnəl, ˈfiːnil] *n.* 【化】苯基.
phen·yl·al·a·nine [ˌfenəlˈælənin] *n.* 【化】苯基丙氨酸.
phen·yl·am·ine [ˌfenələˈmiːn, -ˈæmiːn] *n.* 【化】苯胺 (= aniline).
phen·yl·bu·ta·zone [ˌfenəlˈbjuːtəzəun] *n.* 【化】苯乙丁氮酮.
phen·yl·ene [ˈfenəliːn] *n.* 【化】苯撑,次苯基.
phen·yl·ke·to·nu·ri·a [ˌfenəlˌkiːtəˈnjuəriə, ˌfiːnil-] *n.* 【医】苯酮尿. **-nu·ric** *a.*
phew [ɸː, fjuː] *int.* 唷! 呸! 啐! 〔表示焦躁、惊讶、嫌厌、松一口气等〕— *vt.* 咂(舌).
phi [fai] *n.* 希腊字母表的第二十一字母〔Φ, φ 和英语 ph 相当〕; = 500. ***Phi Beta Kappa***〔美〕①ΦBK 联谊会〔美国大学优秀生的荣誉组织〕. ②ΦBK 联谊会会员. ***Phi Bete*** [beit] = Phi Beta kappa. ***Phi Bete house***〔美俚〕大学图书馆.
phi·al [ˈfaiəl] *n.* 小玻璃瓶; 药瓶.
phi·bete [ˈfaibeit] *n.*〔美〕Phi Beta Kappa 联谊会会员. — *vi.* 用功.
Phil [fil] *n.* 菲尔〔男子名, Phil(l)ip 的昵称〕.
Phil. = ①Philadelphia. ②Philemon. ③Philip. ④Philippians. ⑤Philippine.
phil. = ①philology. ②philosophical. ③philosophy.
phil- *comb. f.*〔用于元音前〕= philo-.
-phil(e) *suf.* ①形容词后缀,表示"对…有好意"、"爱好"、"亲": Russo*phil(e)*. ②名词后缀,表示"对…有好意者"、"爱好…者": biblio*phil(e)*.
Phila. = Philadelphia.
Phila·del·phia [ˌfiləˈdelfjə] *n.* 费拉德尔菲亚〔即费城,美国港市, Pennsylvania 州的首府〕. ***a ~ lawyer***〔美俚〕有手腕的律师; 精明的人.
phil·a·del·phus [ˌfiləˈdelfəs] *n.* 【植】山梅花属植物 (= mock orange).
phi·lan·der [fiˈlændə] *vi.* ①调戏女人,追逐女性. ②玩弄 *(with)*. ~ ***off*** (男女二人)私奔. **-er** *n.* 追逐[玩弄]女性者.
phil·an·thrope [ˈfilənθrəup] *n.*〔古〕= philanthropist.
phi·lan·throp·ic, phi·lan·throp·i·cal [ˌfilənˈθrɔpik, -ikəl] *a.* ①博爱的, 仁爱的. ②慈善的; 慈善事业的. **-throp·i·cal·ly** *ad.*
phi·lan·thro·pism [fiˈlænθrəpizəm] *n.* 博爱主义, 仁爱 (=philanthropy). **-thro·pist** *n.* 博爱主义者; 慈善家.
phi·lan·thro·pize [fiˈlænθrəpaiz] *vt.* 使有善心; 使行善. — *vi.* 行善, 从事慈善事业.
phi·lan·thro·poid [fiˈlænθrəpɔid] *n.* 〔口〕慈善基金会理事[董事].
phi·lan·thro·py [fiˈlænθrəpi] *n.* ①博爱(主义), 慈善, 善心. ②〔常 *pl.*〕慈善(事业、行为、团体).
phil·a·tel·ic, phil·a·tel·i·cal [ˌfiləˈtelik, -ikəl] *a.* 集邮的. **-tel·i·cal·ly** *ad.*
phi·lat·e·list [fiˈlætəlist] *n.* 集邮者,集邮家.
phi·lat·e·ly [fiˈlætəli] *n.* 集邮.
-phile *suf.* =-phil.
phil·har·mon·ic [ˌfilɑːˈmɔnik, filhɑːˈm-] *a.* ①欢喜音乐的. ②交响乐团的, 音乐团体的〔多用作音乐协会、乐团等名称〕. — *n.* ①〔古〕爱音乐的人. ②〔P-〕交响乐团; (交响乐团主持的) 管弦乐队. ③(交响乐团举办的) 音乐会. *the Vienna P-* 维也纳交响乐团.
phil·hel·lene, phil·hel·len·ist [ˈfilheliːn, Am. filˈhelinist] *n.* 爱希腊的人, 希腊之友; (十九世纪)赞成希腊独立运动的人.
phil·hel·le·nic [ˌfilheˈliːnik] *a.* 爱希腊的,亲希腊的.
phil·hel·len·ism [filˈhelinizəm] *n.* 爱希腊,亲希腊; 希腊独立主义.
Phil. I(s). = Philippine Islands.
Phil·(l)ip [ˈfilip] *n.* 菲利普〔男子名〕. ***appeal from ~ drunk to ~ sober*** 请求复审〔因初审在某种影响下不够郑重,故请求复审〕.
Phi·lip·pi [fiˈlipai] *n.* 腓利比〔古代马其顿王菲利浦二世所建的城市, 公元前 42 年安东尼、屋大维联军在此战败布鲁图等〕. ***meet at ~*** 恪守危险的相会信约. ***Thou shalt see me at ~.*** 等着瞧吧! 〔我就要报仇雪耻了〕.
Phi·lip·pic [fiˈlipik] *n.* ①〔常 *pl.*〕《斥菲利浦篇》〔古希腊德摩斯梯尼 (Demosthenes) 痛骂马其顿国王菲利浦二世的十二篇著名演说之一〕; 《斥安东尼篇》〔古罗马西塞罗 (Cicero) 抨击安东尼的演说之一〕. ②〔p-〕猛烈的抨击演说,痛骂,痛斥.
phil·ip·pine [ˈfilipiːn] *a.* 菲律宾 (人) 的. ~ **Islands** 菲律宾群岛〔亚洲〕.
Phil·ip·pine,-pin·a [ˈfilipiːn, -nə] *n.* ①有双核的坚果〔胡桃等〕. ②(二人分双核果的)核果联谊游戏〔习俗〕; 玩双核果游戏的罚物〔通常多为赠品〕.
Phil·ip·pines [ˈfilipiːnz, -painz] *n.*〔the ~〕①菲律宾群岛 (= the Philippine Islands). ②菲律宾〔亚洲〕.
Phil·(l)ips [ˈfilips] *n.* 菲利普斯〔姓氏〕.
Phil·is·tine [ˈfilistain] *n.* ①腓力斯人〔巴勒斯坦西南岸古国腓力斯的居民〕. ②〔p-〕市侩,庸人〔指心地狭窄的实利主义者; 没有教养, 不懂文学、艺术的低级趣味者〕. ③〔p-〕〔谑〕仇敌〔常指司法官、批评家等〕. ④〔p-〕(某科知识的)门外汉; 〔德国学生语〕没有进大学的人. ***fall among ~s*** 大吃苦头, 虎落平阳被犬欺. — *a.* ①腓力斯人的. ②〔p-〕市侩的,庸俗的; 没有文化教养的; 实利主义的. ~ *tastes* 低级趣味.
Phil·is·tin·ism [ˈfilistinizəm, fiˈlis-] *n.* ①腓力斯人的风习. ②〔p-〕庸人习气,市侩习性[作风]; 庸俗,无教养; 偏狭; 实利主义. *free from the slightest trace of ~* 丝毫没有庸人习气.
Phil·lis [ˈfilis] *n.* = Phyllis.
Phil·lpotts [ˈfilpɔts] *n.* 菲尔波茨〔姓氏〕.
Phil·ly [ˈfili] *n.*〔美〕费城〔Philadelphia 市的俗称〕.
philo- *comb. f.* 爱,喜: *philo*biblic.
phil·o·bib·lic [ˌfiləˈbiblik] *a.* ①爱书的, 有爱书癖的. ②爱文学的. ③埋头研究《圣经》的.
phil·o·den·dron [ˌfiləˈdendrən] *n.* ①【植】喜林芋属 *(Philodendron)* 植物〔热带美洲植物〕. ②任何与上述相似的植物〔广义〕.
phi·log·y·ny [fiˈlɔdʒini] *n.* 对女人的爱好, 女性崇拜 *(opp.* misogyny*)*. **-y·nous** [-nəs] *a.* **-y·nist** *n.* 爱好[崇拜]女人的人.
philol. = philological; philology.
phi·lol·o·ger [fiˈlɔlədʒə] *n.* 语文[语言]学家.
phil·o·log·ic, phil·o·log·i·cal [ˌfiləˈlɔdʒik, -ikəl] *a.* 语文[语言]学(上)的. **-i·cal·ly** *ad.*
phi·lol·o·gist [fiˈlɔlədʒist] *n.* 语文学家,语言学家.
phi·lol·o·gize [fiˈlɔlədʒaiz] *vi.* 研究语文[语言]学; 从语文[语言]学上论述[考察].
phi·lol·o·gy [fiˈlɔlədʒi] *n.*①语文学; 语文文献学. ②语言学; 历史比较语言学. ③〔罕〕爱学问, 爱文学. *comparative ~* 比较语言[语文]学.
phil·o·math [ˈfiləmæθ] *n.* 爱学问(尤指数学)的人.
phil·o·mel [ˈfiləmel] *n.*〔诗〕夜莺 (= nightingale).
Phil·o·me·la [ˌfiləuˈmiːlə] *n.* ①【希神】菲洛米拉〔雅典王 Pandion 的女儿,被神化身成夜莺〕. ②〔p-〕= philomel.
phil·o·pe·na [ˌfiləˈpiːnə] *n.* = philippine.
phil·o·pro·gen·i·tive [ˌfilәprəuˈdʒenitiv] *a.* ①爱子女的. ②多子女的.
philos. = ①philosopher. ②philosophical. ③philosophy.
phi·los·o·phas·ter [fiˌlɔsəˈfæstə] *n.* 假哲学家; 半瓶醋哲学家.
phi·los·o·pher [fiˈlɔsəfə] *n.* ①哲学家; 哲人, 贤人. ②思想家; 学者. ③达观者, 逆来顺受者. ④爱卖弄大道理者. ⑤〔古〕炼金术士. *a moral ~* 伦理学家. *a natural ~* 自然哲学家; 物理学家. ***~'s stone*** (空想中的)点金

石. ***take things like a*** ～ 达观世事. ***You are a*** ～. 你真了不起,你真想得开.

phil·o·soph·ic, phil·o·soph·i·cal [ˌfiləˈsɔfik, -kəl] *a.* ①哲学(家)的, 哲学上的; 富于哲理性的. ②通哲学的; 贤明的. ③沉着的, 冷静的; 达观的, 逆来顺受的. ④〔古〕物理学上的. *the American Philosophical Society* 美国科学研究会. *the Philosophical Transactions* 英国皇家学会 *(Royal Society)* 会报. **-i·cal·ly** *ad.* ①在哲学上. ②贤明; 镇定自若, 达观.

phi·los·o·phism [fiˈlɔsəfizəm] *n.* 伪哲学; 诡辩.

phi·los·o·phist [fiˈlɔsəfist] *n.* 伪哲学家; 诡辩家.

phi·los·o·phize [fiˈlɔsəfaiz] *vi.* ①用哲学家的态度研究; 用哲理推究, 思索. ②从事肤浅的说理, 爱卖弄大道理. — *vt.* ①使哲学化, 使理论化. ②(用理论从哲学上)说明.

phi·los·o·phiz·er [fiˈlɔsəfaizə] ①哲理家. ②卖弄大道理的人.

phi·los·o·phy [fiˈlɔsəfi] *n.* ①哲学; 哲理, 哲学体系. ②世界观, 人生观; 宗旨. ③(某一门学科的)基本原理. ④哲学家的态度, 达观, 泰然自若; 悟道, 大悟. ⑤(除医学、法律、神学外的)所有学科; 〔古〕中世纪大学的高等学术. *Marxist* ～ *of dialectical materialism* 马克思主义的辩证唯物论哲学. *critical* ～ 批判哲学. *positive* ～ 实证哲学. *first* ～ (亚里士多德的)第一哲学, 本体论, 实体论. *mental* ～ 心理学〔现在用 psychology〕. *metaphysical* ～ 形而上学. *moral* ～ 伦理学〔现在用 ethics〕. *natural* ～〔古〕自然科学〔现在用 science〕, 物理学〔现在用 physics〕. *the three philosophies* 物理学, 伦理学, 哲学. *the* ～ *of grammar* 语法原理. ***use*** ～ 彻悟, 看破; 采取哲人的态度〔指临危不惧, 达观等〕.

phi·lo·tech·nic, phi·lo·tech·ni·cal [ˌfiləˈteknik, -ikəl] *a.* 爱好工艺的.

Phil. Soc. = Philological Society.

phil·tre, phil·ter [ˈfiltə] *n.* ①媚药, 春药; 有魔力的药. ②诱淫巫术. — *vt.* ①用春药迷住. ②用诱淫巫术蛊惑.

phil·trum [ˈfiltrəm] *n.* ***(pl. -tra*** [-trə]***)*** *n.*【解】人中〔鼻唇间纵沟〕.

phi·mo·sis [faiˈməusis] *n.* ***(pl. -ses*** [-siːz]***)***【医】包茎. **phi·mot·ic** [-ˈmɔtik] *a.*

phiz [fiz] *n.* 〔俚〕脸, 面孔 (= physiognomy). ～ **snapper**〔美俚〕照相师.

phle·bi·tis [fliˈbaitis] *n.*【医】静脉炎.

phleb·o·lite [ˈflebəlait] *n.*【医】静脉石.

phleb·o·lith [ˈflebəliθ] *n.* = phlebolite.

phle·bol·o·gy [fliˈbɔlədʒi] *n.*【医】静脉学, 静脉论.

phleb·o·scle·ro·sis [ˌflebəuskliəˈrəusis] *n.*【医】静脉硬化.

phle·bot·o·mist [fliˈbɔtəmist] *n.* ①用静脉切开放血术治病的医师. ②相信静脉切开术的人.

phle·bot·o·mize [fliˈbɔtəmaiz] *vt., vi.* (使)放血.

phle·bot·o·my [fliˈbɔtəmi] *n.*【医】放血, 静脉切开放血术.

phlegm [flem] *n.* ①痰. ②〔古〕粘液〔古代生理学所称四种体液之一, 认为此种体液型的人多迟钝〕. ③冷淡; 不动感情; 迟钝.

phleg·mat·ic, phleg·mat·i·cal [flegˈmætik, -ikəl] *a.* ①(古代生理学所称)粘液质的. ②迟钝的; 冷淡的; 不动感情的. ③痰多的. *a* ～ *temperament* 迟钝的气质. **-mat·i·cal·ly** *ad.*

phleg·mon [ˈflegmən] *n.*【医】脓性蜂窝织炎.

phlegm·y [ˈflemi] *a.* 痰似的; 含痰的.

phlo·em [ˈfləuem] *n.*【植】韧皮部.

phlo·gis·tic [flɔˈdʒistik] *a.* ①(古代化学所说)燃素的, 热素的. ②【医】炎的; 炎症的; 炎性的.

phlo·gis·ton [flɔˈdʒistən] *n.* (古代化学认为可燃物中存在的)燃素, 热素.

phlog·o·pite [ˈflɔgəpait] *n.*【化】金云母.

phlo·rhi·zin [fləˈrizin] *n.* = phlorizin.

phlo·rid·zin [fləˈrizin] *n.* = phlorizin.

phlor·i·zin [ˈflɔːrizin, fləˈraizin] *n.*【化】根皮甙.

phlox [flɔks] *n.* ①【植】福禄考. ②〔P-〕【植】福禄考属.

phlyc·te·na [flikˈtiːnə] *n.* ***(pl. -nae*** [-niː]***)***【医】水泡; 小泡. **-nar** *a.*

phlyc·ten·ule [flikˈtenjul] *n.*【医】小水泡. **-ten·u·lar** *a.*

Phnom Penh, Phom Penh, Pnom-Penh [pˈnɔm ˈpen] 金边〔柬埔寨首都〕.

-phobe *comb. f.* 恐惧…的人, 反对…的人, 嫌〔厌〕恶…的人: hydro*phobe*; German*ophobe*.

-phobia *comb. f.* =-phobe 对…的恐惧〔嫌恶〕: hydro*phobia*; Anglo*phobia*.

pho·bi·a [ˈfəubjə] *n.* (病态的)恐惧, 憎恶.

pho·bic [ˈfəubik] *a.* ①(有关)病态性恐惧〔憎恶〕的. ②畏缩的, 怕招惹是非的.

pho·cine [ˈfəusain] *a.*【动】海豹的; 似海豹的.

pho·co·me·li·a [ˌfəukəuˈmiːliə, -ˈmiːljə] *n.*【医】短肢畸胎. **-me·lic** [-ˈmiːlik] *a.*

Phoe·be [ˈfiːbi] *n.* ①菲比〔女子名〕. ②【希神】月亮女神 (= Artemis). ③〔诗〕月亮. ④〔p-〕〔美俚〕(骰子的)对五点, 对梅花 (= little P-). ⑤【天】土卫 10.

phoe·be [ˈfiːbi] *n.*【动】(北美洲产)绯鹟.

Phoe·bus [ˈfiːbəs] *n.* ①【希神】太阳神 (=Apollo). ②〔诗〕太阳. **Phoe·be·an** [ˈfiːbiən] *a.*

Phoe·ni·ci·a [fiˈniʃiə, -ʃjə] *n.* 腓尼基〔叙利亚沿岸的古国〕.

Phoe·ni·ci·an [fiˈniʃiən] *a.* 腓尼基(人)的; 腓尼基语的. — *n.* ①腓尼基人. ②腓尼基语.

Phoe·nix [ˈfiːniks] *n.* 菲尼克斯〔美国城市〕.

phoe·nix [ˈfiːniks] *n.* ①【埃神】不死鸟, 长生鸟〔相传此鸟每五百年自焚后再生〕; 毁灭后会再生的事物; 不死的象征. ②(中国古代传说中的)凤凰. ③伟大天才, 绝代佳人, 一代尤物; 完人, 殊品. ④〔the P-〕【天】凤凰座. ⑤【植】海枣; 〔P-〕海枣属. *the Chinese* ～ 凤凰. ～ **tree** 梧桐.

phon [fɔn] *n.*【物】昉〔响度单位〕.

phon- *comb. f.* 〔用于元音前〕声, 音: *phon*ic.

phon. = phonetics.

pho·nate [fəuˈneit, ˈfəuneit] *vt., vi.* 发(音); 发成(声音). **pho·na·tion** [fəuˈneiʃən] *n.*

pho·nau·to·graph [fəuˈnɔːtəgrɑːf] *n.*【物】声波记振仪; 声波振动记录[图表].

phone[1] [fəun] *n.* 〔口〕电话; 电话机〔*telephone* 之略〕. *hang up the* ～ 挂起电话(机). *A* ～ *for you.* 你有一个电话. *Some one wants you on the* ～. 有人打电话给你, 有人叫你接电话. *Please call him to the* ～. 请他来接电话. — *vt.* 〔口〕①给…打电话. ②打电话通知(某事). — *vi.* 〔口〕打电话 ***(to)***. ～ ***up*** 打电话叫人. ～ **book** 电话簿. ～ **meter** 电话计数器.

phone[2] [fəun] *n.*【语音】单音, 音素〔元音或辅音〕. *a* ～ *chart* 语音表, 音素表. **pho·ne·mat·ic** [ˌfəuni(ː)ˈmætik] *a.* 音素的.

-phone *comb. f.* 声音, 说话: tele*phone*, micro*phone*.

pho·neme [ˈfəuniːm] *n.* ①【语音】音素〔如 kiːp (keep), kuːl (cool), kɔːl (call) 中的 k 音〕. ②音, 单音.

phone·me·ter [ˈfəunmiːtə] *n.* (电话的)通话计数器 (= phone meter).

pho·ne·mic [fəuˈniːmik] *a.* ①音素的; 有音素特征的; 以音素为根据的. ②音素学的.

pho·ne·mi·cist [fəuˈniːmisist] *n.* 音素学家.

pho·ne·mi·cize [fəˈniːmisaiz] *vt.* ***(-ciz·ed; -ciz·ing)*** 用音素符号写出〔表示〕. **-mi·ci·za·tion** *n.* 音素化.

pho·ne·mics [fəuˈniːmiks] *n.*【语音】音素学.

pho·nen·do·scope [fəˈnendəuskəup] *n.* 扩音听诊器.

pho·net·ic [fəuˈnetik] *a.* ①语音(上)的; 语音学的. ②表示语音的; 音形一致的. *international* ～ *alphabet* 国际

音标. ~ **notation** 标音法. ~ **signs [symbols]** 音标, 音符. ~ **transcription** 标音(法). ~ **typewriter** 口授打字机, 语音打字机. ~ **value** 音值.

pho·net·i·cal·ly [fəˈnetikəli] *ad.* 根据语音; 在语音上; 语音学上.

pho·ne·ti·cian [ˌfəuniˈtiʃən] *n.* 语音学家, 语音学研究者.

pho·net·i·cism [fəuˈnetisizəm] *n.* 音标标音法; 音标拼字法〔主义〕. **-i·cist** *n.* 语音学家; 主张按照发音拼字的人.

pho·net·i·cize [fəuˈnetisaiz] *vt.* 用音标表(音), 用发音符号写.

pho·net·ics [fəuˈnetiks] *n.* 语音学, 发音学.

pho·net·ist [ˈfəunitist] *n.* ①语音学家, 发音学家. ②主张按照发音拼字的人 (= phoneticist).

phone·vi·sion [ˈfəunˌviʒən] *n.* 【讯】电话电视〔一种收费制电视〕.

pho·ney, pho·n·y [ˈfəuni] *n.* 〔美俚〕①骗子; 冒名顶替的人. ②假货. — *a.* ①假的, 伪造的, 不值钱的. ②假冒的. *a* ~ *writer* 空头文学家. *a* ~ *rap* 〔美俚〕诬告. ~**man** 卖假宝石的人. **phon·i·ly** *ad.* 虚假地. **phon·i·ness** *n.* 虚假.

pho·nic [ˈfəunik, ˈfɔnik] *a.* ①音的, 声音的; 语音的. ②有声的, 浊音的. *a* ~ *symbol* 音符.

pho·nics [ˈfəuniks] *n.* ①声学. ②(以发音为重点的)基础语音教授法, 发音练习. ③〔罕〕= phonetics.

pho·no [ˈfəunəu] *n.* (*pl.* ~*s*) 〔口〕= phonograph.

phono- *comb. f.* 〔用于辅音前〕= phon-: *phono*film, *phono*gram.

pho·no·chem·is·try [ˈfəunəuˈkemistri] *n.* 【化】声化学.

pho·no·deik [ˈfəunədaik] *n.* 【物】声波显示仪.

pho·no·film [ˈfəunəfilm] *n.* 有声电影.

pho·no·gram [ˈfəunəgræm] *n.* ①(速记用的)表音符号; 标音符号. ②(留声机的)唱片; 【影】声带, 录音片. ③【讯】话传电报, 电话电报.

pho·no·graph [ˈfəunəgrɑːf] *n.* ①老式留声机; 机械录音机; 〔美〕留声机, 唱机. ②〔罕〕表音字, 音标字. — *vt.* 使灌音〔录音〕. ~ *needle* 唱针. ~ **record** 唱片. **-er** *n.* 表音速记法专家.

pho·no·graph·ic [ˌfəunəˈgræfik] *a.* ①留声机的, 唱机的. ②表音的, 表音速记法的. **-graph·i·cal·ly** *ad.*

pho·nog·ra·phy [fəuˈnɔgrəfi] *n.* ①表音法. ②表音速记法; 速记法.

pho·no·lite [ˈfəunəlait] *n.* 【矿】响石, 响岩.

pho·no·log·ic, pho·no·log·i·cal [ˌfəunəˈlɔdʒik, -kəl] *a.* ①语音的; 音位学的; 音韵学的. ②按照音位〔音韵〕学原理的.

pho·nol·o·gy [fəuˈnɔlədʒi] *n.* ①音位学; 音韵学. ②语音学〔主指语音的历史研究〕. **-gist** *n.* 音位学家; 音韵学家.

Pho·no·ma·ni·a [ˌfəunəˈmeiniə] *n.* 嗜杀狂; 嗜害狂.

pho·nom·e·ter [fəuˈnɔmitə] *n.* 声强计, 音强度计, 测音计.

pho·no·mo·tor [ˌfəunəˈməutə] *n.* (电唱机或录音机上的)电动机.

pho·non [ˈfəunɔn] *n.* 【物】声子〔晶体点阵振动能的量子〕.

pho·no·phore [ˈfəunəufɔ] *n.* (电)报(电)话两用机.

pho·no·phote [ˈfəunəufəut] *n.* (把音波变成光波的)音波发光机.

pho·no·pore [ˈfəunəupɔː] *n.* = phonophore.

pho·no·re·cord [ˈfəunəuˌrekɔːd] *n.* 唱片 = phonograph record.

pho·no·scope [ˈfəunəuskəup] *n.* 【物】检弦器, 验声器; 微音器; 乐音自记器.

pho·no·type [ˈfəunəutaip] *n.* 音标铅字(体). **-no·typ·y** [-i] *n.* 表音印刷法〔速记法〕.

pho·no·vi·sion [ˈfəunəˌviʒən] *n.* = phonevision.

pho·n·y [ˈfəuni] *a., n.* 〔美俚〕= phoney.

phoo·ie, phoo·ey [ˈfuːi] *int.* 〔美〕呸! 啐! 〔表示讨厌或不信〕.

-phore *comb. f.* 带者, 结者, 运者: sema*phore.*

pho·re·sis [fəuˈriːsis] *n.* 电泳现象 (= cataphoresis).

phor·mi·um [ˈfɔːmiəm] *n.* 【植】新西兰亚麻.

pho·ro·nid [fəˈrəunid] *n.* 帚虫纲 (*Phoronidea*) 动物. — *a.* 【动】帚虫纲的.

pho·ro·nom·ics [ˌfɔrəˈnɔmiks] *n.* 〔罕〕动学.

phos·gene [ˈfɔzdʒiːn] *n.* 【化】光气, 碳酰氯; 【军】毒气 (= ~ gas). ~ **bomb** 光气弹.

phos·gen·ite [ˈfɔzdʒinait] *n.* 【矿】角铅矿.

phosph- *comb. f.* 〔用于元音前〕= pospho-: *phosph*amide.

phos·pha·mide [ˈfɔsfəmaid] *n.* 【化】磷酰胺.

phos·pha·tase [ˈfɔsfəteis] *n.* 【生化】磷酸酶.

phos·phate [ˈfɔsfeit] *n.* ①【化】磷酸盐; 磷酸脂; 磷块石. ②(含有少量磷酸的)汽水. ~ *fertilizer* 磷肥. *calcium* ~ 磷酸钙. ~ *of soda* 磷酸钠. ~ *rock* 磷酸盐岩.

phos·phat·ic [fɔsˈfætik] *a.* 【化】(含)磷酸(盐)的. *a* ~ *deposit* 含磷沉淀物. ~ *manure* 磷肥.

phos·pha·tide, phos·pha·tid [ˈfɔsfətaid, -tid] *n.* 【化】磷脂.

phos·pha·tize [ˈfɔsfətaiz] *vt.* ①使变成磷酸盐, 用磷酸盐处理. ②用磷酸处理. **-za·tion** *n.*

phos·pha·tu·ri·a [ˌfɔsfəˈtjuəriə, -ˈtuər-] *n.* 【医】磷酸盐尿. **-tu·ric** *a.*

phos·phene [ˈfɔsfiːn] *n.* 【医】压眼闪光; 光幻视.

phos·phide [ˈfɔsfaid] *n.* 【化】磷化物. *hydrogen* ~ 磷化氢.

phos·phine [ˈfɔsfiːn] *n.* 【化】①磷化氢; 三氢化磷. ②碱性染革黄棕.

phos·phite [ˈfɔsfait] *n.* 【化】亚磷酸盐.

phospho- *comb. f.* 磷: *phospho*nic.

phos·pho·cre·a·tine [ˌfɔsfəuˈkriətiːn, -tin] *n.* 【化】磷(酸基)肌酸.

phos·pho·lip·id [ˌfɔsfəuˈlipid] *n.* 【化】磷脂 (= phosphatide, phospholipide).

phos·pho·nic [fɔsˈfɔnik] *n.* 【化】磷(酸)的.

phos·pho·ni·um [fɔsˈfəuniəm] *n.* 【化】磷(根).

phos·pho·pro·tein [ˌfɔsfəuˈprəutiːn, -tiːin] *n.* 【化】磷朊.

Phos·phor [ˈfɔsfə] *n.* 〔诗〕晓星, 启明星, 金星.

phos·phor [ˈfɔsfə] *n.* 黄磷; 〔罕〕磷光体. ~ **bronze** 磷青铜. ~ **screen** 荧光屏.

phosphor- *comb. f.* 〔置于元音前〕= phosphoro.

phos·pho·rate [ˈfɔsfəreit] *vt.* 使和磷化合, 给…加磷, 使含磷. **-d** *a.* 含磷的.

phos·pho·resce [ˌfɔsfəˈres] *vi.* 发磷光; 磷似地发光; 发磷火.

phos·pho·res·cence [ˌfɔsfəˈresns] *n.* ①磷光(现象); 磷光性; 鬼火. ②磷光器.

phos·pho·res·cent [ˌfɔsfəˈresnt] *a.* 发磷光的; 磷光质的.

phos·pho·ret·ed, phos·pho·ret·ted [ˈfɔsfəretid] *a.* ①含(低)磷的. ②与磷化合的 (= phosphuret(t)ed).

phos·phor·ic [ˈfɔsfɔrik] *a.* 磷的, 含磷的; 含有五价磷的; 象磷的. ~ **acid** 磷酸.

phos·pho·rism [ˈfɔsfərizəm] *n.* 慢性磷中毒.

phos·phor·ite [ˈfɔsfərait] *n.* ①【化】亚磷脂肟酸. ②【矿】磷灰岩, 磷钙石. ~ **rock** 【地】磷灰岩.

phosphoro- *comb. f.* 磷, 磷光, 含磷的: *phosphoro*scope.

phos·phor·o·graph [ˈfɔsfərəugrɑːf, -græf] *n.* 磷光画; 磷光像.

phos·pho·rog·ra·phy [ˌfɔsfəˈrɔgrəfi] *n.* 磷光画法; 磷光像术.

phos·phor·ol·y·sis [ˌfɔsfəˈrɔlisis] *n.* 【化】磷酸解(作用).

phos·phor·o·scope [fɔsˈfɔːrəskəup, -ˈfɔr-] *n.* 【物】磷光镜.

phos·phor·ous [ˈfɔsfərəs] *a.* 磷的,亚磷的;含有三价磷的;含磷的. ~ **acid** 亚磷酸. ~ **bomb** 含磷(燃烧)弹. ~ **bronze** 磷青铜.

phos·phor·us [ˈfɔsfərəs] *n.* ①【化】磷. ②磷光体(= phosphor). ~ **necrosis**【医】磷毒性颚骨坏死〔俗称 phossy jaw〕. ~ **pentoxide**【化】五氧化二磷.

phos·pho·ryl·ase [ˈfɔsfəriˌleis, fɔsˈfɔːr-] *n.* 【生化】磷酸化酶.

phos·pho·ryl·ate [ˈfɔsfərileit] *vt.* 使磷酸化. **-ryl·a·tion** *n.* 磷酸化.

phos·phu·ret·(t)ed [ˈfɔsfjuretid] *a.* 【化】= phosphoret(t)ed.

phos·sy [ˈfɔsi] *a.* 〔口〕磷的,磷毒性的. ~ **jaw** 〔口〕磷毒性颌疽(= phosphorus necrosis).

phot [fɔt, fəut] *n.* 【物】辐透,厘米烛光〔照明单位,= 1 流明/厘米^2〕.

phot. = ①photograph. ②photographer. ③photographic. ④photography.

phot- *comb. f.* = photo.

pho·tic [ˈfəutik] *a.* ①(关于)光的. ②(有机体)发光(性)的;靠发光(刺激)的. ③透光的(尤指透日光);感光的;受光的. **-s** *n.* 光学.

pho·tism [ˈfəutizəm] *n.* 【心】幻视;光幻觉;发光性.

pho·to [ˈfəutəu] *n.* *(pl. ~s)* 〔口〕照片(= photograph). ~ **finish**〔美赛马〕(因到达终点时前后极接近,只能凭拍摄照片判断胜负的)照相终局;〔喻〕势均力敌的较量. ~ **Joe**〔美空俚〕单座摄影飞机驾驶员. — *vt.* 〔口〕给…照相.

photo- *comb. f.* 光;光电;照相(术): *photo*chemistry, *photo*chrome, *photo*conduction.

pho·to·ac·tin·ic [ˌfəutəuækˈtinik] *a.* (发)光化射线的;能产生光化作用的.

pho·to·ac·ti·vate [ˌfəutəuˈæktiveit] *vt.* 【物】用光使敏化;【化】用光催化. **-ti·va·tion** *n.*

pho·to·ac·tive [ˌfəutəuˈæktiv] *a.* 【物、化】光敏的.

pho·to·ac·tor [ˌfəutəuˈæktə] *n.* 【无】光电变换元件.

pho·to·ad·sorp·tion [ˌfəutəuædˈsɔːpʃən] *n.* 【物】光敏吸附.

pho·to·au·to·tro·phic [ˈfəutəuˌɔːtəˈtrɔfik] *a.* (指植物和某些微生物)光合自养的.

pho·to-beat [ˌfəutəuˈbiːt] *n.* 【物】光拍,光频差拍.

pho·to·bi·ot·ic [ˌfəutəubaiˈɔtik] *a.* 【生】依光生存的.

pho·to·cat·a·list [ˌfəutəuˈkætəlist] *n.* 【化】光催化剂.

pho·to·ca·tal·y·sis [ˌfəutəukəˈtælisis] *n.* 【化】光催化作用.

pho·to·cat·a·lyst [ˌfəutəuˈkætəlist] *n.* 【化】光催化剂.

pho·to·cath·ode [ˌfəutəuˈkæθəud] *n.* 【物】光阴极,光电阴极.

pho·to·cell [ˈfəutəsel] *n.* 【物】光电管,光电池.

pho·to·ce·ram·ic [ˌfəutəusiˈræmik] *a.* 用照相图样装饰陶器的. **-s** *n.* 用照相图样装饰陶器的工艺.

pho·to·chart·ing [ˌfəutəuˈtʃɑːtiŋ] *n.* 摄影制图.

pho·to·chem·is·try [ˌfəutəuˈkemistri] *n.* 光化学. **-chem·i·cal** *a.*

pho·to·chrome [ˈfəutəkrəum] *n.* 【摄】彩色照片.

pho·to·chro·mic [ˌfəutəuˈkrəumik] *a.* 光致变色的,光色的. **-chro·mism** *n.* 光致变色现象.

pho·to·chro·my [ˈfəutəkrəumi] *n.* 【摄】彩色照相术.

pho·to·chron·o·graph [ˌfəutəuˈkrɔnəgrɑːf] *n.* ①活动物体照相机. ②活动物体照片. ③【天、物】活动物体照相计时仪. ④【天】恒星中天摄影仪. **-y** [-krəˈnɔgrəfi] *n.* 活动物体照相术.

pho·to·ci·ne·sis [ˌfəutəusaiˈniːsis] *n.* = photokinesis.

pho·to·co·ag·u·la·tion [ˌfəutəukəuˌægjuˈleiʃən] *n.* 光致凝结〔利用激光等造成瘢组织,用以治疗目疾或实验〕. **-la·tor** *n.* 光致凝结器.

pho·to·com·pose [ˌfəutəukəmˈpəuz] *vt.* 【印】照相排(版),照相排(字).

pho·to·com·po·si·tion [ˌfəutəuˌkɔmpəˈziʃən] *n.* 照相排版;照相排字.

pho·to·con [ˈfəutəkɔn] *n.* 【无】光(电)导元件,光导器件.

pho·to·con·duc·tion [ˌfəutəukənˈdʌkʃən] *n.* 【物】光电导.

pho·to·con·duc·tive [ˌfəutəukənˈdʌktiv] *a.* 【物】光电导的.

pho·to·con·duc·tiv·i·ty [ˌfəutəuˌkɔndʌkˈtiviti] *n.* 【物】光电导性.

pho·to·con·duc·tor [ˌfəutəukənˈdʌktə] *n.* 【物】光电导体.

pho·to·cop·i·er [ˌfəutəuˈkɔpiə] *n.* 影印机.

pho·to·cop·y [ˈfəutəuˌkɔpi] *n.* 影印本,照相复制本. — *vt.* 影印,照相复制.

pho·to·cur·rent [ˈfəutəuˌkəːrənt] *n.* 【物】光电流.

pho·to·de·tec·tor [ˌfəutəudiˈtektə] *n.* 【物】光电探测器.

pho·to·di·ode [ˌfəutəuˈdaiəud] *n.* 【无】光电二极管.

pho·to·dis·in·te·gra·tion [ˌfəutəudisˌintigˈreiʃən] *n.* 【物】光致蜕变.

pho·to·dis·so·ci·a·tion [ˌfəutəudiˌsəusiˈeiʃən, -ʃiː-] *n.* ①【化】光致离解. ②【物】光致蜕变(= photodisintegration).

pho·to·dra·ma [ˈfəutədrɑːmə] *n.* 影片剧〔尤指悲剧或情节曲折紧张的故事影片〕. **pho·to·dra·mat·ic** [ˌfəutədrəˈmætik] *a.*

pho·to·dup·li·cate [ˌfəutəuˈdjuːplikeit] *vt., vi.* 照相复制. — [ˌfəutəuˈdjuːplikit] *n.* 照相复制件.

pho·to·du·pli·ca·tion [ˌfəutəuˌdjuːpliˈkeiʃən] *n.* 照相复制术(= photocopy).

pho·to·dy·nam·ic [fəutəudaiˈnæmik] *a.* 光能作用的;光力学的.

pho·to·dy·nam·ics [ˌfəutəudaiˈnæmiks] *n. pl.* 〔动词用单数〕①(对植物的)光能作用. ②光力学.

pho·to·e·las·tic [ˌfəutəuiˈlæstik] *a.* 【物】光测弹性的.

pho·to·e·las·tic·i·ty [ˌfəutəuˌilæsˈtisiti] *n.* 光测弹性(学).

pho·to·e·lec·tric, pho·to·e·lec·tri·cal [ˌfəutəuiˈlektrik, -trikəl] *a.* 【物】光电的. ~ **cell** 光电管;光电池. ~ **colour analyzer** 光电析色器. ~ **current** 光电流. ~ **effect** 光电效应[作用]. ~ **photometer** 光电光度计.

pho·to·e·lec·tric·i·ty [ˌfəutəuilekˈtrisiti] *n.* 【物】光电(学);光电现象.

pho·to·e·lec·tro·lu·mi·nes·cence [ˌfəutəuiˌlektrəˌljuːmiˈnesns] *n.* 【物】光控电致发光,光控场致发光.

pho·to·e·lec·tro·mo·tive [ˌfəutəuiˌlektrəˈməutiv] *a.* 【物】光电动的. ~ **force** 光电动势.

pho·to·e·lec·tron [ˌfəutəuiˈlektrɔn] *n.* 【物、化】光电子.

pho·to·e·lec·tron·ics [ˌfəutəuilekˈtrɔniks] *n. pl.* 〔用作 sing.〕光电子学.

pho·to·el·e·ment [ˌfəutəuˈelimənt] *n.* 【物】阻挡层光电池;光生伏打电池(= photovoltaic cell).

pho·to·e·mis·sion [ˌfəutəuiˈmiʃən] *n.* 【物】光电放射. **-to·e·mis·sive** [-ˈmisiv] *a.*

pho·to·en·grav·ing [ˌfəutəuinˈgreiviŋ] *n.* 【物】光刻;【印】照相凸版(制版术);照相感光制(凸)版.

pho·to·ex·cit·a·tion [ˌfəutəuˌeksiˈteiʃən] *n.* 【原】光致激发.

pho·to·fin·ish·ing [ˌfəutəuˈfiniʃiŋ] *n.* 冲洗胶卷,洗印照片. **-ish·er** *n.*

pho·to·fis·sion [ˌfəutəuˈfiʃən] *n.*【原】光致(核)裂变.
pho·to·flash [ˈfəutəuflæʃ] *n.* ①(照相用)闪光灯. ②闪光灯照片. ～ **bomb** 照相闪光灯.
pho·to·flood [ˈfəutəuflʌd] *n.* 超压强烈溢光灯〔摄影用〕.
pho·to·flu·o·rog·ra·phy [ˌfəutəufluəˈrɔgrəfi] *n.* 萤光屏图象摄影. **-flu·o·rog·raph·ic** [-ˌfluərəˈgræfik] *a.*
pho·to·flu·or·o·scope [ˌfəutəuˈflu:ərəskəup] *n.* 萤光屏;萤光屏照相机.
pho·tog [fəˈtɔg] *n.* ①= photograph *(n.)*. ②= photographer. ③ = photography.
pho·to·gel·a·tin [ˌfəutəuˈdʒelətin] *a.*【印】珂罗版的. ～ **process**【印】珂罗版制版术.
pho·to·gen [ˈfəutəudʒən] *n.* ①【矿】页岩煤油. ②【生】发光动〔植〕物.
pho·to·gene [ˈfəutəudʒi:n] *n.*【心】后〔余〕象;闭眼留象(= after-image).
pho·to·gen·ic [ˌfəutəuˈdʒenik] *a.* ①【生】发光的;发磷光的. ②由于光而产生的;【医】(疾病)由光导致的〔如皮肤病等〕. ③极适于拍照的,可以拍得很美的,上照的.
pho·to·ge·ol·o·gy [fəutəudʒiˈɔlədʒi] *n.*【地】摄影地质学.
pho·to·glyph [ˈfəutəglif] *n.*【印】照相雕刻版.
pho·tog·ly·phy [fəˈtɔglifi] *n.* 照相雕刻版术.
pho·to·gram [ˈfəutəgræm] *n.* 黑影照片, 物影照片〔将物体放在光源和感光体之间制成〕.
pho·to·gram·me·try [ˌfəutəuˈgræmitri] *n.* 摄影制图法; 摄影测量术. **-met·ric** [-ˈmetrik] *a.* **-gram·met·ri·cal·ly** *ad.* **-gram·me·trist** *n.* 摄影制图〔测量〕者.
pho·to·graph [ˈfəutəgrɑ:f, -græf] *n.* ①照片, 相片. ②栩栩如生的描绘; 逼真的印象. *an instantaneous ～* 瞬时快照. ***have [get] one's ～ taken = sit for one's ～*** 请人拍照. ***have a ～ taken with*** 和…合影. ***take a ～ of*** 拍摄. — *vt.* ①为…照相, 为…摄影. ②逼真地描绘; 把…深刻在印象中. — *vi.* 照相, 被拍照; 现在相片上. ～ *badly* 照得不好;不上照.
pho·tog·ra·pher [fəˈtɔgrəfə] *n.* 照相师; 摄影家; 摄影者.
pho·to·graph·ic, pho·to·graph·i·cal [fəutəˈgræfik, -kəl] *a.* ① 摄影(术)的; 摄影用的; 照相似的. ②(描写或记述)逼真的, 生动的; 能详细记住所见事物的. *a ～ album* 照相簿. ～ **camera** 照相机. ～ **developer** 显像〔影〕剂. ～ **studio** 照相馆, 摄影室. **-graph·i·cal·ly** *ad.*
pho·tog·ra·phy [fəˈtɔgrəfi] *n.* 摄影术; 照相术.
pho·to·gra·vure [ˌfəutəgrəˈvjuə] *n.* 照相凹版(印刷). — *vt.* 用照相凹版印刷.
pho·to·gun [ˈfəutəgʌn] *n.* 光电子枪.
pho·to·he·li·o·graph [ˌfəutəuˈhi:liəugrɑ:f] *n.*【天】太阳照相机.
pho·to·hole [ˈfəutəhəul] *n.*【物】光穴.
pho·to·in·duc·tion [ˌfəutəuinˈdʌkʃən] *n.*【生】光诱导.
pho·to·i·on·i·za·tion [ˌfəutəuˌaiəniˈzeiʃən] *n.* 光致电离(作用).
pho·to·jour·nal·ism [ˌfəutəuˈdʒə:nəlizm] *n.* 摄影新闻工作,摄影报道. **-jour·nal·ist** *n.* 摄影记者.
pho·to·ki·ne·sis [ˌfəutəukiˈni:sis] *n.*【生理】趋光性. **-ki·net·ic** [-ˈnetik] *a.*
pho·to·lith [ˈfəutəliθ] *n.* = photolithography. — *vt.* = photolithograph *(vt.)*. — *a.* = photolithographic.
pho·to·lith·o·graph [ˌfəutəuˈliθəgrɑ:f] *n.* 照相平版(印刷品). — *vt.* 用照相平版印刷. **-o·graph·ic** *a.* 照相平版印刷的. **pho·to·li·thog·ra·phy** *n.* 照相平版印刷术.
pho·tol·o·gy [fəuˈtɔlədʒi] *n.* 光学.
pho·to·lu·mi·nes·cence [ˌfəutəuˌlju:miˈnesns] *n.*【电】光致发光. **-mi·nes·cent** *a.*
pho·tol·y·sis [fəuˈtɔlisis] *n.*【生】光(分)解(作用).
pho·to·lyt·ic [ˌfəutəˈlitik] *a.*
photom. = photometry.
pho·to·mag·net·ic [ˌfəutəumægˈnetik] *a.*【物】光磁的.
pho·to·map [ˈfəutəumæp] *n.* 航空照相地图. — *vt.* 给(城市等)航空摄制地图. — *vi.* 航空照相制图.
pho·to·me·chan·i·cal [ˌfəutəumiˈkænikəl] *a.* 照相制版(工艺)的. **-ly** *ad.*
pho·tom·e·ter [fəuˈtɔmitə] *n.*【物】光度计; 光觉计;【摄】曝光表.
pho·to·met·ric, pho·to·met·ri·cal [ˌfəutəuˈmetrik, -rikəl] *a.* 光度计的;测量光度的;光度学的. ～ *units* 光力〔光度〕单位.
pho·tom·e·try [fəuˈtɔmitri] *n.* 光度学; 光度术.
pho·to·mi·cro·graph [ˌfəutəuˈmaikrəugrɑ:f] *n.* 显微照相;显微照片. — *vt.* 为…拍摄显微照相. **-mi·crog·ra·phy** *n.* 显微照相术.
pho·to·mi·cro·scope [ˌfəutəuˈmaikrəuskəup] *n.* 显微照相机.
pho·to·mix·ing [ˌfəutəuˈmiksiŋ] *n.*【物】光混频.
pho·to·mon·tage [ˌfəutəumɔnˈtɑ:ʒ] *n.*【摄】集成照片;集成照片制作法.
pho·to·mul·ti·pli·er [fəutəuˈmʌltiplaiə] *n.*【电】光电倍增管.
pho·to·mu·ral [ˌfəutəuˈmjuərəl] *n.* (装饰用)大幅照片,壁画式照片.
pho·ton [ˈfəutɔn] *n.* ①【物】光子. ②【医】见光度〔网膜照明单位〕.
pho·to·neg·a·tive [ˌfəutəuˈnegətiv] *a.*【生】负趋光性的.
pho·to·neu·tron [ˌfəutəuˈnju:trɔn, -ˈnu:-] *n.*【物】光激中子.
pho·to-off·set [ˌfəutəuˈɔ:fset] *n.* 照相胶印法.
pho·to·pe·ri·od [ˌfəutəuˈpiəriəd] *n.* 光周期. **-pe·ri·od·ic** [-ˌpiəriˈɔdik] *a.*
pho·to·pe·ri·od·ism [ˌfəutəuˈpiəriədizm] *n.*【生】光周期现象 (= photoperiodicity).
pho·to·phase [ˈfəutəfeiz] *n.*【植】光照(发育)阶段.
pho·toph·i·lous [fəuˈtɔfiləs] *a.*【生】适光的,喜光的 (= photophilic). **pho·to·phi·ly** *n.*
pho·to·pho·bi·a [ˌfəutəuˈfəubiə] *n.*【医】畏光,羞明.
pho·to·phone [ˈfəutəufəun] *n.*【讯】光线电话机;光音机.
pho·to·phore [ˈfəutəufɔ:] *n.*【动】(发光动物的)发光器官.
pho·to·pho·re·sis [ˌfəutəufəˈri:sis] *n.*【物】光致迁动,光泳(现象).
pho·to·pi·a [fəuˈtəupiə] *n.*【医】光适应, 眼对光调节. **-to·pic** [-ˈtəupik, -ˈtɔpik] *a.*
pho·to·plane [ˈfəutəuplein] *n.*【空】摄影飞机.
pho·to·plas·tic [ˌfəutəuˈplæstik] *a.*【物】光范性的.
pho·to·play [ˈfəutəplei] *n.* 电影(剧).
pho·to·play·er [ˈfəutəupleiə] *n.* 电影演员.
pho·to·play·wright [ˌfəutəuˈpleirait] *n.* 电影编剧者.
pho·to·pol·y·mer·i·za·tion [ˈfəutəuˌpɔliməraiˈzeiʃən] *n.*【化】光致聚合(作用).
pho·to·pos·i·tive [ˌfəutəuˈpɔzitiv] *a.*【生】正趋光性的.
pho·to·print [ˈfəutəuprint] *n.* 影印;影印画.
pho·to·pro·ton [ˌfəutəuˈprəutɔn] *n.*【物】光(激)质子.
pho·top·tom·e·ter [ˌfəutɔpˈtɔmitə] *n.*【医】光觉计.
pho·to·ra·di·o·gram [ˌfəutəuˈreidiəugræm] *n.* 无线电传真图片.
pho·to·re·cep·tor [ˌfəutəuriˈseptə] *n.*【生】光感受器, 受光体. **-cep·tion** *n.*【生】光感受. **-cep·tive** *a.*【生】光感受的.
pho·to·re·con·nais·sance [ˌfəutəuriˈkɔnisəns] *n.*【军】(空中)照相侦察. *a ～ satellite* 侦察卫星.
pho·to·re·cor·der [ˌfəutəuriˈkɔ:də] *n.* 摄影〔照相〕记

录器；自动记录照相机．

pho·to·re·duc·tion [ˌfəutəuriˈdʌkʃən] *n.*【化】光致还原．

pho·to·re·pea·ter [ˌfəutəuriˈpiːtə] *n.* 照相复印机．

pho·to·re·sist [ˌfəutəuriˈzist] *n.*【物】光致抗蚀剂．

pho·to·sen·si·tive [ˌfəutəuˈsensitiv] *a.* 感光性的；光敏的．**-si·tiv·i·ty, -ness** *n.*【物】光敏性．

pho·to·sen·si·tize [ˌfəutəuˈsensiˌtaiz] *vt.* 使具有感光性，使光敏．**-si·ti·za·tion** *n.* 光敏作用．**-r** *n.*【化】光敏剂．

pho·to·set [ˈfəutəuˌset] *vt.* *(-set; -set·ting)*【印】照相排版．

pho·to·sphere [ˈfəutəusfiə] *n.*【天】光球；光球层．

pho·to·stat [ˈfəutəustæt] *n.* 直接影印机；直接影印制品．— *vt.* 用直接影印机复制．

pho·to·syn·the·sis [ˌfəutəuˈsinθəsis] *n.*【植】光合作用；光能合成．

pho·to·syn·the·size [ˌfəutəuˈsinθisaiz] *vt., vi.* (使)进行光合作用，(使)进行光能合成．

pho·to·syn·thet·ic [ˌfəutəusinˈθetik] *a.*【植】光合的．**-i·cal·ly** *ad.*

pho·to·tac·tic [ˌfəutəuˈtæktik] *a.*【生】趋光性的．

pho·to·tax·is, pho·to·tax·y [ˌfəutəuˈtæksis, ˈfəutəutæksi] *n.*【生】趋光性．*positive* ～ 向光性．*negative* ～ 背光性．

pho·to·tel·e·gram [ˌfəutəuˈteligræm] *n.*【讯】传真电报．

pho·to·tel·e·graph [ˌfəutəuˈteligrɑːf] *n.*【讯】传真电报(机)．— *vt., vi.* 用电报传真发送(照片)．**-ic** *a.* **-y** *n.* 电传真；光通讯．

pho·to·tel·e·phone [ˌfəutəuˈtelifəun] *n.*【讯】光线电话机．

pho·to·tel·e·scope [ˌfəutəuˈteliskəup] *n.*【天】照相望远镜．

pho·to·ther·a·peu·tics [ˌfəutəuˌθerəˈpjuːtiks] *n.*【医】光线疗法．

pho·to·ther·a·py [ˌfəutəuˈθerəpi] *n.* = phototherapeutics.

pho·to·therm·ic [ˌfəutəuˈθəːmik] *a.* 光热的；关于光和热的．

pho·to·ti·mer [ˈfəutəuˌtaimə] *n.* ①曝光计．②(记录赛跑结果等的)摄影计时器．

pho·tot·o·nus [fəuˈtɔtnəs] *n.*【生】光激性．**-ton·ic** [-ˈtɔnik] *a.*

pho·to·to·pog·ra·phy [ˌfəutəutəˈpɔgrəfi] *n.* = photogrammetry.

pho·to·tox·is [ˌfəutəuˈtɔksis] *n.*【医】光线[波射线]损害．

pho·to·tran·sis·tor [ˌfəutəutrænˈzistə, -ˈsis-] *n.*【无】光电晶体管．

pho·tot·ro·p·ism [fəuˈtɔtrəpizəm] *n.* ①【植】向光性．②【物】光色互变(现象)．

pho·tot·ropy [fəuˈtɔtrəpi] *n.*【物】光色互变(现象)．

pho·to·tube [ˈfəutəutjuːb] *n.*【无】光电管．

pho·to·type [ˈfəutəutaip] *n.*【印】照相凸版；照相凸版制版术；照相凸版印刷品．

pho·to·type·set·ting [ˌfəutəuˈtaipˌsetiŋ] *n.* 照相排版，照相排字 (= photocomposition)．**-set·ter** *n.*

pho·to·ty·pog·ra·phy [ˌfəutəutaiˈpɔgrəfi] *n.*【印】照相排版；照相凸版术．**-ty·po·graph·ic** *a.*

pho·to·typ·y [ˌfəutəuˈtaipi] *n.*【印】照相凸版制版术．

pho·to·var·i·ster [ˌfəutəuˈvɛəristə] *n.*【物】光敏电阻．

pho·to·vi·sion [ˌfəutəuˈviʒən] *n.* 电视．

pho·to·vol·ta·ic [ˌfəutəuvɔlˈteiik] *a.*【物】光电的．

pho·to·zin·co·graph [ˌfəutəuˈziŋkəgrɑːf] *n.* 照相锌版(印制品)．— *vt.* 用照相锌版印制．

pho·to·zin·cog·ra·phy [ˌfəutəuziŋˈkɔgrəfi] *n.* 照相锌版术．

pho·tron·ic [fəuˈtrɔnik] *a.*【物】(用)光电池的．

phr. = phrase.

phras·al [ˈfreizl] *a.* 短语的，片语的．～ *modifier* 短语修饰语．

phrase [freiz] *n.* ①措辞，用语．②成语；名言；警句；格言，箴言．③【语法】短语，片语，词组．④习惯用语．⑤〔*pl.*〕空话，废话．⑥【乐】短句，乐句．⑦【舞】舞式．*an adjective* [*an adverb(ial), a noun*] ～ 形容词[副词、名词]短语．*a set* ～ 固定词组；成语．*an idle* ～ 空话．*We have had enough of* ～*s.* 废话已经够了．*felicity of* ～ 措词恰当．*speak in simple* ～ 用简单的话(表达)．— *vt.*①用话表示；用短语描述；把…叫做…．②〔Scot.〕称赞，恭维；巴结．③【乐】把…分成短句．*Thus he* ～*d it.* 他就是这样说的．～ **book** 成语集；短语集．～**-maker** 擅长创造警句者．～**-monger** 爱用陈词滥调的人，空谈主义者．～**-mongering** 空谈；讲漂亮话．

phra·se·o·gram, phra·se·o·graph [ˈfreiziəgræm, -grɑːf] *n.* 表示短语的速记符号．

phra·se·ol·o·gist [ˌfreiziˈɔlədʒist] *n.* 喜吹咬文嚼字的人；爱用陈腐词藻的人．

phra·se·ol·o·gy [ˌfreiziˈɔlədʒi] *n.* ①用语，措词；熟语．②术语．③〔集合词〕词句，表达方式．**phra·se·ol·o·gist** *n.* ①善于措词造句的人．②满口陈词滥调的人．**-o·log·i·cal** [ˌfreiziəˈlɔdʒikəl] *a.* ①措词的，用语的，表达方式的．②用陈词滥调表达的．③喜欢用陈词滥调的．

phras·ing [ˈfreiziŋ] *n.* ①措词；表达法．②【乐】短句的构成．

phra·try [ˈfreitri] *n.* ①【希腊史】(雅典的)氏族．②【社】宗族分支〔部落中由数个奉同一图腾的氏族组成的族外通婚单位〕．

phre·at·ic [fri(ː)ˈætik] *a.* ①井的，凿井取得的．②【地】自由地下水层的．

phren., phrenol. = phrenology.

phren- *comb. f.* 膈，心灵：*phren*algia.

phre·nal·gi·a [friˈnældʒiə] *n.*【医】①精神痛苦．②膈痛．

phre·net·ic, phre·net·i·cal [friˈnetik, -kəl] *a.* 脑炎的，得脑炎的；狂乱的，发狂的；狂热的 (= frenetic)．

phren·ic [ˈfrenik] *a.* ①【解】横隔膜的．②【生理】精神上的；心理的．

phre·ni·tis [friˈnaitis] *n.*【医】①膈炎；脑炎．②精神错乱，发狂；谵妄．

phreno- *comb. f.* = phren.

phre·nol·o·gy [friˈnɔlədʒi] *n.* 颅相学；骨相学．**phren·o·log·ic, phren·o·log·ical** *a.* **phre·nol·o·gist** *n.* 颅[骨]相学家．

phren·sy [ˈfrenzi] *n., vt.* = frenzy.

Phryg·i·an [ˈfridʒiən] *a.* (小亚细亚古国) 弗利吉亚 (Phrygia) (人)的．—*n.* 弗利吉亚人；弗利吉亚语．～ **cap** 弗利吉亚帽，垂尖圆锥帽 (= cap of liberty)．

phry·nin [ˈfrainin] *n.* 蟾蜍毒．

PHS, P.H.S. = Public Health Service 公共保健服务．

phthal·ein(e) [ˈθæliːn, -iin; ˈfθæl-] *n.*【化】酞．

phthal·ic [ˈθælik] *a.* ～ **acid**【化】酞酸，苯二酸．

phthal·in [ˈθælin] *n.*【化】酞林，酞隐(类)．

phthal·o·cy·a·nine [ˌθæləˈsaiəniːn, ˌfθæl-] *n.* 酞花青(染料)，苯二甲蓝染料．

phthal·yl·sulph·a·thi·a·zole, phthal·yl·sulf·a·thi·a·zole [ˈθælilˌsʌlfəˈθaiəzəul] *n.*【药】羧苯甲酰磺胺噻唑．

phthi·o·col [ˈθaiəkɔl, ˈfθaiə-] *n.*【生化】结核 (菌) 萘醌；结核黄素．

phthi·ri·a·sis [θiˈraiəsis] *n.* 虱病 (= pediculosis)．

phthi·sic [ˈθaisik, ˈtizik] *n.*【医】①肺结核．②肺结核患者．— *a.* (有)肺结核的．

phthis·i·cal [ˈθaisikəl] *a.* = phthisic *(a.)*.

phthis·i·o·log·y [ˌθaisiˈɔlədʒi] *n.* 【医】痨瘵学,肺痨学.
phthi·sis [ˈθaisis, ˈfθaisis] *n.* *(pl.* ***-ses*** [-si:z]*)* 【医】肺结核;消耗性疾病.
phut(t) [fʌt] *ad.*, *n.* 〔口〕啪的一声. ***go [be gone]*** ~ 〔俚〕①(车胎)爆掉,泄气. ②〔喻〕失败,告吹.
phy·co·er·y·thrin [ˌfaikəuˈeriθrin] *n.* 【生化】藻红朊.
phy·col·o·gy [faiˈkɔlədʒi] *n.* 【植】藻类学.
Phy·co·my·cete [ˌfaikəuˈmaisi:t] *n.* 藻菌纲 *(Phycomycetes)* 〔包括霜霉菌;黑霉菌〕. **-ce·tous** [ˈsi:təs] *a.*
phy·co·ph(a)e·in [ˌfaikəuˈfi:in] *n.* 【生化】藻褐素.
phy·cox·an·thin [ˌfaikɔkˈsænθin] *n.* 【生化】藻黄素.
phy·la [ˈfailə] phylum 的复数.
phy·lac·ter·y [fiˈlæktəri] *n.* ①护符, 避邪符. ②(犹太人的)经匣. ***make broad one's ~ [phylacteries]*** 装虔诚;在人前装正经.
phy·le [ˈfaili] *n.* *(pl.* ***-lae*** [-li:]*)* 部落, 宗族〔古雅典人最大的政治划分单位〕.
phy·let·ic [faiˈletik] *a.* ①部落的, 种族的. ②【生】线系的,部的,门的. **phy·let·i·cal·ly** *ad.*
phyll- *comb. f.* 叶: *phyll*ade.
-phyll *comb. f.* 叶: sporo*phyll*.
phyl·lade [ˈfileid] *n.* 【植】鳞状叶.
Phyl·lis [ˈfilis] *n.* 菲莉斯〔女子名〕.
phyllo- *comb. f.* = phyll-.
phyl·lo·ca·line [ˌfiləˈkeilin] *n.* 【生化】成叶素.
phyl·lo·clad, phy·lo·clade [ˈfiləklæd, -ˌkleid] *n.* 叶状枝 = cladophyll.
phyl·lode [ˈfiləud] *n.* 【植】叶状(叶)柄. **phyl·lo·di·al** [-diəl] *a.*
phyl·lo·er·y·thrin [ˌfiləuˈeriθrin] *n.* 【生化】叶红素.
phyl·loid [ˈfilɔid] *a.* 【植】叶状的. — *n.* 叶状枝.
phyl·lome [ˈfiləum] *n.* 【植】叶丛; 初始叶; 叶原体. **-lom·ic** [-ˈlɔmik, -ˈləumik] *a.*
phyl·loph·a·gous [fiˈlɔfəgəs] *a.* 食叶的,以叶为生的.
phyl·lo·pod [ˈfiləpɔd] *n.* 【动】叶脚目 *(Phyllopoda)* 动物〔如丰年虫、兰水丰年虫(卤虾)等〕. — *a.* 叶脚目动物的. **phyl·lop·o·dan** [fiˈlɔpədən] *n.*, *a.* **phyl·lop·o·dous** [-dəs] *a.*
phyl·lo·tax·is [ˌfiləˈtæksis] *n.* 【植】叶序.
phyl·lo·tax·y [ˌfiləˈtæksi] *n.* = phyllotaxis.
-phyllous *comb. f.* 叶…的,…叶的: mono*phyllous*.
phyl·lox·an·thin [ˌfilɔkˈsænθin] *n.* 【生化】叶黄素.
phyl·lox·e·ra [ˌfilɔkˈsiərə] *n.* *(pl.* ***-rae*** [-ri:]*)* 【虫】葡蚜; 〔P-〕根瘤蚜科.
phylo- *comb. f.* 种族: *phylo*geny.
phy·lo·gen·e·sis, phy·log·e·ny [ˌfailəuˈdʒenisis, faiˈlɔdʒini] *n.* ①【生】系统发育(学); 种系发生(学) *(opp.* ontogeny*)*. ②(事物的)发展史. **-gen·et·ic** [ˌfailədʒiˈnetik] *a.* 系统发育的,种系发生的.
phy·lon [ˈfailɔn] *n.* *(pl.* ***-la*** [-lə]*)* 【生】种族.
phy·lum [ˈfailəm] *n.* *(pl.* ***-la*** [-lə]*)* ①(生物分类的)门. ②【语】(泛称)语系.
phys. = ①physical. ②physician. ③physics. ④physiological. ⑤physiology.
physi- *comb. f.* = physio-.
phys·i·at·rics [ˌfiziˈætriks] *n. pl.* 〔动词用单数〕物理治疗,理疗 (= physiatry). **-at·rist** *n.* 理疗医师.
phys·ic [ˈfizik] *n.* ①〔口〕药品,医药;(特指)泻药. ②〔古〕医学; 医术; 医业. ③〔废〕自然科学,物理学. *a dose of ~* 一服药. — *vt.* ①〔口〕给…吃药; 给…吃泻药,使泻. ②治愈. ③〔俚〕虐待(敌人等);处罚. ~ **nut** 麻风树.
phys·i·cal [ˈfizikəl] *a.* ①物质的, 有形的, 形而下的 *(opp.* psychical, spiritual, mental, moral*)*; 确凿的;外界的. ②身体的,肉体的. ③自然的,天然的. ④依据自然规律的;自然科学的;物理学(上)的. ⑤一味追求肉欲的. ⑥〔废〕医药的. ~ **age** 实际年龄,生理龄. ~ **beauty** 肉体美. ~ **chemistry** 物理化学. ~ **climate** 地文气候. ~ **constitution** 体格. ~ **culture [education training]** 体育. ~ **depreciation** 【机】有形损耗. ~ **drill** (普通)体操. ~ **examination** 身体[体格]检查. ~ **exercise** 体操,运动. ~ **force** 力气,膂力. ~ **geography** 地文学,自然地理学. ~ **interpretation** 实际解说. ~ **jerks** 〔俚〕= ~ drill. ~ **laws** 自然法则. ~ **pendulum** 【物】变摆. ~ **sciences** ①物理科学. ②自然科学〔指物理、化学、天文、地理〕. ~ **strength** 体力. ~ **therapy** 【物】物理治疗法,理疗. ~ **world** 外界.
phys·i·cal·ism [ˈfizikəlizm] *n.* 【哲】物理主义. **-cal·ist** *n.* 【哲】物理主义派.
phys·i·cal·i·ty [ˌfiziˈkæliti] *n.* ①肉体性. ②注重肉体〔区别于精神〕.
phys·i·cal·ly [ˈfizikəli] *ad.* ①按照自然规律; 物理上. ②物质上. ③体格上,身体上. *a fine man ~, but a fool mentally* 一个体格好而头脑笨的人.
phy·si·cian [fiˈziʃən] *n.* ①医生, 内科医生 *(opp.* surgeon*)*; 〔美〕(一般)医师; 〔口〕医学博士. ②〔喻〕(精神创伤的) 医治者, 抚慰者. *consult a ~* 请医生看. *one's family ~* 家庭医师. *the ~ in charge* 主任医师.
phys·i·cism [ˈfizisizəm] *n.* ①自然科学研究. ②物理宇宙论,宇宙机械论.
phys·i·cist [ˈfizisist] *n.* ①物理学家;〔古〕自然科学家. ②宇宙机械论者.
phys·i·co·chem·i·cal [ˌfizikəuˈkemikəl] *a.* 物理化学的. **-ly** *ad.*
phys·ics [ˈfiziks] *n. pl.* 〔通常用作单数〕①物理学. ②物理过程;物理现象;物理性质;物理成分. *atomic ~* 原子物理学. *the ~ of flight* 飞行的物理过程.
physio- *comb. f.* 自然,天然; 物理: *physio*gnomy, *physio*graphy, *physio*therapy.
phys·i·o·chem·i·cal [ˌfiziəˈkemikəl] *a.* 生理〔生物〕化学的.
phys·i·oc·racy [ˌfiziˈɔkrəsi] *n.* 重农论,重农主义〔古典政治经济学的一派学说〕.
phys·i·o·crat [ˈfiziəkræt] *n.* 重农论者,重农主义者.
phys·i·og 〔美〕= physiognomy.
phys·i·og·e·ny [fiziˈɔdʒini] *n.* 【生】官能发达; 官能发生学.
phys·i·og·nom·ic, phys·i·og·nom·i·cal [ˌfiziəˈnɔmik, -kəl] *a.* ①观相术的. ②相貌的. **-nom·i·cal·ly** *ad.*
phys·i·og·no·mist [ˌfiziˈɔnəmist] *n.* 相士, 相面先生.
phys·i·og·no·my [ˌfiziˈɔnəmi] *n.* ①观相术, 相法. ②面貌,相貌;〔卑〕面孔,脸. ③(土地等的)形状,外观; 特色,特征.
phys·i·og·ra·phy [ˌfiziˈɔgrəfi] *n.* 地文学,自然地理学;〔美〕地形学;自然现象志. **-ra·pher** *n.* 地文学家,地文学研究者. **phys·i·o·graph·ic, phys·i·o·graph·i·cal** *a.*
physiol. = ①physiological. ②physiologist. ③physiology.
phys·i·ol·a·try [ˌfiziˈɔlətri] *n.* 自然崇拜.
phys·i·o·log·ic, phys·i·o·log·i·cal [ˌfiziəˈlɔdʒik, -kəl] *a.* 生理的,生理学(上)的. *a ~ strain* 【生】生理小种. *~ saline* 生理盐水. **-log·i·cal·ly** *ad.*
phys·i·ol·o·gist [ˌfiziˈɔlədʒist] *n.* 生理学家.
phys·i·ol·o·gy [ˌfiziˈɔlədʒi] *n.* ①生理学. ②生理(机能).
phys·i·o·ther·a·peu·tic [ˈfiziəuˌθerəˈpju:tik] *a.* 物理疗法的,理疗的. **-tics** *n.* 物理疗法,理疗.
phys·i·o·ther·a·py [ˌfiziəuˈθerəpi] *n.* 【医】物理疗法〔热疗、按摩等〕.
phy·sique [fiˈzi:k] *n.* 〔F.〕①体格. ②(土地等的)地形,地势.
phy·so·stig·mine [ˌfaisəuˈstigmi:n, -min] *n.* 【化】毒扁豆碱.
phy·sos·to·mous, phy·sos·to·ma·tous [faiˈsɔstə-

məs, ˌfaisəˈstomətəs] *a.* 【动】通鳔的.
-phyte *comb. f.* 植物: litho*phyte.*
Phy·tin [ˈfaitn] 植酸钙镁〔商标名〕.
phyt(o)- *comb. f.* 植物: *phyto*chemistry.
phy·to·ben·thon [ˌfaitəuˈbenθɔn] *n.* 水底植物.
phy·to·chem·is·try [ˌfaitəuˈkemistri] *n.* 植物化学.
phy·to·chrome [ˈfaitəukrəum] *n.* 植物色素〔如叶绿素〕.
phy·to·cid·al [ˌfaitəuˈsaidəl] *a.* 杀害植物的.
phy·to·cide [ˈfaitəusaid] *n.* 【农】除莠剂.
phy·to·coe·no·sis [ˌfaitəusiˈnəusis] *n.* *(pl.* **-ses** [-siːz]*)* 【植】全层群落.
phy·to·coe·no·si·um [ˌfaitəusiˈnəusiəm] *n.* 【植】植物群落.
phy·to·com·mu·ni·ty [ˌfaitəukəˈmjuːniti] *n.* = phytocoenosium.
phy·to·e·col·o·gy [ˌfaitəuiˈkɔlədʒi] *n.* 植物生态学.
phy·to·flag·el·late [ˌfaitəuflædʒileit, -lit] *n.* 植物状鞭毛虫,匍枝状鞭毛藻.
phy·to·gen·e·sis [ˌfaitəuˈdʒenisis] *n.* 植物发生论. **-to·ge·net·ic, -to·ge·net·i·cal** *a.*
phy·to·gen·ic [ˌfaitəuˈdʒenik] *a.* 植物起源的〔如泥炭,泥炭土,煤〕.
phy·tog·e·nous [faiˈtɔdʒinəs] *a.* = phytogenic.
phy·tog·e·ny [faiˈtɔdʒini] *n.* = phytogenesis.
phy·to·ge·og·ra·phy [ˌfaitəudʒiˈɔgrəfi] *n.* 植物地理学.
phy·tog·ra·phy [faiˈtɔgrəfi] *n.* 叙述植物学.
phy·to·he·mag·glu·ti·nin [ˌfaitəuˌhiːməˈgluːtnin] *n.* 【医】植物血球凝集素.
phy·to·hor·mone [ˌfaitəuˈhɔːməun] *n.* 植物激素 (= plant hormone).
phy·tol·o·gy [faiˈtɔlədʒi] *n.* 植物学 (= botany). **-log·ic, -log·i·cal** *a.*
phy·to·par·a·sit·ol·o·gy [ˌfaitəuˌpærəsaiˈtɔlədʒi] *n.* 植物寄生物学.
phy·to·path·o·gen(e) [ˌfaitəuˈpæθədʒin] *n.* 植物病菌.
phy·to·pa·thol·o·gy [ˌfaitəupæˈθɔlədʒi] *n.* 植物病理学. **-log·ic, -log·i·cal** *a.*
phy·toph·a·gous [faiˈtɔfəgəs] *a.* 【动】吃植物的,草食的.
phy·to·phar·ma·cy [ˌfaitəuˈfɑːməci] *n.* 植物药剂学.
phy·to·plank·ton [ˌfaitəuˈplæŋktən] *n.* 浮游植物; 浮游植物(群落). **-ic** *a.*
phy·to·so·ci·ol·o·gy [ˌfaitəuˌsəusiˈɔlədʒi, -ʃi-] *n.* 植物社会学.
phy·tos·ter·ol [faiˈtɔstərɔːl, -rəul] *n.* 植物甾醇,植物固醇.
phy·to·tax·on·o·my [ˌfaitəutækˈsɔnəmy] *n.* 植物分类学.
phy·to·ther·a·py [ˌfaitəuˈθerəpi] *n.* 植物治疗法,本草疗法.
phy·tot·o·my [faiˈtɔtəmi] *n.* 植物解剖(学).
phy·to·tox·e·mi·a [ˌfaitəutɔkˈsiːmiə] *n.* 植物虫害病毒.
phy·to·tox·ic [ˌfaitəuˈtɔksik] *a.* ①植物性毒素的. ②对植物有毒的. **-tox·ic·i·ty** [-tɔkˈsisiti] *n.* ①植物毒性. ②对植物的毒性.
phy·to·tron [ˈfaitətrɔn] *n.* 人工气候室.
phy·to·zo·on [ˌfaitəuˈzəuɔn] *n.* 【动】植形动物,植虫.
pi[1] [pai] *n.* ①希腊字母表的第十六字母. 〔Π π, 和英语的 p 相当〕. ②【数】圆周率.
Pi[2] [pai] *a.* 〔英学俚〕虔诚的,有道德的,宗教性的 [pious 之略]. **~-jaw** *n.* 〔常蔑〕说教,训话.
pi[3] [pai] *n., vt.* 〔英〕= pie[3].
P.I. = Philippine Islands 菲律宾群岛.
PIA = Pakistan International Airlines 巴基斯坦国际航空公司.
pi·ac·u·lar [paiˈækjulə] *a.* 赎罪的; 须赎罪的; 有罪的; 极恶的.
pi·affe [pjæf, piˈæf] *vi.* (马)用慢步小跑.
pi·af·fer [ˈpjæfə, piˈæfə] *n.* (马的)慢步小跑.
pi·al [ˈpaiəl] *a.* 【解】软(脑脊)膜的.
pi·a ma·ter [ˈpaiə ˈmeitə] 〔L.〕 ①【解】软脑(脊)膜 (*opp.* dura mater 硬脑(脊)膜). ②脑,智慧.
pi·a·nette, pi·a·ni·no [piəˈnet, piəˈniːnəu] *n.* 〔方〕小型竖式钢琴.
pi·an·ism [piːˈænizm, ˈpjæn-, ˈpiːən-] *n.* 弹钢琴术,钢琴技巧; 钢琴演奏. **pi·an·is·tic** *a.*
pi·a·nis·si·mo [pjæˈnisiməu, piəˈn-] *a., ad.* 〔It.〕【乐】很轻的[地]. — *n.* *(pl.* **~s, -mi** [-miː]*)* 须极轻地奏出的乐句[乐段].
pi·an·ist [ˈpiənist, ˈpjænist] *n.* 钢琴家; 钢琴师,钢琴演奏家.
pi·a·no [piˈɑːnəu, ˈpjɑː-] *a., ad.* 〔It.〕【乐】轻轻的[地]; 微弱的[地]. — *n.* 轻奏乐段.
pi·an·o [piˈɑːnəu, ˈpjænəu] *n.* *(pl.* **~s***)* 钢琴; 〔美俚〕囚犯工作席. *a boudoir [cabinet]* ~ 竖钢琴. *an upright* ~ 竖钢琴. *a cottage* ~ 小竖钢琴. *a grand* ~ 大钢琴. *a piccolo* ~ 小竖钢琴. *play [perform] (on) the* ~ 弹钢琴. ~ **accordion** 键盘式手风琴. ~ **duet** 钢琴二重奏(曲). ~ **organ** 手摇式自鸣钢琴. ~ **player** ①弹钢琴的人. ②钢琴自动弹奏机. ~ **stool** 钢琴凳. ~ **system** 分期付款购货法.
pi·an·o·for·te [piˌɑːnəuˈfɔːti, ˌpjæn-] *n.* = piano.
pi·a·no·la [pjæˈnəulə] *n.* 自动钢琴.
pias. = piastre.
pi·as·(s)a·ba, pi·as·(s)a·va [ˌpiːəˈsɑːvə] *n.* 纤维榈(的纤维); 巴西棕(树).
pi·as·ter, pi·as·tre [piˈæstə] *n.* ①〔罕〕比塞塔〔西班牙货币〕. ②皮阿斯特〔阿拉伯联合共和国、黎巴嫩、叙利亚和苏丹的货币单位〕. ③〔美俚〕一元.
pi·at [ˈpaiət] *n.* (英国、加拿大军队中用的)一种短距离反坦克炮 (= projector infantry antitank).
pi·az·za [piˈætsə] *n.* *(pl.* **~s,** 〔It.〕 ***pi·az·ze*** [ˈpjɑːtse]*)* ①(特指意大利都市中的)广场. ②〔美〕游廊,外廊 = verandah. ③〔英〕连拱廊.
pi·bal [ˈpaibəl] *n.* 【气】①测风气球 (= pilot balloon). ②高空测风报告.
pi·broch [ˈpiːbrɔk] *n.* (苏格兰高地人的)风笛曲.
pic [pik] *n.* *(pl.* **~s, *pix*** [piks]*)* 〔picture 之略〕; 〔美俚〕①电影. ②照片. *the* ~ *mob* 电影观众. **~-parlor** *n.* 〔美俚〕电影院.
pi·ca[1] [ˈpaikə] *n.* 【印】12 点活字〔相当我国新 4 号铅字〕.
pi·ca[2] [ˈpaikə] *n.* 【医】异食癖.
pic·a·dor [ˈpikədɔː] *(pl.* **~s, ~es** [ˌpikəˈdɔːriːz]*)* *n.* ①(西班牙的)骑马斗牛士. ②〔喻〕老练机智的论客.
pic·a·ra [ˈpiːkɑːrɑː] *n.* *(pl.* **~s***)* 女流浪者.
pic·a·resque [ˌpikəˈresk] *a.* ①(传奇小说) 以流浪汉、歹徒等的冒险生涯做题材的. ②(经历等)传奇式流浪冒险的. — *n.* ①〔常 the ~〕(16 世纪西班牙的)以歹徒、流浪汉的冒险生涯为题材的故事. ②传奇式流浪冒险的事迹[人物]. *a ~ [picaroon] novel* 歹徒小说.
pi·ca·ro [ˈpiːkɑːrəu] *n.* *(pl.* **~s***)* 流浪汉,亡命徒.
pic·a·roon[1] [ˌpikəˈruːn] *n.* ①歹徒, 强盗; 窃贼. ②海盗; 海盗船. — *vi.* 做强盗; 做海盗. — *vt.* 劫夺.
pic·a·roon[2] [ˌpikəˈruːn] *n.* (加拿大樵夫用的)十字刀.
pic·a·yune [ˌpikəˈjuːn] *n.* ①(原在美国路易斯安那州及南部各州流通的)西班牙小钱币; 〔美〕小钱币〔尤指五分辅币〕. ②〔美口〕不值钱的东西,小人物,不重要的人 — *a.* = picayunish.
pic·a·yun·ish [ˌpikəˈjuːniʃ] *a.* 琐碎的; 微不足道的; 不值钱的.
Pic·ca·dil·ly [ˌpikəˈdili] *n.* 皮卡迪利大街〔伦敦的繁华

街道]. ~ **Circus** 皮卡迪利广场[戏院及娱乐中心].
pic·ca·lil·li [ˈpikəlili] *n. (pl. ~s)* 辣泡菜.
pic·ca·nin·ny, pick·a·nin·ny [ˈpikənini] *n.* 黑种小孩;澳大利亚土著小孩;[谑]小孩. — *a.* 极小的.
Pic·card [piˈkɑːd], **A.** 皮卡德 [1884—1962, 比利时物理学家].
pic·co·lo [ˈpikələu] *n. (pl. ~s)*【乐】短笛. — *a.* (乐器)小型的.
pice [pais] *n. sing., pl.* 旧时印度铜币.
pic·e·ous [ˈpisiəs, ˈpaisi-] *a.* 沥青的,似沥青的;沥青色的(尤指动物).
pich·i·ci·a·go, pich·i·ci·e·go [ˌpitʃisiˈeigəu] *n. (pl. ~s)*【动】铠鼹.
pick[1] [pik] *vt.* ①(用鹤嘴锄等)掘,凿,挖(洞). ②(用手指)挖(鼻孔、耳朵等),挑,剔(牙齿、骨头等). ③摘,掐,采,摘取(花果、棉花等);薅;(草);拔(羽毛等);舐,啄;[口]吃. ④挑选;(细心)选择(用词等). ⑤撬开(锁等). ⑥扒窃,偷,剽窃. ⑦解,拆;扯开(麻絮等),分. ⑧挑…的毛病,找…的碴儿,吵起(架)来,寻找(吵架的机会)*(with)*. ⑨(用指头)弹拨(弦乐器等). ~ *ground* 掘地. ~ *one's teeth* 剔牙. ~ *a thread off one's coat* 从衣服上摘去线头. ~ *a chicken* 拔鸡毛. ~ *a quarrel (with sb.)* 找机会(和某人)吵架. ~ *fault* 挑眼,找碴儿. ~ *sb.'s pocket* 扒窃. — *vi.* ①凿,掘,挖,戳;啄 *(at)*. ②[口](挑肥拣瘦地)吃. ③采摘. ④挑,选. ⑤偷,窃. *Ripe grapes* ~ *easily.* 熟了的葡萄摘起来不难. ~ *at the food* 吃东西挑嘴. *the* ~*ing season* 采摘季节. ***have a bone to ~ with sb.,*** ~ ***a bone*** [美南方 ***crow***] ***with sb.*** 对某人有不满之处;与某人有需要解决的争端;跟…口角[争吵]. ~ ***a hole in*** = ~ holes in. ~ ***acquaintance with*** 偶然和人成为相识. ~ ***and choose*** 挑三拣四,挑肥拣瘦. ~ ***and steal*** 扒窃,偷. ~ ***at [on]*** [美口] ①不断挑剔[指责,骂]某人. ②拣拣吃吃. ~ ***holes in*** 找…的碴儿[漏洞],找…的过失,吹毛求疵. ~ ***in*** ①(在画里)画上(阴影等). ②[英方]承揽,接收(要洗的衣服等). ~ ***oakum*** 拆[撕]填絮;[喻]做苦工. ~ ***off*** ①掐下,摘去,采取. ②一个接一个地瞄准打中. ~ ***on*** [美口]①与…为难,欺负;不断责骂. ②挑中,选中. ~ ***oneself up*** (倒下的人)从地上爬起来;打起精神. ~ ***one's steps*** 小心翼翼地走(险路). ~ ***one's way*** 拣易走处走, 小心走路. ~ ***one's words*** 注意措词,小心说话. ~ ***out*** ①挑选. ②掘出,拔出,啄出. ③闻出,区辨,听出;弄明白,领会,看出(文章等的意思). ④凭听来的调子弹奏(歌曲). ~ ***out with*** ①装饰,使突出. ②(用另一种颜色)衬托(底色). ~ ***over*** 拣,分档挑选;精选. ~ ***sb.'s brains*** 剽窃别人脑力劳动成果. ~ ***spirit*** 提起精神. ~ ***to pieces*** ①拆开;扯碎. ②[喻]刻薄批评,把…骂得一钱不值. ~ ***up*** ①*vt.* 掘起;拾起;(车船等)在半路上搭(人);振起(精神);得到(生活费、知识等);偶然获得,四处收集,想尽办法寻求,听着;(用探照灯等)探出,找到(原来的路);听会,自然学会(言语、游戏等);(抱)起;[口]捉住,逮捕,(跟女人)交起朋友来,选出 (*I ~ed up Beijing last night.* 昨晚上听到北京的广播. ~ *up heart [one's courage]* 振作精神). ②*vi.* (病后)恢复健康,恢复体重,有了精神,有起色;生意好起来;(和偶然碰着的人)成为相识 *(with)*. (~ *up flesh* 病后长肉). ~ ***up on*** [美俚] 同…熟悉起来. — *n.* ①凿,掘. ②选择;选择权. ③[the ~]最好的东西,精华,精选物. ④采摘的农作物. ⑤【绘】修改. ⑥【印】(铅字的)污点. *You can take your* ~. 你可以拣你喜欢的. ***take [have, get] the ~ of*** 任凭挑选;有…的选择权;拣,选. ***the ~ of the bunch [basket]*** 一批中的精选品,精华.
pick[2] [pik] *n.* ①鹤嘴锄,铁镐,铁撬;用于挖掘的尖状物;[口]牙签. ②(弹弦乐器的)拨子. ③撬锁工具;撬锁贼(= ~lock). ~**ax(e)** ① *n.* 鹤嘴锄,镐. ②*vt., vi.* (用鹤嘴锄)掘.
pick[3] [pik] *vt.*【纺】投(梭). — *n.* 纬纱;投梭.
pick·a·back [ˈpikəbæk] *ad.* [口] ①在肩[背]上,背着. ②在铁道平车上. *ride* ~ *on sb.* 骑在某人肩头上. — *a.* ~ **plane** (载于母机背上在空中飞出的)子机,寄生飞机.
pick·a·nin·ny [ˈpikənini] *n.* = piccaninny.
picked[1] [pikt] *a.* ①选净的,精选的,挑选出来的,最好的. ②(果实等)摘下的,摘收的. ③(用锄、镐等)挖掘过的. ~ *to repeat* [美]有再度赛赢的希望.
picked[2] [pikt] *a.* [方]有尖锋的;尖的.
pick·el [ˈpikəl] *n.* (爬山用的)冰斧.
pick·er[1] [ˈpikə] *n.* ①采摘者;摘棉工人,扯拔者;捡拾者,采集者;拣选者;[美]摘棉机. ②扒手,窃贼. ③= pickaxe. ~***s and stealers*** 扒手和窃贼.
picker[2] [ˈpikə] *n.*【纺】清棉机;(织机)皮结.
pick·er·el [ˈpikərəl] *n. (pl. ~(s))* ①【动】小狗鱼. ②[口] = pike, pikeperch.
pick·er·el·weed [ˈpikərəlˌwiːd] *n.* (北美)海寿属(拟)*(Pontederia)* 植物(尤指海寿 *(P. cordata)*).
Pick·er·ing [ˈpikəriŋ] *n.* 皮克林[姓氏].
pick·et [ˈpikit] *n.* ①桩,尖桩;支柱;【电】标橛. ②【军】步哨,哨兵;前哨,警戒哨[队,船,飞机];瞭望者,把风者. ③[*pl.*](工会罢工时的)纠察员. ④【史】(罚罪犯以一足站于桩上的)站桩刑. ⑤[*pl.*][美俚]牙齿. *an outlying* ~ 前哨,前哨队. *a* ~ *fence* 栅栏;[美俚]牙齿. — *vt.* ①用栅栏围上. ②用警戒哨保卫;派…去放哨. ③(把马等)系在桩上. ④(罢工时)派纠察员监视(工厂等). ⑤处…以桩刑. — *vi.* 放哨;担任纠察员(任务). ~**boat** 巡逻船;雷达哨艇. ~ **line** ①【军】哨兵线,警戒线;(罢工时的)纠察线. ②拴马索. ~ **pin** 拴马桩. ~ **rope** 拴马索. ~ **ship** 雷达警戒船. **-er** 纠察员.
Pick·et(t) [ˈpikit] *n.* 皮基特[姓氏].
pick·ing [ˈpikiŋ] *n.* ①(用铁镐等)掘;撬开. ②摘取,采集;选择,挑选. ③[*pl.*] 摘取物,采集物;挑选物;可采物;可检物[垃圾、废品等]. ④[*pl.*] 摘剩的东西,落穗;剩余物. ⑤偷窃;脏品. ⑥[*pl.*] 额外收入,外快. ⑦[*pl.*][英](铺人行道用的)贝壳粉. ⑧未烧透的砖. ⑨【矿】粗选. ~ ***and stealing*** 扒窃.
pick·le [ˈpikl] *n.* ①(腌鱼、菜等用的)盐汁,泡菜水;[*pl.*]酸菜,泡菜,(尤指)泡黄瓜;腌鱼. ②淡酸水,酸洗液[洗金属用]. ③[通例带有形容词]苦境,困境;混乱. ④[口]顽皮孩子. ⑤[美俚]烂醉. ⑥【军】空投鱼雷. ***be in a (sad, fine, nice)*** ~ 处境困难,尴尬,十分混乱. ***have a rod in ~ for sb.*** 蓄谋惩罚某人. ***mixed ~s*** ①十锦酸菜. ②各种不同的人[东西]的集合. ③心情非常混乱. — *vt.* ①把…泡在盐水里,(用盐水等)腌制,腌渍. ②用酸洗液洗(铸造物等). ③使(画)显现古色古香. ④【海】鞭打前用盐(或醋)擦(背). ~ **barrel** *n.* [美空俚]轰炸员练习投弹用的目标. ~ **barrel bombing**【军】极精确的轰炸. **-d** *a.* ①盐腌的,醋泡的. ②[美俚]烂醉的,酩酊大醉的.
pick·ling [ˈpikliŋ] *n.*【化】浸酸,酸洗,浸蚀,浸洗;浸封,浸藏. *electrolytic* ~ 电渍. *a* ~ *process* 浸渍法.
pick·lock [ˈpiklɔk] *n.* ①撬锁具. ②撬锁人,窃贼. ③最优选手.
pick-mat·tock [ˈpikmætək] *n.* (一头尖一头平的)鹤嘴锄,铁镐.
pick-me-up [ˈpikmiːʌp] *n.* [俚]兴奋剂;(尤指)含酒兴奋饮料.
pick-off [ˈpikɔf] *n.*【无】传感器,敏感元件;拣拾器;出件器.
pick·pock·et [ˈpikˌpɔkit] *n.* 扒手. *Beware of ~s!* 谨防扒手!
pick·purse [ˈpikpəːs] *n.* ①[罕]扒手. ②【植】荠菜;大爪草.
pick·some [ˈpiksəm] *a.* 好挑剔的,爱挑三拣四的,吹毛求疵的.

pick•thank [ˈpikθæŋk] *n.* 〔古〕马屁精.

pick•up [ˈpikʌp] *a.* ①〔口〕临时拼凑成的;(菜等)凑合的. ②(球队等)挑选的. — *n.* ①拾起;掘出物. ②〔美俚〕改进,好转;复兴. ③〔美俚〕消息,情报. ④〔美俚〕刺激(品),兴奋剂. ⑤(球戏)回击落地球. ⑥(汽车的)加速度,加快.⑦敞篷小型运货卡车. ⑧〔美俚〕偶然的结识,偶然结识的人;妓女. ⑨临时免费搭乘他人便车的人(= hitchhiker). ⑩随便买的东西;临时准备的菜饭;遗失品.⑪【无】拾波,拾音;唱头,拾波器;电视摄像(管).⑫实况转播地点. *a live* ~ (电视)室内摄影;播送(室内)实况. *an outdoor* ~【电视】室外摄影;实现转播. ~ **coil**【无】拾波线圈.

Pick•wick•i•an [pikˈwikiən, -kjən] *a.* ①(英国作者狄更斯小说《匹克威克外传》中主人公)匹克威克式善意而诙谐的. ②(学句等)别有特殊[专门]意义的. — *n.* 〔the ~〕①匹克威克俱乐部成员. ②爱读《匹克威克外传》的人. ***in a ~ sense*** 有隐晦[影射,微妙,特殊,诙谐]意义的.

pick•y [ˈpiki] *a.* 〔口〕过分讲究的;吹毛求疵的;爱挑剔的.

pic•nic [ˈpiknik] *n.* ①野餐,郊游;各人自带食品的宴会. ②〔俚〕愉快的时间,轻松的工作. ③(猪的)脊肉. *get up a* ~ 发起野餐[旅行]会. *go out on a* ~ 去旅行,去野餐. ***It's no ~.*** 〔口〕这不是一件轻松事. — *vi.* ***(pic•nicked; pic•nick•ing)*** 去郊游,去野餐. ~ **biscuit** 小而甜的饼干.

pic•nick•er [ˈpiknikə] *n.* 野餐者,郊游者.

pic•nick•y [ˈpikniki] *a.* 野餐(式)的.

pic•nom•e•ter [pikˈnɔmitə] *n.* = pycnometer.

pico- *comb. f.* 微微,沙,毫纤〔= 10^{-12}, 略 μμ〕: *pico*farad.

pi•co•far•ad [ˌpikəˈfærəd] *n.*【物】微微法(拉).

pic•o•line [ˈpikəliːn, -lin] *n.*【化】皮考啉,甲基,比啶.

pi•cot [piˈkəu] *n.* (花边、缎带等上的)饰边小环;布边图纹. — *vt.* 在…的边上做上小环.

pic•o•tee [ˌpikəˈtiː] *n.*【英植】红边黄花[白花];荷兰石竹.

pic•o•tite [ˈpikətait] *n.*【矿】铬尖晶石.

pic•quet [ˈpikit] *n.* ①= picket②. ②【军】安铁丝网的乱桩〔旋涡形铁具〕. — *vt., vi.* = picket.

pic•rate [ˈpikreit] *n.*【化】苦(味)酸盐.

pic•ric [pikrik] *a.*【化】苦(味)酸的. ~ **acid**【化】苦(味)酸,2,4,6 三硝基酚.

pic•rite [ˈpikrait] *n.*【矿】橄苦岩. **pic•rit•ic** [-ˈritik] *a.*

pic•ro•tox•in [ˌpikrəˈtɔksin] *n.*【化】苦毒.

Pict [pikt] *n.* 皮克特人〔古代苏格兰东部民族〕. ***~'s houses*** 地下石洞.

Pict•ish [ˈpiktiʃ] *a.* 皮克特人的.

pic•to•graph, pic•to•gram [ˈpiktəgrɑːf, -græm] *n.* ①象形文字,绘画文字;用象形文字所作的记录. ②古代〔史前〕石壁画. ③【统】图表.

pic•to•graph•ic [ˌpiktəˈgræfik] *a.* (用)象形文字的;有象形文字特征的. **-i•cal•ly** *ad.*

pic•tog•ra•phy [pikˈtɔːgrəfi] *n.* 象形文字的使用;象形文字记载法.

pic•to•ri•al [pikˈtɔːriəl] *a.* ①绘画的. ②有图片的;用图片表示的. ③图画似的,形象化的. ~ *art* 绘画. *a* ~ *magazine* 画报. *a* ~ *diagrum* 示意图. *a* ~ *puzzle* 画谜. — *n.* 画报,画刊;画页;图画邮票. **-ly** *ad.*

pic•to•ri•al•ize [pikˈtɔːriəlaiz] *vt.* 用图画表示. **-al•i•za•tion** [pikˌtɔːriəlaiˈzeiʃən] *n.*

pic•ture [ˈpiktʃə] *n.* ①画,图画. ②画像;照片. ③图画似的叙述,写照;画一般美的东西;图画似的风景,美景. ④相似的形象;化身;体现. ⑤心像;情景;局面. ⑥影片;〔the ~s〕电影. ⑦【无】图象. *a* ~ *post-card* 美术明信片. *I had my* ~ *taken.* 我请人照了相了. *She is a* ~. 她象画一样的美丽. *He is the* ~ *of his father.* 他活象他父亲. *He is the very* ~ *of health.* 他是健康的化身(十分健康). ***be (high up) in the ~*** 〔美俚〕出头露面;成为要人;取得成功. ***come into the ~*** ①出现;引起注意. ②被牵涉到. ***give a ~ of*** 把…描绘一番. ***go ~s*** 〔美〕签订演戏合同,入电影界. ***go to the ~s*** 看电影去. ***in the ~*** ①在本题之内的. ②【美体】熟练,有胜利希望. ***out of the ~*** ①在本题之外的,不相干的. ②〔美俚〕喝醉了的. ③不重要的. ***sit for one's ~*** 摆好姿势让人画像[照相]. — *vt.* ①画;用图片表示. ②(形象地)描写. ③想象. ④把…(作为电影)拍摄. ***~ to oneself*** 想象. ~ **book** 图画书. ~ **card** ①花牌〔纸牌中的 K, Q, J〕. ②美术明信片. **~drome [~ hall, ~ palace, ~ theatre]** 〔英〕电影院. ~ **element**【无】象素,象点. ~ **frame** ①画架. ②〔美俚〕绞刑架. ~ **gallery** ①绘画陈列馆,美术馆;画廊. ②〔美马戏用语〕身上刺花的人. **~-goer** 影迷. ~ **hat** (女人戴的)阔边帽. ~ **phone** 电视电话. ~ **play** 电影剧. ~ **puzzle** 画谜. ~ **ratio**【电视】画面(长宽)比. ~ **show** ①绘画展览会. ②电影;电影院. ~ **tube**【电视】显象管 (= kinescope). ~ **window** 风景窗. ~ **writing** (远古时代)用图画记载事件〔通讯〕(的方法);象形文字.

pic•tur•esque [ˌpiktʃəˈresk] *a.* ①(景色等)画似的,美丽的;绚烂的;富于画趣的. ②别致的. ③(语言)生动的,形象化的,逼真的. ④(个性)突出的,独创的. **-ly** *ad.* **-ness** *n.*

pic•tur•ize [ˈpiktʃəraiz] *vt.* ①用图画表示;使绘画化. ②使电影化;把…拍成电影.

pic•ul [ˈpikəl] *n.* ***(pl. ~(s))*** 担,百斤〔中国、泰国等重量单位〕. **~-stick** 扁担.

Pi•cus [ˈpaikəs] *n.*【罗神】田园之神.

pid•dle [ˈpidl] *vi.* 〔英古、美〕①拖遢地处理[工作];鬼混,闲混;浪费 (away)(精力,时间,金钱等). ②〔美俚〕(学生)背错书. ③〔口、儿〕小便,撒尿.

pid•dling [ˈpidliŋ] *a.* 细小的,无价值的,不足道的,琐碎的.

pid•dock [ˈpidək] *n.*【动】星火哈.

pidg•in [ˈpidʒin] *n.* ①(不同语种的人在商业交往中形成的)混杂语言,混杂行话. ②洋泾浜英语〔指旧中国港口等地使用的混杂英语〕. ③〔口〕事务〔business 在半殖民地时代中国的讹音字〕(=pigeon). ~ **English** 洋泾浜英语.

pi-dog [ˈpaidɔg] *n.* = pye-dog.

pie[1] [pai] *n.* ①馅饼;馅饼状物. ②〔美俚〕容易得到的称心东西;容易的工作. ③〔美俚〕不正当的利得,邪财. *a minced* ~ 肉末馅饼. ***a ~ in the sky*** 乌托邦;希望中的报酬;渺茫的幸福. ***(as) easy as ~*** 〔美口〕极容易. ***(as) nice [good] as ~*** 极好. ***cut a ~*** 〔美〕安加干预. ***eat humble ~*** 忍辱含垢. ***have a finger in the ~*** 干预,插手;参与其事;与某事有关系. ***put one's finger into another's ~*** 多管闲事. ~ **book** 〔美俚〕饭票簿. ~ **card** 〔美俚〕工人工会会员证. ~ **chart** 馅饼形统计图〔用大小扇形表示比例〕. ~ **counter** 〔美俚〕(政治上的)资助[分赃]. **~man** 卖[做]馅饼的人. **~-plant** 〔方〕食用大黄〔常用作点心馅〕. ~ **wagon** 〔美俚〕①(警察的)警备车. ②流动小吃车.

pie[2] [pai] *n.* ①【动】喜鹊. ②爱说话的人.

pie[3] [pai] *n.* ①【印】杂色铅字. ②混乱. — *vt.* 使混杂;弄乱(铅字、版面).

pie[4] [pai] *n.* 派〔印度的旧辅币名〕.

pie•bald [ˈpaibɔːld] *a.* ①(马)黑白斑的,有斑纹的 ②驳杂的. — *n.* ①有斑纹的动物(尤指花斑马). ②〔喻〕杂色.

piece [piːs] *n.* ①片;断片,碎片;一部,部分,部件. ②〔作量词〕一片,一幅,一匹,一块,一件,一项,一番,一段,一篇,一出,一首,一张. ③(艺术)作品. ④炮,枪,火器. ⑤货币,钱币;标志物;筹码. ⑥(计件工的)工作(量);事,事项,条款. ⑦〔美俚〕点心,小吃,(饭等的)一口.

⑧棋子. ⑨酒杯,桶. ⑩样品,样本;例子. ⑪〔口〕人;家伙;女人〔多带轻蔑意〕. ⑫(乐器)演奏者〔用以构成复合词〕. *a ~ of paper* 一张纸. *a ~ [two ~s] of bread.* 一块[两块]面包. *a bad ~ of road* 一段坏路. *a fine ~ of painting* 一幅好画. *a night ~* 夜景图;夜想曲. *a ~ of water* 一片池塘[小湖]. *an animal [a war] ~* 动物[战争]画. *a field ~* 野炮. *She is a bold ~.* 她是一个放荡的女人. *What a ~ of folly!* 真混蛋! *a ~ of impudence* 不要脸的话[举动]. *a ~ of work* ①一件作品[产品]. ②费力的工作;难事;〔口〕纷扰. ***a ~ of ...*** 在某种意义[程度]上是个…;还算是一个…. ***a ~ of cake*** 〔口〕轻松[愉快]的事情. ***~ of eight*** 西班牙古银币. ***~ of flesh*** 〔口〕人,(尤指)女人. ***~ of goods*** 〔谑〕东西〔指女人和小孩〕. ***a ~ of one's mind*** 直率的意见;指责(*give sb. a ~ of one's mind* 对某人坦白表示自己的意见;当面指责某人). ***all to ~s*** ①疲惫不堪的,虚弱已极的;神经受撼动的;惊慌而受震动的. ②(破得)粉碎. ③〔俚〕完全,充分,彻底. ***by [on] the ~*** 按件(计酬). ***come to ~s*** 粉碎;(计划)成画饼. ***cut to ~s*** ①切碎;使溃散. ②议论某人,把(某人)批评得体无完肤. ***eat a ~*** 〔口〕吃零食. ***fall [come, go, tumble] to ~s*** 崩碎,垮碎,粉碎. ***go all to ~s*** 气馁沮丧. ***in one ~*** 成整块,没有接缝. ***in ~s*** ①破碎. ②(意见等)分歧,不一致. ***of a [one] ~ (with)*** (和…)同一种类的,同型的;首尾一贯的;调和的. ***~ by ~*** 一件一件;一点一点,逐渐. ***speak one's ~*** ①朗诵. ②〔美口〕诉苦,提意见. ③〔美俚〕求婚. ***take to ~s*** 拆(机器),(机器)拆散. ***tear [break, pull, pick] to [into] ~s*** 把…扯[砸]得粉碎. — *vt.* ①接,补;修理(*up*). ②联结,结合;拼合,拼凑(*together*);串成(*out*). — *vi.* ①【纺】接头. ②〔口〕吃零食. ***~ in*** 插入,添加. ***~ on*** 接合,补足(*to*). ***~ out*** 补足,完成. ***~ together*** 拼合,接合,综合. ***~ up*** 接合,弥缝. **~-broker** 零售商贩. **~-dyed** *a.* 成匹染色的. **~ goods** 〔*pl.*〕【纺】匹头,布匹. **~ rate** 计件工资. **~work** 计件工作,包工工作. **~-worker** 零工,计件工.

pi·èce-de-ré·sis·tance [ˈpjes də reiˈziːstɑ̃ːns] *n.* 〔F.〕①餐中主菜,主要食品. ②主要事件;主要作品.

piece·meal [ˈpiːsmiːl] *ad.* 一件一件,一点一点,逐渐地〔= by ~〕. — *a.* ①一件一件的;逐渐的. ②零零碎碎的. — *n.* 断片,块.

pie·crust [ˈpaikrʌst] *n.* ①烘酥的馅饼皮. ②做馅饼的糊. *Promises are, like ~, made to be broken.* 允诺常常是靠不住的. ***as short as ~*** 性急.

pied [paid] *a.* ①斑驳的,杂色的. ②穿着杂色衣服的. ③〔美俚〕思想混乱的.

pied-à-terre [ˈpjeitɑːˈtεə] *n.* 〔F.〕临时休息所;(备用的)临时寓所.

pied·mont [ˈpiːdmɔnt] *a.* 山麓的,山前地带的. *a ~ stream* 山脚下的溪水. — *n.* 山麓.

Pied·mont [ˈpiːdmənt] *n.* ①皮德蒙特山脉〔意大利〕. ②(美国)皮德蒙特州.

Pied·mon·tese [ˌpiːdmɔnˈtiːz] *a.* (意大利的)皮德蒙特的;意大利人的;意大利文化的. — *n.* (*pl.* ~*e*) 皮德蒙特土人;皮德蒙特居民;意大利土人;意大利居民.

pied·mont·ite [ˈpidməntait] *n.* 【矿】红帘石.

pied noir [pjeˈnəwɑː] *n.* (*pl.* ***pieds noirs***) 〔F.〕(在阿尔及利亚的)欧洲人〔特指法国移民〕.

pie-dog [pai-dɔg] *n.* = pye-dog.

pie-eyed [ˈpaiˈaid] *a.* 〔美俚〕①喝醉了的. ②不漂亮的. ③(因惊讶等)睁大了眼睛的.

Pie·gan [ˈpiːgən] *n.* (*pl.* ~(*s*)) 派岗族人〔黑脚印第安人的一支〕.

pie-pow·der [ˈpaipaudə] *n.* 〔古〕行商.

pier [piə] *n.* ①码头;防波堤. ②桥脚,墩. ③【建】窗间壁,户间壁,扶壁;柱,角柱. *a floating ~* 浮码头. *a landing ~* 码头. *an end ~* 终端(电)杆. **~ glass** 穿衣镜;窗间镜. **~ table** 矮几〔多置于两窗间,常在窗间镜之下〕.

pier·age [ˈpiəridʒ] *n.* 码头费.

Pierce [piəs] *n.* 皮尔斯〔姓氏〕.

pierce [piəs] *vt.* ①刺穿,戳穿,贯穿;刺破,穿(孔);突入,突破. ②深深打动,使感动. ③看穿,看破,洞察. *The wall is ~d by [with] windows.* 墙上开了窗户. *~ the enemy's line* 突破敌人阵线. *His heart was ~d with grief.* 他伤透了心. — *vi.* 刺入,穿入,穿进(*into, through*). *~ through the enemy's line* 突破敌人防线.

pierc·er [ˈpiəsə] *n.* ①穿孔的人[物];钻孔器,锥;(酒桶等的)开口器. ②(昆虫的)产卵管,螯针. ③〔俚〕锐眼.

pierc·ing [ˈpiəsiŋ] *a.* ①刺穿的,贯穿的;尖锐的. ②打动人心的. ③观察敏锐的,洞察的,有眼光的. ④(评论等)尖刻的. *~ cold* 刺骨的寒冷. *a ~ shriek* 尖叫. *a ~ eye* 锐利的眼力. **-ly** *ad.*

pier·head [ˈpiəhed] *n.* 码头外端.

Pi·er·i·an [paiˈeriən, paiˈiər-] *a.* (古马其顿地名,诗神缪斯出生地)皮埃里亚的;缪斯女神的. ***the ~ spring*** 缪斯女神的泉水,诗的源泉;灵感(*drink of the ~ spring* 诗兴大发).

Pi·er·i·des [paiˈeridiːz] *n.* 【希神】= the Muses.

pi·er·i·dine [paiˈeridain, -din] *a.* 【动】粉蝶科(*Pieridae*)的〔包括白蝶〕.

Pi·erre [pi(ː)ˈεə, peə] *n.* 皮埃尔〔男子名, Peter 的异体〕.

Pi·er·rot [ˈpiərəu] *n.* (*fem.* ***pi·er·rette*** [piəˈret]) 〔F.〕①皮耶罗〔古法国哑剧中的白衣丑角〕. ②〔p-〕(搽白粉、穿白衣的)丑角.

Pi·e·ta [ˌpieˈtɑː] *n.* 〔It.〕圣母玛利亚膝上抱着基督尸体的图画[雕刻].

Pi·e·tism [ˈpaiətizəm] *n.* ①虔信派〔17 世纪德国路德教的一个宗派〕;虔信主义. ②〔p-〕虔诚,虔敬. ③假装虔诚.

Pi·e·tist [ˈpaiətist] *n.* 虔信派教徒;〔p-〕虔信的人.

Pi·e·tis·tic, Pi·e·tis·ti·cal [paiəˈtistik, -tikəl] *a.* ①虔信派(教徒)的. ②〔p-〕虔信的;假装虔诚的.

pi·e·ty [ˈpaiəti] *n.* ①虔敬,虔诚. ②孝顺,孝敬. ③忠顺,恭敬;爱国. *filial ~* 孝顺.

piezo- *comb. f.* 压(力): *piezo*crystal.

pi·e·zo·chem·is·try [paiˌiːzəuˈkemistri] *n.* 压力化学,高压化学.

pi·e·zo·crys·tal [paiˌiːzəuˈkristəl] *n.* 【物】压电晶体. **-tal·li·za·tion** *n.* 【物】加压结晶.

pi·e·zo·e·lec·tric [paiˌiːzəuiˈlektrik] *a.* 【物】压电的. **~ constant** 压电常数. **~ crystal** 压电晶体.

pi·e·zo·e·lec·tric·i·ty [paiˌiːzəuilekˈtrisiti] *n.* 【物】压电(学);压电(现象).

pi·e·zom·e·ter [ˌpaiəˈzɔmitə] *n.* 【物】流压计,水压计,压觉计,压力计,压强计.

pi·e·zom·e·try [paiəˈzɔmitri] *n.* 【物】压力测定;流压测量(法).

piff [pif] *int.* 唏,噼〔子弹飞过声〕.

pif·fle [ˈpifl] *vi.* 〔口〕做傻事;讲废话. — *n.* 无聊事,傻事;傻话,废话,梦话.

pig [pig] *n.* ①猪;〔美〕仔猪;猪肉;宰好的小猪;猪皮. ②〔口〕(猪一样)肮脏的人,嘴馋的人,贪心的人,顽固的人. ③〔俚〕警察;密探;荡妇. ④金属块[锭];生铁,铣铁. ⑤〔美俚〕火车头;可疑的酒吧;赛马用的马(尤指劣马). ⑥桔子的瓤. *roast ~* 烤小猪肉. ***bring [drive] one's ~s to a pretty [a fine, the wrong] market*** 卖吃亏,冒险失败;失策,失算;走错门槛,估计错误. ***buy a ~ in a poke [a bag]*** 买下没有过目的东西,不管好坏乱买;不顾后果地承担义务,盲目负责. ***go to ~s and whistles*** 完蛋,失败,毁灭. ***in a ~'s eye*** 很少,难得;刚相反;不会的! ***in ~*** (母猪)怀小猪的. ***make a ~ of oneself*** 狼吞虎咽;大吃大喝. ***~ between sheets*** 〔美〕火腿夹心面包. ***Pig might fly.*** 说不定会发生怪事,

无奇不有. *~'s eyes*〔口〕小眼睛. *~'s wash* 泔脚 (= pigwash). *~'s whisper*〔俚〕①低声的私语. ②一会儿(工夫). ***please the ~s***〔谑〕如果运气好的话〔Please God 的代用语〕. ***teach a ~ to play on a flute*** 教猪吹笛; 做荒谬[不可能办到]的事. ***when ~s fly*** 永不, 决不, 决不可能. — *vt.* (猪)下(仔). — *vi.* ①(猪)生小猪. ②猪一样聚在一块 *(together)*; 过猪一样的生活. *~ it* ①猪一样聚在一块儿生活. ②〔美俚〕停止奔跑; 放慢速度; (因胆小)退却. ~ **bed** ①猪圈. ②【冶】生铁场; 铸床. ~**boat**〔美海俚〕潜水艇. ~**-breeding** 养猪. ~**bucket** 喂猪桶. ~**-eyed** *a.* 眼睛小而凹的. ~ **fight**〔美〕跳舞. ~**fish**【鱼】石鲈. ~**head**〔美〕顽梗的人, 顽固分子. ~**-headed** *a.* 顽固的, 梗得要命的. ~**-herd** 养猪员. ~**iron** ①生铁. ②〔美俚〕私酿的劣酒. ~**-jump** *vi.* (马)举四脚跃起. **P- Latin**〔美〕将英语词尾改成拉丁语式的说法, 倒读隐语〔又作 Hog Latin〕. ~ **lead**【冶】铅锭. ~**nut**〔英〕落花生; 〔美〕光滑山核桃〔喂猪用〕. ~**pen** ①猪圈. ②肮脏的地方. ~**skin** ①猪皮. ②〔口〕马鞍. ③〔美俚〕美式足球 (= football). ~**skinner**〔美俚〕美式足球选手. ~**stick** *vi.* (用标枪)猎野猪. ~**-sticker** ①猎野猪的人; 猎枪. ②〔口〕大号小刀; 〔美口〕刺刀. ~**sty** ①猪圈. ②肮脏的住处. ~**tail**〔口〕①辫子; 有辫子的人. ②卷成细条的烟草. ~**wash** ①泔脚. ②〔俚〕泪水. ③〔俚〕劣酒; 坏汤; 低级咖啡. ~**-weed**【植】藜; 苋属植物.

pi·geon[1] [ˈpidʒin] *n.* ①鸽子〔包括野鸽和家鸽, 诗及美国英语中多用 dove〕; 鸽灰色. ②〔口〕易受欺骗的人, 傻子, 生手. ③(抛入空中作射击飞靶的)土圆盘, 土鸽 (= clay ~). ④〔美〕姑娘; 年轻妇女. ⑤〔英俚〕特别关心的事. *a homing [carrier] ~* 信鸽. *a stool ~* 囮鸽; 囮子; 密探. *~'s blood* 深红色. *~'s milk* ①鸽子用以喂小鸽的部分消化了的食物. ②〔谑〕愚人节那天骗人去拿的没有的东西. ***fly the ~s*** 送货时在路上窃取煤炭. ***It's your ~ to do ...*** 是你的责任. ***pluck a ~***〔俚〕骗去(呆子的)钱. — *vt.* ①用鸽子联络. ②〔俚〕骗, 骗取, 骗(钱). ~ **breat**【医】鸡胸. ~**-breasted** *a.* 鸡胸的. ~ **carrier** ①通信鸽输送兵. ②鸽笼. ~ **company**【军】通信鸽连. ~ **express** 信鸽通信. ~ **fancier** 卖[养]鸽子的人. ~**gram** 鸽信. ~ **hawk**【鸟】灰背隼. ~**-hearted** *a.* 胆小的; 害羞的. ~**hole** ① *n.* 鸽笼的出入孔; 鸽笼的区划; 小房间; (写字台上的)鸽笼式文件架, 分类架, 分信箱. ②*vt.* 把(文件等)搁入分类架; 把(文件等)整理起来保存; 把…留在记忆中; 搁置, 搁下来不管 (*~ hole the request for a new park* 把开辟新公园的请求搁置起来). ~**-livered** *a.* 温顺的. ~**-pea** (印度的)木豆. ~ **shooting** 打鸽子; 飞靶射击. ~**tail** *n.* 〔美〕燕尾服. ~**-toed** *a.* 脚趾内向的. ~**wing** ①一种顿脚的花色舞步. ②鸽翼式花色溜冰动作.

pi·geon[2] [ˈpidʒin] *n.* = pidgin. ~ **English** = pidgin English.

pi·geon·ry [ˈpidʒinri] *n.* 鸽笼, 鸽舍.

pig·ger·y [ˈpigəri] *n.* ①猪场; 猪栏; 肮脏地方. ②猪的习性〔指肮脏、懒惰、贪吃等〕. ③〔总称〕猪.

pig·gie [ˈpigi] *n., a.* = piggy.

pig·gin [ˈpigin] *n.* ①汲水桶, 小手桶. ②长柄杓.

pig·gish [ˈpigiʃ] *a.* 猪似的, 贪吃的, 肮脏的; 利己的; 顽梗的. **-ly** *ad.* **-ness** *n.*

pig·gy [ˈpigi] *n.* 小猪; 〔谑〕孩子. — *a.* 猪似的; 贪心的; 肮脏的. ~**-wig**, ~**-wiggy** *n.* 〔儿〕小猪; 脏孩子.

pig·gy·back [ˈpigibæk] *ad., a.* = pickaback.

pig·let, pig·ling [ˈpiglit, -liŋ] *n.* 小猪(尤指猪仔).

pig·ment [ˈpigmənt] *n.* ①颜料, 色料. ②【生】色素. ~ **granule** 色素粒. ~ **rayon** 无光人造丝.

pig·men·tal, pig·men·ta·ry [pigˈmentl, ˈpigməntəri] *a.* (含有)颜料的; 色素的; 分泌色素的.

pig·men·ta·tion [ˌpigmənˈteiʃən] *n.* ①色素淀积, 着色(作用). ②【医】色素沉着.

pig·my [ˈpigmi] *n., a.* = pygmy.

pi·gno·li·a, pi·gno·li [piˈnjəuliə, -li] *n.* 可食松子.

pig·no·rate [ˈpignəreit] *vt.* 交出[接受]…作为抵押.

pig·nus [ˈpignəs] *n.* *(pl.* ***-no·ra*** [-nərə]*)*〔L.〕【法】①抵押契约, 押据, 当票. ②典当物.

Pig·o·po·lis [ˈpigəpɔlis] *n.* 〔美〕猪市〔辛辛那提市或芝加哥市的别名〕.

Pi·gou [ˈpiguː] *n.* 皮古〔姓氏〕.

pi·ka [ˈpaikə] *n.* 鼠兔科 *(Ochotondae)* 动物〔产于北美洲西部和亚洲高原岩石区〕.

Pike [paik] *n.* 派克〔姓氏〕.

pike[1] [paik] *n.* 【史】长矛, 镖枪. — *vt.* 用长矛戳(伤、死). ***trail a ~*** 当兵, 服役.

pike[2] [paik] *n.* ①矛头, 枪尖, 箭头; (走路时防滑用的)尖头杖. ②〔英方〕(湖畔)尖峰. ③【泳】虾式跳水. ④〔方〕铁镐. ***hit the ~***〔美〕出发, 动身; 前进. **-d** *a.* (有)尖的.

pike[3] [paik] *n.* 【动】梭鱼, 狗鱼.

pike[4] [paik] *n.* ①(收通行税的)关卡; 收税栅; 收费门. ②通行税. ③税道, 收税路; 〔美俚〕大路. — *vi.* 〔美俚〕赶路; 走, 突然离开; 死.

pike[5] [paik] *vi.* 〔美俚〕(跟着大赌客)小心谨慎地赌小钱.

pike[6] [paik] *n.* (由美国 Missiouri 州 Pike 县迁移到太平洋沿岸一带的)流浪农民.

pike·man [ˈpaikmən] *n.* ①枪兵; 使用铁镐的矿工. ②通行税征收处的看守.

pike·perch [ˈpaikˌpəːtʃ] *n.* *(pl.* *~(es))* 鲈鲈属 *(Stizostedion)* 鱼〔如大眼鲈鲈 *(S. Vitreum)*、加拿大鲈鲈 *(S. canadense.)*〕

pik·er [ˈpaikə] *n.* 〔美俚〕①懦夫, 临阵脱逃的人; 小气鬼. ②谨慎小心的小赌客; 小投机商人. ③流浪者.

pik·er·ism [ˈpaikrizəm] *n.* 〔美俚〕①小气, 吝啬. ②胆小.

pike·staff [ˈpaikstɑːf] *n.* *(pl.* ***-staves*** [-steivz]*)* 长矛柄, 枪柄; (旅行者用以防滑的)尖头杖. ***as plain as a ~*** 极明白的.

pil·af(f) [piˈlɑːf] *n.* = pilau.

pi·las·ter [piˈlæstə] *n.* 【建】壁柱, 半露柱.

pil·a·to·ry [piˈleitəri] *n.* 生发剂. — *a.* 刺激生发的.

pi·lau, pi·law [piˈlau, piˈlɔː] *n.* (东方的) 烩肉饭〔米中加鱼或肉及调味品制成〕.

pilch [piltʃ] *n.* 尿布垫.

pil·chard, pil·cher [ˈpiltʃəd, ˈpiltʃə] *n.* 【动】沙脑鱼, 沙丁鱼.

pile[1] [pail] *n.* ①堆积, 堆; 火葬柴堆 (= funeral ~). ②大量, 大批, 大块; 高大建筑物; 〔口〕钱堆, 财产. ③【物】电堆, 电池; 铀堆; (连锁)反应堆. ④【建】桩. ⑤【军】叉枪. *a dry ~*【物】干电池, 干电堆. *an uranium ~* 铀堆. *a ~ of (books)* 一大堆(书籍). ***a ~ of bucks***〔美〕一盘子荞麦饼. ***a ~ of dough*** 一大笔钱. ***a ~ of shot***【数】积弹. ***make a [one's] ~*** 发财. — *vt.* ①堆 *(up; on)*; 积蓄 *(up)*; 堆积; 层积; 【军】叉(枪), 架(枪). ②在…上堆东西. ③【海】使(船)冲上岩礁〔浅滩〕. ④【物】用反应堆处理. — *vi.* ①堆积; 积累. ②拥, 挤; 进(入) *(in into)*; 走出 *(out, off)*. *~ into a car* 挤进车子里. ***P- arms!*** 叉枪! 架枪! *~ in*〔美俚〕挤入(车内、屋内). *~ it on* 夸张. *~ on [up] the (agony)*〔口〕对(悲痛)的刻意渲染〔描绘〕. *~ out*〔美俚〕赶紧跑掉. *~ Pelion on Ossa* 山上有山, 困难重重〔Pelion 及 Ossa 均系希腊山名〕. *~ up* ①堆积; 积聚; (汽车等)挤在一起. ②(使)(船)搁浅. (汽车、飞机等)撞毁. ~**-up** ① *n.* (数辆汽车等的)同时碰撞; (繁重任务等的)堆集. ② *vi.* (数辆汽车等)同时撞挤在一起.

pile[2] [pail] *n.* ①杆木, 木桩, 桥桩. ②箭头; 【徽】楔形; 草叶. *a ~ foundation*【建】打桩屋基. *raise [draw, withdraw] ~* 拔桩. — *vt.* ①打(桩); 把桩打入…; 用桩支撑〔加固〕. ②给…装箭头. ~**driver** 打桩机; 打桩者.

~**-dweller** 湖边桩屋居民．~**-dwelling** 湖边桩屋．

pile[3] [pail] *n.* ①软毛，绒毛；毛茸．②(布、绒的)软面．— *vt.* 使起绒．**-d** *a.* 有绒毛的．

pile[4] [pail] *n.* 痔疮；〔*pl.*〕痔．*blind ~s* 痔核．

pile[5] [pail] *n.* 〔古〕钱币的背面．***cross or ~*** 硬币的正面或反面（= heads or tails，见 head 条)．

pi·le·ate, pi·le·at·ed [ˈpailiit, -tid] *a.* ①【植】有菌盖的．②【动】有羽冠的．

pi·le·ous [ˈpailiəs, ˈpili-] *a.* 有毛的，多毛的，生毛的．

pi·le·um [ˈpailiəm, ˈpili-] *n.* ***(pl. -le·a*** [-ə]***)*** 鸟头的顶部．

pi·le·us [ˈpailiəs, ˈpili-] *n.* ***(pl. -le·i*** [-liai]***)*** ①(古罗马)一种无沿帽．②【植】菌盖．③【动】(水母的)伞状盘；鸟头的顶部（= pileum)．

pile·wort [ˈpailwəːt] *n.* ①白屈菜；小白屈菜（= celandine)．②白屈菜属植物．

pil·fer [ˈpilfə] *vt., vi.* 偷窃，扒；小偷小摸．~**proof** *a.* 防小偷的，安全的．**-er** [ˈpilfərə] *n.* 小偷．

pil·fer·age [ˈpilfəridʒ] *n.* ①小偷小摸，扒窃．②赃品．

pil·gar·lic [pilˈgɑːlik] *n.* ①秃头，秃顶的人．②被人轻视〔奚落〕的人，被人以虚假同情的态度对待的人．

pil·grim [ˈpilgrim] *n.* ①香客，朝圣者，参拜圣地的人．②游历者，旅客，流浪者．③最初的移民；〔美西部〕新来移民；〔P-〕1620 年移居美洲的英国清教徒．*a ~'s staff* 香客手杖．*~('s) signs* 朝山纪念品．*~s on earth* 尘世的过客．*Pilgrim's Progress*《天路历程》〔17 世纪英国作家班扬的寓言式作品〕．*the P- (Fathers)*【美史】1620 年避英国教祸而到美国创立普利茅斯 (Plymouth) 殖民地的新教徒．— *vi.* ①朝山进香，朝圣，参拜圣地．②流浪．~ **shell** 海扇壳．

pil·grim·age [ˈpilgrimidʒ] *n.* ①参拜圣地，朝圣，朝山进香．②人生的旅程，一生．***go on a ~ to*** 去…朝圣．***make one's ~ to*** 参拜．— *vi.* 去朝圣，去参拜圣地．

pil·grim·ize [ˈpilgrimaiz] *vi.* 去朝圣．

pi·li [piˈliː] *n.* 〔Tag.〕①卵橄榄．②卵橄榄树 (*Canarium ovatum*)．

pili- *comb. f.* 毛：*pili*ferous．

pi·lif·er·ous [paiˈlifərəs] *a.*【生】被毛的，有毛的．

pil·i·form [ˈpilifɔːm] *a.* 毛形的．

pil·ing [ˈpailiŋ] *n.* ①打桩，打桩工程．②桩，桩基；桩材．

Pil·i·pi·no, Fi·li·pi·no [ˌpiliˈpiːnəu] *n.* 他加禄语〔1962 年定为菲律宾国语〕（= Tagalog)．

pill[1] [pil] *n.* ①丸；药丸；〔the ~〕(女用口服)避孕丸．②讨厌的东西〔人〕；苦事．③〔俚〕炮弹，子弹；球；〔*pl.*〕〔英俚〕台球戏，弹子戏．④〔美俚〕香烟；切去两端的雪茄烟；(鸦片) 烟泡．⑤投票用小球．⑥【农】粒肥．⑦〔*pl.*〕〔口〕医生．***a bitter ~ to swallow*** 不能不做的苦事，不得不忍受的屈辱．***a ~ to cure an earthquake*** 软弱的措施，姑息手段，弥补政策．***gild [sugar] the ~*** 加糖衣，美化讨厌的东西〔人〕．— *vt.* ①把…作成丸药；给…吃丸药．②〔俚〕投票反对；排斥；不录取；开除．~ **bag**〔美俚〕医生．~ **coll**〔美俚〕药学专科学校．~ **pad**〔美俚〕鸦片窝，吸毒窝．~ **peddler**〔美俚〕医生．~**roller**〔俚〕医生；医科学生．~ **shooter**〔美俚〕医生，药剂师．

pill[2] [pil] *vt.* ①〔古〕抢劫，掠夺．②〔方〕= peel．

pil·lage [ˈpilidʒ] *n.* 抢劫，掠夺；掠夺物．— *vt., vi.* 抢劫，掠夺．**-r** *n.* 抢劫者，掠夺者．

pil·lar [ˈpilə] *n.* ①柱；纪念柱；(柱)墩，柱脚；【矿】(矿井中硬炭层或岩石形成的)矿柱，煤柱．②柱状物〔水柱，火柱等〕．③〔喻〕台柱，栋梁，柱石．*a ~ of the state* 国家的栋梁．***be driven from ~ to post [from post to ~]*** 被逼得四处奔走；到处碰壁，事事失败；被逼得走投无路．— *vt.* ①用柱子装饰〔支持〕．②成为…的栋梁．~**-box**〔英〕邮筒．~**-stone** 隅石，奠基石．

pil·lar·et [ˈpilərit] *n.* 小柱．

pill·box [ˈpilbɔks] *n.* ①(板纸制的) 丸药盒．②〔英俚〕小马车，小汽车，小房屋．③〔军俚〕独立小地堡．④(平底无边)矮圆桶形女帽．

pil·ler [ˈpilə] *n.* 〔美〕药剂师，药商．

pil·lion [ˈpiljən] *n.* ①女用轻鞍；(骑手背后供女人乘用的) 鞍褥．②〔英〕(摩托车的) 后座．— *ad.* 坐在后鞍上．*ride ~* 骑后座．

pil·li·winks [ˈpiliwiŋks] *n.* 古代夹指刑具，拶子．

pil·lo·ry [ˈpiləri] *n.* ①颈手枷．②臭名，笑柄．***be in the ~*** 成笑柄，遭人嘲弄．— *vt.* ①把…上颈手枷示众．②使遭人嘲笑．

pil·low [ˈpiləu] *n.* ①枕头．②【机】轴枕，垫座．③(棒球的) 垒．④花边编织台．⑤〔美俚〕拳击手套．***advise [consult] with one's ~ = take counsel of one's ~*** 躺在床上细想一夜〔明天再说〕．— *vt.* ①用…作枕头，做…的枕头；垫．②把…搁在枕上；使靠在 *(on)*．— *vi.* 把头搁在枕头上，靠在枕上，~ **block**【机】轴台．~ **block bearing**【机】架座．~**case** 枕套．~ **fight** 打闹，小争执．~ **lace** 手编花边．~ **pivot**【机】球面中心支枢．~ **puncher**〔美〕去收拾房间的女佣人．~ **sham** 枕头饰套．~**slip** = ~case．

pil·low·y [ˈpiləui] *a.* 枕头似的；柔软的，一压就凹的．

pill·wort [ˈpilwəːt] *n.*【植】美洲线叶苹．

pi·lo·car·pin(e) [ˌpailəuˈkɑːpi(ː)n] *n.*【化】毛果（芸香)碱〔发汗、利尿剂〕．

pi·lose [ˈpailəus] *a.*【动、植】软毛多的；柔毛状的．**pi·los·i·ty** [-ˈlɔsiti] *n.*【生】细毛被；多毛．

pi·lot [ˈpailət] *n.* ①领港员，舵手；【空】驾驶员，飞行员；领航员；【火箭】起动人员；指导员，领导人；〔美〕向导，带路人，带瞎丐走路的狗〔小孩〕；拳赛〔棒球俱乐部〕干事．②航线指南；罗针盘矫正器；〔美〕(机车前的)排障器．③【交、建】导洞．④【机、电】领示；导频；导向器；指示灯．*a chief ~* 领港长．*an apprentice ~* 领港见习员．*a first [senior] ~* 正〔一级〕驾驶员．*a ~ in command*【空】机长．*a ~'s cockpit* 飞行员座舱．*a ~'s licence* 飞行员执照．*a ~'s log-book* 飞行员日记．*a robot ~*【空】自动驾驶仪．*a ~ balloon* 升力〔风向〕指示气球．***drop the ~*** 辞退好顾问，失去良师益友．— *a.* ①引导的，导向的．②【机、电】辅助的，控制的．③(生产等)小规模试验性质的．*a ~ plant* (小规模)试验厂．— *vt.* ①给(船只)领航〔领港〕*(on, in, over)*．②给…当向导，指导．③驾驶（飞机等)．~ **biscuit**, ~ **bread** (船中用)硬面包；硬饼干．~ **chart** 航空气象简图．~ **chute**【空】引导伞．~ **cloth**【纺】海员蓝色粗呢．~ **engine** 探路机车．~ **fish**【鱼】舟鰤．~ **flag**【海】找领港员或表示已有领港员在船上的信号旗．~**house** 操舵室，驾驶室．~ **jack** = ~ flag．~ **jacket** 海员厚茄克．~**officer**〔英〕空军少尉．~ **tube**【空】空速指示器．~ **whale** 巨头鲸．~ **wheel** 导轮．**-age** *n.* ①领航，领港．②指导，向导．③领港费．④民航机驾驶术（*~ inwards [outwards]* 入港〔出港〕领港费)．**-ing** *n.* 领航，引水．**-less** *a.* 没有领港员〔驾驶员、舵手、领导人〕的．

Pil·sen [ˈpilzin] *n.* = Plzeň．

Pilt·down [ˈpiltdaun] *n.* 皮尔丹〔英国地名〕．~ ***man***【人类】皮尔丹人〔英国考古学家陶逊声称，他于 1911 年在英国 Sussex 州 Piltdown 地方发现史前人化石，称"皮尔丹人"，后经鉴定系伪造〕．

pil·u·lar [ˈpiljulə] *a.* 药丸(状)的．

pil·ule [ˈpiljuːl] *n.* 小药丸．

pil·y [ˈpaili] *a.* 有绒毛的；柔软的．

Pi·ma [ˈpiːmə] *n.* ***(pl. ~(s))***①比马人〔北美印第安人的一个部族，居住在亚利桑那州基拉河及索尔特河流域〕．②比马人的乌托阿芝特克语．③〔美〕比马棉（= ~ cotton)；〔p-〕用比马棉制成的优质衣料．~ **No. 1.**【农】碧玛一号(小麦)．

Pi·man [ˈpiːmən] *n.* (属乌托阿芝特克语系的) 比马语．— *a.* ①比马语的．②比马人的．

pi·men·to [piˈmentəu] *n.* *(pl.* ~*s)* ①【植】多香果(= allspice). ② = pimiento.
pi-me·son [ˈpaiˈmiːzɔn] *n.*【原】π介子.
pi·mien·to [piˈmjentəu] *n.* *(pl.* ~*s)* 甜辣椒.
pim·o·la [pimˈəulə] *n.* 拌有甜辣椒的橄榄.
pimp [pimp] *n.* ①妓院老板,老鸨. ②引人作坏事的人. ③〔美俚〕男妓. *a* ~ *stick*〔美俚〕香烟,烟卷儿. — *vi.* 拉皮条;为妓女拉客;帮助干坏事.
pim·per·nel [ˈpimpənel] *n.*【植】紫蘩蒌;海绿.
pimp·ing [ˈpimpiŋ] *a.* ①细小的,没价值的. ②小气的,卑鄙的. ③病弱的.
pim·ple [ˈpimpl] *n.*【医】丘疹,疙瘩,粉刺;小突起;脓疱.
pim·pled, pim·ply [ˈpimpld, ˈpimpli] *a.* 尽是粉刺的,有疙瘩的.
pim·pon [ˈpimpɔn] *n.*【植】苹婆〔广东凤眼果〕.
pin [pin] *n.* ①别针,扣针,饰针;有别针的徽章. ②钉;楔;栓,销;(弦乐器上调弦的)轸子;发夹. 测针.【电】插头;管脚【海】桨架脚. ③〔*pl.*〕〔口〕腿. ④(装四加仑半的)小桶. ⑤没价值的东西,琐碎东西. ⑥靶心. *a safety* ~ 锁针,安全针;安全栓. *a firing* ~ (枪的)撞针. *You might have heard a* ~ *fall.* (紧张得)连针掉下来也听得见(地寂静). *There is not a* ~ *to choose between.* 没有多大差别,完全一样. ***at a*** ~***'s fee*** 用极少代价. ***be on one's last*** ~***s*** 快死,就要死. ***be on one's*** ~***s*** 站着;健康. ***be quick [slow] on one's*** ~***s*** 腿快[慢]. ***in (a) merry*** ~ 高兴. ***neat as a new*** ~ 清清爽爽的. ***not care a*** ~ 一点也不在乎. ***not worth a*** ~ 毫无价值. ***(sit) on*** ~***s (and needles)*** 如坐针毡[急得要命]. ~***s and needles*** (手脚的)发麻. ***pull the*** ~〔美俚〕①停止工作;走开. ②遗弃妻子,抛弃家属[朋友等]. ***put [keep] in the*** ~〔口、俚〕①停止,作罢. ②戒酒. ***stick*** ~***s into*** *(sb.)* 激励某人;使(人)生气,使(人)烦恼. —*vt.* ①(用钉等)钉住,别住,扣住 *(up; together; on; to)*;刺穿. ②按住;按住使不能动 *(against)*;(用条约等)束缚住 *(to)*. ③(用障壁等)围住,关住 *(up)*;〔俚〕抓住;【军】牵制. ④把…归罪于 *(on)*. ~ ***one's faith on [to]*** 把信念寄托于. ~ ***one's hopes on*** 把希望寄托在…上. ~ ***(sb.) down (to)*** ①强迫(人)承认[履行]条约. ②用…束缚住;阻止;牵制;压住. ~ ***up*** ①钉住,钉起来;(用针)扣住,别住. ②【建】托换…的基础;加固. ~ **artist**〔美俚〕堕胎手术师. ~**ball** ①桌上弹球戏. ②〔美〕球形针插. ~**cushion** ①针插;②【无】栅形失真. ~ **curl** 卷发器〔固定潮湿的发型〕. ~**-curl** *vt.* 以卷发器卷发. ~ **money** (丈夫给妻子的)零用钱. ~**point** ① *n.* 针尖;极尖的顶端;极小的东西;琐事. ②需准确轰炸的小目标;航空照片. ③ *a.* 微小的;极准确的. ④ *vt., vi.* 极精确地测定[瞄准,轰炸];指出;确认. ~**-prick** 针刺(的小孔);使人烦恼的小事情,刺耳的话. ~**tail**【动】针尾鸭;针尾松鸡. ~**-up** ① *n.* 钉在墙上的东西;〔美俚〕被钉在墙上欣赏的女人相片. ② *a.* 可钉在墙上的;(女子)相片可钉在墙上供欣赏的,漂亮的. ~**-wheel** *n.* ①玩具风车. ②彩色焰火. ③〔俚〕直升飞机. ~**work** *n.*【纺】撒纱工艺;(针绣花边的)细小突出饰纹.
Pi·na·cea·e [paiˈneisiː] *n.*〔*pl.*〕【植】松科.
pin·a·co·the·ca [ˌpinəkəuˈθiːkə] *n.* *(pl.* ~*s*, *-cæ* [-siː]*)*〔L.〕(希腊、罗马的)绘画馆.
pin·a·fore [ˈpinəfɔː, -fɔə] *n.* (小孩、女工等的)围裙;围嘴布,涎布;无袖女服.
pi·nang [piˈnæŋ] *n.* 槟榔(树).
pi·nas·ter [paiˈnæstə] *n.*【植】南欧海松.
pi·ña·ta [piˈnjɑːtɑː] *n.*〔Sp.〕彩饰陶罐〔墨西哥人过节时将此种罐悬于天花板上,由儿童用棒击破以取得其中的玩具和糖果〕.
pince-nez [ˈpɛ̃ːnsnei, ˈpæns-] *n.* *(pl.* ***pince-nez*** [ˈpɛ̃ːnsneiz]*)*〔F.〕夹鼻眼镜.
pin·cers [ˈpinsəz] *n. pl.* ①钳子,铁子. ②【动】螯;尾铗. ③【军】钳形攻势[运动](= ~(s) drive 或 ~(s) movement).
pin·cette [pɛ̃ːnˈset] *n.* *(pl.* ~*s)*〔F.〕(外科手术用的)小钳子;小镊子.
pinch [pintʃ] *vt.* ①捏,掐,撮,挟;(鞋子等)夹(脚);掐掉(嫩枝等);修剪 *(out, off, back)*. ②折磨,使苦恼;使消瘦;使萎缩;使缩作一团. ③〔方〕削减,压缩;限制;使缺乏 *(for; in; of)*. ④勒索,夺取 *(from; out of)*;〔俚〕偷;〔俚〕逮捕,抓住. ⑤【英赛马】催(马)快跑;【海】使(帆船)抢风急驶. ⑥加入一撮(粉等). ⑦用杠杆撬动(重物). *be* ~*ed with cold* 冷得缩手缩脚. *be* ~*ed with poverty* 穷困不堪. — *vi.* ①(向里)挤压,收缩 *(in)*;(鞋等)紧,窄. ②俭省,吝啬. ③(渴得、饿得、苦得)要命. ④【地】(矿脉等)狭缩,变薄. ~ ***and save*** 节衣缩食地攒钱. ~ ***and scrape*** 东拼西凑;俭省. ***be*** ~***d for (money)*** 手头拮据,缺钱等. ***know [feel] where the shoe*** ~***es*** 知道问题[困难]在哪里. ~ ***off*** 摘心,打尖;【物】箍断. ~ ***out [back]***【园艺】摘心,摘除(嫩芽). ~ ***pennies*** 吝啬,节俭. — *n.* ①捏,掐,撮,挟;【物】箍缩,收缩. ②紧迫;困难,困苦;剧痛. ③一撮,微量. ④危机,危急. ⑤〔美〕矿脉的狭窄点. ⑥〔俚〕容易事. ⑦撬杆. ⑧〔俚〕盗窃;〔俚〕逮捕,捕捉. *a* ~ *of salt* 一撮盐. *the* ~ *of poverty* 贫困的重压. ***at [in, on, upon] a*** ~ 在危急时. ***when it comes to the*** ~ 一旦危急时. ***with a*** ~ ***of salt*** 有保留地,不全信地. ~**bar** 撬杆. ~**fist** 十分俭省的人;守财奴. ~**-hit** *vi.*【棒球】(吃紧时)代打;〔喻〕代表,代替. ~**-hitter**【棒球】(吃紧时出场的)代打者;(一般的)代理人,替手. ~**penny** *a.* 吝啬的. **-ing** *n.*【农】打尖,摘心.
pinch·beck [ˈpintʃbek] *n.* ①铜锌合金,金色黄铜. ②赝品,冒牌货;廉价宝石. — *a.* ①金色黄铜做的. ②假的;便宜的.
pinch·ers [ˈpintʃəz] *n.*〔*pl.*〕① = pincers. ②〔美俚〕鞋子.
Pinck·ney [ˈpiŋkni] *n.* 平克尼〔姓氏〕.
Pin·dar·ic [pinˈdærik] *a.* ①(古希腊诗人)平达 (Pindar) 的;平达体的. ②格律谨严的. — *n.*〔常 *pl.*〕平达体的诗[颂歌等].
pin·der [ˈpində] *n.*〔美方〕花生 (= peanut).
pin·dling [ˈpindliŋ] *a.*〔美方〕①孱弱的,纤弱的,病弱的. ②易怒的,乖张的.
pine[1] [pain] *n.*【植】①松树;松木. ②〔口〕凤梨,波罗 (= pineapple). *a* ~ *straw*〔美〕枯松叶. *Chinese* ~ 油松. *Oregon* ~ 美国松,洋松. *white* ~ 枞. *a* ~ *tree* 松树. ~ ***tree men***〔美〕缅因 (Maine) 州人的绰号. ***the Pine Tree State***〔美〕缅因州的别名. ~ **barren**〔美南部〕长有松林的沙地. ~ **beauty**【动】松夜蛾. ~ **black** 松烟. ~ **carpet** 松蛾. ~ **cone** 松毬,松果. ~ **marten** 英国黑褐貂. ~ **moth** 松毛虫. ~ **needle** 松叶. ~ **nut** ①松果. ②松子. ~ **overcoat**〔美俚〕(不值钱的)棺材. ~ **resin** 松脂,松香. ~ **tar** 松焦油. ~ **wood** ①〔*pl.*〕松林. ②松木.
pine[2] [pain] *vi.* ①衰弱,憔悴,消瘦 *(out; away)*. ②渴望;恋慕 *(after; for; to do)*. ③〔古〕埋怨,发牢骚.
pin·e·al [paiˈniəl, ˈpainiəl] *a.* ①松毬状的. ②【解】松果腺[体]的. *the* ~ *gland [body]*【解】松果腺[体].
pine·ap·ple [ˈpainæpl] *n.* ①【植】菠萝,凤梨. ②〔俚〕炸弹,手榴弹. ~ **cloth** 波罗纤维布;手帕亚麻布;上浆全丝薄纱.
pi·nene [ˈpainiːn] *n.*【化】蒎烯.
Pi·ner·o [piˈniərəu] *n.* 皮尼罗〔姓氏〕.
pin·er·y [ˈpainəri] *n.* 松林;波罗温室.
pine·sap [ˈpainsæp] *n.* 水晶兰属 *(Monotropa)* 植物〔包括锡仗花,鹿蹄草〕.
pi·ne·tum [paiˈniːtəm] *n.* *(pl.* *-ta* [-tə]*)* ①林,(收集不同种类松树的)松树栽培园. ②关于松树的论文.

pine·y [ˈpaini] *a.* ***(pin·i·er; -i·est)*** = piny. *a ~ wood* 〔美南部〕松林.
pin·feath·er [ˈpinfeðə] *n.* (鸟的)幼羽,新生的羽绒毛. **-ed, -y** *a.*
pin·fish [ˈpinfiʃ] *n.* *(pl. ~(s))* 兔齿鲷.
pin·fold [ˈpinfəuld] *vt.* 把…关入畜栏,监禁. — *n.* ①牛栏. ②禁闭室.
ping [piŋ] *n.* ①砰,咻,〔枪弹飞过空中的声音〕. ②来自回声测距声纳设备的脉冲信号. — *vi.* 咻地响〔飞过〕. ~ **jockey** 雷达兵,声纳兵.
Ping·er [ˈpiŋə] *n.* (研究海流的)声波发射器.
ping-pong [ˈpiŋpɔŋ] *n.* 乒乓球.
pin·guid [ˈpiŋgwid] *a.* 〔谑〕胖的; 脂肪多的; 油腻的; (土)肥.
pin·head [ˈpinhed] *n.* ①针头; 小东西,无聊东西; 傻子,笨人. ②〔美〕鸦片鬼; 〔美〕店员; 〔美〕(铁路)扳道员.
pin·head·ed [ˈpinhedid] *a.* 笨的,愚蠢的,傻的,糊涂的. **-ness** *n.*
pin·hole [ˈpinhəul] *n.* 针孔,小孔,小洞. *a ~ camera* 无透镜照相机〔在暗箱上开小孔,以代替透镜〕.
pin·ing [ˈpainiŋ] *n.* (牛羊的)衰萎病,缺钴病; 【植】憔萎病.
pin·ion[1] [ˈpinjən] *n.* ①(鸟翼的)翼梢; 翅膀; 羽毛; 〔集合词〕翮; 〔诗〕翼. ②(人的)臂膀; 臂绑. — *vt.* ①剪断…的翮毛,捆住…的两翼. ②捆住(两手); 箝制,束缚.
pin·ion[2] [ˈpinjən] *n.* 【机】小齿轮. *a lazy ~* 惰轮. ~ **shaft** 小齿轮轴.
pin·ite [ˈpinait, ˈpainait] *n.* 【化】蒎立醇.
pi·ni·tol [ˈpainitɔːl, ˈpini-; -ˈtəul] *n.* 【化】右旋肌醇甲醚.
pink[1] [piŋk] *n.* ①【植】石竹; 石竹花. ②桃红色,粉红色. ③化身; 精华,极致. ④名流; 穿着入时的人. ⑤〔英〕(猎狐用)红色上衣(料); 猎狐的人. ⑥〔美〕私人侦探. ⑦〔美俚〕汽车驾驶执照; 火急电报. ⑧〔常 P-〕〔美俚〕偏右的左派,左倾分子. — *a.* ①粉红色的. ②有点激进〔左倾〕的. ③面红耳赤的,激怒的. — *vt., vi.* (使)变粉红色. *the Chinese ~* 石竹. *the Indian ~* 茑萝. *wear ~* 穿粉红色衣服. ***in the ~ (of condition)*** 〔口〕极壮健; 〔美俚〕喝醉. ***the ~ of perfection*** 十全十美的东西〔人〕. ***tickle sb. ~*** 〔美俚〕使某人非常高兴. ~ **elephants** (吸毒后)幻觉. ~ **lady** 鸡尾酒〔由白兰地等调制而成〕. ~ **slip** 解雇通知书. ~ **tea** 午后茶会; 社交活动. **-ly** *ad.* **-ness** *n.*
pink[2] [piŋk] *n.* ①〔英〕幼小鲑鱼. ②〔英方〕欧洲鲦鱼.
pink[3] [piŋk] *n.* ①〔废〕小孔. ②〔罕〕刺伤; 〔俚〕血.
pink[4] [piŋk] *vt.* ①刺,扎,戳 *(out)*; 在…穿小孔,穿饰孔. ②在…边作饰褶〔作锯齿饰〕; 〔英方〕装饰 *(out; up)*.
pink[5] [piŋk] *vi.* (发动机)格登格登地响.
pink·en [ˈpiŋkn] *vi.* 成石竹色,成淡红色.
Pink [piŋk] *n.* = Pinkerton.
Pink·er·ton [ˈpiŋkətən] *n.* 平克顿〔姓氏〕.
pink·eye [ˈpiŋk-ai] *n.* ①(马的)流行性感冒; (人的)传染性结膜炎,眼炎,红眼. ②澳洲阔嘴鸭.
pink·eyed [ˈpiŋkaid] *a.* 小眼的; (兔子等)眼发粉红色的.
Pin·ker·ton [ˈpiŋkətən] 〔美〕平克顿私家侦探公司; 便衣侦探.
Pin·kie [ˈpiŋki] 〔美〕(平克顿私家侦探公司的)便衣侦探.
pink·ie[1] [ˈpiŋki] *n.* 〔美东部〕小(手)指.
pink·ie[2] [ˈpiŋkiː] *n.* 尖头帆船.
pink·ish [ˈpiŋkiʃ] *a.* 带粉红色的.
pink·o [ˈpinkəu] *n.* 〔美俚〕准左倾分子.
pink·root [ˈpiŋkˌruːt, -ˌrut] *n.* 【植】浅赤根 *(Spigelia marylandica)* 〔原产美国东南部〕.
Pink·ster, Pinx·ter [ˈpiŋkstə] *n.* 〔美〕= Whitsuntide. ~ *flower* 〔美〕粉红色杜鹃花.
pink·y [ˈpiŋki] *a.* 粉红色的.
pin·na [ˈpinə] *n.* *(pl.* ***pin·næ*** [piniː]*)* ①【动】翅膀,翼,羽毛; 鳍. ②【植】羽片. ③【解】耳郭. **pin·nal** *a.*
pin·nace [ˈpinis, -nəs] *n.* 【海】舰载艇,舢板〔常用作舰船等的供应船〕; 【史】(附随大船的)二桅小船.
pin·na·cle [ˈpinəkl] *n.* ①【建】(哥特式建筑的)小尖塔; 尖柱; 尖端. ②〔美〕小山; 针峰. ③极点,顶点. *a ~ rock* 尖岩. *the ~ of science* 科学尖端,尖端科学. — *vt.* ①使成小尖塔形. ②把…放在高处,举起.
pin·na·cled [ˈpinəkld] *a.* ①小尖塔般耸立的; 有小尖塔的. ②在高处的.
pin·nate, pin·nat·ed [ˈpinit, -id] *a.* ①【植】羽状的,有羽状叶的. ②【动】有鳍的. **-ly** *ad.*
pin·nat·i·fid [piˈnætifid] *a.* 羽状半裂的.
pin·na·tion [ˌpinˈneiʃən] *n.* 【植】羽状.
pin·nat·i·sect [piˈnætisekt] *a.* 【植】羽状全裂的.
pin·ner [ˈpinə] *n.* ①扣别针的人. ②= pinafore. ③【史】〔*pl.*〕(女用帽式)头巾.
pin·ni·grade [ˈpinəgreid] *a.* 用鳍行走的. — *n.* 用鳍〔鳍状肢〕行走的动物.
pin·ni·ped [ˈpiniped] *a.* 鳍足类的. — *n.* 鳍足动物.
pin·nule [ˈpinjuːl] *n.* 【植】①小羽片. ②(棘皮动物的)羽枝. ③【动】小鳍. **-nu·late** [-juleit] **-nu·lat·ed** *a.*
pin·ny [ˈpini] *n.* 〔儿〕围嘴,口水兜.
pi·noch·le, pi·noc·le [ˈpiːnʌkl, -ˌnɔkl] *n.* ①平纳克耳牌戏〔用两副牌从 9 至 K,并加上 A 牌,共 48 张,由二、三或四人同玩〕. ②此种牌戏中的"Q""J"牌组〔由两张黑桃 Q 牌和两张方块 J 牌组成的一副牌〕.
pi·no·le [piˈnəulei] *n.* 〔美〕炒玉米粉.
pi·ñon [ˈpinjən, ˈpiːnjəun] *n.* ***(pl. ~(e)s)*** 〔Sp.〕(美国西部产)矮松〔子可食〕; 矮松子.
pin·set·ter [ˈpinˌsetə] *n.* ①【滚球】球童 (= pin boy). ②自动扶木柱器.
pin·spot·ter [ˈpinˌspɔtə] = pinsetter.
pin·ster [ˈpinstə] *n.* 〔美〕玩滚球 (bowling) 的人.
pin·stripe [ˈpinstraip] *n.* ①细条子,线条. ②隐格布,细条子衣服.
pint [paint] *n.* 品脱〔液量、干量名,〔英〕= 0.57 升弱,〔美〕液量 = 0.47 升强,干量 = 0.55 升〕.
pin·ta [ˈpintə] *n.* 【医】卡拉回线螺旋体斑病,密旋体斑病〔一种热带病,患者皮肤上发各色斑点〕.
pin·ta·do [pinˈtɑːdəu] *n.* *(pl. ~(e)s)* 橙斑马鲛 *(Scomberomorusmaculatus)* 〔常见于佛罗里达州和古巴附近的海洋中〕.
pin·tail [ˈpinteil] *n.* 〔俚〕【鸟】尖尾凫,尖尾鸭(等).
pin·ta·no [pinˈtɑːnəu] *n.* ***(pl. ~s)*** 豆娘鱼属动物(尤指岩豆娘鱼).
pin·tle [ˈpintl] *n.* 【船】舵销. ②(垂直)枢轴; (铰链、枪等的)针栓. *a ~ of the rudder* 舵针.
pin·to [ˈpintəu] *a.* 〔美〕黑白斑纹的. — *n.* ***(pl. ~(e)s)*** ①〔美西部〕黑白斑马. ②斑豆 (= ~ bean). ③墨西哥印第安人.
pint-size [ˈpaintˌsaiz] *a.* 小的; 很小的 (= pint-sized).
pin·wale [ˈpinweil] *a.* (灯芯绒)细棱条的.
pin·worm [ˈpinwəːm] *n.* 【动】蛲虫.
pinx. = pinxit.
pinx·it [ˈpiŋksit] *vt.* *(pl.* ***pinx·erunt*** [piŋkˈsiərʌnt]*)* 〔L.〕(某某)画,…笔〔画家署名用,常略作 pinx 或 pxt.〕.
pin·y [ˈpaini] *a.* ***(pin·ier; -i·est)*** 松树(似)的; 松树繁茂的.
pi·o·let [ˈpiəulei] *n.* 〔F.〕爬山用碎冰斧.
pi·on [ˈpaiɔn] *n.* = pi-meson.
Pion. = Pioneer ②.
pi·o·neer [ˌpaiəˈniə] *n.* ①拓荒者,开辟者; 提倡者; 先锋,先驱. ②【军】轻工兵. ③【生】先驱生物. *a ~ sergeant* 工兵兵长. *the Young Pioneers* 少年先锋队. — *vt., vi.* 开辟,开垦,开(路等); 提倡,做(…的)先锋.
pi·os·i·ty [paiˈɔsiti] *n.* (过分的)假虔诚,表面虔诚.

piou·piou [pju:ˈpju] *n.* 〔F.〕〔军俚〕法国兵.
pi·ous [ˈpaiəs] *a.* ①虔诚的, 信神的. ②以宗教为口实的,以敬神为名的;伪善的. ③〔古〕孝顺的;有善良意向的. *a ~ posture* 假仁假义的姿态. *a ~ fraud* 借宗教名义进行的欺骗. **~-mind** *a.* = pious. **-ly** *ad.* **-ness** *n.*
pip[1] [pip] *n.* ①(苹果、梨等的)果仁, 种子. ②〔俚〕漂亮的人〔物〕. ③〔美〕矮子.
pip[2] [pip] *n.* ①〔英〕(纸牌、骰子上的)点. ②〔英俚〕(军服肩章上的)星;(簇花中的)小花;(草的)根茎;菠萝皮的一小片. ③【讯】尖号信号,(雷达的)反射点;(荧光屏上的)脉冲.
pip[3] [pip] *n.* ①〔the ~〕家禽的舌病. ②〔谑〕(人的)小毛病;〔俚〕梅毒. ③〔俚〕烦躁; 抑郁. ***get [give] sb. the ~*** 使发怒, 使不痛快. ***have the ~*** 〔俚〕不舒服, 发着脾气.
pip[4] [pip] *vt.* (小鸡)啄破(蛋壳)出来. — *vi.* ①(小鸡)破壳而出. ②(小鸡)叽叽地叫.
pip[5] [pip] *vt.* ①〔俚〕反对, 排斥; 打败; 打破(计划等), 妨碍(人). ②射击; 击死; 击伤. — *vi.* 死 *(out)*.
pip[6] [pip] *n.* P字〔广播报时信号〕. *~ emma*=p.m.(午后).
pip·age [ˈpaipidʒ] *n.* ①用管道输送(水、瓦斯、油等). ②用管输送费. ③管道,管道系统.
pi·pal [ˈpi:pəl, paipəl] *n.* 菩提树(= ~tree).
pipe [paip] *n.* ①管, 导管, 筒. ②烟斗, 烟袋; 一袋烟. ③〔古〕笛, 管乐器;【海】(水手长的)哨子(声);〔*pl.*〕风箱. ④尖锐的声音; 鸟叫声; 笛声. ⑤(人体内的)血管;〔口〕气管, 声带, 喉咙;【植】茎;【矿】管状矿脉. ⑥液量名〔=105英加仑,126美加仑〕;(能装1 pipe的)大酒桶. ⑦〔俚〕容易的工作〔学科〕. ⑧〔美俚〕交谈; 短信. ⑨【地】筒状火成砾岩; 火山筒. *a drain ~* 排水管. *a distributing ~* 配水管. *light a ~* 点一袋烟. *smoke a ~* 吸一袋烟. ***dance to sb.'s ~*** 跟着某人亦步亦趋. ***hit the ~*** 吸毒. ***put sb.'s ~ out*** 妨碍某人成功. ***Put that in your ~ and smoke it.*** 〔小声忠告后说〕你仔细想想吧. ***smoke the ~ of peace*** (轮流)吸和睦烟; 言和. ***the Queen's [King's] ~*** 〔英〕走私烟焚毁炉. — *vt.* ①吹(笛);(用尖锐的声音)唱, 叫;【海】(吹水手长哨子)召集 *(up)*, 吹笛子引诱. ②把…装箱用管子输送. ③滚边(在衣服上), 镶花边(在糕饼等上). ④分株繁殖. ⑤〔美俚〕传递(消息等); 谈论, 透露;【电】(用导线或同轴电缆)传送(广播或电视节目等). ⑥〔美俚〕看, 瞧. *~ a song* 唱歌. *~ all hands to work* 吹哨子命令全体船员工作. — *vi.* ①吹笛; 吹口笛. ②叽叽地叫, 高声哭. ③(风)咻咻地吹. ④【矿】掘成圆筒形. ~ ***away***【海】吹哨子命令短艇出发. ~ ***down***【海】①吹哨子停工. ②〔美俚〕停止讲话, 静下来. ③〔俚〕变得较谨慎. ~ ***in*** 用电讯设备传送. ~ ***off*** ①把某人列入黑名单. ②向警察告发. ~ ***one's eye(s)*** 〔口〕流泪; 哭, 号哭. ~ ***up*** 开始吹;〔俚〕开始说〔唱〕; 装饰衣边; 加快速度. **~-clay** ① *n.* (造烟管或磨皮革用的)白粘土;〔喻〕(军队中对服装外貌等的)严格要求. ② *vt.* 用白粘土漂白. ~ **cleaner** 烟斗通条. ~ **course** 〔美俚〕容易对付的课程. ~ **dream** 〔美俚〕黄粱美梦, 空想, 幻想, 痴心妄想; 荒唐话〔计划〕. **~fest** 〔美〕废话, 闲谈. ~ **fitter** 管道安装工 **~fish** 海龙. **~layer** ①铺管工人, 自来水(煤气等)工人. ②〔美俚〕阴险的政客, 阴谋家. **~laying** *n., a.* 〔美〕= wire-pulling. **~-light** 点烟的捻子. ~ **line** ① *n.* 管路, 输油管; 干线, 补给线. ② *vt.* 用油管输(油)(*~line run* 油管输油量). ~ **organ** 管风琴. ~ **rack** 烟斗架;【乐】(风琴的)笛管架. **~stem** ①烟斗杆(管). ②形式上似烟斗杆(管)的东西. **~stone** 北美印第安人制造烟斗用的泥质岩石. ~ **wrench**【机】管板手. **-ful** *n.* 一袋(烟).
pip·er [ˈpaipə] *n.* ①吹笛人;〔Scot.〕风笛手. ②【鸟】鹬鸟; 小鸡; 小鸽;【鱼】鲂鮄; 绿鳍鱼; 海胆. ③气喘的马;〔英〕囮狗. ④制〔铺〕管者. ⑤滚边工;(缝纫机上的)滚边装置. ***drunk as a ~*** 〔口〕烂醉. ***pay the ~*** 负担费用, 承担后果. ***pay the ~ and call the tune*** 出钱而作主, 承担后果而有决定权.
piped [ˈpaipt] *a.* ①有管的; 管状的; 用管输送的. ②(服装)滚边的. ③〔美俚〕烂醉的.
pi·per·a·zin(e) [piˈperəzi(:)n] *n.*【化】哌嗪, 对二氮己环〔痛风药〕.
pi·per·ic [piˈperik] *a.* 胡椒的. *~ acid*【化】胡椒酸.
pi·per·i·dine [piˈperidi(:)n] *n.*【化】哌啶, 氮杂环己烷.
pip·er·ine [ˈpipəri(:)n] *n.*【化】胡椒碱〔解热剂〕.
pip·er·o·nal [ˈpipərənæl] *n.*【化】胡椒醛.
pi·pet, pi·pette [piˈpet] *n.*【化】吸移管, 吸量管, 球管. — *vt.* 用吸量管吸取〔移转〕. *an absorbtion ~* (气体)吸量管.
pip·ing [ˈpaipiŋ] *a.* ①吹笛的; 发锐音的, 高调子的; 滚热沸腾的. ②温和的, 平静的. *the ~ times of peace* 太平时候. — *ad.* 滚热地. *be ~ hot* 滚热的; 才出锅〔炉、蒸笼〕的. — *n.* ①吹笛; 管乐; 笛声; 尖锐声音; 啸鸣;〔口〕哭, 哭声. ②〔集合词〕管系. ③(糕饼的)花边;(衣服的)滚边.
pip·is·trelle, pip·is·trel [ˈpipistrel] *n.* 伏翼属 *(Pipistrellus)* 动物〔北美和东半球大部分地区常见的一种蝙蝠, 尤指伏翼 *(P. pipistrellus)*〕.
pip·it [ˈpipit] *n.*【鸟】鹡鸰科的鸣禽, 鹨.
pip·kin [ˈpipkin] *n.* 小瓦锅; 小汲桶.
pip·pin [ˈpipin] *n.* ①苹果一品种名; 实生苗苹果. ②【植】种子. ③〔美〕美人, 漂亮姑娘; 令人喜爱的人〔物〕. *Newtown P-* 翠玉苹果. *White P-* 青龙苹果.
pip-pip [ˈpipˈpip] *int.* 〔英俚〕再见.
pip·(p)ul [ˈpi:pəl] *n.* 〔pipal 的别字〕【植】菩提树.
pip·py [ˈpipi] *a.* (桔子等)多种子的.
pip·sis·se·wa [pipˈsisiwə] *n.* 伞形梅笠草 *(Chimaphila umbellata)* 〔北美的一种常绿植物〕.
pip·squeak [ˈpipskwi:k] *n.* 〔口〕无足轻重的人, 小人; 无价值的东西, 小东西.
pip·y [ˈpaipi] *a.* ①管状的; 有管的. ②笛声的; 发尖声的;〔口〕爱哭的.
pi·quan·cy [ˈpi:kənsi] *n.* ①辛辣, 开胃. ②泼辣; 痛快; 活泼. ③调皮. ④尖刻.
pi·quant [ˈpi:kənt] *a.* ①辛辣的; 开胃的. ②泼辣的; 痛快的; 使人兴奋的; 有趣的. ③淘气的, 调皮的. ④讽刺的, 尖刻的; 惹人生气的. **-ly** *ad.*
pique[1] [pi:k] *n.* 生气, 不高兴, 呕气. ***in a fit of ~, out of ~*** 赌气地; 愤愤. ***take a ~ against (sb.)*** 对…抱恶感, 生某人的气. — *vt.* ①使愤怒, 使不高兴; 损伤(自尊心), 伤(感情). ②夸耀. ③引起(好奇心、兴趣等). ④【空】俯冲攻击. — *vi.* 发怒, 急躁. ***be ~d at*** 为…生气. ~ ***oneself (up) on*** 夸, 自负 (*~ oneself on having a good memory* 自夸记性好).
pique[2] [pi:k] *n., v.*【牌】揍三十; 得三十分.
pi·qué [ˈpi:kei] *n.* 〔F.〕凹凸织物, 起楞布, 凸纹布. **~-work** 镶花工艺.
pi·quet [piˈket] *n.* ①(用7以上32张牌供二人对玩的)皮克牌. ②[ˈpikit]【军】= picket.
pi·ra·cy [ˈpaiərəsi] *n.* ①海上掠夺, 海盗行为. ②剽窃; 非法翻印; 侵害版权; 侵犯专利权. *literary ~* 侵害著作权, 剽窃.
Pi·rae·us, Peiraiévs [paiˈri(:)əs, ˌpi:reˈefs] *n.* 比雷埃夫斯〔希腊港市〕.
pi·rag·ua [piˈrægwə] *n.* ①独木舟. ②双桅平底船.
Pi·ran·del·lian [ˌpirənˈdeliən] *a.* 皮兰德娄的;(关于)皮兰德娄作品的; 情节离奇荒诞的.
Pi·ran·del·lo [ˈpirəndeləu], **Luigi** 皮兰德娄〔1867—1936, 意大利小说家、剧作家〕.
pi·ra·nha [piˈrɑ:niə, -ræn-] *n.* (南美)比拉鱼.
pi·ra·ru·cu [piˈrɑ:ruku:] *n.* 巨骨舌鱼〔南美洲所产的

一种巨鳞淡水鱼，可食用，有的可重达500磅；为淡水鱼中之最大者〕(= arapaima).

pi·rate [ˈpaiərit] *n.* ①海盗；海盗船. ②(著作等的)剽窃者；侵害版权[专利权]者. ③〔英〕非法行走专有路线的私营公共汽车[马车]. ④未经许可的广播者. *a* ~ *listener* 【讯】偷听者. *a* ~ *river* 夺流河. *swear like a* ~ 破口大骂. — *vt., vi.* ①以海盗方式劫掠，掠夺. ②剽窃，非法翻印. *a* ~*d edition* 翻印本，海盗版，偷印版.

pi·rat·ic, pi·rat·i·cal [paiˈrætik, -ikəl] *a.* ①(象)海盗的. ②剽窃的，侵害著作权的. **-i·cal·ly** *ad.*

pi·ric·u·larrin [piˈrikjuːlærin] *n.* 【生化】稻瘟菌素.

pirn [pəːn] *n.* ①【纺】纬纱管，纡子. ②〔Scot.〕(钓竿上的)线卷. ***wind oneself a bonny [queer]*** ~ 遭到困难. ***wind sb. a*** ~ 使人遭到困难.

pi·ro·gen [piˈrəugən] *n. pl.* 馅饼 (= pirogi).

pi·ro·gi [piˈrəugi] *n. pl.* 〔Russ.〕馅饼 (= piroshki).

pi·rogue [piˈrəug] *n.* = piragua.

pir·ou·ette [ˌpiruˈet] *n.* 【舞蹈】竖趾旋转；【马术】(马的)急转. *turn [perform] a* ~ 用脚尖旋转. — *vi.* 用脚尖旋转；表演旋转舞.

Pi·sa [ˈpiːzə] *n.* 比萨〔意大利城市，城内有著名的比萨斜塔〕. **-n** *a.*

pis all·er [ˈpiːz ˈælei] 〔F.〕不得已而采用的手段，最后手段，应急办法.

pis·ca·ry [ˈpiskəri] *n.* ①【法】(在他人渔区内的)捕鱼权. ②渔场. *the common of* ~ 共渔权.

pis·ca·tol·o·gy [ˌpiskəˈtɔlədʒi] *n.* 捕鱼学.

pis·ca·tor [pisˈkeitə] *n.* 渔夫；钓鱼的人.

pis·ca·to·ri·al, pis·ca·to·ry [ˌpiskəˈtɔːriəl, ˈpiskətəri] *a.* (爱)钓鱼的；(从事)渔业的.

Pis·ces [ˈpisiːz] *n. pl.* ①【动】鱼纲. ②〔the ~〕【天】双鱼座；双鱼宫. ~ **Australis** [ɔsˈtreilis] 【天】南鱼座.

pisci- *comb.f.* 鱼.

pis·ci·cul·tur·al [ˌpisiˈkʌltʃərəl] *a.* 养鱼(术)的.

pis·ci·cul·ture [ˈpisikʌltʃə] *n.* ①养鱼(业)；鱼类养殖. ②养鱼术.

pis·ci·cul·tur·ist [ˌpisiˈkʌltʃərist] *n.* 养鱼专家.

pis·ci·na [piˈsiːnə] *n.* *(pl. -nae* [-niː], *~s)* ①鱼塘，养鱼池. ②〔古罗马〕浴池. ③【宗】洗礼场，洗礼盆.

pis·cine[1] [ˈpisain] *a.* 鱼的，鱼类的；似鱼的.

pis·cine[2] [ˈpisiːn] *n.* ① = piscina. ②公共浴池.

pis·civ·o·rous [piˈsivərəs] *a.* (鸟等)吃鱼的，以鱼为食的.

pis·co [ˈpiskəu] *n.* 皮斯科酒〔秘鲁皮斯科城酿造的白兰地酒，因而得名〕.

pi·sé [ˈpiːzei] *n.* 〔F.〕【建】砌墙粘土.

Pis·gah [ˈpizgə] *n.* 毗斯迦山〔基督教《圣经》传说摩西从此山眺望上帝赐给亚伯拉罕的迦南地方〕. ~ ***sight*** (对得不到的东西)望洋兴叹.

pish [pʃ, piʃ] *int.* 呸! —*n.* 呸〔轻蔑声、嫌恶声〕. — [piʃ] *vt., vi.* (对…)嗤之以鼻，(对…)叫一声"呸". ~ ***away [down]*** 看不起.

pi·si·form [ˈpaisifɔːm] *a.* 豌豆形的. — *n.* 【解】豌豆骨.

pis·mire [ˈpismaiə] *n.* 【虫】蚂蚁.

pi·so·lite [ˈpaisəˌlait] *n.* 【矿】①豆石. ②豆石沉积岩. **-lit·ic** *a.*

piss [pis] 〔卑〕*vi.* 小便，撒尿. — *vt.* ①尿(血). ②撒尿撒脏. *int.* 〔美俚〕呸〔表示厌恶〕. ***be ~d off*** 〔美俚〕①发怒，极厌恶. ②极疲劳. ~ ***off*** 〔俚〕走掉；惹烦；喝醉；极端瘦乏. ~ ***on*** 亵渎. ~ ***pins and needles*** 〔口〕小便极疼痛. — *n.* 〔卑〕尿，小便. *a* ~ *pot* 尿壶. ~ ***and vinegar*** ①精力，活力. ②顽皮，淘气. **·er** *n.* ①小便者. ②〔美俚〕难事，苦差事. ③〔美俚〕淘气鬼〔指男孩〕.

pis·soir [piːˈswɑː] *n.* 〔F.〕男小便池，男小便处〔过去巴黎街上公用的便池〕.

pis·ta·chi·o [pisˈtɑːʃiəu] *n.* *(pl. ~s)* ①【植】阿月浑子；(可作调味香料用的)阿月浑子的子 (= ~-unt). ②淡黄绿色.

pis·ta·reen [ˌpistəˈriːn] *n.* 皮斯塔林〔西班牙的古银币，通用于西班牙在美洲的属地和西印度群岛〕. — *a.* 〔废〕无价值的，贱的，些小的.

piste [piːst] *n.* (板实的)滑雪道.

pis·til [ˈpistil] *n.* 【植】雌蕊 (*opp.* stamen).

pis·til·late [ˈpistilit] *a.* 有雌蕊的；只有雌蕊的 (*opp.* staminate). *a* ~ *flower* 雌花.

pis·tol [ˈpistl] *n.* 手枪. *a revolving* ~ 左轮(手枪). ***best the*** ~ (赛跑时)偷跑. ***hotter than a*** ~ 〔美〕大成功. ***put a*** ~ ***to sb.'s head*** 用手枪对准某人头部加以威胁. — *vt.* (〔英〕*-ll-*) 用手枪射击[打伤]. ~ **carbine** 驳壳枪. ~ **grip [hand]** 手枪形枪把. ~ **route** 〔美〕用手枪打死. ~**-shot** ①手枪射击. ②神枪手. ③手枪射程 (*within [beyond]* ~*-shot* 在手枪射程内[外]). ~**-whip** *vt.* 用手枪柄打(尤指打头部).

pis·tole [pisˈtəul] *n.* 皮斯托尔〔西班牙古金币〕.

pis·to·leer, pis·to·lier [ˌpistəˈliə] *n.* 带[用]手枪的人，手枪手.

pis·tol·graph [ˈpistlgrɑːf] *n.* 快照(机).

pis·ton [ˈpistən] *n.* ①【机】活塞. ②【乐】(管乐器的)直升式活塞. ~**ring** 【机】活塞环. ~**rod** 【机】活塞杆，联杆. ~ **stroke** 活塞冲程. ~ **valve** 活塞阀.

pit[1] [pit] *n.* 〔美〕(桃、杏等的)核. — *vt.* 除去…的核.

pit[2] [pit] *n.* ①坑，凹地，凹处；【矿】矿井；煤坑；【植】纹孔；地下温室，窖；(染)缸. ②〔the ~〕地狱；深渊〔方〕坟墓. ③陷阱；〔喻〕圈套. ④(剧场的)正厅后座〔英国指正面楼厅的下面〕；正厅后座的观众. ⑤斗鸡场，斗狗场(等). ⑥身体的凹窝；心窝，胳肢窝. ⑦麻子. ⑧〔美〕(粮食交易所的)现期交易部. ⑨(汽车赛跑时的)加油站，车胎修理处. ⑩〔美〕棒球联赛的最低位. ⑪【军】散兵坑；靶壕；炮兵掩体. *the* ~ *of the stomach* (腹上部)心窝. *a etching* ~ 【冶】侵蚀陷斑. *the bottomless* ~ = *the* ~ *of darkness* = *the* ~ *of hell* 地狱. *a wheat* ~ 〔美交易所〕现期小麦交易部. ***at the ~'s brink*** 快死. ***dig a ~ for*** 设法使…落在圈套里，陷害. ***shoot [fly] the*** ~①(斗鸡等)飞出斗鸡场. ②不付房租潜逃. —*vt.* ①〔常用 *p.p.*〕弄凹；挖坑；打矿井；使成麻子. ②把(蔬菜等)放在地窖里；坑陷. ③使相斗；抵抗. *a face pitted with smallpox* 麻脸. ~ *John against Paul* 使约翰反对保罗. — *vi.* 成凹；成麻子. ~ **boss** 〔美俚〕(矿井)工头；赌场老板. ~ **coal** 〔英〕煤炭. ~**head** 【矿】矿井口 (*the* ~*head committee* 煤矿主和矿工共同推派代表组成的煤矿委员会. *the* ~*head price* 【商】(煤的)矿山价格). ~**man** 矿工；矿井内机器管理员；下锯木匠；【机】〔*pl.*〕摇杆，连杆. ~**mob** 〔美口〕戏院的乐队. ~**pan** (中美洲)独木舟. ~**prop** 矿井中用的临时木支柱. ~**-saw** 双人竖拉大锯. ~ **sawyer** 下面一个拉大锯的人.

pit·a·pat, pit·pat [ˈpitəˈpæt] *ad.* 劈劈拍拍地(跑等)，(心)卜卜地(跳等). — *vi.* 劈劈拍拍地跑，(心)卜卜地跳. — *n.* 劈劈拍拍的跑声；卜卜卜的心跳声.

Pitcairn [pitˈkɛən] **Island** 皮特凯恩岛〔大洋洲〕.

pitch[1] [pitʃ] *n.* ①沥青；含有沥青的物质；松脂，树脂. ②人工合成沥青；人造树脂. *mineral [Jew's]* ~ 地沥青. ~ *black [darkness]* 漆黑(的). ***Touch ~, and you will be defiled. [You can't touch ~ without being defiled].*** 近朱者赤，近墨者黑. — *vt.* 用沥青涂. ~**blende** 沥青铀矿. ~ **coal** 沥青煤；倾斜煤层. ~**-dark** *a.* 漆黑的，黑暗的. ~ **pine** (北美)油松〔采松脂的松树〕. ~**stone** 【地】松脂石.

pitch[2] [pitʃ] *vt.* ①扔，投，抛，掷；【棒球】投球. ②插(桩等)，搭(帐篷等)，扎(营)，铺(路)，布置(场面等)，安顿(住处). ③〔常用 *p.p.*〕整顿，安排(阵容等)；【乐】为…定音高[定调]. ④〔英〕努力推销(商品)；〔口〕讲(故事). *P- him out!* 把他赶出去! ~ *one's tent* 安顿帐篷. *a*

~ed battle 激战，互有准备的对阵战. ~ ***a note*** 定音高. ~ ***attack*** 攻打. ~ ***(a) woo***〔美〕求爱，搂住亲嘴. ~ ***it strong*** 大吹牛皮. ~ ***oneself***〔口〕坐下来. ~ ***sb. over the bar*** 取消某人的律师资格. — *vi.* ①扔，投，掷；【棒球】作投球员；投球. ②头朝下掉落[倒下] *(on; into)*. ③【地】(地层等)向前方倾斜，倾斜. ④(船)前后颠簸纵摇，俯仰 *(cf.* roll*)*. ⑤搭帐篷，露宿；暂住；定居；布置场面. ⑥选择，决定 *(on; upon)*；偶然碰见 *(on; upon)*. ⑦(蜂等)歇，(马)突然跳起. ⑧【机】咬住. ⑨吹牛，说大话. *I ~ed upon the very house that suited me.* 我找到了合适的房子. ~ ***in***〔美口〕热情参加，拼命干起来. ~ ***into***〔口〕猛烈攻击；大骂；开始大干特干，大吃大嚼. — *n.* ①投掷；投球；投球距离. ②(船的)前后颠簸. ③度，程度；高度；点，顶点，极点；倾斜度；倾斜，坡；【乐】音高；音高标准；【火箭】俯仰；〔喻〕态度. ④【机】节，齿距，节距，螺距，间距；【板球】柱的间隔；【空】螺距〔飞机螺旋桨一次旋转的前进距离〕. ⑤(路边)零售摊；摆售商品量. *the ~ of an arch* 拱高. *the axial ~* 轴节. *the ~ of a saw* 锯齿节，(锯的)齿距. *a concert [French] ~*【乐】高[低]音调. *a high [low] ~ sound* 高[低]音. *cry out at the utmost ~ of one's voice* 尽量地大声叫. *The voices rose to a deafening ~.* 声音大得使人耳朵发聋. ***at concert ~*** 处于高效能状态. ***in there ~ing***〔美口〕拼命地干. ***make a ~ for***〔美口〕为…说项. ~ ***for the tape***〔美〕赛跑的最后冲刺. ***queer the ~ for sb.*** = ***queer sb.'s ~***〔口〕暗中破坏某人计划. ***take up one's ~*** 回到自己原位；保持一定限度. ***to the highest [lowest]*** ~ 到最高[最低]限度. **~-and-toss** 掷钱游戏. **~-down**【火箭】俯冲. ~ **farthing** 投钱戏. **~man**〔美〕摊贩. **~-over**【火箭】转弯. ~ **pipe**【乐】定调管；律管. **~-up**【火箭】上仰. ~ **wheel** (和一个齿轮咬住的另一个)齿轮.

pitch·er[1] [ˈpitʃə] *n.* ①有柄的大水罐，柄盂. ★英国多说 jug. ②【植】瓶状叶. *You are a little ~!* 你是个尖耳小鬼. *She has cracked her ~.* 她失身了. ***Little ~s have long ears.*** 小孩子耳朵尖. ***Pitchers have ears*** 隔墙有耳〔说话要当心〕. ***The ~ goes often to the well but is broken at last.*** 水壶取水，日久必破. ~ **plant**【植】猪笼草，瓶子草. **-ful** (一)满水壶.

pitch·er[2] [ˈpitʃə] *n.* ①投掷的人；【棒球】投手. ②(往车上)投装(干草等)的人；〔英〕装煤人. ③〔英〕铺路石. ④摊贩；搭帐篷卖艺的人.

pitch·fork [ˈpitʃfɔːk] *n.* ①干草叉，草耙. ②【乐】音叉. ***rain ~s.*** 下大雨. — *vt.* ①用耙[叉]掇起. ②(突然或出其不意)推进[硬塞进，抛入] *(into)*.

pitch·ing [ˈpitʃiŋ] *n.* ①铺地石，护堤石. ②扔出；【棒球】投球(法). ③(船的)纵摇或前后簸动；【空】俯仰.

pitch·y [ˈpitʃi] *a.* *(pitch·i·er; -i·est)* ①沥青多的；沥青似的，粘的. ②涂着沥青的. ③漆黑的，黝黑的，黑褐色的. ~ *wool* 原毛，含脂毛.

pit·e·ous [ˈpitiəs, -tjəs] *a.* ①可怜的，凄惨的. ②〔古〕慈悲的. **-ly** *ad.* **-ness** *n.*

pit·fall [ˈpitfɔːl] *n.* 陷坑，陷阱；诱惑；圈套；隐藏的危险；易犯的错误.

pith [piθ] *n.* ①【植】木髓，树心；【解】髓，骨髓. ②体力，力气；精力，精神；(文章的)力. ③精髓，要义，要点；重要. *a man of ~* 精力饱满的人. *a matter of (great) ~ and moment* 非常重要的问题. *the ~ and marrow of an article* 文章的要点〔精华〕. — *vt.* ①除去(茎中的)木髓. ②割去脊髓弄死(牛等). ~ **cavity**【植】髓孔.

pith·e·can·thrope [ˌpiθiˈkænθrəup] *n.*【动】猿人.

pith·e·can·thro·pine [ˌpiθiˈkænθrəpain] *a.* 猿人的 (=pithecanthropoid). — *n.* 猿人.

Pith·e·can·thro·pus[ˌpiθəkænˈθrəupəs] *n.* *(pl.* ***-pi*** [-pai]*)* 猿人属. ~ ***erectus*** [iˈrektəs] 直立猿人. (=Java man).

pi·the·coid [piˈθiːkɔid] *a.* ①(似)猿的. ②狐尾猴的.

pith·less [ˈpiθlis] *a.* 无髓的；没气力的.

pith·y [ˈpiθi] *a.* ①有髓的，有气力的. ②简洁的. **-i·ly** *ad.* **-i·ness** *n.*

pit·i·a·ble [ˈpitiəbl] *a.* ①可怜的. ②可怜又可笑的，卑鄙的，不足取的. **-bly** *ad.* **-ness** *n.*

pit·i·er [ˈpitiə] *n.* 怜悯者.

pit·i·ful [ˈpitiful] *a.* ①慈悲的. ②可怜的. ③可怜又可笑的，卑鄙的. **-ly** *ad.*

pit·i·less [ˈpitilis] *a.* 无情的，冷酷的. **-ly** *ad.*

Pit·man [ˈpitmən] *n.* 皮特曼〔姓氏〕.

pi·tom·e·ter [piˈtɔmitə] *n.* (测量流速的)皮托压差计.

pi·ton [ˈpiːtɔn; *F.* piˈtɔ̃] *n.* *(pl.* ***-tons*** [-tɔnz; *F.* -ˈtɔ̃]*)*【登山】冰用钢锥.

Pitt [pit] *n.* ①皮特〔姓氏〕. ②**William** ~ 威廉·皮特〔1708—78，1759—1806，英国政治家父子〕.

pit·tance [ˈpitəns] *n.* 少量食物；少量收入〔主要用于 *a mere ~*〕.

pit·ted [ˈpitid] *a.* ①有凹痕的；有麻子的. ②【植】具洼点的，具纹孔的.

pit·ter-pat·ter [ˈpitəpætə] *ad.* 拍挞拍挞地，劈劈拍拍地. — *n.* 拍挞拍挞〔连续拍击声，暴雨声〕.

pit·tite [ˈpitait] *n.*【剧】正厅后座的观众.

Pitts·burgh [ˈpitsbəːg] *n.* 匹兹堡〔美国城市〕.

pit·ty-pat [ˈpitipæt] *ad.* = pitapat.

pi·tu·i·ta·ry [piˈtju(ː)itəri] *a.* ①大脑垂体的. ②(分泌)粘液的. ③(由大脑垂体所致的)异常长大的. — *n.* ①【解】大脑垂体. ②【医】大脑垂体制剂. ~ **gland body** 大脑垂体. ~ **membrance** 鼻粘膜.

pi·tu·i·trin [piˈtjuːitrin] *n.* 粘液腺激素.

pit·y [ˈpiti] *n.* ①怜悯，同情. ②可惜的事，憾事. *It is a ~ [a thousand pities] that you cannot come.* 你不能来真是万分遗憾. *What a ~!* 实在可怜！真可惜！*The ~ of it!* 可惜呀！真遗憾！***feel ~ for*** 可怜…. ***for ~'s sake*** 请可怜可怜. ***have [take] ~ (up)on*** = feel ~ for. ***in ~ of*** 因可怜…. ***(the) more's the ~.*** 更可惜了，更冤枉了；可惜，不幸. ***out of ~*** 出于哀怜. — *vt., vi.*(对…)觉得可怜. *He is to be pitied.* 他很值得同情. *I ~ you if you think so.* 你这样想就太可悲了〔有可耻的意思〕.

pit·y·ing·ly [ˈpitiiŋli] *ad.* 怜惜地.

pit·y·ri·a·sis [ˌpitiˈraiəsis] *n.*【医】糠疹，蛇皮癣.

piu [pjuː] *ad.*〔It.〕【乐】更. ~ ***allegro*** [əˈleigrəu] 更快. ~ ***forte*** [ˈfɔːti] 更强.

piv·ot [ˈpivət] *n.* ①【机】交枢，枢轴，支轴，磨经〔磨的回转轴〕；【物】支点，支枢；扇轴儿. ②枢要，中枢，中心点，要点. ④【军】轴兵，基准. ⑤【体】回转运动. — *vt.* ①把…放在枢轴上. ②使绕枢轴旋转. 放在轴上，装尖轴. — *vi.* ①依尖轴旋转；旋转. ②由…而定 *(on; upon)*. ~ **axis** 摆轴. ~ **bearing**【机】立式止推轴承. ~ **bridge** 旋开桥；开合桥. ~ **gun** 旋转炮. ~ **man**【军】基准兵，轴兵.

piv·ot·al [ˈpivətl] *a.* ①枢轴的. ②中枢的，枢要的. *a ~ question* 中心问题. *the ~ strategy* 全局战略方针. **-ly** *ad.*

pix [piks] *n.*〔*sing., pl.*〕〔美俚〕(新闻)照片；影片.

pix·ie [ˈpiksi] = pixy.

pix·i·lat·ed [ˈpiksileitid] *a.*〔美、口〕有点怪的，有点神经病的.

pix·y [ˈpiksi] *n.* 小鬼，妖精. —*a.* 顽皮的.

pi·zen [ˈpaizn] *n.*〔美俚〕威士忌酒；酒.

pizz. = pizzicato.

piz·za [ˈpiːtsə] *n.* (意大利式)烤馅饼.

piz·ze·ri·a [ˌpiːtsəˈriːə] *n.* (意大利的)烤馅饼店.

piz·zi·ca·to [ˌpitsiˈkɑːtəu] *a.*〔It.〕【乐】拨奏的. — *ad.* 拨奏. — *n.* *(pl.* ***-ti*** [-ti(ː)]*)* 拨奏曲.

piz·zle [ˈpizl] *n.* 动物的阴茎〔过去曾做鞭子用〕.

P.J. = ①Police Justice 违警罪法庭法官. ②Presiding

Judge 首席法官. ③Probate Judge. 遗嘱检验法官.

Pj's [ˈpiːˈdʒeiz] *n.* 〔*pl.*〕〔口〕(宽大的)睡衣裤〔pyjamas 的缩略〕.

Pk = pack.

pk. = ①pack. ②park. ③peak. ④peck.

pkg. = package.

pkt. = ①packet. ②pocket.

P.L. = ①Poet Laureate 〔英〕桂冠诗人. ②Primrose League 〔英〕樱草会.

pl. = ①place. ②plate. ③plural.

PLA, P.L.A. = ①People's Liberation Army (中国)人民解放军. ②Port of London Authority〔英〕伦敦港务管理局.

pla·ca·ble [ˈplækəbl] *a.* 可安抚的,易劝解的,宽大的,温和的. **-bil·i·ty** [ˌplækəˈbiliti] *n.*

plac·ard [ˈplækɑːd] *n.* ①招贴,揭示,标语,报单. ②挂图,招贴画,宣传广告画. ③招牌,名牌; 行李牌. — *vt.* ①在…贴招贴,在…贴公告[广告]. ②(用布告等)公布. ③张贴,悬挂.

pla·cate [pləˈkeit] *vt.* 安抚,抚慰; 使和解;〔美〕得到(反对党等的)谅解. **-ca·tion** *n.*

pla·ca·to·ry [ˈpleikətəri] *a.* 安抚的,抚慰的.

place [pleis] *n.* ①地方,场所,处; 所在,位置;〔抽象名词〕空间 *(opp.* time*)*. ②(书中的)处所,页. ③市区; 市,镇,村;〔多用作专有名词〕广场,十字路口; 路,街. ④建筑物; 住处,寓所,住宅;〔英〕乡下大宅院;〔美〕乡下小地产; 本部; 室,办事处. ⑤立场,处境; 地位,身分,资格; 职,官职,本分; 高位. ⑥座位,席位. ⑦【数】位,次序;【赛跑】头二三名,入选;【赛马】第二名 *(opp.* win*)*;【足球】= place-kick. *a ~ of arms* 军队集合处; 要塞; 火药库. *a ~ of business* 营业处. *There is no [not any] ~ for you.* 没有你的位置,没有容纳你的余地. *Put yourself in my ~.* 请你设身处地替我想一想. *Come to my ~ tomorrow.* 明天请你到我家里来. *my ~* 舍间. *at our ~* 在我们家里. *There is always a ~ for you at our table.* 请你随时来吃便饭. *Calculate to 3 ~s of decimals.* 算到小数点第三位. *The mare was beaten for a ~ by a short head.* 那匹母马以不到一头之差跑得第二名. ***a ~ in the sun*** 有利地位; 优越的立场[处境]. ***a wild ~ in the road*** 〔美俚〕小城镇. ***all over the ~*** 到处. ***another ~*** 〔英〕(在下院指)上院,(在上院指)下院. ***As much as my ~ is worth to do*** …做(那种事),我的饭碗就要打破了. ***be no ~ for*** 不是…来的地方; 没有…的余地 (*There is no ~ (left) for doubt.* 没有怀疑的余地. *It is no ~ for you.* 这儿不是你来的地方). ***find [lose] one's ~*** 找到[失去](书中)地方. ***from ~ to ~*** 处处. ***get a ~*** 【赛马】得第三名. ***get ~s*** 〔美俚〕到各处走动. ***give ~ to*** 让位于,被…所代替. ***go ~s*** 〔美俚〕①出去寻乐. ②表演精彩; 成功,胜利. ***have a soft ~ in one's heart for sb.*** 对某人有爱情,对某人有好感. ***in ~*** 得其所,在适当位置; 适当的. ***in ~ of*** 代替. ***in ~s*** 多处,到处,处处. ***in the first [second, last] ~*** 第一[第二,最后]. ***in the next ~*** 其次,第二点. ***keep people in their proper ~s*** 使人安分守己. ***keep sb. in his ~*** 抑制某人; 使某人安分. ***know one's ~*** 识分寸,不越分. ***lose one's ~*** 失去地位,失业. ***make ~*** 腾出地方. ***make ~ for*** 给…留座位. ***out of ~*** 不得其所的; 不适当的; 不相称的; 碍事的; 失着业. ***put sb. in his ~*** 使某人不敢越轨. ***take one's ~*** 就位,就席,就座. ***take ~*** 发生; 举行. ***take the ~ of*** 代替某人,接替某人的位置. ***the high ~*** 祭坛; 偶像. ***the other ~*** 地狱. — *vt.* ①放; 安置; 排列,整顿. ②使就(职); 任命…为(牧师). ③贷(款); 投资. ④发出(订单),订(货); 交…出版. ⑤把(信赖、希望等)寄托于. ⑥定(场所[日期]); 评定(等级). ⑦认出,想起; 了解. ⑧定(赛跑的)跑到次序[向例到第三名为止];【棒球、网球】(把球)打向一定地方. ⑨把声量、音域适当控制着说[唱]. *I will ~ anything at your service.* 任何东西均请随意使用. *~ one's confidence in [on] a friend* 相信朋友,信赖朋友. *I know his face, but I can't quite ~ him.* 我认识他的面孔,可是想不起是谁. *a very difficult person to ~.* 一个很难判断其身分的人物. — *vi.* 【赛马】跑赢〔通常指头、二、三名〕. ***be ~d*** 【体】入选. ***~ oneself on record*** 〔美〕许下诺言,约定. **~ brick** 半烧砖. **~ card** (宴席的)座位牌. **~ hunter** 求职者; 猎官者. **~kick** *v.*【足球】(球置地上)定位踢 *(opp.* dropkick, punt*)* **~man** 〔英〕官吏;〔蔑〕骄横的芝麻官. **~ name** 地名. **-able** *a.* 可被确定位置的. **-less** *a.* 没有固定位置的.

place aux dames [ˈplɑːs əu ˈdɑːm] 〔F.〕妇女座; 请把座位留给妇女; 请让妇女先走.

pla·ce·bo [pləˈsiːbəu] *n.* ①晚祷悼声〔丧歌〕. ②安慰物,安慰剂; 宽心话.

place·ment [ˈpleismənt] *n.* ①放,安置. ②找职业. ③定职位,安排. ④【足球】定位; 定位踢的球位; 定位踢(= place kick).

pla·cen·ta [pləˈsentə] *n.* *(pl.* ~*s*, *-tae* [-tiː]*)* 【解】胎盘;【植】胎座.

pla·cen·tal [pləˈsentl] *a.* 【解】(有)胎盘的;【植】(有)胎座的. — *n.* 【动】有胎盘哺乳动物.

Plac·en·ta·li·a [ˌplæsənˈteiliə] *n.* 〔*pl.*〕【动】有胎盘哺乳类,有胎盘类.

pla·cen·tate [pləˈsenteit] *a.* 【解、动】具有胎盘的;【植】具有胎座的.

plac·en·ta·tion [ˌplæsnˈteiʃən] *n.* ①【解、动】胎盘形成. ②【植】胎座式.

plac·er[1] [ˈpleisə] *n.* ①安置者,调配者. ②第…名. *the sixth ~ in a competition* 比赛中的第六名.

plac·er[2] [ˈpleisə] *n.* 【矿】(含金、铂等的)砂矿,砂积矿床; *(opp.* lode*)*. **~ gold** 砂金. **~ mining** 砂矿开采.

pla·cet [ˈpleiset] *n.* 〔L.〕赞成(票); 许可,认可. *non ~* 不赞成(票).

plac·id [ˈplæsid] *a.* 平静的; 宁静的; 温和的. *in a ~ mood* 心平气和. **-ly** *ad.*

pla·cid·i·ty [plæˈsiditi] *n.* 平静; 宁静; 温和.

pla·cing [ˈpleisiŋ] *n.* (擅自将公司非法)出售,出盘.

plack·et [ˈplækit] *n.* ①(女裙腰上的)开口〔= *~-hole*〕. ②(女裙的)衣袋.

plac·oid [ˈplækɔid] *a.* 【动】板状的; 有盾状鳞的. — *n.* 有盾鳞的鱼.

pla·fond [ˈplæfɔ̃ːŋ] *n.* 〔F.〕①【建】天花板,顶棚. ②顶棚彩画[雕刻].

pla·gal [ˈpleigəl] *a.* 【乐】由下属和弦转成主和弦的. **~ cadence [close]** 变格终止.

plage [plɑːʒ] *n.* 〔F.〕海滨; 海滨游乐地.

pla·gi·a·rism [ˈpleidʒiərizəm] *n.* ①(文章、学说等的)剽窃,抄袭. ②剽窃物.

pla·gi·a·rist [ˈpleidʒiərist] *n.* 剽窃者,抄袭者.

pla·gi·a·rize [ˈpleidʒiəraiz] *vt., vi.* 剽窃,抄袭(别人的文章、学说等).

pla·gi·a·ry [ˈpleidʒjəri] *n.* 〔古〕①剽窃. ②剽窃(物).

pla·gio·clase [ˈpleidʒiəukleis] *n.* 【矿】斜长石.

pla·gi·o·pho·tot·ro·pism [ˌpleidʒiəufəuˈtɔtrəpizəm] 【植】斜屈光性,斜向光性.

pla·gi·o·trop·ic [ˌpleidʒiəˈtrɔpik] *a.* 【植】斜向性的,偏途向性的〔指大多数植物的根与枝而言〕. **-trop·i·cal·ly** *ad.*

pla·gi·ot·ro·pism [ˌpleidʒiˈɔtrəpizəm] *n.* 【植】斜向性.

plague [pleig] *n.* ①时疫,瘟疫,传染病;〔the ~〕鼠疫,黑死病. ②天灾,灾害,祸患; 天罚. ③〔口〕讨厌的人[东西],"祸虫",麻烦事情,疙瘩事. *the black ~* 鼠疫. *the white ~* 肺病. *the ~ of locusts* 蝗灾. *the ~ of hails* 雹灾. ***be at the ~*** 〔*Scot.*〕费事,费心. ***P- (up)on it [him]! = P- take it [him]!*** 该死的(人)! ***What the [a] ~!*** 多讨厌呀! 嗳呀! — *vt.* ①使染瘟疫[得灾

祸等]. ②折磨;〔口〕麻烦，困扰. ***be ~d to death*** 被弄得[问得]烦死了，烦得要死. ~ ***one's life out*** 拼命折磨. ~ **spot**【医】(传染性)疹子；鼠疫斑；瘟疫流行地;〔喻〕罪恶中心. ~**some** *a.*〔口〕麻烦的，讨厌的.

pla·gui·ly [ˈpleigili] *ad.*〔口〕折磨着，烦恼着；非常. *It's so ~ hot.* 天热得要命.

pla·guy, -guey [ˈpleigi] *a.*〔口〕***(-gui·er; -gui·est)*** = plaguesome. — *ad.* = plaguily.

plaice [pleis] *n.*〔*sing. pl.*〕【鱼】鲽.

plaid [plæd] *n.* (苏格兰高地人穿的)方格呢披肩；方格呢，苏格兰呢;〔罕〕格子花. — *a.* 方格花的. **-ed** *a.* 披着方格呢披肩的；用方格呢做的.

plain¹ [plein] *vi.*〔古、诗、英方〕发牢骚，诉苦；叹惜，悲伤；哀悼；悲歌，痛哭.

plain² [plein] *a.* ①平的，平坦的. ②平易的；普通的，简单的. ③明白的，清楚的. ④没有装饰的；平常的；朴素的；单色的，(织品)素净的；【纺】平纹的. ⑤淡泊的，(食物等)清淡的；粗陋的. ⑥爽直的，直率的，坦白的. ⑦丑，难看的. ⑧彻底的，十足的(傻瓜). ⑨单调的，平淡的. ⑩【牌】(2—9点的)普通牌的. ~ *people* (没有衔头等的)普通老百姓，平民. ~ *cloth* 平纹织物. ~ *clothes* 便衣，便服. ~ *rice* 白饭. ~ *silly* 糊涂透了. ***as ~ as a pikestaff [the day, daylight]*** 非常清楚，显而易见. ***as ~ as the nose on one's face*** 清清楚楚看得见，明明白白. ***in ~ English*** 用普通易懂的英语(说). ***in ~ sight*** 视界清楚，一览无遗. ***in ~ terms [words]*** 直说，坦白说. ~ *living* 简朴的生活. ~ *sailing* 顺利（航行）*(cf.* plane sailing*)* *(It's all ~ sailing.* 一帆风顺，进展顺利). ~ *speaking* 打开天窗说亮话. ~ *words*〔美〕日常用语. ***to be ~ with you*** 对你直说〔插入语〕. —*ad.* 平；平易；明白，明瞭；坦白. — *n.* ①平地，平原，旷野. ②〔英方〕(四面被建筑物包围着的)广场，小公园. ③〔*pl.*〕〔美〕(落矶山脉东部的)大草原. ④〔诗〕战场；素织品，单色布. ~ **bond**【商】无担保债款. ~ **chant** = plain-song. ~**clothes man** 便衣警察；侦探. ~ **dealer**〔罕〕率直人，爽直人，老实人. ~**-dealing** *n.*, *a.* 率直(的)，坦白(的)；光明正大(的). ~**-laid** *a.* (绳索)平搓的. ~**-looking** *a.*〔美〕= homely. ~ **song**【宗】平歌，单旋律圣歌；定旋律. ~**-spoken** *a.* 老实说的，直言无隐的. ~ **weave**【纺】平纹组织. ~**-work** 素缝〔刺绣之对〕. **-ly** *ad.* **-ness** *n.*

plains·man [ˈpleinzmən] *n.* *(pl. -men)* 平原居民.

plaint [pleint] *n.* ①〔诗〕悲叹，怨诉. ②委屈；抗议. ③【英法】控诉；诉状. **-ful** *a.* 哀叹的，哀诉的.

plain·tiff [ˈpleintif] *n.*【法】原告 *(opp.* defendant*)*.

plain·tive [ˈpleintiv] *a.* 可怜的，悲哀的，忧郁的；哭诉的. *a ~ melody* 哀调. *a ~ cry* 哀鸣. **-ly** *ad.*

plais·ter [ˈpleistə] *n.* 灰泥；熟石膏；膏药(=plaster).

plait [plæt] *n.* ①褶边. ②辫子；麦杆缏；辫绳. — *vt.* ①在(布上)打褶. ②编，(辫). *~ed yarn* 包芯线.

plan [plæn] *n.* ①计划，设计，方案，规划；方法；进程表，时间表. ②图，图面；平面图，设计图；示意图；图表；(街市)地图. ③雏形，草案；轮廓，梗概. *a ~ of attack [compaign, operations]* 进攻[作战]计划. *I have a ~ for overcoming our difficulties.* 我有克服这些困难的方法. *The better ~ is to peel them after boiling.* 煮后剥皮较好. *a floor ~* 平面图. *a raised ~* 投影图，正面图. *a working ~* 工作图. *a perspective ~* 透视图. ***according to ~*** 按照计划. ***form [lay] a ~*** 拟计划. ***in ~*** 作为平面图. ***give ~ to*** 使…发挥. — *vt., vi.* ①计划，设计. ②制(图)，绘(设计图). ③〔美〕打算 *(to)*. *planned economy* 计划经济. *planned parenthood* 计划生育. ~ ***on***〔口〕打算，想要 *(~ on going to London* 打算去伦敦). ~ ***out*** 想出，计划出.

plan- *comb. f.*〔用于元音前〕= plano-.

pla·nar [ˈpleinə] *a.* ①平面的；在平面上的；平的. ②【数】二维的，二度的.

pla·na·tion [pleiˈneiʃən] *n.*【地】均夷作用.

planch [plɑːntʃ, plæntʃ] *n.*〔废、英方〕板；地板.

plan·ch·et [ˈplɑːnʃit] *n.* 造币坯.

Planck [plɑːŋk], **Max Karl Ernst Ludwig** 普朗克〔1858-1947，德国物理学家〕. ~ **constant**【物】普朗克常数.

planc·ton [ˈplæŋktən] *n.* = plankton.

plane¹ [plein] *n.* 悬铃木属树木. ~ **tree** 美[法]国梧桐.

plane² *n.* ①平面，水平面，面. ②(知识等的)发达程度，水平，阶段. ③【空】机翼面;〔常 *pl.*〕飞机. ④(结晶体的)一面. ⑤【矿】总巷道. *an inclined ~* 斜面. *a ~ of polorization*【矿】偏振(平)面，偏光面. *a ~ of reference*【数】基础(平)面，对照面. *a ~ of symmetry* 对称面. *an elevating ~*【空】升降翼. *a rear ~*【空】尾翼，方向翼. *a robot ~* 无人驾驶飞机. *a rotor ~* 旋翼机. ***on the same ~ as*** 和…同一水准[程度]. — *a.* 平的；在平面上的，平面图的. *a ~ chart* 平面海图. *a ~ figure* 平面图. — *vi.* ①滑行；(比赛船等)在水面上飞一样滑跑. ②〔口〕坐飞机去旅行. ~ **geometry** 平面几何学. ~**-milling machine** 龙门铣床. ~ **table**【测】平板仪，平板绘图器.

plane³ [plein] *n.* 平刨；镘. *a jack ~* 粗刨. — *vt., vi.* 刨平；镘平. **P- tron** 刨刀，刨铁.

plane·load [ˈpleinləud] *n.* 一飞机的人[物]；飞机负载量.

plan·er [ˈpleinə] *n.* ①刨工. ②刨床. ③【印】打塞子.

plane-sailing *n.* [ˈpleinseiliŋ] ①【海】(用平面海图的)平面航法. ②= plain sailing.

plan·et [ˈplænit] *n.* ①【天】行星 *(opp.* fixed star*)*. ②【占星】(左右人命运的)星相. *the major ~s* 大行星. *minor ~s* 小行星. *primary ~s* 一等行星. *secondary ~s* 卫星. ***by ~s***〔方〕不规则；易变. ~**-struck**, ~**-stricken** *a.* ①【占星】(命运)受到行星影响的. ②被诅咒的；带来恐慌的.

plan·e·tar·i·um [ˌplæniˈtɛəriəm] *n.* *(pl. ~s, -ria* [-riə]*)* ①天象仪；太阳系仪. ②天文馆.

plan·e·ta·ry [ˈplænitəri] *a.* ①【天】行星的；由于行星作用的. ②流浪的，不定的. ③俗世的，现世的，地球的. ④【机】行星齿轮的. ~ *days* 一星期. *a ~ gear* (汽车的)行星齿轮. *a ~ hour* 行星时. ~ *motions* 行星运动. *the ~ system* 太阳系.

plan·e·tes·i·mal [ˌplæniˈtesiməl] *n.*, *a.*【天】微星(的). ~ **hypothesis** (行星形成的)微星假说.

plan·e·toid [ˈplænitɔid] *n.* 小行星. **-al** [ˌplæniˈtɔidl] *a*

plan·e·tol·o·gy [ˈplæniˈtɔlədʒi] *n.* 行星学.

plan·form [ˈplænfɔːm] *n.*【空】(飞机的)平面形状.

plan·gent [ˈplændʒənt] *a.* 冲到海边来的，澎湃的，哗啦哗啦响的. **-gen·cy** *n.* (尤指波浪的)澎湃声. **-ly** *ad.*

plani- *comb.f.* 平，平面: *planimeter.*

pla·nim·e·ter [plæˈnimitə] *n.*【数】测面仪，求积仪.

pla·nim·e·try [plæˈnimitri] *n.* 测面(积)学，平面几何.

plan·ish [ˈplæniʃ] *vt.* 弄平；刨平，辗平，打平，鎚光(金属板等)；磨平；研光(纸等). **-ing hammer** 打平锤.

plan·i·sh·er [ˈplæniʃə] *n.* ①平滑器，打平器. ②打平者，研光者.

plan·i·sphere [ˈplænisfiə] *n.* ①平面球体图. ②【天】步天规；星座一览图.

plank [plæŋk] *n.* ①板，厚板〔比 board 厚，通常厚 2—6 英寸，宽 9 英寸以上〕；制板木料 ②木板制成物. ③支持物. ④〔美〕(政纲的)一条. ⑤〔美棒球俚〕=hit. ~ **bed**〔英〕(监狱等里的)木板床. ***burn the ~s*** 长坐，久坐. ***Prick for a soft ~*** (海员)找最舒适的卧处. ***put a ~ in the platform***〔美〕提作政纲之一. ***step off the big ~***〔美俚〕进棺材，死亡. ***walk the ~*** ①【海】走跳板〔海盗处死俘虏的一种办法；把俘虏蒙住眼睛，然后逼使他在一个伸出舷外的跳板上前进，掉落海中〕. ②(转义)被解雇，被迫去职. —*vt.* ①在…上铺板;〔口〕砰一声放下 *(down)*. ②〔口〕立即支付(款项) *(down; out)*. ③〔美〕用菜板端出(烧好的鸡、鱼). ④〔美俚〕打(球). —

vi. 睡光板. ～ **it** 睡光板.
plank·ing [ˈplæŋkiŋ] *n.* ①铺板. ②〔集合词〕木板; 地板;【船】船壳板.
plank-sheer [ˈplæŋkˌʃiə] *n.*【船】舷缘板.
plank·ter [ˈplæŋktə] *n.* 个体浮游生物.
plank·tol·ogy [plæŋkˈtɔlədʒi] *n.* 浮游生物学.
plank·ton [ˈplæŋktən] *n.*【生】浮游生物.
plan·less [ˈplænlis] *a.* 没有图形的; 没有计划的; 没有方案的. **-ly** *ad.* **-ness** *n.*
plan·ner [ˈplænə] *n.* 计划者, 订规划者, 设计者.
plan·ning [ˈplæniŋ] *n.* 计划, 规划. *an overall* ～ 全面规划.
plano-[1] *comb.f.* 平的, 平坦的: *plano*concave.
plano-[2] *comb.f.* 流动, 游动: *plano*gamete.
plan·o·blast [ˈplænəblæst] *n.* 水螅状之水母体.
pla·no-con·cave [ˌpleinəuˈkɔnkeiv] *a.* 平凹的〔一面平一面凹的〕. ～ **lens** 平凹透镜.
pla·no-con·vex [-ˈkɔnveks] *a.* 平凸的. ～ **lens** 平凸透镜.
plan·o·gam·ete [ˈplænəgəmiːt] *n.*【生】游动配子.
pla·nog·ra·phy [pləˈnɔgrəfi, plei-] *n.* 平面印刷; 平印品. **-graph·ic** *a.*
pla·nom·e·ter [pləˈnɔmitə] *n.*【机】测平器, 平面规.
plan·o·spore [ˈplænəspɔː] *n.*【生】游动孢子.
plant [plɑːnt] *n.* ①植物, 草木 *(opp.* animal*)*; 草本; 〔商用语〕树秧, 苗木. ②庄稼, 作物, 收获; (植物的)生育. ③设备, 装置, (工)厂, 车间; (农)场; (研究所、医院、大学等的)全部设备. ④智力工作的工具〔书籍、实验仪器等〕, 方法. ⑤〔俚〕花招, 诈欺; 欺诈者. ⑥〔英俚〕侦探. ⑦(戏剧的)伏线. ⑧〔美俚〕假装观众的演员; (在歹徒等中布置的)内线. ⑨有计划的犯罪; 赃品隐藏库; 歹徒巢窟; 鸦片馆; (逮捕罪犯的) 圈套. *a pot* ～ 盆栽植物. *flowering* ～*s* 显花植物. *ball* ～*s* 带土 (秧) 苗. *cabbage* ～*s* 甘兰秧. *the humble [sensitive]* ～ 含羞草. *a manufacturing* ～ 制造厂. *a water [hydraulic] power* ～ 水力发电厂. *an arms* ～ 兵工厂. *a robotized* ～ 自动化工厂. ***in*** ～ 生长着, 活着. ***lose*** ～ 枯死. ***miss [fail in]*** ～ 长不出; 不发芽. — *vt.* ①栽(树、花), 播(种); 移植(植物); 移民于(某处), 殖(民). ②养(蚝等); 放养(鱼). ③安, 放, 装, 竖, 插; 创立, 建设, 设置, 设立, 树立; 布置(内线). ④刺, 扎, 插进 *(in; on)*; (把子弹)打进; 〔俚〕给与(打击); 〔拳击俚〕看准打. ⑤传播, 散播(新思想等), 灌输 *(in)*. ⑥〔美俚〕埋, 窝藏 (赃品等); 栽(赃). ⑦〔俚〕把(砂金或矿砂等) 放在矿里诱人来买; 图谋(欺骗等). ～ *a garden* 培植庭园. ～ *ideas in mind* 把思想灌输到心中. ～ *one's fists in sb.'s face* 用拳头猛打某人的脸. ～ *soldiers as colonists in the frontier districts* 在边境地区驻军屯垦. ～ ***on*** 〔俚〕拿假东西 (卖)给人; 向某人栽赃(把赃证暗藏在某人处, 使他成为嫌疑犯). ～ ***oneself*** 占一个位置; 站住, 站起来. ～ ***out*** (从盆等中)移植(到地上); 隔相当的距离栽植;【造园】栽种植物遮住…. ～ **cultivation** 作物栽培学. ～ **culture** 作物栽培. ～ **food** 植物养料; 肥料. ～ **hormone** 植物激素. ～ **louse** 蚜虫. ～**-marker** 植物名牌. ～ **percent** 苗木成活率. ～ **racket** 〔美俚〕骗局. ～**-school** 苗圃. ～ **show** 〔美〕黑人乐队的表演. **-let** 树苗, 小树.
plant·a·ble [ˈplɑːntəbl] *a.* ①可以种植的, 可以耕种的. ②能建设[开辟]的; 可殖民的.
Plan·tag·e·net [ˌplænˈtædʒinit] *a.*【英史】金雀花王朝的, 安茹王朝的, 不兰他日奈王朝的〔指由十二世纪亨利二世即位至十五世纪理查三世死的王朝〕.
plan·tain[1] [ˈplæntin] *n.*【植】菜食品种香蕉, 大蕉, 羊角香蕉.
plan·tain[2] [ˈplæntin] *n.*【植】车前草.
plan·tar [ˈplæntə] *a.*【解】蹠的, 脚底的.
plan·ta·tion [plænˈteiʃən] *n.* ①(热带及亚热带地方的)农场, 种植园, 菜园, 橡胶园; 〔英〕造林地; 栽植, 造林. ②【史】移民, 殖民; 〔*pl.*〕殖民地. ③创设, 建设. ④〔P-〕〔美〕*Rhode Island* 的别名. *a coffee [rubber, sugar]* ～ 咖啡〔橡胶, 甘蔗〕园. ～ ***fill in gaps***【林】空隙补植〔自然更新〕. ～ **song** 北美棉花农场中黑人所唱的歌.
plant·er [ˈplɑːntə] *n.* ①种植的人; 耕作的人; 栽培者. ②〔美〕初期移民; (南部地方的)农场主人; 种植园主; 殖民者. ③(机器等的)安装人. ④花盆. ⑤种植器, 播种器. ⑥〔美〕深深插入河底的树.
plan·ti·grade [ˈplæntigreid] *a.*【动】蹠行的; 蹠行类的. — *n.* 蹠行动物.
plant·ing [ˈplɑːntiŋ] *n.* ①种植; 造林; 撒种. ②〔英〕【石工】奠基;【建】基础底层, 基底. *ball* ～ 带土移植. ～ *area* 造林面积. ～ *by suckers* 分蘖造林. ～ *of layers* 压条法.
plan·u·la [ˈplænjulə] *n.* *(pl.* ***-u·lae*** [-liː]*)*【动】浮浪幼体. **-u·loid** [-lɔid] *a.*
plaque [plɑːk] *n.* ①(象牙、陶磁等制的)饰板; 匾. ②(表示地位、名誉的)胸章; 徽章. ③【医】斑; (噬菌体)溶菌斑; 血小板.
pla·quette [plɑːˈket] *n.* 小饰板; 金属印模.
plash[1] [plæʃ] *n.* ①(水的)激溅声, 哗哗声; (光的)闪动. ②积水(小)坑. ③〔方〕倾盆大雨. — *vt., vi.* ①溅泼(水). ②(使)哗啦哗啦的响.
plash[2] [plæʃ] *vt.* 编结(树枝)做树篱. — *n.* 编结成树篱的树枝.
plash·y [ˈplæʃi] *a.* ***(plash·i·er; -i·est)*** ①水坑多的; 尽是泥的, 潮湿的. ②哗啦哗啦响的.
-plasia, -plasis *comb.f.* 形成, 发达: hetero*plasia*.
plasm [ˈplæzm] *n.* = plasma.
-plasm(a) *comb.f.*【生】生成物, 产物: mela*plasm*.
plas·ma [ˈplæzmə] *n.* ①【生理】血浆; 淋巴液. ②【生】原生质. ③(做药膏用的)膏浆. ④【矿】半透明的绿玉髓. ⑤【物】等离子(体); 等离子区. **-mat·ic, -mic** *a.*
plas·ma·gel [ˈplæzmədʒel] *n.*【动】原生质凝胶.
plas·ma·gene [ˈplæzmədʒiːn] *n.*【生】(细) 胞质基因. **-genic** [-ˈdʒenik] *a.*
plas·ma·sol [ˈplæzməsɔːl, -sɔl] *n.*【生】①原生质溶胶. ②质液.
plas·ma·tron [ˈplæzmətrɔn] *n.*【无】①等离子管; 等离子流发生器. ②等离子电焊机.
plas·min [ˈplæzmin] *n.*【化】胞质素, 胞浆素.
plasm(o) *comb.f.* 血浆, 原生质: *plasmo*lysis.
plas·mo·di·um [plæzˈməudiəm] *n.* *(pl.* ***-dia*** [-diə]*)* ①【生】变形体; 原质团; 多核(原生)质体. ②【医】疟原虫.
plas·moid [ˈplæzmɔid] *n.*【物】等离子粒团.
plas·mol·y·sis [plæzˈmɔlisis] *n.*【生】质壁分离; 胞质皱缩.
plas·mo·lyze, -lyse [ˈplæzməˌlaiz] *vt., vi.*【生】(使) 质壁分离; (使)胞质皱缩.
plas·mo·quine [ˈplæzməkwain] *n.*【药】扑疟喹啉.
-plast *comb.f.* 原生质; 原浆: bio*plast*, proto*plast*.
plas·ter [ˈplɑːstə] *n.* ①胶泥, 灰泥, 涂墙泥. ②石膏, (尤指)熟石膏〔又叫 ～ of Paris〕. ③【医】膏药. *adhesive* ～ 橡皮膏. *court* ～ 英国橡皮膏. *a* ～ *figure* 石膏像. ～ *of Paris* 烧石膏, 熟石膏. — *vt.* ①涂胶泥于; (厚厚地)涂抹; 用奶油[发油等]涂 *(with)*. ②在…上敷贴膏药. ③〔谑〕赔偿医药费. ④加石膏除去(葡萄酒的酸味). ⑤粘贴; 使紧贴. ⑥安慰, 抚慰. ⑦在…上加一层掩饰. ⑧〔俚〕狠狠打击(对手等). ～ ***with praise*** 滥夸奖. ～ **board**【建】灰胶纸柏板. ～ **cast** (雕刻师的) 石膏模型;【医】石膏绷带. ～ **stone** (生) 石膏. ～**work** 粉刷墙壁 [天花板等] 的工作. **-ed** *a.* ①涂有灰泥的. ②〔美俚〕喝醉了的.
plas·ter·er [ˈplɑːstərə] *n.* 泥水匠; 石膏工艺品制作人.
plas·ter·ing [ˈplɑːstəriŋ] *n.* ①泥水工作. ②石膏制品. ③贴膏药. ④(葡萄酒的)加石膏除酸.
plas·ter·y [ˈplɑːstəri] *a.* 胶泥[石膏]一样的.

plas·tic [ˈplæstik] *a.* ①造型的；塑造的；给与形态的. ②可塑的，塑性的，受范的；柔软的；〔喻〕温顺的，肯听话的. ③塑料的；塑料制的；合成树脂做的. ④有形成力的，有创造力的. ⑤【医】整形的，成形的，修补的. ⑥【生】有适应力的；能进行新陈代谢的，构成生活组织的. ～ *substances* 可塑性物质. *a* ～ *image* 塑像. *the* ～ *arts* 造型艺术；塑造术. *the* ～ *force of nature* 自然的创造力. — *n.* ①〔常 *pl.*〕塑料；塑料制品；塑胶；电木. ②*pl.* 〔用作 *sing.* 或 *pl.*〕【医】整形外科. *acrylate* [*acrylic*] ～ 玻璃塑料. ～ **clay**【地】第三期下层的中层系. ～ **explosive** 可塑炸药. ～ **flow** 范性[塑性]流变. ～ **operations** 整形外科手术. ～ **sulphur**【化】粘性硫. ～ **surgery**【医】整形外科. **-ti·cal·ly** *ad.*

plas·ti·ca·tion [ˌplæstiˈkeiʃən] *n.*【物】增模，增塑.

plas·ti·cine [ˈplæstisiːn] *n.* 塑像代用粘土.

plas·tic·i·ty [plæsˈtisiti] *n.* ①粘性；可塑性；柔顺性. ②适应性. ③【物】塑性学.

plas·ti·cize [ˈplæstisaiz] *vt., vi.* (使) 成为可塑. **-ci·za·tion** *n.*

plas·ti·ciz·er [ˈplæstisaizə] 增塑剂，增韧剂.

plas·tid [ˈplæstid] *n.*【生】①成形粒. ②质体.

plas·tique [plɑːsˈtiːk] *n.* 〔F.〕①塑料炸弹 (=plastic bomb). ②造型性动作〔指舞蹈或哑剧中极其缓慢的舞姿或动作〕.

plas·ti·sol [ˈplæstisɔːl, -sɔl] *n.*【化】塑料溶胶.

plas·to·gene [ˈplæstədʒiːn] *n.* 质体基因.

plas·tog·raph [ˈplæstəugrɑːf] *n.* 塑性变形图描记器.

plas·tom·e·ter [plæsˈtɔmitə] *n.* 塑性计.

plas·to·some [ˈplæstəsəum]【生】线粒体.

plas·tron [ˈplæstrən] *n.* ①(女服的)胸饰，(男衬衣的)前胸衬领. ②(劈剑用的)护胸革；(中古的)钢制胸甲. ③【动】腹甲；(海胆的)盾板.

-plasty *comb.f.* 形成，长成：auto*plasty*.

-plasy *comb.f.* = plasia.

plat[1] [plæt] *n.* ①(作花坛等的) 一块地. ②〔主美〕地区图，地图. — *vt.* 〔美〕制…的地图.

plat[2] *n., vt.* = plait.

plat [plɑː] *n.* 〔F.〕(菜)一盘；菜单上的菜.

plat du jour [F.plɑ dy ʒuːr] *n.* (*pl.* ***plats du jour***) 〔F.〕今日特制菜[时菜，风味菜].

plat·an(e) [ˈplætən] *n.* = plane tree.

plat·band [ˈplætbænd] *n.* ①花坛的花草边沿. ②【建】平边.

plate[1] [pleit] *n.* ①厚金属板 (*cf.* sheet)；板(片)；(记有姓名等的金属)牌子，(尤指医生的)招牌，藏书牌；【印】印版；图版；另纸印插图. ②金属版，电极版，铅版；金属版画. ③板玻璃；【摄】底片，感光板. ④【史、古】锁金甲. ⑤盘子；盆子；〔英〕金、银餐具；镀金器皿. ⑥(菜的)一盘；一顿饭菜. ⑦(做奖品用的)金杯，银杯；金银奖杯；(教会等的)捐款盘；献金，捐款. ⑧假牙床. ⑨【建】(壁上的)横木；【棒球】投手板；本垒. ⑩【微】平皿，培养皿. ⑪【无】屏极极板，阳极. ⑫(牛的)肋肉. ⑬【动】(幼虫的)盾片；(鱼的)棱鳞. *a negative* ～ 底片；感光板. *a polarizing* ～【物】起偏振片. *a die* ～ 模板. *a die back* ～ 钢板衬片. *a door* ～ 门牌. *a family* ～ 刻有家徽、代代相传的金银餐具. *a* ～ *battery* 板极电池组. *a* ～ *of fish* 一盘鱼. *a theoretical* ～【物】理论屏. ***foul a*** ～ ***with*** 和…共餐. ***put up one's*** ～ 挂牌(行医). ***read one's*** ～ 〔美俚〕①做饭前祷告. ②埋头不吭声吃饭. — *vt.* ①镀；在…上覆盖金属板[装甲]；给(马等)装蹄. ②把…打成薄板；【印】给…制铅版[电版]. ③【造纸】给…上光. *copper* ～*d* 镀铜的. ～ **basket** 〔英〕餐具篮. ～ **dinner** 〔美〕全部菜都盛在一个盘子里的正餐. ～ **glass** (上等)板玻璃. ～ **holder**【摄】干片夹，硬片夹. ～ **iron** 铁板；铁皮. ～**layer** ①(铁路)铺路护路工. ②【印】装版工. ～ **lunch** 〔美〕全部菜都盛在一个盘子里的午餐. ～ **mark** ① = hallmark. ②(印刷时因压力关系压在版画上的)铜版印. ～ **matter** (通讯社发给小报馆的)电版新闻稿. ～ **powder** 擦银粉. ～ **printer** 铜版印刷工人. ～ **printing** 铜版印刷. ～ **rack** 〔英〕(洗后暂放的)餐具架. ～ **wheel**【机】盘轮，无幅轮. **-ful** *n.* 一盘，满盘.

plat·eau [ˈplætəu, plæˈtəu] *n.* (*pl.* ***-x, -s*** [-z]) ①高原，台地，高地；【心】学习高原〔指学习上无进步也无退步的一段〕；〔美喻〕平稳状态[时期]；停滞时期. ②雕花托盘；饰匾；金属板；平顶女帽. ③【物】坪.

plat·ed [ˈpleitid] *a.* ①面上装有金属片的〔如铠甲〕. ②鸳鸯布的〔指织物正反面的质料不同或颜色不同〕. ③镀(金属)的〔尤指镀有稀有金属的〕. *silver-*～ 镀银的.

plate·let [ˈpleitlit] *n.* ①小片；小型板状物. ②【医】血小板，凝血细胞 (= thrombocyte). ～ **laser** 小片状激光器.

plat·(t)en [ˈplætən] *n.* ①(平压印刷机的)压印盘；(打字机的)压纸卷轴. ②【机】台板.

plat·er [ˈpleitə] *n.* ①镀金匠；铁甲工. ②光泽机. ③【赛马】劣等马.

plat·form [ˈplætfɔːm] *n.* ①台，坛；讲坛，主席台. ②步廊；〔英〕(车站的)月台，站台；〔美〕(客车的)上下步梯；楼梯平台. ③【筑城】炮手站台；炮台座；【地】地台，台地；【油】(海洋钻井的)栈桥. ④(政党的)政纲；〔美〕(尤指选定候选人时的)政策宣言. ⑤讨论会(会场)；〔the ～〕演讲，演说. *a* ～ *balance* 台秤. *a launching* ～【宇】发射台. *a* ～ *ticket* 站[月]台票. *support the ministerial* ～ 支持政府党的政纲. ***be at home on the*** ～ 惯于演说. — *vt.* ①把… 放在台上[放在高处；在…设月台]. —*vi.* ①起草政纲. ②站在讲台上演说. ～ **bridge**【铁路】天桥. ～ **car** 平板货车，台车. ～ **carriage** (搬运重物)低架台车，炮车 (等). ～ **scale** [**balance**] 台秤. ～ **truck** 平板大卡车.

plat·form·u·l·a [ˈplætfɔːmjulə] *n.* 〔谑〕演讲八股.

plat·i·na [pləˈtiːnə] *n.*【化】天然铂；铂.

plat·ing [ˈpleitiŋ] *n.* ①(电)镀，喷镀；镀金(术). ②镀层；外覆金属板；【船】(全部)船壳板；(兵舰等的)装甲. ③【摄】晒相. ④悬赏赛马. ～ **bath** 电镀槽.

pla·tin·ic [pləˈtinik] *a.*【化】四价铂的；铂的. ～ **acid** 铂酸. ～ **chloride** 氯化铂，四氯化铂.

plat·i·nif·er·ous [ˌplætiˈnifərəs] *a.* 含铂的；产铂的.

plat·i·ni·rid·i·um [ˌplætinaiˈridiəm] *n.*【矿】铂铱齐 (铂、铱等的自然合金).

plat·i·nite [ˈplætinait] *n.* 代铂齐，代白金，赛白金.

plat·i·nize [ˈplætinaiz] *vt.* 在…上镀铂；使与铂化合. ～*d carbon electrode*【电】镀铂碳电极.

plat·i·no·cy·a·nide [ˌplætnəuˈsaiənaid] *n.*【化】氰亚铂酸盐.

plat·i·node [ˈplætinəud] *n.* 伏打电池 (voltaic cell) 的阴板[阴极].

plat·i·noid [ˈplætinɔid] *a.* 铂状的. — *n.* ①赛白金；合金铂. ②铂系金属.

plat·i·no·type [ˈplætinəutaip] *n.*【摄】铂黑印片术；铂黑照片.

plat·i·nous [ˈplætinəs] *a.*【化】亚铂的，二价铂的. ～ *bromide* 溴化亚铂，二溴化铂.

plat·i·num [ˈplætinəm] *n.*【化】铂白金. ～ *metals* 铂族元素. ～ **black** (做触媒用的)铂黑，铂墨. ～ **blonde** 〔美〕淡金发女人. ～ **lamp** 白金电灯. ～ **sponge** 铂棉.

plat·i·tude [ˈplætitjuːd] *n.* ①单调，平凡，陈腐. ②平凡的话，滥调，俗论. *writings full of* ～*s* 满纸陈词滥调.

plat·i·tu·di·nar·i·an [ˌplætiˌtjuːdiˈnɛəriən] *a.* 平凡的，陈腐的. — *n.* 爱用陈词滥调的人.

plat·i·tu·di·nize [ˌplætiˈtjuːdinaiz] *vi.* 讲[写]陈词滥调.

plat·i·tu·di·nous [ˌplætiˈtjuːdinəs] *a.* 平凡的；陈腐的；陈词滥调式的. ～ *ponderosity* 〔美〕陈腔滥调.

Pla·to [ˈpleitəu] 柏拉图〔公元前 427?—347, 古希腊哲学家〕.

Pla·ton·ic [pləˈtɔnik] *a.* ①柏拉图(学派)的, 柏拉图哲学的. ②〔常 p-〕纯精神的; 纯理论的. — *n.*〔常 *pl.*〕①= Platonist. ②精神恋爱故事. ~ **bodies**【几】五面体. ~ **love** 精神恋爱. ~ **year**【天】柏拉图年〔约 26,000年 的周期,经过此时期各星辰又复归原位〕.

Pla·to·nism [ˈpleitənizəm] *n.* ①柏拉图哲学; 柏拉图主义. ②〔常 p-〕精神恋爱.

Pla·to·nist [ˈpleitənist] *n.* 柏拉图主义者.

Pla·to·nize [ˈpleitənaiz] *vi.* 信奉柏拉图哲学. — *vt.* 使信奉柏拉图哲学; 根据柏拉图哲学解释.

pla·toon [pləˈtuːn] *n.* ①【军】(步兵、工兵等的) 排, 小队. ②(人的) 一群, 一组; 〔美〕警察队. ③【史】排枪(队). *a* ~ *leader* 排长. *a* ~ *sergeant*〔美军〕副排长〔级别与上士相等〕.

Platt·deutsch [ˈplɑːtdɔitʃ] *n.* 德意志北部低地方言.

plat·ten [ˈplætən] *n.* = platen.

plat·ter [ˈplætə] *n.* ①〔美、英古〕长圆形托盘,大浅盘. ②〔美俚〕(留声机)唱片;【运】铁饼;【棒球】本垒. *a* ~ *tosser*〔美〕掷铁饼选手. *on a* ~ ①用盘子端上. ②现成地; 不费力地.

plat·y[1] [ˈpleiti] *a.*【地】板状的, 扁平状的.

plat·y[2] [ˈplæti] *n.* (*pl.* ~*(s)*, *plat·ies*) (中美洲) 剑尾鱼属 (*Xiphophorus*) 鱼.

plat·y-, plat- *comb.f.* 阔, 宽, 扁形, 板状: *platy*cephalous 阔头的.

plat·y·hel·minth [ˌplætiˈhelminθ] *n.* 扁形动物门 (*Platyhelminthes*) 动物〔如绦虫、肝蛭等〕. **-ic** *a.*

plat·y·po·di·a [ˌplætiˈpəudiə] *n.*【医】扁平足.

plat·y·pus [ˈplætipəs] *n.* (*pl.* **-es, pi** [-pai])【动】鸭嘴兽.

plat·yr·rhine [ˈplætirain, -rin] *a.*【动】阔鼻类的. — *n.* 阔鼻类 (*Platyrrhini*) 动物.

plat·yr·rhin·i·an [ˌplætiˈriniən] *a.*, *n.* 阔鼻的(人).

plau·dit [ˈplɔːdit] *n.*〔常 *pl.*〕拍手; 喝采; 称赞, 赞美.

plau·si·ble [ˈplɔːzəbl] *a.* ①(议论)好象有道理的, 表面上讲得通的. ②嘴巧的, 会说话的. **-bil·i·ty** *n.* **-bly** *ad.*

plau·sive [ˈplɔːsiv] *a.* ①〔罕〕赞扬的, 称誉的, 称赞的. ②似有理的; 似诚实的, 似可信的 (= plausible).

play [plei] *vi.* ①玩, 玩耍, 游戏; 闲逛; 〔方〕罢工 (*opp.* work); (动物)跳来跳去, 飞来飞去, 翩翩飞舞. ②(浪、光等)摇动, 闪动, 荡漾, 摇晃, 闪耀; (旗等)翻飞; (微笑等)浮泛(在脸上等); 静静地过去 (*around; about*). ③(机器等)自由运转; (炮等)发射 (*on; upon*); (喷泉等)喷出. ④进行(比赛); 适合打球; 赌; 打赌. ⑤行动, 举动, 处置; 假装; 装扮; 演戏, 做戏; 担任一个角色; (唱片、录音带等)播放; 吹, 奏, 弹(乐器)(*on; upon*). ⑥开玩笑; 嘲弄; 玩弄 (*with; on; upon*); 发生影响. *Bees* ~ *about flowers.* 蜜蜂在花上飞来飞去. *a smile* ~*s on her lips* 她嘴唇上浮泛着微笑. *The sunlight* ~*s on the water.* 阳光在水上荡漾. *The imagination* ~*ed in our minds.* 我们浮想连翩. *The waves* ~*ed on the beach.* 波浪冲上了海滩. *The lawn* ~*s well.* 这块草地很适合打球. *The fountain* ~*s on Sundays.* 喷泉星期天开放. *P-!*【球赛】比赛开始! — *vt.* ①做(游戏), 玩; 打(球等); 赌; 和…竞争[玩耍]〔用此义既表示以球类游戏等为直接宾语而在 with 后接以打玩的对方, 也表示打玩的对方或单位为直接宾语而在 with 或 at 后接以玩打的球类游戏等〕. ②使某人上场担任某角色. ③使轻快地动; 使摇动, 使闪动. ④演(戏), 饰演, 扮演; 弹奏, 吹(乐器、曲子). ⑤做, 行, 干(鬼把戏等); 举动得象…, 模仿. ⑥实行, 使用; 〔罕〕行使, 发挥; 尽(本分等). ⑦开玩笑; 嘲弄, 愚弄. ⑧发射(炮等); 放(水、烟火等); 调摆(上钓的鱼); 得当地操纵. ⑧【板球】打(球);【牌戏】出(牌);【象棋】走动(棋子). *The organist was* ~*ing the congregation out.* 弹风琴的弹着风琴把会众送了出去. ~ *football with them*, ~ *them with football* 同他们比赛足球. *Will you* ~ *me at chess?* 你愿意和我下棋吗? *The coach* ~*ed him at centre.* 教练叫他担任中锋. ~ *a searchlight upon the aeroplane* 向飞机打探照灯. ~ *the host* 作主人. ***be*** ~***ed out***〔美〕筋疲力尽, 累透. ~ ***a double game*** 口蜜腹剑. ~ ***a good stick*** 会使一手好剑. ~ ***a lone hand*** ①〔美〕独个儿工作[旅行、生活], 不靠别人. ②〔美运〕表演不精彩〔引不起观众兴趣〕. ~ ***advantages over sb.*** 〔美〕骗人. ~ ***along with*** 参与, 与…合作. ~ ***at*** 玩, 打; 学…玩[取乐], 比(输赢). ~ ***away*** 赌掉(金钱); 玩掉(时间); 浪费. ~ ***back [forward]***【板球】把球打向后头[前头], 回到三柱门方面. ~ ***ball***〔美口〕开始, 着手; 正正当当做, 光明正大地行动. ~ ***both ends against the middle***〔美俚〕脚踏两只船; 两头卖弄, 从中渔利. ~ ***by ear*** (不会看乐谱)全靠听来的调子弹奏. ~ ***down*** (迎合对方的意思)放低语气. *(to)*; 减弱; 缩小某事的重要性, 轻描淡写. ~ ***fair*** 规规矩矩比赛; 光明正大的行动. ~ ***fast and loose*** 玩弄, 反复无常. ~ ***for kingdom [empire]*** 争天下. ~ ***for love*** (非赌博性地)玩, 打(牌等). ~ ***for money*** 赌钱. ~ ***for time*** 争取时间. ~ ***foul [foully, false]*** 玩(打)得不规矩, 作弊. ~ ***hard*** 行为卑鄙, 不择手段. ~ ***high*** 大赌. ~ ***hookey***〔美〕逃学; 怠工. ~ ***into each other's hands*** 互相渔利, 互相勾结. ~ ***into sb.'s hands [the hands of]*** 故意使…占便宜; 为…谋方便. ~ ***it*** *(low)* ***on*** *(sb.)* = ~ ***low down on*** *(sb.)*〔俚〕用卑劣手段骗人. ~ ***off*** ①(得分相同)进行补赛. ②使某人出丑[出洋相]; 嘲弄某人, 揭某人老底. ③放射 (烟火等). ④以…冒充 *(as)* (~ *off a mere stone as a genuine gem upon sb.* 拿一块假宝石冒充真宝石去骗人). ⑤〔美〕假装有病 (*The man is not ill, he is* ~*ing off.* 这人并不生病, 他是假装的). ~ ***one's hand for all it is worth*** 尽心竭力, 尽全力. ~ ***opposite*** 扮演与主角相对的异性角色. ~ ***out***〔美〕①演完, 做完. ②用完, 输光, 使破产; 使筋疲力竭. ③放出, 放松(绳索等). ~ ***out of the cabbage***〔美、高尔夫球〕从难打的地方把球打出. ~ ***over one's head***〔美运〕得到预料不到的好成绩. ~ ***politics***〔美〕玩弄阴谋诡计, 操纵. ~ ***safe*** 采取稳妥谨慎的措施. ~ ***the market***〔美商〕投机, 买空卖空. ~ ***(the part of)*** 饰演, 扮演. ~ ***the races***〔美〕赌跑马. ~ ***up*** ①〔美〕勇敢行动, 大事渲染. ②开始奏乐, 越发使劲弹奏; (比赛等时)奋战. ③〔口〕嘲弄, 逗弄, 耍戏, 撩. ~ ***(up)on*** ①弹, 奏, 吹(笛子). ②利用 (别人的恐惧心或信赖心). ~ ***(up)on words*** 说俏皮话; 说模棱两可的话. ~ ***up to*** ①做…的配角, 助演; 帮助, 支持. ②〔俚〕谄媚, 拍马屁. ~ ***with*** ①以…自娱. ②玩弄 (火等). — *n.* ①玩耍, 游戏, 娱乐; 比赛. ②玩笑; 玩弄. ③赌博; (游戏, 比赛等的) 方法, 技巧. ④失业; 休业; 罢工. ⑤剧本, 戏剧; 话剧, 戏. ⑥(投机) 交易. ⑦作用; 活动范围; (才智的) 运用;【机】间隙. ⑧波动, 闪动, 飘动. ⑨(对工具等的)使用, 运用. *a high [deep]* ~ 大赌. *fair* ~ 公平的比赛; 光明正大的行为; 君子态度. *foul* ~ 不规矩的比赛; 卑鄙行为; 小人态度. *a benefit* ~ 义演. *All work and no* ~ *makes Jack a dull boy.* 死读书, 不玩耍, 孩子要变傻. *It is your* ~. 轮到你了; 该你发球〔走棋〕了. ***as good as a*** ~ (戏剧似地)有趣. ***at*** ~ 在玩, 正在游戏. ***be in full*** ~ 正在起劲, 正在开足马力转动. ***bring [call] into (full)*** ~ (充分)利用, 使(充分)发挥作用, 使(尽量)活动. ***come into*** ~ 开始活动, 开始起作用. ***give (full)*** ~ ***to*** *(one's speciality)* 发挥 [发扬] (其所长). ***give sb. a*** ~〔美〕努力想得到某人的信任. ***go to the*** ~ 去看戏. ***hold [keep] sb. in*** ~ 使人工作下去; 牵制(敌人等). ***in*** ~ ①开玩笑. ②【球赛】在比赛中; 在工作; (牌)尚未打出. ***make a*** ~ ***for***〔美口〕生方设法引诱. ***make good*** ~ 精神勃勃地 [顺利地]进行 [行动]. ***make*** ~ ①【赛马】调摆追者. ②加紧工作; 起作用, 发生效果. ③(拳击赛中)猛击敌人. ⑤领先. ***out of***

～ 失业;【球赛】死球〔暂停比赛〕. ～ *of colours* 闪色,幻色,变彩,光彩幻现. ～ *of words* 诡辩;玩弄词藻. ～ *on [upon] words* 说双关语,诙俏支话. **～act** *vi.* ①演戏. ②假装; 装扮. ③装腔作势. **～actor** 〔蔑〕演员. **～back** (录音等的)播放,放音. **～bill** 海报;剧场节目单. **～ book** 剧本. **～boy** ①〔美口〕花花公子,荡子,玩要哥儿. ②〔英方〕小丑;滑头. **～-by-～** *a.* (比赛时)现场报道〔评述〕的; 详细叙述的. **～clothes** 平常穿的衣服. **～ club** 高尔夫球棒. **～day** 休息日;〔英〕(煤矿工人等的) 假日. **～fellow** 玩要朋友,游伴. **～game** 儿戏;〔喻〕幼稚的东西. **～girl** 爱交际游乐的女子. **～goer** 爱看戏的人,常看戏的人. **～going** 看戏. **～ground** (学校的)运动场;游乐地;(儿童)游戏场;公园 (*the ～ground of Europe* 欧洲游乐场 〔瑞士的别名〕). **～house** 戏院,剧场;儿童游戏馆. **～land** (＝～ground). **～let** 短剧,独幕剧. **～mate** ＝ playfellow. **～-off** 【运】最后决赛. **～pen** 婴儿圈栏〔供幼儿在内爬着玩的轻便圈栏〕. **～-right** 上演权. **～room** 〔美〕(儿童的) 游戏室. **～-some** *a.* 爱开玩笑的. **～suit** (妇女、儿童)运动衫,运动裤 **～ therapy** 【心】演剧疗法; 游戏疗法. **～thing** 玩具;〔喻〕被玩弄的人〔东西〕,玩物. **～time** 游戏时间,娱乐时间. **～wright, ～writer** 剧作家, 编剧家. **～write** *vi.* 〔美〕写剧本. **～writing** 剧本创作. **-dom** 〔美〕戏剧界. **-ful** *a.* 爱游戏的,爱开玩笑的;滑稽的,开玩笑的.

pla·ya [ˈplɑːjə] *n.* 【地】干盐湖.

play·a·ble [ˈpleiəbl] *a.* 可演奏的;适宜于竞技表演的.

play·er [ˈpleiə] *n.* ①游戏的人;选手;〔英〕【板球】〔*P-*〕职业选手 (*opp.* Gentleman). ②演员;演奏人. ③唱机. ④为了消遣而干…的人;赌徒;懒人. *a seeded* ～ 种子选手. *Players versus Gentlemen* 〔英〕职业选手对业余选手. *a record* ～ 电唱机. ～ **piano** 自动 (演奏的) 钢琴. **-dom** 〔美〕演员界,剧界.

play·ing-card [ˈpleiiŋkɑːd] *n.* (一张)纸牌.

play·ing-field [ˈpleiiŋfiːld] *n.* (野外)运动场.

pla·za [ˈplɑːzə] *n.* 〔Sp.〕(西班牙都市中的)广场; 集市场所.

plbg. ＝ plumbing.

-ple *suf.* 重,倍: tri*ple*.

plea [pliː] *n.* ①恳求,请求,请愿;祷告. ②辩解;托词,口实. ③【法】抗辩, 答辩. *cop a* ～ 避重就轻地主动认罪. *make a* ～ *for* 主张;请求. *on [under] the* ～ *of [that]* 借口…. *The Court of Common Pleas* ①(英国的)高等民事法庭. ②(美国某些州的) 中级民事〔刑事〕法庭.

pleach [pliːtʃ] *vt.* 编结(树枝);编.

plead [pliːd] (*-ed,* 〔美口〕～ [pled]) *vt.* ①辩论,辩护;答辩; 抗辩. ②主张, 解释. — *vi.* ①辩护;辩论;抗辩,解释. ②恳求, 求情. ～ *ignorance* 以不知道情况为借口. ～ *[not] guilty* 〔不〕服罪. ～ *poor mouth* 〔美〕(有人催款〔捐款〕时)装穷. ～ *against* 反驳; 劝人不要…. ～ *for* 恳求 (～ *for sb.'s favour* 替某人说情). ～ *with* 向…恳求,说情 (*for*).

plead·a·ble [ˈpliːdəbl] *a.* 可辩护的,可作为抗辩的理由的.

plead·er [ˈpliːdə] *n.* ①【法】辩护人,律师. ②代为求情者.

plead·ing [ˈpliːdiŋ] *n.* ①辩论,辩护. ②诉讼程序. ③〔*pl.*〕【法】诉状. ④调停,说项. — *a.* 恳求的,请求的. **-ly** *ad.*

pleas·ance [ˈplezəns] *n.* ①(特指邸宅内的)大庭园. ②〔古〕＝ pleasure.

pleas·ant [ˈpleznt] *a.* (*-er; -est*) ①愉快的,快乐的,舒适的,快活的. ②活泼的,可爱的. ③〔古〕滑稽的,有趣的. ～ *spoken* 〔美〕说的有趣,说起来有趣. ～ *to the eye [taste]* 好看〔吃〕. *have [spend] a* ～ *time* 愉快地度过. *make oneself* ～ 处世灵活, 八面玲珑. **-ly** *ad.* **-ness** *n.*

pleas·an·try [ˈplezntri] *n.* 玩笑;幽默,诙谐.

please [pliːz] *vt.* ①使高兴,使欢喜,使快乐,使满足;中…的意. ②〔祈使语气〕请. *One can't* ～ *everybody.* 一个人不可能使人人满意. *Come in,* ～. 请进来. *P- take a seat.* 请坐. — *vi.* ①欢喜,中意;觉得好. ②讨好;讨人喜欢. 有趣. *He is anxious to* ～ 他一心想讨好. *I shall do exactly as I* ～. 我将完全按照我自己的意思去做. *The play* ～*s.* 这戏有趣. *as you* ～ 随你的意思,随你喜欢. *be easily ～d* 容易说话. *be ～d in* 欢喜,爱…. *be ～d to (do)* 乐意;〔敬语〕承蒙;肯 (*He was ～d not to believe me.* 〔带挖苦的敬语〕 他不肯相信我的话). *be ～d with* 喜欢. *if you* ～ ①请劳驾; 对不起 (*I will wash my hands, if you* ～. 对不起, 我要方便一下). ②你看多奇怪,竟… (*Now, if you* ～, *he expects me to pay for it.* 你看多奇怪,他还打算我来掏腰包哩). ～ *God* 如果运气好的话. ～ *oneself* 满意,高兴;随意去做 (*P- yourself.* 请便). *to* ～ *me* 看在我面上.

pleased [pliːzd] *a.* 对…高兴,对…满意 (*with*). *I'm quite* ～ *with your success.* 我为你的成功十分高兴. *be as* ～ *as Punch* 非常高兴.

pleas·ing [ˈpliːziŋ] *a.* 舒适的,愉快的;满意的;惹人喜欢的,可爱的. **-ly** *ad.*

pleas·ur·a·ble [ˈpleʒərəbl] *a.* 令人快乐的,愉快的,舒适的. **-ness** *n.*

pleas·ur·a·b·ly [ˈpleʒərəbli] *ad.* 快乐地,愉快地.

pleas·ure [ˈpleʒə] *n.* ①愉快,快乐,满意;愉快的事情. ②娱乐;(尤指)肉体上的快乐,享受,欢乐. ③意志,欲求,希望. ④恩惠,厚道. *a man of* ～ 逍遥快活的人. *a life given up to* ～ 纵情享受的生活. *It is our* ～ *to submit the balance-sheet.* 现呈上资产负债表. *Is it your* ～ *to go at once?* 你愿意立刻去吗? *ask sb.'s* ～ 问人来意. *at one's* ～; *at* ～ 随意,随时 (*You may go or stay at* ～ 去留都听你的便). *consult sb.'s* ～ 询问〔顾到〕某人的意愿. *do sb. the* ～ *(of)* 讨好某人, 使高兴, 赏光 (*Will you do me the* ～ *of coming to dinner with me?* 请赏光同我一起去吃饭好吗?). *during one's* ～ 在高兴的时候. *for* ～ 为取乐,为消遣. *give* ～ *to* 使…高兴. *have the* ～ *of (doing)* 〔敬语〕幸得…,乞 (*May we have the* ～ *of your company?* 敬请出席). *take (a)* ～ *in* 高兴地;以…为乐;欣然 (*I take* ～ *in sending you a copy.* 兹送上副本一份). *with* ～ 高兴 (*I read of your success with* ～. 看到你成功的消息非常高兴). — *vt.* (使)高兴;(使)欢喜;(使)满意. — *vi.* ①高兴,喜欢. ②游荡,沉溺于享乐;〔口〕游览. ～ **boat** 游船. **～-dome** 富丽堂皇的大厦〔旅馆等〕. ～ **garden,** ～ **ground** 游乐场;公园. ～ **principle** 【心】(精神分析中的)快乐原则. ～ **seeker** *n.* 追求享乐的人. ～ **seeking** *n.* 享乐主义. ～ **trip** 游览.

pleat [pliːt] *n.* (衣服上的)褶. — *vt.* ①使打褶. ②把…编成辫.

pleat·er [ˈpliːtə] *n.* 打褶人; 褶裥机〔尤指缝纫机上打褶用的机件〕.

pleb [pleb] *n.* 〔俚〕①老百姓, 平民. ②〔美〕军官学校〔海军学校〕的一年级生;大学一年级生.

plebe [pliːb] *n.* 〔美俚〕 ＝ pleb②.

ple·be·ian [pliˈbiːən] *n.* 【古罗马史】庶民, 平民 (*opp.* patrician). — *a.* 平民的;下等的,下贱的,鄙俗的. *a ～'s bank* 平民银行. **-ism** *n.* 平民身分〔气习〕. **-ize** *vt.* 使平民化.

pleb·i·scite [ˈplebisit, -sait] *n.* 公民投票;【古罗马史】全民表决. **-sci·tar·y** *a.*

plebs [plebz] *n.* (*pl. plebes* [ˈpliːbiːz]) 〔L.〕①古罗马的下层阶级. ②平民,庶民;百姓.

plec·tog·nath [ˈplektɔgnæθ] *n.* 【动】愈颌类 (固颌类) (*Plectognathi*) 鱼. — *a.* 【动】愈颌类的.

plec·trum [ˈplektrəm] *n.* (*pl.* ～*s, -tra* [-trə]) ①(弦乐

器的)拨子. ②【动】距.

pled [pled] 〔口、方〕plead 的过去式及过去分词.

pledge [pledʒ] *n.* ①公约; 誓约; 〔the ～〕戒酒的誓约; (政党领袖等的)诺言;〔美口〕宣誓入会者. ②【法】抵押权,抵押,典当; 抵押品. ③(表示友谊的)干杯. ④保证; (好意或友情的)表示. *the P- to the Flag* 〔美〕对国旗宣誓. *a ～ of affection [love]* 爱情的象征; 子女. ***be [lie] in ～*** 在抵押中. ***be under ～*** 发了誓. ***give [lay, put] (sth.) to [in] ～*** 抵押, 典当. ***in ～ of good faith*** 当作好意 [信义] 的表示. ***redeem one's ～*** 履行信约. ***take a ～*** 发誓. ***take out of ～*** 赎回. ***take [sign] the ～*** 发誓戒酒. ***under ～ (of secrecy)*** 发誓(守秘密). — *vt.* ①使发誓, 保证. ②典当, 抵押. ③为…干杯. ③〔美口〕 使入会 (作候补会员). *～ oneself to secrecy* 发誓守秘密. *～ one's word [honour]* 发誓; 保证. *～ the honourable guest* 为贵宾干杯. ***be [stand] ～d to*** 对…保证. **-r** *n.*

pledg·ee [pleˈdʒiː] *n.* 接受抵押的人.

pledg·er, pledg·or [ˈpledʒə] *n.* ①抵押者; 典当人. ②(戒酒等的)发誓人. ③举酒干杯的人.

pledg·et [ˈpledʒit] *n.* (包扎伤口用)小拭子.

-plegia, -plegy, *comb. f.* 瘫, 麻痺: hemi*plegia*, para*plegia*.

Pléiade [pleˈjad] 〔F.〕七星社〔十六世纪法国七位喜欢运用古典格式的诗人所组成〕. — *n.* 七名人 (=pleiad).

Plei·a·des, Plei·ads [ˈplaiədiːz, ˈplaiədz] *n.* 〔*pl.*〕①【希神】阿特拉斯 (Atlas) 的七个女儿,后化为天上七星. ②【天】昴(宿)星团;〔喻〕七区头; 七颗明星.

plein-air [ˌpleinˈeə] *a.* (绘画、绘画法)直接利用外光描绘的, 外光主义的, 外光派的〔法国十九世纪的一种印象画派〕. **-ism** *n.* **-ist** *n.*

Plei·o·cene [ˈplaiəsiːn] *a., n.* 【地】上新世(的).

plei·o·tax·y [ˈplaiətæksi] *n.* 【植】花轮增多.

plei·ot·ro·py [plaiˈɔtrəpi] *n.* 【遗】(基因)多效性 (= pleiotropism). **-ic** [ˈplaiəˈtrɔpik] *a.* **-trop·i·cal·ly** *ad.*

Pleis·to·cene [ˈplaistəusiːn] *n., a.* 【地】更新世(的).

Plen. = Plenipotentiary.

ple·na·ry [ˈpliːnəri] *a.* ①十足的,完全的;无条件的,绝对的. ②全体出席的; 有全权的;【法】正式的 (*opp.* summary). *～ indulgence* 【天主】大赦. *～ power [authority]* 全权. *a ～ meeting [session]* 全体会议,大会. **-ri·ly** *ad.*

ple·n·lune [ˈpliːnəluːn] *n.* 【诗】满月,望月; 满月之时.

ple·nip·o·tence [pləˈnipətəns] *n.* 全权; 全部主权. **-o·tent** *a.*

plen·i·po·ten·tia·ry [ˌplenipəˈtenʃəri] *n.* 全权大使, 全权委员. — *a.* 有全权的; (权力等)绝对的. *an ambassador extraordinary and ～* 特命全权大使. *a minister ～* 全权公使.

plen·ish [ˈpleniʃ] *vt.* [Scot.] ①充,充满,充填. ②给(房屋)安置设备. ③养家畜于(农场).

plen·i·ti·tude [ˈplenititjuːd] *n.* = plenitude.

plen·i·tude [ˈplenitjuːd] *n.* ①充分,完全. ②充实,充满; 丰富,多; (权力等的)绝顶; 【医】(胃等的)胀满. *the moon in her ～* 【徽】满月. *in the ～ of his power* 当他权力的最高峰时.

plen·i·tu·di·nous [ˌpleniˈtjuːdinəs, -ˈtuːd-] *a.* ①丰满的,充足的. ②肥壮的,结实的.

plen·te·ous [ˈplentjəs, -tiəs] *a.* 〔诗〕= plentiful. *～ crops* 丰收. *a ～ year.* 丰年.

plen·ti·ful [ˈplentiful] *a.* 丰富的. *a ～ harvest* 丰收. **-ly** *ad.* **-ness** *n.*

plen·ty [ˈplenti] *n.* 多,丰富; 充分. *a year of ～* 丰年. *There is ～ of time.* 时间很充裕. ***in ～*** 多,丰富; 充分 (*live in peace and ～* 过太平富裕的日子. *We are in ～ of time.* 我们有充分时间). ***～ of*** 很多的 (*There is ～ of food.* 食物很充足). — *a.* 〔口、方〕〔通常用作表语〕充裕的,足够的; 很多的. *This is ～.* 这就很多了. ***～ [plentiful] as blackberries*** 很多很多的, 多得不得了. — *ad.* 〔口〕十分,充分. *The house is ～ large enough.* 那房子足够大了.

ple·num [ˈpliːnəm] *n.* (*pl.* **～s, -na** [-nə]) ①充满物质的空间 (*opp.* vacuum); 充实,充满. ②【物】高压间. ③全体会议. — *a.* 增压的. *～ method (of ventilation)* 压力通风法. *～* **gauge** 通风计. *～* **system** 压力通风系统.

ple·och·ro·ism [pliˈɔkrəuizəm] *n.* 【理】多向色性. **-chroic** [-ˈkrəuik] *a.*

ple·och·ro·ma·tism [ˌpli(ː)əˈkrəumətizəm] *n.* 【物】多向色性.

ple·o·mor·phism [ˌpli(ː)əˈmɔːfizəm] *n.* ①【植】多型(现象). ②【动】多态性; 多态现象 (= poly morphism). **-mor·phic, -mor·phous** *a.*

ple·o·nasm [ˈpli(ː)ənæzəm] *n.* 【修】冗词,冗句, 冗言〔如 a false lie〕. **-nas·tic** *a.* 烦冗的; 重复的,赘语的.

ple·o·pha·gous [pli(ː)ˈɔfəgəs] *a.* ①吃多种食物的. ②(寄生虫)寄生于多种动[植]物的.

ple·o·pod [ˈpliːəpɔd] *n.* 【动】(甲壳类幼虫的)腹足; (成虫的)后足.

ple·rome [ˈplirəum], **ple·rom** [ˈplirəm] *n.* 【植】中柱原.

ple·si·o·saur, ple·si·o·sau·rus [ˈpliːsiəsɔː, -ˈsɔːrəs] *n.* (*pl.* **-ri** [-rai]) 【古生】蛇颈龙.

ples·sor [ˈplesə] *n.* 叩诊锤 (= plexor).

pleth·o·ra [ˈpleθərə] *n.* ①过多,过剩. ②【医】多血,多血症,多血质. **-thor·ic** *a.*

ple·thys·mo·graph [pliˈθizməgrɑːf, -græf] *n.* 【医】体积描记器. **-ic** *a.* **-y** *n.*

pleu·ra [ˈpluərə] *n.* (*pl.* **-rae** [-riː]) 【解】胸膜, 肋膜; ①【动】肋部. ②(昆虫的)侧板. **pleu·ral** *a.*

pleu·ri·sy [ˈpluərisi] *n.* 【医】肋膜炎, 胸膜炎. *dry [moist] ～* 干性[湿性]肋膜炎. **-rit·ic** [-ˈritik] *a.*

pleu·ro·dont [ˈpluːrədɔnt] *a.* 偏齿的〔如某些蜥蜴〕. — *n.* 偏齿动物.

pleu·ro·dyn·i·a [ˌpluərəuˈdiniə] *n.* 【医】胸膜痛,肋肌痛.

pleu·ron [ˈpluərɔn] (*pl.* **pleu·ra** [-rə]) *n.* 【动】(甲壳类的)横突起; (昆虫的)侧板.

pleu·ro·pneu·mo·ni·a [ˌpluərəunju(ː)ˈməunjə] *n.* 【医】胸膜肺炎.

pleu·rot·o·my [pluˈrɔtəmi] *n.* (*pl.* **-mies**) 胸膜切开术.

pleus·ton [ˈpluːstɔn] *n.* 水漂生物. **-ic** [-ˈtɔnik] *a.*

plew [pluː] *n.* 海狸皮.

plex·i·form [ˈpleksifɔːm] *a.* 网状的, 丛状的; 复杂的.

plex·i·glass [ˈpleksiglɑːs] *n.* 有机玻璃〔源自商标名〕.

plex·im·e·ter [plekˈsimitə] *n.* 【医】叩诊板.

plex·or [ˈpleksə] *n.* 【医】叩诊锤.

plex·us [ˈpleksəs] *n.* (*pl.* **～(es)**) ①【解】(神经、淋巴管或血管的) 丛. ②纠纷. *the solar ～* 太阳神经丛. *the spinal ～* 脊柱静脉丛.

plf., plff. = plaintiff.

pli·a·ble [ˈplaiəbl] *a.* ①柔韧的,易弯的,柔软的. ②柔顺的; 圆通的. **-bil·i·ty** [ˌplaiəˈbiliti] *n.* 柔韧(性), 柔顺(性). **-ab·ly** *ad.*

pli·ant [ˈplaiənt] *a.* = pliable. **-an·cy, -ness** *n.* **-ly** *ad.*

pli·ca [ˈplaikə] *n.* (*pl.* **pli·cae** [ˈplaisiː]) ①【解】褶,(皱)襞. ②【医】纠发病.

pli·cate, pli·cat·ed [ˈplaikit, ˈplaikeitid] *a.* 【植、动】有皱襞的,有褶的; 折扇状的.

pli·ca·tion [plaiˈkeiʃən] *n.* ①摺,摺叠. ②【植】折扇式. ③【地】皱纹,细褶皱.

pli·ca·ture [ˈplikətʃə] *n.* 摺,摺叠; 皱摺 (= plication).

pli·é [pliːˈei] *n.* 【芭蕾】蹬.

pli·er [ˈplaiə] *n.* ①努力工作的人,勤奋的人. ②定期来回盘运的车[船]. ③【诗】驾驶者;【海】逆风换抢的帆船.

pli·ers [ˈplaiəz] *n.* 〔用作 *sing.*, *pl.*〕钳子, 老虎钳,手钳. *(a) cutting* ～ 钢丝钳. *a pair of* ～ 一把钳子. *a round-rose* ～ 圆头钳.

plight[1] [plait] *n.* 保证;誓约;婚约. —*vt.* ①保证;发誓.②〔～ oneself〕定婚. *She* ～*ed herself to him.* 她和他订婚了. ***～ed lovers*** 山盟海誓的一对爱人. ***～ one's faith [promise, troth, word, honour]*** 牢牢约定,说定,山盟海誓.

plight[2] [plait] *n.* (困难)处境,状况,状态;苦境,悲惨命运. *What a* ～ *to be in!* 真不得了啦! ***in a sorry*** ～ 在狼狈不堪的处境中.

plim [plim] *vt.*, *vi.* ***(plimmed; plim·ming)*** 〔英方〕①(使)膨胀 *(out)*. ②(使)丰满.

plim·soll [ˈplimsəl] *n.* 〔*pl.*〕 ①〔澳〕 橡皮底帆布鞋.

Plim·soll [ˈplimsəl] *n.* ①普利姆索尔〔姓氏〕. ②**Samuel** ～萨·普利姆索尔〔1824—1898,英国船运改革者, 世称 the Sailor's Friend〕.

Plim·soll mark [ˈplimsəlˈmɑːk] *n.* 【海】(商船上显著标明的)载重线标志〔亦作 ～ **line**〕.

pling [pliŋ] *vi.* 〔美〕做叫化子 — *vt.* 乞讨.

plink [pliŋk] *n.* 〔拟声〕轻而尖的玎玲声. — *vt.*, *vi.* ①(使钢琴、班卓琴等) 发出玎玲声. ②(向铁盒或类似目标)射击;乱射. **-er** *n.*

plink-ponk [ˈpliŋk-pɔŋk] *n.* 〔谑〕白葡萄酒.

plinth [plinθ] *n.* ①【建】柱础,柱脚;壁脚板. ②像座,底座.

Plin·y [ˈplini] *n.* 普林尼〔人名〕. ～**"the Elder", Gaius Plinius Secundus** 老普林尼〔23—79, 古罗马政治家,百科辞典编集者〕. ～ **"the Younger", Gaius Plinius Caecilius Secundus** 〔小普林尼62(?)—113 著作家, 政治家,雄辩家〕.

Pli·o·cene [ˈplaiəsiːn] *n.*, *a.* = pleiocene.

pli·o·film [ˈplaiəfilm] *n.* (制雨衣等用的)氢氯化橡胶膜〔源自商标名〕.

pli·o·tron [ˈplaiətrɔn] *n.* 【无】 功率电子管 〔原商标名〕.

plis·sé, plis·se [pliˈsei] *n.* ①褶裥, 打褶〔使棉布、尼龙等起皱的最后一道工序〕. ②(起皱的)纤维织品.

P.L.M. = Paris-Lyons-Mediterranéan Railway. (法国)巴黎-里昂-地中海铁路.

plod [plɔd] *vi.* ***(plod·ded; plod·ding)*** ①沉重地走 *(on; along)*. ②努力从事;勤苦工作[用功] *(at)*. ～ *through the desert* 在沙漠里跋涉. ～ *at one's books* 勤苦读书. *He's plodding away day and night.* 他一天到晚在勤苦工作. ～ *through a task* 苦干到底. *a plodding genius* 勤学苦练的人才. — *vt.* 沉重地走(路). ～ *one's weary way* 拖着疲劳的脚步走. —*n.* ①沉重的脚步[脚声]. ②勤苦工作,辛苦,劳苦.

plod·der [ˈplɔdə] *n.* ①沉重地走的人;勤苦工作的人. ②【化】蜗压机.

Plo·esti [plɔːˈjeʃt(i)] *n.* 普洛耶什蒂〔罗马尼亚城市〕.

-ploid *suf.* 【生】…倍(染色)体: poly*ploid* 多倍体.

plonk[1] [plɔŋk, plʌŋk] =plunk.

plonk[2] [plɔŋk] *n.* 〔澳俚〕廉价的劣等酒.

plop [plɔp] *vt.*, *vi.* ***(plopped; plop·ping)*** (使) 噗通一声掉落,(使)砰一声爆开[弹出];(使)噗噗地沉下去. —*n.* 噗通声; 砰的一声. — *ad.* 噗通一声, 噗噗地,砰的一声. *fall* ～ *into the water* 噗通一声掉落水中. *The cork came out* ～! 塞子砰的一声拔出了.

plo·sion [ˈplouʒən] *n.* 【语音】破裂(发音). **plo·sive** *n.*, *a.* 破裂音(的),爆发音(的).

plot[1] [plɔt] *n.* ①阴谋(事件);策划. ②(小说、戏剧等的)情节. ③【炮兵】 测算表. *hatch a* ～ 策划阴谋. *be privy to a* ～ 参与阴谋. *The* ～ *thickens.* 情节复杂起来了. —*vt.* ①密谋,图谋;策划. ②绘(图); 画(设计图). ③把…记入(海图). ④拟定(剧本等的)情节. — *vi.* 图谋,策划 *(for; against)*.

plot[2] [plɔt] *n.* ①小块土地,一块地;一块地上的作物. ②〔美〕地基;基址图;【军】标绘(图). *an exprimental* ～ 试验田. *reserved private* ～*s* 自留地. *a garden* ～ 园地. *a* ～ *of barley* 一块大麦地. *a radar* ～ 雷达测绘板;雷达情报站. — *vt.* 区划(土地); 划分. ～ *out one's time* 分配自己的时间.

plot·tage [ˈplɔtidʒ] *n.* 一块地皮的面积.

plot·ter [ˈplɔtə] *n.* ①策划者; 阴谋者. ②绘迹器. ③标图员;制图者. *a curve* ～ 曲线描绘器.

plot·ting [ˈplɔtiŋ] *n.* ①测绘;标图. ②标航路. ～ **paper** 方格绘图纸. ～ **scale** 绘图比例尺.

plough, 〔美〕**plow** [plau] *n.* ①犁;犁形器具;排雪机;【矿】煤犁,刨煤机;【建】路犁;(木工用的)沟刨;【印】手动式切书机. ②耕作,农业;耕地. ③〔the P-〕【天】北斗七星. ④〔英俚〕(主考人评定)不及格. *a two-wheeled double-share* ～ 双轮双铧犁. *a cable-towed* ～ 绳索牵引犁. ***be at the*** ～ 在种田. ***beat [follow, hold] the*** ～ 种田. ***go to one's*** ～ 作自己的事. ***look back from the*** ～ 中止,停止. ***put [lay, set] one's hand to the*** ～ 开始工作. ***take a*** ～ 〔英口〕不及格. ***under the*** ～ 在耕作下. — *vt.* ①犁,耕;开(沟), 作(畦);【木工】挖沟(槽). ②使(额头)起皱. ③开(路); 破(浪)前进. ④〔英口〕使不及格. ⑤投(资). *a face* ～*ed with wrinkles* 起皱的脸. —*vi.* ①犁;耕;(土地)适于耕种. ②开路; 分开积雪等前进 *(through)*; 钻研. ③刻苦前进 *(through)*. ④〔英口〕不及格,考落. *The land* ～*s hard after the drought.* 旱后田难犁. ***be*** ～***ed*** 考不及格,考落. ～ ***a [one's] lonely farrow*** = ～ ***one's furrow alone*** (脱离组织)单独行动;过孤独生活,离群索居. ～ ***around*** 〔美口〕试探,打探. ～ ***back*** 把(草等)犁入土中;把(利润)再投资. ～ ***down*** 犁倒. ～ ***into*** 奋力投入(工作). ～ ***in [into] the land*** 犁进去. ～ ***one's way*** 奋力前进. ～ ***the sand(s) [air]*** 白费气力. ～ ***the waves*** 破浪前进. ～ ***under*** 使消失;埋葬掉. ～ ***up*** 犁翻,掘翻. ～ ***with sb.'s heifer [ox]*** ①利用别人的牛给自己耕地. ②利用他人资财. ～**back** 〔主美〕利润再投资;利润再投资额. ～**boy** 耕地时牵牛的孩子;农家子;庄稼汉. ～**head** = ploughshare. ～**land** 〔英〕①(可)耕地. ②= hide[3]. ～**man***(pl.* ～**-men***)* *n.* 耕地人,庄稼汉. ～**share** 犁头;犁铧. ～**staff** 小铲. ～ **tail** 犁柄;农活,耕作 *(at the* ～*tail* 在种田). ～**wright** 制犁 [修犁] 人.

Plough-Mon·day [ˈplauˈmʌndi]【英史】主显节 (Epiphany) 〔1月6日〕后的星期一〔过去英国某些地方在这一日开始耕作〕.

Plov·div [ˈplɔːvdif] *n.* 普罗夫迪夫〔保加利亚城市〕.

plov·er [ˈplʌvə] *n.* 【鸟】鸻科鸟;鸻.

plow [plau] *n.*, *vt.*, *vi.* 〔美〕 = plough.

ploy [plɔi] *n.* ①(为了得到利益而使用的)花招;(挫敌的)策略,手法. ②(社交性的)玩乐.

plu. = plural.

pluck [plʌk] *vt.* ①拔,扯(羽毛等);采,摘,掐(花、果实). ②拉,拖,拉下,拖开. ③振起(勇气等) *(up)*. ④〔口〕抢,夺 *(away; off)*, 诈取,讹诈⑤【地】(冰川)冲走(岩石),拔蚀. ⑥拨响(琴弦). ⑦〔英大学俚〕使不及格. ～ *sb. by the sleeve* 拉…的袖子. — *vi.* 猛拉 *(at)*; 想抓住, 捉 *(at)*. *A drowning man* ～*s at a straw.* 溺水的人会捞救命稻草. ***get*** ～***ed*** 考不及格,落第. ～ ***a pigeon*** 骗取愚人金钱. ～ ***asunder*** 扯开. ～ ***away [off]*** 扯去,撕去. ～ ***down*** 拆毁(建筑物),(把某人)拖下来. ～ ***out*** 拔出;揭露. ～***up*** ①连根拔去,根绝. ②提高,振起(勇气). — *n.* ①拔; 扯. ②(牛等的)内脏. ③〔口〕胆子,勇气. ④〔俚〕不及格. ⑤【摄】鲜明. *a hard* ～*ed man* 冷酷无情的人. *a good-*～*ed man* 有勇气的人.

pluck·less [ˈplʌklis] *a.* 没勇气的.

pluck·y [ˈplʌki] *a.* ***(-i·er; -i·est)*** ①有勇气的，有胆量的．②【摄】清晰的，鲜明的．**-i·ly** *ad.* **-i·ness** *n.*

plug [plʌg] *n.* ①塞子；(龋齿等的)填塞物．②救火龙头，消防栓；(内燃机的)火花塞；【军】火门闩；枪口盖；【海】锚链孔塞子，疏水塞子．③【电】插塞，插头；针形接点；抽水马桶的抽水装置．④板烟．⑤【地】岩颈．⑥〔美俚〕废马，老马；废物；〔美口〕陈货．⑦〔美俚〕用功学生．⑧〔美俚〕高礼帽．⑨〔美俚〕(插在无线电节目里的) 讨厌的广告．⑩〔美俚〕一拳．*chewin'* ～ 橡皮糖．— *vt.* ①塞，填塞，堵 *(up)*．②〔俚〕开枪打死〔打伤〕；〔俚〕用拳头打，殴打．③〔美俚〕反反复复硬叫人听〔看〕；利用无线电做广告．— *vi.* ①〔俚〕勤苦工作；用功．②开枪射击．③【电】插上插头．～ ***along*** 〔美俚〕勤苦工作下去．～ ***(away) at sth.*** 拼命地干着 (某项工作)．～**-in** ①*n.*【无】插座．②*vt.* 接通电源．～ **bush**【无】插头衬套．～ **cock** 旋塞．～ **cord** 【电】①插头 (软) 线．②塞绳．～**-ended trunk** 【无】插头收端中继线．～ **fuse**【电】插塞式熔丝，插入式保险丝．～ **hat** 〔美俚〕高礼帽．～ **rod** 塞杆．～**-ugly** 〔美俚〕(城里的)流氓，恶棍，暴徒．～**-up line** (电话的)障碍试验线．

plug·ger [ˈplʌgə] *n.* ①【医】(牙科医生用)填充器；填塞物．②【矿】凿岩机．③〔美俚〕用功学生；勤苦工作的人．④捧场者；(电台的)商业广告播音员；宣传员．

plum [plʌm] *n.* ①【植】李子；李树；梅．②酒馅巧克力．③(制糕饼用的)葡萄干．④糖果．⑤酱紫色．⑥最好的东西，最好的地方，精华．⑦〔英俚〕十万镑，大财产；(不小的)额外利益，奖品．⑧〔美〕重要职位．— *ad.*〔美〕充分，完全 (= plumb)．～ *ripe* 熟透．～ **cake** 葡萄干糕饼．～ **locoed** 〔美〕思想癫狂的，非常入迷的．～ **pudding [duff]** 葡萄干布丁．～ **tree** 李树；〔美〕利益的来源〔如政治恩惠和职位〕．

plum·age [ˈplu:midʒ] *n.* ①【动】〔集合词〕羽毛．②漂亮衣服．*full-～d* 羽毛长齐的．

plu·mas·sier [plu:ˈmæsiə, -siei] *n.*〔F.〕〔罕〕羽毛制品商，羽毛商人．

plumb [plʌm] *n.* 铅锤，测锤，线砣；垂直．***off*** ～ = ***out of*** ～不垂直，歪斜．— *a.* ①垂直的；公正的．②〔口〕彻底的，完全的，绝对的．～ *nonsense* 荒唐透顶，毫无意义．～ *nuts* 〔美〕完全神经病的；低能到极点的．— *ad.* ①垂直地．②恰恰，正．③〔美口〕完全．*fall* ～ *down* 垂直落下．～ *southwards* 正南，向正南．～ *in the face of* 正对着．— *vt.* ①用铅锤检查(是否垂直)；使垂直 *(up)*．②用测铅测(水深)，测量．③查明；看穿，看出．④给…装铅，灌铅以增加…的重量．⑤给…铺自来水管〔煤气管〕．⑥焊．*No eye can* ～ *those depths.* 谁也看不到那样的深度．— *vi.* ①垂直悬挂．②作(铅)管工．～ **bob** 铅垂，线锤．～ **line** 铅垂线；标准．～**-line** *vt.* ①用铅锤线测量 (…的垂直度)．②探测，检查．～ **rule**【建】垂规．**-less** *a.*〔诗〕深不可测的，无底的(大洋等)．

plum·bag·i·nous [plʌmˈbædʒinəs] *a.* (象) 石墨的，含石墨的．

plum·ba·go [plʌmˈbeigəu] *n.* *(pl.* ～*s)* ①石墨．②【植】琉璃茉莉属的植物．

plum·bate [ˈplʌmbeit] *n.*【化】铅酸盐．

plum·be·ous [ˈplʌmbiəs] *a.* 铅的；似铅的；含铅的；铅色的．*a* ～ *crucible* 石墨坩埚．

plumb·er [ˈplʌmə] *n.* ①管子工，铅工；铅管(铺设)工人．②〔美〕(调查政府人员泄密情况的) 堵防泄密人员．～**-block**【机】轴台．

plumb·er·y [ˈplʌməri] *n.* ①制铅工业；铅器(工艺)．②铅管工；铅(管)厂．

plum·bic [ˈplʌmbik] *a.* ①【化】铅的，含铅的；【化】四价铅的，高铅的．②【医】由于铅毒的．～ **acid** 高铅酸，四氢氧化铅．～ **oxide** 氧化铅．

plum·bif·er·ous [plʌmˈbifərəs] *a.* 产铅的；含铅的．

plumb·ing [ˈplʌmiŋ] *n.* ①制铅工业；铅管制造．②铅管铺设，铅管工程；自来水工程．③管件，铅管类．④铅锤测量．⑤波导设备，波导管．⑥〔the ～〕抽水马桶．

plum·bism [ˈplʌmbizəm] *n.*【医】慢性铅中毒．

plum·bite [ˈplʌmbait] *n.*【化】亚铅酸盐．

plum·bous [ˈplʌmbəs] *a.* 铅的；二价铅的．

plum·bum [ˈplʌmbəm] *n.*【化】铅〔略 Pb〕．

plume [plu:m] *n.* ①(长而美的)羽毛；羽衣．②羽毛饰；荣誉的表征．③【虫】羽状毛；【植】羽状部，羽状圆锥花，冠毛．④【空】卷流．***borrowed*** ～***s*** 借来的衣服；空名 *(adorn oneself with borrowed* ～*s* 穿借来的衣服，虚装门面)．— *vt.* ①(鸟)整理(羽毛)；用羽毛装饰．②〔～ oneself〕借衣服装饰；自夸 *(upon)*．③使形成羽毛状．

plume·let [ˈplu:mlit] *n.* 小羽毛，幼毛；【植】= plumule.

plum·met [ˈplʌmit] *n.* 测锤(钓丝的)坠子；线锤；铅锤线；锤规；重压物．— *vi.* 笔直掉下；骤然跌落．～**-level** 锤准器．

plum·my [ˈplʌmi] *a.* ①李子多的；李子似的；加葡萄干的．②〔英口〕有利的；极好的，高级的．③(声音) 圆润的．

plu·mose, plu·mous [ˈplu:məus, ˈplu:məs] *a.* 羽毛状的；有羽毛的．

plump[1] [plʌmp] *a.* 肥胖的，(女人等)丰满的；(钱包等)鼓起的．— *vt., vi.* (使) 肥胖，(使)膨胀，使(水果等)长饱满 *(out; up)*．**-ly** *ad.* **-ness** *n.*

plump[2] [plʌmp] *vi.* ①噗通地掉落 *(down; into; upon)*．②突然跳进．③(把自己全部选票)投选一人；绝对赞成 *(for)*．— *vt.* ①噗通地放落．②唐突地说出 *(out)*．③为…说好话．— *n.* 沉重的坠落；〔Scot.〕阵雨．— *a.* 直率的，莽撞的；唐突的(话等)；完全的(假话等)．*a* ～ *refusal* 断然拒绝．*a* ～ *lie* (明目张胆的) 大谎话．～ *and plain* 露骨的．— *ad.* ①噗通地，沉重地．②突然，蓦地．③直截了当地，坦白地．*sit down* ～ 噗通一声坐下．*come* ～ *upon the enemy* 突然袭击敌人．*Say it out* ～*!* 老老实实讲出来吧！**-ly** *ad.* **-ness** *n.*

plump[3] [plʌmp] *n.* 〔古〕群，队，丛．

plump·er[1] [ˈplʌmpə] *n.* ①使肥胖〔膨胀〕的东西；(瘪嘴人含用的)鼓腮物．②(鞣皮用的)除酸剂；除酸工人．

plump·er[2] [ˈplʌmpə] *n.* ①急剧重落；猛跌．②把全数选票投选一候选人(的人)．③〔俚〕大谎；特大东西．

plump·y [ˈplʌmpi] *a.* ***(-i·er; -i·est)*** 丰满的，肥胖的．

plu·mule [ˈplu:mju:l] *n.* ①【植】胚芽．②【动】(鸟的)绒毛；(鳞翅目昆虫的)香羽鳞．

plum·y [ˈplu:mi] *a.* ***(-i·er; -i·est)*** ①有羽毛的；似羽毛的；用羽毛装饰的．②绒毛(状)的．

plun·der [ˈplʌndə] *vt., vi.* 掠夺，抢劫；偷，私吞．— *n.* ①抢劫，掠夺．②掠夺物，赃品；〔口〕赚头，利益．③〔美〕家具，行李．～**-bund**〔美口〕剥削公众利益的集团．**-able** *a.* **-er** *n.*

plun·der·age [ˈplʌndəridʒ] *n.*【法】抢劫，掠夺，(尤指)盗用船货；劫掠品．

plun·der·er [ˈplʌndərə] *n.* 抢劫者，掠夺者；盗窃者．

plunge [plʌndʒ] *vt.* ①使投入；插进，扔进；浸入 *(into)*．②使陷入；使遭受；使埋头…，使投身 *(in; into)*．③【园艺】将(花盆)埋入地中．～ *a room into darkness* 突然使屋子一团漆黑．— *vi.* ①跳进，掉进，钻进 *(into)*；冲 *(into; down; up)*；不顾前后地干起来 *(into)*．②下降，急降．③(马)猛烈前冲；跃起后蹄倒竖起来；(船)前后颠簸．④〔俚〕盲目投资；滥赌；借债 *(～ into)*．～ *into the river* 跳入河中．～ *into war* 投入战斗．*plunging deeper and deeper* 愈陷愈深．— *n.* ①跳进，插进．②猛冲，蛮干；冒险，断然手段．③〔俚〕投机，赌博．④〔古〕为难，困难．⑤〔罕〕大雨．⑥(船的)前后颠簸；马跃起后蹄倒竖．***at a*** ～ 进退两难．***take the*** ～ 冒险尝试；蛮干，毅然从事．～ **bath** 大浴池；全身浴．

plung·er [ˈplʌndʒə] *n.* ①跳进水中的人；潜水人；突入者．②【枪炮】(后膛枪的)撞针杆；【机】柱塞，活塞；插棒式铁心；(波导管)短路器．③〔俚〕骑兵．④〔俚〕滥赌的人；盲目的投机家；鲁莽的人．～ **pump** 柱塞泵．

plung·ing [ˈplʌndʒiŋ] *a.* 跳进的;向前猛冲的;俯射的. ~ **fire** (火炮等的)俯射,瞰射.

plunk [plʌŋk] *vt.* ①〔口〕砰地投掷;使砰地坠落;砰砰地弹(弦等). ②〔美〕猛打,猛推,猛戳. —*vi.* ①砰砰地响. ②砰地坠落. ③支持 *(for)*. ~ *down* ①猛地放下;突然落下. ②砰地坐下. ③付款. — *n.* 砰的声音; 啪的打声〔打击〕; 〔美俚〕美元一元. — *ad.* 砰地, 噗通地.

plup. = pluperfect.

plu·per·fect [ˈpluːˈpəːfikt] *n., a.* 【语法】过去完成时(的).

plur. = plural.

plu·ral [ˈpluərəl] *a.* 复数的 *(opp.* singular*)*; 二以上的. — *n.*【语法】复数(形);复数词. ~ **livings**【宗】兼俸. ~ **marriage** 一夫多妻, 一妻多夫. ~ **vote** 双重投票,复投票. **-ly** *ad.*

plu·ral·ism [ˈpluərəlizəm] *n.* ①复数,多种. ②【宗】(在数个教堂)兼职. ③双重投票. ④【哲】多元论. **-ral·ist** *n.* 〔英〕兼职者;双重投票(权)者;多妻主义者;【哲】多元论者. **-ral·is·tic** *a.*

plu·ral·i·ty [pluəˈræliti] *n.* ①复数;多数;大多数;过半数;〔美〕(当选人对次多票者的)超过票数. ②〔英〕兼管数教堂;兼职. ③一夫多妻.

plu·ral·ize [ˈpluərəlaiz] *vt.* 使成复数(形);以复数形表示. — *vi.* ①成为复数. ②〔英〕兼管数教堂;兼数职.

plu·ral·ly [ˈpluərəli] *ad.* 以复数形式.

plu·ri·ax·i·al [ˌpluəriˈæksiəl] *a.* 【植】多轴的.

plus [plʌs] *(opp.* minus*)* *prep.* 加,加上. *Four* ~ *one equals five* 〔4 + 1 = 5〕. 四加一等于五. — *a.* ①【数】加的,正;【电】阳;【植】(菌丝体)阳性的,雄性的;【商】贷方的. ②〔口〕(同等物中)略大[高]的; 标准以上的. ③〔口〕有增益的. ④【高尔夫球】让分的,先加分的. *the* ~ *sign* 加号,正号. *a* ~ *quantity* 正数,正量. *on the* ~ *side of the account*【商】在帐户的贷方. *I found myself* ~ *nearly* £*100.* 我多得了将近百镑. *B* ~ B^+ 的成绩 — *n.* ①【数】加号;正数;正量;正型. ②附加物,多余;剩余;利益. ③【高尔夫球】优者的让步. ~**-fours** 〔*pl.*〕〔俚〕〔英〕(打高尔夫球穿的)灯笼裤.

plush [plʌʃ] *n.* 长毛绒; 〔*pl.*〕长毛绒裤. *on the* ~ 舒服, 舒舒服服的. — *a.* ①长毛绒(做)的. ②〔俚〕豪华的;漂亮的;舒服的. **-ly** *ad.* **-y** *a.*

Plu·tarch [ˈpluːtɑːk] 蒲鲁塔克〔46—120,希腊历史学家,传记作家,以其作品《名人传》著名〕.

plu·tar·chy [ˈpluːtɑːki] *n.* ①富豪统治,财阀统治. ②财阀;财政寡头.

plute [pluːt] *n.* 〔美口〕富豪,财阀,有钱人; 〔*pl.*〕富豪阶级.

plu·te·us [ˈpluːtiəs] *n.* *(pl.* **-te·i** [-ai]*)*【动】长腕幼虫〔海胆类〕.

Plu·to [ˈpluːtəu] *n.* ①【罗神】冥王;阴间之神. ②〔the ~〕【天】冥王星.

plu·to [ˈpluːtəu] *n.* ①放射性检查计. ②【军】海上搜索与救援飞机.

PLUTO = pipeline under the ocean (二次大战时英法两国间的)海底输油管.

plu·toc·ra·cy [pluːˈtɔkrəsi]= plutarchy.

plu·to·crat [ˈpluːtəkræt] *n.* 财阀,富豪政治家. **-ic** *a.* 富豪统治的;财政寡头的,财阀(般)的.

Plu·to·ni·an [pluːˈtəunjən] *a.* ①阴间的,地府的. ②〔罕〕【地】火成的. ③冥王星的.

Plu·ton·ic [pluːˈtɔnik] *a.* ①【罗神】冥王的; 冥府的,阴间的. ②冥王星的. ③〔常 *p-*〕【地】深成的,深发的;深成岩体的; 火成的. ~ **earthquake** 深源地震. ~ **rocks** 深成岩. ~ **theory** 地壳火成论.

plu·to·nism [ˈpluːtəunizm] *n.* ①【地】火成论. ②钚射线伤害.

plu·to·ni·um [pluːˈtəuniəm]【化】钚. ~ **bomb** 钚弹〔使用钚元素的原子弹〕.

Plu·tus [ˈpluːtəs] *n.* 【希神】财神.

plu·vi·al [ˈpluːviəl, -vjəl] *a.* ①雨的,多雨的. ②【地】洪水的,雨成的. **P- age** 洪积时期.

plu·vi·an [ˈpluːviən] *a.* 多雨的;下雨的.

plu·vi·om·e·ter [ˌpluːviˈɔmitə] *n.* 雨量计.

plu·vi·o·met·ric, plu·vi·o·met·ri·cal [ˌpluːviəˈmetrik,-rikəl] *a.* 雨量计的;测定雨量的.

plu·vi·ose [ˈpluːviːəus] *a.* 雨的, 多雨的 (= pluvious). **-os·i·ty** [-ˈɔsiti] *n.* 雨量多.

ply[1] [plai] *vt.* ①勤苦经营,努力从事; 勤用(器具、武器等). ②拼命给…加(煤、柴等);硬逼人(吃菜等); 死劝,硬要 *(with)*; (提质问等)攻击; 缠扰. ③(船等)来回于, 往返于. ~ *an oar* 使劲划. ~ *one's books* 用功读书. ~ *a man with liquor* 硬劝人喝酒. — *vi.* ①(船、马车等)来往,来回兜揽 *(between; from; to)*; (搬运员、船夫等)接客,等客 *(at)*. ②勤苦工作,出力;兜卖 *(in)*. ③赶,向前冲;【海】逆风换抢;〔主诗〕(船)前进. *a* ~*ing taxi* 野鸡汽车. ~ *between* (车船等)来回于…之间,走…线.

ply[2] [plai]*n.* ①襞;股,绹,厚,层. ②倾向,性癖,癖. *three-* ~ *thread* 三股(头的)线. *take a* ~ 有倾向, 有习癖.

Ply·mouth [ˈpliməθ] *n.* ①普利茅斯〔英国港市〕. ②普利茅斯〔蒙特塞拉特岛(英)首府〕. ~ **Brethren**【宗】普里木斯教友会〔1830 年前后形成于英国普利茅斯的基督教的一派〕. ~ **Rock** ①传说中美国第一批移民至美洲登陆处. ②普利茅斯品种鸡.

ply·wood [ˈplaiwud] *n.* 胶合板;层板. *exterior* ~ 耐火胶合板.

Plzeň [ˈpʌlzenjə] *n.* 比尔森〔捷克斯洛伐克城市〕.

PM, P.M. = ①paymaster (发放薪饷的)出纳员; 军需官. ②permanent magnet 永久磁铁. ③police magistrate 违警罪法庭推事. ④postmaster 邮政局长;驿站站长. ⑤postmortem. ⑥prime minister 总理;首相. ⑦provost marshal 宪兵司令 ⑧〔L.〕*post meridiem* 下午,午后(= afternoon). ⑨Pacific Mail 〔英〕太平洋邮船公司. ⑩Past Master (行会、俱乐部等的)前任主持人. ⑪photomultiplier 光电倍增管.

Pm = 【化】promethium.

pm. = premium.

p.m. = ①〔L.〕*post meridiem* 下午,午后(= afternoon). ②postmortem. ③per minute 每分钟. ④〔L.〕*pro memoria* 为了纪念,以作纪念. ⑤purpose made 特制的,特殊用途的.

P.M.G. = ①Pall-Mall Gazette; 〔英〕《蓓尔美尔街官报》. ②Paymaster General 军需部长. ③Postmaster General 邮政部长. ④Provost Marshal General 〔美〕宪兵(总)司令.

pmh = per man-hour 每人每小时.

p.m.h. = production per man-hour 每人每小时的产量.

pmk = postmark 邮戳.

PMLA = Publications of the Modern Language Association of America 《美国现代语言学协会会刊》(期刊名称).

P.M.O. = Principal Medical Officer 〔英〕主治军医.

P.M.R.A.F.N.S. = Princess Mary's Royal Air Force Nursing Service 〔英〕皇家空军玛丽公主护士队.

PN, p.n. = ①promissory note 【商】本票, 期票. ②please note 请注意.

PNA = pentose nucleic acid【生化】戊糖核酸.

pneum. = pneumatic; pneumatic(s).

pneum- = pneumo-.

pneu·ma [ˈnjuːmə] *n.* ①呼吸. ②精神,灵魂. ③〔P-〕【神】圣灵.

pneu·mat·ic [njuːˈmætik] *a.* ① 空气的;似空气的,气体的;空气学(上)的. ②【机】压缩空气推动的;汽动的;风动的. ③装满空气的. ④有气胎的;【动】有气腔的. ⑤〔罕〕

【神】灵的. — *n.* 气胎;〔口〕有气胎的自行车; (风琴的)管. ~ **brake** 气闸;风闸. ~ **cushion** 气枕,气垫. ~ **dispatch** (信件、电报等的)气(力输)送. ~ **drill** 风钻. ~ **hammer** 气(压)锤. ~ **jack**气力起重机, 气压千斤顶. ~ **perforator** 气压钻孔机. ~ **tire** 气胎. **-i·cal·ly** *ad.*

pneu·mat·ic·i·ty [ˌnjuːməˈtisiti] *n.*【生】有气腔.

pneu·mat·ics [njuːˈmætiks] *n.*【物】气体力学.

pneumato- *comb. f.* 空气; 气体; 呼吸; 精神; 圣灵: *pneumato*logy.

pneu·ma·to·gen·i·c [ˌnjuːmətəuˈdʒenik] 气成的. ~ *minerals* 气成矿物.

pneu·ma·tol·o·gy [ˌnjuːməˈtɔlədʒi] *n.* ①【医】气体(治疗)学. ②【物】气体力学. ③【宗】灵物学;圣灵论;〔古〕心理学.

pneu·ma·tol·y·sis [ˌnjuːməˈtɔlisis, ˌnuː-] *n.*【地】气化(作用). **-to·lyt·ic** [-təˈlitik] *a.*

pneu·ma·tom·e·ter [ˌnjuːməˈtɔmitə] *n.*【医】呼吸量测定器.

pneu·ma·to·phore [njuˈmætəufɔː] *n.* ①【植】出水通气根. ②【动】气囊;浮囊. ③【医】救生氧气袋.

pneu·ma·to·ther·a·py [ˌnjuːmətəuˈθerəpi] *n.*【医】气体疗法.

pneu·mec·to·my [njuːˈmektəmi] *n.*【医】肺部分切除术.

pneumo- *comb. f.* 肺. *pneumo*coccus.

pneu·mo·ba·cil·lus [ˌnjuːməubəˈsiləs] *n.* (*pl.* **-li** [-lai]) 肺炎杆菌.

pneu·mo·coc·cus [ˌnjuːməˈkɔkəs, ˌnuː-] *n.* (*pl.* **-coxci** [-ˈkɔksai]) 肺炎双球菌. **-coc·cal** [-ˈkɔkl], **-coc·cic** [-ˈkɔksik] *a.*

pneu·mo·co·ni·o·sis [ˈnjuːməˌkəuniˈəusis, ˈnuː-] *n.*【医】肺尘埃沉着病,肺尘病.

pneu·mo·en·ceph·a·lo·gram [ˌnjuːmoenˈsefələuˈgræm] *n.*【医】脑蛛网膜下腔充气.

pneu·mo·gas·tric [ˌnjuːməˈgæstrik] *a.*【解】①(关于)肺和胃的. ②迷走神经的. *a* ~ *ganglion* 气胃神经节. ~ *nerves* 迷走神经. — *n.* 迷走神经.

pneu·mo·graph[ˈnjuːməgrɑːf] *n.*【医】呼吸描记器.

pneu·mo·nec·to·my [ˌnjuːməˈnektəmi] *n.* (*pl.* **-mies**) 肺切除术.

pneu·mo·ni·a [nju(ː)ˈməunjə] *n.*【医】肺炎; 急性肺炎 (= acute ~). *double* ~ 双肺炎. *single* ~ 单肺炎.

pneu·mon·ic [nju(ː)ˈmɔnik] *a.* 肺的;【医】(患)肺炎的.

pneu·mo·ni·tis [ˌnjuːməuˈnaitis] *n.* 肺炎;局部急性肺炎.

pneu·mo·no·ul·tra·mi·cro·scop·ic·sil·i·co·vol·ca·no·co·ni·o·sis [ˈnjuːmənəuˌʌltrəˌmaikrəsˈkɔpikˈsilikəvɔlˈkeinəuˌkəuniˈəusis] *n.*【医】硅酸盐沉着病, 肺尘病.

pneu·mor·rha·gia [ˌnjuːməuˈrɑːdʒiə] *n.*【医】肺出血.

pneu·mo·tho·rax [ˌnjuːməuˈθɔːræks] *n.*【医】气胸. *artificial* ~ 人工气胸.

pneu·mo·tro·pism [nju(ː)ˈmɔtrəpizəm] *n.*【医】亲肺, 肺向性. **-trop·ic** [-ˈtrɔpik] *a.*

p-n junction [ˈpiːˈenˈdʒʌŋkʃən]【物】p-n 结.

Pnom Penh [ˈnɔmˈpen;pəˈnɔːmˈpen] 金边 (= Phnom Penh).

pnxt. = pinxit (= painted it).

PO, p.o. = ①petty officer 海军军士. ②postal order 〔英〕邮政汇票. ③post office 邮局. ④Pilot Officer 〔英〕空军少尉. ⑤power output 功率输出. ⑥Province of Ontario 〔加拿大〕安大略省. ⑦Public Office (国家机关或社会团体的)办公处.

Po = polonium【化】钋.

po [pəu] *n.* 〔儿语〕便盆 = chamber-pot.

poach[1] [pəutʃ] *vi., vt.* ①〔英〕偷猎,偷偷捕(鱼);(为偷猎而)侵入. ②【赛跑】用不正当手段取得(有利的起步); 【网球】抢打(该由 partner 打的球). ③把(土地)践踏成泥浆. ④【制纸】加水调匀浓度. ⑤【化】漂洗. ⑥把(棒、手指等)戳入 (*into*). — *vi.* ①偷猎,偷偷捕鱼. ②走路陷入泥中. ③【网球】抢打. ~ *in other people's business* 侵犯别人权限. ~ *for fresh ideas* 抄袭(别人著作中的)新观点.

poach[2] [pəutʃ] *vt.* 水煮 (荷包蛋). ~*ed eggs* 水煮荷包蛋.

poach·er[1] [ˈpəutʃə] *n.* ①〔英〕偷猎者. ②侵犯他人权限的人.

poach·er[2] [ˈpəutʃə] *n.* 浅碟煮荷包蛋器.

poach·y [ˈpəutʃi] *a.* (***poach·i·er; poach·i·est***) 潮湿的,湿而软的〔指泥土〕.

POB, P.O.B. = post-office box 邮政信箱.

POC = port of call (沿途)停靠港.

poc·co·sin [pəˈkəussn] *n.* (美国东南部的)沼泽地.

po·chard [ˈpəutʃəd] *n.*【鸟】潜鸭;红头潜鸭.

pock [pɔk] *n.*【医】痘疱,痘疮;痘凹. — *vt.* 使留有痘痕,使有麻点.

pock·et [ˈpɔkit] *n.* ①衣袋;钱袋;(袋鼠等的)袋;小袋;【军】袋形阵地(中的部队). ②金钱,财富,资力;零用钱. ③【台球】球囊;(羊毛等的)一袋〔约 168—224 磅〕;【采】矿穴,窝矿,矿袋;矿石块;【机】套. ④凹处,穴;〔美〕峡谷. ⑤【空】(大气中的)气阱(= air-~). ⑥小航室;煤库. ⑦【赛马、赛跑】被其他马〔人〕挤轧的不利地位. *a deep* ~ 充足的财力. *an empty* ~ 两手空空;穷光蛋. *a high* ~*s* 〔美俚〕高个子,长人. ***be in*** ~ 手头有钱;赚钱;剩下钱 (*I am 5s. in* ~. = *I am in* ~ *by 5s.* 我手头有 5 先令). ***be out of*** ~ 手头没有钱;赔钱. ***have sb. in one's*** ~ 可以左右某人. ***keep one's hands in one's*** ~ 不做事,偷懒. ***line one's*** ~***s*** 赚大钱,肥私囊. ***out-of-~ expenses*** 用现金付出的费用;实际支出. ***pay out of one's own*** ~ 自己掏腰包支付. ***pick a*** ~ 扒窃. *(be prepared to)* ***put one's hand in one's*** ~ (准备)用钱,出钱. ***put one's pride in one's*** ~ 忍辱,抑制自尊心. ***suffer in one's*** ~ 赔钱,亏损. — *a.* ①袖珍的,小型的. ②金钱上的. ③秘密的. *a* ~ *battleship* 袖珍战列舰. *a* ~ *edition* (图书的).袖珍版; 小型的东西. *a* ~ *pistol* 小手枪;〔俚〕小酒瓶. — *vt.* ①把…装在衣袋内; 包藏. ②盗用, 侵吞. ③忍受(侮辱等). ④〔美〕阻挠,搁置(议案等). ⑤抑制,藏住(感情等). ⑥任意摆布, 操纵. ⑦【台球】把球打进(球囊). ⑧【赛跑】自前后妨碍(跑的人),四面挤轧. ~**book** ①皮夹子;〔美、喻〕钱包; 金钱. ②〔英〕笔记簿; 袖珍本. ~ **borough** (英国旧时)由个人〔家族〕操纵的选区. ~ **edition** ①袖珍本〔版〕. ②小东西. ~**-handkerchief** ①(衣袋中的)手帕. ②小型物. ~**-hunter** 〔美〕骗子. ~ **knife** 小刀. ~ **money** 零用钱. ~ **piece** (搁在衣袋里的)吉利钱〔多半是古钱〕. ~**-size(d)** *a.* 尺寸相当小的〔尤指适应于放在口袋中的尺寸〕. ~**veto** *vt.* 〔美〕(总统)搁置议案,拒绝签署. **-ful** *n.* (*pl.* ~**s**) 一袋〔指量〕.

pock·e·ta·ble [ˈpɔkitəbl] *a.* 衣袋里装得下的;可供私用的;能隐藏起来的.

pock·et·y [ˈpɔkiti] *a.* ①有凹入处的; 囊形的,有囊状特征的. ②【矿】袋状分布的.

pock·mark [ˈpɔkmɑːk] *n.* 痘痕, 麻点. — *vt.* ①使布满痘痕. ②使密密麻麻地布满.

pock·marked, pock·pitted, pock·y [ˈpɔːkmɑːkt, -pitid, -pɔki] *a.* 有麻窝的.

po·co [ˈpəukəu; ˈpɔːkəu] *ad.* 〔It.〕【乐】稍,少许,略. ~ ***largo [presto]*** 略慢[快]. ~ ***a*** ~ 渐渐,慢慢.

po·co·cu·ran·te [ˌpəukəukjuəˈrænti] *a.* 〔It.〕无动于衷的; 满不在乎的; 漠不关心的. — *n.* 满不在乎的人; 漠不关心的人.

po·co·cu·ran·tism [ˌpəukəukjuəˈræntizəm] *n.* 满不在乎,不关心,不热心.

pod[1] [pɔd] *n.* ①【植】荚,荚果. ②蚕茧;蝗虫的卵囊. ③(捕鳗鱼的)袋网. ④【空】容器;塔门吊舱;(发动机)吊舱;(翼梢等上的)发射架;(宇宙船的)可分离的舱. ⑤【矿】近圆柱形矿体,扁豆形矿体;透镜形矿体. ⑥〔口〕肚子 (= belly). ~ *bearing plant* = ~*ded plant* 豆科植物. — *vt.* 剥(荚). — *vi.* 成荚,结荚,生荫 *(up)*. ~ **pepper**【植】朝天椒.

pod[2] [pɔd] *n.* (海豹、鲸等的)小群. — *vt.* 把 (海豹等) 赶到一块.

pod[3] [pɔd] *n.*【机】①(某些钻头及螺旋钻的)纵槽;有纵槽的螺旋钻. ②手摇钻的钻头承窝.

POD, P. O. D. = ①pay on delivery【商】货到付款. ②post office department 邮政部门. ③port of debarkation 下船港口, 卸载港口. ④*Pocket Oxford Dictionary* «袖珍牛津词典».

pod(o)-, *comb. f.* 足: *podo*theca.

-pod(e) *suf.* 有足的.

po·dag·ra [ˈpɔdəgrə, pəˈdægrə] *n.*【医】足痛风. **-dag·ral, -dag·ric** *a.*

pod·ded [ˈpɔdid] *a.* ①有荚的;结荚的;生于荚中的. ②〔喻〕富裕的,生活宽裕的,小康的,安乐的,舒适的.

po·des·ta [pəuˈdestə; It. ˌpəudeˈstɑː] *n.* ①【史】中世纪意大利的城镇长官. ②意大利城市小官员. ③法西斯时代意大利的市长.

podge [pɔdʒ] *n.* 矮胖的人.

podg·y [ˈpɔdʒi] *a.* ***(podg·i·er; -i·est)*** 〔英〕矮胖的.

po·di·a·trist [pəuˈdaiətrist] *n.* 足病医生.

podi·a·try [pəuˈdaiətri] *n.*【医】足病学;足医术.

po·dite [ˈpɔdait] *n.*【动】肢节. **po·dit·ic** [pɔˈditik] *a.*

po·di·um [ˈpəudiəm] *n.* *(pl.* ***-dia*** [-diə]*)* ①【建】墩座墙. ②角斗场和前座间的矮墙. ③〔美〕乐队指挥坛. ④屋内墙边的一圈长椅. ⑤【动】足,(乌贼的)管足;【植】叶柄.

-podium *comb. f.* 足;足状部分: pseudo*podium*.

pod·o·car·pus [ˌpɔdəˈkɑːpəs] *n.*【植】罗汉松属 *(Podocarpus)* 植物.

pod·o·phyl·lin [ˌpɔdəˈfilin] *n.*【药】鬼臼树脂〔作泻药〕.

pod·o·phyl·lum [ˌpɔdəˈfiləm] *n.* ①鬼臼属植物. ②鬼臼根〔可作泻剂〕.

pod·o·the·ca [ˈpɔdəθiːkə] *n.* *(pl.* ***-cae*** [-siː]*)* 【鸟】脚鞘.

Po·dunk [ˈpəudʌŋk] *n.* 〔美谑〕小镇.

pod·zol [ˈpɔdzɔːl, -zɔl] *n.* 〔地〕灰壤,灰化土 (= podsol). **-ic** *a.*

pod·zol·i·za·tion, pad·sol·i·za·tion [ˌpɔdzɔːlaiˈzeiʃən] *n.* 灰壤化作用. **pod·zol·ize** [ˈpɔdəzəlaiz] *vt.* 使灰壤化.

Poe [pəu] *n.* ①波〔姓氏〕. ②**Edgar Allan** ~ 爱伦·坡〔1809—1849,美国诗人,短篇小说家,批评家〕.

po·em [ˈpəuim, ˈpəuem] *n.* 诗,韵文 *(opp.* prose*)*; 诗一样的作品;富有诗意的东西. *a prose* ~ 散文诗. *compose a* ~ 作诗. *Their lives are a* ~. 他们的生活就是一首诗.

po·e·sy [ˈpəuizi, ˈpəuezi] *n.* ①〔古、诗〕作诗(法);诗歌,韵文. ②诗才.

po·et [ˈpəuit, ˈpəuet] *n.* 诗人;诗人一样的人,空想家. *a minor* ~ 小诗人. ~ **laureate** 〔英〕桂冠诗人. **Poets Corner** ①诗人区〔伦敦 Westminster Abbey 的南隅,有英国大诗人坟墓和纪念碑〕. ②〔p- corner〕〔美谑〕厕所. ③〔谑〕(报纸上的)诗歌栏. **~'s narcissus**【植】口红水仙.

poet. = ①poetical. ②poetry.

po·et·as·ter [pəuiˈtæstə, pəue-] *n.* 劣等诗人;自封的诗人.

po·et·ess [pəuˈitis] *n.* 女诗人.

po·et·ic, -i·cal [pəuˈetik(əl)] *a.* 诗的,韵文的;有诗意的;诗人(一样)的. ★ poetic 主指内容、本质方面; poetical 主指形式方面. *poetical works* 诗集. *poetic genius [faculty]* 诗才. *a poetical person* 有诗人风度的人. *poetic justice* 劝善惩恶;理想的赏罚. *poetic license* 诗的破格. — *n.* = poetics. **-i·cal·ly** *ad.*

po·et·i·cize [pəuˈetisaiz] *v.* = poetize.

po·et·ics [pəuˈetiks] *n.* ①诗法,诗学,诗论. ②〔the P-〕亚里士多德 (Aristotle) 写的«诗论».

po·et·ize [ˈpəuitaiz, ˈpəuet-] *vi.* ①作诗. ②用诗赞美. — *vt.* 使成诗;使诗化;有诗意地说.

po·et·ry [ˈpəuitri, ˈpəuetri] *n.* ①诗,诗歌,韵文;诗集. ②作诗(法). ③〔P-〕诗神,缪斯神 (= the Muse). ④诗意,诗情;有诗意的事物. *satiric* ~ 讽刺诗. *epic* ~ 叙事诗. *historical* ~ 史诗. *lyric* ~ 抒情诗. *prose* ~ 散文诗.

POGO = polar orbiting geophysical observatory 极轨道地球物理观测卫星.

po·go [ˈpəugəu] *n.* *(pl.* ~*s)* 弹簧单高跷〔一种运动用具,又叫 ~-stick〕;弹簧单高跷游戏.

po·go·ni·a [pəˈgəuniə, -ˈgəunjə] *n.* ①(美洲的)红朱兰 *(Pogonia ophioglossoides)*. ②红朱兰花.

pog·o·nip [ˈpɔgənip] *n.*【气】冻雾.

pog·rom [ˈpɔgrəm] *n.* 〔Russ.〕(有组织的)大屠杀;集体迫害〔尤指帝俄时代对犹太人的大屠杀〕. — *vt.* 大屠杀;集体迫害. **-ist** *n.* 大屠杀的组织者〔参加者〕.

po·gy [ˈpəugi] *n.* *(pl.* ***-gies****)*【动】步鱼;玫瑰海鲫.

po·i [ˈpəui] *n.* *(pl.* ~*es)* (夏威夷的)芋粉酱.

poign·an·cy [ˈpɔinjənsi, ˈpɔinən-] *n.* ①辛辣; 尖锐,刻薄. ②强烈;深刻.

poign·ant [ˈpɔinənt] *a.* ①尖锐的,强烈的;辛辣的;尖酸刻薄的; 痛快的. ②生动的,(记忆等) 活鲜鲜的. *a* ~ *question* 苛刻的质问. ~ *regret* 深沉的懊悔. ~ *remarks* 尖锐的批评. ~ *sarcasm* 尖酸刻薄的讽刺. ~ *tears* 忍不住的眼泪. **-ly** *ad.*

poi·kil·it·ic [ˌpɔikiˈlitik] *a.*【地】嵌晶结构的,嵌晶状的.

poi·kil·o·ther·mal [pɔiˌkiləuˈθəːml, ˌpɔkələu-] *a.*【动】冷血的 (= poikilothermic). **-ther·mism** *n.* 冷血.

poi·lu [ˈpwɑːluː] *n.* 〔F.〕〔俚〕(法国)兵.

Poin·ca·re [pwɛ̃ːŋkɑːˈrei; F. pwɛ̃kɑre] ①普安卡雷(姓氏). ②**J.H.** ~ 普安卡雷〔1854—1912, 法国数学家〕. ③**Raymond** ~ 朋加莱〔1860—1934, 法国政治家,曾代总统〕.

poin·ci·a·na [ˌpɔinsiˈænə] *n.* ①黄蝴蝶属 *(Poinciana)* 植物. ②凤凰木 (= royal poinciana) 〔一种热带树〕.

poin·set·ti·a [pɔinˈsetiə, -ˈsetə] *n.*【植】一品红 *(Euphorbia pulcherrima)*; 猩猩木;大戟属植物.

point [pɔint] *n.* ①尖头, 尖端; 尖头器具; 〔美〕笔尖; 接种针,雕刻针,编织针;小岬,小地角;【拳击】下巴. ②【几】点;【数】小数点;切点;【语】标点; 句号;【乐】点符;(寒暑表等的)度;程度. ③【赛马】标点; 分数. ④时刻,霎那. ⑤地点;位置;目标,目的. ⑥条款,细目;特点,特征;要点,旨趣,〔美〕要领;论点;(故事、笑话等的)高潮,妙处. ⑦〔*pl.*〕【铁路】轨闸,转轨器,道岔扳子;〔英〕〔*pl.*〕路轨总点;〔美〕站;【海】方位;罗经点;两罗经点间的差度〔1 point = $11\frac{1}{4}$ 度〕;【狩】(猎狗)指示猎获物时的姿势. ⑧【印】点〔活字大小的单位,约一英寸的七十二分之一〕;【商】点,磅音〔物价、股票价格涨落的单位〕. ⑨【军】尖兵;【机】岔尖;【板球】三柱门右方前面的防守人. ⑩〔美〕(大学)学分. ⑪【语音】= diacritical mark. ⑫【乐】短促曲调;军号短调讯号;(弦乐器)弓的顶端,弓尖. *the weakest [best, strongest]* ~ 最大缺〔优〕点. *a* ~ *of contact*【机】接触点;【数】切点. *the eye* ~ 出射点. *a full* ~ 句号. *At this* ~ *he got up.* 这时〔说到这里〕他从床上跳了起来. *There is no* ~ *in doing that.* 那没有做的必要. *What is the* ~ *of getting angry?* 发脾气有什么用处呢? *Cotton has gone down several* ~*s.* 棉花跌了好几档了. *a buck of ten* ~*s* 有十叉角的鹿. ***a*** ~ ***of honour*** 体面攸关的事. ***at all*** ~***s*** 充分, 完全, 彻底; 在各方面 *(be beaten* *at all ~s* 彻底被打垮). ***at swords' ~s*** 敌对状态;剑拔弩张. ***at [on] the ~ of*** 将近[就要]…的时候;接近, 靠近 (*at the ~ of death* 濒死时候. *on the ~ of starting* 正要出发的时候). ***at the ~ of the sword*** 用武力;在武力威胁之下. ***away from the ~*** = off the ~. ***be (up)on the ~ of (... ing)*** 正要…的时候,正打算. ***beat on ~s***【拳击】靠得分打胜. ***beside the ~ = off the ~***. ***carry [gain] one's ~*** 达到目的;说服别人. ***catch the ~ of*** 了解[抓住]…的要点. ***come to a ~*** ①(猎狗)停住向猎物所在方向示意. ②变尖. ***come to the ~*** 到紧要关头,说到要点. ***cut to a ~*** 弄尖,削尖. ***from ~ to ~*** 从一个点到另一个点;〔罕〕逐项;详细. ***get one's ~*** 抓住某人话中要点. ***give ~ to*** 按上一个尖;削尖;增强,强调. ***give ~s to sb. = give sb. ~s*** ①让…占优势;让分给对方;〔口〕强过某人. ②给与有益的劝告. ***give the ~***【劈剑】戳进. ***grow to a ~*** 顶端逐渐尖下去. ***in ~*** 适当的;中肯的;当前的,待解决的 (*a case in ~* 恰当的例子). ***in ~ of*** 说到, 关于;就…而言;…上 (*in ~ of fact* 事实上). ***keep to the ~*** 扣住要点;(祈使)别绕圈子,别离题. ***knotty ~*** 难点,困难的地方. ***lack ~*** 抓不住要点. ***make a ~*** ①(比赛)得一分. ②立论;证明论点. ③照预想一样使受到感动. ④(猎狗)作看见猎获物的姿势. ***make a ~ of = make a ~ that ... = make it a ~*** 主张,强调;重视;决心,必定. ***make one's ~*** 达到目的;【猎】对直跑. ***make the ~ that ...*** 大意好象是说. ***miss the ~*** 抓不着要点;不得要领. ***not to put too fine a ~ on it*** 坦白地说,直截了当地说. ***off the ~*** 离开本题,不切要领. ***~ by ~*** 逐一,一点一点地,详细. ***~ for ~*** 一一,细细,正确地. ***~ of order***【议会】议事规程问题. ***~ of view*** 观点,见地,见解. ***potatoes and ~*** 〔谑〕分享马铃薯;看守大肥猪. ***pull a ~***【理】拉尖. ***score a ~*** 得一分;获得利益[有利地位]. ***see one's ~ = get one's ~. see the ~*** 懂得…的要点. ***stand (up)on ~*** 〔罕〕过分刻板[拘泥]. ***strain [stretch] a ~*** 超出范围;破例;通融,作重大让步;牵强附会. ***the ~ run to [sailed from]***【海】目的[出发]地. ***to the ~*** 露骨;中肯,扼要 (*breif and to the ~* 简明扼要). ***to the ~ of ...*** 达到…的程度. *(a joke)* ***without any ~*** (笑话)平平无奇的. — *vt.* ①削尖(铅笔等);弄尖;给…装上尖头;使尖锐;强调,使增加力量. ②指向;使对准;把…对准;注意;指点(路);(猎狗)站住以头指向(猎获物所在处);指出. ③圈点,给…加句点;给…加元音符号;给…打小数点. ④(泥水工)用泥灰涂抹,嵌填(接缝). — *vi.* ①用手指人. ②暗示,指示,表明,显示 *(at; to)*. ③瞄准;对着;面向. ④有…的倾向 *(toward)*. ⑤(猎狗)站住瞻望猎获物所在处. ⑥【海】张帆抢风开行. ⑦(疮等)起脓头. *It is rude to ~.* 用手指人是不礼貌的. ***~ in*** 用锄掏(粪). ***~ off*** 打标点分开. ***~ out*** 指示,指出,提醒. ***~ over*** 用锄播(土). ***~ up*** 〔美〕强调出…;使显眼. ~ **constable** 〔英〕交通警察. ~ **count**【桥牌】数点子. ~ **duty** (警察)值勤;站岗. ~ **lace** 针锈花边. ~ **rationing** 计点配给制.

point-blank [ˈpɔintblæŋk] *a.* ①(枪)近距离平射的,直射的;水平瞄准的. ②直截了当的,干脆的. *a ~ refusal* 直截了当的拒绝. — *ad.* ①平射,直射. ②直截了当地;立即. *fire ~* 平射. *refuse ~* 断然拒绝. — *n.* 直射(点).

point d'ap•pui [ˈpwɛ̃:ndæˈpwi] *n.* 〔F.〕支点;【军】据点;战线据点;集合点;策源地;〔喻〕论据.

point-de•vice, point-de•vise [ˈpɔint dəvais] *a., ad.* 〔古〕极正确的[地];非常精致的[地].

pointe [pwænt] *n. (pl.* ***pointes*** [pwænt] *n.* 〔F.〕【芭蕾】足尖站立的姿式.

point•ed [ˈpɔintid] *a.* ①尖的, 尖角的;尖锐的. ②严厉的;直截了当的. ③显然的. ④中肯的. ⑤突出的. ~ *architecture* 尖拱式建筑(法). **-ly** *ad.*

Pointe-Noire [pwæntˈnwɑ:] *n.* 黑角〔刚果港市〕.

Point•er [ˈpɔintə] *n.* 〔美〕西点 (West Point) 军官学校学员.

point•er [ˈpɔintə] *n.* ①指示者;指示物;(钟、表的)指针;教鞭;〔口〕线索;暗示;点子. ②能站住用鼻尖指示猎获物所在处的猎狗. ③〔*pl.*〕(the P-)【天】(大熊星座中的)两颗指极星. ④【军】(大炮)瞄准手;(捕鲸船桅头的)鲸位指示器. ⑤【商口】广告索引 (= ~ad). ⑥【铁路】闸柄. ~ **fire**【军】直接瞄准射击.

poin•til•lism [ˈpwæntilizəm] *n.*【美】(法国印象派)点画法. **-til•list** *n.* 点画家.

point•ing [ˈpɔintiŋ] *n.* ①弄尖. ②指示;瞄准. ③标点法;标点. ④(砖缝的) 嵌填,勾缝. ⑤【医】脓头,穿头.

point•less [ˈpɔintlis] *a.* ①〔古〕无尖头的,钝的. ②不对劲儿的;无力的. ③不得要领的; 空洞的;无意义的. ④(比赛) 没有得分的. ⑤【植】无芒的. *a ~ sword* 〔古〕钝剑. *a ~ joke* 索然无味的笑话. **-ly** *ad.* **-ness** *n.*

points•man [ˈpɔintsmən] *n. (pl.* ***-men)*** 〔英〕①【铁路】扳道岔人,扳闸员. ②(交通岗上的)交通警察.

point-to-point [ˈpɔinttəˈpɔint] *a.* ①(赛马等) 越过原野的. ②逐点的. ③【无】定向传送的. *a ~ race* 越野赛跑.

point•y [ˈpɔinti] *a.* ***(-i•er; -i•est)*** ①非常尖的. ②多尖的,全是带尖的.

poise [pɔiz] *vt.* ①使重量相等, 使平衡. ②作(投标枪一样的)姿势;使(头等)保持一定姿势[位置]. ③〔罕〕仔细考虑. ④使悬而不决,踌躇. ⑤(鱼等)静静不动. ***~ oneself on*** 在…上面保持身体的重心以免倒下. — *vi.* 保持平衡;悬着. — *n.* ①平衡. ②歪头姿势. ③安定,平静;沉着;自信. ④犹豫不决,踌躇;虚悬. ⑤法码,秤锤. ⑥【化】泊〔粘度单位〕.

poised [pɔizd] *a.* ①沉着的, 有威严的,有自信心的. ②保持平衡的,摇晃的. ③悬空的,盘旋的. *be ~ on the brink of disaster* 濒于灾难.

poi•son [ˈpɔizn] *n.* ①毒;毒药. ②毒害;弊病;有害的主义〔学说、风气 (等)〕. ③〔俚〕劣酒. ④抑制剂. *slow [cumulative] ~* 慢性毒药. *aerial ~* 瘴气. *What's your ~?* 〔俚〕你喝什么(酒)? ***hate like ~*** 〔口〕痛恨;极端厌恶. — *vt.* ①放毒于;涂毒于;毒害;毒杀;使中毒. ②玷污,伤害,败坏(计划、名誉等). ③阻碍;抑制. ④弄坏(机器等). ***~ one's mind*** 对…发生恶感,毒害某人的思想;使沾染上坏习气. — *vi.* 放毒, 投毒. ~ **fang** (蛇等的)毒牙. ~ **gas**【军】毒气. ~ **gland** 毒腺. ~ **hemlock**【植】毒参;芹叶钩吻. ~ **ivy** = ~**-oak** 栎叶毒漆树. ~**-pen** *a.* 〔俚〕恶意中伤的;匿名写的. ~ **sumac**【植】美国毒漆.

poi•son•er [ˈpɔiznə] *n.* 毒害者,毒杀者;放毒者.

poi•son•ing [ˈpɔizniŋ] *n.* 中毒;毒害;布毒;…毒. *mercury-~* 水银毒. *lead-~* 铅中毒.

poi•son•ous [ˈpɔiznəs] *a.* ①有毒的,有害的. ②有恶意的;恶毒的. ③恶臭的. ④〔口〕不愉快的,讨厌的. *a ~ dose* 中毒量. *a ~ gas bomb* 毒气弹. *a ~ smell* 臭味. *an absolutely ~ horse* 一匹极凶猛的马. **-ly** *ad.*

poi•trine [pwɑˈtrin] *n.* 〔F.〕胸部,胸膛〔尤指妇女丰满的乳房〕.

pok•a•ble [ˈpəukəbl] *a.* ①可以戳的. ②能激励的.

poke[1] [pəuk] *vt.* ①(用手指、棍子等)戳,刺 *(in; up; down)*,戳进. ②伸出(头、指等);把…指向[推向]. ③拨,添(火等). ④激励(马等). ⑤〔美俚〕打,殴. — *vi.* ①戳,刺 *(at)*. ②(头等)伸出;好事,多嘴;探听,打听. ③摸索着走;闲逛. ④【板球】小心慢打. *~ (up) the dying fire* 拨燃快熄的火. ***~ about*** ①〔美〕(在书中等)找查. ②闲荡. ③多查多问. ***~ and pry*** 管闲事,探查消息. ***~ fun at*** 〔口〕开…的玩笑,嘲弄. ***~ into*** 干涉;刺探;挑剔. ***~ one's head*** 向前伸头;向前弯腰. ***~ one's nose into*** 干涉,管…的闲事,插手. — *n.* ①戳,刺;〔美俚〕一拳,一击. ②〔美〕(牛等的)颈轭. ③〔美俚〕懒人;讨厌的家伙. ④(救世军女军官等的)帽子的撑边;有撑

边的女帽〔又叫 ~-bonnet〕. ~**nose**〔美〕爱罗罗唆唆打听人家事情的人.

poke[2] [pəuk] *n.* ①〔古〕= pocket. ②〔主方〕小袋；钱袋；钱包；钱〔尤指个人所有的全部钱钞〕. ③(鱼的)鳔. ***buy a pig in a ~*** 瞎买东西，隔山买牛.

poke[3] [pəuk] *n.* = pokeweed.

poke·ber·ry [ˈpəukˌberi] *n.* *(pl. -ries)*【植】美国商陆(= pokeweed).

pok·er[1] [ˈpəukə] *n.* ①戳火的人；火钳，拨火棍. ②烙画用具. ③〔英俚〕(牛津、剑桥大学的)副校长的权标，(队前)持权标的人. ***as stiff as a ~*** (态度)呆板. ***by the holy ~*** 〔谑〕立誓，一定. — *vt.* 用烙画做(图案). ~ **drawing** 烙画术. ~ **picture**, ~ **work** 烙画.

pok·er[2] [ˈpəukə] *n.* 〔罕、美俚〕妖怪.

pok·er[3] [ˈpəukə] *n.*【纸牌】扑克. ~ **face** 一本正经的面容；面无表情的人. ~**-faced** *a.* 扑克面孔的，脸上没有表情的. ~ **pan**〔美〕能毫无表情地表演戏剧的演员.

poke·root [ˈpəukˌru:t, -ˌrut] *n.* = pokeweed.

poke·weed [ˈpəukˌwi:d] *n.*【植】美国商陆 *(Phytolacca americana)*〔产于北美，其根和果有毒〕.

pok·ey [ˈpəuki] *n.* *(pl. ~, pok·ies) n.* 〔美俚〕监狱.

pok·(e)y [ˈpəuki] *a.* ***(pok·i·er; -i·est)*** ①没有神气的；迟钝的；【生】生长缓慢的. ②(房间、场所等)闷人的，窄小的，肮脏的. ③(工作、职业等)微贱的，无聊的. ④无趣味的.

pol [pɔl] *n.* ①老资格的政客，党派政治老手. ②= politician.

Pol. = Poland; Polish.

pol. = political; politician; politics.

po·lac·ca, pola·cre [pəuˈlækə, -ˈlɑ:kə] *n.* (地中海的)三桅商船.

Po·lack [ˈpəulæk] *n.* ①〔蔑〕波兰血统的人. ②〔古〕波兰人. — *a.* 〔口〕= Polish.

Po·land [ˈpəulənd] *n.* 波兰〔欧洲〕.

po·lar [ˈpəulə] *a.* ①(南、北)极的，地极的；近地极的. ②【物、化】(有)极的；磁极的；有磁性的. ③【几】极线的. ④【化】极化的，离子化的；(多)极性的. ⑤中轴一样的；中心的；(象北极星那样)有指向意义的. ⑥(性格)正相反的. — *n.*【几】极线；极面. ~ **circles** 极圈. ~ **bear** 北极熊，白熊. ~ **beaver**〔俚〕白髯人. ~ **body**【解】极体. ~ **cap**【天】极冠. ~ **curve**【数】配曲线. ~ **distance**【天】极距. ~ **front**【气】极锋.

polari- *comb. f.* 极: *polari*scope.

po·lar·im·e·ter [ˌpəuləˈrimitə] *n.*【物】偏振计，旋光计，极化计.

po·lar·i·me·tric [pəuˌlæriˈmetrik] *a.*【物】测定偏振〔旋光、极化〕的.

po·lar·i·me·try [ˌpəuləˈrimitri] *n.*【物】偏振测定法；旋光测定法；极化测定术.

Po·la·ris [pəuˈlɛəris] *n.*【天】北极星.

po·lar·i·scope [pəuˈlæriskəup] *n.* 偏振光镜，旋光计.

po·lar·i·scop·y [pəuˈlæriskəupi] *n.* = polarimetry.

po·lar·i·ty [pəuˈlæriti] *n.* ①【物】(分)极性，磁性引力；(光的)偏极；极体；【数】配极(变换)；【生】(茎与根的)反向性，极性. ②(性格的)正反对. ③(思想、感情等的)归向，倾向. *a ~ inverting amplifier* 倒像放大器.

po·lar·i·za·tion [ˌpəuləraiˈzeiʃən] *n.* ①两级分化. ②【物、天】极化；极化强度. ③【物】偏振(化). *a ~ cell* 极化电池. *atomic ~* 原子极化强度. *orientation ~* 定向极化. *a ~ microscope* 偏振显微镜.

po·lar·ize, po·lar·ise [ˈpəuləraiz] *vt.* ①给与…极性，使归极. ②使(光)偏振. ③使(语言等)有特殊意义〔用途〕. ④使两极分化. *a ~d bell* 极化电铃. *~d light* 偏振. *a polarizing circuit* — *vi.* (物质)偏振；【电】(金属等)极化；两极分化；赋极电路. **-iz·abil·i·ty** [ˌpəuləˌraizəˈbiliti] *n.* **-iz·able** *a.*

po·lar·iz·er [ˈpəuləraizə] *n.*【物】起偏(振)镜，起偏光镜.

po·lar·o·gram [pəuˈlærəgræm] *n.* 极谱.

po·lar·o·graph [pəuˈlærəgrɑ:f] *n.*【物】极谱记录器，极谱仪旋光计.

po·lar·og·ra·phy [ˌpəuləˈrɔgrəfi] *n.*【化】极谱法，极谱学. **-graph·ic, -graph·i·cal·ly** *ad.*

po·lar·oid [ˈpəulərɔid] *n.*【物】(人造)偏振片〔防止闪光用〕.

po·lar·on [ˈpəulərɔn] *n.*【物】极化子.

pol·der [ˈpəuldə] *n.* 堤围泽地，垸，围圩.

pole[1] [pəul] *n.* ①棒，杆，竿〔通常为十英尺以上圆杆〕. ②旗竿；钓竿；【运】(撑竿跳的)竿；桅杆；电线杆；(车的)辕杆；理发师的招牌杆. ③杆〔长度名，等于五码半〕. *a tent ~* 帐篷的中心支柱. *a punt ~* (撑船的)篙子. ***climb up the greasy ~*** 处理困难工作. ***under [with] (bare) ~s***【海】不张帆. ***up the ~***〔俚〕①微狂的. ②进退两难. — *vt.* ①用棒支持；用棒推；用篙撑；架(豆蔓等). ②用(竹)杆挑. — *vi.* 用篙撑船. ~ **jumping [vault]** 撑竿跳.

pole[2] [pəul] *n.* ①【天、地】极；极地；北极星；【物】极点，顶点. ②【电】电极；磁极. ③两极端〔指性格、学说等〕. ④天空. *the North [South] ~* 北〔南〕极. *the positive [negative] ~* 阳〔阴〕极. ***be ~s asunder.*** 截然相反，南辕北辙. (*Our opinions are wide as the ~s asunder* 我们的意见截然相反). ***from ~ to ~*** 全世界 (*English is spoken from ~ to ~.* 英语在世界各国都通用). ~ **piece** 极靴，磁极片. ~ **star**【天】北极星；指导人；指导原理；有吸引力的中心；目标. ~**ward(s)** *ad.* 向极.

Pole [pəul] *n.* 波兰人.

pole·ax(e) [ˈpəulæks] *n.*【史】战斧；钺；【海】短把斧；杀牛斧. — *vt.* 拿斧砍倒.

po·leis [ˈpəuleis] polis 的复数.

pole·cat [ˈpəulkæt] *n.* *(pl. ~(s))* ①【动】鸡貂；臭猫〔鼬类〕. ②〔古〕妓女.

pol. [polit.] econ. = political economy.

po·lem·ic [pɔˈlemik] *n.* ①攻击，驳斥；〔*pl.*〕争论，论战，辩论(术)；〔*pl.*〕(神学上的)论证法. ②争论者，论客. ***~s on paper*** 打笔墨官司. — *a.* 论战的，辩论的；喜欢争论的. *a ~ writer* 爱论战的作者. **-i·cal** *a.* **-ly** *ad.*

po·lem·i·cist [pəˈlemisist] *n.* 争论者，争辩者，善辩论者(= polemist).

po·lem·i·cize [pəuˈlemisaiz] *vi.* = polemize.

pol·e·mist [ˈpɔləmist] *n.* 争论者，善辩论者.

pol·e·mize [ˈpɔlimaiz] *vi.* 争论，辩驳，笔战.

po·len·ta [pəuˈlentə] *n.* 〔It.〕大麦粥；栗粉粥；玉米粥.

pol·er [ˈpəulə] *n.* ①辕马 (= pole horse). ②以竿撑船的人.

po·lice [pəˈli:s] *n.* ①警察；〔集合词〕警务人员. ②治安，公安. ③【火箭】校正，修正. ④〔美军〕(兵营内的)打扫，整顿；内务值勤；内务值勤人员. *ten ~* = ten policemen 十名警察. *the people's ~* 人民警察. *the harbour [marine] ~* 水上警察. *the metropolitan ~ department* 公安厅. *the ~ office* 〔英〕警察局. *a ~ officer* 警官. *the military ~* 〔美〕宪兵队. *mounted ~* 骑巡队. *a ~ agent* (法国等的)警察. *the ~ station* 警察(分)局. *a ~ box [stand]* (警察)岗亭. *a ~ inspector* 巡官. *The ~ are on his track.* 警察正在搜捕他. —*vt.* ①在…实施警察制度；在…设置警察；维持…的秩序. ②统治，管辖. ③【火箭】校正，修正. ④【美军】打扫，整顿. ~ **constable**〔英〕普通警员. ~ **court** 违警罪法庭. ~ **dog** 警犬. ~ **force**〔集合词〕警察(力量). ~ **justice**, ~ **magistrate** 违警罪法庭法官. ~**man** ①警察；【矿山】看守矿井的人. ②【化】淀帚. ~ **offence** 违警罪. ~ **post** 派出所. ~ **state** 警察国家. ~ **trap** (管制车速的)岗哨. **-woman** 女警察.

pol·i·clin·ic [ˌpɔliˈklinik] *n.* (医院的)门诊部；(有教授

作顾问的)学生私人诊所.

pol·i·cy[1] [ˈpɔlisi] *n.* ①政策,政纲;方针,方向;方法. ②策略;权谋;智慧;精明的行为. ③【军】政治,行政. ④〔Scot.〕〔常 *pl.*〕别墅的附属庭园. *a domestic* ~ 国内政策,内政方针. *a foreign* ~ 对外[外交]政策. *non-alignment* ~ 不结盟政策. ~*ies of war and aggression* 侵略政策和战争政策. *a cold war* ~ 冷战政策. *a* ~ *of strength* 实力政策. *the Party's general and specific* ~ 党的方针政策. *Honesty is the best* ~. 正直是最明智的. ***for reasons of*** ~ 出于策略上的原因. ~ **maker** 制订政策的人.

pol·i·cy[2] [ˈpɔlisi] *n.* ①保险单. ②〔美〕(由抽签决定的)彩票. *a life [fire]* ~ 人寿[火灾]保险单. *a floating* ~ 总保(险)单. *a valued* ~ 确定保险单. *an open* ~ 预定保险单. ***play*** ~〔美〕打彩,抽彩. ***take out a*** ~ ***on one's life*** 加入人寿保险. ~ **racket**〔美〕彩票 (= numbers pool). ~ **shop**〔美〕抽彩的商店[场所]. ~ **holder** 保险客户.

pol·ing [ˈpəuliŋ] *n.* ①【冶】还原,吹气. ②【电】立杆,架线路.

po·li·o [ˈpəuliəu] *n.* 脊髓灰质炎 = poliomyelitis.

pol·i·o·my·e·li·tis [ˈpɔliəumaiiˈlaitis] *n.* 脊髓灰质炎,小儿麻痹症. *acute anterior* ~ 小儿麻痹.

po·lis [ˈpəulis, ˈpɔlis] *n.* *(pl.* ***po·leis*** [-leis, -eis]*)*(古希腊的)城邦.

-polis *suf.* 都市: metro*polis*.

Po·lish [ˈpəuliʃ] *a., n.* 波兰(人)的;波兰语(的).

pol·ish [ˈpɔliʃ] *vt.* ①磨光,擦亮,抛光. ②使简练,使醇化,使优美;推敲;润饰(文章等) *(up)*. ~ *one's boots (up)* 擦亮皮鞋. *a* ~*ing mill* 碾米厂. — *vi.* ①发亮. ②变优美. ***be*** ~***ed***〔美俚〕喝醉. ~ ***away [off, out]*** 擦去. ~ ***off*** 很快做好(吃完等);〔口〕很快杀掉. ~ ***the mug***〔美俚〕洗脸. ~ ***up*** 完成;〔口〕改善,改进. — *n.* ①磨擦;光泽. ②擦亮粉,上光剂,亮油,亮漆. ③优美;修养;推敲. *give it a* ~ 把它擦一擦. *Many of his poems lack* ~. 他的诗作有许多是不够精练的. *shoe [boot]* ~ 鞋油.

pol·ished [ˈpɔliʃt] *a.* ①擦亮的,光亮的,磨光的. ②优美的;精练的. ~ *rice* 白米.

pol·ish·er [ˈpɔliʃə] *n.* 磨光工人;磨光器.

polit. = political; politics.

Po·lit·bu·ro [pəˈlitbjuərəu] *n.* ①〔常作 P-〕(共产党)政治局(= political bureau). ②(西方国家类似政治局的)决策控制机构.

po·lite [pəˈlait] *a.* *(-lit·er; -est)* ①有礼貌的;殷勤的,恳切的;斯文的;文雅的;有教养的. ②(文章等)推敲过的,精练的,优美的. ~ *society* 讲究礼貌的场合[交际场所];上流社会. *the* ~ *thing* 规矩礼貌. ~ *letters [literature]* 纯文学. ***do the*** ~〔口〕硬装文雅,竭力做出彬彬有礼的样子. ***say sth.*** ~ ***about*** 恭维. **-ly** *ad.* **-ness** *n.*

pol·i·tesse [ˌpɔliˈtes; F. pɔliˈtɛs] *n.*〔F.〕文雅,斯文;彬彬有礼.

pol·i·tic [ˈpɔlitik] *a.* ①精明的;机敏的,狡猾的;有手腕的. ②(话等)巧妙的,适当的. ③〔古〕政治上的,国家的. *a* ~ *move* 适当的处置. *a body* ~〔罕〕国家. **-ly** *ad.*

po·lit·i·cal [pəˈlitikəl] *a.* ①政治(上)的;政策(上)的;政治学(上)的. ②行政上的;政党的,有政治组织的. *a* ~ *writer* 政论作家;政治记者. *a* ~ *view* 政治见解. *a* ~ *offense [prisoner]* 政治犯[犯人]. ~ *rights* 政权. *a* ~ *party* 政党. *a* ~ *meeting* 政治集会. ~ **economy** 政治经济学. ~ **expedients** 权谋. ~ **science** 政治学. **-ly** *ad.* ①政治上;政策上. ②精明,巧妙.

po·lit·i·cal·ize [pəˈlitiklaiz] *vt.* 使政治化,使具有政治性,使带政治色彩. **-za·tion** *n.*

pol·i·ti·cian [ˌpɔliˈtiʃən] *n.* ①政治家. ②〔蔑〕政客;〔美〕政治贩. *crafty* ~*s* 阴谋家.

po·lit·i·cize [pəˈlitisaiz] *vi.* 从事政治活动;谈论政治. — *vt.* 使政治化;从政治上处理.

pol·i·tick [ˈpɔlitik] *vi.* 进行政治活动;谈论政治. **-er** *n.* 进行政治活动的人.

pol·i·tick·ing [ˈpɔlitikiŋ] *n.* 政治活动〔尤指竞选和拉选票的活动〕.

po·lit·i·co [pəˈlitikəu] *n.* *(pl.* ***-(e)s****)* 政客;专搞党派政治的人.

po·lit·i·co- *comb. f.* 政治…上的: *politico*geographical 政治地理上的.

pol·i·tics [ˈpɔlitiks] *n.* ①〔作单数用〕政治学;政治. ②〔作复数用〕政界;行政工作;政治运动;战略,政策;政见;政治关系;政治斗争;利害,动机,目的. ③〔作单数用〕经营,管理. ④〔作复数用〕政纲,政见. *lunar* ~ 不切实际的问题. *power* ~ 强权政治. *engaged in* ~ 从事政治活动. *It is not practical* ~. 这没有再谈论的价值. *play* ~ 要阴谋诡计,为自己打算. *with [put]* ~ *in command* 政治领先.

Po·l(l)itt [ˈpɔlit] *n.* 波利特〔姓氏〕.

pol·i·ty [ˈpɔliti] *n.* ①政体,国体. ②国家,政府;行政;制度. *civil* ~ 国家行政机构[组织].

Polk [pəuk] *n.* 波克〔姓氏〕.

polk [pɔlk] *vi.*〔口〕跳波尔卡舞.

pol·ka [ˈpɔlkə] *n.* ①(波希米亚的)波尔卡舞(曲). ②女人紧身短上衣. — *vi.* 跳波尔卡舞. ~ **dot** (衣料上的)圆点花纹.

poll[1] [pəul] *n.* ①〔古、谑〕脑袋;人,人数. ②纳税人[选举人]名册. ③投票,投票数;〔*pl.*〕〔美〕投票处. ④人头税. ⑤〔P-〕〔美〕民意测验所. ⑥(锤等的)宽平端. *a gray [snow-white]* ~ 白头. *a heavy [light, poor]* ~ 高[低]得票率. *How stands the* ~? 投票情形怎样? ***at the head of the*** ~ 得票最多. ***go to the*** ~ 到投票处去投票. ***take a*** ~ 投票表决. — *vt.* ①把(选民)登记入名册. ②(候选人)得(票);查(票);投(票). ③作…的民意调查. ④剪短(头发);锯下(家畜的角);〔古〕剪(毛,枝,草等). — *vi.* 投票. *-ing place [booth]* 投票所. ~ **book** 选举人名册. ~ **tax** 人头税.

poll[2] [pɔl] *n.*〔俚〕剑桥 *(Cambridge)* 大学普通毕业生〔又作 ~*man*〕. *go out in the P-* 拿到普通学位. *a* ~ *degree* 普通学位.

poll[3] [pəul] *a.* 【法】当事人一方作成的. *a deed* ~ 单独盖章证书.

Poll [pɔl] *n.* ①〔称呼名〕鹦鹉. ②〔口〕= Mary. ③〔p-〕〔口〕妓女. ~ **parrot** 鹦鹉;瞎说白扯的人.

poll·a·ble [ˈpəuləbl] *a.* 可以修剪的,可以剪去头[角]的;可以投票的.

pol·lack [ˈpɔlək] *n.* 【鱼】绿鳕.

pol·lard [ˈpɔləd] *n.* ①截去了梢的树;脱角鹿[牛],无角兽. ②糠,含有少许面粉的糠. — *vt.* 剪去…的树梢.

polled [pəuld] *a.* 剪去了树梢的;剪了毛[发]的;秃头的;锯了角的;(牛等)无角(品种)的. *the P- Angus* = Aberdeen Angus.

poll·ee [pəuˈliː] *n.*〔美〕受民意测验的人.

pol·len [ˈpɔlin] *n.* ①【植】花粉. ②【虫】粉面. — *vt.* 授粉给;传粉给;用花粉掩盖.

pol·len·o·sis, pol·li·no·sis [ˌpɔliˈnəusis] *n.* 枯草热 (= hay fever).

pol·lex [ˈpɔliks] *n.* *(pl.* ***pol·li·ces*** [-əˈsiːz]*)*【解】拇指. **pol·li·cal** [-ikl] *a.*

pol·li·nate [ˈpɔlineit] *vt.* 【植】给…授粉;传花粉给.

pol·li·na·tion [ˌpɔliˈneiʃən] *n.* 【植】传粉,授粉(作用). *artificial* ~ 人工授粉.

pol·li·nif·er·ous [ˌpɔliˈnifərəs] *a.* 【植】①有花粉的,生花粉的. ②适于传粉的.

pol·lin·i·um [pəˈliniəm] *n.* *(pl.* ***-i·a*** [-ə]*)*【植】花粉块.

pol·li·nize [ˈpɔlinaiz] *vt.* *(-niz·ed; -niz·ing)* =

pollinate. **-r** *n.*

pol·li·no·sis [ˌpɔliˈnəusis] *n.* 【医】花粉病,枯草热.

pol·li·wig, pol·li·wog [ˈpɔliwig, -wɔg] *n.* 〔口〕= tadpole.

Pol·lock [ˈpɔlək] *n.* 波洛克〔姓氏〕.

pol·lock [ˈpɔlək] *n.* = pollack.

pol·loi [ˈpɔlɔi] *n., pl.* 〔Gr.〕人民,民众. ***Hoi ~ = the ~*** 一般民众,群众.

poll·ster [ˈpəulstə] *n.* 〔美〕民意测验所;民意测验录编者;选举预测人.

pol·lu·tant [pəˈluːtənt] *n.* 污染物〔尤指放入水中和空气中的有害的化学物质〕.

pol·lute [pəˈluːt, -ˈljuːt] *vt.* ①弄脏,污染;玷污,亵渎. ②败坏(品性),使堕落.

pol·lu·tion [pəˈluːʃən, -ˈljuː-] *n.* ①污染(作用). ②腐败,堕落. *nocturnal ~* 【医】梦遗(精). **~ disease** 污染病.

Pol·lux [ˈpɔləks] *n.* 【天】北河三(双子座β星).

Pol·ly[1] [ˈpɔli] *n.* = poll parrot.

Pol·ly[2] [ˈpɔli] *n.* 波莉〔女子名, Mary 的昵称〕.

Pol·ly·an·na [ˌpɔliˈænə] *n.* 〔有时亦作 p-〕遇事过分乐观的人〔源出美国作家 Eleanor Porter 所作小说〕.

pol·ly·wog [ˈpɔliwɔg] *n.* = polliwog.

po·lo [ˈpəuləu] *n.* ①马球. ②水球 (= wate ~). **~ shirt** (开领短袖式)马球衬衫. **~ stick** 马球棍. **-ist** *n.* 马球〔水球〕运动员.

Po·lo [ˈpəuləu], **Marco** 马哥孛罗〔1254?—1324, 意大利旅行家〕.

pol·o·naise [ˌpɔləˈneiz] *n.* ①波罗奈〔波兰慢步舞(曲)〕. ②波兰连衫裙;四股装饰花线.

po·lo·ni·um [pəˈləuniəm] *n.* 【化】钋.

po·lo·ny [pəˈləuni] *n.* 半熟干香肠.

pol. sci. = political science.

pol·ter·geist [ˈpɔltəgaist] *n.* 〔G.〕*(pl. ~er* [-ə]*)* (迷信者认为造成各种噪音的)吵闹鬼.

polt·foot [ˈpəultfut] *n., a.* 弯脚(的).

pol·troon [pɔlˈtruːn] *n.* 胆小鬼. — *a.* 胆子小的.

pol·troon·er·y [pɔlˈtruːnəri] *n.* 怯懦.

poly- *comb. f.* 多,复;聚: *poly*gamy; *poly*genesis.

pol·y·a·del·phous [ˌpɔliəˈdelfəs] *a.* 【植】多体雄蕊的.

pol·y·am·ide [ˌpɔliˈæmaid] *n.* 【化】聚酰胺.

pol·y·an·drous [ˌpɔliˈændrəs] *a.* ①一妻多夫的. ②【植】具多种雄蕊的;【动】一雌多雄的.

pol·y·an·dry [ˈpɔliændri, pɔliˈæn-] *n.* ①一妻多夫制. ②【动】多雄,一雌多雄(配合);【植】多雄蕊. **-drist** *n.* 多夫女人. **-drous** *a.*

pol·y·an·thus [ˌpɔliˈænθəs] *n.* 【植】①西樱草. ②多花水仙.

pol·y·ar·ch·y [ˈpɔliɑːki] *n.* 多头政治 *(opp.* oligarchy*)*.

pol·y·a·tom·ic [ˌpɔliəˈtɔmik] *a.* 【化】多原子的,多元的,多碱的,多酸的.

pol·y·au·tog·ra·phy [ˌpɔliɔːˈtɔgrəfi] *n.* 〔古〕石印术.

pol·y·bas·ic [ˌpɔliˈbeisik] *a.* 【化】多碱(价)的;多元的;多代的.

pol·y·bas·ite [ˌpɔliˈbeisait] *n.* 硫锑铜银矿.

pol·y·car·bon·ate resin [ˌpɔliˈkɑːbənit] 聚碳酸脂.

pol·y·car·pel·lar·y [ˌpɔliˈkɑːpiˌlɛəri] *a.* 【植】多心皮的.

pol·y·car·pic [ˌpɔliˈkɑːpik] *a.* 【植】①结多次果的. ②多心皮的 (= polycarpous). **-car·py** [-pi] *n.*

pol·y·cen·trism [ˌpɔliˈsentrizm] *n.* 多中心主义. **-cen·tric** *a.* **-cen·trist** *a., n.* 主张多中心主义的(人).

pol·y·chaete [ˈpɔlikiːt] *n.* 【动】多毛纲 *(polychaeta)* 动物. **-chae·tous** *a.*

pol·y·chlo·ro·prene [ˌpɔliˈklɔ(ː)rəpiːn] *n.* 【化】聚氯丁烯;氯丁橡胶.

pol·y·chres·tic [ˌpɔliˈkrestik] *a.* (药品等)有多种用途的;多能的;(话)有多种意义的.

pol·y·chro·mate [ˌpɔliˈkrəumit] *n.* 【化】多色物质.

pol·y·chro·mat·ic [ˌpɔlikrəuˈmætik] *a.* 多色的;【矿】变色的.

pol·y·chrome [ˈpɔlikrəum] *a.* 多色的;彩饰的;彩印的,多色印刷的. — *n.* ①彩色画;彩像;多色,色彩配合. ②【药】七叶灵.

pol·y·chro·my [ˈpɔlikrəumi] *n.* (雕刻、建筑等的)彩饰;彩画法.

pol·y·clin·ic [ˌpɔliˈklinik] *n.* 综合医院.

pol·y·cot·y·le·don [ˌpɔliˌkɔtəˈliːdən] *n.* 【植】多子叶植物. **-don·ous** *a.*

pol·y·cy·clic [ˌpɔliˈsaiklik, -ˈsiklik] *a.* ①【生】多轮的. ②【化】多环的.

pol·y·cy·the·mi·a [ˌpɔlisaiˈθiːmiə] *n.* 【医】红血球增多(症).

pol·y·dac·tyl [ˌpɔliˈdæktl] *a.* 多指(趾)的〔畸形的〕. — *n.* 多指的人;多趾动物. **-tyl·ism, -ty·ly** *n.* **-tyl·ous** *a.*

pol·y·dip·si·a [ˌpɔliˈdipsiə] 【医】烦渴.

pol·y·dy·mite [pəˈlidimait] *n.* 【矿】辉镍矿.

pol·y·em·bry·o·ny [ˌpɔliˈembriəni] *n.* 【医】多胚,一卵多胎.

pol·y·ene [ˈpɔliiːn] *n.* 【化】聚烯,多烯〔烃〕. **-e·nic** [-ˈiːnik] *a.*

pol·y·es·ter [ˌpɔliˈestə] *n.* 聚酯. **~** *fibres* 聚酯纤维.

pol·y·es·ter·i·fi·ca·tion [ˈpɔliesˌterifiˈkeiʃən] *n.* 【化】聚酯;聚酯化(作用).

pol·y·eth·y·lene [ˌpɔliˈeθiliːn] *n.* 【化】聚乙烯.

pol·y·foam [ˈpɔlifəum] *n.* 泡沫塑料.

pol·y·flu·or·tetra·eth·y·lene [ˈpɔlifluəˌtetrəˈeθiliːn] *n.* 【化】聚四氟乙烯.

po·lyg·a·la [pəˈligələ] *n.* 远志属植物 (= milkwort).

po·lyg·a·mist [pəˈligəmist] *n.* 多配偶论者〔尤指一夫多妻主义者〕,多配偶的人.

po·lyg·amize [pəˈligəmaiz] *vi.* 实行多配偶制.

po·lyg·a·mous [pəˈligəməs] *a.* ①多配偶的;一夫多妻的;一妻多夫的. ②【动】分配性的,一雄多雌的. ③【植】雌雄同株的;杂性的.

po·lyg·a·my [pəˈligəmi] *n.* ①多婚(制);多配偶;一夫多妻;一妻多夫. ②【植】雌雄同株;杂性式. ③【动】多配性,一雄多雌.

pol·y·gene [ˈpɔlidʒiːn] *n.* 【生】多基因. **-gen·ic** [-ˈdʒenik] *a.*

pol·y·genes [ˈpɔlidʒiːnz] *n. pl.* 【遗】多对因子,多基因 (= multiple factors). **-gen·ic** [-ˈdʒenik] *a.*

pol·y·gen·e·sis [ˌpɔliˈdʒenisis] *n.* ①【生】多元发生说. ②有性生殖.

po·lyg·en·y [pəˈlidʒini] *n.* (人种起源的)多源发生. **-gen·ist** *n.* 多元发生说者.

pol·y·glot [ˈpɔliglɔt] *a.* ①数国语言的;用数国语言写的;多种语言混合组成的. ②讲〔懂〕数国语言的. — *n.* ①用数国语言写的书;〔特指〕数国语言对译的圣经. ②会讲数国语言的人.

pol·y·glot·tal, pol·y·glot·tic, pol·y·glot·tous [ˌpɔliˈglɔtl, -tik, -təs] *a.* ①用数国语言写的. ②会讲好几国话的.

pol·y·glot·tism [ˌpɔliˈglɔtizəm] *n.* 数种文字的使用;通晓数种语言.

pol·y·gon [ˈpɔligən] *n.* 【几】多边形,多角形. *a regular ~* 正多边形. **-lyg·o·nal** [ˈpəligənl] *a.* 多边多角形的(地面龟裂).

po·lyg·o·num [pəˈligənəm] *n.* 【植】蓼属 *(Polygonum)* 植物;蓼.

pol·y·graph [ˈpɔligrɑːf] *n.* ①复写器. ②多种波动描记器;测谎器. ③多产作家;论集,著作集. **-ic, -i·cal** *a.*

po·lyg·y·nous [pəˈlidʒinəs] *a.* ①多雌的,一夫多妻的. ②【植】多雌蕊(植物)的;多花柱的.

po·lyg·y·ny [pəˈlidʒini] *n.* 一夫多妻;【植】杂性式;【动】多雌,一雄多雌.
pol·y·hed·ron [ˌpɔliˈhedrən] *n.* *(pl.* ***-dra*** [-drə], *~s)* 【几】多面体;【拓】可剖分空间. **-hed·ral** *a.*
pol·y·his·tor [ˌpɔliˈhistə] *n.* 博学者,博识者,硕学.
pol·y·hy·dric [ˌpɔliˈhaidrik] *a.*【化】多羟(基)的.
pol·y·hy·drox·y [ˌpɔliˈhaidrɔksi] *n.*【化】多羟(基).
pol·y·i·so·prene [ˌpɔliˈaisəuˌpriːn] *n.*【化】聚异戊二烯.
pol·y·math [ˈpɔlimæθ] *n.* 学识渊博的人. **-ic** *a.*
pol·y·mer [ˈpɔlimə] *n.*【化】聚合体,聚合物,多聚物. *high molecular ~s* 高聚物,高分子聚合物. **-ic** *a.*
pol·y·mer·ase [ˈpɔliməreis] *n.*【生化】聚合酶.
pol·y·me·ride [pəˈliməraid] *n.* = polymer.
pol·ym·er·ism [pəˈlimərizəm] *n.*【化】聚合(性),聚合(现象).
pol·y·mer·ize [ˈpɔliməraiz] *vt., vi.*【化】(使)聚合,(使)成同式异量. **-za·tion** *n.* 聚合(作用),聚合度.
po·lym·er·ous [pəˈlimərəs] *a.*【植】多基数的.
pol·y·me·thy·lene [ˌpɔliˈmeθiliːn]【化】聚甲撑,聚亚甲基.
pol·y·morph [ˈpɔlimɔːf] *n.* 多形体;多晶型物.
pol·y·mor·phic [ˌpɔliˈmɔːfik] *a.* = polymorphous.
pol·y·mor·phism [ˌpɔliˈmɔːfizəm] *n.* ①多形性(现象). ②【化】(同质)多晶型(现象);【生】多态性(现象).
pol·y·mor·pho·nu·cle·ar [ˌpɔliˌmɔːfəˈnuːkliə] *a.* 多形核的.
pol·y·mor·phous [ˌpɔliˈmɔːfəs] *a.* ①多形的. ②【化】多晶型的.
pol·y·myx·in [ˌpɔliˈmiksin] *n.*【药】多粘菌素.
Pol·y·ne·sia [ˌpɔliˈniːzjə] *n.* 波利尼西亚〔中太平洋的岛群〕.
Pol·y·ne·si·an [ˌpɔliˈniːziən, -zjən] *a.* ①波利尼西亚(人)的. ②〔p-〕多岛的. — *n.* 波利尼西亚人.
po·lyn·i·a [pəˈliniə] *n.* (北冰洋)冰原中的水圈.
pol·y·no·mi·al [ˌpɔliˈnəumiəl, -mjəl] *a.* ①【动、植】多词学名的. ②【数】多项式的. — *n.* ①【动、植】多词学名. ②【数】多项式. *a ~ expression* 多项式.
pol·y·nu·cle·ar [ˌpɔliˈnjuːkliə, -ˈnuː-] *a.* 多核的 (= polynucleate).
po·lyn·ya [pəˈlinjə, ˈpɔlinjɑː] *n.*【地】冰前沼;冰隙,冰穴〔海水面未结冰处〕.
pol·yp [ˈpɔlip] *n.* ①(水螅型)珊瑚虫;水生小动物. ②【医】鼻息肉;(子宫)蒂肉.
pol·y·par·y [ˌpɔliˈpɛəri] *n.* *(pl.* ***-par·ies)*** (水螅型)珊瑚虫(群栖而成的)岩 (= polyparium).
pol·y·pep·tide [ˌpɔliˈpeptaid] *n.*【化】多肽,缩多氨酸.
pol·y·pet·al·ous [ˌpɔliˈpetələs] *a.*【植】离瓣的.
pol·y·pha·gi·a [ˌpɔliˈfeidʒiə] *n.* ①【医】多食症;贪食. ②【动】杂食性. **-lyph·a·gous** *a.*
pol·y·phase [ˈpɔlifeiz] *a.*【电】多相的. *a ~ dynamo [motor]* 多相发电[电动]机.
Pol·y·phe·mus [ˌpɔliˈfiːməs] *n.*【希神】波吕斐摩斯〔独眼巨人〕.
pol·y·phone [ˈpɔlifəun] *n.* ①多音字母[符号]〔如 lead 中的 ea 既读 [iː] 又读 [e]〕. ②【乐】百音盒.
pol·y·phon·ic, po·lyph·o·nous [ˌpɔliˈfɔnik, pəˈlifənəs] *a.* ①多音的;(标音字)可以发多种音的. ②【乐】复音的;复调的;对位(法)的.
po·lyph·o·ny [pəˈlifəni] *n.* ①多音【语】(一个字母[符号]的)多种发音. ②【乐】复调音乐;对位法. **-pho·nist** [ˈpɔlifəunist] *n.*【乐】复调乐曲作者;口技演员.
pol·y·phy·let·ic [ˌpɔlifaiˈletik] *a.*【生】多源的. **-i·cal·ly** *ad.*
pol·yp·ide, pol·yp·ite [ˈpɔlipaid;-pait] *n.* ①【动】个虫. ②【动】水螅型珊瑚虫;息肉 (= polyp).
pol·y·ploid [ˈpɔliplɔid] *n.*【生】多倍体. — *a.* 多倍体的.
pol·y·pod [ˈpɔlipɔd] *a.*【动】多足(类)的. — *n.* 多足类动物.
Pol·y·po·di·um [ˌpɔliˈpəudiəm, -djəm] *n.*【植】水龙骨属.
pol·y·po·dy [ˈpɔlipəudi] *n.*【植】水龙骨.
pol·y·poid, pol·yp·oi·dal [ˈpɔlipɔid, ˌpɔliˈpɔidəl] *a.*【动】螅形的;【医】息肉[蒂肉]样的.
pol·y·pous [ˈpɔlipəs] *a.* = polypoid.
pol·y·pro·pyl·ene [ˌpɔliˈprəupiliːn] *n.*【化】聚丙二醇酯,聚丙烯.
pol·yp·tych [ˈpɔliptik] *n.* 四联画[雕刻]屏;多联画[雕刻]屏.
pol·y·pus [ˈpɔlipəs] *n.* *(pl.* ***-pi*** [-pai]*)* ①【动】水螅体. ②【医】(鼻子、子宫等的)息肉,蒂肉.
pol·y·rhythm [ˈpɔliˌriðm] *n.*【乐】复合节奏. **-ic** *a.*
pol·y·sac·cha·ride, pol·y·sac·cha·rose [ˌpɔliˈsækəraid, -əs] *n.*【化】多糖(类).
pol·y·sa·pro·bic [ˌpɔlisəˈprəubik] *a.*【生】多腐生活的〔指原生动物〕.
pol·y·se·my [ˌpɔliˈsiːmi] *n.* 一词多义;有多种解释. **-se·mous** [ˈpɔlisiməs] *a.*
pol·y·some [ˈpɔlisəum] *n.*【生】多体〔指染色体〕.
pol·y·so·mic [ˌpɔliˈsəumik] *a.*【遗】多体生物的.
pol·y·stome [ˈpɔlistəum] *a.*【动】多口的;多口类的. — *n.* 多口类动物.
pol·y·style [ˈpɔlistail] *a.*【建】多柱式的. — *n.* 多柱式;多柱式建筑物.
pol·y·sty·rene [ˌpɔliˈstaiəriːn] *n.*【化】聚苯乙烯.
pol·y·sul·phide, pol·y·sul·fide [ˌpɔliˈsʌlfaid] *n.* 多硫化物.
pol·y·syl·lab·ic, pol·y·syl·lab·i·cal [ˌpɔlisiˈlæbik, -ikəl] *a.* 多音节的;多音节词的.
pol·y·syl·la·ble [ˈpɔliˌsiləbl] *n.* 多音节词.
pol·y·syn·de·ton [ˌpɔliˈsinditən] *n.*【修】连词叠用.
pol·y·syn·the·sis, -y·syn·thet·ism [ˌpɔliˈsinθisis, -sinˈθetizəm] *n.* 多数综合,高级综合;【语】多式综合词.
pol·y·syn·thet·ic [ˌpɔlisinˈθetik] *a.*【语】多式综合的.
pol·y·tech·nic [ˌpɔliˈteknik] *a.* 多种工艺的;多种科技的. *a ~ exhibition* 工艺品展览会. *a ~ school* 科技[工艺]学校. — *n.* 综合性工艺学校[大学].
pol·y·the·ism [ˈpɔliθiːizəm] *n.* 多神教;多神论,多神主义 *(opp.* monotheism*)*. **-the·ist** *n.* 多神论者;多神教徒. **-the·is·tic** *a.*
pol·y·thene [ˈpɔliθiːn] *n.* 聚乙烯 (= polyethylene).
pol·y·to·nal·i·ty [ˌpɔlitəuˈnæliti] *n.*【乐】多调性;多音色.
pol·y·troph·ic [ˌpɔliˈtrɔfik] *a.* 多型发酵的;多滋的;(细菌等)广食性的.
pol·y·tropic [ˌpɔliˈtrɔpik] *a.*【动】多花采蜜的.
pol·y·trop·y [ˈpɔlitrɔpi] *n.*【化】多变性.
pol·y·typ·ic [ˌpɔliˈtipik] *a.* ①【生】多型的. ②多分支的.
pol·y·un·sat·u·rat·ed [ˌpɔliʌnˈsætjureitid] *a.*【化】多未饱和的〔指有一个以上的双键或三键有机化合物的;还能溶解更多溶质的〕.
pol·y·u·re·thane [ˌpɔliˈjuəriθein] *n.*【化】聚氨基甲酸脂;聚氨酯(类).
pol·y·u·ri·a [ˌpɔliˈjuəriə] *n.*【医】多尿症. **-u·ric** *a.*
pol·y·va·lent [ˌpɔliˈveilənt] *a.*【化、生】多价的. — *n.*【生】多价(染色)体. **-lence** *n.*
pol·y·vi·nyl [ˌpɔliˈvainil] *n., a.* 聚乙烯化合物[基](的). *~ alcohol* 聚乙烯醇. *~ chloride* 聚氯乙烯. *~ resin* 聚乙烯(基类)树脂.
pol·y·vi·nyl·i·dene [ˌpɔlivaiˈniliˌdiːn] *a.*【化】聚乙烯叉的.

pol·y·wa·ter [ˌpɔliˈwɔːtə] *n.* 聚合水〔如水溶胶、污染水〕.
pol·y·zo·a [ˌpɔliˈzəuə] *n.* 【动】群栖虫,苔藓虫.
pol·y·zo·an [ˌpɔliˈzəuən] *n.* 外肛亚纲动物 (= ectoproct).
pol·y·zo·ar·i·um [ˌpɔlizəuˈɛəriəm] *n.* *(pl.* **-i·a** [-ə]*)* 【动】①苔藓虫的群体. ②苔藓虫群体的骨胳.
pom[1] [pɔm] *n.* = Pomeranian dog.
pom[2] [pɔm] *n.* 砰的一声. — *vi.* 发砰砰声.
pom·ace [ˈpʌmis] *n.* (榨汁后剩下的)苹果渣;鱼渣;蓖麻油渣.
po·ma·ceous [pəuˈmeiʃəs] *a.* 苹果的,梨果的;似苹果的,似梨果的.
po·made [pəˈmɑːd, pəuˈm-] *n.* 润发香脂[香油]. — *vt.* 用润发香脂[香油]搽.
po·man·der [pəuˈmændə] *n.* 香丸;香盒,香袋.
Po·mard [pɔˈmɑː] *n.* = Pommard.
po·ma·tum [pəˈmeitəm] *n., vt.* = pomade.
pom·be [ˈpɔmbi] *n.* 〔Swahili〕(非洲)小米啤酒.
pome [pəum] *n.* 梨果〔如苹果、李、榅桲〕.
pome·gran·ate [ˈpɔmgrænit] *n.* 【植】石榴(树).
pom·e·lo [ˈpɔmiləu] *n.* 【植】柚,栾,文旦; *(pl.* *~s)* 葡萄柚.
Pom·er·a·ni·an [ˌpɔməˈreinjən] *a.* 旧德国波米兰尼亚 (Pomerania) 州的. — *n.* ①波米兰尼亚人. ②尖嘴,竖耳,有光滑长毛的)波米兰尼亚小狗 (= ~ dog).
pom·fret [ˈpɔmfrit] *n.* 【鱼】黑脊鲳鱼,银鲳;乌鲂.
po·mi·cul·ture [ˈpəumikʌltʃə] *n.* 果树栽培.
po·mif·er·ous [pəuˈmifərəs] *a.* 生长梨果的.
Pom·mard [pɔˈmɑː] *n.* 〔F.〕(法国)波马红葡萄酒.
pom·mel [ˈpʌml] *n.* ①(刀把)头. ②鞍头,马鞍前桥. ③球,球形装饰. — *vt.* (*-ll-*) (用刀把头等)打;用拳头连打. ~ *to a jelly* 痛打.
pom·my, pom·mei [ˈpɔmi] *n.* 〔澳、新西兰俚〕〔贬〕英国人〔尤指新来的英国移民〕. — *a.* 英国的.
po·mol·o·gy [pəuˈmɔlədʒi] *n.* 果树学;果树栽培法.
Po·mo·na [pəˈməunə] *n.* 【罗神】果树女神. ~ **green** 嫩绿色.
pomp [pɔmp] *n.* ①华丽,壮观;盛大的仪式,华丽的行列. ②〔*pl.*〕虚荣;浮华;虚饰;浮夸. *do anything with* ~ 体面漂亮地做.
pom·pa·dour [ˈpɔmpəduə] *n.* ①一种往上梳拢的头发样式. ②低领圆角女背心. ③鸭蛋青色. ④【纺】小花卉纹.
pom·pa·no [ˈpɔmpənəu] *n.* 【鱼】(北美)卵鲹.
Pom·pe·i·an [pɔmˈpiːən] *a.* (古意大利)庞贝城 (Pompeii) 的;〔美〕庞贝(壁画)式的. — *n.* 庞贝人.
Pom·peii [pɔmˈpei] *n.* 庞贝〔被维苏威火山灰埋掉的意大利古都〕.
Pom·pey [ˈpɔmpi] 庞培 (Gnaeus Pompeius Magnus) ~ **the Great** 庞培〔106—48 B. C., 罗马将军,第一次三头政治的首领之一〕.
pom·pi·er [ˈpɔmpjə] *n.* 救火梯. — *a.* 救火员用的.
pom·pom [ˈpɔmpɔm] *n.* 〔俚〕高射机关炮;排发炮.
pom·pon [ˈpɔ̃ːmpɔːŋ] *n.* 〔F.〕①(军帽的)毛球;绒球,丝球〔妇女、儿童鞋帽上装饰〕. ②【植】绒球菊花;(生圆形小花的)大丽花.
pom·pos·i·ty [pɔmˈpɔsiti] *n.* ①豪华,华丽. ②自大;夸大;傲慢;自负;摆架子.
pom·po·so [pɔmˈpəusəu] *a., ad.* 〔It.〕【乐】庄重的[地].
pom·pous [ˈpɔmpəs] *a.* ①豪华的,盛大的,壮丽的. ②浮华的;夸大的;自负的;傲慢的. ~ *prolixity* 喜用长字的习惯;冗长的言词. **-ly** *ad.* **-ness** *n.*
pon. = pontoon.
'pon [pɔn] *prep.* = upon.
Pon·ca [ˈpɔŋkə] *n.* ①*(pl.* *~(s))* ①彭加人〔在内布拉斯加州和俄克拉何马州保留地的美洲印第安人部落〕. ②彭加语. — *a.* 彭加人的.
ponce [pɔns] *n.* 〔俚〕= pimp.
pon·ceau [ˈpɔnsəu] *n.* ①【植】丽春花. ②深红,朱红. ③酸性朱,丽春红〔染料商品名〕.
pon·cho [ˈpɔntʃəu] *n.* *(pl.* *-s)* ①(南美人穿的)穗饰披巾. ②(橡胶)雨衣. ~ **cloth** (宿营用)防雨厚毛毯;军用防雨披风.
pond [pɔnd] *n.* 池塘;鱼塘 *the big [herring]* ~ 〔谑〕北大西洋. — *vt.* 把… 挖成池塘;堵(溪流)水成池 *(back; up)*. — *vi.* (水)蓄积成池. ~ **fish** 塘鱼. ~ **life** 池中小动物〔尤指无脊椎动物〕. ~ **lily** 睡莲. ~ **snail** 【贝】生殖于池中的螺〔尤指膀胱螺属〕. ~ **weed** 【植】眼子菜; 角果藻.
pond·age [ˈpɔndidʒ] *n.* (池塘或水库的)蓄水量.
pon·der [ˈpɔndə] *vi.* 仔细考虑;沉思,默想 *(on; over; upon)*. *With the great seriousness he ~ed upon the problem.* 他极其严肃地仔细考虑问题. — *vt.* 衡量,估量. *He ~ed his words thoroughly.* 他说每一句话都要仔细掂量. **-a·tion** [-reiʃən] *n.*
pon·der·a·bil·i·ty [ˌpɔndərəˈbiliti] *n.* 可秤性;可衡量性;可估量性;可估计性.
pon·der·a·ble [ˈpɔndərəbl] *a.* ①可秤的,有重量的;可衡量的. ②可估量的;可估计的. ③值得一秤的;值得一想的. *a ~ body* 有质体. — *n.* 〔the ~s〕①有考虑价值的事件,预先考虑过的事件. ②有重量的东西.
pon·der·ance, pon·der·an·cy [ˈpɔndərəns, -si] *n.* ①重量;重要. ②严重.
pon·der·o·sa (pine) [ˌpɔndəˈrəusə] ①美国黄松 *(Pinus ponderosa)*. ②美国黄松木.
pon·der·os·i·ty [ˌpɔndəˈrɔsiti] *n.* 重, 沉重; 冗长, 呆板.
pon·der·ous [ˈpɔndərəs] *a.* ①极重的;沉重的;笨重的. ②(谈话、文章等)冗长的, 沉闷的 *(opp.* light, gay*)*. **-os·i·ty** *n.* 沉重;冗长,沉闷. **-ly** *ad.* **-ness** *n.*
po·ne[1] [ˈpəuni] *n.* 【牌戏】①(双人牌戏中)发牌者的对手. ②(桥牌戏等玩法中的)庄家右边签牌的人.
pone[2] [pəun] *n.* 〔美南部〕①(椭圆形)玉米饼 (= corn ~). ②玉米面甜糕.
pong [pɔŋ] *vi., n.* 〔英俚〕发恶臭;名誉臭,坏透,讨厌透 (= stink).
pon·gee [pɔnˈdʒiː] *n.* ①类茧绸的织物. ②茧绸,柞丝绸. ③府绸. ~ **silk** 绢.
pon·gid [ˈpɔndʒid] *n.* 类人猿科动物.
pon·go [ˈpɔŋgəu] *n.* (非洲)类人猿;〔俚〕黑猩猩.
pon·iard [ˈpɔnjəd] *n.* 〔古〕短剑, 匕首. *vi., vt.* 用短剑戳.
Pons [pɔnz] *n.* 庞斯〔姓氏〕.
pons [pɔnz] *(pl.* ***pontes*** [-tiːz]*)* *n.* 〔L.〕桥;【解】脑桥. ~ ***asinorum*** [-ˌæsiˈnɔːrəm] = asses' bridge 〔见 ass 条〕. ~ ***Varollii*** [-vəˈrəuliai] 【解】脑桥.
Pon·tic [ˈpɔntik] *a.* ①庞塔斯 *(Pontus)* 的〔庞塔斯原为小亚细亚的国家,位于黑海之南〕. ②黑海的.
pon·ti·fex [ˈpɔntiˌfeks] *n.* *(pl.* ***pon·tif·i·ces*** [pɔnˈtifisiːz]*)* (古罗马的)最高祭司团成员;教长;大祭司.
pon·tiff [ˈpɔntif] *n.* ①【天主】教皇;主教;(古代犹太)大祭司; (古代罗马)高僧团长. ②(某一问题的)权威, 泰斗;自以为是权威的人. *the Supreme [Sovereign] P-* 罗马教皇.
pon·tif·i·cal [pɔnˈtifikəl] *a.* ①教皇 〔大祭司、主教等〕的. ②傲慢武断的. — *n.* ①〔*pl.*〕主教仪典书. ②〔*pl.*〕(天主教的)祭服; (主教的)徽章. *in full ~s* 穿着 (教皇)礼服.
pon·tif·i·ca·li·a [pɔnˌtifiˈkeiliə] *n.* 〔*pl.*〕主教的祭服.
pon·tif·i·cate [pɔnˈtifikit] *n.* 教皇[主教、高僧]的职位 [任期]. — [-keit] *vi.* ①以主教身份执行 (仪式). ②装作绝对正确的样子;发表武断的意见.
pon·ti·fy [ˈpɔntifai] *vi.* 担任教皇;发挥威权 (=pontifi-

cate).

pon·til [ˈpɔntil] *n.* (取熔融玻璃用的)铁杆 (= punty).

Pon·tius Pi·late [ˈpɔntʃəs ˈpailət] *n.* ①彼拉多〔钉死耶稣的古代罗马的犹太总督〕. ②〔美俚〕法官;典当商.

pontlev·is [pɔntˈlevis, pɔ̃:lvi] 〔F.〕吊桥.

pon·ton [ˈpɔntɔn] *n.* 〔美军〕= pontoon.

pon·to·neer, pon·to·nier [ˌpɔntəˈniə] *n.* 【军】架桥兵;浮桥架设人.

pon·toon[1] [pɔnˈtu:n] *n.* ①【军】平底船,浮舟〔架浮桥用〕;趸船;浮桥 (= ~bridge);浮筒;起重机船;驳船. ②(水中工程用)潜水钟〔箱〕;沉箱. — *vt., vi.* (在…上)架浮桥;用浮桥渡(河).

pon·toon[2] [pɔnˈtu:n] *n.* 〔英〕【牌戏】二十一点.

po·ny [ˈpəuni] *n.* ①矮小的马,矮种马;〔口〕矮马. ②〔美大学俚〕(特指拉丁文、希腊文的)注释本;考试作弊用的夹带;自学参考书 (*cf.* 〔英〕crib). ③〔英俚〕二十五镑〔主赌博用语〕. ④小杯子,一小杯;小个子女人;小火车头;小型汽车. ⑤〔美〕少量酒. — *a.* 小(型)的. ***play the ponies*** 〔美俚〕赌赛马. ~ **chorus** 〔美〕少女合唱队. ~ **engine** 小火车头. ~ **express** (美国西部的)用小马快递的邮政制度;〔美〕拉丁文讲座. ~ **tail** 少女或妇女的马尾发型. — *vt., vi.* 〔美俚〕①用注解书学习. ②支付,清偿 (*up*).

POO, P.O.O. = post-office order 〔英〕邮政汇票.

pooch [pu:tʃ] *n.* 〔美俚〕狗,(特指)杂种狗.

pood, poud [pu:d] *n.* 普特〔苏联衡量单位 = 16.38 公斤〕.

poo·dle [ˈpu:dl] *n.* (身上毛修剪成球饰状的) 长卷毛狗 — *vt.* 修剪狗毛使成球饰状.

poof [puf, pu:f] *int.* ①喔哟〔表示突然消失或出现的感叹词〕. ②呸,啐〔表示焦急,讥笑或轻蔑的感叹词〕(= pooh).

pooh [pu:] *int.* 呸! 啐! 〔表示焦急、讥笑、或轻蔑之意〕.

Pooh-Bah [ˈpu:ˈbɑ:] *n.* 公私兼职极多的人〔Gibert 所编歌剧 *The Mikado* 中的人物〕.

poohed [pu:d] *a.* 〔美俚〕筋疲力尽的,累透的.

pooh-pooh [pu:ˈpu:, ˈpu:ˈpu:] *vt.* 轻视,藐视,瞧不起. *He ~ed the idea.* 他藐视那个意见. *the ~ theory* 〔口〕(语言起源的)感叹词说,语言感情反应说. — *int.* 呸呸! 啐啐!

poo·ja [ˈpu:dʒə] *n.* = puja.

poo·ka, phoo·ka [ˈpu:kə, ˈfu:kə] *n.* 〔爱〕马形妖怪.

poo·koo, pu·ku [ˈpu:ku:] *n.* (中非南部产)红羚羊.

pool[1] [pu:l] *n.* ①(天然)水坑,水塘;水池子,沉淀池;游泳池;龙潭. ②〔美〕油田地带;石油层;瓦斯层;煤坑. ③【医】淤血. ***the P- (of London)*** 泰晤士河伦敦桥正下面的水域. — *vt.* ①在…中形成塘〔池〕;使(血)郁积. ②(凿石时)开(楔眼). ③采(煤等);将(煤)从下面挖掘出来.

pool[2] [pu:l] *n.* ①〔英〕赌博性质的台球. ②赌注;放赌注处. ③拼份子赌博;合伙生产〔经营、投资〕(者);合伙人所出的份子. ④【剑术】各场接力联战. ⑤集中备用物资. ⑥〔美俚〕停车场. — *vt.* ①合伙经营,合办;以(资金等)入股;集中(智慧等). ②共享. *~ together our efforts* 协力. — *vi.* 合伙经营. ~ **room** ①台球房. ②(对在远处举行的赛马、拳击等下注的)公开赌场. ~ **table** 台球桌.

poon, poon-wood [pu:n, ˈpu:nwud] *n.* 【植】胡桐〔造船用〕.

poop[1] [pu:p] *n.* 【海】船尾;船尾楼;船尾楼甲板. — *vt.* (浪)冲打(船)尾;使船尾受(浪)冲打.

poop[2] [pu:p] *n., vt.* = pope².

poop[3] [pu:p] *n.* 〔俚〕蠢货,傻子 (= nincompoop).

poop[4] [pu:p] *vi.* 〔俚〕放屁;【军俚】开炮 (*off*). — *n.* 〔俚〕汽车喇叭声;放屁声;炮声.

poop[5] [pu:p] *vt.* 〔口〕〔常用 *p.p.*〕使筋疲力尽;使喘不过气来.

poop[6] [pu:p] *n.* 〔俚〕(官方或非官方的) 情报,消息. ~ *sheet* 专题材料简编.

poop·er [ˈpu:pə] *n.* 翻过船尾的大浪.

poor [puə] *a.* ①穷,贫穷的 (*opp.* rich, wealthy). ②(收获)少,差,不够. ③(衣裳)破旧的,不体面的;卑劣的;(酒等)粗劣的;(演说者等) 拙劣的. ④萎靡的;不健康的;不愉快的;〔口〕瘦;(身体)弱;(精神)差;(土地)贫瘠的. ⑤不幸的 (*opp.* fortunate);不利的 (*opp.* favourable);已故,亡…. ⑥胆小的;可怜的;卑贱的,不足道的,无聊的. *the ~* 穷苦人;贫民阶级. *urban ~* 城市贫民. *a ~ crop of apples* 苹果歉收. *a ~ three days' holiday* 仅仅三天假. *a ~ £1 a week* 一星期仅一镑. *a ~ ore* 贫矿. *~ soil* 瘠地. *in my ~ opinion* 愚见以为;照我的肤浅看法. *~ in spirit* 懦弱的;卑怯的. *a ~ conductor* 不良(电)导体. *~ digestion* 消化不良. *~ health* 身体虚弱. *~ pens* 劣笔. *a ~ speech* 拙劣的演说. *~ So-and-so* 已故某某. *the ~ man's side (of the river)* 〔口〕(伦敦泰晤士河的)南岸. *a ~ crumb [potato]* 〔美〕没趣的人. *My ~ old mother used to say ...* 先母常常说…. *~ fellow [thing]!* 可怜虫! *~ house* 贫民院,养育院. ***as ~ as a church mouse = as ~ as Job's turkey*** 穷到极点;一贫如洗. ***have a ~ chance for*** 做〔得〕某事〔物〕的机会不大. ***have a ~ memory*** 记忆力不好. ~ **box** (教堂的)济贫捐款箱. ~ **law** 贫民救助法,济贫法. ~ **pay** 〔美〕经济上信用不佳的人. ~ **rate** 救贫税. **~-spirited** *a.* 胆小的,懦弱的. ~ **white (trash)** (美国南部各州)穷苦的白种人.

poor·ly *pred., a.* 〔口〕身体不舒服. *He is (looking) very ~.* 他身体好象很不好. — *ad.* 下贱;没有大成就;贫穷;不体面;不够;贫弱;拙劣. ~ ***off*** 日子不好过. ***think ~ of*** 不佩服,不认为好.

poor·mouth [puəˈmauθ] *vi.* 〔口〕哭穷. —*vt.* 把…说得一钱不值.

poor·ness [ˈpuənis] *n.* 贫穷;缺乏;拙劣;不够;粗劣,卑劣;不毛,硗瘠. *~ of supply* 供给差. *~ of character* 人格卑劣.

POP = printing-out paper 【摄】(利用光照直接显影的)印相纸.

pop[1] [pɔp] *vi.* ①砰砰地响;劈劈拍拍地响;砰的一声打出去 (*at*);爆裂. ②突然进去〔出去〕,突然动起来 (*in; out; up*). ③(眼珠) 突出. *~ into one's mind* 忽然想起来. — *vt.* ①使砰砰的响;开枪打,砰的一声打. ②〔美〕(将玉米等) 炒爆. ③突然伸出〔推动、放下〕 (*in, out; down*). ④〔英俚〕典当,抵押. *~ a question* 突然提出质问. *~ corn* 炒玉米. ~ ***in*** 突然进去,突然访问. ~ ***off*** 突然出去;忽然不见;突然死掉(*~ off the hooks* 〔口〕死掉). ~ ***out*** (火,把火)突然灭掉;突然伸出;〔俚〕(突然)死掉. ~ ***the question*** 〔口〕(乘机向女方)要求结婚;求婚. — *n.* ①砰,劈劈拍拍(声);枪声;开枪;〔口〕手枪. ②〔口〕汽水,香槟酒(等). ③斑点〔羊等的记号〕. ④〔英俚〕典当. ⑤〔美俚〕爸爸. 〔口〕大爷,老爹. ~ ***quiz*** 〔美〕突然而来的考试. ***in ~*** (东西) 在当铺里. — *ad.* 砰地(一声);突然,出其不意地. *go ~* 砰地一声响;死掉;破掉. ~ **corn** 炒玉米花;炒用玉米. **~-eyed** *a.* 〔美〕突眼的,眼球突出的;(吓得)睁大了眼睛的. ~ **fly** 【棒球】内野飞球. ~ **gun** 纸枪,木塞枪,汽枪;〔蔑〕没有用〔打不出〕的枪. **~-off** 大声讲话的人;乱说乱讲的人. **~over** (加奶油馅的) 薄空心松饼. ~ **shop** 〔俚〕当铺. ~ **test** 〔美俚〕突然袭击式的测验. **~-up** 【棒球】内野飞球 (= pop fly). ~ **valve** 【机】突开阀.

pop[2] [pɔp] *a.* 〔口〕流行的;普及的;大众的;演唱流行歌曲的. — *n.* 流行音乐〔popular music 之略〕. *a ~ concert* 〔美〕大众音乐会〔主要演奏半古典派音乐或古典派轻音乐〕. ~ **culture** 大众文化. ~ **dao [trio]** 〔美〕流行性的双重唱〔双人戏,三重唱、三人戏〕. ~ **warbler** 【美】流行歌星.

pop. = population; popular(ly).

Pope [pəup] *n.* ①波普〔姓氏〕. ②**Alexander** ～ 蒲伯〔1688—1744,英国诗人〕.

pope[1] [pəup] *n.* ①〔有时作 P-〕罗马教皇. ②教皇一样的人〔自认为或被认为一贯正确的人〕. ③(希腊正教的)教区牧师. **-dom** ①罗马教皇的职权[管区、领地、在职的时期等]. ②教皇政治. ③〔蔑〕= popery.

pope[2] [puːp] *n.* (一打就极痛或发麻的)腿的要害处. *take sb.'s* ～ 打某人腿上要害处. — *vt.* 〔常用 *p.p.*〕打(某人)腿上要害处.

pop·er·y [ˈpəupəri] *n.* 〔蔑〕罗马天主教教义;天主教教皇制度.

pope's-eye [ˈpəups-ai] *n.* (牛、羊等的)腿部淋巴腺.

pope's-head [ˈpəupshed] *n.* 长柄撣帚.

pope's-nose [ˈpəupsnəuz] *n.* 【烹】(煮熟的)鸡[鸭、家禽的]屁股.

pop·in·jay [ˈpɔpindʒei] *n.* ①爱漂亮的人;花花公子;自负的人. ②〔英方〕绿毛啄木鸟;〔古〕鹦鹉;杆上的鸟形靶子.

pop·ish [ˈpəupiʃ] *a.* 〔蔑〕罗马天主教教义的;教皇制度的.

pop·lar [ˈpɔplə] *n.* 【植】杨属;白杨;杨木. *the white [silver]* ～ 银白杨. *the Chinese white* ～ 毛白杨. *the Lombardy* ～ 钻天杨,毛杨. *the trembling* ～ = aspen.

Pop·lar·ism [ˈpɔplərizəm] *n.* 救济过多的济贫政策.

pop·lin [ˈpɔplin] *n.* 府绸;毛葛. ～ *broche* 织花府绸;织花毛葛. *cotton* ～ 棉府绸.

pop·lit·e·al, pop·lit·ic [pɔpˈlitiəl, pɔpˈlitik] *a.* 【解】腿弯部的,腘窝部的.

pop·pa [ˈpɔpə] *n.* 〔美俚〕爸爸.

pop·per [ˈpɔpə] *n.* ①〔美〕爆玉米的锅. ②爆破者. ③爆竹,枪. ④炮手,射手.

pop·pet [ˈpɔpit] *n.* ①〔方〕玩偶;〔英方〕宝宝〔对小孩的爱称〕. ②【机】(车床的)托架;提升阀;【海】(船竣工入水时的)垫架,支架;船舷桨架垫片. ～**head** 【机】随转尾座.

pop·pied [ˈpɔpid] *a.* ①罂粟多的;用罂粟装饰的. ②起麻醉作用的. ③被麻醉了的;昏昏睡的.

pop·ping [ˈpɔpiŋ] *n.* ①爆音. ②【板球】打球员线 (= ～ crease). — *a.* ①(眼睛)鼓出的. ②间歇的. ③活跃的.

pop·ple [ˈpɔpl] *vi.* (海水等)起泡沫;波动;忽沉忽浮;荡漾着微波流动. — *n.* 波动,涟漪.

pop·py[1] [ˈpɔpi] *n.* 【植】罂粟属;鸦片;芙蓉红. *the field [red]* ～ 虞美人. *the garden* ～ 观赏罂粟. *the opium* ～ 可制鸦片的罂粟. *the Californian* ～ 金英花. ～ **cock** 〔美俚〕胡话,废话 (*the* ～ *cock season* 【棒球】春天练球季). ～ **head** 罂粟的头;【建】罂粟状装饰;顶花饰〔特指教堂座位上的〕.

pop·py[2] [ˈpɔpi] *n.* 〔美俚〕爸爸 (= pope[2]).

pop·si·cle [ˈpɔpsikl] *n.* 〔美俚〕①冰棍,棒冰. ②= motorcycle.

pop·sy (-wop·sy) [ˈpɔpsi(wɔpsi)] *n.* 〔称呼〕好宝宝〔尤指女孩〕.

pop·u·lace [ˈpɔpjuləs] *n.* 人民,老百姓;大众;〔蔑〕下层民众,群氓.

pop·u·lar [ˈpɔpjulə] *a.* ①人民的,民众的,大众的,民间的. ②通俗的,普通的,平易的. ③有人望的,得人心的,有名气的;受欢迎的;流行的;大众化的;(民间)流传的;便宜的,低廉的. ④〔美俚〕自以为了不得的,骄傲的. *the* ～ *voice* 群众呼声. *the* ～ *front [P- Front]* 人民阵线. *a* ～ *edition* 普及版,廉价版. ～ *election* 普选. *a* ～ *hero* 众望所归的英雄. ～ *lectures* 通俗讲话. ～ *prices* 廉价. ～ *science* 通俗科学. *a* ～ *song* 流行歌曲. *a* ～ *writer* 受人欢迎的作家. *He is* ～ *in society.* 他在社会上是有名望的. *be* ～ *with* 受…欢迎,在…间名声好. *in* ～ *language* 用普通话;用通俗语言. — *n.* 大众音乐会 (= ～ concert). **-ly** *ad.* 一般地,普通地;通俗地;通过民众地.

pop·u·lar·es [ˌpɔpjuˈlɛəriːz] *n.* 〔L.〕〔*pl.*〕(古罗马的)民众.

pop·u·lar·i·ty [ˌpɔpjuˈlæriti] *n.* 名气,名望;通俗性;大众性;流行;普及. *enjoy general* ～ 享盛名,受欢迎,得众望.

pop·u·lar·i·za·tion [ˌpɔpjuləraiˈzeiʃən] *n.* 通俗化,简单化;普及,推广.

pop·u·lar·ize [ˈpɔpjuləraiz] *vt.* 使通俗化;使大众化;推广,使普及;使流行,使受欢迎. **-er** ①普及者,推广者. ②普及读物.

pop·u·late [ˈpɔpjuleit] *vt.* 使人口聚居在…中;移民于;殖民于;居住于…中. *densely [sparsely]* ～*d* 人口稠密[稀少]的. — *vi.* (人口)繁殖,增加.

pop·u·la·tion [ˌpɔpjuˈleiʃən] *n.* ①人口;人口总数;全体居民;人口的聚居. ②物的全体[总数];【生】虫口;种群(量);群体;族,组,个数;【统】对象总体,全域. ③【物】布居;密度. ④〔罕〕殖民. ～ *dynamics* 群体动态. ～ *explosion* 人口爆炸,人口骤增. *varietal* ～*s* 品种群体.

Pop·u·lism [ˈpɔpjulizəm] *n.* 〔美〕(十九世纪末)人民党主义;〔俄〕(革命前的)民粹主义.

Pop·u·list [ˈpɔpjulist] *a., n.* 〔美〕人民党的(成员);〔俄〕民粹派的(成员).

pop·u·lous [ˈpɔpjuləs] *a.* 人口稠密的,人口多的;挤满的. **-ly** *ad.* 人口稠密地. **-ness** *n.* 人口稠密.

p.o.r. = pay on return【商】返回后付款.

por·bea·gle [ˈpɔːˌbiːgl] *n.* 【鱼】青鲛,鼠鲨.

porce·lain [ˈpɔːsəlin,-lein] *n.* 瓷(料);〔总称〕瓷器. — *a.* ①瓷(器)的. ②精美的. ③脆的;易碎的. *electrical* ～ 绝缘瓷. *a* ～ *shell* 【动】宝贝属贝类;玛瑙贝. *a* ～ *insulator* 【电】陶瓷绝缘子. ～ **clay** 瓷土,高岭土. ～ **enamel** 搪瓷. ～ **glaze** 瓷釉.

porce·lain·ize [ˈpɔːsəlinaiz] *vt.* ①把…做成瓷器. ②涂瓷于(金属器皿).

porce·lain·ous, por·cel·la·ne·ous, por·cel·lan·ic, por·cel·la·nous [ˈpɔːsəlinəs, ˌpɔːsəˈleiniəs, -səˈlænik, pɔːˈselənəs] *a.* 瓷器(似)的,瓷质的.

porch [pɔːtʃ] *n.* ①(有顶棚的)门廊,大门内停车处,门口. ②〔美〕走廊,游廊. ③【无】(脉冲)边沿. ④〔the P-〕公元前 4 世纪斯多噶派哲学家芝诺 (Zeno) 对弟子讲学的柱廊;斯多噶学派,斯多噶哲学. ～ **climber** 〔美〕小偷. ～**ed** *a.* 有门廊的.

por·cine [ˈpɔːsain] *a.* 猪的;象猪的;肮脏的.

por·cu·pine [ˈpɔːkjupain] *n.* ①【动】豪猪,箭猪. ②【纺】梳麻机. ～ **anteater** 【动】食蚁蝟,针鼹. ～ **fish** 【动】鱼虎,针鲀. ～ **grass** 【植】大蓟.

pore[1] [pɔː, pɔə] *vi.* ①注视,细看. ②用心阅读;细心研究 (*on; over*). ③沉思,默想. — *vt.* 因凝视过度而使(眼睛)疲劳. ～ *one's eyes out* 因读书过度以致眼睛疲劳.

pore[2] [pɔː] *n.* 毛孔;气孔,细孔. ***at every*** ～ 全身,浑身. ***sweat from every*** ～ ①极热. ②(因害怕、兴奋等)冒汗,受惊,兴奋.

por·gy [ˈpɔːdʒi] *n.* (*pl.* ～, ***por·gies***) 【动】大西洋鲷;钉头鱼;尖口鲷.

po·rif·er·an [pɔːˈrifərən,pə-] *n.* 海绵动物门[多孔动物门] (*Porifera*). — *a.* 海绵动物门的,多孔动物门的.

po·rif·er·ous [pɔːˈrifərəs] *a.* ①有孔的. ②【动】多孔动物的,海绵动物的.

po·rism [ˈpɔːrizəm] *n.* 【数】不定命题定理;(希腊几何学的)系,系论.

pork [pɔːk] *n.* ①猪肉〔尤指未腌过的〕. ②〔古〕猪 (= hog, swine). ③〔美俚〕支持政党上台所分到的好处,政治分肥. *mess* ～ 上好猪肉. ***P- chops hang high.*** 〔美〕萧条的冬季又来了. ～ **barrel** 〔美俚〕(议员为讨好支持者而私给的)政治分肥〔如促使政府拨款用于地方的水利、公共建筑等福利事项〕. ～ **butcher** (杀猪的)屠户.

~**chop** 猪排. ~ **chopper**〔美俚〕被会员认为是只图私利的工会领导人. ~**pie** ①猪肉馅饼. ②卷边低平顶毡帽 (= porkpie hat).
pork·er [ˈpɔːkə] *n.* 食用猪;肥小猪.
pork·et [ˈpɔːkit] *n.* 乳猪,小猪.
pork·ling [ˈpɔːkliŋ] *n.* 小猪,乳猪.
pork·y [ˈpɔːki] *a.* 猪肉(一样)的;〔口〕肥的.
porn, porno [pɔːn, pɔːnəu] *n.* = pornography.
por·nog·ra·phy [pɔːˈnɔgrəfi] *n.* 春宫, 春画; 色情文学[电影]; 娼妓风俗志. **por·no·graph·ic** [ˌpɔːnəˈgræfik] *a.*
por·o·mer·ic [ˌpɔːrəˈmerik] *n.* 一种人造革〔常用作鞋、行李箱、腰带等的面子〕.
po·ro·plas·tic [ˌpɔrəuˈplæstik] *a.* 多孔而可塑的.
po·ros·i·ty [pɔːˈrɔsiti] *n.* ①多孔性. ②【物】孔积率; 孔度,隙度. ③多孔部分;多孔结构;多孔的东西.
po·rot·ic [pəˈrɔtik] *a.*【医】多孔性的; (骨质) 疏松的. — *n.* 治骨折药,促生骨痂药.
por·ous [ˈpɔːrəs] *a.* ①多孔的; 有气孔的; 〔喻〕漏洞多的. ②能渗透的. ③素烧(瓷)的. **-ly** *ad.* **-ness** *n.*
por·phyr·a·tin [pɔːˈfiərətin] *n.*【化】卟啉的金属络合物.
por·phyr·i·a [pɔːˈfiəriə] *n.*【医】卟啉病.
por·phy·rin [ˈpɔːfərin] *n.*【生化】卟啉(类).
por·phy·rit·ic [ˌpɔːfiˈritik] *a.*【地】斑岩的, 斑状的.
por·phy·roid [ˈpɔːfirɔid] *n.*【矿】残斑岩.
por·phy·rop·sin [ˌpɔːfiˈrɔpsin] *n.*【生化】视紫质.
por·phy·ry [ˈpɔːfiri] *n.*【地】斑岩.
por·poise [ˈpɔːpəs] *n.* ①【动】海豚. ②前后振动; 波动. *a school of ~s* 一群海豚. — *vi.* ①(船) 在水面急行. ②(鱼雷)在水面急驶.
por·rect [pəˈrekt] *a.* (平)伸出的; 延伸的. — *vt.* ①伸出. ②〔教会法用语〕提出(文书等).
por·ridge [ˈpɔridʒ] *n.*〔英〕①粥, 稀饭, 麦片粥. ②(肉菜加大麦等煮的)汤. ***do one's ~***〔英俚〕服刑期. ***keep [save] one's breath to cool one's ~*** 省点力气少开口,少说话〔说也无用〕.
por·ri·go [pɔˈraigəu] *n.*【医】头疮,发癣.
por·rin·ger [ˈpɔrindʒə] *n.* 粥碗,汤钵;(供儿童用的)单柄金属浅杯[浅碗].
port[1] [pɔːt] *n.* ①港;港口;〔喻〕避难港;避难所,休息处. ②(特指有海关的) 港市; 输入港; 通商口岸. ③机场, 航空站. *a close ~* 〔英〕河港. *a free ~* 自由港. *a naval ~* 军港. *an open ~* ①对外贸易港. ②不冻港. *a warmwater [ice-free, non-freezing] ~* 不冻港. *clear a ~* 出港. *enter ~* 入港. *in ~* 在港, 停泊中的. *leave (a) ~* = clear a ~. *make [reach] (a) ~* 入港. *P- Arthur* 旧时外国人对我国旅顺港的称呼. *~ of arrival* 到达港. *~ of call* (沿途)停靠港. *~ of coaling* 装煤港. *~ of delivery* 卸货港,交货港. *~ of departure* 出发港. *~ of destination* 到达港,目的港. *~ of discharge [unloading]* 卸货港. *~ of distress* 避难港. *~ of embarkation* 启航港. *~ of entry* 进口港. *~ office* 港务局. *~ of registry* 船籍港. *~ of sailing* 启航港. *~ of shipment* 装货港. *touch (at) a ~* 靠港. ***any ~ in a storm*** 遇难时任何港口都是好的;〔喻〕穷途之策. ~ **admiral**〔英〕军港司令. ~ **bar** 河[港]口的洲;港口防材; 装货口门闩. ~ **charges** 〔*pl.*〕入港税. ~ **town** 港市.
port[2] [pɔːt] *n.* ①(从前军舰上的)炮门;【海】(商船的)上货口,舱门; (船边的)舷窗. ②〔Scot.〕门, 入口; 城门. ③(工事等的)射击孔; 炮眼; 枪眼; 展望口. ④【机】汽门,汽口;水门. ⑤【徽】门印. *an exhaust ~*【机】排气口. *a stream ~*【机】汽门. ~**hole** ①射击孔;炮眼. ②舷窗; 舱口.
port[3] [pɔːt] *n.* ①态度;举止,样子,风采. ②含意; 意义. ③【军】持枪姿势〔枪筒向上,自左肩至右胯斜持枪〕. — *vt.* ①持(枪). ②〔古〕搬运. ***P- arms!***〔口令〕持枪!
port[4] [pɔːt] *n.* (船、飞机的) 左舷 *(opp.* starboard*). the ~ watch* 床位在左舷的船员的值班. *a ~ engine* 左侧发动机. *a ~ plane [wing]* 左翼. ***on the ~ bow*** 在左舷船首. ***on the ~ quarter*** 在左舷船尾. ***put the helm to ~*** 转左舷. — *vt.*〔主要作命令语〕转(舵)向左〔使船头右转〕. — *vi.* 转舵向左. ***P- the helm!***〔命令〕左舵! ~**side** *a.* 左边的; 左派的;〔美俚〕惯用左手的. ~**sider**〔美俚〕左撇子;【垒球】左手投手.
port[5] [pɔːt] *n.* (葡萄牙)(红)葡萄酒〔有时也作褐色或白酒色 (= ~ wine)〕.
Port. = Portugal; Portuguese.
port. = portable.
por·ta·bil·i·ty [ˌpɔːtəˈbiliti] *n.* 可携带性,轻便.
port·a·ble [ˈpɔːtəbl] *a.* 可搬运的; 便于携带的; 手提式的, 轻便的. *a ~ barometer* 轻便晴雨表. *a ~ railway* 轻便铁路. — *n.* ①手提式打字机[收音机、电视机]. ②活动房屋. **-a·bly** *ad.*
port·age [ˈpɔːtidʒ] *n.* ①搬运; 运输. ②搬运物, 货物. ③水陆联运,联运路线. ④〔古〕运费. *the mariner's ~* (船上准许水手存放所带私货的)物品寄存处〔旧时常以此种方式代替付水手工资〕. — *vt., vi.* 在连水陆路间搬运(船、货物).
Por·tal [ˈpɔːtəl] *n.* 波特尔〔姓氏〕.
por·tal [ˈpɔːtəl] *n.* ①(大建筑物的)入口;正门;桥门;隧道门. ②〔诗〕门,入门. ③【解】门静脉. — *a.*【解】门的;肝门的;门静脉的,关于门脉的. *~ vein* 门脉, 门静脉. ~**-to-**~ 按照从进厂矿到出厂矿的全部时间计算的. ~**-to-**~ **pay** 进出厂统合的计时工资.
por·ta·men·to [ˌpɔːtəˈmentəu] *n.* *(pl.* ***-ti*** [-ti]*)*〔It.〕【乐】滑音,延音.
port·ance [ˈpɔːtns] *n.*〔古〕人的行为,举止或品格.
por·ta·tive [ˈpɔːtətiv] *a.* ①可携带的; 可搬运的. ②有力搬动的;用作支撑的. ③〔古〕携带用的.
Port-au-Prince [ˌpɔːtəuˈprins] *n.* 太子港〔海地首都〕.
port·cul·lis [pɔːtˈkʌlis] *n.* (城堡的) 吊闸, 吊门. — *vt.* ①在…上装吊门. ②用吊门关闭.
Port-de-France [pɔːtdəˈfrɑːns] *n.* 法兰西堡〔尼提尼克岛首府〕.
Porte [pɔːt] *n.* (帝制时代的)土耳其政府 (= the Sublime ~ 或 the Ottoman ~).
porte-co·chère [ˈpɔːtkəuˈʃɛə] *n.*〔F.〕车辆出入门道; 门内停车处.
port(e)·cray·on [pɔːtˈkreiən] *n.*〔F.〕粉笔或蜡笔的(金属)笔夹.
por·te mon·naie [ˈpɔːtˌmʌni] *n.*〔F.〕皮夹子; 小钱包.
por·tend [pɔːˈtend] *vt.* 成为…的前兆,预示,预兆; 给…以警告. *Black clouds ~ a storm.* 乌云为暴风雨的前兆.
Por·te·ño [pɔːˈteinjəu] *n.* (阿根廷首都)布宜诺斯艾利斯人.
por·tent [ˈpɔːtent] *n.* ①预兆,凶兆;不祥之兆. ②怪事,怪物;奇迹.
por·ten·tous [pɔːˈtentəs] *a.* ①预兆的;不吉的. ②可惊的,怪异的;奇特的; 可怕的. ③〔谑〕(沉默等)严肃的. ④〔蔑〕自命不凡的;妄自尊大的. **-ly** *ad.*
Por·ter [ˈpɔːtə] *n.* 波特〔姓氏,男子名〕.
por·ter[1] [ˈpɔːtə] *n.* 看门人,门房.
por·ter[2] [ˈpɔːtə] *n.* ①搬运工人; 〔车站〕行李搬运员; (大饭店等中的)服务员;〔美〕卧车[餐车]服务员. ②(银行、商店中的)杂务工,清洁工. *a ~'s knot* 搬运工肩垫. ~**house**〔美〕①(从前的)小酒馆;饭馆. ②上等牛排 (= ~house steak).
por·ter[3] [ˈpɔːtə] *n.* 〔英〕黑啤酒 (= ~'s beer).
por·ter·age [ˈpɔːtəridʒ] *n.* ①搬运(行李); 搬运业. ②搬运费.
port·fire [ˈpɔːtfaiə] *n.* (烟火、烽火、矿山用炸药等的)点

火装置,导火筒,引火具。

port·fo·li·o [pɔːtˈfəuljəu, -liəu] *n.* *(pl. ~s)* ①纸夹;文件夹;公事包。②部长[大臣]的职位。③[美]有价证券一览表[明细表];(保险)业务量[业务责任]。④(艺术家等的)代表作选辑。*a minister without ~* 不管部部长[大臣]。***hold the ~*** 担任部会政务委员。

Port Harcourt [pɔːt ˈhɑːkət] 哈科特港[尼日利亚港市]。

Por·tia [ˈpɔːʃjə] *n.* ①波西娅[女子名]。②莎士比亚剧《威尼斯商人》中的女主人公;[喻]女律师。

por·ti·co [ˈpɔːtikəu] *n.* *(pl. ~(e)s)*【建】(有圆柱的)门廊。

por·tière [pɔːˈtjɛə] *n.* [F.]门帘,门帷。

por·tion [ˈpɔːʃən] *n.* ①一部分。②一份,一般;(饭菜)一客。③【法】分得的财产。④嫁妆,妆奁。⑤[仅用单数]命运。*one ~ of roast beef* 烤牛肉一客。*a ~ of (land)* 一部分地,若干(土地)。— *vt.* ①把…分成份额;分配 *(out)*。②给…嫁妆。③命运注定。**-less** *a.* 得不到分配物的[尤指遗产]的;没有嫁资的。

Port·land [ˈpɔːtlənd] *n.* ①波特兰[姓氏]。②波特兰[美国港市]。③波特兰监狱[英国 *Dorsetshire* 的监狱](= ~ prison)。~ **cement** 水泥。~ **stone** (英国波特兰岛产的)建筑用石灰石,波特兰石。

port·li·ness [ˈpɔːtlinis] *n.* 肥胖;魁伟。

Port Louis [ˈpɔːt ˈlu(ː)i(s)] 路易港[毛里求斯首都]。

port·ly [ˈpɔːtli] *a.* ①肥胖的;粗壮的;魁梧的。②[方]仪表堂堂的。*a ~ belly* 罗汉肚,大肚子。*a lady of ~ presence* 身量肥胖的女人。

port·man·teau [pɔːtˈmæntəu] *n.* *(pl. ~s, ~x* [-z]*)* ①(两开绞合)旅行皮包[皮箱]。②[喻](两词音为合并的)混成词[=~ word;如 Oxbridge 由 Oxford 和 Cambridge 二字组成]。— *a.* 多用途的;多性质的。

Port Mores·by [pɔːt ˈmɔːzbi] 莫尔斯比港[巴布亚新几内亚首府]。

Por·to [ˈpɔːtu] *n.* 波尔图[葡萄牙港市]。

Port-of-Spain [ˈpɔːtəvˈspein] *n.* 西班牙港[特立尼达和多巴哥首都]。

Porto-Novo [ˈpɔːtəuˈnəuvəu] *n.* 波多诺伏[贝宁首都]。

Por·to Ri·can [ˌpɔːtəuˈriːkən] *a., n.* 波多黎各岛的(人)。

Por·to Ri·co [ˌpɔːtəu ˈriːkəu] *n.* 波多黎各岛[在西印度群岛]。

por·trait [ˈpɔːtrit] *n.* ①肖像,肖像画;相片。②雕像;半身像。③人物描写;生动的描绘。④类型,模型,标本。~ **painter** 肖像画家。

por·trait·ist [ˈpɔːtritist] *n.* 肖像画家,肖像制作者;摄影者。

por·trai·ture [ˈpɔːtritʃə] *n.* ①肖像画法。②肖像画;照相;肖像画集。③生动的描绘;(人物)描写(法)。***in ~*** 所描写的。

por·tray [pɔːˈtrei] *vt.* ①画(人物、风景),画(肖像)。②描绘;描写;描述。③【剧】扮演,饰演。

por·tray·al [pɔːˈtreiəl] *n.* ①画;描写,叙述。②画像;肖像。

port·reeve [ˈpɔːtriːv] *n.* ①【英史】市长;(现在英国某些市镇的)副市长;执行官;副镇长。②港市的长官。

por·tress [ˈpɔːtris] *n.* ①女看门人,女门房。②女杂务工;女帮工。

Port Sa·id [ˈpɔːt ˈsaid] 塞得港[埃及港市]。

Port-Sa·lut [ˈpɔːsæˈluː; F. pɔːrsaˈly] *n.* 一种半硬全脂黄乳酪(= port du salut)。

Ports·mouth [ˈpɔːtsməθ] *n.* 朴次茅斯[英国、美国港市]。

Port Sudan [ˈpɔːt su(ː)ˈdɑːn] 苏丹港[苏丹港市]。

Port Swettenham [ˈpɔːt ˈswetnəm] 巴生港[即瑞天咸港][马来西亚港市]。

Por·tu·gal [ˈpɔːtjugəl] *n.* 葡萄牙[欧洲]。

Por·tu·guese [ˌpɔːtjuˈgiːz] *a.* 葡萄牙的;葡萄牙人的;葡萄牙语的。— *n.* 葡萄牙人[语]。~ **man-of-war**【动】僧帽水母。

por·tu·lac·a [ˌpɔːtjuˈlɑːkə, -ˈlækə] *n.*【植】半支莲 *(Portulaca grandiflora)*。

Port Vila [pɔːt ˈviːlə] *n.* 维拉港[新赫布里底群岛首府]。

pos. = positive; possessive.

po·sa·da [pɔːˈsɑːðɑː] *n.* *(pl. ~s* [-ðɑːs]*)*[Sp.]小旅馆,客栈。

P.O.S.B. = Post-Office Savings Bank 邮政局储蓄银行。

pose[1] [pəuz] *n.* ①(画像、表演、拍照时的)姿态,姿势。②心理状态,精神状态。③矫揉造作;装腔作势;伪装。④(玩骨牌戏时)打的第一张牌。*His diligence is a mere ~.* 他的勤奋不过是装样子罢了。***a dramatic [stage] ~***【剧】亮相。***strike [put on] a ~*** 装腔作势。— *vi.* ①采取某种态度[姿态]。②做作,装腔作势;极力装作…,冒充 *(as)*。③(玩骨牌戏时)打第一张牌。— *vt.* ①(艺术家)使(模特儿等)作某种姿势;使…摆好姿势;把…摆正位置。②拿出(要求等);提出(问题)。***~ … against …*** 把…同…对立起来。***~ for a photograph with*** 摆好姿势同…合影。

pose[2] [pəuz] *vt.* 盘问;(提出难题)难住(人)。

Po·sei·don [pɔˈsaidən] *n.*【希神】①波塞冬[海神]。②海神式导弹(= ~ missile)。

Po·sen [ˈpəuzən] *n.* = Poznan.

pos·er[1] [ˈpəuzə] *n.* 装腔作势的人;伪装者。

pos·er[2] [ˈpəuzə] *n.* ①提出难题的人;考试员。②难题;怪题。

po·seur [pəuˈzəː] *n.* [F.] = poser[1].

po·sey [ˈpəuzi] *n.* = posy.

posh [pɔʃ] *a.* [英俚]①亮晶晶的;漂亮的,优雅的;时髦的;最好的;第一流的。②豪华的;奢侈的。— *vt.* 把…打扮起来 *(up)*。— *int.* 呸[表示蔑视]。**~-looking** *a.* 漂亮的。**-ism** *n.* 奢侈主义。**-ly** *ad.* **-ness** *n.*

pos·it [ˈpɔzit] *vt.* ①[主用被动语态]安置,布置;安排。②【逻】断定;论断;假定。— *n.* ①安置。②论断。

posit. = position; positive.

po·si·tion [pəˈziʃən] *n.* ①位置;方位;地点。②处境,情况;状态,形势,局面。③姿态,姿势。④地位,身份;职位;职务。⑤态度,观点,立场;见解;论点,主张;命题。⑥(音节中的)元音位置。⑦【军】发射阵地;阵地;战略要点。⑧【乐】(左手在提琴指板上的)把位。*the neutral ~*【汽车】空档。*people of ~* 有身份的人们。*What is the ~ of the affairs?* 形势怎么样? *a directory ~* (电话)查号台。*The ~ was stormed.* 阵地遭受猛袭。*~ warfare* 阵地战。***a ready ~***【军】射击准备姿势。***be in a ~ to*** 在可以…的地位;能够…。***be in ~*** 在应有位置,在适当地位,无障碍;照规定姿势。***be out of ~*** 不在应有位置,有障碍;未照规定姿势。***get [go] into ~***【军】进入阵地。***in my ~*** 在我的立场;(对于)象我这样立场的(人)。***jockey for ~*** ①(赛马时)挤其他骑师以占有利位置。②[喻]以(欺诈)手段图谋私利。***maneuver for ~*** 调动军队争取有利地位。***put sb. in a false ~*** 使(某人)处于违反原则行事[被误解]的地位。***presume on one's ~*** 倚仗地位。***take up the ~ that …*** 主张…。— *vt.* ①把…放在适当位置;规定…的位置,给…定位。②【军】屯(兵),驻扎(部队)。~ **buoy** 雾标,指示浮标。~ **light** (飞机的)指示灯;锚位灯。~ **paper** 表明对问题所持见解的论文。

po·si·tion·al [pəˈziʃənəl] *a.* ①位置(上)的;地位的。②【军】阵地的。*~ warfare [fighting]*【军】阵地战。~ **error** (钟表等的)位置误差。

pos·i·tive [ˈpɔzətiv, -zi-] *a.* ①确实的,明确的;确定的;无条件的 *(opp.* qualified, implied, inferential*)*;绝对的,无疑问的,断然的。②有自信的;过份自信的,独断的。③积极的;建设性的;肯定的 *(opp.* negative*)*。④[口]十足的,纯粹的。⑤现实的,实在的,实际的 *(opp.* speculative, theoretical)。⑥【物、数】正的;【物】阳性的;【化】盐基性的。⑦【摄】正片的。⑧【哲】实证的。

⑨【语法】原级的. ⑩【生】(刺激源)向性的,趋性的. ⑪〔用作表语〕一定;确信 *(to do; that)*. ~ *proof [evidence]* 确实的证据. *a* ~ *fact* 无可怀疑的事实. ~ *orders* 绝对命令,强制的命令. *a* ~ *sort of person* 刚愎自用的人. *a* ~ *mind* 实事求是的人. *Are you sure? Yes, I'm* ~. 真的吗?当然了. *She is* ~ *to come tomorrow.* 她明天一定来. *I am* ~ *that he is right.* 我确信他说得对. ***in a*** ~ ***way*** 从正面;由积极方面. ***be*** ~ ***about [of]*** 确信,确知 (~*of the approach of a violent revolutionary storm* 确信一场猛烈的革命风暴的来临). —*n.* ①实在;确实;明确性;绝对性;积极性;正面. ②【语法】原级. ③(电池的)阳极;【摄】正片. ④【数】正量. ~ **adjective [adverb]** 原级形容词[副词]. ~ **charge**【物】阳电荷. ~ **check**【经】积极限制. ~ **column**【电】阳辉区,阳极区. ~ **degree**【语法】原级. ~ **electricity** 阳电,正电. ~ **law**【法】成文法. ~ **number**【数】正数. ~ **organ** 教堂内补助大风琴的小风琴. ~ **philosophy** 实证哲学,实证论. ~ **pole** 正极,阳极. ~ **pressure**【机】正压力. ~ **rays**【理】阳射线,正电射线. ~ **reaction** 阳性反应;正反应;正反力. ~ **sign**【数】正号〔即+〕. **-ly** *ad.* 确实,必定;断然;绝对;积极. **-ness** *n.* = positivity.

pos·i·tiv·ism [ˈpɔzitivizəm] *n.* ①【哲】〔通例 P-〕实证哲学,实证论;实证主义. ②明确性,确实性;积极性.

pos·i·tiv·ist [ˈpɔzitivist] 实证论者;实证主义者.

pos·i·tiv·i·ty [ˌpɔziˈtiviti] *n.* ①确实;确信;积极性. ②【物】正性.

pos·i·tron [ˈpɔzitrɔn] *n.*【物】正电子,阳电子,正子.

pos·i·tro·ni·um [ˌpɔziˈtrəuniəm] *n.*【电】电子偶素,阳[正]电子素.

po·sol·o·gy [pəuˈsɔlədʒi] *n.*【医】配药学,剂量学. **pos·o·log·ic** [ˌpɔsəˈlɔdʒik] *a.* **po·sol·o·gist** [-ˈsɔlədʒist] *n.* 配药学家.

poss. = ①possession. ②possessive. ③possible. ④possibly.

pos·se [ˈpɔsi] *n.* ①武装队;(警察等的)一队;【法】民兵,民团 (= ~ comitatus). ②〔口〕乌合之众,暴徒. ③可能性;潜在力. ***in*** ~ 可能地. ~ **comitatus** [ˌkɔmiˈtaːtəs] (州长、郡长等可随时召集的)地方民团.

pos·sess [pəˈzes] *vt.* ①具有(能力、性质等),掌握(知识等);据有,占有,拥有(财产、房屋等);使占有,使拥有*(of, with)*. ②(鬼等)缠,附;(情欲等)迷住. ③(在身心方面)克制,抑制;保持(镇定等);维持(平衡等). ④使沾染*(with)*;使被任意摆布,支配(人). *What* ~*es you to do such a thing?* 你怎么干出那样的事情来了? ~ *one's mind in peace* 使人心胸保持宁静. ***be*** ~***ed*** 被(鬼等)缠上,迷住. ***be exclusively*** ~***ed by*** 在…把持下. ***be*** ~***ed by [with]*** 被(鬼怪、思想等)缠住,迷住. ***be*** ~***ed of*** 拥有,据有. ***like all*** ~***ed*** 〔美〕疯狂地,猛烈地,拼命地,热烈地. ***like one*** ~***ed*** 象着了魔的人一样. ~ ***oneself*** 自制,镇静. ~ ***oneself of*** 获得;据有,把…占为己有. ~ ***one's soul in patience*** 硬是耐着性子等待. ~ ***sb. of sth.*** 使某人占有[拥有]某物.

pos·ses·sion [pəˈzeʃən] *n.* ①有,所有,拥有;【法】占有. ②〔*pl.*〕占有物,所有物;〔*pl.*〕财产;所有权. ③〔常 *pl.*〕领地,属地,殖民地. ④着迷,着魔. ⑤(足球等比赛中某一队员的)暂时控制住球. ⑥〔罕〕自制,泰然自若. *a man of great* ~*s* 大财主. *personal* ~*s* 个人财物. *The keys are in his* ~. 钥匙他拿着. *He is in full* ~ *of his senses.* 他显得极泰然自若. ***come into sb.'s*** ~, ***come into the*** ~ ***of sb.*** 被某人占有;落入某人手中. ***come into*** ~ ***of sth.*** 获得[占有]某物. ***get*** ~ ***of*** 拿到,占有,占领. ***in*** ~ (物)被据有;(人)据有. ***in*** ~ ***of sth.*** 占有某物. ***in the*** ~ ***of sb.*** 为某人所有. ***P- is nine points of the law.*** 现实占有,败一胜九〔指在诉讼中〕. ***rejoice in the*** ~ ***of*** 幸而有…. ***take*** ~ ***of*** 占领,占有 (*He took* ~ *of his new house.* 他已住进他的新房子了). ***the man in*** ~ 占有者,封查执行官. ~**-minded** *a.* 贪心的,想把一切据为己有的.

pos·ses·sive [pəˈzesiv] *a.* ①所有的,占有的,占有欲的;表示所有的. ②【语法】(词、词组、形态变化等)所属关系的,所有格的. —*n.*【语法】〔the ~〕所有格;所有格的词,物主代词,(表示)所属关系的词(或词组等). *the* ~ *case*【语法】所有格,属格. ~ **adjective**【语法】所有格形容词. ~ **pronoun**【语法】物主代词. **-ly** *ad.* **-ness** *n.*

pos·ses·sor [pəˈzesə] *n.* 持有人,占有人,所有人.

pos·ses·so·ry [pəˈzesəri] *a.* 占有的;所有(者)的;所有性的. ***a*** ~ ***action*** 确认所有权的诉讼. ***a*** ~ ***title to land*** 土地占有权.

pos·set [ˈpɔsit] *n.* 牛奶甜酒〔热牛奶加酒等,旧时常用以治感冒等〕.

pos·si·bil·i·ty [ˌpɔsəˈbiliti] *n.* ①可能,可能性. ②〔常 *pl.*〕可能(发生)的事情;〔*pl.*〕希望. ***a bare*** ~ 万一的事情. ***be within [out of] the bounds [range] of*** ~ …是可能[不可能]的. ***by any*** ~ ①万一,也许〔带条件词〕. ②决不会〔带否定词〕. ***by some*** ~ 或许,也许. ***There is no*** ~ ***of ...*** 没有…的希望[可能].

pos·si·ble [ˈpɔsəbl] *a.* ①可能有的,也许会有[发生]的;潜在的. ②可能实行的,做得到的,想得到的. ③合理的,可以允许的. ④〔口〕相当的,不坏的;可以接受的;还算过得去的. *all the assistance* ~ 尽一切可能支援. *the highest* ~ *speed* 最大速度. *It is* ~ *that he knows.* 他也许知道. ***a*** ~ ***person*** 能胜任(做某事)的人. ***as ... as*** ~ 尽量…,尽可能…. ***if*** ~ 可能的话. ~ ***of*** 可能…的. ***with the least delay*** ~ 尽快. —*n.* ①〔the ~〕可能性,潜在性. ②〔常 *pl.*〕可能的人[物],可能有的事. ③(射击等中)最高分. ④〔*pl.*〕〔俚〕必需物品;金钱. ⑤候补人,预备队员,生力军. ⑥全力. ~*s to probables* 预备队员对候补队员. ***do one's*** ~ 尽全力. ***score a*** ~ (射击等中)得最高分.

pos·si·bly [ˈpɔsəbli] *ad.* ①可能地;合理地. ②或者,也许. ③无论如何,万万,不管怎样〔用于否定句和疑问句〕. *He may* ~ *recover.* 他也许会好. *I cannot* ~ *do it.* 那件事我无论如何也不能做.

pos·sum [ˈpɔsəm] *n.* 〔美口〕鼩,负鼠 (= opossum). *come* ~ *over sb.* 〔口〕欺骗某人,瞒哄某人. ***play [act]*** ~ 装死;装病;装傻;假装不知. —*vi.* 〔美口〕= play ~. ~ **belly** 〔美俚〕火车车箱底下的贮藏室;车辆底部的藏物处.

pos·sy [ˈpɔsi] *n.* 〔军俚〕阵地〔position 的缩略语〕.

Post [pəust] *n.* 波斯特〔姓氏〕.

post[1] [pəust] *n.* ①柱,桩;杆;标竿. ②(赛马等)起跑标,终点标;【矿】矿柱;煤柱;厚砂岩层;厚石灰岩层. ③(剑桥大学的)不及格榜. ④(枪的)准星. *a lamp* ~ 路灯杆. *a sign* ~ 标杆. ***be in the wrong [right] side of the*** ~ 干得不对[对]. ***beat sb. at the*** ~【赛跑】最后一刻胜过某人. ***between you and me and the*** ~ 你知我知,切勿外泄. ***deaf as a*** ~ 全聋. ***kiss the*** ~ 深夜回来被关在门外. ~ ***and railing*** 木栅. —*vt.* ①把(布告等)贴在(柱子等)上 *(up)*;贴出(布告等). ②公布(某船迟到、行踪不明等). ③(出布告)公开揭发[谴责]. ④把…登入榜;(剑桥大学)贴出(不及格榜). ⑤〔美〕公告(地内)禁猎;(出布告等)禁止进入(某地). ***P- no bills.*** (此处)禁止招贴. ~ ***one's land*** 〔美〕贴告示地内禁猎. ~**-mill** 风车.

post[2] [pəust] *n.* ①〔主英〕邮政;邮寄;(一批)邮件 *(cf.* 〔美〕mail*)*;邮件的一次发送[收进]. ②邮政法,邮政制度. ③〔英〕邮政局;邮筒;信箱. ④〔方〕邮递员;快件递送员;邮车;驿站,驿馆;〔古〕驿马. ⑤〔英〕(20 × 16 英寸的)信笺尺寸. ⑥…邮报〔作报名〕. *I had a heavy* ~ *yesterday.* 我昨天收到很多邮件. *Take the letter to the* ~. 请把这封信投到邮筒里. *the Washington P-* 华盛顿邮报. ~ ***and telecommunication*** 邮电. ***by*** ~ 由邮寄 (*send by* ~ 邮寄). ***by return of*** ~【史】回信请交

来人带回;(现指)由下一班回程邮递带回. ***catch [missed] the ~*** 赶上[没有赶上]发信时间. — *vt.* ①[主英]邮寄,投邮. ②用驿马送,急送. ③誊(帐),过(帐);登入(总帐). ④[通例用被动语态]使熟悉;使了解,使懂得(新知识等). — *vi.* ①[古]骑驿马旅行. ②赶紧走,飞快走过. ③【马术】跟着马动. ***be well ~ed up [~ oneself up] in*** 通晓,熟悉. ***~ off [over]*** 赶紧出发. ***~ up sales*** 把销售金额登入总帐. — *ad.* 用急件[驿马];赶紧地,火速地. *ride ~* 骑驿马赶路;催马快跑. **~bag** [英]邮袋. **~ boat** [英]邮船;客船. **~box** [英]信箱;邮筒. **~boy** ①邮递员. ②= postilion. **~ card** [英](不需贴邮票的邮局发行)官制明信片(=[美] postal card);(非邮局发行的)商制明信片[附有图画,需贴邮票]. **~ chaise** [古]驿马车. **~-free** *a.* 免邮费的;邮费付讫的. **~haste** *n., ad.* 赶紧,火速,火急. **~horn** (18、19世纪)驿车上用的喇叭. **~ horse** 驿马. **~house** 驿馆. **~man** 邮递员,邮差. **~mark** ①*n.* 邮戳. ②*vt.* (将邮票)盖销. **~master** 邮政局长. **~mistress** 女邮政局长. **~ office** 邮政局 (*a ~ office box* 邮政信箱[略*P.O.B.*]. *a ~ office order* 邮政汇票[略 *P.O.O.*]. *a ~ office saving bank* 邮政储金局. *a ~ office stamp* 邮政日戳). **~ -paid** *a.* 邮费付讫的. **~rider** ①(过去)骑马投送邮件的人,驿使. ②邮政. **~ road** 驿路. **~ time** 邮件递送[到达、截止]时间;邮件收发时间. **~ town** 有邮局的市镇;(备有驿马的)驿站.

post[3] [pəust] *n.* ①(被指定的)地位,岗位;职位,职守. ②【军】哨所,站;哨兵警戒区;[转义]哨兵,卫兵. ③基地,驻(屯)地;兵营;营区. ④【美军】守备队;复员军人分会. ⑤(特种股票)交易所. ⑥【英军】(睡眠)熄灯号. ⑦商埠;贸易站;租界. *a radar ~* 雷达哨. *the ~ of duty* 工作岗位,职守. *a vigorous, militant command ~* 朝气蓬勃的战斗指挥部. *the first ~* 头遍熄灯号[九点半]. *the last ~* 末次熄灯号[十点]. ***at one's ~*** 在任所;在岗位上. ***fill (up) a ~*** 就任. ***hold a ~ at*** 在…任职. ***keep the ~*** 守住岗位. ***resign [remain at] one's ~*** 退[留]职. ***proceed to one's ~*** 赴任. ***take ~*** 各就各位. ***stick to one's post*** 坚守岗位. — *vt.* ①配置(哨兵等). ②【英史】任命(20门炮以上舰船的舰长等). ③(隆重地)把(国旗)带往指定地. ④把…作赌注. **~ captain**【英史】小军舰的舰长. **~ exchange** [美军]营地服务商店[略作PX].

post [pəust] *ad.* [L.]在后. ***~ bellum*** [ˈbeləm] 战后. ***~ factum*** [ˈfæktəm] 事后. ***~ meridiem*** [məˈridiəm] 午后[略作 P.M., p.m., PM]. ***~ mortem*** [ˈmɔːtem] 死后;事后. ***~ obitum*** [ˈɔbitəm] 死后.

post. = postal.

post- *pref.* 后,次: *post*axial, *post*war.

post·age [ˈpəustidʒ] *n.* 邮费. *~ due* 欠(邮)资. *~ free* 邮寄免费. *~ paid* 邮费付讫. *inland ~* 国内邮资. **~stamp** 邮票. **~ meter** (加盖"邮资已付"的)自动邮资盖印机.

post·al [ˈpəustəl] *a.* 邮政的;邮政局的. *The International [Universal] P- Union* 万国邮政联盟. — *n.* [美口]明信片. **~ card** [美](邮局制的)明信片[上面印有邮票]. **~ clerk** [美]邮局职员. **~ course** 函授课程. **~insurance** 简易保险. **~ matters** 邮件. **~order** [英]邮政汇票. **~ package** 小包邮件. **~ savings** 邮政储金.

post·al·i·za·tion [ˌpəustəlaiˈzeiʃən] *n.* (象邮费那样)远近运费均一化.

post·a·tom·ic [ˈpəustəˈtɔmik] *a.* 第一颗原子弹爆炸之后的;原子能发现以后的.

post·ax·i·al [pəustˈæksiəl] *a.*【解,动】轴后的.

post-bel·lum [pəustˈbeləm] *a.* 战后的;美国南北战争以后的.

post·ca·va [ˌpəustˈkeivə, -kɑː-] *n.* (*pl.* **-vae** [-viː])【解】后腔静脉. **-l** *a.*

post·clas·si·cal [ˈpəustˈklæsikəl] *a.* (希腊、罗马文学艺术的)古典时代后的.

post·date [ˈpəustˈdeit] *vt.* ①把日期填迟(若干天);在…上填事后日期,填迟…的日期. ②在…之后到来,接在…的后面. — [ˈpəustdeit] *n.* (证券等的)事后日期,比实际填迟的日期 (*opp.* predate).

post·di·lu·vi·an [ˌpəustdaiˈluːviən] *a., n.* (基督教《圣经》中所说)世界大洪水 (Deluge) 之后的(人).

post·doc·tor·al [ˌpəustˈdɔktərəl] *a.* (取得博士学位后)从事更高深研究的;从事比博士级工作更高深的研究工作的.

post·en·try [ˈpəustˌentri] *n.* ①(赛马)后补手续书. ②【簿】补记帐目.

post·er[1] [ˈpəustə] *n.* ①(贴在墙壁等上的)广告(画),海报,标语,招贴. ②贴标语[广告、传单等]的人. — *vt.* 贴[传单、广告等];用招贴宣传.

post·er[2] [ˈpəustə] *n.* ①驿马. ②[古]急件递送员;匆匆忙忙的旅客.

poste res·tante [ˈpəust ˈrestɑ̃ːnt] [F.] ①(信封上附注的)留局待领邮件. ②[主英](邮局的)待领邮件科;待领邮件业务.

pos·te·ri·or [pɔsˈtiəriə] *a.* (地位上)后面的 (*opp.* anterior);(时间上)在后的,(次序上)其次的 (*to*) (*opp.* prior);【动】尾部的;【解】背部的;【植】接近茎轴处的. *~ to the year 1972* 一九七二年以后的. *various events that happened ~ to the end of the war* 战后继之发生的种种事件. — *n.* ①后部. ②[*sing.*, [古] *pl.*]臀部,屁股. **-ly** *ad.* 在后部,在背后.

pos·te·ri·or·i·ty [pɔsˌtiəriˈɔriti] *n.* (时间、位置、次序上的)在后.

pos·ter·i·ty [pɔsˈteriti] *n.* [集合词] ①后裔,子孙. ②后世,后代. *write for ~* 为后代写作.

pos·tern [ˈpəustəːn] *n.* ①(城、教堂等的)后门,边门;便门. ②边道;(城堡的)地下暗道;逃路.

post·face [ˈpəusfis] *n.* (刊物等的)编后记.

post·fix [ˈpəustfiks] *n.* ①后加物. ②【语法】后缀;词尾. — [pəustˈfiks] *vt.* 把…加在后面;加后缀于,加词尾于.

post·form [pəustˈfɔːm] *vt.* 把(加工后的薄板材)再制成一定形状.

post·gan·gli·on·ic [ˌpəustˌgæŋgliˈɔnik] *a.*【解】后神经节的.

post·gla·cial [ˈpəustˈgleisjəl] *a.* 冰期后的.

post·grad·u·ate [ˈpəustˈgrædjuit, *Am.* ˌpəustˈgrædʒuit] *a.* 大学毕业后的;大学研究院的. *the ~ course* 研究学科. *the ~ research institute* 研究院. *a ~ student* 研究生. — *n.* 研究生.

post hoc, er·go prop·ter hoc [ˈpəust hɔk ˈəːgəu ˈprɔptə hɔk] [L.]在此之后,因此.

post·hu·mous [ˈpɔstjuməs] *a.* ①父死后生的,遗腹的. ②著作者死后出版的. ③身后的,死后的. *a ~ child* 遗腹子. *one's ~ name* 讳,谥号. *~ works* 遗著. ***confer ~ honours on*** 追赠,谥封,追认…为. **-ly** *ad.* 死后,身后.

post·hyp·not·ic [ˌpəusthipˈnɔtik] *a.* 催眠后的,进入昏睡状态后的时期的. **~ suggestion**【医】催眠后暗示.

pos·tiche [pɔsˈtiːʃ] *a.* [F.] ①伪造的,假冒的,人为的,人造的. ②过份装饰的. — *n.* ①代替物;伪造物. ②虚假;矫饰. ③假发. ④(建筑物等上的)多余的添加物,画蛇添足似的东西.

pos·ti·cous [pɔsˈtaikəs] *a.*【植】在后的;外附的.

pos·til [ˈpɔstil] *n.* (基督教《圣经》的)旁注;注解.

pos·til·(l)i·on [pəsˈtiljən] *n.* (四马以上马车的)前排左马骑手,左马驭者.

post·im·pres·sion·ism [ˈpəustimˈpreʃənizəm] *n.*【美】后期印象派. **-sion·ist** ①*n.*【美】后期印象派画家. ②*a.* 后期印象派的.

post-lib·e·ra·tion [ˈpəustˌlibəˈreiʃən] *a.* 解放后的.
post·li·min·i·um, post·lim·i·ny [ˌpəustliˈminiəm, -ˈlimini] *n.*【国际法】战后财产恢复权;【罗马法】(俘虏等回国后的)公民资格恢复权.
post·lude [ˈpəustljuːd] *n.* ①【乐】(*opp.* prelude) 后奏曲; 尾曲; (乐曲的)结尾部. ②教堂做礼拜后的风琴独奏.
Post·mas·ter-Gen·er·al [ˈpəust*t*mɑːstəˈdʒenərəl] *n.* 〔英〕邮政大臣;〔美〕邮政部长.
post·me·rid·i·an [ˈpəustməˈridiən] *a.* 午后的, 午后发生的 (*opp.* antemeridian).
post·mil·len·ni·al [ˌpəustmiˈleniəl] *a.*【宗】一千至福年(millennium)后的.
post·mil·len·ni·al·ism [ˌpəustmiˈleniəlizəm] *n.*【宗】一千至福年后基督再临说.
post-mor·tem [ˈpəust*t*ˈmɔːtem] *a.* ①死后的. ②事后的. *a ~ table* 验尸台. — *n.* ①尸体解剖, 验尸. ②事后的调查分析 (= ~ examination).
post·na·tal [ˈpəustˈneitl] *a.* 出生后的; 初生婴儿的.
post·na·tus [ˈpəustˈneitəs] *n.* (*pl.* *-nati* [-ˈneitai]) ①某大事件后出生的人; 发表《独立宣言》(1776 年)后出生的美国人. ②〔废〕〔*sing.*〕次子.
post·nup·tial [ˈpəustˈnʌpʃəl] *a.* 结婚后的. **-ly** *ad.* 婚后.
post-o·bit [ˈpəustˈɔbit, Am. pəustˈəubit] *a.* 死后生效的. — *n.* 死后偿还借据〔以应得遗产做抵押的借据〕(= ~ bond).
post·or·bit·al [ˌpəustˈɔːbitl] *a.*【解, 动】眶后的. — *n.* 眶后骨.
post·op·er·a·tive [ˈpəustˈɔpərətiv, -ˈɔprə-; -əreitiv] *a.* 手术后的. **-ly** *ad.*
post·par·tum [ˌpəust*t*ˈpɑːtəm] *a.* 产后的.
post·pone [pəustˈpəun] *vt.* ①使延期, 延缓; 搁置 (*until, till, to, for*). ②把…视为次要, 把…放在次要地位 (*to*). ③【语法】把(某种词等) 放在后面[句尾]. — *vi.*【医】(疟疾等)延迟发作[复发]. *postponing of military service* 缓役. **post·pon·a·ble** *a.* 可延缓的. **-r** *n.* 延迟者, 使延缓者. **-ment** *n.* 延期, 延迟; 搁置.
post·po·si·tion [ˈpəustpəˈziʃən] *n.* ①【语法】后置词. ②后置. **-al** *a.*
post·pos·i·tive [ˈpəustˈpɔzitiv] *a.*【语法】置于词后的, 附加于另一词的; 与前词接合的; 后缀的. — *n.*【语法】后置词. **-ly** *ad.*
post·pran·di·al [ˈpəust*t*ˈprændiəl] *a.* 〔谑〕饭后的.
post·sce·ni·um [ˈpəustˈsiːniəm] *n.* (戏院的)后台.
post·script [ˈpəusskript, ˈpəus-kript] *n.* ①(信的)再者, 又及; 附言〔略作 P.S., PS., PS 或 p.s.〕. ②(书等的)补遗, 附录; 跋. ③英国广播协会 (B.B.C.) 新闻报告的结束语.
pos·tu·lant [ˈpɔstjulənt] *n.* ①【宗】圣职[牧师职]申请人. ②〔罕〕申请者.
pos·tu·late [ˈpɔstjuleit] *vt.* ①(认为当然而)主张, (认为自明之理而)假定; (作为先决条件而) 要求. ②【宗】要求上级任命[指定]. ③根据上级批准而任命[指定]. ④【数】公设, 假设. *the claims ~d* 要求事项. — *vi.* 假定; 要求 (*for*). — [ˈpɔstjulit] *n.* ①假定. ②基本要求; 先决[必要]条件. ③【数】公设, 假设; (作图的)公准. ④基本原理.
pos·tu·la·tion [ˌpɔstjuˈleiʃən] *n.* ①假定. ②要求. ③【宗】须经上级批准的任命[指定]. **-al** *a.*
pos·tu·la·tor [ˈpɔstjuˌleitə] *n.* ①假定者. ②要求者. ③(要求批准圣职的)申请人.
pos·ture [ˈpɔstʃə, -tjuə] *n.* ①姿势, 姿态; 态度. ②精神准备; 心情, 心境. ③形势, 情形 (*of*). *a ~ of defense* 守势. *the present ~ of affairs* 目前形势, 时局. — *vt.* 使作出某种姿势[态度]. — *vi.* 取某种姿势[态度]; 故作姿态. **~-maker** 杂技演员. **~-master** 柔软体操教师.
pos·tur·al *a.*
pos·tur·er [ˈpɔstʃərə] *n.* ①作出某种姿态的人; 装腔作势者. ②杂技演员.
pos·tur·ize, pos·tur·ise [ˈpɔstʃəraiz] *vi.* 取某种姿势, 装作…的样子 (*as*).
post·vac·cin·al [ˌpəustˈvæksinəl] *a.*【医】种牛痘后的, 接种后的.
post·war [ˈpəustˈwɔː] *a.* 战后的 (*opp.* prewar). *~ problems* 战后问题.
po·sy [ˈpəuzi] *n.* ①花束. ②〔古〕(刻在戒指里圈上的)诗句, 题铭.
pot [pɔt] *n.* ①壶, 瓶, 罐; 钵, (深)锅. ②【冶】坩埚. ③一壶[钵、瓶、罐、锅]之量. ④壶中物; 酒; 饮酒; 酗酒. ⑤花盆; 尿壶; 罐状物; 烟囱罩; 捕鱼篓, 捕虾笼;〔美俚〕高顶帽子. ⑥〔俚〕(赌钱时的)巨款; 赌注总额; (一个团体的)基金总额; 纸牌戏的一局. ⑦〔俚〕大人物; 大肚子. ⑧【运】银杯, 银盾, 奖品. ⑨$15\frac{1}{2} \times 12\frac{1}{2}$ 英寸大小的纸张. ⑩【地质】壶穴, 水穴. ⑪〔美俚〕电位计. ⑫〔俚〕(地狱的)深渊. ⑬〔俚〕近距离射击, 随手射击 (= ~-shot). ⑭〔美俚〕大麻叶. *a big ~* 要人, 名人. *brazen and earthen ~s* 阔老和穷人; 名人和无名小卒. *A little ~ is soon hot.* 壶小易热; 量小易怒; 人小火气大. *A watched ~ never boils.* 心急水不沸. ***betray the ~ to the roses*** 露出马脚, 泄露秘密. ***boil the ~*** 挣钱糊口, 谋生. ***call each other ~ and kettle*** 互相谩骂. ***crush a ~*** 设宴. ***go into the melting ~*** 经受锻炼. ***go to ~*** 〔俚〕没落, (营业等)衰落; 被毁坏, 垮掉; 破产; 毁灭. ***If you touch ~, you must touch penny.*** 一律不赊. ***in one's ~, in the ~*** 喝醉. ***make a ~ of money*** 发大财. ***make one's ~s and pans of one's property*** 败尽财产去讨饭. ***make the ~ boil, keep the ~ boiling*** ①谋生, 维持生活, 挣钱糊口. ②保持热度, 继续猛干; 兴致勃勃(玩下去)下去. ***~s and pans*** 炊事用具, 坛坛罐罐. ***put a quart into a pint ~*** 白费劲, 做不可能的事. ***put the ~ in*** 在…中发大财. ***put the ~ on*** 在…上赌巨款. ***The ~ calls the kettle black.*** 乌鸦骂猪黑, 只知责怪人而不知自己有同样的缺点或过失. ***take a ~ at (a bird)*** 用枪乱打(鸟). — *vt.* ①(用锅等)煮, 炖. ②把…装入壶内[罐内](保存). ③把…栽在花盆里. ④删节; 摘录. ⑤(为取得食物)而向(动物)射击; 乱射; 猎获;〔口〕得到. ⑥【台球】把(球)打入袋内. *~ an heiress* 〔俚〕得到一个嗣女. *~ a rabbit* 打兔子. — *vi.* ①射击; 乱射 (*at*). ②〔古〕喝酒. ~ **ale** 酒糟. ~ **barley** 去壳大麦. ~**bellied** *a.* 罗汉肚的; 大肚皮的. ~**belly** 罗汉肚; 大腹便便的人. ~**boil** *vi.* 〔俚〕(为混饭吃而)粗制滥造文艺作品. ~**boiler** 〔俚〕(文学艺术上的) 骗钱作品, 为混饭吃而写作的作品[作者]. ~**-bound** *a.* (植物)根系长满一花盆的; 没有发展余地的. ~**boy** 〔英〕(尤指啤酒馆的)服务员. ~**companion** 酒友. ~ **experiment** 盆栽试验. ~**-gang** 〔美〕聚在一处吃饭的一群无业游民. ~**-garden** 菜地. ~**-hanger** = pot-hook. ~ **hat** 高帽, (硬顶) 礼帽. ~**head** 〔俚〕麻醉品吸者, 吸毒者. ~ **herb** 野菜; 家种蔬菜; 调味香草. ~**holder** (保暖用的) 布壶套. ~**hole** ①【地】锅穴, 壶穴, 地壶〔河床岩石上的壶形洞〕. ②路面的凹窝, 车印. ~**hook** ①锅钩〔挂锅用〕. ②潦草难看的字 (*~hooks and hangers* 初学写字时写成的字; 潦草难看的字). ~**house** ①*n.* 啤酒店; 小酒馆. ②*a.* 小酒馆的, 下等的 (*the manners of a ~house* 作风粗野. *a ~house politician* 小政客). ~**hunter** ①随手乱打的猎人. ②〔口〕以获得奖品为目的的运动员. ~ **lead** (涂赛船底用的) 石墨. ~**-lids** 〔*pl.*〕〔美俚〕铙钹(= cymbals). ~**luck** 便饭, 现成饭菜; 〔美俚〕客人带来的菜 (*take ~luck with friends* 同朋友吃便饭). ~**man** = ~boy. ~ **metal** ①铸铁, 锅铁; 铜铅合金. ②(熔解时着色的) 有色玻璃. ~**pie** 锅贴, 烤馅饼; 加团子的烩肉菜汤. ~ **plant** 盆栽植物. ~ **roast** 〔美〕炖肉, 焖肉. ~**-roast** *vt.* 炖. ~**sherd**

(考古学上有价值的)陶器碎片. ~-shot ①*n.* (为取得食物而进行的)打猎; 近距离狙击; 乱射, 乱打 (*take a ~-shot at a rabbit* 〔喻〕好歹试试看); 肆意[突然]的抨击. ②*vt., vi.* (向…)乱射; 肆意抨击. ~-spinning (化纤的)离心式纺丝. ~-still ①(没有汽套的)罐式蒸馏器. ②非法酒坊. ~stone【矿】粗皂石; 块滑石〔史前人用以做器皿〕. ~-valiant *a.* 酒后胆壮的. ~-valour 酒后之勇. ~waller【英史】(1832年以前)自己成家而具有选举权的人. ~walloper ①= pot-waller. ②〔美俚〕厨师; 洗锅工. ③【海】厨师下手. 〔英俚〕笨手笨脚的人. **-ful** *n.* 一壶, 一锅, 一钵, 一罐.

pot. = potential.

po·ta·ble ['pəutəbl] *a.* 〔谑〕可以喝的, 适合饮用的. ~ *water* 饮用水. — *n.* 〔*pl.*〕饮料, 酒. **-bil·i·ty** [-'biliti], **-ness** *n.*

po·tage [pɔ'tɑːʒ] *n.* 〔F.〕浓汤, 肉汁.

potam(o)- *comb. f.* 河: *potamology.*

po·tam·ic [pəu'tæmik] *a.* 河流的, 江河的.

pot·a·mol·o·gy [ˌpɔtə'mɔlədʒi] *n.* 河流学, 河川学.

pot·a·mom·e·ter [ˌpɔtə'mɔmitə] *n.*【电】水力计.

pot·ash, po·tass ['pɔtæʃ, pɔ'tæs] *n.* ①【化】钾碱, 碳酸钾, 氢氧化钾. ②= potassium. *caustic* ~ 苛性钾碱〔氢氧化钾的俗称〕. *muriate of* ~ 氯化钾. ~ **fertilizer** 钾肥. ~ **soap** 钾皂.

po·tas·si·um [pə'tæsjəm] *n.*【化】钾. ~ **carbonate** 碳酸钾. ~ **chlorate** 氯酸钾. ~ **chloride** 氯化钾. ~ **nitrate** 硝酸钾. ~ **oxide** 氧化钾. ~ **permanganate** 高锰酸钾, 灰锰氧.

po·ta·tion [pəu'teiʃən] *n.* ①一饮; 一杯; 畅饮. ②〔常*pl.*〕喝酒; 酒宴; (酒类)饮料.

po·ta·to [pə'teitəu] *n.* (*pl.* ~*es*) ①【植】马铃薯, 土豆. ②〔美〕甘薯. ③〔俚〕(趾头戳破的)袜子洞. ④〔美俚〕一元钱. ⑤〔美俚〕头; 难看的脸. ⑥〔美俚〕(垒)球. *sweet [Spanish]* ~ 甘薯, 白薯, 山芋. *white [Irish]* ~〔美〕马铃薯. *Canada* ~菊芋. *a* ~ *digger* 马铃薯收获机. ***a hot*** ~ 棘手的问题. ~***es and point*** (肉少得可怜的)一锅马铃薯炖肉. ***quite the*** ~, ***the clean*** ~〔俚〕恰好的, 正合适的事物. ***small*** ~***es [a small*** ~***]*** 〔美俚〕微不足道的人[东西]. ~ **blight** 马铃薯早疫[晚疫]病. ~ **box**〔俚〕嘴. ~ **chip** 炸马铃薯薄片. ~**-head**〔美俚〕笨蛋. ~ **masher** ①熟马铃薯捣烂器. ②木柄手榴弹. ③〔美俚〕鼓槌; 煮熟的鸡[鸭]腿. ④〔俚〕干扰雷达的天线. ~ **plug** 斜面马铃薯培养基. ~ **ring**〔爱〕垫碗、钵的银圈. ~ **trap** = ~ **box**.

po·ta·tory ['pəutətəri] *a.* 饮酒的; 有酒癖的.

pot-au-feu [pɔtəu'fə] *n.* 〔F.〕肉菜汤〔汤中肉菜另盘上桌〕.

pot·e·ca·ry ['pɔtəkəri] *n.* 〔主英方〕药剂师; 药房 (= apothecary).

po·teen [pəu'tiːn] *n.* 〔Ir.〕私造威士忌酒.

po·tence, po·ten·cy ['pəutəns, -tənsi] *n.* ①潜能, 潜力, 能力. ②势; 力量; 权力, 权威, 权势. ③(药品等的)效力, 效验. ④有权势的人; 神力. ⑤生殖力, 性能力.

po·tent ['pəutənt] *a.* ①【诗、修辞】有力的, 强有力的; 有势力的. ②(药等)有效力的; 烈性的; (议论等)使人心服的. ③(茶等)浓的. ④(男性)有生殖力的. **-ly** *ad.*

po·ten·tate ['pəutənteit] *n.* ①有权势的人; 当权者. ②统治者; 君主. ③强盛的国家.

po·ten·tial [pə'tenʃəl] *a.* ①可能的; 【语法】可能语气的. ②潜在的; 有潜势的; 【物】位的, 势的. ③〔罕〕有力的. *The seed is the* ~ *flower and fruit.* 种子是潜在的花和果实. — *n.* ①可能(性); 【语法】可能语气. ②潜在力; 潜势; 【物】位, 势; 电势, 电位. *partial* ~ 化学势. ~ **difference**【物】位差, 势差; 电位差. ~ **energy**【物】位能, 势能. ~ **genius** 有天才素质的人. ~ **hill**【数】位垒, 势垒. ~ **infinity**【数】潜无穷. ~ **mood**【语法】可能语气. ~ **share**【商】权利股. ~ **transformer** (测量用)变压器. **-ly** *ad.* 潜在地, 有潜在可能性地.

po·ten·ti·al·i·ty [pəˌtenʃi'æliti] *n.* 可能性, 潜在的可能; 潜能, 潜势; 〔*pl.*〕潜力. *tap potentialities* 挖掘潜力. *bring all potentialities into full play* 充分发挥一切潜力.

po·ten·tial·ize [pə'tenʃəlaiz] *vt.* ①使具有潜在的可能性; 使成为潜在的. ②【物】使成为势能[位能]. **-i·za·tion** [-ˌtenʃəlai'zeiʃən] *n.*

po·ten·ti·ate [pə'tenʃieit] *vt.* ①赋与…以力量; 使加强; 使(药物等)更有效力. — *vi.* 有加强[提高效力]的作用.

po·ten·til·la [ˌpəutən'tilə] *n.*【植】委陵菜属植物 (= cinquefoil).

po·ten·ti·om·e·ter [pəˌtenʃi'ɔmitə] *n.*【电】电位计, 电势计; 【讯】分压器. *a balance* ~【火箭】随从[伺服]系统电位计.

po·ten·ti·o·stat [pə'tenʃiəstæt] *n.*【物】恒(电)势器.

poth·e·car·y ['pɔθiˌkeri] *n.* 〔英方, 古〕药剂师, 药铺.

po·theen [pɔ'tiːn] *n.* = poteen.

poth·er ['pɔðə] *n.* 〔书〕①喧扰, 骚动; 忙乱. ②弥漫的尘土; 蒙蒙烟雾; 云烟. ③烦恼. ***be in a*** ~ 心神不宁. ***make [raise] a*** ~ 引起骚动. — *vt.* 使烦恼; 使心神不安. — *vi.* 喧扰; 忙乱.

po·tiche [pəu'tiːʃ] *n.* (*pl.* ***po·tiches*** [pəu'tiːʃ]) 〔F.〕瓷(花)瓶; (有盖瓶式)瓷缸.

po·ti·cho·ma·ni·a [ˌpɔtiʃə'meiniə] *n.* ①热衷于花瓶的仿造. ②日本陶器仿造(法).

po·tion ['pəuʃən] *n.* ①(药的)一服, 一剂. ②一服麻醉药[毒药]. *a sleeping* ~ 一服安眠药.

pot·latch ['pɔtˌlætʃ, -ˌlæʃ] *n.* ①〔常用 P-〕冬季赠礼节〔美洲印第安人冬季的一个节日〕; 在该节日里分配或交换的礼物. ②〔美口〕庆宴, 宴会.

Po·to·mac [pə'təumək] *n.* 波托马克河〔美国, 流经华盛顿〕.

po·tom·e·ter [pə'tɔmetə] *n.*【气】蒸腾计.

pot·pour·ri [pəu'puri(ː); F. pɔːpuriː] *n.* 〔F.〕①百花香〔干燥的花瓣加香料, 用于熏房间〕. ②混杂物; 肉菜杂烩. ③【乐】集成曲, 杂曲; (文学作品等的)杂集, 杂录.

Pots·dam ['pɔtsdæm, Ger. 'pɔːtsdɑːm] *n.* 波茨坦〔德意志民主共和国城市, 柏林市西南旧离宫所在地〕. ~ ***Declaration*** (1945年7月盟国敦促日本无条件投降的)波茨坦宣言.

pot·sy ['pɔtsi] *n.* 〔美方〕小孩(独脚)跳踢石子的游戏, "跳房子"游戏, "踢房子"游戏, "跳方"游戏 (= hopscotch).

pot·tage ['pɔtidʒ] *n.* 〔古〕(蔬菜或菜肉)浓汤 (= potage). ***a mess of*** ~ 见 mess 条.

pot·ted ['pɔtid] *a.* ①盆栽的. ②瓶装的; 装成罐头的. ③〔美俚〕喝醉的; 因吸食大麻毒剂而醉倒的. *a* ~ *plant* 盆栽植物. ~ *jam* 瓶装果酱. ~ *meat* 加味罐头碎肉. *a* ~ *play* 短剧.

pot·teen [pɔ'tiːn] *n.* ≐ poteen.

pot·ter[1] ['pɔtə] *n.* ①陶工; 〔英方〕陶器小贩. ②罐头制造人. ~**'s asthma [bronchitis]**【医】陶工喘症[支气管炎]. ~**'s clay** 陶土. ~**'s field** 义冢地, 公共墓地. ~**'s lathe** 陶器旋床. ~**'s wheel** 陶工旋盘. ~**'s work [ware]** 陶器.

pot·ter[2] ['pɔtə] *vi.* ①稀里糊涂地混日子, 吊儿郎当地[磨磨蹭蹭地]做事 (*at; in*). ②慢条斯理地走; 闲逛, 闲荡 (*about*). ~ *over a task* 磨洋工. ~ *about the house all day* 在屋子里整天磨蹭. — *vt.* 混(日子), 浪费(时间) (*away*). ~ ***away one's time*** 混日子, 磨时间.

pot·ter·y ['pɔtəri] *n.* ①〔集合词〕陶器类. ②陶器厂[作坊]. ③陶器制造(法). *a* ~ *casting* 陶器铸坯. ***the Potteries*** 陶器区〔英国斯塔福德郡 (Staffordshire) 北部陶器出产地〕.

pot·ting ['pɔtiŋ] *n.* ①陶器制造. ②装壶, 装瓶. ③盆栽.

pot·tle [ˈpɔtl] *n.* ①〔古〕罐〔液量名 (= 2 quarts)〕. ②(相当于一罐容量的)一壶(葡萄酒). ③(装草莓等的)小果篮.

pot·to [ˈpɔtəu] *n.* *(pl.* ~*s)*【动】(中非的)树熊猴 *(Perodicticus potto)*.

pot·ty[1] [ˈpɔti] *a.* 〔英俚〕①零零碎碎的, 琐碎的; 微不足道的. ②(试题)容易的. ③傻的; 发疯似的; 拼命〔疯狂〕追求的; 着迷的 *(about)*. ④傲慢的; 势利的. *a* ~ *set of questions* 一组容易回答的问题. ***be* ~ *about*** 迷恋. ~ ***little*** 一点点, 琐碎的.

pot·ty[2] [ˈpɔti] *n.* (小孩用的)便罐; 尿壶. **~-chair** (小孩用的)大便坐椅.

pouch [pautʃ] *n.* ①(随身携带的)小袋, 囊; 烟草袋;〔Scot.〕衣袋;〔古〕钱包. ②[pautʃ, puːtʃ]【军】皮制弹药盒. ③邮袋. ④【医】水疱. ⑤【动】(有袋类的)育儿袋, 肚囊; (某些猴子的)颊袋; 囊状部;【虫】翅陷;【解】陷凹; 憩室;【植】短角. ⑥〔口〕酒钱, 小帐. — *vt.* ①把…装入袋中, 把…占为已有. ②把…做成袋状; 使鼓起. ③(鱼、鸟)吞进. ④〔俚〕赏酒钱给…, 付小帐给…. ⑤缩拢(袋口等). ~ *the mouth* 噘着嘴. —*vi.* ①(衣服的一部)成袋状; 膨胀. ②(鸟等)吞食. ③用邮袋递送.

pouched [pautʃt] *a.* 有袋的; 袋形的; 悬垂如袋的. ~ *animals* 有袋类动物.

pouch·y [ˈpautʃi] *a.* 袋状的, 囊状的, 似囊的. **pouch·i·ness** *n.*

poud [puːd] *n.* 普特〔苏联衡量名, = 16.38 公斤〕(= pood).

pou·drette [puːˈdret] *n.* (由粪肥、木炭、石膏混合成的)杂肥.

pouf, pouff, pouffe [puːf] *n.* ①(十八世纪流行的)有高发髻的妇女精巧发饰. ②衣服上四周褶皱中间隆起的部分. ③有厚褥的(睡)椅; 厚实的大坐垫, 蒲团.

pou·lard(e) [puːˈlɑːd] *n.* 割去卵巢催肥的母鸡, 肉鸡; 肥育母鸡. ~ **wheat** 圆锥小麦〔美国的一种饲料〕.

poule [puːl] *n.* 〔F.〕〔俚〕妓女 (= prostitute).

poulp(e) [puːlp] *n.* 〔F.〕【动】章鱼.

poult [pəult] *n.* (鸡、火鸡等的)雏, 幼禽.

poult-de-soie [ˈpuːdəˈswɑː] *n.* 〔F.〕波纹绸, 绉绸.

poul·ter·er [ˈpəultərə] *n.* 〔英〕鸡贩; 家禽贩, 野禽贩.

poul·tice [ˈpəultis] *n.*【医】泥罨〔泥敷〕剂. — *vt.*【医】敷泥罨〔敷〕剂于.

poul·try [ˈpəultri] *n.* 〔集合词〕家禽〔鸡、火鸡、鹅、鸭等〕 *(opp.* game*)*; 鸡类. ~ **farm** 家禽饲养场; 鸡场. **~-man** (以营利为目的的)饲养家禽的人; 家禽商.

pounce[1] [pauns] *vt.* 扑过去抓住. — *vi.* ①猛扑, 飞扑 *(upon)*; 猛抓 *(at)*. ②(对人的过错等)急忙抓住, 攻击 *(on; upon)*. — *n.* ①(猛禽等的)猛扑, 抓. ②(猛禽等的)利爪. ***make a* ~ *(up)on*** 猛扑向. ***on the* ~** 正要扑过去.

pounce[2] [pauns] *n.* ①(从前用来防止墨水洇开的)吸墨粉. ②(绣工撒在镂花模板上以印出图案花样的)印花粉. — *vt.* ①在(纸)上撒吸墨粉. ②用印花粉印出(底样); (在金属板、布等上)打成浮凸花样; 在(布等上)打孔; 在…上作孔饰. ③用擦粉把(纸面、帽子面等)打光.

Pound [paund] *n.* 庞德〔姓氏〕.

pound[1] [paund] *n.* ①磅〔英国重量名, 称一般用品的叫"常衡磅" (avoirdupois ~) = 16 盎司或 453.6 克, 略作 lb. 或 lb. av.; 称金银或药品的叫"金衡磅" (troy ~) = 12 盎司或 373.2 克, 略作 lb. t.; 称药品的叫"药衡磅"(apothecaries' ~, 与金衡磅等重, 略作 lb. ap)〕. ②英镑〔英国货币单位, 又名 ~ sterling, = 20 旧先令, 1971 年取消先令后 = 100 便士, 略作 £ 或 L〕. ③镑〔某些国家的货币单位〕. *five* ~*s [*~*]* 五英镑〔可写作 £ 5〕. *a five-*~ *note* 一张五英镑钞票. *a* ~ *note* 一张一英镑钞票. ***a* ~ *of flesh*** 合法但不合情理的要求; 要求偿还一磅肉〔源出莎士比亚的戏剧《威尼斯商人》〕. ***by the* ~** 按每镑(计价). ***claim one's* ~ *of flesh*** 逼人还债. ***In for a penny, in for a* ~** 一不做, 二不休. ***in the* ~**【商】每镑(贴水多少). ***Mischief comes by* ~*s and goes away by ounces.*** 祸害易来难去. ***penny wise and* ~ *foolish*** 小事聪明, 大事糊涂; 小处精明, 大处马虎. ***pay twenty shillings in the* ~** 全数付清. ~ ***for [and]*** ~ 均等地. — *vt.* 验称(货币等的)重量. ~ **cake** (用面粉、白糖、奶油等主要用料各 1 磅或等量做成的)蛋糕. ~ **foolish** *a.* 大数目上马虎的; 省小失大的. ~ **Scots**【史】1 先令 8 便士. **~s, shillings, and pence** 金钱〔略 L. s. d. 或 £. s. d.〕. ~ **sterling** 英镑.

pound[2] [paund] *n.* ①(收留迷失犬、牛等待领的)官设兽栏. ②(关禁无执照等的家畜的)牲畜栏; (放置充公物品等的)待赎所;〔喻〕监牢, 拘留所. ③养鱼塘, 养龙虾池; 鲜活龙虾出售处. ④〔方〕积水. ⑤【猎】危险地位. — *vt.* ①〔古〕把(走失的牲畜等)关进兽栏 *(up)*;〔喻〕监禁, 拘留 *(up)*. ②〔古〕筑坝拦(水). ~ *the field* 设栅栏使牲畜跳不过去.

pound[3] [paund] *vt.* ①捣碎, 舂烂, 把…捣成粉. ②(连续)猛击; 乱敲; 砰砰砰地乱弹(钢琴等), 乱奏(曲子). ③(不断重复地)灌输 *(into)*. ④(沉重地)沿着…行走; 持续地沿着…移动. — *vi.* ①接连不断地打, 乱打; 打破; 接连不断地开炮*(at; on; away)*; (心)砰砰地跳. ②步子沉重地走*(along)*; 发轰隆声地航行〔飞行〕. ③(持续地)苦干. ~ ***away at*** ①乱打; 接连不断地炮击; 批评, 抨击. ②拼命地干(工作). ~ ***home (to)*** 把(道理等)反复灌输给…. ~ ***one's ear***〔美俚〕睡觉. ~ ***out*** 连续猛打出(字), 猛弹出(曲子等). ~ ***the side walk [pavement]***〔美俚〕①徘徊街头找职业, 找工作做. ②(警察)巡行街道. — *n.* 接连打击; 砰砰的打击(声).

pound·age[1] [ˈpaundidʒ] *n.* ①每英镑应纳的手续费或佣金. ②按磅计算的重量〔收费数〕. ③(企业总收益中的)工资比额.

pound·age[2] [ˈpaundidʒ] *n.* ①(领回走失牲畜时付的)官设兽栏收容费. ②(收容走失牲畜的)官设兽栏. ③拘留, 监禁.

pound·al [ˈpaundl] *n.*【物】磅达〔力的单位〕.

pound·er[1] [ˈpaundə] *n.* ①〔用作复合词〕…磅重的东西〔人〕; 发射…磅重炮弹的炮. ②付…英镑的人; 有…英镑财产〔收入〕的人; …英镑的东西. *a 200-*~ 体重 200 磅的人; 有 200 英镑收入的人. *a ring which is a 2,000* ~ 价值 2,000 英镑的戒指.

pound·er[2] [ˈpaundə] *n.* ①连续猛打的人; 捣〔舂〕的人; 捣〔舂〕的工具, 杵. ②【无】鞭状天线. *a stone* ~ 石硪.

Pou·part [ˈpəupɑːt] *n.* 波帕特〔姓氏〕.

pour [pɔː, pɔə] *vt.* ①注, 倒, 灌, 泻, 喷散(液体、粉粒、光线等); 流(血等); 倾注; 源源不断地输送. ②使冒着(枪林弹雨等); 大施(恩惠等). ③尽情唱(歌); 尽情说, 任意说, 发泄, 倾吐. ④(用话)安抚; 使(锐气、意气等)沮丧. ⑤浪费. *P- yourself another cup of tea.* 请再倒杯茶喝. ~ *out the tea* 倒茶. *The river* ~*s itself into the sea.* 这条河流入大海. — *vi.* ①流出, 注出; 倾泻 *(forth; out; down)*; (雨等)倾盆而下. ②扩大, 传开; 蜂拥而来, 源源而来 *(in)*. ③在茶桌上当主妇〔西方习俗, 招待客人时多由家庭主妇斟茶〕. ***It never rains but it*** ~***s.*** (雨)不下就不下, 一下就大下; 祸不单行. ***in the* ~*ing rain*** 在倾盆大雨之下. ~ ***cold water on*** 泼冷水, 使(人)沮丧, 使(人)扫兴. ~ ***forth abuses on sb.*** 把某人骂得狗血喷头, 大骂某人. ~***ing rain*** 倾盆大雨. ~ ***it on***〔美俚〕①大肆吹捧. ②加油干. ③飞快前进. ~ ***oil on the fire [flames]*** 火上加油. ~ ***oil upon troubled waters*** 平息风波, 排解纠纷, 调停. ~ ***on the coal***〔美俚〕(飞机等)急飞, 急驶. ~ ***oneself out*** 倾诉自己的想法〔感情等〕, 倾诉衷曲. ~ ***out grievances*** 诉苦. — *n.* ①注出, 流出; 大雨. ②【铸】浇注, 灌铸; (已熔金属的)一次浇注量. ~ **point** (润滑油等的)流动点〔保持流动状态的最低温度〕.

pour·boire [ˈpuəbwɑː] *n.* 〔F.〕酒钱, 小帐.

pour·er [ˈpɔːrə] *n.* ①倒(茶等)的人. ②浇铸工.
pour·par·ler [puəˈpɑːlei] *n.*〔F.〕〔常 *pl.*〕(外交上的)预备性谈判,非正式会谈.
pour·point [ˈpuəpɔint] *n.* (14世纪男子穿的)紧身棉马甲.
pousse-ca·fé [ˌpuːskæˈfei, F. puskafe] *n.*〔F.〕(*pl.* ~*s* [-ˈfeiz, F. puskafe]) ①在餐后咖啡之后喝的(甜)酒. ②〔美〕(同一杯里注入比重不同的酒形成的)五色酒.
pous·sette [puːˈset] *vi.* (互相拉着手)跳环舞. —*n.* 拉手环舞〔一种乡村舞蹈〕.
pou sto [ˈpau ˈstəu]〔Gr.〕①立足地,立足点. ②根据地,基础〔来自阿基米德 (Archimedes) 所说他如有一块立足地即可推动地球一语〕.
pout[1] [paut] *n.* ①噘嘴. ②〔常 *pl.*〕生气,不高兴. ***be in the ~s = have the ~s*** 噘着嘴,绷着脸,赌着气. — *vt.* ①噘(嘴);张开(羽毛等). ②噘着嘴说. — *vi.* ①噘嘴,绷脸;发脾气. ②凸起;鼓起;膨胀;胸膛凸出. **-y** *a.* 生气的.
pout[2] [paut] *n.*【动】大头鱼类〔如鳕、棉鳚、鲶等〕.
pout·er [ˈpautə] *n.* ①噘嘴的人,绷脸的人;发脾气的人. ②【动】凸胸鸽.
pov·er·ty [ˈpɔvəti] *n.* ①贫穷. ②缺乏,缺少,贫乏,不足 *(of, in)*;(土地的)贫瘠,不毛. ③虚弱;低劣. *come to ~* 变穷. *~ of blood*【医】贫血. *~ in vitamins* 维生素不足. ***live in genteel ~*** 家贫而要面子摆阔. **~-striken** *a.* 为穷所苦恼的,贫困的;贫穷的;贫乏的;(计谋等)极空泛的.
POW, P.O.W. = prisoner of war 战俘.
pow[1] [pəu, pau] *n.*〔主 Scot.〕脑袋.
pow[2] [pau] *int.* 乓〔表示射击、爆炸声等的拟声词〕.
pow·der [ˈpaudə] *n.* ①粉,粉末. ②(搽脸的)香粉;牙粉;发粉. ③(一服)药粉;粉剂;散. ④尘土,泥屑;雪糁. ⑤炸药,火药;〔喻〕推动力;打击力;(打击对方所需的)力量. ⑥〔美俚〕一杯酒. ⑦〔*pl.*〕〔美俚〕逃跑;溜掉. ⑧〔美俚〕老板的命令. ***burn ~***〔美俚〕射击,开枪. ***food for ~*** 炮灰. ***foolish ~***〔美俚〕海洛英. ***grind [reduce] to ~*** 磨碎;粉碎. ***keep one's ~ dry*** 准备,万一,做好准备. ***take a ~***〔美俚〕逃掉;离开. ***put more ~ into it!*** 加油! 加一把劲! ***put on ~*** 搽粉. ***smell of ~*** 闻过火药味,有实战经验. ***smell ~*** 吸收实战经验. ***wear ~*** 撒发粉. — *vt.* ①把…作成粉,使成粉末,磨碎. ②撒粉于;搽粉于;用粉状物覆盖 *(with)*. ③用圆点图案装饰. — *vi.* ①变成粉末. ②搽香粉[发粉]. ③〔美俚〕逃走. ***~ up***〔美俚〕喝. **~ and shot** ①弹药,军需品. ②费用,劳力 (*not worth ~ and shot* 得不偿失,不值得费力. *waste ~ and shot* 白费力气). **~ blue** 氧化钴〔一种深蓝色颜料〕;(洗衣用的)粉末大青〔花绀蓝〕;深蓝色. **~ box** 化妆盒;粉盒. **~-cart** 弹药车. **~ chamber** (炮弹中的)药室. **~ diagram** 粉末照相,粉末图. **~ down** (昆虫的)粉冉羽. **~ factory [mill]** 火药(制造)厂. **~ flask** 火药瓶,火药筒〔打猎用〕. **~ horn** 牛角制火药筒. **~ keg** (金属制)小型火药箱;易爆炸物. **~ magazine** 火药库. **~ metallurgy**【冶】粉末冶金术. **~ monkey** (从前军舰中)搬火药的少年;〔美谑〕装炸药的人,使用炸药的人. **~ photography** 粉末照相术. **~ puff** ①粉扑〔搽粉用〕;〔转义〕花花公子;〔美俚〕傻姑娘,浅薄无聊的女子;女性化的男子. ②机灵的拳手;轻敲,轻打. **~ rocket** 固体燃料火箭. **~ room** ①〔婉〕妇女盥洗室;女厕所. ②(军舰的)火药室. **~ snow** 雪糁. **~ waggon**〔美〕把枪身切短的猎枪.
pow·dered [ˈpaudəd] *a.* ①弄成粉的. ②涂了白粉的;有小白斑的. ③〔美俚〕喝醉了的. **~ coal** 粉煤,煤末. **~ milk** 奶粉. **~ sugar** (作清凉饮料用的)粉末砂糖.
pow·der·y [ˈpaudəri] *a.* ①粉的,粉状的. ②满是粉的;布满尘埃的. ③容易变成粉的. *~ mildew* 白粉菌,白粉病. **pow·der·i·ness** *n.*
Powel(l) [ˈpəuəl] *n.* 鲍威尔〔姓氏〕.
pow·er [ˈpauə] *n.* ①力,力量;能力;体力,精力;(生理)机能;〔常 *pl.*〕才能. ②势力,权力,权限;威力;政权;权能. ③有力人物,有势力者;有影响的机构. ④兵力;军事力量;大国,强国. ⑤【数】幂,乘方. ⑥(透镜的)放大力. ⑦【法】委任权,委任状. ⑧【机】动力,机力;简单的机械;电力;电(能)源;功率;率;能量;生产率. ⑨〔口,方〕许多,大量. ⑩〔*pl.*〕神,恶魔. *the ~ of vision* 视力. *~ of muscle* 力气. *a man of varied ~s* 多才多艺的人. *the air ~* 空军兵力. *The third ~ of 2 is 8.* 2的三次方是8. *treaty ~s* 缔约国. *the Great (World) Powers* (世界)列强. *super ~s* 超级大国. *the party in ~* 当权政党,执政党. *a ~ of attorney* 委任状. *a full ~* 全权证书. *a ~ of representation*【法】代理权. *dispersive ~*【光】色散率. *mechanical ~* 机械力. *labour ~* 劳动力. *motive ~* 原动力,动力. *~ fuel* 动力燃料. *He did a ~ of work.*〔口〕他做了许多的事情. *I saw a ~ of people.*〔口〕我看见许多人. *It has done me a ~ of good.* 这给我很大的帮助. *~s of darkness* 魔鬼. ***a ~ of*** 许多的. ***be in one's ~*** 在…的权力范围之内. ***beyond one's ~s*** 力量达不到;不能胜任. ***come into ~*** 掌权,上台. ***do all in one's ~*** 尽力做. ***fall into the ~ of*** 落在…手中. ***have (sb.) in one's ~*** 控制住某人,可随意支配[摆布](某人). ***have [hold] ~ over*** 支配,领导. ***in ~*** 执政的,在朝的,当权的. ***More ~ to your elbow [to you].*** 加油干! 好好干! ***out of one's ~*** 力所不及. ***out of ~*** 在野(的). ***tax sb.'s ~s to the utmost*** 需要某人尽力. ***the ~ of the keys***【基督教】司钥权,教皇享有的最高教权. ***the ~s that be***〔谑〕当局. — *vt.*〔美〕给…装发动机,赋与…以动力;用动力发动. **~boat** 机动艇;摩托艇(= motorboat). **~ brake** 机力刹车. **~ dive**【空】全力俯冲. **~ gas** 动力气体. **~ grids** 电力输送网. **~house** 发电厂;〔美〕强有力者. **~ lathe** 动力车床. **~ loom** 机动织机. **~-off**【火箭】(发动机)停车. **~ plant [station]** 发电厂;发动机,动力装置. **~ politics** 强权政治. **~ series**【数】幂级数. **~ shovel** 挖土机;机铲. **~ structure** 权力结构. **~ take-off** 动力输出装置. **~ transmission** 输电.
pow·ered [ˈpauəd] *a.* ①〔构成复合词〕以…为动力的;有…马力的. ②装有发动机的;用动力推动的. *a high-~ engine* 高马力发动机.
pow·er·ful [ˈpauəful] *a.* ①有力的,强大的. ②(药等)有效力的;作用大的. ③有权力的,有势力的;有权威的,有影响的,(演讲等)动人的. ④〔口,方〕很多的,相当的;(头痛等)厉害的. — *ad.*〔美〕非常,很. ***a ~ lot of***〔口〕许许多多. **-ly** *ad.*
pow·er·less [ˈpauəlis] *a.* ①无力的,无能的 *(to do)*. ②无依靠的;虚弱的;无效力的;无权力的. ③无资源的. ④无活动能力的,麻痺的. **-ly** *ad.* **-ness** *n.*
Pow·nall [ˈpaunl] *n.* 波纳尔〔姓氏〕.
pow·wow [ˈpauˌwau] *n.* ①(北美印第安人的)祭司,巫师. ②(北美印第安人的)祛病祈祷;预祝典礼〔出发打猎、打仗前的跳舞、狂欢〕. ③〔美俚〕(政治等方面的)会谈,讨论;社交集会;〔英俚〕(作战时的)军官会议. — *vi.* ①(北美印第安人)做祛病祈祷;举行预祝狂欢. ②〔美俚〕开会;商量 *(about)*. — *vt.* (北美印第安人)用巫术治(病).
Pow·ys [ˈpəuis] *n.* 波伊斯〔姓氏〕.
pox [pɔks] *n.* (*pl.* ~*(es)*) ①【医】痘;(皮)疹;脓疱;〔古〕天花. ②〔俚〕〔the ~〕梅毒. ③瘟疫. ④【植】疮痂病. *chicken ~* 水痘. ***A ~ on [of] you [him]!*** 遭瘟的! 该死的! ***What a ~!*** 嗳呀! **~ marks** 痘瘢,麻瘢.
Poz·nan, Poz·nań [ˈpəuznæn, Pol. ˈpɔznanj] *n.* 波兹南〔波兰城市〕.
poz·z(u)o·la·na [ˌpɔtsəˈlɑːnə, It. ˌpɔːttzɔːˈlɑːnə] *n.*〔It.〕①【地】白榴火山灰〔作胶泥用〕. ②(与火山灰混

合制成的)一种胶合水泥.
poz•zo•la•nic *a.* [ˌpɔtsəˈlɑːnik] *a.*【化】凝硬性的;火山灰的. ～ *action* (水泥的)凝硬作用.
poz•zy [ˈpɔzi] *n.* 〔军俚〕果酱.
PP = ①parcel post 包裹邮递;包裹邮务处;〔总称〕邮包,包裹邮件. ②past participle 过去分词. ③postpaid 邮费付讫的. ④prepaid 已预付. ⑤personal property【律】动产. ⑥power plant 发电站〔厂〕;动力设备.
P.P. = parish priest 教区牧师.
pp =①pages. ②〔L.〕*per procurationem* 由…所代表. ③〔It.〕*pianissimo.*
PPC, ppc = ①〔F.〕*pour prendre congé* 离开;告别 (= to take leave). ②picture postcard 美术明信片.
PPCC = People's Political Consultative Conference 〔中〕人民政治协商会议.
ppd = ①postpaid 邮费付讫的. ②prepaid 已预付.
pph = pamphlet.
PPI = plan position indicator 平面位置雷达指示器.
p.p.i. = ①parcel post insured 挂号邮政包裹. ②picks per inch【纺】纬/英寸.
P.P.M. = picks per minute【纺】纬/分.
ppm, p.p.m. = parts per million 百万分率.
ppr., p.pr. = present participle 现在分词.
P.P.S. = ①Parliamentary Private Secretary 〔英〕政务次官. ②〔L.〕*Post postscrip* 再附言.
PPs, pps = pulses per second 脉冲/秒.
ppt = precipitate 沉淀;沉淀物.
PP-WP = Planned Parenthood-World Population 计划生育-世界人口组织.
P.Q. = ①Province of Quebec 〔加拿大〕魁北克省. ②personality quotient【心】人格商(数).
PR = public relations (通过宣传手段建立的)与公众的联系,对外联络.
P.R. = ①payroll 工资发放名册. ②Parliamentary Reports 〔英〕议会议事录. ③ prize ring 拳击场;拳击(练习). ④proportional representation (选举的)比例代表制.
Pr = praseodymium【化】镨.
Pr. = ①Prince. ②preferred stock〔美〕优先股. ③〔F.〕*Provençal.*
pr. = ①pair. ②power. ③preferred. ④present. ⑤pronoun. ⑥price. ⑦printed. ⑧priest. ⑨primary. ⑩printer.
PRA = Public Roads Administration 〔美旧〕公路管理局.
P.R.A. = President of the Royal Academy 英国皇家艺术学会会长.
praam [prɑːm] *n.* = pram².
prac•tic [ˈpræktik] *a.* = practical.
prac•ti•ca•bil•i•ty [ˌpræktikəˈbiliti] *n.* ①实行的可能性,实用性,可行性. ②实用物.
prac•ti•ca•ble [ˈpræktikəbl] *a.* ①切实可行的,行得通的;实际的;实用的. ②(桥等)可以通行的;适用的;【剧】(窗、门等舞台布景)实际能用的. **-ness** *n.* **-bly** *ad.*
prac•ti•cal [ˈpræktikəl] *a.* ①实地的,事实上的,实际上的 *(opp.* theoretical*)*. ②实践的,实地经验过的,练习过的,经验丰富的,老练的. ③实用的,应用的;注重实用的;〔贬〕只讲实用的. ④(人等)有用的,会做事的,能干的. ⑤有实效的;可行的. ⑥实事求是的,注重实行的. ～ *considerations* 需要切实考虑的事情,实际问题. ～ *duty* 实际工作. *the* ～ *rulers* 事实上的统治者. *a* ～ *joker* 要弄别人的人. ～ *experience* 实际经验. ～ *politics* 实际政治,行得通的政治. ～ *minds* 讲求实际的头脑;注重实际的人. ***be not*** ～ 不实际,不能落实. ***for (all)*** ～ ***purposes*** 实际上. ～ **joke** 恶作剧,戏弄人的鬼把戏. ～ **nurse** 从实际工作中锻炼出来的护士〔未曾正式登记的〕. ～ **piece** 〔美剧〕象实物一样的布景. ～ **unit**【物】实用单位. ～ **wisdom** 常识. **-ness** *n.*
prac•ti•cal•ism [ˈpræktikəlizəm] *n.* 求实主义;实用主义.
prac•ti•cal•i•ty [ˌpræktiˈkæliti] *n.* ①实际;实用;实用性;实践性. ②实物;实例.
prac•ti•cal•ly [ˈpræktikəli] *ad.* ①实际上;实用上;事实上,实质上. ②从实际出发;通过实践. ③[ˈpræktikli]〔口〕差不多;几乎;简直. *P- speaking, there is no more to be done.* 实际地讲,没有别的办法可行了. *It's summer* ～. 这天气简直象夏天了.
prac•tice¹ [ˈpræktis] *n.* ①实行,实践,实施;实际;实用;做法,技术. ②习惯,惯例,常规. ③练习,演习,实习,实验;老练,熟练. ④(医生、律师等的)业务,开业;生意,主顾. ⑤【数】实算. ⑥〔常 *pl.*〕〔古〕策略,诡计,欺诈. ⑦【法】诉讼手续. ⑧【宗】仪式. *A plausible idea, but will it work in* ～? 主意倒好,然而能实行吗? *a common* ～ 风气;常例. *bureaucratic* ～*s* 官僚主义作风. *the old* ～*s* 过去的一套,老一套. *social* ～ 社会实践. *a blank [firing]* ～ 空弹〔实弹〕演习. *sharp* ～ 狡诈〔不正当〕的手段. *The doctor has a large* ～. 这个医生病人很多. ***a matter of common [daily]*** ～ 寻常的事. ***(do)*** ～ *(in music [at the nets])* 练习(音乐〔网球〕). ***in*** ～ ①实际上,事实上;在实践中. ②在不断练习中;练习充足;熟练. ③在开业中. ***in*** ～ ***if not in profession*** 虽不明讲但实际如此. ***It was the*** ～. 这就是当时的习惯. ***make a*** ～ ***of*** 老是;经常进行…;以…为惯用手段. ***out of*** ～ 久不练习,荒疏. ***P- makes perfect.*** 熟能生巧. ***put [bring] in [into]*** ～ 实行. ***reduce to*** ～ 实施. ～ **teacher** (师范学院等的)教学实习生. ～ **teaching** (师范学院学生等的)教学实习.
prac•tice² [ˈpræktis] *vt., vi.* 〔美〕 = practise.
prac•ticed [ˈpræktist] *a.* 〔美〕 = practised.
prac•ti•cian [prækˈtiʃən] *n.* ①实行者,开业者,经营事业者. ②有实际经验的人,熟手.
prac•ti•cum [ˈpræktikəm] *n.* 实习课,实践课.
prac•tise [ˈpræktis] *vt.* ①搞;实行;实践;实施;常做;惯常进行. ②练习,实习;训练,使练习. ③开业从事. ～ *law [medicine]* 开业当律师〔医生〕. ～ *pupils in singing* 教学生唱歌. ～ *economy* 节约. — *vi.* ①实践;实行. ②练习;实习 *(on;at;with)*. ③开业,挂牌行医〔当律师等〕. ④〔古〕策划阴谋. ～ *as a barrister* = ～ *at the bar* 挂牌做律师. ～ *at [on] the piano* 练钢琴. ～ *with the rifle* 练习打步枪. ～ ***on [upon]*** 利用(别人弱点);欺骗(某人).
prac•tised [ˈpræktist] *a.* ①经验丰富的. ②精通的,熟练的;老练的. *a* ～ *hand* 熟手,老手. *the* ～ *in trade* 善于经商的人们.
prac•tis•ing [ˈpræktisiŋ] *a.* 正在从事某种职业〔活动〕的,开业的. *a* ～ *physician [lawyer]* 开业医师〔律师〕.
prac•ti•tion•er [prækˈtiʃənə] *n.* 开业者〔尤指医生、律师等〕;老手. ②从事者,实践者;实习者,练习者. ③〔古〕策士,策划阴谋者. *a private* ～ 开业医生. *a general* ～ 普通医生.
prae- *pref.* 〔多用于拉丁语及与古代罗马事物有关的词前〕〔L.〕= pre-.
prae•co•cial, 〔Am.〕**pre•co•cial** [priˈkəuʃəl] *a.*【动】孤生的〔新孵出来的小鸟即长了羽毛并能自己找食的〕.
prae•dial [priːˈdiəl] *a.* = predial.
prae•fect [ˈpriːfekt] *n.* = prefect.
prae•mu•ni•re [ˌpriːmjuˈnaiəri] *n.* ①(英国古代法律中的)擅自行使教皇司法权罪,蔑视王权罪. ②命令行政司法官传犯蔑视王权罪者的令状.
prae•no•men [priːˈnəumen] *n.* *(pl.* ～*s,* ***prae•nom•i•na*** [priːˈnəuminə]*)*【古罗马】本名,第一个名字〔相当于后来的教名 (Christian name),如 Caius Julius Caesar 的 Caius〕.
prae•pos•tor, pre•pos•ter [priːˈpɔstə] *n.* 〔英〕(某些

公学 (public school) 的)班长,级长.

prae·sid·i·um [priˈsidiəm] *n.* = presidium.

prae·tor,〔Am.〕**pre·ter** [ˈpriːtə] *n.*【罗马史】执政官;(仅次于执政官的)地方长官.

prae·to·ri·an,〔Am.〕**pre·to·ri·an** [priːˈtɔːriən] *n.,a.* ①(古罗马)执政官(的); 地方长官(的). ②〔常作 P-〕(古罗马皇帝的)禁卫军(的).

prag·mat·ic [prægˈmætik] *a.* ①好管闲事的,爱多事的. ②刚愎自用的,独断的;自负的. ③【哲】实用主义的. ④重实效的;实际的. ⑤国务的,国事的;团体事务的. ⑥研究史迹的相互关系的. ~ *lines of thought* 实用主义的想法. *the* ~ *sanction* 构成基本法的诏书,国事诏书. — *n.* ①爱管闲事的人. ②专断的人. ③国事诏书. ④〔废〕实务家,实际家. **prag·mat·i·cal** *a.* **prag·mat·i·cal·ly** *ad.*

prag·mat·i·cism [prægˈmætisizəm] *n.*【哲】实用主义. **-mat·i·cist** *n.* 实用主义者.

prag·mat·ics [prægˈmætiks] *n.* 语用学,(语言)实用学〔研究语言符号和其使用者关系的一种理论,符号学的一个部分〕.

prag·ma·tism [ˈprægmətizəm] *n.* ①【哲】实用主义. ②实用的观点和方法. ③好管闲事;独断(性);自负.

prag·ma·tist [ˈprægmətist] *n.* ①【哲】实用主义者,实用主义哲学的信奉者. ②讲求实际的人. ③爱管闲事的人.

prag·ma·tis·tic [ˌprægməˈtistik] *a.* 实用主义的.

prag·ma·tize [ˈprægmətaiz] *vt.* 把(空想的事物)实际化,使现实化;合理地解释(神话等).

Prague, Pra·ha [prɑːg, ˈprɑːhɑː] *n.* 布拉格〔捷克斯洛伐克首都〕.

Praia [ˈprai-ɑː] *n.* 普拉亚〔佛得角首都〕.

prai·rie [ˈprεəri] *n.* ①(特指美国中西部的)大草原. ②牧场,草原地带. ③〔美方〕林中空地. *the call of the* ~ 大草原的诱惑. ~ *fire* 燎原大火,野火. ~ *oyster [cocktail]* 加调料生吃的蛋. ~ **chicken [hen]** 北美松鸡. ~ **dog [marmot]**【动】(北美产)草原土拨鼠,草原犬鼠. **P-Provinces** 草原诸省〔加拿大的 Manitoba, Saskatchewan, Alberta 诸省的别名〕 ~ **schooner**【美史】(早期在草原地带用的)篷盖大马车. ~ **squirrel** = ~ dog. ~ **value** (不含劳动、资本等的) 自然地价. **P- State**〔美〕草原之乡〔美国伊利诺斯州的别名〕. ~ **wag(g)on** = ~ schooner. ~ **wolf**【动】草原狼.

prais·a·ble [ˈpreizəbl] *a.* 可称赞的; 值得赞扬的,可嘉许的. **-ness** *n.* **prais·a·bly** *ad.*

praise [preiz] *n.* ①称赞;赞扬,表扬;〔*pl.*〕赞词,赞美的话. ②【宗】(对上帝的)崇拜,赞美,尊崇. ③〔古〕值得称赞的人[物];〔古〕可称赞的地方[理由]. ***a service of*** ~ 【宗】赞美礼拜. ***be above [beyond all]*** ~ 赞美不尽的. ***be loud [warm] in sb.'s*** ~***(s)*** 热烈颂扬某人. ***bestow [give]*** ~ 称赞 *(on; upon)*. ***chant [sing] the*** ~***s of sb.*** 颂扬[歌颂]某人. ***P- be to God!*** 感谢上帝! ***in*** ~ ***of*** 称赞[赞美,歌颂]…. ***more*** ~ ***than pudding*** 恭维多而实惠少. ***pudding rather than*** ~ 宁要实惠,不要恭维. ***say in sb.'s*** ~ 称赞某人说. ***sing one's own*** ~***s*** 自吹自擂. ***win high*** ~ 受到高度赞扬. — *vt.* ①称赞,赞扬,表扬,歌颂;吹捧. ②【宗】赞美(上帝). ***God be*** ~***d!*** 谢天谢地. ~ ***sb. to the skies*** 把某人捧上天. **-er** *n.* 赞美者,赞扬者;吹捧者. **-less** *a.* 没有赞扬的.

praise·ful [ˈpreizful] *a.* ①满是称赞话的;赞不绝口的;赞扬的;歌颂的. ②有称赞价值的. **-ness** *n.*

praise·wor·thy [ˈpreizˌwəːði] *a.* 值得赞扬的,值得钦佩的,可嘉许的. **-thi·ly** *ad.* **-thi·ness** *n.*

Pra·krit [ˈprɑːkrit, ˈpræ-] *n.* 帕拉克里语〔印度中部及北部的方言,古时与梵文并存或起源于梵文〕.

pra·line [ˈprɑːliːn] *n.* 果仁糖;胡桃糖,杏仁糖.

prall·tril·er [ˈprɑːltrilə] *n.*【乐】回波音 (= inverted mordent).

pram[1] [præm] *n.* ①〔英口〕婴儿车,童车〔perambulator 的缩称〕. ②〔俚〕(送牛奶的)手推车.

pram[2]**, praam** [prɑːm] *n.* ①(波罗的海沿岸一带的)平底货船;平底炮艇. ②(斯堪的纳维亚一带的)大船上附带的小艇.

prance [prɑːns] *vi.* ①(马)腾跃. ②(人)傲然跃马前行. ③高视阔步,神气十足地走[骑马];欢跃;快活地走[骑马] *(about)*. — *vt.* 使(马)腾跃. — *n.* ①(马的)腾跃. ②昂首阔步;神气十足的态度. ③欢跃;欢跃的舞蹈动作.

pranc·er [ˈprɑːnsə] *n.* ①腾跃前进的人[马]. ②烈性[慓悍]的马;骑烈马者;〔俚〕骑马士官;马贼. ③欢快的舞蹈者,欢跃者.

pran·di·al [ˈprændiəl, -djəl] *a.* 〔谑〕膳食的,正餐的.

prang [præŋ]〔英空俚〕*vt.* ①使(飞机、车辆等)砰地撞坏[坠毁];投弹命中(目标),轰炸. ②撞,击. — *vi.* (飞机)坠毁. — *n.*〔俚〕①(飞机的)猝然坠地,坠毁. ②命中目标的轰炸,炸中. ③大功.

prank[1] [præŋk] *n.* ①开玩笑;恶作剧,鬼把戏. ②不正常的动作;(机器等)不规则的转动. *They are up to their old* ~*s.* 他们又在玩鬼把戏了. ***play*** ~***s on*** 向…开玩笑,戏弄,对…玩鬼把戏.

prank[2] [præŋk] *vt.* ①把…打扮漂亮,盛装 *(up)*. ②装饰. ~ *oneself up [out] with the best clothes* 穿着最漂亮的衣服. *meadows* ~*ed with flowers* 花朵盛开的牧场. — *vi.* 打扮得漂漂亮亮.

prank·ish [ˈpræŋkiʃ] *a.* 爱开玩笑的;顽皮的;恶作剧的.

prank·ster [ˈpræŋkstə] *n.* 开玩笑的人,恶作剧的人.

prase [preiz] *n.*【矿】葱绿玉髓;绿石英.

pra·se·o·dym·i·um [ˌpreiziəuˈdimiəm] *n.*【化】镨.

prate [preit] *vi., vt.* 唠唠叨叨地讲;瞎说,瞎胡诌;空谈;(把无聊事情)大谈特谈. *merely* ~ *about it* 只是空谈[胡扯]一阵. — *n.* 唠叨,多嘴;无聊话. **prat·ing** *a.* **prat·ing·ly** *ad.*

prat·er [ˈpreitə] *n.* 多嘴的人;唠唠叨叨的人;空谈者.

pra·tie [ˈpreiti] *n.* 〔Ir.〕〔常 *pl.*〕马铃薯 (= potato).

pra·tique [ˈprætiːk] *n.* 〔F.〕(检疫后发给的)无疫入港许可证.

prat(t) [præt] *n.* 〔美俚〕屁股. ~ **kick** 〔美俚〕屁股上的裤袋.

prat(t)·fall [ˈprætˌfɔːl] *n.* 〔美俚〕①屁股着地的跌跤. ②倒霉;丢脸;可耻的失败.

prat·in·cole [ˈprætiŋkəul, ˈprætn-] *n.*【动】燕鸻.

Pratt [præt] *n.* 普拉特〔姓氏〕.

prat·tle [ˈprætl] *vi.* ①象小孩般颠三倒四地说话;发出连续而无意义的声音. ②空谈,瞎聊,唠叨. — *vt.* 天真地说;轻率地说. — *n.* ①孩子般颠三倒四的话;连续而无意义的声音. ②空谈,废话,无聊话.

prat·tler [ˈprætlə] *n.* ①喁喁学语的小孩;小孩般幼稚地讲话的人. ②空谈者,瞎聊的人.

prau [prau, ˈprɑːuː] *n.* 马来人的一种快帆船 (=proa).

Prav·da [ˈprɑːvdə] *n.* 〔俄〕《真理报》.

prav·i·ty [ˈpræviti] *n.* 〔古〕①(食物的)腐烂. ②腐败;堕落;邪恶.

prawn [prɔːn] *n.*【动】明虾,对虾;斑节虾. — *vi.* 捉对虾.

prax·e·ol·o·gy [ˌpræksiˈɔlədʒi] *n.* 人类行为学.

prax·is [ˈpræksis] *n.* *(pl. prax·es* [-siːz]*)* ①习惯,惯例,常规. ②练习,实习;实践;应用. ③(语法等的)例题集,练习问题集.

pray [prei] *vi.* ①请求,恳求 *(for)*. ②祷告,祈祷 *(to)*. ~ *for pardon* 请求原谅. *He is past* ~*ing for.* 他是不可救药了. — *vt.* ①请求;恳求;祈求,祈祷. ②请〔I ~ you 之略〕. *What is the use of that,* ~? 请问那有什么用处呢? *Tell me the reason,* ~. 请把理由告诉我吧. *P- come with me.* 请跟我来. ***P- consider that …*** 请想想看. ~ ***down***

[out] 祈祷求神降伏(某人). ～ ***for rain*** 求雨. ～ ***for sb.*** 为某人祈祷. ～ ***in aid of***〔古,雅〕求…帮助. ～***ing insect*** 螳螂.

pray·er[1] [ˈpreiə] *n.* 恳求者;祷告者.

pray·er[2] [prɛə] *n.* ①祈祷,祈求;恳求. ②〔常 *pl.*〕祈祷式;祈祷文,祈祷语句. ③所祈祷[恳求]的事物. ④〔*pl.*〕祝福. ⑤〔口〕极渺茫的成功希望. ***be at one's ～s*** 正在祈祷. ***evening ～*** 晚祷. ***morning ～*** 晨祷. ***say one's ～s = give ～s*** 祈祷,祷告. ***the house of ～*** 教堂. ***the Lord's P-***【宗】主祷文. ***the unspoken ～*** 默祷,心中的愿望. ***wrestle in ～*** 热忱祈祷. ～ **bones**〔美俚〕膝盖. ～ **book** 祈祷书. ～**-machine [～-mill]** = ～-wheel. ～ **meeting** 祷告会. ～ **rug [mat]** (穆斯林祈祷时用的)跪毯. ～**-wheel**【佛教】地藏车,祈祷轮. **-less** *a.* 不祷告的,不虔诚的.

prayer·ful [ˈprɛəful] *a.* 常常祷告的,虔诚的. **-ly** *ad.* **-ness** *n.*

P.R.B. = Pre-Raphaelite Brotherhood〔英〕拉斐尔前派社.

PRC = People's Republic of China 中华人民共和国.

pre- *pref.* 前,先,预先: *pre*history, *pre*pay, *pre*school, *pre*vent.

preach [priːtʃ] *vi.* ①布讲,讲道,布道,传道. ②宣扬,宣传,鼓吹. ③谆谆劝诫,唠叨地劝说. — *vt.*①讲(道);说(教);讲(学). ②教,劝告,规戒. ③提倡,鼓吹,宣传. ④由于说教而(讲得口干舌燥等). *Practise what you ～.* 躬行己言,身体力行,以身作则. ～ ***a funeral***〔口〕致悼辞. ～ ***a sermon*** 讲道;〔喻〕劝诫,说教. ～ ***against*** 对…作反宣传. ～ ***at [to] sb.*** 对某人谆谆告诫. ～ ***down*** 贬损;当众谴责,当众折服[否决掉],驳倒. ～ ***the Gospel*** 布讲福音. ～ ***to deaf ears*** 对聋子讲道;对牛弹琴. ～ ***up*** 称赞,赞扬;推崇;吹捧. —*n.*〔口〕讲道,说教;训诫.

preach·er [ˈpriːtʃə] *n.* ①讲道者;说教者;传教师. ②训诫者,警告者. ③宣传者;鼓吹者. ④〔the P-〕【圣】《传道书》;《传道书》作者.

preach·i·fy [ˈpriːtʃifai] *vi.* 〔口〕(令人生厌地)训诫;说教.

preach·ing [ˈpriːtʃiŋ] *n.* ①讲道;说教;训诫. ②布道术,讲道法. ③有人布道的礼拜. — *a.* 布道的,说教的;训诫的. ～ **shop**〔美俚〕教堂.

preach·ment [ˈpriːtʃmənt] *n.* 〔口〕(冗长的)讲道,说教.

preach·y [ˈpriːtʃi] *a.*〔口〕爱讲道的;喜欢说教的;说教性的;讲道似的. **-i·ly** *ad.* **-i·ness** *n.*

pre·ac·quaint [ˈpriːəˈkweint] *vt.* 预先通知,预告. **pre·ac·quaint·ance** *n.*

pre·act [ˈpriːækt] *vt.* 提前,超前(行动);预作用.

pre·a·dam·ic [ˈpriːəˈdæmik] *a.* preadamite *(a.)*.

pre·ad·am·ite [ˈpriːˈædəmait] *a.* (基督教《圣经》所云人类始祖)亚当以前的. ②亚当以前的人的. — *n.* ①亚当以前的人. ②相信亚当以前已有人存在者.

pre·ad·o·les·cence [ˈpriːædəuˈlesns] *n.* 青春期以前的时期〔约 9—12 岁〕.

pre·ad·o·les·cent [ˈpriːædəuˈlesnt] *a.* 青春期以前一段时期的. — *n.* 处于青春期以前一段时期的少年.

pre·am·ble [priːˈæmbl] *n.* ①序,绪言;(条约等的)前言. ②预兆性事件;开端,端倪. — *vi.* 作序言[绪论]. ***without ～*** 开门见山地,直截了当地.

pre·am·bu·late [priːˈæmbjuleit] *vi.* = preamble *(vi.)*.

pre·am·pli·fi·er [ˈpriːˈæmplifaiə] *n.* 【电】前置放大器.

pre·an·nounce [ˈpriːəˈnauns] *vt.* 预告,事先宣告.

pre·ar·range [ˈpriːəˈreindʒ] *vt.* 预先安排;预先协商;预定. **-ment** *n.*

pre·as·signed [ˈpriːəˈsaind] *a.* 预先指定的;预先分配[分派]的.

pre·a·tom·ic [ˈpriːəˈtɔmik] *a.* 原子弹和原子能使用前的,核时代以前的.

pre·au·di·ence [ˈpriːˈɔːdjəns] *n.* (英国法律中一方律师在法庭上的)优先发言权.

pre·ax·i·al [ˈpriːˈæksiəl] *a.*【解】轴前的.

pre-bat·tle [ˈpriːˈbætl] *a.* 战斗前的,交战前的. ～ **formation** 接敌队形. ～ **intelligence** 战前侦察.

pre·book [ˈpriːbuk] *vt.* 预订;预约.

preb·end [ˈprebənd] *n.* ①牧师会会员的俸禄;供给牧师会会员俸禄的教会财产〔土地、什一税、捐献等〕. ②受俸牧师;名誉受俸牧师. **-al** *a.*

preb·en·da·ry [ˈprebəndəri] *n.*〔英〕受俸牧师;名誉受俸牧师.

prec. = preceded; preceding.

Pre·cam·bri·an [ˈpriːˈkæmbriən] *a.*【地】前寒武纪的. — *n.*〔the ～〕前寒武纪.

pre·can·cel [ˈpriːˈkænsəl] *vt.* ***(～(l)ed, ～(l)ing)*** 在使用前盖销(邮票). —*n.* 在使用前盖销的邮票. **-cel·la·tion** [-ˈleiʃən] *n.*

pre·can·cer·ous [ˈpriːˈkænsərəs] *a.* 可能致癌的;癌症前期的. ***a ～ mole*** 可能致癌的痣.

pre·car·i·ous [priˈkɛəriəs] *a.* ①不确定的,靠不住的;危险的,(生活等)不安定的. ②(推测等)可疑的;前提有问题的,根据不充足的. ③〔古〕由他人摆布的. *a ～ living* 愁吃少穿[朝不保夕]的生活. *a ～ life* 不安定的生活. *the ～ life of a fisherman* 极危险的渔民生活. *～ privileges* 随时均有被取消可能的特权. *a ～ foothold* 不稳定的立足点. *a ～ assumption [assertion]* 靠不住的假定[论断]. **-ly** *ad.* **-ness** *n.*

pre·cast [ˈpriːˈkaːst] *vt., a.*【建】预制(的);预浇铸(的). *～ reinforced concrete beams* 预制钢筋混凝土梁.

prec·a·tive, prec·a·to·ry [ˈprekətiv, -təri] *a.* 恳求的;【语法】祈求的. ～ *words* (遗嘱中的)拜托话,恳求话. **precatory trust**【法】(有约束力的)遗托.

pre·cau·tion [priˈkɔːʃən] *n.* ①小心,警惕,谨防,预防. ②预防措施. ***by way of ～*** 为小心起见,为了预防. ***take ～s against*** 谨防,小心;对…采取预防措施. — *vt.* 使提防;预先警告.

pre·cau·tion·al, pre·cau·tion·a·ry [priˈkɔːʃənəl, -ʃənəri] *a.* 预有戒备的,预防的. ～ *measures* 预防措施.

pre·ca·va [ˌpriːˈkeivə -kaː-] *n.* ***(pl. -vae*** [-viː]***)***【解】前腔静脉. **-val** *a.*

pre·cede [pri(ː)ˈsiːd] *vt.* ①领先于,居先于,在…之先. ②在…之上;优于;比…重要. ③在…前加上;为…加上引言 *(by, with)*. *We were ～d by our guide.* 我们跟着向导走. *Economy ～s every other problem.* 重要的首先是经济问题. — *vi.* 在前面,领先,居先. *the words that ～* 上述的话. **pre·ced·a·ble** *a.*

pre·ced·ence,〔罕〕**pre·ced·en·cy** [pri(ː)ˈsiːdəns, -si] *n.* ①领先,先行,先在;在前. ②上位,上座,上席. ③优先,优越;优先权. ④(按地位的)先后次序. *Economic problems must take ～ of other questions.* 经济问题应作首要问题处理. *the order of ～* 席次,位次. *quarrel about ～* 席次之争. ***give ～ to*** 把主席让给…,承认…的优越. ***take [have the] ～ of [over]*** 在…之上,优于.

prec·e·dent[1] [ˈpresidənt] *n.* ①先例,前例;惯例. ②【法】判例. *There is no ～ for it.* 那是没有前例的. *without ～* 无前例的,空前的. ***have no ～ to go by*** 无先例可循. ***set [create] a ～ for*** 为…开先例. **-less** *a.* 没有前例的.

pre·ce·dent[2] [priˈsiːdənt] *a.* 在前的,在先的;优先的. ***a condition ～*** (财产转让、合同生效等之前的)先决条件.

prec·e·dent·ed [ˈpresidəntid] *a.* 有先例(可援)的 *(opp.* unprecedented*)*.

prec·e·den·tial [ˌpresiˈdenʃəl] *a.* ①先例的,作为先例的. ②有先例的;预先的.

pre·ced·ing [pri(:)ˈsi:diŋ] *a.* ①在前的，在先的 *(opp. following)*. ②上述的. ~ *crops* (轮作中的)前作(物). *the ~ years* 前几年. *in the ~ chapter* 在前章.

pre·cen·sor [ˈpri:ˈsensə] *vt.* (书籍出版、影片放映或新闻发布前)预先审查.

pre·cen·tor [pri(:)ˈsentə] *n.* (教堂歌咏班的)指挥人；领唱人.

pre·cept [ˈpri:sept] *n.* ①训导，告诫；格言，箴言；戒律. ②(技术上的)格式；规程；方案. ③【法】命令书，令状. ***Practice [Example] is better than ~.*** 实例优于口训，以身作则胜于口头训导.

pre·cep·tive [priˈseptiv] *a.* ① 教训的；告诫的. ②【法】令状的.

pre·cep·tor [priˈseptə] *n.* ①训导者，导师. ②教师，(美某些大学的)导师；校长；(带实习生的)辅导医生. ③【史】圣殿骑士团 (Knights Templars) 的教堂长. **-to·ri·al** [-ˈtɔriəl] *a.* (*a preceptorial system* 导师制).

pre·cep·to·ry [priˈseptəri] *n.*【史】圣殿骑士团的教堂；圣殿骑士团地方分团[管辖区]；圣殿骑士团地方分团的产业.

pre·cep·tress [priˈseptris] *n.* 女导师；女教师；女校长.

pre·cess [priˈses] *vi.* 向前运动；【天】(按岁差)向前运行；【机】旋进.

pre·ces·sion [priˈseʃən] *n.* ①前行，先行. ②前进运动，进动；【天】岁差. ~ *of the equinoxes*【天】(分点)岁差. **-al** *a.* 岁差的；进动的.

pre·choose [pri:ˈtʃu:z] *vt.* ***(pre·chose*** [pri:ˈtʃəuz], ***pre·cho·sen*** [pri:ˈtʃəuzən]***)*** 预先选定，预先选择.

pre-Chris·tian [ˈpri:ˈkristjən, ˈpri:ˈkrisʃən] *a.* 基督(教)以前的.

pré·cieuse [preˈsju:z] *n.* [F.] (17 世纪沙龙中的)女学者；社交界附庸风雅和卖弄学问的妇女. — *a.* (妇女)附庸风雅的，过分文雅的，装模作样的.

pré·cieux [preˈsju:] *a.* [F]. = precieuse *(a.)*.

pre·cinct [ˈpri:siŋkt] *n.* ①(建筑物等的) 围地，附近范围；[英](教会的)会内，(寺院的)院内；境域内；[*pl.*]境界. ②[美](县以下的)管区；[美](选举)区；分界，分区. ③[*pl.*](城镇的)周围，附近，郊区. *city ~s* 市区. *an election ~* 选区. *a police ~* 警察管区. *a shopping ~* 商业区.

pre·ci·os·i·ty [ˌpreʃiˈɔsiti] *n.* (措词用句的)过分雕琢，过分讲究；矫揉造作.

pre·cious [ˈpreʃəs] *a.* ①高价的，昂贵的；贵重的；宝贵的，珍贵的. ②可爱的，宝贝的. ③非常，极；大大的，十足的，彻底的. ④[反语]好的，没价值的. ⑤(工艺等)过分精雕细琢的；(文章等)过分讲究的，咬文嚼字的. *the ~ metals* 贵金属. *~ stones* 宝石. *~ memories* 珍贵的纪念品. *My ~ darling!* 我的心肝宝贝! *A ~ friend you have been.* [讽刺话]你真是个宝贝朋友. *a ~ fool* 大傻瓜. ***a ~ deal*** [口]非常，极. ***make a ~ mess of sth.*** 把某事弄成一团糟. — *n.* [称呼用语]可爱的人. ***My ~!*** 我的亲爱的! — *ad.* [口]非常，极. *It is ~ cold.* 冷极了. *There is ~ little of it.* 只有一点点，极少极少. **-ly** *ad.* **-ness** *n.*

prec·i·pice [ˈpresipis] *n.* ①悬崖，绝壁；断崖边. ②危地，危急处境，危机. ***be [stand] on the brink of a ~*** 处于灾难的边缘.

pre·cip·i·ta·ble [priˈsipitəbl] *a.*【化】沉淀性的，能使沉淀的. **pre·cip·i·ta·bil·i·ty** [priˌsipitəˈbiliti] *n.*【化】沉淀性，沉淀度.

pre·cip·i·tance, pre·cip·i·tan·cy [priˈsipitəns, -si] *n.* 急躁；慌张；仓卒；[*pl.*] 轻率行为.

pre·cip·i·tant [priˈsipitənt] *a.* ①很快落下的；陡斜地落下的；倒落的. ②急躁的；(病)急，(行动)突然的；(举动)轻率的. — *n.*【化】沉淀剂，沉淀试药. **-ly** *ad.*

pre·cip·i·tate [priˈsipiteit] *vt.* ①把…倒摔下去，把…猛然扔下. ②使(人)突然陷入(某种状态) *(into)*；使突然发生. ③拼命催促，促成，促使(危机等)早现. ④【化】使沉淀；【物】使(水蒸气)凝结. ~ *sb. into misery* 使某人一下子陷入苦海. ~ *a disaster* 闯下一个大祸. ~ *a war* 发动[挑起]战争. ~ ***oneself into (danger)*** 使自己一下子陷入(危险). ~ ***oneself upon [against]*** 猛袭，突击(敌人). — [priˈsipitit] *a.* ①猛然落下的，倒栽下的；陡斜地落下的；猛冲的；(水流)湍急的. ②慌张的，急躁的，轻率的. — [priˈsipitit] *n.*【化】沉淀物；【物】凝结的水蒸气[指雨、雪、露等]；降水. **-ly** [priˈsipititli] *ad.*

pre·cip·i·tat·ing *a.* ①急落的；猛冲的. ②【化】起沉淀作用的，导致沉淀的.

pre·cip·i·ta·tion [priˌsipiˈteiʃən] *n.* ①猛然摔下，落下. ②猛冲；急躁，轻率，鲁莽. ③【化】沉淀(作用)；降雨(量)；(雨、雪等的)降落. ~ **hardening**【冶】沉淀硬化，弥散硬化.

pre·cip·i·ta·tor [priˈsipiteitə] *n.* ①催促的人[物]，促进者. ②【化】沉淀器；沉淀剂；除尘器；电滤器，滤尘器. ③沉淀器操作者.

pre·cip·i·tin [priˈsipitin] *n.*【生化】沉淀素.

pre·cip·i·tin·o·gen [priˌsipiˈtinədʒən] *n.*【生化】沉淀素原. **-gen·ic** [-ˈdʒenik] *a.*

pre·cip·i·tous [priˈsipitəs] *a.* ①险峻的，绝壁的；陡峭的；急转直下的，突然而来的. ②急躁的，鲁莽的，轻率的；仓卒的. **-ly** *ad.*

pré·cis [ˈpreisi:] *n.* ***(pl. pré·cis*** [ˈpreisi:z]***)*** [F.] (文章或讲话的)摘要，提要；大意，梗概. — *vt.* 作…的摘要，摘取…的大意.

pre·cise [priˈsais] *a.* ①准确的，精确的. ②清楚的，(言语等)清晰的；(区分等)明确的. ③(数量上)恰好的，丝毫不差的. ④[加强语气]恰恰，正当，正是这个[那个]. ⑤合规则的，正式的，正规的；没错的. ⑥古板的，拘泥的，严格的. ***at the ~ moment*** 恰恰在那个时刻. ***to be ~*** [用作插入语]确切地讲. **-ly** *ad.* ①正好，恰恰，恰(*~ly because* 正因为). ②精确地；明白地；严格地. ③刻板地，拘泥(陈规)地，呆板地. ④[表示同意时用]的确那样，一点不错 (*Precisely so.* 正是这样). **-ness** *n.* ①精确，准确，确切. ②呆板，拘泥.

pre·ci·sian [priˈsiʒən] *n.* (尤指宗教方面)严格遵守规则的人；清教徒.

pre·ci·sion [priˈsiʒən] *n.* 精密，精确性；严格；精密度；【修】精确. *arms of ~* 装有瞄准仪的枪炮. — *a.* 精确的，精密的. *~ apparatus* 精密仪器. *a ~ balance* 精密天平. *a ~ fire* 准确射击.

pre·ci·sion·ist [priˈsiʒənist] *n.* 拘泥于道德的人；讲究语言精确的人.

pre·clas·si·cal [ˈpri:ˈklæsikəl] *a.* (特指希腊、罗马文学的)古典时期以前的.

pre·clin·i·cal [ˈpri:ˈklinikəl] *a.*【医】临诊前期的，临床前的.

pre·clude [priˈklu:d] *vt.* ①排除，预防，消灭，杜绝. ②阻断(路等)，阻止；使不可能，妨碍. *A prior engagement will ~ them from coming.* 他们因为有约在先，不能来了. *so as to ~ all doubts* 为了消除疑点. **-clu·sion** [priˈklu:ʒən] *n.* **-clu·sive** [-ˈklu:siv] *a.*

pre·co·cious [priˈkəuʃəs] *a.* ①(人)早熟的，早慧的；发育过早的. ②(植物等)早成的，(花)早开的. **-ly** *ad.* **-ness** *n.*

pre·coc·i·ty [priˈkɔsiti] *n.* (人的)早熟，过早发育；(植物的)早成.

pre·cog·ni·tion [ˈpri:kɔgˈniʃən] *n.* ①预知，预见. ②[Scot.]【法】(对证人或证据的)预先审查.

pre-Co·lum·bi·an [ˈpri:kəˈlʌmbiən] *a.* 哥伦布以前的[指哥伦布发现美洲以前的西半球的任何时期].

pre·com·pose [ˈpri:kəmˈpəuz] *vt.* 预作(诗歌等).

pre·com·pres·sion [ˈpri:kəmˈpreʃən] *n.* 预先压缩，预压力.

pre·con·ceive [ˈpri:kənˈsi:v] *vt.* 预见；事先打好(主意等). *~d prejudices* 先入之见，偏见.

pre·con·cep·tion [ˈpriːkənˈsepʃən] *n.* ①预想，预见. ②先入之见，偏见. **-al** *a.*
pre·con·cert [ˈpriːkənˈsəːt] *vt.* 预定；预先商定；预先同意. *a ~ed plan* 预定的计划. **-ed** [-tid] *a.* 预先商定的.
pre·con·demn [ˈpriːkənˈdem] *vt.* (不调查证据)先预定…有罪.
pre·con·di·tion [ˈpriːkənˈdiʃən] *n.* 前提，先决条件. — *vt.* ①把…预先安排[准备]好. ②预先处理. ③使…先作好思想准备. **-ing** *n.* 预处理.
pre·co·nize [ˈpriːkənaiz] *vt.* ①宣告，声明；公布. ②指名召唤. ③(教皇)正式公布批准任命(新任主教). **pre·co·ni·za·tion** [ˈpriːkənaiˈzeiʃən] *n.*
pre·con·quest [ˈpriːˈkɔŋkwest] *a.* 【英史】诺曼 (Norman) 人征服英国(1066年)前的.
pre·con·scious [ˈpriːˈkɔnʃəs] *n., a.* 【心】前意识(的).
pre·con·sid·er·a·tion [ˈpriːkənˌsidəˈreiʃən] *n.* 预先考察，事先考虑.
pre·con·tract [ˈpriːˈkɔntrækt] *n.* 预约，先约；〔古〕(具有法律效力的)订婚，婚约. — [ˈpriːkənˈtrækt] *vi.* 预约，〔古〕订婚(约). — *vt.* 预先规定；〔古〕同…预订婚约.
pre·cook [ˈpriːˈkuːk] *vt.* 预先烹调，预煮，预烧.
pre·cool [ˈpriːˈkuːl] *vt.* 预先冷冻〔货物打包或装船前进行冷冻〕.
pre·cor·di·al [ˈpriːˈkɔːdjəl] *a.* 【解】心前区的.
pre·cor·di·um [priːˈkɔːdjəm] *n.* (*pl.* **-dia** [-djə]) 【解】心前区.
pre·cos·tal [ˈpriːˈkɔstəl] *a.* 【解】在肋骨前的.
pre·cur·sive [pri(ː)ˈkəːsiv] *a.* = precursory.
pre·cur·sor [pri(ː)ˈkəːsə] *n.* ①前辈，前驱，先锋；前任. ②预兆；先兆. ③预报器. ④【原】前驱波；初级粒子.
pre·cur·sory [pri(ː)ˈkəːsəri] *a.* ①前驱的，先锋的；前辈的，前任的. ②预兆的，预报的. ③开端的，作预备的；初步的.
pred. = predicate; predicative(ly).
pre·da·cious, pre·da·ceous [priˈdeiʃəs] *a.* = predatory.
pre·dac·i·ty [priˈdæsiti] *n.* 【动】捕食性，食肉性.
pre·date [ˈpriːˈdeit] *vt.* ①倒填…的日期，填早于…的日期. ②在日期上早于[先于] (*opp.* postdate). *~ the check by three days* 把支票的日期填早三天.
pre·da·tion [priˈdeiʃən] *n.* ①掠夺的行为. ②捕食其他动物的生存方法.
pred·a·tor [ˈpredətə] *n.* 以掠夺为生的人；捕食其他动物的动物，食肉动物.
pred·a·to·ry [ˈpredətəri] *a.* ①(战争等)以掠夺为目的的，掠夺(性)的；掠夺成性的. ②【动】捕食其他动物的，食肉的. *a ~ war* 掠夺性战争. *a ~ ruffian* 强盗. *~ birds* 食肉禽. **-to·ri·ly** [ˈpredəˈtɔrili] *ad.* **-to·ri·ness** *n.*
pre·dawn [ˈpriːˈdɔːn] *a.* 黎明前的.
pre·de·cease [ˈpriːdiˈsiːs] *vt.* (比某人)先死；死在(某事件)之前. *~ one's father* 比父亲先死. — *vi.* 先死. — *n.* 先死，早死.
pre·de·ces·sor [ˈpriːdisesə] *n.* ①前任；前辈；〔古〕祖先. ②【农】前作；【数】前趋. ③(被取代的)原先的东西. *It will share the fate of its ~.* 它将遭受与前者同样的命运，它将重蹈覆辙.
pre·de·fine [ˈpriːdiˈfain] *vt.* 预先规定[确定].
pre·del·la [priˈdelə] *n.* (*pl.* **-le** [-li]) 祭坛台座[台阶]；祭坛台座垂直面上的绘画[雕刻].
pre·de·pres·sion [ˈpriːdiˈpreʃən] *a.* 经济萧条期以前的. — *n.* 萧条期以前的时期.
pre·des·ig·nate [ˈpriːˈdezigneit] *vt.* 预先指示. **pre·des·ig·na·tion** [-ˈneiʃən] *n.*
pre·des·ti·nar·i·an [pri(ː)ˌdestiˈnɛəriən] *n.* 宿命论者，命定论者. — *a.* 宿命论(者)的；宿命的. **-ism** *n.* 宿命论，命定论.
pre·des·ti·nate [pri(ː)ˈdestineit] *vt.* ①预先注定，命中注定. ②〔古〕预先确定. — [pri(ː)ˈdestinit] *a.* ①被预先注定的；被命运注定的，宿命的. ②〔古〕预定的.
pre·des·ti·na·tion [pri(ː)ˌdestiˈneiʃən] *n.* 前定，预定；命运，前世因缘；【宗】命定论，宿命论.
pre·des·tine [pri(ː)ˈdestin] *vt.* 预先指定，预先决定；命中注定.
pre·de·ter·mi·nate [ˈpriːdiˈtəːminit] *a.* 预定的，先定的. *the ~ will of* …的预定意志.
pre·de·ter·mine [ˈpriːdiˈtəːmin] *vt.* ①预定，先定，注定. ②预先决定…的方向；使先存偏见. **-na·tion** [-ˈneiʃən] *n.*
pre·di·al [ˈpriːdiəl] *a.* ①土地的；与土地有关的；固定资产的，与固定资产有关的；有土地的. ②与耕种有联系的；乡村的. ③佃户的；隶属于土地的. *~ serfs* 农奴. — *n.* 农奴.
pred·i·ca·bil·i·ty [ˌpredikəˈbiliti] *n.* 可断定性；可断定为…的属性.
pred·i·ca·ble [ˈpredikəbl] *a.* 可断定的，可断定为…的属性的 (*of*). *Length is ~ of a line.* 长度是线的属性. — *n.* ①可被作为属性而断定的东西；同类对象的共同属性. ②〔*pl.*〕【逻】宾词；〔the ~〕(特指亚里士多德逻辑学中的)五种宾词〔"类"、"种"、"特异性"、"固有性"、"偶然性"〕.
pre·dic·a·ment [priˈdikəmənt] *n.* ①境遇，状况；穷境，苦境；危境. ②【逻】(可)被论断的事物，种类；〔*pl.*〕(亚里士多德逻辑学中的)十大范畴. *be in an awkward ~* 处困境中.
pred·i·cant [ˈpredikənt] *a.* 讲道的，说教的. — *n.* (天主教多明我会的)说教神父.
pred·i·cate [ˈpredikit] *n.* ①【语法】谓语，②【逻】谓项，谓词，宾词. ③本质；属性. — *a.* 谓语的；谓项的. — [ˈpredikeit] *vt.* ①论断，断言；断定…为某物的属性，断定某物有…的属性 (*about; of*). ②〔美〕使(声明、行动等)依据于 (*on; upon*)，使基于. ③宣言，宣布，声明. ④意味着，具有…的含义. ⑤【语法】表述. — *vi.* 断言 (*of*). *Can anything be ~d about a non-existent thing?* 能够表述不存在的东西吗？ *(We) ~ of the motive that it is good.* (我们)断言这个动机是好的.
pred·i·ca·tion [ˌprediˈkeiʃən] *n.* ①断定；判断. ②【语法】谓语；谓语的表述，述谓.
pred·i·ca·tive [priˈdikətiv] *a.* ①(在某一事物的属性方面)起论断作用的；论断性的. ②【语法】表语的；用作表语的. *a ~ adjective* 表语形容词. — *n.* 【语法】表语；谓语性. **-ca·tiv·i·ty** [priˌdikəˈtiviti] *n.* 谓语性. **-ly** *ad.*
pred·i·ca·to·ry [ˈpredikətəri] *a.* ①说教的，说教性的. ②断定的，论断性的. ③宣言的.
pre·dict [priˈdikt] *vt., vi.* 预言，预告，预报，预示. *~ rain for tomorrow* 预告明天有雨. *~ a good harvest* 预告丰年.
pre·dict·a·ble [priˈdiktəbl] *a.* 可预言的；可预报的. **pre·dict·a·bil·i·ty** [priˌdiktəˈbiliti] *n.* **-a·bly** *ad.*
pre·dic·tion [priˈdikʃən] *n.* ①预言，预告. ②被预言的事物. ③【气】预测，预报. *weather ~* 天气预报.
pre·dic·tive [priˈdiktiv] *a.* 预言性的；(成为)前兆的.
pre·dic·tor [priˈdiktə] *n.* ①预言者；预报者. ②【军】活动目标预测器；水雷发射预测器. ③【气】预报因子.
pre·di·gest [ˈpriːdiˈdʒest, priːdaiˈdʒest] *vt.* 把(食物)弄得容易消化；预先消化. ②使简化易懂. **pre·di·ges·tion** [ˈpriːdiˈdʒestʃən, -dai-] *n.*
pre·di·lec·tion [ˌpriːdiˈlekʃən] *n.* 嗜好，偏好；偏爱 (*for*). *have a ~ for (opera)* 特别爱好(歌剧).
pre·dis·pose [ˈpriːdisˈpəuz] *vt.* ①预先处理[处置，安

排]. ②是…造成…的基础[原因],使先倾向于;使先爱好,使先适应. ③使容易感染;使易接受(病). *A cold ~s one to other diseases.* 伤风容易使人患别的病. **be ~d to** 本来爱好…,有…的倾向;易患…病. **-d** *a.* ①先倾向于…的. ②事先安排好的.

pre·dis·po·si·tion [priːˌdispəˈziʃən] *n.* ①倾向,天性,素质;癖性,资质 *(to)*. ②【医】诱因 *(to)*.

pred·nis·o·lone [predˈnisələun] *n.* 【药】氢化泼尼松,去氢氢化可的松,强的松龙.

pred·ni·sone [ˈprednisəun] *n.* 【药】泼尼松. ~ **acetate** 【药】醋酸泼尼松,去氢可的松,强的松.

pre·dom·i·nance [priˈdɔminəns] *n.* ①优越,优势. ②卓越,出众;显著,突出.

pre·dom·i·nant [priˈdɔminənt] *a.* ①主要的;突出的;最显著的. ②掌握主权的;有力的,有效的. ③占优势的,支配其他的 *(over)*,卓越的. ④流行的. *a ~ idea* 主导思想. *a ~ colour* 主色. — *n.* 【生】特优生物,特优种. **-ly** *ad.*

pre·dom·i·nate [priˈdɔmineit] *vi.* 统治;居支配地位,(数量上)占优势 *(over)*. *a mixed feeling in which jealousy ~s* 嫉妒占优势的复杂感情. *a garden in which dahlias ~* 大丽花最多的花园. — *vt.* 支配,统治. — [priˈdɔminit] *a.* = predominant. **pre·dom·inat·ing·ly** *ad.*

pre·dom·i·na·tion [priˌdɔmiˈneiʃən] *n.* = predominance.

pre·doom [ˈpriːˈduːm] *vt.* 〔古〕命中注定,预先判处.

pre·e·lect [ˈpriːiˈlekt] *vt.* 预选.

pre·e·lec·tion [ˈpriːiˈlekʃən] *n.* ①〔古〕预选;优先的选择. ②预定. — *a.* 选举前的. ~ *promises* 选举前的许诺.

preem [priːm] *n.* 〔美俚〕(电影、戏剧、电视节目等的)初次上演,头轮放映.

pree·mie [ˈpriːmiː] *n.* 〔口〕早产儿〔尤指体重未超过 $5^1/_2$ 磅者而言〕.

pre·em·i·nence [pri(ː)ˈeminəns] *n.* 杰出,卓越.

pre·em·i·nent [pri(ː)ˈeminənt] *a.* 优秀的,杰出的,卓越的;显著的. **-ly** *ad.*

pre·em·pha·sis [ˈpriːˈemfəsis] *n.* 【无】预加重,预修正,(频应)预矫.

pre·empt [pri(ː)ˈem *p*t] *vt.* ①以先买权取得. ②〔美〕为取得先买权预先占据(公地). ③〔喻〕先占,先取. — *vi.* (桥牌中)先发制人地叫牌〔故意叫得很高使对方为难〕.

pre·emp·tion [pri(ː)ˈem *p*ʃən] *n.* ①先买;(个人购买公地的)先买权. ②先取;先占.

pre·emp·tive [pri(ː)ˈem *p*tiv] *a.* ①先买的,有先买权的. ②(桥牌中叫牌、战争等)先发制人的. ***a ~ bid*** 【桥牌】先发制人的叫牌〔故意叫高以阻止对方叫牌〕. ***a ~ war*** 先发制人的战争.

preen [priːn] *vt.* ①(鸟)用嘴理(毛). ②〔~ oneself〕(人)打扮(自己). ③〔~ oneself〕(人)夸耀(自己). — *vi.* ①把自己打扮得漂漂亮亮. ②自满,自负,自我夸耀.

pre·en·gage [ˈpriːinˈgeidʒ] *vt.* ①先订,预约;(以先订的婚约)约束. ②先得,先占. ③使先入为主,使偏向. **-ment** *n.*

pre·es·tab·lish [ˈpriːisˈtæbliʃ] *vt.* 预先设立[制定],预定,先定.

pre·es·ti·mate [pri(ː)ˈestimeit] *vt.* 预测,预估,预算. — [pri(ː)ˈestimit] *n.* 预测,预估,预算.

pre·ex·am·ine [pri(ː)igˈzæmin] *vt.* 预试,预考;预先检查. **pre·ex·am·i·na·tion** [pri(ː)igˌzæmiˈneiʃən] *n.*

pre·ex·ist [ˈpriːigˈzist] *vi.* 先(存)在. — *vt.* 先于…而存在.

pre·ex·ist·ence [ˈpriːigˈzistəns] *n.* ①先在,先存〔尤指所谓灵魂与肉体结合前的存在〕. ②前世. **pre·ex·ist·ent, pre·ex·ist·ing** *a.*

pref. = ①preface; prefaced. ②preference; preferred. ③prefix.

pre·fab [ˈpriːˈfæb] *n.* 〔口〕预制房屋;活动房屋 (= prefabricated house). — *a.* 预制的,预构的 (= prefabricated).

pre·fab·ri·cate [ˈpriːˈfæbrikeit] *vt.* ①预制. ②〔美〕用预制构件建筑[制造]. ③预先构思. *~d parts* 预制构件. *~d structures* 预制结构. *a ~d house* (构件均预先制成,到施工现场装配即建成的)预制房屋,活动房屋.

pre·fab·ri·ca·tion [priːˌfæbriˈkeiʃən] *n.*

pref·ace [ˈprefis] *n.* ①序,绪言;前言;引语;开端. ②〔P-〕【宗】(弥撒的)序诵,序祷. — *vt.* ①给…作序. ②开始,导致;作为…的开端. — *vi.* 作序,写序文. *~ one's remarks by a cough* 先咳嗽一下然后开始讲话.

pref·a·to·ri·al, pref·a·to·ry [ˌprefəˈtɔːriəl, ˈprefətəri] *a.* ①序言的;引言性的. ②位于前面的. *prefatory remarks in a speech* 演说的开场白.

prefd. = preferred stock 〔美〕优先股.

pre·fect [ˈpriːfekt] *n.* ①(古罗马的)行政长官;(陆、海军)司令官;总督. ②(现代法国的)省长;(日本的)县知事. ③(英国某些公立学校、美国某些私立学校负责维持秩序的)班长. ~ ***of police*** 巴黎警察总监. **pre·fec·tor·al** [priˈfektərəl], **pre·fec·to·ri·al** [ˌpriːfekˈtɔːriəl] *a.*

pre·fec·tur·al [ˈpriːfektjurəl] *a.* ①专区的;(日本的)县的;(法国的)省的. ②(日本的)县知事的;(法国的)省的.

pre·fec·ture [ˈpriːfektjuə, -tʃuə] *n.* ①古罗马高级文武长官[法国省长、日本县知事]的职位[任期、管区、官邸]. ②级长的职位[任期]. ③专区;县;府;(法国的)省.

pre·fer [priˈfəː] *vt.* ①(比较起来)喜欢…(而不喜欢…);宁可…(而不…);比起…来还是…好;宁愿选择;更喜欢 *(to, above, before)*. ②提起,提出(声明、请求、控诉等). ③提升,提拔;任命,录用;推荐,介绍. ④【法】给与(某债权人等)优先获得偿付权. ⑤建议;申请. *I ~ water to wine.* 我喜欢水不喜欢酒. *~ working to sitting idle* 喜欢干活而不喜欢闲呆着. *~ the country to the town* 比起城市来还是乡下好. *~ a claim to property* 提出一项财产要求. *~ charge against sb.* 控告某人. *a preferred share [stock]* 【商】优先股. ★ ① ~后接 rather than 的习惯用法: *He preferred to do this rather than that.* 他说宁愿做这个,不愿做那个. ②比较部分常有省略: *~ to wait (rather than go at once)* (与其马上就走)还是等一等的好. *~ to leave it alone = ~ that it should be left alone* 还是听其自然的好. ***~ sb. for*** 提升某人为….

pref·er·a·ble [ˈprefərəbl] *a.* 更可取的;更好的 *(to)*;略胜一筹的. *Poverty is ~ to ill-health.* 贫穷比不健康好一点.

pref·er·a·bly [ˈprefərəbli] *ad.* 宁可,宁愿;最好;更可取地. *I might travel by York or ~ by Preston.* 我想旅途中经过约克,但最好是经过普雷斯顿.

pref·er·ence [ˈprefərəns] *n.* ①优先选择;偏爱. ②优先选择物,偏爱物. ③【法】优先权;特惠〔特指关税〕;(债权人)受优先偿还的权利;选择机会. ④一种牌戏. *This is my ~.* 我喜欢这个. ***by [for] ~*** 喜欢,选择. ***have a ~ for [to]*** 喜欢…,认为…更好. ***in ~ to*** 比…先,比起…来宁愿. ***~ of sth. to [over] another*** 宁要某物而不要另一物. ~ **bond [share, stock]** 〔英〕优先公债[股].

pref·er·en·tial [ˌprefəˈrenʃəl] *a.* ①优先的;优待的;优先选择的;差别制的. ②(国际贸易等方面)特惠的. — *n.* ①优先权. ②特惠税率. ~ **pairing** 【生】偏向配对. ~ **right** 优先权. ~ **shop** 〔美〕优先(雇工会会员的)工厂. ~ **species** 【生】适宜种. ~ **stock** 优先股. ~ **system** = ~ voting ~ **tariff [duties]** 特惠关税. ~ **voting** 选择选票制〔选举者可在选票中注明对被选举人的优先选择次序〕. **-ism** *n.* 关税特惠主义. **-ist** *n.* 关税特惠主义者.

pre·fer·ment [priˈfəːmənt] *n.* ①升级,提升. ②〔古〕

(购置财产等的)优先权. ③(神父等的)高位; 肥缺. ④(控告等的)提出.

pre·fig·u·ra·tion [ˈpriːfigjuˈreiʃən] *n.* ①预示, 预兆. ②预想. ③原型. **pre·fig·u·ra·tive** [ˈpriːˈfigjurətiv] *a.*

pre·fig·ure [ˈpriːˈfigə] *vt.* ①(通过形象)预示,预兆. ②预想; 预见; 预言. **pre·fig·u·ra·tive** *a.*

pre·fix [ˈpriːfiks] *n.* ①【语法】前缀; 前加成分〔如 prefix 的 pre-〕. ②人名前用的尊称〔Mr., Dr., Sir. 等〕. ③【数】首标. — [priːˈfiks] *vt.* ①把…放在前头; 作…的前缀; 给…附加标题. ②〔古〕预先指定,预先任命. *Quotations are ~ed to the chapters.* 各章前头附有引文. **-al** *a.* **pre·fix·al·ly** *ad.*

pre·flight [ˈpriːˈflait] *a.*【空】在起飞之前的. *~ instructions* 起飞前的指示.

pre·form [ˈpriːˈfɔːm] *vt.* ①预先形成〔决定〕. ②把…初步加工, 对(宝石等)粗加工. — [ˈpriːfɔːm] *n.* 初步加工的成品; 压片; 雏形,塑坯预塑; (录音用)盘料; 经过粗琢的宝石.

pre·form·a·tion [ˈpriːfɔːˈmeiʃən] *n.* ①预先形成. ②【生】胚中预存说,预成说 *(opp.* epigenesis*)*.

pre·for·ma·tive [ˈpriːˈfɔːmətiv] *a.* ①使预先形成的. ②【语法】以前缀为特征的; 前缀的. — *n.*【语法】前缀.

pre·fron·tal [ˈpriːˈfrʌntl] *a.*【解】前额的,额叶前部的; 前额骨的. — *n.* 前额骨.

pre·gan·gli·on·ic [priˌgæŋgliˈɔnik] *a.*【动】前神经节的.

pre·gla·cial [ˈpriːˈgleisjəl] *a.*【地】冰河期前的.

preg·na·ble [ˈpregnəbl] *a.* 可攻克的,易占领的; 易受攻击的,有弱点的. *a ~ fortress* 易攻破的堡垒. *a ~ idea* 有毛病的主意. *the only ~ point* 唯一的弱点. **preg·na·bil·i·ty** [ˌpregnəˈbiliti] *n.*

preg·nan·cy [ˈpregnənsi] *n.* ①怀孕,妊娠; 怀孕期; (事件等的)酝酿. ②〔喻〕丰富,丰满; 含蓄, (内容)充实, 富有意义. *~ cell* 孕细胞.

preg·nant [ˈpregnənt] *a.* ①怀着孕的,有孕的,怀胎的. ②意义深长的,(话等)有含蓄的. ③包藏着〔孕育着〕(重大结果)的; 充满…的 *(with)*. ④富于想象的, 富于发明才能的, 聪明的, 有创造力的. ⑤富于成果的. ⑥〔古, 诗〕多产的, 丰饶的. *a ~ construction*【修】简洁体〔如将 *Let him go out* 说成 *Let him out*〕. *the ~ year* 丰年. **-ly** *ad.*

pre·heat [ˈpriːˈhiːt] *vt.* 预热(炉、灶等). **-er** *n.* 预热器.

pre·hen·sile [priˈhensail] *a.* ①【动】(足、尾等)适于抓拿的,适于缠卷的,(有)捕握(力)的. ②善于领悟的, 有洞察力的. *a ~ arm* (头足类的)捉脚. *the ~ tail of a monkey* 猿猴的卷尾. *~ poets* 有特殊洞察力的诗人们.

pre·hen·sion [priˈhenʃən] *n.* ①【动】抓住,捕捉,把握. ②【心】理解,领悟.

pre·his·tor·ic, pre·his·tor·i·cal [ˈpriːhisˈtɔrik, -ikəl] *a.* ①史前的,(有记载的)历史以前的. ②〔口〕陈旧不堪的; 旧式的; 陈腐的. **-i·cal·ly** *ad.*

pre·his·to·ry [ˈpriːˈhistəri] *n.* ①(历史记载以前的)史前史. ②(导致事件、危机等的)背景. ③史前学; 史前考古学.

pre·hu·man [ˈpriːˈhjuːmən] *a.* 人类以前的.

pre·ig·ni·tion [ˈpriːigˈniʃən] *n.*【机】(内燃机内的)提前点火,预燃(作用); 过早点火.

pre·judge [ˈpriːˈdʒʌdʒ] *vt.* 预先判断; 过早判断;【法】不审而判. **-judg(e)·ment** *n.*

pre·ju·di·ca·tion [ˈpriːˌdʒuːdiˈkeiʃən] *n.* ①预先判断; 预先判决; 草率的判断. ②【法】判例.

prej·u·dice [ˈpredʒudis] *n.* ①偏见,成见; 歧视. ②【法】损害, 伤害; 不利. *Divest you of your ~.* 扫除你的偏见. ***be swayed by ~*** 为偏见所左右. ***have a ~ against*** *(sb.)* 对(某人)有偏见. ***have a ~ in favour of …*** 袒护,偏爱. ***in [to the] ~ of*** 有损于,不利于. ***without ~*** ①无偏见. ②【法】不违背; 不使(合法权利等)受损害. — *vt.* ①使抱偏见,使怀成见. ②侵害, 伤害,损害. *His manner ~d his audience against [in favour of] him.* 他的态度使听众对他发生了反感[好感]. *You ~d your chances of success.* 你糟蹋了你的前途.

prej·u·diced [ˈpredʒudist] *a.* 抱有偏见的,有成见的,有偏心的. *a ~ opinion* 偏见. *the least ~ in sizing up situations* 最能不抱偏见地估计形势. *be ~ against [in favour of]* 对…抱反感[好感].

prej·u·di·cial [ˌpredʒuˈdiʃəl] *a.* ①引起偏见的, 有成见的. ②有损害的,不利的. *a course of action ~ to sb.'s interest* 不利于某人的诉讼. **-ly** *ad.*

prel·a·cy [ˈpreləsi] *n.* ①〔the ~〕〔集合词〕主教(团), 高级教士(团) (= prelates). ②主教[高级教士]的地位[职务、管辖区]. ③〔贬〕主教统治,主教监管制.

prel·ate [ˈprelit] *n.* ①高级教士[教长, 主教]. ②〔美〕教士, 牧师. ③【史】修道院长. **pre·lat·ic, pre·lat·i·cal** [priˈlætik(əl)] *a.*

prel·at·ess [ˈprelitis] *n.* ①女修道院长. ②〔谑〕主教太太.

pre·law [ˈpriːˈlɔː] *a.* 〔美〕法科预科的; 修习法科预科的. *a ~ student* 法科预科学生.

pre·lect [priˈlekt] *vi.* (特指大学讲师)讲演,讲述,讲课. **-lec·tion** [-ˈlekʃən] *n.*

pre·lec·tor [priˈlektə] *n.* 〔主英〕(大学)讲师.

pre·li·ba·tion [ˈpriːlaiˈbeiʃən] *n.* 试尝, 预尝〔通常作比喻用〕.

pre·lim [priˈlim] *n., a.* 〔俚〕大学考试(的),初试(的)〔preliminary 的缩略形式〕.

pre·lim·i·na·ry [priˈliminəri] *a.* ①预备的; 初步的, 初级的. ②序言性的,绪言的. *a ~ examination* 初试, 预考〔学生普通说作 prelim〕. *~ expenses* 开办费. *~ hearing*【法】预审. *~ remarks* 前言; 开场白. — *n.* ①〔常 *pl.*〕初步, 开端; 预备行为[步骤、措施], 准备. ②〔*sing.*〕入学初考,预考. ③【体】预赛; 淘汰赛; (主赛前的)次要比赛〔如拳击〕. ④〔常 *pl.*〕正文前的书页〔内容〕. ***without preliminaries*** 直截了当地, 单刀直入地. — *ad.* 预先 (= preliminarily). **pre·lim·i·nar·i·ly** [priˈliminərily, Am. priˌlimiˈnerili] *ad.*

pre·lit·er·ate [priˈlitərit] *a.* 没有文字的社会的, 有文字社会前的.

prel·ude [ˈpreljuːd] *n.* ①【乐】序曲, 前奏曲. ②开场戏; 序幕; 序言. ③前兆, 预兆. — *vt.* ①成为…的序曲[序幕]; 奏(序曲). ②为…作序; 开头; 成为…的前兆. — *vi.* 奏序曲; 唱开场戏; 成为序幕; 成为前兆 *(to)*. *He ~d with some banal remarks.* 他讲了一些老套话作为开场白.

pre·lu·di·al [priˈljuːdiəl] *a.* ①序言(式)的; 序幕(式)的; 序曲(式)的. ②先导的; 前兆的,预兆的.

pre·lu·sion [priˈluːʒən] *n.* 序言 (= prelude *n.*).

pre·lu·sive [priˈljuːsiv] *a.* ①前奏曲的; 序幕的; 序言的 *(to)*. ②先导的; 成为先驱的; 成为前兆的. **-ly** *ad.*

pre·lu·so·ry [priˈljuːsəri] *a.* = prelusive.

prem. = premium.

pre·man [ˈpriːmæn] *n.* *(pl.* ***pre·men*** [ˈpriːˈmen]*)* (假定为人类直系祖先的)一种古灵长类动物.

pre·mar·i·tal [ˈpriːməˈraitəl, priːˈmæritəl] *a.* (结)婚前的.

pre·ma·ture [ˌpreməˈtjuə, ˌpriːməˈtjuə] *a.* ①早熟的; 不成熟的. ②过早的,不到期的; 时机未成熟的. *a ~ birth* 早产. *a ~ death* 夭亡. *a ~ decision* 过早的决定. — *n.* ①早产的婴儿. ②过早爆发的炮弹. ③过早发生的事物.

pre·ma·tu·ri·ty [ˌpreməˈtjuəriti, ˌpriːməˈtjuəriti] *n.* ①早熟(性); 不成熟. ②不到期; 过早, 时机未成熟; (花的)早开.

pre·max·il·la [ˌpriːmækˈsilə] *n.* *(pl.* ***-lae*** [-iː]*)*【解】

切牙骨. **-il·lar·y** [-ˈmæksiləri] *a.*

pre·med [ˈpriːmed] *a.* 〔美〕医科大学预科的〔premedical 的缩略形式〕. — *n.* 医科大学预科(学生).

pre·med·i·cal [ˈpriːˈmedikəl] *a.* 〔美〕医科大学预科的.

pre·med·i·tate [pri(ː)ˈmediteit] *vt., vi.* 预先思考, 预谋, 预先策划.

pre·med·i·tat·ed [pri(ː)ˌmediˈteitid] *a.* 预先想过的, 预先策划的, 有预谋的. *a* ~ *murder* 谋杀. **-ly** *ad.*

pre·med·i·ta·tion [pri(ː)ˌmediˈteiʃən] *n.* 预想, 预谋; 预先策划.

prem·i·er [ˈpremjə, -miə] *n.* 总理, 首相. — *a.* ①第一的, 首位的, 首要的. ②最先的, 最早的. *take the* ~ *place* 占第一位, 占首席. *the* ~ *minister* 〔古〕首相. **-ship** *n.* 首相[总理]的职务[任期].

pre·mière [ˈpremiεə] *n.* 〔F.〕①首次演出; (演出的)第一天, 开场日; 初次的展出. ②(舞蹈、戏剧等的)女主角. ***give*** ~ ***of*** 首次演出. — *vi.* 初次演出; (名演员等)首次登台. — *a.* 首要的, 第一的.

pre·mil·len·ni·al [ˈpriːmiˈleniəl] *a.* 【宗】千年至福期前的; 基督再临以前的; 现世的. **-ism** *n.* 千年至福期前基督再临论.

prem·ise [ˈpremis] *n.* ①【逻】前提〔常作 premiss〕. ②〔*pl.*〕【法】(理由等的)前提, 根据, 缘起部分; 〔*pl.*〕【法】控诉事实; 前述事件; 让渡物件; 证件前款〔如当事人姓名、让渡物件、让渡理由等〕. ③〔*pl.*〕房屋(及其附属基地、建筑等); 院内, 屋内. *the major [minor]* ~【逻】大[小]前提. *business* ~*s* 事务所, 办公室. *the back [front]* ~ 后[前]院. ***on [in] the*** ~***s*** 只供店内喝〔指酒等〕. ***live on the*** ~***s*** 住在楼内. — [priˈmaiz] *vt.* ①预述(条件等); 引导(论述等). ②提出…作为前提[条件]. ③假定. ~ *one's argument with a bit of history* 引证一点历史作为立论的前提. — *vi.* 作出前提.

prem·iss [ˈpremis] *n.* 【逻】前提(= premise *n.*①).

pre·mi·um [ˈpriːmjəm, -miəm] *n.* ①超票面价格, 溢价; 加价; 贴水, 升水. ②奖赏, 奖励; 奖金; 奖状, 奖品; 【桥牌】奖分. ③保险费. ④佣金; (利息、工资等以外的)酬金. ⑤额外费用. ⑥学费; 习艺费. *a* ~ *for* 为…而发的奖金. ***at a*** ~ (股票)以超过票面以上的价格; 〔喻〕非常需要, 极受重视 *(opp.* at a discount*)* (*It sells at a* ~ *of 20 percent* 这是加二卖出的). ***pay a*** ~ ***for*** 付…佣金. ***put [set, place] a*** ~ ***on*** 诱发; 助长, 促进; 鼓励; 奖励. ~ **bond** 溢价债券. **P- Bonds** 〔英〕政府有奖债券〔但无利息〕. ~ **note** 保险费付款期票. ~ **system** 职工奖金制度. ~ **tariff** 保险率表.

pre·mo·lar [ˈpriːˈməulə] *n., a.* 【解】前磨牙(的), 前臼齿(的).

pre·mon·ish [ˈpriːˈmoniʃ] *vt., vi.* 〔罕〕预先警告, 预先劝告.

pre·mo·ni·tion [ˌpriːməˈniʃən] *n.* ①预先的警告[告诫], 预戒. ②预感; 前兆, 征兆.

pre·mon·i·tor [priˈmonitə] *n.* ①预先警告[告诫]者. ②预兆, 征兆.

pre·mon·i·to·ry [priˈmonitəri] *a.* ①预先警告[告诫]的. ②前兆的. ③【医】前驱的, 先兆的, 先期的.

pre·morse [pri(ː)ˈmoːs] *a.* 【植】(叶、根等)啮蚀状的.

pre·mune [pri(ː)ˈmjuːn] *a.* ①显示抗病(力)的. ②【医】预免疫的.

pre·mu·ni·tion [ˌpriːmjuːˈniʃən] *n.* ①〔古〕预防; 抗病(力). ②【医】预免疫.

pre·na·tal [ˈpriːˈneitl] *a.* 出生前的, 胎儿期的.

pre·nom·i·nate [pri(ː)ˈnomineit] *vt.* 〔废〕预先命名, 预先提到. —[pri(ː)ˈnominit] *a.* 〔废〕预先提到的, 预先命名的.

pre·no·tion [pri(ː)ˈnəuʃən] *n.* 〔罕〕先见之明, 预知, 预想.

pren·tice [ˈprentis] *n.* 〔古〕〔口〕定期学徒〔apprentice 之略〕. ~ ***hand*** 生手 (*try one's* ~ *hand at* 做做试试看). — *a.* 〔古〕〔口〕学徒的. — *vt.* 〔古〕〔口〕使做学徒.

pre·nup·tial [pri(ː)ˈnʌpʃəl] *a.* ①结婚前的, 婚礼前的. ②【动】交配前的.

pre·oc·cu·pan·cy [pri(ː)ˈokjupənsi] *n.* ①先占据, 先取; 先占权. ②专心致志, 全神贯注; (事情)极繁忙.

pre·oc·cu·pa·tion [pri(ː)ˌokjuˈpeiʃən] *n.* ①先占据, 先取. ②偏见, 成见. ③专心; 全神贯注; 出神. ④使人全神贯注的事, 首先要做的事, 急务. ***take one's*** ~ ***with*** 全神贯注于, 专心致志于.

pre·oc·cu·pied [pri(ː)ˈokjupaid] *a.* ①专心一意的, 全神贯注的; (为某事)出神的; 心思重重的. ②被先占的. ③【生】(种和属的名称)不能再以新义使用的.

pre·oc·cu·py [pri(ː)ˈokjupai] *vt.* ①先占领, 先取. ②〔常用被动语态〕吸引住, 迷住; 使出神; 使全神贯注; 使专心于; 使抱偏见. *His mind is preoccupied with private cares.* 他一脑袋全是私心.

pre·op·er·a·tive [ˈpriːˈopərətiv] *a.* (外科)手术前的. **-ly** *ad.*

pre·or·dain [ˈpriːoːˈdein] *vt.* ①预先注定, 命该, 命中注定. ②预先规定.

prep [prep] *n.* ①〔学俚〕预备功课; 家庭作业〔*preparation* 之略〕. ②〔美〕预备学校, 预科 *(=* ~ *school)*; 预科学生 *(=* ~ *student)*. — *a.* 〔美口〕预备的, 准备的 (= preparatory). *a* ~ *school* 预备学校. —*vi.* 〔口〕进预备学校; 进行预备学习[训练]; 自修. — *vt.* 预备, 准备, 为(病人)做(手)术前(的)准备.

prep. = ①preposition. ②preparation. ③preparatory.

pre·pack [ˈpriːˈpæk] *n., vt.* = prepackage.

pre·pack·age [pri(ː)ˈpækidʒ] *vt.* (出售前)将(食品或其他商品)按标准重量或单位包装. — *n.* (食品等出售前用透明纸等)预先作好的包装.

pre·paid [ˈpriːˈpeid] *a.* (运费、邮资等)先付的, 付讫的. *a telegram with reply* ~ 复电费先付的电报.

prep·a·ra·tion [ˌprepəˈreiʃən] *n.* ①准备, 预备; 〔常 *pl.*〕准备工作[措施]; 预修, 预习 *(for)*; 预习时间; (对…的)准备. ②(药、菜等的)配制, 备办; 制剂, 配制品; 配制好的食物. ③【乐】准备调(音). ④(进行解剖、病理等实验的)标本. ⑤节日的前夜. *The* ~*s are complete.* 准备妥当了. ~ *of gunpowder* 火药的配制. ~ *of soil* 整地. ***be in*** ~ 在准备中; 在编辑中 (*The dictionary is in* ~. 这部词典在编辑中). ***in*** ~ ***for*** 作为…的准备. ***make*** ~***s against*** 为对付…作准备. ***make*** ~***s for*** 为…作准备. ~**-room** 〔美〕(殡仪馆的)尸体防腐室.

pre·par·a·tive [priˈpærətiv] *a.* 准备的, 预备的, 筹备的 *(to)*. — *n.* ①预备, 准备; 筹备. ②【军、海】(用鼓、号角等发出的)准备信号, 预备号. **-ly** *ad.*

pre·par·a·to·ry [priˈpærətəri] *a.* 准备的, 预备的; 筹备的. *a* ~ *committee for a congress* 大会的筹备委员会. *a* ~ *course* 预科. ~ *formation* 【军】准备姿势. — *n.* 〔英〕(为升入高级中学作准备的)私立预科学校; 〔美〕大学预科. *a* ~ *school* 〔英〕补习学校; 〔美〕大学预科. ~ ***to*** 作为…的准备, 在…之前. — *ad.* 在先前; 作为准备 *(to)*.

pre·par·a·to·ri·ly [priˈpæritərili, Am. priˌpærəˈtoːrili] *ad.*

pre·pare [priˈpεə] *vt.* ①准备, 预备; 筹备; 布置, 备办; 温习(功课). ②锻炼(身体等); 训练. ③编写; 配备, 装备(旅行团、军队等). ④配制, 制造(药等), 调制. ⑤使有准备, 使作准备. ⑥作出, 制订. ⑦【乐】调(音). ~ *lessons* 准备功课. ~ *a boy for an examination* 叫孩子准备考试. ~ *a prescription* 配药. ~ *a meal* 做饭. ~ *oneself for bad news* 对坏消息作好思想准备. — *vi.* ①预备, 作好准备 *(for)*. ②(心中)有思想 *(for)*. ~ *for the worst* 以防万一. ***be*** ~***d for [to (do)]*** 准备着 (*I am* ~*d for anything.* 我已作好应急准备. *My son is preparing for the army.* 我的儿子正准备参军). ~ ***the table*** 布置餐桌, 准备开饭.

pre·pared [priˈpɛəd] *a.* ①有准备的,准备好的. ②精制的, 特别处理过的. ～ *position*【军】既设阵地. **-ly** [priˈpɛədli, Am. priˈpɛəridli] *ad.*

pre·pared·ness [priˈpɛədnis, Am. priˈpɛəridnis] *n.* ①有准备,作好准备. ②〔美〕扩军,备战. *a* ～ *campaign* 扩军运动. *a* ～ *parade* 扩军运动游行. *strengthen* ～ *against war* 加强战备. *P- averts peril.* 有备无患.

pre·par·ing [priˈpɛəriŋ] *a.* 预备的, 准备的; 制备的. ～**-room** *n.* =〔美〕preparation-room.

pre·pay [ˈpriːˈpei] *vt.* *(pre·paid* [ˈpriːˈpeid]*)* 预付,先付(运费、利息、邮资等). ～ *a reply to a telegram* 预付电报复电费. ～**-set** 投币自动售物装置. **-pay·a·ble** *a.* 可预付的. **-ment** *n.*

pre·pense [priˈpens] *a.* 预先考虑过的; 故意的〔用在名词后〕. ***of malice*** ～【法】蓄意伤害〔中伤〕; 预谋 (*to kill a man of malice* ～ 预谋杀人). **-ly** *ad.* 有计划地, 故意.

pre·plan [ˈpriːˈplæn] *vt., vi.* 预先计划[打算,规划].

pre·pon·der·ance, pre·pon·der·an·cy [priˈpɒndərəns, -si] *n.* (数量、重量、力量、影响、重要性上的)优势; 优越. ～ *of force at the crucial point*【军】集中优势兵力于要害目标. ***have the*** ～ ***over*** 比…占优势.

pre·pon·der·ant [priˈpɒndərənt] *a.* (数量、重量、力量、影响、重要性上)占优势的; 压倒的 *(over)*. **-ly** *ad.*

pre·pon·der·ate [priˈpɒndəreit] *vi.* ①数量上超过; 重量超过; (天平)倒向一方. ②(智力、权力等)超过, 压倒 *(over)*. — *vt.* 〔古〕重过; 压倒.

prep·o·si·tion [ˌprepəˈziʃən] *n.*【语法】介词, 前置词.

prep·o·si·tion·al [ˌprepəˈziʃənəl] *a.*【语法】前置词的,介词的. *a* ～ *phrase* 前置词短语. **-ly** *ad.*

pre·pos·i·tive [priˈpɒzitiv] *a.*【语法】前置的; 前缀的. — *n.*【语法】前置[前缀]的词.

pre·pos·i·tor [priˈpɒzitə] *n.* = praepostor.

pre·pos·sess [ˌpriːpəˈzes] *vt.* ①使预先具有; 使充满(某种感情、思想等). ②〔常用被动语态〕(人、态度等)使先有好感; 使偏爱. ③使某人对某事先有反感[偏见] *(against)*. *He is* ～*ed with a queer idea.* 他有一种奇怪的偏见. *She [Her manners]* ～*ed me in her favour.* 她[她的态度] 给我留下了好印象. *I was quite* ～*ed by his appearance.* 他的仪表使我十分喜欢.

pre·pos·sess·ing [ˌpriːpəˈzesiŋ] *a.* 使人喜欢的,可爱的; 有吸引力的; 给人好感的. **-ly** *ad.*

pre·pos·ses·sion [ˌpriːpəˈzeʃən] *n.* ①预先形成的印象[信念]; 偏爱,袒护; 偏见. ②全神贯注; 着迷. ③〔古〕先占,先领.

pre·pos·ter·ous [priˈpɒstərəs] *a.* ①是非颠倒的, 反常的,乖戾的; 十分荒谬的,不合理的, 可笑的; 愚蠢的. ②〔古〕次序颠倒的. *It is* ～*!* 岂有此理! **-ly** *ad.*

pre·pos·tor [priːˈpɒstə] *n.* = praepostor.

pre·po·tence, pre·po·ten·cy [priˈpəutəns, -si] *n.* ①优越的力量[权势]; 优势. ②【生】优先遗传(力).

pre·po·tent [priˈpəutənt] *a.* ①力量极优越的; 优势的. ②【生】有优先遗传力的.

prep·pie [ˈprepi] *a.* 〔美〕①未熟的. ②傻, 笨. — *n.* (大学)预科生.

prep·ping [ˈprepiŋ] *n.* 〔美口〕运动前的练习.

prep·py [ˈprepi] = preppie.

pre·pran·di·al [priːˈprændiəl] *a.* 饭前的.

pre·pref·er·ence [ˈpriːˈprefərəns] *a.* (证券等)最优先的. ～ *shares [stocks]* 最优先股.

pre·prim·er [ˈpriːˈprimə] *n.* ①学前儿童识字书. ②基础入门之书; 初学者所用的书.

prep·ster [ˈprepstə] *n.* 中学校[大学预科]的运动选手.

pre·puce [ˈpriːpjuːs] *n.* ①【解】(阴茎的)包皮. ②【虫】阳(茎)端膜. **pre·pu·tial** [priˈpjuːʃəl] *a.*

Pre-Raph·a·el [ˈpriːˈræfiəl] *a.*【美】①(十九世纪英国) 拉斐尔前派的. ②拉斐尔之前时期的. *the Pre-Raphael Brotherhood* (英国19世纪的) 拉斐尔前派社.

Pre-Raph·a·el·ite [ˈpriːˈræfəlait] *a., n.* 前拉斐尔时期(画派)的(画家).

Pre-Raph·a·el·it·ism [ˈpriːˈræfəlaitizəm] *n.*【美】拉斐尔前派的艺术主张[思潮].

pre·re·cord [ˈpriːriˈkɔːd] *vt.* (无线电与电视)预先录制(广告、节目等).

pre·re·lease [ˈpriːriˈliːs] *n.* ①(电影的)预映. ②(蒸汽机的)提前排汽.

pre·req·ui·site [ˈpriːˈrekwizit] *a.* 必须先具备的, 必要的; 先决条件的 *(to)*. *a* ～ *fund of knowledge* 必须先具有的知识储备. — *n.* 必要条件; 前提; 先决条件 *(for)*.

pre·rog·a·tive [priˈrɒgətiv] *n.* ①特权; 特典; 君权, 帝王的大权〔又作 royal ～〕; 天赋的特权[能力等]. ②【史】优先投票权. ③特性, 特点; 显著的优点. *the* ～ *of mercy* 赦免权. ***within one's*** ～ ***to do*** 是某人的特权[自由] (*It is within his* ～ *to leave* 离席是他的自由). — *a.* ①(有)特权的; 依照特权享有的. ②【罗马史】有优先投票权的. *a* ～ *right* 特权. ～ **court** ①【英史】(审查遗嘱等的)大主教法庭. ②【美史】(英国殖民统治时期)总督委任组成的法庭.

Pres. = President.

pres. = ①present. ②presidency; president. ③presumptive.

pres·age [ˈpresidʒ] *n.* ①预示; 前兆. ②预知, 先见(之明); 预感. ③〔古〕预言. ***of evil*** ～ 不吉利的. — [ˈpresidʒ, priˈseidʒ] *vt.* ①成为…的前兆,预示; 预先警告; 预言. ②预知, 预感. *The lowering clouds* ～ *the storm.* 暗云低沉是暴风雨的前兆. — *vi.* 预言; 〔古〕有预感.

pres·age·a·ble [priˈseidʒəbl] *a.* 能预言的,可预知的.

Presb. = Presbyter(ian).

presby- *comb. f.* ①老, 老者: *presbyopia.* ②长老: *Presbyterian.*

pres·by·cu·sis, pres·by·cou·sis [ˌprezbiˈkjuːsis, ˌpres-] *n.*【医】老年性耳聋.

pres·by·ope [ˈprezbiəup] *n.*【医】老花(眼)者; 远视者.

pres·by·o·pi·a [ˌprezbiˈəupiə, -pjə] *n.*【医】远视(眼), 老花(眼).

pres·by·o·p·ic [ˌprezbiˈɒpik] *a.* 远视眼的, 老花眼的.

pres·by·ter [ˈprezbitə] *n.*【宗】①(早期基督教的)地方教会监察者. ②(基督教长老会的) 长老. ③(英国圣公会的)牧师, 司祭.

pres·byt·er·ate [prezˈbitərit] *n.*【宗】①长老的职位, 长老的职权. ②长老会.

pres·by·te·ri·al [ˌprezbiˈtiəriəl] *a.*【宗】全体长老的; 长老制的.

Pres·by·te·ri·an [ˌprezbiˈtiəriən] *a.*【宗】①〔p-〕长老制的. ②长老会的. *the* ～ *Church* 基督教的长老会. — *n.* ①长老会教友. ②〔p-〕长老制主义者. **-ism** *n.* 长老制, 长老派的信仰[主张].

pres·by·ter·y [ˈprezbitəri] *n.*【宗】①长老会; 长老会教务评议会[管辖区]. ②(大教堂的)司祭席; 祭坛. ③(天主教神父)住宅.

pre·school [ˈpriːˈskuːl] 〔美〕 *a.* (小)学前的,学龄前的 — *n.* 幼儿园, 保育园. **-er** *n.* 学龄前儿童.

pres·ci·ence [ˈpresiəns] *n.* 预知, 先见.

pres·ci·ent [ˈpresiənt] *a.* 预知的, 有先见之明的; 有见识的 *(of)*. **-ly** *ad.*

pre·sci·en·tif·ic [ˈpriːˌsaiənˈtifik] *a.* 近代科学出现前的; 科学方法应用前的.

pre·scind [priˈsind] *vt.* ①(过早或突然地从整体中)割去; 使某甲同某乙分开 *(from)*. ②【哲】 孤立地观察[考虑]; 抽象地思索. ③〔古〕使中断[断绝]. *happiness* ～*ed from pleasure and self-indulgence* 超脱开享乐与自我放纵的幸福. — *vi.* 离开, 脱离; 不加考虑 *(from)*.

Pre·scott [ˈpreskət] *n.* 普雷斯科特〔姓氏〕.

pre·scribe [pris'kraib] *vt.* ①命令,指示,指挥;规定. ②处(方),开(药);劝行(某种疗法等);嘱咐,建议. ③【法】使(过限期而)失效[不合法]. *penalties ~d by law* 法律规定的刑罚. *~ the treatment* 建议采取该种治疗. — *vi.* ①命令,指挥,指令;规定. ②开药,处方 *(for)*. ③【法】(通过长期占有等而)要求(权利等) *(for, to)*;(因过期限而)失效[不合法]. *~ for a patient in a fever* 给热病患者开药方. **-er** *n.* 处方者,开药者;建议者.

pre·script ['pri:skript] *n.* 命令,训令;规定;法令. — [pri'skript, 'pri:skript] *a.* 指示的,命令的;规定的.

pre·scrip·ti·ble [pri'skriptəbl] *a.* ①可以治疗的,有疗效的. ②(根据传统或长期使用等而)要求权利的,(根据长期使用等而)获得权利的. *a ~ illness* 可治疗的疾病.

pre·scrip·tion [pri'skripʃən] *n.* ①命令,训令,指示;规定;法规;(应守的)旧习惯. ②【医】药方,处方;处方的药. ③【法】(依据传统或长期使用等而)要求权利;(由于长期使用等而)获得权利. *a medical ~* 药方. ***make a ~*** 开药方. ***make up the ~*** 抓药,配方. ***the negative ~***【法】可提出诉讼[要求]的法定期限. ***the positive ~***【法】(在法定期内等的)长期使用,长期占有;(由于长期使用等而获得的)权利. ***write out a ~ for*** 为…开药方.

pre·scrip·tive [pri'skriptiv] *a.* ①规定的;指示的,命令的. ②【法】依照时效的,因时效而得的;由于长期使用而获得的. ③惯例的;约定俗成的. *a ~ right*【法】(由于长期使用而获得的)时效权利. *~ grammar* 规范性语法 (*opp.* descriptive grammar). **-ly** *ad.*

pre·se·lec·tive ['pri:si'lektiv] *a.* (汽车齿轮)预选式的.

pres·ence ['prezns] *n.* ①在,存在,实在;存在的人[物]. ②出席,列席,到场;参加;会同 (*opp.* absense). ③(人)面前,眼前;[the ~]御前,驾前;接近. ④见面,谒见;[古]接见室 (= ~-chamber). ⑤鬼,妖怪,精灵. ⑥相貌,姿容;态度,风采,风度. *all foreign military ~* 一切外国的军事存在. *Your ~ is requested.* 请你出席,敬请光临. *a man of (a) noble ~* 有威仪的人. *a man of no ~* 其貌不扬的人. ***be admitted to sb.'s ~*** 被允许谒见[会见]某人. ***be banished from sb.'s ~*** 被斥退. ***in the ~ of*** 在…之前,在…面前;面临着…. ***~ of mind*** 镇静,沉着. ***saving your ~*** (在你面前)说句冒昧的话,恕我冒昧. ***with (great) ~ of mind*** 泰然,毅然,镇定自若地. **~-chamber [room]** (君主、显要人物的)接见厅;客厅,会客室.

pres·ent[1] ['prezənt] *a.* ①在座的,出席的,在场的,到(场)的;现存的,存在的 (*opp.* absent). ②现在的,今天的,当前的,目前的 (*opp.* past, future). ③当面的,该,本,此;意念中的,正在考虑中的. ④[古]立刻有用的,应急的,即刻的. *P-!* (点名时回答)到! *P-, Sir [Ma'am].* 来了[主人、顾客招唤时的回答]! *All ~ assented.* 出席者一致赞成. *those here ~* 在座各位. *the ~ tense*【语法】现在时(态). *the ~ Cabinet* 现(任)内阁. *the ~ volume* 本书. *the ~ writer* 本作者,笔者. *a ~ wit* 机智,急智. ***at the ~ time [day] = in the ~ day*** 在现在,在今天. ***be ~ to the mind*** 放在心里,不忘记. ***in the ~ case*** 在这件事中;在这种情况下. ***~ company excepted*** 在座各人除外. ***the ~ worth of*** *(£100 in 12 years)* (十二年后会变成一百镑的)现在的金额. — *n.* ①现在,目前 (*opp.* past, future). ②【语法】现在时. ③[*pl.*]【法】本文,本证件. ***at ~*** 目前,现在. ***by these ~s***【法】[谑]根据本文件 *(Know all men by these ~s that, ...* (等等)特给此(文件)为证. ***for the ~*** 眼前;暂且. ***until the ~, up to the ~*** 至今,到现在为止. **~ company** 出席者. **~-day** *a.* 现代的,当代的. **~ participle**【语法】现在分词. **~ perfect**【语法】现在完成时(的);现在完成时的动词. **~ tense**【语法】现在时(态).

pres·ent[2] ['preznt] *n.* 赠品,礼物;赠送. *a birthday ~* 寿礼,生日礼物. *a New Year's ~* 年礼. ***make a ~ of sth. to sb.*** 把某物赠送某人 *(Will you make me a ~ of your photograph?* 你可以送我一张照片吗?*)* ***make [give] a ~ to sb.*** 给某人送礼.

pre·sent[3] [pri'zent] *vt.* ①呈献;赠送,给予. ②交出,提出;出示;呈递;交给(收据等);兑(支票等). ③显示;呈现出;陈述;描述. ④提供(机会等);引起(困难等). ⑤引见,介绍;披露,宣布. ⑥上演(戏剧);使扮演. ⑦(拿武器)对准,瞄准 *(at)*;举枪(敬礼). ⑧【法】控告,控诉. ⑨【宗】举荐(牧师任圣职). *~ an album to sb. = ~ sb. with an album* 送某人一本照相簿. *~ an appearance of* 给人以…的印象. *P- my compliments to (him).* 请替我问候(他). *Allow me to ~ Mr. X to you.* 让我给你介绍X先生. ***~ a cheque [bill]*** (为领款)交出支票[票据]. ***P- arms!***【军】举枪! ***~ itself*** 出现;呈现;(主意等)浮现脑中. ***~ oneself*** 出席(会议等),参加(考试等);出现(在听众面前等);到场. — *vi.* ①(举枪)瞄准;举枪致敬. ②【宗】行使牧师推荐权. ③【医】(分娩时婴儿)露出,先露. ***Present!***【军】瞄准! — *n.* ①拿枪对准,瞄准;瞄准时枪的位置;举枪的姿势. ②举枪致敬.

pre·sent·a·bil·i·ty [pri,zentə'biliti] *n.* 漂亮,中看,拿得出;适于赠送.

pre·sent·a·ble [pri'zentəbl] *a.* ①拿得出去的,象样的;漂亮的;见得了人的,中看的;有规矩的,有礼貌的. ②适于赠送的. ③可介绍的,可推荐的.

pres·en·ta·tion [,prezen'teiʃən] *n.* ①赠送,献礼;授予;授予仪式;[罕]赠品,礼物. ②提出;呈递. ③介绍,引见,谒见,[英](特指入宫)晋谒. ④(牧师的)举荐;举荐牧师权. ⑤表现;外观,外貌,仪表;【无】图象;显示,扫描. ⑥【哲】【心】表象,直觉,观念. ⑦发表;表示;展示;陈述,描述. ⑧【剧】演出,上演. ⑨【医】先露,产式,胎位. ⑩【商】(支票等的)提出,交兑 (= presentment). ***give a ~ of*** 对…作陈述. ***payable on ~*** (支票等)交银行即可兑现. ***~ of colours [medals]*** 授军旗[勋章]仪式. ***the ~ of credentials*** 呈递国书. ***~ copy*** 赠本,献本. **~ day** (大学)学位授予日.

pres·en·ta·tion·al [,prezən'teiʃənəl] *a.* ①直觉的;表象(论)的;观念的. ②上演的,演出的. ③(词、语等)描述性的.

pres·en·ta·tion·ism [,prezən'teiʃənizəm] *n.* 【心,哲】表象论,表象主义.

pres·en·ta·tion·ist [,prezən'teiʃənist] *n.* 表象论者,表象主义者.

pre·sent·a·tive [pri'zentətiv] *a.* ①起呈现作用的. ②【宗】有举荐牧师权的. ③【哲】直觉的;表象的;(美术等)抽象的.

pres·ent-day ['prezənt'dei] *a.* 当代的;现在的,当前的. *~ English* 当代英语.

pres·en·tee [,prezən'ti:] *n.* ①受赠者. ②被推荐者,【宗】被举荐为牧师的人. ③(入宫等)晋谒者.

pre·sent·er [pri'zentə] *n.* ①赠送者;呈献者. ②提出者;具呈人. ③推荐者.

pre·sen·ti·ent [pri'senʃiənt, -ʃənt] *a.* 预觉的,预感的 *(of)*.

pre·sen·ti·ment [pri'zentimənt] *n.* (不祥的)预感,预觉. *a ~ of danger* 对危险的预感.

pre·sen·tive [pri'zentiv] *a.*【语法】(文字)直接表达概念的,直(接表)示的 (*opp.* symbolic).

pres·ent·ly ['prezəntli] *ad.* ①不久,一会儿. ②[方,美]现在,目前,眼下. ③[古]马上,立刻;作为直接结果,必然地. *They will be here ~.* 他们马上就到这里. *You will know all about it ~.* 你不久就会了解事情的底细. *He is ~ out of the country.* 他现在出国了.

pre·sent·ment [pri'zentmənt] *n.* ①陈述,叙述;呈示;【心】表象. ②(戏剧的)上演,演出;呈现;展示(物);描写;画,肖像. ③【商】(支票、汇票等的)提出,交兑;出示. ④[罕]赠送(物). ⑤【法】陪审官的报告;【宗】(主教来视察时教区委员的)陈诉.

pre·ser·va·ble [priˈzəːvəbl] *a.* 可保存[保管、保护]的；可储藏的.

pres·er·va·tion [ˌprezə(ː)ˈveiʃən] *n.* ①保存；保管；储藏；保护，防腐. ②保持；维护. *the ~ of one's health* 保持健康. *the ~ of peace* 维护和平. *~ from decay* 防腐. ***be in fair [poor]*** ~ 保存得好[不好].

pre·serv·a·tive [priˈzəːvətiv] *a.* (能)保存的；储藏的；防腐的(*from; against*). —*n.* ①预防法；预防药；防腐剂. ②起维护作用的因素[原则等]，防…物. *Salt is a ~ for meat.* 盐是肉类的防腐剂.

pre·serv·a·tize [priˈzəːvətaiz] *vt.* 给(食品等)施行防腐法，给…加防腐剂.

pre·serve [priˈzəːv] *vt.* ①保存，保藏，防腐；保管(贵重品等)；保留. ②保持，维持；保护，维护. ③腌(肉等)；渍(果物)；把…做成罐头；储藏. ④把…放在心里，不忘记，使(名声、作品等)流传. ⑤禁猎；把…圈为禁猎地. *~ health* 保持健康. *She is well-preserved.* 她保养得好[显得很年轻]. *~order* 维持秩序. *~ fruit* 把水果做成果酱. *~ fruit in sugar* 把水果做成蜜饯. *~ fish in [with] salt* 用盐腌鱼. *These woods are ~d.* 此处林场禁止打猎. —*vi.* ①做蜜饯；做果酱；制罐头. ②禁猎；圈禁地. —*n.* ①[常 *pl.*] 保藏物；糖脯，蜜饯，果酱；罐头. ②[常 *pl.*] 禁猎地；(私有的)猎场，鱼塘. ③独占的活动范围[领域]. ④防护物；[*pl.*] 护目镜；遮光眼镜，防尘眼镜. *poach on another's ~s* 侵犯别人的活动[利益等]范围[领域]. **-d** *a.* ①腌制的，制成蜜饯[果酱、罐头]的. ②得到保存的；受维护的. ③禁猎的. ④[美俚]喝醉的.

pre·serv·er [priˈzəːvə] *n.* ①保存者；保持者；保护者. ②防腐物；防护物. ③罐头制造人；蜜饯制造人. ④[英]禁猎地主管人；鸟兽保护者.

pre·set [ˈpriːˈset] *vt.* ***(pre·set; -set·ting)*** 预先装置；预调，调整.

pre-shrunk [ˈpriːˈʃrʌŋk] *a.* 【纺】(布料等)已预缩的，下水后不会再缩的.

pre·side [priˈzaid] *vi.* ①作会议主席；作议长，作会长(*at; over*). ②统辖；指挥；负责；主持 (*at, over*). ③主奏(*at*). *~ over a meeting* 主持会议. *~ at a public dinner* 主持宴会[充当宴会的主人]. —*vt.* 管理. *~ naval affairs* 主管海军事务. **-r** *n.* 主席，会议主持者.

pres·i·den·cy [ˈprezidənsi] *n.* ①总统[主席、议长等]的职位[任期]. ②统辖；主宰，支配. ③[P-][美]总统直辖的政府机构. ④【史】管辖区[旧英属印度的马德拉斯等三大管区之一]. ⑤(摩门教的)三人评议会.

pres·i·dent [ˈprezidənt] *n.* ①总统. ②总裁；长官；主席；议长；【法】院长；庭长. ③会长；校长；[英]大学院长；[美]大学校长. ④[美](银行等的)行长；董事长；总经理，社长. ⑤【史】州长，知事；(殖民地)总督. *the Lord P- of the Board of Trade* [英]商务大臣. *the Lord P- of the Council* [英]枢密大臣. *the P- of the U.N. General Assembly* 联合国大会主席.

pres·i·dent-e·lect [ˈprezidəntiˈlekt] *n.* 即将就任的总统，新当选(尚未就职)的总统，当选总统.

pres·i·dent·ess [ˈprezidəntis] *n.* ①女总统[总裁、议长、董事长、校长等]. ②总统[总裁、议长、董事长、校长等]的夫人.

pres·i·den·tial [ˌpreziˈdenʃəl] *a.* ①总统[总裁、议长、董事长、校长等](职务)的. ②统辖的，支配的，监督的，指挥的. *the ~ chair* 总统[总裁、议长、校长、董事长等]的职位[地位]. *a ~ election* 总统选举. *~ electors* 总统选举人. *a ~ postmaster* [美]总统任命的邮政局长. *the ~ term* 总统[议长、董事长、校长等]的任期. *a ~ timber* [美]有做总统资格的人. *the ~ year* [口](总统)大选年. ~ **government** 总统制政体. **-ly** *ad.* 以总统[议长、校长等]的资格.

pres·i·dent·ship [ˈprezidəntˌʃip] *n.* [英]总统[议长、会长、社长、总经理、总裁、校长等]的职位[任期].

pre·sid·ing [priˈzaidiŋ] *a.* 主席的，主持会议的，首席的. ~ **judge** 审判长，首席法官. ~ **officer** (选举投票所的)监选员.

pre·sid·i·o [priˈsidiəu] *n.* ***(pl. ~s)*** [Sp.] ①要塞，卫戍区. ②流放地，充军地.

pre·sid·i·um [priˈsidiəm] *n.* ***(pl. pre·sid·i·a*** [priˈsidiə]***)*** 主席团；常务委员会.

pre·sig·ni·fy [ˈpriːˈsignifai] *vt.* 预示，预告.

pre·soak [ˈpriːˈsəuk] *vt.* 事先浸泡；【农】预浸. —*n.* 【农】预浸剂. **-ing** 【农】浸种.

press[1] [pres] *vt.* ①压，按，揿，扳；推动；(用熨斗)熨平；贴(邮票等). ②绞榨，压榨；榨取，挤(葡萄汁等)；压碎. ③使贴紧；压紧；紧抱，紧握. ④坚持；坚决进行；贯彻，严厉执行(法律等). ⑤敦促；谆谆劝说，逼人接受(意见等)；把…强加于人. ⑥强迫；勒索，强募，强要. ⑦催逼；压迫，进逼(敌人等)；使苦恼；使窘迫；虐待，折磨，逼，困. ⑧聚集；拥挤. ⑨强调，加重(语气等). ⑩压倒；抑制(感情等). ⑪[古]使深为感动. ⑫印刷；用模子压制. *~ the trousers* 烫裤子. *Wine is ~ed from the grapes.* 葡萄酒是榨葡萄汁制成的. *~ a child to one's breast* 把孩子紧紧抱在怀里. *~ the argument* 坚持这个论点. *~ home an argument* 反复说明论点使对方接受. *~ sb. into confession* 逼人招供. *~ sb. for money* 向某人勒索钱财. *be hard ~ed* 被逼紧，被紧攻，陷困境. —*vi.* ①压，重压(*on; against*). ②奋勇前进，突进，赶上前 (*on; forward*). ③催迫，勒索，强要；迫切要求 (*for*). ④(事情)紧急；(时间)紧迫. ⑤密集，拥挤 (*up; round*). ⑥侵入，蚕食. ⑦使感觉，给与印象，影响. ⑧承压，受压. *The shoe is ~ing on my toe.* 我的鞋子挤脚. *I must ~ for an answer.* 请速赐复. *The matter ~es.* 事情紧急. *Time is ~ing.* 时间紧迫. *Have you any business that ~es?* 你有什么要紧事没有？ *The argument ~ed upon the judgement.* 那场争论影响到了判决. ***be ~ed for*** 穷于，困于，缺少，缺乏 (*be ~ed for funds* 缺少资金. *be ~ed for time* 时间紧迫). ~ ***an attack*** 强袭. ~ ***about [around] sb.*** 拥挤[密集]在某人周围. ~ ***back*** 推回去，击退. ~ ***for*** 催促，催逼，催索；(时间)迫促；(资金)短少[多用被动式 *be ~ed for*]. ~ ***forward [ahead]*** 突进，推进；奋力前进；向前挤. ~ ***hard upon*** 进逼，压迫，穷追. ~ ***home*** 极力主张. ~ ***on [upon]*** ①向前挤，赶紧向前走. ②坚决推进. ~ ***on [forward] with*** 加紧，决心继续 (*~ on with one's work* 加紧干). ~ ***one's way*** 奋力前进，坚持前进，向前挤. ~ ***sail*** 扯满所有风帆. ~ ***the button*** 按电铃；动手干. ~ ***the matter to a division*** 坚持要把事情弄个明白. ~ ***the words*** 坚持字面意义. ~ ***sb. to death*** 把某人折磨致死. —*n.* ①压；按；揿；挤；紧握；熨. ②绞榨，压榨；冲床，压床，压力机，压榨机；吐丝器. ③印刷机；印刷术；印刷厂，印刷(业)，出版. ④[the ~][集合词](包括报刊、广播、电视、通讯社等的)新闻报道[评论]；报纸；定期刊物，杂志；出版物；出版社；通讯社；新闻界；出版界；[集合词]期刊编者，报馆记者；言论出版. ⑤急迫；紧急；繁忙. ⑥拥挤，杂沓；人丛，群众；白刃战，混战. ⑦柜，衣橱；书箱，书橱. ⑧【机】夹具；(网球拍等的)夹子. ⑨【举重】推举. *a hydraulic ~* 水压机. *a drill [punching] ~* 钻[冲]床. *the ~ of work* 繁忙的工作. *a rotary ~* 滚筒印刷机. *the local ~* 地方报刊. ***a ~ of*** 密集的，拥挤的 (*a ~ of people* 拥挤的人群). ***at ~ time*** 在发稿时，到发稿时为止. ***at (the) ~ , in ~, come to the ~*** 已付印；印刷中. ***correct the ~*** 改正校样；校对. ***freedom [liberty] of the ~*** 言论出版的自由. ***give to the ~*** 在报上发表. ***go to (the) ~*** 付印. ***have a good ~*** 在报上得到好评. ***in (the) ~*** 在印刷中. ***make one's way through the ~*** 挤过人丛. ***off the ~*** 已印好；已发行. ***out of ~*** 绝版，卖光. ~ ***of sail***【海】吃满风的帆. ***send to (the) ~*** 付印. ***stop the ~*** 用重要消息代替已排好的次要消息. ***the Associated P-*** (美国)

联合通讯社〔简称美联社〕. ***the Commercial P-*** 商务印书馆. ***write for the ~*** 给报纸写文章. **~ agent** (剧团等的)新闻广告员; 宣传员. **~board** 皮纸板; 压板. **~ boys**〔美〕体育记者. **~-button** 电钮,按钮. **~ box** 新闻记者席. **~ clipping [cutting]** (一份) 剪报. **~ communique** 新闻公报. **~ compaign [stunt]** (为竞选等而进行的) 报纸宣传. **~ conference** 记者招待会. **~ gallery** (特指英国下院的)记者席. **~ law** 新闻条例; 〔常 *pl.*〕出版法. **~man** ①印刷工人, 印刷厂经营者. ②烫衣人; 熨衣工. ③榨葡萄〔油〕的人. ④〔英〕新闻记者. **~mark** ① *n.* (图书馆书目上的)书架号码. ② *vt.* 在(书上)加号码,给(书)编号. **~ photographer** 摄影记者. **~ proof** 清样; 机样. **~ reader** 清样校对(员). **~ release** ①(通讯社发布的)通讯稿. ②(向记者发布的)新闻稿. **~ representative**〔美〕新闻发布组长. **~ revise** 末校. **~room** ①印刷室. ②(政府机构中的)记者室. **~ telegram** 新闻电报. **~ time** (新闻等的) 截止时间. **~work** ①印刷(工作); 印刷业务. ②〔集合词〕印刷物,印刷品. **-er** 压具, 压者 (尤指熨衣工).

press[2] [pres] *n.*【史】强迫征募, 抓壮丁. — *vt.*【史】①强迫…服兵役〔劳役〕. ②征用. ~ *(things) into the service of* 强制征用 (实物). **~ gang** 抓兵队. **~-gang** *vt.* 强征…入伍〔服劳役〕. **~ money**【史】新兵入伍安家费.

press·ing [ˈpresiŋ] *a.* ①(工作、要求等) 急迫的, 紧急的,迫切的. ②(邀请等)恳切的. *a ~ business* 急事. *a ~ danger* 紧迫的危机,燃眉之急. — *n.* ①压; 按. ②压榨; 催逼. ③冲压; 冲压件; 模压制品. ④唱片; 同一批压制的唱片. *He required no ~.* 他不需要催迫. **-ly** *ad.* **-ness** *n.*

pres·sor [ˈpresə] *a.*【医】加压的, 增高血压的. — *n.* 增压物质.

pres·sure [ˈpreʃə] *n.* ①压; 按; 挤; 榨. ②【物】压力, 压强; 大气压力; 电压. ③精神压力,政治〔经济、舆论等〕压力. ④压迫,强制. ⑤紧急,急迫; 繁重, 繁忙. ⑥艰难, 为难, 困苦. *atmospheric ~* (大) 气压 (力). *downward [up-ward] ~* 向下〔向上〕压力. *high blood ~* 高血压. *~ for money* 金融紧迫; 缺钱. *financial ~* 财政困难. *the ~ of the crowd* 人群的拥挤. *the ~ of affairs* 事务繁忙. ***at high [low] ~*** 紧张〔松懈, 疲塌〕. ***bring ~ to bear upon, exert ~ upon*** 对…施加压力. ***put ~ on [upon]*** … 对…施加压力, 压迫…. ***the ~ of the times*** 不景气, 时势的艰难. ***under the ~ of*** 在…的压力下; 逼不得已. ***work at high ~*** 紧张地工作; 使劲干. — *vt.* ①对…施加压力; 迫使. ②使(机舱等) 增压; 密封. **~ cabin**【空】增压舱, 气密座舱. **~-cook** *vt., vi.* 用高压锅〔压力锅〕烹调. **~ cooker** 高压锅, 加压蒸(汽速)煮器. **~ga(u)ge** 气压计, 压强计; (火炮药室内的)膛压表. **~ group** 压力集团〔对立法者和公众施加压力以影响立法和政策的集团〕. **~ point**【医】压迫止血点. **~suit** 增压(衣)服〔高空飞行用〕. **~ vessel** 压力容器〔锅炉等〕.

pres·sur·ize [ˈpreʃəraiz] *vt.* ①对…加压力; 使压入 (油井等). ②使(机舱) 增压; 密封; 使(飞机中)保持接近于正常气压.

pres·sur·i·za·tion [ˌpreʃəraiˈzeiʃən] *n.* ①压力输送, 挤压. ②气密,密封. ③增压; 加压.

prest [prest] *n.*〔废〕应募金〔= prest money, 尤指发给应募服役英国陆、海军新兵的一笔钱〕. — *a.*〔废〕准备好的.

pre·ster·num [priˈstəːnəm] *n.*【动】(昆虫的)前腹片; 前胸骨; 前腹板 (= manubrium).

pres·ti·dig·i·ta·tion [ˈprestiˌdidʒiˈteiʃən] *n.* 变戏法, 魔术.

pres·ti·dig·i·ta·tor [ˌprestiˈdidʒiteitə] *n.* 变戏法的人,魔术师.

Pres·tige [ˈprestidʒ] *n.* 普雷斯蒂奇〔姓氏〕.

pres·tige [presˈtiːʒ, -ˈtiːdʒ] *n.* 威信, 威望,声望; 声誉; (财势的)显赫. *the political ~ and influence* 政治声势. *national [military] ~* 国家〔军事〕声誉.

pres·tig·ious [ˌpresˈtiːdʒəs, -ˈtidʒjəs] *a.* ①〔古〕魔术的,欺骗的. ②有威信的,有声誉的.

pres·tis·si·mo [presˈtisiməu] *ad., a.*〔It.〕【乐】最快, 极快,更急速. — *n.* 最快速度.

pres·to [ˈprestəu] *ad.* 赶快,快,立刻,转眼之间〔变戏法时用语〕. ***Hey ~, pass!*** 快,变了! 说变就变! ***P-! chango*** [ˈtʃeindʒəu]! 快! 快! 变! 〔魔术师用语〕; 剧变, 迅速的变化. — *a.* 快,迅速的,变戏法似的.

pres·to [ˈprestəu] *a., ad.*〔It.〕【乐】快,急速. — *n.* ***(pl. ~s)*** 急板.

Pres·ton [ˈprestən] *n.* ①普雷斯顿〔男子名〕. ②普雷斯顿〔英国港市〕.

pre·stress [ˈpriːˈstres] *n.* 预应力. *vt.* 对…预加应力. *~ed concrete* 预应力混凝土. **~ unit** 预应力构件.

pre·sum·a·ble [priˈzjuːməbl] *a.* 可推测的,可假定的; 象有的,象是的; 可能的.

pre·sum·a·bly [priˈzjuːməbli] *ad.* 推测起来; 假定; 大概,大抵, 可能. *He knows, ~, what is best for him.* 他总该知道怎样对他最有利吧.

pre·sume [priˈzjuːm] *vt.* ①假定,假设; 推测; 认为, 以为; 想象,猜想. ②敢于, 胆敢, 擅敢〔用于第一人称时多半为客套话〕. ③足以推定,意味着. *I ~ he isn't coming.* 我想他不会来了. *You had better ~ no such thing.* 你最好不要这样想当然. *May I ~ to ask …?* 请问…. — *vi.* ①设想, 推测, 相信. ②擅自行动, 放肆〔用于第一人称时多为客套话〕. ③不正当地利用; 倚靠, 恃 *(on, upon)*. *~ upon sb.'s good nature* 利用某人性情好. *~ upon a short acquaintance* 凭着一面之交就和人亲热起来. *Mr. Johnson, I ~?* 您就是约翰逊先生吧? 〔碰见面熟人时说的话〕. ***You ~.*** 你这人真不客气〔冒昧、脸厚〕.

pre·sumed [priˈzjuːmd] *a.* 假定的; 推测的.

pre·sum·ed·ly [priˈzjuːmidli] *ad.* 据推测,大概.

pre·sum·er [priˈzjuːmə] *n.* ①假定者, 推测者. ②冒昧的人.

pre·sum·ing [priˈzjuːmiŋ] *a.* ①自以为是的, 专横的. ②不客气的; 冒昧的; 放肆的; 傲慢的. **-ly** *ad.*

pre·sump·tion [priˈzʌmpʃən] *n.* ①推测,猜测, 臆断, 假定; 设想,想象. ②专横,自以为是; 不客气, 跋扈, 冒昧,放肆,无礼; 傲慢, 自大. ③【法】事实的推断〔根据已知事实作出的推断〕(= ~ of fact). *The ~ is that he will refuse.* 看起来他会拒绝的. *I have never heard of such ~.* 从来没有听说过如此无礼的事. ***~ of fact***【法】事实的推断. ***~ of law***【法】①法律上的假定. ②(在一定情况下普遍适用的)法定推论.

pre·sump·tive [priˈzʌmptiv] *a.* ①推测的,假定的. ②可据以推定的. ***an heir ~*** 假定继承人〔如有血统更近的继承人出生时,即失去继承权〕. **~ evidence**【法】推定证据. **-ly** *ad.* 据推测.

pre·sump·tu·ous [priˈzʌmptjuəs] *a.* ①放肆的, 不客气的,跋扈的,冒昧的. ②自以为是的, 专横的, 傲慢的. *It is too ~ of you to say so.* 你这样说话太放肆了. **-ly** *ad.*

pre·sup·pose [ˌpriːsəˈpəuz] *vt.* ①预先假定; 预料, 预想; 推测; 猜想. ②以…为前提; 含有. ***Effects ~ causes.*** 有结果必有原因. ***Success ~s diligence.*** 勤勉为成功的先决条件.

pre·sup·po·si·tion [ˌpriːsʌpəˈziʃən] *n.* ①预想(的事), 猜测(的事), 预先假定(的事). ②前提; 先决条件.

pret. = preterit(e).

pre·teen [ˈpriːˈtiːn] *a., n.* 未满十三岁的(孩子), 青春期以前的(孩子).

pre·tence [priˈtens] *n.* ①借口,口实, 托辞, 假托. ②假装,假做作,虚伪. ③虚饰,虚装门面. ④(无理的)要求,虚假的理由*(to)*. ⑤自命，自称；自吹. ⑥〔罕〕目的，企图. *He wished to be relieved of his post on the ~ of ill health.* 他想托病辞职. *There are no ~s about him.* 他一点不虚伪. ***devoid of all ~*** 毫不虚伪〔不做作〕地. ***false ~s*** 【法】欺诈(手段). ***make a ~ of…*** 假装,装做…. ***on the ~ of = under (the) ~ of*** 托辞,借口,拿…做口实. ***on the slightest ~*** 借着一点点口实.

pre•tend [pri'tend] *vt.* ①假托,借口;假装,装做;(戏剧等中)装扮. ②诈,骗…说 *(that)*; 自命,自称; 要求,妄想. *We must not ~ to know when we do not know.* 不要强不知为已知. *~ ignorance* 假装不知道,装聋作哑. — *vi.* ①以…自居;自封,自称;要求,妄想,觊觎 *(to)*; 求婚 *(to)*. ②假装,装作. *~ to beauty [learning]* 自以为是美人[学者]. *It's no use ~ing.* 装假是没用的. *~ to the throne* 觊觎王位. ***~ to a woman [her hand]*** 〔古〕企图和(身分高的)女人结婚.

pre•tend•ed [pri'tendid] *a.* ①虚假的,虚伪的. ②假装的;假冒的;号称为…的,所谓的. ③传说的,听说的. *~ sickness* 假病. *a ~ friend* 虚伪的朋友. **-ly** *ad.*

pre•tend•er [pri'tendə] *n.* ①假装者;冒充者;冒牌学者;骗子. ②妄求者,妄想者,觊觎者;觊觎王位者. *He is a ~ to philosophy.* 他是一个冒牌哲学家. ***the Old P-*** 【英史】老僭君〔指 1715 年觊觎英国王位的詹姆士.爱德华·斯图亚特 (James Edward Stuart), 詹姆士二世的儿子〕. ***the Young P-*** 【英史】小僭君〔指 1745 年觊觎英国王位的查理·爱德华 (Charles Edward), 詹姆士二世之孙,"老僭君"之子〕.

pre•tense [pri'tens] *n.* 〔美〕 = pretence.

pre•ten•sion[1] [pri'tenʃən] *n.* ①抱负,意图;自负;自夸的长处;自命,自称. ②虚饰,假装,做作;虚荣. ③(有根据的)要求;主张;资格;权利. ④借口,托词;口实. ***have no ~s to*** 无权主张[要求],不能称为,说不上是. ***make no ~s to*** 不摆…的架子;不自诩…. ***of the most humble ~s*** (人)极朴实的. ***without ~*** (人)朴实的;不自负的.

pre•ten•sion[2] ['pri:'tenʃən] *vt.* 【建】预张,预拉,给…加预应力. *~ed concrete* 预应力混凝土.

pre•ten•tious [pri'tenʃəs] *a.* ①自负的,狂妄的,自命不凡的;自夸的. ②虚伪的,矫饰的,做作的. *a ~ manner* 妄自尊大,盛气凌人. *~ literary style* 矫揉造作的文体. **-ly** *ad.* **-ness** *n.*

preter- *pref.* 过,超. *preter*natural, *preter*sensual.

pre•ter•hu•man [ˌpri:tə(:)'hju:mən] *a.* 超人的;异乎常人的.

pret•er•ist ['pretərist] *a., n.* ①【基督教】认为«启示录»的预言已经实现的(人). ②发思古之幽情的(人).

pret•er•it(e) ['pretərit] *n.* 【语法】过去〔略作 pret.〕;过去时(态);过去时的动词. — *a.* ①【语法】过去的. ②〔古,谑〕过去的,已往的. *the ~-present tense* 【语法】过去形现在时〔如 can, may, must, shall 等本属过去形,今则用为现在时〕. *the ~ tense* 【语法】过去时(态).

pre•ter•i•tion [ˌpri:tə'riʃən] *n.* ①遗漏,疏漏;忽略;省略,不提 *(of)*. ②【宗】上帝对不宠爱者的忽视. ③【修】暗示忽略法〔例如说 I will not mention his rudeness. 等〕. ④【法】遗嘱中不提某些有继承权者.

pre•ter•mis•sion [ˌpri:tə(:)'miʃən] *n.* 置之不问;疏忽;遗漏;省略.

pre•ter•mit [ˌpri:tə(:)'mit] *vt.* ①对…置之不问;把…忽略过去;遗漏,略去. ②中断,中止.

pre•ter•nat•u•ral [ˌpri:tə(:)'nætʃərəl] *a.* 超自然的;异常的,奇异的,不可思议的. **-ly** *ad.*

pre•ter•sen•su•al [ˌpri:tə(:)'sensjuəl] *a.* 感觉不到的;超感觉的.

pre•test ['pri:test] *n.* (产品等的)预先试验;(对学生等的)预先测验. — *vt., vi.* [pri'test] 预先试验[测验].

pre•text ['pri:tekst] *n.* ①借口,口实,托词. ②假象,掩饰*(for)*. ***find a ~ for*** 为…找口实. ***make a ~ of*** 以…作口实. ***on some ~ or other*** 用某种借口. ***on [under, upon] the ~ of*** 以…为借口,托词. — *vt.* [pri'tekst] 借口,假托.

pre•tone ['pri:təun] *n.* 【语音】重读音节前的音节〔元音〕.

pre•tor ['pri:tə] *n.* = praetor.

Pre•to•ri•a [pri'tɔ:riə] *n.* 比勒陀利亚〔南非(阿扎尼亚)首府〕.

pre•to•ri•an [pri:'tɔ:riən] *n., a.* = praetorian.

pre•treat ['pri:'tri:t] *vt.* 预先处理. **-ment** *n.* 预处理.

pre•tri•al ['pri:'traiəl] *a.* 【法】审判前的. *a ~ motion* 审判前的申请[动议]. — *n.* 〔美〕审判前的预备会议.

pret•ti•fy ['pritifai] *vt.* ①〔蔑〕过分修饰;过分润饰,雕琢(文章等). ②〔蔑〕美化.

pret•ti•ly ['pritili] *ad.* ①漂亮地,可爱地. ②有礼貌地,潇洒地,文雅地. ③优美地;愉快地. ④好地,妙地. ⑤机灵地. ⑥贴切地. ⑦相当多地. *be ~ dressed* 穿得漂亮,穿得花哨. *ask ~* 恭恭敬敬地问.

pret•ti•ness ['pritinis] *n.* ①漂亮,可爱;漂亮的东西. ②(文章、风度等的)优美,潇洒. ③好,妙. ④机灵. ⑤贴切.

pret•ty ['priti] *a.* ①漂亮的,俊俏的,(女子)标致的;(男子)清秀的,潇洒的;(场所、物件等)整洁的,精致的;(花园、山谷等)可爱的;秀丽的,美丽的. ②优柔的,(男性)女人气的. ③优美的;悦耳的;有趣的;(游戏等)愉快的. ④好的,妙的;〔反语〕好〔表示糟糕的,拙劣的〕. ⑤机灵的;巧妙的;狡猾的;贴切的,恰当的. ⑥〔俚,方〕相当的,好多的. ⑦〔古〕(军人等)魁伟的,英勇的. *a ~ fellow* 优柔的[女人气的]家伙. *a ~ child* 可爱的孩子. *a ~ story* 有趣的故事. *a ~ boy* 〔美俚〕(马戏团的)保镖;漂亮男子,女性化的男子. *~ ways* 讨人欢喜的态度. *a ~ sum of money* 相当多的钱. *A ~ mess you have made!* 你弄得真糟! ***a ~ how d'you do*** 麻烦事;〔反语〕好事. ***a ~ kettle of fish*** 乱七八糟. ***a ~ penny*** 一大笔钱. ***Here is a ~ go!*** 这事真糟! ***Here is a ~ mess [business, muddle]!*** 这成个什么样子! — *ad.* 相当,颇,还;〔反〕非常. *I am ~ well.* 我很好. *I am ~ sick of it.* 这个叫我厌烦极了. ***~ much*** ①〔口〕几乎,全部. ②非常. ***~ much the same thing*** 差不多一样. ***~ soft*** 〔美俚〕容易的,便当的;合算的. ***~ soon*** 很快. ***sit ~*** 处于极有利地位;〔美俚〕成功;过舒服日子. — *n.* ①心肝,宝贝〔对子女、妻子的称呼,说作 *my ~! my pretties!*〕 ②〔*pl.*〕〔美〕漂亮东西,衣饰. ③【高尔夫球】球的正规通路. ④(玻璃杯的)凹条花纹. *She has put on all her pretties.* 她打扮得花枝招展. *fill up to the ~* 把酒斟到齐杯子的凹条花纹处(倒满约三分之一杯). **~-pretty** ① *a.* 装饰过分的,漂亮得俗气的;只想漂亮的;矫揉造作的. ② *n.* 〔*pl.*〕小装饰品,中看不中用的便宜货. **-ish** *a.* 有些漂亮的,有点可爱的;好象不错的. **-ism** *n.* (文体、态度等的)矫揉造作,过分讲究修饰.

pre•tu•ber•cu•lous [ˌpri:tju(:)'bə:kjuləs] *a.* 【医】结核(发生前)的.

pre•typ•i•fy [pri'tipifai] *vt.* 预示,预告,预表.

pret•zel ['pretsəl] *n.* ①椒盐卷饼;纽结形盐饼干. ②〔美俚〕(乐器)法国号. *a ~ bender* 〔美俚〕吹法国号的人〔原意为卷盐卷饼的人〕.

prev. = previous(ly).

pre•vail [pri'veil] *vi.* ①胜,压倒,占优势;占上风,胜过 *(over; against)*; 成功,奏效. ②普遍;传开,盛行,流行,普及. ③说服,劝说 *(on; upon; with)*. *This custom does not ~ now.* 这种风俗现在已经不流行了. *Can't I ~ upon you to have another helping of pie?* 你再吃一块馅饼好吗? *I cannot ~ upon him.* 我说服不了他. *~ over [against] the enemy* 战胜敌人.

pre•vail•ing [pri'veiliŋ] *a.* ①盛行的,流行的;当时的,目前的;一般的,普通的. ②占优势的,主要的,有效的,显著的,有势力的,有力的. *the ~ fashions* 流行的式样.

a ~ opinion 普遍的意见. ~ **wind**【气】盛行风. **-ly** *ad.* **-ness** *n.*

prev·a·lence [ˈprevələns] *n.* ①流行，盛行，普遍. ②〔罕〕优势，卓越.

prev·a·lent [ˈprevələnt] *a.* ①流行的，盛行的；一般的，普通的；广布的，蔓延的. ②〔罕〕优势的. *Whooping cough is very ~ just now.* 百日咳正在广泛流行. **-ly** *ad.*

pre·var·i·cate [priˈværikeit] *vi.* 支吾，搪塞，推诿，撒赖. **-ca·tion** *n.* **-ca·tor** *n.* 支吾者，搪塞者，推诿者.

pre·ven·ient [priˈviːnjənt] *a.* ①前，先，以前的；领先的. ②预期的 *(of)*. ③预防的 *(of)* (= preventive).

pre·vent [priˈvent] *vt.* ①阻止，阻挡；制止；妨碍 *(from)*. ②[priːˈvent] 预防；〔古〕先做，预先，迎合(愿望)，预先应付(问题)；【宗】引领. *Rain ~ed the game.* 下雨妨碍了比赛. *~ him from going* = *~ his [him] going* 阻止他走. *~ sb. from injuring himself* 预防某人弄伤自己. — *vi.* 妨碍；阻止. *if nothing ~s* 如果没有什么妨碍的话.

pre·vent·a·ble [priˈventəbl] *a.* 可阻止的；可预防的. **-bil·i·ty** *n.* 预防可能性.

pre·vent·a·tive [priˈventətiv] *a.*, *n.* = preventive.

pre·vent·er [priˈventə] *n.* ①防止者；预防者；防护设备，预防物；预防法，预防药. ②阻止者；妨碍物. ③【海】辅助索，保险索.

pre·ven·tion [priˈvenʃən] *n.* ①阻止，制止；妨碍，阻碍；妨碍物. ②预防；预防法；*P- is better than cure.*【谚】医病不如防病. ***by way of ~*** 作为预防；为预防起见.

pre·ven·tive [priˈventiv] *a.* 预防的 *(of)*；防止的；防护的. — *n.* ①防护物；预防法；预防措施；预防剂. ②〔古〕沿岸缉私员. *~ medicine*【医】预防医学；预防药. *a ~ war*【军】先发制人的战争. *~ maintenance*【机】定期维修. ***the P- Service*** 〔英〕沿岸海关缉私队.

pre·view [ˈpriːˈvjuː] *n.* ①预观；预映，试映；预演，试演；(展览会的)预展；预习. ②(电影)预告片. — *vt.* 预观；预映，试映；预演；预展；预习.

pre·vi·ous [ˈpriːvjəs, -viəs] *a.* ①先，前，以前的 *(opp.* following*)*. ②〔口〕过早的，过急的. *on the ~ night* 在前一晚. *You have been a little too ~s.* 你稍微急了一点. ***P- Examination*** (剑桥大学的) 文学士学位初考. ***~ question*** (议会中的)先决问题[动议]. — *ad.* 在前，在先，在…以前 *(to)*. *He died ~ to my arrival.* 他在我到达以前就故去了. **-ly** *ad.* 在前，在以前；预先 *(previously designated* 预先指定的). **-ness** *n.*

pre·vise [priˈvaiz] *vt.* ①预先警告，预告. ②预知，预先看到.

pre·vi·sion [pri(ː)ˈviʒən] *n.*, *vt.* 预见，预知. **-al** *a.* 有先见之明的，预先就知道的.

pre·vo·cal·ic [ˌpriːvəuˈkælik] *a.* 元音前的.

pre·vo·ca·tion·al [ˌpriːvəuˈkeiʃənl] *a.* 为入职业学校作准备的. *~ courses* 为进入职业学校作准备的课程.

Pre·vost [ˈprevəu, ˈprevəust] *n.* 普雷沃(斯特)〔姓氏〕.

pre·vue [ˈpriːvjuː] *n.*, *vt.* = preview.

pre·war [ˈpriːˈwɔː] *a.* 战前的 *(opp.* postwar*)*. — *ad.* 在战前.

prex(y) [ˈpreks(i)] *n.* 〔美俚〕(大学)校长，(学院)院长；(橄榄球俱乐部的)会长.

prey [prei] *n.* ①被捕食的动物. ②牺牲者，牺牲品. ③捕获；捕食；〔古〕战利品，掠夺品，赃物. *a ~ to circumstances* 境遇的牺牲品. *a beast [bird] of ~* 肉食兽[鸟]，猛兽[禽]. ***become the ~ of*** = ***fall a ~ to*** 被…捕食；成了…的牺牲品；被…所俘；被…折磨 (*He fell a ~ to melancholy.* 他为忧郁所折磨). ***make a ~ of*** 把…当做食物，把…当做捕获物. ***seek after one's ~*** 打食，寻找捕获物；寻求战利品. — *vi.* ①(猛兽、猛禽等)攫食，捕食 *(on, upon)*. ②劫掠，掠夺；诈取 *(on, upon)*. ③(疾病等)使人慢慢衰弱，消耗，折磨；使苦恼，损害 *(on, upon)*. *Foxes ~ on rabbits.* 狐狸捕食兔子. *~ upon the defenseless villages* 抢掠无防备的村庄. *Care ~ed (up)on her health.* 忧虑损害了她的健康.

prez [prez] *n.* 〔美俚〕①= president. ②…大王〔对特别精于自己行业者的称呼〕.

pri. = ①private. ②primary. ③prison.

Pri·am [ˈpraiəm] *n.* 普利安〔荷马史诗《伊利亚特》中被联军围攻的特洛伊国王〕.

pri·ap·ic [praiˈæpik] *a.* ①〔有时作 P-〕阴茎的，崇拜男性生殖器的(= phallic). ②非常雄劲的，很有丈夫气的，很有男性气的.

pri·a·pism [ˈpraiəpizəm] *n.*【医】①胀阳症. ②好色.

Pri·a·pus [praiˈeipəs] *n.* ①【希、罗神】男性生殖神〔酒神和爱神之子〕. ②〔p-〕男性生殖器；(鱼的)交换器.

Price [prais] *n.* 普赖斯〔姓氏〕.

price [prais] *n.* ①价格，价钱；市价；代价；费用. ②报酬；悬赏；交换物；〔美俚〕钱；(为取得某物而付出的)牺牲. ③赌金比率，赌注与赢款的差额. ④〔古〕价值，贵重. *~s (of commodities)* 商品价格，物价. *a cash ~* 现金价格. *a cost ~* 成本价格，原价. *a market ~* 市价. *a famine ~* 缺货时的市价. *a fixed [set, settled] ~* 定价. *a net ~* 实价. *the ~ asked* 开价，喊价. *a reduced [bargain] ~* 廉价；有折扣的价格. *the selling ~* 售价. *the trade ~* 同行价格. *the wholesale [retail] ~* 批发[零售]价格. *a stable ~* 价格稳定. *the ~ of money* 贷款利率；延期日息. *a unit ~* 单价. ***at a ~*** 付很大代价. ***at any ~*** 不惜任何代价. ***at a fair ~*** 售价公平. ***at the ~ of*** 拼着…；以…的代价. ***beyond [above, without] ~*** 无价的，极贵重的. ***fetch a high ~*** 可以卖得高价. ***get a good ~ for*** 好价卖出. ***give a long ~ for*** 高价买. ***make a ~*** 讨价，开价；定价. ***pay a heavy ~*** 付高价. ***raise [reduce] a ~*** 涨[减]价. ***set [put] a ~ on sb.'s head [life]*** 悬赏缉拿某人[悬赏要某人的命]. ***set a ~ (up)on sth.*** 给某物批上价格. ***set high [little, no] ~ on*** 重视[不重视]. ***What ~ …?*** 〔英俚〕①(赛马时走红的马)跑赢的希望怎样？〔喻〕你以为怎么样？有可能…吗？(*What ~ fine weather tomorrow?* 〔口〕明天天气会不会好)？②…算什么东西？…有什么用处[价值]呢？〔嘲笑曾被吹捧而遭到失败的某事物〕. — *vt.* 〔口〕①给…定价. ②问…的价. ③给…估价. ④由于要价过高而使…. ***~ one's goods [oneself] out of market*** 由于要价过高而失掉销路. ~ **control** 价格管制，物价控制. ~ **current** (股票或物品的)行市表. **~-cutter** (为挫败竞争者等的)削价者. ~ **cutting** 减价，削价. ~ **index** 物价指数. ~ **level** 物价水平. ~ **list** 定价表. ~ **tag**, ~ **ticket** 价格标签. ~ **support** 〔美〕①价格维持〔通常由政府采取措施对预定的价格标准的维持〕. ②价格补助金〔为维持一定价格而发放的贷金〕. ~ **war** 价格战〔一再削价的商品竞争〕. ~ **work** 按件计值的工作.

priced [praist] *a.* 有定价的；定价的. *a ~ catalogue* 有定价的目录. *high-~* 高价的. *low-~* 廉价的.

price·less [ˈpraislis] *a.* ①无价的，千金难买的，极贵重的. ②〔英口〕非常有趣的；极荒谬的，不成话的. *a perfectly ~ evening* 一个十分难得的[极愉快的]夜晚. *It's perfectly ~ to hear them abuse each other.* 听他们相骂实在是有趣. *She is ~, isn't it?* 她有些不象话，是吗？

price·y [ˈpraisi] *a.* 〔英口〕昂贵的，高价的.

prick [prik] *vt.* ①扎，刺，戳穿. ②刺伤；扎痛，刺痛；刺激；使痛心，使(良心等)受责备. ③(马、狗等)侧(耳)，竖(耳). ④〔古〕用踢马刺踢(马)，驱策. ⑤在…上穿小孔；在…上穿孔作标记；(在名单等上做小记号)挑选出；选择；选任. ⑥插(苗) *(out; in)*. ⑦【海】缝合(帆、篷)；(在海图上)测量(距离). ⑧追踪(兔等). *The pin ~ed her finger.* 针刺破了她的手指. *My duty ~s me on.* 责任感激励着我. — *vi.* ①扎，刺，被刺；(感到)刺痛. ②〔古〕策马前进 *(on; forward)*. ③(葡萄酒等)变酸. ④(耳朵)耸立，竖立；朝上. *My conscience ~s.* 我受良心责备. ~ ***a bubble*** 戳破肥皂泡; 揭穿真相. ~ ***down*** 选择. ~ ***for a soft plank***【海】在船上找寻舒适的卧处. ~ ***near*** 跟…匹敌,与…并驾齐驱. ~ ***off [out]*** ①(在航海地图上)记上船的位置、进路. ②挑选出. ③移植(幼苗). ~ ***sb. for*** 遴选[选任]某人为. ~ ***up*** ①(用灰泥等)粗涂,打底子. ②【海】(风)厉害起来. ~ ***up oneself*** 打扮自己; 炫耀自己. ~ ***up the [one's] ears*** (狗)竖耳,(人)侧着耳朵听. — *n.* ①扎,刺; 扎痛,刺痛; 刺伤; (良心的)责备,悔恨. ②刺痕; 刺点,刺孔; (箭靶的)靶心;【乐】符点; 野兔的足迹. ③(植物的)刺; (动物)突出的器官. ④尖形器具[武器]; 〔古〕锥, 刺; 踢马刺; (赶牲口用的)刺棍. ***kick against the ~s*** 螳臂挡车,以卵击石; 作无益的抵抗. ***the ~s of conscience*** 良心的责备,内心的悔恨. ~**-eared** *a.* (狗)竖耳的; (人)耳朵显露的(尤指英国十七世纪不戴假发的圆颅党成员). ~ **song** 〔古〕(16、17世纪英国的)乐谱. ~**-up** *a.* 漂亮的.

prick·er [ˈprikə] *n.* ①刺[扎、戳]的人. ②供刺[扎、穿孔]用的工具; 锥子,通针;【电】触针. ③〔古〕轻骑兵.

prick·et [ˈprikit] *n.* ①(双角笔直未生叉的)二岁雄鹿. ②烛台,蜡烛扦.

prick·ing [ˈprikiŋ] *n.* 刺; 刺痕; 刺痛感.

prick·le[1] [ˈprikl] *n.* ①(动植物皮上的)刺,棘. ②刺痛; 刺戳. — *vt., vi.* (使)感到刺痛. *He ~d all over.* 他浑身刺痛.

prick·le[2] [ˈprikl] *n.* 柳条篮子.

prick·ly [ˈprikli] *a.* ①多刺的; 针刺般痛的. ②易动怒的; 敏感的. ③棘手的,难办的. ~**-ash** 花椒. ~ **heat** 痱子. ~ **pear**【植】霸王树; 仙人球〔霸王树的梨状果实〕.

Pride [praid] *n.* 普赖德〔姓氏〕.

pride [praid] *n.* ①自大,骄傲,傲慢. ②自尊(心); 自豪; 得意,自满. ③足以夸耀的东西,引以自豪的人[东西]. ④最优秀部分; 精华[指一部分人等]. ⑤全盛(期); 顶点; 〔诗〕豪华,美观; 装饰. ⑥(马等的)精力,血气. ⑦(禽兽的)群. ⑧〔古〕(牝兽的)交尾期. ⑨(孔雀的)开屏;【徽】孔雀开屏. *a proper ~* 自尊心; 自豪感. *a false ~* 妄自尊大,狂妄. *P- goes before a fall.* = *P- will have a fall.* 骄者必败. *a mother's ~* 母亲的得意孩子. *in the ~ of one's years [life]* 在全盛时期,正年富力强. *a ~ of peacocks* 一群孔雀. ***a peacock in his ~*** 正在开屏的孔雀. ***be puffed up with ~*** 妄自尊大. ***give [yield] ~ of place to*** 使…占第一位,把第一位让给…. ***hold ~ of place*** 占第一位. ***in ~ of grease*** (猎物)正肥,正适宜于狩猎. ~ ***of China*** 楝香. ~ ***of the desert*** 骆驼. ~ ***of one's youth*** 青春. ~ ***of place*** 傲慢; 高位; (尤指鹰的)飞翔. ~ ***of the morning*** 早晨的雾或阵雨〔天晴的预兆〕. ~ ***of the world*** 〔古〕虚荣. ***put one's ~ in one's pocket*** 压抑住自尊心,忍辱. ***take (a) ~ in*** 以…自豪; 对…感到满意. — *vt.* 〔~ *oneself*〕使得意. ~ ***oneself on [upon]*** 以…自豪,自夸…(*She ~s herself on her cooking.* 她自夸会做菜). **-ful** *a.* 骄傲的; 得意的,自傲的.

prie-dieu [ˈpriːdjəː] *n.* ***(pl. prie-dieux*** [ˈpriːdjəː(z)]***)*** 〔F.〕①祷告台. ②祷告椅 (= ~ chair).

pri·er [ˈpraiə] *n.* 刺探[打听]者; 窥探者.

priest [priːst] *n.* ①祭司; 教士; 神父,牧师; 僧人; 术士. ②(学术领域等的)大师,宗师. ③〔主 Ir.〕(用来打死已上钩的鱼的)打鱼槌. ***a ~ of art*** 艺术宗师. ***a ~ of Bacchus*** 酒鬼. ***the ~'s Crown*** 〔英方〕蒲公英. — *vt.* 使成为教士,使做僧人; 任命…为祭司[神父]. ~**craft** 教士[僧侣]的权术[谋略]. ~**-ridden** *a.* 受教士支配[压制]的. **-hood** *n.* ①教士[祭司等的]职位[身分]. ②〔集合词〕全体教士. **-like** *a.* 象教士的; 适于教士的.

priest·ess [ˈpriːstis] *n.* (基督教以外的)尼姑; 女祭司; 女术士.

Priest·ley [ˈpriːstli] *n.* 普里斯特利〔姓氏〕.

priest·ling [ˈpriːstliŋ] *n.* 小教士; 小僧; 小祭司.

priest·ly [ˈpriːstli] *a.* 教士的; 象教士的; 适于教士的. **-li·ness** *n.*

prig[1] [prig] *n.* ①(讲话、态度等)一本正经的人; 爱充学者[教育家]的人. ②讨厌的人.

prig[2] [prig] *n.* 〔俚〕小偷, 扒手. — *vt.* 〔俚〕偷. — *vi.* 〔Scot.〕争论; 讨价还价.

prig·ger·y [ˈprigəri] *n.* ①自负, 自命不凡, 沾沾自喜. ②一本正经,古板.

prig·gish [ˈprigiʃ] *a.* ①骄傲的, 自命不凡的, 自负的. ②一本正经的,死板的. **-ly** *ad.*

prig·gism [ˈprigizəm] *n.* ①自负. ②一本正经; 死板.

prill [pril] *n.* 金属小球,金属颗粒. — *vt.* ①使(固体物)变成小珠状[小颗粒]. ②使(粒状或晶体状材料)变为流体.

prim [prim] *a.* ①整洁的. ②一本正经的; 丝毫不苟的; 古板的. — *vt.* ①使(面孔)摆出一本正经的样子. ②整洁地打扮, 装饰. — *vi.* 装出一本正经的模样. **-ly** *ad.* **-ness** *n.*

prim. = ①primary. ②primate. ③primitive.

pri·ma [ˈpriːmə] *a.* 〔It.〕第一的, 主要的. ~ ***ballerina*** [ˌbæləˈriːnə] 芭蕾舞的主要女演员. ~ ***buffa*** [ˈbufə] (歌舞喜剧的)主要女歌星. ~ ***donna*** [ˈdɔnə] ***(pl. ~ donnas, prime donne*** [ˈpriːmei ˈdɔnei]***)*** ①(歌剧的)首席女演员,音乐会的主要女歌手. ②〔美俚〕爱虚荣的人,傲慢的人,神经质的人(尤指女人).

pri·ma·cy [ˈpraiməsi] *n.* ①第一位,首位; 卓越. ②(英国教会)大主教的职务[地位]; (罗马天主教)教皇的最高权力.

pri·mae·val [praiˈmiːvəl] = primeval.

pri·ma fa·ci·e [ˈpraimə ˈfeiʃii(ː)] 〔L.〕①初看时,一见之下,乍看起来; 据初次印象. ②自明的. ③【法】足以构成案件[事实等]的. ***prima facie case***【法】表面上证据确凿的案件. ***prima facie evidence***【法】表面上确凿的证据,初步证据.

pri·mage[1] [ˈpraimidʒ] *n.* ①运费贴补〔运费以外的费用〕. ②【海】货主送给船长的酬金.

pri·mage[2] [ˈpraimidʒ] *n.* 水分诱出量〔汽锅中随蒸汽排出的水量〕.

pri·mal [ˈpraiməl] *a.* ①第一的,最初的, 原始的. ②首位的,主要的; 根本的. **-ly** *ad.*

pri·ma·quine [ˈpraiməˈkwiːn] *n.*【化】首喹.

pri·ma·ri·ly [ˈpraimərili, Am. praiˈmerili] *ad.* ①首先,最初; 原来. ②主要地; 根本上.

pri·ma·ry [ˈpraiməri] *a.* ①第一的,最初的,初级的; 初等的; 基本的; 基层的. ②主要的,为首的,第一位的. ③原始的,根本的; 原著的,第一手的; (颜色)原色的. ④初步的 *(opp.* secondary*)*; 预备的. ⑤【医】初期的,第一期的. ⑥【电】一次的; 原的; 第一级的. ⑦【生】初生的;【地】原生的,原成的,结晶岩的,最下层的. ⑧【化】伯的; 连上一个碳原子的; (无机盐)一代的. ⑨【语法】语根的; 一级语结的. *a matter of ~ importance* 头等重要的事情. ~ *meaning of a word* 一个词的原义. — *n.* 〔常 *pl.*〕①居首位的事物,主要事物. ②〔美〕候选人选拔会; 初选. ③原色; 原色感. ④(油漆等的)底子. ⑤【天】主星; (有卫星的)惑星. ⑥【电】原线圈; 初级线圈. ⑦【动】〔*pl.*〕鸟翼末节上的羽毛, 初级飞羽; (昆虫的)前翅. ⑧【语法】一级语结〔叶斯帕森用语, 指句中可用作主语、宾语的成分, 包括名词、代词、分句以及不定式结构等〕. ~ **accent**【语音】第一重音. ~ **accumulation**【经】原始积累. ~ **algebra** 准质[准素]代数. ~ **battery [cell]** 一次电池,原电池. ~ **coil** 初级线圈,原线圈. ~ **colours** 原色. ~ **cost** 成本. ~ **cuticula** 外表皮. ~ **education** 初等教育,小学教育. ~ **election** 〔美〕预选(会). ~ **grades** 小学低年级. ~ **group**【地】古生界. ~ **laws** 〔美〕预选会规则. ~ **meeting [assembly]** 〔美〕预选会. ~ **minerals** 原生矿物,未氧化的矿物. ~ **oil**【化】初级油, 原油. ~ **pest** 主要害虫. ~ **products**

农产物,原料品. ～ **road** (公路中的)干线. ～ **salt**【化】一代盐. ～ **school** 小学校. ～ **shock**【医】原发休克. ～ **star**【天】主星. ～ **tenses**【语法】主要时态〔指拉丁文和希腊文语法中的现在、将来、完成和将来完成时〕.

pri·mate[1] [ˈpraimit] *n.* ①(英国教会的)大主教,首席主教,监督长. ②〔古〕首领. *P- of England* 约克大主教. *P- of all England* 坎特伯雷大主教.

pri·mate[2] [ˈpraimeit] *n.* 灵长目动物.

Pri·ma·tes [praiˈmeiti:z] *n.* 〔*pl.*〕【动】灵长目〔包括人、猿等〕.

prime[1] [praim] *a.* ①最初的;第一的,首位的;首要的,主要的;原始的;基本的;原有的. ②最好的,第一流的,头等的;〔英俚〕漂亮的. ③血气旺盛的,青春的. ④【数】质数的,素数的. *the ～ agent* 主因. ***feel ～*** 很神气. ***of ～ importance*** 最重要的. — *ad.* 好极,妙极. — *n.* ①初期,最初. ②春;青春,壮年;盛时,全盛期. ③精华,最好部分 *(of)*; 上等. ④〔古〕黎明. ⑤上撇号,符号〔′〕,(记时的)分号〔例: 6′5″ = 6 分 5 秒〕;英尺号〔3′5″ = 3 英尺 5 英寸〕;重音符号. ⑥【数】质数,素数. ⑦(击剑中八个防御姿势中的)第一姿势〔刺〕. ⑧【天主教】(午前六时的)晨祷. ⑨【乐】同度. ***in ～ of grease*** = in pride of grease〔见 pride 条〕. ***in the ～ of life [manhood]*** 在壮年,年富力强. ***the ～ of the moon*** 新月. ***the ～ of the year*** 春天. ***the ～ of youth*** 青春的全盛期〔12 岁到28岁〕. ～ **cost** 原价,主要成本;进货价格. ～ **meridian** 本初子午线. ～ **minister** 总理;首相. ～ **ministry** 总理〔首相〕的职权〔地位〕. ～ **mover** ①原动力;主导力. ②倡仪者. ③【电】原动机;〔美军俚〕强力牵引车;【哲】第一动因. ～ **number**【数】质数,素数. ～ **number theorem**【数】素数定理. ～ **pump**【机】起动汽油泵. ～ **rate** 最优惠(贷款)利率. ～ **time**〔美〕(电视等观众最多的)黄金时刻. ～ **vertical**【天】卯酉圈. **-ly** *ad.* 〔口〕很好,极好. **-ness** *n.*

prime[2] [praim] *vt.* ①(旧时)为…装雷管,为…装火药;装填,灌注. ②事先为…提供消息〔情报〕;事先给…指示. ③〔口〕使尽量吃,使尽量喝(酒等)*(with)*. ④在…上涂底子,在…上涂头道油漆. ⑤〔英方〕修剪(树枝);采摘(烟叶). ⑥使准备好. ⑦(注入水或油等)使起动,使汽水混合. *fully ～d with the latest news* 掌握了最新的消息. ～ *the pump* 起动油泵;〔美,喻〕采取措施促使事物发展(尤指以政府资金促使就业人数的增加和经济的发展). — *vi.* ①(旧时)装火药(准备开枪);装雷管(准备开炮). ②(水随蒸汽)进入汽缸,汽水共腾. ③事先提供消息. ④涂底子,涂头道漆. ⑤修剪树枝,采摘烟叶.

prim·er[1] [ˈpraimə] *n.* ①初级读本,初学书;初阶,入门(书);(尤指宗教改革前的)小祷告书. ③[ˈprimə]【印刷】10 点或 18 点 活字的旧称. *great ～* 18 点铅字. *long ～* 10 点铅字.

prim·er[2] [ˈpraimə] *n.* ①装填火药者;装雷管者;起动油泵者. ②【机】初给器;发火极;发火药;导火线;爆管,雷管;火帽;底火. ③底漆,首涂油. ④【生化】引物.

pri·me·ro [priˈmɛərəu] *n.* 普利麦罗纸牌戏〔十六与十七世纪流行的一种纸牌戏〕.

pri·meur [pri:ˈmə:] *n.* 〔F.〕〔常 *pl.*〕(果类的)初熟;初上市(的水果、蔬菜);早来的消息.

pri·me·val [praiˈmi:vəl] *a.* 早期的,原始(时代)的,太古的. *a ～ forest* 原始森林. **-ly** *ad.*

prim·ing [ˈpraimiŋ] *n.* ①装雷管,装火药;点火药,起爆药. ②涂底漆;底子,底漆. ③(汽机的)蒸溅,飞沫;汽水并发;(汽缸、唧筒等的)引动水;起动注油. ④引动,起爆,发火,点火. ⑤(知识的)速成灌输. ⑥(事先)提供消息〔情报〕. ⑦(加在啤酒中的)一种浓糖溶液. ～ **can** 注油器. ～ **carburetor** 起爆汽化器. ～ **powder** 起爆药.

pri·mip·a·ra [praiˈmipərə] *n.* *(pl.* ～*s,* *-rae* [-ri:]*)*【医】初产妇;只生过一个孩子的妇女. **pri·mi·par·i·ty** [ˌpraimiˈpæriti] *n.* 初产. **pri·mip·ar·ous** [praiˈmipərəs] *a.* 初产的.

prim·i·tive [ˈprimitiv] *a.* ①原始的,上古的;早期的. ②古风的,老式的;粗糙的,简单的;幼稚的,未开化的,不发达的. ③纯朴的,自然的. ④原来的,基本的,非派生的 *(opp.* derivetive*)*; 最初的,第一位的*(opp.* secondary). ⑤【生】初生的;【地】初期的. ⑥自学出来的;由自学的艺术家创作的. ～ *men* 原始人. *the ～ mode of life* 原始生活方式. *a ～ mode of dressing* 朴素的服装. ～ *colours* 原色. *the ～ chord*【乐】基础和音. ～ *rocks* 原成岩. ～ *soil* 生荒地. — *n.* ①原(始)人;原始事物. ②【语法】原词,根词;【数】本原,原始. ③早期艺术家(作品);模仿早期风格的艺术家;原始派艺术家. ④〔P-〕文艺复兴期前的画家(作品);自学而成的艺术家(作品);风格质朴的艺术家. ⑤〔P-〕〔英〕原始卫理公会派教徒 = P- Methodist. **-ly** *ad.* **-ness** *n.*

prim·i·tiv·ism [ˈprimitivizəm] *n.* ①(生活方式上的)原始主义. ②(艺术或艺术家的)原始风格;尚古主义. **-tiv·ist** *n., a.*

pri·mo[1] [ˈpri:məu, It. ˈpri:mɔ:] *n.* *(pl.* ～*s,* It. *-mi* [-mi]*)*〔It.〕【乐】(重奏或重唱的)第一部,主要部.

pri·mo[2] [ˈpraiməu] *ad., a.* 〔L.〕第一(的),首先(的).

primo- *comb. f.* 始,原始,主部,第一: *primo*genitor, *primo*geniture, *primo*dium.

pri·mo·gen·i·tor [ˌpraiməuˈdʒenitə] *n.* 始祖;祖先.

pri·mo·gen·i·ture [ˌpraiməuˈdʒenitʃə] *n.* 长子身分;【法】长子继承权〔继承法〕.

pri·mor·di·al [praiˈmɔ:djəl] *a.* 原始的,初生的,初发的,最初的;(从)原始时代存在的;基本的. ～ *customs* 原始时代的风俗. ～ *(germ) cell*【植】原生殖细胞. **-ly** *ad.*

pri·mor·di·um [praiˈmɔ:diəm] *n.* *(pl.* ***-di·a*** [-ə]*)*【胚】原基.

primp [primp] *vt., vi.* 〔美〕(过分讲究地)打扮,装饰.

prim·rose [ˈprimrəuz] *n.* ①【植】报春花属;樱草;樱草花. ②樱草色,淡黄色. — *a.* ①樱草的. ②樱草色的,淡黄色的. ③樱草多的. ④华美的;欢乐的. ***the ～ path [way]*** ①享乐之路;追求安逸享受的堕落生活;放荡生活. ②看来容易和恰当却容易出错的行动步骤. **P- dame** 樱草会的女会员. **P- Day** 樱草节〔英国保守党政治家迪斯累利 (Disraeli) 的忌辰〕. **P- League**【英史】樱草会〔为纪念保守党政治家迪斯累利而成立的一个组织〕. ～ **yellow** 樱草色.

prim·u·la [ˈprimjulə] *n.*【植】报春花属植物.

pri·mum mob·i·le [ˈpraimʌm ˈmɔbili:] *n.* 〔L.〕①原动天,第十层天〔古希腊天文学家托勒密的天动说中的最外层天体,带动所有天体转动〕. ②〔喻〕原动力;行动〔运动〕的主因.

pri·mus[1] [ˈpraiməs] *n.* 〔P-〕苏格兰主教派教会的主教. — *a.* 第一的,首位的;(英国男子学校同姓学生中)最年长的,资格最老的. *Jones ～* 最年长的琼斯. ～ ***inter pares*** [intə ˈpɛəri:z] 同事中资格最老的,同辈中居首位的.

pri·mus[2] [ˈpraiməs] *n.* 普利姆斯汽化炉〔一种燃烧汽化油的轻便炉子,商标名〕.

prin. = ①principal; principally. ②principle.

prince [prins] *n.* ①王子;王孙;皇族;亲王. ②(英国以外的)公爵,侯爵,伯爵;…公;…侯. ③(封建时代的)诸侯;(作为小附属国统治者的)公. ④〔诗〕帝王,君主. ⑤宗匠,大家,名家;大王,巨头. ⑥〔口〕好人. *P- Bismarck* 俾斯麦公爵. *a ～ of the blood (royal)* 皇族. *the P- Imperial* 皇太子. *the Crown P-* 皇太子,王储. *the ～ of poets* 诗坛名家. *the ～ of bankers* 银行大王. *a merchant ～* 富商,豪商. ***as happy as a ～*** 极幸福的. ***live like a ～*** 生活(象王侯似地)豪华. ***manners of a ～*** 高贵的态度. ～ ***among men*** 正人君子. ***P- of Denmark*** 丹麦王子〔指莎士比亚笔下的 Hamlet〕 (*Hamlet without the P- of Denmark* 没有 *Hamlet* 的 *Hamlet* 剧,失去了本质〔存在意义〕的东西). ***P- of Peace*** 耶稣. ～

of the air [the world, darkness, evil] 魔王. ***P- of the (Holy Roman) Church*** 【天主教】红衣主教的称号. ***P- of Wales*** 威尔士亲王〔英国皇太子的称号〕. **P- Albert (coat)**〔美口〕大礼服. ~ **bishop** 兼任主教的公[侯]国君主. ~ **charming** 女子理想中的求婚者; 对女子献假殷勤的男子. ~ **consort** 女王的丈夫, 伴君. **P- Regent** 摄政王. ~ **royal** 太子〔王或女王的长子〕. **-dom** 王子[诸侯等]的地位[权力、领土]. **-kin, -let** 幼君; 小公子. **-like** *a.* 象王侯的, 象王子的; 高雅的, 有威严的. **-ling** = -let. **-ship** 王子[诸侯等的]身分[职位].

prince·ly [ˈprinsli] *a.* ①象王侯的, 象贵公子的; 高贵的; 有威仪的. ②堂皇的; 壮丽的; 豪华的; 奢侈的. ③王侯的, 王子的. **-li·ness** *n.*

prin·ceps [ˈprinseps] *a.* 〔L.〕①第一的, 最初的. ②【解】主要的. *editio* ~ 初版.

prin·ce's-feath·er [ˈprinsiz-feðə] *n.*【植】硬穗苋; 荭草.

prin·ce's-met·al [ˈprinsiz-metl] *n.* 黄铜, 一种铜锌合金.

prin·cess[1] [prinˈses] *n.* ①公主; 王妃; 王族女性成员; 亲王夫人. ②(英国以外的)公爵[侯爵]夫人. ③英国国王[女王]的孙女. ④女巨头; 女名家. ⑤〔古〕女王. ★ princess 作定语用时读作 [ˈprinses]. *a ~ of seamstresses* 著名女缝衣师. ***a Crown P-*** 皇太子妃. ***a ~ of the blood*** 女王族. ***P- of wales*** 英国太子之妃. ~ **regent** 女摄政王. ~ **royal** 大公主. **-ship** 公主[王妃等]的身分[地位].

prin·cess[2], **prin·cesse** [prinˈses, ˈprinses] *n., a.* 紧身连衣裙(的). ~ **dress [petticoat, slip]** 紧身连衣裙.

prin·ci·pal [ˈprinsəpəl, -sip-] *a.* ①主要的, 首要的, 最重要的; 第一的. ②领头的; 负责人的, 首长的. ③资本的, 本金的, 作为本钱的. *the ~ actor* 主要演员, 主角. *the ~ boy [girl]* (哑剧中)扮演男[女]主角的女演员. *the ~ offender* 【法】主犯. *the ~ sum* 资本, 本金, 本钱. ~ *operations* 主力战. ~ *clause* 【语法】(复合句中的)主句. ~ *order* 【化】主序模. ~ *parts* 【语法】(动词的)主要变化形式〔现在、过去式及过去分词〕. ~ *sentence* 【语法】主句 (= ~ clause). ~ *tone* 【乐】主音. — *n.* ①长; 长官; 首长; 负责人; 校长; 社长; 会长. ②主动者; 决斗的本人 (*opp.* second); 主要演员, 主角;【法】主犯; 本人; (经纪人、代理人、受委托人所代表的)委托人 (*opp.* agent, surety). ③【商】资本, 本金 (*opp.* interest, dividend); 基本财产 (*opp.* income). ④【建】(主要)屋架; 主构, 主材. ⑤【乐】主音栓; (音乐会的)主奏者, 独奏者, 独唱者, 主演者. ⑥(艺术作品的)主题; 特征. *a lady* ~ 女校长. *I must consult my* ~. 我必须同委托人商量. ~ ***and interest*** 本利. ***a ~ in the first [second] degree*** 主[从]犯.

prin·ci·pal·i·ty [ˌprinsiˈpæliti] *n.* ①公国, 侯国; 封邑. ②公国君主的职位[统治权、领地]. ③〔*pl.*〕【宗】九级天使中的一级. ***the P-*** 英国威尔士 (Wales) 的俗名.

prin·ci·pal·ly [ˈprinsəpəli, -sip-] *ad.* 主要, 大抵.

prin·ci·pate [ˈprinsipit] *n.* ①最高权力. ②古罗马早期帝政〔略带共和政治色彩〕. ③(古罗马帝国)执政者的权力[任期]; 公国君主的统治权. ④公国; 封邑, 领地.

prin·cip·i·um [prinˈsipiəm] *n.* (*pl.* ***-cip·i·a*** [-piə]) 原理, 原则; 〔*pl.*〕基本原理[原则]; 初步; 基础.

prin·ci·ple [ˈprinsəpl, -sipl] *n.* ①原理, 原则. ②主义; 政策; 〔常 *pl.*〕道义, 节操. ③本质, 本体, 根源; 本原, 源泉. ④本性, 本能; 天然的性能; 天赋的才能; 动因, 素因. ⑤【化】素, 要素; 精. *the ~ of dividing to move and uniting to fight* 【军】分进合击原则. *the ~s of political economy* 政治经济学原理. *the first* ~ 第一原理, 本体. *the first ~ of all things* 万物的本原. *a man of* ~ 有原则的人, 正派人. *good [right, moral] ~s* 道义. *a vital* ~ 精力. *guiding ~s* 方针. *the bitter* ~【化】苦味素. *the ~ of causality* 因果律. *the ~ of contradiction*【逻】矛盾律. ***against one's ~*** 违反自己的原则. ***as a matter of ~*** 作为原则的问题. ***by ~*** 按照原则, 原则上. ***in ~*** 原则上, 大体上. ***of ~*** 有原则的. ***on ~*** 按照原则, 根据原则 (*I refuse on ~* 我拒绝是按原则办事[并无恶意]). ***on the ~ of*** 根据…的原则. ***stick to one's ~s*** 坚持原则.

prin·ci·pled [ˈprinsəpld] *a.* 原则的, 原则性的, 有原则的; 有节操的. *high-~* 有高度道德原则的, 原则性强的. *loose-~* 原则性差的, 无主见的, 意志薄弱的.

prin·cox [ˈprinkɔks] *n.* 〔古〕纨袴子, 花花公子.

prink [priŋk] *vt.* ①给…梳妆打扮, 把…打扮漂亮, 把…装饰漂亮(*up*). ②(鸟)用嘴理(毛). — *vi.* ①化妆, 打扮得漂亮(*up*). ②〔英方〕卖俏, 装腔作势; 扭扭捏捏地走.

print [print] *vt.* ①印; 刻; 盖上(印等). ②印刷(书、画等); 把…付印; 出版, 刊行, 发行(书籍等). ③印染, 在(布等上)印花样; 印(花). ④把…写成印刷字体. ⑤把…铭记在心. ⑥【摄】印, 晒印(相片); 复制(电影拷贝等)(*out; off*). ~ *a kiss on her cheek* 在她脸上亲一亲. ~ *a book* 出版一本书. ~ *a newspaper* 发行一种报纸. *~ed matter* 印刷品. *a ~ed circuit* 印刷电路. *~ed goods* 印花布. *P- your name in block capitals.* 请用印刷体大写字母写姓名. ~ *(sth.) on one's memory* 把(某事)铭记在心. — *vi.* ①印刷; 出版; 以印刷为业. ②(相片等)晒出, 现出; 晒相; 复制. ③用印刷体写字. *This paper ~s badly.* 这种纸很难印底片. ~ **out** (印刷机)不断地印出. — *n.* ①印刷; 印刷术; 印刷业. ②图片; 晒图; 版画. ③〔主美〕出版物, 报纸; 印出的字体, 印刷字体. ④痕迹; 印象; 〔*pl.*〕〔美俚〕指纹;【地】印痕. ⑤【摄】(从底片晒出的)相片; 照片; 正片. ⑥印花布; 印花布服装; (用模型制出的)压制品. ⑦印章; 打印器; 印模;【冶】铸模; 型心座. ⑧版本; 印次. *a clear* ~ 清晰的印刷字体. *daily ~s* 日报. *weekly ~s* 周刊(杂志). *write the address in* ~ 用印刷体写住址. *a finger* ~ 指印, 指纹. *a foot* ~ 脚印, 足迹. *cotton* ~ 印花布. *India* ~ 印度花纹印花布. *a ~ of butter* (模压成的)一块黄油. *a blue* ~ 蓝相片; 蓝图. ***appear [come out] in ~*** 印成, 印出来. ***in ~*** 已出版的; (书等)在出售中的; (书等)尚有供应的 (*Is the book in ~?* 这本书还买得到吗?). ***in cold ~*** 已用活字印成(白纸黑字); 〔喻〕不能再更动, 没有变更的余地. ***in large [small] ~*** 用大号[小号]活字印刷的. ***lie like ~*** 撒大谎. ***out of ~*** (书等)已脱销; 已绝版. ***put into ~*** 付印, 出版. ~ **effect** (录音)复制效应, 转印效应. ~ **hand** 用印刷体写的字. **~-out**【自】印出(指以打印方式表示的计算机计算结果). **~-seller** 版画[图片]商. ~ **shop** 版画[图片]店; 印刷所. **~works** (棉布等的)印染厂, 印花布厂.

print·a·ble [ˈprintəbl] *a.* ①可印刷的, 印得出来的; 可翻印的. ②适宜于出版的. **-bil·i·ty** [ˌprintəˈbiliti] *n.*

print·er [ˈprintə] *n.* ①印刷(业)者; 印刷商; 印刷工人, 排字工人. ②印染者; 印花工. ③印刷机;【摄】晒片机, 印像机;【讯】印字机. ***~'s devil*** 印刷厂学徒工. ***~'s dozen*** 十三. ***~'s error*** 排错〔略作 P.E., p.e.〕. ***~'s ink*** 油墨. ***~'s mark*** (版权页等上)出版商的商标. ***~'s pie*** 活字的乱堆; 〔喻〕混乱 (*make ~'s pie of* 搞乱…). ***the public ~*** 〔美〕印刷局局长. **~gram** 印字电报.

print·er·y [ˈprintəri] *n.* ①印染厂. ②印刷所, 印刷厂.

print·ing [ˈprintiŋ] *n.* ①印刷; 版; 印刷术; 印刷业; 印刷品; 〔*pl.*〕供印刷用的纸. ②〔美〕印刷次数, 版次; (书等的一次)印数. ③〔美〕印刷体一样的字. ④【纺】印花, 印染. ⑤【摄】晒片; (电影拷贝等的)复制. *colour* ~ 彩印. *phospher* ~ 荧光屏涂磷. *smoke* ~ 静电印刷. *three-coloured* ~ 三色版印刷(术). ~ **ink** 油墨. ~ **house** 印刷厂. ~ **machine** 印刷机. ~ **office** 印刷所. ~ **paper** 印刷用纸, 道林纸; 相片纸. ~ **press** (电动)印刷机; 印刷厂.

print·less [ˈprintlis] *a.* 无印迹的, 不留印痕的.

print·mak·er [ˈprintˌmeikə] *n.* 制版工人;(尤指)版画制作者. **-mak·ing** *n.* 制版;版画制作.

Pri·or [ˈpraiə] *n.* 普赖尔〔姓氏〕.

pri·or[1] [ˈpraiə] *a.* ①〔用作前置定语〕在前的;优先的. ②〔与 to 连用〕在…之前 (*opp.* posterior);比…优先〔重要〕. ~ *engagement* 预先的约会. ~ *claims* 优先要求权. *This duty is* ~ *to all others.* 这个职务比其他一切职务都重要. — *ad.* 居先, 在前 *(to)*. *I called on her* ~ *to my departure.* 我动身前去看过她. **-ly** *ad.*

pri·or[2] [ˈpraiə] *n.* ①小修道院院长,大修道院的副院长. ②【史】(十三世纪意大利诸共和国的) 行政长官. **-ship** *n.* 小修道院院长〔共和国行政长官〕的职务〔地位、任期〕.

pri·or·ate [ˈpraiərit] *n.* ①= priorship. ②= priory.

pri·or·ess [ˈpraiəris] *n.* 小修女院院长; 大修女院的副院长.

pri·or·i·ty [praiˈɔriti] *n.* ①(时间、顺序上的)先,前. ②较重要;上席;上位;重点,优先(权);先取权. ③优先配给;优先考虑的事. *establish an order of* ~ 确定讨论项目的次序. *give* ~ *to* 把优先权让给…. ~ *of one's claim to another's* 某人的要求比另一人的更重要. ***according to*** ~ 依照次序,依次. ***take*** ~ ***of*** 比…居先;得…的优先权. ~ **construction** 近期〔首期〕建筑.

pri·o·ry [ˈpraiəri] *n.* 小修道院;小的女修道院. ***a*** ~ ***alien*** 从属于外国大修道院的小修道院 (= an alien ~).

Pris·ci·an [ˈpriʃiən] *n.* 普里兴〔六世纪活跃于君士坦丁堡的拉丁语语法学家,被奉为语法学鼻祖〕. ***break [knock]*** ~***'s head*** 违反语法规则,犯语法错误. ***Shade of*** ~***!*** 气死普里兴!〔闹语法笑话时的感叹语〕

Pris·cil·la [priˈsilə] *n.* 普丽西拉〔女子名〕.

prise [praiz] *vt., n.* = prize.

pri·sere [ˈpraisiə] *n.*【植】正常演替系列.

prism [ˈprizəm] *n.* ①【数】棱柱(体), 角柱(体);【物】(结晶)柱. ②棱镜; 棱晶. ③【物】分光光谱;〔*pl.*〕光谱的七色; 折光物体. *an oblique [a regular, a right, a triangular]* ~ 斜〔正、直、三角〕棱柱. *cross* ~*s* 正角棱镜. ~ *glasses* 棱镜双目望远镜. *a reversing* ~ 反像棱镜. *a* ~ *of first [second] order*【物】(结晶)第一〔第二〕柱.

pris·mat·ic, pris·mat·i·cal [prizˈmætik, -kəl] *a.* ①棱柱(形)的. ②用棱镜分析的,分光的. ③虹色的;射出七色光彩的;灿烂的. ④【物】斜方晶系的. ~ *colours* 光谱的七色. ~ *powder* 棱形火药. **-i·cal·ly** *ad.*

pris·moid [ˈprizmɔid] *n.* 平截头棱锥体. **-moi·dal** *a.*

prism·y [ˈprizəmi] *a.* ①棱柱(似)的,棱镜的. ②棱镜七色的,虹色的;五光十色的,灿烂的.

pris·on [ˈprizn] *n.* ①监狱;拘留所,羁押室,禁闭室. ②监禁,禁闭. ***break (out of)*** ~ 越狱. ***cast [put] sb. into*** ~ 把某人下狱,把某人关进牢里. ***escape from*** ~ 越狱逃跑. ***(lie) in*** ~ 在狱中. ***send [take] sb. to*** ~ = cast sb. into ~. — *vt.*〔诗〕〔方〕①监禁; 关押. ②紧紧抱住. ~ **bird**〔口〕囚犯;惯犯,积犯. ~ **breaker** 越狱者. ~ **breaking [breach]** 越狱. ~ **camp** 战俘集中营;苦役拘禁地. ~ **editor** (报上负法律责任的)署名编辑. ~ **fever**【医】斑疹伤寒. ~ **house**〔主喻〕监狱,牢房. ~ **van** 囚车.

pris·on·er [ˈpriznə] *n.* ①囚犯;刑事被告;拘留犯,羁押犯;俘虏. ②被夺去自由的人〔动物〕. *a state [political]* ~ = *a* ~ *of state* 政治犯. *He made her hand a* ~. 他握住她的手不放. *a* ~ *to one's room [chair]* 病人〔困在椅子上的残废者〕. *My work kept me a* ~ *all summer.* 整个夏天,我的工作忙得不可开交. ~ ***at large*** 在无法逃走处(如船上、营房等) 许与相当自由的囚犯;(只准在船上或营房内自由走动的)受约束处分的军人. ~ ***at the bar*** 刑事被告. ***give oneself up a*** ~ 投降;自首;自投罗网. ***make sb.*** ~ 俘虏某人. ~ ***of war*** 战俘. ***take (sb.)*** ~ 俘虏(某人). ***yield oneself*** ~ 投降. ~***s'***〔美 ~'s〕**bars [base]** 抢阵地〔捉俘虏〕游戏.

priss [pris] *vi.* 〔美口〕①做事严肃谨慎. ②穿得讲究整洁.

pris·sy [ˈprisi]〔美口〕*a.* ①严肃谨慎的;刻板的. ②服装讲究整洁的. ③纤柔的;娇气的;缺乏男子气的.

pris·tine [ˈpristain] *a.* ①原始时代的,原始的;太古的;早期的. ②原来的;纯朴的;未受腐蚀的. ~ *innocence* 天真无邪. **-ly** *ad.*

prith·ee [ˈpriði(:)] *int.*〔古、口〕请,求求你〔pray thee 的别字〕.

Pritt [prit] *n.* 普里特〔姓氏〕.

prit·tle-prat·tle [ˈpritl ˈprætl] *n.* ①空谈,废话. ②碎嘴子,饶舌者. — *vi.* 空谈;饶舌.

priv. = private(ly); privative.

pri·va·cy [ˈpraivəsi] *n.* ①隐退,隐避;隐居. ②〔古〕隐居处,隐退处. ③秘密,私下. *He must disturb your* ~. 他一定打搅你的幽静生活了〔真对不起〕. ***in the*** ~ ***of one's thoughts*** 在内心深处. ***in*** ~ 隐避的;秘密地. ***in strict*** ~ 完全私下的〔地〕. ***live in*** ~ 过隐居生活.

pri·vat·do·cent, pri·vat·do·zent [priˈvɑ:tdəuˈtsent] *n.* ***(pl.*** ***-en*** [-ən]***)*** (在德国等的大学中) 无薪俸的讲师〔不支薪俸,仅以学生的学费为报酬者〕.

pri·vate [ˈpraivit] *a.* ①私的,私人的,个人的,私用的,专用的. ②秘密的;保密的;非公开的;(信件等)亲启的. ③(财产等)私有的;私营的;民间的;(学校等)私立的. ④平民的;无官职的;士兵的. ⑤(地方等)隐蔽的,幽僻的. ⑥不宜公开谈论〔显露〕的. ⑦〔古〕隐遁的. ~ *life* 私生活. ~ *coach [teacher, tutor]* 家庭教师;私人教师. ~ *property* 私有财产. ~ *ownership* 私有制. *a* ~ *secretary* 私人秘书. *a* ~ *car* 自备汽车. ~ *business* 个人的事,私事. ~ *affairs* = ~ *concerns* 私事;隐秘的事. *a* ~ *door* 便门. ~ *clothes* 便服. ~ *information* 非正式消息. *Keep the news* ~. 这个消息请守秘密. *We are quite* ~ *here.* 这里就不怕被人看见了. *a* ~ *citizen* 平民. *a* ~ *soldier* 士兵, 列兵. ***a*** ~ ***member (of Parliament)*** 非内阁阁员的普通议员. ***as a*** ~ ***person*** 以个人身分. ***for*** ~ ***reasons*** 仅仅私下地,不能给外人知道. ***for sb.'s*** ~ ***ear*** 秘密地 (*This is for your* ~ *ear.* 这是私下只跟你一个人讲的). ***in one's*** ~ ***capacity*** 以个人身分. — *n.* ①列兵;〔美陆军、海军陆战队〕二等兵;士兵,〔英陆军〕二等兵. ②〔古〕私人,个人. ③〔*pl.*〕阴部, 生殖器. *a basic* ~〔美陆军〕三等兵. *a* ~ *first class*〔美陆军、海军陆战队〕一等兵. ***in*** ~ 秘密地 (*criticism in* ~ 背后批评). ~ **bill [act]**【议会】有关个人利害的议案〔英国也指阁员以外的议员所提的议案〕. ~ **detective**〔美〕人事调查所员,私人侦探. ~ **detective agency**〔美〕私人侦探所,人事调查所. ~ **eye**〔美俚〕= ~ detective. ~ **parts** 阴部,私处. ~ **practice** 私人开业. ~ **school** 私立学校. ~ **secretary** 私人秘书. ~ **soldier** 列兵,士兵. ~ **theatricals** 业余戏剧演出. ~ **view** (绘画等的)预展. ~ **treaty** (买卖双方直接议定条件的) 财产出让契约. **-ly** *ad.* 私下,秘密,一个人.

pri·va·teer [ˌpraivəˈtiə] *n.* ①私掠船〔战时特准掠捕敌方商船的武装民船〕. ②私掠船船长;〔*pl.*〕私掠船船员. — *vi.* 私掠巡航. ~**sman**〔美〕私掠船船长;私掠船船员. **-ing** *n.* 私掠巡航,掠捕敌方商船.

pri·va·tion [praiˈveiʃən] *n.* ①缺乏;(生活必需品的)匮乏;穷困;困难,艰难. ②剥夺;褫夺;没收;丧失. ③【逻】(积极性的)缺性. *suffer many* ~*s* 吃尽苦头,备尝艰辛. *die of* ~ 穷死. *Cold is the* ~ *of heat.* 冷就是缺热性.

pri·va·tism [ˈpraivitizəm] *n.* 利己主义〔只关心与自己直接利益有关的事情〕. **-va·tist, -tis·tic** *a.* **-ti·za·tion** *n.* **-va·tize** [-taiz] *vt.* 使利己主义化,使只顾自己.

priv·a·tive [ˈprivətiv] *a.* ①剥夺的, 褫夺的. ②缺乏某种性质的. ③【语法】表示缺性的;否定的,反义的. — *n.* ①【语法】缺性语〔voiceless, dumb 等〕;否定的前缀〔后

缀〕〔un-, -less 等〕. ②【逻】缺性概念〔blindness, dumbness 等〕.

priv·et [ˈprivit] *n.* 【植】水蜡树,女贞.

priv·i·lege [ˈprividʒ] *n.* ①特权,优惠,特别照顾,特别待遇;特殊荣幸. ②特别处理;特许,特免. ③(对公司股票的)优惠增购权. *the ~ of Parliament* 〔英〕议会〔议员〕的特权. *a breach of ~* 对(国会议员等)特权的侵犯. *water ~* 用水权. *the ~ of citizenship* 公民权. *exclusive ~* 专有特权. ***a bill of ~*** 贵族要求贵族阶级审判的申请书. ***a writ of ~*** (因民事诉讼被扣押的人的)特赦状. ***~ of sb.'s friendship*** 和…交际的光荣. ***the ~ of clergy*** 【史】①教士的特权〔犯罪时可不受普通法院审判〕. ②知识阶级的特权〔初次犯罪时可免予判刑〕. — *vt.* 给…以特权;特许;特免 *(from)*. *~ sb. from arrest* 特免某人不受逮捕. ~ **cab** 特许在车站接客的马车. **-r** *n.* 享受特权者.

priv·i·leged [ˈprividʒd] *a.* ①特权的;有特权的;特殊待遇的. ②特许的;专用的. ③特免的;(由于特殊情况)不受一般法规制约的. ④【天主教】(祭坛等)庆祝大赦的弥撒中特设的. *the ~ few* 少数享受特权者. *a ~ communication* 法律上无论何时皆可拒绝公开的(医生与病人、律师与委托人间等的)通信.

priv·i·ly [ˈprivili] *ad.* 暗中;私下,秘密地.

priv·i·ty [ˈpriviti] *n.* ①暗中参与;私下知悉;默契 *(to)*; 秘密,私事. ②【法】(对同一权利)有合法利益的人之间的相互关系;(对合同等因与当事人的一方有关系而产生的)非当事人的利益. *~ to the plot* 暗中参与阴谋. *with his ~ and consent* 得到他的同意. ***with the ~ of*** 通知,告诉. ***without the ~ of ...*** 不通知,不告诉.

priv·y [ˈprivi] *a.* ①(物、地方等)秘密的;隐蔽的;(行为)暗中参与的,和…有勾结的 *(to)*. ②个人的;私人的. *I was made ~ to it.* 我心里明白那件事. — *n.* ①【法】有利害关系的人. ②〔古〕厕所. ***be ~ to (a plot)*** 参与(阴谋). **P- Council** 枢密院. **P- Councellor [Councillor]** 枢密顾问官. ~ **parts** 阴部. ~ **purse** ①〔英〕(王室的)私财;内库. ②〔*P.P.*〕英国皇室司库〔全称是 *Keeper of the P- Purse*〕. ~ **seal** 〔英〕御玺;〔加 the〕**P- Seal** = Lord P- Seal 掌玺大臣.

prix [priː] *n.* 〔*sing., pl.*〕〔F.〕①奖金;奖品. ②价格. ~ ***fixe*** [fiːks] (一客)份饭;份饭价格. **P- Goncourt** 龚古尔奖金〔法国的文艺奖金〕.

prize[1] [praiz] *n.* ①奖赏;奖品;赠品;奖金. ②争夺物;值得竞争的目标;〔口〕极好的东西. *the Nobel P-* 诺贝尔奖. *Good health is an inestimable ~* 健康是无价之宝. —*a.* ①悬赏的;作为奖品的;得奖的. ②〔口〕非常的;了不起的. *a ~ cup* 奖杯. *a ~ idiot* 可以得奖的大傻瓜,头号傻瓜. *a ~ poem* 得奖诗. ***carry off [gain, take, win] a ~*** 得奖. ***draw a ~ in the lottery*** 摸彩. ***gain the ~s of a profession*** 得到优薪高位. ***pick up a ~ at a sale*** 大减价时买到极好东西. ***play one's ~*** 谋私利. ***run (play) ~s*** (为得奖赏)参加赛跑(比赛). ~ **essay** 得奖论文. ~ **fellow** 得到奖学金的学生. ~ **fellowship** 成绩优异奖学金. ~ **fight(ing)** 职业拳击. ~ **fighter** 职业拳击家. ~**man** 得奖人. ~ **ring** 拳击场;职业拳击赛. ~ **scholarship** = ~ fellowship. ~**winner** 获奖人. **-less** *a.* 未获奖的;成绩平庸的.

prize[2] [praiz] *vt.* ①珍视,宝贵;珍藏. ②〔古〕评价;估价. *~ security above all else* 安全第一.

prize[3] [praiz] *n.* ①捕获(尤指战时在海上捕获敌方的船、货等). ②捕获品,战利品;(战时在海上)捕获的敌船〔货物等〕. ③意外的收获,横财. ***become (the) ~ of [to]*** 为…所捕获. ***make (a) ~ of*** (战时)缉捕(船货等). — *vt.* 捕拿,缉捕;捕获. ~**-court** 处理战时海上捕获物的海军军事法庭. ~ **crew** 战时海上押送捕获船的船员. ~ **master** 捕获船押送官. ~**-money** (战时海上捕获敌方船货者应得的)捕获赏金.

prize[4] [praiz] *vt.* 〔英方〕用杠杆推动;撬开 *(open; out; up; off)*. — *n.* 〔英方〕杠杆,撬棍;杠杆作用.

priz·er [ˈpraizə] *n.* 〔古〕(比赛中)争夺奖品的人.

pro[1] [prəu] *n.* *(pl. ~s)* 〔口〕内行,专家;〔美〕职业选手. *a golf ~* 高尔夫球的职业选手.

pro[2] [prəu] *n.* *(pl. ~s)* 投票赞成者;赞成方面的意见〔理由〕;赞成的(投)票. ***the ~s and cons*** 赞成论与反对论;赞成与反对的理由;赞成者与反对者. — *ad.* 站在赞成方面;正面地 *(opp.* con*)*. ***~ and con*** 赞成与反对. ~**-and-con** *vt., vi.* 辩论.

pro [prəu] *prep.* 〔L.〕①为…的. ②按…,随…,视…. ~ ***bono publico*** [ˈbəunəu ˈpʌblikəu] 为了公益. ~ ***forma*** [ˈfɔːmə] 形式上;【商】估计的,假定的 (*~ forma account sales* 估计卖出计算书. *~ forma invoice* 估价单). ~ ***hac vice*** [hæk ˈvaisi(ː)] 只此一回,只为这个场合. ~ ***memoria*** [miˈmɔːriə] 提醒. ~ ***patria*** [ˈpeitriə] 为祖国. ~ ***rata*** [ˈreitə] 按比例的;成比例地. ~ ***renata*** [riːˈneitə] 【法】临时地〔的〕(*a meeting held ~ renata* 临时举行的会议). ~ ***tanto*** [ˈtæntəu] 至此,到这个程度〔范围〕. ~ ***tem.*** = ~ ***tempore*** [ˈtemperi] 当时(的);暂时(的);临时(的) (*the ~ tem. secretary* 临时秘书).

pro. = ①probation. ②probationer. ③prohibitionist. ④prostitute.

PRO = public relations officer 〔美军〕对外联络官.

pro-[1] *pref.* ①代,副: *pro*noun, *pro*consul. ②亲,赞成,偏袒: *pro*-American. ③出,向前,在前: *pro*duce, *pro*pel, *pro*fane. ④按,照: *pro*portion. ⑤公开: *pro*claim.

pro-[2] *pref.* 〔位置、时间〕前,先: *pro*gnathous, *pro*logue.

pro·a [ˈprəuə] *n.* (马来群岛的)快速帆船.

prob. = probable; probably; problem.

prob·a·bi·lism [ˈprɔbəbilizəm] *n.* ①【哲】盖然论;或然说. ②【宗】盖然说〔一种天主教教义,认为在神学权威有分歧时,可遵从任何一位神学大师的阐释〕.

prob·a·bi·lis·tic [ˌprɔbəbiˈlistik] *a.* ①(天主教教义)盖然论的,或然说的. ②概率的,几率的.

prob·a·bil·i·ty [ˌprɔbəˈbiliti] *n.* ①或有;或然性. ②【哲】盖然性〔在 certainly 和 doubt 或 posibility 之间〕. ③【数】几率,概率,或然率. ④或有的事;可能的结果. ⑤〔*pl.*〕〔美俚〕天气预测. *What are the probabilities?* 有几分把握? *The probabilities are against us [in our favour]* 趋势对我们好象不利〔有利〕. *hit ~* 命中率. ***in all ~*** 很可能,大概,多半,十之八九. ***~ of (missile survival)*** (导弹不被击落的)概率. ***The ~ is that ...*** 大概是…,很可能是…. ***There is every ~ of [that] ...*** 多半有,多半会. ***There is no ~ of [that] ...*** 很难有,很难会.

prob·a·ble [ˈprɔbəbl] *a.* 象有的,象确实的;很可能的,或然的,大概的;有希望的. ★ probable 所指的可能性比 possible 或 likely 所指的要大一些. *Success is possible but hardly ~.* 成功是可能的,但不一定. — *n.* 很可能被选中〔获胜〕的人;很可能的事〔情况〕. ***It is ~ that ...*** 也许是,恐怕是 (*It is ~ that he forgot.* 他也许是忘记了). ~ **candidate** 大有希望的候选人. ~ **cost** 大约的费用. ~ **error** 概差;或然误差;【数】机差;【物】可几〔可能〕误差;【天】或然差. ~ **evidence** 大概确实的证据. ~ **zone** 【军】预期命中地带.

prob·a·bly [ˈprɔbəbli] *ad.* 大概,或许,很可能.

proband [ˈprəubænd] *n.* 家谱中发支始祖 (= propositus).

pro·bang [ˈprəubæŋ] *n.* 【外】除鲠器,食管探子.

pro·bate [ˈprəubit] *n.* 【法】①遗嘱检验. ②验讫的遗嘱. *the ~ court* 遗嘱检验法庭. — [ˈprəubeit] *vt.* 〔美〕①检验(遗嘱). ②对(犯人)予以缓刑. ~ **duty** 立遗嘱人死后的动产税.

pro·ba·tion [prəˈbeiʃən] *n.* ①检定,检验,验证,查验. ②考验(期),见习(期);试用(期);预备期;〔美〕(处罚学

生的)试读期。③察看(以观后效)。④【法】缓刑。***on ~*** ①(作为)试用，作为见习。②察看；【法】缓刑。***place (an offender) on [under] ~*** 对(犯人)缓刑。**~ officer** 缓刑犯的监视官。**~ system** 缓刑制。

pro·ba·tion·al, pro·ba·tion·a·ry [prəˈbeiʃənəl, -ʃənəri] *a.* ①试用的；见习的；(会员等)非正式的；(党员)预备期的。②【法】缓刑(中)的。③察看(以观后效的)。*a probationary officer* = probation officer. *a ~ member* 非正式会员。

pro·ba·tion·er [prəˈbeiʃənə] *n.* ①试用人员，见习生，练习生；试读生；候补牧师；候补会员[党员、社员等]。②缓刑中的罪犯。

pro·ba·tive [ˈprəubətiv] *a.* ①检验的，鉴定的；试验中的。②证明的；作证据用的。*a ~ letter* 证明信。

pro·ba·to·ry [ˈprəubətəri] *a.* = probative.

probe [prəub] *n.* ①【医】探针；探示器，取样器；【物】试探电极。②【医】(对伤处等的)针探，探查；刺探；探索；试探；查究 *(into)*；〔美〕调查；试样。③【空】(飞机)空中加油管。④【宇】探测器；探测飞船。*a lunar ~* 月球探测器。— *vt.* ①用探针[探测器]探查。②刺探；调查，探查，查究。*~ a matter to the bottom* 彻底调查一件事。*~ deeply into* 深入调查。— *vi.* (用探针)探查；探索；查究，深查 *(into)*。

prob·er [ˈprəubə] *n.* 探测器；探示器。

prob·it [ˈprɔbit] *n.* 【统计】正规偏差值〔一种计算平均数的偏差的统计单位〕。

pro·bi·ty [ˈprəubiti] *n.* 正直，诚实。

prob·lem [ˈprɔbləm] *n.* ①问题，课题；疑难问题；令人困惑的情况。②【数、物】习题；作图题。③(象棋的)布局问题。*the ~ of unemployment* 失业问题。*His whole conduct is a ~ to me.* 他的一切行为我都不理解。— *a.* ①成问题的；难处理的。②关于社会问题的。*a ~ child* 【心】问题儿童；难管教的孩子。*a ~ novel [play]* (反映社会问题等的)问题小说[戏剧]。***sleep on [upon, over] a ~*** 把问题留到第二天解决。

prob·lem·at·ic, prob·lem·at·i·cal [ˌprɔbliˈmætik, -ikəl] *a.* ①有问题的；可疑的；疑难的；未定的，未可预断的。②【逻】盖然性的，或然性的。**-i·cal·ly** *ad.*

pro·bos·cid·e·an, pro·bos·cid·i·an [ˌprəubəˈsidiən] *n.* 长鼻目 *(Proboscidea)* 动物〔如象、(第三纪产的)乳齿象〕。— *a.* 长鼻目的。

pro·bos·cis [prəuˈbɔsis] *n.* ***(pl. -cides*** [-sidi:z]***)*** ①(象等的)鼻子。②(昆虫的)喙，吻。③〔谑〕(人的)大鼻子。**~ monkey** 天狗猴。

proc. = ①proceedings. ②process. ③proctor.

pro·caine [ˈprəukein, prəuˈkein] *n.* 【药】普鲁卡因。

pro·cam·bi·um [prəuˈkæmbiəm] *n.* 【植】原形成层。**-bi·al** [-biəl] *a.*

pro·carp [ˈprəukɑ:p] *n.* 【植】果胞系。

pro·ca·the·dral [ˌprəukəˈθi:drəl] *n.* 【宗】作为主教礼拜堂的教区教堂，主教教堂。

pro·ce·dur·al [prəˈsi:dʒərəl] *a.* (法律)程序上的，程序性的。*~ details* 程序上的细节。***reject on ~ grounds*** 根据程序上的理由予以拒绝。

pro·ce·dure [prəˈsi:dʒə] *n.* ①工序，过程，步骤。②程序，手续；方法；诉讼程序；(议会的)议事程序。③行为，行动；传统的做法；(外交、军队等的)礼仪，礼节。④〔罕〕进行。*the code of civil [criminal] ~* 民事[刑事]诉讼法。*legal ~* 法律诉讼程序。*radio ~* 无线电通讯工作规则。*setup ~* 【自】准备程序。

pro·ceed [prəˈsi:d] *vi.* ①前进，进行；出发，赴。②动手，开始，着手。③继续进行；继续做下去；继续讲下去。④发出，发生，出自 *(from)*。⑤办理手续，处置；进行诉讼程序，起诉。⑥〔英大学〕升学位，取(硕士以上)学位 *(to)*。*~ to Beijing* 去北京。*~ to the next business* 着手另一工作。*Please ~ with your story.* 请讲下去。*diseases that ~ from dirt* 因为不清洁引起的疾病。*~ against* 控诉(某人)。***~ on [upon]*** 照…进行。***~ to do sth.*** 开始做某事。***~ to the degree*** 得硕士学位。***~ with one's work*** 继续干下去〔尤指停顿一段时间后〕。— [ˈprəusi:d] *n.* 〔*pl.*〕(从事某种活动或变卖财物等的)收入；货款收入，卖得金额；收益。*gross ~s* 营业总收入。*He sold his house and lives on the ~s.* 他卖了房子靠房款收入过日子。

pro·ceed·ing [prəˈsi:diŋ] *n.* ①进行；进程；程序。②行为，行动；活动；做法，手段；处理。③〔*pl.*〕诉讼程序。④〔*pl.*〕事项，项目。⑤〔*pl.*〕记录，会议录，会报，会刊，学报；(科学文献)汇编。*a high-handed ~* 高压手段。*suspicious ~s* 鬼鬼祟祟的行径。*the ~s of a club* 俱乐部年报。***dispossess ~s*** 〔美口〕(房屋等的)腾让诉讼。***institute [take] legal ~s against*** 对…提起诉讼，控告。***oral ~s*** 口头辩论。

pro·ce·phal·ic [ˌprəusiˈfælik] *a.* 【动】头前部的，与头前部有关的。

pro·cer·coid [prəuˈsə:kɔid] *n.* 【动】原尾幼虫。

pro·cess[1] [ˈprəuses, Am. ˈprɔses] ★后接 of 时，读作 [ˈprəusis]. *n.* ①进行，经过；过程，历程；作用。②处置，方法，步骤；加工处理，工艺程序，工序；制作法。③【摄】照相制版法；照相版图片；三原色印刷。④【法】诉讼程序；法律手续；被告传票，传票。⑤【解】(动植物机体的)突起，隆起，突。*the ~ of growth* 生长过程。*a mental [psychological] ~* 心理作用。*labour-consuming ~* 重体力劳动。*film ~* 影片加工。*offset ~* 胶印法。*legal ~* 法律手续。*vermiform ~* 【解】阑尾[蚓突]。***in ~*** 进行着 *(changes in ~* 正在发生的变化)。***in ~ of time*** 随着时间的推移；逐渐地。***in (the) ~ of*** 在…的过程中 *(in ~ of construction* 正在建筑中)。***serve a ~ on*** 对…发出传票。— *a.* ①经过特殊加工的；(用化学方法等)处理过的。②照相制版的；三色版的。③(电影镜头等)有幻觉效应的。— [ˈprəuses] *vt.* ①加工；处理，办理；初步分类；贮藏(腌肉等)；(用化学方法)处置(废物等)。②用照相版影印。③对…提起诉讼；用传票传审。*a ~ing tax* 〔美〕(农产品)加工税。*a ~ing plant* 炼油厂，石油加工厂。**~ engraving** 【印】三色版。**~ ink** 三色版油墨。**~ plate** 【印】套色版。**~ printing** 彩色套印。**~ server** 递送传票的司法人员。**~ shot** 【摄】伪装镜头〔如地震等的特技镜头〕。**~ing unit** 【计算机】运算器。

pro·cess[2] [prəˈses] *vi.* 〔口〕排队走，列队行进〔procession. 之略〕。

pro·ces·sion [prəˈseʃən, prəu-] *n.* ①(人、车、船等的)行列，队伍。②(队列的)行进；游行，进行，前进，先行；发出；【宗】圣灵的发出。③(运动中)轻易取胜；不认真对付而速败的行为。*a funeral ~* 送葬队伍。*form a ~* 排成行列。*go in ~* 排成队去。*parading ~* 游行队伍。— *vi.* 排队前进。— *vt.* 沿着(街道)列队行进。**-ary** *a.* **-ist** *n.*

pro·ces·sion·al [prəˈseʃənəl] *a.* 队伍的，列队行进的。— *n.* 【宗】列队行进时唱的圣歌，行列仪式书。

pro·ces·sor [ˈprəusesə] *n.* ①〔美〕农产品加工者；进行初步分类的人。②(数据等的)分理者；【自】信息处理机。

pro·cès-ver·bal [ˈprɔseveəˈbal] *n.* ***(pl. -verbaux*** [veəˈbo]***)*** 〔F.〕①官方报告书。②【法】检察官的调查报告书。③(会议)记录，议事录。

pro·chro·nism [ˈprəukrənizəm] *n.* (所记日期比事件实际发生日期早的)记时早的错误。

pro·claim [prəˈkleim] *vt.* ①宣布，公布；宣告，通告，公告。②声明；表示，显示。③赞扬，歌颂。④宣布禁止(集会等)；通告隔离[隔断](某一地区)。*~ him a traitor* 宣布他为叛徒。*~ war* 宣战。*~ a victory* 宣告胜利。*~ one's opinions* 发表意见。*His manners ~ him a scholar.* 从他的举止可以看出他是一个学者。*~ a meeting* 宣布集会为违法，禁止集会。*~ a district* 宣布对(某一地区)加以法律管制。**-er** *n.*

proc·la·ma·tion [ˌprɔkləˈmeiʃən] *n.* ①宣布，公布。②

声明；宣言，布告，公告；宣言书，声明书。③〔古〕自白。*issue [make] a* ～ 发表公告[声明]。～ *of neutrality* 宣布中立。～ *of martial law* 宣布戒严。～ *of war* 宣战。

pro·clam·a·to·ry [prəˈklæmətəri] *a.* 宣言的，布告的，公告的。

pro·cli·max [prəuˈklaimæks] *n.* 【生】原顶极群落。

pro·clit·ic [prəuˈklitik] *a.* 连接发音的〔即一个字与其后面的重读字组成一个语音单位而发音的，如 *once and for all* 中的 *for*〕。— *n.* 连接读音词。

pro·cliv·i·ty [prəˈkliviti] *n.* ①倾向，性癖，脾气 *(to; towards; for; to do)*。②〔古〕敏捷。*a* ～ *to vice* 作恶的倾向。*warlike proclivities* 好战癖。

pro·con·sul [prəuˈkɔnsəl] *n.* 〔古罗马〕地方总督；〔主英〕(殖民地的)总督。

pro-con·sul [prəuˈkɔnsəl] *n.* 代理领事。

pro·con·su·lar [prəuˈkɔnsjulə] *a.* 总督的，总督管辖下的。

pro·con·su·late, pro·con·sul·ship [prəuˈkɔnsjulit, -səlʃip] *n.* 总督的职位[任期]。

pro·cras·ti·nate [prəuˈkræstineit] *vi., vt.* 耽搁，拖延，迁延，因循。

pro·cras·ti·na·tion [prəuˌkræstiˈneiʃən] *n.* 耽搁，拖延，因循。*P- is the thief of time.* 拖延就是浪费时间。

pro·cras·ti·na·tor [prəuˈkræstineitə] *n.* 拖延者。

pro·cre·ant [ˈprəukriənt] *a.* 生殖的；产生的；多产的。

pro·cre·ate [ˈprəukrieit] *vt.* ①生(儿女)，生殖，生育。②产生(新种等)；制造(谣言等)。— *vi.* 生殖。

pro·cre·a·tion [ˌprəukriˈeiʃən] *n.* 生产，生育；生殖。

pro·cre·a·tive [ˈprəukrieitiv] *a.* 生殖的，有生殖力的；产生的；多产的。

pro·cre·a·tor [ˈprəukrieitə] *n.* 生父；生殖者。

Pro·crus·te·an [prəuˈkrʌstiən] *a.* ①【希神】普罗克拉斯提斯的。②〔喻〕用暴力使人就范的；强求一致的。～ *treatment* 粗暴对待。***the ～ bed*** 强求一致的制度[政策]。

Pro·crus·tes [prəuˈkrʌstiːz] 【希神】普罗克拉斯提斯〔传说中的强盗，常使被劫者卧铁床上，比床长者斩去过长部分，比床短者，强行与床拉齐〕。

pro·cryp·tic [prəuˈkriptik] *a.* 【动】有原隐色的，有保护色的。～ **colour** 原隐色。～ **beetle** 有保护色的甲虫。

procs. = proceedings.

proc·to·dae·um, proc·to·de·um [ˌprɔktəˈdiəm] *n.* *(pl. dae·a* [-ə], *-dae·ums)* 【动】肛道。**-dae·al** *a.*

proc·tol·o·gy [prɔkˈtɔlədʒi] *n.* 【医】直肠病学。**-to·log·ic** [-təˈlɔdʒik], **-to·log·i·cal** *a.* **-to·lo·gist** *n.*

proc·tor [ˈprɔktə] *n.* ①代理人；【法】代诉人；(宗教、海事、离婚、遗嘱等的)王室的讼监。②〔英〕(大学的)学监；监考人。***King's [Queen's] P-*** 王室的讼监〔英国对王室有权监察离婚、遗嘱等案件的官员〕。

proc·to·ri·al [prɔkˈtɔːriəl] *a.* ①讼监的；代理人的；代诉的。②学监的。

proc·tor·ize [ˈprɔktəraiz] *vt.* (学监)处罚(学生)。— *vi.* 执行学监任务。

proc·to·scope [ˈprɔktəskəup] *n.* 直肠镜，肛门镜。**-scop·ic** [-ˈskɔpik] *a.* **-tos·copy** [-ˈtɔskəpi] *n.* 直肠镜观察术。

pro·cum·bent [prəuˈkʌmbənt] *a.* ①平伏的。②【植】爬地的，匍匐的；俯卧的。

pro·cur·a·ble [prəˈkjuərəbl, prɔˈk-] *a.* 可以得到的。

proc·u·ra·cy [ˈprɔkjurəsi] *n.* *(pl. -cies)* ①代理(权)。②代理人职位[任务]。

pro·cur·al [prəˈkjuərəl] *n.* 获得，取得。

pro·cur·ance [prəˈkjuərəns] *n.* ①获得，取得；获得[实现]的手段。②代理。

proc·u·ra·tion [ˌprɔkjuəˈreiʃən] *n.* ①获得，取得。②【法】代理(权)；(对代诉人的)委任；〔罕〕委任状；(寺院等献给巡临主教的)巡视费。③(借款的)介绍费，佣金。④娼妓介绍业。

proc·u·ra·tor [ˈprɔkjuəreitə] *n.* ①【法】代理人；代诉人。②〔古罗马〕地方财政官。*a chief* ～ 检察长。**-ship** *n.* 检察官的职位。**-to·ri·al** [-ˈtɔriəl] *a.* **-to·ry** *a.*

pro·cure [prəˈkjuə] *vt.* ①(努力)取得，获得；实现，达成。②〔古，诗〕招致，引起。③介绍(娼妓)。— *vi.* 介绍娼妓，拉皮条。*His pride ～d his downfall.* 骄傲使他身败名裂。**-ment** *n.* ①取得，获得；达成，成就；获；娼妓介绍。②〔美〕(政府的)征购，采购。

pro·cur·er [prəˈkjuərə] *n.* *(fem. -cur·ess* [ˈkjuəris]*)* ①取得者，获得者。②娼妓介绍人，拉皮条者。

Pro·cy·on [ˈprəusiən] 【天】南河三(小犬座 α)。

prod[1] [prɔd] *n.* ①刺针；锥；竹签；刺棒。②刺，戳。③刺激(物)；促使；推动。*give sb. a sharp ～ on the shoulder* 在某人的肩膀上猛戳一下。*under the ～ of conscience* 在道德心的促使下。***on the ～*** 〔美俚〕大发脾气。— *vt.* ***(prod·ded; prod·ding)*** ①刺戳。②刺激起，惹起，促使，激励；使苦恼。～ *a lazy boy into quick action* 催促一个懒男孩动作快一点。*This thought ～ded me out of bed.* 一想起这一点就促使我从被窝爬了起来。— *vi.* 刺，戳 *(at, into)*。*She ～ded into her memory at his suggestion.* 他一提醒，她就想起来了。

prod[2] [prɔd] *n.* 神童，异人，天才 (= prodigy)。

prod. = produce(d); product.

pro·de·li·sion [ˌprəudiˈliʒən] *n.* 首元音的省略〔如 I am 省作 I'm 等〕。

prod·i·gal [ˈprɔdigəl] *a.* ①非常浪费的，挥霍的，奢侈的。②丰富的；大量的；富于 *(of, with)*。③不吝惜的；十分慷慨的。～ *expenses* 冗费。*the ～ son* 浪子。*be ～ of smiles* 笑声不绝。*May is ～ with flowers* 五月里百花盛开。— *n.* ①浪费者；浪子。②【动】军曹鱼。*play the ～* 挥霍；逛荡。**-ly** *ad.*

prod·i·gal·i·ty [ˌprɔdiˈgæliti] *n.* ①浪费，挥霍；奢侈。②慷慨；豪爽。③丰富，大量。*a man of wonderful ～ of ability* 多才多艺的人。

prod·i·gal·ize [ˈprɔdigəlaiz] *vt.* 浪费，挥霍。

pro·di·gious [prəˈdidʒəs] *a.* ①巨大的，庞大的。②可惊的，奇妙的；非常的，异常的。*a ～ opportunity* 绝好的机会。**-ly** *ad.*

prod·i·gy [ˈprɔdidʒi] *n.* ①奇事，奇迹，怪事；奇物，怪物；奇观，壮观。②非凡的人，奇才，天才；神童，天才儿童；绝代美人。③〔古〕预兆。— *a.* 天才的，非凡的。*an infant [child] ～* 神童。*a ～ violinist* 天才提琴家。*a ～ of learning* 非凡的学者。*a ～ of energy* 精力异常充沛的人。

prod·ro·mal, pro·drom·ic [ˈprɔdrəməl, prəˈdrɔmik] *a.* 前驱病状的。

pro·drome [ˈprəudrəum] *n.* ①【医】前驱症状。②序论；序卷 *(to)*。

pro·duce [prəˈdjuːs] *vt.* ①生，产生；生产；结(果实)。②制造；制(图)；创作；作(诗)；出版(书)。③产生，引起。④拿出，提出(证据等)；展现；出示。⑤演出，上演(戏剧等)；(电影)制片；放映；【数】连结，延长(线)，扩展(面)。*The soil ～s grain.* 这块地出产粮食。*a producing lot* 〔美俚〕电影制片厂。～ *one's railroad ticket* 拿出[出示]车票。～ *a play* 公演戏剧。～ *a war* 引起战争。— *vi.* 生产；创作。*With all his scholarship, he seems unable to ～.* 他学识渊博，但好象没有创作力。— [ˈprɔdjuːs] *n.* ①生产，出产；产额，产量。②物产；产品，农产品；制品，作品。③成果，结果。*the agricultural ～* 农产品。*the ～ of the fields* 农作物。

pro·duced [prəˈdjust] *a.* 引长的，畸形伸长的。

pro·duc·er [prəˈdjuːsə] *n.* ①生产者；制造者 *(opp. consumer)*。②〔英影〕制片人；〔美〕(为演出出资的)演出者；舞台监督；(广播等节目的)安排人；〔美〕戏院老板。③发生器；煤气发生炉。④【讯】振荡器。⑤(油)生产井。

pro·duc·i·ble [prəˈdjuːsəbl] *a.* ①可生产[制造]的。②可上演的。③可提出的。④可延长的。 **pro·duc·i-**

bil·i·ty [prəˌdjuːsəˈbiliti] *n.*

prod·uct [ˈprɔdəkt] *n.* ①产物,产品;制品;产量;出产。②结果,成果。③创作,作品。④【化】生成物;【数】积,乘积。*natural ~s* 天然产物。*agricultural ~s* 农产品。*residual ~* 副产物。*40 is the ~ of 5 and 8.* 40是5和8的积。

pro·duc·tion [prəˈdʌkʃən] *n.* ①生产,产生;【物】(粒子的)生成;制造;(电影的)摄制;(戏剧的)演出;著作。②产品,制品;作品;总产量;成果。③提出,提供,拿出。④【数】延长(线)。⑤大事张罗,小题大做。⑥电影制片。*a means of ~* 生产资料。*full ~* 成批生产。*pre-~* 试生产。*line ~* 流水作业法,连续作业法。*standard ~* 标准产额。*go [be put] into ~* 开始生产。***make a ~ of [out of]*** 对…小题大作;*~* **cost** 生产成本;制片费用。*~* **line** 流水作业线。*~* **quota** 生产指标。

pro·duc·tive [prəˈdʌktiv] *a.* ①生产的,生产性的;有生产力的;多产的。②产生[出产]…的 *(of).* *~ labour* 生产劳动。*~ forces* 生产力。*an age ~ of great men* 伟人辈出的时代。*~ of great annoyance* 会产生巨大麻烦的。*~ soil* 沃土,肥地。*a ~ writer* 多产作家。**-ly** *ad.* **-ness** *n.*

pro·duc·tiv·i·ty [ˌprɔdʌkˈtiviti] *n.* ①多产,丰饶。②生产率;生产能力。*labour ~* 劳动生产率。*raise ~* 提高生产率。

pro·em [ˈprəuem] *n.* 开场白;序言;开端。

pro·en·zyme [prəuˈenzaim] *n.* 酶原 (= zymogen)。

prof [prɔf] *n.* 〔美俚〕 = professor.

Prof. = Professor.

pro·fa·na·tion [ˌprɔfəˈneiʃən] *n.* ①亵渎神圣;玷污;滥用,误用;使用亵渎的言语。②〔*pl.*〕亵渎的言语。

pro·fane [prəˈfein] *a.* ①亵渎神圣的,不敬的;好咒骂的。②(与宗教无关或鄙视宗教)世俗的;粗俗的;污秽的。③异教的,邪教的。④未受秘传的;外行的。*~ language* 亵渎的言语。*the ~ (crowd)* 俗众。*~ persons* 俗人。— *vt.* 亵渎,玷污(神圣);滥用,误用。**-ly** *ad.*

pro·fan·i·ty [prəˈfæniti] *n.* = profanation.

pro·fer·ment [prəuˈfəːmənt] *n.* 【化】前酵素,生酶素。

pro·fess [prəˈfes] *vt.* ①表示,明言,声言,宣布;承认;〔~ oneself〕自称。②假装,佯装。③表明信仰。④以…为业;〔英〕教授(化学等)。*~ oneself to be a poet* 自称是诗人。*~ ignorance* 假装[自称]不知道。*~ language* 教授语文。*~ medicine* 行医。— *vi.* 声言,宣言;表明信仰;承认;〔英口〕(在大学)教书。

pro·fessed [prəˈfest] *a.* ①(无神论者)公然表示自己观点的;公开声称的。②专业的,专门的。③假装的,表面上的,自称的。④已立誓信教的。**-ly** *ad.*

pro·fes·sion [prəˈfeʃən] *n.* ①职业,(特指)知识性专门职业 *(opp.* trade, business*)*。②声明,宣言,(信仰等的)自白,表白;入教宣誓;自认,自称。③〔the ~〕同业,同行;〔俚〕戏剧界同人。④信仰表白,立誓信教。*medical ~* 医疗职业。*He is a doctor by ~.* 他的职业是医生。*Spare me these ~s.* 请别逼我讲这件事吧。***by ~*** 职业是。***in practice if not in ~*** 虽不明讲而实际如此。***the (learned) ~s = the three ~s*** 神学、医学及法学三种职业。***the oldest ~*** 〔谑〕卖淫。**-less** *a.* 没有职业的。

pro·fes·sion·al [prəˈfeʃənəl] *a.* ①职业的,专业的,专职的 *(opp.* amateurish*)*;本职的,专门的。②从事(需要知识修养的)专门职业的;业务上的;同行中的。*a ~ politician* 职业政治家。*a ~ singer* 职业歌唱家。*~ education* 职业教育。*~ skill* 专业技术。*a ~ man* 专家。— *n.* (有知识修养的)专门职业者;职业画家[演员等],职业选手[简称 pro];内行,专家 *(opp.* amateur*)*。*~* **competence** 专长,专业知识;专,才 *(have both political integrity and ~ competence* 德才兼备,又红又专*)*。*~* **etiquette** 同行间遵守的规距。*~* **jealousy** 同行间的妒忌。**-ly** *ad.*

pro·fes·sion·al·ism [prəˈfeʃənəlizəm] *n.* 内行派头,专家气派;职业特性;职业选手气派[身分、特性];职业化。

pro·fes·sion·al·ize [prəˈfeʃənəlaiz] *vt.* (使)职业化;(使)专业化;专门处理;用职业选手参加(比赛)。

pro·fes·sor [prəˈfesə] *n.* ①(大学)教授〔略 Prof.〕;〔美口〕(男性)先生,老师。②〔俚、谑〕(魔术、拳击、跳舞等的)专家。③声明者;自称者;表白信仰者。④〔美俚〕(在酒吧间等处)下等场所弹奏钢琴者。*a ~ emeritus* (退职或退休后的)名誉教授。*a ~ extraordinary* 临时教授。*an assistant ~* 助理教授。*an associate ~* 副教授。*a ~'s chair* 讲座;教授的职位。*He is Professor of History at my university.* 他是我们大学的历史教授。

pro·fes·sor·ate [prəˈfesərit] *n.* ①教授的职务[任期]。②(大学的)全体教授;教授会;教师会 (= professoriate [prɔfiˈsɔːriit])。

pro·fes·so·ri·al [ˌprɔfeˈsɔːriəl] *a.* 教授的;教授似的;学者气的,教条式的。*a ~ lecturer* 教授级讲师。**-ly** *ad.*

pro·fes·so·ri·ate [ˌprɔfeˈsɔːriit] *n.* = professorate.

pro·fes·sor·ship [prəˈfesəʃip] *n.* 教授的职务[地位]。

prof·fer [ˈprɔfə] *vt.* ①提供,贡献;提出。②赠送,奉送。③表示愿意,自告奋勇(做某事)。*~ a gift* 献礼物,送礼。*I ~ to help him.* 我愿意帮助他。— *n.* 建议,提议;贡献;提供物。

pro·fi·cien·cy [prəˈfiʃənsi] *n.* 精通,熟练 *(in).* *~ in music* 擅长音乐。*attain ~ in English* 精通英语。

pro·fi·cient [prəˈfiʃənt] *a.* 熟练的,精通…的 *(at; in).* *be ~ at English* 精通英语。— *n.* 熟练者,能手,老手,专家 *(in).* **-ly** *ad.*

pro·file [ˈprəufail, -fiːl] *n.* ①剖面,半面,(雕像等的)侧面;侧面像。②外形,轮廓;外观,形象;型;【空】翼型,翼(剖)面。③(人物)素描;人物简介;传略;简介,简况。④纵断面图,侧面图;【地】断面;(人)形象。*She has a fine ~. = She is fine in ~.* 她侧面看很美。*low ~* 低姿态(形象)。*draw in ~* 画侧面[轮廓]。*soil ~* 土壤剖面图。— *vt.* ①画…的轮廓。②作…的纵断面图,…的侧面图。③【机】铣出…的轮廓。④为(某人)写传略。

pro·fil·ist [ˈprəufailist, -fiːl-] *n.* 侧面图绘制者;侧面像画家。

pro·fil·o·me·ter [ˌprəufiˈlɔmitə] *n.* 【机】轮廓曲线仪;表面光度仪;纵断面测绘器 (= profilograph)。

prof·it [ˈprɔfit] *n.* ①〔常 *pl.*〕赢余,利润,赚头 *(opp.* loss*)*;利润率。②〔常 *pl.*〕红利。③得益,益处。*gross ~(s)* 总利润,毛利。*clear [net] ~* 纯利润,净利。***at a ~*** 获利,赚钱。***in ~*** 〔英方,澳〕(乳牛)在产乳期。***make a ~ on*** 在…上头赚钱。***make one's ~ of*** 利用,使对自己有利。***reap ~s at the expense of others*** 损人利己。***small ~s and quick returns*** 薄利多销。***to one's ~ = with ~*** 有益。— *vt.* 有利于,有益于。*What will it ~ me?* 对我有什么好处呢? — *vi.* 得益;获利,赚钱;利用 *(by; from; of)*;有用。*You may ~ by the experience of others.* 你可以吸取别人的经验教训。*I ~ed by his confusion to make my escape.* 我趁他忙乱的时候逃走了。*~* **and loss**【统】损益。*~* **and loss account** 损益帐。*~***-and-loss** *a.* 损益的 (*~*-and-loss statement 损益计算书)。*~***-hungry** *a.* 贪求利润的。*~* **margin** 利润率。*~* **sharing** 分红制。*~* **taking** (买空卖空)获利了结;(有利可图的)抛售。

prof·i·ta·ble [ˈprɔfitəbl] *a.* ①有益的;有用的。②有利可图的,可赚钱的,合算的。**-it·a·bil·ty** [ˌprɔfitəˈbility] *n.* **-ness** *n.* **-bly** *ad.*

prof·i·teer [ˌprɔfiˈtiə] *n.* (尤指战时的)奸商,发横财的人,暴发户;(生活必需品的)投机商人。— *vi.* 取得不正当的利益,牟取暴利。*profiteering merchants* 奸商。**-ing** *n.* 不当利得,投机活动。

prof·it·less [ˈprɔfitlis] *a.* ①无利的;无利可图的。②无益的,无用的。**-ness** *n.* **-ly** *ad.*

prof·li·ga·cy [ˈprɔfligəsi] *n.* ①放荡;堕落;荒淫。②极度的浪费;恣意的挥霍。

prof·li·gate [ˈprɔfligit] *a.* ①放荡的;堕落的;荒淫的。②

极度浪费的. — *n.* ①放荡的人,浪子. ②恣意挥霍的人.

prof·lu·ent [ˈprɔfluənt] *a.* 词藻丰富文体流畅的; 流利的,流畅的.

pro for·ma [prəuˈfɔːmə] 〔L.〕 形式上.

pro·found [prəˈfaund] *a.* ①(渊等)深. ②(哲理、诗等)深奥的; (意义等)深远的,意味深长的. ③学识渊博的,造诣深的; 深谋远虑的. ④(兴趣等)深厚的; 深刻的; 深切的; 深深的; 极度的,(注意等)充分的; 来自心底的. ⑤谦恭的,谦卑的. *a* ~ *sleep* 熟睡. *a* ~ *scholar* 渊博的学者. *a* ~ *statesman* 深谋远虑的政治家. ~ *sympathy* 深厚的同情. *a* ~ *bow* 深深一躬. ***make a* ~ *curtesy [reverence]*** 恭恭敬敬地打招呼〔行礼〕. ***take a* ~ *interest*** 感到很大的兴趣; 十分关切. — *n.* 〔诗〕〔*the* ~〕深海,大洋; 深渊; (灵魂)深处. **-ly** *ad.* 深深地; 深奥地; 恳切地; 郑重地 (*a* ~*ly scientific attitude* 高度科学的态度).

Prof. Reg. = Regius Professor.

pro·fun·di·ty [prəˈfʌnditi] *n.* ①深,深度; 深处; 〔诗〕深渊. ②深奥; 深刻; 深厚. ③〔常 *pl.*〕深奥的事物; 深刻的思想; 意义深刻的话.

pro·fuse [prəˈfjuːs] *a.* ***(-fus·er; -fus·est)*** ①大方的,豪爽的,十分慷慨的. ②奢侈的,挥霍的,浪费的 ***(in; of)***. ③很多的; 充沛的; 过多的; 极其丰富的. *He was* ~ *in thanks.* 他谢了又谢. ~ *hospitality* 丰盛的款待. **-ly** *ad.* **-ness** *n.*

pro·fu·sion [prəˈfjuːʒən] *n.* ①大量,充沛,丰富. ②豪爽,慷慨,大方. ③浪费,挥霍,奢侈. ***a* ~ *of*** 很多的,大量的. ***in*** ~丰富地,大量地.

prog[1] [prɔg] *n.* 〔俚〕搜寻、偷窃或乞讨来的食物. — *vi.* ①搜寻、偷窃或乞讨食物. ②伺机偷窃.

prog[2] [prɔg] *n.* 〔英〕(大学的)学监. — *vi.* 行使学监的职权,处罚(学生).

pro·gen·i·tive [prəuˈdʒenitiv] *a.* 繁殖的; 有生殖力的.

pro·gen·i·tor [prəˈdʒenitə] *n.* ①(人及动植物的)祖先; 先驱; 前辈. ②(抄本的)原书; 【物】原(始)粒子.

pro·gen·i·tress [prəuˈdʒenitris], **pro·gen·i·trix** [prəuˈdʒenitriks] *n.* (动植物的)雌性祖先; (人的)女性始祖〔先驱,先辈〕.

prog·e·ny [ˈprɔdʒini] *n.* ①子孙,后代. ②成果,结果. ③【物】次级粒子.

pro·ges·ta·tion·al [ˌprəudʒesˈteiʃənl] *a.* 【化】孕酮的,孕激素的.

pro·ges·ter·one [prəuˈdʒestərəun] *n.* 【化】孕(甾)酮,孕激素; 黄体酮〔激素〕.

pro·ges·tin [prəuˈdʒestin] *n.* 孕激素; 黄体制剂; 孕(甾)酮.

prog·gins [ˈprɔginz] *n.* 〔俚〕= prog[2].

pro·glot·tid [prəuˈglɔtid] *n.* 【动】节片.

pro·glot·tis [prəuˈglɔtis] *n.* ***(pl. -tides*** [tidiːz]***)*** (绦虫的)节片.

prog·nath·ic, prog·na·thous [prɔgˈnæθik, prɔgˈneiθəs] *a.* ①突颚的,下巴突出的. ②【动】(昆虫)前口式的. **-thism** *n.* 【解】突颚.

prog·no·sis [prɔgˈnəusis] *n.* ***(pl. -ses*** [-siːz]***)*** ①预测. ②【医】预后,判病结局 ***(opp.*** diagnosis***)***.

prog·nos·tic [prɔgˈnɔstik] *a.* ①预兆的,预示…的*(of)*. ②【医】预后的,(症状)预示后果的. *be* ~ *of failure* 预示失败. — *n.* ①征兆,前兆. ②预测,预知. ③【医】预后症状.

prog·nos·ti·cate [prəgˈnɔstikeit] *vt., vi.* ①由前兆〔症状〕预知,预言,预测. ②预示; 预兆,有…的兆头. **-ca·tion** *n.* ①预言,预测. ②前兆; 症状. **-ca·tor** *n.* 预言者,预测者.

prog·nos·ti·ca·tive [ˌprɔgˈnɔstikeitiv] *a.* 预知的; 能预知…的 *(of)*. ~ *of a dream* 预知未来的梦. *The solar eclipse was thought* ~ *of the fall of the country.* 日蚀过去被认为是国家灭亡的预兆.

pro·gram·mat·ic [ˌprəugrəˈmætik] *a.* ①有纲领的,纲领性的. ②标题音乐的. ③计划性的.

pro·gramme, 〔美〕 **pro·gram** [ˈprəugræm] *n.* ①程序表; 节目单,说明书; (演出)节目; 要目,大纲. ②〔英〕(政党的)纲领,方案. ③规划,计划,打算. ④工作进度表,课程表; 〔美〕时间表. ⑤【自】程序〔用 program〕. ⑥序,绪言. ⑦〔古〕公告,布告. *a theatre [broadcasting, television]* ~ 一个演出〔广播,电视〕节目. *a live* ~ 【电视】实况广播〔电视〕,室内广播节目. *an outdoor* ~ 室外广播节目. *a common* ~ 共同纲领. *What is the* ~ *for today?* 今天有些什么活动? *a television [broadcasting]* ~ 电视〔广播〕节目. *What's on the* ~*?* 有些什么节目? ***a full*** ~ 忙得团团转的工作〔约会(等)〕. ***draw up a* ~ *of work*** 拟定课程表〔工作进度表〕. ***put in the*** ~ 排入节目里. — *vt.* 〔罕〕制定(进度表),排(节目); 拟(计划); 【自】为…编制程序; 使按程序工作. *linear programming* 线性规划. *program(m)ed instruction* 循序渐进的教学(法). *program(m)ed learning* 利用有习题解答的教科书进行的自学; (按书本规定或计算机安排)循序渐进的自学. ~ **girl** 卖戏剧节目单的女子. ~ **music** 标题音乐. ~ **picture** 【影】加映副片; 普通作品.

pro·gram·mer [ˈprəugræmə] *n.* 〔美〕 ①节目编排者; 订计划者. ②【自】程序设计员; 程序设计器.

pro·gress [ˈprəugres] *n.* ①前进,进行. ②上进,进步; 进度; 进展,增长,发展; 经过; 【生】发育,进化. ③〔古〕(特指王侯的)视察,巡行,游历. *the* ~ *of mankind* 人类的进步. ~ *in [of] knowledge* 知识的进步. *the* ~ *of events* 事件的经过. ***in*** ~ 进行中,还没有完的. ***make*** ~ ①进行,前进. ②进步,进展 (*make no* ~ *in one's studies* 研究没有进展). — [prəˈgres] *vi.* 前进,进行; 进步; 发达 *(in)*. ~ *in one's health* 健康在好转. *We are* ~*ing fairly with the work.* 我们正在顺利地进行着工作.

pro·gres·sion [prəˈgreʃən] *n.* ①前进, 进行. ②〔罕〕进步,改进,发展; 进展状态. ③【数】级数; 【乐】(乐音或和弦的)相继进行; (各声部的)和谐进行. *arithmetical* ~ 【数】等差级数,算术级数. *geometrical* ~ 【数】等比级数,几何级数. *in geometrical* ~ 按几何级数,加速度地. ***in*** ~ 连续,相继. ***mode of*** ~ 步法,游法. **-al** *a.*

pro·gres·sion·ist, pro·gress·ist [prəˈgreʃənist, -ˈgresist] *n.* 提倡进步者; 进化论者; 进步党派成员; 革新主义者; 改良主义者.

pro·gres·sive [prəˈgresiv] *a.* ①前进的; 渐进的,发展的; 递增的,累进的. ②进步的,上进的,进取的,改进的; 进步主义的,进步党的. ③【医】进行性的. ④【语法】进行(时)的. ~ *elements* 进步人士. ~ *methods* 新方法. — *n.* 进步分子,进步人士,进步论者; 革新主义者; 改良主义者; 〔P-〕进步党党员. ~ **assimilation** 【语音】顺行同化. ~ **form** (时态之)进行式. ~**-jazz** 渐进式爵士乐〔流行于本世纪五十年代〕. ~ **rate** 累进税率. ~ **taxation** 累进税制. ~ **wave** 【无】行波. **-ly** *ad.* **-ness** *n.*

pro·gres·siv·ism [prəˈgresivizəm] *n.* ①进步人士的政见. ②顺序渐进的教育理论. ③〔P-〕进步党的主义.

pro·hi [ˈprəui] = 〔美〕 prohibition.

pro·hib·it [prəˈhibit] *vt.* 不准许,禁止; 阻止,防止. ~*ed articles [goods]* 违禁品. ~*ed degrees* 同血缘而禁止通婚的. *It was* ~*ed on pain of death.* 违者处死. *P- him from coming [his coming].* 别让他来. *Smoking strictly* ~*ed.* 严禁吸烟. **-er,** 〔美〕 **-or** *n.* 禁止者; 阻止者.

pro·hi·bi·tion [ˌprəuiˈbiʃən, ˌprəuhi-] *n.* ①禁止; 禁令. ②【法】(上级法院禁止下级法院对无权审理的案件起诉的)诉讼中止令. ③〔美〕禁酒; 〔p-〕【美史】禁酒时期. ~ **law** 〔美〕禁酒法. **P- Party** 〔美〕禁酒党. ~ **state** 〔美〕禁酒州. **-ism** *n.* 禁酒主义; 〔美〕保护贸易主义. **-ist** *n.* 禁酒主义者; 〔P-〕〔美〕禁酒党党员; 保护贸易论者.

pro·hib·i·tive [prəˈhibitiv, prəu-] *a.* ①禁止的; 禁止

性的；抑制性的。②(价格)非常高的。*a ~ tax* 寓禁税。*~ inhibition* 超限抑制。*a ~ price* 高得使人不敢买的价格。

pro·hib·i·to·ry [prəˈhibitəri, prəu-] *a.* = prohibitive.

pro·ject [prəˈdʒekt] *vt.* ①投掷，抛出；发射(炮弹等)；喷射。②使突出，使凸出。③设计，规划，计划，打算，筹划。④投影；于…上映。⑤【数】作…的投影图；把…画成投影状。⑥表明…的特点；生动地表演。⑦【心】使(思想、感情)形象化〔具体化〕。⑧【化】投入 *(into; on)*. *~ motion pictures on the screen* 放电影。*~ the rebuilding of a street* 计划改造街道。*~ oneself* 突出自己；使自己显得象…*(as)*；设想自己处于 *(into)*. *a ~ed route* 预定路线。*a ~ed area* 投射面积。— *vi.* 突出，伸出。*The upper storey ~s over the street.* 二楼伸出街上。— [ˈprɔdʒekt] *n.* ①规划，方案，计划，设计。②科研[建设]项目；课外自修项目。③工程；事业，企业。*irrigation ~s* 灌溉工程。*build irrigation ~s* 兴修水利工程。*water conservancy ~s* 水利工程。*abovenorm construction ~s* 限额以上的建设项目。*the ~ method* (要求学生独立思考的)构想教授法。*a ~ engineer* 设计工程师。*a hare-brained ~* 轻率的想法。

pro·jec·tile [ˈprɔdʒektail, prəˈdʒek-] *n.* ①抛射体。②射弹。③导弹，飞弹，火箭。*an atomic ~* 原子炮弹；轰击原子粒子。*a nuclear ~* 核弹头导弹。*a cosmic ~* 宇宙射线粒子。*a rocket ~* 喷气火箭；火箭弹。— [prəˈdʒektail] *a.* ①抛射的，发射的；射弹的。②可抛射的；推进的。③【动】(触角等)能伸出的。*~ force* 推进力。

pro·ject·ing [prəˈdʒektiŋ] *a.* 突出的，凸出的。*a ~ eye* 凸眼。*a ~ tooth* 暴牙。

pro·jec·tion [prəˈdʒekʃən] *n.* ①射出，投掷，发射，喷射。②投射；投影，投影法；(地图)投影图制法；【影】放映。③凸出；凸出部；凸出物。④设计，规划，计划。⑤(根据已知资料或观察所作的)预测，推测，估计。⑥【心】投射；(思想等的)形象化，具体化。⑦【心】想象。⑧【冶】金属的孏变。*central [perspective] ~* 透视投影。*orthogonal [oblique] ~* 正[斜]投影。*a ~ booth [room]* 〔美〕放映室。*a ~ machine* 放映机。*a ~ lantern* 幻灯，映画器。*the ~ of the lower lip* 下唇凸出。**-ist** *n.* ①制投影图的人；地图绘制者。②电影[幻灯]放映员；电视播放员。

pro·jec·tive [prəˈdʒektiv] *a.* ①投影的，射影的。②凸出的，突出的。③【心】投射的。*the ~ power of the mind* 想象力。*~* **geometry** 投影几何。

pro·jec·tor [prəˈdʒektə] *n.* ①设计者，规划人，计划者。②投机公司的发起人，骗子。③投射器，发射装置。④探照灯；幻灯；放映机。⑤放映技师。⑥(制图)投射线。*a flame ~* 【军】喷火器。*a microfilm ~* 缩微胶片放大器。*a supersound ~* 大功率扬声器。

pro·jet [proˈʒei] *n.* 〔F.〕①设计，计划。②(条约或法律的)草案。

prol. = prologue.

pro·lac·tin [prəuˈlæktin] *n.* 【生化】催乳激素。

pro·la·mine [ˈprəuləmiːn, -min; prəuˈlæmin] *n.* 【化】醇溶朊。**-la·min** [-min].

pro·lan [ˈprəulæn] *n.* 【药】绒膜促性腺激素。

pro·lapse [ˈprəulæps] *n.* 【医】= prolapsus. — *vi.* 【医】脱出，脱垂。

pro·lap sus [prəuˈlæpsəs] *n.* 〔L.〕【医】脱肛，(子宫的)脱出，脱垂，下垂。

pro·late [ˈprəuleit] *a.* ①【数】扁长的；延长的；长球形的 *(opp.* oblate*)*. ②扩大的，扩展的。③【语法】=prolative.

pro·la·tive [prəuˈleitiv] *a.* 【语法】补足谓语的，表述性的。*the ~ infinitive* 表述性不定式〔如 He must go, willing to go 的 go, to go〕.

prole [prəul] *a., n.* 〔主英口〕无产阶级的，无产阶级(= proletarian).

pro·leg [ˈprəuleg] *n.* 【动】腹足；原足。

pro·le·gom·e·non [ˌprəuləˈgɔminən] *n.* *(pl. -na* [-nə]*)* 〔常 *pl.*〕序，序言，绪论 *(to)*. **-gom·e·nous** *a.* 序的，绪言的；有长序的，绪言冗长的。

pro·lep·sis [prəuˈlepsis, -ˈliːp-] *n.* *(pl. -lep·ses* [-ˈlepsiːz]*)* ①【修】预辩法。②【语法】预期的叙述；预期描写法。③【哲】感觉概念。④预期；早记日期。

pro·lep·tic [prəuˈleptik, -ˈliːp-] *a.* ①预想的。②预辩的，预驳的。③【语法】预期叙述法的；(形容词)预期描写法的。④【医】提早发作的；早发的。

pro·les [ˈprəuliːz] *n.* 〔集合词〕*pl.* 〔L.〕子孙，后代。

pro·le·taire [ˌprəuleˈtɛə] *n.* = proletarian.

pro·le·tar·i·an [ˌprəuleˈtɛəriən] *n., a.* 无产阶级(的) *(opp.* bourgeoisie*)*；无产者(的)。*~ dictatorship* 无产阶级专政。**-ism** *n.* 无产阶级性；无产者的地位。

pro·le·tar·i·an·ize [ˌprəuliˈtɛəriənaiz] *vt.* *(-iz·ed; -iz·ing)* 使无产阶级化；作为无产阶级对待。**-za·tion** [-ˈzeiʃən] *n.* 无产阶级化。

pro·le·tar·i·at(e) [ˌprəuleˈtɛəriət] *n.* 无产阶级 *(opp.* bourgeoisie*)*；【罗马史】最下层阶级。*the dictatorship of the ~* 无产阶级专政。*the blackcoated ~* 劳动知识分子。

pro·le·ta·ry [ˈprəulitəri] *n., a.* 〔罕〕【史】(古罗马)最下层阶级的公民(的)。

pro·let·cult, pro·let·kult [prəuˈletkʌlt] *n.* 无产阶级文化；无产阶级文化运动。

pro·li·cide [ˈprəulisaid] *n.* 杀害胎儿〔婴儿〕. **-cid·al** [-ˈsaidl] *a.*

pro·lif·er·ate [prəuˈlifəreit] *vi.* ①【生】分芽繁殖，细胞分裂繁殖；增殖；增生；多育。②激增；扩散。— *vt.* 使激增；使扩散。*~ nuclear weapons* 扩散核武器。**-a·tion** [prəuˌlifəˈreiʃən] **-a·tive** *a.*

pro·lif·er·ous [prəuˈlifərəs] *a.* 【植】分芽繁殖的；【动】(珊瑚等的)分枝繁殖的；【医】增生性的；扩散性的；增生的，多育的。

pro·lif·ic [prəˈlifik] *a.* ①多育的，结果实的；有生产力的；富于创造力的；多产…的 *(of)*. ②肥沃的；丰富的；富于…的 *(in)* *a family ~ of children* 多子女的家庭。*a ~ writer* 多产作家。*an age ~ in great poets* 大诗人辈出的时代。**-i·cal·ly** *ad.* **-ness** *n.*

pro·lin(e) [ˈprəuliːn] *n.* 【化】脯氨酸，氮戊氨酸。

pro·lix [ˈprəuliks, prəuˈliks] *a.* 冗长的，罗唆的。**-lix·i·ty** *n.* 冗长，罗唆。

pro·loc·u·tor [prəuˈlɔkjutə] *n.* ①代言人，发言人。②(尤指宗教会议的)议长，主席。

pro·log [ˈprəulɔg] *n., v.* = prologue.

pro·log·ize [ˈprəulɔdʒaiz] = prologuize.

pro·logue [ˈprəulɔg] *n.* ①序，序诗；(戏剧的)开场白；序幕 *(opp.* epilogue*)*. ②序幕性事件 *(to)*. — *vt.* ①作…的序；为…加上序诗；作(戏剧等的)开场白。②成了…的开端。

pro·logu·ize [ˈprəulɔgaiz] *vi.* 作序；作序诗；作开场白。

pro·long [prəˈlɔŋ] *vt.* ①延长；拉长，拖长；引伸。②将(元音等)拉长发音。③拖延，延期。*~ one's life* 延长寿命。

pro·lon·gate [prəuˈlɔŋgeit] *vt.* 延长；拉长；拖延 (= prolong).

pro·lon·ga·tion [ˌprəulɔŋˈgeiʃən] *n.* ①延长；延期。②(发音的)拉长，拖长。③延长部分。

pro·longe [prəuˈlɔndʒ] *n.* 【军】(拉炮用带钩的)缆绳。

pro·lu·sion [prəuˈljuːʒən] *n.* ①序幕，序乐；绪论，绪言。②预演；预习；试讲。**-lu·so·ry** [-ˈluːsəri] *a.*

prom [prɔm] *n.* ①〔英口〕= promenade concert. ②〔美〕(大学的)跳舞会。*a ~ trotter* 〔美〕经常参加舞会的学生。

prom. = promenade; promontory.

prom·e·nade [ˌprɔmiˈnɑːd] *n.* ①散步，(骑马)闲逛，(开车)兜风。②(特指骑马或乘车的)队伍。③散步场所；散步甲板。④〔美〕(大学的)跳舞会〔略 prom〕. ⑤(正式舞会开始前全体参加者的)列队绕场(礼)。— *vi.* ①

散步；运动. ②(骑马，开车)兜风. ③(舞会中)列队(绕场)行进. — *vt.* ①在…散步. ②炫耀地带领着人散步[兜风]. ~ *about* 炫耀地游逛. ~ *the street* 逛街,逛马路. ~ **concert** (部分听众可一面散步一面听的) 逍遥音乐会. ~ **deck** 散步甲板. **-r** *n.*

Pro·me·the·an [prəˈmiːθiən] *a.* ①(象) 普罗米修斯 (Prometheus) 的. ②赋与生命的；有创造力的；勇于创新的.

Pro·me·theus [prəˈmiːθjuːs] *n.* 【希神】普罗米修斯〔因盗取天火给世人而被宙斯神锁在山崖上,每日遭神鹰啄食肝脏,夜间伤口愈合,天明神鹰复来,但他始终坚毅不屈〕.

pro·me·thi·um [prəˈmiːθiəm]【化】钷〔略 Pm；旧名 illinium 钔〕.

prom·i·nence, -cy [ˈprɔminəns, -si] *n.* ①突起；凸出. ②凸出物；突出的部分[地方]. ③显著，杰出，卓越；著名. ④【天】日珥. *give* ~ *to* 重视,突出.

prom·i·nent [ˈprɔminənt] *a.* ①突起的；(眼、牙等)凸出的. ②突出的；显著的；杰出的，卓越的；显眼的. ③重要的；著名的. ~ *eyes* 凸眼. ~ *teeth* 暴牙，虎牙. *a* ~ *paunch* 罗汉肚. *a* ~ *figure* 知名人士. *a* ~ *politician* 杰出的政治家. **-ly** *ad.*

prom·is·cu·i·ty [ˌprɔmisˈkjuːiti] *n.* ①混杂 (性)，混乱,混淆. ②(男女)乱交.

pro·mis·cu·ous [prəˈmiskjuəs] *a.* ①杂乱的，混杂的. ②不加区别的；不分男女的；男女乱交的. ③〔口谑〕偶然的，没有目的的. ~ *bathing* 男女混浴. ~ *sexual relations* 乱交. ~ *hospitality* 不加区别的款待. ***at a*** ~ ***manner*** 胡乱,不分青红皂白地. ***take a*** ~ ***stroll*** 漫步,没有目的地散步. **~-like** *ad.*〔谑〕偶然. **-ly** *ad. (I dropped in ~ly.* 我是随便来串门子的).

prom·ise [ˈprɔmis] *n.* ①允许,诺言；约束,字据；约定事项；允诺的东西. ②(前途有)希望；(有)指望. *an express* ~ 订明的契约. *an implied* ~ 默契. *I claim your* ~. 请把允诺的东西给我吧. *writers of* ~ 有前途[希望]的作家 (*cf.* sterile). *There is every* ~ *of success.* 大有成功的希望. ***the Land of P-***【圣】上帝许给亚伯拉罕的地方〔即迦南〕；福地；想望之乡. ***the P-*** 上帝给亚伯拉罕的允诺. ***afford*** ~ ***of*** (使)有…的希望. ***break a (one's)*** ~ 不守诺言；违约. ***give [show]*** ~ ***of*** 有…的希望，使抱有…的希望. ***keep a (one's)*** ~ 遵守诺言，践约. ***make a*** ~ 约定；许诺. ***put (sb.) off with fair*** ~ 哄开，骗人走开. — *vt.* ①约，约定，订约；约好给，许给；允诺，答应. ②有…的希望；给人以…的指望. ③〔只用于第一人称〕断定，保证. ④〔~ oneself〕指望；指望获得；确信会有. ~ *sb. sth.* 许给某人某物. *I* ~ *you, it will not be so easy.* 包你不会那么容易. *These discussions* ~ *future storm.* 这些争论有引起未来风波的危险. — *vi.* ①允诺；作出保证；②有希望，有指望，有前途. *It is one thing to* ~ *and another to perform.* 约是约做是做. ~ *well* 前途有希望；(庄稼)有丰收希望. ***be ~d to*** 许配给，给…做未婚妻. ***the Promised Land*** = ***the Land of*** ~.

prom·is·ee [ˌprɔmiˈsiː] *n.*【法】受约人.

prom·is·er [ˈprɔmisə] *n.* 作出诺言的人.

prom·is·ing [ˈprɔmisiŋ] *a.* 有出息的；有前途的；有希望的；有指望的. *a* ~ *youth* 有希望的青年. *a* ~ *future* 远大的前途. *a* ~ *sky* 十拿九稳的晴天. *They are intelligent and* ~. 他们聪明有为. ***in a*** ~ ***state [way]*** ①有希望的. ②(病人)在开始复元中. ③〔口〕有孕，有喜.

prom·i·sor [ˈprɔmisə, ˌprɔmiˈsɔː] *n.*【法】立约人，订约者.

prom·is·so·ry [ˈprɔmisəri] *a.* 表示允诺的；约定的；【商】约定支付的. ~ **note**【商】期票；本票.

prom·on·to·ried [ˈprɔməntərid] *a.* 形成海角的；有海角的,有岬的.

prom·on·to·ry [ˈprɔməntəri] *n.* ①海角，岬. ②【解】隆突,荐骨岬.

pro·mor·phol·o·gy [ˌprəumɔːˈfɔlədʒi] *n.* 【生】原形学.

pro·mote [prəˈməut] *vt.* ①增进；提倡，发扬，助长，促进；振兴，奖励；引起. ②提升，使升级，使晋级，提拔. ③发起，创立(企业等)；〔美〕筹划(不正当事业). ④努力使(议案)通过. ⑤宣传，推广(商品等). ⑥〔美俚〕(用不正当手段)获得. ⑦(象棋) 使升格〔如小卒变为女王〕. ~ *digestion* 促进消化. ~ *sb. captain* 提升某人作上尉. *be ~ed to the next grade* 升到下年级. *Milk ~s health.* 牛奶有益于健康.

pro·mot·er [prəˈməutə] *n.* ①增进者，助长者；振兴者，奖励者；后援人；(通常指恶意的)煽动者. ②(企业等)发起人；推销者. ③【化】促进剂，助催化剂. ④(宗教裁判的)起诉人. *~s of progress* 促进派. *a company-~* 投机性公司发起人.

pro·mo·tion [prəˈməuʃən] *n.* ①增进，促进；助长；发扬；振兴，奖励. ②提升；升级. ③(企业等的)发起；举办. ④(商品等的)宣传，推广. ⑤(推销中的)产品. ~ *of disorder* 引起混乱. ~ *expenses*【商】开办费. ~ *shares* 发起人股份. *a* ~ *worker* 推销员. *This electric toothbrush is our latest promotion.* 这种电牙刷是敝公司的最新产品. ***be on one's*** ~ 有缺即可提升的；为了提升而表现自己. ***get [obtain]*** ~ 升级.

pro·mo·tive [prəˈməutiv] *a.* ①促进性的；增进的，助长的，奖励的. ②提升的. ③发起的；创立的. ④宣传的，推广的.

prompt [prɔmpt] *a.* ①敏捷的，迅速的；即刻的，(回答等)及时的. ②【商】即期付款的. *(come to) a* ~ *decision* (作出)迅速的决定. *be* ~ *to obey [carry out an order]* 即刻服从[执行] 命令. ~ *cash payment*【商】即期付现. — *n.* 刺激物；(给演员的)提示，提词；【商】(期货的)付款日期，交割日期. — *vt.* ①刺激，鼓励，怂恿，煽动，唆使，挑拨. ②激起，唤起(思想感情等). ③提醒，指点；给(演员)提词. *~ed by instinct [necessity]* 为本能[需要]所驱使. — *ad.* 准时地，正好. *at seven o'clock* ~ 在七时正. ~**book**【剧】提词用的剧本. ~ **box**【剧】提词人藏身处. ~ **day**【商】交割日. ~ **delivery**【商】即交，即送. ~ **note**【商】期货金额及交割日期通知单. ~ **sale**【商】期货交易. ~ **side** 提白员所在的方面，〔英〕舞台上演员的左方；〔美〕演员的右方. **-ly** *ad.* **-ness** *n.*

prompt·er [ˈprɔmptə] *n.* ①激励者，鼓舞者；唤起者. ②【剧】(台词的)提白员，提词员.

prompt·ing [ˈprɔmptiŋ] *n.* ①刺激，鼓励；煽动；唤起；驱使. ②暗示，提示，提词. *the ~s of conscience* 良心的驱使. *under the ~s of sb. [sth.]* 在某人[某事]的激励下.

prompt·i·tude [ˈprɔmptitjuːd] *n.* 敏捷，迅速，机敏；果断. *with great* ~ 极其敏捷地. *Their own* ~ *in retreating at the critical moment saved them.* 他们自己在危急的时刻迅速退却，这才得以避免被歼灭.

prom·ul·gate [ˈprɔməlgeit] *vt.* ①颁布，公布(法令等). ②传播；宣传；发表. **-ga·tion** [ˌprɔməlˈgeiʃən] *n.* **-ga·tor** *n.*

pro·mulge [prəuˈmʌldʒ] *vt.*〔古〕= promulgate.

pro·my·ce·li·um [ˌprəumaiˈsiːliəm] *n. (pl.* **-li·a** [-ə]*)*【植】先菌丝.

pron. = pronominal; pronoun; pronounced; pronunciation.

pro·na·tal·ist [prəuˈneitəlist] *a.* 鼓励提高人口出生率的；鼓励生育的.

pro·nate [ˈprəuneit] *vt. (-nat·ed;-nat·ing)*①使(手、前肢)翻转向下，旋前；内转. ②使俯，使伏. — *vi.* 俯，伏.

pro·na·tion [prəuˈneiʃən] *n.*【生理】(手的) 旋前(作用)，内转(作用) *(opp.* supination*)*.

pro·na·tor [prəˈneitə] *n.*【解】旋前肌.

prone [prəun] *a.* ①俯伏的；平伏的 *(opp.* erect, supine*)*;

向前弯曲的. ②有…癖的, 易…的, 有…倾向的; 易害…的*(to)*. ③倾斜的, 坡陡的. *lie* ~ 平伏. *fall* ~ 向前跌倒. *a* ~ *surface* 下面. *be* ~ *to anger* 动辄发怒. *be* ~ *to think that* 总认为. ***be less*** ~ ***to*** 不致老是…. ***be*** ~ ***to err*** 易犯过失. ~ **bombing** 俯冲轰炸. ~ **position**【军】卧倒姿势. ~ **pressure method** 俯伏人工呼吸法. **-ly** *ad.*

prone·ness [ˈprəunis] *n.* ①俯伏; 屈, 前屈, 下屈. ②倾向, 脾性, 嗜好.

pro·neph·ros [ˈprəuˈnefrɔs] *n.*【动】前肾. **-neph·ric** *a.*

prong [prɔŋ] *n.* ①尖头; 尖头物; 叉(齿), 股. ②干草叉; (麋鹿的)角. ③【物】射线(径迹); (真空管的)插脚. — *vt.* ①刺; 掘翻(泥土等); 用耙耙. ②给…装上尖头[叉齿等].

pronged [prɔŋd] *a.* 有尖的, 有叉的.

prong·horn [ˈprɔŋhɔːn] *n.* *(pl.* ~*(s))*【动】(美国产)叉角羚.

pro·no·grade [ˈprəunəgreid] *a.* 爬行的, 匍行的.

pronom. = pronominal.

pro·nom·i·nal [prəˈnɔminl, prəu-] *a.*【语法】代(名)词的; 代(名)词性的. ~ **adjective** 代名形容词〔指一个由代名词变成的形容词, 如 my, her 等, 或指有时用作代词有时用作形容词者, 如 each, this 等〕. **-ly** *ad.*

pro·non·ce [prəunɔnˈsei] *a.*〔F.〕显著的; 显眼的; 夸张的.

pro·noun [ˈprəunaun] *n.*【语法】代(名)词. *a personal* ~ 人称代词. *a reflexive* ~ 反身代词〔myself 等〕.

pro·nounce [prəˈnauns] *vt.* ①发音. ②宣判, 宣告(刑罚、赦免等); 演讲, 讲述. ③断言, 断定 *(on; upon)*. *The patient was* ~*d out of danger.* 病人已告脱险. ~ ***a curse (up)on*** 诅咒. ~ ***sentence of death (up)on*** … 宣判…死刑. — *vi.* ①发音. ②发表意见; 作出判断; 表态 *(on)*. *a word difficult to* ~ 发音难的词. ~ *against* 对…表明反对意见. ~ *for* = ~ *in favour of* 表明赞成意见.

pro·nounce·a·ble [prəˈnaunsəbəl] *a.* 可发音的; 读得出的.

pro·nounced [prəˈnaunst] *a.* 决然的, 断然的, 强硬的; 明白的, 显著的. ~ *opinions* 强硬的意见. *a* ~ *improvement* 显著改进. **-ly** *ad.*

pro·nounce·ment [prəˈnaunsmənt] *n.* ①宣告; 表示. ②声明, 公告; 决定, 判决. ~*s on the matter* 对有关问题的表态意见.

pro·nounc·ing [prəˈnaunsiŋ] *a.* 发音的; 表示发音的. *a* ~ *dictionary* 发音词典, 正音词典.

pron·to [ˈprɔntəu] *ad.*〔美俚〕立刻, 马上; 很快地. *They told him to get out of there and* ~. 他们通知他离开那里而且要马上离开. *I thought that you'd be along pretty* ~. 我原来以为你会很快就来的.

pro·nu·cle·us [prəuˈnjuːkliəs, -ˈnuː-] *n.* *(pl.* **-cle·i** [-ai]*)*【动】原核. **-cle·ar** *a.*

pro·nun·ci·a·m(i)en·to [prəˌnʌnsiəˈmentəu] *n.* *(pl.* ~*(e)s)* 宣言(尤指西班牙语国家起义者的宣言); 檄文; 声明; 公告.

pro·nun·ci·a·tion [prəˌnʌnsiˈeiʃən] *n.* 发音(法). *The tongue is one of the organs for* ~. 舌是发音器官之一. *He has a good* ~. 他的发音很好. *An introduction to the* ~ *of American English* 美国英语发音法入门.

proof [pruːf] *n.* ①证明; 证据;【法】证件;【法】(口头或书面)证词, 证言. ②检验, 考验; 验算; 检定的品质[强度等]. ③试管. ④【印】校样, 印样. ⑤(酒精的)标准强度. ⑥(甲胄等的)耐力, 坚牢程度, 不贯穿性. ⑦【摄】样片; 样张. ⑧〔Scot.〕审问. ⑨【数】证, 证明, 证法. *The* ~ *of the pudding is in the eating.* 布丁好坏一吃即知; 空谈不如实验. *Here is* ~ *positive.* 有确实证据. *a foul* ~ 错字很多的校样. *a foundry* ~ (压型前的)清样. *an artist's [engraver's]* ~ 版画印样. *stand a severe* ~ 经受严格的考验. *afford* ~ *of* 提供证据. *armour of* ~ 戳不通的坚牢的铠甲. ***below*** ~ 不合格. ***bring [put] to the*** ~ 试, 试验. ***have*** ~ ***of shot*** 能防弹, 能避弹. ***in*** ~ ***of*** 作…的证据. ~ ***positive of his intention*** 他的企图的确证. ***read the*** ~ 校对. — *a.* ①试验过的, 有保证的; (酒)合标准的, 规定的. ②校样的. ③(子弹等) 不入的, 耐…的, 防…的. *a* ~ *coin* 标准货币, 制钱. *a* ~ *sample* 样品. ~ *against the severest weather* 经得起任何酷烈天气的. ~ *against the pricks of all temptations* 不为任何诱惑所动的. — *vt.* 使经得住, 使(布等)耐久[不漏水(等)]. ~*ed cloth* 防水布. ~ **mark** (枪等的) 验讫记号. ~ **plane** 验电板. ~**read** *vt., vi.* 〔美〕校对. ~**reader** 校对员. ~**reading** 校对. ~ **sheet** 校样. ~ **spirit** 含标准酒精的酒〔英国的标准含酒精成分为 57.1%, 美国为 50%〕. ~**-test** *vt.* 试验, 检验[武器等]. **-less** *a.* 无证据的.

-proof *suf.* 耐, 防(等). *acid-*~ 耐酸的. *air-*~ 密封的. *dust-*~ 防尘的. *fire-*~ 防火的. *radar-*~ 反雷达的. *slander-*~ 听了坏话不会生气的. *sound-*~ 隔音的. *water-*~ 防水的.

Prop. = propeller.

prop. = properly; property; proposition.

prop[1] [prɔp] *n.* ①支柱. ②支持者, 拥护者, 后援者, 后盾, 靠山. ③晾衣绳支柱 (= clothes-~). ④〔美俚〕腿. *pit* ~*s*【矿】坑木. *He is the only* ~ *of mine.* 他是我的唯一的靠山[支柱]. *the main* ~ *of a state* 国家的栋梁. — *vt.* 支持; 把…靠着. *He* ~*ped his cane against the wall.* 他把自己的手杖靠墙立着. ~ *up* (把…)撑住; 给…撑腰. — *vi.* (马等)前腿突然挺直地停住.

prop[2] [prɔp] *n.*【剧】道具 = property.

prop[3] [prɔp] *n.* (英盗贼俚语)钻石别针.

prop[4] [prɔp] *n.*〔口〕【空】螺旋桨 (= propeller).

pro·pae·deu·tic, -ti·cal [ˌprəupiˈdjuːtik, -tikəl] *a.* 初步的, 预备的, 预科的. — *n.* 预备学科[项目], 预科.

pro·pae·deu·tics [ˌprəupiːˈdjuːtiks] *n. pl.* 预备知识, 基础知识.

prop·a·ga·ble [ˈprɔpəgəbl] *a.* ①可传播的; 可宣传的. ②可以繁殖的. *be* ~ *by seed* 种子繁殖的. **-bil·i·ty** [ˌprɔpəgəˈbiliti] *n.* **-ness** *n.*

prop·a·gand [ˌprɔpəˈgænd] *vt.*〔美〕宣传.

prop·a·gan·da [ˌprɔpəˈgændə] *n.* ①〔口〕宣传; 宣传计划; 宣传方法; 传播. ②宣传部, 宣传机关. ③〔the P-〕【天主】布教总会[学校]. ***make*** ~ ***for*** 为…宣传. ***set up a*** ~ ***for*** 设立…的宣传机关. — *vt., vi.* = propagandize.

prop·a·gan·dism [ˌprɔpəˈgændizəm] *n.* 宣传; 宣传事业; 宣传(法).

prop·a·gan·dist [ˌprɔpəˈgændist] *n.* 宣传者; 宣传人员. — *a.* 宣传的. **-ic** *a.*

prop·a·gan·dize [ˌprɔpəˈgændaiz] *vt., vi.* 宣传; 传播; (对…)进行宣传. ~ *Marxism-Leninism* 传播马克思列宁主义.

prop·a·gate [ˈprɔpəgeit] *vt.* ①增殖, 繁殖. ②普及, 传播; 宣传. ③使(光、音、地震等)波及, 传达. ④传染, 使蔓延; 遗传(特征等). ⑤【物】传播. *The weeds* ~ *themselves rapidly.* 杂草繁殖极快. ~ *disease* 传染疾病. — *vi.* 增殖, 繁殖; 普及, 传播, 蔓延. **-ga·tion** *n.*

prop·a·ga·tor [ˈprɔpəgeitə] *n.* 增殖者; 传播者; 宣传者.

pro·pane [ˈprəupein] *n.*【化】丙烷.

pro·pa·none [ˈprəupənəun] *n.*【化】丙酮 (=acetone).

pro·par·ox·y·tone [ˌprəupəːˈrɔksitəun] *a.* 从词尾倒数第三音节上有重音的. — *n.* 从词尾倒数第三音节上有重音的词.

pro pa·tri·a [prəu ˈpeitriə]〔L.〕为了祖国.

pro·pel [prəˈpel] *vt.* 推, 推进, 驱使. *propelling power* 推进力. *be propelled by steam* 由蒸汽推进.

pro·pel·lant [prəˈpelənt] *n.* 推进物, 推进剂; (枪炮的)发射火药; 喷气燃料. *high-energy* ~ 高能燃料. *work*

horse ～【火箭】通用燃料。
pro·pel·lent [prəˈpelənt] *a.* 推进的。— *n.*＝propellant.
pro·pel·ler, pro·pel·lor [prəˈpelə] *n.* ①推进者。②(汽船、飞机的)螺旋桨,推进器;暗轮汽船。
pro·pend [prəuˈpend] *vi.* 〔废〕倾向于，有意于 *(to; toward)*.
pro·pene [ˈprəupi:n] *n.*【化】丙烯 (＝ propylene).
pro·pen·si·ty [prəˈpensiti] *n.* 倾向，嗜好，脾性，癖*(to; for)*. *a* ～ *to extravagance [for gambling]* 奢华［赌博］的癖好。
prop·er [ˈprɔpə] *a.* ①适当的,相当的;正当的,应该的;正式的,正常的。②有礼貌的;规矩的。③固有的，特有的,独特的 *(to)*. ④本来的，真正的；严格意义上的〔用于名词后面〕。⑤【语法】专有的;〔古〕自己的;【天】自身的。⑥【纹】本色的。⑦〔英口〕纯粹的，完全的。⑧〔古〕漂亮的，优美的。⑨【宗】仅限节日应用的。*I dislike* ～ *children.* 我不喜欢一本正经的孩子。*The book hardly belongs to literature* ～. 这本书不好说是纯文学书。*the dictionary* ～ 词典正文。*temperature* ～ *to August* 八月特有的气温。*Ferosity is* ～ *to tigers.* 凶猛是老虎的天性。*a peacock* ～【纹】天然色彩的孔雀（纹章）。*architecture* ～（不包含雕刻、管道等加工工程的）主体纯粹建筑。*There will be a* ～ *row about it.* 这个事情要引起一场大乱子来的。*a* ～ *man* 〔古〕漂亮的男子。*quite a* ～ *book* 一本极好的书。***as you think*** ～ 你认为怎么合适就…。***at a*** ～ ***time*** 在适当的时候。***in the*** ～ ***sense of the word*** 按照这个词的本来意义。***in the*** ～ ***way*** 用适当方法。***paint sb. in sb.'s*** ～ ***colours*** 老老实实批评某人。～ ***for the occasion*** 合时宜。— *ad.* 〔方〕适当地，好好地；非常，很；完完全全地；彻底地。— *n.*〔常 *pl.*〕【宗】特定礼拜仪式，特祷；特赞。～ **circle**【数】真圆，常态圆。～ **function**【数】特征函数，常义函数。～ **mass**【物】静质量。～ **motion**【天】自行。～ **noun**【语法】专有名词。
pro·per·i·spo·me·non [ˈprəuˌperiˈspəuminən] *a.*, *n.* *(pl. -na* [-nə]*)*【希腊语法】词尾倒数第二音节上有变长音符的(词)。
pro·per·din [ˈprəupədin] *n.*（血液中）一种能消灭细菌和病毒的血清。
prop·er·ly *ad.* ①适当,相当;当然,正正当当;整整齐齐。②完全，非常。*He very* ～ *refused.* 他正正当当地拒绝了。*I thrashed him* ～. 我狠狠打了他一顿。～ ***speaking*** ＝ ***to speak*** ～ 严格地说来,本来。
prop·er·tied [ˈprɔpətid] *a.* ①有财产的。②【剧】使用道具的。
prop·er·ty [ˈprɔpəti] *n.* ①财产；资产；所有物；所有地，地产;所有,所有权。②性质,特征,属性,特性;【逻】非本质特性。③〔*pl.*〕【剧】道具;〔英〕服装。*a man of* ～ 有产业者。*real* ～ 不动产。*movable [personal]* ～ 动产。*Is this your* ～? 这是你的东西吗? *The secret is common* ～. 那个秘密人人知道。*literary* ～ 著作权，版权。*the properties of soda* 碳酸钠(苏打)的特性。～ ***in copyright*** 版权所有。～ **animal**〔美〕【影、剧】惯于出演的动物。～ **man [master]**【剧】小道具管理员。～ **owner** 地主，业主。～ **tax** 财产税。
pro·phase [ˈprəufeiz] *n.*【动】(有丝分裂)前期。
proph·e·cy [ˈprɔfisi] *n.* 预言;预言能力;【宗】预言书。
proph·e·sy [ˈprɔfisai] *vt.*, *vi.* 预言,预示。
proph·et [ˈprɔfit] *n.* ①预言者；〔诗〕先知；预告者。②(主义等的)提倡者,主张者。②〔俚〕(赛马输赢的)预测者。*a weather* ～ 天气预报员。*the P-* ①(伊斯兰教祖)穆罕默德。②约瑟·史密斯(Joseph Smith)〔1805—1844,美国摩门教的开山鼻祖〕。***the*** ～***s*** (旧约中的)各预言书或其作者。
proph·et·ess [ˈprɔfitis] *n.* 女预言者。
pro·phet·ic, pro·phet·i·cal [prəˈfetik, -ikəl] *a.* 预言(者)的。**-i·cal·ly** *ad.*

proph·y·lac·tic [ˌprɔfiˈlæktik] *a.*【医】预防(性)的。— *n.* ①【医】预防药;预防法。②避孕用品［药物］。
proph·y·lax·is [ˌprɔfiˈlæksis] *n.*【医】预防(法)。
pro·pine [prəˈpi:n, prəu-] *vt.* 〔Scot.〕〔古〕赠送(礼品)。*n.* 〔Scot.〕〔古〕礼品。
pro·pin·qui·ty [prəˈpiŋkwiti] *n.* ①(地点的)相近，邻近。②(时间的)接近;迫切。③(血统上的)近亲。④(性质、性情等的)近似,类似。
pro·pi·o·nate [ˈprəupiəneit] *n.* 丙酸盐,丙酸酯。
pro·pi·ti·ate [prəˈpiʃieit] *vt.* ①劝解;抚慰;调和,调解。②向…讨好,邀宠于;【宗】向(上帝)赎罪。**-ation** *n.* ①劝解,抚慰。②邀宠;【宗】赎罪。
pro·pi·ti·a·tor [prəˈpiʃieitə] *n.* ①劝解的人，调解人。②邀宠者;【宗】赎罪者。
pro·pi·ti·a·to·ry [prəˈpiʃiətəri] *a.* ①劝解的,调解的。②邀宠的;【宗】赎罪的。— *n.* ＝ mercy-seat. **-to·ri·ly** *ad.*
pro·pi·tious [prəˈpiʃəs] *a.* ①顺利的，幸运的；有利于…的；适合的 *(for; to; towards)*；吉利的。②慈祥的，慈悲的。*a* ～ *sign [omen]* 吉兆。～ *to the undertaking* 有利于任务［事业］的成功。～ *weather for journey* 适合旅行的好天气。～ *wind* 顺风。**-ly** *ad.* **-ness** *n.*
prop·jet [ˈprɔpdʒet] *n.* 涡轮螺桨发动机，涡轮螺桨飞机(＝ turboprop).
prop·man [ˈprɔpmæn] *n.* *(pl.* ***-men)*** 道具管理员 (＝ property man).
prop·o·lis [ˈprɔpəlis] *n.* 蜂胶。
pro·pone [prəˈpəun] *vt.* 〔Scot.〕提议;陈述。
pro·po·nent [prəˈpəunənt] *n.* ①提议者;主张者。②支持者;辩护者。③【法】遗嘱检验申请人。— *a.* 建议的;支持的;辩护的。
pro·por·tion [prəˈpɔ:ʃən] *n.* ①比；比率；【数】比例。②相称,平衡,调和,配合。③份;部分。④〔*pl.*〕大小,面积,容积。*the* ～ *of births to the population* 出生率。*direct [inverse]* ～ 正［反］比例。*a large* ～ *of the earth's surface* 地球表面的大部分。*due [proper]* ～ 调和，相称。***do a sum in [by]*** ～ 按比例计算。***in admirable*** ～ 非常均衡。***in*** ～ ***to [as]*** 与…成比例;与…相称；按…的比例(越…越…)。***of fine*** ～***s*** (高楼等)堂皇的。***of gigantic*** ～***s*** 巨大的。***out of (all)*** ～ ***to*** 和…不相称［不成比例］。***sense of*** ～ 能作出公允判断的能力；辨别轻重缓急的能力。— *vt.* ①使相称，使均衡。②摊派，分配。～ *the expenses to the receipts* 量入为出。
pro·por·tion·a·ble [prəˈpɔ:ʃənəbl] *a.* 可配合的，相称的,相当的,成比例的 *(to)*. **-bly** *ad.*
pro·por·tion·al [prəˈpɔ:ʃənl] *a.* (成)比例的；相称的，平衡的,调和的 *(to)*. *a* ～ *number* 比例数。*a* ～ *error* 相对(比例)误差(率)。— *n.*【数】比例项,比例量。***be directly [inversely, reciprocally]*** ～ ***to*** 与…成正［反］比例。～ **representation**（选举上的）比例代表制。～ **sampling** 比例抽样。**-ist** *n.* ①主张实行比例代表制者。②(人力、物力等的)分派比例的安排者。**-ly** *ad.* 按比例地,相应地,相配合地;比较地。
pro·por·tion·al·i·ty [prəˌpɔ:ʃəˈnæliti] *n.* 比例(性)；均衡(性)；相称。
pro·por·tion·ate [prəˈpɔ:ʃənit] *a.* 相称的，成比例的，相当的。— *vt.* 使相称，使成比例，使相当;使适应 *(to)*. ～ *punishment to crimes* 按罪量刑。**-ly** *ad.*
pro·por·tioned [prəˈpɔ:ʃənd] *a.* 相称的，配合得…的;成比例的。*an evenly* ～ *share* 公平的分配。*well-*～ 相称的,很匀称的。*ill-*～ 不相称的,不成比例的。
pro·por·tion·ment [prəˈpɔ:ʃənmənt] *n.* 比例，相称，调和,匀整。
pro·pos·al [prəˈpəuzəl] *n.* ①申请;提议,建议;提案。②求婚。③〔美〕投标。*a counter* ～ 对案，反提案。*sealed* ～*s* (密封)投标。***agree to a*** ～ 同意某项建议(提案)。***make a*** ～ ***(of marriage)*** 求婚。***make [offer]*** ～***s of***

[for] (peace) 求(和)。

pro·pose [prəˈpəuz] *vt.* ①申请；提议，建议，提出。②推荐，提名。③计划，打算。④求(婚)。～ *a motion* 提出一项动议. *I wish to* ～ *a toast to our friendship*. 我建议为我们的友谊干杯. *We* ～*d him for [as] candidate*. 我们推荐他为候选人. ～ *a riddle* 出谜. *I do not* ～ *to stay long at Shanghai* 我不打算在上海久住. ～ *marriage to a girl* 向一个姑娘求婚. — *vi.* ①打算，作出计划. ②求婚*(to)*. *Man* ～*s, God disposes.* 〔谚〕谋事在人，成事在天.

pro·pos·er [prəˈpəuzə] *n.* 申请者，提议者，建议者，提案国.

prop·o·si·tion [ˌprɔpəˈziʃən] *n.* ①提议，建议；主张. ②【逻】命题；【修】主题；【数】定理. ③〔口〕企业，事业. ④〔口〕商品. ⑤〔口〕事情，工作；家伙. *an absolute [a predicative, a categorical]* ～【逻】定言命题，直言判断. *a major [minor]* ～【逻】大[小]前提. *a paying* ～ 赚钱生意. *a queer* ～ 怪事. *He is a tough* ～. 他是一个难对付的家伙. — *vi.* 〔美俚〕提议，建议. **-al** *a.* **-al·ly** *ad.*

pro·pos·i·tus [prəˈpɔzitəs] *n.* *(pl.* ***-ti*** [-tai]*)* 族谱中发支的始祖.

pro·pound [prəˈpaund] *vt.* ①提议，建议. ②【法】(为求确定合法性向有关方面)提出(遗嘱). **-er** *n.*

propr. = proprietary; proprietor.

pro·prae·tor, pro·pre·tor [prəuˈpriːtə] *n.* 省长〔作过罗马(军事)执政官后被派任为省的行政官〕.

pro·pri·e·ta·ry [prəˈpraiətəri] *a.* ①所有(人)的. ②有财产的. ③专有的，独占的，专利的. — *n.* 〔古〕①所有人，所有团体. ②所有权；所有物. ③专卖药品. ④【美史】(独立前英王特许独占某块殖民地的)领主. ～ **articles** 专利品. ～ **class** 资产阶级；(尤指)地主阶级. ～ **company** ①(亦略作 Pty)(占有其他公司全部或大部分的)控股公司，持股公司. ②土地兴业公司. ～ **medicine** 特许专卖药品. ～ **rights** 所有权.

pro·pri·e·tor [prəˈpraiətə] *n.* ①所有人；业主. ②地主；【美史】(独立前，英王特许独占某块殖民地的)领主. *landed* ～ 地主. *a lord* ～ 大地主. *a peasant* ～ 自耕农. **-ship** *n.* 所有权.

pro·pri·e·to·ri·al [prəˌpraiəˈtɔːriəl] *a.* 所有(权)的. **-ly** *ad.*

pro·pri·e·tress [prəˈpraiətris] *n.* 女所有人[业主，地主等].

pro·pri·e·ty [prəˈpraiəti] *n.* ①妥当，适宜，适当；正当，恰当. ②礼节；〔the proprieties〕礼仪，规矩. *I doubt the* ～ *of the term*. 我怀疑这个术语是否适当. *a breach of* ～ 失礼行为. *observe the proprieties* 遵守礼节；依照社交惯例. ***with*** ～ 按照礼节，正当，适当.

pro·pri·o·cep·tive [ˌprəupriəˈseptiv] *a.* 【动】固有感受的，本体感受的.

pro·pri·o·cep·tor [ˌprəupriəˈseptə] *n.* 【动】本体感受器.

pro·pri·o mo·tu [ˈprəupriəu ˈməutju] 〔L.〕自愿.

pro·proc·tor [prəuˈprɔktə] *n.* 〔英大学〕副学监.

props [prɔps] *n. pl.* 〔英俚〕【剧】小道具.

prop·to·sis [prɔpˈtəusis] *n.* *(pl.* ***-ses*** [-siːz]*)* 【医】突出，脱出，前垂，凸出(尤指眼球凸出).

pro·pul·sion [prəˈpʌlʃən] *n.* 推进(力). *a* ～ *engineer* 动力装置工程师. *jet* ～ 喷气推进. **pro·pul·sive** [prəˈpʌlsiv] *a.* 推进的，促进的，有推进力的.

pro·pul·sor [prəˈpʌlsə] *n.* ①喷气式发动机，推进器. ②推进物；火箭的推进燃料.

pro·pyl [ˈprəupil] *n.* 【化】丙基. **-ic** *a.*

pro·pylae·um [ˌprɔpiˈliːəm] *n.* *(pl.* ***-laea*** [-ˈliːə]*)* 〔常用 *pl.*〕(神殿等的)入口. *the Propylaea* 希腊雅典卫城(Acropolis)的入口.

pro·pyl·ene [ˈprəupiliːn] *n.* 【化】丙烯.

prop·y·lite [ˈprɔpilait] *n.* 【地】青磐岩.

pro·pyne [ˈprəupain] *n.* 【化】丙炔.

pro ra·ta [prəuˈrɑːtə, -ˈreitə] *a., ad.* 按比例的[地].

pro·rate [prəuˈreit] *vt.* 〔美〕按比例分配；摊派.

pro·ro·ga·tion [ˌprəurəˈgeiʃən] *n.* (议会的)闭会；休会.

pro·rogue [prəˈrəug] *vt., vi.* (尤指英国议会)(使)休会；(使)闭会. *Parliament stands* ～*d*. 议会在休会中.

pros. = prosody.

pros- *pref.* ①前，向(…方面)；加之. ②(靠)近.

pro·sage [ˈprəusidʒ] *n.* 无肉香肠；素肠.

pro·sa·ic [prəuˈzeiik] *a.* ①散文的，散文体的 *(opp.* poetic)；没有诗意的. ②单调的，平凡的；使人厌倦的，无聊的. ③如实的. *a* ～ *life* 枯燥无味的生活. **-i·cal·ly** *ad.*

pro·sa·i·cism, pro·sa·ism [ˈprəuzeiisizəm, ˈprəuzeiizəm] *n.* ①散文体. ②平凡，枯燥.

pro·sa·ist [ˈprəuzeiist] *n.* ①散文家. ②平凡的人，没有诗意的人.

Pros. Atty. = prosecuting attorney.

pro·sce·ni·um [prəuˈziːniəm] *n.* *(pl.* ***-nia*** [-niə]*)* ①(舞台的)幕前部分. ②〔古〕(希腊、罗马剧场的)舞台. ③〔泛指〕前部；显著地位. ～ **box** 舞台前部的包厢.

pro·sciut·to [prəˈʃuːtəu, It. prəuˈʃuːttəu] *n.* (意大利的一种熏过的、切得很薄的)五香火腿.

pro·scribe [prəuˈskraib] *vt.* ①使丧失公权，使失去法律保护. ②放逐. ③禁止；排斥. ④〔古〕公布(被处罚者的)姓名；宣布…(公民)为国家的敌人并取消对他的法律保护.

pro·scrip·tion [prəuˈskripʃən] *n.* ①公权剥夺. ②放逐. ③禁止；排斥. ④〔古罗马〕宣布…为公敌的公告. **-tive** *a.*

prose [prəuz] *n.* ①散文 *(opp.* verse*)*. ②平凡，单调，普通. ③干燥无味的话，无聊的议论. ④【天主】续唱. ⑤〔英〕(学生的)译成外语的练习. *a* ～ *-poem* 散文诗. *the* ～ *of life*. 平凡的人生. *I've got 2 French* ～*s to do before tomorrow morning*. 明天上午以前我还要做两道译成法语的练习题. — *vt., vi.* 用散文写；(将诗)译成散文；平淡无趣地写；罗罗唆唆讲.

pro·sect [prəuˈsekt] *vt.* 【医】解剖(尸体)作示范教学.

pro·sec·tor [prəuˈsektə] *n.* (为准备实物示教的)尸体解剖者.

pros·e·cute [ˈprɔsikjuːt] *vt.* ①彻底进行(调查、研究学问等)，推行，执行，从事；经营，做(买卖等). ②控告，对…提起公诉；依照法律手续要求执行(权利). ～ *the war against* 对…作战. — *vi.* ①起诉，告发. ②作检察官. *Trespassers will be* ～*d* 〔告示〕违者法办. **prosecuting attorney** 〔美〕检察官.

pros·e·cu·tion [ˌprɔsiˈkjuːʃən] *n.* ①实行，执行，贯彻；营业. ②控告，起诉，检举. ③〔the ～〕原告及其律师的总称 *(opp.* defense*)*. *the* ～ *of a trade* 从事一门行业. *a criminal* ～ 刑事诉讼. *a malicious* ～ 诬告. *start a* ～ *against sb.* 检举某人. ***the Director of Public P-s*** 〔英〕检察官.

pros·e·cu·tor [ˈprɔsikjuːtə] *n.* *(fem.* ***-trix*** [-triks] *pl.* ***-tri·ces*** [-trisiːz]*)* ①实行者. ②【法】起诉人，告发人，检举人. *a public* ～ 检察官.

pros·e·lyte [ˈprɔsilait] *n.* ①新入教者；(意见、思想、政党等的)改宗者. ②〔古〕从邪教皈依犹太教者. — *vt., vi.* ①(使)改变(意见、思想等). ②〔美〕劝诱(运动员)；搜罗(人员).

pros·e·ly·tism [ˈprɔsilitizəm] *n.* 改宗；(政治信仰等的)改变.

pros·e·ly·tize [ˈprɔsilitaiz] *vt.* 使改宗[转向、变节].

pro·sem·i·nar [prəuˈseminɑː] *n.* (为未毕业的高材生开设的)研究班.

pros·en·ceph·a·lon [ˌprɔsenˈsefəlɔn, -lən] *n.* *(pl.* ***-la*** [-lə]*)* 前脑；壮年人发达的脑部〔包括间脑和大脑半球〕(= forebrain). **-phal·ic** *a.*

pros·en·chy·ma [prɔsˈeŋkimə] *n.* 【植】长轴组织；锐

端细胞组织. **-chym•a•tous** [-ˈkimətəs] *a.*

pros•er [ˈprəuzə] *n.* ①散文家; 写平凡事物的人. ②唠唠叨叨的人.

Pro•ser•pi•na, Pros•er•pine [prəˈsə:pinə, ˈprɔsəpain] *n.* 【罗神】= Persephone.

pros•et•ry [ˈprəuzitri] *n.* 〔美〕散文诗.

pros•i•fy [ˈprəuzifai] *vt.* ①把…改成散文; 使散文化. ②使平庸化. — *vi.* ①写散文. ②变得平庸无奇.

pros•i•ly [ˈprəuzili] *ad.* 散文般地; 平淡无味地, 罗罗唆唆地.

pros•i•ness [ˈprəuzinis] *n.* ①散文体. ②平凡, 单调.

pro•sit [ˈprəusit, ˈprəuzit] *int.* 为…健康干杯! 祝你健康! 〔尤指德国人祝酒时的用语〕.

pro•slav•er•y [prəuˈsleivəri] *a.* 赞成奴隶制度的.

pro•so [ˈprəusəu] *n.* 〔Russ.〕黍, 稷 (= millet).

pro•so•di•al, pro•sod•ic, pro•sod•i•cal [prəˈsəudiəl, -ˈsɔdik, -ikəl] *a.* 诗体学的; 韵律学的; 作诗法的. **-i•cal•ly** *ad.*

pros•o•dist [ˈprɔsədist] *n.* 韵律学者; 诗体学者.

pros•o•dy [ˈprɔsədi] *n.* 韵律学; 作诗法; 诗体学.

pros•o•po•p(o)e•ia [prɔˌsəupəˈpi:ə] *n.* 【修】拟人法; (使虚幻人物)具体化.

pros•pect [ˈprɔspekt] *n.* ①眼界, 风景, 景色; 展望; (房屋的)方向. ②希望, 前途; 远见; 预料. ③形势; 情景, 景色. ④〔美〕可能成为顾客〔应征者〕的人. ⑤探矿有希望的地区. ⑥矿石样品. ⑦试掘; 【地】勘探. *command a fine* ~ 景致好. *a house with a southern* ~. 朝南的房子. *a youth with bright [rosy]* ~*s* 前途远大的青年. *The job offers good* ~*s.* 这工作很有前途. *Socialist modernization opens up broad* ~*s for youth.* 社会主义现代化为青年开辟广阔的前程. *Things offer a gloomy* ~. 形势不佳. *strike a good* ~ 挖到旺矿. ***in*** ~ 可以预料到, 有希望 (*We have a pleasant time in* ~. 我们前途乐观). ***in [within]*** ~ ***(of)*** 可期待, 在望, 有希望. — [prəsˈpekt] *vt.* 勘探(矿藏), 找(金矿等). — *vi.* ①试掘 *(for)*. ②(矿产量)有希望. ~ *a mine* 勘探矿藏. ~ *for oil* 勘探石油矿. *a mine* ~*ing ill [well]* 一个没有〔有〕开采前途的矿山.

pro•spec•tive [prəˈspektiv] *a.* ①将来的, 未来的 *(opp.* retrospective*)*. ②有希望的; 预期的. *my* ~ *son-in-law* 我的将来的女婿. **-ly** *ad.*

pro•spec•tor [prɔsˈpektə] *n.* 探矿者; (指望将来的)投机家.

pro•spec•tus [prəsˈpektəs] *n.* ①(创办学校、公司等的)计划书, 意见书, 发起书. ②(讲义等的)大纲, (计划书等的)样本. ③(即将出版的书等的)内容介绍, 简介.

pros•per [ˈprɔspə] *vi., vt.* (使)兴隆, (使)繁荣; (使)成功. *conditions* ~*ing the business* 使生意兴隆的条件. ~ *in business* 生意兴隆. *Everything he does* ~*s with him.* 他做事样样顺当. *a* ~*ing breeze* 顺风.

pros•per•i•ty [prɔsˈperiti] *n.* 兴隆, 繁荣, 旺盛; 〔*pl.*〕顺遂, 幸福 *(opp.* adversity*)*. *national* ~ 国家的兴旺. *I wish you all* ~. 祝你诸事顺遂.

pros•per•ous [ˈprɔspərəs] *a.* 兴隆的, 繁荣的, 昌隆的; 幸福的, 运气好的; 顺遂的, 良好的. ~ *weather* 绝好天气. *in a* ~ *hour* 恰好, 刚好. *bring a plan to a* ~ *issue* 使计划顺利成功. **-ly** *ad.*

prost [prəust] *int.* 为…健康干杯! 祝你健康! 〔尤指德国人祝酒时的用语〕(= prosit).

pros•ta•glan•din [ˌprɔstəˈglændin] *n.* 【化】前列腺素.

pros•tate [ˈprɔsteit] *n., a.* 【解】前列腺(的).

pros•ta•tec•to•my [ˌprɔstəˈtektəmi] *n.* ***(pl.*** ***-mies)*** 【医】前列腺切除术.

pros•ta•tism [ˈprɔstətizəm] *n.* 前列腺慢性病(尤指前列腺肿大引起对排尿的阻塞).

pros•ta•ti•tis [ˌprɔstəˈtaitis] *n.* 【医】前列腺炎.

pros•the•sis [ˈprɔsθisis] *n.* ***(pl.*** ***pro•the•ses*** [-si:z]***)*** ①【语法】词首增添字母〔音节〕〔如 belove 中的 b〕. ②【医】修复术, 弥补术; 假体. ③【化】取代, 置换. *dental* ~ 假牙.

pros•thet•ic [prɔsˈθetik] *a.* ①【语法】词首增添字母〔音节〕的. ②【医】修复术的. ③【化】非朊基的.

pros•thet•ics [prɔsˈθetiks] *n. pl.* 〔动词用单数〕(假肢、假眼、假牙)装补学, 修复学. **pros•the•tist** [prɔsˈθi:tist] *n.* (假牙等的)装补专家.

pros•tho•don•tics [ˌprɔsθəˈdɔntiks] *n. pl.* 〔动词用单数〕牙修复术 (=prosthodontia). **-don•tic** *a.* **-don•tist** *n.* 镶牙专家.

pros•ti•tute [ˈprɔstitju:t] *n.* 妓女; 卖身投靠的人, 出卖贞操的人. — *a.* 卖淫的; 堕落的. — *vt.* 使卖淫, 卖(身); 出卖(名誉等); 滥用(能力等). ~ *oneself* 沦为娼妓. — *vi.* 卖淫, 卖身.

pros•ti•tu•tion [ˌprɔstiˈtju:ʃən] *n.* 卖淫; 出卖灵魂; 滥用. *illicit* ~ 私娼. *licensed [public]* ~ 公娼(制度).

pro•sto•mi•um [prəuˈstəumiəm] *n.* ***(pl.*** ***-mi•a*** [-ə]***)*** 【动】口前叶.

pros•trate [ˈprɔstreit] *a.* ①(为表示屈服)拜倒在地下的. ②打败了的, 屈服的, 降伏的. ③沮丧的; 筋疲力尽的. ④【植】匍匐性的, 爬地的, 平卧的. *They laid the Republicans* ~. 他们使共和党屈服了. *be* ~ *with fatigue* 疲劳透顶. — [prɔsˈtreit] *vt.* ①使倒伏, 使平卧; 弄倒, (风)吹倒, 吹翻. ②〔~ oneself〕拜倒, 平伏. ③使屈服, 推翻. ④使衰弱, 使筋疲力尽, 使累透. ~ *oneself before sb.* 拜倒人前, 对…五体投地. *be* ~*d by the heat* 热得昏倒.

pros•tra•tion [prɔsˈtreiʃən] *n.* ①拜倒; 平伏. ②疲劳; 【医】虚脱, 衰弱. *general [nervous]* ~ 全身〔神经〕衰弱.

pro•style [ˈprəustail] *a.* 【建】柱廊式的. — *n.* 柱廊; 柱廊式建筑.

pros•y [ˈprəuzi] *a.* ***(-i•er; -i•est)*** 散文(体)的, 枯燥无味的, 罗唆的.

Prot. = Protectorate; Protestant.

prot- *comb. f.* = proto.

pro•t•ac•tin•i•um [ˌprəutækˈtiniəm] *n.* 【化】镤.

pro•tag•o•nist [prəuˈtægənist] *n.* ①(戏剧的)主角; (小说的)主人公. ②领导者, 首唱者, 首创者.

Pro•tag•o•ras [prəuˈtægəræs] *n.* 普罗塔哥拉〔481—411? B.C., 古希腊智者派哲学家〕.

pro•ta•mine, pro•ta•min [ˈprəutəmi:n, -min] *n.* 【化】鱼精朊, 鱼精蛋白; 鱼卵胺.

pro•tan•o•pi•a [ˌprəutəˈnəupiə] *n.* 红色盲. **-tan•op•ic** [-ˈɔpik] *a.*

prot•a•sis [ˈprɔtəsis] *n.* ***(pl.*** ***-a•ses*** [-əsi:z]***)*** 【语法】条件从句 *(opp.* apodosis*)*. **pro•tat•ic** [prəˈtæktik] *a.*

prote- *comb. f.* = proteo-.

Pro•te•an [prəuˈti:ən] *a.* ①【希神】普罗秋斯 (Proteus) 神(似)的. ②〔p-〕千变万化的; 变化不定的; (演员)能演好几种角色的; 【动】变形虫的. *a* ~ *performer* 多面手演员.

pro•te•ase [ˈprəutieis] *n.* 【化】蛋白酶.

pro•tect [prəˈtekt] *vt.* ①保护, 包庇, 守护; 警戒; 防止(危险、损害等). ②【机】装保险器(在枪等上). ③【经】(对外货征收重税)保护(国内产业). ④【商】准备支付(汇票). *a* ~*ed state* 保护国. ~*ed trade* 保护贸易. ~ *sb. from [against] danger* 保护某人免遭危险. — *vi.* 有保护作用.

pro•tec•tion [prəˈtekʃən] *n.* ①保护, 保卫, 防御, 掩护, 包庇, 照顾 *(from; against)*. ②保护者, 防护物 *(against)*; 〔美俚〕(歹徒向人索取的)保护费. ③护照, 通行证; 〔美〕(国籍)护照; 通行证. ③【经】保护贸易制, 保护政策. ~ *against cold* 防寒用具. ~ *against moths [lightning]* 除虫, 避(雷). ~ *at halts* 驻军警戒. ~ *on the move* 行军警戒. ***under the*** ~ ***of*** 在…保护下,

受…保护,托…照顾.

pro·tec·tion·ism [prəˈtekʃənizəm] *n.* 【经】保护贸易主义,保护主义,保护政策. **-ist** *n.* 赞成保护贸易主义者. — *a.* 保护贸易主义的.

pro·tec·tive [prəˈtektiv] *a.* ①保护的,防护的. ②保护贸易的. ~ *clothing* 防毒服. ~ *colouring* 【动】保护色. ~ *mimicry [resemblance]* 【动】保护性拟态. ~ *potential* 自卫能. ~ *reflex* 防卫反射. ~ *system* 保护关税制. ~ *tariff* 保护(性)关税. ~ *trade* 保护贸易. **-ly** *ad.* **-ness** *n.*

pro·tec·tor [prəˈtektə] *n.* ①保护人, 拥护者. ②防护器,保护装置;【棒球】胸甲. ③【英史】摄政;〔the P-〕护国公. *a point* ~ 铅笔套. *Lord P-* 护国公〔英国十七世纪摄政者克伦威尔父子〔Oliver Cromwell 和 Richard Cromwell 的称号〕.

pro·tec·tor·al [prəˈtektərəl] *a.* 保护者的;保护国的;摄政的.

pro·tec·tor·ate [prəˈtektərit] *n.* ①摄政的职位,摄政期间;〔the P-〕护国公执政时期. ②保护领地,保护国;(强国对弱小国家的)保护制度.

pro·tec·to·ry [prəˈtektəri] *n.* 【天主】贫儿收容所,少年感化院.

pro·tec·tress [prəˈtektris] *n.* 女保护者.

pro·té·gé [ˈprəuteʒei, ˈprɔ-] *n.* (*fem.* **-gée** [-ʒei]) 被保护人;手下;门徒.

pro·teid, pro·tein [ˈprəutiːd, -tiːn] *n.* 【化】朊,蛋白(质)〔前者为旧称〕.

pro·tein·aceous, -tein·ic, -tei·nous [ˌprəutiˈneiʃəs, -ˈtinik, ˈprəutinəs] *a.* 朊的,蛋白质的.

pro·tein·ase [ˈprəutineis, ˈprəutiːi-] *n.* 蛋白酶.

pro·tein·ate [ˈprəutineit] *n.* 蛋白化合物.

pro·tein·oid [ˈprəutinɔid] *n.* 【化】类蛋白(质).

pro·tein·u·ri·a [ˌprəutiːnˈjuəriə, ˌprəutiin-] *n.* 蛋白尿(症).

proteo- *comb. f.* 朊,蛋白质: *proteo*lysis.

pro·te·o·clas·tic [ˌprəutiəuˈklastik] *a.* (分)解蛋白的.

pro·te·ol·y·sis [ˌprəutiˈɔlisis] *n.* 【生化】蛋白水解作用. **-lyt·ic** [-ˈlitik] *a.*

pro·te·ose [ˈprəutiəus] *n.* 【化】朊间质,脲.

Prot·er·o·zo·ic [ˌprɔtərəˈzəuik] *n., a.* 【地】元古代〔元古界〕(的).

pro·test [prəˈtest] *vi.* ①声明,断言,坚决主张. ②抗议,声明反对, 提出异议. ③〔古〕说,讲. —*vt.* ①坚决主张,坚决声明,坚持(*that*); 证明说,发誓说. ②【商】拒付(票据). ③〔美〕向…提出抗议. ~ *friendship* 发誓说友情不变. ~ *one's innocence [that one is innocent]* 坚决声明无罪.—[ˈprəutest] *n.* ①声明, 断言. ②抗议(书),不服;(期票等的) 拒付说明. *a* ~ *for non-acceptance [nonpayment]* 拒收[拒付]说明. ***enter [lodge, make] a ~ against*** 向…提出抗议. ***under ~*** 不情愿地, 抗议着,在异议下.

Prot·es·tant [ˈprɔtistənt] *a.* ①新教徒的. ②〔p-〕提出抗议的,表示不服的. — *n.* ①新教徒. ②〔p-〕抗议者.

Prot·es·tant·ism [ˈprɔtistəntizəm] *n.* ①新教;耶稣教. ②〔集合词〕新教徒. ③新教徒的制度[教义].

Prot·es·tant·ize [ˈprɔtistəntaiz] *vt., vi.* (使)改信新教,(使)新教化,(使)成新教徒.

pro·tes·ta·tion [ˌprəutesˈteiʃən] *n.* ①声明,断言,主张(*of; that*). ②抗议,异议(的提出);拒绝(*against*).

pro·test·er [prəˈtestə] *n.* ①声明者. ② 抗议者,提出异议者;拒付(期票等)者.

pro·test·ing·ly [prəˈtestiŋli] *ad.* 抗议地,不服地.

Pro·teus [ˈprəutjuːs] *n.* ①【希神】普罗秋斯,变幻无定的海神. ②〔p-〕容易变的东西;三心二意的[反复无常的]人;【动】变形虫〔亚米巴的旧名〕. ④【动】盲螈属.

pro·tha·la·mi·on, pro·tha·la·mi·um [ˌprəuθəˈleimiən, -əm] *n.* (*pl.* ***-mi·a*** [-ə]) 祝婚歌,洞房赞.

pro·thal·li·um [prəˈθæliəm](*pl.* ***pro·thal·li·a*** [-ˈθæliə]) *n.* 【植】原叶体.

proth·e·sis [ˈprɔθisis] *n.* ①【语法】词首增添字母〔音节〕(= prosthesis). ②【东正教】圣餐桌; 圣餐的准备;圣餐的施舍.

pro·thon·o·tar·y [prəuˈθɔnətəri, ˌprəuθəˈnəutəri] *n.* (*pl.* ***-tar·ies***) ①法院的首席书记. ②【天主】罗马教皇的书记教士.

pro·tho·rax [prəuˈθɔːræks] *n.* (*pl.* ***-rax·es, -ra·ces*** [-əˌsiːz]) 【动】前胸;前胸节. **-rac·ic** [-ˈræsik] *a.*

pro·throm·bin [prəuˈθrɔmbin] *n.* 【生化】凝血酶原.

pro·tist [ˈprəutist] *n.* 【生】原生生物. **-tis·tan** *a., n.*

pro·ti·um [ˈprəutiəm] *n.* 【化】氕.

pro·to- *comb. f.* 第一, 主要, 原始, 最初: *proto*-Arabic 原始阿拉伯人的.

pro·to·ac·tin·i·um [ˌprəutəuækˈtiniəm] *n.* 【化】镤〔protactinium 的旧名〕.

pro·to·col [ˈprəutəkɔl] *n.* ①议定书; 调查书, 始末记. ②(条约等的)草案,草约; (罗马教皇诏书等的) 首尾程式. ③〔the P-〕法国外交部的礼宾司. — *vt., vi.* ①(把…)记入议定书. ②打(草稿),拟(草案).

pro·to·his·to·ry [ˌprəutəuˈhistəri] *n.* ①史前时期. ②史前人类学.

pro·to·hu·man [ˌprəutəuˈhjuːmən] *a.* 古时类人猿的,早期原始人的.

pro·to·lith·ic [ˌprəutəuˈliθik] *a.* 原始石器时代的.

pro·to·mar·tyr [ˌprəutəuˈmɑːtə] *n.* 第一个殉道者〔殉教者〕.

pro·ton [ˈprəutɔn] *n.* 【物】(正)质子; 氕核, 氢核始基;精朊脎. ~ *decay* 质子衰变. ~*-force* 质子间力. ~*-scattering* 质子互致散射.

pro·to·na·tion [ˌprəutəˈneiʃən] *n.* 质子注入.

pro·to·ne·ma [ˌprəutəuˈniːmə] *n.* (*pl.* ***-ma·ta*** [-mətə]) 【植】原丝体. **-l** *a.*

pro·to·ne·phrid·i·um [ˌprəutəuniˈfridiəm] *n.* 【动】原肾;原肾管.

pro·ton·o·tar·y, pro·thon·o·tar·y [prəuˈtɔnətəri] *n.* (*pl.* ***-tar·ies***) = prothonotary.

pro·to·nymph [ˈprəutəuˌnimf] *n.* 【动】第一若虫. **-al** *a.*

pro·to·path·ic [ˌprəutəuˈpæθik] *a.* 【生理】(皮肤的)初感的;原始的,初期的.

pro·to·phyte [ˈprəutəfait] *n.* 【植】原生植物,单细胞植物.

pro·to·plasm [ˈprəutəplæzəm] *n.* 【生】原生质; 原浆;细胞质. **-plas·mat·ic, -ic** *a.*

pro·to·plast [ˈprəutəplæst] *n.* 原人; 原物; 原生动物;【生】原生质体.

pro·to·ste·le [ˈprəutəstiːl -stiːli] *n.* 【生】原生中柱. **-ste·lic** *a.*

pro·to·troph·ic [ˌprəutəuˈtrɔfik] *a.* 【生】原始营养的,原养型的(固氮细菌),不需有机营养的.

pro·to·type [ˈprəutətaip] *n.* ①原型;典型; 样板; 模范,标准. ②试制型式; 样机; 样品;【物】原器. **-typ·al, -typ·ic, -i·cal** *a.*

prot·ox·ide [prəuˈtɔksaid] *n.* 初氧化物,低(价)氧化物.

pro·to·xy·lem [ˈprəutəzailəm, -lem] *n.* 【植】原生木质部.

Pro·to·zo·a [ˌprəutəuˈzəuə] *n. pl.* 【动】原生动物门. **-zo·an** *n., a.* 原生动物(的).

pro·to·zo·an, pro·to·zo·ic [ˌprəutəuˈzəuən, -ik] *n.* 原生动物 (= protozoon). — *a.* 原生动物的.

pro·to·zo·ol·o·gy [ˌprəutəuzəuˈɔlədʒi] *n.* 原生动物学.

pro·to·zo·on [ˌprəutəuˈzəuən] *n.* (*pl.* ***pro·to·zo·a*** [-ə]) 原生动物. **-al** *a.*

pro·tract [prəˈtrækt] *vt.* ①拖长, 延长. ②(用比例尺半圆规) 画(线),画(角),制(图). ③【解】伸出,突出 (*opp.* retract). ~ *one's stay for some weeks* 多逗留几个星期. ~*-ed disease* 拖得很久的病. *a ~ed test* 疲劳试验. *a ~ed* *warfare* 持久战.

pro·tract·ile [prəˈtræktail] *a.* (动物器官等)可伸长的.

pro·trac·tion [prəˈtrækʃən] *n.* ①拖延;伸长,延长. ②制图.

pro·trac·tor [prəˈtræktə] *n.* ①半圆规,分度规,量角器. ②【解】牵引肌. ③【外】异物取除器;钳取器. ④使延长的人. *a bevel(ed)* ~ 角度尺,斜角规,活动量角器.

pro·trude [prəˈtruːd] *vt., vi.* (推)出;(使)突出;(使)伸出 *(beyond)*. ~ *one's tongue* 伸出舌头. *protruding eyes* 凸眼.

pro·trud·ent [prəˈtruːdənt] *a.* 突出的,伸出的.

pro·tru·sile [prəˈtruːsail] *a.* 可突出的,可伸出的.

pro·tru·sion [prəˈtruːʒən] *n.* ①突出,伸出;突起;隆起. ②突起部,隆起物.

pro·tru·sive [prəˈtruːsiv] *a.* 突出的,伸出的;突兀的;触目的.

pro·tu·ber·ance [prəˈtjuːbərəns] *n.* 突起;突出部;瘤,节疤,疙瘩. *a solar* ~【天】日珥. *a* ~ *on a tree* 树节疤. *a cancerous* ~ 癌肿.

pro·tu·ber·ant [prəˈtjuːbərənt] *a.* 凸出的,突起的,隆起的;显著的.

pro·tu·ber·ate [prəuˈtjuːbəreit, ˌ-tuː-] *vi.* *(-at·ed; -at·ing)* 凸出,隆起,突起.

pro·tyle, pro·tyl [ˈprəutail] *n.*【化】(不可分)原质〔想象中认为构成原素的物质〕. *the* ~ *theory* (物质)单元(学)说.

proud [praud] *a.* ①傲慢的,骄傲的. ②有自尊心的,自重的;有见识的. ③自豪的,得意的,高兴的,引以为荣的 *(of)*. ④光荣的,漂亮的,高尚的,堂皇的. ⑤溢出的;涨水的;凸现出来的. ⑥〔古〕勇敢的;〔诗〕(马等)活蹦乱跳的. *a* ~ *man* 傲慢的人. *He is too* ~ *to ask questions.* 他太骄傲,总不问人. *a* ~ *father* (因有好儿子而)得意的父亲. *a* ~ *sight* 壮丽景色. *a* ~ *achievement* 辉煌的成就. *a* ~ *occasion* 隆重的场合. *a* ~ *tailor*〔方〕金翅雀. ***as* ~ *as Punch [a peacock]*** 扬扬得意. ***be* ~ *of*** 以…自豪,对…感觉得意〔光荣〕(*I am* ~ *of his acquaintance.* 我因认识他而觉得自豪). ~ ***flesh*** (伤口长好后凸出的)疤;【医】浮肉. ***too* ~ *to fight*** 战争有违自尊心,不屑战争. — *ad.*〔口〕= proudly. ***do one*** ~〔口〕给面子,使欢喜 (*You do me* ~. (你这样说)令我感到荣幸. *It will do me* ~. 这将使我很满意). ***do oneself*** ~ 干得漂亮,有面子;得意;养尊处优. **~-hearted** *a.* 骄傲的,傲慢的. **-ly** *ad.*

Prou·dhon [pruːˈdɔŋ, F. pruˈdɔ̃], **P·J·** 蒲鲁东〔1809-1865,法国小资产阶级经济学家和社会学家〕.

Prou·dhon·ism [pruːˈdɔːŋizəm] *n.* 普鲁东主义. **-ist** *n.* 蒲鲁东主义者.

Proust [pruːst] *n.* 普鲁斯特〔姓氏〕.

Prov. = ①Proverbs. ②Province. ③Provençal. ④Provence.

prov. = ①provincial. ②provisional. ③provost.

prov·a·ble [ˈpruːvəbl] *a.* 可证明的;可证实的. **-bly** *ad.* **-ness** *n.*

prove [pruːv] *vt.* *(-d; -d,* 〔古、美〕***prov·en***[ˈpruːvən]*)* ①证明,证实;【法】验证,检定. ②试验;检验(武器的效力). ③勘探,探明. ④【数】证,证明,验算,检算. ⑤【印】打(校样). ⑥〔古〕体验. ~ *oneself worthy of confidence* 证明有信用;不负信赖. ~ *a gun* 试炮. *the proving ground*【军】试炮场,打靶场. *I* ~*d the extreme depths of poverty.* 我体验过极贫苦的生活. — *vi.* 结果是…,成为…;试验. *He* ~*d (to be) a swindler* 他原来是个骗子. ~ ***up*** *(on a claim)* 具备(提出某某要求的)条件. ~ ***up to the hilt*** 充分证明.

prov·en [ˈpruːvən] *v.*〔古、美〕prove 的过去分词. —*a.* 被证明了的. ***not*** ~〔Scot.〕【法】证据不足.

prov·e·nance [ˈprɔvinəns] *n.* 起源,出处;原产地. *of doubtful* ~ 出处可疑的.

Prov·en·cal [ˌprɔvɑ̃ːnˈsɑːl] *a.* (法国)普罗旺斯州 (Provence)(人)的. — *n.* 普罗旺斯人[语].

Pro·vence [prɔˈvɑ̃ːns] *n.* 普罗旺斯〔法国东南一地区,中世纪时以诗歌与武侠著称〕.

prov·en·der [ˈprɔvində] *n.* 饲料,粮草,秣;〔谑〕(人的)食物.

pro·ve·ni·ence [prəuˈviːniəns, -ˈviːnjəns] *n.*〔美〕= provenance.

pro·ven·tric·u·lus [ˌprəuvinˈtrikjuləs] *n.* *(pl.* ***-li*** [-ˌlai]*)*【动】①鸟的前胃. ②蚯蚓和龙虾的前胃.

prov·er [ˈpruːvə] *n.* ①试验装置. ②【印】打校样的工人. ③〔古〕证明者.

prov·erb [ˈprɔvəb, -əːb] *n.* ①谚语,古话;俗话;箴言. ②话柄,笑柄. ③人人知道的事情;有名的事情. ④俚谚剧. ⑤〔*pl.*〕俚谚游戏. *His punctuality is a* ~. = *He is a* ~ *for punctuality.* 他严守时间是有名的. *The (Book of) P-s* (基督教《旧约全书》)《箴言》. ***as the* ~ *goes [runs]*** 俗话说. ***pass into a*** ~ ①成为谚语. ②成话柄. ***to a*** ~ 弄到出名 (*He is punctual to a* ~ 他严守时间是人所共知的).

pro·verb [ˈprəuvəːb] *n.*【语法】代动词.

pro·ver·bi·al [prəˈvəːbiəl] *a.* ①谚语(式)的. ②已成话柄的. ③出名的,天下闻名的. *the* ~ *London fog* 有名的伦敦雾.

pro·ver·bi·al·ist [prəˈvəːbjəlist] *n.* 善用谚语的人;谚语作者;集谚者.

pro·ver·bi·al·ly [prəˈvəːbjəli] *ad.* ①如谚语所说. ②广泛地,一般(所知道)地. *Why, medicine is* ~ *nasty.* 药当然难吃啰.

pro·vide [prəˈvaid] *vt.* ①(为某人)提供,供应某物, *(for sb.)*; (以某物)供给某人,(以某物)装备另一物 *(with)*. ②(条约,法律等)规定 *(that)*. ③【宗史】任命,指定…做候补牧师 *(to)*. ④【法】考虑,酌量 *(for)*. ⑤〔古〕准备,预备. ~ *food and clothe for one's family* 为家里人供应衣食. ~ *one's family with food and clothes* 以衣食供应家里人. ~ *children with a good education* 为儿童提供良好的教育条件. ~ *a car with radio* 给汽车装上无线电设备. *Sheep* ~ *us with wool.* 羊供给我们羊毛. *She was* ~*d for, at any rate.* 她总算有了一个着落. — *vi.* ①作准备 *(for)*;预防 *(against)*. ②赡养;提供生计 *(for)*. ③规定 *(for)*;禁止 *(against)*. ~ *for old age* 防老. ~ *against accident* 以防万一. ~ *for one's children* 抚养子女. *The constitution* ~*s for an elected two-chamber legislature.* 宪法规定设置经选举产生的两院制立法机构. ~ ***oneself*** 自备,自办.

pro·vid·ed [prəːˈvaidid] *conj.* 倘若…,只要,在…条件下. *I will come* ~ *(that) I am well enough.* 身体好一定来. —*a.* 预备好的;由…供给的. ~ **school**〔英〕(靠地方税维持的)公立小学校.

Prov·i·dence [ˈprɔvidəns] *n.* 普罗维登斯〔美、加城市〕.

prov·i·dence [ˈprɔvidəns] *n.* ①〔常 *P-*〕神意,天道,天命;〔*P-*〕神,上帝. ②〔罕〕精明,深谋远虑;节约. ③【古】准备. ***a special*** ~ ①天助,天佑. ②自然力,命运. *a visitation of P-* 天灾.

prov·i·dent [ˈprɔvidənt] *a.* ①有先见之明的. ②精明的,节俭的. *He is* ~ *of his money.* 他用钱很节省. **-ly** *ad.*

prov·i·den·tial [ˌprɔviˈdenʃəl] *a.* 神意的;天祐的,幸运的. **-ly** *ad.* 照天意,靠天祐.

pro·vid·er [prəˈvaidə] *n.* ①供给者,准备者. ②需供养家庭的人. *a lion's* ~【动】豺狼 (= jackal);为虎作伥的人,被人利用的人,爪牙. *a universal* ~ 杂货商. *a good* ~ 能使家属丰衣美食的人.

pro·vid·ing [prəˈvaidiŋ] *conj.* = provided.

provinc. = provincial.

prov·ince [ˈprɔvins] *n.* ①省,州;〔*pl.*〕地区,地方;〔the ~s〕乡下. ②本分,职责;(学问等的)范围. ③【宗】大教区;【罗马史】(国外)行省;(旧时)英国在北美的殖民地. *one's native* ～ 故乡. *London and the* ～*s* 〔英〕中央和(全国各)地方. ***be within one's*** ～ 在某人职权内,是某人的本分. ***in the*** ～***s*** 在地方上,在乡下.

pro·vin·cial [prəˈvinʃəl] *a.* ①地方的, 乡下的. ②省的,州的;领地的. ③乡下气的;鄙俗的,粗野的;地方性的, 褊狭的. ④〔英〕大教区的. *a* ～ *accent* 土腔. *a* ～ *paper* 地方报. — *n.* 地方居民,乡下人;【英宗】(管辖教区的)大主教. **-ly** *ad.*

pro·vin·cial·ism [prəˈvinʃəlizəm] *n.* ①乡下气,粗野. ②土腔,方言. ③地区性,褊狭;地方感情,乡土观念. ④地方主义.

pro·vin·cial·ist [prəˈvinʃəlist] *n.* ①地方居民,外省人;乡下人. ②地方主义者.

pro·vin·ci·al·i·ty [prəˌvinʃiˈæliti] *n.* ①地方风尚. ②乡下气,土气;粗野.

pro·vin·cial·ize [prəˈvinʃəlaiz] *vt., vi.* (使)地方化,(使)带乡下气;(使)乡土化人;用方言[土腔]讲.

pro·vi·sion [prəˈviʒən] *n.* ①预备, 准备, 设备 *(for; against)*; 供应,(一批)供应品;生活物资; 贮备物资. ②〔*pl.*〕食品,粮食. ③【法】规定,条项,条款. *an express* ～【法】明文(规定). *the* ～*s of lease* 租借条款. ***according to the*** ～***s of the Act*** 据该法令各条(所说). ***make ample*** ～ ***for*** 充裕地供养. ***make*** ～ 预备,准备 *(against)*. ***run out of*** ～***s*** = ***short of*** ～***s*** 粮食缺乏. — *vt.* 向…供应粮食[必需品]. ～ **merchant** 食品商人. **-er** *n.* 粮食筹办员. **-ment** *n.* 粮食供应.

pro·vi·sion·al [prəˈviʒənl] *a.* 假定的,暂时的,临时的. *a* ～ *consent* 假答应. ～ *charter* 临时执照[证书]. *a* ～ *government* 临时政府. ～ *headquarters* 行营. *the P-37th Division* 暂编第37师. *a* ～ *order* 紧急命令. *a* ～ *treaty* 临时条约. **-ly** *ad.*

pro·vi·sion·al·i·ty [prəˌviʒəˈnæliti] *n.* 临时性, 暂时性.

pro·vi·sion·a·ry [prəˈviʒənəri] *a.* 〔罕〕= provisional.

pro·vi·so [prəˈvaizəu] *n.* ***(pl. -s, -es)*** 附带条款,附文;条件,但书,限制性条款. *I make it a* ～ *that* 以…为附带条件. *with the [a]* ～ *that* 以…为条件.

pro·vi·sor [prəˈvaizə] *n.* ①伙食采办者. ②【宗】(尤其指未出缺的)圣职的被委任者. ③【天主】副主教,代理主教.

pro·vi·so·ry [prəˈvaizəri] *a.* ①有附文的; 有附带条件的. ②临时的,暂定的. *a* ～ *clause* 附文;附带条款;限制性条款,保留条款.

pro·vi·ta·min [prəuˈvaitəmin] *n.* 【生化】维生素原,原维生素.

pro·vo [ˈprəuvəu] *n.* ***(pl. -vos)*** 青年无政府主义者〔在一些欧洲国家内自由地组织起来的无政府主义运动的青年〕.

pro·voc·a·ble, pro·vok·a·ble [prəˈvəukəbl] *a.* 易受刺激[煽动、挑拨]的.

pro·vo·ca·teur [prɔvɔkatœːr] *n.* 〔F.〕 ***(fem. -trice*** [-tris]***)*** 坐探,奸细,内奸 (= agent ～); (故意煽动肇事的)破坏分子,煽动者.

prov·o·ca·tion [ˌprɔvəˈkeiʃən] *n.* ①触怒; 挑拨,挑衅;刺激,煽动;诱发. ②惹人恼火的事;刺激的原因. ③愤怒,发怒,发脾气. ～ *and estrangement* 挑拨离间. ***at the slightest*** ～ = on the slightest ～. ***give*** ～ 激怒,使发怒. ***make*** ～ ***against*** 挑衅. ***on the slightest*** ～ 动不动就…,并不因为什么了不起的事就…. ***under*** ～ 在愤怒下. ***without*** ～ 无缘无故. ～ **method** 诱发试验法.

pro·voc·a·tive [prəˈvɔkətiv] *a.* ①气(人)的, 使人生气的,寻衅的,挑衅的;挑拨性的,刺激性的,(言语、态度等)煽动性的. ②使引起…的*(of)*;引起争论[议论、兴趣等]的. ～ *behaviour* 惹人恼火的行为. *be* ～ *of mirth* 引人发笑. — *n.* 刺激物;兴奋剂. **-ly** *ad.*

pro·voke [prəˈvəuk] *vt.* ①触怒,使愤怒,激怒. ②成为…的原因,引起. ③驱使,逼使;激发,煽动某人做某事 ***(to sth., to do sth.)***. *Don't allow yourself to be* ～*d.* 你不要激动; 你别发火. ～ *riot* 引起骚乱. ～ *indignation* 激起义愤. *This is thought-provoking.* 这是耐人寻味的[颇有启发性的]. ～ *sb. to anger* 惹怒某人. *Oppression* ～*d the people to rebellion.* 压迫逼得老百姓们起来造反了. **-r** *n.*

pro·vok·ing [prəˈvəukiŋ] *a.* 气人的,叫人冒火的,难熬的,叫人焦躁的. **-ly** *ad.*

pro·vo·lo·ne [ˌprəuvəˈləuni, ˌprɔvə-] *n.* 〔It.〕意大利熏干酪〔一种硬的浅色干酪,梨形,通常用烟熏制成〕.

prov·ost [ˈprɔvəst] *n.* ①〔英〕(牛津剑桥等大学某些学院的)院长;〔美〕教务长. ②【史】大教堂主监;修道院长;宗教团体首领. ③〔Scot.〕市长. ④(德国城市新教教会的)牧师. ⑤[prəˈvəu]【军】宪兵司令. ～ **court** 宪兵法庭. ～ **marshal** 宪兵司令. **P- Marshal Department** 宪兵司令部. ～ **sergeant** 宪兵军士.

prow[1] [prau] *n.* 船首,舳;飞机头部;〔诗〕船.

prow[2] [prau] *a.* 〔古〕英勇的,威风凛凛的.

prow·ess [ˈprauis] *n.* 英勇; 威力; 本事. *show one's* ～ 显威风;显本事.

prowl [praul] *vi.* ①(小偷等)鬼鬼祟祟地踱来踱去; (觅食的野兽)悄悄地荡来荡去. ②徘徊 *(about)*. — *vt.* ①在…鬼鬼祟祟地荡来荡去. ②在…徘徊. — *n.* ①(野兽)到处觅食;(小偷)四处探头探脑. ②徘徊;潜行. ***be [go] on the*** ～ (尤指小偷伺机) 踱来踱去. ***take a*** ～ 荡来荡去. ～ **car** 〔美〕警备车.

prowl·er [ˈpraulə] *n.* 荡来荡去的人,徘徊者;秘密警察;小偷(等).

prox. = 〔L.〕*proximo.*

prox·i·mal [ˈprɔksiməl] *a.* ①【解】近身体中心的; 近基的,近轴的 *(opp.* distal*)*. ②最接近的,近似的. **-ly** *ad.*

prox·i·mate [ˈprɔksimit] *a.* ①最接近的; 近似的. ②即将到来〔发生〕的. *the* ～ *cause* 近因, 直接原因. ～ *principles* 近似成分. *the* ～ *grade* 次一级. **-ly** *ad.*

prox·i·me ac·ces·sit [ˈprɔksimi ækˈsesit] ***(pl. accesserunt*** [-ˈsiərənt]***)*** 〔L.〕(赛跑等的) 第二名; 第二. *I was [I got a] proxime accessit.* 我得了第二.

prox·im·e·ter [prɔkˈsimitə] *n.* 【空】着陆高度计.

prox·im·i·ty [prɔkˈsimiti] *n.* 接近,邻近,临近;接近度,距离; 亲近 *(to)*. ～ *of blood* 近亲. ***in close*** ～ ***(to)*** 与…极接近, 紧靠. ***in the*** ～ ***of*** 在…附近. ～ **effect** 邻近效应. ～**-fused** 【火箭】备有近爆引信的,装有近发[无线电]引信的.

prox·i·mo [ˈprɔksiməu] *ad.* 〔L.〕下月〔略 *prox.*〕. ***on the 10th prox.*** 下月十日. ★现在多用 *next month.*

prox·y [ˈprɔksi] *n.* ①代理(权);代表(权);代理投票. ②代理人, 代表人; 代用品. ③(对代理人的)委托书. ***by*** ～ 用代理人, 由代表. ***stand [be]*** ～ ***for*** 做…的代理人,代表….

prs. = ①pairs. ②printers.

prtd. = printed.

prtg. = printing.

prude [pruːd] *n.* 过分拘谨的人; 显得[装作]正经的人〔尤指女人〕.

Pru·dence [ˈpruːdəns] *n.* 普鲁登丝〔女子名〕.

pru·dence [ˈpruːdəns] *n.* ①小心,谨慎. ②精明. ③节俭. ***in common*** ～ 应有的小心. ***use*** ～ 采取慎重态度.

pru·dent [ˈpruːdənt] *a.* ①小心的,慎重的,顾虑周到的,稳健的. ②世故的, 精明的. ③节俭的, 会打算的. *be modest and* ～ 谦虚谨慎. **-ly** *ad.*

pru·den·tial [pru(ː)ˈdenʃəl] *a.* ①谨慎的;考虑周到的. ②备咨询的. *a* ～ *committee* 〔美〕(学校、教会等的) 咨询委员会. — *n.* 〔*pl.*〕必须慎重的事; 慎重的考虑. **-ism** *n.* 谨慎第一. **-ist** *n.* 谨慎小心的人. **-ly** *ad.*

pru·d·er·y [ˈpruːdəri] *n.* 过分拘谨;装正经,假正经.

prud'homme [pruːˈdɔm] *n.* 〔F.〕①【法】劳资纠纷调解委员. ②行家,里手.

prud·ish [ˈpruːdiʃ] *a.* ①过分拘谨的. ②一本正经的,假正经的. **-ly** *ad.*

pru·i·nose [ˈpruːinəus] *a.* 【植】具白粉的,具果霜的.

prune[1] [pruːn] *vt.* ①修剪(树枝),剪除,伐除 *(down)*; 砍去 *(away; off)*. ②省去(费用等); 删掉,除去(多余部分). ~ *a writing of superfluous words* 删去文章中的冗语.

prune[2] [pruːn] *n.* ①洋李脯,梅干. ②深紫红色. ③〔美〕没趣的人,讨厌的人; 蠢货. ***full of ~s*** 〔美俚〕傲慢的; 完全错误的,胡诌的. **~ peddler** 〔美〕食品商,食品店员. **~ picker** 〔美〕果园工人. **~s and prisms** 装腔作势; 矫揉造作的(人或言语).

prune[3] [pruːn] *vt.* 〔罕〕= preen.

pru·nel·la[1] [pru(ː)ˈnelə] *n.* 英国普鲁涅拉斜纹薄呢.

pru·nel·la[2] [pru(ː)ˈnelə] *n.* ①【医】鹅口疮,霉菌性口炎. ②〔P-〕【植】夏枯草属.

prun·ing [ˈpruːniŋ] *n.* ①(树等的)修剪. ②【电】切断分路. ~ **hook** 修枝钩镰. ~ **shears** 剪枝剪.

pru·ri·ence, pru·ri·en·cy [ˈpruəriəns, -ənsi] *n.* ①好色. ②渴望,热望.

pru·ri·ent [ˈpruəriənt] *a.* ①好色的. ②〔罕〕渴想的. ③(枝、芽等)伸得过长的. **-ly** *ad.*

pru·ri·go [pruəˈraigəu] *n.* 【医】痒疹.

pru·ri·tus [pruəˈraitəs] *n.* 瘙痒. **pru·rit·ic** [-ˈritik] *a.*

Prus(s). = Prussia(n).

Prus·sia [ˈprʌʃə] *n.* 【史】普鲁士.

Prus·sian [ˈprʌʃən] *a.* 普鲁士(人)的; 普鲁士式的〔指训练严酷的、军国主义的和妄自尊大的〕. — *n.* ①普鲁士人. ②(古)普鲁士语. ~ **blue** 【化】普鲁士蓝; 绀青色.

Prus·sian·ism [ˈprʌʃənizəm] *n.* 大普鲁士主义〔特指普鲁士统治阶级的专横、黩武主义和严酷纪律性〕.

Prus·sian·ize [ˈprʌʃənaiz] *vt.* 使普鲁士化〔尤指严格的纪律和服从权威方面〕. **-i·za·tion** *n.*

prus·si·ate [ˈprʌʃiit] *n.* 【化】氰化物; 亚铁氰化物; 铁氰化物; 氢氰酸盐.

prus·sic [ˈprʌsik] *a.* 【化】(从)氰化物(得来)的. ~ **acid** 【化】氢氰酸,氰化氢.

pru·ta [ˈpruːtɑ, pruːˈtɑː] *n.* *(pl.* ***pru·tot*** [-ˈtəut]*)* 普鲁达〔以色列的辅币单位,相等于 1/1000 以色列镑〕.

pry[1] [prai] *vi.* 眼睛盯着看,盯; 窥探; 刺探,打听 *(into)*. — *n.* ①窥视; 窥探. ②爱刺探的人. ~ ***about*** 到处窥探. ~ ***into other people's affairs*** 打听别人事情. ~ ***out*** 探出(别人秘密等).

pry[2] [prai] 〔美、英方〕 *n.* 撬具; 杆子,杠杆. — *vt.* (用杠杆等)撬,撬起,撬动; (用尽方法)使脱离.

pry·er [ˈpraiə] *n.* 窥探者,打听(别人事情)者(= prier).

pry·ing [ˈpraiiŋ] *a.* 窥视的; 窥探的; 爱刺探的.

Prynne [prin] *n.* 普林〔姓氏〕.

pryth·ee [ˈpriðiː] *int.* 〔古语、口〕请,求求你(=prithee).

PS., p.s. = postscript.

P.S., PS = ①passenger steamer 客轮. ②permanent secretary 常任书记. ③privy seal 〔英〕御玺; Privy Seal =Lord Privy Seal 〔英〕掌玺大臣. ④public school (英国的)公学; (美国的)公立中学〔小学〕. ⑤police sergeant 警官,巡官. ⑥ prompt side 〔英〕舞台上演员的左方; 〔美〕舞台上演员的右方. ⑦postscript. ⑧per second 每秒.

Ps. =Psalms.

ps. =① pieces. ② pseudonym.

p/s; p/s. = periods per second 周/秒.

psalm [sɑːm] *n.* ①【宗】赞美诗,圣诗,圣歌. ②〔P-〕〔*pl.*〕【圣】《诗篇》. — *vt.* 用赞美诗祝贺. ~ **book** = Psalter. **-ist** *n.* 赞美诗〔诗篇〕作者; 〔the Psalmist〕《诗篇》作者,大卫 (David) 王.

psal·mo·dy [ˈsælmədi, ˈsɑːmə-] *n.* 【宗】唱赞美诗; 赞美诗集. **-ic, -i·cal** *a.* **-dist** *n.* 唱赞美诗的人; 赞美诗作者.

Psal·ter [ˈsɔːltə] *n.* ①【圣】《诗篇》. ②〔p-〕(祷告用的)分印诗篇.

psal·te·ri·um [sɔlˈtiəriəm] *n.* *(pl.* ***-ri·a*** [-ə]*)* 重瓣胃 (= omasum).

psal·ter·y [ˈsɔːltəri] *n.* ①(14—15 世纪的)八弦琴. ②〔P-〕= Psalter.

psam·mite [ˈsæmait] *n.* 〔罕〕【地】砂屑岩(=sandstone). **-mit·ic** [-ˈmitik] *a.*

psam·mon [ˈsæmɔn] *n.* 【生态】适砂〔喜砂〕生物.

psam·mo·phile [ˈsæməfail] *n.* 喜砂性生物〔有机体〕,适砂植物.

psam·mo·phyte [ˈsæməfait] *n.* 砂生植物.

pse·phite [ˈsiːfait] *n.* 砾质岩. **-phit·ic** [-ˈfitik] *a.*

pse·phol·ogy [siˈfɔlədʒi] *n.* 选举学〔对选举结果的统计估价〕. **-log·i·cal** [-ˈlɔdʒikl] *a.* **-gist** *n.*

pse·pho·man·cy [ˈsiːfəmænsi] *n.* 石(子)(占)卜.

pseud. =pseudonym.

pseu·de·pig·ra·pha [ˌsjuːdiˈpigrəfə, ˌsuː-] *n. pl.* 〔亦作 P-〕圣经的模拟作品,圣经的伪仿作品〔所写的虽是经中的人物但不是圣典的正经〕. **-phous** [-fəs] *a.*

pseud(o)- *comb.f.* 伪,拟,假,赝: *pseudo*archaic; *pseudo*-classical; *pseudo*-martyr; *pseudo*-plastic.

pseu·do [ˈpsjuːdəu] *a.* 〔口〕假,伪,冒充的.

pseu·do·al·um [psjuːdəuˈæləm, ˌsuː-] *n.* 假矾.

pseu·do·ar·cha·ic [psjuːdəuɑːˈkɑːik] *a.* 拟古的.

pseu·do·carp [ˈpsjuːdəukɑːp, ˈsuː-] *n.* 假果 (= false fruit). **-ous** *a.*

pseu·do·clas·sic [psjuːdəuˈklæsik, ˌsuː-] *a.* 拟古典的,伪古典的. — *n.* 拟古典的东西.

pseu·do·clas·si·cism [ˈpsjuːdəuˈklæsisizəm] *n.* 拟古体; 拟古典主义; 伪古典主义.

pseu·do-dem·o·crat·ic [ˈpsjuːdəuˌdeməˈkrætik] *a.* 假民主的.

pseu·do·graph [ˈpsjuːdəugrɑːf] *n.* 伪书,冒名著作.

pseu·do·her·maph·ro·dite [psjuːdəuhəˈmæfrədait, ˌsuː-] *n.* 【医】假两性畸形. **-dit·ic** [-ˈditik] *a.* **-dit·ism, -rod·ism** *n.*

Pseu·do·la·rix [psjudəuˈlæriks] *n.* 【植】金钱松属.

pseu·dol·o·gy [psjuːˈdɔlədʒi] *n.* 谎话; 说谎.

pseu·do·mar·tyr [psjuːdəuˈmɑːtə] *n.* 伪殉教者.

pseu·do·morph [ˈpsjuːdəmɔːf] *n.* ①【矿】假晶,假同晶,赝形体. ②假象,伪形. **-ic, -ous** *a.*

pseu·do·nym [ˈpsjuːdənim] *n.* 假名; (特指作者的)笔名.

pseu·do·nym·i·ty [ˌpsjuːdəuˈnimiti] *n.* 使用假名〔笔名〕; 签有假名〔笔名〕.

pseu·don·y·mous [psjuːˈdɔniməs] *a.* 用假名〔笔名〕写的; 签有假名〔笔名〕的; 用假名〔笔名〕的.

pseu·do·plas·tic [ˌpsjuːdəuˈplæstik] *n.* 类塑料,代塑料,假塑性体.

pseu·do·po·di·um [psjuːdəuˈpəudiəm] *n.* *(pl.* ***-di·a*** [-ə]*)* 【动】假足,伪足 (=pseudopod). **-dop·o·dal** [-ˈdɔpədəl] *a.*

pseu·do·preg·nan·cy [ˌpsjuːdəuˈpregnənsi] *n.* *(pl.* ***-cies****)* 【医】假孕. **-preg·nant** *a.*

pseu·do·salt [psjuːdəuˈsɔːlt, suː-] *n.* 假盐〔不能电离的盐〕.

pseu·do·sci·ence [psjuːdəuˈsaiəns] *n.* 假科学,伪科学. **-sci·en·tif·ic** *a.*

pseu·do·scope [ˈpsjuːdəskəup] *n.* 【物】幻视镜 (*opp.* stereoscope).

p.s.f., psf = pounds per square foot 每平方英尺上的磅数,磅/英尺².

pshaw [pʃɔː] *int.* 啐! 哼! 〔表示轻蔑、讨厌、急躁〕. — *n.* 啐〔哼〕的声音. — *vi., vt.* 啐一声 *(at)*; 用鼻子哼的一声应付.

psi [psai] *n.* 希腊语的第二十三字母〔Ψ、ψ,相当于英语的 ps].

p.s.i., psi = pounds per square inch 每平方英寸上的磅数，磅/英寸²。

psia ① pounds per square inch absolute 绝对压强〔磅/英寸²〕. ② pounds per square inch of area 磅/平方英寸面积。

psi·lan·thro·py, psi·lan·thro·pism [psaiˈlænθrəpi, -pizəm] *n.* 耶稣凡夫论。

psi·lo·cin [ˈpsailəsin] *n.* 【生化】裸头草辛，二甲-4-羟色胺。

psi·lo·cy·bin [ˌpsailəˈsaibin] *n.* 【生化】裸头草碱，二甲-4-羟色胺磷酸。

psi·lom·e·lane [psaiˈlɔmilein] *n.* 硬锰矿。

psi·lo·sis [psaiˈləusis] *n.* 【医】脱髮症，秃头病；口炎性腹泻。

psit·ta·cine [ˈpsitəsain, -sin] *a.* 鹦鹉的，似鹦鹉的. **-ly** *ad.*

psit·ta·co·sis [psitəˈkəusis] *n.* 【医】鹦鹉病，鹦鹉热。

P.S.N.C. = Pacific Steam Navigation Company〔英〕太平洋轮船海运公司。

pso·as [ˈpsəuəs] *n.* ***(pl. pso·ai, pso·ae*** [ˈsəuai,-iː]***)*** 【解】腰肌。

pso·cid [ˈpsəusid] *n.* 啮虫科 *(Psocidae)* 昆虫。

pso·phom·e·ter [psəuˈfɔmitə] *n.* 【物】噪声计；测听器。

pso·ra·le·a [psɔ(:)ˈreiliə] *n.* 【植】食用补骨脂 *(Psoralea esculenta)*.

pso·ri·a·sis [psɔ(:)ˈrai-əsis] *n.* 牛皮癣. **pso·ri·at·ic** [ˌpsɔ(:)riˈætik] *a.*

PSS, P.SS. = postscripts.

psst [ps] *int.* 喂！〔引起别人注意的感叹词〕。

PST, P.S.T. = Pacific Standard Time 太平洋标准时间〔美国太平洋沿岸等地采用的西八区时间〕。

psyc [saik] *n.*〔美口〕= psychology.

psych [saik] *vt.* ***(~ed; ~ing)***〔俚〕①使精神纷乱〔失调〕；使感情激动〔常与 *up* 连用〕. ②用精神分析法治疗 (= psycho-analyse). ③用直觉或按照心理学的方法分析……的动机或行动以便智胜(对手). ④〔~ oneself〕使作好精神准备. ~ *a table-tennis opponent* 以心理分析的方法智胜乒乓球对手. ~ ***out***〔美俚〕①吓坏了，吓糊涂了. ②装精神失常进行逃避。

psych. = psychological; psychology.

psy·chas·the·ni·a [ˌsaikəsˈθiːniə] *n.* 精神衰弱症. **-then·ic** [-ˈθenik] *a.*

psy·che [ˈpsaiki(:)] *n.* ①〔*P-*〕【希神】爱神 Eros 所爱的美女〔灵魂的化身〕. ②灵魂，精神. ③【虫】(属衰蛾科的)一种蛾。

psy·che·de·li·a [ˌsaikiˈdiːliə] *n.* ①幻觉剂〔服用后可使人兴奋的一种麻醉剂〕. ②服用幻觉剂的人。

psy·che·del·ic [ˌsaikiˈdelik] *a.* ①引起幻觉的，幻觉的. ②幻觉剂的. — *n.* 幻觉剂. **-cal·ly** *ad.*

psy·chi·at·ric, psy·chi·at·ri·cal [ˌsaikiˈætrik(əl)] *a.* 精神病学的；医精神病的。

psy·chi·a·trist [saiˈkaiətrist] *n.* 精神病医生；精神病学者。

psy·chi·a·try [saiˈkaiətri] *n.* 精神病学；精神病治疗法。

psy·chic, psy·chi·cal [ˈsaikik(əl)] *a.* ①精神的，灵魂的，心理的 (*opp.* physical)；【心】心理(现象)的. ②对超自然力量敏感的；通灵的. ~ *phenomena* 心灵现象. — *n.* ①灵媒；巫师，巫婆；对超自然力量敏感的人；通灵的人. ②精神上的现象；超自然的现象。

psy·chics [ˈsaikiks] *n.*〔口〕心理学；心灵研究。

psy·cho [ˈsaikəu] ***(pl. -chos)*** *n.* ①精神分析(学). ②精神(性)神经病患者. ③精神变态者。

psy·cho(-) *comb. f.* 灵魂，精神，心理：*psycho*analysis, *psycho*biology.

psy·cho·a·cous·tics [ˌsaikəuəˈkuːstiks] *n. pl.*〔动词用单数〕心理声学. **-cous·tic, -cous·ti·cal** *a.*

psy·cho·ac·tive [ˌsaikəuˈæktiv] *a.* (药剂)对神经起显著[特殊]作用的。

psy·cho·a·nal·y·sis [ˌsaikəuəˈnæləsis] *n.* 精神分析(学). **-an·alyst** *n.* 精神分析学家. **-an·alyt·ic(al)** [-əˈlitik(əl)] *a.* 精神分析的。

psy·cho·bi·ol·o·gy [ˌsaikəubaiˈɔlədʒi] *n.* ①心理生物学. ②生物心理学. **-log·i·cal** [-ˈlɔdʒikl] *a.*

psy·cho·chem·i·cal [ˌsaikəuˈkemikl] *n.* 精神病的治疗药物. — *a.* 精神病治疗药物的。

psy·cho·del·ic [ˌsaikəuˈdelik] *a.* 引起幻觉的，幻觉的. —*n.* 幻觉剂的. —*n.* 幻觉剂 (=psychedelic).

psy·cho·dra·ma [ˌsaikəuˈdrɑːmə] *n.* 心理剧〔一种可使患者的感情得以发泄从而达到治疗效果的戏剧〕。

psy·cho·dy·nam·ic [ˌsaikəudaiˈnæmik] *a.* 心理动力的. **-nam·ics** *n.* 心理动力学。

psy·cho·gen·e·sis [ˌsaikəuˈdʒenisis] *n.* 心理发生。

psy·cho·gen·ic [ˌsaikəuˈdʒenik] *a.* 心理发生的，心理(起源)的；由心理冲突引起的. **-al·ly** *ad.*

psy·cho·graph [ˈsaikəgrɑːf] *n.* 【心】心理图案。

psy·cho·ki·ne·sis [ˌsaikəukiˈniːsis] *n.* 【心】(灵学中研究的) 由于思想作用而影响客观事物的能力. **-net·ic** [-ˈnetik] *a.*

psychol. = psychological; psychologist; psychology.

psy·cho·lin·guis·tics [ˌsaikəuliŋˈgwistiks] *n.* 语言心理学。

psy·cho·log·i·cal [ˌsaikəˈlɔdʒikəl] *a.* 心理学(上)的；精神(现象)的. ~ *warfare* 心理战. *the* ~ *moment*【心】心理上的适当瞬间；〔口〕最适当的时机，紧要关头. **-ly** *ad.*

psy·chol·o·gism [saiˈkɔlədʒizəm] *n.* ①心理说，对心理因素的注重. ②心理学专门用语。

psy·chol·o·gist [saiˈkɔlədʒist] *n.* 心理学者；心理学家。

psy·chol·o·gize [saiˈkɔlədʒaiz] *vi.* 研究心理学. — *vt.* 从心理学的角度来解释；用心理学分析。

psy·chol·ogy [saiˈkɔlədʒi] *n.* ①心理学. ②心理. ③心理学论著；心理学体系. *child* ~ 儿童心理学. *comparative [criminal, experimental]* ~ 比较[犯罪，实验]心理学。

psy·chom·e·ter [saiˈkɔmitə] *n.* 用脑时间测定计；智力测验器。

psy·cho·met·rics [ˌsaikəˈmetriks] *n. pl.*〔动词用单数〕心理测验学 (=psychometry). **-tri·cian** *n.*

psy·chom·e·try [saiˈkɔmitri] *n.* ①心理测验(学)；用脑时间测定法；智力测验. ②触物卜卦；心灵占卜术。

psy·cho·mi·met·ic [ˌsaikəumiˈmetik] *a.* 【心】拟精神病的。

psy·cho·mo·tor [ˌsaikəuˈməutə] *a.* ①痉挛的〔精神作用对运动神经(肌)产生影响的〕. ②癫痫病状的〔发作特点是病人出现复杂的行为〕。

psy·cho·neu·ro·sis [ˌsaikəunjuəˈrəusis] *n.* ***(pl. -ses*** [-siːz]***)***【医】精神(性)神经病。

psy·cho·path [ˈsaikəupæθ] *n.* 精神变态者，心理病者。

psy·cho·path·ic [ˌsaikəuˈpæθik] *a.* 精神病态的，心理变态的. — *n.* 精神变态者，心理病者. ~ **hospital** 精神病院。

psy·cho·pa·thol·o·gy [ˌsaikəupəˈθɔlədʒi] *n.* 精神病理学，心理病理学。

psy·chop·a·thy [saiˈkɔpəθi] *n.* 精神变态，心理变态。

psy·cho·phar·ma·col·o·gy [ˌsaikəuˌfɑːməˈkɔlədʒi] *n.* 精神药理学. **-logic, -log·i·cal** *a.*

psy·cho·phys·ics [ˈsaikəuˈfiziks] *n.* 心理物理学，心物学。

psy·cho·phys·i·ol·o·gy [ˈsaikəuˌfiziˈɔlədʒi] *n.* 心理[精神]生理学。

psy·cho·sex·u·al [ˌsaikəuˈsekʃuəl] *a.* (精神上)有性的特性的〔与肉体上相对而言〕. **-sex·u·al·i·ty** [-ˈæliti] *n.*

psy·cho·sis [saiˈkəusis] *n.* *(pl. -ses* [-siːz]*)* ①精神病，精神错乱，精神变态. ②(由于环境、情况等而引起的)精神上极度的紧张、不安.

psy·cho·so·cial [ˌsaikəuˈsəuʃəl] *a.* 社会心理的〔指社会环境影响下的个人心理变化〕.

psy·cho·sur·ger·y [ˌsaikəuˈsəːdʒəri] *n.* 精神(病)外科学.

psy·cho·tech·nol·o·gy [ˈsaikəutekˈnɔlədʒi] *n.* 心理技术学.

psy·cho·ther·a·peu·tics [ˌsaikəuˌθerəˈpjuːtiks] *n.pl.* 〔动词用单数〕心理疗法，精神疗法 (= psychotherapy). **-peu·tic** *a.*

psy·cho·ther·a·py [ˈsaikəuˈθerəpi] *n.* 【医】精神疗法，心理疗法，(尤指)催眠疗法.

psy·chot·ic [saiˈkɔtik] *a.* 精神病的，有精神病的. —*n.* 精神病患者.

psy·cho·tox·ic [ˌsaikəuˈtɔksik] *a.* 【药】精神麻醉品的〔如能损伤大脑的酒精等〕.

psy·cho·trop·ic [ˌsaikəuˈtrɔpik] *a.* (药物)治疗精神病的. —*n.* 治精神病的药.

psy·chrom·e·ter [saiˈkrɔmitə] *n.* (干湿球)湿度计.

psy·chro·phil·ic [ˌsaikrəuˈfilik] *a.* 【生】嗜冷性. **-phile** 点 [-fail] *n.*

psy·co·graph [ˈsaikəugrɑːf,-ˌgræf] *n.* 【心】①性格特点描记图. ②精神作用记录.

psyl·la [ˈsilə] *n.* 叶蝨科 *(Psyllidae)* 昆虫.

psy·war [ˈsaiwɔː] *n.* 心理战 (=psychological warfare).

P.T. = ①Physical Training 体育锻炼. ②post town 设有邮局的市镇. ③Pupil Teacher (小学)见习教师.

Pt = platinum【化】铂.

pt. = ①part. ②payment. ③pint. ④point. ⑤port.

p.t. = potential transformer 变压器，电压互感器.

PTA, P.T.A. = Parent-Teacher Association〔美〕学生家长和教师联谊会.

ptar·mi·gan [ˈtɑːmigən] *(pl. -gan(s))* *n.* 【鸟】雷鸟(松鸡类).

ptbl. = portable.

P T boat [ˈpiː ˈtiː bəut] = patrol torpedo boat〔美〕鱼雷快艇.

Pte. = Private 列兵;〔英〕陆军二等兵;〔美〕陆军〔海军陆战队〕二等兵.

pter·i·dol·o·gy [ˌpteriˈdɔlədʒi] *n.* 蕨类植物学. **-log·i·cal** [-ˈlɔdʒikl] *a.* **-gist** *n.*

pter·i·do·phyte [ˈpteridəuˌfait, təˈridə-] *n.* 蕨类植物 *(Pteridophyta)*. **-phyt·ic** [-ˈfitik], **-doph·y·tous** [-ˈdɔfitəs] *a.*

pter·id·o·sperm [ˈpteridəuspəːm] *n.* 种子蕨 (= seed fern).

ptero- *comb.f.* 翼: *ptero*dactyl.

pter·o·dac·tyl [ˌpterəuˈdæktil] *n.* 【古生】飞龙目动物;翼手龙;无尾飞机.

pter·o·pod [ˈpterəpɔd] *a.* 翼足目的. —*n.* 翼足目 *(Pteropoda)* 动物. **-an** *a., n.*

pter·o·saur [ˈpterəsɔː] *n.* 飞龙目动物 (=pterodactyl).

pte·ryg·i·um [ptəˈridʒiəm] *n.* *(pl. -i·ums, -i·a* [-ə]*)* 【医】翼状胬肉. **-ryg·i·al** *a.*

pter·y·goid [ˈpterigɔid] *a.* ①翅形的. ②翼突的. —*n.* 翼骨或翼突.

pter·y·la [ˈpterilə] *n.* *(pl. -lae* [-ˌliː]*)* 【动】羽区.

Ptg, Ptg. = Portugal; Portuguese.

ptg, ptg. = printing.

ptis·an [ˈtizən, tiˈzæn] *n.* ①大麦(与其他配料同煮的)汤，大麦茶. ②煎汤〔如草药汤药等〕.

PTO, P.T.O., p.t.o. = please turn over 见反面，见下页.

Ptol·e·ma·ic [ˌtɔliˈmeiik] *a.* ①(古埃及)托勒密 (Ptolemy) 王朝的. ②(公元前二世纪古希腊天文学家)托勒密 (Ptolemy) 体系的;天动说的. *the* ~ *system* 托勒密体系，天动说.

Ptol·e·ma·ist [ˌtɔliˈmeiist] *n.* 托勒密体系〔天动说〕信奉者.

pto·ma·in(e) [ˈtəumein] *n.* 【化】尸碱;尸毒. **P- Domain** 〔美军俚〕食堂. ~ **poisoning** 食物中毒. **P-Tillie [Tommy]** 〔美俚〕小酒馆的老板.

pto·sis [ˈptəusis] *n.* 【医】上睑下垂.

pts, pts. = ①parts. ②payments. ③pints. ④points. ⑤ports.

pty·a·lin [ˈtaiəlin] *n.* 唾液淀粉酶.

pty·a·lism [ˈtaiəlizəm] *n.* 唾液分泌过多，多涎.

Pu = plutonium【化】钚.

pub [pʌb] *n.* 〔英〕= public house;〔美〕= publisher. **~-crawl** *vt., vi.* 〔英俚〕(在…)喝通关，从一家喝到一家地逛酒店.

pub. = ①public. ②publication; published; publisher; publishing.

pu·ber·ty [ˈpjuːbə(ː)ti] *n.* ①发身;发情期，青春期;青春，妙龄. ②【植】开花期. *the age of* ~ 发情期〔英法律男 14 岁，女 12 岁〕. *arrive at* ~ 到青春期.

pu·ber·u·lent [pjuˈberulənt] *a.* 【动】柔毛覆盖的.

pu·bes [ˈpjuːbiːz] *n.* 〔*sing., pl.* 同〕①阴毛;阴阜. ②【动，植】柔毛.

pu·bes·cence [pju(ː)ˈbesns] *n.* ①发情期. ②【植，动】短柔毛;柔毛.

pu·bes·cent [pju(ː)ˈbesnt] *a.* ①青春的，妙龄的，发情期的，发身期的. ②【植、动】有柔毛的. —*n.* 发情期的人.

pu·bic [ˈpjuːbik] *a.* 阴毛的;阴阜的. *the* ~ *bone* 耻骨. 【动】*the* ~ *region* 阴部.

pu·bis [ˈpjuːbis] *n.* *(pl. -bes* [-biːz]*)* ①【解】耻骨. ②【动】(昆虫)前胸侧部.

publ. = publication; published; publisher; publishing.

pub·lic [ˈpʌblik] *a.* (*opp.* private) ①公共的，公众的，公用的;人民的，社会的，国家的;政府的，公营的，公立的. ②(会等)公开的，当众的;人人知道的，知名的，突出的. ③〔罕〕国际上的. ④〔英〕大学的，(有别于各分科学院时说的)全校的. ~ *good [benefit, interests]* 公益. ~ *life* 社会生活，公共生活. *at the* ~ *expense* 用公费. *in the* ~ *eye* 公然. *make a* ~ *protest* 提公开抗议. *make* ~ 发表，公布. —*n.* ①〔the~〕人民，国民，公众，社会. ②(某一方面的)大众，群众;…界，…帮，…社会;(文学家等的)爱读者，爱好者. ③〔英口〕酒吧，客栈. *The* ~ *is the best judge.* 公众是最好的判断者. *the British* ~ 英国社会，一般英国人. *the musical [sporting]* ~ 音乐〔运动〕界. ***give to the*** ~ 出版，印行(书等). ***in*** ~ 公然，当众. ***the general*** ~ = ***the*** ~ ***at large*** 公众. ~ **act** 公法. ~ **address system** 扩音装置;有线广播系统. ~ **affairs** 公众事务. ~ **assistance institution** 〔英〕贫民收容所. ~ **auction** 拍卖. ~ **bath** 公共浴室，澡堂. ~ **bidding** 〔美〕投标. ~ **bill** 公共关系法案. ~ **body** 公共团体. ~ **bood** 公债券. ~ **comfort station** 〔美〕公厕. ~ **debt [bond]** 公债. ~ **defender** 公设辩护人〔指律师〕. ~ **domain** 〔美〕官产，公地;公有财产;不受版权〔专利权〕限制的状态. ~ **education** 学校教育;〔英〕公学教育. ~ **enemy** 公敌;社会公敌. ~ **enemy number one** 〔美〕第一号罪犯;万分可恶的人. ~ **examination** 〔英〕大学考试. ~ **funds** 〔英〕公债. ~ **health** 公共卫生. ~ **holiday** 公定假日. ~ **house** 〔英〕客栈;〔英〕酒吧. ~ **latrine** 公厕. ~ **international law** 国际公法. ~ **law** 公法. ~ **lecture** 公开演讲. ~ **library** 公立〔公共〕图书馆. ~ **loan** 公债. **~-minded [-spirited]** 热心公益的. ~ **morality** 风纪. ~ **nuisance** 【法】公妨犯;社会的害物. ~ **offence** 政治犯. **~officer** 公务员. ~ **opinion** 舆论;民意. ~ **opinion poll** 民意测验. ~ **orator** 〔英〕(大学的)代表人，秘书长. ~ **park**

公园. ～ **pay telephone** 公用电话. ～ **peace** 公安. ～ **prosecutor**〔英〕检察官. ～ **relations** (工厂、公司等的)(与)公众(的)关系[联系]. ～ **right** 公权. ～ **sale** 拍卖. ～ **scandal** 众所周知的丑事. ～ **school**〔美〕公立学校;〔英〕公学,私立(寄宿制大学预备)学校. ～ **servant** 公仆,公务员;从事公用事业的个人[团体]. ～**-service corporation**〔美〕公用事业公司. ～ **speaking** 演说(术). ～ **spirit** 热心公益的精神. ～ **street** 公路,大路. ～ **utility** 公用事业. ～ **way** 公路. ～ **welfare** 公安,治安,公共福利. ～ **woman** 妓女. ～ **works**〔美〕公共[市政]工程;公共建筑. **-ly** *ad.* 公然,公开,当众;由公众;由政府(出资、持有等).

pub·li·can [ˈpʌblikən] *n.* ①(古罗马的)收税官. ②〔英〕客栈[酒馆]老板.

pub·li·ca·tion [ˌpʌbliˈkeiʃən] *n.* ①公布,颁布,发布,发表. ②发行,出版. ③发行物,出版物,刊物. *the list of new ～s* 新书[新刊]目录. *a monthly [weekly] ～*月[周]刊.

pub·li·cist [ˈpʌblisist] *n.* ①国际法专家[研究者]. ②政论家,政论学家;政治记者;新闻发布官员.

pub·lic·i·ty [pʌbˈlisiti] *n.* ①公开(性);传开,出名. ②宣传;宣扬. ③(向新闻界散发的)宣传材料;广告. *the ～ department* 宣传部. ***avoid [shun]*** ～避免惹人注意,不想出名. ***court [seek]***～ 自我宣传,求名,沽名钓誉. ***give ～ to*** 公开,宣传,宣扬. ～ **agent [man]** 广告员;(演员等的)宣传员. ～ **hound**〔美〕爱在报上露名的人.

pub·li·cize [ˈpʌblisaiz] *vt.*〔美〕发表,公布;宣传,为…做广告.

pub·lish [ˈpʌbliʃ] *vt.* ①公开,发表,宣布(结婚等). ②公布,颁布. ③发行;出版;刊印. ④出版…的著作. ⑤〔美〕使用(伪钞等). — *vi.* ①出版;发行. ②(著作人)发表著作. **-a·ble** *a.* 可发表的;适于出版的.

pub·lish·er [ˈpʌbliʃə] *n.* ①出版者,发行人,出版社. ②公布者,发表者;〔美〕办报者.

pub·lish·ing [ˈpʌbliʃiŋ] *a., n.* 出版(业)(的). *a ～ house* 出版社.

pub·lish·ment [ˈpʌbliʃment] *n.*〔罕〕= publication.

puc·coon [pəˈkuːn] *n.* ①紫草(=gromwell). ②〔古〕美洲血根草(=bloodroot). ③〔古〕紫草染料.

puce [pjuːs] *a., n.* 深褐色(的).

puck[1] [pʌk] *n.* ①〔P-〕(莎士比亚戏剧《仲夏夜之梦》中的)喜欢恶作剧的小妖精. ②淘气的小孩,顽童.

puck[2] [pʌk] *n.* (冰上运动用的)冰球[硬橡皮圆盘].

puck[3] [pʌk] *n.* ①〔英〕脾脱疽〔相传由蚊母鸟引起的家畜病〕. ②蚊母鸟.

puck·a [ˈpʌkə] *a.*〔印度〕①分量足的. ②纯良的;真正的,可靠的. ③上等的,第一流的. ④坚牢的,(房屋等)永久性的. *a ～ general* 终生陆军上将.

puck·er [ˈpʌkə] *vt.* 折迭,使起皱纹;撅(嘴等),皱(眉头)*(up)*. — *vi.* ①成褶子,皱起来;缩拢 *(up)*. ②〔口〕烦闷,为难. ～ ***up one's brows*** 皱起眉头来. ～ ***up the mouth*** 撅起嘴来. — *n.* ①褶子,襞,皱纹. ②〔口〕狼狈;惶惑. ***in a*** ～ 慌慌张张. ***in ～s*** 起皱,有褶缝.

puck·er·stop·ple [ˈpʌkəˈstɔpl] *v.*〔美〕使着慌,使为难.

puck·er·y [ˈpʌkəri] *a.* 皱起的,易皱褶的.

puck·ish [ˈpʌkiʃ] *a.* 顽皮的,恶作剧的. **-ly** *ad.* **-ness** *n.*

pud [pʌd] *n.*〔儿语〕手手;(小孩的)手;(猫、狗等的)前脚.

pud·ding [ˈpudiŋ] *n.* ①布丁〔西餐中一种甜点心〕;〔喻〕物质的报酬. ②香肠. ③【海】(由帆布等制成的护船用的)船尾碰垫. ④(窃贼给狗吃的)毒肝(等). ⑤〔美卑〕侥幸. *The proof of the ～ is in the eating.* 布丁好坏,一尝便知〔谚语〕. *Indian ～* 玉米布丁. ***more praise than*** ～ 恭维多而实惠少,假恭维. ～ ***rather than praise*** 恭维不如实惠. ～***s and pies*** 眼睛. ～ **cloth** (蒸布丁用的)布丁布. ～ **face** 扁圆呆板的脸. ～**-faced** *a.* 面孔扁圆呆板的. ～**head** 笨人,蠢货. ～**headed** *a.* 愚笨的,蠢的. ～ **heart** 懦夫,精神萎靡的人. ～ **house**〔俚〕胃,肚子. ～ **pie** 肉布丁. ～ **stone**【矿】圆砾岩. **-y** [ˈpudiŋi] *a.* 布丁一样的;沉闷的;迟钝的,愚笨的.

pud·dle [ˈpʌdl] *n.* ①(路上的)水坑. ②(粘土和沙捣成的)胶土. ③〔俚〕混乱. — *vt.* ①弄脏;把…弄得泥糊糊. ②把…做成胶土;用胶土涂塞. ③搅拌(熔铁),搅炼. ④【农】湿土培育(稻秧等). —*vi.* ①搅泥浆;在泥水中泼溅[打滚] *(about; in)*. ②撒尿. ～ **furnace** 搅炼炉,炼铁炉. ～**jumper**〔美俚〕小型(公共)汽车;小火车;小汽艇;〔美军俚〕吉普车(= jeep);小型低空侦察机. ～**-poet** 打油诗人.

pud·dler [ˈpʌdlə] *n.* 搅炼者;搅炼棒;搅炼炉.

pud·dling [ˈpʌdliŋ] *n.* ①涂胶;捣成泥浆;和泥. ②【冶】(铣铁)精炼(法),搅炼炼铁(法),搅炼(作用).

pud·dly [ˈpʌdli] *a.* ①(路等)水坑多的. ②〔罕,方〕尽是泥的,溷浊的;脏的.

pu·den·cy [ˈpjuːdənsi] *n.* 羞怯,害羞;拘谨.

pu·den·dum [pjuːˈdendəm] *n.* ***(pl. -den·da*** [-də]***)*** ①女性外生殖器;阴部. ②〔*pl.*〕外生殖器. **pu·den·dal** [-dl] *a.*

pudge [pʌdʒ] *n.*〔口〕矮胖子;矮胖的动物;短而粗的东西.

pudg·y, [ˈpʌdʒi] *a.* ***(-i·er;-i·est)*** 〔口〕圆胖的;矮胖的. **-i·ly** *ad.* **-i·ness** *n.*

pu·dic·i·ty [pjuːˈdisiti] *n.* 羞怯,害羞;贞洁,淑贞.

puds·y [ˈpʌdzi] *a.* = pudgy.

pu·eb·lo [puˈebləu, ˈpwebləu] *n.*〔*Sp.*〕*(pl. -s)* ①(美国西南部或墨西哥等)印第安人的村庄[集体住所、城镇]. ②〔P-〕住集体住所的印第安人. ③(操西班牙语的美洲国家中的)村庄[城镇].

pu·er·ile [ˈpjuərail] *a.* 孩子气的;幼稚的;不成熟的;傻的. **-ly** *ad.*

pu·er·il·ism [ˈpjuːərilizəm] *n.* 孩子气,幼稚〔尤指成年人〕.

pu·er·il·i·ty [ˌpjuəˈriliti] *n.* ①幼稚;孩子气;愚蠢. ②〔*pl.*〕幼稚的言行. ③【法】幼年〔7—14岁〕.

pu·er·per·al [pju(ː)ˈəːpərəl] *a.*【医】生产的,分娩的. ～ *fever*【医】产褥热.

pu·er·pe·ri·um [ˌpju(ː)əˈpiəriəm] *n.* 产后期,产褥期.

Puer·to Ri·co [ˈpwəːtəu ˈriːkəu] 波多黎各(岛)〔拉丁美洲〕.

puff [pʌf] *n.* ①一吹[喷],噗的一吹[喷];一阵,一股(气味、烟雾等);吹[喷]的声音;(烟等)一喷的分量. ②噗的一声膨胀起来;膨胀起来的东西[部分]. ③被子;鸭绒被. ④夸奖,吹嘘,自我宣传. ⑤粉扑〔又叫 powder-～〕. ⑥(奶油)松饼. ⑦〔美俚〕广告. ⑧〔美俚〕向女性献殷勤的人. *a ～ of the wind* 一阵风. *get a good ～ of one's book* 著作大受称赞. *newspaper ～s* 报纸上的浮夸性广告,吹捧性短文[书评等]. — *vi.* ①噗噗地喷气,噗噗地喷烟 *(out; up)*;噗噗地喷着气开动;喘气;喘着气走. ②膨胀,噗地膨起 *(up; out)*. ③〔古〕哼的一声用鼻音应酬 *(at)*;(拍卖时)把价钱哄抬上去. ～ *and blow [pant]* 喘气. ～ *away at one's cigar* 一口口猛喷着雪茄烟. ～ *out* 喘着气说;(烟)噗噗噗地喷. *the engine ～ed out of the station.* 火车头噗噗地喷着气驶出车站. —*vt.* ①喷(烟等),噗噗地吹去(灰尘等). ②〔口〕使喘气. ③使噗的一下膨起;使自满,使得意 *(up)*;乱夸,瞎吹;(拍卖时)把(价钱)哄抬上去. ～ *out a candle* 吹熄蜡烛. *I was frightfully ～ed by the run.* 我跑得气都喘不过来了. *be ～ed out [up] with self-importance* 自以为了不起而摆架子. ～ **adder** (南非)膨身蛇〔怒时身体膨大的大毒蛇〕. ～**ball**【植】马勃(菌). ～ **box** 粉(扑)盒子. ～**-puff** 噗噗〔烟等喷出声〕;〔儿语〕火车头. **-ing** ① *n.* 噗噗吹;夸奖;【拍卖】虚价. ② *a.* 乱夸奖的.

puff·er [ˈpʌfə] *n.* ①鼓气的人[物]. ②瞎吹乱夸的人. ③拍卖行的囮子,抬价人. ④【鱼】河豚. ⑤〔儿〕火车噗噗,火车头. ⑥【矿】小绞车;小绞车工.

puff·er·y [ˈpʌfəri] *n.* 夸大的称赞,吹嘘,夸奖;吹捧的广告。

puf·fin [ˈpʌfin] *n.* ①【鸟】善知鸟;海鹦。②【植】马勃(菌)。

puff·i·ness [ˈpʌfinis] *n.* ①膨胀。②自夸,自满;夸张。

puff·y [ˈpʌfi] *a.* ***(-i·er; -i·est)*** ①膨起的,肿胀的;肥胖的。②〔罕〕骄傲的,夸大的。③喘气的;容易气急的。④噗一声吹的;一阵的。**-i·ly** *ad.*

pug[1] [pʌg] *n.* ①巴儿狗;狮子鼻。②〔爱称〕狐,兔子,猴子(等)。③〔英〕小火车头。④〔英〕高级仆役,管家。—*a.* 〔美〕①舒服的,贴身的。②往上翘的。

pug[2] [pʌg] *n.* ①(制砖瓦等用的)泥料;隔音土。②捏土机,捣泥机。— *vt.* ①(制砖瓦) 捣[捏](粘土);涂塞泥料。②【建】涂(灰泥)阻止传音。～ **mill** 捣泥机,搅拌机。

pug[3] [pʌg] *n.* 〔印度用英语〕(野兽的)足迹。— *vt.* 寻找(野兽的)足迹。

pug[4] [pʌg] *n.* 〔俚〕(职业)拳击家,拳师。

pugg·a·ree, pugg·ree, pug·gry [ˈpʌgəri,-gri] *n.* 〔印度〕 =pugree.

pug·ging [ˈpʌgiŋ] *n.* ①捏和;捣制窑泥。②【建】隔音层;隔音材料,阻声灰泥。

pugh [pjuː] *int.* 呸!〔表轻蔑、憎恶等〕.

pu·gil·ism [ˈpjuːdʒilizəm] *n.* (空手打的)拳击。

pu·gil·ist [ˈpjuːdʒilist] *n.* ①拳击家,拳师。②(争论中的)劲敌,厉害的对手。**-ic** *a.*

pug·na·cious [pʌgˈneiʃəs] *a.* 爱吵架的,好斗的。**-nac·i·ty** *n.* 好斗性。

pug·ree [ˈpʌgriː] *n.* 〔印度用英语〕轻头巾;帽沿遮阳布。

puis·ne [ˈpjuːni] 〔主英〕 *a.* 晚辈的,年小的;下位的;【法】后的,其次的 *(to)*. — *n.* 陪席法官;晚辈。*a* ～ *judge* 陪席法官。

pu·is·sance [ˈpju(ː)isns] *n.* 〔诗,古〕力,权力,威力,势力,精神。

pu·is·sant [ˈpju(ː)isnt] *a.* 〔诗,古〕 有力的,有势力的,有权力的,强大的。

pu·ja, poo·ja [ˈpuːdʒɑː] *n.* ①(印度教的)偶像礼拜,宗教仪式。②〔印度用英语〕〔常 *pl.*〕祈祷文。

puke [pjuːk] *n.* ①呕吐;呕出物;催吐剂。②绰号。③可唾弃的人;令人作呕的人[事物、情形]。— *vi.* 吐,呕;呕出 *(up)*. *mewling and puking* 哽咽,抽抽噎噎地哭。

puk·ka(h) [ˈpʌkə] *a.* = pucka. ～ **gen** 〔军俚〕可靠的情报 (*opp.* duff gen).

pul [pul] *n.* ***(pl.*** ***～(s))*** 普尔〔阿富汗的货币单位,相当于 1/100 的阿富汗尼〕.

Pu·la [ˈpuːlɑː] *n.* 普拉〔南斯拉夫港市〕.

Pu·las·ki [puˈlæski] *n.* 〔美〕(消防员、伐木工人等用的)斧镐〔源出美国林场主 Edward ～〕.

pul·chri·tude [ˈpʌlkritjuːd] *n.* 〔罕〕体态美,美丽,漂亮(指人)。**-tu·di·nous** *a.*

pule [pjuːl] *vi.* (小鸡等)叽叽地叫;(婴儿等伤心地)抽噎地哭泣。

pu·li [ˈpuːli] *n.* ***(pl.*** ***pu·lik*** **[-liːk],** ***pu·lis)*** 〔Hung.〕匈牙利粗毛狗〔用来看守农场〕.

Pul·it·zer [ˈpulitsə] *n.* 普利策〔姓氏〕. ～ **Prize** 普利策奖金〔美国的一种在文学、艺术和新闻界内颁发的奖金〕.

pull [pul] *vt.* ①拉,拖,牵,曳 (*opp.* push);勒(马)。②拽住,扽;扯破,扯开。③拔去(鸡等的)毛;拔(牙齿、瓶塞等)*(up)*;摘,采(苹果等);搬走,移开。④摇(橹),荡(桨);摆渡(旅客);(船)有…桨。⑤吸引,招徕(顾客);获得(援助等)。⑥〔俚〕 捉拿(罪犯);(警察)突袭 (赌窟等)。⑥抽出(刀子)。⑦完成(计划等)。⑧玩(手段等);干…(勾当)。⑨【印】用手印刷,打(校样)。⑩【赛马】勒马减速而故意跑输;【板球】从三柱门的 *off* 方面把(球)打到 *on* 方面;【高尔夫】把(球)打向左面;【拳击】猛击不中;【运】扭伤(脚筋等);拉伤 (肌肉)。⑪呈现(面容)。⑫～ *a fowl [hide]* 拔鸟毛[皮上的毛]. ～ *sb. by his ear* 扯某人的耳朵. ～ *a cart* 拉车. ～ *a tooth* 拔牙. *The boat ～s four oars.* 这条船有四把桨. ～ *tricks* 要欺诈手段. *a game ～ing a large crowd* 一场吸引了许多人的比赛. ～ *a ligament in one's leg* 扭伤一条腿. *She ～ed the letter to pieces.* 她把信扯成碎片. ～ *a knife* 拔刀. —*vi.* ①拉,拖;被拔;被拉. ②能被拉[拖、拔];(被拖着)动;行驶;(船)被划;划船 *(away; for; out)*. ③一口喝下去 *(at)*;抽烟 *(at)*. ④马咬嚼子不听话. ⑤吃力地前进. ⑥得到后援. ⑦吸引住顾客;(就职等时)提携提携. ⑧(赛跑时)超过对方. *The fish ～s on the line.* 鱼拉钓丝. ～ *up the hill* 吃力地爬山. ～ *at a pipe* 抽烟. *The drawer won't ～ out.* 抽屉拉不开. *a train ～ing out of the station* 一列开出车站的火车. ～ ***a boner*** 〔美俚〕失错,弄错,闹大笑话,出丑. ～ ***a fast one (on sb.)***〔美〕对…行骗,诈取. ～ ***a line*** 〔美俚〕话多起来,嘴碎起来. ～ ***a (long) face*** 板起面孔,拉下面孔. ～ ***a poor mouth*** 〔美俚〕装穷拒绝付款[捐款]. ～ ***a shut-eye*** 〔美俚〕喝醉. ～ ***about*** = ～ ***and haul*** 乱拖;拖来拖去. ～ ***apart [asunder]*** 扯断(索子等);劝开(吵闹). ～ ***at a rope*** 套住绳子拉. ～ ***back*** 拉回来,退;节省,收缩;改变主意,不守诺言. ～ ***caps [wigs]*** 打架. ***P- devil,*** ～ ***baker! [～ dog,*** ～ ***cat!]*** 〔拔河赛〕(鼓励双方)大家加油! ～ ***down*** ①挣钱,赚.②压低,贬低. ③拆坏(房子等);(疾病使人)衰弱;推翻,打倒(政府等) (～ *down one's house about one's ears* 自取灭亡). ～ ***down your jacket!*** 镇定! ～ ***foot*** 〔俚〕逃走. ～ ***for*** 〔美口〕帮助;声援. ～ ***in*** ①使后退,缩(头等). ②节省(费用). ③(火车等)到站;船靠近(海岸). ④逃走,离开. ～ ***in your ears [barber pole, horns, neck]!*** 〔美俚〕不要你管闲事!住嘴! ～ ***it*** =～ foot. ～ ***off*** ①忙着脱(衣服、鞋等). ②(竞争) 得胜, 得(奖). ③做好, 完成; 协定. ④〔美〕干, 实行. ⑤开(船); (船)离开 (*from* shore). ⑥走开, 逃走; 释放 (～ *off one's hat to* 脱帽招呼). ～ ***on*** 穿上 (衣服), 戴 (手套), 穿 (袜子). ～ ***oneself together*** 定定心,恢复精神,重新振作;复元. ～ ***oneself up*** 自制;急忙止住. ～ ***one's freight*** 〔美俚〕急速出发;离开. ～ ***one's leg*** 〔美俚〕①逗,惹,嘲弄.②诓骗. ～ ***sb.'s nose***=～ ***sb. by the nose*** 牵人鼻子[侮辱的动作]. ～ ***sb.'s sleeve*** = ～ ***sb. by the sleeve*** 拉某人袖子使注意. ～ ***one's weight*** 尽自己的力量做. ～ ***out*** ①拔(牙等). ②拖长(谈话等). ③把船划出;(车、船等)开出;(人)出发. ④〔美〕离(职). ⑤【空】(飞机的)改出动作(由俯冲姿势变成水平姿势). ⑥(抽屉等)脱出. ～ ***out of the fire*** 使转败为胜. ～ ***over*** ①(把衣裳)从头上套下来穿. ②推翻(桌子等). ③〔口〕把(车)靠拢路边. ～ ***round*** (使)恢复健康,复元,医好…的病. ～ ***sth. on sb.*** 在…方面欺骗某人. ～ ***the chesnuts out of the fire*** 火中取栗,为他人作牺牲品. ～ ***the iron-man stunt*** 〔美运〕在同一运动会中参加好几个比赛项目. ～ ***the strings [wires]*** 在幕后拉线,在幕后操纵. ～ ***through*** ① *vt.* 使克服困难,使渡过难关 (*Good nursing ～ed him through.* 看护周到使他脱离险境). ② *vi.* 渡过难关,克服困难,脱离险境;(竞争时)赶过,追过. ～ ***to [in] pieces*** ①扯碎. ②批评得一文不值,谩骂. ～ ***together*** ①通力合作,同心协力去做. ②拼凑. ～ ***up*** ① *vt.* 拔出(树、桩等);根绝;勒住(马),拉住(马车等);吃力地攀登;〔口〕制止,责骂,责备 (*He was ～ed up for his error.* 他因过失受到了责骂). ② *vi.* (马、人力车、马车等)停止,刹住. ～ ***up lame*** 〔美〕(赛马的马)跑得慢. ～ ***up to [with]*** …追上,赶上. —*n.* ①拉,拖,牵引. ②【骨牌】抓牌;扣(枪的)扳机. ③拉力,牵引力,(月等的)引力;〔美〕(对人的)吸引力,魅力. ④〔口〕一划,划游. ⑤〔口〕(酒的)一杯,〔英〕(烟的)一口;〔英〕(酒馆中给顾客)额外添加的酒. ⑥把柄,把手,(枪的)拉绳;(啤酒水压机的)挺棍(= beer-～),啤酒泵. ⑦【赛马】(故意要输而)勒住马,放慢. ⑧【印】手印样,校样. ⑨【高尔夫球】左弯球. ⑩

〔俚〕利益,好处;照顾;门路,关系. *A good education gives a man a great* ~. 良好的教育能给人很大好处. *have a* ~ *with the police [on the governor]* 跟警察[州长]有关系. *It's along* ~ *to the top of the building.* 爬上楼顶很吃力. *a* ~ *at a cigar* 吸一口雪茄. *a wooden* ~ *for a drawer* 抽屉的木把手. ***give a*** ~ ***at*** 拉(拖)…. ***have [take] a*** ~ ***at the bottle [a pipe]*** 〔口〕喝一杯[吸一口]. ***have the*** ~ ***of [over]*** 胜过,强于. ***the long*** ~ (酒等的)添送. **~-back** ①〔口〕障碍,不利,弱点. ②反动家伙. ③撤回. **~-over** (无领无扣的)套衫,绒线套衫. **~-through** ①(一头拴有布的)枪筒清扫绳. ②【军口】瘦长汉子. **~-up** ①(马车的)停车处,休息处;停止,休息. ②【空】(飞机的)拉起动作,急升动作(特指从平飞位置转入急升的动作);【体】(单杠)引体向上.

pulled [puld] *a.* ①扯下来的,摘下来的. ②拔去了毛的. ③健康衰退了的,没有精神的. ~ *bread* 面包渣儿. ~ *figs* 用手指拉成扁而圆的无花果果干.

pull·er [ˈpulə] *n.* ①拉的人;摘的人,拔的人. ②拔具,拉出器. ③划手. ④难勒制的马. ⑤〔美〕私酒运入人. **~-in** 〔美俚〕顾客招揽员,拉生意的人.

pul·let [ˈpulit] *n.* ①(孵出后不到一年的)小母鸡. ②〔英〕(食用)毛蛤. ③〔美俚〕小姑娘.

pul·ley [ˈpuli] *n.* 【机】滑车,滑轮;皮带轮. *a compound* ~ 复滑车. *a differential* ~ 差动滑车. *a driven* ~ 从动滑车. *a driving* ~ 主动滑车. *a fast [fixed]* ~ 固定滑车. *an idle [a loose]* ~ 游滑车. *a movable* ~ 动滑车. — *vt.* ①用滑车举起;用滑车推动. ②给…装滑车.

Pull·man[1] [ˈpulmən] *n.* 普尔曼〔姓氏〕.

Pull·man[2], **p-** [ˈpulmən] *n.* ***(pl.*** ~***s)*** 【铁道】(G. M. Pullman 设计的设备特别舒适的)普尔门式火车卧车〔又叫 ~ car〕. *a side door* ~ 〔美〕有盖货车.

pul·lu·late [ˈpʌljuleit] *vi.* ①萌芽,发芽;成长. ②繁殖;发生;发达. **-la·tion** *n.*

pul·ly-haul [ˈpulihɔːl] *vt., vi.* 〔英口〕(竭力)拖,拉. **-y** *n., a.* 〔英口〕拖(的),拉(的).

pul·mom·e·ter [pulˈmɔmitə] *n.* 肺(容)量计.

pul·mo·na·ry [ˈpʌlmənəri] *a.* ①肺的. ②有肺的. ③肺状的,象肺的. ④对肺有影响的. *the* ~ *artery [veins]* 肺动[静]脉. ~ *complaints [diseases]* 肺病. ~ *tuberculosis* 肺结核.

pul·mo·nate [ˈpʌlmənit] *a.* 有肺的;【动】有肺类的. — *n.* 有肺类的(动物).

pul·mon·ic [pʌlˈmɔnik] *a.* ①肺的. ②肺病的;肺炎的. — *n.* ①肺病药. ②肺病病人.

pul·motor [ˈpʌlməutə] *n.* 人工呼吸器.

pulp [pʌlp] *n.* ①果肉;(植物的)髓. ②牙髓. ③纸浆;浆状物;【冶】矿浆. ④〔美俚〕〔常 *pl.*〕庸俗杂志. *a* ~ *cavity* 牙髓腔. *a* ~ *saver* 纸浆回收机. *a* ~ *mill* 纸浆厂. ~ *wood* 制(纸)浆木材. — *a.* 〔美俚〕(杂志)低级趣味的. ***beat one to a*** ~ 打瘫某人,狠揍某人. ***be reduced to*** ~ ①成纸浆,成软块. ②累得瘫软. — *vt.* ①把…捣成浆状;把…制成纸浆. ②取出(咖啡豆的)果肉. — *vi.* 成浆状.

pulped [pʌlpt] *a.* 〔美俚〕被打得要死的.

pulp·er [ˈpʌlpə] *n.* ①(咖啡豆的)果肉采集器. ②搅碎[碎浆]机.

pulp·i·fy [ˈpʌlpifai] *vt.* ①使成纸浆. ②使软烂,使柔软.

pulp·i·ness [ˈpʌlpinis] *n.* ①浆状;果肉状. ②稀烂;柔软性.

pul·pit [ˈpulpit] *n.* ①讲道坛;[the ~]〔集合词〕教士,牧师;传教. ②(捕鲸船的)标枪舌. ③〔英空俚〕飞机驾驶员座位. ④(机器)操纵台. *a* ~ *banger [smiter, thumper]* 〔美俚〕牧师.

pul·pit·eer [ˌpulpiˈtiə] *n.* 〔蔑〕讲道的,说教者. — *vi.* 说教,讲道.

pul·pit·er [ˈpulpitə] *n.* 讲道者,牧师.

pulp·less [ˈpʌlplis] *a.* 无浆的;干燥的.

pulp·ous, pulp·y [ˈpʌlpəs, ˈpʌlpi] *a.* 果肉(状)的,肉多的;浆状的,浆多的;柔软的.

pul·que [ˈpu(ː)lkiː; Sp. ˈpuːlkei] *n.* (墨西哥人所饮的)龙舌兰酒.

pul·sant [ˈpʌlsnt] *a.* ①(心脏)跳动的,(脉)搏动的,有节奏地震动(或鼓动)的. ②发抖的,颤动的.

pul·sar [ˈpʌlsɑː] *n.* 【天】脉冲星.

pul·sate [pʌlˈseit, ˈpʌlseit] *vi.* ①(脉等)搏动,(心脏)跳动,悸动,有规律地拍击;【电】脉动,脉冲,波动. ②震动. — *vt.* 筛选(钻石). *a pulsating [pulsatory] current* 【电】脉冲电流.

pul·sa·tile [ˈpʌlsətail] *a.* ①脉动的,搏动的,跳动的. ②(乐器)敲打的. — *n.* 【乐】敲打乐器〔鼓等〕.

pul·sa·tion [pʌlˈseiʃən] *n.* ①脉搏,悸动;跳动,颤动;【电】脉动. ②【罗马法】(不痛程度的)殴打.

pul·sa·tive, pul·sa·to·ry [ˈpʌlsətiv, -təri] *a.* = pulsatile.

pul·sa·tor [ˈpʌlseitə, pʌlˈseitə] *n.* 〔L.〕脉动器.

pul·sa·to·ry [ˈpʌlsətəri] *a.* 能跳动的;有跳动特征的;跳动的.

pulse[1] [pʌls] *n.* ①脉搏;有节奏的跳动;【物】脉冲(波);脉动. ②意向;倾向. ③【乐】拍子,律动. *His* ~ *was at a hundred.* 他的脉搏(每分钟)一百次. *a galloping* ~ 急脉. *a high* ~ 强脉. *a long [slow]* ~ 缓脉. *a weak* ~ 弱脉. *an action* ~ (火箭)触发脉冲. *a carry* ~ 进位脉冲. *a driving* ~ 起动脉冲. ***feel sb.'s*** ~ = ***have one's fingers on the*** ~ ***of sb.*** 按某人的脉;探某人的意向. ***stir sb.'s*** ~***s*** 鼓动某人的情绪;使人兴奋. ***with quickened*** ~***s*** 心跳得更快地. —*vi.* 脉跳动;震动,脉动. — *vt.* 使发生脉冲;用脉冲输送(血等)*(in; out)*. ~ **code** 【无】脉冲(编)码. ~ **frequency** 【无】脉冲频率. **~-jet** 脉动式空气喷气发动机. **~-on** *n.* 启动. ~ **radar** 脉冲雷达. ~ **ripple [ringing]** 【物】脉动.

pulse[2] [pʌls] *n.* 〔*sing., pl.*〕豆类;豆.

pulse·less [ˈpʌlslis] *a.* ①没有脉搏的. ②没有生气的;不活动的.

pul·sim·e·ter [pʌlˈsimitə] *n.* ①【医】验脉器,脉搏计. ②【物】脉冲计.

pul·som·e·ter [pʌlˈsɔmitə] *n.* ①蒸汽吸水机;气压唧筒. ②【物】脉震计,脉冲计. ③【医】验脉器,脉搏计.

pul·ver·iz·a·ble [ˈpʌlvəraizəbl] *a.* 可以粉碎的.

pul·ver·i·za·tion [ˌpʌlvəraiˈzeiʃən] *n.* 研末(作用),粉碎(作用).

pul·ver·i·za·tor [ˈpʌlvəraizeitə] *n.* 粉碎器.

pul·ver·ize [ˈpʌlvəraiz] *vt.* ①把…磨成粉状,弄碎. ②把(水等)喷成雾. ③粉碎(议论等). ~*d soap stone* 滑石粉. — *vi.* 成粉,碎.

pul·ver·iz·er [ˈpʌlvəraizə] *n.* ①粉碎机,研磨机. ②喷雾器. ③粉碎者.

pul·ver·ous [ˈpʌlvərəs] *a.* 粉的,粉状的,满是粉末的.

pul·ver·u·lent [pʌlˈverjulənt] *a.* ①粉的;灰尘的;满是粉末[灰尘]的. ②(岩石等)脆的. ③【植】如被尘的.

pul·vil·lus [pʌlˈviləs] *n.* ***(pl. -li*** [-ai]***)*** 【动】①垫. ②(昆虫的)毛垫. **pul·vil·lar** *a.*

pul·vi·nate [ˈpʌlvineit, -nit] *a.* ①垫子形的. ②【植】具叶枕的. **-ly** *ad.*

pul·vi·nus [pʌlˈvainəs] *n.* ***(pl. -ni*** [-nai]***)*** 【植】叶座;叶枕.

pu·ma [ˈpjuːmə] *n.* 【动】美洲狮(皮).

pum·e·lo [ˈpʌmiləu] *n.* 柚,文旦= pomelo.

pum·ice [ˈpʌmis] *n.* 轻石,浮石;浮岩;泡沫岩〔亦作 ~ stone, 多用于去污和磨光〕. — *vt.* 用浮石磨,用轻石擦(=pumicate, pumicestone).

pu·mi·ceous [pjuːˈmiʃəs] *a.* 浮石的,象轻石的;轻石质的.

pum·mel [ˈpʌml] *vt.* = pommel.

pum·me·lo [ˈpʌmiləu] *n.* = pomelo.

pump[1] [pʌmp] *n.* (浅口无带的)轻舞鞋.

pump² [pʌmp] *n.* ①泵，抽(水)机，唧筒；抽机作用，抽动；抽运；泵声。②〔口〕盘问，用话套话；盘问者，善于探听消息的人。③〔卑，俚〕反应迟钝的人，呆子。④〔美俚〕心。*a bicycle* ～ 打气筒。*a breast* ～ 吸奶器。⑤〔喻〕(昆虫的)吸盘。*a feed* ～ 给水泵。*a force [pressure]* ～ 压力泵，压水泵。*a fore* ～ 预抽真空泵。*fetch a* ～ 用水灌满抽机排去空气然后抽水。*For all my* ～*s, he did not tell the truth; he is truly a* ～. 盘来问去，总不实说；他实在是个牛皮筋。— *vt.* ①用泵抽(水等)；抽干(井等)；绞(脑筋)。②〔俚〕把(秘密等)盘问出来，诱问出来。③用打气筒(给车胎)打气 *(up)*；把(子弹)打进。④把(功课等)塞进(脑中)，注入。⑤〔口〕使疲倦，使喘气。～ *a ship* 抽出船底的水。*a* ～*ed tree* 腐心木。— *vi.* ①用泵(抽水)，用泵增压，抽动。②被盘问出来。③象泵柄一样)上下运动；(寒暑表水银柱)猛升猛降。④喷出。⑤〔口〕卖力气。***be* ～*ed out*** 累得喘不过气来。***prime the* ～** ①(政府)以增大开支刺激经济复苏。②对(企业等)的经营管理予以支援。～ ***abuses upon sb.*** 破口骂人。～ ***away at*** 努力干。～ ***out*** 抽空。～ **brake** 泵柄；液压制动器。～ **handle** *n.* ①泵柄。②〔俚〕手，手杆，胳臂。③〔俚〕使劲的握手。～**-handle** *vt.* 〔口〕使劲握手。～ **priming** 经济刺激开支。～ **room** ①(温泉等处的)矿泉水饮用处。②(供水处等的)水泵房。**-age** *n.* 泵的抽水量。**-ship** *vi.*, *n.* 〔海俚，卑〕小便，撒尿。

pumped [pʌmpt] *a.* 〔俚〕喘得上气不接下气的。

pump·er [ˈpʌmpə] *n.* ①用泵人；司泵员。②〔美〕用泵抽的油井。

pum·per·nick·el [ˈpumpənikl] *n.* 裸麦粗面包。

pump·kin [ˈpʌmpkin] *n.* ①【植】南瓜；南瓜藤。②〔口〕夜郎自大的蠢货；〔美俚〕〔some ～s〕重要人物，大亨；重要的东西。③〔美俚〕脑袋瓜。***a* ～ *center*** 〔美〕幻想中的典型孤村。～ ***and squash*** 南瓜。～**-ash**【植】绒毛白蜡树。～ **head** 〔美〕笨蛋，傻瓜。～**seed** ①南瓜子；西葫芦子。②太阳鱼〔产于北美〕。

pun¹ [pʌn] *n.* 双关俏皮话，双关语。—*vi.* 用双关语 *(on, upon)*。～ *on a word* 一语双关。— *vt.* 以双关语劝说。

pun² [pʌn] *vt.* 〔英方〕把(土、碎石等)捣结实〔夯实〕*(up)*。

pu·na [ˈpuːnɑː, Sp. ˈpuna] *n.* ①山间高原。②普纳(南美热带高山寒冷旱生植被)。③〔*pl.*〕普那草原，南美安第斯山西部草原。

Pun·a·kha [ˈpunəkə] *n.* 普那卡〔不丹县名〕。

Punch [pʌntʃ] *n.* ①潘趣〔英国木偶戏 Punch and Judy 中的主角，背驼，鼻长而钩，Judy 是他的妻子，时常和他吵架〕。②(英国 1841 年创刊的)《笨拙画报》。***as pleased [proud] as*** ～ 扬扬得意〔神气十足〕。

punch¹ [pʌntʃ] *n.* ①冲压机，冲床，冲孔(机)，穿孔(机)。②打印器；剪票铗；大钢针。③(冲或打出的)孔〔切口〕。*a* ～ *press* 冲床，冲孔机。*a calculating* ～ 穿孔计算机。*a conductor's* ～ 剪票铗。～ ***in (out)*** 用打卡钟在报到卡片上记载上〔下〕班钟点。***put more* ～ *into*** 加强。— *vt.* (用压穿器)穿孔，冲孔；(用打印器)打印；(用票铗)剪票。*have one's ticket* ～*ed* 剪了票。～**(ed) card [tape]**【统计】(统计机上用的)穿孔卡片。

punch² [pʌntʃ] *vt.* ①用拳头打，殴打；(用肘)推；(用棒)捅。②〔美西部〕赶(家畜)。— *vi.* 用拳猛击；用力击；用力按。— *n.* ①拳打，殴打。②〔俚〕(语言、小说等的)力量，效果；精力；魄力。*There was not much* ～ *in his remarks.* 他的话没啥力量。***get a* ～ *on the head*** 头上挨一拳。***pull the* ～*es*** 〔美俚〕故意不用力打，故意让对手打胜。～ **line** (击中要害的)警句，妙语。

punch³ [pʌntʃ] *n.* ①〔英〕(英国 Suffolk 地方产的)矮小肥胖的驮马(= Suffolk punch)。②〔英方〕矮胖子；粗而短的东西。

punch⁴ [pʌntʃ] *n.* ①(果汁、香料、奶、茶、酒等搀和的)香甜混合饮料；多味果汁饮料。②饮香甜混合饮料的聚会。③= ～bowl。④(东印度的)五人会议。～ **bowl** ①混合香甜饮料的大酒钵。②钵状山坳。③〔美俚〕拳击场。～ **ladle** 舀香甜混合饮料用的长柄勺。

punch·board [ˈpʌntʃˌbɔːd] *n.* 抽彩盘。

punch-up [ˈpʌntʃʌp] *n.* 〔主英俚〕①一场吵闹的殴斗；吵闹；怒骂。②打群架；吵闹声；隆隆声。

punch·drunk [ˈpʌntʃdrʌŋk] *a.* ①〔美俚〕(拳赛中)被打得头昏眼花的；惶惑的。②夜郎自大的，过于自信的。③自私的。

pun·cheon¹ [ˈpʌntʃən] *n.* ①短柱；(煤矿坑内的)架柱，支柱。②〔美〕(圆木料对剖成的)半圆木料。②打印器；打孔器。④石凿，凿子。

pun·cheon² [ˈpʌntʃən] *n.* (72—120 加仑的)大桶；一大桶的分量。

punch·er [ˈpʌntʃə] *n.* ①穿孔的人。②穿孔机；打印器。③〔俚〕服务员。④〔美〕= cowboy.

Pun·chinel·lo [ˌpʌntʃiˈneləu] *n.* ***(pl.* ～*(s))*** ①(意大利木偶喜剧的)丑角。②= Punch. ③〔p-〕滑稽人；矮胖子；怪模怪样的男子〔东西〕。

punch·ing-bag, punch·ing·ball [ˈpʌntʃiŋbæg, -bɔːl] *n.* (练习拳击用的)吊袋，吊球。

punch·y [ˈpʌntʃi] *a.* ***(punch·i·er; punch·i·est)*** 〔美口〕①有力的；精力旺盛的，生气勃勃的。②(拳击中)被打得晕头转向的，摇摇晃晃的，惶惑的(=punchdrunk)。

punct. = punctuation.

punc·tate, punc·tat·ed [ˈpʌŋkteit, -teitid] *a.*【动、植】有斑点的，有细孔的，具刻点的，具点的；细孔状。

punc·til·io [pʌŋkˈtiliəu] *n.* ***(pl.* ～*s)*** ①(仪式等的)细节。②死板，拘板，拘泥形式。

punc·til·i·ous [pʌŋkˈtiliəs] *a.* 礼仪烦琐的；死板的，拘泥形式的。**-ly** *ad.*

punc·tu·al [ˈpʌŋktjuəl] *a.* ①严守时刻的，不误限期的，准时的，如期的；准确的。②= punctilious. ③【几】点的。*as* ～ *as the clock* 时间准确(的)。～ *to the minute* 一分不差。*a* ～ *light source* 点光源。**-ly** *ad.* ①按时，如期。②郑重其事地；〔古〕死板地。

punc·tual·i·ty [ˌpʌŋktjuˈæliti] *n.* 严守时间；敏捷，守信用。

punc·tu·ate [ˈpʌŋktjueit] *vt.* ①加标点于，标点(文章)。②加重(语气等)；强调。③间断；不时打断(演说等)。～ *one's talk with sobs* 边哭边讲，抽抽噎噎地讲。*Each word was* ～*d by a blow.* 字字拍桌，慷慨激昂。— *vi.* 点标点。**-a·tor** *n.* 点标点者。

punc·tu·a·tion [ˌpʌŋktʃuˈeiʃən] *n.* ①标点；标点法；全部标点符号。②(Semitic 语)元音点法。③【动】斑点。*close [open]* ～ 精细〔简略〕标点法。～ **marks [points]** 标点符号。

punc·tu·late [ˈpʌŋktjuleit, -lit] *a.*【生】具小点的；有细小孔的。**-la·tion** *n.*

punc·tum [ˈpʌŋktəm] *n.* ***(pl. -ta*** [-tə]***)***【解，植】细穿孔，点，斑点，刻点。

punc·ture [ˈpʌŋktʃə] *n.* ①刺，扎，戳。②穿孔，刺痕，刺伤；扎伤。③【动】刻点；细孔，小点。④(车胎等的)刺孔。— *vt.* ①用针等刺，戳通，穿孔，击穿，打穿。②揭穿。— *vi.* (车胎等)刺破，穿孔。

pun·dit [ˈpʌndit] *n.* ①(印度的)学者，梵学者。②〔谑〕博学的人；空谈家。

pung [pʌŋ] *n.* 〔美方〕方箱形雪车。

pun·gent [ˈpʌndʒənt] *a.* ①辣的，刺鼻的，(味等)刺激性的。②尖酸刻薄的，泼辣的。③【生】尖形的；尖锐的。～ *sarcasm* 尖酸刻薄的讽刺。**pun·gen·cy** [-i] *n.*

Pu·nic [ˈpjuːnik] *a.* ①古迦太基(Carthage)(人)的。②没有信义的，反复无常的。— *n.* 古迦太基语。～ **apple** 石榴。～ **faith** 反叛，背信弃义。*(the)* ～ **Wars** 罗马和迦太基间的三次布匿战役。

pu·ni·ness [ˈpjuːninis] *n.* ①短小；弱小。②次要，不足道。

pun·ish [ˈpʌniʃ] *vt.* ①罚，处罚；惩罚；〔口〕严厉对付，严厉批评。②(比赛)使大败，痛击(对手)；〔～ oneself〕吃

大亏,吃苦头. ③〔口〕【赛马】乱糟踏(马). ④〔口〕大吃大喝,大量消耗. ～ *sb. for his crime* 处罚某人. ～ *sb. with [by] death* 处某人死刑. ～ *an opponent* 严厉抨击〔对付〕反对者. *The enemy was severely* ～*ed.* 敌人被打得惨败. ～ *one's food* 大吃. ～ *the bottle* 喝干(一瓶酒等). — *vi.* 处罚,惩罚.

pun·ish·a·ble [ˈpʌniʃəbl] *a.* 该罚的; 可受惩罚的. **-bly** *ad.*

pun·ish·er [ˈpʌniʃə] *n.* 处罚者,惩罚者.

pun·ish·ing [ˈpʌniʃiŋ] *a.* ①处罚的, 惩罚的. ②猛打的. ③辛苦的. *a* ～ *assault* 猛攻. *a* ～ *blow* 狠狠的一击.

pun·ish·ment [ˈpʌniʃmənt] *n.* ①罚,刑罚 *(for; on)*; 惩罚. ②〔口〕给吃苦头. ③【拳击】痛击;【运】使疲劳. *capital* ～ 死刑. *corporal* ～ 体刑. *disciplinary* ～ 惩戒. *inflict [impose] a* ～ *upon a criminal* 处罚犯人.

pu·ni·tion [pjuːˈniʃən] *n.* = punishment.

pu·ni·tive, pu·ni·to·ry [ˈpjuːnitiv,-təri] *a.* 刑罚的,惩罚的. *a* ～ *expedition* 征伐,讨伐. ～ *actions against* 讨伐…的战争. *a* ～ *force* 讨伐军. ～ *justice* 因果报应. **-ness** *n.* 惩办主义.

Pun·ja·bi [pʌnˈdʒɑːbi] *n.* ①旁遮普人. ②旁遮普语〔旁遮普人讲的印度语〕.

punk¹ [pʌŋk] *n.* 〔古〕妓女,娼妇.

punk² [pʌŋk] *n.* 〔美俚〕①(引火用的)朽木. ②无聊话,无聊人物,无聊东西. ③年轻无知的人; 小伙子. ④不中用的拳师; 面包. — *a.* 〔美俚〕没价值的, 低劣的; 不适当的. *a* ～ *pusher* 〔美〕乡村工人的工头.

pun·ka(h) [ˈpʌnkə] *n.* 〔Hind.〕①(棕榈叶做的)扇子. ②(吊在天花板上的)布风扇. ～**-wallah** 拉布风扇的人.

pun·kie [ˈpʌŋki] *n.* 〔美〕虻的一种.

pun·kin [ˈpʌŋkin] *n.* 〔美〕 = pumpkin. ～**-head** = pumpkin-head.

pun·ner [ˈpʌnə] *n.* (夯地用的)硪,夯.

pun·net [ˈpʌnit] *n.* (阔而浅的)扁篮.

pun·ning·ly [ˈpʌniŋli] *ad.* 一语双关地.

pun·ny [ˈpʌni] *a.* 〔美〕一语双关的.

pun·ster [ˈpʌnstə] *n.* 善于说双关话的人.

punt¹ [pʌnt] 〔英〕 *n.* 方头平底船. — *vt.* ①用篙撑(方头平底船等). ②用平底船装运. —*vi.* ①坐方头平底船走. ②撑方头平底船.

punt² [pʌnt] *vt., vi.* 【足球】踢(从手上放下的未落地的球). — *n.* 踢悬空球. ～**-about** 足球练习(用球).

punt³ [pʌnt] *vi.* (纸牌等)向庄家下赌注; 【赛马】赌. — *n.* = punter.

pun·ter, punt·ist [ˈpʌntə, -ist] *n.* 下赌注的人.

pun·to [ˈpʌntəu] *n.* ①点 (= point). ②【剑术】一刺; 【裁缝】一针.

pun·ty [ˈpʌnti] *n.* (制玻璃时取熔融玻璃用的)铁杆.

pu·ny [ˈpjuːni] *a.* *(-ni·er; -ni·est)* ①短小的; 弱小的, 微弱的. ②不足道的,次要的.

pup¹ [pʌp] *n.* ①小狗,小海豹, 小狐狸(等). ②〔俚〕(狂妄自大的)小伙子. *a conceited [an uppish]* ～ 狂妄自大的小伙子. ***be in*** ～ (母狗)怀胎. ***sell sb. a*** ～ 骗某人; 卖骗人东西给人. — *vi., vt.* (母狗)生(小狗), 下(仔). ～ **tent** 〔美〕楔形帆布小帐篷.

pup² [pʌp] *n.* 〔俚〕低功率干扰发射机.

pup³ [pʌp] *n.* 〔俚〕学生 (= pupil).

pu·pa [ˈpjuːpə] *n.* *(pl.* ～*s, pu·pae* [-piː]*)* 蛹.

pu·pal [ˈpjuːpəl] *a.* 蛹的.

pu·pate [ˈpjuːpeit] *vi.* 【动】化蛹. **-pa·tion** *n.*

pu·pil¹ [ˈpjuːpl, ˈpjuːpil] *n.* ①学生〔指中、小学生,大学生叫 student〕. ②【罗马法】(不满 25 岁的) 被监护人; 【苏格兰法】幼年人〔不满 14 岁(男)或 12 岁 (女)的被监护人〕. ～ **load** 一名教师负责的学生总数. ～ **teacher** (小学校的)实习老师,小先生. **-(l)a·ry** *a.*

pu·pil² [ˈpjuːpl,ˈpjuːpil] *n.* 【解】瞳孔;【物】光瞳. **-ar, -(l)arry** *a.*

pu·pil·(l)age [ˈpjuːpilidʒ] *n.* ①学生身分; 幼年人身分. ②幼年时代,半开化状态.

pu·pil·lar·i·ty, pu·pi·lar·i·ty [ˌpjuːpiˈlæriti] *n.* 【苏格兰法】少年期.

pu·pip·a·rous [pjuˈpipərəs] *a.* 蛹生的.

pup·pet [ˈpʌpit] *n.* ①木偶. ②傀儡; (行动、思想等)受别人操纵的人. *a glove [hand]* ～ (套在手上表演的)布袋木偶. *a* ～ *government* 傀儡政府. ～**play,** ～**show** 木偶戏. ～**valve [clack]**【机】提升阀,随转阀.

pup·pet·eer [ˌpʌpiˈtiːə] *n.* 操纵傀儡的人.

pup·pet·oon [ˈpʌpituːn] *n.* (电影的)木偶片.

pup·pe·try [ˈpʌpitri] *n.* ①〔总称〕木偶, 傀儡. ②木偶戏; 假面宗教戏. ③(小说中的)假想人物. ④虚饰, 假装.

Pup·pis [ˈpʌpis] *n.* 〔the ～〕【天】船尾(星)座.

pup·py [ˈpʌpi] *n.* ① 〔儿语〕小狗〔又叫 ～-dog〕; 幼小的动物. ②狂妄自大的小伙子; 呆笨的花花公子. ③〔*pl.*〕〔美俚〕脚. ～**dom,** ～**hood** 小狗的状态(或时代); 逞能的时代. ～ **love** = calflove. **-ish** *a.* 小狗似的; 爱俏的,爱打扮的; 逞能的. **-ism** *n.* 小狗一般的行为; 傲慢,逞能; 浮华.

pur- *pref.* = pro-.

pur. =①purchaser; purchasing. ②pursuit.

pu·ra·na [puˈrɑːnə] *n.* 〔常用 P-〕印度史诗〔指印度关于创世、神、万物进化等十八篇史诗中任何一篇〕.

Pur·beck [ˈpəːbek] *n.* ①(英国 Dorset 郡的) 珀贝克半岛. ②珀贝克石 (=～ stone [marble]). ～ **marble** 珀贝克大理石〔一级珀贝克石〕. ～ **stone** 珀贝克硬石灰石〔象大理石,建筑用〕.

pur·blind [ˈpəːblaind] *a.* ①半瞎的, 近视眼的. ②(脑筋)迟钝的. ③〔古〕全盲的. — *vt.* ①使成半瞎. ②使愚钝. **-ness** *n.*

Pur·cell [ˈpəːsl] *n.* 珀塞尔〔姓氏〕.

Pur·chas [ˈpəːtʃəs] *n.* 珀切斯〔姓氏〕.

pur·chas·a·ble [ˈpəːtʃəsəbl] *a.* ①可买的; 买得起的, 能买到的. ②可以收买的.

pur·chase [ˈpəːtʃəs] *vt.* ①买,购买. ②努力取得,(付出代价)赢得. ③【法】(用继承以外的方法合法地)购置,取得. ④【海】用滑车(等)举起. *a purchasing agent* 〔美〕办庄,代购人,采购主任. *a purchasing guild [association]* 购买合作社. *purchasing power* 购买力. ～ *freedom with blood* 以血的代价赢得自由. — *n.* ①买进, 购买; 购得物,买进物. ②(靠自己努力、流血等)挣得的〔争取到的〕东西;【法】(非继承性的房屋、地产的)购置, 获得, 取得; 获得物. ③(以全年收益做单位计算的) 价格; (土地等的)每年收益. ④【美史】政府收买〔出售〕的地区. ⑤买卖, 交易;【史】买卖军职的作法. ⑥【机】起重装置, 扩力装置; 复滑车,杠杆; (杠杆等的)支点;〔喻〕人情,门路. ⑦【海】绳索; 绞辘; 滑轮. ⑧紧握,紧抓. ～ *and sale* 买卖. *make a* ～ 买件东西. *It is a recent* ～ *of mine.* 那是我前几天买来的. *I cannot get any* ～ *on it.* 我找不到什么门路. *The estate was sold at ten year's* ～. 田庄以相当于十年间土地收入的价钱售出. ***not worth an hour's*** ～ (人)性命危在旦夕 *(His life is not worth an hour's* ～. 他命在垂危). ～ **tax** 〔英〕消费品零售税.

pur·chas·er [ˈpəːtʃəsə] *n.* 买主,购买人.

pur·dah [ˈpəːdɑː] *n.* 〔印度〕①(印度等地女人闺房用的)帷幔. ②〔the ～〕妇女隔幔的深闺习惯〔制度〕. ③(做帷幔用的)蓝白条花布.

pure [pjuə] *a.* ①纯的,纯粹的; 清一色的 (*opp.* mixed); 单一的,同质的; 道地的;【生】纯血统的, 纯种的. ②纯理论的; 抽象的 (*opp.* applied). ③清洁的, 无垢的; 清白的, 清廉的; 贞淑的; 洗练的, 文雅的. ④十足的, 完全的. ⑤【乐】音调纯正的;【语音】单元音的;【希腊语法】(语根)以元音收尾的, (元音)连接其他元音的, (辅音)不连接其他辅音的. ～ *gold* 纯金. ～ *descent* 纯血统. ～ *of [from] taint* 没有污点的. ～ *white* 纯白. *the* ～

in [of] heart 心地纯洁的人们. *a ~ Englishman* 道地的英国人. ~ *English* 纯正英语. ~ *science* 理论科学,纯(粹)科学. ~ *mathematics* 理论数学. ~ *nonsense* 十足的废话. *a ~ accident* 纯属意外的事件. *out of ~ necessity* 仅仅是由于需要. ~ ***and simple*** 单纯的;纯粹的,十足的. ~**bred** *a.,n.* 纯种的(动物、家畜、植物). ~ **line**【生】纯系. **-ness** *n.* 纯粹;纯度;清白.

pu·rée [ˈpjuərei] *n.*〔F.〕①菜泥;果泥;肉泥;酱. ②(把菜、肉等煮烂捣碎滤过的)纯汁浓汤. — *vt.* 把…做成浓汤[酱等].

pure·ly [ˈpjuəli] *ad.* ①清洁地;纯洁地. ②贞淑地. ③完全,全然,单.

pur·fle [ˈpəːfl] *n.* (衣服的)镶边,花边;【建】边缘饰. — *vt.* ①〔古〕给…装饰边. ②在…边上刺绣. ③美化. ④【徽】用毛皮给…镶边[作里子].

pur·fling [ˈpəːfliŋ] *n.* (特指弦乐器的)镶边.

pur·ga·tion [pəːˈgeiʃən] *n.* ①洗清,净化. ②涤罪,洗罪. ③(吃泻药)通便. ④〔古〕(自行发誓或依审判法)雪冤,证明无罪.

pur·ga·tive [ˈpəːgətiv] *a.* ①洗清的,净化的. ②通便的. ③〔古〕证明无罪的. *a ~ medicine* 泻药. — *n.* 泻药.

pur·ga·to·ri·al [ˌpəːgəˈtɔːriəl] *a.* 炼狱的;(在炼狱中)涤罪的.

pur·ga·to·ry [ˈpəːgətəri] *a.* ①洗清的;净化的. ②涤罪的. — *n.* ①【天主】死后涤罪处,炼狱. ②临时惩罚所[涤罪所];暂时的苦难.

purge [pəːdʒ] *vt.* ①使(身、心)清净 *(of; from)*;清洗,清(党),整(党),肃清,扫除 *(away; off)*. ②(用药)泻,使(人)通便. ③【法】证明…无罪,雪(冤);服满(刑期). ④〔古〕赎(罪). — *vi.* ①变清净. ②证明无罪. ③泻下. ~ *a party of undesirable members* [~ *undesirable members from a party*] 清除党内不合格分子. ~ *one of suspicion* 把某人的嫌疑洗脱干净. ~ *oneself of a charge* 辩明,剖白. — *n.* ①清洗,净化. ②【政】肃整. ③药泻. *the party ~* 清党[整党]运动.

purg·er [ˈpəːdʒə] *n.* ①清洗者. ②泻药. **pur·gee** [-ˈdʒiː] *n.* 被清洗者.

pur·i·fi·ca·tion [ˌpjuərifiˈkeiʃən] *n.* ①清洗,洗净;净化(作用). ②提纯,精制. ③【宗】涤罪;洁身;斋戒;洁礼,祓;【天主】洁杯式. *the P- of the Virgin Mary* = Candlemas.

pu·ri·fi·ca·tor [ˈpjuərifikeitə] *n.*【宗】圣器揩布,圣器帕.

pu·ri·fi·ca·to·ry, pu·ri·fi·ca·tive [ˈpjuərifikeitəri, -tiv] *a.* ①使洁净的;净化的. ②洁身的,涤罪的. ③精炼的,精制的.

pu·ri·fi·er [ˈpjuərifaiə] *n.* ①使洁净的人[物];精炼者. ②精炼用品;清洗装置;净化器,提纯器.

pu·ri·fy [ˈpjuərifai] *vt.* ①使纯净,使洁净,净化;清除 *(from; of)*. ②使清洁身心;涤(罪). ③使(语言)纯正. ④精炼,提纯,精制. — *vi.* 纯净,洁净.

pu·rin(e) [ˈpjuəri(ː)n] *n.*【化】嘌呤,尿(杂)环,四氮杂茚.

pur·ism [ˈpjuərizəm] *n.* 语言纯正;语言纯正癖者所使用的词语. **pur·ist** *n.* 语言纯正癖者. **pur·is·tic** *a.*

Pu·ri·tan [ˈpjuəritən] *n.* ①【宗史】清教徒. ②〔p-〕清教徒似的人;道德上极端拘谨的人. — *a.* 清教徒(似)的,极端拘谨的. ~ *simplicity* 清教徒式的简朴. ***the ~ city*** 〔美〕Boston 市的别名.

pu·ri·tan·ic, pu·ri·tan·i·cal [ˌpjuəriˈtænik,-ikəl] *a.* ①〔P-〕清教徒的;清教主义的. ②〔p-〕宗教[道德]上极端拘谨的. **-i·cal·ly** *ad.*

Pu·ri·tan·ism [ˈpjuəritənizəm] *n.* ①清教;清教徒气质的习俗和教义;清教主义. ②〔p-〕(宗教、道德上)极端的拘谨.

pu·ri·tan·ize [ˈpjuəritənaiz] *vi., vt.* (使)变成清教徒.

pu·ri·ty [ˈpjuəriti] *n.* ①纯净,纯洁,纯粹,清洁;清白,清廉;贞洁. ②(语言等的)纯正. ③【化】纯度.

purk [pəːk] *vt., vi.* 〔美俚〕渗滤 (=percolate).

purl[1] [pəːl] *n.* ①(溪水等的)潺潺声. ②涡纹. — *vi.* (溪水等)潺潺地流;潺潺地响.

purl[2] [pəːl] *n.* ①(绣边等所用)金银丝. ②绣边;金[银]绉边;流苏. ③(编织物的)反编,倒编. — *vt.* ①用金银丝绣. ②用绣边[流苏]装饰;镶以金[银]绉边. ③反编.

purl[3] [pəːl] *n.*【史】苦艾啤酒;搀有杜松子酒的热啤酒.

purl[4] [pəːl] *vt., n.* 〔口,方〕(马等)使(人)翻倒[颠倒].

purl·er [ˈpəːlə] *n.* 〔口〕倒落. ***come [take] a ~*** 头朝地落下,倒栽葱跌下.

pur·lieu [ˈpəːljuː] *n.* ①〔英史〕森林边缘地〔归原主所有〕. ②常出入的场所. ③〔*pl.*〕范围;界限. ④郊外,近郊. ⑤贫民窟. ~ *men*〔古〕御猎场内的土地所有人. ***the dusty ~s of the law*** 律师常出入的场所;法律事务.

pur·lin(e) [ˈpəːlin] *n.*【建】檩(条),桁条.

pur·loin [pəːˈlɔin] *vt., vi.* 偷窃.

pu·ro·my·cin [ˌpjurəuˈmaisn] *n.*【生化】嘌呤霉素.

purp [pəːp] *n.* 〔美俚〕小狗;狗.

pur·ple [ˈpəːpl] *a.* ①紫色的;紫红色的;〔古〕深红色的. ②〔诗〕鲜红的,血腥的. ③帝王的. ④词藻华美的. *turn ~ with rage* 气得脸色发紫. ~ *wine* 红葡萄酒. *a ~ patch [passage]* 浮词丽句. — *n.* ①紫色;〔古〕紫红色 (=Tyrian [royal] ~). ②紫衣;紫袍;〔the~〕帝位,王权,高位;红衣主教的职位. ③【动】紫螺. ④皇族,贵族. ⑤〔*pl.*〕【医】紫斑. ***be born in the ~*** 生在帝王[王侯贵族]家. ***be raised to the ~*** 升为红衣主教. ***marry into the ~*** 嫁到显贵人家. — *vt.* 使成紫色. —*vi.* 变紫. **P- Heart**〔美〕(给受伤兵士的)紫心勋章. ~ **passion** 〔美俚〕暗中被爱着的人.

pur·plish, pur·ply [ˈpəːpliʃ,-pli] *a.* 带紫的.

pur·port [ˈpəːpət,-pɔːt] *n.* ①(文件、演说等的)意义;要旨,大意,要领. ②〔罕〕目的. — *vt.* ①意味着,有…的意义,大意是…. ②声称. ③〔罕〕意欲,意图. *The letter ~s that ...*信上写着…. *a document ~ing to be official* 据称是官方发布的文件.

pur·pose [ˈpəːpəs] *n.* ①目的,宗旨,意向. ②决意,意志,决心. ③用途,效果;意义. ④(讨论中的)论题. *an all ~s army* 〔美〕全能军. *honesty of ~* 认真. *He is wanting in ~.* 他意志薄弱. ***answer the [one's] ~*** 适合目的,管用. ***be at cross ~s*** 彼此不合;观点分歧. ***be firm [infirm, weak] of ~*** 意志坚强[薄弱],有[无]决断力. ***bring about [attain, accomplish, carry] one's ~*** 达到目的. ***for the ~ of*** 为…. ***from the ~***〔古〕不得要领,不中肯. ***miss one's ~*** 达不到目的. ***of set ~*** 有计划地,故意. ***on ~*** 故意;意欲,为要. ***serve the [one's] ~ = answer the [one's] ~.*** ***speak from the ~*** 说得不中肯. ***to no [little] ~*** 全无[很少]效果,完全[几乎]白费,徒,空 (*I laboured to no ~.* 徒劳,无益). ***to some [good] ~*** 相当[很]成功. ***to the ~*** 剀切地,得要领地(*speak to the ~* 讲得剀切,说得中肯). ***to this ~*** 在这一意义上. — *vt.* 想,企图,打算(做);决心(做). *I ~ coming [to come] next week.* 我想下星期来. ***be ~d*** 〔古〕想…,打算,决心. ~**-made** *a.* 特制的,定做的.

pur·pose·ful [ˈpəːpəsful] *a.* ①有目的的;故意的. ②意志坚强的;果断的. ③有意义的,意味深长的. ④重大的. *a ~ character* 果断的性格. **-ly** *ad.* 有目的地,自觉地. **-ness** *n.* 自觉性.

pur·pose·less [ˈpəːpəslis] *a.* ①无目的的;无对象的. ②无决心的. ③无意义的;无益的. **-ly** *ad.*

pur·pose·ly [ˈpəːpəsli] *ad.* 故意;特意.

pur·pos·ive [ˈpəːpəsiv] *a.* = purposeful.

pur·pu·ra [ˈpəːpjurə] *n.* ①【医】紫癜(病). ②〔P-〕【动】荔枝螺属.

pur·pure [ˈpəːpjuə] *n.*【纹】紫色〔以左方上部至右方下部的对角线表之〕.

pur·pu·ric [pəːˈpjuərik] *a.* ①【医】紫癜(性)的. ②【化】红紫(酸)的. ③紫(色)的. ~ **acid**【化】红紫酸.

pur·pu·rin [ˈpəːpjurin] *n.*【化】红紫素.

purr [pəː] *vi.* (猫)得意似地咕噜咕噜叫; (人)高兴得喉咙咕噜咕噜响; (器物)咕噜咕噜响. — *vt.* 咕噜咕噜地叫[说、弄响]. — *n.* 咕噜咕噜的响声.

pur sang [ˈpjuəˈsãːŋ]〔F.〕纯种的; 纯粹的; 真正的,道地的. *The artist pur sang is a rarity.* 真正的艺术家很少.

purse [pəːs] *n.* ①钱包,钱袋. ②金钱; 资财,资力; 国库; 悬赏金,奖金;〔美俚〕拳师的收入. ③钱袋一样的东西; (女用)手提包. ④【解】囊,囊状部. *a cold [a lean, a light, an ill-lined]* ~ 空虚的钱包; 贫穷. *a heavy [long, well-filled, well-lined]* ~ 充实的钱包; 富裕. *sword and* ~ 武力和资财. *the public* ~ 国库. ~*s under the eyes* (老年人眼睛下面的)眼垂,眼泡皮. ***give a*** ~ 赠奖,捐款. ***have a common*** ~ 有公共基金. ***make (up) a*** ~ 募捐. ***one cannot make a silver*** ~ ***out of a sow's ear.*** 巧妇难为无米之炊. ***open one's*** ~ 解囊,出钱. ***put up a*** ~ 赠奖,捐款. —*vt.* ①使缩拢,抽紧. ②〔古〕把…放进钱袋. ~ *(up) one's lips [mouth]* 噘嘴. *vi.* 缩拢,皱起. ~**-bearer** ①保管银钱的人; 出纳员. ②〔英〕在大法官前捧持国玺的人. ③有袋类动物. ~**-crab** (以椰子为食的)椰子蟹. ~ **net** 袋网. ~ **pride** 自负有钱. ~**-proud** *a.* 夸耀富有的. ~ **seine** (用两只船拖的)大型袋网. ~ **strings**〔*pl.*〕钱袋的扣绳; 钱财(*hold the* ~ *strings* 掌管银钱出入. *loosen the* ~ *strings* 乱花钱,浪费. *tighten the* ~ *strings* 扎紧钱袋,节省). **-ful** *n.* 一钱袋.

purs·er [ˈpəːsə] *n.* (轮船、班机等的)事务长;〔古〕(军舰的)军需官; 出纳员.

pur·si·ness [ˈpəːsinis] *n.* ①(因肥胖而引起的)气急; 肥胖. ②(因富有而引起的)傲慢.

purs·lane [ˈpəːslin] *n.*【植】马齿苋.

pur·su·a·ble [pəˈsjuːəbl] *a.* ①可追求的,可追赶的. ②可实行的,可从事的,可继续进行的.

pur·su·ance [pəˈsjuːəns] *n.* ①追,追踪,尾追; 追求. ②奉行,推行; 实行,履行; 贯彻. *the* ~ *of truth* 追求真理. *consistent* ~ *of* 坚定不移地奉行. ***in*** ~ ***of*** 依…, 按…; 履行,推行.

pur·su·ant [pəˈsjuːənt] *a.* ①追赶的. ②依据的,按照的 *(to)*. ③随后的. ~ *to the rules* 按照规则. — *ad.* 依,按照 *(to)*. **-ly** *ad.* 从而,因此.

pur·sue [pəˈsjuː] *vt.* ①追, 追赶, 追踪; 紧跟着, 纠缠;【军】追击. ②求, 追求. ③继续, 奉行, 推行, 实行, 从事; 经营, 贯彻; 采取(方针等). ④走(路等). ~ *the enemy* 追赶敌人. *Detraction* ~*s the great.* 人大招物议,树大惹风吹. ~ *knowledge* 求知. ~ *knowledge under difficulties* 苦学. ~ *a calling* 从事一种职业. ~ *a subject* 继续讨论. ~ *a plan* 贯彻计划. ~ *the proper legal law* 采取法律上的正当手段. — *vi.* ①追,追随 *(after)*. ②继续(说). ③〔Scot.〕起诉 *(for)*.

pur·su·er [pəˈsjuːə] *n.* ①追赶者; 追求者. ②实行者; 研究者. ③〔英〕【法】原告.

pur·suit [pəˈsjuːt] *n.* ①追赶, 追踪; 驱逐,追击; 追求. ②实行; 经营. ③事务; 职业,工作; 研究. ④〔美〕【军】歼击机,驱逐机(= ~ plane). ~ *troops* 追击部队. *daily* ~*s* 日常事务. *mercantile [commercial]* ~*s* 商业. *literary* ~*s* 文学工作[研究]. ***in hot*** ~ 穷追. ***in*** ~ ***of*** 寻求,追求(*in* ~ *of health* 为了健康).

pur·sui·vant [ˈpəːsivənt] *n.* ①纹章院属官;〔废〕王使,国使. ②〔诗〕从者,随员.

pur·sy[1] [ˈpəːsi] *a.* ***(-si·er; -si·est)*** (因肥胖而)气急的; 肥胖的.

pur·sy[2] [ˈpəːsi] *a.* ①缩拢的; 有皱褶的. ②有钱的,夸耀富有的.

pur·te·nance [ˈpəːtinəns] *n.*〔古〕(屠宰后的家畜的)内脏.

pu·ru·lence, -cy [ˈpjuəruləns, -si] *n.* ①化脓,脓性. ②脓,脓液.

pu·ru·lent [ˈpjuərulənt] *a.* 化脓的; 脓性的.

pur·vey [pəːˈvei]〔英〕*vt.* 供给,供应,备办(伙食). — *vi.* (为…)办伙食 *(for)*.

pur·vey·ance [pəˈveiəns] *n.* ①承办[供应]伙食. ②伙食,食物. ③【英史】王室食物徵发权.

pur·vey·or [pəˈveiə] *n.*〔英〕(军队、王室等的)粮食筹办员; 伙食办理员;【史】食物徵发官.

pur·view [ˈpəːvjuː] *n.* ①(法令等的)范围,界限; 应用范围,权限. ②视界,眼界. ③【法】要项,条项 (*opp.* preamble). ***fall within the*** ~ ***of Art.(1)*** 该按第(一)条办理. ***within [outside] the*** ~ ***of*** 在…的范围内[外].

pus [pʌs] *n.* 脓; 脓液.

Pu·san [ˈpuːˈsɑːn] *n.* 釜山[南朝鲜港市].

Pu·sey [ˈpjuːzi] *n.* 普西[姓氏].

Pu·sey·ism [ˈpjuːziizəm] *n.*〔贬〕(E.B. Pusey 等发起的)牛津运动 (Tractarianism). **-ite** *n.* 参加牛津运动的人.

push [puʃ] *vt.* ①推(门等) (*opp.* pull; draw); 推动(车子等); 刺出(剑、手杖等). ②大力推进, 推行. ③使延伸, 使伸出; 发(芽), 生(根) *(out; forth)*. ④强求, 赖着要; 追求(目的等). ⑤驱使, 逼迫, 催促(某事达到…程度, 某人做某事)[后接介词 to, 或 into doing, to do]. ⑥拼命挣(家当), 扩充(营业);〔俗〕增加 *(up)*. ⑦使引人注意; 推荐(人); 推销(货);〔俚〕贩卖(毒品). ⑧【台球】推撞. ⑨使(某人)在金钱等方面受窘, 对难题感到困惑[常用被动结构]. ~ *a car* 推车. *trees* ~*ing their roots into the ground* 深深扎根于土中的树. *They draw some people in,* ~ *others out.* 他们拉拢一些人, 排挤一些人. ~ *one's claims* 竭力要求. ~ *it* 〔口〕死乞白赖地要求. ~ *a person* 推荐人. ~ *one's business* 努力做生意; 扩展事业. ~ *one's wares* 强卖商品. *He* ~*ed me to pay.* 他逼我付款. — *vi.* ①推; 挤. ②推行. ③伸展, 扩展; 增加. ④竭力争取 *(for)*. ⑤〔古〕用角触. *The door* ~*s easily.* 这门一推就开. ~ *past* 挤了过去. *dock* ~*ing far out into the sea* 远远伸入海中的码头. ~ *for higher wages* 争取提高工资. ***be*** ~***ed around*** 被摆布; 被支使; 被欺负. ***be*** ~***ed for*** *(money)* 困于(金钱), 拮据. ~ ***away*** 推开. ~ ***back*** 推回, 捅回. ~ ***in*** ①推进; 推进去. ②(小艇)靠近岸. ~***off*** ①用桨推岸把船撑开. ②〔口〕离去, 回去 (*It is time for us to* ~ *off now.* 现在是我们回去的时候了). ~ ***on*** ①费力地前进. ②赶快完成任务等 *(with)*. ~ ***one's way*** 排开路前进(~ *one's way in the world* 奋斗成名). ~ ***open*** 推开. ~ ***out*** ①*vt.* 推出, 发出(芽等), 伸展(根等). ② *vi.* (岬向海中)突出. ~ ***over*** 推倒. ~ ***round the ale*** 传递啤酒. ~ ***the mark skyward***〔美俚〕创新纪录. ~ ***through*** ①完成(事务). ②冲过, 穿过. ③(树叶等)长出. ~ ***up the daisies***〔美俚〕被埋葬. ~ ***up to*** 逼近. — *n.* ①推, (用剑、棒等)刺, 戳; 推进. ②突进, 冲进; 猛攻, 打击. ③推力;〔口〕精力, 毅力;〔口〕努力, 苦干, 奋发. ④迫切, 紧急, 危机, 紧急关头. ⑤后援, 推荐. ⑥〔俚〕人群; 伙伴; 有力集团. ⑦〔英俚〕贼党, 流氓集团. ⑧【台球】推球;【棒球】轻击. *I gave him a good* ~. 使劲给他一击. *a bell* ~ 电铃按钮. *P- generally succeeds in business.* 在事业中埋头苦干多半成功. ***at a*** ~ 临危; 急迫时. ***at one*** ~ 一推, 一下子. ***at the first*** ~ 第一; 在开始攻击时. ***be in the*** ~ 是集团中一分子; 熟悉情况. ***bring to the*** ~ 使陷绝境. ***come to the*** ~ 临到紧急关头; 陷入绝境. ***get the*** ~〔俚〕被解雇. ***give a*** ~ 给推一把; 给予打击. ***give the*** ~〔俚〕解雇. ***make a*** ~ 奋发, 加油. ~ ***and go***〔口〕精力饱满的, 肯做肯干的 (*a man of* ~ *and go*). ***put to the*** ~ 使陷绝境; 使受到严重考验. ~**ball**【运】推球[球重48磅以上]. ~**-bicycle** [〔俚〕**-bike**]〔英〕自行车, 脚踏车 (*opp.* motorbike). ~ **button**〔美〕电钮, 按钮; 开关. ~**-button** *a.* 按钮的; 按动电钮操纵的. ~ **car**〔美〕(铁路上的)四轮手推车. ~-

cart (商贩的)手推车;坐椅式手推车. ~ **cycle** = ~ bicycle. ~**-down** ①【空】推下. ②【自】后进先出存储器, 迭式存储器. ~**-halfpenny** [-ˈheipəni] = shove-halfpenny. ~**mo·bile**〔美〕手推车. ~ **money**〔美〕推销佣金. ~**over** ①〔美俚〕极简单的工作〔问题〕, 闲差事. ②容易说服的人; 容易打倒的拳击对手, 弱敌. ③年轻荡妇. ④(导弹、火箭)沿弹道水平方向的位移. ~**-pin**〔美〕图钉; (小孩玩的)弹图钉游戏. ~**-pull** *a.*【电子】推挽式的. ~**-up** *n.*【体】俯卧撑.

push·a·ble [ˈpuʃəbl] *a.* 可以推的.

push·er [ˈpuʃə] *n.* ①推者; 挤者. ②推杆; 后推火车头. ③【空】(螺旋桨在后的)推进式飞机.

push·ful [ˈpuʃful] *a.*〔口〕精力充沛的, 富有进取精神的; 肯做肯干的.

push·i·ness [ˈpuʃinis] *n.*〔美〕精神, 精力; 毅力, 冲力.

push·ing [ˈpuʃiŋ] *a.* 推的, 推进的; 奋进的; 活跃的, 有干劲的. **-ly** *ad.*

Push·kin [ˈpuːʃkin], **Alexander Sergeevich** [ɑːlekˈsɑːndə seəˈgejəvitʃ] 普希金或普式庚〔1799—1837, 俄国诗人、散文家、剧作家〕.

Push·tu [ˈpʌʃtuː] *n.* 普什图语 (= Pashto)〔阿富汗和巴基斯坦用的印欧语系伊朗语支的语言, 阿富汗的官方语言之一〕.

push·y [ˈpuʃi] *a.*〔美〕前进的, 有进取精神的, 有干劲的.

pu·sil·la·nim·i·ty [ˌpjuːsiləˈnimiti] *n.* 怯懦; 胆小; 无气力. **-lan·i·mous** [-ˈlæniməs] *a.*

puss [pus] *n.* ①小猫咪〔爱称, 呼唤用语〕. ②〔口〕少女, 小姑娘. ③〔英〕兔子; 老虎. ④〔美俚〕脸, 嘴. *a sly* ~ (要提防的)狡猾女郎;〔美〕姑娘气的青年. ***the ~(-) in(-)the(-)corner***〔美〕抢壁角游戏. ~ **moth** 天社蛾的一种.

puss·ley, puss·ly [ˈpʌsli] *n.*【植】马齿苋 (=purslane).

pus·sy[1] [ˈpʌsi] *a.* 脓多的; 脓一样的 (= pursy).

puss·y[2] [ˈpusi] *n.* ①〔儿〕猫咪(= puss). ②(褪色柳等的)葇荑花序. ③抢壁角游戏. ***play*** ~ 飞机躲在云里. ~ ***gut***〔美〕肥胖的大汉子; 笨汉. ***the ~(-)wants(-)a(-) corner*** ~**cat** 猫咪. ~ **willow**【植】褪色柳.

Puss·y·foot [ˈpusifut] *vi.*〔美俚〕偷偷地走, 轻轻地走; 抱骑墙态度. — *a.*〔美俚〕骑墙的; 主张绝对禁酒的. — *n.*〔美俚〕① 抱骑墙态度的政治家. ②禁酒主义者. ③潜行者.

pus·tu·lant [ˈpʌstjulənt] *a.* 致脓疱形成的. — *n.* 起脓疱剂.

pus·tu·lar [ˈpʌstjulə] *a.*【医】小脓疱的; 有小粒点的, 满布小粒点的.

pus·tu·late [ˈpʌstjuleit] *vt., vi.* (使)生小脓疱. — *a.* 满布小粒点的.

pus·tule [ˈpʌstjuːl] *n.* ①【医】小脓疱. ②【动、植】色点; 小疱.

pus·tu·lous [ˈpʌstʃuləs] *a.* =pustular.

put[1] [put] ***(put; put·ting)*** *vt.* ①搁, 放, 安, 摆; 放进, 加入, 搀进 *(to; in)*. ~ *milk to [in] tea* 加牛奶在茶里. ~ *a saddle on a horse* 把鞍子放在马上. ~ *a man in gaol* 把人关进牢里. ②使贴近, 使接近, 使靠近. ~ *a glass to one's lips* 把杯子贴在嘴唇上. ~ *a cow to a bull* 使母牛跟公牛交尾. ③装, 安. ~ *a handle to a knife* 把刀把安装在刀上. ④套(马拉车), 拴(马). ~ *a horse to a cart* 把马套上车. ⑤做成, 整理成, 使成(某种状态). ~ *a room in order* 收拾房间. ~ *to sleep* 使入睡. ~ *to flight* 打退, 击溃. ~ *a man into a rage* 使人发怒. ~ *to death* 处死. ~ *names in alphabetical order* 依字母次序排列名字. ⑥使转向特定方向. ~ *a horse to a fence* 使马跳过围栅. ~ *one's mind to [on] a problem* 集中心思考虑问题. ~ *the rudder to port* 搬外舵(把舵转向左舷). ⑦使从事. ~ *a boy out in service* 把孩子送去做帮工. ⑧应用, 运用. *put one's skill to good use* 善于运用技术. ⑨委托, 交给, 托付. ~ *a child into his hands* 把孩子托付给他. ⑩写上, 写下来; 记录, 记入, 登记; 盖(印), 签(名). ~ *something on paper* 写到纸上, 留个记录. ⑪叙述, 表明, 说明, 陈述; 翻译. *The case was ~ cleverly.* 事情陈述得很巧妙. *I don't know how to ~ it.* 我不晓得怎样表述才好. *How shall I ~ it?* 我怎样说才好呢? ~ *one's ideas into words* 把思想用言语表现出来. ~ *it into Chinese* 把它翻译成汉语. ⑫提出(问题), 加以(质问); 建议, 提议. ~ *a question to sb.* 向某人提个问题. ~ *a thing before sb.* 向某人建议, 向某人说一件事. ~ *it to sb.* 问某人, 征求某人意见, 要某人承认. ⑬估计; 算定; 认为. ~ *one's income at £3,000 a year* 估计某人收入为一年三千镑. ⑭使负(责任、罪等); 使蒙受(耻辱等); 加以(责难等). *put sb. to trial [shame]* 使某人受考验[蒙耻]. *put sb. in the wrong* 归咎于某人. ⑮使受到(制止等). ~ *a stop [an end, a period] to* 停止, 制止. ⑯抽(税); 下(赌注). ~ *a tax on gasoline* 征收汽油税. ~ *three dollars on the favourite horse* 在热门马上下三元赌注. ⑰掷, 投, 丢, 抛; 捅出(武器), 刺, 戳;〔古〕推, 推进. ~ *the shot*【运】推铅球. ~ *a knife into it* 把小刀戳进去. ⑱为…配(曲等). ~ *that famons poem to music* 为那首名诗配曲. ⑲使渡过(河等). ~ *a boat across a river* 使船渡河. ⑳使(家畜)吃, 限(人)吃 *(to; on; upon)*. — *vi.* ①(船等)前进, 驶向 *(to; for)*; (河水等)流入; 流出. ②(植物)发芽. ③出发; 匆忙离开;〔美口〕逃走 *(for; out)*. ***be ~ to it***〔口〕左右为难, 进退两难. ~ ***about*** ① *vt.* 使转变方向; 公布, 宣布, 散布;〔*Scot.* 口〕使苦恼, 使心烦, 使窘, 使混乱 (= ~ out). ② *vi.* (掉头)折回;【海】掉转航路(方向, 船头) (~ *oneself about* 为难). ~ ***a bug [flea] in one's ear***〔美俚〕通过告知秘密来唆使[煽动]; 使担忧. ~ ***a crimp in***〔美俚〕破坏计划, 妨害, 捣蛋. ~ ***across*** ①美满完成, 弄成功; 堂堂开张. ②〔美俚〕使人接受, 使承认; 欺骗人, 使人上当. ~ ***a half-Nelson on***〔美〕把对方带到不利的地位. ~ ***a large number of runs together*** = ~ ***two and two together*** 推断. ~ ***aside*** 挪开, 撇开; 避开, 扔弃; 排除 (~ *aside one's difficulties* 排除困难). ~ ***asunder*** 分开, 拆散. ~ ***at*** 估量作. ~ *(sb.)* ***at his ease*** 使宽心[放心, 安心]. ~ ***away*** ① *vt.* (a) 拿开, 收掉, 贮存, 留下来(以后用). (b) 排斥; 扔掉, 忘记; 进(医院、监狱等). (c) 抛弃, 放弃. (d)〔俚〕吃光, 喝完 (~ *away a gallon of beer*); (船)开行. (e)〔俚〕当, 押; 葬; 反叛; 告密. ② *vi.* (船)开行 (~ *away for Shanghai* 开往上海). ~ ***back*** ① *vt.* 放在原来地方, 送回; 使退回, 拨慢, 拨回(钟、表的)针; 使退步, 妨碍, 阻碍; 延迟; 羁押(犯人). ② *vi.* 回去, 折回;〔喻〕变年青. ~ ***by*** ①避开(人、质问等); 搁在一边, 推脱, 置之不理. ②积蓄, 储存. ~ ***down*** ①放下. ②镇压; 制止, 使沉默. ③削减, 减, 节省; 降级, 剥夺职权. ④记下; 登记(作申请人) *(Put me down for £5.* 请记下我认5镑). ⑤以为, 认为 *(as; for)*. ⑥归, 担, 推给 *(to) (He ~ the mistake down to me.* 他把错误推给我). ⑦〔口〕大喝. ⑧(飞机)着陆. ~ ***down the drain***〔口〕浪费. ~ ***down in black and white*** 白纸黑字写下. ~ ***for*** 以…为目标前进. ~ ***forth*** ① *vt.* 突出, 长出, 伸出; 放(光); 表现, 发挥, 拿出(力量等); 陈列; 出版, 发行; 建议. ② *vi.* 发芽;〔诗〕出发. ~ ***forward*** ①建议, 提倡; 促进, 振兴; 推举(候补人等). ②使突出, 使显眼. ~ ***heads together*** 讨论, 商量. ~ ... ***home*** ①戳进; 撵走. ②坚持[贯彻]到底. ~ ***in*** ① *vt.* 插(嘴); 替人说(话), 吹嘘吹嘘 (~ *in a word for a friend* 替朋友辩护); 提出(要求、文件等); 加以(打击等); 使就任, 任命, 请(家庭教师等)花费(时间). ② *vi.* (船)入港, 靠码头; 进来, 访问 (~ *in at a port* 入港). ~ *(sb.)* ***in [into] a junk*** 吓(某人). ~ *(sb.)* ***in a fix [hole]*** 使某人陷入绝境. ~ ***in for*** 申请, 做候补人. ~ ***in force*** 实施. ~ ***in hand*** 着手, 动手. ~ ***in mind of*** 提醒, 使想起. ~ ***in motion*** 开动. ~ ***in one's two cents' worth***〔美俚〕发表自己的意见, 参加谈话[讨论]. ~ ***into*** ①插入; 注

入。②(船)入港,开进。~ ***into shape*** 使体现。~ ***it across*** *(him)* 严厉批评[责备]。~ ***it aptly*** 说得好。~ ***it in another way*** 用另一方式说,换句话说。~ ***it on***〔口〕讨高价;乱吹牛;假装。~ ***it on ice***〔美俚〕忘记。~ ***it over***〔美俚〕成功,考试及格。***not to*** ~ ***it past*** *(sb.)*〔美口〕①认为某人能做某事。②认为那是某人的本分。~ ***it*** *(to sb.)* ***that***(向某人)建议。~ ***it to*** *(sb.)* 征求(某人)意见。~ ***it where the flies won't get it***〔美俚〕喝(酒)。~ ***off*** ① *vt.* 拿走,拿开;脱(衣帽等);避开,推辞,推脱(人、要求);搁置;使等;拖,延期 *(till; until; to)*;拿(假货等)骗人,使人上当 *(on; upon)*;排斥,黜免,驱逐,丢弃;谏止 *(from)*;妨碍,反叛,出卖;使为难;使没有精神去…,使厌恶 *(be ~ off one's meals* 不想吃饭)。② *vi.*(船、船员等)离岸,出发,动身。~ ***on*** ①穿上(衣服),戴上(眼镜)。②增加(体重、速度等)(*~ on flesh* 长肉。*~ on the pace* 赶紧走。*~ on weight* 增加体重);(比赛等中)得(分) *(to)*。③装,假装 *(His modesty is all ~ on.* 他的谦虚全是假的)。④赌(*~ £5 on a horse* 赌某马5镑)。⑤使走快,拨快(*~ the clock on* 把钟拨快)。⑥任命。⑦使工作;煽动,教唆,撺掇。⑧上演(剧本)。⑨把(罪)推给。⑩推荐,介绍 *(to)*。~ ***on an act***〔美俚〕假装。~ ***on airs*** 摆架子。~ ***on lugs***〔美俚〕装腔作势,摆架子。~ ***on steam*** ①使劲,加油。②开动,投入生产。~ ***(sb.) on to***〔口〕向某人点明…。~ ***on the dog [ritz]***〔美〕摆架子,逞威。~ ***(sb.) on the pan***〔美俚〕骂,责备。~ ***one's back up*** ①(美橄榄球)抵抗,顶住。②激怒。~ ***oneself out of the way*** 自找麻烦。~ ***oneself outside of***〔美俚〕吃,喝。~ ***oneself over*** *(an audience)*,使(听众)理解[接受、欢迎]。~ ***out*** ① *vt.* 拿出,长出,发出(芽等);迁移,移植(树苗);转让,交出;逐出,赶出,撵走,解雇;伸出(手);熄(火),灭火;表现,表示,发挥;交给(人);出产;完成,作出;发行,出版;使出场(比赛);弄脱(关节),使脱臼;贷出(款子),投资,花费,存款;触怒,惹,使窘,使为难;【棒球】使打出界外,使出局。② *vi.* 开船;〔美〕出发;发芽;突然跑掉。~ ***out of action*** 歼灭,消灭。~ ***out of service*** 关,停止。~ ***(sb.) out of the way*** 除掉(某人);把(某人)关进牢监。~ ***over*** ①(船)渡过去。②延期。③(使戏剧、政策等)成功[得到好评]。④〔美俚〕顺利完成。~ ***paid to***〔口〕认为…已了结[解决]了,毁掉了…。~ ***right*** 订正;医治(病人)。~ ***the acid on***〔美俚〕试。~ ***the bee on***〔美俚〕①骗去…的钱,找借口赖债。②把…打昏过去。~ ***the crimp in***〔美俚〕①领头,打败。②自由驱使。~ ***the cross on***〔美俚〕决定杀死。~ ***the finger on***〔美俚〕向警察局出卖[告密]。~ ***the game on ice***〔美运〕保持胜利。~ ***the heat on***〔美俚〕①使成不愉快的注意对象,使窘,使为难,盘问,折磨。②=~ the finger on. ~ ***the muffler on***〔美俚〕使住嘴,使沉默。~ ***through*** ①完成,做好(工作等)。②戳穿。③使(议案等)通过。④使受(考验等)。⑤接通(电话)*(Put me through to X.* 请接X先生)。~ ***together*** ①编辑;拼拢。②比较考虑,合计。③使结婚。~ ***to it*** 折磨,使为难,使烦恼;强制 *(be ~ to it* 非常困苦)。~ ***to rights***〔美〕整理,整顿。~ ***(sb.) to the door*** 辞退,解雇(某人)。~ ***up*** ① *vt.* (a)挂,升(帆、旗等);贴(广告等);打(伞);吊(蚊帐);撑开(帐篷);盖,造(房子)。(b)作(祷告),提出(请求)。(c)收拾;收藏,插入刀鞘(*~ up the sword* 收刀;停止战争);醃藏;(将汽车等)开进车房。(d)包捆,打包。(e)涨(价)。(f)上演(剧本)。(g)交去拍卖;拿去卖。(h)提名候选人,推荐。(i)留宿;得到食宿。(j)梳(头)。(k)配,配制(药等)。(l)【赛马】雇用…做骑师。(m)鼓动,唆使;(打猎时)赶出野兽。(n)通知,暗示 *(to)*;〔俚〕计划,密谋。(o)公布(结婚的预告)。② *vi.* 投宿(*~ up at an inn* 住旅馆);提名竞选;〔美俚〕付钱;下赌注。~ ***up the shutters*** 停业。~ ***upon*** 欺骗;压迫。~ ***up or shut up!***〔美〕拿出确实证据否则免开尊口!~ ***(sb.) up to*** 唆使(某人)…,煽动(某人)…,告诉,教。~ ***up with*** 忍住,熬住,隐忍迁就。~ ***(sb.) wise***〔美俚〕使(某人)想某事,点醒,点悟。—*n.* ①推;刺,戳;投,掷,扔。②一扔的距离。③【交易所】使按限价卖出(*opp.* call)。~ *and call* 限价买卖,强买,强卖。**~-down** ①平定。②贬低(的话)。③(飞机的)降落。**~-off** ①辩解,遁辞,推诿。③延期,拖延。**~-on**〔美俚〕哄骗,假话。**~-up** *a.*〔美俚〕预谋的,预先商定的(*a ~ job* 阴谋,奸计)。**~-upon** *a.* ①受虐待的。②被愚弄的。

put[2] [put] *a.*〔美口〕固定的,不动的。

put[3] [put] *v., n.* = putt.

pu·ta·men [pjuːˈteimən] *n.* ***(pl. -mi·na*** [-minə]***)***【植】(核果的)内果皮,核;【动】(卵壳内的)硬膜;壳。

pu·ta·tive [ˈpjuːtətiv] *a.* 推断的;假定的。*the ~ author of a book*(真实作者难考的)一本书的假定作者。**-ly** *ad.*

pute [pjuːt] *a.*〔古〕单纯的。

pu·te·al [ˈpjuːtiəl] *n.*(古罗马的)井栏。

put·log, put·lock [ˈputlɔg, -lɔk] *n.*【建】脚手架跳板(短)横木;支踏脚板的横木,踏脚桁。

put-on [ˈputɔn] *a.* 假装的,伪装的。*a ~ smile* 假笑。—*n.*〔俚〕①(利用别人的轻信)欺骗或愚弄人的行为。②(对读者或观众进行戏弄的)滑稽剧,滑稽小说;模仿剧,模仿小说。

put-put, putt-putt [ˈpʌtˈpʌt] *vi.* ***(put-put·ted; put-put·ting)***(汽艇、摩托车等)发出噗噗声 —*n.* ①〔口〕(车辆、发动机等发出的)噗噗声。②移动东西或操作时可能发出的声音。

pu·tre·fa·cient [ˌpjuːtriˈfeiʃənt] *a.* 容易腐败的。—*n.*【医】腐败剂,化脓剂。

pu·tre·fac·tion [ˌpjuːtriˈfækʃən] *n.* ①腐败,腐化(作用)。②腐败物。

pu·tre·fac·tive [ˌpjuːtriˈfæktiv] *a.* ①容易腐败的。②使腐败的,致腐的。

pu·tre·fy [ˈpjuːtrifai] *vt.* 使化脓;〔罕〕使腐烂,使腐败。—*vi.* 化脓;腐烂,腐败,发霉;堕落。

pu·tres·cence [pjuːˈtresns] *n.* ①腐败,腐化,堕落。②正在腐烂的东西。

pu·tres·cent [pjuːˈtresnt] *a.* ①将腐烂的,开始腐烂的。②关于腐烂的。

pu·tres·ci·ble [pjuːˈtresibl] *a.* 会腐败的,容易腐败的。

pu·tres·cine [pjuːˈtresiːn,-in] *n.*【化】腐胺。

pu·trid [ˈpjuːtrid] *a.* ①已腐烂的;恶臭的,脏的;堕落的。②〔口〕(行为、态度等)讨人嫌的,使人不愉快的。*a perfectly ~ book* 极枯燥的书。*turn ~* 烂掉。~ **fever** 斑疹伤寒。~ **sore throat** 白喉;坏疽性咽炎。**-ly** *ad.*

pu·trid·i·ty [pjuːˈtriditi] *n.* ①霉烂,腐败(物)。②堕落。

putsch [putʃ] *n.*〔G.〕仓促起义[暴动],民变,暴动。

putsch·ism [ˈputʃizəm] *n.* 盲动主义。

putsch·ist [ˈputʃist] *n.* 仓促起义的人,盲动主义者。

putt [pʌt] *vt., vi.*【高尔夫球】把(球)轻轻打进洞里。—*n.*【高尔夫球】轻打。

put·tee [ˈpʌti] *n.*(布或皮的)绑腿。

put·ter[1] [ˈpʌtə] *n.*【高尔夫】轻击棒;轻打者。

put·ter[2] [ˈputə] *n.* ①置放者。②【采】搬运工,推车工。

put·ter[3] [ˈputə] *vi., n.*〔美口〕磨蹭,拖拉,偷懒;瞎忙。**-er** *n.* 拖拉者,偷懒者;瞎忙者。

put·tie [ˈpʌti] *n.* = puttee.

put·ti·er [ˈpʌtiə] *n.* 用油灰(装窗玻璃)的人。

put·ting[1] [ˈputiŋ] *n.* 投掷。

put·ting[2] [ˈpʌtiŋ] *n.*【高尔夫球】打球入洞。~ **green [ground]** 离球洞三十码以内的地区。~ **hole** 球洞。

put·to [ˈpuː(t)təu] *n.* ***(pl. put·ti*** [-ti]***)***〔It.〕(巴罗克 *baroque* 新奇艺术风格中的)肥胖的年轻男天使或神童之形象;爱神裸体像(尤指有翅者)。

put·too [ˈpʌtuː] *n.*〔印度〕普妥粗羊绒呢。

put·ty [ˈpʌti] *n.* ①油灰[装窗玻璃等用]。②(擦玻璃或金属用的)去污粉;宝石磨粉〔又叫 jewellers' ~〕。

glazier's ～ 镶玻璃窗的油灰. *plasterers'* ～ 涂底油灰. —*vt.* 用油灰涂固[结合、涂平]. ～**-blower**〔美俚〕(小孩用铁管做的)铁炮. ～ **face**〔美俚〕呆脸; 呆子, 白痴. ～**-head**〔美口〕蠢货. ～**-looking** *a.* 带灰色的. ～ **medal** 油灰(做的)奖章, 微功奖. ～ **powder** (擦玻璃或金属用的)去污粉.

puy [pwi:] *n.* 〔F.〕【地】死火山锥.

puz·zle [ˈpʌzl] *vt.* 使为难, 使迷惑; 使伤脑筋; 使混乱. *I am* ～*d what to do.* 我不知怎样办才好. — *vi.* 为难 *(about; over)*; 伤脑筋 *(over)*. ～ ***one's brains [oneself] about [over] sth.*** 为…大伤脑筋, 拚命想…. ～ ***out*** 解决(难题等). ～ ***through*** 摸索着通过. —*n.* 难题; 迷惑; (字谜、画谜等的)谜. ***in a*** ～ *(about sth.)* (为某件事情)为难. ～**headed** *a.* 昏头昏脑的; 思想混乱的. ～**ring** 益智环[如九连环等]. **-dom** *n.* 为难; 苦境. **-ment** *n.* ①为难, 迷惑. ②难题; 谜.

puz·zler [ˈpʌzlə] *n.* ①使人为难的人[物]. ②难题.

puz·zling [ˈpʌzliŋ] *a.* 使为难的; 费解的; 莫名其妙的. **-ly** *ad.*

PVA = 【化】① polyvinyl acetate 聚醋酸乙烯酯. ② polyvinyl alcohol 聚乙烯醇.

PVC = polyvinyl chloride【化】聚氯乙烯.

Pvt. = Private 列兵;〔英〕陆军二等兵;〔美〕陆军[海军陆战队]二等兵.

PW = prisoner(s) of war 战俘.

PWA, P.W.A. = Public Works Administration〔美〕公共工程署.

P.W.D. =① Psychological Warfare Division〔美〕心理作战部. ② Public Works Department〔美〕公共工程处.

Pwr; pwr = power.

pwt. = pennyweight.

PX = ① please exchange 请交换. ② post exchange〔美〕陆军消费合作社.

pxt; pxt. = 〔L.〕*pinxit* …画, …作[画家署名用语].

pya [pjɑ:] *n.* *(pl. pyas)* 缅分[等于 1/100 缅元 (Burmes-kyat)].

py·ae·mi·a [paiˈi:miə, -mjə] *n.* 【医】脓毒症, 脓血症. **py·ae·mic** *a.*

pyc·nid·i·um [pikˈnidiəm] *n.* *(pl. -i·a [-ə])* 分生孢子器. **-nid·i·al** *a.*

pyc·no·gon·id [ˌpiknəˈgɔnid] *n.* 海蜘蛛类 *(Pycnogonida)* 动物.

pyc·nom·e·ter [pikˈnɔmitə] *n.* 【物】比重瓶; 比重管; 比重计.

Pye [pai] *n.* 派伊[姓氏].

pye-dog, pi(e)-dog [ˈpaidɔg] *n.* (东南亚)野狗.

pye-eyed [ˈpaiaid] *a.* 〔美俚〕醉醺醺的.

py·e·li·tis [ˌpaiəˈlaitis] *n.* 【医】肾盂炎.

py·e·lo·gram [ˈpaiələgræm] *n.* 肾盂 X 线照片.

py·e·log·ra·phy [ˌpaiəˈlɔgrəfi] *n.* 肾盂照相术.

py·e·lo·ne·phri·tis [ˌpaiəˌləuniˈfraitis] *n.* 肾盂肾炎.

py·e·mi·a [paiˈi:miə] *n.* = pyaemia.

py·gid·i·um [paiˈdʒidiəm] *n.* *(pl. -i·a [-ə])*【动】尾节, 尾板; (介壳虫)臀板.

pyg·mae·an, pyg·me·an [pigˈmiən] *a.* ①(在古代历史和传说中所说的, 居住在非洲、亚洲的一种身体矮小的民族) 俾格米人的. ②现代非洲、亚洲的身体矮小的黑人的. ③(人、动物、植物等身体或枝干) 小得奇特的, 侏儒的. ④微不足道的, 无足轻重的人[物]的 (= pygmy).

Pyg·ma·li·on [pigˈmeiljən] *n.* 【希神】皮格梅隆[塞浦路斯国王, 热恋自己雕的少女像].

pyg·moid [ˈpigmɔid] *a.* 似俾格米人的[尤指身体矮小的].

pyg·my [ˈpigmi] *n.* ①矮人; 矮小动物; 智力低劣的人. ②〔P-〕矮小黑人, 俾格米人 (=pagm(a)ean). — *a.* ①矮小的. ②不足道的; 小规模的. ③〔P-〕俾格米人的, 矮小黑人的. *our* ～ *effort* 我们的微小努力.

pyg·my·ism [ˈpigmiizəm] *n.* 矮小, 矮小的状态.

py·ja·mas [pəˈdʒɑ:məz, pi-] *n.* 〔*pl.*〕〔英〕(宽大的)睡衣裤; (印度人等的)宽松裤.

pyk·nic [ˈpiknik] *a.* 肩宽矮胖体型的.

Pyle [pail] *n.* 派尔[姓氏].

py·lon [ˈpailən] *n.* ①(古埃及的)塔门. ②【电】(高压线的)桥塔;【空】(飞机场的)标塔; 标杆, 路标灯; 硬式飞艇的螺桨架; 悬臂, 支架. *a slab* ～【火箭】流线型发射架.

py·lo·rec·to·my [ˌpailəˈrektəmi] *n.* *(pl. -mies)* 幽门切除术.

py·lo·rus [paiˈlɔ:rəs] *n.* *(pl. -ri [rai])*【解】幽门. **py·lor·ic** *a.*

Pym [pim] *n.* 皮姆[姓氏].

pymt; pymt. = payment.

pyo- *comb.f.* 脓: *pyemia.*

py·od [ˈpaiəd] *n.* 热电偶, 温差电偶.

py·o·der·ma [ˌpaiəˈdə:mə] *n.* 脓皮病. **-der·mic** *a.*

py·o·gen·e·sis [ˌpaiəˈdʒenisis] *n.* 【医】酿脓, 生脓. **-gen·ic** *a.*

py·oid [ˈpaiɔid] *a.* 脓的, 脓状的.

py·o·ne·phri·tis [ˌpaiəuniˈfraitis] *n.*【医】化脓性肾炎.

Pyong·yang [ˈpjɔŋˈjæŋ] *n.* 平壤[朝鲜民主主义人民共和国首都].

py·or·rhoe·a [ˌpaiəˈriə] *n.*【医】脓漏, 脓溢, (尤指)齿槽脓漏.

pyorrhoea al·vi·o·la·ris [ˌpaiəˈriə ælˌvi:əˈlɛəris]【医】牙槽脓溢.

py·o·sis [paiˈəusis] *n.* 【医】化脓, 脓溃.

pyr- =pyro-.

pyr·a·can·tha [ˌpirəˈkænθə, ˌpairə-] *n.* 【植】火棘属植物; 欧洲火棘 (firethorn).

py·ral·i·did [paiˈrælidid, pə-] *a.* 【动】螟蛾科的. — *n.* 螟蛾科蛾 (=pyralid).

pyr·a·mid [ˈpirəmid] *n.* ①金字塔. ②【数】角锥, 棱锥;【结晶】锥;【解、动】角锥形器官;【园艺】剪成角锥形的果树. ③【运】叠罗汉. ④〔*pl.*〕〔英〕开盘时使球摆成金字塔形的台球. *a regular [right]* ～ 正[直]角锥. *a truncated* ～ 斜截头角锥. — *vi.* ①成金字塔形状. ②【交易所】用累进式手法扩大交易; 步步升级. —*vt.* ①使成金字塔形状. ②(按累进方式)抬高价格; 用累进方式经营. ③使步步升级. **-ist, -al·ist** *n.* ①埃及金字塔研究者. ②对埃及金字塔持神秘观点者.

py·ram·i·dal [piˈræmidl] *a.* 金字塔状的; 角锥的; 锥体的. — *n.* 【解】楔骨. **-ly** *ad.*

pyr·a·mid·ic, pyr·a·mid·i·cal *a.* = pyramidal.

py·ran [ˈpairæn] *n.* 【化】吡喃, 氧(杂)芑.

py·rar·gy·rite [paiˈrɑ:dʒirait] *n.* 硫锑银矿, 深红银矿.

pyre [ˈpaiə] *n.* 火葬柴堆; 火葬燃料.

py·rene[1] [ˈpairi:n] *n.* ①小坚果. ②分核.

py·rene[2] [ˈpairi:n] *n.* 【化】芘; 嵌二萘.

Pyr·e·nees [ˌpirəˈni:z] *n.* 比利牛斯山脉[法国、西班牙交界处山脉名]. **Pyr·e·ne·an** [ˌpirəˈni:ən] *a., n.* 比利牛斯山的(居民).

py·re·noid [paiˈri:nɔid] *n.* 【植】淀粉核.

py·re·thrin [paiˈri:θrin] *n.* 【化】除虫菊酯.

py·re·thrum [paiˈri:θrəm] *n.* ①【植】红花除虫菊 *(Chrysanthemum coccineum)*. ②除虫菊粉.

py·ret·ic [paiˈretik] *a.* 【医】(害)热病的; 治疗热病的. — *n.* 解热剂, 退热药.

pyr·e·tol·o·gy [ˌpaiərəˈtɔlədʒi] *n.* 热病学.

py·rex [ˈpaiəreks] 派热克斯玻璃, 硼硅酸玻璃[原是一种耐热玻璃的商标名].

py·rex·i·a [paiəˈreksiə] *n.* 【医】热; 发热; 热病.

py·rex·ic [paiəˈreksik] *a.* 热病的.

pyr·he·li·om·e·ter [ˌpaiəhi:liˈɔmitə] *n.*【气】(直接)日

射强度计；日照计，太阳热量计.
pyr·i·din(e) [ˈpiridi:n] *n.* 【化】吡啶，氮(杂)苯〔治喘病用〕.
pyr·i·dox·al [ˌpiəriˈdɔksəl] *n.* 吡哆醛，维生素B_6醛.
pyr·i·dox·a·mine [ˌpiəriˈdɔksəmi(:)n] *n.* 吡哆胺，维生素 B_6 胺.
pyr·i·dox·in(e) [ˌpiəriˈdɔksin, -si(:)n] *n.* 【化】吡哆醇，吡哆素；【药】维生素 B_6，抗皮炎素.
pyr·i·form [ˈpiərifɔ:m] *a.* 梨状的.
py·rim·i·dine [paiˈrimidi:n] *n.* 【化】嘧啶，间二氮(杂)苯.
py·rite [ˈpairait] *n.* *(pl.* ***py·ri·tes*** [paiˈraiti:z]*)* 黄铁矿，天然的二硫化铁.
py·ri·tes [paiˈraiti:z] *n.* 〔*sing.*; *pl.*〕【矿】硫化矿类；黄铁矿 (=iron ~)；白铁矿 (=white iron ~)；黄铜矿 (=copper ~)；黄锡矿 (=tin ~). **py·rit·ic, py·ri·tous** *a.*
py·ri·to·he·dron [piˌraitəˈhi:drən] *n.* 【矿】五角十二面体.
py·ro [ˈpaiərəu] *n.* 【化】焦棓酚，连苯三酚，苯三酚-〔1,2,3〕(=pyrogallol).
pyro- *comb.f.* 火，热，高温，焦: *pyro*chemistry.
py·ro·cat·e·chol [ˌpaiərəuˈkætikɔ:l] *n.* 邻苯二酚 (=pyrocatechin).
py·ro·cer·am [ˌpaiərəusəˈræm] *n.* 派洛塞拉姆钢化玻璃〔一种抗高温的防碎玻璃，用作炊具、火箭锥形头等，原商标名〕.
py·ro·chem·i·cal [ˌpaiərəuˈkemikl] *a.* 高温化学的. **-ly** *ad.*
py·ro·chem·is·try [ˌpaiərəuˈkemistri] *n.* 高温化学.
py·ro·clast·ic [ˌpaiərəuˈklæstik] *n., a.* 【地】火成碎屑物(的).
py·ro·con·den·sa·tion [ˌpaiərəuˌkɔndənˈseiʃən] *n.* 热缩(作用).
py·ro·con·duc·tiv·i·ty [ˌpaiərəuˌkɔndʌkˈtiviti] *n.* 高温导电性.
py·ro·crys·tal·line [ˌpaiərəuˈkristəlin] *a.* 【地】火成晶质.
pyr·o·dy·nam·ics [ˌpaiərəudaiˈnæmiks] *n.* 爆发力学，爆发动力学.
py·ro·e·lec·tric [ˌpaiərəuiˈlektrik] *a.* 热电(学)的. —*n.* 热电物质. **-i·ty** [-ˈtrisiti] *n.* 热电(现象)；热电学.
py·ro·gal·late [ˌpaiərəuˈgæleit] *n.* 【化】焦棓酸盐.
py·ro·gal·lic [ˌpaiərəuˈgælik] *a.* 焦棓性的. ~ *acid* 【化】焦棓酸，焦棓粉.
py·ro·gal·lol [paiərəuˈgæləul,-gəˈləul] *n.* 【化】焦棓酚，焦棓酸，连苯三酚.
py·ro·gen [ˈpaiərədʒin] *n.* ①【医】热原，致热质. ②【化】焦精〔一种染料〕；热精.
py·ro·gen·ic, py·rog·e·nous [ˌpaiərəuˈdʒenik, paiəˈrɔdʒinəs] *a.* ①高热的，高温反应的. ②【地】火成的(=igneous).
py·rog·nos·tics [ˌpaiərɔgˈnɔstiks] *n. pl.* (用吹管测定的)矿物特性〔如可熔性、焰色等〕.
py·ro·graph [ˈpaiərəugrɑ:f] *n.* 烙画；烫画；裂解色谱；热谱.
py·ro·graphy [ˌpaiəˈrɔgrəfi] *n.* 烙画(法)；烫画(法)；裂解色谱法；热谱法.
py·rol·a·try [ˌpaiəˈrɔlətri] *n.* 对火(神)的崇拜；拜火教.
py·ro·lig·ne·ous [ˌpaiərəuˈligni:əs] *a.* 焦木的；干馏木材而得的.
pyr·ol·o·gy [paiəˈrɔlədʒi] *n.* 热工学.
py·ro·lu·site [ˌpaiərəuˈlu:sait] *n.* 软锰矿.
py·rol·y·sis [paiˈrɔlisis] *n.* 热解(作用)，高温分解. —**-lyt·ic** [-ˈlitik] *a.* **-lyt·i·cal·ly** *ad.*
py·ro·man·cy [ˈpaiərəumænsi] *n.* 火占术，火卜.
py·ro·mag·net·ic [ˌpairəumægˈnetik] *a.* 【物】热磁的 (=thermomagnetic).
pyr·o·ma·ni·a [ˌpaiərəuˈmeiniə] *n.* 放火狂. **-ni·ac** *a., n.* 放火狂的；放火狂(者).
py·ro·met·al·lur·gy [ˌpairəumeˈtælədʒi] *n.* 热冶学；热冶术，火法冶金学.
py·ro·met·a·mor·phism [ˌpaiərəuˌmetəˈmɔ:fizəm] *n.* 【地】高热变质.
py·rom·e·ter [ˌpaiəˈrɔmitə] *n.* 【物】高温计. **-rom·e·try** [-ˈrɔmitri] *n.* 高温测定(法)，测高温术.
py·ro·mor·phite [ˌpairəuˈmɔ:fait] *n.* ①【矿】磷氯铅矿. ②【地】火成结晶.
py·rone [ˈpairəun] *n.* ①吡喃酮. ②自吡喃酮中提取的化合物.
py·ro·nine [ˈpairəuni:n, -nin] *n.* 【化】焦宁；二苯氧(杂)芑胺〔染料〕.
py·rope [ˈpairəup] *n.* 镁铝榴石(红榴石).
py·ro·pho·bi·a [ˌpaiərəuˈfəubiə] *n.* 【医】畏火症.
py·ro·phor·ic [ˌpaiərəuˈfɔ:rik] *a.* 引火的；生火花的.
py·ro·phos·phate [ˌpairəuˈfɔsfeit] *n.* 焦磷酸盐(或脂).
py·ro·pho·tom·e·ter [ˌpairəufəuˈtɔmitə] *n.* 高热光度计.
py·ro·phyl·lite [ˌpairəuˈfilait] *n.* 【矿】叶蜡石.
py·ro·sis [paiˈrəusis] *n.* 【医】胃灼热.
py·ro·stat [ˈpairəustæt] *n.* 高温(保持)器.
py·ro·sul·phate, py·ro·sul·fate [ˌpairəuˈsʌlfit] *n.* 焦硫酸盐.
pyrotech. =pyrotechnics.
py·ro·tech·nic, py·ro·tech·ni·cal [ˌpaiərəuˈteknik, -nikəl] *a.* ①烟火制造术的. ②烟火(一般)的；(才智等)辉煌灿烂的，天花乱坠的. ~ **sponge** 发火絮.
py·ro·tech·nics [ˌpaiərəuˈtekniks] *n.* 烟火制造技术；火花；(聪明、才智、口才等的)辉煌灿烂，天花乱坠；善辩的口才.
py·ro·tech·nist [ˌpaiərəuˈteknist] *n.* 烟火制造人.
py·ro·tech·ny [ˈpaiərəutekni] *n.* ①烟火制造术. ②焰火的施放.
py·ro·tox·in [ˌpaiərəuˈtɔksin] *n.* 热毒素.
py·rox·ene [paiˈrɔksi:n] *n.* 【矿】辉石.
py·rox·e·nite [paiˈrɔksinait] *n.* 【矿】辉岩.
py·rox·y·lin(e) [paiˈrɔksilin] *n.* 【化】焦木素，火棉，低氮硝化纤维素.
Pyr·rhic [ˈpirik] *a.* (古希腊伊皮鲁斯 (Epirus) 国王)比鲁斯 (Pyrrhus)王的. ~ **victory** 付出极大牺牲而得到的胜利〔Pyrrhus在 280—279 B.C. 打败了罗马军队，但牺牲极大〕.
pyr·rhic [ˈpirik] *n., a.* ①(古希腊的)战舞(的). ②【韵】二短音步(的)，抑抑格(的).
Pyr·rho·nism [ˈpirənizəm] *n.* (希腊哲学家)庇罗(Pyrrho)的怀疑说；极端怀疑主义. **-nist** *n.* 极端怀疑主义者.
pyr·rho·tite [ˈpiərəutait] *n.* 磁黄铁矿.
pyr·rhu·lox·i·a [ˌpiərəuˈlɔksiə] *n.* 【动】凤头红蜡嘴雀 *(Pyrrhuloxia sinuata)* 〔产于美国西南部和墨西哥北部〕.
pyr·role [ˈpiərəul] *n.* 【化】吡咯.
py·ru·vate [paiˈru:veit] *n.* 丙酮酸盐[酯].
Py·thag·o·ras [paiˈθægərəs] *n.* 毕达哥拉斯 〔?—?497 B.C.，希腊哲学家、数学家〕.
Py·thag·o·re·an [paiˌθægəˈri:ən] *a., n.* 毕达哥拉斯的(信徒)(的)；毕达哥拉斯哲学的. ~ **bean** 莲子. ~ **proposition [theorem]** 【数】毕达哥拉斯定理，勾股定理. ~ **table** (乘法)九九表.
Py·thag·o·re·an·ism [piˌθægəˈri:ənizəm] *n.* 毕达哥拉斯哲学.
Pyth·i·an [ˈpiθiən, -θjən] *a.* ①(古希腊)达尔菲 (Delphi) 地方的. ②(达尔菲地区)阿波罗 (Apollo) 神殿的. ③祀奉阿波罗神的女巫的. ④阿波罗神附身的. ⑤被阿波罗所杀的巨蟒的. ~ **games** 在达尔菲每四年举行一次的古代希腊四大运动会之一. ~ **oracle** 阿波罗神附身所作的宣示. — *n.* 〔the P-〕 ①达尔菲的居民. ②阿波罗神. ③祀奉阿波罗神的女巫.

Py·thon [ˈpaiθən] *n.* ①【动】蚺蛇属,蟒蛇属. ②【希神】(被 Apollo 神杀掉的)巨蟒. ②〔p-〕巫;预言者.

py·tho·ness [ˈpaiθənəs] *n.* ①女巫. ②希腊达尔菲地方祀奉阿波罗神的女巫.

py·thon·ic [paiˈθɔnik] *a.* ①神托的,预言的. ②蚺蛇的,蟒蛇的.

py·u·ri·a [paiˈjuəriə] *n.* 【医】脓尿.

pyx [piks] *n.* ①【天主】圣体容器,圣饼盒. ②(英国造币局的)货币样品箱,货币检查箱. — *vt.* ①(将货币样品)收入货币检查箱. ②检查(铸造的货币). *the trial of the* ~ 货币样品的检查.

pyx·id·i·um [pikˈsidiəm] *n.* *(pl. -id·i·a* [-iə]*)* ①【植】盖果. ②【天】=Pyxis.

pyx·ie [ˈpiksiː] *n.* 【植】沙盖花 *(Pyxidanthera barbulata)* 〔原产于美国大西洋沿岸平原〕.

pyx·is [ˈpiksis] *n.* *(pl. pyx·ides* [ˈpiksidiːz]*)* ①小箱;化妆盒,宝石盒. ②【植】盖果;【解】杯状窝,髀凹.

Pyx·is [ˈpiksis] *n.* 〔the ~〕【天】罗盘(星)座.

Q

Q, q [kjuː] *(pl. Q's, q's* [kjuːz]*)* ①英语字母表第十七字母. ②〔Q〕Q 字形. ③〔Q〕(滑冰动作中的)Q 字形旋转. ④【剧】提示 (=cue). ⑤品质因数, Q 值,佳度. ⑥〔Q〕= queen 〔在国际象棋和纸牌中〕. ***in a merry Q*** 快快活活地. ***mind one's P's and Q's*** 谨言慎行. **Q-boat, Q-ship** 【军】伪装猎潜舰. **Q-correction** 【天】Q 补偿角,北极星高度补偿角. **Q department** 军需部. **Q fever** 【医】Q 热,昆斯兰热. **Q-meter** 【无】Q 表,品质因素表.

Q. = Quebec.

Q., q. =①queen. ②question. ③quart; quarter; quarterly; quarto. ④quasi. ⑤query. ⑥quintal. ⑦quire. ⑧quotient.

Q. and A. = questions and answers 问与答.

Qa·tar [ˈkɑːtər] *n.* 卡塔尔〔亚洲〕.

Q.B., QB = Queen's Bench 英国高等法院.

QC, Q.C. = Queen's Counsel 〔英〕(女王的)王室法律顾问.

q.d. = ①〔L.〕*quasi dicat* 好象应该说 (=as if one should say). ②〔L.〕*quasi dictum* 好象说过了 (=as if said).

Q.E. = 〔L.〕*quod est* 这就是 (= which is).

QEA = Qantas [ˈkwɔntæs] Empire Airways 〔澳〕康达斯帝国航空公司.

Q.E.D., QED = 〔L.〕*quod erat demonstrandum* 【数】这就是所要证明的 (= which was to be demonstrated),证完,证讫.

Q.E.F., QEF = 〔L.〕 *quod erat faciendum* 【数】这就是所要做的 (= which was to be done),作毕,作讫.

Q.E.I., QEI = 〔L.〕*quod erat inveniendum* 【数】这就是所要寻求的 (=which was to be found out),求毕,求讫.

QF, QF. = ①quick-firing 【军】急射的,速射的. ②quick-firer 速射枪[炮].

qin·tar [kinˈtɑː] *n.* 昆塔〔阿尔巴尼亚货币名,等于 1/100 列克〕.

ql. = quintal.

q.l. = 〔L.〕 *quantum libet* 〔药剂处方用语〕随意量 (= as much as is desired).

QM, Q.M. = quartermaster ①【军】军需军官,军需主任. ②【海】(兼管信号等的)舵手,航信士官.

QMC, Q.M.C. = Quartermaster Corps 〔美〕(陆军)军需兵.

QMG, Q.M.G. = Quartermaster General 陆军军需兵司令兼军需局局长.

QMS, Q.M.S. = quartermaster sergeant 军需军士.

qoph [kəuf] *n.* =koph 〔希伯来语第十九个字母〕.

Qo·ran [kəuˈrɑːn, -ˈræn; kɔː-] *n.* 可兰经 (= Koran).

q.p., q.pl. = 〔L.〕 *quantum placet* 〔药剂处方用语〕随意量 (= as much as is desired).

qr. = ①quarter. ②quire.

q.s. = ①〔L.〕*quantum sufficit* 〔药剂处方用语〕适量,足量 (=a sufficient quantity). ②quarter section 约四分之一平方英里的土地〔= 160 英亩〕.

QT, Q.T., q.t. = 〔俚〕 quiet. ***on the*** ~ 秘密地,私下地.

qt. = ①quantity. ②quart.

qto. = quarto.

qts. = quarts.

qu. = ①quasi. ②quart. ③quarter; quarterly. ④queen. ⑤query; question.

qua [kwei] *conj.* 〔L.〕 以…的资格[身分]; 作为. *He does it not ~ father, but ~ judge.* 他不是用父亲身分而是用法官身分处理此事的.

quack[1] [kwæk] *n.* ①嘎嘎〔鸭叫声〕. ②大声闲谈; 嘈杂声,吵闹声. — *vi.* ①(鸭)嘎嘎地叫. ②大声闲谈,聊天.

quack[2] [kwæk] *n.* ①庸医,江湖医生. ②骗子; 大言不惭的人; 假充内行的人. *a ~ doctor.* 庸医. *~ medicines [remedies]* 骗钱药[疗法]. *a ~ politician* 空头政客,骗人的政客. — *vt.* ①卖(假药). ②(用广告等)大肆吹嘘. — *vi.* ①用行医方式骗钱. ②用广告骗人; 大言不惭,吹牛.

quack·er·y [ˈkwækəri] *n.* ①江湖医生的治疗,庸医的医术. ②自我吹嘘,大话; 骗子行为.

quack·ish [ˈkwækiʃ] *a.* ①(象)庸医的; 江湖医生(一样)的; 一知半解的. ②大言不惭的,胡吹的; 骗人的.

quack-quack [kwæk-kwæk] *n.* ①嘎嘎(鸭叫声). ②〔儿〕鸭子.

quack·sal·ver [ˈkwækˌsælvə] *n.* 〔古〕 庸医; 骗子 (= quack[2] *n.*).

quad [kwɔd] *n.* ①四方院子; 〔俚〕监狱. ②=【印】 quadrat. ③= quadruple. ④= quadrant. ⑤【电讯】四心线组. — *vi., vt.* 【印】用空铅填满(字行).

quadr- *comb.f.* = quadri-.

quad·rable [ˈkwɔdrəbl] *a.* 【数】可用有限代数项表示的; 可用等价平方表示的.

quad·ra·ge·nar·i·an [ˌkwɔdrədʒiˈnɛəriən] *a., n.* 四十(多)岁的(人); 四十至四十九岁的(人).

Quad·ra·ges·i·ma [ˌkwɔdrəˈdʒesimə] *n.* 【宗】①四旬斋的第一个礼拜天〔普通叫 ~ Sunday〕. ②〔废〕四旬斋. **-l** *a.*

quad·ran·gle [kwɔˈdræŋgl] *n.* ①四角形, 四边形(特指正方形及矩形). ②(大学等的)四方院子; 围着四方院子的建筑物. ③(美国国家陆地测量局颁布的)标准地形图上的一方格〔通常为南北 27 公里,东西 18—24 公里〕.

quad·ran·gu·lar [kwɔdˈræŋgjulə] *a.* 四角形的; 四边

形的. **-ly** *ad.* 成四边形.

quad·rant [ˈkwɔdrənt] *n.* ①【数】象限; 圆周的四分之一,九十度弧;四分之一圆. ②【天,海】象限仪. ③【生】四分体. ④长度单位 (=10,000 kilometers). ⑤扇形体;【机】扇形齿轮. ~ **elevation**【军】(炮的)仰角; 水平射角. **quad·ran·tal** [kwɔˈdræntl] *a.*

quad·ra·pho·nic [ˌkwɔdrəˈfəunik] *a.* (唱片、录音带等)四轨录音放音的.

quad·rat [ˈkwɔdræt] *n.* ①【印】(用以填空的无字面)空铅,衬铅,嵌块〔略 quad〕. ②【农】样方〔用来进行生态调查的一块长方形地〕. *an em [m]* ~ 全身空铅〔阔铅块〕. *an en [n]* ~ 对开空铅〔狭铅块〕. *a census* ~ 普查样方.

quad·rate [ˈkwɔdrit] *a.* ①【动,解】方骨的. ②正方形的,方形的. ~ *algebra* 方代数. *a* ~ *lobe* (脑髓的)方叶. — *n.* ①正方形; 方形. ②【解】方骨, 方肌. — [kwɔˈdreit] *vt., vi.* ①(使)适合,(使)一致 *(with; to)*. ②【数】将(圆)作成等积正方形; (使)成正方形 *(with)*.

quad·rat·ic [kwəˈdrætik] *a.* ①【数】二次的. ②方形的. — *n.* ①【数】二次方程式; 二次项. ②〔*pl.* 作单数用〕【数】二次方程式论. ~ **equation** 二次方程式.

quad·ra·ture [ˈkwɔdrətʃə] *n.* ①【数】求积分, 求面积. ②【天】矩;(月的)上[下]弦; 方照. ③【物】正交; 转象差; 九十度相位差. *the* ~ *(of the circle)* 圆积法〔作与圆等积的正方形〕. *phase* ~【物】转象相差,九十度相位差.

quad·ren·nial [kwɔˈdrenjəl] *a.* 继续四年的; 每四年一次的. — *n.* ①每四年一次的事件. ②连续四年的时间. ③第四周年; 四周年纪念. **-ly** *ad.*

quad·ren·ni·um [kwɑːˈdreniəm] *n.* *(pl.* ~*s, -nia* [-niə]*)* 四年为一期的时间.

quadri- *comb.f.* ①四,第四: *quadri*lateral. ②【数】平方,二次: *quadric*.

quad·ric [ˈkwɔdrik] *a.*【数】二次的; 二次曲面的. — *n.*【数】二次;二次曲面.

quad·ri·cen·ten·ni·al [ˌkwɔdrisenˈteniəl] *a.* (第)四百周年的. — *n.* 四百周年纪念(日、节).

quad·ri·ceps [ˈkwɑːdriseps] *n.*【解】四头肌. **quad·ri·cip·i·tal** [ˌkwɑːdriˈsipitl] *a.*

quad·ri·fid [ˈkwɔdrifid] *a.*【动,植】四分裂的; 分成四部分的. ~ *petal*【植】四分裂花瓣.

quad·riga [kwəˈdriːgə] *n.* *(pl. -gae* [-dʒiː]*)* 〔古罗马〕四马双轮战车.

quad·ri·lat·er·al [ˌkwɔdriˈlætərəl] *a.* ①四边(形)的. ②四方面的. — *n.* ①【数】四边形. ②方形物,方形地; 【军】(四边有四座堡垒防御的)方形要塞〔地区〕.

quad·rilin·gual [ˈkwɔdriˈliŋgwəl] *a.* 用四种语言(说或写)的; 由四种语言形成的.

qua·drille [kwəˈdril, kə-] *n.* ①四对舞, 方舞; 四对舞曲. ②"打四十张"〔18世纪流行的由四人玩四十张牌的一种牌戏〕. —*a.* (图案等)形成许多大小相等的方格的,方眼的.

quad·ril·lion [kwɔˈdriljən] *num.* 〔英、德〕百万的四次幂〔乘方〕之数〔1 后有 24 个 0 之数〕;〔美、法〕千的五次幂〔乘方〕之数〔1 后有 15 个 0 之数〕.

quad·ri·no·mial [ˌkwɔdriˈnəumiəl] *a.*【数】四项的. — *n.* 四项式.

quad·ri·par·tite [ˌkwɔdriˈpɑːtait] *a.* ①分成四部分的; 由四部分[四人]形成的. ②由四方参加的; 四方面的. *a* ~ *treaty* 四国条约.

quad·ri·ple·gi·a [ˌkwɑːdriˈpliːdʒiə] *n.*【医】四肢麻痹. **quad·ri·ple·gic** [-ˈpliːdʒik, -ˈpledʒik] *n.* 四肢麻痹症患者.

quad·ri·sect [ˈkwɑːdrisekt] *vt.* 把…四等分.

quad·ri·syl·lable [ˈkwɔdriˌsiləbl] *n.*【语音】四音节词. **quad·ri·syl·lab·ic** [-siˈlæbik] *a.* 四音节的.

quad·riv·a·lence, quad·riv·a·len·cy [ˌkwɔdriˈveiləns,-lənsi] *n.*【化】四价.

quad·ri·va·lent [ˌkwɔdriˈveilənt] *a.*【化】四价的.

quad·riv·i·al [kwɔˈdriviəl] *a.* ①四路交叉的. ②(中世纪大学之)四高级学科的〔算术、几何、天文、音乐〕.

quad·riv·ium [kwɔˈdriviəm] *n.*【史】(中世纪大学的)四高级学科〔算术、几何、天文、音乐〕.

quad·rode [ˈkwɔdrəud] *n.*【无】四级管.

quad·roon [kwɔˈdruːn] *n.* ①黑人〔异种〕,(血统占四分之一的)混血儿〔尤指黑白混血儿〕. ②(动、植物)前一代杂交的杂种.

quadru- *comb.f.* = quadri-: *quadru*mana.

quad·ru·ma·na, quad·ru·mane [kwɔˈdruːmənə, kwɔˈdrumein] *n.* (人类之外的)灵长类动物, 四足具有手的功能的动物〔如猿、猴等〕. **-nous** [-nəs] *a.*

quad·rum·vir [kwɔˈdrʌmvə] *n.* 四人团体〔小组〕的成员之一.

quad·rum·vi·rate [kwɔˈdrʌmvərit] *n.* 四人团体〔小组〕.

quad·ru·ped [ˈkwɔdruped] *n.*【动】四足动物 (尤指哺乳动物). — *a.* 有四足的; 四足动物的.

quad·ru·pe·dal [kwɔˈdruːpidəl] *a.*【动】有四足的; 四足动物的.

quad·ru·plane [ˈkwɔdruplein] *n.* 四翼飞机.

quad·rup·le [ˈkwɔdrupl] *a.* ①四倍的. ②四重的; 由四部分组成的. ③【乐】四节拍的. *a size* ~ *to [of] that of the earth* 地球四倍大的大小. — *n.* 四倍, 四倍量. — *vt., vi.* (使)成四倍; 以四乘. ~ **time [rhythm, measure]**【乐】四拍子. **-ness** *n.*

quad·ru·plet [ˈkwɔdruplit] *n.* ①四件一套. ②〔*pl.*〕四胞胎, 四生子. ③四胞胎中的一个孩子. ④四人同乘的自行车.

quad·ru·plex [ˈkwɔdrupleks] *a.* ①四倍的,四重的. ②【电】四心电缆的;(同一线路中)四重信号的;【生】四式的. — *n.* 四工电讯机;【生】四式,四显性组合.

quad·ru·pli·cate [kwɔˈdruːplikit] *a.* ①四倍的, 四重的; 反复四次的. ②(文件等)一式四份的; 第四(份)的. ③【数】四次方的. — *n.* ①一式四份中的一份. ②〔*pl.*〕一式四份的文件. *in* ~ 一式四份地. — [kwɔˈdruːplikeit] *vt.* 使成四倍,使成四重; 使成一式四份. **quad·ru·pli·ca·tion** [kɔˌdruːpliˈkeiʃən] *n.*

quad·ruply [ˈkwɔdrupli] *ad.* 四重地,四倍地.

quae·re [ˈkwiəri] *vt.* 〔L.〕〔用于祈使句〕问,调查; 查询; 敢问, 请问. *Quaere more about it.* 再仔细查查. *But* ~*, is it true?* 不过请问这是真的吗? — *n.* 〔古〕疑问, 询问,问题〔略 qu.〕.

quaes·tio vex·a·ta [ˈkwestʃiəu vekˈsɑːtə] 〔L.〕难题; 争执中的问题.

quaes·tor [ˈkwiːstə] *n.* ①(古罗马的)检察官. ②财务官. **-to·ri·al** [-ˈtɔːriəl] *a.*

quaff [kwɑːf, kwɔf] *vt., vi.* 〔诗〕一口喝干(酒等),咕咚咕咚地喝. ~ ***off [out, up]*** 喝干; 大口大口喝. — *n.* 一饮而尽,痛饮;一饮而尽的酒.

quag [kwæg] *n.* ①泥沼,沼地. ②困境.

quag·ga [ˈkwægə] *n.*【动】南非斑驴〔现已绝种〕.

quag·gy [ˈkwægi] *a.* ①沼泽地的; 泥泞的. ②软的; 松弛的.

quag·mire [ˈkwægmaiə] *n.* = quag.

qua·haug, qua·hog [ˈkwɔːhɔg] *n.* (美国大西洋沿岸所产的)一种圆蛤,帘蛤.

quai [kei] *n.* 〔F.〕 = quay.

Quai d'Orsay [ˌkei dɔːˈsei] ①巴黎塞纳河边一码头. ②〔the ~〕法国外交部〔因法国外交部在上述码头对面而得名〕; 法国外交(政策).

quaich, quaigh [kweik] *n.* 〔Scot.〕双耳小浅酒杯.

quail[1] [kweil] *n.* *(pl.* ~*(s))* ①【动】鹌鹑. ②〔美俚〕女大学生; 漂亮姑娘. *a bevy of* ~*s* 一群鹌鹑〔姑娘〕. *a* ~ *pipe* (引诱鹌鹑的)鹑笛. *a* ~ *call* 鹑笛声. ~**-roost** 〔美俚〕(大学)女生宿舍.

quail² [kweil] *vi.* 沮丧;畏缩 *(at; before; to)*. — *vt.*〔古〕使沮丧;使畏缩.

Quain [kwein] *n.* 奎恩〔姓氏〕.

quaint [kweint] *a.* ①离奇有趣的,古雅的;优雅的;奇妙的. ②(工艺制作等)灵巧的. *a ~ old house* 一座古雅的老房子. **-ly** *ad.* **-ness** *n.*

quake [kweik] *vi.* ①摇动,震动. ②打战,抖,发抖*(with, from, for)*. *~ with fear* 吓得发抖. *~ with cold* 冷得打战. *The earth suddenly began to ~.* 大地突然摇晃. — *n.* ①摇动,震动;〔口〕地震. ②战栗. **quaking ash**【植】白杨. **quaking aspen**【植】颤杨. **quaking concrete** 塑性混凝土. **quak•ing•ly** *ad.*

Quak•er [ˈkweikə] *n.* *(fem. -ess* [-ris]*)* ①(基督教的一个教派)贵格会教徒,教友会教徒,公谊会 (the Society of Friends) 教徒; 象教友派教徒的人. ②〔q-〕发抖的人. ③〔美〕费拉德尔菲亚人. *~ City*〔美〕费拉德尔菲亚 (Philadelphia) 市的别名. *~ gun* 木制假枪. *~ oats* 燕麦片,老人牌麦片. *~s' [~] meeting* ①教友派教徒的祈祷会. ②沉默会;倾向沉默的集会. **~-bird**【动】纯黑信天翁. **~-moth** *n.* 英国夜蛾.

Quak•er•ish [ˈkweikriʃ] *a.* ①象教友派教徒一样的. ②朴实的;严谨的;坚苦的.

Quak•er•ism [ˈkweikrizəm] *n.* 教友派; 教友派教义.

Quak•er•ly [ˈkweikli] *a.* = Quakerish. — *ad.* 象教友派教徒一样地.

quak•y [ˈkweiki] *a.* ①易震动的. ②战栗的.

qual. = qualitative.

qual•i•fi•ca•tion [ˌkwɔlifiˈkeiʃən] *n.* ①授权,批准;资格,职权 *(for)*. ②条件,限制,限定;保留,斟酌. ③身分证明书,执照,工作证. ④形容,评定;称呼,称作,认作. *Nothing but has ~ of some kind.* 无任何性状[限定条件]的东西[事物]是不存在的. *The statement requires ~.* 这项声明须加斟酌. *medical ~s* 医生执照. ***without ~*** 无限制地,无条件地,无保留地. *~* **shares**【商】资格股.

qual•i•fi•ca•to•ry [ˈkwɔlifikətəri] *a.* ①赋与资格的;资格上的. ②带有条件的;有限制的.

qual•i•fied [ˈkwɔlifaid] *a.* ①有资格的,胜任的,适当的;经过检定的,得到许可的. ②有限制的,有条件的. ③〔俚〕十足的,无比的. *a ~ fool* 大傻瓜. ***be ~ for*** 有…的资格;适于担任…. ***in a ~ sense*** 在一定意义上;有点,有些. *~* **acceptance**【商】(票据的)条件承兑. **-ly** *ad.* **-ness** *n.*

qual•i•fi•er [ˈkwɔlifaiə] *n.* ①合格的人[物]. ②限定者. ③【语法】修饰词[如形容词、副词等].

qual•i•fy [ˈkwɔlifai] *vt.* ①使具有资格;授法权予,准予;使适宜,证明…合格. ②限制,斟酌,缓和;(把酒等)搀淡. ③把…当做,把…叫做. ④【语法】限定[形容、修饰]. *~ one's anger* 息怒. *~ spirits with water* 用水搀淡酒. *~ sb. as scoundrel* 把…叫做坏蛋. — *vi.* ①(通过考试、宣誓等)取得资格,具备合格条件. ②〔美〕宣誓就职;宣誓. *~* ***as*** ①取得…的资格. ②宣誓作…. *~* ***oneself for*** 取得…的资格,准备好…的条件. **qualifying examination** (资格)检定考试.

qual•i•ta•tive [ˈkwɔlitətiv] *a.* ①质的,质量上的. ②性质上的. ③【化】定性的,定质的 (*opp.* quantitative) *~* **analysis** 定性分析. *~* **relation** 种别关系. *~* **sound changes**【语音】音质变化. **-ly** *ad.* ①性质上;质量上. ②用定性方法.

qual•i•ty [ˈkwɔliti] *n.* ①质,质量;性质,特质;品质,品位. ②优质,美质,优点. ③才能,能力,技能,素养. ④品种. ⑤身分,地位;〔古、俚〕高位,名门;〔the ~〕〔古〕身分高贵的人们 (*opp.* the common people). ⑥【物】音值,音色;(色泽的)鲜明(性). ⑦【逻】(命题的肯定或否定)性质. *the ~ of inspiring confidence* 受人信任的品质. *This is the best ~ of cigars.* 这是最好的雪茄. ***give a taste of one's ~*** 显本领. ***have many good qualities*** 有许多长处. ***have ~*** 优秀. ***of good [poor] ~*** 优质[劣质]的. — *a.* ①优质的,高级的. ②上流社会的. *~* **of stand**【林】林位. *~* **of steam**【物】蒸汽干度.

qualm [kwɑːm, kwɔːm] *n.* ①一阵眩晕,眼花;恶心. ②不安,疑惧;(良心的)责备. *~s of seasickness* 晕船. *He has no ~s about lying.* 他撒谎毫不内疚.

qualm•ish [ˈkwɑːmiʃ, kwɔː-] *a.* ①有点发晕的,有点恶心的. ②有点不安的;有点受良心责备的.

quan•da•ry [ˈkwɔndəri] *n.* 窘,困惑,左右为难;窘境,狼狈的处境. *I was put in a great [in rather a] ~.* 我简直为难死了.

quand même [kɑ̃ ˈmɛm]〔F.〕即使,纵令,还是,无论如何.

quant [kwɑːnt, kwænt] *n.* (英国平底船用的)平顶篙〔顶端有平顶防止其陷入泥中的篙〕. — *vt., vi.* 用平顶篙撑(船).

quant. = quantitative.

quan•ta [ˈkwɑːntə] quantum 的复数.

quan•tic [ˈkwɔntik] *n.*【数】齐次多项式.

quan•ti•fi•ca•tion [ˌkwɔntifiˈkeiʃən] *n.* 定量;【逻】附量,量化.

quan•ti•fi•er [ˈkwɔntifaiə] *n.*【逻】限量词〔用 all, some 等语词以及前缀、符号等表示〕.

quan•ti•fy [ˈkwɔntifai] *vt.* ①确定…的数量,表示…的数量; 用数量表示 (*opp.* qualify). ②【逻】用量词限定(全称、特称等的命题).

quan•tile [ˈkwɔntail, -til] *n.*【统】分位数.

quan•ti•tate [ˈkwɔntiteit] *vt.* 测定[估计]…的数量;用数量表示. **-ta•tion** *n.*

quan•ti•ta•tive [ˈkwɔntitətiv] *a.* (数)量的;定量的. *the ~ limits that determine the qualities of things.* 决定事物质量的数量界限. *~* **analysis** 定量分析. *~* **inheritance**【生】数量遗传. *~* **sound changes**【语音】音量变化. **-ly** *ad.*

quan•ti•ty [ˈkwɔntiti] *n.* ①量 (*opp.* quality); 分量,数量;额;【物】值,参量. ②〔*pl.*〕大量,大宗,大批,许多. ③定量,定额. ④【数】量;表示量的数字[符号];【逻】(名词、特别是命题主语的)量. ⑤【韵】音节的长短;表示音节长短的符号;【语音】(元音、音节等的)音量. ⑥【法】期限. *a known ~* 已知数. *an unknown ~* 未知数;〔喻〕难预测的人[物]. *a negligible ~* 可忽略的量;〔喻〕无足轻重的人[物]; 可忽略的因素. ***a ~ of*** 一些. ***in quantities*** 大量. ***in ~*** 很多. *~* **goods**【经】数量财. *~* **mark**【语音】(标于元音上的)音量号. *~* **surveyor**【建】估算师,估料师.

quan•tiv•a•lence [ˌkwɔntiˈveiləns] *n.*【化】化合价.

quan•tize [ˈkwɔntaiz] *vt.* ①【数】用基本数的倍数表示. ②【物】使量子化; 用量子论的术语表示. **-za•tion** [ˌkwɔntaiˈzeiʃən] *n.* 量子化.

quan•tiz•er [ˈkwɔntaizə] *n.*【自】数字转换器,编码器;量子化(变化)器. *a binary ~*【自】二进位数字转变器.

quan•tom•e•ter [kwɔnˈtɔmitə] *n.*【自】冲击电流计;电量计;辐射强度测量计;光子计数器,光量计;剂量计.

quan•tum [ˈkwɔntəm] *n.* *(pl. -ta* [-tə]*)* ①量,额;定量,定额;份;总量. ②【物】量子. ***have one's ~ of*** 充分尝到…,充分得到…. *~* ***libet*** [ˈlibet] 随意量〔略 quant. lib. 或 q.l., 药方用语〕;随意. *~* ***meruit*** [ˈmeruit] 按照劳力价值. *~* ***placet*** [ˈpleiset] = *~* *libet.*〔略 q.p.〕. *~* ***sufficit*** [ˈsʌfisit] 足量〔略 quant. suff. 或 q.s., 药方用语〕; 充足的份量,尽量. *~* **chemistry** 量子化学. *~* **electronics** 量子电子学. *~* **equivalence**【物】量子当量. *~* **mechanics** 量子力学. *~* **physics** 量子物理学. *~* **theory**【物】量子论. *~* **yield**【物】量子产量.

qua•qua•ver•sal [ˌkweikwəˈvəːsəl] *a.*【地】(地层从中心)向四方倾斜的. **-ly** *ad.*

quar•an•tine [ˈkwɔrəntiːn] *n.* ①(对港口船舶的)停船检疫,留验;(防传染病而对人、畜等的)隔离,封锁. ②停船期间，检疫期间. ③检疫停船港；检疫所[局]；隔离医院. ④四十日间. ⑤(英国旧时法律规定的)寡妇居留期间〔丈夫死后得留住夫家四十天的期限〕. *a ~ flag* 传染病船旗，检疫旗[黄色]. — *vt.* ①对…进行检疫. ②封锁，隔离；使孤立. ③命令停船留验. ~ *aggressor nations* 孤立侵略国. ~ **measures** 植物检疫工作.

quar·en·den, quar·en·der [ˈkwɔrəndən, -də] *n.* (英国 Devonshire 及 Somersetshire 等地产的)红苹果.

quark [ˈkwɑːk] *n.* 夸克〔假设的带电核粒子，为已知的粒子如质子及中子等的基本构成部分〕.

Quar·les [kwɔːlz] *n.* 夸尔斯〔姓氏〕.

quar·rel[1] [ˈkwɔrəl] *n.* ①争吵，口角，吵闹；不和，不睦；反目. ②吵闹的原因[理由]；怨言. ***espouse sb.'s ~ = fight one's ~s for sb.*** 帮着某人吵闹. ***find ~ in a straw*** 吹毛求疵，找碴儿，鸡蛋里找骨头，寻事生非. ***fix [fasten] a ~ on*** 向某人进行寻衅，向人找碴儿吵闹. ***have a ~ with*** 和…争吵. ***have no ~ against [with]*** 对…无怨言，对某人无所责难. ***in a good ~*** 在理由正大的争论下 (*I will do anything in a good ~.* 只要有理甚么都干). ***make up a ~*** 和解，言归于好. ***pick [seek] a ~ with*** 向…找碴儿吵闹. ***pick ~s*** 闹意气. ***take up another's ~*** 助长别人争吵. — *vi.* ①争吵，争论 (*with; about; for*)；不和. ②责备，埋怨 (*with*). ~ ***with*** 和(人)吵，和…争论；埋怨 (*A bad workman ~s with his tools.* 工人无能，埋怨工具. *Do not ~ with Providence.* 不要怨天). ~ ***with one's bread and butter*** 自暴自弃，厌弃自己的职业. **-er** *n.*

quar·rel[2] [ˈkwɔrəl] *n.* ①【史】方镞箭，角镞箭. ②小块方形[菱形]玻璃. ③(石工的)凿子；方头物.

quar·rel·(l)er [ˈkwɔrələ] *n.* 争吵者；好争吵的人.

quar·rel·some [ˈkwɔrəlsəm] *a.* 好争吵的，好争论的. **-ly** *ad.* **-ness** *n.*

quar·ren·den [ˈkwɔrəndən] *n.* = quarenden.

quar·ri·er [ˈkwɔriə] *n.* = quarryman.

quar·ry[1] [ˈkwɔri] *n.* ①采石场，石坑，石矿. ②知识的泉源；消息[资料、引文等]的出处. ~ *stone* 石块，乱石. — *vt., vi.* ①采(石)，挖掘. ②(从)(书等中)苦心找出(证据等)；苦心寻找(记录等). **quar·ri·er** *n.* 采石工人.

quar·ry[2] [ˈkwɔri] *n.* ①猎获物. ②〔喻〕追求物；复仇的对象，寻找中的仇人.

quar·ry[3] [ˈkwɔri] *n.* ①菱形[方形]玻璃[石、瓦等]. ②机制花砖.

quar·ry·man [ˈkwɔrimən] *n.* (*pl.* ***quar·ry·men*** [-men]) *n.* 采石工人.

quart[1] [kwɔːt] *n.* ①夸脱〔液量单位，=1/4 gallon，约1.14升；干量单位，=1/8 peck〕. ②一夸脱的容器；一夸脱的啤酒. *He still takes his ~.* 他现在还是照常喝大满杯的啤酒. ***try to put a ~ into a pint pot*** 想把一夸脱倒入一品脱的瓶子；想做不可能做的事情.

quart[2] [kɑːt] *n.* ①(剑术中的)右胸开脱〔八种防御姿势中的第四种架式. 手掌向上，剑尖指向对手右胸〕. ②【牌】四张同花顺. ***a ~ major*** 最大的四张同花顺〔ace, king, queen, knave〕. ~ **and tierce** 剑术研究.

quart. = quarterly.

quart- *comb.f.* 四；*quarter.*

quar·tan [ˈkwɔːtən] *a.* (疟疾)每逢第四天发生的，每隔三天发一次的. — *n.*【医】三日疟.

quar·ta·tion [kwɔːˈteiʃən] *n.*【化】(硝酸)析银法.

quarte [kɑːt] *n.* 〔F.〕【剑术】= quart. — *vi., vt.*【剑术】(采用手掌向上、剑尖指向对手右胸的姿式时)将(头部等)仰向后.

quar·ter [ˈkwɔːtə] *n.* ①四分之一. ★ 3/4 通常不说 three-fourths 而说 three ~s. ②一刻钟，十五分钟；一季[四季结帐期之一]；每三个月的付款；〔主 Scot.〕一学期〔一年分四学期〕；【天】弦〔月球公转期的四分之一〕；【乐】四分音符. ③〔英〕夸特〔谷量单位，约2.909公石；衡量单位，1/24英担〕. ④〔美、加拿大〕二角五分(=1/4 dollar)；二角五分银币；1/4 英里；1/4 码；1/4 吋；1/4 磅；1/4 平方英里的土地 (=~-section). ⑤【运】1/4 英里的赛跑；(橄榄球赛的) 1/4 场 (=~-back). ⑥罗盘针四方位基点之一〔东、西、南、北、〕，方位，方角；(机器零件的)相互垂直. ⑦方向，方面；地域，地方；区，市区，街. ⑧(供给、救助、消息的)来源，出处. ⑨〔*pl.*〕寓所，住处；〔*pl.*〕【军】营房，驻地，营盘，宿舍；〔*pl.*〕岗位. ⑩鸟兽四分后的一肢；〔*pl.*〕受刑者被四分肢解后的一肢；〔*pl.*〕(人、马等的)腰，臀部. ⑪【海】船侧后半部〔正横与船尾的中间部分〕，船尾部. ⑫【建】间柱〔柱与柱间的小柱〕；【纹】盾形的四分之一. ⑬英国海峡殖民地征收财产税、所得税的标准单位〔25镑〕. ⑭(特指对投降者的)饶命，免死，慈悲；宽大，宽恕，减轻. *cut an apple in ~s* 把苹果切成四分. *a ~ to [past] nine* 九点差[过]一刻. *the four ~s of the globe* 全世界. *the first [last] ~* 上[下]弦. *What ~ is the wind in?* 风是从哪一方面吹来的？形势如何？*Lies the wind in that ~?* 形势是这样的吗？*I had the news from a good ~.* 这个消息是从可靠方面听来的. *There is no help to be looked for in that ~.* 从那方面得不到什么援助. *workers' living ~s* 工人宿舍. *industrial ~s* 工业区. *residential ~s* 住宅区. *licensed [gay] ~s* (低级下流娱乐场所汇聚的)风化区. ***a bad ~ of an hour*** 不愉快的一刻. ***a ~ and five*** $5\frac{1}{4}$ 吋；***a ~ less five*** $4\frac{3}{4}$ 吋. ***a ~ right [left]***【军】靠右[左] 1/4 直角. ***ask for [cry] ~s*** 请求饶命. ***at close ~s*** ①迫近，逼近，接近；在仔细观察之下. ②【军】短兵相接，白刃战. ***beat to ~s***【海】使各就岗位. ***beat up the ~s of*** 突然访问. ***call to ~s***【军】使各就各位. ***from every ~ [all ~s]*** 从四面八方. ***give ~*** 不杀，饶命. ***Give no ~!*** 格杀勿论！***in all ~s [every ~]*** 到处，处处. ***not a ~*** 完全不是 (*not a ~ so [as] good as* 远不及). ***on the ~***【海】在船尾方面. ***strike the ~s*** (钟)敲一刻钟. ***take up one's ~s*** ①投宿，住宿 (*in, with*). ②(水兵)进入岗位. — *vt.* ①把…四分，把…四等分. ②使住宿；使(军队)扎营；使筹办食宿. ③【海】使各就岗位. ④四裂肢解(动物、罪犯). ⑤将(别家纹章)加在自己盾牌的一角上，将(盾)用纵横线加以四分. ⑥(猎狗为搜寻猎获物)纵横奔跑于(某地区). ⑦使(机器零件)相互垂直. — *vi.* ①驻扎，扎营 (*at, with*). ②变更位置；各就岗位. ③(猎狗)搜找猎物. ④【海】(风从斜后方)吹来. ⑤(机器零件)相互垂直. ~ ***oneself on [with]*** 投宿在…[和…同住]. ~**back** *n.* 〔橄榄球〕四分卫〔在 forwards 和 half-backs 之间〕；进攻时指挥本队的选手. ~ **bell** 每十五分钟一响的铃. ~ **bill**【海】战斗部署表. ~ **binding** (书的)皮脊[布脊]装订. ~ **blood** *n., a.* 四分之一杂种(血统的). ~ **boards** 〔*pl.*〕舰尾的防波板. ~**-bound** *a.* 皮脊[布脊]装订的. ~**-bred** *a.* (牛、马等)四分之一纯血的. ~**-butt**【台球】短小的球棒. ~ **day** 四季结帐日〔英格兰与爱尔兰是 Lady Day (3月25日)，Midsummer Day (6月24日)，Michaelmas (9月29日)，Christmas (12月25日)；苏格兰是 Candlemas (2月2日)，Whitsunday (5月15日)，Lammas (8月1日)，Mastinmas (11月11日)；美国是1、4、7、10月的1日〕. ~**-deck** *n.* ①【海】后甲板. ②〔the ~-deck〕高级船员们，军官们. ~ **horse** 1/4 英里赛跑马. ~**-hour** ①一刻钟的期间. ②(某时的)15分钟前[后]. ~ **jack** = quartermaster. ~ **light** (车辆的)边窗. ~ **line**【海】军舰的雁行式阵形. ~**-master** ①【海】舵手. ②【军】军需(官)〔略 Q.M.〕(~-*master corps* 辎重兵，辎重队. ~*master service* 后方勤务). ~**master-general** 兵站总监〔略 Q.M.G.〕(*Quartermaster-general to the Forces* 〔英〕军需署署长). ~**-master-sergeant** 辎重军士〔略 Q.M.S.〕. ~ **mile** 1/4 英里〔尤指赛跑的距离〕. ~ **miler** 1/4 英里赛跑选手. ~ **note**【乐】四分音符. ~**-phase** *a.*【电】二相的. ~ **plate**【摄】照相干片〔$3\frac{1}{4} \times 4\frac{1}{4}$ 英寸〕；同尺寸的照片. ~**saw** *vt.* 把(木头)打直锯成四块. ~ **section** ①〔美、

加拿大〕【测量】①约 1/4 平方英里的土地(=160英亩). ②四分之一. ~ **sessions** 〔*pl.*〕一年开四次的州法庭. ~**staff** 铁头木棒〔古时英国农民两头包铁的武器〕. ~ **tone**【乐】四分音〔semitone 之半〕. ~**wind**【海】从斜后方吹来的风,船尾风. **-age** *n.* ①按季收付的款项;季度工资[税、津贴]. ②供给军队的住处. ③供宿. ④住宿费. **-ing** [ˈkwɔːtəriŋ] ① *n.* 四等分;(罪犯的)四裂肢解;【军】扎营的分派;【纹】联姻纹章(的配合);【建】间柱;【机】成直角;【天】月球向上弦、满月、下弦的移变. ② *a.*【海】(风)从斜后方吹来的;【机】成直角的. **-ly** ① *a.* 按季的,一年四次的,每季的;【海】(风)向船尾吹的;【纹】(盾面)分为四部分的. ② *ad.* 一年四次,一季一次,按季;【纹】(盾面)纵横四分地. ③ *n.* 季刊,按季出版物.

quar·tered [ˈkwɔːtəd] *a.* ①四分的,四等分的. ②提供住处的. ③(把木头)纵向锯成四片再锯成木板的.

quar·ter·fi·nal [ˌkwɔːtəˈfainl] *a.*【运】复赛的. — *n.* 复赛,四分之一决赛. **-ist** *n.* 参加四分之一决赛的选手[队].

quar·tern [ˈkwɔːtən] *n.* ①夸脱仑〔①液量单位(=1/4 pint, gill). ②谷量单位(= 1/4 peck, stone)〕. ②四等分,四分之一. ③(用 1 quartern 面粉做成、重 4 磅的)大面包,四磅面包〔又作 quartern-loaf〕.

quar·tet, quar·tette [kwɔːˈtet] *n.* ①【乐】四重奏,四重唱;四部合奏[唱]曲;四部合奏[唱]者. ②四件一组,四个一副[一套]. ③【生】四集体;四分孢子;【物】四重线.

quar·tic [ˈkwɔːtik] *a.*【数】四次的. — *n.* 四次齐式;四次(乘)幂.

quar·tile [ˈkwɔːtail, -tl] *n., a.* ①【统】四分位数(的);四分位数一组(的). ②【天】方照(的);弦(的);二天体直径差 90 度(的).

quar·to [ˈkwɔːtəu] *n.* (*pl.* ~*s*) (纸等的)四开〔$7\times8\frac{1}{2}$ 至 10×13 英寸,略作 4 to 或 4°〕;四开书本. *a* ~ *edition* 四开本版. *a* ~ *paper* 四开的纸.

quartz [kwɔːts] *n.*【矿】石英,水晶. *milky* ~ 乳石英. *smoky* ~ 烟水晶. *violet* ~ 紫色英. *water* ~ 泡水晶. ~ **lamp** 石英灯. ~ **clock** 石英晶体钟.

quartz·if·er·ous [kwɔːˈtsifərəs] *a.*【矿】石英质的,含石英的.

quartz·ite [ˈkwɔːtsait] *n.*【矿】石英岩.

qua·sar [ˈkweisaː] *n.*【天】类星体;类星射电源.

quash[1] [kwɔʃ] *vt.*【法】取消,废除,使无效.

quash[2] [kwɔʃ] *vt.* ①捣碎,压碎. ②压制,镇压;平息.

quash·ee, quash·ie [ˈkwɔʃi] *n.* (特指西非)黑人.

qua·si [ˈkwaːzi(ː), ˈkweisai] *ad.* ①在某一意义上,有点,几乎. ②恰如,宛如,就象是. ③就是说,即〔略作 q. 或 qu.,尤用以作语源上的说明〕. *He was* ~ *a prisoner.* 他就象一个犯人. *Earls of Wilbraham,* ~ *wild boar ham* 威尔白莱罕(即'野猪大腿肉')伯爵家. — *a.* 好象是的,似乎是的,类似的. *He was a* ~ *artist.* 他有点儿象画家. *a* ~ *governmental agency* 类似政府机关的一个机构.

quasi- *pref.* 类似,准,拟: *quasi*judicial. ★汉译可较灵活,如 ~*-cholera* 拟似霍乱. ~*-contract* 准契约. ~*-war* 准战争. ~*-conductor* 半导体. ~*-sovereign state* 半独立国.

qua·si·chol·er·a [ˌkwaːzi(ː)ˈkɔlərə] *n.*【医】拟似霍乱.

qua·si-his·tor·i·cal [ˌkwaːzi(ː)hisˈtɔrikəl] *a.* 带有历史性质的.

qua·si-ju·di·cial [ˌkwaːzi(ː)dʒuːˈdiʃəl] *a.* 准司法性的,具有部分立法权的.

qua·si-leg·is·la·tive [ˌkwaːzi(ː)ˈledʒislətive] *a.* 准立法性的,具有部分立法权的.

Qua·si·mo·do [ˌkwaːzi(ː)ˈməudəu] *n.*【基督教】复活节后的第一个星期日.

qua·si-of·fi·cial [ˈkwaːzi(ː)-əˈfiʃəl] *a.* 半官方的.

qua·si-op·ti·cal [ˈkwaːzi(ː)ˈɔptikəl] *a.* 准光(学)的. ~ **wave**【物】准光波.

qua·si-pub·lic [ˈkwaːzi(ː)ˈpʌblik] *a.* (公司、企业等)私营公用事业的.

qua·si-shawl [ˈkwaːziʃɔːl] *n.* 类似围巾的东西.

qua·si-sov·er·eign [ˌkwaːziˈsɔvrin] *a.* 半独立的,半主权的.

quas·qui·cen·ten·ni·al [ˌkwɔskwisenˈteniəl] *n.* 第一百二十五周年纪念日.

quass [kvaːs, kwaːs] *n.* 克瓦斯 (=kvass)〔一种用面包或水果发酵制成的俄式清凉饮料〕.

quas·sia [ˈkwɔʃə] *n.* ①【植】苦树;〔Q-〕苦木属. ②苦树木料[树皮、根];由苦树采取的苦味液. ③啤酒苦味剂. ~**-wood** *n.* 苦木.

qua·ter·cen·te·na·ry [ˌkwætəsenˈtiːnəri] *n.* 四百周年(纪念).

qua·ter·na·ry [kwəˈtəːnəri] *a.* ①四个一组的;由四部分组成的;第四的. ②【化】四元的;四价的;季的.【数】四进制的. ③〔Q-〕【地】第四纪[系]的. — *n.* ①四;四个一组的东西;第四组组成部分. ②〔Q-〕【地】第四纪. ③【数】四进制. *the Pythagorean* ~ 毕达哥拉斯四元数〔即1+2+3+4,结果恰巧是 10〕.

qua·ter·ni·on [kwəˈtəːnjən, -niən] *n.* ①四,四个一组;四组物;四人一组. ②四张对折的一沓纸;对折两次的一张纸. ③【数】四元数;〔*pl.*〕四元法.

qua·ter·ni·ty [kwəˈtəːniti] *n.* ①四,四个一组;四人一组. ②【宗】四位一体.

quat·rain [ˈkwɔtrein] *n.*【韵】四行诗,四行一节的诗.

qua·tre [ˈkaːtə] *n.* (纸牌、骨牌、骰子的)四点.

quat·re·foil [ˈkætrəfɔil] *n.* ①(苜蓿等)四叶片的叶子;四瓣的花朵. ②【建】四叶式;【纹】四叶形. ~ **crossing** (道路的)四叶式交叉.

quat·tro·cen·tist [ˌkwætrəuˈtʃentist] *n.* 十五世纪的意大利艺术家[作家].

quat·tro·cen·to [ˌkwætrəuˈtʃentəu] *n.* 〔常Q-〕十五世纪(风格)〔词义是1400年代,即欧洲文艺复兴的初期〕.

qua·ver [ˈkweivə] *vi.* ①震动,颤动. ②(特指声音)颤抖. — *vt.* 颤抖着说[唱],用颤音演奏 (*out*). — *n.* ①颤音;颤声. ②【乐】八分音符.

qua·ver·ing, qua·ver·ous [ˈkweivəriŋ, -rəs] *a.* 颤抖的;颤声的.

qua·ver·ing·ly [ˈkweivəriŋli] *ad.* 颤抖着声音,用颤声.

qua·ver·y [ˈkweivəri] *a.* 颤音多的,颤声的.

Quay [kwei] *n.* 奎伊〔姓氏〕.

quay [kiː] *n.* 码头,埠头. ~**side** *n.* 码头区〔常作定语,如 ~*side building* 等〕.

quay·age [ˈkiːidʒ] *n.* ①码头使用税[费]. ②码头空位;码头用地,码头面积. ③〔总称〕一组码头.

Que. = Quebec.

quean [kwiːn] *n.* ①〔Scot.〕(未婚)妇女;少女. ②厚脸女人,轻佻妇女(尤指妓女).

quea·sy, quea·zy [ˈkwiːzi] *a.* ①(食物等)使人作呕的,(船等)使人眩晕欲吐的. ②(人)易呕吐的,要呕的,易反胃的. ③心软的;顾虑重重的;(良心等)易不安的. **quea·si·ly** *ad.* **quea·si·ness** *n.*

Quebec [kwiˈbek] *n.* ①魁北克〔加拿大省名〕. ②魁北克〔加拿大港市〕.

que·bra·cho [keiˈbraːtʃəu] *n.* (*pl.* ~*s*)【植】①破斧树 (*Schinopsis lorentzii*)〔产于美洲热带地区〕. ②白坚木 (*Aspidosperma quebracho-blanco*)〔产于南美洲〕. ③破斧树材[树皮];白坚木材[树皮].

Quech·ua [ˈketʃwaː, -wə] *n.* (*pl.* ~*(s)*) ①凯楚阿人〔南美安第斯高原各国的印第安人〕. ②凯楚阿语. **Quech·uan** *n., a.* 凯楚阿人[语](的).

Quech·u·ma·ran [ˈketʃuməraːn] *n.* 凯楚阿马兰语系.

Queen [kwiːn] *n.* 奎恩〔姓氏〕.

queen [kwiːn] *n.* ①皇后,王后. ②女王,女皇,女帝;女

酋长;女首脑.★在位君主是女王时,成语中的King可改用Queen. 如King's Bench[Counsel 等]可说作Queen's Bench [Counsel 等]. ③(因权力、地位、相貌等而被尊崇的)出众的妇女;(神话等中的)女神;圣母马利亚;爱人,情人;心爱的女子〔指妻、女等〕. ④(社交界等的)…皇后,名媛;"美女比赛"第一名,尤物;〔喻〕精华,上品;胜地. ⑤(纸牌或象棋中的)后;(蚂蚁、蜜蜂等的)女王;雌猫(等). ⑥〔美俚〕乱搞同性恋爱的男子,女性化的男人. ⑦〔空军俚〕操纵无人驾驶飞机 (drone) 的指挥机. ***Q- Anne Style*** (18 世纪初期建筑、家具等的)安女王式. ***Q- Anne is dead.*** 老早听腻了;(消息等)早知道了. ***Q- of Grace***【基督教】圣母马利亚. ***~ of hearts*** ①【牌戏】心牌女王. ②美人. ***~ of heaven*** 天后〔希腊神话中主神宙斯之妻朱诺 (Juno) 的别称〕. ***~ of love*** 爱神〔希腊神话中维纳斯 (Venus) 的别称〕. ***~ of night*** ①夜神, 月神〔希腊神话中司狩猎女神、月神狄安娜 (Diana) 的别称〕. ②月. ***~ of the Adriatic*** 亚德里亚海之后〔意大利城市威尼斯 (Venice) 的别称〕. ***~ of (the) May*** 五月女王〔指五月一日花魁日游戏中被选中为女王的女子, = May-queen〕. ***~ of the meadows*** 草原女王〔即【植】绣线菊 = meadow-sweet〕. ***Q- of the seas*** 海上之王〔指旧时英帝国〕. ***Q- of the West*** 西部之王〔美国辛辛那提 (Cincinnati) 市的别名〕. ***~-right colony***【蜂】有王群. ***Queen's Bench*** 英国高等法院. ***Queen's Club*** 英国肯辛顿(Kensington)的运动场. ***Queen's colour*** 英军的团旗. ***Queen's Counsel*** 英国王室法律顾问. ***Queen's omnibus***〔俚〕巡警车, 囚车(= Black Maria). ***~'s ware*** 英国产的奶油色陶器. ***~'s weather*** 晴天. ***to the ~'s taste*** 尽善尽美地, 完美地,使人无可挑剔地. — *vt.* ①立…为女王[王后],使即女王位. ②以女王的身分统治. ③【象棋】使(卒子)达底线后变为王后. — *vi.* ①成为女王;作为女王而统治. ②【象棋】卒子达底线后变为王后. ***~ it*** 做女王统治,象女王一般地动作(*~ it over [among] girls* 在女孩子中称王). ~ **ant** 蚁王,雌蚁. **Q- Bee [Duck]** 无线电操纵的靶机[靶舰]. ~ **bee** 蜂王;〔喻〕社交界女王. ~**cake** 夹有葡萄干的心形小软饼. ~ **consort** 皇后, 王妃. ~ **dowager** (皇)太后〔已故君主之妻〕. ~ **mother** ①(皇)太后〔在位君主之母〕.②(生有太子或公主的)现任女王. ~ **post**【建】双柱架. ~ **regent** ①摄政王. ②〔罕〕女皇. ~ **regnant** (执政的)女皇, 女帝, 女王. ~**-size** 大号的,仅次于特大号的. ~ **wasp** 雌蜂,蜂王. **-dom** ①女王统治的王国. ②〔罕〕女王[王后]的身分[地位].**-hood [-ship]** 女王[王后]的地位[身分,统治期间]. **-less** *a.* 无女王[王后]的. **-like** *a.* = queenly *(a.)*.

queen·ing [ˈkwiːniŋ] *n.* ①立为女王[王后]. ②〔英〕王后苹果〔苹果的一个品种〕.

queen·li·ness [ˈkwiːnlinis] *n.* 女王般的威严;女王般的作风.

queen·ly [ˈkwiːnli] *a.* (象)女王的,俨然女王的, 有威严的. — *ad.* 女王[王后]般地.

Queens·ber·ry [ˈkwiːnzbəri] *n.* 昆斯伯里〔姓氏〕. ~ **rules** 标准拳击规则 (= Marquis ~ of rules).

Queensland [ˈkwiːnzlənd] *n.* 昆士兰〔澳大利亚州名〕.

queer [kwiə] *a.* ①奇妙的,奇怪的. ②〔口〕可疑的,费解的. ③眩晕的,眼花的,(身体)觉得不舒服的;有点神经失常的;〔英俚〕喝醉了的. ④〔美俚〕假的,伪造的;无价值的. ⑤〔美俚〕搞同性恋爱的,(男子)女性化的. ⑥对…着了迷的 *(for, on, about)*. *That's ~!* 那倒奇怪! *a ~ character* 可疑的人物. *a ~ transaction* 不正当的交易. ***a ~ fish [card]*** 怪人,疯子. ***be ~ in the head*** 头脑失常. ***feel ~*** 觉得不舒服. ***in Q- Street***〔俚〕背着债;(财政)陷入绝境;名誉不好. — *n.* ①〔美俚〕〔the ~〕假钞票,伪钞,伪币. ②〔美俚〕搞同性恋爱的男子. ***pass the ~*** 使用伪币. ***on the ~*** 犯伪钞制造罪. — *vt.* ①〔俚〕糟蹋,弄糟,破坏. ②使觉得不舒服;使陷入窘境;使处于危险地位. *Bad food ~ed the party.* 饭菜不好使宴会大为减色. ***~ sb.'s pitch, ~ the pitch for sb.***〔英口〕暗中破坏某人计划. **-ish** *a.* 有点古怪[可疑、不舒服]的. **-ly** *ad.* **-ness** *n.*

quell [kwel] *vt.*〔书〕①镇压(叛乱等),压制;平息. ②镇定,消除,减轻(激动、恐惧等). — *n.*〔古〕屠杀. **quell-a·ble** *a.* 可平定的;可消除的. **-er** *n.* 镇压者,平息者.

quel·que chose [kelkəˈʃəuz]〔F.〕小事,琐事.

Que·moy [ˈkweiˈmɔi] *n.* 金门(岛)〔中国福建省岛屿〕.

quench [kwentʃ] *vt.* ①〔主诗〕熄灭(火、光);扑灭. ②压制,遏制,抑制;解(渴). ③【机】把…淬火,使骤冷;使淬硬;淬炼;【物】淬熄. ④〔俚〕迫使(反对者)沉默,使无话可说. ~ *one's thirst* 解渴. ~ *a fire* 弄灭火. ~ *eyesight* 减弱视力. ~ *an uprising* 镇压起义. ***~ smoking flax*** 弄熄冒着烟的火,中止充满着希望的计划.

quench·a·ble [ˈkwentʃəbl] *a.* ①可熄灭的, 可冷却的. ②镇压得了的;抑制得住的. **-ness** *n.*

quench·er [ˈkwentʃə] *n.* ①熄灭者,扑灭者. ②灭火器;猝灭器;骤冷器;猝火剂. ③抑制者, 压制者[物]. ④〔口〕解渴物,饮料.

quench·ing [ˈkwentʃiŋ] *n.*【机】淬火,【物】淬熄. ~ **effect** 淬炼效应. ~ **machine** 淬火机. ~ **medium** 淬火剂;骤冷剂. ~ **oil** 淬火油.

quench·less [ˈkwentʃlis] *a.* ①难弄熄的;不(可)冷却的. ②难镇压的;难抑制的.

que·nelle [kəˈnel] *n.* 肉丸子;鱼圆子.

Quen·tin [ˈkwentin] *n.* 昆廷〔男子名〕.

quer·ce·tin [ˈkwəːsitin] *n.*【化】栎精;栎皮黄素. **quer-cet·ic** [kwəˈsetik, -ˈsiːt-] *a.*

quer·cine [ˈkwəːsin, -sain] *a.* 栎树的;橡树的;槲树的.

quer·cit·ron [ˈkwəːsitrən, kwəˈsitrən] *n.* ①美洲黑栎的内层皮. ②栎皮粉.

quer·i·mo·ni·ous [ˌkweriˈməuniəs] *a.* = querulous.

que·rist [ˈkwiərist] *n.* 讯问者,质问者.

quern [kwəːn] *n.* 手(推的)磨. ~**stone** 磨石 (= millstone).

quer·u·lous [ˈkweruləs] *a.* 爱抱怨的, 爱发牢骚的;易发脾气的. **-ly** *ad.*

que·ry [ˈkwiəri] *n.* ①质问;询问;疑问,怀疑. ②敢问,请问〔在疑问句前单独使用〕.③【印】(打在原稿或校样上的)疑问号〔?〕〔亦可写作 query, 通常略作 qu. 或 qy.〕. *Query, was the money ever paid?* 请问这钱付过了没有? — *vt.* ①问,询问 *(whether; if)*;质问. ②把…作为问题提出,对…表示怀疑. — *vi.* 质问,询问;表示怀疑,在(校样等上)加疑问符号.

ques. = question.

quest [kwest] *n.* ①找,寻找,搜索,追求,探求. ②(特指中世纪骑士的)追求物. ③〔英方〕审问;〔古〕验尸;验尸陪审团. ***in ~ of*** 为求…,为寻求… *(He has come in ~ of employment.* 他来找工作). — *vi.* ①(狗等)跟踪搜寻,四处找 *(about)*. ②追求,探索. — *vt.*〔诗〕寻求,探索 *(out)*.

ques·tion [ˈkwestʃən] *n.* ①问,询问,发问;质问. ②【语法】疑问句. ③疑问;疑义,疑窦. ④问题;议题;争论点;悬案;(法庭等上的)争端. ⑤(把问题)付表决;付表决的问题. ⑥审问;〔古〕拷问. *a direct ~* 直接疑问句. *an indirect [oblique] ~* 间接疑问句. *a rhetorical ~* 反诘句. *a ~ of time* 时间问题. *leading ~*【法】诱供,诱导询问. *the Eastern ~* 东方问题. *The ~ is ...* 问题是…. ***an open ~*** 未解决的问题,容许讨论的问题. ***a ~ at [in] issue*** 悬案,争持的问题. ***a ~ of ~s*** 首要问题. ***a previous ~*** (议会中的)先决问题[动议]. *a sixty-four dollar ~* 最重要的问题. ***begging (of) the ~*** 用未经证明的假定来辩论. ***beside the ~*** 在本题之外,离题. ***beyond (all) ~*** 毫无疑问;一定,当然. ***call in ~*** 怀疑,表示异议,表示不服;要求…的证据. ***come into ~*** 成为问题,成为有实际重要性. ***foreign to the ~*** = beside the ~. ***in ~*** ①议论中的,该…,本….

②可怀疑,被争论,成为问题的. *make no ~ of* = *make no ~ but that ...* 对…不加怀疑. *out of ~* = beyond ~. *out of the ~* 不在考虑之列,谈不上;根本不可能. *past ~* = beyond ~. *pop the ~* 〔俚〕求婚. *put a ~ to* 向…质问,质问…. *put the ~* 提付表决;要求表决. *put to the ~* 〔古〕加以拷问. *Question!* 〔公开集会等中的叫声〕①请注意正题,离题了!〔促发言人言归本题〕. ②有疑问!有异议!〔表示疑问或不赞成〕. *~s and commands* 问答游戏. *starred ~* 要求口头答复的质问〔因英国国会中要求口头答复时附加星印〕. *That is not the ~.* 那是另外一个问题,那是另外一回事,那是题外话,那和我们的讨论无关. *There is no ~ (but) that ...* 那的确是…的,…是没有怀疑余地的. *There is no ~ of ...* ①…是毫无疑问的. ②…是不可能的. *to the ~* 针对论题;对题,切题. *without ~* 毫无疑问. — *vt.* ①询问;讯问;审问. ②怀疑,对…表示疑问,对…提出疑义. ③争论. ④分析;探究,研究(事实). *~ sb.'s honesty* 怀疑某人是否诚实. — *vi.* 询问;探问;探究. *It cannot be ~ed but that ...,* …无怀疑的余地,…是确实的. ~ **mark,** ~ **stop** 疑问号〔?〕. ~**-master** (广播或电视等中)答问节目的主持人. ~ **time** (英国议会中议员对大臣提问题的)质询时间. **-er** *n.* 询问者;讯问者;审问者. **-less** *a.* ①无疑的. ②无异议的. **-lessly** *ad.* 无疑地,的确.

ques·tion·a·ble [ˈkwestʃənəbl] *a.* 可疑的;(人)靠不住的,(品德等)有问题的. **-a·bly** *ad.*

ques·tion·a·ry [ˈkwestʃənəri] *a.* 询问的,探问的,疑问的. — *n.* 〔美〕= question(n)aire.

ques·tion·ing·ly [ˈkwestʃəniŋli] *ad.* 质问地,象讯问似地,疑惑地,诧异地.

ques·tion·(n)aire [ˌkwestiəˈnεə, -tʃə-] *n.* 〔F.〕①(调查情况用的)一组问题;问题单. ②调查表,征求意见表. ③用调查表进行的调查.

ques·tor [ˈkwestə, ˈkwiːs-] *n.* = quaestor.

Quetta [ˈkwetə] *n.* 奎达〔巴基斯坦城市〕.

quet·zal [ketˈsɑːl, ˈketsəl] *(pl. ~(e)s* [ketˈsɑːleis]*)* *n.* 【动】克沙尔鸟〔中美产,尾特长,羽美,为危地马拉的国鸟〕.

Quet·zal·co·a·tl [ketˌsɑːlkəuˈɑːtl] *n.* (墨西哥印第安人)阿兹台克人信奉的主神.

queue [kjuː] *n.* ①发辫,辫子. ②〔英〕(顺序等车、购物的)行列,长队;车队. *form a ~* 排队. *in a ~* 排成一行. *jump the ~* 不按次序排队;企图获得优惠待遇. — *vt.* 把(头发)梳成辫子. — *vi.* 〔英〕排(成)队,排队等候 *(on; up)*. *~ up at a bus stop* 在公共汽车站排队.

que·zal [ketˈsɑː] *n.* = quetzal.

Quezon City [ˈkeizɔn ˈsiti] 奎松城〔菲律宾城市〕.

quib·ble [ˈkwibl] *n.* ①遁词,狡辩;支吾,模棱两可的说法. ②吹毛求疵的意见. ③〔古〕双关话. — *vi.* ①推托,推委,讲模棱两可的话;狡辩. ②讲双关话. **quibbler** *n.* ①推委〔狡辩〕的人. ②讲双关话的人. **quibblingly** *ad.*

quiche Lor·raine [kiːʃ ləuˈren] *(pl. quiches* [kiːʃ] *Lorraine)* 洛林糕〔用干酪、腌肉等做成的奶旦糕〕.

Quick [kwik] *n.* 奎克〔姓氏〕.

quick [kwik] *a.* ①快,迅速的,急速的 *(opp.* slow);短时间的. ②敏捷的;机敏的,聪明的,伶俐的;(眼睛等)敏锐的. ③生动的,活泼的. ④性急的,易怒的,易发脾气的. ⑤〔古、方〕活着的;(水等)流动的;有孕的(尤指胎动期). ⑥含矿石的;(资本等)生利的;〔美〕(商品等)可立即转换成现金的. ⑦〔古〕(火烧得)旺盛的,(火焰)熊熊的. ⑧(路)弯的;(坡)陡的. *He did a ~ mile.* 他用快步走了一英里. *a ~ march* 【军】急行军. *Q- at meal, ~ at work.* 吃得快,做得快. *Be ~!* 赶快! *a ~ child* 伶俐的孩子. *a ~ eye* 慧眼. *a ~ temper* 急性子. *~ wits* 急智,机智. *a ~ hedge* 活篱,树篱. *~ water* 〔罕〕流水. *in ~ succession* 紧接着. *~ at figures* 算得快. *be ~ on the draw* ①动辄就拿出武器. ②〔美俚〕脑子快. *~ of hearing [sight]* 耳朵[眼睛]尖的. *~ of temper = ~ to take offence* 易怒的. *~ with child* 〔原作 *with ~ child*〕感到胎动. — *ad.* 快速. *as ~ as thought [lightning]* 一眨眼工夫,霎时间,风驰电掣般. — *n.* ①(有感觉的)活肉,(特指指甲下的)肉根,指甲肉;伤口的嫩皮;感情的中枢,感觉最敏锐的地方;痛处. ②要害;本质;核心. ③〔古〕生物,活物. ④彻头彻尾. ⑤〔英〕插条(=quickset). *the ~ and the dead* 生者与死者. *to the ~* ①触到活肉 *(cut the fingernail to the ~* 剪指甲剪着了指甲肉). ②彻骨,入骨,痛切地. ③真正,彻头彻尾;道地 *(He is a cockney to the ~.* 他是道地的伦敦人. *He is a Tory to the ~.* 他是一个彻头彻尾的保守党. *Your coolness cuts me to the ~.* 你的冷淡真使我伤心). ~**-change** *a.* 善变的〔指演员能在同一戏中扮演几种不同的角色〕. ~**-eared** *a.* 耳朵尖[敏锐]的. ~**-eyed** *a.* 眼睛尖的. ~ **fence** 树篱. ~ **fire** 【军】速射. ~**-firer** 速射枪〔炮〕. ~**-firing,** ~**-fire** *a.* 速射的. ~**-freeze** *vt.* 使(生鲜食品)速冻. ~ **grass** (长得极快的)鹅观草. ~ **lime** 生石灰. ~**sand** 流沙;〔喻〕复杂危险的情况. ~**-scented** *a.* 嗅觉敏锐的. ~**set** 〔英〕① *a.* 树篱的. ② *n.* (主指山楂的)树篱;〔集合词〕做树篱用的树,山楂树. ~**-sighted** *a.* 眼睛尖,眼快的. ~**silver** ① *n.* 水银,汞;〔喻〕快活的性格,易变的脾气;三心两意的人. ② *vt.* 涂水银(在玻璃上做镜子). ③ *a.* 水银似的,易变的. ~**step** ①【军】齐步. ②快速进行曲;轻快舞步. ③〔美俚〕拉痢. ~**-tempered** *a.* 性急的,急性子的. ~ **time** 快步〔英国陆军一分钟 128 步;美国陆军一分钟 120 步〕. ~**-witted** *a.* 富于机智的,机敏的;敏捷的. **-ly** *ad.* **-ness** *n.*

quick·en [ˈkwikən] *vt.* ①加快,加速. ②使变活,使复活,使有生命,使苏醒. ③使活跃,使有生气,鼓舞,刺激. ④使(曲线)更弯;使(斜坡)更陡. *~ one's appetite* 开胃,刺激食欲. — *vi.* ①变快,加速. ②变活,苏醒. ③变活泼,变生动. ④感觉胎动;(孕妇)进入胎动期. *The pulse ~s.* 脉搏快起来了;〔喻〕兴奋起来了.

quick·en·ing [ˈkwikəniŋ] *a.* 加快的,使活的,使苏醒的;使活泼的,使振作的. — *n.* 胎动初期〔受孕后第十八周左右〕.

quick·ie [ˈkwiki] 〔美俚〕*n.* ①匆匆做成的事. ②粗制滥造的影片[文艺作品]. ③短促的接吻. ④匆忙的旅行. ⑤(酒的)一饮而干. ⑥未经工会同意的罢工 (= ~ strike). — *a.* 快的,迅速的;简短的. *a ~ training course* 速成训练班.

quid[1] [kwid] *n.* 〔*sing., pl.*〕〔英俚〕一镑金币,金镑;一镑. *half a ~* 半镑.

quid[2] [kwid] *n.* (咀嚼用的)一块烟草块;咀嚼物.

quid·dity [ˈkwiditi] *n.* ①(人、事物的)本质,实质. ②遁辞,诡辩,狡辩. ③莫名其妙的言行,怪癖;怪想法.

quid·nunc [ˈkwidnʌŋk] *n.* ①爱搬弄是非的人;爱闲扯的人. ②爱问长问短的人,爱打听[传播]新闻的人.

quid pro quo [ˈkwid prəu ˈkwəu] 〔L.〕①补偿物;交换物;赔偿;报酬;报复. ②代替物;相等物. ③〔罕〕弄错.

quién sa·be [kiːn ˈsæbi] 〔美〕打在牛身上的秘密烙印〔原意为"有谁会知道呢?"〕.

qui·es·cence, qui·es·cen·cy [kwaiˈesns, -ˈesnsi] *n.* ①不动,静止. ②(蚕等的)休眠,静止期. ③寂静,沉默. ④(疾病的)被遏制状态. *the ~ period* 休眠期.

qui·es·cent [kwaiˈesnt] *a.* ①不动的,静止的. ②(蚕等)静止期的,休眠的. ③寂静的,沉默的. ④(疾病等)被遏制的,无症状的. *a ~ point* 【物】静点. **-ly** *ad.*

qui·et [ˈkwaiət] *a.* ①静的,恬静的,平静的. ②(生物)不动的,安静的. ③肃静的,寂静的. ④(市面)萧条的;(比赛等)松懈的. ⑤(态度、举止等)镇静的,沉着的;温和的. ⑥(社会)太平的,安定的,平稳无事的;(环境、生活方式等)单调的,无变化的;闲适的,从容的. ⑦不显眼的，朴素的，素静的 (*opp*. loud). ⑧秘密的，私下的，暗地里的；转弯抹角的；藏在心里的. ⑨(街道等)僻静的. ⑩非正式的. *a ~ sea* 平静的海. *Be ~! = Keep ~!* 请安静！肃静！*a ~ cup of tea* 安闲享用的一杯茶. *nice ~ people* 稳重的人们. *~ resentment* 闷在肚子里的火气，闷气. *~ colours* 素静的颜色. ***have a ~ dig at (sb.)*** 暗中讽刺某人一下. ***keep (sth.) ~*** (对某事)保守秘密. — *n*. ①寂静，肃静. ②稳静；沉静，沉着. ③沉默. ④安静，休养，静养. ⑤和平，平稳，安定，太平. *rest and ~* 休息. ***at ~*** 平稳地，平静地. ***in ~*** 安静地，和平地. ***on the ~*** 私下，暗地里，秘密〔美俚略作 on the q.t.〕. — *vt*. ①使静，使宁静. ②抚慰，安慰. ③使缓和，平息，使镇定. — *vi*. ①平静，变静，变稳 *(down)*. ~ **conscience** 自问无愧的良心. ~ **irony** 转弯抹角的讽刺. **-ly** *ad*. **-ness** *n*.

qui·et·en [ˈkwaiətn] *vt*., *vi*. 〔俚〕= quiet *(vt*., *vi*.*)*.

qui·et·er [ˈkwaiətə] *n*.【机】防音装置.

qui·et·ism [ˈkwaiətizəm] *n*.【宗】①寂静教〔17 世纪一种基督教的神秘主义教派〕. ②无为主义，清静无为. **-ist** *n*. ①寂静教徒. ②安于清静的人，主张清静无为者. **qui·et·is·tic** *a*.

qui·e·tude [ˈkwaiətjuːd] *n*. 寂静；平静；宁静；沉着.

qui·e·tus [kwaiˈiːtəs] *n*. ①死，灭亡；寂灭；死的解脱. ②(债务、义务等的)偿清，解除，理清；〔古〕清欠收据. ③平息；制止. ④静止状态；休眠. *give a ~ to a rumour* 杜绝谣言. *get one's ~* 死. *give sb. his ~* 杀死.

quiff[1] [kwif] *n*. 〔英俚〕(搽油梳在额前的)一绺卷发.

quiff[2] [kwif] *n*. 〔方、美〕一阵风；一口烟〔whiff 的别字〕.

quiff[3] [kwif] *n*. 〔美俚〕姑娘，女人；轻佻的女子；下等娼妓.

Qui·h(a)i [ˈkwaiˈhi] 〔印度〕久住印度的英国人.

quill [kwil] *n*. ①翮，羽毛管，羽茎；(翼或尾部的)翮羽. ②翮笔，鹅毛笔；翮制弦拨，(钓鱼的)浮漂，羽毛制的牙签. ③〔常 *pl*.〕(猬或豪猪的)刺. ④(芦茎等做的)芦笛. ⑤【纺】线轴；纡管；纬管；【机】套筒轴. ⑥(桂皮或金鸡纳皮等的)一小卷. ⑦(炸药的)导火线. ***drive the ~*** 挥毫，写字. — *vt*. ①在(布)上做管状褶. ②把(线)卷在线轴上. ③(用羽毛管等)刺穿；拔掉…的羽毛管. ④〔俚〕拍…的马屁. ~ **covert** 覆〔鸟翮根部细毛〕. ~ **driver** 〔谑〕吃笔墨饭的；(特指)录事，抄写员. **~wort** *n*.【植】水韭.

quil·lai·a, quil·laj·a, quil·lai [kiˈlaiə, -ˈlai] *n*. 皂树；皂树皮 (= soapbark).

quill·back [ˈkwilbæk] *n*.【动】*(pl. ~(s))* 鲤型亚目鱼属 *(Carpiodes)*.

Quil·ler [ˈkwilə] *n*. 奎勒〔姓氏〕.

Quil·ler-Couch [ˈkwiləˈkuːtʃ] 奎勒-库奇〔姓氏〕.

quil·let [ˈkwilit] *n*. 〔古〕遁辞；细微差别.

quill·ing [ˈkwiliŋ] *n*. ①网眼纱褶裥边〔边饰〕. ②【纺】卷纬(工艺).

quilt [kwilt] *n*. 被子，毛被，驼绒被，鸭绒被；被状物. — *vt*. ①缝(被)，绗(被)，衲(被)；绗缝(衣服). ②用垫料填塞后缝拢；将(钞票等)缝进衣服里. ③在(多层布等)上缝出花样. ④用摘抄等方法编辑；东拼西凑地做. ⑤〔方〕殴打. — *vi*. 制被；缝被. **-er** *n*. ①缝被子的人. ②(缝纫机上的)绗缝附件.

Quilt·er [ˈkwiltə] *n*. 奎尔特〔姓氏〕.

quilt·ing [ˈkwiltiŋ] *n*. ①被子绗缝. ②被子料. ③(衣服上的)管状褶裥. ④〔方〕殴打. ⑤〔美〕= ~ bee. ~ **bee [party]** 〔美〕帮忙绗被子的妇女联谊. ~ **cotton** 棉胎用棉.

quin [kwin] *n*. = quintuplet.

qui·na [ˈkwainə] *n*. 金鸡纳(皮).

qui·na·ry [ˈkwainəri] *a*. 五的；五个的；五个一组的；第五位的. — *n*. 五个一套〔一组〕.

qui·nate[1] [ˈkwaineit] *a*.【植】(复叶)由五枚小叶片组成的.

qui·nate[2] [ˈkwaineit] *n*.【化】奎尼酸.

Qui·nault [ˈkwinəlt] *n*. 奎纳尔特〔姓氏〕.

quince [kwins] *n*.【植】榅桲，榅梨，榅桲树.

quin·cen·te·na·ry, quin·gen·te·na·ry [ˌkwinsenˈtiːnəri, -dʒenˈtiːnəri] *n*., *a*. 第五百周年(的)；五百周年纪念(的).

quin·cun·cial [kwinˈkʌnʃəl] *a*. ①(骰子、纸牌的)五点形的，梅花形的. ②【植】五叶〔五瓣〕叠覆排列的〔二在外，二在内，一个半在外半在内〕. **-ly** *ad*. 成梅花形；迭覆排列地.

quin·cunx [ˈkwinkʌŋks] *n*. ①(五点排列成的)梅花形. ②【植】(果树、灌木的)梅花形栽法. ③【植】五叶〔瓣〕的叠覆排列.

quin·cunx·ci·al [kwinˈkʌnksiəl] *n*. = quincuncial.

Quin·c(e)y [ˈkwinsi] *n*. 昆西〔姓氏〕.

Quin(n) [kwin] *n*. 奎恩〔姓氏〕.

quin·dec·a·gon [kwinˈdekəgɔn] *n*.【数】十五角形，十五边形.

quin·de·cen·ni·al [ˌkwindiˈseniəl] *a*. ①每十五年发生一次的. ②持续十五年的. — *n*. ①十五年期间；十五周年. ②十五周年纪念活动.

quin·i·a [ˈkwiniə] *n*.【医】= quinine.

quin·ic [ˈkwinik] *a*. ~ **acid**【药】金鸡纳酸；【化】奎尼酸.

quin·i·dine [ˈkwinidiːn, -din] *n*.【化】奎尼定.

qui·nine, quin·in [kwiˈniːn, ˈkwiniːn; Am. ˈkwainain] *n*.【药】奎宁；【化】金鸡纳硷. *a Q- Jimmy* 〔美俚〕林场医生.

qui·nin·ism, qui·nism [kwiˈniːnizəm, ˈkwainizəm] *n*. 金鸡纳〔奎宁〕中毒.

quin·nat sal·mon [ˈkwinæt ˈsæmən] *n*. 〔美〕【鱼】大鳞大麻哈鱼〔太平洋沿岸产〕.

qui·no·a [kiˈnəuə] *n*.【植】昆诺阿藜 *(Chenopodium quinoa)*〔产于安第斯山脉地区，印第安人种之以食其粟〕.

quin·oid [ˈkwinɔid] *n*.【化】醌式，醌型.

qui·noi·dine [kwiˈnɔidiːn, -din] *n*.【化】奎诺酊.

quin·o·line [ˈkwinəliːn, -in] *n*.【化】①喹啉，氮(杂)萘. ②喹啉衍生物. **quin·o·lin·ic** *a*.

qui·none [kwiˈnəun, ˈkwinəun] *n*.【化】①醌，苯醌. ②醌类.

qui·non·i·mine [kwiˈnɔnimiːn, -min] *n*.【化】醌亚胺.

quin·o·noid [ˈkwinənɔid, kwiˈnəunɔid] *a*.【化】醌型结构状的.

quinqua- *comb.f*. 五 (= quinque-).

quin·qua·ge·nar·i·an [ˌkwiŋkwədʒiˈnεəriən] *a*., *n*. 五十至五十九岁的(人).

quin·qua·ge·nar·y [ˌkwinkwəˈdʒiːnəri] *a*. 五十岁的. — *n*. 五十岁的人；五十周年纪念.

Quin·qua·ges·i·ma [ˌkwinkwəˈdʒesimə] *n*.【基督教】四旬斋前的星期日，复活节前的第五十日 (= ~ Sunday).

quin·quan·gu·lar [kwiŋˈkwæŋgjulə] *a*. 〔古〕有五角的，五角形的.

quinque- *comb.f*. 五：*quinque*nnial.

quin·que·fo·li·o·late [ˌkwiŋkwəˈfəuliəlit, -leit] *a*.【植】有五小叶的.

quin·quen·ni·ad [kwiŋˈkweniæd] *n*. = quinquennium.

quin·quen·ni·al [kwiŋˈkweniəl, -njəl] *a*. ①每五年(一次)的. ②持续五年的. — *n*. ①五周年纪念；每五年一次的事. ②持续五年的在职期间. ~ **valuation** (决定财产税征收额的)五年一次的估价.

quin·quen·ni·um [kwiŋˈkweniəm] *(pl. ~s, -nia* [-niə]*)* *n*. 五年，五年的时间.

quin·que·par·tite [ˌkwinkwiˈpɑːtait] *a*. 分为五部分的；由五部分组成的.

quin·que·reme [ˈkwiŋkwəriːm] *n*. (古罗马的)五层橹船.

quin·que·va·lence, quin·que·va·len·cy *n*. [ˌkwiŋkwiˈveiləns, -ˈveilənsi] *n*.【化】五价.

quin·que·va·lent, quin·qui·va·lent [ˌkwiŋkwiˈveilənt] *a.*【化】五价(原子)的.
quin·qui·na [kwiŋˈkwainə] *n.* = quina.
quins [kwinz] *n.*〔口〕= quintuplets.
quin·sied [ˈkwinzid] *a.*【医】感染扁桃体周脓肿的.
quin·sy [ˈkwinzi] *n.*【医】扁桃体周脓肿.
quint[1] [kint] *n.* ①【纸牌】同花顺. ②[kwint]【乐】五度;五度音;(提琴的)E 弦[第一弦]. ***a ~ major*** 同花大顺[A, K, Q, J, 10]. ***a ~ minor*** 同花小顺[J, 10, 9, 8, 7].
quint[2] [kwint] *n.*〔美口〕= quintuplet.
quint[3] [kwint] *n.*〔美俚〕男子篮球队.
quin·tain [ˈkwintin] *n.* ①【史】(中世纪的)刺矛靶. ②骑马用刺矛靶练刺.
quin·tal [ˈkwintəl] *n.* ①公担(=100公斤). ②英担[英国为 112 磅,美国为 100 磅].
quin·tan [ˈkwintən] *n.*【医】五日热. — *a.* 每五天的,每逢第五天发生一次的.
Quin·tard [ˈkwintɑ:d] *n.* 昆塔德[姓氏].
quinte [kɛ̃:nt] *n.*〔F.〕【剑】(击剑八种姿势中的)第五种防守架式.
quin·tes·sence [kwinˈtesns] *n.* ①(古代哲学所说的)第五原质[基本物质,指空气、水、火、土之外]. ②精华;精髓;典型,典范. ③(物质的)本体,实体,本质,实质,原质. *the ~ of beauty* 美的典型.
quin·tes·sen·tial [ˌkwintiˈsenʃəl] *a.* ①精华的,精髓的. ②典型的,典范的,最完美的.
quin·tette, quin·tet [kwinˈtet] *n.* ①【乐】五部曲;五部合奏,五重奏;五部合唱;五部合奏队;五部合唱队. ②五人一组;五件一套. ③【物】五重线. ④〔美俚〕男子篮球队.
quin·tile [ˈkwintil, -tail] *a.*【天】(两天体的)五分之一对座的(相隔 72 度). — *n.*【天】五分之一对座.
quin·til·lion [kwinˈtiljən] *num.*〔英、德〕百万的五次幂[乘方][1 后有 30 个 0 的数];〔美、法〕千的六次幂[乘方][1 后有 18 个 0 的数].
quints [kwints] *n.*〔美〕= quintuplets.
quin·tuple [ˈkwintju(:)pl] *a.* ①五的;五倍的,五重的;由五个部分组成的. ②【乐】五拍子的. — *n.* ①五倍量. ②〔罕〕五个一套. — *vt.* 使成五倍,以五乘之. — *vi.* 成为五倍.
quin·tuplet [ˈkwintjuplit] *n.* ①五人一组,五件一套. ②〔*pl.*〕五胞胎;五人自行车.
quin·tu·pli·cate [kwinˈtju:plikit] *a.* ①五倍的,五重的. ②一式五份的;第五(份)的. — *n.* ①五倍的数[量]. ②一式的五份;一式五份中的一份;第五份. — [kwinˈtju:plikeit] *vt.* ①把…作成一式五份. ②使成五倍.
quip [kwip] *n.* ①讥讽,挖苦话. ②妙语;好笑的话. ③奇行;怪物,好笑的东西. ④遁辞 (= quibble). — *vt.* 讥讽,嘲弄. — *vi.* ①讥讽. ②讲妙语[双关语等].
qui·pu [ˈkwi:pu] *n.* (古秘鲁的)结绳语[以颜色和形状各不相同的绳结记事、记数等].
quire[1] [ˈkwaiə] *n.* (纸的)一刀[24 张;略 qr.];(装订时)对折的一叠纸;(中世纪抄本等的)四张对折的纸. ***in ~s*** ①书叶折好尚未装钉的. ②按(纸张)的刀数.
quire[2] [ˈkwaiə] *n., vi., vt.*〔古〕= choir.
Qui·rey [ˈkwaiəri, ˈkwiəri] *n.* 奎厄里[姓氏].
Quir·i·nal [ˈkwirinəl] *n.* 罗马七丘之一;(建在该丘上的)意大利皇宫,〔转义〕意大利政府[宫廷][相对于梵蒂冈教廷而言].
Qui·ri·tes [kwiˈraiti:z] *n.*〔*pl.*〕古罗马平民.
quirk [kwə:k] *n.* ①双关话;遁辞,口实;讥讽话. ②不定心,奇想;奇癖. ③(书写等的)花体. ④三角形物;菱形窗玻璃. ⑤突然的弯曲[扭曲]. ⑥【建】(鸟喙饰的)深槽. ⑦【乐】急转. ⑧〔美俚〕见习空军飞行员. ***a ~ moulding***【建】鸟喙饰. — *vt.* ①嘲讽. ②使弯曲. ③挥鞭急打. ④【建】在(装饰线条等)上作成深槽. — *vi.* ①弯曲,扭曲. ②古怪地说话[行动]. **-y** *a.* ①诡诈的. ②突兀的;离奇的,古怪的.
quirt [kwə:t] *n.*〔美〕(附有长条皮辫的)短柄马鞭. — *vt.* 用马鞭鞭打[驱赶].
quis·le [ˈkwizl] *vi.* 卖国,做卖国贼;当傀儡政府头子.
quis·ling, quis·ler [ˈkwizliŋ, -lə] *n.* 卖国贼,叛国分子,傀儡政府头子[源于挪威法西斯党魁吉斯林 (Vidkun Quisling),他在第二次世界大战时卖国通敌,任纳粹侵占挪威后的傀儡政府头子].
quis·ling·ism [ˈkwizliŋizəm] *n.* 卖国,叛国,通敌.
quis·lin·gite [ˈkwizliŋgait] *n.* 卖国贼,叛国分子. — *a.* 卖国的,叛国的.
quit [kwit] *v.* ***(quit·ted*** [ˈkwitid],〔罕〕***quit)*** *vt.* ①放弃(信仰、行动、工作等);〔美〕停止. ②退出(屋外),离开(本国、军队等);告别(亲友等). ③偿清,还清,偿还(借款等);尽(义务等);〔诗〕报答,酬答. ④解除,免除. ⑤〔~ oneself〕〔古〕使行动,表现. *~ office* 辞职. *Q- your nonsense!* 不要胡说! *Death ~s all scores.* 一死百了. *~ love with hate.* 以恨报爱,恩将仇报. *Q- you like men.*〔古〕举动须如大丈夫. — *vi.* ①(租借人、房客等)迁出租借地,搬出,迁走. ②停止,作罢;认输. ③〔口〕辞职. *give notice to ~* 通知迁出[离职]. *have notice to ~* 接到迁出通知书. ***~ hold of*** 放开,放掉,撂开. ***~ oneself*** 表现得…. ***~ oneself of (fear)*** 消除(恐惧). ***~ score with*** 和…了结债务,结清帐目;向…报复. ***~ the scores*** 报仇雪恨. — *a.*〔仅用作表语〕①被释放,被宣告无罪. ②自由的;摆脱了…的. ③被免除了…的,了清债务的;尽了义务的. ***be ~ for*** 只因…就逃脱[得免] (*He was ~ for a ducking.* 他因钻入水中而逃脱.). ***be [get] ~ of ...*** 免除…,摆脱…,了清… (*get ~ of one's debts* 了清债务). ***~ of (thirty)*** (年龄)(三十)开外. — *n.* ①离开,退出. ②退职,辞职.
qui tam [ˈkwai ˈtæm]〔L.〕【法】要求取得罚金的起诉[此项罚金由起诉人与官方均分].
quitch [kwitʃ] *n.*【植】匍匐根草 (=couch-grass).
quit·claim [ˈkwitkleim] *n.* ①放弃权利[要求]. ②(产权等的)转让契约. — *vt.* (通过转让契约)放弃[转让]对…的合法权利.
quite [kwait] *ad.* ①完全,十分,彻底,真正,的确. ②事实上;差不多;可以说(是…),简直和…一样. ③颇,相当,有点儿,或多或少. ④〔口〕很,极. *~ the opposite* 正相反. *Q- right.* 好,行;完全对. *Oh, ~.* = *Q- so!* 对啦!是啊!不错!正是这样! *I was ~ by myself [~ alone].* 只有我一个人. *He is ~ a man.* 他真是个男子汉. *You are getting ~ a big boy now.* 你已经不小了. *It's ~ too delightful.* 真是太叫人高兴了. ***He [She] isn't ~.***〔英口〕= *He [She] isn't ~ a gentleman [lady].* 他[她]不象是一个绅士[贵妇人],他[她]不象是一个正人君子[正派女人]. ***not~*** 有点不 (*not ~ proper* 有点不妥). ***not ~ the thing to do*** 不太合适,有点不好(但是没有办法). ***not ~ well*** 还有点不好. ***~ a few***〔美〕相当(多)的,很不少. ***~ other [another]*** 完全不同的. ***~ some***〔美〕非常多. ***~ the thing*** 时髦,时新.
Quit·man [ˈkwitmən] *n.* 奎特曼[姓氏].
Quito [ˈki:təu] *n.* 基多[厄瓜多尔首都].
quit·rent [ˈkwitrent] *n.* (封建时代的)免役地税.
quits [kwits] *a.*〔仅用作表语〕(因报复或偿清而)两相抵销了的;恢复原状的;成平局的,不分胜负的;对等的,旗鼓相当的. ***be ~ with*** 向…报复[报仇],和…弄成平局,不分胜负. ***call it ~ = cry ~*** 互无胜负;(打架等时)同意罢休;停做某事声言作罢. ***double or ~*** (连赌两次时的)加倍(输赢),(输赢)相销. ***We are ~ now.*** 现在咱俩清帐了;现在谁也没有对不起谁的地方了.
quit·tance [ˈkwitəns] *n.* ①(债务,义务等的)免除,解除,宽免. ②免除债务[义务]的证书,收据. ③酬报,赔偿;报答;报复. ***Omittance is no ~.*** 不催帐并不就是销帐.
quit·ter [ˈkwitə] *n.*〔美口〕轻易中止[放弃](竞争、计划、

Q

义务等)的人;半途而废的人;懒人;意志薄弱的人,懦夫.
quit·ting-time [ˈkwitiŋtaim] *n.* 〔美〕下班时间.
quit·tor [ˈkwitə] *n.* 马蹄疡,马蹄疽.
quiv·er[1] [ˈkwivə] *vi.* (人、叶、声、光等)轻微地颤抖,震颤,抖动,颤动. — *vt.* 使震颤; 使颤动; (云雀等)抖动(翅膀). — *n.* ①抖动,颤动;颤音. ②一闪.
quiv·er[2] [ˈkwivə] *n.* ①箭袋, 箭筒. ②箭筒中的箭. ③(能装一套东西的)容器. ④大群; 大队. *a* ~ *full of children* 子女多的大家庭. ***have an arrow [a shaft] left in one's*** ~ 还有本钱,还有办法可想. ***have one's*** ~ ***full*** 本钱充足.
quiv·er[3] [ˈkwivə] *a.* 〔古〕迅速的,敏捷的;活泼的.
quiv·er·ful [ˈkwivəful] *n.* ①满箭筒的箭. ②大量, 许多. ③〔谑〕大家庭.
quiv·er·ing [ˈkwivəriŋ] *a.* 颤抖的. **-ly** *ad.*
qui vive [kiːˈviːv] 〔F.〕〔哨兵的查问口令〕你是什么人?你是哪一边的? ***on the qui vive*** 警戒着.
Quix·ote [ˈkwiksət, -səut, Sp. kiˈhɔːte] *n.* ①(堂)吉诃德〔西班牙作家塞万提斯 (Cervantes) 所作小说《堂吉诃德》(Don Quixote) 中的主人翁〕. ②狂热的空想家;愚侠;时代落伍者.
quix·ot·ic, quix·ot·i·cal [kwikˈsɔtik, -kəl] *a.* ①〔q-或 Q-〕(堂)吉诃德式的. ②骑士气派的, 愚侠的; 空想的. — *n.* 〔*pl.*〕= quixotism. **quix·ot·i·cal·ly** *ad.*
quix·ot·ism, quix·ot·ry [ˈkwiksətizəm, -tri] *n.* (堂)吉诃德式的行为〔思想、性格〕;愚蠢的侠义行为,愚妄.
quiz [kwiz] *n.* (*pl.* ***quiz·zes*** [-iz]) ①〔英〕开玩笑,恶作剧;挖苦,嘲笑. ②〔英〕爱开玩笑的人,淘气鬼;挖苦者,嘲弄者. ③〔美〕(教师的)考问,提问;小型考试;测验;(广播节目中的)问答比赛;猜谜;难题. ④〔罕〕怪人,相貌怪的人; 举止奇特的人. ***a drop [shotgun]*** ~ 〔美〕突击测验. — ***[quizzed]*** *vt.* ①对…开玩笑,挖苦,嘲弄. ②冷笑着或无礼地盯着…看,好奇地看,张望. ③〔美〕考问,考试,对(学生)进行测验;给…出难题. ④盘问. ~ **bee [game]** 〔美〕(广播、电视节目中的)问答比赛. ~ **kid** 〔美〕参加电台问答比赛节目的孩子,聪明孩子; 神童. ~ **master** (问答比赛节目的)主持人,提问者. ~ **program(me)** 问答比赛节目. **quizzing glass** 带柄单眼镜.
quiz·zable [ˈkwizəbl] *a.* 可挖苦的,可嘲笑的.
quiz·(z)ee [kwiˈziː] *n.* 参加问答比赛的人,被测验者.
quiz·zer [ˈkwizə] *n.* ①嘲笑者,挖苦者,戏弄者. ②〔美〕主持测验者, 提问者. ③(广播、电视中的)问答比赛节目.
quiz·zi·cal [ˈkwizikəl] *a.* ①专爱挖苦人的. ②问询的,困惑的. ③古怪的,滑稽的. **-ly** *ad.*
quo·ad hoc [ˈkwəuæd ˈhɔk] 〔L.〕①关于这一点,在这一点上. ②到此为止, 到这个程度〔范围〕.
quod [kwɔd] *n.* 监牢, 监狱. *in [out of]* ~ 入〔出〕狱. — *vt.* 把…关进牢里.
quod [kwɔd] *pro.* 〔L.〕= which. ~ ***erat demonstrandum*** [ˈerætˌdemənˈstrændəm] 【数】这就是所要证明的, 证完,证讫〔略作 Q.E.D.〕. ~ ***erat faciendum*** [ˌfeiʃiˈendəm]【数】这就是所要做的,作毕,作讫〔略作 Q.E.F.〕. ~ ***erat inveniendum*** [inˌveniˈendəm] [Q.E.I.] 【数】这就是所要寻求的, 求毕, 求讫. ~ ***est*** [est] 这就是,即. ~ ***vide*** [ˈvidei] 见…, 参看…〔书籍等中的参照用语,略作 q.v.,=which see〕.
quod·li·bet [ˈkwɔdlibet] *n.* ①【乐】幻想曲;各种旋律的随意混合. ②(神学、经院哲学等中的)微妙的争论点;关于微妙问题的辩论.
quoif [kɔif] *n.* = coif.
quoin [kwɔin] *n.* 【建】①(房屋的)突角,外角;(墙壁接合处的)隅石;(拱门等的)楔形石;楔形支持物. ②(夹紧版面或防止圆桶滚动等的)楔子. — *vt.* ①用隅石砌牢;给…装嵌隅石. ②用楔形物支持;打楔子夹紧〔固定〕. **-ing** *n.* (接合墙壁等平面的)外角构件.
quoit [kwɔit] *n.* ①铁环,绳圈. ②〔*pl.*〕〔作单数用〕掷(铁)环〔绳圈〕游戏. *deck* ~*s* (甲板上玩的)掷绳圈. — *vt.* 掷(铁环等),抛(绳圈等).
quo ju·re? [kwəuˈjuəri] 〔L.〕以什么权利?
quo mo·do [kwəuˈməudəu] 〔L.〕①以何种方式? ②用…这样一种形式.
quon·dam [ˈkwɔndæm] *a.* 曾经是(演员、朋友等)的;以前的, 过去的. ~ *lovers* 过去的恋人, 旧情人. *a* ~ *singer* 过去的歌唱家.
Quon·set [ˈkwɔnsit] 〔美〕(用瓦楞铁预制件构成的) 半圆拱形活动房屋〔商标名〕. (= ~ hut).
quor. = quorum.
quo·rum [ˈkwɔːrəm] *n.* ①(英国旧时法庭开庭时必须达到的)法定治安法官人数;〔总称〕治安法官. ②(会议等的)法定人数. ③选出的一群人;特选队员. ***form [lack] a*** ~ 形成〔不足〕法定人数.
quot. = quotation, quoted.
quo·ta [ˈkwəutə] *n.* ①份,担任部分,分得部分. ②定额,比额;(入口货等的)限额,控制额. ***hiring*** ~*s* 〔美〕雇员分配额〔指政府为企业单位等规定的雇员中各人种的比额〕. ~ ***quickie*** 〔英〕(按照影片限额法摄制的)额定影片,廉价影片. ***the*** ~ ***system*** 定额分配制.
quot·a·ble [ˈkwəutəbl] *a.* 可引用的, 有引证价值的. **-a·bil·i·ty** [ˌkwəutəˈbiliti] *n.* **-ness** *n.*
quo·ta·tion [kwəuˈteiʃən] *n.* ①引用, 引证; 引用语, 语录 *(from)*. ②【商】行市,行情,时价;行市表;估价单. ③【印】(填空白的)空铅,嵌块. ④= ~ mark. ~ **mark(s)** 〔*pl.*〕引用号,引号〔即" "或' '〕.
quo·ta·tive [ˈkwəutətiv] *a.* ①引用的, 引证的. ②喜欢引用的.
quote [kwəut] *vt.* ①引用(他人文章); 引证, 引述, 举(例). ②把…放入引号, 用引号把…括起来. ③【商】喊(价),报(价),开(价);给…估价为. *It is* ~*ed at £ 5.* 这在市面上开价 5 镑. — *vi.* ①引用 *(from)*. ②喊价,报价,开价;估价. — *n.* 〔口〕①引用句,引文. ②引号. ③报价,估价表. ~ **mark** = quotation mark.
quot·er [ˈkwəutə] *n.* ①引用者,引证者. ②估价者,报价者,开价者. ③保险单红利计算员.
quote·wor·thy [ˈkwəutˌwəːði] *a.* 有引用价值的, 值得引证的.
quoth [kwəuθ] *vt.* 〔古、谑〕说(= said)〔第一人称和第三人称的直说法过去式, 用如 ~ *I [he, she]* 我〔他, 她〕说. 偶然也用如 ~ *we [they]* 我们〔他们〕说. 常置于主语前, 插在引用语句的前后或当中〕. *Quoth the raven, "Nevermore".* 老鸦说:"决不!"
quoth·a [ˈkwəuθə] *int.* 〔古〕〔带有轻蔑、卑视、讥笑、惊讶等意义〕真的! 的确!
quo·tid·ian [kwəuˈtidiən, ˌkwɔ-] *a.* ①每日的,每天发生的. ②司空见惯的,平凡的. — *n.* ①司空见惯的事,天天发生的事. ②【医】日发疟 (= ~ fever).
quo·tient [ˈkwəuʃənt] *n.* ①【数】商. ②份额,应分得的部分. *intelligence* ~ 智力商. ~ **group** 【数】商群.
quo·ti·e·ty [kwəuˈtaiiti] *n.* 率,系数.
Quo Va·dis [kwəu ˈvɑːdis] *n.* 〔L.〕《君往何处》〔描写罗马暴君尼禄时代的历史小说,1859 年波兰作家显克维支 (Henryk Sienkiewicz) 所作〕.
quo wor·ran·to [ˈkwəu wɔˈræntəu] 〔L.〕【法】①(旧时英国法庭所发)责问某人根据什么行使职权〔享受特权〕的令状. ②(旧时)收回被僭占的职位〔特权〕的诉讼. ③为收回被僭占的职位〔特权〕而提起的公诉.
Quran, Qur'an [kuˈrɑːn] *n.* = Koran.
q.v.[1] = 〔L.〕*quod vide* 参看,另见,见.
q.v.[2] 〔医疗处方〕多少随便 (= as much as you wish).
qy. = query.

R

R, r [ɑː] *(pl. R's, r's* [ɑːz]) ①英语字母表第十八字母. ②〔R〕R字形(之物). ③〔R〕中世纪罗马数字的 80. ④〔R〕〔美〕(电影)需成年人带领入场〔17 岁以下青少年不能单独观看〕,R级(= restricted). R̄ = 80,000. *the 'r' [R] months* 九月到四月〔牡蛎当令的季节,月名都含有 r 字〕. *the three R's* (作为初等教育基础的) 读写算〔reading, writing, arithmetic〕.

R = ①〔L.〕recipe【处方】取. ②radical. ③Reaumur. ④〔L.〕*Rex, Regina*. ⑤radius. ⑥ratio. ⑦resistance. ⑧retree. ⑨roentgen. ⑩range. ⑪registered. ⑫rifle. ⑬regulating.

R. = ①Royal. ②Republic; Republican. ③range. ④radio. ⑤ratio. ⑥resistance. ⑦rabbi. ⑧retarder. ⑨〔L.〕*Rex, Regina*.

r = ①refrigerator. ②rod.

r. = ①railway, railroad. ②right. ③river. ④road. ⑤r(o)uble. ⑥rupee. ⑦rare. ⑧residence. ⑨retired. ⑩rubber. ⑪rabbi. ⑫rood. ⑬runs.

R.A., RA = ①rear admiral 海军少将. ②Regular Army〔美〕正规陆军. ③regular army 常备军,正规军. ④Royal Academecian〔英〕皇家艺术学会会员. ⑤Royal Academy〔英〕皇家艺术学会. ⑥Royal Artillery〔英〕皇家陆军炮兵. ⑦right ascension【天】赤经.

R/A = refer to acceptor【商】询问承兑人.

Ra¹ [rɑː] *n.*【埃神】太阳神.

Ra² = radium【化】镭.

r.a. = radioactive 放射性的.

Ra A = radium A〔即 Po^{218}〕.

R.A.A.F., RAAF = Royal Australian Air Force (皇家)澳大利亚空军.

Ra-B = radium-B【化】镭 B.

Ra·bat [rəˈbɑːt] *n.* 拉巴特〔摩洛哥首都〕.

ra·bat [ˈræbət, rəˈbæt] *n.* (有些牧师服用的,长及前胸,内衬牧师白领的)黑色短披肩.

ra·ba·to [rəˈbeitəu, -ˈbɑːt-] *n. (pl. -tos)* 披肩领子;(细麻布或花边织物)大衬领〔翻下遮住前胸及肩背,流行于十六、十七世纪〕.

rab·bet [ˈræbit] *n.* (木板的)凸凹,槽口;半边槽,半槽[企口]接合〔使榫舌与槽口密接〕. — *vt.* 在…挖槽口;嵌接 — *vi.* 半槽接合 *(on, over)*. ~ **joint** 半槽[企口]接合.

rab·bi, [ˈræbai], **rab·bin** [ˈræbin] *n.* ①犹太法学博士. ②先生, 老师〔犹太人尊称用语〕. ③犹太教教士. *the rabbins* 2—13 世纪的犹太法学家们.

rab·bin·ate [ˈræbinit] *n.* 犹太法学博士[犹太教教士]的身分[职位];〔集合词〕犹太法学博士们;犹太教教士们.

rab·bin·ic(al) [ˈræbinik(əl)] *a.* 犹太法学博士[犹太教教士]的, 犹太法学博士式的; 犹太法学博士的语风的. *rabbinical literature* 犹太教法典 (Talmud) 之后的希伯来文学.

rab·bin·ism [ˈræbinizəm] *n.* 犹太法学博士的学说;犹太法学博士的语风;死钻牛角尖的学风.

rab·bin·ist, rab·bin·ite [ˈræbinist, -ait] *n.* 信奉犹太法学博士学说者;犹太教旧教徒.

rab·bit¹ [ˈræbit] *n.* ①兔,家兔;野兔;兔皮. ②胆小的人,懦夫. ③〔英口〕笨拙的球员. ④【军】由工厂中偷出来的东西. *breed like ~s* 象兔子一样多生孩子. *dead ~* 没价值的东西. *like ~s in a warren* (居民) 稠密,拥挤不堪. *run like a ~* 一溜烟地跑掉. — *vt.* 打兔子,猎兔. — *vi.* 兔子似地聚拢 *(together)*: *go ~ing* 去打兔子. ~ **burrow** 野兔穴. ~ **ears** ①【电视】兔耳形〔室内 V 形〕天线. ②〔美〕(运动员)对场外观众嘲讽的敏感. ~ **fever**【医】兔热病. ~ **fish** 河豚. ~ **food**〔美俚〕生菜; 凉拌菜. ~ **heart**〔美〕懦夫. ~ **hutch** 兔棚. ~ **punch**〔美拳〕向颈背猛打的一拳. ~ **('s) foot**〔美〕(迷信者认为有护符作用,会带来好运的)兔子后足. ~ **twister**〔美〕乡下佬. ~ **warren** 养兔场. **-er** *n.* 捕兔者.

rab·bit² [ˈræbit] *vt.*〔卑〕〔常用命令语气〕咒骂, 诅咒. *Odd ~ it!* = *'Od ~ 'em!* 讨厌! 讨厌的家伙!

rab·bit·ry [ˈræbitri] *n.* 兔群;养兔业.

rab·bit·y [ˈræbiti] *a.* 象兔子一般的;多兔子的.

rab·ble¹ [ˈræbl] *n.* ①临时聚集起来的人,乌合之众,暴民. ②〔the ~〕〔蔑〕低级阶层,贱民. ③(动物等的)一群;(东西)混乱的一堆. *a ~ of books* 一堆乱书. — *vt.* 聚众袭击[暴动].

rab·ble² [ˈræbl] *n.*【冶】(制铁用)搅拌棒;【矿】(长柄)耙. — *vt.* (用拨火棒)搅拌.

rab·ble³ [ˈræbl]〔英方〕*vt., vi.* 急促地说[读],絮絮地说 *(forth; off; out; over)*.

rab·ble·ment [ˈræblmənt] *n.* 一群临时聚集成的人群;喧扰,暴动.

rab·ble-rous·er [ˈræblˌrauzə] *n.* (暴乱、暴动等的)煽动者,蛊惑民心的政客. **-rous·ing** *a., n.*

Rab·e·lais [ˈræbəlei], **François** 拉伯雷〔1490—1533,法国讽刺作家〕.

Rab·e·lai·si·an, Rab·e·lae·si·an [ˌræbəˈleiziən] *a.* (法国讽刺滑稽作家)拉伯雷式的;粗野的. — *n.* 拉伯雷崇拜者[模仿者、研究者].

rab·id [ˈræbid] *a.* ①狂怒的,狂暴的,疯狂的;过激的,激烈的,狂热的. ②恐水病的,患狂犬病的. ~ *hate* 愤恨. *a ~ dog* 疯狗. **-ly** *ad.*

ra·bid·i·ty, rab·id·ness [rəˈbiditi, ˈræbidnis] *n.* ①猛烈;蛮横,不讲理,顽固. ②患狂犬病;疯狂.

ra·bi·es [ˈreibiːz, ˈræ-] *n.*【医】狂犬病.

Ra-C = radium C;【化】镭 C.

R.A.C., RAC = ①Royal Armoured Corps〔英〕皇家装甲兵. ②Royal Automobile Club〔英〕皇家汽车俱乐部.

rac·coon [rəˈkuːn] *n.* = racoon.

race¹ [reis] *n.* ①竞赛;赛跑;赛艇;赛马;〔*pl.*〕赛马会,跑马会;竞赛;疾走. ②路程,行程;经历,人生路程,一辈子,(日、月的)运行;时间的经过. ③急流,急潮;小海峡. ④(水车等的)沟,水道;(织机的)梭道,走梭板;【机】轴承套,夹圈;座圈;【空】螺桨滑流,激流. *a rat ~* 激烈的竞争. *go to the ~s* 看赛马去. *an armament ~* 扩军竞赛. *consolation ~*【体】安慰赛. *His ~ is nearly run* 他的一生快完了. *open ~* 自由参加的赛跑. *play the ~s*〔美〕赌赛马. *ride a ~* 举行赛马,出场赛马. *row a ~* 划船比赛. *run a ~* 赛跑. *sail a ~* 帆船竞赛. *selling ~* 拍卖胜马的赛马. *with a strong ~* 凶猛地, 猛烈地. — *vi.* ①赛跑, 竞走;竞赛 *(with)*;疾走;以赛马为业. ②(螺旋桨、马达等)空转. — *vt.* ①使拼命跑;使赛跑. ②努力想跑过…,和…赛跑. ③为赛马

R

输光(财产) *(away)*; 使(马达等)空转. ~ *the bill through the House* 使议案匆匆[迅速]通过. ~ *against* 和…赛跑,和…竞赛. ~ **about** (比赛用的)快艇,跑车. ~ **ball** 赛马会附带举行的跳舞会. ~**card** 赛马次序表. ~**course** ①〔英〕跑马场,赛马场;赛船水道. ②(水车的)沟. ~ **cup** 奖杯,优胜杯. ~ **glass** (看赛马用的)小型望远镜. ~ **ground** 赛马场;赛跑场. ~ **horse** 赛马的马;【鸟】河鸭;【虫】螳螂(*a ~ horse bill* 〔美〕开给来兑款支票的支票). ~ **meeting** 赛马会;赛跑会. ~ **rotation**【机】空转. ~ **track**【体育】跑道. ~**-way** (矿山等的)导水路,(水车的)水道;电线保护管.

race[2] [reis] *n.* ①人种;种族,民族. ②氏族,家族,家系,系统;门第. ③种类,…们;阶层;〔诗〕子孙,后裔. ④(生物的)类;人类;【动、植】属,种类. ⑤人种的特性;(文体等的)特征;(酒的)特殊风味. *the Jewish ~* 犹太人种. *the white ~* 白(色人)种. *the ~ of poets* 诗人们. *the feathered [finny] ~* 鸟[鱼]类. *The wine has a certain ~.* 这个酒有一种特殊风味. — *a.* 人种的,种族的. *a ~ prejudice* 种族偏见. *the ~ problem* 人种[种族]问题〔美国尤指黑人的问题〕. *a ~ riot* 因种族歧视引起的暴动. ~ **suicide** 种族自杀〔把出生率控制过低而引起某一种族的逐渐消亡〕.

race[3] [reis] *n.* (生姜等的)根.

ra·ce·mate [reiˈsiːmeit, rə-] *n.*【化】外消旋盐,外消旋酒石酸盐.

ra·ceme [rəˈsiːm] *n.*【植】总状花序;【化】外消旋体[物].

ra·ce·mic [rəˈsiːmik] *a.*【化】外消旋的,消旋的;得自葡萄的. ~ **acid**【化】外消旋酸;外消旋酒石酸. ~ **compound**【化】外消旋化合物.

rac·e·mism [ˈræsimizəm, reiˈsiːmizəm] *n.* ①【化】(外)消旋性. ② = racemization.

rac·e·mi·za·tion [ˌræsimiˈzeiʃən] *n.*【化】(外)消旋(作用).

rac·e·mose, rac·e·mous [ˈræsiməus, -məs] *a.*【植】总状的;【解】葡萄状的.

rac·er [ˈreisə] *n.* ①赛跑者;疾走者;赛马者,比赛用快艇,比赛用自行车(等). ②【动】(美洲)黑蛇. ④【军】火炮转台.

race·run·ner [ˈreisrʌnə] *n.*【动】鞭尾蜥 *(Cnemidophorus sexlineatus)*〔主要发现于南美洲和北美洲〕.

Ra·chel [ˈreitʃəl] *n.* ①雷切尔〔女子名〕. ②【圣】拉结〔雅各(Jacob)的妻子〕. ③〔美〕(女)犹太人.

ra·chet = ratchet.

ra·chil·la [rəˈkilə] *n.* *(pl.* **-lae** [-iː]*)*【植】小穗轴;小花轴.

ra·chis [ˈreikis] *n.* *(pl.* ~**es** [ˈreikisiz], ***ra·chi·des*** [ˈreikidiːz]*)*【解】脊椎,脊柱;【植】花序轴,叶轴;【动】羽轴;分脊.

ra·chi·tis [ræˈkaitis] *n.*【医】佝偻病,脊柱炎;【植】萎缩病.

ra·cial [ˈreiʃəl] *a.* 人种(上)的,种族的;种族间的. ~ *antipathies [characteristics, prejudice]* 种族反感[特质,偏见]. **-ly** *ad.*

rac·i·ly [ˈreisili] *ad.* ①保持原味地. ②活泼地. ③爽脆,干脆,痛快;尖锐泼辣地. ④〔美〕近乎淫猥地.

Racine [raˈsiːn], **Jean Baptiste** 莱辛〔1639—1699,法国剧作家〕.

rac·i·ness [ˈreisinis] *n.* ①保持原味. ②活泼,有趣. ③爽气,痛快;尖锐泼辣. ④挑逗性.

rac·ing [ˈreisiŋ] *n.* 竞赛;赛跑;赛马;赛艇;【机】空转. *a ~man* 赛马狂. *the ~ world* 赛马界. *a ~ boat* 竞赛用艇. *a ~ cup* 奖杯. ~ **colours** (赛马)骑师(衣服)的颜色. ~ **form**〔美俚〕赛马消息. ~ **track**【体】滑冰比赛场.

ra·cism [ˈreisizəm] *n.* ①种族主义. ②种族歧视[隔离、迫害].

ra·cist [ˈreisist] *n.* 种族主义者. — *a.* 种族主义的;种族歧视[隔离、迫害]的.

rack[1] [ræk] *n.* ①(火车等的)行李(网)架;各种搁架[枪架、帽架、笔架等];工具架;【海】结绳架;【军】(飞机的)炸弹架;【海】餐具架;防止转动架;【机】齿条,齿轨;饲草架,马槽. ②(从前拉脱犯人四肢关节的)拉肢拷问台,拉肢刑架;拷问;(精神上或肉体上的)巨大痛苦. *a clothes ~* 衣架. *a torpedo net ~* 鱼雷防御网. *a launching ~*【火箭】发射导轨. *an underwing ~*【火箭】翼下发射导轨. ***by ~ of eye*** 依据目测估量,照估计. ***come [stand up] to the [one's] ~*** 听天由命. ***in a high ~*** 在高位. ***live at ~ and manger*** 过豪华[富裕]生活. ***off the ~*** (衣服)做好了的,现成的. ***on the ~*** 正在受拷问;忧虑,害怕(*My ingenuity is on the ~ to find a good excuse.* 我正在绞尽脑汁找借口). ***put sth. on the ~*** 使极度紧张;使受到严格考验. ***put sb. to [on] the ~*** 对…加以拷问. — *vt.* ①对(犯人)拉肢拷问;扭伤. ②使过分紧张,使苦痛,折磨. ③剥削,榨取(佃户);使(地力)变瘦. ④把…做成架子. ⑤把…搁在架子[台子]上;把(马)拴在马槽上. *a cough that ~s one's whole body* 仿佛要扯碎全身的激烈的咳嗽. *a ~ing headache* 要爆烈似的头痛. ***be ~ed with pain*** 苦痛不堪. ***~ one's brains*** 绞尽脑汁,费尽心机. ***~ rent from sb.*** 勒索过高地租剥削某人. ~ ***up*** ①获得(胜利);得(比分)(*~ up 20 points in the first half* 前半场得20分. *~ up a victory* 获得胜利). ②彻底击败. ③把马拴[系]起来喂草料. ~ **car**【铁路】多层平板车皮〔运输汽车用〕. ~ **rail** 齿. ~ **railway**〔美〕~ **railroad** 齿轨铁路. ~**-rent** *vt.* ①收取(盘剥性地租[租金]). ②盘剥性地租,额外地租. ~**-renter** 收取[支付]高额租金的人. ~ **wheel** 大齿轮.

rack[2] [ræk] *n.*〔古〕破坏,荒废. ***go to ~ and ruin [manger]*** 走向毁灭[荒废](= wrack).

rack[3] [ræk] *n.*〔古〕(一片)浮云. — *vi.* (云)随风飘动.

rack[4] [ræk] *n.* (马的)轻跑,小步跑. — *vi.* (马)轻跑.

rack[5] [ræk] *vt.* 把(酒糟中的酒)榨出 *(off)*;(将酒)装成瓶.

rack[6] [ræk] *n.* = arrack.

rack·a·bones [ˈrækəbəunz] *n. pl.*〔用作单数〕〔美〕骨瘦如柴的人[动物].

rack·et[1], **rac·quet** [ˈrækit] *n.* ①(网球等的)球拍. ②〔*pl.*〕〔作单数用〕(四周有围墙的)拍打回力网球. ③球拍形雪鞋;(走泥地时用的)马穿的木鞋. *a ~ swinger*〔美〕网球选手. — *vt.* 用球拍打.

rack·et[2] [ˈrækit] *n.* ①喧骚,吵闹,嚷闹;扰嚷;喧骚嘈杂的集会;狂欢. ②考验,困难的立场[经验],辛酸经历. ③〔俚〕行业,职业,工作;事情. ④〔美俚〕勒索金钱,讹诈,敲诈,骗局. *the publishing ~* 出版业. *What's his ~?* 他做什么工作? *What's your ~?* 请问贵干? *What's the ~?* 甚么事? 怎么啦? *It isn't my ~.* 这不关我事. ***give away the ~*** 没提防把秘密泄漏出去. ***go on a ~*** 纵情欢闹. ***kick up a ~ = make a ~*** 惹乱子,大吵大闹. ***stand the ~ of*** 经受得住考验;负责;偿付[承担]费用. — *vi.* 嚷闹,吵闹;纵情欢闹.

rack·et·eer [ˌrækiˈtiə] *n.*〔美俚〕讹诈钱财的歹徒. — *vi.* 勒索金钱,恐吓,讹诈.

rack·et·y [ˈrækiti] *a.* ①喧闹的;放荡的;寻欢作乐的. ②摇晃的;不可靠的.

rack·ing [ˈrækiŋ] *a.* 拷问的;折磨人的,难忍受的. *a ~ pain* 难以忍受的痛苦.

rack·le [ˈrækl] *a.*〔Scot.〕①不受管束的,刚愎的;任性的,鲁莽的,激烈的. ②精力旺盛的,强健的.

ra·con [ˈreikən] *n.*【无】雷达信标 (= radar beacon).

rac·on·teur [rækɔnˈtəː] *n.*〔F.〕善于讲轶事[故事]的人;爱说话的人,健谈家;说书的.

ra·coon [rəˈkuːn] *n.*【动】浣熊;浣熊毛皮. ~ **dog**【动】貉.

rac·quet [ˈrækit] *n.* = racket[1].

rac·quet·eer [ˌrækiˈtiːə] *n.* 〔美俚〕网球选手.

rac·y [ˈreisi] *a.* ①保持原味的,有风味的,芳醇的,芬芳的;新鲜的;道地的. ②爽气的,痛快的;泼辣的. ③〔美〕猥亵的. ~ *of the soil* 有道地风味的;干脆的,直截了当的;生动活泼的;刺激的. **-i·ly** *ad.* **-i·ness** *n.*

Ra-D = radium-D【化】镭 D.

Rad., rad. = radical; radio.

rad. = 〔L.〕 *radix*【植】根.

rad [ræd] *n.*【物】拉德〔吸收辐射剂量单位〕.

ra·da·me·ter [ˈreidɑːmiːtə] *n.* 防撞雷达设备[装置].

ra·dar [ˈreidə] *n.* 〔美〕【无】〔radio detecting and ranging 之略〕雷达,无线电探测器 (= 〔英〕 radiolocator). *air search* ~ 防空[空中搜索]雷达. *air surface vessel* ~ 飞机用水面舰船搜索雷达. *beam-transmitter* ~ 定向瞄准雷达. *missile* ~ 弹载雷达;跟踪导弹的雷达. *long-range* ~ 远程雷达. ~ *control* 雷达控制. ~ *installation* 雷达装置. *laser* ~ 激光雷达. *a* ~ *set* 雷达装置. ★ radar 是不可数名词. ~ **beacon** 雷达信标. ~ **fence** 雷达警戒网. ~**-homer** 自动瞄准[导航]雷达弹头;自动瞄准雷达. ~**man** 雷达员. ~ **picket** 装有雷达设备的警戒船或飞机. ~**scope** 雷达显示[示波]器. ~ **screen** 雷达荧光屏. ~**-tracking** *a.* 雷达追踪的.

Rad·cliffe [ˈrædklif] *n.* 拉德克利夫〔姓氏〕.

RADCM = radar countermeasures 反雷达措施.

rad·dle[1] [ˈrædl] *n.*【矿】代赭石. — *vt.* 用赭石、胭脂等涂(= ruddle).

rad·dle[2] [ˈrædl] *vt.* 编织;交织.

ra·di·ac [ˈreidiək] *n.* 辐射计. ~ **meter** 辐射剂量计.

ra·dial [ˈreidjəl] *a.* ①光线的;光线状的. ②放射的,辐射(状)的. ③镭的. ④【数】半径的;【物】径向的;【解】桡骨的;【植】射出花的,射出状的. — *n.* ①放射部. ②桡骨神经[动脉]. ③子午线轮胎. ~ **arrangement**【植】间隔排列. ~ **axle** 转向轴. ~ **drill** 旋臂钻床. ~ **engine** 星形发动机. ~ **flux**【物】辐射通量. ~ **heating** 辐射能热. ~ **motion** 径向运动. ~ **(ply) tire** 放射状轮胎. ~ **velocity** 径向速度;【天】视线速度. **-ly** *ad.*

ra·di·al·ized [ˈreidiəlaizd] *a.* 放射(状)的.

ra·di·an [ˈreidjən] *n.*【数】弧度.

ra·di·ance, ra·di·an·cy [ˈreidjəns, -si] *n.* 发光,光辉;(眼睛或脸色的)光彩;辐射;照射(作用).

ra·diant [ˈreidjənt] *a.* ①发光的,放热的. ②放射的,辐射的;【动、植】辐射形的. ③照耀的,辉煌的,灿烂的;满面春风的,容光焕发的;极漂亮的. — *n.* 光源,光点;光体;【天】(流星的)辐射点. ~ *energy* [*heat*] 辐射能[热]. ~ *ray* 辐射线. *the* ~ *sun* 耀眼的太阳. *a* ~ *smile* 满脸微笑. ~ *with joy* 喜形于色. **-ly** *ad.*

ra·di·ate [ˈreidieit] *vi.* ①发光;辐射;射出,发散;放热. ②向周围扩展. — *vt.* ①辐状射出,辐射,放射,发散. ②使向周围扩展. — [ˈreidiit] *a.* 射出的,辐射状的;【动、植】辐射形的.

ra·di·a·tion [ˌreidiˈeiʃən] *n.* ①发光,射光,放热;放射,发射. ②【物】辐射;放射物;幅射线[热、能];照射(作用). ③【动、植】辐射形;【测】射出测量法;【医】射线疗法. *direct* [*indirect*] ~ 直接[间接]放热. *electromagnetic* ~ 电磁辐射. *solar* [*terrestrial*] ~ 太阳[地球]放射热. ~**-meter** 伦琴计, X 射线计. ~**-proof** *a.* 防辐射的. ~**-sickness** 辐射病,射线中毒. ~**-sterilized** *a.* 辐射消毒的. ~**-thermometer** 辐射计.

ra·di·a·tive [ˈreidieitiv] *a.* ①发光的,放热的;放射的,发射的. ②【物】辐射性的.

ra·di·a·tor [ˈreidieitə] *n.* ①辐射体,辐射器,放热物. ②散热器;暖气管;(汽车引擎的)水箱,冷却器;【电】辐射暖房装置;【无】发射天线. *an electric* ~ 电热器. *a full* ~ 黑体,全辐射体. *a spherical* ~ 全向辐射器. *an active* [*reactive*] ~ 有源[无源]辐射器.

rad·i·cal [ˈrædikəl] *a.* ①基本的,根本的;固有的,本来的;重要的,主要的;最初的;彻底的. ②〔常 R-〕激进的,急进的;过激的,极端的. ③【植】根生的;【化】基的,原子团的;【语】根词的;语根的;【数】根的;【乐】根音的. — *n.* ①激进分子,激进主义者;〔R-〕激进党派成员. ②【语】词根;词干;(中国字的)偏旁,部首;【化】根,基,原子团;【数】根数;根号;【乐】根音. *a* ~ *principle* 基本原理. ~ *defects* 生来的缺点. *a* ~ *treatment* 彻底疗法,根治法. ~ *measures* 激烈手段. *a R- party* 激进派. ~ *growths* [*hairs, leaves*] 根生物[根生毛,根生叶]. ~ **centre**【数】等幂心,根轴心. ~ **chic**〔美俚〕(时髦人物)与激进派交往的风尚. ~ **sign**【数】根号. ~ **word**【语】根词. **-ism** 激进主义. **-i·za·tion** [ˌrædikəlaiˈzeiʃən] *n.* 激进. **-ize** *vt., vi.* 使激进,变激进,相信激进主义,成为激进主义者. **-ly** *ad.*

rad·i·cand [ˈrædikænd] *n.*【数】被开方数.

rad·i·cle [ˈrædikl] *n.*【古生】胚根;【化】基;根.

ra·dii [ˈreidiai] *n.* ①radius 的复数. ②辐管;辐部.

ra·dio [ˈreidiəu] *n.* ①无线电讯[电报,电话];无线电,射电. ②无线电广播;无线电(广播)台. ③收音机. *listen (in) to the* ~ 听无线电. ~ *message* 无线电通讯. — *vt., vi.* 用无线电传送[广播],(向…)作无线电广播[传送];用 X 射线拍照;用镭医治. ~ **actor** 广播剧演员. ~**amplifier** 无线电高频放大器. ~ **apparatus** 无线电报[电话]机. ~ **astronomy**【天】射电天文学. ~**autogram** *n.* 无线电传真. ~ **beacon** 无线电航空信标. ~ **beam** 无线电射束. ~**-bearing** 无线电定向[方位]. ~**broadcast** *vi., vt.*【无】(对…)作广播. ~**-broadcaster** 无线电广播员;无线电广播机. ~**broadcasting** 无线电广播 (~*broadcasting station* 广播电台). ~**cast** *vt.* = radiobroadcast. ~ **channel** 无线电波道,射电波道. **R- City**〔美〕纽约市洛克菲勒中心娱乐地区. ~ **communication** 无线电(通)讯,射电通讯. ~ **compass** 无线电罗盘. ~ **compass station** 无线电方位信标站. ~**-controlled** *a.* 无线电控制[操纵]的. ~**detector**【无】无线电探测器,雷达. ~ **direction finder** 无线电探向器. ~**electronics** 无线电电子学. ~ **facsimile** 无线电传真. ~**fication** 无线电化. ~ **field**【无】射电场,无线电场. ~ **frequency**【无】射(电)频(率). ~**goniometer** 无线电测向计,无线电罗盘,无线电方位计. ~ **goniometric station** 无线电测向所. ~**gram** 无线电报;射线照片;〔口〕= radio-gramophone;〔英〕= X-ray, ~**gramophone** 收音、电唱两用机. ~ **intercepts** 无线电情报侦译术. ~ **interference** 无线电干扰. ~**ite**〔美〕无线电广播员. ~ **knife**【医】高频手术刀. ~**-location** 无线电定位(法). ~**locator**〔英〕= radar. ~**man** 无线电员[兵]. ~ **merits** 无线电话的质量. ~ **metal** 无线电高导磁性合金. ~**meteorograph** 无线电气象自记器. ~**meteorography** 无线电气象自记法. ~**moppet**〔美〕电台儿童演员. ~**news** 广播新闻. ~ **operator** 无线电报员. ~**page** *vt.*〔美〕用无线电找(人). ~ **parts** 无线电零件. **R- Beijing** 北京电台. ~**phone** 无线电话(机). ~ **phonograph** 收音电唱两用机. ~**photo,** ~**photograph** 无线电传真照片. ~**photography** 无线电传真(术). ~ **play** 广播剧. ~**press** 广播报. ~**quiet** *a.* 不产生无线电干扰的. ~ **range** 无线电轨[信标],射电轨;无线电航向信标,等信号区无线电信标;无线电测得距离. ~ **range beacon** 航线无线电指标. ~ **receiver** =~-receiving set 无线电接收机. ~ **service code** 无线电电码. ~ **set** 无线电接收[发报]机. ~**sonde** = radiometeorograph. ~ **spectrum**【无】射频频谱. ~**stat** 中放晶体滤波式超外差接收机. ~ **station** 无线电台,广播电台. ~ **studio** 无线电播音室. ~**telegram** 无线电报. ~**telegraph** *n., vt., vi.* 无线电报(机). *v.* 向…发无线电报. ~**telegraphic** *a.* 无线电报(术)的,用在无线电报上的. ~**telegraphy** 无线电报(术). ~ **telemetric** *a.* 无线电遥测的. ~ **telemetry** 无线电遥测学. ~**telephone** *n., vt., vi.* 无线电话(机);打无线电话. ~**telephony** 无线电话(术). ~

telescope【天】射电望远镜. ~**teletype (writer)** 无线电电传打字电报机［设备］. ~**television** 无线电电视. ~**transparent** *a.* 在 X 光照射中不显影的,容许射线通过的. ~ **tube** 无线电真空管.

ra·di·o- [ˈreidiəu] *comb. f.* ①放射;辐射. ②光线. ③半径. ④桡骨. ⑤镭. ⑥无线电.

ra·di·o·ac·tin·i·um [ˈreidiəuækˈtiniəm] *n.*【化】射锕〔略 Rd Ac; 即钍[227]〕.

ra·di·o·ac·ti·vate [ˈreidiəuˈæktiveit] *vt.* 使带放射性.

ra·di·o·ac·tive [ˈreidiəuˈæktiv] *a.*【物】放射性(引起)的. ~ **dating**【地】放射衰变年代鉴定. ~ **decay** 放射衰变. ~ **dust** 放射性尘埃. ~ **fallout** 放射性微粒回降. ~ **isotop** 放射性同位素. ~ **series** 放射系列. **-ac·tiv·i·ty** *n.* [-ækˈtiviti] 放射性;放射(现象).

ra·di·o·as·say [ˈreidiəuəˈsei] *n.* 放射性测量.

ra·di·o·au·to·gram [ˈreidiəuˈɔːtəgræm] *n.* (= radio-autograph).

ra·di·o·au·to·graph [reidiəuˈɔːtəˌgrɑːf, -græf] *n.*【原】放射自显照相［相片］,自动射线照相,射线显迹图(=autoradiograph). **-ic** *a.* **-y** [-ɔːˈtɔgrəfi] *n.* 放射自显照相术,自动射线照相术.

ra·di·o·bi·ol·o·gy [ˈreidiəubaiˈɔlədʒi] *n.* 放射生物学.

ra·di·o·car·bon [ˈreidiəuˈkɑːbən] *n.*【化】放射性碳.

ra·di·o·car·di·o·gram [ˈreidiəuˈkɑːdiəgræm] *n.*【医】放射能心电图.

ra·di·o·car·di·og·ra·phy [ˈreidiəuˌkɑːdiˈɔgrəfi] *n.*【医】放射能心电图测定.

ra·di·o·ce·ram·ic [ˈreidiəusiˈræmik] *n.* 高频瓷.

ra·di·o·chem·is·try [ˈreidiəuˈkemistri] *n.*【化】放射化学.

ra·di·o·el·e·ment [ˈreidiəuˈelimənt] *n.*【化】放射性元素.

ra·di·o·ge·net·ics [ˈreidiəudʒiˈnetiks] *n.* 放射遗传学.

ra·di·o·gen·ic [ˈreidiəuˈdʒenik] *a.* ①【原】放射［辐射］产生的. ②适合于广播的.

ra·di·o·gram [ˌreidiəuˈgræm] *n.* ①无线电报. ②【物】射线照片;收音电唱两用机.

ra·di·o·graph [ˈreidiəugrɑːf] *n.* 射线照片,X 光照片. — *vt.* 给…拍摄射线照片. **-ic** [-ˈgræfik] *a.* **-y** *n.* 射线［X 光］照相术.

ra·di·o·heat·ing [ˈreidiəuˈhiːtiŋ] *n.* 射频加热.

ra·di·o·i·so·tope [ˈreidiəuˈaisətəup] *n.*【原】放射性同位素. **-i·so·top·ic** [ˌreidiəuˌaisəˈtɔpik] *a.*

ra·di·o·la·bel(l)ed [ˈreidiəuˈleibld] *a.*【原】放射性同位素示踪［标记］的.

ra·di·o·lar·i·an [ˌreidiəuˈlɛəriən] *n.*【动】放射目 *(Radiolaria)*〔一种深海单细胞动物〕.

ra·di·o·lo·ca·tion [ˈreidiəuləuˈkeiʃən] *n.* ①无线电定位. ②= radar.

ra·di·ol·o·gy [ˌreidiˈɔlədʒi] *n.*【物】放射学,辐射学;X 线学;【医】放射科,X 线科. **-o·gist** *n.* 放射线学家;【医】放射科医师.

ra·di·o·lu·cent [ˈreidiəuˈluːsnt] *a.* 射线可透射的. **-cenc·y** *n.*

ra·di·o·lu·mi·nes·cence [ˈreidiəuˌljuːmiˈnesns] *n.* 射线［辐射］发光(现象).

ra·di·ol·y·sis [ˌreidiˈɔlisis] *n.*【化】辐射分解,放射性分解,射解作用. **-o·lyt·ic** [-əˈlitik] *a.*

ra·di·om·e·ter [ˌreidiˈɔmitə] *n.*【物】辐射计;放射量测定器;射线检查器.

ra·di·o·mi·crom·e·ter [ˈreidiəumaiˈkrɔmitə] *n.* 辐射微热计.

ra·di·o·mi·met·ic [ˌreidiəumiˈmetik] *a.* 模拟辐射的〔引起与辐照相同作用的〕.

ra·di·on [ˈreidiɔn] *n.*【物】(放)射(微)粒.

ra·di·on·ics [ˌreidiˈɔniks] *n.* 射电电子学;电子管学.

ra·di·o·nu·clide [ˌreidiəuˈnjuːklaid, -ˈnuː-] *n.*【化】放射性核素.

ra·di·o·nym [ˈreidiəunim] *n.*〔美〕无线电民用波段者的绰号.

ra·di·o·paque [ˌreidiəuˈpeik] *a.* (X 线、γ 线等)射线［辐射］透不过的 (= radio-opaque). **-pac·i·ty** [-ˈpæsiti] *n.*

ra·di·o·phare [ˈreidiəufɛə] *n.* ①与船舶通信的无线电台. ②无线电信标. ③雷达探照灯.

ra·di·o·phar·ma·ceu·ti·cal [ˌreidiəuˌfɑːməˈsjuːtik, -ˈsuːt-] *n.*【医】放射性药品,放射性药剂.

ra·di·o·scope [ˈreidiəuskəup] *n.* 放射镜;剂量测定验电器.

ra·di·os·copy [reidiˈɔskəpi] *n.* 放射性试验［检查］;X 光线透视检查法.

ra·di·o·sen·si·tive [ˌreidiəuˈsensitiv] *a.*【医】对辐射敏感的;可被射线杀死［摧毁］的. **-tiv·i·ty** *n.*

ra·di·o·stron·ti·um [ˌreidiəuˈstrɔnʃiən, -tiəm] *n.*【化】放射性锶.

ra·di·o·tel·e·type, ra·di·o·tel·e·type·writ·er [ˌreidiəuˈtelitaip, -raitə] *n.* 无线电电传打字电报机;无线电电传打字电报设备.

ra·di·o·tel·lu·ri·um [ˈreidiəuteˈljuəriəm] *n.*【化】射碲.

ra·di·o·thal·li·um [ˈreidiəuˈθæliəm] *n.*【化】射铊.

ra·di·o·ther·a·peu·tics [ˈreidiəuˌθerəˈpjuːtiks] *n.*【医】放射疗法［治疗］;镭锭［X 线］治疗(科).

ra·di·o·ther·a·py [ˈreidiəuˈθerəpi] *n.* = radiotherapeutics. **-a·pist** *n.* 放射科医师.

ra·di·o·ther·my [ˈreidiəuˈθəːmi] *n.*【医】热放射疗法.

ra·di·o·tho·ri·um [ˈreidiəuˈθɔːriəm] *n.*【化】(放)射(性)钍.

ra·di·o·vi·sion [ˈreidiəuviʒən]〔废〕电视 (= television).

rad·ish [ˈrædiʃ] *n.*【植】小红萝卜(属). *horse* ~ 辣根. *pickled* ~ 盐渍萝卜,萝卜泡菜.

ra·dium [ˈreidjəm] *n.*【化】镭. ~ **emanation** 镭(放)射气,氡(= rodon).

ra·di·um·ther·a·py [ˈreidjəmˈθerəpi] *n.*【医】镭疗法;放射疗法.

ra·di·us [ˈreidjəs] *n.* *(pl.* ***ra·di·i*** [-ai]*)* ①半径;半径范围. ②【解】桡骨. ③(车轮的)辐;【物】辐射线;【无】径向射线;辐射物;(六分仪等的)针;【纺】杼. ④【植】射出花. *within a ~ of three miles* 在周围三英里以内. *the flying ~* 飞行半径;(加一次油的)飞行距离. *a ~ of action*【军】行动［活动］半径［所及范围］;航程;续航距离;续航力. ~ *of convergence*【数】收敛半径. ~ *of curvature*【数】曲率半径 ~ **vector**【数、物】矢径,辐;位置矢量.

ra·dix [ˈreidiks] *n.* *(pl.* ***-es*** *or* ***rad·i·ces*** [-disiːz]*)* ①根本. ②【数】基数;根值;记数根;【植】根;【语】词根.

ra·dome [ˈreidəum] *n.*【无】雷达天线罩;整流罩.

ra·don [ˈreidɔn] *n.*【化】氡〔由镭裂变后生成的放射性元素,旧名 radium emanation〕.

rad·u·la [ˈrædʒulə] *n.* *(pl.* ***-lae*** [-liː]*)*【动】齿舌. **-lar** *a.*

ra·dux [ˈreidʌks] *n.* ①【数】计数制的基数. ②【空】远距双曲线低频导航系统.

RAE; R.A.E. = Royal Aircraft Establishment〔英〕皇家航空研究所.

Rae [rei] *n.* 雷〔姓氏,女子名, Rachel 的昵称〕.

Ra-F = radium-F【化】镭 F.

R.A.F., RAF = Royal Air Force〔英〕皇家空军.

Ra·fael, Raph·a·el [ˈræfeiəl] *n.* 拉斐尔〔男子名〕.

ra·fale [ræˈfɑːl] *n.*〔F.〕【军】(排炮的)迅猛射击.

raff [ræf] *n.* ①社会底层的人(们). ②〔方〕大量,大批,许多. ③垃圾,废料.

raf·fi·a [ˈræfiə] *n.* ①【植】(马达加斯加)酒椰树 *(Raphia ruffia)*. ②酒椰叶的纤维;酒椰纤维帽. ~ **palm** = raffia①.

raf·fi·nate [ˈræfineit] *n.* (石油)(提炼过程中的)残油液.

raf·fi·nose [ˈræfinəus] *n.* (由甜菜根，棉子等提炼的)棉白糖.

raff·ish [ˈræfiʃ] *a.* ①放荡的，颓废的；声名狼藉的. ②粗俗的；艳丽而俗气的.

raf·fle[1] [ˈræfl] *n.* (义卖)抽彩出售. —*vi.* 加入抽彩. ~ *for an auto* 抽彩买汽车. — *vt.* 用抽彩办法出售(商品等) (*off*). ~ *off a piece of furniture* 以抽彩法出售一件家具.

raf·fle[2] [ræfl] *n.* ①废物；杂物；碎屑. ②(船上的)绳索什具. ②〔美俚〕业余窃贼.

raf·fle·si·a [ræˈfliːʒiə, -ʒə, -ziə] *n.* 【植】大花草属 (*Rafflesia*)〔产于马来西亚〕.

raft[1] [rɑːft] *n.* ①筏，桴，槎，木排. ②【军】(登陆用的)浮桥. ③〔美〕(妨碍航行的)流木，浮冰，水鸟群(等). ④【动】(昆虫的)卵筏. ***on a ~*** 〔美俚〕以烤面包垫底 (*Adam and Eve on a ~* 烤面包垫底炒蛋). — *vt.* ①把(木料等)编成筏子. ②筏运(木材等)；用筏子航行. — *vi.* 乘筏子去；使用筏子.

raft[2] [rɑːft] *n.* 〔美口〕大量. *a ~ of trouble* 很多麻烦.

raft·er[1] [ˈrɑːftə] *n.* 【建】椽: *an angle ~* 角椽. ***from cellar to ~*** 遍屋子，屋里到处. — *vt.* ①给…装椽子. ②把(木材)作成椽子. ③〔英〕犁(地)使草泥等顺着一边堆成畦.

rafter[2] [ˈrɑːftə] *n.* 筏夫，撑木排的人.

rafts·man [ˈrɑːftsmən] *n.* (*pl.* ***-men*** [-men]) = rafter[2]

rag [ræg] *n.* ①破布，烂布，碎布；破碎帆布；擦布，抹布. ②〔蔑、谑〕(破旧的)手帕，旗子，帐篷，小块风帆；报纸，钞票，衣服(等)；〔*pl.*〕破烂的衣裳，〔美俚〕衣服. ③少量. ④〔美俚〕卑劣的人. ⑤〔口〕= ragtime. ⑥(橘子的)橘络. ⑦〔the R-〕〔英俚〕陆军〔海军〕俱乐部. *a ~ of cloud* 一片残云. *There is not a ~ of evidence.* 毫无证据. *He has not a ~ to his back.* 他衣不蔽体. ~ *currency [money]* 纸币. ***chew the ~*** 〔美俚〕嚼舌头；发牢骚. ***(be) cooked to ~s*** 煮得稀烂. ***glad ~s*** 〔口〕(个人所有的)最好的一套衣服. ***in ~s*** 成碎片；穿着破衣服 (*go in ~s* 服装破烂，穿着破烂衣服). ***It was like a ~ to a bull.*** 象拿红布给牛看一样(越发使它发火). ***part brass ~s with sb.*** 〔俚〕不再同某人保持亲密关系，同某人疏远了. ***spread every ~ of sail*** 挂起所有的风帆. ***take the ~ off*** 〔美〕强过，超过. ***torn to ~s*** 被撕碎. ***without a ~*** 分文没有. **~-and-bone-man** 收买破烂东西的. ~ **baby** 碎片做成的玩具娃娃. ~ **bag** 放破布的袋；破烂(东西). ~ **cutting** (烟叶的)切丝. ~ **doll** =~ baby. ~ **fair** 旧货市场，旧衣市场. **~man** 收买破布废纸的人；拾破布废纸的人；〔废〕恶魔. ~ **paper** (破布制的)优质纸. ~ **picker** 拾破布废纸的人. **~rug** 碎呢(拼成的)地毯. **~s-rock** 〔美口〕拉格摇摆舞乐. **~tag (and bobtail)** 〔俚〕〔集合词〕衣服褴褛的人们；下层社会；乌合之众. **~-time** ①【美乐】(1890—1915年间流行的)切分乐曲〔大量采用黑人音乐，旋律采用切分法 (syncopation) 作成，以节奏迅速，拍子清楚为特色，可称为最早的爵士音乐〕；爵士音乐〔舞蹈〕. ② *a.* 可笑的，滑稽的；无忧无虑的. **~top** 〔美俚〕敞篷汽车. ~ **trade** 〔美俚〕制衣工业. **~-waggon** 〔蔑〕帆船. **~weed** 【植】豚草(属). ~ **wheel** 抛光布轮. **~wort** 【植】千里光(属).

rag[2] [ræg] *vt.* 〔英俚〕①糟蹋，欺负；骂. ②愚弄，逗，撩，惹；开玩笑. — *vi.* ①吵闹，扰嚷. ②指责；欺负人. ③瞎开玩笑. — *n.* 〔俚〕(大学生等的)顽皮，开玩笑，恶作剧；嚷闹. *I only said it for a ~.* 我不过是说笑罢了.

rag[3] [ræg] *n.* 石板瓦；〔英〕(可作成石板瓦的)石炭页岩.

ra·ga [ˈrɑːgə] *n.* 拉迦〔印度的一些传统曲调，具备特有的音程、韵律和装饰音等，常用以作即席演奏〔唱〕〕.

rag·a·bash [ˈrægəbæʃ] *n.* 不中用的人，废物；乌合之众.

rag·a·muf·fin [ˈrægəˌmʌfin] *n.* ①衣服褴褛的人；流浪儿童. ②【鸟】山雀.

rag·bolt [ˈrægbəult] *n.* 【机】棘螺栓.

rage [reidʒ] *n.* ①愤激，愤怒. ②激烈，猛烈；(风等的)狂暴. ③热望，渴望；热心，热狂，疯狂；〔口〕战争狂. ④〔古〕(诗人、预言者等的)灵感，热情；(音乐的)兴奋. ⑤(战时精神的)昂扬，热烈. ⑥(行动的)白热化. ⑦〔口〕时兴东西. *the ~ of the wind* 风的狂暴. *the ~ of hunger* 非常饿. ***be (all) the ~*** 大流行，风靡一时 (*Table tennis became all the ~ from then.* 从那时以来乒乓球就流行起来). ***burst into a ~ of tears [grief]*** 嚎啕大哭. ***fly into a ~*** 勃然大怒. ***have a ~ for*** 对…具有狂热爱好. ***in a ~*** 一怒之下. —*vi.* ①发怒(*at; upon; against*). ②发狂，(发狂)大嚷大叫. ③〔Scot.〕大骂. ④放肆，尽情做；(风)狂吹，(浪)汹涌；(疫病等)猖獗，(战争)猛烈进行；大流行，风行. — *vt.* 使怒；使狂暴. ~ *oneself* 狂暴起来. ~ *itself out* (暴风雨等)平息下来.

rag·ged [ˈrægid] *a.* ①(衣衫等)破烂的，褴褛的；穷相毕露的. ②外形参差不齐的，凹凸不平的；(毛、发)乱蓬蓬的；粗糙的. ③不调和的；刺耳的. ④不完善的，有缺点的. *a ~ sheep* 乱毛羊. *a ~ hip* (瘦马的)骨架突露的臀部. ~ *sounds* 刺耳的声音. ***on the ~ edge*** 〔美〕在危险状态中，在穷困〔失败〕的边缘. ~ **robin** 【植】布谷鸟剪秋罗. ~ **school** 〔英古〕贫民学校. ~ **time** (赛艇划法或训练中的)不齐整. **-ly** *ad.* **-ness** *n.*

rag·ged·y [ˈrægidi] *a.* 有点破烂的，不大完整的，褴褛样的.

rag·ger [ˈrægə] *n.* ①〔英口〕恶作剧者；胡闹者. ②〔美俚〕新闻记者.

rag·gie [ˈrægiː] *n.* 〔水手俚〕非常友好〔亲密〕的朋友.

rag·ging [ˈrægiŋ] *n.* 〔口〕欺负；开玩笑，恶作剧，(学生的)胡闹.

rag·gle-tag·gle [ˈræglˈtægl] *a.* ①(衣衫等)破烂的. ②(节目等)七拼八凑的；混杂的.

rag·gy [ˈrægi] *a.* 〔美俚〕不公平的，不正当的.

rag·i, rag·gee, rag·gy [ˈrægiː] *n.* 【植】龙爪稷(䅟子，鸭脚粟) (*Eleusine coracana*)〔产于非洲和印度，其粟可食〕.

rag·ing [ˈreidʒiŋ] *a.* 发怒的，愤怒的；狂暴的；猛烈的，猖獗的. **-ly** *ad.*

Rag·lan [ˈræglən] *n.* 拉格伦〔姓氏〕.

rag·lan [ˈræglən] *n.* (袖缝直达领部的)拉格伦式〔套袖〕大衣.

ra·gout [ˈræguː; Am. ræˈguː] *n.* 【烹】浓味蔬菜燉肉. — *vt.* (***-gout·ed*** [-ˈguːd]; ***-gout·ing*** [-guːiŋ]) 把…做成浓味蔬菜燉肉.

rah [rɑː] *int.* = hurrah.

ra·hat la·koum [ˈrɑːhæt ləˈkuːm] *n.* 土耳其甜糕饼.

rah-rah [ˈrɑːˈrɑː] *a.* 〔美口〕①(在大学足球赛中)热烈喝采的，啦啦队的. ②大学(生)的. — *n.* 〔美俚〕传统的大学生精神.

raid [reid] *n.* ①(骑兵队等的)急袭，袭击；突击；(军舰等的)游击；(盗贼、狐等的)侵入. ②(警察的)抄查，围捕. *an air ~* 空袭. *a ~ on a bank* 抢劫银行. *make a ~ into* 侵入，袭击. *make a ~ on [upon]* 抄查，围捕. —*vt., vi.* 攻入，袭击 (*into*)；(警察)抄查，围捕 (*on; upon*). ***~ the market*** (散布谣言等)搅乱市面以便卖出股票等. **~ ing party** 【军】挺进队，突击队.

raid·er [ˈreidə] *n.* 袭击者；侵入者；抄查员；(市场的)扰乱者.

rail[1] [reil] *n.* ①(围栏等的)横木，横档；(钉帽架等用的)横条，栏干，扶手，〔*pl.*〕围栏. ②轨道；钢轨；铁路；〔*pl.*〕铁路股票. *a towel ~* (钉在墙上的)挂毛巾的横木. *a ~ advice* (铁路)到货通知单. *zero-length ~* 【火箭】超短型导轨. ***by ~*** 乘火车，用火车. ***get [go] off the ~s*** 出轨；越轨. ***off the ~s*** 出轨；扰乱秩序；〔喻〕发狂；越轨 (*He is a very reliable person; he has never gone off the ~s.* 他这人十分可靠，从来不越轨逾距). ***ride (sb.) on a ~*** 〔美〕(把人)捆在横杆上抬着赶走〔一种私刑〕. ***run off the ~s*** 出轨，脱轨. — *vt.* ①用围栏围

(in; off), 用栏杆围住,装栏干于. ②在…铺铁轨; 用铁路运输. — *vi.* 坐火车旅行. ~**car** 单节机动有轨车. ~ **chair** (铁路的)轨座. ~ **fence** 栅栏,篱墙. ~**man** ①铁路员工,(装卸货时打信号的)码头工人. ~**-motor** ① *n.*【铁路】摩托交通车,摩托客车. ② *a.* 铁路公路联运的.

rail[2] [reil] *n.*【动】秧鸡.

rail[3] [reil] *vi.* 咒骂; 责备; 抱怨*(against; at)*.

rail·age [ˈreilidʒ] *n.* 铁路运费; 铁路运输.

rail·head [ˈreilhed] *n.*【铁路】轨道终点;【军】军需品的铁路运输终点[兵站基点].

rail·ing[1] [ˈreiliŋ] *n.* 栏干; 围栏,栅栏; 扶手; 做栏干用的木料.

rail·ing[2] [ˈreiliŋ] *n.*, *a.* 咒骂(的),责备(的); 抱怨(的).

rail·ler·y [ˈreiləri] *n.* 挖苦,讥笑.

rail·road [ˈreilrəud] *n.*〔美〕①铁路. ★ 英国说 railway; 市内轻轨铁路美国也说 railway. ②【火箭】轨道设备,滑轨装置. ③(包含车辆、房产、建筑物等说的)铁路设施; 铁路公司;〔集合词〕铁路员工. *a* ~ *bridge* 铁路桥梁. *a* ~ *car* 铁路车辆. *a* ~ *carriage* (铁路)客车车厢. *a* ~ *train* 火车列车. *a* ~ *fare* 火车费. *a* ~ *tariff* 火车运费. *a* ~ *stock* 〔美〕铁路股票. *a* ~ *tie* (铁路)枕木. ~ *trousers* 〔美军俚〕有金线条的裤子. — *vt.* ①在…铺设铁路; 用铁路运输. ②〔美口〕急急忙忙送去; 使(议案等)草草通过. ③捏造罪证拘禁. — *vi.* ①在铁路上服务. ②坐火车旅行. ~ **flat** (没有各间分别进出的走廊的)一间接一间的套房,列车式套房. ~**spike** 铁路道钉. ~ **worm** = apple maggot. **-er** 〔美〕铁路职工; 铁路铺设技术员; 坐火车旅行的人. **-ing** ①铁路建设事业[工程]. ②铁路经营管理. ③〔美俚〕仓卒完成.

rail-split·ter [ˈreilˌsplitə] *n.* 将木头截成横木的人. ***The Rail-Splitter*** 林肯的绰号.

rail·way [ˈreilwei] *n.* ①〔英〕铁路; 铁路系统,铁道部门. ②〔美〕(市内)轻轨(铁路). *an aerial* ~ 高架铁道. *a broad-gauge [narrow-gauge]* ~ 阔轨[狭轨]铁路. *a high level [a surface, an underground, a submarine]* ~ 高架[地下,地上,海底]铁路. *a* ~ *accident* 铁路事故. *a* ~ *engine* 机车,火车头. *a* ~ *man* 铁路员工. *a* ~ *novel* (坐火车旅行时看的)轻松小说. *a* ~ *porter* (车站上的)搬运工;〔美〕卧车服务员. *a* ~ *rug* 火车旅行用绒毯. *a* ~ *station* 火车站. *a* ~ *sub-office* 铁路邮政分局〔略 R.S.O.〕. — *vi.* 〔英〕坐火车旅行. — *vt.* 在…铺设铁路. ~ **letter** 〔英〕由铁道部门运送的信件. ~ **market** 〔英〕铁道股票交易. ~ **sleeper [tie]** (铁路)枕木.

rai·ment [ˈreimənt] *n.* 〔诗〕衣服.

rain[1] [rein] *n.* ①雨; 下雨;〔*pl.*〕阵雨. ②雨天;〔the ~s〕(热带地方的)雨季;〔the ~s〕大西洋北纬 4—10 度的多雨地带. ③(雨一样的)降落物. ④〔俚〕电子流. *a drizzling* ~ 细雨. *fine* ~ 蒙松雨,毛毛雨. *a heavy [light]* ~ 大[小]雨. *It looks like* ~. 象要下雨. ***a* ~ *of*** *(ashes, tears, blows, kisses)* (下雨一样的)一阵(灰,眼泪,打击,吻). ***in the*** ~ 在雨中,冒着雨. ~ ***or shine*** 无论晴雨,风雨无阻; 必然地; 确定不疑地. — *vi.* 下雨〔通例用it为主语〕; 雨一般地落下. *It* ~*s in.* (房屋)漏雨; 雨飘进来. *It has* ~*ed over.* 雨停了. *It never* ~*s but it pours.* 不下则已,一下倾盆;〔喻〕祸不单行; 发生大灾祸. — *vt.* 使象雨一样地落下; 厚施(恩惠等). *It* ~*s blood.* 血流如注. *Her eyes* ~*ed tears.* 眼泪雨般地流. ~ *benefits upon sb.* 给(某人)很大恩惠. ~ ***off*** 〔英〕= ~ out. ~ ***out*** 因下雨阻碍,因下雨而取消 *(The meeting was* ~*ed out.* 大会因雨停开). ~**band** 雨带〔太阳光谱中黄色部分的黑带〕. ~**bow** ①虹. ②〔美俚〕美妙的梦想. ③五彩药片[药丸]〔一种巴比妥类安眠药〕(= ~bow pill) *(all the colours of the* ~*bow* 种种颜色. *a primary* ~*bow* 虹. *a secondary* ~*bow* 霓. *a* ~*bow trout* 虹鳟鱼). ~ **box**【剧】雨声装置,雨声箱. ~ **cap** 雨帽. ~ **cape** 雨披. ~ **check** 〔美〕(比赛因雨停止时的)留待下次补看比赛的票根;〔美俚〕延期举行; 顺延; 死刑的改为无期徒刑 *(Since you can't join us for dinner, we'll give you a* ~ *check.* 既然您不能和我们一起参加宴会,我们就延期举行了). ~ **cloud** 雨云. ~**cloth** 防雨布. ~**coat** 雨衣. ~ **doctor** 祈雨法师. ~**drop** 雨滴. ~**fall** 下雨; 雨量. ~ **forest** (热带多雨地区茂密的)雨林. ~ **gauge** 雨量计. ~ **glass** 晴雨表. ~ **maker** = rain doctor;〔美空俚〕气象学家. ~**making** 人工降雨. ~ **out** (比赛、表演因雨)中断; 暂停;(对大气尘埃的)冲洗,消除. ~**proof** ① *a.* 防雨的,不透雨的. ② *n.* 〔英〕雨衣. ③ *vt.* 使能防雨. ~ **room** 〔俚〕淋浴室. ~ **shadow** (山坡背面降雨极少的)雨影区. ~ **sprout** ①水落管,排水口. ②海龙卷,龙卷风卷起的水柱. ~**-storm** 暴风雨. ~**tight** *a.* = rainproof. ~ **wash** 雨水的冲刷; 被雨水冲走的东西. ~ **water** 雨水. ~**wear** 防雨布. ~**worm** ①蚯蚓. ②【医】爬行疹. **-less** *a.*

rain·i·ness [ˈreininis] *n.* 多雨.

rain·y [ˈreini] *a.* ***(rain·i·er; -i·est)*** 下雨的; 常下雨的,多雨的; 含雨的,象要下雨的. *a* ~ *day* 雨天; 萧条[遭难,穷困]的时候; 万一的时候 *(save [lay up] against a* ~ *day* 以备万一,未雨绸缪). *a* ~ *season* 雨季. *a* ~ *district* 多雨地区. *a* ~ *street* 雨天的湿淋淋街道.

raise [reiz] *vt.* ①抬起,举起(重物等); 升(旗等); 使起立,竖起(柱子等); 捞起,打捞(沉船). ②建造,建立(纪念碑等),造起(房子); 使(雕刻物上的形象等)浮起,凸起. ③踢起,扬起(灰尘等),溅起(泥),喷起(烟);(用酵母等)使膨起;【纺】把(布)拉绒,使起绒. ④抬高(价钱、租金); 增高(温度); 提高(声音); 叫起. ⑤提升,加薪; 使事业成功; 使上进;(一朝有事时)使(市民、国民等)奋起. ⑥引起,掀起(动乱、悲剧等); 惹起,使发(笑等); 提起,提出(问题、异议等). ⑦征收(捐税等),征(兵),招集; 筹(款等). ⑧栽培,种植,出产(谷类等); 饲养(家畜等); 养育,教育(子女). ⑨【军】解除(包围或封锁). ⑩【海】(指船只航近而)使(陆地等)渐渐出现. ⑪【数】使自乘. ⑫使复活,叫醒,提醒; 使出现. ⑬〔美〕任命. ⑭〔美〕增加(赌注). *Not a voice was* ~*d in opposition.* 一声反对都没有. ~ *the white flag* 举[升]起白旗投降. ~ *one's eyes* 抬眼观看,仰视. ~ *a private from the ranks* 把一个列兵提升为下士. ~ *one's spirits* 打起精神. ~ *a smile [blush]* 使微笑[脸红]. ~ *money* 筹款. ~ *cloth* 使布起绒毛. *A deliverer was* ~*d up.* 救星(突然)出现. *Where was he* ~*d?* 他是在哪儿长大的? *stock raising* 家畜饲养. *late raising* 抑制栽培. — *vi.* ①起身,立起. ②升高. ③〔口〕咳出痰. ④提高赌注[叫价]. ***be*** ~***d in the barn*** 缺乏教养,粗野无礼. ~ ***a check*** 〔美〕涂改支票[增加金额]. ~ ***a dust*** 扬起灰尘; 引起骚动; 瞒人眼目. ~ ***Cain [hell, the devil, the mischief]*** 〔俚〕引起风波,闹出问题. ~ ***colour*** 改染. ~ ***oneself*** 长高; 发迹,露头角. ~ ***one's glass to*** 为(某人)举杯祝酒. ~ ***one's hat*** 举帽行礼. ~ ***one's head*** 抬一抬头(表示在座). ~ ***one's voice*** ①在人群中发言 *(No one* ~*d his voice.* 一个不响). ②提高嗓子说;(愤怒着)提高声音. ~ ***one's voice against*** 向…抗议. ~ ***sand*** 〔美〕起风潮,惹出事情. ~ ***the ante*** [ˈænti]〔美〕提价. ~ ***the city against [upon]*** 发动市民抵抗. ~ ***the colours*** 〔美〕走漏计划. ~ ***the lid*** 〔美俚〕熟视无睹,放松禁令. ~ ***the roof*** 〔美俚〕引起风波; 大声叫喊,吵闹. ~ ***the wind*** 起风波;〔喻〕筹款. ~ ***to a [third] power*** 使自乘〔自乘到三次幂〕. — *n.* 〔美〕①升起,抬起; 登高. ②(道路等的)高起处,隆起处;【矿】天井. ③增加; 加价; 加薪,加赌注. ④〔俚〕(钱等的)筹措; 筹募. *make a* ~ 筹办; 筹款,凑钱.

raised [reizd] *a.* ①加高了的; 凸起的,浮雕的; 发过酵的,膨起的,高起的. ②〔美〕受过教育的. *a* ~ *bottom* (升、斗等的)垫高了的底. ~ *tissue* 起毛布. *a* ~ *beach* (因冲积而)上升的海滩. *a book in* ~ *type* 凸字书,点字

书. ～ *work* 浮雕工艺. *a* ～ *cheque* 涂改过的(金额增大了的)支票. ～ *pastry* 发面点心. *a* ～ *pie* 发面馅饼.

rais·er [ˈreizə] *n.* ①举起者, 提出者, 提高者(等). ②(资金等的) 筹集者. ③饲养者, 栽培者. ④(面包厂等的)发酵工人; 酵母.

rai·sin [ˈreizn] *n.* ①〔常 *pl.*〕(无核)葡萄干. ②闪光紫蓝色. ～ **tree**【植】枳椇.

rai·son d'é·tat [rɛzɔŋ deˈtɑ]〔F.〕外交理由, 政治理由.

rai·son d'être [F. ˈreizɔːn ˈdeitr]〔F.〕存在的理由.

rai·son·né [F. rɛzɔne] *a.*〔F.〕合理[有组织地]排列的, 分门别类的. *a catalogue* ～ 分类目录.

raj [rɑːdʒ] *n.*〔印〕主权, 支配, 统治.

Ra·jab [rəˈdʒæb] *n.* (伊斯兰教历)七月.

ra·ja(h) [ˈrɑːdʒə] *n.*〔Hind.〕(印度等的)邦主, 王公; (马来亚的)酋长.

Ra·ja·stha·ni [ˌrɑːdʒəsˈtɑːni] *n.*〔Hind.〕拉贾斯坦语.

Raj·put, Raj·poot [ˈrɑːdʒput] *n.* 拉其普特人〔自称是刹帝利(kshatriya)后裔的印度北部一民族〕.

rake[1] [reik] *n.* ①耙子; 耙地机. ②火钩, 火拨. ③【林】流材挡栅. *a horse* ～ 马拉耙. — *vt.* ①用耙子耙拢, 用耙子耙; 耙除, 扫除 *(off)*; 耙到一块 *(up; together)*;〔废〕在(种子等上)盖上土;〔方〕用土压(火). ②遍搜, 到处找; 探讨. ③掠过, 擦过. ④看透; 俯瞰, 眺望. ⑤【军】扫射, 纵射. — *vi.* ①用耙子工作. ②搜求, 到处找 *(in; into; among)*; 拼命收集. ***as lean [thin] as a*** ～ 瘦得只有皮包骨头. ～ ***among [in, into] old records*** 翻查古老记载[文献等]. ～ ***and scrape*** 拼命攒钱[搜刮]. ～ ***down***〔美〕申斥. ～ ***in the dough***〔美〕发财. ～ ***out*** ①搜集(情报). ②(把火)耙出; 扫除. ～ ***over the coals***〔美俚〕责骂. ～ ***up*** ①搜集; 搜出, 挑剔出来. ②压灭(火).

rake[2] [reik] *n.* ①【海】船首[船尾]的突出部分; 船尾柱; 舵前部的倾斜; (桅、烟囱等)向船尾方向的倾斜(度). ②【矿】罅隙; 倾侧; 斜脉,【空】倾度. — *vi.* (桅杆、烟囱等)倾斜. — *vt.* 使(桅杆等)向后倾斜.

rake[3] [reik] *n.* 荡子, 浪子. — *vi.* 放荡, 游荡. — *a.* 放荡的, 淫乱的, 无赖的. ～**hell**〔古〕荡子, 游荡儿, 浪子; 无赖. ～**-off**〔美俚〕(通常指不合法的)利益; 油水; 佣金, 手续费, 回扣(等).

rak·er [ˈreikə] *n.* ①用耙子耙的人; 耙地机. ②清道夫;【军】纵射炮. ③〔美俚〕大胆的人.

ra·ki, ra·kee [rɑːˈki, ˈræki] *n.* (用葡萄汁制成的)拉基烧酒.

rak·ish[1] [ˈreikiʃ] *a.* ①【海】(象海盗船一样)轻快的. ②时髦的, 漂亮的. **-ly** *ad.*

rak·ish[2] [ˈreikiʃ] *a.* 放荡的, 游荡的. **-ly** *ad.*

râle, rale [rɑːl] *n.*〔F.〕【医】(肺的)水泡音; 罗音; (临死时的)喉鸣.

Ra·le(i)gh[1] [ˈrɔːli] *n.* ①罗利〔姓氏, 男子名〕. ② **Sir Walter** ～ 罗利爵士〔1552?–1618, 英国政治家, 历史家〕.

Ra·le(i)gh[2] [ˈrɔːli] *n.* 罗利〔美国北卡罗来纳州首府〕.

rall. = rallentando [rælenˈtændəu] *a., ad.*〔It.〕【乐】渐慢.

ral·li·car(t) [ˈrælikɑː, -kɑːt] *n.*〔英〕(四人坐)二轮小马车.

Rall's Janet [ˈrɔːlz ˈdʒænit]〔美〕一种晚熟耐藏的苹果〔类似国光苹果〕.

ral·ly[1] [ˈræli] *vt.* ①召集, 纠合, 团结. ②重整(队伍); 挽回(颓势). ②振奋(精神); 集中(力量); 恢复(元气); 激励. ～ *world opinion against nuclear weapons* 重新调动世界舆论反对核武器. ～ *one's followers to action* 纠合追随者行动起来. *They rallied their energies for the counter-attack.* 他们奋起反攻. — *vi.* ①重行集合; 挽回颓势, 重整旗鼓; 恢复气力. ②【网球】(将球)打回去. ～ *from an illness* 病愈恢复. ～ *in price* 物价回升. ～ *round* 聚集在…的周围, 团结在…的周围. — *n.* ①重新集合; 挽回颓势, 重新振作; 恢复气力. ②〔美口〕群众大会[集会]; 示威行动. ③【网球】连续打回. ④汽车竞赛. ～**master** 汽车竞赛的组织者[指挥者]. ～**ing cry** 战斗口号, 呐喊. ～**ing point** 振作点, 恢复点. **-ist** 参加汽车竞赛者.

ral·ly[2] [ˈræli] *n., vt., vi.* 嘲笑, 挖苦.

Ralph [reif, rælf] *n.* 拉尔夫〔男子名〕.

R.A.M. = Royal Academy of Music〔英〕皇家音乐学院.

ram [ræm] *n.* ①(没有阉过的)公羊;〔R-〕【天】白羊宫. ②(从前攻城用的)撞墙车; 撞角〔装在军舰舰首的铁嘴〕; 有撞角的军舰;【建】(打桩用的)撞槌; 夯槌. ③【机】作动筒; (压力机的)压头, 速度头; 压力扬吸机; 活塞. ***milk the*** ～ 作徒劳无益的事. *a* ～ *cat*〔英方〕公猫. *a* ～ *compartment*【海】舰首隔室. *a* ～ *engine* 打桩机. ～ *jet* 冲压喷气(发动机). — *vt.* ①用撞墙车撞; 用撞角撞; 撞 *(against; at; on; into)*. ②撞入; 打入 *(down; in; into)*; 撞倒; 把(地)夯固; (用通条)把(火药)填进(枪炮) *(with)*; 坚持推行; 迫使别人接受, 灌输. ～ *one's head against a wall* 把头撞在墙壁上. ～ ***the argument home*** 反复说明论旨使充分了解. ～ ***up***【火箭】向上运送, 用起重机吊起.

Ram·a·dan [ˌræməˈdɑːn] *n.* ramazan.

Ra·man [ˈrɑːmən] *n.* 拉曼〔姓氏〕.

ra·mark [ˈreimɑːk] *n.*【无】雷达指点标〔连续发射脉冲, 为 radar marker 的缩合词〕.

Ra·ma·ya·na [rɑˈmaiənɑ, rɑˈmɑːjənə] *n.*《罗摩衍那》〔印度古代梵语叙事诗〕.

Ram·a·zan [ræməˈzɑːn] *n.*【伊斯兰教】莱麦丹月, 斋月〔伊斯兰教教历太阴年第九月莱麦丹月禁食戒斋〕.

ram·ble [ˈræmbl] *n.* ①漫步, 散步; 徘徊. ②〔罕〕漫谈, 闲谈. ***on [upon] the*** ～ 在散步. — *vi.* ①漫步, 散步 *(about, over)*; 徘徊. ②闲聊天, 漫谈; 写随笔. ③(草木等)蔓延. ～ ***on*** 长谈. — *vt.* 在…上漫步. *He spent the morning* ～*ling woodland paths.* 他一上午在林间小径漫步.

ram·bler [ˈræmblə] *n.* ①漫步者. ②漫谈者. ③【植】蔓生植物; 攀缘蔷薇;〔the R-〕(十八世纪 Dr. Samual Johnson 主办的)《漫步者》(双周刊).

ram·bling [ˈræmbliŋ] *a.* ①漫步的. ②不着边际的(谈话), 漫无限制的; (思想等)散漫的; (生活等)放浪的. ③(房屋、街市等)不规则的, 不整齐的. ④【植】攀缘的.

Ram·bouil·let [ˈræmbəˌlei, F. rɑ̃buiˈjɛ] *n.*【动】(法国)兰勃羊.

ram·bunc·tious [ræmˈbʌŋkʃəs] *a.*〔美俚〕粗暴的, 蛮横的, 无法无天的.

ram·bu·tan [ræmˈbuːtn] *n.*【植】红毛丹树 *(Nephelium lappaceum)*〔产于马来亚〕; 红毛丹果.

R.A.M.C., RAMC = Royal Army Medical Corps〔英〕皇家陆军军医队.

ram·e·kin, ram·e·quin [ˈræmkin] *n.* ①干酪蛋糕〔以乳酪面包屑、鸡蛋等烘烤而成的食品〕. ②烘烤干酪蛋糕用的烤盘.

ra·men·tum [rəˈmentəm] *n.* ***(pl.*** ***-ta*** [-tə]***)***【植】小鳞片.

ra·mi [ˈreimai] *n.* ramus 的复数.

ram·ie, ram·ee [ˈræmi] *n.*【植】苎麻.

ram·i·fi·ca·tion [ˌræmifiˈkeiʃən] *n.* ①分枝, 分叉; 分歧; 分裂; 分枝状; 分枝式; 分枝法. ②支流, 支派; 分派; 区分, 门类. ③衍生物; 结果, 后果.

ram·i·form [ˈræmiˌfɔːm] *a.* 枝形的, 枝状的.

ram·i·fy [ˈræmifai] *vt.*〔常用被动结构〕使分枝, 使分叉; 分派; 使交错. *Railways are ramfied over the country.* 铁路线分布全国. — *vi.* 生枝, 分叉; 被分派, 分歧; 交错. ～ *into a labyrinth* 分枝成迷宫状.

ram-jet en·gine [ˈræmdʒetˈendʒin]【空】冲压式喷气发动机.

R

ram·mer [ˈræmə] *n.* ①使用夯槌等的人. ②撞槌,夯槌; (枪炮)通条,装填器. ③〔美俚〕臂膊.
ram·mish [ˈræmiʃ] *a.* ①公羊一般的. ②臭气强烈的,膻臊的;气味浓烈的. ③好色的.
Ra·mon [rəˈməun, ˈreimən] *n.* 雷蒙〔男子名, Raymond 的异体〕.
Ra·mo·na [rəˈməunə] *n.* 雷蒙娜〔女子名〕.
ra·mose [rəˈməus], **ra·mous** [ˈreiməs] *a.* 生了枝的,多枝的;枝状的.
ramp[1] [ræmp] *vi.* ①【纹】(狮子等)用后脚直立; 作恫吓姿势;猛扑;暴跳,乱冲. ②【植】(植物)繁茂. — *n.* (纹章上狮子等的)猛扑姿势;〔口〕愤怒.
ramp[2] [ræmp] *vt.*【建】在…设斜面〔斜路、坡〕; 把…弄弯曲(使适于倾斜). — *n.* ①(连结高低互异的两条十字路的) 坡道,斜路;(筑城)斜坡. ②倾斜装置,斜轨;【建】楼梯扶手的弯斜部分. ③【讯】接线夹, 接线端钮. ④【空】(客机的)舷梯.
ramp[3] [ræmp] 〔英俚〕*n., vt.* (向…)索取高价;诈骗,诈取. — *n.* 诈骗,索高价.
ramp[4] [ræmp] *n.*【植】北美野韭 *(Allium tricoccum)*.
ramp·act·or [ˈræmpəktə] *n.* 跳击夯.
ramp·age [ræmˈpeidʒ] *n.* (因发怒等)暴跳;狂暴行为. *be [go] on the* ~ 暴跳如雷,狂怒,处于极端愤激状态. — *vi.*暴跳,暴怒.
ram·pa·geous [ræmˈpeidʒəs] *a.* 暴跳的, 暴怒的, 狂暴的.
ram·pan·cy [ˈræmpənsi] *n.* (疾病等的)蔓延;猖獗;繁茂;(狮子等用后脚)跳起,直立.
ram·pant [ˈræmpənt] *a.* (兽类)跳起的; 直立的;【纹】(狮子用后脚)跳起直立着的. ②蔓延的;猖狂的,猖獗一时的;激烈的;暴怒的;(植物)繁茂的. *a lion* ~【纹】跃立狮形. ~ *gardant*【纹】朝正面用后脚站立着的. ~ *regardant*【纹】用后脚站立着头往后面看的. **-ly** *ad.*
ram·part [ˈræmpɑːt] *n.* 堡垒,壁垒,城墙;防御物. — *vt.* 用堡垒[城墙]围绕,筑城围住;防御,保护.
ram·pike [ˈræmpaik] *n.* 〔加拿大〕高大的死树(尤指被火烧黑了的无枝的树).
ram·pi·on [ˈræmpjən] *n.*【植】匍匐风铃草.
ramps [ræmps] *n.* = ramp[3].
ram·rod [ˈræmrɔd] *n.* ①(火药枪的)通条;推弹杆;洗杆. ②〔俚〕瘦长的人.
Ram·say [ˈræmzi] *n.* ①拉姆齐〔姓氏〕. ②**Sir William** ~ 拉姆齐〔1852—1916,英国化学家,氦的发现者〕.
Rams·den [ˈræmzdən] *n.* 拉姆斯登〔姓氏〕.
ram·shack·le [ˈræmˌʃæk] *a.* ①要倒似的,要塌似的(马车、房子等)摇摇晃晃的. ②无定见的,没主意的;朝三暮四的;放荡的,任性的.
ram·son [ˈræmzən] *n.*【植】熊葱,阔叶葱;〔*pl.*〕熊葱头.
ram·u·lose [ˈræmjuˌləus] *a.* 多小枝的.
ra·mus [ˈreiməs] *n.* *(pl.* **-mi** *[-mai])*【生】支,分支.
ran [ræn] run 的过去式.
R.A.N., RAN = Royal Australian Navy (皇家)澳大利亚海军.
Rance [rɑːns] *n.* 兰斯〔姓氏〕.
ranch(e) [ræntʃ, rɑːntʃ] *n.* 〔美〕大牧场,大农场;〔集合词〕牧场工作人员. — *vi.* 〔美〕经营牧场; 在牧场工作. — *vt.* ①在…经营牧场. ②在牧场饲养. ~ **house** (农场主, 牧场主的) 场内住房; (附有车库的) 平房建筑. ~**man** = rancher.
ranch·er [ˈræntʃə] *n.* 〔美〕牧场主;牧场工人.
ran·che·ria [ˌræntʃəˈriːə] *n.* 〔美〕①(墨西哥的)牧场主〔工人〕的住房. ②牧人小村. ③印第安人村落.
ran·che·ro [rænˈtʃɛərəu] *n.* *(pl.* **-ros***)* ①〔美〕= rancher. ②小农场主.
ranch·ette [ˌrænˈtʃet] *n.* 小农场,小牧场.
ran·cho [ˈræntʃəu] *n.*〔美〕①棚屋,简陋的小房子; 小村庄,(尤指旅客的)投宿地. ②(美西南部)牧场.
ran·cid [ˈrænsid] *a.* ①(指油脂变质后的特有怪味)哈喇的;腐臭的,酸腐的. ②不愉快的, 讨厌的. **-ly** *ad.*
ran·cid·i·ty [rænˈsiditi] *n.* 哈喇; 腐臭; 酸败(度).
ran·cor·ous [ˈræŋkərəs] *a.* 充满〔表示〕仇恨的,憎恨的;有遗恨的. **-ly** *ad.*
ran·cour [ˈræŋkə] *n.* 深仇,怨恨,憎恨.
rand [rænd] *n.* ①(垫在皮鞋后跟上的)斜面衬皮,衬底. ②石桥. ③〔英方〕田边,地头. ④兰特〔南非,博茨瓦纳等国的货币单位〕. **the R-** (南非)河边高地〔尤指德兰士瓦 (Transvaal) 的约翰内斯堡 (Johannesburg) 市附近的产金丘陵〕.
Ran·dal(l) [ˈrændl] *n.* 兰德尔〔= Randolph〕.
ran·dan[1] [rænˈdæn] *n.* (居中一人双桨, 头尾二人单桨的)三人小艇(划法).
ran·dan[2] [rænˈdæn] *n.* 〔俚〕乱闹,傻闹,纵情嬉闹;〔罕〕爱乱闹的人,好纵情嬉闹的人. *go on the* ~ 嬉戏喧闹,狂饮,纵酒取乐.
R and B = rhythm and blues 拍子清楚,节奏简单的勃路斯乐曲.
R & C = receiving and classification 接收与分类.
R and D, R & D = research and development 研究与发展.
Ran·dolph [ˈrændɔlf] *n.* 伦道夫〔姓氏,男子名〕.
ran·dom [ˈrændəm] *n.*〔罕〕胡乱行动;偶然的[随便的]行动[过程]. — *a.* ①任意的,胡乱的,随便的;(话等)信口乱说的;(人等)偶然碰到的. ②随机的;【物】无规则的;(石工)(大小)不齐的. *a* ~ *guess* 瞎猜. *a* ~ *shot* 乱射(的子弹),流弹. *at* ~ 碰运气地;无目标地,漫无目的地. ~ **access**【计】随机存取. ~ **masonry** (随石头不同大小堆砌的)堆砌泥瓦工. ~ **mating** 随机交配. ~ **sampling** 随机取样. ~ **variable**【数、统】随机变数. ~ **walk**【数】随机游动.
ran·dom·ize [ˈrændəmaiz] *vt.* *(-iz·ed; -iz·ing)* ①使形成不规则分布;完全打乱. ②【数、统】使随机化;使不规则化;随机选择. **-i·za·tion** [ˌrændəmaiˈzeiʃən] *n.*
R. & P. Sec = Radio and Panel Section【军】无线电及信号布板通信组.
R and R, R & R ①= rest and recuperation (leave)【美军】(正常例假以外的)休整假期. ②rock'n'roll 摇摆舞(曲).
Ran·dy [ˈrændi] *n.* 兰迪〔男子名, Randolph 的昵称〕.
ran·dy [ˈrændi] *a.* ①〔Scot.〕粗暴的, 吵闹的,(女人)说话大声的. ②〔方〕(牛等) 横暴的. ③〔方〕淫乱的. — *n.* 〔Scot.〕①强横的乞丐;吵闹的女人, 暴躁的女人. ②〔方〕大吵大闹.
ra·nee [rɑːˈniː] *n.* 〔Hind.〕女邦主,王后,王妃,邦主妃(= rani).
rang [ræŋ] ring 的过去式.
range[1] [reindʒ] *vt.* ①排列; 整理(头发等). ②使归类〔班、行、队〕;把…分类. ③加入,站在…的一边〔用被动形或反身形〕*(with; against)*. ④〔古、诗〕在…徘徊,在…走来走去, 到处寻找;【海】巡逻 (沿岸等). ⑤(用枪、望远镜等)对准(目标);瞄准;(炮术)试(炮), 试(射程). ~ *books on a shelf* 把书排列在书架上. ~ *the forest for game* 在森林中跑来跑去猎取猎物. ***be*** ~***d according to size*** 按大小顺序排列. ***be*** ~***d against [among]*** 站在…的反对方面〔…的一伙内〕. ~ ***oneself*** ①(放荡后因结婚而)改过自新. ②得到固定职业. ~ ***oneself on the side of*** 做…的伙伴. ~ ***oneself with*** 做…的伙伴, 与…做伙伴. — *vi.* ①并列, 并行, 成直线 *(with)*; (山脉等) 相连, 连绵; (动植物等) 分布, 蔓延, 散布 *(from... to)*; (子弹)能打到,达到. ②加入,站在…的一边 *(with; against)*; 与…为伍 *(with)*. ③徘徊,走来走去,跋涉 *(in; over; through)*; 【海】巡航. ④(思想、研究等)到达,涉及. ⑤【军】测距,试射测距;射程为. ⑥(在某范围内)变动,升降 *(between; from... to...)*. ~ *north and south* 绵亘南北. *The gun* ~*s 3 miles.* 这

炮能打三英里远. *The thermometer ~s from 45° to 50°.* 温度表的升降幅度是从 45度到 50 度. ***ranging fancy*** 动摇的爱情,水性杨花. — *n.* ①(山脉、房屋等的)排列;连续,绵亘. ②(同种物的)一批,一套,一堆. ③方向;范围,区域;(动植物的)分布[繁殖]区域;生存期间;放牧区域,牧场;知识范围;音域;幅度,差度;限度,极限;【数】变程,量程;值域;全距. ④作用[有效]半径,距离;射程;靶子场,射击场,⑤等级,类别,种类,部类.⑥徜徉,徘徊.⑦(能同时利用余热烧水、烤面包的)多用铁灶;火格子;梯级. ⑧〔美〕公地测量中相距六英里的两子午线间的一排市镇. *a ~ of buildings* 一排房子. *the ~ of politics* 政界. *a high [lower] ~* 大[小]比例,大[小]刻度. *the ~ of a thermometer* 温度表的(升降)幅度. *the ~ of one's voice* 音域;声音所能达到的范围. *the effective ~* 有效射程. *foul the ~ finding* (放烟幕)扰乱测距工作. *a projectile [proving, rocket] ~* 炮兵[军用、火箭]靶场. *a ~ boss* 〔美〕(在某一地段内)看守放牧牲畜的人. *a ~ rider* 〔美〕牧童;山村看守人. *~ cattle* 放牧的牲畜. *a ~ forecast* 【商】(棉花的)收成估计. *a ~ of the cable* 抛锚时所必需的一定长度的锚链. *an electronic ~* 电子炉. ***a low ~ of prices*** 低档价钱. ***at long [short] ~*** 在远距离[近距离]. ***go over the ~*** 〔美〕死. ***in ~ with*** 和…并排着;和…同一方向. ***in the ~ of*** 在…范围内. ***out of one's ~*** 能力达不到的;在知识以外的,不能办到的. ***out of [within] ~*** 在射程外[内]. ***within the ~ of*** 在…的射程内;…能力达得到的,…所能的. ~ **ability** (火箭的)射程. ~ **coal** 块煤. ~ **finder** 测远仪,测距器;【军】(测定由枪炮至目标间距离的)光学测距仪. ~ **hammer**【林】打号槌. ~**land** 牧场,放牧地.~ **oil** 厨房用燃料器.~ **radar** 雷达测距计. ~ **party**【军】监靶官. ~ **pole** 测量标杆. ~**-setting**【军】射程表尺数. ~ **table**【军】射程表;可凑成大桌子的许多小桌子之一. ~ **taker**【军】测距员.

rang·er [ˈreindʒə] *n.* ①荡来荡去的人,徘徊者. ②〔英〕御林看守人,〔美〕护林员. ③【美军】突击队员;(防守广大地域的)游击兵,游骑兵;〔*pl.*〕游骑队. ④〔英〕老资格的女童子军. ~ **district**【林】护林区. **-ing** 试射;定向;测距.

rang·(e)y [ˈreindʒi] *a.* ①〔美〕(动物)走来走去的. ②个子细长的,长脚的. ③广阔的. ④〔澳〕山脉连绵的,多山的.

Ran·goon [ræŋˈguːn] *n.* 仰光〔缅甸首都〕.

ra·ni [ˈrɑːni] *n.* (印度的)王妃;邦主妃;女王;女邦主;公主.

ran·id [ˈrænid] *n.*【动】蛙科 *(Ranidae)*.

rank[1] [ræŋk] *n.* ①列,排;【军】行列;〔*pl.*〕阵线,队伍,军队;〔*pl.*〕士兵,列兵.②阶层,等级,地位;身分;高级,显贵. ③次序,顺序;【统】秩;(棋盘的)横格. ④【语】语结级位〔叶斯帕森语,按语、词和结构在句中所起作用而分为三级,即一级语结 (primary)、二级语结 (secondary) 和三级语结 (tertiary)〕. *the front [rear] ~* 前[后]排. *people of all ~s* 各阶层的人们. *a man of high [no] ~* 地位高[低]的人. *~s and ratings* 官兵. *within the ~s of the people* 在人民内部. ***be in the first ~*** 是第一流的. ***break ~s*** 落伍;走出队伍,出列;溃散. ***close the ~s*** ①使队伍靠拢. ②〔喻〕紧密团结. ***fall into ~*** 排队,列队. ***give first ~ to*** 把…放在第一位. ***keep ~*** 维持秩序. ***other ~s*** 普通士兵们. ***~ and fashion*** 上流社会. ***~ and file*** 队伍,行伍,士兵(群众);民众,老百姓,普通人. ***rise from the ~s*** 由士兵升为军官;行伍出身;布衣起家. ***serve in the ~s*** 服兵役. ***take ~ of*** 在…之上. ***take ~ with*** 和…并列,和…并肩. — *vt.* ①排列,使成横排. ②把…分类,分等级;使归类. ③〔美〕强过,胜过,先于,在…之上. *~ one's ability very high* 把某人能力评得很高. — *vi.* ①并列;位于 *(among; with)*;排列;排队前进 *(off; past)*. ②〔美〕占第一位. ③〔英〕(对破产者财产)有要求权. *~ among the Great Powers* 列名于世界强国之间.

rank[2] [ræŋk] *a.* ①繁茂的,蔓延的;过于肥沃的. ②臭极的,恶臭的. ③〔贬意〕极端(恶劣,下流等)的;真正的,十足的,很厉害的,讨厌的. ④卑鄙的;猥亵的. ⑤〔口〕难制御的,倔强的. ⑥【法】〔古〕过重的,过份的. *a garden ~ with weeds* 杂草滋生的院子. *The land is too ~ to grow corn.* 土地过肥不宜种谷类〔徒长枝叶,结实稀少〕. *tall ~ grass* 长得很高的草. *~ fraud* 大骗局. *~ nonsense* 荒唐到极点的事情[胡说]. *~ pedantry* 好象样样都懂的臭样子. *~ poison* 剧毒. *a ~ traitor* 大叛徒,巨奸. **-ly** *ad.* **-ness** *n.*

rank·er [ˈræŋkə] *n.* 〔英〕兵;(特指)出身行伍的军官.

Ran·kine [ˈræŋkin] *a.* 兰(金)氏温标的〔用华氏度数表示的绝对温标〕. ~ **cycle**【物】兰金循环.~**'s formula**【物】兰金公式.

rank·ing [ˈræŋkiŋ] *n.* 顺序;【统】秩评定. — *a.* 第一流的;首席的;高级的;干部的. *a ~ officer* 高级军官. *a ~ player* 一级选手.

ran·kle [ˈræŋkl] *vi.* ①〔古、诗〕痛. ②红肿. ③(怨恨、失望等)使心痛,压在胸口[心头]. — *vt.* 激怒;使怨恨.

ran·sack [ˈrænsæk] *vt.* ①细搜,遍处搜索,翻来复去地找. ②洗劫,掠夺,劫掠. ③仔细思索.

Ran·som [ˈrænsəm] *n.* 兰瑟姆〔姓氏〕.

ran·som [ˈrænsəm] *n.* ①赎,赎取,赎身. ②赎金;罚款. ③讹诈,威胁. ④〔古〕赎罪. ***a king's ~*** 巨款. ***hold sb. to [for] ~*** 绑票, 勒取赎金. — *vt.* ①赎, 赎回,赎出,赎(身). ②赎(罪). ③向…勒索赎金;绑(某人的)票进行勒索. ④〔现罕〕得赎金后释放(某人). ~ **bill**, ~ **bond**【国际法】(被捕获船舶的)赎回证书〔有此证书的船只此后即通行无阻,可不再受同一国家其他船只的侵袭〕.

rant [rænt] *n.* 大话,夸口话;叫喊,叫声;怒吼;〔Scot.〕欢嚷吵闹. — *vi.* 说粗暴话,大声叫喊;咆哮,怒吼;做戏似地说;说大话;大声讲道[祈祷];怒骂. *~ and rave* 大声叫嚷. — *vt.* 夸口说,大声说. *~ out one's denunciation* 激昂地指责.

ran·tan [ˈræntæn] *n.*〔俚〕敲打声;〔美〕喝酒吵闹.

ran·tan·ker·ous [rænˈtæŋkərəs] *a.* 〔美〕倔强的, 乖僻的.

rant·er [ˈræntə] *n.* ①大言壮语的人;粗声大气(喧闹)的人. ②【宗、史】(英国共和制时代狂热地排斥一切教会,牧师,宗教仪式的)喧骚派教徒; (早期美以美教派大声祈祷或说教的)狂热派教徒[牧师]. ③〔Scot.〕喧嚷的艺人[歌手].

ran·u·la [ˈrænjulə] *n.* 舌下囊肿.

ra·nun·culus [rəˈnʌŋkjuləs] *n.* *(pl. ~es, -li* [-lai]*)*【植】毛茛(属) (= buttercup).

ranz-des-vaches [rɑ̃ːndeivɑːʃ] *n.* 〔F.〕(阿尔卑斯山区牧人用角笛吹奏召集牛羊的)召牛调.

raob [ˈreiəb] *n.* 无线电探空仪观测.

R.A.O.C., RAOC = Royal Army Ordnance Corps〔英〕皇家陆军军械兵.

rap[1] [ræp] *n.* ①重敲,拍;敲(门)声,拍(桌)声(等). ②〔美俚〕监禁,处罚,责骂. ***beat the ~*** 〔美俚〕逃过刑事责任. ***get a ~ on [over] the knuckles*** 受谴责,受申斥,受责骂. ***give sb. a ~ on [over] the knuckles*** 申斥,责骂. ***take the ~*** 挨骂. — *vt.* ①用力敲,嘭嘭地敲[拍].②突然讲,出其不意地说,严厉地说. ③〔美〕斥责,苛评. *~ out* 严厉地说,突然说出;把(意思等)用敲击声表现出来;敲奏(钢琴);击倒. — *vi.* ①敲(门) *(at, on)*. ②发急促尖锐声. ②说粗野话.

rap[2] [ræp] *n.* ①(从前爱尔兰通用的)半辨士私铸货币. ②〔口〕一文(也不),一点儿(也不). *do not care a ~* 一点也不在意.

rap[3] [ræp] *vt.* *(rapped, rapt* [ræpt]*)* ①使心荡神移,使神往,迷住〔多用被动结构〕. ②〔古〕抢去,夺去. ***~ and rend [ren, run, ring, wring]*** (生方设法地)获得;

强夺.

rap[4] [ræp] *vi.* 〔美俚〕自由而坦率地谈论; 交谈 *(to)*; 理解. — *n.* 交谈; 谈论. ~ **session** (非正式的)小组讨论会[座谈会]. ~ **sheet** 〔美俚〕警方档案.

R.A.P. = Regimental Aid Post 〔英〕团救护所.

ra·pa·cious [rəˈpeiʃəs] *a.* ①强夺的, 掠夺的, 剥削性的; 贪婪的. ②【动】(猛禽等)捕食动物的. **-ly** *ad.*

ra·pac·i·ty [rəˈpæsiti] *n.* 强夺, 掠夺(性); 贪婪.

R.A.P.C., RAPC = Royal Army Pay Corps 〔英〕皇家陆军财务队.

rape[1] [reip] *n.* (榨汁后制醋用的)葡萄渣; 制醋用的滤器. ~ *wine* 渣汁葡萄酒, 二汁葡萄酒.

rape[2] [reip] *n.* ①〔古、诗〕强夺, 抢夺, 掠夺. ②【法】强奸. — *vt., vi.* ①抢, 强夺, 掠夺. ②强奸. ~ ***and rend*** = rap and rend.

rape[3] [reip] *n.* 【植】芸苔, 油菜. ~ **cake** 菜子饼. ~ **oil** 菜油. ~ **seed** 菜子.

Raph·a·el [ˈreifl, ˈræfeil] *n.* ①拉斐尔〔姓氏〕. ②**Santi [Sanzio]** ~ 拉斐尔〔1483—1520, 意大利画家〕.

Raph·a·el·esque [ˌræfeiəˈlesk] *a.* 意大利画家、建筑家拉斐尔 (Raphael) 风格的.

ra·phe [ˈreifi] *n.* ①【解】缝际. ②【植】脊; 种脊, 珠脊.

ra·phi·a [ˈreifiə, ˈræfiə] *n.* =raffia.

ra·phide [ˈreifid, ˈræfid] *n.* *(pl.* ***raph·i·des*** [ˈræfidiːz, ˈreifidz]*)* 【植】针晶体.

rap·id [ˈræpid] *a.* ①快, 急(流). ②敏捷的, 麻俐的, 快手快脚的(工人等). ③峻险的(坡等). ④【摄】感光快的. *a* ~ *stream* 急流. *a* ~ *thinker* 颖慧的思想家. *a* ~ *journey* 匆促的旅行. *a* ~ *decline* 急性肺痨. — *n.* 〔常 *pl.*〕急流; 滩, 碛; 湍流. **~-fire, ~-firing** *a.* 速射(用)的. **~-firer** 速射炮[枪]. ~ **transit** 〔美〕高速交通系统. **-ly** *ad.* 快, 迅速, 敏捷, 立刻. **-ness** *n.* 〔罕〕= rapidity.

ra·pid·i·ty [rəˈpiditi] *n.* 迅速, 急速, 敏捷; 速度.

ra·pi·er [ˈreipiə] *n.* (旧时决斗用的)轻巧细长的剑. *a* ~ *thrust* 用剑戳; 妙语, 妙论. *a* ~ *glance* 目光锐利的一瞅.

rap·ine [ˈræpain] *n.* 劫掠, 掠夺; 【林】滥伐.

rap·ist [ˈreipist] *n.* 强奸犯.

rap·pa·ree [ˌræpəˈriː] *n.* ①【史】十七世纪爱尔兰革命时的民兵〔非正规军〕. ②强盗, 海盗, 流寇, 散兵; 游民.

rap·pee [ræˈpiː] *n.* 粗鼻烟.

rap·pel [ræˈpel, rə-] *n.* 坐式下降法〔指登山者用双绳一端系于山上, 一端系在自己身上, 从悬岩陡壁滑下〕. — *vi.* *(-pel·led; -pel·ling)* 用绳绕双腿下降.

rap·pen [ˈrɑːpən] *n.* *(pl. -pen)* 分〔瑞士货币单位"分"的德语名称〕.

rap·per [ˈræpə] *n.* 叩击者[物]; (尤指)敲门者; 敲门锤.

rap·port [ræˈpɔːt] *n.* 〔F.〕①关系; 友好关系; 和好, 和睦, 亲善. ②降神术中的与神鬼灵魂交往. ***be on [in]*** ~ ***with*** 跟…和好(一致).

rap·por·teur [ˌræpɔːˈtuə; F. rapɔrˈtœːr] *n.* 指定为委员会(或大会)起草报告等的人.

rap·proche·ment [ræˈprɔʃmɑ̃ːŋ] *n.* 〔F.〕和解, 和睦; (恢复或建立)友好关系; 恢复国交.

rap·scal·lion [ræpˈskæljən] *n.* 恶棍, 无赖, 流氓.

rapt [ræpt] rap[3] 的过去式及过去分词. — *a.* ①被夺去的 *(away; up)*. ②销魂的, 着迷的; 热心的, 全神贯注的; 发狂似的, 狂喜的. ***be*** ~ ***in wonder*** 惊异得目瞪口呆. ***listen with*** ~ ***attention*** 入迷地听. ~ ***to the seventh heaven*** 欢天喜地.

rap·to·rial [ræpˈtɔːriəl] *a.* 【动】捕食动物的(鸟兽等); 食肉的; 猛禽类的. — *n.* 猛禽. *a* ~ *bird [beast]* 猛禽[兽].

rap·ture [ˈræptʃə] *n.* 狂喜; 〔常 *pl.*〕欢天喜地. *recall childhood's* ~*s of delight* 回忆幼时快乐. ***be in [go into]*** ~***s over [about]***. 狂喜, 欢天喜地. ***fall [go] into*** ~***s over*** 对…发起迷来. ~ ***of the deep*** ①深海晕眩. ②【医】氮麻醉(法) (= nitrogen narcosis).

rap·tured [ˈræptʃəd] *a.* 欢天喜地的, 高兴得不得了的.

rap·turous [ˈræptʃərəs] *a.* 狂喜的, 欢天喜地的; 兴高采烈的, 热烈的. *(a shout of)* ~ *applause* 热烈的鼓掌(喝采). **-ly** *ad.*

ra·ra a·vis [rɛərəˈævis] *(pl.* ***ra·rae a·ves*** [ˈrɛəriːˈeiviːz]*)* 〔L.〕少见的鸟; 稀有事物[人物]; 怪人; 神童; 珍品.

rare[1] [rɛə] *a.* ①稀少的; (空气等)稀薄的; (群岛、星等)稀疏的. ②稀有的, 珍奇的; 极好的, 珍贵的. ③〔口〕非常有趣的. *It is no* ~ *thing.* 那不算什么稀奇. *a* ~ *book* 珍本. ~ *earths* 【化】稀土族. ~ *metals* 稀有金属. *You are a* ~ *one.* 你是一个难得的[了不起的]人. *I had* ~ *fun with him.* = *We had a* ~ *time of it, he and I.* 我和他过得极快乐. *(kind)* ***in a*** ~ ***degree*** 极(亲切的). ***in*** ~ ***cases*** = ***on*** ~ ***occasions*** 难得, 偶尔. ~ ***and*** 〔口〕非常 *(I was* ~ *and hungry.* 我非常饿). — *ad.* 〔口、诗〕非常, 很, 极. *a* ~ *fine view* 极好的风景.

rare[2] [rɛə] *a.* 〔美〕(肉)烹调得嫩的, 半熟的.

rare·bit [ˈrɛəbit] *n.* = Welsh rabbit.

rar·ee show [ˈrɛəriː ʃəu] *n.* ①西洋镜; ②杂耍; 表演.

rar·e·fac·tion [ˌrɛəriˈfækʃən] *n.* 稀少, 稀薄; 纯净; 【化】稀疏(作用). **-tive** *a.*

rar·e·fy [ˈrɛərifai] *vt.* 把(气体)弄稀薄; 使(人格、精神等)纯洁; 使(思想等)精细. ~ *one's earthly desires* 涤除尘俗的欲念. — *vi.* 变稀薄; 变纯洁.

rare·ly [ˈrɛəli] *ad.* 极, 极少有地, 极精彩地; 难得, 很少 *(opp.* often*)*. *I* ~ *meet him.* 我难得遇到他.

rare·ness [ˈrɛənis] *n.* 稀奇; 稀薄; 珍奇, 珍贵.

rare·ripe [ˈrɛəraip] *a.* 早熟的. — *n.* 早熟; 早熟的水果[蔬菜].

rar·i·ty [ˈrɛəriti] *n.* 奇事, 珍品, 奇物; 稀薄, 稀少.

Raro·tonga [ˌrɑːrəuˈtɔŋgə] *n.* 拉罗通加〔库克群岛首都〕.

ras·bo·ra [ræzˈbɔːrə] *n.* 【动】波鱼(属).

R.A.S.C., RASC = Royal Army Service Corps 〔英〕皇家陆军补给与运输勤务队.

ras·cal [ˈrɑːskəl] *n.* ①恶棍, 坏蛋, 流氓. ②〔谑〕家伙. — *a.* 无赖的, 无耻的; 〔罕〕卑鄙的. *the* ~ *rout* 〔古〕平民. *You lucky* ~. 你这幸运的家伙!

ras·cal·dom [ˈrɑːskəldəm] *n.* 流氓[歹徒]集团; 流氓行为; 卑鄙龌龊的事.

ras·cal·ism [ˈrɑːskəlizəm] *n.* 〔罕〕= rascality.

ras·cal·i·ty [rɑːsˈkæliti] *n.* 罪恶勾当; 无赖行为; 流氓行为[习气].

ras·cal·lion [rɑːsˈkæljən] *n.* 恶棍, 流氓, 歹徒.

ras·cal·ly [ˈrɑːskəli] *a.* 恶棍的, 流氓的, 歹徒的; 无赖的; 卑鄙的, 无耻的. — *ad.* 无赖地; 卑鄙地.

rase [reiz] *vt.* 〔罕〕= raze.

rash[1] [ræʃ] *a.* 轻率的, 鲁莽的; 性急的; 过早的, 未成熟的. *be* ~ *enough* 胆敢; 贸然. ~ *advance* 冒进. **-ly** *ad.* **-ness** *n.*

rash[2] [ræʃ] *n.* 【医】①(皮)疹. ②同时大量出现的事件. *a heat* ~ 热疹. *a nettle* ~ 荨麻疹. *the* ~ *of student disturbances* 连续发生的学生闹事事件.

rash·er [ˈræʃə] *n.* 煎咸肉[火腿]片.

ra·so·ri·al [rəˈsɔːriəl] *a.* 【动】搔拨类的[如鸡]; 鹑鸡类的.

rasp [rɑːsp] *n.* ①粗锉, 木锉; 【机】锉机; 锉磨而发出的刺耳声音. ②(心里的)焦急, 烦躁. — *vt.* ①用粗锉锉 *(off; away)*; 粗锉, 粗刮, 粗擦; 把…弄得刺耳地响. ②伤(人感情), 使焦急, 使急躁; 用急躁刺耳的声音说 *(out)*. — *vi.* 锉, 磨擦; 嘎擦嘎擦地响. **-er** [-ə] *n.* ①木锉; 锉刀; (甜菜根的)磨碎器. ②【猎】(难于飞越的)高墙, 障碍. ③〔俚〕令人讨厌的人[东西].

rasp·ber·ry [ˈrɑːzbəri] *n.* ①【植】悬钩子; 木莓, 山莓. ②红光暗紫色. ③〔美俚〕咂舌头嘲笑的声音, 讥笑; 谴责. ***get the*** ~ 被(咂舌头)嘲笑. ***hand [give] sb. the***

～（咂舌头）嘲笑某人. — *a.* 紫红色的. ～**-canes**（次年结果的）悬钩子的新枝. ～ **vinegar** 树莓醋.

rasp·ing [ˈrɑːspiŋ] *a.* 锉的；嘎嘎响的；使人烦躁的. *a* ～ *voice* 刺耳的语声.

rasp·y [ˈrɑːspi, ˈræs-] *a.* ***(rasp·i·er; rasp·i·est)*** ①发刺耳声的；使人烦躁的. ②易怒的. **-i·ness** *n.*

ras·sle [ræsl] *n., vi., vt.* ***(-sled; -sling)***〔方，口〕摔交(= wrestle).

rass·ling [ˈræsliŋ] *n.*〔口，方〕= wrestling.

ras·ter [ˈræstə] *n.*【电视】光栅，(无图象的横线)屏面；【摄】网板. ～ **display**【自】光栅显像〔电子计算机输出的一种图形显像〕.

ra·sure [ˈreiʒə] *n.* 削除，抹掉，作过删除的痕迹（= erasure). *There are many ～s in the manuscript.* 原稿中有许多删除的痕迹.

RAT = rocket-launched antisubmarine torpedo 火箭发射式反潜鱼雷.

rat[1] [ræt] *n.* ①【动】鼠〔比 mouse 要大〕. ②〔俚〕(患难时的)脱党者，退会者，变节者，叛徒，卑劣的人；〔俚〕接受低于工会规定工资的工人，不参加罢工的工人，工贼；〔美俚〕特务. ③〔美口〕(衬在头发下的)假发卷. ④〔*pl.*〕〔美俚〕发酒疯. ⑤〔美俚〕大学新生；下流女人. ***as drunk [poor, weak] as a*** ～ 喝得酩酊大醉〔穷得身无分文，弱得气力毫无〕. ***die like a*** ～ 被毒死. ***have a*** ～ ***in the garret [attic]***〔口〕头脑不正常，有点精神病. ***like a drowned*** ～ 象落汤鸡，浑身湿透. ***like a*** ～ ***in a hole*** 象瓮中之鳖. ***smell a*** ～ 觉得可疑，发觉，看出苗头. — *vi.* ①(特指用狗)捕鼠. ②变节，脱党；〔俚〕接受低于工会规定的工资工作，不参加罢工，接替罢工工人的位置，破坏罢工；〔美俚〕叛变，告密，做特务. ～ ***on*** 出卖. ～**bite fever**【医】鼠咬热. ～ **cheese**（工厂制造的）硬奶酪. ～ **face**〔美〕奸险人物. ～ **fink** 可鄙的人（= fink). ～ **firm** 雇用破坏罢工工人的工厂. ～ **guard**【海】(船索上的)防鼠装置. ～ **poison** 杀鼠药. ～ **race**〔美俚〕费神的日常工作. ～**trap** ①捕鼠夹. ②〔英空俚〕气球防空网. ③(自行车)有齿脚蹬. ④陷入绝境. ⑤〔口〕肮脏破烂的房屋.

rat[2] [ræt] *vt.*〔俚〕诅咒，责骂. ***R- me if I'll do it.*** 绝对〔砍了我的头也〕不干.

rat·a·ble [ˈreitəbl] *a.* ①可估价的，可评价的. ②〔英〕应征税的. ③按比例…的. *the* ～ *value* 征税估价. **-bil·i·ty** [ˌreitəˈbiliti] *n.*〔英〕纳税义务；估价. **-bly** *ad.*

rat·a·fia, rat·a·fee [ˌrætəˈfiə, -fiː] *n.* 果酒〔用樱桃仁等调味的甜酒〕；果酒味饼干.

rat·al [ˈreitl]〔英〕*n.* 征税价格，纳税额. — *a.* 征税价格的，纳税的.

RATAN = radar and television aid to navigation 用于导航的雷达和电视设备.

ra·tan [ræˈtæn] *n.* = rattan.

rat·a·plan [ˌrætəˈplæn] *n.* 冬冬〔鼓声〕. — *vt.* 敲(鼓)，用鼓敲奏. — *vi.* (鼓)冬冬地响.

rat-a-tat [ˈrætəˈtæt] *n.* 砰砰〔敲门声等〕.

ratch·et, ratch [ˈrætʃit, rætʃ] *n.*【机】棘齿，棘爪；(尤指钟表、机器的)棘轮，制轮；棘轮机构. — *vt.* 把…造成棘齿形；于作棘齿，在…上刻锯齿. ～ **brace** 扳钻. ～ **wheel** 棘轮，制轮，闸轮.

rate[1] [reit] *n.* ①比率，率；速度，进度；程度；(钟的快慢)差率. ②价格；行市，行情；估价，评价；费，费用，运费. ③(船或船员的)等级. ④〔常 *pl.*〕捐税；〔英〕地方税. ⑤程度，方式，情况，样子. *the birth [death]* ～ 出生〔死亡〕率. *the seed* ～ 播种率. *the fuel* ～ 燃料消耗率. ～ *cutting* 减低运费〔保险费〕. *the* ～ *of interest* 利率. *the rotation* ～ 转速. ～*s of exchange* = *exchange* ～*s* 外汇率，汇价，汇兑行情. *postal* ～*s* 邮费. *railroad* ～*s* 铁路运费. ～ *of profit* 利润率. ～ *of surplus value* 剩余价值率. *the first* ～ 头等的，上等的. *Things are going first-*～. 事情进行顺畅. ～*s and taxes* 地方税和国税. *the poor* ～〔英〕贫民救济税. ***at a good [terrible]*** ～ 以相当〔惊人〕的速度. ***at a great*** ～ 以高速度，飞快地；大大地，非常地. ***at a high [low]*** ～ 以高〔低〕价 *(live at a high* ～ 生活豪华). ***at all*** ～***s*** 无论如何，一定要. ***at an easy*** ～ 非常容易地，毫不费力地. ***at any*** ～ 总而言之，无论如何. ***at that [this]*** ～〔口〕那〔这〕种样子，照那〔这〕种情形 (*If you go on at that* ～*, you will injure your health.* 你如果照这样子继续下去，你会损害健康的). ***at the*** ～ ***of*** 按…的比例；以…的速度. ***be (come) on the*** ～***s***（贫民）受救济. ***by no*** ～ 决没有…. ***give special*** ～***s*** 给(特惠)折扣. ～ ***of climb***【空】上升速度. — *vt.* ①估价，评价〔常用被动语态〕. ②看做，认为. ③征(地方)税；定(船、船员的)等级；测定(钟表等的)快慢；〔美〕给…批分数；〔美〕按一定运费运输. ④〔美俚〕有…的价值〔资格〕，值得. ～*d age*【保险】标准年龄. ～*d current* 额定电流. ～*d horse-power* 额定马力. ～ **up**（按危险情况）提高保险费. — *vi.* ①被估价，被评价. ②有(某种)价值. ③列于(某一)等级，列入. *The ship* ～*s as a ship of the line.* 这只船列入战列舰级. ～ ***with sb.*** 得某人好评. ～**card**（列举收费标准的）广告费卡. ～**meter** 速率计；(辐射)强度计. ～**payer**〔英〕纳（地方）税人. ～**-war** 减价竞争.

rate[2] [reit] *vt., vi.* 申斥，斥责，骂.

rate[3] [reit] *vt., vi.*〔方〕= ret.

rate·a·ble [ˈreitəbl] *a.* = ratable.

ra·tel [ˈreitel] *n.*【动】(南非)蜜獾.

rat·er[1] [ˈreitə] *n.* ①某一等级的人〔物〕；…吨的比赛艇. ②定等级者；估价者，评价者. *a 10-*～ 十吨快艇. *a first-*～ 一流人物；头等货.

rat·er[2] [ˈreitə] *n.* 责骂者，抱怨者.

rat·fish [ˈrætˌfiʃ] *n.* ***(pl. -fish, -fish·es)***【动】银鲛属 (Chimaera) 的鱼.

rath[1] [rɑːθ] *n.*【考古】(爱尔兰古代族长住所的)围墙，山寨围垣.

rath[2]**, rathe** [reið] *a.*〔诗、古〕快的，敏捷的；比普通时刻早的；早开的，早生的，早熟的.

rat·haus [ˈrɑːthaus] *n.*〔G.〕市〔镇〕议会厅.

rath·er [ˈrɑːðə] *ad.* ①〔与动词连用〕宁愿，宁可，毋宁. ②稍微，有点；相当，颇；比较地说. ★在形容词 + 名词的结构中带有不定冠词时，rather 通常可位于不定冠词之前，也可位于其后. ③〔与 or 连用〕说得更恰当点，更确切地说. ④相反地，反而，倒不如说…更好〔更合理〕. ⑤〔与连词 than 配合〕(与其…)不如(好). ⑥〔用作表语〕更应当，更应该，当然. *I would* ～ *not go.* 我宁可不去. *Which would you* ～ *have, tea or coffee?* 你喜欢喝茶，还是喝咖啡呢？ *I'd* ～ *he was married to somebody else.* 我宁愿他同别的人结婚. *He's done* ～ *well.* 他做得相当好. *This one is* ～ *too large.* 这个稍微大一点. *That is* ～ *an unusual question* (= a ～ unusual question) 这是一个相当异常的问题. *He got home late last night, or* ～ *early this morning.* 他昨天半夜里，更确切地说，今天一清早才回到家. *He was no better, but* ～ *grew worse.* 他的病情未见好转，反而更恶化了. *It's not generosity,* ～ *self-interest.* 这不是慷慨，相反，这是自私. *He is honest* ～ *than clever.* 与其说他聪明，不如说他老实. *It is* ～ *cold than not [otherwise].*（不管怎么说）天就是冷. *I had* ～ *go than stay to be insulted.* 我宁可去，也不愿留着受辱. *He insisted on staying* ～ *than go.* 他坚持要留下来，而不愿意去. *It is* ～ *for us to be here dedicated to the great task remaining before us.* 我们更应当在这里献身于摆在我们面前的伟大事业. — [ˈrɑːˈðəː] *int.* 怎么不，当然. *Have you been here before?* — *R-*！你以前到这儿来过吗？ — 当然来过！ ***had [would]*** ～ ***… than***（与其…）不如. ～ ***than*** 而不. ～ ***too …*** 稍微…一点. (*This one is* ～ *too large.* 这个稍微大一点). ***the*** ～ ***that [because]*** 尤其因为…(就更加).

rat·hole [ˈræthəul] *n.* ①被老鼠咬成的洞。②鼠穴。③狭小龌龊的地方。***(go) down the ~*** 白白浪费。

raths·kel·ler [ˈrɑːts-kelə] *n.* 〔G.〕①〔R-〕市议会厅的地下室餐厅[啤酒厅]。②〔美〕德国式地下室餐馆[咖啡馆、酒吧]。

rat·i·cide [ˈrætisaid] *n.* 杀鼠药。

rat·i·fi·ca·tion [ˌrætifiˈkeiʃən] *n.* 批准,认可;追认。

rat·i·fi·er [ˈrætifaiə] *n.* 批准者,认可者;追认者。

rat·i·fy [ˈrætifai] *vt.* 批准,认可(代理商等);追认。~ *an amendment to a constitution* 批准宪法修正案。

ra·ti·né [ˌrætˈnei], **ra·tine** [ræˈtiːn] *n.*【纺】平纹结子花呢,珠皮大衣呢。

rat·ing[1] [ˈreitiŋ] *n.* ①分等级;定等级;估价;估计;分摊,分配;【电】测定,计算;〔美〕(考试的)批分数。②额定值,定额;参量;工作能力;(商店的)信用程度;〔英〕地方税征收额。③【海】(船舰或海员的)等级;(汽车等的)规格;〔*pl.*〕〔英〕刚入伍的船员。④(电台、电视台经调查确定的)节目受欢迎的程度。*a nominal ~* 标准规格。*a power ~*额定功率。

rat·ing[2] [ˈreitiŋ] *n.* 叱责,斥责: *give a sound ~* 严厉申斥一顿。

ra·ti·o [ˈreiʃiəu] *n.* ***(pl. ~s)*** ①比,比率,比值;比例;系数。②【经】复本位制中金银的法定比价。*the ~ 3:2* (读作 *the ~ of three to two*) 3对2之比。*arithmetical ~* 公差,算术比。*direct ~* 正比。*inverse [reciprocal] ~* 反比。*current ~* 电流比,电流变换系数。*nutritive ~* 营养率。— *vt.* ①用比例方式表达;求出…的比值;使…成比例。②将(相片)按比例放大或缩小。

ra·ti·oc·i·nate [ˌrætiˈɔsineit] *vi.* 推理,推论;推断;用三段论法推论。

ra·ti·oc·i·na·tion [ˌrætiˌɔsiˈneiʃən] *n.* 推理,推论。

ra·ti·oc·i·na·tive [ˌrætiˈɔsineitiv] *a.* 推理的,推论的;爱推论的,好议论的。

ra·tion [ˈræʃən] *n.* ①(供应物等的)限额,定额,定量;饲料配(给)量。②〔常 *pl.*〕(一般人或动物尤指兵员的)每日口粮;食物;军粮,军肉;粮食。*the iron [emergency] ~*【军】紧急用的浓缩食物;随身干粮。***be put on ~s*** 实行配给供应制;计口授粮。***on short ~s*** 处于配给量不足的限制下。— *vt.* (按额定分量)配给;给与…一天口粮;供给(兵士)伙食;限定(粮食等)。*The army is well ~ed.* 部队给养很好。~ **book** 配给供应本。~-**bread** 配给面包;军用面包。~ **export** 限额输出。~ **system** 配给制,供给制。

ra·tion·al [ˈræʃənl] *a.* ①理性的。②推理的;有理性的;懂道理的,讲道理的;合理的,合道理的;纯理论的。③【数】有理的。*the stage of ~ knowledge* 理性认识阶段 (*cf.* perceptual). *Man is a ~ being.* 人是理性动物。*the ~ faculty* 推理力。*a ~ man* 有理性的[言行合理的]人。*~ conduct* 合理的行为。*a ~ explanation* 合乎情理的解释。— *n.* ①【数】有理数。②合理的事物;理性。③懂道理的人,人类。④〔*pl.*〕〔英〕合理的服装(= ~ dress). ~ **expression**【数】有理式。~ **analysis**【化】示构分析。**-ly** *ad.*

ra·ti·o·na·le [ˌræʃiəˈnɑːli] *n.* 理论的说明;基本原理,理论基础 (*of*).

ra·tio·nal·ism [ˈræʃənəlizəm] *n.*【哲】理性主义;唯理论 (*opp.* empiricism).

ra·tion·al·ist [ˈræʃənlist] *n.* 理性主义者,唯理论者。— *a.* = rationalistic.

ra·tion·al·is·tic [ˌræʃənəˈlistik] *a.* 理性主义(者)的;唯理论(者)的。

ra·tion·al·i·ty [ˌræʃəˈnæliti] *n.* 合理性;推理力;理由;〔*pl.*〕合理的意见[行动]。

ra·tion·al·i·za·tion [ˌræʃənəlaiˈzeiʃən] *n.* ①(尤指事业等的)合理化,合理状态。②理论解释。③【数】有理化;【心】文饰(作用)。~ *proposals* 合理化建议。

ra·tion·alize [ˈræʃənəlaiz] *vt.* ①使合理,合理化。②据理[在理论上]解释。③【数】使成为有理数,使消根。④【心】文饰。*a ~d unit*【物】槪理单位。— *vi.* ①据理说明[行动]。②实行合理化。③文过饰非。

ra·tion·ing [ˈræʃəniŋ] *n.* 定量配给。

rat·ite [ˈrætait] *a.*【动】平胸类 (*Ratitae*) 的,无龙骨的。— *n.* 平胸类鸟〔如食火鸡;鸵鸟等〕。

rat·lin(e)s; rat·lings [ˈrætlinz, -liŋz] *n.* 〔*pl.*〕【海】绳梯横索。

rato, RATO [ˈreitəu] *n.* 火箭辅助起飞;起飞辅助火箭。〔rocket-assisted take-off 的首字母缩略词〕。~ **unit** 火箭辅助起飞装置。

ra·toon [ræˈtuːn] *n.*【植】截根苗。— *vi.* 发[长出]截根苗。

rats [ræts] *int.* 〔俚〕瞎扯: *Oh, ~!* 胡说!

rats·bane [ˈrætsbein] *n.* 杀鼠药〔特指亚砷酸〕;某些有毒植物的通称。

RATT = radioteletype.

rat·tail [ˈrætteil] *a.* 鼠尾状的,细长的,一端逐渐变细的 **(= rattailed)**. — *n.*【动】长尾鳕。

rat·tan [rəˈtæn] *n.* 籐,籐条;籐杖。

rat-tat, rat-tat-tat, rat-tat·too [ˈrætˈtæt, -tət-ˈtæt, -təˈtuː] *n.* = rat-a-tat.

rat·teen [ræˈtiːn] *n.*【纺】平纹结子花呢;珠皮大衣呢〔流行于十八世纪英国〕。

rat·ten [ˈrætn] *vt.* (工人在劳资争议时)用瘫痪工厂的战术迫使(资方)同意劳方要求,用隐藏或破坏机件的战术迫使(雇主)同意工会的要求。

rat·ter [ˈrætə] *n.* ①捕鼠者;捕鼠猫[狗];捕鼠机。②〔俚〕叛变者,告密者,变节者,叛徒,工贼(等)。

rat·tish [ˈrætiʃ] *a.* 鼠的,似鼠的,具有老鼠特性的。

rat·tle [ˈrætl] *vi.* ①(硬物相碰或敲打时)格格地响。②卡嗒卡嗒地赶马车。③(人或车)飞跑,疾走 (*along; by; in; out; over; down*). ④(临死的人)喉咙呼噜呼噜地响。⑤喋喋不休地讲 (*on; away; along; about*). *He ~d at the door.* 他把门推得格格地响。— *vt.* ①使格格地响。②急促地讲[吟诵](话、诗等) (*away; off; out; over; through*). ③匆匆忙忙做好,赶着完成(工作等)。④使(人)振作 (*up*). ⑤〔口〕使狼狈[慌张],使烦恼。⑥打草赶出猎物。⑦破口烂骂。~ *a bill through the House* 使议案匆匆通过。*Nothing ~d him.* 什么事都惊动不了他。~ *foxes* 打草赶出狐狸。— *n.* ①卡嗒卡嗒声;格格声。②(喉咙的)呼噜声;〔the ~s〕【医】哮吼〔一种喉炎,= croup〕。③喋喋不休(的话);喋喋不休的人。④格格地响的东西;响荚植物;响环,嘎吱嘎吱响的玩具;(响尾蛇的)音响器官。⑤高声吵闹。⑥响(亮程)度。~-**box** ①响盒[玩具]。②【植】金链花猪屎豆。③〔美〕喋喋不休的人。~**brain,** ~**head,** ~**pate** 糊涂虫。~-**snake**〔美〕【动】响尾蛇 (~*snake and polecat*〔美〕时常吵闹的两个人)。~ **stone** 铃石。~**trap** ①(格格响的)破马车;破汽车。②〔*pl.*〕破烂东西。③〔俚〕嘴;多嘴的人。

rat·tled [ˈrætld] *a.* 〔美俚〕兴奋的;狼狈的;慌张的。

rat·tler [ˈrætlə] *n.* ①格格响的东西。②饶舌者。③〔美〕响尾蛇。④〔口〕极好的东西。⑤倾盆大雨。⑥〔美〕货运列车。⑦〔美俚〕有轨电车。⑧磨砖机。

rat·tling [ˈrætliŋ] *a.* ①格格地[卡嗒卡嗒]响的。②〔口〕活泼的,快活的;迅速的。③〔口〕巨大的,非常好的。④【商】原有响声〔对有松动声的包装的声明〕。~ *fun* 喧嚷;喝酒的嚷闹。*a ~ wind* (吹得窗子)卡嗒卡嗒响的风。*a ~ pile of money* 一大堆钱。— *ad.* 〔口〕极,很,非常: ~ *big distance off* 极远极远。*I had a ~ good dinner.* 吃了一顿极好的饭。***at a ~ pace*** 用很快速度。

rat·tly [ˈrætli] *a.* 作格格响的,吵闹的。

rat·ton [ˈrætən] *n.* 〔Scot.〕老鼠〔尤指褐家鼠;黑家鼠〕。

rat·toon [ræˈtuːn] *n., vi.* (= ratoon).

rat·ty [ˈræti] *a.* ①老鼠似的,老鼠特有的。②老鼠多的。

R

③〔俚〕破烂的;可怜的,悲惨的;可卑的;〔英俚〕爱发脾气的. *a ~ smell* 老鼠臭味. *a ~ house* 闹耗子的房屋.

rau·cous [ˈrɔːkəs] *a.* 沙声的; 粗声的; 吵闹的. **-ly** *ad.* **-ness** *n.*

raugh·ty [ˈrɔːti] *a.* 〔英口〕 = rorty.

raunch [rɔntʃ] *n.* 粗野;粗俗.

raun·chy [ˈrɔːntʃi, ˈrɔn-] *a.* 〔美俚〕 ①质量不好的, 邋遢的,便宜的,草率的. ②赤裸裸地描写两性关系的,猥亵的; 有伤风化的; 粗野的; 粗俗的. **-i·ness** *n.*

rau·wol·fi·a [rɔːˈwulfiə, rau-] *n.* 【植】①萝芙木属 *(Rauwolfia)* 印度萝芙木〔热带有毒植物〕. ②【药】蛇根木 *(Rauwolfia serpentina)* 根部粉剂[浸剂]〔可提取萝芙木硷等〕.

rav·age [ˈrævidʒ] *n.* ①破坏,荒废. ②暴力. ③〔常 *pl.*〕破坏的残迹,灾害,损害. *the ~s of time* 年久荒废. — *vt., vi.* ①摧残,蹂躏,破坏,使荒废. ②劫掠. *a countenance ~d by time* 年老衰颓的面容.

R.A.V.C., RAVC = Royal Army Veterinary Corps 〔英〕皇家陆军兽医队.

rave[1] [reiv] *vi.* ①(狂人一般) 说胡话, 说梦话, 叫喊, 叫嚣,嚷 *(about; against; at; of; for)*. ②(海、风等)狂暴,咆哮; 发狂似地讲; 激赏,狂喜 *(about; of)*: *~ about [of] one's misfortunes* 叹惜自已倒霉. *~ against one's fate* 抱怨自己的命运. *~* ***with fury*** 大发脾气, 激怒. — *vt.* 〔多用反身代词〕(风)使自己咆哮得…, (人)使自己讲得[闹得]…. *~ itself out* (暴风等) 咆哮后停息. *~ oneself hoarse* 叫嚷得嗓子都哑了. *~ oneself to sleep* 闹得疲倦地睡着了. — *n.* ①(人、风、浪的)狂闹; 怒吼; 狂闹声. ②〔俚〕狂热,入迷. ***no ~*** 〔美剧〕不是什么大成功. ***a ~ review*** 〔美〕大加赞赏的评论. **~-up** 疯狂的晚会.

rave[2] [reiv] *n.* 〔常 *pl.*〕(马车、卡车上为便于多装货物而设置的)围子,围栏,围板.

rav·el [ˈrævəl] **(**〔英〕***-ll-*****)** *vt.* ①解开,拆开(缠绕着的东西); 理清, 弄明白(错综复杂的事件) *(out)*. ②使纠缠, 使纷乱. — *vi.* ①(编织物等)散开,脱开;(纠纷、混乱)解决;(困难)解除 *(out)*. ②纠结,缠绕,纷乱: *a hem to prevent its ~ling out* 防止散开的边. *the ~led skein of life* 错综复杂的人生. — *n.* 纠结, 缠绕; (绳、织物等)散开的一端; 错杂,混乱.

rave·lin [ˈrævlin] *n.* 【筑城】半月堡.

ra·vel·ling [ˈrævəliŋ] *n.* 解,拆;解开;散开的线.

rav·el·ment [ˈrævlment] *n.* 缠结,纠缠,混乱.

ra·ven[1] [ˈreivən] *n.* ①【动】渡鸦,大乌鸦. ②〔R-〕【天】乌鸦座. — *a.* 黑而亮的,乌亮的,(头发等)乌黑的: *~ locks [hair]* 黑发.

ra·ven[2] [ˈrævən] *n.* ①强夺,劫掠,抢劫. ②强夺物,赃. — *vi.* ①掠夺,到处抢劫 *(about)*. ②往来捕食 *(for; after)*. — *vt.* 狼吞虎咽地吃.

rav·en·ing [ˈrævniŋ] *a.* 贪婪地捕食的, 掠食的. — *n.* = ravin.

rav·en·ous [ˈrævinəs] *a.* ①贪食的, 贪婪的. ②饿极了的; 渴望的. **-ly** *ad.* **-ness** *n.*

rav·in(e) [ˈrævin] *n.* ①〔诗〕劫掠. ②掠夺物, 赃物. ③大嚼: *a beast [bird] of ~* 猛兽[禽].

ra·vine [rəˈviːn] *n.* 沟壑,深谷,峡谷,山涧.

rav·ing [ˈreiviŋ] *a.* ①说胡话的. ②疯狂的, 怒吼的, 狂暴的. ③令人醉心[痴心]的;〔美口〕非常的,(美人)绝代的. *a ~ lunatic* 胡说胡讲的疯子. *a ~ storm* 凶猛的暴风雨. *a ~ beauty* 绝代佳人. — *ad.* 胡说乱讲地;疯狂地. *be ~ mad* 胡说乱讲地发疯. — *n.* 〔常 *pl.*〕 胡话.

ra·vi·o·li [rævi'əuli] *n.* 〔*pl.*〕〔It.〕【烹】煮合子〔象中国的饺子,但为圆形或方形,煮熟后浇上番茄沙司吃〕.

rav·ish [ˈræviʃ] *vt.* ①强夺; 抢去, 攫去; 〔诗〕(死神)把(人)从人世夺去. ②使心荡神移; 使出神; 使销魂, 使狂喜. ③强奸. **-ing** *a.* 引人入胜的;令人狂喜的,销魂的. **-ing·ly** *ad.* **-ment** *n.*

raw [rɔː] *a.* ①(肉等)生的; 未煮过的; 未加工的,粗的; 不搀水的,(酒精等)纯净的. ②未开化的; 未熟的,生硬的, 无经验的; 未经训练的,不完备的. ③(伤处等)皮肤绽开的, 露出了肉的. ④露骨的; 〔口〕猥亵的. ⑤〔俚〕苛刻的,不当的; 刺痛的,针刺似的. ⑥阴冷的, 湿冷的, 冷冰冰的. *~ brick* (未烧的) 砖坯. *~ fish* 生鱼. *a ~ cocoon* 鲜茧. *~ silk* 生丝. *~ coal* 原煤. *~ cotton* 原棉,籽棉. *~ cloth* (未漂白的)原色布. *~ sugar* 粗糖. *~ spirits* 纯酒. *~ judgement* 不成熟的判断. *a ~ recruit* 生手,新手; 新兵. *a ~ hand* 新手; 莽撞的小伙子. *a nose ~ from rubbing* 擦破了皮的鼻子. *a ~ weather* 阴冷的天气. ***be ~ to one's work*** 对工作还不熟练 ***a. pull ~ one*** 〔美俚〕讲下流的话; 讲逗趣的故事. — *n.* ①擦破了皮的地方,皮开肉绽的地方, 痛处. ②生的食物; 纯酒; 〔*pl.*〕粗糖; 生牡蛎. ***touch sb. on the ~*** 触到某人痛处,触犯,大伤感情. — *vt.* 〔罕〕(特指将马背的皮) 擦破, 使皮开肉绽. *~* **boned** *a.* 瘦削的, 骨瘦如柴的. *~* **crop tillage system** 中耕农作制. *~* **data** 原始数据. *~* **deal** 〔美〕不公平的待遇; 凶狠的处置. **~head** (哄孩子说的) 妖怪 (*~head and bloody bones* 骷髅头和下面交叉的大腿骨〔死的象征〕). **~hide** ① *n.* 生皮; 生皮鞭,皮条; 皮索. ② *a.* 生皮(制)的. ③ *vt.* 〔美〕用皮条抽打,欺负. *~* **material** 原料. *~* **milk** 未经杀菌的牛奶. **~ship** 【海】新服役舰只. *~* **silk** 生丝. **-ness** *n.*

Ra·wal·pin·di [ˌrɑːvəlˈpindiː] *n.* 拉瓦尔品第〔巴基斯坦城市〕.

ra·win [ˈreiwin] *n.* ①无线电高空测候仪,雷达气球,无线电测风仪. ②被测的风. **~sonde** 无线电探空测风仪,雷达气球.

raw·ish [ˈrɔːiʃ] *a.* 有些生的,煮得不很熟的.

Raw·lin·son [ˈrɔːlinsn] *n.* 罗林森〔姓氏〕.

Ray [rei] *n.* 雷〔姓氏,男子名〕〔Raymond 的昵称〕.

ray[1] [rei] *n.* ①光线,射线,热线;〔诗〕光辉,闪烁,曙光,一线光明. ②辐射状物;【植】伞形花序枝,星状毛分枝,伞形花序枝;【动】鳍刺; 【几】半直线. *actinic ~s* 光化射线. *anode [cathode] ~s* 阳极 [阴极] 线. *Becquerel ~s* 柏克勒尔射线〔法人 Becquerel 发现的镭等的放射线; 有 α *rays*, β *rays*, γ *rays*〕. *cosmic ~s* 宇宙线. *electric ~s* 电子束; 电磁波. *H ~s* 氢离子束. *infra-red ~s* 红外线. *ultra-violet ~s* 紫外线. *Rontgen ~s* = X *~s* X 光线. *a star with six ~s* 六角星. *a ~ of hope* 一线希望. *a ~ of truth* 一丝真理. — *vt.* ①放射, 照射, 投射. ②〔俚〕给…照 X 光像片. — *vi.* 放射光线; (思想、希望等)闪现. **-less** *a.*

ray[2] [rei] *n.* 【动】(短鼻) 鹞鱼 (*cf.* skate[2]): *a whip ~* 魟.

ray·a(h) [ˈrɑːjə] *n.* 非穆斯林的土耳其人 (尤指土耳其的基督教徒).

rayl [reil] *n.* 【物】雷(耳)〔1 牛顿/米^2 声压能产生 1 米/秒质点速度的声阻抗率(值)〕.

Ray·leigh [ˈreili] *n.* 雷利〔姓氏〕.

Ray·mond [ˈreimənd] *n.* 雷蒙德〔姓氏,男子名〕.

ray·on [ˈreiɔn] *n.* 人造丝,人造纤维,雷荣; 人造丝织物.

rayon·nant [ˈreiənənt] *a.* ①射出光线的. ②【建】(窗格等)幅射式的.

raze [reiz] *vt.* ①消除,磨灭(记忆等); 毁坏, 毁灭, 夷平(城市房屋等). ②〔罕〕微伤,擦伤.

ra·zee [reiˈziː] *vt., n.* 【史】拆除上面一层[几层]甲板使船身减低(的船).

ra·zon [ˈreizɔn] *n.* 〔俚〕导弹.

ra·zor [ˈreizə] *n.* 剃刀. *a safety ~* 保安剃刀. ***as sharp as a ~*** 厉害的, 机警的. ***on the [a] ~'s edge*** 在锋口上,在危险关头. ***skin a ~*** 做不可能做的事. *~* **back** 尖突的背脊; 尖峰耸立的山脉; 剃刀鲸; 〔美〕半野猪. *~* **bill** 【鸟】尖嘴海鸦. **~edge** ①(剃刀的)刀口; 锐锋; 尖

R

锐的山背. ②危机,危急时候〔情况〕(*on a ~edge [~'s edge]* 在锋口上,在危险关头). ~ **fish**【动】隆头鱼科的一种鱼. ~ **grinder** 剃刀磨石. ~ **shape**〔美〕准备好了的. ~ **shell**【动】竹蛏. ~ **strop** 磨刀皮带,荡刀皮. ~**-thin** *a.* 极薄的、其薄如纸的.

razz [ræz] *n., vt.*〔美俚〕嘲笑;讥笑;逗惹;责备: *give sb. the ~* 嘲笑,奚落. *get the ~* 被嘲笑,被奚落.

raz·zia [ˈræziə] *n.* ①侵略,袭击,劫掠. ②掳掠奴隶的远征.

raz·zle-daz·zle [ˈræzldæzl] *vt.*〔英俚〕①使混乱. ②使酩酊大醉. ③欺骗. — *n.*〔俚〕①烂醉. ②混乱,慌张失措;嬉戏胡闹,喝酒嚷闹. ③波动式旋转木马. *go on the ~* 狂饮,纵酒取乐.

razz·ma·tazz [ˈræzmətæz] *n.*〔俚〕①愉快的精神;精力,活力;兴奋. ②令人眼花缭乱的动作(或场面),卖弄.

R.B. = Rifle Brigade〔英〕步枪旅;步兵旅.

Rb = rubidium【化】铷.

R.B.A. = Royal Society of British Artists 英国皇家艺术家协会.

RBC = red blood cell【解】红血球,红(血)细胞.

RBE = relative biological effectiveness 相关的生物学效力.

R-boat [ɑːbəut] *n.* (德国的)快速扫雷艇.

RC = resistance capacitance (电)阻(电)容.

R.C., RC = ①Red Cross 红十字(会). ②research centre 研究中心. ③right centre (舞台)中央偏右方. ④Roman Catholic 罗马天主教的;罗马天主教徒. ⑤reinforced concrete【建】钢筋混凝土. ⑥Reserve Corps〔美〕后备军.

r.c. = remote control 遥控.

RCA = Radio Corperation of America 美国无线电公司.

R.C.A.F., RCAF = Royal Canadian Air Force (皇家)加拿大空军.

R.C.C. = Radio Chemical Centre〔英〕放射化学中心.

R.C.Ch., RCC, RCCH = Roman Catholic Church 罗马天主教会.

rcd = received.

RCM = ①radar conntermeasures 反雷达措施. ②radio countermeasures 无线电干扰措施.

R.C.M. = Royal College of Music〔英〕皇家音乐专科学校.

R.C.M.P., RCMP = Royal Canadian Mounted Police (皇家)加拿大骑警队.

R.C.N., RCN = Royal Canadian Navy (皇家)加拿大海军.

R.C.O. = Royal College of Organists〔英〕皇家管风琴学院.

r-col·o(u)red [ˈɑːkʌləd] *a.*【语音】带 r 音色彩的〔如 further 中的 u 和 e〕.

R.C.P. = Royal College of Physicians〔英〕皇家内科医师学会.

rcpt. = receipt.

R.C.S. = ①Royal College of Surgeons〔英〕皇家外科医师学会. ②Royal Corps of Signals〔英〕皇家通信兵(部队).

Rct = Recruit.

R.C.V.S. = Royal College of Veterinary Surgeons〔英〕皇家兽医学会.

R.D. = ①Royal Dragoons〔英〕皇家龙骑兵团. ②rural delivery〔美〕乡村免费邮递.

R/D, R.D. = refer to drawer【商】请询问出票人,请与出票人接洽.

Rd., rd. = ①road. ②rod. ③round. ④【物】rutherford. ⑤reduce. ⑥rendered.

RDA = Recommended Dietary Allowance 推荐饮食量.

RdAc =【化】radio-actinium 射锕.

RDB = Research and Development board〔美〕研究发展局.

R.D.C. = Royal Defence Corps〔英〕皇家保卫团.

R.D.C.A. = Rural District Councils' Association〔英〕乡村区议会联合会.

RDF = ①radio direction finder 无线电测向器,无线电定向仪. ②radio direction finding 无线电探向,无线电测向.

RDP = ration distribution point〔美〕给养分配站.

Rd Th = radio-thorium【化】射钍,放射性钍.

RE, R.E. = ①real estate 不动产,房地产. ②Royal Engineers〔英〕皇家陆军工兵. ③Royal Exchange 伦敦交易所. ④rare earths 稀土元素. ⑤Reformed Episcopal (基督教)新主教派的.

re. = ①(with) reference (to). ②rupee.

re[1] [riː; Am. rei] *n.*【乐】全音阶的长音阶第二音〔相当于音名 D〕.

re[2] [riː] *prep.* 关于〔原法律和商业用语,现在用作口语〕: *~ your esteemed favour of 6th inst.*〔商、口〕关于本月六日专函〔旧式信函用语〕. *I want to speak to you ~ your behaviour.*〔口〕关于你的行为,我想跟你谈一谈. ***in ~*** 关于(*in ~ Bardell vs. Pickwick* 关于巴德尔对皮威克的诉讼). ~ *(Brown)* 关于(布劳恩案).

re[3] [riː]〔拉〕事物〔拉丁语 res 的夺格〕. ~ ***infecta*** 事情未成. ~ ***integra*** (事物等)完整如初.

re- *pref.* [ri, re, riː] ①相互,报复: *re*act, *re*venge. ②反对: *re*sist, *re*volt. ③后,在后: *re*lie, *re*main. ④隐退,秘密: *re*cluse, *re*ticent. ⑤离,去,下: *re*miss, *re*side, *re*tail. ⑥反复,加强语气: *re*double, *re*search, *re*solve. ⑦否定: *re*sign, *re*veal. ⑧又,再,从新,重行: *re*adjust, *re*issue, *re*capture, *re*-entrance. ★〔发音〕①表示'再''又'等意义,且其后音节开头字母系元音或 *h* 时读 [riː] (*re*hearse [riˈhəːs] 例外). ②表示其他意义,且重音在其后一音节时读 [ri]: *re*turn [ritəːn]. ③其后为辅音开头的弱音节时读 [re]: *re*collect [ˌrekəˈlekt]. ★加 *hyphen* 的用法: ①欲与原来已有的词有所区别: *re*-pair (*cf.* repair), *re*-cover (*cf.* recover). ②加强'返复''再'的意义: make and *re*-make, search and *re*-search. ③常在元音前,尤其在元音 e 前: *re*-enter, re-assure〔常作 *re*assure〕.

're [ɑ, ə] = are〔如 *we're; you're; they're*〕.

REA =〔美〕Rural Electrification Administration〔美〕农村电气化管理局.

reach [riːtʃ] *vt.* ①到,抵,到达(特定地点,目的地等);(长度等)达到…;(子弹等)打中;扩展到…,延及…;(作为结果或结论而)达到…;〔美俚〕和…通讯,和…得到联络. ②伸(手等) *(out; to; toward)*; 伸手拿;伸手送达,交给,递给;给予. ③取得,打动,感动(人心等);〔美俚〕行贿而收买到. *Your letter ~ed me yesterday.* 你的信昨日到达. *The rule does not ~ the case.* 这条规则不适用于那种情况. *R- me that book.* 请把那本书递给我. *Would you ~ me the salt, please?* 请把盐递给我好吗? *He is liable to be ~ed by flattery.* 他容易被谄媚奉承所打动. ***as far as the eye can ~*** 就眼力所能及,极目,满目. ~ ***bottom*** 到底;查明,打听出来. ~ ***down one's hat*** 伸手脱帽. ~ ***land*** (渡洋而来的船等)好容易到达陆地;找到稳固的立脚点. ~ ***sb.'s conscience*** 打动某人的良心. ~ ***sb.'s ears*** 落入某人耳里,给某人听到. — *vi.* ①伸手抓(东西);(企图拿到某物等而)伸展身体;(手脚)向前伸出;(草木向某方向)伸长,蔓延. ②竭力想得到,竭力想达到(目的等). ③(在时间、空间或程度范围上)扩展,达到 *(to; into)*. ④〔古〕抵达,到达. ⑤【航】横风行驶. ~ ***after [at, for]*** 竭力想达到,竭力想得到〔拿到〕. ~ ***out*** ①伸(手);伸手(拿…) *(for)*. ②(手)伸向前;(草木向…)生长. — *n.* ①伸手(抓东西),伸展身体;手脚所能伸的限度;宽窄,广袤;到达,到达距离;(枪、炮弹等的)射程,所能及的限度,极度. ②理解力,智力;力量.

③区域，领域，范围，有效范围，势力范围；(河流二湾曲间眼所能及的)直线流域，(运河二闸门间的)河段，河流流程；〔美〕岬. ④一次努力；【海】横风行驶；一气进行的航程. *a* ～ *of grassland* 一大片草原. *He has a wonderful* ～ *of imagination.* 他具有很丰富的想象力. *the upper [lower]* ～*es of a river* 河的上[下]流. ***beyond [above] one's*** ～ 达不到，够不着；力量不及. ***have a wide*** ～ 范围宽广. ***make a*** ～ ***for*** *(sb., sth.)* 向…伸出手去；企图抓住. ***out of one's*** ～ = beyond one's ～. ***out of*** ～ ***of danger*** 脱离危险. ***within easy*** ～ ***of*** 在容易达到…的地方，在…的附近 (*My house is within easy* ～ *of the station.* 我家离车站很近[在车站附近]). ***within one's*** ～ 在够得着的地方；力量能做到的；能得到的.

reach-me-down [ˈriːtʃmidaun] *a.* 〔口〕现成的；穿旧了的，别人用过的. — *n.* ①〔常 *pl.*〕现成衣服；旧衣服. ②〔*pl.*〕〔美〕裤子.

re•act[1], **re-act** [ri(ː)ˈækt] *vt.* 再做，重做；再演，重演.

re•act[2] [riˈækt] *vi.* ①反应；发生反作用 *(to)*. ②【化】反应 *(on, upon)*；【物】反拨 *(against; upon)*. ③反抗；【军】反攻. ④反动，倒退，复古. ～ ***against*** 反抗. ～ ***upon*** 对…起反应；作用于… (*Tyranny* ～*s upon the tyrant.* 对于暴虐者反应也是暴虐行动).

re•act•ance [ri(ː)ˈæktəns] *n.* 反作用力；【电】电抗；电抗器.

re•act•ant [riːˈæktənt] *n.* 【化】反应物.

re•ac•tion [ri(ː)ˈækʃən] *n.* ①反作用，反应；反冲；反动力. ②【政】反动，倒退，复古(运动). ③【化】反应，【物】反应力，反作用力；【无】反馈，回授；反向辐射；【医】反应；副作用，后效应；(紧张兴奋后的)无气力，虚脱. ④【商】猛跌. ⑤【军】反击. *action and* ～ 作用与反作用. *the* ～ *of mental on material things* 精神对于物质的反应. *chain* ～ 连锁反应. *nuclear* ～ (原子)核反应. *rocket* ～ 火箭推力[后坐力]. *a* ～ *type wavemeter* 【无】吸收式波长计.

re•ac•tion•ar•y [ri(ː)ˈækʃənəri] *a.* ①反动的，倒退的；保守的. ②【化】反应的. ～ *elements* 反动分子. — *n.* 反动分子；保守分子.

re•ac•tion•ism [ri(ː)ˈækʃənizəm] *n.* 反动思想；极端保守主义；复古主义.

re•ac•tion•ist [ri(ː)ˈækʃənist] *n.* 反动分子，复古主义者，保守主义者. — *a.* 反动的.

re•ac•ti•vate [ri(ː)ˈæktiveit] *vt.* ***(-vat•ed, -vat•ing)*** ①使恢复活动，使复活. ②【海】使复航. — *vi.* 重新活跃起来，重新活动起来. — **re•ac•ti•va•tion** [ri(ː)ˌæktiˈveiʃən] *n.*

re•ac•tive [ri(ː)ˈæktiv] *a.* ①反动的，倒退的，复古的. ②反应的；反作用的；反冲的；【电】电抗的；【化】反应性的，活性的. *a* ～ *current* 无效电流. ～ *power* 无功电力. **re•ac•tiv•i•ty** [ˌri(ː)ækˈtiviti] *n.* **-ly** *ad.* **-ness** *n.*

re•ac•tor [ri(ː)ˈæktə] *n.* ①反应者，被试验者；【医】有(阳性)反应的人[动物]. ②【电】碍圈，扼流圈；电抗器；【化】反应器；【物】反应堆. *a fast* ～ 快中子反应堆.

read[1] [riːd] ***(read*** [red]***)*** *vt.* ①阅读；朗读，诵读；【议会】宣读(议案)；照谱唱[奏] *(aloud; out; off)*. ②辨读，辨认(暗号等)；解答(谜等)；(用计算机等)读出(信息的意义；密码等)；(看脸色等)察觉，了解. ③显示〔钟点，度数等〕. ④能读，看得懂(拉丁语等)；阅悉，读知(某事). ⑤读给人听；读着使…. ⑥把(一段文字)解释为；把(文献中某一字句)读作，写作，印作. ⑦〔主为牛津大学学生语〕学，研究 *(up)*. *R- me (off) the list.* 请把名单给我念一遍. ～ *a bill for the first time* 一读议案. *For "paper"* ～ *"proper."* paper 应(读)作 proper. ～ *a book for sb.* 为某人代读一本书. ～ *the child to sleep* 读书引孩子睡觉. ～ *his silence as consent* 把他的沉默认为是同意. ～ ***a dream*** 解释一个梦. ～ ***men's hearts*** 了解[考察]人们的心理. ～ ***off*** 读(出)；数. ～ ***one's shirt*** 〔美俚〕找衬衫缝中的虱子. ～ ***oneself hoarse*** 读哑嗓子. ～ ***oneself in*** 当众朗读誓约等后而就任. ～ ***out*** 大声读；【自】读出〔指把计算机存储器中的资料取出等〕. ～ ***out of a book*** = ～ from a book. ～ ***sb. a lesson [lecture]*** 训斥某人. ～ ***sb.'s face*** 观察某人的脸色(而猜测他的内心). ～ ***sb.'s hand*** 看某人手相. ～ ***sth. else into sth.,*** ～ ***into sth. sth. else*** 用别种观点[说法]解释某种观点[说法]；把某种观点理解为别种观点〔多指曲解〕(*You are* ～*ing more than was intended into what he said.* 你歪曲了他讲话的真实意图). ～ ***the future*** 预言未来. ～ ***the Scriptures to sb.*** 〔美俚〕对某人下命令；断言，发誓；责斥，命令. ～ ***the signs of the times*** 观察时势. ～ ***to*** 读书给…听 (*Children like to be* ～ *to.* 小孩子喜欢人读书给他们听). ～ ***up*** 专攻(某科目)；重行读一科目. ～ ***up on some subject*** 系统地研究某一科目. — *vi.* ①阅读，读书；学习，勤学，用功；朗读，诵读，宣读；讲读. ②可读，值得读；使(读者或听者)感动. ③(某一文句)具有某种意义，可作某种解释. ④(某一文句)具有某种形式，由某些词组成. *The thermometer* ～*s 90°.* 寒暑表的示度是 90 度. ～ *law* 研究法律. *The ticket* ～*s to Beijing via Shanghai.* 车票上写明经上海到北京. *The play* ～*s better than it acts.* 这出戏阅读比上演有趣. *He who runs may* ～. 跑着的人都能辨读；简明易懂. ***be*** ～ ***out of*** 被宣告开除. ～ ***about*** = ～ of. ～ ***back*** 【军】重复，复述. ～ ***between the lines*** 体会出字里行间之意；看出言外之意. ～ ***for degree [honours]*** 为得学位[为成优等生]而用功. ～ ***from a book*** 选书中一段朗读. ～ ***in a book*** 读一本书读得入迷. ～ ***like*** 可读作…，读了可认为…，可解释作. ～ ***of*** 读知，阅悉(某事). ～ ***through*** (从头到尾)读完. ～ ***to oneself*** 默读. ～ ***with sb.*** 有老师陪着温习功课；(做家庭教师)陪某人读书. — *n.* 读书；(一次的)读书时间. ***have a good [quiet, long, short]*** ～ 舒畅地[安静地，长时间，短时间]读书. ***take a quick [short]*** ～ ***at a book*** 匆匆忙忙读一本书，读[一会儿]书. ～**-in** *n.* ①【自】写入. ②宣读活动〔如议员在国会宣读某种文件以表示反对某议案等〕. ～**-mostly memory** 【计】主读储存器. ～**-only memory** 【计】固定[永久性]只读储存器. ～**-out** ①【机】(仪表等的)测量结果输出值，示值读数；【自】读出. ②(宇宙飞船等的)发回资料. ③宣告开除.

read[2] [red] read 的过去式及过去分词. — *a.* ①被朗读的. ②读知的. ③博识的；博览的；造诣深的：*a well-*～ *man* 博学者. ***(deeply, well)*** ～ ***in*** 精通(某一学科). ***little [slightly]*** ～ ***in*** 略通.

Read(e) [ˈriːd] *n.* 里德〔姓氏〕.

read•a•ble [ˈriːdəbl] *a.* ①易读的. ②值得一读的. *a* ～ *book* 值得一读[读起来有趣]的书. ～ *handwriting* 易读的[易看懂的]笔迹. **-bil•i•ty** [ˌriːdəˈbiliti] *n.* ①(书等)易读；值得读. ②(字迹等的)清晰，清楚. ③【军】清晰程度. **-bly** *ad.*

re•ad•dress [ˈriːəˈdres] *vt.* ①重写(姓名、地址，更改姓名、地址等). ②再讲，再致(辞). ③〔～ oneself〕重新致力于，重新着手 *(in)*.

read•er [ˈriːdə] *n.* ①读者，朗读者. ②讲读者；(英国大学及法学协会的)讲师；〔美〕(大学教授的)助教；读经师〔通常称 lay-～〕. ③读出器，读数镜，读数装置，指示仪表. ④出版社的出版物审稿人〔通常叫 *publisher's* ～〕；阅览者，评阅者；校对人. ⑤好学者. ⑥(谜的)解答人. ⑦(学校用的)读本；文选. *a great* ～ 很爱读书的人；读很多书的人. *gentle* ～*s* 各位读者〔著者对读者的称呼〕. *a French* ～ 法语读本. ～**'s marks** 校对符号. ～**ship** 读者的身分；〔美〕(杂志、报纸的)读者人数 (*cf.* circulation).

read•i•ly [ˈredili] *ad.* 容易地；欣然，爽爽快快地，毫不勉强地，毫不犹豫地. *He would* ～ *die for the cause of communism.* 他为共产主义事业死也甘心.

read•i•ness [ˈredinis] *n.* 容易；迅速；敏捷；欣然允应，愿意；准备，有预备：～ *to assume responsibity* 负责精神.

get (up) everything in ~ for 为…准备齐全. ***hold in ~*** 经常有准备. ***in ~ (for) ...***, 准备妥当. ***~ of wit*** 机敏. ***with ~*** 欣然;爽快地;迅速地.

Read·ing [ˈrediŋ] *n.* 雷丁〔姓氏〕.

read·ing [ˈriːdiŋ] *n.* ①阅读;读书;讲读;朗读,讲读会,读书会;(议会议案的)宣读. ②读物. ③学识,(尤指)书本知识. ④(谜、气候等的)判断,解释;(诗文词句等的)理解含义. ⑤(晴雨表等的)读数,示数,示度. ⑥(考证异本等时所见的)异文;(某节某处的)读法;(剧本人物的)演出法,(音乐的)演奏法. *a penny ~* (从前乡下举办的、门票极低的)朗诵会,歌唱会. *~s from Dickens* 狄更斯作品朗读会[选读]. *~s in politics* 政治读本. *a good [dull] ~* 优良的[无聊的]读物. *the first ~* 初读会〔决定议案可否审议〕. *the second ~* 二读会〔决定议案采纳与否〕. *the third ~* 三读会〔决定所修正议案的成立与否〕. *What is your ~ of the fact?* 你对于这件事情的看法怎样? *a man of vast ~* 博学的人. — *a.* 读书的,爱书的,用功的: *a ~ man* 〔英〕爱读书的人. *~ matter* (报章、杂志的)读物,记事. *the ~ public* 读书界. *~* **book** 读本. *~* **desk** 书桌; 阅览桌. *~* **glass** (看小字用的)放大镜. *~* **lamp** 台灯. *~* **notice** (排在报纸第一页底部的)小广告. *~* **room** (图书馆等的)阅览室;(印刷厂的)校对室.

re·ad·just [ˈriːəˈdʒʌst] *vt.* 重做,再整理,(再)调整. **~ment** *n.*

read·y [ˈredi] *a.* ***(read·i·er; -i·est)*** ①〔用作表语〕准备[预备]…的;下了决心…的;随时可以…的;即将…,动辄…的;已作好准备[预备]的;心中准备好的,打定了主意的. ②现成的,现有的;迅速的,当面的,(答复等)即时的;敏捷的;巧于…的 *(at)*;容易的,轻便的,简便的,立刻可用的;容易得到的. ③【军】摆好放枪姿势的. *clothes ~ for wearing* 准备好了的服装. *~ for sea* 已作好航行准备的. *R-? Go!* (赛跑口令)预备! 跑! *R-, present, fire!* (射击口令)预备! 瞄准! 放! *I am ~ to risk my life.* 我随时可以拼掉这条命. *You are ~ to speak ill of men.* 你动不动就讲人家坏话. *The boat is ~ to sink.* 这只船就要沉了. *a ~ pen [writer]* 敏捷的文笔[作家]. *~ wit* (应对如流,随机应变的)机智. *~ money* 现金. ***be not ~ to*** 来不及. ***too ~ to promise*** 轻易许诺. ***find ~ acceptance*** 被欣然接受,得到爽快的允诺;马上被相信. ***get ... ~*** = make ... ~. ***give a ~ consent*** 马上答应. ***hold oneself ~ to*** 正准备要…. ***make ~*** ①作好准备. ②整装 *(for)*. ***~ about!*** 【海】掉头准备! ***~ all!*** 【军】各就各位! ***~ at excuses*** 随时都能找到借口;善于辩解的. ***~ at [to] hand*** 在手边. ***~ for*** 预备好. ***the readiest way to do it*** 做这事的最简便的方法[捷径]. ***too ~ to suspect*** 疑心太重. — *n.* 〔the ~〕 ①【军】射击准备. ②〔俚〕现金 (= ~ money). ***come to the ~*** 托枪. ***hold the rifle at the ~*** 预备开枪. ***plank down the ~*** 〔俚〕付现款. — *ad.* ①〔多与过去分词连用或用连字符连结,如 *~-made*, *~-built* 等〕;预先,准备好. ②〔多用比较级或最高级〕迅速,欣然,爽快: *be ~ packed* = *be packed ~* 预先包扎好. *the child that answers readiest* 回答最快的孩子. — *vt.* 使预备[准备]好. *~* **up** 〔俚〕即付现款. **~-for-service** 〔美〕 **~-made** ①*a.* (服装等)现成的;预先准备好的,(意见等)听来的. ②*n.* 现成艺术品〔艺术家在实在生活中选出的实物,并不作任何加工〕. **~-mix** *a.* 预先拌好的. *~* **room** (航空母舰上飞行员出发前的)接受命令室. **~-to-wear** *a.* 〔美〕马上就可用的,现成的. **~-witted** *a.* 机敏的,有机智的,能随机应变的.

re·af·firm [ˈriːəˈfəːm] *vt.* 重申,再断言,再肯定.

re·a·gent [ri(ː)ˈeidʒənt] *n.* ①【化】试药,试剂;反应物. ②被试验者. *a ~ bottle* 试药瓶.

re·ag·gre·gate [riˈægrigeit] *vt.* 使重新聚集(为一个整体,一个分子等). — *n.* 重新聚集体[分子]. **-ga·tion** [riˌægriˈgeiʃən] *n.*

re·a·gin [riˈeidʒin] *n.* 【医】反应素.

re·al[1] [riəl, ˈriːəl] *a.* ①真实的,真正的 *(opp.* sham*)*;实际的,现实的 *(opp.* ideal*)*;事实上的,实质上的 *(opp.* nominal*)*;【哲】实在的. ②真诚的. ③【法】不动产的;关于物的. ④【数】 = ~-valued. *a ~ man* 真诚的人;真正的人. *effect a ~ cure* 根治. ***the ~ thing [stuff]*** 道地货,原装货,上等货. — *n.* 〔the ~〕实在;现实;实物;实情;【数】实数. — *ad.* 〔美口〕真,真正,实在: *I am ~ pleased to meet you.* 遇见了你真高兴. *~* **action** 物权诉讼. *~* **capital** 实际资本. *~* **credit** 实际信用. *~* **estate** 不动产,房地产 (*a ~ estate agent [broker]* 房地产经纪人). *~* **green** 〔美俚〕大量的钱,大笔款项. *~* **image** 【物】实象. *~* **life** 现实生活. **~-life** *a.* 实际的,真实的;非想像的. *~* **money** 实价货币;现金. *~* **number** 【数】实数. *~* **property** = ~ estate. *~* **right** 物权. *~* **school** 实业学校. *~* **tennis** 室内网球. *~* **time** (真)实时(间),实际时间. **~-time** *a.* 实时的;快速的. **~-valued** 【数】实数的. *~* **wages** 实质工资〔根据购买力来衡量的工资〕.

re·al[2] [ˈriːəl] *n.* ①*(pl.* ~s [-z];〔Sp.〕 ***-es*** [reɑːles]*)* 从前西班牙及其领地所通用的小银币 (= $^{1}/_{8}$ peso). ②*(pl.* ***reis*** [reis]*)* 从前葡萄牙、巴西的货币单位.

re·al·gar [riˈælgə] *n.* ①【矿】鸡冠石. ②【化】雄黄;二硫化二砷.

re·a·lign [ˌriəˈlain] *vt., vi.* (使)重新排列,(使)重新组合.

re·al·ism [ˈriəlizəm, ˈriːəl-] *n.* ①【文艺】现实主义;写实主义;【哲】实在论,唯实论;【教】实学主义;【法】实体主义. ②现实性.

re·al·ist [ˈriəlist] *n.* 【文艺】现实主义者[作家];【哲】实在论者,唯实论者;【教、数】实学主义者. — *a.* = realistic.

re·al·is·tic [riəˈlistik] *a.* ①【哲】实在论(者)的;【文艺】现实主义的. ②逼真的;栩栩如生的: *a ~ novel* 现实主义的小说. **-ti·cal·ly** *ad.*

re·al·ity [ri(ː)ˈæliti] *n.* ①【哲】现实,实在;实体,本体. ②真实;事实;现实性. ③逼真. *the objective ~* 客观现实[物质世界]. *the subjective ~* 主观的实在[精神世界]. *reproduced with startling ~* 仿造得和原物分辨不出的. ***become a ~*** 实现;成为现实. ***in ~*** 事实上,实际上;实在,真正. ***make sth. a ~*** 实现某事,落实.

re·al·iz·a·ble [ˈriəlaizəbl] *a.* ①可实现的,可实行的;可确实感觉到的. ②可变为不动产的;可换成现钱的.

re·al·i·za·tion [ˌriəlaiˈzeiʃən] *n.* ①(理想等的)实现,实化,实在化;成就;亲身体会,真正认识. ②赚头,实得. ③把钱换成不动产;把财产[商品]换成钱,变卖. ***have a full [a true] ~ of*** 充分认识到某事,真正了解到某事.

re·al·ize [ˈriəlaiz] *vt.* ①实现,实行(希望、计划等). ②实认,实感,领悟,了解,体会. ③使显得逼真;如实表现,写实. ④赚到,实得(若干钱);变卖. ⑤【经】实现〔把商品卖出,收回货币〕. *He could not ~ his own danger.* 他认识不到他自己的危险. — *vi.* 变卖. *The sale of his picture ~d £20,000.* 他的画卖了两万镑.

re·al·ly [ˈriəli] *ad.* 真,真正,实在,果真. *R-?* 真的吗? 哦? 果真吗? *R-!* 实在的! 真的! *~ and truly* 果真,的的确确,千真万确. *Not ~!* 不会吧! *Well, ~!* 哎呀,真是这样[真想不到]! *If that is ~ the case.* 假如真是如此. *Tell me what you ~ think.* 把你的真心话告诉我吧.

realm [relm] *n.* ①王国,国土. ②领域,区域,范围. ③(学术的)部门,界;(动植物分的布)圈,带. *~ of necessity* 必然王国. *the Defense of the R- Act* 英国国防令. *the laws of the ~* 国法. *the coin of the ~* 国币. *persons who are out of the ~* 在国外的人们. *the ~ of poetry* 诗的领域. *ideological ~* 思想领域. *the ~ of sleep* 梦的世界.

Re·al·po·li·tik [reiˈɑːlˌpəuliˈtiːk] *n.* 〔G.〕现实政策;实

力政策. **-er** 现实政治家.

Re·al·schu·le [reːɑːlʃuːle] *n.* 〔G.〕(德国的)实科中学〔与着重古典语教育相对,着重理工,现代语〕.

re·al·tor [ˈriːəltə] *n.* 〔美〕房地产经纪人〔尤指全国房地产同业公会会员〕.

re·al·ty [ˈriəlti, ˈriːəl-] *n.* 不动产,房地产.

ream[1] [riːm] *n.* ①(纸的)令. ★20 刀为一令,计 480 张,称 short ～; 白报纸加损耗为 500 张,称 long ～; 印刷用纸再加印刷损耗为 516 张,称 printer's [perfect] ～. ②〔*pl.*〕〔口〕大量的纸[著述]: *He wrote ～s (and ～s) of verse.* 他写了很多很多的诗.

ream[2] [riːm] *vt.* ①(用绞刀)绞大(枪的口径等). ②折进(子弹壳等的)边. ③挖除(不良部分). ④榨取(果汁).

ream[3] [riːm] *n.* 〔英方〕生奶油.

ream·er [ˈriːmə] *n.* ①【机】扩孔锥,绞刀,绞床; 整孔钻. ②果汁压榨器.

re·an·i·mate [ˈriːˈænimeit] *vt.* 使苏生,使复活; 鼓舞,激励. **-ma·tion** [-ˈmeiʃən] *n.*

reap [riːp] *vt., vi.* ①刈取,收割,采收. ②得到,获得(努力的结果). ③遭到(报应); 得到(报偿). ～ *grain [fruit]* 收割粮食[採收水果]. ～ ***as [what] one sows [has sown]*** 自食其果; 种瓜得瓜种豆得豆; 善因善果, 恶因恶果. ～ ***experience*** 取得经验. ～ ***the fruits of one's actions*** 自作自受. ～ ***where one has not sown*** 不劳而获,侵占别人的劳动成果. ***sow the wind and ～ the whirl wind*** 恶有恶报; 干坏事必将受到严厉的报应. **～ing hook** (收割用)镰刀. **～ing machine** 收割机. **-er** *n.* 收割者; 收获者; 收割机.

re·ap·pear [ˈriːəpiə] *vi.* 再现,再出,再发生. **-ance** *n.*

re·ap·point [ˈriːəˈpɔint] *vt.* ①再任命,使复职. ②重新约定; 重新指定. **-ment** *n.*

re·ap·por·tion [ˈriːəˈpɔːʃən] *vt.* 重新分派,重新分配. **-ment** *n.*

re·ap·praise [ˈriːəˈpreiz] *vt.* ***(-prais·ed, -prais·ing)*** 重新评价,重新估价; 重新鉴定,重新考虑. **re·prais·al** *n.*

rear[1] [riə] *n.* ①后,后部,背面,背后 *(opp.* front); (舰队或军队的)后方; 后尾; 殿后部队, 后卫. ②〔英口〕厕所〔男子专用语〕. ③〔口〕屁股. ***at the ～ of = in (the) ～ of*** 在…之后, 在…的后方, 在…的背后. ***bring [close] up the ～*** 殿后; 走在后头. ***follow in the ～*** 跟在后头. ***front and ～*** 前前后后. ***go to the ～*** 绕到后面. ***hang on the ～ of*** 紧紧尾随(敌人)背后(伺机袭击). ***see (sth.) far in the ～*** 看见(某物)远远在后头. ***send sb. to the ～*** 把某人送到后方. ***take (the enemy) in (the) ～*** 袭击(敌人)后方, 从背后袭击敌人. — *a.* 后(方)的,背面的,背后的,殿后的: *the ～ gate* 后门. *a ～ rank* 【军】后列. ～ *service* 【军】后方勤务. — *vi.* 〔英口〕上厕所去. **～ admiral** 海军少将. **～ guard** 【军】后卫. **～ vassal** 陪臣. **～most** *a.* 最后的.

rear[2] [riə] *vt.* ①举起,竖起,树立(旗竿等); 建设,建立(纪念碑等). ②饲养(家畜等); 抚养,教养(孩子); 栽培(作物). ③〔古〕提高声音(叫喊、歌唱等). ～ *the [its, his] head* 抬头; (人)显露头角; (恶意等)显露出来. *The mountains ～ed their crests into the clouds.* 山顶高耸入云. ～ *pigs* 养猪. — *vi.* ① (马等)用后脚站起. ②〔方〕现出,出现.

rear·er [ˈriərə] *n.* ①养育员,饲养员. ②喜欢用后脚直立起来的马.

re·arm [ˈriːˈɑːm] *vt., vi.* (使)重新武装,(使)重整军备; (使)配备新式武器. **re·ar·ma·ment** *n.*

rear·mouse [ˌriəˌmaus] *n.* = reremouse.

re·ar·range [ˈriːəˈreindʒ] *vt.* 重新整顿,重新布置,重新排列. — *vi.* 【化】(分子)重排. **-ment** *n.*

re·ar·rest [ˈriːəˈrest] *vt., n.* 重新逮捕[拘留].

rear·ward [ˈriəwəd] *ad.* 在后方,向后方. — *n.* 后方,后部,背后; 后卫. *in [at] the ～* 在后卫; 在后部〔背后〕. *in [on] the ～ of* 在…的后方; 在…的后卫. — *a.* 向后方的; 在末尾的.

rear·wards [ˈriəwədz] *ad.* = rearward.

rea·son [ˈriːzn] *n.* ①理由,原因,缘故,动机. ②理性,理智; 智慧; 合理(的行为). ③正常的思想,健全的思想,健全的议论[判断],常识,正常的事物. ④道理,条理; 理论,辩论,推论. ⑤【逻】论据,论点; 前提, 小前提. ⑥理解力,判断力,理性直觉力. ⑦实际的事情,可实行的事情. *bereft of ～* 失去理智,疯狂; 失掉知觉. *It is neither rhyme nor ～.* 莫名其妙. *It is without rhyme or ～* 毫无道理,无缘无故. ***as ～ was*** 根据情理. ***be restored to ～*** 恢复理智. ***bring to ～*** 使明白道理,使服从道理. ***by ～ of*** 凭…的理由,因为. ***by ～ (that)*** 因为, 由于. ***come to ～*** 清醒过来. ***for a ～ of state*** 以国家的利益为理由〔指执政者的借口〕. ***for no other ～ than that [but this]*** 单单因为(这一理由). ***for ～s of*** 因为. ***give ～s for*** 说明…的理由. ***have ～ for [to do]*** 有必须的理由,有理由去(做),…(做)是对的,…(做)是当然的. ***hear ～*** = listen to ～. ***in (all) ～*** 合理; 正当 *(It is not in ～ to expect me to do so.* 要我做这样的事是没有道理的. *I will do anything in ～.* 只要是有道理的事我都答应去做). ***listen to ～*** 服从道理, 听从. ***lose one's ～*** 失去理性,发狂. ***out of all ～*** 不合理, 不对头; 不可理喻的. ***stand to ～*** 得当,合道理. ***There is ～ in ....*** (某事)有道理 *(There is ～ in what you say.* 你讲得有道理). ***with or without ～*** 无论有理与否. ***with ～*** 有道理; 合乎情理. — *vt.* ①论证; 推论, 论断, 推究. ②说服 *(down; out of; into)*; 向…解释. ～ ***oneself into perplexity*** 不能自圆其说. ～ ***out a conclusion*** 推论出一个结论. ～ ***sb. down*** 说服某人. ～ ***sb. into compliance*** 劝某人顺从, 说服某人. ～ ***sb. out of his fears*** 劝人不要怕. — *vi.* ①论究, 推理, 推论, 推究 *(about; of; from; upon)*. ②劝说 *(with)*. ～ *with sb. for [against] sth.* 因赞成[反对]某点同某人讲道理.

rea·son·a·ble [ˈriːznəbl] *a.* ①合理的; 明白道理的, 懂道理的; 有理性的. ②(要求等)适当的; (价钱等)不高的; 适度的: *a ～ man* 明白道理的人. *a ～ creature [being]* 有理智的动物[人]. *You must be ～.* 你别胡说八道,你该讲讲道理. **-bly** *ad.* **-ness** *n.*

rea·son·ing [ˈriːzəniŋ] *n.* 推论,推理; 论究,论断; 理论,论证; 论法. — *a.* 能推理的; 有关推理的. *the ～ power* 推理力. *a ～ creature* 理性动物,人类.

rea·son·less [ˈriːznlis] *a.* 不明道理的; 不合理的, 没有理性的.

re·as·sem·ble [ˈriːəˈsemble] *vt.* 重新召集; 重新装配; 调整. — *vi.* 重新集合.

re·as·sert [ˈriːəˈsəːt] *vt.* 再断言, 再主张, 再申明. ～ ***oneself*** 重申自己的主张. **re·as·ser·tion** *n.*

re·as·sess [ˈriːəˈses] *vt.* ①对…再估价,再估定,再评价. ②再征税. **-ment** *n.*

re·as·sign [ˈriːəˈsain] *vt.* 再指定; 再分配; 再让与; 交还. **-ment** *n.*

re·as·sume [ˈriəˈsjuːm] *vt.* ①再取, 取回. ②再担任, 重就,再接受. ③再设想,再假定. — *vi.* (中断后)再开始说. **re·as·sump·tion** [ˈriːəˈsʌmpʃən] *n.*

re·as·sur·ance [ˈriːəˈʃuərəns] *n.* ①再保证; 自信, 安心. ②〔英〕再保险.

re·as·sure [ˌriːəˈʃuə] *vt.* ①再向…保证; 使安心. ②〔英〕再对…进行保险. *People are ～d.* 人心安定了.

re·a·ta [r(ː)ˈɑːtə] *n.* = riata.

Re·au·mur [ˈreiəmjuə] 列欧穆〔法国姓氏, 特指 René Antoine Ferchault de ～. 法国物理学家, 生物学家, 1683—1757〕. — *a.* 列氏(温度计)的〔略 R.〕— *n.* 列氏温度计〔以零度为冰点, 80 度为沸点〕. *a temperature of more than 55° ～ [55° R.]* 列氏 55 度以上的温度.

reave, reive [riːv] ***(～d, reft*** [reft]***)*** *vt., vi.* 〔古、诗〕掠夺, 劫掠〔多用 reive〕; 抢劫 *(away; from; of)*. *parents (who*

R

were) reft of their children ～ 被夺去了〔死去了〕孩子的父母. ～ *the neighbours of their cattle* 夺取邻人的牲畜.
Reb [reb] *n.* 犹太人的尊称〔相当于"先生",与姓名连用〕.
reb [reb] *n.* 〔美口〕(美国南北战争中的) 南军士兵＝rebel.
Re·ba [ˈriːbə] *n.* 丽巴〔女子名〕〔Rebecca 的昵称〕.
re·bap·tism [riːˈbæptizəm] *n.* 再洗礼;重新命名.
re·bap·tize [ˈriːˈbæptaiz] *vt.* ①给…再施洗礼. ②给…重新取名.
re·bar·ba·rize [ˈriːˈbɑːbəraiz] *vt.* 使重新变野蛮,使回到野蛮时代.
re·bar·ba·tive [riˈbɑːbətiv] *a.* 令人讨厌的; 容貌可怕的,狰狞的.
re·bate[1] [ˈriːbeit, riˈbeit] *n.* ①折扣,回扣. ②〔英古〕减少. *the* ～ *system* 运费回扣制. — [riˈbeit] *vt.* ①给…回扣, 打…的折扣. ②〔英古〕减少; 削弱. ③〔美古〕使钝(刀刃).
re·bate[2] [riˈbeit, ˈræbit] *n., vt.* = rabbet.
re·ba·to [rəˈbɑːtəu] *n.* = rabato.
re·ba·tron [ˈrebətrɔn] *n.*【无】大功率电子聚束(加速)器.
re·bec, re·beck [ˈriːbek] *n.*【乐】雷别克〔中世纪的一种弓拉的梨形三弦乐器,由此演变而成小提琴〕.
Re·bec·ca[1] [riˈbekə] *n.* 丽贝卡〔女子名〕.
Re·bec·ca[2] [riˈbekɑ] *n.*【无】雷别卡〔一种飞机询问应答器〕.
reb·el [ˈrebəl] *n.* 造反者,反叛者;起义者,反抗者;〔美〕(内战时期的) 南方人. — *a.* 造反的, 反叛的. *the* ～ *army* 叛军. — [riˈbel] *vi.* 造反,反叛;反抗,不服从;厌恶 *(against; at)*. *The stomach* ～*s against too much food.* 胃不能接受过多的食物.
reb·el·dom [ˈrebldəm] *n.* ①发难地〔反叛者控制或据守的区域; 尤指美国南北战争中的南方各州〕. ②〔集合词〕叛乱者,起义者. ③叛乱(行为).
re·bel·lion [riˈbeljən] *n.* 造反,叛乱,起义; 反抗. ***rise in*** ～ 造起反来,起义. ***rise in*** ～ ***against*** 起来造…的反. ***the R-*** ①〔英史〕= the Great R- 大叛乱(1642—1660). ②〔美史〕= the Civil War 南北战争.
re·bel·lious [riˈbeljəs] *a.* ①造反的; 反抗的. ②有叛变倾向的; 企图叛变的. ③(事物) 难控制的, 难驾御的; (病)难治的,顽固的. **-ly** *ad.* **-ness** *n.*
re·bel·low [ˈriːˈbeləu] *vi., vt.* 〔诗〕(风等)(使)发回响,(使)回声轰鸣.
re·bind [ˈriːˈbaind] *vt.* ***(re·bound*** [ˈriːˈbaund]***)*** ①重捆,重绑. ②重新装钉.
re·birth [ˈriːˈbəːθ] *n.* 再生,复生,复活;【宗】轮回,转生.
reb·o·ant [ˈrebəuənt] *a.*【诗】大声反响的,回音轰响的.
re·born [ˈriːˈbɔːn] *a.* 再生的,复活的;更新的,复兴的.
re·bound[1] [ˈriːˈbaund] rebind 的过去式和过去分词.
re·bound[2] [riˈbaund] *vi.* ①(球等)弹回,回跳;【篮球】擦板入篮. ②回响;复兴, 重新振作; 回到原地. *Our evil example will* ～ *upon ourselves.* 我们的坏榜样会回到我们自己头上的〔意为结果自己受害〕. — *n.* ①弹回,跳回. ②反应. ③重新振作. *take a ball on the* ～ 抓住反跳回来的球. ***take sb. at [on] the*** ～ 利用某人有某种反应等机会影响某人 (*His courageous words took his depressed supporters on the* ～. 他趁机用豪言壮语鼓舞了那些沮丧消沉的支持者).
re·bo·zo [riˈbəuzəu; *Sp.* reˈbouθəu] *n.* ***(pl. -zos*** [-zəuz, *Sp.* -θəus]***)*** 长披巾〔西班牙和美洲说西班牙语妇女包头和肩〕.
re·branch [ˈriːˈbrɑːntʃ] *vi.* 形成次级分支.
re·broad·cast [ˈriːˈbrɔːdkɑːst] ***(～(ed)) vi., vt., n.***【无】再播送,重播;转播.
re·buff [riˈbʌf] *vt., n.* ①拒绝, 驳斥. ②击退. ③(对希望、计划等的)阻碍,挫折.
re·build [ˈriːˈbild] ***(-built*** [-ˈbilt]***)*** *vt.* 再建,重建;使复原;改建;改造;改变. — *vi.* 重建.
re·buke [riˈbjuːk] *vt., n.* 指责,非难, 谴责,惩戒. *give [administer] a* ～ 谴责. *without* ～ 无可非难, 无可指摘(地).
re·bus [ˈriːbəs] *n.* 谜;画谜,字谜.
re·but [riˈbʌt] *vt.* ①【法】反驳,驳回; 揭露,戳穿. ②〔罕〕击退, 逐回, 阻止(攻击等). — *vi.* 举反证. **rebutting evidence**【法】反证.
re·but·tal [riˈbʌtl], **re·but·ment** [riˈbʌtmənt] *n.*【法】反驳;反证.
re·but·ter [riˈbʌtə] *n.* ①反驳者. ②【法】(被告的)第三答辩;反证.
rec. ①receipt. ②received. ③recipe. ④record; recorded; recorder; recording. ⑤reclamation.
re·cal·ci·trance [riˈkælsitrəns] *n.* 固执; 顽强,顽抗; 难驾御,不听话.
re·cal·ci·trant [riˈkælsitrənt] *a., n.* 倔强的(人),顽抗的(人),不顺从的(人).
re·cal·ci·trate [riˈkælsitreit] *vi.* 反抗, 顽抗; 不顺从;〔罕〕踢回. **-tra·tion** [riˌkælsiˈtreiʃən] *n.*
re·cal·cu·late [riˈkælkjuleit] *vt.* ***(-lat·ed, -lat·ing)*** 重新计算,再核算. **-la·tion** [riˌkælkjuˈleiʃən] *n.*
re·ca·les·cence [ˌrikəˈlesns] *n.*【冶】再辉, 复辉. **re·ca·les·cent** *a.*
re·call [riˈkɔːl] *vt.* ①叫回,召回,召还. ②取消,撤销,撤回. ③使复活;恢复, 挽回, 拿回. ④(使)想起; (使)回忆. ⑤〔美〕(依据一般投票)罢免(官吏). ～ *an ambassador* 召回大使. ～ *a decree* 撤销法令. ～ *sb. to a sense of his duties* 唤起某人责任心. ～ *what was said* 想起说过的事情. ～ ***to life*** 使复活. ～ ***to one's mind*** 回忆,想起. — *n.* ①叫回,(大使等的)召回,召还. ②取消,撤回,撤销. ③恢复. ④回忆, 回想. ⑤【军】归队信号;收操号;集合号(号声). ⑥(音乐会等中的)再演, 再来一次. ⑦【电讯】二次呼叫. ⑧招艇旗;招艇信号. ⑨〔美〕罢免(权). ⑩(制造商因产品有问题等)公开收回出厂产品. ⑪【计】信息检索(能力). *beyond [past]* ～ 收不回的,挽回不了的.
re·cant [riˈkænt] *vt.* 改变,取消, 撤回(主张等). — *vi.* 取消主张;收回前言;撤回声明;公开认错.
re·can·ta·tion [ˌriːkænˈteiʃən] *n.* 撤消, 取消; 改变信仰,改变主张,收回前言〔意见〕: *to exact* ～*s from prisoners of war.* 要战俘认罪. *make a public* ～ 公开认错;(登报)自首.
re·cap[1] [ˈriːkæp, riːˈkæp] *vt.* 翻新,翻造(轮胎). — *n.* 再生轮胎.
re·cap[2] [ˈriˌkæp] *n.* = recapitulation. — *vt., vi.* ***(-capped, -cap·ping)*** = recapitulate.
re·cap·i·tal·ize [ˈriːkəˈpitəlaiz] *vt.* ***(-iz·ed, -iz·ing)*** 再投资;改变〔调整〕资本结构.
re·ca·p·i·tal·i·za·tion [ˈriː-kəˌpitəlaiˈzeiʃən] *n.*【经】资本额的调整.
re·ca·pit·u·late [ˌriːkəˈpitjuleit] *vt., vi.* 扼要重述,概括.
re·ca·pi·tu·la·tion [ˈriː-kəˌpitjuˈleiʃən] *n.* ①扼要的重述. ②【乐】再现部: ～ **theory**【生】重演说,反覆说.
re·ca·pit·u·la·tive, re·capit·u·la·to·ry [ˌriːkəˈpitjuleitiv, ˌriːkəˈpitjuleitəri] *a.* 摘要的,扼要重述的.
re·cap·ture [ˈriːˈkæptʃə] *n.* ①重新获得;收复,夺还;收回物,夺回物. ②征收. — *vt.* ①重新获得;收复,夺还. ②征收. ③想起;再经历;再体验.
re·cast [ˈriːˈkɑːst] *vt.* ①改铸,再铸;改作,改造. ②再计算. ③重新分派(角色). — *n.* ①改铸;重做,改做. ②再计算. ③重新分配角色.
rec·ce [ˈreki], **rec·co** [ˈrekəu], **rec·cy** [ˈreki], **re·con** [ˈriːkɔn] *n.* 〔军俚〕搜索,侦察〔reconnaissance 的缩略〕.
recd., rec'd. = received.
re·cede[1] [ri(ː)ˈsiːd] *vi.* ①后退,退却 *(opp.* proceed*)*. ②

退缩；缩小，减退。③收回意见；退出(某种活动) (from). ④(价值、品质等)跌落，低落；变坏. *the receding tide* 退潮. *a receding forehead* 脱发渐多的前额. ~ ***from one's position.*** 退职. ~ ***in importance*** 重要性减小. ~ ***into the background*** 退居不重要地位；(问题)失去重要性.

re·cede[2] [ri:ˈsi:d] *vt.* 归还(领土等).

re·ceipt [riˈsi:t] *n.* ①接受，接收；收条，收据；〔常 *pl.*〕收入，收益，进款. ②〔旧〕配方，制法. ③〔古〕收税所: *I beg to acknowledge ~ of your letter.* 接奉尊函〔商业信件等用语〕. *a shipping ~* 运货收条. *the gross ~s* 总收入. ***be in ~ of***【商】已收到…. ***on ~ of*** 一俟收到. ***upon (the) ~ of*** = on (the) ~ of. — *vt., vi.* (给…)出收据；(给…)开收条；签收.

re·ceipt·or [riˈsi:tə] *n.* 领收者，领受的人；〔尤指〕【法】受委托而领收有关财产的人.

re·ceiv·a·ble [riˈsi:vəbl] *a.* 应收的，该接收的，该接受的；可信的. *bills ~* 应收票据. *(opp.* bills payable*).* — *n.*〔*pl.*〕应收款项〔票据〕. **-a·bil·i·ty** [riˌsi:vəˈbiliti], **-ble·ness** *n.*

re·ceive [riˈsi:v] *vt.* ①领受，接到，收到，得到(信、命令、请帖等)；接受(欢迎，招待，请愿，建议，惩罚，损伤等). ②承受；顶住，支住(敌人、重量等). ③容纳，收容. ④听从(警告等)，领悟；承认，信任(报告等). ⑤迎接，接见(人)；欢迎，招待，款待. ⑥收买(赃物). ⑦【网球】接(球)，打回. ~ *letters [orders] from sb.* 接到某人的信〔命令等〕. ~ *the enemy's cavalry* 迎击敌人骑兵. ~ *sb. into the Trade Union* 接受某人为工会会员. *a hole large enough to ~ three men* 足够容纳三人的一个大洞. ~ *sb. in audience* 赐见，召见. *He ~d the contents of Jack's pistol.* 他被杰克用手枪打死了. *It deserves more attention than it ~s.* 世人应该更加注意这件事才好. ***be ~ed into sb.'s favour*** 得到某人的宠爱. — *vi.* ①领受，接收. ②接见，接待. ③【通讯】接收，收听，收看电视. ④【网球】接球，打回去. ⑤【宗】受圣餐: *He ~s on Sunday.* 他在礼拜天接见客人. ~ ***with open arms*** 热烈欢迎.

re·ceived [riˈsi:vd] *a.* 被容纳的，被接收的，被公认的；标准的. *R- Standard English* 标准英语. *the ~ text (of a book)* (某书的)标准版本.

re·ceiv·er [riˈsi:və] *n.* ①接受者. ②收税人，收税官. ③招待人. ④窝家，收买贼赃的人. ⑤应战者. ⑥【法】破产案产业管理人，(争执财产等的)委托管理人. ⑦【化】接收器，容器；【机】蓄汽室，收汽室；接受器；接收机，收报机，收音机，收话机，听筒；电视机，(电视)接收机. *a dual range ~* 长短波收音机. *The ~ is as bad as the thief.* 窝家跟贼一样坏.

re·ceiv·ing [riˈsi:viŋ] *n.* ①接收. ②收买贼赃. — *a.* 接受的；收报的. ~ **aerial [antenna]**【无】接收天线. ~ **blanket**〔美〕洗澡后包婴儿的浴巾. ~ **line** 正式场合列队欢迎客人的主人或主宾. ~ **office**〔英〕邮件收寄处. ~ **set**【无】收音机；电视接收机. ~ **order**【法】法院委派破产者产业管理人的委任书. ~ **ship**【海军】新兵练习舰. ~ **station** 收报电台. ~ **teller** (银行的)收款员.

re·cen·cy [ˈri:snsi] *n.* 新近.

re·cen·sion [riˈsenʃən] *n.* 修订；校订本；修订版.

re·cent [ˈri:snt] *a.* ①新近的；近来的. ②近代的. ③[R-]【地】全新世的. **-ly** *ad.*

re·cep·ta·cle [riˈseptəkl] *n.* ①容器. ②贮藏所，仓库. ③【植】花托；囊托；(分泌液的)贮器. ④【电】插座，插孔. *a collection ~* 收钱箱. *a lamp ~*【无】管座.

re·cep·tion [riˈsepʃən] *n.* ①接收；收容. ②接见，招待，欢迎；欢迎会. ③入会，入会许可. ④所受待遇. ⑤承认，公认. ⑥领悟，感受. ⑦【无】接收(力): *a warm ~* 热烈的接待；猛烈的抵抗. *a ~ area* 空袭避难人收容区，躲警报的地区. *a favourable ~* 好评. ***give a ~ to*** 招待，欢迎. ***have a great faculty of ~*** 领会力很强. ***hold a ~*** 举行欢迎会. ~ **centre** (新兵等的)报到站. ~ **chamber** =~ room. ~ **clerk**〔美〕(旅馆等的)接待员. ~ **desk** (旅馆的)接待处. ~ **committee** 接待委员会. ~ **day** 接见日，会客日. ~ **order** (麻疯医院的)病人入院命令. ~ **room** 客厅，会客室，接待室. **-ist** *n.*〔美〕(照相馆、牙科医院等的)接待员.

re·cep·tive [riˈseptiv] *a.* ①接受的，接纳的，容纳的. ②有接受力的，有容纳力的，善于接受的，敏悟的. ③感受的；感官的. **-ly** *ad.* **-ness** *n.*

re·cep·tiv·i·ty [risepˈtiviti] *n.* 感受性；理解力.

re·cep·tor [riˈseptə] *n.*【生】感受器；受体；【化】接受器；受纳体；【电】感受器；接收器.

re·cess [riˈses] *n.* ①休息，歇息；(议会的)休会(期间)；〔美〕(大学等的)短暂的休假. ②隐居处；〔*pl.*〕幽深处，深底. ③(山脉、海岸等的)凹进处，山限，水限；壁龛；壁凹；【解】(器官的)凹处，隐窝. ④【史】条约，条令. *the noon ~* 午休. ***at ~*** 在休息时间. ***go into ~*** 休会. ***in the inmost ~es of*** 在…的最深处. ***in the secret ~es of one's heart*** 在内心深处. — *vt.* 使凹进；把…搁在深处，隐藏. — *vi.*〔美〕(暂时)休会，休课，休庭.

re·ces·sion[1] [riˈseʃən] *n.* ①撤退，后退；退出，退离. ②凹处. ③(工商业的)衰退；(价格的)暴跌. ④(墙壁等的)凹处. ⑤【基督教】(做完礼拜后牧师和唱诗班)退场时的行列.

re·ces·sion[2] [ri:ˈseʃən] *n.* (占领地等的)交还.

re·ces·sion·al [riˈseʃənl] *a.* ①后退的；撤退的. ②(赞美歌等)在礼拜结束后退场时唱的. ③休会〔休课，休庭〕的. — *n.* (礼拜结束后退场时唱的)赞美歌 (=~ hymn)；(礼拜结束时奏的)退场音乐 (=~ music).

re·ces·sive [riˈsesiv] *a.* 后退的，倒退的；逆行的；【生理】衰退的；【生】隐性的: *a ~ character*【生】隐性性状. — *n.*【生】隐性性状. ~ **accent** 逆行重音〔重音由词尾向前移的历史音变〕.

Rech·a·bite [ˈrekəbait] *n.*【圣经】①利甲族(Rechab)的后裔〔见旧约《耶利米书》；相传该族人民不喝酒〕. ②〔转义〕禁酒者.

re·charge [ˈri:ˈtʃɑ:dʒ] *vt.* ①【电】给…再充电；再装填(弹药等)；再装载. ②再袭击. ③重行告发；再控告. — *n.* 再袭击；再装火药.

ré·chauf·fé [riˈʃəufei; F. reʃofe] *n.* *(pl.* ~s [-fe]*)*〔F.〕①回锅菜. ②(文章、小说等的)改头换面之作.

re·cher·ché [rəˈʃɛəʃei] *a.*〔F.〕①考究的，煞费苦心的；精选的，上好的，优秀的；珍贵的，罕有的，难得的. ②(文字等)推敲过的；雕琢的；太讲究的；矫揉造作的.

re·cid·i·vism [riˈsidivizəm] *n.*【法】累犯，惯犯〔指所犯罪行〕.

re·cid·i·vist [riˈsidivist] *n.*【法】累犯，惯犯(指犯罪的人).

rec·i·pe [ˈresipi] *n.* ①【医】处方；照处方配成的药. ②食谱；配方，制法；秘诀，秘法: *a ~ for living long* 长寿秘诀.

re·cip·i·ence [riˈsipiəns], **re·cip·i·en·cy** [riˈsipiənsi] *n.* 接受，领受，容纳.

re·cip·i·ent [riˈsipiənt] *a.* 容纳的，接受的；感受性强的. — *n.* 接受者；感受者；容纳者；容器.

re·cip·ro·cal [riˈsiprəkəl] *a.* ①相互的，交互的；可易的，互易的；酬答的. ②【数】倒数的，反商的. ~ *help* 互助. *on ~ terms* 互惠地，按互惠条件. — *n.* ①互相关联的事物. ②【数】倒数，反商；乘法逆元素. ~ **action** 交互作用. ~ **cone**【数】配极锥面. ~ **cross**【生】正反交，反交. ~ **expression**【数】倒数式. ~ **levelling** 对向水准测量. ~ **love** 相爱. ~ **pronoun**【语法】相互代词. ~**proportion [ratio]** 反比例〔反比〕. ~ **symbiosis**【生】互惠共生. ~ **treaty** 互惠条约. **-ly** *ad.*

re·cip·ro·cate [riˈsiprəkeit] *vt., vi.* ①互换，交换；酬答，报答 *(with).* ②【机】往复，来回: ~ *favours* 互相照应. *a reciprocating engine*【机】往复式发动机. *reciprocating motion* 往复运动.

R

re·cip·ro·ca·tion [riˌsiprəˈkeiʃən] *n.* ①交互作用; 交换; 报答. ②来回, 往复运动.
re·cip·ro·ca·tor [riˈsiprəkeitə] *n.* ①报答者. ②往复机件.
re·c·i·proc·i·ty [ˌresiˈprɔsiti] *n.* 相互关系; 交互作用; 互换; 互惠主义; 相互的利益[义务、权利];【哲】相关性, 相互性;【化】倒易, 可逆性;【数】互反性, 互易性. *a* ~ *treaty* 互惠条约.
re·ci·sion [riˈsiʒən] *n.* 废除, 取消, 撤回.
re·cit·al [riˈsaitl] *n.* ①朗诵, 吟诵. ②叙述; 详述, 细说; 叙事, 故事. ③【法】(契约等中)陈述[证明]事实的部分. ④【乐】独奏[独唱](会).
rec·i·ta·tion [ˌresiˈteiʃən] *n.* ①详述, 叙述. ②朗诵; 朗诵诗文; 背诵的诗[文章]. ③〔美〕背诵; 口头答问. *a* ~ *room*〔美〕教室, 课堂.
rec·i·ta·tive[1] [ˈresiteitiv] *a.* ①朗诵的, 吟诵的. ②叙述的, 讲述的.
rec·i·ta·tive[2] [ˌresitəˈtiːv] *a.*【乐】宣叙调的. — *n.*【乐】宣叙调; (歌剧等中的)宣叙部.
re·cite [riˈsait] *vt., vi.* ①(在听众前) 吟诵, 朗诵 (诗文等). ②讲, 陈述, 细说; 列举. ③【法】在借据 (等) 上复述(事实). ③〔美〕背诵(功课).
re·cit·er [riˈsaitə] *n.* 背诵者, 朗诵者; 朗诵集.
re·cit·ing-note [riˈsaitnəut] *n.*【乐】朗吟符, 朗吟调.
re·civ·i·lize [ˈriːˈsivilaiz] *vt.* 使恢复文明.
reck [rek] *vi., vt.*〔古〕〔仅否定句或疑问句用〕①注意, 留心. ②(与…)发生关系, 相干. *He* ~*s not of danger.* 他不注意危险. *What* ~*s it?* (= It ~s not.) 这有什么关系呢? ***What ~s he [What ~s it, him] if ...?*** 即使…和他又有什么相干? (*What* ~*s he if the sky should fall?* 天垮下来他也不在乎).
reck·less [ˈreklis] *a.* 不注意的; 满不在乎的; 鲁莽的, 轻率的, 不顾一切的. ***be*** ~ ***of*** 不注意 (*be* ~ *of the consequences* 毫不顾及后果). **-ly** *ad.* **-ness** *n.*
reck·on [ˈrekən] *vt.* ①计算; 总计 *(up)*; 合计达…; 算入, 列入, 加入 *(among; in; with)*. ②评定 *(up)*; 断定 *(that)*; 把…看做, 认为 *(as; for; to be)*. ③〔古〕(把某事)归咎于(某人), 把…推到(某人身上) *(to)*. ④〔主美〕想, 料想. *He is not* ~*ed among the leaders.* 他不算领导成员. *It* ~ *53 of them.* (计算起来) 一共是五十三. *R-from 5 to 100.* 由五数到一百. *be* ~*ed as prosperous* 被认为兴隆繁荣. ~ *sb. wise* 认为某人聪明. — *vi.* ①计算; 支付, 结算 *(with, for)*; 正确评定. ②依靠, 指望 *(on; upon)*. ③〔主美〕想, 料想, 想象〔主作插句用〕. *He will come soon, I* ~. 我想他会来的. ~ ***with*** ①和…算帐, 和…结算. ②将…加以考虑, 重视. ~ ***without one's host*** ①不是当着店主人的面结帐; 〔喻〕不考虑重要因素而作出决定. ②打如意算盘, 不顾困难.
reck·on·er [ˈrekənə] *n.* 计算者, 结算人; 计算便览 (= ready ~).
re·ck·on·ing [ˈrekəniŋ] *n.* ①计算, 算帐, 结算; 估计; (酒馆等的) 帐单. ②报应, 惩罚. ③【海】(由天文观测的)船位推算: *Even* ~ *makes lasting [long] friends.* 彼此无帐友情久长. ***a dead*** ~ 仅凭测程器和罗盘进行的船位推算. ***A Dutch*** ~ 单方面有利的结帐; 〔喻〕一厢情愿的事. ***be out in [of] one's*** ~ 计算错误; 估计错误. ***pay the*** ~ 付帐. ***the day of*** ~ ①结帐日. ②报应到来的日子; 最后审判日.
re·clad [ˈriːˈklæd] reclothe 的过去式和过去分词.
re·claim [riˈkleim] *vt.* ①要求归还…; 收回. ②把(鹰)养乖, 叫回. ③矫正, 改正, 使悔改; 教化, 感化. ④开垦, 填筑. ⑤利用; 翻造, 再生, 回收 (废物). ~ *land from the sea* 填海拓地. *a* ~*ed ground* 填筑地. ~*ed (India-) rubber* 再生(橡)胶. — *vi.* ①〔古〕抗辩. ②悔改, 改邪归正. — *n.* ①矫正; 改造; 悔改, 改邪归正; 教化. ②开垦. ③再生 [回收] 利用. ④〔罕〕收回, 取回. ***past [beyond]*** ~ 不可救药, 无法改造.

re·claim [ˈriːˈkleim] *vt.* 要求收回, 要求恢复; 试图取回.
re·claim·a·ble [riˈkleiməbl] *a.* ①可收回[取回]的. ②可养乖的; 可矫正的; 能悔改的. ③可开垦的, 可填筑的. ④可利用[回收]的.
rec·la·ma·tion [ˌrekləˈmeiʃən] *n.* ①收回的请求; 收复, 取回; 矫正; 驯服; 教化. ②开垦, 填筑. ③(废物的)翻造, 再生; 回收; 土壤改良. ~ *of waste land* 开垦荒地. ~ *of desert* 治理沙漠.
ré·clame [ˈreiklɑːm] *n.* 〔F.〕自我宣传, 沽名钓誉; 虚名.
rec·li·nate [ˈreklineit] *a.*【植】(叶片)下垂的, (枝条)拱垂的.
re·cline [riˈklain] *vt.* (将头、身体等) 靠(在某物上). *I lay* ~*d upon the grass.* 我躺在草地上. — *vi.* ①靠, 躺 *(upon)*. ②〔罕〕倚靠, 信赖 *(upon)*. *Being tired out, he* ~*d on the couch.* 他疲倦极了, 横躺在沙发椅上.
re·clin·er [riˈklainə] *n.* ①倚靠者, 斜倚者, 横卧者. ②活动躺椅 (= reclining chair).
re·clo·ser [riːˈkləuzə] *n.*【电】自动开关, 自动接入继电器; 反复充电设备.
re·clothe [ˈriːˈkləuð] *(-d, -clad* [-klæd]*)* *vt.* ①使再穿; 使重新穿. ②使换衣.
re·cluse [riˈkluːs] *a.* 隐居的, 遁世的; 孤寂的, (生活等)寂寞的. — *n.* 隐居者, 隐士, 遁世者. **-clu·sive** *a.*
re·clu·sion [riˈkluːʒən] *n.* ①幽居, 隐退. ②单独监禁.
re·coal [ˈriːˈkəul] *vt., vi.* (给…)再供给煤, (给…)重新添煤, (给…)再装煤.
re·coat [ˈriːˈkəut] *vt.* (用油漆等)重新涂(一层).
rec·og·ni·tion [ˌrekəgˈniʃən] *n.* ①认识; 识出; 识别; 面熟, 认得; 招呼. ②承认, 认可. ③褒奖, 表扬; 感谢, 酬劳. *My* ~ *of him was immediate.* 我一见就认得是他. ***beyond [out of]*** ~ (…得)使人认不出, (…得)完全改了模样, 面目全非. ***escape*** ~ 使人认不出. ***give a passing*** ~ 打一个过路招呼. ***in*** ~ ***of*** 承认…而, 为酬答…而, 按照 (功劳等)… (*He is rewarded in* ~ *of his services.* 他因功受奖). ***receive [meet with] much*** ~ 大受赏识, 大受注意. ***win*** ~ ***from*** 赢得(某人的)赏识, 博得(某人的)好评. ~ **signal**【军】识别讯号.
rec·og·niz·a·ble [ˈrekəgnaizəbl] *a.* ①可认识 [识别] 的. ②面熟的, 好象认得的. ③可承认 [公认] 的. **-bil·i·ty** [ˌrekəgˌnaizəˈbiliti] *n.* **-bly** *ad.*
re·cog·ni·zance [riˈkɔgnizəns] *n.* ①承认. ②【法】保证书, 具结; 保释金. *enter into* ~*s* 具结, 保证.
re·cog·ni·zant [riˈkɔgnizənt] *a.* 认识到的; 表示赏识的; 表示承认…的 *(of)*.
rec·og·nize [ˈrekəgnaiz] *vt.* ①认识; 认别; 认出, 看出; 招呼. ②承认; 赏识; 表扬; 感谢, 酬劳. ③〔美〕认可…发言. ④认清; 确认; 自己承认. ⑤公认. ~ *the independence of a new state* 承认一个新国家. *He* ~*ed that he was beaten.* 他认输了. *He was so much changed that I hardly* ~*d him.* 他变得我几乎认不出了. *I refuse to* ~ *him any longer.* 我以后不再睬他了. ~ *services.* 记功. — *vi.*〔美〕【法】具结, 提交保证书.
re·cog·ni·zee [riˌkɔgniˈziː] *n.*【法】接受具结书的人.
rec·og·niz·er [ˈrekəgˌnaizə] *n.* 承认者.
re·cog·ni·zor [rikɔgniˈzɔː] *n.*【法】写具结书的人.
re·coil [riˈkɔil] *n.* ①反跳, 跳回, 倒退; (枪的)反撞, 反冲, 后坐; 反冲力, 后坐力. ②退缩, 畏缩, 退却 *(from)*. ③报应. — *vi.* ①反跳, 跳回, 倒退, 后坐. ②撤退, 退却, 畏缩 *(from; before; at)*. ~ *(up)on oneself* (害人)反害己, 自食其果. *The advancing troops* ~*ed before the counter-attack.* 前进部队遭遇反攻而退却.
re·coil·less [riˈkɔillis] *a.*【军】无后坐力的.
re·coin [ˈriːˈkɔin] *vt.* 重铸(硬币). **~age** *n.* 重铸; 重铸的硬币.
recol·lect [ˌrekəˈlekt] *vt.* 想起; 回想, 追忆; 想到; 〔~ oneself〕使(自己) 想起一时忘掉的事. — *vi.* 回忆,

记忆.

re-col·lect [ˈriː-kəˈlekt] *vt.* ①再集合. ②使镇定; 鼓(劲),振作(勇气). ***be ~ed*** 沉着. ***~ oneself*** (使自己)镇定下来. — *vi.* 重新集合.

re·col·lec·tion [ˌrekəˈlekʃən] *n.* ①回忆,回想; 记性,记忆力; 〔常 *pl.*〕回想起来的事物. ②心境平静. ③【宗】冥想. ***beyond [past] ~*** 想不出,记不得. ***in one's ~*** 记得. ***have no ~ of*** 无…的记忆,忘记了.

re·col·our, re·col·or [ˈriːˈkʌlə] *vt.* 给…重新着色.

re·com·bi·nant [riˈkɔmbinənt] *n.* 【遗】重组器官, 复合器官.

re·com·bine [ˈriːkəmˈbain] *vt.* 重新结合[化合]; 重组. **re·com·bi·na·tion** [ˈriːˌkɔmbiˈneiʃən] *n.*

re·com·mence [ˈriːkəˈmens] *vt., vi.* (使)重新开始; 从头再做. **-ment** *n.*

rec·om·mend [ˌrekəˈmend] *vt.* ①推荐,推举,介绍. ②(行为、性质)使人欢喜; 使受欢迎. ③劝,劝告,忠告(人) *(to do; that)* 〔现多用 commend〕. ④托, 委托. *Can you ~ me a good cook?* 你可以介绍我一个好厨师吗? *~ sb. as a servant [for a post]* 推荐某人做仆人[就任某职]. *Her manners ~ her to high and low alike.* 她的态度使上上下下的人都喜欢她. *Your plan has very little to ~ it.* 你的计划几乎毫无可取的地方. *I ~ you to take a holiday.* 我劝你休假吧. *the ~ed variety* 优良品种. ***~ one's own person*** 自荐. **-able** *a.* 可以推荐的; 该赞许的; 明智的.

rec·om·men·da·tion [ˌrekəmenˈdeiʃən] *n.* ①推荐,介绍; 介绍信. ②特长; 可取之处. ③劝告. *speak in ~ of sb. [sth.]* 口头推荐某人[某物]. *sb.'s personal ~s* 某人的特长. *long-playing ~s* 受推荐的一些密纹唱片. *follow sb.'s ~s* 听从某人的劝告.

rec·om·mend·a·to·ry [ˌrekəˈmendətəri] *a.* ①推荐的. ②特长的. ③劝告的. *a ~ letter* 介绍信.

re·com·mis·sion [ˈriːkəˈmiʃən] *vt.* 使(已退伍的人员、军舰等)再服役.

re·com·mit [ˈriːkəˈmit] *vt.* ①再干, 再犯(罪); 把…再关进监狱. ②再委托, 再委任. ③重新提出(议案等). **-ment, -tal** *n.*

rec·om·pense [ˈrekəmpəns] *n.* 报应; 报酬; 回报; 回礼; 偿还; 赔偿. — *vt.* 酬答,回报; 偿还, 赔偿: *~ him for his services* = *~ his services* 酬答他的勤劳. *~ (him for) his loss* 赔偿他的损失.

re·com·pose [ˈriː-kəmˈpəuz] *vt.* ①改组(内阁等); 改写(诗文等). ②使安静,使镇定. ③【印】改排,重排: *~ a quarrel* 把争吵平息下来.

re·con [ˈriːkɔn] *n.* = recco; reconnaissance.

rec·on·cil·a·ble [ˈrekənsailəbl] *a.* 有和解 [调停] 希望的; 可顺从的; 可调和的,可使一致的.

rec·on·cile [ˈrekənsail] *vt.* ①使和解,使和好 *(to; with)*; 调停,排解(争端等). ②使顺从, 使满足, 使安心. ③使一致, 使调和 *(to; with)*. ④【宗】使(场所等)洁净. ⑤【造船】使(木板)接缝平滑: *~ persons to each other* = *~ sb. to [with] another man* 使(某人与另一人)和解. *How can you ~ it to your conscience?* 你这样干, 问心无愧吗? *~ one's statement with one's conduct* 使言行一致. ***be ~d*** 言归于好, 和解. ***be ~d to*** = ***~ oneself to*** 甘心…,服从, 顺从 *(one's fate)*.

rec·on·cile·ment [ˈrekənsailmənt], **re·con·cil·i·a·tion** [-siliˈeiʃən] *n.* 调停; 和解,调和,一致; 服从, 顺从.

rec·on·cil·er [ˈrekənsailə] *n.* 调解人.

rec·on·cil·ia·tor·y [ˌrekənˈsiliətəri] *a.* 调解的; 和解的; 调和的; 顺从的.

rec·on·dite [riˈkɔndait, ˈrekən-] *a.* ①奥妙[深奥]的; (作品等)难解的. ②看不出来的,隐藏着的.

re·con·di·tion [ˈriːkənˈdiʃən] *vt.* ①修理, 检修; 修改, 改革. ②重建,恢复; (重行)调整.

re·con·firm [ˈriːkənˈfəːm] *vt.* 再证实; 再确认.

re·con·nais·sance [riˈkɔnisəns] *n.* ①侦察,搜索. ②踏勘; 勘察,探查;【植】概测. ③侦察队; 侦察车. *high ~* 高空侦察. *~ in force* 强行侦察. *a ~ machine [airplane]* 侦察(飞)机.

rec·on·noi·ter, 〔美〕**-ter** [ˌrekəˈnɔitə] *vt., vi.* ①【军】侦察; 搜索. ②踏勘(土地).

re·con·quer [ˈriːˈkɔŋkə] *vt.* 再征服; 夺回,克复.

re·con·sid·er [ˈriː-kənˈsidə] *vt., vi.* 重新考虑. **-a·tion** [ˈriː-kənˌsidəˈreiʃən] *n.*

re·con·sign·ment [ˌrikənˈsainmənt] *n.* ①再交付,再委托; 再寄售,再托卖. ②(在运输中对原提单上的路线、目的地、收货人等的)改变委托事项.

re·con·sti·tute [ˈriːˈkɔnstitjuːt] *vt.* ①重新构成[组成、编制、制定]. ②重新编成. ③恢复(脱水食物的)水分.

re·con·struct [ˈriː-kənˈstrʌkt] *vt.* ①重建, 再建; 改造; 复兴. ②使在想象中重现; 推想; 设想. *~ a crime* (经过调查及推理等)设想犯罪情况. **re·con·struc·tion** *n.* ①重建; 改造; 复兴. ②〔美〕南北战争后南部各州的重建.

Re·con·struc·tion·ism [ˌrikənˈstrʌkʃənizəm] *n.* ①(美国南北战争后)提倡重建的运动. ②【宗】(犹太教)重建运动〔发生于 20 世纪, 目的在于使犹太教传统与时代相适应〕.

re·con·vene [ˈriːkənˈviːn] *vt., vi.* 再召集.

re·con·vert [ˈriː-kənˈvəːt] *vt.* ①使重新皈依; 使恢复党籍,使重新入党. ②使恢复原状. **re·con·ver·sion** *n.*

re·con·vey [ˌrikənˈvei] *vt.* 取回,送还,归还. **-ance** *n.*

re·cord[1] [ˈrekɔːd] *n.* ①记录; 记载. ②【法】案卷; 档案; 证据,证明; 诉状; 公判录. ③履历,经历,阅历. ④成绩; (运动比赛的)最高纪录. ⑤(留声机的)唱片; 录了音的磁带. *a matter of ~* 有案可查的事件. *His ~ is against him.* 他的履历不好(对他不利). *school ~s* 学业成绩. ***a ~ run*** 打破纪录的赛跑. ***bear ~ to*** 给…作证, 保证. ***beat [break, cut] the ~*** 打破前例,打破记录. ***call to ~*** = take to ~. ***go on ~*** ①被记录下来. ②公开表明见解. ***have a good ~*** 履历好; 信誉[名声]好. ***hold the world's ~*** 保持世界纪录. ***in ~*** 有记录在案,纪录上, 被登记 (*the greatest earthquake in [on] ~* 有纪录以来最大的地震,空前的大地震. *It is in ~ that ...* 是有先例的). ***keep to the ~*** ①依据判例判决. ②不扯到题外. ***leave on ~*** 留在纪录上. ***off the ~*** 〔美〕不得发表的; 不可以公开的; 非正式的 (*This is off the ~.* 这是非正式的谈话〔政治家用语〕). ***put [place] on ~*** = leave on ~. ***put [place] oneself on ~*** ①取得卓著的成绩,出类拔萃. ②表示意见,指出. ***set (up) a new ~*** 创新纪录. ***take to ~*** 使…作证人, 求…证明. ***the greatest ... on ~*** 有史以来最大的,前所未闻的. ***travel out of the ~*** ①不依据判例判决. ②扯到题外. — [riˈkɔːd] *vt.* ①记录,记载; 登记,挂号; 叙述,报告; 给…录音; 印记; 永久留下. ②(寒暑表等)表示(度数). ③(鸟)低声唱(歌). *a ~ed statement* 正式声明. — *vi.* ①记录; 登记. ②进行录音; 被录音. ~ **breaker** 打破纪录的人,创新纪录者. **~-breaking** *a.* 打破记录(的),空前的. ~ **changer** 自动换片装置. ~ **holder** (最高)纪录保持人. ~ **library** 收藏唱片的全部. ~ **player** 电唱机. **-a·ble** *a.* 可记录的,值得记录的.

re·cord·er [riˈkɔːdə] *n.* ①记录者,记录员; 市法院法官. ②自动记录器; (电报的)收报机; 录音机; 录音技师. ③〔常 *pl.*〕舌簧八孔直笛. *a wire ~* 钢丝录音器. *a tape ~* 磁带录音机.

re·cord·ing [riˈkɔːdiŋ] *a.* (从事)记录的; 自记的. *a ~ secretary* 记录员. *a ~ altimeter* 【空】自记高度计. *a ~ mechanism* 自记装置. — *n.* (自动)记录,录音; 唱片; 录了音的磁带; 录音的节目. *sound ~* 录音. *disc [film] ~* 唱片[胶片]录音. *wire [tape] ~* 钢丝[磁带]录音. ***play back the ~*** 放录音.

re·cord·ist [riˈkɔːdist] *n.* 录音员.

re·count[1] [riˈkaunt] *vt.* ①详细讲,细述. ②列举.

re·count² [ˈriːˈkaunt] *vt.* 重新点数，再数. — *n.* (投票等的)重数，重计.
re·count·al [riˈkauntl] *n.* 再数，重数；叙述.
re·coup [riˈkuːp] *vt.* ①扣除. ②收回，使赔还；补偿，赔偿. ③重获. ~ *sb. (for) his loss* =~ *sb.'s loss* 赔偿某人损失. ~ *oneself* 收回用费[损失]. — *vi.* 补偿损失.
re·coup·ment [riˈkuːpmənt] *n.* ①扣除. ②赔偿.
re·course [riˈkɔːs] *n.* ①依赖，依靠，利[使]用，求助 *(to)*. ②【法】追索权；偿还要求. ③〔罕〕所依靠的物[人]. *have ~ to ...* 求助于…，依靠…，用…. *without ~* 【法、商】无追索权的；(汇票等)背书人[签证人]不负追索之责.
re·cov·er [riˈkʌvə] *vt.* ①克复，恢复. ②收回，取回，挽回(失去或被夺去之物)；回收(废料)；重新获得[找到](失传的技术等)；找到，搜出(失踪的尸体等). ③使痊愈，使复元；使清醒，使复活. ④赔偿(损失等)；取得(损害赔偿等). ⑤使和解，安抚，怀柔. ⑥使悔改. ⑦填地. ~ *one's feet [legs]* (跌倒后又)站起来. *~ed acid* 回收酸. *~ed wool* 再生毛. ~ *one's losses* 弥补[挽回]损失. ~ *land from the sea* 填海拓地. *R- arms!* 【军】还原！由瞄准转为预备放的口令. *~ed area* 收复区. ~ *oneself* 清醒过来；心定下来；手脚恢复自由；重行站稳. ~ *the meaning of* 发现…的意义. ~ *the wind of* 重新追寻到(猎物的)臭迹. — *vi.* ①恢复；痊愈 *(from; of)*；甦生，清醒. ②【击剑】恢复开始时姿势. ③【法】胜诉. — *n.* 【击剑等】恢复开始时姿势: *at the ~* 恢复开始姿势.
re-cov·er [ˈriːˈkʌvə] *vt.* 重新盖；改装(伞等的)面子，改装[更换]封面.
re·cov·er·a·ble [riˈkʌvərəbl] *a.* 可取回的；可恢复的；可回收的；可医好的. ~ **reserve**【矿】可採储量.
re·cov·er·y [riˈkʌvəri] *n.* ①重获；复得；恢复，收回，回收. ②还原，复原；痊愈；甦生；矫正. ③回缩. ④填地. ⑤【法】胜诉. ~ **room** (观察开过刀的病人或分娩后的孕妇的)恢复室. ~ **plant** (废料)回收设备，再生工厂.
rec·re·ance [ˈrekriəns] *n.* 求饶；怯懦；背叛变节.
rec·re·ant [ˈrekriənt] *a.* 求饶的；怯懦的；不忠的；变节的. — *n.* 胆小鬼，懦夫；背叛者，变节者.
re-create [ˈriːkriˈeit] *vt.* 再创造，再创作；改造，重做.
rec·re·ate [ˈrekrieit] *vt.* 使恢复精神；使得到休养；使得到消遣. ~ **oneself with** 以…消遣 (~ *oneself with baseball* 打棒球消遣). — *vi.* 静养，休养；消遣.
re-cre·a·tion [ˈriːkriˈeiʃən] *n.* 再创造，再创作；重新创造；再创造的事物.
rec·rea·tion [ˌrekriˈeiʃən] *n.* 休养；娱乐，消遣: *a ~ ground* 休养地；娱乐场. *a ~ room* 娱乐室. **-al** *a.*
rec·re·a·tive [ˈrekrieitiv] *a.* 适合休养的；消遣的，娱乐的.
rec·re·ment [ˈrekrimənt] *n.* 〔现罕〕渣滓，废物. **-al** *a.*
re·crim·inate [riˈkrimineit] *vt., vi.* 反责；反(控)诉.
re·crim·i·na·tion [riˌkrimiˈneiʃən] *n.*
re·crim·i·na·tive, -to·ry [riˈkrimineitiv, -təri] *a.* 反责的；反控诉的.
rec room [ˈrekrum] 〔口〕 = recreation room.
re·cross [ˈriːˈkrɔ(ː)s] *vt.* 再横过，再越过，再渡；横越[横渡]回来.
re·cru·desce [ˌriːkruːˈdes] *vi.* (病、痛等)复发；(内乱等)再发作.
re·cru·des·cence [ˌriː-kruːdesns] *n.* 再痛；(病等的)复发.
re·cru·des·cent [ˌriː-kruːˈdesnt] *a.* 又痛起来的(伤等)；复发的(病等)，更加重了的.
re·cruit [riˈkruːt] *vt.* ①添补，补充(兵员)；招募(新兵)，征求(新成员)，征收，吸收(党员). ②补养，保养(身体)，恢复体力. ③把食品装入(船内). ~ ***oneself*** 休养，静养. — *vi.* ①招募新兵[人员]，征求新成员. ②补充；恢复健康；保养. ③装入食品: *a ~ing sergeant* 征兵军士. *~ing ground* 征兵地区. ***go to the country to ~*** 到乡下去休养，易地疗养. — *n.* 新兵，新成员，新加入者，新学生: *a raw ~* 初学者，新手，生手. **-ment** *n.*
Rec. Sec., rec. sec. = recording secretary 记录秘书.
rect. = ①receipt. ②rectangle; rectangular. ③rectified. ④rector; rectory.
rect- *comb. f.* = recti-.
rec·ta [ˈrektə] rectum 的复数.
rec·tal [ˈrektəl] *a.* 【解】直肠的；近直肠的.
rec·tan·gle [ˈrektæŋgl] *n.* 【数】矩形，长方形.
rec·tan·gu·lar [rekˈtæŋgjulə] *a.* 矩形的，长方形的；成直角的. ~ **distribution**【统】均匀分布.
recti- *comb. f.* 直，正；【电】整流.
rec·ti·fi·a·ble [ˈrektifaiəble] *a.* ①可矫正[改正，校正]的；可整顿的. ②【电】可整流的；【化】可精馏的. ③【几】(曲线)可求长的.
rec·ti·fi·ca·tion [ˌrektifiˈkeiʃən] *n.* ①改正，校正，订正；矫正，纠正，整顿. ②【电】整流；矫频；【化】精馏，提纯. ③【数】求长法. ~ **campaign [movement]** 整风运动.
rec·ti·fi·er [ˈrektifaiə] *n.* ①改正者，校正者，订正者，更正者；矫正者，纠正者，整顿者. ②【电】整流器；检波器；检波管；纠[校]正仪；【化】精馏器. *a ignition ~*【机】点火管. *a plate ~*【无】屏极检波器；屏压整流器.
rec·ti·fy [ˈrektifai] *vt.* ①改正，校正，订正，更正；矫正，纠正；整顿. ②【化】精馏，提纯；【电】整流，检波. ③【数】求(曲线的)长. ④【机】调整，拨准(表等). *rectified alcohol [spirits]* 纯酒精. *a ~ing detector*【无】整流检波器. *a ~ing plane*【数】从切[平]面. *a ~ing surface*【数】伸长曲面.
rec·ti·lin·e·al, -e·ar [ˌrektiˈliniəl, -iə] *a.* 直线的；用直围线着的；直线运动的.
rec·ti·tis [rekˈtaitis] *n.* 【医】直肠炎.
rec·ti·tude [ˈrektitjuːd] *n.* ①正直，公正. ②正确. ③〔罕〕直.
rec·to [ˈrektou] *n.* (*pl.* ~*s*) 书籍的右页〔单数页〕；纸张的正面 (*opp.* *verso*).
rec·to·cele [ˈrektəsiːl] *n.* 【医】直肠(向阴道)突出.
rec·tor [ˈrektə] *n.* ①(英国国教中掌管财产及税收的)教区长；〔美〕(新教主教派的)教区牧师；【天主】教区长；修道院院长. ②校长〔尤指德国大学的校长，英格兰限指牛津大学 *Exeter and Lincoln Colleges* 的院长，苏格兰指中学校长〕. *Lord R-* 〔Scot.〕(每三年选举一次的)大学名誉校长〔相当于英格兰的 Chancellor〕. **~ship** = rectorate.
rec·tor·ate [ˈrektərit] *n.* 教区长(等)的职位[任期].
rec·to·ri·al [rekˈtɔːriəl] *a.* 教区长(等)的.
rec·to·ry [ˈrektəri] *n.* 教区长(等)的住宅[职位、辖区、俸禄].
rec·trix [ˈrektriks] *n.* (*pl.* **rec·tri·ces** [ˈrektrisiːz, rekˈtraisiːz]) 【动】尾羽，舵羽.
rec·tum [ˈrektəm] *n.* (*pl.* ***rec·ta*** [ˈrektə]) 【解】直肠.
rec·tus [ˈrektəs] *n.* (*pl.* *-ti* [-tai]) 【解】(眼、颈、大腿等部的)直肌.
re·cum·ben·cy [riˈkʌmbənsi] *n.* ①靠着，斜倚；躺着；休息. ②依靠；依赖.
re·cum·bent [riˈkʌmbənt] *a.* ①靠着的；横卧的. ②不活动的，懒惰的. **-ly** *ad.*
re·cu·per·a·bil·i·ty [riˌkjuːpərəˈbiliti] *n.* ①恢复力，复原力. ②【化】可回收性.
re·cu·per·ate [riˈkjuːpəreit] *vt.* ①恢复(健康、元气)；使复原. ②【化】同流换热；回收. — *vi.* ①(健康)复原；②弥补损失.
re·cu·per·a·tion [riˌkjuːpəˈreiʃən] *n.* ①恢复，复原. ②弥补，挽回. ③【化】同流换热(法)，同流节热，继续收热(法).
re·cu·per·a·tive [riˈkjuːpəreitiv] *a.* ①恢复的，复原的；有复原力的. ②(火炉等)有保热装置的；同流换热的，复热的.

re•cur [riˈkəː] *vi.* ①(问题、困难等)再发生;(疾病等)复发;来来去去,翻来覆去. ②回想;回头讲 *(to)*;(思想等)重新浮现在心上 *(to)*. ③【数】递归,循环. ④〔罕〕倚赖,求助,借助: ～ *in [on, to] the mind [memory]* 又浮现在心上,想起. **recurring decimals** 循环小数.

re•cur•rence [riˈkʌrəns] *n.* ①复回,重现,再发;来去,反覆,隐现. ②【数】递归,循环;回想. ③〔罕〕倚赖: *a ～ formula* 递推〔递演〕公式,循环公式. *have ～ to arms* 用武力解决.

re•cur•rent [riˈkʌrənt] *a.* ①复回的,复现的,再发的. ②时常来的,周期性发作的;循环的;时时想起的;【解、植】逆向的;回归的. — *n.*【解】回归动脉,回归神经,(尤指)上下喉头神经. ～ **fever**【医】回归热. ～ **nerves** 回归神经. ～ **parent** 回交亲本. **-ly** *ad.*

re•cur•sion [riːˈkəːʃən] *n.*【数】递归(式);递推,循环. **-sive** *a.*, **-sively** *ad.*, **-sive•ness** *n.*

re•cur•vate [riˈkəːvit] *a.*【植】反曲的,反弯的.

re•curve [riːˈkəːv] *vt.* 使反曲,使反弯,使向后弯曲. — *vi.* 反弯;(风、水流等)折回.

rec•u•sancy [ˈrekjuzənsi] *n.* 抗拒;不服从;不服权威;【英史】不遵奉国教.

rec•u•sant [ˈrekjuzənt] *a.* ①不服从的,抗拒的. ②【英史】不遵奉国教的. — *n.* ①抗拒者,不顺从舆论〔一般习惯〕的人. ②【英史】不遵奉国教者.

re•cuse [riˈkjuːz] *vt.* *(-cused, -cus•ing)* 〔罕〕宣布反对(审判员、陪审员或法庭),(提出某种理由)要求撤换(审判员等).

rec vee [ˈrekviː] 〔口〕= a recreational vehicle 游玩车辆,家庭旅行汽车.

re•cy•cle [riːˈsaikl] *vt.*, *n.* ①(使)再循环. ②反复应用.

red[1] [red] *a.* **(red•der; red•dest)** ①红色的,赤色的. ②赤热的,(面孔)因…而胀红的 *(with)*. ③血腥的,血淋淋的 *(with)*;(战争等)残酷的. ④〔常 R-〕红的,革命的,共产主义的. ⑤【磁石】(指)北极的. ⑥〔英〕英国的〔由于地图上常把英国领土染成红色〕. ～ *meat* 红肉,牛羊肉 (*cf.* white meat). ～ *wine* 红葡萄酒. *a ～ battle* 血战. *The Chinese R- Army* 中国的红军. ***as ～ as blood [scarlet, a turky-cock]*** 胀红了脸. ***become ～*** = turn ～. ***paint the town ～*** 痛饮;胡闹. ～ ***with (anger)*** (气得)满脸通红. ***turn ～*** 变红,红了脸. — *n.* ①红,赤色;红色绘画颜料. ②红布,红衣;〔美〕印第安人;〔R-〕〔美〕红头发的人;(枱球的)红球. ③共产党(员),共产主义者;左派. ④〔*pl.*〕月经. ⑤〔美〕一分(钱). ⑥〔the ～〕〔美〕赤字,亏空,负债 (*cf.* the black). ⑦〔R-〕【英史】红舰队〔从前英国红、白、蓝三舰队之一〕. ***be in (the) ～*** 〔美〕亏蚀. ***come out of the ～*** 〔美〕开始赚钱,获利. ***go into (the) ～*** 〔美〕出现赤字,发生亏蚀. ***see ～*** 〔口〕激怒,生气. **～-bait** *vt.*〔政俚〕拿红帽子给(人)戴. **～-baiter**〔政俚〕给(人)戴红帽子的人. **～-baiting** *n.*, *a.*〔政俚〕戴红帽子(的). **～ball**〔美〕特快列车. **～-blind** *a.* 红盲的. **～-blooded** *a.*〔美〕健壮的;精神好的;有勇气的;(小说等)情节紧张的. **R- Book** (红皮)社会名人录. ～ **box**〔英〕大臣用红色文件匣. ～ **breast**【鸟】欧鸲,知更鸟. **～brick, ～-brick** ①*a.* (别于牛津和剑桥的)新大学的,新学院的;〔尤指〕地方设立的新大学的. ②*n.* 新大学,新学院. **～bud**【植】紫荆属. **～bug**【动】红恙螨;红蝽. **～cap** ①〔美〕(火车站、飞机场上戴红帽子的)搬运员. ②〔英口〕宪兵. ③〔Scot.〕妖怪,魔鬼. ④〔英〕金翅雀. ～ **cent**〔美口〕铜币 (*I don't care a ～ cent.* 我毫不在乎). **～coat**〔口〕【英史】英国兵,红衣兵. **R- Corners**〔苏联〕红角,文化室. **R- Crescent**〔土耳其〕红新月会〔相当于红十字会〕. ～ **cross** 圣乔治 (St. George) 十字架〔英国国章〕;〔R- C-〕十字军徽章,十字军;〔R- C-〕红十字,红十字会;〔美俚〕吗啡. **R- Cross Society** 红十字会. **～devil**〔美俚〕【药】速可眠〔丙烯戊巴比妥钠〕红色药丸. **～-dog** *vt.* ①= Blitz. ②(在金罗美牌戏中)使(对手)得零分. ③【足球】从边线带(球)插入球门区. ～ **ear**【动】红耳太阳鱼〔产于美国中部和东南部〕. ～ **eye** ①红眼鱼. ②〔美俚〕番茄汁;酒;下等浓威士忌酒. **～fescue**【植】紫羊茅. ～ **fig**【植】红榕. ～ **fish**【动】鲑鱼;海鲋. ～ **flag** 红旗〔革命旗;危险信号旗;开战旗〕;激人发怒的东西;〔the R- F-〕《红旗歌》〔革命歌曲〕. ～ **gold**〔古、诗〕纯金;货币,现金. **R- Guard**〔苏联〕赤卫军. ～ **hands** 血腥的〔杀人的〕手. **～-handed** *a.* 血手淋淋的,残忍的;现行犯的 (*be caught [taken] ～-handed* 当场被捕). ～ **hat** 红帽;红衣主教. **～head** 红头发的人;【动】(美国产)红头啄木鸟 (= redheaded woodpecker). **～headed** *a.* 头发红的;〔美俚〕大怒的. **～legs** 拳参. **～-letter** *a.* 红字的,(日历上)用红字表示的(纪念日,节日等). ～ **light** 红灯;危险信号;【空】红色航空灯. **～-light district**〔美俚〕红灯区,风化区. **(the) R- Sea** 红海. ～ **herring** ①熏青鱼. ②无关紧要的题外的话 (*draw a ～ herring across the track* 提出无关系的问题使人的注意离开本题). **～-hot** ①*a.* 炽热的,灼热的;热烈的;非常激动的. ②*a.* 最新的. ③*n.* 红肠面包. **～-hot miracle**〔美〕意料之外的结果〔如赛跑得胜的马等〕. **R- Indian [man]** (红)印第安人. ～ **ink** 红墨水;〔俚〕赤字;损失;〔俚〕廉价红葡萄酒. **R- International** 第三国际〔1919—1944〕. ～ **knees**【植】蓼. ～ **lamp** 红灯〔医师或药房夜间的门灯;(马路等的)停止通行信号,危险信号〕. ～ **lane**〔儿语〕〔俚〕咽喉. ～ **lattice**〔古〕红格子〔有执照的酒馆的标识〕;〔转义〕酒馆. ～ **lead**【矿】铅丹,红丹,四氧化三铅;〔美俚〕番茄酱. ～ **neck**〔美俚〕乡下佬;(美国)南部农民. ～ **noise**〔美俚〕番茄汤. **～out**【空】红视〔因足向加速头部充血而引起的视野变红〕. ～ **paint**〔美俚〕番茄酱. ～ **pepper** 辣椒. ～ **phosphorus**【化】赤燐,红燐. **～-pole, ～poll** ①【动】金翅雀. ②〔*pl.*〕无角赤牛. ～ **precipitate**【化】红色沉淀物;红色氧化汞. ～ **prussiate**【化】赤血盐,铁氰化物. ～ **rag** ①使人、牛等发怒的东西. ②破红旗〔反动派诅咒"～ *flag*"的话〕. ③(小麦的)锈病. ～ **ribbon Bath** 勋章;(法国)荣誉团勋章;勋章的红绶;佩带红绶勋章者. **～root**【植】西风古;美洲茶. ～ **ruin** 战祸. ～ **sanders [saunders, sandalwood]**【植】紫檀. **～shank**【鸟】赤足鹬 (*run like a ～shank* 飞一样地跑). ～ **shift**【天】红移,红向移动. ～ **shirt**【意史】红衫党人〔十九世纪意大利加里波的之信徒. **～-shirt** ① *vt.*〔美俚〕取消(球员)比赛资格〔一年后可再恢复其资格〕. ② *n.* 大学选手〔通常指延期毕业以进行训练的大学生体育尖子〕. 被取消比赛资格的球员. **～-short** *a.*【冶】(铁)因热而脆的,热脆性的. ～ **skin**〔贬〕(北美)印第安人. ～ **snow** 红雪〔北极和阿尔卑斯山上被红藻染红的雪〕. ～ **soldier** 穿红衣的兵;(皮肤变红的)猪霍乱;患猪霍乱的猪. ～ **spider** 红蜘蛛〔棉花害虫〕. ～ **spruce**【植】云杉. **(the) R- Square** 红场. **～start**【鸟】红尾鸲. ～ **tab**〔俚〕英国参谋军官. ～ **tape** *n.*, *a.* (扎文件的)红带(的);官僚作风(的),文牍主义(的). **～-tapery, ～-typism** *n.* 官样文章,官僚作风,文牍主义. **～-tapist** *n.* 不离俗套的人,官僚〔文牍〕主义者. ～ **tiger** 美洲虎. ～ **top**【植】小糠草,红顶草. ～ **triangle** 红三角〔Y. M. C. A. 的标识〕; = Y. M. C. A. ～ **turkey**〔美俚〕刚煎好的法兰克福香肠. **～ware**【植】掌状昆布〔可食用〕. ～ **water** ①(海湖中因红色微生物造成的)赤潮. ②【兽医】(牛的)血尿病 (= texas fever). **～-wing**【动】红翼歌鸫. **～wood**【植】①〔美〕红杉. ②红树,红木〔作染料用〕. **-ness** *n.* 红,红色.

red[2] [red] *n.* 镇静剂.

re•dact [riˈdækt] *vt.* 编辑,编纂(原稿等);编写;拟订(公告、通告等). ～ *a proclamation* 草拟宣言.

re•dac•tion [riˈdækʃən] *n.* ①编辑;编写;校订,改订. ②改订本. **-tor** *n.* 编辑者;校订者.

re•dan [riˈdæn] *n.*【筑城】凸角堡.

redd[1] [red] *vt., vi.* ***(redd*** 或 ***'red•ded, red•ding)*** 〔口或方〕整理，弄整洁〔常与 *up* 连用〕。
redd[2] [red] *n.* 鳄鱼或鲑的产卵区。
redd[3] [red] *vt.* 整顿，收拾。
red•den [ˈredn] *vt.* 使红；使脸红。— *vi.* 变红；脸红。
red•dish [ˈrediʃ], **red•dy** [ˈredi] *a.* 带红色的，淡红的，微红的。
red•dle [ˈredl] *n., vt.* ***(-dled, -dling)*** = raddle, ruddle.
rede [riːd] *vt.* 〔古、方〕①忠告，劝告。②打算，企图。③解释，说明(谜、梦等)。④讲述。— *n.* ①忠告。②企图。③解释，说明。④故事。
re•deem [riˈdiːm] *vt.* ①买回(已卖之物等)，赎回(典质物等)，赎出(身体)；挽回，恢复(名誉、权利、地位等)。②偿还，还清(债务等)，收回(纸币等)。③赎(罪)；补救，弥补(缺点、过失等)；【宗】(上帝)使免罪；拯救，救出 *(from; out; of)*；超度(众生)。④履行(契约)，尽(义务)。～ *land from the sea* 填海拓地。*a ～ing point [feature]* 足以弥补缺点的特色，可取的地方，长处。～ ***oneself*** 用钱赎回人身。～ ***sth. from*** 补救…的(缺点)。
re•deem•a•ble [riˈdiːməbl] *a.* 可赎回[买回]的；可救的；可偿还的；可赎的，可补救的。*a ～ paper money* 可兑现的纸币。
re•deem•er [riˈdiːmə] *n.* ①买回者，赎当者，赎身者；赎罪者。②〔the R-〕【宗】救世主〔指耶稣基督〕。
re•de•mand [ˌridiˈmɑːnd, -ˈmænd] *vt.* ①再要求，再请求，再询问。②要回，要求交还。
re•demp•tion [riˈdem*p*ʃən] *n.* ①赎回，赎买；赎身。②履行，实践；偿还，(票据的)兑现。③赎罪；【宗】救济，超度。④补救；补偿之物；可取的地方，长处。⑤〔英〕(地位、资格的)出钱购买。*a policy of ～* 赎买政策。*That blow was [proved] his ～.* 他受了那个打击就改过自新了。***beyond [past, without]*** ～ 无恢复希望的，不可救药的；难超度的。***by*** ～ 出钱(获得资格等)。***in the year of our*** ～ … 耶稣纪元…年，公元…年。～ **fund** 偿债基金。
re•demp•tion•er [riˈdem*p*ʃənə] *n.* 〔美〕(殖民地时代)出卖劳力抵作赴美船资的人。
re•demp•tive [riˈdem*p*tiv], **-to•ry** [-təri] *a.* ①赎回的，买回的，赎买的，赎身的。②偿还的。③救世的，拯救的；赎罪的。
Re•demp•tor•ist [riˈdemptərist] *n.* (罗马天主教)传道会会员。
re•de•ploy [ˈriː-diˈplɔi] *vt., vi.* 转移(军队、劳动力等)；(使)重新布署。**-ment** *n.* 转移；(为加强生产力所采取的)调整措施。
re•de•scribe [ridiˈskraib] *vt.* 重新描述，完全重作描述〔尤指对生物学中的分类法〕。**-scrip•tion** *n.*
re•de•vel•op [ridiˈveləp] *vt.* ①再发展。②重点恢复(破败的地区)；恢复(一个地区的)经济发展，促进(一个地区的)经济发展。③【摄】再[重新]显影。— *vi.* 再[重新]发展。**-ment** *n.*
re•di•a [ˈriːdiə] *n.* ***(pl. re•di•ae*** [-diːi]) 【动】雷(迪氏)幼(虫)。
re•dif [reiˈdiːf] *n.* (土耳其的)预备兵。
re•dif•fu•sion [ˈriː-diˈfjuːʒən] *n.* 【无】(电视节目等接收后的)播放，转播。～ **station** (有线)广播台，广播站。
red•in•gote [ˈrediŋgəut] *n.* ①大礼服，长大衣。②女式骑装外衣。
red•in•te•grate [reˈdintigreit] *vi., vt.* (使)复原，(使)复旧，(使)更新。**-gra•tion** [reˌdintiˈgreiʃən] *n.* 恢复原状，复原，复旧，更新；【心】重整作用。
re•di•rect [ˈriː-diˈrekt] *vt.* ①使改寄，更改(信件等)姓名地址。②再查问(证人等)。③使再回到，使折回；使改方向；使改道。
re•di•rec•tion [ˈriː-diˈrekʃən] *n.* ①改寄，更改姓名地址；新姓名地址。②折回；归还。
re•dis•count [riˈdiskaunt] *vt.* 再打折扣，再贴现。— *n.* ①再打折扣，再贴现。②再打折扣(商业)票据，再贴现票据。**-able** *a.* 可再打折扣[贴现]的。
re•dis•cov•er [ˈriː-disˈkʌvə] *vt.* 再发现；重新发现。
re•dis•tribute [ˈriː-disˈtribju(ː)t] *vt.* 重新分配，再分配；重新划分。
re•dis•trict [riˈdistrikt] *vt.* 重新划分(区域)(尤指重划选区)。
re•div•ide [ˈriː-diˈvaid] *vt., vi.* 重新[再]分配[划分]。
red•i•vi•vus [ˌrediˈvaivəs] *a.* 复活的，复生的，再兴的，再生的。*a Napoleon ～* 拿破仑的再世。
Red•mond [ˈredmənd] *n.* 雷德蒙〔姓氏〕。
re•do [ˈriːˈduː] *vt.* ***(re•did*** [ˈriːˈdid]; ***re•done*** [ˈriːˈdʌn]) ①再做，重做。②重新布置[装饰]。
red•o•lence [ˈredəuləns] *n.* ①芬芳，芳香。②怀旧，怀念已往。
red•o•lent [ˈredəulənt] *a.* ①芬芳的，芳香的；有…香味[气味]的 *(of)*。②令人想起[回忆、联想到]…的。～ ***of the past*** 令人想起往事的。
re•dou•ble [ri(ː)ˈdʌbl] *vt.* ①使加倍；加强。②再折迭。③使发反响。④重复，再说。～ *one's efforts* 加倍努力。— *vi.* ①激增，加强。②反响。③重折，重迭。④【桥牌】再加倍。
re•doubt [riˈdaut] *n.* 【军】多面堡，棱堡；(有护墙等的)防守阵地。
re•doubt•a•ble [riˈdautəbl] 〔古〕 **re•doubted** [-id] *a.* (敌手等)可畏的，可怕的；不容轻视的；令人敬畏的。
re•dound [riˈdaund] *vi.* ①抬高，增加(信用、利益等)。②(利益等)归于…，及于… *(to)*；回到…，返还… *(upon)*。③发生，起来。*The sins of the fathers do not ～ to the children.* 父罪不及子。*His praises ～ upon himself.* 他称赞人，人也称赞他。
red•ox [ˈredɔks] *n.* 【化】氧化还原作用 (= oxidation-reduction)。
re•draft [ˈriːˈdrɑːft] *n.* ①【商】(代替退票另加手续费的)新汇票。②新草案，新稿。
re•dress [riˈdres] *n.* ①救济。②调整；调正，纠正，矫正。③赔偿。— *vt.* ①救济(受损害等的人)。②调整；调正，修整；革除(错误，弊病等)；弥补，补救。③赔偿(损害、损失等)；医治(疾病等)。～ *the balance* 恢复平衡；矫正不平衡状态。
re-dress [riːˈdres] *vt.* ①再给…穿上。②重新包扎(伤处)。
re•duce [ˈriˈdjuːs] *vt.* ①减少，减轻，节减；缩短，缩小；降低，贬低；使没落，使落魄。②使降服，征服，克服；攻陷(城市等)。③使衰弱，使退化。④使变为，使成为，迫使，使不得不。⑤把…归类[分类，整理]。⑥【数】简化，约简；化为；缩减；折合。⑦【化】还原；【冶】提炼，精炼；从(原油)中蒸去轻质油。⑧【医】使(脱臼等)复位，使复原。⑨使适合，使适应，使一致。⑩【火箭】整理(测量结果等)；译解(代号等)。⑪【生】使(细胞)减数分裂。⑫【摄】把(底片等)减薄，减低强度。⑬【语音】把(重读音)变为非重读音。～ *production* 减少生产。*a map on ～d scale* 按比例缩小了的地图。～ *wine to two-thirds by boiling* 将葡萄酒煮沸浓缩成三分之二。～ *the temperature* 降低温度。～ *prices* 减低价格。*be ～d to a shadow* 消瘦得像一个影子似的。*be in a very ～d state* 非常衰弱。*be ～d to nothing [to a skeleton]* 瘦成骨架子。*a ～d family* 破落户。～ *sb. to terror [tears]* 使…恐怖[流泪]。～ *to reason* 使明理。～ *the animals to classes* 把动物分类。～ *one's discourse into [to] writing* 把谈话写成文章。～ *a house to ashes* 使房屋化为灰烬。～ *a compound to its components* 将化合物分解成各成分。***at a ～d price*** 廉价。***have the dislocation (shoulder) ～d*** 请人将脱臼(肩骨)复位。***in ～d circumstances*** 没落。***on a ～d scale*** 小规模地。～ ***a fraction*** 【数】约分。～ ***an equation*** 【数】解方程式。～ ***a rule to practice*** 使条文变成实践。～ ***oneself into*** 陷入…的地

步．～ *the establishment* (公司、机关等)裁员．～ *to an absurdity* 使变成荒谬．～ *to assert [asserting] an absurdity* 使陷于不得不讲荒唐话的地步；使窘迫得语无伦次．～ *to discipline* 恢复秩序，平定，使归顺．～ *to order [chaos]* 使秩序井然[乱七八糟]．～ *to powder* 把…弄成碎粉．～ *to subjection* 征服．～ *to the ranks* 把…降为兵．— *vi.* 体重减轻；【生】减数分裂．**reducing agent** 还原剂．**reducing division**【生】减数分裂．

re·duc·er [riːˈdjuːsə] *n.* ①缩小物．②渐缩管；减压阀；退粘剂；【化】还原器，还原剂；【摄】减薄剂．

re·duc·i·ble [riˈdjuːsəbl] *a.* ①可减少的，可缩减的；可贬低的；可降低的．②【数】可简化的，可约的．③【化】可还原的．④【医】(脱臼等)可复位的．

re·duc·ing [riˈdjuːsiŋ] *n.* ①减肥法．②【化】还原，减低．③【数】折合；化简．

re·duc·tase [riˈdʌkteis, -teiz] *n.*【化】还原酶．

re·duc·ti·o ad ab·sur·dum [riˈdʌkʃiəu æd əbˈsəːdəm] [L.] = reduction to absurdity【逻】归谬(证)法，间接证明法．

re·duc·tion[riˈdʌkʃən] *n.* ①缩小，减少；降级，降位；(刑罚等的)轻减；减速；减价，折扣．②(城市、国家等的)陷落，投降，被征服；变成 *(to; into)*．③破落，没落；【物】衰减．④类别；碎矿；提炼．⑤【数】简化，约简，缩减；化归．⑥(测量结果的)整理，(代号等的)译解；【无】订正．⑦【化】还原法，改格法；【摄】减薄：*a 10%* ～ 九折．*great ～s in prices* 大减价．*the ～ of armaments* 裁(减)军(备)．*ascending [descending]* ～ 由小[大]单位改成大[小]单位的换算法．～ *to absurdity = reductio ad absurdum*．～ **division**【生】减数分裂 (= meiosis)．～ **potential**【化】还原电位，还原电势．

re·duc·tion·ism [riˈdʌkʃənizm] *n.* ①简化法；简化论．②归纳主义〔以演绎无生命物质的理化用词来解释一切生物过程的作法〕．**-ist** *n., a.* ①简化论者(的)．②归纳主义者(的)．**-tion·is·tic** *a.*

re·duc·tive [riˈdʌktiv] *a.* ①缩减的；还原的；简化(成)的．②还原艺术的，抽象艺术的．— *n.*【化】还原剂，脱氧剂．

re·duc·tor [riˈdʌktə] *n.*【化】还原器；还原剂；【无】减速器；减压器．

re·dun·dance, -dan·cy [riˈdʌndəns, -si] *n.* ①过多，冗余，过剩(物)，累赘．②冗语．③【自】多余度，冗余度；冗余位；【无】冗余码；多余信息．④【宇航】(在某一配件失灵时能提供备用件的)后备能力．

re·dun·dant [riˈdʌndənt] *a.* ①过多的，冗余的，冗长的(文章等)；累赘的；丰富的(食物等)；过剩的．②后备的〔指特别多配备的配件，以防整个机件中这一配件发生故障〕．～ *words* 冗词，赘语．*a ～ population* 过剩人口．～ **verb** (时态有一种以上拼法的)一态多型动词〔如 light，其过去式可写作 lit 或 lighted〕．**-ly** *ad.*

re·du·pli·cate [riˈdjuːplikeit] *vt.* ①使加倍；重复．②【语法】使重复(音节)；重叠音节形成(派生词)．— *vi.* 重复．— *a.* 重复的；加倍的；重迭的；【植】外向镊合状的．

re·du·pli·ca·tion [riˌdjuːpliˈkeiʃən] *n.* 加倍；重复；【语法】重迭．**-tive** *a.*

re·du·vi·id [riˈdjuːviːid, -duː-] *n.*【动】食虫椿象科 *(Reduviidae)* 昆虫．

re·dye [ˈriːˈdai] *vt.* 重染，再染．

ree·bok [ˈriːbɔk] *n.*【动】(南非)尖角羚羊．

re-ech·o [ri(ː)ˈekəu] *vt., vi.* ①(使)再发回声，(使)回声传回，反响．②响遍，轰传，哄动．— *n.* *(pl. -es)* 回声的反响，再回声．

reech·y [ˈriːtʃi] *a.*〔古、方〕烟熏的，煤烟熏黑的，污秽的，败坏的，恶臭的．

Reed [riːd] *n.* ①里德〔姓氏，男子名〕．②**Walter** ～ 里德〔1851—1902，美国军医，黄热病原发现者〕．

reed [riːd] *n.* ①【植】芦苇，芦秆，苇丛；〔主英〕盖屋顶用的麦秸．②芦笛，牧笛．③牧歌．④〔诗〕矢，箭．⑤〔常 *pl.*〕【乐】簧片；簧[管]乐器．⑥【纺】杼，筘，钢筘；【建】芦饰；小凸嵌线；【矿山】引火管：*the ～s* 乐队中的簧乐器．***a broken [bruised]*** ～ 折断的芦苇杆；〔喻〕不可靠的人[物]．***lean on a*** ～ 倚赖不可靠的人[物]．***let out a*** ～【海】解开缩帆带；〔喻〕饭后松开衣服．***take in*** ～【海】收缩帆篷；减少用费．— *vt.* ①用茅草[麦秸、芦苇]盖(屋顶)；用芦苇装饰；把簧装(在乐器上)．～ **mace**〔英〕【植】香蒲．～ **organ**【乐】簧风琴．～ **pipe** 牧笛；舌管，簧管．～ **stop**【乐】簧管音栓．

reed·ed [ˈriːdid] *a.* ①芦苇覆盖的；芦苇丛生的．②有沟的，有凹槽的．

reed·ing [ˈriːdiŋ] *n.*【建】小凸嵌线，芦饰，小凸嵌线装饰〔如圆柱上的装饰〕．

re·ed·u·cate, re-ed·u·cate [riˈedʒu(ː)keit] *vt.* *(-cated, -cat·ing)* 再教育．**-ca·tion** [riˌedʒu(ː)ˈkeiʃən] *n.* **-ca·tive** *a.*

reed·y [ˈriːdi] *a.* *(-i·er; -i·est)* ①多芦苇的，芦苇丛生的；芦苇做的；芦苇状的．②细长的．③象芦笛声音的．

reef[1] [riːf] *n.* ①【地】暗礁，礁脉；沙洲．②【矿】矿脉；含金石英脉．

reef[2] [riːf] *n.*【海】(便于减少受风面积的)缩帆部，叠帆部．***let [shake, take] out the ～s*** 放开帆篷．***take in a*** ～ 收缩帆篷；〔喻〕缩减(用费等)；慎重行事．— *vt.* 收缩(帆篷)．～ **knot**【海】缩帆结，平结，方结．～**-point**【海】缩帆索．

reef·er [ˈriːfə] *n.* ①缩帆者．②〔英俚〕海军候补士官生；〔美俚〕海军学校学员．③平结，方结，缩帆结 (= reef-knot)．④(水手穿的)对襟双排钮短上衣 *(= ～ jacket)*．⑤〔美俚〕大麻卷烟 (= marijuana cigarette)．⑥〔美俚〕冰箱，冷藏汽车；冷藏车箱；冷藏船．

reek [riːk] *n.* ①〔主 Scot.〕烟．②热气，水蒸汽．③恶臭；腐臭的空气．④雾．*the ～ of tobacco* 烟臭味．*amid ～ and squalor* 在恶臭和污秽之中．— *vi.* 冒烟；冒水蒸气，冒热气；冒血腥气；放恶臭，冲鼻子 *(of; with)*．～ *of garlic* 发出大蒜的臭气．～ *with gore* 染满淤血．***～ of affectation*** 摆臭架子．～ ***of blood*** 冒血腥气．～ ***of murder*** 杀气腾腾．— *vt.* 用烟熏；散发(烟、水汽等)；发出…的气息．*Her manner ～s prosperity.* 她的风度显出有钱的样子．

reek·ing [ˈriːkiŋ] *a.* 冒烟的，烟雾腾腾的，热气腾腾的；发臭的；冒血腥气的；新鲜的(血等)．

reek·y [ˈriːki] *a.* 冒烟的，烟雾沉沉的，烟熏熏的；熏黑的；冒蒸汽的；发臭的．

reel[1] [riːl] *n.* ①【纺】卷线车，纺车；绕线筒．②〔英〕(钓丝的)卷轴，线框；(线、铁丝、胶片、纸、铅管等的)一卷；【机】线轴；电缆盘，影片盘，磁带盘；(影片的)一盘，卷〔1,000—2,000 英尺〕．③刈割机上的夹秆器．*a picture in six ～s* 六盘长的影片．*two ～s of motion picture film* 两盘电影片．～ *boss*〔美〕影片公司的经理．***off the*** ～ (线等)陆续放长；滔滔不绝地，继续不断地 *(tell a story off the ～* 滔滔不绝地讲故事)．— *vt.*【纺】捲(线)，纺(线)，缫(丝) *(off)*．②收卷轴拉近(鱼、测程线等) *(in; up)*．— *vi.* (蟋蟀等)唧唧地叫．～ ***in [up]*** (将上钓的鱼、测程线等)收卷轴拉近[拉起]．～ ***off*** 从纺车上把线拉出；(用茧)缫(丝)；滔滔不绝地讲．***～ing frame and comber***【纺】梳麻机．

reel[2] [riːl] *n.* 摇摆，蹒跚；眩晕．***the ～ of vice and folly around us*** 在我们周围乱动的邪恶和愚蠢．***without a ～ or a stagger*** 脚步稳定地．— *vi.* 摇摆，摇摇摆摆地走 *(about; along)*；眼花，眩晕；摇动，动摇．*My brain ～s* 我的头晕．*The drunkard ～ed down the street.* 那醉汉在街上摇摇欲倒地走．— *vt.* ①使眩晕．②在…上蹒跚而行．

reel[3] [riːl] *n.* (苏格兰高地人的)双人对舞(曲)；〔美〕弗吉尼亚舞〔一种乡村舞蹈，Virginia Reel 的简称〕．— *vi.* 跳双人对舞．

re-elect [ˈriːiˈlekt] *vt.* 重选,改选.
re-elec·tion [ˈriːiˈlekʃən] *n.* 重选,改选.
reel·er [ˈriːlə] *n.* ①【纺】摇纱工;缫丝工;【纺】摇纱机;缫丝机. ②〔英俚〕警察. ③…卷的影片. *a three-reeler.* 一部三卷胶片组成的影片.
re-el·i·gi·ble [ˈriːˈelidʒəbl] *a.* 可以重选的;可改选的;可再任命的.
reel·ing·ly [ˈriːliŋli] *ad.* 摇摇摆摆地,蹒跚地;头晕眼花地;动摇不定地.
re-en·able [ˈriːiˈneibl] *vt.* 使再能…;重新授权给.
re-en·act [ˈriːiˈnækt] *vt.* ①再制定,再用法律规定. ②再扮演. **-ment** *n.*
re-en·force [riːinˈfɔːs] *vt.* = reinforce.
re-en·gine [ˈriːˈendʒin] *vt.* 更换(船只等的)发动机.
re-en·ter [ˈriːˈentə] *vt.* ①再进入;再加入;再登记. ②【雕刻】加深(不清楚的线条等);加印印刷品的颜色. ③【法】收回(贷出物). ④(角等)凹入. *The spacecraft ~ed the atmosphere* 宇宙飞船重返大气层. — *vi.* ①再入,又进去. ②收回所有权;重新占有.
re-en·trant [riːˈentrənt] *a., n.* ①再进去(的). ②【筑城】凹角(的). ~ **angle** 凹角.
re-en·try [riːˈentri] *n.* ①再进入. ②【法】所有权的收回. ③【宇】重返大气层. ④【牌戏】可以重占优势的大牌 (= ~ **card**).
Reese [riːs] *n.* 里斯〔姓氏〕.
re-estab·lish [ˈriːisˈtæbliʃ] *vt.* 重建;使复原;使复职,使复位. **-ment** *n.*
reeve[1] [riːv] ***(-d or rove)*** *vt.* ①【海】穿(绳入孔等)(through);穿(绳)入孔结牢 *(in; on; round; to)*. ②把(棍子等)插进(洞内). ③(船)穿过(浮水、浅滩等).
reeve[2] [riːv] *n.* ①〔英史〕地方官,镇长,区长;〔加拿大〕(村会的)主席. ②【采】矿工领班.
reeve[3] *n.* 【动】雌流苏鹬 *(cf.* ruff).
re-ex·am·ine [ˈriːigˈzæmin] *vt.* ①再考试,重考,复试;复查,再调查,再检查,再审查;再审. **-i·na·tion** *n.*
re-ex·change [ˈriːiksˈtʃeindʒ] *n.* ①再交换,再交易. ②【商】退汇(要求);要求退汇的金额. — *vt.* 再交换;掉换;换回.
re-ex·port [ˈriːeksˈpɔːt] *vt.* (将进口货)再输出,再出口. — [riːˈekspɔːt] *n.* 再输出,再出口;再出口的货物;〔*pl.*〕再出口额. **-a·tion** *n.*
ref. = ①referee. ②reference; referred. ③reformation; reformed; reformer. ④refining. ⑤refunding. ⑥refrigeration; refrigerator. ⑦refrain.
re·face [ˈriːˈfeis] *vt.* ①重修(房屋等的)门面. ②换(衣服的)面子.
re·fash·ion [ˈriːˈfæʃən] *vt.* 再作,重作,改制,改做;改变(形式等);给…以新形式. **-ment** *n.*
re·fect [riˈfekt] *vt.* 〔废〕(通过饮食)使精力恢复,使精神振作.
re·fec·tion [riˈfekʃən] *n.* 消遣,休养;(吃饮食)恢复精神,提神;小吃;茶点.
re·fec·to·ry [riˈfektəri] *n.* (神学院、修道院等的)饭厅,食堂. *a ~ table* 长条餐桌.
re·fer[1] [riˈfəː] *vt.* ①把…提交,交付,委托,付托(事件、问题等) *(to)*. ②叫…去打听,叫某人参看,叫某人查询,叫某人注意 *(to)*;叫…到某处或某人处 *(to)* 查询某事 *(for)*. 让…过目;使…参看;使…注意(事实等) *(to)*. ③把某人叫做 *(as)*, 将…归因于…,认为…是起因于〔由于〕…;将…归入,认为…属于(某物、某类、某地、某人、某时代等) *(to)*. ~ *oneself to* 依赖,求助于. *The dispute was ~red to the United Nations.* 这项争论已提交联合国. ~ *a bill to a committee* 把议案提交委员会. *For further particulars I ~ you to my secretary.* 详细情况请问我的秘书. *She often ~s questions to me.* 她常拿问题来问我. ~ *sb. to the dictionary* 叫某人去查字典. *All these are referred to as animals.* 这些都叫做动物. *Zoologists ~ barnacles to Crustancea.* 动物学家把螺蛳归入甲壳类. — *vi.* ①借助,参考,参看,引证,引用;翻阅,查看(帐簿等) *(to)*. ②有关系,涉及 *(to)*;说到,提到;打听,查询〔特别是品行、能力等〕*(to)*. ③使注意,指点,指示. *The asterisk ~s to a footnote.* 星号表示参看附注. *all the documents referring to this matter* 有关这一事件的一切文件. ~ *to a dictionary* 查阅词典. *The figure ~s to chapters [pages].* 数字表示章数〔页码〕. ~ *to drawer* 【商】请与出票人接洽〔略 R.D., R/D〕.
re·fer·a·ble [riˈfəːrəbl] *a.* 可交付的;可归因于…的;可归入…的;可借助的,可倚赖的;可参考的;可说及的,与…有关的 *(to)*. *This disease is ~ to microbes.* 这个病是由细菌引起的.
ref·er·ee [ˌrefəˈriː] *n.* 公断人,仲裁人;【法】(受法庭委托的)审查人,鉴定人;(足球等的)裁判员. — *vt., vi.* (为…)担任仲裁;(为…)担任裁判.
ref·er·ence [ˈrefərəns] *n.* ①(对委员、审查人等的)委托;委托项目〔范围〕. ②说到,论到,提到. ③参考;参考书;附注,引证;基准,依据;关系. ④(关于人品、能力等的)查询,咨询,询商;可供查问的人;证明人,介绍人;(身份、能力等的)证明书,介绍书,服务经历,鉴定书. ⑤参看符号〔如 asterisk*, obelisk†, section§, parallel ‖, paragraph ¶ 等〕(= ~ **marks**). *the commission's terms of ~* 委员会的职权. *R- was made to me.* 提到了我;所指的是我. *You make no ~ to your plan in your letter.* 你信里没有提到你的计划. *a book of ~ = a ~ book* 参考书. *Who are your ~s?* 你的证明人都是谁? ***bear ~ to*** = have ~ to. ***give a ~ to*** 提到,介绍. ***have ~ to*** 和…有关系. ***in ~ to*** 关于. ***load one's pages with ~s*** (在著作中)引用大量参考资料〔文献〕. ***make ~ to*** 说到,涉及,提到;参考;查问;介绍. ***with ~ to*** 关于. ***without ~ to*** 不管,不论 (*without ~ to age or sex* 无论男女老少). — *vt.* 加注,附加注脚;给(书等)列出参考书目〔注明资料来源〕. ~ **Bible** 附有参读章节注释的圣经. ~ **buoy** 基准浮标. ~ **frame** 参考系;座标系统;(电子计算机的)计算系统. ~ **gauge** 校对量规. ~ **library** (不外借图书的)参考书阅览室. ~ **mark** 参照符号;【建】参考标记. ~ **point** 控制点;衡量的标准. ~ **pressure** 参考压力. ~ **room** 图书参考室.
ref·er·en·dary [ˌrefəˈrendəri] *n.* 【英史】(宫廷、教廷中负有审查或顾问职责的)审查官,咨询官;〔罕〕公断人. — *a.* 公民投票的.
ref·er·en·dum [ˌrefəˈrendəm] ***(pl. -s, -da*** [-də]***)*** ①(决定政策可否等的)公民表决;投票(权);公民所投的票. ②(大使对本国政府的)请示书.
ref·er·ent [ˈrefrənt] *n.* ①被谈到的事物、概念等. ②【语】语词所指的对象.
ref·er·en·tial [ˌrefəˈrenʃəl] *a.* 参考(用)的,有参考文献的,有附注〔傍注〕的;咨询的;有关的.
re·fer·ra·ble, -ri·ble [riˈfəːrəbl] *a.* = referable.
ref·er·ral [riˈfəːrəl] *n.* ①介绍,指引,指点,指示;职业介绍,工作〔职务〕指派. ②受指点〔指示〕者,被介绍〔指派〕者. ③(对病人、病症等的)转诊〔转科〕介绍.
re·fill [ˈriːˈfil] *vt., vi.* 再装满;再灌满;再填;再补充.
re·fi·nance [ˈrifiˈnæns, riˈfainæns] *vt.* ***(-nanc·ed, -nanc·ing)*** 对…再供给资金.
re·fine [riˈfain] *vt.* ①精炼,精制,提炼;纯化,提纯. ②使高尚,使优美,使精致;使优雅;琢磨(文章等),推敲. ③除去缺点,改善,美化. — *vi.* ①变纯粹,澄清;(言语、举动等)变高尚,变优雅. ②改善;弄得更好,精益求精 *(on, upon)*. ③应用精密的语言〔思想〕;细加区别;详细讲 *(on, upon)*.
re·fined [riˈfaind] *a.* 精炼的,精制的;高尚的,优雅的,洗炼的;极微妙的,精密的,正确的. ~ *salt* 精盐. ~ *sugar* 精制糖. ~ *distinctions* 微妙的区别. ~ *cruelty* 阴险刻毒的残忍. **-ly** *ad.*
re·fine·ment [riˈfainmənt] *n.* ①精炼,提炼,提纯,纯化,

精制；净化；纯净，精美．②高尚，优雅；改善．③(思想、推理、议论等的)精密，微妙；细微的区别；极致．*a person of* ～ 高尚的人．*a* ～ *of cruelty* 阴险刻毒之极的残忍．

re·fin·er [riˈfainə] *n.* ①精炼者，精制者，提炼者．②精炼机，精制机，精研机；(纤维的)匀浆机．③过于精细的人，精密地推论的人．

re·fin·er·y [riˈfainəri] *n.* 精炼厂；炼糖厂；精炼设备．*a sugar* ～ 制糖厂．

re·fin·ish [ˈriˈfiniʃ] *vt.* 再修整，再修光，再抛光；修整(木、金属物的)表面．**-er** *n.*

re·fit [ˈriːˈfit] *vt.* 整修(船等)；重新装修，改装．— *vi.* (船等)进行整修，进行改装．— *n.* (特指船的)整修；改装．**-ment** *n.*

refl. = ①reflection; reflective(ly). ②reflex; reflexive.

re·flate [riˈfleit] *vt., vi.* (使)通货再膨胀．**re·fla·tion** *n.*

re·flect [riˈflekt] *vt.* ①【物，计】反射(光、热、声音等)．②(镜子等)映现(影像等)；反响，反照；〔喻〕反映；表现．③招致，带来，博得(信用等)；使蒙受(羞辱等) *(on, upon)*．④转移(视线等)；折转(纸角等)；(球等)弹回．⑤反省，沉思熟虑，仔细想．*The sidewalks* ～ *heat on a hot day.* 在热天，人行道反射热气．*Her actions* ～ *her thought.* 她的行为反映她的思想．*clouds* ～*ed in the water* 映在水里的云影．*His conduct* ～*ed great credit (up)on him.* 他的行为给他带来了很大荣誉．～ *the eyes from* 把眼睛避开．～ *how to get out of a difficulty* 盘算怎样渡过难关．— *vi.* ①【物，计】反射．②反映；反响．③反省，熟虑，沉思，仔细想，回顾 *(on, upon)*．④反应；非难，谴责，中伤，诽谤；(行为等)发生坏影响，丢脸 *(on, upon)*．*His conduct* ～*s on his parents.* 他的行为使他父母丢脸．**-ing·ly** *ad.*

re·flec·tance [riˈflektəns] *n.* 【物】反射比；反射能力〔系数〕．

re·flec·tion [riˈflekʃən] *n.* ①【物，计】反射；反射波〔光，热，音，色〕．②反映；反影，映象，(映在水等中的)影像；〔喻〕学人样的人，极像…的人，逼肖的形象〔言语、动作、思想〕．③反省，熟虑，沉思，回顾；〔*pl.*〕感想，意见；【心】(神经等的)反射作用．④非难，谴责；丢脸，耻辱 *(on, upon)*．⑤折转；弹回；【解】翻转(处)，折转(处)．*theory of reflection* 反映论．*an angle of* ～ 反射角．*He is simply a* ～ *of his father.* 他完全是他父亲的复本．*I have a few* ～*s to offer on what you have said.* 我对你的发言提供几点意见．***be lost in*** ～ 沉思．***cast a*** ～ ***on*** 谴责…，成为…的耻辱．***on [upon]*** ～ 仔细想，反省；对…不利，使…名誉受影响，使…蒙受耻辱；中伤，影射 (*On* ～, *I doubt whether I was right.* 细细想起来我倒怀疑我讲的是否正确了)．***without (due)*** ～ 不经思考，轻率．**-al** *a.*

re·flec·tive [riˈflektiv] *a.* ①反射的，反照的，反映的，反光的．②能反省的；反省性的，熟虑的．③反射性的，相互的．④〔罕〕【语法】= reflexive. ～ **power** 反射率〔力〕．**-ly** *ad.*

re·flec·tor [riˈflektə] *n.* ①反射物，反射器；反光镜；【原】反射层；【天】反射望远镜．②(习惯、感情等的)反映(者)．③〔罕〕反省者，回想者，沉思者：*a* ～ *lamp* 反光灯．*The newspaper is a true* ～ *of public opinion.* 报纸是舆论的真实反映(者)．

re·flec·tor·ize [riˈflektəˌraiz] *vt.* *(-iz·ed, -iz·ing)* ①使能反射光线．②装反射器(或反射镜)．

re·flect·os·cope [riˈflekˈtəskəup] *n.* 超声探伤仪；反射测试仪．

re·flet [rəˈfle] *n.* (陶瓷器物表面的)光泽，光彩．

re·flex [ˈriːfleks] *a.* ①反射的，反射性的，有反应的，有反射作用的．②反作用的(效果、影响等)．③反省的；回想的．④(叶、茎等)折转的，反曲的．⑤【无】来复式的．⑥【数】优角的．— *n.* ①(光、热的)反射，(本质等的)反映，显现；反射光；(镜子等反映的)影像，映像．②【生理，心】反射作用．③【无】来复；来复式收音机〔接收机〕．来复式增幅装置．～ *action* 反射作用，反射运动．～ *angle* 优角．～ *arc*【生】反射弧．～ *camera* 反光镜照相机．～ *condenser* 回流冷凝器．～ *receiver* 来复式收音机 — [riˈfleks] *vt.* 把…折转〔折回〕；【无】加来复式增幅装置．

re·flex·i·ble [riˈfleksəble] *a.* 可反射的；可折射性的．

re·flex·ion [riˈflekʃən] *n.* = reflection.

re·flex·ive [riˈfleksiv] *a.* ① = reflex. ② = reflective. ③【语法】反身的．— *n.*【语法】反身动词〔代词〕．～ *law* 自反律．**-ly** *ad.*

re·float [ˈriːˈfləut] *vt.* 使(沉没或搁浅的船)再浮起来；打捞．— *vi.* 再浮起．～*ing operations* 打捞工程．

re·float·a·tion [ˈriːfləuˈteiʃən] *n.* (沉船、搁浅的船)打捞；离礁．

ref·lu·ence [ˈrefluəns] *n.* 倒流，逆流；退潮．

ref·lu·ent [ˈrefluənt] *a.* (潮水、血液等)逆流的，倒流的，回流的；退潮的．

re·flux [ˈriː-flʌks] *n.* ①回流，反流，倒流，逆流；退潮．②【化】回流加热：*the flux and* ～ *of the tides [fortune]* 潮水的涨落；〔喻〕(人、事物的)荣枯盛衰．

re·focil·late [riːˈfɔːsileit] *vt.* 使振作精神，使复苏．

re·foot [ˈriːˈfut] *vt.* 换(袜子等的)底子．

re·for·est [ˈriːˈfɔrist] *vt., vi.* 重新造林．

re·form [riˈfɔːm] *vt.* ①改革，改良，革新(制度、事业等)．②矫正(品行等)，使悔改；改造；改正(错误等)．③救济，救治，铲除(弊害、紊乱等)．④【化】重整〔指将石油等裂化〕．～ ***oneself*** 改过自新，自我改造．— *vi.* 改过自新，改邪归正；改善，面目一新．～ ***through labour*** 劳动改造．— *n.* ①(社会、政治等的)改革，改良，改进，改造，革新．②(谬误的)改正；(品行等的)感化，矫正，悔改．*agrarian (land)* ～ 土地改革．*democratic* ～*s* 民主改革．**R- Bill [Act]** (1832 年英国的)选举法修正法案〔条令〕．**R- Church** (基督教)新教．～ **school** 〔美〕教养〔改造〕院．

re-form [ˈriːˈfɔːm] *vt., vi.* 再作，重作；改编(军队等)；(飞机在攻击后)重新编队．**-ism** *n.* 改良主义．**-ist** *n., a.* 改良主义者〔的〕．

re·form·a·ble [riˈfɔːməbl] *a.* 可改革的；可改正的；可革除的；可矫正的，可感化的．

ref·or·ma·tion [ˌrefəˈmeiʃən] *n.* ①改造；改革，改良，改善，革新；矫正．②〔the R-〕(欧洲 16—18 世纪)宗教改革(运动)，基督教改革(运动)．

re-for·ma·tion [ˈriːfɔːˈmeiʃən] *n.* 再构成；重新组成；重作，再作，再造．

re·form·a·tive [riˈfɔːmətiv] *a.* ①改革的，改良的；改造的．②= reformatory.

re·form·a·to·ry [riˈfɔːmətəri] *a.* 起改革〔革新〕作用的；起改良作用的．— *n.* 教养院；〔英〕妓女改造所．

re·formed [riˈfɔːmd] *a.* 改正了的，改造了的；〔R-〕【宗】改革派的．

re·form·er [riˈfɔːmə] *n.* 改革者，革新者；〔R-〕宗教改革者；选举法修正论者．

re·fract [riˈfrækt] *vt.*【物】(水、玻璃等)折射(光线等)；【化】分析(硝石)；测定…的折射度．*a* ～*ing angle* 折射棱角．～*ing power* 折射率〔力〕．*a* ～*ing telescope* 折射望远镜．

re·fract·a·ble [riˈfræktəbl] *a.* 可折射的，折射性的．

re·frac·tion = [riˈfrækʃən] *n.* (光、音波等的)屈折，折射；折射作用；折射度；【天】濛气差，折光差；【化】硝石杂物含有率(测定)．*astronomical* ～ 空中屈折．*terrestrial* ～ 地上屈折．*index of* ～ 折射率，屈折率．**-al** *a.*

re·frac·tive [riˈfræktiv] *a.* 折射(光线等)的，有屈折〔折射〕力的：～ *index* 折射率，屈折率；折光指数．

re·frac·tom·e·ter [ˌriːfrækˈtɔmitə] *n.*【物】折射计；屈光计．

re·frac·tor [riˈfræktə] *n.* 折射器；折射望远镜；折射透镜．

re•frac•to•ri•ly [riˈfræktərili] *ad.* 倔强地，顽强地，执拗地；顽固地；难熔化地.

re•frac•to•ry [riˈfræktəri] *a.* ①不听话的，难驾驭的，倔强的，执拗的. ②加工困难的；难处理的；【医】难医的，难治疗的(病、伤等)；无刺激反应的(神经)；不感受病毒的，能抵抗(疾病等)的. ③耐熔的，耐火的(矿、金属等). — *n.* ①倔强的人. ②耐火矿石[金属]；耐熔质：*～ matter* 耐火材料. *a ～ brick* 火砖.

re•frain[1] [riˈfrein] *vi.* ①抑制，自制，忍住. ②戒除(烟、酒等). ③避免；避开. *～ from (smoking)* 戒烟. *I cannot ～ from laughing.* 我忍不住好笑. *～ from unprincipled argument* 不作无原则的争论. — *vt.* 抑制. *～ oneself* 抑制自己，忍住.

re•frain[2] [riˈfrein] *n.* (诗歌、乐曲每节收尾的)迭句，反复句，迭句的乐曲；口头禅. ***take up the ～ of*** 为…帮腔.

re•frame [ˈriːˈfreim] *vt.* ①再构造；重新制订. ②给某物装上新框架.

re•fran•gi•ble [riˈfrændʒibl] *a.* 屈折(性)的，可折射的. **-bil•i•ty, -ness** *n.*

re•fresh [riˈfreʃ] *vt.* ①(磨光表面等)使变新，使焕然一新；翻新. ②(雨、微风等)使清新；使爽快，使清凉. ③(娱乐、饮食、休息等)使(人)心神爽快，使神清气爽，使精神振作，使精神恢复. ④恢复(记忆)，使重新明了；使(火等)再旺盛；充电(入电池)；(给船)补装. *～ oneself with a cup of tea* 喝一杯茶提神. *～ a storage battery* 给蓄电池充电. — *vi.* ①(因饮食、休养等)恢复精神，觉得神清气爽，觉得爽快. ②〔口〕吃东西，喝一杯(酒)；(船等)补装粮食[饮用水](等).

re•fresh•er [ˈriˈfreʃə] *n.* ①使心神清爽的东西[人]；饮料，食物；〔口〕冷饮料；酒；使恢复记忆的东西. ②〔英〕(诉讼长期不决时的)律师额外酬劳. ③〔美〕(温习性的)补修科 (= ～ course). ④最新科技资料. — *a.* 〔美〕温习的，进修的；最新的(科技资料).

re•fresh•ing [riˈfreʃiŋ] *a.* 使人身心爽快的，使人精神振作的；使人耳目一新的. *a ～ breeze* 使人凉爽的微风；清风. *a ～ drink* 清凉饮料. *～ innocence* 可爱的天真. **-ly** *ad.*

re•fresh•ment [riˈfreʃmənt] *n.* ①提神；精神恢复，身心爽快，心旷神怡. ②〔常 *pl.*〕提神物；饮食，点心. *take some ～s* 吃点东西. *Refreshments provided* 备有茶点. *～* **car** (火车的)餐车. *～* **room** (车站、火车中的)餐室. **R- Sunday** 四旬斋 *(Lent)* 中的第四个礼拜天.

re•frig•er•ant [riˈfridʒərənt] *a.* 解热的，使清凉的；冷却的. — *n.* 清凉剂，凉药；清凉饮料；冷却剂，冷冻剂，致冷剂.

re•frig•er•ate [riˈfridʒəreit] *vt.* ①解热，消热，使冷，使清凉. ②冷藏，冷冻，冰镇(鱼、肉等). *a refrigerating machine* 冷冻机，冷冻装置. *a ～d van* 冷藏车.

re•frig•e•ra•tion [riˌfridʒəˈreiʃən] *n.* 消热，清凉；冷却(法)；冷藏(法)，冰冻，致冷；致冷学.

re•frig•er•a•tive [riˈfridʒəreitiv] *a.* 消热的，清凉的；致冷的，冷却的.

re•frig•er•a•tor [riˈfridʒəreitə] *n.* (电)冰箱；致冷器，冷藏库；制冰机；冷冻机. *～ car* 【铁道】冷藏车(厢).

re•frig•er•a•to•ry [riˈfridʒərətəri] *a.* 致冷的；消热的；冷却的. —*n.* 冷却器，(电)冰箱；冷藏室；制冰机；冰冻机.

re•frin•gent [riˈfrindʒənt] *a.* 【物】折射的. **-gen•cy, -gence** *n.*

reft [reft] *v. reave* 的过去式及过去分词. — *a.* 〔诗〕被夺去的，被掠夺的；失去了的.

re•fu•el [riːˈfjuəl] *vt., vi.* (给…)加油[燃料]. *～ station* 加油站.

ref•uge [ˈrefjuːdʒ] *n.* ①避难；庇护，保护；庇护者；避难所，隐匿处，藏身处；〔英〕(马路中的)安全岛. ②可倚靠的人[物]；慰藉物. ③口实，借口. ④权宜之计；应急办法；【医】救急(疗)法. *a harbour of ～* 避风港. *a house of ～* 难民收容所. *He is the ～ of the distressed.* 他是不幸者的朋友. ***the last ～*** 最后的托词. ***find a ～*** 找到避难所[躲避处]. ***give ～ to*** 隐匿，包庇，庇护. ***seek ～ in flight*** 逃难. ***seek ～ with sb.*** 求某人庇护，逃难到某人处. ***take ～ in*** 避难到；求助于…，求安慰于…，用…支吾过去. — *vt.* 〔古〕庇护. —*vi.* 躲避，避难.

ref•u•gee [ˌrefju(ː)ˈdʒiː] *n.* (特指逃避战祸或政治、宗教迫害的)难民，避难者，亡命者；逃亡者. — *a.* 避难的，逃难的. — *vi.* 避难，逃难.

re•ful•gence [riˈfʌldʒəns] *n.* 辉煌，灿烂.

re•ful•gent [riˈfʌldʒənt] *a.* 辉煌的，灿烂的. **-ly** *ad.*

re•fund [riːˈfʌnd] *vt., vi.* 赔还，偿还. — [ˈriːfʌnd] *n.* 赔还，偿还；退款. **-ment** *n.*

re•fur•bish [riːˈfəːbiʃ] *vt.* ①重新擦亮. ②再刷新；整修；翻新.

re•fur•nish [ˈriːˈfəːniʃ] *vt.* ①再供给；供给新装备. ②【植】剪顶枝嫁接(果树等).

re•fus•a•ble [riːˈfjuːzəbl] *a.* 可拒绝的.

re•fus•al [riˈfjuːzəl] *n.* ①拒绝，谢绝，固辞，不允，不承认. ②优先取舍[选择]权；优先购买权. *a ～ to obey orders* 违抗命令. *the ～ of an invitation* 谢绝邀请. ***ask for the ～ of*** 要求优先权. ***buy the ～ of*** 付定钱，买得优先权. ***give sb. a flat ～*** 断然拒绝. ***give the ～ of*** 给与优先[选择]权 (*I will give you the ～ of my offer till the end of the month.* 对我提议[要价]是否采纳[同意]请于本月底以前决定). ***have the ～ of*** 获得先买权；获得取舍权. ***take no ～*** 不许说不，逼人答应.

re•fuse[1] [riˈfjuːz] *vt.* ①拒绝，谢绝，固辞，辞退，推辞，不受. ②不肯(承认、服从等)；拒婚〔主指女子拒绝男子〕. ③(马)不肯跳过(沟、篱等)而突然停住；(机件等)发生故障失效. ④【牌戏】因无同花的牌而出别的牌. ⑤【军】(交战前)撤回(翼军)，撤出(不重要的阵地). ⑥否认，放弃. *～ sb. satisfaction* 拒不赔偿；拒绝某人的要求. *～ sb. money* 拒绝借钱给某人. *～ a suitor* 拒绝求婚者. *～ a gift* 拒受礼物. *～ one's consent* 不同意，不答应. *～ to burn* (柴等)烧不着. *～ to shut* (门等)关不上. — *vi.* ①拒绝. ②(马)不肯跃过. ③(纸牌)打不出同花牌.

ref•use[2] [ˈrefjuːs] *n.* 废料，糟粕，渣滓，垃圾；废物. — *a.* 无用的，无价值的，垃圾的，废料的：*kitchen ～* 厨房垃圾. *～ oil* 废油. *a ～ consumer [destructor]* 垃圾焚毁炉. **～-up** 垃圾堆.

re•fus•er [riˈfjuːzə] *n.* 拒绝者，推辞者；不信奉国教者；不肯跳过沟渠[篱笆等]的马.

ref•ut•a•ble [ˈrefjutəbl, riˈfjuːt-] *a.* 可驳倒的；有错误的. **-bly** *ad.*

ref•u•tal [riˈfjuːtəl] *n.* 驳斥，反驳.

ref•u•ta•tion [ˌrefjuːˈteiʃən] *n.* 驳斥，驳倒.

re•fute [riˈfjuːt] *vt.* 驳斥，驳倒(某论点，对方). *His doctrine was ～d down to the last point.* 他的学说被驳得体无完肤.

Reg. = ①Regina. ②Regiment.

reg. = ①Regent. ②regiment. ③region. ④register; registered; registrar; registry. ⑤regular; regulation; regulator.

re•gain [riˈgein] *vt.* ①取回，夺回，收复，恢复(失物、失地、健康等)；回收. ②再到，回到(某地、某种状态)：*～ consciousness* 清醒过来；恢复知觉. *～ one's feet [footing, legs]* (跌倒的人)重新站起来. — *n.* ①收回；复得；夺回，收复；恢复. ②(纤维的)回潮(率).

re•gal[1] [ˈriːgəl] *a.* ①王的；帝王(般)的. ②庄严的，堂皇的，凛然的：*the ～ office* 王位. *live in ～ splendour* 生活得象帝王一样奢华. **-ly** *ad.*

re•gal[2] [ˈriːgəl] *n.* (16 世纪可携带搬动的)小风琴.

re•gale [riˈgeil] *vt.* 盛宴招待，款待；使欢悦，使快乐；使心满意足 *(with)*. *～ oneself with drink [a cigar]* (高兴地)喝酒，抽[雪茄]. — *vi.* 享受好滋味；吃喝，享用

(on)；大大欢喜. — *n.*〔古〕盛宴；山珍海味，佳肴. **~ment** *n.*

re·ga·lia[1] [riˈgeiliə] *(sing.* ***rega·le*** [riˈgeili:]*)* *n.*〔*pl.*〕①王室徽章；王位的标记〔王冠、王节、宝剑等〕；(等级、协会等的)标记，纹章；勋章. ②〔史、古〕王室特权，王权. ③华丽的服装. ***in full*** **~** 威风凛凛.

re·ga·li·a[2] [riˈgeiljə] *n.* (古巴产的)优质大雪茄烟.

re·gal·ism [ˈri:gəlizəm] *n.* 王权至上论〔尤指宗教事务方面〕.

re·gal·i·ty [ri:ˈgæliti] *n.* 王位；国王的地位〔身分〕；〔*pl.*〕王权；王国.

re·gard [riˈgɑ:d] *n.* ①注重，注意，留意；考虑，关心 *(to)*；注目，注视，凝视；牵挂，惦念 *(for)*. ②尊重，尊敬；敬意，好意，厚意，好感；名誉，声名. ③事项，关系. ④〔*pl.*〕致意，问候，请安：*Give my (best) ~s to ....* 请代问候…. *With kindest ~s to you all.* 向各位问候. ***have a ~ for*** 尊敬；考虑到，顾到；重视. ***have ~ to*** 顾到，注意 (*R- must be had to his wishes.* 须照顾到他的愿望). ***hold sb. in high [low]*** **~** 尊敬[藐视]某人. ***in sb.'s*** **~** 关于某人，对于某人. ***in ~ of*** 关于，对于；为了答复…；关于，在…方面；取决于…的，…对…的影响. ***in this [that]*** **~** 在这[那]一点上，关于这[那]件事. ***pay (no) ~ to*** (不)考虑；(未)顾到；(不)尊敬；(不)注意. ***turn one's ~ on sb.*** 把目光[注意力]转向某人. ***with ~ to [of]*** = in ~ to. ***with ~ to*** 关于；对于；为了答复. ***without ~ to [for]*** 不顾…，与…无关，不遵守. — *vt.* ①看，瞧，注视，凝视，注意；关心. ②考察，考虑；顾虑；(用爱情、憎恨等)对待，看待. ③〔主要用于否定句〕重视，尊重；尊敬，敬重. ④把…看做，把…视为，把…认为 (as ...). ⑤和…有关系. *Many passed, but none ~ed her.* 许多人走过去了，没有一人注意她. *~ a matter from every point of view* 从各方面去考察一个问题. *~ a situation with anxiety* 担忧局势. *He does not ~ my advice.* 他不重视我的劝告. *~ him as a friend* 把他看做朋友. *The matter does not ~ you at all.* 这事和你毫无关系. ***as ~s*** 关于，至于. — *vi.*〔罕〕注意，留意.

re·gard·ant [riˈgɑ:dənt] *a.* ①【纹】回头向后看的(动物的姿态) *(cf.* gardant*)*. ②〔古、诗〕注视的，留心的，谨慎的. *keep a ~ eye upon* 对…仔细观察.

re·gard·ful [riˈgɑ:dful] *a.* ①对…留心，注意周到，谨慎 *(of)*. ②表示敬意的，恭敬的 *(for)*. *be ~ of one's promises* 守约.

re·gard·ing [riˈgɑ:diŋ] *prep.* 关于. *~ the future of reform* 关于改革的前途.

re·gard·less [riˈgɑ:dlis] *a.* ①不重视的，不尊敬的；不注意的，不留心的，不顾虑的，不关心的. ②不受注意的；毫无价值的. ***~ of*** 不管，不顾，不拘，不注意 (*I shall go ~ of the weather.* 无论天气好坏我都要去). — *ad.*〔口〕〔用于省略句中〕不顾一切地；无论如何；不惜费用地. ***be got up [be dressed]*** **~** 不惜化费地打扮. **-ly** *ad.*

re·gat·ta [riˈgætə] *n.* ①(威尼斯大运河上举行的)狭长平底船的比赛. ②赛艇会.

re·ge·late [ˈri:dʒileit, ˌri:dʒiˈleit] *vi.*【物】(已溶解的碎冰)再凝冻，重新冻结，复冰. **-la·tion** *n.*【物】复冰(现象).

re·gen·cy [ˈri:dʒənsi] *n.* ①摄政；摄政期间；摄政管辖区；摄政权；摄政团. ②〔古〕政权，统治. ③〔美〕(州立大学)评议员的职位. *the R-*【史】英国 (1811—1820 年的或法国1715—1723 年的)摄政时期.

re·gen·er·a·cy [riˈdʒenərəsi] *n.* ①再生，新生，更生，复生. ②刷新，革新. ③悔悟，洗心.

re·gen·er·ate [riˈdʒenəriit] *a.* ①再生的，新生的. ②革新的. ③改造了的，回心转意的. —[-nəreit] *vt.* ①使再生，使复生，使新生. ②使悔悟. ③改造，革新(社会、国家等). ④回收(废热、废料等)；【无】使回授，使反馈. *~d rubber* 再生橡胶. — *vi.* ①再生. ②悔悟. *Nails are constantly regenerating.* 指甲不断地新生.

re·gen·er·a·tion [riˌdʒenəˈreiʃən] *n.* ①再生，新生. ②悔悟. ③改造，革新. ④回收. ⑤【化】交流换热(法)；【物】正回授[反馈]放大. ***~ through one's own efforts*** 自力更生.

re·gen·er·a·tive [riˈdʒenərətiv] *a.* ①再生的；使更生的. ②使悔悟的. ③更新的. ④【机】回热式的；【电】回授的，反馈的；【化】交流换热(的). *a ~ furnace* 回热炉；交流换热炉.

re·gen·er·a·tor [riˈdʒenəreitə] *n.* ①(使)新生的人[物]. ②更新者；改革者. ③【机】交流换热器，蓄热器；回热器；【电】再生器；再发器.

re·gen·e·sis [ri:ˈdʒenisis] *n.* 再生，新生；更新.

re·gent [ˈri:dʒənt] *a.* ①摄政的〔通常用于名词后〕. ②〔美〕担任(大学)评议员职位的. ③〔罕〕统治的. — *n.* ①摄政者. ②〔罕〕统治者，支配者. ③〔美〕(州立大学的)评议员，(Harvard 大学的)学监；〔英史〕(牛津、剑桥大学)辅导讨论的文学士. *the Prince R-* 摄政王. *the Queen R-* 摄政女王. **~ship** 摄政王的地位[任期].

re·ger·mi·nate [ˈri:ˈdʒə:mineit] *vi.* 再发芽；重新生长. **re·ger·mi·na·tion** *n.*

re·ges [ˈri:dʒi:z] *n.* rex 的复数.

reg·gae [ˈreˌgei] *n.*【乐】一种源出西印度群岛，带有勃鲁斯音乐成分的，节拍强烈的通俗音乐.

reg·i·cid·al [ˌredʒiˈsaidl] *a.* 弑君的.

reg·i·cide [ˈredʒisaid] *n.* 弑君(行为)；弑君者. *the Regicides* ① 处死英王 查里一世 (Charles I) 的国会议员团. ②处死法王 路易十四 (Louis XIV) 的革命党员.

ré·gie [reiˈʒi:] *n.*〔F.〕(烟、盐等的)专卖局；(公共事业的)官营，官办. **-book** (记有舞台导演说明的)导演须知.

re·gime, ré·gime [reiˈʒi:m] *n.* ①制度，社会组织；政权，政体；统治(时期). ②管理；方法；状态. ③【医】养生法；(病人等的)生活规则. *the Parliamentary ~* 议会制度. *establish a new ~* 建立新秩序. ***during the ... ~*** 在…统治时代. ***under the ~ of*** 在…的制度下.

reg·i·men [ˈredʒimen] *n.* ①【医】摄生，食物疗法，养生法；(给病人等特定的)生活规则. ②支配，统治；政体，政权；社会制度. ③管理办法；事物的所处状况. ④【语法】支配. *the water ~* 水分状况.

reg·i·ment [ˈredʒimənt] *n.* ①【军】团. ②〔常 *pl.*〕大群，大量. ③〔罕〕统治，支配. — *vt.* ①把…编成团. ②使(职工、劳动者等)受组织训练，组织起来；组织化，系统化；把…编成组；编入(团、团体). *an education that ~s children* 使儿童受到组织训练的教育.

reg·i·men·tal [ˌredʒiˈmentl] *a.*【军】团的. — *n.*〔*pl.*〕军服；特种团队的军服和徽章. *a ~ colour* 团旗，军旗. *a ~ district* 团管区. *~ headquarters* 团本部.

reg·i·men·ta·tion [ˌredʒimenˈteiʃən] *n.* ①【军】团的编制. ②编制，类别；组织化，规格化；组织训练.

Re·gi·na[1] [riˈdʒainə] *n.*〔L.〕女王〔略 R.，或 Reg.〕. ★用于布告等的署名或在王室对臣民的诉讼案件中用作女王称号〔*cf. Rex*〕.

Re·gi·na[2] [riˈdʒainə] *n.* 丽贾纳〔女子名〕.

re·gi·nal [riˈdʒai(ə)l] *a.*〔L.〕女王(一样)的；拥护女王的.

Reg·i·nald [ˈredʒinəld] *n.* 雷金纳德〔男子名〕.

re·gion [ˈri:dʒən] *n.* ①地方，地域，地带；地区；行政区，管辖区，区；左近，邻近；(大气、海水等的)层，界，境. ②【解、动】(身体的)局部，部位. ③(学问等的)范围，领域. ④〔罕〕天空. *a fertile ~* 肥沃地带. *a desert ~* 沙漠地带. *forest ~s* 森林地带. *the lower [infernal, nether] ~s* 地狱. *the middle [lower, upper] ~ of the air* 大气的中[下、上]层. *the operating ~* 工作范围. ***in the ~ of*** 在…附近；在…的左右 (*in the ~ of 45 dollars* 四十五美元左右).

re·gion·al [ˈri:dʒənəl] *a.* 地方(性)的；地方主义的；区域(性)的；局部的. **-ism** *n.* 地方习惯，地方制度；地方主

义. **-ly** *ad.*

ré·gis·seur [ˌreiʒiˈsəː] *n.* 〔F.〕导演;舞台监督.

reg·is·ter [ˈredʒistə] *n.* ①记录,注册,登记,挂号. ②(人口动态,户籍等的)登记簿,注册簿;【商】船籍登记簿;海关证明书. ③自动记录器;【自】寄存器;自动记录的数. ④〔美〕记录员,登记员,注册员. ⑤(暖房的)通风装置;调温装置. ⑥【印】所印纸张两面行、线等位置的相符;彩色版各种颜色的准确套合;【摄】感光板[软片]与焦点玻璃片间的位置的相符. ⑦【乐】(人声与乐器的)声域,音区;音掣;声域的一部分;(风琴的)整调器,音栓. ⑧【语言】语域,使用域;专用语言,特殊场合使用语言. *a hotel* ～ 住客登记簿. *a* ～ *of members* 股东登记名簿. *a line* ～ (电话)用户计次器. *a cash* ～ 现金出纳机. *a program* ～ (计算机的)程序寄存器. *in close* ～【电视】精确配准. ***be on the*** ～〔美〕有嫌疑,被怀疑;受到注意. — *vt.* ①记录,登记,注册;(信件等)挂号. ②牢记心上. ③(寒暑表等)示度,指示;(机器等)自动记录;【印、电视】对准,套准,配准. ④〔美〕(电影演员等)做(喜、怒等的)表情. ～ *a letter* 把信交付挂号寄发. ～ *oneself* (在选举人名册等上)登记自己姓名. ～ *luggage on a railway*〔英〕把行李交铁路托运. ～ *a vow* 立誓. ～ ***a bull's eye*** 打中(靶子的)黑圈. — *vi.* ①〔美〕登记姓名. ②【印、电视】对准,套准,配准. ③(电影演员)做表情. ④〔口〕留下印象;受到注意. ～ ***at a hotel***〔美〕住旅馆时登记. ～ ***at the congress*** 向大会报到. ～ **office** = registry③.

reg·is·tered [ˈredʒistəd] *a.* 登记过的,注过册的;记名的;挂号的. *a* ～ *design [trade-mark]* 注册图案[商标]. *a* ～ *letter* 挂号信. ～ *post* [〔美〕 mail] 挂号邮件. *a* ～ *reader* 预约读者,订阅者. *a* ～ *nurse*〔美〕领有执照的护士. ～ *horses [cattle, dogs]* (其血统业经登记认可的)立案马[牛、狗]. ～ *ballots* 记名投票. *a* ～ *bond* 记名债券[证券]. *a* ～ *certificate of shares* 记名股票.

reg·is·tra·ble [ˈredʒistrəbl] *a.* ①可注册的;(邮件)可挂号的. ②(感情)可表达的. ③(印刷品)可对齐的,可套准的.

reg·is·trant [ˈredʒistrənt] *n.* (商标,专利权等的)登记者;注册人;挂号人;被登记者;被注册者.

reg·is·trar [ˌredʒisˈtrɑː] *n.* 记录员,登记员,注册员,户籍员;(专管学生学籍、成绩等的)注册干事;负责登记股票转让的信托公司. *the Registrar-General*〔英〕(伦敦)户籍处[注册处]处长.

reg·is·tra·tion [ˌredʒisˈtreiʃən] *n.* ①记录,登记,注册;〔美〕签到,报到;(信件等的)挂号;记名;(寒暑表等的)示度,读数. ②【乐】音栓配合法. ③【印、电视】(正反面版面的)对准,(彩色的)套准,(图像的)配准. *a* ～ *fee* 挂号费;登记费.

reg·is·try [ˈredʒistri] *n.* ①记录,登记,注册;(船舶登记证上的)国籍. ②记录簿,登记簿. ③记录处,登记处,注册处;〔英〕户籍处. ④佣工介绍所〔又叫 *servants'* ～ *(office)*〕. *a* ～ *fee*〔美〕= a registration fee. *be married at a* ～ (不举行仪式)登记结婚.

re·gi·us [ˈriːdʒiəs] *a.* 〔L.〕王的;钦定的: *a R- professor* (牛津、剑桥)钦定讲座教授.

reg·nal [ˈregnl] *a.* (某王)在位时的,统治时期的,朝代的;王国的;王的: *the* ～ *day* 即位纪念日. *the third* ～ *year* 即位第三年.

reg·nant [ˈregnənt] *a.* ①〔通例用于名词后〕(帝王等)在位的,统治的,支配的. ②优势的,有力的;流行的;广泛的. *the Queen R-* 执政[当朝]女王.

reg·o·lith [ˈregəliθ] *n.*【地】风化层,土被,表皮土(= mantlerock).

re·gorge [riˈgɔːdʒ] *vt.* ①吐出. ②〔罕〕吞回. ③使倒流. — *vi.* 倒流,涌回.

reg·o·sol [ˈregəˌsɔːl, -sɔl] *n.*【地】表面土,浮土.

re·grant [riˈgrænt] *vt.* 重新许可,再答应,再承认;再次授与. — *n.* 再答应,重新承认;再次的补助金.

re·grate [riˈgreit] *vt.* 囤积;售出(商品等). **-tor** *n.* 囤积居奇者.

re·gress [ˈriːgres] *n.* ①回归,退回. ②【法】复归(权). ③退化,退步. ④回顾. ⑤【天】= regression. — [riˈgres] *vi.* ①后退,倒退;退回;【天】退行. ②复归,回归.

re·gres·sion [riˈgreʃən] *n.* ①复归,回归. ②退步,退化. ③【天】退行. **-sive** *a.* **-sive·ly** *ad.*

re·gret [riˈgret] *n.* ①遗憾,抱歉;后悔,悔恨;痛惜,惋惜,哀悼 *(at; for; over; of)*. ②〔常 *pl.*〕〔美〕(对于邀请等的)婉言辞谢〔回帖〕. ***express*** ～ ***at*** 惋惜…,表示…可惜. ***express*** ～ ***for*** 对[为]…表示抱歉,为…道歉. ***have no*** ～***s*** 没有遗憾,没有后悔. ***hear with*** ～ ***of [that]*** 听到觉得后悔[惋惜、失望]. ***(much) to my*** ～ 非常抱歉. ***refuse with many*** ～***s [much*** ～***]*** 非常抱歉地谢绝. ***send*** ～***s [a*** ～***]*** (尤指对请帖)发出辞谢信. — *vt.* ①怀念,想念(快乐的童年、故乡等);悼念,哀悼(死去的亲友等). ②悔恨,后悔,懊悔(过错、失去的机会等);以(不能…)为憾,抱歉,抱憾. *I* ～ *that I did not take your advice.* 我懊悔没有听你的劝告. ***I*** ～ ***(to say) that*** 我很遗憾…,很抱歉… (*I* ～ *to say that I am unable to help you.* 我很抱歉不能帮助你). ***It is to be regretted that*** ... 使人遗憾的是…;真可惜…;真可怜….

re·gret·ful [riˈgretful] *a.* ①悔恨的,后悔的,婉惜的,有遗憾的,抱歉的. ②怀念的;依依不舍的,依恋的: *a* ～ *apology* 道歉. **-ly** *ad.*

re·gret·a·ble, re·gret·ta·ble [riˈgretəbl] *a.* 使人后悔的,可惜的,可悲的,可叹息的,令人抱歉的,令人遗憾的,令人过意不去的. **-bly** *ad.*

re·group [ˈriːˈgruːp] *vt.* ①重新聚合;重行编组. ②【军】变更(军队)的部署. — *vi.* ①重行组合. ②【军】变更部署.

re·gs〔美〕= regulations 海军学校规则.

Regt. = ①Regent. ②Regiment.

reg·u·la·ble [ˈregjuləbl] *a.* 可调整的,可调节的;可控制的.

reg·u·lar[1] [ˈregjulə] *a.* ①有规则的,有规律的;有秩序的,井井有条的,整齐的;正规的,正式的. ②端正的,匀称的,调和的,和谐的;首尾一贯的,一律的. ③不变的,一定的;常例的,平常的;习惯的,非偶然的;定期的,定时的. ④【军】常备的,正规的. ⑤合格的,得到营业执照的,挂牌的(医师等),公认的. ⑥【语法】按规则变化的. ⑦【数】等边等角的;【结晶】等轴的;〔立体〕各面大小形状相等的;【植】整齐的(花). ⑧【宗】受教规束缚的;属于教团的. ⑨〔口〕十足的,真正的,名符其实的,彻底的. ⑩〔美口〕诚实的,可靠的. ～ *procedure* 正规手续. *a* ～ *member* 正式会员. ～ *people* 生活有规律的人〔尤指大便、月经有定时的〕. *a* ～ *pulse* 规则脉. ～ *features* 端正的面貌. *a* ～ *customer* 老主顾. ～ *holidays* 正式假日. ～ *service* 定期航行,定期开车(等). *the* ～ *army* 正规军,常备军. *a* ～ *verb* 规则动词. *a* ～ *hero* 真正的英雄. *a* ～ *rascal* 十足的恶棍. *a* ～ *fellow [guy]*〔美口〕受大家欢迎的人;(用钱)手松的人;有趣的家伙. ***keep*** ～ ***hours*** 过有规律的生活. — *ad.* ①有规则地,定期地,经常地. ②完全,非常: *He comes* ～. 他经常来. *It happens* ～. 这经常发生. *He is* ～ *angry.*〔卑〕那家伙生气极了. — *n.* ①〔常 *pl.*〕正规兵,常备兵;(球队的)正式队员. ②〔口〕长期雇工;固定职工;老主顾,常客. ③【宗】修道士. ④〔美〕(某党派的)忠诚支持者. ⑤〔俚〕〔*pl.*〕赃物的份儿. ～ **bedtime** 规定[通常]的睡眠时间. ～ **coast** 平直岸. ～ **contributor** 定期[经常]撰稿人. ～ **course** (学校的)本科. ～ **curve**【数】正弧. ～ **five**【篮球】主力队员. ～ **forest**【林】同龄林. ～ **marriage** (按仪式举行的)正规[合法]结婚. ～ **planting**【农】方形种植. ～ **practitioner** 合格的开业医生[律师]. ～ **publications** 定期刊物. ～ **stock**【交易所】现货. ～ **reflection**【物】单向反射. ～ **subscriber** (期刊)长期订户. ～ **way** (交易所的)普通交易. **-ly** *ad.*

reg·u·lar·i·ty [ˌregjuˈlæriti] *n.* 有规则; 整齐(度); 调和; 一定不变; 正规; (合乎)规格; 规律性; 经常, 定期.

reg·u·lar·i·za·tion [ˌregjulәraiˈzeiʃәn] *n.* 正规化, 秩序化, 组织化; 整理, 调整; 合法化.

reg·u·lar·ize [ˈregjulәraiz] *vt.* ①使有规律; 使规则化, 使有秩序, 使有组织. ②整理, 调整. ③使合法.

reg·u·late [ˈregjuleit] *vt.* ①规定, 管制, 控制. ②整顿; 使有条理, 使整齐. ③调节(温度、速度等); 调准, 校准, 对准(机器、钟表等); 【化】调节.

reg·u·la·tion [ˌregjuˈleiʃәn] *n.* ①规则, 规程, 规章, 条例. ②控制, 管理, 限制, (情欲等的)节制. ③调整, 调节, 整顿. ④校准; 稳定; 【电】变动率; 【火箭】导向; 【生】调整〔指胚胎发育物质的重新分配〕; (维持早期胚胎正常发育的)调节机制. — *a.* ①正规的, 规定的, 正式的. ②正常的, 普通的. *In many cases ~s alone will not work.* 单靠行政命令, 在许多情况下就行不通. *detailed ~s* 详细规定[章程], 细则. *laws and ~s* 法令. *draft ~s* 条例草案. *staff ~s* 人事条例. *a ~ cap* [*uniform*] 制帽[制服]. *a ~ game* 正式比赛. *~ speed* 规定速率. *the ~ mourning* 正式悼念仪式. *of the ~ size* 普通大小[尺寸]的.

reg·u·la·tive [ˈregjuleitiv] *a.* ①管理的; 管制的, 规定的. ②调整的; 调节的; 整理的. **-ly** *ad.*

reg·u·la·tor [ˈregjuleitә] *n.* ①管理者. ②调整者; 整理者. ③校准者; 【机】调整器, 校准器, 调节器; 【无】稳定器; 【化】调节剂; 【代】调整子; (钟表的)整时器; 标准钟. ④原则, 标准. ⑤【英史】选举调查[监视]委员.

Reg·u·lus [ˈregjulәs] *n.* 雷古拉斯〔Marcas Atilius ~, 罗马大将〕.

reg·u·lus [ˈregjulәs] *n.* ①【天】(狮子座 a) 轩辕十四. ②[r-] ***(-lus·es, -li*** [-lai]***)*** 【化、冶】a) 锑块. b) 金属渣. c) 熔块.

re·gur·gi·tate [ri(ː)ˈgәːdʒiteit] *vt., vi.* ①(使)掷还, (使)丢回; (使)喷回; (使)回流. ②(婴儿)吐(奶); (使)反胃; (使)反哺; (使)反刍. **-ta·tion** *n.* 回流, 回涌; 【动】反刍; 反胃, 回吐; 【医】心脏瓣口(血液)反流.

re·gust·ed [riˈgʌstid] *a.* 〔美俚〕= disgusted.

re·ha·bil·i·tant [ˌriːhәˈbilitent] *n.* 在康复中的病残者.

re·ha·bil·i·tate [ˌriːhәˈbiliteit] *vt.* ①使复原; 使复权[复职, 复位]. ②使恢复. ③改善, 复兴, 修理. *~ oneself* 恢复名誉, 昭雪.

re·ha·bil·i·ta·tion [ˈriːhәˌbiliˈteiʃәn] *n.* ①复权, 复职, 复位. ②善后; 平反, 恢复名誉, 昭雪. ③恢复, 复兴, 改善.

re·han·dle [ˈriːˈhændl] *vt.* ①再处理. ②改造; 改铸. ③重新整顿.

re·hash [ˈriːˈhæʃ] *vt.* ①重新剁碎(肉等). ②(特指利用旧文学材料)改作, 重作, 重讲. — *n.* (旧东西的)改作; 用旧材料改编的作品. *~ of platitude* 滥调翻新.

re·hear [ˈriːˈhiә] ***(-heard*** [-ˈhәːd]***)*** *vt.* ①再听. ②【法】复审, 再审.

re·hears·al [riˈhәːsәl] *n.* ①背诵. ②(经验等的)详述, 复述. ③(音乐演出等的)练习; 排练; 排演. *a ~ of one's experiences* 介绍经验. *a (full) dress ~* 【剧】彩排. *a full ~* 【剧】全体排演. *a public ~* 【剧】公开预演.

re·hearse [riˈhәːs] *vt.* ①背诵; 反复讲, 再三讲; 讲述, 详述; 学嘴, 照样讲(别人讲的话). ②练习, 排练; 排演, 预演. ③列举; 总计. — *vi.* ①朗诵, 背诵. ②练习, 预演, 排演.

re·heat [ˈriːˈhiːt] *vt.* 再热, 对…重新加热.

re·house [ˈriːˈhauz] *vt.* 供给新房子, 给…安排新房子.

re·hu·man·ize [ˈriːˈhjuːmәnaiz] *vt.* 使改邪归正, 使成正经人.

re·hy·drate [riˈhaiˌdreit] *vt.* ***(-drat·ed, -drat·ing)*** 【化】再水合, 再水化. **-dra·tion** *n.*

Reich [raik] *n.* 〔G.〕帝国, 国; 德国, (德意志)帝国. *the First R-* 第一(神圣罗马)帝国〔962—1806〕. *the Second R-* (德国 Bismarck 当权时代的) 第二帝国〔1871—1919〕. *the Third R-* (纳粹统治下的)第三帝国〔1933—1945〕.

Reichs·mark [ˈraiksmɑːk] *n.* ***(pl. -s, ~)*** 〔G.〕德国马克.

Reichstag [ˈraikstɑːg] *n.* 〔G.〕(旧德意志帝国)国会; (旧德意志共和国)国民议会.

Reichsweshr [ˈraiksvεә] *n.* 〔G.〕(1919 年组成的德国)国防军; 德国军队.

Reid [riːd] *n.* 里德〔姓氏, 男子名〕.

re·i·fy [ˈriːifai] *vt.* ***(-fi·ed, -fy·ing)*** 【哲】使(抽象的概念)具体化. **-ca·tion** *n.*

reign [rein] *n.* ①(帝王等的)统治, 支配; 朝代, 在位时代; 统治权, 支配权. ②势力, 权势. ③领域, 范围. *during five successive ~s* 一连五个统治者统治时代中. *His ~ was a gentle one.* 他在位时期很太平. *Night resumes her ~.* 黑夜重临. *the ~ of law in nature* 自然规律的支配. ***the R- of Terror*** 【法史】恐怖时期〔1793—1794〕. ***under [in] the ~ of*** …在位时期. — *vi.* ①掌握权力, 统治, 君临, 支配 *(over)*. ②称霸, 有巨大势力. ③盛行, 大大流行, 通行. *the ~ing beauty* 绝代佳人, 当代第一美女. *~ing sovereign* 在位君主.

re·im·burse [ˌriːimˈbәːs] *vt.* 偿还, 付还, 赔还, 赔偿, 补偿. **-ment** *n.*

re·im·port [ˈriːimˈpɔːt] *vt.* 再输入(输出品等), 再进口. — [ˈriːˈimpɔːt] *n.* 再输入, 再进口; 〔常 *pl.*〕再进口货. **-ta·tion** [ˌriːimpɔːˈteiʃәn] *n.* 再进口货.

re·im·pose [ˈriːimˈpәuz] *vt.* 再征收(停征的税等). **reimposition** *n.*

re·im·pres·sion [ˌriimˈpreʃәn] *n.* 【印】再版, 重版.

rein [rein] *n.* ①(皮)韁, 韁绳. ②〔常 *pl.*〕驾驭(法); 统治(手段); 拘束物; 控制(权), 箝制, 牵制. ***assume [drop] the ~s of government*** 执掌[放弃]政权. ***draw ~*** = draw in the reins 收紧韁绳(勒住马); 放弃努力; 节省费用. ***drive [ride] with a loose ~*** 放松缰绳; 放任, 纵容. ***gather up one's ~s*** 勒紧韁绳. ***give ~ [the ~s] to*** 让马自由走; 使…自由发挥; 给…自由, 放任, 纵容 (*He gave ~ to his fancy.* 他一味空想). ***hold a ~ on*** *(one's appetites)* 抑制(食欲). ***hold [keep] a tight ~ over [on]*** 紧紧地控制, 对…严加约束. ***hold the ~s*** 掌握(政权等). ***take the ~s*** 掌权, 支配, 有决定权, 作领导人. ***throw (up) the ~s to*** = give ~ to. — *vt.* ①给(马)套上缰绳; 用缰绳勒住. ②控制, 支配, 约束; 箝制; 抑制(情欲等). ***~ back*** 勒(马)后退. ***~ in [up]*** 勒住(马); 控制, 约束, 抑制. *Rein your tongue.* 住嘴! — *vi.* ①(马)顺从缰绳. ②勒缰绳使马止步[慢行] *(in, up)*; 止住; 放慢 *(in, up)*. *a horse that ~s well* 易于驾驭的马.

re·in·car·nate [riːˈinkɑːneit] *vt.* ①再赋与新的肉体. ②使化身, 使转生. — [-ˈkɑːnit] *a.* 再具肉身的; 化身的, 转生的.

re·in·car·na·tion [ˈriːˌinkɑːˈneiʃәn] *n.* 再具肉体; 化身, 再生; 再投胎; 再体现.

rein·deer [ˈreindiә] *n.* ***(pl. ~, -s)*** 【动】驯鹿.

reinf. = reinforced.

re·in·fect [ˈriːinˈfekt] *vt.* 使再感染. **-fec·tion** *n.*

re·in·force [ˌriːinˈfɔːs] *vt.* 增兵, 增援. ②增强, 加固, 补强; 补充, 增加; 添加, 补足. *~ a fortress* 增援要塞. *~ a party* 加强党的力量[组织]. *~d concrete* 钢筋混凝土. *reinforcing bar(s) [iron]* 钢筋. *~ one's health* 增进健康. *~ provisions* 补充粮食. — *vi.* 求援; 得到援助. — *n.* 加固物.

re·in·force·ment [ˌriːinˈfɔːsment] *n.* ①增强, 加固; 补强物, 强化物; 补给品. ②增援, 支援; 〔*pl.*〕增援部队, 援军, 救援舰. *a stub ~* 【电】撑杆; 帮桩, 接腿. *a concrete ~ worker* 钢筋工人.

re·ink [ˈriːˈiŋk] *vt.* 重新加墨水[油墨]于.

rein·less [ˈreinlis] *a.* 无缰的；不受勒制的，无拘束的，放纵的，自由的。

reins [reinz] *n.* 〔*pl.*〕〔古〕①肾脏；腰部。②感情，爱情、激情。

re·in·state [ˈriːinˈsteit] *vt.* ①使复原；使恢复；使复任，使复位，使复职。②使恢复健康。③修补，修理。*be ~d in an office [to lost privileges]* 复职〔恢复特权〕。**-ment** *n.*

re·in·sur·ance [ˌriːinˈʃuərəns] *n.* 再保险，转保险；分保；再保险金额。

re·in·sure [ˈriːinˈʃuə] *vt.* 再保险；再承受保险；分保。*the ~d* 再保险者。

re·in·te·grate [ˈriːˈintigreit] *vt.* 使重新完整，恢复；重建，复兴；再统一，再团结。**-gra·tion** [ˈriːˌintiˈgreiʃən] *n.*

re·in·ter [ˈriːinˈtəː] *vt.* 重埋，改葬。

re·in·ter·pret [ˌriinˈtəːprit] *vt.* 再解释〔尤指给…以不同的解释〕。**-ation** *n.*

re·in·tro·duce [ˈriːˌintrəˈdjuːs] *vt.* 再介绍；再提出；再引入。

re·in·vest [ˈriːinˈvest] *vt.* ①再投资于；重新投资于。②再授与；再委任 (*with*)；归还。③再围攻。**-ment** *n.*

re·in·vig·or·ate [ˈreːinˈvigəreit] *vt.* 使恢复生气，使再活跃，使恢复精神〔体力〕，使重新振作。**-or·a·tion** [ˌriː-inˈvigəreiʃən] *n.*

reis [reis] *n. pl.* real②的复数。

re·is·sue [ˈriːˈisjuː, ˈriˈiʃjuː] *vt., vi.* 再发出（证券、汇票等），再发行（书籍等）；重行发布。— *n.* 重新发行；改版。

re·it·er·ate [riːˈitəreit] *vt.* 反复；反复讲；反复做；重申；重作。

re·it·er·a·tion [riːˌitəˈreiʃən] *n.* 反复；重复；重申；〔主英〕【印】反面印刷。

re·it·er·a·tive [riːˈitərətiv] *a.* 反复的。— *n.* 【语法】反复动作词〔如从 prate 变成的 prattle 等〕；重叠语〔如 dillydally, pell-mell 等〕。

reive [riːv] *v.* = reave.

reiv·er [ˈriːvə] *n.* 抢夺者，掠夺者。

re·ject [riˈdʒekt] *vt.* (*opp.* accept) ①拒绝，抵制；不受理，不接受；驳回，否决，否认。②退掉；丢弃，除去，滤去。③(胃)吐出，呕出（食物）。④【物】拒斥。*His view has been ~ed.* 他的意见已被否决了。*Sorting-machine ~s all defective specimens.* 精选机挑除一切有疵瑕的制品。*~ a literary contribution* 退稿。*~ a vote* 否决所投之票〔视为无效〕。— [ˈriːdʒekt] *n.* 废品，下脚料；不合格者；被剔除者。*reduction in the number of ~s and seconds* 废品次品率降低。

re·jec·ta·men·ta [riˌdʒektəˈmentə] *n.* 〔L.〕(*pl.*) ①垃圾，废物。②(被冲到岸上的)海草，漂浮物。③排泄物。

re·ject·er [ˈriˈdʒektə] *n.* 丢弃者；排除者；拒绝者；否决者；呕吐者。

re·jec·tion [riˈdʒekʃən] *n.* ①抛弃，排除，退回；废弃。②抵制；拒斥；拒绝；排泄物，呕出物。③【统】否定；否决；【法】驳回；【电讯】阻碍。*~ and waste* 返工和浪费。

re·jec·tor [riˈdʒektə] *n.* ①= rejecter. ②【无】带阻滤波器；抑制器。

re·jig·ger [ˈriːˈdʒigə] *vt.* 〔英口〕重新安排；更新装备（工厂等）。

re·joice [riˈdʒɔis] *vi.* ①欢喜，高兴，快乐，欢乐(*at; in; to do; over*)。②欢呼，宴乐；庆祝，欢庆。*~ in* 〔谑〕拥有，享有（*~ in health* 身体健康。*~ in the name of* 名叫…。*~ in one's youth* 年轻）。— *vt.* 使欢喜，使高兴，使快乐。***be ~d to hear [at hearing]*** 听到而欢喜〔高兴〕（*I am ~d to hear of your success.* 听到你的成功我很高兴）。

re·joic·ing [riˈdʒɔisiŋ] *n.* ①喜悦，欢喜，高兴。②〔*pl.*〕欢呼，欢声；庆祝；欢庆；宴乐。**-ly** *ad.*

re·join[1] [ˈriːˈdʒɔin] *vt.* ①使再接合，使再聚合 (*to, with*)。②再参加，再加入，重返（队伍等）；重逢。*~ one's colours* 重归队伍。*~ one's regiment [ship]* 归队。— *vi.* 照原样接合；再结合，重逢，复聚，重聚。

re·join[2] [riˈdʒɔin] *vt.* (再)回答说，答应，答复。— *vi.* ①回答，答辩。②【法】(被告)再次答辩，抗辩。

re·join·der [riˈdʒɔində] *n.* ①回答，答辩；回嘴。②(被告的)第二答辩。

re·ju·ve·nate [riˈdʒuːvineit] *vi., vt.* ①(使)回复青春，(使)恢复精神，(使)复壮，(使)年轻化；(使)翻身。②【化】(使)(粘胶)嫩化；【地】(使)回春；(使)再生。**-nation** *n.* 恢复过程；复壮作用〔现象〕；嫩化。

re·ju·ve·na·tor [riˈdʒuːvineitə] *n.* ①回复青春的人。②复活器；复壮剂；【化】嫩化剂。

re·ju·ve·nesce [ˌriːdʒuːviˈnes] *vi., vt.* (使)回复青春；【生】(使)复壮。

re·ju·ve·nes·cence [ˌriːdʒuːviˈnesns] *n.* 回复青春，回春，更新；【生】复壮(现象)。

re·ju·ve·nes·cent [ˌriːdʒuːviˈnesnt] *a.* (使)回复青春的；(使)恢复活力的；(使)复壮的。

re·ju·ve·nize [riˈdʒuːvinaiz] *v.* = rejuvenate.

re·kin·dle [ˈriːˈkindl] *vt., vi.* ①再点火；重新燃起；重新燃烧。②〔喻〕使再振作精神；使重新激起〔引起〕。

REL = rate of energy loss 能量损耗率。

-rel, -er·el *suf.* '小'，'少'，'轻'：cocker*el*.

rel. = ①relative; relatively. ②religion; religious.

re·lapse [riˈlæps] *n.* ①复旧，故态复萌；退步，堕落；累犯。②【医】再发，旧病复发。— *vi.* ①回复（原来坏习惯等），故态复萌；(重新)堕落，退步；恶化；沉陷。②(病)再发，复发 (*into*)。*relapsing fever* 【医】回归热。

re·late [riˈleit] *vt.* ①讲，叙述（故事等）。②把…与…关联起来；显示…与…的关系；使联系 (*to, with*)。③〔通例用被动语态〕使结成亲戚。*Curious to ~, the giraffe has no voice.* 说来奇怪，长颈鹿不会出声。***be ~d to*** 和…有(亲戚)关系。— *vi.* ①关联，有关系 (*to*)。②符合 (*with*)。③与…相适应；与…友好相处。*These remarks ~ to the socialist modernization.* 这些话涉及社会主义的现代化。*unable to ~ to one's environment* 不能适应环境。*~ well to people* 人缘好。

re·lat·ed [riˈleited] *a.* ①所叙述的，所说的。②相关的，有关系的〔尤指有亲戚关系的〕。③【乐】和声的。**-ness** *n.*

re·la·tion [riˈleiʃən] *n.* ①说话，叙述，报告；故事。②关系，联系；〔*pl.*〕(利害)关系，交情；〔*pl.*〕国际关系。③亲戚关系；亲戚。④【法】告发；追溯效力。⑤比率，比数。⑥〔*pl.*〕男女关系；性关系。*diplomatic ~* 外交关系。*the ~s of production* 生产关系。*social ~s* 社会关系。*the ~ between cause and effect* 因果关系。*the ~ of father and son* 父子关系。*Is he any ~ to you?* 他是你的亲戚吗？***bear no ~ to = be out of all ~ to*** 和…无关；和…完全不称。*The outlay seems to bear no ~ to the object aimed at.* 这费用似乎和预期目的完全不相称。***have ~s with*** 和…有(某种)关系。***have ~ to*** 有关；和…有关系(*The report has ~ to a state of things now past.* 这个报告是关于现在已经过去的事件的。) ***in [with] ~ to*** 关于…，就…而论。***make ~ to*** 提及…，读到…。***~ by marriage*** 姻亲，裙带关系。

re·la·tion·al [reˈleiʃənəl] *a.* 有关系的；亲戚的；(特指语法上)表示关系的。**-ly** *ad.*

re·la·tion·ship [riˈleiʃənʃip] *n.* ①亲戚，亲戚关系。②关系，联系。

rel·a·tive [ˈrelətiv] *a.* ①关于…的，与…有关系〔联系〕的。②相对的；相关的；以(他物)为准的，相应的，成比例的 (*to*)；相比较的。③附条件的。④切合本问题的(例证)。⑤【乐】关系的〔指有相同调号的〕；【语法】表示关系的。— *n.* ①亲戚，亲属。②关系物；有关事项。③相对物。④【语法】关系词。*What are the ~ merits of the two?* 两者相较的优劣如何？*~ velocity* 相对速度。*to assign tasks according to their ~ importance and urgency* 按轻重缓急安排工作。*a different yet ~ reason* 虽不同

但有连带关系的理由. *without some more ~ proof* 倘无更恰当的证据. ***be ~ to*** 和…相应,和…成比例,和…有关系,随…为转移 (*Value is ~ to demand.* 价值随需要为转移. ~ **adjective [adverb, pronoun]** 关系形容词[副词,代名词]. ~ **terms** 相对词语〔例: *strong, weak*〕.

rel·a·tive·ly [ˈrelətivli] *ad.* ①关系上; 相对; 相互. ②比较上; 按…比例说,比较…地. *an engine ~ powerful to its weight* 就重量而论马力较大的发动机.

rel·a·tiv·ism [ˈrelətivizəm] *n.* 相对性; 相对主义, 相对论.

rel·a·tiv·ist [ˈrelətivist] *n.* 相对论者.

rel·a·tiv·is·tic [ˌreləti ˈvistik] *a.* 相对论(性质)的.

rel·a·tiv·i·ty [ˌreləˈtiviti] *n.* 相关(性); 互相依存; 相对性; 相对论: *the general [restricted, special] theory of ~* 广义[狭义]相对论.

rel·a·tiv·ize [ˈreləti ˌvaiz] *vt.* ***(-iz·ed, -iz·ing)*** 把…相对起来考虑,把…作为相对物描述,把…作为相对物处理. **-i·za·tion** *n.*

re·la·tor [riˈleitə] *n.* 〔L.〕 ①叙述者, 讲说者. ②【法】原告,告发人.

re·lax [riˈlæks] *vt.* ①松弛(肌肉等),放松(紧握的手等); 使软弱无力. ②缓和, 放宽, 减轻(刑罚等). ③使松懈, 减少(注意、努力等). ④使休息; 使(心里)轻松,使舒畅, 宽(心). — *vi.* ①松弛; 放松. ②缓和,放宽. ③变得不拘束; 变得从容. ④休养; 休息; 娱乐. ⑤通便. *thinking that ~es the will to fight* 松懈战斗意志的思想. *a ~ed throat* 咽喉炎. *a ~ing climate* 使人懒洋洋的气候. *You must not ~ in your efforts.* 你不能松气; 你要继续努力. ~ *one's attention* 疏忽,懈怠. ~ *one's pace* 放慢步伐. ~ *the bowels* 通便.

re·lax·ant [riˈlæksənt] *a.* 放松的, 弛缓的〔尤指减轻肌肉的紧张程度〕. — *n.* 【医】弛缓剂.

re·lax·a·tion [ˌriːlækˈseiʃən] *n.* ①(精神等的) 松弛; 放松;【物】张弛; 弛豫. ②(刑罚等的)减轻, 放宽. ③休养,休息,解闷,娱乐. ④松懈; 宽舒; 缓和. ⑤衰弱,精力减退.

re·lax·ed [riˈlæksid] *a.* ①松懈的,不严格的. ②放松的, 得到安宁的. ③随意的,自在的,不拘束的.

re·lax·ed·ly [riˈlæksidli] *ad.* 松弛地.

re·lax·in [riˈlæksin] *n.* 【医】松弛激素.

re·lay [riˈlei] *n.* ①接替的马; 驿马; 接替的狗; (备有接替马匹的)旅馆. ②接替; 接替人员; 补给供应. ③分程递送; 传达; 转运; 【军】递骑; 【体】接力赛跑. ④[ˈriːlei]【电】替续器; 【机】继动器; 【无】转播的无线电节目: *work in [by] ~s* 轮班工作. *a fresh ~ of workers* 刚接班的一批工人. *a key ~* 键控继电器. *a radar ~* 雷达中继站. — *vt.* ①用驿马递送; 分程递送; 使接替. ②供给接替马匹; 供给新材料. ③[riːˈlei] 传达; 【无】转播. — *vi.* ①得到接替[补充]. ②传达; [riːˈlei] 转播: *a ~ing station* 【无】转播电台. ~ **broadcast** 【无】转播. ~ **race** 接力赛跑. ~ **station** 【电信】中继站 [局].

re-lay [ˈriːˈlei] *vt.* ***(-laid, -lay·ing)*** ①再放, 重放; 重铺. ②再征收(税等). ③再给穿上,使重穿; 重涂.

re·lease [riˈliːs] *vt.* ①放(箭等), 投(炸弹); 解放, 释放(囚犯、俘虏等); 使免除; 救出; 解除(痛苦、债务等) *(from)*. ②【法】放弃; 让与(权利、财产等). ③【机】吐出, 放出;【农】推广. ④【物,电】释放; 断开; 断路器. ⑤发表(消息); 发行(新影片、书刊等). *This medicine will give you ~ from pain.* 这药吃后会减轻你的疼痛. *He is ~d at five o'clock.* 他五点钟就下班了. — *n.* ①(炸弹等的)投掷,投下. ②释放; 解放; 解除,免除. ③救出, 救济; 安慰. ④【法】弃权,让渡(证书). ⑤【机】放气装置; 放气时间; 吐出,放出. ⑥发表; 发售(物); (影片的)发行上映. ⑦发布的消息; 发行的书[刊物、影片等]. *a news ~* 新闻稿. *a happy ~* 幸福的解放〔尤指久病后的死〕.

re-lease [riːˈliːs] *vt.* 重订契约出租; 再出租.

re·leas·ee [riˌliːˈsiː] *n.* 【法】(权利或财产的)受让人; 被免除债务者.

re·lea·sor [riˈliːsə] *n.* 【法】放弃权利者; (权利或财产的)让与人.

rel·e·gate [ˈreligeit] *vt.* ①命令撤离, 驱逐(出境); 〔古〕充军; 降职, 贬黜; 丢弃,束之高阁. ②使归属(某类、某级). ③委托,移交(事件); 指示(某人向某人打听).

rel·e·ga·tion [ˌreliˈgeiʃən] *n.* 充军; 降职, 贬黜; 归属; (事件的)移交,委托; 指示问讯处.

re·lent [riˈlent] *vi.* 变温和, 变宽厚; 心平气和; 发慈悲心,动怜悯心 *(towards)*; 减弱, 缓和. **-ing·ly** *ad.* 温和地; 心平气和地; 怀着怜悯心; 宽厚地,随和地.

re·lent·less [riˈlentlis] *a.* ①狠心的,冷酷的,残忍的,惨酷的,毫不留情的. ②坚韧的,不屈不挠的; 不懈的. **-ly** *ad.*

re·let [riˈlet] *vt.* ***(-let, -let·ting)*** 再出租; 续租; 转租.

rel·e·vance, -van·cy [ˈrelivəns, -si] *n.* ①有关系; 适当,适切. ②实质性; 现实意义; 实质作用. *His answer bore little ~* 他的回答无关痛痒. ***have ~ to*** 和…有关.

rel·e·vant [ˈrelivənt] *a.* ①有关的; 适当的,贴切的,中肯的 *(to)*. ②成比例的; 相应的. ③有重大意义[作用]的; 实质性的. ***not ~ to the present question*** 和目前的问题无关的. **-ly** *ad.*

re·le·vé [ˌrəlˈve] *n.* 〔F.〕 (正餐上用的)开胃菜.

re·li·a·bil·i·ty [riˌlaiəˈbiliti] *n.* 可靠性, 安全性, 确实(性). ~ **trials** (汽车等的)耐用[可靠]试验.

re·li·a·ble [riˈlaiəbl] *a.* 可靠的,确实的. *It is reported on ~ authority that* …据可靠方面消息…. **-bly** *ad.*

re·li·ance [riˈlaiəns] *n.* 信赖,信任; 信心; 依靠 *(in; on, upon)*; 所信赖的人[物]; 寄托. *No ~ is to be placed on his word.* 他的话靠不住. ***have [place] ~ upon*** 信赖…. ***in ~ on*** 信赖…而 (*I waited in ~ on your promise* 我相信你答应过的话而等待着).

re·li·ant [riˈlaiənt] *a.* 信赖的, 信任的, 依靠的 *(on; upon)*; 信赖自己的; 依靠自己的; 自力更生的.

rel·ic [ˈrelik] *n.* ①〔常 *pl.*〕 遗物; 遗跡; 遗风. ②(殉教者的)圣骨,圣物,遗宝. ③纪念物,遗念; 〔*pl.*〕〔古、诗〕遗骨,遗骸; 尸体. ④【古生】残遗体; 残遗种〔如水杉〕; 【地】残余. *unearthed ~s* 出土文物. ~ *species* 【生】孑遗种. ~ *fauna* 残遗动物群.

rel·ict [ˈrelikt] *n.* ①〔古〕寡妇. ②【古生】残遗体; 残遗种;【地】残余.

re·lief[1] [riˈliːf] *n.* ①(难民、贫民等的)救助,救济,救护; 救济品. ②(痛苦、忧虑等的)解除,减轻;【化】减压. ③慰藉,安慰,安心; 解闷,消遣. ④调班,换班,替换; 替换者,接班者; 接班兵; 救援,解围; 救兵, 援兵; 【军】换防; 接防部队;【机】退切;【电】卸载; 释放;【机】保险; 放泄; 离隙. *a ~ fund* 救济(基)金. *This medicine will give you ~.* 这药会使你舒服的. *A comic scene follows by way of ~.* 接着来一个喜剧场面以资调剂. ***feel a sense of ~*** 放下心,如释重负. ***find ~ from*** 从…中摆脱出来. ***for the ~ of*** 为了救济…. ***give a sigh of ~*** 宽慰地舒一口气. ***to my great ~*** 使我大为欣喜[放心]的是. ~ **valve** 保险阀,安全阀. ~ **works** 失业救助工程〔如修筑道路等〕.

re·lief[2] [riˈliːf] *n.* ①【雕刻】凸起,浮起,浮雕; 浮雕品; 【绘画】人物凸现,轮廓鲜明. ②鲜明,生动,显著,卓越. ③地形,地势,起伏; 【筑城】壁高; 【摄】调剂画面. *high [grand] ~* 高[深]浮雕. *low ~* 低[浅]浮雕. *His deeds stand out in ~.* 他功绩显赫. *micro-~* 小区地形,小区起伏. ***blank wall without ~*** (无门无窗的)平墙. ***bring [throw] into ~*** 使突出,使鲜明,使显著. ***bring out the fact in full ~*** 把事实十分鲜明地摆出来. ***in ~*** 浮雕一般; 鲜明地,显著地. ***stand out in bold [strong] ~*** 鲜明地突现出来 *The snowy Alps stand out in bold ~ against the blue sky.* 白雪皑皑的阿尔卑斯山在蓝色天空的衬托下鲜明地耸立着. ~ **map**

模型地图；立体地图．～ **printing** 凸版印刷．～ **telescope**【军】体视望远镜．～ **television** 立体电视．

re·li·er [ri'laiə] *n.* 信赖者；依靠者．

re·liev·a·ble [ri'li:vəbl] *a.* ①可减轻的；可解除的，可安慰的．②可援救的．③可刻成浮雕的．

re·lieve [ri'li:v] *vt.* ①(从危险、苦痛等中)救出，使脱离，解脱．②救济，救助(难民等)；供应食品[物资]给．③援救(被围城市等)．④使安心，使放心，安慰．⑤减少，减轻，缓和，除去(忧虑、恐惧等)．⑥使调班[换班]，使(哨兵、卫兵等)交班休息；免除(职务)，免职 *(from; of)*．⑦使变化多趣，使能消愁解闷．⑧使浮现，使突出；使显目，衬托，使互相对照．*I am [feel] much ～d to hear it.* 我听了感到十分宽慰．～ *sb. from pain* 解除某人的痛苦．*You shall be ～d at 10.30.* 你十点半钟下班．*a black bodice ～d with white lace* 用白花边作衬托的黑胸衣．***be ～d of*** 被解除…，消失 (*He was ～d of his post [of his post at his own request]* 他撤职[辞职]了)．*Let me ～ you of your bag.* 让我替你拿这个提包．～ ***guard*** 换岗．～ ***nature [the bowels, oneself]*** 解手，大便，小便．～ ***sb. of his purse***〔谑〕扒去某人钱包．— *vi.* ①救济．②接班，接防．③突出．④解除．

re·liev·er [ri'li:və] *n.* 解除苦痛的人；救助者，救济者；救济物；慰藉物；缓和装置；接替者．

re·lie·vo [ri'li:vəu] *n.* *(pl. -s)*【雕刻】浮雕；浮雕品．*in* ～ = in relief.

re·li·gion [ri'lidʒən] *n.* ①宗教；宗派．②信仰．③宗教[修道]生活．④心爱的事物；一心追求的目标．⑤有关良心的事；(自己感到)应做的事．⑥〔罕〕宗派仪式；〔罕〕教团，僧团：*liberty of* ～ 宗教自由．*the established* ～〔英〕国教．*the Mohammedan* ～ 伊斯兰教．***enter into*** ～ 加入教团，做修士；做教士；出家．***experience [get]*** ～〔美俗、谑〕皈依宗教．***lead the life of*** ～ 过修士生活．***make a*** ～ ***of*** *(doing)* = ***make it*** ～ ***to*** *(do)* 自己认为必须做….

re·li·gion·ism [ri'lidʒənizəm] *n.* ①笃信宗教；狂热信仰．②伪装的虔信宗教(模样)．

re·li·gion·ist [ri'lidʒənist] *n.* ①宗教家；热心宗教的人，宗教狂；笃信宗教的人．②假信徒．

re·li·gi·os·i·ty [riˌlidʒi'ɔsiti] *n.* ①信仰宗教的特性〔尤指笃信宗教，宗教狂〕．②虚伪的虔信态度．— **re·li·gi·ose** [-ˌəus] *a.*

re·li·gious [ri'lidʒəs] *a.* ①宗教(上)的．②笃信的，虔诚的．③修道(院)的；(属于)教团的．④严正的，认真的；凭良心的．⑤【诗】神圣的．— *n.* 修士，修女；出家人．*a* ～ *house* 修道院．*a* ～ *question* 宗教问题．*the* ～ 笃信宗教的人；修士，修女．***with*** ～ ***care [exactitude]*** 非常细心[严谨]地．**-ly** *ad.* **-ness** *n.*

re·line ['ri:'lain] *vt.* ①换(衣服的)里子，换衬里．②重新划线．③【军】换(炮的)内筒．

re·lin·quish [ri'liŋkwiʃ] *vt.* ①作罢，废除，撤回；放弃(计划、政策、信仰、希望等)．②放开，放松(所握之物)．③让出(权利、财产等)．～ *bad habits* 戒除不良习惯．**-ment** *n.*

rel·i·quary ['relikwəri] *n.* 圣骨盒，遗骨盒；圣物盒；遗物盒．

rel·ique ['relik] *n.*〔美、古〕= relic.

re·liq·uiae [ri'likwii:] *n.*〔L.〕〔*pl.*〕①遗骨，遗物；遗著．②【地】化石；【植】(经久不落的)枯叶，残花．

rel·ish ['reliʃ] *n.* ①味，味道，滋味，风味，美味．②嗜好，兴趣 *(for)*；食欲，胃口；玩味，赏玩．③调味品，佐料；引起兴趣的东西．④(…的)气味，痕跡 *(of)*；少量．⑤意味，寓意，含意．*Hunger gives* ～ *to any food.* 肚子饿了什么都好吃．*give* ～ *to* 添加滋味；增加兴趣．*(has no* ～ *[loses its* ～*] when one is ill)* 病中什么都不好吃．***have no*** ～ ***for*** 不喜欢，对…不感兴趣．***with*** ～ 津津有味地，有趣地．— *vt.* ①津津有味地吃，品味，领略；喜欢，爱好，享受．②加味，调味．*Hunger will* ～ *the plainest fare.* 肚饿糠好吃，饥不择食．*He does not* ～ *my advice* 他不喜欢听我的劝告．— *vi.* 有(…的)味道，有…的风味 *(of)*；有(…的)气味 *(of)*.

re·live ['ri:'liv] *vi.* 再生，甦醒，复活．— *vt.* (尤指凭想象)使再现，重新生活，重新体验．～ *one's life* 重新生活．

re·load ['ri:'ləud] *vt., vi.* 再装货；再装填；再装弹．

re·lo·cate [ri:'ləukeit] *vt.* ①重新安置[配置]，改放．②【军】调动．③〔美〕强制疏散．**relocation** *n.*

Rel. Pron.; rel pron. = relative pronoun 关系代词．

re·lu·cent [ri'lju:sənt] *a.* ①返照的，反射的．②光辉的，明亮的．

re·luct [ri'lʌkt] *vi.*〔罕〕①作斗争 *(against)*；反抗、反对 *(at)*．②不愿意，勉强．

re·luc·tance, -tan·cy [ri'lʌktəns, -si] *n.* ①厌恶，嫌厌．②不情愿，勉强．③〔罕〕抵抗，反抗 *(to; at)*．④【电】磁阻．***with*** ～ 不情愿地，勉强地．***without*** ～ 欣然，甘愿．

re·luc·tant [ri'lʌktənt] *a.* ①厌恶的，嫌厌的，不高兴的；不情愿的，勉强的(同意、答复等)．②难处理的；难加工的；难得到的．③〔罕〕反抗的，抵抗的．*be* ～ *to discard* 舍不得丢弃．*give sb.* ～ *assistance.* 勉勉强强帮人的忙．～ *followers* 胁从分子．*The soil is hard and* ～ *to the plough.* 地硬难耕．**-ly** *ad.*

rel·uc·tiv·i·ty [ˌreləkˈtiviti] *n.*【物】磁阻率．

re·lume, re·lu·mine [ri'lju:m] *vt.*〔古，诗〕再点燃；使重新照亮；使重新明亮．

re·ly [ri'lai] *vi.* ①倚赖，依靠，仗恃．②信任，信赖 *(on, upon)*．～ *on one's own efforts* 依靠自己努力．～ *on the poor peasants and farm labourers* 依靠贫雇农．～ ***upon a broken reed*** 倚靠不可靠的东西．～ ***upon it*** 放心吧 (*You may* ～ *upon it that he will be here.* 请相信他一定会来的．)

REM [rem] (= rapid eye movement) *n.* ***(pl. REMS)***【心】眼的迅速跳动〔指人做梦时眼的跳动〕.

rem. = remittance.

rem [rem] (= roentgen equivalent, man) *n.* ***(pl. rem)***【物】雷姆，人体伦琴当量．

re·main [ri'mein] *vi.* ①剩余，剩下；遗留，留下；活着(未死)．②逗留(在某处) *(in; at; with)*．③搁着不动，搁置；尚待…；留待…；依然，仍然…；继续存在，现存．④终属，归于 *(with)*．*This* ～*ed over from yesterday's dinner.* 这是昨天晚饭吃剩的．*I* ～*ed three weeks in Paris.* 我在巴黎逗留了三个星期．*She* ～*s unmarried.* 她仍然没有结婚．*Much [Little] now* ～*s to be done.* 还有许多事[没有什么事]待做．***I*** ～ ***yours truly [sincerely, etc.]*** 你永远忠实的，谨上[信尾客套语]．***It*** ～***s to be proved that ...,*** (...)尚待证明．***Nothing*** ～***s but to*** 只要…就行了 (*Nothing* ～*s but to draw the moral.* 只要引出其中的教训就行了．) ～ ***abroad*** 滞留在国外．～ ***at home*** 留在家里，留在国内．～ ***at one's post*** 留在岗位上．～ ***faithful*** 保持忠诚．～ ***with*** 在…的权限内，在…的手里，属于，归于，终属．— *n.*〔常 *pl.*〕①剩余物；遗物，遗跡；余额．②残余人物；遗属．③遗体，遗骨．④遗稿．⑤遗风．⑥【古生】化石．*the* ～*s [a* ～*] of a temple* 一座寺庙的遗跡．*the* ～*s of an army* 残兵败将；残部．

re·main·der [ri'meində] *n.* ①剩余物，残余，剩余；剩下的人，残留者，其余的人．②【数】余部，余项；余数．③【法】残留权．④(爵位等的)继承权．⑤卖剩的书籍、商品存货；处理品．⑥〔*pl.*〕遗址，遗迹，废墟；遗风，遗痕．*the* ～ *of one's life* 余生，晚年．— *a.* 剩余的；留存下的：*the* ～ *biscuit* 吃剩的饼干．*If you divide 10 by 3. the* ～ *is 1.* 用三除十，余数是一．— *vt.*〔美〕作处理品廉价出售．**-ship** *n.*【法】残留权，继承权．

re·make ['ri:'meik] *vt.* 再作，再制；重造，改造，改作，修改，翻新．— *n.* 重制；翻新；改造，修改；重制物；重新摄制的影片．

re·man ['ri:'mæn] *vt.* ①(给船只、军舰、炮台等)重新配

备人员. ②使重新象男子汉;使重新有勇气.

remand [riˈmɑːnd] *n.* ①召回; 送回. ②【法】还押(命令);被还押者;案件的发回. — *vt.* ①送回,送还;叫回,召回,命令归回. ②【法】还押(被告、嫌疑犯);押候;发回(案件)至下级法院. ~ **home**〔英〕青少年拘留所.

rem·a·nence [ˈremənəns] *n.* 【电】剩余磁感应; 剩磁,顽磁.

rem·a·nent [ˈremənənt] *a.*〔现罕〕残余的,剩余的.

re·mark [riˈmɑːk] *n.* ①注意,观察. ②话,言语; 评论,意见. *worthy of* ~ 值得注意. *the ~s column* 备注栏. *a theme of general* ~ 议论纷纷的事情. *Did you make a ~?* 你有没有说过什么话[发表意见]? ***make a ~ on*** 就…说一说〔表示一点意见〕. ***make no ~*** 什么也不说. ***make ~s*** 说东道西;评论;演说. ***pass a ~*** 表示一点意见,略陈所见. ***pass without ~*** 置之不理,置若罔闻,默认. — *vt.* ①注意到, 看见, 觉得,发觉. ②说,讲;陈述(注意到的事情等). *I ~ed the heat as soon as I entered the room.* 一进房间就觉得热. *as ~ed above* 如上所述;前面已说过. — *vi.*①留意. ②评论,谈论,议论 *(on, upon)*.

re·mark·a·ble [riˈmɑːkəbl] *a.* 值得注意的,惊人的;显著的;非凡的,非常(好)的,异常的,出众的, 奇异的. *He is ~ for precocity.* 他早熟得惊人. *She makes herself too ~.*她这人锋芒毕露. *a ~ work* 极出色的工作[作品]. **-bly** *ad.*

Re·marque [rəˈmɑːk] *n.* ①雷马克〔姓氏〕. ② **Erich Maria** ~雷马克〔1898—1970,美国小说家,原籍德国,《西线无战事》的作者〕.

re·marque [riˈmɑːk] *n.* 〔F.〕【印】①(注在印版边上的)轮廓略图[记号]. ②带有轮廓略图的印版或校样.

re·mar·riage [ˈriːˈmæridʒ] *n.* 再娶;再嫁;再婚.

re·mar·ry [ˈriːˈmæri] *vt., vi.* (使男或女)再结婚;再娶;再嫁.

re·mast [ˈriːˈmɑːst] *vt.* 换船桅.

re·match [ˈriːˈmætʃ] *n.* (体育运动项目的)复赛;重赛.

rem·blai [rɑ̃ːmˈblei] *n.*〔F.〕填筑(铁道路基的)土方.

Rem·brandt [ˈrembrænt], **van Rijn [Ryn]** 伦布兰〔1609—1669,荷兰画家〕.

R.E.M.E.,Reme [ˈriːmi] = Royal Electrical and Mechanical Engineers 〔英口〕皇家电气和机械工程师部队.

re·me·di·a·ble [riˈmiːdiəbl] *a.* 可医治的; 可挽回的,可补救的;可纠正的;可修补的. **-bly** *ad.*

re·me·di·al [riˈmiːdjəl] *a.* ①医治(用)的, 治疗上的. ②挽回的, 补救的; 纠正(用)的; 修补(用)的; 补习的. **-ly** *ad.*

re·me·di·a·tion [riˌmidiˈeiʃən] *n.* 【教】补习, 辅导. **-al** *a.*

rem·e·di·less [ˈremidilis] *a.* 治不好的;不能挽回的;无法纠正的;无法修补的.

rem·e·dy [ˈremidi] *n.* ①医药;药品;医疗,疗法. ②补救(法),纠正(法) *(for)*. ③【法】(损失的)赔偿;补偿. ④(硬币的)公差. ***be past [beyond]*** ~ 无可救药的, 医不好的. ***There is no ~ but*** ... 除…外别无办法. — *vt.* ①医治,疗治. ②补救, 纠正,改善, 减轻,克服,消除(弊病等). ③修补,修理;赔偿.

re·mem·ber [riˈmembə] *vt.* ①记起,想起,回忆起 *(opp.* forget*)*;记着,记得;记着去…;谙记. ②牢记, 记住, 铭记;铭感,感谢;酬劳,赏赐,送礼. ③致意,问候. *I can't ~ your name.* 我想不起你的名字了.*I ~ seeing him once.* = *I ~ that I saw him once.* 我记得见过他一次. *Please ~ to call me at six.* 请别忘记六点钟叫我. *~ a child on its birthday* 给孩子生日送礼. ***~ sb. in one's will*** 在遗嘱中把财产一部分赠给某人. ***R- me to*** ... 请向…致意. ~ ***oneself*** 醒悟,反省,检查自己过失;想起,记起. — *vi.* 记起,想起, 追想, 回忆; 记着,记得;有记忆力. ***if I ~ right(ly)*** 我没记错的话;我记得的确是那样的. ***~ of***〔美〕记得…,想起….

re·mem·brance [riˈmembrəns] *n.* ①记忆;回忆,回想;记忆力. ②纪念,追忆;纪念品;纪念碑;备忘录. ③〔*pl.*〕致意,问候. ***bear [keep] in ~*** 记在心里,记着. ***bring to ~*** 使记起[想起]. ***call to ~*** 想起. ***come to ~*** 回忆起,想起. ***escape one's ~*** 记不起了;忘记. ***give my ~s to*** 请代问候…. ***have in ~*** 记得. ***have no ~ of*** 一点也不记得…. ***in ~ of*** 为纪念…;回忆…. ***pass from sb.'s ~*** 忘记. ***put in ~*** 使想起. **R- Day**〔英〕休战纪念日.

re·mem·branc·er [riˈmembrənsə] *n.* ①使想起的人[物],提醒者;纪念品;备忘录. ②记录官. *the City R-*〔英〕伦敦市议会代表. *the King's [Queen's] R-*〔英〕皇室债款的征收官[旧时英国的高等法院官吏].

re·mex [ˈriːmeks] *n.* ***(pl. rem·i·ges*** [ˈremidʒiːz]***)*** (鸟的)飞羽.

rem·i·ges [ˈremiˌdʒiːz] *n. pl.* ***(sing. re·mex*** [ˈriːmeks]***)*** 【动】飞羽. **-g·i·al** [riˈmidʒiəl] *a.*

re·mil·i·ta·rize [ˈriːˈmilitəraiz] *vt.* 使重新武装, 再武装. **-za·tion** *n.*

re·mind [riˈmaind] *vt.* 使想起,使记起,提醒 *(of; that; how)*. *You ~ me of your father.* 你使我想起你的父亲. *Please ~ me to call her up before ten.* 请提醒我在十点以前给她打电话.

re·mind·er [riˈmaində] *n.* ①使人回想起其他东西的东西;提醒者,提醒物.②提示,信号,通知. ③【商】催询单. *a ~ slip* 催询单. *a ~ tray* 意见箱. *a gentle ~* 暗示.

re·mind·ful [riˈmaindful] *a.* 留意的, 注意的; 使想起的;提醒注意…的 *(of)*.

Rem·ing·ton [ˈremiŋtən] *n.* 雷明顿〔姓氏〕.

rem·i·nisce [ˌremiˈnis] *vi.* 追忆[缅怀]往事 *(of)*. — *vt.* 追忆[怀旧]地说[写](往事).

rem·i·nis·cence [ˌremiˈnisns] *n.* ①回想, 追忆, 回忆,怀念; 记忆力, 回想力; 怀念的事物; 一星半点的回忆线索,暗示者;潜在意识. ②〔*pl.*〕回忆往事的谈话; 经验谈; 回忆录. ③引起联想的相似物. *The scene awakens ~s of my youth.* 这景象唤起我年轻时的往事. *~ of the war* 大战回忆录.

rem·i·nis·cent, rem·i·nis·cent·i·al [ˌremiˈnisnt, -snʃəl] *a.* ①怀旧的,回忆的. ②喜谈往事的. ③暗示…的,提醒的;使人联想…的 *(of)*. *The old man was ~.* 那老年人爱谈往事. *His writings were ~ of ancient classical writers.* 他的作品很象古代的古典作家. — *n.* 回忆者,回忆录作者;追记前事者. **-ly** *ad.*

re·mint [ˈriːˈmint] *vt.* 改铸;重铸(货币).

re·mise¹ [rəˈmiːz] *n.* ①【击剑】再刺, 重刺. ②(高级)出租马车;马车房. — *vi.*【击剑】再刺,重刺.

re·mise² [riˈmaiz] *vt.* ***(-mised, -mising)***【法】让渡,让与(权利、财产等),立契出让.

re·miss [riˈmis] *a.* ①怠慢的, 疏忽的, 不留心的. ②慢吞吞的,迟缓的,倦怠的: *be ~ in one's duties* 玩忽职守. **-ness** *n.*

re·mis·si·ble [riˈmisibl] *a.* 可宽恕的, 可饶恕的; 可赦免的. **-bil·i·ty** *n.*

re·mis·sion [riˈmiʃən] *n.* 宽恕,饶恕;(负债、捐税等的)免除;免罪,赦免. ②(怒气、紧张等的)缓和,松弛,减退;(病痛等的)减轻,平息. ③〔罕〕寄钱,汇款;(事件的)交付;延期: **R- Thursday**【宗】洗足星期四. **-sive** *a.*

re·mit [riˈmit] *vt.* ***(-mit·ted*** [-ˈmitid]; ***-mit·ting*** [-ˈmitiŋ]***)*** ①汇寄,付(款); 送交(行李等); 开发(支票). ②【法】(将案件)发回下级法院; (把事件)移转(某方面取决) *(to)*; 指示(某人)去问(某人)[参考(某书)]. ③使复原,恢复原状. ④饶恕, 赦免, 免除, 减轻(罚金、捐税等). ⑤缓和,减退,停止(苦痛、注意、努力等). ⑥展期,延期(以便重新调查). ⑦〔古〕再拘押. ⑧〔古〕释放(犯人). ⑨〔古〕放弃. *~ one's anger* 消除怒气. *~ the siege* 解围. *I ~ money to my family every month.* 我

每月给家里汇款. ~ *one's efforts* 轻松,不费劲. — *vi.* ①汇款,寄款,付款. ②(病痛等)减退,和缓,减轻. *kindly ~.*【商】祈即付款. *Her pain began to ~.* 她的疼痛开始缓和了.

re·mit·tal [riˈmitl] *n.* ①赦免; 免除. ②减轻. ③【法】(案件的)发回,移转.

re·mit·tance [riˈmitəns] *n.* ①汇款; 汇款额; 支付(金额). ②【法】(案件的)发回,移转. *make ~* 汇款, 开发(支票等). *a ~ man*〔英〕侨居外国靠本国汇款生活的人[游手好闲不务正业的懒人].

re·mit·tee [riˌmiˈtiː] *n.* 汇款领取人.

re·mit·tent [riˈmitənt] *a.* 弛张的; 忽轻忽重的(病等). — *n.*【医】弛张热 (= ~ fever).

re·mit·ter [riˈmitə] *n.* ①汇款人, 出票人. ②【法】(诉讼案件的)移转. ③〔罕〕复权,复位,复旧.

rem·nant [ˈremnənt] *n.* ①剩余,残余;余物,残屑;剩货;零头;碎布;〔常 *pl.*〕残存者,幸存者. ②余烬;遗迹,遗风. *the ~s of a feast* 筵席的残汤剩菜. *a ~ of the feudal times* 封建时代的遗留物,封建残余. — *a.* 剩余的,残余的,残留的.

re·mod·el [ˈriːˈmɔdl] (〔英〕*-ll-*) *vt.* 重新塑造; 重作, 改造; 改作 (剧本); 改编(军队); 改变(行为等): *~ a barn into a house* 把谷仓改成住宅. *a ~led army* 经过改编的军队.

re·mo·lade [ˌreiməˈlɑːd] *n.* = rémoulade.

re·mold [ˈriːˈməuld] *vt.*〔美〕= remould.

re·mon·e·tize [ˈriːˈmʌnitaiz] *vt.* 把(某种金属)重新作货币通用.

re·mon·strance [riˈmɔnstrəns] *n.* 抗议;抗辩;规谏,规劝,诤谏,忠告, 劝告;【史】谏书. *the Grand R-*【英史】(1641 年的)大抗议书. ***make ~ with sb. against [on] his …*** 对某人…的抗议[劝告]. ***say in ~ that*** 抗议说….

re·mon·strant [riˈmɔnstrənt] *a.* 抗议的; 诤谏的, 忠告的. — *n.* 抗议者;诤谏者,忠告者.

re·mon·strate [riˈmɔnstreit] *vi.* 表示异议, 抗议; 抗辩 *(against)*; 忠告,规劝,诤谏, 苦谏 *(with; on, upon)*. — *vt.* 抗议 [抗辩] 地说. **-stra·tion** [ˌrimɔnsˈtreiʃən] *n.* **-stra·tive** [-ˈmɔn-] *a.* **-tor** *n.*

rem·on·toir, rem·on·toire [ˌremənˈtwɑː] *n.* (钟表的)摆锤均衡键.

rem·o·ra [ˈremərə] *n.* ①【动】鲫鱼. ②阻碍,障碍物.

re·morse [riˈmɔːs] *n.* ①(对罪恶的)后悔,悔恨,良心的责备,自责. ②〔古〕慈悲,怜悯;同情心. ***without ~*** ①毫不后悔地,毫无遗憾地. ②无情地;不宽恕地.

re·morse·ful [riˈmɔːsf*u*l] *a.* ①后悔的, 悔恨的, 深受良心责备的. ②〔古〕慈悲的;怜悯的. **-ly** *ad.*

re·morse·less [riˈmɔːslis] *a.* ①无情的;无慈悲心的;冷酷的;残忍的. ②不懊悔的,不悔恨的. **-ly** *ad.*

re·mote [riˈməut] *a.* ***(-mot·er; -est)*** ①遥远的, 远距离的;偏僻的,边鄙的 *(from)*. ②很久以前[以后]的. ③疏远的;远缘的,(血缘)关系淡薄的(亲戚等),远房的;间接的. ④大不相同的,悬殊的, 别种的 *(from)*. ⑤细微的,稀少的, 漠然的, 模糊的(观念等); 看上去决不会发生的,可能性极少的. ⑥稀毛的. ⑦遥控的. *a ~ village ~ from a city* 离城市远的一个乡村. *the ~ regions of the earth* 天涯地角. *a ~ ancestor* 远祖. *a ~ kinsman* 远亲. *a ~ cause* 远因. *a ~ effect* 间接影响. *be ~ and cold in one's manner* 态度冷淡. *a ~ resemblance* 微似. *~ sensing* 遥感. ***have only a very ~ [have not the ~st] conception [idea] of what he means*** 对他的意思只有一点点了解 [全无了解]. ***live ~*** 住在偏僻的乡下. **~ ages** 古代. **~ control**【无】遥控. **~ damages**【法】间接损害. **~ possibility** 极少的可能性. **-ly** *ad.* **-ness** *n.*

re·mo·tion [riˈməuʃən] *n.* ①移动. ②〔废〕分离,离开.

re·mou·lade [ˌreiməˈlɑːd] *n.* 加料的蛋黄酱〔用作凉菜或色拉的调味品〕.

re·mould [riːˈməuld] *vt.* 改型,重造,改造,改铸,改塑. *to ~ our world outlook* 改造我们的世界观. *ideological ~ing* 思想改造.

re·mount [riːˈmaunt] *n.* 新马, 接替的马; 新补充的马群;新马的补充. — *vi., vt.* ①再骑(马). ②再登上(山、梯等). ③重新供给马;重新安置(炮);重镶(宝石等);重新裱装(照片等). ④回溯,回到(某时代、地点等).

re·mov·a·ble [riˈmuːvəbl] *a.* ①可移动的; 可拆装的. ②可去除的; 可撤职的. — *n.*〔英〕(爱尔兰的)非终身治安法官 (= ~ magistrate). **-bil·i·ty** *n.*

re·mov·al [riːˈmuːvəl] *n.* ①移动,迁移;撤退;折卸. ②排除;除去;切除;杀害;【林】皆伐,终伐. ③撤职;调职. **~ sod right** 林地刈草权. **~ van** 搬运卡车〔特别是供搬家用〕.

re·move [riˈmuːv] *vt.* ①移动, 迁移. ②拿走, 撤去, 收拾(碗碟等);脱掉(衣服等),拿下(眼镜等); 扫除, 消除, 除去,洗清(疑虑、污点等);〔委婉话〕除掉,杀掉,暗杀. ③使退出,使离开(某处); 免职, 撤职. ④【法】移交(案件). ⑤窃取,偷. *There was soup and fish, ~d by boiled chicken and bacon.* 接在汤和鱼之后, 换上来的是煮鸡和咸肉. *This will ~ the last doubts.* 这会将最后的疑虑一扫而光. *~ sb. from office* 免去某人职务. *Truth has ~d from the earth.* 真理荡然无存. ***be ~d from school*** 被勒令退学, 被开除. ***~ a name from a list*** 把姓名从名单中勾消,开除. ***~ furniture*** 替人搬家(为业). ***~ oneself*** 走开,离开. ***~ one's hat*** 脱帽〔打招呼,表示敬意〕. — *vi.* ①移动;搬家,迁居 *(from… to)*. ②〔诗〕跑开,离去,消失. — *n.* ①移动;〔英〕迁移,搬家〔美国通常说 move〕. ②距离,路程,间隔;阶段,等级;亲戚等次. ③〔英〕(学校的)升级;(charterhouse 学校等的)中间学级,中班. ④〔英〕下一道菜;收去的杯盘;收碗[盘]: *action but one ~ from crime* 差一点就犯罪的行为. *He is but one ~ [few ~s] from me.* 他和我隔着一代[两三代]. *Three ~s are as bad as a fire.* 搬家三次等于失火一次.

re·moved [riˈmuːvd] *a.* ①(亲族关系)隔了…代的. ②远离的; 远隔的; 无关的(与 *from* 连用). *They are not many degrees ~ from the brute.* 他们跟禽兽相差不远. *a first cousin once ~* 嫡堂[嫡表]兄弟[姐妹]的子女. *a first cousin twice ~* 嫡堂[嫡表]兄弟[姐妹]的孙子女. *a cousin forty times ~* 很远的本家[亲戚].

re·mov·er [riˈmuːvə] *n.* ①搬运工; 搬家公司. ②脱离器;【化】脱膜剂; 去…剂. ③【法】(案件的) 移送. ④〔罕〕迁居者;调差者.

Rem·sen [ˈremsn] *n.* 雷姆森〔姓氏〕.

re·mu·da [riˈmuːdə] *n.* (大牧场里供牧人每日外出乘骑的)加鞍备用马群.

re·mu·ner·ate [riˈmjuːnəreit] *vt.* 报酬,酬劳;给…赔偿[补偿]. *His trouble is sufficiently ~d.* 他的辛苦得到十分优厚的报酬.

re·mu·ner·a·tion [riˌmjuːnəˈreiʃən] *n.* 报酬, 酬劳; 赔偿,补偿.

re·mu·ner·a·tive [riˈmjuːnərətiv] *a.* 有报酬的; 有利的,合算的. *~ work* 有报酬的工作.

Re·na [ˈriːnə] *n.* 丽娜〔女子名〕.

re·nais·sance [rəˈneisəns; F. rənsɑ̃ːs,〔美又〕reneˈsɑ̃ːns] *n.* ①复兴;新生;复活. ②〔the R-〕(14—16 世纪欧洲的) 文艺复兴(期); 文艺复兴期 (的美术、建筑)式样. — *a.*〔R-〕文艺复兴(时代)的,文艺复兴式的. *R- architecture* 文艺复兴时期[风格]的建筑.

re·nal [ˈriːnl] *a.* 肾脏(部)的. *~ calculus*【医】肾结石. *~ capsule* 肾上腺. *~ colic* 肾绞痛. *~ corpulse* 肾小体,肾球.

re·name [ˈriːˈneim] *vt.* 给…重新命名;给…改名.

Ren·ard [ˈrenəd] *n.* = Reynard.

re·nas·cence [riˈnæsns] *n.* ①更生,再生;复活,复兴. ②

〔R-〕 = Renaissance.

re·nas·cent [ri'næsnt] *a.* 新生的,再生的; 复兴的,复活的;四季青春的.

ren·con·tre [ren'kɔntə] *n.* ①偶遇, 邂逅. ②决斗, 冲突;遭遇战;论战,论争.

ren·coun·ter [ren'kauntə] *n.* = rencontre. — *vt., vi.* ①偶然碰见,邂逅. ②(与…)交战,(与…)冲突.

rend [rend] ***(rent*** [rent]***)*** *vt.* ①割裂,劈开; 使分裂,使分离. ②〔古〕(因愤怒)扯破,撕碎(头发、衣服等). ③(悲伤等)撕裂,扯乱(心肠等); 伤…的感情. ④剥(树皮). ⑤抢去,强夺 *(off, away, from, out of, up)*. ⑥(声音)刺破,响彻. *The party was rent in two.* 这个政党分裂成两派. *Her heart was rent by conflicting emotions.* 她的心被矛盾的感情搅乱. *Infants were rent from their mother's arms.* 婴儿从母亲手里被抢走. ***be rent in two*** 分成两份. **~ *apart [asunder]* = ~ *in [to] pieces*** 〔古、诗〕扯碎. **~ *one's garments [hair]*** 扯破衣服[扯乱头发]. — *vi.* 裂开,劈开,寸断,分裂. **~ *the air*** (喊声等)震天.

ren·der ['rendə] *vt.* ①报答,报复; 归还,付还; 交付,交纳. ②提出,开出,拿出(帐单、理由等). ③给与(帮忙等); 表示(敬意等). ④让与,让出,放弃; 移交,托付. ⑤致使. ⑥表现,描写(个性等),演出,演奏(音乐等); 翻译 *(into)*. ⑦反映,反响,反应. ⑧提取(脂肪),炼(油). ⑨放出,放松(滑车上的索子). ⑩【建】给…初涂[打底];粉刷;给…抹灰. ~ *good for evil* 以德报怨. *You have ~ed great service.* 你们作了很大的贡献[帮了很大的忙]. ~ *a bill* 开出帐单. ~ *judgement* 宣判. ~ *sb. famous* 使某人出名. *My efforts were ~ed futile.* 我的努力全落空了. *Poetry can never be adequately ~ed in another language.* 诗从来不能贴贴切切翻译成另一种语言. ***an account ~ed***【商】开出而未付帐单. **~ *a fortress*** = ~ up a fortress. **~ *an account of*** 讲述…,说明…. **~ *(sb.) a service*** 帮(某人)忙. **~ *good for evil*** 以德报怨. **~ *him service* = ~ *service to sb.*** 为某人效劳[服务]. **~ *oneself up to*** 投降. **~ *thanks to*** 感谢,报答. **~ *up*** 放弃,让出. **~ *up a fortress*** 放弃要塞. — *n.* ①〔罕〕(地租、房租等)缴纳. ②【建】(墙壁的)初涂,打底;粉刷;抹灰. ③精制油.

ren·der·ing ['rendəriŋ] *n.* ①翻译,译文;表现,描绘;演出,演奏. ②提炼,炼油,熬油. ③(墙壁的)初涂,打底;粉刷;抹灰. ④(滑车上绳索的)放出.

ren·dez-vous ['rɔndivuː] *n.* 〔*sing., pl.*〕①【军】指定集合地;集合基地;集合,结集. ②约会,聚会;约会地点[时间]; 幽会处. ③宇宙飞船的会合(点). — *vi.* (尤指在约定地点)会合,会见,集合,聚会.

ren·di·tion [ren'diʃən] *n.* ①〔美〕翻译; 重显,再现,复制; 演出, 演奏. ②施行;给予. ③〔罕〕(犯人的)引渡; (城市等的)放弃.

ren·dzi·na [ren'dʒiːnə] *n.* 黑色石灰土.

Re·ne ['renei] *n.* 雷内〔男子名〕.

ren·e·gade ['renigeid] *n.* 叛教者,改信伊斯兰教的基督教徒;变节者,叛徒,脱党者. — *a.* 叛教的,变节的. — *vi.* 背叛,变节;脱党;背教.

ren·e·ga·do [ˌreni'geidəu, -'gɑː-] *n.* ***(pl. -does)*** 〔古语〕= renegade.

re·ne·go·ti·ate [ˌriːni'gəuʃiːeit] *vi., vt.* ***(-at·ed, -at·ing)*** 重新商议,重新谈判〔尤指对契约的复审,以免订约一方获得超额利润〕. **-a·ble** *a.* **-a·tion** *n.*

re·neg(u)e [ri'niːg] *vt.* 否认;放弃 *(one's country)*; 拒绝. — *vi.* ①【牌戏】有某种花色的牌可跟而(故意或无意)违反规则出另一花色的牌. ②〔喻〕食言,背信,违约. — *n.* 【牌戏】有某种花色的牌可跟而违反规则不跟.

re·new [ri'njuː] *vt.* ①翻新(旧物),更新. ②使(精神)一新;使复活,使甦生;恢复(青春等); 再兴,重建. ③重新想起;重新开始,再开始(攻击等); 重做;反复. ④重订,更改(契约等);换取(新的东西),更换; 再补给, 补充. *a coat ~ed in places* 东缝西补的上衣. ~ *correspondence [efforts, game]* 再开始通讯[努力、游戏]. ~ *the garrison* 增援守军. *A snake ~s its skin.* 蛇蜕皮. ~ *one's health* 恢复健康. ~ *one's old friendship with* 和…重温旧情. ~ *one's youth* 回复青春. — *vi.* 恢复原状;重新开始;继续;展期.

re·new·a·ble [ri'njuː(ː)əbl] *a.* ①可翻新的. ②可恢复[复活]的; 可再生的. ③(契约等)可延期[更新]的. ④可重新开始的. *a ~ natural resource* 可再生的自然资源.

re·new·al [ri'nju(ː)əl] *n.* ①更新. ②复活; 恢复,复新. ③再开始. ④重做; (票据等的)更换; (契约等的)重订,延期. **~ *of term of office*** 连任.

ren·i·form ['reniˌfɔːm, 'riːni-] *a.* 肾形的.

re·nig [ri'nig] *v., n.* 〔美俚〕= reneg(u)e.

re·nin ['riːnin] *n.*【生化】肾素,高血压蛋白原酶.

re·ni·tent [ri'naitnt, 'renitənt] *a.* ①抵抗压力的. ②顽抗的. **re·ni·ten·cy** *n.*

Renminbi ['ren'min'biː] *n.* 〔Chin.〕人民币.

Renmin Ribao ['ren'min 'ribau] 〔Chin.〕人民日报 = the People's Daily.

ren·net[1] ['renit] *n.* ①(晒干的)小牛皱胃的内膜〔制干酪用〕;(小牛皱胃中的)凝乳. ②【化】= rennin.

ren·net[2] ['renit] *n.* 〔英〕(原产法国的)王后苹果.

ren·nin ['renin] *n.*【生化】(粗制)凝乳酶.

Re·no ['riːnəu] 离诺〔美国有名的"离婚城市",在内华达州西部,凡欲离婚者,只须在该市住满三个月,即可离婚〕. **go to Reno** 离婚.

re·no·gram ['riːnəˌgræm] *n.*【医】肾爱克斯线(造影)照片.

re·nog·ra·phy [riː'nɔgrəfi] *n.*【医】肾爱克斯线照相术,肾造影照片. **-no·graph·ic** *a.*

re·nounce [ri'nauns] *vt.* ①抛弃, 放弃, 背弃. ②不承认,否认;与(儿子等)断绝关系. ~ *the world* 退隐. ~ *one's peerage* 放弃贵族地位. — *vi.* ①【法】放弃权利[财产、地位等]. ②【牌戏】(因打不出应跟的花色而)垫牌. ③正式投降.

re·no·vas·cu·lar [ˌrinə'væskjulə] *a.*【医】肾血管的. ~ *hypertension* 肾血管高血压.

ren·o·vate ['renəuveit] *vt.* ①弄新,刷新,革新; 翻新; 重做,改做,再制. ②修理,修补; 改善. ③恢复; 使精神一新. ④弄干净, 使清洁. *a ~d tyre* 再生轮胎. — *a.* 恢复的,革新的,翻新的.

ren·o·va·tion [ˌrenəu'veiʃən] *n.* ①革新; 更新, 复壮. ②修理,修补. ③清扫. **-va·tor** *n.* 革新者; 修理者(等).

re·nown [ri'naun] *n.* ①声誉,名望,声望. ②〔古〕传说,传闻. *a man of ~* 知名之士,名人. *have great ~ for* 因…出名. *of great [high] ~* 有名.

re·nowned [ri'naund] *a.* 有名的,著名的,有声望的.

rens·se·laer·ite ['rensiləˌrait, ˌrensi'liəˌrait] *n.*【化】假晶滑石.

rent[1] [rent] *n.* 地租;房租;〔美〕(一般的)租借; 租金, 租费;〔口、美〕出租地; 出租房屋;〔美〕***for*** ~ 出租的. **For R-** 召租〔广告用语〕. — *vt.* 付地租[房租等]; 租用,把…租给某人(to); 向…租入 (from),向某人收租. ~ *one's tenants low* 向租户收低价租金. — *vi.* 出租: *This apartment ~s cheaply.* 这套公寓房间租价便宜. ~ **charge**【法】地租. **~-free** *a., ad.* 不收租金的[地],不付租金. ~ **roll** 租册; 租金总额. ~ **service**【史】地租服役; 代替租金的劳役. ~ **strike** (租户因房租过高,房屋失修等)拒付房租.

rent[2] [rent] *n.* ①(衣服等的)裂缝,破缝,绽线处; (云等的)裂隙; 谷, 峡谷;【地】断口. ②(意见等的)分裂,分歧;(关系等的)破裂.

rent[3] [rent] *v.* rend 的过去式及过去分词. — *a.* 撕裂的; 分裂的.

rent·a·ble ['rentəbl] *a.* 可出租的,可租借的.

rent·al ['rentl] *n.* 地租总额,租金总额; 租费,收入;〔罕〕

租折,租册. ~ **library** ①〔美〕收取租借费的图书馆.②(商店附设的)租书处.

rente [F. rɑ̃:t] *n.* 〔F.〕年金,每年的收入,定期收入;〔*pl.*〕长期公债;公债年利.

-rent·ed [-ˈrentid] *a., suf.* 租金…的; *high- [low-] ~* 租金高[低]的.

rent·er [ˈrentə] *n.* 承租人,租户,佃户,房客;〔美〕(一般)出租人;租借人;【影】影片经租商.

ren·tier [ˈrɔntiei] *n.* 〔F.〕领年金的人;靠债券[地租、房租]利息生活的人.

re·num·ber [ˈriːˈnʌmbə] *vt.* 重编…的号码,重新编号.

re·nun·ci·a·tion [riˌnʌnsiˈeiʃən] *n.* ①放弃,抛弃,废弃;弃权;否认状;【法】(对权利等的)放弃声明书. ②不承认,拒绝,否认. ③断念;自制;出家. **-tive** *a.*

ren·voi [renˈvɔi] *n.* (政府对外国人,特别是外交官)驱逐出境.

re·oc·cu·py [ˈriːˈɔkjupai] *vt.* ①再占领,收复;再占用;再住. ②再从事. *the reoccupied area* 收复区. **-pa·tion** *n.*

re·om·e·ter [riˈɔmitə] *n.* = rheometer.

re·o·pen [ˈriːˈəupən] *vt.* ①再开,重开. ②再开始;重新进行(辩论、讨论、考虑等). *The matter is settled and cannot be ~ed.* 这件事已经作了决定,不能再予讨论. — *vi.* 再开,重开. *School ~s on Monday.* 星期一开学.

re·or·der [riˈɔːdə] *n.* 再定货. — *vt.* ①再订购,再定货. ②重新整理;重新整顿,重新安排. — *vi.* 再订购同类货品.

re·or·gan·ize [ˈriːˈɔːgənaiz] *vt., vi.* 改组,改编,整编;改造,改革;整理. **-zation** *n.*

reo·vi·rus [ˌriːəuˈvaiərəs] *n.* 【医】呼吸道肠道病毒.

rep[1] [rep] *n.* 【纺】棱纹平布.

rep[2] [rep] *n.* ①〔俚〕浪子;堕落者. ②〔美俚〕代表. ③〔美俚〕名誉;名声,名气.

rep[3] [rep] *n.* 〔学俚〕默唱,背诵的诗句(等)〔repetition之略〕.

rep[4] [rep] *n.* 【原】物体伦琴当量〔电离辐射剂量〕.

Rep. = ①Representative. ②Republic; Republican.

rep. = ①repeat. ②report; reported; reporter. ③repair. ④representative. ⑤reprint.

re·pack·age [riˈpækidʒ] *vt.* ***(-aged; -ag·ing)*** 重新打包,重新包装.

repaid [riːˈpeid, ri-] repay 的过去式及过去分词.

re·paint [riːˈpeint] *vt.* ①重新涂(油漆). ②重画. — [ˈriːpeint] *n.* (画面)重新着色的部分;重新漆过的高尔夫球.

re·pair[1] [riˈpɛə] *n.* ①(房屋、衣服等的)修理,修补;〔*pl.*〕修理工作. ②(健康等的)恢复;(错误等的)改正,订正,矫正;(伤害等的)赔偿,补偿. *The shop is closed during ~s.* 本店进行装修,暂停营业. *Repairs done while you wait.* 修理来件,立等可取. *big [capital, heavy] ~* 大修. *operating ~* 日常维护检修. *permanent ~* 大[治本、永久]修理. ***beyond ~*** 无法修理(的). ***in bad ~*** 维修不善,失修. ***in good ~*** 维修良好,修理认真,完好可用. ***in ~*** 维修良好 (*Keep roads in ~* 保持道路的维修良好). ***out of ~*** 长年缺乏维修,失修. ***past ~*** (= beyond ~). ***under ~s*** 在修理中(的). — *vt.* ①修理,修补. ②赔偿,补偿. ③使恢复;改正,订正,矫正;治疗. *a ~ing lease* 租户自负修理责任的租约. *~ a mistake* 改正错误. *~ a wound* 治伤. **~man** 修理工. **~ planting** 补植. **~ ship** 修理船.

re·pair[2] [riˈpɛə] *n.* ①常去之处,人来人往的地方,热闹场所. ②依赖,依靠. ***have ~ to*** 依靠,依赖. ***a place of great [little] ~*** 游人杂沓[稀少]的地方,热闹[僻静]场所. — *vi.* ①去,往,赴,时常去 *(to)*; 大伙儿去; 群集,聚拢. ②依靠,依赖 *(to; for)*.

re·pair·a·ble [riˈpɛərəbl] *a.* 可修理的; 可赔偿[补偿]的; 可挽回[恢复]的.

re·pair·er [riˈpɛərə] *n.* 修理工人,修补者.

re·pand [riˈpænd] *a.* 【植】残波状的〔指叶缘〕.

re·pa·per [ˈriːˈpeipə] *vt.* ①重新用纸裱糊(墙壁等). ②用纸重新包;重新供给纸张.

rep·a·ra·ble [ˈrepərəbl] *a.* 可修补的; 可赔偿的; 应由(某人)修理[赔偿]的. **-bly** *ad.*

rep·a·ra·tion [ˌrepəˈreiʃən] *n.* 赔偿(款项); 修理〔现在多用 repair〕;〔*pl.*〕修理工作,维修工程〔现在多用 repairs〕. ***demand ~ for*** 要求赔偿. ***make ~ for*** 对…作出赔偿. ***~s in kind*** 货物赔偿.

rep·a·ra·tive, re·par·a·to·ry [ˈrepərətiv, riˈpærətəri] *a.* 修理的; 赔偿的; 恢复的; 弥补的.

rep·ar·tee [ˌrepɑːˈtiː] *n.* 敏捷的回答; 巧妙的回答; 应对敏捷(的才能).

re·par·ti·tion [ˈriːpɑːˈtiʃən] *n.* ①分配,区分,摊分. ②再分配,再区分,再分割,再瓜分. — *vt.* (再)分配,(再)区分,(再)分割.

re·pass [ˈriːˈpɑːs] *vt., vi.* 再通过[经过],再渡过(河、海等); 在回程中又通过[渡过]; 再通过(议案等). *pass and ~* 往返. **-age** *n.*

re·past [riˈpɑːst] *n.* 膳食,饭餐; 饮食; 就餐时间. *a dainty [rich] ~* 盛餐,筵席. *a light [slight] ~* 便餐. — *vi.* 就餐; 设宴.

re·pat·ri·ate [riːˈpætrieit] *vt.* 遣送回国,送回本国. — *vi.* 回国. — *n.* 被送回本国的人.

re·pat·ri·ation [ˈriːˌpætriˈeiʃən] *n.* 遣送回国,遣返.

re·pay [ri(ː)ˈpei] *vt., vi.* ***(-paid*** [-ˈpeid]***)*** ①付还,偿还. ②报答,回敬; 报复. *~ a visit* 回访. *~ a salutation* 答礼. **-ment** *n.* ①偿还. ②报答; 报复,复仇. ③赔款.

re·pay·a·ble [ri(ː)ˈpeiəbl, ri-] *a.* 可付还的; 可报答的; 应报复的.

re·peal [riˈpiːl] *n.* (法令等的)废除,作废,取消,撤销,撤回;【英史】撤销合并运动;〔美〕废除禁酒法. — *vt.* 废除,作废,取消,撤销,撤回(法律、判决、决议等); 召回.

re·peal·er [riˈpiːlə] *n.* 废除[撤销]者,撤销论者;【英史】合并撤销论者.

re·peat [riˈpiːt] *n.* ①再说,再做,重演,(尤指应听众要求的)再演; 重播. ②【乐】复奏[复唱]部分; 反复符号. ③【商】(同样货物的)再供给; 再定货. ④拷贝,复制. ⑤(花纸等的)重复的花样. — *vt.* ①反复; 重说,再三讲; 重做. ②照样传达(别人的话),照样讲; 复述,背诵,复诵. *~ an error* 一错再错. *History ~s itself.* 历史反复重演. *Please don't ~ this to anybody.* 请不要对别人再提此事. **~ *oneself*** 反复做[讲]同样事情. — *vi.* ①重复说[做]. ②(枪)连打. ③(小数等)循环. ④〔美〕在同一选举中投几次票〔违法行为〕.

re·peat·ed [riˈpiːtid] *a.* 反复的,再三的. **-ly** *ad.*

re·peat·er [riˈpiːtə] *n.* ①重复某一行动者; 重复发生的事物. ②背诵者; 复述者. ③连珠枪,连发枪. ④【数】循环小数. ⑤〔美〕在同一选举中投几次票者. ⑥〔美〕重考者; 重修(某课程)者; 留班生. ⑦(每小时或每15分钟报时一次的)自鸣钟. ⑧【电】重发器,转发器,(替续)增音机,中继器; 复示器. ⑨累犯,惯犯. *a reverse ~* 【机】反围盘.

re·peat·ing [riˈpiːtiŋ] *a.* 反复的; 循环的; 连发的. *a ~ instrument* 复测仪. *a ~ rifle* 连发枪. *a ~ watch* 打簧表. *a ~ ship* 信号船.

re·pel [riˈpel] *vt.* ***(-pelled*** [-ˈpeld], ***-pel·ling*** [-ˈpeliŋ]***)*** ①逐退,击退(敌军等). ②反驳; 抵抗(诱惑等); 抵制; 拒绝,推却(请求、建议等). ③【物】反拨,排斥,弹回. ④使厌恶,使不快,使反感. *Water ~s oil.* 水排斥油. *A study which ~s you is invaluable.* 使你望而生畏的研究倒是大有用处的. — *vi.* ①被排斥,被击退. ②引起反感. *Evil odors invariably ~.* 臭味总是使人不愉快.

re·pel·lent [riˈpelənt] *a.* ①排斥的; 防水的;【化】防止的; 相斥的. ②拒人于千里之外的(表情等),令人厌恶的. — *n.* ①反拨力,排拒力. ②防水布. ③【医】消肿药; 驱虫剂. *moth* ~ 防蛀剂. **-lency, -lence** *n.* **-ly** *ad.*
re·pent[1] [riˈpent] *vt.* (对某事或行为感到)悔恨,后悔,〔古〕使后悔〔多用于无人称句,有时用反身代词〕. ~ *one's injustice to another* 对于对某人的不公正的态度感到悔恨. ~ *an imprudent act* 后悔行为粗暴. ~ *have said slanderous and false things about sb.* 后悔对某人说了些污蔑不实之词. *He repenteth him of the evil.* 他对罪恶感到后悔. *It* ~*s me that I did it.* 我很后悔做了这事. *R- what's past; avoid what is to come.* 痛悔过去,慎防将来. — *vi.* 后悔;【宗】忏悔(of); 悔悟; 悔改.~ *of having missed a good opportunity to learn* 后悔失去一个学习的好机会. *too late to* ~ 后悔已晚. *I have nothing to* ~ *of.* 我没有什么后悔的. *A man who* ~*s of his thoughtlessness.* 一个对自己的粗心大意有所悔悟的人.
re·pent[2] [ˈriːpənt] *a.*【植】匍匐生根的;【动】爬行的.
re·pent·ant [riˈpentənt] *a.* 对…感到懊悔[忏悔] *(of)*. *be* ~ *of sth.* 对…表示后悔. **-tance** *n.*
re·peo·ple [ˈriːˈpiːpl] *vt.* 使人重新居住,使新居民住于;给…重新提供家畜.
re·per·cus·sion [ˌriːpə(ː)ˈkʌʃən] *n.* ①反击,击退. ②弹回;返回;(事件、声音的)反响,影响. ③散肿法; 消疹法;浮动诊(胎)法. ④【乐】(赋格曲中间插段后的)主题的再现,答句,(音调或和弦的)重复.
rep·er·toire [ˈrepətwɑː] *n.* ①(排好待演的)常备剧目,演奏节目; 保留节目. ②全部技能; 所有组成部分. *instruction* ~【计算机】指令系统. ~ **company** 拥有大量常备剧目的剧团.
rep·er·to·ry [ˈrepətəri] *n.* ①= repertoire. ②仓库,贮藏所,宝库;(尤指知识等的)贮藏,搜集;贮藏物.
re·pe·ruse [ˈriːpəˈruːz] *vt.* 重读,再读,重新细读,重新审读. **-ru·sal** *n.*
rep·e·tend [ˈrepiˌtend, ˌrepiˈtend] *n.* ①重复的声音(词、短语);(诗与乐曲的)迭句,副歌. ②【数】小数的循环节.
rep·e·ti·tion [ˌrepiˈtiʃən] *n.* ①反复,重复;重说,再讲;背诵;背诵文(诗);再现,再演. ②【乐】复唱,复奏,重奏. ③副本,拷贝;模仿物. **-al, -ar·y** *a.* 反复的.
rep·e·ti·tious [ˌrepiˈtiʃəs] *a.* 反复的,重复的;啰嗦的. **-ness** *n.*
re·pet·i·tive [riˈpetitiv] *a.* 反复的,重复的,重说的; 复唱的,复奏的. **-ly** *ad.*
re·phrase [riˈfreiz] *vt.* *(-phras·ed, -phras·ing)* 改变说法;重新措词.
re·pine [riˈpain] *vt.* 发牢骚,诉苦 *(at; against)*; 渴望改变困难处境等而想望,向往 *(for)*.
repl. = replacement (补充).
re·place [ri(ː)ˈpleis] *vt.* ①放回原处[原位].②还,送还,赔还(钱、书等). ③使复职[复位]. ④代替,接任,取代. ⑤调换,替换;给与替手[代用品]. ⑥【化】置换. *The socialist system will eventually* ~ *the capitalist system.* 社会主义制度终究要代替资本主义制度. *a thing hard to* ~ 难替换之物. **-able** *a.* 可放回原处的; 可替换的,可代替的. **-ment** *n.* 复位,归还;【军】补充;替换,替代,代换;替换物;代替物; 代替者; 补充人员[兵员];【化】移位;置换;取代;【地】交代(作用).
re·plant [ˈriːˈplɑːnt] *vt.* ①改种;移植,补种,补播. ②使复位. **-ta·tion** *n.*
re·play [ˈriːˈplei] *vt.* 重新举行(比赛);重演;再播放. — [ˈriːplei] *n.* 重赛;重演;(录音、电影等的)重放.
re·plead·er [riˈpliːdə] *n.*【法】①第二次申诉. ②再诉权. ③法院要求诉讼双方进行第二次申诉的令状.
re·plen·ish [riˈpleniʃ] *vt.* ①再斟满,再装满 *(with)*. ②装足,装满,补充(钱袋等);加强. ③〔古〕使牲口[人和动物]众多. ~ *the fire* 添燃料,加火. ~ *the earth* 使土地上充满生物. **-er** *n.* 补充者;【电】补电器;【摄】显像剂,显影剂. **-ment** *n.* 再斟满,再装满,新补给;充满,充实,补充;供给.
re·plete [riˈpliːt] *a.* ①充分供应的,饱满的; 吃饱了的;塞满的*(with)*. ②〔罕〕充分的,完全的. ~ *state of soil* 土壤充水状态.
re·ple·tion [riˈpliːʃən] *n.* ①充满,充实,吃饱;满足. ②【医】多血. *to* ~ 饱,满满,充分.
re·plev·in [riˈplevin] *n.*【法】没收物[扣押物]的发还[收回]; 收回(不该没收的)物件的诉讼; 发还物件的命令. — *vt.* = replevy.
re·plev·y [riˈplevi] *vt.* ①【法】经诉讼收回(被没收的物件等) ②凭令状取回(被扣押物品). ③〔罕〕保释;准许保释.
rep·li·ca [ˈreplikə, riˈpliːkə] *n.* ①复制品〔特指由原作者自己照前一作品作成的〕;摹本,拷贝. ②逼肖的东西,一模一样的东西. ③【乐】(主题的)反复;(乐谱中的)重复句. *a* ~ *of his father* 跟父亲长得一模一样的子女. ~**ble** *a.* 可重复[重演]的,可反复再现的.
rep·li·cate [ˈreplikit] *a.*【植】折转的. — *n.*【统】重复实验中的一次. — [-ˈkeit] *vt.* ①【植】折转. ②重复,反复,复制. ③〔罕〕回答.
rep·li·ca·tion [ˌrepliˈkeiʃən] *n.* ①(尤指对答辩的)回答;【法】(原告对被告抗辩的)答辩. ②(绘画等的)复制,摹写;拷贝,复制品. ③【统】重复(实验). ③【植】折转;折缝. ④反响. **-ca·tive** *a.*
re·pli·er [riˈplaiə] *n.* 回答者,答复者.
re·ply [riˈplai] *n.* 答复,回答;(用行动等)应战;反响;【法】(原告对被告抗辩的)答辩. ***in*** ~ ***(to)*** 为答复…,作为…的答复. ***make*** ~ 回答. ~ ***paid*** 附回信邮费;(拍电人已将)回电费付讫. — *vi.* 答复,回答 (to);【法】(原告)答辩; 应付,应战; 反响. ~ *to the enemy's fire* 对敌人炮火加以回击. ~ ***for*** 代表…答辩[回答,答谢祝酒]. — *vt.* 回答. *He replied that he would not do that.* 他回答说他不愿做那件事.
re·pon·dez s'il vous plaît [repõde sil vuː plɛ]〔F.〕乞赐复〔请帖用语,通常略作 R.S.V.P.〕.
re·port [riˈpɔːt] *vt.* ①告知,报告,汇报;报道(新闻、调查结果等);发表,公布,发表公报. ②传达(人的话);转述;传说,传闻; 品评. ③记录(讲演等以备发表). ④(向当局)报到(等);揭发,告发(某人不法行为等). *It is* ~*ed that* ... 据说…,据传…. *He was* ~*ed killed* 据说他已阵亡[被杀]. ~*ed speech*【语法】间接引语. ***be badly (well)*** ~***ed of*** 名气坏[好]. ***move to*** ~ ***progress*** (以妨碍议事为目的而)提议中止讨论. ~ ***oneself*** 报到,到差;出席. ~ ***progress*** 报告经过. — *vi.* ①报告,呈报,回报 *(on)*; 作报告,打报告,就…提出报告 *(on; upon)*. ②(新闻记者)采访,访问,通讯,报道. ③报到,到差. ~ ***for duty [work]*** 报到,上班,上工. ~ ***for the Times*** 担任泰晤士报的通讯记者,给泰晤士报写通讯. ~ ***to at*** 到…报到; 到校, 上学. ~ ***to the police*** 向警察报告. — *n.* ①(调查、研究后的) 报告(书) *(on)*;(政府机关等的)公报;(学校的)成绩报告单;(报纸等的)通讯,报道. ②【议会】记录;速记;【法】〔*pl.*〕审判记录;意见书;(给上级法院的)申请书;案件[判例]汇编. ③传说,传闻,社会上的评论,名气,名声. ④响声,爆炸声,枪炮声. *idle* ~*s* 无根据的传说. *a matter of common* ~ 大家都知道的传闻. *The rifle went off with a loud* ~. 枪砰的一声打了出去. ***a*** ~ ***on*** 关于…的报告. ***as*** ~ ***has it [goes]*** 据说. ***have a good [bad]*** ~ (学生)成绩好[不好]. ***make*** ~ 报告(调查结果等). ***of good*** ~ 名声好的,评价好的. ***The*** ~ ***goes [runs, has it] that ...*** 据说,据传. ***through good and evil*** ~ 不顾毁誉褒贬;不管名声好坏. ~ **card** (学生)成绩报告单. ~ **stage** (英国议会)委员会的报告会;第三读会.
re·port·age [ˌrepɔːˈtɑːdʒ] *n.* ①新闻采访,新闻报导. ②报告文学,报导文体.
re·port·ed·ly [riˈpɔːtidli] *ad.* 据报导,据传说.
re·port·er [riˈpɔːtə] *n.* 报告者;呈报者;采访记者,新闻通讯员; 审判[议事]记录员; 指示器. **-tori·al** [ˌrepə-

ˈtɔ:riəl] *a.*

re·pos·al [riˈpəuzəl] *n.* (信用等的)托付,信托.

re·pose[1] [riˈpəuz] *vt.* 把(希望等)寄托在…;〔罕〕委托. ～ *trust [confidence] in [on] sb. [sth.]* 信任某人[某情况].

re·pose[2] [riˈpəuz] *vi.* ①休息,安歇;睡,安睡;〔喻〕永眠,长逝. ②躺着,横卧;蕴藏;处于. ③建立于,基于 *(on; upon)*. ④倚靠,信赖 *(on; in)*. *The statue ～s on a pedestal* 雕像安在台座上. *The scheme ～s on a revival of trade.* 这个计划以活跃贸易为基础. **～ in sleep [death]** 睡着[永眠]. **～ on a bed of down [roses]** 过奢侈生活. **～ on the past** 留恋过去;缅怀往昔. — *vt.* 使休息,使安睡 *(on; in)*. ～ *one's head on the pillow* 将头靠枕休息. ～ *oneself* 休息,歇息,睡觉. ～ *oneself on a bed* 躺在床上. — *n.* ①休息,睡眠;静止;平静,安静;休养,静养;永眠,长逝. ②(色彩等的)恬静;(态度的)镇静,悠闲,泰然自若. ③信用,信赖. *make [seek, take]* ～ 休息. *a volcano in* ～ 休止的火山.

re·pose·ful [riˈpəuzful] *a.* 平静的,安静的;泰然自若的. **-ly** *ad.*

re·pos·it [riˈpɔzit] *vt.* ①保存,贮藏. ②〔罕〕使复位,放回原位;归还;取代;改变…的位置.

re·po·si·tion[1] [ˌri:pəˈziʃən] *n.* ①安置,保存,保藏. ②【医】复位术.

re·po·si·tion[2] [ˌri:pəˈziʃən] *vt.* 换位;改变位置〔主张、态度、立场等〕.

re·pos·i·to·ry [riˈpɔzitəri] *n.* ①〔英〕仓库,贮藏所;〔罕〕(美术品等的)陈列所[室],博物馆;店铺;墓室;贮物器;(知识等的)宝库;学识见闻广博的人. ②受人信托的人,心腹,亲信. *He was a ～ of all her secrets.* 她的一切秘密她都告诉他;他是她完全信赖的人. *The book [man] is a ～ of curious information.* 这书里有[这人晓得]许多奇事.

re·pos·sess [ˈri:pəˈzes] *vt.* 再占有,取回,复得(被夺之物);使恢复. **～ oneself of** 使自己重新占有…;取回,恢复.

re·post [ri:ˈpəust] *n., v.* = riposte.

re·pot [ˈri:ˈpɔt] *vt.* 移植到别的花盆里,换盆.

re·pous·sé [ripu:ˈsei] 〔F.〕 *a.* ①(金属细工所锤成或冲压出)凸纹形的. ②凸纹饰的. — *n.* ①凸纹(面). ②凸纹制作(术).

repp [rep] *n.* = rep[1].

repr. = representing; reprinted; reproduction.

rep·re·hend [repriˈhend] *vt.* 责难,指摘,谴责;申斥.

rep·re·hen·si·ble [ˌrepriˈhensəbl] *a.* 应受谴责的. **-bly** *ad.*

rep·re·hen·sion [ˌrepriˈhenʃən] *n.* 谴责;指摘;申斥.

rep·re·sent [ˌrepriˈzent] *vt.* ①(用文章等)描述;(用绘画等)表现,描写,描画;象征,意指,表示,意味. ②把…讲述为 *(as)*;声称自己是 *(oneself as; to be)*;认为…是 *(as)*. ③相当于,比拟. ④上演(戏等);扮演(某角色). ⑤代表,代理;被选为议员. ～ *ideas by words* 用言语表示思想. *I am not what you ～ me to be.* 我并不是象你所说的那种人. *They ～ed him as the chief conspirator.* 他们说他是主谋者. *He ～ed himself as a philosopher.* 他声称自己是哲学家. *We ～ed this plan easy, but it was not.* 我们原以为这计划很容易,但实际并非如此. *Camels are ～ed in the New World by llamas.* 在美洲相当于骆驼的是美洲驼. *members ～ing urban constituencies* 市选议员. **～ sth. to oneself** 想象出某事物. **～ oneself as [to be]** 声称自己是…. — *vi.* 提出异议.

re-pre·sent [ˈri:priˈzent] *vt.* 再赠送;再提出;再上演(戏剧等).

rep·re·sen·ta·tion [ˌreprizenˈteiʃən] *n.* ①表示,表现,描画,描写;画像,肖像;雕像,想像,想像力;【心】表象. ②上演,演出;扮演. ③〔常 *pl.*〕说明,陈述;主张,断定;建议,提议;抗议. ④代理,代表;选举区民代表;〔集合词〕代表人. ⑤【物】图像;显像;描绘;扫描. ⑥【法】(权利、债务的)继承;(促使另一方订契约的)陈述. *a symbolic ～* 象征性的图象,象征物. *a coded ～* 代码. **make a ～ against** 向…抗议. **make a ～ to** 向…说明. **make ～ to** 向…交涉.

rep·re·sen·ta·tion·al [ˌreprizenˈteiʃənl] *a.* ①表现的,再现的,表象的. ②扮演的,反映客观现实的艺术的. **-ly** *ad.*

rep·re·sen·ta·tion·al·ism [ˌreprizenˈteiʃənlizm] *n.* ①表现论. ②【哲】再现说〔头脑只有通过概念或思想才能理解客观事物的理论〕. **-tion·al·ist** *n., a.*

rep·re·sent·a·tive [ˌrepriˈzentətiv] *a.* ①表示的;表现的,描写的;象征的. ②能代表…的;可作…的典型[模范]的 *(of)*. ③代理的,代表的,代议制的. ④相当[类似](另一种属)的. ～ *art* 描绘自然或生活的艺术. *a ～ body* 代表团. *a ～ chamber [house]* 代议院. **in a ～ capacity** 以代表资格. — *n.* ①代表,代理(人);继任者,继承人;议员;〔美〕众议员;驻外代表〔大使,公使,领事〕. ②类似物;样本,标本;典型. *a legal [personal] ～* 遗嘱执行人,法定代理人. *a real [natural] ～* 承继人. *the House of Representatives* 〔美〕众议院. **-ly** *ad.*

re·press [riˈpres] *vt.* ①镇压(叛乱等). ②抑制,压抑(欲望等);忍住,熬住,止住(笑、眼泪等);【心】把(冲动等)压入(潜意识). **-er, -or** *n.* **-i·ble** *a.*

re-press [ri:ˈpres] *vt.* 再压.

re·pressed [riˈprest] *a.* ①被抑制的,受约束的. ②被镇压的.

re·pres·sion [riˈpreʃən] *n.* ①镇压;制止. ②抑制. *the ～ of a cough* 制止咳嗽. *R- made him behave worse.* 受抑制使他表现得更糟.

re·prieve [riˈpri:v] *n.* 【法】缓刑;死刑缓刑期[命令];〔喻〕(死、痛苦等的)暂免,暂止,暂减,暂缓. — *vt.*【法】缓期执行(死刑),暂缓处刑;暂免,暂缓,暂止.

rep·ri·mand [ˈreprima:nd] *n.* (特指当权者进行的)严责,谴责,惩戒;申斥. — [ˈre-; repriˈma:nd] *vt.* 申斥,谴责,惩戒.

re·print [ˈri:ˈprint] *n.* ①再版;重印;翻版. ②(刊物中论文的)单行本,抽印材料. ③已不通用的邮票的重印版. — [ˈri:print, -ˈprint] *vt.* ①再版;重印;翻印. ②(刊物中论文的)单独抽印. ③转载.

re·pris·al [riˈpraizəl] *n.* ①(特指国家间的)暴力性报复,报复行为;【史】(对敌国人民、财产的)报复性劫掠. ②〔罕〕〔主 *pl.*〕赔偿,赔款. *letters [a commission] of ～* 报复性拘捕证. *make ～(s)* 进行报复.

re·prise [riˈpraiz] *n.* ①【法】〔常 *pl.*〕从贵族所有地每年收入中扣除的费用[租费、恩俸等]. ②【乐】反复(句)〔尤指奏鸣曲乐章的主题〕. *beyond [above, besides] ～s* 付完租费(等)后剩下的.

re·pro [ˈri:prəu] *n.* *(pl. -pros)* reproduction proof 的缩略词 (= repro proof).

re·proach [riˈprəutʃ] *n.* ①责备,责骂,谴责;耻辱,污辱 *(to)*. ②〔*pl.*〕【宗】应答圣歌. *a term of ～* 侮蔑话;责难的话. *the mute ～ in his eyes* 他眼睛里现出的无言谴责. *The state of the roads is a ～ to civilization.* 道路的这种状态是文明的耻辱. **beyond ～** 无可非议地,漂亮地,出色地. **bring down ～ upon** 玷污,毁损. **bring [draw] ～ (up) on** 使成为…的耻辱. **heap ～es on** 痛骂,痛责. — *vt.* 责备,责骂,谴责;使丢脸;损伤…的体面. *His eyes ～ me.* 他用眼睛责备我. **-a·ble** *a.* 应受责备的;可责备的. **-less** *a.*

re·proach·ful [riˈprəutʃful] *a.* 谴责的;责备的;应受斥责的;〔古〕可耻的. **-ly** *ad.* **-ness** *n.*

rep·ro·bate [ˈreprəubeit] *vt.* ①拒绝,排斥. ②谴责. ③【宗】(上帝)摈弃;(天)罚. — *a.* 为上帝摈弃的;邪恶的,堕落的. — *n.* 为上帝摈弃的人;堕落的人;恶棍.

rep·ro·ba·tion [ˌreprəuˈbeiʃən] *n.* ①拒绝,排斥. ②反对,异议;斥责. ③【宗】摈弃.
re·pro·cess [ˈriːˈprəuses] *vt.* 重新处理;再加工;使再生;回收(废料).
re·pro·duce [ˌriːprəˈdjuːs] *vt.* ①再生产;再现. ②复制,复写;仿造. ③再演;再版;转载;翻印. ④生殖,繁殖. ~ *oneself* 生殖,繁殖. — *vi.* ①繁殖,生殖. ②进行再生产;复制.
re·pro·duce·a·ble, re·pro·duc·i·ble [ˌriːprəˈdjuːsəbl,-ibl] *a.* 能再生产的;能复制的;能繁殖的.
re·pro·duc·er [ˌriːprəˈdjuːsə] *n.* ①再现设备. ②扬声器.
re·pro·duc·tion [ˌriːprəˈdʌkʃən] *n.* ①再生产,再现;【心】再生作用. ②复制(品),复写,仿造;转载;翻印. ③生殖,繁殖. ~ *by division [ramification, gemmae]* 分裂[分枝、芽胞]生殖. ~ *by tending treatments* 【林】抚育更新. ~ **proof** 【印】照相制版用样张.
re·pro·duc·tive [ˈriːprəˈdʌktiv] *a.* ①生殖的. ②再生产的,再现的. ③多产的. ~ *organs* 生殖器官. **-ly** *ad.*
re·pro·gram [ˈriːˈprəugræm] *vt.* 改编[重编](程序),程序重调.
re·prog·ra·phy [riːˈprɔgræfi] *n.* 复印,翻印. **-pher** *n.* **-graph·ic** *a.*
re·proof¹ [riˈpruːf] *n.* 责备,谴责. ***in ~ of*** 对…加以责备.
re·proof² [riˈpruːf] *vt.* ①重新上防水胶. ②【印】重新打样.
re·prov·al [riˈpruːvəl] *n.* = reproof¹.
re·prove [riˈpruːv] *vt.* 责骂,谴责,训斥 *(for)*. ~ *sb. to his face* 当面责备某人.
re-prove [riːˈpruːv] *vt., vi.* 再证明.
re·prov·ing·ly [riˈpruːviŋli] *ad.* 谴责地.
re·pro·vi·sion [ˈriːprəˈviʒən] *vt.* 再给…食品,补充粮食给….
reps [reps] *n.* = rep¹.
rep·tant [ˈreptənt] *a.* 【植】匍匐的;【动】爬行的.
rep·tile [ˈreptail] *a.* ①匍匐的,爬行的;爬虫类的. ②卑劣的. — *n.* ①爬虫,爬行动物. ②卑劣的人.
Rep·til·ia [repˈtiliə] *n.* 〔*pl.*〕【动】爬虫纲.
rep·til·i·an [repˈtiliən] *a.* ①(象)爬行动物的;(象)爬虫类的. ②卑劣的. — *n.* 爬行动物;爬虫.
Repub. = Republic; Republican.
re·pub·lic [riˈpʌblik] *n.* ①共和国;共和政体. ②…圈,…界,…坛. ③〔古〕国家. *the People's R- of China* 中华人民共和国. *the ~ of letters* 文学界,文坛.
re·pub·li·can [riˈpʌblikən] *a.* ①共和政体的,共和国的;共和主义的;〔*R-*〕〔美〕共和党的. ②【动】群栖的(鸟等). — *n.* 共和主义者;拥护共和政体者;〔*R-*〕〔美〕共和党员. *the R- Party* 〔美〕共和党. **-ism** *n.* 共和政体;共和主义;(美国)共和党的政策. **-ize** *vt.* 使成共和政体,使成共和国.
re·pub·li·ca·tion [ˈriːˌpʌbliˈkeiʃən] *n.* 再版(的书);再发表,再发行.
re·pub·lish [ˈriːˈpʌbliʃ] *vt.* ①再出版;再发表;再发行. ②【法】重行订立(遗嘱).
re·pu·di·ate [riˈpjuːdieit] *vt.* ①(古代)休(妻),与(妻)离婚,遗弃(妻子);逐(子),断绝(父子)关系. ②不承认,不接受,否定,批判,推翻(建议);驳斥,驳倒;拒绝(要求等). ③(尤指政府等)拒付(公债等);赖(债).
re·pu·di·a·tion [riˌpjuːdiˈeiʃən] *n.* ①休妻;逐子. ②拒绝;(国家、政府的)赖债,拒付公债. ③推翻,批判,驳斥.
re·pu·di·a·tor [riˈpjuːdieitə] *n.* 抛弃者;否认者;拒绝支付者,赖债者.
re·pugn [riˈpjuːn] *vt., vi.* 〔罕〕(使)厌恶;反对 *(against)*.
re·pug·nance, -nan·cy [riˈpʌgnəns, -si] *n.* 厌恶,反感 *(to, against; towards)*;反对;矛盾,冲突 *(of; between; to; with)*.
re·pug·nant [riˈpʌgnənt] *a.* ①令人厌恶的,令人讨厌的 *(to)*,不得人心的. ②冲突的 *(to)*;与…不一致的,不调和的 *(with)*. ③反抗的;抱反感的.
re·pulse [riˈpʌls] *vt.* ①反击[打退](敌人等);推开;驳倒;挫败(对方). ②排斥;拒绝,谢绝. — *n.* 反击;打退;击退;拒绝;【物】拒斥. *meet with [suffer] (a) ~* 被拒绝[击退].
re·pul·sion [riˈpʌlʃən] *n.* ①反击,反驳. ②排斥,拒绝. ③嫌恶,嫌忌. ④【物】反斥,推斥;斥力. ⑤【医】(疮肿等的)消散;分离倾向,分散性. *feel ~ for sb.* 觉得某人讨厌.
re·pul·sive [riˈpʌlsiv] *a.* ①(令人)厌恶的,讨厌的 *(to)*. ②情绪上有抵触的;排斥的;【物】推斥的,斥力的. *a ~ smell* 讨厌的气味. *~ forces* 斥力. **-ly** *ad.*
rep·u·ta·ble [ˈrepjutəbl] *a.* 名气好的,有名声的;可尊敬的,高尚的;规范的. *a man of ~ character* 人格高尚的人. **-bly** *ad.*
rep·u·ta·tion [ˌrepju(ː)ˈteiʃən] *n.* 名气,名声;名誉,名望,信誉,声望. *a man of ~* 有名望的人. *a man of no ~* 默默无闻的人;没有声望的人. *build up a ~* 博得名声. *enjoy a high ~ as a man of science* 享有盛名的科学家. ***have a good [poor] ~*** 名誉好[坏]. ***have a ~ for*** = have the ~ of 因…而著名,以…闻名,有…的名气. ***live up to one's ~*** 不负盛名;行为与名声相符. ***lose [ruin] one's ~*** 名誉扫地.
re·pute [riˈpjuːt] *n.* 名誉,名声,声望,信用. *know sb. by ~* 由传闻中知道某人. *authors of ~* 有名的作家们. ***of good [bad] ~*** 名誉好[坏]的,有[无]信用的. ***through good and evil ~*** 不管毁誉褒贬,不管人家怎样讲,不管舆论如何. — *vt.* ①〔古、诗〕以为,认为. ②看做;称为;评价. *He is ~d [as, to be] honest.* 一般都认为他老实. *He is ill [well] ~d of.* 他名誉不好[好].
re·put·ed [riˈpjuːtid] *a.* ①名誉好的,有名气的. ②号称…的,被称为…的,据说是…的. ~ *gin* 驰名的杜松子酒. *sb.'s ~ father* 据说是某人的父亲〔真假不明〕. *a ~ pint* 号称一品脱装的(酒等). **-ly** *ad.* 据一般批评,据说.
re·quest [riˈkwest] *n.* ①请求,恳求,恳请;要求,需要. ②要求物,需要品,请求之事;请求文,请愿书. *I have a ~ to make of you.* 我有事求你. *You shall have your ~.* 你要的东西会给你的,会答应你的请求的. ***at sb.'s ~*** 应某人请求. ***be in (great) ~*** (非常)需要. ***by ~*** 照需要;依照请求;应邀,如嘱 (*She will sing by ~.* 她将应邀歌唱.) ***come into ~*** 出现需要,受人需要. ***make (a) ~ for*** 请求,恳请. ***on ~*** 承索(即寄等). — *vt.* (郑重或正式)请求,要求,恳求,恳请 *(sth.; sb. ... to do; that ...)*. ~ *a loan from the bank* 请求银行借款. *Your presence is immediately ~ed,* 即请光临[驾临,出席]. *May I ~ your attention?* 请您注意! *Gentlemen are ~ed not to smoke.* 先生们请勿吸烟. *I ~ them to stop making such a noise.* 我请求他们别这样吵闹. *I ~ (of him) that he (should) leave.* 我恳请他离开. *We ~ that no flowers be sent.* 敬辞花圈〔讣文中用语〕. ***as ~ed*** 依照请求.
re·quick·en [ˈriːˈkwikən] *vt., vi.* (使)苏醒;(使)重新振作.
req·ui·em [ˈrekwiem] *n.* ①〔R- 〕【宗】安魂弥撒(曲). ②安魂曲,挽歌. ③安息,平安,平静.
re·qui·es·cat in pace [ˌrekwiˈeskæt in ˈpeisiː] 〔L.〕 愿灵安眠〔基督教徒墓碑用语,略 R.I.P.〕.
re·quire [riˈkwaiə] *vt.* ①需要. ②要求;请求,命令. *Will you ~ breakfast earlier than usual?* 〔英〕你需要比平常早一点开早饭吗? *They ~ me to come.* 他们要我来. *He ~s medical care.* 他需要治疗. *The emergency ~s that it should be done.* 事情紧急,非这样做不可. *All passengers are ~d to show their tickets.* 所有乘客都必须出示车票. ***It ~s that*** ... 有…的必要. — *vi.* 需要;请求,要求. ***if circumstance ~*** 遇必要时.

re•quired [riˈkwaiəd] *a.* 〔美〕必修的(大学课程).
re•quire•ment [riˈkwaiəmənt] *n.* ①要求，需要. ②要求物,必需品;需要量;必要条件，资格 *(for)*. *the detail ~s* 详细规格. *meet the ~s of the times* 适应当时需要. *the first ~* 第一要件.
req•ui•site [ˈrekwizit] *a.* 必要的,必需的,需要的 *(to; for)*. — *n.* 必需品;要素，要件 *(for; of)*. *a quality ~ to a scientist* 科学家必不可少的品质. *the number of votes ~ for him to be elected* 他当选的不可少的票数.
req•ui•si•tion [ˌrekwiˈziʃən] *n.* ①要求,请求,命令,必要条件;【国际法】引渡犯人的要求. ②需要;【军】征购,征用,征发. ③通知书;调拨单;申请书,请求书;召唤书. *be in [under] ~* 另有需要，现在无空. ***bring [call, place] into ~ = put in ~ = lay under ~*** 征收,征发，征用. *~ **of land*** 征用土地. — *vt.* 要求;强制使用;【军】征发;命令征发;召集.
re•quit•al [riˈkwaitl] *n.* 报答;报复,复仇;罚;报答的行动;酬谢之物;〔罕〕赔偿，补偿. ***in ~ of [for]*** 作为…的报酬,为酬谢…,为报复….
re•quite [riˈkwait] *vt.* 报答,酬谢,报酬;报复 *(for;with)*; 补偿. *~ **like for like*** 用同样手段报答,以恩报恩，以怨报怨;以牙还牙.
re•ra•di•a•tion [ˌrireidiːˈeiʃən] *n.* 【物】再幅射.
re•read [ˈriːˈriːd] *(-read [-ˈred])* *vt.* 重新读，再读.
rere-arch [ˈriəˈɑːtʃ] *n.* 【建】背拱,内拱 (= rear arch).
re•re•cord [ˈriːriˈkɔːd] *vt.* (录音)再录,重录.
re•re•cord•ing [ˈriːriˈkɔːdiŋ] *n.* 再录音.
rere•dos [ˈriədɔs] *n.* 〔英〕祭坛背后的装饰品(= altarpiece).
re•re•fine [ˈriːrəˈfain] *vt.* 再精炼. *~d oil* 再生润滑油.
re•re•lease [ˈriːriˈliːs] *n.* 【影】= reissue.
rere•mouse [ˈriəˌmaus] *n.* *(pl. -mice [-ˌmais])* 〔古语〕蝙蝠 (= bat).
re•route [riˈruːt, -ˈraut] *vt.* *(-rout•ed, -rout•ing)* 按新路线发送,改道发送.
re•run [ˈriːˈrʌn] *vt.* *(-ran, -run•ning)* 重新开动，重新进行〔尤指首轮放映后的影片或电视片的再度上映〕. — [ˈriːˌrʌn] *n.* ①再开动，再进行. ②再度上映的影片或电视片.
res [riːz] *n.* 〔*sing., pl.*〕〔L.〕物,实体,物件;事,事件;财产. *~ **angusta domi*** [-æŋˈgʌstə dəuˈmai] 家境贫困. *~ **judicata*** [dʒuːdiˈkeitə] 已决事件.
res. = ①reserve. ②residence. ③resort. ④resolution.
re•sad•dle [ˈriːˈsædl] *vt.* 给…再装鞍子.
re•sail [ˈriːˈseil] *vt.* 再航行. — *vi.* 开回;再航行.
re•sal•a•ble [riˈseiləbl] *a.* 可再卖的,可转卖的.
re•sale [ˈriːseil] *n.* 再卖;转卖.
re•scind [riˈsind] *vt.* ①废除,作废,取消,撤销,解除. ②〔古、主喻〕扫除,删除.
re•scis•sion [riˈsiʒən] *n.* ①取消,撤销,解除，废除. ②【法】解约. **-scis•so•ry** [-ˈsisəri] *a.*
re•script [ˈriːskript] *n.* ①(罗马皇帝或教皇的)书面答复;诏书,政令布告. ②再写，重写;重写的东西;〔美〕【法】副本.
res•cue [ˈreskjuː] *vt.* ①救,援救，营救，救出(俘虏等). ②【法】劫出(囚犯)，夺回(没收物). ③维护. *He ~d the child from drowning.* 他救起了一个溺水的孩子. — *n.* ①援救,营救,救济. ②【法】(囚犯的)劫出,(没收物的)非法夺回. *a ~ party* 援救队. *a ~ home* 娼妓救济所,济良所. *~ work* (对妇女、儿童的)救济事业. ***go (come) to the ~*** 进行援救,营救.
res•cu•er [ˈreskju(ː)ə] *n.* 救助者,援救者;救星.
re-search [riːˈsəːtʃ] *vt., vi.* 再调查，再搜索 *(sth., into sth.)*.
re•search [riˈsəːtʃ] *n.* ①仔细搜索 *(for, after)*. ②〔常 *pl.*〕研究,调查,探测;追究. *literary [scientific] ~es* 文学[科学]研究. *basic ~* 理论研究. *a scholar of great ~* 非常有研究的学者. *be engaged in ~* 从事研究. *scholastic ~* 繁琐的追究. — *vt., vi.* 追究;调查，研究 *sth., into sth.*
re•seat [ˈriːˈsiːt] *vt.* ①使再坐下;使复职. ②增设座位;换装座面. *~ oneself* (站起来后)又坐下来. *The boy's trousers want ~ing* 这个孩子的裤子后座部得修换了.
re•seau, réseau [reiˈzəu] *n.* *(pl. -seaux [-ˈzəuz, -zəu])* ①网状物;【天】网格;【气】世界气象网. ②(花边织物的)网眼地纹组织. ③【摄】滤(光)屏.
re•sect [ri(ː)ˈsekt] *vt.*【医】切除. **-tion** *n.* 切除(术).
re•s•e•da [ˈresidə] *n.* ①【植】木樨草. ②灰绿色.
re•seg•re•ga•tion [ˈriːˌsegriˈgeiʃən] *n.* 恢复种族隔离.
re•sell [ˈriːˈsel] *(**re•sold** [ˈriːˈsəuld])* *vt.* 再出售;转卖.
re•sem•blance [riˈzembləns] *n.* 相似 *(to; between; of)*; 相似性;相似点;相似程度;外表,外观,外形,样子;肖像,像. *He has a strong ~ to his father.* 他极象他父亲. *He was of fine ~* 他外表很好.
re•sem•ble [riˈzembl] *vt.* ①像，类似，相似. ②〔古〕比拟,譬喻 (to). ③〔罕〕使像(某人，物). ④〔古〕仿造,摹写,画肖像. *They ~ each other in shape.* 他们形态相像.
re•send [riˈsend] *vt.* *(-sent, -send•ing)* 再送，再寄;重派;再发;退还,送还.
re•sent [riˈzent] *vt.* 憎恶,愤恨,憎恨.
re•sent•ful [riˈzentful] *a.* 愤怒的,愤慨的;易发脾气的,易怒的;显然不满的. **-ly** *ad.* **-ness** *n.*
re•sent•ment [riˈzentmənt] *n.* 愤怒,愤慨;怨恨，憎恨. *harbor [cherish] ~ (against)* 对…怀恨.
re•ser•pine [riˈsəːpin, -piːn; ˈresəˌpiːn] *n.*【药】利血平. **re•ser•pi•nized** *a.* 用利血平治疗[处理]过的,被投给过利血平的.
res•er•va•tion [ˌrezə(ː)ˈveiʃən] *n.* ①(权利等的)保留;保留下来的权利;条件，限制，除外条件，但书. ②〔常 *pl.*〕(房间、座位等的)包定,租定,预定,预约. ③〔古〕隐讳. ④保留地;专用地;禁猎地;〔美、加拿大〕(给印第安人指定的)居留地. ⑤【宗】留给 (病人等的)一部分圣餐. ⑥(教皇对)圣职任命权的保留;(高级圣职者对)特殊罪恶赦免权的保留. ⑦【法】(让与或贷借财产时的)特殊权益保留权;保留权益. ***make ~s*** 定座，定房间(等);附保留条件;声明. ***without ~*** 直率地，坦白地;无条件地. ***with ~s*** 有保留地 *(I agree with you, but with some ~s.* 我同意你，不过有几点要保留[除外]). ***write for ~s*** 写信去预定座位(等).
re•serve [riˈzəːv] *vt.* ①保留;留下(以备后用、享受等). ②预定,预约,租定,包，定(座位、房间等). ③贮藏，储备. ④把…除外,附加但书,限制. ⑤改期(宣判等). ⑥订约保留(某种权益). ⑦〔罕〕让活着;救命. ⑧【宗】留出(部分圣餐);保留(特赦权). ⑨注定. *All rights ~d.* 所有权利全部保留;版权所有,不许翻印. *This discovery was ~d for Columbus.* 一直等到哥伦布才来完成这一发现. *A great future is ~d for you.* 远大的前程等着你. *All seats ~d.* 所有座位必须预定. *~ **oneself for*** 养精蓄锐以待. — *n.* ①贮藏,保存;保留;储备，预备. ②备用人力[资源];贮藏物. ③保留地;预备林;猎区. ④【军】〔常 *pl.*〕后备兵;后援部队;后援舰队;预备舰队;【运】预备队员，候补选手;(博览会等的)预备奖品. ⑤【商】准备金,公积金. ⑥自制,虚心,谨慎;斟酌，限制，条件，例外. ⑦缄默;隐讳,隔阂，冷淡，不坦白. ⑧【染】防染物;(电镀用的)防镀剂. ⑨【采】埋藏量，(石油)贮量. ⑩限价，最低价格. ⑪【生化】(溶液、血液等的酸或碱的)储量. *He has a great ~ of energy.* 他绰有余力;他精力充裕. *the first ~* 预备役[军]. *the second ~* 后备役[军]. *the gold ~* (发钞银行的)黄金准备. *proved ~* 【采】探明贮量. *~ cell* 补充细胞. ***be placed on the ~*** (军舰)被编入后备舰队. ***break down all ~*** (无保留地)消除一切隔阂. ***call up the ~s*** 召集预备役. ***in ~*** 留下的,预备的,备用的. ***have [keep] in ~*** 留作预备. ***place a ~ upon a house*** 给房子标上拍卖的最低价格. ***place to*** ～ 留作备用款[公积]. ***with all*** ～ ***[all proper*** ～***s]*** 有保留地(*We publish this with all* ～. 本处公布此事确否待证). ***throw off*** ～ 消除隔阂. ***with*** ～ 有保留地;有条件地;有限制地. ***without*** ～ 不客气地,坦白地,直言不讳地;无限制地,无保留地.(*sale without* ～ 不限价拍卖). — *a.* 后备的,准备的,多余的. *one's* ～ *strength* 潜力. *a* ～ *bank* 〔美〕准备银行,储备银行. *a* ～ *city* 〔美〕(市内国立银行保有一定黄金储备的)准备市. *a* ～ *fund* 储备金,公积金. *a* ～ *tank* 【机】后备油箱. *a* ～ *tooth* 永久齿. *a* ～ *price* 最低拍卖限价. ～ *speed* 〔美军〕最大速度. ～ **clause** 保留条款〔职业运动员与某一团体签订的合同中,该团体保有自动延长合同期限,以及解约前该运动员一切活动全部受约束的条款〕. ～ **officer** 预备军官.

re·served [riˈzəːvd] *a.* ①保留的,留作专用的;包定的,预定的,预约的. ②有隔阂的,有保留的;缄默的;有节制的,谨慎的;冷淡的. ③贮藏着的,保存着的. *a* ～ *seat* 预定的座位. *a* ～ *car* 包定的汽车. *a* ～ *army* 后备军 (*opp. active army*). *a* ～ *price* 最低拍卖价格. **-ly** *ad.*

re·serv·ist [riˈzəːvist] *n.* 后备役军人.

res·er·voir [ˈrezəvwɑː] *n.* ①贮藏所;贮气筒;贮水池,水库;贮水槽,水槽;贮存器;贮油器,油筒,油箱;贮墨管;【解】贮液囊. ②(知识、精力等的)贮藏,蓄积. *an air* ～ 气槽. *a depositing [settling]* ～ 澄清池. *a distributing* ～ 配水池. *a receiving* ～ 集水池. *a storing* ～ 贮水池. *a seminal* ～【解】贮精囊. *the Ming Tomb R-* 十三陵水库. *a* ～*-pen* 自来水笔. — *vt.* 贮藏;设贮藏所[贮水槽].

re·set [ˈriːˈset] *vt., n.* 重新安放,重新安装;重排(铅字);重镶,重嵌(宝石);重磨(刀具等);【电讯】重调,重安设;【物】(使)复位,转接;零位设置;【医】重接(断骨),接骨;【园艺】移栽(植物). *a* ～ *button* 重复起动按钮.

re·set·tle [ˈriːˈsetl] *vt.* 使重新安居;使在新地方定居;使再殖民; ～ *oneself* 再坐下来 (*in, on*); 使(纠纷等)恢复安定,再度澄清. — *vi.* 再坐下,再就席. **-ment** *n.*

resh [reiʃ] *n.* 希伯来语第二十个字母.

re·shape [ˈriːˈʃeip] *vt.* 给…以新形态[新方针]; 改造. — *vi.* 采取新形式;打开新局面. *Affairs are gradually reshaping themselves.* 事情在慢慢地转变着.

re·ship [ˈriːˈʃip] *vt.* 把…再装上船;重新装船;把…改装别船. ～ *oneself* 再上船,换搭另一船. — *vi.* 再上船;(船员)签订另一次航行合同.

re·ship·ment [ˈriːˈʃipmənt] *n.* (货物的)重装,转载,换船;重装货物;重装量.

re·shuf·fle [ˈriːˈʃʌfl] *vt.* ①重新洗(牌). ②〔喻〕改组(政府等),重新安排[布置](事件). — *n.* ①(牌的)重洗. ②〔喻〕(政府等的)改组;重新配置,(事件的)重新安排.

re·sid [riˈzid] *n.*【石油】残油,渣油.

re·side [riˈzaid] *vi.* ①住,居住 (*in; at*); (官吏)留驻,驻在. ②(性质)存在,具备 (*in*); (权力、权利等)属于,归于 (*in*). *The real power* ～*s in the people.* 真正的权力属于人民;真正的力量在于人民.

res·i·dence [ˈrezidəns] *n.* ①居住,居留;驻在;居住期间;宅邸,公馆;(权利等的)所在. ②(污染物质等在介质中的)留存,滞留. *R- is required.* 须居住在任所. *an official* ～ 官邸. *Desirable family* ～ *for sale* 优良住宅出售〔广告文〕. ***have [keep] one's*** ～ 住,居住. ***in*** ～ (官吏)驻在(任地);住在官邸;(大学教职人员)寄宿(校内). ***take up one's*** ～ ***(in)*** 住入…,住进….

res·i·dent [ˈrezidənt] *a.* ①居住的 (*at; in; abroad*). ②驻节的. ③【动】不迁徙的(鸟兽等) (*opp.* migratory). ④固有的;内在的. *the* ～ *population* 居民,现住人口. ～ *aliens* 外侨. *the* ～ *physician of a hospital* 住院医生. *a* ～ *minister* = *a minister* ～ 驻节公使〔地位仅次于全权公使〕. *a* ～ *tutor* 住家家庭教师. ***be*** ～ ***at [in]*** 住在…. ～ ***in the nerves [nation]*** 神经[国民]所固有的. ***whether*** ～ ***at home or abroad*** 无论住在家内家外. — *n.* 住户,居民,侨民;驻扎官;驻节公使;【动】留鸟. *foreign* ～*s* 外侨. *summer* ～*s* 避暑客.

res·i·den·tial [ˌreziˈdenʃəl] *a.* 住宅的,适宜作住宅的;关于居住的. *a* ～ *district [quarter, section]* 住宅区. **-ly** *ad.*

res·i·den·tia·ry [ˌreziˈdenʃəri] *a.* 居住的(人民等);应留在任地的,驻在的. — *n.* 居住者;【宗】住守教堂的牧师〔又名 canon ～〕;住院僧.

re·sid·u·al [riˈzidjuəl] *a.* 残余的,剩下的;残留的;残渣的;未加说明的;【数】残数的,留数的. — *n.* ①残余;【数】残数,留数;余差;渣滓;【地】残丘;【心】记忆痕迹;【医】后遗症. ②上演税〔商业电影等每次重新上演付给作家及演员等的酬金〕. ～ *property*【法】剩余财产,余产. ～ *products* 副产物. *a* ～ *error* 【数】残差. ～ *oil*【石油】残油.

re·sid·u·a·ry [riˈzidjuəri] *a.* 残余的,剩余的;残渣的;【法】接受[处理]剩余财产的,余产的. ～ *odds and ends* 剩下的零碎东西,零头. *a* ～ *estate*【法】余产. *a* ～ *legatee* 余产承受人.

res·i·due [ˈrezidjuː] *n.* 残余,残渣;余款;【林】废材,木屑;【法】剩余遗产,余产;【化】残基;滤渣;余渣,残余物;【数】残数,留数,余数. ***for the*** ～ 至于其余;说到其他.

re·sid·u·um [riˈzidjuəm] *n.* (*pl.* ***re·sid·u·a*** [riˈzidjuə]) ①残余,剩余物;【化】残渣,残留物;残留产物;残(渣)油副产品;【数】剩余;残差. ②【法】余产. ③社会底. ④社会渣滓.

re·sign [riˈzain] *vt.* ①辞去(职务). ②放弃,抛弃(权利等);让出(工作等). ③〔用反身代词或用被动语态〕委身给,听从,服从. ④委托,把…交托给 (*to*). *He* ～*ed his seat to a lady.* 他把坐位让给了一个女人. *be* ～*ed to one's fate.* 听天由命了. ～ ***one's child to sb.'s care*** 委托某人照顾自己的孩子. ***be*** ～***ed to a state of lagging behind*** 甘居下游,自甘落后. ***not*** ～ ***oneself to*** 不甘心. ～ ***oneself to*** 听任(某种影响);只好(做某事) (*to sth., to do*) (～ *oneself to waiting [to wait] till next morning* 只好等到明天再说. ～ *oneself to extinction* 束手待毙. ～ *oneself to another's guidance* 听任别人指导. *We must* ～ *ourselves to doing without a domestic help.* 我们只好不用仆人). — *vi.* ①辞职,退职,退出 (*from*). ②服从. ～ *(from) one's office* 〔美〕辞职. ～ *to one's fate* 听天由命.

re-sign [riːˈsain] *vt.* 重新签署.

res·ig·na·tion [ˌrezigˈneiʃən] *n.* ①辞职,退职,让位;辞呈. ②抛弃,断念. ③(对于命运等的)听从,服从,听任. ***accept sb.'s*** ～ 准予辞职. ***give in [hand in] one's*** ～ = send in one's ～. ***meet one's fate with*** ～ 听天由命. ～ ***under instruction*** 着令免职. ***send in [tender] one's*** ～ 提出辞呈.

re·signed [riˈzaind] *a.* ①〔被动用法〕已辞职的,已告退的;已放弃的. ②〔反身被动用法〕听从…的(摆布);(断了某念头而)决心[只好]做某事的〔后接介词 to,美国口语中可接不定式〕. *be* ～ *to die* 决心一死. **-ly** *ad.*

re·sile [riˈzail] *vi.* ①跳回,弹回;有弹力,能恢复原状;很快就恢复(精神),恢复愉快情绪. ②折回,回来. ③(契约等)被撤回,取消 (*from*); 畏缩,躲避,怕 (*from*).

re·sil·i·ence, -en·cy [riˈziliəns, -si] *n.* 跳回,弹回;弹性;恢复力;精神恢复(力).

re·sil·i·ent [riˈziliənt] *a.* ①跳回的,弹回的;有弹性的. ②能立刻恢复精神的;心情开朗的. ～ *steel* 弹性钢.

res·in [ˈrezin] *n.* 树脂,松脂;树脂状沉淀物. ～ *opal*【矿】脂光蛋白石. *acrylate [acrylic]* ～ 玻璃状可塑物. — *vt.* 涂树脂;用树脂处理. ～ *tapping* 采收树脂.

res·in·ate [ˈreziˌneit] *vt.* (***-at·ed, -at·ing***) 用树脂浸透[处理].

res·in·if·er·ous [ˌreziˈnifərəs] *a.*【化】含有树脂的,含

脂的.

res•in•oid [ˈreznˌɔid] *a.*【化】似树脂的. — *n.* ①树脂型物. ②树胶脂 (= gum resin).

res•in•ous [ˈrezinəs] *a.* ①树脂质的; 含树脂的; 用树脂做的. ②〔罕〕【电】阴电性的, 负电性的. ~ *electricity* 阴电.

res•i•pis•cence [ˌresiˈpisəns] *n.* 认错,悔过自新.

re•sist [riˈzist] *vt.* ①抵抗,反抗,抗拒,敌对;抵御,阻止,击退(敌人、侵略等);妨碍,阻碍. ②忍耐(艰苦等);抵制(疾病等);〔主与否定语连用〕忍住(笑等). ③反对,不赞成(提案等);蔑视,违背(法律等). ~*ing force* 抵抗力. ~ *heat* 耐热. *a cement that will* ~ *damp* 抗[耐]湿水泥. ~ *law* 违抗法律. *I cannot* ~ *a Joke.* 我听了一个笑话总忍不住要笑出来; 我想起一个笑话总忍不住要说出来. *I can never* ~ *strawberries and cream.* 我一看见奶油草莓就非吃不可. — *vi.* 抵抗; 反对; 抵制. —*n.* 防染剂,(印染花布用的)排色物; 防蚀用涂料; 防腐剂.

re•sist•ance [reˈzistəns] *n.* ①抵抗,反抗,抗拒,抵御,敌对; 抵抗力,反抗力; 阻力;【生】抗病性. ②【电】电阻; 阻抗; 电阻器. *electric* ~ 电阻. *abrasive* ~ 耐磨力[度]. *dead* ~ 吸收[消耗,镇流]电阻. *passive* ~ 无源电阻; 消极抵抗. ***a piece of*** ~ 主要品,压轴,出类拔萃的东西; 主菜,压桌菜 (= pièce de résistance). ***make some [no]*** ~ 进行[不]抵抗. ***offer [put up]*** ~ ***to [against]*** 抵抗. ~ ***welding*** 电阻焊接, 电焊. ***take the line of least*** ~ 采取阻力最小的路线; 采取最省力的方法. ~**-box** 电阻箱[器].

re•sist•ant [riˈzistənt] *a.* 抵抗的; 耐久的, 稳定的. — *n.* 抵抗者; 有抵抗力的东西; 防染剂,防腐剂.

re•sist•i•ble [riˈzistəbl] *a.* 可抵抗的,可反抗的,可反对的; 抵抗得住的.

re•sis•tive [riˈzistiv] *a.* = resistant.

re•sis•tiv•i•ty [ˌri:zisˈtiviti] *n.* 抵抗力; 抵抗(性);【电】电阻率; 电阻系数,比阻.

re•sist•less [riˈzistlis] *a.* ①不可抗的; 不可避免的. ②不抵抗的; 无抵抗力的. **-ly** *ad.*

re•sist•o•jet [riˈzistəˌdʒet] *n.* 电阻加热电离式发动机.

re•sis•tor [riˈzistə] *n.*【电】电阻(器).

re•sole [ˈri:ˈsəul] *vt.* 给(鞋)换底[换前掌].

re•sol•u•ble [riˈzɔljubl] *a.* ①可分解的,可溶解的 *(into)*. ②可解决的.

res•o•lute [ˈrezəlju:t] *a.* 坚决的, 毅然的; 坚定的. — *vi.* 〔美〕决议. **-ly** *ad.*

res•o•lu•tion [ˌrezəˈlju:ʃən] *n.* ①决心,果断; 坚定,刚毅. ②(议会等的)决定,决议(案);【法】〔罕〕判决; (疑问等的)解决,解答. ③分解,溶解; 解析,离析; 变形,变化,转化. ④【医】(疮肿等的)消散; 〔罕〕松弛. ⑤【乐】由不谐和音转变为谐和音;【诗】用二短音节代替一长音节. ⑥【机】分解力;【自】分辨(力). *a man of no* ~ *of character* 意志不坚定的人. *visual* ~ 目力分辨率. *come to a* ~ = *form [make, take] a* ~ 决心. *make good* ~*s* 下定改好的决心. *pass a* ~ *in favour of [against]* 通过赞同[反对]…的决议.

res•o•lu•tive [ˈrezəlju:tiv] *a.* 使溶解的; 使分解的;【医】消散的;【法】解除的. — *n.* 消散药. *a* ~ *clause [condition]*【法】解除条款[条件].

re•solva•bil•i•ty [riˌzɔlvəˈbiliti] *n.* ①分解[溶解]的可能; 可分析性; 可溶解性. ②可解决性.

re•solv•a•ble [riˈzɔlvəbl] *a.* ①可解析的; 可溶解的. ②可解决的.

re•solve [riˈzɔlv] *vt.* ①(使)下决心, 决意. ②决定; 决议. ③使分解,使解体; 解析,溶解(化合物). ④使消释; 解释(疑惑等),解决(问题等); 分辨. ⑤变成, 转化为. ⑥消退(炎症等). ⑦【乐】使不谐和音转变为谐和音. *This discovery* ~*d us to go.* 是这一发现使我们决心去的. *I* ~*d to give up smoking.* = *I* ~*d that I would give up smoking.* 我决心戒烟了. *It was* ~*d that* ... (会议)议决…. ~ *doubts* 使疑惑冰释. *be* ~*d to (do)* ... 决心(做…). ~ *itself into* 分解成, 还原; 终归成为 (*The House* ~*d itself into a committee.* 整个议会已改变成委员会了.) *resolving power*【物】分辨本领; 分辨率. —*vi.*①决心,决定 *(on, upon)*. ②分解,解体; 溶解; 解析; 分辨; 还原. ③归结于,变成, 成为 *(into)*. ④(疮肿)消散. ⑤【乐】变成谐和音. ⑥【法】失效,消失. *She* ~*d on making an early start.* 她决定早早出发. — *n.* 决心,坚定,不屈不挠,刚毅;〔美〕(议会等的)议决. *a man of* ~ 刚毅的人. *deeds of high* ~ 果敢的行为. ***keep one's*** ~ 坚持. ***make a*** ~ 下决心.

re•solved [riˈzɔlvd] *a.* 坚决的,断然的; 决心的. **-ly** *ad.*

re•solv•ent [riˈzɔlvənt] *a.*【医、化】使分解的; 有溶解力的; 消散性的. — *n.* ①分解物; 溶剂; 消散药;【数】预解(式). ②(事件等的)解决办法.

re•solv•er [riˈzɔlvə] *n.* ①下决心者. ②解决者; 解答者. ③分解器;【化】溶剂,溶媒.

res•o•nance [ˈrezənəns] *n.* ①回声,反响;【物】共鸣,共振;【无】(波长的)调谐. ②【化】中介(现象). ③【医】叩响. *atomic* ~ 原子共振. *fission* ~ 裂变反应共振. ~ **box,** ~ **chamber**【物】共振箱. ~ **level**【物】共振级.

res•o•nant [ˈrezənənt] *a.* 共振的; 能共鸣的; 反响的,有回声的. **-ly** *ad.*

res•o•nate [ˈrezəˌneit] *vi.* ***(-nat•ed, -nat•ing)*** ①回响,共鸣,反响. ②产生共鸣,产生反响; 产生共振. — *vt.* 使共鸣,使反响,使共振.

re•sona•tor [ˈrezəneitə] *n.* 谐振器,共鸣器.

re•sorb [riˈsɔ:b] *vt.* ①再吸收,再吸入,重新吸收,再吞. ②消溶. **-sorp•tion** [-ˈsɔ:pʃən] *n.* **-sorp•tive** *a.*

res•or•cin•ol [riˈzɔ:siˌnəul, -nɔ:l] *n.*【化】间苯二酚,雷琐辛 (= resorcin).

re•sort [riˈzɔ:t] *n.* ①热闹场所, 娱乐场; 常去[人多]的地方,胜地. ②常去; 人多; 人群. ③倚靠, 凭藉; 手段. *a place of great* ~ 人们常去的热闹地方. *a place of public* ~ 娱乐场所. *a fashionable* ~ 高级游乐地. *a holiday* ~ 假日游乐地. *a health* ~ 疗养地. *a pleasure* ~ 游乐胜地. *a* ~ *of thieves* 贼窝. *a summer [winter]* ~ 避暑[避寒]地. *A carriage was the only* ~. 乘马车是唯一的办法. *He encouraged the* ~ *of scholars.* 他鼓励学者常去访问. ***have*** ~ ***to*** *(force)* 用(武力), 动(武). ***in the last*** ~ 作为最后的一着[手段], 终于. ***without*** ~ 无计可施. — *vi.* ①去, 常去, 群往, 会集 *(to)*. ②倚靠,凭藉,采用(某种手段). *the inn to which he was known to* ~. 他常去的客栈. ~ ***to (armed force),*** 使用(武力), 诉诸(武力). ***without*** ~***ing to (force)*** 不使用(武力).

re-sort [ˈri:ˈsɔ:t] *vt.* 把…再分类,再分级.

re•sound [riˈzaund] *vi.* 回响; 反响 (with); (名声等)轰传,传遍 *(through)*. *Radios* ~ *from every house.* 家家户户传出收音机的广播声. — *vt.* ①反响; 使回响. ②高声响; 使(某地)充满声响. ③赞扬; 传播.

re•sound•ing [riˈzaundiŋ] *a.* ①反响的, 共鸣的; 响亮的,宏亮的. ②彻底的, 完全的. ③夸张的, 虚夸的. *a* ~ *victory* 彻底的胜利,完全的胜利. **-ly** *ad.*

re•source [riˈsɔ:s] *n.* ①〔*pl.*〕资源; 物力, 财力. ②方法,手段; 机智,智谋, 才略. ③消遣, 娱乐. *natural* ~*s* 自然资源. *hidden* ~*s* 地下资源. *Flight was his only* ~. 他只有逃走一法. *Reading is a great* ~ *in illness.* 读书是病中极好消遣. *He is lost without* ~. 他彻底完蛋[失败]了. ***a man of no*** ~***s*** 无资力的人; 毫无办法的人; 闲极无聊的人: ***at the end of one's*** ~***s*** 山穷水尽; 无计可施. ***be full of*** ~***(s)*** 富有机智. *be thrown on one's own* ~*s* 除独自努力外别无他法. **-ful** *a.* **-ful•ly** *ad.*

re•spect [risˈpekt] *n.* ①尊敬, 尊重; 〔*pl.*〕敬意, 问候,请安. ②注意,关心. ③关系; 着眼点, 方面; 细目. ④〔古〕偏袒; 事由,动机,目的. ***give one's*** ~***s to*** 向…致

候. ***have ~ for*** 尊敬; 尊重, 重视. ***have ~ to*** 关心; 筹划; 与…有关系. ***hold in ~*** 尊敬. ***in all ~s = in every ~*** 无论从哪方面(哪一点)来看; 在各方面. ***in no ~*** 无论在哪方面(哪一点)都不是…; 完全不是…. ***in ~ that*** 因为…; 如果考虑到…. ***in ~ to [of]*** 关于, 就…来说; 对…有影响的. ***in that [this] ~*** 在那一[这一]方面. ***no ~ of persons with*** 对…无所偏袒. ***pay one's ~s to*** 向…请安, 向…致敬〔常作反语用〕; 拜望, 拜访. ***pay ~ to*** 斟酌, 考虑, 关心. ***send one's ~s to*** 向…问候. ***win the ~ of all*** 处处受人尊敬. ***with all ~ for your opinion*** 你的意见很好可是…. ***with ~ to = in ~ to. without ~ to [of]*** 不考虑…, 不管…. — *vt.* ①尊敬; 尊重; 不侵犯, 不妨害. ②注意, 重视, 关心. ③关于. ~ *sb.'s silence* 尊重别人的沉默; 不随便跟人谈话. ~ *privileges [property, neutral territory]* 尊重[或不侵犯]特权[所有权、中立地带]. ***as ~s*** 关于, 说到. ~ ***oneself*** 自重.

re•spect•a•bil•ity [ris͵pektəˈbiliti] *n.* ①可尊敬, 人格高尚, 品行端正; 威望; 尊严, 体面. ②可尊重的事物; 可尊敬的人; 有身分[名望]的人; 〔谑〕一本正经的人. ③〔*pl.*〕礼仪, 习俗.

re•spect•a•ble [risˈpektəbl] *a.* ①可尊敬的, 可尊重的, 人格高尚的, 品行端正的; 有身分的, 有相当地位的, 有名望的. ②相当大的, 可观的, 不少的(数量等). ③不难看的, 体面的, 大方的, 相当好的. ④(举止、态度等)过分高雅的, 一本正经的, 装腔作势的. *the* ~ 有身分的人们. *a ~ income* 相当大的[不少的]收入. ~ *clothes* 体面的[相当好的]衣服. *a ~ hill* 相当大的小山. *a ~ painter* 相当有名的画家. *a ~ minority* 不小的少数. *He is too ~ for my taste* 那个人太高雅了, 我不喜欢. **-bly** *ad.*

re•spect•ant [risˈpektənt] *a.*【徽】(动物)面对面的; 向后看的.

re•spect•er [risˈpektə] *n.* 尊重者; 势利的人. ***be no ~ of persons*** 对任何人一律看待. (*The law is no ~ of persons.* 法律面前人人平等). ~ ***of persons*** 势利鬼, 趋炎附势的人.

re•spect•ful [risˈpektful] *a.* ①尊重人的, 表示敬意的; 谦恭的, 有礼貌的, 殷勤的. ②〔古〕可尊敬的. ***be ~ of tradition*** 尊重传统. ***be ~ to age*** 尊敬老人. ***keep [stand] at a ~ distance*** 有礼貌地离着一点; 〔喻〕保持一定距离; 敬而远之.

re•spect•ful•ly [risˈpektfuli] *ad.* 恭敬地, 殷勤地. *Yours (very)* ~ = ~ *yours* 谨上, 敬礼〔信末用语〕.

re•spect•ing [risˈpektiŋ] *prep.* 关于…; 由于, 鉴于. *I am at a loss ~ his whereabouts.* 关于他的下落, 我一无所知.

re•spec•tive [risˈpektiv] *a.* 各自的, 各个的, 各有分别的. *A and B contributed the ~ sums of 4d. and 3d.* A和B的捐款分别是四辨士和三辨士. *All men have their ~ duties.* 各人有各人的职责.

re•spec•tive•ly [risˈpektivli] *ad.* 各自, 各别, 分别. *The first and second prizes went to Mary and George ~.* 头奖归玛丽所得, 二奖归乔治所得.

re•spell [ˈriːˈspel] *vt.* 再拼(单词); 以别种形式(尤指按语音系统)另拼(单词).

re•spir•a•ble [ˈrespiərəbl, risˈpaiərəbl] *a.* ①可呼吸的, 适于呼吸的. ②能呼吸的. **-bil•i•ty** *n.*

res•pi•ra•tion [respiˈreiʃən] *n.* 呼吸; 【生理】呼吸作用. *artificial* ~ 人工呼吸.

res•pi•ra•tor [ˈrespəreitə] *n.* ①口罩; 【军】防尘口罩; 防毒面具; 【化】滤毒罐. ②〔美〕人工呼吸装置. *a canister* ~ 防毒面具.

re•spir•a•to•ry [risˈpaiərətəri] *a.* 呼吸(作用)的. ~ *organs* 呼吸器官.

re•spire [risˈpaiə] *vi.* ①呼吸. ②休息; 透一口气. ③〔罕〕生存, 生活. — *vt.* ①呼吸. ②〔罕〕散发(香气等), 表现(情绪等); 悄悄透露(爱情等).

res•pi•rom•e•ter [͵respiˈrɔmitə] *n.* 【医】呼吸(运动)计; **-try** *n.*【医】呼吸(运动)计量(法). **-tric** *a.*

res•pite [ˈrespait; Am. ˈrespit] *n.* ①延期; 【法】缓刑. ②暂停; 休息, 休养; 休息期间. *grand a ~ to a condemned man* 对判刑的人宣布缓刑. ***put in ~*** 延期, 暂缓. ***toil without ~*** 不断地工作. — *vt.* ①延期; 缓期执行(死刑). ②使休息, 使(苦痛等)暂时停止, 使缓和一下. ③【军】停付(军人)薪饷; 停付(薪金).

re•splend•ence, -en•cy [risˈplendəns, -si] *n.* 辉煌, 光辉, 光彩.

re•splend•ent [risˈplendənt] *a.* 辉煌的, 灿烂的. ~ *with jewels* 带着耀眼的宝石. ~ *achievements* 辉煌的成就. ~ *in full uniform* 穿着耀眼的全副盛装.

re•spond [risˈpɔnd] *vi.* ①答, 回答; 响应(to). ②【宗】(会众对牧师)唱和[例行应答]. ③答应(要求等), 应付(敌人等), (对刺激等)感应, 反应. ④【法】承担责任; 〔美〕负责, 赔偿. ⑤〔罕〕符合(希望等). ~ *by a nod* 点头答应. ~ *for the masses* 代表群众致谢辞. ~ *to the cheers of the crowd* 向欢呼的群众挥手致意. ~ *with a left hander*【拳击】用左手回击. ~ *in damages* 赔偿损失. ~ *to the controls* (飞机)好驾驶, 对操纵反应灵敏. ~ *unsoundly to* 对…不起劲. —*vt.* 回答, 响应; 〔美〕应负…的责任, 履行; 〔古〕一致, 符合. ~ *the judgement of the court* 履行法院判决. *His great deeds ~ed his great speeches.* 他的巨大事业体现[符合]了他的豪言壮语. — *n.*【宗】应唱圣歌; 【建】(柱、拱基等的)对称; 壁联.

re•spond•ence, -en•cy [risˈpɔndəns, -si] *n.* ①相应, 适合, 符合. ②作答; 回答; 反应, 响应.

re•spond•ent [risˈpɔndənt] *a.* ①回答的; 有反应的, 响应的, 感应的. ②【法】被告的. ③〔古〕符合的. — *n.* ①回答者; 答辩者; 提案辩护者. ②【法】(特指离婚诉讼的)被告. ③【生理】(对外来刺激的)反应, 反射. *The knee jerk is a typical ~* 膝反射是一种典型反射.

res•pon•den•tia [͵responˈdenʃiə] *n.* 船货抵押借款; 冒险借款.

re•spond•er [riˈspɔndə] *n.* ①响应者, 回答者. ②【电】应答机.

re•sponse [riˈspɔns] *n.* ①回答, 答复. ②【宗】应唱圣歌. ③(因刺激等引起的)感应, 反应, 反响; 应验; 【物】响应; 【无】灵敏度, 感扰性; 特性曲线. *His oratorical efforts evoked no ~ in his audience.* 他的雄辩在听众中不起反响. ***call forth no ~ in sb.'s breast*** 在某人心中不起反应. ***in ~ to*** 应…而, 答…而. ***make no ~*** 不回答.

re•spon•si•bil•i•ty [ri͵spɔnsəˈbiliti] *n.* ①责任; 责任心; 职责, 义务 *(of; for)*; 负担. ②〔美〕义务履行能力, 偿付能力. ③【无】响应性[度]. *The person with overall ~ in the locality* 一个地区的总负责人. ***be relieved of one's ~ [responsibilities]*** (被)解除责任. ***decline all ~ for*** 声明对…不负任何责任. ***lack of ~*** 无人负责现象. ***on one's own ~*** 自作主张地. ***take [assume] the ~ of [for]*** 负起…的责任. ***take the ~ upon oneself*** 自己承担起责任来.

re•spon•si•ble [riˈspɔnsəbl] *a.* ①有责任的, 应负责任的 *(to sb.; for a thing)*. ②能负责的, 可靠的; 懂道理的, 明白是非的. ③责任重的(地位等). *have a ~ position* 担任要职. ~ *government* 责任政府制. *I am not ~ to you for my actions* 我的行为我没有向你说明的义务. *a ~ face* 一本正经的面孔. ***hold sb. ~ for*** 使某人负担…的责任. ***make oneself ~ for*** 负起…的责任. ~ ***for*** 为…负责; 是造成…的原因. **-bly** *ad.*

re•spon•sion [risˈpɔnʃən] *n.* ①〔*pl.*〕〔英〕(牛津大学) B.A. 学位初试〔俗称 smalls〕. ②大学的公开讨论会. ③〔罕〕回答.

re•spon•sive [risˈpɔnsiv] *a.* 回答的; 表示回答的; 反应迅速的, 易反应的, 共鸣的, 敏感的; 唱应答歌的. *a ~ glance* 带有回答意义的一瞥. **-ly** *ad.* **-ness** *n.*

re·spon·so·ry [ris'pɔnsəri] *n.* 【宗】应答歌.

res·pu·bli·ca [res'pʌblikə,-'pu:bli:-]〔L.〕*n.* 国家,联邦,共和国.

res·sen·ti·ment [rə,sɑ̃ti'mɑ̃] *n.* 【社】(阶级、阶层、或集团间的)仇恨,憎恶.

rest[1] [rest] *n.* ①休息,休养;【军】稍息. ②停止,静止;安静,安稳;安心. ③睡眠;长眠,死. ④休息处,安歇处,住处;床. ⑤台,架,托,支柱;(枪炮的)瞄准台. ⑥停顿;【乐】休止;休止符. *the day of* ~ 休息日;假日;星期日;【宗】安息日. *a good night's* ~ 一夜的充分休息;一晚好睡. *a tripod* ~ 三脚架. *an eighth* ~ 八分休止符. ***at*** ~ 静止的,安宁的,心情安定的;长眠,死;解决了的,不必再谈的 (*a volcano at* ~ 静止的火山). ***bring a machine to*** ~ 停止机器. ***go to one's*** ~ 永眠,死. ***go to*** ~ 去睡;去休息. ***lay to*** ~ 安葬;完全消除;完全解决. ***put at*** ~ 使安心;使休息;予以解决. ***retire to*** ~ 去睡;去休息. ***set at*** ~ = put at ~. ***set sb.'s mind at*** ~ 安定人心,使安心. ***set up one's*** ~ 居住,定居. ***take a*** ~ 休息一下. ***take (one's)*** ~ 休息,睡觉,就寝. — *vi.* ①休息,歇息;静止,停止;〔美〕【法】停止举证. ②躺,靠 *(on; upon; against)*. ③搁在,安置在(台上等);根据,以…为基础 *(on; upon)*. ④睡;长眠,死. ⑤信赖;安心,满足(于某事) *(on; upon)*. ⑥(成功、决定)系于,在于,在…的权限内 *(with)*. ⑦归于. *I* ~*ed well.* 我睡得好. *I am* ~*ed and refreshed.* 我精神恢复了. *I cannot* ~ *under an imputation.* 我不能甘受诬陷. *Science* ~*s on phenomena.* 科学以现象为根据. *The matter cannot* ~ *here.* 这个事情不能就此搁置不管. ~ ***in oneself*** 依靠[信赖]自己. ~ ***in peace*** 安静永眠. ~ ***in pieces*** 〔美〕炸死. ~ ***on [upon]*** 被支持在…上,搁在…上,以…为基础;依靠,信任;(目光等)停留在…上,落在…上. ~ ***on one's arms*** 枕戈待旦,警惕着. ~ ***on one's oars*** (停划)靠着桨暂时休息;喘一口气,休息一下. ~ ***on [in] sb.'s promise*** 相信[指望]某人的诺言. ~ ***with*** 取决于,属于…的权限. (*The decision* ~*s with you* = *It* ~*s with you to decide.* 决定在你. *The honours* ~*ed with him.* 荣誉归他.)— *vt.* ①使休息,使歇息,(使)休养;使轻松;使恢复精神;使平静;【军】使稍息. ②安放,搁置;把…靠在 *(on; against)*. ③〔美〕【法】对…停止举证. ~ *the ladder against the wall* 把梯子靠在墙上. ~ ***oneself*** 休养. ~ ***the [sb.'s] case*** 〔美〕对某人某案停止举证. ~ **cure** 【医】(特指精神病的)卧床疗养法. ~ **day** 休息日;假日;〔军〕星期日;【宗】安息日. ~ **energy**【物】静能. ~ **house** 客栈;休养所;〔美俚〕监狱. ~ **mass**【物】静质量. ~ **period**【生】休眠期. ~ **room** (车站、戏院的)休息室;〔美〕厕所. **-ful** *a.* 平静的,安静的,悠闲的.

rest[2] [rest] *n.* ①〔the ~〕其余,其他,残余部分. ②〔the ~〕〔作复数处理〕残留的人;其余的人[物]. ③〔英〕【银行】〔the ~〕公积金,准备金. ④【网球】连续回击(时间). *You know the* ~ = *The* ~ *needs no telling.* 其余不必再说. ***among the*** ~ 其中;尤其 (*myself among the* ~ 我也是其中之一). ***and (all) the*** ~ ***(of it)*** 其他一切,等等. ***as to the*** ~ 至于其余各点[其他方面]. ***for the*** ~ 其后,至于其余 (*for the* ~ *of one's life* 今后一辈子. *for the* ~ *of the day* 在这天的其余时间). — *vi.* 〔与表语连用〕依然是,仍旧是;保持;〔古〕留下. *The mistakes* ~ *uncorrected.* 错误仍旧没有更正. ~ ***assured*** 请放心 (*R- [You may* ~*] assured that I will do my best* 请放心,我一定尽力.) ~ ***satisfied [content]*** 满意[心满意足].

re·stamp [ri:'stæmp] *vt.* 另[重新]盖印;另贴邮票.

re·start [ri:'stɑ:t] *vt., vi.* 重新开始.

re·state ['ri:'steit] *vt.* 重申;再声明;重新陈述. **-ment** *n.*

res·tau·rant ['restərɔ̃:ŋ, 'restərɔnt] *n.* 餐馆;(大旅馆等的)餐厅. *a* ~ *car* 餐车.

res·tau·ra·teur ['restɔ(:)rə'tə:] *n.* 〔F.〕餐馆老板.

rest·har·row ['resthærəu] *n.* 【植】芒柄花(属).

res·ti·form ['resti,fɔ:m] *a.* 【解】索状的.

rest·ing ['restiŋ] *a.* ①不动的,静止的;沉默的. ②【植】休眠的,静止的. ③【生理】静止的,不积极分裂的. ~ **place** ['restiŋpleis] *n.* ①休息所[室]. ②坟墓. ③【建】= landing. *the last* ~ 坟墓.

res·ti·tute ['restitju:t] *vt., vi.* ①赔偿(损失等);归还(夺去物等). ②〔罕〕恢复,复旧.

res·ti·tu·tion [,resti'tju:ʃən] *n.* ①赔偿;归还;复职. ②恢复;【物】(因弹性体的)复原;【化】复原取代(作用). ③【法】要求恢复原状的诉讼. ***make*** ~ 赔偿损失,归还. ~ **nucleus** 再组核. ~ **of conjugal rights**【法】夫妇同居权的恢复. ~ **suit**【法】恢复夫妇同居权的诉讼.

res·tive ['restiv] *a.* 烈性的(马);难驾驭的;不听话的. *a* ~ *person* 倔强的人. **-ly** *ad.* **-ness** *n.*

rest·less ['restlis] *a.* 不安定的,坐卧不宁的;动作不停的;得不到休息的,不休息的;不睡的. *a* ~ *heart* 烦乱不宁的心. *a* ~ *child* 不肯安静的孩子. *a man of* ~ *energy* 精力充沛[不停活动]的人. ~ *waves* 动荡不停的波浪. ~ **cavy** (拉丁美洲)野豚鼠. **-ly** *ad.*

re·stock ['ri:'stɔk] *vt.* 使重新进货;再储存.

re·stor·a·ble [ris'tɔ:rəbl] *a.* 可恢复原状的,可复原的;可再兴的;可归还的.

res·to·ra·tion [,restə'reiʃən] *n.* ①(领土等的)恢复,光复;复位,复职;复旧,复古;复兴;归还. ②【建】修复,照原样修复的建筑物;(受损美术品等的)修复,修补;(古动物的)再造,复原. ③复辟;〔the R-〕(英国 1660 年查理二世的,法国大革命后布尔蓬王朝的)复辟;(日本的)明治维新. *the* ~ *of peace [health]* 和平[健康]的恢复. *the* ~ *of a picture* 画的修复.

re·stor·a·tive [ris'tɔ:rətiv] *a.* 复原的;复兴的;恢复健康[元气]的;滋补的. — *n.* 恢复剂,补药;补品. **-ly** *ad.* **-ness** *n.*

re·store [ris'tɔ:] *vt.* ①拿回原处,恢复原状;复旧;恢复;复活,复兴,再兴(制度、习惯等);使复位,使复职,使复辟. ②归还. ③修理,修补,重建,修复;再造,复原(古生物);补正,校补(书籍中的缺失文字等). ④使恢复健康[元气],使恢复意识. ~ *order* 恢复秩序. ~ *to its owner* (把拾物等)归还原主. ~ *sb. to life* 使人苏醒过来. *be* ~*d out of all recognition* 修复得一点也认不出.

re·stor·er [ris'tɔ:rə] *n.* 复原者;修补者;修建者;【无】恢复设备;复位器. *a hair* ~ 生发药. *tired nature's sweet* ~ 睡眠.

re·strain [ris'trein] *vt.* ①压抑,抑制. ②制止,防止,禁止. ③拘束,束缚;羁押,监禁. ④限定,限制. *She* ~*ed tears with difficulty.* 她好容易才忍住了眼泪. ~ *sb. from interference* 制止某人干涉. ~ *sb. of his liberty* 剥夺某人自由,束缚某人自由. ~ *oneself* 自制;克己,忍耐. **-er** *n.* 抑制者;【化】抑制剂.

re·strain·a·ble [ris'trenəbl] *a.* 可抑制的,可遏制的,可制止的.

re·strain·ed [ris'treind] *a.* 受限制的;受约束的;克制的,谨严的;忍耐的,拘束的. **-ly** [-li] *ad.*

re·straint [ri'streint] *n.* ①(活动等的)克制,抑制,制止;禁止. ②拘束,束缚,桎梏;拘束力,牵制力;羁押,监禁. ③自制;拘泥;(表现、记述的)严谨. ④限制. ***be beyond*** ~ 不能抑制. ***be held in*** ~ 受监禁. ***be under*** ~ (尤指精神病人)被拘禁中. ***free from*** ~ 无束缚的,自由的. ***in*** ~ ***of*** 以便制止. ***keep under*** ~ 抑制,束缚. ***place under*** ~ 监禁. ***put under*** ~ 拘禁,送进疯人院. ~ ***of princes***【海上保险】出港[入港]的禁止. ***with*** ~ 用克制态度. ***without*** ~ 无拘束地,自由地;放纵地,肆无忌惮地.

re·strict [ris'trikt] *vt.* 限制,限定 *(to; within; in)*;制止,禁止. *I am* ~*ed by time.* 我受时间限制. *I am* ~*ed to advising.* 我只限于劝导. **-ed** *a.* 有限制的,范围狭窄的;〔美军〕一般保密的 (*It has a very* ~*ed application.*

它的应用范围很窄. *a ~ed area* 禁止通行地区;〔美军〕闲人止步(地区). *~ed materials* (内部)参考资料). **-ed-ly** *ad.*

re·stric·tion [risˈtrikʃən] *n.* ①限制,限定. ②拘束,束缚;自制. ③【逻】限定. *impose [lay down, place, put] ~s on* 加以限制. *remove [withdraw] ~s* 取消限制. *without ~s* 无限制地.

re·stric·tion·ism [riˈstrikʃənizm] *n.* 限制主义〔如限制贸易的政策,限制移民的政策等〕. **-ist** *n., a.*

re·stric·tive [risˈtriktiv] *a.* 限制的;限定的,特定的.— *n.*【语法】限制性词语. **-ly** *ad.* **-ness** *n.*

re·struc·ture [riˈstrʌktʃə] *vt.* *(-tured; -tur·ing)* 重新组织,调整,改组.

re·stud·y [ˈriːstʌdi] *vt., n.* 再学习; 重新学习; 重新估计;重新研究.

re·stuff [ˈriːˈstʌf] *vt.* 再充填,重新填塞.

re·sult [riˈzʌlt] *n.* ①结果,效果,效验,成效;成绩;〔*pl.*〕【体】比分. ②【数】计算的结果,答案. ③〔美〕(立法机构等的)决议,决定. *to lead to good ~s* 引出好的结果. *The ~ was that ...,* 结果是…. ***as a ~ of*** 作为…的结果. ***bring about [yield] good ~s*** 得到好结果[好成绩]. ***give out the ~s*** 发表成绩. ***in the ~*** 结果. ***meet with good ~s*** 取得好结果. ***without ~*** 无效地,毫无结果地. — *vi.* ①结果为 *(in)*, 由…而造成[产生] *(from)*. ②归结为, 导致 *(in)*. *Love ~s in marriage.* 恋爱终归于结婚. *Nothing has ~ed from my efforts.* 我的努力毫无结果. *~ in (failure)* 终于(失败).

re·sult·ant [riˈzʌltənt] *a.* ①〔尤指由若干相反力量所造成〕作为最后结果的; 作为后果而产生的. ②【物】组合的,合成的. — *n.* ①结果;后果. ②合力,合成力;合成[运动];【物】合量;组合;【化】生成物,(反应)产物;【数】结式;消元式.

re·sult·ful [riˈzʌltful] *a.* 有结果的,有效果[效验]的,有效的.

re·sult·less [riˈzʌltlis] *a.* 无结果的, 无效果[效验]的,无益的.

re·sum·a·ble [riˈzjuːməbl] *a.* 能恢复的;能取回的;能再开始的.

re·sume [riˈzjuːm] *vt.* ①拿回,取回,收回(给人的东西等);恢复(自由等); 重占(场所等);再穿用(衣服等);再开始用(烟管等). ②重新开始(已停的事),继续(中断的谈话等). ③扼要说,摘要叙述.④重新获得工作*(work)*,复职 *(office)*,收复失地 *(lost territory)*.*~ a pipe*(把烟斗再点着)又抽起烟斗来了. *The House ~d work.* 议会(休会后)又开会了. ***~ one's seat*** 回位,回到原座,归席.***~ one's spirits*** 恢复精神. ***~ the thread of one's discourse*** 言归正传,回到谈话的本题. — *vi.* 重新开始;再讲,继续讲;扼要讲. *Let us ~ where we left off.* 让我们回头来再接下去讲. *Well, to ~* 好,接下去讲.

ré·su·mé [ˈrezju(ː)mei] *n.* 〔F.〕 摘要, 梗概;(求职时等所写的)个人简历.

re·sum·mon [ˈriːˈsʌmən] *vt.* 再[重新]召集;【法】再传唤. **-s** *n.* 再召集;【法】再传唤.

re·sump·tion [riˈzʌmpʃən] *n.* ①取回,收回;再占领. ②再开始,继续;再使用. ③〔罕〕摘要,概要.

re·sump·tive [riˈzʌmptiv] *a.* ①恢复的, 取回的, 收回的; 恢复精神的. ②再开始的. ③摘要的. — *n.*〔古〕补药. **-ly** *ad.*

re·su·pi·nate [riˈsjuːpineit] *a.*【植】(叶等)翻转的,颠倒的;仰卧的;【古生】双曲形. **-na·tion** *n.*

re·su·pine [ˌrisjuˈpain, -su-] *a.* 仰卧的.

re·sur·face [riˈsəːfis] *vt.* *(-faced; -fac·ing)* 重换新面,铺新路面. — *vi.* 重新露面,(潜艇)重新露出水面.

re·surge [riˈsəːdʒ] *vi.* 再起;复活,苏醒.

re·sur·gent [riˈsəːdʒənt] *a., n.* 复活的[者];复兴(的). **-gence** *n.* 复活.

res·ur·rect [reˌzəˈrekt] *vt.* 使复活; 复兴;〔口〕掘墓偷(尸),偷挖(尸体). — *vi.* 复活.

res·ur·rec·tion [ˌrezəˈrekʃən] *n.* ①〔the R-〕【宗】耶稣的复活; (最后审判日的)人类的复活〔又叫 general ~〕. ②复活;复兴;再起,恢复,再用,再流行. ③〔口〕掘墓偷尸,发掘尸体. *~ man* (掘墓)盗尸者. *~ pie*〔英俚〕用剩菜做的馅饼. **-al** *a.* 复活的; 耶稣复活的;复活节的. **-ism** *n.* (为解剖而)掘墓盗尸. **-ist** 偷尸人.

re·sur·vey [ˈriːsə(ː)ˈvei] *vt.* 再[重新]测量,再勘查;复查;再看一遍. — [ˈriːˈsəːvei] *n.* 再测量; 再勘查;复查.

re·sus·ci·tate [riˈsʌsiteit] *vi., vt.* (使)复活;(使)复兴;(使)恢复精力.

re·sus·ci·ta·tion [riˌsʌsiˈteiʃən] *n.* 复活, 回生; 复兴,再兴. **-ta·tive** *a.*

re·sus·ci·ta·tor [riˈsʌsiˌteitə] *n.* 使苏醒(或复活)的人[物];〔尤指〕【医】复苏器.

ret [ret] *vt., vi.* ***(ret·ted*** [ˈretid], ***ret·ting*** [ˈretiŋ]***)*** 沤(麻、肥料等);受潮湿腐烂. *flax ~ting* 亚麻浸洗[脱胶].

ret. = ①retired. ②returned.

re·ta·ble [riˈteibl] *n.* 祭坛后部的高架〔供放十字架、灯、装饰品等〕.

re·tail [ˈriːteil, riːˈteil] *n., a.* 零售(的). *a ~ dealer* 零售商人. *a ~ shop* 零售店. *~ trade* 零售业. *the ~ sales department* 零售营业部. ***at [by] ~*** 零卖. — *ad.* 零卖. *He buys wholesale and sells ~.* 他整买零卖. — [riːˈteil] *vi.* 零售,零卖. — *vt.* ①零售,零卖. ②传播,转述,到处宣扬(丑事、新闻等).

re·tail·er [riːˈteilə] *n.* ①零售店, 零售商. ②到处散布闲话的人.

re·tain [riˈtein] *vt.* ①保留;保持;保有;维持. ②留住;挡住. ③记住. ④雇用,聘用(律师等). *~ an appearance of youth* 保有年青的外貌. *~ one's presence of mind* 镇定自若. *~ed object*【语法】保留宾语〔如: He was given a book 中的 book, 和 A book was given him 中的 him〕. *~ing fee* 预约辩护费. *~ing force*【军】牵制队. *~ing wall* (防止沙土崩溃的)护堤壁,撑壁. *~-ing works* 拦水工程;蓄水工程. **-able** *a.* 能保持[保有,留住].

re·tain·er [riˈteinə] *n.* ①【史】(诸侯等的)家臣,侍从,随从;门客. ②随军商人(等). ③保持者;保留者. ④保留物;保留权;预约辩护费;律师的预聘. ⑤【机】承盘;导圈,护圈;挡板;(滚动轴承的)保持架. ***become ~ of*** 投靠.

re·take [ˈriːˈteik] *vt.* *(-took; -taken)* 再取;重新拿起;夺回,抢回,克服;【摄】再摄影,改拍,重拍,补摄. — *n.*【摄】改拍,重拍;补摄;重拍的场面.

re·tal·i·ate [riˈtælieit] *vi.* (向某人)报复 *(upon, against)*;为某事进行反击;倒算 *(for)*. — *vt.* 征收报复关税.

re·tal·i·a·tion [riˌtæliˈeiʃən] *n.* 报复;反击;倒算.

re·tal·i·a·tive, re·tal·i·a·to·ry [riˈtæliətiv, -lieitəri] *a.* 报复(性)的.

re·tard [riˈtɑːd] *vt.* 弄慢,延缓,延迟,使停滞;推迟;使耽误,妨碍,阻止;【物、工】减速. *Lack of science and education ~s social progress.* 缺乏科学和教育会妨碍社会进步. — *vi.* (潮水涨退等)迟延;耽误;迟到. — *n.* 迟延,迟滞,耽误;妨碍,阻止. ***in ~*** 迟延,耽阁,阻碍. ***keep at ~*** 使迟延,耽误,阻碍,妨碍发达[进步].

re·tard·ant [riˈtɑːdnt] *n.* 阻止物,迟延物〔指化学上的抑止剂〕. — *a.* (使)延迟的.

re·tar·date [riˈtɑːdeit] *n.* 智力发展迟于正常的人[儿童],智力迟钝者.

re·tar·da·tion [ˌriːtɑːˈdeiʃən] *n.* 迟延, 推迟, 迟滞;阻碍;迟延程度, 妨碍量;【物】减速度; 妨碍物;【心】发育迟缓;迟钝.

re·tard·a·tive, re·tard·a·to·ry [riˈtɑːdətiv, -təri] *a.* 减速的,使迟延的,阻碍的.

re·tard·ed [riˈtɑːdid] *a.* 发展迟缓的〔尤指智力迟钝的〕.

re·tard·er [riˈtɑːdə] *n.* 延迟者[器];【化】延迟剂,阻滞剂.

retch [riːtʃ, retʃ] *vi.* 作呕,发恶心,干呕. — *vt.* 呕吐. — *n.* 恶心;要呕时的声音.

retd; retd. = ①retained. ②returned.

re·te [ˈriːtiː] *n. (pl. -ti·a* [-iə]*)*【解】网,膜层.

re·tell [ˈriːˈtel] *vt. (-told* [-ˈtəuld]*)* 再讲,重讲,重述;重数;(用不同方式)复述.

re·tene [ˈriːtiːn, ˈretiːn] *n.*【化】惹烯,1—甲—7—异丙基菲.

re·ten·tion [riˈtenʃən] *n.* ①保留,保持,(意见等的)保留. ②保持力,记忆力;保留物. ③〔古〕拘押,监禁,扣留. ④【医】分泌闭止,停滞;闭尿;固位. ⑤【保险】保有额. ~ *of snow* 积雪. *the seizure and* ~ *of power* 权力[政权]的夺取和保持.

re·ten·tive [riˈtentiv] *a.*①保持(热等)的,(对…)有保持力的*(of)*;保持湿气的,易潮湿的.②记性好的,记忆力强的. ③【医】固位的. *a* ~ *faculty* 记忆力. *a* ~ *memory* 好记性.

re·ten·tiv·i·ty [ˌriːtenˈtiviti] *n.* ①保持力. ②【物】顽磁性.

re·ten·ue [rətəˈnuː; F. retny] *n.*【法】克制,节制;谨慎.

re·think [riˈθiŋk] *vt. (-thought* [-ˈθɔːt]; *think·ing* [-ˈθiŋkiŋ]*)* 再思考,重新考虑.

re·ti·a [ˈriːʃiə] rete 的复数.

re·ti·a·ri·us [riʃiˈɛəriəs] *n. (pl. -ri·i* [-ˌai]*)* (古罗马持三叉戟和网的)角斗士.

re·ti·a·ry [ˈriːʃ*i*əri] *n.* ①结网蜘蛛. ②(古罗马)持三叉戟带网角斗士. —*a.* 网(状)的;结网的;以网为武器的;巧于纠缠的.

ret·i·cence, ret·i·cency [ˈretisəns, -si] *n.* 沉默,缄默;寡言;含蓄;保留.

ret·i·cent [ˈretisənt] *a.* 沉默的;爱缄默的;有保留的,含蓄的 *(of, about, on)*. *be* ~ *about [on] the matter* 对该问题保持沉默. *be* ~ *of one's opinion* 有保留意见. **-ly** *ad.*

ret·i·cle [ˈretikl] *n.*【光】(光学仪器上的)分划板,标线片;标线,十字线.

ret·i·cul *comb.f.* 网,小网: *reticular*.

re·tic·u·la [riˈtikjuələ] reticulum 的复数.

re·tic·u·lar [riˈtikjulə] *a.* ①网状的. ②【生】网状结缔[组织]的. ③复杂的,错综的,交错的. **-ly** *ad.*

re·tic·u·late [riˈtikjulit] *a.* 网状的. — [-leit] *vt., vi.* (使)成网状.

re·tic·u·la·tion [riˌtikjuˈleiʃən] *n.* 网状,格子状;网状物,网状组织;(绘画等的)方眼复写法.

ret·i·cule [ˈretikjuːl] *n.* ①(女用)网状手提包. ②【光】(光学仪器上的)十字线,标线片 (= reticle).

re·tic·u·lo·cyte [riˈtikjuləuˌsait] *n.*【解】网织红血球,网状细胞. **-cy·tic** [-ˈsitik] *a.*

re·tic·u·lo·en·do·the·li·al [ritikjuləuˌendəuˈθiːliəl] *a.*【解】网状内皮组织的.

re·tic·u·lose [riˈtikjuləus] *a.* (= reticulate *a.*)

re·tic·u·lum [riˈtikjuləm] *n. (pl. re·tic·u·la* [-lə]*)* ①网状物,网状构造[组织]. ②(反刍动物的)蜂巢胃. ③〔R-〕【天】网罟座.

re·ti·form [ˈriːtifɔːm] *a.* 网状的;有交叉线的.

ret·i·na [ˈretinə] *n. (pl.* ~*s, -nae* [-niː]*)*【解】视网膜. **-l** *a.*

ret·i·nac·u·lum [ˌretiˈnækjuləm] *n. (pl. -u·la* [-lə]*)*【生】支持带. **-u·lar** [-lə] *a.*

ret·ine [ˈretiːn] *n.*【生化】抑制碱〔抑制体内细胞生长的物质〕.

ret·in·ene [ˈretiniːn] *n.*【生化】视黄素,视黄醛.

ret·i·ni·tis [ˌretiˈnaitis] *n.*【医】视网膜炎.

ret·i·nos·co·py [ˌretiˈnɔskəpi] *n.* 爱克斯线透视检查法;视网膜镜检法 (=skiascopy). **-scop·ic** [-ˈskɔːpik] *a.*

ret·i·nue [ˈretinjuː] *n.* 〔集合词〕随员,扈从.

ret·i·nu·la [riˈtinjulə] *n. (pl. ret·i·nu·lae* [-liː]*)* (昆虫复眼的)小网膜.

re·tire [riˈtaiə] *vi.* ①后退,退却;(部队等主动)撤退;退去,离开. ②退隐,退休,退职,退役,告退. ③就寝,去睡觉. ④(浪等)向后退,(海岸等)缩进. *He* ~*d from office in disgrace.* 他受处分撤职. ~ ***for the night*** 上床去睡,就寝. ~ ***from the service*** 辞职;退役. ~ ***from the world*** 退隐;出家,做和尚. ~ ***in disorder*** 溃退. ~ ***in good order*** 秩序良好地退却. ~ ***into oneself*** 不和人交际,退隐;沉默. ~ ***on a pension*** 领退休金退休. ~ ***to bed [to rest]*** 去就寝. ~ ***under the age clause*** 因年老退休. — *vt.* ①【军】(令)撤退. ②收回(纸币等). ③使退职,使告退. — *n.* 退隐;〔罕〕退隐所;【军】退兵信号. *sound the [a]* ~ 吹退兵号.

re·tired [riˈtaiəd] *a.* ①告退的,退职的,退休的,退役的;歇了业的. ②退隐的;与世隔绝的. ③秘密的;僻远的;幽静的. *a* ~ *general* 退职将军. *the* ~ *list* 退伍军官[退职人员]名册. ~ *pay* = *a* ~ *allowance* 退休金,退职金. *a* ~ *life* 退隐生活. *a* ~ *valley* 幽谷. ***go on the*** ~ ***list*** 退休,退职,退役. ***place [put] on the*** ~ ***list*** 使退职,使退役. **-ness** *n.*

re·tir·ee [riˌtaiəˈriː] *n.* 退休者,退职者 (= retirant).

re·tire·ment [riˈtaiəmənt] *n.* ①退休,退职,退役. ②退却 *(from)*. ③退休[隐]处;幽静地方,偏僻地方. ④(通货等的)收回. *live in* ~ 过退休生活. ~ **pay** 退休金,退役补贴.

re·tir·ing [riˈtaiəriŋ] *a.* 退休的,退职的;不爱交际的,谦让的;退却的. ~ *pension* 退休金;养老金. *a* ~ *room.* 休息室,〔尤指〕厕所. ~ *board*【军】退役调查委员会. **-ly** *ad.*

re·told [riːˈtəuld] retell 的过去式及过去分词.

re·took [ˈriːˈtuk] retake 的过去式.

re·tool [ˈriːˈtuːl] *vt., vi.* ①改进[更换较好的]工具,在机器上作改进〔以适应新产品的生产〕. ②(为适应新形势)重新组织.

re·tor·sion [riˈtɔːʃən] *n.*【国际法】报复,反斥,回报〔尤指国际法中受害国对侵害国的报复〕.

re·tort[1] [riˈtɔːt] *vt.* ①回嘴,反责. ②反驳;照样报复. *He* ~*ed the invectives [sarcasm] on her.* 他用恶言还击她. ~ *blow for blow* 以牙还牙. — *vi.* 反击,回嘴,反驳 *(on, upon, against) She* ~*ed upon him, saying he was to blame.* 她反驳他,说他不好. — *n.* 回嘴,反责;(议论的)反攻,反驳;报复. *quick at* ~ 善于回嘴的.

re·tort[2] [riˈtɔːt] *n.*【化】干馏釜,甑,杀菌釜.

re·tor·tion [riˈtɔːʃən] *n.* ①扭转,拧转. ②【国际法】= retorsion.

re·touch [ˈriːˈtʌtʃ] *vt., n.* ①再碰[接]触. ②润色,修饰,修改(文章,绘画等). ③【摄,印】修描(底片,照片,照相版等).

re·trace [riˈtreis] *vt.* ①折回,折返,退回. ②探源,调查追溯. ③回想,回忆;回顾,回头看,重看. ④重新再描摹. ~ *one's steps* 折回;重做. ~ *a book* 再重头阅读,再回到前面某处重新阅读. ~ *one's steps [ways]* 顺原路返回.

re·tract[1] [riˈtrækt] *vt.* 缩进. *A cat* ~*s its claws.* 猫缩进它的爪子. ~ *one's tongue* 缩进舌头.

re·tract[2] [riˈtrækt] *vt.* 取消;撤消,撤回,收回(命令、前言等). — *vi.* 取消前言,食言,撤回. ~ *from an engagement* 取消约会.

re·tract·a·ble [riˈtræktəbl] *a.* ①能缩进的;伸缩自如的. ②可取消的,可撤回的. *a* ~ *landing wheel [gear]*【空】伸缩起落轮[架].

re·trac·ta·tion [ˌriːtrækˈteiʃən] *n.* ①(意见等的)取消,撤回. ②缩进;缩回. ③【拓】保核收缩.

re·trac·tile [riˈtræktail] *a.* (爪等的)伸缩自如的;能缩进的.

re·trac·til·i·ty [riːtrækˈtiliti] *n.* 伸缩性；可缩进性．

re·trac·tion [riˈtrækʃən] *n.* ①(爪等的)缩进 *(opp.* protrusion*)*．②缩回；取消，撤回．

re·trac·tive [riˈtræktiv] *a.* (能)缩进的．

re·trac·tor [riˈtræktə] *n.* ①取消前言者，食言者．②【解】牵缩肌；【外】牵开器，牵开绷带．③(枪炮的)抽筒器，抽(弹)壳．

re·tread [ˈriːˈtred] *vt.*【汽车】翻新修补，热补(轮胎)．— *n.* ①热补过的轮胎．②〔美俚〕再服兵役者．*a ~ing plant* 轮胎修补厂．

re-tread [ˈriːtred] ***(re·trod*** [ˈriːˈtrɔd]***; re·trod·den*** [ˈriːˈtrɔdn], ***re·trod)*** *vt.* 再踏上；重走，再走上(路途)，走回头路．

re·treat [riˈtriːt] *n.* ①退却；退兵；退却信号，(日没时的)回营号〔鼓〕．②隐退；隐退处，躲藏处，避难处；(兽、盗贼等的)潜伏处，巢窟．③(醉汉、疯子等的)收容所．④【宗】静修；默想．⑤【空】(翼等的)向后倾斜．*He lives in a quiet ~.* 他住在一个幽静的地方．*a mountain ~* 山庄．*a summer ~* 避暑地．***beat a ~*** 发出收兵的信号；撤退，退却，放弃不干，打退堂鼓．***be in full ~*** 总退却，全线溃败．***be beyond ~*** 没有后退的可能．***blow [sound] the [a] ~*** 吹退却号，下令退却．***cover the ~*** 掩护退却．***cut off the ~*** 截断退路．***go into ~*** 到修道院里静修(一个时期)．***make a ~*** 撤退．***make good one's ~*** 安全撤退；顺利地脱身．— *vi.* ①后退，退却，撤退．②隐退．③退缩；(眼睛等)凹进．④撤回，撤销，作罢，放弃．⑤【空】向后倾斜．*~ before the enemy* 被迫撤退．— *vt.* 使退回，缩回(象棋的棋子等)．

re·treat·ism [riˈtriːtizəm] *n.* 退却主义，逃跑主义．

re·tree [riˈtriː] *n.* 次品纸张〔在包装外面英国标有XX，美国标有R记号〕．

re·trench [riˈtrentʃ] *vt.* ①节省，减省；削减，缩减，减少(经费等)；删除，省略(字句等)；截去，割去，修剪．②【筑城】设内郭，筑内墙．— *vi.* 俭约，节省．**-ment** *n.* ①节约，缩减，紧缩；删除，省略．②【筑城】内郭，内墙；内线防御工事．

re·tri·al [ˈriːˈtraiəl] *n.* ①【法】再审；复审．②再实验；再试验；重新实验〔试验〕．

re·tri·bu·tion [ˌretriˈbjuːʃən] *n.* 报复；惩罚；报应；果报；报酬，报答．*the day of ~* 最后的审判日；报应到来的时候．

re·trib·u·tive, re·trib·u·to·ry [riˈtribjutiv, -təri] *a.* 报应的；报复的；惩罚的．**-tive·ly** *ad.*

re·triev·al [riˈtriːvəl] *n.* (可)取回，(可)恢复，(可)挽回；(可)修补，(可)修正，(可)更正；(可)弥补，(可)补偿．*beyond ~* 不能补救的，不能挽回的．

re·trieve [riˈtriːv] *vt.* ①取回，恢复，挽回(失物、名誉等)．②补偿，弥补(损失等)；更正(错误等)．③(从灾难中等)救出，拯救 *(from)*．④想起(忘记的事情)．⑤(猎狗将猎获物)找回；拉回(钓鱼线)．*~ freedom* 恢复自由．*~ one's character* 恢复名誉．*~ an error* 更正错误．— *vi.* (猎狗)找回猎获物；拉回钓鱼线，恢复；精神恢复．— *n.* 恢复，挽回．*beyond [past] ~* 无可挽回地，无法补救地．**-ment** *n.* = retrieval. **-vable** *a.*

re·triev·er [riˈtriːvə] *n.* 恢复者；重新得到者；衔回猎物的犬．

retro- *pref.* 向后，倒退，追溯：*retro*gress, *retro*rocket.

ret·ro·act [ˌretrəuˈækt] *vi.* ①逆动；反作用．②【法】追溯(既往)，有追溯效力．

ret·ro·ac·tion [ˌretrəuˈækʃən] *n.* ①逆动；反作用．②【法】追溯效力．③【化】逆反应．

ret·ro·ac·tive [ˌretrəuˈæktiv] *a.* ①逆动的；反作用的．②【法】追溯既往的，有追溯力的．③补发增加工资的．*a ~ law* 有追溯力的法律．**-tiv·i·ty** [-ˈtiviti] *n.* **-ly** *ad.*

ret·ro·cede[1] [ˌretrəuˈsiːd] *vt.* 交还，退还．

ret·ro·cede[2] [ˌretrəuˈsiːd] *vi.* ①后退，退却．②【医】(疾病)内攻；(器官)内移．

ret·ro·ces·sion [ˌretrəuˈseʃən] *n.* ①交还；后退．②【医】(疾病)内攻；(器官等)内移．③【保险】再再保险，三重保险．

ret·ro·choir [ˈretrəukwaiə] *n.* (大教堂的)祭坛后面的地方；圣歌队席位的后面．

ret·ro·cog·ni·tion [ˌretrəukɔgniʃən] *n.* (超过常态感知能力的)异常回溯性知觉．

re·trod·den [ˈriːˈtrɔdn] retread 的过去分词．

re·trode [ˈriˈtrɔd] retread 的过去式和过去分词．

ret·ro·fire [ˈretrəˌfaiə] *vt., vi., n.* ***(-fired; -fir·ing)*** (制动火箭的)点火发动．

ret·ro·fit [ˈretrəˌfit] *n.* (飞机等的)式样翻新．— *vt., vi.* ***(-fit·ted; -fit·ting)*** (对…)作翻新改进．

ret·ro·flex [ˈretrəufleks] *a.* 反曲的，翻转的；【语音】卷舌的．— *n.*【语音】卷舌音．

ret·ro·flex·ion, -flec·tion [ˌretrəuˈflekʃən] *n.* ①翻转，反曲．②【医】子宫后屈．③【语音】卷舌(音)．

ret·ro·gra·da·tion [ˌretrəugrəˈdeiʃən] *n.* 后退，倒退；逆行；退步，退化；退减(作用)．

ret·ro·grade [ˈretrəugreid] *a.* 后退的，倒退的；反的，倒转的；逆行的；退步的，退化的．— *vi.* 后退，倒退；逆行；退步，退化；堕落．*~ metamorphosis [development]*【生】退化．*~ motion*【天】逆行．*in a ~ order* 以相反次序，颠倒地．— *ad.* 后退地；向后地；颠倒地．*flow ~* 倒流．

ret·ro·gress [ˈretrəugres, ˌretrəuˈgres] *vi.* *(opp.* progress*)* ①倒退，退步，衰退．②【生】退化．

ret·ro·gres·sion [ˌretrəuˈgreʃən] *n.* 后退，倒退，退步，消退，堕落，衰微；【生】退化；【天】逆行(运动)；【化】逆反应．*Persist in progress and oppose ~!* 坚持进步，反对倒退！**-sive** *a.*

ret·ro·len·tal [ˌretrəuˈlentl] *a.*【解】眼晶状体后面的．

ret·ro·pack [ˈretrəupæk] *n.* 制动〔减速〕发动机；(由火箭组成的)制动〔减速〕装置．

ret·ro-rock·et [ˈretrəurɔkit] *n.* 制动火箭，减速火箭．

re·trorse [riˈtrɔːs] *a.*【生】下向的，倒向的．**-ly** *ad.*

ret·ro·spect [ˈretrəuspekt] *n.* ①回顾 *(opp.* prospect*)*．②怀旧，追忆．③追溯力．④对证，参照．*It is pleasant in (the) ~.* 回想起来令人愉快．*The ~ was depressing.* 回想起来令人沮丧．— *vi., vt.* 〔罕〕回顾；回想，追忆．— *a.* = retrospective.

ret·ro·spec·tion [ˌretrəuˈspekʃən] *n.* 回顾，回想；(过去事实等的)对证．

ret·ro·spec·tive [ˌretrəuˈspektiv] *a.* ①回顾的，怀旧的；爱追溯既往的．②【法】有追溯力的．*a ~ law*【法】追溯法．**-ly** *ad.*

re·trous·sé [rəˈtruːsei] *a.* 〔F.〕(鼻子)朝上翘的；尖端向上弯的．

ret·ro·ver·sion [ˌretrəuˈvəːʃən] *n.* ①回顾；向后转，倒退．②(器官的)翻转，后倾〔特指子宫的后倾〕．

ret·ro·vert [ˌretrəuˈvəːt] *vt.* 使翻转；使后倾．**-ed** *a.* (子宫等)后倾的．

re·try [ˈriːˈtrai] *vt.* ①(重新)再试．②【法】再审，重审．

ret·si·na [ˈretsinə] *n.* (带松脂香味的)希腊红(白)葡萄酒．

ret·ter·y [ˈretəri] *n.* 沤麻场．

ret·ting [ˈretiŋ] *n.* (亚麻)浸渍(法)，沤麻．

re·turn [riˈtəːn] *vi.* ①回转，回来，回去，返回，折回 (to)．②再来，又来；复发；回复；恢复．③回头说正经话，回到本题，言归正传．④送还，归还(原主)．⑤回答，回嘴，回骂．*He has gone never to ~.* 他一去不回．*The property ~ed to the original owner* 财产已归还原主．*~ to duty* 回到岗位．***~ from a digression*** 把说开去的话拉回来，言归正传．***~ home*** 回家；回乡；回国．***~ to dust*** 死．***~ to one's muttons*** 回到本题，言归正传．***~ to oneself*** 苏醒；醒悟．— *vt.* ①归还，送还，送〔放〕回(原处)；(光、声等)反射，反响．②报复；回礼，报答，酬答．③回答说；反驳道；答辩；回骂．④汇报，报告，呈报．⑤选举(为议员

等). ⑥【牌戏】(响应搭档者)跟出(同花色的牌);【网球】将(球)打回. ⑦【法】(陪审员)答复. ⑧【建】(使墙壁、嵌线等)向侧面转延. ~ *one's income at $ 200* 申报收入额是二百元. ~ *a soldier as killed* 呈报某兵士已阵亡. *a ~ing officer*〔英〕负责选举的官员. ~ *a compliment* 回礼,还礼;报复. ~ ***sb. to Parliament*** 选举某人为议员. ~ ***a profit*** 产生收益[利润]. ~ ***a visit*** 回拜. ~ ***good for evil*** 以德报怨. ~ ***kindness with ingratitude*** 恩将仇报. ~ ***like for like*** 以牙还牙,以眼还眼,一报还一报. ~ ***swords*** 纳剑入鞘. ~ ***thanks*** (对宴会,祝酒等)答谢. ***To*** ~ 〔用作插入语〕闲语休讲,言归正传. — *n.* ①归来,回去;回家,还乡,归国;复归,回归;再发,复发;来回,回程;【电】回路. ②退还,归还,付还,送还. ③还报,报复;还礼,报答;回答,答复;回骂,反唇相讥. ④报告(书),汇报,申报;〔主 *pl.*〕统计表;【物】输出量. ⑤(议员的)选出,当选. ⑥〔常 *pl.*〕赢利,利润,赚头;报酬. ⑦【法】送回. ⑧【建】(嵌线等的)转延,侧面. ⑨〔*pl.*〕〔英〕(用废料制成的)再生板烟. ⑩〔口〕= ~ ticket 来回票. *(I wish you) Many happy ~s (of the day)!* (敬祝)多福多寿. *election ~s* 选举结果,选举报告书. *official ~s* 公报. *Small profits and quick ~s.* 薄利多卖〔商店广告用语〕. *a third-class ~ (ticket) (to) London* (到)伦敦(的)三等来回(票)一张. ***at (the) ~ of the year*** 过了年就. ***bring [yield] a prompt [quick]*** ~ 利润回来得快. ***by ~ (of post)*** 请即回示. ***in*** ~ 作报复[报酬,回答,报答];作替换. ***in ~ for*** 作…的报酬[回礼]. ***make a*** ~ 作报告[汇报]. ***make ~ for*** 报答…. ***secure a*** ~ 当选(为议员). ***without*** ~ 无赚头,无利润. ***write in*** ~ 写回信. ~ **circuit**【电】回路. ~ **game [match]** (同样两个球队的)再赛. ~ **of health [an illness]** 恢复健康;〔旧病〕复发. ~ **passenger [voyage, cargo]** 回程的乘客[行程,货载]. ~ **postcard** 来回明信片. ~ **ticket** 〔主英〕来回票. ~ **visit** 回访,答拜,回拜.

re·turn·a·ble [riˈtəːnəbl] *a.* ①可返回的. ②可回答的;应返还的. ③应报告的. ④可多次利用的;可回收的. ⑤【法】应送回[答辩]的.

re·turned [riˈtəːnd] *a.* 被送回的;已归来的;已回国的. ~ *empties* 退回的空箱[空桶(等)];〔英谑〕归国牧师. *a ~ overseas Chinese* 归国华侨. *a ~ soldier* 回国兵.

re·turn·ee [ritəːˈniː] *n.* ①(服刑后)释放回来的人. ②(从国外服役后)回国军人. ③从国外回来的人. ④回校复学的学生.

re·turn·less [riˈtəːnlis] *a.* ①回不来的. ②没有报酬的,赚不到钱的. ③没有报告的;没有回答的.

re·tuse [riˈtjuːs] *a.*【植】(叶)微凹形的;凹端的.

ret·zi·na [ˈretsinə] *n.* = retsina.

Reu·ben [ˈruːbin] *n.* 鲁本〔男子名〕.

re·une [riːˈjuːn] *vi.*〔美俚〕重新聚会.

re·u·ni·fy [ˈriːˈjuːniˌfai] *vt., vi.* *(-fi·ed; fy·ing)* (使)重新统一,(使)重新团结. **-fi·cation** [ˌriːjuːnifiˈkeiʃən] *n.*

Ré·un·ion [riːˈjuːnjən] *n.* 留尼汪(岛)〔非洲〕.

re·un·ion [ˈriːˈjuːnjən] *n.* ①复合,再结合,再合并,再统一;和解. ②重聚;(亲友等的)聚会,恳亲会. *a family ~* 亲属的团聚. *a college ~* (大学)校友联欢会. **-ist** *n.*

re·u·nite [ˈriːjuːˈnait] *vt., vi.* (使)再联合;(使)重聚;(使)再结合.

re-up [ˈriːˈʌp] *vt., vi.* *(-upped; -up·ping)*〔美俚〕再服兵役,再入伍.

re·used [ˈriːˈjuːzd] *a.* 再生的. ~ *wool*【纺】旧呢片再生毛.

Reu·ters [ˈrɔitəz] *n.* (英国)路透(通讯)社.

rev [rev] *n.*〔口〕(发动机的)旋转. — *vi., vt.* (使)变速. ~ ***down [up]*** 使(马达)转得慢点[快点].

Rev. = ①Revelation. ②Reverend.

rev; rev. = ①revenue. ②reverse(d). ③review(ed). ④revised; revision. ⑤revolution.

re·va·lo·ri·za·tion [riːˌvæləraiˈzeiʃən] *n.*【经】(通货膨胀后对资产或通货的)重行估价.

re·val·u·ate [ˈriːˈvæljueit] *vt.* *(-at·ed; -at·ing)* 再估价,重新评价[估价]. **-a·tion** *n.*

re·val·ue [ˈriːˈvæljuː] *vt.* 对(货币等)再估价;对…重新估价[评价].

re·vamp [ˈriːˈvæmp] *vt.* 补钉,补缀;修理,修补;〔美口〕改制;翻新;改装(书等);给(鞋等)换新面.

re·vanche [rəˈvɑ̃ːnʃ; F. rəvɑ̃ːʃ] *n.*〔F.〕报复;复仇战.

re·vanch·ism [riˈvɑːnʃizəm, -ˈvɑːntʃ-] *n.* (促使战败国企图收复失地的)复仇主义. **-ist** *a., n.*

re·veal [riˈviːl] *vt.* ①显露,揭露,揭发,剖明;告诉,透露,泄露(秘密等);给…看. ②(神)默示,启示. ~ *a secret* 泄露秘密. *~ed religion*【宗】天启宗教〔指信仰有一个有意志的神的任何宗教,如犹太教,基督教等〕. *A man's work ~s him.* 由作家的作品可看出作家其人. *It was soon ~ed to him how much he needed her cooperation.* 他很快就明白他是多么需要同她合作. ~ ***itself*** 出现. ~ ***oneself*** 讲出姓名,表明身分. ~ ***one's identity*** 揭示身分. — *n.* ①显露,启示. ②【建】窗侧壁[外抱];门侧. ③(汽车的)窗框. **-a·ble** *a.* **-ment** *n.*

re·veal·er [riˈviːlə] *n.* 显示者;揭露者;【宗】启示者.

re·veil·le [riˈvæli] *n.*【军】起床号,起床鼓;(一天的第一次)列队,集合.

rev·el [ˈrevl] (〔英〕*-ll-*) *vi.* ①欢宴,纵酒狂欢,闹饮. ②狂喜,得意扬扬;极爱,沉迷(艺术等) (in). — *vt.* 宴饮作乐浪费掉(钱、时间). ~ *in luxury [mischief, vice]* 爱奢华[捣蛋,干坏事]. ~ *away the time* 狂欢作乐虚度光阴. ~ *it* 纵酒狂欢;欢宴. — *n.*〔常 *pl.*〕宴会;狂欢,欢乐. *the Master of the Revels* (王室、法学院等的)宴会主持人. ~ *rout*〔古〕参加宴会的人们.

rev·e·la·tion [ˌreviˈleiʃən] *n.* ①揭发,暴露;泄露;显示;被揭露出来的事物;意外的发现[新事,新经验]. ②【宗】天启,启示,默示;圣经;〔the Revelations〕(基督教《圣经》中的)《启示录》. *It was a ~ to me.* 这真是一件料想不到的事情. *What a ~!* 这真是一个意外! **-al** *a.* ①暴露的;显示的. ②意外发现的. ③天启的,启示的. **-ist** *n.* 启示论者;启示录作者.

rev·e·la·tor [ˈrevileitə] *n.*〔美〕= revealer.

rev·e·la·to·ry [ˈrevilətəri, riˈvelətəri] *a.* ①揭露的. ②能启示…的 *(of)*. *a ~ account of their home life* 对他们家庭生活的揭露性的叙述. *a poem ~ of his deep, personal sorrow* 能表明他的深沉的个人悲痛的一首诗.

rev·el·(l)er [ˈrevlə] *n.* 参加欢宴的人,纵酒狂欢的人,大喝大闹的人;荡子.

rev·el·ry [ˈrevlri] *n.* 纵酒狂欢,宴饮作乐;欢宴.

rev·e·nant [ˈrevənɑ̃ːŋ] *n.*〔F.〕①幽灵. ②久别归来的人.

re·venge [riˈvendʒ] *n.* 报仇,雪恨;仇恨;报仇[报复]的机会;【运】雪耻赛(的机会). *a counter-attack in ~* 反攻倒算. *give sb. his ~* 给输方一个雪耻赛的机会. ***get*** ~ 报仇. ***have [take] one's*** ~ 复仇,报仇. ***in ~ of [for]*** 为报复…而. ***meditate*** ~ 企图报仇. ***seek one's ~ (up) on*** 找机会向…报仇. ***threaten*** ~ 声言要报仇,以报仇威胁. — *vt.* 〔~ oneself 或用被动语态〕报复,报仇;替…报仇. ***be ~d (up)on sb.*** = ~ ***oneself (up)on sb.*** 对…进行报复[报仇]. ~ ***a wrong*** 申冤雪恨. ~ ***wrong with wrong*** 以牙还牙,报仇. — *vi.* 报仇 *(upon, on)*.

re·venge·ful [riˈvendʒ*ful*] *a.* 仇恨深的,不共戴天的,一心要报仇的;报仇的,报复的. **-ly** *ad.*

rev·e·nue [ˈrevinjuː] *n.* ①(国家的)岁入;税收;(土地、财产等的)收入,收益,所得;(个人的)固定收入;*(pl.)* 总收入;收入项目;财源. ②税务署;〔美俚〕税务官. *the Public R-* 国库岁入. *defraud the ~* 漏税,逃税. ~ **cutter** (海关的)缉私船. ~ **duty** =~ **tax.** ~ **officer** 税务员. ~ **stamp** 印花税票. ~ **tax** 税收.

re•verb [riˈvəːb] *n.* = reverberation③.

re•ver•ber•ant [riˈvəːbərənt] *a.* 反响的；回荡的；【物】交混回响的；反射的.

re•ver•ber•ate [riˈvəːbəreit] *vi.* ①反响，混响；反射；(球等)弹回．②(反射炉)返焰．③〔罕〕抱反感．— *vt.* ①使反响；使回荡；使反射．②使返焰；用返焰〔反射〕炉处理．*a reverberating peal of thunder* 雷的隆隆声．**-ative** *a.*

re•ver•ber•a•tion [riˌvəːbəˈreiʃən] *n.* ①反响，回荡，余韵；反射；反射热，反射光．②(反射炉的)返焰；返焰炉处理法．③【物】交混回响，混响，余响．

re•ver•ber•a•tor [riˈvəːbəreitə] *n.* 反射炉，反焰炉；反射器，反射灯，反射镜．

re•ver•ber•a•to•ry [riˈvəːbərətəri] *a.* ①回响的．②反射的．③返焰(炉)的，发射炉的．— *n.* 反射炉，反焰炉．

re•vere[1] [riˈviə] *vt.* 尊敬，崇敬．

re•vere[2] [riˈviə] *n.* = revers.

Re•vere [riˈviə] *n.* 里维尔〔姓氏〕．

rev•er•ence [ˈrevərəns] *n.* ①尊敬，崇敬．②威望；〔古〕敬礼，鞠躬．③〔your R-; his R-〕〔古、谑〕大师；尊敬的…阁下．***at the ~ of*** 对…尊敬地．***bow in humble ~*** 必恭必敬地鞠躬．***do [make] ~ to*** 〔废〕= *pay ~ to.* ***feel ~ for*** 觉得…可敬．***hold … in [regard … with] ~*** 敬畏某人，尊敬某人．***make a profound ~*** 恭恭敬敬行礼，深深鞠躬．***pay ~ to*** 尊敬，向…致敬．***saving your ~*** 〔古〕恕我冒昧(地讲)；请原谅．— *vt.* 尊敬，崇敬；敬畏．

rev•er•end [ˈrevərənd] *a.* ①应受尊敬的，可尊敬的，可敬畏的．②大师，法师〔对僧侣、牧师的尊称、略作 Rev. 或 the Rev.；对教长用 the Very R-，对主教 (bishop) 用 Right R-，对大主教 (archbishop) 用 *Most* R-〕．③教士的，圣职的．④〔古〕恭敬的，表示敬畏的．*the ~ gentleman* 那个牧师．— *n.* 〔常 *pl.*〕教士，牧师．*the ~s and right ~s* 牧师和主教们．

rev•er•ent [ˈrevərənt] *a.* ①尊敬的，虔诚的，谦恭的．②〔美俚〕(威士忌酒)烈性的．**-ly** *ad.*

rev•er•en•tial [ˌrevəˈrenʃəl] *a.* 表示尊敬的，出于虔诚的．**-ly** *ad.*

rev•er•ie [ˈrevəri] *n.* ①冥想，沉思；空想，幻想，白日梦；梦想，妄想，奇想．②【乐】幻想曲．***be lost in (a) ~*** 想得出神，正在做白日梦．***fall into (a) ~*** = ***indulge in ~*** 沉溺于不实际的空想中．

re•vers [riˈviə, riˈvɛə; 〔*pl.*〕 riˈviəz, riˈvɛəz] *n.* 〔*sing., pl.*〕〔F.〕翻领，翻边，翻袖(等)．

re•ver•sal [riˈvəːsəl] *n.* ①颠倒，倒转，反转，逆转，反向；反复．②【法】撤消．③【摄】正负片之间的转换．*That would be a ~ of the order of host and guest.* 这就主客颠倒了．*a ~ of wind* 风向突然逆转．*a thrust ~* 【火箭】推力反向装置．

re•verse [riˈvəːs] *vt.* ①使颠倒，使倒转，使反转；使翻转；翻(案)．②掉换，交换．③使成正相反的东西，完全改变．④【机】使倒退，使绕行，使倒开，*~ an engine* 倒车．*~ a motion [policy]* 使运动倒转〔完全改变政策〕．*~ an order* 颠倒次序．*~ positions* 掉换位置．*R- arms!* 倒枪！〔行葬礼时使枪口向地的命令〕．*a ~d line* 【物】自蚀(光线)谱．*~ the verdict* 翻案．*~ the charge* 让接电话的人付电费．*~ oneself* 完全改变自己主张，使逆转．⑤【法】撤消；推翻．— *vi.* 颠倒，倒转，反转，倒退；逆转；反向；【机】回动；(跳舞时)向左转．— *a.* ①反对的，相反的，倒转的，颠倒的；翻转的，反面的，背后的；朝后的；反捲的；反向的，倒开的，回动的，逆流的．②【生】倒捲的，左捲的．***in the ~ direction*** 朝着相反的方向．***in ~ order*** 次序颠倒地．— *n.* ①反对，相反．②(硬币等的)反面，背面 *(opp.* obverse*)*．③倒转，颠倒；反向；【机】回动；回动装置〔齿轮〕．④(枪等的)托尾．⑤逆境，倒霉，不幸，挫折，失败．⑥【剑术】倒击，倒刺．⑦【跳舞】左转．*the very ~* 正相反．*the ~s of fortune* 运气不佳；灾难，不幸．*With others the ~ (of this) happens.* 其他各人遭遇完全相反．***in ~*** 相反；【军】在阵后，在〔从〕背面．***meet with ~s*** 遭受挫折；倒霉；失败；吃败仗．***on the ~*** (汽车)倒开着．***quite the ~*** 正相反．***suffer [sustain, have] a ~*** 遭受失败；被打败，吃败仗．***take in ~*** 从背面攻击．**-d** *a.* 颠倒的；撤销了的．— *ad.* = reversely，颠倒地，翻转地，反对地，(和这)相反地，在另一方面．*~* **fire** 背面火力〔炮击〕．*~* **turn** 【空】(方向的)急转．

re•vers•i•bil•i•ty [riˌvəːsəˈbiliti] *n.* 可逆(性)；正反〔表里〕两用；(命令、判决等)可撤销性．

re•vers•i•ble [riˈvəːsəbl] *a.* ①可转换〔掉换〕的；可翻转的，正反〔表里〕两用的；可逆的．②可取消的，可废弃的．— *n.* (正反一样的)双面织物；晴雨两用大衣；正反两用式上衣．*a ~ carpet* 双面地毯．

re•vers•ing [riˈvəːsiŋ] *a.* 回动的，倒进的．*a ~ key* 【电】换向电钥．*a ~ lever* 【机】回动杆．

re•ver•sion [riˈvəːʃən] *n.* ①回复；复原；逆演；颠倒，反转．②【生】回复变异；返祖(现象)，返祖遗传，隔世遗传．③【橡胶】(硫化)还原．④未来〔复归〕享有权；继承权；(约满后财产还给原主的)复归，财产复归．⑤(可在一定期间后或死后得到的)复归储金〔退休金、恤金、人寿保险金等〕．⑥〔古〕剩余．***in ~*** 以让与人死亡〔约定期间届满〕为条件(的)；将来应归某人所有的；将来应实现的．*~* ***to type*** 隔世遗传，间歇遗传，返祖性．**-al** [-ʃənl], **-ary** [-ʃnəri] *a.* ①回复的，复原的，复归的．②隔世遗传的，返祖遗传的．③将来应享有的，应继承的；归属原主的．**-er** *n.* 有将来享有权的人，继承权人．

re•vert [riˈvəːt] *vi.* ①恢复原状；回复(归习惯等)；复辟，复归(原主等) *(to)*．②回到原来话题 *(to)*．③回想 *(to)*．④【生】回复变异；返祖遗传，隔世遗传 *(to)*．⑤归属，继承．— *vt.* 使颠倒，使绕行，使(眼睛等)转向后．— *n.* ①恢复原来信仰的人．②归属，继承．

re•vert•i•ble [riˈvəːtəbl] *a.* 可回复的；(财产等)应归还的，可归复的；可逆的；可回溯的．**-i•bil•i•ty** *n.*

rev•er•y [ˈrevəri] *n.* = reverie.

re•vest [riˈvest] *vt.* ①使重新具有(财产、权力、职位)；再授予(给予)(财产、权力、职位等)．②重新投资．— *vi.* 重新拥有，重归原主〔指财产、权力等〕．

re•vet [riˈvet] *vt.* (用砖石等)遮护，铺盖(堤防等)．*~ a trench* 用砂包、鹿砦等巩固壕沟．**-ment** *n.* 【筑城】被覆；拥壁；护岸．

re•view [riˈvjuː] *vt.* ①再看，再阅，复阅；重行检查，再检查；检查；审查，观察．②检阅(军队)．③评论(新书等)．④温习，复习(功课等)．⑤【法】复审，再审．⑥回顾；回忆；写回忆录．⑦〔古〕校改，校订，修订，改订．— *vi.* 评论，写评论；做评论员．— *n.* ①(再)检查；检阅；观察，校阅．②复习，温习；习题．③评论；书评；评论杂志．④阅兵；阅兵式，阅舰式．⑤【法】复审．⑥回顾，回忆；反省．⑦= *revue. the Board of R-* (影片等的)审查局．*a court of ~* 复审法庭．***give a general ~ of*** 概括地谈谈．***hold a military ~*** 举行阅兵式．***in ~*** 检查中．***pass [march] in ~*** ①(队伍行进)受检阅．②(被)检查；(被)回顾 (*pass events in ~* 对事件一一检查)．***the years under ~*** 回顾中那些年代．**-able** *a.* 应检查的，可评论的．

re•view•al [riˈvjuːəl] *n.* 复查；校阅；评论；复习．

re•view•er [riˈvjuːə] *n.* ①评论家，评论员，评论作者．②校阅者．③检阅者；阅兵者．

re•vile [riˈvail] *vt., vi.* 辱骂，漫骂；诽谤．**-r** *n.* 漫骂者．

re•vis•al [riˈvaizəl] *n.* 修订，校订；修订本；【印】校对．

re•vise [riˈvaiz] *vt.* ①修订，校订；校阅．②再检查；修正，改变(意见等)．③【生】对…重新分类．*~d and enlarged* 修订增补的．*a ~d edition* 修订版．*the Revised Version* (基督教)《圣经》钦定英译本的修订本〔1881—1885 年出版，略 R. V. 或 Rev. *Ver.*〕*the Revised Standard Version* (基督教)《圣经》修订版标准英译本〔1952年出版于美国〕．— *n.* ①校订，订正．②【印】再校样．

re·vis·er, re·vis·or [riˈvaizə] *n.* ①校订者,修订者;修正者;检查员. ②【印】校对员.

re·vi·sion [riˈviʒən] *n.* ①校订,订正,修订;修改,修正. ②【印】校对;再校. ③校订本;修订本. ④复审;上诉. ⑤〔R-〕= (the) Revised Version. **-al,-ary** *a.* ①校订的,校正的,修订的;修改的,修正的. ②校对的. **-ism** *n.* 修正主义. **-ist** ①*n.* 修正主义者. ②*a.* 修正主义的.

re·vis·it [ˈriːˈvizit] *vt., n.* 再访问;再参观;重临,重游,回到.

re·vi·so·ry [riˈvaizəri] *a.* ①校订的;修订的,修改的,修正的. ②校对的.

re·vi·tal·ize [ˈriːˈvaitəlaiz] *vt.* 使恢复元气;使有新的活力;使新生;复兴.

re·viv·a·ble [riˈvaivəbl] *a.* 能苏醒的,能复生的;可复兴的;可恢复的.

re·viv·al [riˈvaivəl] *n.* ①苏醒;更生,再生,复活;复兴;再流行. ②【宗】信仰复兴;〔R-〕文艺复兴;【剧】(旧戏等的)重新上演. ③【法】(契约等的)再生效. *the ~ of learning [letters, literature]* 文艺复兴. **-ism** *n.* ①【宗】信仰复兴运动. ②复兴精神. **-ist** *n.* ①【宗】信仰复兴运动者. ②复兴者.

re·vive [riˈvaiv] *vi.* ①苏醒,更生,再生,复活. ②恢复,更新;恢复精神,振奋. ③复兴,再兴;再流行;再生效. ④【化】再生,复原;(金属)还原. — *vt.* ①使苏醒,使复活. ②使恢复;使(重新)振作精神,使重新活跃. ③使复兴,使再兴;使再流行;使再生效. ④回想起;重新上演(旧戏等). ⑤【化】使再生,复原,还原. *~ an old play* 重演旧戏(使再受人欢迎).

re·viv·er [riˈvaivə] *n.* 使复活[复兴]者;〔俚〕刺激性饮料,兴奋剂;酒;生色剂.

re·viv·i·fi·ca·tion [ri(ː)ˌvivifiˈkeiʃən] *n.* ①苏醒,复活. ②【化】复原(作用),再生(作用).

re·viv·i·fy [ri(ː)ˈvivifai] *vt.* ①使苏醒,使复活;使恢复精神,使振作,使有生气. ②【化】使复原,使再生. — *vi.* = revive.

rev·i·vis·cence [ˌreviˈvisns] *n.* 苏醒,复活;再生;精神[活力]的恢复.

re·vi·vis·cent [ˌreviˈvaisənt] *a.* 苏醒的,复活的;恢复精力的.

re·vi·vor [riˈvaivə] *n.* 【法】恢复诉讼.

rev·o·ca·ble [ˈrevəkəbl] *a.* 可废除[撤销,解除]的. **-bly** *ad.*

rev·o·ca·tion [ˌrevəˈkeiʃən] *n.* 废除,取消,解除;(对契约、建议等)撤销;〔古〕召还,唤回.

rev·o·ca·to·ry [ˈrevəkətəri] *a.* 废除的,撤销的,解除的. *a ~ action* 【法】解除契约诉讼.

re·voice [riˈvɔis] *vt.* ***(-voic·ed; -voic·ing)*** ①(用语言)重新表达,应答;把(声音)反射回来. ②调校(风琴管等).

re·vok·a·ble [riˈvəukəbl] *a.* = revocable.

re·voke [riˈvəuk] *vt.* ①取消,撤销,收回,作废,废除,解除(命令、权利、诺言等). ②〔古〕唤回,召还. *~ verbal evidence* 翻供. — *vi.* 【牌戏】(不跟出同样花色的牌而)犯规另出他牌.— *n.* ①【牌戏】(不跟出同样花色的牌)犯规另出他牌. ②〔罕〕取消,废弃. ***beyond ~*** 不能取消的. ***make a ~*** 【牌戏】犯规另出他牌.

re·volt [riˈvəult] *n.* ①反叛,造反;起义. ②反抗,反对. ③反感,对抗情绪,厌恶. ***in ~*** 反抗着;造着反. ***raise a righteous ~*** 起义. ***rise in ~*** 起来反抗,起义,造反. ***rouse [stir up] the people to ~*** 鼓动人民造反[反抗]. — *vi.* ①反抗;反叛;起义;造反. ②恶心,感觉不快,反感,嫌恶 *(at; against; from)*. *~ against authority* 反抗当局. *~ from one's allegiance* 反叛,对…不再忠诚. *~ to the enemy* 投敌. *Common sense ~s against [at, from] such measures.* 这种处置违反常情. *The stomach ~s at such food.* 这种食物使人恶心. — *vt.* 使恶心;使嫌恶;使反感.

re·volt·ed [riˈvəultid] *a.* 反叛的;造反的;起义的;起来反抗的.

re·volt·ing [riˈvəultiŋ] *pred., a.* ①反叛的;造反的;叛乱的;反抗的;起义的. ②使人厌恶的,令人恶心的. *It is ~ to ...* 那是违反…的. *This is ~ to me.* 这使我讨厌死了.

rev·o·lute[1] [ˈrevəljuːt] *a.* 【植】外卷的;【动】后旋的.

rev·o·lute[2] [ˈrevəljuːt] *vi.* 〔俚〕干革命.

rev·o·lu·tion [ˌrevəˈluːʃən] *n.* ①革命;剧烈的变革. ②回转,绕转,旋转;转数;周期;一转;【天】运行,周转,公转. *bourgeois-democratic ~* 资产阶级民主革命. *the Chinese ~* 中国革命. *the industrial ~* 产业革命,工业革命. *national-democratic ~* 民族民主革命. *new-democratic ~* 新民主主义革命. *palace ~* 宫廷政变. *the October Socialist R-* 十月社会主义革命. *proletarian ~* 无产阶级革命. *Socialist ~* 社会主义革命. *Violent ~* 暴力革命. 〔*the R-*〕= *the English [French] ~* 英国[法国]革命. *technical ~* 技术革命. *the ~ of the seasons* 季节的循环. *the ~ of the moon around the earth* 月球绕着地球的公转. *The earth completes one ~ each day.* 地球每天完成一次自转. **~s per minute** 〔略 r. p. m.〕【物】每分钟转数. **-ism** *n.* 革命主义[学说、原理]. **-ist** *n., a.* 革命者(的),革命家(的),革命论者(的).

rev·o·lu·tion·a·ry [ˌrevəˈljuːʃənəri] *a.* ①革命的,大变革的,革命性的. ②旋转的. *the R- War* 〔美〕独立战争. *~ sweep* 革命气概. — *n.* 革命家[者].

rev·o·lu·tion·ize [ˌrevəˈljuːʃənaiz] *vt.* 使革命化;引起革命;鼓吹革命思想;革新;彻底改革. **-i·za·tion** [-ˈzeiʃən] *n.* **-d** *a.* 革命化的;被彻底改革的.

re·volve [riˈvɔlv] *vi.* 旋转,绕转;运行,周转;【天】公转,循环. *The earth ~s both round [about] the sun and on its own axis.* 地球又公转又自转. *Seasons ~.* 时令循环周而复始. *a mechanism for revolving the turntable* 回转桌的回转装置. — *vt.* ①使旋转;使周转. ②细想,转念头,盘算. *~ a problem (in one's mind)* 反复思考问题.

re·volv·er [riˈvɔlvə] *n.* ①旋转者;旋转式装置. ②【冶】转炉. ③转[左]轮手枪. *a six-chambered ~* 六响左轮. *the policy of the big ~* (用报复关税等)威吓政策.

re·volv·ing [riˈvɔlviŋ] *a.* 回转的;周转性的;旋转(式)的,轮转式的;循环的. — *n.* 【游泳】滚泳. *a ~ bookstand* 旋转书架. *a ~ door* 旋转门. ***~ fund*** (贷借经常保持平衡的)周转基金.

Rev. stat. = revised statutes 经过修订的(新)章程(法规).

re·vue [riˈvjuː] *n.* 〔F.〕①时事讽刺剧,活报剧. ②轻歌舞剧.

re·vul·sion [riˈvʌlʃən] *n.* ①(感情等的)激变,急变;突发变乱. ②〔罕〕(资本等的)突然收回;突然的分离. ③嫌恶,反感. ④【医】(尤指用相反刺激剂的)诱导(法).

re·vul·sive [riˈvʌlsiv] *a.* 【医】诱导的. — *n.* 【医】诱导药[剂];诱导器具.

Rev. Ver. = Revised Version 〔见 revise 条〕.

re·ward [riˈwɔːd] *n.* ①报酬,酬劳,奖赏,酬金 (for). ②报答;报应;惩罚. *offer [give] ~ to sb. for sth.* 为某事给某人以报酬. *in ~ for* 为酬答…,作为…的奖赏. — *vt.* ①酬劳,奖赏 *(for; with)*. ②报答;惩罚. ***be ~ed by success*** 获得了成功. ***~ sb. for sth.*** 为某事报答某人. ***~ according to sb.'s deserts*** 论功行赏;给予应得的赏罚. —*vi.* ①报答. ②报复. **-ing** *a.* 有价值的,有益的. **-less** *a.* 无报酬的,白费气力的,徒劳的.

re·wind [riˈwaind] *vt.* ***(-wound; -wind·ing)*** 重新卷绕〔尤指倒卷影片等〕. — *n.* ①重卷物. ②重卷.

re·wire [riˈwaiə] *vt., vi.* ***(-wir·ed; -wir·ing)*** ①再接电线,接新电线〔尤指给房子、马达等装新线〕. ②再发报,重新发报.

re·word [ˈriːˈwəːd] *vt.* 重说;改说;改变…的措词.

re·work [riˈwəːk] *vt.* 再作;重做;重写;再工作;再加工.

re·write [ˈriːˈrait] *vt.* (*-wrote* [ˈriːˈrəut], *-writ·ten* [ˈriːˈritn]) 书面答复；重写；再写；改写，修改. — [ˈriːrait] *n.* 改写[重写]的文稿. **-man** *n.* (报馆等的) 改写加工编辑.
Rex [reks] *n.* 雷克斯〔男子名〕.
Rex [reks] *n.* 〔L.〕 ①〔英〕王，君主〔略 R.，常用于诉讼案件中，如：George R. = King George Rex V. Jones 国王对琼斯，即对琼斯提出公诉的刑事案件〕. ②〔俚〕控制导弹的脉冲系统. ③(比利时的法西斯党)国王党，列克斯党.
rex·ine [ˈreksiːn] *n.* 人造封面布；人造革沙发套.
Rey·kja·vik [ˈreikjəviːk] *n.* 雷克雅未克〔冰岛首都〕.
Rey·nard [ˈrenəd] *n.* (民间故事中的)列那狐；〔r-〕狐狸. ~ *the Fox* (中世纪流行的)《列那狐故事》.
Reyn·old [ˈrenəld] *n.* 雷诺〔男子名，Reginald 的异体〕.
Reyn·olds [ˈrenəldz] *n.* 雷诺兹〔姓氏〕.
RF = ①radio frequency 射频，无线电频率. ②range finder【摄，军】(测定目标距离的)测距计，光学测距仪. ③rapid-fire (枪等)速射的. ④〔F.〕*République Française* 法兰西共和国.
R.F. = ①right field (棒球)右外场. ②right fielder (棒球)右场手.
R.F.A. = Royal Field Artillery〔英〕皇家野战炮兵.
RFC = Reconstruction Finance Corporation〔美旧〕复兴金融公司.
R.F.C = Royal Flying Corps〔英旧〕皇家陆军航空队.
R.F.D. = Rural Free Delivery〔美〕乡村免费邮递.
RG = registered (bonds).
R.G.A. = Royal Garrison Artillery〔英〕皇家要塞炮兵.
R.G.S. = Royal Geographical Society〔英〕皇家地理学会.
R.H. = ①relative humidity 相对湿度. ②right-handed 右手的，右方的.
R.H. = ①Royal Highlanders〔英〕皇家苏格兰高地团. ②Royal Highness〔英〕殿下.
Rh = Rhodium【化】铑.
R.H.A. = Royal Horse Artillery〔英〕皇家骑炮兵.
rhab·do·coele [ˈræbdəˌsiːl] *n.*【动】单肠类 (*Rhabdocoela*) 动物.
rhab·do·man·cy [ˈræbdəmænsi] *n.* 棍卜〔用探矿杖占测矿物的迷信活动〕.
rhab·do·my·o·ma [ˈræbdəumaiˈəumə] *n.* (*pl.* *-ma·ta* [mətə])【医】横纹肌瘤.
rha·chis [ˈreikis] *n.* = rachis.
Rhad·a·man·thine [ˌrædəˈmænθain] *a.* ①象冥府判官似的. ②铁面无私的.
Rhad·a·man·thus [ˌrædəˈmænθəs] *n.*【希神】拉达曼斯〔宙斯 (Zeus) 神与欧罗巴(Europa)之子，阴间的判官；铁面无私的法官〕.
Rhae·to-Ro·man·ic [ˌriːtəurəuˈmænik] *n.* (瑞士东南部和意大利北部所讲的)拉蒂亚罗曼斯方言. — *a.* 拉蒂亚罗曼斯方言的.
rham·nose [ˈræmnəus] *n.*【化】鼠李糖.
rhap·so·dic, rhap·sod·i·cal [ræpˈsɔdik(əl)] *a.* ①狂文的；狂诗的. ②热狂的；狂喜的；夸张的. ③狂乱的，混乱的. **-cal·ly** *ad.*
rhap·so·dist [ˈræpsədist] *n.* ①〔古希腊〕吟诵史诗者；吟游诗人. ②狂热的写作者[说话者]；狂诗[狂想曲]作者.
rhap·so·dize [ˈræpsədaiz] *vi.* 用狂诗[狂文]描写；吟诵狂诗；作狂文[狂诗]；作狂想曲；狂热地讲 (*about; on; over*). —*vt.* 狂热地吟诵；狂热地说.
rhap·s·o·dy [ˈræpsədi] *n.* ①〔古希腊〕适于一次吟诵的史诗[叙事诗]的一节〔尤指荷马史诗 Odyssey 或 Iliad 中的〕. ②狂文，狂诗；狂话；【乐】狂想曲. ③狂喜. ***go into rhapsodies*** 狂热地说[写]；夸张地说.
rhat·a·ny [ˈrætni] *n.* (*pl.* *-nies*)【植】拉檀根〔南美一种豆科植物的根，含丹宁酸，可用于鞣革〕.
rhd. = railhead 铁路终点.
rhe [ri] *n.*【物】流值〔流度绝对单位，动力粘单位厘泊的倒数，有时亦指厘沲的倒数〕.
Rhe·a [riə, ˈriːə] *n.* ①丽亚〔女子名〕. ②【希神】宙斯的母亲. ③〔r-〕【动】(南美产)三趾鸵鸟.
Rhein [rain] *n.* 〔G.〕 = Rhine.
Rhein·gold [ˈrainˌgəuld *G.* ˈrainˌgɔːlt] (北欧神话)莱茵金〔秘藏的黄金，原由莱茵仙女守护，后为尼柏龙矮人和西格夫里特所得〕.
Rhe·n·ish [ˈriːniʃ, ˈren-] *a.* 来因(Rhine)河的. — *n.* 来因白葡萄酒 (= Rhine wine).
rhe·ni·um [ˈriːniəm] *n.*【化】铼〔Re〕.
rheo- *comb. f.* 流：*rheology*.
rhe·o·base [ˈriəˌbeis] *n.*【生理】基强度. **-bas·ic** *a.*
rhe·ol·o·gy [riˈɔlədʒi] *n.*【物、化】(研究物质流动、变形、弹性、粘性、可塑性的)流变学；液流学；河流学.
rhe·om·e·ter [riːˈɔmitə] *n.*【电】电流计；【医】血流速度计；【物】流变仪.
rhe·o·phile [ˈriəˌfail] *n.*【生】急流生物〔生活在流水中的动物或植物〕. **-oph·i·ly** [ˈɔfili] *n.*
rhe·o·scope [ˈriːəskəup] *n.*【电】验电器.
rhe·o·stat [ˈriːəstæt] *n.*【电】变阻器；电阻箱.
rhe·o·tax·is [ˌriəˈtæksis] *n.*【动】趋流性. **-tac·tic** *a.*
rhe·o·tome [ˈriːətəum] *n.*【电】周期断流器.
rhe·o·tron [ˈriːətrɔn] *n.*【物】= betatron.
rhe·o·trope [ˈriːətrəup] *n.*【电】电流转换开关.
rhe·ot·ro·pism [riˈɔtrəpizm] *n.*【生】向流性. **-trop·ic** [-əˈtrɔpik] *a.*
rhe·sus [ˈriːsəs] *n.*【动】(印度)恒河猴，罗猴 (= ~ monkey). **R- factor**【医】(在人和罗猴红血球中发现的)凝血素，Rh 因子 (=Rh factor).
rhet. = rhetoric(al).
rhe·tor [ˈriːtə] *n.* 〔古希腊〕修辞学教师[大师]；雄辩家，演说家.
rhet·o·ric [ˈretərik] *n.* 修辞学；辩论法；雄辩术；华丽的文词；花言巧语；辩才；修辞学书.
rhe·tor·i·cal [riˈtɔrikəl] *a.* (符合)修词学的；修辞上的；华丽的，夸张的(文风). *a ~ question* 修辞性疑问(句)，(不期望得到回答的)反问，反诘〔例如：*Who cares?* (= *Nobody cares*)〕. **-ly** *ad.*
rhet·o·ri·cian [ˌretəˈriʃən] *n.* ①修辞学者；雄辩家. ②说话浮夸的人；词藻华丽浮夸的作家.
Rhe·um [ˈriːʌm] *n.*【植】大黄属.
rheum, rheu·ma [ruːm, ˈruːmə] *n.*【医】①稀粘液，粘膜分泌物〔鼻涕、泪等〕. ②(鼻粘膜)感冒. ③〔*pl.*〕风湿痛. ~ **epidemic** 流行性感冒. **-y** *a.*
rheu·mat·ic [ru(ː)ˈmætik] *a.*【医】(害)风湿病的. — *n.* ①风湿病人. ②〔*pl.*〕〔口〕风湿痛. ~ *fever* [*gout*] 急性关节风湿病. *a ~ paper* 风湿膏药. ~ *walk* 风湿病人的步态. **-i·cal·ly** *ad.*
rheu·ma·tism [ˈruːmətizəm] *n.*【医】风湿病. *acute* [*chronic*] ~ 急性[慢性]关节风湿病. *articular* [*muscular*] ~ 关节[肌肉]风湿病.
rheu·ma·tiz [ˈruːmətiz] *n.* 〔口〕= rheumatism.
rheu·ma·toid [ˈruːmətɔid] *a.* 风湿性的；害风湿病的；患风湿性关节炎的；类风湿病的. ~ **arthritis** 风湿性关节炎.
rheu·ma·tol·o·gy [ˌruːməˈtɔlədʒi] *n.*【医】风湿病学. **-tol·o·gist** *n.*
rheum·y [ˈruːmi] *a.* ①分泌粘液的；粘膜分泌液的；粘液过多的. ②鼻粘膜感冒[鼻炎、鼻伤风]的. ③潮湿的；多湿气的(空气)；阴冷的.
R.H.G. = Royal Horse Guards.〔英〕皇家近卫骑兵团.
rhig·o·lene [ˈrigəliːn] *n.*【药】列哥凌〔局部麻醉药〕.
rhi·nal [ˈrainl] *a.*【解】鼻(腔)的. ~ *cavities* 鼻腔.
Rhine [rain] *n.* 来因河. ~ *wine* (来因)白葡萄酒. ~-

stone 莱茵水晶石；假金钢钻．
rhi·nen·ceph·a·lon [ˌrainen'sefəˌlɔn] *n.* (*pl.* **-la** [-lə]) 【解】嗅脑．**-phal·ic** [-'fælik] *a.*
rhi·ni·tis [rai'naitis] *n.* 【医】鼻(粘膜)炎．
rhi·no[1] ['rainəu] *n.* 〔英俚〕钱．*ready* ～ 现钱．
rhi·no[2] ['rainəu] *n.* (*pl.* **-s**) ①〔口〕＝rhinoceros．②〔美海军口〕(可作登陆浮桥用的)自动箱船．
rhino *comb. f.* 鼻，鼻腔：*rhino*laryngology．
rhi·noc·e·ros [rai'nɔsərəs] (*pl.* **-es, rhinoceros**) *n.* 【动】犀牛．
rhi·no·lar·yn·gol·o·gy [ˌrainəuˌlærin'gɔlədʒi] *n.* 鼻喉科学．**-ogist** *n.*
rhi·nol·o·gy [rai'nɔlədʒi] *n.* 【医】鼻科学．
rhi·no·phar·yn·gi·tis [ˌrainəuˌfærin'dʒaitis] *n.* 【医】鼻咽炎．
rhi·no·plas·ty ['rainə'plæsti] *n.* 【医】鼻成形术．**-plastic** *a.*
rhi·nor·rhe·a [ˌrainə'riə] *n.* 【医】鼻液溢．
rhi·no·scope ['rainəskəup] *n.* 【医】鼻(窥)镜．
rhi·nos·co·py [rai'nɔskəpi] *n.* 【医】鼻镜检查法；鼻腔检查．
rhi·no·vi·rus ['rainəu'vairəs] *n.* 【医】鼻病毒．
rhi·zo·bi·um [rai'zəubiəm] *n.* (*pl.* **-bi·a** [-ə]) 【生】根瘤菌(属)〔如豆和车轴草根部所生〕．
rhi·zo·cal·ine [ˌraizəu'keili:n] *n.* 【植】成根素．
rhi·zo·car·pous [ˌraizə'kɑ:pəs] *a.* 【植】根部多年生而茎叶每年生的〔指多年生草本植物而言〕．
rhi·zo·ceph·a·lan [ˌraizə'sefələn] *n.* 【动】根头目 (*Rhizocephala*)．**-ceph·a·lous** *a.*
rhi·zoc·to·ni·a [ˌraizɔk'təuniə] *n.* 【生】丝核菌．
rhi·zo·gen·ic [ˌraizə'dʒenik] *a.* 【植】生根的 (＝rhizogenous, rhizogenetic)．
rhi·zoid ['raizɔid] *a.* 【植】似根的．— *n.* 假根．**-al** *a.*
rhi·zo·ma, rhi·zo·me [rai'zəumə] *n.* (*pl.* **-ta** [-tə]) 【植】根茎，地下茎．
rhi·zo·mor·phous [ˌraizə'mɔ:fəs] *a.* 【植】似根的，根形的．
rhi·zo·pod ['raizəˌpɔd] *n.* 【动】肉足(虫)纲 (*Sarcodina*) 动物．**-al, -ous** *a.*
rhi·zo·pus ['raizəpəs] *n.* 【生】根霉属 (*Rhizopus*) 菌；根霉．
rhi·zo·sphere ['raizəˌsfiə] *n.* 【生态】根围．
rhi·zot·o·my [rai'zɔtəmi] *n.* (*pl.* **-mies**) 【医】神经根切断术．
rho [rəu] *n.* ①希腊语第十七个字母〔ρ 相当于英语的 r〕．②【原】ρ 介子 (＝rho meson)．
rhod- *comb. f.* 玫瑰，红．
Rho·da ['rəudə] *n.* 罗达〔女子名〕．
rho·da·mine ['rəudə'mi:n,-min] *n.* 【染】若丹明，玫瑰精，盐基桃红，啰呢．
Rhode Island ['rəud'ailənd] *n.* 罗德艾兰州〔美国州名〕．***Rhode Island Red*** 〔美〕罗德艾兰州红鸡〔卵肉兼用品种〕．**Rhode Island White** 〔美〕罗德艾兰州白鸡〔与罗德艾兰州红鸡近似，但为白羽〕．
Rhodes [rəudz] *n.* 罗兹〔姓氏〕．
Rho·de·sia [rəu'di:zjə] *n.* 罗得西亚〔津巴布韦的旧称〕．
Rho·di·an ['rəudiən, -djən] *a.* (地中海的)罗得岛的；罗得骑士的．— *n.* 罗得岛人；罗得骑士．*the* ～ *law* 罗得海商法〔世界最古的海上法〕．
rho·dic ['rəudik] *a.* 【化】铑的〔尤指四价的〕．
rho·di·um ['rəudiəm, -djəm] *n.* 【化】铑．
rhodo- *comb. f.* ＝rhod-．
rho·do·chro·site [ˌrəudə'krəusait] *n.* 【矿】菱锰矿．
Rho·do·den·dron [ˌrəudə'dendrən] *n.* 【植】杜鹃花属．〔r-〕杜鹃花．
rho·do·lite ['rəudəˌlait] *n.* 【矿】红榴石〔柘榴石 (*garnet*) 的变种，常用作宝石〕．
rho·do·my·cin [rəudə'maisin] *n.* 〔L.〕【化】玫红霉素．
rho·do·nite ['rəudənˌait] *n.* 【矿】蔷薇辉石〔有时用作装饰品〕．
rho·do·plast ['rəudəˌplæst] *n.* 【生】藻红体．
rho·dop·sin [rəu'dɔpsin] *n.* 【生理】(眼球视网膜上的)视玫红质，视紫红质．
rho·dous ['rəudəs] *a.* 铑的；含铑的．
rhomb [rɔm] *n.* 【数】菱形，斜方形；【结晶】斜方六面体．
rhom·ben·ceph·a·lon [ˌrɔmben'sefəˌlən] *n.* 【解】后脑 (＝hindbrain)．
rhom·bi ['rɔmbai] *n.* rhombus 的复数．
rhom·bic, rhom·bic·al ['rɔmbik(əl)] *a.* 菱形的；斜方形的，正交(晶)的．
rhom·b(o) *comb. f.* 菱形：*rhomb*hedron．
rhom·bo·hed·ral [ˌrɔmbə'hedrəl] *a.* 斜方六面体的；【化】菱形的；三角晶的．
rhom·bo·hed·ron [ˌrɔmbə'hedrən] *n.* (*pl.* **-dra** [-drə]) 【结晶】斜方六面体，菱面体．
rhom·boid ['rɔmbɔid] *n., a.* 【数】偏菱形(的)；长斜方形(的)．
rhom·boi·dal ['rɔmbɔidl] *a.* 【数】偏菱形的，长斜方形的．
rhom·boi·de·us [rɔm'bɔidiəs] *n.* (*pl.* **-de·i** [-ˌai]) 【解】脊胛肌．
rhom·bus ['rɔmbəs] *n.* (*pl.* **-bi** [-bai], **-es**) 【数】菱形，斜方形；菱面体．
rhon·chus ['rɔŋkəs] *n.* (*pl.* **-chi** [kai]) 【医】干罗音；鼻音；(临死时的)喉鸣 (＝râle)．**-chal, -chi·al** *a.*
Rhon·dda ['rɔndə] *n.* 朗达〔姓氏〕．
rho·ta·cism ['rəutəsizm] *n.* 以 r 取代其他音或变他音为 r．
R.Hq ＝ Regimental Headquarter【军】团部．
R.H.S. ＝①Royal Historical Society〔英〕皇家历史学会．②Royal Horticultural Society〔英〕皇家园艺学会．③Royal Humane Society．〔英〕皇家人文科学学会．
rhu·barb ['ru:bɑ:b] *n.* ①【植】大黄；食用大黄；大黄根〔药用〕．②〔美俚〕争吵；激烈的争论；(比赛中的)抱怨．～**ing** ①*a.*〔英〕(舞台后部演员)造成人声嘈杂效果的．②*n.* 嘈杂的人声．
rhumb [rʌm] *n.* 【海】罗盘方位；罗盘方位二点间的角距；罗盘方位线；恒角线 (＝～ line)．
rhum·ba ['rʌ:mbə] *n.* ＝rumba．
rhyme [raim] *n.* ①韵，脚韵．②同韵语．③〔常 *pl.*〕韵文，诗．*single* [*male, masculine*] ～ 单韵，阳性韵〔如 disdain, complain, 仅末音节押韵〕．*double* [*female, feminine*] ～ 二重韵，阴性韵〔如 motion 和 notion，前后两个音节都押韵〕．*imperfect* ～ 不完全韵 [*love, move; phase, race* 等]．*a nursery* ～ 摇篮曲．*a* ～ *slinger*〔美〕诗人．***neither*** ～ ***nor reason, without*** ～ ***or reason*** 杂乱无章；莫名其妙；无缘无故．— *vi.* 作诗，作韵文；押韵；(和某字)叶韵，同属一韵(*to; with*)；(诗、音乐)和谐．— *vt.* 用韵文[诗]写；写(诗、韵文)；把(故事、感想等)作成诗；写(押韵诗)；使押韵；用…作韵脚；使合韵．～*d verse* 押韵诗 (*opp. blank verse* 无韵诗)．*a rhyming dictionary* 诗韵辞典，韵府．
rhyme·less ['raimlis] *a.* 无韵的；不押韵的．
rhym·er, rhym·ist, rhyme·ster ['raimə, -ist, -stə] *n.* 作诗的人；打油诗人．
rhyn·cho·ce·pha·li·an [ˌriŋkəusi'feiliən] *a.* 【动】喙头目 (*Rhynchocephalia*) 的．— *n.* 【动】喙头目．
rhy·o·lite ['raiəˌlait] *n.* 【地】流纹岩．
Rhys [ri:s] *n.* 里斯〔姓氏〕．
rhythm ['riðəm, 'riθəm] *n.* 【诗】抑扬，节奏；韵律；【乐】节拍；节奏的格调；律动；【美】(色彩变化、浓淡配置等的)调和，匀称，和谐；有节奏的变化，有规律的循环运动；【医】节律；周期性．*the* ～ *of a sentence* 文句的抑扬顿挫．***play*** [***sing***] ***in quick*** ～ 用快调奏乐[歌唱]．

rhyth·mic, rhyth·mi·cal [ˈriðmik(-əl)] *a.* 有抑扬顿挫[节奏、韵律]的；韵律[节奏、配合]匀整和谐的，格调优美的；周期性的，间歇的，有规则地循环的. **-cal·ly** *ad.* 有节奏地；按照拍子.

rhyth·mic·i·ty [riðˈmisiti] *n.* 速度均匀，韵律，节奏性.

rhyth·mics [ˈriðmiks] *n. pl.* 〔动词用单数〕韵律学.

rhyth·mist [ˈriðmist] *n.* 通韵律的人，作韵文的人；富有韵律的诗人[作曲家]；有节奏感的人.

rhythm·less [ˈriðəmlis] *a.* 无韵律[节奏]的；不合拍子的.

rhy·ton [ˈraitɔn] *n.* (一种古希腊的)角状杯.

R.I., RI = ①Rhode Island 罗德艾兰〔美国州名〕. ②Rotary International "扶轮国际". ③〔L.〕*Rex et Imperator* (=King & Emperor)国王和皇帝. ④〔L.〕*Regina et Imperatrix* (Queen & Empress) 女王和女皇. ⑤Royal Institution 〔英〕皇家学会.

R.I.A. = Royal Irish Academy 爱尔兰皇家研究院.

ri·a [ˈriə] *n.*【地】溺河.

ri·al [ˈraiəl] *n.* 里亚尔〔伊朗货币单位〕.

rial·to [riˈæltəu] *n.* *(pl. ~s)* ①交易所；市场. ②(威尼斯的)里亚尔托岛〔商业中心区〕；(威尼斯大运河上通里亚尔托岛的)大石桥. ③〔R-〕纽约百老汇戏院区. *What news on the R-?* 有什么新闻没有?

ri·ant [ˈraiənt] *a.* (主要指风貌、风景等)含笑的，喜气扬溢的，欢乐的；悦目的.

ri·a·ta [riˈɑːtə] *n.* 〔美〕(牧童用的)套索.

rib[1] [rib] *n.* ①【解】肋骨；【烹】排骨. ②(船等的)肋材；(叶)主脉；叶肋. ③(昆虫的)翅脉；(鸟的)羽翮. ④【空】(翼)肋；【建】(圆拱的)弯梁，肋拱；(桥的)横梁；伞骨，扇骨；【采】矿壁；【机】力骨，变梁；【装订】书背凸带. ⑤【谑】心上人，妻子；〔美俚〕姑娘，少女. ⑥(布上的)棱线，棱纹，凸条，罗纹，山嘴；(在沙滩上的)浪痕，铁. *false [floating] ~* 【解】假肋，游肋，浮肋. *true [sternal] ~* 【解】真肋. *cooling ~s* 散热片. *~s of beef* 大块牛排. *Poke sb. in the ~s* (用肘)碰触某人肋骨一下使注意. ***smite under the fifth ~*** 戳进心脏，戳死. — *vt.* ①装肋骨，装肋材；用肋骨[肋材]包围. ②起棱；【农】作垄. ~ **flange** 肋凸缘.

rib[2] [rib] *vt.* 〔俚〕开…的玩笑，戏弄. — *n.* 〔俚〕开玩笑，戏弄；讽刺[滑稽]诗文. *tickle the ~s* 使人大笑.

rib- *comb.f.* 表示"有关核糖的".

rib·ald [ˈribəld] *n.* 讲下流猥亵话的人；开下流玩笑的人. — *a.* 下流的，猥亵的，嘴脏的，不敬的；开下流玩笑的.

rib·ald·ry [ˈribəldri] *n.* 下流；下流话，猥亵话；下流的笑话.

rib·and [ˈribənd] *n.* 〔古、英〕= ribbon.

rib·band [ˈribbænd] *n.*【船】带板；木桁.

rib·bed [ribd] *a.* 呈肋骨形的；用肋状物支撑的；起棱的；有罗纹的.

rib·bing [ˈribiŋ] *n.* ①〔集合词〕叶肋，肋材，翅脉，垄. ②肋材的装配[排列]；(建筑等)肋材构架；作垄. ③〔美俚〕开玩笑，挖苦.

rib·ble-rab·ble [ˈribəlˌræbl] *n.* ①瞎嚷，胡言乱语. ②暴民.

rib·bon [ˈribən] *n.* ①缎带，丝带；带. ②(勋章的)饰带，绶带；【军】勋表〔佩于军服左上袋上方代表所得勋章的彩色条带〕；帽带. ③带状物；(打字机的)墨带；(钟表的)发条；钢条卷尺；带状切片；【木工】条板；碎片；【船】= ribband. ④〔*pl.*〕〔口〕缰绳. *the blue ~* (英国 Garter 勋章的)蓝绶带；最高荣誉的标记；禁酒会会员的徽章. *the red ~ (Bath* 勋章的)红绶带. *a ~ of road* 一条道路. ***be torn to ~s*** 撕成碎片. ***handle [take] the ~s*** 牵马，赶马车. ***hang in ~s*** 裂成碎片吊着. ~ ***brake*** 【机】带状制动器. ~ ***building*** [development] (从都市通到郊外干道两旁的)带状建筑. ~ **fish** 【动】带鱼. — *vt.* ①装上丝带，用丝带装饰；加上带状条纹. ②把…撕成长带，撕碎. — *vi.* 形成带状.

ri·bes [ˈraibiːz] *n.*【植】醋栗.

rib·grass [ˈribˌgrɑːs, -græs] *n.*【植】长叶车前草 *(Plantago lanceolata).*

ri·bi·tol [ˈraibitɔl] *n.*【化】核糖醇.

ri·bo·fla·vin [raibəuˈfleivin] *n.*【化】核黄素，维生素 B_2，维生素 G.

ri·bo·nu·cle·ase [ˌraibəuˈnjuːkliˌeis, -ˈnuː-] *n.*【生化】核糖核酸酶.

ri·bo·nu·cle·ic acid[raibəunjuˈkliːik ˈæsid] *n.*【生化】核糖核酸〔略 RNA〕.

ri·bose [ˈraibəus] *n.*【化】核糖.

ri·bo·side [ˈraibəsaid] *n.*【化】核糖甙.

ri·bo·some [ˈraibəˌsəum] *n.*【生化】核糖体. **-so·mal** *a.*

ri·bo·tide [ˈraibətaid] *n.*【化】核糖酸.

rib·wort [ˈribˌwəːt] *n.*【植】长叶车前草 *(Plantago lanceolata).*

R.I.C. = Royal Irish Constabulary 爱尔兰皇家警察.

Ri·car·do [riˈkɑːdəu] *n.* ①里卡多〔姓氏〕. ②David ~ 大卫·李嘉图〔1772—1823，英国经济学家〕. **-dian** *a.* 李嘉图学说[学派]的.

Rice [rais, riːs] *n.* 赖斯〔姓氏〕.

rice [rais] *n.* 稻，水稻；米；米饭. *a ~ seeding bed* 秧田. *broken ~* 碎米. *cargo ~* 糙米. *cleaned ~* 白米. *polished ~* 〔英〕= *faced ~* 〔美〕上白米. *glutinous ~* 糯米. *~ bran* 米糠. *~ in the husk* 谷子，稻子. *early [middle-season, late] ~* 早[中、晚]稻. *~ sprouts* 稻秧. *paddy ~* 水稻. *upland ~* 陆稻，旱稻. *~ blast* 稻瘟病. *Canada [India, wild] ~* 菰. *false ~* 鞘糠草. — *vt.* 用压粒器把(熟马铃薯等)压成碎粒. **~bird**【动】(美国产)禾花雀；芙蓉鸟；爪哇麻雀. ~ **flour** 米粉. ~ **milk** 米粉牛奶. ~ **paper** 卷烟纸；通草纸；宣纸. ~ **pud·ding** 米饭布丁. **~-stem** 稻秆 *(a ~-stem borer* 水稻螟虫). ~ **transplanter** 水稻插秧机. ~ **water** (供病员喝的)稀粥，米汤.

ric·er [ˈraisə] *n.* (把熟马铃薯压成碎粒的)压粒器.

rich [ritʃ] *a.* ①富有的，富裕的，有钱的. ②富于…的 *(in)*；丰富的，大量的 *(in; with)*. ③肥沃的，丰饶的；出产丰富的(土地等). ④华美的，奢侈的，高价的，昂贵的. ⑤富有某种美好之处的 *(with)*. ⑥富有滋味的；意味深长的. ⑦芳醇的，芳烈的(酒等)；浓厚的，油腻的. ⑧浓艳的，鲜艳的(颜色). ⑨洪亮的，圆润的(声音等)；强烈的(香等). ⑩〔口〕好笑的，有趣的；荒唐的. ⑪〔和过去分词连用〕= richly. *the ~* 富人；有钱人. *~ and poor* 有钱人和穷人. *a ~ ore* 富矿，好矿. *a ~ mine* 贮量丰富的矿山. *a ~ harvest [crop]* 丰收. *~ soil* 沃土，肥壤. *~ dresses* 华美的衣服. *~ dishes* 丰富的菜餚. *~ milk* 浓厚的牛奶. *~ allusions* 意味深长的典故[喻指]. *be ~-clad* 穿得漂亮华贵. *a ~-bound book* 装订豪华的书. *That's ~!* 〔口〕真有意思！真可笑！真荒唐！ ***as ~ as a Jew [as Croesus]*** 非常有钱的. ***be ~ in...*** 富于…. **-ness** *n.*

Rich·ard [ˈritʃəd] *n.* 理查德〔姓氏，男子名〕. ~ ***Roe*** 【法】诉讼中不知姓名的当事人(参见 John Doe). ***~'s himself again.*** 又是好好的理查德了〔指从疾病、失望、恐怖中恢复正常〕.

Rich·ards [ˈritʃədz] *n.* 理查兹〔姓氏〕.

Rich·ard·son [ˈritʃədsn] *n.* 理查森〔姓氏〕.

rich·en [ˈritʃn] *vt.* 使富有；使浓；使(混合燃料)可燃成分更高.

rich·es [ˈritʃiz] *n.* 〔*sing., pl.*〕〔常 *pl.*〕财富，财宝；丰富. *the ~ of knowledge* 知识的宝库.

rich·ly [ˈritʃli] *ad.* 富裕地；丰饶地；浓厚地；浓郁地；华美地；〔主要和 deserve 连用〕充分地；完全地；彻底地. *He ~ deserves a thrashing.* 他挨揍活该.

Richter scale [ˈriʃtə skeil]【地】里氏地震强度表〔强度分级〕.

ri·cin [ˈraisin, ˈris-] *n.*【生化】蓖麻蛋白；蓖麻子白蛋白〔会凝集红血球〕.

ric·in·o·le·in [ˌraisinˈəuliːin] *n.*【生化】甘油三蓖麻醇酸酯.

rick[1] [rik] *n., vt.*〔英〕禾堆,干草堆；堆成草堆. ~ **barton**〔英〕干草堆积场.

rick[2] [rik] *v., n.*〔英〕= wrick.

rick·ets [ˈrikits] *n.*〔*sing., pl.*〕【医】软骨病,佝偻病.

rick·ett·si·a [riˈketsiə] *n.* (*pl.* **-si·ae** [-iː], **-si·as**)【微】立克次氏体. **-l** *a.*

rick·et·y [ˈrikiti] *a.* (**-et·i·er; -i·est**) ①佝偻病〔软骨病〕的；患佝偻病；似佝偻病的. ②蹒跚的,东倒西歪的,摇晃的；虚弱的.

rick·ey [ˈriki] *n.*〔美〕利克酒；利克水〔酸橙汁、糖、酒、汽水的混合饮料〕.

rick·rack, ric·rac [ˈrikræk] *n.* 波状[曲折]花边.

rick·sha, rick·shaw [ˈrikʃə, -ʃɔː] *n.* 人力车,黄包车. *a ~ man* 人力车夫.

rick·y-tick [ˈrikiˈtik] *a.*〔俚〕①【乐】单调而快速的〔如二十世纪二十年代的一种民间音乐〕. ②老式的,过时的 (= ricky-ticky).

ric·o·chet [ˈrikəʃet, -ʃei] *n.* (石片、枪弹等接触地面、水面后的)跳飞；漂；跳飞的石片；【军】跳弹. ~ *fire [firing]* 跳弹射击,跳射. *a ~ shot* 跳弹. —*vi.*(〔英〕*-tt-*) 跳飞；漂掠. — *vt.* 使跳飞,用跳弹射击.

ri·cot·ta [riˈkɔtə; It. riːˈkəutɑː] *n.* (意大利制)乳清干酪.

ric·tus [ˈriktəs] *n.* ①【动】嘴裂,(鸟或动物)张嘴时的阔度. ②(此种)裂口. ③露齿裂嘴,龇牙咧咀. **-tal** *a.*

rid[1] [rid] (**rid** [rid], **rid·ded** [ˈridid]; **rid·ding**) *vt.* ①使脱除,使摇脱 (*of; from*). ②〔方〕除去,扫除；收拾干净(房间、饭桌) (up)；打发掉(工作等) (*off, away*). ③〔古〕救,救出. *The world is well ~ of him.* 那个家伙死得好. *He is ~ of fever.* 他的烧退了. **get [be] ~ of** 摆脱；除去,驱除,拔除(眼中钉) (*I can't get ~ of this cold.* 伤风总是不好.)

rid[2] [rid] *v.*〔古〕*ride* 的过去式和过去分词.

rid·a·ble [ˈraidəbl] *a.* 可以骑的(马)；可以骑马过去的(路、河等).

rid·dance [ˈridəns] *n.* 摆脱；除去,驱除. *a good ~* 拔除得好；可喜的摆脱. *He is a good ~.* 他这家伙不在的好. *make clean ~ of* 把…扫除干净[一扫而光].

rid·den [ridn] *ride* 的过去分词. — *a.* 受…支配的,受…虐待的,受…折磨的；…横行的. *a country ~ by soldiers* 军人跋扈的国家.

ri·dent [ˈraidnt] *a.*〔罕〕笑的.

rid·dle[1] [ˈridl] *n.* 谜；谜语,哑谜；莫名其妙的事情,闷葫芦；莫名其妙的人. *propound [propose, ask] a ~* 出谜. *solve [find out, guess] a ~* 解谜,猜谜. *speak in ~s* 令人摸不着头脑地说. — *vt.* 解(谜),猜. *Riddle me a [my] ~, what is this? = Riddle me, ~ me what it is.* 给你猜一个谜,你猜这是什么谜? — *vi.* 出谜；令人摸不着头脑地说.

rid·dle[2] [ˈridl] *n.* 粗筛. —*vt.* 用筛分选(卵石等),筛分. ②(子弹等把船等)打得枪眼象筛子一样. ③精查,细查(证据、真伪)；连连质问(使人为难),(列举事实)问倒(人). *The door was ~d with shot.* 门被子弹打得尽是窟窿.

rid·dling [ˈridliŋ] *a.* 谜似的,费解的,莫名其妙的,令人摸不着头脑的.

ride [raid] (**rode** [rəud]; **ridden** [ˈridn]) *vi.* ①骑(马)去,坐(车)去；骑,乘,坐；骑马；骑自行车去(旅行). ②当骑兵,在骑兵队服务. ③(骑师赛马前穿着骑装)在马上有若干重量. ④(马乖乖地)给骑(等),骑(乘,坐)着(舒服、不舒服等). ⑤揹,揹去,(车等)载,载去. ⑥浮,漂,像浮(在空中、水上),(船)停泊；(月、太阳)上升,挂；被支持着动；【导弹】乘波. ⑦(折断的骨头等)叠上；【彩印】套上. ⑧〔美俚〕(事情)进展顺利. ~ *in [on] a carriage [train, ship]* 坐车[火车,船]. ~ *on a bicycle* 骑着自行车走. *He ~s in Life Guards.* 他在近卫骑兵队服务. ~ *12 stone* (指赛马骑师)穿着骑装有12 呖重. ~ *well [hard]* (道路等)好[不好]骑行,(车)好[不好]乘坐. *Let it ~* 〔美俚〕听其自然. — *vt.* ①骑,乘,坐,跨；驾御(马等)；破(浪)前进(等). ②乘马[车等]经过(某处). ③支配,控制. ④压迫；使痛苦,折磨[通常用过去分词, *cf.* ridden]. ⑤〔美〕给坐着去,载去,载运. ⑥系(船),使停泊. ~ *a bicycle* 骑自行车. *Spectacles ~ his nose* 眼镜架在鼻子上. *I was ridden by a nightmare* 我被梦魇压住了. ~ **a gravy train**〔美〕多取,多拿. ~ **a man down like the main-tack** 使人过分疲劳. ~ **a method [jest] to death** 把一种方法用得过多以致失却效用,(笑话)讲得过分反而乏味. ~ **a race** 赛马,赛车. ~ **and tie** 两人轮流骑一匹马〔一人骑至某处即拴马留给另一人,自己徒步前进〕. ~ **at** 骑马驶向. ~ **at single anchor** 抛单锚停船. ~ **at the ring** 跑马(用枪)挑(取高悬的)圈[环]. ~ **away** = ~ off. ~ **bareback** 骑没鞍子的马. ~ **behind** 骑在背后. ~ **bodkin** 乘在两人当中. ~ **double** 两人骑一匹马[一辆自行车]. ~ **down** 骑马穷追[赶上]；骑马踏坏[撞倒]；克服；打败；把马骑死；过度驱使. ~ **for a fall** 蛮干,自讨苦吃,自取灭亡. ~ **herd**〔美西部〕(牧童)骑马看管牧群；(一般)看管,保护. ~ **off** 岔开去. ~ **off on (side issues)** 岔到枝节问题上去；回避要点. ~ **(sb.) on a rail** 令人骑在木棍上杠着赶走〔作为惩罚〕. ~ **sb. off**【马球】驱马插入球和对手中间阻止对手打球. ~ **one's horse at a fence** 策马向篱笆跑去〔准备跳过去〕. ~ **one's horse to the enemy** 骑马向敌人冲锋. ~ **one's horse to death** 把马骑死；把自己的得意话讲得过分而惹人讨厌. ~ **on the wind [waves]** (船)迎风[破浪]前进. ~ **out** ①(船等)安然冲过风暴. ②平安渡过困难. ~ **over** 蹂躏；威吓,压倒；跳(越)过；(赛马)从容胜过；骑马而来. ~ **roughshod over** 大摆架子,趾高气扬；蹂躏,欺凌,为所欲为,横行霸道. ~ **rusty** 变顽固；倔强地反抗. ~ **sth. to death** (把某事物)使用过份,反而得不到效果. ~ **the beam** 沿着波束所示航线飞行. ~ **the bumpers [buffers]**〔美俚〕(站在货车与货车连接处)偷乘火车. ~ **the deck**〔美俚〕(扒在客车顶上)偷乘火车. ~ **the fence** 骑马巡视牧场周围并检修篱笆. ~ **the goat**〔口〕加入秘密团体. ~ **the line**〔美俚〕(在无篱笆的牧场与牧场间)做看守. ~ **the rods [tickets]**〔美俚〕(钻在棚车里面)偷乘火车. ~ **the shoe leather express**〔美俚〕走路去. ~ **the whirlwind** (天使)御旋风；叱咤风云；趁革命机会. ~ **to hog [pig]** 猎野猪. ~ **to hounds** (猎狐时)骑马紧跟着猎狗追赶；猎狐. ~ **up** (身上的衣服等)向上拱,缩上去；(衣领)露出(衣外)；(领带)松开,走样. ~ **up to** 骑马[坐车]赶到…跟前. — *n.* ①骑乘,乘坐；骑马旅行；乘车[船等]旅行；搭乘时间. ②(森林等中的)马道；跑马场. ③【军】补充骑兵队. ④〔美俚〕汽车；轻松自由的节奏. **give sb. a ~** 让(人)骑马[乘车]. **go for a ~** 去骑一骑,乘车转一圈. **have [take] a long ~** 骑马[乘车]走很远一段路. **take for a ~**〔美俚〕用汽车诱出杀害；欺骗.

rid·er [ˈraidə] *n.* ①骑马的人；善于骑马的人；骑师；〔古〕跑生意的,行商. ②〔古〕骑士,武士；驯马师；马贼. ③附款；附笔；(特指议会三读会的)追加条款. ④(精密天平上的)游(动砝)码. ⑤制导器；【数】系；〔口〕乘波导弹；【几】应用问题；(机械装置的)上部；夹层；【海】(加固船体的)盖顶木料[钢板]；【园艺】接穗；【建】(支墙)斜撑. *by way of ~* 作为…的追加,作为附款. *the ~'s boue* (屁股上骑马磨擦成的)老繭. **-ship** 全体乘客；乘客数. **-less** *a.* 没人骑的；没主人的(马)；无附款的,无追加条款的.

ridge [ridʒ] *n.* ①【动】脊；脊背. ②山脊；岭,岗；分水岭,山脉. ③屋脊；(犁沟与犁沟间的)犁垄；田塍；鼻梁；隆起线；【筑城】斜堤脊；【铸造】沟,注沟；(气象圈上)狭长的高压带(脊). — *vt.* 装屋脊；作垄,培土；使(面上)起皱纹；

种在垄上. — *vi.* 成垄; 起皱纹. ~**beam**, ~**piece**, ~**pole** 栋梁; 栋木. ~ **roof**=gable roof. ~ **tile** 脊瓦. ~**tree**【建】栋木. ~**way** 山顶上的路, 山脊路; 田塍路.

Ridge [ridʒ] *n.* 里奇〔姓氏〕.

ridg·y [ˈridʒi] *a.* *(-·er; -i·est)* 有脊的; 成垄的; 隆起的.

rid·i·cule [ˈridikjuːl] *n.* 嘲笑, 愚弄, 揶揄; 〔古〕笑柄. ***bring into ~ = cast [pour] ~ upon = cover with ~ = hold up to ~ = turn into [to] ~*** 嘲笑, 讽刺, 挖苦. (*He was held up to ~.* 他被人嘲弄. *He turns everything into ~.* 他把一切都当作笑话看待. *pour ~ on sb.* 嘲笑某人). — *vt.* 嘲笑, 奚落; 愚弄; 讥刺, 挖苦.

ri·dic·u·lous [riˈdikjuləs] *a.* 可笑的, 滑稽的; 该嘲笑的; 荒谬的. ~ *in dress [shape]* 衣服[形状]好笑的. *the* ~ 可笑的事物. **-ly** *ad.* **-ness** *n.*

rid·ing[1] [ˈraidiŋ] *n.* 区〔英国约克郡的行政区, 有东西北三区〕. *the Three Ridings* (英国)约克郡.

rid·ing[2] [ˈraidiŋ] *n.* 骑马; 乘车; 马道, 跑马场. *take a* ~ 骑马, 乘车. ~ ***hawse full***【海】船在停泊中前后簸动致海水由锚链孔打入. ***radar beam*** ~ 波束导航. ~ **bitts**【海】系缆柱. ~**-habit** 女骑装. ~ **lamp**, ~ **light**【海】锚位灯, 停泊灯. ~ **master** 马术教练[教官]. ~ **school** 马术学校. ~ **suit** 骑装.

Rid·ley [ˈridli] *n.* 里德利〔姓氏〕.

ri·dot·to [riˈdɔtəu] *n.* *(pl. -tos)* 舞蹈会, 歌舞会〔十八世纪英国流行的社交聚会, 常为一种化装舞会〕.

Rid·path [ˈridpɑːθ] *n.* 里德帕斯〔姓氏〕.

Ri·el [riˈel, riːl] *n.* 瑞尔〔柬埔寨货币单位〕.

Ries·ling [ˈriːzliŋ] *n.* 一种浓烈的莱茵白葡萄酒.

ri·fa·ci·men·to 〔It.〕 [riˌfɑtʃiˈmentəu] *n.* *(pl. ri·fa·ci·men·ti [-ˈmentiː])* 改编, 改写.

rif·am·pi·cin [ˌrifæmˈpaisən] *n.*【药】利福平 (=rifampin).

rif·a·my·cin [ˌrifəˈmaisən] *n.*【药】利福霉素.

rife [raif] *a.* 〔用作 *Pred.*〕流行的, 盛行的; 普遍的; 大量的, 丰富的. ***be [grow, wax]*** ~ ***with*** *(idioms)* 富于, 充满(习语等). ***used to be*** ~ 过去很盛行.

Riff [rif] *n.* ①= Rif, Er. ②(北非的)里弗族. **-i·an** *n., a.* 里弗人(的).

riff [rif] *n.* (爵士音乐的)即兴反复片段. — *vi.* 反复演奏即兴段.

rif·fle [ˈrifl] *n.* ①【采】(沙金采集槽的)捕砂沟. ②〔美〕(河中)急流; 波纹. ***make the*** ~ 成功地渡过河流或急滩; 成功地战胜困难; 成功, 胜利. — *vt., vi.* ①流过(浅滩); 使起涟漪. ②(用拇指)翻(书页等). ③快速洗(纸牌).

riff·raff [ˈrifræf] *n.* 地痞, 流氓; (人类的)渣滓; 废物, 碎屑.

ri·fle[1] [ˈraifl] *n.* 步枪; 来复枪, 膛线枪〔和滑膛枪区别〕; 来复线, 膛线; 〔*pl.*〕步枪队. — *vt.* 在(枪膛)内制来复线; 用步枪[来复枪]射击. ~**bird** (叫声象枪声一样的)嘘鸣飞鸟. ~ **corps** 志愿步枪队. ~**-green** *n., a.* 暗绿色(的). ~ **ground** 步枪射击[打靶]场. ~**man** ①步兵; 步枪射手. ②= ~ **bird**. ~**-pit**【军】散兵壕. ~**-range** 步枪射击[打靶]场; 步枪射程. ~ **scope** 步枪上的望远瞄准器. ~**shot** 步枪子弹; 步枪射手; 步枪射程.

ri·fle[2] [ˈraifl] *vt.* 搜劫; 抢劫一空; 偷去; (顺手)带走. ~ *the drawers and show cases* 翻箱倒柜, 抢劫一空. ~ *a person of his belongings* 搜劫某人的行李. — *vi.* 搜劫; 抢劫; 掠夺.

ri·fle·ry [ˈraifləri] *n.* 步枪打靶(练习).

ri·fling [ˈraifliŋ] *n.* ①(在枪膛里)制来复线. ②来复线, 膛线.

rift [rift] *n.* ①裂口, 罅隙, 空隙, 裂缝. ②【地】断裂; 断层线; 长狭谷; 河流浅石滩. ③分裂, 不和. *a little* ~ *within the lute* 嫌隙; 最初的分歧; 发狂的预兆〔神志开始不清〕. — *vt., vi.* 破开, 裂开, 劈开. ~ **valley**【地】地堑; 裂谷.

rig[1] [rig] *n.* ①【海】索具, 装具, 装备; 舣装; 帆缆的配备; 帆装, 帆具, 索具; 帆式. ②〔口〕服装. ③〔美〕设备, 装配, 配备; 配好了马的马车; 准备好的马车. ④钻探设备〔平台〕; 凿井机器;【矿】钻塔, 钻车. ⑤〔口〕钓鱼用具〔设备〕. *a working* ~ 工作服. *a* ~ *of the day* 时装. *a test* ~【空】试验台. — *vt.* ①【海】装上索具〔帆桩, 帆桁等〕; 配备, 装备;【空】装机身[机翼]. ②〔口〕穿(美服) *(out; up)*. ③临时赶造, 草草做成 (up). — *vi.* (船)装上索具 *(out; up)*. ~ ***out*** 装饰, 打扮. ~ ***up a tent*** 赶忙撑起一个帐篷. ~ ***up a military force*** 调兵遣将.

rig[2] [rig] 〔口〕*n.* ①捣蛋, 恶作剧; 嘲弄, 戏弄; 欺骗. ②阴谋, 诡计. ③【商】垄断, 囤积. *run a [the]* ~, *run one's* ~*s* 恶作剧, 捣蛋 (upon). — *vt.* 用不正当手段操纵, 控制; (为欺骗目的而)事先决定[安排]; 〔口〕欺骗. ~ *the market* 操纵市价, 垄断(证券等)市价. ~ *an election* 操纵选举.

rig[3] [rig] *n.* 发育不全[部分阉割]的动物.

Ri·ga [ˈriːgə] *n.* 里加〔苏联港市〕.

rig·a·ma·role [ˈrigəməˌrəul] *n.* 冗长的废话, 无聊的罗唆话, 没条理的文章, 烦琐的仪式程序 (=rigmarole).

ri·ga·to·ni [ˌrigəˈtəuni; It. ˌriːgɑːˈtəuniː] *n.* 小肉龙〔一种条状肉馅的面食〕.

Ri·gel [ˈraidʒl, -gl] *n.*【天】参宿七.

rig·ger [ˈrigə] *n.* ①装配工人;【海】索具装配人;【空】机身装配员. ②【机】束带滑车;【建】脚手架安全装置. ③骗子; 垄断市价[操纵物价]的人.

rig·ging [ˈrigiŋ] *n.* ①【海】索具; 装置, 设备;【空】机身装配; (舞台用)索具; 传动用装置. ②〔口〕衣服, 服装. *a* ~ *band*【空】装配带, 座带. *a* ~ *shop*【空】装配厂. ***climb the*** ~ 〔美俚〕发脾气; 发怒.

right [rait] *a.* ①右, 右方的, 右侧的, 右派的 *(opp.* left*)*. ②正当的, 当然的 *(opp.* wrong*)*. ③不错的; 正确的; 真的, 真正的; (布的)正面的. ④笔直的, 直角的 *(opp.* olique*)*. ⑤恰好的, 合适的, 适当的, 得当的, 妥当的, 顺当的, 顺利的; 秩序井然的, 井井有条的. ⑥健康的, 健全的; 精神正常的. ⑦〔罕〕(人、性格)正直的; 公正的; 〔美〕同情的; 有好意的. ⑧〔古〕合法的. ~ *and left* 左右的, 两方的. *the R- Wing(s)* 右派, 保守派. *That's* ~ 好; 〔口〕就是那样. *R-!* 〔口〕= *R- you are.* 说得对; 〔回答命令、提议〕是, 知道了, 对. *R- oh!* = righto. *the* ~ *side of cloth* 布的正面. ~ *arm* 得力助手. *Mr. [Miss] R-* 〔口〕很相配的丈夫[妻子]. ~ *amount* 需要量, 适量. *a* ~ *angle* 直角. *a* ~ *line* 直线. *I am not quite* ~ 我身体不大舒服. *He is not* ~ *in his head* 他神志不正常. ***a fault on the ~ side*** 可以原谅的过失, 小缺点. ***act a ~ part*** 采取正当行动. ***all*** ~ 好; 圆满; 确实. ***All's*** ~ 万事顺利, 一切都好. ***as ~ as a trivet [as rain]*** 非常健康; 〔美〕好极了. ***at [on, to] one's ~ hand*** 在右方. ***at ~ angles with*** 和…成直角. ***do the ~ thing*** 做正确的事情, 做得对. ***get it*** ~ (使)真正[正确]理解, (使)了解清楚. ***get on the ~ side of*** 得到…的喜爱[宠爱]. ***get [make]*** ~ 改正, 弄正, 弄好. ***give the ~ hand of fellowship*** 接纳为友; 同意入伙. ***in one's ~ mind [senses]*** 精神正常. ***on the ~ side of (fifty)*** (50岁)以下, (50岁)不到. ***put oneself*** ~ 说明自己的正确立场[真正用意] *(I put myself ~ with him.* 我向他说明他对我的误解). ***put one's ~ hand to the work*** 认真[尽力]做事. ***put*** ~ 改正, 恢复健康[秩序], 弄好; 修理; 矫正, 订正. ***put the (~) saddle on the ~ horse*** 责备应该责备的人. ***R- capitulationism*** 右倾投降主义. ~ ***D. A.*** 〔美俚〕老实公正的地方检察官 *[D. A. = district attorney]*. ~ ***forward*** = ~ ***in***. ~ ***guy*** 〔美俚〕忠实可靠的人. ~ ***half back***【足球】右前卫. ~ ***in***【足球】右内锋. ***R- opportunism*** 右倾机会主义. ~ ***or wrong*** 无论对与不对, 无论怎样, 一定. ~ ***side out*** 正面向外. ~ ***side up*** 正面朝上. ***set oneself*** ~ = put oneself ~. ***set*** ~ = put ~. ***the***

~ man in the ~ place 人地两宜；人得其位，位得其人．*the ~ way* 正路 *(to)*；最正当[适当、有效]的方式[做法]；真相；〔用作状语〕正当地，适当地．— *ad.* ①一直，笔直；一直，始终．②正当地，公正地；正确地，准确地；无误地；真实地，真正地．③适当地，得当地；正好地，恰好地；当然地；顺当地，顺利地；完全，全然；恰好，正好．④立刻，马上．⑤向右，向右侧．⑥〔古、俗〕非常，很．⑦〔尊称〕：*the R- Honourable*，见 honourable 条．*It sank ~ to the bottom* 直沉到底．*I guessed ~* 我猜中了．*It serves you ~* 真是活该，真是报应．*~ well* 非常好．***be rotten ~ through*** 完全腐烂．***come ~*** 改正，变好；实现．***do a thing ~*** 好好干，认真做．***go ~*** 进行得顺利．***go ~ home*** 直接回家．***go ~ on*** 一直前进，向前突进．***if I remember ~*** 如果我没有记错的话．***look neither ~ nor left*** 目不斜视．***Right about!***〔口令〕向后转！***~ along***〔美〕不停地，不断地．***~ and left*** 向左又向右；向四面八方，从四面八方；(拳击等的)乱打．***~ away***〔美〕立刻，马上．***~ down*** 一直朝下；明明白白地，不隐瞒地；很，十分；无风．***Right dress!***〔口令〕向右看齐！***~ here***〔美〕现在就在这里；即刻．***~ in the middle of one's work*** 正在工作中．***~ in the wind's eye*** 迎风．***~ now***〔美〕现在，目前；方才，刚刚．***~ off***〔美〕即刻；全然．***~ off the bat***〔美俚〕立刻．***~ off the reel***〔美俚〕立刻；慌忙；新鲜的．***~ on***〔美俚〕①对啊！②老于世故．***~ on time*** 准时．***~ opposite*** 正对面，正相反．***~ out of the feed box***〔美俚〕最新情报〔尤指关于赛马的〕．***~ over (the way)*** 在(道路的)正对过．***~ smart (of)***〔美〕大量的，很多的．***~ straight***〔美〕即刻．***~ there*** 就在那里．***Right turn!***〔口令〕向右转！***~ up and down***【海】风平浪静；直率认真地．***send sb. to the ~ about*** 一口谢绝，拒绝(某人)．***turn out ~*** 顺利起来；碰巧．***turn ~*** 转往右面．***turn ~ round*** 转一个圈．— *n.* ①右，右面，右边，右侧；【军】右翼；右边的东西；〔美〕【海军】右舷．②〔R-〕【政】(从主席台上看去)右座议员[党员]；右翼[右派](分子)；保守派，保守分子．③正，正当；正义，公理，公道；公正；正当行为；正确，准确，无误；〔*pl.*〕正当状态[秩序]；〔*pl.*〕事情的真相．④权利；〔常 *pl.*〕(董事对新股的)优惠权．⑤正面．*~(s) and wrong(s)* 是非曲直．*the ~s of a matter [the case]* 事情的真相．*absolute ~s* 绝对权．*civil ~s* 公民权．*the ~ of flights beyond*【空】以远权．*the ~ of visit (and search)*【法】(交战国在公海上的)搜查权．***be in ~ with*** = *get in ~ with*．***the Bill of Rights***【英史】①《权利法案》〔1689年公布的英国君主立宪制的根本法文件〕．②《人权法案》〔1789年美国通过的美国宪法的第一次修正案〕．***bring to ~s*** 使复原状，改正；规劝．***by (good) ~*** 正当地，当然．***by ~ of ...*** 依…，以…的权限[理由]．***by ~s*** 根据正当权利．***claim a ~ to*** 要求…的权利．***confuse ~ with wrong*** 混淆是非．***do (sb.) ~*** 公平对待(某人)，正当批评(某人)．***get in ~ with***〔美〕得到…的喜爱．***go to the ~ about*** 向后转；扭转[转变]局面[主义、政策等]．***have a [the] ~ to do [of doing]*** 有权做…；应该做…．***have a [no] ~ to (sth.)*** 有[没有]要求(某事物)的权利．***have a [no] ~ to do [of doing]*** 有[没有]做…的资格[权利]，应该[不应该]做…．***have ~***〔罕〕正当，有理．***in one's (own) ~*** 依据自己的权利；依据自己生来应有的权利．***in ~ of*** = by ~ of. ***in the ~*** 有理，正当．***keep to the ~*** 靠右边走；走正路．***of ~*** = by ~．***put to ~s*** = set to ~s．***~ of way*** 通行权；(车、船)先行权；(消防车等的)优先通行权；〔美〕铁路[公路、电路]用地．***set to ~s*** 整理，整顿，改正，纠正．***sit on the R-*** 是右座[右方，右翼，右派，保守党]议员．***stand on [upon] one's ~s*** 坚持自己权利．***to the ~*** 向右面．***turn to the ~*** 向右拐(弯)．***turn to the ~ about*** = go to the ~ about. — *vt.* ①弄直，扶直，竖立，扶起，扶正．②改正，修正，纠正，改善；整理．③〔美〕把(舵)转向右舷．④使复权，使恢复名誉；报复；救济，拯救(被压迫者等)．*~ itself* 恢复常态，(重新)站平，摆平．*~ oneself* 辩明，表白，伸雪．— *vi.*(歪斜的船等)复原，恢复正常；站平，摆平．**~-about** ① *n.* 反相的方向；向后转；(态度、主义、政策等的)转变，改变．②*a.*, *ad.* 向后转的[地]．③*vi.*, *vt.* (使)向后转．*(~-about face [turn]!*【军】〔口令〕向后转！*send to the ~-about* 拒绝；使溃退；驱逐；立刻解聘[免职]．*)* **~-angled** *a.* 直角的．**~-down** *a.*, *ad.* 彻底的[地]；真正的[地] *(a ~-down scoundrel* 十足的恶棍．*I was ~-down sorry.* 十分抱歉*)*．**~ hand** *n.* ①亲信；得力的助手．②〔古〕有实权的地位；荣誉地位．**~-hand** *a.* 右手的；右边的；用右手的；非常得力的，心腹的，倚为股肱的 (*a ~-hand man* 自己右边的同排的人；心腹，左右手，得力的助手；〔美〕没趣味的主人)．**~-handed** *a.* 惯用右手的；用右手的；向右旋转的，右旋性的；〔罕〕可原谅的 *(~-handed screw* 右旋螺钉．*~-handed fault* 可原谅的过失[缺点]*)*．*ad.* 用右手．**~-hander** 惯用右手的人；向右旋转的东西；〔口〕用右手的一击．**~ heart**【生】右心房．**~-hearted** *a.* 正直的，诚实的．**~-minded** *a.* 有正义感的；公正的；**~-mindedness** 正直，正义感，诚实的．**~ sailing**【海】(直向)基点方位航行法．**~-to-work** *a.* (法律等)禁止强行要求工人加入工会的；禁止工会垄断雇用工人的．**~-ward** *ad.*, *a.* 向右，向右边；向右的，右的．**~wards** *ad.* 向右．**~ whale**【动】露脊鲸．**~-wing** *a.* 右翼的．**~-winger** 右翼分子．

right·en [ˈraitn] *vt.* 使恢复正常，整顿．*lack the agility to ~ oneself at once* 缺乏立刻恢复正常的敏捷性．

right·eous [ˈraitʃəs] *a.* ①正直的，公正的，正义的．②正当的，当然的，〔the ~〕好人，正人君子．*~ indignation* 义愤．**-ly** *ad.* **-ness** *n.*

right·ful [ˈraitful] *a.* ①正直的，正义的．②正当的，当然的；合法的；正统的．③恰当的，合适的．*a ~ cause* 正义．*one's ~ position* 当然的地位．**-ly** *ad.* **-ness** *n.*

right·ism [ˈraitizəm] *n.* ①〔常 R-〕右派纲领[言论、观点]．②对右派观点的赞同；右派思潮．

right·ist [ˈraitist] *n.*, *a.* 右派分子(的)，右倾分子(的)，保守分子(的)．*~ ideas* 右倾[派]思想．

right·ly [ˈraitli] *ad.* 正义地，正直地，正当地；正确地；恰当地；当然．

right·ness [ˈraitnis] *n.* 正直，诚实；正义，公正；正确(性)；恰当．

right·o [ˈraitəu, ˈraiˈtəu] *int.*〔主英口〕是！对！好！

rig·id [ˈridʒid] *a.* ①坚硬的，强直的，硬性的，僵硬的 *(opp.* flexible, elastic*)*．②坚定的，固定不动的．③严格的，严正的，严肃的，严厉的；严密的(实验等)．④刚直的；顽固的；不屈的．⑤【物】刚性的；【空】硬式的(飞船)．*~ in one's views* 意志坚定．*~ discipline* 严格的训练．*~ adherence to rules* 严守规则．*a ~ body*【物】刚体．**-ly** *ad.* **-ness** *n.*

ri·gid·i·fy [riˈdʒidiˌfai], *vt.*, *vi.* **(-fi·ed; -fy·ing)** 使[变]坚硬，使[变]顽固，(使)僵化，使[变]坚固．**-fi·ca·tion** [ˌridʒidifiˈkeiʃən] *n.*

ri·gid·i·ty [riˈdʒiditi] *n.* ①坚硬，强直；僵硬；【物】刚性，刚度．②刚直；顽固，强硬．③严格，严励，严峻，严肃；严密，精密．

rig·ma·role [ˈrigmərəul] *n.* 鬼话，冗长的废话，无聊的罗唆话；冗长的文章．— *a.* 乱七八糟的，条理不清的；无聊的．

rig·or [ˈrigə] *n.*〔美〕= rigour.

rig·or [ˈraigɔː] *n.*〔L.〕【医】寒战，发冷，冷颤；强直，僵硬．*~ mortis*【医】尸僵[死后僵硬]．

rig·or·ism [ˈrigərizm] *n.* 过分严厉，严肃主义，严格主义．**-ist** *n.*

rig·or·ous [ˈrigərəs] *a.* ①严格的，严肃的；严厉的．②严峻的，严酷的，苛刻的；酷烈的，凛烈的．③严密的，精确的．

rig·our [ˈrigə] *n.* ①严格，严肃；严厉，严酷，苛刻；苛刻

行为；横暴行为．②(法律等的)严格执行；严密，精密．③艰苦，困苦；〔常 *pl.*〕(气候等的)酷烈，凛烈．*execute a law with ~* 严厉执法．*with the utmost ~ of the law* 最严格地依法(办理等)．*the ~ of winter [punishment]* 冬天的严寒[处罚的严厉]．**-ism** *n.*

rig-out [ˈrigˈaut] *n.* 〔英俚〕一套服装．

Rigs•dag [ˈrigzdɑːg] *n.* (丹麦的)国会．

Rig-ve•da [rigˈveidə] *n.* 〔Sans.〕梨俱吠陀〔印度最古经典四吠陀之一〕；赞颂．

R.I.I.A. = Royal Institute of International Affairs. 〔英〕皇家国际问题研究所．

rijst•ta•fel, rijs•ta•fel [ˈraisˌtɑːfəl] *n.* 〔D.〕【烹】印尼式饭菜〔以米饭为主食，配有各种菜餚和各种调味酱汁的吃法〕．

Riks•dag [ˈriksdɑːg] *n.* (瑞典或芬兰的)国会．

rile [rail] *vt.* ①〔美〕搅浑，搅浊．②〔口〕惹怒，激怒，使急躁．

Ri•ley [ˈraili] *n.* 赖利〔姓氏，男子名〕．

ri•li•e•vo [riliˈeivəu] *n.* 〔It.〕浮雕，凸雕．

rill[1] [ril] *n.* 〔诗〕小河，小溪，细流．— *vi.* 象小河一般流．

rille, rill[2] [ril] *n.* 【天】(月面)谷，沟纹．

rill•et [ˈrilit] *n.* 小溪，细流．

rim [rim] *n.* ①(圆形器皿的)边，缘；轮圈，辋圈，轮辋，轮缘；眼镜框，帽边(等)．②【海】水面，海面．*the golden ~* 王冠．*the sea's ~* 水平线．— *vt.* 装边(缘)，装轮圈；〔美俚〕欺骗，诳骗．**~-brake** 轮圈煞车．**~land** 【地理】(中心地区的)边缘地带．

rimble-ramble [ˈrimblræmbl] *n., vi.* 〔美〕(说)没意思的话，(说)傻话．

rime[1] [raim] *n.* ①〔诗〕白霜，雾凇．②结晶，凝结的外壳．— *vt.* 使盖上霜．

rime[2] [raim] *n., vi., vt.* = rhyme.

rime riche [riːmˈriːʃ] ***(pl. rimes riches*** [riːmˈriːʃ]***)*** 【诗】(完)全韵 (= perfect rhyme).

rim•fire [ˈrimˌfaiə] *a.* 弹药筒的，子弹筒的〔指底火装在底部边上的弹药筒〕．

rim•i•fon [ˈrimifən] *n.* 【药】雷米封，异烟肼〔肺结核特效药〕．

rim•less [ˈrimlis] *a.* 无边(缘)的；(眼镜)无框的．

ri•mose, ri•mous [ˈraiməus, -məs] *a.* 【植】有裂缝的，多罅裂的．

rim•ple [ˈrimpl] *n., vt., vi.* ***(-pled; -pling)*** 〔罕〕皱纹；皱起；生皱；弄皱．

rim•y [ˈraimi] *a.* 下了霜的，白霜[雾凇]盖满了的．

rind [raind] *n.* ①外皮，果皮，菜皮；树皮；皮壳；熏肉皮；干酪皮；鲸皮．②外观，外表．— *vt.* 剥…皮；削…皮．**~ gall** 树皮上的伤痕．

rin•der•pest [ˈrindəpest] *n.* 【兽医】牛瘟，牛疫．

Rine•hart [ˈrainhɑːt] *n.* 赖恩哈特〔姓氏〕．

ring[1] [riŋ] *n.* ①圈，环，轮；戒指，指环，耳环，鼻圈，镯子(等)；【运】吊环．②轮状物；【植】年轮；(羊齿类的)环带．③赛马场，竞技场，运动场；(赛马的)赌客席；马戏场；(动物展览会的)陈列场；〔the ~〕拳击场，拳师帮伙．③〔主美〕(政治、商业上的)党派，圈子，帮，集团．④【化、数】环，圈．*a betrothal ~* 订婚戒指．*a heavy ~* 承力环．*a ~ counter* 环形计数器．*an annual ~*【植】年轮．*an inner ~* 骨干分子小圈子．***be in the ~ for*** 参加…的竞选．***close the ~ around*** 【军】缩紧包围．***hold [keep] the ~*** 保持中立，保持不干涉态度．***in a ~*** 成圈地，团团地．***lead the ~*** 领头，发起．***make a ~*** 围成圈；结成小集团操纵市场．***make [run] ~s round sb.*** 〔俚〕抢在某人之前；容易地击败某人，大大地胜过．***meet in the ~*** 比赛拳击[摔跤]．***puff out ~s of smoke*** 喷烟成圈圈，吐烟圈．***ride [run] at the ~*** 跑马挑圈．***~s in water*** 一圈一圈的水纹．***sit in a ~*** 坐成一圈．***toss one's hat in the ~*** 参加竞选．— *vt.* ①给套上环；给戴上戒指，给穿上鼻圈．②围住，包围 *(in; round; about)*．③【园艺】环剥(树皮)；把(洋葱)切成圈．④使马兜着圈子跑．⑤(投环游戏)套住．**~ *a quoit*** (投环游戏)投环．**~ *(up) cattle*** 骑马把牛圈赶在一块儿．— *vi.* 成环状；(鹰等)盘旋飞翔；(狐、兔等)兜圈子奔跑．**~ armour** 连环甲，锁子甲．**~ bolt** 【机】环端螺栓．**~-dove** 【动】斑尾林鸽．**~-fence** 围墙，围栅；束缚，限制．**~-finger** 无名指〔尤指左手的，结婚戒指通常戴在这里〕．**~ hunt** 烧火围猎．**~lead•er** (尤指暴动、违法行为等的)领头人，首领．**~like** *a.* 似环的，环状的．**~-lock** 密码锁；暗码锁．**~-man** 〔英〕(赛马的)马票掮客．**~-master** 马戏团领班．**~neck** 颈上有环纹的鸟、蛇等．**~-necked** *a.* 【动】颈上有环纹的．**~ net** (捕鱼用)围网．**~ road** 环形道路；环城公路．**~side** (马戏场等的)场缘前座；可以近望的地点．**~-streaked** *a.* (身上)有环纹的．**~-tailed** *a.* 尾上有环纹的．**~toss** 投环游戏，套圈游戏．**~worm** 【医】轮癣，金钱癣．

ring[2] [riŋ] *vt.* ***(rang*** [ræŋ]***; rung*** [rʌŋ]***)*** ①鸣，敲(钟)，摇[按](铃)；敲钟[摇铃]报知，敲钟[按铃]叫(人)；给…打电话．②使响遍；大声讲，唠唠叨叨讲，说来说去．**~** *an alarm* 敲警钟．***~ down*** 【剧】鸣铃闭幕；使[宣布]结束，使[宣布]告终．***~ in [out]*** 打铃上班[下班]；(鸣钟)迎进(新年)，[送出(旧岁)]；以不正当手段引入．***~ a bell*** 引起反应[共鸣]．***~ one's own bell*** 自夸自赞．***~ sb.'s praises*** 大声夸赞某人．***~ the bell*** 〔口〕成功；得…赞许 *(with)*．***~ (the) changes*** 变花样形式收到同样效果；用正常的程序作出不同花样形式；把同一事情翻来覆去地说 (*He likes to ~ the changes on his old story.* 他喜欢翻来复去地说他的老一套)．***~ the glim*** 〔美俚〕开灯．***~ the knell*** 敲丧钟；宣告废除[没落] *(of)*．***~ up*** 〔Eng.〕打电话给某人 *(sb.)*；【剧】鸣铃开幕 *(the curtain)*．***~ up a win*** 〔美〕记录胜利；得胜．— *vi.* ①(钟、铃等)鸣，响；敲钟，摇铃，敲钟[摇铃]叫人 *(for)*．②反响，鸣响，响遍；名气大．**~** *at the door* 按门铃．**~** *for the nurse* 按铃叫护士．*the woods rang with their shouts* 树林里响遍了他们的叫声．*a shot rang out* 传来一声枪响．*ears ~.* 耳朵叫，耳鸣．***~ again*** 轰响，反响．***~ false [true]*** 似乎是假的[真的]；可以断定是假货[真货]．***~ in one's ears*** (语声等)还留在耳朵里，声犹在耳．***~ in one's heart [fancy]*** 铭记在心，留在记忆里．***~ off*** 挂断电话；〔美〕停止说话；静默．***~ to [for] dinner*** 摇吃饭铃．***~ with one's fame*** 名声传遍．— *n.* ①(钟、铃等的)鸣，响；鸣声，响声；(性质、真伪等的)声音；(文章、言语等的)韵调，格调，腔调，口气．②(教堂的)一套钟，钟声．*There is a ~ at the door* 有人按门铃．*Give me a ~ this afternoon.* 今天下午给我一个电话．*His words have the ~ of truth.* 他的话听来象是真的．***answer sb.'s ~*** 答应某人铃声．***give the bell a ~*** 按一按铃．***have a ~ of*** 有…的声音，有…的风韵[意味]，有…的腔调，是…的口气．***have a false ~*** 声音不对，是假钱，是假货，品质低劣．***have the true [right] ~*** 声音好[对]，是真币，是真品，有实力，有真正价值．

ring-a-ding [ˈriŋəˌdiŋ] *a.* 〔拟声〕〔俚〕疯狂刺激的，振奋的．— *n.* 〔俚〕①疯狂的刺激性，狂饮．②具有疯狂刺激性的人[物]．

ringed [riŋd] *a.* ①(镶)有环[轮、圈]的；轮状的；用环[圈]装饰的．②被包围的．③戴着戒指的．④正式结[订]了婚的．

rin•gent [ˈrindʒənt] *a.* 【植、动】开口(状)的．

ring•er [ˈriŋə] *n.* ①敲钟[摇铃]的人；鸣钟[铃]装置；电铃．②〔口〕成功(者)．③〔美俚〕冒名(用捏造的记录)出场比赛的人[动物]；〔喻〕极相象的人；骗子．*That man is a ~ for so-and-so.* 那个人很象某人．

ring•hals [ˈriŋhæls] *n.* ***(pl. -hals, -hals•es)*** 【动】唾蛇 *(Haemachates haemachatus)*〔产于南非〕．

ring·let [ˈriŋlit] *n.* ①小环;小圈. ②(长)卷发.
ring·let·ed [ˈriŋlitid] *a.* 有(长)卷发的; 成(长)卷发状的.
ring·ster [ˈriŋstə] *n.* 〔美口〕同党(的人);(政治等)集团的成员.
rink [riŋk] *n.* (室内)溜冰场;(冰上)溜石遊戏场;(草地)木球场. *a skating* ～ 溜冰场. — *vi.* (在溜冰场中)溜冰〔尤指穿四轮溜冰鞋溜冰〕. **-er** *n.*
rink·y-dink [ˈriŋkiˈdiŋk] *a., n.* 〔俚〕劣等的(东西),便宜的(东西),破旧的(东西),陈腐的(东西) (= rinky-tink).
rinse [rins] *n.* 嗽洗; 漂洗, 漂清. — *vt.* 嗽(口); (用清水)刷; 涮掉, 冲洗掉 *(out; away)*; 用开水冲服 *(down)*. — *vi.* 漂净. ～ *out one's mouth with water* 用水嗽口. ～ *(the soap) out of washed clothes* 把洗过的衣服(中的肥皂水)漂去. *give sth. a* ～ 漂清〔冲洗〕某物.
rins·ing [ˈrinsiŋ] *n.* 〔常用复数〕①(冲洗,漂清用的)清水;漂洗池;漂洗过东西的水. ②残渣,渣滓,剩余物 (= dregs). ③冲洗,漂清.
RINT [rint] = radio intelligence【军】无线电侦察.
Rio de Ja·nei·ro [ˈri(ː)əu də dʒəˈniərəu] *n.* 里约热内卢〔巴西港市,州名〕.
Ri·o Gran·de [riəudəˈgrɑːndei] *n.* (美国和墨西哥之间的)格兰得河.
ri·ot [ˈraiət] *n.* ①骚乱;暴动;暴乱,骚动;混乱. ②放荡;闹饮,嘈闹的宴会,喝酒狂闹. ③(植物、疫病等的)蔓延. ④五色缤纷; 喧嚣嘈杂. ⑤〔美口〕非常成功的戏剧. ⑥(想象、感情等的) 奔放. ⑦(猎狗) 闻错猎物臭味乱追. *The garden was a* ～ *of colour.* 园花竞艳,五色缤纷. *a* ～ *of sound* 声音嘈杂. *a* ～ *of emotion* 感情的奔放. *race* ～ 〔美〕种族骚动. ***get up a*** ～ = ***raise [start] a*** ～ 闹乱子,挑起暴动. ***read the R- Act*** 下令解散;〔口〕严重警告〔告诫〕. ***run*** ～ 猎狗认错猎物臭味乱跑,〔转义〕追来追去; 越出常轨, 放肆, 横行无忌; 放纵自己的想像; 猖獗;(花)盛开. *His tongue runs* ～. 他胡言乱语,讲话放肆. — *vi.* ①骚乱; 暴动. ②闹饮; 喝酒狂斗; 放荡 *(in)*. — *vt.* 花天酒地地混 (日子); 挥霍;因放荡花光 *(out; away)*. **R- Act**【英史】骚乱取缔令. ～ **call** (警察因发生骚乱的)紧急召集. ～ **gun** (驱散骚乱人群用的)连发短枪. ～ **police** 防暴警察.
ri·ot·er [ˈraiətə] *n.* ①闹乱子的人,骚乱者,暴徒. ②闹饮者,喝酒狂闹的人;放荡的人.
ri·ot·ous [ˈraiətəs] *a.* 扰乱性的;暴动的;闹饮的,喝酒狂闹的; 放荡的; 吵闹的; 奔放不羁的; 五色缤纷的;(植物等)茂盛的. ～ *fancy* 胡思乱想;想入非非.
rip[1] [rip] *vt.* ***(ripped; rip·ping)*** ①扯裂,割裂(up); 剥去,拆去,割掉, 扯掉 *(off; away; out)*; 划破; 撕开, 割开 *(open)*. ②劈开,直锯,解(木材);凿开(洞穴等). ③使绽线. ④暴露;穷究, 寻根究底. — *vi.* ①裂开, 破开; 绽开. ②〔口〕突进,横撞直闯; 任意行动. ③〔口〕乱说乱讲,乱骂. ～ *(the seams of) a garment* 拆衣裳. ～ *open a bag* 拆开袋子. *let things* ～ 搁置不管,任其自然;开足马力. *Let her [it]* ～. 别管它,让它去. ～ ***and tear*** 狂怒;胡闹. ～ ***into*** 攻击, 批评. ～ ***off*** 扯掉;〔口〕偷窃;骗取. ～ ***out*** *(an oath)* 〔口〕狠狠发出咒骂语. ～ ***out [off] the lining*** 扯去里子. ～ ***up the back*** 〔口〕背后中伤. — *n.* ①扯裂;绽线;破绽;裂口,裂缝. ②= **ripsaw.** ～ **cord** 【空】开伞索;(气球放气的)拉索. ～**-off** 〔口〕偷窃;骗取. ～ **panel** 【空】(气球的)裂瓣;【机】裂幅. ～**-roaring [-roarious]** *a.* 〔美俚〕(非常热闹的);喧闹的. ～ **saw** 粗齿锯. ～ **snorter** 〔俚〕喧闹狂暴的人〔事物〕;突出的人〔物〕.
rip[2] [rip] *n.* 劣马,废马;废物;〔口〕浪子,荡子.
rip[3] [rip] *n.* 巨澜. ～ **current,** ～**-tide** 岸边巨澜的回流,激流.
rip[4] [rip] *n.* 清管器;刮板,刮刀.
R.I.P. = 〔L.〕 *Requiescat [Requiescant] in pace* (= May he / she [they] rest in peace). 愿灵安眠〔墓碑用语〕.
ri·pa·r·i·an [raiˈpɛəriən] *a.* 河岸〔河边〕的;【动】岸栖的. — *n.* 河岸土地所有人.
ripe [raip] *a.* ①成熟的. ②成人的; 圆熟的,老练的. ③时机成熟的, 已准备妥当的. ④红润丰满的 (嘴唇等). ⑤已养肥(可宰食)的(动物); 醇美可口的(酒); 熟透的. ⑥【医】(疖等)已化脓的; (白内障等) 可开刀的. ⑦〔俚〕喝得烂醉的. *Soon* ～, *soon rotten.* 熟得早,烂得快;〔喻〕早慧早衰. *a person of* ～ *years* 成年人,大人. ***at the*** ～ ***age of*** 以…的高龄. ***be*** ～ ***for*** …的时机成熟; 渴想…. ***die at a*** ～ ***age*** 享高年而死. ***an opportunity*** ～ ***to be seized*** 时机成熟,可乘的好机会. — *vt., vi.* 〔主诗〕= ripen. ～ **beauty** 妙龄. ～ **wine** 醇酒. **-ly** *ad.* **-ness** *n.*
rip·en [ˈraipən] *vi.* 成熟;长成 *(into)*. — *vt.* 使成熟;催熟;【医】使(疖等)化脓〔适于开刀〕. **-er** *n.* 【化】催熟剂.
Ri·pley [ˈripli] *n.* 里普利〔姓氏〕.
Rip·man [ˈripmən] *n.* 里普曼〔姓氏〕.
ri·post(e) [riˈpəust] *n.* ①【剑术】敏捷的回刺. ②机敏迅速的回答〔应对〕. — *vt., vi.* ①敏捷回刺. ②机敏迅速的应对〔回答〕.
rip·per [ˈripə] *n.* ①扯裂者; 拆缝线用具; 拆屋顶用具; 粗齿锯. ②〔英俚〕非常好的人〔物〕.
rip·ping [ˈripiŋ] *a.* ①扯裂的. ②〔英俚〕非常好的,绝妙的. *a* ～ *pace* 极快的速度. *We had a* ～ *good time* 我们过了一段快活极了的时光. — *ad.* 〔英俚〕极好地,绝妙地.
rip·ple[1] [ˈripl] *n.* ①涟漪,皱波,涟波;涟波声,潺潺声;细小急流;(头发等的)波浪形,卷曲;(沙上的)波痕 (= ～ mark);【物】脉动,波动. ②〔美俚〕钱. ～ *cloth* 波纹细呢,绒毛织物. *a* ～ *of laughter* 一阵(嘻嘻哈哈的)笑声. *a* ～ *of conversation* 咕咕哝哝的谈话声. *make the* ～ 〔美〕发财. — *vt.* 使起涟漪〔波纹〕; 卷(头发), (把头发) 弄成波浪形; 使作潺潺声. — *vi.* 起涟漪〔波纹〕;作潺潺声. ***rippling through*** 【物】行波传送. ～ **mark** (砂岩等上的)波痕;【植】波状纹.
rip·ple[2] [ˈripl] *n., vt.* 麻梳;用麻梳梳(去麻子).
rip·plet [ˈriplit] *n.* 小涟漪,小波纹.
rip·ply [ˈripli] *a.* 起涟漪的,有波纹的;潺潺响的.
rip·rap [ˈripˌræp] *n.* ①(防冲)乱石筑成的地基或堤坝. ②(防冲)乱石. — *vt.* ***(-rap·ped; -rap·ping)*** ①在…上堆(防冲)乱石. ②用(防冲)乱石加固.
Rip·u·ar·i·an [ˌripjuˈwɛəriən] *n., a.* (四世纪初叶移居于)莱茵河畔的佛朗克族人(的).
Rip van winkle [ˈripvæn ˈwiŋkl] 里普·万·温克尔〔美国作家欧文 (W. Irving) 作 *Sketch Book* 中一篇故事题名及其主人公;时代落伍的人〕.
rise [raiz] *vi.* ***(rose*** [rəuz]; ***risen*** [ˈrizn]***)*** *(opp.* fall, sink*)* ①上升,升起;(日、帆等)现出, 出来; (地势)向上斜, 隆起. ②起身〔口语说 get up〕; 起立,立起〔口语说 stand up〕,耸起;直立;浮起. ③(声音等)提高,变高;(面包等)膨胀,发起来;(物价等) 高涨, 腾贵; 增大; 涨水, 涨潮, 起浪. ④反抗;义愤;恶心. ⑤兴起;起源,发端;发生. ⑥(植物) 出芽, 生长. ⑦成功, 发迹, 出头, 高升, 升进;上进. ⑧苏醒, 复活. ⑨撤离, 退出, 撤退; 散会. *Morning [Dawn]* ～*s.* 天亮了. *The tide* ～*s.* 潮水上涨. *The tower* ～*s 80 feet.* 塔高80英尺. *The house rose at the actors.* 全场起立对演员鼓掌喝彩. *The wind rose rapidly.* 风突然吹了起来. *His anger rose at that remark.* 听见那话他就生气了. *My gorge [stomach]* ～*s at it.* 我一看见这东西就恶心. *I can't* ～ *to it.* 没有干那个的气力〔情绪〕. *My heart* ～*s.* 我的情绪好起来了. *They rose from a siege.* 他们停止(对某地的)围困而撤走. ～ ***above*** 凌驾…之上;超越…;摆脱. ～ ***again (from the dead)*** 死而复生. ～ ***and fall*** 盛衰,兴亡. ～ ***before [in] the mind*** (想象等)在头脑里浮现,在心里发生. ～ ***from the ranks*** (军官)出身行伍;布衣起家. ～ ***from the table*** 吃好了饭离开饭桌. ～ ***in sb.'s***

opinion [estimation] 受某人器重,在某人心目中信用[声誉]增加. ***~ in arms [rebellion]*** 武装起义[反抗,暴动]. ***~ in the world*** 出头,发迹. ***~ (1,000 feet) out of the sea*** 拔海(1,000英尺). ***~ to a fence*** 马耸身跃起准备过篱笆. ***~ to fame*** 出名. ***~ to greatness*** 成为伟大人物. ***~ to one's eyes*** 哭肿眼睛. ***~ to one's feet*** 站起来. ***~ to the bait [fly]*** (鱼)上钩;(人)被诱惑,上当. ***~ to the occasion [emergency]*** 随机应变;起而应付紧急事件. ***~ to the requirement*** 符合要求,胜任. ***~ with the larks*** 早起,黎明即起. — *vt.* ①举高,提高,抬高,擢升;[美]登(山). ②(将鱼)诱出水面;使(鸟)飞起;使(兽)跳起;【海】驶近(另一船)使慢慢在地平线上出现. ③[俗]养育,饲养. ④[罕]使苏醒,使复活. — *n.* ①上升;(日、月、星的)出来;(鱼吞饵时的)浮出;【猎】鸟出窝. ②斜坡;隆起(地). ③涨价,腾贵;增加(量);涨水;升级;加薪. ④苏醒,复活. ⑤发迹,出头;上进,进步. ⑥起源,发源;兴起,发生. ⑦【建】倾斜高,梯高,矢高. *a ~ of land* 高地. *He asks for a ~.* 他要求加薪. ***at ~ of sun [day]*** 日出时候. ***buy for the ~*** 看涨而买进. ***get a ~ from*** [美俚]惹怒人. ***get [have, take] a ~ out of sb.*** 激怒某人;挖苦某人;把某人当笑柄. ***give ~ to*** 使发生,引起,惹起. ***have a ~ in life = make a ~*** 发迹,出头. ***on the ~*** 在涨;在增加;好转. ***~ and fall*** 盛衰;兴亡;高低,抑扬. ***take its one's ~ in [among, from]*** 始于,发端于.

ris·en [ˈrizn] rise 的过去分词. — *a.* 升起的;复活的. *the ~ sun* 升起的太阳.

ris·er [ˈraizə] *n.* 起来的人;反抗者,起义者;【空】起飞装置;【机】(铸件)冒口;上升装置;【建】(梯级的)起步板,登板. *an early [a late] ~* 起得早[晚]的人.

ris·i·ble [ˈrizibl] *a.* ①能笑的;善笑的;爱笑的. ②可笑的. *a ~ animal* 会笑的动物.

ris·i·bil·i·ty [ˌriziˈbiliti] *n.* ①可笑性. ②笑癖. ③[美][*pl.*]对可笑事物的敏感性.

ris·ing [ˈraiziŋ] *a.* ①上升的;渐渐上升的(坡等). ②上涨的,腾贵的;增大的,增加的;涨水的. ③升进的;新进的,前途有望的(作家等);如日之升的,勃兴的,正在发展中的. *the ~ sun* 朝日. *a ~ ground* 台地. *a ~ market* 上涨的行情. *a ~ novelist* 新进小说作家. *the ~ generation* 年轻的一代. — *prep.* (年龄)将近…的;[美口](数量)不下…的;…以上的,超过…的. *he is ~ ten* 他快十岁了. *~ (of) a thousand men were killed.* 一千以上的人被杀害了. — *n.* ①上升;起床;起立;出现;苏醒,复活. ②坡,坡地;高地. ③起义,反抗. ④[方]瘤,疙肿,疙瘩. ⑤闭会,散会. *the ~ of the sun* 日出. *the ~ of the mother* 子宫病;歇斯底里.

risk [risk] *n.* ①风险,危险;冒险. ②【保险】(损失的)风险(率);保险金额;被保险人,被保险物. ***at all ~s = at any [whatever] ~*** 无论冒什么危险,一定,无论如何. ***at one's own ~*** 对可能发生的后果自己负责,自担风险. ***at owner's [buyer's] ~*** 由所有人[购买者]负责. ***at the ~ of*** 冒着…的危险. ***run ~s [a ~]*** 冒险. ***run [take] the ~ of*** 冒…的危险. ***take a ~ [~s]*** 冒险;【保险】承保…的险. ***take no ~s*** 慎重行事. — *vt.* 冒…的危险;拼着,赌着(性命);好歹试试看,冒险去干. *~ a battle* 冒险一战. *~ one's fortune [life]* 拼着财产[性命]. *~ the jump* 大着胆子跳跳看. *~ sb.'s anger* 冒着某人可能会生气的风险;抱着受某人责备的决心试试看. *~ it* 豁出去. ~ **capital** 冒风险投资的资本(= venture capital).

risk·ful [ˈriskfəl] *a.* 危险(多)的.

risk·i·ly [ˈriskili] *ad.* ①冒险地. ②近乎淫猥地.

risk-mo·ney [ˈriskmʌni] *n.* (由于出纳工作中难免少收多付等差错,银行等给出纳员的)差错补贴.

risk·y [ˈriski] *a.* ***(-i·er; -i·est)*** ①危险的;冒险的,孤注一掷的. ②[口]近乎猥亵的(作品等; =[F.] ***risqué***).

Ri·sor·gi·men·to [riˌsɔːdʒiˈmentəu] *n.* [It.](十九世纪为解放和统一意大利的)复兴运动,复兴时代.

ri·sot·to [riˈsɔtəu] *n.* [It.]洋葱、鸡肉等煨饭.

ris·qué [riˈskei] *a.* [F.] 近乎淫猥的;有伤风化的.

ris·sole [ˈrisəul] *n.* [F.] 炸肉卷,炸丸子;油炸包子.

Ri·ta [ˈriːtə] *n.* 丽塔[女子名, Margaret 的昵称].

ri·tar·dan·do [ˌriːtɑːˈdændəu] *a., ad.* [It.]【乐】渐缓[略 rit., ritard.].

Rit·chie [ˈritʃi] *n.* 里奇[姓氏].

rite [rait] *n.* 仪式,典礼,礼仪;习惯,惯例: [R-]【宗】礼拜式. *the burial [funeral] ~s* 丧礼. *the conjugal [marriage, nuptial] ~s* 婚礼. *the ~s of hospitality* 招待客人的礼节. *the ~ of passage* (某些民族习俗中的)进年庆祝仪式[如成年典礼之类];一生中值得庆祝的大事(=[F.] le rite de passage).

ri·tor·nel·lo [ˌritəˈneləu; It. ˌriːtɔːˈneləu] *n.* ***(pl. -los;*** It. ***-li*** [-li]***)*** 【乐】①间奏. ②副歌.

rit·u·al [ˈritjuəl] *a.* 仪式的,礼仪的;典礼的;宗教仪式的. *~ murder* 杀人祭神[以人为牺牲]. — *n.* 仪式;典礼. **-ism** *n.* 教会仪式,礼拜式;仪式主义;仪式学,仪式研究. **-ist** *n.* 精通仪式的人;墨守教会仪式者;仪式主义者.

rit·u·al·is·tic [ˌritjuəˈlistik] *a.* 仪式的;仪式主义的. **-ti·cal·ly** *ad.*

rit·u·al·ize [ˈritʃuəˌlaiz] *vi.* ***(-iz·ed; -iz·ing)*** 参加仪式,参加典礼. — *vt.* ①使进行仪式,使奉行仪式. ②使仪式化. **-za·tion** *n.*

Ritz [rits] *n.* ①里兹大饭店[以豪华著称的瑞士大旅馆]. ②[r-][美俚]豪华,摆场;炫耀. ***put on ritz*** 摆阔气,讲豪华.

ritz·y [ˈritsi] *a.* ***(-i·er; -i·est)*** [美俚]时新的,时髦的,最新式的,漂亮的,高级的;骄傲的. **ritz·i·ly** *ad.*

Riv. = river.

riv·age [ˈrividʒ] *n.* [古]河岸,海滨.

ri·val [ˈraivəl] *n.* 竞争者,对手,敌手;匹敌者,对等的人[物]. *a ~ in love* 情敌. *without a ~* 无与匹敌,无敌. — *a.* 竞争的,对抗的. *~ suitors* 情敌;相竞争的求婚者. — *vt., vi.* ([英] ***-ll-***) 竞争,对抗;匹敌.

ri·val·ry, ri·val·ship [ˈraivəlri, -ʃip] *n.* 竞争,对抗. *friendly ~* 友谊竞赛. ***contend in ~*** 互相倾轧[争胜]. ***enter into ~ with*** 和…开始竞争.

rive [raiv] *vt.* ***(~d; riv·en, ~d)*** ①扯裂,撕开,劈开. ②扭去,拧去 *(from; away; off)*. ③使苦恼,使烦恼. — *vi.* 裂开,分裂. — *n.* [英方]裂缝,裂罅;[废]裂片,碎片.

riv·el [ˈrivəl] *vt., vi.* ([英] ***-ll-***) [古]弄皱;皱起来,皱缩;干瘪.

riv·en [ˈrivən] rive 的过去分词.

riv·er[1] [ˈrivə] *n.* ①河,江. *~ Thames* 或 *the R- Thames* 泰晤士河;[美] *the Hudson R-* 哈得孙河. *the ~ of Jordan* 约旦河. *the Yangtze R-* 长江,扬子江. ②巨流;[*pl.*]大量. ③[the ~]生与死的界河,阴阳河. ***a ~ rat*** [美俚]住在河边低地的人. ***a ~ novel*** = roman-fleuve. ***He at last crossed the ~.*** 他终于死了. ***~s of blood*** 血流成河,大量的血[杀伤]. ***over the ~*** [美俚]再会[由法语 *au revoir* 变来]. ***row sb. up Salt River*** [美政俚]使失败;使落选. ***sell down the ~*** [美]陷害,欺骗. ***send up the ~*** [美俚]关进监狱. **~ basin** (江河的)流域. **~bed** 河床. **~ boat** 江轮;内河船只. **~-god** 河神. **~-head** 河源. **~-horse**【动】河马. **~ sand** 河沙. **~-side** 河边,河畔. **~ wall** 河堤. **~-word(s)** *a., ad.* 向河的[地].

riv·er[2] [ˈraivə] *n.* 劈木工人.

riv·er·ain [ˈrivərein] *a.* 河的,河边的;住在河边的. — *n.* 住在河边的人.

riv·er·ine [ˈraivərain, -in] *a.* ①河岸上的,水滨的,靠近河边的. ②河流的,河状的.

riv·et [ˈrivit] *n.* 铆钉. — *vt.* ①(用铆钉)铆,铆接

(down; in; on; together); 敲打(螺栓)使成铆钉头. ②固结,加深(爱情、友谊等). ③集中(目光、注意力) *(on; upon)*; 吸住人心,使心醉. ~ *one's attention [eyes] upon* 集中注意…. ~ **gun** (自动) 铆钉枪. **-ed** *a.* 用铆钉钉牢的; 〔美俚〕结了婚的 (*a* ~*ed error* 根深蒂固的错误. ~*ed hatred* 深恨). **-er** *n.* 铆工(工人); 铆钉枪.

Riv·i·er·a [ˌriviˈɛərə] *n.* 〔the ~〕 ①里维埃拉〔法国东南部和意大利西北部沿地中海的假日游憩胜地〕. ②(气候温和的)沿海游憩胜地.

riv·i·ère [riviˈɛə] *n.* 〔F.〕 宝石项链.

riv·u·let [ˈrivjulit] *n.* 小河,溪流.

Ri·yadh [riːˈjɑːd] *n.* 利雅得〔沙特阿拉伯首都〕.

ri·yal [riˈjɑːl, -ˈjɔːl] *n.* *(pl. -yals)* 里亚尔〔沙特阿拉伯、卡塔尔、也门货币单位〕.

R.M., RM = ①Royal Marines 〔英〕皇家海军陆战队. ②resident magistrate 〔爱〕受薪治安推事.

rm. = ①ream. ②room.

R.M.A., RMA = Royal Military Academy 〔英〕皇家陆军军官学校.

RMB = Renminbi (中国的)人民币.

R.M.C., RMC = Royal Military College 〔英〕皇家陆军学院.

R.M.L.I. = Royal Marine Light Infantry 〔英〕皇家海军陆战队轻步兵.

RMS = root-mean-square 【数】均方根(值).

R.M.S., RMS = ①Royal Mail Steamer 英国邮船. ②Royal Mail Service 英国邮政. ③Railway Mail Service 铁道邮政.

rms. = rooms.

Rmt = remount 新补充的马匹.

R.N., RN = ①registered nurse 注册护士. ②Royal Navy 〔英〕皇家海军.

Rn = radon 【化】氡.

RNA = ribonucleic acid 【生化】核糖核酸.

R.N.C. = Royal Naval College 〔英〕皇家海军学院.

R.N.D. = Royal Naval Division 〔英〕皇家海军局.

R.N.R. = Royal Naval Reserve 〔英〕皇家海军后备队.

R.N.S.S. = Royal Naval Scientific Service 〔英〕皇家海军科学研究部.

R.N.V.R. = Royal Naval Volunteer Reserve 〔英〕皇家海军志愿后备队.

R.N.Z.A.F., RNZAF = Royal New Zealand Air Force (皇家)新西兰空军.

R.N.Z.N., RNZN = Royal New Zealand Navy (皇家)新西兰海军.

roach[1] [rəutʃ] *n.* 【鱼】斜齿鳊,(欧洲)石斑鱼. ***sound as a*** ~ 非常健壮.

roach[2] [rəutʃ] *n.* ①蟑螂 (= cockroach). ②〔美俚〕大麻制成的烟卷烟蒂. ~ *clip* 大麻烟卷夹子.

roach[3] [rəutʃ] *vt.* ①梳(发)使成拱状. ②切短(马鬃等)使竖立. — *n.* 【海】横帆下缘的弧形切口. ~ **back** 弓形背〔尤指马背〕.

road [rəud] *n.* ①路,道路;街〔略 Rd.〕; 公路; 行车道; 路程,行程. ②〔美〕铁路. ③方法,手段,办法; (走向成功、失败等的)道路,途径. ④【海】〔常 *pl.*〕(开放)锚地,海中停泊处. ⑤〔the ~〕〔美剧俚〕纽约以外的任何地方〔巡回剧团经常旅行的路线和演出的城镇〕; 〔美推销员俚〕旅行路程. *a main* ~ 大街,干道. *a beaten* ~ 走惯了的路; 〔喻〕惯例,常规办法. *royal* ~ 捷径. *by* ~ 经由公路(而非铁路,空路). *the rule of the* ~ 交通规则. *a gentleman [knight] of the* ~ 〔谑〕拦路强盗. *All* ~*s lead to Rome* 条条道路通罗马. ***break a*** ~ 开路前进; 排除困难前进. ***for the*** ~ 为了送行,祝一路平安. ***get out of the [sb.'s]*** ~ 不妨碍; 让开道路给…走过. ***get sth. out of sb.'s [the]*** ~ 扫清,消除,赶走. ***give*** *(sb.)* ***the*** ~ 让路; 给通过; 辞退某人. ***go on the*** ~ = *take the* ~. ***go over the*** ~ 〔美俚〕被判徒刑. ***hit the*** ~ 〔美俚〕上路; 离去. ***in sb.'s*** ~ 拦着…的路; 〔口〕阻碍着. ***on the*** ~ 在旅行中; 〔美〕(剧团等)在巡回演出中. ***out of the common*** ~ ***of*** 离开…常规,逸出…的常轨. ~ ***agent*** 〔美〕拦路强盗; 小贩. ***take the*** ~ 出发,启程,动身; 流浪; 〔古〕做强盗; (剧团)去巡回演出. ***take the*** ~ ***of sb.*** 居某人之上. ***take to the*** ~ 出发旅行; 〔英古〕做拦路强盗. — *vt.* (狗)闻着臭迹追. ~**bed** 〔美〕①(铁路)路基,路床. ②铺路材料〔碎石,沙子〕. ③供车辆行驶的路面部分; 行车道. ~**block** 【军】路障. ~**book** 路程〔旅行〕指南. ~ **discipline** 【军】行军纪律. ~ **hog** *vi., n.* 乱开汽车(的人); 妨碍其他车辆行驶(的司机); 〔美〕流浪人. ~**house** 〔美〕小旅馆,客栈. ~ **lamp** 路灯. ~ **louse**, 〔*pl.*〕 ~ **lice** 〔美俚〕微型汽车. ~ **map** 街道地图,路线图,行车地图. ~**mender** = ~ man. ~ **metal** 铺路碎石. ~ **roller** 压路机. ~ **runner** 【动】槲鸡. ~ **scraper** 平路机. ~ **sense** 安全行车本领. ~**show** 巡回演出; 〔美俚〕【影】(予售剧票的)特别献映. ~**side** *n., a.* 路傍(的),路边(的)(树木等). ~ **sister** 〔美〕流浪女人. ~ **sprin·kler** 撒水车. ~**stead** 【海】(开敞)锚地. ~**ster** ①早期无后座的敞篷汽车; 跑车. ②可以走长途的车马〔自行车〕. ③停泊在海中的船. ④走惯某条路的人; 徒步旅行者; 流浪者; 马车夫; 拦路强盗. ~**test** *vt., n.* 对(车辆)进行路上试车; 实骑试验(自行车等),实作试验(才能等). ~**-train** (运货)汽车队. ~**way** 道路; 车行道; 【林】运材路; 铁路. ~**work** 【运】越野长跑训练. ~**worthy** *a.* 适于走长途的(马、车等); (人)能旅行的. **-er** *n.* ①修路工人; 清道夫. ②= ~ster. **-man** *n.* 修路工人.

road·a·bil·i·ty [ˌrəudəˈbiliti] *n.* (车辆的)行车稳定性; 行车舒适性; (行车时的)操纵灵便性.

Road Town [ˈrəud taun] *n.* 罗得城〔英属维尔京群岛首府〕.

roam [rəum] *n., vi., vt.* 漫游,游历,游荡,漫步,闲逛.

roan[1] [rəun] *a., n.* 灰斑〔白斑〕栗色皮毛的(马); 花毛的(马或其他动物).

roan[2] [rəun] *n.* (装订书籍用的)柔软羊皮.

roar [rɔː, rɔə] *vi.* ①(猛兽尤指狮子)吼,咆哮; (海、风等)呼啸,怒号; (人)喊叫,呼号,吆喝; 〔美〕诉苦. ②狂笑,哄笑,大笑. ③轰鸣,反响. ④(马)喘鸣. ~ *with laughter* 哄堂大笑. *You need not* ~. 你不必那么大声嚷嚷. — *vt.* ①大声讲〔唱〕. ②大声喊叫而造成某情况. ③使轰鸣. ~ *out an order* 大声发出命令. ~ *down* 哄下; 大声压倒某人讲话声. ~ *oneself hoarse* 喊哑嗓子. *The driver pressed on the accelerator, savagely* ~*ing the engine.* 司机踩下油门踏板,漫不经心地让引擎轰鸣. — *n.* 吼(声),咆哮; 怒号; 叫唤,呼叫; 喧哗,鼓噪,大笑声; 轰鸣. *a* ~ *of anger* 怒骂声. *in a* ~ 大声鼓噪着. *set the table in a* ~ 引起全桌(的人)哄堂大笑.

roar·er [ˈrɔːrə] *n.* ①吼者,咆哮者; 怒号者. ②【兽医】患喘鸣症的马. ③〔美俚〕极好的人物〔东西〕; 暴风雨; 吵闹多言的人; 鲁莽〔好动武〕的人; 强壮的人; 低劣的运动员〔拳击家〕; 喷油井.

roar·ing [ˈrɔːriŋ] *n.* 咆哮,怒号,喧噪; 【兽医】(马的)喘鸣症. — *a.* ①吼叫的,咆哮的,怒号的,轰鸣的; 暴风雨的(夜等). ②喧哗的,鼓噪的,吵闹的. ③〔口〕兴旺的,(生意)兴隆的. ~ *applause* 雷鸣一般的鼓掌喝彩. *a* ~ *night* 暴风雨之夜; 纵酒狂闹之夜. ***drive a*** ~ ***trade*** 生意兴隆. ***in*** ~ ***health*** 非常健康,精神饱满. ~ **blade** 〔古〕荡子,浪子. ~ **forties** (北纬 40° 左右的)大西洋暴风雨带. ~ **game** (苏格兰人玩的)冰上滚石戏.

roast [rəust] *vt.* ①(在火上)烤,炙,烧(肉); 烘; (用文火)焙; (用热沙)炒. ②【冶】锻烧,焙烧. ③〔俚〕讥刺,挖苦; 〔美〕责备. ~ *oneself* 挨着火烤身子. ~ *one's hands* 烘手. — *vi.* 烤; 炙; 烘; 炒; 烤好; 变热; 烤得发烫. — *a.* 烤的,烘的,炒的. ~ *beef* 烤牛肉. ~ *ducks* 烤鸭. — *n.* ①烤肉,烧肉; 烤食聚餐会; 烤,烘,炒. ②〔俚〕挖苦,愚弄; 逗乐. ③【冶】锻烧,焙烧. *a cold* ~ 〔古〕没价值的东西. ***rule the*** ~ 当家; 做主人; 执牛耳,指挥.

roast·er [ˈrəustə] *n.* 烤[烘、炒]的人[用器]；锻烧炉，焙烧炉；烤用的食物[鸡、小猪等]。

roast·ing [ˈrəustiŋ] *a.* ①适于烤食的；烤肉用的。②天气酷热的。～ *jack* 旋转烤肉叉。*a* ～ *July* 炎热的七月。～**-spit**〔俚〕刺刀。

Rob [rɔb] *n.* 罗布[男子名，Robert 的昵称]。

Rob. = Robert.

rob [rɔb] *vt.* 强夺，掠夺；盗劫；抢夺，夺取，剥夺，使丧失 *(of)*；【矿】滥掘。～ ***sb. of*** 使…丧失，剥夺…的…（～ *sb. of his money* 抢人钱财。*The shock* ～*bed him of speech* 他震惊得说不出话来）。～ *a safe* 盗劫金库[保险柜]。～ ***Peter to pay Paul*** 抢了东家给西家；东挪西借；借钱还债。— *vi.* 抢劫，劫掠；掠夺。

rob·a·lo [ˈrɔbəˌləu, ˈrəubə-] *n.* *(pl.* ***-los, -lo)***【动】锯盖鱼科鱼[尤指锯盖鱼]。

rob·and [ˈrɔbənd] *n.*【海】系帆绳索。

rob·ber [ˈrɔbə] *n.* 盗贼，强盗。～ **baron** ①(封建时代)对路过自己领地的旅客进行抢劫的封建主。②【美史】十九世纪末靠残酷剥削致富的美国资本家。～ **fly**【动】食虫虻，盗蝇。

rob·ber·y [ˈrɔbəri] *n.* 抢夺，劫夺；【法】强盗[盗劫]罪。*daylight* ～ 白昼抢劫，光天化日之下的抢劫；明目张胆的掠夺，剥削。*To ask such prices is sheer* ～. 要这样的价钱简直是明火执仗的抢劫。

Rob·bins [ˈrɔbinz] *n.* 罗宾斯[姓氏]。

robe [rəub] *n.* ①长袍，罩袍；晨衣，浴衣；〔商店用语〕长连衣裙。②〔*pl.*〕衣服。③〔常 *pl.*〕礼服，法衣，官服，制服。④〔诗〕被盖。⑤〔美〕(毛皮)短围裙。*the long* ～（法官、牧师的）长袍。*the short* ～〔废〕军服。～*s of office* = *official* ～*s* 制服。*gentlemen of the long* ～ 律师们，法官们。*the* ～ *of night* 夜幕。*both* ～*s* 长袍阶级和兵士，文人和武人。*either* ～ 文人或武人。***follow the*** ～ 充任律师。— *vt., vi.*（给…）穿上，装扮；穿法衣。

robe-de-cham·bre [rɔbdəˈʃɑːmbr]〔F.〕*n.* *(pl.* ***-cham·bres*** [-br]) 晨衣；化妆时穿的长衣。

Rob·ert [ˈrɔbət] *n.* ①罗伯特[男子名，昵称为，Bert, Bertie, Bobby, Dob, Dobbin, Rob, Robin]。②〔英口〕警察。

Ro·ber·ta [rəuˈbəːtə] *n.* 罗伯塔[女子名]。

Ro·berts [ˈrɔbəts] *n.* 罗伯茨[姓氏]。

Ro·bert·son [ˈrɔbətsn] *n.* 罗伯逊[姓氏]。

Robe·son [ˈrəubsn] *n.* ①罗伯逊[姓氏]。②**Paul** ～ 罗伯逊[1898— 美国黑人歌唱家]。

Rob·in [ˈrɔbin] *n.* 罗宾[男子名，女子名，Robert 和 Roberta 的昵称]。

rob·in [ˈrɔbin] *n.*【动】鸲鸟，知更鸟〔又叫 ～ redbreast〕；〔美〕鸫。～*s egg blue*〔美〕绿兰色。～ **snow**〔美〕春天的小雪。

Rob·in Good·fel·low [ˈrɔbinˈgudfeləu]（英国民间传说中专门跟人捣蛋的）小妖怪，小精灵。

Rob·in Hood [ˈrɔbinˈhud] 罗宾汉[英国中古传说中的绿林好汉]。***sell Robin Hood's pennyworth*** 象盗贼一般廉价卖东西给人。

Rob·ins [ˈrəubinz, ˈrɔbinz] *n.* 罗宾斯[姓氏]。

Rob·in·son [ˈrɔbinsn] *n.* 鲁宾逊[姓氏]。

Rob·inson Cru·soe [ˈrɔbinsn ˈkruːsəu] 鲁宾逊[英国小说家 Daniel Defoe 所著《鲁宾逊漂流记》一书中主人公]。*Robinson Crusoe and Friday*〔美〕教堂[剧场]过道中两旁的两个座位。

ro·ble [ˈrəublei] *n.*【植】(美国西南部的)栎树[尤指加州白栎 *(Quercus lobata)*]。

ro·blitz [ˈrəublits] *n.* 无人飞机闪击轰炸。

ro·bomb [ˈrəubɔm] *n.* = robot bomb.

rob·o·rant [ˈrɔbərənt] *a.* 起强壮作用的。— *n.*【医】强壮剂。

ro·bot [ˈrəubɔt, ˈrɔbət] *n.* ①机器人。②自动机，自动仪器，自动控制导弹，遥控设备。*an electronic* ～ 电子自动装置。*a* ～ *airplane* 无线电操纵飞机，无人飞机。*a* ～ *bomb* 自动操纵的飞弹。*a* ～ *bomber* 遥控轰炸机，无人驾驶轰炸机。

ro·bot·is·tic [ˌrəubəˈtistik] *a.* 机器人似的；自动化的。

ro·bot·ize [ˈrəubətaiz] *vt.* ①使自动化。②使象机器人一样地行事。

ro·bur·ite [ˈrəubəˌrait] *n.*【化】罗必赖特[一种炸药]。

ro·bust [rəˈbʌst] *a.* ①强壮的，强健的；雄壮的，粗壮的。②费力的(运动等)。③坚定的；健全的。**-ly** *ad.* **-ness** *n.*

ro·bus·tious [rəuˈbʌstʃəs] *a.* ①强壮的。②粗野的；刚愎自用的。③〔美〕猛烈的。

roc [rɔk] *n.* ①(阿刺伯、波斯传说中的)大怪鸟。②〔R-〕〔俚〕(海军用)无线电制导的电视瞄准导弹，"大鹏"式制导炸弹。*a* ～*'s egg* 乌有之物。

R.O.C. = Royal Observer Corps〔英〕皇家对空观察队(民防组织)。

Ro·ca [ˈrəukɑ] *n.* 罗卡角[在葡萄牙西部，欧洲大陆的最西端]。

roc·am·bole [ˈrɔkəmˌbəul] *n.*【植】葫蒜 *(Allium scorodoprasum)*〔欧洲的一种圆葱〕。

Ro·chelle [rəuˈʃel] *n.* 罗谢尔[姓氏，女子名]。～ **salt** 罗谢尔盐，四水(合)酒石酸钾钠。

roche mou·ton·née [rɔʃ mutɔne]【地】羊背石。

roch·et [ˈrɔtʃit] *n.*【宗】紧身法衣。

rock[1] [rɔk] *n.* ①岩，岩石，磐石，岩壁；卵石；〔常 *pl.*〕〔美口〕石子儿；暗礁，岩礁。②〔the R-〕直布罗陀 (Gibraltar) 的别名。③〔喻〕靠山，护符。④〔喻〕隐藏的危险[困难]，祸根。⑤= ～-cake, ～-candy. ⑥〔英〕硬糖果；硬干酪。⑦〔美〕用来投掷的石头；〔美俚〕金刚钻，宝石(等)；〔美俚〕一块钱；〔*pl.*〕钱。*a needle of* ～ 巉岩。*a sunken* ～ 暗礁。*Rocks ahead!* 前面有暗礁！危险！*an almond* ～ 杏仁味硬糖。***as firm as a*** ～ = like a ～ 安如磐石，坚定不移，屹然不动。***built [founded] on*** ～ 建立在岩石上的；基础坚固的。***driven on the*** ～ 触礁。***on the*** ～***s*** 触礁；搁浅；手头拮据；进退两难；〔美俚〕分文没有的，破了产的。***run [strike] upon the*** ～***s*** = ***thrown on the*** ～ 触礁。***see*** ～***s ahead*** 看到前途的暗礁，看到前途的危险。***split on a*** ～ 在暗礁上撞得粉碎；完全破灭[失败]。***the Rock of Ages***【宗】永久的磐石[原为基督教会一首赞美诗的题目，现指耶稣和基督教]。～ **and rye** 加有冰糖和水果片装瓶的裸麦威士忌酒。～**away** 四轮轻便马车。～ **bass**【动】岩阳鱼，岩鲈。～ **bot·tom** *n., a.* 岩底(的)；最底下(的)，底细，底蕴，真相（～*-bottom prices*〔俚〕最低价钱）。～**-bound** *a.* 岩炮围着的，岩多的。～ **brake**【植】岩珠蕨。～ **cake** 糖衣脆皮小饼。～ **candy**〔美〕冰糖(=〔英〕sugar candy)。～**-climbing**【爬山】爬岩(术)。～ **cod**【动】岩鳕；鲳。～ **cork** 软木状石绵。～**-crusher** 碎石机；【牌戏】一手实力强大的好牌。～ **crystal**【矿】石英，水晶。～ ***dove***, ～***-pi·geon***【动】野鸽。～ **drill** 凿岩机；开石钻。**R- English** 直布罗陀英语。**R- fever**【医】马尔他热病。～ **fish**【鱼】生活在海底岩石间的鱼类之一[石鲳；鲳；石斑鱼等]。～ **floor**【地】岩原。～ **garden**（种植岩生植物的）岩石[假山]庭园。～ **goat** 野山羊。～**-hewn** *a.* 岩石凿成的。～ **hind**【动】岩石斑鱼。～**-hound**〔美口〕奇石采集者。～ **leather** 一种石棉。～ **maple**【植】糖槭树。～ **oil** 石油。～ **rabbit** ①=hyrax. ②=pika. ～**-ribbed** *a.* 有岩层的；多岩脊的；岩石突露的；顽强的；坚定不移的；僵硬的。～**rose**【植】①*n.* 岩蔷薇属。②*a.* 半日花科的。～ **salmon**【动】角鲨。～ **salt** 岩盐。**R- scorpion** 磐石蠍[直布罗陀人的绰号，有贬意]。～ **slide**【地】岩滑，塌方。～ **snake** 锦蛇。～ **squirrel**【动】岩黄鼠；巨松鼠。～ **tar** 礁油。～ **tripe**【植】石耳属。～ **wool** 石棉，石绒。～ **work** 粗面石工；岩壁；爬岩术；石块砌筑；堆石工艺；假山。

rock[2] [rɔk] *vt.* ①摇，摇动，使振动。②【采】摇选。③摇引…入睡；抚慰。④使感动，打动；使震动，使震惊。*He* ～*ed* *back and forth in his chair.* 他坐在椅子上前前后后地摇. ～ *the baby to sleep* 摇婴儿睡觉. *a* ～*ing gait* 摇摇摆摆的步态.— *vi.* ①摇动,动摇,振动;摇摆;蹒跚. ②感动;震动. — *n.* ①摇,动摇. ②摇摆;摇摆舞曲. ～ **and roll** 摇摆舞(曲). ～**shaft** 摇臂轴.

rock³ [rɔk] *n.* 〔古〕(手纺用)卷线杆. **R- day** 开纺日〔Twelfth day 的翌日〕.

Rock·e·fel·ler [ˈrɔkifelə] *n.* 洛克菲勒〔姓氏〕.

rock·er [ˈrɔkə] *n.* ①摇的人;摇摇篮的人. ②摇杆,摇轴;〔美〕摇椅;摇木马;【动】摇移器;【化】振荡器;【采】摇选台. ③【溜冰】弯底冰鞋;【航】龙骨弯曲的船. ④〔俚〕头,脑袋. ⑤= *rocking-turn.* ***off one's*** ～ 〔俚〕发疯.

rock·er·y [ˈrɔkəri] *n.* 假山;有假山的园林.

rock·et¹ [ˈrɔkit] *n.* 火箭;火箭弹,火箭发动机;火箭式投射器;〔英俚〕斥责. *a carrier [freight]* ～ 载运火箭. *an antitank* ～ 反坦克火箭. *a moon* ～ 月球火箭. *an outer-space* ～ 外层空间宇宙火箭. *a photon* ～ 光子火箭. *a sounding* ～ 探测火箭. *a* ～ *signal* 火箭信号. — *vt.* 用火箭运载;用火箭轰击. — *vi.* (鸟等)直升飞起;(马或骑手)向前猛冲,(物价)猛涨. ～ **base** 火箭(发射或试验)基地. ～ **bomb** 火箭(推动的)炸弹. ～ **jet** 火箭喷管;火箭喷气流. ～ **launcher [gun]** 火箭发射装置[发射筒]. ～ **motor** 火箭发动机. ～ **plane** 火箭(发射)飞机. ～**-propelled** 火箭推进的. ～ **propulsion** 火箭推进. ～ **range** 火箭靶场;火箭试验区. ～ **ship** 火箭宇宙飞船. ～**sonde** 【气】火箭探空仪. ～ **target** 火箭靶机.

rock·et² [ˈrɔkit] *n.* 【植】芝麻菜;紫花南芥.

rock·et·eer [ˌrɔkiˈtiə] *n.* 〔美〕火箭专家;火箭制造人.

rock·et·er [ˈrɔkitə] *n.* ①惊起向上直飞的猎鸟. ②= rocketeer.

rock·et·ry [ˈrɔkitri] *n.* ①火箭学;火箭技术;火箭研究. ②火箭〔总称〕.

rock·i·ly [ˈrɔkili] *ad.* 岩石一般;多岩.

rock·i·ness [ˈrɔkinis] *n.* ①坚如岩石,坚硬性. ②冷酷无情. ③摇晃性.

rock·ing [ˈrɔkiŋ] *a.* 摇动的,来回摇摆的. ～ **chair** 摇椅. ～ **horse** 摇木马. ～ **turn** 【溜冰】摇转〔从弧线外侧扭转身体用同侧冰鞋刃滑回来〕.

Rock·ing·ham [ˈrɔkiŋəm] *n.* 罗金厄姆〔姓氏〕.

rock 'n' roll [ˈrɔknˈrəul] *n.* 摇摆舞(曲)(=rock-and-roll).

rock·oon [rɔˈkuːn, ˈrɔkuːn] *n.* ①(由气球带到空中发射的)气球火箭. ②火箭(探空)气球.

rock·y¹ [ˈrɔki] *a.* ***(-i·er; -i·est)*** ①岩石的;岩石重叠的,岩石多的. ②磐石一般的;泰然不动的;冷酷的,无情的,铁石心肠的. ③障碍重重的;困难的. the *R- Mountains* = 〔口〕 *the Rockies* 〔美〕 落矶山脉. ～ **desert** 沙漠,戈壁.

rock·y² [ˈrɔki] *a.* ①摇摆的;不稳的;不安定的. ②〔俚〕头晕目眩的;(因虚弱,酒醉,被猛击等)站不稳的. **-i·ly** *ad.* **-i·ness** *n.*

ro·co·co [rəˈkəukəu] *n.* 【美】(法国 18 世纪以浮华纤巧为特色的)罗可可式;罗可可式建筑;浮华纤巧俗气的装饰. — *a.* 罗可可式的;俗不可耐的;浮华纤巧的.

rod [rɔd] *n.* ①枝,一节树枝. ②棍棒;杆;竿;钓竿. ③杖,魔杖;鞭,体罚. ④职标,权标;笏;权力,威力. ⑤【机】杆,拉杆,推杆,连杆;测量杆,照尺;避雷针. ⑥〔主、美〕杆〔$=5^1/_2$码 = 5.0292 公尺〕;平方杆〔$=30^1/_4$平方码〕;【解】(网膜内的)杆状体;【生】杆状菌,杆状染色体. ⑦〔美俚〕(左轮)手枪. ⑧【圣】种族;家系;血统;子孙. ⑨〔美俚〕旧汽车改装成的跑车〔= hot rod〕. *a calculating* ～ 计算尺. ***give the*** ～ 鞭打. ***have a*** ～ ***in pickle for sb.*** 伺机惩罚(某人). ***kiss the*** ～ 俯首受罚,甘心受刑. ***make a*** ～ ***for one's own back [for oneself]*** 自找麻烦,自找苦吃,自作孽. ***ride [take] the*** ～***s*** (躲在货车车厢下的棒轴上)偷乘火车. ～ **cell** 【生】杆细胞. ～ **license** 〔加拿大〕鲑鱼税. ～**man**(用钓竿)钓鱼者;【测】标杆员,立尺员;〔美俚〕执枪强盗.

rode [rəud] ride 的过去式.

ro·dent [ˈrəudənt] *a.* ①咬的,嚼的;【动】齧齿目的. ②【医】侵蚀性的(溃疡等). — *n.* 【动】齧齿动物.

ro·den·tial [rəuˈdenʃəl] *a.* ①【动】齧齿目的. ②【医】侵蚀性的.

ro·dent·i·cide [rəuˈdentiˌsaid] *n.* 杀鼠剂,杀啮齿类剂.

ro·de·o [rəuˈdeiəu] 〔美〕 *n.* ①(集中牛马的)圈地;(为打烙印的)驱集牛马. ②牧人马术表演;摩托车花式表演.

Rod·er·ic(k) [ˈrɔdərik] *n.* 罗德里克〔男子名〕.

Rod·ger [ˈrɔdʒə, ˈrəudʒə] *n.* 罗杰〔男子名〕.

Rod·gers [ˈrɔdʒəz] *n.* 罗杰斯〔姓氏〕.

Rod·ney [ˈrɔdni] *n.* 罗德尼〔姓氏,男子名〕.

rod·o·mon·tade [rɔdəmɔnˈteid] *n.,* 大话. — *vi.* 吹牛,说大话. — *a.* 说大话的,吹牛的.

roe¹ [rəu] *n.* ***(pl.*** ～***s,*** 〔集合词〕～***)*** 【动】牝麅鹿,獐(= ～ deer). ～**buck** 雄獐.

roe² [rəu] *n.* (鱼类、甲壳类、两栖类的)卵,卵块. *hard* ～ 卵. *soft* ～ (雄)鱼精.

Roent·gen [ˈrentgən], **Wilhelm Conrad** 伦琴〔1845—1923,德国物理学家,伦琴射线的发现者〕.

roent·gen [ˈrentgən, ˈrɔntjən, ˈrʌntdʒən] *n.* 伦琴射线,爱克斯[X]射线. — *a.* 伦琴(射线)的,X 射线的. *a* ～ *photogram [photograph]* X 〔爱克斯〕射线照片. ～ *rays* 爱克斯[X]射线.

roent·gen·ize [ˈrentgənaiz] *vt.* 爱克斯线照射.

roentgeno- *comb. f.* 伦琴射线的: *roentgeno*gram.

roent·gen·o·gram, roent·gen·o·graph [ˈrentgənəgræm, -dʒə-, ˈrʌt-, ˈrɔtgen-; ˈrɔntˈgenəgrɑːf] *n.* 伦琴射线照片.

roent·gen·og·ra·phy [ˌrentgeˈnɔgrəfi] *n.* 爱克斯射线〔伦琴射线〕拍摄技术.

roent·gen·ol·o·gy [ˌrɔntgeˈnɔlədʒi] *n.* 爱克斯射线学.

roent·gen·o·sco·py [ˌrɔntgənˈɔskəupi] *n.* 爱克斯射线透视术;荧光屏检查.

roent·gen·o·ther·a·py [ˌrɔntgənəˈθerəpi] *n.* 爱克斯射线疗法.

roe·stone [ˈrəustəun] *n.* 【矿】鲕状岩,鱼卵石.

Rog. = Roger.

ro·ga·tion [rəuˈgeiʃən] *n.* ①〔古罗马〕法案的提出;法律草案. ②〔*pl.*〕【宗】连祷,祈求. ～ **flower** 【植】= milkwort.

Rog·er [ˈrɔdʒə] *n.* 罗杰〔男子名〕. *Jolly* ～ (黑底白骷髅的)海盗旗.

rog·er [ˈrɔdʒə] *int.* 知道了! 收到了! 〔无线电话通讯用语〕;〔俚〕好! 对! 行!

Rog·ers [ˈrɔdʒəz, ˈrəudʒəz] *n.* 罗杰斯〔姓氏,男子名〕.

Ro·get [ˈrɔʒei] *n.* 罗热〔姓氏〕.

rogue [rəug] *n.* ①歹徒,恶棍;流氓,无赖;乞丐;骗子. ②爱捉弄人者;淘气孩子,小淘气. ③傢伙〔爱称〕. ④离群的象,离群的野兽;(赛马或行猎时的)腿懒的马. ⑤【生】变劣;【园艺】变劣了的实生苗;劣种. *a* ～ *and vagabond* 身体健壮的乞丐. *a* ～*s' gallery* (警察局里的)前科犯相片陈列室. ～*'s yarn* 〔英海军〕标识(用)绳股. ***play the*** ～ 行恶作剧,淘气. — *vt.* ①骗,欺诈. ②【农】间苗;【育种】去劣;去杂,淘汰. — *vi.* ①流浪,游荡;行骗. ②【农】淘汰劣种〔杂种〕.

ro·guer·y [ˈrəugəri] *n.* ①流氓〔无赖〕行为;坏行为;欺骗. ②淘气,捣鬼.

ro·guish [ˈrəugiʃ] *a.* ①流氓的,无赖的. ②淘气的,捣鬼的,恶作剧的. **-ly** *ad.* **-ness** *n.*

roi [rwɑ] *n.* ***(pl.*** ～***s*** [rwɑ]***)*** 〔F.〕王. ***le*** ～ ***le veut*** [ləˈrwɑːləˈvə] 照准 〔= the king wills it〕. ***le*** ～***s' avisera*** [ləˈrwɑːsɑːˈviːzərɑː] 缓议〔= the king will consider〕. ～ ***fai·ne·ant*** [-ˈfeineiɑ̃ːŋ] ***(pl. rois fai·ne·ants*** [fɛnex]. 徒拥虚名的国王〔议长〕,傀儡(首领).

roil [rɔil] *vt.* 〔美〕①搅浑;搅乱. ②惹怒,使生气. — *vi.*

动荡.

roil·y [ˈrɔili] *a.* ①浑浊的. ②生气的,易怒的. ③动荡的.

roi·nek [ˈrɔinek] *n.* 〔南非〕新来移民;〔南非、蔑〕英国兵.

roist·er [ˈrɔistə] *vi.* ①摆架子,欺侮人. ②嚷闹;闹饮. **-er** *n.* 喧闹者;闹饮者.

Ro·land [ˈrəulənd] *n.* ①罗兰〔男子名〕. ② 勇士罗兰〔与奥利佛(Oliver)各为查理大帝手下十二勇士之一〕;〔喻〕勇将. ***a ~ for an Oliver*** 旗鼓相当;势均力敌.

role, *rôle* [rəul] *n.* ①(演员扮演的)角色. ②任务;作用. *the leading ~* 主角. ***fill the ~ of*** 担负…的任务. ***play an important ~ in*** 在…中起重要作用.

Rolf(e) [rɔlf, rəuf] *n.* 罗尔夫〔男子名, Rudolph 的异体〕.

roll [rəul] *vt.* ①滚,转,推滚(桶、车轮等),使(烟、尘土)滚滚上升,滚滚推进(浪、水等);滚动,溜转(眼睛). ②卷,卷成圆球,弄圆;包卷,卷拢,卷捆,卷起 *(in; into; up)*. ③滚压(草地);辗,轧,辗平,辗薄;用面棍辗薄〔擀薄〕. ④擂(鼓);用卷舌发(*r* 音). ⑤使左右摇摆. ⑥(在心里)盘算,翻来复去细想. ⑦〔美俚〕趁人睡着〔喝醉〕时偷窃. *The chimney ~s up smoke.* 烟囱滚滚冒烟. *She ~ed the string into a ball.* 她把线卷成一团. *The boy ~ed himself up in a blanket.* 这孩子拿毯子把身体裹了起来. *He ~ed himself from side to side.* 他左右摇晃. — *vi.* ①滚转,旋转,滚去,滚动前进;坐车去. ②彷徨,流浪. ③波动,起伏,弯转;(岁月)周而复始,移变. ④横摇,摆动,左右颠簸 *(opp.* pitch*)*;(船)左右摇摆着航行,(人)踉踉跄跄地走. ⑤卷起;变圆;卷拢 *(up; together)*;展延. ⑥(雷)隆隆地响;(言语)滔滔不绝;(鸟)啭. ⑦(动物)打滚;(眼睛)转动. ⑧(烟)滚滚上升;(雾)消散. *The carriage ~ed along.* 马车隆隆走过. *Bills ~ up.* 帐单堆积. *Years ~ on [by].* 岁月流逝. ***~ around*** 〔美口〕(时光)流逝;周而复始;按时到临. ***be ~ing in luxury [money]*** 十分奢华〔有钱〕. ***~ sb. over*** 把某人打翻〔撞倒〕在地. ***~ and pitch*** (船)左右前后摇摆. ***~ back*** 使退却,击退;压平(物价). ***~ down*** 滚下来;流下来. ***~ed gold*** (辗压成的)金箔. ***~ed steel*** 轧过的薄钢板. ***~ in*** ①(予约者、捐款等)滚滚而来;(浪)滚滚打来;大量进来. ②〔俚〕飘然到来;到达. ③〔美〕睡;退下. ***~ into*** 卷成(一团);交混成(一体). ***~ one's own*** 〔美俚〕卷自己的香烟;自行生活. ***~ oneself up*** 卷成一团. ***~ out*** ①滚出;动身,离开. ②伸出,展开. ③〔美〕起床. ④不及格被开除. ⑤朗诵;声音宏亮地唱. ***~ over*** 使滚;滚;〔美棒球〕得分. ***~ the bones*** 闲谈;吹牛. ***~ up*** ①卷起(袖子);包卷. ②积贮,攒(钱). ③缩成圆球,团拢. ④(烟等)袅袅上升. ⑤(车)前进;到达;〔澳〕蜂拥而来;〔口〕(人)出现(某处),登场;来到约定地点. ⑥〔美〕起床 *(A carriage ~ed up to the inn.* 一辆马车驶至旅店前停下). ***~ your hoop*** 〔美〕当心自己的事. — *n.* ①滚,滚动,旋转;波动,起伏;摇摆,蹒跚. ②(雷等的)轰鸣,隆隆声,(鼓的)疾擂,连敲;(诗、散文等的)朗朗可诵的格调. ③卷物,卷轴;纸;卷;一卷. ④(学校、军队等的)点名簿;名单,细目单;公文,案卷;记录;目录. ⑤卷制品,面包卷,肉卷,烟卷(等). ⑥滚筒机、辗压机、压路机,卷扬辘轳;【装订】压型机. ⑦【建】(柱头的)漩涡饰. ⑧【空】侧滚. ⑨〔美俚〕一卷钞票,钱. ⑩【乐】(和弦)琶音. *the ~ of thunder* 雷鸣. *a toilet ~* 一卷手纸. *a ~ of printing-paper* 一卷印刷用纸. *a ~ of cloth* 一卷呢绒,成卷的一匹布. *a ~ of bread* (早点用的)面包卷儿. *He has ~s of fat on him* 他浑身胖得圆滚滚的. *(vote)* ***by ~ call*** 唱名(表决). ***call the ~*** 点名. ***in the ~ of*** 载于…名单〔目录〕中,跻身…之列. ***on the ~s*** 在名单中. ***on the ~s of fame*** 在名人录里,在名人之列. ***the ~ of honour*** 阵亡将士名簿〔单〕. ***strike off the ~s*** 消去(律师)名册中名字;开除. **~ angle** 倾斜角 **~away** *a.* 附有轮子并可折叠推动搬移的 *(a ~away bed* 有轮子、可搬移的床). **~back** 压平物价;击退. **~ bar**【机】辗棍,辗杆. **~booster**【火箭】绕纵轴助推器〔加速器〕. **~call** 点名;【军】点名号. **~ cumulus** 层积云. **~ film** 摄影胶卷. **~-mop** 腌鲱鱼. **~-out** (新飞机)初次出厂〔展出〕. **~past** (军事检阅中)重武器行进. **~-top desk** 拉盖书桌. **~way** 滚木坡;(在河岸上)一堆待运圆木.

Rol·land [rɔːˈlæŋ], **Romain** 罗曼罗兰〔1866—1931,法国小说家,音乐评论家,剧作家〕.

roll·a·way [ˈrəuləˌwei] *a.* 可折叠滚动的. *a ~ bed* 带轱辘的折叠床.

roll·er [ˈrəulə] *n.* ①使滚转的人;滚转物;滚筒;【印】墨辊,印色辊;(地图等的)轴,卷轴;辊子,转子,滚轴,滚子,辊;轧滚;镇压器,压路机;〔方〕擀面棍;布卷,绷带卷. ②(暴风雨后打来的)大浪. ③【动】啭舌金丝雀;鷃鸽. **~ bandage** 绷带卷. **~ bearing**【机】滚柱轴承. **~ lap**【纺】皮辊花. **~-skate** 四轮滑行鞋. **~ towel** (套在横木架或滚筒上供擦手用的)环状毛巾.

roll·ey [ˈrɔli] *n.* = rulley.

rol·lick [ˈrɔlik] *vi.* 嘻嘻哈哈地闹着玩,欢闹. — *n.* 嬉戏;说笑;欢闹;高兴. **-ing, -some** *a.*

Rol·lin [ˈrɔlin] *n.* 罗林〔男子名, Rol(l)and 的异体〕.

roll·ing [ˈrəuliŋ] *a.* ①旋转的;滚动的;波动的,起伏的;滔滔地流的;隆隆响的. ②卷起的. ③左右摇摆的. ④〔美〕起伏不平的(土地等). ⑤〔美俚〕有钱的,钱多的. *the ~ smoke* 滚滚浓烟. *the ~ sea* 波涛滚滚的大海. *a ~ collar* 翻领. *the ~ seasons* 周而复始的季节. — *n.* ①滚动;旋转;横摇. ②辗压,轧. ③轰鸣,隆隆声;啭鸣声. **~ barrage**【军】徐进弹、幕射击. **~ bridge** 滚轮活动桥. **~ hitch**【海】轮结〔一种绳结〕. **~ hospital**【军】随军医院. **~ kitchen** (设置在卡车上的)流动厨房〔俗叫 *soup-kitchen*〕. **~ mill** 轧钢厂;轧钢机. **~ pin** 擀面棍. **~ press** 滚筒印刷机;轧光机;(橡胶)压延机. **~ stock** (铁路或汽车运输机构的)全部车辆. **~ stone** 无定居的人;见异思迁的人. **~ strike** 持续罢工.

Rol·lo [ˈrɔləu] *n.* 罗洛〔男子名〕(L. = Rolf).

ro·ly-po·ly [ˈrəuliˈpəuli] *n.* ①〔英〕果酱布丁卷. ②滚园肥胖的人〔动物〕. ③滚球. — *a.* 胖得园滚滚的(孩子等).

Rom [rəum] *n.* *(pl.* ***Ro·ma*** [ˈrəumə]*)* = gypsy.

Rom. = ①Roman. ②Romance. ③Romanic. ④*Romans* (基督教《圣经》,《新约》中的)《罗马人书》*(= Epistle to the Romans)*.

rom. =【印】roman.

Ro·ma·ic [rəuˈmeiik] *n., a.* 现代希腊语(的);有关现代希腊的.

ro·maine [rəuˈmein] *n.*【植】长叶莴苣.

Ro·man [ˈrəumən] *a.* ①(古)罗马的;(古)罗马人的;(古代)罗马人气概〔风度〕. ②(罗马)天主教的. ③〔r-〕罗马字的,罗马体铅字的;正体字的;罗马数字的. **~ *arch*** 半圆拱. **~ *architecture*** 罗马式建筑. **~ *balance [beam, steelyard]*** (普通的)天平. **~ *candle*** 手持燃放的焰火筒. **~ *Catholic*** 罗马天主教的;天主教徒. **~ *Catholicism*** 天主教. **~ *cement*** 天然水泥. **~ *Curia*** 罗马教廷. **~ *holiday*** 以看别人受苦为乐的娱乐. **~ *Law*** 罗马法. **~ *letter [type]*** 罗马字体,正体(铅)字. **~ *mosaic*** 镶嵌玻璃. **~ *nose*** 鼻梁高的鼻子. **~ *numerals*** 罗马数字〔I = 1, V = 5, X = 10, L = 50, C = 100, D = 500, M = 1000,从大到小顺列者为各数相加之和: MDCLXVI = 1666. 大小倒列者为二数相减之差: XC = 90, MCM = 1900〕. **~ *order***【建】罗马柱型,混成柱型. **~ *pitch*** 25°的屋顶斜面. **~ *school*** 拉斐尔(Raphael)画派. **~ *vitriol*** 罗马矾〔即硫酸铜〕. — *n.* ①(古)罗马人. ②天主教徒. ③拉丁语. ④〔r-〕【印】罗马字,罗马体铅字,正体铅字〔略 rom.〕. *an Emperor of the ~s* 神圣罗马帝国皇帝.

ro·man [rɔˈmɑ̃] *n.* 〔F.〕(中世纪在法国发展起来的)韵文小说;传奇小说. ***~ à clef*** [nɑˈklei] 影射小说. ***~-fleuve*** [flœːv] 家世小说 =〔英〕saga novel.

ro·mance [rəˈmæns, ro-] *n.* ①中世纪骑士故事;冒险故

事,传奇,虚构小说. ②小说般的事蹟; 浪漫史, 风流事蹟,恋爱故事. ③传奇式的生活〔世界、情调等〕; 空想癖; 杜撰,虚构. ④【乐】浪漫曲. ⑤〔R-〕= *R- language* 罗曼(斯)语,拉丁系语言〔包括意大利语、葡萄牙语、罗马尼亚语、法兰西语、西班牙语等〕. — *a.* 〔R-〕 拉丁系语言的. *the ~s about King Arthur.* 亚瑟王故事. *travel in search of ~* 寻找奇遇的旅行. — *vi.* ①讲〔写〕虚构故事. ②吹牛; 空想,妄想. ③〔口〕谈情说爱; 追求异性. — *vt.* 〔口〕和…恋爱; 追求(异性).

ro•manc•er [rəˈmænsə] *n.* ①= romancist. ②爱空想的人; 爱瞎吹的人.

ro•manc•ist [rəuˈmænsist] *n.* 虚构故事作者,传奇小说作家.

Rom•an•es [ˈrɔmənez] *n.* 【语言】(吉普赛的)罗马乃斯语,吉普赛语.

Ro•man•esque [ˌrəuməˈnesk] *n.* ①【建】罗马式建筑; 罗马式绘画〔雕刻〕. ②〔罕〕拉丁系语言. — *a.* ①【建】罗马式的; 罗马风格的. ②拉丁语系的. ③〔r-〕 传奇小说的; 空想的.

Ro•ma•nia [rəuˈmeinjə] *n.* 罗马尼亚〔欧洲〕.

Ro•ma•nian [ˈrəuˈmeinjən, rəuˈmeiniən] *a.* 罗马尼亚的. — *n.* ①罗马尼亚人. ②罗马尼亚语.

Ro•man•ic [rəuˈmænik] *a.* ①(古代)罗马(人)的. ②拉丁语系的. — *n.* 拉丁系语言.

Ro•man•ish [ˈrəumaniʃ] *a.* 〔蔑〕罗马天主教(徒)的.

Ro•man•ism [ˈrəumənizəm] *n.* ①〔常蔑〕天主教. ②(罗马天主教) 教义 〔教规〕. ③古罗马气质 〔制度〕. ④【建】罗马式.

Ro•man•ist [ˈrəumənist] *n.* ①天主教徒. ②古罗马掌故学家. ③罗马法学者〔专家〕. ④拉丁系语言学者.

Ro•man•ize [ˈrəumənaiz] *vt.* ①使罗马化; 使拉丁化. ②使天主教化. ③〔r-〕 用罗马字写,用罗马体〔正体〕铅字印刷. — *vi.* ①(古)罗马化; 拉丁化. ②成为天主教徒. ③使用拉丁字母. **-i•za•tion** [-ˈzeiʃən].

Ro•ma•no- [rəuˈmeinəu] *pref.* 罗马的.

Ro•mansh, R(o)u•mansh [rəuˈmænʃ, ruːˈmænʃ] *n., a.* 瑞士东部所用拉丁语系方言(的).

ro•man•tic [rəˈmæntik] *a.* ①【文艺】〔常 R-〕浪漫主义的(*opp.* Classical, Realistic 等). ②传奇(式)的; 小说般的; 情节离奇的. ③空想的,虚构的; 怪诞的,想入非非的; 不实际的,难实行的(计画等). ④谈情说爱的,多情的,风流的,香艳的. — *n.* ①浪漫主义者,浪漫派诗人〔艺术家〕. ②〔*pl.*〕浪漫思想〔行为〕. *the R- school* 【文艺】浪漫(主义)派. **-ti•cal•ly** *ad.*

ro•man•ti•cism [rəˈmæntisizəm] *n.* ①传奇小说体裁; 虚构,空想; 传奇性; 浪漫精神〔倾向〕. ②浪漫主义 (*opp.* classicism 等). **-cist** *n.* 浪漫主义者〔作家,艺术家〕.

ro•man•ti•cize [rəˈmæntisaiz] *vt.,vi.* (使)浪漫化,(使)幻想化.

Rom•a•ny [ˈrɔməni] *n., a.* 吉普赛 (Gipsy) (的); 吉普赛语(的). *deep ~* 纯粹的吉普赛语. *~ rye* 与吉普赛人结伙,能说吉普赛话的非吉普赛人.

ro•maunt [rəuˈmɔnt, -ˈmɔːnt] *n.* 〔古〕传奇诗或故事; 骑士故事.

Rom. Cath. = Roman Catholic.

Rome [rəum] *n.* ①罗马〔意大利首都〕. ②古罗马城; 罗马城邦; 古罗马(帝国). *All roads lead to ~* 条条道路通罗马; 殊途同归. *Do in [at] ~ as ~ does [as the Romans do].* 入国问禁,入境从俗. *fiddle while ~ is burning* 罗马大火漠不关心. *~ was not built in a day.* 罗马不是一天建成的; 伟业非一日之功.

Ro•me•o [ˈrəumiəu] *n.* 罗米欧〔莎士比亚戏剧《罗米欧与朱丽叶》中的男主人公〕.

Rome•ward [ˈrəumwəd] *a.,ad.* 向天主教(的); 向罗马.

Rome•wards [ˈrəumwədz] *ad.* = Romeward.

Rom•ish [ˈrəumiʃ] *a.* = Romanish.

Rom•ney [ˈrɔmni] *n.* 罗姆尼〔姓氏〕.

romp [rɔmp] *n.* ①乱蹦乱闹; 顽皮嬉闹; 顽皮嬉闹的孩子〔尤指女孩〕; 顽童. ②【赛马】轻快的飞跑; 轻易的胜利. — *vi.* ①顽皮嬉闹; 〔美学生语〕跳舞. ②轻易地取胜; 【赛马】轻快地飞跑 *(along; past)*. ***~ away with it*** 〔美剧〕获得大成功. **~ home** = **~ *in*** 〔俚〕(赛马时)轻松愉快地得胜.

romp•er [ˈrɔmpə] *n.* ①嬉戏的人,顽皮不羁的女孩. ②〔*pl.*〕(小孩穿的一种宽松)连裤外衣.

romp•ish, romp•y [ˈrɔmpiʃ, -i] *a.* 顽皮嬉闹的,乱蹦乱闹的.

Rom•u•lus [ˈrɔmjuləs] *n.* 【古罗马传说】古罗马的建国者〔Mars 的儿子,古罗马人的守护神〕.

Ro•na, Rho•na [ˈrəunə] *n.* 罗娜〔女子名〕.

Ron•ald [ˈrɔnəld] *n.* 罗纳德〔男子名, Reginald 的异体〕.

Ron•da [ˈrɔndə] *n.* 朗达〔女子名〕.

ron•deau [ˈrɔndəu] *n.* ①【诗】二韵叠句短诗〔主体由 13 行或 10 行构成,其最初二行在中间及末尾构成重复出现的叠句, 基本形式为"a a b b a, a a b 叠句, a a b b a 叠句"〕. ②【乐】回旋曲 (= rondo).

ron•del [ˈrɔndl] *n.* 【诗】由 14 行构成的二韵叠句短诗〔最初二行与第 6,7 行及第 13,14 行相同〕.

ron•de•let [ˈrɔndeˌlet] *n.* 【诗】五行或七行短叠句诗.

ron•do [ˈrɔndəu] *n.* ***(pl. ~s)*** 〔It.〕【乐】回旋曲.

ron•dure [ˈrɔndʒə] *n.* 〔罕,诗〕圆形,圆形物,弧线.

Ro•ne•o [ˈrəuniəu] *n., vt.* (用)复写机(复写)〔商标名〕.

Ron•nie [ˈrɔni] *n.* ①罗尼〔男子名, Ronald 的昵称〕. ②罗妮〔女子名, Veronica 的昵称〕.

Rönt•gen *n.* = Roentgen.

rood [ruːd] *n.* ①【宗】十字架上的基督像; 〔the ~〕〔古〕(处死耶稣的)十字架. ②长度单位〔= $5^1/_2$—8 码〕; 地积单位(= $^1/_4$ 英亩). *Not a ~ remained to him.* 没有寸土留给他. ***by the (holy) ~*** 的确,一定. **~ arch** (教堂里)十字架隔屏正中的圆拱. **~ loft** (教堂里的)十字架神龛. **~ screen** (教堂里设置在圣坛与会堂之间,以示分隔的)十字架隔屏.

roof [ruːf] *n.* ①屋顶,房屋; 家屋. ②(放行李的)车顶; 笠形罩. ③上颚. ④最高部,顶部; 【矿】顶板. ⑤【空】(飞机)机身上的包皮; 担任空中掩护的飞机; 〔口〕(飞机的)绝对上升限度. *the ~ of heaven* 天空. *the ~ of the world* 世界的屋脊. ***full to the ~*** 塞满一屋. ***hit the ~ [ceiling]*** 勃然大怒〔狂怒〕. ***left [be] without a ~*** 无家可归. ***raise the ~*** 〔俚〕喧闹; 闹翻了天; 大声诉苦〔发怨言〕. ***under sb.'s ~*** 寄住某人家里. ***under a ~ of foliage*** 在树荫下. ***under the ~ of*** 住在…的家里,寄…的篱下, 在…的照应下. — *vt.* 给…盖屋顶; 象屋顶一样盖着; 放入屋里; 保护,庇护. **~ garden** 屋顶花园. **~ spotter** (对敌机的)屋顶了望员. **~ top** 屋顶. **~ tree** 栋梁; 屋脊梁. **-less** *a.* 无屋顶的; 无家的,无住处的.

roof•age [ˈruːfidʒ] *n.* 屋顶用材〔用料〕.

roofed [ruːft] *a.* 有屋顶的; …屋顶的. *a ~ wagon* 有盖货车. *a thatch-~ house* 茅草顶房. *a flat-~ house* 平顶房.

roof•er [ˈruːfə] *n.* ①〔口〕盖屋顶的人; 盖屋顶的厚板. ②〔英、口〕客人给主人道谢的信.

roof•ing [ˈruːfiŋ] *n.* ①屋顶; 盖屋顶; 屋顶用材料. ②覆盖; 保护. *~ felt* 【建】油毛毡.

rook[1] [ruk] *n.* ①【鸟】白嘴鸦; 〔北英〕乌鸦. ②赌棍; 骗子. — *vt.* (用赌博)骗(钱),诈骗; 敲竹杠. *They ~ed me £10 for my berth.* 他们敲了我十英镑的卧铺费.

rook[2] [ruk] *n.* 【国际象棋】车,堡垒.

rook•er•y [ˈrukəri] *n.* 〔英〕①白嘴鸦〔海豹、企鹅等〕群(的栖居处). ②公寓; 贫民窟. ③同类人〔物〕的集中处.

rook•ie, rook•y[1] [ˈruki] *n.* 〔军俚〕新兵; 新手,新队员,新来者. *a ~ cop* 〔美俚〕新来的警察.

rook•y[2] [ˈruki] *a.* 有白嘴鸦的; 白嘴鸦多的.

room [rum, ru:m] *n.* ①室,房间. ②场所,席位,位置,地位,空间. ③余地,余裕;机会. ④〔*pl.*〕一套房间;寄宿舍;出租的房间. ⑤屋子里的人们;一屋子[满座](的人们). *an upper* ~ 顶楼房间. *a single [double]* ~ 单人[双人]房间. *a strong* ~ 保险库. *There is* ~ *for one more.* 还可以容纳一个人. *I would rather have his* ~ *than his company.* 他不在反而好. ~ *for doubt* 怀疑的余地. *set the* ~ *in a roar* 使一屋子的人哄然大笑. ***give*** ~ 腾地方(位置),让开,移开,挪开一点. ***in sb.'s*** ~ = ***in the*** ~ ***of sb.*** 处于某人的地位,代替某人,代…而. ***leave*** ~ ***for evasion*** 留下推诿余地. ***make*** ~ ***for*** 让地位[位置]给…. ***no*** ~ ***to turn in*** = ***no*** ~ ***to swing a cat*** 地方狭窄;无转身余地. ***parcels*** ~ 衣帽[物件]寄存处. ~ ***to rent*** 〔美俚〕傻瓜. ***take*** ~***s at*** 在…租房间. ***take up too much*** ~ 占用地位过多. — *vi.* 〔美〕占有[租有]房间,在房间里;投宿,住宿,寓居,同住 *(at; with; together)*. — *vt.* 留…住宿,留住(客人). ~*(ing) house* 〔美〕公寓;供寄宿的房屋. ~ ***and board*** (供)膳宿,吃住 *(He receives wages plus* ~ *and board.* 他除享受膳宿待遇外,还领有工资). ~ **clerk** (旅馆里的)预定、登记房间的职员. ~ **mate** 〔美〕同房间的人. ~**-to-room** *a.* 室对室的 (~*-to-*~ *telephone* 各室互通电话). ~ **service** 送酒菜等到房间的旅馆的服务(部).

roomed [ru(:)md] *a.* 有…间房间的.

room·er [ˈru:mə] *n.* 〔美〕(旅馆、公寓里的)寄宿者,房客.

room·ette [ru(:)ˈmet] *n.* 〔美〕(铁路卧车的)单人小室.

room·ful [ˈru(:)mfəl] *n.* 满房间;一屋子的人;满场的人,满座.

room·ie [ˈru:mi] *n.* 住在同一房间里的人.

room·y [ˈru:mi] *a.* *(-i·er; -i·est)* 宽敞的,广阔的;有很多空间的. **-i·ly** *ad.* **-i·ness** *n.*

roor·back, roor·bach [ˈruəbæk] *n.* 〔美〕(中伤选举中的政敌或可能出任本人所想获得的职位的人的)诽谤性谣言.

roose [ru:z; Scot. röz] *n., vt., vi.* 〔英方〕称赞,赞美.

Roo·se·velt [ˈrəuzəvelt, ˈru:svelt] *n.* ①罗斯福〔姓氏〕. ②**Franklin Delano** ~ 佛兰克林·迪拉诺·罗斯福〔1882—1945, 1933—1945 任美国第三十二任总统〕. ③**Theodore** ~ 赛奥多尔·罗斯福〔1858—1917,美国第二十六任总统〕.

roost [ru:st] *n.* ①栖架;鸡埘,鸡棚,鸡舍;同栖的一群家禽. ②歇息处;卧室;床;〔口〕旅舍. ***at*** ~ 歇着;睡着. ***come home to*** ~ 还归原主;得到恶报 *(Curses come home to* ~. 害人反害己.) ***go to*** ~ 去歇;去睡. ***rule the*** ~ 当家,作主;跋扈,称雄,居首. — *vi.* 栖息;进窝;〔美〕歇着;睡着;投宿;过夜;〔口〕就座,坐下. — *vt.* 为…设置栖息处;把…送去栖息.

roost·er [ˈru:stə] *n.* ①〔美、方〕雄鸡. ②狂妄自负的人. ③飞机问答机.

Root [ru:t] *n.* 鲁特〔姓氏〕.

root[1] [ru:t] *n.* ①(草木、毛发等的)根;根菜,食用菜根;根茎,地下茎;块根;有根植物,草木,草;〔*pl.*〕根菜类;(山)麓. ②根本,根源,原因;本质;基础,根柢;【语】词根;根词;【数】根数,根. ③祖先;【圣】子孙;【乐】和弦基音. *the* ~ *of a tooth* 牙根. *the* ~ *of all evil* 祸根. *the* ~ *of a gem* 玉根〔毛玉的非玉部分〕. *a cubic [second, square]* ~ 立方[平方]根. ***at (the)*** ~ 根本上. ***be at the*** ~ ***of*** 是…的根本[基础]. ***by the*** ~***(s)*** 连根,从根部,从根源 *(pull up by the* ~*s* 连根拔除,根除). ***get at [go to] the*** ~ ***of*** 追究…的根底,追查…的真相. ***lay the axe to the*** ~ ***of*** 根本改革;治本. ~ ***and branch*** 完全,都;彻底地,急进地. ***strike at the*** ~ ***of*** 打击…的根部,彻底摧毁. ***strike [take]*** ~ 生根;扎根;固定,固着. ***to the*** ~***(s)*** 充分地;竭力地;彻底地. — *vi., vt.* (使)生根;(使)固定,(使)固着;〔喻〕深深种下,使根深蒂固. *Terror* ~*ed him to the spot.* 吓得他呆立不动. ~ ***up [out]*** 连根拔除(杂草等);肃清(反革命等). — *a.* 根的;根本的. *a* ~ *idea* 根本思想. ~ **borer** 馈根害虫. ~ **cellar** 块根储藏窖. ~ **climber** 根部攀缘植物. ~ **crop** 块根作物〔马铃薯、萝卜等〕. ~ **infinitive**【语法】动词的无 "to" 不定式. ~**let** 幼根,细根,根枝. ~ **nodule (bacteria)** 根瘤(菌). ~ **rot** 根腐病. ~ **stock** ①【植】根茎;砧木. ②根源,起源. ~**-tubercle** 根瘤.

root[2] [ru:t] *vt., vi.* (猪等)用鼻子掘(地);搜寻 *(for)*: *R-, hog, or die.* 〔美〕拼命干啊,不然就得饿死.

root[3] [ru:t] *vi.* 〔美俚〕应援,声援;支持,赞助;欢呼,喝采.

root·age [ˈrutidʒ] *n.* 生根;固定;根源.

root·ed [ˈru:tid] *a.* 生了根的;有根的;根深蒂固的;固定的. **-ly** *ad.*

root·er [ˈru:tə] *n.* 〔美俚〕(比赛时的)声援者,啦啦队;拔根者,拔根器.

root·le [ˈru:tl] *vt.* (猪)用嘴拱土 — *vi.* 翻,寻找.

root·less [ˈru:tlis, ˈrut-] *a.* 无根的. **-ly** *ad.* **ness** *n.*

root·y[1] [ˈru:ti] *a.* ①根多的;根状的.

root·y[2] [ˈru:ti] *n.* 〔英军俚〕面包.

ROP = ①〔常作 rop〕run-of-paper (由编辑)随意决定登载位置的. ②record of production 生产纪录.

rope [rəup] *n.* ①(通常指 1—10 英寸以上粗细的)索子,麻索〔*cf.* cable; cord〕. ②绳〔长度名 = 20 英尺〕. ③套索;测量索;绞首索;〔the ~〕绞刑;缢死. ④一串;(啤酒等液体中的)丝状粘质,菌丝束. ⑤干扰雷达用的长反射器. ⑥〔*pl.*〕(拳击的)围栏索. ⑦〔*pl.* the ~s〕秘诀,内幕. ⑧〔美俚〕劣质雪茄烟;项圈. ~ *of sand* 靠不住的东西. ***be at [come to] the end of one's*** ~ 山穷水尽,日暮途穷;智穷力竭;一精二光. ***be outside the*** ~***s*** 〔俚〕不懂秘诀[内情];是门外汉. ***dance on the*** ~***s*** 〔俚〕被绞死. ***get on to the*** ~***s*** 熟识适当手续. ***give sb. a*** ~***'s end*** 鞭打某人. ***give (sb.) (plenty of)*** ~ 放任. ***give (sb.)*** ~ ***enough (to hang himself)*** 放任(某人)使他自取灭亡. ***give the calf more*** ~ 〔美〕给予较多的自由,听其自便,别管. ***know the*** ~***s*** 熟悉内幕,懂得秘诀. ***learn the*** ~***s*** 摸到窍门[线索],弄清内幕. ***name not a*** ~ ***in his house that hanged himself*** 在有人吊死的人家莫说绳子;要避免提及别人的忌讳[隐痛]. ***on the high*** ~***s*** 得意扬扬;精神饱满;骄傲. ***on the*** ~ (登山者)互相用绳子联系着. ***on the*** ~***s*** 被击倒在(拳击场的)围栏索上;〔俚〕使窘困[毫无办法];即将完蛋. ***put (sb.) (up) to the*** ~***s*** 把窍门[线索]指点给(某人). ***show sb. the*** ~***s*** 指点某人窍门[线索]. — *vt.* ①用绳绑(捆、缚). ②(爬山者等)用绳系住(身体). ③拉绳分隔,制索子围住 *(in; off)*. ④用绳拉;拉运;〔美俚〕引诱. ⑤勒着马慢跑. ⑥〔美西部〕用套索捕捉(牛马等). — *vi.* ①拧成绳. ②生粘丝. ③〔英〕故意让对方赛赢. ~ ***in*** 〔美俚〕引诱,诱惑,诱入圈套. ~**-dancer** 走钢索的演员. ~**dancing** 走钢索. ~ **end** (打人的)鞭子. ~ **ferry**【军】绳渡. ~ **ladder** 绳梯. ~**manship** 走索技术;爬绳技术. ~ **quoit** (投环戏用的)(麻索)环. ~**'s-end** (笞刑用的)鞭子. ~ **skipping** 跳绳. ~**-walk** = ropery. ~**walker** 走钢索的演员. ~**walking** 走钢索. ~**way** 架空索道. ~ **yard** = ropery. ~ **yarn** 旧索子解开的绳线;无足轻重的小事物 *(Rope-Yarn Sunday*【军】星期五下午的衣物缝补假;一星期内不工作的一个下午).

rop·ery [ˈrəupəri] *n.* 绳厂,制索厂.

rop·i·ness [ˈrəupinis] *n.* 可拉成丝;粘性.

rop·y [ˈrəupi] *a.* *(-i·er; -i·est)* ①像绳子的;可做绳子的;能拉长的. ②胶粘的,粘韧的. ③坚牢的,粗壮结实的.

Roque·fort [ˈrɔkfɔ:] *n.* (洛克福)羊乳干酪.

ro·que·laure [ˈrɔkəˈlɔ:, ˈrəukə-; F. rɔkˈlɔr] *n.* 一种

十八世纪男式齐膝外套.

ro·quet [ˈrəuki, -kei] *n., v.* 【槌球】(使)自己的球碰到(别人的球).

ror·qual [ˈrɔːkwəl] *n.* 【动】鳁鲸 = finback.

ror·ty [ˈrɔːti] *a.* 〔英俚〕愉快的,快乐的,有趣的;喜爱娱乐的. *have a ~ time* 过得愉快.

Ro·sa [ˈrəuzə] *n.* 罗莎〔女子名〕.

ro·sace [ˈrəuzeis] *n.* 蔷薇花〔圆花〕图样;【建】圆花窗;圆浮雕;圆花饰.

ro·sa·ceous [rəuˈzeiʃəs] *a.* 【植】蔷薇科的;蔷薇花形的;玫瑰色的,玫瑰香的.

Ros·a·lie [ˈrɔzəli] *n.* 罗莎莉〔女子名〕.

Ros·a·lind [ˈrɔzəlind] *n.* 罗莎琳德〔女子名〕.

Ros·a·line [ˈrɔzəlin] *n.* = Rosalind.

ros·an·i·line [rəuˈzænilin, -ˌiːn, -ˌain] *n.* 【化】品红碱,玫苯胺.

ro·sa·r·i·an [rəuˈzɛəriən] *n.* ①蔷薇〔玫瑰〕栽培者. ②〔R-〕【天主】念珠祈祷会会员.

Ro·sa·rio [rəuˈsɑːrjəu] *n.* 罗萨里奥〔阿根廷港市〕.

ro·sar·i·um [rəuˈzɛəriəm] *n.* *(pl.* ***ro·sar·i·a*** [-iə]*)*〔L.〕蔷薇〔玫瑰〕园,蔷薇花坛.

ro·sa·ry [ˈrəuzəri] *n.* ①【天主】念珠;念珠祈祷. ②蔷薇冠. ③玫瑰园;蔷薇花坛. ④佳句集.

Ros·coe [ˈrɔskəu] *n.* ①罗斯科〔姓氏,男子名〕. ②〔r-〕〔美俚〕手枪,左轮.

ros·coe·lite [ˈrɔskəulait] *n.* 【矿】钒云母.

Rose [rəuz] *n.* 罗斯〔姓氏,女子名〕.

rose¹ [rəuz] *n.* ①【植】蔷薇,玫瑰;蔷薇科植物;蔷薇〔玫瑰〕花. ②蔷薇〔玫瑰〕色,淡红色;〔*pl.*〕玫瑰色的脸色;玫瑰香,玫瑰香料. ③〔喻〕舒服,安乐,愉快. ④【纹】(象征英国的)五瓣蔷薇花样;(装饰等)蔷薇花样;玫瑰结. ⑤【建】圆花饰,车轮窗,圆花窗. ⑥玫瑰形钻石;(喷壶的)莲蓬头,喷咀. ⑦【医】〔the ~〕丹毒. ⑧【海】(罗盘等的)刻度盘;罗经卡. ⑨【机】停座器;【电】灯线盒. *Every ~ has its thorn. = No ~ without a thorn.* 没有无刺的玫瑰,没有十全十美的幸福. *the Alpine ~* 【植】石南. *the Chinese ~ = the ~ of China* 【植】月季花. *the ~ of May* 【植】白水仙. *a blue ~* 蓝玫瑰,虚有之物,办不到的事. *She has quite lost her ~s.* 她脸上的玫瑰色完全消失了. *It is not all ~s = It is no bed of ~s.* 并非一切都轻松愉快〔十全十美〕;未必完全安逸. *a wind ~* 【空】风图. ***a [the] bed of ~s*** 称心如意的境遇;安乐窝. ***as welcome as the ~ in May*** 象五月的玫瑰那样可爱〔受欢迎〕. ***gather (life's) ~s*** 追求欢乐. ***the Golden ~*** 【宗】金玫瑰〔教皇于四旬斋中对某国元首或城市特别颁赠,象征祝福的赠物〕. ***path strewn with ~s*** 欢乐的一生,一帆风顺的遭遇. ***the ~ of (the party)*** (一群人中)最漂亮的美人. ***the white ~ of innocence [virginity]*** 白玫瑰似的纯洁. ***under the ~*** 秘密地;暗中地;私下地. ***the Wars of the Roses*** 【英史】蔷薇战争. — *vt.* ①(运动等把脸色等)弄红,使成玫瑰色〔通常用被动语态〕;把(羊毛等)染成玫瑰色. ②使有玫瑰香味. **~-acacia** 【植】毛洋槐. **~ aphid** 【动】蔷薇长管蚜. **~ apple** 【植】蒲桃. **~ bay** 【植】夹竹桃;石南. **~bed** 玫瑰花坛〔圃〕. **~ beetle** 【动】吉丁虫. **~ bit** 【机】梅花钻. **~-breasted grosbeak** 【动】红斑胸腊嘴雀. **~ bud** 玫瑰的蓓朵;美丽的少女;〔美俗〕初次出入社交场所的少女. **~bush** 蔷薇〔玫瑰〕丛. **~ campion** 【植】毛缕 (= mullein pink). **~chafer [bug]** 【动】蔷薇鳃〔玫瑰〕金龟子. **~-colo(u)red** *a.* 玫瑰色的;乐观的. **~-diamond** 二十四面钻石. **~ drop** 酒糟鼻. **~ engine** 车制曲线花样的车床附件. **~ fever [cold]** 【医】枯草热. **~fish** 许多红色食用鱼的通称〔如鲈鲉,拟石首鱼,无鳔鲉等〕. **~ geranium** 【植】头状天竺葵. **~ leaf** 玫瑰花瓣 (*a crumpled ~ leaf* 幸福中的小折磨). **~ mallow** 【植】木槿属. **~mary** 【植】迷迭香(属). **~ moss** 【植】半支莲 (= portulaca). **~ of Jericho** 【植】含生草. **~ of Sharon** 【植】木槿;〔主英〕大萼金丝桃. **~ oil** 玫瑰油,玫瑰香水. **~ola** 【医】蔷薇〔玫瑰〕疹. **~ pink** ①*n.* 玫瑰色;玫瑰色颜料. ②*a.* = ~coloured. **~-pipe** 滤吸管. **~-rash** 【医】= ~ola. **~ quartz** 【矿】蔷薇石英. **~-red** *a.* 玫瑰红的. **~ scale** 【动】蔷薇白边蚧. **~ slug** 【动】蔷薇粘叶蜂. **~ water** 玫瑰香水;奉承话;温和的处置,优柔的办法〔手段〕. **~water** *a.* 像玫瑰香水的;温和的,感伤的;优雅的,优美的. **~ window** 【建】车轮窗,圆花窗. **~ wood** 【植】黄檀(属);花梨树;黄檀〔花梨〕木;青龙木.

rose² [rəuz] rise 的过去式.

rosé [rəuˈzei] *n.* 玫瑰葡萄酒.

ro·se·ate [ˈrəuziit] *a.* =rose-coloured.

Rose·bery [ˈrəuzbəri] *n.* 罗斯伯里〔姓氏〕.

Rose·mar·y [ˈrəuzməri] *n.* 罗斯玛丽〔女子名〕.

rose·mar·y [ˈrəuzməri] *n.* *(pl.* ***-mar·ies****)* ①【植】迷迭香. ②艾菊(= costmary).

ro·se·o·la [rəuˈziːələ] *n.* 【医】蔷薇疹;玫瑰疹.

ro·ser·y [ˈrəuzəri] *n.* 蔷薇园,玫瑰园;玫瑰花坛〔花圃〕.

Ro·setta [rəuˈzetə] *n.* 罗塞塔(女子名).

Rosetta stone [rəuˈzetəstəun] 罗塞塔石〔1799 年在埃及 Rosetta 地方发现的碑石. 用象形文字,古埃及俗语,和古希腊语三种文字写成,由此得到解释古埃及象形文字的初步依据〕.

ro·sette [rəuˈzet] *n.* ①玫瑰花结,蔷薇花缨縌;蔷薇花饰. ②【建】圆花饰;圆花窗;【电】插座,(天花板)接线盒. ③【植】莲座(叶)丛 (=rose-diamond). *peanut ~* 花生丛簇病.

Rosh Ha·sha·na [ˌrɔʃhəˈʃɑːnə] *n.* 犹太新年.

Ro·si·cru·cian [ˌrəuzikruˈʃən, ˌrɔzi-] *n.* ①炼金〔占星〕术士〔十七、十八世纪一些自称属于会玄术的秘密会社的人〕. ②其它类似会社的成员. — *a.* 玄术〔炼金术、占星术等〕的. **-ism** *n.*

ros·in [ˈrɔzin] *n.* 松脂,松香;树脂. — *vt.* 用松脂擦(提琴弓弦);用松脂封. **~ oil** 【化】树脂油,松香油. **~-weed** 【植】松香草 (Silphium laciniatum);松脂植物的泛称.

ros·i·nan·te, ro·zi·nan·te [ˌrɔziˈnænti] *n.* 老弱瘦马,不中用的马.

Ross [rɔs] *n.* 罗斯〔姓氏,男子名〕.

Ross. =〔Scot.〕Ross and Cromarty 罗斯克罗马太郡〔苏格兰北部一个郡〕.

ross [rɔs] *n.* (树皮上)粗糙带鳞状的表面.

Ros·set·ti [rɔˈseti] *n.* 罗塞蒂〔姓氏〕.

ros·tel·late [ˈrɔstlˌeit, -it] *a.* ①【植】有蕊喙的;有小喙的. ②【动】有顶突的;有小喙的(虱).

ros·tel·lum [rɔsˈteləm] *n.* *(pl.* ***-tel·la*** [-ə]*)* ①【植】蕊喙;小喙. ②【动】a) 顶突. b) 小喙(虱). **-tel·lar** [-ə] *a.*

ros·ter [ˈrəustə] *n.* 【军】花名册,勤务薄;名册;登记簿.

Ros·tock [ˈrɔstɔk] *n.* 罗斯托克〔东德港市〕.

Ros·tov [ˈrɔstɔv] *n.* 罗斯托夫〔苏联港市〕(=~-on-Don 顿河畔罗斯托夫).

ros·tra [ˈrɔstrə] *n.* rostrum 的复数.

ros·tral [ˈrɔstrəl] *a.* ①【动】喙的,嘴的;有嘴的. ②【建】附有喙形船首装饰的(圆柱等). *a ~ column* (雕有敌舰舰首花样的)海战纪念柱. *a ~ crown* 【古罗马】(赠给海战中第一个跃登敌舰的将士的)海战功勋冠.

ros·trate, ros·trat·ed [ˈrɔstreit, -tid] *a.* ①【动】有喙的,有嘴状突起的. ②【建】有嘴状装饰的,有喙形船首装饰的.

ros·tri·form [ˈrɔstrifɔːm] *a.* 喙形,嘴状.

ros·trum [ˈrɔstrəm] *n.* *(pl.* ***-tra, -s****)* ①(古罗马装在舰首用以撞击敌舰的)喙形舰首. ②〔*pl.*〕(有敌舰舰首装饰的)舰首讲坛;讲坛;主席台;检阅台. ③【动】喙,嘴;嘴状突起. ④【医】镊子,钳子. *take the ~* 登坛.

ros·y [ˈrəuzi] *a.* ***(-i·er;-t·esi)*** ①蔷薇[玫瑰]色的；粉红色的；玫瑰一样香的；用蔷薇装饰的．②光明的，有希望的；会幸福的；情况好的，乐观的；[美]滥醉的．*a ~ blush (face)* 玫瑰红的(脸)．*~ about the gills* (酒后等)脸色红润．*~ cheeks* 红润的脸颊．*~ finch*【动】粉红岭雀．*the ~ future* 光明的将来．*~ views* 乐观的想法．**-i·ly** *ad.* **-i·ness** *n.*

rot [rɔt] *vi.* ①腐烂；朽坏；枯萎；(尤指囚犯)虚弱，消瘦；(羊)生肝蛭病；腐败，堕落．②[英俚]说胡话，说讽刺话，说挖苦话．***be only rotting*** 一味胡说；只不过是开玩笑．***~ off [away]*** (树枝等)枯死，凋落．— *vt.* ①使腐朽[烂]；使枯萎；沤制(亚麻等)．②糟蹋，弄糟；完全破坏(计划等)．③[英俚]讽刺，挖苦，取笑．*~ it [um, 'em]* 糟了！胡说！见鬼！*R- it! I forgot to bring my book with me.* 糟了！忘记带书来了．*Rot the luck!* 弄糟了！— *n.* ①腐朽，腐烂；腐败，堕落．②【植】腐烂病；【兽医】[*the* ~] 羊肝蛭病，羊瘟；【医】消耗性疾病．③[英俚]胡话，无聊(愚蠢、糊涂、荒唐)的事情．④(板球赛等的)料不到的失败．⑤令人沮丧的事；失败．*the black ~ on sweet potato*【农】甘薯黑斑病．*Don't talk ~!* 别胡说！*It is perfect ~ to trust him.* 相信他简直是荒唐．*Rot!* [俚]胡说，废话；蠢话，蠢事(=tommyrot)．*What ~ that it is not open on Sundays!* 星期天老不开演[开门]真是荒唐！*A ~ set in* 士气不振而成败局．

ro·ta [ˈrəutə] *n.* ①[主英]花名册，勤务簿．②[英]值班，轮班．③轮唱．④[R-]【天主】最高法庭．

ro·ta- *comb. f.* 表示"旋转"，"转动"，"轮转"．

ro·ta·me·ter [ˈrəutəˌmiːtə] *n.* 转子流量计，转子流速计．

Ro·ta·r·i·an [rəuˈtɛəriən] *a., n.* 扶轮社 (Rotary Club) 的(社员)；扶轮社社员(的)；"扶轮国际"的(成员)．

ro·ta·ry [ˈrəutəri] *a.* 旋转的，轮转的．*a ~ press [machine]* 轮转印刷机．*a ~ fan* 扇[吹]风机．*the R- Club* 扶轮社["扶轮国际" (R- International) 的旧称；现指"扶轮国际"的各地分社]．*~ Cultivator*【农】旋(转中)耕机．— *n.* ①轮转(印刷)机．②环行交叉路．③[the R-]"扶轮国际"．**~-wing aircraft**【空】旋翼飞机．

ro·ta·scope [ˈrəutəskəup] *n.* (高速)转动机械观察仪．

ro·tat·a·ble [ˈrəuteitəbl] *a.* 可旋转[转动，轮转]的．

ro·tate [rəuˈteit] *vi.* ①旋转；轮转；循环；②【天】自转．③轮流，交替，轮换．— *vt.* ①使旋转[轮转]；使循环．②使轮流，使轮换；使交替．③【农】轮作．

ro·ta·tion [rəuˈteiʃən] *n.* ①旋转，轮转；循环．②【天】自转．③【物】旋度．④轮流，轮换；交替．⑤【农】轮作；【林】轮伐(期)．***by [in]*** ~ 轮换，轮流．

ro·ta·tion·al [rəuˈteiʃənəl] *a.* ①旋转的；轮流的，循环的．②【农】轮作的．~ **inertia**【物】转动惯量．~ **grazing**【农】循环[轮换]放牧．

ro·ta·tive [ˈrəutətiv] *a.* 旋转的，转动的；循环的，轮流的．

ro·ta·tor [rəuˈteitə] *n.* ① ***(pl. ~s)*** ①旋转器，旋转部．②【冶】旋转反射炉．③【物，电】转子．④***(pl. ~es)***【解】rotatory (轴)转肌．

ro·ta·to·ry [ˈrəutətəri] *a.* ①(使)旋转的，(使)循环的．②使轮流的．③【物】旋光的．~ **dispersion**【物】旋光色散．~ **power** 旋光力，旋光本领．

ROTC = Reserve Officers' Training Corps [美]后备军官训练队．

rotch(e) [rɔtʃ] *n.*【动】扁脚海雀 *(Plantus alle)* [产于北极和北大西洋沿岸]．

rote[1] [rəut] *n.* ①死记，死背．②机械方法；刻板办法；固定程序．***by*** ~ 死记；机械地 *(do by ~* 呆板地做．*have [get, learn] by ~* 死记)．

rote[2] [rəut] *n.*【乐】=rotte.

ro·te·none [ˈrəutnˌəun] *n.*【化】鱼藤酮．

rot·gut [ˈrɔtgʌt] *n.* [美俚]劣酒；下等威士忌酒．— *a.* 劣质的．

Roth·en·stein [ˈrəuθənstain] *n.* 罗森斯坦[姓氏]．

rô·ti [ˈrɔti] *n.* [F.] 烤肉．

ro·ti·fer [ˈrəutifə] *n.*【动】轮虫纲 **-al, -ous** *a.* **-an** *a., n.*

ro·ti·form [ˈrəutiˌfɔːm] *a.* 轮形的，轮状的．

ro·tis·ser·ie [rəuˈtisəriː] *n.* ①熟肉店，烤肉店．②电转烤肉架．

rot·l [ˈrɔtl] *n.* ***(pl. ar·tal*** [ˈɑːtɑːl], ***rotls)*** 罗特尔[穆斯林国家重量单位，标准因地而异，差别约在一磅到五磅之间]．

ro·to [ˈrəutəu] *n.* ***(pl. -tos)*** [美] = rotogravure.

ro·to·chute [ˈrəutəʃuːt] *n.*【空】(减速)螺旋桨降落伞．

ro·to·graph [ˈrəutəgrɑːf] *n.*【摄】①轮转印片机；旋印照片．②(将正本转为反像而直接拍摄的)翻拍照片．

ro·to·gra·vure [ˌrəutəgrəˈvjuə] *n.* [美]①轮转凹板印刷术[品]．②(报纸的)凹版图画副刊．

ro·tor [ˈrəutə] *n.* ①【电机】转子 (*cf.* stator)；动片，转片．②【空】水平旋翼．③【物】旋度．④(风筒船的)风筒，旋转圆筒．**~craft**【空】旋翼飞机 (= rotary-wing aircraft, ~ plane)．

ro·to·till [ˈrəutətil] *vt.* 使用旋耕机碎土．

Ro·to·till·er [ˈrəutəˌtilə] *n.* 旋耕机商标名，旋转碎土器商标名；[r-] 旋耕机，旋转碎土器．

rot·te [ˈrɔtə] *n.* 洛特琴[中世纪的一种弹拨乐器]．

rot·ten [ˈrɔtn] *a.* ①腐败的，腐朽的；腐烂的；不干净的，邋遢的；臭的．②腐朽的，堕落的．③破烂的；不坚固的，不牢的，脆的，易碎的；虚弱的，不健全的．④[俚]劣等的，无用的，不可靠的；坏的，不愉快的．⑤(羊)患肝蛭病的；害了羊瘟的．⑥[古、方]潮湿的，下雨的．*a ~ municipal government* 腐败的市政府．*a ~ show* [美]蹩脚的演出．*a ~ deal* [美]不公平的待遇．*~ to the core* 腐败透顶．*~ weather* 恶劣的天气．***Something is ~ in the state of Denmark*** 这里有点古怪[不对头]的事情．~ **borough**【英史】(有权选民太少的)有名无实的选举区．**R- Row** (伦敦 *Hyde Park* 中的) 练马林荫路[常简称 the Row]．~ **stone** 磨石．**-ly** *ad.* **-ness** *n.*

rot·ter [ˈrɔtə] *n.* ①[英俚]没用的人，废物；无赖，下流坯．②自动瞄准干扰发射机．

Rot·ter·dam [ˈrɔtədæm] *n.* 鹿特丹[荷兰港市]．

ro·tund [rəuˈtʌnd] *a.* ***(-er; -est)*** ①近圆形的．②胖得圆滚滚的，胀得圆圆的；张得圆圆的(嘴等)．③(声音)洪亮的，圆润的．④铺张的，华丽的(文体等)．**-ly** *ad.*

ro·tun·da [rəuˈtʌndə] *n.* (有圆顶的) 圆形建筑物；圆形大厅．

ro·tun·di·ty [rəuˈtʌnditi] *n.* ①球状，圆形；圆物．②肥胖．③(声音的)洪亮．④(言语的)圆熟．⑤(文体等的)铺张，华丽．

ro·tu·rier [F. rotyrje] *n.* [F.] 平民．

r(o)u·ble [ˈruːbl] *n.* 卢布[苏联货币单位]．

rou·é [ruːˈei] *n.* [F.] 荡子，浪子．

Rou·en [ˈruːɑ̃ːŋ] *n.* 鲁昂[法国城市]．

rouge[1] [ruːʒ] *n.* ①胭脂，唇膏，口红．②红粉，过氧化铁粉，铁丹．— *vt., vi.* (在…上)搽胭脂，搽口红；弄红；变红．— *a.* [罕] 红的只用于: ***R- Croix*** [krwɑː] [英] 纹章局四属官之一，其纹章为圣乔治红十字．***R- Dragon*** [英]纹章局四属官之一，其纹章为亨利七世赤龙．

rouge[2] [ruːdʒ] *n.*【橄榄球】[Eton 校语] ①扭夺 (= scrummage)．②一分[带球越过球门界线三次]．

rouge-et-noir [ˈruːʒeˈnwɑːr] *n.* [F.] (用纸牌玩的) 猜红黑．

rough [rʌf] *a.* ①粗糙的 (*opp.* smooth)；凹凸的，崎岖不平的 (*opp.* level)．②粗毛的，多毛的，蓬乱的 (头发)．③狂暴的(风雨等)；汹涌的(海水等)；激烈的．④粗鲁的，粗暴的，无礼的．⑤粗陋的，粗杂的．⑥未完成的，未加工的，未琢磨的；粗制的．⑦草率的，粗枝大叶的，大体的．⑧刺耳的，难听的(声音)；刺眼的；难看的．⑨涩的，难吃的．⑩[口]辛苦的，难受的，难忍的(on)．⑪【希腊语法】带"h"音的，送气的．*a ~ skin* 粗糙的皮肤．*a ~ road* 崎岖不平的道路. *a ~ weather* 狂风暴雨的天气. *~ manners* 粗暴的态度. *~ work* 粗暴的举动; 粗活. *~ word* 粗话. *~ accommodation* 粗陋的设备. *the ~er sex* 男性. *a ~ circle* 不精确的圆. *a ~ estimate* 粗略的估计. *a ~ guess* 瞎猜. *~ music* (捣蛋的) 大声喧闹. *a ~ landscape* 荒芜 [极难看] 的景色. *~ claret* 味涩的红葡萄酒. *~ coal* 粗煤, 原煤. *~ materials* 原料. *~ rice* 糙米. *~ coating* 粗抹的底子; 灰泥粗糙的表面. *a ~ leaf*【植】(在子叶之后生出的)真叶, 糙叶. *~ makeshifts* 勉强临时对付办法. *a ~ life* 艰苦的生活. *a ~ but hearty welcome* 虽然不周到但是诚心诚意的欢迎. ***be ~ on sb.*** 对某人粗暴苛刻; 欺侮某人; 使某人倒霉. ***call sb. ~ names round*** 乱七八糟的, 庞杂的. ***~ and tough*** 强壮的, 结实的. ***~ going*** 〔美、运〕苦战. ***give sb. a lick with the ~ side of one's tongue*** 严厉责备, 申斥. ***have a ~ time (of it)*** 吃苦头, 受苦受难, 备尝辛酸. — *ad.* 〔口〕粗, 粗糙地; 粗暴地; 粗话谩骂某人; 用坏话骂某人. *play ~* (比赛中) 动作粗暴. *treat sb. ~* 对人态度粗暴. ***cut up ~*** 狂暴起来, 闹起来, 暴跳起来. ***live ~*** 艰苦地生活. — *n.* ①粗糙的东西, 崎岖不平的地面; (马蹄上的)防滑钉; 〔the ~〕【高尔夫球】障碍区域. ②未加工[粗加工]状态. ③〔英〕粗暴的人. ④虐待; 艰难困苦. ⑤粗矿, 废矿. ⑥草图; 要略. ***in the ~*** 未加工(的), 未完成(的); 杂乱的[地]; 无准备的[地]; 大体上; 处于日常状态; 〔美高尔夫球〕处于障碍地区. ***over ~ and smooth*** 不管甘苦难易; 无论高低起伏; 到处. ***take the ~ with the smooth*** 是好是歹, 一起承受. ***the ~(s) and the smooth(s)*** 人世的苦乐; 幸与不幸. — *vt.* ①弄粗, 弄粗糙; 弄成崎岖不平; 使(羽、毛等)倒竖 *(up)*; 弄成乱七八糟, 搅乱. ②粗制, 草草作成, 使略具雏形 *(out)*. ③(铁蹄上)装防滑钉; 粗暴地对待, 虐待; 讲粗鲁话, 粗暴地说; 惹怒, 使发脾气. ④写概略 *(in)*; 拟定大体的计划 *(out)*. ⑤驯(马); 使(动物)受饥寒. ***~ sb. up the wrong way*** 惹怒某人. ***~ it*** 胡闹; 含辛茹苦, 忍受辛苦. —*vi.* 变粗糙; 粗鲁行事. **~-and-ready** *a.* 只管快不管好的; 潦草塞责的 *(the ~-and-ready rule* 只管快不管好的作法[主张]). **~-and-tum·ble** ①*a.* 乱七八糟的, 混乱的, 杂乱的; 莽撞的. ② *n.* 混战; 乱斗, 漫无计划的生活. **~ bluegrass**【植】粗茎莓系草. **~cast** *vt., n.*【建】粗作, 粗制; 粗涂, 打底子; 打底用灰泥; (拟定) 大体方案. *~ cut* 粗切的烟叶. **~-cut** 乱切的; 粗切的. **~ diamond**〔喻〕外表粗鲁的人. **-dry** *vt.* 晒干(衣服)不烫. **~ fish** 非食用鱼, 无经济价值的鱼. **~-footed** *a.* 脚上有羽毛的 (鸟). **~-hearted** *a.* 无同情心的, 硬心肠的. **~-hew *(~-hewed; ~-hewn, ~-hewed)*** *vt.* 粗切, 粗削; 粗制. **~-hewn** *a.* 粗制的; 粗糙的; 粗鲁的. **~ house** ① *n.* 〔原美俚〕(学生的) 乱闹. ②*vt., vi.* 吵闹, 叫嚣; 虐待. **~-legged** *a.* 脚上有毛的(马、鸟等). **~ luck** 恶运, 倒霉. **~ neck**〔美俚〕粗暴的人, 蛮横的人. **~ quarter (of the town)** 城市的贫民区. **~ rice** 稻谷. **~ rider** *n.* 驯马人; 劣马骑手; 非正规的骑兵; 〔R-R-〕【美史】美西战争时的义勇骑兵. **~ scuff**〔美俚〕粗暴的人, 暴徒. **~shod** *a.* 穿钉靴的; 钉着防滑铁蹄的(马); 残酷无情的 *(ride ~shod over* 对…大摆架子; 骑在…脖子上作威作福, 对…恣意妄为, 对…横行霸道). **~spo·ken** *a.* 说话粗鲁的. **~ stuff**〔美俚〕暴力行为; 下流行为; 色情文字. **~-up**〔俚〕动武; 打架. **~ wrought** *a.* 潦草作成的, 粗制的.

rough·age [ˈrʌfidʒ] *n.* ①素材, (粗)原料. ②粗糙食物中的纤维质, 富于纤维质的粗食, 食用糠; (美国西部)粗草料.

rough·en [ˈrʌfən] *vt.* 弄粗糙, 使崎岖不平. — *vi.* 变粗糙, 变得崎岖不平.

rough·ish [ˈrʌfiʃ] *a.* ①有点粗糙的. ②有点粗暴的; 有点不好听的.

rough·ly [ˈrʌfli] *ad.* 粗糙地; 粗暴地; 粗俗地; 粗略地. *~ estimated* 粗略地估计起来. *~ speaking* 粗略地说来.

rough·ness [ˈrʌfnis] *n.* ①粗糙; 凹凸不平, 崎岖; 蓬乱. ②粗暴; 狂风暴雨. ③未加工. ④难听, 刺耳; 味涩; 不调和. ⑤概略. ⑥【工】粗糙程度.

rou·lade [ruːˈlɑːd] *n.* ①【乐】华彩经过句. ②(牛肉片馅的)肉卷.

rou·leau [ruːˈləu] *n.* *(pl.* ***~s, ~x*** *[-z])* ①一卷东西; (用纸卷包着的)一卷硬币; 〔*pl.*〕一卷丝带. ②【军】柴捆. ③【医】缗线状红血球簇.

rou·lette [ru(ː)ˈlet] *n.* ①轮盘赌; (轮盘赌用的) 转轮. ②(雕刻家的)点线压制轮; 粗网纹压制轮; (邮票)骑缝虚线压制轮. ③【数】一般旋轮线. ④转轮式卷发器.

roum [ruːm] *n.* room 的一种旧拼写法.

Roum. = **Rouma·ni·a(n)** = Rumania(n).

Rou·mansh [ru(ː)ˈmænʃ] *n.* = Romansh.

roun·ce·val, roun·ci·val [ˈraunsivəl] *n.*【植】大豌豆.

round[1] [raund] *a.* ①圆形的; 球形的; 圆筒形的; 弧形的, 半圆(形)的. ②兜圈子的, 一周的; 来回的. ③完全的; 十足的; 完整的, 无零头的. ④数目不小的, 巨额的. ⑤流畅的, 嘹亮的. ⑥轻快的, 迅速的; 活泼的. ⑦率直的, 坦白的; 不客气的, 严厉的; 断然的, 毅然的. ⑧【语音】圆唇音的, 撮口音的. *a ~ face* 圆脸. *a ~ dance.* 圆舞. *a ~ arch*【建】半圆拱. *a ~ lie* 十足的谎话. *a ~ dozen* 恰好[整整]一打. *a ~ number* 整数〔10, 100, 1000 等〕. *a good ~ whipping* 一顿狠打. *~ dealing* 光明正大的做法. *a ~ unvarnished tale* 坦白话, 真情实话. *~* hand 圆体楷书〔*cf.* running hand〕; 楷书书法. ***at a ~ pace*** 轻快矫健的步子. ***be ~ with*** 对…露骨地讲, 老老实实跟…讲. ***bring up with a ~ turn***【海】套住索子使(船)停止; 使突然停止, 突然阻止. ***have a ~ scolding*** 被大骂一顿. ***in good ~ terms*** 直率地(说). ***in ~ numbers*** 大概算起来, 大略. — *n.* ①圆形物, 球; 环. ②(散步、喝酒等的)一圈, 一巡, 一转; (人的)一团, 一伙. ③巡视, 巡逻; 巡视路线; 巡逻区域; 【军】巡逻队. ④环行路, 圆路. ⑤周围, 范围. ⑥周转; 循环. ⑦牛腿肉. ⑧(梯子、椅子脚等的) 横档. ⑨【建】圆形嵌线; 【雕】〔the ~〕立体雕刻 (*opp.* relief). ⑩(工作的)一件; (比赛的)一次, 一回(合), 一场, 一局, (谈判等的)一轮. (欢呼的)一阵, (弹药的)一发, 一颗; (枪炮等的)(一次)齐发; 排射; (事情、行动等的)一连串, 一系列. ⑪【乐】轮唱; 圆舞(曲). *this earthly ~* (这个)地球. *The news goes the ~.* 消息传遍. *the ~ of knowledge* 知识的范围. *the daily ~ (of life)* 日常生活[工作、事务]. *three ~s of cheers* 三次欢呼. *a live ~* 实弹. *a training ~* 教体[试验]用导弹. ***draw from the ~*** 照着立体模型描绘. ***go for a good ~*** 兜一个大圈子. ***go [make] one's ~s*** ①兜圈子, 巡回; 走遍. ②(医生)巡视病房; (邮递员) 按户投送. ***go [pace, walk] the ~(s)*** 巡回, 走遍; 传遍. ***make the ~ of*** 巡视. ***in all the ~ of Nature*** 在自然界的整个范围内; 在世界各处. ***in the ~*** 雕刻成立体(的), 栩栩如生的, 表现无余的. ***play a ~*** 赛一次. ***~ after ~ of cheers*** 一阵一阵欢呼. ***serve out a ~ of brandy to all hands*** 拿白兰地酒给全体喝一巡. ***take a ~*** 走一转, 兜个圈子; 散步. — *ad.* ①旋转, 回转, 团团转, 循环往复, 周而复始; 兜着圈子. ②(在)周围, 在附近; 到处; 在四方. ③走整整一圈; 从头至尾; 传遍; 挨次. ④朝反方向; 转过来. ⑤绕弯儿地, 绕道, 迂回. ⑥到某(指定)地点. *turn ~* 旋转, 团团转. *three inches ~* 周围三英寸. *all the neighbours for a mile ~* 周围一英里以内的人们. *Glasses (went) ~* 每人都给了一杯酒. *spread destruction ~* 向四面八方进行破坏. *all the country ~* 全国. ***all ~*** 周围, 到处; 四面八方. ***all the year ~*** 一年到头. ***ask sb. ~*** 邀人来家. ***bring ~*** ①使苏醒回来. ②说服过来. ③拿到…去 (to). ***come ~*** (从某处)转来, 兜回来; 恢复(神志); 复元; 到来, 来到 *(May Day soon comes ~ again* 劳动节很快又要来了). ***come ~ to sb.'s view*** 同意某人意见. ***cut round [around]*** 〔俚〕故意卖弄 [显示]. ***go a long way ~*** 绕远路走,

兜着圈子去. ***go*** **~** 绕着走; 迂回着走; 运行; (食物等)人人分到 *(enough food to go ~* 食品充足人人有份) ***hand*** **~**传递给每一个人. ***look*** **~** 往周围一看; 回头看. ***order a carriage*** **~** 叫马车过来. ***right*** **~** 周围, 到处; 四面八方. **~ *about*** 成圆圈, 在周围, 在四面八方; 绕着, 迂回着; 向相反方向; 大约. **~ *and*** **~** = (加强语气的) *round*. ***show one*** **~** 带人到处游览. ***sleep the clock*** **~** 连续睡一整天. ***turn (short)*** **~** (忽然) 转过身来. ***win (sb.)*** **~** 把某人拉到[争取到]自己方面. — *prep.* 在…的周围; 在…的四面八方; 在…各处; 向…四周; 围(绕)着…; 绕过; 在…的附近; (在时间方面)横贯过. *a tour ~ the world* 环球旅行. *~ the corner* 在拐弯的地方. *the country ~ Beijing* 北京近郊. ***argue*** **~** ***and*** **~** ***a subject*** 只在问题表面兜圈子[不深入问题核心]. ***get [come]*** **~** ***sb.*** 智胜某人; 诱骗人. ***go*** **~** ***the papers*** 报上普遍登载. **~** ***the clock*** = ***the clock*** **~** 整天整夜; 昼夜不停地. — *vt.* ①弄圆, 弄成圆形; 使涨得圆圆的. ②完成, 使圆满. ③环绕; (船)绕过(某处), 迂回(某处); 拐(弯); 包围, 围住; 〔罕〕使旋转. ④骑马赶拢(畜群) *(up)*. ⑤【语音】发圆唇音. ⑥使成整数; 【数】把…四舍五入. **~ *in*** 【海】(把索缆)拉上来. **~ *off*** 弄圆; 完成, 使成熟; 使完美; 使圆满; 愉快地渡过. **~ *on sb.*** 骂某人, 说某人坏话, 攻击某人; 告某人的密, 出卖某人. **~ *on one's heels*** 用脚后跟支住而转身, 转过身来. **~ *out*** ①〔美〕= *round off*. ②使胖得圆滚滚的. **~ *to*** ①【海】使船掉头迎风停下. ②恢复健康[体力]. **~ *up*** 弄成圆球; 使数目恰好; 使成一个整数; 赶拢, 赶在一块儿; 兜捕, 逮捕. — *vi.* ①变圆; 弯曲. ②成熟, 长饱满. ③巡视, 巡逻; 绕转, 拐弯; 回过头来. **~about** ① *a.* 绕大圈子的, 迂回的(路等); 转弯抹角的, 委婉的; 包围着的, 广泛包含的; 长胖了的. ② *n.* 迂回曲折的路, 远路; 转弯抹角的说法, 婉转的说法; 周游, 圆形物, 圆场, 圆形阵营; 团团围住的树篱; 圆背靠椅; 〔英〕旋转木马; 〔英〕环状交叉路; 〔美〕(男用)短上衣 *(lose on the swings what you make on the ~-about* 转木马得来打秋千失去; 一手得来, 一手失去; 结果落空). **~ angle** 【数】(360度)周角. **~-arm** *a., ad.* 手臂齐肩的[地]. **~ clam** 【动】(北美)蛤蜊 (=quahog). **Roundhead** 【英史】圆头党人[1642—1652 英国内战时反对贵族的清教徒议会党人]. **~heel(s)** 〔俚〕性行为随便的女人. **~house** ①【海】后甲板舱室. ②〔美〕(中央有调车转台的)圆形机车库. ③【史】拘留所. ④〔美俚〕把胳臂弯成弧形打出去的一拳; 〔美棒球俚〕大弯球. **~let** 小圆圈. **~-off** 舍去零数. **~ robin** ①(看不出签名人先后的)环形签名请愿[抗议]书. ②【运】循环赛. **~ shot** (旧时的)圆球形炮弹. **~-shouldered** *a.* 弯腰曲背的. **~ steak** 一刀[一块]牛腿肉. **~ table** 圆桌会议, 协商会议; 出席圆桌会议的人们. **~-the-clock** *a., ad.* 昼夜不停的(地); 连续二十四小时的(地). **~ top** 桅楼. **~ trip** 〔英〕周游; 〔美〕来回(的旅程). **~-trip** *a.* 〔美〕来回的. **~up** ①〔美、澳〕畜群驱集; 赶拢一块的牲畜, 赶拢家畜的人; 兜捕, 围捕, 逮捕(犯人). ②综述; 摘要. **~ worm** 蛔虫.

round[2] [raund] *vi., vt.* 〔古〕低声讲, 悄悄地说. **~ *sb. in the ear*** 对着某人耳朵悄悄地讲.

round·ed [ˈraundid] *a.* ①圆的; 丰满的, 匀称的. ②(兴趣)多样的; (能力)强的, 多面的. ③【语音】圆唇的. ④【数】四舍五入的. *a well ~ person* 有多方面兴趣[能力]的人. **-ness** *n.*

roun·del [ˈraundl] *n.* ①圆形物; 环; 小圆盘; 圆楯; 圆形纹章; 【建】小圆窗, 串珠花边; 【筑城】圆形棱堡. ②【诗】= rondeau. ③圆舞.

roun·de·lay [ˈraundilei] *n.* ①鸟的啼啭声. ②【乐】反复重唱的民歌, 回旋曲. ③圆舞.

round·er [ˈraundə] *n.* ①〔口〕绕行者, 巡行者. ②〔美俚〕累犯; 无业游民; 酒鬼; 〔美〕乱花钱的人. ③加工成圆形的人[工具]. ④〔英〕〔*pl.*〕〔作单数用〕软球粗棒球. ⑤〔英〕〔R-〕卫理公会牧师.

round·ish [ˈraundiʃ] *a.* 稍圆的, 圆圆的.

round·ly [ˈraundli] *ad.* ①圆圆地, 滚圆地. ②充分, 完全, 全面地. ③坦白地, 率直地, 露骨地; 严厉地, 毫不容情地; 断然. ④迅速地; 大略. *go ~ to work* 热心工作. *scold ~* 严厉谴责. *He ~ asserted that it is true.* 他(完全)断言这是真的.

round·ness [ˈraundnis] *n.* ①圆, 圆形; 球形; 圆筒状. ②完满, 圆满; 完整; 丰富. ③率直, 坦率; 严厉.

rounds·man [ˈraundzmən] *n.* *(pl. -men)* 〔英〕推销员, 跑街; 〔美〕巡官; 看夜人.

roup[1] [ruːp] *n., vt.* 〔Scot.〕拍卖.

roup[2] [ruːp] *n.* 【兽医】①(家禽的)感冒; 鸡瘟[疫]. ②(家禽的)哑声病; 哑声. **-y** *a.*

rouse[1] [rauz] *vt.* ①叫(人)起来; 使跳起来, 赶出(猎物). ②叫醒; 使觉醒; 惊醒; 鼓励, 鼓舞, 激励, 振起. ③激发(感情); 惹怒, 使发脾气. ④搅动[液体使发酵, 如在啤酒制造中]. ⑤【海】用力拉 *(up)*. — *vi.* ①醒来; 跳起来, 飞起来; 【军】起床. ②奋起; 活动起来. **~ *and bitt [shine]!*** 【军】起床! **~ *oneself*** 振作精神, 奋起. **~ *to action*** 使奋起. ***want rousing*** 需要刺激, 懒惰. — *n.* ①觉醒; 奋起. ②〔英〕【军】起床号. **~about** =roustabout ②.

rouse[2] [rauz] 〔英古〕*n.* 满杯; 干杯; 闹饮. ***give a*** **~** 举杯祝酒. ***take one's*** **~** 乱喝乱闹.

rous·er [ˈrauzə] *n.* ①唤起者; 使觉醒者; 使惊醒的东西. ②〔俚〕惊人的话[行为]; 大谎.

rous·ing [ˈrauziŋ] *a.* ①(使)觉醒的; 鼓励的, 使兴奋的. ②烧起的(火); 活泼的, 兴旺的(贸易等). ③〔口〕惊人的, 异常的. *a ~ lie* 弥天大谎. *~ cheers* 热烈的欢呼.

Rous·seau [ˈruːsəu], **Jean Jacques** 卢梭 [1712—1778, 法国哲学家, 启蒙思想家]. **-ism** *n.* 卢梭的学说[社会契约说].

roust [raust] *vt.* ①撵出, 赶出, 驱逐 *(out)*. ②唤醒; 激动, 鼓舞 *(up)*. — *vi.* ①勤快地工作. ②〔俚〕扒窃.

roust·a·bout [ˈraustəbaut] *n.* ①〔美〕码头工人; (矿山、牧场等的)杂工; (炼油厂的)非[半]熟练工人; 〔美〕马戏团场地工. ②〔澳〕干零碎杂活的人[尤指牧羊场的打杂工 = rouseabout].

rout[1] [raut] *n.* ①混乱的群众[集会]; 【法】非法集会. ②〔英〕盛大的晚会. ③〔古〕团队. ④溃败, 溃散. *put to ~* 打垮, 击溃. — *vt.* ①打垮, 击破, 击溃; 使溃退. ②逐出, 赶出.

rout[2] [raut] *vt., vi.* ①=root. ②(从床上)唤起, 拉出. ③挖掘出; 刳刨. **-er** *n.* 刳刨者; 刳刨工具.

route [ruːt] *n.* ①路; 路线, 路程; 航线. ②【军】[raut] 出发令, 开拔令. ***en*** **~** 〔F.〕 =*on* **~**. ***give the*** **~** 下令出发. ***on*** **~** 在途中. ***on the*** **~** 在途中. ***take one's*** **~** 向…行进. — *vt.* ①给…规定路线[次序, 程序]. ②由某一路线发送. **~ formation** 【军】行军队形. **~man** 专在某一条路线上营业的推销员. **~ march** 【军】便步行军. **~-proving flight** 【空】新航线试飞.

rou·ter [ˈrautə] *n.* 刳刨者, 刳刨工具[尤指 a) 刳空刨 (= router plane). b) 一种刳刨机].

rou·tine [ruːˈtiːn] *n.* 例行公事, 日常工作; 常规; 惯例; 程序. *the day's ~ = daily ~* 日常工作. *He can only follow the old ~.* 他只会照常规办事. *a test ~* 检验程序. *the input ~* 【计】输入程序. **~-car** 定期汽车. **~-time** 授课时间. — *a.* 日常的, 常规的, 一定不变的.

rou·tin·eer [ˌruːˈtiniə] *n.* ①墨守成规者; 事务主义者. ②【无】定期测试装置.

rou·tin·ism [ruːˈtiːnizm] *n.* 墨守成规, 事务主义. **-ist** *n.*

rou·tin·ize [ruːˈtinaiz] *vt.* *(-ized, -iz·ing)* 使程序化, 常规化, 习惯化. **-za·tion** [-ˈzeiʃən] *n.*

roux [ruː] *n.* 油脂(尤指黄油)面粉糊[用于加浓羹汤等].

rove[1] [rəuv] *vi.* ①盘桓, 徘徊, 流浪, 漂泊. ②(眼睛)转来转去. ③(爱情、权利等)不断地变动. ④【弓术】随走随选目标射箭; 用活饵钓(鱼). — *vt., n.* 徘徊(于), 流浪

(于). **on the ～** 徘徊着,流浪着. **～ the woods** 漫游森林. *His eyes ～d round the room.* 他的眼睛环视着房间的每个角落.

rove[2] [rəuv] *vt.* 穿过孔拉; 梳; 纺(成粗纱). — *n.* 粗纱; 【船】(敲弯钉头用的)垫圈.

rove[3] [rəuv] *reeve* 的过去式及过去分词.

rov·en [ˈrəuvn] reeve (①穿(绳索). ②穿(绳)入孔系牢)过去分词的异体.

rove-o·ver [ˈrəuvˌəuvə] *a.* 【韵】转接韵的〔前一行末尾的超韵律音节与第二行的第一音节组成一个音步, 形成不间断的韵〕. — *n.* 转接韵诗.

rov·er [ˈrəuvə] *n.* ①徘徊者, 漫游者, 漂泊者, 流浪者. ②海盗; 海盗船. ③【弓术】远处的临时目标. ④〔英〕(音乐会等的)站位. ⑤(橄榄球的) 外场守场员. ⑥(17 岁以上的)童子军. *shoot at ～s* 乱射; 射远处的临时目标.

rov·ing[1] [ˈrəuviŋ] *n.* ①粗纱. ②粗纺.

rov·ing[2] [ˈrəuviŋ] *a.* 流浪的; 流动的; 无定所的, 不固定的. *a ～ ambassador* 巡回大使. *a ～ correspondent* 流动通讯员. *a ～ mission* 巡回特派团. *a ～ patrol* 游动哨. *～-rebel ideology* 流寇主义.

row[1] [rəu] *n.* ①(一)排, (一)行; 一排(座位); 行列, 横列. ②(两旁或一旁有房屋的)路, 街〔英国常用作某种行业占用的街道、地区〕. ③【无】天线阵. ④〔*the R-*〕〔英〕＝*Rotten R-* 伦敦海德公园中的骑马道. ***It doesn't amount to a ～ of beans.*** 〔美、俚〕这实在不算什么. **at the end of one's ～** 〔美〕沦落不堪; 万不得已. **have a hard [long] ～ to hoe** 〔美〕有麻烦事, 有巨大任务. **hoe one's own ～** 〔美〕做自己的事情, 自扫门前雪. **in a ～** 成一排; 连续, 一连串. **in ～s** 排列着. **in the front ～** 在头排; 〔美〕胜人一等的, 优秀的. — *vt.* 使成行, 使成排 *(up)*. **～ house** 联立[成排]房屋的一幢.

row[2] [rəu] *vt.* ①划(船); 用…划; 划运; 摆渡. ②划船去参加(竞渡等); 赛划. *Shall I ～ you to the shore?* 要我来把你划运到岸边吗? *The boat ～s six oars.* 小艇用六把桨划. **look one way and ～ another** 〔俚〕看东划西, 声东击西. **～ a fast stroke** 拼命划. **～ a race** 竞渡, 赛艇. **～ bow [stroks, five] (in the boat)** 担任(小艇)前桨手[整调手, 五号划手]. **～down** 划着赶上. **～dry** 不溅水地划; 空划. **～ in the eight** 作八人小艇选手出场. **～ in the Oxford boat** 作牛津大学选手去赛艇. **～ in the same boat** 同划小船; 同干一工作, 有同一处境, 抱同样见解. **～ out** 使划累. **～ over** 划赢. **～ 30 to the minute** 一分钟划三十次. **～ up Salt River** 〔美〕使反对党失败. **～ wet** 水花四溅地划. — *vi.* ①划船; 荡桨, 摇橹. ②参加竞渡[赛艇]; 赛划. — *n.* 划, 一划; 划船, 划船旅行; 划程.

row[3] [rau] *n.* 〔口〕吵嚷, 吵架, 争吵; 谴责; 打架; *What is the ～?* 吵嚷些什么? 怎么啦? *We've had awful ～s now and then.* 我们常常争吵的很厉害. **get into a ～** 挨骂, 被斥责. **have a ～ with** 和…争吵. **Hold your ～!** 〔口〕住口! 别吵! **kick up a ～ ＝ make a ～** 起哄, 吵闹; 抗议. **make a ～ about** 因…谴责. **pick a ～ with** 和…争吵. — *vt.* 〔口〕责骂, 申斥, 责备. **～ *sb.* up** 〔美〕责备某人. — *vi.* 〔口〕争吵, 吵闹.

row·an, row·an·ber·ry [ˈrəuən, ˈrau-; -beri] *n.* 【植】①欧洲花楸 *(Sorbus aucuparia)*. ②美洲花楸. ③花楸果.

row·an·tree [ˈrəuəntriː, ˈrauən-] *n.* ①(欧洲) 山楸. ②(美洲)花楸.

row·boat [ˈraubəut] *n.* 用桨划的船; 划艇, 划子.

row-de-dow, row·dy·dow [ˈraudiˈdau] *n.* 〔口〕吵闹, 喧嚷.

row·dy [ˈraudi] *n.* 凶暴的人; 无赖; 〔美俚〕钱. *a young ～* 阿飞. — *a.* ***(-di·er; -di·est)*** 凶暴的, 粗暴的; 吵闹的. **-ism** *n.* 吵闹 [粗暴] 的行为; 流氓作风. **-di·ly** *ad.* **-di·ness** *n.*, **～ish** *a.* 有点吵闹的; 有点粗暴的.

row·dy-dow·dy [ˈraudiˈdaudi] *a.* 喧哗的, 吵闹的.

Rowe [rəu] *n.* 罗〔姓氏〕.

row·el [ˈrauəl] *n.* (踢马刺上的)齿轮, 距轮; 【兽医】插环打脓. — *vt.* (〔英〕*-ll-*) 用距轮刺; 插入插环打脓器.

row·en [ˈrauən] *n.* ①留茬(放牧)田. ②二茬作物; 再生草.

Ro·we·na [rəuˈiːnə] *n.* 罗伊娜〔女子名〕.

row·er [ˈrəuə] *n.* 划船的人, 划手.

row·ing [ˈrəuiŋ] *n.* 划船. *a ～ boat* 划艇. *a ～ club* 划船俱乐部. **～-machine** 练划台.

Row·land [ˈrəulənd] *n.* 罗兰〔男子名〕.

Row·ley [ˈrəuli] *n.* 罗利〔姓氏〕.

row·lock [ˈrʌlək] *n.* 桨架, 桨叉.

Rox·burgh(e) [ˈrɔksbərə] *n.* 【印】罗克斯布拉装订式〔烫金皮书脊, 布或纸封面, 外切口与底切口为毛边的书籍装订〕.

rox·y [ˈrɔksi] *n.* 〔美学生语〕地质学教授.

Roy [rɔi] *n.* 罗伊〔男子名〕.

roy·al [ˈrɔiəl] *a.* ①王的, 女王的; 王室的; 〔*R-*〕(英国)皇家的. ②受王保护的, 敕立的, 敕许的, 敕定的. ③象王的; 高贵的, 庄严的; 大模大样的. ④极好的, 极佳的, 无上的, 高级的, 盛大的(宴会、欢迎等). ⑤大形的, 非常大的; 非常重要的, 地位非常高的. ⑥浓艳的 (颜色等) *His[Her] R- Highness* 殿下〔间接提到时用〕. *the Princess R-* 大公主. *a ～ princess* 公主. *the ～ family [household]* 王室, 皇家, 皇族. *the ～ blood* 王族. *a ～ feast* 盛宴. *a battle ～* 大规模的战争; 大混战. **have a ～ time** 非常愉快. **in ～ spirits** 精神很好. **live in ～ state[splendor]** 生活豪华. **R- Academician** (英国) 皇家艺术院院士. **R- Academy** (英国) 皇家艺术院 〔略 R. A.〕. **R- Air Force** (英国)皇家空军〔略R.A.F.〕 **R- Anthem** 英国国歌. **～ arch** 共济会 **(Freemasonry)** 中的一种级别. **R- Army** (英国)皇家陆军. **R- Army Medical Corps** (英国)皇家陆军医疗队〔略 R.A.M.C.〕. **R- Army Ordnance Corps** (英国)皇家陆军军械队. 〔略 R.A.O.C.〕. **R- Army Pay Corps** (英国)皇家陆军财务队〔略 R.A. P.C.〕. **R- Army Service Corps** (英国) 皇家陆军补给与运输勤务队〔略 R.A.S.C.〕. **R- Army Veterinary Corps** (英国)皇家陆军兽医队〔略 R.A.V.C.〕. **R- Artillery** (英国)皇家陆军炮兵〔略 R.A.〕. **～ blue** 品兰, 红光兰. **R- Botanic Gardens** (伦敦) 皇家植物园. **～ burgh** 〔*Scot.*〕 敕许自治邑. **R- Canadian Mounted Police** 加拿大骑警. **～ cell** (白蚁巢中的)王房. **R- Corps of Signals** (英国)皇家通讯兵〔略R.C.S.〕. **R- Courts of Justice** (伦敦)高等法院. **～ duke** 大公〔对公爵的王子〕. **R- Enginners** (英国) 皇家陆军工兵〔略 R.E.〕. **～ evil** 瘰疬. **R- Exchange** 伦敦交易所 〔略 R.E.〕. **～-fern** 【植】王紫萁. **R- Field Artillery** (英国)皇家陆军野战炮兵〔略 R.F.A.〕. **～ flush** 【牌戏】最大的五张同花顺. **R- Flying Corps** (英国) 皇家飞行队〔略 R.F.C.〕. **R- Humane Society** 英国溺水者营救会〔略 R.H.S.〕. **R- Institution** 英国科学知识普及会〔略R. I.〕. **R- Irish Constabulary** 爱尔兰皇家警察队〔略 R.I. C.〕. **～ jelly** (昆虫的)王浆. **R- Marine** (英国)皇家海军陆战队〔略 R.M.〕. **R- Marine Artillery** (英国) 皇家海军陆战炮兵〔略 R.M.A.〕. **R- Martyr** 【英史】查理 *(Charles)* 一世. **～ mast** 【船】最上桅. **R- Military College** (英国)皇家陆军军官学校〔略 R.M.C.〕. **R-** Naval Air Service (英国) 皇家海军航空队〔略 R.N. A.S.〕. **R- Naval Reserve** (英国) 皇家海军后备队. 〔略 R.N.R.〕. **R- Navy** (英国)皇家海军〔略 R.N.〕. **～octavo** 八开纸 ($6\frac{1}{2}\times10$英寸). **～ palm** (古巴) 大椰子. **～ paper** 24×19 英寸的纸; 25×20 英寸的印刷纸. **～ purple** 深紫色. **～ road** 捷径 *(There is no ～ road to knowledge* 学问上没有平坦的大道〔捷径〕). **～ sail** 【船】最上桅帆. **R- Society** (英国) 皇家学会. **～ stag** 有十二以上角叉的鹿. **～ standard** 〔英〕王旗. — *n.* ①〔口〕王族, 皇族. ②＝ ～ paper. ③【海】

= ~ mast; = ~ sail. ④ = ~ stag. ⑤〔*pl.*〕〔*the Royals*〕(英国)皇家步兵第一团 (=the R- Scots); (英国)皇家海军陆战队(= the R- Marines).

roy·al·ism [ˈrɔiəlizəm] *n.* 尊王主义,保王主义;保皇,忠君.

roy·al·ist [ˈrɔiəlist] *n.* 保皇党员;【英史】保王党,查利一世党;【美史】(独立战争时的)英国军队,英国方面的人;〔*R-*〕〔美〕死而后已的人. *an economic* ~ 保守的实业家. — *a.* = **roy·al·is·tic** 尊王主义的,保皇党员的.

Roy·al(l) [ˈrɔiəl] *n.* 罗亚尔〔姓氏,男子名〕.

roy·al·ly [ˈrɔiəli] *ad.* 作为王,像王;庄严地,高贵地;挥金如土地.

roy·al·ty [ˈrɔiəlti] *n.* ①为王;王位;王德,王威;王道,王者;〔集合词〕皇族,王族;〔常 *pl.*〕王的特权,王权;王国;王的领土. ②版税;上演税;铸币税;矿区使用费;特许权使用费. ③堂皇,庄严,高贵.

Royce [rɔis] *n.* 罗伊斯〔姓氏,男子名〕.

roys·ter [ˈrɔistə] *vi.* = *roister.*

roz·zer [ˈrɔzə] *n.* 〔英俚〕警察.

RP =① *radiophotography* 无线电传真术. ②rocket projectile 火箭弹. ③ refilling point 补给所.

R.P. = ① replay paid 回电费付讫. ② regius Professor 〔英〕(英国大学中担任希腊文等)钦定讲座的教授.

r.p. = relative poisoning 相对中毒.

RPF = 〔*F.*〕 *Rassemblement du Peuple Français* (=*Reunion of French People*). 法兰西人民联盟.

r.p.m., rpm = revolutions per minute 每分钟转数.

R.P.O. = Railway Post Office 铁路邮局.

RPS = revolutions per second 转/秒.

rpt = report.

R.Q. = respiratory quotient 【医】呼吸商.

R.R. =①railroad. ②Right Reverend 可尊敬的…〔对主教的尊称〕. ③rural road 乡村道路.

Rr = rear.

R.R.C. =①Royal Red Cross 英国红十字会. ②Rubber Reserve Commission 〔美〕橡胶储备委员会.

RR Ly·rae variables [ˌɑːˌɑː ˈlairi ˈvɛəriəblz]【天】天琴 RR 型(变)星.

RRS = Radiation Research Society. 〔美〕辐射研究学会.

RS = Revised Statutes〔加拿大〕《修整法案》〔指 1867 年加拿大由英殖民地变为自治领的法案〕.

R.S., RS =①Royal Society〔英〕皇家学会. ②Recording Secretary 秘书记录员. ③ Royal Scots 〔英〕皇家苏格兰团.

Rs =①rupees. ②rivers.

r.s. = reed space【纺】筘幅.

RSC =Reactor Safeguards Committee 反应堆安全技术委员会.

R.S.F.S.R. = Russian Soviet Federative Socialist Republic 俄罗斯苏维埃联邦社会主义共和国.

R.S.M. = ① Regimental Sergeant Major〔英〕团部军士长. ②Royal Society of Medicine〔英〕皇家医学会.

R.S.O. = Railway Sub-Office 铁路分局.

R.S.S. = 〔L.〕*Regiae Societatis Socius*〔英〕皇家学会会员.

RSVP, r.s.v.p. = 〔F.〕 *répondez s'il vous plaît* (请帖等用语)请答复 (=please reply).

RT, R.T., R/T =①radiotelegraphy 无线电报术. ②radiotelephony 无线电话(术).

rt. = right.

R.T.C. = Royal Tanks Corps. 〔英〕皇家坦克兵.

Rt. Hon. =Right Honourable. 〔英〕可尊敬的〔对有爵位者的尊称〕.

R.T.R. = Royal Tank Regiment 〔英〕皇家坦克团.

Rt. Rev. =Right Reverend 尊敬的〔对主教的尊称〕.

RTT = radioteletype.

R.U. = Rugby Union 〔英〕橄榄球联合会.

Ru = ruthenium【化】钌.

Ru·an·da [ruˈwɔndə] *n.* ① ***(pl. -das, -da)*** 卢旺达人〔住在卢旺达和刚果的班图人〕. ②卢旺达人用的班图语.

ruat·cae·lum [ˈruːætˈsiːləm] 〔L.〕 即使天塌下来也罢.

rub[1] [rʌb] *vt.* ①擦,摩擦;使相擦;抚摩;揩拭;把…摩擦得(干净,光亮等). ②用…擦;擦上,涂上 (on, over). ③触痛,惹怒(某人). ④擦掉,擦去 (out, off). ⑤拓印,摹拓(碑石等). ⑥〔美俚〕杀害. ~ ***away*** 擦掉,揩掉;消除. ~ ***down*** ①用力擦遍(全身),擦干净;按摩. ②彻底梳刷(马毛). ③〔口〕(警察等对人)全身搜查. ~ ***in*** 把…用力擦进去;〔俚〕反反复复说. ~ ***it in*** 〔美俚〕反反复复提别人的不愉快的事情;(故意)触人痛处. ~ ***noses*** 用鼻互擦〔某些民族寒暄方式〕. ~ ***off*** 擦掉,擦去. ~ ***one's hands*** 搓手〔满足等的表情〕. ~ ***out*** ①擦掉,磨去(~ *out the pencil marks from the picture* 擦掉插图上的铅笔印). ②〔美俚〕杀死. ~ ***shoulders*** 肩肩相擦,接触;交际 (with). ~ ***(sb.) the right way*** 迎合(某人),使…高兴〔满意〕. ~ *(sb., the hairs, the fur)* ***the wrong way*** 惹怒(某人),使焦急. ~ ***up*** 擦,磨擦;温习;拌和,调(颜料等);想起. — *vi.* ①摩擦,擦到 (on, against). ②被擦掉 (off, out). ③(皮肤等)擦痛,擦破;(衣服等)磨损. ④引得恼火〔烦恼〕. ~ ***against one's grain*** 使人生气〔烦恼〕.~ ***along*** ①(两人或两人以上)平安相处. ②(一个人)过得去. —*n.* ①擦,磨擦. ②障碍, 阻碍, 困难. ③【滚木球戏】(场所的)不平坦,崎岖;球碰到障碍物滚歪. ④伤害感情的东西;暗讽,讥刺,挖苦. ⑤〔方〕磨(刀)石. *There's the* ~. 问题难就难在这里. *a* ~ *of [on] the green* 球碰到障碍物滚歪. ***give a thing a*** ~ ***with*** 用…擦,用…磨. ~***s and worries of life*** 人世的辛酸. ~**down** ①擦全身. ②按摩 (*have a* ~*down with a wet towel* 用湿毛巾擦全身). ~ **rail** (汽车等防止擦坏的)摩擦横档. ~ **stone** 磨石,磨刀石.

rub[2] *n.* 〔*the* ~〕 = *rubber.*[2]

rub. = ruble.

rub·a·dub [ˈrʌbədʌb] *n.* 冬冬(鼓声). — *vi.* (鼓)冬冬地响.

Ru·bai·ya·t [ˈruːbiˌjɑːt,-bai-] 《鲁拜集》〔古波斯诗人我默·伽亚谟所作的每节四行的长诗〕. ~ **stanza** 抑扬格五音步的四行诗节〔韵律为 a a b a〕.

ru·basse [ruːˈbɑːs, -ˈbæs] *n.* 【矿】红水晶.

ru·ba·to [ruːˈbɑːtəu] *a., ad.*【乐】表演者随意改变音符的; 节奏自由的. — *n.* ***(pl. -tos)*** ①表演者随意改变音符的时值. ②节奏自由的演奏风格.

rub·ba·boo, rub·a·boo [ˈrʌbəˌbuː] *n.* 烩干肉饼,烩牛肉干〔有时加面粉使汤更加浓稠〕.

rub·ber[1] [ˈrʌbə] *n.* ①摩擦者; 磨者; 磨擦物,磨光器;按摩师;(土耳其浴室的)擦背人;(洗澡用)毛巾.②擦具;粗锉;磨石,砥石,磨砂.③橡胶;橡胶状物;橡皮;橡皮擦子;黑板擦;〔英〕抹布,搌布.④〔*pl.*〕橡皮鞋;〔美〕橡皮套鞋;【棒球】〔俚〕本垒. ⑤挖苦,讥讽;阻碍,困难;不幸,倒楣. ⑥〔美俚〕职业刺客,凶手. ~ *cement* 树胶胶水. *reclaimed* ~ 再生橡胶. *a* ~ *check [cheque]* 〔美俚〕空头支票. ~ *cloth* 橡皮布. ~ *drink* 〔美〕 酒醉呕吐前的最后一口〔一杯〕酒. ~ *heel* 〔美俚〕侦探. ~ *insertion sheets* 夹布橡皮. ~ *insulated copper wire* 皮(电)线. ~ *joint* 〔美俚〕低级下流的舞厅. ~ *plant* 橡胶植物. ~ *sole* 橡胶(鞋) 底. ~ *solution* 橡胶胶水. — *vt.* 涂橡皮于…. — *vi.* 〔美俚〕 = *rubberneck.* ~ **stamp** *n.* ①橡皮图章;〔喻〕瞎盖图章(的人). ②机器一样传达命令的人. ③陈腔滥调.

rub·ber[2] *n.*【纸牌】(三盘或其他成单的盘数构成的)一局;〔*the* ~〕 三盘两胜,三盘分输赢. *have a* ~ *of bridge* 打三盘〔一局〕桥牌.

rub·ber·ize [ˈrʌbəraiz] *vt.* 给…涂上橡胶,用橡胶处理.

rub·ber·neck [ˈrʌbənek] *n.* 〔美俚〕 ①橡皮套管. ②伸长脖子看的人,好围观的;游览者. *Two cars had smashed together and a cluster of* ~*s had gathered around.* 两辆

汽车相撞，一群好奇的人围拢起来观看。— *a.* 〔美俚〕供游览用的。*a* ~ *bus* 游览汽车。— *vi.* 好奇观览，伸长脖子看；游览，观光。*She ~ed through Shanghai last month.* 她上月游览了上海。**-er** *n.*

rub·ber-stamp [ˌrʌbəˈstæmp] *vt.* ①盖橡皮图章。②〔口〕不加思考就赞同[批准]（计划、建议、文件等）。*They expect the board to ~ their findings.* 他们期望理事会能不加思考就赞同他们的调查结论。— *a.* ①盖橡皮图章的。②〔口〕不加思索而批准的；为形式而批准的。

rub·ber·y [ˈrʌbri] *a.* （形态、性质等）似橡胶的。**-i·ness** *n.*

rub·bing [ˈrʌbiŋ] *n.* 磨擦；研磨；按摩；摹拓（片）。~ *from a tablet* 碑板等的拓本。

rub·bish [ˈrʌbiʃ] *n.* 碎屑，垃圾，废物；拙劣的作品，无聊的想法，荒唐的事情。*a good riddance of bad* ~ 眼中钉[讨厌的人]离开好。*He is talking* ~. 他在说废话。*This book is* ~. 这本书不行。*Oh,* ~! 〔蔑〕真无聊！废话！

rub·bish·ing, rub·bish·y [ˈrʌbiʃiŋ,-ʃi] *a.* 碎屑的，垃圾的，废物的；无聊的，没价值的。

rub·ble [ˈrʌbl] *n.* 【建】毛石，块石；碎石，卵石，转石；碎砖，瓦砾。~**work** 【建】毛石工（程）；乱石工（程）。**-bly** *a.* 由毛石砌成的；碎石状的，碎石多的。

rube [ruːb] *n.* 〔美俚〕乡下佬，土包子。

ru·be·fa·cient [ruːbiˈfeiʃənt] *a., n.* 【医】（使皮肤）发红的；发红药[外用]。

ru·be·fac·tion [rubiˈfækʃən] *n.* （用引赤药后）皮肤的发红。

ru·be·fy [ˈruːbifai] *vt.* 使红；使（皮肤）发红。

Rube Gold·berg [ˈruːb ˈgəuldbəːg] ① (Reuben L. Goldberg) (1883—1970) 美国漫画家。②〔美〕杀鸡用牛刀的，小题大做的〔喻用繁琐办法做简单的事〕。

ru·bel·la [ruːˈbelə] *n.* 【医】风疹，流行性蔷薇疹。

ru·bel·lite [ruːˈbelait] *n.* 【矿】红电气石，红碧玺〔用作宝石〕。

Ru·ben [ˈruːbin] *n.* 鲁宾〔男子名〕。

Ru·bens [ˈruːbəz], **Peter Paul** 茹宾斯〔1577—1640，荷兰画家〕。

ru·be·o·la [ruːˈbiːələ, ˌruːbiˈəulə] *n.* 【医】麻疹。

ru·bes·cent [ruːˈbesnt] *a.* 变红的，发红的。**-cence** *n.*

Ru·bi·con [ˈruːbikən] *n.* （原为意大利一河名）〔*r-*〕【皮克牌】比对手早得百分。***cross [pass] the*** ~ 采取断然手段[行动]；下重大决心；破釜沉舟。

ru·bi·cund [ˈruːbikənd] *a.* （脸色等）红润的。

ru·bi·cun·di·ty [ˌruːbiˈkʌnditi] *n.* 发红，红。

ru·bid·i·um [ru(ː)ˈbidiəm] *n.* 【化】铷 *[Rb]*.

ru·bied [ˈruːbiːd] *a.* 红玉色的，深红的。

ru·big·i·nous, ru·big·i·nose [ruːˈbidʒinəs, -nəus] *a.* 锈色的，赤褐色的，棕红色的。

ru·ble [ˈruːbl] *n.* = *rouble.*

ru·bric [ˈruːbrik] *n.* ①红字，红色印刷；红字标题。②礼拜规程；规程，例式。— *a.* ①用红字写[刻]的。②印红字的：*a* ~ *day* 节日。**-i·ty** [ruːbˈrisiti] *n.* ①变红。②礼教。

ru·bri·cal [ˈruːbrikəl] *a.* 礼拜规程的；用红色印刷[标明]的；朱红的。

ru·bri·cate [ˈruːbrikeit] *vt.* 用红字写，用红色印刷，加红字标题；制定礼拜规程。**-ca·tor** *n.* 加红字标题的人。

ru·bri·ca·tion [ˌruːbriˈkeiʃən] *n.* 红色印刷；红字标题；用红字写的东西。

ru·bri·cian [ruːˈbriʃən] *n.* 墨守教仪者。

Ru·by [ˈruːbi] *n.* 鲁比〔女子名〕。

ru·by [ˈruːbi] *n.* ①〔矿〕红宝石，红玉；（钟表里的）宝石（轴承）。②红宝石色，鲜红色。③〔英〕细铅字〔相当于美国的 agate, 中国的七号铅字〕。④红葡萄酒；（脸上的）红酒刺；【拳击】血；〔*pl.*〕嘴。***above rubies*** 极贵重的。— *vt.* 弄红；把…涂染成红色。— *a.* 红宝石（色）的，鲜红色的。~ **copper** 赤铜矿。~ **glass** 红玻璃。~ **laser** 红宝石光激射器。~ **wedding** 红宝石婚〔结婚后第 45 年〕。

ruche [ruːʃ] *n.* 〔F.〕（花边、纱等的）褶带，褶边，褶饰。**ruch·ing** *n.* 褶裥饰边（料）。

ruck[1], **ruck·le** [rʌk,ˈrʌkl] *vt.* 弄皱。— *vi.* 变绉，起绉。— *n.* 绉，褶。

ruck[2] [rʌk] *n.* 多数，多量；群；散乱的人群；【赛马】落伍马群；【美俚】碎屑，废物；〔*the* ~〕群众；一般的人，普通人；一般事物。— *vt.* 把…堆起来。

ruck·le [ˈrʌkl] *n.* （尤指人将死时的）喉鸣，喘鸣。— *vi.* 发喉鸣声。

ruck·sack [ˈruksæk] *n.* 帆布背包。

ruck·us [ˈrʌkəs] *n.* 〔美口〕吵闹，吵嚷；乱动，骚动。*raise a* ~ 引起一场争吵。

ruc·tion [ˈrʌkʃən] *n.* 〔常 *pl.*〕〔口〕吵闹，骚动。

Rud·beck·i·a [rʌdˈbekiə] *n.* 【植】金光菊属。

rudd [rʌd] *n.* 【鱼】赤睛鱼。

rud·der [ˈrʌdə] *n.* （船等的）舵；【空】方向舵；指针；领导人，指导者；麦芽浆搅拌棒；【动】尾羽。*an internal* ~【火箭】燃气舵。~**fish** 追船鱼。~**post** [ˈrʌdəˌpəust] *n.* 【船】①舵柱。②上舵杆，舵头。~**stock** [ˈrʌdəˌstɔk] *n.* 【船】上舵杆，舵头。**-less** *a.* 无舵的，无领导者的。

rud·de·va·tor [ˈrʌdəveitə] *n.* 【空】方向升降舵。

rud·di·ness [ˈrʌdinis] *n.* 红色，红。

rud·dle [ˈrʌdl] *n.* 【矿】代赭石，红土；赭色。— *vt.* 用红土（在羊身上作记号）；涂红土。

rud·dle·man [ˈrʌdlmən] *n.* ***(pl. -men*** [-men]***)*** 卖代赭石（赤铁矿）的人。

rud·dock [ˈrʌdək] *n.* 【鸟】知更鸟，欧鸲。

rud·dy [ˈrʌdi] *a.* ***(-di·er; -di·est)*** ①红的；微红的；红润的；血色好的。②〔俚〕讨厌的，可恶的。— *ad.* 非常，很。~ *health* 强壮，健康。*a* ~ *youth* 容光焕发的少年。— *vt., vi.* （使）变红。~ **duck** （北美）红鸭。~ **squirrel** 红松鼠。

rude [ruːd] *a.* ①粗陋的，粗笨的，未加工的。②原始的，朦昧的，野蛮的。③粗暴的，粗鲁的，无礼的。④残暴的，猛烈的；厉害的；突然的。⑤芜杂的；荒凉的；大略的，不正确的；不成样子的，难看的；不熟的，拙劣的；未完成的，粗制的。⑥强壮的，健壮的。*(opp. delicate)*. *a* ~ *beginning* 草率的开始。~ *cotton* 原棉。*a* ~ *drawing* 草图。*a* ~ *plenty* 粗糙物品一大堆。~ *produce* 天然产物。~ *petroleum* 原油。~ *fare* 粗陋的食物。~ *savages* 未开化的野蛮人。~ *simplicity* 质朴。*a* ~ *man* 粗人。~ *classification* 大致的分类。*a* ~ *blast* 一阵狂风。~ *scenery* 荒野景色。~ *times* 原始时代。~ *health* 健壮。~ *version* 粗略的译文。*a* ~ *writer* 拙劣的作家。**be ~ to** 对…粗暴无礼。***say ~ things*** 说无礼话。**-ly** *ad.* **-ness** *n.*

ru·der·al [ˈruːdərəl] *n.* 宅旁杂草，道旁杂草。— *a.* 杂草似的。

rudes·by [ˈruːdzbi] *n.* ***(pl. -bies)*** 〔古语〕鲁莽汉，粗鲁的人。

ru·di·ment [ˈruːdimənt] *n.* ①基本，基本原理[知识]；〔*pl.*〕初步，入门。②【生】（器官的）原基；退化[痕迹]器官。*the ~s of grammar* 语法入门。*the ~s of civilization* 文明的萌芽。

ru·di·men·tal, -ta·ry [ˌruːdiˈmentl, -təri] *a.* 根本的，基本的；初步的，开端的；原状的，发育不全的；残留的。*a rudimentary knowledge* 初步知识，起码的知识。*a rudimentary organ* 退化器官，痕迹器官。**-ta·ri·ly** [-ˈtærili] *ad.*

Ru·dolph, Ru·dolf [ˈruːdɔlf] *n.* 鲁道夫〔男子名〕。

Ru·dy [ˈruːdi] *n.* 鲁迪〔男子名，Rudolph 的昵称〕。

rue[1] [ruː] *n.* 〔古〕悲叹；悔恨；后悔。— *vt., vi.* 悲叹；后悔，懊悔，悔恨。*You shall ~ it.* 你要后悔的。~ *the loss of opportunities* 后悔失掉机会。

rue[2] [ruː] *n.* 【植】芸香。

rue·ful [ˈruːfəl] *a.* 悲伤的；可怜的；悔恨的；沮丧的。*the knight of the R- Countenance* 愁容骑士〔指唐·吉诃德

(Don Quixote)〕. **-ly** *ad.* **-ness** *n.*

ru·fes·cent [ruːˈfesnt] *a.* 带红色的,带有红色的. — **ru·fes·cence** *n.*

ruff[1] [rʌf] *n.* ①(伊利莎白 (Elizabeth) 时代流行的)皱领;绉领状物. ②鸟兽的颈毛. ③【鸟】有绉领状颈毛家鸽;流苏鹬.

ruff[2] [rʌf] *n.* 【鱼】鲈鲋.

ruff[3] [rʌf] *n.* 勒弗牌戏〔一种早期的纸牌戏〕. — *vt.* 用王牌胜过. — *vi.* 出王牌.

ruf·fi·an [ˈrʌfjən, -fiən] *n.* 暴徒,恶棍,流氓;〔俚〕无线电盲目投弹系统. — *a.* 凶恶的, 残暴的. **-ism** *n.* 流氓习气;暴徒行为. **-ly** *a.* 流氓般的,歹徒似的;凶恶的,残忍的,凶暴的.

ruf·fle[1] [ˈrʌfl] *vt.* ①(将布、纸等)弄皱; 兴波作浪;(鸟发怒等时)颤动身体竖起羽毛;搅乱,扰乱,弄乱(头髦);洗(牌). ②使着急,使发躁,使发脾气,惹怒. ③做褶纹;加褶边. ～ *up the feathers [plumage]* 颤动身体竖起羽毛;惹怒,使生气;发怒,生气. — *vi.* ①起皱,变皱;生浪,起浪;(旗等)飘动. ②生气,发脾气,着急,发躁. ③自大,摆架子. — *n.* ①褶边;褶边状物;皱纹;(鸟的)颈毛;(兽的)头毛. ②兴波作浪,微波,波纹. ③动摇,混乱;急躁;〔罕〕吵闹,骚动. ***put in a*** ～ 使躁急不安;激怒. ***without*** ～ ***or excitement*** 不吵不闹.

ruf·fle[2] [ˈrʌfl] *n.* 【军】(鼓的)轻擂声. — *vt.* 轻擂,轻击(铜鼓).

ruf·fler [ˈrʌflə] *n.* 起皱机;(缝纫机上的)打裥装置;〔俚〕骄傲自大的人.

ru·fous [ˈruːfəs] *a.* 赤褐色的.

Ru·fus [ˈruːfəs] *n.* 鲁弗斯〔男子名〕.

rug [rʌg] *n.* (整块皮制成的)皮毡; 小地毯〔尤指 *hearth-*～〕. 〔英〕(围盖膝的)围毯,车毯;〔美俚〕男子假发;〔俚〕反雷达干扰发射机. ***cut a*** ～〔美俚〕跳摇摆舞. ***pull the*** ～ ***from under*** 破坏…的计划. — *vt.* 用厚毯包. ～ **joint**〔美俚〕高级豪华的夜总会.

ru·ga [ˈruːgə] *n.* ***(pl.-gae [-dʒiː])*** 【生,解】皱,皱褶.

ru·gate [ˈruːgeit] *a.* 皱的,有折痕的.

Rug·bei·an [rʌgˈbi(ː)ən] *n.* (英国) 拉格比市市立学校的学生[毕业生].

Rug·by [ˈrʌgbi] *n.* ①拉格比市〔英格兰中部城市〕. ②橄榄球;橄榄球戏 *(cf. socker* = ～ football).

rug·ged [ˈrʌgid] *a.* *(superl.* ～***est)*** ①毛蓬松的;凹凸不平的,高低不平的,崎岖的;嵯峨的. ②有皱纹的,皱眉蹙额的(脸等). ③粗鲁的,粗暴的. ④粗眉大鼻的,丑陋的;刺耳的,难听的;严厉的,严格的(教师等). ⑤辛苦的,艰难的(生活等);〔罕〕狂风暴雨的,恶劣的(气候). ⑥〔美口〕强壮的,结实的. *a* ～ *beard* 蓬松的胡子. *a* ～ *life* 艰难的生活. ～ *manners* 粗鲁而朴实的态度. *a* ～ *road* 崎岖不平的路. ～ *honesty* 率直,坦白. ～ *kindness* 粗鲁而朴实的好意. **-ly** *ad.* **-ness** *n.*

rug·ge·dize [ˈrʌgidaiz] *vt.* 使(机器等)坚固;使耐用. **-di·za·tion** [ˌrʌgidaiˈzeiʃən] *n.*

rug·ger [ˈrʌgə] *n.* 〔英俚〕rugby *(football)* (橄榄球;橄榄球戏)的变体.

ru·gose, ru·gous [ˈruːgəus,-gəs] *a.* 【生】有皱纹的,多皱的,皱层的.

ru·gos·i·ty [ruːˈgɔsiti] *n.* 皱纹,皱纹多(状态).

Ruhr [ruə] *n.* ①鲁尔〔联邦德国一地区〕. ②〔the ～〕鲁尔河〔来因河支流〕.

ru·in [ˈruin,ˈruːin] *n.* ①毁灭,灭亡;瓦解,崩溃;没落,破产,败落;(女人的)堕落;没落者,破产者;毁坏,破坏. ②〔*pl.*〕废墟,遗迹,旧址;毁灭[灭亡]的原因,祸根. ③〔*pl.*〕损失. ④〔卑〕劣等杜松子酒〔通常叫 *blue* ～〕. *the crash of* ～ 可怕的倒塌声. *He is but the* ～ *of what he was.* 他现在(穷困潦倒)不象当年那样容光焕发了. ***be the*** ～ ***of*** 成为…毁灭的原因. ***bring to*** ～ 使失败,使没落. ***come [fall, go] to*** ～ 毁灭,灭亡;崩溃;破坏掉. ***lay in*** ～ 使荒废,弄成废墟. ***lie in*** ～***s*** 成为废墟. ***go to rack and*** ～ 陷于毁灭. — *vt.* ①使破产;诱奸. ②破坏,毁灭. ③使没落,使堕落. ～ ***oneself*** 毁掉自己. ～ ***one's prospects*** 断送某人前程. — *vi.* 破产; 堕落; 变成废墟;〔古、诗〕倒栽葱落下来.

ru·in·ate [ˈruːəˌneit] *vt., vi.* ***(-at·ed, -at·ing)*** 〔古语〕使破产,灭亡,毁坏,瓦解,崩溃;堕落. — *a.*〔古〕破坏了的,毁坏了的,破产的,没落的,堕落的.

ru·in·a·tion [ru(ː)iˈneiʃən] *n.* 毁灭,灭亡; 没落,破产;毁坏; 毁灭的原因,祸根. *The olive is spoken of as the* ～ *of martini.* 有人认为橄榄会使马丁尼酒走味.

ru·ined [ˈru(ː)ind] *a.* 破坏了的,毁坏了的,灭亡了的;破产的,没落的;堕落的. *a* ～ *city* 一座破坏了的城市. ～ *hopes* 破灭了的希望.

ru·in·ous [ˈruinəs,ˈruːinəs] *a.* 破坏性的, 招致毁灭的;没落的;破坏的;已成废墟的. *a* ～ *heap* 倾圮的一堆,废墟. **-ly** *ad.*

rul·a·ble [ˈruːləbl] *a.* 可统治的;〔美〕规章上允许的.

rule [ruːl] *n.* ①规则,规定;法则,定律;章程,规章;标准;(教会等的)教规,条例,教条;常例,惯例. ②统治,支配;【法】命令;(对某一案的)裁决,裁定. ③尺,画线板;【印】线,线条. ④【数】解法. ⑤〔*the* ～*s*〕【英史】(允许囚犯交付保证金后迁往居住的)狱旁特区. *the* ～*(s) of the road* 交通规则. *a hard and fast* ～ 严厉的规则;精密的标准. *Exception proves the* ～ 有例外就证明有规则. *a carpenter's* ～ (木工)折尺. *a dotted [wave]* ～【印】点线,[波]线. *the golden* ～ 金科玉律. *make it a* ～ *to (rise early)* 惯于(早起),照例(起得早). *R- Britannia* 英国的爱国国歌. ～ *of force* 武力政治. ～ *of three* 比例的运算法则. ～ *of thumb* 手工业方式; 靠经验估计. ～ *test* (石油产品的) 简单评价法. ～*s of decorum* 礼法. ***as a*** ～ 通常,照例. ***break*** ～***s*** 破例,犯规. ***by*** ～ 按规则. ***by*** ～ ***and line*** 准确地,精密地. ***work to*** ～ (故意)死扣规章而降低生产. — *vt.* 统治,控制,支配;管理;规定; 判决; (用尺) 画线. *the* ～*d class* 被统治阶级. ～ *paper with lines* 在纸上画线. ～*d paper* 划线纸. ～ *the roast [roost]* 当领袖. ***be*** ～***d by*** 听从…的忠告[指导]. ～ ***against*** 不许;否决. ～ ***off*** 划线隔开;不准参加比赛. ～ ***out*** ①(用直线)划去. ②排除在外; 拒绝考虑;使…不可能. *Bad weather* ～*d the picnic out for that day.* 天气不好使那天的野餐告吹了. — *vi.* 控制,统治,支配 *(over)*; 裁决,决定;【商】(价格)稳定, 经常. *prices* ～*d high.* 行市一直高. *Crops* ～ *good.* 庄稼情况一般都不错. ～ ***over*** 治理…,统治…. ～**-drill·er** 教法呆板的教员. ～ **joint** 肘垫;(曲尺等只能朝单一方向弯折的)活动接头. ～ **mon·ger** 拘泥规则的人. ～**-of-three** *a.* 按比例计算的. **-less** *a.* 无规则的,无约束的.

rul·er [ˈruːlə] *n.* ①统治者,支配者. ②尺,画线板. ～**ship** *n.* 统治者的地位[职权].

rul·ing [ˈruːliŋ] *a.* 统治的,支配的,管辖的;主要的,主导的,优势的,有力的;普遍的, 流行的,一般的,平均的(价格等);划线用的. — *n.* 统治,管辖;【法】判决;(用尺的)划线[量度]; 划出的线. *a* ～ *passion* 占统治地位的感情,主要动机. *the* ～ *class* 统治阶级. *the* ～ *spirit* 主动者,首脑. *the* ～ *price* 市价,时价. *accept the* ～ 服从判决. *give a final* ～ 作出最后决定. ～**pen** 直线笔,鸭嘴笔.

rul·ley [ˈrʌli] *n.* 〔英〕四轮卡车.

rum[1] [rʌm] *n.* 朗姆酒, 甘蔗酒;〔美俚〕酒. *a* ～ *hound* 〔美俚〕酒鬼,醉鬼. ～ **row**〔美口〕酒类走私船. ～**run·ner**〔美口〕酒类走私贩;酒类走私船. ～**-running**〔美口〕酒类走私.

rum[2] [rʌm] *a.* ***(-mer; -mest)***〔英俚〕奇怪的;难对付的,危险的;蹩脚的. *feel* ～ 觉得不妙;觉得害怕,觉得奇怪. *a* ～ *go* 可疑的情况. *a* ～ *start* 惊人事件. *a* ～ *customer* 危险的家伙;奇怪的家伙. **-ly** *ad.*

Rum. = Rumania.

Rumania(n), [ruːˈmeiniə(n)] *n., a.* 罗马尼亚(人)(的),

罗马尼亚语(的).

rum•ba [ˈruːmbə] *n.* ①(古巴的)伦巴舞〔交际舞的一种〕. ②伦巴舞曲. — *vi.* 跳伦巴舞.

rum•ble[1] [ˈrʌmbl] *n.* (闷雷、电车、肚子等的)隆隆声,辘辘声;噪声;吵闹声,喧哗声;(随员坐的)马车后座;(汽车车篷后的)活动座位[又叫 ~ **seat**]. — *vt., vi.* (使)隆隆[辘辘]地响; (使)车子轱辘轱辘地跑 *(along; by)*;闹,为患. *My guts* ~. 〔俚〕我的肚子咕噜咕噜地响. **-bling** *n.* & *a.* 〔俚〕打闹;隆隆声(的),辘辘声(的). **~-tumble** *n.* 咯噔咯噔动动摇摇的车;咯噔咯噔的摇动,厉害的摇动.

rum•ble[2] [ˈrʌmbl] *vt.* 〔英俚〕看穿,看破.

rum•bus•tious [rəmˈbʌstʃəs] *a.* 〔英口〕吵闹的,喧嚣的.

ru•men [ˈruːmen] *n.* *(pl.* ***ru•mi•na*** [-minə]) 【动】(反刍动物的)瘤胃.

ru•mi•nant [ˈruːminənt] *a.* 反刍的;反刍动物的;沉思默想的,左思右想的. — *n.* 反刍动物.

ru•mi•nate [ˈruːmineit] *vi., vt.* 反刍;深思,沉思,左思右想 *(about; of; on, upon; over)*. **-na•tor** *n.* 沉思默想的人,好思考的人.

ru•mi•na•tion [ˌruːmiˈneiʃən] *n.* 反刍;思索;沉思,默想.

ru•mi•na•tive [ˈruminətiv] *a.* 沉思默想的,左思右想的. **-ly** *ad.*

rum•mage [ˈrʌmidʒ] *vt., vi.* 翻查,抄查,搜查;搜出,抄出 *(out; up)*;(为搜查)乱翻,翻箱倒柜;(海关人员)检查(船内). — *n.* (尤指海关人员的翻查,搜查,搜遍(船内). 查遍,抄遍,杂物,七零八碎的东西. ~ **sale** 捐品拍卖;处理品廉价出售.

rum•mag•er [ˈrʌmidʒə] *n.* 翻查人,搜查人;检查人.

rum•mer [ˈrʌmə] *n.* 大酒杯.

rum•my[1] [ˈrʌmi] *a.* *(-mi•er; -mi•est)*〔英俚〕 =rum[2].

rum•my[2] [ˈrʌmi] *n.* ①兰米牌戏. ②〔俚〕怪人.

rum•my[3] [ˈrʌmi] *n.* 〔美俚〕酒徒,无赖. — *a.* 兰姆酒(一样)的.

ru•mour, 〔美〕**ru•mor** [ˈruːmə] *n.* 谣言,传闻,流言. *R- has it that [says that]* 据谣传…. *the author of the* ~ 造谣者. *The* ~ *ran that* … 谣传…. *start a* ~ 造谣. *spike a* ~ 辟谣. — *vt.* 〔常用被动语态〕谣传. *It is* ~*ed that* … 谣传…,听说….

ru•mour•mon•ger [ˈruːməˈmʌŋgə,-ˌmɔŋ] *n.* 传布谣言者,造谣者,谣言贩子. **~ing** *n.* 造谣.

rump [rʌmp] *n.* (鸟兽的)臀部,尾部;〔谑〕(人的)臀部;〔英〕(牛的)大腿肉;残余物,渣滓; [the R-] = ***R-Parliament*** 【英史】残余议会. ~ **steak** 〔英〕牛腿扒.

rum•ple [ˈrʌmpl] *vt.* (把织物、纸等)弄皱;(把头发等)弄乱. — *vi.* 变绉,起绉. — *n.* 〔罕〕绉纹,褶子. **-ply** *a.* 弄皱的,弄乱的.

rum•pus [ˈrʌmpəs] *n.* ①〔口〕喧噪;吵闹. ②〔英俚〕比赛. = ***room*** (地下)晚会室,游戏室,娱乐室. *raise a* ~ 引起骚乱.

run[1] [rʌn] ***(ran*** [ræn] ***run)*** *vi.* ①跑,奔,驰;【空】滑行. ②赶,赶去. ③逃,逃走,逃亡. ④参加赛跑;当候选人,参加竞选. ⑤(时间)经过,过去. ⑥(事等)进行;运转,运行;(火车、船等)走,开行,行驶;(路)通到(某地). ⑦来回跑,往来. ⑧(植物)爬,蔓延;(鱼群)回游,溯流而上(产卵);(孩子等)长大,生长,发达. ⑨(河、血、鼻涕等)流;(墨水等)渗开;(金属、蜡烛等)熔化,熔解. ⑩变(冷、热、干、胖等);陷入(危险、负债等),染上(邪恶等). ⑪很快地蔓延,扩大;传闻,传布;(谈话等)涉及,谈到(某题目);略一过目,匆匆浏览. ⑫(机器等)转动,开动;滑走,滑动;(旅馆等)营业. ⑬倾向,偏向. ⑭有效力;通用,适用;(戏等)连演;继续. ⑮写着,说明. ⑯【乐】急奏. ⑰(诗句、口才等)流畅,流利. ⑱平均是,大体是. *He who* ~*s may read (it).* 跑着都读得出,明显易懂. *The train* ~*s daily.* 火车每天开行. *The river* ~*s clear [thick]* 这条河流清沏[混浊]. *Shelves ran round the walls.* 架子靠墙四面摆满. *The child's nose* ~*s.* 这孩子流鼻涕. *A thought ran through my mind.* 我脑子里闪过一个念头. *His eyes ran down the page.* 他看了看这一页. *His letter* ~*s as follows.* 他的信这样写着. *So the story rans.* 据说(事情)就是这样的. *The play will* ~ *(for) thirty nights.* 这戏将连演一个月. *How your tongue* ~*s!* 瞧,你讲个没完. — *vt.* ①使跑;跑去. ②(使)逃走;想逃开. ③催赶;追,追赶,追猎. ④使(船)来回行驶,(用车、船)运输;开(会、车等);经营,办,管理(旅馆、学校等);指挥. ⑤把(绳子等)穿过,通过(某物);刺;戳;撞,碰;突破(封锁线);顺利通过(岗哨等). ⑥流(血、泪等);倒,注(水、铅等入桶,模形等);铸(子弹等);熔化(金属等). ⑦举…做候选人;举出(候选人);和…赛跑,使(马)参加赛跑. ⑧使处(于) *(into)*;冒(危险等) *(risks, the risk of)*;陷使入(困难、负债等). ⑨划,划定(界线等);砌(隔墙),装(隔板). ⑩急急忙忙地缝. ⑪想下去,思索. ⑫走私,秘密输入[出]. ⑬〔口〕欺负,挖苦. ⑭〔口〕生(热). ⑮〔美〕登(广告);(比赛)连续得分. *We will* ~ *you for $ 50 a side.* 我们各赌50元来赛跑吧. *The fever must* ~ *its course.* 这种热病要经过一定过程才会好. ~ *a race* 赛跑. ~ *errands* (为别人)跑腿,跑差使. ~ *cattle* 把家畜赶到牧场. ~ *a scent* 追赶猎物. ~ *a hare to earth [ground]* 把兔子追到洞里. ~ *a hotel* 经营旅馆. ~ *a cord through* 穿绳子. ~ *a cart into a wall* 把车撞到墙上. ~ *sb. into trouble* 使某人为难. ~ *a blockade* 冲破封锁. ~ *the rapids* 过急滩. ***cut and*** ~ 〔口〕奔逃. ***have*** ~ ***one's course*** 了结一生. ***let things*** ~ ***their course*** 听其自然. ~ ***a simile too far*** 把一个明喻用得太牵强. ~ ***across*** 遇到,碰见. ~ ***after*** 碰上,撞上;偶然遇见,碰见;终于对…不利. ~ ***aground*** 〔船〕搁浅. ~ ***ahead of*** 赶过,超过. ~ ***at*** 向…扑过去,攻击…. ~ ***at the nose [mouth]*** 流鼻涕[口水]. ~ ***away*** 逃,逃走,逃脱;私奔;(事情)进行不顺利,弄不好,失去控制. ~ ***away from*** 学生从(学校)逃出,逃学;水兵从(船里)逃出;放弃(主义等);远远超过(其他竞争者). ~ ***away with*** 拐走,偷去;带着…逃跑,和…私奔;贸然接受(别人意见等);消耗(金钱时间等) *(Don't let your feelings* ~ *away with you.* 你不要被感情驱使[不要感情用事]). ~ ***away with it*** 〔美〕好好儿地做成功,顺利办妥. ~ ***back*** 跑回来;(家谱等)上溯到 (to). ~ ***back over the past*** 想起过去,回顾过去. ~ ***before*** 被(敌人)追着逃走;好过,胜过;预料,预想 (~ *before one's horse to market* 市场未到先想赚钱). ~ ***before the wind*** 【海】顺风行驶. ~ ***behind*** 跑在…的后头,落后 (~ *behind one's expenses* 钱不够用,入不敷出). ~ ***by the name of*** 通用…这个名字,以…这个名字见知于世. ~ ***close*** 赶上,追上,紧逼;是…的劲敌,不在…之下. ~ ***down*** ①跑下来,下乡;(钟表等)停止;衰弱 *(I am[feel]much* ~ *down.* 累极了). ②追上,赶上(人、猎物);找出,搜出;讲坏话,诽谤;撞倒;【海】撞沉;压倒,威压;【化】馏出. ~ ***dry*** 干;(奶、水等)不出;在干燥的情况下操作;干涸. ~ ***false*** (猎狗不跟着臭迹跑而)直朝着猎物奔去. ~ ***(money) fine*** 尽量省钱. ~ ***for*** 去叫(…);参加…的竞选,做…的候选人. ~ ***for an office*** 做候补人;钻营做官,运动做官,〔美〕参加竞选. ~ ***for it*** 逃出,逃脱(危险). ~ ***for one's life*** 拚命逃跑;好容易逃脱. ~ ***foul of*** 与…撞上;与…冲突. ~ ***full*** 【海】一帆风顺地行驶. ~ ***hard*** = ~ close. ~ ***high*** (市价等)上涨;(海浪等)汹涌;激昂. ~ ***idle*** (机器)空转,白转. ~ ***in*** ①跑进;(火车)进站;流入;注入;〔口〕(到某处)顺便访问一下 *(to)*;互相扭住;一致,同意 *(with)*. ②赶进;捉进牢里;〔口〕(使)某人当选;【印】(不分段的)接排,连排;【机】试车;试转. ~ ***into*** ①跑进,陷入,冲进;(河)注入(海);撞上;到达;和…合并;倾向 (~ *into a lot of money* 要花费很多钱. *the readers* ~ *into millions* 读者人数多到以百万计. ~ *into five editions* 出到第五版). ②戳进,插进 (~ *something into the ground* 把某物插入地里). ③使陷入 (~ *sb. into* 使人

陷入…). ~ ***its course*** 跑到,跑完;(病)痊愈. ~ ***low*** 消耗尽;缺乏. ~ ***neck and neck*** 并肩跑. ~ ***off*** ①逃走;流出,溢出;(火车等)出轨;(话等)离题,越轨. ②放出;使流出;流利地念[写,叙述];举行(赛跑的)决赛;【印】印刷;(用机器)制造. ~ ***off at the mouth***〔美俚〕刺刺不休,说个不完. ~ ***off with*** =~ away with. ~ ***on*** ①〔*on* 副词〕继续,继续作用[有效];说个不停.【印】印完;(排印材料)不另行,接排;连排. ②〔*on* 前置词〕(话等)牵涉到(某问题);搁(浅),触(礁);(到银行去)挤兑. ~ ***sb. off his legs*** 使某人疲于奔命. ~ ***out*** ①跑出;跑累;突出;流出;冲出;(钟等)停止,终止,尽,满期;花光,用光;(稿子付排结果)超出预定篇幅;【海】(绳子)散开;扩张. ②【棒球】使跑垒者出场;决定…的胜负. ③【机】溢流;偏转. ④【空】放下(起落架襟翼). ⑤【印】把(一段的第一行)排成向左伸出. ⑥【印】用空铅[点线]填入. ~ ***out of*** 用光…,缺乏. ~ ***over*** ①溢出;泛出;(人)走近 (*to*). ②略一过目,匆匆忙忙看一遍;想想看;概括地讲;匆匆排练,急奏(乐谱). ③(车辆等)辗过(人). ~ ***ragged***〔美俚〕工作过度,筋疲力尽,累透. ~ ***short*** 用完;缺乏. ~ ***small*** 大概都小,生得小. ~ ***the streets*** 荡马路;流浪街头. ~ ***the show***〔口〕总管[主管]某事;称霸,逞威,发挥权势;新奇玩意儿大展览. ~ ***through*** ①扎穿,刺穿,戳穿;穿过. ②匆匆忙忙看一遍. ③不间断地排练,略一过目. ④花光,浪费(财产等);(将文字等)划线涂掉. ⑤普及到,遍达;(铁路)贯通,贯串. ~ ***time fine*** 尽量省时间. ~ ***to*** (数量等)达…;陷于(毁灭、衰亡等);〔口〕(人)有(购买、支付等的)资力,(钱)足够(应付事业、费用等). ~ ***to arms*** 急忙拿起武器. ~ ***to extremes*** 走极端. ~ ***to fat*** 发胖. ~ ***to leaves*** 生叶子,变成叶子. ~ ***to meet one's troubles*** 杞忧,自苦. ~ ***to seed*** (菜)开了花不能吃;要结子了;〔转为〕盛时已过. ~ ***together*** 混合. ~ ***up*** ①跑上去;赶快;迅速长大;(价格)上涨,腾贵;(债款等)增加;(数目)达到…;(弄湿的布等)缩短;末赛跑输. ②抬高(市价等);升(旗等);盖,造,急造(房屋等);增加(费用、债款等). ~ ***up against*** 撞上,碰上. ~ ***up to*** 跑到;匆匆忙忙去;(数目)达到. ~ ***upon*** 偶然碰到,意外地碰见;(思想等)时时刻刻集中(在某问题上). ~ ***wide*** (鱼)成群游回近海. ~ ***wild*** 蔓延;狂暴起来;放肆起来,撒起野来;放荡. ~ ***with the hare and hunt with the hound(s)*** 一面跟着兔子跑一面帮着猎狗咬,两边讨好,骑墙. — *n.* ①跑,奔跑;逃亡,逃走;跑拢;赛跑;打猎;航行;(短期)旅行;跑速;跑的气力;【空】滑行;滑行距离. ②进行;行程;航程;船舶一昼夜的航程;【空】(投弹前的)直线飞行;【铁路】区间. ③延续,继续,蝉联;联结;(戏的)连演;【美】(给杂志)连载,发表. ④流出,淌;流量;【美】小河,水路;水管. ⑥(银行的)挤兑 (*on*);订购踊跃,畅销;流行. ⑥(山脉、水理等的)方向,趋向,(矿脉的)走向,方位;(市场的)趋势;(事件的)经过;(工厂的)作业,工作,工作时间,产额. ⑦(普通的)人,物,事件;种类,类型,品质. ⑧(动物的)通路;(牛、羊的)圈,放牧场. ⑨(产卵期的鱼的)迁徙,洄游,奔上水;迁徙中的鱼群(鸟群、兽群). ⑩使用的自由,出入的自由. ⑪【球戏】得分,一分;【棒球】场分,得分. ⑫【乐】急奏;律动;〔美〕(袜子的)梯形抽丝[绽线]. ⑬〔美〕【纺】纶(1 盎司长 100 码为 1 纶). ⑭【船】船尾尖部. *The train makes a ~ of 100 miles in 2 hours.* 火车两小时跑 100 英里. *a ~ on the Continent* 到欧洲大陆去的短期旅行. *a ~ of a mile* 一英里路程. *a ~ of wet weather* 阴雨连绵. *a ~ of luck* 一连串的好运气. *There was a great ~ to see the new comer.* 许多人跑拢来看新来的人. *a great ~ on the new novel* 新出版小说的畅销. *the ~ of events* 事态的趋势;形势. *the heat ~*【电】发热试验. *the common ~ of mankind* 普通人,常人. *It's all in the day's ~.* 应看作正常[普通]的事. *the ordinary [common] ~* 普通人,普通物品[事件]. *the ~ of the mine* 粗煤. *a poultry ~* 养鸡场. ***at a ~*** 跑着. ***a bill at the long ~*** 长期支票. ***by the ~*** = ***with a ~*** 突然,忽然. ***get the ~ upon***〔美〕奚落,挖苦. ***give a good ~*** 使尽量跑. ***have a good [great] ~*** 大受欢迎,非常流行,盛行. ***have a long [short] ~*** 影片放映时间长[短]. ***have a ~ for one's money*** 不白费力;不白花钱. ***have the ~ of one's teeth*** (多半作为劳动报酬)可免费吃饭. ***in the long ~*** 最后,结果,归根到底. ***keep the ~ of***〔美〕和…并肩而行[并驾齐驱],不落…之后. ***let sb. have his ~*** 给某人自由,听任某人自由去做. ***level ~*** 水平飞行. ***no ~ left*** 气力用完了. (***no more ~ left in him*** 他再也跑不动了.) ***put sb. to the ~*** 使…逃走. ***Sunday ~***〔美俚〕①长距离. ②(流动售货员的)星期日的旅行.

run² [rʌn] run 的过去分词.

run³ [rʌn] *a.* 刚出海的,刚捉上来的(鱼);榨取的(蜜等);熔化的,液化的;铸的;〔俚〕走私的. ~ *goods* 私货.

run·a·bout [ˈrʌnəbaut] *n.* ①流浪者,游民. ②〔美〕无盖小马车;轻快小汽车;小汽艇;小型飞机;幼童. *trial ~*【机】试车. — *a.* 徘徊的,流浪的,跑来跑去的. ~ ***on sentence*** ①(该用连接词)错用逗号的句子. ②乱加从句的冗长句子. ***on the ~*** 在逃走中;在跑着时. ***take a ~ to the city*** 到城里去一趟. ~ ***of gold*** 富金脉.

run·a·gate [ˈrʌnəgeit] *n.*〔罕〕游民,瘪三;逃亡者,亡命者;变节者,叛徒.

run·a·round [ˈrʌnəraund] *n.* ①〔俚〕借口. ②躲闪,回避,逃避. ③藐视,冷待.

run·a·way [ˈrʌnəwei] *n.* 逃走者,逃亡者;阻不住的奔马,逃马;逃走,逃亡,私奔. — *a.* 逃走的,逃亡的,私奔的;容易跑赢的(马);节节上涨的(物价). *a ~ chin* 凹下巴. *a ~ ring* 按铃逃[按了铃就逃,和人家开玩笑].

run·back [ˈrʌnˌbæk] *n.*【足球】断球后带球回跑.

run·ci·ble [ˈrʌnsəbl] *a.* 有利刃的.

run·ci·nate [ˈrʌnsinit] *a.*【植】下向锯齿形的;倒向羽裂的.

Run·di [ˈruːndi] *n.* ①*(pl. -dis, -di)* 布隆迪人[住在布隆迪的班图人]. ②布隆迪人用的班图语[布隆迪和卢旺达所用的两种商业语言之一].

run·dle [ˈrʌndl] *n.* ①梯级. ②灯笼齿轮的齿. ③绞盘头.

rund·let [ˈrʌndlit] *n.*〔古语〕①小桶. ②隆勒[液体容量单位[相当于 18 美国加仑].

run-down [rʌnˈdaun] *a.*〔美〕伤身体的,累人的;荒废的;(钟等)停了的. — *n.* 削减人员,裁员.

Rund·rei·se [ˈruntraizə] *n.*〔G.〕环游. *a ~ ticket* 环游车票.

rune [ruːn] *n.*〔常 *pl.*〕北欧古字;北欧古诗;芬兰古诗;神秘;神秘的符号.

rung¹ [rʌŋ] *ring* 的过去时及过去分词.

rung² *n.* ①梯级,梯子(等)的横档;车辐;〔罕〕(船的)地板料. ②(地位等的上升)一级. *the lowest [topmost] ~ of Fortune's ladder* 倒楣[幸运]之至.

ru·nic [ˈruːnik] *a.* ①北欧古字的;古北欧人的;古北欧风的. ②(符号等)有神秘性[魔术性]的. — *n.* 北欧古字碑文.

run-in¹ [ˈrʌnin] *n.* 插入物;(印件上的)插补段落,(主要词目下的)附加词目;【军】(发动机)试车;【军】飞机向目标(或指定地点)的飞行.

run-in² [ˈrʌnin] *n.*〔美〕争论,口角;第二道门;〔橄榄球〕抢球冲进对方球门界线拿球触地.

run·let¹ [ˈrʌnlit] *n.* = rundlet.

run·let², run·nel [ˈrʌnlit,ˈrʌnl] *n.* 小河,水沟.

run·ner [ˈrʌnə] *n.* ①跑的人;赛跑者;交通员;通讯员,情报员;使者;(银行等的)收款员;善跑的马;乘用马;赛跑马. ②逃走的人;破坏封锁的船;走私者,买卖私货的人. ③(火车等的)司机. ④〔美〕接客员;兜揽员,推销员,跑街. ⑤(习车、溜冰鞋等的)滑走部;【机】转子,滚子;【冶】流道. ⑥【英史】警察,巡捕;【植】纤匐枝,蔓;蔓生草本植物;【鸟】走禽类鸟;秧鸡;鲹属的鱼;黑蛇. ⑦(铺走廊的)长条地毡,(铺在条桌中部的)长条桌布;(袜子的)梯形绽线. ⑧【海】游动绞辘. ~ **bean** 〔英〕红花菜豆.
run·ner-up [ˈrʌnərˈʌp] *n.* 【运】亚军,第二名;决赛失败者;(在竞选等中)占第二位的人;(拍卖时)喊高货价的人;【高尔夫球】末赛输者.
run·ning [ˈrʌniŋ] *a.* ①跑的,边跑边走的;流动的,流体的;【机】操作中的;现在的,现行的;【植】纤匐的,攀缘的. ②继续的,连接的. ③草草的,仓率的;出脓的(伤等). *a ~ fight* (海上的)追击战. *four days ~* 接连四天. *the ~ month* 本月. ***at the ~ pace*** 用跑步. —*n.* ①奔跑;赛跑;跑力;【棒球】跑垒. ②流出;出脓. ③开动,运转;经营,管理. ④【植】匍匐,长纤匐枝. ⑤〔口〕短期旅行. *idle ~*【机】空转. ***in the ~*** 参加赛跑;有胜的希望. ***make the ~*** 使(熟练马)带领着(生马)跑;向导. ***out of the ~*** 不参加赛跑;没有胜的希望. ***take up the ~*** (马)从半路起尽力跑;率先领导. ~ **account** 流水帐. ~ **board** 〔美〕(汽车两旁的)踏(脚)板. ~ **commentary [comments]** (散见书中的)评注,注解;(电台的)时事评述. ~ **cost** 运转费用[成本];营业费用. ~ **fire** 连续炮火. ~ **frequency** 转速. ~ **gear** 【机】驱动装置;【海】驱动船具. ~ **hand** 草书. ~ **head [line, title]** 栏外标题,书楣标题. ~ **knot [noose]** 一扯就紧的活结[套绳]. ~ **mate** (熟马带着跑的)练跑马;〔美〕副职候选人;〔口〕(某人的)密友. ~ **meter** 延米,纵长米. ~ **plate** 【机】踏板. ~ **repair** 验修. ~ **shed** 〔英〕圆形机车车库. ~ **test** 试探性试验,行车试验. ~ **time** 操作时间. ~ **water** 流水;自来水.
run·ny [ˈrʌni] *a.* ***(-ni·er, -ni·est)*** ①液状的. ②流粘液的. ***a ~ nose*** 流鼻涕的鼻子. **-ni·ness** *n.*
run-off [rʌnˈɔːf] *n.* (同分者之间的)决赛;〔美〕(地表)径流,径流量.
run-of-paper [ˈrʌnəvpeipə] *a.* (由报纸编辑)随意决定刊载位置的.
run-of-the-mill [ˈrʌnəv ðəˈmil] *a.* 普通的,一般性的,不突出的,不出色的.
run-of-the-mine, run-of-mine [ˈrʌnəv ðəˈmain] *a.* ①(煤)不按规格、质量分等级的. ②普通的,不出色的.
run·on [ˈrʌnɔn] *n., a.* 追加(的),连续接排(的). *~ entries* 接排词目.
run-o·ver [ˈrʌnəuvə] *a.* 超篇幅而需转页的.
runˊo·ver [ˈrʌnəuvə] *n.* 超篇幅的排印材料;(报刊等文章的)转页部分.
runt [rʌnt] *n.* ①小牛;矮小的家畜. ①矮人;〔蔑〕矮子. ③特大品种家鸽. ④〔苏格兰、英方〕植物的硬茎;腐朽的根;老牛,干瘪老太婆.
run·way [ˈrʌnwei] *n.* 〔主美〕跑道;飞机跑道;河床;(滑运木材等用的)滑路;(窗框等的)滑沟;〔美〕动物来往的路;【剧】演员由观众席间上场的通道.
Run·yon [ˈrʌnjən] *n.* 拉尼恩〔姓氏〕.
ru·pee [ruːˈpiː] *n.* (印度等国的货币单位)卢比;卢比银币.
Ru·pert [ˈruːpət] *n.* 鲁珀特〔姓氏,男子名〕.
ru·pes·trine, ru·pic·o·lous, ru·pic·o·line [ruːˈpestrin, -ˈpikələs,-ˈlain] *a.* 【生】生长或居住在岩石丛中的.
ru·pi·ah [ruːˈpiːə] *n.* 卢比,盾〔印尼货币单位〕.
rup·ture [ˈrʌptʃə] *n.* 裂断,破裂;决裂,断绝,闹翻;【医】脱肠,疝. ***come to a ~*** (交涉)破裂,决裂;闹翻脸. ***have a ~*** 有疝气. —*vt.* 弄破,使破裂;断绝(关系等);使不和,闹翻;【医】使患脱肠症. ***~d duck*** 〔美俚〕二次大战从军纪念章. —*vi.* 裂开,破裂;断绝.
ru·ral [ˈruərəl] *a.* 乡下的,农村(风味)的 (*opp.* urban);地方的;农业的. *~ life* 农村生活. *a ~ district* 〔英〕地方自治区. ~ **dean** 〔英〕(主管若干教区的)乡村牧师. ~ **free delivery** 〔美〕农村地区免费邮递. ~ **route** (乡村免费邮递区的)邮道. *~ economy* 农业经济. **-ly** *ad.*
ru·ral·ist [ˈruərəlist] *n.* 过田园生活的人,提倡田园生活的人.
ru·ral·ism, ru·ral·i·ty [ˈruərəlizm,ruəˈræliti] *n.* ①田舍风味,乡村风味. ②田园生活. ③农村习语,乡村特色.
ru·ral·ize [ˈruərəlaiz] *vt.,vi.* 弄[变]成乡村风味;(使)田园化;过田园生活.
Rus. = Russia; Russian.
ruse [ruːz] *n.* 策术,谋略,阴谋诡计.
ru·sé [ˈruːzei] *a.* 〔F.〕玩弄策术的,狡猾的.
Rush [rʌʃ] *n.* 拉什〔姓氏〕.
rush[1] [rʌʃ] *vi.* ①向前猛进,冲,突进;突击,冲击,袭击*(on; upon)*. ②匆匆忙忙地走[通过、旅行]. ③迫不及待地要,冒冒失失地做;突然出现[发生]. —*vt.* ①使向前冲,使猛进;突破,冲破;赶,驱;催促;赶紧做[执行、进行];赶紧送,急送. ②冲锋夺取,袭击;冲破;【足球】带球冲到球门;〔美俚〕热烈地追求;拼命巴结;〔美学生语〕款待(新,会员). *He ~es into things.* 他做事冒失. *R- this order please.* 请赶快办理订货单. ***~ a bill through*** 使议案匆匆通过. ***~ at*** 向…冲过去. ***~ headlong*** 冒进. ***~ harvest*** 抢收. ***~ plant*** 抢种. ***~ in*** 冲进,跑进,跳进,踏进. ***~ into extremes*** 走极端. ***~ in upon one's mind*** 忽然浮现在心里. ***~ out*** 赶制出来. ***~ out of the room*** 冲出屋子. ***~ to a conclusion*** 轻率下结论. ***~ to arms*** 急取武器. —*n.* ①突进,猛进;突击,突破. ②蜂拥而至;激增,猛长;繁忙. ③抢购,抢订. ④【足球】带球冲破敌阵冲到球门(的人). ⑤〔美〕(大学各年级学生间抢夺旗子等的)揪扭,乱斗;〔美学生活〕上好成绩,几乎得一百分. ⑥【影】试映影片. ⑦〔美俚〕热烈的追求,殷勤,体贴. *a ~ of water* 奔流. *a ~ of wind* 一阵急风. *a ~ of blood to the head* 脑溢血. *a great ~ of work* 工作繁忙. *a ~ of buds* 芽猛长. ***be in a ~*** 大忙特忙. ***with a ~*** 哄地一下子,猛地 *(They came in with a ~.* 他们一哄而入). —*a.* 〔主美〕猛冲的,蜂拥而来的;赶紧完成[执行]的(命令等). ~ **hours** (上班、下班时)交通拥挤的时刻;(公共车辆)高峰时间. ~ **job** 急件. ~ **order** 加急订单.
rush[2] [rʌʃ] *n.* 【植】灯心草,蔺;没价值的东西. ***not care a ~*** 满不在乎. ***not worth a ~*** 毫无价值. —*vt.* 铺灯心草;用灯心草做. ~**bearing** 〔英〕献堂纪念节. ~-**candle** 灯心草蜡烛. ~**light** 灯心草蜡烛;黯淡的亮光;微光;微弱的知识;微不足道的人.
rush·ee [rʌˈʃiː] *n.* (大学生联谊会的)拉进对象.
rush·y [rʌʃi] *a.* ***(-i·er;-i·est)*** 灯心草多的;灯心草做的;铺满灯心草的.
rusk [rʌsk] *n.* ①干面包片,脆饼干. ②〔R-〕腊斯克〔姓氏〕.
Rus·kin [ˈrʌskin] *n.* ①拉斯金〔姓氏〕. ②**John** ~约翰·拉斯金〔1819—1900,美国作家,美术评论家,社会改革家〕.
Russ [rʌs] *a., n.* 〔古〕= Russia(n).
Russ. =Russia(n).
Rus·sell [ˈrʌsl] *n.* ①拉塞尔〔姓氏〕. ②**Bertrand** ~ 贝特兰·罗素〔1872—1970,英国数学家、哲学家〕.
rus·set [ˈrʌsit] *a.* 枯叶色的,黄褐色的,赤褐色的;手织的;〔古〕乡下式的,简陋的. —*n.* 枯叶色,黄褐色,赤褐色;赤褐色手织土布(衣服);赤褐色冬苹果.
rus·set·y [ˈrʌsiti] *a.* 枯叶色的,赤褐色的.
Rus·sia [ˈrʌʃə] *n.* ① = the Russian Empire. ②=Soviet Union. ③〔r-〕=~ leather (做书皮用的)俄国皮.
Russian [ˈrʌʃən] *a., n.* 俄国的;俄国人(的),俄语(的). ~ **boots** 长统靴. ~ **dandelion** 橡胶草. ~ **olive**【植】沙枣. ~ **Revolution** 俄国革命. ~ **Socialist Federative Soviet Republic** 俄罗斯苏维埃联邦社会主义共和国〔略 R.S.F.S.R.〕.
Rus·sian·ize [ˈrʌʃənaiz] *vt.* 使俄罗斯化.
Rus·sify [ˈrʌsifai] *vt.* = Russianize.
Rus·so- *comb. f.* 俄国. *the ~-Japanese War* 日俄战争.
rust [rʌst] *n.* ①锈;锈色. ②铁锈;【植】锈菌,锈病. ③荒废,停滞,无活动. *a life of ~* 疲塌懒散的生活. *the*

~ *of idleness* 懒癖;惰性. *talents left to* ~ 白有才能,怀才无用. **be in** ~ 生着锈. **gather** ~ 生锈. **get [rub] the** ~ **off** 把锈擦掉. **keep from** ~ 使不生锈. — *vi.* 生锈;【植】害锈病;(不用的结果)变钝,变荒废,变呆;变成锈色. *Better wear out than* ~ *out.* 与其锈坏不如用坏,与其闲死不如忙死. — *vt.* 使生锈,使腐蚀;使钝,使弱. ~**-coloured** *a.* 铁锈色的,赤褐色的. ~**proof** *a.* 抗锈的,防锈的,不锈的. **-a·ble** *a.* 会生锈的. **-less** *a.* 无锈的,不锈的.

rus·tic [ˈrʌstik] *a.* ①乡村的,乡下的. ②质朴的,朴素的. ③粗鲁的,没礼貌的. ④(石工等)粗面的;圆木造的;(古代拉丁字体)粗俗体的. ~ *simplicity* 纯朴. *a* ~ *bridge* 独木桥. ~ *tobacco* 黄花烟. *a* ~ *seat* 粗木椅. ~ *work* (用天然树根树枝等建造成的)圆木结构;【石工】粗面石堆砌. — *n.* 乡下人,农夫;粗汉.

rus·ti·cal [ˈrʌstikəl] *a.* 〔古〕乡村的,土气的,粗俗的,做工粗糙的〔rustic 的变体〕.

rus·ti·cal·ly [rʌsˈtikəli] *ad.* 照乡下式样;质朴地,不加修饰地,粗鲁地.

rus·ti·cate [ˈrʌstikeit] *vi.* 到乡下去,下乡;在乡下住.— *vt.* ①使在乡下住,把…送到乡下去. ②〔英大学〕勒令…停学. ③使成粗面石堆砌.

rus·ti·ca·tion [ˌrʌstiˈkeiʃən] *n.* 下乡;乡村生活.

rus·tic·i·ty [rʌsˈtisiti] *n.* ①乡下式,乡村风味;乡村生活;质朴,朴素. ②粗鲁,撒野,没礼貌. *He was ashamed of his own* ~ *in that distinguished company.* 在那伙人当中他因自己粗俗而惭愧.

rust·ily [ˈrʌstili] *ad.* 生着锈;用哑声.

rust·i·ness [ˈrʌstinis] *n.* 生锈.

rus·tle [ˈrʌsl] *vi.* ①(树叶、纸等)沙沙地[飒飒地]响;绸衣沙沙沙地摩擦着走 (*along*). ②〔美俚〕快快干,勤奋工作;〔原美西部〕偷牲畜. — *vt.* ①使作沙沙[飒飒]声,沙沙地抖动[抖落]. ②〔美俚〕快干,迅速取到;〔原美西部〕偷(牛马等). ~ ***in silks*** 穿着绸衫. — *n.* 沙沙声,飒飒声.

rus·tler [ˈrʌslə] *n.* 〔美俚〕活动分子,活跃分子;偷牲畜的贼.

rus·tling [ˈrʌsliŋ] *n.* 沙沙[飒飒]的声音;〔美〕偷牲畜. **-ly** *ad.*

rust·y[1] [ˈrʌsti] *a.* ①生了锈的,上锈的;腐蚀了的. ②由锈而成的,因锈而生的;【植】患锈病的. ③锈色的;褪了色的;陈旧的. ④(因不使用)变得不能用的,变荒疏的,变拙劣了的,变钝了的. *His Greek is a little* ~. 他的希腊语丢生了. *He is getting* ~. 他渐渐落伍了. ***cut up*** ~ 发脾气的. **-i·ly** *ad.* **-i·ness** *n.*

rust·y[2] [ˈrʌsti] *a.* 〔方〕发脾气的,恼怒的. *He turned* ~. 他发火了.

rust·y[3] [ˈrʌsti] *a.* 有腐烂臭味的,开始腐烂的.

rut[1] [rʌt] *n.* ①车辙,车印. ②定例,常例,常轨,惯例,老规矩. ***get into a*** ~ 陷入一定格式. ***go on in the same old*** ~ 老是干同一样事情. ***move in a*** ~ 照惯例行动,干老工作. — *vt.* 在…上留下车印;在…挖沟.

rut[2] [rʌt] *n.* (雄鹿、雄羊等的)发淫,发风,起兴;发淫期,发淫期的鸣声. ***at [or] the*** ~ 在发淫. ***go to (the)*** ~发淫. — *vi.* 发淫,起兴,动情.

ru·ta·ba·ga [ruːtəˈbeigə] *n.* 【植】芜菁甘蓝.

ruth [ruːθ] *n.* 〔古〕同情,怜悯;悔恨. **-ful** *a.* 充满同情的,悲哀的.

Ruth [ruːθ] *n.* ①露丝〔女子名〕. ②【圣】大卫的女祖先 ③【圣】《路得记》〔旧约全书的一篇〕.

ru·the·ni·um [ruːˈθiːniəm] *n.* 【化】钌.

Ruth·er·ford [ˈrʌðəfəd] *n.* ①卢瑟福〔姓氏〕. ②**r-**卢〔放射性强度单位,略作 rd.〕

ruth·less [ˈruːθlis] *a.* 无情的,残忍的. **-ly** *ad.* **-ness** *n.*

ru·ti·lant [ˈruːtilənt] *a.* 发红色火光的.

ru·tile [ˈruːtiːl] *n.* 【矿】金红石.

ru·tin [ˈruːtin] *n.* 【药】芸香苷;卢丁.

Rut·land [ˈrʌtlənd] *n.* 拉特兰市〔美国佛蒙特州西部一城市〕.

Rut·ledge [ˈrʌtlidʒ] *n.* 拉特利奇〔姓氏〕.

rut·tish [ˈrʌtiʃ] *a.* 发淫的;好色的.

rut·ty [ˈrʌti] *a.* 车印多的.

R.V. = Revised Version (of the Bible).

R.V.O. = Royal Victorian Order.

R.W. =Right Worshipful; Right Worthy.

Rwan·da [ruːˈɑːndə] *n.* 卢旺达〔非洲〕.

R.W.S. = Royal Society of Painters in water-colours.

Rx [ˈɑːreks] *n.* ①处方. ②〔喻〕解决方案.

Ry. = Railway(s).

-ry, -ery *suf.* 构成名词: ①表示'性质、行为'. 例: pedant*ry*, brave*ry*. ②表示'境遇,身分'. 例: slave*ry*. ③表示'货物的种类'. 例: perfume*ry*. ④表示'制造所、饲养所' 例: bake*ry*.

Ry·der [ˈraidə] *n.* 赖德〔姓氏〕.

rye [rai] *n.* 【植】①裸麦〔面包原料、牲畜饲料〕;〔美俗〕裸麦威士忌酒. ②绅士,(特指)吉卜赛绅士,和吉卜赛人要好的人. ~ **bread** 黑面包. ~ **grass** *n.* 【植】毒麦〔做粮草用〕.

ryke [raik] *vi.* 〔Scot.〕到,达.

Ry·land [ˈrailənd] *n.* 赖兰〔姓氏,男子名〕.

ry·ot [ˈraiət] *n.* 〔英印〕农夫.

R.Y.S. = Royal Yacht Squadron.

Ryu·kyu [ˈrjuːˈkjuː] *n.* 琉球(群岛)〔日本〕. **-an** *n.* 琉球民族;琉球人.

ryve [raiv] *vi.* 戳通.

S

S,s [es] (*pl.* ***S's, s's Ss ss*** [ˈesiz]) ①英语字母表第十九字母. ②S 字形, S 形物. ③〔S〕【化】元素硫的符号 (= sulphur). ④〔S〕〔美〕(学业成绩的)良好等级(= satisfactory). ⑤〔S〕中世纪罗马数字中的 7 或 70. *the collar of S [SS, Ss, esses]*, S 字状连锁颈章〔最早为英国兰加斯特王族以后为伦敦市长等权贵所佩用〕. *an S-hook* S 形钩子. *an S curve* S 形曲线.

S.,s. = ①saint. ②school. ③society. ④Sabbath. ⑤Saturday. ⑥Saxon. ⑦Senate. ⑧September. ⑨〔It.〕*Signor.* ⑩Socialist. ⑪south; southern. ⑫Submarine. ⑬Sunday. ⑭second(s). ⑮section. ⑯see. ⑰series. ⑱shilling(s). ⑲sign. ⑳singular. ㉑son. ㉒steamer. ㉓substantive.

's 〔〔浊辅音后〕z, 〔清辅音后〕s〕〔口〕= is, has, does, us: *He's a boy. He's done it. What's he say about it? Let's go.*

-'s 〔〔浊辅音后〕z, 〔清辅音后〕s, 〔咝音后〕iz〕①〔古〕= God's: *'sblood* (= God's blood)! 真的! 啐! ②字

母、数字等略语的复数: 3's, *M.P.'s*. ③作名词所有格: *cat's, Tom's*. ④加于数字、字母、缩写词之后构成复数: *Ph.D.'s [Ph.D.s]* 哲学博士们. *1980's [1980s]* 二十世纪八十年代.

-s 〔浊辅音后〕z, 〔清辅音后〕s〕 *suf.* ①名词复数在词末加 -s: *cats, dogs.* ②行为动词第三人称单数现在一般时在词末加 -s: *He jumps. It rains.* ④副词词尾: *always, indoors, needs, forwards.*

S.A. = ①Salvation Army【宗】救世军. ②Sex appeal 性感. ③Small-arms 轻武器. ④South Africa 南非. ⑤South America 南美洲. ⑥South Australia 南澳大利亚. ⑦〔G〕 *Sturmabteilung* (= Storm detachment) 〔旧〕(希特勒德国的)冲锋队.

Sa =【化】元素钐的符号(= Samarium).

Sa. = Saturday.

s.a. = ①(〔L〕 *secundum artem* = according to art, in accordance with the rules of the art) 依常规. ②(〔L〕 *sine anno* = without year or date) 无年代,无日期. ③ small-arms 轻武器. ④subject to approval 有待批准.

SAA, S.A.A. = small arms ammunition 轻兵器弹药,轻武器弹药.

SAAM = small arms ammunition 轻兵器弹药, 轻武器弹药.

Saar [sɑː] *n.* ①〔the ~〕萨尔河〔西欧〕. ②萨尔〔西德州名〕(= ~land).

Saar·brück·en [ˈsɑːbrukən] *n.* 萨尔布吕肯〔西德城市〕.

SAB =Science Advisory Board 〔美〕科学咨询委员会, 科学顾问委员会.

Sab. = Sabbath.

Sa·ba [ˈseibə] *n.*【史】塞巴〔阿拉伯南部一古国, 今也门〕.

Sa·ba·e·an [səˈbi(ː)ən] *a., n.* ① 塞巴地方的(人). ② 〔误用〕= Sabian.

sab·a·dil·la [ˈsæbəˌdilə] *n.* ①【植】沙巴藜芦〔*Schoenocaulon officinale* 墨西哥和中美产有毒百合科植物〕. ② 沙巴达子〔沙巴藜芦的干熟种子,用以杀灭害虫〕.

Sa·bah [ˈsɑːbɑː] *n.* 沙巴〔马来西亚州名〕.

Sa·ba·han [səˈbɑːhən] *n.*沙巴人. — *a.* 沙巴的.

Sa·ba·ism [ˈseibiizəm] *n.* 拜星; 星辰崇拜.

Sab·a·oth [sæˈbeiɔθ, ˈsæbeiɔθ] *n.* 〔*pl.*〕【圣】万军; 万民. ***the Lord of ~***【圣】上帝.

sab·bat [ˈsæbət] *n.* 〔常作 S-〕= Sabbath ④.

Sab·ba·tar·i·an [ˌsæbəˈtɛəriən] *a.* (严守) 安息日的. — *n.* ①严守安息日的犹太人. ②严守星期日为安息日的基督教徒. ③认定星期六为安息日的基督教徒. **-ism** *n.* 严守安息日习惯.

Sab·bath [ˈsæbəθ] *n.* ①安息日〔犹太人及少数基督教徒是星期六, 一般基督教徒是星期日〕. ②〔s.〕休息; 静寂. ③安息年; 休息时. ④(传说中每年一次在夜半举行的)魔女的聚会; 恶魔的聚会 (= Witches' Sabbath). ***the great [holy] ~*** 复活节前一日. ***a s- of sound*** 静寂. ***keep [break] the ~*** 守〔不守〕安息日的. ***~-day's journey*** 安息日行程〔约三分之二英里〕; 〔喻〕轻便旅行. **~-breaker** 不守安息日的人. **~ day** 安息日. **~ School** 星期日〔安息日〕学校, 主日学校, 星期日教授宗教课程的学校.

Sab·bat·ic [səˈbætik] *a., n.* = sabbatical.

Sab·bat·ical [səˈbætikəl] *a.* ①安息日(般)的. ②〔s-〕安息的, 休息的. ***s-leave*** 〔美〕(大学教授每七年得享受一年的)休假. **~ *year*** (古代犹太人每七年休耕一年的)安息年; 〔美〕(大学教授的)休假年. — *n.* ①(古犹太人的)安息年; (大学教授的)休假年; 休假. ②〔*pl.*〕星期天穿的衣服, 节日服装. **-ly** *ad.*

Sa·be·an [səˈbi(ː)ən] *a., n.* = Sabaean.

Sa·bel·li·an [səˈbeliən] *n.* ①塞贝里人〔包括塞宾人和萨摩奈人在内的古意大利一个部族集团中的成员〕. ② 塞贝里语.

sa·ber [ˈseibə] *n., vt.* 〔美〕= sabre.

Sa·bi·an [ˈseibiən] *n., a.* ①萨比教徒(的)〔在古兰经中, 与伊斯兰教徒、犹太教徒和基督教徒并列, 信仰真主〕. ②〔误用〕拜星教徒(的). **-ism** *n.* ①萨比教. ②=Sabaism 〔误用〕.

Sa·bin [sæbin, ˈseibin] *n.* 萨宾〔姓氏〕.

sa·bin [ˈseibin] *n.*【声】沙平, 赛宾〔声吸收单位〕.

Sa·bine [ˈsæbain] *n., a.* ①萨拜恩〔姓氏〕. ②〔古代意大利住在亚平宁 (Apennines) 山区的〕塞宾人(的). ③塞宾语(的).

sa·ble [ˈseibl] *n.* ①【动】黑貂; 黑〔紫〕貂皮; (黑)貂(尾)毛画笔; 〔常 *pl.*〕 黑貂皮大衣. ②【徽、诗】黑色; 〔*pl.*〕【诗】丧服. — *a.* ①黑貂皮(制)的. ②【诗】黑的; 阴暗的; 阴森可怕的. ***His S- Majesty [Excellency]***【谑】魔王. **~ antelope** *n.*【动】貂羚. **~fish** *n.*【动】裸盖鱼.

sa·bled [ˈseibld] *a.* ①穿着丧服的. ②黑色的.

SABMIS = seaborne anti-ballistic missile intercept system 舰载反弹道导弹截击系统.

sab·ot [ˈsæbəu] *n.* ①(法、比等国农民穿的)木鞋, 木屐; 木底鞋. ②【军】炮弹软壳;【机】镗杆, 衬套;【建】桩靴. **-ed** *a.* 穿木鞋的〔指农民〕.

sab·o·tage [ˈsæbətɑːʒ, ˈsæbətidʒ, ˈsæbətɑːdʒ] *n.* 怠工; (劳资纠纷、战争中的)胡乱破坏. ***engage in ~*** 从事破坏. —*vt., vi.* (对…) 怠工 (*on*); 破坏, 阻挠. ~ *peace* 破坏和平.

sab·o·teur [ˌsæbəˈtəː] *n.* 〔F.〕怠工者, 破坏者.

sa·bra [ˈsɑːbrə] *n.* 在以色列出生的人.

sa·bre, 〔美〕**sa·ber** [ˈseibə] *n.* ①(骑兵的)军刀, 马刀. ②骑兵; 〔*pl.*〕骑兵队. ③〔the ~〕武力; 军法; 黩武政治. *have 3000 ~s* 有三千骑兵. *by the ~* 用武力. — *vt.* ①用军刀斩〔砍、杀〕. ②把… 用骑兵武装起来. ~ *one's way*(用军刀)杀开一条路. **~-cut** 用军刀斩; 军刀伤口〔疤〕. **~ jet** 佩刀式喷气战斗机〔F-86 型战斗机〕. **~-rattler** 卤莽的黩武主义者, 张牙舞爪的人. **~-rattling** *a.* 耀武扬威的, 张牙舞爪的. **~ saw** 轻便〔手提〕电锯. **~-toothed** *a.* 有军刀式上犬齿的. **~-toothed tiger**【古生】剑齿虎.

sab·re·tache [ˈsæbətæʃ] *n.* 【军】(挂在骑兵军官佩刀带左方的)佩囊.

sab·u·lite [ˈsæbjulait] *n.* 一种烈性炸药〔爆炸力约为普通炸药的三倍〕.

sab·u·lous [ˈsæbjuləs] *a.* ①多沙的; 含沙的; 沙质的; 沙状的. ②【医】(尿)沉淀多的, 有粒状物的.

SAC = Strategic Air Command 〔美〕战略空军司令部.

sac [sæk] *n.* ①【生】囊, 液囊. ②上衣 (= sack). ~ **fungus** 子囊菌.

sac·a·ton [ˌsækəˈtəun] *n.* 〔美〕【植】赖特氏鼠尾粟 *(Sporobolus wrightii)* 〔一种粗草, 美国西南部和墨西哥作饲料用〕.

sac·cade [sæˈkɑːd] *n.* ①(阅读等时眼睛的)飞快跳阅, 扫视. ②急速勒马.

sac·cadic [sæˈkɑːdik] *a.* 跳阅的, 扫视的.

sac·cate [ˈsækeit] *a.*【生】囊状的, 有囊的.

sac·char- *comb. f.* 糖的, 糖精的: *saccharase.*

sac·cha·rase [ˈsækəreis] *n.*【生化】蔗糖酶 (= invertase).

sac·cha·rate [ˈsækəreit] *n.* ①【化】糖质酸盐. ②糖合物, 糖与金属氧化物的化合物.

sac·char·ic [sæˈkærik] *a.*【化】①糖合物的. ②从糖合物取得的. ③糖质的. ~ **acid**【化】糖质酸; 糖二酸.

sac·cha·ride [ˈsækəraid] *n.*【化】糖化物; 糖类.

sac·cha·rif·er·ous [ˌsækəˈrifərəs] *a.*【化】含糖的; 产糖的.

sac·char·i·fy [ˈsækərifai] *vt.*【化】 把…制成糖; 使糖化.

sac·cha·rim·e·ter [ˌsækəˈrimitə] *n.*【化】(比重)糖量计.

sac·cha·rin [ˈsækərin] *n.* 糖精.
sac·cha·rine [ˈsækərain, -riːn] *a.* ①糖(质)的. ②太甜的. ③(十分)甜蜜的. ④巴结的,逢迎的,讨好的,奉承的. — [ˈsækərin]*n.* 糖精 (= saccharin). ~ **diabetes** 糖尿病. ~ **sorghum** 甜高粱.
sac·cha·rize [ˈsækəraiz] *vt.* 糖化;使发酵.
sac·cha·ro- *comb. f.* = sacchar-.〔用于辅音前〕.
sac·cha·roid [ˈsækərɔid] *a.* ①糖块状的;糖质物,糖晶. ②【地】结构纹理象砂糖状的. — *n.* 粒状物;砂糖状物.
sac·cha·roi·dal [ˈsækərɔidl] *a.* = saccharoid *a.*
sac·cha·rom·e·ter [ˌsækəˈrɔmitə] *n.* = saccharimeter.
sac·cha·ro·my·cete [ˌsækərəuˈmaisiːt] *n.* 【植】酵母菌.
sac·cha·rose [ˈsækərəus] *n.* 【化】蔗糖.
sac·cu·lar [ˈsækjulə] *a.* 【生】囊状的.
sac·culate(d) [ˈsækjuleit(id)] *a.* 成囊的; 袋状的; 分成囊状的. **-la·tion** [ˌsækjuˈleiʃən] *n.*
sac·cule [ˈsækjuːl] *n.* 【生】小囊,〔尤指〕耳迷路的球囊.
sac·cu·lus [ˈsækjuləs] *n. (pl. **-li** [-lai])* 〔L〕= saccule.
sac·er·do·tal [ˌsæsəˈdəutl] *a.* ①僧侣的; 祭司的; 祭司制的. ②主张僧侣掌握大权的. **-do·cy** [-ˈdəusi] *n.* 〔罕〕(= sacerdotalism). **-ism** *n.* 祭司制度,僧侣政治. **-ly** *ad.*
sa·chem [ˈseitʃəm] *n.* ①(某些北美印第安人的)酋长. ②〔谑〕大老板,首领,巨头. ③〔美〕(纽约市民主党组织)坦慕尼协会 (Tammany Society) 的干事.
sa·chet [ˈsæʃei] *n.* ①香囊;香袋. ②香粉.
sack[1] [sæk] *n.* ①(通常指亚麻或大麻等制的)袋, 包; 麻袋; 硬纸袋. ②(旧时妇女穿的)宽身长袍; 宽短外衣. ③〔美俚〕床, 卧铺, 铺位. ④【棒球】垒. ⑤撒克〔重量单位, = 101.6 公斤〕. ⑥〔the ~〕〔英俚〕解雇,革职. *Nothing comes out of the ~ but what was in it.* 袋子里有什么才能倒出什么;无中不能生有. ***a sad ~*** 〔美俚〕①好心办错事的兵〔人〕. ②难处的人,讨人厌的女孩. ***buy a cat in the ~*** 买封在口袋里的猫; 不看清货物瞎买. ***get [have] the ~*** 〔俚〕被解雇;被拒绝. ***give (sb.) the ~*** 〔英俚〕解雇(某人); 抛弃(情人等). ***hit the ~*** 〔美俚〕就寝, 睡觉. ***hold the ~*** ①被留下来独担罪责. ②只分得最差的一份, 两手空空, 上当受骗. — *vt.* ①把…装进袋里; 装袋运输. ②〔口〕解雇; 把…驱逐出校, 开除; 抛弃(情人等). ③〔口〕侵吞. ④〔口〕〔竞赛〕打败; 胜过. ~ ***in [out]*** 〔美俚〕上床睡觉, 睡个痛快. ~**but** 中世纪低音喇叭. ~**cloth** ①(粗)麻布, 麻袋布. ②丧服 (*~-cloth and ashes* 悲哀, 深深懊悔). ~ **coat** 〔美〕男式便装短上衣. ~**-race** 【运】袋囊赛跑〔腿上套着袋子的跳跃式竞走〕. ~ **suit**〔美〕= ~ coat. ~ **time** 〔美俚〕睡眠时间. **-er** *n.* ①制(或装) 袋工人. ②【棒球】守垒员. **-ful** *n.* ①满袋, 一袋. ②一大堆. **-ing** *n.* ①袋布, 粗麻布. ②〔美俚〕守垒.
sack[2] [sæk] *vt.* 抢劫; 掠夺. — *n.* 掠夺(物). *put to the ~* 掠夺. **-er** *n.* 掠夺者.
sack[3] [sæk] *n.* (从前西班牙输出的) 白葡萄酒. ***one half-pennyworth of bread to an intolerable deal of ~*** 吃的面包太少, 喝的汤汤水水太多; 无关紧要的东西太多.
sack·less [ˈsæklis] *a.* 〔古〕无罪的. ②〔Scot.〕垂头丧气的, 软弱的; 头脑愚钝的.
Sack·ville [ˈsækvil] *n.* 萨克维尔〔姓氏〕.
sack·y [ˈsæki] *a.* (衣服)宽大的, 像布袋似的.
sacque [sæk] *n.* ①(妇女穿的)宽短外衣. ②〔古〕(妇女穿的)宽长服. ③(婴儿的) 短上衣〔通常系在脖子上〕(= sack[1]).
sa·cral [ˈseikrəl] *a.* 【解】骶骨〔荐骨〕的. *the ~ vertebrae* 腰椎.
sa·cral·ize [ˈsækrəlaiz, ˈseikrəlaiz] *vt.* 使神圣化; 使神圣. **-za·tion**[-ˈzeʃən] *n.*
sac·ra·ment [ˈsækrəmənt] *n.* ①圣礼. ②神圣的东西; 神秘; 神圣的宣誓; (古罗马军队的) 入队宣誓. ③〔the S-〕圣餐(礼); 圣体; 圣餐面包〔英国国教、罗马天主教通常把这叫做 the Blessed [Holy] S-〕. *the ~ of the altar* 圣餐面包; 圣物. ***administer the ~*** 行圣餐礼. ***go to ~*** 参加圣餐礼. ***take the ~s*** 发誓, 宣誓. — *vt.* 〔主用被动语态〕使发誓, 使宣誓.
sac·ra·men·tal [ˌsækrəˈmentl] *a.* ①神圣的. ②圣礼的; 圣餐礼的; 重视圣礼的; 重视圣餐礼的. ③发过誓的. ④象征性的. — *n.* ①类似圣礼的仪式(如用圣水等). ②〔*pl.*〕圣餐礼用具(如十字架等). ~ **elements** 圣餐礼的面包和葡萄酒. ~ **rites** 圣餐礼. ~ **wafers** 圣饼, 圣餐面包. **-ism** *n.* 重视圣礼 (的信仰, 教义). **-ist** *n.* 重视圣礼者.
sac·ra·men·tar·i·an [ˌsækəmenˈtɛəriən] *a.* ①重视圣礼的; 圣餐的. ②圣餐形式论者的. — *n.* 重视圣礼者; 圣餐形式论者.
sac·ra·men·ta·ry [ˌsækrəˈmentəri] *n.* ①= sacramentarian *(n.)*. ②〔*pl.*〕圣礼书. —*a.* = sacramentarian *(a.)*.
Sac·ra·men·to [ˌsækrəˈmentəu] *n.* 萨克拉门托〔美国城市〕.
sa·crar·i·um [səˈkrɛəriəm] *n.* *(pl. **-ri·a** [-riə])* ① (古罗马)神龛. ②【宗】圣堂. ③【天主】(带有排水设备用以处理洗礼圣水用的)水盆.
sa·cré [ˈsækrei] *vi.* *(~d; ~ing)* 〔法国人〕骂一声该死的〔傻瓜(等)〕; 骂人, 咒人.
sa·cred [ˈseikrid] *a.* 神圣的 *(opp.* profane); 宗教的 *(opp.* secular); 上帝的, 神的. ②(动物、植物等)被崇为神物的; 不可侵犯的. ③献给…的; 供献给…的. *a ~ disease* 疯癫. *a ~ number* (宗教上) 神秘的数字〔特指 7〕. *a ~ place* 【法】坟墓. *the ~ cat* (古埃及的) 神猫. *the ~ beetle* = scarab. *a monument ~ to the memory of sb.* (某人的)纪念碑. ***be ~ from*** 免除, 不受. ***hold ~*** 尊重, 保护. ~ **baboon** 【动】阿拉伯狒狒; 阿比西尼亚猩猩 (= hamadryad). ~ **book [writing]** 圣典, 宗教经典〔包括一个宗教的律法, 如可兰经, 圣经〕. ~ **college** 罗马教廷枢密院. ~ **cow** ①(印度的) 神牛. ②〔喻〕不可批评〔冒犯〕的人或物. ~ **mushroom** 祭神菌〔美洲几种可以引起幻觉的菌类之一, 常被用于印第安人的祭神仪式中〕. ~ **music [poetry]** 圣乐〔诗〕. **-ly** *ad.*
sac·ri·fice [ˈsækrifais] *n.* ①牺牲, 供品, 祭品. ②供奉, 献祭; 〔喻〕损失. ③供作牺牲, 牺牲行为, 献身, 舍身. ④【宗】基督的献身〔指耶稣之钉死在十字架上〕; 圣餐. ⑤【商】大贱卖. ⑥【棒球】(为了他人进垒而特意轻击的) 牺牲打 (= ~bunt, ~ hit). ***at the ~ of*** 以…为牺牲, 牺牲…而. ***fall a ~ to*** 成为…的牺牲. ***fear no ~*** 不怕牺牲. ***make all ~s*** 不惜一切牺牲. ***make ~s [a ~] to*** 为…牺牲. ***make the ~ of*** 以…为牺牲. ***sell at a ~*** 亏本出售. ***the great [last] ~*** 阵亡, 战死, 为国捐躯. — *vt.* ①牺牲; 把…奉献给… *(for; to)*. ②廉价卖出. —*vi.* ①牺牲, 献祭. ②【棒球】作牺牲打. ~ **fly** 【棒球】(为了使跑垒的人得分而打出的) 牺牲飞球.
sac·ri·fi·cial [ˌsækriˈfiʃəl] *a.* ①(供作)牺牲的, 供奉的, 献祭的. ②〔罕〕献身的, 舍身的. ③〔俚〕亏本卖的. **-ly** *ad.*
sac·ri·lege [ˈsækrilidʒ] *n.* ①亵渎(神物); 窃取圣物. ②【法】渎圣罪.
sac·ri·le·gious [ˌsækriˈlidʒəs] *a.* 亵渎(神物)的; 窃取圣物的; 有罪孽的. **-ly** *ad.*
sa·cring [ˈseikriŋ] *n.* 【宗, 古】圣餐礼. ~ **bell** 圣餐铃.
sac·rist [ˈseikrist] *n.* 【宗】圣器保管人.
sac·ris·tan [ˈsækristən] *n.* ①= sacrist. ②〔古〕教堂司事(= sexton).
sac·ris·ty [ˈsækristi] *n.* (教堂的)圣器(保藏)室.
sac·ro·il·i·ac [ˌseikrəuˈiliæk; ˌsækrəu-] *a.* 【解】骶骼的; 骶骨与骼骨之间的关节的. — *n.* 骶骨与骼骨之间

S

的关节(或软骨)。

sac·ro·sanct [ˈsækrəusæŋkt] *a.* 神圣不可侵犯的.

sac·ro·sanc·ti·ty [ˌsækrəuˈsæŋktiti] *n.* 神圣不可侵犯.

sa·cro·sci·at·ic [ˌseikəusaiˈætik] *a.* 【解】骶骨和坐骨的.

sa·crum [ˈseikrəm] *n.* *(pl. ~s, sa·cra* [-krə]*)* 【解】骶骨,荐骨.

sad [sæ:d, sæd] *a.* ①悲哀的,悲伤的;悽惨的,可悲的,可怜的.②〔俚、谑〕糟透了的,不可救药的.③〔古〕认真的.④黯淡的,(颜色等)阴郁的.⑤〔罕、方〕(面包、饼等)发得不好的;粘糊糊的.⑥〔美俚〕二流的,次等的. *feel ~* 悲伤. *a sadder and a wiser man* 吃过苦学了乖的人;饱经忧患的人. ***in ~ earnest*** 〔古〕认真地. ***It is ~ that…*** 遗憾的是…. ***make ~ work of it*** 大失败,弄得糟透. *~* **dog** 〔蔑、谑〕不可救药的家伙,糟透了的家伙,无赖,流氓. *~* ***to say*** 可悲的是. ~**-coloured** *a.* 黯淡的,阴郁的. ~ **sack** 〔美口〕冒失鬼. **-ly** *ad.*

sad·den [ˈsædn] *vt.* 使悲哀,使悲伤;使阴郁;使黯淡. —*vi.* 悲伤(起来);阴郁(起来);黯淡起来. *Do not ~ your friends and gladden your enemies.* 勿使亲者痛仇者快.

sad·dle [ˈsædl] *n.* ①马鞍;(自行车等的)鞍.②(羊等的)带肋[脊]骨的肉.③鞍形架,鞍状物.④【地】鞍部;马鞍形山;鞍状构造.⑤【物】谐振曲线的凹谷.⑥【船】圆枕木;【机】凹座,轴鞍,鞍座板;滑动座架;滑板;锅炉座.⑦【电】电线杆的托架;【建】浮桥的托架;(门口的)踏板. *an axle ~* 【机】轴鞍. *a cylinder ~* 鞍形汽缸座. *the Gr. Saddle* (长江口外的)马鞍山群岛. ***be at home in the ~*** 善于骑马. ***be cast out of the ~*** 免职. ***for the ~*** (马)骑用的. ***get into the ~*** 骑上马;就职. ***in the ~*** 骑着马;在职;统辖着,控制着,掌着权. ***lost the ~*** 从马上摔下来. ***put the ~ on the right [wrong] horse*** ①责备应该[不该]责备的人.②夸奖应该[不该]夸奖的人. — *vt.* ①加鞍,上鞍.②给背上,使负担(责任等). *~ sb. with a task* 使某人担负某一任务. ~**back** ①鞍状峰.②【建】两山头房顶.③【动】鞍背动物;黑背鸥;北海豹. ~**-backed** *a.* ①鞍状的;(动物等)背部呈鞍形的.②(鸟、鱼)背部有鞍状花纹的.③【地】有鞍部的. ~**-bag** 鞍囊,马褡裢. ~ **block (anesthesia)** 【医】鞍基麻醉〔产妇分娩时的腰脊麻醉,有久乘鞍马的麻木感觉〕. ~**-bow** 鞍的前穹;鞍的后穹. ~**-cloth** 鞍垫[褥]. ~**function** 【数】鞍式函数. ~**-horse** 骑用马. ~ **roof** 【建】两山头房顶. ~ **shoe** 〔美〕鞍背鞋〔深色鞋背和白色鞋帮的皮鞋〕. ~ **soap** 皮革皂. ~ **sore** 鞍疮. ~**-tree** ①鞍框.②【植】(北美)鞍叶桉(树);美国鹅掌楸. **-less** *a.*

sad·dler [ˈsædlə] *n.* ①鞍工,马具师;马具制造[贩卖]人.②【军】(骑兵团的)鞍工兵.③〔美俚〕骑用马.

sad·dler·y [ˈsædləri] *n.* ①〔总称〕鞍具;马具.②(放)马具室.③马具店;马具业.

Sad·du·cee [ˈsædjusi:] *n.* 撒都该人〔基督时代犹太教中以僧侣、贵族为主的派别中的人,只承认摩西五书之成文法而不承认传说律法及复活、来世等教义〕. **-an** *a.* 撒都该人的. **-ism** *n.*

sa·dhe [ˈsɑ:di:, ˈtsɑ:-] *n.* 〔Heb.〕希伯来语字母表的第十八个字母(= tsadi).

sa·dhu [ˈsɑ:du:] *n.* (印度的)圣人,哲人;苦行高僧,苦行者,禁欲主义者.

Sa·die [ˈseidi] *n.* 塞迪〔女子名, Sara(h) 的昵称〕.

sad·i·ron [ˈsædaiən] *n.* (实心)熨斗,烙铁.

sa·dism [ˈsɑ:dizm] *n.* ①【心】(对异性的)残暴色情狂,施虐淫. *(opp.* masochism*)*.②〔美〕残忍癖. **sa·dist** *n., a.* 残暴色情狂者(的),施虐淫者(的);〔美〕有残忍癖者(的). **sa·dis·tic** [-ˈdistik] *a.*

sad·ness [ˈsædnis] *n.* ①悲哀,悲伤,忧愁,忧伤.②愁眉苦脸,心境恶劣,心情恶劣.③认真. ***in sober [good] ~*** 认真地.

sad·o·mas·o·chism [ˌseidəuˈmæsəkizəm; ˌsædəuˈmæzə-] *n.* 【心,医】施虐一受虐狂. **-chist** *n.* **-chis·tic** *a.*

sae [sei] *ad.* 〔Scot.〕= so.

SAF = Strategic Air Force 〔美〕战略空军.

sa·fa·ri [səˈfɑ:ri] *n.* (徒步)旅行(队),(科学考察,游猎)远征(队)〔特指在非洲东部〕.

safe [seif] *a.* ①安全的,安稳的;无危险的.②确实的,一定的.③安全,平安〔作 *arrive, come* 等的表语用〕.④谨慎的,稳健的,可靠的;小心翼翼的.⑤【棒球】不会死的,安全的〔安抵某垒的〕*(opp.* out*)*.⑥【自】稳定的. *I saw him ~ home.* 我送他平平安安地到了家里. *It is ~ to get warmer as the day goes on.* 天气确实一天比一天暖和了. *He is ~ to get in.* 他肯定会当选. *get a person ~* 抓牢某人. *a ~ [good] catch* 【棒球】灵巧的接球员. *a ~ first* 稳拿第一的人. *S- bind, ~ find.* 藏得牢,找得着. ***be ~ from*** *(attack; infection)* 没有受到(攻击、传染)的危险. ***It is ~ to say that …*** 不妨说,说…准不会错. ***on the ~ side*** 谨慎[安全,可靠]地 *(It's best to err on the ~ side.* 即使错,最好也错在谨慎上面). ***play ~*** 采取四平八稳的办法. *~* ***and sound*** 平安无恙,安全. —*n.* ①保险箱,安全容器,纱厨,纱罩;〔美俚〕冰箱.②马鞍防擦皮. ~**-blowing** 爆破保险箱进行盗窃. ~**-conduct** ①*n.* (特指战时的)通行证,(军用)护照;安全证〔免受逮捕或伤害〕.②*vt.* 发护照给;护送,保卫. ~ **cracking** 撬盗保险箱. ~ **deposit** 保险仓库,信托仓库. ~**-deposit** *a.* 安全保管的 (*a ~-deposit company* 信托公司. *a ~-deposit box [vault]* 银行地下室中备人租用的保险箱). ~**guard** ①保护,捍卫,守护.②防护设施,装置;安全保护物,防护物 *(against)*.③卫兵;警卫船.④通行证;(军用)护照,安全证〔免受逮捕或伤害〕(= ~-conduct).⑤【机】护轮轨条;排障器.⑥保护措施,保证条款.⑦(美反弹道导弹系统的)卫兵式导弹 (*~guarding duties* 〔英〕保护关税. *~-guard against* 防止). ~**keeping** 保护,保管 (*be in ~-keeping with sb.* 在某人处保管着). ~ **light**【摄】(暗房用)安全灯. ~ **load** 【工】安全载荷. ~ **one** =~ **'un** 【赛马】包跑第一的马,稳赢的马. ~ **operation** 安全操作. ~ **seat** (候选人准能被选出的)可靠的选举区. ~ **winner** 稳赢的人[马]. **-ly** *ad.*

sefe·ty [seifti] *n.* ①安全;平安,稳妥,保险.②(枪等的)保险器,安全瓣;〔口〕低座自行车 (= ~-bicycle).③安全设备,保险装置.④【棒球】安全打. *public ~* 公安. *~ explosive* 安全炸药. *a gun at ~* 上了保险的枪. *a ~ device [apparatus]* 保险装置. *There is ~ in numbers.* 人多保险;大家一致行动起来成功的希望较大. *coefficient [factor] of ~* 安全系数. ***flee for ~*** 避难. ***in ~*** 平安地. ***play for ~*** 稳扎稳打,谨慎行事. ***S- first!*** 安全第一! ***Seek ~ in flight*** 避难. ***with ~*** 安全地,平安地. ~ **action** 保安措施. ~**-arresting** 安全制动. ~ **belt** 安全带;【海】救生带. ~ **bicycle** (低座的)安全自行车. ~ **check** 安全检查. ~ **curtain** (戏院的)消防幕. ~ **cut-off** 保安开关. ~ **cut out** 保安断路器. ~ **film** (电影等用)不燃性[安全]胶片. ~ **fuse** 【电】安全熔断器,保险丝;保险信管,安全导火线. ~ **glass** 不碎玻璃(= triplex glass). ~ **island [zone]** (马路中间的)安全岛[地带]. ~ **lamp** (矿山用)安全灯. ~**-light** 【摄】(暗室用)安全灯. ~ **match** 安全火柴. ~ **pin** 保险销,安全销,别针. ~ **razor** 保险剃刀. ~ **relay** 保安继电器,闭销继电器. ~ **valve** 保险阀;〔喻〕缓和紧张状态的手段 (*sit on the ~ valve* 按住保险阀;压住性子;采取高压性的权宜措施). ~ **switch** 紧急开关,保险开关. ~ **zone** = ~ island.

saf·fi·an [ˈseifiən] *n.* 一种着色的特制山羊革,摩洛哥革 (=~ leather).

saf·flow·er [ˈsæflauə] *n.* ①【植】红花.②红花染料. ~ **oil** 红花油.

saf·fron [ˈsæfrən] *n., a.* ①【植】藏红花(色的),番红花(色的).②深黄(色的),橘黄(色的). ~ **oil** 藏红花油.

~-tritonia【植】观音兰. **-y** *a.*
S.Afr. = South Africa(n).
saf·ra·nin(e) [ˈsæfrənin] *n.*【化】(碱性)藏红(染料),盐基桃花.
saf·role [ˈseifrəul] *n.*【化】黄樟脑,黄樟素.
sag [sæg] *vi.* ①(桥、梁等)陷下,压弯;(门)成一边高一边低状;(蜡烛等)弯曲;(绳、天花板等)松弛,下垂;(裙子下摆等)松垂,弛垂;(土地等)下陷,陷没. ②(物价等)下跌. ③〔喻〕委顿;消衰;(情绪)低落;疲沓,松懈. ④【海】漂流(特指船向下风流去). — *vt.* 使下陷,压弯;使下垂〔下落〕,【海】使漂流. — *n.* ①弯下,下垂;下沉,下陷. ②垂度. ③(物价的)下跌. ④【海】随风漂流.
sa·ga [ˈsɑːgə] *n.* ①(中世纪冰岛或挪威的)散文体叙事〔故事〕;北欧英雄传说. ②〔口〕长篇故事;冒险故事,英雄故事. ③〔多卷本〕家世小说〔= ~ novel〕.
sa·ga·cious [səˈgeiʃəs] *a.* ①聪明的,明智的,敏锐的;精明的. ②(动物等)灵敏的,〔特指〕嗅觉敏锐的. **-ly** *ad.* **-ness** *n.*
sa·gac·i·ty [səˈgæsiti] *n.* 聪明,明智;敏锐,精明.
sag·a·more [ˈsægəmɔː] *n.* 北美印第安部落的首长〔次于酋长的二头目〕.
SAGE = semiautomatic ground environment 半自动地面防空警备体系.
Sage [seidʒ] *n.* 塞奇〔姓氏〕.
sage[1] [seidʒ] *a.* ①聪明的,明智的,贤明的;精明的. ②〔谑〕象煞聪明的;道貌岸然的. — *n.*〔常谑〕圣人,贤人,哲人. *the ~ of the village*〔谑〕三家村学究. ***seven ~s*** 希腊七贤〔有几种说法,通常指 *Solon, Thales, Pittacus, Bias, Chilo, Periander* 及 *Cleobulus*〕. **-ly** *ad.* **-ness** *n.*
sage[2] [seidʒ] *n.*【植】①鼠尾草(属);鼠尾草〔洋苏〕叶〔药用、食用〕. ②一串红〔又称 Scarlet~〕. ③ = sagebrush. **~ cock**【动】雄性艾草鸡. **~ green** 灰绿色. **~ grouse**【动】(北美西部荒漠地带的)艾草鸡. **~ hen**【动】母艾草鸡;〔S- H-〕〔美俚〕Nevada 州人的浑名. **~ oil** 洋苏叶油. **~ rat** 原鼠;〔美俚〕艾原居民. **~ tea**【药】鼠尾草煎汁〔用作健胃剂〕.
sage·brush [ˈseidʒbrʌʃ] *n.* ①蒿(属). ②【植】山艾〔美国西南荒漠地带所产的一种灰绿色灌木〕. **S- state**〔美〕*Nevada* 州的别名.
sag·ger, sag·gar [ˈsægə] *n.* ①(陶瓷工业用的)烧箱,烧盆. ②(制造烧箱的)粘土. — *vt.* 用烧箱〔盆〕烘.
sag·gy [ˈsægi] *a.* *(-gi·er, -gi·est)* 倾斜的;松弛的;下垂的.
Sagh·a·lien [ˌsægəˈliːn] *n.* 库页岛(= Sakhalin).
Sa·git·ta [səˈdʒitə] *n.* ①【天】天箭(星)座. ②〔s-〕【数】矢. ③〔s-〕【动】箭虫.
sag·it·tal [ˈsædʒitl] *a.* ①箭的,矢状的. ②【解】颅顶骨矢状合缝的;纵分的;矢形面的,纵分面的. **-ly** *ad.*
Sag·it·tar·i·us [ˌsædʒiˈteəriəs] *n.*【天】人马(星)座.
sag·it·tar·y [ˈsædʒitəri] *n.* *(pl. -tar·ies)* ①弓箭手. ②【希神】半人半马的怪物. ③【天】人马(星座)(= centaur).
sag·it·tate [ˈsædʒiteit] *a.*【植】镞形的,箭头形的.
sa·go [ˈseigəu] *n.* *(pl. ~s)* ①西〔壳,谷〕米〔用西米椰子茎髓做成的淀粉质食品〕. ②【植】西〔壳,谷〕米椰子(= ~ palm).
Sa·hap·tin [sɑːˈhæptin] *n.* ①*(pl. ~(s))* 萨哈泼丁人〔北美印第安一个部族集团的成员〕. ②萨哈泼丁语. ③由萨哈泼丁语和内珀西 *(Nez Percé)* 语组成的语族. 亦作 **sa·hap·tian** [-tiən].
Sa·ha·ra [səˈhɑːrə] *n.* ①(非洲)撒哈拉大沙漠. ②〔s-〕沙漠,荒野. **Saha·ran, Saha·rian, Sahar·ic** *a.*
Sa·hib [ˈsɑːhib] *n.* ①大人,老爷〔旧时印度人对欧洲人的尊称〕;〔S-〕先生(=Mr., Sir, 用于职称或人名后): *colonel S-* 上校先生;*Jones S-* 琼斯先生. ②〔口〕绅士: *a pucka [pukka] ~*〔常谑〕真正的欧洲人;*Jone S-* 地道的绅士.
said [sed] say 的过去式及过去分词. — *a.* 上述的. *the ~ witness* 该证人.
Sa·i·da [ˈsɑːidɑː] *n.* 赛伊达〔即 Sidon 西顿,黎巴嫩港市〕.
sai·ga [ˈsaigə] *n.*【动】高鼻羚羊〔赛加羚羊〕*(Saiga tatarica)*〔产于俄罗斯东南部和西伯利亚西南部草原〕.
Sai·gon [saiˈgɔn] *n.* 西贡〔越南港市,胡志明市的旧称〕.
sail [seil] *n.* ①帆,〔集合词〕(船上)全部风帆,全帆(= sails). ②帆船;〔集合名词〕船只(= ships);【空】滑翔机. ③〔*pl.*〕缝帆员;〔英海军俚〕帆具官. ④扬帆行驶,航行. ⑤航行距离,航程;航行力. ⑥帆形物;(风车等的)翼板;〔诗〕(鸟的)翼;(鹦鹉螺的)触手. *a set ~* 已张开的风帆. *a riding ~* 停泊用小帆. *a ~ taken aback* (逆风吹翻过来的)反帆,逆帆. *a ~ well taut* 绷紧了的帆. *a shoulder-of-mutton [leg-of-mutton] ~* 三角帆. *S-ho!* 看,有船! *a fleet of twenty ~* 二十只船的一个船队〔舰队〕. *ten days' ~ from ...* 离…有十天航程. ***at full ~(s)*** 张起所有的帆;开足马力. ***back [brace aback] the ~s*** 使成反帆〔逆帆〕. ***be under ~*** 在航行中. ***bend the ~*** 将(帆)绑在桁上〔支索上〕. ***brail [clue] up a ~*** 卷帆. ***bring a ~ to*** 将帆绑在桁上. ***carry a press of ~*** 张满风帆. ***carry a ~*** 张着风帆. ***carry ~ well*** 张满风帆. ***crowd [clap on] (all) ~(s)*** 扯起异常多(所有)的风帆. ***douse ~*** = strike ~. ***fill the ~s*** 使帆吃满风,(风)满帆. ***furl a ~*** 叠帆,收卷风帆. ***get in a ~*** 收下一张帆. ***get under ~*** 开船. ***go for a ~*** 乘船游览. ***haul down a ~*** 落帆,下帆. ***haul in one's ~s*** 退出比赛,回避. ***hoist a ~*** 张起一张帆. ***hoist ~*** 扯起所有风帆;〔喻〕逃跑. ***in full ~*** 张满帆的. ***in ~*** 坐着帆船. ***keep full ~s*** 张着所有的风帆. ***lower a ~*** 落下一张帆. ***lower one's ~*** (下帆)投降;认输,甘拜下风. ***make ~*** 急加帆;扬帆,出航,开船;〔口〕逃跑. ***more ~ than ballast*** 华而不实. ***put on [pack (on)] all ~*** 扯起所有的帆;竭尽全力. ***set ~ for*** 开船,驶往…,乘船往…. ***shorten ~*** 减(少风)帆;抑制(欲望、野心等),放慢速度. ***solar ~*** 太阳反射器〔在星际飞行中利用太阳能的一种设备〕. ***spread the ~s*** 张帆. ***strike ~***〔为行敬礼或因急风〕急下帆;屈服,投降;认输;减少排场. ***take in ~*** = shorten ~. ***take the wind out of one's ~s [the ~s of]*** 抢(他船)上风;〔喻〕先发制人. ***trim the [one's] ~s*** 调整风帆;临机应变地处置,机动处理. ***under ~*** 扬帆而驶;航行中. ***with all ~s set*** = ***with every ~ set out*** 张起全部风帆. — *vi.* ①扬帆行驶,航行;开船;坐船旅行. ②(水禽)游泳;(鸟、云等)轻快地飞,浮游. ③(尤指妇女)步态优美地走. — *vt.* ①扬帆行驶,航行. ②驾驶(船);漂浮(玩具船). ③(鸟等)飞行(空中). ***~ a race*** 进行帆船比赛. ***~ against the wind*** 逆风驶船;处逆境;违抗潮流. ***~ away*** ①〔美〕慌忙启程. ②逸散,挥发. ***~ before the wind*** 顺风驶船;一帆风顺;走运,处顺境. ***~ close to [near] the wind*** ①切风〔几乎逆风〕行驶. ②俭约地处事,简朴地生活. ③冒昧地行动;几乎犯法〔违背道德准则〕. ***~ in*** ①驶入港口;〔口〕毅然出面(*~ in and settle the dispute* 毅然出面排解纠纷). ②开始行动;攻击,责叱. ***~ in company*** = ~ under convoy. ***~ in the same boat*** 同乘一船;干同一工作,有同一处境,抱同样见解. ***~ into*** ①大摇大摆地〔庄严地〕走进,突然闯入. ②〔俚〕攻击,辱骂,殴打. ③精力充沛,效率高地投入(某项工作). ***~ large*** 满帆行驶. ***~ on one's bottom*** 自主地航行;〔喻〕独立自主. ***~ one's own boat*** 独立自主地行动;走自己的路. ***~ out*** 开船. ***~ over*** 跳过;【建】突出. ***~ right before the wind*** 顺风行驶;一帆风顺. ***~ round*** 返航. ***~ under convoy*** 在护送下结队航行. ***~ under false colours*** (海盗等)挂着冒牌旗子航行. ***~ under the Chinese flag*** 搭乘中国船. **~ arm** 风车翼板. **~ axle** 转动风车翼板的轴. **~board** 小型风帆船,风帆滑水板. **~-boat**〔美〕帆船(=〔英〕-ing boat). **~cloth**

S

帆布；篷布；苫布．~**-fish**【动】东方旗鱼〔背鳍如帆〕．~**-flying**【空】滑翔飞行．~**-maker** 缝帆员；〔英海军〕缝帆兵；〔美海军〕掌帆长．~ **needle** 缝帆用的针．~**-plane** ①*n.* 滑翔机．②*vi.* 滑翔飞行．

sail·er [ˈseilə] *n.* 帆船．*a good [fast]* ~ 速度快的船．*a heavy [bad, poor, slow]* ~ 速度慢的船．

sail·ing [ˈseiliŋ] *n.* ①扬帆行驶，航行；开船．②航行方法，航海术；滑翔．*fixed* ~*s* 定期航行．*Hours of* ~ *will be announced daily.* 开船时刻每日公布．*aerial* ~ 航空术，飞行．*current* ~ 潮流航法．*great-circle* ~ 大圈航法．*Mercator's* ~ 马氏航法，渐长纬度航法．*middle-latitude* ~ 中分纬度航法．*parallel* ~ 等距航法．*plane* ~ 平面航法．***plain [smooth]*** ~ 一帆风顺，轻而易举．~**-boat** 〔美〕帆船．~ **flight**【空】滑翔飞行．~**-master** 〔英〕(游艇的)、〔美〕(军舰的)领航员．~ **orders** 〔*pl.*〕(给船长的)开船命令．~ **ship,** ~ **vessel** 帆船．

sail·or [ˈseilə] *n.* ①海员，航海者；水手，水兵．②〔美〕老兄．③〔口〕= ~ hat. *a leading* ~〔英〕一等水兵．*an able [full]* ~〔英〕二等水兵．*an ordinary* ~ 新水兵．*a bad [good]* ~ 晕船[不晕船]的人．*What kind of (a)* ~ *are you?* 你晕船不晕船？~ **boy** 小水手；见习水手．~ **collar** 水手领〔领口背部宽而方〕．~ **hat** 水手帽；狭檐草帽〔妇女或儿童用〕~**'s book** 航海指南．~**'s choice** 〔美〕黑棘鲷鱼；海摩伦鱼．~**s' home** 海员旅舍〔收费低廉〕．~**'s knot** 水手结，水手领结．~ **suit** 男童的水手装．

sail·or·ing [ˈseiləriŋ] *n.* 海员生活；航海(生涯)；水手工作．

sail·or·ly [ˈseiləli] *a.* 象水手的．

sail·or·man [ˈseiləmæn] *n.* 〔谑〕= sailor.

sain [sein] *vt.* 〔古，方〕划十字于…之上以祈福避灾．

sain·foin [ˈseinfɔin] *n.*【植】红豆草，驴喜豆．

Sains·bury [ˈseinzbəri] *n.* 塞恩斯伯里〔姓氏〕．

saint [seint, 弱 sənt] *n.* ①神圣的人；圣者；(教会正式尊崇的)圣徒．②道德崇高的人；圣人；圣者[徒]似的人．③(被认为已进入天堂的)死者．④上帝的选民，基督教教徒．⑤〔S-〕[sənt, sint, snt]〔用于人名，地名前，单数略作 **St., S.** 复数略作 **SS** 或 **Sts.**〕圣…．*I am no* ~. 我不是圣人．*He is a* ~ *of a man.* 他是一个圣人．***All saints' Day*** 万圣节〔11月1日〕．***It would provoke [try the patience of] a*** ~ 这话[事、行为等]连圣徒听了都会生气〔葬礼用语〕．***keep St. Monday***〔英〕星期天喝醉星期一请假．***play the*** ~ 假装信徒．***St. Agnes's Eve*** 圣女埃格尼斯节前夜〔一月二十日之夜，传说少女在这天夜晚行某种仪式就可以看到未来丈夫的模样〕．***St. Andrew's cross*** X形十字架(形)．***St. Anthony's cross*** T 形十字架(形)．***St. Anthony's fire*** 皮肤病，皮炎；丹毒；麦角中毒．***St. Bernard*** 圣比纳品种救护犬．***St. George's cross*** 白底红色希腊教会十字架(形)．***St. James's*** (伦敦)圣詹姆士宫；圣詹姆士宫附近的高级住宅区；英国宫廷．***St. John's-bread***【植】稻子豆(= carob)．***St. John's-wort***【植】小连翘．***St. Lubbock's Day***〔英〕(St. Lubbock 法案中所规定的)公假日．***St. Luke's summer = St. Martin's summer*** 晚秋〔10月18日前后〕风和日暖的天气．***St. Michael*** (大西洋东部 *Azores* 群岛的)子少皮薄的桔子．***St. Peter's chair*** 教皇的职位．***St. Vitus's dance***【医】舞蹈病〔主要指小孩的抽搐〕．***the departed*** ~ 蒙上帝召唤弃我而去的故人(指死者)．— *vt.* 〔通例用被动语态〕(教会正式宣布)…列[尊]为圣徒；把…视为圣徒[圣者]．

Saint-Denis [seint ˈdenis] 圣但尼〔留尼汪岛(法)首府〕．

saint·dom [ˈseintdəm] *n.* ①圣徒身分[地位]．②〔集合词〕圣徒．③圣洁．

saint·ed [seintid] *a.* ①列为圣徒的，成为神圣的．②神圣的．③升了天的〔称呼死者的委婉说法〕．*my* ~ *mother* 先母．

saint·ess [seintis] *n.* 女圣徒，圣女．

saint·hood [ˈseinthud] *n.* = saintdom.

saint·ly [seintli] *a.* 象圣徒的；道德高尚的；神圣的；圣洁的．

Saints·bury [ˈseintsbəri] *n.* 森茨伯里〔姓氏〕．

saint's-day [ˈseintsdei] *n.* 纪念某一圣徒的日子〔节假日〕．

saint·ship [ˈseintʃip] *n.* 圣徒的地位[品格]．

Saint-Si·mon [sæŋsiˈmɔŋ; F. sɛ̃simɔ̃], **C.H.** 圣西门〔1760—1825，法国空想社会主义者〕．

Saint-Si·mon·ian [sən-siˈməuniən] *n., a.* 圣西门主义者(的)；空想社会主义者(的)．**Saint-Si·mon·ism** *n.* 圣西门主义，空想社会主义．

Saint-Si·mon·ist *n.* = Saint-Simonian *(n.)*.

Sai·pan [saiˈpɑːn] *n.* ①塞班岛〔西太平洋〕．②塞班〔马里亚纳群岛、加罗林群岛、马绍尔群岛(美托管)首府〕．

saith [seθ] says 的古体．

sake [seik] *n.* 缘故，理由，目的，关系．★现常在 for the ~ of ..., for ... 's ~中应用；修饰sake 的名词的尾音是[s] 时，常省去所有格的 s: *for goodness'* ~. *for the* ~ *of health* 为了健康．***art for art's*** ~ 为艺术而艺术．***for all [both] our*** ~***s*** 为了大家[你我双方]．***for any*** ~ 无论如何，好歹．***for appearance'*** ~ = ***for the*** ~ ***of appearance*** 为了面子，面子上．***for form's*** ~ 形式上．***for God's [Christ's, goodness', heaven's, mercy's]*** ~千万，务请．***for old*** ~***'s*** ~ 为了老交情，看从前交情的面上．***for pete's*** ~〔俚〕= for God's ~. ***for the*** ~ ***of [for one's*** ~ ***]*** 为…起见，为了…．***Sakes (alive)!***〔方，美俚〕天呀！吓我一跳！***without*** ~无缘无故，毫无理由地．

sa·ke, sa·ké, sa·ki [ˈsɑːki] *n.* 〔Jap.〕酒．

sa·ker [ˈseikə] *n.*【动】猎隼〔用于放鹰行猎〕．

Sa·kha·lin [ˌsækəˈliːn; 俄 səxaˈljin] *n.* 萨哈林岛〔即库页岛〕．

sa·ki [ˈsɑːki] *n.*【动】(南美)粗尾猿．

sa·ki·a [ˈsækiə] *n.* 〔Arab.〕水车〔用于农田灌溉〕．

Sal [sɑːl] *n.*【植】〔印度〕娑罗双树；柳安(亦作 Saltree)．

sal[1] [sæl] *n.* ①【化、药】盐．②【地】硅铝带，硅铝质．~ **ammoniac** 氯化铵，硇砂．~ **soda** 苏打，十水(合)碳酸钠．

sal[2] [sæl] *n.* 〔俚〕= salary.

Sa·la [ˈsɑːˈlɑː] *n.* 撒拉族，撒拉族人．

sa·laam [səˈlɑːm] *n.* 额手礼〔伊斯兰教用右手摩额鞠躬的礼〕；敬礼，敬意．— *vt., vi.* (向…)行额手礼．

sal·a·bil·i·ty [ˌseiləˈbiliti] *n.* 畅销；销路．

sal·a·ble [ˈseiləbl] *a.* 有销路的；畅销的．

sa·la·cious [səˈleiʃəs] *a.* ①(人)好色的，淫荡的．②(书、画、写作、言谈)诲淫的．**-ly** *ad.* ~**-ness** *n.* **sa·lac·i·ty** *n.*

sal·ad [ˈsæləd] *n.* ①色拉〔凉拌杂菜〕；色拉用蔬菜．②〔美、方〕(特指)莴笋，生菜．~ **days** 没有经验的少年时代，少不更事的时期．~ **dressing** 色拉用调料〔植物油、醋、香料等的混合〕．~ **oil** 色拉油〔多用净纯橄榄油〕．

Sa·lade [səˈlɑːd] *n.* = sallet.

sal·a·man·der [ˈsæləmændə] *n.* ①(传说中的)火蛇；火怪，火精．②〔俗〕能耐高热的人[物]，不怕炮火的军人；吞火的魔术师．③【动】蝾螈．④拨火棒．⑤〔美俚〕耐火保险箱〔又称~safe〕．⑥【徽】火兽．⑦〔口〕(烤肉或烘糕饼等用的)烤盘．⑧【冶】(高炉)炉底铁块．

sal·a·man·drine, -dri·an [ˌsæləˈmændrin, -driən] *a.* ①象火蛇[蝾螈等]一样的．②耐火的，耐热的．— *n.* ①耐火物，耐热的人．②蝾螈类．

sa·la·mi [səˈlɑːmi(ː)] *n.* (意大利式)蒜味咸腊肠．

sal·an·gane [ˈsæləŋgein] *n.*【鸟】(筑食用"燕窝"的)金丝燕．

sa·lar·i·at(e) [səˈlɛəriæt] *n.* 薪水阶级，薪水阶层．

sal·a·ried [ˈsælərid] *a.* ①拿薪金的．②有薪金的．*a* ~ *man* 靠薪水生活者．*a* ~ *office* 有薪金的职位．

sal·a·ry [ˈsæləri] *n.* 薪水，薪金，薪俸. ★ salary 指公职人员、职员等按年、按月计算的"年薪"或"月薪"；工人等拿的"工资"叫做 wages 一般按日、按时或按件计算. *a ~ man = a salaried* man. ***draw one's ~*** 领薪水. — *vt.* 〔常用被动语态〕发…薪水，付…薪水.

sale [seil] *n.* ①卖，出卖，出售. ②拍卖；贱卖(尤指季末存货的大减价). ③销路. ④销数，销售额. ⑤【法】买卖契约. *a ~ for [on] cash = a cash ~* 现金出售. *a ~ on credit [account]* 赊销. *a public [an open] ~* 拍卖. *forced ~* 强制拍卖. *a trade ~* 同行拍卖. *the season of ~s.* 出清存货的季节. *a grand [bargain] ~* 大廉价. ***at ~*** (书店同行间)照定价七折. ***dispose of (sth.) by ~*** 卖掉(某物). ***dull of ~*** 滞销，销路不好. ***easy of ~*** 畅销，销路好. ***find no ~*** 无销路. ***have [meet with, command] a ready [good] ~*** 畅销. ***for [on] ~*** 出售(的). ***no ~*** 〔美俚〕不；我不赞成，我不来. ***not for ~*** 非卖品；不出售的. ***offer for ~*** 供应销售. ***on ~*** = for ~. ***put up for ~*** 拿出拍卖. ***~ by area*** 【林】场地上立木全部出卖. ***~ by bulk*** 估堆卖，成批出售. ***~ of work*** (教友等举行慈善性质的)义卖. ***~ or [and] return*** 剩货保退〔指批发给零售商的货物〕. **~ price** 廉价. **~-ring** 聚集在拍卖人周围的人. **~-room** 〔英〕= **~sroom** 〔美〕 **~s departments** 营业部. **~s resistance** 〔美俚〕无销路，无定购户，滞销，(公众的)不愿购买. **~s talk** ①兜售的话. ②〔喻〕游说. **~s tax** 营业税. **~ yard** 买卖家畜的围场.

sale·a·ble [ˈseiləbl] *a.* = salable.

sal·ep [ˈsælep] *n.* 色列普淀粉〔从兰科植物球根提制，可供药用及食用〕.

sal·e·ra·tus [ˌsæliˈreitəs] *n.* 〔美〕(烹调用)小苏打，发酵粉.

sales·clerk [ˈseilzklɑːk] *n.* 〔美〕= salesperson.

sales·girl [ˈseilzgəːl] *n.* 〔美〕女售货员，女店员.

sales·la·dy [ˈseilzleidi] *n.* 〔美〕= saleswoman.

sales·man [ˈseilzmən] *n.* ***(pl. -men)*** ①售货员，店员. ②〔美〕推销员，跑街. *a dead ~* 〔英〕肉店，屠户. *an insurance ~* 〔美〕保险公司的跑街. **-ship** *n.* 售货术；推销术.

sales·per·son [seilspəːsn] *n.* ***(pl. -people)*** 〔美〕①店员，营业员，售货员. ②推销员.

sales·room [ˈseilzrum] *n.* 〔美〕①货品陈设室；售货处. ②拍卖处，拍卖物.

sales·woman [ˈseilzwumən] *n.* ***(pl. -wom·en)*** ①女店员. ②〔美〕女推销员，女跑街.

sali- *comb. f.* 盐: *sali*ferous.

Sa·li·an [ˈseiliən] *a.* ①【古罗马】战神祭司的. ②(四世纪时居于 Ijssel 河沿岸、作为法兰克人一支的)撒利族的. *a ~ hymn* 战神赞歌. — *n.* 撒利族.

Sal·ic [ˈsælik] *a.* ①撒利族的. ②撒利人法典的. **~ law** 【法】撒利族法典〔尤指其中禁止妇女继承土地的规定〕；撒利法〔法国和西班牙禁止女性继承王位的法律〕.

sal·i·cin [ˈsælisin] *n.* 【化】水杨甙；柳醇.

sal·i·cyl [ˈsælisil] *n.* 【化】水杨基，邻羟苄基.

sa·lic·y·late [sæˈlisileit] *n.* 【化】水杨酸盐〔脂〕. — *vt.* 加水杨酸.

sal·i·cyl·ic [ˌsæliˈsilik] *a.* 【化】水杨酸的. **~ acid** 水杨酸，**~ aldehyde** 水杨醛. **~ amide** 水杨酰胺.

sa·li·ence, -cy [ˈseiljəns, -si] *n.* ①凸出，突起. ②跃起，跳跃. ③喷出，射出，发出. ④【军】突出部，突角. ⑤〔喻〕特征，特点，特色，卓越，显著.

sa·li·ent [ˈseiljənt] *a.* ①显著的，卓越的，惹人注目的. ②凸出的，突起的. ③跃起的，跳跃的. ④(泉水等)喷出的，涌出的. ⑤【徽】前脚腾空作跳跃状的. — *n.* 凸角；(筑城)突出部. *a ~ feature* (海岸线、脸形的)突出部分. *~ features [points, characteristics]* 特色，特征，特点. **-ly** *ad.*

sa·li·en·ti·an [ˌseiliˈenʃiən] *n.* 【动】无尾目动物〔包括蛙、蟾等〕. — *a.* 无尾目的.

sa·lif·er·ous [səˈlifərəs] *a.* (地层)含〔产〕盐的.

sal·i·fi·a·ble [ˈsælifaiəbl] *a.* 【化】能变成盐的.

sal·i·fi·ca·tion [ˌsælifiˈkeiʃən] *n.* 【化】成盐作用.

sal·i·fy [ˈsælifai] *vt.* ①使变咸，使含有盐分；【化】盐化. ②使成盐；使与盐化合.

Sa·li·i [sæliai] *n. pl.* 撒利族法兰克人.

sa·lim·e·ter [sæˈlimitə] *n.* 【化】盐(液比)重计.

sa·li·na [səˈlainə] *n.* 【地】盐沼，盐地，盐湖，盐碱滩.

sa·line [ˈseilain, səˈlain] *a.* ①盐的；含盐的；盐性的，咸的. ②盐渍的. — [səˈlain] *n.* ①盐沼，咸湖，盐泉；盐皮；盐碱滩；盐田，盐地，制盐所，盐场. ②【医】盐水；含盐泻药. *~ matter* 盐分. *~ taste* 咸味. *normal ~* 生理盐水.

sa·lin·i·ty [səˈliniti] *n.* 盐分；盐浓度，咸度；含盐量.

sal·i·nom·e·ter [ˌsæliˈnɔmitə] *n.* ①【化】盐(液比)重计，盐液密度(比重)计. ②【化】(电导)调浓器.

Sa·lique [səˈliːk] *a.* = Salic.

Salis·bur·y [ˈsɔːlzbəri] *n.* ①索尔兹伯里〔津巴布韦(原罗得西亚)首都〕. ②索尔兹伯里〔英国城市〕. ③(英格兰 Wiltshire 郡的)索尔兹伯里平原〔又称 ~ Plain〕. ***as plain as ~*** 明明白白地. **~ steak** 汉堡牛排，牛肉饼(= Hamburger).

Sa·lish [ˈseiliʃ] *n.* ①撒利希语族〔北美印第安语，包括十五个语支〕. ②讲此语族语言的人. ③"平头" 印第安人(= flathead). ④撒利希语. 亦作 **Sa·lish·an** [-ən].

sa·li·va [səˈlaivə] *n.* 涎，唾液. *eject ~* 吐唾沫.

sal·i·var·y [ˈsælivəri] *a.* (分泌)唾液的. *a ~ gland* 【解】涎腺，唾(液)腺.

sal·i·vate [ˈsæliveit] *vt., vi.* (使)分泌(过多)唾液，(使)流口水. **-va·tion** [ˌsæliˈveiʃən] *n.* 【医】流涎，多涎(症).

salle [sɑːl, sæl] *n.* 〔F.〕大厅. ***~ à manger*** [ˈsæləˈmɑ̃ːnʒei] 餐厅；茶室，咖啡室. ***~ d'attente*** [ˈsældæˈtɑ̃ːnt] (车站的)候车室.

sal·len·ders [ˈsæləndəz] *n. pl.* 马跗关节的干性皮疹.

sal·let [ˈsælit] *n.* 特指15世纪带护颈的轻盔.

sal·low[1] [ˈsæləu] *a.* (肤色)灰黄的. — *n.* 灰黄色，土色. — *vt., vi.* (使)成〔变成〕灰黄色. **-ish** *a.* 略带灰黄色的. **-ness** *n.*

sal·low[2] [ˈsæləu] *n.* ①【植】阔叶柳，黄华柳，山毛柳. ②柳枝，柳条.

sal·ly [ˈsæli] *n.* ①(被围军队的)突围，出击. ②远足；外出；旅行. ③(感情等的)迸发，突发. ④(脱口而出的)俏皮话，警句. ⑤戏谑，开玩笑，恶作剧. ⑨【建】凸出部；钝角. *make a ~ into* 到…去逛. *a ~ wit* 脱口而出的俏皮话〔警句〕. — *vi.* ①突围，冲出，出击 *(out)*. ②动身，出发 *(forth, off, out)*. **~ port** 【筑城】暗门，(碉堡等的)出击口；(备失事用的)太平门.

Sal·ly [ˈsæli] *n.* 萨莉〔女子名，Sarah 的昵称〕. **~ Lunn, s- lunn** 萨莉·伦恩饼〔一种趁热抹上黄油食用的茶点，源于1797年英国巴思(Bath)一位名叫萨利·伦恩的女子沿街出卖的甜饼〕.

sal·ma·gun·di [ˌsælməˈgʌndi] *n.* ①酸辣鱼肉杂烩〔意大利菜肴〕. ②〔喻〕杂凑，大杂烩.

sal·mi [ˈsælmi] *n.* 五香野味〔烧天鹨、鸫等，加大量调味烧烤后并以葡萄酒蒸煮〕.

salm·on [ˈsæmən] *n.* ***(pl. ~,*** 〔罕〕***~s)*** ①鲑，大麻哈鱼. ②鲑肉色，橙红色，淡红色. *chum [dog] ~* 大麻哈鱼. — *a.* 鲑肉色的，橙〔淡〕红色的. **~ colo(u)r** 鲑肉色，橙〔淡〕红色. **~ trout** 【鱼】①(一种似鲑的)鳟(= brown trout). ②硬头鳟 (= steel head).

sal·mo·nel·la [ˌsælməˈnelə] *n.* ***(pl. -nel·lae*** [-iː], ***-nel·la, -nel·las)*** 【生】沙门氏菌属.

sal·mo·nel·lo·sis [ˌsælməˈneləusis] *n.* 【医】沙门氏菌病〔沙门氏菌属引起的传染病〕.

sal·mo·noid [ˈsælmənɔid] *a.* 【动】①似鲑的. ②鲑鱼

属的,鲑亚目的〔包括鲑鱼、白鲑等〕. — *n.* 鲑科鱼;(尤指)鲑鱼.

sal·ol [ˈsæləul,-ɔːl] *n.* 【化】萨罗,水杨酸苯酯〔用作保护皮肤的药剂〕.

Sa·lo·me [səˈləumi] *n.* ①萨洛米〔女子名〕. ②【圣经】莎乐美〔希律王 (Herod) 之女,以其舞使希律王着迷,允其所请将施洗者约翰斩首并将首级赐给她,见马太福音〕. ③《莎乐美》〔王尔德 (Oscar Wilde) 根据圣经故事用法文写的剧本〕.

Sa·lo·mon·ic, Sa·lo·moni·an [ˌsæləˈmɔnik, -ˈməunjən] *a.* 所罗门 (Solomon) 王的,所罗门王似的.

sal·on [ˈsælɔ̃ːŋ] *n.* 〔F.〕①沙龙,客厅. ②(尤指巴黎资产阶级妇女客厅中举行的)招待会. ③名流集会. ④美术展览所; 〔the S-〕(每年举行一次在世美术家作品的)巴黎美术展览会. ⑤(营业性的)厅,院. *a beauty* ~ 美容院. *literary* ~*s* 文艺沙龙. ~ **music** 一种室内轻音乐.

Sa·lo·ni·ka, Sa·lo·ni·ca [səˈlɔnikə] *n.* 萨洛尼卡〔希腊港市〕.

sa·loon [səˈluːn] *n.* ①(旅馆、轮船等的)大厅,客厅. ②(旅客机的)客室; 〔英〕(火车的)客厅式豪华车厢〔又叫 ~ car, ~ carriage〕. ③大轿车〔又叫 ~ car = 〔美〕*sedan*〕. ④〔英〕高级酒店(= ~-bar);〔美〕酒吧 (= 〔英〕public house). ⑤〔英〕(公众出入的)…厅,…店,…场(等). *a dining* ~ 〔英〕餐车;〔美〕(轮船的)餐厅. *a* ~ *cabin* 头等舱. *a family* ~ 专用客车. *a refreshment* ~ 饮食店. *a hair-dressing* ~ = *a hair dresser's* ~ 理发店〔馆〕. *a shooting-*~ 靶子厅. ~ **deck** 头等船客专用甲板. ~**keeper** 〔美〕酒吧老板,酒店主人. ~ **pistol [rifle]** 打靶枪.

sa·loon·ist [səˈluːnist] *n.* ①〔美〕= saloon-keeper. ②酒吧的老主顾,酒店的常客.

sa·loop [səˈluːp] *n.* ①色列普茶〔用 salep 或 sassafras 做的热饮料〕. ②= salep.

Sal·op [ˈsæləp] *n.* 【动】英国希罗普郡 (Shropshire) 绵羊.

Sa·lo·pi·an [səˈləupiən, -pjən] *a.* ①希罗普郡 (Shropshire) 的. ②希罗普郡人的. ③Shrewsbury 公学的. — *n.* ①希罗普郡居民. ②Shrewsbury 公学的学生.

sal·pa [ˈsælpə] *n.* *(pl.* ~*s,-pae* [-piː]*)* 【动】萨尔帕属的被囊动物,萨尔帕. 亦作 **salp**.

sal·pi·glos·sis [ˌsælpiˈglɔsis] *n.* 喇叭舌草〔一种茄科观赏植物,原产南美智利等地〕.

sal·pin·gec·to·my [ˌsælpinˈdʒektəmi] *n.* *(pl. -mies)* 【医】输卵管切除术.

salping- *comb. f.* 【医】输卵管的,耳咽管的: *salping*itis.

sal·pin·gi·tis [ˌsælpinˈdʒaitis] *n.* 【医】输卵管炎;耳咽管炎.

salpingo- *comb. f.* = salping.

sal·pin·gos·to·my [ˌsælpinˈgɔstəmi] 【医】输卵管造口术.

sal·pinx [ˈsælpiŋks] *n.* *(pl.* **sal·pin·ges** [-pindʒiːz]*)* ①【解】输卵管 (= Fallopian tube). ②咽鼓管,欧氏管 (=Eustachian tube). — **sal·pin·gi·an** [-ˈpindʒiən] *a.*

sal·si·fy [ˈsælsifi] *n.* 【植】婆罗门参〔其根可食,有牡蛎的味道〕.

SALT [sɔːlt] = Strategic Arms Limitation Talks 限制战略武器会谈.

salt [sɔːlt] *n.* ①盐,食盐. ②【化】盐; 酸类和盐基化合物. ③〔*pl.*〕盐剂,药用盐,〔特指〕泻盐. (= Epsom ~s). ④俏皮话,讽刺;机智. ⑤要素,精华. ⑥趣味,滋味,风味,刺激(品). ⑦(老练的〔富有经验的〕) 水手〔通例叫 old ~〕. ⑧〔俚〕(餐桌上的) 小盐缸,盐瓶(=~-cellar). ⑨现实〔慎重、有保留〕的态度. ⑩盐沼;盐碱滩(= ~ marsh). *common [culinary, table]* ~ 食盐. *white* ~ 精盐. *a dose of* ~ 一付泻药. *smelling* ~*s* (提神的)嗅盐,碳酸铵. ***above [below, beneath, under] the*** ~ 坐上席〔下席〕〔从前长餐桌中间摆盐缸,上面一半算是上席〕;受〔不受〕尊敬. ***be faithful [true] to one's*** ~ 忠于自己的职位. ***cast [lay, put, throw, drop a pinch of]*** ~ ***on the tail of*** 诱捕; 巧妙地捕捉. ***earn one's*** ~ 自立,自食其力. ***eat sb.'s*** ~ = ***eat*** ~ ***with sb.*** 做某人的(食)客; 吃某人的饭; 依赖某人. ***in*** ~ 撒了盐的;盐腌的. ***not made of*** ~ 不是盐做的,遇水不溶的. ***spill*** ~ 把盐撒落在餐桌上〔被认为是恶兆〕. ***the*** ~ ***of the earth*** 社会中坚〔源出《圣经》〕. ***with a grain of*** ~ 有保留地,须打折扣的,须视为是夸大的 (*His statement must be taken with a grain of* ~. 他的话要打一个折扣听取〔不能全信〕.) ***worth one's*** ~ 称职,胜任,不是吃白饭的. — *a.* ①盐的,含盐份的. ②咸的, 有咸味的. ③盐腌的, 盐渍的. ④(土地等)灌进海水的; 生长于咸水中的. ⑤(眼泪等)饱含痛苦的. ⑥(俏皮话等)犀利的,痛快的,辛辣的,尖刻的. ⑦(话等)猥亵的, 下流的. ⑧〔俚〕(帐款等)浮报的,以少报多的. *The dish is too* ~. 这盘菜太咸. *a* ~ *pasture* 海水淹过的牧场. ***as*** ~ ***as fire*** 极咸. ***rather too*** ~ 〔俚〕太贪暴利. — *vt.* ①给…加盐,给…调味. ②撒盐 (使路上的雪溶化). ③〔口〕(以盐)腌;保存. ④储蓄. ⑤使(话等)有风趣〔力量〕. ⑥〔用被动语态〕使(马或人)服水土. ⑦以盐喂…, 给(羊等) 盐吃. ⑧【化】用盐类处理. ⑨〔俚〕给(劣矿)移入别处良矿石作伪装; 〔商俚〕(用伪品)冒充,(用劣货)骗卖. ⑩虚报,浮报(价钱),浮记(帐款). ~ *a mine* 移入别处良矿伪装 矿山〔使人误以富矿购买〕. ~ *an account* 〔商俚〕浮报帐款. ~ *books* 浮记盈余. ~ *prices* 讨虚价,开虚价. ~ ***away [down]*** ①腌制. ②积蓄,储蓄. ③〔美〕投资. ④〔美俚〕大骂一顿. ~ ***in*** 盐(助)溶. ~ ***out*** 【化】盐析; 加盐分离. ~**-and-pepper** (黑白点相间的)椒盐色(织物),芝麻呢. ~**box** 斜盖盐箱; (17—19 世纪初美国新英格兰地区的一种)盐箱形楼房. ~**bush** 【植】滨藜属 *(Atriplex)* 植物〔生于盐碱地或沙漠〕. ~ **cake** 盐饼,芒硝,粗制硫酸钠. ~**-cat** 盐块(喂鸽子的)含盐饲料. ~**cellar** (餐桌上的)盐瓶, 小盐缸;〔俚〕脖子基部两边的窝, 脖根窝. ~ **dome** 【地】盐丘, 盐穹. ~ **glaze** 【化】盐釉. ~ **grass** 【植】盐草属 *(Distichlis)* 植物〔尤指拉美海滨盐草 *(Distichlis spicata)*〕 ~ **horse [junk]** 【海】腌牛肉. ~ **lake** 咸水湖. **S- Lake City** 〔美〕盐湖城. ~ **lick** 动物爱舐食的含盐地. ~ **marsh** 盐泽,盐沼. ~ **mine** 岩盐产地,岩盐坑. ~**pan** ①盐锅. ②盐田. ③〔*pl.*〕= ~works. ~**peter**, ~**-petre** 【化】硝石,芒〔火〕硝,钾硝,硝酸钾 (*Chile* ~*peter* 智利硝,硝酸钠. ~ *peter rot* 湿墙上生的白斑). ~ **pit** 盐田. ~ **rheum** 〔美〕湿疹. **S- River** (美国 Arizona 中部的)咸河;〔美喻〕政治上失败,政治生命结束 (*row sb. up S- River* 结束某人的政治生命). ~ **spoon** 盐匙. ~ **temperature** 【冶】盐浴温度. ~ **water** *n.* ①咸水,海水. ②〔谑〕泪. ~**-water** *a.* ①咸水的. ②(鱼等)咸水产的. ~ **well** 盐井. ~**works** 〔*sing. pl.*〕盐场. ~**wort** 【植】(生于海边或盐沼)藜科植物,尤指猪毛菜和海蓬子. **-less** ①无盐的,无咸味的. ②无味道的. **-ness** *n.*

sal·tant [ˈsæltənt] *a.* ①跳跃的, 舞蹈的. ②【徽】(兽)跳跃状的; — *n.* 【生】突变形,菌落突变型.

sal·ta·rel·lo [ˌsætəˈreləu] *n.* ①萨尔塔列洛舞〔意大利的一种轻快的舞蹈名〕. ②萨尔塔列洛舞曲.

sal·ta·tion [sælˈteiʃən] *n.* ①跳, 跳跃. ②舞蹈. ③脉动. ④【生】突变;菌落局变; 不连继变异. ⑤【地】河底滚沙.

sal·ta·to·ri·al [ˌsæltəˈtɔːriəl] *a.* ①跳跃的;舞蹈的. ②(动物) 适于跳跃的. ~ *exercises* 跳跃运动. ~ *legs* 善跳的腿.

sal·ta·to·ry [ˈsæltətəri] *a.* ①跳跃的. ②舞蹈的. ③跃进的. *the* ~ *art* 舞蹈(艺)术. *her* ~ *talent* 她的舞蹈才能.

salt·ed [ˈsɔːltid] *a.* ①腌的;加了盐的,有咸味的. ②〔俚〕(马等) 得过瘟病而有免疫性的. ③有经验的, 熟练的. ④〔俚〕(矿山等)伪装过的. ⑤〔俚〕冒销的,骗卖的.

salt·er [ˈsɔːltə] *n.* ①制盐者. ②卖盐者，盐商. ③盐田〔盐井〕职工. ④腌制者. ⑤干货商.
salt·ern [ˈsɔːltən] *n.* 盐田;盐场.
salt·er·y [ˈsɔːltəri] *n.* ①盐场. ②腌鱼厂.
sal·tier [ˈsæltiə] *n.* = saltire.
sal·ti·grade [ˈsæltigreid] *a.* ①有适应于跳跃的腿的. ②借跳跃移动的.
salt·ine [sɔːlˈtiːn] *n.* (盐精)梳打饼干.
sal·tire [ˈsæltaiə] *n.* 【徽】X形十字; 圣安得列 (St. Andrew)十字. — *a.* 成X形的.
salt·ish [ˈsɔːltiʃ] *a.* 带有咸味的,略带咸味的.
sal·tus [ˈsæltəs] *n.* ①急变,急转;中断.②【逻】跳越(推论步骤而作)判断,速断,逻辑的飞跃.
salt·y [ˈsɔːlti] *a.* ***(-i·er; -i·est)*** ①有盐味的; 有海洋味的. ②富有(航海)经验的. ③刺激的,辛辣的,有趣的,富于机智的. ④(马等)难驾御的. **-i·ness** *n.* 咸性.
sa·lu·bri·ous [səˈljuːbriəs] *a.* (气候等)有益健康的. **-ly** *ad.* **-ness** *n.*
sa·lu·bri·ty [səˈljuːbriti] *n.* 有益健康.
sa·lud [sɑːˈluːd] *int.* 〔Sp.〕祝你健康,干杯,敬酒.
salu·ki [səˈluːki, səˈluːgi] *n.* (猎羚羊用的)萨路基猎狗〔亦作 Saluki. 产于波斯和阿拉伯等地〕.
Sa·lus·bury [ˈsɔːlzbəri] *n.* 索尔兹伯里〔姓氏〕(= Salisbury).
sal·u·ta·ry [ˈsæljutəri] *a.* ①有益健康的. ②有益的.
sal·u·ta·tion [ˌsælju(ː)ˈteiʃən] *n.* ①问候,致意,祝贺,道别,招呼〔现多用 greeting, welcome〕. ②(书信开始的)称呼,敬称. ③〔罕〕敬礼〔现用 salute〕. *a word of* ~ 欢迎辞(等). *the Angelic S-* = the Ave Maria. **-al** *a.*
sa·lu·ta·to·ri·an [səˌluːtəˈtɔːriən] *n.* 〔美〕行毕业礼时代表致辞的(第二名)毕业生 (cf. valedictorian).
sa·lu·ta·to·ry [səˈluːtətəri] *a.* 行礼的,致意的,致敬的,祝贺的. — *n.* 〔美〕(通常由第二名毕业生作的)毕业致辞;欢迎词;祝词.
sa·lute [səˈluːt, -ˈljuːt] *vt.* ①向…敬礼,向…(放礼炮)致敬,向…致意. ②欢迎,祝贺. ③〔古〕对(来人)吻手,吻脸〔表示敬意〕. ④(景象,声音等)迎着…的面而来,呈现在…的面前. ~ *a flag* 向国旗致敬. *The lark ~s the dawn.* 云雀(以歌声)迎接天明. ~ *sb. with cheers* 欢呼迎接. ~ *the enemy with a volley* 用排炮〔密集火力〕迎接敌人. — *vi.* ①行礼,点头,招呼,致敬. ②祝贺. ③放礼炮. *Salute!* 〔信末用语〕敬礼! — *n.* ①行礼,招呼,敬礼. ②礼炮,举枪,举刀(礼). ③喝彩; 〔古〕表示致敬的吻手或吻脸〔又称 chaste ~〕. *a ~ of 21 guns* 二十一响的礼炮. ***acknowledge a ~*** 答礼. ***at the ~*** 以敬礼姿势. ***come to the ~*** 【军】行敬礼. ***exchange ~s*** 交换礼炮. ***fire a ~*** 鸣礼炮. ***national ~*** ①为国旗〔国家元首〕鸣放的 21 响礼炮. ②〔美〕〔独立纪念日鸣放相当于所有州数的〕国庆礼炮(= ~ to the Union). ***stand at (the) ~*** (比赛前的)立正敬礼; 立正致敬. ***take the ~*** (元首、将军等高级官员)接受敬礼,还礼,行答礼.
salv. = salvage.
Salv. = Salvador.
sal·va·ble [ˈsælvəbl] *a.* ①可挽救的,可抢救的. ②(船、货等)可打捞的.
Sal·va·dor [ˈsælvədɔː] *n.* 萨尔瓦多〔拉丁美洲〕.
Sal·va·do·ran [ˌsælvəˈdɔːrən], **-do·ri·an**[-ˈdɔːriən] *a.*, *n.* 萨尔瓦多的〔人〕.
sal·vage [ˈsælvidʒ] *n.* ①(海上遇险的)海员海难救助,船舶救助,货物救助. ②【商】海难救助酬金,救货费,救难费. ③被救船舶,(海难的)被救财货. ④【保险】(可抵补一部分损失额的)残余财货. ⑤沉船打捞工作,救难工作. ⑥(从火灾或其他灾难中抢救出来的)被救货物,被救财产. ⑦救济;救助;救难. ⑧废物利用. ⑨〔美俚〕偷. *a ~ boat* 海难救助船. *a ~ company* 海难救援公司. ~ *corps* (保险公司的)救火队. ~ *money [charges]* 援救费. — *vt.* ①(从海难、火灾等中)救出. ②打捞(沉船). ③抢救(财产). ④把…(从危难中)解救出来; 解决…的困难. ⑤【医】救,治. ⑥〔美、俚〕把…据为已有; 偷. ~ **archaeology** 古物抢救工程.
sal·var·san, S- [ˈsælvəsən] *n.* 【药】"六〇六",洒尔佛散〔= arsphenamine, 治梅毒的特效药,最先由 Paul Ehrlich (1854—1915)加以运用〕.
sal·va·tion [sælˈveiʃən] *n.* ①救助,拯救,救济. ②救济者; 救济品; 救助的工具. ③解救办法,救济措施. ④【宗】得救,超度. ⑤救星,救世主. ⑥救出来的东西,劫余之物. ***be the ~ of*** 是…的劫余之物. ***find ~*** ①信教,皈依; 改宗. ②〔谑〕找到改变态度的借口. ***S- Army*** (1865 年创建的基督教)救世军. ***work out one's own ~*** 独立自救,自寻出路. **-ism** 救世主义〔救世军的教义〕. **-ist** ① *n.* 救世军传道师. ② *a.* 救世军(式)的.
salve[1] [sɑːv] *n.* ①药膏;软膏.②缓和物,安慰物〔同 for 连用〕. ③安慰. ④〔俚〕奉承. — *vt.* ①〔古〕用药膏医治,给…敷药膏. ②缓和(恶劣感情等); 减轻(痛苦); 安慰(良心等). ③〔古〕掩饰,遮掩(缺点等). ④解除(困难等);消除(疑惑、矛盾等). ⑤〔美俚〕奉承. ~ *a sore* 减轻痛苦.
salve[2] [sælv] *vt.* 营救(难船),抢救(火灾中物资); 救助,救护.
sal·ve [ˈsælvi] 〔L.〕 *int.* 万岁! 好! 有福了! 〔原意为"你好!"欢呼祝贺或祝人安好的呼声或用语〕.
sal·ver [sælvə] *n.* (金、银、铜制的或电镀的,端食品或放置信件,名片等的)托盘,盘子. **~form, ~-shaped** *a.* 【植】高脚托盘状的,(花冠)管状的〔上端边缘扁平展开〕.
sal·vi·a [ˈsælviə, -vjə] *n.* 【植】鼠尾草(属).
sal·vif·ic [sælˈvifik] *a.* 救人的, 救世的, 救苦救难的. **-ally** *ad.*
sal·vo[1] [ˈsælvəu] *n.* ***(pl. ~s)*** ①〔英〕保留;保留条款. ②口实,遁词,托词. ③(名誉等的)保全手段,(感情等的)缓和方法.
sal·vo[2] [ˈsælvəu] *n.* ***(pl. ~s, ~es)*** ①(礼炮或射击的)齐发,齐鸣,齐射,(炸弹、伞兵等的)齐投, 连续投. ②一阵(热烈鼓掌);齐声欢呼,同声喝彩. ③突然爆发. ④【军】(炮兵的)翼次射. *The ~es of the October Revolution brought us Marxism-Leninism.* 十月革命一声炮响, 给我们送来了马列主义. ~ **bombing** 齐投轰炸. ~ **fire** 集中射击. **~-switch** *n.* 齐投开关.
sal vo·la·ti·le [sæl vəuˈlætili] 【化】碳酸铵(水),挥发盐〔一种提神药,主要成分是碳酸铵〕.
sal·vor [ˈsælvə] *n.* ①救难者, 救助人员, 打捞人员. ②救援船,打捞船.
Sam [sæm] *n.* 萨姆〔男子名, Samuel 的昵称〕. ~ ***Browne (belt)*** (军官的)皮带, 武装带. ~ ***Hill*** 〔美卑〕地狱; 魔鬼. ***stand ~*** 〔俚〕会钞,付(酒)账. ***take one's ~ upon it*** 〔俚〕保证; 敢于承担. ***Uncle ~*** 山姆大叔〔美国、美国人的绰号〕. ***upon my ~*** 〔英俚〕我敢发誓,我敢断言.
SAM = surface-to-air missile, 地对空导弹.
S. Am., S. Amer. = South America.
sam·a·ra [ˈsæmərə, səˈmɑːrə] *n.* 【植】翅果,翼果〔如槭,枫等果实〕.
Sa·ma·ri·a [səˈmɛəriə] *n.* 撒马利亚〔古代巴勒斯坦与约旦河间一个地区,同名的王国或其首都〕.
Sa·mar·i·tan [səˈmæritən] *n.*, *a.* ①撒玛利亚人(的); 撒玛利亚语(的). ②乐善好施者(的). *a good ~* 乐善好施的人. *a ~ fund* 贫民救济基金. *a ~ home* 养育院. **-ism** *n.* 慈善;乐善好施.
sa·mar·i·um [səˈmɛəriəm] *n.* 【化】钐〔稀有金属元素,化学符号为Sm 或 Sa〕.
sa·mar·skite [səˈmɑːskait, ˈsæməskait] *n.* 【矿】铌钇矿.
Sa·ma-Ve·da [ˈsɑːməˈveidə, -viː-] *n.* 娑摩吠陀〔古印度亚尔耶民族的赞歌四吠陀之一〕.
sam·ba [ˈsæmbə] *n.* 〔美〕桑巴舞〔巴西一种轻快的二拍

子舞〕. — *vi.* 跳桑巴舞.

sam•bar, sam•bur [ˈsɑːmbə, ˈsæm-] *n.* *(pl.* ~*(s))* 【动】水鹿,里鹿 *(Cervus Unicolor)* 〔产于印度的一种大鹿〕.

sam•bo [ˈsæmbəu] *n.* *(pl.* ~*s,* ~*es)* ①〔拉丁美洲〕北美印第安人或黑白混血儿与黑人的后裔. ②〔S-〕〔美,侮辱性用语〕黑人.

sam•buke [ˈsæmbjuːk] *n.* 桑布克琴〔一种近似竖琴的三角形古弦乐器名〕.

Sam•dech [ˈsæmdek] *n.* 〔高棉语〕陛下,殿下〔对国王、亲王、王子、公主等的敬称,放在称号的前面〕.

same [seim] *a.* 〔常 the ~〕①相同的,同样的,同种的 *(as)*; 同一个 *(with; that; who; which)*. ②(和以前)一样,没有变化. ③上述的,该,那个〔和 this, these, that, those 等连用,常用轻蔑意〕. ④〔不用 the〕〔罕〕单调的,千篇一律的. *eat the* ~ *(sort of) food every day.* 每天吃同样的东西. *It is the* ~ *old game.* 老是那一手. *It is the* ~ *with me.* 我也是那样. *She has been always the* ~ *to me.* 她对我始终如一. *The life is perhaps a little* ~. 那种生活也许有点单调. — *pro.* ①同一事〔物〕;〔古〕同一人〔常可不用 the〕. ②【法、商】该人(等) (= he, him, she, her, they, them 等). ③上述之物,该物. *We have heard from Mr. Jones and have written to* ~.【商】琼斯君有信来,已复讫. — *ad.* 一样, 相同地,不变. *I think the* ~ *of him as you do.* 我对他的看法和你对他的看法一样. ***about the*** ~ = much the ~. ***all [just] the*** ~ ①完全一样 *(It's all the* ~ *to me.* 那对我完全一样). ②然而还是,仍然 *(I like him all the* ~. (虽有缺点)我仍然喜欢他). ***at the*** ~ ***time*** 同时;〔俚〕〔可省去 the〕然而,可是,还是. ***much the*** ~ 差不多完全一样;一丘之貉. ***not quite the*** ~ 有点两样. ***one and the*** ~ ***(= the very*** ~***)*** 完全相同的,同一的;就是那个. ~ ***here*** 〔口〕我也一样. ***the*** ~ ①同样地 (= in the ~ way, in the ~ manner); ②同一事物;上述事物;该人,那个人 *(I wish you the* ~. = *(The)* ~ *to you!* 彼此彼此〔对恭贺年禧时的答话〕). ***the very*** ~ 正是这个,完全相同〔加强语气〕. **-ness** *n.*

sa•mekh, sa•mech [ˈsɑːmeh] *n.* 希伯来语的第十五个字母.

Sa•mi•an [ˈseimiən] *a.* ①萨姆斯(Samos)岛的. ②萨姆斯岛居民的. — *n.* 萨姆斯岛上的居民.

sam•iel [ˈsæmjel] *n.* = simoom.

sam•ite [ˈsæmait] *n.* (中世纪一种织有金银线的) 锦绣〔织锦〕.

sa•mi•sen [ˈsæmisən] *n.* 〔Jap.〕日本三弦.

Saml. = Samuel.

sam•let [ˈsæmlit] *n.* 幼鲑.

Sam•my [ˈsæmi] *n.* ①〔俚〕美国兵〔第一次世界大战时对美国远征军大兵的称呼,即对 Uncle Sam 的昵称〕. ②Samuel 或 Samantha 的昵称. ③〔俚〕笨蛋,傻子,蠢货. ***stand*** ~ = stand Sam.

Sam Neua [ˈsæm nuə] 桑怒〔老挝城市〕.

Sam•nite [ˈsæmnait] *a.* ①撒姆尼 (Samnium) 的. ②撒姆尼人的. ③撒姆尼语的. — *n.* ①撒姆尼人〔意大利中部古撒本 (Sabine) 民族的人〕. ②撒姆尼语.

Sa•mo•a [səˈməuə] *n.* 萨摩亚群岛〔南太平洋中一群岛〕.

Sa•mo•an [səˈməuən] *n., a.* ①萨摩亚岛人(的). ②萨摩亚语(的).

Sa•mos [ˈseimɔs] *n.* 萨姆斯岛〔爱琴海〕.

SAMOS = satellite antimissile observation system 卫星反导弹观察系统.

sam•o•var [ˈsæməuvɑː] *n.* (俄国式)茶炊,茶汤壶,水火壶. *Chinese* ~ 火锅.

Sam•oy•ed(e) [ˌsæmɔiˈed] *n.* (西伯利亚西北部的)撒摩耶人. ②撒摩耶语. ③撒摩耶种狗. — *a.* ①撒摩耶人的. ③撒摩耶语的.

Sam•oy•ed•ic [ˌsæmɔiˈedik] *a.* ①撒摩耶人的. — *n.* 撒摩耶语.

samp [sæmp] *n.* ①〔美〕玉米碴[粗粉]. ②〔美〕玉米粥.

sam•pan [ˈsæmpæn] *n.* 〔中〕舢板; 用橹摇的小木船. (= sanpan). ★ 这个词在英语中已不限于指很小的舢板,也指用橹或使帆的各种不大的木船.

sam•phire [ˈsæmfaiə] *n.*【植】①(欧洲海滨的)一种伞形科植物,海马齿. ②欧洲海蓬子, 钾猪毛菜, 厚岸草(= glasswort).

sam•ple [ˈsɑːmpl] *n.* ①样品,货样. ②标本; 榜样,实例. ③【统计】典型取样,抽样检查. ④【讯】信号瞬时值. ⑤【冶】〔*pl.*〕锌华. *That is a fair* ~ *of his manners.* 那就是他的典型态度. *a light* ~ 光脉冲. ***up to*** ~ ①和样品一样[相符]. ②可以接受的, 可以同意的. — *vt.* ①从…取样, 从…抽样; 提供…货样. ②对…进行抽样检查. ~ **card** (衣料等的)样本卡. ~ **copy** 样书. ~ **fair** 样品展览会. ~ **room** ①样品陈列室. ②矿石样品分析室. ③〔美方〕酒吧.

sam•pler [ˈsɑːmplə] *n.* ①样品检查员; 试饮人(等); 抽样者. ②取样器,选样器. ③刺绣图案样本;(文学作品等的)范本.

sam•pling [ˈsæmpliŋ] *n.* ①取样(品),取标(本)〔指行动或程序〕. ②样品,标本. ~ **cock** 取样阀. ~ **well** 取样井.

sam•sa•ra [səmˈsɑːrə] *n.*【佛教,印度教】轮回.

Sam•son [ˈsæmsn], **Samp•son** [ˈsæpsn] *n.* ① 萨姆森〔男子名〕. ②【圣】参孙〔旧约传说中的力大无比的勇士〕. ③大力士. ~ **post**【海】(船上的)吊杆柱.

Sam•u•el [ˈsæmjuəl] ①塞缪尔〔男子名〕. ②撒母耳〔《圣经》中人物,希伯来先知和法官〕. ③《撒母耳记》〔《圣经》旧约全书篇名〕.

Sam•u•rai [ˈsæmurai] *n.* 〔Jap.〕①(日本封建时代的)武士;〔*pl.*〕武士阶级. ②日本陆军军官;〔*pl.*〕日本军阀.

san [sæn] *n.* 〔口〕 = ①sanatorium. ②sanitary. ③sanitation.

Sa•nʻa, Sa-naa [sɑːˈnɑː] *n.* 萨那〔也门首都〕.

san•a•tive [ˈsænətiv] *a.* ①有疗效的; 有益健康的. ②〔喻〕起纠正作用的.

san•a•to•ri•um [ˌsænəˈtɔːriəm] *n.* *(pl.* ~*s,* ***-ria*** [-riə]*)* 〔主英〕①疗养院. ②(学校等机构中的)隔离病房. ③疗养地,休养地(= 〔美〕 sanitarium).

san•a•to•ry [ˈsænətəri] *a.* = sanative.

san•be•ni•to [ˌsænbeˈniːtəu] *n.* *(pl.* ~*s)* 【宗史】①(黄色的) 悔罪服. ②(黑色的) 地狱服〔被宗教裁判所判处火刑的异端者受刑时所穿〕.

San•cho Pan•za [ˈsænkəu ˈpænzə] 桑科·潘萨〔西班牙作家塞万提斯著名小说《堂吉诃德》中人物,堂吉诃德的仆人,无文化而有实际经验和富于常识,和堂吉诃德的耽于幻想形成对比〕.

San Cle•mente [ˌsæn kliˈmenti] 〔美〕圣克利门蒂(岛).

sanc•ti•fi•ca•tion [ˌsæŋktifiˈkeiʃən] *n.* ①神圣化,净化; 奉献. ②圣洁.

sanc•ti•fy [ˈsæŋktifai] *vt.* ①使神圣; 使净化; 把…奉献给神. ②使圣洁; 使纯洁. ③使神圣不可侵犯. ④使成为正当; 认可; 批准. ⑤崇奉. ⑥使能产生幸福. *sanctified airs* 神圣不可侵犯的神态; 道貌岸然.

sanc•ti•mo•ni•ous [ˌsæŋktiˈməunjəs, -niəs] *a.* 假装神圣[虔诚]的; 伪善的. **-ly** *ad.* **-ness** *n.*

sanc•ti•mo•ny [ˈsæŋktiməni] *n.* 假装神圣[虔诚]; 伪善.

sanc•tion [ˈsæŋkʃən] *n.* ①批准; 准许; 承认. ②赏罚; 处罚;【法】惩罚. ③〔主 *pl.*〕(对侵略者等的) 制裁; 良心制裁,制裁力,约束力. ④【史】法令. *social* ~ 社会的制裁. *moral* ~ 道德制裁. *punitive [vindicatory]* ~ 惩罚. ***give*** ~ ***to*** 批准, 同意. ***suffer the last*** ~ ***of the law*** 被处死刑. ***take*** ~***s against*** 对…采取制裁手段. — *vt.* ①批准; 认可; 承认. ②支持, 赞许.

sanc•ti•ty [ˈsæŋktiti] *n.* ①神圣、圣洁. ②尊严. ③〔*pl.*〕神圣的义务[感情(等)]. *the* ~ *of an oath* 誓言的神圣

性. *the sanctities of the home* 对家庭的神圣义务[感情].

sanc·tu·a·ry [ˈsæŋktjuəri] *n.* ①圣所,圣堂;礼拜堂,神殿;至圣所〔犹太神殿内院藏经处〕;(教堂的)内殿. ②(罪犯等的)避难所;庇护所. ③(中世教堂等特有的)犯人庇护权. ④禁猎期,禁猎区. *break* ~ 侵入教堂逮捕罪犯〔行凶〕. *take* ~ (逃入教堂)得到庇护. *a bird* ~ 鸟类禁猎地.

sanc·tum [ˈsæŋktəm] *n.* ①圣所;内殿. ②〔口〕私室,书房. ~ ***sanctorum*** ①至圣所. ②〔谑〕密室,私室.

sanc·tus [ˈsæŋktəs] *n.*【宗】三圣颂[曲]. ~ **bell** (唱三圣颂时的)圣铃,圣钟.

sand [sænd] *n.* ①沙. ②〔*pl.*〕沙滩,沙洲,沙地,沙漠. ③〔*pl.*〕沙粒;(计时用的沙漏中的)细沙. ④光阴,时间,寿命. ⑤〔美俚〕勇气,毅力,胆量,坚毅. ⑥【医】砂状结石. ⑦【地】含石油砂层. ⑧粗矿石;尾矿;【冶】模砂. ⑨沙色;带红的黄色. ⑩〔美俚〕砂糖. *quick* ~ 流沙. *play on the ~s* 在沙滩上玩耍. *The ~s [His ~s] are running out.* 期限快到[他的命数将尽]. *a man with plenty of ~ in him* 坚毅的人,刚强的人. ***built on*** ~ 不稳固的;不安定的. ***footprints on the ~s of time*** 留在人世变迁的沙滩上的脚印. ***have ~ in one's craw*** 〔美口〕有勇气[决断,毅力]. ***knock the ~ from under*** 〔美〕使失去立足之地;(设法)占上风. ***make ropes of*** ~ 用沙结绳;做不可能[徒劳无功]的事. ***numberless as the ~(s)*** 多如恒河沙数. ***number [plough, sow] the ~s*** 白费气力,徒劳. ***put ~ in the wheels [machine]*** 捣乱,暗中破坏. — *vt.* ①撒沙于,铺沙于,把…埋进沙里;用沙搀入. ②用沙[砂纸]擦[磨光]. ③使(船)开上沙滩. ~ ***up*** 用沙填塞(油井等). ~**bag** ①*n.* 沙包,沙袋. ②*vt.* 用沙包堵塞,堆上[放上]沙包;用沙包打,用沙包把…击昏[倒];〔美〕强迫,强制. ~**-bank** 沙丘;沙洲. ~ **bar** 沙洲,沙堤. ~ **bath** ①沙浴. ②【化】沙浴器. ③【地】沙盘〔用于土质分析〕. ~**blast** ①【机】喷沙. ②喷沙器. ③ *vt., vi.* 以喷沙器清洗[打磨]. ~**-blind** 〔古〕视力极差的,半盲的,被沙蒙住眼睛的 (~*-blind ostriches* 〔喻〕对外界事情视若无睹的人). ~**-box** ①(火车机车上的)沙箱. ②(翻砂用的)砂型. ~ **box tree**【植】(美洲热带的)沙匣树 (*Hura crepitans*). ~**-break** 防沙林. ~**-bur(r)**【植】①蒺藜草属 (*Cenchrus*) 植物. ②龙葵 (*Solanum rostratum*). ~**-casting**【机】沙型铸造. ~ **cloud** 沙烟,沙漠热风. ~ **crack**【兽医】裂蹄;(热沙上行人的)脚裂. ~**culture**【农】沙基培养. ~ **dab**【动】(北美洲西海岸)沙鲆. ~ **dollar**【动】沙海胆,饼海胆. ~ **drift** 流沙. ~**-eel**【鱼】玉筋鱼. ~**-flea** = sandhopper. ~**-fly**【虫】白蛉. ~**-glass** (计时用的)沙漏. ~**-grouse**【鸟】沙鸡. ~**-hill** 沙丘. ~**-hiller** 〔美俚〕(住在 Georgia 州等砂丘松林中的)穷白种人. ~**-hog**〔美俚〕挖沙工,水底工作的工人,隧道工人. ~**-hopper**【动】沙蚤,矶蚤. ~ **jack**【建】沙箱千斤顶. ~ **la(u)nce**【动】= ~-eel. ~ **lily**【植】白文殊兰 (*Leucocrinum montanum*). **-man** (童话中的)睡魔. ~**-painting** "洒沙画符"治病法〔那伐鹤印第安人一种巫术〕;"洒沙符"的图案. ~**paper** ①*n.* 砂纸. ② *vt.* 用砂纸擦[磨光]. ~**piper** *n.*【鸟】矶鹞. ~**-pump**【机】扬沙泵,抽沙泵. ~ **shoe** 〔英〕(沙滩上穿的)橡皮底布鞋. ~ **sink** (消除海面油污的)沙沉法. ~**-stone**【地】沙岩. ~**-storm**【气】沙(风)暴. ~ **trap** ①【高尔夫球】障碍沙坑. ②分沙器. ~ **verbena**【植】叶子花属 (*Abronia*) 植物,(尤指)黄叶子花,大花粉红叶子花. ~**wort**【植】蚤缀属. 鹅不食属 (Arenoria) 植物.

san·dal[1] [ˈsændl] *n.* ①草带鞋;草鞋. ②凉鞋. ③便鞋. — *vt.* 使穿上凉鞋;给鞋上系襻.

san·dal[2] [ˈsændl] *n.*【植】檀香木;白檀. *red* ~ 紫檀. ~**wood** *n.* 檀香木.

san·da·rac [ˈsændəræk] *n.* ①【化】山达(树)脂. ②【植】北非山达树 (*Tetraclinus articulata*),山达木.

sand·er·ling [ˈsændəliŋ] *n.*【动】三趾鹬 (*Crocethia alba*).

san·dhi [ˈsɑːndhiː, ˈsæn-,sʌn-] *n.*【语音】连音(变读),连接音变(例: *"t"* 在 *picture* 中读为 [tʃ]; *"am"* 在 *I am glad* 中读为 [ʼm]).

Sand·hurst [ˈsændhəːst] *n.* ①桑赫斯特〔英格兰南部一小镇〕. ②英国陆军军官学校〔在桑赫斯特〕. *a* ~ *man* 〔英〕桑赫斯特陆军军官学校的学生[出身者].

San Di·e·go [sæn di(ː)ˈeigəu] *n.* 圣地亚哥〔美国 California 州南西海岸一港口,为著名的海军、海运基地〕.

Sand·i·ness [ˈsændinis] *n.* ①沙质;多沙. ②沙色. ③流沙,不稳定状态.

san·di·ver [ˈsændivə] *n.* 浮沫〔玻璃熔液的浮渣废料如硫酸盐等〕.

sand·lot [ˈsændlɔt] *n.* (市郊)空旷沙地〔供儿童进行游戏或运动之用〕. — *a.* (市郊)空旷沙地的. **-lotter** *n.* 在空旷沙地上游戏的人.

Sand·wich [ˈsænwitʃ, -dʒ] *n.* 三维治〔英国五港之一〕.

sand·wich [ˈsænwidʒ, -witʃ] *n.* 三明治,夹心面包片;三明治层状结构[物]. ***ride [sit]*** ~ 夹坐二人中间. —*vt.* ①把…夹[挤]在(两层[者])中间. ②将…做成三明治. ~ *an appointment in between two board meetings* 在两个重要会议的中间安排插入一次约会. ~ **board** ①挂在身体前后的广告牌. ②胶合板. ~ **boat** *n.* (牛津及剑桥大学划船赛中)一天中优组中最后、劣组中最前的船. ~ **man** *n.* ***(pl. -men)*** 身体前后挂着广告牌(在街头游行)的广告人. ~ **shop** 小吃店.

sand·y [ˈsændi] *a.* ***(-i·er; -i·est)*** ①沙的,沙质的,多沙的. ②沙状的,(头发等)沙色的. ③(感觉等)粗涩的. ④不稳固的,不稳定的.

Sand·y [ˈsændi] *n.* ①桑迪〔男子名, Alexander 的昵称〕. ②苏格兰人的绰号.

sane [sein] *a.* ①神志清楚的,头脑清楚的;精神健全的 (*opp.* insane). ②明智的;合乎情理的,稳健的. ③〔罕〕健康的. *a* ~ *policy* 明智的政策. **-ly** *ad.* **-ness** *n.*

San Fair·y Ann [ˈsæn ˈfɛəri ˈæn] 〔军口〕不要紧,别怕 (=〔F.〕*ça ne fait rien* [sɑ nə fɛ rjɛ̃]).

san·for·ized [ˈsænfəraizd] *a.*【纺】(棉布)经过预缩水处理过的〔原为商标名桑福赖,指经机械方法抽缩使缩水率大为降低的〕.

San Fran·cis·co [ˌsæn frənˈsiskəu] *n.* 旧金山,三藩市〔美国港市〕.

sang[1] [sæŋ] *sing* 的过去式.

sang[2] [sæŋ] *n.* 〔美口〕参,人参. (= ginseng).

san·ga·ree [ˌsæŋgəˈriː] *n.* 西班牙式桑格里酒〔用葡萄酒加水、糖、香料的一种冷饮〕.

sang-froid [ˈsɑ̃ːŋˈfrwɑː] *n.* 〔F.〕冷静,沉着,镇定 (= cold blood).

San·graal, -grail, -greal [sænˈgreil] *n.*【宗】圣杯〔传说中耶稣在最后的晚餐时所用的杯〕(= Grail).

san·gri·a [sɑːnˈgriːɑː] *n.* = sangaree.

san·gui·na·ri·a [ˌsæŋgwiˈnɛəriə] *n.* ①【植】血根草(属) (= bloodroot). ②美洲血根草〔含生物碱,医用作催吐剂,祛痰剂〕.

san·gui·nar·y [ˈsæŋgwinəri] *a.* ①血腥的,血淋淋的;血迹斑斑的. ②残暴的;嗜血的,好杀的,动辄判死刑的. ③(话)粗暴的,难听的 (=〔英〕bloody). *a* ~ *battle* 血战. ~ *suppression* 血腥镇压. ~ *hands* 沾满鲜血的双手. *a* ~ *fool* 大傻瓜. ~ *language* 不堪入耳的话. **-ri·ly** *ad.*

san·guine [ˈsæŋgwin] *a.* ①血红色的;(脸色等)有血色的,红润的;多血质的. ②乐观的;充满自信[希望]的. ③〔罕〕嗜血的,血腥的;残忍的;流血的. *a* ~ *lip* 红润的嘴唇. *a* ~ *person* 乐观自信的人. *a* ~ *nature [disposition]* 乐观开朗的性格. ~ *slaughter* 血腥的屠杀. ***be ~ of*** 自信,对…抱乐观. — *n.* ①血红色,自信;抱乐观. ②(用氧化铁染色的)红粉笔. ③红粉笔画.

san·guin·e·ous [sæŋˈgwiniəs] *a.* ①血的,含有血的. ②【植】血红色的;(动物)有血的. ③多血的,多血质的.

S

④乐观的,自信的. ⑤〔罕〕血腥的,残忍的.

san·guin·in [ˈsæŋgwinin] *n.* 【生化】血素.

san·guin·o·lent [sæŋˈgwinələnt] *a.* ①血的,含血的,染上血的. ②残酷的.

San·he·drim [ˈsænidrim], **-hed·rin** [sænˈhedrin] *n.* ①【犹太史】最高法院〔古犹太国的最高法院兼参议会,由71人组成,兼管宗教事务〕. ②〔S-〕会议,协议会.

san·i·cle [ˈsænikl] *n.* 【植】变豆菜〔原被认为具有愈合伤口的疗效〕.

sa·ni·es [ˈseinii:z] *n.* 〔L.〕【医】稀脓,血脓. **-ni·ous** *a.*

san·i·fy [ˈsænifai] *vt.* ①使卫生化,使健康化. ②使具有卫生设备.

san·i·tar·i·an [ˌsæniˈtɛəriən] *a.* (公共)卫生的. — *n.* (公共)卫生学家;保健专家.

san·i·ta·rist [ˈsænitərist] *n.* = sanitarian.

san·i·tar·i·um [ˌsæniˈtɛəriəm] *n.* ***(pl.*** *~s, **-i·a*** **[-riə])** 〔美〕= sanatorium.

san·i·ta·ry [ˈsænitəri] *a.* 卫生(上)的. *a ~ cup* 卫生纸杯(用过一次就废弃). *a ~ engineer* 卫生技师,卫生工程学家;(厕所等的)管道工人. *a ~ inspector* 卫生检查官. *~ regulations* 卫生规则. *~ science* 公共卫生学. *a ~ towel [napkin, belt]* 月经带. — *n.* (有卫生设备的)公共厕所. ~ **cordon** 防疫地带、传染病流行区边界上布置的防疫警卫人员. ~ **engineering** 卫生工程学〔如给水排水〕. **-ri·ly** *ad.* **-ri·ness** *n.*

san·i·ta·tion [ˌsæniˈteiʃən] *n.* ①公共卫生,环境卫生. ②卫生设备,(尤指)下水道设备,卫生状况改善. *environmental ~* 环境卫生. ~**man** 〔美〕环境卫生员.

san·i·tize [ˈsænitaiz] *vt.* ***(-tiz·ed; -tiz·ing)*** ①使卫生〔如以灭菌、消毒方法〕. ②使免除有害的东西,使具有良好外观,使消除不良印象. **-r** *n.* (食物加工设备所用的)消毒杀菌剂.

san·i·ty [ˈsæniti] *n.* ①神志清楚,头脑清楚,精神健全, *(opp.* insanity*)*. ②明智;合乎情理;稳健. *lose one's ~* 失去理智,发狂.

san·jak [ˈsændʒæk] *n.* 〔Turk.〕州,行政区.

San Jo·sé [ˌsɑ:n həuˈsei] *n.* 圣约瑟〔哥斯达黎加首都〕.

San Jo·se scale [ˈsænhəuˈzeiskeil] *n.* 数蝇【动】〔一种有害于果树的甲虫〕.

San Juan [sænˈhwɑ:n] *n.* 圣胡安〔波多黎各首府,在西印度群岛〕.

sank [sæŋk] sink 的过去式.

San·khya [ˈsɑ:ŋkjə] *n.* 僧佉,数论(派)〔印度哲学六正统派中最古一派〕**(= Samkhya).**

San Ma·ri·no [ˌsæn məˈri:nəu] *n.* 圣马力诺〔意大利半岛东部的一小国〕.

san·nup [ˈsænʌp] *n.* 〔美〕印第安人的已婚男子.

sans[1] [sænz] *prep.* 〔古、诗〕无. *~ teeth, ~ eyes, ~ taste, ~ everything* 无齿,无眼,无味,无一切〔指老人,莎士比亚: *As You Like it* II vii. 166 中用语〕.

sans[2] [sɑ̃] *prep.* [F.] = without 〔主要用在下列成语中〕. ***~ cérémonie*** [ˈseremɔni:] 不拘礼节,没礼貌地. ***~ doute*** [ˈdu:t] 无疑. ***~ façon*** [ˈfæsɔ̃:ŋ] 坦率地,不客气地. ***~ gêne*** [ˈʒein] 不拘束. ***~ pareil*** [ˈpæˈrei] 无比的. ***~ peur et ~ reproche*** [ˈpə: ei rəˈprɔʃ] 无所畏惧,无可非议〔指骑士的性格〕. ***~ phrase*** [ˈfrɑ:z] 不罗唆地,直截了当地. ***~ souci*** [su:ˈsi:] 无忧无虑,逍遥自在.

Sans., Sansk. = Sanskrit.

San Sal·va·dor [sænˈsælvədɔ:] *n.* 圣萨尔瓦多〔萨尔瓦多首都〕.

sans-cu·lotte [ˌsænzkjuˈlɔt] *n.* ①【史】无套裤汉〔法国大革命时期贵族阶级对急进的共和主义者的蔑称〕. ②下层阶级的人;缺乏教养的人. ③急进主义者;过激分子. **-tic, -tish** *a.,* **tism** *n.* 急进共和主义.

san·sei, S- [ˈsɑ:nsei] *n.* ***(pl.*** *~(s)*) 〔美〕第三代美籍日人〔其祖父为日本移民〕.

san·ser·if [sænˈserif] *a., n.* 【印】没有衬线的(铅字).

san·se·vi·e·ri·a [ˌsænsiˈviəriə, -viˈi:riə] *n.* 【植】虎尾兰属植物.

San·skrit [ˈsænskrit] *n., a.* 梵语(的),梵文(的). **-ist** *n.* 梵语学家. **-ic** *a.*

sans·ser·if [sænˈserif] *n.* = sanserif.

San·ta ①[ˈsæntə] 〔美〕= Santa Claus. ②[ˈsæntə, ˈsɑ:ntɑ] *n.* 〔Sp., It.〕= Saint.

San·ta Claus, Santa Klaus [ˌsæntəˈklɔ:z] 圣诞老人.

San·ta Cruz de Te·ne·rife [ˌsæntə ˌkru:z də tenəˈri:f] *n.* 特纳里夫圣克鲁斯〔西班牙加那利 (Canary) 群岛中特纳里夫岛的一海港〕.

San·ta Ger·tru·dis [ˈsætəgəˈtru:dis] *n.* 〔美〕【动】圣格特鲁地斯菜牛〔美国德克萨斯州的一种杂交肉用牛,可在炎热而饲料稀少的环境里繁殖〕.

San·ta Is·a·bel [ˈsæntəˈizəbel] *n.* 圣伊萨贝尔〔赤道几内亚首都的旧称,现称马拉博 (Malabo)〕.

San·ta Ma·ri·a [ˈsætə məˈriə; *Sp.* ˈsɑ:ntɑ: mɑ:ˈri:ɑ:] ①圣玛利亚号〔1492年哥伦布航海用的旗舰〕. ②圣玛利亚〔危地马拉西南部的一个活火山〕.

San·tia·go [ˌsæntiˈɑ:gəu] *n.* 圣地亚哥〔智利首都〕.

San·to Do·min·go [ˈsæntəu dəˈmiŋgəu] *n.* 圣多明各〔多米尼加首都,位于海地岛东部〕.

san·ton [ˈsæntən] *n.* (伊斯兰教的)修士,隐士.

san·ton·i·ca [sænˈtɔnikə] *n.* 【植】蒿属植物; (尤指)山道年草;山道年花.

san·to·nin [ˈsæntənin] *n.* 【药】山道年〔驱蛔虫药〕.

São To·mé [sɑ̃u tɔ:ˈme] *n.* 圣多美〔圣多美和普林西比首都〕. **São Tomé and Principe** [principə] 圣多美和普林西比〔非洲〕.

sap[1] [ˈsæp] *n.* ①树液,(树皮下的)白木质. ②体液,生命液;元气,精力,活力. *the ~ of life* 元气,精力. *the ~ of youth* 青年的活力. —*vt.* 榨取…的树液;去除…的白木质;使衰弱〔衰竭〕. ~ **green** 暗绿色,一种暗绿色的颜料. ~ **sucker** 一种以树汁为食的啄木鸟. ~**wood** (树皮下较软的)白木质,边材〔心材外增生的木质部〕.

sap[2] [sæp] *n.* ①【军】(袭击敌人用的)坑道,对壕. ②坑道的挖掘. ③暗中的破坏,逐步的损坏,削弱. — *vt., vi.* ①(在…下面)挖掘使倒塌;(使)逐渐损坏,(使)逐渐削弱. ②挖坑道进攻〔逼近〕. ③(水等)逐渐浸蚀. ④暗中颠覆. ~ *a wall* 挖墙脚. ~ *a line of trenches* 挖掘坑道逐渐逼近(敌方)防线. ~**head** 【军】坑道头.

sap[3] [sæp] *n.* ①〔英学生俚〕用功读书的人;埋头工作的人. ②〔口〕讨厌的工作,苦活. ③〔美、俚〕= saphead. ④〔美俚〕棍子. *It is such a ~.* 这事真麻烦. — *vt.* 〔美俚〕用棍子打. — *vi.* 〔英学生俚〕死用功. ~**head** 〔美口〕傻瓜,笨蛋.

SAP = semi-armour-piercing 半穿甲.

sap·a·jou [ˈsæpədʒu:] *n.* 【动】卷尾猴 (= capuchin).

sap·an·wood, sap·pan·wood [ˈsæpənwud] *n.* 【植】(可提取红染料的)苏方,苏木.

sap·ful [ˈsæpful] *a.* 树液多的.

sa·phe·na [səˈfi:nə] *n.* 【解】隐静脉. **-nous** [-nəs] *a.*

sap·id [ˈsæpid] *a.* ①(食物等)有味道的,有风味的,滋味好的. ②(书等)有趣味的. *(opp.* insipid*)*. **-i·ty** *n.* ①味道,风味,滋味. ②(书等的)趣味.

sa·pi·ence, -en·cy [ˈseipiəns, -si] *n.* 〔常讽〕(外表上的)学识丰富;智慧;精明.

sa·pi·ens [ˈsæpiəns] *a.* 〔L.〕(类似)现代人的. ***homo ~*** 人类.

sa·pi·ent [ˈseipiənt] *a.* 〔常讽〕①(貌似)学识丰富的,有高深知识的. ②聪明的,明智的;精明的. — *n.* 早期人类,史前人.

sa·pi·en·tial [ˌseipiˈenʃəl] *a.* 〔罕〕智慧的;有智慧的;使人增长智慧的.

sap·less [ˈsæplis] *a.* ①无树液的;枯萎的. ②没有元气的,没有精力的,没有活力的. ③乏味的,没趣味的.

sap·ling [ˈsæpliŋ] *n.* ①(直径 3—4 英寸的)树苗; 幼树. ②年轻人. ③【动】仔灵猩〔一岁以内的〕. *grow ~s* 培育树苗.

sap·o·dil·la [ˌsæpəˈdilə] *n.* 【植】人心果(树)〔美洲热带所产的一种大常青树〕. — *a.* 山榄科 (*Sapotaceae*) 的.

sap·o·na·ceous [ˈsæpəuˈneiʃəs] *a.* ①皂质〔状〕的. ②难于捕捉的; 善于闪避的, 圆滑的.

sa·pon·i·fi·ca·tion [səˌpɔnifiˈkeiʃən] *n.* 【化】皂化(作用).

sa·pon·i·fy [səˈpɔnifai] *vt., vi.* 【化】(使)皂化, (使)碱解. **-i·fi·a·ble** *a.* 可皂化的. **-i·fi·er** *n.* 皂化剂.

sap·o·nin [ˈsæpənin] *n.* 【化】皂角苷.

sap·o·nite [ˈsæpənait] *n.* 【矿】皂石.

sa·por [ˈseipɔː] *n.* ①(物质中能产生味觉的)滋味; 味. ②风味. 亦作 **sa·pour.**

sa·po·ta [səˈpəutə] *n.* = sapodilla.

sa·po·te [səˈpəutiː] *n.* 【植】①美洲几种热带树或其果实. ② 美果榄 (= marmalade tree) 〔产于美洲热带地区〕. ③= sapodilla.

sap·per [ˈsæpə] *n.* ①坑道〔地雷〕工兵. ②挖掘者〔器〕.

Sap·phic [ˈsæfik] *a.* ①希腊女诗人莎孚(Sappho) 的; 莎孚式(诗体)的. ②〔亦作 s-〕 女性同性恋的. —*n.*〔*pl.*〕莎孚式诗(体). *~ vice* = Sapphism.

sap·phire [ˈsæfaiə] *n.* ①【矿】蓝宝石. ②天蓝色, 蔚蓝色. — *a.* 天蓝色的, 蔚蓝色的.

sap·phir·ine [ˈsæfərain] *a.* ①象蓝宝石的. ②蓝宝石色的, 天蓝色的. ③蓝宝石制的. — *n.* 【矿】假蓝宝石.

sap·phism [ˈsæfizəm] *n.* 女子(间的)同性恋.

Sap·pho [ˈsæfəu] *n.* 莎孚〔公元前六世纪前后的希腊女诗人〕.

Sa·ppo·ro [səˈpɔːrəu] *n.* 扎幌〔日本城市〕.

sap·py [ˈsæpi] *a.* (*-pi·er; -pi·est*) ①多树液的; 似白木质的, 含大量白木质的. ②精力充沛的; 年富力壮的. ③〔俚〕愚蠢的; 傻; 易于伤感到愚蠢程度的.

sapr- *comb. f.* 〔辅音前用 sapro〕 腐败, 死: *sap*raemia *sap*rophagous.

sa·pr(a)e·mi·a [sæˈpriːmiə] *n.* 【医】腐血症, 脓毒中毒. **sap·r(a)e·mic** *a.*

sapro- *comb. f.* 腐(败), 死: *sapro*be; *sapro*pel.

sap·robe [ˈsæprəub] *n.* 【生】污水生物.

sap·ro·bic [sæˈprəubik] *a.* 【生】①污水生物的. ②腐生植物的. **-bi·cal·ly** *ad.*

sap·ro·gen·ic [ˌsæprəuˈdʒenik] *a.* 【植】腐生的 (= saprogenous).

sap·ro·lite [ˈsæprəulait] *n.* 【地】腐泥土. **-lit·ic** [ˌsæprəuˈlitik] *a.*

sap·ro·pel [ˈsæprəupel] *n.* 【地】 湖泥(腐殖质); 腐殖泥. **-ic** [-ˈpelik] *a.*

sa·proph·a·gous [səˈprɔfəgəs] *a.* 【动】食腐的.

sap·ro·phyte [ˈsæprəufait] *n.* 【生】腐生(植)物; 腐物寄生物; 死物寄生菌.

sap·ro·zo·ic [ˌsæprəuˈzəuik] *a.* 【生】①食腐的. ②腐生(植)物的; 腐物寄生(动)物的. — *n.* 腐物寄生物.

sap·sa·go [sæpˈseigəu] *n.* 【美】瑞士(产)绿干酪.

Sar. = ①Sardinia. ②Sardinian.

S.A.R. =① Sons of the American Revolution. ② South African Republic.

sar·a·band [ˈsærəbænd] *n.* ①(西班牙慢拍子)撒拉本舞. ②撒拉本舞曲.

Sar·a·cen [ˈsærəsn] *n.* 撒拉逊人 〔原为叙利亚附近一游牧民族, 后特指抵抗十字军的伊斯兰教阿拉伯人, 现泛指伊斯兰教徒或阿拉伯人〕. — *a.* 撒拉逊人的. *~* **corn [wheat]** 荞麦. **-ic** [ˌsærəˈsenik] *a.*

Sar·ah [ˈseərə] *n.* 萨拉〔女子名, 昵称 Sadie, Sal〕.

SARAH = search and rescue and homing 搜索救援的归航无线电信标.

Sa·ra·je·vo [ˌsærəˈjeivu] *n.* 萨拉热窝〔南斯拉夫一城市〕.

sa·ran [səˈræn] *n.* 【化】萨冉树脂; 莎纶〔氯乙烯, 二氯乙烯共聚纤维〕.

sa·rape [səˈrɑːpi] *n.* = serape.

Sar·a·to·ga [ˌsærəˈtəugə] *n.* ①萨拉托加〔美纽约州东部一村落, 附近有温泉疗养地〕. ②〔美〕女用旅行箱 〔= *~* trunk〕. *~* **chips [potato]** 〔美〕油炸土豆片.

Sa·ra·wak [səˈrɑːwək] *n.* 沙捞越〔马来西亚的一个邦〕.

sarc- *comb. f.* 〔用于元音前〕 = sarco-.

sar·casm [ˈsɑːkæzəm] *n.* ①讽刺, 讥讽, 挖苦. ②讽刺话, 挖苦话. *squelch sb. with biting ~* 用尖刻的挖苦话压服人.

sar·cas·tic, -ti·cal [sɑːˈkæstik(əl)] *a.* 讽刺的, 讥讽的, 挖苦的. **-ti·cal·ly** *ad.*

sarce·net [ˈsɑːsnet] *n.* = sarsenet.

sarco- *comb. f.* 肉: *sarco*carp; *sarco*logy.

sar·co·carp [ˈsɑːkəukɑːp] *n.* 【植】①(桃、杏等的)果肉. ②肉(质)果皮. ③多果肉的果子.

sar·code [ˈsɑːkəud] *n.* 【生】原生质. **-cod·ic** [sɑːˈkɔdik] *a.*

sar·coid [ˈsɑːkɔid] *a.* 肉的, 肉状的.

sar·coid·o·sis [ˌsɑːkɔiˈdəusis] *n.* 【医】肉样瘤病, 类肉瘤病.

sar·col·o·gy [sɑːˈkɔlədʒi] *n.* 【医】软组织解剖学; 肌肉学.

sar·co·ma [sɑːˈkəumə] *n.* (*pl. ~s, -ta* [-tə]) 【医】肉瘤.

sar·coph·a·gus [sɑːˈkɔfəgəs] *n.* (*pl. -gi* [-gai, -dʒai], *~es*) (雕花大理石)石棺.

sar·co·sine [ˈsɑːkəsiːn] *n.* 【化】肌氨酸.

sar·cous [ˈsɑːkəs] *a.* 肉的, 肌肉(组成)的.

sard [sɑːd] *n.* 【矿】肉红玉髓, 黄玉髓.

sar·da·na [sɑːˈdɑːnə] *n.* ①萨达纳舞〔西班牙加泰隆尼亚的一种民间舞蹈〕. ②萨达纳舞曲.

Sar·da·na·pa·li·an [ˌsɑːdənəˈpeiliən] *a.* 亚述(Assyria)王沙达那帕鲁斯 (Sardanapalus) 似的, 荒淫的; 穷奢极欲的.

sar·dine[1] [sɑːˈdiːn] *n.* (*pl. ~(s)*) ①【鱼】鳁鱼, 沙丁鱼. ②〔俚〕庸碌无能的人. *be packed like ~s* 拥挤不堪. **~-fit** *a.* 拥挤不堪的.

sar·dine[2] [ˈsɑːdain] *n.* = sard.

Sar·din·ia [sɑːˈdinjə] *n.* 撒丁(岛)〔意大利在地中海上的一大岛〕.

Sar·din·i·an [sɑːˈdiniən] *a.* ①撒丁(岛)的. ②撒丁(岛)人的. ③撒丁(岛)语的. — *n.* ①撒丁(岛)人. ②撒丁(岛)语.

sar·di·us [ˈsɑːdiəs] *n.* ①= sard. ②【圣】希伯来高级祭司胸饰上的宝石.

sar·don·ic [sɑːˈdɔnik] *a.* 嘲笑的, 讥笑的, 冷笑的, 讥讽的. *a ~ laugh [chuckle, smile]* 冷笑. **-al·ly** *ad.*

sar·do·nyx [ˈsɑːdəniks] *n.* 【矿】缠丝玛瑙.

sar·gas·so [sɑːˈgæsəu] *n.* (*pl. ~(e)s*) 【植】果囊马尾藻(= *~* weed).

sar·gas·sum [sɑːˈgæsəm] *n.* = sargasso.

sarge [sɑːdʒ] *n.* 〔美俚〕 = sergeant.

sa·ri, sa·ree [ˈsɑːriː] *n.* (*pl. -ris*) (印度女人披在身上的)卷布, 莎丽服.

sark [sɑːk] *n.* 〔Scot.〕 衬衣.

Sar·ma·tian [sɑːˈmɑːʃən] *a.* (古时东欧地区维斯杜拉河和伏尔加河之间的) 萨尔马提亚的; 萨尔马提亚人的. — *n.* 萨尔马提亚人.

sar·men·tose [sɑːˈmentəus] *a.* 【植】具长匐茎的.

sa·rod, sa·rode [səˈrəud] *n.* 萨洛德琴 〔类似琵琶的一种印度乐器〕.

sa·rong [ˈsɑːrɔŋ] *n.* (马来民族男女所著的)围裙, 莎笼.

sar·os [ˈseərɔs] *n.* 【天】(日食和月食的)沙罗周期〔计 18 年又 $11^1/_2$ 天, 为日蚀和月蚀关系的反复周期〕.

sar·ra·ce·ni·a [ˌsærəˈsiːniə] *n.* 【植】美洲瓶子植

物。

sar·sa·pa·ril·la [ˌsɑːsəpəˈrilə] *n.* ①【植】菝葜；菝葜根〔美洲产的热带植物〕。②菝葜精（香料）。③菝葜（为香料所做的）汽水。

sarse·net [ˈsɑːsnit] *n.* 里子薄绸〔素纺，棉布〕；平纹丝带（= sarcenet, sarsnet）。

sar·tor [ˈsɑːtə] *n.* 裁缝，成衣匠〔文学或幽默用语〕。

sar·to·ri·al [sɑːˈtɔːriəl] *a.* ①裁缝的；缝纫的；衣服的〔文学或幽默用语〕。②【解】裁缝肌的。 *a ~ triumph* 〔谑〕缝制得极好的衣服。 *the ~ art* 〔谑〕裁缝艺术。

sar·to·ri·us [sɑːˈtɔriəs] *n.* 【解】（大腿上的）缝匠肌。

SAS = Scandinavian Airlines System 斯堪的纳维亚航空公司。

sas 〔口〕 = sarsaparilla.

SASE = self-addressed stamped envelope 回邮信封。

Sa·se·bo [ˈsɑːsəbɔː] *n.* 佐世保〔日本港市〕。

sash[1] [sæʃ] *n.* ①（妇女、儿童用的）饰带，腰带。②【军】肩带，绶带，值星带。— *vt.* 用饰带装饰；给…系上腰带〔饰带〕。

sash[2] [sæʃ] *n.* 窗框，门框；门窗的框格；吊窗；一组这样的窗框。— *vt.* 在…上装吊窗；给…装上框格。 ~ **cord,** ~ **line** 吊窗绳。 ~ **pocket** 吊窗锤的滑槽。 ~ **pulley** 吊窗滑轮。 ~ **rope,** ~ **tape** = ~ line. ~ **weights** 〔*pl.*〕吊窗锤。 ~ **window** 吊窗；上下拉动的窗。

sa·shay [sæˈʃei] *vi.* ①〔美口〕走〔特指漫不经心或大摇大摆地〕。②（舞蹈中）用快滑步前进。 ③斜向行进〔移动〕。

sa·shi·mi [sɑːˈʃiːmiː] *n.* 〔*pl.*〕生鱼片〔日本菜肴中一种料理添饰的配菜〕。

sas·ka·toon [ˌsæskəˈtuːn] *n.* 〔主加〕 = juneberry.

sass [sæs] *n.* ①蔬菜；（餐末吃的）煮水果。②〔美俚〕唐突；顶嘴。— *vt.* 对…说唐突话，和…顶嘴，对…出言不逊。 ~**-box** 〔美〕说话唐突的人，冒失鬼〔亦作 savce〕。

sas·sa·by [ˈsæsəbi] *n.* ***(pl. -bies)*** 【动】（南非产的）大羚羊。

sas·sa·fras [ˈsæsəfræs] *n.* ①【植】檫树属；黄樟，美洲檫木。②檫木的根和皮〔含芳香挥发油〕。

Sas·sa·nid [ˈsæsənid] *n.* ***(pl. ~s, Sas·san·i·dae*** [sæˈsænidiː]***)*** 萨珊王（朝）〔公元 226？—641 年间波斯萨珊王朝，或其中任何一个君主〕（=Sassanian, Sasanian）。

Sas·se·nach [ˈsæsənæk] *n., a.* 〔Scot; Ir. 贬〕撒克逊（血统的）人（的）；苏格兰〔苏格兰低地〕人（的）。

sass·y [ˈsæsi] *a.* ***(-i·er, -i·est)*** ①〔美方〕莽撞的，冒昧的；脸皮厚的，不顾一切的，唐突的，孟浪的，无礼的。②漂亮的，时髦的，俊俏的，很帅的（= saucy）。

sas·sy bark 【植】①基尼格木皮。②基尼格木 *(Erythrophleum guineense)* 〔产于非洲〕（= sassywood）。

Sat. = ①Saturday. ②Saturn.

sat [sæt] sit 的过去式及过去分词。

SAT= Scholastic Aptitude Test 学术才能测验。

Sa·tan [ˈseitən] *n.* 撒但，[s-] 恶魔，魔王。

sa·tang [sɑːˈtæŋ] *n.* ***(sing., pl.)*** 萨当〔泰国货币名，硬币，等于 1/100 铢 (Thai baht)〕。

sa·tan·ic, -i·cal [səˈtænik, -ikəl] *a.* ①恶魔的；魔王的。②似恶魔的；邪恶的；蔑视（宗教）道德的。③丑恶的，极恶劣的。 ***His S-Majesty*** 〔谑〕魔王。~ ***energy*** 超人的精力。 **-i·cal·ly** *ad.*

Sa·tan·ism [ˈseitənizəm] *n.* ①恶魔主义，魔鬼崇拜。②魔鬼行为；恶魔性格；穷凶极恶。

Sa·tan·ist [ˈseitənist] *n.* ①恶魔主义〔崇拜〕者。②本性邪恶者。

S.A.T.B. = soprano, alto, tenor, bass.

satch·el [ˈsætʃəl] *n.* ①小背包；（小学生用的）书包。②【军】图囊。~ **charges** 【军】炸药包。

satch·el(l)·ed [ˈsætʃəld] *a.* 背〔有〕着小背包〔书包〕的。

SATCOM =〔美〕 Satellite Communication Agency.（陆军）卫星通信机构。

SATCOMA = Satellite Communications Centre 卫星通信中心。

sate[1] [seit] *vt.* 〔主用被动语态〕①使饱，喂饱。②使心满意足。③使餍足，使腻。 ***be ~d with*** 吃饱，饱享，吃腻，餍足。 ***~ oneself with*** ①饱餐。②大量享受。

sate[2] [sæt, seit] sit 的古体过去式及过去分词（= sat）。

sat·een [sæˈtiːn] *n.* 【纺】棉缎，缎纹布；纬缎；横贡。

sate·less [ˈseitlis] *a.* 〔诗〕①不知饱的。②无餍的，不知足的。

sat·el·lite [ˈsætəlait] *n.* ①【天】卫星；人造卫星；〔喻〕卫星国。②随从，帮闲者，食客。③【生】随体（指染色体）；陪簇虫；【地】伴生矿物；伴线。④附属社区，卫星区，郊区。⑤附属品。 *an artificial [earth]* ~ 人造〔地球〕卫星。 *a multistage* ~ 多级人造卫星。 ~ **DNA** 【生】随体脱氧核糖核酸。 ~ **town** 卫星城。 **-lit·ic** [ˌsætəˈlitik] *a.* 卫星的。

sat·el·oid [ˈsætəlɔid] *n.* ①（因速度较慢而不能作长时间轨道运行的）太空船。②（一种半飞机、半人造卫星式）有人驾驶的太空船。

sa·tem [ˈsɑːtəm, ˈseit-] *a.* 【语言】咝音语言的〔指原始印欧语中阻塞音已变为咝音的语言，而有别于腭音语言 (centum)〕。

sa·ti [səˈtiː] *n.* = suttee.

sa·ti·a·ble [ˈseiʃiəbl] *a.* 可使饱的，可使餍足的；可使满足的。 **-bly** *ad.*

sa·ti·ate [ˈseiʃieit] *vt.* = sate[1]. — [ˈseiʃiit] *a.* 〔诗〕饱足的，吃饱的；满足的。

sa·ti·a·tion [ˌseiʃiˈeiʃən] *n.* = satiety.

sa·ti·e·ty [səˈtaiəti] *n.* ①饱食；餍足，饱足。②许多，过多 *(of)*. ***to ~*** 饱饱地，充分地。

sat·in [ˈsætin] *n.* ①缎子；【纺】缎纹；经缎组织；经面缎纹。②〔俚〕杜松子酒。 *the ~ of a fine skin* 缎子一样的皮肤。 *the ~ of the coat of a horse* 缎子一样光滑柔软的马毛。 ~ *cloth* 有光缎纹细呢。 ~ *double face* 双面缎。 *figured* ~ 花缎。 ~ *finish* （银器等的）擦光整理。 *white* ~ 〔俚〕杜松子酒。 — *vt.* 对（纸等）作加光处理〔使具缎状光泽〕。 ~ **paper** 蜡光纸。 ~ **stitch** （使现缎子光泽的）缎纹刺绣法。 ~ **straw** （打草帽用的）柔软麦稭。 ~ **wood** 缎栋。

sat·i·net, sat·i·nette [ˌsætiˈnet] *n.* 【纺】①充缎子；缎纹棉毛呢；棉毛缎。②全丝薄缎。

sat·in·y [ˈsætini] *a.* 似缎的；光滑的。

sat·ire [ˈsætaiə] *n.* ①讽刺诗〔文〕；讽刺作品；②讽刺。 *His action is a ~ on his boastful pretension.* 他的行动是对他自我吹嘘〔卖弄〕的一个讽刺。

sa·tir·ic, -i·cal [səˈtirik, -kəl] *a.* 讽刺的。

sat·i·rist [ˈsætirist] *n.* 讽刺诗〔文〕作者；善于讽刺的人。

sat·i·rize sat·i·rise [ˈsætiraiz] *vt.* ①讽刺，写文章讽刺；挖苦。②违反。 *This detestable custom ~s humanity.* 这个可厌的风俗违反人性。

sat·is [ˈsætis] *n., ad.* 〔L.〕足够，充分，（考试成绩等）及格。 ***jam*** [dʒæm] ~ 已够，已及格。 ~ ***superque*** [sjuːˈpəːkwi] 足够并已超出；十二分，及格以上。

sat·is·fac·tion [ˌsætisˈfækʃən] *n.* ①满足，满意，舒服 *(at; with)*. ②〔a ~〕使（欲望等）满足的事物。③偿还，赔偿，义务的履行 *(for)*. ④赔偿物。⑤【宗】苦行赎罪。⑥（雪耻，挽回名誉损失的）决斗；报复。 *I heard the news with great [much] ~.* 我听了这个消息非常满意。 *It will be a great ~ to you to know that ...* 你如果听到…一定很满意。 ***demand ~*** 要求道歉〔决斗，赔偿〕。 ***enter (up) ~*** 在法院备案表明已偿清应付款项。 ***give ~*** 使满足〔满意〕；赔偿；答应决斗。 ***in full and complete ~*** 照数还讫，全数还清。 ***in ~ of*** 作为…的赔偿。 ***make ~ for*** 赔偿，偿还（*~ for a debt [crime]* 还债，赎〔罪〕）。 ***to sb.'s ~ = to the ~ of*** 使…满意地，…得使…满意。

sat·is·fac·to·ry [ˌsætisˈfæktəri] *a.* ①令人满足〔满意〕的，称心如意的 *(to)*；圆满的。②【神】赎罪的。 *His* *behaviour is anything but* ~. 他的行为实在不能令人满意. ~ *results* 圆满的结果. **-ri·ly** *ad.*

sat·is·fi·a·ble [ˈsætisfaiəbl] *a.* ①可使满足[满意]的. ②能偿还[赔偿]的.

sat·is·fy [ˈsætisfai] *vt.* ①使满足,使满意,使果腹;符合(标准),达到(要求). ②赔偿,偿清;履行(义务);答应(要求),赎(罪). ③使确信;消除(恐怖、疑惑等);使安心. ④【数】满足…的条件;【化】使饱和. ~ *one's desire [hunger]* 满足欲望[饥饿]. ~ *one's aspirations* 实现抱负. ~ *one's creditor* 对债权人清偿欠款. ~ *one's fears [doubts]* 消除恐怖[疑虑]. ***be satisfied*** ①满足,满意,吃饱. ②欢喜 *(with)*. ③深信,确信 *(of; that)* (*I'm satisfied he is the thief.* 我确信他就是贼.) ***rest satisfied*** 满足于 *(with)*. ~ ***oneself*** ①满意. ②查明,证明,确实弄明白 *(of; that)*. ~ **the examiners** 考试及格. — *vi.* ①令人满意. ②【宗】(基督)为世人赎罪.

sat·is·fy·ing [ˈsætisfaiiŋ] *a.* ①使人满足的,令人满意的. ②充分的;可以相信的,确实的. **-ly** *ad.*

sat·rap [ˈsætrəp] *n.* ①(作为古波斯地方长官的)州长,总督. ②(殖民地等的)总督. ③暴吏.

sat·u·ra·ble [ˈsætʃərəbl] *a.* 可饱和[浸透]的.

sat·u·rant [ˈsætʃərənt] *a.* 使饱和的. — *n.* ①【化】饱和剂,浸渍剂. ②【医】制酸剂.

sat·u·rate [ˈsætʃəreit] *vt.* ①使浸透,使渗透,浸;使渗进,使湿透. ②使满,【化】使饱和. ③【军】饱和轰炸. ~*d compound* 饱和化合物. ***be ~d by*** 被…浸透[湿透]. ***be ~d with*** 充分渗透着,充满着. ~ ***oneself (in)*** 埋头(在…中),精通. — [-rit] *a.* 〔诗〕浸透的,渗透的,颜色浓[深]的;饱和的.

sat·u·rat·ed [ˈsætʃəreitid] *a.* ①饱和的. ②充满…了的. ③浸透的,湿透的. ④(颜色)未被白色弄淡的. ⑤〔美俚〕喝醉了的. ~ **rock**【地】饱和岩. ~ **colo(u)r** 彰色,饱和色. ~**solution**【化】饱和溶液. ~ **steam** 饱和蒸汽. ~ **steel**【冶】共析钢.

sat·u·ra·tion [ˌsætʃəˈreiʃən] *n.* ①浸透,浸润. ②充满;饱和. ③【化】饱和(状态). ④饱和剂. ⑤【物】磁性饱和. ⑥【色】浓度,章度. ⑦【商】(市场的)饱和供应,足量供应. ~ **bombing**【空】饱和轰炸. ~ **point** 饱和点. ~ **pressure** 饱和压力.

Sat·ur·day [ˈsætədi] *n.* ①星期六. ②【犹太教】安息日. ~ **night special** 〔美俚〕周末特备品〔指手枪,因罪犯常在周末作案〕. ~**-to-Monday** *n., a.* 周末(的). **-s** *ad.* 〔美〕每星期六.

Sat·urn [ˈsætə(:)n] *n.* ①【古罗马】农神. ②【天】土星. ③【炼金术】铅. ④(美国的)土星运载火箭. *the ~'s ring*【天】土星环. ~ **salt**【化】醋酸铅.

Sat·ur·na·li·a [ˌsætəːˈneiljə] *n.* 〔*sing., pl.*〕【古罗马】农神节〔十二月中旬〕;〔s-〕〔用作 *sing.*〕放肆欢闹,纵情狂欢. *a s- of crime* 恣意胡为. **-li·an** *a.*

Sa·tur·ni·an [sæˈtəːniən] *a.* ①【古罗马】农神的. ②【天】土星的. ③黄金时代的,繁荣昌盛的,快乐的,幸福的. — *n.* (想象中的)土星居民. ~ **age** 农神时代,黄金时代. ~ **verse**(未受希腊诗体影响以前的)古拉丁诗体.

sa·tur·nic [səˈtəːnik] *a.* ①铅毒的,铅毒性的. ②【医】中了铅毒的.

sa·tur·ni·id [səˈtəːniːid] *n.* 【动】(天蚕蛾科 *(Saturniidae)* 的)天蚕蛾. — *a.* 天蚕蛾科的.

sat·ur·nine [ˈsætə(:)nain] *a.* ①阴沉的,不愉快的;性情乖僻的;沉默寡言的;忧郁的,严肃的. ②讥诮的,讥讽的. ③铅的;铅中毒的. *a man of ~ temper* 性格阴沉的人. *a ~ patient* 铅中毒病人. *a ~ symptom* 铅中毒症状. ~**ly** *ad.*

sat·ur·nism [ˈsætə(:)nizəm] *n.* 【医】(慢性)铅中毒.

sat·yr [ˈsætə] *n.* ①〔常作 S-〕【希神】(淫逸放纵半人半兽的)森林之神〔人形,有马或山羊般的耳朵和尾巴〕. ②淫欲无度的男人,色鬼,色情狂者. ③〔罕〕猩猩. ④【昆】蛇眼蝶. ~ **play**【古希腊】森林之神滑稽短歌剧〔其中合唱队化装成森林之神模样〕. **-ic** [səˈtirik] *a.* ①森林之神的. ②色情狂的.

sat·y·ri·a·sis [ˌsætiˈraiəsis] *n.* 【医】男性淫狂,色情狂,求雌狂.

sau [sau] *n.* 〔越南语〕分〔越南货币名,等于1/100盾〕.

sauce [sɔːs] *n.* ①调味汁,酱油. ②刺激物,趣味. ③〔方〕(鱼肉的)配菜[蔬菜等] (= garden-~). ④〔美〕(文火)煮的水果;(果)酱. ⑤〔俚〕冒昧,莽撞,唐突,无礼. ⑥〔美俚〕烈酒. *apple ~* 苹果酱. *mint ~* 薄荷酱. *tomato ~* 蕃茄酱. *What's ~ for the goose is ~ for the gander.* 可以用到乙方的,也可以用到甲方;害人害自己. *Hunger is the best ~.* 饥饿是最好的调味品. *The ~ is better than the fish.* 配菜比鱼还好;喧宾夺主. *None of your ~! = Give me none of your ~! = Don't come with any of your ~! = I don't want any of your ~!* 不要无礼!说话留神点〔别对我胡说八道〕! ***more ~ than fig*** 十分无礼. ***serve the same ~ to (sb.) = serve (sb.) with the same ~*** 即以其人之道还治其人之身. ***sweet meat and sour ~*** 美味的肉和酸味的配菜;苦乐相间. — *vt.* ①给…加调味汁[品],给…加滋味. ②〔俚〕对…说冒昧话. *a sermon ~d with wit* 有风趣的说教. ~**boat** (船形)调味汁碟. ~**box** 〔口〕冒失鬼,〔尤指〕莽撞无礼的孩子. ~**pan** 有柄小平底锅. ~**pot** (一般的)煮锅.

sau·cer [ˈsɔːsə] *n.* ①茶杯托,茶碟. ②(放花盆的)垫盘(等);茶碟状的器物. ③浅碟形盆地. ④〔美〕拳击场. ~ **eyes** (睁得)又圆又大的眼睛. ~**-eyed** *a.*(天生或因惊讶等睁得)大而圆的眼睛的. ~**man** 星球人,外太空人.

sau·cy [ˈsɔːsi] *a.* (**-ci·er; -ci·est**) ①冒失的,莽撞的,没礼貌的,不客气的. ②〔俚〕灵活的;愉快的;轻快的;活泼的. ③漂亮的,俊俏的,时髦的. **sau·ci·ly** *ad.* **sau·ci·ness** *n.*

Sa·u·di A·ra·bi·a [ˈsaudi əˈreibjə] 沙特阿拉伯〔位于阿拉伯半岛,首都 Riyadh〕. **Saudi Arabian** 沙特阿拉伯人.

sau·er·bra·ten [ˈsauəbrɑːtn, ˈzauə-] *n.* 〔美〕洋葱醋渍牛肉〔菜名〕.

sau·er·kraut [ˈsauəkraut] *n.* 〔G.〕泡(白)菜.

sau·ger [ˈsɔːgə] *n.* 〔美〕【动】鲕鲈 *(stizostedion canadense)* 〔产于美洲〕.

Sauk [sɔːk] *n.* ①*(pl. ~s, ~)* 索克人〔以前居住于密执安州一带的北美印第安人〕. ②福克斯人〔以前居住于威斯康星州一带的北美印第安人〕;福克斯人和索克人所操的阿尔衮琴语.

Saul [sɔːl] *n.* 索尔〔男子名〕.

saul [sɔːl] *n.* = sal¹.

Sau·mur [ˈsəumjuə] *n.* (法国产)梭缪尔白葡萄酒.

sau·na [ˈsaunə, ˈsɔːnə] *n.* 〔Finn.〕①(芬兰)蒸汽浴. ②(芬兰)蒸汽浴室.

Saun·dra [ˈsɔːndrə] *n.* 桑德拉〔女子名, Sandra 的异体〕.

saun·ter [ˈsɔːntə] *n., vi.* 闲逛,闲荡;混日子. ~ ***through life*** 闲混一辈子;过闲荡生活.

sau·rel [ˈsɔːrəl] *n.* 【鱼】竹筴鱼 *(Trachurus symmetricus)* 〔产于欧、美〕.

sau·ri·an [ˈsɔːriən] *a., n.* 【动】蜥蜴类的(动物).

sau·roid [ˈsɔːrɔid] *a., n.* 蜥蜴状的(动物).

sau·ro·pod [ˈsɔːrəpɔd] *n.* 蜥脚类亚目动物〔如雷龙〕. — *a.* 蜥脚类亚目的.

sau·ry [ˈsɔːri] *n.* 【鱼】长颌竹刀鱼,针鱼,鱵鱼. ~ **pike** 竹刀鱼.

sau·sage [ˈsɔsidʒ] *n.* ①香肠,腊肠. ②〔军俚〕腊肠形[圆柱形]观测气球 (= ~ balloon). ③〔口〕德国人. *a Bologna ~* 大红肠. ***not have a ~*** 〔俚〕不名一文. ~ **machine** 做香肠用的绞肉机. ~ **meat** 香[腊]肠用肉馅. ~ **roll** (裹上湿面粉然后油煎的)香[腊]肠

肉馅卷.

sau·té [ˈsəutei] *a.* *(pl.~(e)s)*〔F.〕【烹】(嫩)煎的,(油)炸的,炒的. —*n.* (嫩)煎[炸、炒]的菜餚. —*vt.* *(-(e)d, ~ing)* 嫩煎.

Sau·terne [səuˈtəːn] *n.* (法国 Sauterne 地区产的)一种白葡萄酒.

sauve qui peut [F. səuv kiː pəː]〔F.〕四散溃逃,总崩溃.

sav·a·ble [ˈseivəbl] *a.* ①可拯救的. ②可节省的. ③【宗】可得救的.

Sav·age [ˈsævidʒ] *n.* 萨维奇〔姓氏〕.

sav·age [ˈsævidʒ] *a.* ①荒野的;野性的. ②野蛮的;未开化的. ③凶猛的;残酷的;粗暴的;猛烈的. ④【徽】裸体的. ⑤〔口〕愤怒的;暴躁的. *a ~ beast* 野[猛]兽. *a ~ man* 残暴的人;粗野的人. *~ manners* 粗暴的态度. *a ~ criticism* 粗暴的批评. ***as ~ as a meat oxe***〔美〕①暴跳如雷的. ②狼吞虎咽的. ***get ~ with*** 向…大发脾气. ***make a ~ attack upon*** 猛烈攻击. ***make sb. ~*** 使大发脾气,惹怒. —*n.* ①野蛮人;残暴的人;粗野的人. ②野兽. ③〔美〕有拘捕狂的警察. ④〔*pl.*〕〔美俚〕雇员. — *vt.* ①(马,狗)乱咬[乱踏]. ②用暴力攻击,痛打,痛骂. **-ly** *ad.* **-ness** *n.*

sav·age·ry [ˈsævidʒəri] *n.* ①野蛮,残暴,凶猛. ②野蛮状态;蛮荒[蒙昧]状态. ③荒野. ④〔集合词〕野蛮人,野兽.

sa·van·na, sa·van·nah [səˈvænə] *n.* (美国东南部无树)大平原. ②(亚洲)热带大草原.

sa·vant [ˈsævənt] *n.* 学者;(特指)著名大科学家.

sa·vate [səˈvɑːt] *n.*〔F.〕(可以用脚和头的)法式拳击.

save[1] [seiv] *vt.* ①救,拯救,救济;保全. ②储蓄,贮存;保留. ③节约;节省. ④不误,赶上. ⑤〔美卑〕杀,干掉. ⑥救(球),阻碍球赛对方得(分). ⑦【宗】为…赎罪. *~ sb. from danger* 救某人脱离危险. *~ sb. from drowning* 把某人从水里救出来. *God ~ the King!* 上帝保佑国王;国王万岁. *S- [God ~] me from my friends.* 请别那样做!别管闲事! *A stitch in time ~s nine.* 及时一针抵得事后九针. *~ time* 节省时间. *~ the dinner-hour* 赶上吃饭时间. *~ the gate* 关门前赶回. *~ the train* 赶上火车. ***~ appearance [hono(u)r]*** 保全体面,保全面子. ***~ one's bacon*** 见 bacon 条. ***~ one's breath*** 缄默. ***~ one's face*** 保全面子. ***~ one's pains*** 不滥费气力,节省精力. ***~ one's pocket*** 免掉出钱. ***~ one's skin,*** 见 skin 条. ***~ oneself*** 偷懒. ***~ oneself trouble*** 省事. ***~ the situation*** 挽回局势,度过难关,化险为夷. ***~ the tide*** 趁潮涨时出[入]港;抓住时机. ***~ up*** 贮(蓄). ***S- us!*** 哎呀! —*vi.* ①救,拯救;救济. ②贮存,储蓄. ③节约,节省. ④(鱼、水果等)不易坏,搁得住. ⑤【足球】阻止对方得分. *food that will ~* 搁置不坏的食物. — *n.*【足球等】救球;阻碍对方得分. *a fine ~* 球救得漂亮.

save[2] [seiv] *prep.* 除…以外,除了. *all ~ him* 除他以外都. *the last ~ one* 倒数第二. *I am well ~ that I have a cold.* 除了感冒,我没什么毛病. ***~ and except***〔加强语气〕除了…,除…以外. ***~ errors***【商】有错不在此限. ***~ that*** 此外. — *conj.* ①若不是;只是. ②除去,除了.

save-all [ˈseivɔːl] *n.* ①【机】省费器;承油碟;防溅器;挡雾罩. ②【建】承漏布. ③节约装置. ④(有插烛钉的)烛碟;烛台底盘. ⑤工作服;工装,围裙;罩衫. ⑥储蓄箱;扑满. ⑦【海】附加风帆;脚帆. ⑧(防止货物落水的)安全网. ⑨〔方〕极端俭省的人;吝啬鬼.

sav·e·loy [ˈsævilɔi] *n.*〔英〕(熟的)五香辣味干腊肠.

Sa·vels [ˈsævəlz] *n.* 萨弗尔斯〔姓氏〕.

sav·er [ˈseivə] *n.* ①救助者,救星. ②省费器,节约装置. ③俭省的人. *oil ~*【矿】节油装置.

sav·in, sav·ine [ˈsævin] *n.*【植】①新疆圆柏 *(Juniperus sabina)*. ②铅笔柏 (= red cedar).

sav·ing[1] [ˈseiviŋ] *a.* ①救助的,救济的,挽救的,援救的,搭救的,拯救的. ②可取的;保存的,储蓄的. ③俭省的,节省的,节约的;俭约的,节俭的. ④无损失的,不赔不赚的. ⑤【法】保留的,除外的. ⑥补偿的;补不足的. — *n.* ①救助,救济,挽救,援救,搭救,拯救. ②〔*pl.*〕储蓄(金). ③俭省,节省,节约. ④【法】保留,除外. ⑤【化】滤屑. *He has the ~ (grace of) modesty.* 他有谦逊这一个可取的地方. ***From ~ comes having. = S- is getting.*** 节约就是增加收入. **~ bargain** 不赔不赚的交易. **~ clause** 保留条款.

sav·ing[2] [ˈseiviŋ] — *prep.* 除…以外. *~ your reverence [presence]*〔古〕恕我冒昧地讲;说句失敬的话,您别多心.

sav·io(u)r [ˈseivjə] *n.* ①救济者,救助者,拯救者. ②〔the S-〕救世主,救星.

sa·voir-faire [ˈsævwɑːˈfeə] *n.*〔F.〕机警,圆滑,手腕;处世术.

sa·voir-vi·vre [ˈsævwɑːˈviːvr] *n.*〔F.〕彬彬有礼,举止得体;善于待人接物,熟悉人情事故;有教养.

sa·vor·y [ˈseivəri] *n.* ①【植】香草,木质薄荷〔烹调用〕. ②〔美〕= savoury.

sa·vo(u)r [ˈseivə] *n.* ①味,味道,滋味;风味;〔古〕香,香味. ②气味,一点儿,几分. ③兴味,趣味. ④〔喻〕特点;意味. ⑤〔诗〕名声,名气. *a book without ~* 枯燥无味的书. — *vt.* ①〔罕〕给…增加滋味[趣味],使有味[有趣味]. ②〔古〕尝味;欣赏…的味;玩味;鉴赏. ③〔罕、诗〕有…的气味. — *vi.* 有…味道;有…的气味*(of)*. *conduct ~ing insolence* 蛮横的举动. *The offer ~s of impertinence.* 这个提议有点不客气[无礼]. **-less** *a.* 没有滋味的,没有味道的,不好吃的.

sa·vo(u)r·y [ˈseivəri] *a.* ①有滋味的,好吃的;【烹】咸味的;辣味(而不是甜味)的. ②〔常和否定词连用〕舒适宜人的,令人愉快的;体面的;名声好的. *have to live in a not very ~ district* 不得不住在一个不大舒服的地段. *have not a very ~ reputation* 名誉不大好. — *n.* (饭前或饭后有助胃纳的)美味小盘菜肴. **sa·vo(u)r·i·ly** *ad.* **-i·ness** *n.*

sa·voy [səˈvɔi] *n.*【植】皱叶甘兰,一种卷心菜.

Sa·voy·ard [səˈvɔiɑːd] *a.* (法国)萨伏依 (Savoy) 地方的. — *n.* ①萨伏依人. ②萨伏依歌剧的演员[导演,爱好者].

Savoy [səˈvɔi] **Operas** 萨伏伊轻歌剧〔指英国 Gilbert 作词、Sullivan 作曲的十多个轰动一时的轻歌剧,因这些歌剧最初在伦敦萨伏伊剧场演出而得此名〕.

Sav·vy [ˈsævi] *vt., vi.*〔俚〕知道;懂得;领悟. *S-? No ~.* 懂吗?不懂. — *n.*〔俚〕见识;理解力;处世才能,机智;精明;本领,专门技能. — *a.* 精明的;能干的;有见识的.

saw[1] [sɔː] see 的过去式.

saw[2] [sɔː] *n.* 格言,谚语〔通常冠用 old 或 wise〕.

saw[3] [sɔː] *n.* ①锯,锯机. ②【动】锯齿状器官[部分]. ③〔*pl.*〕(昆虫的)产卵锯. ④〔美俚〕十元钞票. *a circular ~* 圆锯. *a hand back ~* 手锯. *a chain ~* 链锯. *a crosscut ~* 横割锯;两人对拉的锯. — ***(-ed; -n)*** *vt.* 锯,锯开;锯成. — *vi.* 用锯;锯. ***~ a horse's mouth*** 勒紧缰绳. ***~ a log into boards = ~ boards out of a log*** 把木头锯成木板. ***~ crossway [lengthways, longway] of the grain*** 横[顺]着木理锯. ***~ the air with one's hands*** 用手左右挥动. ***~ up*** 锯断,锯掉. ***~ wood***〔美俚〕(在别人疲塌磨蹭的时候)埋头工作. ***S- your timber!***〔卑〕干你的事去! **~ blade** 锯带,锯条. **~bones**〔谑〕外科医生. **~buck** ①〔美〕锯台,锯木架. ②〔美〕十年刑期;十块钱,十元钞票. **~ chain** 锯链. **~doctor** 锯齿制作器[机];= saw set. **~dust** *n.* 锯屑 *(let the ~dust out of* (象弄出布娃娃里面锯屑那样)说出…的缺点,戳穿绣花枕头). **~fish**【鱼】锯鳐. **~fly**【动】叶蜂,锯蜂. **~ gin** 锯齿轧棉机. **~ grass**【植】锯齿草;牙买加砖子苗 (Cladium jamaicensis). **~horse** = **~buck.** **~ log**〔美〕锯材. **~mill** ①锯

木厂. ②大型锯机. ～ **pit** (上下各立一人的)锯木坑. ～ **set** 锯钳，锯齿修整器［机］. ～**tooth** 锯齿. ～-**toothed** *a.* 锯齿状的.

saw·der [ˈsɔːdə] *vt., n.* 〔俚〕奉承，谄媚.

sawed-off [ˈsɔːdɔːf] *a.* ①〔美俚〕锯短了的. ②身材矮小的；受排斥的. *a* ～ *gun* 〔美俚〕(匪徒等为了便于隐藏携带)锯短的枪.

sawn [sɔːn] saw 的过去分词.

saw·n(e)y [ˈsɔːni] *n.* ①〔俚蔑〕苏格兰人. ②〔s-〕笨人，蠢货，傻瓜.

saw-whet owl [ˈsɔːˌwet aul] 【动】阿加底亚枭 (*Aegolius acadica*) 〔产于北美〕.

saw·yer [ˈsɔːjə] *n.* ①锯木者，锯工. ②〔美〕(在河里擦来擦去的)漂流树［圆木］. ③(幼虫蛀入树木里的)蛀树甲虫.

Saw·yer(s) [ˈsɔːjə(z)] *n.* 索耶(斯)〔姓氏〕.

sax[1] [sæks] *n.* ①石板瓦工用的凿刀. ②〔Scot.〕＝ six.

sax[2] [sæks] *n.* 〔俚〕＝ saxophone.

Sax. ＝ Saxon; Saxony.

sax·a·tile [ˈsæksətil] *a.* ＝ saxicolous.

saxe [sæks] *n.* ①萨克森蓝〔一种鲜艳淡蓝色〕(＝～ blue, Saxon blue, Saxony blue). ②〔德制〕蛋白照相纸.

sax·horn [ˈsækshɔːn] *n.* 【乐】萨克斯号.

sax·ic·o·lous [sækˈsikələs], **sax·ic·o·line** [sækˈsikəlain] *a.* 【生，生态】生活［成长］于岩石上［岩石间］的.

sax·i·frage [ˈsæksifridʒ] *n.* 【植】虎耳草(属).

Sax·on [ˈsæksn] *n., a.* ①(原住德国、一部分于5—6世纪移居英国的)撒克逊人(的)；盎格鲁撒克逊人(的). ②英格兰人(的). ③苏格兰低地人(的). ④撒克逊语(的)；盎格鲁撒克逊语(的)，纯粹英语(的). ～ **blue** ＝ saxe (blue).

Sax·on·ism [ˈsæksənizəm] *n.* ①盎格鲁撒克逊语. ②盎格鲁撒克逊性格. ③英国风. ④英国国粹主义.

Sax·on·ist [ˈsæksənist] *n.* ①盎格鲁撒克逊语学家. ②英国国粹主义者. ③外来语排斥论者.

Sax·on·y [ˈsæksəni] *n.* ①萨克森〔德意志民主共和国一地区〕. ②光毛呢. **Lower** ～ 下萨克森〔德意志联邦共和国州名〕.

sax·o·phone [ˈsæksəfəun] *n.* 【乐】萨克斯管. **-phon·ist** [-ˈfəunist] *n.* 萨克斯管吹奏者.

Sax·ton [ˈsækstn] *n.* 萨克斯顿〔姓氏〕.

sax·tu·ba [ˈsækstjuːbə] *n.* 【乐】(大型)低音萨克斯号.

say [sei] (***said*** [sed]; 第三人称单数陈述语气现在时 ***says*** [sez]) *vt., vi.* ①说，讲；表达，表明，宣示；声明，主张，断定. *Say all you know and* ～ *it without reserve.* 知无不言，言无不尽. *S- no more.* 别再说了. *Never* ～ *die!* 不可气馁！*Do you mean what you* ～? 你是说真的吗？你说的是当真的吗？*I mean what I* ～. 我说了是算数的. *S- what you mean.* 把你的意思说明白. *Do you* ～ *so?* 那是真的吗？*You don't* ～ *(so)!* 未必吧！不至于吧！真的！*You may well* ～ *so.* 你那样说可能(固然)对；你不妨那么说. *Who shall I* ～, *sir?* (传达者问来客)你是哪一位？请问尊姓？*I'll* ～ *so.* 〔美俚〕你说得很对；我也同意. *He said "Yes" ＝ "Yes," said he.* 他说'是'. ②背，背诵，念，诵读. *to be said or sung* 供诵读或歌唱. ～ *one's lessons* 背功课，背书. ③〔祈使句〕假定(说)，比如说，就说，姑且说，大约 (＝ *let us* ～). *a few of them,* ～ *a dozen* 其中几个人，假定［比如说］一打左右吧. *a couple of hours,* ～ *from four to six* 两个钟头的时间，比方说从四点到六点. ④〔美口〕＝ I say〔见下〕. ⑤〔俚〕反驳. ***as much as to*** ～ 等于说；好象是说…一样地；象要说…似地. ***as to*** ～〔插入语〕也就是说. ***Easier said than done.*** 〔谚〕说着容易做时难. ***have nothing to*** ～ ***for oneself*** 〔口〕总是不开口；没话可说，一言不发. ***have something to*** ～ ***for oneself*** 有要辩白的话. ***have something [nothing] to*** ～ ***to[with]*** 要［不］对［和］…争辩，有话要说［没话可说］，有［没有］关系. ***hear*** ～ 听说，据说. ***I cannot*** ～. 我不知道. ***I cannot*** ～ ***much for ...*** 对…不以为…怎样好；对…不敢恭维. ***I dare*** ～〔插入语〕大概；许是；我想. ***I*** ～ ＝〔美口〕～ 喂，喂喂；哎呀；我是说 …〔加强语气〕；哎呀！(*I* ～, *John* ＝〔美〕～, *John* 喂，约翰. *I* ～, *what a beauty!* 哎呀！好漂亮的人［东西］)；***I should*** ～ ***(that)*** 大概，许是. ***I should*** ～ ***not*** 我以为不是那样. ***(It) goes without*** ～***ing that*** 当然不用说…. ***It is said that ...*** 据说，听说. ***(let us)*** ～ 比如说；大约. ***may well*** ～ ***that*** …很可以说. ***mean what one*** ～***s*** 是当真的. ***No sooner said than done.*** 一说就做；说到做到. ***not to*** ～ ***...,*** 虽不能说…；即使不说 (*It is warm, not to* ～ *hot.* 虽说不上热，但也很暖和了). ～ ***a good word for*** 替…说好话，替…说情，替…辩护，推奖. ***S- away!*** 完全说出来吧；尽量说吧！～ ***for oneself*** 分辩，争辩. ***S- on.*** 说下去，继续说吧. ～ ***nay*** 否认；拒绝. ～ ***one's prayers*** 祷告. ～ ***one's say [word]*** 说出自己的想法；把话说完；畅所欲言. ～ ***out*** 坦白说出，直说. ～ ***over [again]*** ①再说，反复说. ②背诵…. ～ ***something*** ＝ ～ ***grace*** 饭前后的祷告；即席演说几句. ～ ***something of*** 批评. ～ ***the word*** (下)命令. ～ ***to do*** 〔美俚，英卑〕叫，命 (*He said (for me) to tell you not to come.* 他叫(我)告诉你不要来. *They said to telephone.* 他们叫(我)打电话.) ～ ***(sth.) to oneself*** 暗自思量，心想，心中盘算★'自言自语'是 talk to oneself. ***so to*** ～〔插入语〕①好比，活象是，恰如，正象. ②可以这么说. ***That is*** ～***ing a great deal.*** 这可了不得. ***that is (to*** ～***)***〔插入语〕即，换句话说，(也)就是说；至少. ***They*** ～ ***...*** 据说，听说. ***There is no saying ...*** 很难说，说不准. ***though I*** ～ ***it (who should not)*** 虽然不应该由我来说；我来说虽然不大好. ***to*** ～ ***nothing of***〔插入语〕更不用说，更不待言，更不必说. ***to*** ～ ***the least of it*** 至少［插入语］可以(这样)说；退一步说. ***What do you*** ～ ***to (a walk)? ＝ What*** ～ ***you to (a walk)?*** (去散散步)你说怎么样［以为怎么样］？(散步)好不好？***What I*** ～ ***is ...*** 我的意思是…. ***when all is said (and done)*** 结果；毕竟. —*n.* ①该说的事情；想说的事情；话；言词. ②〔口〕轮到发言，发言的机会，发言权；〔*the* ～〕〔美〕最后决定权. ③〔the ～〕〔口〕格言，谚语. *It is now my* ～. 现在该我发言［发表意见］了. ***have a [some]*** ～ 有发言权. ***have the*** ～〔美〕要想怎样就怎样，有最后决定权. **-er** *n.* 发言人；〔古〕诗人.

Sa·yers [ˈseiəz, sɛəz] *n.* 塞耶斯〔姓氏〕.

say·est [ˈseiist], **sayst** [seist] *vt., vi.* 〔古〕say 的第二人称单数陈述语气现在式.

say·ing [ˈseiiŋ] *n.* ①话；言语. ②格言；谚语. *There is no* ～ *(what may happen).* 不知道(会发生什么事情). ***As the*** ～ ***is [goes]*** 俗话说(得好)；谚语说；常言道. ***It goes without*** ～ ***that ...*** 不用说；不消说；很明显；不言而喻. ～ ***and doing*** 言行.

say-so [ˈsei-səu] *n.* 〔美口〕①无证据的断言. ②最后决定权. ③谣传，道听途说.

say·yid, say·id [ˈsɑːjid] *n.* 赛义德〔穆斯林的一种尊称，尤用于对穆罕默德的后代〕.

Saz·e·rac [ˈsæzəræk] *n.* 〔美〕〔常用 s-〕萨塞拉克鸡尾酒〔一种有苦味(原加苦艾酒)的威士忌鸡尾酒〕.

S.B.,SB ＝ ①〔L.〕*Scientiae Baccalaureus* 理学士 (＝ Bachelor of Science). ②simultaneous broadcast(ing) 【无】同时广播. ③sales book 销货帐簿. ④South Britain〔英〕南不列颠. ⑤Special Branch (of Police) (警察局的)特别科.

Sb ＝ stibium 【化】锑 (＝ antimony).

sb. ＝ ①somebody. ②substantive.

SBA ＝ Small Business Administration〔美〕小企业管理局.

S-band S波段〔一种无线电超高频波段〕.
SbE, S by E = south by east 南偏东.
sbir·ro [ˈsbirəu, ˈzbirəu] *(pl. -ri* [-ri]*)* *n.* 〔It.〕警察.
'sblood [zblʌd] *int.* 〔古〕该死的！糟了！啐！(= God's blood!).
SbW, S by W = south by west 南偏西.
SC,S.C. = ①Sanitary Corps【军】环境卫生队. ②Signal Corps〔美〕陆军通信兵. ③South Carolina 南卡罗来纳〔美国州名〕. ④Supreme Court 最高法院. ⑤Security Council (of the United Nations)(联合国)安全理事会.
s.c. = ①small capitals【印】小体大写字母. ②supercalendered (纸张)特别光洁的. ③special constable〔英〕临时警察.
sc. = ①scale. ②scene. ③scilicet. ④screw. ⑤scruple. ⑥scandium. ⑦sculptor. ⑧special circular.
Sc. = ①Scotch. ②Scots. ③Scottish.
scab [skæb] *n.* ①痂, 疮痂. ②(羊等的)疥癣〔又叫 ~ rubbers〕. ③【植】疮痂病, 斑点病, (葡萄)黑豆病, (苹果)黑星病. ④〔俚、原美〕不加入工会的工人; 工贼. ⑤〔俚〕恶棍, 无赖. ⑥(金属等材料表面的)结疤; 铸件表面粘砂; 瑕, 疵, 孔, 眼. — *vi.* ①(伤口)生痂, (疮)结疤. ②〔俚〕破坏罢工. ~ *on strikers* 出卖罢工工人; 当工贼. ~**land** 荒瘠不毛的火山地带; 表土被洪水冲走的不毛之地. ~**wort** *n.*【植】土木星(= elecampane).
scab·bard [skæbəd] *n.* 鞘, 剑鞘. ***fling [throw] away the*** ~ 丢开剑鞘, 断然处置, 决死战斗, 奋斗无底. — *vt.* 把(剑)插进鞘中. ~ **fish** (大)刀鱼, 安哥拉带鱼.
scab·bed [skæbd, -id] *a.* ①有痂的; 满是疙痂的. ②生疥癣的. ③【植】感染斑点病等的〔*cf.* scab〕. ④不足取的, 低劣的, 下贱的, 卑鄙的.
scab·ble [ˈskæbl] *vt.* *(-bled, -bling)* (对采下的石头)作粗糙修整〔使粗具形态〕.
scab·by [skæbi] *a.* *(-bi·er; -bi·est)* ①结(满)痂的. ②长(满)疥癣的. ③〔口〕下贱的, 卑鄙的. ④少得可怜的. ⑤【植】感染斑点病等的〔*cf.* scab〕. ⑥【印】不鲜明的. ⑦【翻砂】(表面)有疤的. ~ *sixpence* 少得可怜的六个便士. **-bi·ly** *ad.* **-bi·ness** *n.*
sca·bi·es [ˈskeibii:z] *n.* 【医】疥疮; 疥螨病. **-et·ic** [ˌskeibiˈetik] *a.*
sca·bi·o·sa [ˌskeibiˈəusə] *n.* 山萝卜属 *(scabiosa)* 植物〔如: 轮锋菊(松虫草) *(Scabiosa atropurpurea)*〕.
sca·bi·ous [ˈskeibiəs] *n.*【植】山萝卜(属). — *a.*〔罕〕生疥癣的; 结满痂的.
sca·brous [skeibrəs] *a.* ①【动、植】粗糙的. ②多障碍的; 困难重重的. ③有伤风化的, 猥亵的; 品行恶劣的. **-ly** *ad.*
scad[1] [skæd] *n.*【鱼】竹筴鱼; 圈纹大眼鲷.
scad[2] [skædz] *n.*〔美俚〕极大数量, 大量, 许多〔美语多用复数〕. ~*s of money* 大量金钱.
scaf·fold [ˈskæfəld] *n.* ①【建】脚手架. ②(临时搭的)台架, 支架; 陈列台, 展览台; 露天舞台, 看台. ③绞架, 断头台; 〔the ~〕死刑. ④【解】骨骼, 骨架. ⑤(露葬用的)尸架. *a flying* ~ 悬空脚手架. *go to [mount] the* ~ 被处死刑. *send sb. to the* ~ 把某人处死刑. — *vt.* ①搭脚手架于(某处); 使站在脚手架上. ②把…绞死, 把…处死刑. ~**ing**【建】①脚手架; 台架. ②脚手架〔台架〕材料. ③储料台. ④【解】骨骼.
scag [skæg] *n.*〔美俚〕海洛因.
scagl·io·la [skælˈjəulə] *n.*【建】人造大理石; 仿云石.
scal·a·ble [ˈskeiləbl] *a.* ①可攀登的. ②可秤的. ③可剥去鳞片的.
sca·lade [skəˈleid] *n.*〔古〕用梯子攀登;【军】(用云梯)爬城 (= escalade).
scal·age [ˈskeilidʒ] *n.* ①缩减〔下降〕率. ②(对大圆木的)可用材估量.
sca·lar [ˈskeilə] *n.*【数】数量; 标量, 无向量; 实量; 纯量 *(opp.* vector*)*. — *a.* ①梯阶状的, 分等级的. ②【数】数量的; 标量的; 无向向量的. ③【生】= scalariform. ~ **product** 数(量)积.
sca·la·re [skəˈlεəri, -ˈlɑ:-] *n.*【动】天使鱼属 *(Pterophyllum)* 的鱼;〔尤指〕天使鱼 *Pterophyllum scalare)*.
sca·lar·i·form [skəˈlærifɔ:m] *a.*【动】梯状的;【植】阶纹的. *a* ~ *vessel* 梯纹导管.
scal·a·wag [ˈskæləwæg] *n.* ①〔美口〕流氓, 无赖. ②〔贬〕(美国南北战争后重建时期)参加共和党的南部白人. ③不中用的牲口, 瘦小的家畜.
scald[1] [skɔ:ld] *n.* 烫伤; 晒焦. ~*s and burns* 烫伤和烧伤. — *vt.* ①烫伤, 晒焦. ②把…放在滚水中过一下, 嫩煮; 用开水消毒, 烫. ③热(牛奶). *be* ~*ed to death* 被滚水烫死. *the* ~*ed cream* 用热牛奶提取的奶油. ~*ing tears* 热泪, 血泪. ~ *(out) a cup* 烫一烫杯子.
scald[2] [skɔ:ld] *n.*〔口〕头癣. ~**-head** *n.*〔口〕癞痢头.
scald[3] [skɔ:ld] *n.* (古代北欧的)吟唱诗人.
scale[1] [skeil] *n.* ①(尺、秤等上刻划的)分度, 度数; 标, 标度; 刻度; 尺寸; 尺, 尺度. ②【乐】(标度)音阶; 音列. ③等级(表), 级别(表), 品级. ④【数】计数法, 进位法, 换算法. ⑤比例; 比例尺; 缩尺程度. ⑥率, 税率. ⑦规模; 大小. ⑧阶梯, 梯子. *a proportional [proportionate]* ~ 比例尺. *a reduced* ~ 缩尺. *an enlarged* ~ 放大尺. *a folding* ~ 折尺. *a calculating [sliding]* ~ 计算尺. *the binary [ternary, decimal]* ~【数】二〔三, 十〕进法. *a chromatic [diatonic]* ~ 半〔全〕音阶. *the social* ~ 社会地位(等级). *rate* ~ 定价, 价目表. *visibility* ~ 能见度. *the* ~ *of hardness*【物】硬度(表). *a rate* ~ 价目表. *Kelvin temperature* ~ 开氏〔绝对〕温标. *lower* ~ 低读数; 刻度下段. *natural* ~ 实物大小; 自然数; 自然量; 固有量. *oil* ~ 油表. *circular* ~ 刻度盘, 图标度. *colour* ~ 彩色温标. *be high [low] in the* ~ *of civilization* 文化程度高〔低〕. *full* ~ *test*【火箭】实物试验. ***in*** ~ 按照一定尺度, 在一定限度〔范围〕内. ***on a large[small]*** ~ 大〔小〕规模地. ***on an extensive*** ~ 广泛地〔的〕. ***play [sing, run over] one's*** ~***s*** 奏〔唱、练习〕音阶. ***sink in the*** ~ 降级. ***to a*** ~ 按一定比例. — *vt.* ①用梯子爬上; 爬越, 攀登(山等). ②用缩尺制图; (用比例尺)设计〔测量〕, 按比例排列〔绘制, 制造〕. ③相机决定〔判断〕;〔美〕大略估计, 约略计算(林木的可用材等); (按比例)增减. — *vi.* 变成梯子, 成梯形; 逐步攀登; 逐渐增高. ~ *the height of scientific knowledge* 攀登科学知识的高峰. ~ ***down*** 按比例缩小〔减少, 减低〕. ~ ***up*** (按比例)增加, 扩大, 升高. ~**-down** (按比例)缩减, 降低;【无】分频. ~ **model** 比例模型.
scale[2] [skeil] *n.* ①称盘, 天平盘. ②〔*pl.*〕秤, 磅秤, 天平〔常说 *a pair of* ~*s*〕. ③(骑师、拳师等的)体重检查(器). ④〔the Scales〕【天】天平座; 天平宫 (= Libra). ⑤正义, 裁判. *a beam and* ~*s* 天平. *a beam* ~ (杆)秤. *a platform* ~ 台秤. *a clerk of the* ~*s* 体重检查员. ***go to*** ~ 量体重. ***go to*** ~ ***at*** 体重(多少). ***hang in the*** ~ 未作决定. ***hold the*** ~***s even*** 公平裁判. ***throw one's sword into the*** ~ 用武力解决. ***turn [tip] the*** ~***s*** ①使平衡(局势)发生变化. ②起决定作用. ③扭转局面; 转变为有利的情势. ***turn the*** ~ ***at ... pounds*** 重(若干)磅, 有(若干)磅重. — *vt.* 用秤称; 把…过秤. — *vi.* 重(若干), 有(若干)重.
scale[3] [skeil] *n.* ①鳞〔有时也用作集合词〕. ②鳞状物. ③【植】鳞苞, 鳞片; 甲鳞; 翅瓣. ④齿垢. ⑤水锈, 锅垢. ⑥氧化铁皮, 铁鳞; 锈皮. ⑦【医】鳞癣. ⑧(眼睛的)翳, 阴翳. ⑨皮, 壳; 薄皮; 刀鞘. ⑩= ~ insect. *boiler* ~ 锅炉水垢. *Scales fall from one's eyes.* 眼睛的阴翳消掉, 发觉错误, 觉醒. *anvil* ~ 锻渣. *forge* ~ 锻铁鳞, 氧化皮. *mill* ~ 轧屑; 轧钢鳞皮. — *vt.* ①剥…鳞. ②刮掉…的锅垢; 给…去锈. ③【炮】清扫(炮筒). — *vi.* ①(鳞一般)剥落 *(off; away)* ②生锈垢. ~ **armo(u)r** 鳞甲. ~ **board** (玻璃框、镜子等的)背板. ~ **deposits** 炉管积垢.

~ **insect**介壳虫. ~ **moss** 叶苔科植物,叶苔 (= liverwort).

scaled [skeild] *a.* ①屋瓦排列成鳞状的. ②【动】有鳞的,有鳞(状)斑(点)的; (鸟)有鳞羽的. ③刮去了鳞的,已去鳞的. ④鳞状排列的(羽毛等). ⑤用云梯登城而占领的.

sca·lene [ˈskeiliːn] *n., a.* ①【数】不等边(三角形)(的). ②【解】斜角肌(的).

sca·le·nus [skeiˈliːnəs] *n.* 〔L.〕【解】斜角肌.

scal·er [ˈskeilə] *n.* ①刮鳞器. ②【齿】牙垢刮除器. ③攀登者, 爬城士兵. ④〔美〕测树者, 检尺员. ⑤【电】定标器; 计数器.

scal·ing[1] [ˈskeiliŋ] *n.* ①〔古〕攀登; 升高. ②测量; 排列; 绘制. ③【电】定标; 电子法计算电脉冲. ~ **circuit**【电】定标电路. ~**-ladder** ①(攻城用) 云梯, 爬城梯. ②消防梯.

scal·ing[2] [ˈskeiliŋ] *n.* ①起皮; 去锈. ②结成水垢.

scal·la·wag [ˈskæləwæg] *n.* = scalawag.

scal·lion [ˈskæljən] *n.*【植】①亚实基隆葱. ②韭葱. ③大葱.

scal·lop [ˈskɔləp] *n.*【贝】①扇贝[海扇]. ②扇贝肉; 干贝. ③扇贝壳〔又叫 ~ shell, 因从前用作朝拜圣地的纪念章, 所以又叫 pilgrim shell〕. ④(烤贝类和鱼类用的)扇贝壳状平锅; 扇贝形盘碟. ⑤扇贝状薄肉片. ⑥〔*pl.*〕扇(贝)形. — *vt.* ①使成[切成]扇形; 饰以扇形花样. ②烤, 焙〔一种烹调法: 和以调料, 牛乳和稀薄湿面在烤箱中〕.

scal·lop·ing [ˈskɔləpiŋ] *n.* ①扇贝采捕业. ②扇状花样饰物.

scal·ly·wag [ˈskæliwæg] *n.* 〔美〕 = scalawag.

sca·lo·gram [ˈskeiləgræm] *n.* 〔美〕(进行心理学或社会学调查测验用、问题按难易排列的)程度测验(表).

scal·op·pi·ne [ˌskɑːləˈpiːni, ˌskæl-] *n.* 加酒和香料的煎炒牛肉片.

scalp [skælp] *n.* ①(带有头发的) 头皮. ②圆秃秃的山顶. ③(无下颚的)鲸头. ④胜利品〔源于印第安人把敌人头皮剥下作为战利品〕. ⑤做股票小投机所得的微小赢利. ⑥〔俚〕抢帽子. ***have the ~ of ...*** 打败(某人), 打倒 (某人). ***out for ~s*** 去剥头皮; 〔喻〕去出征; 挑战; 寻衅; 抨击, 决心袭击敌人. ***take a ~*** 剥取头皮. ***take sb.'s ~s*** 剥掉头皮; 战胜某人, 向某人报仇. — *vt.* ①剥取…头皮. ②倒卖 (黄牛票); 以(某物) 屯积居奇牟取暴利. ③剥去 (表面上的一层, 如地面), 筛去 (矿砂或谷物表面一层质量低劣的部分). ④夺取(对方的势力); 击败; 使屈辱. — *vi.* ①炒股票〔进行投机取巧牟利活动〕. ②倒买黄牛票. ~ **lock** 印第安人故意留在头皮上向敌人挑战的一撮头发.

scal·pel [ˈskælpəl] *n.* 外科用小手术刀,解剖刀.

scalp·er [ˈskælpə] *n.* ①剥取头皮者. ②【外】骨锉, 刮骨刀; 解剖刀〔又叫 scalping iron〕. ③雕刻刀. ④〔美〕进行投机活动者; (车站、戏院等处的)卖飞票的人, 黄牛. ⑤【股】抢帽子的人, 搞股票小投机的人. ⑥筛选机.

scal·y [ˈskeili] *a.* ***(-i·er; -i·est)*** ①有鳞的; 鳞状的. ②【植】有鳞苞的, 有鳞片的. ③有锅垢的; 鳞状剥落的. ④被介壳虫蛀坏了的. ⑤〔俚〕卑劣的, 吝啬的. ~ **anteater** = pangolin. ~ **bum** 〔美〕邋遢鬼; 卑劣的人. ~ **lentinus** 松菌. **-i·ness** *n.*

scam [skæm] *n., vt.* 〔美俚〕诓骗, 诈骗.

scam·mo·ny [ˈskæməni] *n.* ①【植】墨牵牛子. ②墨牵牛子脂〔泻药〕.

scamp[1] [skæmp] *n.* ①恶棍, 无赖; 流氓. ②顽皮的家伙. ③〔古〕拦路强盗.

scamp[2] [skæmp] *vt.* 草率地做(工作), 胡乱地做, 不得当地做. **-er** *n.*

scam·per [ˈskæmpə] *vi.* ①(小孩子、小走兽) 跳跳蹦蹦 *(about)*. ②(受惊的动物) 奔逃; 惊奔 *(off; away)*. ③浏览; 涉猎 *(through)*. ④匆匆忙忙旅行[走过]. — *n.* ①奔跑, 疾走. ②匆匆忙忙旅行[浏览, 涉猎]. *a ~ through Europe [Dickens]* 匆匆忙忙旅行欧洲[浏览狄更斯的小说]. ***be (up)on the ~*** 东奔西走, 瞎蹦乱跳. ***put sb. to the ~*** 使(某人)东奔西跑.

scam·pi [ˈskæmpi] *n.* ***(pl. ~(s))***【动】食虫虾〔可食用〕.

scamp·ish [ˈskæmpiʃ] *a.* 无赖的; 淘气顽皮的.

scan [skæn] *vt.* ①细看, 细察; 审视. ②〔口〕大略一阅; 浏览. ③按韵节念, 按句调读, 标出(诗)的格律 (指划分音步). ④【视】扫描; 扫掠; 搜索. — *vi.* ① (诗) 符合格律, 读起来抑扬顿挫. ②【无】扫描. *This line does not ~*. 这一行不合节律. — *n.* ①细看; 细察. ②扫视, 浏览. ③【电视】扫描; 扫掠. ④眼界; 视野. **scan·na·ble** *a.* ①可细察的. ②可标出的, 可扫描[掠]的.

Scan., Scand. = Scandinavian.

scan·dal [ˈskændl] *n.* ①丑闻; 丑名; 丑事, 丑行, 丢脸的事件; 舞弊案件; 耻辱. ②(社会上的)反感, 物议; 诽谤, 诋毁. *It is a ~ that such things should be possible.* 竟会有这样的事情真是丢脸. *a case of ~* 毁谤事件. ***be a ~ to*** 是…的耻辱. ***cause [raise] a ~*** 引起公愤[物议]. ***spread about ~*** 传播丑闻〔讲人家的坏话〕, 毁谤人. ***talk ~*** 传播丑闻; 说人坏话. ~ **monger** 喜欢传播丑闻的人. ~ **power** 〔美〕臭名; 名声臭的人. ~ **sheet** 〔俚〕黄色小报.

scan·dal·ize [ˈskændəlaiz] *vt.* ①使…愤慨. ②使…震惊; 使…起反感. ③中伤, 诽谤. ④使…受耻辱. ***be ~d at*** 对…大为愤慨. **-iz·er** *n.* 诽谤者, 恶意中伤者. **-iz·ing** *a.*

scan·dal·ous [ˈskændələs] *a.* ①可耻的, 丢脸的; 出丑的, 令人发生反感的. ②毁谤的, (恶意)中伤的. **-ly** *ad.*

scan·dent [ˈskændənt] *a.* 攀缘的〔如藤〕.

scan·di·a [ˈskændiə] *n.*【化】钪氧.

Scan·di·an [ˈskændiən] *a., n.* = scandinavian.

Scan·di·na·via [ˌskændiˈneivjə, -viə] *n.* 斯堪的纳维亚 (瑞典、挪威、丹麦、冰岛的泛称).

Scan·di·na·vi·an [ˌskændiˈneivjən] *n., a.* ①斯堪的纳维亚(人)的, 北欧(人)的. ②斯堪的纳维亚语(的), 北欧语(的).

scan·di·um [ˈskændiəm] *n.*【化】钪〔化学符号为 Sc〕.

scan·ner [ˈskænə] *n.* ①细辨诗行韵律的人. ②细查者. ③【电视】扫描器[设备]; 扫掠器[设备, 机构]. ④【无】扫掠天线. ⑤析象器. *a disc ~* 析象圆盘. *a film ~* 电视电影机. *a follow ~* 跟踪扫掠设备.

scan·ning [ˈskænniŋ] *n.* ①细看, 细察, 审视. ②【电视】扫描, 扫掠; 搜索. ~ **agent** 象素, 元象. ~ **beam** 扫描光线. ~ **disk**【电视】扫描盘. ~ **element** 象素, 元象. ~ **line** 扫描线. ~ **yoke** 扫描线圈; 致偏磁轭; 偏转系统.

scan·sion [ˈskænʃən] *n.* 按(轻重)节奏 [韵律] 念; 节奏[韵律]分析.

scan·so·ri·al [skænˈsɔːriəl] *a.* ①攀爬的, (适于)攀附的. ②【动】攀禽类的.

scant [skænt] *a.* ①缺乏的, 不足的, 不够的 *(of)*. ②恰好够的. ③将近的. ④俭约的, 节省的; 吝啬的. ★英国现在常用的是 scanty. *a ~ attendance* 出席者[听众]稀少. *a ~ supply of food* 食品供应不足. *a ~ halfhour* 恰好[仅仅]半小时. *a ~ five yards* 刚够五码 ***be ~ of money*** 钱不够[缺钱]. ***fat and ~ of breath*** 胖得喘气. ***with ~ courtesy*** 不太礼貌地, 有点不客气地. — *vt.* 〔英古、美〕①限制; 缩减. ②尅扣; 吝惜. ③不客气地对待. — *ad.* 〔美方〕好容易才, 几乎不[没有]. **-ly** *ad.* **-ness** *n.*

scant·ling [skæntliŋ] *n.* ①小木块, 小石料; 〔集合〕小块材料. ②(木材的)宽厚度, (石料的)体积. ③【建】标品; 量度; 建筑尺寸. ④略图, 草图. ⑤【船】船材尺度, 船体各部的尺寸. ⑥少量, 少许, 一点点 *(of)*. ⑤桶架. ⑥〔古〕样品, 样本.

scant·y [ˈskænti] *a.* ***(-i·er, -i·est)*** ①缺乏的, (数量)

S

不足[不多]的 *(opp.* ample*)*.②狭小的,稀疏的.③吝啬的,俭省的. *Crops are very ~ this year.* 今年收成极少. ***be ~ of** (words; praise)*, 难得(开口), 不大(称赞). **-i·ly** *ad.* **-i·ness** *n.*

SCAP [skæp] = Supreme Commander of the Allied Powers 盟军最高司令.

SCAPA [ˈskæpə] = Society for Checking the Abuses of Public Advertizing 公共广告弊端遏制协会.

Scap·a Flow [ˈskæpə ˈfləu] 〔英〕斯卡帕弗洛〔苏格兰北部 Orkney 群岛间的水域;英国海军基地〕.

scape[1] [skeip] *n.* ①【植】(水仙等的)花葶〔指郁金香等由地面或地面下抽出的花梗〕. ②【昆】柄节〔膝形触角的长基节〕; 独角根;【动】羽轴. ③【建】柱身; 柱根特大部分.

scape[2] [skeip] *n., vt., vi.* 〔方〕= escape. ~ **wheel**【机】擒纵轮 (= escape wheel).

scape[3] [skeip] *n.* = landscape.

-scape *suf.* 景: sea*scape* 海景.

scape·goat [ˈskeipgəut] *n.* ①(古代犹太教祭礼中替人承担罪过的)替罪羊. ②〔喻〕替(人负)罪者; 代人受过者. ***be made the ~ for*** ①做…的替罪者. ②承担…的罪名; 代…受过.

scape·grace [skeipgreis] *n.* ①轻浮的人; 莽撞的人. ②无赖; 恶棍. ③顽童; 淘气鬼.

scaph·oid [ˈskæfɔid] *a.* 船形的〔尤指船形骨的〕.

scaph·o·pod [ˈskæfəˌpɔd] *n.*【动】掘足纲 *(Scaphopoda)* 软体动物.

scap·o·lite [ˈskæpəˌlait] *n.*【矿】方柱石.

sca·pose [ˈskeipəus] *a.*【植】具花葶的; 有根生花梗的.

s. caps. = small capitals.

scap·u·la [ˈskæpjulə] *n.* *(pl.* **-læ** [-li:]*)*【解】肩胛骨; 肩板; 髆. ~ *medal*【天主】肩衣徽章〔用来代表肩衣〕.

scap·u·lar [ˈskæpjulə] *a.* 肩胛骨的; 肩的. — *n.* ①【解】肩胛(骨). ②【动】肩羽,肩翼; 肩衣,肩布. ③【医】肩绷带. ④【宗】肩衣; 无袖法衣. ⑤一种无袖工作服.

SCAR = subcalibre aircraft rocket 机载次口径火箭.

S.Car = Scout Car 巡逻车.

scar[1] [skɑ:] *n.* ①创伤; 伤痕; 疤; 痕迹. ②〔喻〕(精神上或内心的)创伤. ③【植】叶柄痕; 瘢痕. ④(金属等材料表面的)斑疤; 痕. *a vaccination ~* 牛痘疤. *He jests at ~s that never felt a wound.* 〔谚〕没有受过伤的人总爱嘲笑别人的伤疤; 未经痛苦的人不会同情别人. — *vt.* ①使留伤痕. ②〔喻〕使留痕迹; 弄丑. — *vi.* 长疤; 结疤; 成疤,〔伤口〕愈合 *(over)*. ~ **tissue**【医】瘢痕组织.

scar[2] [skɑ:] *n.* 〔英〕①巉岩,露岩; 断崖; 峭壁. ②(海中的)孤岩; 暗礁.

scar·ab [ˈskærəb] *n.* ①【动】金龟子科甲虫; 圣甲虫. ②(古埃及人当做丰饶、再生象征的)甲虫形宝石〔古埃及人作为护符〕.

scar·a·bae·id [ˌskærəˈbi:id] *n.*【动】金龟子. — *a.* 金龟子科甲虫的.

Scar·a·mouch [ˈskærəmautʃ] *n.* ①(古意大利喜剧中)懦弱而好夸口的丑角. ②〔s-〕只会吹牛的胆小鬼 [懦夫]; 无赖(汉).

scarce [skεəs] *a.* *(-er; -est)* ①〔用作 表语.〕(生活必需品) 缺乏, 不足 *(of)*. ②稀有的, 罕见的, 珍贵的, 难得的. *We are ~ of provisions.* 我们缺乏粮食. *a ~ book* 珍本; 难得的书. ~ *metals* 稀有金属. ~ *times* 市面萧条, 困难时节. ***make oneself ~*** 〔口〕悄悄走[躲]开; 退避; 溜掉; 不露面. — *ad.* 〔古诗〕= scarcely.

scarce·ly [skεəsli] *ad.* ①简直不[没有],几乎不[没有]. ②好容易; 勉强. ③将近, 刚刚, 才. ④的确没有, 不至于; 一定不, 决不. ⑤(刚)一…就〔与 before 或 when 连用〕. ⑥不…的几乎没有〔与 but 连用〕. *I ~ saw him.* 我简直没看见他. *I ~ know him.* 我简直不认识他. *I need ~ say.* 用不着说,不必说. *He is ~ old enough for the office.* 他担任这个职务稍嫌年轻一点. *He can ~ write his own name.* 他勉强能写自己的名字. *He is ~ seventeen years old.* 他还不到[将近]十七岁. *He can ~ have said so.* 他不至于这样说. *S- had we reached home, before it began raining.* 我们(刚)一到家就下起雨来了. *He had ~ escaped when he was recaptured.* 他一逃就被逮住了. *There is ~ a man but has his weak side.* 无缺点的人几乎没有. ~ ***any*** 简直没有. ~ ***ever*** 偶然,极少. ~ ***less*** 简直相等,简直一样.

scarce·ment [ˈskεəsmənt] *n.*【建】(墙上,堤岸上或扶壁上的)壁阶. ②【矿】梯架.

scar·ci·ty [ˈskεəsiti] *n.* ①缺乏,缺少,不足. ②稀罕; 少见. ③【经】匮乏,萧条. *a ~ of rain* 雨水缺乏. *a year of great ~* 大荒年. ~ **price** 缺货市价. ~ **value**【经】稀少价值.

scare [skεə] *vt.* 吓, 吓唬; 吓走,吓跑 *(away, off)*. — *vi.* 吓, 吃惊, 惊吓, 惶恐. ***be more ~d than hurt*** 无事自扰,自找烦恼; 虚惊. ***be (as) ~d as a rabbit*** 吓得要命; 惊惶失措. ***be ~d stiff [hollow]*** 吓一大跳. ***~ the pants off of*** 〔美俚〕吓坏…; 把…吓得魂不附体. ***~ up [out]*** 〔美〕①(将猎物)吓出来; (将钱财)敲诈出来; 找出,得到. ②筹措,张罗. — *n.* 吓唬; 恐怖,(商界的)恐慌. ***get a ~*** 吓一跳,吓坏. ***throw a ~ into sb.*** 〔美〕使…吓一大跳,吓坏…. **~crow** *n.* ①稻草人. ②骨瘦如柴的人,衣衫褴褛的人. ③威吓物. **~head(ing)** *n.* 报纸上的煽动性 [耸人听闻] 大标题. ~ **monger [merchant]** *n.* 散布恐怖谣言 [骇人听闻消息] 的人. **scar·er** [ˈskεərə] 吓人的人; 吓人的事物.

scared [skεəd] *a.* ①吃惊的, 吓坏的. ②〔方〕怕, 不敢 (=afraid). *a ~ look* 吃惊的面孔. ***I'd** be ~ to do that* 〔方〕我怕做那件事.

scared·y-cat [ˈskεədikæt] *n.* 易受惊吓的人.

scarf[1] [skɑ:f] *n.* *(pl.* **~s**, 〔英又作〕***scarves****)* ①围巾; 头巾. ②领巾; 领带, 领结. ③披巾; 腰巾. ④桌巾,台巾. ⑤(高级军政人员的)绶带. *red ~* 红围巾; 红领巾. — *vt.* ①围 (围巾). ②打 (领带). ③披 (披巾). ④盖 (台巾). ⑤用围巾[台布]围[盖].

scarf[2] [skɑ:f] *vt.* ①嵌接(木材、金属、皮革). ②割取(鲸鱼的)油脂和皮. — *n.* ①(木材、金属、皮革的)嵌接. ②嵌接处; (嵌接的)斜面; 截面; 切口; 接榫. ③(刻在木头等上的)槽, 凹线. ④(在鲸鱼尸体上的) 纵向切割. ~ **joint** 嵌接. **~skin**【解】(特指)指甲根上的角质表皮; ~ **weld**【机】嵌焊; 斜面焊接.

scar·i·fi·ca·tion [ˌskεərifiˈkeiʃən] *n.* ①【医】多次划破(法). ②刺破,划破. ③划(破的)痕(迹). ④放血(法). ⑤【农】松土. ⑥严厉批评.

scar·i·fi·ca·tor [ˈskεərifikeitə] *n.*【医】刺破器, 划痕器,放血器.

scar·i·fi·er [ˈskεərifaiə] *n.* ①【医】划痕器, 放血器; 划皮肤的划刀. ②划破者,放血者. ③【农】松土器. ④(道路工程用的)翻路机.

scar·i·fy [ˈskεərifai] *vt.* ①【医】刺破,多次划破(皮肤). ②给…放血. ③【农】松土; 对 (硬皮种子)作破皮处理(使易于发芽). ④严厉批评;〔口〕虐待,欺负,折磨.

scar·la·ti·na [ˌskɑ:ləˈti:nə] *n.*【医】(轻症的)猩红热.

scar·let [ˈskɑ:lit] *n.* ①深红色,猩红,鲜红. ②红布; (大主教、英国高等法院法官、英国陆军军官等的)红衣. ③象征罪恶的深红色. — *a.* ①深红的, 猩红的, 鲜红的. ②面红耳赤的. ③罪恶昭彰的; 淫荡的. ***turn ~*** 变得面红耳赤. ***wear ~*** ①穿深红衣服. ②(市长等) 穿制服. ~ **fever** ①猩红热. ②〔谑〕(妇女的) 军人热 [崇拜]. ~ **hat** 红衣主教的帽子[职位]. ~ **letter** 红A字〔美国殖民时期给被判通奸罪者佩戴的耻辱标记〕. ~ **pimpernel** = pimpernel【植】海丝 *(Anagallis arvensis)*. ~ **rash** 蔷薇疹. ~ **runner**【植】红花菜豆〔美洲热带产〕. ~ **sage**【植】一串红 *(Salvia splendens)*. ~ **woman [whore]** ①异教的罗马〔源出《新约》启示录; 宗教改革时期新教徒用来指罗马天主教会〕. ②世俗精神. ③娼妓,淫妇.

scarp [skɑːp] *n.* ①陡坡; 险坡; 悬崖. ②【筑城】(城墙的)内斜坡; (外壕的)内削壁. — *vt.* ①使成陡坡. ②在…设斜坡;在…设内削壁. ③垂直切断(山腰等). ④〔俚〕偷.

scar·per [ˈskɑːpə] *vi.* ①〔英俚〕逃走; 溜掉. ②撤退,撤营.

scarves [skɑːvz] *n.* 〔英〕scarf[1] 的复数.

scar·y [ˈskɛəri] *a.* ***(-i·er; -i·est)*** ①(马等)易受惊的,胆怯的. ②可怕的,吓人的.

scat[1] [skæt] *int.* 〔口〕嘘; 〔赶猫等的呼声〕 — *vi.* 〔口〕走开〔常用命令式〕. **~back** 〔足球俚〕迅速敏捷的后卫.

scat[2] [skæt] *n.* 〔英方〕砰〔枪声、打击声,爆炸声等〕. ***go ~*** 〔俚〕①粉碎. ②破产; 完蛋.

scat[3] [skæt] *n.* (爵士音乐中)无意义的狂叫. — *vi.* (歌唱中间)作即兴的狂叫.

scathe [skeið] *n.* 损害,损伤. ***keep from ~*** 使避免伤害;保护. ***without ~*** 平安地;无损伤地. — *vt.* ①严厉批评. ②〔古方〕损害,损伤. ③使枯萎. **-less** *a.* 无伤,平安.

scath·ing [ˈskeiðiŋ] *a.* ①伤害(性)的,引起剧痛的. ②(眼光)严厉的;尖刻的,苛刻的;(批评等)严厉的. **-ly** *ad.*

sca·tol·o·gy [skəˈtɔlədʒi] *n.* ①粪便研究;【医】粪便诊断. ②【古生】粪石学〔研究粪便化石之学〕. ③粪便学〔研究古时以粪便占卜疾病的民俗学的一科〕. ④猥亵描写;对猥亵情节的兴趣.

scat·ter [ˈskætə] *vt.* ①散布,撒(种),散播. ②使散乱;逐散,驱散,击溃;使化为乌有,摧毁(希望等);消除(恐怖等). ③【物、军】扩散,散射(光、热等). ④挥霍,浪费(财产). — *vi.* ①分散. ②四散,溃散. ③扩散;(子弹炮火等)散射. ~ *seed* 播种. ~ *the crowd* 驱散群众. ***~ about*** 散布,撒布. ***~ to the winds*** 挥霍浪费. — *n.* ①撒布;散播. ②散播物. **~brain** *n.* ①思想不集中的人,思想混乱的人. ②轻率[浮躁]的人. **~brained** *a.* 轻率的,浮躁的. **~good** *n.* 挥霍无度的人. **~gun** 〔美俚〕猎枪;机枪. ~ **rug**(铺覆部分地板的)小幅地毯. ~ **shot** ①大型铅弹. ②(猎枪等)散弹的扩散范围. **~shot** *a.* ①扩散很广的. ②一般的,广泛的. **-a·tion** [ˌskætəˈreiʃən] *n.*

scat·tered [ˈskætəd] *a.* ①(人家等)疏疏落落的;分散的,散乱的. ②(思想等)不集中的,散漫的. ③【植】星散的,参差的,散生的. ④【物】(光)散射的.

scat·ter·ing [ˈskætəriŋ] *a.* ①分散在不同方向的,分散在不同范围的. ②广泛扩散的. ③(选票)数量分散的,不集中的. — *n.* ①散乱. ②在媒介质中的散播. ③【物】散射. ~ **layer** 能使声波散射的海中浮游生物层. **-ly** *ad.*

scat·ty [ˈskæti] *a.* ***(-ti·er; -ti·est)*** ①〔俗〕疯疯癫癫的. ②〔俚〕低能的;意志薄弱的. ③轻率的,浮躁的,粗心的.

scaup [skɔːp] *n.* 【鸟】斑背潜鸭 (= ~ duck).

scaur [skɔː] *n.* 〔Scot.〕 = Scar[2].

scav·enge [ˈskævindʒ] *vt., vi.* ①清除(污物或杂质),打扫(街道等). ②【动】吃(腐肉等). ③【机】排除(内燃机等的)废气;给[从](内燃机汽缸)扫气. ④【冶】清除(杂质);纯化(金属液). ⑤(从…中)提取有用物质;在废物中提取(有用物质). ~ **trunk**【冶】吹气管.

scav·en·ger [ˈskævindʒə] *n.* ①清道夫;清扫工. ②食腐动物〔指食腐物腐尸〕; ③(纱厂)花屑清扫人. ④黄色作家,猥亵文章作者. ⑤清除剂,净化剂. ⑥【矿】选池. ⑦吹洗泵,清理泵. — *vi.* ①做清道夫. ②排除废气. ~ **hunter** 觅物游戏. **~'s cart** 扫街车. **~'s daughter**【英史】铁箍刑具.

Sc. B. = 〔L.〕 *Scientiae Baccalaureus* 理学士 (= Bachelor of Science).

Sc. D. = 〔L.〕 *Scientiae Doctor* 理学博士 (= Doctor of Science).

sce·na [ˈʃeinə] *n.* 〔It.〕 ①(歌剧的)一场. ②(古代剧场的)舞台. ③(精致的戏剧性的)叙唱,宣叙调[部]〔下接咏叹调〕.

sce·na·ri·o [siˈnɑːriəu] *n.* ***(pl. -s)*** 〔It.〕 ①【剧】剧情说明. ②歌剧脚本;电影剧本. ③方案. *a ~ editor* 电影剧本编辑. *a ~ writer* 电影剧[脚]本作者.

sce·na·rist [siˈnɑːrist] *n.* 电影剧[脚]本作者.

sce·nar·ize [ˈsiːnəraiz] *vt.* 〔美影〕把(小说等)改编成电影剧本.

scend [send] = send[2].

scene [siːn] *n.* ①(戏剧的)一场,一幕. ②〔常 *pl.*〕场(舞台的)布景. ③【影】场面;出事地点,现场;〔古〕舞台. ④事件,史实,插话. ⑤吵闹;发脾气. ⑥景色,景致,风景. ⑦〔*pl.*〕光景,实况. Act III, S- ii 第三幕第二场. *moving ~s* 激动人心的场面. *a set ~* 背景;大道具. *a ~ of disaster* 肇祸现场[情景]. *a ~ of action* 出事地点. *the ~ of operations* 军事行动的地点;战场. ***a carpenter's ~*** (换布景时演的)插幕. ***be quickly on the ~*** 立刻到达出事地点. ***behind the ~s*** 知道内幕;秘密地,暗中. ***change of ~*** 场面的变化;转地. ***come on the ~*** 出现,登场. ***have a nice ~ with*** 和…大吵一场. ***lay [place] the ~ in*** 取…做场面,用…做舞台. ***make a ~*** 吵架 (*Please don't make a ~.* 别吵架.) ***make the ~*** 〔美俚〕在某地露面;参加某项活动. ***on the ~*** 在出事地点,当场. ***paint ~s*** 画布景. ***quit the ~*** 退场,离场;离开人间,死. ***shift [change] the ~s*** ①换幕,换景. ②改变环境,转移地点. ~ **dock** (舞台旁边的)布景存放处. **~man** [ˈsiːnmən] *n.* ***(pl. -men)*** = ~shifter. ~ **master** 剧院中控制数条灯光电路的开关. ~ **painter** 布景画师,画布景者. **~shifter**【剧】移置布景者. **~stealer** 在舞台上抢出风头的配角演员,喧宾夺主的配角.

scen·er·y [ˈsiːnəri] *n.* ①景色,景致,风光,风景. ★ scene 是局部景色, scenery 是全景. ②舞台面,(舞台)布景. ③背景. ④〔罕〕风景画. *landscape ~* = *~ of a landscape* 自然景色. *paint ~* 画背景. ~ **wagon** (有脚轮的)布景台.

sce·nic [ˈsiːnik] *a.* ①布景的,背景的. ②舞台的;戏剧的. ③戏剧性的,(表情等)戏剧式的. ④画一般的;(画等)表现实景的. ⑤风景的,风光明媚的,风景佳美的;景色优美的. *~ persons* 戏剧演员. *~ poets* (特指希腊罗马的)戏剧作者. *a ~ railway* (游览区里的)游览小铁路. *a ~ bas-relief* 神采栩栩的浮雕. — *n.* ①风景影片;实景电影. ②风景照片[图片]. **-i·cal** *a.* = scenic. **-i·cal·ly** *ad.*

sce·no·graph [ˈsiːnəgrɑːf, -græf, ˈsen-] *n.* 透视图.

sce·nog·ra·phy [siːˈnɔgrəfi] *n.* ①透视(图)法. ②〔尤指〕古希腊舞台布景画法. ③配景图法;写景术. **-graph·ic** [ˌsiːnəˈgræfik] *a.*

scent [sent] *n.* ①香,气味,香气. ②〔口〕香水. ③(野兽的)臭迹,遗臭. ④迹,踪迹;线索〔只用单数〕. ⑤〔a~〕嗅觉,敏锐的感觉. ⑥"狗捉兔子"游戏(hare and hounds)中兔子撒在地上代表踪迹的纸片. *a dog of good ~* 嗅觉敏锐的狗. *a burning ~* (动物走后留下的)强烈的臭迹. *a cold [hot] ~* 微弱的[强烈的]臭迹. *a false ~* 错误的臭迹;错误的线索. ***be off the ~ [get the wrong ~]*** ①【猎】失去猎物的臭迹,追错方向. ②〔转义〕迷失方向;抓住错误的线索,作错误的判断. ***cast about for the ~*** (猎狗)寻找(猎物等). ***follow up the ~*** (猎狗)闻着臭迹追赶. ***get ~ of*** 闻出;发觉. ***have a keen ~ for an error*** 有发现错误的敏锐感觉. ***have no ~ for*** 对于…没有敏感. ***hunt by ~*** 凭嗅觉追赶,循臭迹追猎. ***on the right [wrong] ~*** 线索正确[错误],得[不得]法. ***on the ~ of*** 获得…的线索 (*be hot on the ~ of an important discovery* 及时抓紧重大发现的线索追查). ***put sb. off the ~*** (用替身等)使人追错方向而逃逸;使人迷失线索. ***put [throw] sb. on the ~*** (自己做向导)使人跟着追,使人跟踪追赶. ***put [throw] sb. on a***

wrong ～ = put sb. off the ～. ***recover the*** ～ (猎狗)重新嗅到臭迹. ***take the*** ～ ***of*** = get ～ of. — *vt.* ①闻,嗅,闻出. ②察觉,发觉,看破(阴谋等). ③使香,使臭;在…上洒香水. ～ *spring in the air* 空气中感到春天的气息. *The flower* ～*s the air.* 花散布芳香. ～ *one's person* 往身上洒香水. — *vi.* ①闻着气味追赶. ②发出气味;发出香味. ～ **bag** ①香袋;香囊. ②【动】臭腺. ～ **bottle**①香水瓶. ②〔俚〕厕所. ～ **gland**【动】臭腺,麝香分泌腺.

scent·ed [ˈsentid] *a.* ①洒了香水的,加有香料的. ②馥郁的,芳香的. ③有…嗅觉的. ～ *soap* 香皂. *keen-*～ 嗅觉敏锐的.

scent·less [ˈsentlis] *a.* ①不香的,无香气的,无气味的. ②不臭的. ③(行猎时)失去了臭迹的. ④无嗅觉的.

scen·tom·e·ter [sinˈtɔmitə] *n.* (记录空气中尘埃污染物等的)气味计.

scep·sis [ˈskepsis] *n.* ①怀疑. ②怀疑哲学;怀疑主义.

scep·ter [ˈseptə]〔美〕= sceptre.

scep·tic [ˈskeptik] *n.* ①怀疑者;抱怀疑态度者. ②怀疑基督教(真理)的人;怀疑宗教教条者;无神论者. ③【哲】怀疑论者,不可知论者. — *a.* = sceptical. **scep·ti·cal** *a.* ①怀疑(论)的. ②怀疑论者的. ③〔口〕怀疑,不相信 *(of;about)*.

scep·tic·ism [ˈskeptisizəm] *n.* ①怀疑(态度). ②怀疑论,怀疑主义. ③怀疑宗教(教条).

scep·tre, scep·ter [ˈseptə] *n.* ①(帝王的)权杖,权标;王节. ②〔the ～〕王权,王位. *lay down the* ～ 退位. *wield the* ～掌权,统治. — *vt.* 授…以权杖;授…以王节;授…以王[君]权.

scep·tred, scep·tered [ˈseptəd] *a.* ①成了帝王的;有王权的. ②持王节的.

sch. = ①school. ②scholar.

scha·den·freu·de [ˈʃɑːdənfrɔidə] *n.* 〔G.〕幸灾乐祸.

Schanz·e [ˈʃæntsə] *n.*〔G.〕【滑雪】跳台.

schap·pe [ʃæp,ˈʃɑːpə] *n.*【纺】绢丝[废丝]织物.

schat·chen [ˈʃɑːtkən] *n.* (犹太)媒人.

sched·ule [ˈʃedjuːl; Am. ˈskedʒul] *n.* ①目录. ②表(格);清单,明细表. ③〔美〕程序表,计划表;进度表;时间表. ④〔美〕预定日期,预定计划. *a* ～ *of prices* 定价表. *a train* ～ 火车时刻表. *a design* ～设计计算表,进度表. ***according to*** ～ 按照预定计划[时间表]. ***behind [ahead of]*** ～ ***(time)*** 比预定时间晚[早]. ***file [give in] one's*** ～ (宣布)破产. ***on*** ～ ***(time)*** ①按时间表,准时. ②按照预定计划. — *vt.* ①为…作目录. ②将…列表,把…记入表格. ③将…列入程序表[计划表,进度表]; 为…规定时间表[进度计划]. ⑤排定,安排. *Supper is* ～*d for six o'clock.* 晚餐预定六时开始. ***be*** ～***d to*** *(sail today)* 预定(本日开船). ～*d time* (火车等的)时刻表,预定时间. **Scheduled Caste [Class]** (在印度,原先属于"不可接触"贱民阶层的)在册种姓.

scheel·ite [ˈʃiːlait] *n.*【矿】白钨矿.

sche·ma [ˈskiːmə] *n.* *(pl.* ～*ta* [-tə]*)* ①图解;图表;略图. ②摘要,一览;大要,大意;纲要,要略. ③【逻】(三段论法的)格. ④【修】词采;词藻;修辞手段. ⑤(康德哲学的)先验图式. ⑥(东正教教士穿的)法衣.

sche·mat·ic [skiˈmætik, skə-] *a.* 要领的;纲要的. ②图解的,(按照)图式[公式]的. — *n.* 简图〔如电路图〕. **-i·cal·ly** *ad.*

sche·ma·tism [ˈskiːmətizəm] *n.* ①系统分类(或说明)方案;系统性的组合;(事物的)特定系统性安排. ②设计.

sche·ma·tize [ˈskiːmətaiz] *vi., vt.* *(-tiz·ed, -tiz·ing)* (使)构成计划;按计划(或方案)安排(工作等). **-ti·za·tion** [ˌskiːmətaiˈzeiʃən] *n.*

scheme [skiːm] *n.* ①计划;方案;路线;设计. ②系统;配合;组织. ③纲目;表;清单;分类表;大纲. ④谋划,策划;诡计,奸计,阴谋. ⑤图,图式,图型,图解,图表;图纸,设计图,流程图;示意图;线路图. ⑥电路. *a* ～ *of distribution*【法】分红表. *a* ～ *of scantling*【造船】船体各部明细表. *a* ～ *of wiring*【电】线路图. *bubble* ～ 空头计划(在资本主义社会里人们用这种空头计划诱人认股,进行诈骗取利). ～ *of a symphony* 交响乐的结构. *under the present* ～ *of society* 在现社会机构下. ***contrive [form, lay] a*** ～ 计划,拟方案,策划. ***in the*** ～ ***of things*** 在事物发展过程中. ***prepare a*** ～ ***of***… 作…的计划. *(a painter's)* ～ ***of colour*** (某画家的)着色法. — *vt., vi.* ①计划;设计. ②策划;阴谋;图谋;策动*(for; to)*. ～ ***to do [for] sth.*** 策划某事. ～ ***for power*** 策动夺取政权. **-er** 计划者;阴谋家,野心家. **-ing** *a.* ①计划的. ②策划的;机诈的,诡计多端的.

scher·zan·do [skeəˈtsændəu] *a., ad.*〔It.〕【乐】戏谑的[地];玩笑的[地];愉快的[地];谐谑的[地];幽默的[地]. — *n.* 谐谑[幽默]的段落.

scher·zo [ˈskeətsəu] *n.*〔It.〕【乐】谐谑曲.

Schick [ʃik] **test**【医】希克氏白喉免疫性检验.

Schie·dam [ˈskiːdæm, ˈʃiː-] *n.* ①斯希丹〔荷兰西南部一城市名〕. ②斯希丹地方所产的杜松子酒.

schil·ling [ˈʃiliŋ] *n.* 先令〔奥地利货币单位,等于 100 格罗申 *(Groschen)*〕.

schip·per·ke [ˈʃipəki, ˈskip-] *n.* 一种无尾小黑狗〔原产于比利时,一种在运河上守卫载货船的守卫犬〕.

schism [ˈsizəm] *n.* ①分裂. ②(特指教会的)分立;(教会的)分派. ③宗派;派别;派系. ④【宗】犯宗派分立罪.

schis·mat·ic [sizˈmætik] *n.* 教会分立(论)者;分裂宗教者. — *a.* ①分裂的. ②派别的,宗派的. ③教会分立论者的;犯宗派分立罪的. **-i·cal·ly** *ad.*

schis·ma·tize [ˈsizmətaiz] *vt., vi.* (引诱…)从事(宗教)分裂活动.

schist [ʃist] *n.*【地】片岩;页岩;板岩.

schis·tose [ˈʃistəus] *a.* 页(片)岩的;页(片)岩质的;页(片)岩状的.

schis·to·some [ˈʃistəsəum] *n.* 血吸虫;裂体吸虫.

schis·to·so·mia·sis [ˌʃistəsəuˈmaiəsis] *n.*【医】血吸虫[裂体吸虫]病.

schist·ous [ˈʃistəs] *a.* = schistose.

schiz [skits], **schiz·o** [ˈskitsəu] *n.*〔美俚〕= schizophrenia*(n.)*.

schizo- *comb. f.* 分裂;裂开;解离: *schizo*genesis.

schiz·o·carp [ˈskizəkɑːp] *n.*【植】裂果,分果,分离果. **-car·pous, -car·pic** *a.*

schi·zo·gen·e·sis [ˌskidzəuˈdʒenisis] *n.*【生】裂配生殖;直裂增殖.

schi·zog·o·ny [skiˈzɔgəni] *n.*【动】裂配生殖;直裂增殖〔= schizogenesis〕.

Schiz·oid [ˈskizɔid] *n.*【医】类精神分裂症患者. — *a.* ①类精神分裂症(患者)的. ②〔转义〕支离分裂的;自相矛盾的.

schiz·o·my·cete [ˌskidzəumaiˈsiːt] *n.*【生】裂殖菌类.

schiz·o·my·co·sis [ˌskizəumaiˈkəusiz] *n.*【医】裂殖菌病.

schiz·ont [ˈskizɔnt] *n.*【生】裂殖体.

schiz·o·phrene [ˈskizəufriːn] *n.*【医】精神分裂症患者.

schiz·o·phre·ni·a [ˌskizəuˈfriːniə] *n.*【医】精神分裂症.

schiz·o·phren·ic [ˌskizəuˈfrenik] *a.*【医】患精神分裂症的. — *n.* 精神分裂症患者.

schiz·o·phyte [ˈskizəfait] *n.*【植】分裂植物;分裂菌 *(Schizophyta)*. **-phy·tic** [-fitik] *a.*

schiz·o·pod [ˈskizəpɔd] *n.* 裂足类动物〔婿虾类和糠虾类的总称〕. — *a.* 裂足类动物的 (= schizopodous).

schiz·o·thy·mi·a [ˌskizəuˈθaimiə] *n.*【心】(濒临精神)分裂气质[状态]〔一种精神分裂情绪状态;没有精神分裂症那样严重〕. **-thy·mic** *a., n.*

schiz·(z)y [ˈskizi] *a.* 精神分裂的.

schlep, schlepp [ʃlep]〔美俚〕*vt.* ***(schlep·ped; schlep-***

*ping)*拖，带，运．— *vi.* 拖曳着走；费力地走．— *n.* 不中用[不起作用]的人；无足轻重的人；没有工作效力的人．

schlock [ʃlɔk] *n.*〔美俚〕贱货；不值钱的东西；次品，劣等品．— *a.* 价贱的；不值钱的；次劣的．

schloss [ʃlɔːs] *n.*〔G.〕城堡，堡垒．

schmaltz [ʃmɑːlts] *n.*〔G.〕〔美俚〕①脆弱的感情；伤感．②极度伤感[渲染、夸张]的音乐[文艺作品]．③感伤的风格．④(鸡的)脂肪，油腻．～ **herring**【动】鲱鱼．**-y** *a.*

schmalz [ʃmɔːlts]〔G.〕= schmaltz.

schmo [ʃməu] *n.* *(pl.* ～*(e)s)*〔美俚〕呆子，笨蛋，傻瓜，愚人．亦作 **schmoe**．

schmooze [ʃmuːz] *vi.* *(schmooz·ed, schmooz·ing)*〔美俚〕聊天，扯皮，说闲话，搬弄是非．— *n.* 闲谈，闲话，流言蜚语．亦作 **schmoos** [ʃmuːs].

schmuck [ʃmʌk] *n.*〔美俚〕笨蛋，粗鄙的人，愚人．

Schna·bel [ˈʃnɑːbəl] *n.* 施纳贝尔〔姓氏〕．

schnap(p)s [ʃnæps] *n.* ①荷兰杜松子酒．②烈酒．

schnau·zer [ˈʃnauzə] *n.* (德国种)刚毛㹴犬．

schnit·zel [ˈʃnitsl] *n.* 肉片；炸肉片〔尤指小牛肉片〕．

schnook [ʃnuk] *n.*〔美俚〕易受骗的人；头脑简单的人；可怜虫．

schnor·kel, schnor·kle [ˈʃnɔːkl] *n.* = snorkel.

schnor·rer [ˈʃnɔrə] *n.*〔美俚〕乞丐，叫化子；过寄生生活者，食客．

schnoz·zle [ˈʃnɔzl], **schnoz·zo·la** [ʃnɔˈzəulə] *n.*〔美俚〕鼻子．

Scho·field [ˈskəufiːld] *n.* 斯科菲尔德〔姓氏〕．

schol. = scholarship.

schol·ar [ˈskɔlə] *n.* ①学者；古典学者；〔俚〕有文化的人，有某种文科知识的人．②公费生，领有奖学金的学生．③学生；门徒；学习者．*He is no* ～．他不是一个学者[有学问的人]．*I am a poor hand as a* ～．= *I am not much of a* ～．我没有什么文化．*a general* ～ 博学的人．*an apt* ～ 颖悟的学生．～**-bureaucrat** (中国旧时的)士大夫．**-ship** ①学问，学识．②学业成绩，学习成就．③奖学金．～ **tyrant** 学阀．**-ly** *a.* ①学者派头的，学究气的．②有学问的，博学的．

scho·las·tic [skəˈlæstik] *a.* ①学校的，(学校)教育的．②(象)学生的．③(象)学者的；学究的；烦琐的；卖弄学问的．④教师的．⑤学术的．⑥〔常 S-〕经院[烦琐]哲学(派，家)的．～ *attainments* 学业成绩．*a* ～ *attire* 校服．～ *education* 学校教育．*a* ～ *institution* 学校．～ *philosophy* 经院哲学，烦琐哲学．— *n.* ①有学者派头的人，卖弄学问的人．②经院[烦琐]哲学家．**-ti·cal·ly** *ad.*

scho·las·ti·cate [skəˈlæstikeit, -kit] *n.*【天主】神学院(尤指耶稣会神学院)．

scho·las·ti·cism [skəˈlæstisizəm] *n.* ①经院哲学；烦琐哲学．②墨守成规．

scho·li·a [ˈskəuliə] *n.* scholium 的复数．

scho·li·ast [ˈskəuliæst] *n.* (古典著作的)注释者；评注者．**-li·as·tic** [ˌskəuliˈæstik] *a.*

scho·li·um [ˈskəuliəm] *n.* *(pl.* ～*s, -li·a)* ①〔常 *pl.*〕(对于古典著作的)傍注．②注释，注解，评注．

school[1] [skuːl] *n.* ①学校；〔美〕(大学的)学部，学院；学系；校舍；讲堂，教室．②研究所，训练所，养成所．③〔不用冠词〕学，学业；上课；功课；授课(时间)；学期．④全体学生；全体师生．⑤〔喻〕经验；锻炼所，修养所；学习[修养]环境．⑥学派，(画家等的)流派；派别；(机械等的)型．⑦(牛津大学等的)学位考试科目；〔*pl.*〕大学毕业考试．⑧(中世大学的)学科；学会；〔the ～s〕〔集合词〕大学，学界．⑨(哲学家、艺术家等的)门徒．⑩(大学的)讲堂；〔*pl.*〕(牛津大学等的)考场．⑪锻炼；【乐】教授规程；【军】训练(规程)．*a continuation* ～ 职业补习学校；成人学校．*a medical [law]* ～ 医[法]学部[学院]．*an artisan* ～ 技工学校．*a trade [vocational]* ～ 职业学校．*a national* ～〔英〕公立学校．*the chemistry* ～ 化学教室．*a sixth form* ～〔英〕六年级教室．*S- begins at nine o'clock.* 九点钟开始上课．*The whole* ～ *was punished.* 全校学生都受处罚了．*Let a hundred flowers blossom, let a hundred* ～*s of thought contend.* 百花齐放，百家争鸣．*two* ～*s of aviating apparatus* 飞行机的两大类型．***after*** ～ 下课后，放学后 (*I will tell you after* ～ 下课后跟你讲．) ***at*** ～ ①在学校．②在求学．③在上课．***be dismissed [expelled] from*** ～ 被开除学籍．***begin [start]*** ～ 开始求学．***finish*** ～ 完成学业．***go to*** ～ 到校上课；上学去；开始求学．***go to*** ～ ***to (sb.)*** 受教于某人，跟某人学习，模仿(某人)．***have no*** ～ ***today*** 今天无课．***in*** ～ 在上[求]学．***in the hard*** ～ ***of adversity*** 经受逆境的艰苦锻炼．***in the*** ～***s*** = ***in for one's*** ～***s*** (某人)正在考试，正在考(牛津大学)学位考试．***keep a*** ～ 办(私立)学校．***leave*** ～ ①退学．②(毕业)离校．③放学回家．***old*** ～ ***tie***〔英〕毕业后沿用不舍的母校特殊图案的领带；〔转义〕感情用事的地方[怀旧]观念．***put [send] a child to*** ～ 送孩子进学校．～ ***age*** 学龄；义务教育年限．～ ***fee(s)*** 学费．～ ***pence***〔英〕小学校的每周学费．***stay away from*** ～ 旷课 (= cut ～)．***teach*** ～〔古〕教学，教书，当教师〔现普通说作 ***teach in a*** ～〕．***tell tales out of*** ～，见 tale 条．— *vt.* ①〔罕〕给…上学，把…送进学校；在…学习．②教，教授；教育，教导，教训；训练，锻炼．③约束，克制．④训诫．*a well* ～*ed man* 受过良好教育的人；有教养的人．～ *a horse* 驯马．～ *oneself to patience* 锻炼[养成]忍耐力[性]．*be* ～*ed in war* 受过战争训练；富有战争经验．～ *one's temper* 克制脾气．*He will not be* ～*ed.* 他不听人劝导．～ **aeroplane**【空】教练机，练习机．～ **age** ①入学年龄．②接受义务教育的年限．～**-ager** 学龄儿童．～ **bag** 书包．～ **board** (地方上管理公立学校的)教育委员会．～**-book** ①*n.*教科书．② *a.*〔美〕教科书式的，过于简略的．～ **boy** (小学、中学的)学生．～ **bus** 校车．～ **commissioner**〔美〕督学．～ **committee**〔美〕(由居民中选出人组成参与管理学校事务的)学校委员会．～ **day** 授课日，上课日；～**-days** 学生时代．～ **edition** 书籍作教科书用的版本．～ **fellow** 同学；校友．～ **girl** (小学、中学的)女(学)生．～**house** ①校舍；小学教员宿舍．②(S- House)〔英〕(public school 的)校长住宅．③全体寄宿生．～ **inspector** 视学员；督学．～ **ma'am,** ～ **marm**〔美口〕= schoolmistress ①女教师．②卖弄学问的女人．③架子十足[傲慢]的女人．～**man** ①〔S-〕经院哲学家；烦琐哲学家．②〔*pl.*〕〔美俚〕教师；学者．～**master** ①教师；(男)教员．②校长．～ **mastering** ①当教员．②学校教育．～ **masterly** *a.* ①教员派头的，教员似的．②卖弄学问的．～**mate** *n.* 同学．～ **miss** ①女学生．②女学生脾气的姑娘．～**mistress** *n.* ①女教员．②女校长．～**room** 教室，讲堂．～**ship**【军】教练舰，练习舰，教练船．～**teacher** 教师〔尤指小学教员〕．～**teaching**①教学．②职业．～**time** ①(学校的)上课时间．②(家里的)用功时间；自修时间．③训练期间．④求学时代，学生时代．～**work** 课堂作业，课外作业．～ **yard** ①校园．②(学校的)运动场．～ **year** 学年．

school[2] [skuːl] *n.* (鱼、鲸等水族动物的)群；队．*a* ～ *of dolphins* 一群海豚．— *vi.* (鱼)成群结队地游，成群前进．～ ***up***成群游近水面；集在水面附近．

school·ing [ˈskuːliŋ] *n.* ①学校教育；教育．②学费．③训练，锻炼；驯马，练马．*He did not get much* ～．他没有上过多少学[受过多少学校教育]．*to shorten the length of* ～ 缩短学制[学习期限]．*a man with less* ～ 文化水平较低的人．*pay for the* ～ *of one's children* 付孩子的学费．

schoon·er [ˈskuːnə] *n.* ①双桅[三桅、四桅]纵帆船．②

〔美〕(拓荒者用的)有篷四轮大马车,大篷车. ③〔美〕大啤酒杯(=prairie ~). **~rigged** 有纵帆装置的;纵帆式的.

Scho·pen·hau·er [ˈʃoupənhauə] 叔本华, **Arthur**〔1788—1860,德国厌世哲学家〕.

schorl [ʃɔːl] *n.* 〔G.〕【地】黑电气石(黑碧珊) **-a·ceous** [ʃɔːˈleiʃəs] *a.*

schot·tisch(e) [ʃɔˈtiːʃ, Am. ˈʃɔtiʃ] *n.* 【乐】一种类似波尔卡(polka)的苏格兰慢步圆舞. ②苏格兰慢步圆舞曲.

schtick, schtik [ʃtik] *n.* 〔美俚〕= **shtick.**

schul [ʃuːl] *n.* = shul.

Schu·man(n) [ˈʃuːmən] *n.* ①舒曼〔姓氏〕. ② **Robert** ~ 罗伯特·舒曼〔1810—1856,德国作曲家〕.

Schurz [ʃurts] *n.* 舒尔茨〔姓氏〕.

schuss [ʃus] *n.* 〔G.〕(滑雪)直下. — *vi.* (滑雪)全速直下. **-er** *n.* 直线全速滑雪者.

schutz·mine [ˈʃutsmiːnə] *n.* 〔G.〕【军】榴霰地雷.

Schutz·staf·fel [ˈʃutsˈʃtɑːfəl] *n.* 〔G.〕(纳粹的)党卫队,黑衫队(略 S.S. 或 SS.).

Schuy·ler [ˈskailə] *n.* 斯凯勒〔姓氏〕.

schwa [ʃwɑː; G. ʃvɑː] *n.* ①(英语弱读音节中的)中性元音〔如 *ago* 中的 *a*, *agent* 的 *e*, *sanity* 中的 *i* 等〕. ②国际音标中的 [ə] 符号.

Schwa·be [ʃwɑːb] *n.* 施瓦布〔姓氏〕.

Schwann [ʃwɔn] *n.* 施沃恩〔姓氏〕.

Schwer·punkt [ˈʃveːrpuŋkt] *n.* 〔G.〕【军】重点突破战术.

sci. = science; scientific.

sci·ae·nid [saiˈiːnid] *n.* 石首鱼科 *(Sciaenidea)* 的鱼〔包括石首鱼,黄花鱼〕. **sci·ae·noid** [-nɔid] *a., n.*

sci·a·gram [ˈsaiəgræm] *n.* X 射线照片〔= skiagram〕

sci·a·graph [ˈsaiəgrɑːf] *n.* ①(特指用 X 射线照射的)投影图,X 射线照片. ②房屋纵断面图. — *vt.* 对…作 X 射线摄影;对…摄制投影图.

sci·ag·ra·phy [saiˈægrəfi] *n.* ①投影法;X 线照相术. ②房屋纵断面图. ③【天】星影计时法.

sci·am·a·chy [saiˈæməki] *n.* 假想战,模拟战;同想象的敌人作战,同影子作战.

sci·am·e·try [saiˈæmitri] *n.* ①【天】日月蚀的数学理论. ②【物】射线的数学研究.

sci·at·ic [saiˈætik] *a.* ①【生理,医】坐骨(神经)的. ②坐骨神经(痛)的.

sci·at·i·ca [saiˈætikə] *n.*【医】坐骨神经痛.

sci·ence [ˈsaiəns] *n.* ①科学;科学研究. ②(一门)科学,学科. ③自然科学. ④学;学问;〔古〕知识. ⑤(拳术、马术等的)技术,专门技巧;〔the ~〕〔卑〕拳术. ⑥〔有时作 S-〕信仰疗法,基督教精神疗法〔又称 Christian S-〕. *the pure* ~ 纯理论科学. *the* ~ *of history* 历史学. *social* ~ 社会科学. *the most advanced branches of* ~ *and technology* 尖端科学技术. *physical* ~ 自然科学,物理(科)学. *natural* ~ 自然科学. *borderline [boundary]* ~ 边缘科学. ~ *and learning [scholarship]* 自然科学和人文科学;学术;学艺. *the Academy of S-* 科学院. *a man of* ~ 科学家. *a bachelor of* ~ 理学士. *a doctor of* ~ 理学博士. ***the noble* ~ *(of defence)*** 自卫术,拳术,剑术. ~ **fiction** 科学(幻想)小说.

sci·en·ti·a est po·ten·ti·a [skiːˈentiːɑː est pəuˈtentiːɑː] 〔L.〕知识就是力量.

sci·en·tial [saiˈenʃəl] *a.* ①知识的,学问的. ②有知识的,有学问的;学识丰富的.

sci·en·tif·ic [ˌsaiənˈtifik] *a.* ①(自然)科学(上)的,学术(上)的,科学性的;从事科学工作的. ②应用科学的. ③精通学理的,有学问的. ④合乎科学的;方法正确的;有系统的. ⑤有专长的. ⑥有本事的;技术纯熟的;有技巧的. ~ *and learned circles* 学术界. ~ *studies [~ researches]* 科学研究. *a* ~ *method* 科学方法. ~ *experiments* 科学实验. *a* ~ *man* 科学家. ~ *socialism* 科学社会主义. ~ *farming* 科学种田. **-i·cal·ly** *ad.*

sci·en·tism [ˈsaiəntizəm] *n.* ①科学信念;科学态度;科学方法. ②唯科学主义. **sci·en·tis·tic** [ˌsaiənˈtistik] *a.*

sci·en·tist [ˈsaiəntist] *n.* ①科学家,自然科学家,科学工作者. ★ 有人爱用 man of science 来代替此字. ②【宗】〔S-〕信仰疗法者,基督教精神疗法者(= Christian S-).

sci.fa. = 〔L.〕*scire facias.*

sci-fi [ˈsaiˈfai] *a., n.* = **science fiction.**

scil. = 〔L.〕*scilicet* (= namely).

sci·li·cet [ˈsailiset] *ad.* 〔L.〕即,就是,换句话说〔缩写 sc., 或 scil, 或 SS., 或 ss.〕.

Scil·la [ˈsilə] *n.*【希神】(居于意大利墨西拿 (Messina) 海峡岩礁上的)六头女妖;意大利墨西拿海峡上的岩礁(= Scylla).

scil·la [ˈsilə] *n.*【植】绵枣儿属 *(Scilla)* 植物;〔尤指〕西伯利亚绵枣儿 *(Scilla sibirica)*; 海葱 (= squill).

scim·e·tar, scim·i·tar, -ter [ˈsimitə] *n.* (阿拉伯人的)单刃短弯刀,偃月刀;半月形镰刀.

scin·coid [ˈsinkɔid] *a.*【动】①石龙子科的. ②石龙子科动物状的. — *n.* 石龙子蜥蜴.

scin·ti·gram [ˈsintəgræm] *n.*【激】闪烁(曲线),闪烁图.

scin·tig·ra·phy [sinˈtigrəfi] *n.*【物理】闪烁录像术.

scin·til·la [sinˈtilə] *n.* ①火花;闪烁. ②微分子. ③〔通例用于否定〕微量;极少,一点. ***not a* ~ *of*** 一丁点…也没有.

scin·til·lant [ˈsintilənt] *a.* 发火花的;闪烁的.

scin·til·late [ˈsintileit] *vi.* ①发(出)火花;发闪光. ②闪烁. ③(才气)焕发. — *vt.* 发(出)(火花等). *Her eyes* ~ *anger.* 她的眼睛闪烁着愤怒的光芒.

scin·til·la·tion [ˌsintiˈleiʃən] *n.* ①放射闪光,发出火花. ②闪光;火花. ③【天、物】闪烁(现象). ④(才气的)焕发,(天才)横溢. ~ **camara** 闪烁摄影机. ~ **counter** 【物】= scintillometer.

scin·til·la·tor [ˈsintileitə] *n.* ①闪烁者,闪烁物. ②【物】闪烁体,闪烁器.

scin·til·lome·ter [ˌsintiˈlɔmitə] *n.*【物】闪烁计数器(= scintillation counter).

scin·til·lo·scope [sinˈtiləskəup] *n.*【物】闪烁(观察)镜.

scin·ti·scan·ner [ˈsintiˌskænə] *n.*【物】闪烁扫描器.

sci·o·cra·cy [ˈsaiəkrəsi] *n.* 科学民主统治.

sci·o·graph [ˈsaiəgrɑːf] *n.* = skiagraph. **-ic** *a.*

sci·o·lism [ˈsaiəlizəm] *n.* 一知半解;浅学. **sci·o·list** *n.* 学识肤浅的人,一知半解的人,半瓶醋. **-lis·tic** [ˌsaiəˈlistik] *a.* 学识肤浅(者)的,一知半解(者)的,半瓶醋的.

sciol·to [ˈʃɔltəu] *ad.* 〔It.〕【乐】①自由地;敏捷地;无拘束地. ②断音地;断开地,分开地.

sci·om·a·chy [saiˈɔməki] *n.* = sciamachy.

sci·o·man·cy [ˈsaiəmənsi] *n.* 扶乩;关亡.

sci·on [ˈsaiən] *n.* ①【植】接穗;(栽种或接枝用的)幼枝,幼芽. ②(主指贵族等的)子孙;后裔. *a* ~ *of a noble family [royal stock]* 贵族[皇族]家庭的子弟.

sci·op·tic [saiˈɔptik], **sci·op·tric** [saiˈɔptrik] *a.* 用暗箱(成像)的.

sci·re fa·ci·as [ˈsaiəri ˈfeiʃiæs] 〔L.〕【法】请告知;请说明理由〔法院命令关系人说明某项成案何以不应执行的书状〕.

scir·rhous [ˈsirəs] *a.*【医】硬(性)癌的.

scir·rhus [ˈsirəs] *n.* ***(pl. scir·rhi*** [ˈsirai], ***~es)***【医】硬(性)癌.

scis·sel [ˈsisəl] *n.*【机】①(金属板[片]的)切屑;截屑. ②(冲压后的)金属板余料.

scis·sile [ˈsisil] *a.* 可被切割[分裂](成片)的.

scis·sion [ˈsiʒən, ˈsiʃən] *n.* ①切断,割断;剪断. ②分离,分裂,裂开. ③【物】裂变.

scis·sor [ˈsizə] *vt.* ①(用剪刀)剪,剪断,剪下〔与 off,

up, out 连用〕. ②删除,削减. ~ *out a paragraph from a newspaper* 从报纸上剪下一段新闻. ~ *up a newspaper* 把报纸剪碎. ~ *off a piece of cloth* 剪下一块布来. *items ~ed* 削除了的项目. ~**bill**〔美工俚〕①对本阶级利益不关心的工人; 不参加工会的工人. ②庄稼汉; 没知识的人. ~**-bird** = ~tail. ~**-cut** 剪纸. ~**tail**【鸟】(美西南及墨西哥产的)铁尾鸟. ~ **tooth**(食肉动物的)裂齿.

scis·sor·ing [ˈsizəriŋ] *n.* ①剪. ②〔*pl.*〕剪下来的东西.

scis·sors [ˈsizəz] *n. pl.* ①〔亦可用作单数〕(一把)剪刀,剪子. ②〔用作单数〕【体】交叉,两腿前后错跃;【摔跤】= ~ hold. *a pair of* ~ 一把剪刀. *I want some* ~ 我要几把剪刀. *The* ~ *aren't sharp.* 这把剪刀不快. *A* ~ *was lying on the table.* 一把剪刀放在桌子上. ~ ***and paste*** 剪贴工作,编纂工作; 东鳞西爪凑合成的东西. ~**bird** = scissortail. ~ **chair**(打开后成X形的)折椅. ~ **hold**【摔跤】脚搭勾. ~ **kick**(游泳,尤指侧泳的)剪水动作. ~**tail** = scissortail.

scis·sure [ˈsiʒə] *n.*〔现罕〕裂口;(身体上或器官上的)纵切口,裂隙.

sci·u·rid [saiˈjuərid] *n.* 松鼠科 *(Sciuridae)* 动物〔包括松鼠、黄鼠、土拨鼠等〕. **sci·u·roid** [saiˈjuərɔid] *a.* ①(似)松鼠的. ②松鼠尾巴状的.

sclaff [sklæf] *vt.*【高尔夫球】用球棒擦〔刮〕地,把球棒擦着地面打(球). — *n.* ①用球棒擦地一击. ②〔Scot.〕轻拍,轻击.

scle·ra [ˈskliərə] *n.*【解】(眼球的)巩膜.

scle·re·id [ˈskli:riid] *n.*【植】石细胞,硬化细胞.

scle·ren·chy·ma [skliəˈreŋkimə] *n.* ①【植】厚壁组织. ②【动】石核组织.

scle·ri·a·sis [skliəˈraiəsis] *n.*【医】①硬皮病. ②睑硬结.

scle·rite [ˈskliərait] *n.*【古生】(骨)片; 灰质体.

scle·rit·is [skliˈraitis] *n.*【医】巩膜炎〔亦作 sclerotitis〕.

scle·ro- *comb. f.* 硬,厚〔在元音前作 scler〕: *scleroma.*

scler·o·der·ma [ˌskliərəuˈdə:mə] *n.*【医】硬皮病; 皮硬化症.

scler·o·der·ma·tous [ˌskliərəuˈdə:mətəs] *a.* ①硬皮病的; 皮硬化症的. ②【动】长着硬皮的〔如角质鳞片〕.

scler·oid [ˈskliərɔid] *a.*【生】硬的; 硬化的, 硬结的.

scle·ro·ma [skliəˈrəumə] *n. (pl.* ***-ma·ta*** [-mətə]*)*【医】硬结.

scle·rom·e·ter [skliəˈrɔmitə] *n.*【机】硬度计〔测矿的硬度〕.

scle·ro·pro·tein [ˌskliərəuˈprəuti:n] *n.*【生化】硬蛋白.

scle·rosed [skliˈrəust, ˈskliərəuzd] *a.*【医】患硬化症的; 硬化的, 硬结的.

scle·ro·sis [skliəˈrəusis] *n. (pl.* ***-ses*** [-si:z]*)* ①【医】硬化(症). ②【植】细胞壁硬化. **-ro·sal** *a.*

scle·rot·ic [skliəˈrɔtik] *a.* ①硬的,厚的; 硬性的. ②【解】巩膜的. ③【医】硬化的; 硬结的. — *n.* ①【解】巩膜. ②硬结药,硬化剂. ~ *cells* 石细胞.

scle·ro·ti·tis [ˌskliərəuˈtaitis] *n.*【医】巩膜炎.

scle·ro·ti·um [skliˈrəuʃiəm] *n. (pl.* ***-ti·a*** [-ʃiə]*)*【生】硬化体; 菌核. **scle·ro·tial** [-ʃiəl] *a.*

scle·rot·o·my [skliˈrɔtəmi] *n. (pl.* ***mies****)*【医】巩膜切开术.

scle·rous [ˈskliərəs] *a.* 硬化的; 骨的, 多骨的; 骨质的.

Sc. M. =〔L.〕*Scientiae Magister* 理学硕士 (= Master of Science).

scobs [skɔbz] *n.*〔*sing., pl.*〕①(角、金属等的)锯屑; 锯末; 剉屑; 刨花.

scoff[1] [skɔf] *n.*(特指对宗教的)嘲笑; 嘲弄; 冷笑*(at)*. ②笑柄*(of)*. — *vi., vt.* 嘲笑; 嘲弄; 冷笑. **-er** *n.* 嘲笑者. **-ing·ly** *ad.* 嘲笑地.

scoff[2] [skɔf] *vt., vi.* ①〔俚〕狼吞虎咽地吃; 饱食. ②掠夺,攫取. — *n.*〔俚〕食物; 伙食, 饭餐.

scoff·law [ˈskɔ:flɔ:] *n.*〔美口〕惯犯〔尤指违犯交通规则和禁酒法者〕.

scold [skəuld] *vt., vi.* 责骂; 叱责. — *n.* 唠唠叨叨〔吵吵嚷嚷,高声〕骂人的人〔妇女〕,〔特指〕(好骂人的)泼妇. *a common* ~ 整天骂人吵得四邻不安的泼妇. **-er** *n.* 责骂者.

scold·ing [ˈskəuldiŋ] *n.* 责骂,叱责,斥责. ***get[receive] a good*** ~ 挨一顿大骂. ***give sb. a good*** ~ 把某人大骂一顿. — *a.* 责骂的,叱责的,斥责的;(女人等)爱骂人的.

scol·e·cite [ˈskɔlisait, ˈskəul-] *n.*【地】钙沸石.

sco·lex [ˈskəuleks] *n. (pl.* ***sco·le·ces***[skəuˈli:si:z]*)*【动】(绦虫的)头节,头结.

scol·i·o·sis [ˌskɔliˈəusis] *n.*【医】脊柱侧凸.

scol·lop [ˈskɔləp] *n., vt., vi.* = scallop.

scol·o·pen·dra [ˌskɔləuˈpendrə] *n.* ①〔S-〕【动】蜈蚣属. ②蜈蚣. **-drid** [-drid] *a.*

scol·o·pen·drine [ˌskɔləuˈpendrain] *a.*【动】蜈蚣(属)的.

Scom·ber [ˈskɔmbə] *n. (pl.* ***-bri*** [-bri]*)*【动】鲭鱼(属).

scom·brid [ˈskɔmbrid], **scom·broid** [-brɔid] *a., n.*【动】鲭鱼科(的); 鲭鱼(科).

scon [skɔn] *n.* = scone.

sconce[1] [skɔns] *n.* ①(孤立的)小堡垒. ②隐身处; 保护所; 避难处〔室〕. ③盔. ④〔口〕头,脑袋. ⑤才智,智慧,智力,脑力. ⑥人头税; 特指牛津大学学生违反席间礼貌〔吃饭规矩〕时的(轻微)惩罚〔或罚出啤酒钱,或喝啤酒〕. ⑦浮冰的碎块. — *vt.* ①筑堡垒守护. ②对…征收人头税. ③对…施以薄惩〔特指牛津大学学生违反席间礼貌〔吃饭规矩〕时被罚出啤酒钱,或喝啤酒〕.

sconce[2] [skɔns] *n.*(钉在墙上的)烛台; 灯台.

scone [skɔn, skəun] *n.*〔Scot.〕〔英〕(大麦或燕麦等制的)甜烙饼,烤饼〔圆或扇形的〕.

scoop [sku:p] *n.* ①勺,杓; 戽斗; 大匙; 勺状物〔工具〕;【医】匙. ②铲; 铲斗;〔英〕煤斗. ③捞(鱼)网,挡网 (= scoop-net);【空】收集器. ④【机】洞,穴,口,凹进处. ⑤舀子. ⑥(一)舀(之量),(一)铲(之量). ⑦〔俚〕(能给一份报纸产生好处的)(独家)内幕(特快)消息,独家新闻,本报特讯,特稿; 秘闻. ⑧〔口〕(由投机而抢先赚取的)一大笔钱,暴利. ⑨汤匙形墁刀. *an air* ~【空】(戽斗式)空气吸入孔,进气孔. ***at a [one]*** ~ 一勺,一舀,一铲,一下子. ***get a*** ~ ***on other papers*** 登出特快消息〔特讯〕压倒他报. ***in [with] one*** ~ 一勺;一舀;一铲;一下子. ***make a*** ~ 舀一杓; 铲一铲. ***make a big*** ~〔口〕发大财; 抢先得到新闻. ***on the*** ~ 饮酒过度; 乐而忘返. — *vt.* ①舀*(out of)*. ②挖,掘,淘; 淘空,挖空; 通过淘挖而做成. ③〔口〕扒进; 大赚一笔. ④比…抢先登出特外消息. ~ *a rival paper.* 用特快消息压倒一家相竞争的报纸. ~ ***in*** ①舀进. ②〔口〕赚到. ~ ***out***【军】接应〔轰炸机返航时由战斗机接应,击退敌机追击〕. ~ **channel** 水槽. ~**full** 一(满)勺之量. ~ **neck**(开得较低的)圆领口. ~ **net** 捞(鱼)网,挡网. ~ **-wheel** 斗式挖泥转轮; 汲水车; 戽水水车. **-er** *n.* 舀〔掘、掏〕的人;(雕刻用的)凿刀.

scoot [sku:t]〔口〕*vi., vt.* ①(使)迅速跑开. ②(使)溜走. ③(使)射出;(使)喷出. — *n.* 迅速跑开; 溜走; 疾走.

scoot·er[1] [ˈsku:tə] *n.* ①踏板车〔儿童一脚踏在板上,一脚在地上撑着跑的玩具车〕. ②(象踏板车似的)小型摩托车. ③水上冰上两用的平底小帆船. ④〔Scot.〕水枪,喷水器. ⑤【农】开垄犁. *a motor* ~〔美〕摩托两用(水上冰上)艇.

scoot·er[2] [ˈsku:tə] *n.* = scoter.

scop [skɔp, skəup] *n.* 古代盎格鲁撒克逊的(吟游)诗人.

sco·pa [ˈskəupə] *n.*【动】(蜂等昆虫足上的)花粉刷〔栉〕.

scope [skəup] *n.* ①(活动)范围. ②眼界,视界; 视野; 见识. ③力量,能力. ④发挥能力的"用武之地"; 余地; 机会. ⑤广度,广袤,地域. ⑥【数】分野,辖域. ⑦(箭式导弹等的)射程. ⑧【海】(抛出的)锚缆长度. ⑨观测设备; 显示器; 阴极射线管. ⑩〔美俚〕潜望镜. ⑪〔古〕目的. ⑫(算命用的)星占图,天宫图. ***beyond[outside] sb.'s*** ~ 越出某人力量范围之外. ***give line and ~*** 先纵后擒;先给自由后压制. ***give ~ to [for]*** 给与…以…的自由;给…以发挥…的机会. ***have (an) ample [(a) full, (a) large] ~ (for)*** 有充分发挥能力的机会[活动的余地]. ***have (a) free ~*** 有…的自由. ***have no ~ for the imagination*** 无想象的余地. ***of wide ~*** 广泛的,广大的 (*a mind of wide ~* 见识广大的人. *an undertaking of wide ~* 范围广大的事业). ***seek ~ for*** 寻求发挥…的机会; 找…(活动的)机会. ***within the ~ of*** 在…的范围内;在…所及的地方.

-scope *suf.* 看的东西,看的器械,…镜,…指示器: tele*scope*.

sco·pol·am·in(e) [skəuˈpɔləmin, ˌskəupəˈlæmin] *n.* 【化】莨菪胺.

sco·po·phil·i·a [ˌskəupəuˈfiliə], **scop·to·phil·i·a** [ˌskɔptəuˈfiliə] *n.* 【医】视淫.

scop·u·la [ˈskɔpjulə] *n.* (*pl.* **~s, -lae** [-liː]) = scopa.

-scopy *suf.* 看,观察,看的方法: micro*scopy*.

scor·bu·tic [skɔːˈbjuːtik] *a.* 【医】①坏血症的. ②患坏血症的. — *n.* ①患坏血症者. ②坏血症特效药.

scorch [skɔːtʃ] *vt.* ①灼伤;晒焦;烘焦;烧焦. ②使枯萎. ③(军队撤退前)烧光(地面物). ④使(心里)着急, 使焦急. ⑤大骂. ⑥【化】使(橡胶)过早硫化;焦化. *a ~ed earth policy* 焦土政策. — *vi.* ①焦;萎,枯. ②令人感到灼痛,挖苦. ③〔俚〕(汽车等)高速疾驰. — *n.* ①烧焦. ②〔俚〕(汽车等的) 高速疾驰. **~-pencil** *n.* 烧画(所用的)笔.

scorch·er [ˈskɔːtʃə] *n.* ①极热的东西. ②〔口〕象火热一样的大热天. ③尖酸刻薄的话; 严厉之斥责;痛骂. ④〔俚〕触目的人或物. ⑤高速驾驶汽车(等)的人. ⑥〔俚〕特级品,极品,热门货. *a week of ~s* 酷热的一周.

scorch·ing [ˈskɔːtʃiŋ] *a.* ①烧焦似的, 灼热的, 象烧一般的,非常热的. ②尖酸刻薄的;苛刻的. *a ~ day* 大热天. — *ad.* 〔口语〕灼热地;热得灼人. **-ly** *ad.*

score [skɔː, skɔə] *n.* ①斫痕,截痕,刻痕,划线;痕,抓痕,鞭痕;裂缝;记号. ②对号筹片. ③计算; 百分数, 成份; 【运】比数. ④得分; 得分记录. ⑤(酒馆等的)帐目, 欠款. ⑥旧仇,宿怨. ⑦〔*sing.*, *pl.*〕二十, 二十人, 二十磅重. ⑧〔*pl.*〕许多. ⑨〔俚〕成功, 幸运. ⑩驳倒别人的议论, 打倒别人的动作. ⑪受骗者, 欺诈的目标. ⑫论点,理由,缘故,根据. ⑬(现实的)真相. ⑭【运】起步线; (射手站立的)打靶线,起射线. ⑮【乐】总谱, 乐谱; (电影歌舞等的)配乐. ⑯【造船】(滑车的)带槽. *a clean ~* 全胜得分. *a team ~* 团体分. *win by a ~ of 10 to 9* 以十比九得胜. *five ~ of herring* 一捆鲱鱼[100尾]. *~-(s) of times* 几十次, 屡次. *~(s) of years ago* 几十年前. *He is too fond of making cheap ~s.* 他总喜欢投机取巧(压倒别人). *What's the ~?* 现在几分? 形势怎样? *What a ~!* 真运气! *the ~* 真情;事实;情况. *from the ~* 从起步线,从打靶线. *a compressed [close, shot] ~* (由高音部和低音部压缩成的声乐的)二段总谱. ***by ~s*** 大批地,很多,许多. ***clear ~s [a ~]*** ①付清账款;还债. ②报仇,雪耻;泄愤. ***Death pays all ~s.*** 【谚】一死百了. ***get of [go off] at (full)~*** (马)全速向前猛冲;(人)精神十足地开始讲[做]. ***have an old ~ to settle with sb.*** 跟某人有老帐要算[有宿怨]. ***in ~*** 【乐】用总谱,以总谱方式排列. ***in ~s*** 很多,大批,大群. ***keep the ~*** (比赛等)记分数. ***make a good ~*** 得分很多,大成功. ***make a ~ in*** 在…上划一个记号. ***make a ~ off*** (*an awkward heckler*) 驳倒(难对付的诘问者), 说得…没话讲. ***make a ~ off one's own bat*** 独力做, 靠自己力量做. ***on a new ~*** 重新. ***on that ~*** 因此, 因那理由;在那一点上. ***on the same ~*** 用同样理由. ***on the ~ of*** 因为, 为了. ***pay off [settle] old ~s [an old ~]*** ①报复宿仇. ②还清旧账. ***pay one's ~*** 清账,还清债务. ***play to the ~*** 随机应变,见机行事. ***quit ~s with sb.*** 跟某人结清前账;向某人报复. ***run up (a) ~(s) to*** 对…负债累累. ***settle ~s with sb.*** 向某人清算. ***start at (full) ~*** = get of at (full) ~. ***three ~ (years) and ten*** (人生)七十年;一辈子. ***tie the ~*** 打成平局. ***wear off ~*** = ***clear ~***. — *vt.* ①在…上作斫痕[截痕、刻痕],打记号于,划线于. ②用线划掉〔又作 ~ out〕. ③计算. ④记…的帐. ⑤不忘记,记住(怨恨). ⑥记…的数,给…批分数. ⑦得到(胜利等);【运】获得(分数等). ⑧〔美口〕刻薄地批评,骂,责备. ⑨(议论等时)说败,击败. ⑩【乐】把…写成总谱,为…配乐. ⑪将(马)带到起跑线. *a heart ~d by sorrow and remorse* 饱经忧患的人. *~ a game [goal, point]* 胜一局[进一球,得一分]. — *vi.* ①记分数. ②得分,得胜(*against*). ③成功,得利. ④划线(*in*);(马)来到起跑线. ⑤借款,赊买. *Who will ~?* 不晓得哪个会赢? ***~ against*** = ~ over. ***~ off*** (*sb.*) 〔俚〕打败;驳倒(某人);羞辱(某人);使丢脸. ***~ out*** (用线)划掉;删去 (*The name and date have been ~d out.* 名字和日期已经划掉了.) ***~ over*** 打败,击败. ***~ under*** 在…字下划线; 强调. ***~ up*** ①把…(作记号)记下; 记帐. ②赊,欠下. **~ board** 【运】记分牌;比赛经过记录表;记录. **~ book** 【运】记分薄,比赛成绩薄. **~ card** 【运】记分卡;参加比赛的运动员登记卡. **~ keeper** 【运】记分员; 记帐员. **~pad** (每页都印有格子的) 记分簿. **~ sheet** 【棒球】记分单. **-less** 【运】未得分的.

scor·er [ˈskɔːrə] *n.* ①加斫痕[刻痕]的人. ②刻线条用的东西. ③作记号的人. ④算帐的人,帐房. ⑤【运】记分员;得分者.

sco·ri·a [ˈskɔːriə] *n.* (*pl.* **-ri·ae** [-riiː]) ①【冶】矿渣;金属渣;铅析(法)渣. ②【地】〔常 *pl.*〕火山岩渣, 熔岩渣,溶岩灰. **-ri·a·ceous** [ˌskɔːriˈeiʃəs] *a.*

sco·ri·fy [ˈskɔːrifai] *vt.* 【冶】(用烧熔试金法)析取;使成矿渣,煅烧,使渣化. **-fi·ca·tion** [ˌskɔːrifiˈkeiʃən] *n.* 【冶】渣化法,铅析金银法. **-fi·er** *n.* 【冶】煅烧皿;渣化皿;试金坩埚.

scorn [skɔːn] *n.* ①藐视;侮弄;嘲笑. ②受侮弄[嘲笑]的人,被轻视的东西. ③笑柄. ***feel [have] ~ for*** 对…抱藐视心理, ***hold in ~*** 藐视, 瞧不起. ***laugh sb. to ~*** 嘲笑, 挖苦(某人). ***point the finger of ~ at sb.*** 轻蔑地指点某人,嘲笑某人,轻蔑地批评某人. ***think [hold] it ~ to (do)*** 不屑(做). ***think ~ of*** 藐视,蔑视,瞧不起. — *vt.*, *vi.* ①蔑视, 嘲笑, 侮弄. ②不屑. *~ lying [to tell a lie]* 不屑说谎.

scorn·er [ˈskɔːnə] *n.* 藐视者,轻蔑者,嘲笑者.

scorn·ful [ˈskɔːnful] *a.* ①藐视的, 嘲笑的; 傲慢的. ②〔罕〕当做笑柄的. *~ remarks* 挖苦话. ***be ~ of*** 藐视. **-ly** *ad.* **-ness** *n.*

scor·pae·nid [skɔːˈpiːnid] *n.* 【动】鲉科 (*Scorpaenidae*) 鱼. **scor·pae·noid** [-nɔid] *a.*, *n.* 【动】鲉科的(鱼).

Scor·pi·o [ˈskɔːpiəu, -pjəu] *n.* ①【动】蝎属. ②【天】天蝎座,天蝎宫.

scor·pi·oid [ˈskɔːpiɔid] *a.* 【动】①似蝎的. ②蝎科的. ③末端弯曲如蝎尾的;拳卷的.

scor·pi·on [ˈskɔːpjən, -piən] *n.* ①【动】蝎. ②蠍子般的家伙; 黑心肠的人. ③蝎尾鞭. ④(古代)弩炮. ⑤〔S-〕= Scorpio. **~fish** *n.* 【动】锯鲉. **~ fly** 【动】蝎虫类 (*Mecoptera*) 昆虫. **S-'s Heart** 【天】天蝎宫的主星.

Scot. = ①Scotch. ②Scotland. ③Scottish.

Scot [skɔt] *n.* ①苏格兰人. ②〔*pl.*〕盖尔人〔五世纪时从爱尔兰移居到苏格兰的一个高卢部族〕.

scot[1] [skɔt] *n.* 估定的[已缴付的]款项,帐款;税金. ***pay (one's) ~ and lot*** 缴纳按能力负担的教区税,缴清税款;付清所欠;尽应尽的义务. ***~ free*** 免予支付; 未受损害,未受惩罚.

scot[2], **Scot** [skɔt] *n.* 〔误用〕= God. *Great ~!* 真是!糟糕! 哎呀!

Scotch [skɔtʃ] *a.* ①苏格兰(人、语)的. ★除 Scotch whisky [fir, tweeds, girl] 等常用词组外,苏格兰人自己喜欢用 Scottish 或 Scots, 很少用 Scotch; 英格兰人对

苏格兰人说恭维话时用 Scots. ②〔美俚〕节约的; 俭约的; 节俭的; 朴素的, 小气的. — *n.* ①〔the ～〕苏格兰人. ②苏格兰语; 苏格兰土腔. ③〔口〕苏格兰威士忌酒 (= ～ whisky); 〔美俚〕威士忌酒. *a small* ～ 酒味淡的苏格兰威士忌酒. *broad* ～ 苏格兰土话, 粗鄙的苏格兰话. ***flying*** ～ 开往苏格兰的特别快车. ***out of all*** ～ 〔卑〕过度地, 非常地. ～ ***and English***(分成两组的)儿童捉人游戏. ～ ***and soda*** 威士忌苏打. ～ **blessing** 〔方〕严厉的申斥. ～ **broth** 羊肉, 野菜. (大)麦片汤. ～ **cap** 苏格兰人戴的无边帽 (= Glengarry). ～ **catch [snap]**【乐】(后随一长音符的)重拍短音符. ～ **cousin** 远亲. ～ **fiddle** 〔卑〕疥癣. ～ **fir**【植】银松. ～ **grain** 苏格兰纹理〔一种制革法〕. ～ **Highlander** 苏格兰高地人. ～**-Irish** 苏格兰-爱尔兰裔的〔指住在爱尔兰北部的苏格兰低地人后裔, 尤指移居美国的这种人的后裔〕. ～**man** 苏格兰人. ～ **mist** (苏格兰山地的)山霭. ～ **pine**【植】欧洲赤松 *(Pinus sylvestris)*. ～ **tape** ①苏格兰胶带〔一种透明薄胶带, 亦其商标名〕② *vt.* 用透明胶带封口〔贴〕. ～ **terrier**【动】苏格兰㹴犬 (= Scottish terrier). ～ **thistle**【植】苏格兰刺蓟 *(Onopordum acanthium)*. ～ **verdict**【法】苏格兰式判决〔对"未证实"刑事案作非无罪判决〕; 〔转义〕非最后的决定, 未最后定局的事. ～ **whisky** 苏格兰威士忌酒. ～ **woman** 苏格兰女人. ～ **woodcock** 涂鳀酱的烤面包加鸡蛋的食物.

scotch [skɔtʃ] *n.* ①浅刻. ②擦伤, 轻伤. ③玩儿童跳格游戏(hopscotch)时地上划的线. ④止车楔, 垫楔, 车辖. — *vt.* ①轻轻切. ②在…上加刻痕. ③使受微伤; 伤及. ④将(蛇等)弄得半死. ⑤压碎; 粉碎; 打破(阴谋等). ⑥扑灭; 消除(谣言等); 弹压, 镇压(暴动等). *We have ～ed the snake, not killed it.* 我们将蛇弄得半死, 没有把它完全弄死.

sco·ter [ˈskəutə] *n.*【动】黑凫.

sco·tia [ˈskəuʃə] *n.*【建】(柱基的)凹圆线饰〔凹形边饰〕.

Sco·tia [ˈskəuʃə] 〔诗〕 = Scotland 〔苏格兰的拉丁名称〕.

Sco·tism [ˈskəutizəm] *n.*【哲】(Duns Scotus 的) 斯科塔斯哲学〔主张哲学与神学各不相关〕.

Scot·land [ˈskɔtlənd] *n.* 苏格兰. ～ **Yard** ①伦敦警察厅〔采用旧地址名, 现已迁移, 改称 New ～ Yard〕. ②伦敦警察厅侦缉处. ③伦敦警察 *(call in ～ yard* 向伦敦警察厅报警).

scot·o·graph [ˈskɔtəugrɑːf] *n.* ①暗处写字器; 盲人写字器. ②X 光线照片.

sco·to·ma [skəˈtəumə] *n.* *(pl. ～ta* [-tə]*)*【医】(网膜上的)暗点; 盲点. **sco·tom·a·tous** [skəˈtɔmətəs] *a.*

sco·to·pi·a [skəˈtəupiə] *n.* **sco·to·pic** [-ˈtəupik, -ˈtɔpik] *a.*【医】①暗光适应. ②暗视力.

Scots [skɔts] *a.* 〔*Scot.*〕苏格兰(人)的〔*cf.* Scotch〕. *the ～ language* 苏格兰(低地英)语. *the ～ law* 苏格兰法. *pounds ～* 苏格兰镑. *a ～ mile* 苏格兰英里. *～ greys* 苏格兰龙骑兵第二团. — *n.* ①〔the ～〕苏格兰民族. ②苏格兰(英)语, 苏格兰方言. *speak broad ～* 讲苏格兰土话. ～**man** 苏格兰人. ～**woman** 苏格兰女人.

Scott [skɔt] *n.* ①斯科特 (司各脱)〔姓氏, 男子名〕. ② **Robert Falcan** ～ 罗伯特·弗·斯科特〔1868—1912, 英国 1912 年到达南极的南极探险家〕. ③**Sir Walter** ～ 瓦尔特·司各脱〔1771—1832, 苏格兰诗人及小说家〕.

Scot·(t)i·ce [ˈskɔtisi] *ad.* 用苏格兰语; 用苏格兰方言.

Scot·(t)i·cism [ˈskɔtisizəm] *n.* 苏格兰语(法), 苏格兰方言; 苏格兰语化; 苏格兰发音.

Scot·(t)i·cize [ˈskɔtisaiz] *vi., vt.* ①(使)(言语、习惯等)苏格兰化. ②(把…)翻译成苏格兰语.

Scot·tie, Scot·ty [ˈskɔtiː] *n.* ***(pl. -ties)***〔口〕= **scottish terrier.**

Scot·tish [ˈskɔtiʃ] *a., n.* = Scotch. ～ **Gaelic** 苏格兰高地凯尔特语. ～ **rite** 苏格兰仪式〔共济会一种仪式制度〕.

scoun·drel [ˈskaundrəl] *n.* 恶棍, 无赖. — *a.* 恶棍(般)的, 无赖的; 卑鄙的. **-ism** *n.* ①卑劣; 无赖. ②下流举动; 恶棍〔无赖〕行为. **-ly** *a.* 无赖的, 恶棍的; 凶横的; 卑劣的.

scour[1] [ˈskauə] *vt., vi.* ①(用沙等)擦亮, 擦光; 擦掉(锈、污点等) *(off; away; out)*; 洗涤. ②肃清(海盗等); 扫荡. ③洗刷; 冲刷; 冲洗(管道等). ④疏浚(河底等). ⑤(用泻药)泻; 打(虫). ⑥【冶】侵蚀, 烧蚀. — *n.* ①磨擦, 去锈. ②洗去. ③疏浚. ④扫除, 扫荡. ⑤〔常 *pl.*〕(家畜的)泻药. ⑥洗涤剂. *give it a ～* 洗一洗. ～**-ing-rush**【植】木贼; 笔管草; 锁眼草. ～**ing-stock** 漂布机. **-ings** ①(机床的)切屑; 残屑. ②擦洗下来的污垢. ③谷皮. ④社会渣滓. **-er** [ˈskauərə] *n.* 擦洗者; 洗刷器.

scour[2] [skauə] *vt.* (急急忙忙来回)搜寻 *(about)*. — *vi.* 飞快地跑过, 奔跑, 搜寻着跑过 *(away, off)*. ～ ***along*** 跑过, 搜索, 出没. ～ ***the coast*** 沿海岸搜索, 出没在沿岸(一带).

scourge [skəːdʒ] *n.* ①天罚, 天灾, 灾难, 灾害〔瘟疫、战争等〕. ②苦难的根源, 引起灾害的事物, 带来灾害的人. ③鞭, 笞. *the ～ of Heaven* 灾殃, 祸患. ***the white*** ～ 肺痨. — *vt.* ①折磨, 磨难, 使苦恼; 严罚, 重惩, 重责. ②鞭打; 鞭笞.

scouse [skaus] *n.* = lobscouse.

scout[1] [skaut] *n.* ①守望员; 侦察员; 斥候. ②侦察舰; 侦察机; 搜索救援机. ③童子军. ④【军】侦察, 守望, 观察. ⑤(牛津大学的)校工〔剑桥大学称 gyp, 都伯林大学称 skip〕. ⑥〔古〕【板球】外场守场员. ⑦【动】海乌; 海鸠; 善知鸟. ⑧〔俚〕家伙. *a good old ～* 有趣的家伙. ***be in [on] the*** ～ 在侦察中. — *vi., vt.* ①侦察 *(about; round)*. ②寻找; 搜索 (out; up). ～ **bomber** 侦察轰炸机. ～ **car** 轻装甲巡逻车. ～**craft** ①侦察术. ②童子军活动. ～ **cruiser** 侦察巡洋舰. ～**hood** ①童子军身份. ②童子军的精神〔作风〕. ～**master** ①侦察队长. ②童子军领队; 〔S-〕〔美俚〕广告公司经理. ～ **plane** 侦察机.

scout[2] [skaut] *vt., vi.* ①认为荒唐而拒绝(提议, 意见等). ②讥笑, 嘲弄. ③轻视.

scow [skau] *vt.* 〔美〕用敞舱驳船驳运; 用方头驳船驳运. — *n.* 敞舱驳船, 方头驳船, 大型平底输送船.

scowl [skaul] *n.* ①愁容; 皱着眉头的脸; 不高兴的脸; 绷着的脸; 怒容; 不豫之色. ②(天空)晦暗; 阴沉; 就要发生暴风雨的样子. — *vi.* ①皱眉头; 绷脸; 瞪着眼看; 怒视 *(at; on)*. ②(天气)变坏; 阴沉起来; 象要下雨. — *vt.* 用怒容(对人)把…压下去; 用怒容表示; 皱眉拒绝 *(away)*; 对…绷脸使…. ～ *sb. into silence* 绷着脸使某人无话可说. ～ *down* 瞪眼怒视, 瞪着眼睛使沉默. **-ing·ly** *ad.*

SCP = single-cell protein 单细胞蛋白.

SCR = ①silicon controlled rectifier【无】硅可控整流器, 可控硅. ②semiconductor controlled rectifier 半导体可控整流器.

scr. = scruple.

scrab·ble [ˈskræbl] *vi., vt.* ①(用爪)扒找, 乱扒; 匆匆忙忙地扒集. ②(为生活)挣扎〔争夺〕. ③七颠八倒地写; 乱写, 乱涂. — *n.* ①(乱)扒. ②争夺; 挣扎; 奋斗. ③乱写, 乱涂. ④胡乱写下来的东西, 乱写的字.

scrab·bly [skræbli] *a.* ***(-bli·er; -bli·est)***〔口〕①有抓刮声的. ②长满矮树丛的. ③矮小的. ④多短硬毛的. ⑤不足取的, 没价值的. ⑥次要的; 不重要的. ⑦下贱的; 贫穷的.

scrag [skræg] *n.* ①骨瘦如柴的人〔动物〕. ②矮小枯萎的树木〔植物〕. ③〔英〕肉类的多骨部分, 排骨. ④(烧汤用的)羊〔小牛〕颈肉. ⑤〔俚〕(人的)颈, 脖子. ⑥糟粕, 碎块, 碎片, 碎屑. — *vt.* ①〔俚〕掐…脖子, 勒…颈, 绞死(罪犯等). ②【橄榄球】抱住(对方队员的)脖子. ～**-end** 羊颈肉.

scrag·gly [ˈskrægli] *a.* ***(-gli·er; -gli·est)*** ①稀疏的，稀少的；短小的。②不规则的；不整齐的；参差的；散乱的。③破烂的。*a ~ beard* 参差不齐的胡子；稀稀拉拉的胡子。**scrag·gli·ness** *n.*

scrag·gy [ˈskrægi] *a.* ***(-gi·er; -gi·est)*** ①骨瘦如柴的，瘦削的。②凹凸不平的，高低不平[齐]的。**-gi·ly** *ad.*

scram [skræm] *vi.* 〔美俚〕快离开；滚(开)〔通常用于命令语气〕。—*n.* ①急速离开。②紧急刹车。

scram·ble [ˈskræmbl] *vi.* ①爬，爬上去，攀登；攀缘 *(about; up; down; through)*。②争先恐后地抢；互相争夺；竭力搜求 *(for)*。③【空】争先恐后地起飞；紧急起飞(应战)。④(蔓草等)蔓延，繁生。⑤【无】扰频；【讯】保密。⑥〔美足球俚〕(没有挡截队员保护下)单独带球冲锋陷阵。— *vt.* ①攀登；爬(上)。②炒[搅拌](鸡蛋、牛奶等)。③搅乱；把…打乱。④【无】改变…的频率使不被窃听。⑤把…胡乱扔(在一堆)；撒(钱等让大家来抢)。⑥匆忙凑合，凑拢，收集。⑦【空】命令…紧急起飞。*~d egg* 炒鸡蛋。***~ after*** 搜求，拼命找。***~ along [on]*** 爬向前；勉强对付过去。***~ for a living*** 勉强度日。***~ for office*** 争夺职位；抢官做。***~ into one's clothes*** 急急忙忙穿上衣服。***~ the dope***〔美〕比赛中出现与预料相反的成绩。***~ through*** 勉强设法通过。***~ up*** 爬上去；扒拢。— *n.* ①爬上，攀登；攀缘。②争取；(互相)争夺。③【空】紧急起飞。④混乱的动作[活动]。⑤【无】扰频；倒频。*a ~ for office* 抢官位；争权。***in a ~*** 急忙；赶忙。**scram·bler** ①爬行者；攀缘者；争先恐后(抢夺)者；攀缘植物。②【无】扰频器；倒频器；保密器(scrambler phone 防窃听电话)。

scram·jet [ˈskræmdʒet] *n.* 超音速冲压式喷气发动机[飞机]。

scran [skræn] *n.* ①〔俚〕食物，粮食。②(食物)屑；残羹剩饭。***Bad ~ to you!***〔Ir.〕见你的鬼去吧！去你的！***out on the ~***〔卑〕做乞丐，去讨饭。

scran·nel [ˈskrænl] *a.* 〔英古〕①细(小的)；弱。②难听的，刺耳的。

scran·ny [ˈskræni] *a.* 〔英方〕瘦骨嶙峋的(= scraggy)。

scrap[1] [skræp] *n.* ①小片；小块；破片；切剩剪剩的碎片；碎屑；零头。②〔集体词〕废料。③〔*pl.*〕破烂东西；残羹剩饭。④(报纸剪下的)零杂资料；断片；断简；残篇。⑤【冶】碎铁，铁屑。⑥〔*pl.*〕剩余物；油渣；金属渣。⑦少许，一点点。*a ~ of cloth* 一小块布。*a few ~s of news* (零零碎碎的)两三条消息。*a ~ of paper* 一小块碎纸；〔讽〕废纸一样的条约。*dry ~* (干)鱼渣。*green ~* 生鱼渣。*~s of Latin* 一点点拉丁语知识。***do not care a ~*** 一点不在乎。***not a ~*** 一点也没有…。— *vt.* 〔俚〕①把…作为废料拆毁；撕毁。②废弃；撕毁。**~basket** 废纸篓。**~book** 剪贴簿；贴报簿。**~ cake** (饲料用)鱼渣。**~ iron** 废铁。

scrap[2] [skræp] *n.* ①打架 *(with)*；扭打；争吵；口角。②拳赛。— *vi.* 打架。

scrape [skreip] *vt.* ①刮，削，擦，搔；刮去，削去，擦去 *(away; off; out)*；擦过 *(against; past)*。②磨擦，打磨。③挖出，挖空 *(up; out)*。④凑；收集；勉强凑拢。⑤搜刮；积攒；一点一点地储蓄 *(together; up)*。⑥(乱)弹拨(弦乐器)；使咯吱咯吱地响。⑦(行礼时)将(右脚)向后一退。⑧用脚擦地板发声以妨碍(演讲者等)。⑨(用平地机)平地。*~ one's boots* 刮净鞋底。*~ one's chin* 剃胡子。*~ one's plate* 刮光盘中食物。— *vi.* ①刮；削；擦；搔；*(against)*。②积攒；一点一点地积蓄。③乱弹，瞎弹 *(on)*。④将右脚向后退一下鞠躬。⑤(鸡等)刨地。*the scrapings and scourings of the street* ①街道上的垃圾。②街上的流氓无赖。***bow and ~*** ①打躬作揖[屈膝]；一面鞠躬一面将脚向后一退。②奉承；巴结。***pinch and ~ = ~ and screw*** 省吃省用地贮蓄；节约；俭省。***~ along*** ①擦过去。②勉勉强强过下去。***~ (up) an acquaintance with …*** 老着脸皮去接近[结识](某人)。***~ down*** ①擦掉，刮去；弄平。②用脚擦地板轰走(演讲者等)。***~ off*** 刮去。***~ out a mark*** 擦掉记号。***~ the mug***〔美俚〕刮胡子。***~ through*** ①好容易完成。②(考试)勉强及格。③勉强对付过去。④勉强通过。***~ together [up]*** ①一点一点地贮蓄。②设法凑拢 (*I pay the bill scraping up the money we had.* 我把我们所有的钱凑起来付清了帐。) — *n.* ①刮；削；擦；刮痕；擦伤。②刮削声；摩擦声；乱弹声。③打扦。④(自己招来的)困难，困境，窘境。⑤刮胡子；修面。⑥(在面包上)涂点奶油。*a ~ of a pen* ①大笔一挥。②签字。*bread and ~* 涂了一点点奶油的面包。*a fine [pretty] ~* 为难的事情，困境。***be in a ~*** 正在困难中，正在为难。***get into a ~*** 陷入困境。***out of all ~*** 脱离困难，脱离窘境。**~ iron**【林】树脂收集器。**-penny** *n.* 吝啬鬼。

scrap·er [ˈskreipə] *n.* ①刮(削)的人，擦的人。②擦具；搔具；刮刀；刮削器。③刮土器；泥擦。④鞋擦。⑤橡皮擦。⑥【医】刮器；刮刀。⑦【军】(扫除炮口内火药的)通条刮子。⑧〔罕〕吝啬鬼；悭吝人；财迷。⑨〔蔑〕理发匠。

scrap-heap [ˈskræphi:p] *n.* 垃圾[废料]堆，废铜烂铁堆。***fit the ~*** 毫无用处的；该废弃的。***go to the ~*** 变成废物，荒废，被废弃，没落。***throw [toss, cast] on the ~*** 废弃。**~ policy** 喜新厌旧[用旧就扔]政策。

scrap·ing [ˈskreipiŋ] *n.* ①刮，削，擦。②刮声，削声，擦声。③〔常用 *pl.*〕刮屑。

scrap·per[1] [ˈskræpə] *n.* ①刮(或擦)的人。②刮刀；削刮器，刮土机，铲运机。③吝啬鬼，守财奴。

scrap·per[2] [ˈskræpə] *n.* 〔口〕①爱打架[吵架]的人；会打架[吵架]的人。②(职业)拳击家。

scrap·ple [ˈskræpl] *n.* 〔美〕【烹】玉米面肉末饼。

scrap·py[1] [ˈskræpi] *a.* ***(-pi·er; -pi·est)*** ①碎料的；剩余的；零碎的。②片断的；不连贯的；杂乱无章的。*a ~ dinner* 一顿拼拼凑凑的饭菜。**-pi·ly** *ad.*

scrap·py[2] [ˈskræpi] *a.* 〔俚〕①爱吵架的；好打架的。②斗志旺盛的。

scratch [skrætʃ] *vt., vi.* ①(用爪、针等)搔；搔(痒)；抓；抓(表面)；刨；用爪刨[扒，挖](洞)。②抓伤[破]；刮坏。③刺刺地抓；作刮擦声。④潦草地写；涂写；乱画。④涂掉；勾消；勾划掉 *(out; out of)*。⑤停止；丢弃。⑥(将马)从名单中勾消掉；(使)退出比赛；〔美〕(把…)从候补人名单中删掉。⑦刨拢在一块，凑合。⑧勉强维持[对付，糊口]。〔美俚〕伪造(支票)。*S- my back and I will ~ yours.* = *S- me and I will ~ you.*〔口，谚〕你捧我我就捧你；互相迎合，互吹互捧。*~ one's head* 搔首；为难 *(over)*。*~ a match on a box* 在火柴盒上擦火柴。*My pen ~es.* 我的钢笔写起来刮纸。***~ about for*** 到处竭力搜寻。***~ for oneself***〔美〕为自己的利益奔走。***~ one's head*** ①搔头皮。②(对某事)迷惑不解 *(over)*。***~ the surface of*** ①搔…的表面。②有一些…的肤浅知识。***~ together [up]*** 刨在一块；凑拢 (*~ up some money* 凑点钱)。***~ (sb.) where he itches*** ①给(某人)抓痒。②迎合人意。— *n.* ①抓；搔。②抓痕；搔痕；划痕。③抓伤；擦伤；微伤。④【地】擦痕；【建】刮痕。⑤搔声；刮擦声。⑥〔口〕拙笔；乱写。⑦【台球】造成罚分的一击；空球(亦要罚分)。⑧【运】(不接受让步待遇者的)平赛起步线；平赛起跑时间[开始时间]。⑨【运】零分；平局。⑩【拳】拳击开始线。⑪〔*pl.*〕马脚葡萄疮。⑫半假发[又称 ~ wig]。⑬〔美俚〕伪造者；假造的支票[钞票]。*a mere ~* 一点儿擦伤。*a ~ man* 不接受让步待遇的赛跑者。*the Old S-* 恶魔。***bring to the ~*** 使决定；使实行；使决心。***by the ~ of a pen*** 动一动笔，签一个字 (*The business could be settled by the ~ of a pen.* 那件事大笔一挥签一个字就可以办成)。***come (up) to (the) ~*** ①站到拳击开始线上，走[踏]上起步线。②挺身迎敌，决意奋斗；坚决行动。③能胜任，称职。***no great ~***〔俚〕没有什么了不得。***on the ~*** 在起步线上没有让步地，平等地。***start from [at, on] ~*** ①从起步线跑；从零开始。②从头做起；白手起家。***up to ~*** 合格;称职;处于良好状态. — *a.* ①[俚]东拼西凑的;(船员、球队等)临时凑成的; 凑合的; 庞杂的,各种各样的. ②碰巧的; 偶然的. ③平等比赛的; (赛跑等)无让步的. ④随便写的; 打草稿用的. *a ~ race* (无让步条件的)平赛. ~ **back** (抓痒用的)麻姑爪. ~**-block** = scratch-pad. ~ **board** 刮板. ~ **brush** 钢丝刷. ~ **cat** 狠毒的女人;凶狠的小孩. ~ **coat** 【建】打底子的水泥层;(涂灰)打底. ~ **hardness** 擦硬度,刻画硬度. ~ **hit** 【棒球】触击. ~ **line** 【运】起跑线,起跳线,投掷线. ~ **man** 比赛时让别人的人. ~**-pad** [美]便条本;拍纸簿. ~**-pad memory** 便笺式存储器; 高速暂存存储器. ~ **paper** 便条纸. ~ **test** ①【医】抓挠试验[把能引起过敏反应的物质放在微微挠破的皮肤上,试验病人所产生的反应]. ②刮痕[硬度]试验.

scratch·er [ˈskrætʃə] *n.* ①抓扒者,抓扒工具. ②制金属模具工人. ③树木刮痕器. ④【建】划痕器;拉毛爪子. ⑤[美俚] 伪造者.

scratch·y [ˈskrætʃi] *a.* *(-i·er; -i·est)* ①草率的;潦草的(书、画等). ②(钢笔等)会刮纸的;瑟瑟响的. ③东拼西凑的; (船员、球队等)拼凑成的. ④使人发痒的; 搔人的,扎人的. ⑤稀少的. **-i·ly** *ad.* **-i·ness** *n.*

scrawl [skrɔːl] *n.* ①潦草书写;乱写;乱涂;瞎画. ②草草写成的信. — *vt., vi.* 潦草书写;乱写,乱涂;瞎画. ~ *all over the wall* 满墙乱写乱画. **-y** *ad.*

scraw·ny [ˈskrɔːni] *a.* *(-ni·er; -ni·est)* [美] 骨瘦如柴的,瘦骨嶙嶙的.

screak [skriːk] *vi.* 尖叫;发出尖锐刺耳声. — *n.* 尖叫声; 尖锐刺耳声; 吱吱嘎嘎声[因摩擦而发出的尖锐的刺耳声].

scream [skriːm] *n.* ①(恐怖、苦痛的)尖叫声,惊叫声,拼命的叫喊声;尖(高)声大笑;(枭、汽笛等的)尖叫声. ②[俚]非常可笑的人[事情];笑柄. ③[美]伙伴. ④[不用冠词]花哨, 夸张. *a ~ of laughter* 哄笑. — *vi.* ①尖声喊叫,拼命叫喊,绝叫;叫喊;呜呜地叫. ②(颜色)花哨刺眼[不协调]. ③(字)花哨潦草. — *vt.* ①喊叫着说出. ②[~ oneself] 尖叫得使变…. ~ ***oneself hoarse*** 叫哑嗓子. ~ ***out*** 尖声喊叫,发尖声. ~ ***with laughter*** 格格地大笑.

scream·er [ˈskriːmə] *n.* ①(尖声)喊叫的人;尖声怪气说话的人. ②发尖锐刺耳声音的东西. ③[俚]使人笑破肚皮的话[唱歌](等). ④令人惊叹[愕]的东西. ⑤极标致的女人. ⑥[美俚](报纸上)耸人听闻的[惊人的]大字标题;横贯全页的大标题. ⑦恐怖(影)片;恐怖场面. ⑧[俚] 花哨刺眼的东西;【印】[俚] 惊叹号. ~ **bomb** 啸声炸弹.

scream·ing [ˈskriːmiŋ] *a.* ①尖声怪气地叫的,尖声喊叫的. ②发尖锐刺耳声音的. ③使人笑破肚皮的; 非常可笑的. ④令人惊叹[愕]的. ⑤耸人听闻的. ⑥花哨刺眼的. ~ **meemies** [ˈmiːmiːz] [俚] 神经极度紧张(的状态);歇斯底里.

scream·y [ˈskriːmi] *a.* *(-i·er; -i·est)* 尖叫的; 悲鸣的;哀号的;怪叫的;尖声怪气的, **-i·ly** *ad.*

scree [skriː] *n.* [常 *pl.*][英]山脚碎岩;岩屑堆;碎石堆.

screech [skriːtʃ] *n.* (表示恐怖、苦痛、愤怒等的)尖叫声;尖锐刺耳的声音. — *vt.* 尖声喊叫出 *(out)*. —*vi.* 发出尖锐刺耳的声音. ~**owl** ①叫声很尖的枭;仓鸮. ②凶事预言者. **-y** *a.*

screed [skriːd] *n.* ①【建】样板;(混凝土修正机的)整平板;准条. ②冗长的议论[文章,演讲,书信]. ③[Scot.] ①裂口,裂缝. ②碎片;裂片. — *vt., vi.* [Scot.] ①(使)裂开;撕破. ②喋喋不休地讲.

screen [skriːn] *n.* ①屏风;围屏;屏幕;簾;幔;帐(等). ②矮墙,隔板. ③荧光屏;【电】屏蔽.【物】栅,网,帘栅极. ④(电视的)屏幕;(电影的)银幕;电视屏; [the ~] 电影(界). ⑤粗筛;煤筛. ⑥滤网;过滤器. ⑦【印】网纹玻璃;网屏,网板[照相制版将银粒浓淡色调转变为网目的工具]. ⑧【摄】滤光器; 网孔. ⑨掩蔽物; 警戒幕. ⑩【军】掩护部队,掩护舰;屏护[前卫]部队. ⑪掩护. ⑫【气】百叶箱. ⑬(金属,塑料等制成的)纱窗;饰窗;纱门. ⑭【心】屏隔,屏障[一种隐蔽或掩饰形式]. *a folding ~* 折叠屏风. *a smoke ~* 烟幕. *make a ~ version of* 将…编成电影(剧本). *put on a ~ of indifference* 假装不知道的样子;假装冷淡. ~ *mesh* 筛眼;网孔. ~*play* 电影剧(本) [脚本] ~ *time* 放映时间. *show [throw] on the ~* 放映. *silk ~ method* 丝网漏印法. *under ~ of night* 乘黑; 在夜幕掩护下. — *vt.* ①遮;遮蔽;隔开;藏匿;庇护. ②【无】屏蔽. ③筛选(煤炭等); 甄别. ④把(小说)拍成电影;把…放映在银幕上. —*vi.*拍电影,在银幕上出现. ~ *off* 用幕(屏)隔开;隔出. ~ ***out*** ①筛去. ②筛选;选拔;甄别. ~**actor** 电影演员. ~ **constant** 【电】屏蔽常数. ~ **face** 适于上银幕 [演电影]的脸. ~ **gride [tube]** 【无】筛栅管. **ground** ~ 地网. **lamp** ~ 灯罩. ~ **land** 电影界 [美国说法多作 ~**-dom**]. **luminescent** ~ 荧光膜. ~ **memory** 【心】屏隔回忆 [回忆一件有关系而不太痛苦的事来屏隔一件回忆起来令人痛苦的事]. ~ **pass** 【足球】过人短传. ~ **riddle** 振动筛. ~ **test** 【影】试镜头[测验某人是否适于当电影演员]; 试映片断镜头[检查已拍的镜头在银幕上的效果]. ~**washer,** ~**wiper** (汽车)挡风玻璃刷子. ~ **writer** 电影编剧人[作者].

screen·ing [ˈskriːniŋ] ①做装帘[纱窗]. ②审查;甄别;放映. ③[*pl.*] 筛屑;筛渣. ~ *effect* 【无】屏蔽效应. ~ *committee* 考选[甄别]委员会. ~ *test* 选拔考试;甄别考试.

screeve [skriːv] *vi.* [俚]在路边画图求乞;告地状. —*n.* 马路图画. **-r** [俚] 马路画家;告地状者.

screw [skruː] *n.* ①螺旋;螺钉. ②螺旋桨;暗轮. ③暗轮轮船. ④螺旋状物. ⑤拔塞器; 螺丝钻子. ⑥螺旋的一拧; 螺旋的一转. ⑦[英俚](力争而得的)薪水;工钱. ⑧爱出难题的教员;难题. ⑨压迫; 暴力. ⑩吝啬鬼; 守财奴; 善于讨价还价的人. ⑪跑乏了[老弱]的马; 驽马. ⑫[英](烟丝的)卷纸;一卷;(盐、烟草、茶叶等的)一包. ⑬【几何】螺旋体;螺体. ⑭【台球】拧;转;【网球】削;搓. ⑮[卑] 钥匙;[尤指]万能钥匙. ⑯[卑] 监狱看守人. *a female [an interior] ~* 阴螺旋. *a male [an external] ~* 阳螺旋. *a poor ~* 菲薄的薪水. *draw a ~* [俚]领薪水. *raise sb.'s ~* [俚]加薪. ***a ~ loose*** ①毛病;故障. ②有毛病的东西 (*He has a ~ loose.* 他头脑有点不对头). ***apply the ~ to*** = put the ~ on. ***give a nut a good ~*** 扭紧螺母. ***give another turn to the ~*** = put the ~ on. ***have a ~ loose*** 疯疯癫癫的;乖僻;古怪;精神不正常. ***put a ~ on a tennis ball*** (网球)削球. ***put the ~ on [put ... under the ~]*** 加以强制;强迫;施加压力;催促;催索(债务). ***tighten the ~s*** 拧紧螺丝;加强控制. ***turn the ~s at sb. [sth.]*** 对某人[某事]施加压力[加强控制]. — *vt.* ①用螺丝拧紧[钉紧];拧紧. ②加强(效率),鼓起(勇气) *(up)*. ③拧;扭;扭歪(嘴,脸等). ④勒索;强逼;勉强付出. ⑤虐待;欺压. ⑥[美]严格考试. ⑦【台球】拧(球);【网球】搓(球);削(球). ⑧[美俚] 与…发生性关系. *His head is ~ed on the right way.* 他头脑清楚. *I am ~ed down by fixed rules.* 我被清规戒律束缚住了. ~ *up a piece of paper into a ball* 把纸揉成一团. — *vi.* ①起螺丝的作用;扭转;拧转. ②催促; 强逼; 勒索. ③拼命俭省. ④严格考试. ⑤[美俚]走掉;离开;出去. ⑥[美俚]性交. *The top ~s on [off].* 这个盖子可以拧上[拧下]. ~ ***around*** [俚]胡混,鬼混. ~ ***down*** ①用螺丝拧紧;用螺钉钉住. ②使减低价钱. ~ ***in*** 拧进去. ~ ***into*** 很会奉承;巴结. ~ ***off*** 拔螺丝. ~ ***oneself up to*** *(doing sth.)* 勉强做(某事). ~ ***out*** 勒索;逼出. ~ ***up*** ①拧紧;钉上. ②卷成螺丝状. ③扭歪(嘴、脸等). ④强迫. ⑤非法抬高 (地租等). ⑥弄糟. ⑦鼓起(勇气). ~ ***up discipline*** 严格训练[管教]. ~ **armer** [棒球俚]左手投球员[投手]. ~ **auger** 螺旋锥. ~**ball** ① *n.* [美俚] (棒球的)怪球; [转义]

怪人；白痴；怪事；怪东西；旋转球。② *a.* 古怪的；不合情理的；有怪僻的；不安定的，不能预测的。～ **base** 螺钉脚。～ **bean**【植】螺丝豆(树)。～ **bolt** 螺栓。～ **cap** 螺丝帽；螺旋盖〔有螺纹的瓶盖〕。～ **coupling** 螺旋联结。～ **driver** ①螺丝起子；螺丝刀；赶锥。②〔美俚〕桔汁和伏特加酒的混合饮料〔鸡尾酒〕。～ **eye** ①环首木螺钉。②螺丝眼。～ **gear** ①螺轮。②螺轮联动装置。～ **gearing** 螺轮联动。～ **hook** 螺丝钩。～ **jack** 螺旋起动机；螺旋千斤顶；绞盘(= jack ～)。～ **key** = ～ wrench. ～**loose** ① *a.* 脾气古怪的。② *n.* 脾气古怪的人。～ **nut** 螺帽。～ **pile** 螺旋桩。～ **pine**【植】露兜树(属) *(Pandanns)*. ～ **press** 螺旋压榨机。～ **propeller** 螺旋桨。～ **thread** 螺纹；螺丝线。～**-topped** *a.* (瓶等)有螺旋盖的；口上有螺丝的。～**-up** 〔美俚〕弄糟的事情。～ **worm**【动】螺旋蛆。～ **wrench** 有螺丝的扳拑；活络扳子。**-ed** *a.* ①用螺丝拧紧的。②有螺纹的。③扭曲的。④〔俚〕喝醉了的。

screw·y [ˈskruːi] *a.* ①螺旋形的。②〔美俚〕神经有点不对头的；古怪的；特别的。③〔俚〕吝啬的。④〔俚〕喝醉了的；微醉的。⑤不中用的；(马)老弱的。⑥扭曲的。⑦不实际的。⑧(容易)使人误解的。

scrib·al [ˈskraibəl] *a.* ①笔写的；抄写(者)的。②(犹太)法学家的。*a* ～ *error* 笔误。

scrib·ble[1] [ˈskribl] *vt., vi.* ①胡写；乱写；潦草地写。②滥写(文学作品等)。*No scribbling!* 禁止涂写。*scribbling block* 〔英〕便笺簿(= scratch-pad). *scribbling paper* 便条纸。— *n.* ①胡写；乱写；潦草书写。②拙劣文字；粗制滥造的文章。**-r** *n.* ①乱写〔书写潦草〕的人。②拙劣的作者；粗制滥造的作家。

scrib·ble[2] [skribl] *vt.*【纺】粗梳；预梳；头道梳理(羊毛等)。**-r** *n.* 粗〔预〕梳机。

scribe [skraib] *n.* ①能写一笔好字的人；书法家。②抄写员；书记；文牍员。③新闻记者。④【史】书吏。⑤【犹太史】法学家。⑥【谑】作家；〔美〕电影剧本作家。⑦= scriber. *a ring* ～ 〔美〕报道有奖拳赛的新闻记者。— *vi.* ①缮写；做抄写员。— *vt.* 用划线器划线；【木工】雕合；使配合。～**-awl**【机】画针。

scrib·er [ˈskraibə] *n.* ①【建】划线〔片〕器。②书写者；刻划者。

scrim [skrim] *n.* (作窗帘等用的)条纹稀棉布〔麻布〕。

scrim·mage [ˈskrimidʒ] *n.* ①扭打；混战；小战斗，小冲突。②【橄榄球】扭夺；并列争球。③(分成两队)练球。— *vi.* ①扭打；参加混战。②【橄榄球】投入〔加入〕扭夺；并列争球。—*vt.*【橄榄球】(练球时)与(对方)对抗。**scrimmager** *n.* ①扭打者；扭夺者。②【橄榄球】前锋。

scrimp [skrimp] *vt., vi.* ①过份缩减。②节省；俭省。③吝啬。④少给；克扣。**-y** *a.*

scrim·shank [ˈskrimʃæŋk] *vi.* 〔英军俚〕玩忽职务；逃避任务；回避责任；偷懒。**-er** *n.* 玩忽职守者。

scrim·shaw [ˈskrimʃɔː] *vt., vi.* (在漫长的航程中水手于暇时)在(贝壳，鲸牙等上)做精致手工〔雕刻、采画等〕。— *n.* (水手做的这种)精致工艺品。

scrip[1] [skrip] *n.* ①纸片；纸条。②字条；收条。③临时单据；(以备换取正式股票等有价证券的)临时凭证。④(市政府等在非常时期发行的)临时通货；军用券。⑤股票，证券。⑥〔美俚〕(从前的)辅币。～ **dividend** 日后兑现的股票红利证书。

scrip[2] [skrip] *n.* 〔英古〕旅行袋，朝香袋。

Scripps [skrips] *n.* 斯克里普斯〔姓氏〕。

scrip·sit [ˈskripsit] 〔L.〕(某人)著，撰。

script [skript] *n.* ①手写的文件 *(opp.* print*)*；稿本；手迹；笔迹。②【印】书写体(铅字)；【法】原本，正本 *(opp.* copy*)*. ③【影，剧】脚本；(广播节目等的)底稿。④〔英〕考卷。— *vt.* 〔美俚〕把…改编成电影剧本；把…写成广播稿。— *vi.* 写电影脚本〔广播稿等〕。～ **writer** 剧本〔电影脚本，广播剧，广播节目稿〕作者。**-er** *n.* = ～ writer.

Script. = Scripture.

scrip·to·ri·um [skripˈtɔːriəm] *n.* *(pl.*～*s; -ri·a* [-riə]*)* ①(修道院内的)缮写室。②〔美〕电影剧本作者事务室。

scrip·tur·al, S- [ˈskriptʃərəl] *a.* ①圣经的；根据圣经的。②经文的；经典的。**-ly** *ad.* 按照圣经，从圣经上。

scrip·ture [ˈskriptʃə] *n.* ①〔S-〕(基督教)圣经〔通常说作 Holy Scripture 或 the Scriptures〕②〔S-〕〔罕〕圣经的一句〔一节〕。③经文；经典；圣典。④书写的文件；文稿；著作。⑤〔英古〕铭。*Buddhist* ～*s* 佛经。*a* ～ *text* 采自圣经的一段引文。

scrive·ner [ˈskrivnə] *n.* 〔古〕①代笔人，抄写员。②公证人。③掮客；放债者。～**'s cramp [palsy]** =【医】书写痉挛(writer's cramp.)

scro·bic·u·late [skrəuˈbikjulit] *a.* ①【生】具粒陷的。②有小凹的；有浅槽的。

scrod [skrɔd] *n.* 〔美〕小鳕鱼〔特指已切开去骨准备烹调的〕。

scrof·u·la [ˈskrɔfjulə] *n.*【医】淋巴结结核；瘰疬。

scrof·u·lous [ˈskrɔfjuləs] *a.* ①(生)淋巴结结核的；瘰疬(性)的。②道德败坏的；腐化堕落的。

scroll [skrəul] *n.* ①(写在羊皮纸等上的)古代文书手卷；书卷；画卷；卷轴。②〔古〕表；目录；文稿；阅件。③涡卷形的东西；【建】旋涡；涡卷形装饰〔花样〕；涡卷。④【空】涡形边。⑤【机】涡形管，盘香牙；平面螺丝。⑥【乐】(提琴等上的)涡卷形头。⑦【数】涡卷。⑧(签名后面的)花押；花字。⑨细长的旗。⑩【解】甲介骨。***on the*** ～ ***of fame*** 名垂史册；留名后世。— *vt., vi.* 〔罕〕〔通例用被动语态〕①用涡卷花样装饰。②(使)成卷形，(把…)卷成卷轴形。③在(卷轴)上题字；题记；铭刻。～ **chuck** (车床的)三爪卡盘，三爪自动定心卡盘。～ **head**【海】船头涡卷装饰。～ **painting** 卷轴画。～**saw** 线锯；钢丝锯；云形截锯。～**shears** 涡形剪床；曲线剪床。～ **wheel** 涡形齿轮。～**work** 涡卷装饰；云形花样。

scrooch, scrootch [skrutʃ] *vi.* 〔口〕蹲下；蜷缩；耸起；挤成一团。

scroop [skruːp] *n.* 轧轧(的响)声。— *vi.* 作轧轧声；轧轧地响。

scro·tum [ˈskrəutəm] *n.* *(pl.* ***-ta*** [-tə]，～*s)*【解】阴囊。

scrouge [skraudʒ, skruːdʒ] *v., n.* 〔口〕压榨；勒索；榨取；剥削。

scrounge [skraundʒ] *vi., vt.* 〔口〕①觅取。②乞取；乞讨。③骗取；偷，擅自攫取。～ ***around*** (用不正当的方法)搜寻 *(*～ *around for sth. to eat* 到处找东西吃*)*.

scrub[1] [skrʌb] *vt., vi.* ①用力擦洗，擦净；擦洗(地板等)，擦去(污斑)等；用力摩擦。②【化】(使)(气体)净化；(从气体中)分离出，提出。③〔口〕(临时宣布)取消；废弃；中止；去除；消除。— *n.* ①擦；擦洗。②擦(洗)者。～**(-)brush** 〔美〕〔英〕洗衣刷；板刷；硬毛刷；洗船刷(= scrubbing-brush)。～**bing tower** 涤气塔。～**-up** 彻底擦洗。

scrub[2] [skrʌb] *n.* ①矮小的树木；灌木；灌丛(地带)。②瘦小的家畜；杂种(家畜)。③矮小的人〔物〕；不中用的人。④〔口〕二流运动员。〔*pl.*〕二流球队。— *a.* 〔美〕①矮小的。②不中用的，低劣的；次等的。③由预备队员组成的；二流球队的。

scrub·ber [ˈskrʌbə] *n.* ①擦洗员；擦洗甲板的水手。②板刷；刷帚；擦布。③【化】煤气洗净器；涤气器；清洁器；洗涤器；滤清器；【制革】洗皮机。

scrub·by [ˈskrʌbi] *a.* ①灌丛繁茂的；尽是矮树的；杂木丛生的。②矮小的；低劣的；次等的。③难看的；不成样子的。**-bi·ness** *n.*

scruff [skrʌf] *n.* 颈背。***take*** *(sb.)* ***by the*** ～ ***of the neck*** 抓住(某人)颈背。

scruff·y [ˈskrʌfi] *a.* ***(scruff·i·er; scruff·i·est)*** ①褴褛的；蓬乱的；邋遢的；杂乱的。②卑鄙的，可鄙的。**scruff·i·ly** *ad.* **scruff·i·ness** *n.*

scrum [skrʌm], **scrum·mage** [skrʌmidʒ] *n.*【橄榄球】= scrimmage.

scrump·tious [ˈskrʌmpʃəs] *a.* 〔俚〕①极好的;头等的;第一流的.②吸引人的;令人愉快的;很讨人喜欢的.③美味的;好吃的.④〔罕〕好挑剔的,吹毛求疵的.

scrunch [skrʌntʃ] *v., n.* = crunch.

scru·ple[1] [ˈskru:pl] *n.* 〔否定、成语外常用 *pl.*〕(对事情正当与否的)考虑;顾虑;迟疑;犹豫;思量;顾忌;自责;良心的责备. *a man of no* ~ 肆无忌惮[无所不为]的坏蛋. ~*s of conscience* 良心的责备. ***do not care a*** ~ 毫不在乎. ***do not stick at*** ~***s*** 不加思量,不迟疑. ***have little*** ~ ***about doing…*** 做…毫无顾忌. ***have no*** ~***s about*** 毫不踌躇,不惜. ***have*** ~***s about*** 对…有所顾忌;对…踌躇. ***make no*** ~ ***of doing [to do]…*** 做…毫不迟疑[没有顾忌]… ***stand on*** ~ 有所顾忌,顾虑. ***without*** ~ 毫无顾忌地. — *vi., vt.* 顾虑;迟疑;犹豫;思量;顾忌;怀疑;疑心;〔罕〕(对…)感到良心的责备. *Don't* ~ *to ask for anything you want.* 你要什么请尽量讲. ~ *at nothing (to do)* 肆无忌惮;毫无顾忌.

scru·ple[2] [ˈskru:pl] *n.* ①药量单位 (=20 grains; = 1.296 g).②微量.

scru·pu·los·i·ty [ˌskru:pjuˈlɔsiti] *n.* 仔细周到;顾虑;犹豫;踌躇;小心谨慎.

scru·pu·lous [ˈskru:pjuləs] *a.* ①顾虑多的,小心谨慎的,步步留心的.②谨严的,认真负责的;一丝不苟的;无懈可击的;细心的.③正确的;彻底的;完全的. *a* ~ *proof-reader* 认真负责[一丝不苟]的校对员. ***be*** ~ ***about*** 对…不马虎;对…很注意. ***not over*** ~ 不过份客气;不过份拘谨. ***pay*** ~ ***attention to*** 细心注意. **-ly** *ad.*

scru·ta·ble [ˈskru:təbl] *a.* 可辨认的;可理解的.

scru·ta·tor [skru:ˈteitə] *n.* (精细的)检查者;调查者;观察者.

scru·tin [skrytɛ̃] 〔F.〕投票. ~ *d'arrondissement* 对个别候选人投票(法). ~ *de liste* 对成批名单投票(法).

scru·ti·neer [ˌskru:tiˈniə] *n.* 〔英〕检查者;〔特指〕检票人;监票者.

scru·ti·nize [ˈskrutinaiz] *vt., vi.* ①细看;细读.②细察;审查;彻查. **-niz·ing·ly** *ad.* 细看地,仔细检查地.

scru·ti·ny [ˈskru:tini] *n.* ①细看;细读.②仔细检查[考察];复查;彻查.③选票检查[复查]. ***demand a*** ~ 要求(重新)检查(选票). ***make a*** ~ ***into*** 细查;彻查. ***not bear*** ~ 经不住复查. ***subject to the*** ~ ***of*** 可由[有待]…进行复查[彻查、追究].

scry [skrai] *vi.* 使用水晶球占卜. **-er** *n.* 水晶球占卜师.

scu·ba [ˈsku:bə] *n.* 〔美〕水肺[潜水者用的水下呼吸器].

scud [skʌd] *n.* ①飞跑.②飞云;雨云〔=showery ~〕;(随风移行的)阵雨;(被风吹来的)飞沫[雾、雨、雪].③〔学生语〕飞毛腿.④【矿】白云岩. — *vi.* ①飞跑;疾行;掠过;飞过.②【海】顺风疾驶. ~ ***over the sky*** (云等)飞过天空. ~ ***under bare poles*** 不张帆顺风行驶.

scuff [skʌf] *vi.* ①拖着脚走;(偏促不安地)拖脚.②用脚碰触试探. — *vt.* ①拖着(脚)走.②磨损(鞋底、鞋面、地板等).③拳打,打伤;攻击. — *n.* ①拖脚行走;拖步.②拖着脚走的声音.③拖鞋.④〔美〕(鞋面上磨损的)疤痕,白瘢.

scuf·fle [ˈskʌfl] *vi.* ①扭打,乱斗,混战 (*with*).②拖脚行走. — *n.* ①扭打,混战.②拖脚行走,拖步;拖着脚走的声音. ~ **hoe** 板锄.

scull [skʌl] *n.* ①〔美〕(一人或二人用短桨[橹]划的比赛用)轻便小艇;小划艇[英国 skuller 或 skiff].②船的尾橹.③轻便短桨[又称 ~ing oar]. — *vt., vi.* ①用短桨划;划(轻便小艇).②用短橹摇(船).

scull·er [ˈskʌlə] *n.* ①用短桨划小船的人.②〔英〕= scull ①.

scul·ler·y [ˈskʌləri] *n.* 〔英〕碗碟洗涤室;餐具存放室 ~**-maid** 女佣.

scul·lion [ˈskʌljən] *n.* ①〔古〕厨房下手;(大宅厨房中)洗盘碟的帮工.②地位低微的人.

sculp [skʌlp] *vt., vi.* 〔口〕= sculpture.

sculp. = sculptor.

scul·pin [ˈskʌlpin] *n.* ***(pl.*** ~***(s))*** ①【动】锯鲉.②〔美俚〕不中用的人;不成器的家伙.③不中用的东西. — *a.* 〔美〕不中用的.

sculps. = sculpsit.

sculp·se·runt [ˈskʌlˈpsiərʌnt] 〔L.〕某某等人谨刻 〔(= They sculptured).

sculp·sit [ˈskʌlpsit] 〔L.〕他[她]雕刻(此作品),(某某)谨刻 (= He [She] sculptured).

sculpt [skʌlpt] *vt., vi.* ①雕;刻;塑(模型).②雕塑 (= sculp).③做(发式).

sculp·tor [ˈskʌlptə] *(fem.* ***-tress*** [-tris]*)* *n.* 雕刻[塑]家[师];雕刻[塑]工人. **-tress** [-tris] 女雕刻[塑]家[工人].

sculp·tur·al [ˈskʌlptʃərəl] *a.* 雕刻[塑]的. **-ly** *ad.*

sculp·ture [ˈskʌlptʃə] *n.* ①雕刻(术);雕塑(术).②雕像;雕刻[塑]物[品].③【动、植】(好象雕刻成的)刻纹;【地】刻蚀. *clay* ~*s* 泥塑(像). *a* ~*d pillar* 雕花柱. — *vt.* ①雕刻[塑].②〔通例用被动语态〕雕饰.③【地】刻蚀. — *vi.* ①雕刻.②以雕刻为职业.

sculp·tur·esque [ˌskʌlptʃəˈresk] *a.* ①象雕刻一般的,有雕刻风味的.②精致的;肃穆的.③秀丽的,眉清目秀的. **-ly** *ad.* **-ness** *n.*

scum [skʌm] *n.* ①(煮沸或发酵时发生的)浮渣,浮垢;沫子;渣滓,碎屑,(清炉)渣块.②卑贱的人;下贱的人.③〔美学俚〕(服侍高年级生的)一年级大学生. *the* ~ *of the earth [of mankind]* 人类的渣滓. *the* ~ *of society* 社会的渣滓. — *vt.* 去除(浮渣),撇去(沫子). — *vi.* 形成泡沫;生浮皮 *(over)*;变得满是浮渣.

scum·ble [ˈskʌmbl] *vt.* 【油画】(薄涂暗色)使(油画等)变柔和暗淡;【铅笔画】(用粉笔涂擦或用指尖轻擦)使(轮廓或线条)柔和. — *n.* ①(线条的)暗淡[柔和];暗色.②薄涂(彩色或粉);轻擦.③薄涂的彩色[粉].

scum·my [ˈskʌmi] *a.* ***(-mi·er; -mi·est)*** 生[有]浮渣[浮皮、沫子]的.②〔美〕卑劣的;卑贱的;无价值的.

scun·ner [ˈskʌnə] 〔Scot.〕*vt., vi.* (对…)讨厌;厌恶. — *n.* 厌恶. ***take a*** ~ ***against*** 对…抱反感;厌恶.

scup [skʌp] *n.* 〔美〕【鱼】尖口鲷.

scup·per [ˈskʌpə] *n.* 【海】(甲板的)排水孔;(屋顶等的)排水口;泄水口;水沟. — *vt.* ①〔英俚〕(用袭击办法)杀伤;杀死,使击溃.②使(船)沉没.

scup·per·nong [ˈskʌpənɔŋ] *n.* ①(美国南部)一种栽培种野葡萄.②(美国南部)野葡萄酒.

scurf [skə:f] *n.* ①皮屑;头皮;头垢.②鳞片状附着物;附着物的残垢.③【植】粗皮病;糠秕. **-y** *a.* ***(-i·er; -i·est)*** ①尽是皮屑的;象皮屑的.②【植】糠秕状的;有糠秕的.

scur·ril(e) [ˈskʌril] *a.* 〔古〕= scurrilous.

scur·ril·i·ty [skʌˈriliti] *n.* ①粗俗;下流.②粗话,漫骂;下流行为. **-ril·ous** [ˈskʌriləs] *a.* **-ly** *ad.* **-ness** *n.*

scur·ry [ˈskʌri] *vi.* 急匆匆地走;急赶 *(away; off)*. — *vt.* 使急赶;催促. — *n.* ①快步急跑;疾走.②仓皇奔跑声.③骤雨;骤雪.④短距离赛马.

scur·vied [ˈskə:vid] *a.* 患坏血病的.

scur·vy [ˈskə:vi] *a.* ***(-vi·er; -vi·est)*** ①〔废〕= scurfy.②卑鄙的;无耻的;下流的. — *n.* 【医】坏血病. ~**-grass**, ~ **weed** (对坏血病有特效的)辣根菜;坏血病草. **-vi·ly** *ad.* **-vi·ness** *n.*

scut [skʌt] *n.* ①(兔、鹿的)短尾.②短尾兽.③〔俚〕可鄙的人;(卑鄙)小人.

scu·ta [ˈskju:tə] *n.* scutum 的复数.

scu·tate [ˈskju:teit] *a.* ①【动】盾形的,有鳞甲[大鳞]的,有盾片的.②【植】(椭圆)盾状的 (= peltate).

scutch [skʌtʃ] *vt.* ①〔Scot.〕鞭打.②【纺】(梳)打(棉花、麻等);清(棉);开(布)幅. — *n.* ①【纺】梳打器;清棉机;打麻机;开幅机 (= scutcher).②【建】砖工锤.

scutch·eon [ˈskʌtʃən] *n.* ①= escutcheon.②钥匙孔

盖. ③姓名牌子. ④盾形标牌;盾饰.
scutch·er [ˈskʌtʃə] *n.* ①【纺】打棉机,展棉机;打麻机;(染整)开幅机. ②打棉者;打麻者.
scute [skju:t] *n.*【动】= scutum.
scu·tel·late [ˈskju:təleit] *a.*【生】①盾状的;小盾片状的. ②有小鳞片[盾片]覆盖[保护]的.
scu·tel·la·tion [ˌskju:təlˈeiʃən] *n.*【动】(鸟腿,鱼身的)鳞片的排列[性状].
scu·tel·lum [skju:ˈteləm] *n.* *(pl.* ***-tel·la*** [-ə]*)* ①【植】盾片. ②【动】小盾片;菱状鳞片.
scu·ti·form [ˈskjutiˌfɔ:m] *a.* 盾形的.
scut·ter [ˈskʌtə] *vi.*〔英〕= scurry.
scut·tle[1] [ˈskʌtl] *n.* ①煤桶;煤斗;煤箱〔又作 coalscuttle〕. ②满煤桶(的分量). ③筐〔装谷物、蔬菜等〕.
scut·tle[2] [ˈskʌtl] *n.* ①【船】小舱口;舷窗;船底孔洞. ②【建】天窗;气窗. ③(汽车的)前窗. — *vt.* ①在(船底)凿孔(使船沉没);凿沉. ②破坏(计划);毁坏. ③(完全)放弃. ~**butt**, ~**cosk** ①(甲板上的)饮用自来水,饮用喷泉;饮水柜台. ②〔美海军俚〕谣言;闲话.
scut·tle[3] [ˈskʌtl] *vi.*〔匆匆忙忙地〕快走,〔慌慌张张地〕急奔 *(away; off)*. — *n.* 疾走;快跑.
scu·tum [ˈskju:təm] *n.* *(pl.* ***-ta*** [-tə]*)* ①古罗马的长盾. ②【动】鳞甲;盾片,盾板. ③【解】髌骨. ④〔美〕雨衣. ⑤〔S-〕【天】盾牌座.
Scyl·la [ˈsilə] *n.* ①(意大利 Messina 海峡中著名大旋涡 Charybdis 对面的)锡拉巨岩. ②(住在锡拉巨岩上的)六头十二手的女怪. ***between*** ~ ***and Charybdis*** 进退两难;左右为难;前有虎后有狼;腹背受敌.
scy·phi·form [ˈsaifîfɔ:m] *a.*【植、动】酒杯状的;杯形的.
scy·pho·zo·an [ˌsaifəˈzəuən] *n., a.*【动】钵水母纲 *(Scyphozoa)* 动物(的).
scy·phus [ˈsaifəs] *n.* *(pl.* ***scy·phi*** [-fai]*)* ①(古希腊)双耳平底杯. ②【植】(某些花的)杯状部.
scythe [saið] *n.* (长柄)大镰刀;(古代装在战车车轮轴上的)战车镰刀. — *vt.* 用大镰刀割(草等). ~**man** ①使用大镰刀的人. ②时间与死亡的拟人化.
Scyth·i·a [ˈsiðiə] *n.* 塞西亚〔黑海与里海间东北部一古地名〕. **Scyth·i·an** [ˈsiðiən] *a., n.* 塞西亚的;塞西亚人[语](的).
S.D., SD = South Dakota 南达科他〔美国州名〕.
s.d. = several dates;〔L.〕*sine die.*
S.D. = ①Doctor of Science. ②single decker. ③sight-draft (即期汇票).
S/D = sea-damaged.
S. Dak. = South Dakota 南达科他〔美国州名〕.
s.dev. = standard deviation 标准偏差.
SDR = Special Drawing Rights (国际货币基金组织的)特别提款权.
SDS = Students for a Democratic Society〔美〕学生争取民主社会组织.
S.E., SE, s.e. = southeast; southeastern.
S/E = stock exchange 证券交易所.
Se = selenium【化】硒.
se- *pref.* 离隔,离去,分开,不用.
SEA = Southeast Asia 东南亚.
sea [si:] *n.* ①海;海洋;内海;大(淡水)湖. ②〔*pl.* 或与不定冠词连用〕海面(状态);浪,波涛;大浪;潮流. ③很多;大量;茫茫一片. ④海事;海上生活;航海. *the high ~s* 公海 (*opp.* the closed ~ 领海). *Praise the ~, but keep on land.* 隔岸观火. *There's as good fish in the ~ as ever came out.* 世上富源如鱼虾,日日取用无尽期. *The ~ gets up [goes down].* 波浪大起来[平静下去]了. *a long ~* (通常的)波涛滚滚的海. *a high [rough, heavy] ~* 巨浪汹涌[怒涛滔天]的海. *a quarter ~* 冲上船尾的大浪. *a full ~* 高潮. *A high ~ is running = The ~ is running high.* (海上)怒涛汹涌. *a ~ of trouble* 无限的麻烦. ***above the ~*** 海拔. ***across the ~(s)*** 远隔重洋;渡过大海;到海外;在海外. ***arm of the ~*** 海湾. ***a ~ of …*** 大量的. ***at full ~*** 满潮,在高潮上;绝顶;极端. ***at ~*** ①在海上;在航海中. ②迷惑;茫然;不知如何是好. ***be (all) at ~*** 如堕五里雾中;(简直)不晓得怎样才好;茫然. ***be buried at ~*** 葬身海中. ***between the devil and the deep ~*** 腹背受敌;进退两难. ***beyond the ~(s)*** = across the ~(s). ***by ~*** 由海路;经海路;乘船. ***by the ~*** 在海边. ***command of the ~*** 制海权. ***follow the ~*** 当海员;做水手. ***freedom of the ~s*** 海上通航权. ***go (down) to the ~*** 到海边去. ***go to ~ = follow the ~*** 当海员;做水手. ***half ~s over*** 酒喝得太多;有点醉. ***head the ~*** 迎浪行驶. ***keep the ~*** ①(船)在海中;在继续航行中. ②保持制海权. ***on the ~*** ①在海(岸)上. ②乘船;在海面的船上. ③临海;在海岸;在海边. ***out to ~*** 离港. ***put (out) to ~*** 开船出航;离港出海. ***over the ~(s)*** = across the ~(s). ***ship a ~*** (小艇)冒浪(前进). ***stand to ~*** 离陆驶向海中. ***take the ~*** 乘船;在船上服务;出海;开船;下水. ***take to ~*** 启航. ***the closed ~*** 领海. ***the high ~s*** 公海. ***the mistrss of the ~(s)*** 海上霸主;最强海军国. ***the narrow ~s*** 英法海峡. ***the seven ~s*** (世界)七大洋〔即北冰洋,南冰洋,北大西洋,南大西洋,北太平洋,南太平洋及印度洋〕;全球. ***wish sb. at the bottom of the ~*** 希望某人葬身鱼腹;咒(某人)不得好死. ~ **air** 海[海上,海边]的空气. ~**-air** *a.* 海空的. ~ **anchor** 海上风暴时用的浮锚;海锚. ~ **anemone**【动】海葵. ~ **bag** 水手旅行袋. ~ **bank** 防波堤;海岸的护堤. ~**-bar** 海燕. ~**barrow**【动】(海鳐鱼的)卵壳. ~ **bass**【鱼】巴西刺鲈. ~ **bathing** 海水浴. ~ **bear** ①白熊;北极熊. ②腽肭兽;海狗. ~**-beaver** 海獭. ~ **bed** 海底. ~ **bells**【植】海滨牵牛花. ~ **bird** 海鸟. ~ **biscuit** [~ **bread**]【海】(可以久藏的)硬饼干;硬面包. ~ **board** 海岸;海滨;沿海地方. ~ **boat** ①远洋轮船;能耐波浪的船. ②(大轮船上的)救生艇. ~ **book** 航海图. ~ **boots** (海员用的)高统防雨靴. ~**-born** *a.* ①〔诗〕从海里生出来的 *(the ~-born city = Venice. the ~-born goddess* = Aphrodite*)*. ②海中出产的. ~**-borne** *a.* 用海轮装运的;海运的;〔船〕浮在海上的 (*~-borne articles* 舶来品. *~-borne commerce* 海上贸易. *~-borne goods* 海运货物). ~**bream**【动】鲷;棘鬣鱼. ~ **breeze** (白天从海上吹到陆上的)海(上和)风. ~ **brief** = sea letter. ~ **brown** 海豹皮色的. ~ **calf**【动】海豹. ~ **captain** ①船长;舰长. ②海军上校. ③〔诗〕大航海者. ④海上名将. ~ **catfish**【动】海鲶. ~ **change** ①(因海的作用而发生的)变形. ②重大[显著]的变化〔转变〕. ~ **chest** ①水手用的贮物箱. ②【船】通海吸水箱. ~ **chestnut**【动】海胆. ~ **clutter** 海波干扰. ~ **coal**【英史】(被海水从沉积物中冲刷出来的)煤;从纽卡塞海运来的煤. ~**coast** 海岸;海边;海滨. ~ **cock** ①(船壳上的)海底阀;通海[船底]旋塞. ②〔谑〕海盗. ③【动】黑腹鹬. ~ **cook** 船上厨师〔对新水手的蔑称〕~ **cow**【动】①海牛. ②海象. ③河马. ~**craft** ①航行海上的船只. ②航海术. ~ **crawfish [crayfish]**【动】= spring lobster. ~ **crow**【鸟】海鸥. ~ **cucumber**【动】海参. ~ **damage** 海损. ~ **devil**【鱼】华脐鱼;鮟鱇. ~**dog** ①【动】海豹;【鱼】角鲛. ②【转义】海盗;老练水手[海员]. ~ **drome**【空】海上机场. ~ **duck**【海】海鸭. ~**dust** ①沙漠中的砖红色灰尘;从干旱陆地吹向海上的红尘. ②〔俚〕盐. ~ **duty** 出海[海上]勤务. ~ **eagle**【动】一种捕食鱼类的鹰;白尾鹰;〔美方〕鹗. ~**-ear**【动】石决明;(也误用为)鲍鱼. ~ **earth** 海底电缆接地. ~ **echo** 海水反射的回波. ~ **elephant**【动】海象;大海豹. ~ **fan**【动】石帆;海团扇;柳珊瑚. ~**farer**〔诗〕①海员;水手. ②航海者;海上旅行者. ~**faring** *a., n.* ①航海事业(的). ②水手工作(的) (*a ~faring life*

水手生活;航海生活. *a ~-faring man* 水手;海员). ~ **farming** 海产养殖. ~ **feather**【动】海鳃;海羊;海羽(= ~ pen). ~ **fern**【动】石帆. ~ **fight** 海战. ~-**floor** 海底;海床. ~ **flower**【动】= sea anemone. ~ **foam** ①海面泡沫. ②【矿】海泡石. ~ **food**〔美〕海味;鱼 (*a ~-food caterer* 鱼贩). ~ **force** 海军. ~ **fox**【鱼】长尾鲛. ~ **fret**〔英〕海雾. ~ **front** ①海岸;海边. ②海滨马路. ③海岸区. ④(都市、房屋的)向海的一面. ~ **gauge** ①【海】吃水[船入水的深度]. ②气压测深器;自记海深计. ~**girt** *a.* 四面环海的. ~-**god** 海神. ~-**goddess** 海的女神. ~ **going** *a.* ①(适于)航行远洋的. ②从事航海业的 (*a ~going vessel* 远洋轮船. *a ~ going hack*〔美〕旧式汽车. *a ~-going pipe line* 海底油管). ~**grape** ①马尾藻. ②乌贼鱼等类海生动物. ③海葡萄〔美国弗罗里达州沿海的一种结葡萄状果实的植物〕. ~-**green** *n., a.* ①海绿色(的). ②潮浸(的). ~ **gull**【鸟】海鸥. ~**haul** =~lift. ~ **hare**【动】海兔;雨虎. ~ **hedgehog**【动】①海胆. ②海豚;鱼虎. ~ **hog**【动】海豚. ~ **holly**【植】海滨刺芹. ~ **horse** ①【神话】(拖海神战车的)半马半鱼的怪物. ②【动】海马;龙落子;马头鱼;海象. ③〔转义〕白色的浪峰. ~-**island (cotton)** 海岛棉. ~ **jeep**〔美海军〕水陆两用吉普车. ~-**jelly**【动】水母. ~ **kale**【植】欧洲海甘兰. ~ **king** (古代北欧的)海盗王. ~**lamprey**【动】海七鳃鳗. ~ **lane** 航路;海上航线. ~ **lavender**【植】匙叶草属植物. ~ **lawyer** ①〔海俚〕好讲歪理的水手[人]. ②【鱼】鲨鱼. ~**legs**〔*pl.*〕①〔口〕(惯于船颠簸时仍能站稳不晕船的)水手腿. ②不晕船 (*get [have, find] one's ~ legs on* 在船上能不晕船地正常行走. *get [have] one's ~ legs off* 登陆后能毫无晕船感觉地正常行走). ~ **leopard**【动】(南冰洋)海豹(类). ~ **letter** (海关发给非交战国船只的)中立国船舶证. ~ **level** 海(平)面标准[平均]海面 (*above ~ level* 海拔). ~**lift** *n.* 海上运输. ~**lily**【植】海百合. ~ **line** ①水平线;海岸线. ②〔*pl.*〕深海渔业用钓绳. ~ **lion** ①【动】海狮. ②【徽】半狮半鱼的怪物. **S- Lord** 海军大臣〔英〕〔海军部四个海军首长之一〕. ~ **maid(en)** ①美人鱼. ②海中女神. ~ **mark** ①潮汛线. ②航海标;航标[如灯塔等]. ~ **mat**【贝】网贝. ~ **mew**【鸟】海鸥〔特指产于欧洲的一种〕. ~ **mile** 海里;浬. ~**monster** ①海怪. ②【鱼】银鲨鱼. ~**mount** 海底山. ~ **mouse**【动】海毛虫,鳞沙蚕属动物. ~ **needle**【鱼】海针鱼. ~ **nettle**【动】刺水母. ~ **nymph** 海妖. ~ **onion**【植】棉枣儿;海葱;(欧洲)春棉枣儿. ~ **otter**【动】海獭. ~ **pass** = sea letter. ~ **pen**【动】海鳃. ~ **pie** ①咸肉馅饼. ②捉蠔者. ③〔英〕【鸟】长嘴鹬. ~ **piece** 海景画. ~ **pig**【动】海豚;儒艮. ~ **pink**【植】海簪. ~ **plane** 水上(飞)机. ~ **plant** 海草;海藻. ~ **port** 海港;海口;商埠. ~ **power** ①海军力量. ②制海权. ③海军强国. ~ **purse**【动】(鳐鱼等的)角质卵壳[卵袋]. ~ **quake** *n.* 海啸;海底地震. ~ **raven**【动】绒林父鱼. ~ **return** (雷达)海面反射讯号. ~ **robin**【鱼】鸦鲂鮄. ~ **room** ①足够行船的水面. ②(足够)自由行动的余地. ~ **rover** ①海盗. ②海盗船. ~ **salt** 海盐. ~ **scallop**【动】扇贝. ~ **scape** ①海景. ②海景画. ~ **scorpion**【动】广鳍类动物. ~ **serpent**【动】海蛇. ~ **service** ①海上勤务. ②海军. ~ **shell** 海软体动物的壳;贝壳;海贝. ~**shore** ①*n.* 海岸;海滨;【法】满潮线与退潮线间之地. ②*a.* 海滨的. ~ **sick** *a.* 晕船的. ~ **sickness** 晕船. ~**side** *n., a.* (特指充作游泳场、休养地等的)海边(的);海滨(的) (*go to the ~side* 到海边去游泳. *a ~side hotel* 海滨旅馆. *a ~side resort* 海水浴场). ~**sider**〔美〕住在海边的人;去洗海水澡的人. ~ **sleeve**【动】乌贼;墨鱼. ~**slug**【动】海参 (= nudibranch). ~ **snake**【动】海蛇. ~ **spider**【动】①蜘蛛蟹. ②鲿鱼. ③海盘车(鱼)〔海蜘蛛类动物〕*(= pycnogonid)*. ~ **squirt**【动】海鞘(类动物) *(= ascidian)*. ~ **stock**, ~ **stores** 船上食粮. ~ **swallow**【动】海鸥,海燕 (= stormy petrel). ~ **tangle**【植】墨角藻;褐色藻. ~ **term** 航海用语. ~ **train** ①运载火车的轮渡. ②海上运输队. ~ **trout**【动】海鳟. ~ **trumpet**【植】荒布〔南太平洋的一种海带〕. ~ **urchin**【动】海胆. ~ **wall** 防波堤;海堤. ~ **walnut**【动】栉水母门动物. ~ **ware** 海草〔尤指肥田用的〕. ~**way**【海】①航路;航道;海路. ②外海;外洋;公海;大海. ③(船冒浪)航行. ④波涛汹涌的海(面). (*in a ~way* 在惊涛骇浪中. *make ~way* 航行). ~**weed** 海草;海藻. ~ **whale**【动】鰛鲸. ~ **whip**【动】海鞭子〔柳珊瑚属动物〕. ~ **wife** 濑鱼. ~**worthiness** 适于航海;适航性. ~**worthy** *a.* 适于航海的(船),耐航[风浪]的(船). ~ **wrack** 海藻;海草〔尤指浪潮送上岸来的海藻〕. -**ward** *a., n., ad.* 朝海(的);向海(的);海那一边(的). -**wards** *ad.* 向海;向海那一边.

Sea·bee [ˈsiːbiː] *n.*〔美俚〕①海军工程营成员. ②〔*pl.*〕海军工程营〔源于美 1941 年成立的 Construction Battalion 两词词首 C, B 两字母的读音〕.

Sea·borg [ˈsiːbɔːg] *n.* 西博格〔姓氏〕.

S.E.A.C. = Southeast Asia Command〔英归〕东南亚司令部.

seal[1] [siːl] *n.*〔*sing., pl.*〕【动】①海豹. ②海豹毛皮(制品). ③海豹皮色[灰黄深褐色]. ④〔Seals〕〔美〕海豹突击队〔美国的一支海陆空军突击队〕. *the common [harbor] ~* (斑纹)海豹. *the fur ~* 膃肭兽,海狗. — *vi.* 猎海豹.

seal[2] [siːl] *n.* ①(打在火漆,铅等上的)火漆封印;封蜡;封铅;封条. ②捺印;封缄. ③印;图章;戳记;纪念邮戳. ④图记;记号. ⑤保证;严守秘密的誓约;守秘密的义务. ⑥密封;隔离;堵塞. ⑦【机】密封垫;焊接. ⑧【物】绝缘. ⑨征候;预兆. ⑩(下水道的)s形防臭弯管(= ~pipe). *the privy ~* 御玺. *Lord Keeper of the Great [Privy] S-* 掌玺大臣. *the ~s* 英国上议院议长[国务大臣]的公章;上议院议长[国务大臣]的官职. *a bond under sb.'s hand and ~* 有某人签名盖章的字据. *the ~ of love* 爱情的保证[接吻、结婚等]. *the ~ of death* 死的征兆. ***a ~ upon sb.'s lips*** 堵嘴钱. ***affix [put, set] one's ~ to*** 在…上盖印;对…表示同意;保证;批准. ***break the ~*** 开封;拆信. ***conduit ~*** 线管壳. ***pass the ~s*** 得到批准. ***put the ~ upon*** = ***put ... under ~*** 在…封上火漆印[打上封印]. ***receive the ~s*** 接印;接任. ***set one's ~ to*** ①=affix one's ~ to. ②批准;赞同. ***take off the ~*** 拆信;开封. ***under [with] a flying ~*** 以开口信. ***the great ~*** = ***the ~ of state*** 国玺. ***under my hand and ~*** 经我签名盖章. ***under ~*** 盖有印鉴(的). ***under the ~ of secrecy*** (约定)保守秘密. — *vt.* ①盖印于;打印于;在(度量衡器、商品等上)加上检验封印. ②〔常作~ up〕在…上打上封印;封;密封(信等). ③关进;关闭;密闭(容器、窗等). ④【电】使(插头与插孔等)紧密接触. ⑤用水泥等充填. ⑥闭(嘴);缄(口等);守(秘密). ⑦证明. ⑧保证 (*with*). ⑨决定;确定;注定(命运);解决. ⑩〔英海军〕接受;采用. ⑪在…上划十字;给…施洗礼;(摩门教徒)举行(结婚[过继]仪式). *The treaty has been signed and ~ed.* 条约已经签字盖章[签订]. *a ~ed letter* 密信. *~ing pliers* 铅印钳. *~ing wire* 铅印铅丝. *My lips are ~ed.* 我的嘴被封住了[我已经不好开口了]. ***a ~ed book*** 加上封印[不能打开]的书;谜,不可理解的事物. ***as good as ~ed*** (命运)是注定了[算完蛋了]. ~ ***in*** ①封入. ②焊死. ~ ***off*** = ① ~ up. ②烫开;脱焊. ~ ***on*** 焊上. ~ ***up*** ①封;密封. ②确定. ~ **ring** 印章戒指.

Sea·lab [ˈsiːˌlæb] *n.* (美海军)海底实验室.

seal·ant [ˈsiːlənt] *n.* 封蜡;火漆;密封胶.

seal·er[1] [ˈsiːlə] *n.* ①海豹猎船. ②海豹猎人.

seal·er[2] [ˈsiːlə] *n.* ①盖印人;密封人. ②密封器;封口机. ③封口机操作者. ④(度量衡器等的)检验员. ⑤保

护层.

seal·er·y [ˈsiːləri] *n.* ①海豹群集地;海豹猎场. ②捕海豹业.

seal-fishery [ˈsiːlfiʃəri] *n.* ①猎海豹业. ②海豹猎场.

seal·flow·er [ˈsiːlˈflauə] *n.* 【植】荷包牡丹.

seal·ing [ˈsiːliŋ] *n.* 猎海豹业.

sealing-wax [ˈsiːliŋwæks] *n.* 火漆;封蜡.

seal·skin [ˈsiːlskin] *n.* ①海豹皮. ②海豹皮大衣.

seal·wort [ˈsiːlwəːt] *n.* 【植】黄精;平铺漆姑草.

seam [ˈsiːm] *n.* ①缝;线缝. ②接口;接缝;接合处;接合线. ③裂缝. ④(脸上的)皱纹. ⑤伤痕. ⑥【船】(船板间的)缝隙. ⑦【地,矿】层;矿层;节理;煤层. ⑧(铸件等的)接痕. ⑨【解】缝合. — *vt.* ①缝拢;缝合;接合;合拢. ②〔主用被动语态〕使生裂缝[皱纹、伤痕]. ③【编织】在(袜子等上)做棱线. *be ~ed with care [old age]* 因忧虑[年老]而生了皱纹的. *be ~ed with wounds* 有伤痕的. — *vi.* ①生裂缝;裂开. ②【编织】做棱线. **-er** ①缝纫机. ②缝纫工. **-less** *a.* 无缝的 (*a ~less steel pipe* 无缝钢管. *a ~less tubing mill* 无缝钢管厂).

sea·man [ˈsiːmən] *n.* *(pl. -men)* ①水手;船员;海员. ②水兵. *a merchant ~* 商船船员. *a good [poor] ~* 能干的[不行的]船员. *a leading ~* 〔英〕一等水兵. *an able [able-bodied] ~* 〔英〕二等水兵. *an ordinary ~* 〔英〕 = *an apprentice ~* 〔美〕三等水兵. *~ recruit* 〔美〕候补水兵〔低于三等水兵〕. **-like, -ly** *a.* 象水手的. **-ship** *n.* 海员技术;航海技术.

seam·ster [ˈsemstə; ˈsiːm-] *n.* 〔古〕裁缝 (= tailor).

seam·stress [ˈsemstris, Am. siːmstris] *n.* 女裁缝,女缝工.

seam·y [ˈsiːmi] *a.* ***(-i·er; -i·est)*** ①有缝的;有裂缝的. ②粗糙不光洁的;难看的;丑恶的;令人不快的. ***the ~ side*** (衣裳等的)里面;(社会等的)丑恶的一面;阴暗面. **-i·ness** *n.*

Sean [ʃɔːn] *n.* 肖恩〔男子名, John 的异体〕.

Sean·ad Eir·eann [ˈʃænəðˈεərən] 〔Ir.〕爱尔兰共和国参议院.

sé·ance [ˈseiɑ̃ːns] *n.* 〔F.〕①集会,会议. ②降神(术)会.

sear[1] [siə] *a.* 〔诗〕干枯的;干瘪的;枯萎的. *the ~ and yellow leaf* 〔喻〕老年;老境. — *vt.* ①使干枯;使凋萎. ②烧焦;烧灼. ③加烙印于. ④使憔悴. ⑤使失去感觉;使麻木. *a countenance ~ed by grief and weeping* 因悲伤哭泣而憔悴的脸. *a ~ed conscience* 麻木了的良心. — *vi.* ①枯萎;凋谢. ②灼伤. ③变得麻木不仁. — *n.* 烙印;焦痕. **~ing iron** 烙铁.

sear[2] [siə] *n.* 扣机〔枪炮的一种保险装置〕.

search [səːtʃ] *vt.* ①搜查;检查(身体、衣袋等);搜索,搜寻;找;寻找. ②调查;查究;探求;追求;根究 (*into*). ③(冷风等)到处侵入,刺透. ④【军】使(火力)向纵深展开. *~ sb.* 搜查身体. *~ a book* 在一本书里查找材料. *~ one's memory* 竭力回忆. *The shrapnel was ~ing every cranny.* 榴霰弹正在四散开来. — *vi.* ①搜寻,搜查 *(for)*;探求. ②【计】觅数,检索. ***~ after [for]*** 寻找;寻求,追求;探求 (*~ after health* 讲究健康;保养. *~ a house for papers* 在一座房屋里搜查文件). ***~ into*** 调查;研究;根究. ***S- me!*** 〔美〕我不知道. ***~ out*** 搜出;查出;探出;找出. — *n.* ①搜索;搜寻;寻找. ②探索;探求 *(after; for)*;调查;检查. ***in ~ of*** 寻找;去找;追求;为了寻求;试图发现. ***make a ~ after [for]*** (去)找;寻求;追求. **~ coil** 【无】搜索线圈;探测线圈. **~ light** *n.* ①探照灯(光). ②= flash light (*play a ~-light on* 用探照灯照). **~ party** 搜索队. **~ warrant** (住宅)搜查证.

search·er [ˈsəːtʃə] *n.* ①搜寻者;搜查者;探求者;调查者,检查者. ②海关检查员;船舶检查员;囚犯检查员. ③【无】搜索器;大炮检查器. ④【医】探针;膀胱(石)探杆.

search·ing [ˈsəːtʃiŋ] *a.* ①搜查的;搜索的. ②仔细的;彻底的;严格的. ③(目光等)锐利的. ④(冷风)刺骨的. *a ~ examination* 仔细严格的考试. *a ~ look* 锐利的眼光. *~ wind* 刺骨寒风. — *n.* 搜寻;搜查;搜索;探索;调查;探究. *the ~(s) of heart* 反复扪心自问. **~ gunfire** 【军】纵深射击.

Sea·shore [ˈsiː-ʃɔː] *n.* 西肖尔〔姓氏〕.

sea·son [ˈsiːzn] *n.* ①季;季节;〔美〕雨季. ②(水果、鱼类等的)旺季;流行季节;时令;活动期. ③好时机;适当时机. ④一时;暂时. ⑤社交季节;某种活动的季节[期间]. ⑥〔英口〕(电车等的)季票;月票. ⑦【林】干材法. *the (four) ~s* 四季. *a dry [wet, rainy] ~* 旱[雨]季. *the ~ of occurrence* (热带的)暴风雨季节. *a close [an open] ~* 禁猎[打猎]期. *rush ~* 旺季;忙季. *the harvest ~* 收获期. *the strawberry ~* 草莓旺季. *a dead [a dull, an off] ~ (in trade)* (营业的)淡季. *the height of the ~* (流行的)极盛时期. *There is a ~ for work and for play.* 玩也好,工作也好,都有个时候. *the (London) ~* 伦敦社交季节[初夏时期]. ***at all ~s*** 一年四季;一年到头. ***for a ~*** 一时;一会儿;暂时. ***in due ~*** 在适当的时候. ***good ~*** 恰好;尽早;及早;及时地. ***in ~*** ①时机正好的;恰合时宜的 (*a word in ~* 合时宜的话). ②尽早;及早. ③(水果等)正旺;当令;应时. ④(狩猎)在猎期. ⑤(动物)在发情期中. ***in ~ and out of ~*** 始终;不断;任何时候;一年到头. ***out of ~*** ①过时的. ②失去时机. ③过了旺季. ④在禁猎期. — *vt.* ①使熟练;使(习)惯. ②风干;晒干(木材);晾干;对…进行干燥处理;使陈化. ③使适应(气候等). ④给…加味[调味]. ⑤给…增加趣味. ⑥缓和,调和. *a ~ed soldier* (有经验的)老兵. *~ tobacco* 晒烟叶. *cattle ~ed to diseases* 免疫家畜. *highly ~ed dishes* 佐料多味道浓的菜肴. *~ed wood* 干材. *conversation ~ed with humour* 有风趣的谈话. — *vi.* ①熟练;习惯. ②(木材)变干;陈化. ***~ oneself to (cold),*** 练得不怕(寒冷). **~ opener** 球季的揭幕比赛.

sea·son·a·ble [ˈsiːznəbl] *a.* 当令的;合时的;及时的. *a ~ weather* 合时的气候. *a ~ aid* 及时的援助. **-a·bly** *ad.*

sea·son·al [ˈsiːzənl] *a.* 季节(性)的. **-ly** *ad.*

sea·son·ing [ˈsiːzniŋ] *n.* ①调味品;调味剂;佐料. ②调和;缓和. ③处理(法);气候处理;风干;干燥(处理);木材干燥法;老化. ④【物】(磁控管的)不稳定性;时效.

season-ticket [ˈsiːznˈtikit] *n.* 月季票;长期票;定期车票 (=〔美〕 commutation-ticket).

seat [siːt] *n.* ①座;座位;席位;席次. ②椅子;凳子. ③(椅子等的)座部;垫子. ④臀部;裤裆. ⑤地位;场所;位置;所在地;中心地. ⑥邸宅;别墅. ⑦王座;主教座;王权,主教权. ⑧议员席. ⑨(交易所等的)会员资格. ⑩(马、脚踏车等的)骑法;坐法;骑乘姿势. *S- must be booked in advance.* 座位必须预定. *the ~ of disease* 病源;病灶;患部. *the ~ of war* 战场. *the county ~* 县城(行政机构所在地). *the ~ of learning* 学术中心地. *the ~ of soul* 神经中枢. *a safe ~* 稳可当选的选举区. ***have a good ~*** 骑法不错. ***have a ~*** 〔美〕 = take a ~. ***keep one's ~*** 留在原位不动. ***lose one's ~*** 失去原有的位置[席位];落选. ***on the anxious ~*** 〔美〕提心吊胆. ***take a ~*** 就座;入座. ***take one's ~ in the House of Commons*** (当选后)开始充当众议院议员. ***vacate [resign] one's ~*** 辞去议员职. ***win a ~ in Congress*** 获得国会议员席位;当选为议员. — *vt.* ①使…坐下,使…就座. ②在…设座位;给…装座位. ③给(机器等)装底座;给…装座子[垫子]. ④给…掉换[修补]垫子[座子]. ⑤安装;安置. ⑥安插(职位);派…做议员. ⑦安牢;使固定. ⑧住;住定. *Pray be ~ed.* 请坐下. *The hall is ~ed for 5000.* 这个讲堂坐得下五千人. ***be ~ed*** ①坐着. ②坐落在;位于…. ***~ a candidate*** 选举候补人. ***~ oneself*** 坐下;就座;入席. ***~ oneself along (Medilerrancan coast)*** 定居于(地中海沿岸). ~

angle【机】支座角钢. ~**belt**(汽车、飞机上的)座位安全带. ~ **clay** 耐火土. ~ **earth**【农艺】根土. ~ **frame** 座架. ~**mate** (飞机、公共车辆等上的)邻座者. ~**(-)mile** 客运里程 (指一名旅客一英里的旅程). ~**-pack** *a.* 座仓式 (~*-pack parachute* 可作座垫用的座仓式降落伞). ~**work** 课堂作业[学生在课堂座位上做的功课].

seat·ed [ˈsi:tid] *a.* ①(有)…座位的. ②(有)…座垫的. ③根深的; 固定的. *a deep-~disease* 痼疾.

seat·er [ˈsi:tə] *n.* 有(若干) 座位的飞机[汽车等]. *a Four-~* 四座飞机[汽车等].

seat·ing [ˈsi:tiŋ] *n.* ①座位(设备); 座位数. ②椅料; 椅垫; 椅布. ③骑姿, 骑法. *a ~ capacity* 座(位)数; 容纳量.

SEATO [ˈsi:təu, si(:)ˈætəu] = Southeast Asia Treaty Organization 东南亚条约组织.

Se·at·tle [siˈætl] *n.* 西雅图[美西北部港口].

se·ba·ceous [siˈbeiʃəs] *a.* 脂肪(状)的; 脂肪多的; 分泌脂肪的. ~ **cyst**【医】脂腺囊肿. ~ **glands**【解】皮脂腺.

se·bac·ic [siˈbæsik] *a.* 含脂的. ~ **acid**【化】癸二酸.

Se·bas·tian [siˈbæstjən] *n.* 塞巴斯蒂安[男子名].

Se·bas·to·pol [siˈbæstəpl] *n.* = Sevastopol.

S.E.bE = South-east by East 东南偏东.

se·bif·er·ous [siˈbifərəs] *a.*【生】生脂肪的, 分泌脂肪的, 多脂肪的(= sebiparous).

seb·or·rhe·a, seb·or·rhoe·a [ˌsebəˈri:ə] *n.*【医】皮脂溢. **-rhe·ic, -rhoe·ic** *a.*

S.E.bS = South-east by South 东南偏南.

se·bum [ˈsi:bəm] *n.*【医】(皮脂腺中分泌的)脂肪; 皮脂.

sec. =①secant. ②second; seconds; secondary. ③secretary. ④secured; security. ⑤sector; section, sections. ⑥[L.] *secundum.*

S.E.C. = ①Supreme Economic Council ②Securities and Exchange Commission [美]证券与汇兑委员会. ③Social Economic Council [荷]社会经济理事会.

SECAM = *Séquence de Couleurs avec Mémoire* [F.] 彩色顺序存储; (法国)"色康"五彩电视系统 (= Colo(u)r Sequence with Memory).

se·cant [ˈsi:kənt] *a.* 分[交]割的; (横)切的, 交叉的. — *n.*【数】正割; 割线. *a ~ line* 切线; 割线.

sec·a·teur [ˈsekətə:] *n.* [常用 *pl.*]修枝铗[钳]; 整枝剪[大剪刀].

sec·co [ˈsekəu] *a.* [It.] ①【乐】无伴奏的; 简朴的. ②干燥的; 无水分的. — *n.* 干(灰泥)壁画[画法]; (= secco painting; tempera).

se·cede [siˈsi:d] *vi.* (从教会、政党等)退出; 脱离 *(from).*

se·ced·er [siˈsi:də] *n.* 退出者; 脱离者; 退党者.

se·cern [siˈsə:n] *vt.* 分; 区分; 鉴别. — *vi.* 分开; 分离. **-ment** *n.*

se·cern·ent [siˈsə:nənt] *a.*【生】分泌(性)的. — *n.* ①【生理】分泌器官; 分泌作用. ②分泌促进剂[药物].

se·ces·sion [siˈseʃən] *n.* ①(从教会、政党等的)脱离; 退出; 分裂. ②【建】直线式; 直线派. ③[S-]【美史】(1861年南方十一州的)脱离联邦. ***the War of S-*** [美] 南北战争. **-ism** *n.* ①脱离论; 分离论; 分裂主义; [常 S-]【美史】(南北战争时的) 分离主义 (*national ~ism* 民族分裂主义). ②【建】直线式; 分离式. **-ist** *n.* ①脱离论者; 【美史】(南北战争时的)分离主义者; 分裂主义者. ②【建】直线派建筑家.

Seck·el [ˈsekəl] *n.* [美]红棕皮小甜梨.

se·clude [siˈklu:d] *vt.* ①使分离; 隔离; 隔绝(人、场所等). ②使隐退; 使隐居. ~ *oneself from the world* 隐退; 与世隔绝.

se·clud·ed [siˈklu:did] *a.* 与世隔绝的; 偏僻的; 幽静的; 隐退的. *a ~ place* 与外界隔绝的所在.

se·clu·sion [siˈklu:ʒən] *n.* ①隔离; 隔绝; 隐退. ②偏僻的地方. *a policy of ~* 闭关自守政策. *live in ~* 过退隐生活.

se·clu·sive [siˈklu:siv] *a.* ①爱僻静的; 隐居性的; 隔离性的. ②退隐的. **-ly** *ad.*

sec·ond[1] [ˈsekənd] *a.* ①第二的; 第二次的; 二等(的). ②次等的; 较差的; 劣于…的*(to).* ③[美] 较年轻的. ④另一(个)的; 又一(个)的; 别的; 类似的. ⑤次(的); 副(的); 从属的; 辅助的. ⑥【乐】第二度音程的; 低音部的. *a ~ cabin* 二等舱. *the ~ (largest) town in the country* 国内第二(大)城市. *a ~ time* 再(一次). *a ~ coat* 第二层 (油漆等). *a ~ pair of boots* 另一双皮鞋. *a ~ helping* (食物)再来一份. ***be the ~ to come*** 第二个来. ***come in ~*** (赛跑时)跑得第二. ***come ~ (in one's estimation, affection)*** 得第二; 占第二位. ***every ~ day*** 隔一天; 隔日. ***in the ~ place*** 第二(点); 其次. ***on ~ thoughts*** 经重新考虑后. ***~ to none*** 不比任何人[东西]差; 最好的; 第一等的. ***Shall [Will] never be ~*** 决不后人. — *n.* ①第二人[物]; 次一等的人[物]; 副. ②跑第二的人; 第二名. ③(某月的)二日; 初二; 二号; (火车等的)二等车. ④辅助人[者]; 助手; 副手; (决斗的)帮手. ⑤其他的人[物]. ⑥[*pl.*]【商】二级品; 次品; 二等货; 次等品; 次货. ⑦粗面粉; 粗面粉做的面包. ⑧【乐】第二度音程; 第二音; 二度; 低音部(声音); 低音部乐器. ⑨【汽车】第二速度. ⑩【商】汇票的第二联[又称 ~ of exchange]. ⑪【棒球】二垒. *a good [poor] ~* 跟第一件差不多[差得远]的第二件衣服. *the ~ in command* 副司令官. *He [She] will soon take a ~.* 他[她]就要第二次结婚了. ***act as a most useful ~*** 大力支援[辅助]; 成为左右手. ***get into a ~*** 坐上二等车. — *vt.* ①辅助; 支援; 支持; 赞成(提议). ②[siˈkɔnd]【英军】暂时调派担任特殊职务. ~ *words with deeds* 用行动辅助言语. *be ~ed for service on the staff* 被暂时调到参谋部工作. — *vi.* 附议; 附和. ~ **advent** [S- Advent] 基督再临. ~ **ballot** 决选投票. ~ **banana** [美俚](戏剧、杂耍中的)配角; 次要人物. ~ **base**【棒球】第二垒. ~ **baseman**【棒球】二垒手. ~ **chamber** 上(议)院. **S- Chamber** (荷兰)众议院. ~ **childhood** 老耄(智力衰退)期. ~**-coming-of-Christ head** [美新闻] 横贯全页的红字大标题. ~ **contact**【天】食既. ~ **cousin** 远房堂[表]兄弟姊妹. ~**-cut file** 中细锉. ~**-degree burn** 二级烧伤. ~ **division** 低级文官; (监狱里的)中等待遇. ~**drawer** *a.* [美口]次等的, 第二流的. **S- Empire** 法兰西第二帝国(1852 —1870). ~ **endoderm**【生】后成内胚层. ~ **estate** 第二等级[贵族]. ~**fiddle** ①(乐队的)第二小提琴(演奏者). ②第二把手; [美俚]二等角色. ~ **floor** [美]二楼; [英]三楼. ~ **front** 第二战场. ~ **growth**【植】次生生长. ~**-guess** *vi., vt.* ①事后批评[劝告]. ②预言; 猜测. ~**-guesser** 事后聪明的人. **S- International**【史】第二国际. ~ **lieutenant** 少尉[陆军, 海军陆战队, [美] 空军]. ~ **mate [officer]**【海】二副. ~ **mortgage** 二次抵押. ~ **nature** 第二天性 (*Habit is a ~ nature.* 习惯是第二天性.) ~ **nerves**【解】视神经. ~**-pair back [front]** [英]三楼后[前]房. ~ **papers** [美] (外国侨民要求加入美国国籍的)第二次申请书. ~ **person**【语法】第二人称. ~ **pilot** 副驾驶员. ~**-rate** ① *a.* 第二流的; 二等的; 次等的. ②*n.* 次等货; 次级品; 二等战舰; 二流人物. ~**-rater** 二流人物; 二等角色; 次等货. ~ **reading** (议会中对提案的)二读. **S- Republic** (法兰西)第二共和国(1848—1852). ~ **root** 次生根. ~ **self** 第二自我(指心腹朋友等). ~ **sight** ①超级视力; 千里眼. ②卓见; 预见力. ~ **soprano** 次高音. ~ **sound**【物】第二声. ~ **speed** 二档速度. ~**stor(e)y** = ~ floor. ~**-stor(e)y** *a.* ①第二层楼的. ②[俚](贼)从二层楼进屋的. ~**-stor(e)y man** [俚](从楼上进屋的)夜盗, 窃贼. ~**-strike** *a.* (核子武力)反击的; 报复的. ~**-string** *a.* ①【体】(指球员)后备的. ②[转义]次等的, 第二流的. ~**-stringer** 后备球员. ~ **teeth** 成人齿; 永久齿. ~ **thoughts** [[美]

thought〕重新考虑;重想. ~**-timer** 第二次犯罪的罪犯. ~ **wind** 重新振作; 精神恢复; 恢复元气. **S- World War** 第二次世界大战(1939—45).

sec·ond[2] [ˈsekənd] *n.* ①秒 (= 1/60分); 秒(针). ②片刻; 一瞬间. ③弧秒(= 1/3600弧度). *He was done in a few ~s.* 他一会儿就累倒了. *Wait a ~!* 等一下! *in a ~* 立刻.

sec·ond·a·ri·ly [ˈsekəndərili] *ad.* ①在第二; 其次. ②从属地,在第二位.

sec·ond·a·ry [ˈsekəndəri] *a.* ①第二(位)的,第二次的; 中级的 *(opp.* primary*).* ②副(的); 从属的; 附属的; 辅助的; 补充的; 次要的; 次等的; 代理的. ③【医】继发(性)的, 第二期的. ④【地】中世代的; 次生的. ⑤【电】(产生)感应电流的; 次级电流的. ⑥【化】仲的, 次的; 副的, 二代的. ⑦中等教育[学校]的. ⑧〔语音〕次重音的. ⑨间接的; 非原始的. *Of the two contradictory aspects, one must be principal and the other ~.* 矛盾着的两方面中, 必有一方面是主要的, 他方面是次要的. *a ~ cause* 副因. *~ action* 副作用. *a ~ product* 副产物. *the S-strata*【地】中世层. *be of ~ importance* 不大重要. — *n.* ①助手; 副手; 帮手; 代理人; 被委任者; 次要的人; 次要的东西. ②【天】双星中较小较暗的一个; 卫星. ③副低气压. ④【电】次级[二次] 绕组[线圈]. ⑤【动】(鸟的)次级飞羽; 腕羽; (昆虫的)后翅. ⑥【地】中世代. ⑦【语音】次重音. ~ **battery** = ~cell. ~ **carbon atom**【化】仲碳原子. ~ **cell** 蓄电池; 副电池. ~ **circle**【天】第二圈, 副圈. ~ **coil**【电】副线圈. ~ **colour** 等和色; 合成色. ~ **contact** 辅助触点. ~ **current**【电】二次电流, 次级线圈电流. ~ **diagonal**【数】次对角线. ~ **education [school]** 中等教育 [学校]. ~ **electron**【物】次级电子. ~ **emission**【物】次级发射. ~ **evidence** 补证. ~ **fan**【矿】局部 (辅助) 扇风机. ~ **fever**【医】后热. ~ **foci** 共轭焦点. ~ **forest**【林】再生林. ~ **gas** 精洗煤气. ~ **generator** 蓄电池; 变压器; 变量器. ~ **inductance** 二次电路电感. ~ **line** 支线. ~ **metal** 再用 [生] 金属. ~ **planet**【天】卫星. ~ **protection tube**【冶】热电偶护管. ~ **radiation**【原】次级辐射. ~ **sex characteristic**【生】第二性征. ~ **syphilis**【医】第二期梅毒. ~ **union**【医】二次愈合, 化脓愈合.

sec·ond-best [ˈsekəndˈbest] *a.* 第二等的, 第二流的, 第二位的. — *n.* 第二等的东西. *one's ~ clothes* 第二件好衣裳. ***come off ~*** 输; 被击败; 被…胜过.

sec·ond-chop [ˈsekəndˈtʃɔp] *n.* 〔俚〕二等货; 下等货.

sec·ond-class [ˈsekəndˈklɑːs] *a.* ①〔英〕第二等的, 次级的. ②第二类的. ③第三流的. *a ~ carriage* 二等(客)车. *~ matter*〔美〕第二类邮件〔新闻纸类、定期刊物等〕. — *ad.* 乘二等车地; 坐二等舱地. *travel [go] ~* 坐二等车[舱]旅行.

sec·ond·er [ˈsekəndə] *n.* ①后援者. ②(尤指动议的)附议者; 赞成者.

sec·ond-hand[1] [ˈsekəndˈhænd] *a.* ①用过的; 旧的; 做旧货买卖的. ②第二手的; 间接(得来)的; (由旁人那里)听[借]来的; (学说等)不是独创的. *~ books [clothes]* 旧书[衣]. *~ witness* 陈述传闻情况的证人. — *ad.* 从旧货店(买到); 从第二手; 间接(地). *buy ~* 买旧货. — *n.* 旧货. ***at ~*** ①用旧货. ②间接(地); 辗转(得来地). ~ **tap**【机】中丝锥; 二丝锥.

sec·ond-hand[2] [ˈsekənd-ˈhænd] *n.* (钟表的)秒针.

sec·ond·ly [ˈsekəndli] *ad.* 第二; 其次.

se·con·do [seˈkɔndəu] *n.* 〔It.〕【乐】(协奏曲的) 第二部〔尤指四手联弹钢琴曲中的较低音部〕.

se·cre·cy [ˈsiːkrisi] *n.* ①秘密(状态); 隐蔽(状态); 守秘密. ②保密; 保密能力. *I can rely on his ~.* 我相信他不会泄漏秘密. ***in [with] ~*** 秘密地; 暗中. ***in the ~ of one's own heart*** 在内心深处. ***with the utmost ~*** 极秘密地.

se·cret [ˈsiːkrit] *a.* ①秘密的; 机密的; 隐秘的. ②僻远的. ③隐藏的; 看不见的. ④神秘的; 奥妙的; 不可思议的. ⑤隐居的. ⑥〔罕〕沉默寡言的. *a ~ code* 暗号. *a ~ door* 暗门. *a ~ errand* 密使. *a ~ passage* 秘密通道. *a ~ valley* 僻静的山谷; 幽谷. *the ~ workings of nature* 鬼斧神工. ***a ~ passion [sorrow]***〔美学生语〕意中人. ***be ~ in one's habits*** 有一切喜欢背着人做的习惯. ***keep (sth.)*** ~ 保守 (某事) 秘密. — *n.* ①秘密的事情; 秘密; 机密. ②秘诀; 隐蔽的真义. ③〔*pl.*〕神秘; 奇迹. ④〔*pl.*〕私处; 阴部〔又称 ~ parts〕. *an open ~* 公开的秘密. *the ~ of success* 成功的秘诀. ***be in the ~*** 知道秘密; 知道内情; 参与秘密. ***in ~*** 秘密地; 偷偷摸摸地. ***keep a [the] ~*** (保) 守秘密. ***keep sth. ~ from (sb.)*** 不把(某事)告诉(某人). ***let out a ~*** 泄漏秘密. ***let sb. into the ~*** 告诉秘密; 传授秘诀. ***make a [no] ~ of*** 隐秘[不隐秘]; 把[不把]…保守秘密. ~ **agent** 特务; 间谍. ~ **ballot** 无记名投票. ~ **ink** 隐显墨水. ~ **joint**【机】暗接. ~ **nail** 暗钉. ~ **police** 秘密警察. ~ **process** (虽非专利却受法律保护的) 秘密制造方法. ~ **service** ①特务组织; 特务机构; 情报机关; 情报部门. ②特务工作. ③〔美〕(财政部的)特工处〔缩写为 S.S.〕. ~ **society** 秘密会社; 帮会. **-ly** *ad.*

sec·re·taire [ˌsekriˈtɛə] *n.* = escritoire.

sec·re·tar·i·al [ˌsekrəˈtɛəriəl] *a.* ①秘书的; 书记的. ②部长的; 大臣的.

sec·re·tar·i·at(e) [ˌsekrəˈtɛəriət] *n.* ①书记 [秘书、部长]的职务. ②秘书长办公室; 秘书处, 书记处. ③秘书处[书记处]全体工作人员. *S- of the State Council* 国务院秘书厅. *S- of the Premier of the State Council = the Premier's S-* 国务院总理办公室. *United Nations S-* 联合国秘书处.

sec·re·tar·y [ˈsekrətri] *n.* ①秘书; 书记; 干事. ②[S-]〔美〕部长;〔英〕大臣. ③(上部附有书橱的)写字台. ④书写体大写铅字. *a private ~* 秘书. *the Party S-* 书记. *an honorary ~* 名誉干事. *the S- of State*〔美〕国务卿;〔英〕大臣〔也有单称 Minister 的〕. *the S- of Defense*〔美〕国防部部长. *the S- of State for Home [Foreign] Affairs = the Home [Foreign] S-*〔英〕内务[外交]大臣. *a general ~* 秘书长; 总书记. ~ **bird** 鹭鹰; (南非产)食蛇鸟. ~**-general** 秘书长; 书记长; 总书记. **-ship** 书记[秘书、部长、大臣]的职位[任期].

se·crete [siˈkriːt] *vt.* ①藏, 隐藏; 隐匿〔通常指物〕. ②侵吞. ③【生理】分泌. *a secreting cell* 分泌细胞.

se·cre·tin [siˈkriːtn] *n.*【生】分泌素.

se·cre·tion [siˈkriːʃən] *n.* ①隐匿; 藏匿; 隐藏. ②【生理】分泌. ③分泌物; 分泌液. ④树液.

se·cre·tive [siˈkriːtiv] *a.* ①遮遮掩掩的; 躲躲闪闪的; 沉默寡言的; 守口如瓶的; 秘而不宣的; 不坦率的; 隐秘的. ②【生】(促进)分泌的. **-ly** *ad.* **-ness** *n.*

se·cre·to·ry [siˈkriːtəri] *a.*【生】(促进) 分泌的. — *n.* 分泌器官.

secs. = ①seconds. ②sections.

sect [sekt] *n.* ①派(别); 宗派; 教派〔尤指教义不同的分裂教派〕. ②(哲学等的)学派; 党派; 团体.

sect. = section(al).

sec·tar·i·an [sekˈtɛəriən] *a.* 宗派的; 分裂教派的; 派系的; 学派的; 宗派主义的. *Cadres should guard against ~ tendencies.* 干部应该防止宗派主义的倾向. — *n.* ①宗派主义者. ②某宗派[教派]成员. ~**ism** *n.* 宗派主义.

sec·ta·ry [ˈsektəri] *n.* ①〔古〕某宗派成员. ②【英史】分裂教派[长老派(等)]信徒.

sec·tile [ˈsektail] *a.* (矿物等)可切开的; (云母等)可剖成片的;【植】(叶子)可分的.

sec·tion [ˈsekʃən] *n.* ①(外科、解剖的)切断; 切割; 切开. ②【外科】切片,【金相】磨石. ③(果子的)瓣. ④【数】截口. ⑤截面(图); 剖面(图); 断面(图). ⑥段; 断片; 部分. ⑦部件; 零件. ⑧部门; 部; 处; 科; 组; 股;【工】工段. ⑨木材的切口．⑩(文章等的)节[段落]；(条文等的)款；条；项．⑪轮廓．⑫【乐】(乐队的)乐器组．⑬(团体的)派；党；(社会的)阶层；界．⑭区域；地段；分区；区划．⑮【矿】采区；【生】派；亚属．⑯(铁路的)区间．⑰〔美〕一平方英里的面积．⑱【军】班；(炮兵)排；〔英〕小队；〔美〕小分队．*a vertical* ～ 纵断面．*a cross [transverse]* ～ 横断面．*a horizontal* ～ 水平断面．*an oblique* ～ 斜断面．*a microscopic* ～ (显微镜检查用的)切片．*an accounts* ～ 会计科．*a* ～ *leader*【军】班长；(炮兵)排长．***build in*** ～***s*** 分段制造．***convey in*** ～***s*** 拆开搬运．— *vt.* 解，拆(船等)；把…分(成)节[段、组]，区分；作截面图；(做显微镜检查用)将…切(成)片．*body* ～ 机身；床身．～ **crew** = ～ gang．～ **cutter** 切片机．～ **cutting** 切片法．**S- Eight** 美国陆军条例第八节〔不合军队要求(尤指精神不正常)而开除军籍〕；据此开除军籍的士兵．～ **gang**【铁路】工务段养路班．～ **hand [man]**【铁路】护路工．～ **mark** 分节号[即§]．～ **paper** (制图用)(方)格纸．～ **plane** 剖面．

sec·tion·al [ˈsekʃənəl] *a.* ①部分的；区分的；部门的；段落的；(分)节的；分项的；有区分的；分级的．②地方性(强)的；地段的；区域的．③局部的；断面(图)的．～ *quarrels* 派系间的争吵．*a* ～ *chief* 科[股，组]长．*a* ～ *boat* 可以拆开的小船．*a* ～ *plan of a building* 建筑物的断面图．**-ism** *n.* 地方主义；本位主义．**-ly** *ad.*

sec·tion·al·ize [ˈsekʃənəlaiz] *vt.* ***(-iz·ed, -iz·ing)*** ①把…分成段[区]；把…划成区〔尤指地理区划〕．②使具有地方性；使成党派性．**-al·i·za·tion** [-ˈzeiʃən] *n.*

sec·tor [ˈsektə] *n.* ①【数】扇形(面)．②函数尺；两脚规．③防(御分)区；扇形战区；方面战区；阵线．④【机】扇形齿轮．*a* ～ *of a sphere* 扇形圆锥．～ **gear**【机】扇形齿轮．～ **scan** 监视某一有限地区的雷达扫描．

sec·to·ri·al [sekˈtɔːriəl] *a.* ①扇形的．②【植】扇形嵌合体的．③【动】适于裂食肉类的．— *n.* (食肉动物的)裂齿．

sec·u·lar [ˈsekjulə] *a.* ①现世的；此世的；尘世的；俗界的；世俗的；非宗教(性)的．②【天主】修道院外的．③一世纪一次的；一代一次的．④长期的；长久的；不朽的；〔诗〕古老的．～ *affairs* 俗事；世事．～ *education* 普通教育〔与宗教教育相对〕．*the* ～ *acceleration*【天】长期加速度．～ *arm [power]* 俗权．*a* ～ *equation*【数】特征方程．*a* ～ *change* 缓慢变化．～ *depression*【地】缓慢下降．～ *fame* 不朽的名声．*the* ～ *bird* 不死鸟 (= phoenix)．*the* ～ *oaks* 古老的橡树．*a* ～ *phenomenon* 百年一度的奇异现象．—*n.*①【宗】俗僧；教区牧师；俗人．②〔美〕(黑人中间流行的)俗歌 *(opp.* spiritual*)*．**-ism** *n.* 现世主义；世俗论；宗教与教育分离论．**-ist** *n.* 世俗论者；宗教与教育分离论者．

sec·u·lar·i·ty [ˌsekjuˈlæriti] *n.* ①= secularism．②世俗性，现世性；对于世俗事务的关念；俗心；俗事．

sec·u·lar·i·za·tion [ˌsekjuləraiˈzeiʃən] *n.* ①世俗化；还俗．②脱离[不隶属于]教会；使教育与宗教分离．③改作俗用．

sec·u·lar·ize [ˈsekjuləraiz] *vt.* ①使世俗化；使还俗．②使脱离[不隶属于]教会；使(教育)和宗教分离．③使改作俗用．

se·cund [ˈsiːkʌnd] *a.*【动、植】偏向一边[侧，方]的；只有一边的；只生在一边的．

sec·un·dines [ˈsekʌndainz] *n. pl.* ①【医】胞衣；胎盘；胎膜 (= afterbirth)．②【植】内种皮；(胚珠的)内珠被〔内包皮〕．

se·cun·do [siˈkʌndəu] *ad.*〔L.〕其次；第二．

se·cun·dum [siˈkʌndəm] *prep.*〔L.〕依据；根据．～ ***artem*** [ˈɑːtem]〔L.〕人工地；科学地；技术地；巧妙地．～ ***legem*** [ˈliːdʒem]〔L.〕根据法律；从法律．～ ***naturam*** [nəˈtjuərəm]〔L.〕自然地；天然地．～ ***quid*** [kwid]〔L.〕只在某点上；只在某一方面；不是绝对的；不是一般的；有限制地．～ ***usum*** [ˈjuːsəm]〔L.〕根据惯例．

se·cur·a·ble [siˈkjuərəbl] *a.* ①能拿到手的；能获得的．②可保安全的．

se·cure [siˈkjuə] *a.* ***(-cur·er; -cur·est)*** ①安心的；不必担心的；有把握的．②可靠的．③安全的．④坚固的；牢固的．⑤必定的；拿稳的．⑥不怕逃走的；关得牢靠的．⑦〔古〕过分自信的；自负的．*a* ～ *place* 安全地方．*I have got him* ～ 我牢牢地逮住了他．*a* ～ *fool* 糊涂虫．***be*** ～ ***against [from]*** 没有…的危险．***be*** ～ ***of*** 对…有信心的，认为…靠得住的．***feel*** ～ ***(about, as to)*** (对…)放心；认为不要紧．***have one's mind*** ～ 放下心．***keep*** *(a prisoner)* ～ 把(犯人)关牢．— *vt.* ①使确实可靠；把…弄稳当．②使安全；防护；保卫；妥善保管．③搞到；把…拿到手；得到；获得．④吸引住．⑤招致；促成．⑥紧闭；关牢；关进；绑住 *(to)*．⑦保证；担保；保险．⑧指定把财产遗赠给… *(to)*．⑨【海】吩咐…停止工作；使停止(操作)．～ *a vein* (做外科手术时)防止静脉出血．～ *valuables* 将贵重物品收藏妥当．*a fully* ～*d loan* 有十足担保的借款．～ *oneself against [from] loss* 防止损失．～ *oneself against accidents* 投保人身意外险．～ *oneself against the cold* 作好御寒准备．～ ***arms!***【军】倒挟枪(以免雨水淋湿枪机)．～***(sth.) from sb.*** 从(某人处)拿到(某物)．～***one's ends*** 达到目的．—*vi.* ①作出保证；承诺保险〔开出保险单〕．②【海】停止工作；值勤完毕．③抛锚停靠．**-ly** *ad.* **-ness** *n.*

securi- *comb. f.* 斧：*securiform*.

se·cu·r·i·ty [siˈkjuəriti] *n.* ①安全(感)；安稳；稳妥；平安．②确实；确信；把握；可靠性；安心．③【军】防御物．④保护；防护；保卫；防御 *(against; from)*；治安，安全防卫．⑤【法】保证，担保；抵押．⑥担保品；保证金；借用证 *(for)*．⑦担保人；保证人．⑧〔*pl.*〕证券；债券；公债；股票．⑨〔古〕疏忽；大意．*public* ～ 公安．*public* ～ *organs* 保卫机关；公安机关．*What* ～ *can you offer for it?* 你对这件事能拿什么做担保呢？*S- is the greatest enemy.* 疏忽[麻痹大意]是最大的敌人．***give*** ～ ***against*** 保护；使无…之忧．***go [enter into, give]*** ～ ***for*** 做…的保人．***in*** ～ 安全．***in*** ～ ***for*** 作…的担保．***on good*** ～ 有可靠的抵押．～ **analyst** 股市分析家．～ **blanket** 安乐毯〔给小孩抓摸使感觉舒适安全的小绒毯〕．～ **clearance** (对参加机密工作的人进行的)忠诚调查．**S-Council** (联合国的)安全理事会．～ **police** 秘密警察．～ **risk**〔美〕(不适合参加国家机密工作的)不可靠分子．

secy., sec'y = secretary.

Se·dan [siˈdæn; F. sədɑ̃] *n.* 色当〔法国东北部一城市，1870年普法战争战场〕．

se·dan [siˈdæn] *n.* ①轿子．②〔美〕轿[汽]车．～ **chair** 轿子．

se·date [siˈdeit] *a.* ***(-dat·er; -dat·est)*** 沉着的；安详的；镇静的；平静的；静肃的 *(opp.* excitable*)*．— *vt.* 使服镇静剂而安静下来．**-ly** *ad.*

se·da·tion [siˈdeiʃən] *n.*【医】①镇静．②镇静状态．

sed·a·tive [ˈsedətiv] *a.* 镇静的；镇定的；止痛的．— *n.*【医】镇静剂；止痛药．

se de·fen·den·do [siː ˌdefənˈdendəu]〔L.〕为了自卫，自卫；正当防卫．

sed·en·ta·ri·ly [ˈsedəntərili] *ad.* ①坐着地；不活动地．②需要坐着的．③定居不动地．

sed·en·ta·ri·ness [ˈsedəntərinis] *n.* ①坐着；不活动．②定居．

sed·en·ta·ry [ˈsedntəri] *a.* ①坐定不动的；坐着做的．②坐成的；(病)坐出来的．③【动】定居一地的；定栖的(鸟)；(贝壳等)固定附着的；(昆虫)静止的．～ *habits* 常坐的习惯．*a* ～ *posture* 坐着的姿势．*a* ～ *statue* 坐像．— *n.* ①爱坐的人；坐着工作的人．②【动】坐巢蜘蛛．～ **soil** 原地土壤，原生土．

Se·der [ˈseidə] *n.* *(pl.* ***Se·dar·im*** [siˈdɑːrim] ～***s****)*【犹】犹太人出埃及节(祝宴)．

se·de·runt [siˈdiərʌnt] *vi.*〔L.〕(某某等人)出席 (=

There sat ...). ~ A, B, ..., 出席人甲、乙(等等). — *n.* 集会;会议;联欢会;座谈会.

sedge [sedʒ] *n.*【植】薹(属);菅茅;蓑衣草. *the sweet ~* 菖蒲. *a ~ warbler [wren]*【动】苇滨雀.

Sedg•wick [ˈsedʒwik] *n.* 塞奇威克〔姓氏〕.

sedg•y [ˈsedʒi] *a.* *(-i•er; -i•est)* ①薹属植物丛生的. ②似薹的.

se•di•le [seˈdaili] *n.* *(pl. -dil•ia [-ˈdailiə])*〔多用 *pl.*〕(教堂南侧的一排座位)祭司席;牧师席.

se•dil•i•a [seˈdailiə] *n.* sedile 的复数.

sed•i•ment [ˈsedimənt] *n.* ①沉淀(物); 沉渣. ②【地】沉积物.

sed•i•men•tal, sed•i•men•ta•ry [ˌsediˈmentl, -təri] *a.* ①沉淀[沉积](物)的;沉淀性的. ②沉淀[沉积]成的;水成的. ~ **clay** 沉积黏土. ~ **deposit**【地】沉积矿床;成层沉积. ~ **rocks**【地】沉积岩;水成岩.

sed•i•men•ta•tion [ˌsedimenˈteiʃən] *n.* ①沉淀[沉积、沉降](作用). ②沉积学,沉积法. ~ **rate [test]** (血液等的)沉降速度[检查]. ~ **velocity** 沉降速度.

se•di•tion [siˈdiʃən] *n.* ①煽动暴乱[闹事]的言论[行动]. ②扰乱治安;暴动;骚乱. *a ~ bill* 危害治安煽动取缔法. *stir up a ~* 煽起暴动. *a speech abounding in ~* 富有煽动性的演说.

se•di•tion•ar•y [siˈdiʃənəri] *a.* = seditious. — *n.* *(pl. -ar•ies)* 骚乱煽动者;煽动分子.

se•di•tious [siˈdiʃəs] *a.* 煽动(性)的;扰乱治安的;煽动叛变的. *a ~ demagogue* 煽动家. *a ~ harangue* 煽动性演说. **-ly** *ad.* **-ness** *n.*

se•duce [siˈdju:s] *vt.* ①诱使…堕落;诱坏;使入歧途. ②勾引;诱奸(妇女);挑唆,诱出(人). ③使入迷; 迷惑;吸引. *The beauty of the evening ~d me abroad.* 傍晚的美景把我吸引到户外去了.

se•duce•a•ble [siˈdju:səbl], **se•duc•i•ble** [-ibl] *a.* ①可引诱的;可诱惑的. ②易被勾引的;可诱奸的.

se•duce•ment [siˈdju:smənt] *n.*〔罕〕= seduction.

se•duc•er [siˈdju:sə] *n.* ①诱惑者. ②勾引者;〔特指〕诱奸者.

se•duc•tion [siˈdʌkʃən] *n.* ①引诱;诱惑. ②勾引;诱奸. ③〔常 *pl.*〕诱惑物;吸引力;魅力. *the ~s of country life* 乡村生活的吸引力.

se•duc•tive [siˈdʌktiv] *a.* ①引诱的;诱惑的. ②勾引的;诱奸的. ③吸引人的,富有魅力的. **-ly** *ad.*

se•duc•tress [siˈdʌktris] *n.* 有勾引力的女人;勾引男人的女人.

se•du•li•ty [siˈdju:liti] *n.* 勤勉;勤奋;坚持努力;恒心.

sed•u•lous [ˈsedjuləs] *a.* ①勤勉的; 孜孜不倦的. ②小心周到的. *~ attention* 密切注意. *~ flattery* 百般奉承. *with ~ care* 小心周到地(注意着).

Se•dum [ˈsi:dəm] *n.*【植】景天属植物.

see[1] [si:] *n.*【宗】主教的职位[权力]; 主教的辖区. *the Apostolic [Holy, Papal] S- = S- of Rome* 教皇的职位;罗马教廷;〔有时指〕教皇.

see[2] [si:] *(saw* [sɔ:]; *seen* [si:n]) *vt.* ①看见; 看到. ②细看;观察. ③观看;参观. ④查看; 检查. ⑤看出;看破;明白;领会;领悟;认为. ⑥体验; 经历. ⑦遇见;会见;访问; 谒见. ⑧学懂. ⑨(护)送;陪送. ⑩留心;留神;注意;考虑; 负责,务必使…. ⑪帮助;设法. ⑫〔美俚〕收买;贿赂. ⑬让;允许;任凭;听凭. ⑭看上;喜欢;同意. ⑮(纸牌赌博中)与(对方)下同样赌注 (要求对方摊牌);〔转义〕接受…的挑战. *S- p. 5.* 见第五页;参看第五页. *Let us ~ a great deal of each other.* 我们以后经常见见面吧. *I have seen nothing of him these days.* 我近来简直没有看见他. *I ~ you.*〔美〕我明白你的意思. *Well, I'll ~ what I can do.* 好的,我想想办法看. *He will never ~ fifty again.* 他已五十(岁)出头了. *I am ~ing no one today.* 我今天谁都不(会)见. *I saw him as far as the station.* 我一直送他到车站. *I don't see being made use of.* 我是不愿意受人利用的. — *vi.* ①看见;看;视. ②查看;检查; 想一想. ③明白;懂;理解;看透. ④注意,小心;留神;照顾;监督. *S-?*〔口〕= *Do you ~?* 明白了吧? *You shall ~.* 你不久就会明白的; 以后告诉你. *You ~.* 你知道;你说;你想;你看; 就这样,是不是. *I ~.* 原来如此;明白了. *Let me ~.* 让我想想看. ***as far as I can ~*** 就我所知;根据我的判断. ***as I ~ it*** 据我看;我以为. ***do not ~ it in that light*** 不那样想. ***first ~ the light (of day)*** 呱呱堕地;诞生. ***have seen better [best] days*** 过过好日子;过去情况不错(*She must have seen better days.* 她过去生活得不错,现在不行了. *He was dressed in an old coat that had seen better days.* 他穿着一套本来是很不错的旧西装). ***I'll be ~ing you.***〔美俚〕再见. ***I will ~ that ...*** 一定设法使…. ***I will ~ you blowed [damned, hanged] (first, before)*** 无论如何这种事情我是不干的. ***live to ~ ...*** 活着看到…. ***~ a doctor*** 去看医生. ***~ about*** 注意;查看;查询;留意于;留神. ***~ after*** 照料; 照应;照看. ***~ at a glance*** 一见就知道; 一看就明白. ***~ company*** 接见客人. ***~ (sb.) coming***〔俚〕使某人上当(*He saw you coming.* 你上他当了). ***~ ... done*** 监督…(的)完成. ***~ double*** 见 double. ***S- everything clear!***【海】预备〔放小船时的口令〕! ***~ eye to eye*** 见 eye 条. ***~ fit [good] (to do)*** 觉得…是适当的[好的]. ***~ for oneself*** 自己去看; 亲眼看. ***~ here***〔美〕喂喂. ***~ (sb.) home*** 送(某人)到家. ***~ if [whether]*** …看看是否. ***~ into*** ①调查; 检查. ②看透彻; 领会; 了解; 彻底理解. ***~ it*** 了解;理会;明白. ***~ justice done*** ①设法使事情处理得公平合理. ②报了仇. ***~ life*** 体验生活; 见世面. ***~ much [little] of*** 常常[很少]见到某人. ***~ no further than one's nose*** 前头漆黑[看不见]. ***~ sb. off*** 送(某人)启行;为某人送行. ***~ one's way (clear) to do(ing) ...*** 有可能[有意思]做…. ***~ out*** ①把…送到大门口. ②看到底;听到底;〔俚〕看穿;看破. ③做到底;取胜,完成;贯彻. ***~ out of the corners of one's eyes*** 偷看;侧目而视. ***~ over*** 查看; 检查;视察. ***~ red*** 见 red 条. ***~ the devil***〔卑〕喝醉. ***~ the good of*** 知道…的好处;尝到甜头. ***~ the inspector*** 收买[贿赂]检查员. ***~ the last of*** 赶走…; 和…断绝关系. ***~ the red light*** 发现危险在前. ***~ the time when*** 遭遇…. ***~ the use of*** 知道…的用途[价值]. ***~ things*** 发生幻觉. ***~ through*** ①看透; 看穿; 识破. ②坚持; 贯彻(*~ through a brick wall [a millstone]* 眼睛尖;眼光厉害). ***~ (sb.) through (his troubles)*** 帮助某人(渡过难关). ***~ (sth.) through [out]*** ①办好某事; 将(某事)做到底. ②看到底;看完. ***~ to*** 注意;留心; 当心, 负责;检查(*~ to one's business* 注意自己的事; 照看; 照料). ***~ (to it) that ...*** 留心使…;设法使;务必使;注意使;努力使;保证. ***~ visions*** 看见幻景;想象丰富地预想到未来景象; 有先见之明,有眼力;未卜先知. ***~ well and good***〔口〕觉得好;认为不要紧. ***~ which way the cat jumps*** 见 cat 条. ***~ with*** 同意. ***~ with half an eye*** 一看就明白[了解]. ***you ~***〔插入语〕是不是;你瞧;你听我说. ***S- you later.*** 再见. **~-through** ① *a.* (物件等)透明的,可以看到内部的;(衣服等)透视的,极薄的. ② *n.* 透视装,极薄的衣服.

see•catch [ˈsi:kætʃ] *n.*〔美〕【动】(阿拉斯加海域)成年雄海豹(= seecathie).

seed [si:d] *n.* *(pl. ~(s))* ①〔集合词〕【植】种;种子. ②颗粒;晶粒. ③〔*pl.* 通例 seed〕【生理】精液;鱼精;鱼卵;蠔(等的)卵. ④子孙;苗裔;后裔;种族. ⑤〔*pl.* 通例 ~s〕萌芽;根本;根源. ⑥(玻璃中的)气泡. *the ~s of disease* 病因;病根. ***go [run] to ~*** ①花谢结子. ②消瘦; 失去活力; 衰颓[落];〔美〕成为废料. ***in ~*** ①在结实[结子]时期. ②播着种的. ***raise up ~*** 繁殖子嗣. — *vi.* ①播种. ②结实;结出种子;成熟;脱籽. — *vt.* ①播(种);去…的核;脱…的籽;弄去…的种子. ②催促发育[成长];

催化；催促加速．③用种子花样装饰；把…做成点花底子．④【运】从(运动员)中挑选种子选手．~*ing stage* 出苗期．~*ing time* 播种期．~ ***down*** 撒种；播种．~ ***the draw***【运】安排种子选手分布在各组出场．~ **bearer** 母树．~**bed** ①苗床．②〔喻〕发源地；温床．~ **breeding** 良种繁殖．~ **cake** 撒有芬香种子(如芝麻)的糕饼．~ **case** 种皮．~**coat** 种皮．~ **coral** (装饰用)珊瑚珠．~ **corn** (作种用的)谷种；〔美〕玉米种．~ **crystal** 籽晶；晶种．~ **dressing**【农】拌种．~ **farm** 采种圃．~ **fat** 植物油．~ **fern** 种子蕨．~ **fish** 产卵期的鱼．~ **huller** 去壳机,去皮机．~ **manure** 种肥．~ **leaf**【植】子叶．~ **money** (用以吸引更多资金的)种子基金,股金．~ **oyster** (繁殖用)蠔种．~ **pearl** 小粒珍珠；米珠．~ **plant**【植】种子植物 (= spermatophyte). ~ **plot** 苗床；策源地．~ **pod**【植】荚果．~**production** 种子繁殖．~ **shrimp**【动】= ostracod. ~ **sower** 播种机．~ **subassembly** ①种子配件．②点火装置．~ **time** 播种时期〔晚春及初夏〕. ~ **tuber** 种薯．~ **vessel**【植】(囊)果皮．

seed·er [ˈsiːdə] *n.* ①播种者；播种机．②除核器；去核机．

seed·ing-machine [ˈsiːdiŋməʃiːn] *n.* 播种机．

seed·ling [ˈsiːdliŋ] *n.*【植】①种子繁殖．②实生苗．

seeds·man [ˈsiːdzmən] *n.* *(pl. -men)* ①播种者．②卖种子者；种子商．

seed·y [ˈsiːdi] *a.* *(-i·er; -i·est)* ①种子多的．②结子的．③(玻璃)多气泡的．④(白兰地酒)带草香的．⑤〔口〕消瘦的；憔悴的．⑥破旧的；褴褛的．⑦不很高尚的；下流的；低级的．⑧不愉快的；没精打采的；(脸色等)难看的．**-i·ly** *ad.* **-i·ness** *n.*

See·ger [ˈsiːɡə] *n.* 西格〔姓氏〕.

see·ing [ˈsiːiŋ] see 的现在分词．— *n.* 视觉；视力；看．*S- is believing.* 百闻不如一见．—*conj.* 因为，既然，鉴于．~ ***(that)*** 因为…；既然；鉴于；从…一点来看(~ *his youth and inexperience* 因为他年轻没经验)．**S- Eye**〔美新泽西州〕①能给瞎子带路的狗．②能给瞎子领路的狗的训练所．

seek [siːk] *vt.* *(sought* [sɔːt]*)* ①找；寻觅．②谋求(名誉等)；图谋；请求；求得．③寻求；探求；追求；调查；研究．④〔古〕去；赴．— *vi.* ①找；搜索；寻觅．②寻求；探求；要求．***be not far to*** ~ ①在近处；就在旁边．②很明白；很简单．***be (much) to*** ~ 还(很)需要探求；还(非常)不够；(非常)缺乏(*He is to ~ in intelligence.* 他才智不够)．***be yet to*** ~ 还没有，还得找找看．***deliberately*** ~ ***all means*** 处心积虑．~ ***a lady's hand in marriage*** 向女人求婚．~ ***after [for]*** 求；寻求；探究．~ ***by all means*** 处心积虑．***S- dead!*** 去找！〔命令猎狗去找打中的猎物．〕~ ***one's bed*** 就寝．~ ***out*** 找出；寻求；想获得．~ ***safety in flight*** 逃难．~ ***sb.'s life*** 图谋杀害某人．~ ***the truth from facts*** 实事求是．~ ***through*** 找遍．

seek·er [ˈsiːkə] *n.* ①搜索者；探求者．②【火箭】自导导弹；自动导引的弹头．③〔S-〕(英国17世纪的)求正教徒．

seel [siːl] *vt.* ①〔古〕拿线缝(鹰的眼睛等)；闭(眼睛)．②弄瞎；使眼睛发花．③蒙骗．

seem [siːm] *vi.* ①好象；似乎；好象是．②〔与人称代词连用〕〔口〕(感到)好象，(觉得)似乎．③〔与引导代词 it 连用〕看来好象．*He ~s (to be) deaf.* 他好象是聋子．*I do not ~ to like him.*〔口〕不知道什么缘故我总是不欢喜他．*Be what you ~ (to be).* 表里要一致；言行必须一致．*She ~ed an old woman.* 她看上去象个老太婆．*I ~ed to see a dog.* 我好象看到了一条狗．***It ~s*** 据说，据传；好象，似乎．***It ~s to me that ...*** 我想，我以为，据我看．***It should*** (or ***would***) ~ = it ~s. ★ seem 和 appear 在应用上常无差别，但前者似可导致某种结论，后者仅仅显示某一客观现象：He *seems* to be sick, for he *appears* pale. **-er** *n.* 装模作样的人，做作的人．

seem·ing [ˈsiːmiŋ] *a.* 表面的；外表上的；外观上的．*with ~ sincerity* 好象很诚实地．— *n.* 外观；表面；外表．*the ~ and the real* 外表和实际．**-ly** *ad.*

seem·ly [ˈsiːmli] *a.* *(-li·er; -li·est)* ①合宜的；适当的；得体的．②好看的；美貌的．— *ad.* 合宜地；适当地．**-li·ness** *n.*

seen [siːn] see 的过去分词．— *a.* ①看得见．②〔古〕懂得；熟悉的；精通的．*be well [ill] ~ in music* 精通音乐．

seep[1] [siːp] *vi.*〔美 Scot.〕渗出；漏出；(观念等)渗入．~**age** *n.*〔美 Scot.〕①漏水；渗流．②渗漏；渗出(现象)．③【矿】油苗．**-y** *a.* 排水不良的；湿气很重的．

seep[2] [siːp] *n.* 水陆两用吉普车．

se·er [ˈsiːə, siə] *n.* ①观看者．②预言者；先知；幻想家．③晶球占卜者．

seer·band [ˈsiəbænd] *n.* 印度缠头纱．

seer·fish [ˈsiəfiʃ] *n.* (印度)鲭鱼．

seer·suck·er [ˈsiəsʌkə] *n.* (印度)泡泡纱．

see·saw [ˈsiːˈsɔː, ˈsi-sɔː] *n.* ①跷跷板(戏)．②上下动；前后动；动摇；变动．— *ad., a.* 上下动地[的]；前后动地[的]；交互地[的]；拉锯性地[的]．— *vi.* ①玩跷跷板戏；一上一下地玩；上下动；前后动；动摇．②交替；(温度等)升降；涨落．~ **battle [game]** 拉锯战．~ **circuit**【无】跷跷板放大电路．~ **policy** 观望政策．~ **switch**【电】交互转换开关．

seethe [siːð] *vi.* *(~d* [-d]，〔古〕***sod*** [sɔd]; ***~d***〔古〕***sod·den*** [ˈsɔdn]*)* ①煮滚；沸滚．②沸腾；激昂．— *vt.*〔古〕煮；浸(在水等中)．*seething waters* 波涛汹涌的海面．*be sodden to the skin* 浑身湿透．

seg [seɡ] *n.*〔美俚〕种族隔离主义者．

se·gar [siˈɡɑː] *n.* cigar 的别字．

seg·gie [ˈseɡi] *n.*〔美俚〕= seg.

seg·ment [ˈseɡmənt] *n.* ①(自然形成的)段落；断片；部分；分节；段；节．②【数】(线)段；弓形．③圆缺；球缺．④环节；切片．⑤【生】分裂片；体节；环节；【植】细裂片；全裂片．⑥【电】整流子片；【计】程序段；【机】扇形体；弧层；拼合轮缘．*a ~ of an orange* 桔子的一片．*the jointed ~s of a bamboo stem* 一根竹子的许多节段．***in ~s*** 成节[段]，分节[段]．— *vi.*【生】分裂．*guide ~* 弓形座．*mica ~* 云母片．— *vt.* 分割，分裂；【生】使分裂．*a ~ed worm* 环虫．~ **gear**【机】弓形齿轮．

seg·men·tal, seg·men·ta·ry [seɡˈmentl, ˈseɡməntəri] *a.* ①节的；段的；分节的；分段的；部分的；线段的；弓形的．②圆缺的；球缺的．③【生】环节的；体节的；分节的．~ **organ**【生】环节器官．~ **phonemes**【语音】分解音素〔指音节中的元音、辅音和半元音〕.

seg·men·ta·tion [ˌseɡmənˈteiʃən] *n.* ①分割；切断．②【生】(细胞)分裂；(动物)分节；断裂．~ **cavity**【生】囊胚腔；分裂腔；卵裂腔．

se·gno [ˈsenjəu] *n.*〔It.〕【乐】记号〔尤指再奏部分开始或终了的记号〕.

seg·re·gate [ˈseɡriɡeit] *vt.* ①分开；分离；隔开，对…实行种族隔离．②【生】使分异；使变成其他种属、类别 *(from, under)*. ~ *boys and [from] girls* 把男孩和女孩分开．*segregating harvest*【农】分段收割．~*d junction* 中继线分线束．— *vi.* ①分开；分离 *(from)*. ②【化】分凝；【物、冶】偏析；熔析；【生】分异；(成熟分裂时等位基因)分离．③实行种族隔离．— [-ɡit] *a.* ①分离的；隔离(开)的；单独的．②实行种族隔离的．③【冶】偏析的．

seg·re·ga·tion [ˌseɡriˈɡeiʃən] *n.* ①分离；分开；隔离．②【化】分凝；【物、冶】偏析；熔析；【生】分异．【机械】离析性．③(等位基因)分离．*racial ~* 种族隔离．**-ist** *n.* (种族)隔离主义者．

seg·re·ga·tive [ˈseɡriɡeitiv] *a.* 分离的；分开的；易分离的；隔离性的．②(人)不合群的；不欢喜交际的．

se·gue [ˈseɡwei, ˈseiɡwei] *vi.* *(-gued, -gue·ing)*【乐】继

续如前；延续；连续；不间断；（伴奏者）跟随独奏〔独唱〕者表情演奏. — *n.*【乐】继续如前.

se·gui·dil·la [ˌsegəˈdiːljə] *n.* ①塞圭地拉舞〔一种有响板伴奏的西班牙舞蹈〕. ②塞圭地拉舞曲〔歌词、诗节〕.

sei·cen·to [seˈtʃentəu] *n.* 〔It.〕〔常 S-〕第十七世纪〔指意大利文艺的一个分期〕.

seiche [seiʃ] *n.* 〔Swiss F.〕【地】湖震；假潮；湖面；波动；湖啸.

sei·del [ˈzaidl, ˈsai-] *n.* *(pl.* ~*(s))* 大啤酒杯〔有时指连盖大啤酒杯〕.

Seid·litz [ˈsedlits] *n.* 塞得利兹〔捷克斯洛伐克的著名碱质矿泉地〕. ~ **powder**【化】塞得利兹粉〔一种轻泻剂，也可用以制成碱质矿泉水〕.

sei·gneur [seiˈnjəː,siːˈnjə] *n.* 封建领主；庄园主；诸侯；贵族；显贵.

sei·gneur·y [ˈseinjəri, ˈsiːn-] *n.* *(pl.* ***-gneur·ies)*** ①领主权. ②贵族庄园.

seign·ior [ˈseinjə,ˈsiːnjə] *n.* ①君主；封建领主；庄园主；贵族；乡绅. ②(用作尊称)先生〔= Sir〕. ~**age** *n.* ①君权；领主权. ②铸币税. ③硬币铸造利差.

seign·ior·al [ˈseinjərəl ,ˈsiːn-] *a.* = seignorial. **sei-gnio·rial** [-riəl] *a.* = seignorial.

seign·ior·y [ˈseinjəri,ˈsiːn-] *n.* ①君权；领主权. ②领地. ③(中古意大利共和国的)市政议会.

seign·or·al [ˈseinjərəl,ˈsiːn-] *a.* = seignorial.

sei·gno·ri·al [seiˈnjɔːriəl,siː-] *a.* ①君主的；领主的；庄园主的. ②掌握大权的，有主权的.

Seil [zail] *n.* 〔G.〕(登山运动用)爬山绳索.

seine [sein, siːn] *n.* (捕鱼用)拖拉大围网；拉网. — *vt., vi.* 用拖网捕(鱼).

Seine [sein] *n.* (流经巴黎的)塞纳河.

sei·ri·a·sis [saiəˈraiəsis] *n.*【医】日射病，中暑.

seise, sei·sin [siːz, -zin] = seize②, seizin.

seism [ˈsaizəm] *n.* 地震.

seis·mal [ˈsaizməl] *a.* 地震(引起)的.

seis·mic, -mi·cal [ˈsaizmik, -ikəl] *a.* 地震(性)的；由地震引起的；易生地震的. *a* ~ *area* 震域；震区. *the* ~ *centre [focus, orgin, vertical]* 震源；震中. *a* ~ *detector* 地震检波器. *a* ~ *ray* 地震线. *a* ~ *region* 地震区. **-cal·ly** *ad.*

seis·mic·i·ty [saizˈmisiti] *n.*【地】①震态；震状. ②震级.

seis·mics [ˈsaizmiks] *n.* 地震探测(法).

seis·mism [ˈsaizmizm] *n.*【地】地震(现象).

seismo- *comb. f.* 表示"地震"：*seismo*gram.

seis·mo·gram [ˈsaizməgræm] *n.*【地】震波图；地震波曲线.

seis·mo·graph [ˈsaizməgrɑːf] *n.* 地震仪.

seis·mog·ra·pher [saizˈmɔgrəfə] *n.* 地震学者，地震检测专家.

seis·mog·ra·phy [saizˈmɔgrəfi] *n.* ①地震验〔检〕测法；地震记录法. ②地震仪使用法. ③地震学.

seismol. = ①seismology. ②seismological.

seis·mo·log·ic, -i·cal [ˌsaizməˈlɔdʒik, -ikəl] *a.* 地震学(上)的. **-ly** *ad.*

seis·mol·o·gist [saizˈmɔlədʒist] *n.* 地震学家.

seis·mol·o·gy [saizˈmɔlədʒi] *n.* 地震学.

seis·mom·e·ter [saizˈmɔmitə] *n.*【地】(比 seismograph 精密的)测震仪；地震计；测震表.

seis·mo·met·ric [ˌsaizməˈmetrik] *a.* = seismometrical.

seis·mo·met·ri·cal [ˌsaizməˈmetrikl] *a.* ①地震仪〔计，表〕的. ②地震检测术的.

seis·mo·scope [ˈsaizməskəup] *n.* 地震波显示仪.

seis·mo·scop·ic [ˌsaizməˈskɔpic] *a.* 地震波显示仪的；地震波显示仪记录的.

sei·ty [ˈsiːti] *n.* 自身；自我；个性.

seiz·a·ble [ˈsiːzəbl] *a.* ①可抓住〔捉到，拿到，捕捉，夺取，抢到，劫掠，掠夺，占领〕的. ②可没收的.

seize [siːz] *vt.* ①抓；捉；捕；夺；抢；劫掠；掠夺. ②〔通例用被动语态〕【法】查封；充公；没收；扣押. ③依法占有(终身或世袭领地等)(= seise). ④(心中)明白；了解. ⑤〔通例用被动语态〕(病等)侵袭. ⑥【海】(用细索)绑住；捆上*(up)*. ~ *the point* 抓要点. ~ *an opportunity* = ~ *the occasion* 抓牢机会；乘机. ~ *a fortress* 夺取要塞. *the struggle to* ~ *power* 争夺政权的斗争. *I cannot* ~ *your meaning.* 我不明白你的意思. — *vi.* ①抓住；捉住；夺取 *(on, upon)*. ②利用；采用 *(on, upon)*. ③(机器因过热或过压而)停止转动；停住*(up)*. ***be*** ~***d of*** 占有着…；〔喻〕拥有(情报等)；知道(消息等)；(很)晓得. ***be*** ~***d with*** 被…侵扰；害；患；得 (*be* ~*d with gout* 害痛风症. *be* ~*d with a panic* 起恐慌. *be* ~*d with terror* 害怕). ~ ***hold of*** 抓住；捉住；逮住；占领. ~ ***on [upon]*** 猛扑；袭击；利用；采用(提议). ***stand*** ~***d of*** = be ~d of. ~ ***up*** (机器由于过热、摩擦、压力等)失灵；轧住. ~ ***sb. up***【海】把某人绑在索具上(以便鞭打).

seiz·er [ˈsiːzə] *n.* ①抓〔捉，捕〕(…)的人. ②没收者；扣押者. ③(捕捉猎物的)猎犬.

sei·zin(e) [ˈsiːzin] *n.*【法】①(终身或世袭领地等的)依法占有. ②占有物；所有地；财产. ~ ***in deed [fact]*** 事实上的占有.

seiz·ing [ˈsiːziŋ] *n.* ①捕捉；强夺. ②所有；占有；强占. ③查封；没收；扣押. ④【海】(用细绳索)捆绑；捆扎；捆结. ⑤〔*pl.*〕捆(扎用的细绳)索. ⑥卡住；材料粘附在模子上.

sei·zor [ˈsiːzə] *n.*【法】(尤指终身或世袭领地的)占有人；扣押者.

sei·zure [ˈsiːʒə] *n.* ①捉拿；捕捉. ②夺取；占领；掠夺；篡夺. ③查封；没收；充公. ④捕获物；没收物；扣押物. ⑤(疾病的)突然发作；〔特指〕脑溢血. *the* ~ *of power* 夺取政权. *die from a* ~ *of apoplexy* 中风而死.

se·jant [ˈsiːdʒənt] *a.*【徽】(狮子等)前腿伸直地坐着的.

Sejm [seim] *n.* 波兰议会.

sel. = selected; selection(s); selector.

se·la·chi·an [siˈleikiən] *n.*【动】鲨类(亚纲) *(Selachii)* 的鱼. — *a.* 鲨类(亚纲)的.

se·la·dang [seiˈlɑːdɑːŋ] *n.*【动】马来犎.

sel·a·gi·nel·la [ˌselədʒiˈnelə] *n.*【植】卷柏属 *(Selaginalla)* 植物.

Sel·den [ˈseldən] *n.* 塞尔登〔姓氏〕.

sel·dom [ˈseldəm] *ad.* 不常；很少；难得…. *He* ~, *if ever, goes out.* = *He* ~ *or never goes out.* 他很少出门. *It is* ~ *that a man lives to be a hundred years old.* 人生百岁古来稀. ***not*** ~ 往往；时常. ~ ***or never*** = ***very*** ~ 很少；简直不. — *a.* 不常的；稀少的.

se·lect [siˈlekt] *vt.* 选；选择；挑选；选拔. *Her father let her* ~ *her own birthday present.* 她的父亲让她自己挑选生日礼品. — *vi.* 挑选，选择. — *a.* ①挑选出来的；精选的；极好的. ②〔口〕爱挑三拣四的；挑剔的. ③苛择的；入会条件苛刻的. *a* ~ *crew* 一批精选的水手. *be* ~ *in choosing one's friends* 择友谨慎. ~ *wines* 精选的酒. — *n.* ①〔口〕精选品；顶好的货色. ②〔常 *pl.*〕被挑选者. ~ **committee** (英国下院受命进行某一特别调查工作的)小型特别委员会. ~ **school** (学生经过挑选的)私立学校. ~ **society** 上流社会.

se·lect·ed [siˈlektid] *a.* 挑选出来的；精选的. ~ **clientele** 〔美〕= restricted clientele.

se·lect·ee [ˌselekˈtiː] *n.* 选征合格的士兵；应征兵.

se·lec·tion [siˈlekʃən] *n.* ①选择；挑选；选拔. ②拔萃；选择物；精选物〔品〕；文选. ③【无】分离；(自动电话)拨号. ④【生】选择，淘汰. ~*s from great poets* 名家诗选. *mass* ~ 混合选种. *artificial [natural, reproductive, sexual]* ~ 人为〔自然，生殖，雌雄〕淘汰. *natural* ~ 自然淘汰. ~ **committee** 提案处理委员会.

se·lec·tive [siˈlektiv] *a.* ①选择的；挑选的；有选择性的；淘汰的。②【无】选择性的。～ **amplifier**【无】选频放大器。～ **hardening**【冶】局部淬火；局部硬化；选择硬化。～ **lever**（汽车等的）选速杆。【电】～ **relay** 选择(性）继电器；谐振继电器。**S-Service**〔美〕选征兵役制。**-ly** *ad.*
se·lec·tiv·i·ty [silekˈtiviti] *n.* ①选择；精选。②【无】选择性；选择度；【物】选择能力；选择率。
se·lect·man [siˈlektmæn] *n.* *(pl. -men)*〔美〕〔美国新英格兰 (New England)地区除罗得岛(Rhode Island)外各州的〕市政委员。
se·lec·tor [siˈlektə] *n.* ①选择者；挑选者；选拔者；精选者。②【无】选择器；选波器；调谐旋钮；波段开关。③【计】选数器；选数管。④分离机。⑤〔澳〕选取公地定居下来的人；小农。
se·lec·tron [siˈlektrɔn] *n.* ①【计】选数管。②【化】聚酯树脂。
sel·e·nate [ˈselineit] *n.*【化】硒酸盐。
Se·le·ne [siˈliːni] *n.*【希神】(月之女神)塞妮涅。
se·len·ic [siˈlenik] *a.*【化】①(正)硒的；四价硒的。②六价硒的。～ **acid** 硒酸。
sel·e·nide [ˈselinaid] *n.*【化】硒化物。
se·le·ni·ous [siˈliːniəs] *a.*【化】二价硒的，亚硒的；四价硒的。
sel·e·nite[1] [ˈselinait] *n.* ①【矿】透明石膏。②【化】亚硒酸盐。
sel·e·nite[2], **S-** [siˈliːnait] *n.*（旧时想象中的)月中居民。
se·le·ni·um [siˈliːniəm, -njəm] *n.*【化】硒。*a* ～ *cell*【电】硒电池。
sel·e·nod·es·ist [ˌseliˈnɔdist] *n.* 月球学家。
sel·e·nod·e·sy [ˌseliˈnɔdisi] *n.*【天】月面测量学。
se·le·no·graph [siˈliːnəgrɑːf] *n.*【天】月面图。
sel·e·nog·ra·pher [ˌseliˈnɔgrəfə] *n.* 月面学家。
sel·e·nog·ra·phic [siˌliːnəˈgræfik] *a.* 月面学的。
se·le·nog·raph·y [ˌseliˈnɔgrəfi] *n.*【天】月面学。
se·le·nol·o·gy [ˌseliˈnɔlədʒi] *n.*【天】月球学。
Se·leu·cid [siˈluːsid] *n.* *(pl. ～s, -ci·dae* [-siˌdiː]*)* 塞琉古王朝的一代君王。— *a.* 塞琉古王朝的 (= seleucidan)。
self [self] *n.* *(pl. selves*[selvz]*)* ①自己；自身；本身；【哲】自我；我。②本性；本质。③私利；私心，私欲。④【俗】我；我自己；本人。⑤本身〔某种抽象性质的体现〕。⑥【园艺】单色花；原色花〔未经人工培育变色的〕。⑦【商、谑】我〔你、他〕自己 (= myself, yourself, himself)。*my poor [humble]* ～〔自称〕敝人，在下，不才。*one's second* ～ 密友。*our two selves* 我们两个。*our noble selves!*〔谑〕(干杯时)祝各位健康；*your good selves*【商】您；您处；您店。*your honoured selves* 阁下。*Your Royal S-* 殿下。*S- is a bad guide to happiness.* 利己心带不来幸福。*S- do,* ～ *have.* 自作自受。*a ticket admitting* ～ *and friend* 限本人和朋友用的入场券。*Please accept our thanks to Mr. Jones and* ～. 谢谢您和琼斯。***by one's*** ～ 单独。***have no thought of*** ～ 没有个人打算。***one's better*** ～ 良心；本性中良好的一面。***pay to*** ～〔支票用语〕认票不认人。***rise above*** ～ 舍己为人。***pity's*** ～ 极令人遗憾〔怜悯〕的(事物或人）— *a.* ①〔古〕同样的；这；那。②纯净的；一样的；单一的；(颜色等)同一的；(弓等)用一根木头做的；同样材料的。*the* ～ *way* 用同样方法。*at that* ～ *moment* 正在那同一时刻。*a* ～ *button* 用与衣料相同的材料制成的钮扣。— *vt.* 使近亲繁殖；使同种繁殖；【植】使自花授精。— *vi.*【植】自花授精。
-self *suf.* 自己：my*self*, him*self*.
self- *pref.* ①自己；自我。②自行；自动：*self*-control, *self*-conscious.
self-a·ban·don [ˈselfəˈbændən] *n.* 自暴自弃；放肆。
self-a·base·ment [ˈself-əˈbeismənt] *n.* 自贬，自卑，自我菲薄。
self-ab·hor·rence [ˈselfəbˈhɔːrəns] *n.* 自我憎恶。
self·ab·ne·ga·tion [ˈselfəbniˈgeiʃən] *n.* 克己，自制；自我牺牲。
self-ab·sorbed [ˈselfəbˈsɔːbd] *a.* 只顾自己的；自私的。
self-ab·sorp·tion [ˈselfəbˈsɔːpʃən] *n.* ①只顾自己；自私自利。②【物】自吸收。
self-a·buse [ˈselfəˈbjuːs] *n.* ①自暴自弃。②手淫。
self-act·ing [ˈselfˈæktiŋ] *a.* 自动的。
self-ac·tu·al·i·za·tion [ˈselfæktjuəlaiˈzeiʃən] *n.* 充分发展自己的才能；充分实现自己的抱负。
self·ac·tu·al·ize [ˈselfˈæktjuəlaiz] *vi.* 充分认识自己的抱负，自我认识；充分发展自己的才能。
self-ad·dressed [ˈselfəˈdrest] *a.* 写明发信人自己的地址的。*a* ～ *envelope* 写明发信人姓名地址的信封。
self-ad·just·ing [ˈselfəˈdʒʌstiŋ] *a.* 自动调节的。
self-ad·vance·ment [ˈselfədˈvɑːnsmənt] *n.* 对自身利益的促进。
self-af·fec·ted [ˈselfəˈfektid] *a.* 自负的。
self-af·fir·ma·tion [ˈselfˌæfə(ː)ˈmeiʃən] *n.* 自己证明；自行断定；自己作主；【心】自我肯定。
self-ag·gran·dize·ment [ˈselfəˈgrændizmənt] *n.*（不择手段地)自我扩张(权势、财富等)。
self-a·nal·y·sis [ˈselfəˈnælisis] *n.* 自我精神分析。
self-an·ni·hi·la·tion [ˈselfˌənaiəˈleiʃən] *n.* ①自毁，自杀。②【神学】自我消融，自我消失〔消失于与神融合的神秘状态中〕。
self-ap·point·ed [ˈself-əˈpɔintid] *a.* 自己作主的；自行推荐〔任命〕的；自封的。～ *duties* 自己喜欢做的职务。
self-ap·pre·ci·a·tion [selfəˌpriːʃiˈeiʃən] *n.* 自我欣赏。
self-as·ser·tion [ˈselfəˈsəːʃən] *n.* ①自作主张；坚持己见；一意孤行。②任性；自负；逞能。
self-as·ser·tive [ˈselfəˈsəːtiv] *a.* ①自作主张的，坚持己见的；一意孤行的。②任性的；自负的；逞能的。
self-as·sumed [ˈselfəˈsjuːmd] *a.* 独断独行的；专断的；僭越的。
self-as·sur·ance [ˈselfəˈʃuərəns] *n.* ①自信，自恃。②自足；自满。
self-as·sured [ˈselfəˈʃuəd] *a.* ①自信的。②自满自足的。
self-be·tray·al [ˈselfbitreiəl] *n.* 自我暴露。
self-bind·er [ˈselfˈbaində] *n.* ①【农】自动束禾〔草〕机。②自动装钉器〔机〕。③活页夹。
self-bred [ˈselfˈbred] *n.*【生】自交系。
self-cen·tred [ˈselfˈsentəd] *a.* ①自我本位〔中心〕的；自私自利的。②自给自足的。③作为中心而固定不动的。
self-clos·ing [ˈselfˈkləuziŋ] *a.* 自动关闭的。*a* ～ *door* 自动关闭的门。
self-col·lect·ed [ˈselfkəˈlektid] *a.* 沉着的；冷静的。
self-col·o(u)red [ˈselfˈkʌləd] *a.* ①单色的；纯色的。②天然色的；(织物)本色的。
self-com·mand [ˈselfkəˈmɑːnd] *n.* 自制；克己；沉着，镇定自若。
self-com·pat·i·ble [ˈselfkəmˈpætəbl] *a.*【植】能自花传粉的。
self-com·pla·cen·cy [ˈselfkəmˈpleisnsi] *n.* 自我陶醉；自满；自得。
self-com·pla·cent [ˈselfkəmˈpleisnt] *a.* 自我陶醉的，自满自得的。
self-com·posed [ˈselfkəmˈpəuzd] *a.* 镇定自若的；冷静的。
self-con·ceit [ˈselfkənˈsiːt] *n.* 自负；自大，自夸。**-ed** *a.*
self-con·cept [ˈselfkənˈsept] = self-image.
self-con·cern [ˈselfkənˈsəːn] *n.* 只顾自己，自私自利。**-ed** *a.*
self-con·demned [ˈselfkənˈdemd] *a.* 受良心责备的；自责的。
self-con·fessed [ˈselfkənˈfest] *a.* 自(动承)认的。*He is*

a ～ *drunkard*. 他自己承认自己是个醉鬼.
self-con·fi·dence [ˈselfˈkɔnfidəns] *n.* 自信;自恃.
self-con·fi·dent [ˈselfˈkɔnfidənt] *a.* 自信(力强)的;自恃的. **-ly** *ad.*
self-con·scious [ˈselfˈkɔnʃəs] *a.* ①自觉的. ②怕难为情的;害羞的. **-ly** *ad.* **-ness** *n.*
self-con·se·quence [ˈselfˈkɔnsikwəns] *n.* 妄自尊大.
self-con·sist·ent [ˈselfkənˈsistənt] *a.* 前后照应的,首尾一贯的,无自我矛盾现象的.
self-con·sti·tuted [ˈselfˈkɔnstitju:tid] *a.* 自定的;自我任命的,(保护人等)自许的;(机构等)自行设立的.
self-con·tained [selfkənˈteind] *a.* ①沉默寡言的;不爱说话的. ②独立的;自恃的;自足的;自治的;自制的. ③【机】(本身)设备齐全的;整套装在一起的;装备在一个容器里的. ④(公寓等)独门独户的;出入各别的. ⑤〔喻〕独立的. ～ *and self-sufficient* 自给自足的.
self-con·tempt [ˈselfkənˈtempt] *n.* 自我轻蔑.
self-con·tent, self-con·tent·ment [ˈselfkənˈtent, -mənt] *n.* 自满.
self-con·tent·ed [ˈselfkənˈtentid] *a.* 自满的.
self-con·tra·dic·tion [ˈselfˌkɔntrəˈdikʃən] *n.* 自相矛盾.
self-con·tra·dic·to·ry [ˈselfˌkɔntrəˈdiktəri] *a.* 自相矛盾的;前后矛盾的.
self-con·trol [ˈselfkənˈtrəul] *n.* 克己;自制. **-ed** *a.*
self-crit·i·cal [ˈselfˈkritikəl] *a.* 自我批评[判]的.
self-crit·i·cism [ˈselfˈkritisizəm] *n.* 自我批评.
self-cul·ti·va·tion [ˈselfˌkʌltiˈveiʃən] *n.* 自我修养.
self-cul·ture [ˈselfˈkʌltʃə] *n.* 自修;自我修养.
self-de·cep·tion [ˈselfdiˈsepʃən] *n.* 自欺.
self-de·feat·ing [ˈselfdiˈfi:tiŋ] *a.* 弄巧成拙的;自我拆台的,使自己失败的.
self-de·fence, 〔美〕**-se** [ˈselfdiˈfens] *n.* 自卫(术);【法】自卫权;正当权利.
self-de·lu·sion [ˈselfdiˈlu:ʒən] *n.* = self-deception.
self-de·ni·al [ˈselfdiˈnaiəl] *n.* 自我牺牲;克己,无私.
self-de·ny·ing [ˈselfdiˈnaiiŋ] *a.* 克己的;无私的;自我牺牲的.
self-de·pend·ence [ˈselfdiˈpendəns] *n.* 依靠自己;自力更生. **-pend·ent** [-ˈpendənt] *a.*
self-des·truc·tion [ˈselfdisˈtrʌkʃən] *n.* 自毁;自杀.
self-de·ter·mi·na·tion [ˈselfdiˌtə:miˈneiʃən] *n.* ①自决. ②民族自决. ③【哲】(强调意志自由的)自我决定.
self-de·termin·ing [ˈselfdiˈtə:miniŋ] *a.* 自决的;民族自决的;自我决定的.
self-de·vo·tion [ˈselfdiˈvəuʃən] *n.* 自我牺牲;献身.
self-dis·ci·pline [ˈselfˈdisiplin] *n.* 自律;自我约束.
self-dis·ci·plined [ˈselfˈdisiplind] *a.* 自律的;自己约束自己的;自动守纪律的.
self-dis·trust [ˈselfdisˈtrʌst] *n.* 自疑;无自信 (*opp.* self-confidence).
self-doubt [ˈselfˈdaut] *n.* 自疑;对自己缺乏信心.
self-dram·a·tiz·ing [ˈselfˈdræmətaiziŋ] *a.* (象演员般)装腔作势的;自吹自擂的;大摇大摆的.
self-dram·ti·za·tion [ˈselfˌdræmətaiˈzeiʃən] *n.* 装腔作势;自吹自擂;大摇大摆.
self-drive [ˈselfˈdraiv] *a.* 〔英〕租来自己驾驶的. ～ **car** 〔英〕出租汽车.
self-driv·en [ˈselfˈdrivn] *a.* (车辆等)自动推进的.
self-ed·u·cated [ˈselfˈedju(:)keitid,-ˈedʒu(:)-] *a.* 自修的;自学的;自我教育的.
self-ef·face·ment [ˈselfiˈfeismənt] *n.* 谦让,避免出风头.
self-em·ployed [ˈselfimˈplɔid] *a.* ①自己经营的;不受雇于别人的. ②不专为某一雇主工作的.
self-en·er·giz·ing [ˈselfˈenədʒaiziŋ] *a.* 【机,电】自激的;自给供电的;自身增大能量的.
self-en·er·gy [ˈselfˈenədʒi] *n.* 固有能量.
self-es·teem [ˈselfisˈti:m] *n.* ①自重;自尊. ②自大;自满 (*opp.* diffidence).
self-ev·i·dent [ˈselfˈevidənt] *a.* 自明的,不需证明的;不言而喻的.
self-ex·am·i·na·tion [ˈselfigˌzæmiˈneiʃən] *n.* 自我检查,反省.
self-ex·ci·ta·tion [ˈselfˌeksiˈteiʃən] *n.* 【物】自激;自励磁.
self-ex·cit·er [ˈselfikˈsaitə] *n.* 自激发动机.
self-ex·e·cut·ing [ˈselfˈeksikjutiŋ] *a.* 【法】(法律条约等在特定条件下)自动生效的.
self-ex·ist·ent [ˈselfigˈzistənt] *a.* 自存的,独立存在的.
self-ex·plain·ing, self-ex·plan·a·to·ry [ˈselfiksˈpleiniŋ -ˈplænətəri] *a.* (意义)不解自明的.
self-ex·pres·sion [ˈselfiksˈpreʃən] *n.* 自我表现.
self-faced [ˈselfˈfeist] *a.* (石面)未加雕凿的,天然的.
self-feed·er [ˈselfˈfi:də] *n.* ①【机】自动给料器,自给器. ②【农】(牲畜的)自动喂饲槽.
self-fer·ti·li·za·tion [ˈselfˌfə:tilaiˈzeiʃən] *n.* ①【植】自花传粉[授粉] (*opp.* cross-fertilization). ②【动】自体受精.
self-for·get·ful [ˈselffəˈgetful] *a.* 忘我的,无私的.
self-ful·fill·ment [ˈselffulˈfilmənt] *n.* 自力完成;自力达到期望[目标].
self-gen·er·at·ing [ˈselfˈdʒenəreitiŋ] *a.* 【生】自生的;自然发生的.
self-giv·en [ˈselfˈgivn] *a.* ①出自本身的. ②自封的.
self-giv·ing [ˈselfˈgiviŋ] *a.* 舍己为人的,无私的.
self-glo·ri·fi·ca·tion [ˈselfˌglɔrifiˈkeiʃən] *n.* 自我陶醉,自命不凡,自负.
self-gov·ern·ing [ˈselfˈgʌvəniŋ] *a.* ①自治的,②自制的. *a* ～ *colony* 自治殖民地. *a* ～ *dominion* 自治领. *a* ～ *man* 一个能自我克制的人.
self-gov·ern·ment [ˈselfˈgʌvənmənt] *n.* ①自治. ②自制,克己.
self-guid·ed [ˈselfˈgaidid] *a.* 自导的,自动导向的.
self-hard·en·ing [ˈselfˈhɑ:dniŋ] *a.* 自(动)硬(化)的;空气硬化的〔特指钢在空气中自行冷却而硬化〕.
self-hate, self-hatred [ˈselfˈheit, -trid] *n.* 怨恨自己;仇恨自己人.
self-heal [ˈselfˈhi:l] *n.* 有医疗作用的植物〔特指夏枯草〕.
self-help [ˈselfˈhelp] *n.* ①自助. ②【法】自救行为.
self-hood [ˈselfhud] *n.* ①个性,自我. ②自我中心,自私.
self-hu·mil·i·a·tion [ˈselfhju:ˌmiliˈeiʃən] *n.* 自辱,自我丢丑;自卑.
self-hyp·no·sis [ˈselfhipˈnəusis] *n.* 自我催眠.
self-i·den·ti·ty [ˈselfaiˈdentiti] *n.* 自我同一性,自我同一感.
self-ig·nite [ˈselfigˈnait] *vi.* 自燃,自动点火. **-nition** [-ˈniʃən] *n.*
self-im·age [ˈselfˈimidʒ] *n.* 自我形象;对自己的看法〔估价〕.
self-im·por·tance [ˈselfimˈpɔ:təns] *n.* 妄自尊大. **-tant** [-tənt] *a.*
self-im·posed [ˈselfimˈpəuzd] *a.* 自愿承担的,自己强加的. *a* ～ *task* 自己要做的工作.
self-im·prove·ment [ˈselfimˈpru:vmənt] *n.* 自我改进〔改善〕.
self-in·clu·sive [ˈselfinˈklu:siv] *a.* 包括自己在内的;自含的.
self-in·crim·i·na·tion [ˈselfˌinkrimiˈneiʃən] *n.* (因自己的供词、答词而)牵连;自陷法网;自认犯罪.
self-in·duc·tion [ˈselfinˈdʌkʃən] *n.* 【电】自感应.
self-in·dul·gence [ˈselfinˈdʌldʒəns] *n.* 自我放纵,任性;纵欲.
self-in·dul·gent [ˈselfinˈdʌldʒənt] *a.* 自我放纵的,任性

的；纵欲的。
self-in·flict·ed [ˈselfinˈfliklid] *a.* 自己造成的，自使蒙受的。
self-in·i·ti·at·ed [ˈselfiniʃiˈeitid] *a.* 自己发起的；从自己开始的。
self-in·sur·ance [ˈselfinˈʃuərəns] *n.* 自我保险。
self-in·ter·est [ˈselfˈintərist] *n.* ①自身利益. ②私心，自私自利。
self·ish [ˈselfiʃ] *a.* 自私自利的，只顾自己的；利己的 *(opp.* atruistic*)*. **-ly** *ad.* **-ness** *n.*
self-jus·ti·fi·ca·tion [ˈselfˌdʒʌstifiˈkeiʃən] *n.* 自我证明(正当，合理)；自我辩明。
self-know·ing [ˈselfˈnəuiŋ] *a.* 有自知之明的。
self-know·ledge [ˈselfˈnɔledʒ] *a.* 自知之明；自觉。
self·less [ˈselflis] *a.* 忘我的，无私的. *a* ~ *man* 一个无私的人。
self-liq·ui·dat·ing [ˈselfˌlikwiˈdeitiŋ] *a.* ①能自行收回成本并产生利润的. ②能使货物迅速变为现款的。
self-load·er [ˈselfˈləudə] *n.* 自动装弹的武器，半自动武器。
self-load·ing [ˈselfˈləudiŋ] *a.* 自动装载的；自动装弹进膛的。
self-love [ˈselfˈlʌv] *n.* ①自我怜爱. ②自负，自大. ③自私。
self-made [ˈselfˈmeid] *a.* ①独自做的，自己搞的. ②自力更生的，靠自己努力而成功的。
self-mail·er [ˈselfmeilə] *n.* 邮简。
self-mas·ter·y [ˈselfˈmɑːstəri] *n.* 自制，约束自己，沉着。
self-mor·ti·fi·ca·tion [ˈselfˌmɔːtifiˈkeiʃən] *n.* 禁欲(主义)。
self-mo·tion [ˈselfˈməuʃən] *n.* 自动。
self-mov·ing [ˈselfˈmuːviŋ] *a.* 自动的。
self-mur·der [ˈselfˈməːdə] *n.* 自杀；自我毁灭。
self-noise [ˈselfˈnɔiz] *n.* (船破浪前进时产生的)自噪声。
self-o·pin·ion·at·ed, self-o·pin·ioned [ˈselfəˈpinijəneitid, -ˈpinjənd] *a.* 固执己见的，刚愎自用的；自负的。
self-or·gan·i·za·tion [ˈselfˌɔːgənaiˈzeiʃən] *n.* 组织工会；加入工会。
self-os·cil·lation [ˈselfˌɔsiˈleiʃən] *n.*【物】自激振荡。
self-par·tial·i·ty [ˈselfˌpɑːʃiˈæliti] *n.* ①自视过高. ②徇私，自我偏袒。
self-per·pet·u·a·ting [ˈselfpəˌpetjuˈeitiŋ] *a.* ①使自身长存不废的. ②恋栈的，想尽办法保留自己官职的。
self-pit·y [ˈselfˈpiti] *n.* 自怜。
self-poise [ˈselfˈpɔiz] *n.* ①自动平衡. ②镇定. **-d** *a.*
self-pol·li·nate [ˈselfˈpɔlineit] *vt., vi.*【植】(使)自花授[传]粉的. **-d** *a.*
self-pol·lu·tion [ˈselfpəˈluːʃən] *n.* 手淫。
self-por·trait [ˈselfˈpɔːtreit] *n.* 自画像；自我描述。
self-pos·sessed [ˈselfpəˈzest] *a.* 有自制力的；沉着的，冷静的。
self-pos·ses·sion [ˈselfpəˈzeʃən] *n.* 沉着，冷静，泰然自若。
self-praise [ˈselfˈpreiz] *n.* 自我称赞，自我吹嘘。
self-pres·er·va·tion [ˈselfˌprezəˈveiʃən] *n.* 自我保存，自卫本能。
self-pride [ˈselfˈpraid] *n.* 自负。
self-pro·claimed [ˈselfprəˈkleimd] *a.* 自称的，自封的。
self-pro·duced [ˈselfprəˈdjuːst] *a.* 本身产生的。
self-pro·nounc·ing [ˈselfprəˈnaunsiŋ] *a.* 在原词上标注读音符号的. *a* ~ *dictionary* 标音词典。
self-pro·pelled [ˈselfprəˈpeld] *a.* ①自动推进的，自己开动的；【军】(火炮)自行的. ②装备有自行火炮的。
self-pro·tec·tion [ˈselfprəˈtekʃən] *n.* 自我防护，自卫. *a means of* ~ *against riot* 防备暴乱的自卫手段。
self-ques·tion·ing [ˈselfˈkwesʃəniŋ] *n.* 反省。
self-re·act·ing [ˈselfriːˈæktiŋ] *a.* 自动适应的，自动调整的。
self-read·ing [ˈselfˈriːdiŋ] *a.* 易读的。
self-re·al·i·za·tion [ˈselfˌriəlaiˈzeiʃən] *n.* 本人才能的充分发挥。
self-re·cord·ing [ˈselfriˈkɔːdiŋ] *a.* 自动记录的，自记的。
self-re·flec·tion [ˈselfrifˈlekʃən] *n.* 反省。
self-re·gard [ˈselfriˈgɑːd] *n.* ①利己，利己心. ②自尊，自尊心。
self-reg·is·ter·ing [ˈselfˈredʒistəriŋ] *a.* 自动记录的. *a* ~ *anemometer* (自记)风力计。
self-reg·u·la·tion [ˈselfˌreguˈleiʃən] *n.*【自】自动调整，自动调节。
self-re·li·ance [ˈselfriˈlains] *n.* 依靠自己；自力更生。
self-re·nun·ci·a·tion [ˈselfriˌnʌnʃiˈeiʃən] *n.* 献身；舍己，牺牲自己；大公无私。
self·rep·li·cat·ing [ˈselfˈreplikeitiŋ] *a.* 自我复制的。
self-re·proach [ˈselfriˈprəutʃ] *n.* 自责；后悔。
self-re·spect [ˈselfrisˈpekt] *n.* 自尊，自尊心；自重. *lose one's* ~ 丧失自尊心。
self-re·straint [ˈselfrisˈtreint] *n.* 自我克制，自我约束。
self-re·veal·ing [ˈselfriˈviːliŋ] *a.* 无意中流露的，自我暴露的。
self-rev·e·la·tion [ˈselfˌreviˈleiʃən] *n.* 无意中的流露；自我暴露。
self-right·eous [ˈselfˈraitʃəs] *a.* 自以为是的；自以为有道德的；伪善的。
self-rule, self-rul·ing [ˈselfˈruːl, -liŋ] *n.* = self-government.
self-sac·ri·fice [ˈselfˈsækrifais] *n.* 牺牲自己；自我牺牲。
self-same [ˈselfseim] *a.* 完全相同的，一样的. *We arrived here on the* ~ *day.* 我们恰好是同天到达这里的。
self-sat·is·fac·tion [ˈselfˌsætisˈfækʃən] *n.* 自鸣得意；自满。
self-sat·is·fied [ˈselfˈsætisfaid] *a.* 自满的，自鸣得意的。
self-seal·ing [ˈselfˈsiːliŋ] *a.* 自动封闭的；自行封口的；自固的. ~ **tank** 自封式油箱. ~ **tire** 自封式轮胎。
self-seek·er [ˈselfˈsiːkə] *n.* 追求私利的人；只求自己享乐的人。
self-seek·ing [ˈselfˈsiːkiŋ] *a.* 追求私利的；只求自己享乐的。
self-serv·ice [ˈselfˈsəːvis] *n., a.* 无人售货(的)；顾客自己取用(的). *a* ~ *cafeteria* 顾客自己取用食物的餐馆。
self-serv·ing [ˈselfˈsəːrviŋ] *a.* 为个人利益服务的；图私利的。
self-slaugh·ter [ˈselfˈslɔːtə] *n.* 自杀。
self-slay·er [ˈselfˈsleiə] *n.* 自杀者。
self-sow [ˈselfˈsəu] *vi.*【植】(植物利用风、水等自然力)自然播种。
self-sown [ˈselfˈsəun] *a.* 自然播种的，自然生长的。
self-start·er [ˈselfˈstɑːtə] *n.* ①【机】(内燃机的)自动起动装置. ②〔美口〕工作主动的人，自行发起某项计划等的人。
self-steer·ing [ˈselfˈstiəriŋ] *a.* (船)自操纵的，自动化驾驶的。
self-stud·y [ˈselfˈstʌdi] *n.* ①自我研究. ②自学。
self-styled [ˈselfˈstaild] *a.* 自称的，自封的. *a* ~ *authority on history* 自封的历史界权威。
self-suf·fi·cient [ˈselfsʌˈfiʃənt] *a.* ①自给自足的. ②过于自信的；傲慢的. **-cien·cy** [-ʃənsi] *n.*
self-sug·ges·tion [ˈselfsəˈdʒestʃən] *n.*【心】自觉暗示，自我暗示。
self-sup·port·ing [ˈselfsəˈpɔːtiŋ] *a.* ①自立的，自给的，自谋生活的. ②【建】自承的. *a* ~ *student* 工读生。
self-sur·ren·der [ˈselfsəˈrendə] *n.* 自动屈从；沉溺，放任。
self-sus·tain·ing [ˈselfsəsˈteiniŋ] *a.* ①自给的，自立的。

②【建】自承的. ③自保持的.

self-taught [ˈselfˈtaut] *a.* 自学的, 自修的; 自学而获得的. *Japanese Self-Taught* 《日语自修读本》.

self-tim•er [ˈselfˈtaimə] *n.*【摄】自拍器,快门自动关闭装置.

self-tor•ture [ˈselfˈtɔːtʃə] *n.* 苦行; 自我折磨.

self-ward(s) [ˈselfwəːd(z)] *ad., a.* ①向自己地[的]; 朝着自己地[的]. ②内向地[的].

self-will [ˈselfˈwil] *n.* 任性; 固执己见. **-ed** *a.* 任性的; 执拗的.

self-wind•ing [ˈselfˈwaindiŋ] *a.* (钟等)自动上发条的.

self-wrong [ˈselfˈrɔːŋ] *n.* 自作孽; 自我戕害.

Sel•juk [selˈdʒuːk] *n.* (土耳其的)塞尔柱王朝; 塞尔柱朝君主[臣民]. — *a.* = Seljukian.

sel•juk•i•an [selˈdʒuːkiən] *a.* 塞尔柱王朝的,塞尔柱王朝时代人的.

sell [sel]*(sold* [səuld]*)* *vt.* ①卖,售 *(opp.* buy*)*; 促进…的销路,使好卖. ②〔喻〕出卖(朋友,节操),背叛(祖国). ③〔口〕〔通例用被动语态〕欺骗; 使失望. ④〔美〕宣传; 推荐; 说服; 使接受; 使赞成. *Do you ~ wine?* 有葡萄酒卖吗? *S- it for what it will bring.* 随市卖出. *The good quality will ~goods.* 高质量会促进货品销路. *Sold again!* 〔俚〕又上了一次当! *~ an idea to the public* 〔美〕对公众宣传某一种主张; 使公众接受一种观念. — *vi.* ①卖出,售出. ②销售 (=be sold). ③〔口〕得到承认[采纳]; 得到赞同. ④当店员; 做推销员. *The book ~s for ten dollars.* 此书售价十美元. *~ by the dozen* 按打出售. *~ at 10 for one yuan* 一块钱十个. *Beef ~s very dear.* 牛肉很贵. *a doctrine that will ~* 一种能被接受的学说. *To S-.* 〔标示〕出售. ***be sold on*** 〔美〕热中于…, 给…迷住. ***made to ~*** (不考究品质地)造来卖的. ***~ a bargain*** 愚弄, 欺骗. ***~ a match [game]*** 受贿赂故意输掉, 出卖比赛. ***~(sb.) a pup*** 〔美俚〕欺骗(某人). ***~ at a bargain*** 廉价卖出. ***~ at a Loss [sacrifice]*** 亏本卖出. ***~ at a profit*** 赚钱卖出. ***~ by public auction*** 拍卖. ***~ by retail*** 零售. ***~(by) wholesale*** 批发, 批售. ***~ down the river*** 〔美谑〕出卖. ***~ high*** 以高价卖出. ***~ like wildfire [hot cakes, T-shirts]*** 畅销. ***~ off*** (打折扣) 销完; 卖清(存货). ***~ one's life dear(ly)*** 使敌人蒙受巨大损失而后死. ***~ oneself*** ①卖身; 出卖人格. ②〔俚〕自我宣传, 自荐. ***~ out*** ①卖完; 脱销. ②〔美口〕欺骗. ③〔美俚〕出卖; 背叛. ***~ short***【交易所】卖空. ***~ time*** 接受播送广告业务. ***~ up*** 拍卖; 变卖 (债务人的财产以抵债). ***~ well*** 易于销售, 行销. — *n.* ①卖, 销售(术). ②〔俚〕欺骗; 诳骗. ③失望. *What a ~!* 多失望! 上当啦! **-a•ble** *a.* 可以出售的.

sell•er [ˈselə] *n.* ①卖主,卖方. ②行销货. *a good ~* 易于销售的货品. *a best ~* 畅销品; 畅销书. *a ~s' market* (缺货时)有利于卖方的市场.

sell•ing [ˈseliŋ] *n.* 出售; 卖. *a ~ price* 售价. *a ~ agent* 代销商店. *a ~ race* 出售(胜马的)赛马. —*a.* ①出售的, 卖的. ②销路好的. *a low ~ price* 使货物易销的低价.

sell-off [ˈselɔːf] *n.* 廉价抛售; 出清存货.

sell•out [ˈselaut] *n.* 〔美〕①满座的演出; 入场券全数销完的一场戏[比赛](等). ②(商品)售缺, 脱销. ③〔美俚〕出卖; 背叛; 告密.

Sel•ma [ˈselmə] *n.* 塞尔玛〔女子名〕.

sel•syn [ˈselsin] *n.*【电】①自动同步机,自整角机. ②直流自协调. *~ generator* 自动同步发电机.

Selt•zer [ˈseltsə] *n.* 塞尔查水〔一种德国矿泉水,亦作 ~ water〕; [s-]仿制的矿泉水.

sel•va [ˈselvə] *n.* ***(pl.*** ***~s)*** (南美亚马孙河流域) 热带雨林.

sel•vage, sel•vedge [ˈselvidʒ, ˈselvedʒ] *n.* ①【纺】织边; 布边; 纸边. ②【矿】(包围矿脉的)粘皮. ③【地】断层泥. ④锁的孔板. ⑤边缘; 断片. *make the best use of the ~s of one's time* 尽量利用片断[零碎]的时间.

sel•vaged [ˈselvidʒd] *a.* (织物)有织边的.

sel•va•gee [ˌselvəˈdʒiː] *n.*【海】(外缠细绳的)束环索.

selves [selvz] self 的复数.

SEM = scanning electron microscope 扫描电子显微镜.

Sem. = Seminary; Semitic.

sem. = semicolon.

se•man•teme [siˈmæntiːm] *n.*【语】义素〔语义单位〕.

se•man•tic [siˈmæntik] *a.* 语义(学)的.

se•man•ti•cist [siˈmæntisist] *n.* 语义学家.

se•man•tics [siˈmæntiks] *n.* ①【语】语义学. ②【哲】语义哲学; 语义学派.

sem•a•phore [ˈseməfɔː, -fɔə] *n.* ①(铁路的)臂板信号(机),信号(灯); 信号装置. ②(军队的)旗语通信(法). — *vt.* 打信号(机)通知. — *vi.* 打信号; 打旗语.

sem•a•phor•ic(al) [ˌseməˈfɔrik(əl)] *a.* ①臂板信号(机)的; 信号灯的; 信号装置的. ②用旗语通信的. **-cal•ly** *ad.*

se•ma•si•ol•o•gy [siˌmeisiˈɔlədʒi] *n.* = semantics ①.

se•mat•ic [siˈmætik] *a.*【生】(毒蛇等的颜色)预告危险的, 有警告作用的; 引起其他动物警戒的. *~ colours [coloration]* 警戒色.

sem•bla•ble [ˈsembləbl] *a.*〔古〕①相似的. ②合适的. ③显而易见的; 外观上的; 外表的; 表面的; 非真实的. — *n.*〔古〕①类似物. ②相似; 类似.

sem•blance [ˈsembləns] *n.* ①外观; 外貌, 外表; 样子. ②类似; 相似. ③貌似物. ④肖像. ⑤假装; 伪装. ***have no ~ of*** 一点不象…. ***have the ~ of*** 象…. ***in ~*** 外貌是; 外表上. ***in the ~ of*** 以…的姿态. ***make ~ (that, as if)*** 假装. ***put on a [make] ~ of*** 装做…(的样子). ***to the ~ of*** 象…似地. ***under the ~ of*** 装着…(的样子); 在…的幌子下. ***without even the ~ of*** 连象…的地方也没有,一点…的味道也没有.

se•mé [ˈsemei] *a.*〔F.〕【徽】(星、百合花等)小花纹星罗棋布的; 碎花纹的.

se•mei•ol•og•ra•phy [ˌsiːmaiˈɔgrəfi] *n.*【医】症状记录.

se•mei•ol•o•gy [ˌsiːmaiˈɔlədʒi], **se•mei•ot•ics** [-ˈɔtiks] *n.* ①【医】症状学. ②符号学. ③手势语言(= semiology).

sem•eme [ˈsemiːm] *n.*【语】词义要素; 义素.

se•men [ˈsiːmen] *n.* ***(pl. sem•i•na*** [ˈseminə], ***~s)*** ①【生理】精液. ②【植】种子; 胚种.

se•mes•ter [siˈmestə] *n.* 六个月的时期; (美、德等国学校课程的)半学年; 一学期. **-tral** [-trəl] *a.*

sem•i [ˈsemi] 〔口〕= semitrailer.

sem•i- *pref.* ①"半"; "部分". ②一半; (一段时期中)出现两次的: *semi*-colony, *semi*monthly.

sem•i-ab•stract [ˈsemiˈæbstrækt] *a.* (艺术品等)半抽象的.

sem•i•air-cooled [ˈsemiˈɛəkuːld] *a.* 半气冷的.

sem•i•an•nual [ˈsemiˈænjuəl] *a.* 半年一次的, 一年两次的. **-ly** *ad.*

sem•i•a•quat•ic [ˈsemiəˈkwætik] *a.*【植】半水生的; 近水生的;【动】半水栖的.

sem•i•ar•id [ˈsemiˈærid] *a.* 半干旱的.

sem•i•au•to•mat•ed [ˈsemiˌɔːtəˈmeitid] *a.* =semiautomatic.

sem•i•au•to•mat•ic [ˈsemiˌɔːtəˈmætik] *a.* (机器、武器等)半自动的.

sem•i•breve [ˈsemibriːv] *n.*【乐】全音符.

sem•i•cen•ten•ni•al [ˈsemisenˈtenjəl] *a.* ①五十年一度的. ②持续半个世纪的. —*n.* 五十周年; 五十周年纪念.

sem•i•cho•rus [ˈsemiˌkɔːrəs] *n.*【音】小合唱〔指部分合唱队员的合唱〕.

sem•i•cir•cle [ˈsemiˌsəːkl] *n.* ①半圆. ②半圆形体. *sit in a ~* 坐成半圆形.

sem•i•cir•cu•lar [ˈsemiˈsəːkjulə] *a.* 半圆形的. ~

canal【解】(耳的)半规管.
sem·i·civ·i·lized [ˈsemiˈsivilaizd] *a.* 半文明的，半开化的.
sem·i·clas·si·cal [ˈsemiˈklæsikəl] *a.* 半古典的. —*n.* 半古典的音乐[作品等].
sem·i·co·lon [ˈsemiˈkəulən] *n.* 分号〔;〕.
sem·i·co·lo·ni·al [ˈsemikəˈləunjəl] *a.* 半殖民地的.
sem·i·col·o·ny [ˈsemiˈkələni] *n.* 半殖民地.
sem·i·con·duc·tor [ˈsemikənˈdʌktə] *n.*【物】半导体.
sem·i·con·scious [ˈsemiˈkɔnʃəs] *a.* 半自觉的；半意识的；半知觉的.
sem·i·con·ser·va·tive [ˈsemikənˈsəːvətiv] *a.*【遗传】半保留的；半保守的.
sem·i·cyl·in·der [ˈsemiˈsilində] *n.* 半圆柱体.
sem·i·dai·ly [ˈsemiˈdeili] *a., ad.* 一天两次的[地].
sem·i·dem·i·sem·i·qua·ver [ˈsemiˈdemisemiˌkweivə] *n.*【乐】六十四分音符.
sem·i·de·tached [ˈsemidiˈtætʃt] *a.* 半分离的；(房屋)一侧与他屋相接的.
sem·i·di·am·e·ter [ˈsemidaiˈæmitə] *n.* 半径；【天】(天体的)视半径.
sem·i·di·ur·nal [ˈsemidaiˈəːnl] *a.* ①半天的；半天内做完的. ②半天一次的，一天两次的，每隔十二小时的.
sem·i·dome [ˈsemidəum] *n.*【建】半圆屋顶；半圆形天花板. **-d** *a.*
sem·i·dou·ble [ˈsemiˈdʌbl] *a.*【植】半重瓣的.
sem·i·el·lip·ti·cal [ˈsemiˈiliptikəl] *a.* 半椭圆(形)的.
sem·i·feu·dal [ˈsemiˈfjuːdl] *a.* 半封建的.
sem·i·fi·nal [ˈsemiˈfainl] *n., a.*【体】半决赛(的).
sem·i·fi·nal·ist [ˈsemiˈfainəlist] *n.* 半决赛选手.
sem·i·fin·ished [ˈsemiˈfiniʃt] *a.* ①【机】半加工的；半光制的. ②半完成的；半成品的.
sem·i·fin·ishing [ˈsemiˈfiniʃiŋ] *n.* 半精加工.
sem·i·for·mal [ˈsemiˈfɔːməl] *a.* 半正式的〔指衣着等〕.
sem·i·in·fi·nite [ˈsemiˈinfinit] *a.*【数】半无穷的，半无限的.
sem·i·lit·er·ate [ˈsemiˈlitərit] *a.* 半文盲的；略知阅读和书写的；识字而不会书写的.
sem·i·lu·nar [ˈsemiˈljuːnə] *a.* 半月形的.
sem·i·man·u·fac·tures [ˈsemiˌmænjuˈfæktʃəz] *n. pl.* 半成品.
sem·i·met·al [ˈsemiˈmetl] *n.*【物】半金属.
sem·i·me·tal·lic [ˈsemimiˈtælik] *a.* 半金属的.
sem·i·month·ly [ˈsemiˈmʌnθli] *a. ad.* 一月两次的[地]. — *n.* 半月刊.
sem·i·na [ˈseminə] *n.* semen 的复数.
se·mi·nal [ˈsiːminl, ˈse-] *a.* ①精液的. ②【生】胚种的，种子的. ③繁殖的，再生的，生殖的；生产(性)的；有力的. ④潜在的；(思想等)含蓄的. ⑤胚胎的；萌芽状态的；待发育的；将大为发展的. ⑥根本的，基本的. ～ *fluid [semen]* 精液. ～ *power* 生殖力. *the* ～ *principle* 基本原则. *in a* ～ *state* 在胚胎状态中的；处于待发达状态中的. ～ **cup**【昆】卵突杯. ～ **duct**【解】输精管. ～ **leaf**【植】子叶. ～ **receptacle [reservoir]**【解】受[蓄]精囊. **-ly** *ad.*
sem·i·nar [ˈseminɑː] *n.* ①(大学的)研究班；研究小组. ②研究室；研究科目. ③〔美〕(专家)讨论会；讲习会.
sem·i·nar·i·an [ˌsemiˈnɛəriən] *n.* 神学院学生.
sem·i·nar·ist [ˈsemiˌnɛərist] *n.* =seminarian.
sem·i·na·ry [ˈseminəri] *n.* ①高等中学；女子中学〔学院〕. ②神学校[院]；养成所. ③发源地；温床. ④= seminar. *a* ～ *of revolution* 革命的温床. *a* ～ *of vice* 罪恶的渊薮.
sem·i·na·tion [ˌsemiˈneiʃən] *n.* =dissemination.
sem·i·nif·er·ous [ˌsemiˈnifərəs] *a.* ①【植】生种子的，结子的. ②生精液的，输精的. ～ *tubes* 输精管.
sem·i·niv·o·rous [ˌsemiˈnivərəs] *a.* 食种子为生的.
Sem·i·nole [ˈseminəul] *n. (pl.* ～, ～*s)* (印第安人的)塞米诺尔族；塞米诺尔语.
sem·i·no·ma [ˈsemiˈnəumə] *n.*【医】睾丸肿瘍.
sem·i·oc·ca·sion·al·ly [ˈsemiəˈkeiʒənlli] *ad.*〔美口〕偶然地.
sem·i·of·fi·cial [ˈsemiəˈfiʃəl] *a.* 半官方的. *a* ～ *statement* 半官方的声明. **-ly** *ad.*
se·mi·ol·o·gy [ˌsemiˈɔlədʒi] *n.* ①【医】症状学. ②符号学. ③手势语言. **-o·log·ic** [-əˈlɔdʒik], **-o·log·i·cal** *a.* **-o·log·ist** *n.*
se·mi·ot·ic [ˌsemiˈɔtik] *n.* 〔常用复数，动词用单数〕【哲】符号论；符号学. — *a.* = semiotical.
se·mi·ot·i·cal [ˌsemiˈɔtikəl] *a.* ①与符号有关的；符号学的. ②症状学的. **-ti·cian** *n.* 符号学专家；症状学研究者.
sem·i·o·vip·a·rous [ˈsemiəuˈvipərəs] *a.*【动】半卵生的〔如袋鼠等，未完全发育即出生，因而需在母体袋中生活一段时期〕.
sem·i·pal·mate [ˈsemiˈpælmit] *a.*【动】半蹼足[趾]的.
sem·i·par·a·site [ˈsemiˈpærəsait] *n.*【动】半寄生(= hemiparasite).
sem·i·per·me·a·ble [ˈsemiˈpəːmjəbl] *a.* 半渗透的.
sem·i·post·al [ˈsemiˈpəustəl] *a.* 半邮政的. — *n.* 半邮政邮票〔售价高于票面值，其收益多用于非邮政的公用事业〕.
sem·i·pre·cious [ˈsemiˈpreʃəs] *a.* (宝石)半珍贵的；不算太珍贵的〔指石榴石，绿松石，蛋白石等〕.
sem·i·pri·vate [ˈsemiˈpraivit] *a.* 半私用的；〔尤指〕(医院病房)私人半专用的〔指资本主义国家医院病房的等级，大体分为普通病房，私人半专用病房，私人专用病房〕.
sem·i·pro [ˈsemiprəu] *n., a.* 半职业性选手(的)〔semi-professional 之略〕.
sem·i·pro·duc·tion [ˈsemiprəˈdʌkʃən] *n.*【经】中间生产.
sem·i·pro·fes·sion·al [ˈsemiprəˈfeʃənl] *a.* 半职业性的；〔尤指〕(体育等)半职业性活动的；由半职业性运动员从事的. — *n.* 半职业性运动员. **-ly** *ad.*
sem·i·pub·lic [ˈsemiˈpʌblik] *a.* 半公开的.
sem·i·qua·ver [ˈsemiˌkweivə] *n.*【乐】十六分音符.
sem·i·re·li·gious [ˈsemiˈrilidʒəs] *a.* 半宗教性的.
sem·i·re·tired [ˈsemiriˈtaiəd] *a.* 半退休的.
sem·i·rev·o·lu·tion [ˈsemiˌrevəˈluːʃən] *n.* 半回转.
sem·i·rig·id [ˈsemiˈridʒid] *a.* (飞艇)半硬式的.
sem·i·sav·age [ˈsemiˈsævidʒ] *a.* 半野蛮的. — *n.* 半野蛮人.
sem·i·sil·low [ˈsemiˌsailəu] *n.*【农】半休闲.
sem·i·skilled [ˈsemiˈskild] *a.* (工人)半熟练的；只需有限训练即可操作的.
sem·i·soft [ˈsemiˈsɔft] *a.* 半软的〔如干酪〕.
sem·i·som·nus [ˈsemiˈsɔmnəs] *n.*【医】半[轻]昏迷；昏睡.
sem·i·star [ˈsemiˈstɑː] *n.*〔美俚〕二流电影明星；二流演员.
sem·i·starved [ˈsemiˈstɑːvd] *a.* 半饥饿的.
sem·i·steel [ˈsemiˈstiːl] *n.*【冶】高级铸铁；钢性铸铁；半钢质.
sem·i·syn·the·tic [ˈsemisinˈθetik] *a.*【化】半合成的.
Sem·ite [ˈsiːmait, ˈse-] *n.* 闪族(人)，闪米特族(人)〔古代包括希伯来人、亚述人、腓尼基人、阿拉伯人、巴比伦人等〕；〔今特指〕犹太人. — *a.* = Semitic.
Se·mit·ic [siˈmitik, seˈm-] *a.* 闪族(语言)的；〔今特指〕犹太人的. — *n.* 闪语〔希伯莱语、阿拉伯语等〕.
Se·mit·ics [siˈmitiks, seˈm-] *n. pl.* 〔动词用单数〕闪族学〔研究闪族的文化、语言、文学等的科学〕.
Sem·it·ism [ˈsemitizəm] *n.* ①闪语表达方式. ②闪族人气质；闪族人性格；闪族人思想. ②亲犹太人思想

〔主义〕.

Sem·i·to-Ha·mit·ic [ˈsemitəuhæˈmitik] *a.* 亚非语系的，闪含语系的 (= Afro-Asiatic).

sem·i·tone [ˈsemitəun] *n.*【乐】半音；半音程. *a major [minor]* ~ 长[短]半音.

sem·i·trail·er [ˈsemiˌtreilə] *n.* 半拖车；单轴拖车；双轮拖车，挂车.

sem·i·trans·par·ent [ˈsemitrænsˈpɛərənt] *a.* 半透明的.

sem·i·trop·i·c(al) [ˈsemiˈtrɔpikəl] *a.* 副热带的；亚热带的.

sem·i·tur·bu·lent [ˈsemiˈtə:bjulənt] *a.* 半湍流的.

sem·i·u·ni·form [ˈsemiˈju:nifɔ:m] *a.* 半均匀的.

sem·i·vo·cal [ˈsemiˈvəukəl] *a.*【语音】半元音的.

sem·i·vow·el [ˈsemiˈvauəl] *n.*【语音】半元音〔英语 w, y 的发音〕；半元音字母〔指如 w, y〕.

sem·i·week·ly [ˈsemiˈwi:kli] *ad., a.* 每半周一次(的)；一周两次(的). — *n.* 半周刊；三日刊.

sem·i·works [ˈsemiwə:ks] *n. pl.* 〔用作 *sing.* 或 *pl.*〕(试制新产品或试行新工艺的)小规模工厂.

sem·i·year·ly [ˈsemiˈjə:li] *a., ad.* 一年两次的[地]；半年一次的[地]. — *n.* 半年刊.

sem·o·la [ˈsemələ], **sem·o·li·na** [ˌseməˈli:nə] *n.* (做布丁等用的)粗粒面粉.

sem·per [ˈsempə] *ad.* 〔L.〕经常；永远. ~ *fidelis* [fiˈdeilis] 永远忠诚〔美海军陆战队箴言〕 ~ *paratus* [pəˈreitəs] 永远有准备；时刻准备着 〔美海岸警卫队箴言〕.

sem·per·vi·vum [ˌsempəˈvaivəm] *n.*【植】长生草属(*Sempervivum*)植物.

sem·pi·ter·nal [ˈsempiˈtə:nl] *a.* 〔诗〕永久的；永远的.

sem·pli·ce [ˈsemplitʃi] *a., ad.* 〔It.〕【乐】单纯的[地]；自然的[地]；真实的[地]；无装饰音的[地].

sem·pre [ˈsempri] *ad.* 〔It.〕【乐】自始至终(按照指示的色调演奏). ~ ***forte***【音】始终强音地. ~ ***piano***【音】始终柔和地.

semp·stress [ˈsem*p*stris] *n.* = seamstress.

sen [sen] *n.* (*sing., pl.*) ①钱〔日本辅币的单位，等于1/100日元〕. ②仙〔印度尼西亚等的辅币单位〕.

Sen. = ①Senate. ②Senator. ③Senior.

sen., senr. = senior.

se·na·ry [ˈsi:nəri] *a.* 六(个)的；六进制的；以六为基础的. ~ *division* 六分. ~ *scale*【数】六进制.

sen·ate [ˈsenit] *n.* ①(古罗马的)元老院. ②[S-](美、法等国议会的)参议院；上(议)院. ③立法机构(全体成员)；立法程序. ④(剑桥大学等的)评议会；理事会. ~ **house** ①参议院议事厅. ②(剑桥大学等的)评议会办公处 (*a* ~ *house examination* 剑桥大学等的学位考试. *a* ~ *house problem* 上述考试中的数学题).

sen·a·tor [ˈsenətə] *n.* ①参议员；上(议)院议员. ②(古罗马)元老院议员. (剑桥 等大学的)评议员；理事. ③〔美〕参议员〔对现任或前任参议员的尊称〕. **-ship** *n.* 参议员〔上议院议员〕的地位[职务，任期].

sen·a·to·ri·al [ˌsenəˈtɔ:riəl] *a.* ①参议院[员]的；上(议)院的. ②元老院(议员)的. ③〔美〕有参议员选举权的. ④(大学)评议会的. ~ **courtesy** 〔美〕参议院礼貌否决〔当总统任命某州官员受到该州参议员反对时，参议院为对这些参议员表示尊重而对总统任命不予认可〕. ~ **district** 〔美〕参议员选举区. **-ly** *ad.*

se·na·tus [siˈneitəs] *n.* 〔L.〕①(古罗马的)元老院. ②(苏格兰某些大学的)评议会.

send[1] [send] *vt.* (***sent*** [sent]) ①送；寄. ②打发；派；遣(使者等). ③发(信). ④放；投；掷；射(球、箭等). ⑤传递(酒等). ⑥【电】传导；输送. ⑦(神等)赏；赐；降；施. ⑧促使；使处于；使陷入；使(变)成…. ⑨〔美俚〕(尤指奏摇摆音乐)使兴奋；使心荡神移. ~ *a messenger* 派人送信. *S- help at once!* 请立刻派帮手来！ ~ *a person mad* 使人发狂. *These records used to* ~ *her.* 这些唱片过去往往使她听得如醉如痴. *God* ~ *it may (not) be so!* 但望(不)是这样. — *vi.* ①派人；遣人. ②送音讯；寄信；【电】播送. ③〔美俚〕如醉如狂地唱[奏]爵士即兴音乐. *If you want me, please* ~. 假若有事找我，请即告知. ~ ***along*** 随即发送；使加紧；促进. ~ ***and do*** 派人去做. ~ ***away*** ①撵走；开除；解雇. ②把…送到远处；写信[派人]至远方. ③派人去拿 [去请] (*for*). ~ ***down*** ①〔英大学俚〕勒令退学；开除. ②使下降；使下落；使减少. ③使到(饭厅)去. ~ ***(sb.) flying*** 解雇某人；撵走某人；打走某人；把某人打倒在地. ~ ***for*** 派人去叫[请]；遣人去拿；乞求(~ *for a doctor* 派人去请医生. ~ *for a book* 派人去拿一本书). ~ ***forth [out]*** ①送出；发送. ②发出(香气). ③长[生]出(芽，枝等). ④派遣. ⑤出口. ~ ***in*** ①送. ②拿出；提出. ③递(名片). ④参加展览. (~ *in one's papers* (海陆军人等)提出辞呈；呈请辞职. ~ *in one's jacket* 辞职. ~ *in one's name* 申请参加(比赛)). ~ ***off*** ①寄出；发(信、货等). ②驱逐；撵走. ③送别(出走、旅行等的人). ④差遣；辞退. ~ ***on*** ①转送；转寄(信等)；②预送；先送(*Please* ~ *the letter on to my mother.* 请将此信转送家母). ~ ***one's love*** (*to sb.*)向(某人)问安. ~ ***out*** = ~ ***forth.*** ~ ***over*** 播送. ~ ***packing*** 解雇；撵走；开除 (*He was sent packing for stealing.* 他因盗窃被开除). ~ ***round*** ①传递；使传阅. ②派遣(*A notice was being sent round to the representatives.* 在代表中传阅一项通知). ~ ***through*** 报告；通知(消息等). ~ ***(sb.) to school***〔美俚〕把某人送入感化院. ~ ***up*** ①弄上去；使上升. ②提出(报告等). ③传递(球等). ④检举. ⑤〔美口〕把某人送进监牢. ⑥端出(饭菜). ⑦【海】扬(帆). ⑧冷笑；〔英〕(采用模仿办法)使显得可笑. ~ ***word*** 通知；报知；转告. **~-out** *n.* 送出[输出]量. **~-up** (装作严肃的)讽刺性模仿；讽刺.

send[2] [send] *n.* 〔海〕①波浪的推(进)力. ②船的纵摇. ③〔美俚〕摇摆音乐化；摇摆乐的即兴演奏. ④〔Scot.〕使者. — *vi.* 【海】(船被波浪推着)前进；(纵摇时)船头[船尾]向上翘起.

Sen·dai [ˈsenˈdai] *n.* 仙台〔日本城市〕.

sen·dal [ˈsendl] *n.* ①森丹绸〔中世纪产的一种薄绸，做衣服、旗帜等用〕. ②森丹绸袍.

send·er [ˈsendə] *n.* ①发送人；送货人. ②【讯】发射机；发送机；发报机；发射器. ③(天线)引向器；记发器. ④(电报)电键. ⑤〔美俚〕能使人兴奋若狂的爵士即兴音乐演奏者. *a multi-class* ~ 万用记发器[记录器]. *a* ~ *decoder* 发报机译码器. *the* ~ *of a letter* 发信人.

send·ing [ˈsendiŋ] *n.* ①发送，派遣；【讯】发射. ②信件 ③神赐，天降. ~ **set** 发射机 ~ **station** 发射台；发信局.

send-off [ˈsendˈɔ:f] *n.* ①送别；欢送. ②发动；起动. ③〔美俚〕(开创事业时的)鼓励. (吹捧性质的)推荐；介绍. ④〔美俚〕送葬；葬礼. *a* ~ *party* 欢送会. *give (sb.) a fine* ~ 〔口〕盛大欢送(某人).

Sen·e·ca [ˈsenikə] *n.* ①印第安人的塞尼加族. ②**Lucius** ~卢修斯·塞尼加〔公元前4？—公元65，罗马政治家，哲学家，作家〕.

sen·e·ga [ˈsenigə] *n.*【植】美远志；美远志根〔治蛇毒咬伤，亦用作祛痰药〕.

Sen·e·gal [ˌseniˈgɔ:l] *n.* ①塞内加尔〔非洲〕. ②〔the ~〕塞内加尔河〔非洲〕. **~ese** [ˈseligəˈli:z]① *n.* 塞内加尔人. ② *a.* 塞内加尔(人)的.

se·nesce [siˈnes] *vi.* 开始衰老.

se·nes·cent [ˈsenisnt] *a.* 衰老的；开始衰老的.

sen·es·chal [ˈseniʃəl] *n.* (中世纪贵族的)管家；执事.

se·nhor [seˈnjɔ:] *n.* (*pl.* ~*s,* ***se·nho·res*** [seˈnjɔ:ri:z]) ①〔Portu.〕先生(= Mr., Sir)；绅士. ***se·nhor·a*** [seˈnjɔ:rə] *n.*〔Portu.〕夫人；太太，***se·nho·ri·ta*** [ˌsenjɔ:ˈri:tə] *n.* 〔Portu.〕小姐.

se·nile [ˈsi:nail] *a.* ①老年的；因年老发生的；衰老的. ②【地】老年期的. ~ *atrophy* 老衰性萎缩. ~ *dementia*

老年性痴呆. ～ *river* 老年河.

se·nil·i·ty [si'niliti] *n.* 老迈;衰老;老耄.

Sen·ior ['si:njə] *n.* 西尼尔〔姓氏〕.

sen·ior ['si:njə] *(opp.* junior*)* *a.* ①年长的;(同名两人中)年纪较大的. ★ 略作 Sen., Senr. 或 Sr., 附在姓名后,以区别父子或两个同姓的人: *John Smith, Sr.* 老〔大〕约翰·史密斯. ②前辈的;先辈的;资格老的;资深的. ③上席的;上级的;高级的. ④〔美〕(中学)最高年级的;(大学)四年级的;毕业班的:〔英〕高年级的. *a ～ statesman* 富有资历的政治家. *a ～ officer* 高级军官. *a ～ man* 高班(学)生. *a ～ citizen* 老年人〔尤指退休老人〕. *a ～ counsel* 首席律师. *the ～ partner* (股份公司的)董事长;主持人;(商行的)主要合并人. *the ～ branch of a family* 一个家族的嫡系. **～ in office** 上级的. ***the ～ service*** 〔英〕海军. — *n.* ①年长者. ②前辈;上司;上级;资历深者. ③〔英〕高班生;〔美〕(中学)最高年级生,(大学)四年级生;毕业班生;〔英〕高年级生. *Paul is his brother's ～ by two years.* 保罗比弟弟大两岁. ～ **high school** 〔美〕高级中学(10—12年级).

sen·i·o·res pri·o·res [ˌsi:ni'ɔ:ri:z prai'ɔ:ri:z] 〔L.〕让年长者居先;先老后小.

sen·i·or·i·ty [ˌsi:ni'ɔriti] *n.* ①年长;上级,前辈. ②老资格;年资深;资历. *Promotion goes by ～.* 按资历晋升. *the first on the ～ list* 资格最老的成员. ～**rule** 〔美〕资深通例〔国会中由多数党资历最老议员任委员会主席的规定〕.

sen·na ['senə] *n.* ①【植】山扁豆属植物;番泻树. ②【药】番泻叶〔缓泻剂〕.

sen·net ['senit] *n.* 〔古〕(演员上下场的)喇叭奏鸣;号角.

sen·night, se'n·night ['senait] *n.* 〔古〕一星期. *Tuesday ～* 一星期前〔后〕的星期二.

sen·nit ['senit] *n.* ①【海】(通常由三根至九根打成的)扁索. ②草帽辫.

se·ñor [se'njɔ:] *n.* 〔Sp.〕*(pl.* ***se·ñores*** [-'njɔ:res]*)* ①先生〔与姓氏连用〕. ②绅士.

se·ño·ra [se'njɔ:rə] *n.* 〔Sp.〕①太太,夫人〔与姓氏连用〕. ②女士.

se·ño·ri·ta [ˌsenjə'ri:tə] *n.* 〔Sp.〕①小姐〔与姓氏连用〕. ②女士.

sen·sate ['senseit] *a.* ①有感觉的;有知觉力的. ②由感官知觉到的,感觉到的. ～ *matters* 可感知的物质. —*vt., vi.* 〔罕〕感觉,感知. **-ly** *ad.*

sen·sa·tion [sen'seiʃən] *n.* ①感觉;知觉. ②兴奋的感情;感动;激动. ③轰动;轰动一时的事物. *a ～ of fear* 恐怖感. *a disagreeable ～* 不愉快的感觉. *create [cause, make] a ～* 使感动;动人视听;引起世人注意;引起轰动. *a literary ～* 轰动文坛的作品. *a ～ of the first magnitude* 最为轰动的大事件. *three days' ～* 一时的轰动;昙花一现的声名. *the latest ～* (戏剧、事件等)最新的轰动一时的事物.

sen·sa·tion·al [sen'seiʃənəl] *a.* ①感觉的;感情的;感动的;知觉的;有感觉的. ②使感动的;轰动世间的;惊动社会的;耸人听闻的;令人激动的. ③投合时好的. ④非常的;异常的;(胜利等)巨大的. ⑤出名的. ⑥【哲】感觉论的. *a ～ crime* 骇人听闻的罪行. *a ～ victory* 巨大的胜利. *a ～ novel* 轰动一时的小说. **-ism** *n.* ①【哲】感觉论. ②【伦】官能主义. ③(文艺上)耸人听闻的手法. ④投合时好的行为. **-ist** *n.* ①感觉论者;官能主义者. ②采用耸人听闻手法的人. **-ly** *ad.*

sen·sa·tion·al·ize [sen'seiʃənlˌaiz] *vt.* *(-ized, -iz·ing)* 使引起轰动;耸人听闻地报道〔渲染〕.

sense [sens] *n.* ①感官;官能. ②感觉;知觉;…感;…心. ③意念;观念;意识. ④感觉器;【计】感受;读出. ⑤〔*pl.*〕理智;理性. ⑥思考;辨别力;判断力;见识. ⑦【数】指向;向旨;方向. ⑧意味;意义. ⑨公众意见〔情绪〕;舆论. *the ～s = the five ～s* 五官. *a sixth ～ = the muscular ～* 第六官能,运动觉;〔口〕直觉. *a ～ of duty* 责任感. *a ～ of honour* 名誉心. *a ～ of time* 时间的观念. *the moral ～* 道德观念. *a man of ～* 有理智的人. *common ～* 常识;通情达理. *good ～* 健全的见识;明智的判断;切合实际的想法;通情达理. *～ of current* 【电】电流方向. *～ of organization* 组织性. ***against all ～s*** 荒谬绝伦. ***be lost [dead] to all ～ of shame*** 全不知耻. ***bring sb. to his ～s*** 使某人醒悟过来. ***come to one's ～s*** 恢复理性;恢复知觉;苏醒过来;醒悟过来. ***have a keen ～ of duty*** 责任心极强. ***have more ～ than to = have too much ～ to*** 因为有头脑所以不会做…. ***have no ～ of humour*** 不懂幽默. ***have the ～ to (do)*** 有…做的头脑 (*He had not the ～ to do so.* 他没有这样做的脑筋). ***in all ～s*** (= in every ～) 在任何一点上;在各种意义上;彻头彻尾. ***in a broad [narrow] ～*** 在广〔狭〕义上. ***in a ～*** 在某种意义上;有一点儿. ***in every ～*** = in all ～s. ***in no ～*** 决不是. ***in one's ～s*** 精神正常;头脑清醒;有理智. ***in some ～*** 在某种意义上;在某种程度上. ***in the direct ～ of the word*** 按照这个词的原义. ***in the true ～*** 名副其实的. ***lose one's ～s*** 昏过去;发痴;发疯. ***make ～*** (话等)有意义;合理;有道理;讲得通(*What you say doesn't make ～ to me.* 你说的话我不能理解). ***make ～ of*** 了解〔弄懂〕…的意义 (*Can you make ～ of what she says?* 你懂得她说的是什么意思吗?). ***make ～ out of nonsense*** 弄清胡涂话的意义. ***out of one's (right) ～*** (神智)失常;发疯;(醉得)胡里胡涂 (*It almost frightened me out of my ～s.* 几乎把我魂都吓掉了). ***speak [talk] ～*** 讲得有理;说有意义的话. ***stand to ～*** 〔口〕有道理;说得有理. ***take leave of one's ～s*** 精神失常;发疯. ***take the ～ of*** 弄明白…的意向 (*take the ～ of the meeting* 问清到会群众的意见). ***talk ～*** = speak ～. ***There is no [some] ～ in doing*** … 做…是没有〔有一些〕道理的〔意义的〕(=It doesn't make ～ to do…). — *vt.* ①感觉到;觉得;〔美口〕发觉. ②了解;理会;明白. ③【自】自动检测. ～ **antenna** 辨向天线. ～ **cell** 感觉细胞. ～ **centre** 感觉中枢. ～ **datum** 感性材料;感性资料. ～ **detector [finder]** 【电】探向器;定向器;单值无线电测向器. ～ **organ** 感(觉器)官. ～ **perception** 感性知觉. ～**-preserving** *a.* 【拓】保向的. ～ **signal** 探向信号. ～ **stress** = sentense stress. ～ **winding [wire]** 【计】读出线,读出绕组.

sense·less ['senslis] *a.* ①无知觉的,无感觉的,不省人事的. ②无知的;愚蠢的. ③无意义的. *a ～ person* 胡涂虫. *a ～ argument* 谬论. ***fall ～*** 晕倒;失去知觉. ***knock sb. ～*** 把某人打得晕过去. **-ly** *ad.*

sen·si·bil·i·ty [ˌsensi'biliti] *n.* ①感性,感觉(力). ②敏感(性);灵敏度. ③感受性;感光性;感光度;感度. ④〔常 *pl.*〕感情;(诗歌的)感伤情调. *wound sb.'s sensibilities* 伤人感情.

sen·si·ble ['sensəbl, -sibl] *a.* ①能感觉到的;可觉察的;明显的. ②发觉;觉悟;明白;感知;知道 *(of)*. ③懂事的;有常识的;通情达理的;明智的;合情合理的;有理智的;(人、方法等)聪明的. ④有知觉的. ⑤(计划等)切合实际的;实用的. ⑥(数量等)相当大的. ⑦〔古〕易感的;敏感的 *(to)*. *a ～ change for the better [worse]* 显著变好〔坏〕. *He was ～ enough to mind his own business.* 他很聪明,不管别人闲事. *I'm very ～ of your kindness.* 我深感您的好意. ～ *clothing* 实用的衣服. *a ～ idea* 明智的意见. *a ～ man* 聪明人. *a ～ plan* 切合实际的计划. *a ～ proposal* 合理的建议. *a ～ reduction in price* 大幅度降价. ～ **heat** 【物】显热 (*opp.* latent heat). **-ness** *n.* 懂事;明智.

sen·si·bly ['sensəbli, -si-] *ad.* ①能感觉到地. ②显著地;明显地. ③敏感地;易感觉地. ④聪明地,乖巧地.

sens·ing ['sensiŋ] *n.* ①感觉. ②【无】测向;偏航显示;【计】读出. *remote ～* 遥感. ～ *elements* 灵敏部件. ～ *units* 传感器.

sen·si·tive [ˈsensitiv] *a.* ①有感觉的. ②敏感的, 感觉灵敏的; 敏锐的. ③易受伤的. ④(神经)过敏的, 神经质的. ⑤易于发生反应的. ⑥(软片等)感光的. ⑦(市场等)易波动的; 易受影响的. ⑧极机密的; 极微妙的. ⑨〔罕〕感觉的; 感官的. ~ *faculty* 感性; 感(觉)官(能). *a* ~ *position* 一个涉及高度机密而微妙的职位. ***be* ~ *to*** 对…敏感; 易感受…. ~ ***about one's appearance*** 关心外表; 注意修饰. ~ **paper**【摄】感光纸. ~ **plant**【植】含羞草. ~ **strain**【植】敏感晶系〔菌株〕. **-ly** *ad.*

sen·si·tiv·i·ty [ˌsensiˈtiviti] *n.* ①敏感(性); 感受性. ②(仪器等的)灵敏性. ③【摄】感光度.

sen·si·ti·za·tion [ˌsensitaiˈzeiʃən] *n.* ①【医】敏感(作用); 感受(作用); 致敏(感). ②【物】敏化, 激活. ③【摄】感光.

sen·si·tize [ˈsensitaiz] *vt., vi.* ①(使)〔变〕敏感. ②【物】(使)敏化; 激活. ③(使)(照相底片)具感光力; (使)(照相底片)易于感光.

sen·si·tom·e·ter [ˌsensiˈtɔmitə] *n.*【物, 摄】感光计; 曝光表.

sen·sor [ˈsensə] *n.* ①=sensory (*n.*). ②【自】感受器; 传感器; 灵敏元件, 控制仪板上显示温度、幅射量等变动的装置.

sen·so·ri·al [senˈsɔːriəl] *a.* = sensory (*a.*).

sen·so·ri·mo·tor [ˌsensəriˈməutə] *a.*【生理, 心】感觉运动的.

sen·so·ri·um [senˈsɔːriəm] *n.* (*pl.* ~*s*, *-ri·a* [-riə]) ①【解】感觉中枢. ②【医】意识; (整个人体的)感官系统.

sen·so·ry [ˈsensəri] *a.* ①感觉(上)的. ②【生理】感官的; 知觉器官的. — *n.* 感觉器官〔又作 ~ organs〕.

sen·su·al [ˈsensjuəl] *a.* ①肉体(上)的; 官能的. ②肉欲的. ③色情的; 淫荡的; 肉感的; 耽于肉欲的. ④【哲】感觉论的. *a* ~ *attraction* [*charm*] 肉欲上的吸引力. ~ *appetites* 肉欲. ~ *pleasures* 肉体〔官能〕上的快乐. *a* ~ *person* 好色的人. **-ism** *n.* ①【哲】感觉论. ②【美】官能主义; ③【伦】纵欲主义. ④肉欲主义; 好色. **-ist** ①【哲】感觉论者. ②肉欲主义者; 纵欲者; 好色者. **-ly** *ad.* **-ness** *n.*

sen·su·al·i·ty [ˌsensjuˈæliti] *n.* ①纵欲; 淫荡; 好色. ②感觉性; 感能.

sen·su·al·ize [ˈsensjuəlaiz] *vt.* 使荒淫; 使耽于声色.

sen·su·ous [ˈsensjuəs] *a.* ①感觉(上)的; 感官的. ②敏感的. ③官能享受的; (引起)美感的; 审美的. ★与 sensual 不同之处在于它不含丑恶意义.

sen·sur·round [sensəˈraund] *n.* (一座电影院内的)现场包围音响.

sent [sent] send 的过去式及过去分词. ***be* ~ *down south*** 〔美〕被送进监狱. ***be* ~ *off in disgrace*** 碰一鼻子灰走了. ***be* ~ *to the showers*** 〔美〕在比赛中被替换下场.

sen·tence [ˈsentəns] *n.* ①【法】宣判; 判决. ②判刑. ③【语法】句(子). ④【逻】命题. ⑤【乐】乐句. ⑥〔古〕名言; 格言. ⑦意见; 主张. *a* ~ *of death* 死刑. *a dark* ~ 难懂的文句. ***pass* ~ *upon* [*on*] *sb.*** 对某人判刑. ***serve a* ~** 服刑. ***under* ~ *of*** 被判决; 受…宣判. —*vt.* 宣判; 判决; 处刑. *be* ~*d to death* 被判处死刑. *be* ~*d for theft* 因盗窃罪被判刑. ~ **stress** [**accent**] 句子的重音. ~ **word** 相当于句子的单词〔Come! Certainly, 等〕.

sen·ten·tial [senˈtenʃəl] *a.* ①【法】判决的; 判断的. ②【语法】句子的. *a* ~ *analysis* 句子分析. *a* ~ *pause* 句的停顿.

sen·ten·tious [senˈtenʃəs] *a.* ①格言(多)的; 警句(多)的. ②简洁的. ③(故作)庄重的; 说教式的. **a** ~ **essayist** 爱用警句的杂文家. **-ly** *ad.* **-ness** *n.*

sen·tience, -en·cy [ˈsenʃəns,-si] *n.* ①感觉力〔性〕; 知觉(能)力. ②感觉; 知觉. ③直觉; 单纯的感性.

sen·tient [ˈsenʃənt] *a.* ①感觉的; 知觉的. ②有感觉〔知觉〕力的. ~ *cells* 感觉细胞. — *n.* 〔罕〕①有知觉〔感觉(力)〕的人〔物〕. ②意识; 心 (= mind).

sen·ti·ment [ˈsentimənt] *n.* ①(思想)感情; 情操. ②【艺术】情趣; 情感. ③情绪. ④感情上的弱点; 感伤. ⑤〔常 *pl.*〕意见; 观点. ⑥感想; 简短的致词. *patriotic* ~ 爱国心. *hostile* ~*s* 敌意. *a man of* ~ 感情用事的人. *a man of tender* [*noble*] ~ 多愁善感〔情操高尚〕的人. *general* ~ 一般意见; 舆论. *These are my* ~*s.* =〔谑〕*Them's my* ~*s* 这就是我的想法. ***ascertain sb.'s* ~*s on* [*regarding*] ...** 查明(某人)对于…的意见. ***free from* ~** 不带感伤情绪; 不夹杂个人好恶. ***give* [*propose*] *a* ~** 发表感想. ***run to* ~*s*** 感情用事.

sen·ti·men·tal [ˌsentiˈmentl] *a.* ①感情的; 情绪的; 情操的. ②感情用事的; 多愁善感的; 感伤的; 充满柔情的; 动情的. *a* ~ *girl* 多愁善感的姑娘. *a* ~ *drunkard* 酒后易动感情的人. ~ *considerations* [*motives*] 人情; 情面. *a* ~ *patriot* 慷慨悲歌之士. *strike a* ~ *note* (演讲等时)作出感情激动的姿态. ~ **damage**【保险】推定损害. **-ism** *n.* ①感情主义; 感伤主义. ②多愁善感; 故作多情. ③感情用事的言行; 牢骚. **-ist** *n.* 感情主义者; 感伤主义者; 多愁善感的人; 故作多情的人; 感情用事的人. **-ly** *ad.*

sen·ti·men·tal·i·ty [ˌsentimenˈtæliti] *n.* ①感伤性; 多愁善感; 柔情. ②故作多情.

sen·ti·men·tal·ize [ˌsentiˈmentəlaiz] *vi.* (*-ized, -izing*) 伤感; 感伤地想; 感伤地行事. ~ *over* [*about*] *the past* 思往事而伤感. — *vt.* ①使伤感; 使有感情. ②对…伤感; 感伤地看待〔处理〕. **-za·tion** *n.*

sen·ti·nel [ˈsentinl] *n.* ①哨兵; 步哨. ②看守人. *post* [*station*] *a* ~ 放(步)哨; 设看守(人). ***stand* ~ (*over*)** 站岗; 放哨; 守卫. —*vt.* (〔英〕*-ll-*) ①在…设岗哨. ②警戒, 守卫.

sen·try [ˈsentri] *n.*【军】①哨兵; 岗哨; 步哨. ②看守, 警卫. ③〔古〕望楼. *a* ~ *on colours* 军旗卫兵. ***be on* ~** 站岗, 看守. ***come off* ~** 下岗; 交班; 退哨. ***go on* ~** 上岗; 接班; 上哨. ***keep* ~** 警备; ***post on* ~** 放步哨; 使上哨. ***relieve a* ~** 换哨; 换班; 换防. ***stand* ~** 站岗; 看守; 放哨. —*vt.* 在…设岗哨. —*vi.* 站岗, 放哨. ~ **box** ①哨房; 岗亭. ②【无】调谐部分. ~ **duty** 步哨勤务. ~ **go** ①步哨勤务; 步哨线. ②换哨命令.

Se·nus·si, Se·nu·si [siˈnuːsi] *n.* (*pl.* *-si*) 北非穆斯林的一个战斗性同道会(的会员). **-si·an** *a.*

sen·za [ˈsentsə] *prep.* 〔It.〕〔略 s.〕【乐】无. ~ ***sordino*** 无弱音器. ~ ***stromenti*** 无乐器地. ~ ***tempo*** 不拘节拍地.

s.e.o.o. = 〔F.〕sauf erreur ou omission 错误遗漏不在此限.

Se·oul [səul] *n.* 汉城〔南朝鲜城市〕.

sep. = ①sepal. ②separate. ③septic.

Sep. = September.

sep·al [ˈsepəl, ˈsiːpl] *n.*【植】萼片.

se·pal·oid [ˈsiːplˌɔid] *a.*【植】萼片状的 (= sepaline).

sep·a·ra·bil·i·ty [ˌsepərəˈbiliti] *n.* 可分(离)性.

sep·a·ra·ble [ˈsepərəbl] *a.* 可分(离)的; 可分隔的; 可分开的 (*from; into; between*). **-bly** *ad.*

sep·a·rate[1] [ˈsepəreit] *vt.* ①分; 分开; 分离; 隔开; 隔离; 切断; 割断. ②区别; 分别; 识别. ③使脱离关系; 使分居. ④开革; 开除; 遣散; 使退役. ⑤【化】离析, 从…中提取. ~ *milk* 提取奶油. ***be* ~*d by*** 被…隔断. ***be* ~*d from*** 和…分离开; 和…分散. ~ ***into*** 分离成. — *vi.* ①分开; 离开; 分离; 脱离. ②(公司等)解散. ③分居. ④【化】离析, 析出.

sep·a·rate[2] [ˈseprit] *a.* ①分开的; 分离的 (*from*). ②各别的; 各自的; 各个的; 单独的; 独立的, 不相连的. ③分别开的; 分居的. ④离开肉体的. *a book in three* ~ *volumes* 分为三卷的书. ~ *houses* 独立式住宅. — *n.* ①(杂志论文的)抽印本; 单行本. ②〔*pl.*〕可以不配套单独穿的妇女服装. ③分开的事物. ~ **estate**[**property**]

(妻子的)独有财产. ～ **maintenance** (夫妻分居后妻子的)赡养费. ～ **school** (加拿大的)非公立学校(尤指天主教学校). **-ly** *ad.*

sep·a·ra·tion [ˌsepəˈreiʃən] *n.* ①分离;分类;分开. ②隔开;间隔;脱离. ③(夫妇的)分居. ④分隔物. ⑤【化】离析;析出;释出. ⑥【矿】分选. ⑦【电】(导线的)间距;间隙. ⑧【海】(装货的)隔票垫料. ⑨【地】(断层引起的)离距. ～ *of powers* (政府)权能的分立. *contact* ～ 【电】接点间隙. *judicial* ～ 【法】(法庭判定的)夫妇分居. ～ **allowance** (政府给出征军人家属的)分居津贴. ～ **centre** 【军】复员转业中心. ～ **coal** 精选煤. ～ **energy** 【物】结合能. ～ **pay** 遣散费. **-ist** *n.* ＝separatist.

sep·a·ra·tism [ˈsepərətizəm] *n.* ①(政治、宗教上的)分离主义;脱离主义. ②分离;分裂;脱离;隔离. *feudal* ～ 封建割据. **-tist** *n.* ①分离主义者. ②脱离国教的人. ③主张独立[自治]者.

sep·a·ra·tive [ˈsepərətiv] *a.* ①倾向分离的;分离(性)的. ②【动、植】区别性的. ③区别的;分别的.

sep·a·ra·tor [ˈsepəreitə] *n.* ①分离者. ②分离器;液体分离器;分液器;离析器;脱脂器. ③(蓄电池的)隔板. ④分离片;垫圈;隔离物;隔片. ⑤【矿】分选机. ⑥(数据项目)分隔标志. *an electric* ～ 滤波器.

sep·a·ra·to·ry [ˈsepərətəri] *a.* 使分离的;分离用的;离析用的. *a* ～ *funnel* 分液漏斗.

Se·phard [siˈfɑ:d] *n.* ＝ Sephardi.

Se·phar·di [seˈfɑ:di] *n.* *(pl.* **-dim** [-dim]*)* 西班牙[葡萄牙]籍的犹太人(的后裔). **-dic** *a.*

se·pi·a [ˈsi:pjə] *n.* *(pl.* ～*s,* **-pi·ae** [-pii:]*)* ①【动】乌贼;〔S-〕乌贼属. ②乌贼的墨汁;乌贼墨色;深褐色. ③用乌贼墨制成的深褐色颜料[墨水];用乌贼墨颜料[墨水]绘制的画. — *a.* 乌贼墨的;深棕色的;深褐色的.

se·pi·o·lite [ˈsi:piəlait] *n.* 【矿】海泡石.

se·poy [ˈsi:pɔi] *n.* 旧时英国军队中的印度兵.

sep·pu·ku [seˈpu:ku:] *n.* 〔日〕切腹自杀.

sep·sis [ˈsepsis] *n.* 【医】①腐败;腐败作用;败血. ②脓毒病;败血症.

sept [sept] *n.* (爱尔兰)氏族;(苏格兰)氏族中的部落.

Sept. ＝ ①September. ②Septuagint.

sept-, septa-, septem-, septi- *comb. f.* 七: *sept*angle, *septem*partite.

sep·ta [ˈseptə] *n.* septum 的复数.

sep·tal[1] [ˈseptl] *a.* 氏族(sept)的.

sep·tal[2] [ˈseptl] *a.* 【生】中隔 (septum)的;隔膜的;芽胞壁的.

sep·tan [ˈseptən] *a.* 【医】每七天复发一次的. ～ **fever** 【医】七日热.

sep·tan·gle [ˈseptæŋgl] *n.* 七角形,七边形.

sep·tan·gu·lar [sepˈtæŋgjulə] *a.* 七角(形)的,七边(形)的.

sep·tar·i·um [sepˈtɛəriəm] *n.* *(pl.* **-i·a** [-ə]*)* 【矿】龟背石;裂心结核;核桃心结核. **-tar·i·an** *a.*

sep·tate [ˈsepteit] *a.* 【生】有中隔[隔膜]的;分隔的.

Sep·tem·ber [sepˈtembə, səp-] *n.* 九月.

sep·tem·par·ti·te [ˌseptemˈpɑ:tait] *a.* ①由七部分组成的;分成七部分的. ②【植】七深裂的;七裂的.

sep·te·na·ry [sepˈti:nəri] *a.* ①七的;七个的;由七个组成的;以七为基础的. ②乘[除]以七的. ③七进制的. ④七年一次的;为期七年的;七年一度的. — *n.* ①七;七个. ②七年间. ③七进制. ④七个一套;七个一组. ⑤【诗】七音步的诗行.

sep·ten·nate [sepˈtenit] *n.* ①七年;七年期间;为期七年. ②七年的任期.

sep·ten·ni·al [sepˈtennjəl, -niəl] *a.* ①七年的;每七年的;七年一次的. ②继续七年的. **-ly** *ad.*

sep·ten·tri·o·nal [sepˈtentriənl] *a.* 〔古〕①北方的;北部的. ②来自北方的. ③北风的.

Sep·ten·tri·o·nes [septentriˈəuni:z] *n.* 北斗七星;大熊座.

sep·tette, 〔美〕**sep·tet** [sepˈtet] *n.* ①七人小组;七人一组;七个一组. ②【乐】七重奏[唱],七部合奏[唱]曲.

sept·foil [ˈseptfɔil] *n.* ①七叶形饰物〔尤指天主教七种圣物的象征〕. ②【建筑】七叶形. ③【植】直立委陵菜.

sep·tic [ˈseptik] *a.* 【医】①脓毒性的;败血症的. ②腐败性的;使[致]腐败的;使[致]败血的. — *n.* 引起腐败的东西;腐败物. ～ **poisoning** 腐败物中毒;败血症. ～ **tank** 化粪池.

sep·ti·cae·mi·a, 〔美〕 **-ce·mi·a** [ˌseptiˈsi:miə] *n.* 【医】败血症. **-cae·mic** *a.*

sep·ti·ci·dal [ˌseptiˈsaidl] *a.* 【植】胞间开裂的. **-ly** *ad.*

sep·tif·ra·gal [sepˈtifrəgəl] *a.* 【植】胞轴开裂的. **-ly** *ad.*

sep·ti·lat·er·al [ˌseptiˈlætərəl] *a.* 七边(形)的;七面的.

sep·til·lion [sepˈtiljən] *num.* 〔英〕100 万的 7 乘方[7 次幂][1 后有 42 个 0 的数];〔法,美〕1,000 的 8 乘方[8 次幂][1 后有 24 个 0 的数].

sep·ti·mal [ˈseptiməl] *a.* 七的.

sep·time [ˈsepti:m] *n.* 【剑】(八种防御姿势中的)第七个姿势.

sep·tu·a·ge·nar·i·an [ˌseptjuədʒiˈnɛəriən], **sep·tu·ag·e·na·ry** [-ˈdʒi:nəri] *a., n.* 七十岁的(人);七十至八十岁的(人).

Sep·tu·a·ges·i·ma [ˌseptjuəˈdʒesimə] *n.* 【宗】四旬斋〔Lent〕前的第三个星期日(亦作 Septuagesima Sunday).

Sep·tu·a·gint [ˈseptjuədʒint] *n.* 希腊文《旧约全书》〔相传公元前三世纪(270 年)七十二位犹太学者于亚历山大用七十二日译成〕.

sep·tum [ˈseptəm] *n.* *(pl.* **-ta** [-tə]*)* 【解、动、植】隔壁;中隔;隔膜;芽胞壁;胞片;(珊瑚的)隔片.

sep·tu·ple [ˈseptjupl] *n., a.* 七倍(的);七的. —*vt.* 以七倍之;用七乘;使变成七倍.

sep·tu·plet [sepˈtʌplit, -ˈtju:plit, -ˈtu:-; ˈseptuplit] *n.* ①一胎七个中的一个. ②(同样的)七个一组. ③七胞胎〔用作复数〕.

sep·ul·cher [ˈsepəlkə] *n.* 〔美〕＝ sepulchre.

se·pul·chral [siˈpʌlkrəl] *a.* ①坟墓的. ②葬礼的. ③阴森的;阴沉的. *a* ～ *monument* 墓碑. *a* ～ *mound* 冢. *a* ～ *stone* 墓石,墓碑. *a* ～ *voice* 阴[低]沉的声音.

sep·ul·chre [ˈsepəlkə] *n.* (尤指石岩凿成的)坟墓;地下坟墓;冢. *the* ～ *of one's hopes* 〔喻〕绝望. ***the whited*** ～ 伪君子;伪善者;虚有其表的人〔见《圣经》"马太福音"〕. ***the Holy*** ～ 【宗】圣墓;耶稣墓. — *vt.* 埋葬.

sep·ul·ture [ˈsepəltʃə] 〔古〕 *n.* ①埋葬. ②坟墓;墓地.

seq. ＝ ①sequel. ②sequence. ③squentes; sequentia 〔L. ＝ the following〕.

se·qua·cious [siˈkweiʃəs] *a.* ①随从的;顺从的;盲从的,附和的. ②缺乏独创精神的. ③〔喻〕奴性的. ④〔罕〕(论证等)推论上有条不紊的;合乎逻辑推论的;前后一贯的. **-ly** *ad.* **se·quac·i·ty** [siˈkwæsiti] *n.*

se·quel [ˈsi:kwəl] *n.* ①继续,后续. ②后果;结果;结局. ③续集;续篇. ④〔罕〕推论. *the* ～ *of a novel* 小说的续篇. ***as a*** ～ ***to [of]*** 作为…的后果;由于…结果. ***in the*** ～ 结果;到后来. **-ize** *vi.* (作品等)写续篇;(电影等)拍续集.

se·que·la [siˈkwi:lə] *n.* *(pl.* **-lae** [-li:]*)* ①〔常 *pl.*〕【医】后遗症;续发症;后发病;遗患. ②结果;后果.

se·quence [ˈsi:kwəns] *n.* ①继续;接续;连续. ②顺序;程序;次第;关系;关联. ③后果;结果;接着发生的事;后事;后文. ④【数】数列;序列;数贯. ⑤【无、计】指令序列;定序. ⑥【计】顺序机〔将信息项目排成顺序的机器〕. ⑦【乐】用不同音调反复演奏一组乐句. ⑧【天主】宣讲福音前唱的圣歌. ⑨【牌】顺. ⑩【影】(描述同一主题的)连续镜头;片断,插曲;场景. *a logical* ～ 条理;

逻辑顺序. *a causal [physical]* ~ 因果关系. *the natural* ~ *to [for] folly* 愚笨行为的必然结果. ***in rapid*** ~一个接着一个; 紧接着. ***in regular*** ~ 挨次; 按次序; 逐一; 有条不紊地. ***in*** ~ 挨次; 顺次; 逐一. ~ ***of tenses*** 【语法】时态的配合 [接续, 呼应]. **~-controlled** 程序控制的.

se•quent [ˈsiːkwənt] *a.* ①继续的; 连续的; 随着…而发生的 *(on; upon; to)*. ②继起的; 继承的. ③结果的. *a ~ order* 连续的顺序. *a ~ king* 继位的国王. — *n.* 接着发生的事; 后果; 结果. **-ly** *ad.*

se•quen•tes [siˈkwentiːz], ***se•quen•ti•a*** [-ʃiə] 〔L.〕以下 (= the following). ★ 略作 Seq. 或 Seqq., 用于引文页数[章数、行数]之后, 其前常加用 et (= &): *P. 10 (et) seq(q)* 第十页以下.

se•quen•tial [siˈkwenʃəl] *a.* ①继续的; 连续的; 随着…而发生的 *(to)*. ②结果的. ③〔美俚〕(避孕丸)按期服食的. —*n.* 〔*pl.*〕〔美俚〕按期服食的避孕丸. ~ **analysis** 【统计】序列分析. **-ly** *ad.*

se•ques•ter [siˈkwestə] *vt.* ①使分开; 使隔离; 使退隐. ②【法】扣押; 没收; 查封 (= sequestrate). ③【国际法】接收; 扣押(敌产). ~ *oneself from the world* 退隐. — *vi.* 弃权; 【法】(遗孀)放弃(对亡夫财产等的)要求. — *n.* 【化】螯合剂, 金属封锁剂. **~ed** *a.* 退隐的; (人、生活孤独的); (房子等)僻静的.

se•ques•trant [siˈkwestrənt] *n.* 【化】多价螯合作用.

se•ques•trate [siˈkwestreit] *vt.* 【法】①查封; 没收. ②假扣押, 把…暂交第三者保管; 暂行保管(有争议物). ③〔古〕隔离, 分离. **-tra•ble** *a.* ①可查封的; 可扣押的; 可没收的. ②〔古〕可隔离的; 可分离的.

se•ques•tra•tion [siˌkwesˈtreiʃən] *n.* ①隐退; 隐居. ②【法】假扣押; 假执行; 暂时查封; 没收; 争执物的保管. ③〔古〕分隔, 分开. ④【化】多价螯合作用.

se•ques•tra•tor [ˈsiːkwestreitə] *n.* ①【法】财产查封人; 没收者. ②有争议财产的暂行保管人.

se•ques•trum [siˈkwestrəm] *n.* *(pl. ~,-tra* [-trə]*)*【医】腐骨片; 坏骨片; 死骨片.

se•quin [ˈsiːkwin] *n.* ①古代威尼斯[马耳他、土耳其]的金币名. ②装饰衣服用的圆形小金属片.

se•quoi•a [siˈkwɔiə] *n.* 【植】红杉[又称 redwood]; [S-] 红杉属. **S- National Park** 美国国家加州红杉公园〔以其高大的红杉著称〕.

ser. = ①serial. ②series. ③service. ④sermon.

ser [siə] *n.* 西阿[印度重量单位, 2.057 磅] (= seer).

se•ra [ˈsiərə] *n.* serum 的复数.

se•rac [ˈseræk] *n.* 〔常 *pl.*〕【地】冰雪柱; 冰塔.

se•ragl•io [seˈrɑːliəu] *n.* *(pl. ~s)* ①(伊斯兰教国家的)后宫; 闺房. ②(一群)妻, 妾. ③〔the (old) S-〕【史】(土耳其)宫廷.

se•ra•i [seˈrɑːi, -ˈrei] *n.* *(pl. ~s)* ①(伊朗等国家的)旅店; (队商)客栈. ②(土耳其等伊斯兰教国家的)宫殿; 后宫.

ser•al [ˈsiərəl] *a.* 【生态】演替系列的.

se•rang [səˈræŋ] *n.* 〔英印〕(东印度的)水手长.

se•ra•pe [səˈrɑːpi] *n.* 〔美〕(拉丁美洲人的)披肩毛毯; 披身毛毯.

ser•aph [ˈserəf] *n.* *(pl. ~s,* **-a•phim** [-im]*)* ①【宗】六翼天使〔最高位天使〕. ②(《圣经》旧约)撒拉弗. **-ic, -i•cal** *a.* [seˈræfik(əl)] 天使般的; 纯洁的.

Serb [səːb] *a.* 塞尔维亚(人)的; 塞尔维亚语的. — *n.* ①塞尔维亚人. ②塞尔维亚语.

Ser•bia [ˈsəːbjə, -biə] *n.* 塞尔维亚〔南斯拉夫一地区〕.

Ser•bi•an [ˈsəːbjən,-biən] *a., n.* =Serb.

Ser•bo-cro•a•tian [ˌsəːbəukrəuˈeiʃən] *n.* 塞尔维亚-克罗地亚语[人]. — *a.* 塞尔维亚-克罗地亚语的; 塞尔维亚-克罗地亚人的.

Ser•bo•ni•an [səːˈbəunjən, -niən] *a.* 古埃及塞波尼斯 (Serbonis) 大沼泽的. ~ ***bog*** ①(旧时尼罗河三角洲与苏彝士运河之间的)危险的沼泽. ②困境; 绝境.

sere[1] [siə] *a.* 〔诗〕干枯的(= sear).

sere[2] [siə] *n.* 【生】植生系列; 演替系列.

se•rein [sərɛ̃ːŋ; F. sərɛ̃] *n.* 〔F.〕【气】(热带地方日落后晴空落下的)晴空雨.

ser•e•nade [ˌseriˈneid] *n.* 【乐】①小夜曲. ②= serenata ②. — *vt., vi.* (对…)唱[奏]小夜曲. ~ *one's ladylove* 对情娘唱[奏]小夜曲. **-r** *n.*

ser•e•na•ta [ˈseriˈnɑːtə] *n.* *(pl. ~s, -te* [-te]*)*【乐】①合唱剧. ②(介乎组曲与交响乐之间的)多乐章器乐曲.

ser•en•dip•i•ty [ˌserənˈdipiti] *n.* 易于偶然发现珍宝的运气〔源出英国作家 H.Walpole 所著童话 *The Three Princes of Serendip*〕.

se•rene [siˈriːn] *a.* ①清澈的; 晴朗的; (天空等)明朗的. ②(海、生活等)宁静的; 安定的; (一生等)没有风波的. ③沉着的; (性情)沉静的; (人、脸色、性格等)安详的. ④[S-] 殿下〔欧洲大陆对王公的尊称, 说作 *His S- Highness, Your S- Highness* 等〕. — *n.* 〔诗、古〕晴朗(天空); 平静(的海). — *vt.* 〔诗〕使(海、脸色等)平静; 宁静; 使(天空)明朗. ***All*** ~! 〔俚〕百事顺利; 一切都好. ***the*** ~ ***drop*** = ***the drop*** ~ 【医】黑蒙.

se•ren•i•ty [siˈreniti] *n.* ①晴朗. ②宁静; 平静. ③安详; 从容. ④[S-] 殿下. *His S-* = His Serene Highness.

serf [səːf] *n.* ①农奴. ②奴隶. ③象奴隶一样的人.

serf•age [ˈsəːfidʒ] *n.* = serfdom.

serf•dom [ˈsəːfdəm] *n.* ①农奴身分; 农奴的境遇[地位]. ②农奴制. ③奴役.

serf•hood [ˈsəːfhud] *n.* ①〔总称〕农奴; 奴隶. ② = serfdom.

Serg(t) 【军】= sergeant.

serge [səːdʒ] *n.* (粗)哔叽. ~ *cloth* 哔叽呢.

ser•gean•cy [ˈsɑːdʒənsi] *n.* 军士等 (sergeant)的职位.

ser•geant [ˈsɑːdʒənt] *n.* ①【军】军士; (英陆军、空军、海军陆战队; 美陆军、海军陆战队) 中士. ②警官, 巡官. ③【英史】(在皇家法庭具有特权的)高级律师. ④〔S-〕〔美〕一种地对地导弹. ***colour*** ~ (英海军陆战队)上士. ***master*** ~ (美陆军[空军、海军陆战队])军士长. ~ ***at arms*** =〔英〕serjeant-at-arms, (议会、法院等的)卫士. ***staff*** ~ (英陆军)上士; (美空军)参谋军士. ***technical*** ~ (美空军[海军陆战队])技术军士. **~-at-law**【英史】(在皇家法庭具有特权的) 高级律师. ~ **aviation**(军士级)航空长. ~ **first [1st] class** (美陆军)上士. ~ **fish** 【动】①军曹鱼(属). ②军曹鱼(科). ~ **major** 军士长. **~-ship** =sergeancy.

se•ri•al [ˈsiəriəl] *a.* ①连续的; 一连串的; 一系列的. ②按期出版的; (小说等)连载的; 连续刊行的; 连续广播的. ③分期偿付的. ④【计】串行的; 串联的. *a ~ number* ①序号; 编号. ②【军】军号; 入伍编号. *a ~ publication* 陆续出版的成套出版物. *a ~ story* 连载小说. ~ *rights* 连续刊载的版权. — *n.* ①连载小说; 连续广播; 连续电视; 连本影片. ②定期刊物. ③【军】行军梯队. ***in*** ~ ***order*** 顺次. ***write in*** ~***s*** 写连载小说(等).

se•ri•al•ism [ˈsiəriəlizəm] *n.* 【乐】十二音阶体系; 十二音阶体系作曲技法. **se•ri•al•ist** *n.*

se•ri•al•ize [ˈsiəriəlaiz] *vt.* ***(-iz•ed, -iz•ing)*** ①使连续. ②连载; 连续出版; 分集[分期]顺次出版. **-za•tion** [ˌsiəriəlaiˈzeiʃən] *n.*

se•ri•al•ly [ˈsiəriəli] *ad.* 顺次; 连续(地); 连续登载(地). *The novel will appear* ~. 这篇小说将连续登载.

se•ri•ate [ˈsiəriit] *a.* ①顺序的; 连续的. ②【植】轮的; 列的; 层的. —[ˈsiərieit] *vt.* (按)顺序排列; 使连续. **-ly** *ad.*

se•ri•a•tim [ˌsiəriˈeitim] *a., ad.* 〔L.〕连续(地); 顺次(地); 逐一[条](地). *discuss* ~ 逐条讨论.

se•ri•a•tion [ˌsiəriˈeiʃən] *n.* 顺次排列.

Ser•ic [ˈserik, ˈsiərik] *a.* ①〔古、诗〕= Chinese. ②〔s-〕②丝绸的; 丝制的.

ser·i·cate, ser·i·cat·ed, se·ri·ceous [ˈserikit, -keitid, siˈriʃəs] *a.* ①丝(状)的; 象丝的. ②【动、植】有丝状柔毛的; 有绢毛的; 有丝光的.
ser·i·cin [ˈserisin] *n.*【纺】丝胶.
ser·i·cite [ˈserisait] *n.*【矿】丝[绢]云母.
ser·i(ci)·cul·tur·al [ˌseri(si)ˈkʌltʃərəl] *a.* 养蚕的; 蚕丝业的.
ser·i·(ci)cul·ture [ˈseri(si)kʌltʃə] *n.* 养蚕; 养蚕业.
ser·i·(ci)cul·tur·ist [ˌseri(si)ˈkʌltʃərist] *n.* 养蚕家; 蚕丝(业)者.
ser·i·e·ma [ˌseriˈi:mə, -ˈeimə] *n.*【动】叫鹤.
se·ries [ˈsiəri:z] *n.* [*sing., pl.*] ①连续; 系列. ②套; 辑; 丛刊; 丛书. ③【生】区; 族. ④【植】轮; 列; 层; 系. ⑤【动】列; 组. ⑥【数】级数. ⑦【化】系; 系列; 组. ⑧【电】串联 (*opp.* parallel). ⑨【地】统; (岩系的)段. ⑩【乐】音列. ⑪【商】货物分类法. ⑫[美体]由同队进行的一连串比赛. ⑬【语音】交替的一组元音字母[如 sing, sang, sung]. *a* ~ (*of books*) 丛书. *the first* ~ 第一辑. *a* ~ *of victories* 连战连胜. *a* ~ *of misfortunes* 一连串的不幸. *a* ~ *of years* 连年. *an arithmetical* [*a geometrical*] ~ 等差[等比]级数. *a* ~ *and parallel circuit* 混联电路. *a* ~ *circuit* 串联电路. ***a* ~ *of*** 一系列; 许多. ***in*** ~ ①连续; 逐次. ②按顺序排列. ③作为丛书.【电】成串联; 串联的. ***in*** ~ ***with*** 与…串连; 与…相连. ***round robin*** ~【运】循环赛. ~ **aiding** (线圈等的)正向串联; 相助串联. ~ **dynamo [generator]** 串励发电机. ~ **machine** 串行计算机; 串励电机. ~ **modulation** 串馈式屏极调剂; 阳极调剂 ~ **motor** 串励电动机. ~**-multiple connection** 串并联. ~ **opposing** (线圈等的)反向串联. ~**-parallel** *a.* 串并联的; 混联的. ~ **reactor** 串联电感器; 串联扼流圈. ~ **resonance** 串联[电压]谐振. ~ **winding** 串联绕组, 串联绕法. ~**-wound** *a.* 串绕的; 串联的; 串激的.
ser·if [ˈserif] *n.*【印】衬线[如字母 I 上下两端的细横线] (*cf.* sanserif).
ser·i·graph [ˈserigrɑ:f, -græf] *n.* ①【纺】绢网印花. ②【纺】(试验绞丝用的)生丝复式强伸力机. **-er** [siˈrigrəfə] *n.* 绢网印花者. **-y** [siˈrigrəfi] *n.* 绢网印花工艺.
ser·in[1] [ˈserin] *n.*【动】金丝雀 (*Serinus canarius*).
ser·in[2] [ˈserin] *n.* =serine.
ser·ine [ˈsi:ri:n] *n.*【化】丝氨酸; 血清蛋白.
se·rin·ga [siˈriŋgə] *n.*【植】三叶胶属 (*Hevea*) 植物[产于巴西].
se·ri·o·com·ic, -i·cal [ˈsiəriəuˈkɔmik, -ikəl] *a.* 装作庄重其实是滑稽的; 半庄半谐的. **-i·cal·ly** *ad.*
se·ri·ous [ˈsiəriəs] *a.* ①严肃的; 一本正经的; (人、脸等)庄重的. ②认真的; 真诚的; 恳切的. ③重要的; 重大的. ④危险的; 严重的. ⑤[古]宗教的; 伦理学的; [谑]虔诚的. ⑥热中的, 很感兴趣的. *You cannot be* ~. 你是说着玩儿的吧. *Are you* ~? 你(说的)是真的吗? *a* ~ *opponent* 须认真对待的敌手; 劲敌. ~ *damage* 严重的损害. ***and now to be*** ~ 现在来谈正经的 [用作插入语]. ***make a*** ~ ***attempt*** 认真试一试. ***pretending to be*** ~ 象煞有介事地. ~ ***advice for sb.*** 正告某人. ~ ***money*** [美]巨款. ***take for*** ~ 当真. ***think in a*** ~ ***light*** 认真想. ***to be*** ~ 别开玩笑 [用作插入语]. ***to talk*** ~ 说正经的[用作插入语].
se·ri·ous·ly [ˈsiəriəsli] *ad.* 严肃; 认真; 严重. ~ *ill* 害着重病. ~ *speaking* 老实讲; 认真说来. *Do you* ~ *mean what you say?* 你这话是不是当真的? *be* ~ *offended* [*affected*] 大怒 [受重大影响]. ***now*** ~ 说正经的. ***take*** ~ 重视; 认真(想); 当真.
se·ri·ous-mind·ed [ˈsiəriəsˈmaindid] *a.* 认真的; 严肃的; 热诚的; 一本正经的.
se·ri·ous·ness [ˈsiəriəsnis] *n.* ①严肃; 认真. ②严重; 重大. ***in all*** ~ 郑重地; 十分认真地 (*tell sb. in all* ~ 正告某人). ***with affected*** ~ 象煞有介事地.
ser·iph [ˈserif] *n.* = serif.
ser·jeant [ˈsɑ:dʒənt] *n.* [英] = sergeant.
ser·mon [ˈsə:mən] *n.* ①【宗】布道; 讲道; 说教. ②训诫; 训导. ③唠叨得令人厌烦的长篇演讲. ④(受自然界的启发而作的) 道德上的反省. *preach* [*deliver*] *a* ~ 讲道. *a lay* ~ 非宗教家的宗教谈. **-ic, -i·cal** [sə:ˈmɔnik(əl)] *a.*
ser·mon·et(te) [ˌsə:məˈnet] *n.* 简短的讲道.
ser·mon·ize [ˈsə:mənaiz] *vi.* ①讲道, 布道; 说教. ②写作讲道稿. ③训诫, 训导. —*vt.* ①对…布道. ②训诫, 对…说教. **-r** *n.* 布道者, 训诫者.
sero- *comb. f.* 浆液; 血清: *sero*sity.
se·rol·o·gy [siəˈrɔlədʒi] *n.*【医】血清学. **-log·i·cal** [ˌsiərəˈlɔdʒikəl] *a.*
se·ro·sa [siˈrəusə, -zə] *n.* (*pl.* ~***s***, ***-sae*** [-si:]) ①【动】浆膜 (= serous membrane); 绒(毛)膜 (= chorion). ②【动】(昆虫的)胚膜. **-l** *a.*
se·ros·i·ty [siˈrɔsiti] *n.* ①【医】浆液; 滑液. ②浆液性; 浆液状.
se·rot·i·nal [seˈrɔtinæl], **se·rot·i·nous** [siˈrɔtinəs] *a.* ①夏末的; 晚夏的. ②【植】晚熟的; 迟季的.
se·ro·to·nin [ˌsiərəˈtəunin, ˌser-] *n.*【生化】5-羟色胺[血管收缩素].
se·rous [ˈsiərəs] *a.* ①如水的; 稀薄的. ②【医】(象)浆液的; 血浆(般)的; 血清的. ~ *fluid* 浆液. ~ **cavity** 浆液膜腔. ~ **gland**【解】浆液腺. ~ **membrane** 浆膜.
ser·ow [ˈserəu] *n.* 鬣羚属(*Capricornis*)动物[产于南亚].
Ser·pens [ˈsə:penz] *n.*【天】巨蛇座.
ser·pent [ˈsə:pənt] *n.* ①大毒蛇. ②奸人; 阴险的人. ③蛇状焰火. ④【乐】蛇状管. ⑤[the S-]【天】巨蛇座. ***the (Old) S-*** 撒旦; 恶魔. **S- Bearer**=Serpens. ~**-charmer** (吹笛)耍蛇的人. ~ **eater**【动】食蛇鸟. ~**'s tongue** *n.* ①鲨牙化石. ②双尖剑. ③【植】瓶尔小草属的一种.
ser·pen·tar·i·um [ˌsə:pənˈtɛəriəm] *n.* (动物园的)蛇馆.
ser·pen·tine [ˈsə:pəntain] *a.* ①蛇一般的. ②蜿蜒的; 弯弯曲曲的; 盘旋的; 螺旋形的. ③阴险的; 奸险的; 狡猾的. *a* ~ *pipe* 蛇管. *a* ~ *verse* 头尾词相同的诗. *the* ~ *turnings* [*windings*] (河流、道路的)蜿蜒; 曲折. ~ ***windings*** 转弯抹角地逢迎 [巴结]. — *n.* ①【矿】蛇纹岩. ②(古代的)蛇形大炮. ③【滑冰】S 形曲线; 蛇形线. ④[the S-] (伦敦海德公园的)曲折蜿蜒的水池. —*vi.* 蜿蜒地流; 迂回曲折前进; 缠绕. **-d** *a.* ①有蛇(栖息)的. ②蛇形的, 弯曲的.
ser·pi·go [sə:ˈpaigəu] *n.*【医】匐行疹; 圈癣. **-pig·i·nous** [-ˈpidʒinəs] *a.*【医】(皮肤病等)匐行的.
ser·ra·nid [səˈreinid, -ˈæ-, -ˈɑ-] *n.* 鮨科 (*Serranidae*) 的鱼[包括锯鮨]. — *a.* 鮨科的 (= serranoid).
ser·ra·noid [ˈserənɔid] *a.*【鱼】鮨科的.
ser·rate [ˈserit] *a.*【生】锯齿形的; 有锯齿的. — *vt.* 使成锯齿状. —*n.*【军】飞机的反截击雷达设备.
ser·ra·tion [seˈreiʃən] *n.* 锯齿(状); 锯齿形(突起).
ser·ried [ˈserid] *a.* (行列等)密集的; 排紧的; 拥挤的.
ser·ru·late, -lat·ed [ˈserjuleit, -id] *a.* 细锯齿形的.
ser·ru·la·tion [ˌserjuˈleiʃən] *n.* ①锯齿状; 锯齿形. ②细小锯齿.
ser·tu·lar·i·an [ˌsə:tjuˈlɛəriən] *n.*【动】海桧叶属水母[体形分枝如桧叶].
se·r·um [ˈsiərəm] *n.* (*pl.* ~***s***, ***-ra*** [-rə]) ①【医】血清. ②血浆. ③浆液; 树液. ④乳清; 乳浆. ~ **albumin**【生化】血清白蛋白. ~ **disease** 血清病. ~ **globulin**【生化】血清球蛋白.
ser·val [ˈsə:vəl] *n.*【动】(非洲)长脚山猫; 薮猫.
serv·ant [ˈsə:vənt] *n.* ①仆人; 佣人; 雇工. ②[美]奴仆; 奴隶. ③随员; 献身…的人; 追随者; 信徒. ④官吏;

公务员；服务员；雇员. ⑤有用之物 *an indoor* ～ 内勤. 用人[厨役等]. *an outdoor* ～ 外勤用人 [园丁等]. *an upper* ～ 管家. *All our cadres are* ～*s of the people.* 我们一切工作干部都是人民的勤务员. *Fire and water may be good* ～*s, but bad masters.* 水火是忠仆，但一旦逞凶则危害极大. *a* ～ *of art* 献身艺术的人. *a civil* ～ 文官. *the* ～*s of a railway company* 铁路公司职员. ***His [Her] Majesty's*** ～***s*** = ***the king's [queen's]*** ～***s*** 〔英〕官吏；公务员；演员. ***the*** ～ ***of the*** ～***s*** 上帝最卑下的仆人〔罗马教皇的自称〕. ～ **girl,** ～ **maid** *n.* 女仆.

serve [sə:v] *vt.* ①(为…)服务；为…尽力[效劳]. ②侍候；招待(客等). ③端上；摆出(食物)；斟(酒). ④服(刑，役)；供[奉](职)，经历，度过. ⑤符合；对…有用，对…适用；适合(目的). ⑥满足(欲望、食欲、要求、需要)；供给. ⑦分派，分配. ⑧对待；处理. ⑨操作；发射(大炮)；使用(枪). ⑩主演. ⑪开动. ⑫【海】卷缠(绳索等). ⑬【法】送达(命令等). ⑭【网球】开(球)；发(球). ⑮(种马等)与(母畜)交配. *to* ～ *the people heart and soul* 全心全意地为人民服务. ～ *coffee hot* 把咖啡趁热端上桌(供饮用). *First come, first* ～*d.* 先到的先招待. *S- the ladies first.* 女客先得到供应[招待]. *Lunch is* ～*d now.* 现在开午饭了. *Is there anyone to* ～ *me?* 〔顾客叫服务员〕有人接[招]待(我)吗？ *What can we* ～ *you with?* 〔店员对顾客〕给您拿点什么？您要些什么？ — *vi.* ①服务；服役；供[奉]职. ②有用；合用；可作…用；作为 (*as, for*)；足够；适宜. ③侍候；服侍；端菜；斟酒. ④【网球】开球；发球. ⑤(举行弥撒时)充当助祭. ***as memory*** ～***s*** 每逢想起的时候. ***as occasion*** ～***s*** 一有机会. ***make the past*** ～ ***the present and foreign works*** ～ ***China*** 古为今用，洋为中用. ～ ***a gun*** 炮击. ～ ***an attachment*** 送达查封令 (*on, upon*). ～ ***sb. a bad turn*** 使人吃苦头. ～ ***sb. a trick [***～ ***a trick on sb.]*** 欺骗某人. ～ ***at table*** 侍应人吃饭[上菜等]. ～ ***behind a counter*** 做店员；站柜台. ～ ***for nothing*** 毫不中用. ～ ***in the ranks*** 服兵役. ～ ***one's apprenticeship*** 当学徒. ～ ***one's sentence*** = ～ time. ～ ***one's time*** 做满任期[规定期限]；服刑. ～ ***sb.'s turn [need]*** 对某人合用；够某人用. ～ ***oneself of*** 利用. ～ ***out*** ①分给；分配(食粮等). ②端出(饭菜等)；斟(酒等). ③做到期满. ～ ***(sb.) out*** 使自食其果；给予报复. ～ ***(sb.) right*** 给(某人)该得的待遇 (*It* ～*s him [you] right.* 他[你]活该. *He is rightly [well]* ～*d.* 他算得到报应了.) ～ ***round*** ①挨次分派(食物). ②摑上. ～***tables*** 张罗膳食(而忽视精神需要). ～ ***the Devil*** 干坏事；犯罪. ～ ***the need [turn]*** 有用；合用；够用. ～ ***the purpose of*** 可用于；可充当；合乎…的目的. ～ ***the time*** 骑墙观望. ～ ***time*** 服刑. ～ ***under sb.*** 在某人下面工作. ～ ***up*** 端出(饭菜等)；上(菜). ～ ***(sb.) with*** 拿出…给(某人)；提供；供给. ***when the tide*** ～***s*** 方便的时候. — *n.* 【网球】开球；发球. *Whose* ～ *is it?* 该谁发球？

serv·er [ˈsə:və] *n.* ①服务者；工作者；侍候者；服役者. ②【网球】开球人；发球人. ③上菜用的器具〔如托盘，手推小车等〕；布菜用的火匙、叉子等. ④助祭〔做弥撒时神父的助手〕.

Ser·vi·an [ˈsə:vjən, -viən] *a., n.* = Serbian.

Ser·vice [ˈsə:vis] *n.* 塞维斯〔姓氏〕.

serv·ice [ˈsə:vis] *n.* ①服务；工作；公务；职务；事务；业务；行政部门(人员)，服务机构(人员). ②事业；公用事业；(交通，供水，供电等)公共设施(业务). ③仪式；(宗教)礼拜仪式(乐曲). 【宗】功德，修行〔祈祷、行善等〕. ④【军】勤务；服役；兵役(期间). ⑤军种；勤务部队. ⑥利益；有用. ⑦照顾；帮助. ⑧〔常 *pl.*〕贡献，功劳. ⑨(厂方对售出机械等的)维修(服务). ⑩服务业；服务公司. ⑪(用膳时的)侍候；招待；上菜；斟酒. ⑫(全套)餐具；茶具. ⑬【海】(防止绳索磨损而进行的)卷缠；缠索材料〔纱线、帆布或金属丝〕. ⑭装弹发射(大炮). ⑮(传票等的)送达；执行. ⑯【网球】开球；发球；开球方式[方面]. ⑰国债利息. ⑱(种马等)与母畜的交配. ⑲= service tree. *public* ～ 公务. *government* ～ 行政事务；政府机关；公务员. *postal* ～ 邮政业务. *There is a good* ～ *of trains.* 火车客运业务良好. *the U.S. Information S-* 美国新闻处. *the secret* ～*s* 特务机关. *the reporting* ～ (会议的)报到处. *a marriage [burial]* ～ 婚[丧]礼. *the civil* ～ 文官. *the (fighting)* ～*s* 陆海空军. *the united* ～*s* 陆海军. *the junior [senior]* ～ 〔英〕陆[海]军. *Will you do me a* ～? 帮我一个忙好吗？ *My* ～ *to you!* 祝你健康；敬你一杯；干一杯吧. *a* ～ *of glass* 一套玻璃茶具. *a table* ～ 一套餐具. *Whose* ～ *is it?* 该谁开球？ *Personal* ～【法】直接送达当事人. ***at your*** ～ 敬候差遣，请随意(使用) (*I am at your* ～. 您有事请随时吩咐好了. *I am so-and-so at your* ～. 我叫某某，有事请随时吩咐.) ***be of*** ～ ***to*** 对…有用[有帮助]. ***enter into*** ～ = go into ～. ***enter the*** ～ 入伍. ***enter [go] upon*** ～ 参加战斗；上火线；服现役. ***(give) my*** ～ ***to*** 请向(某人)致候. ***give*** ～ ***to*** 为…效劳. ***go into*** ～ = ***go (out) to*** ～ 去帮工；去做仆人. ***have seen*** ～ ①上过火线[参加过战斗]. ②已经用旧. ***in active*** ～ 在职；在现役. ***in*** ～ 在帮工；被雇用着；在军中服役. ***of no*** ～ 无用. ***on His [Her] Majesty's S-*** 〔英〕公事〔公文免费邮递印记，略 O. H. M. S.〕. ***on*** ～ 在职(的)；在役(的). ***out of*** ～ ①退职；退役. ②已不能用的；已作废的. ***pay lip*** ～ ***to*** 空口说白话；嘴上说得好听. ***place at sb.'s*** ～ 听任某人使用. ***present one's*** ～ ***to*** 向…致敬. ***render a*** ～ 帮忙；效劳，尽力；贡献. ***retire from*** ～ 退役；退职. ～ ***by substitution*** 【法】代理送达. ***take sb. into one's*** ～ 雇用某人. ***take*** ～ ***with*** 在…处做事[服务]. ***take the*** ～ 发球，开球. — *vt.* ①为…做后勤[第二线、辅助性]服务工作；满足(顾客)需要. ②检修；维修，保养(车辆、仪器、电视机等). ③支付(公债等)的利息并提存偿债基金. ④(种马等)与(母畜)交配. ～ *an automobile* 修理汽车. ～ *the needs of customers* 满足许多顾客的需要. — *a.* ①武装部队的；服现役用的. ②服务性的；为提供后勤[资料等]服务的. ③仆人用的；仆人的. ～ **area** ①服务区域. ②供水区域. ③【无】广播区域. ～**berry** 花楸(树)果(实). ～ **book** 【宗】祈祷书. ～ **break** (网球等)对方发球而己方取胜局. ～ **call**【军】集合号；上班[上操等]号；下班号. ～ **cap** 〔美〕军礼帽. ～ **car** 〔美婉〕殡仪车. ～ **ceiling** 【空】实际(上)升限(度). ～ **club** (机关团体的)福利部；【军】军官俱乐部. ～ **counter** 服务台. ～ **court** 【网球】发球时球应落入的地方[内场]. ～ **depot** = ① ～ station. ②【军】后勤仓库. ～ **diagram** 行车图表. ～ **dress** 军便服 (*opp.* full dress). ～ **elevator** 运货电梯；服务人员电梯. ～ **entrance** 服务人员出入处. ～ **flat** 〔英〕能包饭的公寓. ～ **hatch** 递送饭菜的小窗. ～ **interruption** (电话)不通. ～ **lift** 运货电梯，服务人员使用的电梯. ～ **line** ①【电】用户进线. ②【网球】发球线. **-man** *n.* ***(pl.-men)*** ①军人. ②维修人员. ～ **meter** 【电话】通话次数计. ～ **module** (宇宙飞船的)机械舱〔包括机械系统和燃料储备等〕. ～ **parts** 备用零件. ～ **pipe** (由总管通入屋内的)自来水[煤气]输送管. ～ **record** 服务经历. ～ **round** 作战用炮弹，实弹. ～ **stairway** (房屋后部) 勤杂人员使用的楼梯. ～ **station** 服务站；修理站；加油站；(飞机的)停留处. ～ **stripe** 〔美〕军龄臂章. ～ **telegram** 【讯】公电. ～ **tree** 【植】花楸树；治疝花楸. ～ **water** 家用[自来]水. ～ **yard** 后院；杂作场.

serv·ice·a·ble [ˈsə:visəbl] *a.* ①合用的；有用的；便利的，适于平时使用的 (*to*). ②经用的；耐用的. ③正常的，能操作的. **-bly** *ad.*

serv·i·cing [ˈsə:visiŋ] *n.* 维修.

ser·vi·ette [ˌsə:viˈet] *n.* 餐巾.

serv·ile [ˈsə:vail] *a.* ①奴隶的. ②奴性的；奴颜婢膝的；卑屈的；屈从的；隶属的. ③无创造性的；无独立精神的. ④【语】附属性的〔指本身不发音，只表示在它之前的元音字母发长音的字母,如 stone 一词中的 e 字母;或指词中表示派生关系[词性变化、语法关系等]的部分,如 mother's, sees, students 等词中的 s]. ~ *flattery* 卑躬屈膝的奉承. ~ *labour* 奴隶般的劳动. —*n.* 奴隶. ~ **letter** 除表示另一字母的发音外别无作用的字母〔如 manag*e*able, sal*e*able 中的 *e* 等〕. ~ **works**【宗】礼拜六禁止做的卑下工作. **-ly** *ad.* **-ness** *n.*

ser·vil·i·ty [səːˈviliti] *n.* ①奴隶处境. ②奴颜婢膝;奴性;卑屈;屈从. ③隶属.

ser·ving [ˈsəːviŋ] *n.* ①服务;服侍,伺候;上菜. ②(食物的)一份;一客. — *a.* 用于上菜的. *a* ~ *spoon* 布菜匙;分菜匙.

ser·vi·tor [ˈsəːvitə] *n.* ①〔古、诗〕仆从;跟班;侍从. ②【史】(牛津大学的)工读生.

ser·vi·tude [ˈsəːvitjuːd] *n.* ①奴役;奴隶状态;(刑罚)劳役. ②【法】地役(权);使用权. *in* ~ *to one's evil passions* 变成邪念的俘虏(为非作歹). *penal* ~ *for life* 终身劳役;无期徒刑. ~ *to by-product* 副产物使用权.

ser·vo [ˈsəːvəu] *n.* 〔用作定语或前缀〕①【自】伺服. ②伺服系统;随动系统;伺服机械;从动系统. ③【空】舵机〔自动驾驶仪附件〕. *an on-off* ~ 继电随动系统. ~ **actuator** 伺服执行机构;伺服拖动装置. ~ **amplifier** 跟踪系统放大器;伺服放大器. ~**-analog computer** 伺服模拟计算机. ~ **control** 伺服控制;随动控制. ~**-driven** *a.* 伺服拖动的. ~**-gear** 助力机构;伺服机构;伺服系统. ~**-link** 助力传动装置;助力系统;伺服系统. ~ **mechanism** 伺服机构;随动系统. ~ **modulation** 伺服调剂. ~ **motor** 伺服电动机;继动器. ~**-position** 伺服活塞. ~ **potentimeter** 伺服电位计. ~**-recorder** 伺服记录器. ~**-stabilization** 伺服稳定. ~**-system** 随动系统,跟踪系统. ~ **valve** 伺服(操纵)阀.

ses·a·me [ˈsesəmi] *n.* 【植】芝麻;脂麻. ~ *oil* 芝麻油;香油. ~ *soy* 芝麻酱. *open* ~ 开门咒〔源于《天方夜谈》〕;(过难关的)秘诀;窍门.

ses·a·min [ˈsesəmin] *n.*【生化】芝麻明;脂麻素.

ses·a·moid [ˈsesəmɔid] *a.* 芝麻(籽)形的;【解】籽骨的. ~ *bone* 籽骨. ~ *cartilage* 籽软骨. — *n.*【解】籽骨;籽软骨.

sesqui- *comb. f.* 表示"一个半": *sesquioxide.*

ses·qui·car·bon·ate [ˌseskwiˈkɑːbənit, -neit] *n.*【化】倍半碳酸盐.

ses·qui·cen·ten·ni·al [ˌseskwisenˈteniəl] *n., a.* 一百五十年纪念(的).

ses·qui·ox·ide [ˌseskwiˈɔksaid] *n.*【化】倍半氧化物;三氧化二…. *nickle* ~ 三氧化二镍.

ses·qui·pe·da·li·an [ˈseskwipiˈdeiliən] *a.* ①一英尺半(长)的. ②(词、语)极长的;多音节的. ③好用长词的. —*n.* 长词.

ses·sile [ˈsesail] *a.* 【生】①无柄的;无腹柄的. ②固着的;座生的. *a* ~ *leaf* 无柄叶. ~ *medusa* 座生水母.

ses·sion [ˈseʃən] *n.* ①会议;会议的一次[一届];开会;(法庭的)开庭. ②开会期;开庭期. ③〔美、Scot.〕学期. ④〔美〕授课时间. ⑤〔*pl.*〕〔英〕(处理轻微案件的)治安法庭. ⑥【商】(证券交易等的)市;盘. ⑦(为某项活动或目的集合在一起的)一段时间. ⑧基督教长老会的地区性执行理事会. ⑨〔美〕地方刑事法院 (=the court of ~). *be in* ~ 在开会中;在会议中;在开庭中. *the autumn* ~ (英国国会暑天休会后的)秋季会期. *the plenary [full]* ~ 全体会议. *between* ~*s* 休会期间. *the conference now in* ~ 现在召开的会议. *petty* ~*s* 即决审判;即决法庭. *quarter* ~*s* 〔英〕(每三月一次、审理轻微刑事案件及民事案件的)四季法庭. *the morning* ~ 【商】(交易所的)早市. **-al** *a.*

ses·ter·ti·um [sesˈtəːtiəm] *n.* (*pl.* **-ti·a** [-ʃiə]) 塞斯特帖姆〔古罗马货币单位,等于 1,000 塞斯特斯 (*sesterce*)〕.

ses·tet [sesˈtet] *n.* ①【乐】六重唱(曲);六重奏(曲);六人演出小组. ②【诗】十四行诗的最后六行,六行诗节.

ses·ti·na [sesˈtiːnə] *n.* (*pl.* ~*s*, **-ne** [-niː]) 六节诗〔一种抒情诗的格式,每节六行,最后另加一节为三行;第一节六行的末一词,按不同次序在其他五节各行的末尾重复之,并出现在最后一节三行的中间及末尾〕.

Set [set] *n.* 【埃神】赛特〔古埃及神话中兽头人身象征邪恶的神〕.

set [set] *vt.* (*set;set·ting*) ①放;搁;贴;靠. ~ *a cup on the table* 把杯子放在桌上. ~ *it against the wall* 把它靠在墙上. ~ *eyes on* 注视;碰见. ②安置;布置;安排;设置;装置. ~ *a guard at the gate* 派卫兵守门. ③使固定. ~ *a butterfly* 钉住蝴蝶(做标本). ~ *a cutting tool on a carriage* 把切削刀具固定在刀架上. ④镶;嵌. ~ *a jewel* 镶宝石. *an island* ~ *in a sea of silver* 镶在银色海面上的一个岛. ⑤种植. ~ *seed [plants]* 播种;种(植物). ⑥扬(帆);扯上;扯开. ~ *sail* 张帆;开船. ⑦设(陷井);张(罗网). ⑧点燃;放(火). ~ *fire to* 放火. ⑨签(字);盖(章). ~ *seal [signature] to the deed* 在证书上盖章[签字]. ~ *one's hand to a document* 在文件上签字. ⑩树立(榜样、模范). ~ *an example* 树立榜样;示范;以身作则. ~ *the fashion* 树立新型样板;开风气. ⑪规定;约定;择定(日子等);指定(地点);划定(界限);确定;决定;制定;颁布. ~ *a price* 定价钱. ~ *the atomic mass of hydrogen at 1 atomic mass unit* 把氢原子量定为一个原子量单位. ⑫创造(记录). ~ *a new production record* 创造新的生产记录. ⑬使坚固;使凝结;弄硬;使牢固. ~ *the white of an egg by boiling it* 煮蛋使蛋白凝固. *Cold* ~*s jellies.* 果子冻[肉冻]因冷而冻结. ⑭使(头发)成波浪形;卷(头发). ~ *one's hair* 把头发卷[作]成波浪形. ⑮接骨;整骨. ~ *the broken bone* 正骨. ⑯锉(锯齿);抢(梯刀);对(钟、表);拨准(钟的指针);校正(仪器);调整. ~ *a clock [watch]* 对钟[表]. ~ *an alarm clock* 拨好闹钟. ⑰提出(问题,任务);出(题目);指定(作业). ~ *an examination paper* 出考试题目. ⑱排(铅字). ⑲使从事;使…[指定]做某事[某动作]. ~ *him to the task* 使[指定]他做那件工作. ⑳专心;集中;倾注. ~ *one's heart on* … 一心要;迷恋. ~ *one's affections on* 爱上;热爱. ㉑使处于某种状态. ~ *his mind at ease* 使他安心. ~ *a question at rest* 使问题得到解决. ~ *machines in motion* 使机器开动. ~ *the bell a-ring* 把钟敲响. ~ *right* 矫正;弄正. ~ *things going* 使事情进行下去. ~ *affairs in order* 使事情就绪. ㉒为(诗、词)谱曲;改写(乐曲);配(布景). ~ *piano music for the violin* 改钢琴曲成小提琴曲. ~ *word to music* 将歌词编成曲子. ㉓使(母鸡)孵蛋. ~ *a hen* 使一母鸡孵蛋. ㉔〔桥牌〕打败(对手). ㉕使朝某一方向. ~ *one's feet homeward* 朝回家的方向走. ㉖使移动. ~ *a match to fire* 以火柴点火. ~ *a pen to paper* 提笔写字,著书立说. ㉗〔方〕使坐下. ㉘释放. ~ *a prisoner free* 释放犯人. ㉙(猎狗)以鼻指着(猎物)以指示其位置. ㉚使(颜色)固着. — *vi.* ①(太阳等)(沉)落;偏西. *The sun has* ~. 太阳落了. *His star has* ~. 他的命运完了. ②(液体等)凝固;凝结;固定. *The jelly has* ~. 冷冻凝结起来了. *His character has* ~. 他的性格固定下来了. *His face* ~. 他绷起面孔. *Her eyes* ~. 她的眼睛定住了. ③着手,从事. ④开始活动;开始工作. ⑤(水、风等)流向;吹向;(感情、意见等)倾向. *The tide* ~*s in [out].* 湖水涨[退]了. ⑥结果实;结子儿. ⑦植树;插树. ⑧(母鸡)孵卵. ⑨(衣服等)合身;适合. *The coat* ~*s badly.* 这件上衣不合身. ⑩(猎犬)站住指示猎物所在. ⑪(跳舞)采取面对面姿势. ⑫(骨)接合;(金属)永久变形. ⑬〔方〕坐. ⑭(头发)卷成波浪形. ⑮攻击 (*upon*). ⑯(颜色)固着. ***be hard*** ~ ①处于为难境地 (*for; to*). ②(蛋)在孵化中. ③感到饥饿. ***be sharp [keen]*** ~ ①很饿. ②渴求. ③(脸)表情严肃. ~ ***a case*** 假定. ~ ***a limit to*** (规定)限制;缩减(冗费). ~ ***a thief [rogue] to catch a thief [rogue]*** 以毒攻毒. ~ ***about*** ①开始;下手;着手. ②〔口〕攻击. ③散布(谣言). ④〔俚〕接连殴打;乱

打. ~ ***abroad*** 散布；推广；宣扬；公开发表. ~ ***afloat*** ①落水；使下水. ②着手；开始. ~ ***against*** ①比较；对照. ②使对抗；使反对；使猜忌. ③使平衡. ④使不和；离间. ⑤赌. ~ ***agoing [going]*** 使动；开动；使开行. ~ ***apart*** ①留出(充当别用). ②分开；分离. ~ ***aside*** 拨出；搁置；驳回. ~ ***at*** 袭击；嗾使(狗等). ~ ***at ease [rest]*** 使安心；安慰；抚慰. ~ ***at large [liberty]*** 释放；解放. ~ ***at odds,*** ~ ***at variance*** 挑拨离间；使争吵；使打架. ~ ***back*** ①阻碍；阻止. ②使挫折；使退步. ③拨回(钟表的针). ④〔美口〕使(某人)花钱 (*How much did it ~ you back?* 它使你花了多少钱?) ~ ***before*** ①摆在…前面；拿出；盛出(食物)；(把酒)斟出. ②告诉(事实等)；陈述；说明；劝导. ~ ***by*** ①搁在一旁；拿开；搁起；藏起；保留. ②尊重；珍重. ~ ***by the compass*** 按罗针仪测定(方位). ~ ***by the heels*** ①上脚镣. ②拘禁；监禁；逮捕；使不能活动[无能，无用]. ③弄翻；弄倒. ~ ***down*** ①搁下；丢下. ②让乘客下车；把东西卸下车. ③记入；登记. ④定；设；制定. ⑤归于；归功于. ⑥认为是由于 *(to)*；认为；视为；看作*(as)*. ⑦〔俚〕谴责. ⑧〔美〕着陆；降落. ~ ***foot*** 踏上；进入. ~ ***forth*** ①显示；明示. ②排列；陈列. ③公开；发行；公布. ④陈述；宣布；说明. ⑤表彰；颂扬；赞扬. ⑥出发. ~ ***forward*** ①促进；助长. ②提出；宣布；声明. ③出发；启程. ④拨快(钟、表). ~ ***free*** ①释放. ②【化】使游离. ~ ***going*** 开动；展开. ~ ***in*** ①固定；停当. ②涨潮. ③进来；来到. ④开始 (*The rainy season has ~ in.* 雨季开始了.) ~ ***in order*** 整顿；整理. ~ ***(a friend) in the world*** 提拔(朋友). ~ ***little [light] by*** 轻视. ~ ***loose*** 解开；释放. ~ ***off*** ①分；分割；划开；区划. ②装饰；使更鲜明；衬托出；使显得更美丽；表扬. ③使爆发；发射(焰火)；燃放. ④出发；动身. ⑤扣除；抵销. ⑥对照；对比. ⑦使开始(做某事). ⑧【印】(墨未干)弄污(次页). ~ ***off against*** 使和…对抗；使对照；扣除；抵销. ~ ***on*** ①前进. ②嗾使；挑唆；挑拨；煽动；鼓动. ③使跟踪追赶. ④【火箭】定位；调节. ⑤置放(在上)；端上(桌子). ⑥决心要拿到. ⑦埋头；专心(工作等). ⑧攻击；袭击. ⑨出发；动身. ⑩着手；开始. ~ ***... on foot*** 开始；着手. ~ ***(sb.) on his feet*** 使站立；帮助人独立谋生. ~ ***(sb.) on his way*** 送人上路(以免走错). ~ ***one's face against*** (坚决)反对. ~ ***one's face to*** 正视；决心去做；着手做. ~ ***one's hand to*** ①抓住；握住. ②着手做；开始做. ~ ***one's hand [name, signature, seal] to a document*** 在文件上签名[盖章]. ~ ***one's hand to the plough*** 开始工作；开始做. ~ ***one's teeth*** 咬紧牙关；〔喻〕下定决心(干). ~ ***one's wits to another's*** 和人闹意见，跟人辩论. ~ ***oneself against*** 反对，与…相对抗. ~ ***oneself right*** 自行改正；表明自己的正当. ~ ***oneself to do*** 竭力设法. ~ ***oneself up in opposition to*** 同…唱对台戏[相对抗]. ~ ***out*** ①出发；动身. ②开始 (~ *out in business* 动手做事). ③(潮水)退落. ④分派；发布. ⑤分界，区划；限定. ⑥陈列；敍装；准备好使出去. ⑦修饰；装饰. ⑧表示；申述；陈述. ⑨测定(位置). ⑩【石工】(把上面的石头)砌出一点. ⑪隔开一定距离栽植. ⑫【印】用完(架上铅字)；(把字)排稀. ~ ***over*** ①放在…上. ②支配. ③定为…的监督人. ④移交；递交. ~ ***people by the ear*** 使争吵. ~ ***store [much] by*** 尊重；敬重. ~ ***the axe to*** ①动手斫倒[破坏]. ②摧毁. ~ ***the Thames on fire*** 做不平凡的事. ~ ***to*** ①认真着手；动手做. ②打起来. ③吃起来. ~ ***up*** ①竖起；摆正. ②建立；创立；发起；开办 (~ *up for oneself* 独自经营). ③供给；供应；预备；准备好拿出；〔美口〕摆(菜等). ④提高(声音)；喊叫. ⑤提出；提议；提倡；主张；示；提示；揭示. ⑥假装. ⑦胜过；使获胜 *(over, about)*；使掌握权力. ⑧使自立. ⑨振起精神；恢复(健康)；复元. ⑩敬(一杯)；请吃(酒)；使醉. ⑪使高兴；使兴高采烈；使扬扬得意. ⑫拿出拍卖. ⑬排版；拼版；把剥制的标本等拼拢；裱装. ⑭装置；装备. ⑮【军】训练；锻炼. ⑯【海】扯紧索具. ~ ***up against*** 和…对抗. ~ ***up for*** 自称为；装作；摆…的架子. ~ ***upon*** = ~ on. ~ ***upside down*** 弄颠倒. — *a.* ①确定的. ②固定的；不动的；装好的. ③强硬的；(意见等)坚决的；决心的；急切的. ④顽固的；固执的；不变的. ⑤既定的；预定的；规定的；指定的；正式的. ⑥凝结的；凝固的. ⑦安好的；装好的；造成的，做成的. ⑧准备就绪的；(赛跑等)作好预备姿势的；(拳击等)拿好架子准备出击的. ⑨(两军)对垒的. ~ *eyes* 凝视不动的眼睛. *deep ~ eyes* 深陷的眼睛. *a ~ battle* 正式的战斗. *a ~ discourse* 正式演说，准备过的演说. *a ~ distance* 一定的距离. *a ~ machine* 安好的机器. *a ~ screw* 定位螺钉. *a ~ smile* 假笑. ***all*** ~ 〔美俚〕准备妥当；准备就绪. ***at the ~ time*** 在规定时间. ***be ~ in one's opinions*** 意见坚定. ***get*** ~ 〔赛跑口令〕预备(On your mark! Get ~! Go! 各就各位! 预备! 跑!). ***in ~ terms*** 用陈套. ***of [on, upon] ~ purpose*** 故意. ~ ***form for all cases*** = ~ ***method for different cases*** 千篇一律. ***with ~ teeth*** 咬紧牙关. — *n.* ①〔诗〕(太阳等的)下沉；日没. ②机组；(成套)设备；电子仪器. ③(餐具等的)套；(同类事物的)批，组，副，对；(由若干卷书组成的)部，集. ④【数】集(合)；【运】(网球等竞技比赛的)一局，一盘. ⑤【物】变定；【机】(弹簧等因使用过度形成的)变形. ⑥打印具；练铁完成器；螺旋钳；平起子；附钩螺旋钳；(铆钉的)打头器；(垫在桩头上使间接受力的)桩头垫；钳子；扣子；【木工】敲钉楔；锯齿；剉锯器. ⑦(墙壁的)末次粉刷. ⑧(铺路用)花岗石. ⑨型；形. ⑩【园艺】插条；苗木；树苗；幼树；树秧. ⑪刚结成的果实；种用小块茎[块根]. ⑫一窝(蛋). ⑬同伴；同类的人；党；派；集团；阶层；界. ⑭(风、潮水等的)方向，进路；倾向，趋势. ⑮【心】定向. ⑯歪斜；弯曲构造；弯曲；转弯. ⑰形状；形势；姿势；体态；态度. ⑱【猎】猎犬发现猎物时的蹲立不动姿势. ⑲(液体的)凝结；硬化. ⑳【捕鲸】戳刺；打进. ㉑【剧】舞台装置；布景. ㉒【影】发声装置. ㉓【无】接收机. ㉔【矿】巷道支架. ㉕锯齿的倾角；铅字宽度. ㉖卷做头发. ㉗一窝蛋. ㉘〔英〕(獾的)洞穴. ㉙猎狗发现猎物时的蹲立姿势. ㉚(篮球)远距离投篮. *a dinner ~* 一套餐具. *a radio ~* 收音机. *a television ~* 电视机. *an extension ~* 【电话】分机. *a head ~* 听筒；耳机. *a complete ~* 全副；全套. *Jones and his ~* 琼斯和他的同伙. *He is not of my ~.* 他不是我的同道. *the best ~* 权贵阶层. *the fast ~* 一伙放荡人物. *a literary [political] ~* 一班文艺界[政治界]人士. ***a dead*** ~ ①难关；死路；挫折. ②猛烈的攻击；反对的态度. ③(恋爱中人等的)如痴如迷的态度；死死地纠缠. ④【猎】猎狗发见猎物时的蹲立姿势. **~-aside** *n.* ①〔美〕联邦政府下令储备的军用物资. ②任何储备的物品. **~back** *n.* ①挫折；倒退；(病的)复发，逆流. ②延迟；阻碍. ③向后运动；后退；逆转. ④【建】(高楼上层壁面的)缩进；收进；上层壁面逐渐收进的高楼. ⑤后棱角. ⑥制动器. **~-down** *n.* ①申斥；斥责；辱骂；反驳；拒绝. ②(电车、火车等的)一段(路)；搭乘. **~-fair** ① *a.* (天气)晴定了的. ② *n.* 镘平的灰泥面. **~-in** ① *n.* (潮等的)上涨；开始；(冰霜雨雪的)来临，降落. ② *a.* 套入的；嵌装在里面的；附建在墙壁上的. **~off** *n.* ①扣除；抵销. ②装饰；装饰品；陪衬物 *(to)*. ③(旅行的)出发. ④【建】墙壁的凸出部. ⑤【印】粘脏 (未干油墨粘到另一张印张上). **~out** *n.* ①开始. (*at the first ~out* 最初，起头). ②出发；动身. ③准备；预备；布置. ④设备；装备. ⑤(餐具等的)一套. ⑥开饭；摆桌子. ⑦陈列. ⑧【印】排松[使字母之间有空隙]；排完(架上铅字). ~ **phrase** 成语；陈套. **~piece** *n.* ①按传统格式制作的艺术作品. ②大架焰火；花式焰火[构成较复杂画面的]. ③一套可移动的、立体的舞台布景. ④精心布置的行动 [局势]. ~ **scene** 舞台立体布景. ~ **screw** 固定[定位]螺丝；弹簧调节螺丝. ~ **square** 三角板. ~ **theory** 【数】集(合)论. **~-to** *n.* *(pl. ~-tos)*

殴斗；拳赛；争论；较量．～**up** *n.* ①组织；机构；构造；体制．②体格；身体的构造．③〔美〕(身体的)姿势；姿态．④布置好的餐桌［餐具］．⑤(科学仪器等的)装置；装配；配置；调整；准备．⑥(选定的)摄影机位置；某一位置的胶片拍摄长度．⑦〔美俚〕(故意布置得)容易做的工作；布置得一面倒的比赛．⑧〔美俚〕本领不行的拳击选手．⑨〔美台球〕易于得分的球．⑩〔美俚〕拿烈酒请客；混有威士忌酒的汽水．⑪计划；方案．⑫【无】调定．⑬〔计〕运算电路的构成．

se·ta·ceous [si'teiʃəs] *a.* ①具［有］刚毛的．②鬃毛状的；鬃状的．**-ly** *ad.*

SETAF＝Southern European Task Force（北大西洋公约组织的）南欧特遣部队．

Seth [seθ] *n.* ①塞斯〔男子名〕．②＝Set.

se·tif·er·ous [se'tifərəs] *a.*【生】具刚毛的，生刚毛的．

se·ti·form ['si:tiˌfɔ:m] *a.* 刚毛状的．

se·tig·er·ous [se'tidʒərəs] *a.* ＝setiferous.

se·ton ['si:tn] *n.*【医】①串线(法)；泄液线．②排液．

se·tose ['si:təus] *a.* ＝ setaceous.

set·te·cen·to [ˌsette'tʃentou] *n.*〔It.〕(意大利文艺的)十八世纪(时期)．

set·tee [se'ti:] *n.* ①长靠椅；中、小型长沙发．②三角帆船．

set·ter ['setə] *n.* ①安放者；安装者；嵌镶者；排字者；作曲者．②教唆者，嗾使者；为警察作谍报的人；(盗贼的)眼线．③塞特种猎狗．④【无】调节器；给定装置．～**-forth** 发行者；说明者．～**-off** 装饰物品．～**-on** 攻击者；教唆者；煽动者．

set·ting ['setiŋ] *n.* ①安装；装配；装置；安放．②(机器的)底座．③调整．④整齿．⑤剉锯子．⑥配乐；谱曲．⑦(果树的)坐果．⑧【印】排字．⑨镶嵌；镶嵌物；镶嵌(宝石等)的框子．⑩【剧，影】剧景；布景；舞台面．⑪背景；(花园的)布置；环境．⑫(天体的)没落；(日、月的)沉落．⑬(潮水、风等的)方向．⑭凝结；凝固；硬化．⑮炮床．⑯一套餐具．⑰【空】定位；【建】下沉．*a ～ hen* 伏窝的母鸡．*a circle ～*【测】度盘位置．*a ～ of butterflies* 一组蝴蝶标本．*with a sea ～*用海作背景．*a ～ chamber* 沉淀室．*a ～ tank* 澄水池．～ **box** 昆虫标本板．～ **lotion** 卷发水．～ **needle** 制标本用的木柄针．～ **rule**【印】排字尺．～ **stick** 排字托盘．～ **up**【无】调定．～**-up exercises** 不需要使用器械的健身操．

set·tle[1] ['setl] *vt.* ①安排；使妥贴；使安定，处理好，办好；决定；解决，确定．②使平静；使镇定．③调停；排解．④设定；派定；安牢；放定．⑤使就职．⑥使坐下．⑦使守规矩，使就范．⑧使坚固；使坚实；使地干硬．⑨使澄清；使沉淀；使降；【地】沉降．⑩支付；清算；清偿；结清(款项、帐目等)．⑪使住定；安顿；使定居．⑫殖民(某地)．⑬赠予．⑭【法】指定；授与；让渡；和解．⑮【动】使受孕．*～ a daughter by marriage* 嫁女儿．*That ～s the matter.* 这样问题就解决了．*The Government is quite ～d in power.* 政权稳固．*～ a claim* 结清债务．— *vi.* ①稳定；固定；平安；平静．②了结；解决．③偿付；清算；结算．④决定，确定．⑤安家；成家；安居；定居；侨居．⑥栖息．⑦变坚固；变结实．⑧澄清；沉淀；下沉；沉降．⑨和解．⑩【动】受孕；怀胎．***The weather has ～d at last.*** 天气终于稳定下来了．*～ down to dinner* 坐定下来用餐．***～ an account*** 清算；〔美、运〕雪耻，挣回面子．***～ down*** ①平静下来；恢复镇静．②沉淀；沉．③定居；成家；移居．④定下心来；定心去做．***～ for*** 满足于，对…感到满意．***～ in*** ①搬入（新住所）；使某人搬进（新住所）．②定居；殖民．③在家从容休息（*～ in Shanghai* 长住上海）．***～ into shape*** 逐渐成形，（事情）有了眉目．***～ on [upon]*** ①授与；赠与(财产、遗产等)．②决定；选定(*They have ～ed on you as my successor.* 他们已选定你为我的继承人)．③(鸟等)停在；歇落在．***～ one's affairs*** (在遗嘱等中)安排自己后事．***～ oneself*** 成家；择定住处；安家．***～ oneself (down)*** 定心去做．***～ sb. hash*** 〔美俚〕征服［收拾］某人．***～ the score*** 〔美运〕挣回面子．***～ up*** ①决定．②解决；支付．***～ with*** ①与…和解．②决定；讲定．③收拾．④付清，清算．⑤与…成交．

set·tle[2] ['setl] *n.* 高背长靠椅［座位下为柜子］．

set·tled ['setld] *a.* ①固定(下来)的；确定不变的；稳定(下来)的．②根深蒂固的；坚固的；安定的．③安居在一个地方的；有居民的．④深切的．⑤决定的．⑥终身借用的．⑦算清了的；已付清的．⑧【化】沉降的；澄清的．*a ～ abode* 固定的住所．*a ～ melancholy* 深愁．*～ conviction* 确信．*a ～ government* 稳定的政府．*～ weather* 稳定的天气．*～ estate* 终身租地．

set·tle·ment ['setlmənt] *n.* ①解决．②决定．③镇定；安定．④固定；定着．⑤澄清；沉淀；沉淀物；沉积物；【地】沉陷．⑥和解．⑦整理；清理．⑧支付；清算；清偿；结帐；决算．⑨殖民；殖民地；居留地；租界；(新)住宅区；居民点．⑩〔美〕部落；村落．⑪殖民团体；(一地的)居民社会．⑫居住权．⑬成家；有家属．⑭【法】(财产的)授与；让渡；处理．⑮(房屋等的)下沉．⑯(作为慈善事业的)贫民区社会改良团体．*a ～ out of court*【法】(自行)和解．*terms of ～* 和解条件．*the International S-* (解放前上海等处的)公共租界．*a marriage ～*【法】结婚时的财产授与处理．*a social ～* 社会服务处．***come to a ～*** ①解决．②决定．③和解．***make a ～ on [upon]*** 授财产给．***reach a ～*** ＝ come to a ～．～ **duty** 遗产税．～ **worker** 贫民区社会改良团体工作人员．

set·tler ['setlə] *n.* ①居留者；定居者．②移居者；殖民者，开拓者．③〔口〕决定性打击；定论；最后解决者．④赠予者；调停者．⑤【化】澄清器．⑥【冶】前床；沉积槽．

set·tling [-tliŋ] *n.* ①固定；安置．②沉淀．③〔*pl.*〕沉淀物；渣滓．④决定；解决．⑤结帐；清算；决算．⑥移住；殖民．⑦镇静．～ **day** *n.*〔英〕(交易所等的)清算日；交割日；结帐日．～ **tank** 沉淀槽．

set·tlor ['setlə] *n.*【法】财产授与人．

Se·vas·to·pol [si'væstəpl] *n.* 塞瓦斯托波尔〔苏联港市，海军基地〕．

sev·en ['sevən] *num.*，七；第七(章、卷、页等)．—*n.* ①七个东西．②七个一组．③七岁．④七点钟．⑤七个人；第七个人［物］．⑥〔喻〕十分，很多．*be frightened out of one's ～ senses* 吓得魂飞魄散．***at sixes and sevens*** 乱七八糟．***seventy times ～***巨额数目．～ **deadly sins**【宗】七大罪〔即 pride, covetousness, lust, anger, gluttony, envy, sloth, 据云犯此等罪者即下地狱〕．～**fold** *a., ad.* ①七倍的［地］；七重的［地］；七折的［地］．②非常的［地］．～**-hilled city** 罗马（的别名）．**S- Hills** 罗马七丘〔罗马城即建于此七座小山丘上及其附近〕．～**night** 七昼夜；一周；一星期．～ **principal virtues** 七美德〔即 faith, hope, charity, prudence, justice, fortitude, temperance〕．**S- Sages** 希腊七贤〔有几种说法，最通常指 Bias, Chilon, Cleobulus, Periander, Pittacus, Solon, Thales〕．～ **seas** 七大洋〔指南、北大平洋，南、北大西洋，印度洋，南、北冰洋〕；全球．～**-up** 七点儿〔二人到四人玩的一种牌戏，七点成局〕．

sev·en·teen ['sevən'ti:n] *num.* (基数词)十七；第十七．—*n.* ①十七个．②十七的数［物、人］．③十七的记号．④十七岁．⑤十八世纪．*sweet ～* 十七芳龄，妙龄．～**-year locust**【动】〔美〕十七年蝉〔幼虫在地下 13—17 年才成虫．〕

sev·en·teenth ['sevən'ti:nθ] *num.* ①第十七(的)．②十七号(的)．③十七分之一(的)．—*n.*〔the ～〕(月的)十七日．

sev·enth ['sevənθ] *num.* ①第七．②七号．③七分之一．—*n.* ①(月的)七日．②【乐】第七音［程、度］；第七和音．*a ～ part* 七分之一．*the ～ of May* 5月7日．**S- Art** 第七艺术〔指电影〕．**S- Avenue** 纽约市第七街；纽约市妇女服装中心．～ **chord**【乐】七和音．～**-day** *a.* 以星期六为安息日的．～ **heaven** ①七重天．

②极乐世界 (*be in the ~ heaven* 欢天喜地地; 在无上的幸福中). **~-inning touch**〔美〕努力; 奋发; 使劲. **-ly** *ad.*

sev·en·ti·eth [ˈsevəntiiθ] *num.* ①第七十(的). ②七十号(的); 第七十次(的). ③七十分之一(的).

sev·en·ty [ˈsevənti] *num.* (基数词)七十; 第七十(页等); 七十个. —*n.* ①七十个东西. ②七十的记号. ③七十多岁. ④〔*pl.*〕(世纪的)七十年代. *the nineteen ~* 1970 年. *the nineteen seventies* 二十世纪七十年代 (略 1970's). ⑤〔*pl.*〕七十到七十九岁的时期. ⑥〔俚〕快转速唱片. ***the S-*** ①翻译希腊文旧约《圣约》的七十二个译者〔常作LXX〕. ②古犹太的高等参议院. **~-eight** ①*num.* 七十八(个). ② *n.* 每分钟七十八转的唱片, 快转速唱片. **~-five** *n.*【军】法国的 75 厘米大炮. **~ fold** *a., ad.* 七十倍 (的、地). **~-four** *n.*【史】装有 74 门大炮的军舰. **~-three** (73) *n.*〔美〕祝平安〔Best wishes 的电报记号〕.

sev·er [ˈsevə] *vt.* ①切断; 割断. ②断绝; 分隔开; 使不和; 离间. ③【法】分割(产业等); 分别处理(权益等). ④区别. *~ diplomatic relations with* 和…断绝外交关系. *~ friends* 离间朋友. — *vi.* ①分离; 分裂; ②分开; 断. *The rope ~ed under the strain* 索子拉断了. ***~ one's connection with*** 和…断绝关系. ***~ oneself from*** 退(会); 脱离; 和…分离.

sev·er·a·ble [ˈsevərəbl] *a.* 可分开的;〔尤指〕【法】权益(或职责范围) 可分开的〔指契约〕. **sev·er·a·bil·i·ty** [ˌsevərəˈbiliti] *n.*

sev·er·al [ˈsevrəl] *a.* ①几个的; (二以上)多个的; 数个的. ②各不相同的; 种种的. ③各自的, 各个的. ④专有的, 独占的, 个人的. ⑤【法】有连带责任的. ⑥〔方〕大量的. *Each has his ~ ideal.* 各人有各人的理想. *They went their ~ ways.* 他们各走各的去了. *S- men, ~ minds.* 各人有各人的想法. *three ~ items* 三个各不相同的项目. *a ~ estate* 个人的财产. *a joint and ~ responsibility* 连带责任. *myself and ~ others* 我和其他几个人. ***each [every] ~*** 各别的, 各个的 (*Each ~ ship sank her opponent.* 各舰分别击沉了敌舰. *each ~ part* 各部分). ***for ~ days*** 好几天. ***~ times*** 屡次; 好几次. — *pron.* 几个, 数个; 数人. *S- have given their consent.* 有几个人已表示同意. *~ of us* 我们当中的几个人. **~-fold** *a., ad.* ①有几部分的[地]; 有几方面的[地]. ②好几倍的[地].

sev·er·al·ly [ˈsevrəli] *ad.* 各自; 分别; 个别(地). *conjunctly [jointly] and ~* 【法】负连带责任地. *The bond was signed jointly and ~.* 证书上有联名签字. *exeunt ~* 【剧】分别退场.

sev·er·al·ty [ˈsevərəlti] *n.* (*pl.* **-ties**) ①各自; 各个; 单独. ②个人拥有的财产. ③个人拥有财产; (土地的)个人所有权.

sev·er·ance [ˈsevərəns] *n.* ①切断; 隔断. ②分离, 隔离. ③(关系等) 断绝. ④区别, 差别. **~ pay** (雇主违约辞退工人时的)解雇费; 遣散费.

se·vere [siˈviə] *a.* (**-ver·er; -ver·est**) ①(面孔等)严肃的; 严正的; (训练等)严格的; 严厉的; (批评家等)苛刻的. ②猛烈的; 剧烈的; (暴风等)凶猛的; 凛烈的; 厉害的, (疾病等)严重的. ③困难的; 艰难的; (工作等)极难的. ④(建筑)简朴的; 简练的; (文艺作品)严谨的; 朴素的; 朴实的. ⑤精确的. *a ~ pain* 剧痛. *a ~ wound* 重伤. *a ~ sickness [disease]* 重病. ***be ~ on [upon]*** 猛烈攻击; 严厉对付.

se·vere·ly [siˈviəli] *ad.* ①猛烈地; 剧烈地. ②严密地; 严格地. ③严重地. ④严厉地; 苛刻地. ⑤简洁地. ***be ~ ill [wounded]*** 患重病[负重伤]. ***leave [let] ~ alone*** (因讨厌而)敬而远之.

se·ver·i·ty [siˈveriti] *n.* ①严肃; 严正; 严格; 严厉; 苛刻. ②严重. ③厉害; 猛烈. ④严密. ⑤纯洁. ⑥简朴; 简练. ⑦【机】刚度; 硬度. **~ factor** 硬[刚]度系数.

Se·ville[ˈsevil, səˈvil], **Se·vil·la** [seiˈviːjaː] *n.* 塞维利亚〔西班牙城市〕. **-vil·li·an** *a.*

Sè·vres [ˈseivr] *n.* ①塞夫勒〔法国城市〕. ②塞夫勒 (产的)陶器.

sew [səu] *vt.* (**-ed; -ed, sewn**[səun]) ①缝; 缝合; 缝制; 缝做; 缝补. ②装订(书籍). *~ a garment* 缝外套. *~ a buttonhole* 锁钮扣眼. — *vi.* 缝纫; 做针线活. ***be ~ed up*** ①【海】搁浅; 停顿. ②喝醉. **~ *in*** 缝进(*~ money in a bag* 把钱缝进袋里). **~ *on*** 缝上. **~ *up*** ①缝拢; 缝合. ②把…缝入; 缝进. ③〔卑〕使累极. ④〔俚〕使大醉. ⑤使(船)搁浅; 使无可如何. ⑥诈欺. ⑦〔美俚〕绝对控制住; 垄断; 压住. ⑧解决, 确定; 〔美俚〕成功地完成(协商、合约等).

sew·age [ˈsju(ː)idʒ] *n.* ①阴沟污物; 污水. ②下水道. —*vt.* ①用污水灌溉[作肥料]. ②装设下水道于(某地). **~-farm** ①污水利用农场; 污水灌溉田. ②污物处理场. **~ tank** 化粪池; 污水(沉淀)池.

se·wan [ˈsiːwən] *n.* 西文〔北美阿尔衮琴印第安人所用的贝壳货币〕.

Se·ward [ˈsiːwəd] *n.* ①西沃德〔姓氏〕. ②**W. H.** ~威廉·西沃德〔1801-1872, 美国政治家, 曾任国务卿〕. **~'s Folly** ①阿拉斯加的别称. ②暂时看来愚蠢、日后显示出极为合算的行为〔源出西沃德用巨款从俄国购买阿拉斯加之举〕.

se·wel·lel [sjuːˈwelel, siˈwelel] *n.* 【动】(美国西海岸的)鼠獭.

sew·er[1] [ˈsəuə] *n.* ①缝纫者; 缝工; 成衣师. ②缝纫机.

sew·er[2] [ˈsjuə] *n.* 阴沟; 污水管道; 下水道; 排水管. *the trunk ~* 下水干道. — *vt.* ①从…排污水. ②在…开阴沟; 装设下水道于. **~ gas**【化】阴沟气; 沟道气. **~ rat**【动】褐鼠.

sew·er[3] [ˈsjuːə] *n.* (中世纪贵族第宅中的)侍膳管家〔家仆〕.

sewer·age [ˈsjuəridʒ] *n.* ①污水; 污物 (= sewage). ②暗沟工事; 下水设备; 下水道系统, 排水系统; 沟渠系统. ③下水处理; 污水. ④肮脏思想〔言行〕.

sew·ing [ˈsəuiŋ] *n.* ①缝纫. ②(书的)装订. ③缝纫物; 针线活. ④〔*pl.*〕(缝纫用)线. **~ circle** 妇女义务缝纫组. **~cotton** 缝纫棉线. **~ machine** ①缝纫机. ②【装订】穿线订书机. **~ needle** (缝纫用)针. **~ press**【印】锁线装订机. **~ thread** (缝纫用)线.

sewn [səun] sew 的过去分词. **~-up** *a.* ①〔俚〕累极了的. ②〔俚〕大醉的.

sex [seks] *n.* ①性; (男女的)性别; 〔集合词〕男性, 女性. ②性的活动[器官]; 性交; 性欲; 色情. *persons of both ~es* 男男女女. *the two ~* 男女; 雌雄. *without distinction of age or ~* 不分男女老幼. ***have ~*** 〔美俚〕发生性行为. ***the fair [gentle, softer, weaker] ~*** 女性; 妇女. ***the male [rough, sterner, stronger] ~*** 男性; 男人. ***the ~***〔谑〕女人. —*vt.* ①区别(小鸡等)的性别. ②增强…的性感; 刺激起…的性欲. **~ *it up*** 〔美俚〕两性间的热烈爱抚. **~ *up*** 〔美口〕①勾引(异性). ②增加吸引力(*~ up the movie with some fighting scenes* 加几场打斗镜头以加强影片的吸引力). — *a.* 性的; 与性有关的. **~ appeal** 性的吸引力; 性感. **~ cell** 生殖细胞. **~ education** 性教育. **~ hormone** 性激素. **~ impulse** 性的冲动. **~ instinct** 性的本能. **~ linkage**【遗】伴性遗传; 性连锁. **~linked** *a.*【遗】伴性遗传的; 性连锁的. **~ pot** 〔美俚〕性感女人. **~ ratio** 男女人口比例. **~ urge** (病态的)性欲.

sex-, sexi- *comb. f.* 六: *sex*angle, *sexi* llion.

sex·a·ge·nar·i·an [ˌseksədʒiˈnɛəriən] *a., n.* 六十至六十九岁的(人); 六十多岁的(人).

sex·ag·e·na·ry [sekˈsædʒinəri] *n.* ①六十个 (东西). ②= sexagenarian (*n.*). —*a.* ①六十的. ②= sexagenarian (*a.*).

Sex·a·ges·i·ma [ˌseksəˈdʒesimə] *n.* 【宗】四旬节前第二个星期日〔亦作 S- Sunday〕.

sex·a·ges·i·mal [ˌseksəˈdʒesiməl] *a.* 六十的; 以六十为基础的; 六十进位的. — *n.*【数】六十分数〔以六十

为分母的分数〕.
sex·an·gle ['seks,æŋgl] *n.*【数】六角形.
sex·an·gu·lar [seks'ægjulə] *a.* 六角的.
sex·cen·te·na·ry [,sekssen'ti:nəri] *a.* 六百年的. — *n.* 六百年纪念.
sexed [sekst] *a.* ①性别的; 有性别的. ②有性欲的; 性感的. ~**-up** *a.*〔美俚〕①性感的. ②吸引人的.
sex·en·ni·al [sek'senjəl, -niəl] *a.* 六年间的; 连续六年的; 每六年的,六年一次[度]的. — *n.* 六周年纪念. **-ly** *ad.*
sex·foil ['seksfɔil] *n.*【建】六叶[六瓣花]形(装饰图案);【植】六瓣花,六叶复叶.
sexi- *comb. f.* =sex-.
sex·il·lion [sek'siljən] *n.* = sextillion.
sex·i·ly ['seksili] *ad.*〔口〕性感地.
sex·i·ness ['seksinis] *n.*〔口〕性吸引力; 性感.
sex·ism ['seksizm] *n.* 性别歧视〔尤指歧视妇女〕. **-ist** *n.* 实行性别歧视的人.
sex·i·va·lent ['seksi,veilənt] *a.*【化】①(有)六价的. ②(有)六种价的.
sex·less ['sekslis] *a.* 无性别的; 无性的; 中性的; 无性感的.
sex·ol·o·gy [sek'sɔlədʒi] *n.*【医】性行为学. **sex·ol·o·gist** *n.* 性行为学研究家.
sex·par·tite [seks'pɑ:tait] *a.* ①分成六部(分)的. ②【植】六深裂的. ~ **vault**【建】六肋拱穹.
sex·ploit·a·tion [,seksplɔi'teiʃən] *n.*〔美〕(电影等大肆宣扬色情的)性泛滥.
sex·ploit·er ['seksplɔitə] *n.*〔美〕色情电影.
sext [sekst] *n.* ①【宗】第六时 [正午] 祈祷(仪)式. ②【乐】第六度音程.
sex·tan ['sekstən] *a.* 隔六天发作一次的. *a* ~ *fever*【医】六日热. — *n.*【医】六日热.
Sex·tans ['sekstənz]【天】六分仪(星)座.
sex·tant ['sekstənt] *n.* ①六分仪. ②【天】〔S-〕六分仪(星)座(= Sextans). ③〔罕〕圆的六分之一.
sex·tet, sex·tette [seks'tet] *n.* ①六人[物]的一组. ②【乐】六重唱; 六重奏; 六重唱[奏]表演者. ③六行诗节. ④曲棍球队.
sex·tile ['sekstl] *n.*【天】(二天体互距的)六十度之位置. — *a.*【天】(二天体互距)六十度之位置的.
sex·til·lion [seks'tiljən] *n.* ①〔英、德〕100万的6次幂[乘方]〔1后有36个0的数〕. ②〔美、法〕1,000的7次幂[乘方]〔1后有21个0的数〕.
sex·to ['sekstəu] *n.* *(pl. ~es)* 六开本(的书).
sex·to·dec·i·mo ['sekstəu'desiməu] *n.* *(pl. ~s)* 十六开(的书[纸])(略16 *mo* 或16°, 通常读作 sixteenmo).
sex·ton ['sekstən] *n.* 教堂司事〔担任教堂内外管理、敲钟、墓地等工作〕.
sex·tu·ple ['sekstjupl] *a.* ①六倍的; 六重的. ②【乐】六拍子的. — *vt., vi.* (使)变成六倍.
sex·tu·plet [seks'tjuplit, -'tu:plit, -'tʌplit; 'sekstuplit] *n.* ①一胎六个之一. ②(同一类的)六个一组. ③〔*pl.*〕一胎六个. ④【乐】六连音.
sex·tu·plic·ate [seks'tju:plikeit] *vt.* ①使成六倍. ②把…打印成六份. —[seks'tju:plikit] *a.* ①重复六次的. ②第六的. — *n.* ①第六个同类物. ②相同的六份.
sex·u·al ['seksjuəl] *a.* ①性的; 有性别的. ②性欲的. ③生殖的;【生】有性的. ~ *affinity* 异性间的吸引力. ~ *appetite* 性欲. ~ *perversion* 变态性欲. ~ *intercourse [commerce]* 性交. ~ *diseases* 性病. ~ **generation**【生】有性世代. ~ **organs** 性器官; 生殖器. ~ **reproduction**【生】有性生殖. ~ **selection**【生】性选择; 雌性淘汰. ~ **spore**【植】有性胞子. **-ly** *ad.*
sex·u·al·i·ty [,seksju'æliti] *n.* ①性别; 有性状态. ②性欲; 性生活[行为].
sex·u·al·ize ['seksjuəlaiz] *vt.* *(-iz·ed, -iz·ing)* 给以性的特征; 使有性别.
sex·y ['seksi] *a.* *(-i·er; -i·est)*〔美俚〕①有性的吸引力的; 性感的; 色情的. ②因加装饰而更为有趣的.
Sey·chelles [sei'ʃelz] *n.* 塞舌尔(群岛)〔非洲〕.
Sey·mour ['si:mɔ:r, 'seimɔ:] *n.* 西摩〔姓氏, 男子名〕.
Sezyou [sez'ju:] (= says you)〔美俚〕你说你的吧(我可不信).
sf. = 〔It.〕 *sforzando.*
S.F. = ①San Francisco. ②Sinn Fein〔爱尔兰〕新芬党.
s.f. = ①selffeeding 自动送料; 自动进给. ②sinkingfund 减债资金. ③square foot. ④*sub fine [finem]*〔L.〕(【乐】到末尾). ⑤semi-finished 半加工的; 半光制的. ⑥=square foot 平方英尺. ⑦=science fiction 科幻小说.
Sfax [sfɑ:ks] *n.* 斯法克斯〔突尼斯港市〕.
Sfc = sergeant first class (〔陆军〕上士).
S.F.C. = specific fuel consumption 单位耗油率.
sfer·ics ['sfiəriks, ,sfer-] *n. pl.* 〔动词用单数〕【无】①低频天电 (= atmospherics). ②低频天电学, 天电学. ③远程雷电 ④风暴电子探测器.
sfor·zan·do [sfɔ:'tsɑ:ndəu]〔It.〕*a., ad.*【乐】强调; 着重; 力; 突出. — *n.* *(pl. -dos)* 特强符号 "sf".
sfor·za·to [sfɔ:r'tsɑ:təu] 〔It.〕 *a., ad.* = sforzando.
sfz = 〔It.〕 *sforzando.*
s.g. = specific gravity【物】比重.
SG = sweep generator 扫描[扫频]振荡器.
sg. = signature.
S.G. = ①Solicitor-General ②〔L.〕【海】*salutis gratia* (为安全起见). ③【海】ship and goods 船货. ④screen grid【电】帘栅极. ⑤signal generator 信号发生器. ⑥spark gap【电】火花隙.
sgd. = signed.
s.g.d.g. = 〔F.〕 *Sans garantie du gouvernment* (〔F.〕 = without Government guarantee) 政府不予担保.
sgl. = single 单独的; 单一的; 纯粹的; 单纯的.
SGR = sodium graphite reactor 石墨慢化钠冷反应堆; 纳石墨反应堆.
sgraf·fi·to [skræ'fi:təu; It. zgrɑ:f'fi:təu] *n.* *(pl. -fi·ti* [-ti:])【建】①五彩拉毛粉饰法. ②五彩拉毛粉饰. ③五彩拉毛粉饰陶瓷.
Sgt., sgt. = sergeant.
Sgt. Maj. = Sergeant Major.
sh. = 〔美〕 ①share. ② sheet. ③shilling. ④shunt.
S.H. = School House.
SHA = sideral hour angle【海】赤经共轭量; 恒星时角.
shab·by ['ʃæbi] *a.* *(-bi·er; bi·est)* ①(衣衫)褴褛的; 破旧的. ②失修的. ③腌臜的. ④卑劣的; 卑鄙的. ⑤吝啬的. ⑥低劣的; 拙劣的; 简陋的. *a* ~ *street* 腌臜的马路. *a* ~ *fellow* 卑鄙的家伙; 小气鬼. ~**-gen·teel** *a.* 穷要面子的; 摆穷架子的. **-bi·ly** *ad.* **-bi·ness** *n.*
shab·rach, shab·rack ['ʃæbræk] *n.* (骑兵用的)鞍被[鞍褥].
Sha·bu·oth [ʃɑ:'vu:əut, ʃə'vu:əus] *n.* = Shavuot.
shack[1] [ʃæk] *n.* ①〔美、加〕窝棚; 圆木小屋. ②(派某种用场的)小室, 房间; 〔美俚〕无线电收发室. — *vi.* 居住; 暂住. ~ ***up*** ①住下. ②过夜; 宿泊. ③(与人)姘居; 同居. ~ **job**〔美俚〕情妇, 姘头.
shack[2] [ʃæk] *n.* ①〔美〕游民. ②驽马; 废马. ③【铁路】〔美俚〕制动员. ~ **fever**〔美俚〕(游民)想打瞌睡的疲乏.
shack[3] [ʃæk] *n.* ①〔方〕落穗; 落实. ②收获后茬地上的放牧自由权.
shack[4] [ʃæk] *vt.* 〔美口〕追到、捡起并把(球)丢回去; 取回来.
shack·le ['ʃækl] *n.* ①〔常 *pl.*〕手铐; 脚镣; 〔*pl.*〕桎梏. ②〔*pl.*〕束缚(物); 羁绊(物); 阻碍(物); 碍手碍脚的东西. ③枷形装饰. ④【机】钩环; 【铁路】(车厢间的)钩链. ⑤【电】绝缘器. ⑥【海】十五英尺长的缆绳[锚链].

the ~s of convention 陈规旧习的束缚. — *vt.* ①给…上手铐[上脚镣]. ②束缚;拘束. ③妨碍;阻碍. ④用钩链连结. ⑤【电】在…装绝缘器. ~ **bone** 〔Scot.〕①动物的膝或肘关节. ②手腕,腕关节.

Shack·le·ton [ˈʃækltən] *n.* ①沙克尔顿〔姓氏〕. **Sir Ernest Henry** ~ 沙克尔顿〔1874—1922, 英国南极探险家〕.

shad [ʃæd] *n.* 【鱼】(美洲)河鲱.

shad·berry [ˈʃædberi], **shad·bush** [ˈʃædbuʃ] *n.* 【植】唐棣〔又叫 shadblow〕.

shad·chan, shad·chen [ˈʃɑːtkhən] *n.* = schatchen.

shad·dock [ˈʃædək] *n.* 【植】柚子.

shade [ʃeid] *n.* ①荫; 阴处; 树阴. ②〔*pl.*〕阴暗, 幽暗. ③遮阳;遮棚;天幔;阳伞;灯罩;簾;幕;屏风;挡风物;遮尘物;挡热隔子;玻璃罩. ④〔*pl.*〕〔美俚〕太阳眼镜. ⑤(画的)阴暗部分;朦胧色;晕色;明暗; 浓淡; 色调. ⑥〔诗〕〔主 *pl.*〕隐居处; 僻远处. ⑦幽灵; 阴魂. ⑧〔the ~s〕〔诗〕黄泉;冥府;阴间;死;坟墓. ⑨〔*pl.*〕酒窖;地下室酒吧间;旅馆的酒吧间. ⑩些许;少许. ⑪愁容,面色阴郁. ⑫〔美俚〕窝赃犯. *the ~ of night* 夜色苍茫. *the same colour in a light ~*. 同样颜色浅一点的. *This picture shows fine effects of light and ~*. 这幅画的明暗效果很好. *people of all ~s (of opinions)* (意见)千差万别的人们. ***a ~ of*** 少许;微微(*a ~ of difference* 微微一点区别). ***cast into the ~*** 使失色;使相形见绌. ***delicate ~s of meaning*** 意义的细微层次. ***fall into the ~*** ①被夺去光彩;黯然失色. ②被踢下来. ***go down to the ~s*** 死. ***in [into] the ~*** ①在阴处;在树阴下;在暗处. ②没落;衰微 (*in the ~ of obscurity* 避着人眼; 被人遗忘). ***not a ~ of doubt*** 毫不怀疑. ***put into the ~*** = cast into the ~. ***S- of Priscian [Plato, Soyer]!*** 活见鬼!〔普里兴、柏拉图, 索雅三人各为语法、哲学、烹饪之祖; 语法家、哲学家、厨师闹笑话时的叹声〕. ***the shadow of a ~*** 幻影;虚中之虚. ***throw into the ~*** = cast into the ~. ***under the ~ of*** *(a tree)* 在(树)阴底下. ***without light and ~*** (画)没有明暗的;(文章等)单调的. —*vt.* ①遮(光);阴蔽;遮蔽;覆盖;隐藏;在…装遮阳篷[天棚](等). ②使暗;使失色;使黯淡. ③在(画上)画阴影;使色采具有明暗层次. ④使(意见,方法等)逐渐改变. ⑤〔美〕略减(物价). ⑥使(风琴管)音调缓和. ~ *one's eyes with one's hand* 用手挡住射向眼睛的直射光. *a ~d lamp* 装有灯罩的灯. ~ **density** 【林】郁闭度. — *vi.*(色彩、意见、意义等)逐渐变化 *(away; off; into)*.

shad·i·ly [ˈʃeidəli] *ad.* ①多荫地;阴暗地. ②暧昧地;可疑地.

shad·i·ness [ˈʃeidinis] *n.* ①多阴;阴暗. ②暧昧;可疑.

shad·ing [ˈʃeidiŋ] *n.* ①阴蔽. ②【绘画】阴影;明暗;浓淡. ③〔喻〕隐微的渐变;细微差别[层次].

sha·doof [ʃɑːˈduːf, ʃəˈduːf] *n.* (中东地区农民用的)汲水吊杆;桔槔.

shad·ow [ˈʃædəu] *n.* ①(阴)影;影象;阴暗;黑暗. ②影子;形影相随的人. ③跟着客人来的人;不速之客;食客. ④〔美俚〕侦探. ⑤鬼;幽灵;幻影. ⑥迹象; 苗头; 前兆;预兆. ⑦少许;一点点. ⑧隐藏处;庇护;保护;隐退(处) ⑧(电波传播)静区. ⑨〔美俚〕〔贬〕黑人. ⑩郁郁寡欢(的神色). ⑪没落,微贱. ⑫(友谊等的)暂时中断. *Coming events cast their ~s before.* 事未发生; 先有苗头. *May your ~ never grow less!* 祝你永远健康! *the ~s of old age* 老态. *the ~ of a name* 虚名. *the ~ of death* 死的前兆. ***be afraid of one's own ~*** 风声鹤唳; 草木皆兵. ***be the ~ of one's former self*** = ***be worn to a ~*** 瘦成皮包骨头. ***cast ~s*** 投影; 预兆. ***catch [grasp] at ~s, run after ~s*** 捕风捉影; 徒劳. ***fight with one's own ~*** 和自己的影子作战,进行毫无结果的斗争. ***have only the ~ of*** *(freedom)* 获得有名无实的(自由). ***in the ~*** 在阴处;在暗处. ***in the ~ of*** 在…的附近〔身边〕;与…很接近. ***live in the ~*** 隐姓埋名. ***quarrel with one's own ~*** 容易为小事情而发莫名其妙的脾气. ***under [in] the ~ of*** ①在…的附近[身边]. ②与…很接近. ③在…的保护下. ***within the ~ of*** 在…的身边. ***without a ~ of doubt*** 毫不怀疑地. — *vt.* ①把影子投在…上; 用自身的影子遮住; 遮阴; 遮暗; 遮住; 遮蔽; 遮盖; 隐藏;隐匿. ②保护; 庇护. ③(在画上)画阴影; 使朦胧; 使阴暗. ④尾随; 跟牢; 盯牢; 盯梢. ⑤暗暗表示; 预示; 成为…的前兆. *He is ~ed by the police.* 他被警察盯住了. ~ *forth some future occurrence* 预示将来的事. — *vi.* 渐变; 变阴暗. ~ **aircraft** 侦察机. ~ **angle** 影锥角. ~ **area** 投影面积. ~ **bands** 【无】影带. ~ box〔美〕(挂在墙上,有玻璃盖的) 陈列框. ~**box** *vi.* ①作拳击练习;与假想的对手作拳斗. ②避免作出直接的决定行动. ~ **cabinet** ①〔英〕(假拟的由在野党人士组成的)影子内阁. ②总统[首相]的智囊团. ~ **dance** 影舞〔不见舞者本人,只见其映在幕布上的影子〕. ~ **effect** 【无】阴影效应; 屏蔽效果. ~ **factory** 战时可转产军需品的民用工厂. ~-**land** ①鬼世界,阴府. ②想象中的世界,幻境. ~ **mask** ①投影掩模;障板. ②(彩色显象管的)遮蔽屏. ~ **play** 影子戏. ~ **silk** 闪光绸. ~ **tone** 半色调.

shad·ow·graph [ˈʃædəugrɑːf] *n.* ①(用阴影在墙上作成的)投影画;描影;影象图. ②【摄】(逆光)影象;逆光摄影;阴影摄影. ③放射线照相(= radiograph); X光摄影. ④=shadow play.

shad·ow·y [ˈʃædəui] *a.* ①多阴影的;多荫的;郁苍的;阴暗的. ②朦胧的;模糊的. ③影子一般的;虚幻的. ④前兆性的;暗中表示的;爱空想的. *a ~ hope* 微薄暗淡的希望. **shad·ow·i·ness** *n.*

shad·y [ˈʃeidi] *a.* ***(-i·er; -i·est)*** ①多阴影的; 有荫的; 荫蔽的;成荫的;背阴的;遮阴的; ②(年龄)过了盛年的. ③不可靠的;不明不白的;可疑的. ④阴暗的;秘密的;背着人的. *a ~ character* 可疑的人物[性格]. ***keep ~*** 〔美〕避开人眼;藏匿. ***on the ~ side of*** ①在…的黑暗一面;在…的背阴方面;在下坡路上. ②〔年龄〕…多岁;超过;大于 (*on the ~ side of forty* 已过四十). **-i·ly** *ad.* **-i·ness** *n.*

SHAEF=Supreme Headquarters Allied Expeditionary Force (二次大战期间)盟军最高统帅部.

shaft [ʃɑːft] *n.* ①箭; 箭杆. ②(枪、槌、斧等的)柄;矛. ③【植】干;茎;柄. ④【动】羽轴;羽干. ⑤(古生物的)主突起茎. ⑥〔the ~s〕辕;车杠;车把. ⑦烛台杆;鞭柄; 棍棒; 旗竿. ⑧【建】柱身. ⑨(露出屋面的)烟囱. ⑩轴;旋转轴. ⑪【冶】炉身. ⑫【矿】矿井; 竖坑; 通风管道;升降井. ⑬光线;电光. ⑭柱;柱身. ⑮〔美〕纪念标; 尖塔. ⑯〔美俚〕大腿. ~ *excavation* 井筒掘进;竖井. *~s of satire [ridicule, envy]* 尖锐的讽刺〔嘲笑, 嫉妒〕. ~ *walls* 炉墙. ***get the ~*** 〔俚〕受骗. ***give (sb.) the ~*** 〔俚〕欺骗(某人). ***have a ~ left in one's quiver*** 还有本钱, 还有计可施. ~ **bearing** 【机】轴承. ~ **horse** 辕马. ~ **house** 【矿】(竖坑口升降机器用的)粗架. ~ **sinking** 【矿】凿井.

Shaftes·bur·y [ˈɹɑːftsbəri] *n.* 沙夫茨伯里[姓氏].

shaft·ing [ˈʃɑːftiŋ] *n.* 【机】①轴系. ②传动轴. ③轴材.

shag[1] [ʃæg] *n.* ①粗毛. ②【纺】长绒;长绒粗呢. ③粗烟丝. ④杂[蓬]乱的一丛[毛发,草丛,灌木等].

shag[2] [ʃæg] *n.* 【动】欧洲鸬鹚[鹈鹕];绿鸬鹚;有冠鸬鹚.

shag[3] [ʃæg] 〔美〕 *vt.* ***(shag·ged, shg·ging)*** ①追赶; 追回. ②钉在…后面;紧跟在后面;推拥.

shag·a·nap·pi [ˈʃægəˌnæpi] *n.* 生皮带;〔总称〕皮条.

shag·bark [ˈʃægbɑːk] *n.* 〔美〕【植】①小糙皮山核桃树. ②这种树的木材. ③这种树结的核桃.

shagged [ʃægid] *a.* ①〔英口〕累坏了;累垮了. ②有〔似〕粗毛的. ③有粗植物的. ④表面粗糙的.

shag·gy [ˈʃægi] *a.* ***(gi·er; gi·est)*** ①多粗毛的; 毛发蓬松的. ②【动、植】有绒毛的;草木丛生的. ③粗野的;不整洁的. ~ **dog story** ①冗长繁琐叙述后有一个意外结尾的故事。②以一个会说话动物为主角的故事［笑话等］。**-gi·ly** *ad.* **-gi·ness** *n.*

sha·green [ˈʃægriːn] *n.* ①鲨革。②表面呈粒状的皮革。

shah [ʃɑː] *n.* 〔Per.〕王；伊朗国王的称号。～**dom** 伊朗国王的领土；王位。

Sha·hap·ti·an [ʃɑːˈhæptiən] *n.* = Sahaptin.

shai·tan [ʃaiˈtɑːn] *n.* ①魔鬼；〔尤指〕〔常用 S-〕撒旦〔穆斯林用语〕。②恶人；坏人。

shake [ʃeik] ***(shook*** [ʃuk]; ***shak·en*** [ˈʃeikən]) *vt.* ①摇；摇动；摇撼。②动摇(信念、决心等)；使(人心)动摇。③挥(拳)。④摇醒(睡着的人)*(up)*。⑤摇落*(from; out of)*。⑥使战慄；使发抖。⑦减损；减少；挫折(勇气等)。⑧〔俚〕摆脱。⑨【乐】使发颤声；使抖颤。⑩〔美俚〕=～down. *To be shaken before taking.*【药】服前摇匀。*His resolution is not to be shaken by anything.* 他的决心是怎么也动摇不了的。*The ranks were shaken, but not broken.* 队伍动摇了，但未崩溃。—*vi.* ①发抖；抖颤；战慄；震颤。②动；震动；摇曳；摆动；动摇。③【乐】发颤声。④〔美俗〕〔用命令语气〕握手。***be shaken at*** 被…惊吓。***deserve a good shaking*** 该好好的揍一顿。～***a foot [leg]*** ①跳舞。②〔美俚〕赶快〔通常用命令语气〕。～***a loose leg*** 漫游；闲荡；徘徊。～***a stick at*** 〔美俚〕数不清(*There are as many taverns as you can ～ a stick at.* 有无数小酒馆)。～***down*** ①(将果实从树上)摇下来；摇下去；摇平(米谷等)。②把(毯子等)做成临时床铺。③使安定[稳定]下来。④整理使有秩序。⑤精简；缩减。⑥〔美俚〕勒索；敲诈；纳(贿)。⑦【俚】搜查；搜(身)；搜索(武器或钱)。～***hands*** 握手。～***in one's shoes*** 吓得发抖；战慄。～***it up!*** 〔美俚〕赶快！～***off*** ①抖去；弹去；拍去(灰尘等)。②医好(疾病)。③抛弃(坏习惯)；摆脱(坏朋友)。④撵走；断绝关系。⑤推开；拆开；消除；避开；巧妙逃避。～***on it*** 〔美〕口头约定；致祝辞。～***on to*** 承认；答应。～***one's bones*** 〔卑〕跳舞。～***one's finger at*** 拿食指抖颤地指着〔表示威胁，警告，责备〕。～***one's fist [stick] in sb. face [at sb.]*** 挥拳［棍子］威胁。～***one's head*** 摇头〔表示拒绝，否定，谴责，失望〕。～***one's sides with laughter*** 捧腹大笑。～***oneself free [loose] from*** 摆脱。～***oneself together*** 奋发；拿出勇气。～***out*** 抖开；展开(旗子等)摊开；晒干(毯子等)；抖掉(灰尘)。～***sb. by the hand*** 和人握手。～***the dust from one's feet*** 愤然离开。～***the jinx*** 〔美〕连败后打胜。～***up*** ①摇匀；摇动；抖匀(枕头等)。②摇醒。③打击；鞭挞。④震动。⑤激起。—*n.* ①震动；摇动；动摇。②握手。③打击。④冲动；激动。⑤发抖；战慄；震惊；〔口〕地震。⑥(木材的)轮裂，心裂；裂口；裂缝；(由圆木锯成的)盖屋板。⑦【乐】颤音。⑧〔口〕片刻；一刹那；一瞬间；⑨【物】(精密计时单位)百分之一微秒。⑩〔美口〕牛奶冰淇淋搅合饮料(= milk-～)。⑪驱逐；撵走；解雇。⑫〔the ～s〕〔俚〕发冷，疟疾；酒精中毒性精神病人。⑬【造纸】抄纸机。⑭〔美俚〕敲诈，勒索；贿赂。⑮命运；运气，***a brace of ～s*** 片刻。***a fair*** ～〔美〕正常的交易；公正的处置［安排，待遇］。***all of a*** ～ 颤抖，索索发抖。***give (sth.) a good*** ～ 使劲地摇。***give a*** ～ ①摇一摇。②逐出；撵走。***have the ～s*** 发寒热；发疟疾。***in half a*** ～ 立刻；马上；忽然。***in a brace [couple] of ～s*** = ***in the ～ of a lamb's tail*** = ***in two ～s*** = ***in half a*** ～〔俚〕忽然；马上，立刻。***no great ～s*** 并不出色；并不重要；平凡。***on the*** ～〔美俚〕参与犯罪活动(尤指行贿、受贿等)。***put sb. on the*** ～ = ***put the ～ on sb.*** 〔美俚〕向某人勒索钱财。

shake·down [ˈʃeikˈdaun] *n.* ①摇落。②临时铺的地铺。③〔美俚〕敲诈，勒索。④狂舞。

shak·en [ˈʃeikən] shake 的过去分词。—*a.* ①摇晃的；动摇的。②受震的。③颓丧的；虚弱的。④撞碎了的；开了裂的。

shake·out [ˈʃeikˌaut] *n.* ①抛售(债券等)。②(行情下跌中赢利微薄行业、产品等的被淘汰。③股票的暴跌。

shak·er [ˈʃeikə] *n.* ①摇的人[物]；震动的人[物]。②震荡器；【纺】混合器；振动(试验)器。③打绒机。④振子；筛。⑤(盖上有细孔的)细孔瓶，胡椒粉缸，盐缸。⑥〔S-〕震教徒〔十八世纪基督教的一个教派，做礼拜等时颤抖狂舞〕。*a cocktail* ～ 鸡尾酒混和器。*a pepper* ～(盖上有小孔的)胡椒瓶。

Shake·speare, Shak·spear(e) [ˈʃeikspiə], **William** 莎士比亚〔1564—1616，英国诗人，戏剧家〕。

Shake·spear·e·an, -i·an [ʃeikˈspiəriən] *a.* 莎士比亚(时代)的；莎士比亚作的；莎士比亚风格的。—*n.* 莎士比亚研究者[崇拜者]。**-spear·i·a·na** [ˌʃeikspiəriˈɑːnə] *n.* 莎士比亚文学[研究文献、言行录]。～ **sonnet** (按莎士比亚十四行诗格律作的)英国十四行诗。**-spear·i·an·ism** 莎士比亚语风[文体]。

shake-up [ˈʃeikˈʌp] *n.* ①〔美口〕动乱；骚动。②摇动；震动；激动；搅动。③〔俚〕机构的大改组；人员大变动。

shak·o [ˈʃækəu] *n.* *(pl.* ～*s)* (通常前面有一簇羽毛帽缨的)步兵筒状军帽。

shako·dër [ˈʃkəudə] *n.* 斯库台〔阿尔巴尼亚城市〕。

Shak·spere [ˈʃeikspi] = Shakespeare.

Shak·ti [ˈʃʌkti] *n.* 【印度教】= Sakti. **-tism** *n.* = Saktism.

shak·y [ˈʃeiki] *a.* ①震动的；摇动的。②(手等)发抖的；震撼的；战慄的。③有裂口的；龟裂的。④(房子、椅子等)摇摇晃晃的。⑤(地位、信用等)动摇的；不稳的；不可靠的；靠不住的。⑥(投票人等)三心二意的。⑦(老人等)衰弱的；有病的。***feel*** ～ 不舒服。***look*** ～ 脸色不好。**-i·ly** *ad.* **-i·ness** *n.*

shale [ʃeil] *n.* 【矿】页岩。*oil* ～ 油母页岩。～ *oil* 页岩油。

shall [强 ʃæl；弱 ʃəl, ʃl] *v. aux.* ★ 在现代英语(尤其在美国英语)中有用 will 代 shall 的趋势；目前在美国(口头语)中第一人称用 will 的也很普通，因此本来是 I will 之略的 I'll 也可视作是 I shall 的缩略形式：*I'll go there tomorrow.* ①〔单纯未来，用于第一人称单复数〕将要，会。*I ～ arrive by the first train tomorrow.* 我将于明天搭头班车到达。*I ～ be back soon.* 我马上就会回来。*You must do this. — (I) shan't* 你必须做这件事。—(我)不干〔句中加强 shall 的语势，有表示决心、意志之意〕。②[ʃæl]〔意志未来，在陈述句中用于第二人称或第三人称，表示说话者的意志、命令、约定、决心、警告、威吓、预言等〕必须；应该；要；得；给。*You ～ do what you are told.* 叫你做什么你就该做什么。*He shan't have any; he has been most rude.* 什么也不给他，他太没礼貌了。*He ～ be punished.* 他得受处罚。*You ～ die. (= I will make you die.)* 我要杀死你。③疑问句：(a)〔单纯未来〕*S- you ...?* (b)〔单纯未来或问对方的意愿〕*S- I [we] ...?* (c)〔问对方的意愿〕*S- he [she, it, they] ...?* (d)〔问意愿〕*Will you ...?* (e)〔问意愿或单纯未来〕*Shall he [she, they] ...?* …吗；…好吗；叫…好吗；是不是想…；会…吗；*S- you go?* 你去吗。*S- I be in your way?* 我会妨碍你吗？*S- I get you some more tea?* 再来点茶好吗？*Have another cigar — S- I?* 再抽一支雪茄——好吗？*S- he make a speech?* 叫［请］他演说好吗？④〔在以 if, when 等词开始的从句中，第一人称表示未来，第二或第三人称表示不能确定〕将；便，就。*When I ～ see her, I ～ give her your message.* 我见到她就把你的信交给她。*If he ～ come, we ～ be save.* 要是他来，我们就有救了。

shal·loon [ʃəˈluːn] *n.* 【纺】二上二下斜纹组织；夏龙绒〔作里子或女服用〕。

shal·lop [ˈʃæləp] *n.* ①〔诗〕轻舟；小船。②小型战船。③(四角帆的)双桅船。

shal·lot [ʃəˈlɔt] *n.* 【植】冬葱；冻葱；亚实基隆葱；青葱。

shal·low [ˈʃæləu] *a.* *(～er; ～est)* (水、器物等)浅的。②浅薄的；③肤浅的；表面的；皮毛的。④(呼吸)浅短

的. — *n.*〔常 *pl.*〕浅处; 浅滩. — *vt., vi.* (使)变浅; (使)变浅薄. **~-brained, ~-headed, ~-pated** *a.* (知识)肤浅的; 浅薄的; 头脑简单的; 愚蠢的. **~-hearted** *a.* 薄情的. **-ly** *ad.* **-ness** *n.*

sha·lom [ʃɑːˈləum] *n., int.* 舍拉姆〔犹太人传统的招呼、道别语,意为"平安"〕.

shalt [强 ʃælt; 弱 ʃəlt, ʃlt] *v. aux.*〔古〕shall 的第二人称单数陈述语气现在时〔主语为 thou 时用〕.

shal·y [ˈʃeili] *a.*【矿】页岩的; 含页岩的; 页岩状的.

sham [ʃæm] *n.* ①假冒; 虚伪; 欺诈. ②虚伪的事; 伪(装)物; 赝品. ③骗子; 欺骗者. ④(起床后做装饰用的)枕头套; 床单. *a pillow* ~(作装饰用的)绣花枕套. *a sheet* ~ 装饰性床单. — *a.* 假的; 虚伪的; 仿制的. *a* ~ *fight* 演习战; 模拟战. *a* ~ *gentleman* 伪君子. ***a ~ plea*** 【法】(以拖延时间为目的的)虚伪的抗辩. — *vt., vi.* 假装,冒充. ~ *illness [ill]* 装病. ~ *sleep [asleep]* 装睡. *She is not ill, she is only shamming.* 她没有病,是在装病. ~ ***Abraham*** 装病.

sha·man [ˈʃæmən] *n.* 萨满教巫师; 黄教僧. **-ism** *n.*【宗】(西伯利亚北部等处的)萨满教,黄教. **-ist** *n.* 萨满〔黄〕教徒.

sham·ble [ˈʃæmbl] *vi.* 蹒跚; 踉踉跄跄地走; 拖着脚步走. — *n.* 蹒跚; 踉跄; 蹒跚的脚步.

sham·bles [ˈʃæmblz] *n. pl.*〔用作单或复〕①屠(宰)场; 宰牛场. ②肉铺; 肉摊; 肉市. ③屠杀场(所). ④(被轰炸后的)废墟. ⑤大混乱. *Her desk is a* ~. 她的桌子上乱七八糟.

shame [ʃeim] *n.* ①耻辱; 羞耻; 羞愧. ②廉耻心; 羞耻心. ③可耻的事〔人, 物〕. ④侮辱; 凌辱. ⑤不贞. ⑥〔口〕太岂有此理的事情; 不应该的事情; 令人惋惜的事. *flush with* ~ 羞得脸红. *a burning [crying]* ~ 奇耻大辱. *a life of* ~ 卖笑生活. *What a* ~ *to treat you like that!* 那样对待你实在太不应该了. ***bring a blush of ~ to sb.'s cheek*** 使人脸红; 使丢脸. ***bring sb. to ~*** 使人脸红; 侮辱; 欺负. ***bring ~ on*** = ***bring to ~*** 使丢脸; 侮辱. ***cannot do it for very ~*** 不好意思做. ***cry ~ upon*** 指责…可耻. ***dead to ~*** 不知耻; 不怕难为情. ***Fie for ~!*** = For ~! ***for ~*** = ***from [out of] ~*** 知耻而; 羞得; 红着脸. ***For ~!*** 真丢脸! 好不要脸! 真可耻! ***lost to ~*** = past ~. ***past ~*** 无耻; 不要脸. ***put to ~*** 给丢脸; 使脸红; 侮辱. ***S- on you!*** = For ~! ***to the ~ of*** 自觉惭愧地, 很惭愧地. ***without ~*** 无耻. ***What a ~!*** 真丢脸! 〔口〕真遗憾. — *vt.* ①使羞愧; 使害羞; 使丢脸; 侮辱; 凌辱. ②使相形见绌; 使黯然失色; 〔主用被动语态〕使感觉羞耻而 *(into; out of doing). He was ~d into working [out of his bad habits]* 他羞愧得开始工作了〔改了他的坏习惯了〕. **~faced** *a.* ①害羞的; 发怯的. ②可耻的; 丢人的. ③〔诗〕谦逊的; 脸皮薄的. ④不惹眼的,朴素的. ~ **reel** *n.*〔Scot.〕婚礼后的跳舞.

shame·ful [ˈʃeimful] *a.* ①可耻的; 丢脸的. ②猥亵的. **-ly** *ad.* **-ness** *n.*

shame·less [ˈʃeimlis] *a.* ①无耻的; 不要脸的. ②猥亵的,伤风败俗的. **-ly** *ad.* **-ness** *n.*

sham·mer [ˈʃæmə] *n.* 冒充者; 骗子; 说谎者.

sham·my [ˈʃæmi] *n.* = chamois.

Sha·mo [ˈʃɑːˈməu]〔Chin.〕沙漠〔特指大戈壁〕.

sham·oy [ˈʃæmɔi] = shammy.

sham·poo [ʃæmˈpuː] *n.* ①洗头; 洗发. ②洗发剂. ~ *powder* 洗发粉. — *vt.* ①(用肥皂等)洗(头〔头发〕). ②给…洗头发. ③〔罕〕给…浴后按摩身体.

sham·rock [ˈʃæmrɔk] *n.*【植】①白花酢浆草 (= white clover)〔爱尔兰的国花〕. ②三叶苜蓿. ③天兰.

sham·us [ˈʃæməs] *n. (pl. ~es)*〔美俚〕①警察. ②私家侦探.

Shan [ʃɑːn, ʃæn] *n.* ①*(pl. ~(s))* (居住在东南亚的)掸人. ②掸族泰语.

shan·dry·dan [ˈʃændridæn] *n.* ①二轮轻马车. ②破旧马车.

shan·dy(gaff) [ˈʃændi(gæf)] *n.*〔英〕①啤酒与姜汁混合饮料. ②啤酒与柠檬汽水混合饮料.

Shang·hai [ˈʃæŋˈhai] *n.* ①上海. ②(上海)浦东鸡.

shang·hai [ʃæŋˈhai] *vt.* ①(用酒或麻醉剂) 使…失去知觉而把人劫掠到船上去当水手. ②〔美俚〕(以武力或其他卑劣手段)强迫…干苦活. ③拐骗,诱拐; 胁迫. **-er** *n.* 拐骗者.

Shan·gri-La, Shan·gri·la [ʃæŋgriːˈlɑː] *n.*〔美〕①香格里拉; 世外桃源. ②二次大战时美国的空军秘密基地. ③〔美军俚〕厕所.

shank [ʃæŋk] *n.* ①胫,小腿; 胫骨. ②(鸟的)跗骨; (昆虫的)胫节; (牛羊的)腿肉. ③轴; 轮轴; 杆,柄; 钥匙柄. ④锚身. 钉身. ⑤小刀、凿等插入柄内的部分. ⑥鞋底的中腰; 袜子的统. ⑦【印】铅字身. ⑧【植】秆; 花梗; 叶柄. ⑨〔美口〕末梢; 后部; 剩余部分; 剩余. ⑩最后一段时间. ⑪【铸造】浇包手柄. ⑫【矿】钻杆尾; 钎尾; 钎柄. *a long [thin]* ~〔蔑〕长〔细〕脚杆. ***ride [go] ~'s [~s'] mare [pony]*** 步行; 走; 骑两脚马去. ***~s of the evening***〔口〕黄昏将尽时; 夜晚最好时.

shan·ny [ˈʃæni], *n. (pl. -nies, ~y)*【动】线鳚科 *(stichaeidal)* 的鱼〔尤指北鳚 *Lumpenus maculatus*〕.

sha'n't, shan't [ʃɑːnt]〔口〕= shall not. *I* ~.〔口〕我不干. *Now we* ~ *be long.* 我们马上就好了; 不用再等多久了.

shan·tey [ˈʃɑːnti, ˈʃæn-] *n. (pl. ~s)* = chantey.

Shan·tung [ʃænˈtʌŋ] *n.* ①山东. ②(s-) (山东)茧绸.

shan·ty[1] [ˈʃænti] *n.* ①〔美〕简陋的(临时)小屋; 棚屋. ②下等酒馆. **~-man**〔美〕①伐木工. ②乡巴佬. ~ **town** ①(城市)贫民窟. ②棚户区.

shan·ty[2] [ˈʃænti] *n.* = shantey.

shap·able [ˈʃeipəbl] *a.* ①可成形〔成型〕的; 可塑造的. ②样子好(看)的.

SHAPE, Shape = Supreme Headquarters, Allied Powers in Europe (北大西洋公约组织的) 欧洲盟军最高司令部.

shape [ʃeip] *n.* ①形状; 样子; 形态; 外形; 模样. ②形式; 定型; 模型. ③种类. ④(没有实体的) 朦胧的形象〔人影〕; 轮廓. ⑤幽灵. ⑥状态; 情况. ⑦【剧】戏剧服装; (用来充抵手脚等形状的)戏装衬垫. ⑧(女人的)姿态身段. ⑨〔口〕造法; 做法; 成绩. ⑩具体化; 体现; 实现. ⑪【军】(海上远距离联系用的)锥形信号标. *a hat* ~ 帽型. *a fiend in human* ~ 人形的魔鬼; 人面兽心的人. ***be in bad ~*** 混乱; 紊乱. ***get...into ~*** ①使成一定形状. ②整顿; 使具体化. ***give ~ (to)*** 给与一定的形状; 弄成一个样子; 使…成形; 修整; 实现. ***in any ~ or form*** 以任何形式〔任何种类〕; 不论种类方法如何; 无论怎样都; 随便哪样的. ***in good ~*** 完整无损. ***in no ~*** 决不; 无论如何不; 完全不. ***in the ~ of*** 以…的形状; 呈…的形状; 以…的形式; 作为… (*He has nothing in the ~ of money.* 什么钱他都没有.) ***keep ... in ~*** 使…保持原形; 不使走样. ***lick...into ~*** 塑造; 使象样; 使有效能. ***put ... in ~*** 使…成形. ***put ... into ~*** = get ... into ~. ***put ... out of ~*** 使变样; 使走样. ***settle ... into ~*** 有头绪; 上正轨. ***take ~*** 成形; 形成; 具体化; 有显著发展; 实现 *(in)*. ***take the ~ of*** 呈…形状; 成…形状. — *vt.* ①使成形; 使具有某种形状; 形成, 构成, 塑造. ②使适合; 使符合. ③使具体化; 实现. ④说明; 表明. ⑤设计; 计划; 图谋; 想象; 设想. ⑥使朝向; 使向一定方向发展. ⑦(修)刨; 把(锯齿)锉匀. ~ *one's course* 确定方针〔办法〕. ~ *clay into balls* 把黏土搓成圆球. *The hat is ~d to your head.* 这顶帽子你戴正好. ~ *a question* 提问题. — *vi.* ①形成; 成形; 成型. ②有前途; 成长; 发展; 发达; 发生. *It is shaping well.* 发展得很好; (形状)长得很好. *Let time* ~. 听其自然发展吧. ~ ***the destiny of*** 决定…的命运. ~ ***up*** = ~ ***out***〔美〕①发展; 成形; 具体化; 显示…的倾向. ②进入准备

状态。③协调；合适；举止得体。*wear to one's* ～（衣服）穿过一段时间后变得合身。～ **factor** 波形因数；波形系数。～**d brick** 异形砖。

shape·less [ˈʃeiplis] *a.* ①无定形的；不成样子的，没样子的。②形状丑陋的。**-ly** *ad.*

shape·li·ness [ˈʃeiplinis] *n.* 相称；漂亮；美。

shape·ly [ˈʃeipli] *a.* ***(-li·er; li·est)*** ①有样子的；模样儿好的。②美观的；井井有条的。

shap·er [ˈʃeipə] *n.* ①造形者；定形物。②整形器；【机】成形机；〔口〕牛头刨床。③(脉冲)形成电路。*a hydraulic* ～ 液压牛头刨床。*a vertical* ～ 立式牛头刨床。*a gear* ～ 刨齿机。～ **amplifier** 脉冲形成放大器。

shape-up [ˈʃeipʌp] *n.* 〔美口〕①(旧时每天由工头从聚集在码头上的工人中)选雇码头临时工。②健康增进。

Sha·piro [ʃəˈpirəu] *n.* 夏皮罗〔姓氏〕。

shard [ʃɑːd] *n.* ①碎陶瓷片。②薄硬壳；【动】(昆虫的)甲；鞘翅。*break into* ～*s* 粉碎，砸碎。

share[1] [ʃɛə] *n.* ①一份；份儿。②份额；分配额；分担量。③股；股份。④〔*pl.*〕〔主英〕股票。*a fair* ～ 应得的份儿；应负担的部分。*ordinary* ～*s* 普通股。*a* ～ *certificate (to bearer)* (不记名)股票。***bear [take] one's*** ～ ***of*** 负担…的部分；付…的份。***come in for a*** ～ 得到分配；分得一分。***fall to sb.'s*** ～ 由某人负担。***go*** ～***s (with...)*** 平分；分享；均摊；分担；合伙经营；共同负责。***have [take] a [one's]*** ～ ***in*** 分担；参加。***on [upon]*** ～***s*** ①共负盈亏。②利害与共；同甘共苦。***the lion's*** ～ 最大[最好]的一份；绝大部分。—*vt.* ①均分；均摊；平分；分配；分派。②共有；分[同]享，共负，参加，分担。～ *losses* 共同负担损失。～ *the blame [responsibility]* 共负责任；共同负责。—*vi.* 受分配；共享；分享；参与(*in*)。～ *in the profits* 分享收益。～ *with sb. in distress* 与某人共患难。～ ***and*** ～ ***alike*** 平均分配；平均分担；一切与别人分享。～ ***out*** 分配；分给。～ ***sb.'s joys and sorrows*** 和某人同甘共苦［休戚相关］。～ ***weal and woe*** 同甘共苦。～**broke** 股票经纪人。～ **capital** 股份资本。～ **certificate** 股票。～**crop** *vi.* 〔美南部〕充当分成制佃农。～ **cropper** 〔美南部〕分成制佃户。～ **holder** 〔英〕股东。～ **list** 〔英〕股票行市表。～**-out** *n.* 分配物；配给品；分摊。～**d time** 接受校外生课时〔公立中小学校让教会及私立学校学生来校听某些课程的安排措施〕。

share[2] [ʃɛə] *n.* 犁头；犁铧；(播种机等的)刃（= plough-～）。～**bone** 【解】耻骨。

shar·er [ˈʃɛərə] *n.* ①分配者；分派者；分[共]享者；分担者；②参与者；关系人 *(in; of)*.

shark[1] [ʃɑːk] *n.* 【鱼】鲨鱼。～ **sucker** 【鱼】鲫鱼(= *remora*).

shark[2] [ʃɑːk] *n.* ①贪得无厌的人；骗子。②高利贷。③〔口〕海关人员。④〔美俚〕老手，专家；〔美学生语〕优秀学生 *(in* mathematics*)*。— *vt.* ①用不正当手段攫取；榨取；骗取；勒索 *(up)*。②狼吞虎咽。— *vi.* 骗；诈欺；诳骗。*He* ～*s for a living.* 他靠诈骗过日子。**-er** *n.* 骗子。

shark·skin [ˈʃɑːkskin] *n.* ①鲨鱼皮；鲨皮革。②【纺】鲨皮布；雪克斯金细呢。

Sharp [ʃɑːp] *n.* 夏普〔姓氏〕。

sharp [ʃɑːp] *a.* ①锐利的；锋利。②尖锐；成锐角的。③陡急的；急转的。④敏锐的；聪明的；精明的；机警的；狡黠的；狡猾的。⑤敏捷的；轻快的。⑥剧烈的；猛烈的。⑦尖酸的；刻薄的；苛刻的。⑧(严寒)象刀割的；刺骨的；(风等)凛冽的。⑨峻峻的。陡削的。⑩急剧的；激烈的。⑪【乐】偏高的，升半音的；婴音的。⑫【语音】无声音的；清音的；气音的〔p, t, k 等〕；尖声的。⑬苦涩的；酸；辣。⑭准确的；清晰的；轮廓鲜明的；明显的。⑮瘦削的。⑯(衣服等)很讲究的；时髦的；漂亮的。*a* ～ *turn* 急转弯。～ *wine* 酸酒。*a short and* ～ *life* 短促而有为的一生。*a* ～ *remark* 严厉［尖刻］的话。～ *freezer* (食品)硬化室。～ *practice* 诈欺；诳骗。～ *tongue* 语言恶毒［刻薄］；利嘴。～ *work* 敏速的工作。***as*** ～ ***as a razor*** 厉害的；机警的。***be*** ～ ***at figures*** 算盘精明；擅长计算。***be*** ～ ***upon*** 苛待。***keep a*** ～ ***lookout*** 严密监视。～ ***as a needle*** 非常锐利。***S- is the word!*** 赶快，快点。 ***S- stomachs make short graces.*** 肚饿礼仪差〔饿着肚子，饭前感恩祈祷也说得短〕。 ***take a*** ～ ***walk*** 快步走。— *ad.* ①尖锐地；锐利地。②机警地。③急速地；急剧地；突然地。④(时间)整；准。⑤【乐】偏高地；升半音地。*at three o'clock* ～ 三时整；准三时。***Look*** ～***!*** 赶快！留神！当心！注意！— *n.* ①【乐】升音，升号(即 ♯)。②〔口〕骗子。③〔美谑〕专家。④〔*pl.*〕(缝纫用)细长针。⑤〔*pl.*〕〔英〕粗面粉。*a political* ～ 政治家。— *vt., vi.* ①〔古、卑〕磨利；磨快；磨。②【乐】(使)提高音调；(使)提高半音。③〔俚〕骗，诈欺。～**-angled** 尖角的；锐角的。～**-cut** *a.* ①用快刀切的。②干净利落的；分明的。③轮廓鲜明的。～ **cut-off** 〔无〕锐截止。～**-eared** *a.* 耳灵的，听觉敏锐的。～**-edged** 尖缘的；刀刃锋利的；锐利的。～**-eyed** *a.* 目光锐利的。～**-nosed** *a.* ①有尖鼻的。②嗅觉敏锐的。～**-pointed** 削尖的；尖锐的。～ **sand** 尖角砂。～**-set** *a.* ①非常饿的。②渴望的 *(upon; after)*。③成锐角的，锐利的。④使边缘锋利的。～**-shooter** ①神枪手；狙击兵。②【棒球俚】投球名手。～**-sighted** *a.* ①目光锐利的。②观察力敏锐的；机警的；敏捷的。～**-tongued** *a.* 说话尖酸刻薄的；挖苦的。～ **tuning** 〔无〕锐调(谐)。～**-witted** *a.* 敏捷的；机灵的；聪明的。

sharp·en [ˈʃɑːpən] *vt.* ①磨锐利；磨快；磨尖；削尖；修尖(铅笔等)。②使锐利；使敏锐；磨练(才智等)。③加深；加重；加强(苦痛等)；使剧烈；使尖锐。④加辣。⑤【乐】使提高音调；使提高半音。～ *one's tongue* 磨练说话的能力。*a* ～*ing stone* 磨石。～*ing tools* 磨刀器。—*vi.* 变锐利；变尖；变锋利；变尖锐；加剧。～***one's knife for sb.*** 准备惩罚[攻击]某人。

sharp·en·er [ˈʃɑːpnə] *n.* ①磨的人；削的人；磨削者。②磨具；磨床；刃磨器；削刀；削具。③锐化器；锐化电路。*a knife-*～ 磨刀石；磨刀器。*a pencil-*～ 修铅笔刀[器]。

sharp·er [ˈʃɑːpə] *n.* ①磨具；削具。②骗子〔尤指以赌博行欺骗者〕。*a knife* ～ 磨刀石，磨刀器。*a pencil* ～ 卷笔刀。*a card* ～ 扑克牌赌棍。

sharp·ie [ˈʃɑːpi] *n.* 〔美〕①三角帆平底船。②骗子；机灵精明的人；时髦人物。

sharp·ly [ˈʃɑːpli] *ad.* ①锐利的。②高音地；锐声地。③刀割似地。④严厉地；严酷地。⑤苛刻地；刻薄地。⑥厉害地；剧烈地。⑦敏捷地；机灵地。⑧峻峻地。

sharp·ness [ʃɑːpnis] *n.* ①锐利；尖锐。②锐度。③高音；锐音。④严厉；剧烈。⑤严酷；刻薄。⑥敏捷；机灵。

sharp·y [ˈʃɑːpi] *n.* 〔美俚〕服装华丽的人〔尤指男子〕。

Shar·(r)on [ˈʃɛərɔn, ˈʃɛərən] *n.* 莎伦〔女子名〕。

shash·lik [ˈʃɑːʃlik] *n.* 烤羊肉串。

Shas·ter [ˈʃæstə], **Shas·tra** [-trə] *n.* 〔Ind.〕神圣的著作；圣典。

shat·ter [ˈʃætə] *vt.* ①使四面八方散开；使粉碎；把…打得落花流水。②破坏；捣毁；破灭(希望等)。③损害；损伤；糟蹋。*her* ～*ed hopes* 她那些破灭了的希望。*a* ～*ing blow* 毁灭性打击。*his* ～*ed nerves* 他那因心灵受创伤而变得极度衰弱的神经。— *vi.* 破碎；碎裂；粉碎；纷纷散落。— *n.* ①破片；碎片。②破损；粉碎。③(过早的)落花；落果。～**proof** *a.* (玻璃等)防碎的；不会四散粉碎的。～ **cones** 【地】震裂锥。**-ing** *n.* 脱粒，落粒(性)。

shave [ʃeiv] *vt.* ***(-d; -d, shav·en*** [ˈʃeivn]***)*** ①剃(头发)；刮(脸)。②削，刨；把…切成薄片。③擦过；掠过。④修剪(草坪)。⑤骗取；强夺。⑥〔口〕削减(价格)；杀价买进(期票)。⑦〔美俚〕险胜，勉强胜过。⑧〔美俚〕减少；减轻。～*n and shorn* 剃了头刮了脸。*The car* ～*d a wall.* 车子擦墙开过。～ *the sentence to one year* 把刑期减为一年。— *vi.* ①剃胡须；修面。②勉强通过；善于讲价。～ ***a note*** 〔美〕杀价收购票据。～ ***off*** 剃掉；

削去. ~ ***through*** 勉强通过;〔口〕勉强考及格. — *n.* ①刮脸; 剃胡子; 修面. ②削片; 薄片. ③擦过,掠过. ④〔口〕侥幸逃过; 幸免. ④票据的煞价收买. ⑤诈欺. ⑥剃刀,刮刀,削刀;刨刀. ***be a close*** ~ 侥幸逃过; 九死一生. ***by a [close, narrow]*** ~ 差一点点; 险些儿; 几几乎. ***clean*** ~ ①剃光胡子. ②〔英〕欺骗. ***have a close*** ~ ***of it*** = be a close ~. ***take a*** ~ ***off*** 削一下.

shave·ling [ˈʃeivliŋ] *n.* ①〔蔑〕剃去(顶部)头发的人. (剃发的)和尚; 修士. ②小伙子; 青年人.

shav·en [ˈʃeivən] shave 的过去分词. —*a.* ①修过脸的; 刮过脸的. ②修剪过的.

shav·er [ˈʃeivə] *n.* ①剃者; 削者; 刮者; 刨者. ②理发师; 剃头者; 刮脸者. ③剃具; 刮刀. ④〔古〕骗子; 掠夺者; 〔美〕高利贷者; 煞价收买的人; 善于讲价的人. ⑤〔口〕年轻人,小伙子. ⑥家伙. *an electric* ~ 电动剃刀.

shave·tail [ˈʃeivteil] *n.* ①〔美军俚〕没有驯服的骡子. ②〔美军俚〕(新任职的) 陆军少尉. *a* ~ *general*〔美军俚〕旅长.

Sha·vi·an [ˈʃeivjən, -viən] *n., a.* ①英国戏剧家肖伯纳 (Bernard Shaw) 作品风格(的). ②肖伯纳研究家〔崇拜者〕(的).

shav·ing [ˈʃeiviŋ] *n.* ①剃; 剃胡子; 修面. ②〔*pl.*〕削屑; 刮屑; 刨花. ③票据的煞价收买; 诈欺. ~*s of wood* 刨花. ~ **board** 刨花板. ~ **brush** 修面刷. ~ **cream** 刮胡膏. ~ **horse** 削架; 刨工台. ~ **lotion** 修面用的香水. ~**-shop** 不可靠的银行. ~ **soap** 刮胡皂.

Sha·vu·ot [ʃɑːˈvuːəut, ʃəˈvuːəut] *n.* 【犹太教】五旬节〔犹太历九月的第六,七日〕.

Shaw [ʃɔː] *n.* ①肖〔姓氏〕. ②**George Bernard** ~ 肖伯纳〔1856—1950, 英国剧作家,批评家〕.

shaw [ʃɔː] *n.* 小树林; 丛林.

shawl [ʃɔːl] *n.* 披肩; 围巾. ~ **pattern** *n.* (东方)披肩花样.

shawm [ʃɔːm] *n.* 【乐】古双簧管.

Shaw·nee [ʃɔːˈniː] *n.* ①肖尼〔美国城市〕. ②肖尼人〔美国印第安人的一族〕.

shay [ʃei] *n.* 〔口〕轻便马车 = chaise.

Shaw·wal [ʃɔːˈwɔːl] *n.* (穆斯林历)的十月.

she [ʃiː, 弱 ʃi] *pro.* 她〔人称代名词、第三人称、阴性、单数; 所有格是 her 和 hers, 宾格是 her, 复数是 they〕★ 船舶、国家、月亮、火车等也常比拟作阴性而说作 she. — [ʃiː] *n. (pl.* ~*s* [ʃiːz]*) (opp.* he*).* 女人; 女子;〔蔑〕女的; 〔口〕雌. *Is it a he or a* ~*?* 这是男是女? 是雄是雌? — *a.* 女的; 雌的; 母的. *a* ~*-cat* 雌猫. *a* ~*-napper* 女侦探. *a* ~ *stuff*〔美〕(母牛除外的)母畜. ~**devil** 狠毒女人. ~**gal**〔美口〕温柔的女子.

shea [ʃiː] *n.* 【植】牛油树 *(Butyrospermum parkii)*〔产于非洲,其籽含油脂,可食用、制皂等〕.

sheaf [ʃiːf] *n. (pl.* **sheaves** [ʃiːvz]*)* ①(谷类等的)束; 捆; 扎. ②【军】火制正面; 射面. *a* ~ *of papers* 一扎文件. *a* ~ *of arrows* 一束箭〔通常是24枝〕. *a* ~ *of fire* 【军】集束弹道. — *vt., vi.* 捆束; 捆扎.

sheal·ing [ˈʃiːliŋ] *n.* 〔Scot.〕= shieling.

shear [ʃiə] *vt., vi.* ***(~ed,*** 〔古〕***shore*** [ʃɔː]***; shorn*** [ʃɔːn], ***~ed)*** ①剪(羊毛等); 修剪(树木); 剪(呢绒的)长毛. ②〔诗〕(用剑)斩. ③【机】剪断, 切断;【矿】截割.【物】(使)切变. ④剥夺; 抢夺; 骗取. ⑤〔Scot.〕(用镰刀)收割(庄稼). ⑥飞越, 如割开一般地越过. ~ *sheep* = ~ *wool from a sheep* 剪羊毛. ~*ed of one's rights.* 被剥夺权利. *a cruiser* ~*ing through the water* 破浪前进的巡洋舰. ***a shorn lamb*** 钱被人骗去的笨人. ***come home shorn*** 输〔亏蚀〕得精光回来. ~ ***off*** ①剪下来. ②折断. ~ ***off sb.'s plume*** 下掉某人的架子〔威风〕; 挫某人的骄气. — *n.* ①剪; 切; 刈割. ②剪下的东西. ③【机】剪断; 剪力; 剪床. ④【物】切变; 切力; 剪力. ⑤(羊的)剪毛次数; (羊的)年岁. ⑥【矿】截割; 直立截槽. *a sheep of two* ~*s* 两岁(剪过两次毛)的羊. ~ **diagram** 剪力图. ~ **hog**〔英〕剪过第一次毛的羊. ~ **hulk** 起重机船〔亦作 sheer hulk, sheerhulk〕. ~**ing force** 剪力. ~**ing strain**【物】剪应变. ~**ing strength**【物】抗剪强度; 抗切强度. ~**ing stress**【物】切胁强; 切应力; 剪应力. ~ **legs**〔亦作 ~ legs〕〔*pl.*〕= shears. ~**ling** 剪了一次毛的羊; 一岁羊. ~ **steel** 刃钢; 剪钢. ~ **ware**【物】切变波; 剪力波. ~**-water**【鸟】海鸥. **-er** [ˈʃiərə] *n.* ①剪切者; 剪切工; 剪羊毛者. ②可剪毛的羊. ③剪切机, 剪床;【矿】直立槽截煤机. **-ing** [ˈʃiəriŋ] *n.* ①剪羊毛. ②剪断, 切断. ③剪下的羊毛.

shears [ʃiəz] *n. pl.* ①大剪刀. ②【机】剪床; 剪切机. ③起重三角架; 人字起重架; 起重机叉柱. *a pair of* ~ 一把大剪刀.

sheat·fish [ˈʃiːtfiʃ] *n.* 【鱼】一种须鲶.

sheath [ʃiːθ] *n. (pl.* ~*s* [ʃiːðz]*)* ①(刀剑的)鞘. ②护套; 外皮; 外壳; 包装. ③【生,解】鞘; 兜. ④【植】叶鞘. ⑤茎衣; 箨; 笋叶. ⑥【昆】翅鞘. ⑦(电缆的)铠装. ⑧【无】阳极; 正电压电极; (电子管的)屏极. ⑨(河边)防泛石堤. ⑩女式紧身衣服. — *vt.* = sheathe. ~**bill**【鸟】鞘嘴鸥. ~ **knife** (海员用)带鞘短刀.

sheathe [ʃiːð] *vt.* ①把…插入鞘; 装…入鞘. ②覆盖; 包; 套; 藏. ③把(爪)缩回; 把(剑)刺入肉体. ~ *the sword* 把剑插回鞘里; 讲和. **sheath·er** *n.*

sheath·ing [ˈʃiːðiŋ] *n.* ①外壳; 鞘套; 外层覆盖; 护板; 护套; 护皮. ②【电】甲套. ③【建】盖板; 望板; (屋顶瓦下的)夹衬板〔亦作 ~ board〕. ④【船】覆材; 船底包板. ⑤【空】(螺旋桨)包端. — *a.* 有外层〔外壳, 包皮等〕覆盖的.

sheave[1] [ʃiːv] *n.* 【机】滑车轮; 起重滑轮; 绳轮; 槽轮; 绞缆轮; 滑车; 凸轮盘.

sheave[2] [ʃiːv] *vt.* 捆; 束(作物等).

sheaves [ʃiːvz] sheaf 和 sheave 的复数.

She·ba [ˈʃiːbə] *n.* ①【圣】希巴〔阿剌伯南部一古王国, 今也门地区,以经营香料、宝石贸易著称〕. ②〔美口〕美女; 情妇.

she·bang [ʃiˈbæŋ] *n.* 〔美俚〕①小屋; 居处; 房屋; 陋屋; 茅屋; 店铺. ②妓院; 下等酒吧; 赌场. ③东西; 事情; 勾当〔常与 whole 连用〕. ***I'm sick of the whole*** ~. 我对整个这件事发腻了.

She·bat [ʃəˈvɑːt] *n.* 〔Heb.〕(犹太历)五月.

shed[1] [ʃed] ***(shed)*** *vt.* ①流出; 落下; 倾注. ②散发(光、热、香等); 放射. ③(屋顶、油布等)把(雨水)排泻掉. ④【生】排出(孢子等). ⑤(鸟)脱(毛); (树)落(叶); 脱落; (蛇)蜕(皮); 褪; (鹿)换(角等). ⑥放弃; 摆脱(恶习). ⑦【电】减少(负荷). ~ *tears* 流泪. ~ *blood* 流血; 杀. — *vi.* ①流出; 溢出. ②散发. ③脱毛; 脱壳; 脱换; 脱落; 蝉退. ~ ***light on*** ①照亮. ②阐明; 解释; 将…弄明白. ~ ***one's blood for*** 献身. ~ ***the blood of*** 使流血; 杀伤; 杀死. — *n.* ①脱落物; 蜕落的皮壳. ②微量的小雪. ③分水岭. ④【纺】(织机的)梭口; 梭道.

shed[2] [ʃed] *n.* ①小屋; 棚屋. ②堆房; 库房. ③车房. ④〔美〕有盖汽车. *a cattle* ~ 牛槛. *a locomotive [an engine]* ~ 机车库.

she'd [ʃiːd, 弱 ʃid] = she had [would].

shed·der [ˈʃedə] *n.* ①脱落者; 放射者. ②流出…的人〔物〕; 使流出…的人〔物〕. ③蜕壳期的虾〔蟹〕. ④卸件装置; 推〔拨、抛〕料机. *a* ~ *of blood* 流血者; 杀人者.

sheen [ʃiːn] *n.* ①光辉; 光彩; 光泽. ②华服; 有光泽的织物. — *a.*【诗】华丽的; 光辉的; 有光泽的. — *vi.* 发亮; 发光彩; 照耀; 闪闪发光.

sheen·y[1] [ˈʃiːni] *a.* 发光的; 闪烁的; 光亮的; 有光泽的.

shee·ny[2] [ˈʃiːni] *n.* 〔俚蔑〕犹太人.

sheep [ʃiːp] *n.* 〔*sing., pl.*〕①羊; 绵羊. ②羊皮(革). ③怯懦的人; 羞怯的人; 胆小鬼; 蠢人. ④〔谑〕〔总称〕信徒; 教友; 教区居民. *keep* ~ 养羊. ***a black*** ~ 家庭中的不肖子; 败类; 不肖之徒; 害群之马; 拒绝参加罢工的工人. *a lost* ~ 迷途羔羊；迷失正道的人. *a wolf in ~'s clothing* 披着羊皮的狼；口蜜腹剑的人. *cast[make] ~'s eyes at* 向…送媚眼；向…递秋波. *count* ~ 数羊〔心里计数以求入睡〕. *follow like* ~ 盲从. *one may as well be hanged for a* ~ *as a lamb* 一不做，二不休. *return to one's* ~ *[muttons]* 回到本题. ~ *and goats* 善人与恶人. ~ *herder* 牧羊人；〔美〕怀俄明州人〔绰号〕. ~ *that have no shepherd* 乌合之众. *separate the* ~ *from the goats* 区别好人和坏人. ~**berry**【植】荚迷(属)；荚迷果；羊莓. ~**cot(e)** 羊栏；羊舍；羊圈. ~**-dip** *n.* 洗羊药水；羊消毒液. ~ **dog** 牧羊狗[犬]. ~ **fescue**【植】羊茅. ~**fold**〔英〕羊栏；羊舍；羊圈. ~**herder**〔美〕牧羊人. ~ **hook** 牧羊杖. ~**ked**【动】羊虱蝇 (= ~ tick). ~ **laurel**【植】狭叶山月桂. ~**like** *a.* ①温顺的；驯良的. ②怯懦的. ~**man**〔古英〕= shepherd；〔美〕牧羊业者. ~**pen**〔英〕= ~fold. ~ **range** 牧羊场. ~ **-run** 大牧羊场. ~**shank** ①羊胫；羊的小腿. ②纤弱而细的东西. ③无价值的东西；不重要的东西. ④【海】(将长绳暂时缩短的)缩结. ~**shead** [ˈʃiːpshed] ①(食用的)羊头. ②【动】羊鲷；淡水石首鱼；红隆头鱼. ③愚蠢的人. ~**shearer** 剪羊毛的人；剪羊毛机. ~**shearing** ①剪羊毛. ②剪羊毛时期. ③剪羊毛节目. ~**skin** ①羊皮；羊革. ②羊皮衣服(等). ③羊皮纸. ④〔美〕毕业文凭. ~ **sorrel**【植】小酸模. ~ **station**〔澳〕牧羊场. ~ **tick** = ~ ked. ~**walk**〔英〕牧羊场.

sheep·ish [ˈʃiːpiʃ] *a.* ①羞怯的；腼腆的. ②(象绵羊一样)驯顺的；胆怯的；愚钝的. **-ly** *ad.* **-ness** *n.*

sheer[1] [ʃiə] *a.* ①纯粹的；十足的；全然的；没有搀杂的；不搀水的；绝对的；真正的. ②透明的；(纱等)极薄的. ③崄峻的；陡峭的；垂直的. *a* ~ *impossibility* 绝对不可能. ~ *silk* 薄绸. ~ *nonsense* 胡说八道；完全瞎扯. *by the* ~ *force of one's will* 全靠意志力. — *ad.* 完全；绝对；①十足；全然；彻底. ②垂直地；峻峭地；笔直地. *torn* ~ *out by the root* 连根拔除. *The rock rises* ~ *from the water.* 岩石笔直地从水面矗立起来. *fall 300 feet* ~ 垂直坠落[低落]三百英尺. — *n.* 透明薄纱，透明薄料的衣服.

sheer[2] [ʃiə] *n.* ①【海】舷弧. ②以单锚系泊的船位. ③偏航；偏荡；转向；避开；弯曲进行. *break* ~ 抛单锚时船位移动而使锚链绞结. *have little [a straight]* ~ 甲板弧度不大. — *vi., vt.*【海】(使)偏航；(使)偏荡；避开；(使)转向. ~ *off*【海】离开；躲开. ~ **hulk** = shear hulk. ~ **legs** = shear legs.

sheers [ʃiəz] *n. pl.* = shears.

sheet[1] [ʃiːt] *n.* ①〔常 *pl.*〕被单；褥单. ②裹尸布. ③(忏悔者穿的)白衣；忏悔服. ④一张(纸)；纸张；(尤指黄色)报纸；〔*pl.*〕书页；印刷品. ⑤表格；图表；单子；票笺；文件；罪犯的记录单. ⑥(一)片；(一)块；(一)层；薄片；薄板. ⑦(烤面包的)铁板. ⑧(水、雪、冰、火、颜色等的)广大的面；一片(汪洋、原野等). ⑨〔诗〕帆. ⑩邮票的印张〔美国每一印张有邮票400枚〕. ⑪【地】岩席；岩床；【空】涡面；【数】叶. *a bed* ~ 床单. *a fly* ~ 传单. *an operation* ~ 使用说明书；施工说明书；工艺规范. *a work* ~ 工作单. *a log* ~ 纪录表. *a* ~ *of fire* 一片火海. ~*s of rain* 倾盆大雨. *a blank* ~ ①一张白纸. ②纯洁的心灵. *a clean* ~ ①清白的历史. ②历史清白的人；品行善良的人. *as white as a* ~ (脸色)刷白. *(get) between the* ~*s* 就寝；(睡)在床上. *in* ~*s* ①成薄板[薄片]. ②【装订】散页；印好放着不加装订. ③(大雨)倾盆；(大雾)濛濛. *pale as a* ~ (脸色)苍白. *put on a white* ~ 穿上白色忏悔服，忏悔；悔改. ~*s hot from the press* 刚印好的印刷品. *stand in a white* ~ = put on a white ~. — *vt.* ①给…盖被单；在…上铺被单. ②(用裹尸布)包(死尸)；覆盖. ②把(铁板等)延展成薄片；铺开；展开；伸开；扩展；使成一大片. *The lake was* ~*ed with ice.* 湖面结一层冰. — *vi.* 大片地落下；成片地铺开；大片地流动. ~ **erosion** 土壤的整块被水冲走. ~ **glass** 薄玻璃板. ~ **ice** 水面的冰层. ~ **iron** 薄铁板；铁板. ~ **lightning** 片状闪电. ~ **metal** 薄金属板. ~ **music** 散页乐谱；单张乐谱. ~**-steel mill** 薄板厂.

sheet[2] [ʃiːt] *n.*【海】①缭绳；帆脚索. ②〔*pl.*〕(船头或船尾的)空位. *be [have] a* ~ *[three* ~*s] in the wind'(s eye)*〔俚〕有点醉[大醉]. *with flowing* ~*s* (横风时)放松帆脚索. — *vt.* 用帆脚索扣紧(帆). ~ *home* 用帆脚索扣住(风帆). ~ **anchor** ①【海】(船首的)副锚；紧急备用大锚. ②紧急时的靠山；最后的依靠；最后手段. ~ **bend**【海】单索花〔一种绳结，用于把一条绳系在绳环上〕.

sheet·ing [ˈʃiːtiŋ] *n.* ①被单料子；床单布. ②薄板轧制；〔集合词〕金属薄板；(塑料)薄膜；薄片；【建】挡板；护堤板；护墙板；板栅. ③(用被单)覆盖；铺被单；做护板.

Shef·field [ˈʃefiːld] *n.* 设菲尔德〔英国城市〕.

sheik, sheikh [ʃeik, ʃiːk] *n.* ①(阿拉伯国家的)家长，村长，族长；酋长. ②伊斯兰教教主. ③〔美口〕美男子；使妇女倾倒的男子. ~**dom** (阿拉伯)酋长统辖的领土，酋长国. **S- ul** [ul] **Islam** (土耳其的)伊斯兰教法典权威.

Shei·la [ˈʃiːlə] *n.* 希拉〔女子名，Cecilia 的异体〕.

she·kar·ry [ʃiˈkæri] *n.* = shikaree, shikari.

shek·el [ˈʃekl] *n.* ①锡克尔〔古巴比伦及希伯来的衡量单位，约 1/2 盎司〕. ②重一个锡克尔的古希伯来金币或银币. ③〔*pl.*〕〔美俚〕钱.

Shel·by [ˈʃelbi] *n.* 谢尔比〔姓氏，男子名〕.

Shel·don [ˈʃeldən] *n.* 谢尔登〔姓氏，男子名〕.

shel·drake [ˈʃeldreik] *n.*【鸟】冠鸭；麻鸭；翘鼻麻鸭.

shel·duck [ˈʃeldʌk] *n.* sheldrake 的雌性.

shelf [ʃelf] *n.* *(pl. shelves* [ʃelvz]*)* ①搁架；搁料架；搁板. ②沙洲；暗礁. ③格；层. ④【矿】平层；锡沙矿基岩；【海】承梁架[材]；【地】(大)陆棚，大陆架〔又作 continental ~〕. ⑤搁板状物；突出的扁平岩石. ⑥〔俚〕(同伙中的)告密者. *off the* ~ ①现货供应 *(All of those parts can be purchased off the* ~*.* 所有这些零件都有现货供应*)*. ②〔俚〕复活. **be on the** ~ ①被搁置；束之高阁；无人问津的；废弃的；闲置的. ②(因年老)而没有人雇用；(妇女无人过问)没有结婚的机会[希望]；〔美俚〕退休的，退出体育界的. ③〔商业用语〕推迟的；(计划等)缓行的. ④〔古〕在当铺内. ⑤〔盗贼俚〕被流放. ⑥〔俚〕死了. ~ **ice** 陆棚冰 (=ice ~). ~ **life** 贮藏寿命；货架寿命〔商品储放不变质的期限〕.

She·lia [ˈʃiːljə] *n.* 希莉亚〔女子名，Sheila 的异体〕.

shell [ʃel] *n.* *(pl.* ~*s,* ②义为 ~*)* ①壳；介壳；甲壳；贝. ②(昆虫的)翅鞘；蛹的蜕皮. ③【植】种子的外皮；荚. ④【地】地壳；薄硬岩层. ⑤【解】外耳. ⑥【机】(汽)锅身. ⑦【建】薄壳(屋顶)；房屋的框架；内部未竣工的建筑物. ⑧船体；骨架. ⑨子弹壳；炮弹；猎枪子弹；爆破筒. ⑩(滑车等的)外框；内棺. ⑪外观；外表；外形. ⑫单人赛用艇. ⑬〔英〕(学校的)中级班〔四、五年级〕. ⑭〔诗〕竖琴；七弦琴. ⑮= ~ jacket. ⑯【物】(原子的)电子壳层. ⑰(刀剑的)护手. ⑱(象钻进壳中似的)沉默；冷淡. *the* ~ *of an egg [a walnut]* 蛋[胡桃]壳. *Beetles have* ~*s.* 甲虫有硬壳. *an illuminating* ~ 照明弹. *a tear* ~ 催泪弹. *the* ~ *of a pipe* 管壁. *You're scarcely out of the* ~ *yet.* 你还乳臭未干. *cast the* ~ 脱壳；蜕皮. *come out of one's* ~ 不再羞怯沉默. *go [retire] into one's* ~ 缄默起来；害羞起来；对人持冷淡态度；保持距离. *in the* ~ 在萌芽[潜伏]时期. — *vt.* ①由壳中剥出(豌豆等)；〔美〕剥(玉米)；给…脱粒. ②用壳体包被；用介壳铺(路). ③轰击；炮击[轰]. ④〔棒球俚〕(投手)使(对方)获得多次安全打或得分. ~ *oysters* 去牡蛎壳. — *vi.* ①脱壳；蜕壳；(金属等)剥落；(果实等)脱落. ②炮击. ③采集贝壳. *as easy as* ~*ing peas*〔口〕非常容易. ~ *out*〔俚〕交出；付出；付款，捐献

(*S- out your money!* 拿出钱来!)~**back**〔俚〕老水手;绕越赤道的航海者. ~ **bark** = shagbark. ~ **bean** 去荚而食的豆〔有别于刀豆、豇豆等〕. ~ **burst** 炮弹的爆炸. ~**fire** 炮火; 炮轰. ~**fish** 甲壳类动物. ~ **game** ①一种骗人的打赌游戏. ②欺骗. ~ **heap** 贝塚;介壳堆.~ **jacket**〔美〕(热带的)简单礼服;〔英〕(热带地方穿的)陆军军官的常服;圆领露臂装;背心装. ~ **lime** 贝壳灰. ~ **mound** = ~ heap. ~**proof** [ˈʃelpruːf] *a.* 防弹的. ~ **road** 贝壳铺的路. ~ **shock**【医】炮弹休克;弹震症. ~ **structure** (原子、原子核的)壳层构造. ~ **work** 贝壳工艺品.

she'll [ʃiːl, 弱 ʃil] = she will [shall].

shel•lac(k) [ʃəˈlæk] *n.* ①紫胶; 虫胶; 虫漆; 洋干漆; 漆片. ②含虫胶的唱片原料;虫胶制剂; 虫胶清漆. — *vt.* ①给…涂紫胶;以虫胶处理. ②〔美俚〕打; 揍; 大败(对方); 彻底击败. **-ed** *a.* ①〔美俚〕喝醉了的. ②〔美棒球俚〕大败的. **-ing** ①殴打; 鞭笞. ②彻底失败; 〔美运〕全盘赛输;大败.

shelled [ʃeld] *a.* ①脱壳的;脱皮的. ②有[带]壳的. ~ *egg* 带壳的蛋.

shel•ler [ˈʃelə] *n.* ①剥壳者;脱粒者. ②剥壳器;脱粒机.

Shel•ley[1] [ˈʃeli] *n.* ①谢利〔姓氏〕. ② **Percy Bysshe** ~ 雪莱〔1792—1822,英国诗人〕.

Shel•ley[2] [ˈʃeli] *n.* 谢莉〔女子名〕.

shell•ing [ˈʃeliŋ] *n.* ①去壳;去皮. ②去壳的谷物;谷壳. ③用壳荚施肥. ④贝壳采集. ⑤炮击.

shell•y [ˈʃeli] *a.* ①有壳的; 贝壳多的. ②贝壳一样的. ③由贝壳铺成[制成]的.

shel•ta [ˈʃeltə] *n.* 小炉匠切口〔以爱尔兰语和盖尔语为基础,现今尚在英国、爱尔兰等地的补锅匠、游民间使用〕.

shel•ter [ˈʃeltə] *n.* ①隐藏所;庇护所; 避难所; 躲避处; 蔽身之处. ②保护;庇护;隐蔽, 遮蔽;屏障. ③掩护物; 遮蔽物;掩蔽部. ④百叶箱. *an Anderson* ~〔英〕(上面盖铁板的)家庭防空壕. *an air-raid* ~防空洞. *a bus* ~ 公共汽车站候车亭. *a cabman's* ~ (十字路口上) 等候雇客的马车棚. ***be a ~ from*** 成为躲避…的处所. ***find ~*** = take ~. ***fly to sb. for*** ~ = seek ~ at sb.'s house 逃进某人家里避难. ***give ~ to*** 庇护. ***lend the ~ of one's name and position to*** 利用自己的名誉地位庇护(某人). ***take ~*** 避难;躲避; 躲雨. ***under the ~ of*** 在…的庇护下. — *vt.* ①遮蔽; 隐蔽; 隐匿. ②保护;包庇;掩护. ~ *sb. for the night* 留人住一宿. —*vi.* 躲避,避难. ~***ed trades*** (不受外国竞争影响的)国内受保护行业〔建筑业、内地运输业等〕. ~ ***oneself behind (a hedge; superiors)*** 躲在(篱笆,上司)背后. ~ **area**【军】战地宿营地区. ~ **belt** 防风林带. ~ **half** 双人帐篷的半幅〔三角形帆布〕. ~ **tent** 军用双人帐篷. ~ **trench**【军】掩蔽壕. **-less** *a.* 没有隐藏处的;无处避难的;无依无靠的;无保护的;任风吹雨打的.

shel•tie, shel•ty [ˈʃelti] *n.* *(pl. -ties)* = ①shetland pony. ②shetland sheepdog.

shelve[1] [ʃelv] *vt.* ①装搁架于. ②把…放在架[搁板]上. ③搁置(议案等). ④罢免;解雇;使(军官等)退役.

shelve[2] [ʃelv] *vi.* 逐渐倾斜;成斜坡(尤指海岸).

shelves [ʃelvz] shelf 的复数.

shelv•ing[1] [ˈʃelviŋ] *n.* ①【建】架子料. ②〔总称〕架子; 一组搁架. ③搁置;延误. ④免职;解职.

shelv•ing[2] [ˈʃelviŋ] *n.* (海岸等)的倾斜(度).

She•ma [ʃəˈmɑː] *n.*【犹太教】施玛篇〔晨祷和晚祷中的祷文,申述对上帝的笃信〕.

she•male [ˈʃiːmeil] *n.* 〔美俚〕女人;女性.

Shem•ite [ˈʃemait] = Semite.

Shem•it•ic [ʃeˈmitik] *a.* = Semetic.

she•nan•i•gan [ʃəˈnænigən] *n.*〔美口〕〔常 *pl.*〕①鬼把戏; 诡计; 欺骗. ②恶作剧; 胡闹. ③无聊的话;无意义的话;胡说. *Cut out the ~s!* 别胡说了!

Shen•stone [ˈʃenstən] *n.* 申斯通〔姓氏〕.

shent [ʃent], *a.* 〔古、方〕①受辱的;丢脸的; 羞愧的. ②失去的;打败的;失败了的. ③被伤害的;毁坏的;损坏了的. ④受斥责的;受谴责的.

she-oak [ˈʃiːəuk] *n.* ①【植】(澳洲)木麻黄属 *(Casuarina)* 的一种. ②〔澳俚〕强烈啤酒.

She•ol [ˈʃiːəul] *n.* ①【圣】(希伯来人的)阴间. ②[s-]冥府;地狱.

Shep•hard [ˈʃepəd] *n.* 谢泼德〔姓氏〕.

shep•herd [ˈʃepəd] *n.* ①牧羊人; 牧羊者. ②牧羊狗〔犬〕(= ~ dog). ③牧师. ④保护者; 指导者. ***S-Kings*** 古埃及希克索["牧人"]王朝的国王, 见 *Hyksos*. ***the (good) Shepherd*** 基督. — *vt.* ①牧(羊);放牧. ②照看. ③领导,指导. ~ **dog** 牧羊狗〔犬〕. ~**ess** 牧羊女;乡下姑娘. ~ **god** 牧羊神. ~**'s crook** (有钩的)牧羊杖. ~**'s pie** 肉馅土豆饼. ~**'s plaid [check]** 黑白方格花呢. ~**'s-pouch**, ~**'s-purse**【植】荠菜. ~**'s trade** ①写田园诗. ②耶稣的业绩.

sher•bet [ˈʃəːbət] *n.* 〔英〕冰冻果汁水;〔美〕果汁牛奶冻.

sherd [ʃəːd] *n.* = shard.

she•reef [ʃəˈriːf] *n.* ①穆罕默德的女儿法蒂玛 (Fatima) 的后裔. ②(阿拉伯国家的)君主;王公,酋长. ③麦加的地方〔行政〕长官.

Sher•i•dan [ˈʃeridn] *n.* 谢里登〔姓氏,男子名〕.

she•rif [ʃəˈriːf] *n.* = shereef.

sher•iff [ˈʃerif] *n.* 〔英〕(任期一年的)名誉郡长〔正式名称为 High S-〕; (某些城市的)行政司法长官;〔美〕县的行政司法长官. ***dance at the ~'s ball*** 被处绞刑. ***~'s hotel***〔俚〕监狱. ~**'s sale** 强制拍卖. ~**hood** ~**ship** 郡长等的任期[职权]. ~**dom** 郡长等的辖区. ~**wick** = ~dom.

sher•lock [ˈʃəːlɔk] *n.* 〔俚〕①私家侦探. ②善于看破奥祕的人〔亦作 Sherlock〕.

S- Holmes [həumz] 夏洛克·福尔摩斯〔英国作家柯南道尔 (Conan Doyle) 作品中名侦探〕.

Sher•man [ˈʃəːmən] *n.* 谢尔曼〔姓氏,男子名〕.

Sher•pa [ˈʃəːpə,ʃɛə-] *n.* *(pl. -pas, -pa)* 谢尔巴人〔喜马拉雅山区尼泊尔一个部族的成员〕; [s-]〔英俚〕搬运工〔因谢尔巴人常从事此项职业〕.

Sher•riff [ˈʃerif] *n.* 谢里夫〔姓氏〕.

Sher•rill [ˈʃeril] *n.* 谢里尔〔姓氏〕.

Sher•rill [ˈʃeril] *n.* 谢丽尔〔女子名〕.

Sher•ring•ton [ˈʃeriŋtn] *n.* 谢灵顿〔姓氏〕.

sher•ris [ˈʃeris] *n.* 〔古〕= sherry.

Sher•ry, Sher•rie [ˈʃeri] *n.* 谢丽〔女子名〕.

sher•ry [ˈʃeri] *n.* 雪利酒〔西班牙南部所产的白葡萄酒〕. *brown* ~ 黑雪利酒. ~ **cobbler** (加糖水, 柠檬)冰雪利酒. ~**-glass** 雪利酒酒杯.

Sher•win [ˈʃəːwin] *n.* 舍温〔姓氏,男子名〕.

Sher•wood [ˈʃəːwud] *n.* 舍伍德〔姓氏,男子名〕.

she's [ʃiːz, 弱 ʃiz] = she is [has].

Shet•land [ˈʃetlənd] *n.* (苏格兰东北的)设得兰群岛. ~ **pony** 设得兰矮种马. ~ **sheepdog** 设得兰牧羊狗. ~ **wool** 设得兰产的细羊毛.

She•vu•oth [ʃəˈvuːəut] *n.* 〔Heb.〕= Shavuot.

shew [ʃəu] *v.* 〔英古〕= show. ~**bread** 犹太教徒用作祭品的无酵饼,陈设饼〔见《圣经》《出埃及记》(= show-bread).

shewn [ʃəun] *v.* 〔英方〕= shown.

s.h.f., shf = superhigh frequency【无】超高频.

Shi•ah [ˈʃiːə] *n.* *(sing., pl.)* ①【伊斯兰教】什叶派 (= the Shiites). ②什叶派教徒 (= Shiite).

shib•bo•leth [ˈʃibəleθ] *n.* ①【犹太史】(基利德人 [Gileadite] 用来鉴别逃亡的厄弗雷姆人〔Ephraimite〕的)检验用词〔看其能否正确地读出该词音,因厄弗雷姆人发不出 sh 音〕. ②(社团成员间彼此辨认的)切口; 对口话; 黑话; 口令. ③(一阶层、一团体的)特殊语言、习惯、服装(等).

shick•er [ˈʃikə] *a.* 喝醉的. — *n.* 醉汉; 酒鬼 (= shikker).
shied [ʃaid] shy 的过去式和过去分词.
shield [ʃiːld] *n.* ①盾; 盾牌. ②罩; 屏, 屏蔽. ③防御物; 保护物. ④防御; 保护. ⑤保护者; 庇护者[人]. ⑥盾形物;【徽】盾形徽;〔美〕警察[侦探]徽章. ⑦【动、植】(甲壳等的)盾状部; 背甲; 头胸甲; 龟甲板. ⑧【地】地盾. ⑨【矿】掩护支架. ⑩【电】屏蔽铠装. ⑪【炮】钢盾; 防盾. ⑫(机器等的)铠装; (隧道用的)铠框. ⑬〔the S-〕【天】盾牌座. *a heat* ~ 热屏. ***be sb's ~ and buckler*** 充当某人的保护者. ***both sides of the ~*** ①盾的正反两面. ②事物的表里. ***S- of David*** 大卫王的盾牌〔犹太教的六芒星形标志〕. ***the other side of the ~*** ①盾的反面. ②问题[事情]的另一面. — *vt.* ①用盾挡住; 防护; 防御; 保护; 屏蔽. ②庇护; 掩盖. ③挡开; 避开. ~ *a country from invasion* 保护一个国家不受侵犯. *In old society officials ~ one another* 旧社会官官相护. —*vi.* ①起盾的作用; 起保护作用; 防御. ②充当保护者. ~**back** (英国十八世纪流行的)盾形背椅子. ~ **bearer** 携盾侍从. ~ **hand**〔古〕左手. ~ **law**〔美〕新闻保障法〔保护新闻从业人员可拒绝说出机密消息来源的法律〕.
shiel•ing [ˈʃiːliŋ] *n.* ①〔Scot.〕(夏季)羊棚. ②(山区的)夏季牧场. ③牧羊人住的小屋. ④运动员的休息棚.
shi•er [ˈʃaiə] *a.* shy 的比较级. — *n.* 易受惊的马.
shi•est [ˈʃaiist], *a.* shy 的最高级.
shift [ʃift] *vt.* ①变动; 改变; 搬移; 移动; 转移; 变换; 替换, 更换. ②推卸; 转嫁. ③消除; 撤除. ④【语】变换(语音). ⑤〔方〕换(衣); 使换衣服. ⑥〔汽车〕变(速); 换(排档). ~ *all the blame on others* 把一切错误归于别人. — *vi.* ①变; 移; 动; (风)改变方向; 漂移. ②想种种办法; 筹划; 策划; 设法. ③瞒骗; 强辩; 托词闪避. ④挣生活; 糊口. ⑤〔口〕走开. ⑥【机】变速; 调档. ⑦【语】辅音变换. ⑧〔方〕换衣服. ~ ***about*** 搬来搬去; 屡变位置. ~ ***for oneself*** 独立谋生. ~ ***off*** 拖延; 消除; 整顿; 逃避; 推托(责任等); (用借口等)把…打发走. ~ ***oneself*** 换衣服(= ~ one's clothes). ~ ***one's ground*** 改变论据[立场]. — *n.* ①变迁; 变化; 变换; 替换; 更换; 掉换; 更易; 转移; 代用. ②谋划; 办法; 计划; 手段; 权宜之计. ③哄骗; 欺诈. ④班; 轮[换]班; 轮值. ⑤轮班职工. ⑥轮值时间; 轮班工作时间. ⑦〔古〕女汗衫. ⑧【农】轮作; 轮作农作物; 轮作的农地. ⑨【矿】断层; 断层变位; 平移. ⑩【语】辅音变换. ⑪〔方〕换衣服; (常更换的)衬衣. ⑫〔足球〕开赛前球员阵势的变动. ⑬(堆砖瓦的) 互接法. ⑭汽车排挡. *the ~ of responsibility* 责任的转嫁. *an eight-hour ~* 八小时的工作班. *work in three ~s of eight hours* 每班八小时分三班轮流工作. *the day-~* 日班. *the night-~* 夜班. ***be put [reduced] to the ~s*** 被逼得走投无路. ***for a ~*** 出于权宜之计; 将就地; 为眼前打算. ***full of ~s and devices*** 足智多谋. ***live by ~(s*** 东拼西凑过日子. ***make (a) ~*** ①拼拼凑凑过日子 ②尽力设法利用[应付] (*with*); 安于某事物; (没有…也)勉强对付过去 (*without*). ③尽力做到〔与不定式连用〕. ***one's*** (*or* **the**) ***last*** ~ 最后的手段[办法]. ~ ***of crops*** 轮作. ***the ~s and changes of life*** (人生的) 祸福荣枯. ***try every ~ available*** 想尽办法. ~ **key**〔打字机〕大写字体按键. ~ **register**【自】移位寄存器.
shift•er [ˈʃiftə] *n.* ①【电】移动装置; 移相器; 倒相器; 移带器. ②开关. ③(印字电报机等的) 换行器. ④搬移工. ⑤回避论点者. ⑥(铁矿中的)领班. ⑦(煤矿中的)辅助工. *a phase ~*【测】调相器.
shift•ing [ˈʃiftiŋ] *a.* ①变动的; 移动的; 多[易]变的. ②想尽办法的; 尽量设法的. ③用权谋的; 哄骗的; 狡赖的; 诡诈的. ~ *cultivation* 轮作. ~ *sand* 流沙. ~ *wind* 方向不定的风. — *n.* ①转移; 移动; 移位; 偏移. ②变化; 转变. ③狡赖; 遁词诈术等的使用. *gear* ~ 调档. *phase* ~ 相位移. ~ **arm** 变速臂. ~ **ga(u)ge** 划线规; 根距. ~ **spanner** 活动扳手.
shift•less [ˈʃiftlis] *a.* ①没办法的; 走投无路的; 无计算的; 无计谋生的. ②没用的; 不中用的; 无能的. ③偷懒的; 懒惰的; 得过且过的. **-ly** *ad.*
shift•y [ˈʃifti] *a.* ***(-i•er; -i•est)*** ①变动的; 多变的; 不稳定的. ②策略多的; 足智多谋的; 办法多的; 善于应变的. ③会哄骗的; 诡诈的; 不老实的; 不正直的; 靠不住的. **-i-ly** *ad.* **-i•ness** *n.*
shi•gel•la [ʃiˈgelə] *n.* *(pl.* ***-gel•lae*** [-iː], *~s)*【生】志贺氏菌属.
shi•gel•lo•sis [ˌʃigəˈləusis] *n.*【医】志贺氏菌痢疾.
shi•kar [ʃikɑː] *n.*〔Ind.〕打猎; 狩猎.
shi•kar•ee, shi•kar•i [ʃiˈkɑːri], **shi•kar•ry** [-kæ-] *n.*〔Ind.〕猎人; 做向导的猎人.
Shi•ko•ku [ʃiˈkəukuː] *n.* 四国〔日本主要岛屿之一〕.
shill [ʃil], **shil•la•ber** [ˈʃiləbə] *n.*〔美俚〕(道旁摊贩引诱顾客的)假购物同伙; (勾引赌客入局的)赌棍同伙.
shil•la•lah, shil•le•la(g)h [ʃiˈleilə], **shil•la•ly** [-li] *n.* (爱尔兰人鞭笞时用的)橡树棒.
shil•ling [ˈʃiliŋ] *n.* 先令〔旧英国货币单位, 一镑的 $^1/_{20}$, 十二便士为一先令, 略 s., sh.〕. *2 ~s 6 pence*〔略 2s. 6d. 或2/6〕二先令六辨士. ***cut off sb. with a ~ = cut off one's heir with a ~*** 取消某人的继承权. ***long ~s*** 高额工资; 高薪. ***pay twenty ~s in the pound*** 全数付清. ~ ***shocker***〔英〕一先令一本的黄色[侦探, 惊险]小说. ***take the King's [Queen's] ~***〔英〕入伍; 从军, 当兵. ***want two-pence in the ~*** 一先令短少两辨士; 〔口〕智力不足. ~ **mark** 书写[印刷]的"/"记号.
Shil•luk [ʃiˈluːk] *n.* ① *(pl. ~(s))* 希鲁克人〔苏丹的尼罗特人〕. ②希鲁克语.
shil•ly-shal•ly [ˈʃiliʃæli] *n., vi.* 磨蹭; 支支吾吾; 游移不定; 踌躇不决; 优柔寡断. — *a., ad.* 踌躇不定的[地]; 优柔寡断的[地].
shi•ly [ˈʃaili] *ad.* = shyly.
shim [ʃim] *n.*【机】①薄垫片; 楔形填隙片; 衬垫; 夹铁. ②补偿棒; 粗调棒. —*vt.* 用薄垫片填入; 拿填隙片塞; 向…中插夹铁.
shim•mer [ˈʃimə] *n.* 微光; 闪光. — *vi., vt.* (使)微微发亮[发光]; (使)闪烁; (使)发闪光. **-y** *a.* 发微光的; 闪烁的.
shim•my[1] [ˈʃimi] *n.*〔口〕女式无袖衬衫 (= chemise).
shim•my[2] [ˈʃimi] *n.* ①〔美〕西迷舞〔身体颤动着跳的一种狐步舞〕. ②【机】震动; 摆动; 振动. ③(机车前轮的)不正常振动[急剧摇荡]. — *vi.* ①跳西迷舞. ②(汽车)震颤; 震动; 摆动.
Shi•mo•no•se•ki [ˌʃiməunəuˈseki] *n.* 下关〔即马关, 日本港市〕.
shin[1] [ʃin] *n.* ①【解】胫;【昆】胫节; 外胫; 脚杆骨; 胫骨; ②牛的小腿肉. — *vt.* ①〔美〕爬(树等). ②(比球时)踢…的外胫. ~ *oneself against a rock* 脚杆骨撞在岩石上. —*vi.* ①攀爬 *(up)*. ②〔美〕(为借钱而)到处奔走; 跑来跑去 *(about)*; 快步走. ~**bone** 胫骨 (= tibia). ~ **guard** (运动员用的)护胫. ~**plaster** ①〔美〕贴外胫的膏药. ②〔美口〕私营银行发行的钞票. ③(旧指)贬值的钞票; 滥发的纸币.
shin[2] [ʃiːn] *n.* 希伯来语第二十一个字母.
shin•dig [ˈʃindig] *n.*〔美俚〕盛大舞会〔社交集会〕. ~ **dancer** (夜总会等处)表演色情舞蹈的舞女.
shin•dy [ˈʃindi] *n.* ①〔口〕纠纷; 吵闹; 骚动; 喧嚣; 喧哗. ②〔美俚〕盛大宴会; 舞会. ***kick up a ~*** 引起骚动.
shine [ʃain] ***(shone*** [ʃɔn; Am. ʃəun]***)*** *vi.* ①发光; 发亮; 照耀; 闪耀; (太阳)照耀. ②出众; 杰出; 出风头. ③(情感等)明显流露. *a shining painter* 卓越的画家. *She ~s in dancing.* 她跳舞极好. — *vt.* ①使发光; 使发亮; 使照耀. ②〔过去及过去分词 ~d〕〔口〕擦亮(皮鞋等); 磨光; 以灯等照耀. ~ *one's shoes* 擦皮鞋. *S- your light over here.* 把灯朝这里照照. ***improve the shining hour*** 抓紧时间. ~ ***in society*** 在交际场中出风头. ~

round = ～ ***up to***〔美俚〕竭力[百般]讨好[巴结]某人[异性]. — *n.* ①阳光;晴天;华丽. ②光;光辉;光亮;〔口〕光泽;光采. ③〔美俚〕爱好;喜爱. ④〔常 *pl.*〕恶作剧;鬼把戏;诡计. ⑤〔英俚〕纠纷;骚动;吵闹;混乱. ⑥〔美俚,蔑〕黑人. ***(come) rain or*** ～ ①不论晴雨. ②不管怎样. ***keep up [make] a*** ～ 引起(大)风潮;引起(大)骚动. ***make no end of a*** ～〔口〕大闹. ***put a good*** ～ ***on*** 将…擦得晶亮. ***take a*** ～ ***to***〔美俚〕喜爱;爱上;看中. ***take the*** ～ ***off [out of]*** 消除…的光泽;使…黯然无光[失色];使相形见绌;胜过. ～**less** *a.* 无光泽的.

shin·er [ˈʃainə] *n.* ①发光物;闪耀发亮的东西;发光体〔日、月等〕;丝质礼帽. ②出色[杰出]的人物;衣着漂亮的人. ③〔美〕(作饵用)银色小鱼. ④〔英俚〕钱币;〔尤指〕一镑金币;〔*pl.*〕钱. ⑤〔俚〕受伤后青肿的黑眼圈;眼睛. ⑥擦皮鞋者.

shin·gle[1] [ˈʃiŋgl] *n.* ①屋顶板;木瓦板. ②(女式)短发. ③〔美口〕(医师、律师等的)小招牌. ***hang out one's*** ～ 挂牌;开业. — *vt.* ①用木瓦板盖(屋顶). ②把(女子头发)剪短. ③【冶】锻;压, ④〔美俚〕责打(孩子等).

shin·gle[2] [ˈʃiŋgl] *n.*〔*sing.*, *pl.*〕扁砾石;砂砾;〔英〕(海滨的)圆卵石;砂石;砂石海滩.

shin·gles [ˈʃiŋglz] *n.*〔*sing.*, *pl.*〕【医】带状匍行疹;缠腰龙.

shin·gly [ˈʃingli] *a.* 多砂石的;似海滩圆卵石的;铺满圆卵石的.

shin·i·ness [ˈʃaininis] *n.* 光泽;光彩;闪亮.

shin·ing [ˈʃainiŋ] *a.* ①发光的;反光的;闪光的;光亮的;照耀的. ②灿烂的;显赫的;杰出的;卓越的;辉煌的.

shin·leaf [ˈʃinˌliːf] *n.*【植】鹿蹄草属 *(Pyrola)* 植物.

shin·ny,[1] **shin·ney** [ˈʃini] **shin·ty** [-ti] *n.*〔美〕①(儿童玩的)简式曲棍球戏. ②曲棍球球棍. — *vi.* ①玩简式曲棍球. ②击球.

shin·ny[2] [ˈʃini] *vi.*〔美俚〕攀爬(树等)*(up)*.

Shin·to [ˈʃintəu] *n.* (日本的)神道;神道教. **-ism** *n.* **-ist** *n. a.* **-is·tic** *a.*

shin·ty [ˈʃinti] *n.* = shinny.

shin·y [ˈʃaini] *a.* ***(-i·er; -i·est)*** ①晴朗的;发光的;辉煌的;光亮的;闪闪发亮的;有光泽的. ②磨亮的;磨光的;磨损的. **-i·ness** *n.*

ship [ʃip] *n.* ①船;大船;海船;舰〔作阴性看,代名词用 she, her〕. ②三桅船;全装帆船. ③船形物. ④〔俚〕赛艇. ⑤〔美〕飞船;飞机. ⑥全体船员. *His Majesty's* ～〔英军舰〕. *a capital* ～ 主力舰. *a* ～*'s company* 船员. *a* ～*'s husband* (在岸上代表船方处理事务的)船舶代理人. *a* ～*'s lawyer*〔美〕次等律师. ～*'s papers* 船证;船照. *a space* ～ 宇宙飞船. ***burn one's*** ～ 破釜沉舟. ***clear a*** ～ 卸货. ***gauge a*** ～ 量船的吃水量. ***go on board a*** ～ 乘船. ***heave a*** ～ ***to***【海】停船. ***jump*** ～ ①弃船潜逃. ②背弃;潜逃. ***launch a*** ～ 使船下水. ***on board a*** ～ 在船上;在[往]船内. ***lose [spoil] the*** ～ ***for a ha'p'orth*** (= halfpennyworth) ***of tar*** 因小失大. ***speak a*** ～【海】给别的船打招呼[发信号]. ***take*** ～〔古〕乘船;搭船. ***when one's*** ～ ***comes home*** 如果变成富翁;如果有了钱;当某人时来运转;当某人发财时. ***wind a*** ～【海】掉转船头. — *vt.* ①装上船;用船运;装货;卸货;(用船、铁路、马车等)装运;运送;送、②雇(水手). ③装上;安上(船具). ④〔口语〕解雇;赶走;撵走;摆脱. ⑤(自船舷侧)灌进(海水). — *vi.* ①上船;乘船. ②在船上工作;做水手[水兵]. ～ *as bo'sun* 做水手长. ～ ***a sea [water]*** 冒着波浪,波浪打上甲板. ～ ***oars*** 把桨安在桨架上,～ ***off*** 送往;遣送. ～ ***out*** ①坐船到国外去. ②送(某人上船)到海外去. ～ ***over***〔美〕重新再进海军服役. ～ **airplane [aeroplane]** 舰上飞机. ～ **biscuit** (船上用的)硬饼干. ～**board** 船上,舷侧;船. ～ **bread** = ～ biscuit. ～ **breaker** 废船包拆人. ～ ～ **breaking** 废船拆卸业. ～ **broker** 船舶经纪人;水险掮客. ～**builder** 造船技师;造船工人;船匠. ～ **building** ①造船术[学]. ②造船业. ～ **canal** (可航行海船的)海船运河. ～ **chandler** 船具商. ～ **chandlery** ①船具. ②船具业. ～ **fever**【医】伤寒. ～**fitter** ①造船装配工[安装工]. ②(美海军)下士;安装技工. ～ **letter** 交普通船运送的信件. ～**load** ①船货. ②一只船的载货量. ～**man** ①水手;海员. ②船长. ～**-master** 船长;船主. ～**mate** 同船水手;水手同伴. ～ **money**【英史】造舰税. ～ **of the desert** 骆驼. ～ **of the line**〔古〕(备有七十五门炮以上的)战列舰. ～ **of war** (= ～-of-war) 战舰. ～ **owner** 船主. ～ **plane** 舰载飞机. ～ **railway** 移船轨道. ～**-rigged** 三桅(上备有)横帆的;有横[方形]帆的. ～**'s articles** 雇用船员条例. ～**'s bell** (每隔半小时的)船上敲钟. ～ **boat** 救生艇. ～**'s boy** 船轮服务员 (= cabin boy). ～**'s company** 全体船员. ～**shape** *a., ad.* 井然有序的[地]. ～**'s husband** 船舶代理人;随船押货人. ～ **side** 码头的靠船一侧. ～ **station** 船上电台. ～**way** 造船台. ～ **worm** 凿船虫;船蛆. ～**wreck** *n., vt., vi.* ①船只失事;失事船. ②灭亡;毁灭;失败;挫折. ③使(船)失事 *(make* ～ *wreck of* 破坏;糟蹋;把…弄得一塌糊涂). ～ **wright** 造船工;船匠. ～**yard** 造船厂;船坞.

-ship *suf.*〔附在形容词或名词后,作成抽象名词后〕表示状态、情况、性质、资格、身分、职、术等: hard*ship*, leader*ship*, member*ship*, scholar*ship*.

ship·ment [ˈʃipmənt] *n.* ①装货;船运;装运. ②装载的货物;载货. ③载货量.

ship·pa·ble [ˈʃipəbl] *a.* 可以装运的;适于装船的;可以运输的;可船运的.

ship·pen [ˈʃipən] *n.* 牛棚;马房.

ship·per [ˈʃipə] *n.* 发货人;交运货物者;运货者;托运人;货主.

ship·ping [ˈʃipiŋ] *n.* ①装货;船运;海运;航运;装运;运输. ②航行. ③航运业;运输业. ④〔集合词〕(某一范围内的)全部船舶. ⑤船舶总吨数. *line* ～ 定期航运 ～ **a·gent** 运输[船运]代理商. ～ **ar·ti·cles**〔*pl.*〕船员雇用合同. ～ **bill [note]** 舱单;船货清单;装船通知单. **S- Board**〔美〕船务局. ～ **clerk** (码头上的)理货员;运务员. ～ **room** (工厂等的)发货仓库.

ship·pon [ˈʃipən] *n.* = shippen.

Shi·raz [ʃiəˈrɑːz] *n.* 设拉子[伊朗城市].

shire [ˈʃaiə] *n.* ①(英国的)郡(= county). ②〔the S-s〕(尤指以猎狐出名的)英国中部各郡地区. ③= ～ horse 英国中部出产的、高大有力的拉车马. *a knight of the* ～【英史】郡选议员. ***come from the*** ～***s***〔英〕是中部地方的(人). ***get in the*** ～ ***what one loses in the hundred*** 失之东隅,收之桑榆. ～ **horse** (英国中部出产的、高大有力的)拉车马;大种马. ～ ***town*** ①郡的行政机关所在地;郡的首府. ②中级法院所在地.

-shire [-ʃiə, -ʃə] *suf.*〔英〕…州. Berk*shire*, York*shire*, Lanca*shire*.

shirk [ʃəːk] *n.* 逃避者;偷懒者. — *vi. vt.* 逃避;躲避;规避(义务、责任等);怠忽;偷懒. *(from)*. ～ *military service* 逃避兵役. ～ ***off [out]*** 逃开. ～**er** 逃避者;偷懒者.

shir(r) [ʃəː]〔美〕*n.* 抽褶;(抽褶、松紧带里的)松紧线;象皮筋. — *vt.* 把…抽上褶子;【烹】(把奶油和上面包屑)焙烤(蛋).

shir·(r)ing [ˈʃəːriŋ] *n.* 抽褶(饰边).

Shir·ley [ˈʃəːli] *n.* 雪莉[女子名].

shirt [ʃəːt] *n.* ①(男式)衬衫. ②(仿男式的)女用衬衫. ③内衣;汗衫. *T-*～ 短袖圆领口汗衫. ***get sb.'s*** ～ ***out [off]***〔俚〕惹怒;使发脾气. ***give away the*** ～ ***off one's back*** 送掉身上所有的东西;不顾自己尽力接济[帮助]别人. ***give sb. a wet*** ～ 使(某)人工作到汗流浃背. ***hang onto sb.'s*** ～***s*** 依靠某人. ***have not a*** ～ ***to one's back*** 连衬衫都没有,穷极. ***have one's*** ～ ***out [off]*** 发脾气. ***keep one's*** ～ ***on***〔俚〕保持冷静;不发脾气. ***lose one's***

～〔俚〕失去一切；搞得精光。***put one's ～ on [upon]*** *(a horse)*〔俚〕把全部赌本押在（一匹马上）。***Near [close] is my ～, but nearer [closer] is my skin.*** 为人不如为己。～ **band** 衬衫的领口［袖口］。～**-dress** ＝ ～ waist, blouse. ～ **front** 衬衫的胸部。～ ***hunt***〔美〕捉虱子。～ **maker** ①制衬衣者。②简易妇女上衣。～ **sleeves** 衬衫袖子 (*in one's ～-sleeves* 不穿外衣)。～**-sleeve** *a.* 不穿外衣的，衣著随便的；不拘礼貌的，随便的。～ **tail** *n.* ①衬衣的下摆。②〔美新闻语〕排在主要新闻下的小新闻；不重要的小事物。*a.* ①〔口〕(亲戚)远房的。②小的；短的。③幼小的。④非正式的；随便的。～ **waist**〔美〕＝ blouse. ～ **waister** 连衣裙。

shir·ting [ˈʃəːtiŋ] *n.* 衬衫料子。

shirt·y [ˈʃəːti] *a.*〔俚〕脾气不好的；发怒的；被激怒的。

shish ke·bab [ˈʃiʃ kəˌbɑːb] 烤羊肉串 (＝ shish kabob).

shit [ʃit]〔英卑〕*vi.* 拉屎；通便。— *vt.* 对…胡言乱语；对…胡作非为。— *n.* ①大粪。②通便。③假装；伪装。④胡说；大话。— *int.* 狗屎！狗屁！ **-ty** *a.* 不舒服。

shit·tah [ˈʃitə] *n.* (*pl.* **shit·tahs, shittim**)【植】塞伊尔相思树 *(Acacia seyal)*〔产于亚洲〕。

shit·tim (wood) [ˈʃitim] *n.* 塞伊尔相思树木。

shiv [ʃiv] *n.*〔俚〕刀；剃刀；弹簧刀。

Shiva [ʃiːvə] ＝ Siva.

shiv·a·ree [ˌʃivəˈriː] *n.*〔美〕＝ charivari.

shive [ʃaiv] *n.* ①碎片；断片。②亚麻硬外皮。③〔*pl.*〕下脚麻。④(大口瓶的)扁薄软木塞。⑤〔美俚〕剃刀；小刀。⑥布上的线头。

shiv·er[1] [ˈʃivə] *vi., vt.* ①(使)发抖；(使)打颤；(使)迎风飘动。— *n.* 发抖；颤抖。***give sb. the ～s*** 使人不寒而栗；使人毛骨悚然。***the ～s*** ①〔口谑〕发冷；战栗；冷颤。②【医】疟疾。

shiv·er[2] [ˈʃivə] *n.*〔常 *pl.*〕碎块；破片；碎片。— *vt., vi.* 打碎；敲碎；破碎。***break [burst] into ～s*** 粉碎。***shiver my timbers!*** 粉身碎骨！他妈的！〔水手骂人的话。〕

shiv·er·ing·ly [ˈʃivəriŋli] *ad.* 发着抖；颤抖着。

shiv·er·y[1] [ˈʃivəri] *a.* ①颤抖的；战栗的；易发抖的；使人打冷颤的；毛骨悚然的。②寒冷的。

shiv·er·y[2] [ˈʃivəri] *a.* 易碎的；脆弱的。

shi·voo [ʃiˈvuː] *n.*〔澳俚〕兴高采烈［吵吵嚷嚷］的庆祝(宴)会。

Shi·zu·o·ka [ʃiˈzuəukɑː] *n.* 静冈〔日本城市〕。

shlep, shlepp [ʃlep]〔美俚〕*n., vt., vi.* ＝ schlep.

shmaltz [ʃmɑːts] *n.*〔美俚〕＝ schmaltz. **-y** *a.*

shmuck [ʃmʌk] *n.*〔美俚〕＝ schmuck.

shnook [ʃnuk] *n.*〔美俚〕＝ schnook.

sho *a.*〔南美、方〕＝ sure.

shoal[1] [ʃəul] *n.* ①(尤指潮退时露出的)沙洲；浅滩。②〔常 *pl.*〕潜在的危险［危机，困难］；隐患；陷井。***the ～s*** 海的浅水部分。— *vi. vt.* ①变浅；变成浅滩；使浅。②驶入浅水的地方。— *a.* (水)浅的；(船)吃水浅的。

shoal[2] [ʃəul] *n.* ①(鱼)群。②〔*pl.*〕〔口〕大群；大量；许多。***in ～s*** 成群；许多。***～s of*** 许多的；大群的(人)；充分的(时间)。— *vi.* (鱼)成群；(鱼)成群集聚。

shoal·er [ˈʃəulə] *n.* 沿海贸易商船［水手］。

shoal·y [ˈʃəuli] *a.* ①多浅滩的。②多潜在危险的；隐患重重的；尽是陷井的。

shoat [ʃəut] *n.* ①小猪。②〔美俚〕懒鬼；无用的人。

shock[1] [ʃɔk] *n.* ①冲突；冲撞；冲击；突击。②震动；冲动；激动。③感动；愤慨；惊愕；震惊。④地震。⑤【医】休克；震荡。⑥【电】电击；电震。⑦【物】冲波；激波；突跃波；爆音。⑧(对信用、安全等的)打击。⑨〔口〕晕厥。*the ～ of arms* 军队的冲突。*give a terrible ～ to sb.* 使人非常震惊；给与巨大打击。*electric ～* 电振荡；电震；触电。*expansion ～* 膨胀突跃。— *vt.* ①冲击；使震动；使震荡；激动。②使震惊；使惊骇，使毛骨悚然；使愤慨。— *vi.* ①冲突；震动。②震惊；震骇；觉得毛骨悚然。***be ～ed to learn*** 听见…感到震惊［极度愤慨］。～ **absorber** 减震器；缓冲器。～ **action** 突袭。～ **excitation** 冲击激励；震激。～ **free** 无冲激的；无激波的。～ **load** 冲击负载；突加荷载。～ **mount** 减震器；防震座。～**-proof** *a.* 防震的；不怕震的；防电击的。～**-resistant** 抗震的。～ **stall**【空】激波失速；激波分离。～ **strength** 抗震强度。～ **tactics** 突击战术。～ **troops** 突击部队。～ **wave**【物】冲击波；激波。～ **workers** 突击工人；突击手。

shock[2] [ʃɔk] *n.* 禾束堆；〔美〕玉米杆堆；干草堆。— *vt., vi.* 将…堆成捆堆〔堆成禾束堆〕；捆堆禾束。

shock[3] [ʃɔk] *n.* ①蓬乱的一堆(毛发)。②长毛蓬松的狗；狮子狗。— *a.* 蓬乱的；茂密的。～**-head,** ～**headed** *a.* 头发乱蓬蓬的。

shock·er [ˈʃɔkə] *n.* ①使人震惊的东西［人］。②〔英口〕恶劣的东西；不值钱的惊险小说〔常作 *shilling ～*〕；〔美〕耸人听闻的影片［小说，等］。

shock·ing [ˈʃɔkiŋ] *a.* ①使人震惊的；骇人听闻的；触目惊心的；令人毛骨悚然的。②〔口〕非常粗陋的；非常坏的(菜、声音等)。— *ad.*〔口〕极度［说不出地］(坏)。**-ly** *ad.* **-ness** *n.*

Shock·ley [ˈʃɔkli] *n.* 肖克利〔姓氏〕。

shod [ʃɔd] shoe 的过去式及过去分词。— *a.* 穿着鞋的；装有轮胎［铁蹄］的；有金属包头的。

shod·den [ˈʃɔdn] shoe 的过去分词。

shod·dy [ˈʃɔdi] *a.* ①长弹毛的；软再生毛的。②劣等的；假的；冒充的；虚有其表的。— *n.* ①(拿旧货重制的)翻造呢绒；回纺绒线。【纺】长弹毛；软再生毛；软再生毛织物。②冒充物；不值钱的东西；(暴发户等的)虚矫假饰。*～ clothes* 再生呢绒。*a ～ character* 虚有其表的人物。**-di·ly** *ad.* **-di·ness** *n.*

shoe [ʃuː] *n.* (*pl.* ～s,〔古〕**shoon**) ①鞋〔一般指鞋帮不到踝骨的鞋子；过踝骨的靴子叫 boots；在美国也叫鞋子为 low ～s, 叫靴子为 ～s〕。②鞋形物。③蹄铁。④(汽车的)轮胎，外胎。⑤(汽车轮的)制动器，刹车。⑥【机】闸瓦。⑦(手杖等的)金属箍。⑧(中国从前的)马蹄银(等)。⑨【建】桩靴。⑩【电】端；靴；管头；触屐。⑪【空】尾撑；【火箭】导向板；发射导轨。⑫〔*pl.*〕所处的地位［境遇］。*a pair of ～s* 一双鞋子。*high ～s* 长筒［高帮］鞋。*the ～ is on the other foot.* 责任在别人身上；情况完全相反了，现在不是这样了。***another pair of ～s*** 另一回事；另一个问题。***cast aside like an old ～*** 弃若敝屣。***fill sb.'s ～s*** 接替某人；步某人后尘。***die in one's ～s*** 横死；惨死；(尤指)被绞死。***in another's ～s*** 处于别人的地位。***in one's ～s*** 穿着鞋子。***know [feel] where the ～ pinches*** (由经验)知道困难［症结］之所在。***lick sb's ～s*** 巴结某人。***look after [wait for] dead men's ～s*** 窥伺［等待］遗产。***over ～s over boots.*** 一不作，二不休。***over [up to] the ～s*** 深深钻进去；深深陷入。***put the ～ on the right foot*** 责备应该责备的人；责备得当。***shake in one's ～s*** 发抖；害怕；颤栗。～ ***of the launcher*** 发射导轨；起动导轨。***stand in sb.'s ～s*** 代替［取得］某人职位，处于某人位置［境遇］。***The ～ is on the other foot.*** 情况完全不同了。***where the ～ pinches*** 症结所在；困难所在，痛苦之处。— *vt.* (**shod** [ʃɔd]; **shod, shod·den** [ˈʃɔdn]) 给…穿鞋；给(马)钉蹄铁；给…装上鞋状物；装金属片包覆。*neatly shod feet* 穿着象样的鞋子的脚。*～ a horse* 给马钉蹄铁。*a staff shod with iron* 端部包上铁皮的棍子。～**black,** ～**boy** 擦鞋子的(人)。～**-blacking** 黑鞋油。～**brush** 鞋刷。～ **buckle** 鞋扣。～**horn** 鞋拔。～**lace** 鞋带。～ **leather** ①鞋用皮革。②〔口〕(集合名词) 鞋 (*save ～ leather* 节省鞋子，尽量少走路)。～**less** *a.* ①没有鞋的；不穿鞋的。②没有钉蹄铁的。～ **lift** ＝ shoehorn. ～**-maker** 鞋店；鞋匠。～**making** ①制鞋；补鞋。②制鞋业。～**pac,** ～**pak** 派克高统保温、防水靴。～ **pol·ish** 鞋油。～**shine** ①擦皮鞋。②擦亮的鞋面光泽。③擦皮鞋者。～**shop** 鞋店。

~ **store** = ~ shop. ~**-string** ①〔美〕【无】电线. ②鞋带 *(on a ~-string* 〔美口〕用很少的本钱. *walk on one's ~-string* 〔美〕陷入贫困. ~**string potatoes** 拔土豆丝. **steel** ~ 钢挡板(上下)模板. ~ **tree**〔美〕鞋楦.

shoe·bill [ˈʃuːbil] *n.* 【动】鹭 *(Balaeniceps rex)* 〔发现于中非白尼罗河沿岸〕.

sho·er [ˈʃuːə] *n.* 钉蹄铁工人; 挂掌匠.

sho·far [ˈʃəufə 〔Heb.〕 ʃəuˈfɑː] *n. (pl. -fars;* 〔Heb.〕 *-frot* [-ˈfrəut]*)* (犹太教徒礼拜时用的)羊角号.

sho·ji [ˈʃəudʒi] *n. (pl. sho·ji, -jis)* 〔Jap.〕拉门〔日本式拉动开关的门扇〕(= shoji screen).

Sho·na [ˈʃəunɑː] *n.* ①*(pl. Sho·nas, Sho·na)* 修纳人〔罗得西亚与邻近的莫桑比克的农民〕. ②修纳语.

shone [ʃɔn] shine 的过去式及过去分词.

shoo [ʃuː] *int.* 嘘! 〔驱赶禽类的嘘声〕. — *vi., vt.* 发'嘘!'声驱赶.

shoo·fly [ˈʃuːˌflai] *n.* 〔美〕①舒弗莱舞〔曳步舞〕. ②(小孩的) 动物状摇椅〔如摇动木马等〕. ③糖浆馅饼 (= shoofly pie). ④(铁路的)临时轨道; 临时便道. ⑤(印刷机)拨离爪〔使在印的纸离开滚筒转移到纸台的装置〕.

shoo-in [ˈʃuːin] *n.* 〔美口〕十拿九稳的取胜者.

shook[1] [ʃuk] shake 的过去式.

shook[2] [ʃuk] *n.* ①一套装配木桶〔木箱等〕的木板. ②禾捆.

shoon [ʃuːn] *n.* 〔古〕 shoe 的复数.

shoot [ʃuːt] *vt.* *(shot* [ʃɔt]*)* ①发射; 射(箭); 开(枪); 放(炮); 放射(光线). ②射中; 打中; 射死; 打死; 射伤; 打伤; 〔喻〕毁坏. ③投; 掷; 抛出; 倒出; 撒(网等). ④爆破; 使爆炸. ⑤〔美俚〕递送; 传递. ⑥【纺】投(梭). ⑦发(芽); 发出 *(forth; out; up)*. ⑧突出; 伸出; 突入. ⑨闩(门); 上(门栓); 拔出(门栓). ⑩【足球】射门. 【篮球】投篮; 击(球). ⑪掷(骰子). ⑫飞速通过; 迅速投送〔派遣〕; 迅速推进. ⑬拍摄. ⑭把…刨光. ⑮〔通例用 p.p.〕织入异色纬纱. ⑯测量(天体的)高度. ⑰给…注射〔打针〕. — *vi.* ①射箭; 放枪; 放炮. ②射击; (子弹)打中; 击中. ③出猎; 拿枪打猎. ④迅速移动; 箭一般地飞行; 射出. ⑤(船)飞也似地开行; (车)疾驰(而过). ⑥(光)闪发. ⑦(牙齿等)感到剧痛; 急痛. ⑧(草木)发芽; 生长; 长大; 发育. ⑨高耸; *(up)*; 落下; 流下. ⑩冲出; 突出; 伸出. ⑪〔足球〕射门; 〔篮球〕投篮; 打球. ⑫掷骰子等. ⑬【纺】投梭. ⑭〔美〕拍电影, 拍照; 摄影. ⑮〔美俚〕讲吧; 快讲. ~ *out one's tongue* 伸出舌头. ~ *rubbish* 倒垃圾. *S- the salt to me.* 把盐递给我. ~ *edges* 刨齐边缘. ***I'll be shot if ...*** 如果是…的话打死我好了; 决不是…. ~ ***a bolt*** 拉开〔插上〕插梢. ~ ***a covert [an estate]*** 在猎场〔庄园〕打猎. ~ ***ahead*** 疾进; 超过; 追过. ~ ***a line*** 〔俚〕吹牛. ~ ***a match*** 参加竞射. ~ ***a tie*** 射击比赛比分相同时重行射击. ~ ***away*** ①继续不停地发射子弹; 打光, 射完(子弹等). ②打掉, 击毁. ③象子弹出膛一样飞快地离去. ~ ***craps*** 〔美俚〕 掷骰子. ~ ***disc*** 掷骰子. ~ ***down*** ①射落; 打下来; 射倒. ②击死; 打死. ③〔口〕严厉谴责; 〔俚〕驳倒. ④遗弃. ~ ***fire*** (眼睛)闪闪发光; 发亮. ~ ***for [at]*** 力争; 切望. ~ ***forth*** 射出; 弄出. ~ ***into*** 〔美〕使人相信; 想左右某人. ~ ***off*** ①〔及物用法〕发射(子弹); 击毁, 打掉(腿等); 使爆炸. ②不及物用法〕象子弹出膛一样飞快离去; 吹嘘 *(about)*. (~ *off firecrackers* 放鞭炮. *have one's leg shot off* 一条腿给打断了). *The driver without a word shot off before he could rightly be seated.* 他还没有坐稳当司机就一言不发驱车飞驶了). ~ ***off one's bazoo*** 〔美俚〕 自夸. ~ ***off one's [the] mouth [face]*** 〔美俚〕象连珠炮似地讲; 信口开河; 瞎说乱讲; 瞎吹牛; 夸口. ~ ***one's cookies*** 〔美俚〕呕吐. ~ ***one's wad*** 〔美〕说想说的; 做想做的. ~ ***out*** ①射出; 投出; 发出. ②突出; 伸出; 高耸. ③用武力解决. ~ ***over [to] a dog*** 用狗打猎. ~ ***sb. full of daylight*** 〔美俚〕把某人打得全身都是枪眼. ~ ***straight*** 正打中. ~ ***the baloney*** = ~ ***the bull*** 〔美俚〕 胡说; 瞎说. ~ ***the breeze*** 〔美俚〕说大话; 夸大; 胡扯; 吹牛; 畅谈. ~ ***the bull*** 【俚】漫谈; 夸张. ~ ***the moon*** 〔英俚〕(为了逃避清偿房租)在夜间带着自己的东西潜逃. ~ ***the Niagara*** 冒极大风险; 企图做冒险的事. ~ ***the sun*** 【海】用六分仪测太阳高度. ~ ***the works*** 〔美俚〕孤注一掷; 〔喻〕倾全力而为; 尽人事. ~ ***up*** ①上冒; 喷出; 欣欣向荣; 猛长; 暴腾; 猛跳; 高耸; 涨价. ②〔俚〕注射麻碎剂. ③〔美俚〕乱射; 乱放枪; 乱放枪吓人. ④〔美卑〕抛弃. ***shot between wind and water*** 被击中吃水线附近; 击中要害. — *int.* 哼! 嗜! 〔反感、失望声〕 — *n.* ①射击; 发射; 开枪; 放炮; (火箭等的)试射. ②〔棒球俚〕快球的小弯球. ③打靶会; 狩猎; 〔英〕游猎会. ④游猎地; 猎场. ⑤迅速的移动〔动作〕. ⑥急流; 奔流; 喷泉; 富矿体. ⑦光线; 光道. ⑧芽; 苗; 新梢; 嫩枝; 徒长枝. ⑨(滑运木材; 煤等的)滑水路; 滑槽; 泻槽; 斜槽. ⑩垃圾场. ⑪摄影; 拍电影. ⑫推力; (冰块, 土块)崩落. ⑬(划桨时) 两划间的间隔时间. *transplant rice ~s* 插秧. *take a ~* 〔美〕经由急流航行; 抄近路. *the whole ~* 所有的东西; 全部; 一切. ***be on the*** ~ 〔美〕预备射击; 备战.

shoot·er [ˈsuːtə] *n.* ①射手; 弓手; 炮手; 猎者; 爆破手. ②流星; 火器; 枪; 〔美〕手枪. *a sharp ~* 狙击兵. *a six-~* 六响〔六发子弹〕枪. *a pea~* (用豆作子弹的)玩具豆子枪.

shoot·ing [ˈsuːtiŋ] *n.* ①发射; 射击; 射出, 发出. ②射杀; 枪杀. ③打鸟; 狩猎, 打猎. ④狩猎权, 猎场. ⑤摄影. ⑥刺痛; 剧痛. ⑦〔美俚〕兴奋; 骚动; 乱子. ⑧〔足球〕射门; 〔篮球〕投篮. *Why all the ~?* 〔美俚〕 怎么这样闹法? *trouble ~* 故障检修. ~ **box,** 狩猎小屋. ~ **gallery** ①(游艺场所的) 打靶场. ②〔美俚〕注射麻醉剂的秘密处所. ~ **iron** 〔俚〕枪. ~ **off** (比分相等时)延长射击比赛. ~**range** 靶子场; 射击场. ~ **script** (电影)摄影台本; 分镜头脚本. ~ **star** ①流星; 陨星. ②【植】美国樱草. ~ **stick** 猎人手杖〔握手处可折下当座子〕. ~ **war** 实战; 热战 *(opp.* cold war).

shoot-the-chute [ˈʃuːtðəˈʃuːt] *n.* = chute-the-chute.

shop [ʃɔp] *n.* ①〔英〕铺子; 店铺; (零售)商店〔美国主要说 store〕; (大商店里的)特殊部门. ②〔*pl.*〕工厂; 工场; 车间; 修理所. ③(本人的)职业; 本行; 业务. ④〔俚〕工作; 职业. ⑤事务所; 办事处; 机构; 场所. ⑥家; 自己的家. ⑦房屋; 建筑物. ⑧学校; 大学(等); 〔the S-〕〔英俚〕〔废〕陆军军官学校. *closed ~* 〔美〕不得雇用非工会会员的企业. *back [repair] ~s* 修理厂〔车间〕. *Shop!* 〔在店门口〕喂! 有没有人! *Cut the ~!* 别讲本行的事! *How are they all at your ~?* 〔俚〕府上各位好吗? ***all over the*** ~ 〔俚〕零乱; 杂乱; 到处; 任意; 盲目. ***come [go] to the wrong*** ~ 〔俚〕找错门道, 找错了人〔指求助、打听消息等〕. ***keep(a)*** ~ 开店; 照管店务. ***set up*** ~ 开店; 开始营业. ***shut up*** ~ ①停止(工作、游戏等). ②歇业; 关店; 宣告破产. ***sink the*** ~ 不谈自己职业上的〔本行的, 专门的〕事情. ***smell of the*** ~ 商人气息; 行业气息. ***talk*** ~ 动不动谈自己职业上的事情; 三句不离本行; 说行话. ***the other*** ~ 作为竞争劲敌的企业、学校或是其他机构. — *vi.* ①买东西(去). ②到处寻找. — *vt.* ①〔俚〕逮捕; 投入监狱. ②〔俚〕密告; 出卖(某人). ③选购(商品); 挑选(商品). ④送往修理所修理. ⑤〔美〕解雇. *go shopping* 去买东西. ~ *around* ①到处选购; 到一家一家店铺访求〔买东西〕. ②〔美〕找事〔好职位〕. ~ **assistant** 〔英〕店员. ~**boy** 〔英〕店伙计. ~**-call** (对厂主不满时的)厂内集会. ~ **card** 营业卡; 营业证. ~ **chairman,** ~ **deputy** = ~ steward. ~ **drawing** 制造图. ~ **girl** 〔英〕 女店员. ~ **hours** 营业时间. ~ **keeper** ①〔英〕零售商人; 店主, 老板. ②〔俚〕冷货; 陈货. ~**lifter** 店铺扒手. ~ **lifting** 入店行窃. ~**-made** 〔美〕定做的. ~**man** ①店铺商人; 零售商. ②店员; 伙计. ~ **steward** (一个工厂的) 工人代表. ~**talk** 行话; 非工作时间谈论本行的谈话. ~ **truck** 修理车 ~-

union 工会. ~-**walker**〔英〕(百货商店等的)巡视员;招待员. ~**window** (商店的)橱窗 *(put all one's goods in the ~window = have everything in the ~window* 全部摆出来给人看;浅薄;内容空虚). ~**worn** [ˈʃɔpwɔːn] 店里摆旧的;滞销的;陈旧的.

sho·phar [ˈʃəufɑː, Heb. ʃəuˈfɑː] *n.* = shofar.

shoppe [ʃɔp] *n.* = shop.

shop·per [ˈʃɔpə] *n.* ①买东西的人;顾客. ②(商店雇用的)代客选购货物的人. ③(商店雇用的)打听行情的人. ④〔美〕购物指南〔登载当地各商店广告的传单〕.

shop·ping [ˈʃɔpiŋ] *n.* 买东西. *do one's ~* 买东西. ~ **centre** 购物中心;市郊商店区.

shop·py [ˈʃɔpi] *a.* ①商人的;生意人(似)的. ②象零售店的;职业气味的(会话等). ③商店多的. ④三句不离本行的.

sho·ran [ˈʃɔːræn] (= short-range navigation) *n.*【空】①近程无线电导航系统;肖兰系统. ②短程无线电导航法. ③近距助航仪.

shore[1] [ʃɔː, ʃɔə] *n.* ①岸;海岸;滨. ②【法】满潮线和退潮线中间的地区. ③〔常 *pl.*〕陆(地). *a ~ line* 滨线;海岸线. *a ~ fish* 近海鱼. *~ to ship service* 水陆联络设备. *one's native ~(s)* 故乡;故国. ***go on ~*** 上岸. ***in ~*** 近岸. ***off ~*** ①离岸. ②在离海岸不远处. ***on ~*** 在岸上. ***put on ~*** 使上岸;起(货)上岸. ***within these ~s*** 在这个国家内. ~-**based** [ˈʃɔːbeist] 以陆地为基地的;以海岸为基地的. ~ **bird** 水鸟;沙禽;涉禽. ~ ***dinner*** 〔美〕由海鲜菜餚组成的一顿饭. ~ **leave** (船员)上岸假(期). ~ **reef** 裙礁.

shore[2] [ʃɔː] *n.* (房屋、树木、修建中房屋等的)支柱;斜撑柱. — *vt.* 用支柱[斜撑]撑住 *(up)*.

shore[3] [ʃɔː] *v.*〔古〕shear 的过去式.

shor·ing [ˈʃɔːriŋ] *n.*〔集合词〕支柱;斜撑柱.

shorn [ʃɔːn] shear 的过去分词. — *a.* ①被剪过的. ②被拿去的;被夺去的;被剥去的. *shaven and ~* 修过面剪过发的. *closely ~* 剪短的(头发等). *~ of (one's money)* 被抢去了(钱).

Short [ʃɔːt] *n.* 肖特〔姓氏〕.

short [ʃɔːt] *a.* ①短的;短暂的 *(opp.* long*)*. ②矮的;低的 *(opp.* tall*)*. ③短期的. ④简短的;简略的;缩写的. ⑤【语音】短音的. ⑥不足的;不够的;短少的. ⑦不及的;达不到的. ⑧(见闻等)浅陋的. ⑨简慢的;唐突的;无礼的;急性子的;不高兴的;发着脾气的. ⑩〔口〕不掺水的,强烈的(酒等);〔威士忌〕纯的. ⑪【商】卖空的;抛空的;无存货的. ⑫〔金属〕脆的;易裂的;易碎的;松脆的(饼等). ⑬波涛汹涌的(海). ⑭(智力等)弱的;(记忆力)差的. *a ~ life and a merry one* 短暂光辉的一生. *a ~ mile distance* 不到一英里的距离. *In speaking one should be ~ and to the point.* 说话要简洁扼要. *He was very ~ with me.* 他对我很冷淡. *~ memory* 善忘. *a ~ temper* 急性子. *something ~* 烈酒. ***come [drop, fall] ~ (of)*** 在某方面有所不足;在某方面差一点、有缺陷;辜负期待,达不到目的. ***in the ~ run*** 在短时期里. ***little ~ of*** 几乎;简直 *(It is little ~ of a miracle* 简直是奇迹). ***make [let] a long story ~*** 说得简单些. ***make ~ work of*** 迅速处理[破坏、消费];杀死. ***nothing ~ of*** 完全是;不折不扣的是;简直可以说;除…外,别无…. ***run ~ (of)*** 缺乏. ***~ and sweet*** ①(说话)扼要的. ②短而愉快的. ***~ arm drill*** 〔美军俚〕花柳病检查. ***~ of*** 缺少;达不到;除了;只要不是 *(be ~ of money* 缺少钱.) ***~ of breath [puff]*** 喘着气. — *ad.* ①简短地;简单地. ②缺乏;不足. ③脆. ④突然;忽然. ⑤简慢地;唐突地. ***be taken ~*** 忽然想解手[大、小便]. ***bring [pull] up ~*** 忽然停止. ***cut ~*** 突然停止;突然阻止. ***sell ~*** 卖空. ***take sb. up ~*** 阻断(某人)谈话. — *n.* ①概略;要点;不足;缺乏. ②【语音】短音节;【乐】短音符. ③【商】卖空;(交易所的)空方;空头. ④【棒球】游击手. ⑤〔*pl.*〕(运动)短袴. ⑥不到规定长度的东西[鱼等]. ⑦〔*pl.*〕短少的数额;【印】短少部数;追加部数. ⑧次货;废料;次粉;细麸子. ⑨(报刊的)短讯;短篇;(电影的)短片 (= ~ piece *or* film). ⑩【电】= ~-circuit. ⑪〔美俚〕汽车. ⑫〔*pl.*〕短期票据〔债券〕. *The long and ~ of it is ...* 总而言之;简单地说. ***at (the) ~*** 简单地;立即. ***for ~*** 简称〔简称人名时用〕. ***in ~*** 简单地说;总之. — *vt.* ①故意少给;欺骗. ②【电】使短路. ~-**arm**, ~-**armed** *a.* ①胳臂短的;蜷起手臂的(一击等). ②短距离的. ~ **bill** 短期票据. ~ **bit**〔美〕一角;十分〔美元〕. ~**bread** 松脆的酥饼. ~**cake** [ˈʃɔːtkeik]〔美〕松饼;脆饼. ~**change** [ˈʃɔːtˈtʃeindʒ] ①故意少给找头. ②欺骗. ~ **circuit** ①【电】短路;漏电. ②*vt., vi.* 使短路;漏电. ~ **clothes [coats]** 童装. ~**coming** [ʃɔːtˈkʌmiŋ] ①不足;缺乏. ②(谷类等的)歉收. ③短处;缺点;忽略;玩忽. ~-**common** [ˈʃɔːtˈkɔmənz]〔*pl.* 作单数用〕分量不足的粮食. ~ **contract**【商】买空卖空. ~ **covering**【商】卖空. ~ **crop** 低产. ~ **cut** 近路;捷径. ~ -**date**, ~-**dated** *a.* ①短期的. ②时间很短的. ~-**day** *a.*【植】短日照的. ~-**day plant**【植】短日照的植物. ~ **division**【数】(不写明演算过程的)简短除法. ~ **end** 处于劣势的一方. ~ **ender** (竞赛中)没有希望获胜的一方. ~-**fall** ①不足;短缺;亏空. ②短缺之量. ~ **field**〔棒球〕内野二垒与三垒间的地区. ~-**fired** *a.*〔陶器等〕火候不足的. ~**hand** ①速记;速记法. ②速记记录文字. ~**handed** [ˈʃɔːtˈhændid] *a.* 人手不足的. ~**hand-writer** 速记员. ~ **head** ①短颅人. ②(赛马)险胜. ~**horn** [ˈʃɔːthɔːn] ①短角菜牛. ②〔美〕(特指西部牧场中的)东部的人;新来的人;生手. ~-**horned grasshopper**【动】短角蚱蜢. ~ **iron** 脆性铁. ~-**legged** [ˈʃɔːtˌlegid] *a.* 腿短的. ~-**lived** [ˈʃɔːtˈlivd] *a.* 短命的;一时的;昙花一现的. ~ **order** 快菜〔很快做好的一道菜〕. ~ **position** ①【商】空头户;做空头. ②全部售完;售缺. ~-**range** 短射程的;短期的. ~ **residuum** 浓缩残铀. ~ **rib** 假肋骨. ~ **round**【军】近弹. ~ **sale**【商】卖空. ~ **sea** 波浪汹涌的海;三角浪. ~ **seller**【商】卖空的人;空头. **short ~s** 热裤. ~ **shrift** ①(死刑犯临刑前的)短促忏悔. ②不耐烦;漠不关心. ~-**sighted** *a.* ①近视(眼)的. ②眼光短浅的. ~ **snort** (喝酒)一口喝尽;快饮. ~-**spoken** [ˈʃɔːtˈspəukən] *a.* (寒暄等)冷淡的,马马虎虎的;简慢的. ~-**stop** [ˈʃɔːtstɔp]【棒球】游击手;②【摄】速显液. ~ **subject** 正片放映前的短片. ~-**tempered** *a.* 急性子的;暴躁的;易怒的. ~-**term** [ˈʃɔːttəːm] *a.* 短期的. ~ **ton** 短吨,美吨〔= 2000 磅或 0.907 公吨〕. ~-**wave** [ˈʃɔːtweiv] ① *n.* 短波;短波无线电发射机. ② *vt.* 用短波无线电发射[播送]. ~-**winded** [ˈʃɔːtˈwindid] *a.* ①气促的;喘气的. ②简短的;短促的.

short·i·a [ˈʃɔːtiə] *n.*〔美〕【植】枝草叶岩扇 *(shortia* galacifolia*)*.

short·ie [ˈʃɔːti] *n.*〔口〕= shorty.

short·age [ˈʃɔːtidʒ] *n.* 不足,缺少;不足额;〔美〕缺点,缺陷. *owing to ~ of staff* 由于人员的缺少. *a ~ of 50 tons* 五十吨的短缺额. ***cover [make up for] the ~*** 弥补不足.

short·en [ˈʃɔːtn] *vt.* 弄短,缩短;减少;加上使糕饼松脆的油脂;【海】收(帆),缩(帆);给(脱去长的婴孩服)改穿短衣. *~ one's arm [sword]* 缩回胳臂[剑]. *have a coat ~ed* 把上衣改短. *~ the arm of* 限制…的力量. *~ a child* 给孩子改穿短衣. — *vi.* 变短,缩短,缩小.

short·en·ing [ˈʃɔːtniŋ] *n.* 缩短;加在湿面里使糕饼松脆的油脂.

short·ly [ˈʃɔːtli] *ad.* 立刻,马上,不久;简单;简短. *answer ~* 简短地回答. *~ after* …之后立即. *~ before* …之前不久. *to put it ~* 简言之.

short·ness [ˈʃɔːtnis] *n.* 短;不足,缺少;简单;脆性. *~ of breath* 喘气. ***for ~*** = for short.

short·y [ˈʃɔːti] *n.* 〔口〕矮子,矮小的动物;小东西;〔俚〕酒。

Sho·sho·ne [ʃəuˈʃəuniː] *n.* ① *(pl. -sho·nes, -sho·ne)* 绶绶尼族人〔美国北部的一种印第安人〕。②绶绶尼语(= Shoshoni)。

shot¹ [ʃɔt] shoot 的过去式及过去分词。—*a.* ①打〔发射〕出去的;被射中的;发了芽的。②〔美俚〕坏得不能再使用的,注定要失败的。③【纺】杂色的,闪光的,色采幻变的。④〔俚〕喝醉了的。~ *cloth* 闪光绸。*crimson* ~ *with gold* 闪金光的深红色。*half* ~ 醉得差不多了。~ ***through with*** 充满…的。~ ***to pieces*** 破烂不堪的;毁坏了的。

shot² [ʃɔt] *n. (pl. ~s)* ①〔*pl.* ~〕弹,子弹,炮弹;散弹;【运】铅球。②射击,打枪,开炮;枪声,炮声;(网的)一撒;〔口〕(烈酒的)一口;〔俚〕(吗啡等的)注射;〔俚〕(酒吧等的)帐。③射程;瞄准,狙击。④射手,枪手。⑤猜测,推测。⑥【矿】炸破,爆破;炸药;【运】射门,投篮,(网球,台球)一击;【纺】投梭;(电影和摄影的)拍摄距离;拍摄;镜头;照片;〔美〕【无】广播节目。*a ~ of distress* 遇难信号炮。*a pot* ~ 容易的狙击。*a bad* ~ 不行的射击手;猜错,搞错。*a dead* ~ 神枪手。*a good* ~ 好枪手,好射手;猜对。*Good ~!* 打得好;好球! *a crane [zoon]* ~【影】俯瞰摄影。*a long* ~ 长射程;远程摄影;远景(镜头);大胆的企图[猜测]。*a mid* ~【影】中景。*a follow* ~【影】跟镜头;*a model* ~【影】模型摄影。*a big* ~〔美俚〕名人。~ *beer* 加有酒精的啤酒。***as a*** ~ 作为猜测 *(As a ~ I should say she's about forty.* 看来她怕有四十岁左右了)。***at a*** ~ 一枪就。***get [have, make] a ~ at*** 射击;推测,猜测。***have a ~ for [at]*** 尝试,试试看。***in*** ~ 在射程内。***like a*** ~〔口〕(象子弹一样)快,立刻。***not ... by a long*** ~ 绝对没有希望的,绝对不行的。***not worth powder and*** ~〔口〕不值得费力。***off like a*** ~ 子弹一样地,立刻。***out of*** ~ 在射程外。***pay [stand] the*** ~〔俚〕付帐。***put the*** ~ 掷铅球。***within ear-~ [rifle-~]*** 在听得见[子弹打得到]的距离内。***within*** ~ = in ~。—*vt.* 装弹药;装沙子、石子摇洗(瓶子等);用铁锤吊着使沉下,加铅粒使沉重;(用喷射法)使成颗粒。~ **effect**【电】散粒效应。~**gun** *n., a.* 散弹枪,鸟枪,猎枪;〔美俚〕强制的,用武力的。~ **hole** 弹孔,弹痕。~**-proof** *a.* 防弹的。~**-put(ting)**【运】(掷)铅球。~ **tower** 制弹塔;〔美俚〕厕所。~**weld·ing**【机】点焊。

shote [ʃəut] *n.* = shoat.

shott [ʃɔt] *n.* 北非盐湖盆地。

should [强 ʃud; 弱 ʃəd, ʃd] *aux.v.* shall 的过去式。①〔在间接引语中用作 shall 的过去式〕将,会。*He said he ~ succeed in the examination* (= He said, "I *shall* succeed in the examination")。他说了他会考取的。②(a)〔在虚拟语气的现在时条件句中〕万一…的话,如果…的话。*If I ~ fail I would try again.* 万一失败我还要试一试。(b)〔在表示与过去事实相反的虚拟语气的主句中〕就会 *If he had said so, I ~ have been angry.* 他要是这样说了,我就生气了。(c)〔省略虚拟的条件〕不妨会,倒是。*It is beautiful, I ~ say.* 啊,真漂亮。*I ~ like to go* (假如有人劝)我也许会去的。*She is under thirty, I ~ think.* 我想她还不到三十(岁)。*It ~ seem* 好象是,总象是〔比 it seems 委婉〕。③(a)〔不问人称,表示义务、责任〕应该,必须。*We ~ not do such a thing.* 我们不应该做这种事情。*You ~ not speak so loud; it is bad manners.* 说话声音别那么大;这没礼貌。*Why in the world ~ I go?* 为什么一定要我去。*You are not behaving as you ~.* 你的行为不得当。(b)〔说话者的意志、许诺〕*If the book were in the library, it ~ be at your service.* 这本书如果在图书馆里,那你就可以拿去看。*You ~ do it if we could make you.* 你如果肯的话,这件事就请你做了。(c)〔确实或可能有的未来或期待〕会。*They ~ arrive by one o'clock, I think.* 我想他们一点钟以前总会到的。*If the farmers can get continuous sunshine, they ~ have a satisfactory harvest.* 天气如果继续好下去,农民们就会得到满意的收获了。④〔在表示当然、意外、遗憾等意的句子中〕竟会…(是)。*It is natural [proper, necessary] that he ~ do so.* 他这样做是当然[适当,必要]的。*It is surprising that he ~ have been so foolish.* 真想不到他会那样愚蠢。*It is a pity that he ~ miss such a golden opportunity.* 真可惜,他竟会失去这样一个绝好的机会。*I wonder such a man as he ~ have succeeded.* 想不到他那样的人竟会成功。*They ~ not have been allowed to come.* 原不该让他们来的。⑤〔表示踌躇、委婉、谦逊、客气〕可,好象是,倒,大概是。*I ~ hardly think so.* 我倒并不那样想。*S- you like tea?* 你欢喜茶吗?⑥〔和 why, who, how 等连用,表示理由不易了解或吃惊〕*Why ~ he resign?* 他为什么要辞职呢? *Who ~ do it?* 谁才会做呢? *Who ~ write it but himself?* 你当是谁写的,是他自己呀。⑦(a)〔在表示意志、提议、意向、决定、命令等的从句中〕*It was proposed that we ~ act at once.* 有人提议我们必须立刻行动。*I was determined that he ~ write his letters first.* 我已决定让他先写他的信。(b)〔在 lest 后的状语从句中〕*I stayed in lest I ~ catch cold.* 我怕伤风,所以待在屋里。⑧〔在让步状语从句中〕即使。*S- he fail, he would try again* 即使他失败了,他也会再努力一试的。

should·a [ˈʃudə]〔美俚〕= should have.

shoul·der [ˈʃəuldə] *n.* ①肩,肩膀;〔*pl.*〕双肩;肩背;〔喻〕担当的能力;【动】(昆虫的)肩角,前角,中胸角,侧角。②肩胛关节;(牛等连前腿的)肩肉;(衣服、家具等的)肩部;【筑城】(棱堡面与侧面所成的)肩角;【印】(铅字的)字肩;【建】用来支持的凸出部;路肩〔路两侧不铺装柏油的部分〕。③掮枪的姿势。④【地】山肩,谷肩;峁;【海】吃水线的凸出处〔弯曲部〕。***clap [tap] sb. upon the*** ~ 拍人的肩膀;逮捕。***come to the*** ~ 掮枪。***dislocate [put out] one's*** ~ 肩胛关节脱臼。***give [show, turn] the cold ~ to*** 冷落某人,对某人表示冷淡;躲避某人,对某人表示讨厌,同某人断绝往来。***have a head upon one's ~s***〔口〕懂事,懂道理。***have broad ~s*** 肩膀阔而强壮;能掮重物,能担负重任。***lay the blame on the right ~s*** 指责应负责任的人。***over the*** ~ 讥讽,挖苦。***overleap one's ~s***〔美〕大显身手;超越自己的成绩或正常状态。***put on sb.'s ~s [put on the ~s of sb. shift on to other ~s]*** 叫人家负责任,把责任推给别人。***put an old head on young ~s*** 叫年轻人懂事,使年轻人认真负责。***put [set] one's ~ to the wheel*** 积极工作,勤奋工作;帮助人。***rub ~s with*** 和…接触;并肩,协力,团结一致。***~ to ~*** 密集;并肩,协力,互相帮助。***straight from the*** ~ 直截了当地,不留情地,开诚布公地。***with one's ~ to collar*** 紧张地(工作),拚命地(干)。—*vt.* 掮在肩上,掮,担;掮起;(司机的)安全带。—*vi.* 用肩膀推,使劲推。~ **belt** 背带;肩带。~ **blade,** ~ **bone** 肩胛骨。~ **brace** 驼背矫正器。~ **girdle**【动】(脊椎动物的)肩带 (= pectoral girdle)。~ **harness** (汽车驾驶者的)安全带。~ **knot** 肩章;肩饰。~ **loop**〔美〕(陆军的)肩章。~ **mark**〔美〕(海军的)肩章。~ **patch**【军】(所属部队)番号臂章。~**-pegged** *a.* 肩膀强壮的〔指马〕。~ **strap**【军】肩章;(裤子等的)背带,吊带。

shoul·dered [ˈʃəuldəd] *a.*〔用以构成复合词〕肩膀…的;背着的。

should·est [ˈʃudist] *aux.v.*〔古〕= shouldst.

should·n't [ˈʃudnt] = should not.

shouldst *aux.v.* [强 ʃudst; 弱 ʃədst, ʃdst]〔古〕= should〔主词为 thou 时用〕。

shout [ʃaut] *vi.* 呼喊,叫喊;喝叫 *(at)*;喊,叫 *(to)*;〔澳俚〕付请客喝酒的帐。—*vt.* 大声讲,呼喊出;高声呼喊使…,喊跑,喊走,呼喊着鼓励,呼喊着助威。*It's all over bar [but] the ~ing.* 场赛终止,只是呼喊声不绝。*Now you're ~ing.*〔美俚〕说得真恰当,说得好极了。~ ***for*** 大声叫唤(侍者);〔美政〕竭力支持。~ ***for [with] joy*** 欢呼。~ ***sb. down*** 大声喝倒某人;〔美〕打败某人。~ ***out***

大声嚷,呼喊. ～ ***something rude*** 大骂. ～ ***with laughter*** 大声笑. ***within ～ing distance*** 在大声喊叫时听得见的距离内. —*n.* 呼喊,叫喊,呐喊;〔澳俚〕付请客帐,会钞. *give a ～ of warning* 大喊危险. *It's my ～.* 〔口〕我请我请. *the last ～*〔美俚〕最新式样,最时髦的东西.

shout·er [ˈʃautə] *n.* 叫喊的人;〔美〕后援者,支持者.

shove [ʃʌv] *vt.* 推,推动,推进;使劲猛推;推开;卖掉;〔口〕乱放,乱塞. —*vi.* 推,推进,推出;推挤. *Don't ～, wait your turn.* 别推,顺次等候好了. *S- it in your pocket.* 把它放在你的口袋里. ～ ***across***〔美〕杀. ～ ***along*** 推着走. ～ ***in*** 推进. ～ ***off*** (拿篙子)把船撑开;〔美俚〕乘船离开;分别,走掉. ～ ***on*** 推着往前走. ～ ***one's clothes on***〔口〕穿上衣服. ～ ***out*** (拿篙子)把船撑开. ～ ***past*** 推开…往前走. ～ ***publicity***〔美运〕指挥宣传. ～ ***the queer*** (美)付给伪币. —*n.* 推,推出,推开;【地】走向滑移.

shov·el [ˈʃʌvl] *n.* 铲,铁锹,(舀糖用的)杓子(= ～-hat.) —*vt.* 拿铲子铲,拿杓子舀. —*vi.* 用铲子工作. ～ ***food into one's mouth*** =～ ***up [down] food*** 大口大口吃. ～ *up [in] money* 大大赚钱. **～bill**【鸟】阔嘴鸭,琵琶嘴鸭. **～board** (在甲板等上玩的)推盘游戏;作这种游戏场地. **～ful** 满铲. ～ **hat** (教士戴的)宽边铲形帽. ～ **head**【动】窄头双髻鲨. **～-nosed** *a.* 宽头的;宽喙的;宽扁鼻的. **～-nosed [～nose] shark**【动】双髻鲨,犁骨鳐. **～-nosed sturgeon**【动】铲鲟. ～ **stiff**〔美〕用铁锹的工人;生手工人.

shov·el·ler [ˈsʌvlə]〔美〕**shov·el·er** *n.* ①用铲子铲的人;推土机驾驶员. ② = shovel-bill.

show [ʃəu] *vt.* (*～ed; shown* [ʃəun],〔罕〕*～ed*) ①给看,示,出示;显示,显出;陈列,展出,供参观;炫耀,卖弄. ②教,告诉;指示,指出. ③带领,指引,向导,领导参观;说明;证明. ④给与,施与. ⑤【法】陈述;申辩. —*vi.* ①显现;呈现;显眼;〔口〕露脸,出来,跑出来. ②〔口〕展览,演出,放映(电影). ③〔美俚〕(赛马)跑第…名. *S- your tickets, please!* 请把票拿出来! *S- me a liar, and I'll ～ you a thief.* 撒谎是做贼的第一步. *It ～s you better.* 这使你格外显眼. *He didn't ～ all day yesterday.*〔美俚〕他昨天整天没露面. ～ *that he is no fool* 证明他不笨. ***have sth. to ～ for*** 在…方面有可显示的成绩. ～ ***a leg*** 起床. ～ ***sth. the fire*** 把…稍微热一热. ～ ***cause*** 讲理由. ～ ***daylight*** 有洞,有窟窿. ～ ***fight*** 反抗;顽强抵抗. ～ ***in*** 领进(客等). ～ ***off*** 卖弄,夸示(学问等);展览,陈列;使显眼. ～ ***oneself*** 出现,露面. ～ ***oneself off as*** 夸耀,标榜. ～ ***one's cards [colours]*** 摊牌,公开自己的计划,吐露自己的真实打算. ～ ***one's hand*** 摊牌;表明思想[目的]. ～ ***one's heels*** 一溜烟地逃走;〔美运〕追过;大显比赛的优越本领. ～ ***sb. the door*** 叫人走,逐出,撵跑;〔美〕拒绝要求. ～***sb. to the door*** 送到门口. ～ ***out*** 送出(客人). ～ ***sb. over [round]*** 带着[遍处]参观. ～ ***the wing*** (用飞行访问)显示空军力量. ～ ***up*** 显眼;暴露,揭发;嘲笑;〔口〕出席,到场,露面(*He never ～s up at balls.* 他从来不参加舞会). —*n.* ①表示;显示;展览;展览会;展览物,陈列品;演出;景像,壮观;洋相,丑相;出丑的人;就任(等)游行. ②卖弄,夸示,炫耀;粉饰,盛装,铺张;外观,外貌,装扮,假装;样子;痕迹,征象. ③〔俚〕机会;事情,事件;团体,机关. ④【医】(临产时)破水,见红;(月经开始时)现血;【矿】初现浮散矿;(矿脉,石油,天然气的)迹象. ⑤〔美赛马俚〕第三名. *an one-horse ～* 小公司,小商店;小事;小东西. *a road ～* 巡回演出. (新影片的)故意提高票价的盛大演出. *variety ～s* 杂耍. *a ～ of gold* 金矿迹象. *He is fond of ～.* 他爱漂亮. *a fine ～ of blossom on the trees this year* 今年花开得很壮观. *I have no ～ of trying.* 我没有干的机会. *The dinner was a dull ～.* 这个宴会乏味. ***boss the ～*** 操纵;主持(演出). ***for ～*** 为夸示,为给人家看. ***give away the (whole) ～*** 露马脚,讲滑了嘴泄漏秘密;失言;叛变;揭穿内幕(等). ***give sb. a fair ～*** 给与表现机会. ***have a [the] ～ of*** 好象. ***in dumb ～*** 打着手势(表示),用手比划着. ***in opən ～*** 公然. ***in ～*** 外表是,外观是,表面是. ***make a good ～*** 好看,有看头;大出洋相. ***make a ～ of*** 卖弄,夸示,展览,装门面,装样子. ***make a ～ of oneself*** 丢丑,弄出笑话. ***on ～*** 成为展览物;被陈列着. ***put on a ～*** 假装;装病(*He is not really ill she's just putting on a ～.* 他不是真病,他不过是装病罢了. ***put up a good[bad] ～*** 演出好[不好],干得(不)好. ***run the ～*** 操纵;主持(演出). ～ ***of hands*** 举手(表决). ～ ***of reason*** 似乎有理. ***stand a ～*** 有可能,有希望. ～ **bill** 海报,招贴,广告. ～ **boat**〔原美〕演戏船. **～bread** (犹太教的)供神面包. ～ **business** [biz-] 娱乐性行业〔指戏院、电影院,电视等〕. ～ **card** 广告牌;货样纸板. **～case** 陈列箱,陈列橱;〔美俚〕应接室;(试片)影戏院(*a ～-case try*〔美剧〕试片会). **～down**〔美〕摊牌;〔喻〕最后的较量;公布,暴露;〔美俚〕危机. ～ **girl** 歌舞团女演员,夜总会歌舞女郎. **～man** ①开展览会的人,(马戏团等的)老板. ②〔美〕出风头的人物;编剧家. ～ **man·ship** (马戏等的)经营术;杂剧演出技巧. **～-off** 夸耀;卖弄;〔美〕自大的人,爱吹牛的人. **～piece** 样品;陈列品,展品. ～ **place** 可参观的场所[建筑物],名胜. **S- Sunday**〔英〕节日前夜的星期天. **～room** 货品陈列室. **～up**〔口〕暴露,揭发. ～ **window** 橱窗,陈列窗.

show·er[1] [ˈʃauə] *n.* ①阵雨;(风雪等的)一阵. ②淋浴;(弹)雨(等),阵雨一样涌到的东西(信等);【物】簇射;(美)(为新娘等举行的)送礼会;大批礼物. *a ～ stick*〔美〕雨伞. *be caught in a ～* 遇到阵雨. *Letters come in ～s.* 信件象阵雨一样涌到. *a labile ～*【物】晶霰. *a meson ～*【物】介子簇射. *send sb. to the ～s*〔美〕拒绝要求;散会. —*vt.* 把…给阵雨淋湿;使湿透;阵雨似地倾注(炮弹等);大量给与(礼物等) *(upon)*. —*vi.* 下阵雨;阵雨似地落下. ～ ***affections upon*** 对…倾注爱意. ～ **bath** 淋浴(装置);湿透.

show·er[2] [ˈʃəuə] *n.* 出示者;表示者;展出者;指示者[器].

show·er·y [ˈʃauəri] *a.* 阵雨般的;多阵雨的. **-i·ness** *n.*

show·ing [ˈʃəuiŋ] *n.* 表现;展览(会);〔口〕外观,外表;主张. ***make a good [bad] ～*** 表现好[不好]. ***on one's own ～*** 按照自己主张.

Show-me [ˈʃəumi] *a.* 没有证据不相信;需要有证明的. *a ～ attitude* 存疑态度. *Show-me State*〔美〕米苏里州〔别名,由美国谚语 I'm from Missouri (不见不信)而来〕.

shown [ʃəun] show 的过去分词.

show·y [ˈʃəui] *a.* 华美的,华丽的;炫耀的;显眼的;好看的. **-i·ly** *ad.* **-i·ness** *n.*

shp, SHP = shaft horsepower【机】轴马力.

shpt. = shipment.

shr. = share(s).

shram [ʃræm] *vt.*〔英方〕使冷得麻木.

shrank [ʃræŋk] shrink 的过去式.

shrap·nel [ˈʃræpnəl] *n. sing., pl.* ①榴霰弹. ②〔集合词〕榴霰弹片.

shred [ʃred] *n.* 裂片,碎片;破布条;少量. *left without a ～ of reputation* 名誉扫地. *not a ～ of evidence* 毫无证据. *without a ～ of clothing on him* 一丝不挂. ***in ～s and tatters*** 破烂不堪,穿得破破烂烂. ***tear to ～s*** 扯碎,扯得稀烂. —(*～ded,*〔古〕*shred*) *vt., vi.* 撕碎,切碎;切成丝;破碎.

shrew [ʃru:] *n.* 泼妇,悍妇;【动】鼩鼱[又叫 ～-mouse].

shrewd [ʃru:d] *a.* 敏捷的,机灵的,机敏的,精明的;锐利的;〔古〕严酷的,刺骨的,猛烈的(风等);狡猾的,油滑的;〔古〕刻毒的. ***do (one) a ～ turn*** 给(某人)吃一个苦头. ***have a ～ tongue*** 说话刻薄. **-ly** *ad.* **-ness** *n.*

shrew·ish [ˈʃru:iʃ] *a.* 泼妇似的,爱骂人的;刻薄的. **-ly** *ad.* **-ness** *n.*

shriek [ʃri:k] *n.* 尖锐的喊声[笑声];〔美〕引起人注意的事物;怪有趣的东西. —*vi.* 尖声叫喊,惊喊;引人注意. —*vt.* 尖声讲,令人吃惊地说;动人听闻地报导[描述].

give [utter] a ~ 发出尖叫,惊喊. a ~ing heading 惊人的标题. ~ out 尖声哭叫. ~ with laughter 高声大笑. ~ with pain 痛得绝叫. ~ curses at sb. 尖声锐气地咒人.

shriev·al·ty [ˈʃriːvəlti] n. sheriff 的职位[任期].

shrieve [ʃriːv], n. 〔废〕=sheriff.

shrift [ʃrift] n. (对牧师所作的)忏悔;认罪. short ~ 死刑执行前的短暂忏悔时间. give [get] short ~ 很快解决掉[处死];不耐烦地摆脱掉;对…简慢无礼[漠不关心].

shrike [ʃraik] n.【鸟】伯劳,百舌鸟.

shrill [ʃril] a. 尖声的,刺耳的;强烈的,刺激的,哀诉的;怒汹汹的;讨厌的,过度的. — n. 尖锐的声音. — vt., vi.〔诗〕【修】发尖锐音;尖声锐气地讲[唱] (out). — ad. = **shrilly** ad. 用尖锐的声音.

shrimp [ʃrimp] n. (pl. ~s,〔集合词〕~) ①【动】褐虾,河虾. ②〔俚〕矮子;微不足道的人. — vi. 捕捉褐虾. ~ **sauce** 虾油. ~ **plant**【植】麒麟吐珠. **-er** n. 捕虾者;捕虾器.

shrine [ʃrain] n. 神龛;神祠,庙;神殿;圣地. the ~ of art 艺术圣地. — vt.〔诗〕安置在神龛里;祀在祠堂里;奉为神圣.

shrink [ʃriŋk] vi. (**shrank** [ʃræŋk]; **shrunk** [ʃrʌŋk],〔罕〕**shrunken** [ˈʃrʌŋkən]) ①皱缩;缩短,收缩. ②变小,减小. ③退缩,畏缩,害怕. — vt. ①使皱缩,弄皱;使缩短. ②缩进,拉回. ~ **away** 衰退;退缩,退避. ~ **back** 退缩,畏缩,害怕. ~ **fit**【机】热配合,冷缩配合;烧嵌. ~ **from (do)ing** 畏缩不…. ~ **into oneself** 踌躇. ~ **to nothing** 渐渐缩小到没有. ~ **up** 缩拢,缩成一团. ~**ing violet** 非常怕羞的人;谦逊的人. — n. 皱缩;收缩,缩水;畏缩;退缩;〔美俚〕精神病科医师.

shrink·age [ˈʃrinkidʒ] n. 皱缩;缩水;减缩,减少;【物】缩误;缩减量;(肉类在运输、加工过程中的)重量的损耗. ~ **theory**【地】冷缩说.

shrink·ing [ˈʃrinkiŋ] a. 畏缩的,退缩的,踌躇的,犹豫不决的. **-ly** ad.

shrive [ʃraiv] vt. (~d,〔古〕**shrove** [ʃrəuv]; ~d,〔古〕**shriven** [ˈʃrivən]) 听忏悔而赦免…的罪. — vi. 听忏悔;忏悔赎罪. ~ oneself 忏悔以求赎罪.

shriv·el [ˈʃrivl] vt., vi. (**shriv·elled**; **shriv·el·ling** [ˈʃrivliŋ]) (使)皱缩;(使)干瘪;(使)枯萎;(使)无能为力,(使)失效.

shriv·en [ˈʃrivən]〔古〕shrive 的过去分词.

shroff [ʃrɔf] n. (旧中国、印度的)银钱兑换商;钱兑店;货币鉴定人,收帐员. — vt. 鉴别(钱币).

Shrop·shire [ˈʃrɔpʃiə] n. ①(英国)什罗郡. ②(黑头黑脚白毛无角)肉用羊.

shroud [ʃraud] n. ①裹尸布,尸衣. ②覆盖物,屏蔽,掩蔽(物),幕,帐. ③【空】罩,侧板;【机】护罩;套管;(水车的)侧板. ④〔pl.〕【海】支桅索;【空】= ~ line 降落伞的吊伞索. a ~ ring【机】覆环. wrapped in a ~ of mystery 笼罩着神秘的气氛. — vt. 用裹尸布覆盖;覆盖,隐藏. ~**-laid** a. 四单股向右绞成的(绳索).

shrove [ʃrəuv]〔古〕shrive 的过去式.

Shrove·tide [ˈʃrəuvtaid] n. 忏悔节.

shrub[1] [ʃrʌb] n. 灌木,灌木丛.

shrub[2] [ʃrʌb] n. 果汁甜酒〔果汁加糖及少量 rum 酒等做成的饮料,通常叫 rum-~〕;冰果汁水.

shrub·ber·y [ˈʃrʌbəri] n. ①〔集合词〕灌木丛;灌木丛生的地方;(公园等中的)灌木丛中的路;〔美俚〕络腮胡.

shrub·by [ˈʃrʌbi] a. 灌木状的;多灌木的.

shrug [ʃrʌg] vt., vi. (**shrugged**, **shrug·ging**) 耸(肩);耸肩. ~ one's shoulders 耸耸肩膀〔表示不快、绝望、惊愕、疑惑、冷笑等〕. ~ **off** (耸肩)表示轻蔑[不屑];摆脱;扭身脱掉(衣服). —n. 耸肩.

shrunk [ʃrʌŋk] shrink 的过去式及过去分词. — a. 浸缩过的,缩过水的,不会再缩的(毛织品).

shrunk·en [ˈʃrʌŋkən]〔罕〕shrink 的过去分词. — a. 皱缩的. ~ grains 不饱满的籽粒,瘪籽.

shs. = shares.

shtet·l [ˈʃtetl] n. (pl. **shtet·lach** [-lɑːkh], **shtet·ls** [-lz]) (东欧早先的,尤其是俄国的)犹太村社.

shtg. = shortage.

sh.tn, sh.ton. = short ton 短吨.

shtick [ʃtik] n.〔美俚〕①滑稽场面. ②引人注意的小噱头. ③特别才能,特色.

shuck [ʃʌk] n. 壳,皮,荚;贝壳;〔pl.〕〔美口〕不值一提的东西;骗局. **light a ~**〔美俚〕急匆匆跑掉. **not worth ~s** 毫无价值. — vt. 剥壳,剥皮,剥荚. ~ **off**〔美口〕脱掉(上衣等);舍弃;摆脱;无限期拖延.

shucks [ʃʌks] int.〔美俚〕呸!哼!〔表示藐视、失望、厌恶等〕.

shud·der [ˈʃʌdə] vi. 发抖,打颤,战栗 (at; to do). — n. 发抖,战栗. ~ **at the thought of** = ~ **to think of** 一想到…就发抖[毛骨悚然].

shuf·fle [ˈʃʌfl] vt. ①(尤指走路时,把脚)在地上拖曳;滑来滑去. ②(笨拙地)穿上,披上,脱去;狡猾地进行(某事). ③混和,搅乱;洗(纸牌);移来移去;反复挪动. ④推诿,推开;〔美〕使火车转轨. — vi. ①洗纸牌. ②拖着脚步走[舞蹈];把脚挪来挪去;移动;推诿自己职责,推托,搪塞;蒙混. ③笨拙地穿衣[脱衣]. ~ cards 洗纸牌. ~ the cards〔喻〕改变机构人事;改变政策. ~ **off** 脱掉,丢弃,抛弃 (~ off this mortal coil 死). ~ **off (a duty) upon [onto]** 把(责任)推给…. ~ **through** 搪塞过去. — n. 拖着脚走;(舞蹈的)拖步;搅乱,混合;洗牌;轮到洗牌;混蒙;推托,敷衍. double ~ 一脚迅速拖动两次的舞步. ~**board** n. = shovel-board.

shul [ʃuːl] n. = synagogue.

Shu·lam·ite [ˈʃuːləˌmait] 书拉密〔旧约雅歌中所赞美的少女〕.

shun [ʃʌn] vt. 避开,躲开(危险等). Materialists face truth, whereas idealists ~ it. 唯物主义者面向真理,唯心主义者则逃避真理.

'shun [ʃʌn] int. 立正!〔attention 之略〕.

shune [ʃuːn] n.〔Scot.〕shoe 的复数.

shunt [ʃʌnt] vt. ①逃避,躲开,闪开;〔口〕将(工作、义务等)推给别人;拖延,搁置(计划、讨论等). ②【铁路】把(车)开到岔轨上,调车;【电】在…上装分路器,使分路[流]. —vi. 退到旁边,闪开,躲开;(车)转入岔轨;改变话题,把话闪开;改变意思. — n.【铁路】侧避;调车;调轨;转轨;轨闸;【电】分路[分流]器. a ~ing station【铁路】调度站. a ~ (wound) dynamo【电】并激发电机. ~ **winding**【电】并激绕组,分流绕组,并联线圈;分线组;分线法.

shunt·er [ˈʃʌntə] n.【铁路】扳道员,转辙员,扳闸员;道岔机;调车机车;〔俚〕有能力的组织者.

shush [ʃʌʃ] int. 嘘!别响!安静. — vt. 叫…别出声.

Shu·shan [ˈʃuːʃɑːn] 苏沙 (Susa)〔伊朗西部废墟古城在圣经里的名称〕.

shut [ʃʌt] vt. (**shut** [ʃʌt]) ①关闭 (opp. open);把…关在门外,排斥;关进,围进 (in; into);关上(箱子等),闭上(嘴等) (up);封闭,封锁;停止开放[营业];叠拢,合拢(伞、小刀等);挟住,挟进. ②使暗,隐藏. —vi. 关闭;塞住;(店铺等)关门. S- the door after you. 随手关门. ~ the door against sb. 把某人关在门外. ~ a book 合上书. The door ~ with a bang. 门砰地一声关上了. **be ~ of** (sb.)〔英俚〕摆脱,甩开(某人). ~ **down** ①关闭;关拢(窗等);停业,停工;停止,阻止,禁止. ②(夜色、迷雾等)浓暗起来. ~ **down on**〔口语〕禁止,压制. ~ **in** ①把…关进去,监禁;围住;遮住. ②(夜等)降临,迫近 (The night has ~ in. 天黑了.) ~ **off** 阻断,关上(自来水、收音机,煤气等);使不接触,使隔离,使隔开. ~ **one's eyes [ears] to** 假装没有看见[听见];拒绝看[听]. ~ **one's face [head]**〔俚〕默不作声. ~ **one's heart to** 对…漠不关心. ~ **one's lights (off)** 死. ~ **one's mind to** 死不答应. ~ **one's**

mouth 闭嘴不响，不开口 (*S- your mouth*〔口〕别响. ~ *sb.'s mouth* 叫某人莫开口). ~ ***one's teeth*** 咬紧牙关. ~ ***out*** 不让进来,关在外头;遮得看不见;【棒球】不让得分. ~ ***the door in sb.'s face*** 闭门不纳. ~ ***the door on[upon](sb.)*** 把…关在门外,限制,绝对不许…进来[出去]; 完全不把…当做问题, 根本不理睬 (*~the door on the proposals* 对建议根本不理睬). ~ ***together*** 接合,(尤指)钎合(金属物). ~ ***up*** ①关上,关住;监禁;密封,密藏; 停止. ②不许开口, 使人哑口无言; 不响 (*~ up shop* 关店. *S- up!*〔俚〕住嘴; 别说.) — *n.* ①〔主诗〕关闭, 闭锁, 终止, 完结. ②焊接缝. ③【语音】闭锁音. ④【机】冷塞. — *a.* 紧闭的; 声音低沉的, 闭锁音(l,p,t,k,b,d 等)的. **~down** 停工,停业. **~-eye**〔美俚〕酒;睡眠. **~-in** ① *a.* 闭居家中的;孤僻的. ② *n.* 病弱不外出的人. **~-off** 中止;堵塞;中断;关闭器〔如阀门〕. **~out** 关在外面;锁闭厂门;【棒球】得零分.

Shute [ʃu:t] *n.* 舒特〔姓氏〕.

shut·ter [ˈʃʌtə] *n.* ①百叶窗; 护窗板; (照相机上的)快门,(光)闸; 光盘;【火箭】(调节喷气口的)鱼鳞板; 风琴里的开关;开闭器;关闭者. ②〔*pl.*〕〔美拳〕眼睛. ***put up the ~s*** 关上护窗板;关铺子. ***take down the ~s*** 打开护窗板〔百叶窗〕. — *vt.* ①给…装上百叶窗. ②使关上百叶窗. ③装光闸于(照相机上).

shut·ter·bug [ˈʃʌtəˌbʌg] *n.*〔美俚〕摄影迷,摄影爱好者.

shut·tle [ˈʃʌtl] *n.* (织机的)梭; (缝纫机的)滑梭; (编织用的)梭形针; 穿梭般来回; 短程来回运输(线, 工具),【空】穿梭式来回不停的民航运输机〔轰炸机〕;〔美〕短程盘运火车〔又叫 ~-train〕; 穿梭旅行; 穿梭外交(活动). — *vt., vi.* (使)作穿梭式来回运动; (使)前后移动, (使)来回如梭. ~ **armature**【电】梭形电枢. ~ **bus**〔美〕区间(公共汽)车. **~-bombing**【空】穿梭轰炸.

shut·tle·cock [ˈʃʌtlkɔk] *n.* ①羽毛球. ②羽毛球运动. ③争论之点; 犹豫的人. — *vt.* 抛来抛去, 打来打去, 往返递送. — *vi.* 来回走动, 穿梭似往返.

s.h.v. = 〔L.〕*sub hac voce [hoc verbo]* 在此词下,参见该词.

shy^{1} [ʃai] *a.* ***(~er; ~ est,*** 〔罕〕***shi·er; shi·est)*** ①胆小的, 见人就躲避的. ②怕羞的,羞怯的. ③畏缩的;存戒心的, 小心的,谨防…的 *(of)*. ④不易捉摸的; (话等) 难懂的, 费解的. ⑤(植物)很少开花结子的;(动物)很少下仔的. ⑥〔口〕【牌】还没有出赌注的; ⑦〔俚〕缺少,不足 *(of)*. *This made him ~ of trying it again.* 这使他不敢再试了. *She was ~ two months of her nineteenth birthday.* 她差两个月就是十九岁的生日. ***fight ~ of*** 厌恶…,避开…. ***look ~ at [on]*** 怀疑. ***of ~ disposition*** 怯懦的. — *n. (pl. shies)* (马)惊退,惊逸. — *vi.* ①惊退,惊逸,畏缩 *(at)*. ②避开 *(away from)* *He isn't the man to ~ at difficulties.* 他不是在困难面前畏缩的人. *Her eyes ~ away from mine.* 她一见我盯她就把自己的眼睛避开了. —*vt.* 避开(某人). *He has shied us lately.* 他近来对我们不理睬了. **-ly** *ad.* **-ness** *n.*

shy^{2} [ʃai] *n.* ①投扔,乱丢. ②〔口〕嘲弄. ③〔口〕尝试;企图; 目标; 机会. *three shies a penny* 一辨士投掷三次. ***have a ~ at*** ①试图投中某物. ②挖苦,嘲弄. ③想得到,想(做). — *vt., vi.* (用石子、球等)乱投 *(at)*.

-shy [-ʃai] *comb. f.* 怕…的,讨厌…的: gun-*shy*, work-*shy*.

shy·er [ˈʃaiə] *n.* 畏缩不前的人;胆小的马,易受惊的马.

shy·ster [ˈʃaistə] *n.*〔美〕讼棍;手段卑鄙的人〔政客〕.

si [si:] *n.*【乐】长音阶的第七音.

SI = 【化】silicon.

S.I. = ①Sandwich Islands〔旧〕桑威奇群岛〔美, 现称 Hawaiian Islands 夏威夷群岛〕. ②short interest 短期债券总额. ③Staten Island.〔美〕斯塔腾岛.

SIA = Singapore Airlines 新加坡航空公司.

si·al [ˈsaiæl] *n.*【地】硅铝带,硅铝层. **-ic** *a.*

si·al·a·gogue [saiˈæləˌgɔg] *n.*【化】催涎剂. **-gog·ic** *a.*

si·a·lid, si·al·i·dan [ˈsaiəlid, -ˈælidən] *a.*【动】蛇蛉科 *(Sialidae)* 的动物. — *n.* 蛇蛉科昆虫.

si·a·loid [ˈsaiəˌlɔid] *a.* 似唾液的.

Si·am [ˈsaiæm, saiˈæm] *n.* 暹罗〔泰国(Thailand) 的旧称〕.

si·a·mang [ˈsi:əˌmæŋ],【动】*n.* 合趾猿 *(Symphalangus syndactylus)*〔产于马来半岛和苏门达腊〕.

Si·a·mese [saiəˈmi:z, ˈsaiə-] *a.* ①暹罗的; 暹罗人〔语〕的. ②孪生的;相似的;〔s-〕【建】(管道)二重联接的. —*n.*〔*sing., pl.*〕暹罗人; 暹罗语; 暹罗猫. *the ~ twins* 连体双胞胎;情投意合的朋友,如胶似漆的朋友. —〔s-〕*vt.* 连接;结合. *They are ~d to France.* 他们同法国相连.

sib [sib]〔英古〕*a.* 有血缘关系的 *(to)*; 近亲的. — *n.* 血亲;〔集合词〕亲族;〔常 *pl.*〕兄弟姊妹;【人类】氏族;【生】(同科、属)亲缘动植物;【选种】同系.

Sib. = Siberia; Siberian.

Si·ber·i·a [saiˈbiəriə] *n.* 西伯利亚〔苏联一地区〕.

Si·be·ri·an [saiˈbiəriən] *a., n.* 西伯利亚的(人). ~ ***husky*** 爱斯基摩狗.

sib·i·lance, -cy [ˈsibiləns, -si] *n.* 发咝音; 齿音, 咝音〔s,ʃ,z,ʒ 等〕.

sib·i·lant [ˈsibilənt] *a.* 发咝音的,作咝咝声的. — *n.* 咝音(字).

sib·i·late [ˈsibileit] *vt., vi.* 发咝音;咝咝地说. **sib·i·la·tion** [ˌsibiˈleiʃən] *n.* 发咝音;咝音;作咝咝声.

sib·ling [ˈsibliŋ] *n.* ①〔常 *pl.*〕兄弟姊妹; 同胞. ②【人类】氏族成员.【生】同科,同属.

sib·yl [ˈsibil] *n.* (古代的)女巫;女卜者,女预言者,女术士. **-byl·ic** *a.*

sib·yl·line [siˈbilain] *a.* 女巫的; 预言的, 神秘的. ~ ***books*** (古罗马)《西彼拉占语集》;〔转义〕起初不想买后来反愿出高价收买的东西.

SIC = specific inductive capacity 电容率.

sic^{1} [sik] *a.*〔Scot.〕= such.

sic^{2} [sik] *vt.* ***(~ked; ~king)*** = sick^{2}.

sic [sik] *ad.*〔L.〕原文如此〔对引文错误、可疑处的附注〕. ~ ***jubeo*** [ˈju:biəu] 这是我的意思, 这是我的命令. ~ ***passim*** [ˈpæsim] 以下同此〔仿此〕. ~ ***transit gloria mundi*** [ˈtransit glɔuri:ə mundi:] 尘世繁华转眼即逝. ~ ***volo***, ~ ***vos non vobis*** [ˈvəus nɔn ˈvəubis]〔L.〕你这样做原来并不是为了自己〔指某人做某事而另一人获得利益〕

Si·ca·ni·an [siˈkeiniən] *a.* = Sicilian.

sic·ca·tive [ˈsikətiv] *a.* 促使干燥的. — *n.* (加在油漆中的)干燥剂.

sice^{1} [sais] *n.* = syce.

sice^{2} [sais] *n.*〔英俚〕六辨士;(骰子的)六点.

Si·cil·i·an [siˈsiljən, -liən] *a.* 西西里岛的, 西西里岛人的. — *n.* 西西里岛人;西西里方言.

Sic·i·ly [ˈsisili] *n.* 西西里(岛)〔意大利〕.

sick^{1} [sik] *a.* ①病的,有病的,身体不舒服的;〔美,英古〕虚弱的. ②〔用作表语〕〔英口〕使人作呕的, 恶心的; 厌倦, 厌恶(人生等) *(of)*; 发腻 *(to)*; 失望 *(at)*; 想望着,怀念着 *(for)*. ③不健康的; 有病容的; 精神不振的, 苍白的. ④在月经期中. ⑤(情况)失常的;(船)需要修理的. ⑥【农】地力变瘦了的,不适于栽种…的;带有病菌的(土地). ⑦(铁)发脆的;(葡萄酒)变了味的. ~ *of love [a fever]* 害着相思病[热病]. *the ~* 病人,病员. *It makes me ~ to think of that.* 一想起这件事我就发腻. *He was ~ with me for being so late.* 他怪我这样迟. *a boat ~ of paint* 需要重行油漆的船. *tomato-~* 不能栽番茄的. ***be ~ at heart*** 觉得讨厌,心中烦闷,悲观. ***be ~ of doing nothing*** 闲得发腻. ***be ~ to dead of*** …腻得要命. ***fall [get] ~*** 生病. ***feel [turn] ~*** 觉得要呕,作呕,恶心. ***go [report] ~*** 请病假. ***make sb. ~*** 使人作呕;〔美〕使生病. ~ ***as a dog***〔美〕病重的. ~ ***into death*** 病得要死. ~ **bay** (军舰等的) 病房. **~bed** 病床. ~ **benefit** 疾病补助. ~ **call**【军】伤病员集合(准备就诊),伤病员集合号. ~ **flag** 检疫旗. ~ **headache** 呕

吐性头痛. ~ **leave** 病假. ~ **list** (尤指陆海军的)病员名单. ~**room** 病房. ~**-worker** 补缺工人.

sick² [sik] *vt.* 追击;攻击;(纵狗)追击;〔美〕嗾使(狗等)去咬[去攻击]. *He ~ed the dog on me.* 他嗾狗来咬我.

sick·en [ˈsikn] *vt.* 使生病;使作呕,使恶心;使厌倦. — *vi.* 患病;觉得要吐,想呕,恶心 *(at)*; 厌倦,厌恶 *(of)*.

sick·en·er [ˈsikənə] *n.* 致病之物;过量的药物;催吐物;呕吐红菇;令人讨厌的东西;厌倦的感觉;〔学生俚〕讨厌的家伙.

sick·er [ˈsikə] *n.* 〔美军俚〕住院病人.

sick·ish [ˈsikiʃ] *a.* 象要生病似的,有点不舒服的;象要吐的. **-ly** *ad.* **-ness** *n.*

sick·le [ˈsikl] *n.* 镰刀,小镰刀;装在斗鸡脚上的镰刀形距铁;〔the S-〕【天】(狮子座中的)镰形星群. ~ **alfalfa** 黄花苜蓿. ~ **bar** (刈草用)切割器. ~**bill**【动】杓鹬. ~ **cell** (**anemia** 或 **disease**)【医】镰形血球(贫血). ~ **feather** (公鸡的)镰形羽尾. ~ **mia**【医】镰状血球贫血.

sick·li·ness [ˈsiklinis] *n.* ①疾病,多病. ②恶心, 呕吐. ③苍白;(光色的)暗淡. *There is little ~ here this year.* 今年这里的疾病很少. *a sudden ~ of disgust* 厌恶得突然呕吐发作.

sick·ly [ˈsikli] *a.* ①有病的,病态的;虚弱的,(面容等)苍白的;多愁善感的. ②令人作呕的;(风土等)有碍健康的;疾病流行的;易引起疾病的. ③令人生厌的;(笑样等)阴沉的. ④(光或色)暗淡的,微弱的;惨淡的. *a ~ child* 一个多病的孩子. *a ~ season* 疾病流行的季节. *a ~ moonlight* 暗淡的月光. — *vt.* 使现病容.

sick·ness [ˈsiknis] *n.* 病,疾病;恶心,呕吐. *a ceylon ~* 脚气病. *a country ~* 思乡病. *a falling ~* 癫痫.

sic pas·sim [sikˈpæsim] *n.* 〔L.〕全书下同〔注释中有某种特殊规定时的行文用语〕.

Sid·dhar·tha [sidˈdɑːtə] 悉昙多〔佛教始祖释迦牟尼的本名〕.

Sid·dons [ˈsidnz] *n.* 西登斯〔姓氏〕.

sid·dur [siˈduə, ˈsiduə] *n.* *(pl.* ***-dur·im*** [-ˈiːm], ***-durs****)* 犹太教祈祷书.

side [said] *n.* ①(左右上下等的)边, 侧面; (事物内外等的)面,方面;(人、物等的)旁, 旁边. ②〔数〕(三角形等的)边;(立体的)面. ③(身体的)侧边, 胁;(牛羊等从脊骨一分为二的)半片;肋肉. ④(父方、母方等的)方, 血统;(一个集团中的)派别,(敌对的)一方. ⑤【海】舷侧;【徽】纵线;【台球】侧击转球;【印】页. ⑥〔俚〕(摆)架子,傲慢,自大. ⑦(比赛的)队. ⑧〔美俚〕一段[一页,一份]台词. ⑨河岸,山坡. *the right [wrong] ~* (纸、布等的)正[反]面. *the flat ~* (刀)背. *the near [off] ~* (马、车的)靠近[远离]路边的一边. *Let's play ~s.* 我们来分成两方比赛吧. *No ~!*【橄榄球】比赛完毕! *Which ~ are you on?* 你属于哪一派? *The school has a strong ~.* 该校有实力雄厚的一队. *He is English on his mother's ~.* 他的母系是英国血统. *a ~ of bacon* 一块熏肋肉. *six ~s of dialog* 〔美剧〕六页台词. ***by sb.'s ~ = by the ~ of*** 在…的旁边;在…的附近;和…比较. ***change ~s*** (改变立场) 投到对方去. ***clear ~***【海】露出在水面上的部分. ***from all ~s*** 从各方面;到处;从四面八方. ***from ~ to ~*** 左右(摇等). ***have lots of ~*** 架子十足. ***have [put on] too much ~*** 太摆架子,太傲慢. ***hold [shake, burst, split] one's ~ (with [for] laughter)***捧腹大笑. ***look on all ~s*** 到处细看. ***off [on] ~***【橄榄球】违犯规则[合规则]的地位. ***on all ~s*** 四方八面, 到处. ***on one ~*** 在一旁,在一边;斜着. ***on the high ~*** 相当高. ***on the other ~*** 反对方面的;在对面. ***on the right ~ = on the ~ of the angels*** 在正对面. ***on the right [better, bright] ~ of*** 未过…岁. ***on the ... ~*** 趋向于…, 稍微…一点 (*Prices were on the high ~* 物价稍微高一点). ***on the ~*** 顺便,附带;作为副业;〔美口〕略略添上,稍为加上. ***on the ~ of*** 站在…一边, 袒护…, 帮着…. ***on the small ~*** 相当小. ***on the wrong [shady] ~ of*** 过了…岁. ***on the wrong ~ of the door*** 被关在门外, 被拒绝入内. ***on this ~ of*** 在…的这一边;未到(某时日). ***on this ~ (of) the grave*** 在现世. ***place [put] on one ~*** 放到一边;忽视,不当回事. ***put on ~*** ①乱摆架子. ②【台球】侧击使旋转, 给球一捻. ***~ by ~*** 并排着,并肩,连接着 *(with)*. ***~ door trade*** 〔美拳〕临时买票入场的观众. ***stand by sb's ~*** 站在某人方面, 伙同某人. ***take ~s [a ~]*** 左袒, 偏袒; 拥护(某方面). — *a.* ①旁,旁边的,侧面的;横. ②次要的,枝节的,副的;片面的. *a ~ mark* 旁注. *a ~ issue* 枝节问题. *a ~ job* 副业. — *vi.* ①支持;偏袒,附和,站在…的一边*(with)*. ②宽度仅有…. ③〔英俚〕摆架子. — *vt.* ①支持;站在…的一边. ②(将宰了的猪等)对半切开;刨平(木料等的)侧面;装上侧面;【建】钉上披叠板. ③〔俚〕收拾开;放到一边,推开. *We should ~ with the people.* 我们要站在人民方面. ~**arm** *ad., a.* 挥臂(的). ~ **arms** 腰佩武器[刺刀,佩剑,手枪等]. ~**band**【无】边(频)带. ~**board** 餐具柜. ~ **bone** 髀骨;【兽医】环骨肿. ~**-burns** 〔*pl.*〕〔美〕短腮巴胡子. ~**car** ①(摩托车的)边车;(爱尔兰的)轻便三轮马车. ②〔常 S-〕鸡尾酒. ~ **chain**【化】侧链. ~ **check** (马缰绳的)侧勒. ~**-circuit**【电】实线电路. ~ **crops** 杂粮. ~ **dish**【烹】添菜,小菜. ~ **drum** (军用)小鼓. ~ **effect** (药物)副作用. ~ **elevation** 侧视图. ~ **entrance** 侧门. ~**-kick** 〔美俚〕老伙伴,朋友;死党. ~ **light** ①侧面光;边窗;舷窗;舷灯. ②(报刊上的)杂闻;间接的说明 (*let in [throw] a ~ light on [upon]* … 间接说明,偶然证明). ~ **line** 旁线,横线;副业,兼职;(本业以外的)兼售商品. ~**long** *ad., a.* 打横,打斜;横,斜 (*give sb. a ~long glance* 斜眼看人,瞟人). ~**man** (爵士音乐)乐队队员,伴奏者. ~ **meat** 肋肉〔尤指腌的或烟熏过的〕. ~ **money** 横财. ~**note** 旁注. ~**piece** 侧部,边件. ~**saddle** 女鞍. ~ **shaft**【机】侧轴,副轴. ~ **show** 余兴;枝节问题,小问题,小事件. ~ **slip** ①旁枝;私生子. ②舞台上首和下首的槽〔大道具出入用〕. ③【空】(机翼)侧滑;沿横轴方向的运动. ~**splitter** 〔俚〕叫人笑痛肚皮的笑话. ~**-splitting** *a.* 笑痛肚皮的. ~ **step** ①*n.* 向旁边避让一步;(上车下车的)踏板. ②*vt., vi.* 向旁边避让;靠向旁边;〔美俚〕逃避,规避. ~ **stroke** 侧击,横击;侧泳,横泳;附带行动. ~**swipe** ①*vt., vi.* 擦边撞击. ②*n.* 擦撞. ~ **tone** 侧音. ~**track** ①*n.* 〔主美〕【铁路】(等候交车的)岔道,侧线. ②*vt.* 〔主美〕转入侧线;〔转义〕降到从属地位;避让;扣压,拖延(事件);转变(话题). ~ **view** 侧面图;侧面形状. ~ **walk** 〔美〕人行道 (=〔英〕*pavement*). ~**walk superintendent** 〔美口〕站在路边看拆建房屋的闲人. ~**wall** 轮胎壁. ~**ward** ①*a.* 旁,横,侧面的. ②*ad.* = ~wards. ~**wards** *ad.* 横,斜,向旁边,从旁边. ~**way** ①*n.* 小路,岔路;人行道. ②*ad., a.* = ~ways. ~**ways** *ad., a.* 旁,横,斜着,从旁边. ~**-wheel** *a.* 有明轮的(船). ~ **wheeler** 〔美〕明轮船. ~**whiskers** 络腮胡子. ~ **wind** 〔英〕①*n.* 侧风;间接的影响[手段、方法]. ②*a.* 间接的. ~**winder** *n.* 〔美〕 ①响尾蛇(导弹) ②横击,侧击. ~**wise** *ad., a.* = ~ ways.

sid·er [ˈsaidə] *n.* 帮派成员.

si·de·re·al [saiˈdiəriəl] *a.*【天】星的,恒星的;星座的. ~ *light* 星光. *a ~ revolution* 周天. ~ **day** 恒星日〔23时56分〕. ~ **hour** 恒星时〔恒星日的1/24〕. ~ **year** 恒星年〔365日6时9分9秒〕.

sid·er·ite [ˈsidərait] *n.*【矿】菱铁矿;陨铁.

sid·e·rog·ra·phy [ˌsidəˈrɔgrəfi] *n.* 雕钢术;钢板雕刻(复制)术.

sid·er·o·lite [ˈsidərəlait] *n.* 铁陨石.

sid·er·o·sis [ˌsidəˈrəusis] *n.*【医】(因吸进铁粉发生的)铁质沉着病,铁尘肺.

si·des·man [ˈsaidzmən] *n.* 党羽,同党;副教区委员;教会副执事.

si·di [ˈsiːdi] *n.* 〔印度和非洲东部用语〕埃塞俄比亚人；黑人.

sid·ing [ˈsaidiŋ] *n.* ①偏袒,附和,支持. ②【铁路】(等候交车等用的)岔道,侧线；〔美〕【建】披叠板；【船】(船材的)边宽；(运河等的)让船处.

si·dle [ˈsaidl] *vi.* (羞怯或偷偷地)侧身而行； 侧身挨近 *(up)*.

Sid·ney, Syd·ney [ˈsidni] *n.* 西德尼〔姓氏,男子名〕.

Si·don [ˈsaidn] *n.* 西顿〔即 Saida 赛达〕〔黎巴嫩港市〕.

sid·y [ˈsaidi] *a.* 〔口〕高视阔步的,趾高气扬的,傲慢的.

Sie·bold [ˈziːbɔlt] **P.F. von** 席博尔特〔1796—1866, 德国博物学家〕.

siè·cle [ˈsjekl] *n. (pl. -cles* [-kl]*)* 〔F.〕百年,一世纪；年代,时代.

siege [siːdʒ] *n.* ①包围,围攻； 被围攻； 围攻期间. ②说服,劝诱；强求；长期努力；长期折磨；不断袭击. ③炉底,炉床. *a regular ~* 正攻法. *a state of ~*戒严. *~ warfare* 包围战. ***lay ~ to*** 包围,围攻. ***lay ~ to a lady's heart*** 生方设法地追求女人. ***press [push] the ~*** 猛烈围攻. ***raise the ~ of*** 解…的围；停止围攻. ***stand a ~*** 抵御围攻. ***under heavy ~ by*** 在…的重重包围之中. ***undergo a ~*** 被围攻. — *vt.* 〔古〕围攻,包围. **~-basket** 堡篮；弹盾. **~ gun** 攻城炮. **~ money, ~ piece** (受围城市临时发行的)应急货币. **~ train** 攻城炮兵连. **~works** 〔*pl.*〕攻城设施.

Sieg·fried [ˈsiːgfriːd] *n.* 西格弗里德〔男子名〕.

Sieg Heil [ˈziːkˈhail] 〔G.〕胜利〔德国法西斯分子见面时招呼用语〕.

si·en·na [siˈenə] *n.* 浓黄土〔一种矿物颜料〕；赭石；赭色. *raw ~* 生赭石〔黄色颜料〕. *burnt ~* 煅赭石〔红黄色颜料〕.

Si·en(n)·ese [ˌsaiəˈniːz, ˌsiː-] *a.* (意大利都市)西爱那(Sienna)的. *the ~ school* (13、14世纪的)西爱那画派. — *n. (sing., pl.)* 西爱那人.

Si·er·ra [ˈsiərə] 通讯中用以代表字母 S 的词.

si·er·ra [ˈsiərə, siˈerə] *n.* ①〔美〕【地】锯齿山脊；岭. ②西班牙鲐鱼.

Si·er·ra Le·one [ˈsiərə liˈəun] 塞拉利昂〔旧译塞拉勒窝内〕〔非洲〕.

si·es·ta [siˈestə] *n.* (特指西班牙、拉丁美洲等国的)午睡；〔美剧〕闭场(期间). — *vi.* 午睡.

sieur [sjœːr] *n.* 〔古法〕先生〔相当于 sir 的尊称〕.

sieve [siv] *n.* ①(细眼)筛. ②(约装一 bushel 的)粗筐. ③〔喻〕嘴松的人,守不住秘密的人,嘴不严的人. *a head [memory] like a ~* 记性糟透了. *draw water with a ~* = *pour water into a ~* 白费气力，徒劳. *as leaky as a ~* 嘴松,容易泄漏秘密. —*vt.* 筛，筛选. **~ tube**【植】筛管.

sif·fleur [siˈfləː] *n. (pl. ~s; fem. siffleuse,* [-øːz]*)* 〔F.〕口哨音乐家.

sift [sift] *vt.* ①筛,筛分；精选；细查；清理. ②在…上撒(胡椒等) *(over; upon)*. — *vi.* ①被筛下. ②精选；详查 *(into)*. ③落进. *~ the flour from the bran* 把面粉从麦麸中筛出来.

sift·er [ˈsiftə] *n.* 筛者；精选者；细选者；筛子；撒粉器.

sift·ings [ˈsiftiŋz] *n. pl.* ①筛出来的东西，似筛下来的东西. ②筛除物；杂质.

SIG = Signal Corps 通信兵(部队).

Sig. = Signor; signal; signature.

sigh [sai] *n.* 叹气，叹息(声)；(风、树的)啸声，呜咽声. *draw [fetch, heave] a ~* 叹气,抽口气. — *vi.* ①叹气，叹息. ②悲叹；渴慕 *(for)*. ③(风等)呜咽呼啸. — *vt.* 叹息着说 *(forth; out)*.

sigh·ing·ly [ˈsaiiŋli] *ad.* 叹息地；呼啸着；哀鸣着.

sight [sait] *n.* ①视力，视觉. ②眼界，视域，视界，视距. ③观看；壮观，奇观；风景；〔the ~s〕名胜. ④光景，情景；视察，观察. ⑤意见，见解. ⑥视门，窥孔；瞄准，照准；(枪、炮的)准心，瞄准器. ⑦〔a ~〕〔口〕许多，大量. ⑧〔口语〕机会. ⑨〔美〕直线，直路. ⑩〔美〕说笑话逗同伴快活的牧童. *have long ~* 看得远. *have far ~* 有远见. *short ~ [near ~]* 近视；眼光短浅，缺乏远见. *Get out of my ~!* 滚开! *I cannot bear the ~ of him.* = *I hate the very ~ of him.* 我连看也不要看他. *a beautiful ~* 美景. *a bill payable at long [Short] ~* 见票后远期〔短期〕照付的票据. *a perfect ~* 实实在在的壮观；十足的笑话. *see [do] the ~s of Beijing* 游览北京名胜古迹. *a radar ~* 雷达瞄准器. ***a(long) ~ better*** 〔口〕比…好得多,远胜. ***a ~ for sore eyes*** 看着舒服的东西；佳客，珍品(等). ***a ~ of*** 非常多的. ***at first ~*** 一见就；乍看起来 (*love at first ~* 一见倾心). ***at ~*** 一看见就；见(票)即(付) (*play music at ~* 一看见乐谱就演奏得出. *read at ~* 读得流利). ***at the ~ of*** 一看见就. ***be in ~*** 看得见，在眼前. ***catch [have, gain, get] ~ of*** 发见，看出. ***come in ~*** 呈现在眼前；可以望见. ***find favour in sb.'s ~*** 受某人欢迎，得某人宠爱，被某人看中. ***go [get] out of ~*** 看不见了. ***in full of ~***【商】暂时入口申请书. ***in one's own ~*** 由自己的眼光看来，照自己的见解. ***in sb.'s ~*** 在某人面前；照某人的眼光看来，由某人来看 (*Do what is right in your ~.* 你认为该做的就做吧). ***in ~*** 看得见 (*Peace is in ~.* 和平不远了). ***in [within] ~ of*** 在看得见…的地方. ***in the ~ of*** 由…看来. ***keep sth. in ~*** = ***keep ~ of sth.*** 看守物件. ***know by ~*** 曾经见过，见过面. ***line of ~*** 瞄准线，视线. ***lose one's ~*** 失明，成瞎子. ***lose ~ of*** 看不见了…，看漏了…；忘了…；失踪了. ***make a ~ of oneself*** 打扮得故意使人注意；给人取笑. ***not by a long ~*** 远不及. ***on ~*** = at ~. ***out of ~*** ①在看不见的地方，看不见. ②〔口语〕(瘦得)不成样子. ③〔口〕好到极点，非常出色；无可争辩地，毫无问题地，绝对地 (*Out of ~, out of mind.* 离久情疏). ***put out of ~*** 藏起；用尽；吃掉，喝掉. ***~ unseen*** 〔美商〕不看现货. ***take a ~ of*** 看. ***take ~*** 瞄准. ***upon ~*** = at ~. — *a.* 一看就能做〔演奏，翻译〕的，不必预先准备的；【商】见票即照付的. *~ translation* 看到原文就下笔的翻译. — *vt.* ①看见；观测(天体等)；熟视. ②给…装瞄准器. ③调准瞄准器；瞄准. ④出示，给看(票据等). — *vi.* 瞄准；(向某一方向)察看. ***~ing board*** 测视牌. ***~ing pendant*** 瞄准锤. ***~ing shot*** 试射，练射. **~ gag** 哑剧；不说话而充分表示意义的可笑场面. **~line**【剧】(观众)视线〔剧场中每一座位都能无阻地看清舞台面的线〕. **~ reading** 见谱即奏〔唱〕；见文即译〔读，理解〕. **~-worthy** *a.* 值得看的.

sight·ed [ˈsaitid] 〔用以构成复合词〕*a.* …视的，眼光…的，…视眼的. *near- [far-] ~* 近〔远〕视的.

sight·less [ˈsaitlis] *a.* 无视力的，盲，瞎；〔罕、诗〕看不见的.

sight·ly [ˈsaitli] *a.* 好看的；显眼的；〔美〕可以眺望风景的.

sight·see [ˈsaitsiː] *vt.* ***(-saw, -seen, -sing)*** 〔美〕游览，参观. **-r** *n.* 游览者，参观者.

sight·see·ing [ˈsaitsiːiŋ] *n.* 游览，观光. — *a.* 游览的，参观的. *a ~ car* 游览汽车. *a ~ party* 参观团.

sig·il [ˈsidʒil; 常读 ˈsig-] *n.* ①印，印章. ②(被认为有神秘意义或力量的)图谶，图象.

sig·ma [ˈsigmə] *n.* 希腊字母表的第十八字母〔Σ, σ, ς, 相当于英语的 s〕【动，植】S〔Σ〕形；【心】千分之一秒.

sig·mate [ˈsigmeit] *vt.* 加 *S* 字在…的词尾. — *a.* S 形的；Σ 形的.

sig·moid [ˈsigmɔid] *a., n.* S〔Σ〕形的；【医】乙状的，乙状结肠. *the ~ flexure*【解】S 状弯曲. **~oscope**【医】乙状结肠窥镜.

Sig·mund [ˈsigmənd] *n.* 西格蒙德〔男子名〕.

sign [sain] *n.* ①记号，符号. ②信号，暗号. ③(示意的)姿势，手势；表示. ④招牌，广告(牌). ⑤形迹、痕迹〔常与 no 连用〕；〔美〕(野兽的)足迹. ⑥证据；预兆，朕兆；性状；【医】症状. ⑦【圣】奇迹. ⑧【天】(黄道十二宫的)

官.⑨〔罕〕徽章;旗. *deaf-and-dumb ~s* 聋哑人的手势;聋哑字母. *talk in ~s* 用手势说. *~ of assent* 同意的表示. *a call ~* 呼号. *~s and wonders* 奇迹. *~ and countersign* 问答口令;暗语问答,暗号. ***bear the ~ of the times*** 带有时代的特征. ***give the high ~*** 〔美〕发出信号〔尤指危险的信号〕. ***in ~ of*** 作为…的记号. ***make a ~ to*** 对…作暗号[打手势]. ***make no ~ of*** 没有…的样子[征象]. ***show a ~ of*** 现出…的样子或形迹,有…的征兆. ***~ of the cross*** 划押,作为签名的十字记号;用手划的十字. ***There are ~s of*** 有…的征象.— *vt.* ①用信号表示,做姿势通知;预示.②签名于,署名于,画押于;签名盖章约定;〔美〕使签名,使订约;(签名)雇用;加记号于.③画十字于.— *vi.* 用姿势通知,打手势,使眼色,做暗号;签名;订契约 *(on)*. *~ed and sealed* 签了名盖了章. *~ed, sealed, and delivered* 【法】已签名盖章交还,决定. *The treaty was ~ed today.* 条约今天签了字了. *He ~ed to me to enter the garden.* 他招手要我进园里. ***~ assent*** (用动作)表示同意. ***~ away [off]*** 在证书上签字让与(财产等).***~ off***【无】①广播完毕.②签字发誓戒绝;废除(契约);断绝(关系).③〔美俚〕停止讲话,住嘴,停止. ***~ on*** 签字聘用[就聘];签字承认. ***~ over*** = ~ away. ***~ up*** 〔美口〕签字应征[应聘,受雇];(报名)参加. ~ **board** 招牌;〔美〕招贴板,布告板. ~ **language** 手势语. ~ **manual** ①(国王的)亲笔署名.②特征,特性. ~ **painter** 写招牌的(人). ~**post** 招牌柱,广告柱;路标;明显的表示[线索,症状].

sig·nal [ˈsignl] *n.* ①信号,暗号;信号器.②动机,导火线 *(for)*.③预兆,征象. *call ~*【无】呼号. *an alarm ~* 警报(器). *an information ~* 〔美〕暴风警报(旗). *an international code of ~s* 国际通用信号. *a ~ of distress = a distress ~* 船只失事信号.— *a.* ①暗号的,作信号用的.②显著的,非常的,优越的. *a ~ victory [defeat]* 大胜[败].— *vt., vi.* (〔英〕*-ll-*) 发信号[警报]给(人、船等);用信号[警报]通知(暴风、危险等);用动作[手势]示意;预示. *a ~ing bomb* 信号弹. ~ **book** (尤指陆海军等的)信号通信手册. ~ **box** (铁路的)信号房. ~ **code** 信号密码. ~ **corps** 通信队;〔S- C-〕〔美陆军〕通信兵团. ~ **fire** 烽火,烽烟. ~ **flag** 信号旗. ~ **generator** 发(信)号机. ~ **gun** 号炮. ~ **lamp** 信号灯. ~**man** 信号员. ~**ment** 特征描述〔如缉捕令中对逃犯的描述〕. **-officer**【军】通信主任;信号军官. ~ **plate** 信号板. ~ **rocket** 信号火箭. ~ **station** 信号所,望楼.

sig·nal·ize [ˈsignəlaiz] *vt.* ①用信号通知.②使著名;使显眼;表明;显示.③在…设置交通信号. *~ a victory by public rejoicing* 万众欢腾庆祝胜利. *~ oneself by* 因…著名.

sig·nal·ly [ˈsignəli] *ad.* 显著,大大,非常.

sig·na·to·ry [ˈsignətəri] *a.* 签署的,签约的.— *n.* 签字人;签约国,缔盟国. *the ~ powers to a treaty* 条约签字国,缔约国.

sig·na·ture [ˈsignitʃə, -nətʃə] *n.* ①签名,署名,画押,盖章.②【乐】记号〔调号或拍子记号〕;【无】(广播节目开始或完毕的)信号曲;【代数】符号差;【印】装钉用折叠号码;【医古】外征;【药】(注明在药瓶上的)用法说明〔略 S, sig.〕;〔古〕象征,特征. *add one's ~ to* 在…上签字. *a time ~*【乐】拍子记号. *a key ~*【乐】调号. *bear the ~* 有署名,签过字. *over sb.'s ~* 经某人签名,有某人签字为凭. ~ **drive** 签名运动. ~ **tune** (无线电广播或电影的)信号(歌)曲.

sign·er [ˈsainə] 签名人;(用手势)示意者;〔S-〕美国独立宣言署名人.

sig·net [ˈsignit] *n.* ①印;图章,〔the ~〕玺.②〔喻〕痕迹,影象. ***writer to the ~*** 〔Scot.〕【法】律师. ~ **ring** 图章戒指.

sig·nif·i·cance [sigˈnifikəns] *n.* ①有意义,意味深长;意义,旨趣.②重要(性),紧要,重大;【统】显著性. *a word of great ~* 意味深长的一个词. ***of no [little] ~*** 不重要的,无关紧要的.

sig·nif·i·cant [sigˈnifikənt] *a.* ①有意义的;大有讲究的,意味深长的.②表明…的 *(of)*;③重要的,重大的,值得注意的.④有效的,有影响的.⑤非偶然的.⑥【语】有区别的;有实义的. *a historically ~ meeting* 一次有历史意义的会议. *a ~ wink* 意味深长的眼色. *a gesture ~ of consent* 说明同意的姿态. *~ figures*【物】有效数字. **-ly** *ad.*

sig·ni·fi·ca·tion [ˌsignifiˈkeiʃən] *n.* 意义,含意;〔罕〕表示;正式通知; *a primary ~* 本义.

sig·nif·i·ca·tive [sigˈnifikətiv, -keit-] *a.* ①有意义的,意味深长的.②表示…的*(of)*.③为…提供推定证据的. *~ of approval* 表示答应了的.

sig·ni·fy [ˈsignifai] *vt.* ①表示,象征;意味.②成为预照,预示.③〔常用于否定句〕有重大关系[影响]. *Please ~.* 请表示意见. *What does it ~?* 那是什么意思呢?这有什么关系呢? *What does K. G. ~?* K. G. 是什么意思?— *vi.* ①有重要性,要紧.②〔美俚〕装模作样,装腔作势. *It does not ~.* 没有什么关系. ***~ little*** 不大重要,没有什么关系 *(to)*. ***~ much*** 很重要,有很大关系 *(to)*.

si·gnior [ˈsi:njɔ:] *n.* 〔英〕=〔It.〕Signor.

si·gnor [ˈsi:njɔ:] ***si·gno·re*** [si:ˈnjɔ:re] *n.* 〔It.〕*(pl. si·gno·ri* [-ri]*)* ①〔S-〕= Mr. 或 Sir. ②(特指意大利的)贵族,绅士.

Si·gno·ra [si:ˈnjɔ:rə] *n.* *(pl. -re* [-re]*)* 〔It.〕夫人,太太〔相当于 Madam, Mrs.〕.

si·gno·re [si:ˈnjəure] *n.* *(pl. si·gno·ri* [-ri:]*)* ①〔S-〕先生〔意大利尊称呼语,单独使用,不连姓名〕.②绅士,贵族.

Si·gno·ri·na [ˌsi:njəˈri:nə] *n.* 〔It.〕*(pl. -ne* [-nei]*)* ①小姐〔对少女的尊称〕.②姑娘,少女.

si·gno·ri·no [sinjəuˈri:nəu; E. ˌsinjəˈri:nəu] *n.* *(pl. -ri·ni* [-ni:]; E. *-ri·nos)* ①〔S-〕少爷〔对青年男子的尊称〕.②青年男子,少年.

sig·no·ry [ˈsi:njəri] *n.* = seigniory.

Si·grid [ˈsigrid] *n.* 西格丽德〔女子名〕.

Sikh [si:k] *n.* (印度的)锡克教徒.— *a.* 锡克教徒的,锡克教徒似的. **-ism** *n.*

Sik·kim [ˈsikim] *n.* 锡金〔亚洲〕.

sil [sil] *n.* 〔美〕傻子 (= Silly person).

si·lage [ˈsailidʒ] *n.* 青贮饲料. *a ~ cutter* 切草机.— *vt.* 青贮 (= ensilage).

Si·las [ˈsailəs] *n.* 赛拉斯〔男子名〕.

Si·las·tic [siˈlæstik]【化】硅橡胶〔原为商标名〕.

si·lence [ˈsailəns] *n.* ①沉默,无言;无表示;无声,沉静,肃静,寂静;【乐】停止.②忘却,湮没;无表示;无音讯. *a man of ~* 沉默寡言的人. *S- gives consent.* 沉默即承认,没有表示就是承认. *I beg pardon for my long ~.* 长久没有写信给你,请原谅. *The rest is ~.* 其余就不知道了. ***break ~*** 打破沉默,开口讲话. ***buy sb.'s ~*** 收买某人使不开口[守秘密]. ***in ~*** 沉默着,静静地. ***keep ~*** 保持沉默,不开口. ***observe a moment's ~ in honour of*** 为(某人等)静默一分钟. ***pass a matter with ~ = pass over a matter in ~*** 不过问某事. ***pass into ~*** 被遗忘. ***put to ~ = reduce to ~*** 把…驳得哑口无言.— *vt.* ①使(嘈杂声音等)静下来;堵住…的嘴,使无言;使(敌人的炮台等)沉默,打哑.②把…说得无话可对,使哑口无言;使停止;使安静.— *int.* 请静一静,嘘,喂.

si·lenc·er [ˈsailənsə] *n.* ①使沉默的人.②【机】消音装置,消声器;【炮】消音器.③压倒对方的议论.

si·lent [ˈsailənt] *a.* ①沉默的,无言的;寡言的;无声的,寂静的.②未作记述的,没有提及的;未说出的.③音讯不通的;静止的,不活动的.④【语音】不发音的.⑤【商】匿[隐]名的. *a ~ thought [agreement]* 默想[认]. *a ~ film* 默片. *S- waters run deep.* 静流水深. *History is ~ about it.* 史书上没有记述这件事情. *~ partner* 〔美〕匿名

合伙人. ~ *as the grave* 没有一点声音. ~ **butler** 〔美〕烟灰盒. ~ **drama** 哑剧. **[the] S- Service** 英国海军. ~ **service** 〔美〕海军；潜艇部队. **-ly** *ad.* 默然，寂然，不声不响. **-ness** *n.*

Si·le·nus [saiˈliːnəs] *n.* ①【希神】塞列努斯〔森林神的首领，酒神的养父〕. ②〔S-〕= satyr. ③愉快的醉汉.

Si·le·sia [saiˈliːzjə] *n.* ①西里西亚〔中欧东部一地区〕. ②〔s-〕(作窗帘或衣里用的)一种牢固而轻软的亚麻布〔斜纹布〕.

si·le·si·a [saiˈliːzjə] *n.* 亚麻布；薄斜纹布.

Si·lex [ˈsaileks] *n.* ①〔美〕玻璃咖啡壶〔商标名〕. ②〔s-〕=silica. ③无水硅酸制成的耐热玻璃.

sil·hou·ette [ˌsilu(ː)ˈet] *n.* 侧面影象，剪影；轮廓，廓影. *in* ~ = *on* ~ 象影画一样，成剪影；仅现轮廓. —*vt.* 〔常用被动语态〕给…画侧面影象；使映出影子；使仅现轮廓.

sil·i·ca [ˈsilikə] *n.* 【化】硅石，二氧化硅. ~ **gel** (氧化)硅胶.

sil·i·cate [ˈsilikit] *n.* 【化】硅酸盐(脂).

si·li·ceous [siˈliʃəs] *a.* = silicious.

si·lic·ic [siˈlisik] *a.* 【化】硅酸的，硅的，硅石的. ~ *acid* 硅酸(类)；形成各种硅酸盐的酸.

sil·i·cide [ˈsiliˌsaid] *n.* 【化】硅化物.

sil·i·cif·er·ous [ˌsiliˈsifərəs] *a.* 【化】含硅的，含硅土的，生硅土的.

si·lic·i·fy [siˈlisifai] *vt., vi.* 【化】(使)硅化.

si·li·cious [siˈliʃəs] *a.* 硅质的，含硅的(= siliceous). ~ *sand stone* 玻璃砂.

si·li·ci·um [siˈliʃiəm] *n.* 【化】硅〔旧名矽〕. ~ **steel** 【冶】硅钢.

sil·i·cle [ˈsilikl] *n.* 【植】角，短荚. **-cu·lar** *a.*

sil·i·con [ˈsilikən] *n.* = silicium. ~ **carbide** 【化】碳化硅，金刚砂. ~ **controlled rectifier** 硅(可)控整流器. ~ **transistor** 硅晶体管.

sil·i·cone [ˈsilikəun] *n.* 【化】①硅有机树脂. ②硅黄；聚硅酮. ~ **rubber** 硅(氧)橡胶，硅酮橡胶.

sil·i·co·sis [ˌsiliˈkəusis] *n.* 【医】石末沉着病，硅〔矽〕肺.

si·lic·u·la [siˈlikjulə] *n.* *(pl. -lae* [-ˌliː]) = silicle.

si·lic·u·lose [siˈlikjuˌləus] *a.* 【植】①有短角的. ②短角形的.

sil·i·qua [ˈsilikwə] *n.* *(pl. -quae* [-kwiː]) ①= silique. ②【解】长角状包被.

si·lique [siˈliːk] *n.* 【植】长角(果)〔十字花科的长形果实〕.

silk [silk] *n.* ①蚕丝，丝；绸，绢，缎；〔*pl.*〕绸衣〔特指拳师、骑师在比赛时所穿的〕. ②丝状物. ③〔英〕皇室律师的绸袍；〔口〕皇室律师. ④(宝石等的)绢丝光泽. ⑤玉米的须. ⑥降落伞. *artificial* ~ (= artificial fibre) 人造丝. *raw* ~ 生丝. *air* ~ 空心丝. ***hit the*** ~ 用降落伞降落. ***sit among the ~s = take (the)*** ~ 当皇室律师. ***thrown*** ~ 丝经，搓好的丝. ~ **conditioning** 生丝检查. ~ **cotton (tree)** 木棉(树). ~ **gland** 【动】丝腺. ~ **gown** 皇室律师绸袍. ~ **hat** 大礼帽. ~ **mill** 丝厂；织绸厂. ~ **paper** 薄纸. ~**screen** (丝绢网印花用的)丝绢网. ~**screen process** 【纺】丝绢网印花法. ~**-stocking** ① *n.* 有闲阶级(的人)；贵族. ②〔美〕*a.* 穿着长统丝袜的；奢华的；贵族(一样)的. ~**weed** 【植】丝状绿藻. ~**worm** 蚕 (*a ~worm egg raising station* 种蚕场).

silk·en [ˈsilkən] *a.* ①丝(制)的；丝一样的；绸缎的；〔诗〕柔软的，光滑的，有丝光的；优雅的. ②穿着绸衣的，奢华的. ③圆滑的. ~ *rustling* 绸衣的簌簌声. *her* ~ *locks* 她的柔软光滑的头发.

silk·y [ˈsilki] *a.* ①丝一样的，象绸缎的；光滑的，有丝光的. ②优雅的，温柔的；善于奉承的，圆滑的. ③(酒)舐着舒服的. **-i·ness** *n.*

sill [sil] *n.* ①【建】基石，基木；沓板；梱，门槛，窗台. ②【地】岩床，岩层，海底山脊；平巷底，矿山巷道的底面；底梁. ③【机】(车体底框的)梁.

sil·la·bub [ˈsiləbʌb] *n.* 一种用牛奶与葡萄酒合成的甜饮料；华而不实的东西；空洞无物的话.

sil·ler [ˈsilə] *n.* 〔Scot.〕银；金钱.

sil·li·man·ite [ˈsilimənait] *n.* 〔美〕【地】硅线石 (= fibrolite).

sil·ly [ˈsili] *a.* *(-li·er; -li·est)* ①傻的，愚蠢的；无聊的，无意义的，头昏眼花的，稀里胡涂的. ②【板球】逼近三柱门的. ③〔古〕单纯的，天真的；无知的；不中用的. —*n.* 〔儿、口〕傻子，蠢货. *a ~ laugh* 傻笑. *Don't be ~!* 别傻了. *Don't be a ~!* 别胡说! ***be knocked ~*** 被打得失去知觉. ***go ~*** 〔口〕成傻瓜. ***the ~ season*** 〔新闻用语〕新闻饥荒期〔8，9月〕. ~ **Billy** 笨蛋. ~ **milk** 〔美〕酒. **-li·ly** *ad.* **-li·ness** *n.*

si·lo [ˈsailəu] *n.* *(pl. ~s)* 青贮塔；【导弹】井状地下仓库，发射井. *an upright ~* 青贮塔. — *vt.* 用青贮塔贮藏(牧草等).

si·lox·ane [siˈlɔksein] *n.* 【化】硅氧烷.

silt [silt] *n.* 泥沙，淤泥(沉积处). ~ *content* 淤泥含量. *the total volume of ~* 淤泥总量. — *vt., vi.* (用淤泥)阻塞 (*up*)；淤积. **-y** *a.*

Si·lu·ri·an [saiˈljuəriən, si-] *n., a.* ①(Wales 南部古代英国住民) 西留尔 (Silures) 人(的). 西留尔人居住地方. ②【地】志留纪(的)，志留系(的).

si·lu·rid [siˈluərid, sai-] *n.* 【动】鲇科 *(Siluridae)* 的鱼：鲇鱼，鲶. — *a.* 鲇科的.

sil·va, sil·van = sylva, sylvan.

sil·ver [ˈsilvə] *n.* ①银；银币；钱. ②银(白)色. ③银器；银丝，银边带. ④〔美〕【摄】银盐；硝酸银. — *a.* ①银的，银制的；象银的；银白的，(头发等)发银光的. ②银声的，清亮的；雄辩的. ③和平的，平静的；寂静的. ④银本位的. ⑤25周年的. *native* ~ 天然银. *fine [pure, refined]* ~ 纯银. *a ~ tongue* 能言善辩. *a ~ jubilee* 二十五周年纪念. ***be born with a ~ spoon in one's mouth*** 生于富有家庭. — *vt.* 包银，镀银；使成银白色；涂银，涂锡汞合金(在镜子等上)；【摄】涂硝酸银子. — *vi.* 变成银一样；(头发)变白；发银光. ~ **age** 白银时代〔神话传说中最幸福的黄金时代后情况稍差的时代；文学史上指：(1) 罗马 Augustus 皇帝到 Hadrian 皇帝期间(公元 14—138) 的拉丁文学隆盛时代；(2) Anne 女皇在位时(1701—15)的英国文学隆盛时代〕. ~ **bath** 【化】银锅；银浴器；【摄】银盐溶液槽. ~ **bell** 【植】四翅银钟花树(又叫 ~-bell tree) ~ **berry** 【植】银果胡颓子. ~ **birch** 【植】纸皮桦(= paper birch). ~ **bromide** 【化】溴化银. ~ **bullets** 〔美〕市民认购的战时公债. ~ **certificate** 〔美〕银元券〔旧时一种可以兑换现银的纸币〕. ~ **chloride** 【化】氯化银. ~ **fish** *n.* 【鱼】银鱼；【虫】蠹鱼. ~ **foil** 银箔. ~ **fox** 【动】银狐. ~**-gilt** *a.* 镀银的. ~**-grey** *n., a.* 银灰色(的). ~ **hake** 【动】银元须鳕. ~ **iodide** 【化】碘化银. ~ **Latin** 白银时代的拉丁语. ~ **leaf** 银箔. ~ **lining** (失望或不幸中的)一线希望，一点慰藉. ~ **nitrate** 【化】硝酸银. ~ **paper** 上等薄纸；银箔纸；锡纸；【摄】银感光纸. ~ **perch** 【动】石首鱼；类石首鱼. ~ **plate** 银餐具. ~**-plated** *a.* 包银的，镀银的. ~ **point** ①银笔画. ②银的熔点. ~ **protein** 【化】蛋白银. ~ **salmon** 【动】银大马哈鱼(= coho). ~ **screen** 银幕；电影界. ~ **side** 牛腿肉的最好部分. ~**side(s)** 【动】银汉鱼. ~**smith** 银(器)匠. ~ **solder** 银焊条. ~ **standard** 银本位. **S- State** 银州〔美国内华达的别名〕. **S- Streak** 银条纹〔英吉利海峡的别名〕. ~**tail** 〔澳俚〕有钱人. ~**-tongued** *a.* 口才流利. ~ **thaw [frost]** 【气】雨淞 (= glitter ice). ~**ware** 银器，银制品；〔美运〕优胜杯. ~ **wedding** (婚后二十五周年的)银婚礼. ~**weed** 【植】①鹅绒委陵菜. ②银叶花属.

sil·ver·i·ness [ˈsilvərinis] *n.* ①象银，银光，银色，银白. ②声如银铃，银声.

sil·ver·ing [ˈsilvəriŋ] *n.* ①镀银，包银. ②镀上的银层；银色光泽. ③【摄】用硝酸银使感光.

sil·ver·ly [ˈsilvəli] *ad.* 象银一样地.
sil·vern [ˈsilvən] *a.* ①银的, 银制的; 象银的. ②银铃般的, 清脆响亮的. ③第二位的, 次好的. ④银白的.
sil·ver·y [ˈsilvəri] *a.* ①象银一样的, 银色的, 银白的. ②银铃一般的, 清脆响亮的. ③含银的; 包银的, 镀银的.
Sil·via [ˈsilviə] *n.* 西尔维娅〔女子名〕.
sil·vi·cal [ˈsilvikl] *a.* 森林的; 造林学的; 森林生态学的.
sil·vic·o·lous [silˈvikələs] *a.* 生长于林地的.
sil·vics [ˈsilviks] *n. pl.* 〔动词用单数〕森林生态学.
sil·vi·cul·ture [ˈsilvikʌltʃə] *n.* 造林学, 造林法. **-turist** *n.* 林学家.
s'il vous plaît [sil vu plɛ] 〔F.〕 (= if you please) 请.
Sim [sim] *n.* Simeon 和 Simon 的爱称.
sim. = 〔It.〕 *simile.*
si·ma [ˈsaimə] *n.* 【地】硅镁带, 硅镁层.
si·mar [siˈmɑː] *n.* (中世纪后期妇女穿的)宽长袍.
Sim·birsk [simˈbiəsk] *n.* 辛比尔斯克〔(Ulyanovsk 苏联乌里扬诺夫斯克)的旧称〕.
Sim·fe·ro·pol [ˌsimfiˈrəupl] *n.* 辛菲罗波尔〔苏联城市〕.
sim·i·an [ˈsimiən] *n., a.* 猿(的), 类人猿(的); 象猿猴的.
sim·i·lar [ˈsimilə] *a.* ①近似的, 相似的, 类似的(*to*). ②【乐】平行前进的. ~ *triangles*【数】相似三角形. ~ *permutations*【数】同班排列. *be* ~ *to* 象, 类似. — *n.* 类似物, 相象的人; 相似物. **-ly** *ad.*
sim·i·lar·i·ty [ˌsimiˈlæriti] *n.* ①类似, 相象, 相似. ②类似点; 类似物, 相似物.
sim·i·le [ˈsimili] *n.* 【修】直喻, 明喻.
sim·i·le [ˈsiːmilei] *n.* 〔It.〕【乐】同样, 同上〔略 *sim.*〕.
si·mil·i·tude [siˈmilitjuːd] *n.* ①类似, 相似(*between*). ②类似物, 一模一样的人. ③样子. ④外貌; 〔罕〕比喻; 【数】相似. ***assume the*** ~ ***of*** 装成…的样子. ***in*** ~***s*** 用比喻. ***in the*** ~ ***of*** 模仿着, 以…的姿态. ***speak [talk] in*** ~***s*** 用比喻说.
sim·i·lize [ˈsimilaiz] *vi., vt.* 用比喻说明.
sim·i·ous [ˈsimiəs] *a.* = simian.
sim·i·tar [ˈsimitə] *n.* = scimitar.
Sim·la [ˈsimlə] *n.* 西姆拉〔印度城市〕.
sim·mer [ˈsimə] *vi.* 徐徐沸腾, 慢慢烧滚; (危机等)处于酝酿中. — *vt.* (用文火)燉, 煨; 拼命忍住笑; 压住怒火. ~ ***down*** 用文火熬浓; 冷掉; 平定下来. ~ ***with anger*** 怒火中烧. — *n.* ①徐徐沸腾. ②勉强忍住的笑〔积怒〕. ***at a [on the]*** ~ 在文火上慢慢煨着; 快要沸腾, 快要爆发. ***bring*** *(water)* ***to a*** ~ 使(水)烧滚.
sim·o·le·on [siˈməuliən] *n.* 〔美俚〕一美元.
Si·mon [ˈsaimən] *n.* 西蒙〔姓氏, 爱称: Sim〕. ~ **Pure** 真物, 真人 (*the real* ~ *Pure* 真物, 真人). **s- pure** ①*n.* 〔美俚〕业余选手. ②*a.* 真正的, 道地的, 原原本本的; 业余的, 非职业性的.
sim·o·ny [ˈsaiməni] *n.* 圣职买卖(罪).
si·moom, si·moon [siˈmuːm, -ˈmuːn] *n.* 【气】西蒙风, 带沙风暴〔非洲和阿拉伯地方的干热风〕.
simp [simp] *n.* 〔美俚〕 = simpleton.
sim·pa·ti·co [simˈpɑːtikəu, -ˈpæt-] *a.* 同情的, 性情随和的; 相容的, 和谐的; 意气相投的.
sim·per [ˈsimpə] *n., vi.* 假笑; 傻笑. — *vt.* 傻〔假〕笑着说.
sim·ple [ˈsimpl] *a.* (*-pler; -plest*) ①单纯的; 简单的, 简易的; 轻便的. ②质朴的, 自然的, 天真的; 朴素的; 率直的, 坦白的, 露骨的. ③无知的, 头脑简单的, 愚蠢的. ④普通的, 平常的. ⑤卑贱的, 身分低微的, 无足轻重的. ⑥完全的, 纯粹的. *a* ~ *(mode of) life* 简单的生活. ~ *diet* 简单的饮食, 粗茶淡饭. ~ *beauty* 纯朴的美. *Mine is a* ~ *nothing.* 我的东西实在不象样子〔不足一道〕. *You must be very* ~ *to be taken in by such a story.* 你会上这种话的当, 太老实了. *a* ~ *soldier* 普通一兵. *a* ~ *peasant* 一个普通农民. *twist of the wrist* 〔美〕易如反掌的事; 轻而易举的办法. ***gentle and*** ~ 〔方〕贵贱, 上下. ***pure and*** ~ 绝对的, 完全的, 纯粹的, 十足的 (*It is a mistake pure and* ~. 这是纯粹的错误). — *n.* ①头脑简单的人; 单纯之物, 单体. ②〔古〕药用植物; 药草制剂. ~ **equation**【代】一次方程式. ~ **harmonic motion**【物】简谐运动〔略 S.H.M.〕. ~**-hearted** *a.* 纯洁的; 天真的. ~ **leaf**【植】单叶. ~**-minded** *a.* 轻信的, 易上当的; 头脑迟钝〔简单〕的 (=~-hearted). ~ **pendulum**【物】单摆. ~ **sentence**【语法】简单句. **Simple Simon** ①傻瓜西蒙〔一首儿歌里的人物〕. ②傻瓜, 笨人. **-ness** *n.* 〔罕〕 = simplicity.
sim·ple·ton [ˈsimpltən] *n.* 笨人, 傻子.
sim·plex [ˈsimpleks] *a.* 单纯的, 单一的. 【无】单工的; 单缸的. — *n.* (*pl.* ***-plex·es, -pli·ces*** [-pləsiːz])【数】单纯形.
sim·pli·ci·ter [simˈplisitə] *ad.* 〔L.〕绝对地, 无条件地, 完全地, 纯然; 普遍地, 无限地.
sim·plic·i·ty [simˈplisiti] *n.* ①单纯; 简单, 简易; 轻便. ②质朴; 天真; 朴素; 诚实. ③无知, 愚钝. ④卑贱.
sim·pli·fi·ca·tion [ˌsimplifiˈkeiʃən] *n.* 简单化; 单一化; 单纯化.
sim·pli·fy [ˈsimplifai] *vt.* 简化; 使简易; 使单纯.
sim·plism [ˈsimplizəm] *n.* 过分简单化; (看问题)片面(性)、一刀切. *an astonishing* ~ *in dealing with international issues* 在处理国际问题上令人吃惊的片面简单.
sim·plist [ˈsimplist] *n.* 简单化者; 把问题看得过于简单的人. — *a.* = simplistic.
sim·plis·tic [simˈplistik] *a.* 把复杂问题搞得过于简单的; 简单化的. **-ly** *ad.*
sim·ply [ˈsimpli] *ad.* ①简单地; 明白易懂地; 坦白地, 露骨地; 朴素地; 天真地; 率直地. ②单单, 仅仅. ③〔加强语气〕真正, 的确, 绝对; 非常, 极. *It is* ~ *a question of time.* 这不过是时间的问题罢了. *The cold was* ~ *awful.* 冷得真厉害. *It is* ~ *beautiful.* 这个的确是美.
Simp·son [ˈsimpsn] *n.* 辛普森〔姓氏〕.
sim·u·la·crum [ˌsimjuˈleikrəm] *n.* (*pl.* ***-cra*** [-krə]) 象; 影, 幻影; 伪品, 假象.
sim·u·lant [ˈsimjulənt] *a.* ①模拟的; 伪装的, 看起来象…的. ②【生】拟态的. *colouration* ~ *of surroundings* 保护色.
sim·u·lar [ˈsimjulɑ] *a., n.* 〔古〕 = simulant.
sim·u·late [ˈsimjuleit] *vt.* 假装, 冒充, 装做; 模拟; 模化; 【生】拟(态), 拟(色). ~ *death* 装死. ~ *Jove* (演员)装扮作乔夫神. — *a.* = **sim·u·lat·ed** [-id] 假装的, 装成的; 模仿的; 拟态的. ~ *rain* 人工降雨.
sim·u·la·tion [ˌsimjuˈleiʃən] *n.* 假装; 模拟; 装病, 装疯; 【生】拟态, 拟色.
sim·u·la·tor [ˈsimjuleitə] *n.* ①模仿的人, 假装的人. ②模拟器, 仿真器, 模拟装置〔设备〕; 模拟计算机; 模拟宇航机.
sim·ul·cast [ˈsiməlkɑːst] *vi., vt. n.* (广播和电视)同时联播(节目).
sim·ul·ta·ne·i·ty [ˌsiməltəˈniəti] *n.* 同时, 同时性, 同时发生〔存在〕.
sim·ul·ta·ne·ous [ˌsiməlˈteinjəs] *a.* 同时发生的, 同时做的, 同时的 (*with*). ~ *development of heavy and light industries* 重工业和轻工业同时并举. ~ ***broadcast***【无】联(合广)播. ~ **equations**【数】联立方程式. **-ly** *ad.* 同时, 一齐.
sin[1] [sin] *n.* ①(道德上的)罪, 罪恶(*against*); 过失; 违背常情. ②无礼貌, 粗卤. *setting* ~*s* 容易陷入的罪恶〔恶习〕. *It is a* ~ *to be indoors on such a fine day.* 这样好的天气待在家里实在不对〔罪过〕. ***commit a*** ~ 犯罪. ***for my*** ~***s*** 〔谑〕自作自受, 活该. ***like*** ~ 〔俚〕厉害地, 猛烈地 (*hate sb. like* ~ 恨死某人). ***live in open*** ~ 过明目张胆的罪恶生活. ***visit the*** ~***s [a*** ~***]*** *(upon a sinner)* 使(犯罪者)受报复. — *vi.* 犯罪 (*against*); 违犯(礼仪、教规等)(*against*). ~ ***in one's ill health*** 因干坏事而招致

健康损坏. — *vt.* 犯(罪恶). **be more sinned against than sinning** 受到超过应得程度的惩罚. ~ **away one's health** 因干坏事而损坏健康. ~ **one's mercies** 对幸运无动于衷[不感激]. ~**-offering** 赎罪祭品.

sin² [sain] *n.* 【数】 = sine¹.

sin³ [siːn] *n.* = shin².

Si·nai [ˈsainiai] *n.* 西奈(半岛)〔埃及〕; (西奈半岛上的)西奈山.

Sin·an·thro·pus *n.* [ˌsinænˈθrəupəs]〔L.〕【考古】中国猿人 (= Peking Man).

sin·a·pism [ˈsinəpizəm] *n.* 【医】芥子泥.

since [sins] *conj.* ①…以来, 以后, 自从…的时候起. ★ (1) 主句中动词用现在完成时时, since 所引导的从句须用过去式: *We have both changed ~ we parted.* 分别以来彼此都变了. (2) 主句主语为 *it*, 动词用现在[过去]式时, since 引导的从句须用过去[过去完成]时: *It is two years ~ we parted.* 我们分别以来有两年了. *It was two years ~ we had parted.* 那时我们已经分别两年了. ②因为, 所以, 既是. ★ 在表示原因的几个连词中, 语气最强的词是 because, 其次是 since, 再其次是 as, for. because 是直接说明问话 why? 的'理由''原因'. since 是站在'时间'立场用'既是…就…'的意义去说明事件关系中的自然结果的; 表达这一理由的 since 通常放在句首, 但在省略句中也可放在句中: *S- force is no remedy, let us try conciliation.* 武力既不中用, 就想法和解吧. *That is a useless, ~ impossible, proposal.* 既然不可能, 那就是一个没用的提议. — *prep.* …以来, …以后, …之后, 自从. *S- seeing you I have had good news.* 见面以后得到(你的)不少好消息. ~ **then** 其后, 从此一直. — *ad.* ①以后, 此后, 以来. ★由前置词惯用短语 ~ *then*, ~ *that* 略去 then (时), that (事)而形成: *I have not seen him ~ (= ~ then).* (那时)以后没见过他. ②(距今几年)以前; (从那时候起几年)以前. ★ 由 *conj.* ①义转变成的: *It is two years ~ (we parted).* = *We parted two years ~* (= ago). 我们是在两年以前分别的. *It was two years ~ (we had parted).* = *We had parted two years ~* (= before). 我们是在那以前两年分别的. **ever ~** 从那时起, 此后一直. **long ~** 好久以前, 已久. **not long ~** 就在不久, 未久.

sin·cere [sinˈsiə] *a.* (**-cer·er; cer·est**) ①真挚的; 真诚的. ②〔古〕纯粹的, 不混杂…的 *(of)*.

sincere·ly [sinˈsiəli] *ad.* 真挚地, 真诚地; 诚实地. ***Yours ~*** 谨启[信的结尾语].

sin·cer·i·ty [sinˈseriti] *n.* 真挚, 真实; 诚实, 诚意; 纯粹. *meet it in all ~* 开诚相见.

sin·ci·put [ˈsinsipʌt] *n.* 【解】前顶〔颅顶的前半部〕.

Sin·clair [ˈsiŋklεə] *n.* 辛克莱〔姓氏〕.

Sind [sind] *n.* 信德〔巴基斯坦省名〕.

sine [sain] *n.* 【数】正弦〔略 sin〕. ~ *curve* 正弦曲线. ~ *wave* 正弦波.

si·ne [ˈsaini] *prep.* 〔L.〕无. ~ ***die*** [daiiː] 无限期地, 无期; 日期不定. ~ ***qua non*** [kweiˈnɔn] 必要条件[资格]. ~ ***prole*** [ˈprəuli] 【法】无后嗣[子女]的.

si·ne·cure [ˈsainikjuə] *n.* 闲职, 挂名差事, 〔尤指〕领干薪的牧师职. *hardly a ~ = not a ~ = no ~* 繁忙的差事. **-cur·ist** *n.* 冗员; 担任挂名差事的人; 领干薪的牧师.

sin·ew [ˈsinjuː] *n.* ①【解】腱. ②〔*pl.*〕肌肉, 筋肌; 体力; 精力. ③〔常 *pl.*〕中坚, 主力, 资源, 支持的人[或物]. *the ~s of war* 军费[军备]; 军事力量. — *vt.* 用腱连结; (好象使用肌筋似的)给…以力量, 支持.

sin·ew·y [ˈsinju(ː)i] *a.* 腱的, 腱质的; 肌肉发达的; 强壮有力的; 遒劲的.

sin·fo·ni·a [ˌsinfəˈni(ː)ə] *n.* 〔It.〕【乐】①= symphony. ②〔古〕器乐曲; (初期意大利歌剧的)序曲.

sin·ful [ˈsinful] *a.* 有罪的, 罪孽深重的; 该遭天罚的; 不道德的, 邪恶的. **-ly** *ad.* **-ness** *n.*

sing [siŋ] *vi.* (**sang** [sæŋ], 〔罕, 美〕 **sung** [sʌŋ]; **sung**) ①歌唱; (鸟、虫、风、壶; 箭、子弹等)唱歌似的鸣叫; 耳鸣; 〔诗〕作诗; 歌颂, 赞美 *(of)*. ②〔美俚〕向警察局自首. ~ *in [out of] tune* 唱得合[不合]调. ~ *for the peasants* 为农民歌唱. — *vt.* ①唱, 歌唱; 吟诵. ②唱着使…. ③称赞, 歌颂. ~ *sb. into good humour* 用歌唱使某人心情好转. ~ *the harvest home* 唱着歌把庄稼收回家里. *The song has been sung to death.* 这个歌听腻了. ***give sb. something to ~ for*** 惩罚某人, 叫人吃吃苦头, 使(顽皮小孩)哭出声来. ***make sb.'s head ~*** 把某人脑袋打得发响. ~ ***another song [tune]*** 〔口〕改变调子[论调、方针、态度(等)]; 沮丧; 变谦恭. ~ ***by ear*** 不看谱学唱. ~ ***for joy*** 快乐极了. ~ ***for one's supper*** 付出力气以取得酬劳; 做应做的事情 (不是吃白饭). ~***ing the blues*** 〔美运〕垂头丧气. ~ ***low*** 谨慎小心地说. ~ ***of*** 歌(功), 颂(德), 唱歌庆贺. ~ ***sb.'s praises*** 竭力称赞某人. ~ ***out*** 〔俚〕大声说, 喊叫 (*S- out if you want anything.* 你要什么就大声说吧.) ~ ***small*** 变得垂头丧气, 变得低声下气. ~ ***the same [old] song [tune]*** 翻来复去老是那一套. ~ ***to the piano*** 合着钢琴唱. ~ ***up*** 使劲地唱. — *n.* ①(风、小河、开水壶等的)嗖嗖声, 玲玲声. ②〔美口〕歌唱会. ***on the ~*** (开水壶等)嘘嘘地响.

Sing. = Singapore.

sing. = singular.

sing-a·long [ˈsiŋəˌlɔːŋ] *n.* 〔口〕(非正式的)歌咏会.

Sin·ga·pore [ˌsiŋgəˈpɔː] *n.* ①新加坡〔亚洲〕. ②新加坡〔新加坡首都〕.

singe [sindʒ] *vt.* (**~d; ~ing**) ① 烧焦; 燎(猪、布等的)毛, 烧茸. ②损害(名誉等). *I can smell something ~ing.* 有东西烧焦了. ~*d cat* 〔美〕给人不良印象的人. ~ ***hair*** 烧燎毛发的末梢. ~ ***one's feathers [wings]*** 弄坏名誉; (事业, 冒险)失败, 亏损. ~ ***sb.'s beard*** 侮辱. — *vi.* 烧焦. — *n.* 烧焦; 燎毛, 烧茸.

Sing·er [ˈsiŋə] *n.* ①辛格〔姓氏〕. ②**I.M.** ~ 辛格〔1811—1875, 美国发明家〕.

sing·er¹ [ˈsiŋə] *n.* 歌手; 鸣禽; 诗人.

sing·er² [ˈsiŋə] *n.* (屠宰场的)燎毛工人; 燎毛器, 燎发器.

Sin·gha·lese [ˌsiŋgəˈliːz] *a., n.* = Cinhalese.

sing·ing [ˈsiŋiŋ] *n.* 唱歌, 声乐; 鸟鸣; 耳鸣; 【物, 无】振鸣, 嘤鸣, 啸声. ~ **bird** 鸣禽. ~ **school** ①(特指 18 世纪美国的)成人音乐教习所. ②〔美俚〕(警察的)拷问; (警察局的)询讯室. ~ **voice** 歌声, 乐声.

sin·gle [ˈsiŋgl] *a.* ①仅只一个的, 单独的; 单式的, 【植】(花等)单瓣的. 【无】单工的, 单次的. ②独身的, 单身的; 孤独的; 一人用的. ③一人对一人的; 单层的. ④纯真的, 单纯的; 诚实的. ⑤一次的; 唯一的; 无比的. ⑥〔英〕(酒等)味淡的, 力弱的. — *n.* 一个 (*opp.* double). 【棒球】单打; 〔美俚〕一垒手〔*pl.*〕【网球】单打比赛; 〔*pl.*〕多股线; 【植】单瓣花; 〔英〕单程票. *each ~ person* 每一个人. *a ~ life* 独身生活. *a ~ man* 单身汉. *a ~ woman* 单身女人; 〔婉〕妓女. *a ~ bed* 单人床. *a ~ flower* 单瓣花. *a ~ premium* 一次付清的保险费. *a ~ heart* 专一[真诚]的心. ~ *devotion* 全心全意的献身精神. ~ *ale* 淡啤酒. ~*s silk* 多股生丝, 缫制生丝. ***with a ~ eye*** 诚心诚意地, 一心一意地. ***work with a ~ purpose*** 同心协力地工作. — *vt.* 拣出, 选拔. ~ *out the biggest apples* 拣出最大的苹果. — *vi.* ①【棒球】作一垒手. ②(马)单步行进. ~**-acting** *a.* 单作用的, 单动的. ~**-action** *a.* (枪)单发的. ~ **blessedness** 〔谑〕独身状态. ~ **bond** 【化】单键. ~**-breasted** *a.* (上衣等)单排钮的. ~ **entry** 单式簿记. ~ **eyed** *a.* ①独眼的. ②纯真的, 赤诚的, 诚实的. ~ **file** 单行, 一路纵队. ~ **foot** 单步〔马的一种步法〕. ~**-handed** ① *a.* 只有一只手的, 单手的; 单独的; 能使用一只手的; 可以单独做的. ② *ad.* 只手; 单独, 独力. ~**-hearted** *a.* 有诚意的; 诚实的, 真心的; 一心一意的. ~**-minded** *a.* = single-hearted. ~**-phase** *a.* 【电】单相的. ~ **seater** 单座车〔飞机〕.

~**-side-band**〔无〕单边带的. ~**-space** *vt.* 不空行地打字〔抄写〕. ~**standard** ①(尤指男女)应同样遵守的道德标准. ②(货币的)单本位制. ~**stick**(练习用)剑形木棍; 单棍(搏斗), 剑术. ~**-sticker**〔美口〕单桅帆船. ~ **tax** 单一税[制]. ~**ticket** 单程车票. ~**-track** *a.* 单轨的; 单向的; 死心眼的. ~ **tree** 车前横木 = whiffletree. **-ness** *n.* 单一,单独; 诚意.

sin·glet [ˈsiŋglit] *n.* ①(男式)汗衫; 背心. ②【物】单线; 独态; 单纯. ~ *state* 独态.

sin·gle·ton [ˈsiŋgltən] *n.* 【牌】(某一花色的)单张; 孤张; 手拿孤张的人; 〔美俚〕只有一个影片的演出; 独一无二的(人或物).

sin·gly [ˈsiŋgli] *ad.* ①各自地,分别地; 单独地, 独自地. ②诚实地,真诚地.

sing·song [ˈsiŋsɔŋ] *n.* 单调; 拙劣的歌唱; 声调平板的诗; 〔英口〕临时凑成的歌咏会. — *a.* 单调的; 毫不精采的, 平淡无味的. — *vt., vi.* 用单调的声音读[说].

sing·spiel [ˈziŋ,ʃpi:l] *n.* (*pl.* ***-spiel·en*** [-ən]) 小歌剧〔德国十八世纪的一种歌剧〕.

sin·gu·lar [ˈsiŋgjulə] *a.* ①唯一的,独一的,单独的,一人的,一个的;【法】各自的,各个的;【逻】单称的;【语法】单数的. ②奇特的, 特别的, 异常的; 非凡的, 卓越的. ~ *clothes* 奇装异服. ~ *nature* 奇特性. *a most* ~ *phenomenon* 一个最奇特的现象. ***all and*** ~ 所有的人; 一律; 完完全全一个不漏. ***be dressed in*** ~ ***fashion*** 穿着奇装异服. — *n.*【语法】单数; 单数的词. ~ **number** 【语法】单数. ~ **successor**【法】特定继承人. **-ly** *ad.* ①异常; 格外. ②单独; 个别; 【语法】用单数. **-ness** *n.* =singularity.

sin·gu·lar·i·ty [ˌsingjuˈlæriti] *n.* ①奇特; 特别; 非凡, 异常; 奇特的东西; 怪癖,特性. ②〔罕〕独一,单一,独个. ③【物】奇点.

sin·gu·lar·ize [ˈsiŋgləraiz] *vt.* 使成单数; 使奇特.

Sin·ha·lese [ˌsinhəˈli:z] *a., n.* = Cinhalese.

Sin·i·cism [ˈsinisizəm] *n.* 中国式,中国风味,中国习惯; 中国语(风).

Sin·i·co-Ja·pan·ese [ˈsinikəudʒæpəˈni:z] *n., a.* 中日的; 日语里面的汉字(的); 仿中国古文的日语文体(的).

sin·is·ter [ˈsinistə] *a.* ①不吉的,凶险的,不祥的; 有害的; 阴险的,险恶的; 邪恶的. ②〔谑〕左的 (*opp.* dexter);【徽】(盾章)左边的. *a* ~ *design* 阴险的计划,阴谋. **-ly** *ad.*

sin·is·tral [siˈnistrəl] *a.* (opp. dextral) 向左的,(贝壳等)左旋的;(比目鱼)左边朝上的; 用左手的.

sin·is·tro·dex·tral [ˌsinistrəuˈdekstrəl] *a.* 从左向右行的,从左向右指的.

sin·is·trorse [ˈsinisˌtrɔ:s, ˈsinisˈtrɔ:s] *a.* 【植】左旋的. **-ly** *ad.*

sin·is·trous [ˈsinistrəs] *a.* = sinister.

Si·nit·ic [siˈnitik] *n.*【语言】汉语族. — *a.* 中国的; 中国人的; 汉语的,中国文化的.

sink[1] [siŋk] *vi.* (***sank*** [sæŋk], 〔古、美〕 ***sunk*** [sʌŋk]; ***sunk, sunken*** [ˈsʌŋkən]) ①下沉, 沉没. ②(日、月等) 沉入地平线下; 低落; 下垂; 下沉, 坍下去, 塌下去, 下陷. ③(声音等) 低落; (火势) 减弱; (病人等) 衰弱; (精神等) 沮丧, 销沉; 衰颓, 沦落, 败落, 堕落 (*into; under*). ④(物价等) 跌落, 减少, 退落. ⑤(水等) 沁进, 渗下, 渗入; (教训等) 深入 (心里等) (*in; into; through*). ⑥(眶、双颊等)凹[陷]下去; (眼睛)低垂; (坡等) 斜下去. ⑦(鱼) 游入水底深处. *The sun* ~*s in the west.* 太阳落在西方. *The floods are* ~*ing rapidly.* 洪水正在急退中〔水位迅速降低〕. *He is*~*ing fast.* 他迅速地一天比一天更衰弱〔快要去世〕. *The dye* ~*s in well.* 这个染料容易吃进去〔渗进去〕. *The war now sank into peace.* 战争平定了. — *vt.* ①弄沉,使 沉没; 击沉; 使下沉. ②使衰弱,使没落,使败落; 损害,毁坏(名誉等); 使颓然下垂,垂下来. ③使降低; 使低落; 使减弱; 使沮丧,使颓丧. ④掘,凿,挖(井等),(把桩, 管子等)向下挖掘, 打进, 插进, 埋入(地下等); (将石头等)嵌入(墙壁等); 【铸造】雕,刻. ⑤减少,减低(力量等),使(股票等)跌价; 糟踏掉,丧失,荡尽(财产等). ⑥偿还(国债等); 投资给(难于收回的事业). ⑦使看不见, 隐藏. ⑧不重视, 不理, 不当做问题. ⑨【印】低行(排). ~ *a ship* 把船弄沉. ~ *one's head upon one's breast* 颓丧地垂下头来. ~ *a well* 掘井. ~ *a stone in the wall* 把石头嵌进墙里. ~ *minor differences* 不计较微小的差异. ~ *a die* 雕一个印模. ***One's heart*** ~***s within one.*** 消沉,灰心. ~ ***a fact*** 息事宁人. ~ ***down*** 沉没; 晕过去, 昏倒. ~ ***in another's estimation*** 声望降低; 失去别人(对他)的信任〔尊重〕. ~ ***into absurdity*** 做荒唐事. ~***into a chair*** 深深地坐进椅子里. ~ ***into a faint*** 晕过去. ~ ***into oblivion*** 被忘掉. ~ ***into the grave*** 死掉. ~ ***one's identity*** 隐瞒身分. ~ ***oneself [one's own interests]*** 舍己为人. ~ ***or swim*** 孤注一掷,不管好歹. ~ ***out of sight*** 隐没不见. ~ ***to the elbow***〔美拳〕打得着实. ~ ***tooth into***〔美俚〕吃. ~ ***under*** 受不了…而倒下去. — *n.* ①(厨房的)洗涤槽; 水斗,水槽,水池; 阴沟; 渗水坑;【地】落水洞; 〔美俚〕海洋. ②巢窟, 藏垢纳污之所. ③洼地, 湖沼. ④【物】中子吸收剂; 变换器,换能器; 转发器. ⑤【剧】布景起落口. ~ **unit** = kitchen unit.

sink·age [ˈsiŋkidʒ] *n.* ①下沉. ②下沉度. ③下沉地带; 低洼地.

sink·er [ˈsiŋkə] *n.* ①沉下的人[物]. ②(钓丝等的)坠子. ③掘井〔矿井〕的人; 开模工(人). ③〔美俚〕银元. ④〔美口〕饼干,炸面圈. = doughnut. ~*s and suds* 〔美口〕炸面圈和咖啡. ***hook, line, and*** ~〔美口〕完全地,全部地.

sink·hole [ˈsiŋkhəul] *n.* ①阴沟口; 污水池; 吸尘孔. ②藏垢纳污之所. ③【地】灰岩坑; 落水洞.

sink·ing [siŋkiŋ] *n.* ①沉没; 沉下; 低陷,塌下,凹下. ②试掘; 投资. ③【建】孔,凹处. ④(饥饿、劳苦等造成的)衰弱. *a* ~ *in the stomach* 空腹时胃的虚脱感. *a* ~ *at the heart* 情绪低落. ~ **fund** 偿债基金.

sin·less [ˈsinlis] *a.* 无罪的,无辜的; 清白的,圣洁的. **-ly** *ad.* **-ness** *n.*

sin·ner [ˈsinə] *n.* ①(宗教、道德上的)罪人,有罪的人, 罪孽深重的人. ②不信神的人. ③〔谑〕坏人, 顽皮鬼. *as I am a* ~〔断定时说〕正象我是罪人一样,的确. *a young* ~〔谑〕小家伙.

Sinn Fein [ˈʃinˈfein] ①〔爱〕新芬党〔20 世纪初以争取民族独立和恢复民族文化为目的的爱国主义组织〕. ②新芬党党员(= Sinn Feiner).

Sino- *comb. f.* 表示 ①中国(的): *Sino*logy. ②"中国和…": *Sino*-Japanese.

Si·no·gram [ˈsainəugræm] *n.* 汉字.

Si·nol·o·gist, Sin·o·logue [siˈnɔlədʒist, ˈsinəlɔg] *n.* ①汉学家. ②中国问题专家.

Si·nol·o·gy [siˈnɔlədʒi] *n.* ①汉学〔研究中国语言、文学、历史、风俗习惯等〕. ②中国问题研究.

Si·no·ma·ni·a [ˌsainəˈmeinjə] *n.* 中国热.

Sin·o·phile, Sin·o·phil [ˈsinəfil, ˈsinəfail; ˈsinəfil] *a.* 喜爱中国的; 亲华的. — *n.* 喜爱中国的人; 亲华人士.

Sin·o·phobe [ˈsinəfəub, ˈsain-] *a.* 厌恶中国的; 排华的. — *n.* 厌恶中国的人; 排华的人.

sin·o·ple [ˈsinəpl] *n.*【地】铁水铝英石; 铁石英; 朱砂〔黑海南岸 Sinope 产〕.

Si·no-Ti·bet·an [ˌsainəutiˈbetn] *a.*【语言】汉藏语系的. — *n.* 汉藏语系〔包括汉语、藏语、缅甸语等〕.

SINS = ship's inertial navigation system 船舰惯性导航系统.

sin·ter [ˈsintə] *n.* ①【地】泉华〔矿泉四周沉淀的结晶岩石〕. ②铁的锈皮; 【冶】熔渣, 烧结物. — *vt.* 烧结. ~ **glass**【化】烧结玻璃, 多孔玻璃. ~ **process** 烧结法.

sin·u·ate [ˈsinjuwit, -ˌweit] *a.* ①= sinuous ②【植】具

弯缘的;具深波状的(指边缘). — *vi.* *(-at·ed, -at·ing)* 蜿蜒,弯曲,曲折. *The snake ~ed along the ground.* 那蛇缘着地面蜿蜒爬行. **-ly** *ad.*

sin·u·a·tion [ˌsinjuˈeiʃən] *n.* 波状,蜿蜒,弯曲.

Si·nui·ju [ˈʃiniːdʒuː] *n.* 新义州〔朝鲜民主主义人民共和国城市〕.

sin·u·os·i·ty [ˌsinjuˈɔsiti] *n.* ①蜿蜒,弯曲,起伏. ②(情节等)曲折,错综复杂. ③柔软动作; ④〔常 *pl.*〕(河流、道路的)弯曲处.

sin·u·ous [ˈsinjuəs] *a.* ①弯曲的,波状的,蜿蜒的(河流等). ②曲折的,错综复杂的. ③动作柔软的. ④转弯抹角的,间接的; 不老实的. ⑤【植】(叶子)具弯缘的, 具深波状边缘的. **-ly** *ad.*

si·nus [ˈsainəs] *n.* *(pl. ~, ~es* [-siz]*)* ①弯曲; 湾; 穴, 凹. ②【解】窦,【医】瘘. ③【植】弯缺, 深裂. ④【动】(软体动物的)弯; (腕足类的)中槽,凹.

si·nus·i·tis [ˌsainəˈsaitis] *n.*【医】窦炎.

si·nu·soid [ˈsainəˌsɔid] *n.* 【数】正弦曲线 (= sine curve). **-al** *a.*

Si·on [ˈsaiən] *n.* = Zion.

-sion *com. f.* 表示"行为,状态","性质": expan*sion*.

Siou·an [ˈsuːən] *n.* *(pl. ~(s))* ①(印第安人) 苏语组. ②说苏语的印第安人, 苏族人. — *a.* 苏语组的; 苏族人的.

Sioux [suː] *n.* *(pl. ~* [-(z)]*)*〔北美〕苏族〔印第安人的一族,自称达可塔 (Dakota) 族〕. — *a.* 苏族的.

sip [sip] *vi.* 啜饮,一点一点地喝. ~ *at one's drink* 细细饮酒. —*vt.* ①呷,啜饮. ②从…中呷吸. ~ *tea* 呷茶,啜茗. — *n.* 啜, 一啜之量. *take a ~* 吸一口. *drink brandy in ~s* 细饮白兰地. **-per** *n.* 吸者; 饮者; 吸浆管.

si·phon [ˈsaifən] *n.* ①虹吸; 吸水管, 弯管; 虹吸管〔瓶〕. ②苏打水瓶(= ~ bottle). ③【建】存水弯. ④【动】呼吸管;【昆】管形口器; (蚊幼虫)管形突; (头足类)体管; (软体动物)水管; (软体、棘皮动物)虹管. — *vt.* ①用虹吸管吸,虹吸. ②吮吸 (民脂民膏等) (*off*). —*vi.* 通过虹吸管. ~ **barometer** 虹吸气压计. ~ **cup**【机】虹吸上油壶. ~ **gauge** 虹吸压力计. ~ **recorder** 虹吸(管)记录器;【无】波纹收报机. **-al** *a.*

si·phon·age [ˈsaifənidʒ] *n.*【物】虹吸能力,虹吸作用.

si·pho·no·phore [saiˈfɔnəˌfɔː, ˈsaifənə-] *n.*【动】管水母目*(Siphonophore)*动物.

si·pho·no·stele [saiˈfɔnəˌstiːl, ˈsaifənə-; saiˌfɔnəˈstiːli] *n.*【植】管状中柱. **-ste·lic** [-ˈstiːlik] *a.*

si·phun·cle [ˈsaifʌŋk] *n.* 【动】体管(指硬体); (蚜虫)腹管.

sip·pet [ˈsipit] *n.* ①(浸在汤汁里的)小片炸[烤]面包; 〔*pl.*〕浸过肉汁的面包片. ②小片,碎片.

sir [强 səː; 弱 sə] *n.* 先生,阁下,君 ①〔一般对职务或年龄比自己大的男子的尊称〕; 议长〔议员对议会主席的称呼〕. ②〔商业信件抬头用语〕先生; 〔*pl.*〕各位,执事诸君〔通常用 Gentlemen〕. ③〔S-〕〔英〕爵士〔对爵士 (Knight) 或从男爵 (baronet) 的称呼,用于姓名前或名字前,但不用于姓氏前,如 Sir Henry Smith, 日常招呼时称作 Sir Henry, 不称作 Sir Smith〕. ④〔美口〕不分性别,用以强调肯定或否定〔如 *Yes, sir; No, sir*〕. ⑤〔谑〕喂,老兄!〔挖苦或申斥时用〕. ⑥〔谑〕大人, 先生〔如 ~ critic 评论先生. S- Oracle 神示老爷〕. *Good morning, ~.* 先生,早. *Get out, ~!* 喂! 出去!〔挖苦话〕. *Will you be quiet, ~!* 喂,老兄,静一点!〔挖苦话〕. — *vt.* 称…为先生. *Don't ~ me quite so much.* 别那样先生先生的叫我.

sir·car, sir·kar [ˈsəːkə] *n.* 〔印度英语〕①政府; 政府首脑. ②主人,老爷. ③总管; 帐房先生.

sir·dar [ˈsəːdɑː] *n.* ①(印度、巴基斯坦、阿富汗等的)首长,贵族,首领. ②高级军官,将军; (旧时埃及军队中的英国)总司令. ③(印度的)达官贵人,居重要职位的人.

sire [ˈsaiə] *n.* ①〔古〕陛下 = Your majesty ②〔诗〕父; (男性) 祖先. ③(四足哺乳动物的) 种畜〔尤指种马〕. — *vt.* ①(指种马等雄性动物的)生殖. ②产生; 创作, 创办. *~d by* …种的.

Siree [səːˈriː] *n.* = sirree.

si·ren [ˈsaiərin] *n.* ①〔或 S-〕【希神】莎琳〔传说中半人半鸟的海妖, 常用歌声诱惑过路的航海者而使航船触礁身死〕. ②歌声美妙的女歌手. ③妖妇, 妖女; 诱惑者〔物〕. ④【动】土鳗属两栖动物; 海牛目动物. ⑤汽笛,警报器. *an air-raid ~* 空袭警报器. *an ambulance (a fire) ~* 救护(救火)车上的警报器. *a ~ bomb* 啸声(炸)弹. *a ~ disk* 验音盘. — *a.* 海妖一样的,诱惑的,迷人的. — *vi.* (警车、救火车等)响着警报器驱车前进.

si·re·ni·an [saiəˈriːniən] *n., a.*【动】海牛目动物(的).

si·ri·a·sis [siˈraiəsis] *n.*【医】①日射病, 中暑. ②日光浴.

Sir·i·us [ˈsiriəs] *n.*【天】天狼星.

sir·loin [ˈsəːlɔin] *n.* 牛的上腰部肉,牛腰肉.

si·roc·co [siˈrɔkəu] *n.* *(pl. ~s)* ①【气】西洛可风〔欧洲南部从利比亚沙漠吹来的一种常带沙尘, 间或带雨的热风〕. ②(泛指从炎热或干旱地区吹来的)热风.

sir·ra(h) [ˈsirə] *n.* 〔古〕你这家伙, 小子, 老兄〔气愤时对男人的轻蔑称呼语〕.

sir·ree [səˈriː] *n.* 〔美口〕= sir 〔用在 "yes" 或 "no" 后,加重语气〕.

sir-rev·er·ence [ˌsəːˈrevərəns] *int.* 〔废〕请原谅; 抱歉.

sir·up [ˈsirəp] *n.* = syrup.

sir·vent(es) [siəˈvent; F. sirˈvɑːŋt] *n.* *(pl. -ventes* [-ˈvents; F. sirˈvɑ̃t]*)* 感兴诗〔十二、十三世纪法国普洛温斯抒情诗的一种,常具讽刺性〕.

sis [sis] *n.* 〔美口〕= sister.

sis·al [ˈsisəl] *n.* ①【植】〔中美〕西沙尔龙舌兰. ②西沙尔麻, 波尔麻〔用于制绳、麻袋布等,又叫 ~ grass, ~ hemp〕.

sis·kin [ˈsiskin] *n.*【鸟】金翅雀.

Sis·ley [ˈsisli] *n.* 西斯利〔姓氏〕.

sis·si·fied [ˈsisiˌfaid] *a.* 〔口〕= sissy.

sis·soo [ˈsisuː] *n.*【植】印度黄檀.

sis·sy [ˈsisi] *n.*〔美〕①〔口〕女子气的男孩或男子. ②懦弱的人,胆小鬼. ③姊妹, 少女, ④〔俚〕搞同性爱的人. ~ *beer*〔美〕(酒精成分在 3.2%以下的)淡啤酒. — *a.*〔美〕女人似的,柔弱的. **-ish** *a.*

sister [ˈsistə] *n.* ①姊,妹. ②情同手足的女子; 女同事,女同志,女同学,女社友,女会友. ③〔英〕护士长; (一般)护士. ④【天主】修女. ⑤〔喻〕姊妹; 同类的事物⑥(同一母体出生的)同胞雌性动物. *a full [whole] ~* 同胞姊妹. *a half ~* 异父〔母〕姊妹. *elder [younger] ~* 姊姊〔妹妹〕. ~ *arts* (具有某种共同点的) 姊妹艺术. ~ *ships* (同型的) 姊妹船, 姊妹舰. *Fatal S-s [S-s three, three S-s]*【希神、罗神】命运三女神. *S- of Mercy* 慈善姐妹会〔尤指 1827 年创建于都柏林教育慈善组织〕. ***be like ~s*** 象姊妹一样, 非常亲密. ***waste and its ~ want*** 浪费及其同胎姊妹——匮乏. — *a.*姐妹的; 同类(型)的. — *vt.* 如姐妹般相待. **~-german** *n. (pl. ~s-german)* 同胞姊妹, 同父母的姐妹. ~ **hood** *n.* 姊妹关系; 妇女团体, 妇女会; 护士长的职务. ~ **hook**【机】双抱钩. **~-in-law** [ˈsistərinlɔː] *n.* *(pl. sisters-)*〔配偶的姊妹〕姑, 姨; 嫂, 弟媳. ~ **uterine** (同母异父的)姐妹. **-ly** *a.* 姊妹般的.

sis·tern *n.* 〔*pl.*〕〔美方〕= sisters.

Sis·tine [ˈsistain] *a.* 罗马教皇西斯廷 (特指 Sixtus 四世或五世)的. ~ **Chapel** (罗马教廷中的主要教堂) 西斯廷教堂. ~ **Madonna** (意大利画家 Raphael 画的) 西斯廷圣母像. ~ **Vulgate** (教皇 Sixtus 五世时代改订的)拉丁语译本圣经.

sis·troid [ˈsistrɔid] *a.*【数】凸边角的.

sis·trum [ˈsistrəm], *n.* *(pl. -trum, -tra* [-trə]*)* 铁摇子〔古埃及祭祀司繁殖女神爱希丝 *(Isis)* 时使用〕.

Sis·y·phe·an [ˌsisiˈfi(ː)ən] *a.* 象西昔孚斯 (Sisyphus) 的；徒劳无益的。

Sis·y·phus [ˈsisifəs] *n.*【希神】西昔孚斯〔希腊古时国王，因作恶多端，死后堕入地狱，被罚推石上山，但推上又滚下，永远如此，劳苦无已〕。*the stone of* ～ 徒劳。

sit [sit] *v.* ***(sat*** [sæt]，〔古〕***sate*** [sæt, seit]; ***sat*** [sæt]***)*** *vi.* ①坐，就座。②(鸟等) 栖息，憩息，进窝；(鸡等) 伏窝，孵蛋。③(房屋等) 座落，位于；【军】扎营，驻扎。④(衣服) 合身，适合。⑤(风)来自，吹来。⑥就职，做议员［委员］；出席。⑦以某一姿势坐定让人画肖像［照相］；充当模特儿。⑧(议会、法庭等)开会，开庭。⑨应试 *(for)*。⑩临时替人照看 (婴孩)。⑪被搁置不用 *The coat does not* ～ *properly across the shoulders.* 上衣不怎样合身。*His principles* ～ *loosely on him.* 他的原则对己没有约束力。*The law court will* ～ *to-day.* 法院今天要开庭了。— *vt.* ①〔～ oneself〕使坐，使就座。②骑(马)；(用身体或桨) 调平 (小船)。③(车辆等)可供…坐。④(鸡等)孵(卵)。***make sb.*** ～ ***up***〔俚〕使大吃一惊；虐待，虐使，折磨。～ ***at home*** 闲居家中。～ ***at one's feet*** 师事(某人)，拜某人为师。～ ***back*** 松劲休息；不活动。～ ***by*** 袖手旁观。～ ***down*** 坐下；住定；占有；(坐下来)开始工作(谈判等)；结束发言；(飞机等)降落。～ ***down before*** *(a place)*【军】扎营围攻(某地)。～ ***down hard (up) on***〔美俚〕断然反对，痛斥，痛骂。～ ***down under*** 温顺地忍受(侮辱等)。～ ***down with*** 只好满足于，不得不忍受。～ ***for*** ①坐着〔让人画肖像或照相〕。②〔英〕参加(学位、奖学金等)考试；作…候选人 ～ ***heavy on*** 重压；(食物)不消化。～ ***her***〔美〕骑稳(牛、马)不要被摔下。～ ***in***〔美〕参加；列席；出席；代理。～ ***in judgement on*** 审判，裁判；(高高在上地)批评，评断。～ ***in parliament*** 当议员。～ ***lightly on*** (食物等) 不滞胃，不使人难受。～ ***like a bump on a log.***〔美〕饱食终日无所用心，整天不做事，木头木脑。～ ***loosely on*** (主义等) 不受人注意。～ ***on*** ①审理(案件等)；调查。②〔俚〕压制，责备 (*He wants sitting on.* 那个家伙得骂一顿才行)。～ ***on a committee*** 充当(委员会的)委员。～ ***on one's hands*** 不鼓掌赞许；(应行动时)袖手旁观。～ ***on one's knees*** 跪下。～ ***on the bench*** 做法官。～ ***on two chairs*** 脚踏两只船。～ ***out*** ①坐一旁不加入(跳舞比赛等)。②(在宴会中)坐到(众人)走完；坐到(戏)完。～ ***over*** *(a player)*【运】(有利地)排在某选手之后；(打桥牌时)坐在某人左边占有利地位。～ ***through*** = ～ out (～ *through a long sermon* 耐心听完一篇冗长的说教)。～ ***tight*** ①屹然不动；稳守不动。②固执己见；坚持自己的主张。③〔美〕耐心等候。～ ***to*** 坐着给…画像［拍照］。～ ***under*** 听…的训导。～ ***up*** ①坐起来；(狗)用后脚站起。②熬夜。③端坐，坐正。④吓一跳；奋起(～ *up all night* 通夜不睡。～ *up at work* 做夜工。～ *up late at night* 熬到深夜)。～ ***up and take notice***〔英口〕(突然)引起兴趣来；〔美俚〕发觉，注意起来，怀疑起来。～ ***upon*** = ～ on. ～ ***well on*** (衣服)很合身。～**-in** 占座抗议，静坐示威。～ **up,** ～**-up**【运】仰卧起坐。

si·tar [siˈtɑː] *n.* 西塔尔琴〔印度的一种六弦乐器〕。**-ist** *n.* 西塔尔琴演奏者。

sit·come [ˈsitkʌm] *n.* (广播、电视中的) 系列幽默剧 (= situation comedy)。

sit-down (strike) [ˈsitdaun] *n.*〔美〕静坐罢工。**-er** *n.*

site [sait] *n.* ①地点，位置，地基。②场所，现场。③遗址。*construction* ～ 建筑工地。*firing [launching]* ～ (火箭等)发射场。*historic* ～*s* 历史遗址。*nuclear test* ～ 核试验场。*the* ～ *of a battle* 战场。— *vt.* 给与位置，为…选定地点；安放；使坐落。**-ed** [ˈsaitid] *a.* 地点［位置］…的 (*a well-*～ *factory* 地点好的工厂)。

sith [siθ] *ad., conj., prep.*〔古〕= since.

sitio-, sito- *comb. f.* 表示"食物"：*sito*logy.

si·tol·o·gy [saiˈtɔlədʒi] *n.* 营养学。

si·to·pho·bia [ˌsaitəˈfəubjə] *n.*【医】恐食症。

si·tos·ter·ol [saiˈtɔstərəul, -rɔːl] *n.*【化】谷甾醇。

sit·ten [ˈsitn]，【废】sit 的过去分词。

sit·ter [ˈsitə] *n.* ①坐的人；坐着给人画像［照相］的人，模特儿。②孵卵鸡。③栖息不动［容易命中］猎物；胡里胡涂命中的射击；容易的工作。④〔美口〕临时替人照看孩子的人。

sit·ting [ˈsitiŋ] *n.* ①坐，就座，就席，坐的姿势；充当(绘画［摄影］的)模特儿。②开会，开庭；会期，开庭期间。③(坐)一次，一气，一股劲儿。④孵卵；孵卵数；孵卵期。*Can you give me six* ～*s?* 你可以让我画六次吗？*The* ～ *is open [is called to order].* 现在开会了。*an opening [a final]* ～ 开幕［闭幕］会。— *a.* ①坐着的，就座的。②孵卵中的(雌鸟)。③易于命中的。④租占着田地［房屋］的。***at a [one]*** ～ 一气，一口气，一下子。***be holding a*** ～ 在开会。***to be*** ～ 开会。～ **duck**〔美〕易于命中［易受攻击］的目标；容易上钩的对象。～ **room** 起居室。～ **pretty**〔美俚〕占着良好位置。～ **tenant** 现在租占着土地［房屋］的租户。

sit·u·ate [ˈsitjueit] *a.*〔古〕= situated. — *vt.* 使某设施等位于［坐落］某地，确定某事发生于某地某时 *(in, at, on)*。使人处于某境地〔多用被动结构，见下条〕。～ *a factory in a suitable site* 把工厂建在一个适中的地点。*Their apartments were* ～*d on the first floor.* 他们的住房在二楼。*He can't* ～ *his recollection in any place or at any time.* 他想不起在什么地方，也想不起在什么时间了。

sit·u·at·ed [ˈsitjueitid] *a.* ①位于…的，坐落在…的 *(at; on)*。②处于…地位［境遇、状态］的。*a pleasantly* ～ *house* 一所地址优美的住宅。*be awkwardly* ～ 处于困难的地位，处境尴尬。*thus* ～ 在这种状况下。

sit·u·a·tion [ˌsitjuˈeiʃən] *n.* ①(房屋建筑等的)地点，位置；场所。②形势，局面；情况，关系。③(戏剧等的)紧张场面，危急关头。④境遇，处境；在一定时间内作用于生物的内外总刺激。⑤【心】情境。⑥(特指仆役等的) 职业，职位，地位，工作。⑦〔古〕健康状况。*the close quarter* ～ (同航向或同速度二船间的) 最小安全距离。*the domestic* ～ 国内形势。*the international* ～ 国际形势。*the current* ～ 时局。*the political* ～ 政局。*the actual* ～ *at a given time and place* 当时当地的实际情况。*a difficult* ～ 困难处境。*a thrilling [tense]* ～ 紧张的场面。*cope [do] with the* ～ 应付局势，应付当前的情况。*hold a* ～ 有职业。*look for a* ～ 找事，谋职。*save the* ～ 挽回局势，解救危局。*throw up a* ～ 放弃职位。～ **comedy**【剧】(广播、电视中的)系列幽默剧。～ **ethics** 境遇伦理学。～**s vacant [wanted]** 事求人［人求事］〔报纸上的招聘栏标题〕。**-al** *a.* **-al·ly** *ad.* **-ism** *n.*【心】情境决定行为论。

si·tus [ˈsaitəs] *n.* ①地点，部位〔尤指动植物器官生来的原位置〕。②〔军〕位置。*analysis* ～【数】拓朴(学)。

Sit·well [ˈsitwəl] *n.* 西特韦尔〔姓氏〕。

Sitz bath [ˈsitsbɑːθ, ˈzits-]【医】坐浴(疗法)；坐浴盆。

sitz·krieg [ˈzitskriːk] *n.*〔G.〕对峙战，胶着战〔源出第二次世界大战德国在西部战线采取的非进攻性的战术〕。

sitz·mark [ˈsitsˌmɑːk, ˈzits-] *n.* 滑雪者摔跤后在雪地上留下的痕迹。

Si·va [ˈsivə, ˈsiːvə] *n.* 湿婆〔印度教三个主神之一，破坏神〕。**-ism** *n.* 湿婆教。**-is·tic** *a.* 湿婆似的；湿婆教的。**-ite** ① *n.* 湿婆教徒。②湿婆教的。

Si·van [siːˈvɑːn, ˈsivən] *n.* (犹太历)九月。

Si·vyer [ˈsiviə] *n.* 西维尔〔姓氏〕。

SIW = self-inflicted wound 自伤〔尤指为逃避兵役等的自伤〕。

si·wash [siˈwɔʃ], *n.* ①(阿拉斯加、西北加拿大的)锡沃斯族印第安人。②阿拉斯加狗。③〔S-〕规模小的内地蹩脚大学。④〔美俚〕印第安人；〔蔑〕西部的人。

six [siks] *num.* (基数)六；第六(页章等)。—*n.* ①六个人［物］。②六人一组；由六个单位组成的东西；六个汽缸的发动机[汽车]. ③六的记号. ④六点钟. ⑤六岁. ⑥〔英〕六便士; 六先令; 六点的纸牌, (骰子的)六点. ⑦〔*pl.*〕一磅重六支装的蜡烛;六分利公债;(手套、鞋子的)六号. ~ *and* ~ 六先令六便士. *two and* ~ 二先令六便士. ~ *and eight (pence)* 六先令八便士〔英国以前付给律师的一般报酬〕. *It is* ~ *of one and half-a-dozen of the other.* 半斤八两; 难兄难弟. ~ *feet above contradiction* 〔美〕傲慢的. *a* ~ *monther* 〔美剧〕定期半年的契约. ~ *ways to [for] Sunday* 〔美俚〕在许多方面;完全,彻底. ***at* ~*es and sevens*** 乱七八糟; 意见不一致. ~ ***to one*** 六比一;优劣悬殊. **~-bits**〔美〕0.75 美元. **~-by**〔美俚〕大卡车. **~-by-six** 〔美军俚〕六轮卡车. ~ **chamber** 六响枪. **~-fold** *a., ad.* 六倍的,六重的,六折的; 成六倍; 成六重. **~-footer** 〔口〕身长六英尺的人; 六英尺长的东西. **~-gun**〔美〕六响枪. ~**mo** *n.* (纸张)六开. ~ **o** ~ 霉毒特效药六〇六 (=arsphenamine). **~-pack** *n.* 六瓶[六罐头]装的食品纸匣. ~**pence**〔英〕六便士 (银币); 微不足道的东西 (*It doesn't matter* ~*pence.* 这没什么关系. *I don't care(a)* ~*pence about it.* 这事我一点儿也不在乎. *the same old* ~*pence* 老笨蛋). ~**penny** *a.* 〔英〕六便士的; 便宜的, 不值钱的. ~**penny nail** 三英寸半长的钉子. ~**pennyworth**〔英〕价格六便士的东西; 六便士的数量. ~ **score** *n., a.* 一百二十. **~-shooter** 〔俚〕六响枪. **-er**【板球】(得)六分(的一)打.

sixte [sikst] *n.*【剑术】第六个招架法.

six·teen [ˈsiksˈtiːn] *num.* (基数)十六; 第十六〔表示章、页等次第时用于该词的后面〕. —*n.* ①十六个人[物]. ②十六的记号. ③【印】十六开. ④十六岁; 十六点钟. *in* ~*s*【印】以十六开. *in* ~ *sixties* 在十七世纪的六十年代[略作 in 1660's].

six·teen·mo [siksˈtiːnməu] *n.* *(pl.* ~*s)* = sextodecimo.

six·teenth [ˈsiksˈtiːnθ] *num.* (序数)第十六(的), 十六号(的); 十六分之一(的)〔常冠于所限定的词之前〕. — *n.* ①(月的) 第十六日. ②【乐】十六分音符. ③十六分之一. *three* ~*s* 十六分之三. *the* ~ 十六号.

sixth [siksθ] *num.* 第六(的), 六号(的); 六分之一(的). — *n.* ①(月的)第六日. ②【乐】六度音程,六度和音; 第六音. ③六年级. ④六分之一. *the* ~ *of April* 四月六日. *the* ~ *hour* 正午. ~ ***form***〔英〕(高中) 六年级. ***~-former*** 六年级学生. ~ ***sense*** 第六官能, 直觉. **-ly** *ad.*

six·ti·eth [ˈsikstiiθ] *num.* 第六十(的), 六十号(的); 六十分之一(的).

Six·tine [ˈsikstiːn, -tin], *a.* = sistine.

six·ty [ˈsiksti] *num.* (基数)六十, 第六十. — *n.* ①六十个人[物]. ②六十镑. ③六十的记号. ④六十岁;〔*pl.*〕六十到六十九岁的时期. ⑤〔*pl.*〕(世纪的)六十年代. ***a [one]*** ~ 六十分之一. ***in eighteen sixties*** 在十九世纪六十年代[略作 in 1860's]. ***in eighteen*** ~ 在 1860 年〔略 in 1860〕. ***in the sixties*** 六十多岁(的); 在六十年代. ***like*** ~〔美俚〕飞快地,剧烈地,大大地 (*run like* ~ 飞跑. *ache like* ~ 剧痛). **~-four-mo** *n.* 64 开的纸; 64 开本. **~-four dollar question** 〔美俚〕重大问题,难题.

siz·a·ble [ˈsaizəbl] *a.* 相当大的,大的. **-ness** *n.* **-a·bly** *ad.*

siz·ar[1] [ˈsaizə] *n.* (剑桥等大学的)减费生, 靠服侍其他学生来津贴学费的学生.

size[1] [saiz] *n.* ①大小,尺寸; 规模; 身材. ②(鞋帽等的)尺码, 号; (纸张的)开. ③巨大, 大量; 相当大的份量. ④〔口〕实情,真相. ⑤(人的)能力, 才干, 身价; (物的)质量,特性. ⑥量珠尺, 珍珠筛. ⑦〔古〕(饭食、酒类的)定量;份饭. *full [natural, real]* ~ 如实物大. *life* ~ 如真人一般大[指雕象等]. *a* ~ *seven hat* 七(号)大的帽子. *What* ~ *do you take in gloves?* 您手套尺码要多大? *That's about the* ~ *of it.* 〔口〕实际情况大致就那么样. *a man of a considerable* ~ 相当有才干的人. ***be of a*** ~ 大小相同. ***cut down to*** ~ 把重要性[威望等]降至合适的程度,还…的本来面目. ***for*** ~ 试试尺码,试试是否合适; 按不同尺码. ***of all*** ~***s*** 大小尺码齐全. ***be (half, twice) the*** ~ ***of*** 如…的(一半,一倍)大小. ***of some*** ~ 相当大. ~ ***and strength*** 大小强弱. ***take the*** ~ ***of*** 量…的尺寸. — *vt.* ①依大小排列; 量大小; 测定大小;【军】量身段,依身长排列. ②筛分,分粒. ③按规定尺寸制作; 使…大小合适. — *vi.* ①(在大小、质量等方面)相同, 不相上下 (*up to, up with*). ②领取定食. ~ *a company* 按身段高低排列一连士兵. ~ ***down*** 由大到小排列. ~ ***up*** 够标准, 合尺寸; 估量, 测量;〔口〕品评, 鉴定(人物等). ~ **stick** (鞋匠用的)量脚尺. **~-up** 估量,估计.

size[2] [saiz] *n.* (用面粉、树胶、树脂等配制的)胶料,浆糊〔用于给纸张、皮革、织物等浆洗上光〕. — *vt.* 给…上胶,对…上浆. *a sizing machine* 浆纱机.

size·a·ble [ˈsaizəbl] *a.* = sizable.

(-)sized [saizd] *a.* 〔构成复合词〕①有…大小的,…大小的,…号的,…开的. ②依据大小排列的. *small-*~ 小型的,小号的. *medium-*~ 中等大小的, 中型的, 中号的.

siz·er [ˈsaizə] *n.* ①分粒器,整粒器; 大小分档拣理器. ②〔英俚〕极大的东西. ③【化】上胶器,填料器. *an egg* ~ 鸡蛋拣理器.

siz·ing [ˈsaiziŋ] *n.* 胶料; 填料; 上胶,上浆.

siz·y [ˈsaizi] *a.* 胶水的,浆糊的; 胶水[浆糊]般的; 胶质的; 粘性的.

sizz [siz] *n.* 咝咝声. *vt., vi.* (使)发咝咝声.

siz·zle [ˈsizl] *vi.* ①〔口〕(油炸时)嘘嘘地响, 嗞嗞响. ②表现喜人,进行顺利. ③〔口〕闷热得要命. ④非常愤怒. *The oil lamp* ~*d softly on his table.* 油灯在他桌上发出轻微的嗞嗞声. *Sales immediately began to* ~. 销售情况立即出现喜人景象. —*vt.* ①把…烧得嗞嗞响; 烧之使焦. ②恶言相骂. *They used to* ~ *each other.* 他们过去常常互相谩骂. — *n.* (油炸鱼等时发出的)嘘嘘声, 嗞嗞声.

siz·zard [ˈsizə] *n.* 〔美口〕(夏季的)闷热.

siz·zler [ˈsizlə] *n.* 〔口〕嗞嗞发烫的东西,大热天.

s.j. = *sub judice* 【法】审理中的; 在考虑中的 (〔L.〕= under consideration).

SJ = Society of Jesus.

sjam·bok [ˈʃæmbɔk] *n., vt.* 〔南非〕犀[河马]皮鞭; 用犀皮鞭打.

SJC = Supreme Judicial Court 〔美〕最高法院.

SJD = 〔L.〕 *Scientiae Juridicae Doctor* 法理学博士 (= Doctor of Juridical Science).

skag [skæg] *n.* 〔美俚〕烟丝; 香烟(头); 海洛因.

Skag·er·ra(c)k [ˈskægəræk] *n.* (丹麦北端的)斯卡格拉克海峡.

skald [skɔːld] *n.* 古代北欧的诗人. = scald.

skate[1] [skeit] *n.* ①(刃式)冰鞋 (= ice ~); (轮式)溜冰鞋 (= roll ~). ②滑冰,溜冰. ③〔美俚〕足够喝醉的酒量. ***have a*** ~ ***on*** 〔美俚〕喝醉. — *vi.* ①滑冰, 溜冰; 飞跑. ②掠过, 触及 (*over*). ~ ***over [on] thin ice*** 处理难题; 巧妙地处理难局.

skate[2] [skeit, skit] *n.*【动】鳐鱼.

skate[3] [skeit] *n.* ①〔美俚〕老马,瘦马. ②人,家伙. *cheap* ~ 〔美〕吝啬鬼; 心肠卑鄙的人. *good* ~ 讨人喜欢的人.

skate·board [ˈskeitˌbɔːd] *n.* 滑板〔小长方木板两端有轮,儿童用以在斜坡上滑着玩的玩具〕. —*vi.* ***(-boarded, -board·ing)*** 作滑板运动, 滑滑板. **-er** *n.* 玩滑板的人.

skat·er [ˈskeitə] *n.* 滑冰的人,溜冰的人.

skat·ing [ˈskeitiŋ] *n.* 滑冰, 溜冰; ~ **rink** 滑冰场; 溜冰场.

skat·ole [ˈskætəul] *n.*【化】粪臭素.

ske·an [skiːn] *n.* (古苏格兰和爱尔兰人的)双刃短剑.

Skeat [skiːt] *n.* ①斯基特〔姓氏〕. ②**Walter William** ~

沃尔特·威廉·斯基特〔1835—1912,英国语言学家〕.

ske·dad·dle [skiˈdædl] *vi.* 〔口〕仓惶逃走,匆忙离去. —*n.* 溃逃,逃走.

skee [ʃiː, skiː] *n., vi.* = ski.

skee·sicks [ˈskiːziks] *n. pl.* 〔美俚〕恶棍,流氓;〔对孩子的爱称〕小鬼,小坏蛋.

skeet [skiːt] *n.* 飞靶射击,打飞靶〔从不同角度射击抛掷的泥鸽或泥盘〕. **-er** *n.* 飞靶射击者.

skeet·er [ˈskiːtə] *n.* ①〔美俚〕蚊子. ②小型冰上滑行船.

skeg [skeg] *n.*【船】导流尾鳍.

skein [skein] *n.* ①(丝、纱、线等的)(一)束,(一)绞;绞纱,绞丝. ②(野禽的)一群. ③纠缠,混乱(的一团). *the ravelled [tangled]* ~ 错综复杂(的一团).

skel·e·tal [ˈskelitl] *a.* 骨胳的,骸骨的. **-ly** *adv.*

skel·e·ton [ˈskelitən] *n.* ①骨胳,骷髅;(房屋、伞、扇子等的)骨架;残骸;(叶子的)脉络,筋. ②骨瘦如柴的人〔动物〕. ③梗概,轮廓,概略. ④骨干,基干;【军】(官多兵少的)基干团〔连〕;因战斗伤亡以致缺额极多的部队〔= ~ company, ~ regiment〕. ⑤不可外扬的丑事. *a mere [walking]* ~ 瘦得象骷髅一样的人. *a* ~ *structure* 骨架,结构. — *a.* ①骨胳的. ②只剩骨架的;瘦得皮包骨头的. ③概括的. *a* ~ *army* 基干部队;官多兵少的部队. *a ~-drill* 假想演习. *a* ~ *hand* 青筋暴起的手. ***be reduced to a*** ~ (因病)瘦得象骷髅,瘦得只剩一把骨头. ***be worn to a*** ~ (因生活困苦)瘦得象骷髅. ***family*** ~ = ~ ***in the cupboard [closet, house]*** (不可外扬的)家丑. ~ ***at the feast [banquet]*** 扫兴的东西. ~ **crew**【海】基干船员. ~ **crystals** 骸晶. ~ **drawing**【工】草图,骨架图. ~ **face** 字体细小的铅字. ~ **key** (可以开各种锁的)万能钥匙.

skel·e·ton·ize [ˈskelitənaiz] *vt.* ①使成骨胳,使成骷髅. ②把…节略成为概要. ③大量裁减;把…编成基干部队. ~ *a news story* 节略一篇新闻报导. ~ *a regiment* 编成基干团. ~ *a leaf* 把叶子弄成脉络. — *vi.* ①节略,缩略. ②瘦得不象人样.

skel·lum [ˈskeləm] *n.* 〔古〕〔Scot.〕恶棍;无赖;流氓.

skelp [skelp] *vt.* 〔英方〕打,掌击. — *vi.* 赶快走;催促;硬挤过去. — *n.* 〔英方〕一击,一巴掌.

Skel·ton [ˈskeltn] *n.* 斯克尔顿〔姓氏〕.

skene [skiːn] *n.* = skean.

skep [skep] *n.* ①柳条筐(篮). ②(用草辫或柳条编的)蜜蜂箱.

skep·sis [ˈskepsis] *n.* 〔Am.〕= scepsis.

skep·tic(al) [ˈskeptik, -kəl] 〔Am.〕= sceptic(al). **-ly** *ad.*

skep·ti·cism [ˈskeptisizəm]〔Am.〕= scepticism.

sker·ry [ˈskeri] *n.* ***(pl. -ries)*** 〔Scot.〕岩岛,(岩)礁.

sketch [sketʃ] *n.* ①草图,粗样,略图;素描,速写;草稿. ②概略,大意,大要,纲领. ③短篇作品,小品文〔如特写、随笔、见闻录等〕. ④(滑稽)短剧;独幕剧;短曲、短小器乐曲〔尤指钢琴曲〕. ⑤滑稽;丑态. *I never saw such a* ~. 从来没有见过这种丑态. ***make a*** ~ 速写,画草图. ~ ***map*** 草图,略图,示意地图. — *vt.* ①给…绘草图;给…作速写. ②草拟,拟订;记述…的概要,说出…的大意. — *vi.* 绘草图,作速写. ~ ***(out) a plan [scheme]*** 草拟计划. ~ **block** *n.* 速写素描簿. ~ **book** *n.* 速写簿;小品文集,短文集,随笔集.

sketch·y [ˈsketʃi] *a.* ①速写的,略图似的. ②粗略的,简略的;粗枝大叶的. ③未完成的,不完全的;贫乏的,肤浅的. **-i·ly** *ad.* **-i·ness** *n.*

skew [skjuː] *vi.* ①走偏,斜进;歪斜. ②斜视(*at*). —*vt.* ①使歪斜,使偏. ②曲解,歪曲. *-ed statistical data* 歪曲的统计资料. —*a.* ①斜的,歪的,偏的;弯曲的. ②误用的,曲解的. ③【数】敧斜的;挠的;非对称的. *a* ~ *bridge* 斜桥. *a* ~ *curve* 挠曲线,空间曲线. ~ *lines*【物】敧斜(直)线. *a* ~ *wheel* 歪轮. — *n.* ①歪斜,扭曲. ②【建】斜砌石;斜交;【机】歪轮;【统】敧斜. ***on the*** ~〔口〕歪斜地 (*wear one's hat on the* ~ 歪戴帽子). ~ **back**【建】拱座,底座,斜块. **~-bald** *a.* 特指马白色与他色夹杂的. ~ **polygon** 挠多边形. **-ness** 偏斜,不对称;【统】偏斜度.

skew·er [ˈskjuə] *n.* ①串肉扦,烤肉叉;扦状物,叉状物. ②〔谑〕剑,刀. ③扣针;卷线针. — *vt.* 用串肉扦串起来.

ski [ʃiː, ski] *n.* ***(pl. ~(s))*** ①滑雪板〔鞋,雪橇〕. ②(导弹的)推进装置. ③滑水橇 (= water ~). — *vi.* ***(~ed, ~'d)*** 滑雪;坐雪橇. ~ **bob** 单人滑雪车. ~ **boot** 滑雪靴. ~ **joring** 由马或车辆拖曳的滑雪运动. ~ **jump** 飞跃滑雪;飞跃滑雪助滑道. ~ **lift** (把滑雪者送上高坡的)滑雪运送机. ~ **meister** [ˈskiˌmaistə] 滑雪能手,职业滑雪运动员;滑雪教练员. ~ **mobile** 履带式雪上汽车. ~ **pants** 滑雪裤. **~-plane** (能在雪地上降落的)雪上飞机. ~ **run** 滑雪坡,滑雪道. ~ **stick [pole]** 滑雪杖. ~ **suit** 滑雪服. ~ **tow** = ~ lift. ~ **troops** 滑雪部队.

ski·a·gram [ˈskaiəgræm] = skiagram.

ski·a·graph [ˈskaiəgrɑːf] = sciagraph.

ski·ag·ra·phy [skaiˈægrəfi] = sciagraphy.

ski·a·scope [ˈskaiəˌskəup] *n.*【医】爱克斯射线透视镜;视网膜镜.

ski·as·co·py [skaiˈæskəpi] *n.*【医】爱克斯射线透视检查法;视网膜镜检法.

ski·a·tron [sˈkaiətrɔn] *n.*【电】暗迹管.

skib·by [ˈskibi] *n.* 〔美蔑〕日本佬;东方人.

skid [skid] *n.* ①制动器,刹车(= ~-pan). ②(搬移重物用的)滑动垫木,滑道. ③(支承重物的)低平台,垫木. ④(飞机的)起落橇,滑橇;【海】(上下货物时保护船舷的)垫板,护舷木. ⑤(车辆)高速行驶时或在结冰的道上打滑,溜滑;〔*pl.* 喻〕下坡路. *hit the ~s* 〔美俚〕走下坡路;变弱;被打败. *put the ~s under* 〔美俚〕使失败,使走下坡路;摆脱,除去. ***on the ~s*** 〔美俚〕快要失败〔打败〕;快要被解雇;正在衰落. — *vi.* ①(车辆)刹着车滑行,打滑;滑向一侧. ②在滑材上拖;刹车. ③【空】(飞机转弯时)外滑;④急剧下降. ⑤〔美俚〕败北. *skidding dog*【林】曳运铁钉. — *vt.* ①用刹车刹住;使减慢. ②用垫木支承;用滑材拖. ③使滑行〔打滑〕. ~ **fin** (飞机的)翼上垂直面. **~-fin antenna**【无】附翼天线,翅形天线. ~ **pad** 〔美〕试车场. ~ **road** ①木材滑送道. ②城镇中伐木工人经常出入的地区. ③= ~ row. ~ **row** (城市中流浪汉、酒鬼等经常出入的)地区〔多小酒店、小旅店和职业介绍所等〕.

skid·dy [ˈskidi] *a.* 溜滑(面)的.

ski·doo [skiˈduː] *vi.* 〔美俚〕出去! 走开!

skid·proof [ˈskidˌpruːf] *a.* 防滑的,抗滑的.

ski·er [ˈʃiːə, ˈskiːə] *n.* 滑雪者.

skiff [skif] *n.* 小艇,小船.

ski·ing [ˈʃiːiŋ, ˈskiːiŋ] *n.* 滑雪术,滑雪运动.

skil·ful [ˈskilfəl] *a.* = skillful.

skill[1] [skil] *n.* ①技巧,技艺,技能. ②本领;手艺,(专门)技术. ③巧妙,熟练. ④〔古〕知识,理解力,判断能力. *a specialized* ~ 专门技能. *basic ~s* 基本功. *have no ~ in* 没有…的技能. *knowledge and* ~ 知识和技能. *language ~s* 掌握语言的能力.

skill[2] [skil] *vi.* 〔古〕〔常用 it 为主语〕起作用;有助于;有影响. *It ~s not.* 这毫无用处;不起作用.

skilled [skild] *a.* ①= skillful *(in)*. ②需要技巧的;有技巧的. ~ *hands [workers]* 熟练工人. ~ *labour* 熟练劳动;技工;熟手(工人). ~ *in chemistry* 精于化学. ~ *in keeping accounts* 善于管理帐目.

skil·let [ˈskilit] *n.* ①〔英〕长柄(矮脚)小锅. ②〔美〕长柄平底锅 (= frying pan). ***put on the*** ~〔美〕挨骂,受责备.

skil·ley [ˈskili] *n.* 〔美俚〕= gravy.

skill·ful [ˈskilful] *a.* ①熟练的,灵巧的;擅长于 ***(at; in)***. ②制作精巧的. **-ly** *ad.* **-ness** *n.*

skil·ling [ˈskiliŋ] *n.* 斯吉林〔斯堪的纳维亚旧铜币和货币单位〕.

skil·ly [ˈskili] *n.* 〔英俚〕稀薄的麦片粥.

skim [skim] *vt.* ①撇取(牛奶等的)乳皮[奶油]; 撇去浮沫;【机】撇渣. ②使掠过,使擦过,使滑过. ③略读,快读. ④使蒙上一层薄膜. ~ *the cream (off milk)* 撇取奶油;〔喻〕提取精华. —*vi.* ①掠过,擦过. ②浏览,略读. ③结上薄的覆盖层; 涂上最后一层(漆、泥灰等). ④〔美俚〕瞒税,漏税. ~ ***it down***〔美俚〕我可不信! 别吹牛! — *a.* 撇去奶油的;用脱脂乳做的. — *n.* 撇去浮沫; 脱脂乳. ~ **gate** 撇渣口;除渣器. ~**milk** 脱脂乳.

skim·ble-scam·ble [ˈskimblˌskæmbl] *a.* 随口说的,杂乱无章的,互不关联的,毫无意义的.

skim·mer [ˈskimə] *n.* ①撇乳器;撇取浮沫的杓子,网杓,漏杓. ②马马虎虎阅读的人. ③【机】刮路机; 铲削器. ④蜻蜓;【鸟】撇水鸟. ⑤〔美〕帽子,平顶宽边草帽.

skim·ming [ˈskimiŋ] *n.* ①撇沫,撇取(奶油). ②〔*pl.*〕浮渣; 撇取的奶油;【化】蒸去轻油. ③(赌场的)抽头. ~ **dish** 撇取奶油的扁平盘子;平底快船.

skimp [skimp] *vt.* ①〔口〕马马虎虎做,敷衍了事. ②少给,克扣;一点一点地[吝啬地]给(食物、金钱等). — *vi.* 俭省,吝啬. ~ *and screw* 吝啬. — *a.* 少的,不足的.

skimp·ing·ly [ˈskimpiŋli] *ad.* 吝啬地,小气地.

skimp·y [ˈskimpi] *a.* ①吝啬的,小气的. ②勉强够数的;短缺的,不足的;不充分的,不够大的. ③马马虎虎的,敷衍了事的. **-i·ly** *ad.* **-i·ness** *n.*

skin[1] [skin] *n.* ①(人体的)皮,皮肤. ②〔口〕皮肉;肉体,性命. ③兽皮,(特指小牛、山羊等小动物的)皮革.【解】真皮. ④皮制品,(装酒等的)皮囊. ⑤(果实、葱等的)皮,壳; 奶皮. ⑥【海】(叠起来的)帆的上部; (船体的)外板,壳板. ⑦〔俚〕骗子;〔美口〕吝啬鬼,小气鬼. ⑧〔谑〕人,家伙;马,〔尤指〕瘦马. ⑨〔美俚〕〔*pl.*〕一套鼓〔尤指爵士乐队的〕. ⑩〔美俚〕一美元. *the true [inner]* ~ 真皮. *green [raw, undressed]* ~ 生皮. *clean ~s* 〔澳〕无烙印的野牛. *a bad old* ~〔俚〕老坏蛋. ***be in sb's*** ~ 变做某人 (*I would not be in your* ~. 我无论如何不愿意是你). ***be no ~ off sb's back [nose]***〔美口〕与某人无关;对某人没影响. ***by [with] the ~ of one's teeth***〔口〕好容易才,幸而. ***cast the*** ~ 脱皮. ***change one's*** ~ 改变性格、作风等; 改头换面,装出新的面貌. ***fly [jump, leap] out of one's*** ~ 惊喜若狂;大吃一惊. ***get off with a whole*** ~ 平安脱险,安然无恙. ***get under sb's*** ~ 抓住某人的心;使某人高兴[发怒,厌烦]. ***have a thick [thin]*** ~ 感觉迟钝[敏锐];面皮厚[薄]. ***in a bad*** ~〔俚〕情绪不好;发着脾气. ***in [with] a whole*** ~ 平安无事地. ***in one's*** ~〔谑〕一丝不挂地. ***save one's*** ~ 平安逃脱,未受损伤. ***~ and bone(s)***, (瘦得只剩)皮包骨. ***wet(ted) to the*** ~ 浑身湿透. ***wear next to the*** ~ 贴身穿着. — *vt.* ①剥…的皮;削…的皮; 使脱去贴身衣服;(拿皮)覆盖(伤口),使愈合 *(over)*; 擦伤(皮). ②〔口〕抢夺,骗取;(严厉)批评;责斥;〔美俚〕(比赛中)击败,胜过. ③〔口〕(用鞭)驱赶(牲口). *a skinned rabbit* 瘦鬼. *a skinned diamond*〔美〕不长草的棒球场. — *vi.* ①长皮 *(over)*; (伤口)愈合; 长出新皮. ②〔美俚〕(考试等时)作弊,夹带. ③〔口〕攀爬 *(up, down)*; 勉强挤过去 *(by, through)*. ④〔俚〕逃走,溜掉. ***keep one's eyes skinned***〔口〕把眼睛看牢,小心提防. ***~ a flea for its hide (and tallow)***〔口〕非常俭省. ***~ a flint*** 非常吝啬. ***~ a razor*** 做不可能的事情. ***~ a wicked eye***〔美〕不怀好意地盯着. ***~ alive***〔美俚〕活剥;折磨;严责;使大败. ***~ off*** 脱下(衣服等). ***~ out*** (猎狗)老远老远地乱跑. ***~ the [a] cat*** 两脚由双手间穿上去翻坐铁杆上. ***~ the lamb*** 全赢,满贯. ~-**bound** *a.* 皮绷得紧紧的;【医】患硬皮症的. ~-**deep** *a.* 只有一层皮深度的,肤浅的,皮毛的 (*Beauty is but ~-deep.* 美不过是外表罢了. *a ~-deep wound* 擦伤表皮). ~ **diving** (不穿潜水服而只带面罩、紧身衣、橡皮脚掌等的)潜泳,潜水. ~ **effect**【无】集肤效应. ~ **flick** 裸体黄色影片. ~**flint**〔美〕小气鬼,吝啬鬼. ~ **friction** 表皮摩擦. ~-**ful** 满皮囊,满肚子 (*have a ~-ful* 喝饱一肚皮酒). ~ **game**〔美俚〕欺骗. ~ **glue** 皮胶. ~ **grafting**【医】表皮移植; 植皮术. ~**head**〔美俚〕光头; 剃光头的人; 海军陆战队新兵; 短发青年暴徒. ~ **pop(ping)** 皮下注射麻醉毒品. ~ **test**【医】皮肤试验. ~**tight** *a.* 紧包着身子的.

skink [skiŋk] *n.*【动】石龙子科动物.

skinned [ˈskind] *a.*〔常构成复合词〕①有…皮的. ②没有草皮的. *a ~-racetrack* 无草皮的跑道. *dark-~* 有黝黑皮肤的.

skin·ner [ˈskinə] *n.* ①剥皮者,皮革工人. ②皮革商,皮毛商. ③〔俚〕骗子;〔美〕赶牲口的人.

skin·ny [ˈskini] *a.* ①皮的; 皮状的,皮质的. ②瘦削的,皮包骨的. ③不够大的; 不够好的; 低劣的. ④〔俚〕吝啬的. ~**dip** *n., vi.* 裸体游泳. **-ni·ly** *ad.* **-ni·ness** *n.*

skip[1] [skip] *vi.* ***(skip·ped, skip·ping)*** ①(小羊、小孩等)跳,蹦 *(about)*; 跳绳. ②跳来蹦去; 在表面上掠过. ③跳着读[看]; 跳过,略过,遗漏. ④很快地改变(话题、职业等) *(off; from)*;【乐】急转. ⑤回跳,弹回; 发跳弹射击. ⑥【机】不发火. ⑦〔口〕匆匆离开; 潜逃,逃亡. ⑧〔美〕(学校里)跳级. ~ *over [across] to Japan for a week* 去日本匆匆忙忙旅行一个星期. ~ *(over) the dull parts of a book* 跳过书中无聊的地方. ~ *from golf to theology* 从谈高尔夫球跳到谈神学. — *vt.* ①使跳; 跳过. ②跳读,跳看; 漏去,省去; 忽略. ③投掷(砖片等)使掠水跳飞. ④〔常以 it 为宾语〕〔口〕悄悄离开,匆匆离开(某地); 逃亡. ⑤(学校里)使跳级;不出席(学校、教堂、会议等). ~ *two days* 缺席两天. ***~ for joy*** 喜欢得跳. ***~ it***〔美俚〕忘掉,不再提起,别提了. ***~ one's bail***〔口〕保释中逃亡. ***~ the cinders***〔美〕顺着铁路走. — *n.* ①轻跳,跳跃. ②读漏,看漏,遗漏,省略; 漏看的东西,略过的东西. ③(计算机的)空白指令;【自】跳跃(进位). ④〔俚〕可以跳过不读的部分. ~ **band**【无】短波段. ~ **bombing**【军】跳弹轰炸〔一种超低空轰炸〕. ~ **distance**【无】越距,跳跃距离.

skip[2] [skip] *n.* (Dublin 大学的) 校役,校工.

skip[3] [skip] *n.* = skipper[1]. — *vi.* 充当队长[船长等].

skip[4] [skip] *n.*【矿】箕斗,翻斗车,斜井用四轮车,料车; 起重箱.

skip·jack [ˈskipdʒæk] *n.* ①趾高气扬的纨袴子弟; 暴发户. ②鲣,(各种)飞鱼; 叩头虫. ③跳跃玩具.

skip·per[1] [ˈskipə] *n.* ①(小商船、渔船等的)船长. ②(滚球,冰上溜石等游戏的)队长. ③〔空军俚〕机长,正驾驶员. *~'s daughters* 高白浪. — *vi.* 充当船长,充当队长.

skip·per[2] [ˈskipə] *n.* ①跳跃者. ②【鱼】飞鱼(类); 长颌竹刀鱼;【虫】叩头虫; 酪蛆; 水蝇; 弄(花)蝶.

skip·pet [ˈskipit] *n.* 封印护套.

skip·ping·ly [ˈskipiŋli] *ad.* 跳着,蹦着; 跳过,漏去,省去.

skip·ping-rope [ˈskipiŋrəup] *n.* 跳绳用的绳.

skirl [skə:l] *n.*〔Scot.〕尖锐声; 风笛声. —*vi.*(风笛)发尖锐声. — *vt.* 用风笛演奏.

skir·mish [ˈskə:miʃ] *n.* ①【军】小接触,小战斗,小冲突. ②小争论. ③〔美运〕比赛. — *vi.* ①进行小规模战斗; 进行小争论. ②搜索,侦察. *a ~(ing) line* 散兵线.

skir·mish·er [ˈskə:miʃə] *n.*【军】散兵.

skirr [skə:] *vi.*〔拟声〕飕飕地动(飞,跑等). — *vt.* ①走遍(某地)搜索. ②飞越过; 使掠过. — *n.* 飕飕声.

skirt [skə:t] *n.* ①女裙; (衣服的)裙,下摆. ②〔俚〕女人,姑娘. ③物件的裙状部分; 套筒; 缘,边,端; 马鞍两边下垂部分; 〔*pl.*〕郊区. ④(牛的)横膈膜. ⑤【建】壁脚板. *a divided* ~ (女人骑马用的)裙裤. *on the ~s of a city* 在市郊. ***clear sb's ~s*** 为某人洗去耻辱; 表明某人清白无辜. *like a bit of* ~〔口〕喜欢与女人作伴. — *vt.* ①用裙子覆盖, 使穿裙子. ②给…装边; 给…装防护罩. ③沿着…边缘; 和…接界; 绕过…的边缘. ④避开(危险等); 回避(问题等). — *vi.* ①位处边缘; 沿边走 (*along, around*). ~ **chaser**〔俚〕色情狂者. ~ **dancing [dance]** (优美地摆着裙子跳的)裙子舞.

skirt·ing [ˈskəːtiŋ] *n.* ①边缘. ②裙料. ③〔英〕【建】踢脚板, 壁脚板〔又叫 ~-board〕.

skit [skit] *n.* ①讽刺话[文]; 讽刺剧, 滑稽短剧; 幽默故事. ②〔*pl.*〕〔口〕多数, 很多 (*of*).

skit·ter [ˈskitə] *vi.* ①(水鸟等)轻轻掠过(水面或地面). ②轻快地将钓饵在水面上拉动. — *vt.* 使轻轻掠过.

skit·tish [ˈskitiʃ] *a.* ①易惊的(马等). ②羞怯的; 胆小的. ③(尤指女人) 轻佻的; ④不可靠的, 反复无常的. **-ly** *ad.* **-ness** *n.*

skit·tle [ˈskitl] *n.*〔英〕九柱戏用的小柱;〔*pl.*〕九柱戏〔类似 ninepins〕. *Life is not all beer and ~s.* 人生并不完全是吃喝玩乐. ***Knock over like ~s*** 一下子打倒, 驳倒. ***Skittles!*** 别胡说! 胡说! — *vi.* 做九柱戏游戏. — *vt.* 耽误(时机); 失误. ~ **alley [ground]** 九柱戏场. ~ **ball** 九柱戏的球.

skiv [skiv] *n.*〔俚〕一镑(金币).

skive [skaiv] *vt.* (把皮革等)割成薄片; 磨(宝石). — *n.* (磨宝石用的)钻石轮.

skiv·er [ˈskaivə], *n.* ①装订书籍用皮革, 帽里子革〔一种切割成薄片的羊皮革〕. ②割革工. ③割革刀.

skiv·vy [ˈskivi] *n.* ①〔英口, 蔑〕女用人. ②〔美俚〕(水手等的)短袖内衣; 汗衫.

skoal [skəul] *int.* (祝酒词)祝您健康! (一杯酒).

skoo·kum [ˈskuːkʌm] *a.*〔美俚〕极好的, 顶刮刮的; 强壮的, 有力的.

Sko·p(l)je [ˈskəuplje] *n.* 斯科普里〔南斯拉夫城市〕.

Skr., Skt. = Sanskrit.

sku·a [ˈskjuːə] *n.* ①【鸟】贼鸥〔挪威产〕. ②〔S-〕【英空军】大鸥式飞机.

skul(l)·dug·ger·y [skʌlˈdʌgəri] *n.*〔美口〕欺骗, 欺诈, 诡计; 卑鄙的行为.

skulk [skʌlk] *vi.* ①躲躲闪闪地走 (*about; through*). ②偷偷避开, 躲避; 躲藏 (*behind*); 潜逃 (*away*). ③偷懒; 装病; 逃避责任. ~ ***after*** 躲躲闪闪地跟在后头. — *n.* ① = **-er** ①. ②〔古〕狐群. **-er** *n.* ①躲藏者. ②装病者; 逃避责任者. **-ing·ly** *ad.* 偷偷摸摸地; 躲躲闪闪地; 懦怯地.

skull [skʌl] *n.* ①颅骨, 头骨, 脑壳, 头盖骨. ②头脑; 智能. ③【冶】渣壳; 熔铁上的浮渣. *an empty* ~ 头脑空空. *thick* ~ 笨头笨脑. ~ ***and crossbones*** 骷髅枯骨图〔由一个骷髅和两根交叉的枯骨组成, 作为死的象征; 过去为海盗旗标记; 现作毒药瓶上的标记〕. ~**cap** *n.* ①(无沿绒制室内戴的)便帽. ②古时的铁盔. ③【植】黄芩属植物, 美黄芩, 并头草. ④【解】前顶部. ~**-drag** *vi.* 〔美俚〕用功. ~**duggery**〔美俚〕= skulduggery. ~ **practice [session]** ①〔俚〕咨询会, 交流会, 非正式的学术讨论会. ②(运动员的)策略研究会议.

skunk [skʌŋk] *n.* ①【动】臭鼬; 臭鼬皮. ②〔俚〕臭名昭彰的卑劣家伙. ③〔美俚〕得零分. ***hotter than a*** ~ 烂醉. — *vt.* ①〔美俚〕击败〔尤指使对方得零分〕. ②欺骗. ~ **cabbage**, ~**weed** *n.*【植】臭菘(属植物).

sky [skai] *n.* ①〔常 *pl.*〕 ②【宗】天国. ③〔常 *pl.*〕天气; 气候, 风土. ④天蓝色. ⑤〔口〕画展室的顶列画. *a cloudy* ~ 阴云密布的天空. *blue* ~ 蓝天. *If the ~ fall(s), we shall catch larks.* 天垮了好捉云雀; 不必预先担忧. *He is in the ~.* 他在天上〔死了〕. ~ *piece*〔美俚〕帽子. ~ *police*〔美俚〕牧师. ~ *scout*〔美军俚〕随军牧师. ***be raised to the skies*** 升天了, 死了. ***in the skies*** 高兴, 得意扬扬. ***laud sb. to the skies*** 把(某人)捧上天. ***out of a clear [blue]*** ~ 晴天霹雳一样地, 突然. ***to the skies*** 无保留地; 过分地. ***The ~ is the limit.*** 没有限制. ***under a foreign*** ~ 在异乡, 在异国. ***under the open*** ~ 露天, 在野外. — *vt.* (将画)挂在最高一排;【板球】(将球)高打, 打上去. ~ *one*〔美棒球〕打大飞球. ~ **blue** *a.* 天蓝色的, 蔚蓝的. ~**-borne** *a.* 空运的; 空降的. ~**-clad** *a.*〔俚〕裸体的. ~ **diving**【空】张伞跳伞前的准备活动. ~**-gun** 高射炮. ~**-high** *a., ad.* 极高的; 天一样高. ~ **jack**〔口〕空中劫持(飞机). ~ **lab** 太空实验室. ~ **lark** ① *n.*【鸟】云雀, 天鹨, 告天子. ② *n., vi.*〔口〕闹着玩, 嬉戏; 寻欢作乐. ~**larker** *n.*〔美〕轻薄子, 轻薄女人. ~ **lift** *v., n.* 空运. ~ **light** 天窗. ~**line** 天边, 天涯, 地平线; (山、大厦等) 空中轮廓; 展览会场的顶层. ~**lounge** 把旅客从城里送往机场的车辆. ~**man**〔美俚〕飞行员; 伞兵. ~**master** 巨型客机. ~**motel** [ˈskaiməˌtel] (机场附近的) 汽车旅馆. ~ **parlor** 阁楼; 最上层的房间. ~ **pilot**〔俚〕(尤指船上的)牧师;【空】飞行员, 驾驶员. ~**rocket** ① *n.* 流星焰火; 高空探测火箭. ② *vi., vt.* 突然出现; (使) 腾空而起; (使) 直线上升; (物价) 猛涨. ~**sail**【海】第三层帆. ~**scape** 天空风景 (画). ~**scraper** ①摩天楼; 非常高的烟囱. ②【海】第三层帆 (skysail) 上的三角帆. ③〔美棒球〕钻高飞球. ~ **screen** "空网"〔一种用来观测导弹横偏差的光学仪器〕. ~**-shot** 朝天拍摄成的镜头〔画面〕. ~**sign** (设在高楼大厦顶上的) 空中广告. ~**-sweeper** (装有雷达瞄准设备的)一种口径 75 毫米的高射炮. ~**trooper** 伞兵. ~ **truck**〔口〕运输机. ~**ward(s)** *ad.* 向天空. ~ **wave** 天(空电)波. ~**-ways** 高架公路; 航线. ~ **winder** *n.*〔俚〕飞行员, 空军. ~**-writing** (飞机放烟飞成的)天空文字; 空中广告.

Skye (terrier) [skai] *n.* 匐狗〔一种身长脚短的长毛猎狐狗〕.

sky·ey [ˈskaii] *a.* ①〔诗〕天空的, 在天上的, 从天上来的. ②象天空的; 天蓝色的, 蔚蓝的. ③极高的; 高耸云霄的.

sky·o·graph [ˈskaiəgræf] *n.* 空摄地图.

Sl = ①slightly. ②slow.

S.L. = ①Solicitor-at-Law〔英〕初级律师. ②Support Line〔美〕支承线.

SL = ①sea level 海拔. ②south latitude 南纬. ③lens spectrometer 透镜分光计.

slab[1] [slæb] *n.* ①平板, 厚板; (圆木解成板时外面两块带皮的)背板. ②(面包等的)片, 厚块; 铁块; 土块. ③混凝土路面;【地】板层. ④〔棒球俚〕投球员足标, 投手板; 难看的人. *a ~ of marble* 一块云石板. ~ *of moo*〔美〕牛排. *a ~ milling*【机】平面铣. — *vt.* ①把…分成厚片, 使成厚板. ②铺石板. ③将(木材)锯去背板. ④在…涂上一厚层. ~**-sided** *a.* ①〔美〕侧面平坦的. ②细长的, 瘦的, 高的. ~**stone** (铺路)石板. ~ **top** 木板〔石板〕顶〔桌面〕. ~ **top** *a.* 以厚木板或石板为顶的.

slab[2] [slæb] *a.*〔古〕浓稠的, 粘的, 半流体的. ~ *porridge* 稠粥.

slab·ber [ˈslæbə] *v., n.* = slobber, slaver.

slack[1] [slæk] *a.* ①松的, 宽松的(衣服、绳子等). ②行动迟缓的; 无精神的, 无气力的. ③马马虎虎的, 懒惰的; 松弛的, 松懈的, 不紧张的. ④(商业等)呆滞的, 清淡的, 萧条的. ⑤温的, 微热的; (面包等)未烘干的, 烤得不透的; (石灰等)熟化的. ⑥【语音】松弛的, 开口音的. ⑦不坚实的, 软弱的; 不完善的. ⑧漏水的, 透水的. *He is ~ in study.* 他学习松懈. *I feel ~.* 我觉得发软. *a ~ market* 呆滞的市场. ~ *muscles* 松弛的肌肉. *a ~ oven* 微温的烤箱. *at a ~ pace* 慢条斯理地. *Keep a ~ hand [rein]* 松着手[缰绳]; 宽大统治. ~ *lime* 消[熟]石灰. ~ *season [time]*【商】淡季. ~ *water* (停止涨退的)平潮(期); 静流. ~ *weather* 使人倦怠的天气. ~ ***in stays***【海】(调头时)转得慢的(船). — *ad.* ①松弛地; 缓慢地. ②无力地, 宽松地, 不活泼地. ③不充分地; 不透地. ④呆滞地, 清淡地. — *n.* ①(绳、带、帆等的)松弛部分. ②空隙, 空间余宽. ③轨幅, 轨间距离. ④萧条(时期), 淡季. ⑤静止; 停滞; 平潮期. ⑥〔*pl.*〕(水手等的)宽裤,工装；〔美〕（男女）运动裤，女裤。⑦〔口〕闲散，休息。***have a good*** ~ 舒舒服服地休息一下。***pull in [up] the*** ~ 勒紧松弛部分。— *vi.* ①怠惰，偷懒；松懈，放松。②放慢；减少，和缓，减弱，虚弱；停止。③（石灰）熟化。④〔口〕休息，懒散。— *vt.* ①放松；松懈，怠忽。②使缓慢，放慢；减少，使缓和。③熟化（石灰）。~ ***off*** 放松，松劲；偷工，怠工，敷衍了事。~ ***up*** 放慢，慢下来。**-ly** *ad.* **-ness** *n.*

slack[2] [slæk] *n.* 粉煤，煤屑。

slack·en [ˈslækən] *vt.* ①松弛，松劲，放松。②放慢，使慢下来；削弱；减少。— *vi.* ①（绳索等）变松弛，松劲。②（风等）变弱，减弱。③〔口〕怠惰，休息。

slack·er [ˈslækə] *n.* ①战时逃避兵役的人。②〔口〕逃避责任的人；懒鬼，敷衍塞责的人；怠惰的人。③【林】架空集材机。

slacks [slæks] *n. pl.* （宽松的）裤子。

slag [slæg] *n.* ①矿渣，铁渣，炉渣，熔渣。②火山岩渣。— *vt., vi.* （使）起溶渣；（使）成熔渣。~ **heap** 熔渣堆。~ **wool** 渣棉，渣绒〔将熔化的炉渣用蒸汽或压缩空气吹散而成，用作防火、隔热、隔音材料〕。**-gy** *n.*

slain [slein] slay 的过去分词。

slake [sleik] *vt.* ①消除，扑灭（火等），平息（怒气）；解（渴）；满足，②熟化，消化（石灰）。~*d lime* 消〔熟〕石灰。— *vi.* ①〔古〕消除，平息；缓和，松，停。②（石灰）熟化。~ ***one's last of blood*** 满足血腥欲望。

sla·lom [ˈslɑːləm] *n.* 〔挪威〕障碍滑雪（赛）。— *vi.* 进行障碍滑雪赛。

SLAM = ①supersonic low altitude missile 低空超音速导弹。②strategic low altitude missile 低空战略导弹。

slam [slæm] *vt.* ①砰地关上（门等），砰地放下；砰地丢下。②〔口〕猛打；猛击；【牌】以满贯击败对方。③〔美口〕侮辱；猛烈抨击。— *vi.* ①发出砰声，砰地关上。②猛攻；使劲干。③〔美口〕侮辱，猛烈抨击。~ *the door* 砰地一声关上门；〔喻〕断然拒绝〔考虑、商讨〕。~ *down the lid of a trunk* 砰的一声关上箱盖。~ *the door in sb's face* 把某人砰的一声关在门外；拒绝听取某人的意见。~ *off* 〔美俚〕离去；死。— *n.* ①砰的〔轰的〕声音。②猛击，猛攻。③【牌戏】满贯。④〔美口〕侮辱，猛烈抨击。*a grand* ~ 【桥牌】大满贯。*a little [small]* ~ 【桥牌】小满贯。*with a* ~ 轰的一声。**~-bang** *ad., vt., vi.* 砰地（关上）。

slan·der [ˈslɑːndə] *n.* ①诽谤，诋毁；【法】毁谤。②（口头）诽谤罪。— *vt.* 讲坏话，污蔑，诽谤。**-er** *n.*

slan·der·ous [ˈslɑːndərəs] *a.* 毁谤的，污蔑的，毁坏名誉的；造谣中伤的。**-ly** *ad.*

slang[1] [slæŋ] *n.* 俚语；（盗贼等的）黑话，切口，隐语；行话，专门语。*army* ~ 军队俚语。*art* ~ 艺术上的行话。*back* ~ 倒读隐语。*doctors'* ~ 医生行话。*schoolboy* ~ 学生俚语。— *vt.* 用粗话烂骂。— *vi.* 用俚语，用粗俗的话。

slang[2] [slæŋ] 〔方，古〕sling 的过去式。

slan·gu·age [ˈslæŋgwidʒ] *n.* 〔谑〕多俚语的话〔作品〕；俚语。

slang·y [ˈslæŋi] *a.* 鄙俗的，俚语多的；滥用俚语的。

slank [slæŋk] 〔古〕slink 的过去式及过去分词。

slant [slɑːnt] *a.* 倾斜的，歪斜的。— *n.* ①倾斜；歪斜；斜坡；斜线，斜向，斜面；斜线号（/），②（对某事的）倾向性；观点，态度，意见；偏见，偏向，歪曲。③〔口〕斜眼看。④〔古、美〕挖苦，讽刺。⑤〔俚〕机会。*I need to get your* ~ *on the situation.* 请说说您对于情况的意见。*on the [a]* ~ 倾斜着，倾斜地。***a*** ~ ***of wind*** 【海】一阵风；顺风。***have a*** ~ ***on*** 〔美〕喝醉。— *vi.* ①倾斜，歪斜；倾向；斜向前进；②〔美俚〕走开。— *vt.* ①使倾斜，弄歪斜。②使具有倾向性；使带某种色彩；加以歪曲。~ **rhyme** 借押韵，不完全韵〔用音韵相近，但不属于同一韵部的词借押，如：lid, lad; wait, made.〕

slan·ten·dic·u·lar, slan·ting·dic·u·lar [ˌslɑːntinˈdikjulə, -iŋ-] *a.* 〔谑〕倾斜的；间接的，转弯抹角的。

slant·ing [ˈslɑːntiŋ] *a.* 倾斜的，歪斜的。**-ly** *ad.*

slant·ways [ˈslɑːntweiz] *ad.* 倾斜地，歪斜地。

slant·wise [ˈslɑːntwaiz] *ad., a.* 倾斜地〔的〕，歪斜地〔的〕。

slap [slæp] *n.* ①一巴掌，一拍；击拍声。②侮辱；拒绝。③【机】松动（声）。*a* ~ *in the face* 脸上一巴掌，一个耳光；〔喻〕（意外的）拒绝〔侮辱、失望、责备等〕。— *vt.* ①（用巴掌或其他扁平东西）打，拍；啪的一声关上（门等）。②啪的一声放下 *(down)*；猛掷；漫不经心扔掉。③攻击，侮辱。④任意涂；任意课税；强加。~ *on* 啪的一声穿上〔戴上〕。~ *(sb.) on the back* 拍拍（某人）脊背〔表示赞许等〕。~ *a defeat on* 〔美运〕打败对手。~ ***down*** 〔美俚〕粗暴地压制，制止，镇压。— *ad.* ①啪的一下。②猛然，突然。③直接，一直，迎面。*The tail came* ~ *off.* 尾巴忽然掉了下来。***run*** ~ ***into*** 迎面相撞。**~-bang** ① *ad.* 突然；猛然。② *a.* 匆促的，草率的，鲁莽的。**~dash** ① *a., ad.* 匆促的〔地〕，草率的〔地〕，鲁莽的〔地〕。② *n.* 鲁莽；草率；草率做成的东西。③ *vt.* 乱做，瞎做；乱七八糟地涂抹（墙壁等）；起草，草拟。**~dashery** *n.* 草率；脏乱。**~happy** *a.* 〔美俚〕（因受击）头昏目眩的；胜利冲昏头脑的，愚蠢的。**~jack** *n.* 〔美〕= flapjack; griddlecake. **~man** 〔美俚〕便衣警官。**~stick** *n.* （滑稽戏里打人时能发出响声的）敲板，击板；低级滑稽戏。*a.* 低级滑稽戏的。**~-up** *a.* 〔俚〕第一流的，上等的；最新式的；铺张的。

slap·ping [ˈslæpiŋ] *a.* 〔俚〕非常快的；（马、人）魁梧的；极好的。*a* ~ *pace* 快步，*a* ~ *horse* 高大的马。*a* ~ *dinner* 美肴佳餐。

slash [slæʃ] *vt.* ①深深砍入，深深切进；割下，割开；乱砍，乱斩；鞭打；〔喻〕严厉地批评〔谴责〕。②【军】砍（树）成鹿砦。③在（织物上）开裂缝，在（衣服上）开叉。④〔美、俚〕减（薪），减少。⑤猛动，猛挥，猛拉。— *vi.* ①乱砍，乱斩，挥击 *(at)*。②乱用鞭子抽；飞跑，冲过去；〔喻〕严厉地批评〔谴责〕。— *n.* ①深砍，深切；乱砍，乱斩；刀痕，伤痕，鞭痕。②衣服上开的叉〔缝〕。③【军】鹿砦。④（树木被砍后的）林中空地；（树林砍伐后留下的）枝桠，废材；〔*pl.*〕长满灌木的低洼地。⑤〔美、俚〕减薪，减少。⑥斜线号（/）。~ **pine** 〔美〕（佛罗里达产的）坚硬松木；加利比松（木）。~ **pocket** 斜口插袋。

sla·sher [ˈslæʃə] *n.* 断木机；〔美俚〕衣裳时髦的花花公子，香喷喷的纨袴子。

slash·ing [ˈslæʃiŋ] *a.* ①乱斩的，猛砍的。②不客气的，严厉的，厉害的（批评等）。③冲劲十足的；飞快的（步子等）。④〔口〕巨大的（财产等）。⑤倾泻的，急降的。⑥（颜色）鲜明的。*a* ~ *rain* 一阵倾盆大雨。*a* ~ *success* 巨大的战功。— *n.* 〔美〕伐木区域；〔*pl.*〕废材，残木。

slat[1] [slæt] *n.* ①（金属、木材的）板条；狭板；〔俚〕〔*pl.*〕肋骨。— *vt.* 用板条制作；装上板条。***hit the ~s*** 〔美俚〕（躺下）睡觉。

slat[2] [slæt] *vi.* 〔英，美方〕（帆、索等）劈拍劈拍地碰撞；敲打；猛烈拍动。—*vt.* 〔英、美方〕猛投，猛掷；打，击，以拳连接。—*n.* 拍打声；猛烈的一击。

S. lat. = south latitude 南纬。

slatch [slætʃ] *n.* （一段时间的）清静；安静无事的间隔。

slate[1] [sleit] *n.* ①（建筑用）板石；石板，石板瓦；板岩。②（书写用）石板。③鼠灰色；石板色，暗蓝灰色。④〔美〕候补人〔候选人〕名单；内定名单。⑤（操行等的）记录。*There is a loose* ~ *in his house.* = *He has a* ~ *off.* 他精神有点不对。*a clean* ~ 良好的经历，历史清白。***break [smash] the*** ~ 〔美〕取消候选人名单。***clean the*** ~ 勾销往事；了脱义务；免除义务。***make up the*** ~ 〔美〕拟定（候选人）名单。***start with a clean*** ~ （改过）自新；重新开始。***under the same*** ~ 在同一屋顶下，在一家。***wipe off the*** ~ 勾销往事。— *vt.* ①用石板瓦盖（屋顶）。②〔美口〕提名…做候补人〔候选人〕。~ **club** 〔英〕（每人每星期拿出少数钱组织的）互助会。**~-colo(u)red**

石板色的,暗蓝灰色的. ~ **pencil** 石笔.

slate² [sleit] *vt.* ①〔口〕(在报刊上)抨击,谴责. ②责骂(部下等);痛打,鞭打,拳打.

slat·er [ˈsleitə] *n.* ①石板瓦匠;(用石板作刀口的)刮毛器. ②抨击者. ③【动】鼠妇〔一种陆栖等足类甲虫〕;水栖等足类动物.

Slat·er [ˈsleitə] *n.* 斯莱特〔姓氏〕.

slath·er [ˈsleiðə, ˈslæðə] *n.* 〔美俚〕大量. — *vt.* 大量耗用;挥霍.

slat·ing¹ [ˈsleitiŋ] *n.* ①盖石板瓦;石板瓦活. ②(盖屋顶用的)石板瓦.

slat·ing² [ˈsleitiŋ] *n.* 严厉的批评,责骂.

slat·tern [ˈslætə(ː)n] *n.* ①懒散女人,邋遢女人. ②行为不检的女人;荡妇,妓女. —*a.* 懒散的;邋遢的,不整洁的.

slat·tern·ly [ˈslætə(ː)nli] *a., ad.* ①懒散的〔地〕;邋遢的(地),不整洁的(地). ②(女人)行为放荡的〔地〕. **-li·ness** *n.*

slat·ting [ˈslætiŋ] *n.* 条板料,条板.

slat·y [ˈsleiti] *a.* ①板岩(质)的,石板状的. ③蓝灰色的.

slaugh·ter [ˈslɔːtə] *n.* ①屠宰. ②(大)屠杀;杀戮,残杀. ③大减价,大贱卖. — *vt.* ①屠宰;(大)屠杀. ②大减价,大贱卖. ~**house** *n.* 屠场. **-er** *n.* 屠夫,屠宰工人;刽子手,屠杀者.

slaugh·ter·ous [ˈslɔːtərəs] *a.* 好杀的,凶暴的,残忍的;破坏性的. **-ly** *ad.*

Slav [slɑːv, slæv] *n.* 斯拉夫人;〔the ~s〕斯拉夫民族. — *a.* 斯拉夫民族的;斯拉夫语的. **-ist** *n.*

Slav. = Slavic; Slavonian; Slavonic.

slave [sleiv] *n.* ①奴隶. ②…的奴隶,耽迷…的人*(of; to)*. ③奴隶一般工作的人,苦工. ④【动】奴隶蚁(= ~ ant). ⑤【机】从动装置. ⑥卑劣的人. ⑦〔*pl.*〕〔美〕职业棒球选手. *a ~ to duty* 拚命尽本分工作的人. *be a ~ of [to] drink = a ~ to the bottle* 酒的奴隶,酒鬼. *a willing ~* 甘心情愿唯命是从的人. *the ~ of one's wife's caprices* 悉听妻子左右的男人. *the ~s of fashion* 拚命赶时髦的人们. — *vi.* (象奴隶一样)拚命工作,牛马似地工作,做苦工. ~**-born** *a.* 生于奴隶家庭的. ~ **driver** 奴隶监督人;残酷的老板〔监工〕. ~**-grown** *a.* 使用奴隶种植的. ~**holder** 蓄奴者,奴隶主. ~ **hunter** 捕捞奴隶去贩卖的人. ~ **labo(u)r** 奴隶劳动;强迫劳动. ~**-making ant**【动】蓄奴蚁. ~ **market** 奴隶市场;〔美俚〕职业介绍所. ~**-pusher**〔美〕残酷的老板. ~**robot** 机器人. ~ **ship** 贩奴船. ~ **state** (美国南北战争前)实行奴隶制度的州. ~ **station** (双曲线导航系统中受主台控制的)辅助电台. ~ **trade [traffic]** 奴隶贩卖.

slav·er¹ [ˈsleivə] *n.* 买卖奴隶者,奴隶贩子;贩奴船.

slav·er² [ˈslævə] *vi.* ①淌口水,垂涎. ②奉承,谄媚. —*vt.* 口水淌湿…;流涎弄脏(衣服等). — *n.* ①口水,唾液.吐沫. ②奉承,谄媚.

slav·er·y¹ [ˈsleivəri] *n.* ①奴隶身分,奴隶状态. ②奴隶制;占有奴隶. ③苦役;奴隶般的劳动. ④束缚;屈从;耽迷(酒色等) *(to)*.

slav·er·y² [ˈslævəri] *a.* 流口水的;被口水弄脏的.

slav·ey [ˈslɑːvi, ˈsleivi] *n.* 〔英俚〕(做粗笨杂事的)女工.

Slav·ic [ˈslævik, ˈslɑːv-] *a., n.* = Slavonic.

Slav·i·cist [ˈslɑːvisist, ˈslævisist] *n.* 斯拉夫语言、文化的研究者 (= slavist).

Slav·i·cize [ˈslævisaiz] *vt.* 使斯拉夫化.

slav·ish [ˈsleiviʃ] *a.* ①奴隶(一样)的;奴性的,卑屈的. ②无独创性的;盲从的,模仿的. *a ~ flatterer* 卑躬屈节地奉承者. **-ly** *ad.* **-ness** *n.*

Slav·ism [ˈslɑːvizəm] *n.* 斯拉夫人特点,斯拉夫式;斯拉夫主义;斯拉夫语风.

slav·oc·ra·cy [sleiˈvɔkrəsi] *n.* 〔美〕蓄奴派,蓄奴集团〔美国南北战争前,南方的奴隶主与拥护奴隶制度的统治集团〕.

Sla·vo·ni·a [sləˈvəuniə] *n.* 斯拉沃尼亚〔南斯拉夫多瑙河 (Danube) 与萨瓦 (Sava) 二河间地区〕. **Sla·vo·ni·an** [sləˈvəunjən, -niən] *a.* 斯拉沃尼亚的;斯拉沃尼亚人的;斯拉夫民族的;斯拉夫语的. — *n.* 斯拉沃尼亚人;斯拉夫人;斯拉夫语.

Sla·von·ic [sləˈvɔnik] *a.* 斯拉夫民族的,斯拉夫人〔语〕的. — *n.* 斯拉夫语.

Slav·o·nize [ˈslævənaiz,-ˈslɑː-] *vt.* 使斯拉夫化.

Slav·o·phil(e) [ˈslævəfil] *n.* 亲斯拉夫人的人;斯拉夫文化优越论者.

Slav·oph·i·lism [sləˈvɔfiləzm] *n.* 十九世纪中叶俄国知识分子中主张斯拉夫文化,俄罗斯文化优越论.

Slav·o·phobe [ˈslævəfəub] *n.* 憎恨〔畏惧〕斯拉夫人〔文化〕的人.

Slav·o·phobi·a [ˈslævəfəubjə] *n.* 对南斯拉夫人〔文化〕的憎恨〔畏惧〕.

slaw [slɔː] *n.* 〔美〕= coleslaw.

slay [slei] *(slew* [sluː]*; slain* [slein]*)* *vt.* ①杀死;杀害;毁灭. ②〔美俚〕使(异性)迷恋(自己);给人强烈的好印象;使…发生好感〔愉快,喜欢,快乐〕. *The slaves slew their master with swords.* 奴隶们用乱刀砍死主人. *Your jokes ~ me.* 你的笑话使我笑破肚皮. *slay'em*〔美俚〕迅速给人强烈好印象的人. — *vi.* 造成死亡. *No other infection so quickly ~s.* 再没有别的疾病会造成如此迅速的死亡.

slay·er [ˈsleiə] *n.* 杀人者,凶手.

SLBM = ①submarine-launched ballistic missile 潜艇发射的弹道导弹. ②sea-launched ballistic missile 海上发射的弹道导弹. ③satellite-launched ballistic missile 人造卫星发射的弹道导弹.

sld. = sailed; sealed; sold.

sleave [sliːv] *n.* ①细丝. ②乱丝;纠缠. — *vt.* 解开乱丝,理丝. ~*d silk*【纺】丝吐. —*vi.* 分成细丝.

sleaz·y [ˈsliːzi] *a.* ①【织】质地薄的. ②〔转义〕质量差的;低劣的;卑劣的. ③不整洁的;破旧的;未修理的. **-zi·ness** *n.*

sled [sled] *n.* ①(小)雪橇,滑橇,滑板. ②【空】滑轨;空气动力车. ③〔美〕采棉机. — *vt.* ①用雪橇运. ②用采棉机采. — *vi.* 乘雪橇. *hard ~ding*〔美〕困难的工作;难局. *smooth ~ding*〔美〕顺利轻松的工作. **-plane** 雪上飞机. **-der** 乘雪橇者;拉雪橇的动物.

sledge¹ [sledʒ] *n.* 雪橇;〔英〕(从前送犯人赴刑场用的)席橇. — *vt., vi.* 用雪橇运;坐雪橇走.

sledge² [sledʒ] = sledgehammer.

sledge·ham·mer [ˈsledʒˌhæmə] *n.* ①用双手抡打的长柄大铁锤. ②〔美〕连续猛击的拳击家. —*vt.* 用大锤连续猛击. — *vi.* 象用大锤猛击. — *a.* 象用大锤猛击的;猛烈的,重大的,致命的. *a ~ blow* 重大的打击,致命的打击. *a ~ argument* 激烈的争论;驳得对方哑口无言的论点.

sleek [sliːk] *a.* ①(毛发等)光滑的,柔滑的;油滑的,有光泽的;整洁的. ②(动植物)喂养得好的,长得好的,健康的. ③嘴甜的,花言巧语的,圆滑的. ④非常时髦的,豪华的;兴旺的. *~ dark hair* 柔滑乌黑的头发. *as ~ as a cat*〔喻〕象猫一样圆滑谄媚. — *vt.* ①使光滑,使有光泽. ②〔口〕使整洁. — *vi.* ①〔口〕滑动. ②〔口〕打扮整洁,打扮漂亮 (*up*). **-ly** *ad.* **-ness** *n.*

sleek·it [ˈsliːkit] *a.* 〔Scot.〕①光滑的,柔滑的. ②圆滑的,诡诈的. ③手巧的,能干的.

sleek·y [ˈsliːki] *a.* = sleek.

sleep [sliːp] *vi.* *(slept; slept* [slept]*)* ①睡,睡眠,睡着. ②被埋葬着;长眠. ③麻痹,发麻. ④(陀螺)稳定地飞速旋转. ⑤静止,过闲静日子,醉生梦死. ⑥过夜,住宿. ⑦发生性关系. ⑧【动】冬眠,蛰伏;【植】(花叶)夜间闭合. — *vt.* ①睡(觉). ②用睡眠消除. ③可住,供给…住宿. *~ well [badly]* 睡得好〔不好〕. *~ late* (早晨)起得晚,睡懒觉. *She slept eight hours* 她睡了八小时. *The sails* ~. 风帆被风鼓胀得静止不动. ~ *a sound sleep* 熟睡一觉. *This hotel* ~*s 500 guests*. 这旅馆可供五百人住宿. *I shall* ~ *in New York tonight*. 今晚在纽约过夜. *Let* ~*ing dogs lie* 不要打草惊蛇; 可能发生麻烦的地方别去碰它. ~ ***around*** 〔俚〕到处乱搞男女关系. ~ ***away*** ①= ~ off. ②在睡眠中打发日子, 把时间浪费在睡眠中. ~ ***in*** ①〔英〕(用人)住在东家家里. ②睡过头. ③睡懒觉. ~ ***off*** 睡过(时候); 睡掉(忧愁等), 用睡眠治好(头痛等). ~ ***on [upon, over]*** ... 将…睡着想一晚; 将…拖到明天. ~ ***one's last (sleep)*** 长眠. ~ ***out*** ①(佣工)睡在自己家里, 日作夜归. ②睡过. ③露宿. ~ ***over*** ①寄宿别人家. ②忽略, 不注意. ~ ***over one's work [happiness]*** 沉醉在工作〔幸福〕中. ~ ***rough*** 在公园〔车站等处〕过夜. ~ ***the clock round*** 一睡十二个钟头. ~ ***the sleep of the just*** 〔谑〕酣睡, 安心睡眠. ~ ***with one's fathers*** 死去. — *n.* ①睡眠. ②长眠, 死. ③昏迷, 麻痹; 静止, 静寂. ④【动】冬眠, 蛰伏; 【植】(花、叶) 夜间闭合. ⑤夜. ⑥睡意. *He talks in his* ~. 他说梦话. *a dead* ~ 熟睡. *the beauty* ~ (午夜前入睡的) 头觉. *a broken* ~ 不眠之夜. *Not ten* ~*s have passed since the last of our fighting men returned*. 自从我们最后一个战斗员回来至今还不到十天. ***be dying with*** ~ 瞌睡得要死. ***fall on*** ~ 〔古〕就眠; 死. ***go to*** ~ 入睡, 睡着. ***last*** ~ 死, 长眠. ***lay sb to*** ~ 使…入睡; 埋葬. ***put [send] to*** ~ 哄(孩子)睡; 使麻醉. ***the*** ~ ***that knows not breaking [no waking]*** 永眠, 长逝, 死. ~**-in** *a., n.* 住宿在雇主家的(佣工). ~**-out** *a., n.* 不住宿在雇主家的(佣工). ~ **producer** 〔美剧〕使人打瞌睡的戏. ~**walking** 梦游病. ~**wear** 睡衣.

sleep·er [ˈsliːpə] *n.* ①睡眠者; 懒人; 死人. ②有(卧)铺(设备的)飞机; 【铁路】〔美〕卧车, 卧铺. 〔英〕枕木. ③冬眠动物. ④【建】小阁栅; 【船】机座垫. ⑤〔美〕长期不受人注意而一举受人瞩目的人或物. ⑥〔常 *pl.*〕小儿睡衣裤. ⑦在耳上作了记号而未打烙印的小牛. *a good* ~ 睡眠好的人. *a heavy* ~ 不易惊醒〔睡眠酣畅〕的人. *a light* ~ 易惊醒〔睡眠不酣〕的人.

sleep·i·ly [ˈsliːpili] *ad.* 想睡地, 瞌睡地; 静寂地.

sleep·i·ness [ˈsliːpinis] *n.* 想睡, 睏倦.

sleep·ing [ˈsliːpiŋ] *n.* 睡眠; 休止, 静止. — *a.* 睡着的; 睡眠用的. *a* ~ *beauty* ①(童话中的)睡美人; 〔转义〕贪睡的美人, 懒美人. ②【植】白花酢浆草 (= ~ clover). ~ **bag**, ~ **sack** 睡袋〔旅行等用〕. ~ **car**, ~**-carriage** 卧车. ~ **draught [pill, potion, tablet]** 安眠药(片), 催眠剂. ~**-dropsy** 【医】睡眠病. ~ **-partner** (不参与经营的)匿名合伙人. ~ **rent** 固定的租金; 不依获利多寡而增减的资金. ~ **saloon** 〔英〕(高级)卧车. ~ **sickness** (热带)嗜眠病; 嗜眠性脑炎. ~ **suit** 睡衣裤. ~**walker** 梦游病者. ~**walking** 梦游(病).

sleep·less [ˈsliːplis] *a.* ①不眠的, 睡不着的; 醒着的. ②无休止的, 不停的; 活跃的; 警觉的. *a* ~ *night* 不眠之夜. ~ *wind* 刮个不停的风. **-ly** *ad.* **-ness** *n.*

sleep·y [ˈsliːpi] *a.* ①想睡的, 瞌睡的; 嗜睡的. ②困乏的(声音等); 懒散的; 寂静的. ③使睡的, 催眠的. ④睡着的, 不活动的; 感觉迟钝的, 水果等(因开始干枯腐烂而变得)乏味的. *a* ~ *song* 催人入眠的歌. *a* ~ *little town* 呆滞的小城镇. *a* ~ *valley* 寂静的山谷. *feel* ~ 想睡. ~ *sickness* 〔口〕嗜眠性脑炎. ~**head** 贪睡的人; (终日)昏昏欲睡的人; 懒鬼. **-i·ly** *ad.* **-i·ness** *n.*

sleet [sliːt] *n.* ①冻雨, 雨夹雪, 霙. ②雨淞, 冰凌. — *vi.* 下雨夹雪; 下冻雨. **-y** *a.* 雨淞一样的.

sleeve [sliːv] *n.* ①袖子, 袖套. ②【机】套筒, 套管, 套. ③唱片套. ④【气】风(向)袋. *Every man has a fool in his* ~. 〔谚〕人人都有不够聪明之处. ***hang on sb.'s*** ~ 听从某人. ***hang [pin] one's judgement [opinion] (up) on sb.'s*** ~ 依靠某人给自己出主意. ***have a plan [a card, something] up one's*** ~ 别有用心, 另有应急计划, 另有秘诀. ***laugh [smile] in [up] one's*** ~ 暗笑, 在肚子里笑. ***roll [turn] up one's*** ~***s*** (为工作或搏斗) 卷起袖子; 磨拳擦掌. ***wear one's heart on one's*** ~ 开诚布公, 坦率. ***work in one's*** ~***s*** 脱去上衣做活, 只穿着衬衫工作. — *vt.* 给…装袖子, 给…装套筒. ~ **button** 袖口钮. ~ **emblem** (军队中文职人员佩戴的)袖章. ~ ~ **fish** 【动】枪鲗, 鱿鱼. ~ **let** 袖套. ~ **link** 袖钮. ~ **nut** 【机】套筒螺母. ~ **target** 【空】筒形拖靶 〔飞机在飞行中拖曳的靶子〕. ~ **valve** 【机】套阀. **-less** *a.*

sleigh [slei] *n.* (马拉的)雪橇; 雪车. — *vi.* 坐雪橇(走), 用雪橇运送. ~ **bells** 雪橇铃〔挂在拉雪橇牲口身上的小铃〕.

sleight [slait] *n.* ①技巧, 手法. ②〔古〕诡计, 奸诈; 〔罕〕手段, 策略. ~ ***of hand*** ①(在变魔术时蒙蔽观众的)手法. ②戏法, 花招, 特技. ***resorted to a*** ~ ***of hand*** 耍了一个花招. ***turn out to be a clumsy*** ~ ***of hand*** 弄巧成拙.

slen·der [ˈslendə] *a.* ①细, 细长的, 苗条的. ②柔弱的, 纤弱的. ③狭, 窄; 微薄的, 微小的, 不足的. ④微弱的, 薄弱的(基础等). ⑤【语音】细弱的. *a* ~ *girl* 身段苗条的少女. *a* ~ *cheque* 小额支票. ~ *hopes* 渺茫的希望. ~ *means* 小小本钱, 小额财产. **-ly** *ad.*

slen·der·ize [ˈslendəraiz] *vt., vi.* 使〔变〕细长.

slept [slept] sleep 的过去式及过去分词.

sleuth [sluːθ] *n.* ①〔古〕(人或兽的)足迹, 臭迹. ②= sleuthhound. ③〔美口〕侦探.

sleuth·hound [ˈsluːθhaund] *n.* ①警犬, 嗅觉敏锐的猎狗. ②〔口〕厉害的侦探.

slew[1] [sluː] slay 的过去式.

slew[2], **slue** [sluː] *n.* 〔美, 加拿大〕泥淖; 沼地.

slew[3] [sluː] *vt.* 使回转, 使旋转 *(around, round)*. —*vi.* 旋转; 滑溜. —*n.* 回转, 旋转, 旋转后的位置.

slew[4] [sluː] *n.* 〔常 *pl.*〕〔美口〕大量, 大批, 大群 *(of)*.

slice [slais] *n.* ①薄片, 切片, 一片; 一部分. ②餐刀, (切薄片用的)菜刀; 锅铲; 火铲; 刮子. ③【印】油墨铲. ④【建】泥板, 泥刀. ⑤【海】进水台用楔. ⑥【无】限幅, 削波. ⑦【运】(高尔夫球)左〔右〕曲球; (乒乓球)削球, 左旋球. *a* ~ *of bread* 一片面包. *a* ~ *of luck* 幸运. —*vt.* ①把…切成薄片. ②切下, 切去; 切开, 分开 *(away, from, off)*. ③用(火铲)铲; 用(泥刀)铺. ④(高尔夫球)使球曲向左〔右〕边; (乒乓球)削球. — *vi.* ①切. ②打左〔右〕曲球. ~ **bar** 炉钎. ~**-of-life** *a.* 栩栩如生地反映实际生活的一个片断的. **-r** *n.* 切片机.

slick [slik] *a.* ①光滑的, 滑溜的. ②熟练的, 灵巧的. ③聪明的, 机灵的; 圆滑的, 口齿伶俐的; 狡猾的, 诡诈的. ④〔口〕(文体等)华而不实的. ⑤陈腐的, 老一套的; 平凡的, 无独创性的. ⑥〔美俚〕极好的, 第一流的; 吸引人的, 好玩的. ⑦纯然的, 单纯的. *a* ~ *alibi* 圆滑的托词. *a* ~ *style of writing* 花俏的文体, 华而不实的文体. *a story* ~ *of the* ~ *variety* 老一套的故事. *He did it out of* ~ *perversity*. 他全然是出于不合情理的想法做了这件事的. ***(as)*** ~ ***as a whistle*** 敏捷地; 干净利落地. — *ad.* ①润滑地(转动); 自如地, 灵活地. ②熟练地, 巧妙地. ③直接地, 径直地; 正面; 恰好地, 恰巧地. *go* ~ 运转自如, 进行顺利. *run* ~ *into sth.* 迎面撞上某物. — *vt.* ①使光亮; 使滑溜. ②使美观; 整顿, 使齐整. ③占…的便宜; 揩…的油. ~ *the flour on a board with a spatula* 用抹刀把擀面板上的麦块刮平. *turn out to be* ~*ed* 结果吃了亏. ~***ed up*** 〔美〕干净的, 整洁的; 流线型的, 吸引人的. —*vi.* 打扮整洁, 打扮漂亮 *(up)*. — *n.* ①〔美〕(水上有一层油膜的)平滑面; 油膜. ②平滑器; 刮刀; 修型镘刀. ③〔美俚〕(装璜漂亮、内容浅薄的) 通俗杂志〔= ~ paper〕. ④没有花纹的汽车轮胎. ~ **chick** 〔美俚〕束装漂亮的女子. ~ **paper** (装璜漂亮而内容浅薄的) 通俗杂志. ~**-paper** *a.* 装璜漂亮而内容浅薄的.

slick·en·side [ˈsliknˌsaid] *n.* 〔常用作 *pl.*〕【地】擦痕面, 断面擦痕.

slick·er [ˈslikə] *n.* ①〔美〕(宽大的)油布雨衣. ②〔美口〕狡猾的骗子. ③【工】刮子,刮刀. ④〔美俚〕衣着漂亮行为假诈的城里人.

slide [slaid] *vi.* (*slid* [slid]; *slid*, 〔美〕 *slid·den* [ˈslidn]) ①滑; (在雪或冰上)滑动; 滑倒, 滑掉. ②改变位置, 脱离原来位置; 不知不觉陷入 (*into*). ③【棒球】溜进; 【乐】滑动. ④偷偷进入; 潜逃, 偷偷溜掉. ⑤流, 流逝; 放任自流. *The book slid off my knee.* 书由我膝头上滑落. ~ *into bad habit* 渐渐养成坏习惯. *The economy slid from recession to depression.* 经济由退缩进入萧条. ~ *from grave to gay* 渐渐由严肃中欢闹起来. — *vt.* ①使滑动; 使滑倒; 滑溜地进行. ②用滑冰(等)消磨(时间). ③偷偷[轻轻]放进去, 使溜进去 (*in, into*). ***let things [it]*** ~ 听其自然; 放任不管. ~ ***away*** 偷偷跑掉, 溜掉. ~ ***over*** 略过, 回避 (*He slid over the delicate subject.* 他对那个困难问题一点而过). — *n.* ①滑动; 滑道, 滑坡, 滑轨; 滑面. ②土崩, 山崩; 雪崩. ③【地】(层面)断层; 冲断面; 褶皱. ④【棒球】溜进. ⑤滑动的部分; 【机】滑板; 滑盖; 滑座; 【物】滑动片; 幻灯片; (显微镜的)载片; 【摄】(照相机的)拉盖. ⑤【乐】滑音, 延音; 长号的U形伸缩管. ⑥(妇女保持头发整齐的)发夹 (= hair ~). *a nodal* ~ 【物】测节器. ~ **bar** 【机】滑杆. ~ **block** 【机】滑块. ~ **carriage** 【军】滑动炮架. ~ **door** 拉门. ~ **fastener** 拉链, 拉锁. ~ **knot** 止滑结. ~ **rule** 计算尺. ~ **trombone** = trombone. ~ **valve** 【机】滑阀. ~**way** 滑道, 滑坡. **-r** ①滑动的人或物; (器械的)滑动部分. ②【棒球】曲线球.

slid·ing [ˈslaidiŋ] *a.* 滑动的; 易变的, 不稳定的. —*n.* 滑动. ~ **door** 拉门. ~ **rule** 计算尺. ~ **scale** ①计算尺. ②【经】(按物价涨落折算工资、税款等的)折价计算法. ~ **seat** (赛艇的)滑座.

slight [slait] *a.* ①轻微的, 细微的; 微小的, 少量的. ②纤细的, 细长的; 苗条的, 瘦小的. ③不结实的; 脆弱的. ④〔罕〕轻蔑的. ⑤不足取的, (辩解等)无聊的. *a* ~ *cold* 轻微的伤风. *a* ~ *criticism* 无力的批评, 轻微的批评. *I have not the* ~*est doubt.* 我没有丝毫怀疑. *She takes offence at the* ~*est thing.* 她极易发怒. ***make*** ~ ***of*** 轻视. ***not in the*** ~***est*** 一点不 (= not at all). — *n.* 轻蔑, 怠慢, 侮辱; 忽视. *suffer* ~*s* 受到怠慢. ***put a*** ~ ***on [upon] sb.*** 蔑视某人, 瞧不起某人. — *vt.* ①轻视, 蔑视, 藐视. ②玩忽; 怠慢. ~ *one's work* 玩忽职守. *feet* ~*ed* 感觉受到藐视.

slight·ing [ˈslaitiŋ] *a.* 轻蔑的, 无礼的. *a* ~ *remark* 轻蔑的话. **-ly** *ad.*

slight·ly [ˈslaitli] *ad.* ①轻微地, 轻轻地. ②细长地, 苗条地. ③有一点, 略; 脆弱地. ④〔罕〕轻蔑地. *be* ~ *wounded* 受了轻伤的. *be* ~ *deaf* 有一点聋. *be* ~ *built* (建筑物等)不牢固的; (体格)瘦弱的, 细长的. *I knew him* ~. 我略为认识他.

sli·ly [ˈslaili] *ad.* = slyly.

slim [slim] *a.* ①纤细的, 苗条的; 微弱的. ②不足取的, 琐细的, 无价值的; (议论等)不充实的, 空洞的. ③〔方〕狡猾的, 油滑的. *a* ~ *excuse* 理由不充分的借口. *very* ~ *chances of success* 成功的希望很渺茫. *the* ~*mest (of) evidence* 最不充分的证据. — *vt., vi.* (使)变细, (使)减肥. (用运动等)减轻体重. *He feels like dieting to* ~ *down.* 他很想节制饮食来减肥. ~**ming exercises** 保持身材苗条的体操. **-ly** *ad.*

slime [slaim] *n.* ①软而滑的东西. ②粘土, 稀泥. ③粘质; (蜗牛等的)粘液. ④沥青; 〔*pl.*〕【矿】矿泥; 煤泥. ⑤〔转义〕令人不愉快的粘腻的东西. ⑥谄媚; 堕落. ~ *flux* 【林】伤口流液. — *vt.* ①(用稀泥等)涂, 糊; (尤指蛇吞蛙等时)分泌粘液使粘滑. ②清除粘液[稀泥等]. ③把(矿石)研磨成矿泥. — *vi.* ①弄得泥糊糊; 变粘滑. ②〔英俚〕滑脱, 用狡猾手段脱身溜掉 (*away; through etc.*). ~ **mold [fungus]** 【生】粘菌 (= myxomycete). ~ **pit** ①产沥青的矿井. ②贮矿泥的坑.

slim·ming [ˈslimiŋ] *n.* 减轻体重; 减肥; 减食疗法.

slim·nas·tics [ˌslimˈnæstik] *n.* 健美操.

slim·sy [ˈslimsi], **slim·zy** [ˈslimzi] *a.* 〔美〕脆弱的, 薄弱的; 不结实的; 不耐穿的.

slim·y [ˈslaimi] *a.* ①粘糊糊的; (分泌)粘液的; 泥泞的. ②〔口〕谄媚的; 可鄙的; 讨厌的. **-i·ly** *ad.* **-i·ness** *n.*

sling[1] [sliŋ] *n.* ①投石器; 弹弓. ②投掷; 打击, 一击. ③【医】悬带; 【海】钩索, 吊锁, 吊索, 吊链; 一吊货, 一关; 【军】(枪的)背带. ④后跟用带绊住的女鞋. *have [carry] one's arm in a* ~ 用悬带吊着手臂. — *vt.* (*slung* [slʌŋ], 〔古〕 *slang* [slæŋ]; *slung*) ①用投石器投; 投掷, 扔. ②用悬带吊挂; 吊起 (辘轳等). ~ *a door open* 把门推开. ~ *abuse* 〔俚〕谩骂. ~ *arms* 把枪用背带挂在肩膀上. ~ *a sword from a belt* 把佩刀吊在带子上. ~ *type* 排字. — *vi.* 用投石器投; 大踏步走. ~ ***chin music*** 〔美〕说(空话). ~ ***one's hook*** 〔俚〕逃走, 离去. ~ ***ink*** 〔俚〕(卖稿人)赶写(稿件); 做新闻记者. ~ ***mud at sb.*** 谩骂, 毁谤. ~ ***over*** 使劲拥抱. ~ ***oneself up*** 溜上. ~ ***(the) woo*** 〔美俚〕= pitch (a) woo. ~ **cart** (装有千斤吊的)吊搬车. ~ **dog** 吊钩. ~**shot** 弹弓 [玩具]. **-er** 用投石器者; 投掷装置; 吊环, 吊索; 吊装工. (*-er ring* 【空】分液环; 防冻液洒射环).

sling[2] [sliŋ] *n.* 〔美〕果汁甜酒〔用烈酒、糖、果子露掺水混合而成的饮料〕.

slink[1] [sliŋk] (*slunk* [slʌŋk], 〔罕〕 *slank* [slæŋk]; *slunk*) *vi.* 偷偷地走进, 溜走, 潜逃 (*away; by; off*). — *n.* 鬼鬼祟祟的人. **-y** *a.* ①偷偷摸摸的, 行动诡秘的. ②〔俚〕动作[线条]柔和优美的.

slink[2] [sliŋk] (*slunk* [slʌŋk], 〔罕〕 *slank* [slæŋk]; *slunk*) *vt.* (动物, 尤指家畜)早产, 流产. — *n.* 早产的小牛. — *a.* 早产的, 不足月的(小牛等).

slip[1] [slip] *vi.* (~*ped*, 〔古〕 *slipt* [slipt]; ~*ped*) ①滑(动); 滑倒, 跌交. ②滑脱, 松脱; (骨等)脱节, 脱落. ③溜, 溜走, 潜逃 (*away, off*); 悄悄走; (时间)不知不觉地过去, 逝去 (*by; away*). ④疏忽; 遗忘; 弄错. ⑤(机会等)被错过, 被放走. ⑥〔口〕(健康)变坏, (质量)下降. ⑦【空】侧滑. ⑧〔美俚〕颓丧, 垂头丧气. ⑨匆忙地穿上[脱去] (*into [out of]*). *Mind you don't* ~. 当心别滑倒. *He often* ~*s in his grammar.* 他常常犯语法错误. *Mistakes will* ~ *in.* (注意是注意但)错误难防. — *vt.* ①使滑动; 偷偷放进, 偷偷地搁到. ②错过, 放走 (机会等); 解开, 脱去 (*off; down*); 放走(狗等); 放开. ③省去(某事项等); 漏掉, 遗漏. ④不留神地说出, 漏出(话等). ⑤(牲畜)早产. ⑥〔美俚〕付(款); 偷偷地塞 (钱). ***let*** ~ ***the dogs of war*** 挑起战争. ~ ***along*** 〔俚〕急急忙忙地走, 飞也似地跑. ~ ***down to the wire*** 〔美运〕比赢. ~ ***from one's memory*** 遗忘. ~ ***into*** 急急穿上; 〔俚〕痛殴; 竞赛; 攻击. ~ ***me five*** 〔美俚〕握手. ~ ***off*** 急急脱掉; 偷偷拿走; 偷偷跑掉, 溜掉. ~ ***on*** 一下子穿上. ~ ***over*** 对…漫不经心. ~ ***out of joint*** 脱节, 脱榫. ~ ***sth. over on sb.*** 用欺骗手段把某物塞给他人; 用欺骗手段胜过他人 (*try to* ~ *sth. over on one's customers by substituting inferior merchandise for that ordered* 将所订购的商品以次品代替企图欺骗顾客). ~ ***the anchor*** 【海】斩断锚链. ~ ***the leash*** 〔美〕摆脱束缚, 得到自由. ~ ***through sb.'s fingers*** 从某人的掌握中逃脱. ~ ***up*** 滑一跤; 〔美〕弄错; 失败. — *n.* ①滑动; 滑倒, 失足, 跌跤. ②滑脱; 滑落. ③【地】(岩层的)滑距; 山崩, 断层. ④【船】滑台, 滑路; 船台; 两码头间的水区. ⑤【机】滑程, 滑率; 滑动量; 润滑性 [度]; 空转; 转差. ⑥【空】侧滑. ⑦过失, 错误; 失败; 错过, 遗漏; 意外事故. ⑧溜走, 不告而别. ⑨〔常 *pl.*〕狗带. ⑩女人套裙; (幼孩的)外衣, 围涎; 〔*pl.*〕(男式)游泳裤, 枕套. ⑪〔美〕系船处; 停泊处. ⑫〔俚〕(牲畜)流产. ⑬【剧】舞台边门. ⑭【陶器】泥釉, 滑泥. ⑮【鱼】小比目鱼. ⑯【板球】外

场员;〔*pl.*〕外场员防区. ~ *of the memory* 遗忘. *a ~ of the pen* 写错. *a ~ of the tongue* 失言. *a deposit [withdrawal] ~* 存款[取款]单. *There's many a ~ between the cup and the lip.* 〔谚〕杯已到口还会失手,往往事败垂成;凡事都难以十拿九稳. *give sb. the ~* 趁某人不防溜掉,甩掉某人. ~ **carriage**〔英〕滑脱车厢〔快车经过不停的车站时解下的车厢〕. ~**case** 书套. ~ **clay** 易熔土,易滑土. ~ **cover** 椅套,沙发套. ~**-horn**〔美俚〕= trombone. ~**knot** 滑结,蝶结. ~ **noose** 滑结[蝶结]套. ~**-on** ①*a.* 易穿脱的. ②*n.* 无带扣便鞋;套衫,宽松的外套. ~ **over** = pullover. ~**page**【机】滑动(量);滑程;动力传递损耗. ~**-ped disk**【医】脱出的脊椎盘〔常引起坐骨神经痛〕. ~**ring**【电】滑环,汇流[电]环. ~ **sheet**【印】衬纸〔用于防止刚印好的纸页上的湿油墨染污另一页〕. ~**shod** *a.* 穿着塌跟鞋的;不齐整的,乱七八糟的,懒散的;潦草的,疏漏的,粗糙草率的. ~**-shods**〔美〕鞋子. ~**slop** ①*n.* 无味的食物、谈话、著作(等). ②*a.* 淡(酒等);无聊的,没有价值的;潦草的. ③*vi.* 趴踏趴踏地走;写无聊文章. ~**-stick**〔美俚〕= slide rule. ~ **stitch**【纺】暗针. ~ **stream**【空】滑流,切向流;向后气流. ~**-up**〔口〕失败,错误;不幸事故. ~**way**【船】滑台;滑路;船台.

slip[2] [slip] *n.* ①【园艺】插条,插穗;幼枝;〔喻〕子孙,后裔. ②木条,纸条,(土地等的)一长条;(条形)传票,便条;【印】长条排样[校样]. ③瘦长的青年人. ④【机】楔形磨石. ⑤〔美〕条凳座位. *an inventory count ~* 盘存点料单. *an issue ~* 领料单. — *vt.* 剪取插条.

slip·per [ˈslipə] *n.* ①(常 *pl.*) 拖鞋;(室内)便鞋. ②(马车的)刹车;【机】滑动部分;滑屐. ③(小孩的)围涎;放猎狗的猎人. *a bed-~* 床上便器. ***take one's ~ to*** 用拖鞋打…. — *vt.* (用拖鞋)打(孩子等). —*vi.* 穿着拖鞋走. *She ~ed across the room from her bed.* 她下床穿着拖鞋走过房间.

slip·per·y [ˈslipəri] *a.* ①滑,滑溜的. ②易滑脱的. ③狡猾的,不可靠的;易变的. ④含糊的;难以解释的. *a ~ customer* 滑头. *a ~ situation* 变化不定的形势. *~ as an eel dipped in butter* 狡猾极了的,极不可靠的. ~ **elm**【植】(北美)滑榆(木,皮). **-per·i·ly** *ad.*

slip·ping [slipiŋ] *a.* ①〔美俚〕渐渐松弛的,渐渐不行了的,渐渐吃不开了的,渐渐变懒的. ②电视图象水平偏移的.

slip·py [ˈslipi]*a.* 麻俐的,手脚灵活的;〔口,方〕=slippery. ~**-ring**【电】汇电环.

slipt [slipt] *v.*〔古〕slip[1] 的过去式.

slit [slit] *n.* ①狭长切口;裂缝,狭缝. ②(自动售货机的)投钱口. — *vt.* ***(slit, ~ted)*** ①切开,割开;扯裂,剖开,切成长条. ②使成狭缝. *He appears to have two ~s for eyes.* 他眯细着眼睛. ~ *a hide into thongs* 把兽皮切成皮条. — *vi.* 纵切,纵裂. ~ **trench**【军】避弹,狭壕. **slit·ter** *n.*

slith·er [ˈsliðə] *vi.* 滑动;滑行;蜿蜒地滑行. —*vt.* 使滑动,使滑行. — *n.* 滑动;滑行. **-y** *a.*

sliv·er [ˈslivə, ˈslaivə] *n.* ①长条,裂片,细片;碎料. ②【纺】条子,梳条,棉条. ③(作鱼饵用的)小鱼片. — *vt.* ①把…剖成长条,把…切成薄片. ②把(鱼)剖成两半. — *vi.* 切开;裂开.

sli·vo·vitz [ˈslivəˌvits] *n.* 梅子白兰地〔尤指东欧的〕.

Sloan [sləun] *n.* 斯隆〔姓氏〕.

slob [slɔb] *n.* ①〔英方〕泥,(河底)烂泥. ②〔口〕懒汉;蠢汉,笨蛋,无用的人;邋遢[粗鲁]的人;〔美俚〕大胖子. ~ **ice**〔纽芬兰的〕混杂着雪的浮冰.

slob·ber [ˈslɔbə] *vi.* ①淌口水,垂涎. ②(说话时)感情迸发,过分伤感. —*vt.* ①口水淌湿. ②哭诉;过分伤感〔令人讨厌〕地说[写]. ③将(工作)敷衍了事,马马虎虎做. *~ over sb.* 将人弄得尽是口水,流着口水接吻;拚命宠爱;哭诉. ~ *a bibful*〔美〕倾诉满肚皮牢骚;唠叨一大堆. — *n.* 口水;哭诉;唠叨. *all of a ~* 淌着口水. ~**-gulluious** *a.*〔美俚〕上好的;美味的.

Slo·cum [ˈsləukəm] *n.* 斯洛克姆〔姓氏〕.

sloe [sləu] *n.*【植】黑刺李(树或果);〔美〕野梅. ~**-eyed** 眼睛黑而大的;长着杏眼的. ~ **gin** 野梅红金酒.

slog [slɔg] *vt.* (打板球或拳击等时)猛击. — *vi.* ①猛击. ②顽强地行进,吃力地走 *(on)*. ③拼命工作,苦干 *(away)*. — *n.* ①乱打,猛击. ②苦干. ③吃力地行进.

slo·gan [ˈsləugən] *n.* ①(原为苏格兰高地和爱尔兰氏族号召战斗的)呐喊;集合信号. ②口号,标语. ③(商业广告上用的)短语. **-eer** ①*vi.* 拟定标语口号;使用标语口号. ② *n.* 标语口号拟制[使用]者. **-istic** *a.* **-ize** *vt.* 使成标语口号;以标语口号方式表达;标语口号化.

slog·ger [ˈslɔgə] *n.* (棒球等的)猛击者.

sloid [slɔid] *n.* = sloyd.

sloop [slu:p] *n.* ①多帆单桅小船. ②【军】海岸炮舰;(尤指二次大战中担任反潜任务的)小型护航舰. *a ~ of war*〔英〕古代的炮艇.

slop[1] [slɔp] *n.* ①稀泥;半融化的雪;泥浆. ②泼落的水;弄湿了的地方;水坑. ③〔*pl.*〕(粥等)流体食物;(作饲料的)泔水. ④不值钱的感伤. ⑤(酿造过程中的)釜馏物;废液;废油. ⑥〔俚〕不整洁的人. ⑦不含酒精的饮料. ⑧〔*pl.*〕人体排泄物. *live on ~s* 吃稀的过日子. — *vi.* ①泼出,撒出,溢出. ②在泥浆[化了的雪]中走. — *vt.* ①泼出,撒出;泼脏. ②用泔水喂(猪等). ③溅污,弄脏. ④咂咂地吃;贪婪地喝. ***get ~ped*** 喝醉. ~ ***over*** ①泼出,溅出,溢出. ②滔滔不停地说. ③变得极感伤,感情太流露. ~ ***up***〔美〕喝(啤)酒. ***(be) slopped over [up]***〔美〕喝醉了的. ***(be)slopped to the ear*** 喝得烂醉的. ~ **basin [bowl]**〔英〕(餐桌上)倒剩茶等用的盆. ~ **chute** 船后部的垃圾筒. ~ **jar** 盛污水[小便]的缸[桶]. ~ **pail** 污水桶. ~ **sink** 倒泔水或冲洗拖把的水池.

slop[2] [slɔp] *n.*〔*pl.*〕(宽大的)罩衣[工作服],(价钱低廉的)现成衣服;〔*pl.*〕〔水手用语〕衣服,卧具;〔俚〕裁缝. ~ **chest** (船上)准备发给海员的贮藏品. ~ **room** (船上的)被服室. ~ **seller**〔美〕现成服装商. ~ **shop**〔美〕现成服装店. ~**work** 现成衣服缝制工作;现成衣服,便宜衣服;马马虎虎的工作 *(No ~ ever dropped from his pen.* 他从不草率写文章*)*.

slop[3] [slɔp] *n.*〔英俚〕警察〔由倒读 police 转化而成〕.

slope [sləup] *n.* ①倾斜,坡度;坡,斜坡,斜面;【印】斜体. ②【军】掮枪的姿势. ③【数】斜率. ④【矿】斜井. ⑤经济衰退. ⑥〔美军俚〕〔贬〕东方人. *a gentle ~* 缓坡. — *vt.* 弄斜,使倾斜,使成斜坡. — *vi.* ①倾斜,成斜坡. ②〔口〕逃亡;来,去. ~ ***about***〔俚〕闲荡. ***S- arms!***〔口令〕掮枪; ~ ***off***〔俚〕离去;逃亡. **-wise** *ad.* 倾斜着.

slop·ing [sləupiŋ] *a.* 倾斜的,成斜坡的. **-ly** *ad.* **-ness** *n.*

slop·pi·ness [ˈslɔpinis] *n.* ①泥泞;潮湿;稀薄. ②懒散;(工作)草率;易伤感;(外表)邋遢.

slop·py [ˈslɔpi] *a.* ①稀薄的,(食品)流质的. ②雨多的(天气);水坑多的;泥泞的;被污水溅污的,满是污水的. ③懒散的;(工作)草率的. ④易伤感的;含泪的. ⑤(外表)邋遢的;喝醉的. ~ *joe* 碎牛肉饼. **-pi·ly** *ad.*

slosh [slɔʃ] *n.* = ①slush. ②溅泼声. ③〔美〕稀薄的食物[饮料]. ④〔俚〕胡话. — *vi.* 在水[泥]中挣扎[乱走];到处乱溅;发出液体晃动声. — *vt.* 搅动;溅泼;〔英俚〕打. **-ed** *a.*〔主英俚〕喝醉了的.

slot[1] [slɔt] *n.* ①狭缝,窄孔;【机】槽沟;自动售货机,自动售货机投钱口. ②【空】翼缝. ③〔美口〕(集体或系列中的)位置,职位. ~ **car** 遥控电动玩具汽车. ~ **drills**【机】铣槽. ~ **machine** 自动售货机(等);吃角子老虎〔赌具〕. ~ **man** 负责新闻编排的报纸编辑.

slot[2] [slɔt] *n.* (鹿等的)足迹,臭迹. — *vt.* 跟着足迹追赶.

slot[3] [slɔt] *n.*〔英方〕门闩;〔方〕条板.

sloth [sləuθ] *n.* ①懒惰,怠惰. ②【动】树懒〔产于南美洲的一种哺乳动物,行动迟缓〕. ~ **bear**【动】(印度等地的)懒熊.
sloth·ful [ˈsləuθfəl] *a.* 偷懒的,懒惰的.
slouch [slautʃ] *n.* ①没精打采[垂头丧气]的姿态[步调]. ②(帽边等的)下垂,耷拉. ③萎靡不振的人; 不整洁的人; 不中用的人; 〔美〕无价值的场所[人、物]. *a ~ hat* 垂边帽,阔软边呢帽. *He is no ~.* 他不是不中用的人. — *vi.* ①没精打采地走[坐,站]. ②耷拉, 低垂. — *vt.* 使低垂. **-y** *a.* **-i·ly** *ad.* **-i·ness** *n.*
slough[1] [slau] *n.* ①低洼泥泞的地方,泥潭,泥坑; 泥沼. ②绝望的境地;堕落; 道德败坏. ③[slu:] 〔美、加拿大〕沼泽地中的小溪, 叉流, 河湾. *the ~ of despond* 失望的泥沼; 绝境; 异常沮丧的状态. — *vt.* ①使陷入泥沼; 〔喻〕使陷入泥坑; 使堕落, 使沉沦. ②〔美俚〕逮捕; 监禁 *(up, in)*. — *vi.* 在泥浆中跋涉.
slough[2] [slʌf] *n.* ①(蛇等蜕的)皮,壳; (动物身上)定时脱落的外表部分. ②被丢弃的东西(习惯、嗜好, 成见等). ③【医】腐肉,痂; 脱落. — *vi.* ①长痂, 生痂. ②(蛇皮等的)脱落;(蛇等)蜕皮. ③(标点等)漏掉. ③(岩石、河岸等)崩塌. — *vt.* ①脱落(皮等). ②抛弃, 丢弃 *(off)*. ③【牌】丢掉(没用的牌). *~ (off) bad habits* 戒掉坏习惯. *~* ***over*** 当作微不足道;轻视.
slough·y[1] [ˈslaui] *a.* 泥泞的;泥沼一样的.
slough·y[2] [ˈslʌfi] *a.* 蛇脱皮似的; 腐肉似的, 疙痂似的; 脱落的.
Slo·vak [ˈsləuvæk] *n.* 斯洛伐克人;斯洛伐克语. —*a.* 斯洛伐克的,斯洛伐克人的,斯洛伐克语的.
Slo·va·ki·a [sləuˈvækiə] *n.* 斯洛伐克[捷克斯洛伐克一地区].
Slo·va·ki·an [sləuˈvækiən] *n., a.* = Slovak.
slov·en [ˈslʌvən] *n.* 不修边幅的人,邋遢鬼, 懒鬼; 字迹[工作]潦草的人. — *a.* = ①slovenly. ②未开垦的;未开化的.
Slo·vene [ˈsləuvi:n], **Slo·ve·ni·an** [sləuˈvi:njən] *n.* 斯洛文尼亚人,斯洛文尼亚语. —*a.* 斯洛文尼亚的, 斯洛文尼亚人的,斯洛文尼亚语的.
Slo·ve·ni·a [sləuˈvi:njə] *n.* 斯洛文尼亚 〔南斯拉夫一地区〕.
slov·en·ly [ˈslʌvənli] *a., ad.* 邋遢的[地],不修边幅的[地], 不整洁的[地]; 懒散的[地]; 草率的[地].
slow [sləu] *a.* ①慢的,缓慢的 *(opp.* fast; quick; rapid; swift*)*. ②迟钝的,笨的; 没精神的,不活泼的; (表演等)没趣的. ③不激烈的,不尖锐的; 温和的,低下的. ④要求很长时间的, 逐步的. ⑤慢于…的,慢了的;晚于…的 *(on)*. ⑥落后的; 落后于时代的. ⑦作用缓慢的. ⑧(商业)吊滞的. ⑨(路面等) 妨碍前进(或行动的); 使减速的. *a ~ train* 慢车. *~ poison* 缓效毒药. *~ fire* 文火. *a ~ oven* 火力小的炉灶. *a ~ student* 学得慢的学生. *He was ~ to anger [wrath].* 他不轻易发怒. *His clock is slow.* 他的钟慢. *My watch is five minutes ~.* 我的表慢五分钟. *a ~ convalescence* 缓慢的恢复健康. *~ music* 哀乐. *find life ~ in the country* 觉得乡间生活沉闷. *a ~ town* 落后的城镇. *a ~ season* 淡季. *~ in action* 行动缓慢. *~ at account* 不善于算帐. ***~ and steady [sure]*** 慢而稳,稳步的. ***~ as (cold) molasses (in January)*** 〔美〕极缓慢的; 极迟钝的. ***~ as the seven-year itch*** 〔美〕极缓慢的. ***~ of speech [wit]*** 嘴钝[迟钝]的. — *ad.* 缓慢地; 慢慢. *go ~* 慢慢走; 慢慢做; 耽误; 小心地进行. *How ~ you read!* 你读得真慢! — *vt.* 使慢,开慢, 拖延 *(down; up; off)*; 使呆滞. — *vi.* 放慢,慢起来, 减(低)速(度). *~ down [up] (a motor-car)* 减低(汽车)速度. ~ **burn** 〔美俚〕渐渐的发怒. ~ **coach** 迟钝的人,慢性子的人; 时代落伍者. ~**-down** 减缓,减速; 减退. ~ **match** 慢燃引信头, 火绳, 导火线. ~**-motion camera (picture)**【影】(拍慢镜头的)高速摄影机, 用高速摄影机拍摄的(影片). ~**-moving** *a.* 动作缓慢的, 无进展的; 滞销的. ~**poke** 〔美俚〕做事慎重的人, 慢性子的人. ~ **starter** 〔美拳〕初防守后猛攻的拳击手. ~ **time** ①〔口〕(与夏季时间区别的)标准时间. ②【军】慢步[每步75厘米每分钟75步的步调]. ~**-up** 减缓. ~**-witted** *a.* 迟钝的, 笨的. ~ **worm**【动】蛇蜥. **-ly** *ad.* **-ness** *n.*
sloyd [slɔid] *n.* 以木雕手工为基础的手工教育 (= sloid).
S.L.P. = Socialist Labor Party 〔美〕社会主义工人党.
slub [slʌb] *n.*【纺】头道粗纺的棉纱[羊毛]; 纱节, 大肚纱[疵点]. — *vt., vi.*【纺】轻捻, 粗纺.
slub·ber [ˈslʌbə] *vt.* ①敷衍了事, 马马虎虎做; 乱七八糟地做. ②〔英方〕弄脏, 玷污. — *n.* 〔美〕卑鄙的人.
sludge [slʌdʒ] *n.* ①泥, 泥浆, 烂泥. ②(锅炉等的)泥状沉积物. ③半溶的雪; 浮冰. ④【矿】矿泥; 煤泥; 淤渣; 钻泥. ⑤【油】(油灌底部的)酸渣; 碱渣. ⑥【医】血泥, 红血球在血管中凝集. ⑦〔美俚〕胡说; 脏话; 猥亵行为. — *vt.* ①涂上污泥; 清除污泥. ②【医】使成血泥. ~ **worm**【动】正颤蚓.
sludg·y [ˈslʌdʒi] *a.* 有淤泥的; 泥泞的.
slue[1] [slu:] *vt.* 使斜向;【海】使转,使回转. — *vi.* 回转. — *n.* 回转; 回转后的方向.
slue[2] [slu:] *n.* = slew[2].
slue[3] [slu:] *n.* = slew[4].
slue·foot [ˈslu:fut] *n.* 〔美俚〕侦探.
slug[1] [slʌg] *n.* ①【动】蛞蝓,蜒蚰,鼻涕虫; 蛞蝓状幼虫. ②动作缓慢的人[动物,车,船]; 懒人. ③金属块[棒]; (气枪的)子弹. ④(开动自动售货机等的)代硬币的金属片; 〔美〕【电话】5分代币. ⑤【印】大嵌条. ⑥【物】斯勒格, 斯(质量单位). ⑦【无】铁心; 波导调配柱; 〔美口〕一口[一杯]酒. *a sea ~* 海参. — *vi.* ①捕杀蛞蝓. ②偷懒; 睡着. ③〔美〕喝一口酒. *~ indoors* 懒散在家里,偷懒在家. —*vt.* 在…中插嵌片. ~ **abed** *n.* 〔古〕睡懒觉的人.
slug[2] [slʌg] *v., n.* 〔美口〕 = slog. ~ **-nutty** *a.* 〔美俚〕 = punch-drunk.
slug·fest [ˈslʌgfest] *n.* 〔美俚〕拳赛.
slug·gard [ˈslʌgəd] *n.* 懒人. — *a.* = **-ly** 懒人的, 懒.
slug·ger [ˈslʌgə] *n.* ①〔美口〕(棒球拳击等的)猛击者. ②(不善于自卫的)职业拳击家.
slug·ging [ˈslʌgiŋ] *n.* 〔美俚〕打得猛的拳赛[棒球赛].
slug·gish [ˈslʌgiʃ] *a.* ①偷懒的, 懒惰的(人). ②(流水等)动得缓慢的,停滞的; 惰性的; 呆钝的, 不活泼的. ③(市场等)清淡的, 萧条的. **-ly** *ad.*
sluice [slu:s] *n.* ①水闸,水门,水闸门〔又称 ~-gate, ~-valve〕; 闸沟, 泄水道〔又称 ~-way〕; 闸口. ②(被闸门拦住或从闸门流出的)蓄水; 泄水. ③【林】(流放木材的)斜水槽. ④【矿】(洗金矿等用的)流矿槽;〔转义〕根本, 源泉. *open [let loose] the ~s* 开水闸, 让水流出; 〔喻〕将想说的话说出来; 让感情发泄出来. *have a ~* 〔俚〕洗澡. — *vt.* ①开闸灌溉,开闸放(水). ②冲洗,好好地洗. — *vi.* 流出,奔流.
slum[1] [slʌm] *n.* ①〔常 *pl.*〕贫民窟, 贫民区. — *vi.* 到贫民区去[观光,游玩等]; 在贫民区发展保险业务[从事慈善事业]. ~**dweller** 贫民窟居民. ~**lord** 〔俚〕贫民窟外出房东〔尤指勒索高价而不管房屋维修的屋主〕.
slum[2] [slʌm] *n.* = slumgullion.
slum·ber [ˈslʌmbə] *n.* ①微睡; 安眠, 熟睡; 打盹儿. ②蛰伏[静止]状态. —*vi.* ①睡眠, 微睡. ②蛰伏; 处于静止状态. — *vt.* (用睡眠)消磨(时间) *(away)*. *a ~(ing)-robe* 〔美〕睡衣. *a ~ bum* 〔美俚〕夜间看门人.
slum·ber·er [ˈslʌmbərə] *n.* 睡眠者; 微睡者.
slum·ber·ous, slum·brous [slʌmbərəs, -brəs] *a.* ①瞌睡的, 昏昏欲睡的. ②催眠的, 使人瞌睡的. ③睡着的,打着盹儿的; 寂静的.
slum·gul·lion [slʌmˈgʌliən] *n.* ①〔美俚〕淡饮料. ②燉肉; 马铃薯洋葱燉肉. ③原油渣. ④【采】洗矿沟中淤积的红泥浆. ⑤(捕鲸船甲板上的)残余血油. ⑥〔美蔑〕不中用的家伙; 仆役.
slum·mer [ˈslʌmə] *n.* 贫民区居民; 出入贫民区从事慈善事业[发展保险业务]的人.

slum·my [ˈslʌmi] *a.* 贫民区的.

slump [slʌmp] *n.* ①〔方〕陷入,掉下;〔方〕沼地. ②【商】(物价等的)暴跌;(事业的)衰败,低落;(精神等的)销沉,萎靡. — *vi.* ①〔方〕掉下,陷入(泥、雪等中); 崩坍. ②失败,挫折. ③【商】暴跌; 衰败; 销沉. ~ *into a chair* 倒在椅子里. *hit a* ~〔美〕(选手成绩)猛落.

slung [slʌŋ] sling 的过去式及过去分词. ~ **shot**〔美〕(弹弓上用的)石弹.

slunk [slʌŋk] slink 的过去式及过去分词.

slur [slə:] *vt.* 藐视,轻视;忽略,略过 *(over)*. ②急促而不清楚地讲[写]. ③【乐】圆润地接连唱[演奏]; 加连接线. ④弄脏,玷污;诬蔑,诽谤;掩饰,隐瞒;假装没看见. ⑤【印】涂污,印模糊. — *n.* 污点;耻辱; 毁谤,诬蔑,污辱;【乐】连接线;【印】污点,模糊不清处. ***put a ~ upon*** =〔美〕***cast ~s at*** 毁谤,诬蔑.

slurb [slə:b] *n.*【俚】市郊贫民区.

slurp [slə:p] *vt., vi.*【俚】咕噜咕噜地喝;叭嗒叭嗒地吃. — *n.*〔俚〕咕噜[叭嗒]声[吃喝或吸吮].

slur·ry [ˈslə:ri] *n.* ①泥浆;灰泥,水泥浆. ②膏剂;【机】型心粘合液. ~ *seed treatment*【农】拌种处理.

slush [slʌʃ] *n.* ①烂泥; 污水. ②半融雪(冰); 雪水. ③薄胶泥;搪瓷液料;脂膏. ④【机】机油; 抗蚀润滑油; 白铅石灰,油灰. ⑤水泥砂浆;纸浆. ⑥过于感情用事的言语[文字];哭诉;废话. ⑦〔美俚〕贿赂;伪钞. — *vt.* ①使溅上泥浆[雪水],溅污. ②涂润滑油于; 给…灌上泥浆; 给…嵌上油灰; 冲洗(甲板). — *vi.* ①(在泥浆等中)吃力地行走. ②发出溅泼声. **-y** *a.* 泥泞的. **-i·ness** *n.*

slut [slʌt] *n.* ①母狗. ②邋遢女人,懒女人. ③放荡的女人,妓女. ④〔谑〕少女,顽皮女孩. **-tish** *a.* **-tish·ly** *ad.* **-tish·ness** *n.*

slut·ter·y [ˈslʌtəri] *n.* 邋遢; 龌龊; 放荡 (= stuttishness).

sly [slai] *a.* ***(~er, sli·er; ~est, sli·est)*** ①狡猾的,狡诈的. ②顽皮的;淘气的. ③秘密的,暗中的,偷偷摸摸的. ④〔方〕灵活的,巧妙的. *He is a ~ dog.* 他是一个狡猾的家伙. ***on [upon] the ~***〔口〕秘密地,偷偷地. **~boots** *n.*〔*sing., pl.*〕顽皮的家伙[小孩、动物等];狡猾的人. **-ly** *ad.* **-ness** *n.*

slype [slaip] *n.*〔英〕(从教堂通到别院的)走廊.

SM, S.M. =①〔L.〕*Scientiae Magister* 理科硕士(=master of science). ②Sergeant Major【军】军士长. ③Soldier's Medal〔美〕军人奖章(因作战以外的英勇事迹而被授予的奖章). ④strategic missile 战略导弹. ⑤submarine minelayer 布雷潜水艇. ⑥short metre〔诗〕短韵律. ⑦Special Message〔美〕特别咨文. ⑧square metre 平方米.

Sm =【化】samarium.

SMA = Surplus Marketing Administration.〔美〕(军用)剩余物资销售管理局.

smack[1] [smæk] *n.* ①味,滋味,风味;气味. ②遗痕. ③些微,一点点. *a ~ of wine to each* 每人一点酒. — *vi.* 有味,有…的风味;有…的气味;有点象…的地方 *(of)*. *Southern cookery ~s of oil.* 南方口味油重. *His gait ~s of the sea.* 他走路的样子有点象海员. ***a wet ~*** 讨厌的人,使人扫兴的人.

smack[2] [smæk] *n.* ①咂嘴(声); 接吻(声); 鼓舌(声). ②用掌拍打(声);鞭声,劈拍声. *get a ~ in the eye* 遭受突如其来的打击[挫折].〔喻〕感到出乎意料的失望. *have a ~ at*〔口〕去试,去尝试. *tickets at three dollars a ~* 三元一张的票. — *vt., vi.* ①咂(嘴),有声响地吻. ②啪的一声用手掌猛击; (使)劈拍地响. ~ *one's lips over* 咂嘴;满足. ~ ***down***〔美俚〕(对不守本分的人)责斥,使屈辱. — *ad.* ①啪的一下;使劲;猛地. ②准确地,恰好,正好. *hit sb. ~ in the face* 啪的打一个耳光. *go ~ into the ditch* 啪的一跤摔在沟中. *run ~ into* 正好撞在.

smack[3] [smæk] *n.* 单桅小帆船;(有鱼池设备的)渔船.

smack[4] [smæk] *n.*〔俚〕海洛因.

smack·er [ˈsmækə] *n.* ①咂嘴的人;鞭打的人. ②啪的一击;殴打. ③极大的东西;绝好的东西. ④〔美俚〕一元. ⑤嘴巴,嘴唇;〔口〕大声接吻.

smack·ing [ˈsmækiŋ] *a.* 活泼的,精神勃勃的; 兴旺的; 尖锐的.

smacks·man [ˈsmæksmən] *n.* (有鱼池设备的)渔船的船主[船员].

small[1] [smɔ:l] *a.* ①小 *(opp.* large*)*; 少 *(opp.* large, numerous*)*; 细小的; 窄小的; 琐细的,些微的; 少额的(收入等);小规模的. ②吝啬的,小器的,小心眼儿的. ③难为情的,觉得羞耻的;低级的,贫穷的;卑劣的. ④(雨)细微的;(声音)微弱的;(酒等)清淡的. ★*little* 含有可怜可爱的意思, small 只照实叙述事实. *a ~ (bottle of) soda (water)* 一小瓶苏打水. *a ~ audience* 人数不多的听众[观众]. ~ *years* 小时候, 幼年. ~ *arms* 轻便武器,〔尤指〕步枪. ~ *errors* 小过, 小错. ~ *rain* 细雨. *He has ~ French and less German.* 他不大懂法语, 德语更不行. *It is ~ of you to say so.* 你这样说那就小气了. *a ~ nature* 小心眼. ~ *cares and worries* 无谓的操心烦恼. ~ *punkins*〔美〕无足轻重的;所谓要人;〔讽〕小要人[其实是不足道的小人物]. ***and ~ blame to him*** 对他没有多少可以责备的地方. ***and ~ wonder*** 没有什么奇怪的. ***and such ~ deer*** 其他闲杂人等,其他的人们. ***be great in ~ matters*** 小事聪明. ***by ~ and ~*** 慢慢地,一点一点地. ***feel ~*** 觉得难为情,觉得羞耻. ***in a ~ way*** 小规模地;朴素地. ***in ~ numbers*** 少. ***It is ~ wonder that***(这件事)并不足怪. ***live in a ~ way*** 简朴谨慎地过日子. ***look ~*** 显得渺小,自惭形秽. ***of no ~ consequence*** 重大的. ***on the ~ side*** 比较小. — *n.* ①〔the~〕细小部分,〔尤指〕腰部. ②小物,琐碎东西;身分低的人. ③〔*pl.*〕小商品;〔英口〕小件洗濯物;〔英牛津大学〕〔*pl.*〕= responsions. *(the) great and (the) ~* 身分高高低低的人们. ***a. ~ and early*** 人少而早散的晚会. ***in ~*** =〔罕〕***in the ~*** 小规模. — *ad.* 小声地, 轻轻地 (讲等). **~-beer** ①*n.* 淡啤酒. ②*a.* 无价值的,微不足道的 (*think no ~-beer of oneself* 自负). **~-bore** ①小口径枪的. ②眼界狭窄的. ~ **calorie**【物】小卡. ~ **capitals [caps]**【印】小体大写字母. ~ **change** 找头; 无聊话; 〔美〕无用的人[东西]. ~ **clothes** 〔*pl.*〕〔古〕短裤,小件衣服. ~ **fry** 小鱼; 微不足道的人[物]. ~ **game** 小猎狗. ~ **helm**【海】小舵〔指舵和龙骨线成很小的角度〕. ~ **holder** (耕地 1—50 英亩的) 小自耕农. ~ **holding** 小自耕农地,小地产. ~ **hours** 夜半后一、两点钟的时间,深更半夜. ~ **letter** 小写体(字母). **~-minded** *a.* 气量狭窄的,小心眼的,小气的. **~mouth (black) bass**【动】小口黑鲈. ~ **potatoes**〔作单数用〕〔美俚〕小人物. **~pox**【医】天花. **~-scale** *a.* 小比例尺的(地图);小规模的(*-scale business operations* 小规模商业活动). ~ **stores** (船上供应船员的)小卖部. **~-sword** 尖头刺剑〔劈剑用〕. ~ **talk** 闲谈 *n.* **~-talk** *vi.* 聊天 *(They like to ~-talk.* 他们喜欢聊天*)*. ~ **time** ①短时间. ②〔美〕小职业棒球队. ③一天反复小演同一戏剧的流动演出;薪水少的职位. **~-time** *a.*〔美口〕不重要的,不成功的, 不出色的, 劣等的 (*~-time stuff* 劣货; 笨举; 琐事). **~-timer** 小剧团从业人员;小规模事业组织的从业人员. **~-town** 小市镇的; 乡土气的,内地色彩的,简单朴实的. ~ **wares** 杂货,小东西;狭幅衣料. **-smal·ly** *ad.* 小规模地.

small·age [ˈsmɔ:lidʒ] *n.*〔罕〕【植】芹菜 *(Apium graveolens)*.

small·ish [ˈsmɔ:liʃ] *a.* 略小的,有点小的.

small·ness [ˈsmɔ:lnis] *n.* 小,少;些微;小规模;低贱;吝啬,小气;卑鄙.

smalt [smɔ:lt] *n.* ①【化】大青,花绀青,藤紫〔颜料〕. ②(用钴、钾碱、硅石制成的)蓝玻璃. ③大青色.

smal·tite [ˈsmɔːtait] *n.*【矿】砷钴矿.
smal·to [ˈsmɑːltəu; *It.* ˈzmɑːltəu] *n.* *(pl.* **-tos, -ti** [tiː]*)* ①用于镶嵌工艺的色玻璃或搪瓷. ②一块色玻璃, 一块搪瓷.
smar·agd [ˈsmærægd] *n.*〔现罕〕= emerald. **-ine** *a.*
sma·rag·dite [sməːrægdait] *n.*【矿】绿闪石.
smarm·y [ˈsmɑːmi]〔英口〕*a.* 满口恭维话的, 爱拍马的.
smart [smɑːt] *a.* ①灵敏的,灵巧的,敏捷的;聪明的,伶俐的. ②漂亮的, 衣冠楚楚的, 潇洒的; 时髦的 *(opp.* shabby, dingy*)*. ③精明的,狡猾的. ④刺痛的,厉害的,强烈的,猛烈的;尖锐的;辛辣的;活泼的, 有力的; 爽快的,痛快的;〔口〕粗鲁的,无礼的. ⑤〔口〕可观的,相当大[多]的. *a ~ saying* 漂亮话. *~ clothes* 漂亮的衣服. *~ dealings* 狡猾的手段. *~ frost* 严霜. *a ~ skirmish* 猛烈的小接触. *walking a ~ pace* 轻快的步伐行走. *a ~ few* 相当多(的). ***as ~ as a new pin [threepence]*** 〔口〕非常潇洒的[时髦的]. ***as ~ as a steel trap***〔美俚〕(做生意等)非常精明的. ***be ~ (about it)*** 做得麻利. ***make a ~ job of it*** 办得巧妙. ***right ~***〔美口〕极大的, 许许多多的 (*a right ~ rain* 暴雨).***~ as threepence***〔英俚〕穿着得漂亮. — *ad.* = smartly. — *vi.* ①刺痛;作痛. ②痛苦,伤心,悲痛;愤慨 *(under)*. ③受罚,受罪 *(for)*. *~ under an injustice* 因受委曲而感痛心. *The eyes ~ with smoke.* 眼睛给烟熏得痛. *~ from an insult* 因受辱而愤慨. *~ with mortification* 因屈辱而痛心. *~ for* 因…受罚,因…吃苦头. — *n.* 疼痛;苦痛; 悲痛; 愤慨. *feel the ~ of one's folly* 痛恨自己愚蠢. ~ **alec, ~aleck** [-ˈælik], ~ **ellick** [-ˈelik] *n.* 自作聪明的人. **~-aleckry, ~-aleckism** 自作聪明,自以为样样都懂; 刚愎自用. **~-alecky [~-aleck, ~-alec]** *a.* 自作聪明的,自以为样样都懂的. ~ **bomb** (装有激光制导器的)灵敏炸弹. ~ **chance**〔美〕绝好的机会;大量. ~ **money** ①赔偿金,罚金. ②〔英〕伤兵抚恤金. ③(知道内情者投下的)可操胜算的赌注[投资]. ~ **set**〔美〕时髦人士. **~weed**【植】蓼车.
smart·en [ˈsmɑːtn] *vt.* ①使漂亮潇洒,打扮 *(up)*. ②使活泼, 使轻快. ③使强烈; 使清醒[了解情况]. ④使聪明, 使精明*(up)*. — *vi.* ①变得漂亮潇洒. ②变强烈. ***~ oneself*** (漂漂亮亮地)打扮. ***~ up***〔美俚〕劝告;说明.
smartie [ˈsmɑːti] *n.* = smarty.
smart·ish [ˈsmɑːtiʃ] *a.* ①相当漂亮的. ②〔口〕相当的. — *ad.*〔口语〕厉害. ***a ~ few*** 许多.
smart·ly [ˈsmɑːtli] *ad.* ①华美地,漂亮地. ②一阵一阵刺痛地;厉害地,剧烈地,猛烈地. ③聪明地; 精明地; 机敏地;伶俐地.
smart·y [ˈsmɑːti] *n.* 自作聪明的人 (= smart aleck). **~-pants** = smarty.
smash [smæʃ] *vt.* ①打碎,打破,打烂;压碎,捣烂;碰撞. ②使破产;击溃. ③猛击; 猛掷;【网球】从上往下猛杀, 猛扣. ④使(原子、原子核)发生裂变. *~ up the furniture* 捣毁家俱. *~ an egg* 打破蛋. *~ the record* 打破纪录. *~ the jinx*〔美运〕连败后的胜利. — *vi.* ①碎裂,粉碎;压碎. ②猛冲, 猛撞 *(against, into, through)*. ③破产,倒闭 *(up)*; 瓦解, 垮掉. ④扣球, 杀球. ⑤〔俚〕使用伪造的货币. *~ in a door* (从外面)打破门户. *~ into a wall* 撞在墙上. — *n.* ①破碎,粉碎;全部毁灭;破产;(火车等的)猛撞, 重击; 破碎声, 重击声. ②【网球】杀球,扣球. ③甜酒薄荷水. ④〔美〕大成功. *the ~ of two automobiles* 两车相撞. ***all to ~*** (完全)粉碎;全部崩溃. ***come [go] (to) ~*** 粉碎;破产. ***play ~***〔美〕破产. — *ad.* 轰然. ***run [go] ~ into*** 和…迎面相撞. ~ **hit** 最佳电影;演出极为成功的戏剧.
smashed [smæʃt] *a.*【俚】沉醉的;烂醉如泥的.
smash·er [ˈsmæʃə] *n.* ①打碎者,击破器,破碎器. ②〔俚〕猛烈的打击,崩溃;厉害的回答,使人无可答辩的议论. ③绝好的东西; 漂亮的人[物]. ④〔俚〕用假钱的人;赝币,伪币.
smash·ing [ˈsmæʃiŋ] *a.* ①凶猛的,沉重的, 惨重的, 粉碎性的(打击等). ②活泼的, (商业情况等)兴旺的. ③〔俚〕漂亮的,突出的,不一般的. *a ~ success* 极大的成功. *a ~ victory* 巨大胜利. *have a ~ time* 玩得非常痛快.
smash·up [smæʃʌp] *n.* ①〔口〕破碎, 粉碎. ②〔美〕(火车等的)猛撞. ③失败,破产;崩溃,破灭.
smat·ter [ˈsmætə] *n.*〔美,英古〕肤浅的知识 (= smattering). — *vt.* 一知半解地谈论;肤浅地研究, 涉猎. — *vi.* 一知半解地瞎说, 装懂, 充内行. **-er** *n.* 一知半解的人.
smat·ter·ing [ˈsmætəriŋ] *n.* ①肤浅的知识,一知半解;半瓶子醋. ②少数, 少量. *to rest content with a ~ of knowledge* 满足于一知半解.
smaze [smeiz] *n.*【气】烟霾,烟雾.
S.M.C. = spermatocyte; sperm mother-cell【生】精母细胞.
sm.c., sm. caps. = small capitals【印】小号大写字母.
smear [smiə] *vt.* ①搽上,涂上,抹上(油、漆等). ②涂去,抹掉. ③(油、墨水等)抹脏,涂污,弄得模糊不明,涂得不能辨认出. ④〔美〕(尤指政客)诽谤, 糟蹋(名誉). ⑤〔美俚〕打倒, 打垮, 击破. *~ the address on a letter* 把信上的地址弄得看不清楚. *~ the record*〔美运〕大胜. *~ a wet signature* 把一个墨迹未乾的签名弄糊涂. *~ a word* 涂掉一个字. — *n.* ①油迹,污点,污斑. ②【生】涂片;涂料;釉. ③〔美口〕诽谤,中伤. *a ~ camera* 扫描摄影机. **~-bund** 诽谤集团. ~ **case**〔美〕乡下干酪. **~-caster**〔美〕诽谤者.
smear·y [ˈsmiəri] *a.* 弄脏的,易涂污的; 油污的; 涂用的. **~i·ness** *n.*
smec·tic [ˈsmektik] *a.* ①【化】碟状液晶分子的, 近晶的. ②净化的.
Smed·ley [ˈsmedli] *n.* 斯梅德利〔姓氏〕.
smeech [smiːtʃ] *n.*〔方〕焦臭;浓烟.
smeg·ma [ˈsmegmə] *n.*【医】阴垢; 包皮垢. **~tic** *a.*
smell [smel] *vt.* *(***smelt,**〔美〕***~ed*** [-d]*)* ①闻, 嗅. ②闻出; 发觉, 查出 *(out)*. ③发出…的气味. *~ trouble* 觉察出困难. *~ the milk to tell if it's sour* 闻一下牛奶,看是否发酸了. — *vi.* ①有嗅觉; 有难闻的气味; 有某种气味[样子] *(of)*. ②闻闻看 *(at; of; to)*; 想闻出 *(about)*. *You ~ wine.* 你身上一股酒味. *You shall ~ of the whip.* 要你尝尝鞭子的味儿. *Meat began to ~.* 肉开始发臭了. *a ~ing committee*〔美俚〕调查委员. ***~ about [round]*** 到处嗅寻, 到处打听. ***~ a rat*** 怀疑起来. ***~ of drink*** 有酒臭, 有酒气. ***~ of the inkhorn*** 有学究气. ***~ of the lamp*** 显然是用功到深夜; (著作上)表现出下过苦工夫. ***~ out*** ①闻出. ②细心研究出;察觉. ***~ powder*** 体验实际战斗生活. ***~ the ground***【海】水渐浅,渐渐减低速度. ***~ up*** (使)发散臭气,(使)充满臭气. — *n.* 嗅觉;香,臭;气味;闻,嗅. *What a lot of ~s!* 真难闻! ***have a ~ of = take a ~ at*** (将…)闻闻看. **~age**〔集合词〕有香味的植物. **~-feast** 逢人家请客就去大吃的人; 食客. **~ing-bottle** (装有炭酸铵的)嗅盐瓶. **~ing-salts** (从前治昏厥、头痛用的)炭酸铵醒药,嗅盐. **-er** ①嗅的人;发出臭气的人[东西]. ②〔俚〕鼻子; 〔俚〕间谍. ③〔俚〕(对准鼻子的)猛击. ④(动物的)触角,触须. **-less** *a.* 无臭的, 无气味的. **-y** *a.*〔口〕有臭味的,发臭的.
smelt[1] [smelt] smell 的过去式及过去分词.
smelt[2] [smelt] *n.* *(pl.* *~s,*〔集合词〕*~)*【鱼】胡瓜鱼(属).
smelt[3] [smelt] *vt.*【冶】熔炼; 提炼; 冶炼. — *vi.* 受熔炼. **~ing-furnace** 熔炉. **-er** *n.* ①熔铸工,冶炼者. ②冶炼厂;熔炉.
smelt·er·y [ˈsmeltəri] *n.* 冶炼厂.

smew [smju:] *n.* 【鸟】鸦鸥,斑头秋沙鸭.

SMG, smg = submachine gun 冲锋枪,轻型自动枪,半自动枪.

smice [smais] *n.* 冰雾.

smidg·en [ˈsmidʒən] *n.* 〔美口〕一丁点儿 (= smidgin, smidgeon).

smi·lax [ˈsmailæks] *n.* 【植】①〔S-〕菝葜属. ②圆叶菝葜.

smile [smail] *vi.* ①微笑 *(at; on; upon)* (*opp.* frown). ②讥笑,冷笑 *(at)*. ③眉开眼笑,现笑脸;表示友好态度;(天气等)变晴朗;呈现乐观气象. — *vt.* ①作某种笑容;以微笑表示. ②以微笑促使. *I should* ~. 〔美口〕好得很,我很高兴. *She* ~*s her consent.* 她以微笑表示同意. ~ *a forced smile* 强作笑容. **come up smiling** (对失败、灾难等)不屈服地挺身迎接. ~ **sb. into good humor** 微笑着使人高兴起来. ~ **at** 看着…微笑; (对威胁等)一笑置之,无视,嘲笑 (*She* ~*d at his threats.* 她对他的威胁一笑置之). ~ **away** 笑着忘掉;一笑置之. ~ **on** 向…微笑 (*Fortune* ~*d on us.* 好运来了.) ~ **upon** = ~ on. — *n.* ①微笑;冷笑;笑脸;喜气;友好态度. ②〔美俚〕一杯威士忌酒. *He was all* ~*s when I met him next.* 第二次碰见时他已经满脸笑容[不生气]了. *a forced* ~ 勉强的笑容. *a best Sunday* ~ 〔口〕非常快乐的笑. *a bitter* ~ 苦笑. *crack a* ~ 展颜微笑. *have a* ~ 喝一杯威士忌. **the** ~**s of fortune** 好运. **-r** *n.* **-less** *a.*

smile·age [ˈsmaileidʒ] *n.* 〔美俚〕持久的愉快心情;不绝的微笑.

smil·ing [ˈsmailiŋ] *a.* 微笑的,含笑的,亲切的;明媚的(风景等);表示好感的;呈现乐观气象的. **-ly** *ad.*

smirch [smə:tʃ] *vt.* 沾污,损坏(名誉等). — *n.* 污斑,污点 *(on; upon)*.

smirk [smə:k] *n.* 傻笑;假笑. — *vi.* 假笑,嘻嘻地傻笑 *(at; on; upon)*. — *vt.* 假笑着说.

smite [smait] *vt.* (**smote** [sməut]; **smit·ten** [smitn], 〔古〕**smit** [smit]) ①打,重击;杀死. ②破坏,毁灭 *(with)*;打败;惩罚. ③(疾病等)侵袭,袭击 *(with)*. ④使深深感动;迷住;使心中苦恼. — *vi.* 打,重击,撞;突然来临 *(on; into)*. ~ *a person dead* 打死某人. *My conscience* ~*s me.* 我良心上过意不去. *be smitten by the charms of* 被…的魅力迷住. *be smitten with palsy* 害中风病. ~ *on the door* 敲门. *His knees smote together* 他的双膝互撞. — *n.* 〔口〕打,打击;【板球】猛击;尝试,企图;一点儿. *It didn't do a* ~ *of good.* 一点儿效果也没有. *have a* ~ *at it* 试试看.

Smith [smiθ] *n.* ①史密斯〔姓氏〕. ② **Adam** ~ 亚当·史密斯〔1723—1790,英国经济学家〕.

smith [smiθ] *n.* ①铁匠,冶工,锻工;金属工匠. ②〔通常用以构成复合词〕…的制造者. 〔*cf.* gold*smith* 金匠, silver*smith,* 银匠, tune*smith* 作曲者〕.

smith·er·eens [ˈsmiðəˈri:nz] *n.* 〔*pl.*〕〔口〕碎片,碎粉. *break [smash] into [to]* ~ 粉碎. *It should be smashed to* ~ 应当彻底摧毁.

smith·er·y [ˈsmiθəri] *n.* 锻冶术;铁匠铺,铁工厂,锻工车间;铁匠业.

Smith·field (Market) [ˈsmiθfi:ld] *n.* 伦敦肉市场.

Smith·son [ˈsmiθsn] *n.* 史密森〔姓氏〕.

Smith·so·nian Institution [smiθˈsəunjən] 因出资创办人史密森得名,(设在华盛顿的)美国国立博物馆 (= S- Institute).

smith·son·ite [ˈsmiθsəˌnait] *n.* 【矿】菱锌矿.

smith·y [ˈsmiði, ˈsmiθi] *n.* ①铁匠铺;锻工车间;锻铁炉. ②铁匠,锻工.

smit·ten [ˈsmitn] smite 的过去分词.

S.M.M. = 〔L.〕*Sancta Mater Maria* (= Holy Mother Maria) 【宗】圣母玛利亚.

smock [smɔk] *n.* 〔古〕女衬衣;(孩子、妇女、画家等的)罩衫 (= smockfrock). — *vt.* 给…穿上罩衫;用褶裥装饰. ~ **frock** (欧洲农民干活时穿的)长罩衫.

smock·ing [smɔkiŋ] *n.* 规则几何图案的抽褶.

smog [smɔg] *n.* 烟雾 〔= smoke + fog〕. **-gy** *a.*

smok·a·ble [ˈsməukəbl] *a.* 可吸的;可抽的. — *n.* 〔*pl.* 集合词〕各种烟(香烟,雪茄烟等).

smoke [sməuk] *n.* ①烟,烟尘,烟柱;雾;水气,蒸气;尘雾. ②没有实体[意义、现实性]的事物;空谈;空虚. ③模糊视线的东西. ④抽烟;香烟、雪茄烟;〔俚〕内含大麻叶毒品的香烟. ⑤烟色,暗灰色. ⑥〔美俚〕劣质酒. ⑦〔俚〕黑人. ⑧〔俚〕铁道救火员. *No* ~ *[There is no* ~*] without fire.* 无火不生烟,无风不起浪. *a box of good* ~*s* 〔俚〕一盒上好雪茄烟. *have a* ~ 抽一口烟. **end up in** ~ 烟消云散,不成功,终成泡影. **from** ~ **into smother** 越来越坏. **go up in** ~ ①烧尽. ②〔喻〕毫无结果,化为乌有. **like (a)** ~ **(on fire)** 〔俚〕无阻碍地,迅速地,轻易地. *watch my* ~ 〔美俚〕看我的本领,看我做得多快. — *vi.* ①烟,熏;冒烟;冒水蒸气;(烟似地)袅袅上升. ②吸烟,抽烟. ③迅速地走(致使尘土飞扬). ④发火,生气 *(against)*;〔学生语〕脸红. ⑤〔古〕受苦,受罚. ⑥〔美俚〕开枪. —*vt.* ①用烟熏,熏脏,熏黑;熏走,熏死(虫等);熏制. ②吸(烟),抽(烟);抽烟而…. ③〔古〕发觉;怀疑;〔美〕查明,使说出秘密. ④〔古〕嘲弄,欺负,欺骗. ⑤〔美俚〕开枪打,射击. *That oil-lamp* ~*s badly.* 那盏油灯烟冒得很厉害. *You must not* ~ *in this carriage.* 车内不可抽烟. ~ *oneself sick* 抽烟抽得不舒服. *The milk has been* ~*d.* 牛奶带烟味儿了. *Put that in your pipe and* ~ *it.* 仔细想想(我的话)吧. ~ *like a chimmney* 烟瘾很大. *Their swords* ~*d with blood.* 冒血腥气. ~ **abatement** 防烟法. ~ **ball** = ~ bomb. ~ **bell** 烟罩. ~ **bomb** 烟幕弹. ~ **box** (汽锅的)烟室,烟箱. ~**chaser** 森林灭火员. ~ **consumer** 完全燃烧装置. ~ **curtain** 【军】烟幕. ~**-dried** *a.* 熏制的. ~**-fest** 〔美〕抽烟叙谈会. ~**-filled room** (旅馆中)政客们进行商谈的密室. ~ **helmet,** ~ **mask** 救火帽;防毒面具. ~**house** 熏制所;熏肉贮藏所. ~ **jack** (借烟囱内气体上升力驱动的)自动旋转烤肉装置. ~ **jumper** 森林跳伞灭火员. ~**-oh** = smoko. ~ **pipe** (金属的)烟囱筒. ~ **projector** 烟幕放射器. ~**proof** *a.* 不透烟的,防烟的. ~ **ring** 吸烟者吐出的烟圈. ~ **room** 〔主英〕吸烟室. ~**-screen** 【军】烟幕;障眼法. ~ **seasoning** 熏干. ~ **shell** 发烟炮弹. ~ **signal** 狼烟;征兆,象征. ~**stack** 烟囱. ~**stone** 【矿】烟晶. ~ **tracer** 曳烟弹. ~**tree** 【植】黄栌(属). ~**-up** 〔美俚〕广告宣传;学生成绩不及格通知;轰炸. ~ **wag(g)on** 〔美俚〕手枪;火车.

smoke·less [ˈsməuklis] *a.* 无烟的. ~ *powder* 无烟火药.

smok·er [ˈsməukə] *n.* ①熏制(肉类)者. ②吸烟者;吸烟室;〔口〕允许吸烟的车厢;允许吸烟的音乐会;〔美〕男子非正式的聚会. ③冒烟的东西;施放烟幕的船只[飞机]. ④养蜂用熏箱. ⑤〔学生语〕害羞的人. ⑥〔美俚〕蒸汽火车头. *a heavy* ~ 烟瘾大的人. ~**'s heart [throat]** 吸烟过度而生的心脏病[喉病]. **-y** *n.* 吸烟室.

Smok·ey [ˈsməuki] 护林熊〔森林防火标志,是一头穿着护林人员制服的漫画熊〕.

smok·i·ly [ˈsməukili] *ad.* 冒着烟;烟雾弥漫;如烟.

smok·ing [ˈsməukiŋ] *n.* ①冒烟;冒水蒸气,冒汗. ②吸烟. — *a.* ①冒烟的,熏的;冒水蒸气的,朦胧的. ②吸烟用的. — *ad.* 冒着热气. *No* ~ 禁止吸烟. *a* ~ *steed* 冒汗的马. ~ *hot soup* 热气腾腾的汤. ~ **cap** 吸烟帽. ~ **car,** ~ **carriage,** ~ **compartment** (火车等的)吸烟室. ~ **concert** 允许吸烟的音乐会. ~ **jacket** (吸烟时套在外面的)吸烟服. ~ **lamp** (船上的)允许吸烟信号灯. ~ **mixture** 杂拌烟丝. ~ **room** 吸烟室. ~**-room** *a.* 淫秽的,只适合男子的 (*a* ~*-room talk* 避开女人讲的话).

smo·ko [ˈsməukəu] 〔Austral.〕 *n.* ①工间休息和抽烟时

间;吃茶点时间. ②允许抽烟的音乐会.

smok·y [ˈsməuki] *a.* ①冒烟的;熏的;如烟的;烟雾弥漫的. ②熏黑了的,熏污了的. ③不高兴的,不开心的;〔美俚〕雾深的. ~ **quartz**【矿】烟晶. **-i·ly** *ad.* **-i·ness** *n.*

smol·der [ˈsməuldə] *vi., n.* = smoulder.

Smol·lett [ˈsmɔlit] *n.* 斯莫利特〔姓氏〕.

smolt [sməult] *n.* 初次由河入海的小鲑.

smooch[1] [smuːtʃ] *v., n.* 〔美俚〕接吻;拥抱,爱抚;〔美〕= smutch.

smooch[2] [smuːtʃ] *n., vt.* 弄脏. — *n.* 污迹.

smooth [smuːð] *a.* ①滑溜的, 平滑的, 光滑的(表面) *(opp.* rough*)*. ②流利的,流畅的(文章等);柔嫩的,柔和的,悦耳的(声音、调子等);进行顺利的(事情);口齿伶俐的(人);温和的,圆滑的(态度等). ③平静的,安稳的(航海等). ④无毛的,无须的(脸等). ⑤【语音】不送气的. ⑥调匀的(液体,浆糊等);易上口的,和淡的,温和的(酒等). ⑦〔美俚〕极好的,绝妙的,可爱的,迷人的. *make* ~ 弄平滑;扫除障碍. *run* ~ 进行顺利 (*The course of true love never did run* ~. 恋爱无坦途;好事多磨). — *ad.* = smoothly. *a* ~ *skin* 光滑的皮肤. *a* ~ *chin* 没有须的下巴. ~ *temper* 温和的脾气. ~ *manners* 文明礼貌的态度[举止]. *a* ~ *flight* 平稳的飞行. *The way is now* ~. 路平坦了;困难扫除了. *a* ~ *cocktail* 柔和可口的鸡尾酒. ***get to [reach]*** ~ ***water*** 到达平静的海面;度过困难到达顺境. ***in*** ~ ***water*** 处身顺境. ***speak*** ~ ***words*** 圆滑地搪塞. — *vt.* ①弄平滑,弄光滑,烫平,垫平,校平 *(away; down; out; over)*. ②抹平,抚平(发等);使流利,使流畅;使容易;消除(障碍等). ③掩饰,粉饰,遮掩. ④使柔和;缓和,镇定. ⑤使(文体,举止)高雅,使(面部表情)平和;使(晚年等)平安. — *vi.* ①变平滑,变光滑. ②变平静,变缓和 *(down)*. ~ ***away [over]*** 使容易,排除,解决(困难等);调解,调停;掩饰,粉饰. ~ ***the way*** 铺平道路,排除障碍,使容易做. — *n.* ①〔口〕光滑部分,平滑的水面[地面];(事情的)平易方面,愉快方面. ②抚平,抹平. ③〔美〕平地;草原;一角银币. ④修光[磨平]的工具. *give a* ~ *to the hair* 把头发抹平. ***take the rough with the*** ~ 安然自偷,不介意人世苦乐浮沉. ~**bore** 滑膛枪,滑膛炮. ~ **breathing**【语音】不送气符号[希腊文中做在打头的不送气元音前的"'"];不送气音. ~**dogfish**【动】星鲨. ~**-drying** *a.* (指织物)免烫, 干后自然平滑不皱的. ~ **face** ①没胡子的脸. ②伪善的人,谄媚的人. ~**-faced** *a.* 表面平滑的; 刮得光滑的(脸), 没胡须的,讨人欢喜的,和颜悦色的; 装老实的, 装谦恭的. ~ **hound**【动】星鲨属鲨鱼. ~**ing**【统】修匀. ~**ing iron** 烙铁,熨斗. ~ **move**〔美〕聪明的[爽快的、狡猾的]行动. ~ **muscle**【解】平滑肌. ~**-paper magazine**〔美〕高级杂志. ~**ing plane** (木匠的)细刨. ~**-shaven** *a.* 胡须刮得光光的,不留胡须的. ~**-spoken,** ~**-tongued** *a.* 油嘴滑舌的,甜言蜜语的;娓娓动听的,能说会道的. ~ **things** 恭维话. **-ly** *ad.* **-ness** *n.*

smooth·en [ˈsmuːðən] *vt., vi.* = smooth.

smooth·ie [ˈsmuːði] *n.* 〔美俚〕*n.* 圆滑的人;会迎合人的人;举止文雅的人.

smor·gas·bord [ˈsmɔːgəsbɔːd] *n.* 〔Sw.〕①瑞典式餐前冷菜;瑞典式冷菜宴会;瑞典式冷菜餐馆. ②大杂烩.

smor·zan·do [smɔrtsaːndəu] *a.* 〔It.〕【乐】(音响)逐渐消失,减弱音响和减慢速度.

smote [sməut] smite 的过去式.

smoth·er [ˈsmʌðə] *vt.* ①使透不过气来,使窒息;闷死,扼杀;盖熄,闷住(火等). ②抑制住(感情),止住;隐蔽,遮掩(罪恶等);扣压(报告等);笼罩,覆盖. ③【烹】蒸,闷,煨. ④密密地涂上[浇上]. ⑤〔美运〕使对方大败. — *vi.* ①透不过气来,窒息;闷死. ②用文火闷烧,微燃,闷燃,熏,冒烟;给包住,隐藏;(事实等)被捂住. ③被抑制,被忍住. ~ *a yawn* 忍住呵欠. ~ *a scandal* 掩盖丑事. ~ *the patient in blankets* 把病人包在毯子里. ~ *a salad with oil* 在生菜上浇满油. ~ ***sb. with (kisses)*** (吻得)透不过气来. ~ ***up*** 蒙蔽过去,含糊了结;压制. — *n.* ①窒息物;窒息状态,被抑制状态. ②浓烟,浓雾,浓尘;冒烟;冒着烟的火. ③制止,抑制. ④一片混乱,一大堆乱七八糟的东西. ~***ed mate*** (国际象棋)用马将死对方王的一着. **-er** *n.* **-y** *a.*

smo(u)l·der [ˈsməuldə] *vi.* ①慢燃;用文火闷烧,熏烧. ②(愤怒等)在心中燃烧;表现出闷在心里的愤怒[仇恨];郁积. — *n.* 慢燃,无焰闷燃. *The* ~ *will soon be a flame.* 闷火很快变为烈焰.

smouse [smaus] *n.* 〔俚〕犹太人;(南非的)商贩.

s.m.p = 〔L.〕*sine mascula prole* 无男性后代(= without male issue).

Smri·ti [ˈsmriti] *n.* 印度传统的宗教教义.

smudge[1] [smʌdʒ] *n.* ①污点, 污斑, 污迹. ②模糊的字迹. — *vt.* ①弄脏,涂污,玷污. ②涂去,使模糊. — *vi.* 变脏,被弄脏;变模糊.

smudge[2] [smʌdʒ] *n.* (为驱虫或防止农作物冻伤而生的)冒浓烟的火堆,浓烟. —*vt.* 使冒浓烟;用烟熏(驱虫).

smudg·y [ˈsmʌdʒi] *a.* 弄脏了的;熏黑了的;不鲜明的. **-i·ly** *ad.* **-i·ness** *n.*

smug [smʌg] *a.* ①整洁的;体面的. ②沾沾自喜的,自以为是的(人). *the* ~ *calculation* 如意算盘. — *n.* ①自命不凡的人,沾沾自喜的人. ②〔英大学俚〕死用功不活动的学生,书呆子. **-ly** *ad.* **-ness** *n.*

smug·gle [ˈsmʌgl] *vt.* 走私,私运,做走私生意;偷偷拿进[拿出] *(in; out; over)*. — *vi.* 走私. ~*d goods* 走私货. ~ *a clause into the bill* 偷偷在议案上添了一项条款.

smug·gler [ˈsmʌglə] *n.* 走私者;走私船;私酒酿造者.

smug·gling [ˈsmʌgliŋ] *n.* 走私; 秘密买卖. *a* ~ *ring [gang]* 走私集团.

smut [smʌt] *n.* ①煤烟,煤炱;(含大量泥质的)劣煤. ②污点;污斑;污物. ③【植】黑穗病,黑粉病. ④猥亵的言语[文字];〔美〕〔*pl.*〕猥亵的图片. *covered (kernel)* ~ 坚黑穗病. *loose (kernel)* ~ 散黑穗病. *long* ~ 角黑穗病. *head* ~ 黑穗病. — *vt.*①(用煤烟等)弄脏,弄黑. ②使患黑穗病[黑粉病]. — *vi.* ①变黑;弄脏. ②患黑穗病[黑粉病]. ***brother*** ~〔卑〕你 *(Ditto, brother* ~. 你也一样〔反击口气〕). ~ **ball**【微】马勃菌科的菌. ~ **mill** (清除患黑穗病谷粒的)清谷机. **-ty** *a.*

smutch [smʌtʃ] *n.* ①污点,污迹. ②炭炱;尘垢;污物. —*vi.* 〔英古,美〕= smudge. — *vt.* (用煤烟等)弄脏,弄黑. **-y** *a.*

smut·ty [ˈsmʌti] *a.* ①给煤灰弄黑的, 熏黑的. ②患黑穗病[黑粉病]的;猥亵的. **-ti·ly** *ad.* **-ti·ness** *n.*

Smyr·na [ˈsməːnə] *n.* 士麦那〔即 Izmir 伊兹密尔〕〔土耳其港市〕.

Smyr·ni·ot(e) [ˈsməːniət] *a., n.* (土耳其西部海港)士麦那的(人).

Smyth [smiθ, smaiθ] *n.* 史密斯[姓氏].

S/N = shipping note 装船通知书.

Sn = 【化】stannum (=tin); sanitary.

s.n. = ① 〔L.〕*secundum naturam* 自然地. ②*sine nomine* 无名称;姓名不详.

snack [snæk] *n.* ①快餐;小吃;点心. ②一口;一份. ***go*** ~***s*** 〔口〕均分,分派,摊分. ***Snacks!*** 平均分呀! — *vi.* 吃快餐[小吃,点心]. ~ **bar,** ~ **counter,** ~ **stand** 快餐馆[部、摊]. ~ **table** 供单人用的小餐桌.

snack·er·y [ˈsnækəri] *n.* 快餐馆,小吃馆.

snack·e·teer [ˈsnækeˈtiːə] *n.* 〔美俚〕经常急匆匆地吃一顿快餐的人;爱吃闲食的人.

snaf·fle[1] [ˈsnæfl] *n.* 圈嚼子〔无勒索的轻马衔〕, 轻勒马衔. ***ride (sb.) in [on, with] the*** ~ 轻轻地控制,用温和手段控制. — *vt.* 装上圈嚼子;〔俚〕控制.

snaf·fle[2] [ˈsnæfl] *vt.* 〔英俚〕盗用,偷.

sna·fu [snæˈfuː, ˈsnæfuː] *n.* 〔美军俚〕情况混乱. — *a.*

混乱的. — *vt.* 搅乱,使混乱.

snag [snæg] *n.* ①残干,残根;根株;水中隐树,沉树;暗礁;〔喻〕障碍. ②暴牙,歪牙;缺牙;牙根. ③意外的[隐蔽的]阻碍,困难. — *vt.* ①在沉树上绊住;碰在沉树[暗礁]上撞坏. ②妨碍,阻挠. ③清除沉树[其它障碍物]. ④迅速抓住. ⑤【织】擦毛,抽丝. ⑥偷取,夺取. — *vi.* 撞在沉树上(绊住);形成暗礁,阻碍. *come up against a* ~= *strike a* ~ 撞上沉树[暗礁]. *run into* ~*s* 碰钉子. ~ *a pickup*〔美〕拦到(而搭上)一辆顺路的(汽车等). ~ *the current*〔美俚〕了解(情况).

snag·ged, snag·gy [ˈsnægid, ˈsnægi] *a.* 根株多的;沉树多的;〔美俚〕脾气坏的,弯扭的.

snag·gle·tooth [ˈsnægltu:θ] *n. (pl. -teeth)* 不整齐的牙齿;歪牙;破齿. **-ed** *a.*

snail [sneil] *n.* ①【动】蜗牛. ②动作缓慢的人[动物],懒人. ③【机】涡形轮. ④〔美〕肉桂面包卷. ~*s and slugs*【动】腹足类. ***at a*** ~***'s pace [gallop]*** 慢条斯理地,非常慢地. **-clover, -trefoil** *n.*【植】苜蓿属;蜗牛苜蓿. ~**-paced,** ~**-slow** *a.* 慢得象蜗牛的.

snake [sneik] *n.* ①蛇. ②冷酷阴险的人,卑鄙的人,虚伪的人. ③〔美俚〕西弗吉尼亚 (West Virginia) 人的绰号. ④(劣质)威士忌酒;〔*pl.*〕〔美俚〕震颤性酒疯[谵妄]. ⑤〔美俚〕男阿飞. *a black* ~ 长鞭子;运煤火车. *a poor* ~ 穷人,干苦活的人. *a* ~ *in one's bosom* 恩将仇报的人 (*warm [cherish] a* ~ *in one's bosom* 爱护忘恩负义的人,养虎贻患). *a* ~ *in the grass* 潜伏着的危险,隐患;暗藏的敌人. ***be above*** ~〔美〕活着,生存着. ***have*** ~***s in one's boots***〔美俚〕烂醉如泥;患震颤性酒狂病[谵妄]. ***raise [wake]*** ~***s*** 无故惊扰人;惹事,引起不愉快的事. ***see*** ~***s*** 喝醉酒;患震颤性酒狂病[谵妄]. —*vi.* ①弯曲;蜿蜒;弯弯曲曲地走. ②偷偷行进,偷偷溜走. — *vt.* ①扭弯;扭转. ②迂回地取(道). ③〔美〕拖,拉,拖出来. ~**bird**【动】蛇鹈. ~**bite** (毒)蛇的咬伤. ~ **charmer** 弄蛇人. ~ **charming** 弄蛇. ~ **dance** ①蛇舞〔印第安人的一种宗教仪式〕. ②蜿蜒前进的队伍. ~ **doctor**〔美〕①蜻蜓. ②美洲翅虫的幼虫. ~ **eater**【动】①猬. ②鹭鹰. ~ **feeder**〔美〕蜻蜓. ~ **fence**〔美〕弯弯曲曲的栅栏. ~**-fly** *n.* 蛇蛉亚目昆虫;骆驼虫. ~**('s)-head**【植】贝母. ~**-locked** *a.* 蛇发的. ~**mouth**【植】红朱兰(花). ~ **oil** 蛇油〔江湖医生的一种万应药〕. ~ **pit** ①蛇窖. ②恐怖和混乱的地方. ③精神病医院. ~**root**【植】蛇根草;蛇根草的根〔能治蛇咬伤〕. ~**'s eyes** 〔美俚〕一对么 〔两粒骰子都是么点〕. ~ **skin** 蛇皮(皮革). ~ **stone**【古生】菊石;蛇石. ~ **weed**【植】拳参. ~**wood**【植】①蛇根木. ②马钱子(又名番木鳖).

snak·y [ˈsneiki] *a.* ①(象)蛇的;蛇多的;弯弯曲曲的,蜿蜒的. ②狡猾的,阴险的;冷酷的,残忍的. *a* ~ *rod* (*Mercury* 神的)蛇杖. ~ *locks [hair]* (复仇女神 Furies 的)蛇发. **-i·ly** *ad.*

SNAP = ①systems for nuclear auxiliary power 核辅助电力系统. ②subsystem for nuclear auxiliary power (原子)核温差电池,核热电池,核热电堆.

snap [snæp] ***(snapped*** [snæpt]***; snap·ping*** [ˈsnæpiŋ]***).*** *vt.* ①猛地咬住;猛扑. ②突然折断. ③砰地关上(盖子等) *(down)*. ④使(鞭子等)劈拍地响;弹击. ⑤〔口〕急速拍摄;急速射击;急速投掷[传球]. ⑥厉声说,吆喝着说 *(out)*. ⑦〔美〕突然伸出. — *vi.* ①抢夺,抓住;猛地咬住,猛扑;连声应承住*(at)*;突然折断. ②劈拍地[砰地、格达地]响;(门)卡搭一声关上. ③突然发亮〔指眼睛,因忿怒而闪亮〕. ④谩骂 *(at)*. ~ *a pistol* 卡搭一声扳动手枪的扳机. *He was snapped falling off his horse.* 他正摔下马的时候给照下相来了. *The bolt snapped into its place.* 门闩卡搭一声扣上了. *The door snapped to.* 门卡搭一声关上了. ~ ***at a chance*** 抓住机会. ~ ***at an offer*** 抢先答应. ~ ***into it***〔美俚〕急忙开始[干起来]. ~ ***one's fingers at*** 用两个指头叭地一弹〔表示不关心,轻蔑〕. ~ ***sb.head [nose] off*** 怒冲冲地[鲁莽地]打断某人的话;恶狠狠地回答. ~ ***out***〔美〕起来;精明地干;【火箭】排出,放出. ~ ***out of it***〔美俚〕突然摆脱某种不好的状态;变更办法;(尤指)停止抱怨[忧虑、悲伤等]而迅速振作起来. ~ ***short*** 突然折断;突然打断别人的话;喝阻. ~ ***to attention*** (兵士)急忙采取立正姿势. ~ ***up*** 咬住;突然插嘴. ~ ***up an offer*** 抢着答应. — *n.* ①猛咬,猛扑. ②拍地一下折断;砰地关上;(鞭等的)劈拍声;弹指. ③揿钮,按扣;【无】揿钮接头. ④急促而粗暴的言语. ⑤(天气的)急变;(特指)骤冷;〔口〕【摄】快照;【棒球】急投. ⑥〔口〕精力,元气,气力. ⑦脆薄饼干. ⑧【剧】演员的临时雇用;〔美俚〕容易的工作;容易对付的人. *a cold* ~〔美〕骤冷. *There is no* ~ *left in him.* 他一点精力都没有了. *a style without much* ~ 不很生动的文章风格. ***in a*** ~ 立刻,马上. ***not care a*** ~ 毫不在乎. ***not worth a*** ~ 毫无价值,毫无用处. ***with a*** ~ 拍地一下子,突然. — *a.* 一碰就锁上的(锁等);突然的;〔美俚〕容易的. *a* ~ *lock* 弹簧锁. *a* ~ *division* 临时[当场]表决. *take a* ~ *vote* 举行临时[仓卒的]表决[投票]. *a* ~ *assignment* 容易的工作. — *ad.* 砰[拍]地一下,突然. *S-! went an oar.* 卡喳一声,折断了一支桨. ~ **back** ①(橄揽球)快速传球. ②很快恢复过来. ~ **bean** 青豆,菜豆. ~ **bolt** 自动门栓. ~**-brim hat** 帽顶纵摺,前沿下垂的男帽. ~ **dragon**【植】金鱼草(属);(从燃有白兰地酒的盘子中)抢吃葡萄干等(游戏),这样抢到的食物. ~ **ping beetle**【动】叩头虫. ~ **ping turtle**【动】鳄鱼科动物,〔尤指〕啮龟. ~**-roll**【空】(飞行特技)快滚. ~**shoot** *vt.* 快镜拍摄. ~ **shooter** 快枪手. ~**shooter** 快镜拍摄者. ~ **shot** *n., v.* 仓卒的射击;急射;(拍)快照.

snap·per [ˈsnæpə] *n.* ①咬人的狗[动物];拍拍响的东西. ②偷窃者;爱骂人的人. ③揿纽,按扣.〔*cf.* snap 条〕. ④【动】〔北美〕麝香鳖,啮龟 (= snapping turtle);新西兰真鲷;叩头虫. ⑤〔俚〕= whopper. ⑥*(pl.)* 牙齿. ~**-up** *(pl.* ~*s-up)* *n.* 争夺者. *a* ~*-up of bargains* 争购便宜货者.

snap·pish [ˈsnæpiʃ] *a.* ①爱咬人的(狗等). ②暴躁的,爱骂人的. **-ly** *ad.* **-ness** *n.*

snap·py [ˈsnæpi] *a.* ①活泼的,精神饱满的;敏捷的. ②漂亮的,时髦的;聪明的. ③(天气)冷飕飕的. ④〔罕〕= snappish. ⑤发出劈拍声的. *a short,* ~ *article* 简短而有力的文章. *Make it* ~*!*〔口〕直截了当地干;快干.

snare[1] [snɛə] *n.* ①绊子,圈套,罗网,陷阱. ②诱惑. ③【外科】(肿瘤等的)勒除器. *fall into the* ~ 落入圈套,上当. *lay a* ~ 设圈套. — *vt.* 安圈套;(用圈套等)捕捉,套住,绊住,陷害;诱惑. **-r** *n.*

snare[2] [snɛə] *n.* (绷在小鼓下面的)肠线,响弦.

snarl[1] [snɑ:l] *vi.* (狗等)嗥叫,咆哮;骂 *(at; against)*. — *vt.* 咆哮着说,怒喝 *(out)*. — *n.* 嗥叫,咆哮;谩骂. **-ly** *a.*

snarl[2] [snɑ:l]〔英古,美〕*n.* ①缠结,缠乱. ②混乱,纠纷. ③乱糟糟一群. — *vt.* ①使(线、发等)缠结,弄乱. ②使为难,使惶惑. ③(在金属薄片上)打出浮凸花纹. — *vi.* 缠结. *a* ~*ed skein* 乱丝;杂乱的工作. ~ *traffic* 使交通混乱. *a* ~*ing-iron* 敲花器. ***get all*** ~***ed up*** 乱成一团. **-y** *a.*

snarl·er [ˈsnɑ:lə] *n.* 嗥叫的狗[动物];乱骂人[咆哮]的人.

snatch [snætʃ] *vt.* ①抢,抓住;抢去,夺去,攫取 *(away; off; up; down; from)*. ②趁机获得;侥幸救出;杀死. ③〔美俚〕诱拐,绑架. — *vi.* 攫取,抢夺,抓住 *(at)*. ~ *a hurried meal* 急急忙忙吃饭. ~ *an opportunity* 抓住机会. *He was* ~*ed away by premature death.* 他突然夭亡. *The handbag was* ~*ed from its owner.* 手提包从物主手中夺走. *He was* ~*ed from the jaws of death.* 他侥幸得救,从死亡中抢救出来. ~ *a kiss* 冷不防接一个吻. ~ *a nap* 抓空小睡. ~ *at an offer* 抢先答应. ~ *at the chance of* 抓住机会. — *n.* ①抢夺,抓住,攫取;【举重】抓举.

②小片,破片;一节,两三句;(膳食的)一口;(工作等的)一阵子,一下工夫. ③〔美俚〕诱拐,绑架. *a ~ of sleep* 短短一觉. *~es of song* 断断续续的歌唱. ***by (fits and) ~es = in ~es*** 断断续续地. ***make a ~ at*** 动手想攫取. ~ **block**【海】扣绳滑轮;凹口滑轮.

snatch·er [ˈsnætʃə] *n.* 〔美俚〕= kidnapper.

snatch·y [ˈsnætʃi] *a.* 不完全的;不连续的;断断续续的,间歇的,不定的. **-i·ly** *ad.*

snath, snathe [snæθ, sneið] *n.* 〔美〕大镰刀的长柄.

snaz·zy [ˈsnæzi] *a.* 〔美俚〕漂亮的,时髦的; 显眼的; 动人的.

SNCC = Student National Coordinating Committee 〔美〕学生全国统一行动委员会.

sneak [sni:k] *vi.* ①偷偷逃走,偷偷跑来 *(about; away; in; off; out; past; round)*. ②行动鬼祟[神秘,卑怯];〔口〕偷窃. ③〔学俚〕告密,告发. ~ ***out of*** *(a room)* 偷偷地溜出(屋子),逃走. ~ ***up and down*** 偷偷跑来跑去. — *vt.* ①偷偷地做[通过];〔口〕偷窃,隐藏. ~ *a look at sth.* 偷看某物. ~ *smoke* 偷吸烟. — *n.* ①鬼鬼祟祟的人,卑怯的人. ②小偷;〔英〕〔学俚〕告密的人. ③溜走,偷偷摸摸的举动. ④【板球】滚球;〔*pl.*〕橡皮底帆布鞋. — *a.* 不声不响进行的;偷偷的. *a ~ attack* 偷袭. ~ *raid*【空】偷袭. ~ *raider* 偷袭者. ~ **current**【电】潜行电流,寄生电流. ~ **thief** (溜进屋去行窃的)小偷. ~ **preview**【影】(用于估计观众反应的)突击试映.

sneak·er [ˈsni:kə] *n.* 〔美〕鬼鬼祟祟的人,〔口〕*(pl.)* 橡皮底帆布鞋.

sneak·ing [ˈsni:kiŋ] *a.*①偷偷逃走[进入]的,潜逃的;偷偷摸摸的. ②不知不觉在心里产生的;别人不知道的;卑怯的. ~ *notion [suspicion]*〔美〕不知不觉在心里产生的想法[疑惑]. *have a ~ affection for him* 暗暗爱慕他. *have a ~ feeling it is not right* 心里感到不对头. **-ly** *ad.*

sneak·y [ˈsni:ki] *a.* 鬼鬼祟祟的; 卑怯的. **-i·ly** *ad.* ~ **pete** 〔美俚〕劣等的酒;酒脚.

sneer [sniə] *n.* ①嘲笑,冷笑,讥笑. ②鄙视; 冷语. —*vi.* 讥诮,嘲笑,冷笑 *(at)*. — *vt.* 轻蔑地笑着说出,冷笑着说; 讥诮着予以打消 *(away; down)*; 嘲笑得使…. ~ *sb. out of countenance* 嘲笑得使某人张皇失措. ~ *down a proposal* 对提案嗤之以鼻,予以否定. **-er** *n.*

sneer·ing·ly [ˈsniəriŋli] *ad.* 嘲笑地,冷笑地,鄙视地.

sneeze [sni:z] *n.* 打喷嚏,喷嚏(声);轻视. —*vi.* 打喷嚏. ***not to be ~d at*** 不可轻视,相当不错,值得考虑. ~ **weed**【植】堆心菊(属). ~ **wort**【植】珠蓍.

snell[1] [snel] *a.* 〔方〕①活泼的,敏捷的. ②精明的,伶俐的. ③厉害的;锐利的;猛烈的.

snell[2] [snel] *n.* 〔美〕(一端系钓钩一端连结在钓丝上的)根线. — *vt.* 把钓钩系在钓丝上.

snick [snik] *vt.* ①作细刻痕于; 微微割开[伤]. ②猛击. ③【板球】削(球). — *n.* 细刻痕;【板球】削球.

snick·er [ˈsnikə] *vi., n.* = snigger.

snick·er-snee [ˈsnikəˈsni:] *n.* 短刀,砍刀.

snide [snaid] *a.* 〔口〕①假的,伪造的. ②劣等的; 卑劣的. ③恶意的,嘲弄的;贬抑的. — *n.* 人造宝石;假钱,伪币. ~ *remarks* 暗讽的话. *a ~ trick* 狡诈的伎俩. **-ly** *ad.* **-ness** *n.*

snides·man [ˈsnaidzmən] *n.* 使用假钱的人.

sniff [snif] *vi.* ①(伤风鼻阻时)呼呼地吸(气); 嗅. ②嗤之以鼻,蔑视,轻视 *(at)*. — *vt.* ①用力吸;嗅,闻. ②嗅到,闻出,发觉. ~ *(out) peril [danger]* 发觉危险. ~ *at a flower* 嗅花. ~ ***up*** 用鼻子吸入,闻. — *n.* ①吸,嗅,闻;吸气(声). ②嗤之以鼻. ③从鼻子吸入的东西. *a ~ of fresh air* 吸一口新鲜空气. **-er** 嗅探者;嗅探器.

snif·fle [ˈsnifl] *vi., n.* = snuffle.

snif·fy [ˈsnifi] *a.* 〔口〕瞧不起人的,傲慢的;〔美〕微臭的.

snift·er [ˈsniftə] *n.* ①〔Scot.〕(用鼻子)嗅,闻,吸(气). ②突然的暴风. ③〔美〕高脚小口酒杯;〔美俚〕一小杯酒,一口酒. ④有可加因 *(cocaine)* 瘾的人. ⑤*(pl.)* 伤风鼻塞. — *vi.* 闻,嗅;吸气.

snift [snift] *vi., vt.* 〔方〕(=sniff).

snift·ing valve [ˈsniftiŋvælv]【机】喷气阀,吸气阀.

snift·y [ˈsnifti] *a.* ①傲慢的, 轻蔑的. ②〔俚〕有吸引人的气味的. ③〔美俚〕下贱的,卑劣的 (= nifty).

snig·ger [ˈsnigə] *vi.* 嘻皮笑脸地笑,吃吃地笑,窃笑 *(at; over)*. — *vt.* 嘻皮笑脸地说. — *n.* 窃笑.

snig·gle [ˈsnigl] *vi.,vt.* (把钓钩放进鳗洞里)钓(鳗). ~ *for eels* 钓鳗.

snip [snip] *vt.* 剪,剪断,剪去;剪做. — *vi.* 剪. — *n.* ①一剪;剪切声,(剪下的)片断,小片,一份. ②〔英口〕裁缝. ③〔美口〕藐小的人;傲慢无礼的人. ④〔*pl.*〕(剪金属薄片的)大剪;铁丝剪. ***go ~s*** 均分;分摊. **~-snap** 喀嚓喀嚓〔剪刀声〕*(Snip-snap went the scissors and her golden locks fell.* 剪刀喀嚓一响她的金发便掉下来了).

snipe [snaip] *n. (sing., pl.)* ①【鸟】鹬,沙锥鸟. ②〔美俚〕烟屁股,香烟头; 雪茄烟头. ③狙击. ④可鄙的人. *a ~ hunter* 〔美俚〕被众人开玩笑的人. *a ~ shooter* 〔美俚〕拾烟屁股的人. — *vi.* 打沙锥鸟; 狙击*(at)*; 中伤,暗害. — *vt.* 狙击.

snip·er [ˈsnaipə] *n.*【军】狙击兵, 狙击射手. ~ **scope**【军】红外线瞄准镜,夜袭镜〔利用红外线作用能在暗处看见目标〕.

snip·pet [ˈsnipit] *n.* ①小片;小片断. ②*(pl.)* (消息,知识等)的片断;摘录,零星的东西. ③〔美口〕年青人,不足道的人. *~s of news* 零星消息.

snip·py [ˈsnipi] *a.* ①脾气急躁的; 言语唐突的. ②无礼的;骄傲的;摆架子的. ③零碎的. **-pi·ly** *ad.* **-pi·ness** *n.*

snit [snit] *n.* 一阵怒气,呕气.

snitch[1] [snitʃ] *n.* 〔美俚〕贼. — *vt.* 偷,扒. — *vi.* 进行小偷小摸.

snitch[2] [snitʃ] *vi.* 〔俚〕告发,告密*(on)*. — *n.* = **snitcher** 〔俚〕告密者,告发者.

sniv·el [ˈsnivl] *vi.* ***(sniv·el(l)ed*** [ˈsnivəld], ***sniv·el(l)-ing*** [ˈsnivəliŋ]) 流鼻涕;吸鼻涕. ②啜泣,抽噎地哭,哭鼻子;哭诉. ③假哭,哭着装后悔[同情,失望]. — *n.* ①流鼻涕,吸鼻涕(声). ②啜泣;哭鼻子,哭诉. ③假哭;假话,假作慈悲,装可怜相. ④〔古〕鼻涕. ⑤*(pl.)* 〔方〕伤风.

sniv·el·(l)er [ˈsnivlə] *n.* 爱哭的人;哭诉者;假哭者.

S.N.O. = senior naval officer 〔英〕高级海军军官.

snob [snɔb] *n.* ①假绅士;谄上傲下的人,势利小人;附庸风雅之徒;假内行. ②〔学俚〕街坊;〔英方〕不参加罢工的工人,工贼. ③〔古〕身分低贱的人,无教养的人; 皮匠,鞋匠. ~ **appeal** (商品引起顾客要派头的)吸引力.

snob·ber·y [ˈsnɔbəri] *n.* 摆绅士架子;势利,谄上傲下;附庸风雅;假充内行;〔*pl.*〕势利行为.

snob·bish [ˈsnɔbiʃ] *a.* 谄上傲下的,势利的;假充内行的.

snob·oc·ra·cy [snɔˈbɔkrəsi] *n.* 〔谑〕俗不可耐的人们,势利的人们.

snood [snu(:)d] *n.* ①〔Scot.〕(未婚女子用的)束发带,头带. ②〔美〕袋状发网; 袋形帽. ③= snell[2]. ***lose one's silken ~*** 已非未婚的少女. — *vt.* 用束发带[发网]束(发).

snook[1] [snuk] *n.* *(pl.* ***snook, snooks)***【动】①锯盖鱼科 (Centropomidae)的鱼〔尤指锯盖鱼 *(Centro Pomus undecimalis)* 产于大西洋热带地区〕. ②类似锯盖鱼科的鱼.

snook[2] [snu:k, snuk] *n.* 〔俚〕拿拇指按着鼻尖,招动其余四指表示轻蔑的动作. *cock [cut, make] ~s [a ~] at* 用上述动作表示瞧不起[轻蔑]. *Snooks!* 这有什么了不起! 去你的!

snook·er [ˈsnu:kə] *n.* ①一种落袋撞球戏〔使用十五个红球,六个其他颜色的球〕. ②〔英俚〕Woolwich 陆军军官学校的新生. — *vt.* 〔俚〕击败,挫败.

snoop [snu:p] *vi.* ①〔美口〕探听,窥探. ②偷窃,抽偷(货物等);管闲事. **-y** *a.*

snoop·er [ˈsnuːpə] *n.* 窥探者，探听者；装有雷达的飞机（= sneak-thief）. ~**scope** 红外线夜望镜，夜间探测器.

snoot [snuːt] *n.* ①〔美俚〕(人的)鼻子；脸；愁眉苦相的脸，(表示某种感情的)鬼脸. ②【火箭】(翼的)前缘；喷嘴，小孔. — *vt.* 轻蔑地对待；对之表示厌恶；讥笑.

snoot·y [ˈsnuːti] *a.*〔美口〕自大的，傲慢的，势利的. **-i·ly** *ad.* **-i·ness** *n.*

snooze [snuːz]〔口〕*vi., vt.* (尤指在白天)打瞌睡，睡午觉，懒散地混过 *(away)*. — *n.* 打瞌睡，午睡.

snore [snɔː, snɔə] *n.* 鼾声，呼噜. — *vi., vt.* 打鼾，打呼噜；在鼾声中混过 *(away; out)*. ~ *oneself awake* 打鼾弄醒. **-r** *n.*

snor·kel [ˈsnɔːkl] *n.* ①(潜艇或潜水者的)通气管. ②(救火车上的)水力起重机. —*vi.* 使用通气管潜泳〔航〕.

snort[1] [snɔːt] *vi.* ①(马等)喷响鼻子. ②(表示不同意、轻蔑、惊愕、焦躁等时)哼鼻子，喷鼻息. ③(轻蔑、愤怒时)狂笑，高声大笑. ④(汽锅)喷汽. — *vt.* ①喷着鼻息说. ②(喷鼻息似地)喷出. ③吸入(粉末状毒品). —*n.* ①鼻息，鼻息声；(汽锅)喷汽声. ②〔美俚〕一口酒.

snort[2] [snɔːt] *n.* = snorkel.

snort·er [ˈsnɔːtə] *n.* ①鼻息粗的人[动物]；声音吵闹的汽车(等). ②〔俚〕暴风. ③极大的东西；极好的东西；令人咋舌的人[事物]，使人捏把汗的表演. ④〔口〕申斥. ⑤〔美〕一小杯酒.

snort·y [ˈsnɔːti] *a.* 鼻息粗的；轻蔑的；愤怒的；不以为然的.

snot [snɔt] *n.* ①〔卑〕鼻涕. ②〔俚〕傲慢无礼的(年轻)人，卑贱的人. ③〔*pl.*〕蠓. ~ **rag** *n.*〔俚〕手绢儿，手帕.

snot·ty [ˈsnɔti] *a.* ①〔卑〕尽是鼻涕的. ②无礼的；急躁的. — *n.*〔英海军俚〕= midshipman.

snout [snaut] *n.* ①(猪、象等的)鼻子；猪鼻形的东西；〔蔑〕(人的)大鼻子. ②(断岩的)露头. ③(软管等的)嘴；【动】吻状突起，吸盘；(船的)冲角. ④〔俚〕烟草. — *vt.* 装管嘴. ~ **beetle**【动】象鼻虫. **-y** *a.*

Snow [snəu] *n.* 斯诺[姓氏].

snow [snəu] *n.* ①雪；下雪；〔*pl.*〕积雪. ②雪白色；雪白的[象雪花的]东西；白花；〔*pl.*〕白发；泡沫. ③〔美俚〕银币；海洛因，可卡因 *(cocaine)* 粉(等)；白布丁. ④【无】雪花干扰[效应]. *a heavy (fall of)* ~ 一场大雪. *a ~ flier*〔美〕冬季到暖和的南方去的流浪者. — *vi.* 下雪；(花瓣等)雪一般地落下来. — *vt.* ①使象雪一般地落下来. ②用雪封住，用雪覆盖. ③使雪白；使有白发. ④〔俚〕用花言巧语欺骗. *It ~s.* 下雪. *Complaints [Congratulations] came ~ing in.* 抗议[贺电]象雪片似地飞来. *It ~ed petitions.* 请愿书纷至沓来. ***be ~ed in [up, over]*** ①被大雪封住；被花言巧语蒙蔽住. ②〔美俚〕被毒品麻醉. ***be ~ed under*** 埋在雪里；〔美〕被彻底打败，被压倒. ~ **ball** ①*n.* 雪球；雪战；〔谑〕白发黑人；〔英〕滚雪球募捐法[甲捐后劝乙捐，乙又劝丙捐的方法]；【烹】苹果馅稻米布丁；【植】荚蒾属. ②*vi., vt.* 扔雪球；打雪仗；(使)滚雪球般迅速增长. ~**-balling** *a.* 滚雪球一样(迅速增长)的. ~ **bank** 堤状大雪堆. ~ **bell**【植】安息香属植物. ~ **berry**【植】①北美雪球(浆果). ②白浆果. ~ **bird** ①= junco. ②【动】雪鹀. ③〔美俚〕有白面[可卡因]瘾的人. ~**-blind** *a.* 雪盲的. ~ **blindness** 雪盲(症). ~ **blink**【气】雪照云光. ~ **blower** 吹雪机，螺桨式除雪机. ~**-bound** *a.* 给雪围住的，给雪封住的. ~**-broth** ①雪水，融雪. ②冰镇酒类. ~ **bunny** 初学滑雪的(女)人. ~ **bunting**【动】雪鹀. ~ **bush**【植】山白刺美洲茶. ~**-cap** ①(山上的)雪顶. ②(产于中美洲的)白头蜂鸟. ~**-capped** *a.* 顶上积雪的. ~**-clad** *a.* 大雪覆盖的. ~ **cruiser** (极地探险用的)大雪车. ~ **drift** 吹雪；雪堆；【植】香雪球. ~ **drop**【植】雪花莲属. ~**fall** 下雪(量). ~ **fence** (铁路的)避雪墙. ~ **field** 雪原；万年雪. ~ **flake** 雪片；【动】雪鹀；【植】雪片莲属；〔俚〕投掷反射带的导弹. ~ **gauge** 雪量计. ~**-goggles** (滑雪、登山用)墨镜. ~ **goose**【动】雪雁. ~ **grouse**【动】雷鸟属鸟. ~ **ice** 冻雪. ~**-in-summer**【植】绒毛卷耳. ~ **job**〔俚〕花言巧语欺骗[劝诱]. ~ **leopard**【动】雪豹. ~ **line**, ~ **limit** 雪线. ~ **man** 雪人. ~ **mobile** 机动雪车. ~ **mold**【植】雪腐病. ~**-on-the-mountain** *n.*【植】银边翠. ~ **plant**【植】赤雪藻. ~ **plough**, ~ **plow** 雪犁，扫雪机；滑雪板制动器. ~ **plume** (由山顶吹下来的)雪縋. ~ **scape** 雪景. ~ **shed** (保护铁道的)防雪廊. ~ **shoe** ①*n.* 雪鞋. ②*vi.* 穿雪鞋走. ~**shoe hare [rabbit]**【动】美洲兔. ~ **slide**, ~ **slip** 雪崩. ~ **storm** 雪暴，暴风雪；【无】“雪花”干扰. ~**suit** 儿童风雪服. ~ **sweeper** 扫雪器. ~ **tire** 雪地防滑轮胎. ~ **train**〔美〕(开到冬季运动场去的)雪地专车. ~**-white** *a.* 雪白的.

Snow·den [ˈsnəudn] *n.* 斯诺登[姓氏].

snow·y [ˈsnəui] *a.* 雪(样)白的；多雪的. **-i·ly** *ad.* **-i·ness** *n.*

SNPO = Space Nuclear Propulsion Office〔美〕航天核推进办事处.

SNSE = Society of Nuclear Scientists and Engineers〔美〕核子科学家工程师学会.

snub [snʌb] *n.* ①故意怠慢；斥责. ②〔罕〕狮子鼻. — *a.* 狮子鼻的. — *vt.* ①【海】勒住缆索突然刹住；突然制止(别人发言). ②故意怠慢，故意冷落. ③叱止，断然拒绝；责骂. ④压熄(香烟等). *being snubbed* 碰一鼻子灰. ~**-nosed** *a.* 狮子鼻的.

snub·ber [ˈsnʌbə] *n.* ①突然制止[阻止]的人；断然拒绝的人；责骂人的人. ②【机】减振器；缓冲器；减声器；【船】锚链制止器.

snub·by [ˈsnʌbi] *a.* ①故意怠慢的；好斥责人的. ②(有点象)狮子鼻的，(鼻子)朝天的.

snuck [snʌk]〔美口〕sneak 的过去式.

snuff[1] [snʌf] *n.* 烛花，灯花. — *vt.* 剪烛花，剪灯花. — *vi.* 死去 *(out)*. ***go off like the ~ of a candle*** 突然死掉. ~ ***it***〔美俚〕死. ~ ***out*** 弄熄，吹熄(蜡烛等)；压灭(希望等)；消灭，扫除；扑灭，镇压；〔俚〕死.

snuff[2] [snʌf] *vt.* ①(伤风鼻阻时)呼呼地吸(气)；吸入. ②闻，嗅；闻出，嗅出. — *vi.* ①(伤风鼻阻时)呼呼地吸气；吸鼻烟；哼鼻子，嗤之以鼻；(狗、马等)喷鼻子. ②动怒，愤怒. — *n.* ①吸鼻子；喷鼻子；闻，嗅. ②气息，气味. ③鼻烟；【医】鼻吸药，鼻粉，闻药. ④动怒，生气. ~ *tobacco* 吸鼻烟. *take a (pinch of)* ~ 吸(一撮)鼻烟. ***beat to*** ~ 打得要死，痛殴. ***give sb.*** ~ 痛骂. ***in high*** ~ 趾高气扬地，傲然. ***put (sb.) up to*** ~〔俚〕给(人)出主意. ***take it in*** ~ 动怒，生气，发火. ***up to*** ~〔俚〕①精明的，不易受骗的；老油条. ②〔美俚〕符合一般标准的，有效力的，万应的. ~**-and-butter** *n., a.*〔英〕黄褐色(的)；欧洲人和印度人的混血种(的). ~**-box** *n.* 鼻烟盒. ~**-colo(u)red** *a.* 鼻烟色的，黄褐色的. ~ **mill**〔苏格兰〕鼻烟盒；碾鼻烟器. ~ **stick** 鼻烟勺. ~**-taker** 吸鼻烟者. ~**-taking** 吸鼻烟.

snuff·er [ˈsnʌfə] *n.* ①剪烛花的人；〔*pl.*〕烛花剪子〔常作 a pair of ~s〕. ②喷鼻子的[动物]；吸鼻烟的人. ③海豚.

snuf·fle [ˈsnʌfl] *n.* ①鼻声，鼻音，鼻塞声；抽鼻子；哽咽声. ②〔the ~s〕鼻伤风. ③哀诉. — *vi.* ①抽鼻子；喷鼻子. ②用鼻音讲[唱] *(out)*. ③嗅，闻；嗅寻. ④〔罕〕哀诉. — *vt.* ①用鼻音讲[唱] *(out)*. ②嗅着去找；抽着鼻子嗅. **-r** *n.* ①抽鼻子的人. ②哀诉的人.

snuff·y [ˈsnʌfi] *a.* ①鼻烟色的；象鼻烟的；给鼻烟弄脏了的；吸鼻烟的. ②〔口〕生气的；脾气不好的；不讨人喜欢的；傲慢的，目空一切的. **-i·ness** *n.*

snug [snʌg] *a.* ①温暖而舒适的(房屋等)，不受寒冷侵袭的. ②合身的，恰好的，整洁的(衣服等). ③温和的(气候)；舒服的，畅快的；生活安乐的(人)；可以温饱的(收入，地位). ④建造得很好，宜于航海的(船只). ⑥隐密的. *a ~ little cottage* 舒适的小农舍. *a ~ shop* 小巧整洁的商店. ***as ~ as a bug in a rug*** 非常舒适地，极安乐地. ***lie ~ for some time*** 暂时躲避着. ***lie ~ in bed*** 舒舒服服地躺在床上. — *vi.* 〔方〕舒适地蜷伏；偎依. — *vt.* ①弄整洁，弄舒服；使紧贴合身. ②藏好；隐藏. ③【海】作好暴风来袭的准备 *(down)*. **-ly** *ad.* **-ness** *n.*

snug·ger·y [ˈsnʌgəri] *n.* 〔口〕温暖舒服的地方；私室，书房；(旅馆的)酒吧间.

snug·gies [ˈsnʌgi:z] *n.* 〔*pl.*〕女式保暖长内衣.

snug·gle [ˈsnʌgl] *vi.* ①舒适地蜷伏；偎依. ②挨近，紧靠 *(up; to)*. — *vt.* ①(将孩子等)紧抱. ②使舒服温暖. *~ down in bed* 舒舒服服地睡在床上. *~ up to sb.* 偎依[紧靠]着某人.

S.O. = ①Stationery Office 〔英〕文书局. ②Staff Officer 参谋. ③suboffice 分局(处，社，公司). ④【商】shipping order 运货单.

S.O., s/o = seller's option 卖主选择权.

so[1] [强 səu; 弱 səu, sə] *ad.* ①〔表示方式、方法、情况等〕那么，那样；这么，这样. *You will never do it ~.* 你那样做不行. *They may do ~, if they please.* 随他们的便. *Hold the knife ~.* 这样持刀. *He is not a child and should not be treated ~.* 他不是小孩，不要这样对待. ②〔表示程度〕到那个程度，那样，那么. *Why are you panting ~?* 你为什么那么喘气？ *Don't walk ~ fast.* 别走得那么快. *He didn't expect to live ~ long.* 他没想到会活得那么长命. ③〔表示强调〕非常，很，极，十分. *I am ~ glad to see you.* 我看见你非常高兴. *Thank you ~ much.* 多谢多谢. *He is ever ~ angry.* 他气得不得了. ④〔代替表语或谓语，使用倒装语序〕也…. *You are young and ~ am I.* 你年轻，我也年轻. *Tom speaks French and ~ does his brother.* 汤姆会讲法语，他的兄弟也会讲法语. ⑤〔语气〕原来，那么. *So you are back again at last!* 那么你终于回来了！ *So you are Comrade Chang.* 原来你就是张同志. ⑥〔用作表语〕 ⓐ 那样的. *But it is ~.* 可是倒是那样的. *Is that ~?* 是那样吗？ *Not ~.* 不是那样. *How ~?* 怎么会那样呢？ *Quite ~ = Just ~* 正是那样. ⓑ 不错，真的. *You said it was good, and ~ it is.* 你说过它好，它真好呀！ *Nineteen fifty? So it is.* 1950 年？正是. *It was cold yesterday. So it was.* 昨天天气冷. 是的. *We have all worked hard. So we have.* 我们都努力工作. 是的. ⑦〔代替形容词〕这么，那么. *He is complacent — ~ much so that he does not know what he is worth.* 他很自满——自满得忘乎所以. *They wanted fifty dollars but John could not pay ~ much.* 他们要五十元美金，可是约翰付不起那么多. ⑧〔关联副词〕ⓐ〔so ... that 结构〕…得…，这样…以便；如此…以致. *We have ~ arranged matters that one of us is always on duty.* 我们已经做了安排，使得我们之中总有一个人在值班. *It was ~ happened that I couldn't attend the meeting.* 碰巧我无法参加会议. *He was ~ angry that he couldn't speak.* 他很生气，气得连话也讲不出了. *He was ~ ill that we had to send for a doctor.* 他病得很厉害，我们不能不请了一位医生来. *It is ~ small that you cannot see it.* 小得你看不出来. ⓑ〔so that 结构，口语常将 that 省略〕以便，为了；所以. *Speak clearly, ~ that they may understand you.* 说话说清楚，以便他们能够听得懂你的意思. *Finish this ~ (that) you can start another.* 把这个做完，好开始另一个. *All precautions have been taken, ~ that we expect to succeed.* 已经采取了各项预防措施，所以我们有希望成功. *Nothing was heard of him, ~ that people thought that he was dead.* 再没有听到关于他的什么消息，所以人们认为他已经死了. ⓒ〔as ..., so ... 结构〕象…那样，…也…. *As you treat me, ~ will I treat you.* 我象你对待我那样对待你[你怎样对待我，我也怎样对待你]. ⓓ〔so... as...结构〕象…一样. 〔not so ... as ... 结构〕没有…那样. *They must ~ walk as he walked.* 他们必须照他的步法走. 他怎样走，他们也一定要怎样走. *I am not ~ tall as he.* 我没有他高. *He was not ~ much angry as disappointed.* 生气还是其次，他倒是失望得厉害. *He is not ~ old as you think.* 他的年纪没有你以为的那么大. — *conj.* ①〔古〕只要…，要是，既是. *So it is done, it matters not how.* 只要成功，怎样办都行. ②〔口〕那样就… (= so that). *Turn it from time to time ~ it may be cooked alike on both sides.* 常常翻翻，那样两面就烤得匀了. — *int.* 好，那样行了；别动；别吵；停住，〔命牛马〕缩！〔又作 soh〕. *A little more to the right, ~!* 再靠右一点儿，行了！ *If that will content him, ~.* 倘若那会满足他，那就行了. *If you agreed, ~; if not, ~.* 要是同意，好；要是不同意，也好. — *pro.* ①〔用作 say, call, speak, tell, think, hope, expect, suppose, imagine, fear, hear, do 等动词的宾语〕 *I think ~.* 我想是这样. *I suppose ~.* = *So I suppose.* 我想大概是那样. *I told you ~.* 我不是跟你说过是这样了吗？ *Do you say ~?* = *You don't say ~.* 真的吗〔表示惊奇〕. *So he says.* 他这样说. ②〔用在 or 之后〕左右，上下，约. *two hundred or ~* 两百上下. *an hour or ~* 一个钟头左右. *He is forty or ~.* 他大概是四十岁. ***and ~*** 〔英古，美〕所以，从此(就…了)；〔古〕其次 *(And ~ to dinner)*. ***and ~ forth*** = ***and ~ on*** 等等. ***even ~*** 〔古〕确是那样. ***ever ~*** 非常，很 (*He is ever ~ clever.* 他很聪明. *He has ever ~ many children.* 他有不少孩子. *That is ever ~ much better.* 〔口〕那个好得多). ***ever [never] ~ bad*** 无论怎样坏. ***every ~ often*** 〔美〕时时. ***if ~*** 要是那样的话. ***in ~ far as*** 到…的程度 (*You will succeed in ~ far as you persevere.* 你能坚持，便会得到相应的成功). ***~ and in no other way = ~ and ~ only*** 别无他法. ***~ and ~*** 某某，这么这么，如此这般〔参看 *so-and-so*〕. ***~ ... as to*** …得… (*He was ~ angry as to be unable to say.* 他愤怒得话都说不出了). ***~ be it*** 那样也好，算啦；不管喽. ***~ far*** 就是那么些；到现在为止，到此刻为止，到这里[那点，这点，那个程度]为止 (*So far for today.* 今天就是那么些了. *So far so good.* 到这里为止，一切还好，到那点为止，一切还好). ***~ far as*** 就…而论，在…的范围内 (*~ far as I know* 就我所知. *~ far as I am concerned* 至于我. *~ far as the style goes* 若就文章风格来讲. *~ far as in me lies* 尽我力量所及). ***~ far from*** 非但不…反而 (*So far from loving him, I hate him.* 非但不爱他，反而恨他). ***~ goes the story*** 据说. ***~ long!*** 〔口〕再见. ***~ long as*** 只要. ***~ many*** 很多(的)；和…一样多的，同样多的；全都是 (*You have ~ many.* 你有很不少. *~ many apples and ~ many pears* 这么多的苹果和同样多的梨). ***~ much*** 和…一样多；就只那么多；多少 (*It is only ~ much rubbish.* 全是废物. *At ~ much a week [a head]* 每礼拜[每人]多少(钱). *~ much brandy and ~ much water* 一半白兰地一半水). ***~ much for,*** …的事情[话]就是这么些[至此为止]；…不过如此 (*So much for him, now about ...* 他的事情就这样好了，下面且说…罢. *So much for his learning.* 〔蔑〕那家伙的学问不过如此). ***~ much more*** 更加. ***~ much ~ that*** …到要…，因为非常…. ***~ much the better*** 反而好. ***~ please you*** 〔古〕= if you please. *~ ~* 〔口〕既不算好也不算坏，勉勉强强，还好 (*How are you getting along? Oh, ~ ~.* 近来怎么样？唉，勉勉强强). ***~ styled [termed]*** 叫做…的，所谓. ***~ that's that*** 〔口〕所以是这样. ***~ then*** 原来如此，那么，所以. ***~ to say [speak]*** 好比，如同，可谓. ***So what?*** 那么又怎样呢？那怎么样了呢？结果怎样呢？那有什么关系呢？你想怎么样呢？ **~-and-~** [ˈsəuənsəu] *n.* 某某人，某某事 (*Mr. ~-and-~* 某某先生. *He asked them to do ~-and-~.* 他叫他们做某事). **~-called** *a.* 所谓的，号称的〔常含贬义〕.

So[2] [səu] *n.* 【乐】= sol[1].

soak [səuk] *vt.* ①浸，泡；弄湿，使湿透. ②沉浸在 (工作,

学习中)〔用反身代词〕.③浸出;吸出;吸收*(in; up)*;〔俚〕使大醉. ④〔口〕向…敲竹杠,敲榨;多要价钱;征重税. ⑤〔俚〕典当,典押(东西). ⑥重击,痛殴. —*vi.* ①浸泡. ②渗透,印进 *(into)*. ③〔口〕大喝,狂饮. ④经受长时间热处理. *Blotting paper ~s up ink.* 吸墨纸能吸墨水. ~ *the rich* 向富人征重税. — *n.* ①浸,泡;浸液,浸渍. ②〔口〕大雨. ③〔俚〕狂喝滥饮的人,酒鬼;酒宴;狂饮. ④〔俚〕典当. ⑤殴打. ***in*** ~ 〔俚〕(东西)在典押中[当铺里]. ~ ***it*** 使为难,〔美〕处罚 *(to)*. ~ ***oneself in*** 沉浸在,埋头于,专心(研究). ~ ***out*** 浸泡掉,吸出.

soak·age [ˈsəukidʒ] *n.* ①浸,泡;浸渍;浸湿性,吸水量. ②电容器的静电荷.

soak·er [ˈsəukə] *n.* 浸渍的人,泡的人[物];【化】浸渍剂;(石油)裂化反应室;〔俚〕酒鬼;〔口〕倾盆大雨;〔*pl.*〕婴儿用的尿布垫.

so-and-so [ˈsəuən*d*səu] *n.* 某某人;某某东西. — *ad.* 如此这般;相当. *Mr. S-* 某先生. *He says ~ would be offended.* 他说某某人恐怕要生气.

soap [səup] *n.* ①肥皂. ②【化】脂肪酸盐. ③〔美俚〕钱(尤指贿赂);奉承,假恭维;胡话. *a cake [cube, tablet] of ~* 一块肥皂. *hard ~* 硬肥皂. *marine ~* 海水皂,船用肥皂. *medical ~* 药皂. *soft ~* 软肥皂,钾肥皂;〔俚〕奉承话. *toilet ~* 香皂. ***How are you off for ~?*** 〔俚〕你身上有钱吗? ***no ~*** 〔美俚〕无结果,不成功;不接受(建议,要求等). ***wash one's hands in invisible ~*** 搓手[表示忸怩,为难的表情]. — *vt.* ①用肥皂搓洗,上肥皂. ②〔俚〕拍马屁,奉承. ~ ***the ways*** 使事情顺利进行. ~**bark** 【植】皂树;皂树皮;金龟树属含皂甙的树. ~**berry** = ~-nut. ~ **boiler** 肥皂锅;肥皂制造者. ~ **boiling** 肥皂制造(业). ~**-box** ①*n.* 〔美〕(街头演说用的)肥皂箱. ②*vi.* (站在肥皂箱上)(作)街头演说,煽动. ~**boxer** 街头演说家. ~ **bubble** 肥皂泡;短暂而空虚的好景. ~ **dish** 肥皂缸[碟]. ~ **earth** 【化】皂石. ~ **flakes** 肥皂片. ~**-nut** 【植】无患子. ~ **opera** 〔美〕内容常为家务事的日间广播剧〔常系肥皂商人主办,对象为家庭妇女〕. ~ **plant** 制皂植物. ~ **powder** 肥皂粉. ~**stone** 【化】皂石. ~ **suds** *sing., pl.* (起泡的)肥皂水,肥皂泡. ~**wort** 肥皂草.

soap·y [ˈsəupi] *a.* ①肥皂状的,肥皂质的;尽是肥皂的. ②〔俚〕满口奉承话的;油滑的. ~ *water* 肥皂水. ~ *feeling* 滑腻的感觉. **-i·ly** *ad.* **-i·ness** *n.* **-less** *a.*

soar [sɔː, sɔə] *n.* ①高飞,翱翔,飞升. ②上升高度;高飞范围. — *vi.* ①高飞,翱翔,飞上去. ②耸立,屹立. ③(物价)飞涨,暴腾,猛增;(思想等)向上. ④【空】滑翔. — *vt.* 〔诗〕飞翔到,高飞到. *beyond the ~ of fancy* 出乎意想之外;想象不到. *The temperature ~ed to 80°.* 温度猛升到 80 度. **-er** *n.*

soar·ing [ˈsɔːriŋ, ˈsɔər-] *a.* 高飞的,翱翔的(鹰等);高耸云霄的(尖塔等);高超的(思想等). *a ~ eagle* 凌空翱翔的鹰. *a ~ flight* 高空飞行;滑翔飞行. *a ~ plane* 滑翔机. *a ~ ambition* 远大的抱负,雄心壮志. ~ *spire* 高入云霄的尖顶.

SOB, S.O.B., s.o.b. [ˈeˌsəuˈbiː] *n.* 〔美俚〕(骂人语)畜生,狗娘养的〔son of a bitch 的缩略〕.

sob [sɔb] *vi.* ①抽噎,啜泣;哽咽,呜咽. ②(风等)发出呜咽声. — *vt.* ①抽噎着说,哭诉 *(out)*. ②哭得使… — *n.* 抽噎(声),啜泣(声);哽咽,呜咽;(风等的)呜咽声. ~ **sister** 〔美俚〕写感伤文章的女记者;演感伤角色的女演员;感伤而不实际的人. ~ **story** 〔美俚〕感伤故事. ~ **stuff** 〔美新闻、剧〕感伤材料,感伤文章[故事].

sob·bing·ly [ˈsɔbiŋli] *ad.* 啜泣地,呜咽地,抽抽噎噎地.

sob·by [ˈsɔbi] *a., n.* 〔美俚〕引人感伤的 = sob sister.

so·ber [ˈsəubə] *a.* ①没有醉的,清醒的,没有喝酒的;节酒的,饮食有节制的. ②严肃的,认真的,冷静的;稳重的,非极端的;非想象的,不夸张的;神志清醒的. ③朴素的,素净的,不鲜艳的(颜色、衣服等). *a ~ truth* 不夸大或歪曲的事实真相. *Who are the moderate and ~?* 谁是温和冷静派呢? ***as ~ as a judge*** 挺严肃的. ***become ~*** 酒醒. ***in one's ~ senses*** 神志清醒地,冷静地,沉着地. ***in ~ earnest*** 非常认真[严肃]地. ***in ~ fact*** 事实上. ***lead a ~ life*** 认真过日子,不喝酒过日子. — *vt.* 使酒醒;使严肃,使认真;使冷静,使沉着;使忧郁. — *vi.* 酒醒 *(up; off)*;变严肃,变认真,变清醒 *(down)*. ~**-blooded** *a.* 严肃的,沉着的. ~**headed,** ~**-minded** *a.* 沉着的,头脑冷静的. ~**-sides** 〔口〕沉着的人,严肃的人. ~**water** 〔谑〕苏打水. **-ly** *ad.* **-ness** *n.*

so·ber·ize [ˈsəubəraiz] *vt.* 〔古〕使清醒,使庄重严肃.

sob·fest [ˈsɔbfest] *n.* 〔美〕伤心落泪的场合;互相倾吐苦情.

so·bri·e·ty [səuˈbraiəti] *n.* 节酒;清醒;认真;节制;谨严;冷静,沉着,稳健.

so·bri·quet [ˈsəubrikei] *n.* 非正式的名字[头衔];诨名,绰号.

Soc. = ①Socialist. ②Society.

soc·age [ˈsɔkidʒ] *n.* 无兵役租佃(制)〔英国中世纪一种租佃制度,佃户不对领主服兵役,只缴地租或服其他劳役〕.

so-called [ˈsəuˈkɔːld] *a.* 所谓的,号称的.〔英国习惯常含有不信或轻视之意〕.

soc·cer [ˈsɔkə] *n.* 〔英口〕英式足球(= football, association football).

So·chi [ˈsəutʃi] *n.* 索契〔苏联港市〕.

so·cia·bil·i·ty [ˌsəuʃəˈbiliti] *n.* ①爱交际;会交际;讨人欢喜,和气. ②社交性格[心理,倾向,气氛]. ③【生】群集度.

so·cia·ble [ˈsəuʃəbl] *a.* ①爱交际的;会交际的;讨人欢喜的,和气的. ②喜欢群居的;社交性的;宜于交际的. — *n.* ①〔美〕恳亲会,联谊会,联欢会. ②〔英〕对座四轮马车;双座三轮自行车;(二人座)S形椅子. **-bly** *ad.*

so·cial [ˈsəuʃəl] *a.* ①社会的,社会上的. ②交际的,社交的;喜欢交际的. ③合群的;【动】群居的;【植】丛生的. ④【史】同盟国间的. ⑤一定社会阶层[地位]的;上流社会的. ⑥社会性的. ~ *customs* 社会习俗. ~ *history* 社会历史. ~ *problem* 社会问题. ~ *reforms* 社会改革. *her busy ~ life* 她繁忙的社交生活. *Man is a ~ animal.* 人是群居动物. ~ *advancement* 社会地位的提高. *one's ~ equals [inferiors, superiors]* 社会地位与自己相同[比自己低、比自己高]的人们. ~ *order* 社会秩序. ~ *origin* 出身. ~ *politics* 社会政策. ~ *problem* 社会问题. ~ *rank* 社会等级,社会地位. ~ *register* 〔美〕社会名人录. ~ *student* 社会学研究家. *the ~ evil* 卖淫. — *n.* **a ~ gathering** 联欢会,联谊会. ~ **anthropology** 社会人类学. ~ **climber** 向上爬的人,企图进入上流社会的人. ~**-chauvinism** 社会沙文主义. ~**-chauvinist** *n.* 社会沙文主义者. *a.* 社会沙文主义的. ~ **contract [compact]** 民约论,社会契约论. ~ **dancing** 交际舞,交谊舞. ~ **Darwinism** 社会达尔文主义. ~ **democracy** 社会民主主义. ~ **democrat** 社会民主党人. ~ **disease** 性病,花柳病,(肺病等)社会性疾病. ~ **engineering** 社会工程学. ~ **gospel** 社会福音;〔美〕社会福音运动. ~**-imperialism** 社会帝国主义. ~**-imperialist** *n.* 社会帝国主义者. *a.* 社会帝国主义的. ~ **insurance** 社会保险. ~**-minded** *a.* 关心社会的;热心于社会福利的. ~ **psychology** 社会心理学. ~ **science** 社会科学. ~ **secretary** 交际秘书. ~ **security** 社会福利,〔美〕政府的公共福利计划. ~ **service** 社会慈善救济事业. ~ **studies** 社会学科〔指中学、大学中的历史、地理、经济、人类学、社会学等课程〕. ~ **welfare** 社会福利;社会福利救济. ~ **work** 社会福利工作. ~ **worker** 社会福利工作者. **-ly** *ad.* 社会上;社交上,交际上;和睦地,亲密地.

so·cial·ism [ˈsəuʃəlizəm] *n.* 社会主义. *scientific ~* 科学社会主义. *utopian ~* 空想社会主义. *Christian S-* 基督教社会主义〔企图用基督教的教义来实现社会主

义〕.

so·cial·ist [ˈsəuʃəlist] *n.* 社会主义者. — *a.* ①社会主义的. ②〔S〕社会党的. *the ~ revolution* 社会主义革命. *~ enthusiasm [initiative]* 社会主义的积极性. *~ consciousness* 社会主义觉悟. *~ tendencies* 社会主义倾向. *S- Party* 社会党. **~-minded** *a.* 有社会主义觉悟的.

so·cial·is·tic [ˌsəuʃəˈlistik] *a.* 社会主义(者)的.

so·cial·ite [ˈsəuʃəlait] *n.* 〔美〕社会名流,社交界的知名人士.

so·ci·al·i·ty [ˌsəuʃiˈæliti] *n.* 社会性;爱交际;社会的风俗习惯;群居性.

so·cial·i·za·tion [ˌsəuʃəlaiˈzeiʃən] *n.* 社会(主义)化.

so·cial·ize [ˈsəuʃəlaiz] *vt.* ①使社会化;使社会主义化. ②使适应社会需要的;使适合于过社会生活. ③使参加集体学习,使(学习)组织化. — *vi.* 〔美口〕参加社交活动. *~d medicine* 〔美〕公费医疗制,社会化的医疗制度.

so·ci·e·tal [səˈsaiətl] *a.* 社会的. **-ly** *ad.*

so·ci·e·ty [səˈsaiəti] *n.* ①社会. ②会,社;协会,学会,公会,团体. ③交际,社交;社交界〔特指上流社会〕;社交场所. ④群居,群栖. ⑤〔美〕教区居民. *primitive ~* 原始社会. *class ~* 阶级社会. *slavery ~* 奴隶社会. *feudalist ~* 封建社会. *semi-feudal and semi-colonial ~* 半封建半殖民地社会. *capitalist ~* 资本主义社会. *socialist ~* 社会主义社会. *communist ~* 共产主义社会. *a building ~* 建筑协会. *a charitable ~* 慈善团体. *I enjoy your ~.* 和您交往真高兴. *avoid [seek] the ~ of* 避免〔追求〕和…来往〔相处〕. *be quit of sb.'s ~* 和…断绝来往. *go into ~* 入交际界;常赴宴会. *live in ~* 出入交际界. ~ **beauty** 交际花. ~ **editor** 社会栏编辑. ~ **gossip** 社交界的流言蜚语. ~ **house** 加入公会的印刷所. ~ **lady** 社交界〔上流社会〕妇女;〔英〕出入宫廷的妇女. **Society of Friends** (基督教)公谊会. **Society of Jesus** (天主)耶稣会. ~ **verse** 社交诗〔一种轻松,有风趣的诗〕.

So·cin·i·an·ism [səuˈsiniənizəm] *n.* 索西奴斯教义〔16世纪意大利神学家 *Faustus Socinus* 所主张,否认三位一体,耶稣的神性等,而以唯理论来解释罪恶和得救〕.

so·ci·o·cul·tu·ral [ˌsəusiəuˈkʌltʃərəl] *a.* 社会文化的;涉及社会文化因素的.

so·ci·o·e·co·nom·ic [ˈsəusiəuˌiːkəˈnɔmik] *a.* 社会经济(学)的.

so·ci·o·gram [ˈsəusiəˌgræm, ˈsəuʃi-] *n.* 【社会学】社会关系分析表〔图〕.

sociol. = sociology; sociological; sociologist.

so·ci·o·lin·gwis·tics [ˌsəusjəuˈliŋgwistiks] *n.* 社会语言学.

so·ci·o·log·i·cal [ˌsəusjəˈlɔdʒikəl] *a.* 社会学(上)的. **-ly** *ad.*

so·ci·ol·o·gist [ˌsəusiˈɔlədʒist] *n.* 社会学家.

so·ci·ol·o·gy [ˌsəusiˈɔlədʒi] *n.* 社会学.

so·ci·om·e·try [ˌsəusiˈɔmitri] *n.* ①社会关系计量学. ②社会群体心理测定法. **-met·ric** [-ˈmetrik] *a.*

so·ci·o·path [ˈsəusiəˌpæθ, -ʃi-] *n.* 极端反社会的人〔精神病患者的一种类型〕;不爱社交的人. **-ic** *a.*

so·ci·o·po·lit·i·cal [ˌsəusiəupəˈlitikl] *a.* 社会和政治的.

sock[1] [sɔk] *n.* (*pl.* *~s,*【商】*sox*) ①短袜. ②鞋内的皮革衬垫. ③(古希腊,罗马喜剧演员穿的)轻便软鞋;〔喻〕喜剧;【美剧】大成功. ④〔美俚〕钱袋;银柜;准备金,存款;巨款. ⑤= windsock. *an associate of the ~ and buskin* 戏剧演员. ***old ~s*** (男子之间的亲热称呼)老兄. ***Pull up your ~s!*** 〔英俚〕鼓起劲来!加紧努力! ***Put a ~ in [into] it!*** 〔俚〕别讲话! — *vt.* ①给…穿上短袜. ②〔美俚〕储蓄(钱). *~ **away*** 把钱存放一边. *~ **in*** 关闭(机场);禁止(飞机)起落.

sock[2] [sɔk] *vt.* 〔俚〕用力打击,殴打. *~ **it to sb.*** 〔美俚〕猛揍某人. — *n.* 拳打;拳头. *~ peddler* 〔美〕拳击选手. ***give sb. ~(s)*** 痛殴. — *ad.* 正好,对准,迎面. *He hit me ~ in the eye.* 他一拳正好打在我的眼睛上.

sock[3] [sɔk] *n.* 〔英学俚〕食品,零食,点心. — *vt., vi.* (请…)吃零食.

sock·dol·a·ger, sock·dol·o·ger [sɔkˈdɔlədʒə] 〔美俚〕*n.* 决定性的一击〔回答〕;大成功;异常大的东西.

sock·er [ˈsɔkə] *n.* 〔英俚〕英式足球 (= soccer). *~ **eleven*** = *~ **team*** 足球队.

sock·er·in·o [sɔkəˈriːnəu] *n.* 〔美俚〕大成功.

sock·et [ˈsɔkit] *n.* ①(承物或藏物的)孔,洞,窝,凹处,承口. ②【解】(眼)窝,腔;(齿)槽;【地】牙槽;(烛台的)烛窝;轴孔;【机】承窝,座;套节;轴承. ③【电】插口,插座,管座. *the eye ~* 眼窝. *an electric bulb ~* 电灯泡插座. *a ~ pipe* 套管. *a reducing ~* 异径管节,大小头. *a screw ~* 螺丝插口. *~ wrench* 套筒扳手. — *vt.* ①给…配插座〔承口等〕;使装入插座,用插座固定住. ②用球棒的后跟击(高尔夫球).

sock·eye [ˈsɔkˌai] *n.* 【动】红大麻哈鱼 (*Oncorhynchus nerka*) 〔产于北太平洋,常用作罐头食品〕.

sock·o [ˈsɔkəu] 〔美俚〕*n.* ①大成功〔特指演出等〕. ②猛击,重拳〔尤指打在下巴上的〕. — *vt.* 猛击,使一举成功. — *a., ad.* 非常成功的(地),极为卖座的(地).

soc·le [ˈsɔkl] *n.* ①【建】(石象、石柱等的)座石,柱脚. ②(电子管的)管脚,管底.

Soc·ra·tes [ˈsɔkrətiːz] *n.* 苏格拉底〔公元前470?—399,古希腊哲学家〕.

So·crat·ic [sɔˈkrætik] *a.* 苏格拉底的,苏格拉底哲学的,信奉苏格拉底的. — *n.* 苏格拉底的信徒. ~ **method** 苏格拉底问答法〔对话法〕.

sod[1] [sɔd] *n.* ①(切成方块的)草皮;草根泥;草地. ②土地,故乡,本国. *a ~ buster* 〔美〕乡下人;农民;农科大学生. *a ~ widow* 〔美〕寡妇. *the old ~* 祖国,故乡. ***turn the ~*** 挖地. ***under the ~*** 在坟墓里,长眠地下. — *vt.* 铺草皮,用草皮覆盖.

sod[2] [sɔd] *n.* ①〔卑〕〔谑〕人,家伙〔尤作骂人语〕. ②〔英俚〕鸡奸者,兽奸者〔系 sodomite 的简写〕.

sod[3] [sɔd] *v.* 〔古〕seethe 的过去式及过去分词;煮熟的.

so·da [ˈsəudə] *n.* ①【化】苏打,碱,碳酸钠;碳酸氢钠,小苏打;氢氧化钠;氧化钠;(化合物中的)钠. ②苏打水,汽水. *washing ~* 洗涤用苏打〔使水软化〕. *baking ~* 烹调用苏打,小苏打. *caustic ~* 烧碱,苛性钠. ~ **ash** 无水碳酸钠,纯碱,苏打灰. ~ **biscuit [cracker]** 苏打饼干. ~ **fountain** (装有龙头的)散装苏打汽水容器〔柜台〕;〔美〕冷饮小卖部〔多半附设在药房中,兼卖冰淇淋、点心等〕. ~ **jerk [jerker, squirt]** 冷饮柜台售货员. ~ **lime**【化】碱石灰. ~ **mica** 钠云母. ~ **nitrate** 智利硝石. ~ **pop** 苏打汽水. **~-water** 苏打水.

so·da·lite [ˈsəudəlˌait] *n.* 【矿】方钠石.

so·dal·i·ty [səuˈdæliti] *n.* ①联谊会,兄弟会,团体. ②(罗马天主教徒间宗教性或慈善性的)会社.

sod·den [ˈsɔdn] *a.* ①湿润的,发潮的;没有烤透的(面包等);浸透了的,泡涨了的. ②(因沉迷于酒而变得)呆头呆脑的,无表情的,麻木的. *~ ground* 浸透水的土地. *~ features* 呆头呆脑的样子. *~ minds* 迟钝的脑子. — *vt.* ①浸,泡,弄湿. ②使呆头呆脑,使(头脑)麻木. —*vi.* 浸透;变软;腐败. **-ly** *ad.* **-ness** *n.*

Sod·dy [ˈsɔdi] *n.* 索迪〔姓氏〕.

sod·dy[1] [ˈsɔdi] *a.* 草皮的;铺满草皮的;草地多的. *~ soil* 生草土.

sod·dy[2] [sɔdi] *n.* 〔美西部〕(草泥墙的)窝棚.

so·dik [ˈsəudik] *a.* 钠的,含钠的.

so·di·um [ˈsəudjəm, -diəm] *n.* 钠. ~ **benzoate**【化】苯甲酸钠,安息香酸钠. ~ **bicarbonate**【化】碳酸氢钠,小苏打. ~ **borate**【化】硼砂. ~ **bromide**【化】溴化钠. ~ **carbonate**【化】碳酸钠,纯碱. ~ **chlorate**【化】氯酸钠. ~ **chloride** 氯化钠,食盐. ~ **cyanide**【化】

氰化钠. ～ **dichromate**【化】重铬酸钠. ～ **hydrosulphite**【纺】保险粉. ～ **fluoroacetate**【化】氟醋酸钠〔一种毒鼠药〕. ～ **hydroxide**【化】氢氧化钠,烧碱. ～ **nitrate** 硝酸钠,智利硝石. ～ **pentothal**【药】喷妥撒钠. ～ **perborate**【化】过氧化钠. ～ **phosphate**【化】磷酸钠. ～ **propionate**【化】丙酸钠. ～ **silicate**【化】硅酸钠,水玻璃. ～ **sulfate**【化】硫酸钠. ～ **thiosulfate**【化】硫代硫酸钠,大苏打. ～**-vapor lamp** 钠蒸气灯.

sod·om·ite [ˈsɔdəmait] *n.* ①鸡奸者;兽奸者. ②反常的性交.

sod·om·y [ˈsɔdəmi] *n.* 鸡奸;兽奸.

SOED, S.O.E.D. = Shorter Oxford English Dictionary. 《简编牛津英语词典》.

so·ev·er [səuˈevə] *ad.* ①无论〔用于 how 后的形容词之后或最高级形容词之后〕. ②不论何种,任何,完全(没有)〔用于名词后面,与否定语连用〕. *How great ～ he may be* 无论他怎样伟大. *the most selfish ～ in this world* 天下最自私的. *He has no home ～.* 他完全没有家.

SOF = sound on film.

so·fa [ˈsəufə] *n.* 沙发. *a ～ lizard* 〔美〕待在家里不爱参加社交集会的人. ～ **bed** (兼可作床的)两用沙发.

so·far [ˈsəufɑː] *n.* (测定水下物体距离的)声发,声波定位(仪).

Soff [səuf] *n.* 索夫〔姓氏〕.

sof·fit [ˈsɔfit] *n.* ①【建】拱腹;楼梯(或柱上楣等的)下部. ②【剧】上部布景,天空布景.

So·fi·a [ˈsəufjə] *n.* 索非亚〔保加利亚首都〕.

So·fi(sm) [ˈsəufi(zm)] = Sufi(sm).

So·fos [sɔˈfəuz] 〔苏联〕 = Sovkhos.

soft [sɔft] *a.* ①软的,柔软的 *(opp.* hard, tough*)*; 柔滑的(皮肤,毛发等); 悦耳的,好听的,柔和的(声音等); 不刺目的(光等); 不明亮的,水汪汪的(眼睛等). ②温柔的,温和的,和蔼的,厚道的,宽大的(行动、态度等); 软弱的,不强健的,不坚强的,吃不了苦的,娇嫩的. ③平静的,安稳的,平安的,和平的. ④〔英〕潮湿的,下雨的,解冻的,沉闷的,阴郁的(天气等); 线条柔和的,模糊的(轮廓); 不陡削的,坡度小的. ⑤愚钝的,痴呆的,低能的. ⑥【语音】(辅音)带声的,浊的; 不送气的; 软音的 〔gin 的 g, city 的 c〕. ⑦【化】软化的. ⑧无矿盐的(水); 不含酒精的(饮料); 易消化的(食物); 毒性不大的(麻醉品). ⑨〔口〕舒服的,轻松的. ⑩【商】不稳定的,下跌的(市场,价格等); 长期低率的(贷款等); 纸币的; 黄金后盾不足的,难以兑成外币的(货币). ⑪【军】无遮蔽而易受攻击的(军事目标,基地等). ⑫易磁化和消磁的(铁等). — *n.* ①柔软(部分). ②〔口〕拙笨;傻子. ③(the ～)〔美俚〕钱〔尤指纸币〕. *A ～ answer turnth away wrath.* 温和的回答可以消解怒气. *S- and fair goes far.* 〔谚〕柔能克刚. ～ *breezes* 和风. ～ *fire* 文火. ～ *hat* 呢帽. ～ *manners* 温和的举动. ～ *sentence* 宽大的判决. ～ *soil [ground]* 软土[地]. *as ～ as velvet* 象天鹅绒一样柔滑. ～ *whispers* 低声的耳语. *in a ～ voice* 低声地. ～ *nonsense* 傻话. ～ *nothings* 情话. ～ *things* 恭维话;温柔话,心里话. *a ～ tongue* 动听的说话能力. *a ～ slope* 缓坡,平坦的斜坡. *I think he is a bit ～.* 我看他有点笨. *a ～ job* 轻松的工作. *a ～ thing* 〔口〕好差事,舒适而报酬丰厚的工作. ～ *market* 〔美俚〕便宜的价钱; 疲软的行市. ～ *money* 纸币;支票. *an aboveground ～ launching site* 地面上易受敌攻击的发射场. ～ *iron* 易磁化的铁. ～ *X rays* 软性 X 射线. ～ *stuff* 〔美俚〕奉承(话). ～ *heel* 〔美俚〕侦探. ～ *jack* 〔美俚〕轻易得来的钱财. ***appeal to the ～er side of sb.'s character*** 打动某人的慈悲心. ***be ～ (up) on sb.*** 爱着某人 (*He has been ～ on her for years.* 多年来他一直爱恋着她). ***go ～*** ①软化. ②变痴愚,变狂乱 (*He's gone ～.* 他变得痴呆[有点狂乱]了). ***have a ～ place in one's head*** 〔口〕愚笨. ***plead guilty to the ～ impeachment*** 〔口〕自认糊涂. ***the ～ [softer] sex*** 女性. — *ad.* = softly. *lie ～* (在柔软的床上)静静地躺着. *Play [Speak] ～er, please.* 请弹[说]得轻一点. — *int.* 〔古〕别响! *S-! someone comes.* 别响! 有人来了. ～**back** 平装书,纸版书. 【体】 ～**ball** 软式棒球,垒球. ～**-boiled** *a.* 半熟的(蛋等); 心肠软的. ～**bound** *a.* 软封面的. ～ **chancre** 【医】软下疳. ～ **coal** 烟煤. ～ **core** ①*a.* 比较隐晦的. ② *n.* 比较隐晦的黄色内容. ～ **cover** = paperback. ～ **currency** 软性通货,不硬挺的通货〔不能兑现或市场价格不高的纸币等〕. ～ **drinks** 不含酒精的饮料. ～**-finned** *a.*【动】软鳍的. ～ **fly**【棒球】容易接的飞球. ～**-footed** *a.* 脚步轻的. ～ **goods** 纺织品,非耐用品. ～**-head** 笨人,蠢人;无主见的人. ～**-headed** *a.* 笨拙的; 无主见的. ～**-hearted** *a.* 心肠软的,仁慈的. ～**-land** *vi., vt.* (使)软着陆. ～**-lander** 软着陆装置. ～**-landing** 软着陆. ～ **line** 温和路线. ～**-liner** 实行温和路线者,温和路线支持[主张]者. ～ **palate** 软颚. ～ **pedal** ① *n.* (用以减弱音量的)钢琴踏板;减弱效果的东西. ② *vt.* 在演奏…时使用减音踏板;降低(意见、批评等)调子; 对…不予张扬,秘而不宣; 禁止讨论. ～**-rayed** *a.* (鱼鳍)有软条的. ～ **rot** 【植】软腐病. ～ **rush**【植】灯心草. ～ **sawder** ① *n.* 奉承,谄媚. ②*vt.* 奉承,谄媚. ～ **sell** 〔美〕劝诱推销,非强行推销. ～**-shell** *a.* 软壳的;脆壳的. ～**-shell clam**【动】沙海螂. ～**-shelled** *a.* 软壳的. ～**-shelled turtle**【动】鳖,北美龟属动物. ～**-shoe** *a.* 软鞋踢跶舞. ～ **shoulder** (沿公路的)路边软地. ～ **snap** 不需花费多少力气的事. ～ **soap** 软皂,半液体皂;奉承,拍马屁. ～**-soap** *vt., vi.* 使用软皂; 奉承,阿谀. ～**-soaper** 奉承者,拍马者. ～ **solder** 软焊料〔用于易熔金属〕. ～**-spoken** *a.* 说话温柔的,中听的,会说话的. ～ **spot** 性格中易受打动之处,弱点;软弱不振的经济部门[企业]. ～ **steel** 软钢. ～ **touch** 耳朵软的人,轻易上当的人;〔美俚〕一打就败的拳击手,可轻易击败的对手. ～ **tube**【无】软性(电子)管,低真空管. ～ **underbelly** 软弱[易受伤害]的部位. ～ **ware** (计算机的)软件,软设备;程序设备;语言设备;程序系统; 设计计算方法; 计算程序; 程序编排手段;方案;资料图纸. ～ **water** 软水. ～ **wheat** 软麦〔一种低蛋白、软粒心小麦面粉,宜于做糕点〕. ～**-witted** *a.* 半痴半呆的,愚蠢的. ～ **wood** 软(木)材;针叶树材;针叶树.

sof·ten [ˈsɔ(ː)fn] *vt.* ①使软化,弄软. ②减轻,减弱(抵抗或反对). ③使(心)变温和;使柔弱;使不闪闪发光;使柔和;使婉转. — *vi.* ①变软;变温和,变柔和; 变弱,变柔弱. ②变静,变安稳,融和. ～ *water* 使硬水软化成软水. ***be ～ed into tears*** 感动得流泪. ～***up*** 〔美俚〕(用恭维话等)软化;【军】(进攻前用猛烈轰炸、炮击等)削弱(对方的抵抗力),破坏(对方的士气). **-er** *n.* 使软化[变柔和]的人[物];软化剂,软水剂. **-ing** *n.* 【无】真空恶化;漏气.

soft·ie [ˈsɔ(ː)fti] *n.* 〔口〕软心肠的人;柔弱的人;懦夫;轻信者;笨人. ***go ～*** 爱上,看中.

soft·ish [ˈsɔftiʃ] *a.* 有点柔软[柔和、仁慈、柔弱]的.

soft·ly [ˈsɔftli] *ad.* 柔软地;轻轻地,低声地,静静地;温和地;宽大地,松弛地.

soft·ness [ˈsɔftnis] *n.* 柔软;温柔;柔和;柔软;【农】粉质性.

soft·y [ˈsɔfti] 〔口〕 *n.* = softie.

Sog·di·an [ˈsɔgdiən] *n.* ①古索格代亚纳人〔居住在索格代亚纳的伊朗人〕. ②古索格代亚纳语〔已消亡,属伊朗语〕.

sog·getto [sɔˈdʒətəu] *n.* 〔It.〕【乐】主题.

sog·gy [ˈsɔgi] *a.* ①浸水的,湿润的,潮湿的. ②未烤透的. ③迟钝的,不活泼的;沉闷的,乏味的. *a ～ lawn* 潮湿的草地. *a ～ bread* 未烤透的面包. ～ *prose* 枯燥无味的散文. **-gi·ly** *ad.* **-gi·ness** *n.*

so·ho [səuˈhəu] *int.* 缩啊! 〔命马止步声〕;来啦! 〔发见猎物时的叫声〕.

soi-di·sant [ˈswɑːdiːˈzɑ̃ːŋ] *a.* 〔F.〕所谓的,自称的,冒充的. *a ~ artist* 自命的艺术家.

soi·gné [swɑːˈnjei] *a. (fem. soignée)* 〔F.〕打扮得极考究的;整洁的;时髦的. *a ~ restaurant* 高雅的饭店.

soil[1] [sɔil] *n.* ①泥土,土壤;土质. ②土地;国土. ③滋生地,温床. ④农业生活,务农. *clayey [sandy] ~* 粘[砂]壤. *poor [rich] ~* 瘦[肥]土. *high ~* 轻质土. *alluvial ~* 冲积土. *arable ~* 耕地. *a tiller [child, son] of the ~* 农民;本地人. *the lord of the ~* 领主,地主. *~ conservation* 土壤保持. *~ invaders*【农】土壤寄居菌. *on foreign ~* 在外国. *one's native [parent] ~* 故乡,祖国. ~ **bank**〔美〕联邦休耕地补助制. ~**borne** *a.* 由土壤传播的,在土壤中传播的. ~ **conservation** 土壤保持. ~ **science** 土壤学.

soil[2] [sɔil] *n.* ①脏东西,污物,污秽,污斑. ②粪尿,肥料. *a ~ pipe* 污水管. *night ~* 粪便. — *vt.* ①弄脏,弄污;污染,污损. ②污辱,败坏. ③给…上粪[施肥]. — *vi.* 被弄脏,变脏. *~ one's hands with* 〔喻〕因…弄脏手;染手. *It ~s easily.* 那东西容易脏. *~ a field* 给田施肥. *~ed clothes* 脏衣服.

soil[3] [sɔil] *vt.* (给畜舍内畜牲)喂青草[青饲料](用青饲料给畜牲)通便;催肥. *~ing crops* 青饲料作物.

soil·age [ˈsɔilidʒ] *n.* ①青饲料作物. ②弄脏;肮脏,污秽.

soil·ure [ˈsɔiljuə] *n.* 〔古语〕①污涂,污染. ②污秽,污斑.

soi·rée [ˈswɑːrei] *n.* 晚会,晚上举行的聚会.

soi·xante-quinze [F. swɑːsɑ̃ntkɛ̃z] *n.* 〔F.〕法国 75 毫米口径的炮.

so·ja [ˈsəujə, ˈsəudʒə] *n.*【植】大豆.

so·journ [ˈsɔdʒə(ː)n, ˈsəudʒəːn] *n.* 旅居,侨居;逗留,寄居. —*vi.* 旅居,逗留. *a ~ in the country* 在乡间逗留. **-er** *n.*

soke [səuk] *n.*【英史】①区域审判权. ②司法管辖区.

so·ko [ˈsəukəu] *n.* 黑猩猩.

so·kol [ˈsəukɔːl] *n.* 索科尔〔意为"鹰",捷克斯洛伐克的体育运动组织〕.

Sol [sɔl] *n.* ①男子名〔Solomon 的爱称〕. ②【罗神】太阳神;太阳. ③〔s-〕(炼金术中的)金.

sol[1] [sɔl] *n.*【乐】全音阶第五音.

sol[2] [səul] *n. (pl. ~s)* 索尔〔秘鲁货币单位〕.

sol[3] [sɔl] *n.*【化】溶胶,液胶.

Sol. = Solicitor; Solomon.

sol. = solicitor; soluble; solution.

S.O.L. 〔美〕倒霉的;为难的 (= short of luck).

so·la[1] [ˈsəulə] *n.*【植】(印度合萌属的)合欢草;(用合欢草的轻茎制成的)遮阳帽 (= ~ topi).

so·la[2] [ˈsəulə] *a.* solus 的阴性.

sol·ace [ˈsɔləs] *n.* 安慰;安慰物. — *vt.* ①安慰,抚慰. ②缓和,减轻. ③使高兴,使快活. ***~ oneself with*** 拿…来自慰.

so·lan [ˈsəulən] *n.*【动】塘鹅 (= ~-goose).

so·la·nin(e) [ˈsəuləˌniːn, -nin] *n.*【化】茄碱.

so·lar [ˈsəulə] *a.* 太阳的,根据太阳运行测量的;因太阳作用产生的. — *n.* = solarium. *the ~ system* 太阳系. *a ~ spot* 太阳黑点. *~ light* 日光. *~ energy* 太阳能. *a ~ battery* 太阳能电池. *~ heat* 太阳热. *~ calendar* 阳历. *a ~ spectrum* 太阳光谱. ~ **constant** 太阳常数〔太阳幅射的基准量〕. ~ **corona** 日冕. ~**cycle** 太阳周期〔一般以 28 年为一个周期,日历上月日和星期的一定排列重复出现〕;太阳活动周〔以 11 年左右为周期,太阳的一些主要现象重复出现〕. ~ **day** 太阳日. ~ **eclipse** 日蚀. ~ **eyepiece** 太阳望远镜. ~ **fever** = dengue. ~ **flare** 耀斑. ~ **flowers** 只在白天开一个时候的花. ~ **furnace** 太阳炉. ~ **month** 太阳月. ~ **oil** 煤油;页岩油. ~ **plexus**【解】太阳(神经)丛;〔口〕心窝儿. ~ **prominences** 日珥. ~ **sail** 太阳帆〔星际航行中利用太阳能作为动力的一种设备〕. ~ **time** 太阳时. ~ **wind** 太阳风,辐射微粒流. ~ **year** 太阳年.

so·lar·ism [ˈsəulərizəm] *n.* (神话中的)太阳中心说.

so·lar·i·um [səuˈlɛəriəm] *n. (pl. -ria [-riə])* 太阳钟,日晷;日光浴室[治疗室].

so·lar·ize [ˈsəuləraiz] *vt.* ①用日光曝晒;使受日光作用. ③【摄】使(胶片)曝光过久. —*vi.* (因曝光过久)胶片受损坏.

so·late [ˈsɔleit] *vi.*【化】(凝胶)液化,成为液胶. **-lation** *n.*

so·la·ti·um [səuˈleiʃjəm, -ʃiəm] *n. (pl. -tia [-ʃiə])* 赔偿;安慰金.

sold [səuld] sell 的过去式及过去分词.

sold·er [ˈsɔldə, ˈsɔ(ː)-] *n.* ①焊药,焊剂;焊锡. ②结合物,联接因素. *hard ~* 硬焊药. *soft ~* 软焊药. — *vt., vi.* 焊;接合;锡焊;焊接;(使)结合. ~**ing iron** 焊铁,烙铁. ~ **paste** 焊药.

sol·dier [ˈsəul dʒə] *n.* ①军人;(陆军)士兵 (*opp.* officer);战士,勇士. ②富有军事经验[军事技术]的人;军事家,军事指挥员. ③为某事业献身的人. ④〔口〕偷懒[装病]的人,懒汉. ⑤【动】(群居性昆虫)兵虫;兵蚁;寄居蟹;〔俚〕熏鲱鱼. *a ~ of the carpet* 游手好闲,贪图享受的人 (= carpet knight). *the great ~s of history* 历史名将. *~ of fortune* 雇用军人;(追求名利的)冒险家. *a great ~* 勇将. *a militia ~* 民兵. *a private [common] ~* 兵. *tin [toy] ~s* 玩具兵. ***come the old ~ over sb.*** 拿老资格派头指挥某人,教训某人;欺骗,哄骗. ***go for a ~*** 参军. ***no ~*** 没有指挥能力的军官,没有做军人资格的人. ***old ~*** 老兵;老资格,老手;〔俚〕(酒席等的)空瓶;雪茄烟头[屁股]. ***play at ~s*** 玩军队游戏. — *vi.* ①当兵. ②〔口〕偷懒,装病. — *vt.* 〔美〕逃避,规避. *He has ~ed all over the world.* 他做军人,走遍了全世界. ~**s and sailors** 陆军和海军. ~ **ant**【动】兵蚁. ~ **colour**〔美〕全部清一色. ~ **crab**【动】寄居蟹. ~**'s heart** 军人病〔一种心脏病〕. ~**s' home**〔美〕美退伍军人收容所. ~**'s medal**〔美〕军人奖章〔对非战斗英勇行动授予的奖章〕. ~**'s wind**【海】顺风. **-like, -ly** *a.* 象军人的,象武士的,勇敢的,英勇的. **-ship** *n.* 军人身分[品质];军事才干.

sol·dier·y [ˈsəuldʒəri] *n.* ①〔集合词〕军人,军队. ②军事训练,军事知识[科学].

sol·do [ˈsɔldəu] *n. (pl. -di [-diː])* 索尔多〔意大利铜币, = $^{1}/_{20}$ lira〕.

sole[1] [səul] *n.* ①脚底,蹠;鞋底;鞋底皮;袜底. ②【农】犁底;垄沟底;蹄底;【筑城】(炮眼的)底面;【船】底板;(高尔夫球棒的)底部. — *vt.* 装鞋底,换鞋底;(高尔夫球)使棒底接触地面. ~**channel** *n.* 鞋底缝线的凹槽.

sole[2] [səul] *n. (pl. ~s,* 〔集合词〕*~)*【动】鳎科的鱼;舌鳎;箬鳎鱼,板鱼.

sole[3] [səul] *a.* ①单独的,单一的,唯一的. ②孤独的;独立的;独占的. ③【法】未婚的,独身的〔主要用于妇女〕. *She was her mother's ~ confident.* 她是母亲唯一信任的人. *~ reason* 唯一的理由. *~ rights to a patent* 专利独享的权利. *a feme ~* 独身女人. ***have [be in] ~ charge of*** 单独掌管,是…的总负责人. ***have the ~ responsibility of*** 单独负…的责任. ***have the ~ right of*** 有…的独占权. ***on one's own ~ responsibility*** 单独负责地. ~ **trader** 个体商人;不靠丈夫而独立经商的妻子. **-ness** *n.*

sol·e·cism [ˈsɔlisizəm] *n.* ①违反语法;文理不通. ②失礼,无礼. ③误谬,背理.

sol·e·cist [ˈsɔlisist] *n.* 违反语法的人;失礼的人,不合情理的人.

sol·e·cis·tic [ˌsɔliˈsistik] *a.* 违反语法的;不通的;无礼貌[不合情理]的.

sole·ly [ˈsəu(l)li] *ad.* 独自,单独;单只;完全. *~ because [on account] of* 完全为了. *~ for your sake* 只为了你.

sol·emn [ˈsɔləm] *a.* ①严肃的,庄严的. ②仪式隆重的,庄重的. ③一本正经的,装腔作势的. ④重大的,严重的. ⑤按照仪式的,合仪式的;神圣的,宗教上的. ⑥黝暗阴沉的. *a ~ feast day* 隆重的节日. *give a ~ warning* 提出严重警告. *put on a ~ face* 装出一本正经的面孔. *a ~ oath*【法】正式的誓约. ***in ~ form*** 正式的[地].

so·lem·ni·fy [səˈlemniˌfai] *vt.* 使严肃,使庄重.

so·lem·ni·ty [səˈlemniti] *n.* ①庄严,严肃,庄重,隆重. ②一本正经,装腔作势. ③〔常 *pl.*〕仪式;【法】正式.

sol·em·ni·sa·tion,〔Am.〕**-za·tion** [ˌsɔləmnaiˈzeiʃən] *n.* 庄严化;举行典礼[仪式]. *~ of marriage* 举行婚礼.

sol·em·nize [ˈsɔləmnaiz] *vt.* 使庄严;举行典礼. *~ a marriage* 举行婚礼.

so·len [ˈsəulən] *n.*【贝】竹蛏.

so·le·no·cyte [səˈliːnəˌsait] *n.*【生】火焰细胞,管细胞.

so·le·no·glyph [səˈliːnəˌglif] *n.*【动】管牙类 *(solenoglypha)* 毒蛇.

so·le·noid [ˈsəulinɔid] *n.*【电】螺线管;圆筒形线圈.

sol-fa [sɔlˈfɑː] *n.*【乐】唱名;视唱法. — *vt., vi.* 视唱〔指用唱名来唱,通常看谱即唱〕. ~ **syllables** 七唱名(即 do, re, mi, fa 等).

sol·fa·ta·ra [ˌsəulfəˈtɑːrə] *n.*【地】硫质喷气孔.

sol·fége [sɔlˈfeʒ] *n.*【乐】①= solfeggio. ②音乐基础理论教学.

sol·feg·gio [sɔlˈfedʒəu, -ˈfedʒiːˌəu] *n. (pl.* ***-feg·gios, -feg·gi*** [-ˈfedʒi]*)*【乐】①视唱练习. ②视唱音阶使用〔尤指看谱视唱〕.

so·li [ˈsəuliː] solo 的复数.

so·lic·it [səˈlisit] *vt.* ①恳求,乞求,请求;征求;要求,恳求给予. ②【法】教唆;诱惑;(妓女)拉(客);送贿赂请求. ③提起(注意);诱发,引发. — *vi.* ①请求,恳求,征求 *(for)*. ②(妓女)拉客. *~ sb. for a thing = ~ a thing of sb.* 向某人乞求一件东西. *We ~ you for your favours [custom]. = We ~ favours [custom] of [from] you.*【商】请予惠顾. *~ for funds* 征求捐款;募捐. **-ant** *n.* 请求者;征求者.

so·lic·i·ta·tion [səˌlisiˈteiʃən] *n.* ①恳求,请求,恳请;征求. ②诱惑;【法】教唆(罪);(妓女等的)拉客. ③诱发,引发.

so·lic·i·tor [səˈlisitə] *n.* ①恳求者,催促者;求婚者;〔美〕掮客,推销员;募捐人. ②〔英〕初级律师. 〔美〕(为一个城市或部门负责法律事务的)法务官. *a S- of the treasury* 〔美〕财政部法务官. ~ **general**〔英〕【法】副检察长;〔美〕司法部副部长;(若干州的)首席司法官.

so·lic·it·ous [səˈlisitəs] *a.* ①热切要求[希望]…的,渴望[热心]…的 *(to do; of)*. ②担心的,挂念的,惦记的. ③非常关心[注意]的,非常考究的. *~ to please* 渴望讨人欢喜. *~ of his help* 渴望得到他的帮助. *be ~ about [for, concerning] (sb.'s health)* 挂念(某人健康). *~ in matters of dress* 非常讲究衣着. *a ~ inquiry about his health* 对他健康关切的询问. **-ly** *ad.* **-ness** *n.*

so·lic·i·tude [səˈlisitjuːd] *n.* ①切望,热心;挂念,担心,关心,渴望. ②〔*pl.*〕担心的事情. *show the warmest ~ for* … 向…表示最亲切的关怀. *with the warm ~ of* 在…的亲切关怀下.

sol·id [ˈsɔlid] *a.* ①固体的;实心的,实质的,密实的. ②【数】立体的,立方的,三维的. ③结实的,坚强的,坚固的,牢靠的 *(opp.* flimsy, slender, slight*)*;有力的,强健的;扎扎实实的,非浮浅的(学习);确实的,可靠的,忠实的;稳健的. ④慎重的,严肃的;(财政上)稳固的,有资产的. ⑤团结的,全体一致的. ⑥纯粹的,全体同质的,十足的(金、银等);全部一样的,齐一的,没有浓淡的(颜色等). ⑦完整的,完全的;连续无间断的. ⑧【哲】(有)实体的. ⑨【印】(行间)密排的. ⑩〔美乐俚〕极好的,表演精采的. ⑪〔美口语〕亲密的,融洽的*(with)*. ⑫〔美口〕〔用于 good 之后以加强语气〕着实的,有力的. *a ~ body* 固体. *~ food* 固体食物[面包、肉等]. *a ~ figure* 立体形. *a ~ bath*【医】(沙浴等)固体浴. *a ~ bulb*【植】球茎. *a ~ bullet* 实心子弹. *~ comfort* 真正的安慰. *~ compound*【语】连写复合词. *~ content*【林】实积. *~ earth [ground]* 大地. *a ~ man* 稳健的人;有资产的人. *~ gold* 足赤(金). *~ ivory*〔美〕头脑迟钝的人. *~ measure* 体积,容积. *a ~ problem*【数】三次方程式问题,解析几何问题. *a ~ vote* 全场一致的投票. *for a ~ hour* 整整一小时. *~ colo(u)r* 单色. *a ~ matter*【印】实排印件. *a good ~ blow* 着着实实的一击. ***be [go] ~ for [in favour of]*** 团结一致援助[拥护、赞成]. ***be ~ with***〔美俚〕确实可以得到…的援助[拥护]. ***get ~ with***〔美俚〕得到…的宠信. — *n.* 固体;【火箭】固体燃料,火箭火药;【数】立体. — *ad.* 一致. *vote ~* 全场一致投票. ~ **angle**【几】隅角. **~-drawn** *a.*【冶】整体拉伸制成的(管子等). ~ **earthing**【无】固定接地. ~ **fuel [propellant]**【火箭】固体[态]燃料. ~ **geometry** 立体几何. **~-hoofed** *a.* 有单蹄的. **~-horned** *a.* 有实角的. ~ **motor**【机】固体燃料发动机. **~-looking** *a.* 看来很富足的(*~-looking well-fed citizens* 看上去日子过得很富裕的老百姓). **~-state** *a.* 固态的,固态学的;固态元件[器件]的(*~-state physics* 固态物理学. *a ~-state circuit* 固体电路). **-ly** *ad.* **-ness** *n.*

sol·i·da·go [ˌsɔliˈdeigəu] *n. (pl.* ***-gos****)*【植】秋麒麟草(= goldenrod).

sol·i·da·rism [ˈsɔlidərizəm] *n.* ①团结一致. ②社会连带主义〔一种社会学理论,认为利害相关的社会组织是以社会成员的相互依存为基础的〕.

sol·i·da·rist [ˈsɔlidərist] *n.* 社会连带主义者 **-ris·tic** *a.*

sol·i·dar·i·ty [ˌsɔliˈdæriti] *n.* 团结一致,共同一致;共同责任;休戚相关. ***in ~ with*** 声援.

sol·i·dar·ize [ˈsɔlidəraiz] *vi.* 团结一致.

sol·i·dar·y [ˈsɔlidəri] *a.* ①团结一致的. ②休戚相关的.

so·lid·i·fi·a·ble [səˈlidifaiəbl] *a.* 可固化的,能凝固的;能团结一致的.

so·lid·i·fi·ca·tion [ˌsəlidifiˈkeiʃən] *n.* 团结;凝固;【化】固体化(作用).

so·lid·i·fy [səˈlidifai] *vt.* ①使凝固,固化. ②使硬;使结晶. ③使团结. — *vi.* ①变硬,结晶. ②凝固. ③团结. *the ~ing point*【物】(凝)固点.

so·lid·i·ty [səˈliditi] *n.* ①固态;固体;【物】硬度,强度;【空】稠度;充实. ②坚固,坚牢;牢靠,稳固;殷实;确实. ③【数】体积. ④完整性,连续性.

sol·i·dus [ˈsɔlidəs] *n.* 〔L.〕*(pl.* ***-di*** [-dai]*)* ①索里达〔Constantine 大帝发行的金币;欧洲后来称之为 bezant,略 s. 或 S.〕. ②(表示 shilling, 分数等的)斜线分隔符号(/)〔原为 s 的长体ʃ: 7/6 = 7s. 6d. 2/3=三分之二〕.

sol·i·fid·i·an [ˌsɔliˈfidiən] *n., a.* 唯信论者(的). **-ism** *n.* 唯信论.

so·lil·o·quist [səˈliləkwist] *n.* ①自言自语者. ②【剧】独白者.

so·lil·o·quize [səˈliləkwaiz] *vi.* 自言自语;【剧】独白.

so·lil·o·quy [səˈliləkwi] *n. (pl.* ***-quies****)* 自言自语,【剧】独白.

sol·i·ped [ˈsɔliped] *n.* 单蹄兽[马等]. — *a.* 单蹄的.

sol·ip·sism [ˈsɔlipsizəm] *n.*【哲】唯我论. **-sist** *n.*【哲】唯我论者.

sol·i·taire [ˌsɔliˈtɛə] *n.* ①独粒宝石的首饰[戒指,耳环等],独粒宝石[钻石]. ②单人纸牌戏;单人球戏;单人象棋. ③〔罕〕隐士.

sol·i·ta·ri·ly [ˈsɔlitərili] *ad.* 孤独寂寞地;孤立地.

sol·i·ta·ry [ˈsɔlitəri] *a.* ①独个儿的,孤独的;独居的. ②寂寞的;冷落的,僻远的,人烟稀少的. ③孤立的;单独的,唯一的. ④【解、植】分离的,单生的. ⑤【动】孤栖的 *(opp.* social, gregarious*)*. *~ confinement [imprisonment]* 单独监禁. *a ~ life* 孤独生活. *a ~ ramble* 独自漫步. *a ~ exception* 唯一的例外. *a ~ place* 冷僻的地方. — *n.* 独居者;隐士;单独监禁. **-ri·ly** *ad.* **-ri·ness** *n.*

sol•i•tude [ˈsɔlitju:d] *n.* 孤独,独居;寂寞(的地方),幽静(的地方),荒野. ***in*** ~ 独个儿;孤独地;寂寞地.
sol•ler•et [ˈsɔləˌret, ˌsɔləˈret] *n.* 铁靴〔欧洲中世纪盔甲〕.
sol•mi•za•tion [ˌsɔlmiˈzeiʃən] *n.*【乐】= solfa.
so•lo [ˈsəuləu] *n.* *(pl. ~s, -li* [-li]*)* ①【乐】独奏(曲);独唱(曲);独唱[奏];单人舞. ②单独表演;【空】单飞. ③单人纸牌戏;一种惠斯特纸牌戏(由一人对抗三人). — *a.* 独唱[奏]的;单独的,单人的. — *ad.* 独,单独. — *vi.* 独唱,独奏;单飞.
so•lo•ist [ˈsəuləuist] *n.* 独奏者;独唱者.
So•lo man [ˈsəuləu] 梭罗人〔爪哇猿人的一种〕.
Sol•o•mon [ˈsɔləmən] *n.* ①所罗门(男子名) (H. = peaceable)〔爱称 Sol〕. ②圣人,贤人. **Solomon Is.** 所罗门群岛. **~'s seal** 六角星形(☆). **~'s-seal**【植】萎蕤;黄精属植物.
So•lon [ˈsəulɔn] *n.* ①梭仑〔古雅典的立法者〕. ②〔s-〕贤人;明智的立法家;〔美口〕议员. **-lo•ni•an, -lon•ic** *a.*
sol•on•chak [ˌsɔlənˈtʃæk] *n.* 盐土.
sol•o•nets, sol•o•netz [ˈsɔ:ləˌnets] *n.* *(pl. **-netses, -netz, -netzes**)* 碱土.
so-long [ˈsəuˈlɔŋ] *int.* 〔口〕再会,再见.
sol•stice [ˈsɔlstis] *n.*【天】至,至点;最高点. *the summer [winter]* ~ 夏[冬]至.
sol•sti•tial [sɔlˈstiʃəl] *a.* 至的,夏至的,冬至的.
sol•u•bil•i•ty [ˌsɔljuˈbiliti] *n.* ①【化】溶(解)度,溶(解)性;(可)溶性. ②可解释性,可解(决)性.
sol•u•ble [ˈsɔljubl] *a.* ①可溶的,易溶解的 *(in)*. ②能解释的,能解决的;【数】可解的. ~ *glass*【化】水玻璃,溶性玻璃. ~ *oil* 溶性油. ~ *tar* 轻木焦油.
so•lus [ˈsəuləs] *a.* *(fem. **sola**)* 独自,单独〔主,舞台指挥用语〕. *I found myself* ~. 〔谑〕我那时是孤零零一个人. *Enter the king* ~. 国王单独登场.
sol•ute [ˈsɔlju:t] *n.*【化】溶质;溶解物.
so•lu•tion [səˈlju:ʃən] *n.* ①溶解;溶液,溶体,溶剂. ②(补轮胎用的)橡胶水;〔美〕药水. ③解决,解答 *(of; for; to)*;解释;(数学等的)解法,解式. ④免除,解除. ⑤【医】消散,消退. *a nitrate of silver* ~ 硝酸银溶液. *chemical* ~ 化学溶解. *mechanical* ~ 机械溶解.
so•lu•tion•ist [səˈlu:ʃənist] *n.* (报刊上的)疑难解答专家.
So•lu•tre•an, So•lu•tri•an [səˈlu:triən] *a.* 索鲁特期的〔指欧洲旧石器时代前期文化,因遗址在法国小村索鲁特而得名〕.
solv•a•ble [ˈsɔlvəbl] *a.* ①可解释[解答,解决]的. ②可溶解的. **-bil•i•ty** [ˌsɔlvəˈbiliti] *n.* ①可解释[解答,解决]. ②溶解能力;溶剂化度.
sol•vate [ˈsɔlveit] *n.*【化】溶剂化物. — *vt.* 使(分子,离子)变成溶剂化物. **-va•tion** [sɔlˈveiʃən] *n.*
Sol•vay process [ˈsɔlvei]【化】苏尔未法〔制苏打的一种方法〕.
solve [sɔlv] *vt.* ①解释,说明,解答,解决;调停. ②清偿(债务). ③〔古〕解开,松开(结子).
sol•ven•cy [ˈsɔlvənsi] *n.* ①【化】溶解本领. ②偿付能力.
sol•vent [ˈsɔlvənt] *a.* ①有溶解力的,可溶解的;〔喻〕使(信仰等)瓦解[削弱]的 *(of)*. ②有偿付能力的. — *n.* ①【化】溶剂,溶媒 *(of; for)*. ②解释,说明. ③使瓦解[削弱]的东西. ~ *action* 溶解作用. *Water is the commonest* ~. 水是最普通的溶剂. *Alcohol is a* ~ *of resinous substances.* 酒精是树脂性物质的溶媒. *science as a* ~ *of superstition* 作为破除迷信手段的科学.
sol•vol•y•sis [sɔlˈvɔlisis] *n.*【化】溶剂分解(作用).
Som. = Somaliland; Somerset(shire).
so•ma[1] [ˈsəumə] *n.* *(pl. **~ta*** [-tə]*)*【生】(动植物的)躯体[干];体细胞.
so•ma[2] [ˈsəumə] *n.* ①苏麻液〔吠陀仪式的文献中提到的能令人致醉的一种植物液汁〕. ②【植】苏麻 *(Sarcostemma acidum)*〔一种马利筋属植物,据猜测即上述液汁的来源〕.
So•ma•li [səuˈmɑ:li] *n.* *(pl. ~, ~s)* ①(非洲)索马里人[语]. ②(非洲)索马里.
So•ma•li•a [səuˈmɑ:liə] *n.* 索马里〔非洲〕.
So•ma•li•land [səˈmɑ:lilænd] *n.* 索马里〔非洲国家〕.
so•ma•scope [ˈsəuməskəup] *n.*【医】超声波检查仪.
so•mat•ic [səuˈmætik] *a.* ①身体的,肉体的. ②【生、解】体的. ③躯体的;体壁的;体细胞的. *a* ~ *cell* 体细胞,营养细胞. ~ *anthropology* 人体学.
so•ma•tol•o•gy [ˌsəuməˈtɔlədʒi] *n.* 人类躯体学.
so•ma•to•plasm [ˈsəumətəˌplæzm, səuˈmætə-] *n.*【生】体质,体细胞. **-plas•tic** *a.*
so•ma•to•pleure [ˈsəumətəˌpluə] *n.*【胎生学】胚体壁. **-pleu•ral** *a.*
so•ma•to•type [ˈsəumətəˌtaip] *n.* 体型;体格.
som•bre,〔美〕**som•ber** [ˈsɔmbə] *a.* ①昏暗的;浅黑的,幽暗的;阴沉的. ②忧郁的. ③暗淡的,不鲜艳的(颜色等). *a* ~ *countenance* 忧郁[阴沉]的面容. *a* ~ *sky* 阴沉的天空. *a man of* ~ *character* 性格忧郁的人. ~ *clothes* 暗色的衣服. *a* ~ *hue* 暗淡的颜色.
som•bre•ro [sɔmˈbrɛərəu] *n.* *(pl. ~s)* 墨西哥阔边帽.
som•brous [ˈsɔmbrəs] *a.* 〔诗〕= sombre.
some [强 sʌm; 弱 səm, sm] *a.* 〔和表示否定、疑问的 any 对应的肯定词〕①ⓐ [sʌm]〔用于单数普通名词前〕(有)一个(人、物、时间). *He went to* ~ *place in Africa.* 他到非洲一个地方去了. *S- fool or other has broken it.* 是一个蠢家伙把它弄坏了. *We must find* ~ *way out of it.* 得想一个方法逃脱才行. ★ some 是指完全不知道的事物而言,a certain 则是在知道而故意不说时、或轻蔑地说'某一个…'时用. ⓑ [sʌm]〔强调〕了不起的,极好的. *He is* ~ *scholar.* 他是了不起的学者. *I call that* ~ *picture.* 我觉得那是很不错的画. *This is* ~ *war.* 这是很象样的战争. ②〔用于复数普通名词或物质、抽象名词前表示数量〕ⓐ〔一般〕[səm, sm] 若干(的),多少(的),一些(的),几分(的),一点儿(的). *I want* ~ *money.* 我需要一点钱. *I saw* ~ *people I knew.* 我看见了几个熟人. ★ 表示疑问、条件时虽用 any, 但表示劝导、拜托而期待 yes 时则用 some: *May I give you* ~ *tea?* 您喝茶吗? *Will you buy me* ~ *books?* 请您给我买几本书好吗? ⓑ [sʌm]〔强调〕有的(人、物). *S- people do not like that sort of thing.* 有的人不喜欢那种事. *All wood is not hard,* ~ *wood is soft.* 木料不一定都硬,也有软的. ⓒ [sʌm] 相当多的,不少的. *I stayed there for* ~ *days.* 我在那儿待了好多天了. *You'll need* ~ *courage to face this.* 应付这件事情得有相当勇气. ③ⓐ〔用于数词前〕大约. ~ *40 tons in weight* 约重四十吨. ⓑ〔用于距离、时间的单数名词前〕左右. ~ *mile [hour] or so* 一英里[一个钟头]左右. ***after*** ~ ***time*** 过了一会,不久之后. ***in*** ~ ***degree*** 多少,几分. ***in*** ~ ***way or other*** 设法,想法子. ~ ***day*** 改天,他日;(今后)有一天. ~ ***days ago*** 几天前. ~ ***few [little]*** 少许,一点,少数,几个. ~ ***more*** [səˈmɔ:] 再…一点. ~ ***one*** [ˈsʌm wʌn] 有人; [ˈsʌmˈwʌn] 某一个(人). ~ ***other day*** 改天,过天. ~ ***punkins***〔美〕名流;摆架子的人. ~ ***time*** 暂时,一会儿 (= ~ day). ~ ***time ago*** 先前,不久以前. ~ ***time or other*** 迟早,早晚. — *pro.* 有些人;有的东西;若干(数量);若干部分,多少,几分,有些 *(of)*. *Some of it is spoiled.* 其中有些已经坏了. ***and (then)*** ~ 〔美俚〕(比那个)还要多一些. ~ ***of these days*** 近日内. — *ad.* 〔英俚,美口〕几分,稍微;〔美口〕很,非常,相当. *look* ~〔美口〕很不错. *That's going* ~. 〔美口〕那很不错,那个倒好极啦. *Do you like it?* —— *Some!* 你喜欢那个吗?——当然.
-some *comb. f.* 表示①"易于…的","使人…的","有…倾

向的": weari*some*, quarrel*some*. ②〔附加数词后〕"…个一组": two*some*, four*some*. ③"体","染色体": chromo*some*, mono*some*.

some·bod·y [ˈsʌmbədi] *n.* 有相当身分的人,重要人物. *think oneself to be (a) ~* 自以为是个大人物. *nobodies posing as somebodies* 冒充大人物的小人物. — *pro.* 某人,有人. *S- has disclosed the secret.* 有人把秘密泄露出去了. *General S-* 某某将军. *Call a taxi, ~!* 什么人去叫部出租汽车来吧! *~ **else*** 别人; 了不起的人物. *~ **or other*** 某一个人〔不知道是哪一个〕.

some·day [ˈsʌmdei] *ad.* (今后)有一天,改日,有朝一日.

some·how [ˈsʌmhau] *ad.* 设法,想办法,想个方法; 不知道怎样,不晓得什么缘故. *I must get it finished ~.* 我总得想办法把它做完才行. *He ~ dropped behind.* 他不晓得怎么落后了. *~ **or other*** 设法,想办法; 不晓得为什么.

some·one [ˈsʌmwʌn] *pro.* 有人,某人〔同 somebody, 但多用于书面语,特别是疑问句或否定句的场合〕. *S- wants to see you.* 有人想会见你. *Why can't she go to the dance with ~ else?* 她为啥不能同别人去参加舞会呢? *Would ~ please tell me what it is?* 这是什么东西,请哪位告诉我一下. — *n.* 不知姓名的人. *Was that ~ else aware of the accident?* 另外那个不知姓名的人也知道这件事故吗?

some·place [ˈsʌmpleis] *ad.* 〔美〕= somewhere.

som·er·sault, som·er·set [ˈsʌməsɔ(:)lt, -set] *n.* ①筋斗. ②(意见等的) 颠倒; 一百八十度的转变. *cut [make, throw, turn] ~s* 翻筋斗. — *vi.* 翻筋斗.

Som·er·ville [ˈsʌməvil] *n.* 萨默维尔〔姓氏〕.

some·thing [ˈsʌmθiŋ] *pron.* ①某物,某事. ②若干,几分; 该类事物〔表示的是模糊的概念〕. ③实有物 (*opp.* nothing). ④重要事物[人]. ⑤〔口〕喝的,吃的. *There is ~ in him.* 他这个人是有些道理的. *Here is ~ for you.* 送你一点东西. *What's his name? Jim something.* 他叫什么名字? 吉姆什么的. *It is ~ to have got so far.* 弄到那个地步,挺什么(了不起)的了. *You've got ~ there.* 〔口〕你的话有点道理; 那是一个好主意. *take [have] a drop of ~* 喝一点(酒). *S- is better than nothing.* 聊胜于无. *He is [has] ~ in the Customs.* 他在海关里有一个差事[有点地位]. *He lost his train or (did) ~.* 他也许没赶上火车或是什么的啦. *I caught the five ~ train.* 我赶上五点多的火车. *Theory is ~, but practice is everything.* 理论虽重要,实践更重要. ***be ~ of a [an]*** … 有一点…,有些象…的地方(*I am ~ of a musician.* 我有一点点音乐知识). ***have ~ of the … in one*** 有…的天分. ***have ~ on one's mind*** 有心事. ***know ~ of everything and everything of ~*** 通百艺而专一长. ***make ~ of*** 将…训练成相当的人物; 利用…. ***or ~*** 大概是…之类的 (*He is a scientist or ~.* 他大概是科学家之类的人物. *She's got a cold or ~.* 她大概是受了凉). ***see ~ of (him)*** 和(他)有些来往; 有点认识(他). ***~ damp*** 〔俚〕酒. ***~ for nothing*** 不费劲得到的好处,轻易得来的利益. ***~ good*** 好东西; 赛马的内幕消息. ***~ of*** 在某种意义(或程度)上. ***~ of the kind*** 类似的事物. ***~ on the hip*** 〔美俚〕酒. ***~ short*** 〔俚〕酒. ***~ to write home about*** 值得大书特书的事情. ***~ tells me*** 〔口〕我认为… (*S- tells me my watch isn't quite right.* 我觉得我的手表走得不准). ***think ~ of oneself*** 自以为了不起,自命不凡. — *ad.* 〔古〕几分,有点,多少,相当. ***~ like*** 〔口〕大约,约; 有几分象…的,有点象…的; 〔口〕了不起的,极好的,伟大的 (*It must be ~ like six o'clock.* 现在一定是六点钟模样了. *That's ~ like!* 〔口〕那倒是极好的东西!). — *n., a., vt.* 〔委婉话〕= hell, devilish, damn. *What the ~ are you doing here?* 你究竟在这儿干什么? *You ~ villain!* 你这大坏蛋! *I'll see you ~ed first!* 该死的东西!

some·time [ˈsʌmtaim] *ad.* ①改天,哪一天; (今后)有一天. ②〔古〕从前,往昔. — *a.* 以前的. *He was ~ mayor of …* 他以前是…市长. *(the) ~ professor at …* 前任…教授. ***~ ago*** 先前,不久以前. ***~ or other*** 迟早.

some·times [ˈsʌmtaimz, səmˈtaimz] *ad.* 常常,往往,有时. *~ rich, ~ poor* 有时富,有时穷. ★ 本词可用在句首、句尾、动词前、助动词及 be, have 后: ~ he seemed depressed; I go there ~; I ~ go; I am ~ late.

some·way(s) [ˈsʌmwei(z)] *ad.* 设法,想办法; 不知道什么缘故.

some·what [ˈsʌm*h*wɔt] *ad., n.* 一点儿,稍微,有点,多少. *He answered ~ hastily.* 他回答得轻率了一点儿. *He is ~ of a connoisseur.* 他多少总是一个鉴定家.

some·when [ˈsʌm*h*wen] *a.* 〔罕〕= sometime.

some·where [ˈsʌm*h*wɛə] *ad.* 某处,在[到]某处,不知道在[到]什么地方. ***I'll see you ~ (in hell) first!*** 混蛋! 讨厌! (等). ***~ about*** 大约,约略,几乎; 在…的附近,在…的时候 (*~ about here* 在这附近. *~ about fifty* 约五十岁).

some·whith·er [ˈsʌm*h*wiðə] *ad.* 〔古〕到某处,不知道到什么地方.

some·wise [ˈsʌmˌwaiz] *ad.* 〔古〕某种程度地,不知怎地〔通常构成词组: *in ~*〕.

so·mite [ˈsəumait] *n.* ①【动】体节,环节. ②【解】原节,原椎,初椎. **-mit·ic** [-ˈmitik], **-mi·tal** [-mitl] *a.*

som·me·lier [ˌsʌmilˈjei; F.sɔmˈlje] *n.* (*pl.* **-liers** [-jeiz; F. -ˈlje]) (饭店的)酒侍者; 斟酒服务员.

som·nam·bu·late [sɔmˈnæmbjuleit] *vi., vt.* 梦行,梦游. **-lation** *n.* **-lator** *n.*

som·nam·bu·lism [sɔmˈnæmbjulizəm] *n.* ①梦行,梦游(症). ②梦游者的恍惚状态. *artificial ~* 催眠术.

som·nam·bu·list [sɔmˈnæmbjulist] *n.* 梦游(症)者.

som·ni- *comb. f.* 表示"睡眠": *somni*ferous, *somni*loquy.

som·nif·er·ous [sɔmˈnifərəs] *a.* 使睡眠的,催眠的; 麻醉的.

som·nil·o·quence, som·nil·o·quy [ˈsɔmˈniləkwəns, -kwi] *n.* 说梦话,梦呓.

som·nil·o·quous [sɔmˈniləkwəs] *a.* (说)梦话的,梦呓的.

som·no·lence, -cy [ˈsɔmnələns, -si] *n.* ①思睡,困倦. ②嗜眠状态; 幻梦; 恍惚. ③【医】嗜眠(症).

som·no·lent [ˈsɔmnələnt] *a.* ①想睡的,困倦的. ②催眠的. **-ly** *ad.*

Som·nus [ˈsɔmnəs] *n.* 【罗神】睡神.

son [sʌn] *n.* ①儿子; 〔*pl.*〕后裔,子孙. ②国人,国民,居民. ③女婿,养子. ④一分子,会员,党员; 子弟; (某一专业或品质的)继承者,从事…的人. ⑤〔年长者对年轻人的称呼〕年轻人; 朋友. ⑥〔S-〕(与冠词 the 连用) 耶稣基督. *a ~ of China* 中国人. *a ~ of man* 任何人. *the ~s of men [Adam]* 人类. *the ~s of Abraham* 亚伯拉罕的子孙,犹太人. *a ~ of the Muses* 诗人. *a ~ of the Mars* 军人. *my ~* 小伙子. *old ~* 老朋友. ***a favourite ~*** ①宠儿,爱子. ②〔美俚〕本州代表支持的总统候选人,政界红人. ***every mother's ~*** 每一个人,大家. ***his father's ~*** (容貌、性格)象父亲的人. ***~ and heir*** 长子. ***~ of a bitch*** 〔卑〕狗娘养的,婊子养的. ***~ of a gun*** 王八蛋,狗崽子; 家伙; 讨厌的工作,完成不了的任务. ***a ~ of Bacchus*** 酒鬼. ***a ~ of dripping*** 厨子. ***a ~ of ebony*** 黑人. ***Son of God*** 天使; 精神上依附上帝的人. ***a ~ of Momus*** 爱嘲弄的人,滑稽的人. ***~ of the morning*** 趁早赶路的人,旅客. ***~ of the soil*** 本地人; 农民. ***~ of toil*** 劳动者,工人. ***The Son of God [Man]*** 耶稣基督. ***the Sons of Liberty*** 〔美史〕自由子弟会. ***the Sons of the Revolution*** 〔美〕革命子弟会. **~-in-law** (*pl.* **~s-in-law**) 女婿. **-less** *a.* 无后嗣的. **-ly** *a.* 儿子般的; 孝顺的. **-ship** *n.* 儿子身份.

so·nance, -cy [ˈsəunəns, -si] *n.*【语音】有声音;发浊音,发成节音.

so·nant [ˈsəunənt] *a.*【语音】有声音的,浊音的;成(音)节的. — *n.* 浊音 *(opp.* surd*)*;成节音.

so·nar [ˈsəunɑː] (= sound operation navigation and range) *n.* 声纳,声波导航和测距系统,音响定位器;潜艇探察仪.

so·na·ta [səˈnɑːtə] *n.*【乐】奏鸣曲.

so·na·ti·na [ˌsɔnəˈtiːnə] *n.*【乐】小奏鸣曲.

sonde [sɔnd] *n.* 探测装置;探头;探针.

Son·dra [ˈsɔːndrə] *n.* 桑德拉〔女子名, Sandra 的异体〕.

son et lu·mière [sõ ne lyˈmjɛːr] ①照明配音技巧〔表现历史景象,尤指晚上在纪念碑前用特殊的照明效果和现场或录音的解说,音乐等〕. ②这种景象.

song [sɔŋ] *n.* ①歌,声乐,唱歌. ②歌曲;歌曲集;歌词. ③诗歌,短诗,抒情诗;韵文. ④鸟叫声,鸟语. *a folk* ~ 民歌. *a love* ~ 爱情歌曲. *a popular* ~ 流行歌曲. ***break [burst forth] into*** ~ 唱出. ***for a (mere)*** ~ = ***for an old*** ~ 非常便宜地,简直等于白送地. ***go for a*** ~ 贱价抛出. ***not worth an old*** ~ 毫无价值的,白送也不要的. ***nothing to make a*** ~ ***about***〔俚〕没价值的东西,不值一顾. ***sing the*** ~ ***to death*** 反复唱得腻死人. ~ ***and dance***〔美〕歌舞表演;〔口〕(对质问的)解释;演说;空洞的废话;遁词. ~ **bird** 鸣鸟,鸣禽;女歌手,歌女. ~**-book** 歌曲集. ~**-plugging** 通过反复广播使歌曲流行. ~**-smith** 作曲家. ~ **sparrow**【动】歌鹀. ~ **thrush**【动】歌鸫. ~**writer** 流行歌曲作家.

song·fest [ˈsɔːŋˌfest] *n.*〔美〕民歌演唱联欢会.

song·ster [ˈsɔŋstə] *n.* *(fem.* **song·stress** [-tris]*)* ①歌手;歌女;歌曲作者;诗人. ②鸣禽.

So·nia, So·nya [ˈsəunjə] *n.* 索尼娅〔女子名, Sophia 的昵称〕.

son·ic [ˈsɔnik] *a.* ①【物】(利用)音波的;声音的;音速的. ②能发声音的. ~ *barrier*【空】声垒,音障. ~ *boom*【空】声震. ~ *depth finder* 音响测深仪. ~ *mine* 感音水雷. **-i·cal·ly** *ad.*

son·i·cate [ˈsɔniˌkeit] *vt.* ***(-cat·ed, -cat·ing)*** 使(细胞,病毒等)经声波处理. **-ca·tion** *n.* **-ca·tor** *n.*

son·ics [ˈsɔniks] *n.*〔动词用单数〕声能学.

so·nif·er·ous [səuˈnifərəs] *a.* 发声音的,有声音的;传声的.

son·net [ˈsɔnit] *n.* 十四行诗;短诗,商籁体.

son·net·eer [ˌsɔniˈtiə] *n.* 十四行诗人;〔蔑〕拙劣的诗人,歪诗作者. — *vi.* 作十四行诗.

son·net·ize [ˈsɔniˌtaiz] *vt., vi.* 写十四行诗,写小诗,写短诗.

son·ny [ˈsʌni] *n.*〔口〕〔爱称〕宝宝;孩子,年轻人.

son·o·buoy [ˈsɔnəbɔi] *n.*【军】声纳浮标;航空侦潜仪. *a radar* ~ 雷达声纳浮标.

so·nom·e·ter [səuˈnɔmitə] *n.*【物】弦音计;振动频率计;【医】听力计.

so·no·rant [səˈnɔːrənt, səu-] *n.*【语音】响辅音.

so·no·rif·ic [ˌsəunəˈrifik] *a.* 发声音的.

so·nor·i·ty [səˈnɔriti] *n.* ①洪亮,响亮(度). ②洪亮的音调,响亮的语声〔声调〕.

so·no·rous [səˈnɔːrəs] *a.* 响亮的,洪亮的. **-ly** *ad.* **-ness** *n.*

son·ship [ˈsʌnʃip] *n.* 为人子,儿子身份.

son·sie, son·sy [ˈsɔnsi] *a.*〔英方〕①来喜(的),致福(的),幸运的. ②好看的;体态丰满的,胖得圆滚滚的,血色好的. ③性情温和的,脾气好的. ④舒服的,惬意的.

Soo·fee, Soo·fee·ism [ˈsuːfi, ˈsuːfizəm] = Sufi, Sufism.

soo·gan [ˈsuːgæn] *n.*〔美俚〕毯子,被单.

sook [suːk] *n.* = souk.

sool [suːl] *vt.*〔Aus.〕①嗾(狗)去咬. ②(猎狗)撕咬(猎物). ③敦促,力劝.

soon [suːn] *ad.* ①立刻,即刻,马上;一会儿,不久,没多时. ②快,早. ③高兴地,欣然. ④宁愿,不如〔用 sooner 形,常和 would, should, had 等连用〕. *You spoke too* ~. 你说得太急了〔忍一下就好了〕. *S- got,* ~ *gone [spent].* 来得容易去得快. *You will* ~ *get the better of that fellow.* 象他那样的家伙你是不难胜过他的. *S-learned,* ~ *forgotten.* 学得快,忘得快. *Winter has come rather* ~ *this year.* 今年冬天来得早. ~ *at five o'clock* 一到五点钟就. ***as*** ~ … ***as***〔和 would, could 等连用〕要是能…的话就会…,与其…不如… (*He could as* ~ *write an epic as drive a car.* 他要是能开汽车就会写叙事诗啦. *I would just as* ~ *take a walk (as stay at home).* 我(与其待在家里)还不如去散步). ***as*** ~ ***as*** 一…就… (*He got there as* ~ *as he graduated.* 他一毕业就去那里了). ***as*** ~ ***as possible*** 尽快. ***at the*** ~***est*** 无论怎样快. ***none too*** ~ 在恰到好处的时候. ***no*** ~***er*** … ***than*** … 一…就… (*No* ~*er said than done.* 一说就实行了;风驰电掣地做了). ~***er or later*** = ~ ***or late*** 迟早,早晚. ***The*** ~***er the better*** 越快[早]越好! ***would*** ~***er*** … ***(than)*** (与其)…不如 (*I would* ~*er die than do it.* 与其做这事,不如死掉好).

soon·er [suːnə] *n.* ①〔美〕(在政府开放西部前)抢先取得占有权的人;用不正当手段先下手的人. ②〔*pl.*〕俄克拉何马 (Oklahoma) 州人的绰号;〔S-〕~ **State** 捷足州〔俄克拉何马州的别名〕.

soot [sut] *n.* 煤烟(灰),烟垢,油烟;锅灰. — *vt.* 煤烟弄脏,弄得尽是煤烟.

sooth [suːθ] *n.*〔古〕事实,实际. ***for*** ~ 事实上,的确. ***in (good)*** ~ 其实,真实地. ~ ***to say*** = ***to tell the*** ~ 老实说,说老实话. — *a.* ①〔古〕真实的,真正的. ②〔诗〕抚慰的;光滑的. ~ **fast** *a.*〔古〕说实话的,忠实的;真实的. ~ **say** *vi.* 预言,预示. ~ **sayer** *n.* ①占卜者,预言者. ②【虫】螳螂. ~ **saying** *n.* 占卜,预言.

soothe [suːð] *vt.* ①安慰,劝慰,抚慰;使镇定(神经、感情),使平静. ②缓和,减轻,减少(痛苦等). ③奉承. ~ *a crying baby* 哄哭着的孩子. **-er** *n.* ①安慰者[物];奉承拍马者. ②(哄婴儿的)橡皮假奶头.

sooth·ing [ˈsuːðiŋ] *a.* ①安慰性的. ②缓和的,减轻(痛苦)的;起镇定作用的. **-ly** *ad.*

soot·i·ness [ˈsutinis] *n.* 烟垢,尽是烟垢;烟垢状,乌黑.

soot·y [ˈsuti] *a.* ①煤烟的,煤灰的;(尽是)烟垢的;烟垢状的. ②给煤烟弄脏的,覆盖着烟炱的. ③乌黑的. ~ *smoke* 浓黑的乌烟. *a* ~ *tern*【鸟】乌燕鸥. ~ **mold**【生】烟霉(菌).

SOP, S.O.P. = standing [standard] operating procedure【军】标准作战规定;〔美俚〕标准操作规定,标准做法.

sop [sɔp] *n.* ①(泡在肉汤、牛奶等里的)面包片;湿透的东西. ②(出于让步,息事宁人而给与的)东西;贿赂,让步. ③〔英俚〕傻瓜,懦夫;〔美俚〕酒鬼. *The ground is a mere* ~. 地面湿透啦. ***give [throw] a*** ~ ***to Cerberus***〔喻〕用贿赂收买. ~ ***in the pan*** 煎面包;一口好吃的东西,好滋味. — *vt.* 泡在肉汤[牛奶等]里;使湿透;用贿赂收买 *(up)*. — *vi.* 泡;湿透.

sop. = soprano.

soph [sɔf] *n.*〔美口〕= sophomore.

So·phi·a [səˈfaiə] *n.* 索菲娅〔女子名〕.

So·phie [ˈsəufi] *n.* 索菲〔女子名〕.

soph·ism [ˈsɔfizəm] *n.* 诡辩.

soph·ist [ˈsɔfist] *n.* ①〔常 S-〕(古希腊以教授修辞学、哲学为职业并以善于诡辩出名的)智者;诡辩学者. ②诡辩家;博学者.

soph·ist·er [ˈsɔfistə] *n.* ①诡辩家 (= sohpist). ②大学的二年级学生 (junior ~);(英国某些大学的)三年级学生 (senior ~).

so·phis·tic, -ti·cal [səˈfistik, -tikəl] *a.* (古希腊)诡辩

学派的；诡辩的，强辞夺理的．～ *reasoning* 诡辩式推理．**-ti·cal·ly** *ad.*
so·phis·ti·cate [səˈfistikeit] *vt.* ①用诡辩欺骗；使迷惑；强辞夺理，牵强附会；窜改．②把杂物搀入(酒、烟等)降低品质，搀杂，搀低，搀坏，伪造．③使(人)世故，使(人)懂事；使失去天真纯朴．④使复杂，使精致．⑤〔古〕使堕落，使腐化．— *vi.* 强辞夺理，诡辩．— *n.* 世故深的人．
so·phis·ti·cat·ed [səˈfistikeitid] *a.* ①非自然状态的；搀杂的，不纯真的；矫揉造作的；伪造的．②老于世故的，世故深的；富有经验的，老练的．③(技术、产品等)复杂的，尖端的，高级的；微妙的．④(文学作品等)理智上吸引人的，深奥微妙的，精致的．*a* ～ *oil* 搀假的油．～ *electronic devices* 尖端的电子装置．*a* ～ *adolescent* 老于世故的青少年．*a* ～ *columnist* 老练的专栏作家．*a* ～ *novel* 思想内容深奥的小说．
so·phis·ti·ca·tion [səˌfistiˈkeiʃən] *n.* ①玩弄诡辩；诡辩；牵强附会．②丧失天真，变世故．③伪品；搀杂品；伪造．
so·phis·ti·ca·tor [səˈfistikeitə] *n.* ①诡辩者，强辞夺理的人．②搀杂者．
soph·ist·ry [ˈsɔfistri] *n.* ①诡辩(法)．②似是而非的推理[论证]；诡辩法的应用．
soph·o·more [ˈsɔfəmɔː, -mɔə] *n.* 〔美〕大学[中学]二年级学生．②第二年的工作人员．③自以为有学问而实际上幼稚浅薄的人．**-mor·ic, -mor·i·cal** *a.* 〔美〕二年级学生(气派)的；幼稚而自大的．
So·phy [ˈsəufi] *n.* 〔古〕(16—17 世纪)波斯统治者．
sophy *comb. f.* 表示"知识"，"学问"：philo*sophy*.
so·pite [ˈsəupait] *vt.* ①使入睡．②〔古〕结束，解决．
sopor [ˈsəupə] *n.* 〔L.〕【医】迷睡，酣睡．
so·po·rif·er·ous [ˌsəupəˈrifərəs] *a.* 引起迷睡[酣睡]的；催眠的．**-ly** *ad.* **-ness** *n.*
so·po·rif·ic, -i·cal [səupəˈrifik] *a.* 催眠的；令人思睡的，嗜眠的；酣睡的，迷睡的．— *n.* 安眠药．**-i·cal·ly** *ad.*
sop·o·rose [ˈsɔpərəus] *a.* 迷睡的，酣睡的；嗜眠的．
sop·ping [ˈsɔpiŋ] *a.* 湿透的，浸透的．— *ad.* 湿透．
sop·py [ˈsɔpi] *a.* ①浸湿的，泡湿的，湿透的．②多雨的，潮湿的(路，天气等)．③〔英口〕感情柔弱的，易动感情的；易感伤的．***be*** ～ ***on*** 对(女人等)易动情的．
so·pra·ni·no [ˌsəuprəˈniːnəu] *a.* 【乐】特高音乐器的．— *n.* 特高音乐器〔尤指英国八孔笛 *(recorder)*〕．
so·pra·no [səˈprɑːnəu] *n.* *(pl.* ～*s, -ni* [-niː]*)* ①【乐】女高音，高音部．②女高音歌手；唱最高音者．—*a.* 女高音的；最高音的．**-pran·ist** *n.* 女高音歌手；唱最高音者．
-sor *comb. f.* ＝ -or.
so·ra [ˈsɔːrə] *n.* 〔美〕【动】秧鸡 *(Porzana carolina)*〔多见于北美洲沼泽〕(＝sora rail).
Sorb [sɔːb] *n.* 索布人〔德国境内一种少数民族〕；温德人；索布语．
sorb[1] [sɔːb] *n.* 【植】①花锹树，山梨树．②花锹果，山梨果〔产于欧洲〕．
sorb[2] [sɔːb] *vt.* 吸附，吸收．
sor·bate [ˈsɔːbeit] ①吸着物．②【化】山梨酸醋．
sor·be·fa·cient [ˌsɔːbiˈfeiʃənt] *a.* 【医】促进吸收的．*n.* 吸收促进药．
sor·bent [ˈsɔːbənt] *n.* 【化】吸着剂．
sor·bet [ˈsɔːbət] *n.* 果汁冰水．
Sor·bi·an [ˈsɔːbiən] *a.* 索布人的；索布语的．—*n.* ①索布语．②＝ sorb.
sor·bic acid [ˈsɔːbik] 【化】山梨酸，已二烯酸；已邻隔二烯酸．
sor·bi·tol [ˈsɔːbiˌtɔːl, -ˌtəul] *n.* 【化】山梨糖醇；葡已六醇．
Sor·bonne [sɔːˈbɔn] *n.* (巴黎) 索本神学院；(16—17 世纪)巴黎大学神学院；(现在)巴黎大学的文理学院，〔泛指〕巴黎大学．

Sor·bonn·ist [sɔːˈbɔnist] *n.* 巴黎大学的神学家〔神学院学生〕；巴黎大学文理学院毕业生[学生]．
sor·bose [ˈsɔːbəus] *n.* 【化】山梨糖．
sor·cer·er [ˈsɔːsərə] *n.* *(fem.* ***-ceress*** [-ris]*)* 巫师，术士．
sor·cer·y [ˈsɔːsəri] *n.* 巫术；邪术，妖术．
sor·did [ˈsɔːdid] *a.* ①肮脏的，邋遢的，不清洁的；破烂不堪的．②心地不纯的，卑鄙的；贪鄙的，贪婪的，啬吝的．③可怜的，悲惨的．④【植、动】泥色的；色彩暗淡的．～ *slum* 污秽的贫民窟．～ *motives* 卑鄙的动机．*live in* ～ *poverty* 生活在贫困中．**-ly** *ad.* **-ness** *n.*
sor·dine [ˈsɔːdiːn] *n.* 【乐】弱音器；弱音踏板．
sor·di·no [sɔːˈdiːnəu] *n.* *(pl. sordini* [-ˈdiːniː]*)* 〔It.〕【乐】＝ sordine.
sor·dor [ˈsɔːdə] *n.* 不幸；悲惨；卑鄙；肮脏；污秽；下贱．
sore [sɔː, sɔə] *a.* ①痛的，疼痛发炎的；(一碰就)疼痛的；受了伤的，皮肤擦破了的，发肿的，生着疮的．②辛苦的，吃力的(工作等)；激烈的，猛烈的，厉害的．③痛心的，伤心的；悲哀的．④〔俚〕恼怒的，恼火的，动辄发脾气的．⑤〔古〕痛切的，迫切的．— *ad.* 〔古、诗〕＝ sorely. *a* ～ *throat* 喉痛．*a* ～ *subject* 使人难堪的话题．～ *distress* 非常贫困．*a* ～ *loser* 一输就恼火的人．***a sight for*** ～ ***eyes*** 受欢迎的，悦目的人[物、景致(等)]．***be*** ～ ***about*** 对…痛心[发愁，觉得难过，生气，觉得不高兴，觉得厌恶]．***be*** ～ ***up*** 〔美俚〕发怒．***feel*** ～ 痛；生气．***get (sb.)*** ～〔口〕(使人)生气，动怒．***in*** ～ ***need of*** 极端需要….***like a bear with a*** ～ ***head*** 脾气极大的，拗性的．— *n.* ①一碰就疼的地方，(伤)痛处；疮肿，溃疡．②一想起来就难过的事情，伤心事．*a hard* ～ 下疳．*an open* ～ 积弊．*bed* ～*s* 褥疮．*old* ～*s* 旧伤；旧恨，难过的[伤心的]回忆(等)．～ **place [point, spot]**〔主喻〕触及痛处的问题，一提起来就叫人难为情、生气、痛苦、起反感的问题．～ **throat** 咽喉炎．**-ness** *n.*
sore·back [ˈsɔːbæk] *n.* 〔美〕弗吉尼亚州人的绰号．
sore·head [ˈsɔːhed] *n.* 〔美口〕脾气大[牢骚多]的人，〔尤指〕落魄政客．
sore·ly [ˈsɔːli] *ad.* ①疼痛地；痛苦地．②严厉地；猛烈地，激烈地，厉害地．③非常，很．*be* ～ *oppressed* 痛受压迫．
sor·ghum [ˈsɔːgəm] *n.* ①【植】蜀黍，高粱；〔S-〕蜀黍(属)．②高粱糖浆．③甜得发腻的东西；过度描述柔情．令人肉麻的文字．*sweet* ～ 甜高粱．
sor·go, sor·gho [ˈsɔːgəu] *n.* 【植】芦粟，甜高粱 (＝ sweet sorghum).
so·ri [ˈsəurai] *n.* sorus 的复数．
sor·i·cine [ˈsɔːriˌsain, -sin, ˈsɔr-] *a.* 鼩鼱的，似鼩鼱的．
so·ri·tes [səuˈraitiːz] *n.* ①【逻】复合三段论．②诡辩推理．
sorn [sɔːn] *vi.* 〔Scot.〕①不请自去地赖着吃赖着住 *(on)*，强求膳宿．②乞求，强求．**-er** *n.* 强求膳宿的人．
so·rop·ti·mist [sɔːˈrɔptimist] *n.* 国际妇女俱乐部成员；职业妇女福利互助会会员．
so·ror·al [səˈrɔːrəl] *a.* 姐妹的，姐妹般的．**-ly** *ad.*
so·ro·rate [səˈrɔːrit, -eit] *n.* 内妹填房的风俗〔妻子不育或死亡，丈夫娶其一个妹或几个妹为妻〕．
so·ror·i·cide [səˈrɔːriˌsaid] *n.* ①杀害亲姐妹的行为．②杀害亲姐妹者．**-cid·al** *a.*
so·ror·i·ty [səˈrɔriti] *n.* 妇女社团；〔美〕大学女生联谊会．
so·ro·sis [səˈrəusis] *n.* ①【植】聚花果，椹果[菠萝、桑果]等．②妇女俱乐部．
sorp·tion [ˈsɔːpʃən] *n.* 【化】吸着(作用)．**-tive** *a.*
sor·ra [ˈsɔrə] *ad.* 〔爱俚〕＝ not; never.
sor·rel[1] [ˈsɔrəl] *a.* 红褐色的，栗色的(马等)．— *n.* ①红褐色，栗色．②栗色的动物．③三岁的雄鹿．
sor·rel[2] [ˈsɔrəl] *n.* 含酸液的植物〔如酸模、酢浆草等属的植物〕．

sor·row [ˈsɔrəu] *n.* ①悲哀,悲痛,伤心;忧伤,哀悼,悲叹;悔恨,惋惜,遗憾,抱歉。②可悲的事情,伤心事,不幸;魔鬼。③悲哀的原因,伤心的原故。*S- comes unsent for.* 悲哀不招自来。*the Man of S-s* 耶稣。*the muckle* ～〔Scot.〕魔鬼 *He has had many ～s.* 他遭遇过种种不幸。***cause much ～ to*** 使…非常伤心;给…造成许多烦恼。***express one's ～ for one's mistake*** 对错误表示遗憾。— *vi.* 悲痛,悲叹,惋惜,哀悼(*for; at; over*)。— *ad.*〔爱口〕〔常作 sorra〕= not; never. ～ ***a bit*** 一点儿也没有。～ **drowner**〔美〕酒。～**-striken** *a.* 哀伤的,悲痛的。

sor·row·ful [ˈsɔrəufəl] *a.* ①悲伤的,悲叹的;悲惨的。②可悲的,可怜的;悔恨的;可惜的,抱歉的。**-ly** *ad.* **-ness** *n.*

sor·ry [ˈsɔri] *a.* ①〔用作 *pred.*〕可怜的,觉得难过的(*for; to do; that* …);懊悔的,觉得过意不去的(*for*);抱歉的,对不起的,遗憾的;惋惜的,可惜的。②拙劣的,卑劣的;不中用的,没价值的;不成样子的,不体面的;可悲的,悲惨的。③悲哀的,悲伤的。*I am ～ for you.* 我很替你难过。*I am ～ for it.* 很抱歉,对不起。*I am ～ about it.* 那很遗憾。*I am (so) ～.* =〔口〕*So ～!* = *S-!* 对不起。*You will be ～ for this some day.* 你有一天要懊悔这件事的。*Say you are ～ and I will forgive you.* 你说你错了我便饶你。*I'm ～ for him but it's his own fault.* 可惜那是他自己不对(怨谁呢)。*I am ～ to say that I cannot come.* 很遗憾,我不能来。*in a ～ state [plight]* 处在可怜的境地中。*a ～ excuse* 卑劣的借口。*a ～ end* 可悲的结局。***cut a ～ figure*** 出丑。***make a ～ spectacle of oneself*** 出洋相。***(feel) ～ for oneself***〔口〕垂头丧气,灰心失望。**-ri·ly** *ad.* **-ri·ness** *n.*

sort [sɔːt] *n.* ①种类,类别,品种;种。②品质,本性,性质。③方法,情形,样子,程度。④某种人[物]。⑤【印】〔主 *pl.*〕一套铅字;〔*pl.*〕【纺】并级毛,同型毛。⑥〔古〕(一)群,(一)伙。*all [several, these, those] ～s of hats* 所有各种[种种,这几种,那几种]帽子。*He is a good [bad] ～ (of a fellow).*〔口〕他是好[坏]人。*He is the right ～.* = *He's my ～.* 他倒是挺合适的人,他正是我需要的人。*Queer ～ (of a thing) this!*〔口〕这(东西)倒挺妙。*I don't believe anything of the ～.* 我不相信这种事情。*He is not my ～.* 他那种人我不喜欢。*That's your ～.* 就是这个样呀;〔俚〕那样做挺好。*This copy is hard [runs] on ～s.*【印】这件稿子要用几种铅字排。***after [in] a ～*** 有些,有几分,稍为。***all of a ～*** 差不多,大同小异。***all ～(s) of*** = ***of all ～s*** 一切种类的,各种各样的。***a ～ of*** 一种;可以说是…的东西 (*cf.* of a ～)。***in any ～*** 无论如何,必须。***in a ～ of way*** 略为,比较。***in some ～*** 多少,稍为。***no ～ of*** 毫无。***nothing of the ～*** 根本没有那种事情,决没有那种事情。***of a ～*** 同一种[类];相当的;勉强称得上的,较差的,所谓的 (*a war of a ～* 所谓的战争。*a poet of a ～* 蹩脚的诗人)。***of every ～ and kind*** 各种各样的。***of one's ～*** 和某人同样身份[性质、品性]的。***of ～s***〔口〕①= of a ～. ②各种各样的;未经挑选的。***of the ～*** 那样的。***out of ～s*** 觉得不舒服;情绪不好;没有精神;【印】铅字不全。～ ***of*** = ***～o'***〔美口〕〔用作状语〕几分,有点,稍微 (*～ of moist* 有点湿。*I ～ of expected it.* 我料到几分了。*Now ～ of turn round!* 来稍微转动一下吧)。— *vt.* 分类;整顿,整理;分选,拣 (*out*)。— *vi.*〔英古〕一致,相配,适合(*with*)。～ *letters* 拣信。*a ～ing room [clerk]* (邮局)拣信室[员]。～ *out* 清理。

sort·a [ˈsɔːtə] *ad.*〔美俚〕= sort of.

sort·er[1] [ˈsɔːtə] *n.* ①分类者;选别者,分选者;(邮局)拣信员。②【自】分类器;分类装置;清选机,选别机;(纤维长度)分析器。

sort·er[2] [ˈsɔːtə] *ad.*〔方,俚〕= sort of.

sor·tes [ˈsɔːtiːz] *n. pl.*〔L.〕签,阄;(翻书)占卜。～ *Homericae* [hoˈmerisiː] 翻荷马诗占卜。

sor·tie [ˈsɔːti(ː)] *n.* ①【军】出击;突围;出港。②出击部队。③(飞机出动的)架次。

sor·ti·lege [ˈsɔːtilidʒ] *n.* ①(抽签)占卜,阄占。②巫术,妖术。

sor·ti·tion [sɔːˈtiʃən] *n.* 抽签,拈阄。

so·rus [ˈsɔːrəs] *n.* (*pl.* ***-ri*** [-rai])【植】孢子堆;(蕨类的)囊群。

-sory *comb. f.* = -ory.

SOS, S.o.S. [ˈesəuˈes] (= Save Our Souls [Ship]; Suspend Other Service)【讯】失事信号,呼救信号;发失事信号 (= Service of Supply);【军】后勤部,供应署 (= silicon on sapphire);硅,蓝宝石技术。

so-so [ˈsəusəu] *a., ad.* 一般的(地),还过得去的(地),不好也不坏的(地),马马虎虎的(地)。～ *reaction*〔美〕(观众的)不怎样热烈的喝彩。

sos·te·nu·to [ˌsɔstəˈnuːtəu] *ad.*〔It.〕【乐】自制地,沉着地;集中地并且节奏准确地;保持速度〔通常是中速〕。— *n.* (*pl.* ***～s, -ti***) 象上述那样演奏[演唱](部分)。

sot [sɔt] *n.* 酒鬼。— *vi.* 滥喝,拼命喝酒。

so·te·ri·ol·o·gy [səuˌtiəriˈɔlədʒi] *n.*【宗】灵魂拯救〔尤指信耶稣灵魂得救〕;灵魂拯救论[学]。**-log·i·cal** [-ˈlɔdʒikl] *a.*

So·thic [ˈsəuθik] *a.*【天】天狼星的。***S- Cycle [period]*** (古埃及历法)天狼星周期〔= 1460 天狼星年〕。***S- year*** (古埃及历法)天狼星年〔= $365^1/_4$ 日〕。

So·tho [ˈsəuθəu] *n.* ①(*pl.* ***So·thos, So·tho***) (南非)梭托人。②梭托语。

sot·ted [ˈsɔtid] *a.* 醉得稀里糊涂的,昏昏沉沉的。

sot·tish [ˈsɔtiʃ] *a.* ①酒鬼似的,滥喝酒的。②(因饮酒过多而)愚蠢的,迟钝的,糊涂的。

sot·to vo·ce [ˈsɔtəuˈvəutʃi]〔It.〕低声地;把声音压住。

sou [suː] *n.* (*pl.* ***～s***) 苏〔法国旧铜币;合五生丁〕。*He hasn't a ～.*〔口〕他一个钱也没有。

sou·bise [suːˈbiːz] *n.* 苏比斯调味汁〔主要成份为融化黄油和洋葱〕。

sou·brette [suːˈbret] *n.*〔F.〕①【剧】喜剧中风骚的女仆或轻佻的女人;饰同上角色的女演员;在喜歌剧中担任配角的女高音演员。②女仆。

sou·bri·quet [ˈsəubrikei] *n.* = sobriquet.

sou·chong [ˈsuːˈʃɔŋ, -tʃɔŋ] *n.*〔Chin.〕小种毛尖[红茶]。

Sou·dan [su(ː)ˈdæn] *n.* = Sudan.

Sou·da·nese [ˌsuːdəˈniːz] *a., n.* = Sudanese.

souf·flé [ˈsuːflei] *a., n.*〔F.〕【烹】与打松了的蛋白和奶油搅拌在一起而焙烤的(甜食或菜肴)。

sough [sau] *n.* 飕飕,飒飒〔风等的声音〕。— *vi.* (风)飕飕地响,飒飒地吹。

sought [sɔːt] seek 的过去式及过去分词。

souk [suːk] *n.* (北非和中东的)露天市场。

soul [səul] *n.* ①灵魂,心灵 (*opp.* body);精神;气魄;热情;道义力量。②精华,精髓,要素。③化身,典型。④领唱者,领袖,首脑,中心人物。⑤人。⑥〔美〕(黑人表演激起的)强烈感情。⑦(美国)黑人文化的特征;黑人种族的自豪感。*His whole ～ revolted from it.* 他十分讨厌它。*Not a ～ was to be seen.* 一个人也没有。*Be a good ～ and help me.* 好孩子来帮帮我的忙。*There's a good ～.* 好孩子〔安慰小孩子、仆人等的话〕。*a good ～*〔口〕好人。*a thirsty ～* 酒徒。*Poor ～!*〔插入句〕可怜! — *a.*〔美〕黑人的,黑人文化的,黑人控制的。*a ～ radio station* 黑人广播电台。***All Souls' day*** 万灵节。***by my ～*** 真的,的的确确。***cannot call one's ～ one's own*** 完全受别人支配。***for my ～*** = ***for the ～ of me*** 一定;无论如何也。***have no ～*** 没有骨气;(作品等)没有感情。***in my ～ of ～s*** 天地良心。***keep body and ～ together*** 苟延残喘。***possess one's ～ in patience*** 忍耐。***sell one's ～ for*** 为了…出卖灵魂,作出一切牺牲去得到…。***～ and body*** 热心地。***～ aviator***〔美〕牧师。***the ～***

of hono(u)r 诚实的人. *the very life and* ~ *of*…的灵魂[领袖等]. *to save my* ~=for the ~ of me. *upon (or 'pon, on, 'on) my* ~ = by my ~. *with one's heart and* ~ 全神贯注;全心全意. ~ **brother** 〔美〕黑人男子. ~**-destroying** *a.* 消磨精神的, 毁灭灵魂的. ~ **food** 〔口〕美国南部黑人的传统食物〔如小肠,火腿胫,玉米面包,萝卜缨等〕. ~ **kiss** (舌接触舌的)接吻,深深的亲吻. ~ **mate** 意气相投的朋友;情人. ~ **music** 激情的爵士音乐. ~**-searching** 反省,内省. ~ **sister** 〔美〕黑人女子.

soul·ful ['səulfəl] *a.* 精神[灵魂]上的;热情的,充满生气的. **-ly** *ad.*

soul·less ['səullis] *a.* ①缺乏高尚精神的,没有灵魂的. ②卑鄙的;残酷的;无情的. ③没有表情的,发呆的. **-ly** *ad.*

sound[1] [saund] *a.* ①健全的;强壮的,正常的;完好的,无疵的,没有腐烂的(船、牙齿等). ②正确的;正当的,合法的;合理的,见解正确的;合逻辑的. ③坚牢的,坚固的;确实的,安全的,可靠的,稳当的;正派的;正统的. ④有偿付能力的,资金充实的(公司等). ③严厉的,厉害的;充分的(睡眠等). ④【法】有效的. — *ad.* 充分地. *A* ~ *mind in a* ~ *body.* 有健全的身体才有健全的精神. ~ *fruit* 完好的水果. ~ *argument* 有充分根据的论点. *a* ~ *policy* 健全的政策. *a* ~ *opinion* 合理的意见. *a* ~ *analysis* 中肯的分析. *a* ~ *investment* 稳妥的投资. *I gave him a* ~ *beating.* 我把他痛打了一顿. *The child is* ~ *already.* 〔口〕孩子已经睡熟了. *sleep a* ~ *sleep* 睡一个畅快的觉. ***as*** ~ ***as a bull [colt, roach]*** 很健全[健康]. ~ ***in wind and limb*** 〔口〕身体健全的.

sound[2] [saund] *n.* ①音,响,音响;声音;发音. ②噪音,闹声,各种声音. ③音调;语调;笔调,含意. ④听力的范围. ⑤(唱片、电影等的)录音材料. ⑥音乐风格. ⑦〔古〕谣传,名声;意义;印象. ***out of*** ~ ***of*** 在听不见…的地方. ~ ***and fury*** 喧嚣吵嚷. ***within*** ~ ***of*** 在听得见…的地方. — *vi.* ①响;反响,鸣响;发声音,发音;用声音传播;传播;召唤. ②听来象,令人觉得. ③【法】具有…的性质,具有…要求 *(in).* *The bugle* ~*s to battle.* 号角召唤去战斗. *His voice* ~*s as if he had a cold.* 他的声音听着象伤了风似的. *His story* ~*s incredible.* 他的故事听起来难以令人置信. *This* ~*s like a fiction.* 这简直象编成的故事一样. *Strange as it may* ~. 也许听起来奇怪. *The plan* ~*s good.* 这个计划听着不错. *How does this proposal* ~ *to you?* 你以为这个提案怎样? *His action* ~*s in damages.* 他的诉讼具有要求赔偿的性质. — *vt.* ①弄响(电铃等). ②吹号命令,吹…号;吹号[打钟](等)通知,吹号庆祝. ③(用语言)表达,发表. ④宣告;传布. ⑤敲(听声音)检(查);【医】敲诊. ~ *the charge [retreat]* 吹冲锋[退却]号. ~ *an alarm* 发出紧急警报. ~ *the lungs* 听诊肺音. ~ ***sb.'s [one's own] praises*** 夸奖某人[自己]. ~ ***off*** ①〔美俚〕大声说;呱拉呱拉地说;说大话;发牢骚. ②【军】依次报数;呼行军口令(一、二、一等);奏序曲. ~ **arrester** 隔音装置. ~ **barrier** 【空】音障,声垒. ~ **box** (乐器的)共鸣匣;留声机唱头. ~ **camera** 电影录音摄影机. ~ **detector** 检声器;测音器;【无】伴音信号检波器. ~ **effects** (广播、电视节目、电影等的)音响效果. ~ **engineer** 声工程师. ~ **film,** ~ **(motion) picture** 有声电影. ~ **locator** 【物】声波定位器. ~**man** 音响效果操作者. ~ **poiiution** 噪音污染. ~ **projector** 有声电影放映机. ~**proof** ①*a.* 防音的,隔音的. ②*vt.* 防音,隔音;设防音装置. ~ **ranging** 音源探测(法),声波测距(法). ~ **recorder** 录音机. ~ **recording** 录音. ~ **recordist** 〔美〕【影】录音技师. ~ **spectrograph** 分音仪. ~ **tosser** 〔美〕【无】播音员. ~ **track** 【影】音带,声带;声迹. ~ **truck** 广播车. ~ **wave** 音波;声波.

sound[3] [saund] *vi.* ①测水深;探测(上层空气). ②试探(别人的意见);调查(可能性). ③(鱼或鲸鱼)突然潜入海底. — *vt.* ①测量(海深);锤测;探测. ②【外】用探针检查(尿道等). ③试探(别人的意见) *(out).* ~ *(out) sb. on [about] a question* 打听某人对某一个问题的意见. — *n.* 【医】探子,探条,探针.

sound[4] [saund] *n.* ①港,海峡;海湾. ②【动】气胞,鳔. ③乌贼,鱿鱼.

sound·er ['saundə] *n.* ①发声物[者];【电】发声器,(发)声(收)码器. ②测深员;测深器;【外】探针. *an echo* ~ 回声[回波]探测器. *a* ~ *key* 【电】发声电钥.

sound·ing[1] ['saundiŋ] *n.* ①声距测量,测深. ②【气】探空,测高. ③〔*pl.*〕测锤到达的水底;(测得的)水深;〔*pl.*〕底质[测锤附带上来的泥沙]. ④【医】探通术,探针诊断. ⑤【影】发声. *air* ~ 大气探测. *rocket* ~ 用火箭探测大气. ***be in [come into]*** ~***s*** 在测锤到达的地方;在(进入)水浅的地方〔指鲸鱼〕. ***be out of [off]*** ~***s*** 在测锤下达不到的地方. ***get off [on]*** ~***s*** 到测锤达不到的地方去;碰到不得意的事情. ***get on*** ~***s*** 来到测锤能达到的地方;做着得意的事,渐入佳境. ***strike*** ~***s*** 测量水深. ***take*** ~***s in*** 测…的水深. ~ **balloon** 【空】探空气球. ~ **lead** 测深铅锤. ~ **line** 测深索. ~ **rocket** 探空火箭. ~ **rod** (量水舱用)量水尺.

sound·ing[2] ['saundiŋ] *a.* ①作声的,响亮的. ②夸张的,言过其实的;空洞的,唱高调的. ③堂堂的,给人深刻印象的. ~ *rhetoric* 空洞的言词. ~ *promise* 好听的语言. *a* ~ *oratory* 夸张的演说. *a* ~ *title* 堂皇的头衔. ~ **board** ①共鸣[共振]板. ②(设在舞台上方或后方增加音响洪亮度的)回声结构. ③用来扩散舆论的人或物,"传声筒". ④(用来测验外界对某种意见的反应的)反应灵敏的人.

sound·less ['saundlis] *a.* ①深不可测的,无底的. ②无声的,寂静的;不响的. **-ly** *ad.*

sound·ly ['saundli] *ad.* ①完好地,无疵地;健全地;稳健地;坚固地;壮健地;正确地;正当地;确实地. ②严厉地,厉害地. ③酣畅地. *sleep* ~ 酣睡.

sound·ness ['saundnis] *n.* ①完好;健全;稳健,确实. ②坚固;公正,正当. ③坚固性,坚固度.

soup[1] [su:p] *n.* ①(浓)汤. ②浓汤般的东西;浓雾;硝化甘油;显影液. ③【法】〔英俚〕分配给资历较浅的律师承办的刑事案件. ④〔美俚〕电. ⑤〔口〕不幸的境遇,困境. *eat* ~ 喝汤. *a* ~ *hound* 爱参加宴会做客的人. ***in the*** ~ 〔俚〕受困,在困难中. ~ **and fish** 〔俚〕晚礼服. ~ **kitchen** (救济贫民的)施食处;〔美俚〕(汽车式)流动食堂. ~ **maigre** 菜汤. ~ **plate** 汤盘. ~ **spoon** 汤匙.

soup[2] [su:p] *n.* 〔空俚〕(发动机的)马力;加大了的马力[效率]. — *vt.* 加大马力. ~ ***up*** 加大马力;加快(飞机)速度. ~**ed-up** *a.* ①加大马力的. ②加工后变得吸引人的.

soup·çon ['su:psɔ̃:ŋ] *n.* 〔F.〕怀疑,嫌疑;(可疑的)痕迹;少量,一点点 *(of).* ***not a*** ~ ***of*** 一点没有.

soup·er·y ['su:pəri] *n.* 〔美〕餐厅,食堂.

soup·fin shark ['su:pfin ʃɑ:k] *n.* 翅鲨〔其翅可作中菜"鱼翅"〕.

soup·y ['su:pi] *a.* ①浓汤似的. ②〔美口〕雾浓的;阴雨的(天气). ③〔美俚〕故作多情的,过于多愁善感的.

sour ['sauə] *a.* ①酸的,酸味的;变酸了的,酸腐的. ②发酵的. ③乖张的,乖戾的;愁眉不展的,愠怒的,不开心的;尖酸刻薄的;令人厌恶的,乏味的. ④坏的,错的;敌对的;不再迷恋的. ⑤【农】酸性土壤的,瘦瘠的,冷湿的,不毛的(土地等). ⑥没有达到一般[预期]标准[质量]的. ⑦酸性反应的. *a* ~ *fellow* 脾气乖张的人. ~ *looks* 一肚子不高兴的样子. ~ *cream* 酸奶油. ~ *milk* 酸奶. *be* ~ *on* 〔美俚〕嫌恶,憎厌. ~ *grapes* 酸葡萄〔可望而不可及之物〕. — *n.* ①酸味,酸东西. ②讨厌的东西;痛苦,苦恼. ③〔美〕酸味饮料;酸味鸡尾酒. *The sweet and* ~ *together.* 有苦有乐. ***get in*** ~ 〔美俚〕不和,失去…的好感;遇到麻烦. ***take the sweet with the*** ~ 对人生苦乐满不在乎. ***the sweet and*** ~ ***of life*** 人生的苦乐. — *vt.* ①弄酸;使酸败;败坏. ②使性情乖僻,使情绪不好. ③(漂白时)用弱酸处理;使(土地等)冷湿,使不毛. — *vi.* ①变酸;酸败. ②性情变乖僻,情绪不好. ~ **on**〔美〕讨厌;憎恶. ~ **ball** ①(夹心)酸糖球〔水果糖〕. ②〔俚〕诉苦者;老是口出怨言的人. ~ **cherry**【植】(欧洲)酸樱桃(树). ~**crout**, ~**krout** *n.* = sauerkraut. ~ **gum**〔美〕= black gum【植】多花紫树. ~**-humus** 粗腐殖质. ~ **mash** 酸麦芽汁〔造威士忌酒用〕. ~ **orange**【植】酸橙(树). ~ **salt** 酸味盐〔调味等用,如柠檬酸、酒石酸结晶体〕. ~ **sop**【植】刺果番荔枝(树). ~ **top**〔美俚〕脾气别扭的人. ~**wood** 一种开白花,叶有酸味的欧石南属小树. **-ly** *ad.* **-ness** *n.*

source [sɔːs] *n.* ①源头,水源,源泉. ②根源,本源;来源. ③原因;出处;原始资料. ④提供消息的人. ⑤血统. *the* ~ *of wealth* 富源. *historical* ~*s* 史料. *a reliable [an authoritative]* ~ 可靠[权威]人士. ***draw [have] from a good*** ~ 由可靠方面听到[得到]. ***take its*** ~ ***at*** 发源于,出自,起于. ***trace to its*** ~ 追根寻源. ~ **book**〔美〕原始资料集,史料集. ~ **language** 始发语言(*opp.* target language). ~**-material** 原始资料.

sour·dine [suəˈdiːn] *n.*【乐】弱音器;噪音抑制器.

sour·dough [ˈsauədəu] *n.* ①〔美西北部、加拿大〕〔口〕探矿者;垦荒者;在阿拉斯加过冬的人;老资格,老手. ②发面底子,酵种,面肥.

sour·puss [ˈsauəpus]〔美俚〕面色阴沉的人;性情乖戾的人.

sou·sa·phone [ˈsuːzəfəun] *n.* 大号〔一种大型的吹奏乐器,主要用于军乐队〕.

souse[1] [saus] *n.* ①盐渍品,腌货;腌猪耳[脚、头]. ②腌渍用的盐水. ③腌浸,泡. ④浸透,湿透. ⑤〔美俚〕酒鬼,狂饮. *get a thorough* ~ *in a thunderstorm* 在雷雨中淋得浑身湿透. *give (sb.) a* ~ (把人)浸入水里. — *vt.* ①腌,泡在盐水里;浸入水里. ②使湿透,泼(水). ③〔俚〕灌醉. —*vi.* ①泡在水里;被湿透. ②喝醉. ***be*** ~***d to the skin*** 浑身湿透. ~ ***it***〔美俚〕住嘴,不做声. ~ ***oneself***〔美〕洗手洗脸.

souse[2] [saus] *vi.*〔古〕(鹰等)猛扑下来. — *vt.* 扑在…上面,向…飞扑;猛地扑下而撞倒. — *n.* (鹰在拦截鸟时的)猛扑. — *ad.* 扑通一声;飞扑地,倒栽葱地.

soused [saust] *a.* 腌渍的;〔俚〕喝醉了的.

sou·tache [ˈsuːtɑːʃ] *n.*〔F.〕【纺】绠带状条子织物.

sou·tane [suːˈtɑːn] *n.* (天主教)祭司的法衣.

South [sauθ] *n.* 索斯〔姓氏〕.

south [sauθ] *n.* ①南;南方. ②南国居民. ③〔诗〕南风. ④〔the S-〕(一国或一地区的)南方,南部,〔美〕南部各州;【美史】南部邦联;地球的南部〔尤指南极地区〕. — *a.* ①南的,南方的. ②在南的,向南的;自南方的. — *ad.* 向南方;在南方;自南方. *the far* ~ = the South Pole 南极. *the* ~ *country* 南英格兰. *the S- Downs (of Hampshire and Sussex)* 南方草原. *S- Island* 南岛〔新西兰两主岛之一〕. *S- Pole* 南极. *the S- Sea* 南太平洋. *the S- Seas* 南洋. *a* ~ *aspect* 南面. *a* ~ *window* 南面的窗子. *down* ~ (向)南部各州;(向)南方边疆地方. — [sauð, sauθ] *vi.* ①转向南方. ②【天】(天体)向南走;越过子午线,过南北线. ~ **bound** *a.* 向南走的,往南去的. ~ **by east** 南偏东〔正南偏东 11°15′〕. ~ **by west** 南偏西〔正南偏西 11°15′〕. ~**land**〔美〕美国南部(各州) = Dixie. ~**paw** *a.*, *n.*〔美〕左撇子;【棒球】惯用左手的;左手投球员.

South Africa [sauθ ˈæfrikə] 南非.

South·amp·ton [sauθˈæm*p*tən] *n.* 南安普敦〔英国港市〕.

South Carolina [ˈsauθ ˌkærəˈlainə] 南卡罗来纳〔美国州名〕.

South Dakota [ˈsauθ dəˈkəutə] 南达科他〔美国州名〕.

South·down [ˈsauθdaun] *a.* 英国南岗 (South Downs) 的. — *n.* 英国南岗羊;南岗羊肉.

south·east [ˈsauθˈiːst] *n.* ①东南〔泛指东南方向;正东以南 45°;略作 S E〕. ②〔S-〕(美国)东南部. ~ *by east* 东南偏东. ~ *by south* 东南偏南. —*a.* ①位于东南的;向东南的. ②来自东南的. —*ad.* 在东南;向东南;从东南.

south·east·er [ˈsauθiːstə] *n.* 东南大风.

south·east·er·ly [sauθˈiːstəli] *a.* 向[在、自]东南的. ~ *gale* 东南烈风. — *ad.* 向[在、自]东南. — *n.* 东南大风.

south·east·ern [sauθˈiːstən] *a.* ①向[在、自]东南的. ②东南部的;〔S-〕美国东南部的.

south·east·ern·most [sauθˈiːstənməust] *a.* 东南端的;最东南的.

south·east·ward [sauθˈiːstwəd] *a.*, *ad.* 向东南的[地]. **-ly** *a.*, *ad.* 向东南的[地],自东南的[地].

south·east·wards [sauθˈiːstwədz] *ad.* 向东南.

South·end-on-Sea [ˈsauθˈendɔnˈsiː] 滨海绍森德〔英国港市〕.

south·er [ˈsauðə] *n.* 南风,南暴风.

south·er·ly [ˈsʌðəli] *a.*, *ad.* 南,在南(的);向南(的);从南方来(的). *a* ~ *course* 南方航线. *sail* ~ (船)向南航行.

south·ern [ˈsʌðən] *a.* *(superl.* ~ ***most)*** ①南的,在南的;向南的;从南的. ②南方的,南部的,南国的. ③朝南的,向南的. ④〔S-〕〔美〕南部各州的,从南部各州来的;有南方地区特征的. — *n.* 南方人,南部人;〔S-〕美国南部方言. *a* ~ *aspect* 南向. *a* ~ *course* 南方航线. ~ *trade* 南洋贸易. **the S- Cross**【天】南十字座. ~ **hemisphere** 南半球. ~ **lights** 南极光. ~**wood**【植】青蒿. **-er** *n.* 南方人;〔S-〕南部英格兰人;〔美〕南部各州的人.

Southey [ˈsauði, ˈsʌði] *n.* 索西〔姓氏〕.

south·ing [ˈsauðiŋ] *n.* ①【海】南向,南进;南航. ②【天】南向纬度差;南中(天);南赤纬.

south·ron [ˈsʌðrən] *n.* 南方人;〔S-〕〔Scot. 蔑〕英格兰人;〔美〕南部各州的人.

south-south·east [ˈsauθsauθˈist] *n.* 东南南(正东以南 22°30′;略作 SSE). — *ad.*, *a.* ①在[向]东南南方(的);②来自东南南方(的).

south-south·west [ˈsauθsauθˈwest] *n.* 西南南(正南以西 22°30′;略作 SSW). — *ad.*, *a.* ①在[向]西南南方(的). ②来自西南南方(的).

south·ward [ˈsauθwəd] *ad.*, *a.* 向南方(的). — *n.* 向南方向,南方地区. **-ly** *ad.*, *a.* 向南方(的);来自南方(的).

south·wards [ˈsauθwədz] *ad.* 向南方.

South·well [ˈsauθwəl] *n.* 索斯韦尔〔姓氏〕.

south·west [ˈsauθˈwest] *n.* ①西南〔泛指西南方向,或指正西以南 45°;略作 SW〕;~ *by south* 西南偏南(即西南偏南 11°15′,写为 S 33°45′ W). ~ *by west* 西南偏西(即西南偏西 11°45′,写为 S 56°15′W). ②〔S-〕一国或一地区的西南部. — *a.* ①位于西南的;向西南的. ②来自西南的. *a* ~ *wind* 西南风. — *ad.* 在西南;向西南;从西南.

South West Africa [sauθ west ˈæfrikə] *n.* 西南非洲.

south·west·er [sauθˈwestə] *n.* ①西南大风,西南大风暴. ②海员用的防水帽.

south·west·er·ly [sauθˈwestəli] *ad.*, *a.* ①在(或向)西南(的). ②来自西南(的).

south·west·ern [sauθˈwestən] *a.* ①(在)西南的;向西南的. ②来自西南的. *a* ~ *wind* 西南风. ③〔S-〕一国或一地区的西南部的. **-er** *n.* 西南人,住在西南部的人;〔S-〕美国西南部人.

south·west·ward [sauθˈwestwəd] *ad.*, *a.* 向西南(的). — *n.* 西南方向;西南地区. **-ly** *ad.*, *a.* 向西南(的);来自西南(的).

south·west·wards [sauθ'westwədz] *ad.* 向西南.

sou·ve·nir ['suːvəniə] *n.* ①回忆，追忆. ②纪念品[礼物]. *This year book ekes out souvenir of my life in the university.* 这本年鉴帮助我追忆大学生活. ~**sheet** (印在纸片上的)纪念邮票.

sou'·west ['sau'west]【海】= southwest.

sou'·west·er ['sau'westə] *n.* = southwester.

sov., sovs. = sovereign(s).

sov·er·eign ['sɔvrin] *a.* ①握有主权的，独立自主的. ②元首的，国王的. ③拥有最高权力的. ④最高的，最上的. ⑤优秀的，极好的. ⑥完全的. ⑦有特效的(药). —*n.* ①主权者；君主，元首. ②主权国，独立国. ③〔英口〕金镑〔= 20 先令〕. *a ~ state* 主权国家. *~ authority [power]* 主权[最高权力]. *a ~ prince* 君主，元首. *a ~ remedy* 特效药. *the ~ good* 至善. *show a ~ contempt for useless formalities* 表现出对无味的形式的完全蔑视. **-ly** *ad.*

sov·er·eign·ty ['sɔvrinti] *n.* ①主权，宗主权. ②君权，统治权. ③主权国家. *S- will not suffer any infringement.* 主权不容侵犯.

so·vi·et ['səuviet] *n.* ①〔苏联〕苏维埃，代表会(议). ②〔the S-〕= S- Russia. ③〔*pl.*〕苏联人. — *a.* 苏维埃的；〔S-〕苏联的. *the S- Government* 苏联政府. *the S- people* 苏联人民. *The Russian S- Federated Socialist Republic* 俄罗斯苏维埃联邦社会主义共和国〔苏联一加盟共和国，略 R. S. F. S. R.〕. *S- Union, the Union of S- Socialist Republics* 苏维埃社会主义共和国联盟〔略 U. S. S. R. (苏联)〕.

So·vi·et·ism ['səuvietizəm] *n.* ①苏维埃主义[制度]. ②反映苏维埃主义特点的事物.

So·vi·et·ist ['səuvietist] *n.* 苏维埃主义者.

So·vi·et·ize ['səuvietaiz] *vt.* ①使苏维埃化. ②把…纳入苏联轨道. ③对…灌输苏联思想；使符合苏联政策. ~**-zation** *n.*

So·vi·et·ol·o·gist [ˌsəuvie'tɔlədʒist] *n.* 研究苏维埃制度的专家；苏联问题专家.

sov·khos ['səuvkəuz] (〔*pl.*〕 ***sovkhozy sovkhozes*** [sɔv'kɔzi, -'kɔziz]) *n.*〔苏联〕国营农场.

sov·ran ['sɔvrən] *n., a.*〔诗〕= sovereign.

sow[1] [səu] *vt.* ***(~ed; ~ed, sown)*** ①播，撒；播种，种. ②散播，传播；惹起. ③ 使密布. *Let's sow our field with rice.* 让我们在田里种稻子吧. *Tom handed in a paper sown with grammatical mistakes.* 汤姆交上去一份满是语法错误的读书报告. — *vi.* 播种. *You must reap what you have sown.* = *As a man ~s, so he shall reap.* 种瓜得瓜种豆得豆. ~ ***discord*** 散播不和，挑拨离间. ~ ***the sand*** 白费气力. ~ ***the seeds of*** *(revolution)* 播下(革命)的种子.

sow[2] [sau] *n.* 母猪；【冶】高炉铁水沟；炉底结块；火铸型；沟铁；大型铸铁；【军】攻城掩舍(= ~ bug). — *a.*〔美〕雌的. *You cannot make a silk purse out of a ~'s ear.* 猪耳朵做不出丝钱袋来. *~ bosom*〔美〕腌肋肉，咸肉. *a ~ cat*〔美〕母猫. ***as drunk as a (David's, Davy's) ~*** 烂醉如泥的. ***get [have, take] the wrong [right] ~ by the ear***〔俚〕弄错[弄对]人，拿错[拿对]东西；见解错误[不错]，论断错误[不错]，解答错误[不错](等). ~ **back** 山背，沙丘. ~**belly**〔口〕咸猪肉. ~**bread**【植】野生仙客来. ~ **bug**【虫】土鳖，地鳖，蛜蝛. ~**-gelder** 割母猪卵巢的人；〔英俚〕下流人物，肮脏鬼. ~ **thistle**【植】苦苣菜属.

so·war [səu'wɑː] *n.* (印度的)骑兵；传令骑兵.

sow·ens ['səuənz, suː-] *n. pl.*〔Scot.〕发酵燕麦麸粥.

sow·er ['səuə] *n.* ①播种者；播种机. ②散布者；提倡者，发起人，创办人.

sown [səun] sow[1] 的过去分词.

sox [sɔks] *n.*〔美俚〕短袜 (= socks).

soy [sɔi] *n.* ①中国酱油. ②大豆，黄豆. ~**-bean**〔美〕= soya-bean.

so·ya(-bean) ['sɔiə(biːn)] *n.* 大豆；〔英〕= soybean. ~ *cake* 豆饼.

so·zin ['səuzin] *n.*【生化】(动物体内的)抗菌素，抗毒素.

soz·zled ['sɔzld] *a.*〔俚〕烂醉的.

SP = shore patrol (美国海军或海军陆战队的)岸上宪兵，基地宪兵.

S.P. = ①small pica. ②supraprotest. ③single phase. ④stirrup pump 镫式(手摇)灭火泵.

Sp. =Spain; Spaniard; Spanish.

sp. =①special; specialist. ②species. ③specific. ④spell; spelled; spelling. ⑤spirit. ⑥specimen.

s.p. =〔L.〕*sine prole* 无子女 (= without issue).

spa [spɑː] *n.* ①矿泉，温泉；温泉疗养地. ②游乐胜地[豪华旅馆]. ③〔美〕(新英格兰的药房等附设的)冷饮部.

space [speis] *n.* ①空间；太空. ②空隙，空地；场地；(火车轮船飞机中的)座位；余地；篇幅. ③空白；间隔；距离. ④(一段)时间；片刻，一会儿. ⑤【乐】(谱表的)线间空白，线间；区间. ⑥【印】隔条，衬条，空铅；空铅间隔；印刷物(或书写)的行间空白，打字稿一格或一行的宽度. ⑦【电】开键. ⑧电台(电视)为广告节目留出的时间. ⑨〔美〕一年徒刑. *celestial ~* 天空. *outer ~* 外层空间；星际[宇宙]空间. *leave a ~* 留空白. *blank ~* 空白. *an open ~* 空地. *a dangerous ~* 危险区域. *a delivery ~* 扩散器. *a compression ~* 高压室. *S- forbids.* 限于篇幅. *a long [short] ~* 长[短]时间. *Let us rest a ~.* 休息一会儿吧. *Your luggage occupies too much ~.* 你的行李占地太多了. *The reading room affords an ample ~ for 500 people.* 阅览室面积可能容五百人. *Please leave a wider ~ between the lines.* 行间的空请留得大一些. *vanish into ~* 在空中消失. ***the ~ of*** (多少年)之间. ***for a ~*** 暂时. ***for the ~ of a mile [two years]*** 一英里的距离[两年]间. ***in ~*** 片刻就，一会儿就. — *vt., vi.* 留间隔；【印】行间[字间]衬空铅. *In designing the houses, ~ out them from 10 to 12 yards apart.* 在设计房子时，家与家之间留间隔十至十二码. ~***d crop*** 宽行栽培. ~***d emphasis*** 加宽字母间间隔所表示的强调. ~ ***out***【印】加宽行间[词间]间隔排匀. **S- Age** 宇宙空间时代. ~ **bar** (打字机的)间隔档，空档. ~**-charge**【热离子学】空间电荷. ~ **craft** 宇宙飞行器. ~ **current**【无】(管内)空间电流. ~ **fiction** 宇航冒险小说. ~ **flight** 宇宙飞行，星际飞行. ~ **heater** 小型供暖器〔装于室内，供一室用〕. ~ **lattice**【原】空间栅格[点阵]. **-less** 无限的；无空隙[间隔、余地]的. ~**man** 宇宙空间科学工作者，宇航员，太空人. ~ **model** 立体模型. ~**-out** *a.* 遨游太空的；(因吸毒而)呆若木鸡的. ~**port** 宇航站〔飞船装配、试验、发射中心〕. ~**-ship** 宇宙飞船. ~ **shuttle** 航天飞行，航天飞机. ~ **sickness** 宇航病. ~ **station [platform]** 宇航站，空间站. ~ **suit** 宇宙飞行服. ~ **time**【数，物】时空(连续体)；时空关系. ~ **walk** *n., v.* 空间行走，宇宙行走〔指宇航员离开飞船在外活动〕. ~ **writer** 按篇幅计算稿酬的记者或撰稿人，〔美〕= ~**man.**

spac·er ['speisə] *n.* ①留间隔者[器]. ②隔离物. ③垫片，垫圈；衬垫，衬套；撑挡；隔板；(打字机跳格的)间隔档. ④【印】空铅，衬条. ⑤【影】暗帧.

spa·cial ['speiʃəl] *a.* = spatial.

spac·ing ['speisiŋ] *n.* ①(留)间隔，间距. ②【印】(词间、行间等)调节间隔. ③【农】植距.

spa·cious ['speiʃəs] *a.* ①宽，广阔的，宽敞的. ②(知识)广博的；宽裕的. *a ~ room* 宽大的房间. *It's quite beyond me to speak on a ~ topic like this.* 我实在讲不了这般博大广泛的题目. **-ly** *ad.* **-ness** *n.*

spa·cis·ter ['speiˌsistə] *n.*【无】空间电荷晶体管，宽阔管.

Spack·le ['spækl] 一种抹墙粉的商标名. — *n.*〔s-〕抹墙粉. — *vt.* ***(-led, -ling)***〔s-〕上抹墙粉于….

spade[1] [speid] *n.* ①铲；锹；(剖鲸鱼用的)铲刀. ②【军】(撑住炮架,制止它因后坐力而移动的)驻锄. ***call a ~ a ~*** 直言不讳,有啥说啥. — *vt.* 拿铲子铲；拿铲刀切开. *Orders came that we should ~ the trench in an hour.* 有命令我们必须在一小时之内挖好战壕. ~**fish**【动】细鳞白鲳；白鲟；匙吻鲟. ~**foot toad**【动】锄足蟾(科动物). ~ **husbandry** 深耕细作. ~**-warfare** 堑壕战. ~**work** ①铲工，铲活. ②需要努力的准备工作. **-r** *n.* 铲具；用铲子的人.

spade[2] [speid] *n.* (纸牌的)黑桃；黑桃牌；〔*pl.*〕一副黑桃. ***in ~*** 〔口〕①肯定地；明确地；非常强烈地；绝对地. ②直率地. *He told me the whole story in ~s and there's no doubt about it.* 他明确地把整个经过都对我讲了，一点也不含糊.

spade[3] [speid] *n.* = spado. — *vt.*〔方〕= spay.

spadg•er [ˈspædʒə] *n.*〔英俚〕麻雀；〔美俚〕孩童.

spa•di•ceous [speiˈdiʃəs] *a.* ①浅褐色的，栗色的. ②【植】生肉穗花序的,肉穗花序状的.

spa•di•cose [ˈspeidikəus] *a.* 肉穗花序的.

spa•dix [ˈspeidiks] *n.* (*pl.* **-di•ces** [speiˈdaisi:z])【植】肉穗[佛焰]花序.

spa•do [ˈspeidəu] *n.*〔L.〕(*pl.* **-dones** [speiˈdəuni:z]) 阉人；阉兽，骟过的马；【法】无生育能力者.

spae [spei] *vi., vt.*〔苏格兰〕预言. ~wife 女算命者.

spa•ghet•ti [spəˈgeti] *n.*〔It.〕①(意大利式)实心面条. ②【电】漆布绝缘管,绝缘套管.

spa-hi (spa•hee) [ˈspɑ:hi:]【史】①土耳其的非正规骑兵. ②(过去法国陆军中的)阿尔及利亚骑兵.

Spain [spein] *n.* 西班牙〔欧洲〕.

spake [speik]〔古〕speak 的过去式.

spald•er [ˈspɔ:ldə] *n.* 击碎(矿)石的工人.

Spal•ding [ˈspɔ:ldiŋ] *n.* 斯波尔丁〔姓氏〕.

spall [spɔ:l] *n.* 碎片，裂片；碎(矿)石. — *vt., vi.* ①削，割，(弄)碎. ②粗研(生矿). ③剥落；裂开. ④【原】分裂,蜕变. **-ation** [spɔˈleiʃən] *n.*【原】分裂,蜕变.

spal•peen [spælˈpi:n] *n.* ①〔爱〕短工工人. ②〔爱〕饭桶，懒汉；无赖；恶棍. ③〔爱〕孩童,少年.

Spam, spam [spæm] *n.* (美国)罐头猪肉[火腿](= *sp*iced h*am*).

Sp.Am. =Spanish American 通用西班牙语的美洲人.

span[1] [spæn] *n.* ①一拃[手指张开时,拇指尖至小指尖的长度,通常九英寸]. ②(常有短的涵义的)一段时间；很小的间隔；片刻，顷刻. ③广度；全长，从一头到一头. ④跨度；(桥礅间的)礅距. ⑤【空】翼展；(气流)宽度. ⑥【海】跨绳. *the ~ of a man's life* 一个人的一生. *the whole ~ of English history* 英国历史的全程. *the ~ of memory* 记忆所及. — *vt.* ①(用拇指和小指)拃,用拃量. ②(眼睛)观测,看到. ③(记忆等)到,及. ④横跨,跨越,(桥)跨(在河上),架(桥在河上)；弥补. ⑤【海】绑住,系住. — *vi.* (在水中)时浮时沉地向前游泳；(尺蠖)段段移进. *His political life ~s half a century.* 他的政治生活长达半个世纪. *Imagination will ~ the gap in our knowledge.* 想象会弥补知识的不足. *Over there is a small stream ~-ned by a wooden bridge.* 那边有一条架着木桥的小溪. ~ **dogs** 木材抓起机. ~**-new** *a.* 崭新的. ~**-roof** 等斜屋顶.

span[2] [spæn] *n.*〔美，南非〕一对共轭牛，共轭马. — *vt.* (把两头牲畜)并排套在车上.

span[3] [spæn]〔古〕spin 的过去式.

span•cel [ˈspænsl] *n.* 绊脚索. — *vt.* (**-celed, -celled; -cel•ing, -cel•ling**) 用绊脚索羁绊.

span•dex [ˈspændiks] *n.*【纺】斯潘德克斯弹性纤维〔用于腰带、游泳衣等〕.

span•drel [ˈspændrəl], **span•dril** [-dril] *n.*【建】(三角)拱肩,拱上空间；上下层窗空间.

spang [spæŋ] *ad.* ①恰好，笔直，直接；猛然. *It fell ~ into my lap.* 它正好落在我的怀里. ②完全地. *You've poured too much water into the flower pot. It runs ~ full to the edge.* 你往花盆里浇水太多了,都流到盆沿上了.

span•gle [ˈspæŋgl] *n.*〔常 *pl.*〕①亮晶晶的东西，(戏装上的) 闪光装饰. ②(槠树叶子背面的) 菌状瘤. — *vt., vi.* 用亮晶晶的东西装饰；(使)闪闪发光，闪耀.

span•gled [ˈspæŋgld] *a.* 装饰着…的，…灿烂的. *star-~ heavens [skies]* 星光灿烂的天空. *the Star-Spangled Banner* 星条旗(美国国旗)；美国国歌.

Span•iard [ˈspænjəd] *n.* 西班牙人.

span•iel [ˈspænjəl] *n.* ①长毛垂耳狗. ②卑躬屈膝的谄媚者,走狗. ③〔俚〕无线电制导的导弹. *the field ~* 猎兔(等)长耳猎犬. *the Japanese ~* (日本)哈巴狗.

Span•ish [ˈspæniʃ] *n.* ①西班牙语. ②〔the ~〕西班牙人. ③〔美〕新墨西哥 (New Mexico) 州的别名. — *a.* 西班牙的；西班牙人[语]的；西班牙式的. ***walk ~***〔美俚〕踮着脚尖走,鬼头鬼脑地走；提心吊胆地走. ~ **America** (讲西班牙语的) 拉丁美洲各国. ~ **athlete**〔美〕吹牛者. ~ **bayonet**【植】丝兰属植物；千手兰；麟凤兰. ~ **catarrh**【医】流行性感冒. ~ **coin**〔卑〕奉承话,假恭维话. ~ ***fly***【动】斑蝥. ~ **Inquisition** (中世纪天主教审判异端的)西班牙宗教法庭. ~ **mackerel**【动】(大西洋)马鲛(属). ~ **Main**【史】南美洲北岸〔从巴拿马海峡到 Orinoco 河间的区域〕；南美北东部 Caribbean Sea 沿岸一带. ~ **moss**〔美〕【植】铁兰. ~ **needles**〔美〕【植】鬼针草(籽,果). ~ **trot**〔美〕缓步. ~**white** 硝酸铋.

spank [spæŋk] *vt.* ①(用巴掌、拖鞋等)打(屁股等). ②赶…前进，催打. ③(在比赛中)击败. — *vi.* (马、船等)飞跑,急驶 (*along*). — *n.* 拍打,一巴掌.

spank•er [ˈspæŋkə] *n.* ①大踏步急走的人；飞跑的马. ②【船】后樯纵帆. ③〔俚〕极好的东西,了不起的人.

spank•ing [ˈspæŋkiŋ] *a.* ①急走的，飞跑的. ②(风)猛烈的；强烈的. ③〔口〕极好的，最新式的；了不起的. *a ~ pair of horses* 一对飞跑的马. *a house of ~ modernistic conveniences* 一所有最新式的现代化设备的房子. — *ad.* 显著地,突出地. — *n.* 打屁股,拍打.

span•less [ˈspænlis] *a.* 不可测量[计量]的.

span•ner [ˈspænə] *n.* ①span[1] 的人. ②〔英〕(螺钉)扳钳,扳子,扳头；【建】(桥梁的)交叉支撑,横拉条. ③【动】= spanworm. *a shifting ~* 活络扳头. ***throw a ~ in the works*** 捣乱,妨碍或阻挠人家的计划.

span•worm [ˈspænwə:m] *n.*【动】尺蠖.

Spar, SPAR [spɑ:] *n.* 美国海岸警卫队妇女队员.

spar[1] [spɑ:] *n.* ①【船】圆材[桅、桁等]. ②圆木；【空】翼梁. — *vt.* ①装圆材. ②用圆材使(船)脱离浅滩. ~ **buoy**【船】杆状浮标. ~ **deck**【船】轻甲板. ~ **varnish**【化】桅杆清漆.

spar[2] [spɑ:] *n.*【矿】(不含金属成分的) 晶石. *calcareous ~* 重晶石. *cube ~* 硬石膏. *fluor [Derbyshire] ~* 萤石. *heavy ~* 重晶石. *Iceland ~* 方解石,冰洲石. *pearl ~* 白云石. *satin ~* 石膏.

spar[3] [spɑ:] *vi.* (***sparred; spar•ring***) ①(鸡)用脚踢斗. ②(拳击中)拳斗；拳打. ③争吵. ④(小规模)战斗. *The grocer ~ed with her outside his store.* 杂货商在店外和她吵起来了. ~ *at each other* 对骂. — *n.* ①拳斗. ②斗鸡. ③吵嘴. ~**mate** = sparring partner.

spar•a•ble [ˈspærəbl] *n.* 无头小鞋钉.

spare[1] [spɛə] *vi.* 节省，俭省. — *vt.* ①不用，抽出，省掉. ②出让,割爱,分让. ③宽恕，饶(命)；救命；不伤害，不损害；使某人免遭(麻烦等). *Have you any ticket to ~?* 你有多余的票子出让吗? *I cannot ~ time for it.* 那件事情我匀不出时间来. *We can ~ you for tomorrow.* 明天可以不要你帮忙了. *Can you ~ me a few minutes?* 你能抽几分钟和我谈谈吗?［你能给我几分钟去办点事吗?］ *S- him the trouble.* 别麻烦他吧. *His satiric poem ~ed neither the politicians nor the merchants.* 政客们和商人们都未能免于遭受他的诗篇的讽刺. ***... and to ~*** 多余

的，剩余的；过多的，很多的 (= enough and to ~) (*There are cases (enough) and to ~ of such a thing happening.* 有很多情况都可以发生这种事情). ***enough and to ~*** 过多的，很多的. ***if one is ~d*** 要是不死的话. ***not ~ oneself*** 不宽容自己，严格要求自己；很卖力很干，不疲塌. ***~ no efforts*** (*Let's ~ no efforts to push ahead with the four modernizations.* 让我们竭尽全力地推进四化运动). ***~ no expense*** 不惜工本. ***~ sb.'s blushes*** 不使丢脸害羞. ***~ sb.'s feelings*** 不使难过；不惹怒某人. ***~ oneself the trouble*** 不必自找麻烦，不必操心，不必费神 (*He might have ~d himself the trouble.* 他本来可以不用自找麻烦嘛. *You may ~ yourself the trouble.* 你不必费神). ***time to ~*** 余暇. — *a.* ①多余的，剩下的(钱等)，空闲的(时间等)；可以出让的. ②预备的，备用的，替换用的. ③薄弱的，简陋的；粗陋的；俭约的；瘦的. *a ~ bed* 客床，闲床. *a ~ ticket* (备)退票，多余的票，剩票. *~ cash* 剩款. *a ~ part* 备件，零件. *a ~ room* 闲房. *a ~ tire* 预备轮胎；〔美俚〕讨厌的人. *a ~ man* 【运】预备队员. *a ~ crew* 【海】预备船员. — *n.* ①节省，俭省. ②预备品，替换品. ③准备金，预备房间(等). ④〔*pl.*〕(机器等的)备件. ⑤〔美〕〔十柱戏〕(头两个球把十柱打得)全倒. ***make ~*** 节省. **~hand** 替班工人. **~ part** (机器的)备件. **~-set** *a.* 体型瘦细的. **~time** *a.* 业余的(学校)；*n.* 业余时间. **-ly** *ad.* **-ness** *n.* **-r** *n.*

spare·rib [ˈspɛərib] *n.* (猪的)排骨.

spar·ga·no·sis [ˌspɑːgəˈnəusis] *n.* 【医】裂头蚴病.

spar·ga·num [ˈspɑːgeinəm] *n.* 【生】裂头蚴.

sparge [spɑːdʒ] *vt., vi.* ***(sparged; sparg·ing)*** ①洒，撒，喷雾(于). ②(用压缩空气经过喷雾器)搅动(液体). **-r** *n.* ①喷洒器. ②【电】配电器.

spar·go·sis [ˈspɑːgəusis] *n.* 【医】象皮肿.

spar·id [ˈspærid] *n.* 【动】鲷科 *(Sparidae)* 鱼.

spar·ing [ˈspɛəriŋ] *a.* ①节省的；(对…)爱惜，舍不得 *(of)*；节制着的. ②(某方面)贫乏[不足]. ③〔古〕慈悲的，宽大的. *Be ~ of your epithets.* 不要乱用形容词；不要随便议论人. *This guide to the Museum is ~ of information.* 这本博物馆指南内容不丰富. ***be ~ of oneself*** 不卖力，不肯吃苦，懒惰. **-ly** *ad.*

spark[1] [spɑːk] *n.* ①火花；火星. ②(钻石等的)闪光；(目光的)闪耀. ③生气，活力，(才智的)焕发. ④〔美〕小钻石；小宝石. ⑤〔通常用于否定句〕一丝，一分，一点点. ⑥【电】电花，瞬态放电. ⑦【机】(内燃机火花塞的)控制放电装置. ⑧〔*pl.*〕〔口语〕(船上的)无线电技术员. *A single ~ can start a prairie fire.* 星星之火可以燎原. *There was a wild ~ in his eyes.* 他的两眼炯炯发光. *The vital ~ in him makes him an artist.* 他的生气勃勃的活力使得他成为一个艺术家. *fairy ~s* 燐光，鬼火. *a ~ of wit* 才气的焕发. *the vital ~ = the ~ of life* 生气. ***as the ~s fly upward*** 合乎道理，的确，不错. ***have not a ~ of interest*** 毫无趣味. ***strike ~s out of sb.*** 激发某人的聪明才智. **~ arrester** 火花避雷器. **~ chamber** 【原】火花室〔用于探测带电逊原子粒子〕. **~ coil** 【电】点火[发火]线圈. **~ gap** 【电】放电器，火花隙. **~ guard** 〔美〕火炉围板. **~ plug** *vt.* 发动；激励. **~ plug** ① = sparking plug. ②鼓励同伴的人，活跃分子；好领袖. **~ transmitter** 【电】火花式发电机. **~ telegraphy** 【电】电花电报. — *vi., vt.* 发火花，飞火星儿；使闪耀，使闪光；用眼神表示(喜悦等)；〔美〕鼓舞，激励. *Joseph is a player who can ~ his team to victory.* 约瑟是个能激励他的队员取胜的运动员. *The discovery ~ed us to further study.* 这个发现鼓舞我们作进一步的研究.

spark[2] [spɑːk] *n.* 愉快的年轻人；翩翩少年；纨袴子弟，花花公子；求爱者；情郎. — *vi.* 讨好女人，追逐女性. — *vt.* 〔美〕求爱，求婚.

spark·ing-plug [ˈspɑːkiŋplʌg] *n.* (内燃机的)火花塞.

spar·kle [ˈspɑːkl] *n.* ①火花，火星；闪光；光彩. ②生气，活力. ③(酒等的)气泡. ④【化】发泡. — *vt., vi.* ①发火花，迸火星；闪亮，闪耀. ②(才智等)焕发；活跃. ③起泡. *Listening to the radio, father's eyes ~d with joy.* 爸爸听着无线电眼色喜悦. *Dr. Wang's speech at the party ~s with wit.* 王博士在会上的演说，妙语如珠.

spar·kler [ˈspɑːklə] *n.* 闪亮的东西；宝石；才华焕发的人；〔口〕亮晶晶的眼睛.

spark·let [ˈspɑːklit] *n.* ①小火花，小火星，小闪光. ②(妇女衣服上的)闪光装饰. ③(自制汽水用的)碳酸胶丸，发泡剂.

spar·kling [ˈspɑːkliŋ] *a.* ①发火花的；迸火星的；闪亮的；灿烂的；活泼的. ②才华焕发的. ③有汽泡的(香槟酒等). *When I skate, I'm fearful of the ~ ice.* 我滑冰的时候很怕那闪亮的冰. *Dr. Johnson was famous for his ~ conversation.* 约翰逊博士以他的才华焕发的谈话而知名. *~ wine* 香槟酒；汽酒. **-ly** *ad.*

Sparks [spɑːks] *n.* 斯帕克斯〔姓氏〕.

spar·ling [ˈspɑːliŋ] *n.* ***(pl. ~, -lings)*** 【动】(欧洲) 胡瓜鱼 *(Osmerus eperlanus)*.

spar·oid [ˈspɛərɔid, ˈspær-] *a.* 【动】鲷科的. — *n.* = sparid (鲷科鱼).

spar·ring [ˈspɑːriŋ] *n.* ①拳击. ②争论，辩论. **~ partner** (职业拳击手的)练拳对手.

spar·row [ˈspærəu] *n.* ①【鸟】麻雀. ②〔美〕个子小的人. **~bill** 无头小鞋钉. **~grass** *n.* 〔口〕= asparagus. **~ hawk** 食雀鹰，鹞. **~ tongue** 【植】萹蓄.

spar·ry [ˈspɑːri] *a.* 晶石的，似晶石的，多晶石的. **~ iron** 菱铁矿.

sparse [spɑːs] *a.* ①(树木分布等)稀的；(交通车辆等)稀疏的. ②(人口、毛发等)稀少的. ③(雨量)稀缺的；瘦小的. *~ beard* 稀疏的胡须. *a country of ~ population.* 人口稀少的小国. **-si·ty** [ˈspɑːsiti] *n.* **-ly** *ad.* **-ness** *n.*

Spar·ta [ˈspɑːtə] *n.* 斯巴达〔古希腊南部一个城邦〕.

Spar·ta·cist [ˈspɑːtəsist] *n.* 【史】(德国)斯巴达克同盟成员.

Spar·tan [ˈspɑːtən] *a.* (希腊)斯巴达的；斯巴达式的〔刻苦耐劳、严于律己、战争中视死如归〕. — *n.* 斯巴达；斯巴达式的人. *a ~ dog* 英国种警犬；残忍的人. **-ism** *n.* 斯巴达主义〔精神、方式、性格〕. *Didn't you notice a ~ brevity in his speech?* 难道你没有注意到他讲话的那种斯巴达式的"简短"吗？

spar·te·ine [ˈspɑːtiˌiːn, -tiːin] *n.* 【化】鹰爪豆碱.

spa·score [ˈspeiskɔː] *n.* 人造卫星位置显示屏.

spasm [spæzəm] *n.* ①痉挛，抽搐. ②一阵(感情发作或一阵动作)；(地震等的)一震. *a ~ of the stomach* 胃痉挛. *have a ~ of grief* 一阵悲伤. *a ~ of coughing* 一阵咳嗽. *a ~ of pain* 疼痛一阵.

spas·mod·ic, -i·cal [spæzˈmɔdik, -ikəl] *a.* ①痉挛(性)的；抽搐的. ②阵发性的，一会儿做一会儿停的，间歇的；勤惰无常的. *~ efforts* 时作时止的努力. *a ~ worker* (做事)忽冷忽热的工作者. **-i·cal·ly** *ad.*

spas·tic [ˈspæstik] *a.* ①【医】痉挛(性)的. ②患大脑性麻痹的. *~ paralysis* 【医】痉挛性麻痹. — *n.* 患大脑性麻痹者.

spat[1] [spæt] 〔古〕spit 的过去式及过去分词.

spat[2] [spæt] *n.* 蠔〔牡蛎〕卵；贝苗；〔集合词〕幼蠔. — *vi., vt.* (蠔等)产卵.

spat[3] [spæt] *n.* 〔常 *pl.*〕①鞋罩. ②= spatterdashes.

spat[4] [spæt] *n.* ①掌击，拍打，一个巴掌. ②大雨(等)的声音. ③〔美口〕口斗，争论；小冲突，小争斗. — *vt., vi.* ***(spat·ted*** [ˈspætid]; ***spat·ting*** [ˈspætiŋ]***)*** 〔口〕①用巴掌打. ②(雨点等)啪啪地落下. ③小冲突，争吵. *Bullets were ~ting the car.* 枪弹象雨点般打在汽车上. *Mary is ~ting with mother again.* 玛丽又在和妈妈吵架了.

spatch·cock [ˈspætʃkɔk] *n.* 杀后马上切成小块下锅煮的鸡肉. — *vt.* (把鸡)杀后就下锅；〔口〕把(文句等)增补[插入] *(in; into)*. *I'm busy ~ing more examples into my book.* 我在忙着给我的书增补更多的例句.

spate [speit] *n.* ①洪水,突然泛滥,猛涨;〔苏格兰〕倾盆大雨. ②大量. *The river is in* ～. 河水猛涨. *Refugees crossed the border in full* ～. 难民大量地越过了边境.

spa·tha·ceous [spəˈθeiʃəs] *a.*【植】①有佛焰苞的. ②佛焰苞质的.

spathe [speið] *n.*【植】佛焰苞.

spath·ic [ˈspæθik] *a.*【矿】象晶石的,方解石状的;薄层状的.

spa·those[1] [ˈspeiθəus, ˈspæθəus] *a.* = spathaceous.

spath·ose[2] [ˈspæθəus] *a.* = spathic.

spath·u·late [ˈspæθjulit] *a.*【植】匙形的,抹刀形的.

spa·tial [ˈspeiʃəl] *a.* ①空间的;在空间中存在[发生,占有位置]的. ②占大篇幅的. *too* ～ *a theme for a book like this* 要占很大篇幅,不是这本书所能容得下的主题. **-i·ty** [ˌspeʃiˈæliti] *n.* 空间性. **-ly** *ad.*

spa·tial·ize [ˈspeiʃəlaiz] *vt.* 予以形态[形状];使形状化;使空间化. *Man invented writing to* ～, *i.e. preserve, language.* 人类发明了文字,才能给予语言以形态,也就是,才能把语言保存下来. *cognitive disposition to* ～ *everything* 使每一事物都形象化的认识倾向. **-tial·i·za·tion** *n.*

spa·ti·og·ra·phy [ˌspeiʃiˈɔgrəfi] *n.* 太空学.

spa·ti·o·nau·tics [ˌspeiʃiəuˈnɔ:tiks] *n.* 宇宙航行学.

spa·ti·o·tem·po·ral [ˌspeiʃiəuˈtempərəl] *a.* ①存在于时间和空间的. ②时空的. **-ly** *ad.*

spat·ter [ˈspætə] *vt.* ①泼,溅,洒. ②泼脏,溅脏. ③诽谤,诋毁. ～ *mud on sb.'s clothes* 溅泥在某人衣服上. *mistakes* ～*ed through the whole of the article.* 文章中俯拾皆是的错误. — *vi.* ①溅,洒. ②喷散;喷唾沫,滴下. ③(子弹)雨般射来. ④诽谤. *Rain* ～*ed down on the roof.* 雨滴滴嗒嗒地落在屋顶上. — *n.* ①泼,溅. ②(雨等的)滴滴嗒嗒声. ③泼溅的污迹. ④点滴,少量. *When he finished his recitation, there was a* ～ *of applause.* 他朗诵完了以后,有阵稀稀落落的掌声. ～**dashes** *n.*〔常 *pl.*〕(从前雨天骑马用的)皮绑腿. ～**dock**【植】黄花圆叶萍蓬草;睡莲.

spat·u·la [ˈspætjulə] *n.* ①〔L.〕(涂油漆、涂药等用的)抹刀;刮铲. ②【医】压舌片;调药刀. ③【动】(瘿蚊幼虫的)胸骨;匙突.

spat·u·lar [ˈspætjulə] *a.* 抹刀似的.

spat·u·late [ˈspætjulit] *a.* ①抹刀形的,刮铲状的. ②【植】(树叶等)匙形的.

spav·in [ˈspævin]【兽医】跗节内肿. **-ed** *a.* 跛的;残废的.

spawn [spɔ:n] *n.* ①(鱼等的)卵,子. ②(繁殖菌类植物的)丝;菌. ③〔蔑〕小子,小鬼. ④产物,结果. ⑤【植】菌种体,菌砖. — *vt.* ①(使)产卵. ②〔蔑〕生(子). ③用菌砖栽. ④引起,酿成. *Quarrels are often* ～*ed by misunderstanding.* 争吵常常是误会酿成的. — *vi.* ①(鱼)产卵;(卵)产下来. ②大量生育. *shoot* ～ 产卵. *you* ～ *of the devil!* 你这小鬼!

spay [spei] *vt.* 割去(牲畜的)卵巢.

spdl. =【纺】spindle.

S.P.E. = Society for Pure English〔英〕纯正英语学会.

speak [spi:k] ***(spoke*** [spəuk], 〔古〕***spake*** [speik]; ***spo·ken*** [ˈspəukn]) *vi.* ①讲,说,说话;谈话 *(to; with).* ②演说,讲演;发言,陈述,声明. ③表明;(以讲话外的方式)表达,表现;辩解 *(for),* 驳 *(against).* ④〔口〕(乐器、枪炮等)响. ⑤【海】(船)发响,冲水,破浪. ⑥〔英〕(狗)吠. — *vt.* ①讲,说,说出,(用书面)声明;朗诵. ②宣告. ③〔古〕证明. ④(脸、眼睛等)表示,表现(悲哀、感情等). ⑤【海】(从船上)高声喊,(用旗语等方式)招呼. ⑥〔古〕向…说话 (= ～ to sb.). *The child cannot* ～ *yet.* 孩子还不会说话. *I'll* ～ *to the teacher about it.* 这件事我要和教员谈谈. *Professor Wang is going to* ～ *on Old English tomorrow.* 王教授明天要作关于古英语的讲演. *S- of the devil, and he is sure to appear.* = *S- of angels, and you will hear their wings.* 说鬼就见鬼,说到曹操曹操就到. *strictly* ～*ing* 严格地讲. *English spoken here.* 本处通用英语〔商店告白等〕用语. *Facts* ～ *louder than words.* 事实胜于雄辩. *The portrait* ～*s.* 这张画十分逼真. *This* ～*s him generous.* 这表明他宽大. *In the poem, Tate is* ～*ing his usual blind optimism.* 在这首诗里,泰特表达出了他通常的那种盲目的乐观主义. *We spoke a ship or two.* 我们(的船)对一两只船通过话了. ～ *sb. fair* 很有礼貌地同某人说话. ***as they [men]*** ～ 俗语说. ***generally*** ～***ing*** 一般地说来. ***nothing to*** ～ ***of*** 不值一说,没有说的价值. ***not to*** ～ ***of*** (更)不用说,当然. ***so to*** ～ 可以说. ～ ***a good word for*** 给…说好话,劝解. ～ ***about*** 讲起,说到. ～ ***against*** 说…的坏话;作不利于…的陈述. ～ ***aside*** 向旁边说,独言独语. ～ ***at*** 暗讽,指桑骂槐. ～ ***by the book*** 正确讲. ～ ***for*** 代表…讲话,为…辩护;订购 (～ *for the new farm tool* 订购新式农具);要求得到 (～ *for more cheese* 要求多给点干酪). ～ ***for itself*** 不说自明 (*There is no need for me to praise it; it* ～*s for itself.* 无需我来称赞,那是不说自明的). ～ ***for oneself*** 为自己辩护,陈述自己意见. ～ ***highly of*** 称赞. ～ ***ill [evil] of*** 诽谤,诋毁,说…坏话. ～ ***in meeting*** 〔美〕发表意见. ～ ***not a word of*** 全未谈到. ～ ***of*** 讲起,谈到;特别推荐说. ～ ***on*** 继续讲;演讲(某问题等). ～ ***one's piece*** 〔美〕说想说的话;【拳】在报上宣传. ～ ***out [up]*** 大声讲;老老实实讲,明白地讲 (*S- out — don't be afraid.* 照直说——别怕. *S- out — we can't hear.* 大声说——我们听不见). ～ ***to*** 向…说;说到 (*He* ～*s to the point.* 他说到点子上.) 招呼;恳求;申斥,忠告;证明 (*I can* ～ *to his honesty.* 我可以证明他是老实的). ～ ***together*** 商量. ～ ***under one's breath*** 悄悄地说. ～ ***United States*** 说美国话. ～ ***up*** 极力辩护;明说;提高声音说 (*We should* ～ *up about each other's mistakes.* 我们要公开讲明彼此的错误). ～ ***upon*** = ～ on. ～ ***volumes (for)*** 表示重要意义;为…的有力证据. ～ ***well for*** 证明…好[有效]. ～ ***well of*** 称赞,说…好话. ～ ***with*** 和…谈话;和…商量;〔古〕= talk to. ～ ***without book*** 凭记忆讲. **-a·ble** *a.* 可以交谈的;可以出口的.

speak·eas·y [ˈspi:ki:zi] *n.* *(pl.* ***-eas·ies****)*〔美俚〕非法秘密酒店.

speak·er [ˈspi:kə] *n.* ①说话人;演说者;雄辩家. ②广播员. ③扩音器,扬声器;喇叭,话筒. ④〔S-〕英国下议院、美国众议院议长〔美国正式叫做 the S- of the House〕. ⑤(会议的)主席. *Blame not the* ～ *but be warned by his words.* 言者无罪,闻者足戒. *a fine [no]* ～ 演说漂亮[不行]的人. *Mr. S-!* 〔招呼〕议长先生! ～**-phone** 扬声器电话(由电话线连接的对讲装置). ～**ship** 议长的职位、任期.

speak·ies [ˈspi:kiz] *n.* 〔*pl.*〕〔美口〕有声电影;话剧.

speak·ing [ˈspi:kiŋ] *a.* ①发言的,交谈的,说话的. ②栩栩如生的,活现的,逼真的. ③雄辩的,说明问题的,富于表情的. ～ *acquaintance* 见面谈几句的朋友,泛泛之交. *a* ～ *look* 富有表情[意味深长]的样子[眼神]. *a* ～ *likeness [portrait]* 栩栩如生的画像. ***not on*** ～ ***terms (with)*** (和…)不是相互交谈的朋友(点头之交);(和…)见了面也不开口,(和…)不和. — *n.* 谈话;传说;〔*pl.*〕演说,雄辩(术),语言. ***at the [this] present*** ～〔美〕现在,眼下. ～ ***in tongues*** 出神地喃喃作声〔不自觉地发出无确定意义的声音,有人认为是由于宗教体验而造成 (= glossolalia)〕. ～ **trumpet** 传话筒;扩音器. ～ **tube** 通话管.

spear[1] [spiə] *n.* ①矛,标枪,鱼叉. ②持矛者[兵]. — *vt.* 用标枪戳,用鱼叉叉鱼;叉;〔美俚〕得到,捕到. *Papa knows how to* ～ *salmon.* 爸爸知道怎样叉鲑鱼. *S- the cake and put it on the plate, Tom.* 汤姆,叉起蛋糕放在盘子上. — *vi.* 刺,戳. — *a.* 父系的,右边的. ～ *half* = ～ *side* 父系 (*opp.* distaff [spindle] side). ～ *hand* 右手 (*opp.* shield hand). ～**fish** ① *n.*【动】四鳍旗鱼(属),旗鱼. ②*vi.*

用鱼叉捕鱼. ～ **grass**【植】针茅(属). ～**man**, ～**sman** *n.* *(pl. -men)* 持矛枪的人[兵]. ～**point** 矛头,枪尖 (～*point against* ～*point* 针锋相对的[地]).

spear² [spiə] *n.* (植物的)长形的叶片[嫩芽]. — *vi.* (植物)长出长叶片[嫩芽].

spear·head [ˈspiəhed] *n.* 矛头,枪尖;前锋,尖端,先锋. — *vt.* 〔美口〕带头;当…的先锋. *act as the* ～ *of* 当…的先锋. ～ *the drive for modernization* 争当现代化运动的先锋.

spear·mint [ˈspiəmint] *n.*【植】绿薄荷,留兰香.

spec [spek] *n.* 〔口〕投机(事业)〔speculation 的缩略〕. ***on*** ～ 投机,冒险 (*do a thing on* ～ 冒险干).

spec. = ①special; specially. ②specification. ③specimen.

spe·cial [ˈspeʃəl] *a.* *(opp.* general, ordinary, usual*)* ①特别的,特殊的. ②专门的;专用的;特设的. ③额外的,临时附加的. ④特别亲密的(朋友). — *n.* ①特别的人,特别警卫员,特使. ②特别考试. ③特别的东西;临时(列)车,专车;新闻号外,特刊,特稿,特别通讯,特约稿;特制影片. ④〔美〕选科生;特别生 (*opp.* regular student). ⑤【医】特别护士. ⑥〔美〕特制品. *a* ～ *case* 特例. ～ *duty* 特殊任务. *a* ～ *purpose computer* 专用计算机. ～ *anatomy* 解剖学各论. *a* ～ *constable* 临时警察. *in* ～ 格外,特别. *one's* ～ *chair* 专用椅子. ～ **agent** ①特别代理人. ②特务. ～ **areas** 〔英〕萧条地区. ～ **assessment** (对房地产征收的)公用事业专用税. ～ **correspondent** 特派记者. ～ **course** 选科. ～ **delivery [handling]** 〔美〕快递〔英国叫 express delivery〕. ～ **edition** 号外,专刊. ～ **effects** (影片和电视中的)特技. ～ **hospital** 专科医院. ～ **pleading**【法】①不直接答复对方而另提出事实以抵销的间接答辩法. ②只讲有利之点回避不利之点的诡辩法. ～ **privilege** 特权,特典. ～ **steel** 特种钢. **-ism** *n.* (学科等)专精一门;专业;特例. **-ist** *n.* 专家;专科医生 (*a -ist in diseases of the heart* 心脏病专家). **-ly** *ad.* **-ness** *n.* 特殊,专门.

spe·cial·is·tic [ˌspeʃiəˈlistik] *a.* 专家的,专门学科的.

spe·ci·al·i·ty [ˌspeʃiˈæliti] *n.* 〔英〕 = specialty.

spe·cial·ize [ˈspeʃəlaiz] *vt.* ①(使)特殊化;(使)专门化. ②专门研究;专门从事. ③专用于…;限定(意义范围等),指定(受款人). ④特别加指明,列举. ⑤【生】分化;(使)特化,(使)专化. —*vi.* ①专门研究,专攻. ②逐条详述. ③【生】分化,特化,专化. *I'll have to ask you to examine the account and* ～ *each item.* 我得请你检查一下帐目逐项详列. *any* ～*d skill* 任何业务专长. *We* ～ *in glass making.* 我们专门从事制造玻璃. **-i·za·tion** *n.* ①特化,特殊化;专门化. ②(意义的)限定,限制. ③【生】特化(作用),专化性. **-d** *n.* 指定受款人的支票.

spe·cial·ty [ˈspeʃəlti] *n.* 〔美〕(=〔英〕speciality) ①特性,特质. ②专门,专门研究,专业;专长. ③特制品;特级产品;创制品,新出品. ④〔*pl.*〕特点;特别事项. ⑤【法】盖印,盖印证书[契约]. ⑥钢琴伴奏团体合唱歌. *Biochemistry is his* ～. 生物化学是他的专业[专长]. *Walnut is a local* ～ *here.* 核桃是此地的土特产. ***in*** ～ 特别,专门. ***make a*** ～ ***of*** 以…为专业;专攻某学科.

spe·ci·ate [ˈspiːʃieit] *vt.*【生】生物形成.

spe·ci·a·tion [ˌspiːʃiˈeiʃən, -siː-] *n.*【生】物种形成.

spe·cie [ˈspiːʃi] *n.* 〔*sing., pl.*〕硬币 *(opp.* paper money*)*. *in* ～ 用实物;以同样方法;用硬币. ～ *held [holding] abroad* 流出国外的硬币. ～ *money* 硬币. ～ *par* 法定平价. ～ *payment* 硬币支付. ～ **point** 硬币输送点. ～ **reserve** 硬币准备. ～ **shipment** 硬币装运. **the S-Bank** (日本的)正金银行.

spe·cies [ˈspiːʃiz] *n.* *(sing., pl.)* ①种类;【生】(物)种. ②【逻】种. ③【原】核素. ④【法】形式. ⑤【宗】圣餐物. *a* ～ *of folly* 一种愚蠢行为. *the four* ～【数】四则,加减乘除. *The Origin of S-* 物种源始〔Darwin 著〕. *the [our]* ～ 人类.

spe·cif. = specific(ally).

spec·i·fi·a·ble [ˈspesiˌfaiəbl] *a.* 可列举的,能详细说明的.

spe·cif·ic, -al [spiˈsifik, -əl] *a.* ①特殊的;特有的;特定的,专门的. ②明确的,具体的. ③【生】种的;【细菌】专性的. ④【医】有特效的;由特种病菌(病毒)引起的,特异型的. ⑤【商】按数量征税的. ⑥【物】比的. *I want a* ～ *analysis of the problem.* 我要一个对这问题的专门的分析. *This tells you that there is a* ～ *distinction between the right and the wrong.* 这件事告诉你是与非是有明确的区别的. — *n.* ①特殊用途的事物. ②详论;细节. ③特性. ④特效药 (*for*). *a* ～ *sum of money* 一定金额. ～ **activity** 放射性比度. ～ **capacity** 电离率. ～ **characters**【生】种特性. ～ **duty**【商】从量税. ～ **gravity** 比重. ～ **heat** 比热. ～ **mass** 密度. ～ **name**【生】种名. ～ **performance** 照规定严格执行. ～ **remedy [medicine]** 特效药. ～ **surface** 单位表面. ～ **volume** 体积度.

spe·cif·ic·al·ly [speiˈsifikəli] *ad.* ①按种别地,按类别地,按特性地. ②特别地,明确地,各别地;尤其. *I told him* ～ *not to miss Professor Chang's lecture.* 我曾特别地嘱咐他不要缺张教授的课.

spec·i·fi·ca·tion [ˌspesifiˈkeiʃən] *n.* ①详细说明,逐一登记,详记. ②〔*pl.*〕规范,规格. ③清单,明细单. ④【法】(申报新发明时的)设计说明书. ⑤【法】用来料加工制成新产品所取得的权利. *Can you send the job* ～ *to me at once?* 你能把工程作业的详细说明马上送来吗? *a signal* ～ 信号规格;信号技术条件. *working* ～*s* 操作规程. ***fall short of*** ～***s*** 不合规格.

spe·ci·fic·i·ty [ˌspesiˈfisiti] *n.* ①特异性,特征;种别性. ②特效. ③【化】专一性. ④【生】专化性.

spec·i·fy [ˈspesifai] *vt.* ①指定;具体说明,详细说明. ②逐一登记,详列;列入清单;分类;特殊化. *at a time and place to be specified* 在指定的时间地点. *specified weight* 规定重量. ～ *those to whom invitations are to be sent* 具体开明应加邀请的人名.

spec·i·men [ˈspesimin, -mən] *n.* ①样本,样品,实例,例子;标本;雏形. ②供检查用的材料,试料. ③〔口〕怪人. *a* ～ *copy* (新书)样本. *a* ～ *page* 样张. ～*s in spirits* 泡在酒精中的标本. *stuffed* ～*s*【动】剥制标本. *queer* ～ 怪人. *What a* ～*!* 真是一个怪家伙!

spe·ci·ol·o·gy [ˌspiːʃiˈɔlədʒi] *n.*【生】物种学. **-log·i·cal** [-ˈlɔ-] *a.*

spe·ci·os·i·ty [ˌspiːʃiˈɔsiti] *n.* ①〔罕〕外表美观[华而不实](的人[物]). ②貌似有理[似是而非](的言行).

spe·cious [ˈspiːʃəs] ①外表美观的. ②貌似有理的. *We wouldn't accept his* ～ *claim.* 我们不会接受他那貌似有理的要求的. **-ly** *ad.* **-ness** *n.*

speck¹ [spek] *n.* ①斑点;污点;缺点. ②(水果的)疵斑. ③微片,微粒. ④有烂斑的东西[鱼,水果等]. *You can't eat fish covered with dark* ～*s.* 你可不能吃满是黑斑的鱼. *Now you put a* ～ *of orange juice in the water.* 现在你在水里放一点点橘子汁. — *vt.* 〔常用 *p.p.*〕加斑点;玷污.

speck² [spek] *n.* 〔美、南非〕(海豹等的)脂肪;肥肉.

speck·le [ˈspekl] *n.* 斑点;斑纹〔常用 *p.p.*〕. — *vt.* ①加斑点. ②玷污. ③点缀. *a* ～*d group [lot]* 驳杂的人群. ～*d trout* 斑鲑,斑鳟[指各种鲑鱼,鳟鱼,因地而异]. *dark hair* ～*d with gray* 斑白的头发.

specks, specs [speks] *n.* 〔*pl.*〕〔口〕眼镜.

spec·ta·cle [ˈspektəkl] *n.* ①观览物,展览物. ②光景,景象,状况;奇观,壮观. ③惨状,悲惨景况. ④阅兵典礼. ⑤表演,场面,场面富丽的影片[戏剧]. ⑥〔*pl.*〕眼镜. ⑦【铁路】信号灯灯框. *On June 1st, the kids of the kindergarten made a very amusing* ～. 六一那天,幼儿园的孩子们作了很有意思的表演. *Such a* ～ *has seldom been seen of late years.* 这样的壮观近年来很少见哪. *a pair of* ～*s* 一副眼镜;〔板球俚〕两次吃零分. *I cannot see things through your* ～*s.* 我的看法和你的不一样.

make a ~ of oneself 出洋相；大大出丑. ***see all things through rosy ~s*** 事事(过分)乐观. ***wear [take off] ~s*** 戴上[取下]眼镜. ~ **plate**【机】双孔板.

spec·ta·cled [ˈspektəkld] *a.* 戴着眼镜的；【动】有眼镜状斑纹的. *a ~ bear*【动】眼镜熊.

spec·tac·u·lar [spekˈtækjulə] *a.* ①场面富丽的，壮观的；观赏品的，展览物的. ②引人注意的，轰动一时的，惊人的. *The Beijing Opera Troupe is going to give a ~ play.* 北京京剧团即将上演一出场面富丽的戏. *At night Wang Fu Jing street is a ~ display of lights.* 晚上，王府井大街呈现着壮观的灯火. *in a ~ fashion* 惊人地，壮观地. — *n.* ①盛大的场面；壮观，展览物. ②〔美〕一小时半以上的大场面电视节目. ③特大的霓虹灯广告. **-ly** *ad.*

spec·tate [ˈspekteit] *vi.* 出席观看.

spec·ta·tor [spekˈteitə] *n.* (*fem.* ***-tress*** [-tris]) ①(比赛等的)观众；旁观者. ②〔*pl.*〕〔美〕女运动鞋. *The S-*〔英〕《旁观者》[期刊名]. — *a.*〔美〕①能吸引观众的. ②观看用的；运动用的；华美的，漂亮的. *such ~ spots as boxing* 象拳斗之类的能吸引观众的运动. ~ **frock** 运动(上)衣.

spec·ta·to·rit·is [ˌspekˈteitəraitis] *n.* 运动不足病.

spec·ter [ˈspektə] *n.*〔美〕= spectre.

spec·tra [ˈspektrə] spectrum 的复数.

spec·tral [ˈspektrəl] *a.* ①鬼的；鬼怪(似)的. ②【物】光谱的. *a ~ apparatus* 分光器. *~ analysis* 光谱分析. *~ colours* 谱色. *~ line* 光谱线.

spec·tre [ˈspektə] *n.* ①幽灵；鬼影. ②恐怖的根源，(纠缠不去的)心中暗鬼. *There is no denying that the ~ of unemployment and want is constantly haunting them.* 失业和贫乏的幽灵一直在对他们作祟是不能否认的.

spectro- *comb. f.* 光谱的: *spectro*scope.

spec·tro·chem·is·try [ˌspektrəˈkemistri] *n.* 光谱化学. **-chem·i·cal** *a.*

spec·tro·gram [ˈspektrəˌgræm] *n.*【物】光谱图.

spec·tro·graph [ˌspektrə*u*grɑːf] *n.*【物】摄谱仪，分光摄谱仪. **-ic** *a.* **-i·cal·ly** *ad.* **-y** *n.*

spec·tro·he·li·o·gram [ˌspektrəˈhiːliəˈgræm] *n.*【天】太阳单色光照片.

spec·tro·he·li·o·graph [ˌspektrəˈhiːliəˌgrɑːf, -ˌgræf] *n.*【天】太阳单色光照相仪，日射光谱计.

spec·tro·he·li·o·scope [ˌspektrəˈhiːliəˌskəup] *n.*【天】太阳单色光观测镜.

spec·trom·e·ter [spekˈtrɔmitə] *n.*【物】分光仪，分光计. *a mass ~* 质谱仪. *a sound ~* 声频频谱计.

spec·tro·me·tric [spektrəˈmetrik] *a.* 光谱测定的，度谱的.

spec·tro·pho·to-e·lec·tric [spektrəfəutə*u*iˈlektrik] *a.*【物】分光光电作用的.

spec·tro·pho·tom·e·ter [ˌspektrəufəˈtɔmitə] *n.*【天】分光光度计. **-pho·to·met·ric** [-ˈfəutəmeˈtrik] *a.* **-pho·tom·e·try** *n.*

spec·tro·scope [ˈspektrəskəup] *n.*【物】分光镜，分光器. **-scop·ic, -i·cal** *a.* **-i·cal·ly** *ad.*

spec·tros·co·py [spekˈtrɔskəpi] *n.*【物】分光术，光谱学. **-ist** *n.*

spec·trum [ˈspektrəm] *n.* (*pl.* ***-tra*** [-trə]) ①【物】谱，光谱；波谱；能谱，质谱. ②【无】射频频谱；无线电(信号)频谱. ③【心】(眼睛的)余象，残象. ④〔转义〕范围，幅度；(连续的)系列. *an absorption ~* 吸收(光)谱. *a bright line ~* 线状光谱. *an optical ~* 光谱. *a solar ~* 太阳光谱. ***a wide ~ of opinion*** 意见的不同幅度甚大. ~ **analysis** 光谱分析. ~ **distribution** 光谱分布.

spec·u·la [ˈspekjulə] speculum 的复数.

spec·u·lar [ˈspekjulə] *a.* ①镜子的；镜子似的，反射的. ②【医】用窥器(检查)的，镜检的. *~ cobalt ore* 辉钴矿. *~ iron* 镜铁矿. *~ orb* 眼睛；透镜. *~ reflection*【物】单向反射. *~ surface* 反射面. *~ stone* 云母.

spec·u·late [ˈspekjuleit] *vi.* ①沉思，思索；设想，推测 (*about; on, upon*). ②投机 (*in*). *It was a quiet evening and Tom was ~ing about the origin of the universe.* 那末个静悄悄的暮间，汤姆在沉思着宇宙的起源. *~ in stocks* 做股票投机. ***~ on a rise [fall]*** 做多头[空头]投机，赌涨[跌].

spec·u·la·tion [ˌspekjuˈleiʃən] *n.* ①沉思，思索，考虑. ②推测；空谈. ③投机；投机事业[买卖]. ④一种纸牌戏. ***buy sth. as a ~*** 投机购买某物. ***engage in ~*** 做投机生意. ***much given to ~*** 想入非非. ***Much ~ is rife concerning [as to]*** ... 关于…有许多推测. ***on ~*** 投机，碰运气地. ***spread the ~ that*** 散播空气说.

spec·u·la·tive [ˈspekjulətiv, -leit-] *a.* ①思索的；思辨的；推理的；纯理论的；(专事)推测的. ②投机(性质)的；冒风险的. ~ **geometry** 理论几何学. ~ **market** 投机市场. **-ly** *ad.* **-ness** *n.*

spec·u·la·tor [ˈspekjuleitə] *n.* ①投机者，投机商人；〔美〕垄断收买(戏票)的人. ②思辨者；纯[抽象]理论家，空谈者.

spec·u·lum [ˈspekjuləm] *n.* (*pl.* ***-la*** [-lə], ***~s***) ①(古代的)金属镜；反射镜. ②【医】窥器，诊察镜；开张器. ③【天】行星相对位置图谱. ④【动】(鸟的)翼斑，翼镜. ⑤(鳞翅目翅的)透明斑；(鳞翅目幼虫的)颈斑. ⑥【动】灿点，眼状斑. *~ metal* 镜齐，镜用(铜锡)合金. *a nasal ~*【医】鼻镜.

sped [sped] speed 的过去式及过去分词.

speech [spiːtʃ] *n.* ①言语；说话；谈话；说话能力(或方式). ②民族语言，方言，专门语言；〔罕〕流言. ③演说，演讲；发言. ④【语】词(类)；引语；用语. ⑤(乐器的)音，音色. *Everybody has the right to give ~ to his feelings.* 人人有说出他的感情的权利. *Speech is silver, silence is gold.*〔谚〕畅言是银，沉默是金. *a man of rapid [slow] ~* 口齿流利[迟钝]的人. *an opening [a closing] ~* 开幕[闭幕]辞. *parts of ~*【语法】词类. *a ~ community* 使用某种特有语言(或方言)的集团. *freedom of ~* 言论自由. ***deliver [make] a ~*** 演说. ***find one's ~*** 能说话；说得出话. ***give ~ to*** 说出. ***have ~ of (a person)*** 和…谈话. ***lose one's ~*** 不能说话，说不出话. **~-amplifier** 音频放大器. ~ **centre** 言语中枢. ~ **clinic** 言语矫正所. **~-day**〔英〕学校毕业授奖典礼日. ~ **disorder** 语言失常[紊乱]. ~ **form** 语言形态. ~ **maker** 演说家. ~ **organ** 发言器官. ~ **reading** 聋哑人的视话法. **~-way** (某民族地区集团)特有的言语方式. **~writer** 讲演稿撰写人.

speech·i·fy [ˈspiːtʃifai] *vi.*〔谑、蔑〕(滔滔不绝地)演说，高谈阔论. **-fi·er** *n.*〔谑、蔑〕滔滔不绝的演说者. **-fi·cation** *n.*

speech·less [ˈspiːtʃlis] *a.* ①不会说话的；哑的. ②说不出话来的. ③言语表达不出的；无言的. ④〔英俚〕烂醉的. *A gorilla is just a ~ animal.* 猩猩只不过是一种不会说话的动物. *The fact that she grew pale showed her ~ fright.* 她面无人色说明了她说不出来的恐惧. ***~ with [from] fear*** 吓得说不出话来. **-ly** *ad.* **-ness** *n.*

speed [spiːd] *n.* ①快，迅速. ②速率，速度. ③(汽车的)变速器，排档. ④(胶片，照相纸)感光速度. ⑤〔古〕兴隆，成功. ⑥〔美〕甲基苯异丙胺(类毒品). *More haste, less [worse] ~.* 越急越慢，欲速反迟. *The ship has a ~ of 30 knots.* 这条船时速 30 海里. *Let's accelerate the ~ of our socialist construction.* 让我们加速我们社会主义建设的速度. *a top ~* 最大速度. *a ~ of escape [escape ~]*【火箭】第二宇宙速度，逃逸速度〔克服地球引力的速度〕. *a horse of ~* 快马. ***(at) full ~ = at the top of one's ~*** 用全速，开足马力. ***make ~*** 赶快，赶紧，加快. ***put on full ~*** 用全速，开足马力. ***with ~*** 迅速，赶快. ***wish (sb.) good ~ = wish good ~ (to sb.)*** 祝…成功. ***with all ~*** 用全速，开足马力. — *vt.* (**sped** [sped], ***~ed***) (常用 ***~ed***) ①催，使赶快，促进，快速送传. ②〔古〕使

成功，使成就，使兴隆．③祝愿成功，祝一路平安．④调节速度，使保持一定速度．*Speed our boat forward. It's getting dark.* 使我们的小船快速前进，天黑起来了．*It's time we sped the parting guests.* 现在是我们去祝离别客人一路平安的时候了．— *vi.* ①迅速前进，快行 *(along; down; up; across)*．②进行；过日子．③〔美〕(汽车司机)用规定以上的速度驾驶．④〔古〕成功，兴隆．*The car sped directly to the village.* 汽车一直地疾驶进入村子里．*I should like to know how you speed.* 我很想知道您的好情况．*God ~ you!* 祝成功；~ ***ill*** 不顺利．~ ***up*** 加快(机器等的)速度；使加紧做 *(sth.)* (~ *up the work* 加紧工作)．~ ***well*** 顺利．**~ball** ①快速球类运动．②(俚)掺海洛因、吗啡的可卡因．**~-baller** *n.*【棒球】速球投球员．**~bird, ~boat** 高速快艇．**~ brake**【空】气动减速刹车，减速器．**~-change gear**【机】变速齿轮．**~cop**〔美俚〕取缔超速汽车的警察．**~-down** 减速．**~flash** = ~ light．**~-fiend, ~-hog** = speeder①．**~ freak** 毒瘾很深的人．**~ indicator** 速度计．**~ing**〔美〕(违犯规定的)超速行驶．**~ light** 闪光管，频闪放电器．**~ limit** 速度限制．**~-merchant** *n.*〔美〕= speeder①，汽车司机；【棒球】速球投球员．**~ multiplier**【机】倍速器．**~-reading** (掠过一些段落的)快速阅读．**~ scout**【军】高速侦察机．**~ shop** 高速赛车部件店．**~-track** = ~ way．**~ trap** (汽车)速度监查所．**~-up** ①加快速度；(机械等的)能率促进．②(火车等的)高速度化．**~-way** ①摩托车汽车赛跑道．②〔美〕高速公路．**~ well**【植】(药用)婆婆纳(属)．

speed·er [ˈspiːdə] *n.* ①违法超速开车者．②【机】调速装置；加速器．

speed·i·ly [ˈspiːdili] *ad.* 快，迅速，赶快，赶紧．

speed·i·ness [ˈspiːdinis] *n.* 迅速．

speed·ing [ˈspiːdiŋ] *n.* 超速行驶．

speed·om·e·ter [spiːˈdɔmitə] *n.*【机】示速器；(汽车等的)速度计，里程计．

speed·ster [ˈspiːdstə] *n.* ① =speeder. ②双人座高速汽车；快艇．

speed·y [ˈspiːdi] *a.* ***(-i·er; -i·est)*** 快的，迅速的；敏捷的．*a ~ answer* 敏捷的回答．*a ~ retribution* 迅速的报应．

speiss [spais] *n.*【冶】硬渣，黄渣．

spe·lae·an, spe·le·an [spiˈliən] *a.* ①洞穴的，洞穴状的．②穴居的．

spe·l(a)e·ol·o·gy [ˌspi(ː)liˈɔlədʒi] *n.* 洞穴学．**-gist** *n.*

spell[1] [spel] ***(spelled*** [spelt, -d], ***spelt)*** *vt.*①(用字母)拼写；边拼边读．②费力地读出、读懂 *(out; over)*．③拼作；拼作…而读作…．④认真研究出，琢磨 *(out)*．⑤指示，是…的表现，有…的意义；招致，带来，意味．— *vi.* 拼写；读；〔诗〕研究．*How do you ~ your name?* 你的名字是怎样拼的？ *You've ~ed this word wrong.* 你把这个字拼错了．*Can you ~ out this word in the manuscript?* 你能认出手稿中的这个字吗？*Our failure is likely to ~ heavy losses.* 我们的失败可能招致重大的损失．~ ***danger*** 招致〔意味着〕危险．~ ***backward*** 倒拼；曲解，误解．~ ***down*** 在拼字比赛中胜过(某人)．~ ***out*** ①详细说明，清楚地说明．②【印】正式拼写，全文拼写出来．~ ***over*** 思考，考虑．~ ***short*** 随随便便讲，漫不经心地讲．**-able** *a.* 可拼写的．**~down** 拼字比赛〔尤指失误者即淘汰的〕．

spell[2] [spel] *n.* ①轮班，换班；替班；服务时间．②(天气等)一段(持续的)时间，休息一段时间．③(工作的)一段时间．④(疾病等的)一次发作时间．⑤〔口〕短距离，暂时．⑥〔美口〕心里不愉快的时候，烦闷的时候．*Each one of them does a six hours' ~ of duty.* 他们每个人值六小时的班．*Let's take a ~ and have some tea.* 咱们休息一会儿喝点茶．*a ~ of coughing* 一阵咳嗽．*a ~ of fine weather* 连日好天气．*a hot ~* 连热不已．*a ~ of service in Hongkong* 在香港工作的一段时间．*a ~ of bad luck* 一连串的坏运气．*a breathing ~* 喘息的机会．***by ~s*** 轮流，轮班，断断续续地．***for a ~*** 暂时．***give a ~*** 使换班休息．***have a ~ = keep a ~ = take a ~*** 换班，接班 (*have a ~ at the oars* 换班划桨)．***take by ~ = take ~ and [for] ~*** 轮流．— *vt.*〔英罕，美〕使换班休息．

spell[3] [spel] *n.* ①符咒，咒语．②吸引力，诱惑力，魔力，魅力．***be bound by a ~ = be under the ~*** 给符咒镇住；被…迷住．***break a ~*** 破除魔力〔吸引力，诱惑力〕．***cast [lay, put]*** *(sb.)* ***under a ~ = cast [lay, put] a ~ (up)on [over]*** *(sb.)* 迷住；蛊惑．— *vt.* ***(~ed*** [spelt, -d], ***spelt*** [spelt]***)*** ①念咒镇住，用符咒镇服．②蛊惑，迷惑．**~bind** *vt.* 迷惑〔诱惑〕．**~-binder**〔美口语〕(使听者入迷的)雄辩家(*an air ~-binder* 广播演说家)．**~bound** *a.* ①被符咒镇住的．②被迷住的，着了迷的．

spell·er [ˈspelə] *n.* 拼字者；拼写者；〔美〕拼字书．

spell·ing [ˈspeliŋ] *n.* 拼字；拼写法．*In English there are often several ~s for one sound.* 英语一个音常常有几种拼写法．*Don't make a mistake in your ~.* 不要在拼法上出错．**~ bee [-match]** *n.*〔美〕拼写比赛．**~ book** 拼写课本．**~ pronounciation** 拼写读音法〔指按拼写读音，而不是一般公认的读音的误读〕．

spelt[1] [spelt] spell[1] 和 spell[3] 的过去式及过去分词．

spelt[2] [spelt] *n.*【植】(作饲料用的)斯佩耳特小麦．

spel·ter [ˈspeltə] *n.*【商】锌块；锌合金焊料，硬钎料．

spe·lunk·er [spiˈlʌŋkə] *n.* 洞窟学家，洞窟探险家．**-lunk·ing** *n.*

spence, spense [spens] *n.*〔主 Scot.〕①食品贮藏室．②(学校等的)食品供应部．③(乡间的)内室，起居室．

spen·cer[1] [ˈspensə] *n.* (19世纪男女通用的)短大衣；毛线短褂．

spen·cer[2] [ˈspensə] *n.*【船】(风暴时用的)小斜桁帆．

Spen·cer [ˈspensə] *n.* ①斯潘塞〔姓氏，男子名〕．② **Herbert ~** 斯宾塞〔1820—1903，英国实证主义哲学家〕．

Spen·ce·ri·an [spenˈsiəriən] *a.* 英国斯宾塞哲学的；美国人罗吉·斯宾塞(Rogers Spencer)体书法的．— *n.* 斯宾塞派的哲学家；【书法】斯宾塞体．

spend [spend] *vt.* ***(spent***[spent]***)***①用(钱)，花费．②乱花；浪费；过(日子)．③消磨(时间)，度过，过日子；用光，用尽(子弹、气力、财产等)；消耗；使筋疲力尽，使极度衰弱；费(很多心血等)．④献出(生命等)；【海】失去(桅)．*How much have you spent on books this term?* 这学期你在买书上用了多少钱？*Father is going to ~ the winter in Guangdong.* 父亲将要在广东过冬．*His life is a life honestly spent in the faithful service of Communism.* 他的一生是忠心耿耿地奉献给共产主义的一生．— *vi.* ①用钱，花钱；浪费．②耗尽，用尽，用完；筋疲力尽，极度衰弱．③(鱼等)产卵，下子．*Don't ~ without the thought of the next day.* 不要只顾眼前不想明天地花钱．~ ***and be spent*** 出钱又出力，尽全力．~ ***itself [oneself]*** 耗尽；筋疲力尽，衰弱(*The storm has spent itself.* 暴风雨已过去了)．~ ***one's blood*** 费尽心血．~ ***one's breath [words] (in vain)*** 白费唇舌，说也无用．~ ***one's last*** 动用最后存品〔存款〕．**-able** *a.* 可花费的．**-er** *n.* 挥霍者，浪费者．

Spen·der [ˈspendə] *n.* 斯彭德〔姓氏〕．

spend·ing [ˈspendiŋ] *n.* 经费，开销．~ *money*〔美〕零用钱．

spend·thrift [ˈspendθrift] *n.* 乱花钱的人，浪费者；浪子，败家子．— *a.* 乱花钱的；挥霍的，浪费的．*no ~*〔美〕吝啬(鬼)．

Spen·ser[1] [ˈspensə] *n.* ①斯潘塞〔姓氏〕．②Edmund ~ 爱德门·斯宾塞〔1552?—1599，英国诗人〕．

Spen·se·ri·an [spenˈsiəriən] *a.* (英国诗人)斯宾塞体的．— *n.* 斯宾塞(Spenser)派诗人．**~ stanza** 斯宾

塞体〔斯氏在 *Faerie Queene* 中所用的诗体〕.

spent [spent] spend 的过去式及过去分词. — *a.* ①筋疲力尽的,冲势已完的,衰弱了的. ②产了卵的(鱼). *a ~ arrow* 冲力已完的箭. *~ gas* 废气. *~ material* 废料. *~ residue* 废物.

sperm[1] [spəːm] *n.* 【生】精子;精液.

sperm[2] [spəːm] *n.* ①= ~ whale 抹香鲸. ②= ~ oil 鲸蜡;鲸脑(油).

sperm(a)-, -sperm *comb. f.* 精子,精液: *sperma*duct.

sper·ma·cet·i [ˌspəːməˈseti, -məˈsiːti] *n.* 鲸蜡,鲸脑油.

sper·ma·duct [ˈspəːmədʌkt] *n.* 【解】输精管.

sper·ma·go·ni·um [ˌspəːməˈgəuniəm] *n.* *(pl.* ***-ni·a*** [-ə]*)* 【植】精原细胞.

sper·ma·ry [ˈspəːməri] *n.* ①【动】睾丸;精巢. ②【植】雄器,(蕨苔的)精子器;花粉管.

sper·ma·the·ca [ˌspəːməˈθiːkə] *n.* 【动】(雌虫的)受精囊.

sper·mat·ic [spəːˈmætik] *a.* ①精子[液]的;精囊的,睾丸的;精巢的;生殖的. ②产生的,发生的. *~ fluid* 精液. *a ~ duct* 输精管. *~ cord* 【解】精索.

sper·ma·tid [ˈspəːmətid] *n.* 【动】精子细胞.

sper·ma·ti·um [spəˈmeiʃiəm] *n.* *(pl.* ***-ti·a*** [-ə]*)* 【植】①不动精子. ②(锈菌)性孢子.

sper·mat·o·blast [ˈspəːmətəublæst] *n.* 精子细胞.

sper·mat·o·cyte [spəˈmætəˌsait, ˈspəːmətə-] *n.* ①【植】精母细胞. ②【动】精母细胞.

sper·mat·o·gen·e·sis [spəmætəˈdʒenisis, ˌspəːmətəu-] *n.* 精子发生. **-ge·netic** [-dʒiˈnetik] *a.*

sper·ma·tog·e·nous [spəːməˈtɔdʒənəs] *a.* 产生精子[精液]的. **-e·ny** *n.* = spermatogenesis.

sper·mat·o·go·ni·um [spəmætəˈgəuniəm] *n.* *(pl.* ***-ni·a*** [-ə]*)* 【动】精原细胞. **-go·ni·al** *a.*

sper·ma·tol·o·gy [ˌspəːməˈtɔlədʒi] *n.* 精子学. **-log·i·cal** *a.* **-o·gist** *n.*

sper·ma·to·phore [ˈspəːmətəfɔː, -fɔə] *n.* 【生】精子托;精原细胞;精子包囊;(低等植物的)精子孢蒴.

sper·ma·to·phyte [ˈspəːmətəfait] *n.* 【植】种子植物(门).

sper·ma·tor·rh(o)e·a [ˌspəːmətəuˈriːə] *n.* 【医】精溢[漏].

sper·mat·o·zo·id [spəˌmætəˈzəuid, ˌspəːmətə-] *n.* 【植】游动精子.

sper·ma·to·zo·on [ˌspəːmətəuˈzəuɔn] *n.* *(pl.* ***-zoa*** [-ˈzəuə]*)* 【生】精子. **-zo·al, -zo·an** *a.*

sperm·i·cide [ˈspəːmiˌsaid] *n.* 【医】杀精子剂. **-i·ci·dal** *a.*

sperm·ine [ˈspəːmiːn] *n.* 【生化】精胺,精素,精硷〔作补药用〕.

sper·mi·o·gen·e·sis [ˌspəːmiəuˈdʒenisis] *n.* 【动】①精子形成. ② =spermatogenesis.

sper·mo·blast [ˈspəːməblæst] *n.* 【生】精子细胞.

sper·mo·go·ni·um [ˌspəːməˈgəuniəm] *n.* *(pl.* ***-ni·a*** [-ə]*)* = spermagonium.

sper·mo·lo·gy [spəːˈmɔlədʒi] *n.* ①精子学. ②种子学. **-log·i·cal** *a.* **-o·gist** *n.*

sper·mo·phile [ˈspəːməˌfail, -fil] *n.* 【动】欧黄鼠.

sper·mous [ˈspəːməs] *a.* 精子的;精子状的.

sper·ry·lite [ˈsperiˌlait] *n.* 【矿】砷铂矿.

spes·sar·tite, spes·sart·ine [ˈspesəˌtait,-tin] *n.* 【地】锰铝榴矿;闪斜煌斑岩.

spew [spjuː] *vt.* ①呕吐. ②喷;涌;渗. — *vi.* ①呕吐. ②涌出. ③渗出. *This is an active volcano which ~s out lava every year.* 这是个每年喷熔岩的活火山. *One of the ways to purify water is to make it ~ slowly from the soil.* 净化水的方法之一是让它从土中慢慢地渗出. — *n.* 吐[呕]出物;喷出物,渗出物.

sp.gr. = specific gravity 【物】比重.

sphac·e·late [ˈsfæsileit] *vt., vi.* (使)生坏疽;(使)形成腐肉;(使)生枯斑;(使)腐烂,坏死. — *a.* 【植】枯萎了的.

sphac·e·la·tion [ˌsfæsiˈleiʃən] *n.* 【医】(生)坏疽;腐肉形成.

sphac·el·us [ˈsfæsiləs] *n.* 【医】坏疽,坏死组织;腐肉.

sphag·num [ˈsfægnəm] *n.* *(pl.* ***-na*** [-nə]*)* 【植】水藓,泥炭藓.

sphal·er·ite [ˈsfeiliˌrait] *n.* 【矿】闪锌矿.

sphene [sfiːn] *n.* 【化】榍石.

sphe·no·don [ˈsfiːnəˌdɔn] *n.* 【动】斑点楔齿蜥(= tuatara).

sphe·no·gram [ˈsfiːnəugræm] *n.* 楔形文字.

sphe·nog·ra·phy [sfiˈnɔgrəfi] *n.* 〔罕〕①楔形文字书写术. ②楔形文字学. **-ra·pher** *n.* **-ra·phist** *n.* **-graph·ic** *a.*

sphe·noid [ˈsfiːnɔid] *a.* 楔状的;【解】蝶骨的. — *n.* 楔状骨,蝶骨;【地】楔;【化】半面晶形. **-al** *a.*

spher·al [ˈsfiərəl] *a.* ①球的,球状的. ②球面的;天体的. ③匀称的,对称的.

sphere [sfiə] *n.* ①球;球体,圆体,球面,球形. ②天体;星,行星. ③地球仪,天体仪. ④【天】天球;天空. ⑤(活动)范围,领域;本分,职分. ⑥身分,地位. ⑦〔美俚〕棒球. *the geometry of ~s* 球面几何学. *a ~ of fortress* 要塞地带. *a ~ of influence* 势力范围. *I take up a second foreign language to widen my ~ of knowledge.* 我选修一种第二外语来扩大我的知识面. ***be beyond [out of] one's ~*** 在本人的(某种)范围外,越分. ***be in one's ~*** 在本人的(某种)范围内,不越分. ***remain in one's proper ~*** 守本分,安分守己. — *vt.* ①使成球形. ②放在球内;使处于天体之间. ③包围,围住. ④〔诗〕捧上天,极力赞扬.

spher·i·cal [ˈsferikəl] *a.* 球的;球面的;球形的,圆的;天体的;天空的. *a ~ bush* 【机】球面衬. *a ~ conic section* 【数】球锥曲线. *a ~ sector* 球心角体. *~ geometry* 球面几何学. *a ~ triangle* 球面[弧]三角形. **-ly** *ad.*

sphe·ric·i·ty [sfeˈrisiti] *n.* 球状;球面;球体;球(形)度.

spher·ics [ˈsferiks] *n.* ①【数】球面几何学;球面三角学. ②【气】远距离电气测候法;(低频)天电;(低频)天电学(= sferics).

sphe·roid [ˈsfiərɔid] *n.* ①扁球体;回转扁圆体. ②〔美〕棒球用球.

sphe·roi·dal [sfiəˈrɔidl], **sphe·roi·dic** [sfiəˈrɔidik] *a.* 扁球体的;回转扁圆体的. *~ state* 【物】球腾态. **-roi·dal·ly** *ad.*

sphe·roi·di·city [ˌsfiərɔiˈdisiti] *n.* 球形,扁球形,椭球形.

sphe·rom·e·ter [sfiəˈrɔmitə] *n.* 球径计,测球仪.

spher·u·lar [ˈsferjulə] *a.* 小球(状)的,小球似的.

spher·u·late [ˈsferjulit] *a.* 布满小球体的.

spher·ule [ˈsferjuːl] *n.* 小球(体).

spher·u·lite [ˈsferjuˌlait, ˈsfiər-] *n.* 【地】球粒. **-lit·ic** [-ˈlitik] *a.* **-lit·ize** *vt.* 使成球粒.

spher·y [ˈsfiəri] *a.* ***(spher·i·er; spher·i·est)*** 【诗】①圆体的,似球的. ②天体的,关于天体的.

sphinc·ter [ˈsfiŋktə] *n.* 【解】括约肌. *~ ani* 肛门括约肌. **-ter·al** *a.*

sphin·gid [ˈsfindʒid] *n.* = hawkmoth.

sphin·go·my·e·lin [ˌsfiŋgəuˈmaiəlin] *n.* 【生化】(神经)鞘磷脂.

sphin·go·sine [ˈsfiŋgəusi(ː)n] *n.* 【生化】(神经)鞘氨醇.

sphinx [sfiŋks] *n.* *(pl.* ***~es, sphin·ges*** [ˈsfindʒiːz]*)* ①〔S-〕【希神】斯芬克斯〔有翼的狮身女面怪物〕. ②【古埃及】狮身人面[鹰头,羊头]巨象. ③莫名其妙的事,谜似的人[物]. ④【动】天蛾;一种非洲狒狒.

sphra·gis·tics [sfrəˈdʒistiks] *n.* 印章学.

sp.ht. = specific heat 比热.
sphyg·mic [ˈsfigmik] *a.* 【生理】脉搏的.
sphyg·mo·gram [ˈsfigməˌgræm] *n.* 【医】脉搏描记,脉搏曲线.
sphyg·mo·graph [ˈsfigməgrɑːf] *n.* 【医】脉搏描记器. **-ic** *a.*
sphyg·mo·gra·phy [sfigˈmɔgrəfi] *n.* 【医】脉搏描记法.
sphyg·mo·ma·nom·e·ter [ˌsfigməuməˈnɔmitə] *n.* 【医】血压计. **-mo·man·o·met·ric** [-ˈmetrik] *a.*
sphyg·mom·e·ter [sfigˈmɔmitə] *n.* 【医】脉搏计.
sphyg·mo·phone [ˈsfigməfəun] *n.* 【医】脉搏计.
sphyg·mo·scope [ˈsfigməskəup] *n.* 【医】脉搏检视器.
sphyg·mus [ˈsfigməs] *n.* 【医】脉搏.
spic, S- [spik] *n.* 〔美俚〕墨西哥人;拉丁美洲人.
spi·ca [ˈspaikə] *n.* *(pl. -cae* [-siː]*)* ①【植】(谷类的)穗. ②【医】人字形绷扎法. ③〔S-〕【天】角宿一〔室女座 α 星〕,天门.
spi·cate, -cat·ed [ˈspaikeit, -ted] *a.* 有穗的; 穗状排列的, 穗状花序的.
spic·ca·to [spiˈkɑːtəu] *a.* 【乐】〔弦乐器演奏术语〕用跳弓演奏的,分开的,断续的. — *n.* 跳弓演奏; 跳弓技术; 须用跳弓演奏的段落.
spice [spais] *n.* ①香料,调味料. ②香气,香味;〔诗〕芳香. ③情趣,风味. *Please add more ~ to the cake.* 请给蛋糕多加点香料. *Henry's worn-out joke lacks ~ for anyone.* 亨利的老掉牙的笑话谁听起来也乏味. *a ~ of life* 生活的情趣. *a ~ of humour* 幽默味. — *vt.* ①加香料[佐料] *(with)*. ②添趣味 *(with)*. ~ **box** 香料盒. ~**ber·ry** 【植】①菱叶番樱桃 *(Eugenia rhombea)*〔产于加勒比地区〕. ②香料植物〔尤指鹿蹄草; 鹿蹄草油, 鹿蹄草香〕. ~**bush** 【植】①黄果山胡椒. ②西美蜡梅.
spic·e·ry [ˈspaisəri] *n.* ①〔集合名词〕香料, 调味品. ②香辣味,芳香,香味,香气.
spi·ci·form [ˈspaisifɔːm] *a.* 穗状的.
spick [spik] *n.* 〔美俚〕= spic.
spick-and-span [ˈspikəndˈspæn] *a.* ①崭新的, 新做的(衣服). ②漂亮的;干干净净的,整洁的.
spic·u·la [ˈspikjulə] *n.* *(pl. spic·u·lae* [ˈspikjuliː]*)* ①针状体,刺. ②【动】(海绵动物的)骨针; (海参的)骨片; (昆虫的)螫刺,针突,产卵器. ③【植】交合刺. **-r** *a.* = spiculate.
spic·u·late [ˈspikjuˌleit] *a.* ①针骨状(的), 针状的. ②有针状体覆盖的;有针状体的 (= spicular).
spic·ule [ˈspikjuːl] *n.* ①针状体;【植】交合刺; 穗状花序. ②【动】(海绵动物的)骨针; (海参的)骨片; (昆虫的)螫刺;针突;产卵器.
spic·u·lum [ˈspikjuləm] *n.* *(pl. -la* [-lə]*)* 〔L.〕针骨,针状体;〔尤指〕(海盘车鱼等低级动物中的)交合刺.
spic·y [ˈspaisi] *a.* *(-i·er; -i·est)* ①加有香料的; 香的. ②出产香料的. ③辛辣的;痛快的;有风味的;有趣味的. ④漂亮的(服装等). ⑤(故事等)猥亵的, 下流的. *The hillside is green, the air ~.* 山坡青碧空气芬芳. *a ~ magazine* 淫秽下流的杂志. **-i·ly** *ad.* **-i·ness** *n.*
spi·der [ˈspaidə] *n.* ①【动】蜘蛛. ②带柄三脚平底锅. ③三脚架. ④【机】星形轮;十字叉;(螺旋桨的)辐射架; 星形接头. ⑤(中耕机的)泥土粉碎器. ⑥设圈套者和入圈套者. ⑦〔美俚〕缫丝工人. *a ~ and a fly* 设圈套者和落入圈套者. ~ **crab** 【动】蜘蛛蟹,尖头蟹. ~ **line** (光学仪器) 交叉瞄准线, 叉丝. ~ **mite** 【动】叶螨. ~ **monkey** 【动】蛛猿. ~ **wasp** 【动】(幼虫食蜘蛛的)黄蜂. ~ **web** 蜘蛛网, 蜘蛛网状的东西. ~ **web coil** 【电】蛛网形线圈. ~**wort** 【植】紫露草属. —*a.* 鸭跖草科的.
spi·der·y [ˈspaidəri] *a.* ①蜘蛛(网)似的. ②(象蜘蛛脚一样)细长的(腿,轮辐,笔划等). ③多蜘蛛的.
spie·gel·ei·sen [ˈspiːgˌlaizn] *n.* 【矿】镜铁 (= spiegel 或 spiegel iron).
spiel [spiːl] *n.* ①〔美俚〕招徕生意的讲话或演说. ②〔美俚〕流利夸张的演说、讲话. — *vi.* ①演奏音乐. ②流利夸张的说话或演说. — *vt.* 流利夸张地讲, 背得烂熟般地讲. *Henry is ~ing about the same old story —his innovation in techniques.* 亨利在夸夸地谈着他的老调——他对工艺上的革新. ~ ***off*** 〔美俚〕象背诵那样滔滔不绝地讲.
spiel·er [ˈspiːlə] *n.* ①〔美俚〕能说会道的演说家, 讲话者. ②商业宣传员. ③广告播音员. ④〔澳俚〕骗子.
spi·er [ˈspaiə] *n.* 侦探,间谍.
spiff [spif] *a.* 〔俚〕整洁的;漂亮的; 上等的; 时新的. — *n.* 〔美俚〕推销佣金;〔*pl.*〕额外的钱. — *vt.* 〔俚〕使整洁[漂亮]. *The parlour has to be ~ed up a bit before the guests arrive.* 客人们来到之前,得把客厅搞得整洁一点.
spif·fy [ˈspifi] *a.* *(-fi·er; -fi·est)* ①〔俚〕整洁的; 漂亮的; 时新的; 衣冠楚楚的. ②绝妙的. ③喝醉了的. *You're sure ~ in your new dress.* 你穿上这身新衣服真是漂亮. *The ~ thing is to hit the sack at once.* 最妙不过的事是马上睡觉去.
spif(f)·li·cate [ˈspiflikeit] *vt.* ①〔俚〕痛打. ②使惊慌, 使混乱,使狼狈. ③粗暴地对待. ④使完蛋,干掉,杀死. **-cation** [ˌspifliˈkeiʃən] *n.*
spif·li·cat·ed [ˈspiflikeitid] *a.* 〔俚〕慌张的, 混乱的,为难的;喝得烂醉的.
spig·ot [ˈspigət] *n.* ①〔美〕龙头;放液嘴. ②(桶等的)塞子. ③(管子的)联接器;套管. *a ~ joint* 【机】套管接合,接嘴.
spig·ot·ty, spig·go·ty [ˈspigəti] *a.* 〔美俚〕怪有趣的; 有点怪的. — *n.*〔美俚〕墨西哥人;南欧人;南洋群岛人.
spik [spik] *n.* 〔美俚〕= spic.
spike[1] [spaik] *n.* ①(围墙等上尖头向外或向上的) 长钉, 尖铁(等). ②有尖端的细长东西;鞋底尖钉;(运动员的) 钉鞋;高跟女鞋的细长的跟. ③(铁路上的)道钉. ④【火箭】销钉. ⑤【讯】尖峰信号; 测试信号. ⑥【动】(不到六英寸的)幼鲐. ⑦【炮】火门栓. ⑧〔口〕顽固的高教会派. ⑨〔美俚〕皮下注射用的针头. *a dog ~* 狗头钉. *a jog ~* 鬼钉. *a ~ nail* 小钉. *a ~ tooth harrow* 钉齿耙. *a ~ puller* 拔钉钳. *an antenna ~* 【无】天线杆. *a ~ top* 枯梢. ***hang up one's ~s*** 〔口〕退休,退出职业运动界. — *vt.* ①打上桩子. ②用大钉钉;打上钉子,用尖物刺. ③把头弄尖. ④塞住(大炮)火门. ⑤阻挡, 抑制,挫败. ⑥【棒球】用鞋底钉伤(人). ⑦【排球】在网边跳起猛扣. ⑧〔美俚〕掺入烈酒;增强…的效果、生气、风味或美观;为女子[男子]大学生联谊会干杯. *~ an attempt* 挫败一企图. *recite a humorous poem to ~ one's lecture* 背一首滑稽诗来使他的演讲有生气. *~ a rumo(u)r*〔美〕辟谣;制止谣言. *~d beer*〔美〕加了烈酒的啤酒. *~* ***sb.'s gun*** 破坏某人的计划. ~ **coat** 燕尾服. ~ **heel** 女皮鞋的高后跟. ~ **team** 〔美〕中间一匹在前、套在一起的三马队. ~**-tooth harrow** 有多排铁齿的整土耙.
spike[2] [spaik] *n.* (谷类的)穗;【植】穗状花序. ~**let** 小穗;小穗状花. ~ **lavender**【植】欧洲宽叶熏衣草. **-d** *a.*
spike·nard [ˈspaiknɑːd] *n.* ①【植】甘松. ②甘松香油. ③美洲楤木.
spik·y [ˈspaiki] *a.* ①大钉似的,尖而长的;锐利的. ②打了尖桩[钉]的. ③〔俚〕难应付的, 尖刻的. ④〔英口〕顽固的(高教会派). *a ~ roller* 羊角碾.
spile [spail] *n.* ①塞子. ②(桶的)气孔塞, 木塞, 小塞. ③〔美〕(采糖枫汁用的)插管. ④(篱笆的)木头桩子; 支柱. — *vt.* ①插塞子. ②(桶盖上)开小孔. ③装插管, 用插管引导. ④打桩支承. ~**hole** (桶的)通气孔.
spil·ing [ˈspailiŋ] *n.* 〔集合词〕木桩, 木材; 桩基, 桩材; 打桩.
spill[1] [spil] *vt.* *(~ed, spilt)* ①使溢出,使溅出,使(血)流出, 撒出; 倒出. ②〔俚〕泄漏(秘密等). ③【海】使风从…漏出. ④使(从马鞍、马车上)摔下来,使跌下来. — *vi.* ①泼出,溢出,泻出,涌流. ②泄漏出. ③倾覆,倾跌,摔下.

④【海】漏风. ⑤〔卑〕输掉(钱), 浪费. *Take care not to ~ a drop of the medicine.* 注意一滴药也不要洒. *You've ~ed ink all over the carpet.* 你把墨水溅在整个的地毯上了. ~ ***one's guts*** 把自己知道的一切都说了出去. ~ ***over*** 溢出. ~ ***the beans*** = ~ ***it*** 〔美俚〕泄漏秘密. ~ ***the blood of*** 杀死. ~ ***the dope*** 泄漏情报. ~ ***the mazuma*** 〔美〕(任意)花钱, 挥霍浪费. — *n.* ①溢出(量); 溅出; 涌出; 撒出, 撒落. ②〔口〕滚下, 摔下, 跌下. ③(雨等的)倾盆下注. ④溢洪道, 溢水口 (= **spillway**). ⑤因某种商品供应不足而引起的对其他商品的需求.

spill² [spil] *n.* ①木片. ②(引火用)纸捻儿, 引柴. ③小塞子. ④金属细棒; 销子. ⑤锥形[圆筒形]纸包.

spill·age [ˈspilidʒ] *n.* 溢出, 溢出量.

spil·ler¹ [ˈspilə] *n.* 使溢出者, 使溅出者.

spil·ler² [ˈspilə] *n.* (从大鱼网中取出鱼的)堕落网.

spil·li·kin [ˈspilikn] *n.* 〔主英〕①(抽杆游戏用的)杆子. ②〔*pl.* 动词用单数〕抽杆游戏 (= spilikin).

spill·o·ver [ˈspilˌəuvə] *n.* ①溢出, 泻出. ②溢出物, 泻出物; 过多, 外流人口.

spill·way [ˈspilwei] *n.* (水库的)溢水口, 溢洪道; 溢洪堰. a conduit ~ 溢洪道; 溢水管.

spi·lo·site [ˈspailəsait] *n.* 【地】绿点板岩.

spilt [spilt] spill 的过去式及过去分词. *It is no use crying over the ~ milk.* 为洒了的牛奶而哀号是无益的; 〔喻〕往者不谏.

spilth [spilθ] *n.* ①泻出(物), 溢出(物). ②过剩物, 废物, 垃圾.

spin [spin] *vt.* ***(spun***[spʌn], 〔古〕***span***[spæn]; ***spun)*** ①纺. ②使(陀螺等)旋转; 使(车轮)打空转[在冰上, 沙中]. ③(蜘蛛、蚕等)吐(丝), 结(网), (蚕)结(茧). ④转镟床(等)旋制; 钻孔. ⑤编造; 讲(故事等). ⑥〔俚〕〔常用 *p.p.*〕使过度疲劳. ⑦〔美俚〕欺骗. ⑧〔英〕使考不及格. ⑨(通过离心力作用)抛出, 丢开 (*off*). *Cotton is spun into thread.* 把棉花纺成线. *Silkworms ~s.* 蚕作茧. *Old sailors like to ~ yarns.* 老海员们喜欢讲故事. — *vi.* ①纺, 纺绩. ②(陀螺等)旋转; 眼花, 眩晕; (车轮)因打滑而空转. ③吐丝, 作茧, 象丝一般地流出. ④〔口〕(车、船等)飞驶, 飞跑. ⑤〔俚〕考不取. ⑥【空】旋冲. ⑦〔美俚〕跳舞. *My head ~s.* 我头晕. ~ ***in*** 〔美俚〕上床, 睡午觉. ~ ***out*** ①拉长, 拖长, 延长, 拖延; 使(钱等)勉强再维持一段时间. ②磨度过. ③使汽车作回形滑行. ~ ***the bottle*** 〔美〕转瓶游戏[瓶口所向的人须被人亲吻]. ~ ***your wheels*** 〔美空军俚〕劳而无功. — *n.* ①兜一圈; 自旋, 自转. ②飞跑, 飞过, 疾驶; 划一划. ③【空】旋冲; 螺旋, 旋转; 【物】自转. ④眩晕, 心里乱. ⑤〔澳〕运气. *isotopic ~* 同位旋. *nuclear ~* 核自旋. *go for a ~ in a car* 坐汽车溜一溜. *get into a flat ~* 穷下来. ~**cast** *vi.* 用匙形诱饵钓鱼. ~ **casting** 用匙形诱饵钓鱼. ~**-drier** 旋转式脱水机. ~ **flip** 【物】自旋转向. ~ **off** ①母公司收回子公司全部股本使之脱离的做法. ②有用的副产品 (= spinoff).

spi·na·ceous [spiˈneiʃəs] *a.* (象)菠菜的.

spin·ach, spin·age [ˈspinidʒ] *n.* ①【植】菠菜. ②〔俚〕胡说八道, 〔美俚〕不加修剪的胡子; 杂乱的蔓生物.

spi·nal [ˈspainl] *a.* ①【生】针的, 刺的; 棘状突起的. ②【解】脊骨的, 脊柱的, 脊髓的. ~ *anaesthesia* 脊髓(椎)麻醉. ~ *canal* 脊管, 椎管. ~ *column* 脊柱. ~ *cord [marrow]* 脊髓. ~ *nerve* 【解】(脊)髓神经. —*n.* 【医】脊髓麻醉 (= ~anaesthesia); 脊髓麻醉药. **-ly** *ad.* 在脊骨方面, 沿着脊骨.

spi·nate(d) [ˈspaine(i)t, -netid] *a.* ①刺一样的, 有刺的. ②有脊的.

spin·dle [ˈspindl] *n.* ①锭子, 纺锤. ②(机器的)(主)轴; 门锁的转轴. ③细长的人[物]; 长茎. ④〔美〕松叶. ⑤锭〔线长单位, 棉纱为 45,360 英尺, 麻丝为 43,200 英尺〕. ⑥(剑)柄. ⑦【生】纺锤状细胞. ⑧【解】纺锤状部分, 纺锤状器官. ⑨【数】纺锤状体. ⑩【生】纺锤体, 梭. ⑪【海】杆状警标. ⑫(报馆编辑室的)原稿[校样]插钉. ⑬液体比重计. ⑭(栏杆的)纺锤形立柱, 螺旋扶梯的中柱. *the number of ~s* 【纺】锭数. *ring ~s* 【纺】细纱锭. *the ~s in operation* 【纺】开工锭数, ~ *oil* 【机】锭子油, 轴润滑油. *a live [dead] ~* 动[死]轴. *the ~ side* 母系, 母方. — *vi.* ①长成细长茎. ②长(变)得细长. — *vt.* ①装锭子于, 使成锭子. ②用纺锤形铿打眼(穿孔). —*a.* ①象锭子的. ②〔古〕〔家族〕母系的, 母方的 (the ~ side 母系, 母方). ~**legs** 腿细长的人. ~**-legged,** ~**-shanked** *a.* 腿细长的. ~ **oil** 【机】锭子油, 轴润滑油. ~**-shanks** 细长的腿; 腿细长的人. ~ **tree** 【植】卫矛.

spin·dling spin·dly [ˈspiŋdliŋ, -dli] *a.* 纺锤形的; 细长的. — *n.* 细长物; 瘦高个子.

spin·drift [ˈspindrift] *n.* 【海】(大风吹起的)浪花, 浪沫.

spine [spain] *n.* ①【解】脊骨, 脊柱. ②【植】针, 刺. ③【动】棘状突起刺, 壳针. ④(书)背; (山)脊. ⑤〔英方〕草地. ⑥【地】火山栓, 熔岩塔. ⑦〔美〕(由中心和支持因素转为)勇气, 骨气, 毅力. ⑧〔美俚〕铁路上货车的平顶. *a man who lacks ~ and starch* 一个缺少骨气的人.

spi·nel(le) [spiˈnel] *n.* 【矿】尖晶石.

spine·less [ˈspainlis] *a.* ①无脊骨的. ②没骨气[勇气]的, 优柔寡断的. ③【生】无刺的. **-ly** *ad.* **-ness** *n.*

spi·nes·cent [spaiˈnesnt] *a.* ①有刺的, 具刺的, 多刺的. ②成为有刺的; 刺状的.

spi·net [spiˈnet] *n.* 【乐】(16—18 世纪的)键琴.

Spin·garn [ˈspingɑːn, ˈspiŋən] *n.* 斯平加恩〔姓氏〕.

spini- *comb. f.* 脊; 刺: *spinitis.*

spi·nif·er·ous [spaiˈnifərəs] *a.* 有刺的.

spin·i·fex [ˈspiniˌfeks] *n.* 【植】鬣刺属 *(Spinifex)* 植物.

spin·i·ness [ˈspaininis] *n.* ①多针, 多刺. ②困难重重. ③刺状.

spi·ni·tis [spiˈnaitis] *n.* 【医】脊髓炎.

spin·na·ker [ˈspinəkə] *n.* 【赛艇】大三角帆.

spin·ner [ˈspinə] *n.* ①纺纱工人. ②纺纱机. ③【空、机】机头罩, 螺旋毂盖, 桨毂整流罩. ④【钓鱼】旋转(诱鱼)器; 旋转匙状诱饵. ⑤【橄榄球】带球人的旋转动作(急转身假动作). ⑥〔方〕蜘蛛; (= spinneret.) ⑦〔美俚〕卡车司机.

spin·ner·et, spin·ner·ette [ˌspinəˈret] *n.* ①【动】(蜘蛛、蚕等的)吐丝器. ②【纺】喷丝头.

spin·ner·y [ˈspinəri] *n.* 纱厂.

spin·ney [ˈspini] *n.* 〔英〕树丛, 灌木丛[林].

spin·ning [ˈspiniŋ] *n.* ①纺; 精纺; 棉纱. ②旋转, 自旋; 旋压. ③用旋转匙状诱饵钓鱼. — *a.* 纺纱的; 旋转的. *a ~ electron* 自旋电子. *a ~ flight* 螺旋飞行. *a ~ roll* 【空】螺旋侧滚. ~ *nose dive* 【空】垂直螺旋俯冲. ~ *time* 〔美〕睡觉时间. ~ **frame** 精纺机. ~ **jenny** (初期的)多轴纺纱机. ~ **machine** 纺纱机, 纺丝机. ~ **mill** 纱厂. ~ **mule** 纺棉机. ~ **wheel** 纺车.

spin·off [ˈspinˌɔːf] *n.* ①(母公司把其子公司所有的股份分发给股票持有人的)抽资摆脱(做法). ②副产品; 附带的发展; 附带的利益 (= spin-off).

spi·nor [ˈspinə] *n.* 【数】旋量.

spi·nose [ˈspainəus] *a.* 有刺的, 多刺的.

spi·nos·i·ty [spaiˈnɔsiti] *n.* ①有刺(物), 多刺(物). ②棘手的问题. ③尖刻的话.

spi·nous [ˈspinəs] *a.* ①多刺的; 刺状的, 尖细如刺的. ②棘手的.

Spi·no·za [spiˈnəuzə], **Ben·e·dict** 斯宾诺沙〔1632—1677, 荷兰哲学家〕.

Spi·no·zism [spiˈnəuzizm] *n.* 斯宾诺莎哲学. **-no·zist** *n.*

spin·ster [ˈspinstə] *n.* ①(尤指中年的)未婚女人, 老处女. ②〔美〕纺纱妇女. — *a.* 未婚的. **-hood** *n.* 未婚女子(老处女)的身分.

spin·thar·i·scope [spinˈθæriˈskəup] *n.* 【原】(计算质

点数用的)闪烁镜.

spin·to [ˈspiːntəu] *a., n.* 〔It.〕【乐】抒情但带有强烈戏剧成份的(歌手,歌喉).

spi·nule [ˈspainjuːl] *n.* 【生】小刺. **-u·lose, -u·lous** [-njuləus, -njuləs] *a.*

spin·y [ˈspaini] *a.* ***(-i·er; -i·est)*** ①有刺的,多刺的,刺状的,细尖如刺的. ②困难重重的,麻烦的. **~-anteater**【动】针鼹. **~ dogfish**【动】(白斑)角鲨. **~-finned** *a.*【动】棘鳍的. **~-headed worm**【动】棘头纲动物. **~ lobster** 龙虾. **~ rayed**【动】有尖硬鳍的. **-i·ness** *n.*

spi·ra·cle [ˈspaiərəkl] *n.* ①【动】(昆虫类的)呼吸孔,气门; (鲸类的)喷水孔. ②通气孔. **-rac·u·lar** [-ˈrækjulə] *a.*

spi·rae·a [spaiˈri(ː)ə] *n.*【植】绣线菊(属).

spi·ral [ˈspaiərəl] *a.* ①螺旋形的,盘旋的,盘旋上升的. ②【数】螺线的. *Experts watch the ~ development in industry with keen interest.* 专家们以很大的兴趣观察工业的螺旋式的发展. — *n.* ①螺旋形物. ②螺簧;【物】蜷线. ③【数】螺(旋)线. ④【空】盘旋,盘旋降落〔又叫 ~ down〕. ⑤(足球运动的)旋球. ⑥(物价等)不断加剧上升或下降. ~ *galaxy*【天】螺旋星系. *a ~ line* 螺线. *a ~ spring* 螺(旋弹)簧, 蜷簧. *a ~ stair* 螺旋梯. *an inflationary [a vicious] ~* 恶性通货膨胀. — *vt., vi.* ①(〔英〕 ***-ll-***) 使成螺旋形. ②【空】盘旋降落〔上升〕. ③(物价)螺旋上升〔跌落〕. **-ly** *ad.*

spi·ral·i·ty [spaiˈræliti] *n.* 螺旋形,螺状.

spi·rant [ˈspaiərənt] *n., a.*【语音】摩擦音(的).

spire[1] [ˈspaiə] *n.* ①塔尖;尖塔;尖峰;锥形体. ②【植】幼叶;幼苗〔禾等的〕纤茎. *Have you ever seen the beautiful ~s of rocks in Guilin?* 你看过桂林的美丽的塔状尖峰吗? — *vt.* 装尖塔. — *vi.* ①(塔状)耸立. ②发芽. *Price ~s up almost every week.* 物价几乎每周高涨.

spire[2] [spaiə] *n.* ①螺旋,螺线. ②【动】螺旋部;(软体动物的)螺塔. — *vi.* 螺旋形上升. **-d** *a.*

spi·re·a [spaiˈri(ː)ə] *n.* = spiraea.

spire·let [ˈspailit] *n.* 小尖塔.

spi·reme [ˈspairiːm] *n.*【生】染色质纽.

spi·rif·er·ous [spaiˈrifərəs] *a.*【动】有螺旋部〔螺塔〕的,螺旋部〔螺塔〕结构的〔如某些贝壳〕;有螺旋形〔螺塔〕附属物的〔如腕足纲〕.

Spi·ril·lum [spaiəˈriləm] *n.* ***(pl. -ril·la*** [-lə]***)***【生】螺旋菌.

spir·it [ˈspirit] *n.* ①精神,心灵,灵魂 *(opp.* body, flesh*)*. ②灵,神;天使,妖精,魔鬼(等);鬼怪,幽灵. ③〔只用 *sing.*〕元气,志气;气概,气魄;勇气. ④〔*pl.*〕情绪,心情,兴致. ⑤(具有突出精神力量的)人物. ⑥(时代)精神,潮流,风气. ⑦〔常 *sing.*〕态度. ⑧(法律、文件等的)精神 *(opp.* letter 文字). ⑨〔常 *pl.*〕精(华). ⑩〔常 *pl.*〕酒精,醇. ⑪【医】酯剂,酒剂,药酒. *It is our duty to cultivate the ~ of boldness and fearlessness.* 我们的责任是培育大无畏的精神. *The editorial voices the ~s of the Chinese people.* 社论表达了中国人民的心情. *a man of ~* 精神饱满的人. *an unbending ~* 倔强的人. *a bold ~* 大胆的人. *a master ~* 杰出人物. *the leading ~* 领袖. *a teenager of ~* 意志坚强的少年. *Leave this to some more inquiring ~.* 把这个交给更有研究的人去干吧. *He never drinks ~s.* 他从来不喝烈酒. *~(s) and water* 搀水酒精. *~(s) of ammonia*【药】卤精〔10%的氨水溶于酒精中〕. *~(s) of hartshorn*【化】鹿精〔氢氧化铵的旧称〕;鹿角酒. *~(s) of turpentine* 松节油. *~(s) of wine* 纯酒精. ***be full of animal ~s*** 血气旺盛. ***break sb.'s ~s*** 挫折…锐气,使…垂头丧气. ***catch sb.'s ~*** 引起…兴趣. ***give up the ~*** 死. ***have a high ~*** 精神好,有进取心. ***in good ~s*** 精神好,高兴,兴致好. ***in high ~s*** 情绪极好,兴高采烈,兴致勃勃 (*He is in high ~s today.* 他今天很高兴). ***in low ~s*** 意气消沉,垂头丧气,怏怏不乐. ***in ~s*** 愉快地,活泼地. ***in (the) ~*** 心中,在内心;在精神上. ***keep up one's ~s*** 打起精神. ***lead the life of the ~*** 过崇尚精神的生活. ***lose one's ~s*** 气馁,败兴,垂头丧气. ***meek in ~*** 性情温柔. ***out of ~s*** 郁郁不乐,气闷. ***raise sb.'s ~*** 发扬…锐气,使…扬眉吐气. ***Party ~*** 党性. ***recover one's ~s*** 恢复精神. ***take in a wrong ~*** 误会 (*He takes criticism in the wrong ~.* 他误会这个批评了). ***the poor in ~*** 谦虚的人. ***to one's ~*** 到心里. — *vt.* ①鼓励,鼓舞 *(up; on)*;使精神振作. ②拐带,诱拐,拐去 *(away; off)*. **~ up** 打起精神,拿出精神. **~ blue**【化】醇溶青. **~ colours** 醇溶染料. **~ ga(u)ge** 酒精比重计. **~ gum**【剧】化妆发胶. **~ lamp** 酒精灯. **~ level**【物】(气泡)酒精水准器. **~ rapper**(自称能与死者通信息的)招魂术巫师. **~ room**【海】食物贮藏室. **~ stove**(烹饪用的)酒精炉. **~ writing** 被认为是人在神鬼缠身时写出来的东西.

spir·it·ed [ˈspiritid] *a.* ①精神饱满的,生气勃勃的,活泼的;勇敢的;猛烈的. ②〔构成复合词〕精神…的,有…心的,心地…的. *a ~ girl* 活泼的姑娘. *a ~ attack* 猛攻. *high [low] ~* 精神极好〔萎靡〕的. *public-~* 热心公益的. **-ly** *ad.* **-ness** *n.*

spir·it·ism [ˈspiritizəm] *n.* = spiritualism.

spir·it·ist [ˈspiritist] *n.* 信招魂术的人;【哲】唯灵论者. — *a.* 招魂术的;【哲】唯灵论的.

spir·it·less [ˈspiritlis] *a.* ①无精打采的,垂头丧气的;灰心的,冷淡的. ②无生命的,死的. **-ly** *ad.* **-ness** *n.*

spi·ri·to·so [ˌspiriˈtəusəu] *a.* 〔It.〕【乐】有精神的;热烈的;有兴致的.

spir·it·ous [ˈspiəritəs] *a.* ① =spirituous. ②〔废〕活泼的,情绪高昂的.

spir·it·u·al [ˈspiritjuəl] *a.* ①精神(上)的;心灵的. ②神的,灵的,神圣的;宗教的,信仰上的,超乎世俗的. ③高尚的,崇高的,崇尚精神的. ④唯灵论的,招魂论的,鬼的. — *n.* ①〔*pl.*〕教会事务. ②〔美〕(黑人的)圣歌. *the ~ man* 心灵;为圣灵所嘉佑的人. *a ~ corporation* 宗教团体. *the Lords ~* 英国上院有神职的议员〔主教〕. *negro ~* = *~ songs* 〔美〕圣歌,赞美歌. **~ bouquet**【天主】精神花束〔做特定的善事或参加弥撒为别人或死者祈祷〕. **-ly** *ad.*

spir·it·u·al·ism [ˈspiritjuəlizəm] *n.* ①【哲】唯灵论. ②招魂术 (= spiritism). ③观念论;精神至上主义. **-al·is·tic** [ˌspiritjuəˈlistik] *a.*

spir·it·u·al·ist [ˈspiritjuəlist] *n.* ①唯灵论者. ②迷信招魂术者. ③招魂术巫师.

spir·it·u·al·i·ty [ˌspiritjuˈæliti] *n.* ①精神(性);灵性. ②〔*pl.*〕教堂或教士的事务、权利、或收入. ③〔总称〕教士.

spir·it·u·al·i·za·tion [ˌspiritjuəlaiˈzeiʃən] *n.* 精神化;赋予精神意义;从精神上解释.

spir·it·u·al·ize [ˈspiritυəlaiz] *vt.* ①使精神化;赋予精神意义;从精神上来解释. ②以精神来鼓舞.

spir·it·u·al·ty [ˌspiritjuˈælti] *n.* ①属于教堂的事物. ②教士,牧师.

spi·ri·tu·el *mas.*, ***spi·ri·tu·elle*** *fem.* [ˌspiritjuˈel] *a.* 〔F.〕优雅而伶俐的;有风趣的.

spir·it·u·o·sity [ˌspiritjuˈɔsiti] *n.* 含酒精性.

spir·it·u·ous [ˈspiritjuəs] *a.* 含酒精的,酒精成分高的;蒸馏过的 *(opp.* fermented*)*.

spir·i·tus as·per [ˈspiəritəs ˈæspə] 〔L.〕 = rough breathing 〔语音〕送气音.

spir·i·valve [ˈspaiərivælv] *a.* 有螺状壳的;(壳)螺状的.

spir·ke·ting [ˈspəːkitiŋ] *n.*【船】内部腰板.

spiro-[1] *comb. f.* 螺线形,蜷线形;螺旋形: *spiro*chaetic.

spiro-[2] *comb. f.* 呼吸: *spiro*graph.

spi·ro·chae·ta, spi·ro·chae·te, spi·ro·che·te [ˌspaiərəˈkiːtə, -ˈkiːt] *n.*【微】螺旋体,波体. **~l** *a.* 由螺旋体引起的.

spi·ro·ch(a)etic [ˌspaiərəˈkiːtik] *a.*【微】螺旋体的;由

螺旋体引起的.

spi·ro·che·to·sis [ˌspairəkiːˈtəusis] *n.* 【医】波体病, 螺旋体病.

spi·ro·graph [ˈspairəˌgrɑːf, -ˌgræf] *n.* 呼吸描记器. **-ic** *a.*

spi·ro·gy·ra [ˌspairəˈdʒairə] *n.*【植】水绵属 *(spirogyra)* 植物.

spi·roid [ˈspairɔid] *a.* 螺旋状的,成螺旋形的.

spi·rom·e·ter [spaiəˈrɔmitə] *n.* 【医】呼吸量测定器, 肺活量计.

spi·rom·e·tric [ˌspaiərəˈmetrik] *a.* (使用)呼吸量测定器的,呼吸量测定法的.

spi·rom·e·try [ˌspaiəˈrɔmitri] *n.*【医】呼吸量测定法.

spi·ro·phore [ˈspaiərəufɔː]【医】人工呼吸器.

spi·ro·scope [ˈspaiərəuskəup] *n.* 【医】呼吸量测定器.

spirt [spəːt] *v., n.* = spurt[1].

spir·u·la [ˈspi(ə)rjulə, -ulə] *n.* *(pl. -lae* [-ˌliː]*)*【动】团鲗属 *(spirula)* 动物;团鲗.

spir·y[1] [ˈspaiəri] *a.* 塔尖(形)的.

spir·y[2] [ˈspaiəri] *a.* 螺旋式的.

spit[1] [spit] *vt.* *(spat* [spæt],〔古〕*spit; spit·ting)* ①吐(唾沫等),咯(血)*(out; forth; up)*. ②(唾弃地)说,发(牢骚)*(out)*. ③(雨、雪) 哗啦或霏霏地落下. ④(昆虫)产卵. ⑤点燃(导火线等). — *vi.* ①吐唾沫,吐痰. ②唾弃,蔑视. ③(猫等)呼噜呼噜地叫. ④(雨、雪)哗啦哗啦或霏霏地下. ⑤(沸水)滚腾.⑥(蜡烛等)喷出火花,枪发出火舌,(发动机等)劈啪地响. *Please don't ~ in the bus.* 请不要在公共汽车中吐痰. *I simply spat my contempt and threw the drug back to the quack.* 我愤怒地表示了我的蔑视把药扔回给那个江湖医生. *The rain spat icily down and we all felt rather chilly.* 雨冰冷地哗啦哗啦地下着,我们都觉得冷飕飕的. ~ *blood* 吐血,咯血. ~ **at** 向…啐唾沫;藐视,侮辱. ~ ***in sb.'s face*** 啐唾沫在人脸上,唾弃某人. ~ ***in [on] one's hands*** 啐唾沫在手掌上,加紧努力. ~ ***it out***〔俚〕毫无保留地讲;大声说[唱];打败. ~***on [upon]*** 藐视,侮辱 (= ~ ***at***). ~***swapping***〔美俚〕接吻. ~ ***up*** 咳出;呕出. — *n.* ①涎,唾液,啐唾沫. ②(雨、雪等的)哗啦哗啦或霏霏地下降. ③(猫) 呼噜呼噜地叫. ④喷火式战斗机;【动】(昆虫的) 唾状泡沫,吹泡. ⑤〔口〕极相象的人,一模一样的物. *He's the ~ of his dad.* 他活象他爹. ***be the very [the dead]*** ~ ***of*** 和…完全一样,和…一模一样. ~ **and image** 极相象的人. ~ **and polish**〔英口〕极注意整洁;〔英海军俚〕擦洗打扫整理内务. ~**-and-polish** *a.* 注重表面;整洁的 *(a ~-and-polish band* 仪容整洁的乐队*)*. ~**ball** *n.* (小孩用唾沫裹成扔人的)纸团;【棒球】(用唾沫濡湿一部分扔投的)唾球. ~ **box** 痰匣. ~ **devil** 喷火不倒翁[玩具]. ~ **kit**〔美〕痰盂.

spit[2] [spit] *n.* ①烤肉铁签;(海关关员的)查货铁签. ②岬,沙嘴;狭长的暗礁. — *vt.* *(spit·ted; spit·ting)*用铁签穿过(肉片等);(以刀矛等)刺,戳.

spit[3] [spit] *n.*〔英〕一铲的深度[分量].

spit·al [ˈspitl] *n.*〔废〕①病院,医院〔尤指为贫民或麻疯病人等开设的医院〕. ②(旅行者的)道边窝棚.

spitch·cock [ˈspitʃkɔk] *n.* 烤鳝[鳗]. — *vt.* 剖开后烤(鳗、鳝等).

spitch·er [ˈspitʃə] *vt.*〔军俚〕击沉(敌人的潜艇).

spite [spait] *n.* 恶意;怨恨;遗恨. ***bear sb. a ~ = have a ~ against sb.*** 怀恨某人. ***from ~ = in ~*** 为泄愤. ***in ~ of*** =〔罕〕~ ***of*** 不管,不顾;〔古〕无视. ***in ~ of oneself*** 不知不觉的,不由的. ***in ~ of sb.'s nose [teeth]*** 不管某人反对. ***in ~ of you*** 对不起…. ***out of ~*** 为泄恨,为出气. ***owe sb. a ~*** 怀恨某人. ***spite [vent] one's ~*** 解恨,出气. ***vent personal ~*** 泄私愤. — *vt.* 欺负,虐待,妨碍,刁难;泄愤. *cut off one's nose to ~ one's face* 为了泄忿[损人]反而害己.

spite·ful [ˈspaitful] *a.* 怀恨的,怨恨深的;有恶意的,心毒的. **-ly** *ad.* **-ness** *n.*

spit·fire [ˈspitfaiə] *n.* ①喷火的东西. ②〔英〕喷火式战斗机. ③【海】船头三角帆. ④〔特指〕大炮. ⑤〔口〕脾气暴躁的人〔尤指女人及小孩〕. ⑥咬人的狗[猫].

spit·ter[1] [ˈspitə] *n.* ①啐唾沫的人. ②〔俚〕=spitball.

spit·ter[2] [ˈspitə] *n.* ①用铁签烤肉的人. ②开始长角的幼鹿.

spit·tle [ˈspitl] *n.* ①唾沫,涎沫. ②(沫蝉的)泡沫状分泌物. ~**-bug,** ~**-insect**【动】沫蝉 (=froghopper).

spit·toon [spiˈtuːn] *n.* 痰盂.

spitz, spitz-dog [spits, -dɔg] *n.* 尖嘴丝毛狗;〔美〕= spitzenberg.

spit·zen·berg, -burg [ˈspitsənbəːg] *n.* 〔美〕红黄色晚熟种尖头苹果.

spiv [spiv] *n.* 〔英口语〕①不务正业靠投机取巧度日的人. ②懒汉.

spiz·zer·inc·tum [ˌspizəˈriŋktəm] *n.* 〔美方〕劲儿,雄心.

splanch·nic [ˈsplæŋknik] *a.* 内脏的.

splanch·nol·o·gy [splæŋkˈnɔlədʒi] *n.* 内脏学.

splanch·no·tomy [splæŋkˈnɔtəmi] *n.* 内脏解剖术,内脏解剖学.

splash [splæʃ] *vt.* ①溅,泼(水等);(把衣服等)溅污[湿],泼污[湿]. ②淌水走;溅着水[泥]走.③泼洒得使到处是斑点. ④〔美俚〕以显示地位展示[发表],吹嘘. ⑤〔美俚〕击落敌机. ⑥〔俚〕挥霍钱财. — *vi.* ①溅泼,溅起水[泥];蹚着水[泥]前进. ②发出溅泼[拍激]声. ③〔美俚〕洗澡,游泳. ~ *a page with ink* = ~ *ink on a page* 书页上溅满墨水斑迹. ~ *(one's way) through the mud* 溅着泥向前进. ~ *through the stream* 蹚着水过小河. *Across the surface of the river was ~ed the flaming gold of the sunrise.* 江面之上布满了初升的太阳的熔金之色. *On the wall of the parlour was ~ed his certificate of merit.* 在客厅的墙上高悬着他的奖状. — *n.* ①溅,泼. ②溅起的泥(水);飞溅声,水的拍激声.③游泳,玩水. ④溅污的斑点,污迹. ⑤斑点;色斑,光斑. ⑥〔口〕显著的展示炫耀. ⑦(米粉制成的)香粉. ⑧〔英口〕(搀威士忌用的)少量汽水(等). ⑨〔美俚〕被击落的飞机. ⑩〔美俚〕一杯水[汤]. ⑪〔美俚〕下流行为. *a ~ dam* 积水坝. *a ~ fan* 〔美〕游泳迷. ***make [cut] a ~*** 发出泼溅声;引人注意,引起哄动. ***with a ~*** 啪嚓[噗通]一声. ~**board** *n.* (车的) 挡泥板;(水闸或溢洪道的)挡水板. ~**down** (宇宙飞船在水面上)溅落. ~ **guard** (卡车后轮的)防溅板[帘]. ~ **headline** (报纸等)显眼的大字标题.

splash·er [ˈsplæʃə] *n.* ①溅泼者. ②(车的)挡泥板,轮罩. ③(洗脸架的)遮水板. ④【冶】折焰板. ⑤〔俚〕挥霍者.

splash·y [ˌsplæʃi] *a.* ①易溅的;污水多;泥泞的. ②溅泼的,溅泼着通过的. ③有色斑的. ④〔口〕炫耀的,铺张的,惹人注目的. *a ~ wedding* 铺张的婚礼. **-i·ness** *n.*

splat[1] [splæt] *n.* (椅背的)中靠板.

splat[2] [splæt] *n., int.* 淅沥声;哗啦哗啦响.

splat·ter [ˈsplætə] *vi., vt.* ①溅(水等). ②啪嚓啪嚓[拨拉拨拉]地响,唠叨,急促不清楚地结结巴巴地讲. ③【讯】边带噪声;相邻信道的干扰. ~ **dash**〔口〕嘈杂声,喧闹;〔*pl.*〕= spats. — *n.* 溅泼.

splay [splei] *vt., vi.* ①伸展开;张开(手掌等). ②【建】(使)斜削,(使)开成八字形. ③(把桶等)造成喇叭状. ④使(马的肩骨等)脱节,脱臼. — *a.* ①向外张开的,八字形的,宽扁的. ②难看的,没样子的,笨重的. — *n.* ①展开. ②【建】斜削;斜面(度). ③(枪眼等的)喇叭口. ~**-foot** *n., a.* 八字脚(的),平蹠外翻脚(的). ~**mouth** 大嘴,阔嘴.

spleen [spliːn] *n.* ①【解】脾(脏). ②愤怒,发脾气. ③〔古〕忧郁,愁闷,消沉,颓丧. ***in a fit of (the)*** ~ 发脾气,发怒. ***bear [have, take] a ~ against*** 恨,怨恨. ***vent one's ~ upon [on]*** 向…发脾气,拿…出气. ~

wort【植】(从前用以治忧郁症的) 药铁角蕨. **-less** *a.* 脾切除的.
spleen•ful [ˈspliːnful] *a.* 脾气坏的, 发脾气的, 不高兴的; 忧郁的; 恶意的; 怀恨的. **-ly** *ad.*
spleen•ish [ˈspliːniʃ] *a.* = spleenful.
spleen•y [ˈspliːni] *a.* = spleenful.
sple•nal•gi•a [spliˈnældʒiə] *n.*【医】脾痛.
sple•nal•gic [spliˈnældʒik] *a.*【医】脾痛的.
splen•dent [ˈsplendənt] *a.* ①发亮的,光亮的,有光泽的(矿物等). ②豪华的; 辉煌的,显著的,宏大的.
splen•did [ˈsplendid] *a.* ①发亮的, 光亮的, 有光彩的, 灿烂的. ②华丽的,壮丽的,壮观的,辉煌的. ③杰出的, 显著的,伟大的, 名声赫赫的. ④〔口〕极好的,上等的. *What about going there together?* — *Yes, ~!* 一道去怎么样? ——不错, 很好! *~ sight* 壮观. *a ~ victory* 大胜. *a ~ chance* 极好的机会. *a ~ figure in history* 历史上的杰出人物. *a ~ dish of ice cream* 一杯极好的冰激凌. **-ly** *ad.* **-ness** *n.*
splen•dif•er•ous [splenˈdifərəs] *a.* 〔口、谑〕极好的, 了不起的,壮丽的,豪华的. **-ly** *ad.* **-ness** *n.*
splen•dour, 〔美〕**-dor** [ˈsplendə] *n.* ①光辉, 光耀, 光彩. ②豪华, 壮丽. ③(名声等的)杰出,显赫,显著. *the ~ of the sunrise* 日出的光辉. *the ~ of his achievements* 他的功绩辉煌.
sple•nec•to•my [spliˈnektəmi] *n.*【医】脾切除术.
sple•net•ic(al) [spliˈnetik(l)] *a.* ①脾的; 位于脾附近的, 脾病的. ②易发脾气的,脾气坏的. ③恶意的, 怀恨的. *a letter ~ in tone* 一封发脾气语调的信. — *n.* ①生脾病的人. ②易发脾气的人,脾气坏的人. ③脾病药. **-i•cal•ly** *ad.*
sple•ni•al [ˈspliːniəl] *a.*【解】夹肌的.
splen•ic, -i•cal [ˈsplenik, -ikəl] *a.* 脾脏的. ~ **fever**【兽医】=anthrax, 炭疽.
sple•ni•tis [spliˈnaitis] *n.*【医】脾炎.
sple•ni•us [ˈspliːniəs] *n.* *(pl. -nii* [-niai]*)*【解】(颈部的)夹肌.
sple•ni•za•tion [ˌspliːnaiˈzeiʃən] *n.*【医】脾样变.
sple•noid [ˈspliːnɔid] *a.*【解】脾样的.
sple•no•meg•a•ly [ˌspliːnəˈmegəli, ˌsplenə-] *n.*【医】脾大.
sple•no•tomy [spliˈnɔtəmi] *n.*【医】脾切开术.
splent [splent] *n.* = splint.
spleu•chan [ˈspluːhən] *n.* 〔Scot., Irish〕钱袋, 烟袋.
splice [splais] *vt.* ①拼接,叠接(木板等); 粘接. ②绞接, 编接, 捻接(绳子等). ③〔俚〕使结婚. ④【机】接头. *get ~d* 结婚. — *n.* ①拼〔绞、捻、叠〕接(处). ②接头; 接枝. ③〔俚〕结婚. ④〔俚〕食客. ***not by a long ~*** 〔美〕简直不是…. ***sit on the ~*** 〔板球俚〕小心取守势. ***~ the main brace*** 〔海员俚〕喝酒. **splicer** *n.*
spline [splain] *n.* ①【机】花键; 方栓; 止转楔; 齿槽, 齿条, 键槽条. ②【建】塞缝片. ③活动曲线规. — *vt.* ①开键槽于. ②用花键(或方栓)联接.
splint [splint] *n.* ①薄木条; 藤条. ②〔口〕碎片, 裂片. ③【医】夹板. ④【解】腓骨〔又叫 *~-bone*〕. ⑤【兽医】炮骨瘤. ⑥(铠甲的)金属叶. ⑦烟煤. — *vt.* 用夹板夹. ~ **ar•mo(u)r** 百叶锁子甲. ~ **coal** 硬烟煤.
splin•ter [ˈsplintə] *n.* ①碎片,裂片; 木片; (炮弹的)破片; (碎木片等的)刺. ②分裂出来的小派别. ③微末的事物,微不足道的事情. ④〔美俚〕极瘦的人. — *vt.* ①劈成碎片. ②割裂,使分裂,扯裂. — *vi.* 裂开, 劈开; 分裂. *run a ~ into one's thumb.* 拇指上扎了根刺. *Opinions are ~ed now.* 意见现在纷纭了. ~ **bar** 〔英〕马车的横档. ~ **deck**【军】防弹片甲板. ~ **netting** (军舰的)弹片防御网. ~ **party**【政】分裂小派别. **~proof** 防弹片的.
splin•ter•y [ˈsplintri] *a.* 裂片(似)的,多片状的; 易碎裂的; 碎裂的; 粗糙的(岩石等).
Split [split] *n.* 斯普利特〔南斯拉夫港市〕.
split [split] *vt.* *(split)* ①劈开,切开,割裂,扯裂; 剖分. ②使分裂,使分离; 分解; 分配. ③【海】扯破(帆). — *vi.* ①裂开,劈开; 分离,分开. ②(党派等)分裂. ③分担; 分享. ④〔口〕大笑. ⑤〔口〕逃跑,开小差; 走开. ⑥〔美俚〕分赃. ⑦告密. *~ the grapefruit in two.* 把柚子剖成两半. *~ a compound into its elements.* 把一个化合物分解成元素. *Mother said her headache was ~ting.* 妈妈说她头痛欲裂. *The club ~ on the journey question into two groups.* 俱乐部在外出旅行的问题分裂为两派. ***be ~ by parties and factions*** 分裂成一些派别. ***~ a bottle of wine*** 〔口〕两人分喝一瓶葡萄酒. ***~ across*** 分裂成二. ***~ away*** 分离. ***~ fair*** 〔俚〕讲真话. ***~ off*** 劈开; 分开; 分裂出来. ***~ on*** 〔俚〕告密,出卖(朋友). ***~ on [upon] a rock*** 搁浅,触礁; 遭遇意外灾难; 意见分歧, 不和. ***~ one's infinitives*** 在动词原形和 to 之间插入副词〔例: Allow me to heartily congratulate you〕. ***~ one's sides*** 捧腹大笑. ***~ one's vote [*** 〔美〕***ticket]*** 同时投几个党的候选人的票. ***~ open*** 裂开,劈开,绷破,爆裂. ***~ straws [words, hairs]*** 作过分仔细的烦琐分析〔考查〕; 详细区分. ***~ the difference*** 互相让步, 折中; 妥协. ***~ up*** (使)分裂,(使)分离,〔美俚〕吵架, 离婚. ***~ with sb.*** 〔俚〕和某人闹翻; 同某物决裂. — *a.* 裂开的, 劈开的; 分离的, 分裂的. *a ~ anode* 双瓣阳极. *a ~ antenna* 隙缝天线. *~ order*【商】散分定货. *a ~ second [minute]* 片刻,一转眼的功夫. *~ cable*【电】分股电缆. *~ foot* 双层袜底. — *n.* ①劈裂,分裂; 裂缝, 罅隙; 裂片,破片,碎片; (劈开的)柳条; 薄板; 薄皮. ②分裂, 分化; 派别. ③〔美俚〕(往往是赃物的)份儿. ④【矿】分裂通气,分裂气流. ⑤〔俚〕密告者, 奸细; 便衣警察. ⑥半杯酒; 半瓶汽水. ⑦〔*pl.*〕(劈)一字腿(两腿左右成一直线伸开坐下的表演),劈叉. ⑧水果片,冰淇淋,糖浆等做成的甜食. *That may lead to a serious ~ in our class.* 那可能导致我们班的严重分裂. ***(at) full ~*** 拼命,飞快地. ***run like ~*** 〔美〕飞一样地跑. ~ **gear**【机】拼合齿轮. ~ **infinitive**【语法】分离不定式〔在 to 和动词原形之间有副词插入的结构〕. **~-level** *a.*【建】错层式的. **~-off** ①分裂; 分裂出去的东西〔派别〕. ②母公司向子公司的部分股本转移. ~ **pea** 〔美〕剖开的干豌豆. ~ **personality** 人格分裂〔精神分裂症的俗称〕. ~ **pin**【机】开尾销. ~ **reel** (一卷中收入两三部短片的)部分影片. ~ **shift** 〔美〕(中间间歇比通常长久的)两班制. ~ **ticket [vote]** 〔美〕(一部分投给反对党候选人的)分裂选票. **~-up** ①分裂; (股本的)分散转移. ②〔美俚〕吵架; 离婚.
split•ter [ˈsplitə] *n.* ①劈(切、割)的(工)人. ②爱作无谓的分析的人. ③劈裂机,分离器,分解器,分裂机.
split•ting [ˈsplitiŋ] *a.* ①要爆裂似的; 剧烈的(疼痛等). ②〔口〕飞也似的, 极快的. ③〔口〕笑痛肚皮的. — *n.* 【物】裂距; 分裂. *at a ~ pace* 飞也似地. *a ~ laugh* 大笑. *a ~ attack* 突破攻势.
split•tism [ˈsplitizəm] *n.* 分裂主义.
splodge [splɔdʒ] *n., vt.* = splotch.
splore [splɔː] *n.* 〔苏格兰〕①闹饮; 嬉戏. ②大混乱.
splosh [splɔʃ] *n.* ①〔口〕泼下的大量的水. ②〔俚〕金钱. — *vt., vi.* 泼,溅. — *ad.* 劈劈啪啪地. **-y** *a.*
splotch [splɔtʃ] *n.* 污点, 斑点. *a ~ of blue paint* 蓝色油漆的污迹. — *vt.* 弄脏; 沾污.
splotch•y [ˈsplɔtʃi] *a.* *(-i•er; -i•est)* 弄脏了的, 有污点的,有斑点的.
splurge [spləːdʒ] *n.* 夸示, 炫耀, 卖弄; 摆阔; 挥霍. —*vi.* ①夸示,卖弄,炫耀. ②*vt.* 挥霍. *~ it* 〔美〕生活奢华; 任意挥霍. *The victory meeting should be one without any ~.* 庆功会应该开成一个毫不炫耀摆阔的会. *Millionaires swarmed into Nice to ~ billions during the summer holidays.* 暑假时, 百万富翁们群趋尼斯挥霍了亿万巨款. **-r** *n.*

splut·ter [ˈsplʌtə] *v., n.* = sputter.
Spode [spəud] *n.* 斯波德陶瓷〔得名于英国陶瓷匠 *Josiah Spode* (1754—1827)〕.
spod·u·mene [ˈspɔdʒuˌmiːn] *n.*【地】锂辉石.
spof·fish [ˈspɔfiʃ], **spof·fy** [ˈspɔfi] *a.*〔英俚〕爱管闲事的；大惊小怪的；小题大做的.
spoil [spɔil] *vt.* *(~ed, spoilt)* ①〔*p.p.* 用 *~ed*〕〔古〕抢劫,掠夺,强夺 *(of)*. ②损怀,弄坏,糟蹋；把(酒、肉等)放坏. ③娇养坏,惯坏,溺爱坏,宠坏(孩子等)；奉承. ④妨碍,破坏(兴趣等). ⑤〔俚〕杀害,伤害.— *vi.* ①(食物等)变坏,糟蹋；腐败. ②抢劫,掠夺. *Our holidays were spoilt by bad weather.* 我们的假期给坏天气毁了. *~ a story in the telling* 笨嘴说坏了(好)故事. *a ~ed child* 惯坏了的孩子. *a spoilt child of fortune* 任性的人,唯我独尊的自私者. *The rain ~ed the hay crop.* 这场雨使种的牧草毁坏了. *Meat will soon ~ in warm weather.* 天热肉会很快地变得腐坏的. ***be ~ing for a fight*** 一心想打架；很想显一显本事. ***~ sb.'s appetite*** 弄坏胃口.— *n.* ①抢劫,掠夺,强夺. ②掠夺物；〔常 *pl.*〕战利品；猎获物；(搜集家的)获得物. ③〔常 *pl.*〕〔美〕(胜利政党分给党员的)官位,职位. ④弃泥,掘出的泥土. ⑤废品,次品. *the ~s of war* 战利品. *the ~ of office*〔美〕猎官,追求官职. ***~s system***〔美〕(胜利后分与党员、支持者物质利益和职位的)政党分肥制. **~sport** 妨碍人家欢娱的人,扫人兴的人,插嘴阻挠的人. **-er** ①掠夺者；破坏者；溺爱者. ②【火箭】阻流板,扰流器.
spoil·age [ˈspɔilidʒ] *n.* ①损坏；(食物等)腐坏. ②损坏物；【印】印坏的纸张. ③因损坏所受的损失.
spoils·man [ˈspɔilzmən] *n.* *(pl. -men)*〔美〕①为个人利益而为某政党效劳的人. ②赞成政党分肥制的人.
spoils·mon·ger [ˈspɔilzmʌŋgə] *n.*〔美〕卖官鬻爵的政党分肥制政客.
spoilt [spɔilt] spoil 的过去式及过去分词.
spoke[1] [spəuk] *n.* ①(车轮的)辐条. ②【船】舵轮把柄. ③扶梯棍梯级,梯磴. ④(下坡时防止车轮猛转的)木棒(等)煞车. ***put a ~ in sb.'s wheel***〔口〕阻挠〔破坏〕某人的计划.— *vt.* ①给…装上辐条. ②用木棒煞车煞住. ③阻挠,妨碍. *We might easily ~ their scheme if we choose.* 我们要是愿意干的话,可以很容易地阻碍他们计划的进行. ~ **wise** *ad.* 象(车轮上的)辐条一样地,象辐射状.
spoke[2] speak 的过去式.
spo·ken [ˈspəukən] speak 的过去分词. — *a.* ①口头讲的 *(opp.* written*)*；口语的 *(opp.* literary*)*. ②〔构成复合词〕口头…的,说话…的. *a ~ message* 口信. *pleasant-~* 说话中听的. ~ **language** 口语. ~ **title**【影】对白字幕.
spoke·shave [ˈspəukʃeiv] *n.* (制造车辐等用的)辐刀；【机】辐刨片.
spokes·man [ˈspəuksmən] *n.* *(pl. -men)* 发言人；代言人.
spokes·per·son [ˈspəukspəːsn] *n.* 发言人,代言人；辩护士.
spokes·wo·man [ˈspəuksˌwumən] *n.* *(pl. spokeswomen)* 女发言人,女代言人.
spo·li·a o·pi·ma [ˈspəuliə əuˈpaimə]〔L.〕古罗马将军单骑与敌将决斗所夺得的武器；〔喻〕无上的成功或荣誉.
spo·li·ate [ˈspəulieit] *vt., vi.* 抢劫,掠夺.
spo·li·a·tion [ˌspəuliˈeiʃən] *n.* ①(尤指交战国对中立国船只的)抢劫,掠夺. ②【宗】(教堂俸禄的)冒领；〔美〕腐败,腐朽. ③【法】(文件、票据等的)销毁,窜改. **-a·tor** *n.* **-a·tory** *a.* 抢劫的,掠夺的,毁灭文件票据的,窜改文件票据的.
spon·da·ic [spɔnˈdeiik] *a.* (诗句)扬扬格的.
spon·dee [ˈspɔndiː] *n.* (诗句的)扬扬格.
spon·du·lic(k)s, spondu·lix [spɔnˈdjuːliks] *n.*〔*pl.*〕〔美俚〕钱,钞票.
spon·dyl·ar·thri·tis [ˌspɔdilˌɑːˈθraitis] *n.*【医】(脊)椎关节炎.
spon·dyl(e) [ˈspɔndil] *n.*【解】脊椎,椎关节.
spon·dy·li·tis [ˌspɔndiˈlaitis] *n.*【医】脊椎炎.
sponge [spʌndʒ] *n.* ①海绵. ②海绵动物；海绵状的东西〔如泡沫塑料等〕；金属绵. ③加有发酵粉的生面包；海绵布丁,蛋糕. ④【医】外科用纱布,棉球. ⑤枪刷. ⑥(擦身用)海绵揩. ⑦〔古、美口〕食客,寄生者,吃闲饭的. ⑧一堆蟹子. ⑨〔俚〕大量的人. ⑩知识丰富的人. ***have a ~ down*** 洗一个用海绵擦洗的澡. ***pass the [a] ~ over*** 抹去,勾销；忘却(旧怨),不再提起. ***throw [toss, chuck] up the ~***【拳击】扔掉擦身用的海绵认输；〔口〕认输；投降.— *vt.* ①用海绵揩〔擦〕；消除(债务等),忘却(往事等) *(out; off; away)*；用海绵擦洗 *(over; down)*；用海绵弄湿；用海绵吸 *(up)*. ②占…的便宜,厚着脸骗吃(饭等)；乞讨,骗取,敲诈.— *vi.* ①(海绵等)吸收. ②采集海绵. ③敲诈. ④寄食,依赖他人过日子 *(on; upon)*. *Please ~ my back with alcohol.* 请用酒精擦擦我的背. *Every evening Tom would go to the White Bear to ~ drinks.* 每天晚上汤姆都到白熊酒馆去讨酒吃. *A young-man like you shouldn't ~ on your uncle.* 象你这样的小伙子不该寄食在叔叔家里. ~ **bath** 海绵擦浴. ~ **cake** 海绵(松)蛋糕. ~ **cloth** ①【纺】海绵布. ②(熨衣用的)润湿布. ~ **cucumber,** ~ **gourd**【植】丝瓜. ~ **rubber** 海绵状橡皮. ~ **tree,**【植】金合欢.
spong·er [ˈspʌŋdʒə] *n.* ①用海绵擦洗的人. ②海绵采集人；海绵采集船. ③寄生食客,依赖他人生活的人,吸血鬼；寄生虫.
spong·i·form [ˈspʌŋdʒiˈfɔːm] *a.* 海绵组织的,海绵状的.
spon·gin [ˈspʌndʒin] *n.*【化】海绵硬蛋白.
spong·i·ness [ˈspʌŋdʒinis] *n.* 海绵状,海绵质.
spong·ing-house [ˈspɔndʒiŋhaus] *n.*【英史】负债人拘留所.
spon·gi·o·pi·lin(e) [ˈspɔndʒiəupilin] *n.*【医】(敷药用)海绵毡.
spong·y [ˈspʌndʒi] *a.* *(-gi·er; -gi·est)* ①海绵状的,海绵质的. ②多孔的,吸水的. ③松软有弹性的. **-gi·ly** *ad.* **-gi·ness** *n.*
spon·sion [ˈspɔnʃən] *n.* ①【法】(为他人所作的)担保,保证. ②【国际法】未经受权的代表所作的约定〔行为〕.
spon·son [ˈspɔnsn] *n.* ①(舷侧)突出部. ②(军舰,坦克的)突出炮座. ③(水上飞机的)翼梢浮筒.
spon·sor [ˈspɔnsə] *n.* ①【宗】教父,教母. ②发起者,主办者,倡议者. ③(船只的)命名人；保证人. ④在广播〔电视〕作广告节目的资助人. *a ~ for a class tea party* 本班茶话会的发起人.— *vt.* ①发起,主办,倡议. ②做…的保人,担保. ③做广告节目的资助人. *The meeting was ~ed by five departments.* 会议是五个系倡议召开的. *a ~ed programme* 插有广告的广播〔电视〕节目. **-ship** ①教父〔母〕身分. ②保证人身分. ③发起,主办；支援；倡议.
spon·so·ri·al [spɔnˈsɔːriəl] *a.* 保证人的；教父的,教母的；主办人的.
spon·ta·ne·i·ty [ˌspɔntəˈniːiti] *n.* ①自发(性)；自生. ②〔*pl.*〕自发行为〔行动〕.
spon·ta·ne·ous [spɔnˈteinjəs, -niəs] *a.* ①自发的,一时冲动的. ②天然发生的(电等)；自生的,天然产生的(草木等),不依赖人工的. ③本能的,自动的. ④(文体)自然流畅的. *~ expression of gratitude* 自发的感激的表示. *~ offer of help* 自动提供的帮助. *~ growth of wood* 树木的天然生长. *~ recovery from indigestion* 消化不良症的自然痊愈. *a ~ writer* 文笔自然流畅的作家. *~ combustion* 自燃. *~ generation* 自然发生. **-ly** *ad.* **-ness** *n.*
spon·toon [spɔnˈtuːn] *n.* 短矛,戟；〔美方〕警棍.
spoof [spuːf]〔俚〕*n.* ①玩笑性的哄骗,戏弄. ②幽默的讽刺诗〔文章〕.— *a.* 假的,扯谎的,骗人的.— *vt.* ①

哄骗，戏弄．②开…的玩笑．— *vi.* 欺骗，哄骗，开玩笑．*Nobody likes those clumsy ~s of yours.* 谁都不喜欢你那拙笨的玩笑．*Don't let them ~ you.* 不要让他们哄骗你了．**-er** *n.* **-ing** *n.* ①哄骗．②【军】电子欺骗．

spook [spu:k] *n.* 〔口〕①鬼．②〔美俚〕出没无常行踪古怪的人〔精神病人，密探等〕．③〔美俚〕代笔者．④〔美俚〕黑人．— *vt.* ①鬼怪般地出没于．②惊吓．— *vi.* (因受惊吓而)逃窜．*At night, he would creep out of the house like a ~.* 夜间，他常常象幽灵一般地从家里偷偷地出来．*When our car drove forward, the deer ~ed.* 我们的汽车向前开动时，鹿群吓得逃散了．

spook·ish, spook·y [ˈspu:kiʃ, -i] *a.* ①鬼似的．②有点怪的，不可思议的．③稍微地有些神经质的，(容易)害怕的．*Did your ~ brother take his night stroll yesterday?* 你那个鬼似的哥哥昨天又在夜里散步了吗？*This mule is rather ~.* 这匹骡子很容易受惊．

spool [spu:l] *n.* ①【纺】有边筒子；轴线；线管，线板，线框；短管；卷筒．②(胶片，录音带等的)卷轴；卷轴状物品．③卷络的数量〔长度〕．— *vt.* 绕在卷轴上；【纺】络纱，络筒．*S- the film for use.* 把胶卷卷上待用．~ **cotton** 木纱团，线团．**-er**【纺】络纱机，筒子车；绕卷轴〔筒子〕工人．**-ing** *n.*【纺】络纱，络筒．

spoon[1] [spu:n] *n.* ①匙，调羹．②一匙的量．③匙状物；匙桨．④【杓球】匙棒，三号高尔夫球棒．⑤挖土机，泥铲．⑥(钓鱼用)匙状假饵 (= ~ bait). *It takes a long ~ to sup with him.* 和他打交道要小心．*a wooden ~*【史】末席．~ *bread* 〔美〕(用匙吃的)湿软奶蛋面包．***be born with a silver [wooden] ~ in one's mouth*** 生在富有〔贫穷〕的人家．***be past the ~*** 已经不是孩子(是大人了)．***hang up the ~*** 〔俚〕死．***make a ~ or spoil a horn*** 不计成功失败；破釜沉舟，背城借一．***stick one's ~ in the wall*** 〔俚〕死．— *vt., vi.* ①拿匙舀，舀取 *(into; off; out; up)*．②将球轻轻向上打去．③用匙状假饵钓鱼．④〔美俚〕面对背地侧身贴着睡．*You're to ~ the tomatoes into the jars, Mary and Jack is to ~ out bowls of porridge.* 玛丽，你把西红柿舀进罐子里，贾克用匙子舀粥．~ **bait** 匙钩，匙状假饵〔附装在钓丝上用以诱鱼游近的金属片〕．~**bill** *n.*【鸟】篦鹭；阔嘴鸭．~**-fashion** *ad.* 面对背地匙一样地(侧身贴着)．~**-fed** *a.* ①用匙喂的(小孩、病人等)．②娇养的．③受到补助金等保护的(产业等)．④受填鸭式教育的；无独立思考〔行动〕能力的，被当做孩子看待的；〔美〕奢华的．~ **food**, ~ **meat** 流体食物；汤类；面包粥．~ **net** 捞网．**-ful** *n.* 一匙的量，一满匙．

spoon[2] [spu:n] *n.* 〔俚〕傻子，呆子；迷恋者，痴情汉．— *vi., vt.* ①痴爱，迷恋．②〔美〕向…求爱．③〔口〕谈情说爱，动手动脚．***be ~s on*** 痴爱，迷恋．***on the ~*** 迷恋着．

spoon·drift [ˈspu:ndrift] *n.* = spindrift.

spoon·er·ism [ˈspu:nərizəm] *n.* 首音调换法〔如将 well-oiled bicycle 俏皮地改成 well-boiled icicle 之类；有时并非故意而系首音误置〕．

spoon·y, spoon·ey [ˈspu:ni] 〔俚〕 *a.* ***(-i·er; -i·est)*** ①傻气的；愚蠢的．②过于多愁善感的．③痴恋的，迷恋的 *(on; upon)*．— *n.* ①傻子．②痴情汉．**-i·ly** *ad.* **-i·ness** *n.*

spoor [spuə] *n.* (野兽的)脚迹，臭迹．— *vt., vi.* 跟着脚迹〔臭迹〕追．**-er** *n.* 跟踪者．

spo·rad·ic, -i·cal [spəˈrædik, -ikəl] *a.* 不时〔个别〕发生的；分散的；零星的；特发的，散发的．*a ~ case* 散发病例．*a ~ disease* 单发病．~ *fighting.* 零星战斗．*sporadic mutation*【生】自然突变．**-cal·ly** *ad.* **-cal·ness** *n.*

spo·ran·gi·al [spɔ:ˈrændʒiəl] *a.*【生】孢子囊的；孢蒴的．

spo·ran·gi·o·spore [spəˈrændʒiəspɔ:] *n.*【生】孢囊孢子．

spo·ran·gi·um [spəˈrændʒiəm] *n.* *(pl.* **-gia** [-dʒiə]*)*【生】孢子囊；(苔藓植物的)孢蒴．

spore [spɔ: spɔə] *n.* ①【生】孢子；胚种．②(事物的)根源，原因．— *vi.* 长孢子．~ **case** 芽孢〔孢子〕囊；孢蒴．~ **fruit** 子实体；子囊果．

spo·ri·ci·dal [ˌspɔ:riˈsaidl] *a.* 杀孢子的．

spo·ri·cide [ˈspɔ:risaid] *n.* 杀孢子剂．

spo·rif·er·ous [spɔ:ˈrifərəs] *a.*【生】带孢子的．

spo·ro·carp [ˈspɔ:rəˌkɑ:p] *n.*【植】孢子果；子实体．

spo·ro·cyst [ˈspɔ:rəˈsist] *n.* ①【植】孢子被．②【动】孢子囊，胞蚴．**-tic** *a.*

spo·ro·gen·e·sis [ˌspɔ:rəˈdʒenisis] *n.*【生】①孢子发生．②胞子形成．**-gen·ic** [-ˈdʒenik] *a.* **-rog·e·nous** [-ˈrɔdʒinəs] *a.*

spo·ro·ge·ny [spəˈrɔdʒini] *n.* (= sporogenesis).

spo·ro·go·ni·um [ˌspɔ:rəˈgəuniəm] *n.* *(pl.* **-ni·a** [-ə]*)*【植】(苔藓的)孢子体．

spo·rog·o·ny [spɔ:ˈrɔgəni] *n.*【生】孢子发生，孢子生殖，孢子形成．

spo·ro·phore [ˈspɔ:rəˌfɔ:] *n.*【植】孢囊柱；子实体．**-phor·ic, -roph·o·rous** [-ˈfɔrik, -ˈrɔfərəs] *a.*

spo·ro·phyll [ˈspɔ:rəˌfil] *n.*【生】胞子叶．**-phyll·a·ry** [-ˈfiləri] *a.*

spo·ro·phyte [ˈspɔ:rəˌfait] *n.*【生】孢子体．**-phyt·ic** [-ˈfitik] *a.*

spo·ro·zo·an [ˌspɔ:rəˈzəuən] *n.*【生】孢子虫类 *(Sporozoa)* 的虫 (= sporozoon). — *a.* 孢子虫类的 (= sporozoic, sporozoal).

spo·ro·zo·ite [ˌspɔ:rəˈzəuait] *n.*【生】孢子虫，孢子体，子孢子．

spor·ran [ˈspɔrən] *n.* (苏格兰人系在裙前做装饰的)毛皮袋．

sport [spɔ:t] *n.* ①娱乐，消遣；游戏，玩耍．②〔常 *pl.*〕运动，运动比赛；打猎，赛马，钓鱼，游泳(等)．③〔*pl.*〕运动会．④闹着玩儿，玩笑；戏谑；嘲笑，嘲笑对象，玩弄品，玩物．⑤= sportsman；有体育道德精神的人；运动员．⑥〔美俚〕讨人喜欢的人．⑦爱漂亮〔吃喝玩乐〕的人；好色之徒，赌徒．⑧【生】突变；【植】芽变．⑨变态或畸形的人或动植物．*Fishing affords great ~ to us.* 钓鱼使我们有很好的消遣．*I had fine ~ with my new skates.* 我穿着新冰鞋溜冰玩得痛快极了．*It is fine ~ to sail in a boat* 驾着小舟游览是很好的娱乐．*What ~!* 真有趣呀！*athletic ~s* 体育运动，运动会．*the ~ of kings* 〔美〕赛马；打猎．*a ~ of terms [wit, words]* 双关话，俏皮话．*the ~ of the fortune* 被命运玩弄的人．*the ~ of nature* 突变种，畸形．*He is an old ~.* 他是一个有趣的人〔爽快人〕．*Be a good ~!* (象运动家一样)努力干！***for [in]~*** 闹着玩地．***have good ~*** 打了一次好猎〔猎获甚多〕．***make ~ of*** 戏弄，愚弄．***say in ~*** 说着玩儿．— *vt.* ①〔口〕炫耀，夸示．②【生】突变为，芽变出．③〔英〕关门〔表示无暇接待来客〕．④玩过(时候)，浪费．— *vi.* ①运动，打猎(等)．②玩要，游戏；嬉戏．③闹玩儿，开玩笑．④【生】发生突变，【植】芽变．*James proudly ~s his new watch* 詹姆斯骄傲地夸示他的新表．~ *a moustache* 捻弄胡子．*Grandpa is ~ing with us.* 爷爷在和我们开玩笑呢．~ *the Union Jack* 挂出英国国旗．~ ***on the cinders*** 〔美〕赛跑，参加径赛．~ ***one's oak [timber, door]*** 〔英大学生俚〕锁上门〔谢绝来客〕．~ ***silk*** 穿(骑师)绸衫；做骑师；(骑师或马)参加赛马．— *a.* 〔常作 ~s〕适于户外运动的，运动(比赛)用的，户外穿的(裙子等)．*a ~s shirt* 运动衬衣．~*s requisites* 运动用具．*a ~s editor* 体育栏编辑．*a ~s page* 体育版．~**(s) car** 赛车〔一指比赛用汽车；通常用来指称操纵灵活的高速双座汽车〕．~**s cast** *n., v.* 〔美，无〕(播送)体育运动节目．~ **caster** *n.* 体育节目广播员．~**s dom** 〔美〕运动界．~**s jacket** 猎装〔户外活动或非正式场合穿着的粗花呢男上衣〕．~**s wear** 运动服装．~**s writer** 体育运动专栏作家．

sport·ful [ˈspɔ:tful] *a.* ①游戏的，玩要的．②有趣的，

愉快的,高兴的. ③开玩笑的. **-ly** *ad.* **-ness** *n.*

sport·ing [ˈspɔːtiŋ] *a.* ①运动的,有关体育运动的,象运动家的; 喜欢运动的; 喜欢打猎的; 运动用的. ②有体育道德的,光明正大的,公平的. ③放荡的, 好赌的; 投机的,赌博性质的. ④【生】突变的; 芽变的; 畸形的. — *n.* 运动, 比赛; 打猎. *a ~ section* (报纸的)体育运动栏. *a ~ editor* 体育运动栏新闻编辑. *~ goods* 〔美〕体育运动用具. *the ~ world* 体育运动界. *a ~ man* 体育运动家; 打猎者; 赌徒. *~ conduct* 正大光明的行为. *a ~ scope* 望远镜. *a ~ thing to do* 危险工作. *a ~ chance* 冒险. *~* **girl (woman)** 妓女. *~* **house** 〔美,口〕妓院; 赌场. *~* **page** (报纸的)体育版. **-ly** *ad.*

spor·tive [ˈspɔːtiv] *a.* ①嬉戏的; 游戏的; 闹着玩的; 愉快的,高兴的,玩乐的. ②运动[打猎、赛马(等)]的. ③好色的. ④【生】突[芽]变的; 〔古〕色情的. **-ly** *ad.* **-ness** *n.*

sports·man [ˈspɔːtsmən] *n.* *(pl. -men)* ①运动家, 运动员; 爱好运动的人(如打猎,钓鱼). ②有运动员品质[道德]的人; 直爽[正大光明]的人. ③〔美〕赌徒. *~***like** *a.* 象运动家的, 合乎运动员道德精神的; 直爽的. **-ly** *ad.* **-ship** *n.* 运动员精神; 运动员风格; 体育[运动]道德; 正大光明,直爽; 打猎[赛马(等)]技术.

sports·wom·an [ˈspɔːtswumən] *n.* *(pl. -wom·en)* 女运动员,女运动爱好者,女运动家.

sport·sy [ˈspɔːtsi] *a.* ①运动时穿的. ②运动服般的.

sport·y [ˈspɔːti] *a.* *(-i·er; -i·est)* 〔口〕①运动员一样的. ②有体育道德精神的, 正大光明的, 直爽的. ③(服装)花哨的, 华美的. **-i·ly** *ad.* **-i·ness** *n.*

spor·u·lar [ˈspɔrjulə] *a.* 小孢子的.

spor·u·late [ˈspɔrjuleit] *vi.* 形成孢子.

spor·u·la·tion [ˌspɔːrjuˈleiʃən] *n.* 【生】孢子形成.

spor·ule [ˈspɔrjuːl] *n.* 【生】(小)孢子.

SPOT [spɔt] (= satellite positioning and tracking) 人造卫星定位及跟踪.

spot [spɔt] *n.* ①斑点; 污点; 疵点, 缺点. ②地点; 场所, 现场; 部位; 位置; 职位; 地位. ③处境(尤指困境、窘境). ④一小片, 少量, 少许; 〔口〕一杯酒. ⑤〔*pl.*〕【交易所】现货. ⑥〔美俚〕小额纸币〔常与数词连用〕. ⑦〔美俚〕非法酒店; 没有执照的酒吧; 夜总会. ⑧〔美俚〕舞台聚光灯 = spotlight. ⑨〔常接数词〕短期徒刑. ⑩【台球】〔特指红球〕最初放置处, 置球点 (= ~ -ball). ⑪〔俚〕目标. ⑫【鸟】头上有黑斑的黑尾家鸽. ⑬太阳的黑点, 肺部等处的阴影. ⑭【鱼】黄鲻. ⑮〔*pl.*〕金钱豹. ⑯【无】给某一节目指定的时间; 广播中插入的简短公告[广告]. *solar ~s = ~s in the sun* 太阳黑点; 〔喻〕白玉微瑕. *John's face was covered with ~s* 约翰的脸上全是雀斑. *a tender [sore] ~* 容易触痛之处, 不愿别人提起的事情[问题]. *the meeting on the ~* 现场会议. *a ~ of leave* 短暂的休假. *Let's take a ~ of lunch* 吃一点午餐. ***have a ~*** 喝一杯. ***hit the high ~s*** 〔美俚〕走马看花地浏览; 提纲挈领, 概括要点. ***hit the ~*** 〔口〕正合要求; 恰到好处. ***in a ~*** 〔美俚〕处在困境中. ***in ~s*** 〔美〕时时; 在某几点上,到某程度. ***knock the ~s off [out of]*** 〔俚〕彻底击败,超过,凌驾. ***on (upon) the ~*** 当场,在现场; 立刻; 【商】用现货[现款]; (人)准备妥当,没有疏忽; (射击等)姿势好; 〔美俚〕处境危险的; 注定要被暗杀的; 【运】在困难环境中苦斗的. ***price on ~*** 现货价格; 现金售价. ***put one's finger on sb.'s weak ~*** 指出某人(性格等上)的缺点. ***put (sb.) on the ~*** 〔美俚〕决定暗杀(某人). ***touch the (tender) ~*** 碰到痛处. ***upon the ~*** = on the ~. ***without ~ or stain*** 毫无缺点. — *vt.* ①弄上斑点; 弄上污点, 弄脏, 污辱. ②散布, 点缀, 布置. ③在…上用点子作记号. ④〔口〕认出, 发见, 找到, 预先认准、猜中(谁会在比赛中获胜等), 看出, 记认(惯犯等). ⑤准确地定出…的位置, 使准确地打中目标. ⑥把…置于需要(或指定)的地点上. ⑦使处于聚光灯下, 集中照射. ⑧把节目排在特定的时间. ⑨除去污点 (*out*). ⑩比赛中给对方以礼让(如下棋让两个棋子). ⑪〔美俚〕暗杀, 杀死. *Lookouts were spotted all along the coast.* 沿岸一带都布置了监视哨. *I spotted him at once as an American.* 我一见就看出他是个美国人. *calicoes ~ted with beautiful flowers* 满幅美丽花朵的印花布. *Everybody ~s the Fighting Irish as the winner.* 人人都猜准诺特丹大学会得胜. *We've spotted the enemy battery position.* 我们已经测定敌炮连阵地. *He knows how to ~ genial smiles on the audience.* 他知道怎样向观众们投送亲切的微笑. *Our performance is spotted at 10.* 我们的表演排定在十点钟上场. — *vi.* ①沾上污点; 给污点弄脏; 易染污点, 易脏. ②【军】从空中侦察敌方目标. ③〔口〕下小雨. *This kind of cloth tends to ~ in the rain.* 这种布容易在雨中弄脏. *We spent the whole morning ~ting* 我们花了整个早上侦察敌方目标. —*a.* 〔只作定语〕①现场的. ②现货的; 付现的; 专做现货生意的. ③插在电台[电视]节目之间播送的. ④局限于某些项目的; 任选的; 抽样的. *~ coverage of the parliamentary debate* 议会辩论的现场采访. *a ~ transaction* 现货交易 (*with*). *~ cotton* 现货棉花. *~ delivery* 现货交付; *a ~ sensational news* 一桩插在电视节目中广播的耸人听闻的消息. *~ announcement (broadcasting)* 插在节目中的公告 [广播]. *~* **answer** 当机立断的回答. *~* **ball** 【台球】置球点上的球; 有黑点的白球 *~* **cash** 【商】货到即付的现金. *~* **check** 抽样调查; 抽查. *(a ~ check on prices* 对物价的抽查*)*. *~***-check** *vt., vi.* 抽查, 抽样. *~***light** ①*n.* 聚光灯; (汽车上的)反光灯, 探路灯; 【视】点光; 〔喻〕(世人的)视听, 注意. ② *v.* 把光线集中在…, 使显著(*a ~light hunter* 〔美剧〕(演剧时)好到舞台中央去 [好出风头]的演员). *~* **news** 最新消息. *~* **pass** 【体】定点长传球. *~* **test** 当场试测. *~* **welding** 点焊.

spot·less [ˈspɔtlis] *a.* ①纯洁的; 没有污点的; 无瑕疵的. ②极其清洁的. **-ly** *ad.* **-ness** *n.*

spot·ted [ˈspɔtid] *a.* ①有斑点的. ②有污点[缺点]的. ③削去树皮打上记号的. ④〔口〕受注意的. *~* **adder** 【动】①黑边乳蛇. ②黄背锦蛇. *~* **dog** 〔俚〕葡萄干布丁. *~* **fever** 脑脊髓膜炎; 斑疹伤寒; 落基山热. *~* **girl** 〔美俚〕马戏团里的长颈鹿. *~* **sandpiper** 【动】斑点矶鹞. **-ness** *n.*

spot·ter [ˈspɔtə] *n.* ①〔美〕(对雇工等的) 秘密监视人; 私人雇佣的侦探. ②【机】测位仪; 定心钻. ③【军】监靶员; 弹着及爆炸点观测员; 弹着观察机[气球]. ④【铁路】检路器. ⑤【空】观察机, 侦察机; 敌机监视员. ⑥【无】搜索雷达, 警戒雷达站. ⑦把物件放到指定地点上的人[机器], 指定货物放置地点的人.

spot·ti·ness [ˈspɔtinis] *n.* 斑点多, 污点多; 有斑疹.

spot·ting [ˈspɔtiŋ] *n.* 配置, 装设; 落弹观测.

spot·ty [ˈspɔti] *a.* *(-ti·er; -ti·est)* ①多斑点的. ②尽是污点的; (质量)参差不一的, 不规则的. *In his youth, Wang received only a ~ secondary education.* 王年轻时只受过不正规的中等教育. *Medical care in those hospitals is rather ~.* 那些医院的医疗质量参差不齐. **-i·ly** *ad.*

spous·al [ˈspauzəl] *n., a.* 〔常 *pl.*〕 结婚, 婚礼(的).

spouse [spauz] *n.* 配偶, 夫, 妻; 〔*pl.*〕 夫妇. — *vt.* 〔古〕嫁, 娶, 和…结婚.

spout [spaut] *vt.* ①喷出, (鲸)喷水. ②滔滔不绝地讲, 吟诵, 朗诵. ③〔俚〕典押. — *vi.* ①喷出, 喷射. ②高谈阔论. *Water ~ed from the break of the pipe.* 水从管子的裂口喷出. — *n.* ①喷管, 喷嘴; 喷口; (茶壶等的)嘴; (鲸类的)喷水孔. ②水柱, 喷流. ③(装谷类时用的)架槽, 斜槽. ④【冶】斜槽; 流出槽. ⑤【气】龙卷. ⑥(过去当铺传送东西用的)筒子; 〔俚〕当铺. *Little Tony broke the ~ off the teapot.* 小唐尼把茶壶嘴打下来了. ***put [shove, pop] up the ~*** 拿去当押. *~* ***opinions*** 哇啦哇啦地提意见. ***up the ~*** 在当押中; 〔喻〕经济拮据, 穷困. **-er** *n.* 喷油井; 捕鲸船; 说话滔滔不绝的人; 照管流出槽的工人. **-less** *a.* 无喷嘴的.

S.P.Q.R. = 〔L.〕 *Senatus Populusque Romanus* (= the

Senate and the People); small profits, quick returns 薄利多得.

SPR = Swimming Pool Reactor 浸没式反应堆.

sprad·dle [ˈsprædl] *vt., vi.* ***(-dled; -dling)*** 〔方,口〕叉开腿站立[行走].

sprag [spræg] *n.* ①(防止车轮滑动的)制轮木. ②【矿】煤面防护柱. *bottom* ~ 底部支撑; *face* ~ 工作面斜支柱.

sprain [sprein] *n.* 扭伤. — *vt.* 扭,扭伤,挨伤. ~ *one's wrist* 扭伤手腕.

sprang [spræŋ] spring 的过去式.

sprat [spræt] *n.* ①【鱼】西鲱. ②瘦子;小个子;年轻人,小人物,小孩子;〔英俚〕= sixpence. ***Jack*** ~ 矮子,侏儒. ***throw [fling away] a ~ to catch a herring [whale]*** 用小虾钓大鱼,用小本赚大钱;抛砖引玉. —*vi.* ***(sprat·ted, sprat·ting)*** 捕西鲱.

sprawl [sprɔːl] *vt.* ①懒散(或拙笨地)伸开(手足). ②使蔓生,使散漫地伸开;潦草地书写. —*vi.* ①手脚伸开(成大字形)躺[坐]着. ②(难看地)爬行. ③(陆地、蔓藤等)不规则地延伸,蔓延;(建筑物)无计划地延伸;(字体军队)向四面八方散开;不整齐,散漫. *In our garden, bushes are allowed to* ~ *as they will.* 在我们园子里,灌木丛爱怎么蔓延就怎么蔓延. *Father was* ~*ed out in a sofa.* 爸爸手足伸开地躺在沙发上. — *n.* ①手脚伸开躺卧(的姿势). ②蔓延;散乱. ③〔美〕毅力. ***go ~ing*** 爬行. ***send sb. ~ing*** 打倒在地. ***~ one's last*** 临死作最后挣扎. **-er** *n.*

spray[1] [sprei] *n.* ①浪花,水花,水雾;雾状物. ②【医】喷雾(药)[液]. ③喷雾器;消毒器. — *vt.* 喷,喷射,使起浪花;喷雾(入咽喉等).— *vi.* 喷,(象浪花般)溅散. ~ *an insecticide upon plants* = ~ *plants with an insecticide* 用杀虫药喷洒作物. ~ **can** 喷雾壶[罐]. ~ **fountain** 喷水池. ~ **gun** 喷(漆)枪. ~**ing car** 喷水车. ~**-paint** *vt.* 喷漆. ~ **painting** 喷漆. ~ **method** 喷漆法. ~ **needle** 喷雾针. ~ **nozzle** 喷雾嘴.

spray[2] [sprei] *n.* ①小树枝,小花枝. ②枝状花样[装饰],枝状物. ~ **drain** (以小树枝填在沟漕内,上面覆土而形成的)排水暗沟.

spray·er [ˈspreiə] *n.* ①喷雾的人[东西]. ②喷雾器;喷油机;喷漆器. ③喷水车.

spread [spred] *vt.* ***(spread)*** ①伸开,伸长(手臂等),展开,张开(帆等),打开(地图等);铺开(毡子等),展宽,展延(金属等). ②撒,施,敷,涂;被覆;上胶. ③散布,流传,传播;普及. ④把…分期,使延长;拖延(时间). ⑤敲平,铆(钉子等). ⑥详细记载,记录. ⑦展出,展示. ⑧布置,安排. — *vi.* ①伸开,伸长;扩大,扩张;(金属等)展延. ②传开,传播,蔓延开;拖延,继续. ③(花、叶等)开放. ④(墨水等)渗开,散开;展开. ~ *the news* 传播消息. ~ *manure over a field* 在田里撒粪肥. ~ *butter on bread* = ~ *bread with butter* 在面包上涂奶油. ~ *resolutions upon the minutes* 把决议记录在记录(本)里. ~ *the matter on the records* 把情况记录下来. ~ *tea on the table* 把茶点摆在桌子上. ~ *the table* 摆饭桌准备吃饭;开饭. *It is time to* ~ *for dinner.* 是(摆桌子)开饭的时候了. *Coloured banners* ~ *in the wind.* 彩旗迎风招展. *This is a prescribed course which* ~*s over two semesters.* 这是门两个学期学完的必修课. *A scene of rich harvest* ~ *out before us.* 一片丰收景象展示在我们面前. ~ ***oneself*** 〔口〕舒展身体四肢(躺下);竭力去做,努力,奋发;做得过分;滔滔不绝地讲. ~ ***oneself thin*** 〔口〕企图同时做很多事情而分散精力. ~ ***out*** 张开,伸开,铺开;扩大,扩张,展开,伸长. ~ ***to*** 传到,波及,蔓延到. — *n.* ①伸展,扩展;扩展度[幅度],(金属的)展宽,延伸;跨距. ②【机】轮距. ③传播,普及;蔓延,流行. ④(一片)广阔的土地[水域];〔美〕大牧场;范围. ⑤扩散,扩张,展开;展度;(动植物的)分布. ⑥展性;【数】展形. ⑦〔美〕桌布;床单. ⑧〔口〕(丰盛的)酒席,宴会. ⑨〔美〕涂味品〔涂面包的黄油、果酱等〕. ⑩(报上占大量篇幅或整版的)文章[广告];连占两版的大幅插图. ⑪〔美商〕原价和卖价的差额,进销价差. *the* ~ *of the great metropolis* 大都市的扩展. *the gradual* ~ *of higher education* 高等教育的逐渐普及. *a* ~ *of 100,000 acres* 十万英亩的一大片土地. *the wide* ~ *of his answer and yours* 他的答案和你的答案的很大的距离. ***give (sb.) a regular ~*** 请(某人)吃酒席. ***no end of a ~*** 各种各样好吃的东西. — *a.* ①扩大的,伸展的,广大的;大幅的. ②(宝石)薄而无光泽的. ~ **eagle** *n.* ①【徽】展翼鹰〔美国国徽〕. ②美国人对于本国的自夸自赞;自夸者. ③【股】(在买卖双方间)吃盘子,加码子. ④【溜冰】横一字型. ⑤【海】将水手绑在索具上处罚. ~**-eagle** ①*a.* 张翼鹰似的;自夸的,沙文主义的. ②*vt.*, *vi.* 伸开四肢跳下〔跌下、躺下〕;【海】把四肢作大字形绑起来,绑起四肢鞭打. ~**-ea·glism** (美国的)自夸自赞的沙文主义;夸耀本国. ~ **head** (报纸上占两栏以上的)大标题. ~**-over** (system)〔英〕对工作时间根据特殊需要而作调整的制度. ~**ing factor** 扩散素〔促使另一种物质通过机体组织扩散的物质,如透明质酸酶〕.

spread·er [ˈspredə] *n.* ①散布者,传播者. ②展延器,展播器;展着剂. ②【电】开隔体,撑挡. ③【化】涂胶机;扩张器. ④【纺】分纱器;分绞箱.

sprech·stim·me [ˈʃpreˌʃtimmə] *n.* 〔G.〕(半象说话,半象唱歌)吟唱.

spree [spriː] *n.* ①欢闹,狂欢〔尤指狂饮〕. ②无节制的狂热行为. ***go on a ~*** 痛饮,喝得兴高采烈. ***be on the ~*** 在狂欢中,喝得兴高采烈. — *vi.* 狂欢,纵乐,喝得兴高采烈〔常作 ~ *it*〕.

sprig [sprig] *n.* ①小(树)枝. ②小枝状花样饰物. ③〔谑〕子孙. ④〔主蔑〕小伙子,少年,小家伙. ⑤无头钉,扁头钉,⑥嵌玻璃针. — *vt.* ①用小枝装饰,加小枝花样. ②剪除小枝. ③使(草)蔓生. ④钉扁头钉.

sprig·gy [ˈsprigi] *a.* 多小枝的,多嫩枝的;小枝似的.

spright·ful [ˈspraitful] *a.* = sprightly(a). **-ly** *ad.* **-ness** *n.*

spright·li·ness [ˈspraitlinis] *n.* 活泼,生气勃勃,轻松愉快.

spright·ly [ˈspraitli] *a.* ***(-li·er; -li·est)*** 活泼的,生气勃勃的,轻快的.

spring [spriŋ] *n.* ①春季,春天. ②青春;初期. ③〔*pl.*〕大潮时期. ④泉. ⑤源头,水源,根源,本源;发生;动机,原动力. ⑥跳跃;弹回,反跳. ⑦弹力;弹性. ⑧发条,弹簧,(汽车的)钢板. ⑨活力,精力,元气. ⑩【船】(桅杆等的)裂缝;缆索,系船索. ⑪(甲板的)上翘;转向锚索;倒缆. ⑫【构球】棒的弯曲. ⑬【建】起拱点,起拱面. ⑭〔美俚〕年轻无经验的人,年轻幼稚的女子. *the* ~ *of life* 青春(时代). *hot* ~*s* 温泉. *the* ~*s of one's conduct* 行为的动机. *The custom had its* ~ *in Beijing.* 这个风俗起源于北京. *a hair* ~发丝弹簧. ***set every ~ in motion*** = ***set all ~s going*** 开动所有发条;尽全力. ***with a ~*** 一跳,一骨碌(起来等). — *vi.* ***(sprang*** [spræŋ], ***sprung*** [sprʌŋ]***; sprung)*** ①跳,跃. ②跳出;涌出[上];发源. ③起源于,发生;发芽. ④(木板等)弯曲,反翘,歪,裂开;(地雷)炸开. ⑤高出,耸立. ⑥【建】(拱等)开始,升起. ⑦【海】拼命划船使飞跃向前. ⑧出身. — *vt.* ①使跳起来;惊起;跳过. ②使爆炸,使炸裂,使弯曲;使破裂,使折断. ③弹出;突然提出. ④〔主用 ***p.p.***〕装弹簧. ⑤扭伤(腿等),使跛. ⑥【建】开始砌(拱洞等). ⑦【海】用锚缆转变方向. ⑧〔美俚〕(从监狱)释放出去,保释出去. *They sprang to the new task.* 他们争先恐后地去做这件新的工作. *The doors* ~ *open.* 门砰的一声开了. *The lid sprang to.* 盖子砰的一下盖上了. *The dawn began to* ~. 天开始亮了. *The river* ~*s in the Alps.* 这条河发源于阿尔卑斯山脉. *He* ~*s from poor peasant family.* 他是贫农出身. *Many new factories have sprung up in my home town.* 我的家乡新建了许多工厂.

A twenty storied building ~s high above the city. 一座二十层的高楼高耸于城的上空. *The mistake sprang from his absent-mindedness.* 这错误是由于他的心不在焉造成的. *S- ahead hard!*【海】拼命划. *The ship's timbers are sprung.* 船上材料的接头部分松了. *I've sprung my table-tennis bat.* 我把我的乒乓球拍打裂了. *It was Old Sun who sprang the new proposal on them.* 是老孙突然向他们提出那新建议的. ~ *a butt*【海】船因动摇致外部接头变松. ***get sprung***〔口〕大醉. ~ ***a blue book***〔美〕临时测验. ~ ***a leak*** 生漏缝. ~ ***a mine***【军】使地雷爆炸. ~ ***a mine upon*** 突然袭击. ~ ***a somersault*** 翻觔斗. ~ ***a surprise on*** 使…吃一惊. ~ ***an arch***【建】砌拱洞. ~ ***at*** 扑到. ~ ... ***for a quid*** 勒索一镑. ~ ***forth*** 跳出,冲出,突出;涌出,喷出. ~ ***into fame*** 一举成名. ~ ***off*** 裂开. ~ ***on*** 扑向,袭击. ~ ***out of*** 跳出,冲出. ~ ***over*** 跳过. ~ ***to attention*** 跳起来作立正姿势. ~ ***to one's feet*** 立即站起. ~ ***up*** 跳上来;发生;萌芽,生长;出现. ~ ***up like a mushroom*** 有如雨后春笋迅速大量产生. ~ ***upon*** = ~ on. ~ **bal·ance** 弹簧秤,磅秤. ~ **beam** 大桁,系梁. ~ **beauty**【植】春美草. ~ **bed** 弹簧床. ~ **binder** 弹簧活页夹. ~ **blade knife** 弹簧折合刀. ~**-board** 跳板;出发点,发端. ~ **bok**, ~ **buck** *(pl.* ~*s,*〔集合词〕~*)*【动】南非小羚羊. ~ **carriage**, ~ **cart** 弹簧马车,装有弹簧的运货马车. ~ **chicken** 童子鸡;〔美俚〕年轻人,天真的人. ~**-cleaning** 春季大扫除. ~ **fever**〔美〕春困〔某些人在春季初暖时出现的困倦状态〕. **S- Gardens** 园林春〔伦敦市议会所在地〕. ~ **gun** 弹簧枪,伏击枪. ~**halt**【兽医】= stringhalt. ~**head** 源头,水源;车上的弹簧头. ~**house**〔美〕(建筑在泉水、小溪上的)肉类乳品冷藏所. ~**like** *a.* 象春天的. ~ **lock** 弹簧锁. ~ **mattress** 弹簧床垫. ~ **peeper**【动】〔美〕小雨蛙. ~ **steel**【冶】弹簧钢. ~**tail**【动】弹尾目昆虫. ~**-tide** 大潮,子午潮,朔望潮;舆论,趋势;〔诗〕= springtime. ~**time** 春天,春季;青春;初期;早期;全盛期. ~**water** 泉水. **S- Wheat Belt** 春麦带〔美国明尼苏达州的别名〕. ~**wood**【植】早材,春材.

spring·al [ˈspriŋəl] *n.*〔古〕活跃的小伙子,年轻人(= springald).

springe [sprindʒ] *n.* 圈套,陷阱. — *vt., vi.* 设圈套[陷阱]捉捕.

spring·er [ˈspriŋə] *n.* ①跳的人,跳的东西. ②【动】猎,能哄起猎获物的长耳小猎犬〔又叫 ~ *spaniel*〕. ③逆鳍鲸. ④【建】起拱石,拱底石. ⑤= spring chicken.

Spring·hall [ˈspriŋhɔ:l] *n.* 斯普林霍尔〔姓氏〕.

spring·i·ness [ˈspri:ŋinis] *n.* 有弹力,弹性;多泉水,湿润;轻快.

spring·ing [ˈspriŋiŋ] *n.*【建】起拱点.

spring·i·za·tion [ˌspriŋiˈzeiʃən] *n.* = vernalization.

spring·less [ˈspriŋlis] *a.* 无弹簧的;无泉水的.

spring·let [ˈspri:ŋlit] *n.* 小泉,小河,小溪.

spring·y [ˈspri:ŋi] *a.* *(-i·er; -i·est)* ①有弹力[性]的. ②轻快的. ③多泉水的;湿润的. *All the kids went up the hill with ~ steps.* 所有的小孩子都以轻快的步伐上了小山. **-i·ly** *ad.*

sprin·kle [ˈspriŋkl] *vt.* ①洒;撒;喷淋. ②撒布,使散布. ③点缀. — *vi.* ①洒,喷淋;撒;散布在. ②〔主语为 it〕下疏稀的雨. ~ *salt on a dish* = ~ *a dish with salt* 在菜餚上撒盐. *His coat was ~-d with cigarette ashes.* 他的上衣撒满了纸烟灰. — *n.* ①洒;撒. ②小雨. ③少量;疏稀散布的东西. ④〔常 *pl.*〕撒在面上的一层东西. ⑤洒水器. *Let's cover the cakes with chocolate ~s.* 咱们把蛋糕用巧克力末撒上.

sprin·kler [ˈspriŋklə] *n.* ①洒水车,洒水器,喷壶;洒水装置. ②(草坪、高尔夫球场的)地下灌浇系统. ~ *system* 自动喷水消防系统.

sprin·kling [ˈspri:ŋkliŋ] *n.* ①洒,撒,撒布;喷雾(工作). ②(雨等的)点滴;少量;零星. *Don't you have a ~ of common sense?* 你难道一点儿常识也没有吗? *a smart ~*〔美俚〕很多,许多. ~**-can**〔美〕= watering-can [-pot]. ~**-cart**〔美〕= watering-cart.

sprint [sprint] *vt., vi.* 全速奔跑(短距离). — *n.* ①全速疾跑. ②短距离赛跑(= ~ race). ③短时间的紧张活动;长距离赛跑中的冲刺. ④不超过一英里的赛马. *Smith's ~ at the finish was really wonderful.* 史密斯的终点冲刺确实是了不起. ~ **car** 短程泥路赛车.

sprint·er [ˈsprintə] *n.* 短跑运动员.

sprit [sprit] *n.*【船】(撑帆用)斜杠,横杠;第一斜桅. ~ **sail** 斜杠帆.

sprite [sprait] *n.* ①妖怪,小妖精. ②捣蛋鬼,爱恶作剧的人. ③〔古〕鬼魂.

spritz [sprits; G. ʃprits] *vt., vi.* 喷水. — *n.* 水花,喷雾.

sprock·et [ˈsprɔkit] *n.*【机】链轮齿,扣链齿;链轮〔又叫 ~ wheel〕.

sprout [spraut] *vi.* ①出芽,发芽,萌芽;抽条. ②很快地生长. — *vt.* ①使发芽;使生长. ②〔美方〕摘去(马铃薯等的)芽. — *n.* ①幼芽;新梢,嫩枝. ②〔*pl.*〕【植】汤菜(= *Brussels* sprouts). ③幼苗状物,年轻人;〔美俚〕后代. *bamboo ~* 竹笋. *bean ~s* 豆芽. *a ~ who isn't old enough to go to school* 一个岁数小还不能上学的娃娃. *The spring rain has ~ed the seeds.* 春雨使种子发了芽. *Peach trees ~ed their new leaves.* 桃树长出新叶来了. ~ **forest**, ~ **land** 萌芽林.

spruce[1] [spru:s] *n.*【植】云杉(属),云杉木〔又叫 ~ *fir*〕. ~ *beer* 云杉酒. ~ *grouse*【动】云杉鸡.

spruce[2] [spru:s] *a.* 整洁的,潇洒的;漂亮的. — *vt., vi.* (弄)整洁,(把)打扮漂亮 *(up)*. *My study looks ~.* 我的书房看起来挺漂亮. *Mother told us to ~ the parlour for Christmas.* 妈妈要我们把客厅收拾整洁过圣诞节. *You really must ~ up a bit, Albert.* 阿尔培,你可是得把自己搞得整洁一点了. **-ly** *ad.* **-ness** *n.*

sprue[1] [spru:] *n.*【铸造】浇口,注入口;熔渣.

sprue[2] [spru:] *n.*【医】口炎性腹泻.

spruit [spreit, spru:t] *n.* (南非用语)(只有在雨季才有水的)干涸小河.

sprung [sprʌŋ] spring 的过去式及过去分词. — *a.*〔口〕微醉的.

spry [sprai] *a.* *(-er; -est* or *spri·er; spri·est)* 活泼的,生气勃勃的;敏捷的,轻快的. *When Teacher Ma was 70 years old, he was as ~ as a kitten.* 马老师七十岁的时候,还轻快敏捷地象只小猫一般. **-ly** *ad.* **-ness** *n.*

s.p.s. =〔L.〕*sine prole superstite* 无后代,无子孙(= without surviving issue).

spt. = seaport.

Sp. Trs. = Special Troops 特种兵.

spud [spʌd] *n.* ①除草锄. ②(栎树)剥皮器,剥皮刀. ③〔俚〕马铃薯. ④短而粗的东西. — *vt.* ***(spud·ded*** [ˈspʌdid; ***spud·ding*** [ˈspʌdiŋ]*)* 用除草锄锄(草等) *(up;out)*.

spudder [ˈspʌdə] *n.* (剥树皮用的)铲凿;草锄.

spud·dle [spʌdl] *vi.* 轻掘,翻掘.

spud·dy [ˈspʌdi] *a.* 粗而短的;矮胖的.

spue [spju:] *vt., vi.* = spew.

spug [spʌg] *n.* ①〔Scot., 英方〕家雀. ②〔美俚〕反对赠送虚伪礼物的人.

spume [spju:m] *n.* 泡沫,浮沫. —*vt., vi.* (使)起泡沫.

spu·mes·cence [spjuˈmesns] *n.* 起泡;泡沫状态. **-cent** *a.* 似泡沫的;发出泡沫的.

spu·mo·ne, spu·mo·ni [spəˈməuni] *n.*〔It.〕意大利式多层不同颜色加蜜饯的冰激凌.

spu·mous, spum·y [ˈspju:məs, ˈspju:mi] *a.* 泡沫的,多泡沫的,泡沫状的,被泡沫覆盖的.

spun [spʌn] spin 的过去式及过去分词. — *a.* ①纺成

的;拉成丝状的. ②〔俚〕精疲力尽的. ③【海】细油麻绳(由二至四股绳条捻成). ~ **cotton** 棉纱. ~ **glass** 玻璃纤维. ~ **gold** 金丝. ~ **silk** 纺丝. ~ **string**【乐】钢丝弦. ~ **sugar** 棉花糖. ~ **yarn** 精纺纱,细纱;麻纱.

spunge [spʌndʒ] *n., v.* 〔古〕 = sponge.

spunk [spʌŋk] *n.* ①〔口〕精神,生气;勇气,胆量. ②急躁,愤怒. ③引火木柴,火绒. ④〔英方〕火星,小火焰. — *vi.* 点着,烧起来. *Grandpa told a story with rare ~ last night.* 昨天晚上祖父极其生动地讲了个故事. *get sb's ~ up* 给某人打气,鼓励某人. ~ ***out*** 〔美〕被揭穿,给人晓得;失败. ~ ***up*** 〔美〕打起精神. —*vt.* 鼓励某人 *(up)*.

spunk·y [ˈspʌŋki] *a.* ***(-i·er; -i·est)*** 〔口〕①精神十足的,勇气倍增的. ②易怒的. ③〔英方〕灿烂的. ④火绒的. **-i·ly** *ad.* **-i·ness** *n.*

spur [spəː] *n.* ①踢马刺,靴刺,马扎子;【史】金踢马刺〔骑士 *(knight)* 所用〕. ②刺激物,鼓励品,促进器;教唆,挑拨,煽动,鼓舞,刺激. ③树根;【动】(鸟类、虫类等的)距;(斗鸡时加于鸡腿上的)距铁;【植】花距;短枝;(军舰的)冲角. ④(攀爬用)刺铁;(登山用)铁钉助爬器. ⑤山嘴,山鼻子;石嘴,尖坡,悬岩;支脉,横岭;【建】凸壁;支撑物;【铁路】支线;【代】迹(数). ***clap [give] ~s to*** = put ~s to. ***need the ~*** 需要用靴刺踢,需加激励. ***on [upon] the ~*** 用足速力,飞快地,火急. ***on the ~ of the moment*** 一时兴起[冲动];当场,即席. ***put [set] ~s to*** 用靴刺踢;激励. ***win one's ~s*** (由古时因功被封为骑士转为)得到荣誉,飞黄腾达,出名. ***with whip and ~ = with ~ and yard*** 快马加鞭地,立刻,马上. — *vt.* ①用靴刺踢;装靴刺[刺铁等]. ②刺激,推动,教唆,煽动,鞭策,鼓舞. ③斗鸡时用距铁踢[踢伤]. — *vi.* ①用靴刺踢马,催马前进;驱赶 *(on)*. ②疾驰. *Professor Smith's new book ~s interest in his course.* 史密斯教授的新书鼓起了大家对他的课的兴趣. ***booted and spurred*** 穿了靴子上了靴刺. ~ ***sb. up to [on to, into] action*** 激励某人. ~ **gall** ①*n.* (马腹的)靴刺伤. ②*vt.* 用靴刺踢伤;弄伤. ~ **gear,** ~ **wheel**【机】正齿轮. ~ **line [track]** 〔美铁路〕短叉道,支路.

spurge [spəːdʒ] *n.*【植】大戟(属)植物. ~ **laurel**【植】桂叶芫花.

spu·ri·ous [ˈspjuəriəs] *a.* ①假的,乱真的,伪造的. ②欺骗性的;谬误的. ③私生的. *When you go to the fair, beware of the quacks selling ~ medicinal herbs.* 你赶集的时候,当心卖假草药的江湖医生. *a ~ fruit* (草莓,无花果等的)假果. ~ *oscillation* 【物】乱真振荡. **-ly** *ad.* **-ness** *n.*

spur·less [ˈspəːlis] *a.* ①没有踢马刺的(靴跟等). ②没有距的(鸡脚等). ③没有花距的.

spurn [spəːn] *vi.* ①〔古〕踢,踢走,赶走,驱逐;一脚踢开. ②蔑视,唾弃. —*vt.* ①践踏;一脚踢开. ②轻蔑地拒绝,摒弃,唾弃. *As an armyman, I ~ fearlessly at all danger and the enemy.* 作为一个军人,一切危险和敌人丝毫不在我的眼下. *He ~ed my suggestion that he shouldn't go and see the brawl of the hoodlums.* 他冷然地拒绝了我提的不要去看阿飞们吵架的建议. ~ ***at sb.*** 〔罕〕不理睬某人. ~ ***sb's affection*** 拒绝某人的爱情. ~ ***the ground*** 跳起来. — *n.* ①踢开. ②拒绝;唾弃;不理睬;藐视.

spurred [spəːd] *a.* 有靴刺的,装上靴刺的;有距的〔指鸟〕.

spur·ri·er [ˈspəːriə] *n.* 踢马刺[距铁等]制造人.

spur·rite [ˈspəːrait] *n.*【化】灰硅钙石.

spur·ry, spur·rey [ˈspəːri] *n.*【植】大爪草属 *(Spergula)* 植物;大爪草 *(S. arvensis)* 〔产于北美洲〕.

spurt [spəːt] *vt.* 喷射. — *vi.* 喷出,迸出 *(up; out; down)*. ②突然拚命努力,在赛跑中最后冲刺;突发. ③发芽,生长. — *n.* ①突然喷出,突发,突然爆发[冲出等]. ②短促突然的爆发或激增,(怒气、精力等的)迸发. ③短时间. ④(营业的)突然兴隆. ⑤(赛跑)最后冲刺;最后死拚.

sput·nik [ˈsputnik] *n.* (苏联)人造地球卫星. *a ~ spaceship* 卫星式宇宙飞船.

sput·ter [ˈspʌtə] *vi., vt.* ①飞溅唾沫;(食渣等)飞溅. ②唾沫飞溅地说;激动地争吵. ③(湿柴)劈劈啪啪地爆裂. ④爆响着停熄掉,停息 *(out)*. — *n.* ①急语;吵闹,争论. ②喷溅声. ③劈啪声. *Jack ran up to the referee, ~ing protest.* 贾克跑到裁判跟前,唾沫飞溅地提出抗议. *Fat ~s in the frying pan.* 肥油在炸锅里劈啪劈啪地响. *After the talk with the party secretary, his excitement ~ed out.* 和支书谈过话以后他的激动已经消失了. **~-bridget, -budget** 〔美〕动不动就吵闹的人. **-er** *n.* ①语无伦次[说话气急败坏]的人. ②发劈啪声的东西.

sput·ter·ing·ly [ˈspʌtəriŋli] *ad.* ①唾沫飞溅地. ②气急败坏地,语无伦次地. ③劈啪作响地.

spu·tum [ˈspjuːtəm] *n.* ***(pl. -ta*** [-tə]***)*** 唾液;痰.

sp. vol. = specific volume 比容.

spy [spai] *n.* 间谍,密探,侦察,侦探;特务. ***set spies after [upon]*** 派密探监视. — *vt.* ***(spied)*** ①侦察,暗中侦查(监视). ②察见,发现. ③仔细察看. *vi.* ①做密探间谍. ②暗中监视,侦查 *(on, upon* 某人 *into)*. *I ~ strangers.* 〔英议会〕请禁止旁听;请举行秘密会议. ~ *out the secret of the enemy special agent* 侦查出敌特的秘密. ~ *on (upon) the movements of the terrorists* 暗中监视恐怖分子的活动. ~ *all the exhibits with an artist* 和一位艺术家一起仔细观查全部展览品. ~ *into a complicated affair* 侦察一桩复杂离奇的事件. ~ **glass** 小望远镜. **~-hole** 窥[监]视孔.

sq = ①sequence. ②〔L.〕*sequens* = (the following one). ③〔L.〕*sequentia* (= the following ones).

Sq. = ①Squadron. ②Square.

sq. = square.

sq. ft = square foot [feet].

sq. in. = square inch(es).

sq. mi. = square mile(s).

sqn. = squadron.

sq(q). = 〔L.〕*sequentes, sequentia.*

squab [skwɔb] *a.* ①(鸟类)还未生毛的,刚出蛋壳的. ②(人)矮胖的. — *ad.* 〔口〕沉重地,咕咚地. — *n.* ①小鸽子,小鸟,雏. ②〔美俚〕少女,小姑娘. ③矮胖子. ④厚垫子;沙发. **~-chick** 雏鸟. ~ **pie** 羊肉饼.

squab·ble [ˈskwɔbl] *n.* (为小事)口角,争论. *a ~ over property right* 关于产权方面的争论. — *vi.* 争论,争吵. — *vt.*【印】搅乱(排好的铅字). ~ *with sb. about [over] sth.* 为了某件事情和人争吵. **-bler** *n.*

squab·by [ˈskwɔbi] *a.* 矮胖的.

Squac·co [ˈkwɔːkəu] *n.* 竖冠池鹭〔产于南欧、非洲等地〕.

squad [skwɔd] *n.* 〔军〕班. ②小组,小队. *an awkward ~* 一小队新兵. *a beef ~* 〔美俚〕大力士打手队. *a flying ~* 紧急任务执行小组〔如警察局的特勤队〕. *a ~ car* (装有无线电话的)警备车. *a ~ drill* 班教练. *a ~ leader* 班长. *a goon ~* 〔美俚〕打手队. *a vice ~* 〔美〕(取缔卖淫、赌博等的)警察缉捕队. ~ *room* ①【军】士兵寝室. ②(警察局点名分配任务的)集合厅. — *vt.* 成立(军队)班的建制;把某士兵编入班的建制内;把人员分成小队.

squad·ron [ˈskwɔdrən] *n.*【军】①骑兵中队;(各特种兵的)连. ②分舰队. ③空军中队. ④团体,一组,一群. ⑤(归时军队)方阵. — *vt.* 编成中队[分舰队]. *a detached ~* 分遣小舰队. *a flying ~* 游击分舰队. *a standing ~* 常备舰队. *a missile ~* 导弹中队. ~ **leader** *n.* ①空军中队长. ②〔英〕少校.

squail [skweil] *n.* ①〔英〕(推盘游戏用的)小圆盘. ②〔*pl.*〕推盘游戏;九柱戏. — *vi., vt.* ①投掷铅头棒打鸟或击落树上的果子. ②〔英方〕用投掷棒子的方法打击

(人、物).

squail·er [ˈskweilə] *n.* 〔英方〕(投击野禽、松鼠等用)铅头棒.

squa·lene [ˈskweiliːn] *n.* 【化】角鲨烯,三十碳六烯.

squal·id [ˈskwɔlid] *a.* ①肮脏的,邋遢的. ②(道德品质)卑劣的. ③贫困的,悲惨的,可怜的. ~ *dress* 肮脏的衣服. ~ *affairs* 伤风败俗的坏事. ~ *motive* 卑鄙的动机. **-ly** *ad.* **-ness** *n.*

squa·lid·i·ty [skwɔˈliditi] *n.* 肮脏,邋遢;卑劣;贫困.

squall[1] [skwɔːl] *vi.* (因疼痛、害怕而起的)大声喊叫,怪叫;嚎哭. — *vt.* 刺耳地大声说,尖声锐气地说. — *n.* 尖叫,怪叫;大声哭泣. *Mother knows how to comfort a ~ing baby. Let her do it.* 妈妈知道怎样哄好大声嚎哭的小孩,还是让她做吧. *An old woman rushed out of the house on fire and ~ed.* 一个年老妇女从失火的房子里冲了出来大声地喊叫.

squall[2] [skɔl] *n.* ①(带有雨、雪、雹等的)暴风,飑. ②〔口〕麻烦,困难,打扰. *a black* ~【气】乌云飑. *a thick* ~ 带雨雪冰雹的狂风. *a white* ~ 无云飑. ***look out for*** *~s* 谨防危险,随时警惕. — *vi.* 〔主语为 it〕刮狂风,起风暴[飑].

squall·y [ˈskɔli] *a.* ***(-i·er; -i·est)*** ①(象要)起风暴的. ②可怕的,厉害的;不安全的. ***look*** ~ 象要刮狂风;〔喻〕形势险恶.

squa·loid [ˈskweilɔid] *a.* 似鲨鱼的.

squal·or [ˈskwɔlə] *n.* ①肮脏,邋遢. ②(道德品质等的)卑劣. ③贫困.

squam [skwɔm] *n.* 〔美〕(渔夫戴的)油布帽子.

squa·ma [ˈskweimə] *n.* ***(pl. -mae*** [-miː]***)*** ①【植】鳞片;【动】鳞. ②(昆虫的)腋瓣;负须叶;鳞形节;刺缘突.

squa·mate [ˈskweimeit] *a.* 有鳞的,鳞斑的.

squa·ma·tion [skwəˈmeiʃən, ˈskwei-] *n.* ①有鳞,多鳞. ②鳞列.

squa·mo·sal [skwəˈməusl] *a.* ①= squamous. — *n.* 【解】鳞状骨.

squa·mose [ˈskweiməus] *a.* = squamous. **-ly** *ad.* **-ness** *n.*

squa·mous [ˈskweiməs] *a.* ①鳞状的,覆以鳞的,由鳞片组成的. ②【解】鳞状骨的. **-ly** *ad.*

squam·u·le [ˈskweimjuːli] *n.* 【生】小鳞片.

squam·u·lose [ˈskwæmjuˌləus, ˈskweimju-] *a.* 有细鳞的,覆以细鳞的,由细鳞组成的.

squan·der [ˈskwɔndə] *vt.* ①挥霍,浪费;乱用(时间、金钱等). ②驱散,使散开. *vi.* ①浪费. ②浪荡,漂泊. ③四散. *To ~ the collective fund is a crime.* 浪费集体的钱是犯罪. *Don't ~ your time in reading those dime novels.* 不要把你的时间浪费在读那些粗造滥制的小说上. *Many of the enemy were ~ed.* 多数敌军都被驱散了. *n.* 浪费,挥霍. **-er** *n.*

squan·der·ing·ly [ˈskwɔndəriŋli] *ad.* 浪费地;滥用乱花地.

squan·der·ma·ni·a [ˈskɔndəˈmeinjə] *n.* 浪费狂.

square [skwɛə] *n.* ①正方形,四方块,四角;方形物. ②(方形)广场;〔美〕(四面都是马路的)方阵建筑;街区;(方阵建筑中任何一面)一排房子的长度. ③画线板;丁字规,直角尺,矩尺. ④【数】平方,二次幂,自乘. ⑤【军】方阵. ⑥【天】矩象. ⑦(象棋盘等的)小方格纵横字谜〔每方格填一字母〕. ⑧一方〔房屋面积单位,一方为一百平方英尺〕. ⑨含苞未放的棉蕾. ⑩〔俚〕古板守旧的人. ⑪〔美俚〕拳击场. ⑫〔美俚〕丰富的饭菜〔又叫 ~ meal〕. *Tian An Men Square* 天安门广场. *a house a few ~s up* 两三个街区外的一所房屋. *bring six to* ~ 使 6 自乘. *a set* ~ 三角板. ***by the*** ~ 恰好地. ***on the*** ~ 成直角;诚实地,规规矩矩地;平等地;同等地;〔美俚〕诚实的,公正的,可靠的. ***out of*** ~ 不成直角,斜;没有秩序地,不规则地;不公平地. — *a.* ①正方形的;四方的,四角的;成直角的,矩形的. ②宽而结实的(体格、肩膀、船等). ③适合的,正好的. ④规规矩矩的;光明正大的,正直的,公平的(交易等). ⑤同高的,同水准的;平等的,同等的;笔直的,平行的,水平的. ⑥结清贷借的,两讫的. ⑦坚决的,断然的(拒绝等),干脆的. ⑧【数】平方的,等边的. ⑨〔俚〕充实的,令人满意[满足]的,吃得饱的(饭). ⑩【海】和龙骨成直角的(帆桁). ⑪〔美俚〕古板守旧的,老派朴质的. *a man of ~ frame* 肩膀宽阔的人. *a ~ deal = ~ dealing* 〔口〕公平的交易[处理]. *a ~ eater* 吃得净光的人. ***all*** ~ 两清,彼此不欠;扯平,不分胜负;一切安排妥当,很好,很满意. ***call it*** ~ 当作已清帐[不必再提]. ***get*** *(things)* ~〔口〕整顿. ***get*** ~ ***with***〔口〕和…清算;向…报仇[报复]. ***keep*** ... ~ ***to*** 使…与…成直角. ***make a*** ~ ***meal*** 饱餐一顿. ***make accounts*** ~ 结清,付清. ~ ***with the world***〔美俚〕与人无借贷关系. — *ad.* ①四四方方地;成直角地;成方形地;笔直地,端正地. ②正直地,公正地,规规矩矩地. ③坚定地,坚实不动的. *stand* ~ 端正地站着. *play fair and* ~ 表现得公公道道. — *vt.* ①弄成方形;使成直角. ②检验…的平直度. ③抬平(肩膀等). ④调正,修正. ⑤把(纸张等)划分成方格. ⑥使方正,使符合,使一致. ⑦扯平,使贷借相抵,算清,结清. ⑧【数】使作自乘. ⑨【海】使和桅[龙骨]成直角. ⑩〔口〕笼络,贿赂,收买. — *vi.* ①成直角. ②符合,调和,一致. ③结清. ④【高尔夫球】分数相同. ⑤【拳】摆好进攻架势. ~ *accounts* 清算,结清,付清. ~ *one's shoulders* (吵架前等)抬起肩膀. *Your idea and mine do not ~.* 你跟我的意见不一致. ~ ***a rap*** 〔美〕贿赂官吏. ~ ***away*** ①扬帆顺风驶行. ②(拳击中)摆好架势. ③〔口〕准备停当,整理好. ~ ***it***〔美〕改过自新. ~ ***off***〔美〕(拳击中)摆好架势. ~ ***oneself***〔口〕认错,赔不是,赔偿损失. ~ ***the circle*** 作面积等于一个圆的正方形;做异想天开的事. ~ ***up***〔口〕清帐;【拳击】摆好进攻架势. **~-built** *a.* 四方的;(肩膀)宽阔的. **~d circle** 拳击台. ~ **dance** (四对男女跳的)方舞. ~ **face** 廉价烈酒. ~ **head**〔美〕在美、加拿大的北欧人;〔蔑〕德国人. ~ **John**〔美俚〕守法良民,不吸毒的人. ~ **knot** 平结. ~ **leg**【板球】打手左方的外场守场员. ~ **man** 石匠,木匠. ~ **measure**【数】平方积,面积. ~ **number**【数】平方数. ~ **one** 起点. **~-rigged** *a.*【海】横帆的. ~ **room**〔美〕最好的房间. ~ **root**【数】平方根. ~ **rule** 直角尺. ~ **sail**【海】横帆. ~ **shooter**〔美〕公平正直的人,老实人. **~-shouldered** 平肩的,阔肩的. **~-toed** ①(鞋)方头的. ②古板的,守旧的. ~ **toes** 古板的人.

squar·er [ˈskwɛərə] *n.* ①锯木方工人,凿石方工人. ②方形剥刀. ③【无】平方电路.

square·ly [ˈskwɛəli] *ad.* ①成方形. ②规规矩矩地;公正地. ③断然地. ④笔直地,对准地. ⑤〔俚〕吃得饱饱地. *face the crisis* ~ 正视危机,断然应付危机. *hit sb. ~ in the left eye* 正好打在某人的左眼.

square·ness [ˈskwɛənis] *n.* ①方形;方正. ②正直,公正.

squar·ish [ˈskwɛəriʃ] *a.* 近似方形的,有点方的. **-ly** *ad.*

squar·rose [ˈskwærəus, ˈskwɔr-] *a.* ①【生】粗糙的,具有糙鳞的,糠秕状的. ②【植】末梢成直角突出的;开展的,伸展的. ③多皮屑的. **-ly** *ad.*

squar·son [ˈskɑːsn] *n.* 〔英谑〕兼做牧师的地主.

squash[1] [skwɔʃ] *vt.* ①压扁;压碎,压烂;压挤进去. ②镇压(叛乱等);压制;压服;〔口〕使缄默,使住口. — *vi.* ①压扁;压碎,压烂;落下砸扁;挤进去 *(into)*. ②发溅泼声,发咯吱声. — *n.* ①扁片;易压碎(烂、扁)的东西. ②〔英〕果汁汽水. ③〔口〕拥挤的人群. ④(在筑有围墙的场地上玩的,兼有手球和网球特点的)墙球;短柄墙球球拍. ⑤趴跶〔重软东西落下声〕,(行走泥沼地的)咯吱声. *Let me ~ the mosquito on the wall.* 让我来把墙上的蚊子揿死. *No capitalist can ~ the strike.* 哪个资本家谁也不能压制罢工. *fall ~ing to the ground* 趴跶一声掉在地上. *We all managed to ~ into the bus.* 我们都设法挤进了公共汽车. *The crash reduced the car to ~.* 汽车经过这次碰撞变成一堆稀巴烂的东西了. ~ **hat** 软呢帽〔可以折叠的宽边呢帽〕. ~ **racquets** 小型墙球戏. ~ **tennis** 大型墙球戏.

squash[2] [skɔʃ] *n.* 【植】南瓜,倭瓜;笋瓜;西葫芦. ~ **bug** 【虫】南瓜虫.

squash·y [ˈskɔʃi] *a.* *(-i·er; -i·est)* ①易压碎[压扁]的. ②软而湿的. ③(道路)泥泞的. ④(水果)熟透了的. ~ *cantaloupes* 熟透了的甜瓜. **-i·ly** *ad.* **-i·ness** *n.*

squat [skwɔt] *vi.* *(~·ted, squat)* ①蹲;坐. ②〔美俚〕大便. ③(动物)爬在地上,蹲伏. ④〔口〕坐 *(down, on)*. ⑤【海】(高速航行中)船尾下坐. ⑥〔美〕非法擅自占住空地、空房、公地等. ⑦〔美〕依法在公地上定居〔以图取得所有权〕. ⑧〔美商〕违约. ⑨〔美俚〕被处电刑. — *vt.* ①使蹲下. ②占住;霸占. *Under the shade of a tree, she ~ted down on the ground.* 在树荫之下,她蹲坐在地上. *He ~ted down as a Japanese.* 他象日本人似的蹲坐着. ~ ***on*** 〔美〕停止;拚命反对;责难. ~ ***oneself*** 蹲下. ~ **hot** 被电刑处死,坐电椅. **take a** ~ 大便. — *a.* ①蹲着的. ②矮胖的. — *n.* ①蹲;蹲伏的位置[姿势]. ②矮胖子. *the hot* ~ 〔俚〕电椅.

squat·ter [ˈskwɔtə] *n.* ①蹲着的人[动物]. ②〔美〕擅自占住者;在公地上定住者. ③〔澳〕牧羊场主. ~ **sovereignty** 【美史】人民主权论〔南北战争前的一种政治思想,主张各州人民有权处理其内政,并决定是否容许奴隶制 = popular sovereignty〕.

squat·ty [ˈskwɔti] *a.* *(-ti·er; -ti·est)* ①蹲着的. ②矮胖的.

squat·ter [ˈskɔtə] *vi.* 涉水而行,蹚水.

squaw [skwɔ:] *n.* ①北美印地安女人,印第安人的妻子. ②〔俚谑〕老婆. ③〔贬〕女子气的男人. ④蹲跪人形靶. *the ~ with the papoose on her back* 揹着孩子的印第安女人; (北斗七星中的)开阳双星. ~ **fish** 【动】①(美国西部河流中的)折唇鱼. ②(北美洲太平洋海岸的)海鲫. ~**man** 娶印地安女人做妻子的白人.

squawk [skwɔ:k] *n.* ①嘎嘎〔鸟、鸡、鸭等的叫声〕. ②【鸟】黑冠夜苍鹭. ③〔美俚〕粗厉的叫声. ④大声诉苦,抗议. — *vi.* ①(鸡、鸭、鸟等)嘎嘎地叫. ②〔美俚〕(粗声大声地诉苦,发牢骚,抗议. ③〔美俚〕自首;告密. *This is the third time the tourists ~ed about the service of the hotel.* 这是旅客们第三次对饭店的服务发牢骚了. *The dog barked and the hens ~ed in terror.* 狗吠了,鸡也吓得嘎嘎地叫了起来. — *vt.* 粗声叫出. ~ **box** (内部联系用)对讲机. ~ **sheet** 飞行员关于飞机在飞行时各种缺点的报告. **-er** *n.*

squawk·ies [ˈskwɔki:z] *n.* 〔*pl.*〕〔美谑〕有声电影.

squeak [skwi:k] *vi.* ①(鼠等)叽叽的叫;(婴儿)哇哇的哭;发尖锐声,作轧轹声. ②〔俚〕告密. ③非常侥幸成功[获胜]. —*vt.* 以短促尖锐声发出(报时信号等). — *n.* ①叽叽声〔鼠等的叫声〕;刺耳的尖锐声,轧轹声. ②〔口〕困难通过的危机,极难得的机会. ③机会. *When I entered the room, Little Tom gave a startled ~.* 我进屋的时候,小汤姆吓了一跳哇哇地哭了. *a ~ stick* 〔美俚〕= clarinet. *I had a ~ of it.* 我好容易才得救[成功]了. *We've pulled you through a narrow [near, tight] ~.* 我们侥幸地助你通过了难关. **-er** *n.*

squeak·y [ˈskwi:ki] *a.* *(-i·er; -i·est)* 发刺耳声的,叽叽叫的,哇哇哭的,发轧轹声的. **-i·ly** *ad.* **-i·ness** *n.*

squeal [skwi:l] *vi.* ①(婴儿等因痛苦、恐怖、发怒、欢喜等)哇哇地叫,尖声呼叫,号叫. ②〔俚〕激烈抗议 *(against)*. ③〔俚〕告密. — *n.* ①尖叫(声). ②〔美〕抗议. *The kids ~ed with delight at the sight of the Christmas tree.* 娃娃们看到圣诞树喜欢得尖声高叫起来. *The accountant says she's going to ~ on the manager for graft and embezzlement.* 会计说她就要告发经理贪污公款.

squeal·er [ˈskwi:lə] *n.* ①发尖叫声的动物,雏鸟等. ②〔学生语〕吵闹的初级生. ③〔美俚〕告密者.

squeal·ing [ˈskwi:liŋ] *n.* 【无】啸声,振鸣声;号叫(声).

squeam·ish [ˈskwi:miʃ] *a.* ①易呕吐的. ②易受惊的,易生气的,神经质的. ③过分讲究细节的,好吹毛求疵的,过于拘谨的. **-ly** *ad.* **-ness** *n.*

squee·gee [ˈskwi:ˈdʒi:] *n.* ①(横木上装有橡皮条用以扫甲板、地板上积水,擦玻璃的)橡皮扫帚. ②【摄】(压去相片上水分的)橡皮滚子. ③(自命的)重要人物. — *vt.* ①用橡皮扫帚扫除,拭清. ②【摄】用橡皮滚子压去水分.

squeez·a·bil·i·ty [skwi:zəˈbiliti] *n.* ①可压榨,可榨取. ②可敲诈,可勒索.

squee·zable [ˈskwi:zəbl] *a.* ①可压榨的,可榨取的. ②可敲诈的,可勒索的.

squeeze [skwi:z] *vt.* ①挤,压,塞;压出,挤出 *(out; from)*. ②压迫,压榨,剥削(人民等);榨取;勒索,敲诈 *(from)*. ③握紧(手等);紧抱. ④压进,挤入 *(into)*. ⑤拓印(碑文等). ⑥使(利润等)缩减. ⑦勉强赢得(赚得). ⑧压印(硬币等). ⑨(桥牌中)逼对方出牌. — *vi.* ①压;挤;挤过 *(through)*;榨. ②压榨. ③勉强通过[赢得]. ④拓印(碑文等). ~ *a lemon dry* 挤干柠檬. *a ~d lemon [orange]* 〔喻〕被榨干后(被抛弃)的人. *S-yourselves a little.* 请各位再挤紧一点. *Can you ~ past?* 你挤得过去吗? ~ *money from the people* 勒索人民的钱. ~ *the shorts* 【交易所】杀空头. ~*ing bulls [bears]* 忍痛补卖[买]的多头[空头]. ~ ***in*** 挤入. ~ ***off*** 扳枪机射击. ***Squeeze one!*** 〔美俚〕来一瓶橘子汁. ~ ***one's waist in*** 勒紧腰杆. ~ ***one's way through a crowd*** 在人群中挤过去. ~ ***out*** 榨取,挤出,勒索;排斥,排挤. ~ ***out a tear*** 干哭,装哭. ~ ***to death*** 压死. — *n.* ①挤压,压榨;〔口〕压力. ②握紧,抱紧;塞紧;拥挤. ②〔口〕榨取,勒索,敲诈;贿赂. ③榨出的少量东西. ④密集的一群人. ⑤佣金,回扣. ⑥(桥碑中)被扔出的牌. ⑦(碑铭等的)拓印. *We all got in, but it was a (tight) ~.* 我们都进去了,可是太拥挤了. *a ~ of people on the square* 广场上密集的一群人. ***at [upon] a ~*** 在危急中. ***be in a tight ~*** 陷入困境. ***put a ~ on sb.*** 对某人施加压力. ~ **bottle** 软塑料挤瓶〔挤捏之下,内装之物可以挤出来,如塑料胶水瓶等〕. ~ **play** 【棒球】(迫使三垒跑者跑回本垒的)轻打战术;【桥牌】迫使对方吐出能起重要作用的牌的出法;〔喻〕施加压力.

squeez·er [ˈskwi:zə] *n.* ①压榨者;榨取者,剥削者,敲诈者,勒索者. ②压铆机;压榨机. ③【织】轧水机. ④〔*pl.*〕右上角记有花式和点数的纸牌. ⑤〔美俚〕吝啬者,小气的人.

squeg [skweg] *vi.* *(squegged; squeg·ging)* 【无】作非常不规则的振荡.

squelch [skweltʃ] *vt.* ①压碎. ②镇压,压服,压制. ③使哑口无言;使不知所措不再作声. ④在泥水中(使)发出格喳声. —*vi.* ①格喳格喳地作响. ②格喳格喳地响着走,涉水而行. *Five proposals were made and each was ~ed by the manager.* 提出了五项建议,每一个都被经理压了回去. *I could hear his broken shoes ~ing in the water.* 我可以听到他的破鞋在水中格喳格喳作响. — *n.* ①压碎. ②镇压,压制. ③〔口〕压倒对方的议论[回答];反驳得对方不再作声. ④格喳格喳声. ⑤【无】噪声抑制(电路);无噪声(电路);【空】静音. ~ *circuit* 【无】噪声抑制[无噪声]电路.

sque·teague [skwi:ˈti:g] *n.* *(pl. sque·teague)* = weakfish.

squib [skwib] *n.* ①爆筒;导火管;爆竹,甩砲. ②【军】电气导火管;小型点火器. ③(讽刺或幽默的)讲话,短文. ④补白. ⑤胡乱写成的短文. — *vi., vt.* ①扔爆筒;放爆竹. ②发表或作讽刺短文 *(against; at; on; upon)*. ③信口地讲,随便地写. *Don't spend your time on writing this sort of ~s.* 不要花时间写这路的讽刺短文了. *A newspaperman says they want versified ~s.* 一个报馆人说他们要幽默的讽刺诗.

squid[1] [skwid] *n.* *(pl. ~s,* 〔集合词〕 *~)* (食用或作饵

用)枪乌鲗，柔鱼，鱿鱼. — *vi.* ①(降落伞)成乌鲗状. ②捕乌鲗;用乌鲗作饵捕鱼.

squid[2] [skwid] *n.* 反潜多筒迫击炮.

squiffed [skwift] *a.* 喝醉了的.

squiff·er [ˈskwifə] *n.* 〔英俚〕六角小手风琴.

squif·fy [ˈskwifi] *a.* = squiffed.

squig·gle [ˈskwigl] *n.* ①蜿曲线. ②(无法辨认的)曲里拐弯的字迹. — *vt.* ***(-gled; -gling)*** ①形成蜿曲线. ②潦草地书写. — *vi.* ①作蜿曲线. ②蜿蜒瞟动. **-gly** *a.*

squil·gee [ˈskwilˈdʒiː] *n., vt.* = squeegee.

squill [skwil] *n.* ①【植】绵枣儿属植物;海葱;海葱根. ②【动】虾蛄. ~**-fiis**【动】虾蛄.

squil·la [ˈskwilə] *n.* ***(pl. -las, lae*** [-iː]***)***【动】虾蛄属*(squilla)*动物.

squinch [skwintʃ] *n.*【建】突角拱.

squin·ny [ˈskwini] *n., vi., vt.* ***(-nied; -ny·ing)*** 〔罕〕= squint.

squint [skwint] *a.* 斜着眼的,斜视的;细眯着眼看的. — *n.* ①斜视眼;斜视. ②一瞥,一瞟. ③倾向(某一政策等) *(to; towards)*. ④【建】斜孔小窗;窥视窗. ⑤(教会的)圣体遥拜窗. ⑥【无】斜倾,偏斜〔指天线方向性〕;斜视角;两波束轴间夹角. *have a bad* ~ 斜视得厉害. *Let me have a* ~ *at it.* 让我看一看. *His speech shows a* ~ *to your view.* 他的演说表现出倾向于你的看法. — *vi.* ①斜着眼看,眯着眼看. ②成斜视眼. ③倾向. ④偏斜,偏斜正确方向. ~ ***at*** 瞟一瞟,瞟眼偷看一下; 看,窥视. *He lost his glasses and had to* ~ *into the dark.* 他把眼镜丢了,不得不眯着眼在黑地上走. ⑤有间接关系(或意义). — *vt.* 斜视;眯眼睛看. ~**-eyed** *a* ①斜眼的. ②斜视的. ③侧目而视的,恶意的. ~**ing modifier**【语法】歧义修饰语〔指误放位置的副词,解释为修饰不同的两个词都可以〕. **-ing·ly** *ad.* **-y** *a.*

squint·er [ˈskwintə] *n.* 斜视者;斜视眼.

squire [ˈskwaiə] *n.* ①〔英〕(地主阶级的)乡绅,老爷〔敬称用〕. ②殷勤伺候妇女的人;献殷勤以追求妇女的人. ③骑士的随从;扈从. ④〔美〕对治安官,法官的敬称;律师,法官. — *vt.* ①在社交场合作为保护者与特定的一个妇女作伴. ②护卫,侍从. ~**arch** 〔英〕地主. ~**archy** 〔英〕地主政治;地主势力;〔集合词〕地主阶级. ~**let**, ~**ling** 小地主.

squir·een [ˌskwaiəˈriːn] *n.* 〔爱〕乡绅;小地主.

squir·ess [ˈskwaires] *n.* 地主夫人,女地主.

squirm [skwəːm] *vi.* ①蠕动;蠢动. ②折腾;展转反侧地不安,觉得不好意思. — *n.* ①蠢动,蠕动;折腾. ②〔罕〕【海】绳索的扭曲. **-y** *a.*

squir·rel [ˈskwirəl] *n.*【动】①松鼠. ②松鼠毛皮. ③〔美俚〕心理学家. ④威士忌酒. ⑤怪人,疯子. ⑥乱开车的人. ⑦追随人家后面想成为其中的一分子的人. ~ **cage** 松鼠笼子;〔喻〕无目的而又无尽头的单调生活〔活动〕. ~ **corn**【植】加拿大荷包牡丹. ~ **dew** 〔美〕酒. ~ **dumplings** 〔美俚〕面条. ~ **fish** 鳂属的鱼. **a** ~ **food** 〔美俚〕坚果〔松子,核桃等〕;精神不健全的人. ~ **hawk** 捕食松鼠的大鹰. ~ **monkey** 鼠猴. **a** ~ **shooter** 〔美俚〕(边远地区的)乡下人.

squir·rel·(l)y [ˈskwəːrəli] *a.* 〔美俚〕古怪的;疯狂的,毫无意义的.

squirt [skwəːt] *vt., vi.* ①喷射,喷湿;喷出. ②注射;(使)迸出. — *n.* ①喷,细的喷流. ②水枪;注射器. ③〔口〕忽然高升的人;傲慢无礼的年轻人. ④〔俚〕喷气式飞机. ~ **gun** 喷射器,水枪. ~**ing cucumber**【植】喷瓜.

squish [skwiʃ] *vt.* 〔方〕= squash[1]. — *n.* ①= squash[1]. ②〔口〕= marmalade.

squish·y [ˈskwiʃi] *a.* 〔美俚〕湿软的;粘糊糊的;易压扁的;发出泥浆的咯吱声的.

sq. yd. = square yard(s).

S.R. = ①solid rocket 固体(燃料)火箭. ②Southern Railway 〔英〕南方铁路. ③Shipping Receipt 船货收据. ④specific resistance 电阻率. ⑤star route 〔美〕星号邮线.

Sr. = ①Senior. ②Sir. ③〔Pg.〕*Senhor.* ④〔Sp.〕*Señor.* ⑤【化】strontium.

Sra = ①〔Port.〕Senhor. ②〔Sp.〕Señora.

SRAAM = short-range air-to-air missile 近程空对空导弹.

SRAM = short-range attack missile 近程攻击导弹.

SRBM = short-range ballistic missile 近程弹道导弹.

Sres. = 〔Sp.〕Señores.

Sri Lanka [sri ˈlæŋkə] 斯里兰卡〔亚洲〕.

S.R.N. = State Registered Nurse 〔英〕合格护士.

S.R.O. = ①standing room only 只有站票〔戏院或车辆售票处用语〕. ②Statutory Rules and Orders 成文法令.

S.R.S. = Statistics and Reports Section 统计报告部.

Srta = Señorita.

S.S = ①sections. ②shortstop. ③【处方】*semis* (〔L.〕= a half).

SS., ss. = ①scilicet. ②Saints. ③〔G.〕*Schutzstaffel.*

S.S., SS = ①steamship. ②〔G.〕*Schutzstaffel.*

S.S. = ①Secretary of State 〔美〕国务卿. ②Secret Service 〔英〕特工处. ③short stick 短码尺〔1 码 = $35\frac{1}{2}$ 英寸〕. ④simplified spelling 简易拼写法. ⑤Statistical Society 〔英〕(皇家)统计学会. ⑥Sunday-school 主日学校.

S/S = steamship.

SSB(N) = ship, submarine, ballistic (nuclear-powered) (核动力)弹道导弹潜艇.

SSCAE = Special Senate Committee on Atomic Energy 〔美〕参议院原子能特别委员会.

S.S.E., SSE,s.s.e. = south-southeast.

SSgt, SSGT = staff sergeant 〔英〕陆军上士;〔美〕空军〔海军陆战队〕参谋军士.

SSM = ①surface-to-surface missile 地对地导弹. ②staff sergeant major 军士长.

SSP =【生】subspecies 亚种.

SST = supersonic transport【空】超音速运输机.

S.S.W., SSW,s.s.w. = south-southwest 西南南.

ST = sulphathiazole.

S.T. = summer time.

St = Saturday.

St.[1] [sənt, sint, snt] (= Saint).

St.[2] = ①Street. ②Strait.

st. = ①stanza. ②〔L.〕*stet* 〔校对符号〕不删. ③stone (重量单位). ④strong. ⑤statute.

s.t. = short ton 短吨.

-st *comb. f.* 〔在古语和诗作中接在动词后,构成陈述语气第二人称单数〕: did*st*.

STA = station.

S.T.A. Sail Training Association 〔英〕航海训练协会.

sta. = ①station(ary). ②stator.

stab. = stable.

stab[1] [stæb] *vt.* ***(stab·bed*** [stæbd]***, stab·bing)*** ①刺,戳,刺入,刺伤. ②伤害,刺痛(感情等). ③用线钉(书). ④【建】把墙面凿粗糙(以涂灰泥). — *vi.* 刺,刺伤. *He was* ~*bed by a terrorist with a sword.* 他被一个恐怖分子用匕首刺伤了. *Mother's scold* ~*bed her to the heart.* 妈妈的责骂刺伤了她的心. *A sharp pain* ~*bed at his right knee.* 他的右膝感觉到一阵剧痛. ~ ***sb. in the back*** 背后暗害〔中伤〕某人. ~ ***the pill*** 〔美棒球〕捕接快球. — *n.* ①刺,戳,刺痛,刺伤. ②一种突然强烈的感觉. ③背后骂〔害〕人,暗害,中伤. ④试图,努力. *I have a sharp* ~ *of pain in the stomach.* 我的胃突然感觉一阵剧痛. ***a*** ~ ***in the back*** 背后一刀,伤人的暗箭,中伤,诽谤. ***have [make, take] a*** ~ ***at [on]*** *(sth.)* 〔美

俚〕试图做某事，对某物有企图. ~ **culture**【医】穿刺培养.
stab² [stæb] *a.* 周薪制，时薪制. *a* ~ *hand* 周薪工人.
stab³ [stæb]〔俚〕= established; establishment.
Sta·bat Ma·ter [ˈstɑːbæt ˈmɑːtə]〔L.〕【宗】圣母悼歌.
stab·ber [ˈstæbə] *n.* ①穿刺器. ②(虱的)口针. ③穿索针，锥. ④刺客.
stab·bing [ˈstæbiŋ] *a.* 刺穿的；伤感情的. **-ly** *ad.*
sta·bile [ˈsteibl, -bil] *a.* ①稳定的，固定的，空位的. ②【医】抗温热的，稳定性的. — *n.* 静态抽象雕塑〔通常为用金属、铁丝、木头等制作的结构〕.
sta·bil·i·ty [stəˈbiliti] *n.* ①稳定，稳定性，稳度. ②(船等的)复原力. ③巩固；坚定，持久不变. *secure financial* ~ 确保财政上的稳定.
sta·bi·li·za·tion [ˌsteibilaiˈzeiʃən] *n.* 稳定(作用)，币值的稳定；坚定，固定. *effect economic* ~ 实现经济的稳定. **-za·tor** *n.* = stabilizer.
sta·bi·lize [ˈsteibilaiz] *vt.* 使稳定；使安定；使固定.—*vi.* 稳定，安定. ~ *the currency* 稳定货币. *a* ~*d warfare* 阵地战. *a stabilizing apparatus* 稳定装置. *stabilizing fins*【空】稳定叶片. *Prices have* ~*d.* 物价已经稳定了.
sta·bi·liz·er [ˈsteibilaizə] *n.* ①稳定器，平衡器，止摇机. ②(防止火药自然分解的)稳定剂. ③【空】稳定〔安定〕面. ④【医】定安剂.
sta·ble¹ [ˈsteibl] *a.* ①稳定的；安定的；固定的. ②意志坚定的，有恒心的. ~ *currency* 稳定的通货. *a* ~ *economy* 稳定的经济. ~ *equilibrium*【物】稳〔安〕定平衡，(船的)复原力. ~ *opinions* 坚定的意见. **-bly** *ad.* **-ness** *n.*
sta·ble² [steibl] *n.* ①厩，马厩，马棚；〔罕〕牛栏，牛棚. ②〔集合词〕同一个人所有的〔一个马厩内的〕全部马匹或牛. ③〔集合词〕同一个经理人掌握的全部运动员〔演员，作家等〕. ④〔常 *pl.*〕【军】马厩值勤；马匹的查看(等)；〔常用~-call〕马厩值勤号. ⑤〔美俚〕妓院，属于一个把头的全部妓女. ⑥大学生用的一套解答书. *the whole* ~ 厩内所有马. *a* ~ *police*〔美军俚〕马房兵. *back the wrong* ~ 赌错马；失算，考虑错. ~ *manure* 厩肥. — *vt., vi.* 关进马厩(或牛棚)里，拴在马厩(牛棚)里；(马牛)关在棚里. *lock [shut] the* ~ *door when [after] the horse is stolen.*〔谚〕贼走关门. *smell of the* ~ (一个人的言行)带有所从事职业的味道. ~**boy** 马夫. ~ **companion, -man** 马夫.〔美俚〕同厩的马；同学；俱乐部同人. ~**mate** ①同一马主的马. ②受雇于同一老板的拳击手. ~**push**〔美俚〕内幕新闻；来自有影响人士的消息. ~**r** *n.* 厩主，棚主.
sta·bling [ˈsteibliŋ] *n.* ①马厩，牛棚. ②马厩或牛棚(设备).
stab·lish [ˈstæbliʃ] *vt.*〔古〕= establish.
stac·ca·to [stəˈkɑːtəu] *a.* ①〔It.〕【乐】断奏的 (*opp.* legato). ②断续的，不连贯的. — *ad.* 断奏地，奏成断音地，不连贯地. — *n.* ①断奏. ②断续的一段音乐. ③不连贯的东西(如说话，发动机的声音等). ~ *mark* 断音符号. *Maybe I'm a backnumber. I can never enjoy a play of* ~ *scenes.* 也许我是个落伍的人了，我欣赏不了一出场面互不连贯的戏.
stack [stæk] *n.* ①(麦秆等的)堆，垛；干草堆. ②积材，层积，堆积；〔英〕一堆〔木材等的计量单位，= 108 立方英尺〕. ③〔常 *pl.*〕(图书馆的)许多书架；书库 (= ~ room). ④【无】迭式存储器. ⑤枪架. ⑥烟囱；一排〔一群〕烟囱，车船的烟突. ⑦【机】管组. ⑧〔英〕(突出海面的)浪蚀岩柱，海中孤峰. ⑨(赌博时的)一堆筹码. ⑩〔口〕许多，大量. *a precariously ballanced* ~ *of books* 眼看就要倒下来的一堆书. *a* ~ *of postcards [old newspapers, shoeboxes]* 一大堆明信片〔旧报纸、鞋盒〕. *a* ~ *of rice straw* 稻草垛. *a considerable* ~ *of evidence* 大量的证明材料. *have* ~*s of work to do* 有许多工作要做. ~ *of arms* 枪架. — *vt.* ①堆叠，堆垛，堆积，堆起. ②【空】指令飞机作分层盘旋飞行等待依次着陆. ③【军】架(枪). ④秘密地预先安排好，内定. ⑤〔美俚〕把房间弄得乱七八糟. ⑥【桥牌】洗牌作弊. *S- arms!*【军】架枪! ***be nicely*** ~***ed up*** 体态丰满匀称的〔指妇女〕. — *vi.* 成堆，堆起来. ***blow one's*** ~〔俚〕大发脾气 (*When he came in and saw the mess he blew his* ~. 他一进屋里看见那个混乱情况就大发一顿脾气). ***have the cards*** ~***ed against sb.*** 把某人的处境被弄得极端不利. ~ ***the pins***〔美，运〕准备下一次比赛. ~ ***up*** ①总起来，加起来 (*He is all abroad as to how things* ~ *up today.* 他对当前总的形势毫无所知). ②(飞机)分层盘旋飞行. ③与某人相称〔比较〕(*to*)；与…较量〔争输赢〕(*with, against*) (*She doesn't* ~ *up to you, honey.* 她不如你，小宝贝儿)! ④牵强附会，表面似乎合理 (*Your story just doesn't* ~ *up.* 你讲的简直是胡说八道). ~ ***up the velvet***〔美，剧〕赚到钱，营业情况好. ~ **funnel** 烟囱内的尖塔形通风设备. ~ **room** 书库. ~ **up**【空】分层盘旋飞行. **-er** *n.* ①堆垛者. ②可升降摄象机台.
stac·te [ˈstæktiː] *n.* (古犹太人用来制造香料的)没药.
stac·tom·e·ter [stækˈtɔmitə] *n.* 滴量计.
stad·dle [ˈstædl] *n.* ①〔古，方〕底部，底撑架；〔尤指〕草垛的底. ②根底，基础.
stade [steid] *n.* (古希腊罗马的)赛跑场〔长 607 英尺，周围有台阶式看台〕.
stad·hold·er, stad·thold·er [ˈstædˌhəuldə] *n.*【史】荷兰的省长，荷兰联合省的最高行政长官.
sta·di·a¹ [ˈsteidiə] *n.*【测，土木】视距(测量)；视距仪.
sta·di·a² [ˈsteidiə] *n.* stadium 的复数.
sta·di·um [ˈsteidiəm] *n.* ***(pl. -dia*** [-diə]***)*** ①斯达地〔古希腊、罗马长度单位，约 = 600 希腊尺，合 607 英尺；赛跑场的跑道以这个长度为准〕. ②【古希腊】赛跑场；***(pl.*** ~***s)*** (现在的)运动场，体育场. ③【医】(疾病的第…)期. ④【生】龄期(尤指前后二次换羽或脱皮之间的). *an indoor* ~ 室内体育馆.
staff¹ [stɑːf] *n.* ***(pl. staves,*** ~***s)*** ①〔*pl.* 通常作 staves〕棍，棒，杖，竿；旗竿；(枪、戟等的)柄. ②支柱. ③权标，权杖，指挥棒. ④(测量或造船用的)标竿，标尺. ⑤【机】小轴杆. ⑥〔*pl.* 通常作 ~s〕【铁道】路签. ⑦【医】导引探子. ⑧【音】五线谱. ⑨(全体)职员，干部，工作人员；编辑部. ⑩【军】参谋(人员)；参谋机构. *Bread is the* ~ *of life.* 面包是生活的必需品〔主要支持物〕. *A son should be the* ~ *of his father's old age.* 儿子是父亲老年的依靠. *the editorial* ~ 编辑部(职员). *the medical* ~ 全体医务人员. *the teaching* ~ 全体教员. *the domestic* ~ 用人. *a* ~*-author* = *a* ~*-writer* 影片公司属下的作家. *the general and his* ~ 将军和他的参谋(部). *the Headquarters of the General S*~ 总参谋部. *the Chief of the General S*~ 总参谋长. *a military [naval]* ~ *college* 陆〔海〕军参谋学院. ***be on the*** ~ 在职，是职员〔部员、干部〕. — *vt.* 给…调配干部. *What we need is a hospital and a finely* ~*ed one.* 我们需要一所医院而且是医务人员充实的医院. ~ **cuts** 裁减人员. ~ **locator** 值勤号铃. ~ **officer** 参谋. ~ **record**【商】工作记录. ~ **sergeant**〔英陆军〕上士；〔美空军〕参谋军士. ~ **work** 参谋工作；组织，经营.
staff² [stæf] *n.*【建】纤维灰浆.
staff·er [ˈstɑːfə, ˈstæfə] *n.* 职员，工作人员〔如报刊的编辑人员〕.
staff-tree [ˈstɑːfˈtriː] *n.*【植】南蛇藤属 (*Celastrus*) 植物〔包括美洲南蛇藤 (*Celastrus scandens*)〕. — *a.* 卫茅科 (*Celastraceae*) 的.
stag [stæg] *n.* ①牡(赤)鹿，雄狐，公火鸡(等). ②阉过的雄畜〔牛、猪〕. ③刚长大的雄家禽. ④【商】非会员股票经纪人. ⑤非真心投资，遇有有利机会即行出售股票的认股者. ⑥〔美〕不带女伴的舞客；单身出外交际的男人；全是男人的社交集会〔又叫 ~ party (*opp.* hen party)，忌说 cock party〕. ⑦〔苏格兰〕小马. ⑧〔英〕告密者.

— *vi.* ①不带女伴单身赴会。②〔商俚〕买进新股(等)见利即抛。③不带女伴参加舞会。— *vt.* ①〔美俚〕密探，盯梢；告密；叛变。②截短长裤。— *a.* ①全是男人(集会等)的。②无异性伴侣的。~ *it* 〔美俚〕单身(不带女伴)赴会。*Jack says he goes ~ every Saturday night.* 贾克说他每个星期六晚上不带女伴去跳舞。~ **beetle**【虫】锹螂；锹形甲虫；鹿角甲虫。~**-evil** 马的破伤风。~ **horn** 公鹿的角；【植】石松；鹿角大珊瑚。~ **hound**【动】鹿猩[猎鹿猎狗]。~ **muck** 〔美俚〕糊涂虫。

stage [steidʒ] *n.* ①讲台；舞台；戏院，剧场；〔the ~〕戏剧，戏剧艺术，戏剧文学；〔the ~〕戏剧业，剧坛。②(活动)舞台；活动范围(场所)；注意中心。③(显微镜的)镜台。④(发展的)阶段，时期，程度，步骤。⑤【影】室内摄影场。⑥(建筑用的)脚手架；栈桥，浮码头，趸船。⑦站，驿站；一站路的行程；驿马车，公共马车[汽车]。⑧【地】(地层的)阶，段，层；(地文的)期。⑨浮码头，趸船(= landing ~)。*a ~ hog* 〔美〕爱到舞台正面去表现自己的演员。~ *attitude* 表演(艺术)。~ *presentation* 上演，上场。*theory of the development of revolution by ~s* 革命发展阶段论。*in the early ~s* 在初期。*the larval ~* 幼虫期。*The proposal has not yet passed the discussion ~.* 这个提案还没有通过讨论阶段。*The disease now occupies the centre of the medical ~.* 这种病现在是医学界的注意中心。***at the ~ of being*** 暂时，在目前。***be on the ~*** 过演员生活。***bring on [to] the ~*** 上演(戏剧)；扮演。***come on [upon] the ~*** 上舞台，进入社会(活动)。***go on the ~*** 做演员。***hold the ~*** 继续上演；引人注目。***put on the ~*** 上演；扮演。***quit the ~*** 退出舞台；辞职，退出…界。***take to the ~*** 做演员。***travel by long [easy, short] ~s*** 匆匆[从容]旅行；赶着[拖拖拉拉地]做。— *vt.* ①演出，搬上舞台，上演。②〔美〕筹办，举行，发起(某事)。— *vi.* ①坐公共马车旅行。②(剧本)适于上演，上舞台。~ *a comeback* 〔美〕卷土重来，恢复原有地位；再度走红，复辟；(花)重开。*This play ~s only one woman character among the armymen.* 这出戏只有一个女角色在男性军人之中。*Teachers of the Arts College are going to ~ an exhibition.* 艺术学院的教师们在筹划着要举办一个展览。~ *a meet* 〔美〕举行比赛。~ **box** (舞台旁)特别包厢。~ **coach** 公共马车，驿站马车。~ **craft** 戏剧作法，编剧法；编剧才能；戏剧演出法。~ **direction** 舞台说明，演出说明[准备]。~ **director** (戏剧)导演。~ **door** 后台口。~ **effect** 舞台效果。~ **fever** (想做戏剧演员的)演员狂，舞台狂。~ **fright** (特指初上舞台时的)怯场。~**hand** 舞台[布景，道具，照明]管理员。~ **manage** *vt.* ①舞台监督。②作戏剧性安排[尤指背后操纵]。~ **manager** 舞台监督；戏剧导演；戏院经理。~ **play** (话剧)剧本。~ **player** (舞台)演员。~ **right** 上演权。~ **setting** 舞台装置。~**-struck** *a.* 一心想做戏剧演员的。~ **whisper** (舞台上的)高声私语；故意给人听见的私语。

stag·er [ˈsteidʒə] *n.* ①演员。②公共马车的马。③经验丰富的人[动物]，识途老马，内行。*an old ~* 老手，内行。

stage·wise[1] [ˈsteidʒwaiz] *a.* ①有戏剧知识的。②有戏剧效果的。*a ~ director* 善于制造戏剧效果的导演。

stage·wise[2] [ˈsteidʒwaiz] *ad.* 在舞台上；在戏剧方面。

stage·y [ˈsteidʒi] *a.* ***(stag·i·er; stag·i·est)*** = stagy.

stag·fla·tion [stægˈfleiʃən] *n.*【经济】经济停滞与通货膨胀，停滞膨胀。

stag·gard [ˈstægəd] *n.* 四岁牡鹿。

stag·ger [ˈstægə] *vi.* ①蹒跚，摇摇晃晃。②逡巡，犹豫，动摇。— *vt.* ①使摇晃。②使逡巡，犹豫，动摇。③使吃一惊，使吓一跳。④使(辐条等)左右交错；使(复翼飞机的上下翼)前后交错。④〔口〕使(上下班、吃饭时间等)错开(以减轻交通拥挤情况)。*Grandma managed to ~ upstairs.* 奶奶好不容易地摇晃晃地上了楼。*For a moment I ~ed at the price.* 我听了价钱迟疑了一会儿。*I was positively ~ed by the news.* 我真的给这消息吓了一跳。~ *office hours* 错开上下班时间。~ ***along*** 摇摇晃晃地走。~ ***around the lot*** 〔美〕比赛成绩不行。~ ***in*** 〔美〕(特指赛跑)跑得末名；【棒球】(以很少的比分)勉强得胜。~ ***to one's feet*** 摇摇摆摆地站起来。~***ed wings***【空】交错翼。— *n.* ①蹒跚，摇晃，动摇，摆动；摆动误差。②〔*pl.*〕眼花，眩晕，酒醉；〔复数用作单数〕(马等的)晕倒症〔又叫 *blind ~s*〕。③斜罩，交错；(上下班等的)交错制。④〔美〕企图，努力。⑤【空】(双翼机)斜罩，前伸角。~ **bush**【植】马氏南烛〔北美洲东部一种灌木，开白色或粉红色花，牲畜食之中毒〕。~ **juice [soup]** 〔美俚〕酒。~ **wires**【空】斜罩线。

stag·ger·er [ˈstægərə] *n.* ①摆晃[蹒跚，犹豫]的人。②难题，难关。

stag·ger·ing [ˈstægəriŋ] *a.* ①摇晃的。②(令人)犹豫的。③令人吃惊的；压倒的；数目大得令人吃惊的。*The external debts of that country are ~.* 那个国家的外债大得惊人。**-ly** *ad.*

stag·gy [ˈstægi] *a.* (雌畜或阉过的雄畜)象成年雄畜的。

stag·ing [ˈsteidʒiŋ] *n.* ①脚手架。②【工】构架，台架。③驿马车旅行。④驿[公共]马车业。⑤【剧】上演。⑥【军】(人员或物资的)分段运输；中间集结。⑦【宇】宇宙飞船与火箭脱离。~ **area**【军】集结待运地区。~ **base**【军】飞机中间停留基地；舰船中间补给基地；前进基地。~ **post**【军】补给站。

Stag·i·rite [ˈstædʒirait] *n.* (古希腊马其顿的)斯塔吉利亚(Stageira)城的人。*the S-* 亚里斯多德的别称。

stag·nan·cy [ˈstægnənsi] ①停滞不动，淤积不流，滞止。②迟钝，呆滞。③不景气，不振，萧条。

stag·nant [ˈstægnənt] *a.* ①停滞的，不流动的。②(水等因不流动而)污浊的。③迟钝的，呆笨的。④萧条的，不景气的。*The room was small and the air ~.* 屋子小空气污浊。*The market is extremely ~.* 市场极为萧条。*Without criticism and self criticism, a man will become ~.* 一个人没有批评自我批评会变得迟钝的。**-ly** *ad.*

stag·nate [ˈstægneit] *vt., vi.* ①(使)(水等)停滞不流。②(使)不动，(使)不活动。③(使)迟钝。(使)不活泼。④(使)变萧条。

stag·na·tion [stægˈneiʃən] *n.* ①停滞，不流，不动；滞止。②萧条。③迟钝。*a ~ point*【数】静点，驻点。

stag·nico·lous [stægˈnikələs] *a.* 生活于沼泽地的，生活于死水中的。

stag·y [ˈsteidʒi] *a.* ***(-i·er; -i·est)*** ①做戏似的。②戏剧(性)的；舞台的。③不真实的，做作的，缺乏真实感的。**-i·ly** *ad.* **-i·ness** *n.*

staid [steid] *a.* ①固定的，不动的，稳定的。②认真的，踏实的，沉着的 *(opp.* frivolous, flighty*)*。— *v.* 〔古、美〕stay[1] 的过去式及过去分词。*your ~ opinion* 你的坚决的意见。*a ~ person* 一个沉着踏实的人。**-ly** *ad.* **-ness** *n.*

stain [stein] *vt.* ①弄脏，染污 *(with)*；沾污，玷污(名誉等)。②(在玻璃、生物切片等上面)染色。③(在糊墙纸上等)着色，印上颜色。— *vi.* 变肮脏，染污；生锈。*It is ~ed with ink.* 它让墨水弄脏了。*hands ~ed with blood* 沾满血的手；凶手。~*ed glass* 彩色玻璃，彩画玻璃。*This fabric ~s easily.* 这种织品容易弄脏。—*n.* ①污点；变色；锈；瑕疵 *(on; upon; of)*。②色斑。③色素，染色剂，着色剂。***without a ~ on one's character*** 性格上没有缺点。~ **fungus** 变色菌。**-able** *a.*

stained [steind] *a.* ①玷污的；褪色的。*a ~ hat* 一顶褪了色的帽子。②着色的，染色的。*a bookcase ~ and waxed* 着色打蜡的书橱。

stain·er [ˈsteinə] *n.* ①(木材皮革等的)着[染]色工。②上釉工人。③染料，色料，着色液。

stain·less [ˈsteinlis] *a.* ①不会脏的，不会染污的。②不生锈的。③无疵瑕的，纯洁的。~ **steel** 不锈钢。**-ly** *ad.*

stair [stɛə] *n.* ①(梯子的)一级。②〔常 *pl.*〕楼梯，阶梯。*the top ~ but one* 上面第二磴。*a flight [pair] of ~s* 一段楼梯。*He lives up two pairs of ~s* 他住在三层(即

再上去二层)楼上. *a winding* ~ 回转楼梯. ***below [down]*** ~***s*** ①在房子最下层. ②在地下室. ③在仆人房间. ④做着底下人工作. ***up*** ~***s*** 在[向]楼上. ***walk up the*** ~***s*** 上楼梯. ~ **carpet** 楼梯地毯. ~**case** 楼梯; 楼梯间[室]. ~**head** 楼梯顶端, 梯口. ~ **rod** 楼梯地毯夹条. ~**way** 〔美〕= staircase. ~**well**【建】楼梯井.

staith(e) [steiθ, -ð] *n.* 〔英〕(尤指煤炭)装卸转运码头.

stake[1] [steik] *n.* ①(标)桩; 竖管, 支柱. ②火刑柱〔人绑在柱上, 周围堆满木柴烧死〕; 〔*the* ~〕火刑. ③桩砧, 圆头砧, 小铁砧. ④(装在车辆四周, 防止所装货物散落的)栅柱. *tether a horse to a* ~ 把马拴在木桩上. ***pull up*** ~***s*** 〔美口〕离开; 收摊子. — *vt.* ①用桩撑持. ③立桩, 用桩分开, 用桩标出或围住. ③拴(马)在桩上; 拿桩戳. ~ ***off [out]*** 立标桩分(界). ~ ***off [out] a claim*** 树立标桩表示所有权; 提出要求. ~ ***out*** (警方对嫌疑犯)布设监视哨; 置于监视之下. ~ ***up [in]*** 设桩圈起来. ~ **boat** 航标艇, 赛船标志起点的标艇. ~ **body** 有栅柱的(平板)车身. ~ **net** 挂在桩上的渔网. ~-**out** (警方对嫌疑犯)布置监视哨; 设有监视哨的地区. ~ **truck** 有栅柱的卡车.

stake[2] [steik] *n.* ①赌博; 赌注, 赌金. ②〔*pl.*〕【运】奖金, 奖品; 有奖赛马. ③利害关系; 风险. ④下在投机生意上的股本. ⑤〔美口〕= grubstake. *enter for the Maiden Stakes.* 【赛马】把赌注押在生马上. *My honour is at* ~. 我的声名在危险中. *He has a deep* ~ *in the business.* 他和这个商店有极大的利害关系. **at** ~ 被赌着; 在危险中; 利害〔生死〕攸关. — *vt.* ①赌. ②〔美口语〕= grubstake. ③〔美俚〕(有偿地)对…给以经济援助. ~ *one's future on a single chance* 拿个人前途作孤注一掷. *I* ~ *my reputation on his honesty.* 我拿名誉担保他诚实. ~ **holder** 赌金保管者.

Sta·kha·noff [stəˈhɑːnɔːf], **Alexei Grigorievich** 斯达哈诺夫〔苏联煤矿工人, 1935 年创始采煤合理化的方法, 产量大增, 全国推行, 形成一个很大的运动〕.

Sta·kha·no·vism [stəˈhɑːnəvizəm] *n.* 〔苏联〕斯达哈诺夫运动.

Sta·kha·no·vite [stəˈhɑːnəvait] *n.* 斯达哈诺夫式工作者.

stal·ac·tic(al) [stəˈlæktik] *a.* = stalactitic(al). **-cal·ly** *ad.*

sta·lac·ti·form [stəˈlæktiˌfɔːm] *a.* 钟乳石状的.

sta·lac·tite [ˈstæləktait] *n.*【地】钟乳石; 钟乳石状物.

stal·ac·tit·ic, -i·cal [ˌstæləkˈtitik(əl)] *a.* 钟乳石的; 钟乳石状的; 钟乳石质的. **-i·cal·ly** *ad.*

sta·lag·mite [ˈstæləgmait] *n.*【地】石笋.

stal·ag·mit·ic(al) [ˌstæləgˈmitik(əl)] *a.* (多)石笋的; 石笋状的; 石笋质的. **-cal·ly** *ad.*

stal·ag·mom·e·ter [ˌstæləgˈmɔmitə] *n.* (表面张力)滴重计.

stale[1] [steil] *a.* ①陈旧的; 腐败了的, 变坏了的; 走了气的, 走了味的(酒等); 干瘪的, 霉臭的. ②不新鲜的; 陈腐的(俏皮话等). ③(因过劳)弄垮了的, 泄了气的(学生、运动员等). ④停滞的, 不流的. ⑤冷淡的, 萧条的, 呆涩的(市场等). ⑥【法】(因不行使权利而)过期失效的. — *vt.* 使陈旧; 使没有味道, 使走气, 使失时效, 用旧, 用坏. — *vi.* 变陈旧; 走气, 走味, 失时效. *The bread is too* ~ *to eat.* 面包太陈不能吃了. *Nobody likes your* ~ *jokes.* 谁也不喜欢听你那些陈旧的笑话. ~ *beer* 走气啤酒. ~ *flesh* 不新鲜的肉. *a* ~ *cheque* 过期支票. *get rid of the* ~ *and take in the fresh* 吐故纳新. **go** ~ 〔美〕(运动员等)筋疲力尽, 丧失元气. **-ly** *ad.* **-ness** *n.*

stale[2] [steil] *n.* (牛马的)尿. — *vi.* (牛马)撒尿.

stale[3] [steil] *n.* 〔英古〕①囮子, (猎人做掩蔽用的)假马. ②笑柄; 受人愚弄成为笑谈的人.

stale·mate [steilˈmeit] *n.* ①【国际象棋】僵局, 王棋受困. ②僵持, 相持, 困境. *His tricks will bring us into a* ~. 他的花招会使我们陷入僵局. ***break the*** ~ 打开僵局. — *vt.* 使成僵局, 使王棋受困; 使束手无策, 使相持.

Sta·lin [ˈstɑːlin], **Joseph Vissarionovitch** [ˈdʒəuzif visariəˈnəuvitʃ] 约瑟夫·维萨里奥诺维奇·斯大林〔1879—1953, 苏联党和国家领导人〕.

Sta·lin·a·bad [stɑːlinɑˈbɑːt] (苏联塔吉克斯坦首都)斯大林纳巴德〔现称杜尚别〕.

Sta·lin·grad [ˈstɑːlingræd] *n.* 斯大林格勒〔现称伏尔加格勒〕〔苏联城市〕.

stalk[1] [stɔːk] *n.* ①【植】茎, 柄, 秆, 梗, 轴. ②【动】(无脊椎动物的)茎状部, 梗节, 肉茎, 羽毛管. ③酒杯脚; 寒暑表管. ④【建】叶梗饰. ⑤(工厂等的)高烟囱. ~-**eyed**【动】(无脊椎动物)柄眼的. **-y** *a.* **-i·ness** *n.*

stalk[2] [stɔːk] *vi.*, *vt.* ①高视阔步, 大踏步走. ②(疾病等)蔓延, 猖獗. ③偷偷地走, 蹑手蹑脚地走; (用东西掩蔽着身体)偷偷走近, 偷偷接近. ④搜索, 追踪. — *n.* ①高视阔步; 猖獗, 弥漫. ②偷偷接近, 潜随. ③狙击. *I saw Bob* ~*ing out from the kitchen.* 我看见伯普蹑手蹑脚从厨房里出来. *The parade* ~*ed along the highway.* 游行队伍沿着公路阔步前进. *I'm afraid famine will* ~ *the land over.* 恐怕饥荒要在那个地方蔓延起来. **-er** *n.*

stalk·ing-horse [ˈstɔːkiŋhɔːs] *n.* ①(猎人)掩蔽用假马. ②(为掩蔽有力候补者设置的打掩护的另一名)假候补者. ③口实, 借口; 掩饰物.

stall[1] [stɔːl] *n.* ①畜舍的一个隔栏; 马房, 牛棚. ②(房舍内的)分隔小间; 〔美〕汽车间. ③售货摊; 棚店; 售品陈列台. ④〔英〕〔常 *pl.*〕(戏院楼下)正厅前座(观众). ⑤(教堂里的)牧师席; 教徒们的长排坐椅. ⑥【矿】矿坑; 采煤道; 泥窑; 敞式矿沙焙烧炉. ⑦【空】失速; 失举. ⑧橡皮手脚指护套. ⑨小分隔间(a shower ~ 淋浴隔间). — *vt.* ①关进马房(牛栏); 关着养肥. ②把(畜舍)分成小格. ③〔美〕使(马、车)陷入泥中〔雪中〕, 使进退不得, (使机车等)停顿, 停止. ④【空】使失速. ⑤〔古〕授予(职位). — *vi.* ①住在畜舍内. ②陷入泥中〔雪中〕. ③【空】失速; 失举. ③(发动机)发生障碍, 停止, 停顿. *a* ~*ed ox* 关着养肥了的牛. *Heavy rain* ~*ed traffic.* 大雨使交通停顿. ~ *down landing*【空】失速降落. ~-**feed** *vt.* 把牲畜关着养肥. ~-**in** 阻塞交通示威.

stall[2] [stɔːl] 〔美俚〕*n.* ①口实, 借口; 拖延, 搪塞, 敷衍; 欺骗办法. ②(盗贼或扒手的)同党. — *vi.*, *vt.* ①欺骗; 逃避. ②拖延; 支吾, 敷衍. ~ *for a while* 暂时拖一下. ~*ing tactics* 缓兵之计. *He knows how to* ~ *off the applicants for the houses.* 他很晓得怎样敷衍打发申请住房的人.

stall·age [ˈstɔːlidʒ] *n.* ①(售货摊的)摆摊权. ②摆摊税. ③摆摊场所〔位置〕.

stal·lion [ˈstæljən] *n.* 公马; 种马.

stall·o·me·ter [stɔːˈlɔmitə] *n.* 失速信号器, 气流分离指示器.

stal·wart [ˈstɔːlwət] *a.* ①高大强健的, 壮健的. ②绝对忠实的, 可靠的; 坚定的, 刚强的. — *n.* ①高大健壮的人. ②忠实于…的人, 忠实的成员. **-ly** *ad.* **-ness** *n.*

sta·men [ˈsteimen] *n.* *(pl.* ~*s, stam·ina* [ˈstæminə]*)* 【植】雄蕊.

stam·i·na [ˈstæminə] *n.* 毅力, 持久力; 精力, 体力. *exhibit enough* ~ *to master Greek and Latin* 表现出掌握希腊语拉丁语的充足的毅力. *a drilling machine with* ~ *and correctness of design* 一架有持久力设计准确的钻机.

stam·i·nal [ˈstæminəl] *a.* ①雄蕊的. ②有毅力的, 有持久力的, 有耐力的.

stam·i·nate [ˈstæminit] *a.* 【植】(只)有雄蕊的 *(opp.* pistilate*)*. *a* ~ *flower* 雄花.

sta·min·e·al [stəˈminjəl] *a.* 雄蕊的 (= staminal).

stam·i·nif·er·ous [ˌstæmiˈnifərəs] *a.* 有雄蕊的. *a* ~ *plant* 雄株.

stam·i·node [ˈstæmiˌnəud] *n.*【植】退化雄蕊 (= staminodium).

stam·i·no·dy [ˈstæmiˌnəudi] *n.* 【植】(花的器官的)雄蕊显著化.

stam·mel [ˈstæml] *n.* ①中世纪苦行僧所穿用的一种粗毛布. ②染此种布所用的红色.

stam·mer [ˈstæmə] *vi., vt.* 口吃;结巴着说 *(out).* — *n.* 口吃,结巴. **-er** *n. He ~ed out an excuse.* 他结结巴巴地讲了个借口. *He ~s but not so badly as you say.* 他口吃但不像你说的那么厉害.

stam·mer·ing [ˈstæməriŋ] *a.* (患)口吃的. *n.* 口吃. **-ly** *ad.*

stamp [stæmp] *n.* ①戳子,图章,戳记,印记. ②邮票,印花(税). ③〔常用 *sing.*〕标记;特征;记号,痕迹. ④压型器;压断器;杵子;捣击机. ⑤跺脚,踏脚;【摔角】把势. ⑥性质,特征;类型;种类. ⑦〔美俚〕钞票. *Every article bears the ~ of the maker.* 每一种货品上都有制造者标记. *stick a ~ (on a letter)* 贴邮票. *men of that ~* 那种(类型的)人. *bear the ~ of a Marxist* 带有马克思主义者的特征. *Your ~ of impatience won't give me a scare.* 你那不耐烦的跺脚吓不了我. *put to ~* (交)付印(刷). — *vt.* ①盖戳,打图章;印刷,压印. ②贴邮票,贴印花. ③跺,踏(脚);踏碎;跺碎;捣碎. ④铭记(心中);使不朽. ⑤标出,表示. ⑥压断,压滚. — *vi.* ①捣碎. ②踩踏,踏脚,跺脚;【摔角】摆把势. *~ a document with the address and date* 给文件盖上地址和日戳. *~ one's name on the page of history* 留名青史. *~ one's feet* 跺脚,踏脚. *~ the grass flat* 踏平草地. *~ upstairs* 咄咄咄地上楼梯. *This alone ~s him (as) a swindler.* 这一件事就表明他是一个骗子. ***be ~ed with the brand of a class*** 打上阶级的烙印. *~* ***about the room*** 踏着脚在屋里走来走去. *~* ***down*** = *~* ***to the ground*** 蹂躏,践踏. *~* ***on*** 拒绝. *~* ***out*** 踏灭(火);根绝,扑灭(暴动等). *~* ***with rage*** 发怒跺脚. **~-album** 集邮簿. **~ collector** 集邮家. **~ duty [tax]** 印花税. **-ing** *n.* 冲击,冲压;冲压件;碎矿;跺脚声. **~ing ground** 常到的地方,落脚处. **~-machine** 邮票印刷机. **~mill** 捣碎机,捣岩机,碎矿机. **~-note** (海关发的)装货执照. **~-office** 印花税务局. **~ tax** 印花税.

stamp·age [ˈstæmpidʒ] *n.* 跺脚;邮资;盖印.

stam·pede [stæmˈpiːd] *n.* ①(畜群的)惊跑,乱窜;(军队的)总崩溃,溃逃. ②〔美〕(人群)蜂拥上前;(选举中)突然一面倒. — *vi., vt.* (使)惊逃,(使)争先恐后逃走,(使)溃散;(使)蜂拥上前;(使大群人)突然采取某种行动. *There was a ~ of panic-stricken crowd from the burning hotel.* 从失火的旅馆中跑出来乱窜的惊惶失措的人群. *I won't allow myself to be ~ed by fear.* 我不会容许我自己被恐惧吓跑的.

stamp·er [ˈstæmpə] *n.* ①盖章人. ②打印器. ③压模. ④模压工,冲压工. ⑤捣碎机. ⑥〔卑〕〔*pl.*〕脚;靴子. *a backed ~* 复制模. *a master ~* 原模.

Stan [stæn] *n.* 斯坦(男子名)〔Stanley 的昵称〕.

stance [stæns] *n.* ①(高尔夫球,板球)击球的姿势;(运动员的)始发姿势. ②站立姿势;安放的姿势〔位置〕;〔Scot.〕(建筑物的)位置. ③姿态,态度,立场,地位. *If I were you, I'd take a moderate ~ towards your brother's affairs.* 要是我是你,我就会对你弟弟的事件采取温和的姿态.

stanch[1] [stɑːntʃ] *vt.* ①使伤口止血;止血;使不漏水. ②停住,止住. — *vi.* 血液止住;水停漏. *~ a cut* 使伤口止血. *~ a leak* 堵水漏. **-er** *n.* 止血药.

stanch[2] [stɑːntʃ] *a.* (= staunch).

stan·chion [ˈstɑːnʃən] *n.* ①支柱,柱子;标桩,标柱. ②(拴牲畜的)套架,(畜栏中)限制它们活动的枷. — *vt.* 用柱子支撑;装上支柱;把(牲畜)拴在套架上〔枷上〕.

stand [stænd] *vi.* ***(stood*** *[stud]****)*** ①站立,站起来***(up)***;站住,站定 *(opp.* sit, lie, kneel, couch, squat*).* ②(房子等)在,坐落(某处),位于. ③(高度、价格、温度,数量等)达到,处于(某种程度,情况). ④固持,固守,坚守,坚持;在实行,(仍然)有效,维持原状,不变更. ⑤持久,耐久;不剥落,不褪,不变;不倒;不散;不渗开,不阴;不流,不动,停滞;踌躇. ⑥可代用;帮. ⑦〔美〕(公马)可作种马. ⑧〔英〕做候选人〔候补者〕*(for.)* ⑨向(某方向)行驶;【海】取某一航向. — *vt.* ①竖起,竖立,使立起,使站立;弄直. ②坚持;耐,忍耐,忍受;顶住,接受. ③费用,要(多少钱). ④〔口〕请客,付帐,会钞. ⑤【军】排成(某种队形). ⑥可容纳(若干人)站立. *S- easy!* 稍息! *S- from under!* 注意脚底下! *The thermometer ~s at 80°.* 寒暑表的读数为八十度. *Food ~s higher than ever.* 食品比从前更贵了. *The agreement ~s.* 契约在有效中. *His resolution will ~.* 他的决心不会动摇. *That translation may ~.* 那个译文可靠. *Let the word ~.* 【校刊】此字不改. *let all ~* 【海】装备全部不动. *~ a ladder against the wall* 把梯子靠在墙上. *He ~s his ground* 他坚持己见. *I cannot ~ great heat.* 我受不住高温. *I will ~ you a dinner.* 我要请你吃一顿饭. *The matter ~s thus.* 事情就是这样. ***as affairs [things matters] now ~*** 按照现状, 事实上. *~* ***a (good, fair) chance*** (很)有希望,(很)有成功可能. *~* ***a good deal of wear*** 耐久,经久,持久. *~* ***a show*** 有一个(希望不大的)可能. *~* ***against*** 抵抗,反抗;靠在. *~* ***alone*** 孤立;卓越,无与伦比. *~* ***aside*** 站开;避开;不参加. *~* ***at*** 犹豫不决,踌躇. *~* ***at attention [ease]*** 立正〔稍息〕. *~* ***at bay*** 陷入绝境. *~* ***away*** 不接近,离着. *~* ***back*** 退后,靠后站,缩在后头,位于靠后一点的地方. *~* ***behind*** 后援,做后盾. *~* ***by*** ①站在旁边;袖手旁观. ②待机;等待;【无】(发报台)准备发送信号;(收报台)处于调谐状态;等待下次收听(例: *Please ~ by*). ③站在一起,帮助,援助(例: *~ by one's friends* 支持某人的朋友). ④维持,遵守(例: *~ by one's promise* 遵守诺言). *~* ***clear*** 站开,让开,躲开. *~* ***convicted of …*** 罪状明显,被判…. *~* ***corrected*** 接受修改,承认错误. *~* ***down*** ①【法】退出证人席位. ②暂时辞退. ③【军】不在值勤中. *~* ***fast [firm]*** 固执,固守,坚持不屈. *~* ***fire*** 冒炮火,站在攻击的正面. *~* ***firmly on*** 确信,深信. *~* ***for*** ①(为主义等)挺身奋斗. ②主张(*We ~ for reform and renovation.* 我们主张改革和革新). ③支持,拥护,帮助. ④代表做候补人,做候选人. (*CP ~ for Communist Party.* CP 是英语共产党的缩写). ⑤〔美口〕忍耐,忍受 (*I won't ~ for such nonsense!* 我不能容忍这样的胡言乱语)! ⑥允许. ⑦【海】驶向. ⑧可代…之用,可当…用 (*This box may ~ for a desk.* 这个箱子可当书桌用). *~* ***for nothing*** 毫无用处. *~* ***good*** 依然真实[有效]. *~* ***in*** ①加入,参加. ②〔口〕使花费 (*It stood me in a lot of money.* 花费我不少钱). ③【影】(在工作人员考虑拍摄办法时)代替名演员站位置 *(for).* *~* ***in for the shore*** 驶向海岸. *~* ***in the way of*** 妨碍,阻挠. *~* ***in with***〔美俚〕帮助,左袒;和…共同行动;分担 (*I'll ~ in with you in this expense.* 我和你分担这笔费用). *~* ***off*** ①离着,远离. ②【海】离岸驶行. ③〔美〕疏远,避开(债主或攻击者);延期. ④(因市面萧条等)暂时解雇. *~* ***off and on***【海】一忽儿接近海岸一忽儿远离海岸航行. *~* ***on*** = *~* upon ①坚持,拘泥. ②【海】向一个方向笔直航行. *~* ***on one's hand [head]*** 倒立;讲怪话. *~* ***sb. in (good) stead*** 紧急时对某人(非常)有用[便利]. *~* ***one's friend*** 袒护朋友,帮助朋友. *~* ***sb. up***〔美俚〕(失约)使人失望. *~* ***or fall*** *(with, together, by)* 共命运,共浮沉. *~* ***out*** 突出;浮出,显著,显眼 (*Red plums ~ out against the white snow.* 红梅衬着白雪十分醒目). 抵抗到底,坚持到底;支持到底 (*This is the third time we stood out against the enemy attacks* 这是我们第三次顶住敌人的进犯了).【海】离岸向海中航行. *~* ***out (of war)*** 不参加战争. *~* ***over*** ①(工作、讨论等)延期, 展期 *(Payment will ~ over till next month.* 付款展期到下月. *I object to letting the matter ~ over any longer.* 我反对再把这事推延下去). ②密切注意;监督. *~* ***pat*** (扑

克）不再换牌；反对任何变更；固执己党政策；坚决不改变主张．～ ***still*** 站住；搁置不动．～ ***to*** 守(约、条件等)；坚决主张，坚持〔常用作 ～ *to it that*〕；（尤指在天亮前或日落后防备敌人进攻）进入阵地；就活动岗位．～ ***to lose [win]*** 看来会输[赢]．～ ***to one's colours [guns]*** 坚持．～ ***to reason*** 合乎道理，有理．～ ***under*** 忍受．～ ***up*** 站起来，起立；持久；露头角；〔美俚〕背约．～ ***up for*** 拥护，辩护（～ *up for the truth* 坚持真理）．～ ***up on one's hind legs*** 〔美运〕显示力量[勇气]．～ ***up to*** 勇敢地抵抗，顶住；经得起，受得住．～ ***up with*** 和…双双站起，和…跳舞；（结婚时）陪侍(新郎新妇)．～ ***upon*** 依靠，倚赖，信赖；要看…怎样，视…如何而定；不改变；坚持，主张，拘泥(礼貌)．～ ***well with*** 同某人相处得好；得到某人的好感[好评]．～ ***with*** 和…一致；主张，坚持．～ ***without hitching*** 〔美〕服从命令，全部照办．— *n.* ①起立，站立；停止，静止．②立场，地位；位置；态度．③看台；讲坛，音乐坛；台，架，小桌子；〔美〕(法庭的)证人席．④〔美〕货摊；售货台．⑤停车场，等车处；（鸟的）栖木；（旅行剧团等的）留宿地，上演地．⑥（采伐后）留下的幼树，根生树；（一地区上的）林木，林分；庄稼，青苗，植株．⑦一套，一副，一组．⑧抵抗，反抗；防御．*a* ～ *for flowers* 花插．*a service* ～ 工作梯架．*a hat* ～ 帽架．*a fruit* ～ 水果摊．*a good* ～ *of wheat* 一块生长良好的麦苗．*approbation of varietal* ～ 品种鉴定．***be at a*** ～ 停顿，僵持；不知所措．***be brought to a*** ～ ＝ ***come to a*** ～ 停顿，弄僵．***make a*** ～ 站住 *(at)*；抵抗到底，阻击 *(against; for)*．***put [bring] to a*** ～ 使停顿；使为难；阻止．***take a [one's]*** ～ 困守(城池等)；决定态度，立定脚跟．***take a*** ～ ***for [against]*** 赞成[反对]．**～away** *a.* (衣、裙等）不贴住身子的．**～-by** ①（紧急时的）可依靠(的人物)，助力．②【军】一级战斗准备．③备用品，备用设备．④救援船只．⑤党羽．⑥【无】(呼号)准备发报[收报]．～ **camera** 放在三脚架上的摄影机．**～-down** ①休止，暂停；停工；临时解雇时期．**～-fast** *a.* 稳固的(地位)．**～-in** ①〔美影〕(开拍前)代替名演员站位置的人；替身．②有利地位．③〔美俚〕照顾，偏袒；门路，线索．**～-messenger** 〔美〕(服装等的)活人广告．**～-off** ①离岸驶去；离开，避开；隔开；孤立．②〔口〕*a.* 冷淡的．③支付延期；抵销，平衡；（橄榄球的）half back；〔美运〕不分胜负，和局．④〔英〕闲散，停工．⑤有支座托脚的．**～-offish** *a.* 疏远的，有隔阂的，冷淡的；傲慢的．～ **oil**【化】熟油．～ **out** *a., n.* ①杰出的(人物)；出色的．②【运】优秀的选手．③〔口〕坚持己见的人；孤立主义者．～ **pat** ①*a.*〔美〕不要求换牌的；〔转义〕固执本党政策的，主张维持现状的，顽固的．②*n.* ＝～patter．～ **patter** 〔美〕顽固分子，死硬派．～ **pat-tism** 保守主义，反对变革．～ **pipe** 配水塔，竖管，水鹤．**～point** 立场，立脚点；见地，论点，观点（*class* ～*-point* 阶级立场．～*point of class struggle* 阶级斗争观点）．～ **still** ①停止，停顿，搁浅，*come (be brought to) to a* ～ 停顿下来．②【电】静止．**stand-to**〔英〕【军】战斗准备．**～-up** *a.* ①站立的；（衣领）直立的 *(opp.* turn-down*)*；站着的（a ～ meal 立餐）．②光明正大的，敢说敢干的，坦率正直的，不要手段的，凭真功夫的．③〔美〕不守会面约言的．

stand·ard [ˈstændəd] *n.* ①标准，水准，规格，模范．②旗；军旗，队旗；【徽】标帜，标记；旗标，象标．③【植】旗瓣．④金[银]的纯度标准；（硬币的）法定纯度比例；（作为货币价值标准的）本位．⑤（度量衡的）原基；原器．⑥〔英〕(小学的)学年，年级．⑦直立支柱；灯台；烛台，电杆，垂直的水管(电管)．⑧【林】中年木〔胸径 1—2 英尺〕；保残木，第一代上木；【园艺】直立式整枝，嫁接于树干上的灌木．⑨高脚杯，大杯．*the* ～ *of living* 生活水平[标准]．*conform to the* ～*s of the present-day society* 合乎当前社会的准则．*the gold [silver]* ～（货币的）金[银]本位制．***below*** ～ 标准以下的，不合格的．***come up to the*** ～ 够标准．***fall short of the*** ～ 不够标准．***join the*** ～ ***of*** 加入…的军队．***raise the*** ～ ***of revolution*** 举起革命的旗帜．***under the*** ～ ***of*** 在…旗下，参加…的军队．***up to*** ～ 达到标准的．***up to the*** ～ 合格达到标准．— *a.* ①标准的，模范的，规范化的．②公认为优秀的，权威的．③合格的，普通一般的．④装支柱的．⑤不依附他物生长的．～ *money* 本位货币．*the* ～ *meridian* 本初子午线．～ *English* 标准英语．*the* ～ *gauge* 标准轨距；标准样板；法定度量表．～ *solution* 定规液，标准溶液．*a* ～ *tree* 自然树．*a* ～ *writer* 标准作家，权威作家．*the* ～ *model of a bicycle* 普通型的自行车．*a* ～ *lamp*（支柱可以伸缩的）落地灯．**～-bearer**【军】旗手；带头者，倡导者；领导者，领袖（*the Republican* ～*-bearer*〔美〕共和党领袖，共和党的总统候选人）．～ **candle** 标准烛光．～ **deviation**【统】标准(偏)差．～ **error**【统】标准误差，均方差．～ **ga(u)ge** 标准量规；标准轨距（＝1.435 米）．～ **time** 标准时间．

standard·bred [ˈstændədˈbred] *n.* 〔常用S-〕美洲的良种马〔用于小跑，溜跑，尤其是驾车赛跑者〕．

stand·ard·ize [ˈstændədaiz] *vt.* ①使合标准；使标准化，使统一；作为标准．②使与标准比较，用标准校检．～ *English speech* 使英语标准化．～*d products* 标准化产品．**-i·za·tion** *n.* **-iz·er** *n.*

stand·ee [stænˈdiː] *n.* 〔美〕①（戏院中的）站立看客．②（电车的）站立乘客．

stand·er-by [ˈstændəˈbai] *n.* （〔*pl.*〕 ***standers-by***）旁观者（＝ bystander）．

stand·ing [ˈstændiŋ] *a.* ①直立的；站着的．②【林】未伐的．③【农】尚未收割的．④停伫的；停滞的，不在运转的，不流动的．⑤持续的，长期有效的，标准的，不退的(颜色)．⑥常备的，常设的．⑦【印】已排好的．⑧有垫脚的，有脚的(杯子等)．⑨（由法律习惯）确立的，永久的．*a* ～ *tree* 立木．～ *corn* 尚未收割的庄稼[玉米]．*a* ～ *jump* 立定跳远．*a* ～ *ovation* 起立欢呼．*a* ～ *dish*（饭馆里）常备的菜肴．*a* ～ *factory* 停工的工厂．*a* ～ *order* 长期订单．～ *operation procedure*【军】标准作战程序．*a* ～ *committee* 常务委员会．～ *orders* 议事规则；【军】标准作战规定．— *n.* ①起立，站立；站立处．②持续，继续，期间．③立场；地位，身分．*social* ～ 社会地位．*a man of high* ～ 身分高的人．*an illness of long* ～ 长期疾病．***be in good*** ～ 身分相当好．～ **room**（公共汽车、戏院的）站席空位（*Standing room only!* 本院只有站票出售！）～ **rules**（团体、机构、企业的）办事[经营]规则．～ **wave**【物】驻波，定波．

Stand·ish [ˈstændiʃ] *n.* 斯坦迪什〔姓氏〕．

stand·ish [ˈstændiʃ] *n.* 〔古〕墨水缸；笔座．

Stand·ley [ˈstændli] *n.* 斯坦德利〔姓氏〕．

stane [stein] *n., a., vt.* 〔苏格兰，英方〕＝ stone．

Stan·ford [ˈstænfəd] *n.* 斯坦福〔姓氏，男子名〕．

stang[1] [stæŋ]〔古语〕sting 的过去式和过去分词．

stang[2] [stæŋ] *n., vt., vi.* 〔苏格兰、英方〕＝ sting．

stan·hope [ˈstænəp] *n.* 无篷高座马车．

stank[1] [stæŋk] stink 的过去式．

stank[2] [stæŋk] *n.* ①〔英方〕池塘；水沟．②〔英〕坝，堰．

Stan·ley [ˈstænli] *n.* ①斯坦利〔姓氏，男子名〕．②**Henry Morton** ～ 斯坦利〔1841—1904，英国的非洲探险家〕．

Stan·ley [ˈstænli] *n.* 斯坦利港〔马尔维纳斯群岛(福克兰群岛)首府〕．

stan·na·ry [ˈstænəri]〔英〕*a.* 锡矿的，采锡的．— *n.* 〔常 *pl.*〕锡矿；锡矿产地．

stan·nate [ˈstænit] *n.*【化】锡酸盐．

stan·nic [ˈstænik] *a.*【化】(正)锡的；四价锡的．

stan·ni·fer·ous [stæˈnifərəs] *a.*【化】亚锡的，二价锡的．

stan·nite [ˈstænait] *n.*【矿】黄锡矿．

stan·nous [ˈstænəs] *a.*【化】亚锡的；含锡的；二价锡(的)．

stan·num [ˈstænəm] *n.*【化】锡．

St. An·thony's fire [snt'æntəniz'faiə] 丹毒型皮肤炎.

Stan·ton ['stɑːntən, 'stæntən] *n.* 斯坦顿〔姓氏,男子名〕.

STANVAC〔缩〕Standard Vacuum Oil Company 美孚真空石油公司〔美国〕.

stan·za ['stænzə] *n.* ①【韵】(诗的)节. ②〔美〕运动比赛的段落〔如局、盘、场等〕. ③(戏剧等在某一地点的)演出期〔通常为一星期〕. *The troupe has agreed to be held over for another* ~. 剧团已经同意续演一期. **-i·c** *a.*

sta·pe·dial [stə'piːdiəl] *a.* 镫骨的,靠近镫骨的.

sta·pes ['steipiːz] *n.* *(pl. stapes, stapedes* [stə'piːdiːz]*)*【解】镫骨;【医】镫形绷带.

staph [stæf] *n.* staphylococcus 的缩略词.

staph·y·lo·coc·cus [ˌstæfiləu'kɔkəs] *n.* *(pl.* **-coc·ci** [-'kɔksai]*)*【微】葡萄球菌. **-coc·cal, -coc·cic** *a.*

staph·y·lo·plas·ty ['stæfiləuˌplæsti] *n.*【医】悬雍垂成形术. **-plas·tic** *a.*

staph·y·lor·rha·phy [ˌstæfi'lɔːrəfi] *n.* *(pl.* **-phies***)*【医】软腭缝术.

sta·ple[1] ['steipl] *n.* ①主要产物(或商品),大宗出产,名产;重要商品. ②销路稳定的商品,常用品,广泛采用的东西. ③主要成分;特色;(谈话等的)要项,主题. ④原材料. ⑤(棉、麻、羊毛等的)纤维,(织物的)质地,底子. ⑥来源地,中心. ⑦【史】(出口商品的)特定市场,贸易中心城点. *Tea and silk are the ~s of East China.* 茶和丝绸是华东的主要商品. *Dry goods are ~s of the store.* 织品是这家商店销路稳定的商品. *I'm trying to make an analysis of the ~s of his talk.* 我在试行分析他的谈话的要旨. — *a.* ①主要的,常产的,大宗生产的. ②经常需要的,经常用的. ③纺织纤维的. *cotton of fine [short]* ~ 细[粗]绒棉. *the ~ commodities* 主要商品. ~ *goods* 大路货,主要货品. ~ *linen* 大宗生产亚麻织品. ~ *fibre* 人造短纤维,切断纤维. — *vt.* 分拣,分齐(纤维等),(依长短)分类(羊毛等);分级;穿吊眼(结网). *We'll have to ~ synthetic fibre this afternoon.* 今天下午咱们得把合成纤维分分档.

sta·ple[2] [steipl] *n.* ①卡钉,U 字钉,肘钉,骑马钉;钉书钉. ②钩环,锁环. ③【乐】(双簧管等置有簧片的)嘴套. — *vt.* 用骑马钉钉住.

sta·pler ['steiplə] *n.* ①买卖大宗土产的商人;批发商. ②按纤维长短分类的工人. ③纤维切断机,羊毛分选机. ④【装钉】铁丝钉书机.

star [stɑː] *n.* ①星;【天】恒星 *(opp.* planet*)*. ②星状物;星(形勋)章. ③【印】星形号〔*〕. ④【占星术】〔常 *pl.*〕命星;〔*pl.*〕命运,运气. ⑤名演员,明星;〔口语〕著名人物. ⑥【林】棁. ⑦【动】海星. ⑧(马额等的)白斑. ⑨〔卑〕初次坐牢的犯人. *a falling [shooting]* ~ 流星. *a fixed* ~ 恒星. *this* ~〔诗〕地球. *His ~ was in the ascendant.* 他(那时)正在走运. *My ~s!* = 〔谑〕*My ~s and garters!* 哎呀!天哪!〔表示吃惊〕. *The ~s were against it.* 那注定要失败的. *the S- Chamber*【英史】星法院〔以暴虐专横著称〕. ***be born under a lucky [an unlucky]*** ~ 生在幸福[不幸]中. ***curse one's ~s*** 怨恨自己不走运. ***march by the ~s***【军】看星行进. ***see ~s***〔口〕眼里冒金星. ***all ~ cast***【剧】全部角色由名演员扮演. ***thank one's ~s*** 觉得运气好,觉得幸福. ***trust to one's*** ~ 相信自己的运气. —*vt.* ***(Starred; star·ring)*** ①用星(形物)装饰;加星号. ②使…成为明星[名演员],使演主角. — *vi.* ①星一般地辉跃. ②作出杰出成就. ③(演员)主演*(in)*;成为明星[名演员]. ④(打台球或玩 domino 输掉而失权的人)出钱购买继续游戏的权利. *the five-starred national flag of the People's Republic of China* 五星红旗〔中华人民共和国国旗〕. *They ~red her for the first time.* 他们第一次以她为主角. *She has ~red in many pictures.* 她已主演多部影片. ~ **apple**【植】星苹果(树). ~**backs**〔美〕预订的座位. ~ **cluster**【天】星团. ~**-crossed** *a.* 命运不佳的. ~**dom** ①明星的地位. ②一群明星 ~**drift**【天】星流. ~ **dust** 宇宙尘. ~**fish**【动】海星,海盘车. ~**finch**【鸟】= redstart. ~**flower**【植】①七瓣莲(属). ②星形花植物〔如伞形虎眼万年青〕. ~**gaze** *vi.* ①凝视星辰. ②想入非非,做白日梦. ~**gazer** 占星家;〔谑〕天文家;空想家,梦想家;【动】眼镜鱼;〔谑〕专爱看女明星的人. ~**gazing** 凝视,空想,心不在焉. ~ **grass**【植】星形花草本植物〔包括小金梅草属和肺筋草属〕. ~**king** 红星苹果. ~**less** 无星的. ~**let** 小星;童星,儿童演员. ~**like** 象星那样亮的,星形的. ~**light** ① *n.* 星光. ② *a.* 星光灿烂的,有星光的. ~**lit** *a.* = ~light. ~ **man** 初次坐牢的犯人. ~ **metal** 精锑,星纹锑. ~**-nosed mole**【动】北美星鼻鼹鼠. ~**-of-Bethlehem**【植】伞形虎眼万年青(属). **Star of David** 犹太教六芒星形标志,意为"大卫王的盾"牌. ~ **role**〔美运〕名选手. ~ **route** 星形邮线〔偏僻地区专门雇用人员邮递的路线;〔美〕铁道两旁的路. **Stars and Bars**【美史】1861 年美国南部联邦旗. ~**s of the show**〔美〕某一场比赛中出场的名选手. ~ **sapphire**【矿】星彩蓝宝石. ~ **shell** 照明弹. ~**-spangled** 镶有星星的,星印的 *(the Star-Spangled Banner* 美国星条旗;美国国歌*)*. ~ **streaming**【天】星流. ~ **studded** 星罗棋布的;星星点缀着的. ~ **system** ①【天】天河系. ②以少数明星做台柱的明星制度. ~ **thistle**【植】矢车菊(属). ~ **turn**〔主英〕①演出的主要节目;主要演员. ②被他人广为宣传的人. **the S-s and Stripes** 星条旗〔美国国旗〕.

star·board ['stɑːbəd, -bɔːd] *n.*【海,空】(船,飞机的)右舷 *(opp.* port[4]*)*. — *a.* (在)右舷的. — *vt.* 转向右舷. *sight a steamer to* ~. 在右舷方向看见一艘轮船. *S- (the helm)!* 舵柄转向右!

starch [stɑːtʃ] *n.* ①【化】淀粉;〔*pl.*〕淀粉质食物. ②古板,僵硬,严格,拘泥,形式主义. ③〔美俚〕精力,元气. ~***-sweet corn*** 甜(粉种)玉米. ***take the ~ out of***〔美俚〕压服,使屈服,使气馁;使…不僵硬. — *vt.* ①(给衣服)上浆,浆硬. ②使僵硬. *a man of ~ed manners* 古板僵硬的人. ~ *the shirts* 浆衬衣. **-less** *a.* 不含淀粉的;未上浆的.

starched ['stɑːtʃit] *a.* 浆过的;古板的,僵硬的,拘泥的. **-ly** *ad.* **-ness** *n.*

starch·i·ly ['stɑːtʃili] *ad.* 古板地,僵硬地,拘泥地.

starch·i·ness ['stɑːtʃinis] *n.* 淀粉质,淀粉性;古板,僵硬,拘泥.

starch·y ['stɑːtʃi] *a.* ***(-i·er; -i·est)*** ①淀粉(质)的;上过浆的,像浆过的. ②古板的,拘泥的,严格的;〔美〕严肃的,高傲的.

stare [steə] *vt., vi.* ①盯着看,目不转睛地看 *(at)*,凝视;盯眼看得…;瞪眼看,张大眼睛看. ②(颜色)太显眼*(out)*. ③(毛)倒竖. *She ~ed thoughtfully into the distance, deliberating the state of affairs.* 她深思地凝视着远方,考虑当前的情况. *The green hat ~s out unpleasantly.* 绿帽子怪惹眼的. ~ **at** 目不转睛地看,盯着看,凝视. ~ ***sb. down*** = ~ ***sb. out of countenance*** 盯得人局促不安. ~ ***sb. in the face*** 盯眼看人;(死、不幸等)就在眼前;(事实等)摆在面前,明明白白. ~ ***sb. into silence*** 用眼睛瞪得某人哑口无言. ~ ***sb. up and down*** 将人浑身上下打量一番. ~ ***with surprise*** 吓[惊奇]得目瞪口呆. — *n.* 凝视. *Having heard what I said, James looked at me with cold ~.* 听了我讲的话以后,詹姆斯冷然地盯着我. *With an angry ~, mother silenced Mary.* 妈妈生气地盯了一眼,吓得玛丽不讲话了.

sta·re de·ci·sis ['stɑːri di'saisis] *n.*〔L.〕照章办事.

star·ing ['steəriŋ] *a.* ①盯着看的,瞪眼看的,凝视的,目不转睛的;太显眼的. ②怪俗气的. ③倒竖的(头发等). *stark ~ mad* 完全发狂的. *a ~ sheet*【工】检验单. — *ad.*〔口〕显然,全然,完完全全. **-ly** *ad.*

stark [stɑːk] *a.* ①僵硬的,严格的,顽固不化的,刻板的.

②完全的,全然的,绝对的,真正的.③一丝不挂的,赤裸裸的.④荒凉的,不毛的. *There the dead man lay, ~ and stiff.* 那个死人躺在那里,僵硬直挺. *He gave a ~ denial to the rumour.* 他对谣言加以完全的否认. **-ly** *ad.* 完全,全然,简直. *~ naked* 一丝不挂.

Stark(e) [stɑːk] *n.* 斯塔克〔姓氏〕.

star·ling[1] [ˈstɑːliŋ] *n.*【鸟】燕八哥,高粱头,欧椋鸟;椋鸟科的鸟.

star·ling[2] [ˈstɑːliŋ] *n.*【建】杀水桩;桥墩尖端.

starred [stɑːd] *a.* 〔构成复合词〕①用星装饰的;戴着星章的.②标有星号的.③成了明星[主角]的,…主演的.④命运…的. *the Five-Starred Red Flag* 五星红旗. *a five-~-general*〔美〕五星上将,元帅. *a four-~-general*〔美〕四星上将,大将.

star·ry [ˈstɑːri] *a.* **(*-ri·er; -ri·est*)** ①星的;多星的.②被星照亮的,星一样闪亮的,明亮的;灿烂的.③星形的.④高如天上之星的. *~ eyes* 明亮的眼睛. *~ light* 星光. *a ~ night* 星夜. *a ~ program* 许多明星演出的节目. *a wrist-watch ~ with gold and gem* 一只被黄金和宝石照得闪亮的手表. **~-eyed** *a.*〔美俚〕(看待事物)过分乐观的;不实际的(梦想家). **-ri·ness** *n.*

start [stɑːt] *vi.* ①〔美〕出发,动身,起程.②(机器)开动;开始,着手,下手,发生.③突然出现,涌出;鼓出,突出.④跳起,惊起,吃惊,吓一跳.⑤(船材、钉等)松动,翘曲,歪,脱落.⑥参加比赛.— *vt.* ①使出发,使动身,对(比赛者)发出起跑等信号;使参加比赛.②开动(机器等),开始;创办,开办;着手,下手.③引起;使从事.④惊动;惊起,吓出(猎物).④突然开始讲;提出(问题等).⑤使脱节,使松动,弄歪,弄翘曲.⑥说出(痛苦等).⑦领头(跳舞等),开始雇用某人.⑧【海】开桶取酒;把酒从桶里倒出.⑨生(火). *~ from Beijing* 从北京出发. *~ for home* 动身回家. *~ on a journey* 起程旅行. *~ on a task* 着手工作. *~ work(ing)* =〔口〕*~ to work* 开始工作. *Knowledge ~s with practice.* 认识从实践开始. *A screw has ~ed. Tighten it.* 一个螺丝松了,把它拧紧. *~ a newspaper* 创办报纸. *Your advice ~ed me thinking seriously.* 你的意见引起了我的认真考虑. *Mary has ~ed a baby.*〔口〕玛丽已经怀孕. ***get the engine to ~*** 开动机器. *~ **after*** 尾追,追逐,追赶. *~ **another hare*** 赶出另外一只野兔;〔喻〕提出意料不到的事情. *~ **something*** 制造麻烦(骚乱). *~ **against*** 起来和…竞选,和…对抗. *~ **aside*** 跳往一旁,跳开. *~ **back*** 惊退,畏缩. *~ **for*** 往…出发,起程,动身 (*I'm going to ~ for Shanghai.* 我即将动身去上海). *~ **from scratch***〔美〕赤手空拳地开始. *~ **from taw***〔美〕白手起家. *~ **in***〔口〕开始,动手 (*It ~ed in to rain.* 开始下雨了. *He ~ed in on the cake.* 他吃起蛋糕来了). *~ **in life*** 开始到社会上做事[谋生]. *~ **off*** 出发,动身 (*When shall we ~ off?* 我们什么时候出发?) *~ **off with*** 从…开始,用…开始. (*What shall we ~ off with?* 我们从什么谈起?) *~ **out*** 跳出;开始,着手;〔俚〕企图,计划 *(to do).* (*I'll ~ out to write my paper tomorrow.* 我计划明天写读书报告). *~ **up*** ①惊跳起来 (*Suddenly he ~ed up from the chair.* 突然间他从椅子上惊跳起来).②突然出现.③突然发动.④开始工作.⑤开办,开张. *~ **with a bang***〔美俚〕一开始就顺利,旗开得胜. ***to ~ with*** 首先,第一.— *n.* ①出发,动身,起程;起飞,起动;出发点.②着手,开始.③惊跳,惊起;吃惊;〔口〕惊人的事.④(赛跑的)起跑(点);起跑信号;〔转义〕先跑权,优先地位,有利条件 **(*opp.*** handicap**)**.⑤〔*pl.*〕发作,冲动;努力.⑥松动,脱节,弯曲.⑦〔古〕(思想、感情等的)爆发. *It is a difficult work at the ~.* 那是一件开头困难的工作. *make an early ~* 早点动身. *What a ~ you gave me!* 你吓了我一跳! *He gave me a ~ of ten yards.* 他让我先跑十码. ***a rum ~***〔口〕惊人事件. ***at the ~*** 开始,当初. ***at the very ~*** 一开始. ***awake with a ~*** 突然醒来,惊醒. ***by fits and ~s*** 一阵一阵地,间歇地. ***from ~ to finish*** 自始至终,彻头彻尾. ***get a ~*** 吃惊,吓一跳. ***get [have] the ~ of*** 比…占先,比…先走一着,先发制人. ***give sb. a ~ in life*** 让某人到社会上谋生,给人职业. ***give a ~ of*** 因…而愣了一下,因…而震颤了一下. ***make a ~ on a job*** 开始工作. ***make good [bad] ~*** 开头儿好[不好]. ***take a fresh ~*** 重新开始.

start·er [ˈstɑːtə] *n.* ①出发者;开始者.②参加赛跑的人(或马).③(赛跑等的)起跑发号员;(火车等的)开车发号员.④起动装置,始动杆,起动机(器).⑤〔口〕原因,诱因.⑥〔俚〕无花果干.⑦【农】催肥饲料.⑧酵母. ***as a ~ = for a ~*** 首先. *~ **fertilizer*** 基肥,底肥.

start·ing [ˈstɑːtiŋ] *n.* 出发;开始;【机】开动,起动;开车. ***at ~*** 最初,开头. *~ **material*** 原材料. *~ **motor*** 起动电动机. *~ **deck**【空】起飞甲板. *~ **gate** (赛马的)起跑栅门. *~ **point**, ~ **post** 起点,起跑点,出发点,出发标. *~ **rail**【空】跑道,起飞道.

star·tle [ˈstɑːtl] *vi., vt.* (使)大吃一惊,(使)震惊,(使)吓一跳,(使)惊跳. ***be ~d at*** 给…吓一跳. *~ **from sleep*** 惊醒.— *n.*〔美〕吃惊,震惊;惊跳.

star·tler [ˈstɑːtlə] *n.* 吓人的人,做惊人事情的人;可惊的事物.

star·tling [ˈstɑːtliŋ] *a.* 可惊的,吓人的. *a ~ scandal* 一件使人触目心惊的丑闻. *~ news* 惊人的消息.

star·va·tion [stɑːˈveiʃən] *n.* 饥饿;饿死;绝食. *~ **cure [diet]*** 绝食疗法,断食疗法. *~ **wages** 资本主义社会中难以维持温饱生活的工资.

starve [stɑːv] *vi.* ①饥饿,为饥饿所苦;饿死;绝食.②〔英罕〕冻死.③〔口〕饿得要命.④因缺乏而极需要,渴望 *(for).* — *vt.* ①(使)饿死;使饥饿.②(使)冻死.③使渴望.④使极度缺乏. *~ a cold* 用绝食医伤风. *~ the enemy into surrender* 使敌人因饥饿而投降. *be ~d to death* 饿死. *My hands are ~ving while I write.* 我写字的时候,手冻得要命.

starve·ling [ˈstɑːvliŋ] *n.* ①饥饿者.②饿瘦了的人[动物];营养不良的人[动物].— *a.* ①饥饿的.②营养不良的.③极贫困的,匮乏的.

stash [stæʃ] *vt., vi.*〔美俚〕①隐藏;藏匿.②贮藏.③〔英〕停止.— *n.* 隐[贮]藏物;隐[贮]藏处. *Mother has ~ed some money for future use.* 妈妈藏起来一些钱准备将来花用. *It's a slack season and we're going to ~ business.* 现在是生意萧条的季节,咱们不久就要停业了.

sta·sis [ˈsteisis] *n.* **(*pl.* *sta·ses*** [-siːz]**)** ①【医】壅滞,郁积.②静态平衡;停滞.

stat. = statics; stationary; statistical; statistics; statuary; statue; statute.

-stat, *comb. f.* 稳定器[计],固定装置: aero*stat,* thermo*stat.*

state [steit] *n.* ①〔常作 S-〕国,国家;〔通例作 S-〕(美国、澳洲的)州;〔the States〕美国[美侨用语].②国务,政权,政府.③身分,地位,资格,社会阶层.④状况,情形,情况,形势.⑤〔口〕难看的样子,邋遢相.⑥忧虑,兴奋,激动[状态].⑦优越的生活;盛大的仪式;尊严,气派.⑧〔*pl.*〕(Jersey 及 Guernsey 的) 议会.⑨〔古〕宝座;(宝座上的)华盖;(餐桌的)上席.⑩版画制作中的任一阶段. *fight for the S-* 为国家作战. *affairs of ~* 国事. *Have you been to the States?* 你到过美国没有? *What's the ~ of affairs?* 有什么情况? *the ~ of the case* 实情,真相. *What a ~ you are in!* 你怎么这样激动[狼狈]. *a visit of ~* 正式访问. ***a ~ of siege*** 戒严状态. ***be in a ~*** 不太好,不振. ***be in a ~ of grace***【宗】蒙受神恩. ***in a good ~ of repair*** 修理得很好. ***in a great ~*** 威风凛凛. ***in a ~ of nature.*** ①处于原始(未开化)状态.②一丝不挂地,裸体.③【宗】有罪. ***in a terrible ~*** 情况恶劣;非常激动. ***in easy [great] ~*** 很轻松[严重]的样子. ***in ~*** 堂皇地,庄严地,正式地,郑重地. ***keep up one's ~*** 保持尊严,摆架子. ***live in ~*** 过豪华生活. ***lie in ~***

殡殓后任人瞻仰. — *a.* 国家的, 国务的,公务的;〔美〕州的,仪式用的;来宾用的;正式的;华丽的,壮丽的. ~ *service* 国务, 公务. *a* ~ *call* 〔口〕国事访问. *a* ~ *apartment* 大礼堂,大厅;贵宾室. — *vt.* ①讲, 说明, 陈述. ②〔常用 *p.p.*〕规定,指定(日期、地点、价钱等). ③【数】用符号或代数式表示(问题、关系等). ~ *one's case* 陈述自己主张[立场]. *I'll* ~. 〔美〕实在是那样. *It is ~d that ...* 据说. ~ *an account* 开帐单,算帐. ~ **aid** 〔美〕州政府对地方公共事业的补助费. ~ **bank** 国家(或州立)银行. ~ **capitalism** 国家资本主义. **S- Council** (中华人民共和国的)国务院. ~ **craft** 管理国家的本领. ~ **criminal** 政治犯. ***S- Department*** 〔美〕国务院. ***S- Dinner*** 〔美〕总统邀请的晚宴. ~ ***documents [papers]*** 公文. **S- flower** (代表某国某州的)花. ~ ***functionary*** 官吏. ~ ***funeral*** 国葬. ~ ***land*** 公地. ~ ***ownership*** 国有. ~ ***policy*** 国策. ~ ***prison*** 政治犯监狱;〔美〕州立监狱. ~ ***socialism*** 国家社会主义. ~ ***trial*** (政治)案件. ~**'s evidence** 政府证言;〔美〕刑事同案犯的证言[证人] (*turn ~'s evidence*〔美〕作共犯证言). **States General**(荷兰及革命前法国的)国会. **Statehouse** 〔美〕州议会大楼;州的首府. ~ **medicine** 国家公费医疗. **State(s') Rights** 〔美〕州权. ~ **trial** 由国家起诉的案件(尤指政治案件)的审问. ~**wide** *a.* 全国范围的. *ad.* 在全国范围内.

stat•ed [ˈsteitid] *a.* ①规定的,固定的,一定的,定期的(会议等). ②被宣称的; 作过说明的. ③【数】用符号或代数式表示的. *The ~ office hours are from 8 a.m. to 6 p.m.* 规定办公时间是上午八时至下午六时. *These are all ~ exceptions.* 这些都是已经说明的例外. *at ~ intervals* 定期. ~ *clerk* 【宗】(基督教长老会中推选出来的)书记,执事. **-ly** *ad.*

state•less [ˈsteitlis] *a.* 无国家的; 无国籍的; 无公民权的.

state•li•ness [ˈsteitlinis] *n.* 庄严,堂皇,雄壮,华贵.

state•ly [ˈsteitli] *a.* (建筑等)庄严的,堂皇的;宏伟的,华贵的. *the ~ Altar of Heaven* 宏伟堂皇的天坛. **-li•ness** *n.*

state•ment [ˈsteitmənt] *n.* ①陈述,声明;声明书. ②【法】供述; 交待. ③【商】贷借对照表; (财务)报告书. *Statements should be based on facts.* 说话要有根据. *prepare an official ~* 准备一项正式声明. *make a detailed ~ of profit and loss.* 出具详细的损益计算书. *issue a ~* 发表一个声明. *a random ~* 胡乱的供词. *a bank ~* 银行报告单[结单].

stat•er[1] [ˈsteitə] *n.* 陈述者.

stat•er[2] [ˈsteitə] *n.* (古希腊、波斯的)金银硬币.

state•room [ˈsteitrum] *n.* (宫殿、大厦等的)大厅;(轮船的)单间卧舱,特等舱;〔美〕(火车的)单间卧铺,包房.

state•side [ˈsteit-said] *a., ad.* 〔美〕(不包括阿拉斯加州和夏威夷州在内的)美国国内(的),在美国大陆(的).

states•man [ˈsteitsmən] *n.* ***(pl. -men)*** ①政治家. ②〔北英〕自耕农. *a proletarian* ~ 无产阶级政治家. *an elder* ~ 政界元老. ~**ship** 治理国家的本领[手腕]; 政治家风度. ~**like, -ly** *a.* 象政治家的, 政治家风度的.

stat•ic[1], **-i•cal** [ˈstætik, -ikəl] *a.* 静止的, 静态的, 静力的. ②【物】天电的,静电的. ③【无】静态特性. ④固定的,不活泼的,变化小的. ⑤使安静的. ~ *draft* 【机】静力通风. ~ *electricity* 静电. ~ *energy* 静能, 位能. ~ *sensation* 静位觉,平衡感觉. ~ *tube* 【化】静止管. *a ~ population* 固定不变的人口. *a play full of ~ characters* 一出满是不活泼的人物的戏. **i•cal•ly** *ad.*

stat•ic[2] [ˈstætik] *n.* ①〔美〕【物】天电; 静电; 天电[静电]干扰. ②〔俚〕恶言,口角,争吵.

stat•i•ce [ˈstætiˌsi] *n.* ①【植】匙叶草属植物 (= sea lavender). ②〔Scot.〕营生,工作,活计.

stat•ics [ˈstætiks] *n.* 【物】静力学;【无】静电(干扰).

sta•tion [ˈsteiʃən] *n.* ①站,台,车站;航空站,机场. ②派出所;署,局,所. ③【无】电台,电视台. ④驻地,部戍地,根据地,警备区域; 基地;〔集合词〕基地全体人员. ⑤停泊地;军港;〔美〕空军兵站. ⑥部位, 位置, 场所. ⑦地位; 身分; 职位, 岗位. ⑧停留, 停驻; 站立(姿势). ⑨【生】= habitat. ⑩【宗】耶稣受难十四处之一(或其图画之一幅). ⑪【测】测点,测站,标准距离. ⑫〔澳〕牧场. ⑬〔美〕邮政局;〔海关用语〕仓库. *a midway* ~ 错车车站. *a ~ agent* 〔美〕(火车站)站长. *a power* ~ 发电厂. *an atomic* ~ 原子能发电站. *an air* ~ 飞机场. *a broadcasting* ~ 广播电台. *people of* ~ 有地位的人. ~ *call letters* 电台呼号. ~ *in life* 【法】身分. ~ *waggon* 〔美〕车站接送汽车, 客货两用汽车, 面包车. ***take up a convenient*** ~ 占有利地位. ***take up one's appointed*** ~ 各就指定岗位. — *vt.* 驻扎,安置,配置,设置. ~ *a guard at the gate* 门口设置一个警卫员. ~ **bill** 船上人员应急岗位部署表. ~ **break** 【无】(电台)播音间歇〔通常指插入商业广告的时间〕. ~**-calendar** 〔英〕火车出站时刻指示牌. ~ **house** 〔美〕派出所;车站. ~ **indicator** 火车发车到车公告牌; 停车车站揭示板. ~**master** (火车站)站长; 〔美空军口语〕军用机场司令官. ~ **pointer** 【测】示点器,三脚分度规,三杆分度仪.

sta•tion•a•ry [ˈsteiʃənəri] *a.* 不动的,静止的,不变的;不增不减的, 固定的, 装定的. — *n.* ①不动的人; 固定物. ②〔*pl.*〕驻军. ~ *air* (呼吸时留在肺中的)静气. *a ~ engine* 固定式发动机. *a ~ engineer* 固定动力机技师. ~ *radiant* 【天】不动辐射点. ~ *parasitism* 永寄生(现象). ~ *states* 【物】定态. *a ~ temperature* 不变的温度. ~ *troops* 驻军. ~ *vibration* 【物】驻波,定波;【无】稳定振荡. ~ *wave* 【物】定波,驻波. **-ar•i•ness** *n.*

stat•ion•er [ˈsteiʃənə] *n.* ①文具商. ②〔古〕书商,出版商. Stationers' Hall 伦敦书籍出版业公会(会所). ***entered at the Stationers' Hall*** 版权登记讫.

sta•tion•er•y [ˈsteiʃənəri] *n.* 文具; (尤指)信纸. ~ ***and envelopes*** 信纸和信封. — *a.* 文具的. *a ~ case* 文具合. **S- Office** (英国政府)文书局〔出版政府文件等〕.

stat•ism [ˈsteitizəm] *n.* 中央集权下的经济统治;经济的国家统制; 国治主义 (*opp.* anarchism), 国家主义.

stat•ist [ˈsteitist] *n.* ①国治[国家]主义者,主张国家(中央集权下)统制经济者. ②= statistician.

sta•tis•tic, -ti•cal [stəˈtistik, (-əl)] *a.* 统计(上)的,统计学(上)的. ~ *data* 统计资料; ~ *figures* 统计数字. *n.* 〔只 *sing.*〕①统计资料中的一项. ②(对总体具有代表性的)典型统计量. **-ti•cal•ly** *ad.*

stat•is•ti•cian [ˌstætisˈtiʃən] *n.* 统计工作者; 统计学家.

sta•tis•tics [stəˈtistiks] *n.* ①统计学, 统计法〔用作单数〕. ②统计数字[资料], 统计表〔用作复数〕. *Government statistics indicate that prices have gone down.* 政府统计指出物价已经下降. *You may consult the ~ on population issued by the government.* 你可以查一查政府发表的人口统计. *the vital* ~ (出生、结婚、死亡等)人口动态统计. *collect [take]* ~ 进行统计.

stat•i•tron [ˈsteititrən] *n.* 静电加速器[发生器, 振荡器].

stat•o•blast [ˈstætəˌblæst] *n.* 【动】休眠芽.

stat•o•cyst [ˈstætəˌsist] *n.* ①【植】平衡囊. ②【动】平衡器,(昆虫的)平衡胞.

stat•ol•a•try [steiˈtɔlətri] *n.* 中央集权论.

stat•o•lith [ˈstætəˌliθ] *n.* ①【植】平衡石. ②【动】耳石,听石. **-ic** *a.*

sta•tor [ˈsteitə] *n.* 【电】(固)定子;【空】导向叶片压气机.

stat•o•scope [ˈstætəskəup] *n.* 【空】微动气压计; 灵敏高度表.

stat•u•a•ry [ˈstætjuəri] *n.* ①雕像家,塑像家,雕刻家. ②雕塑艺术. ③〔集合词〕雕像,塑像. — *a.* 雕像的; 适合雕像用的(大理石等).

stat•ue [ˈstætjuː] *n.* 雕像,铸像,塑像. — *vt.* ①用雕像装饰. ②〔古〕为…雕塑. *a ~ to (of) Liu Hu-lan* 刘胡

兰的塑像. *the Statue of Liberty* (美国纽约的)自由女神铜像. *a ~d garden* 用雕像装饰的花园.

stat·u·esque [ˌstætjuˈesk] *a.* 雕像般的;雕像一样庄严优美的(轮廓). **-ly** *ad.* **-ness** *n.*

stat·u·ette [ˌstætjuˈet] *n.* 小雕[塑]像.

sta·ture [ˈstætʃə] *n.* ①(特指人的)身长,身材. ②才干,(道德精神的)器量;发展、成长的状况或高度. *the lofty moral ~ of a revolutionary martyr.* 一个革命先烈的崇高精神境界. *a scholar of world ~* 世界性的学者. *be of mean ~* 个子矮小. *be small in ~* 身材小.

sta·tus [ˈsteitəs] *n.* ①情形,状况,状态. ②地位;资格;【法】身分. ③重要地位,要人身分. ④(器材的)本性. *the ~ of world affairs* 世界形势. *the international ~* 国际局势. *the ~ of a citizen* 市民[公民]的身分. *class ~* 阶级成分. *social ~* 社会地位. *a ~ seeker* 想往上爬的人. *the alert ~*【军】待机状态. *~ lymphaticus* 浆液质,淋巴质. *~ **quo*** [kwəu] 〔L.〕现状,维持现状. *~ **quo ante*** [ˈænti] 〔L.〕原状,以前状况. *~ **quo ante bellum*** 〔L.〕战前状况. ~ **symbol** 社会地位表征〔指能表示某种身份的用品,作风等〕.

stat·u·ta·ble [ˈstætjutəbl] *a.* = statutory.

stat·u·ta·bly [ˈstætjutəbli] *ad.* 依照法令,法令上.

stat·ute [ˈstætjuːt] *n.* ①【法】法令,法规;成文法. ②(学校,公司等的)规则,章程,条例. *The Academic Council has passed a ~ of marking system.* 教务会议已经通过了一项记分制度章程. ~ **book** 法令全书. ~ **law** 成文法. ~ **mile** 法定英里 (=5,280英尺或1,609.3 m). **~s at large** 一般法规,法令全书.

stat·u·to·ry [ˈstætjutəri] *a.* ①法令的,有关法令的. ②法定的;依照法令的;可依法处罚的. *a ~ provision* 法令条款. *a ~ meeting* 第一次股东大会. *a ~ minimum* 法定最小限度. ~ **tariffs** 国定税率. ~ **rape**【法】强奸幼女(罪).

staunch[1] [stɔːntʃ] *vt.* 制止(出血),止(血). — *vi.* (血)停止 (= stanch[1]).

staunch[2] [stɔːntʃ] *a.* ①坚固的;坚定的;忠实可靠的. ②不漏水的,耐航的;不漏气的. *a ~ defender of peace and democracy* 和平民主的坚定保卫者. *a ~ ally* 坚定可靠的同盟者. *a ~ cabin* 不漏水的舱. **-ly** *ad.* **-ness** *n.*

stau·ro·lite [ˈstɔːrəˌlait] *n.*【矿】十字石. **-lit·ic** [-ˈlitik] *a.*

stau·ro·scope [ˈstɔːrəskəup] *n.* 十字镜〔测定光在晶体中偏振平面方向的仪器〕.

Sta·vang·er [stəˈvæŋə] *n.* 斯塔万格〔挪威港市〕.

stave [steiv] *n.* ①(桶等的)侧板,狭板,桶板. ②(车)辐;梯级(横木);横档. ③棒,棍. ④诗句,诗节. ⑤【乐】五线谱 (= staff). — *vt.* ①装桶板;换桶板;拆桶板;穿孔(在桶、船等上);敲破(箱匣等) *(in)*; 装梯级,装横档. ②压扁,打坏,压牢. ③挡开,避开,延缓 *(off)*. — *vi.* ①穿孔. ②破碎. ③快步走动. ④〔美俚〕突进,猛冲. ~ ***in*** 冲过,冲破;压扁(帽子等);拆散. ~ ***it out*** 争[抵抗]到成功为止. ~ ***off*** 挡开;避开,勉强阻止(失败、毁灭、暴露等);延宕,拖延 (*measures to ~ off an attack* 缓兵之计). *The boat's hull has been ~d in by the tremendous seas.* 小船壳让巨浪打穿了. *Glad that you've ~d off the trouble.* 很高兴你避开了这件麻烦事儿.

stav·er [ˈsteivə] *n.* 〔美俚〕活动家,精力充沛的干将,积极苦干的工作者.

staves [ˈsteivəz] staff[1] 和 stave 的复数.

staves·a·cre [ˈsteivzˌeikə] *n.* ①【植】斯塔维翠雀,虱草 *(Delphinium staphisagria)* 〔产于欧、亚两洲,其籽含生物碱,可作外敷用防腐剂〕. ②斯塔维翠雀子,虱草子.

stav·ing [ˈsteiviŋ] *a.* 〔俚〕特大的,特好的.

stay[1] [stei] *vi.* *(~ed,* 〔古美〕 ***staid)*** ①停留;暂住,逗留. ②保持下去;持久,坚持. ③站住,停止,中止,暂停. ④并驾齐驱*(with)*. — *vt.* ①阻止,制止,平息,暂时满足一下. ②坚持,停留到…完,等待到(某一刻); 留着度过(某一段时间). ③(判决等)延期,延缓. ④留等. *S-where you are.* 请原位勿动. *I don't live here, I'm only ~ing.* 〔口〕我不住在这里,我只是耽搁几天罢了. *My temperature ~s around 39°.* 我的体温老在三十九度左右. *Tell him to ~ a minute.* 告诉他停一会儿. *He'll try to ~ with his rival.* 他会尽力和他的敌手并驾齐驱的. *The court has decided to ~ the procedding.* 法庭已决定暂缓进行这诉讼程序. *Keep on, Tom! S~ the course.* 汤姆,接着干,跑完全程. *Oh, you must ~ dinner, Jane.* 简妮呀,你一定要留下吃饭. ***be unable to ~ to the end of a race*** 不能坚持到比赛完结. ***come to ~*** 稳定下来 (*The fine weather has come to ~.* 天气晴定了). ~ ***at home*** = ~ in. ~ ***away*** 不在家里;长时间内不在,离开一个时期. ~ ***away from school*** 缺课. ~***-down strike*** (矿工)井内罢工. ~ ***in*** 在家里,不外出. ~ ***in the clear*** 〔美〕别碰电线. ~***-in strike*** 留厂罢工. ~***ing power*** 耐久力,持久力. ~ ***on in*** 赖着不走. ~ ***one's [sb.'s] hand*** (使某人)住手不作某事. ~ ***one's stomach*** 忍住饥饿. ~ ***out*** 在外头,不在家;不干涉,不插手. ~ ***overnight*** 住一晚. ~ ***put*** 〔美〕安装牢固,原位不动. ~ ***the course*** (赛跑的马)跑到终点;坚持到底. ~ ***up late [all night]*** 很晚[终夜]未睡. ~ ***with it*** 〔美〕忍耐,容忍. — *n.* ①停留,逗留(期间). ②遏制,抑制;妨碍,阻止. ③延缓;【法】延期. ④持久(力),忍耐(力). *the ~ of judgement* 延缓判决. *The horse has good pace but no ~.* 这马脚步倒快就是没有持久力. ***make a long ~*** 长住,长期逗留. ***put a ~ on*** 抑制;妨碍. ~***-at-home*** *a., n.* 不爱出门的(人). **-er,** 逗留者;有持久力者;遏制者[物].

stay[2] [stei] *n.* ①【海】(船桅的)支索. ②【机】牵条,拉线;牵条,支撑物. ③支柱;倚靠. ④〔*pl.*〕〔英〕(妇女的)紧身褡,胸衣. *the ~ of one's old age* 老年时候的依靠. ***be in ~s***【海】(船)在掉头,正在掉换[抢风,转向上风]方向. ***be quick [slack] in ~s*** (船头)掉得快[掉不过去]. ***miss [lose] ~s***【海】掉头没有成功. — *vt.*【海】①用支索[支柱]固定. ②把(船)掉过头来(向上风). ③支持. — *vi.*【海】转向上风. *Your friendship has ~ed me.* 你的友谊支持了我. *Grandma put her hand on the chair to ~ her from falling.* 奶奶把手放在椅子上撑住自己不致摔倒. ~ **bar [rod]** 撑杆. ~ **bolt** 牵条螺栓. ~ **tube** 牵管. ~ **lace** 〔英〕紧身褡的带子. ~ **sail**【海】(用支索拉紧的)长三角帆,支索帆. **-er** *n.* 支持者,支撑物.

St. Clair [ˈsiŋkleə] *n.* 圣克莱尔〔姓氏〕.

STD = standard.

Std = standard.

St. Dft. =【商】sight draft 见票即付的汇票.

Ste. = 〔F.〕Sainte〔Saint 的女性〕; Stephen.

stead [sted] *n.* ①代替. ②用处,好处,有帮助. *in sb.'s ~* 代某人. *in (the) ~ of* = instead of. *stand sb. in good ~* 对某人很有用,对某人很有帮助. — *vt.* 对…有用[有利,有帮助].

stead·fast [ˈstedfəst] *a.* 坚定的(信仰),不动摇的,不变的(意志,朋友). *be ~ to Marxism-Leninism* 坚信马列主义. *our ~ ally in peace or war* 无论在战争中或和平中我们坚定的盟国. *a ~ gaze* 凝视. **-ly** *ad.* **-ness** *n.*

stead·i·ly [ˈstedili] *ad.* 稳定地;坚定地;坚固地;不断地.

stead·i·ness [ˈstedinis] *n.* ①稳固,稳当. ②坚定,不变;始终如一;有规则. ③【物】定常性;恒定性;均匀.

stead·ing [ˈstediŋ] *n.* ①〔英〕小农场. ②〔苏格兰〕农庄,农场的建筑物.

stead·y [ˈstedi] *a.* ①稳固的,平稳的,稳定的,不变的(脚步、努力等). ②坚定的,扎实的,牢靠的(船等). ③有规则的,没有激变的(水流、气候等). ④镇定的,沉着的,从容的;有节制的;稳健的. ⑤(船)不畏风浪依旧前进的. *A young nurse dressed his wounds with ~ hands.* 一个青年护士稳稳当当地扎裹他的伤处. *He is making ~ pro-*

gress in English. 他在英语学习中取得稳定的进步。*I know she is ~ in her purpose.* 我晓得她是意志坚定的。*Slow and ~ wins the race.* 慢而稳事必成。*Steady!* 别急！镇定！留心！*Steady! = Keep her ~!*【海】(船头)方向照旧。*a ~ theatergoer* 戏院常客。*~ hand* 不抖颤的手；稳定的统治，不可动摇的命令。*~ load*【工】稳恒负载。*~ wind* 持续而方向不变的风。—*vt., vi.* (使)稳固；(使)稳定，(使)坚定；(使)沉着；变稳重；稳定地动，稳定地前进。*Danger steadies some people.* 有的人在危险时候反而沉着。*~ on* 停划，把牢(桨)；沉着，镇定。— *ad.* 经常地；坚定地；持续不变地。***go ~***〔美口〕经常只和某一异性朋友约会出游；(二人)成为情人。— *n.* ①【机】固定中心架；台，承。②〔美俚〕未婚夫[妻]，(关系确定的)情人。**~-going** *a.* 稳定的；扎扎实实的，稳重的 *(opp.* easy-going*)*。**~-state** 恒稳的。**~-state theory**【天】稳恒态学说〔宇宙论的一种，认为随着宇宙的发展和星系的分出，新物质经常不断地在产生〕。

steak [steik] *n.* (做牛排等用的)大块肉片；牛排；大块鱼片。~ **house** 牛排餐馆。~ **knife** 吃牛排时用的餐刀。~ **tartare** 鞑靼式生拌牛肉末〔加洋葱葱花、生鸡蛋、胡椒粉生拌，配欧芹菜生吃〕。

steal [sti:l] ***(stole*** [stəul]***; stolen*** ['stəulən]***)*** *vt.* ①偷，窃取；剽窃(别人文字)；【棒球】偷垒。②偷偷地做；暗暗拉拢，笼络；突然做。③僭据，侵占。— *vi.* ①偷东西，做贼。②偷偷走近[出去]，溜 *(along; by; down; from; into; out of)*。③(船、烟等)悄悄地动；(水、泪等)静静地流。④(棒球)偷垒。*The purse has been stolen from my pocket.* 有人从我的口袋里把钱包偷走了。*She stole a glance at George when he was writing the letter.* 乔治写信时，她偷偷地看了他一眼。*Father was angry and I stole softly out of the room.* 爸爸生气了，我轻轻地溜出了房间。*The years ~ by.* 岁月不知不觉地过去了。*~ sb.'s heart* 在不知不觉间抓牢对方爱情。*The feeling ~s (in) upon me* 我在不知不觉之间发生这种感情。*~* ***a march on*** 偷偷抢在…的前头，占先。*~* ***away*** 溜掉。*~* ***in*** 偷偷跑进，溜进；(将货物)走私运入；偷偷放进(人或物)。*~* ***off*** 偷去，拿跑。*~* ***on*** ①(睡魔、感觉等)袭来。②不知不觉地跑来 (*The winter has stolen on us.* 冬天悄悄地来了)。*~* ***sb.'s thunder*** 抢先做某人想做的事〔发表论点等〕；剽窃别人的发明[研究成果等]抢先利用。*~* ***one's way*** 偷偷地来[去]。*~* ***out*** 偷偷地溜出去。*~* ***over*** = *~* on. *~* ***round to the back door*** 偷偷地绕到后门。*~* ***the glory***〔美运〕创最高记录。*~* ***the headlines***〔美运〕赛得精采；创光荣记录。*~* ***the show [the limelight]***〔美剧〕把观众的注意力都吸引到自己身上；使旁的演员都黯然失色地一个人取得很大的成功。— *n.* ①〔口〕偷窃；赃物。②意外之财；诈欺。③不正当的获得[交易]。④【棒球】偷垒。**-er** *n.* ①偷取者，偷干者。②僭据者。③(棒球)偷垒者。④【船】合并挡板。

steal·ing ['sti:liŋ] *n.* ①偷盗，盗窃；欺骗。②【棒球】偷垒。③〔*pl.*〕赃物。**-ly** *ad.* 偷偷地，不知不觉地，暗中。

stealth [stelθ] *n.* ①秘密行动，背人的活动，不为人知的活动。②行窃。***by ~*** 秘密，鬼祟，暗中 (*eat things by ~* 偷偷吃东西。*do good by ~* 暗中做好事)。

stealth·y ['steilθi] *a.* ***(-i·er; -i·est)*** 偷偷的，秘密的；鬼鬼祟祟的；不声不响的。*a ~ glance* 偷看。*a ~ murder* 暗杀。*~ footsteps* 蹑足。**-i·ly** *ad.* **-i·ness** *n.*

steam [sti:m] *n.* ①蒸汽，水蒸气，水气，雾，蒸气压力。②〔口〕精神，精力，气力。③轮船，乘轮船旅行。*dry ~* 干蒸汽。*high ~* 高压汽。*a ~ limit curve* 汽液界线。*In our plant, technical innovation gets up ~.* 我们厂的技术革新的劲头增加了。*Now, Tom, let the ~ off and come to an agreement.* 好了，汤姆，吐吐怨气达成协议吧。*Playing football is one of the ways of letting off youthful ~.* 踢足球是青年人散发精力的方法之一。***at full ~*** 放足蒸气；开足马力，尽力。***by ~*** 坐轮船。***get up ~*** 冒水蒸气；振作精神，拿出干劲；愤怒。***have ~ on*** 冒着水蒸气。***let off ~*** 发泄多余的精力；发牢骚。***put on ~*** 拿出精神。***run out of ~***〔口〕泄气；失去势头。***under its [her] own ~***〔指船〕依靠本身的蒸汽力。***under ~*** 被汽力推动着；在航行中；拿出精神。***work off ~*** 拿出精力[干劲]工作；发泄某种感情。—*vi.* ①蒸发，冒水汽；出汗；被水汽弄模糊。②用汽力开动[行驶]；航行。③〔口〕大大进步[进展]。— *vt.* ①蒸，煮；蒸软(木材)。②使蒸发；散发。③用蒸汽力开动。— *vi.* ①发蒸汽；蒸发。②利用蒸汽行驶。③凝结蒸汽。④〔口〕发脾气。⑤〔口〕疾行。*~ the meat* 蒸肉。*a ~ed bun* 馒头。*~ a ship through the straight* 把轮船开进海峡。*The train ~ed into the station.* 火车冒着蒸汽开进车站。*That would make him ~ again.* 那会使得他又发火了。*~* ***along [ahead]*** 拼命开。*~* ***away*** 蒸发；(人)去得快，(工作)做得快。*~* ***up*** (玻璃)蒙上蒸汽而模糊；制造蒸汽；〔口〕拿出精神；鼓励；〔美〕喝酒；喝醉；兴奋，愤怒。

~ **bath** 蒸汽浴。~**boat** 汽艇，汽船，轮船。~ **boiler** 蒸汽锅炉。~ **box** ①= ~ chest. ②蒸笼。~ **brake** 蒸汽制动机，汽闸。~ **chest**【机】汽柜；【化】蒸气箱。~ **coal** 蒸汽锅炉用煤。~ **-cork** 汽管旋塞。~ **colo(u)r** 蒸汽染色。~ **consump·tion** (蒸)汽(消)耗量。~ **cooling** 蒸汽冷却(法)。~ **crane** 汽力起重机。~**cylinder** 汽缸。~ **dome** 聚汽室。~**engine** 蒸汽机 (*like a ~ engine* 精力充沛，精神勃勃)。~ **fiddle**〔美俚〕= calliope. ~ **fitter** 汽管装配工人。~**-gas** 过热蒸汽。~ **gauge** 汽表，汽压计。~ **hammer** 汽锤。~ **heat** 汽热；蒸汽热量。~ **heat-ed** 用蒸气加热的，蒸气取暖的。~ **heater** 蒸汽加热器。~ **heating** 汽热装置。~ **iron** 蒸汽熨衣器。~ **jacket** 汽套。~ **launch** 汽艇，小火轮。~ **navvy**〔英〕汽力挖掘机。~ **packet** 定期轮船。~ **plough** 汽锄，汽犁。~ **port** 汽门，汽口。~ **power** 蒸汽力。~ **pressure** 蒸汽压力。~ **rate** 耗汽率；汽率。~**-roll** ① *vt.* 用蒸汽碾路机压平[压碎]；施以高压。② *vi.*〔口〕以不可抗拒之势推进。~**roller** ① *n.* 蒸汽碾路机；高压手段；(无可反抗的)压倒的力量，不可抗力。② *vt., vi.* = ~ roll. ③ *a.* 强制(性)的，高压的。~ **room** 蒸汽浴室。~**-ship** 轮船。★ 和船名连用时略作 s.s. (the s.s Queen Mary 玛丽皇后轮)。~**-shovel** = ~ navy. ~ **table** 具有用蒸汽或热水保暖设备的餐桌或食品柜；蒸汽表。~**tight** *a.* 不漏汽的，汽密的；防止蒸汽的，耐汽的。~ **tug** (小)拖轮。~ **turbine** 蒸汽涡轮。~**-whistle** 汽笛。~ **winch** 蒸汽绞车，蒸汽起货机。

steam·er ['sti:mə] *n.* ①汽船，轮船。②蒸汽汽车；蒸汽机。③汽锅；蒸锅，蒸笼。④蒸…的人[物]；【动】沙海螂 (= soft-shell clam)。~ *chair* 甲板躺椅，帆布躺椅。~ *rug* 甲板躺椅上用毛毯〔盖腰、腹、膝腿部〕。~ *trunk* 轮船衣箱〔宽而扁，原设计供放在船舱铺位下〕。

steam·i·ness ['sti:minis] *n.* 蒸汽多，冒水气；蒸汽[雾气]弥漫状态。

steam·ing ['sti:miŋ] *a.* ①热气腾腾的。②〔美〕兴奋的；兴致勃勃的。— *ad.* 热气腾腾地。*a ~ runner* 跑得热气腾腾的人。*The tea is ~ hot.* 茶汽蒙蒙地烫。

steam·y ['sti:mi] *a.* ***(-i·er; -i·est)*** 蒸汽的，蒸汽似的，蒸汽多的；雾深的，水气蒙蒙的，潮湿的。**-i·ly** *ad.* **-i·ness** *n.*

ste·ap·sin [sti'æpsin] *n.*【生化】胰脂酶。

ste·a·rate ['stiəˌreit] *n.*【化】硬脂酸盐，硬脂酸脂。

ste·ar·ic [sti'ærik] *a.*【化】(取自)硬脂的；似硬脂的。~ ***acid*** 硬脂酸。

ste·a·rin(e) ['stiərin] *n.* 硬脂(精)；甘油(三)硬脂酸脂；商用硬脂酸。

ste·a·rop·tene [ˌstiə'rɔpti:n] *n.*【化】硬脂萜，硬脂脑。

ste·a·tite ['stiətait] *n.*【矿】块滑石，冻石，皂石。

ste·a·tol·y·sis [ˌstiə'tɔlisis] *n.*【化】脂肪分解。

ste·a·to·pyg·i·a [ˌstiətəu'pidʒiə, -'paidʒiə] *n.* 臀部特

别肥突〔尤指妇女由于臀部脂肪层厚所致,如非洲霍屯督妇女〕. **-pyg·ic, -py·gous** [-ˈpaigəs] *a.*

ste·at·or·rhe·a, -or·rhoe·a [ˌstiətəˈriːə] *n.* 【医】脂肪痢,脂溢.

sted·fast [ˈstedfəst] *a.* = steadfast.

Steed [stiːd] *n.* 斯蒂德〔姓氏〕.

steed [stiːd] *n.* ①〔诗〕(骏)马. ②〔谑〕驽马 = nag. ③〔美〕(学生的)解答书.

steek [stiːk] *vt.* 〔苏〕关门〔窗〕; 关闭; 监禁. —*n.* (缝纫)一针. —*vi.* 缝.

steel [stiːl] *n.* ①钢,钢铁. ②钢制品; 刀,剑,打火镰; (女人胸衣等中的)松紧钢条〔丝〕; 钢磨; 〔美〕剃刀,小刀; 钢骨. ③【医】铁剂. ④钢铁般的坚强,坚硬. ⑤钢铁工业; 〔*pl.*〕钢铁工业股票. — *a.* ①钢制的,搀有钢的. ②钢一样的; 坚硬的,冷酷的. ③钢铁业的. *high-grade* ~ 优质钢. *low [mild, soft]* ~ 软钢. *high [hard]* ~ 硬钢. *medium* ~ 中钢. *small* ~ *shape* 小型钢材. *a cold* ~ 利器,刀剑. *a grip of* ~ 牢牢握紧. *muscles of* ~ 结实的肌肉. *a heart of* ~ 铁石心肠,冷酷的心. *off the* ~ 〔美〕离开铁路线(的). ***a foe worthy of sb.'s*** ~ 需要认真对付的敌人,够格的对手; 劲敌. — *vt.* ①钢化,用钢包上,用钢作刀口. ②使象钢铁一般; 锤炼; 锻炼,使坚硬,使坚强. ③使冷酷. ④〔美俚〕(用刀)刺杀. ~ *oneself in the revolution* 在革命中锤炼自己. ~ *one's willpower and physical strength* 锻炼一个人的意志和体质. ~ **ball** 钢珠. ~ **band** 钢带. ~ **bar** 钢条. ~ **blue** 钢青色. ~ **casting** 铸钢件,铸钢. ~**-clad** *a.* 装甲的,披甲的. ~ **diaphragm** 钢膜片. ~ **engraving** 【印】钢板雕刻(术); 钢板印刷品. ~ **grey** 青灰色. ~ **guitar** 夏威夷吉他. ~**head** 【动】硬头鳟. **S- Helmets** (德国历史的)钢盔团. ~ **ingot** 钢锭,钢块. ~**making** 炼钢. ~ **mill** 炼钢厂. ~ **plate** 钢板. ~ **product [section]** 钢材. ~ **rule** 钢尺. **S- State** 钢州〔美国宾夕伐州的别名〕. ~**-trap** *a.* 极快的,直接的. ~**-wire** 钢丝. ~ **wool** 钢丝绒. ~**work** 钢铁工程,钢制品,钢结构. ~**worker** 炼钢工人. ~**works** 〔用作 *sing.*〕炼钢厂. ~**yard** 秤,提秤. ~**-like** *a.* 钢铁般的.

Steele [stiːl] *n.* 斯蒂尔〔姓氏〕.

Steel·op·o·lis [stiːˈlɔpəlis] *n.* 钢都〔英国 Sheffield 的别名〕.

steel·y [ˈstiːli] *a.* *(-i·er; -i·est)* 钢的; 含钢的,钢制的; 钢色的; 硬如钢铁的. ②顽强的; 无情的,冷酷的; 极严格的. *a* ~ *northwester.* 刺骨的西北风. ~ *fortitude* 刚强不屈. **-i·ness** *a.*

steen [stiːn] *a.* = um(p)teen.

steen·bok, steen·buck [ˈstiːnbɔk, -bʌk] *n.* (非洲)小羚羊.

steep¹ [stiːp] *a.* ①陡急的,峻峭的,崄峨的. ②〔口〕(要求等)过分的,过当的,过高的; 夸张的, 极端的. ③〔古〕极高的. ④急剧升降的,急转直下的. ⑤难以接受的,不合理的. *a* ~ *dive* 【空】垂直俯冲. *an impassably* ~ *mountain* 一个无路可以攀登的峻峭的山. *a* ~ *fall in market value* 市场价值的急剧下降. *a* ~ *demand* 一个难以接受的要求. — *n.* 倾斜〔16°—26°〕, 陡坡; 绝壁,悬崖. **-ly** *ad.* **-ness** *n.*

steep² [stiːp] *vt.* ①泡,浸 *(in)*; 浸湿,浸透. ②使专心一意,使埋头. ③(雾、烟、光等)包覆, 笼罩(山野、树木等). — *vi.* (在水中)浸泡. — *n.* 浸,泡; 泡种子的水,浸渍液. ~ *tea in boiling water* 泡茶. ***be*** ~***ed in*** 埋头于,专心于. ***be*** ~***ed in prejudice*** 偏见很深. *Dried vegetable* ~*s slowly.* 晾干的菜浸渍得慢.

steep·en [ˈstiːpən] *vt., vi.* 使陡峭,使崄峨,变崄峨,越来越崄峨.

steep·er [ˈstiːpə] *n.* 浸渍者; 浸渍器.

stee·ple [ˈstiːpl] *n.* (特指礼拜堂的)尖塔,尖顶; (女用)尖塔形头巾. *a* ~ *head rivet* 【机】尖头铆钉. ~**d** *a.* 有尖顶的,尖塔形的. ~ **bush** 〔美〕【植】绒毛绣线菊. ~**chase** 越野赛马〔跑〕; 障碍赛马〔跑〕. ~**-crowned** *a.* 尖塔形的(帽等). ~ **jack** *n.* 尖塔修理工人,烟囱修理工人,高空作业工人. ~ **top** *n.* ①尖塔状顶部. ②北极鲸.

steep·y [ˈstiːpi] *a.* 〔诗〕崄峨的,陡峭的.

steer¹ [stiə] *vt., vi.* ①掌舵; 驾驶(船、车) *(for; towards)*; 〔主口、诗〕(使)向、沿着(某方)行进 *(for; to)*. ②指导,领导; 操纵,控制,筹划. ③〔美俚〕建议,劝告,忠告. ④〔美俚〕替赌场〔妓院〕拉客. ~ *one's flight heavenwards* 飞向空中. *We must* ~ *our efforts towards solving the problem.* 我们必须把努力导向解决问题. *Thanks to your help, we've* ~*ed clear of the difficulties.* 多亏你的帮忙,我们已经避免了困难. *Where are you* ~*ing for?* 你上哪儿去? ~ ***by*** = ~ past. ~ ***sb. clear of*** 设法使某人躲开. ~ ***clear of*** 机灵地脱身,避开. ~ ***a steady course*** 坚定地不断前进. ~ ***one's country to*** 领导国家向…方面前进. ~ ***one's way to*** 向…方前进. ~ ***past*** 避过,躲过. — *n.* ①关于行路(或驾驶)的指示. ②〔美俚〕建议,劝告,忠告. ~**-able** *a.* ①可驾驶的; 易操纵的. ②〔天线等〕易改变位置的.

steer² [stiə] *n.* 公牛; (食用)阉牛; 〔美〕食用牛.

steer·age [ˈstiəridʒ] *n.* ①驾驶,掌舵. ②操纵,领导. ③【海】舵(的)效(力),舵能; 驾驶装置. ④船尾; (商船的)三等客舱,统舱. ⑤〔美〕(军舰的)下级军官室. ***have an easy [a bad]*** ~ 顺手〔不顺手〕. ***go*** ~ = ***travel*** ~ 搭三等舱走. ~ **passenger** 三等舱乘客. ~ **way** 【海】舵效速率〔足够使舵生效的低速〕.

steer·er [ˈstiərə] *n.* ①舵手,司机. ②具有某种驾驶性能的船(车). ③〔美俚〕(赌场的)囮子; (妓院等坏地方的)拉客的人.

steer·ing [ˈstiəriŋ] *n.* ①掌舵; 驾驶; 转向. ②指导,领导; 操纵,控制. *a* ~ *handle* 舵把, 方向盘. *current* ~ *logic* 电流控制逻辑. ~ **committee** 〔美〕(团体、机构的)指导委员会. ~ **engine** 转向舵机. ~ **gear** 【海】操舵装置. ~ **house** 舵室. ~ **wheel** 【海】舵轮,驾驶盘; (汽车的)方向盘.

steers·man [ˈstiəzmən] *n.* *(pl. -men)* 舵手; (汽车)司机.

steeve [stiːv] *n.* ①【船】艏斜桅仰角. ②起重桅; 吊杆. — *vt.* ①用起重桅装货. ②使(艏斜桅)倾斜. — *vi.* (艏斜桅)倾斜.

Stef·ans·son [ˈstefənsn], **Vilhajalmur** [ˈvilhjaulmə] 斯蒂芬森〔1879—1962 美国北极探险家〕.

Stef·fens [ˈstefənz] *n.* 斯蒂芬斯〔姓氏〕.

steg·o·sau·rus [ˌstegəˈsɔːrəs] *n.* *(pl. -ri* [-ai]*)* 〔美〕【动】剑龙〔产于北美〕.

Stein [stain] *n.* 斯坦〔姓氏〕.

stein [stain] *n.* (陶制有盖)啤酒杯; 玻璃等制的啤酒杯. 一啤酒杯的容量.

Stein·beck [ˈstainbek] *n.* 斯坦贝克〔姓氏〕.

Stein·beck [ˈstainbek], **John Ernest** *n.* 斯坦贝克〔1902—1968,美国作家〕.

stein·bo(c)k [ˈstainbɔk] *n.* = ①steenbok. ②ibex.

Stein·metz [ˈstainmets], **Charles Proteus** 斯坦梅茨〔1865—1923,美国电工学家、发明家〕.

ste·la [ˈstiːlə] *n.* *(pl. -lae* [-liː]*)* = stele ①.

ste·le [ˈstiːli] *n.* *(pl. -lae* [-liː], *~s)* ①【考古】(刻有文字或图案的)石版,石柱. ②【植】中柱.

Stel·la [ˈstelə] *n.* 斯特拉〔姓氏〕.

stel·lar [ˈstelə] *a.* ①(恒)星的. ②星似的,星形的,星光灿烂的; 星多的. ③〔美〕主要的,第一流的. ④【影】名演员的,明星的. ~ *photography* 天体摄影术. ~ *photometry* 星体光度学.

stel·lar·a·tor [ˈsteləˌreitə] *n.* 【物】仿星器〔一种等离子体实验装置〕.

stel·lat·e(d) [ˈsteleit(id)] *a.* 象星的,星形的,放线状的. ~ *diaphram* 【植】星形隔膜. *a* ~ *ornament* 星形装饰品. **-ly** *ad.*

stel·len·bosch [ˈstelənbɔʃ] *vt.* 〔英军俚〕调充闲职.
stel·lif·er·ous [steˈlifərəs] *a.* 〔罕〕有星的,布满星的.
stel·li·form [ˈstelifɔːm] *a.* 星形的.
stel·li·fy [ˈstelifai] *vt.* 使成星状,使成明星,把…列入明星群中.
Stel·lite [ˈstelait] *n.* 司太立特硬质合金,钨铬钴合金.
stel·lu·lar, stel·lu·late [ˈsteljulə, -lit] *a.* 小星形的;星点花样的.
St. El. mo's fire [sntˈelməuz] = corposant. (暴风雨时在桅顶上或教堂尖塔上常见的)放电辉光球.
stem[1] [stem] *n.* ①(草木的)茎,干,梗;叶柄,花梗,果柄. ②(工具的)柄,把,杆. ③高酒杯的脚,烟斗柄;鸦片烟枪. ④〔*pl.*〕〔美俚〕腿. ⑤(手表,怀表的)转柄. ⑥【动】羽轴. ⑦【语】词干. ⑧【化】母体. ⑨〔美俚〕主要大街,干道. ⑩种族,血统,家系. ⑪【船】艏柱;艏材;艏,船头. ⑫【无】电子管心柱;晶体管管座. ⑬【乐】符尾. *Don't eat the ~ of a mushroom.* 不要吃蘑菇的梗. *a terrestrial [an aerial] ~* 【植】地上茎. *a subterranean [an underground] ~* 【植】地下茎. ***from ~ to stern*** 从船头到船尾,全船,全舰;从头到尾,到处,全部. ***give the ~*** 撞击. ***~ for ~*** 并排着;靠拢. ***~ on*** 把船头向着. ***~ to ~*** 船头对着船头. — *vt.* ①除掉梗茎. ②装上柄、杆;(给假花等)装上梗柄. — *vi.* 〔美〕起源于,(由…)发生,来自 *(from; out of)*. *Correct decisions ~ from correct judgements* 正确的决心来源于正确的判断. *Our hopes ~ from our previous achievements.* 我们的希望源于我们从前的成就. **~less** *a.* 【植】无茎[柄、梗]的. **~let** 小茎,小干,小梗. **~like** *a.* 茎[柄]状的. **~med** *a.* ①有茎[梗、柄]的. ②去掉茎[梗、柄]的. **~son** 【船】副艏材. **~ware** 高脚器皿,高脚杯. **~-winder** 〔美口〕有转柄的表;〔俚〕第一流人物[东西]. **~-winding** 〔表〕上弦,上发条.
stem[2] [stem] *vt.* ①(船)逆(风)开行. ②抵抗,反抗,逆(流)而行,顶着水面上. ③闸住,堵住(水等);遏止,防止,压住. ④【滑雪】转动滑雪展以停止滑行. —*vi.* ①堵住,止住. ②逆行. ③转动滑雪展停止滑行. *Debris have ~med the current.* 破瓦片之类的东西堵住了水流. *This is the way to ~ the flow of the blood.* 这才是制止流血的方法. — *n.* ①堵塞物,坝,止住. ②转动滑雪展停止滑行.
stem·ma [ˈstemə] *n.* *(pl.* ***-mata*** [-mətə]*)* ①世系,家谱. ②【动】(昆虫的)侧单眼,小眼面〔属复眼的一部分〕.
stem·med [stemd] *a.* 〔常用以构成复合词〕①有茎[梗]的;装有小柄的. ②去掉茎(或梗)的. *blue-~ grass* 蓝色茎的草.
stem·mer [ˈstemə] *n.* ①〔美〕剔除梗子的工人;(烟厂中)抽梗童工. ②抽梗机. ③【矿】炮棍,塞药棒;导火线留孔针. ④〔俚〕在街头行乞的游民.
stem·ple [ˈstempl] *n.* 【矿】①(用作梯级的)井筒内横木. ②巷道横梁. ③(不用柱腿的)嵌入梁.
sten [sten] *n.* 〔英〕轻机关枪〔= **sten gun**〕.
stench [stentʃ] *n.* 臭气,恶臭. *The ~ of the rotton fish is fearful.* 烂鱼的臭味太难闻了. —*vt., vi.* (使)发恶臭. **-ful** *a.* 充满恶臭的. **-y** *a.* 恶臭的.
sten·cil [ˈstensl, -sil] *n.* ①(镂花)模板,型板,漏(字)板. ②(油印)蜡纸. ③刷印上的文字[符号等]. — *vt.* (〔英〕***-ll-***) 用模板[蜡纸]刷印. *My job is to cut ~s and sort up mails.* 我的工作是刻蜡板和把来信分类. **~ paper** 钢板蜡纸. **~ pen** (刻蜡纸的)铁笔. **~ plate** 模板,型板. **-(l)er** *n.* 刻模板者,刻蜡纸者.
steno- *comb. f.* 小,少,薄,狭: *stenography.*
steno [ˈstenəu] *n.* 〔美口〕= stenographer, stenography.
sten·o·bath [ˈstenəˌbæθ] *n.* 【生】狭窄水带生物. **-ic** *a.*
sten·o·chro·my [steˈnɔkrəmi] *n.* 一次印成的彩色印刷术.
sten·o·graph [ˈstenəgrɑːf] *n.* 速记文字〔用速记法写成的文件〕;速记机. — *vt.* 速记. **-er, -ist** *n.* 速记员. **-y** *n.* 速记法;用速记法写成的文件.
sten·o·graph·ic, -i·cal [ˌstenəˈgræfik, -ikəl] *a.* 速记(术)的. **-cal·ly** *ad.*
sten·o·ha·line [ˌstenəˈheilain, -ˈhælain] *a.* 【生】狭盐性的;固定盐度生物的.
sten·o·hy·gric [ˌstenəˈhaigrik] *a.* 【生】狭湿性的.
ste·no·ky [stəˈnəuki] *n.* 【生】狭栖性. **-no·kous** [-kəs] *a.*
ste·noph·a·gous [stəˈnɔfəgəs] *a.* 【生】狭食性的.
ste·nosed [stəˈnəust, -ˈnəuzd] *a.* 患(器官)狭窄症的.
ste·no·sis [stiˈnəusis] *n.* 【医】(器官)狭窄. **-not·ic** [-ˈnɔtik] *a.*
sten·o·therm [ˈstənəˌθəːm] *n.* 【生】狭温性生物. **-al, -ous, -ic** *a.*
sten·o·top·ic [ˌstenəˈtɔpik] *a.* 【生态】窄幅分布的.
sten·o·type [ˈstenətaip] *n.* ①〔S-〕速记打字机〔商品名〕. ②(速记打字机用的)速记符号. — *vt.* 用速记机记录. **-typ·ic** *a.*
sten·o·typ·y [ˈstenəˌtaipi] *n.* 速记打字. **-typ·ist** *n.*
Sten·tor [ˈstentɔː] *n.* ①(荷马叙事诗 *Iliad* 中)声音宏亮的传令使者. ②〔s-〕声音宏亮的人. ③〔s-〕【动】喇叭虫. ④〔s-〕【动】吼猿.
sten·to·ri·an [stenˈtɔːriən] *a.* 声音极洪亮的.
sten·to·ro·pho·nic [ˌstentərəˈfɔnik] *a.* 声音洪亮的.
step [step] *vi.* ①走;跨步. ②踩,踏上 *(on)*. ③跳舞,轻快地走,合着步调走. ④跨入,踏进. ⑤走上. — *vt.* ①跨,踏,踏入;走(…步). ②(用脚)步测(量) *(out)*. ③跳舞. ④使成梯级;使成梯级状. ⑤【海】(将桅杆)竖立在桅座上. *S- this way.* 请打这边走. *Will you ~ inside?* 请进来. *~ on sb.'s toe* 踩着某人脚趾. ***~ across*** 走过,横穿过. ***~ aside*** ①走到一旁. ②避到一旁;让给别人,让步. ③走错路;走入邪道 (*"Step aside!" barked the policeman.* "躲开点!"警察大声喊着说). ***~ back*** ①后退;后退一步. ②回想,回顾 (*Henry remained silent, stepping back into the first time he met her.* 亨利继续沉默着,回想他第一次和她相会的时候). ***~ down*** ①走下,下(车). ②辞退. ③退出. ④【电】下降 (*I'm old enough to ~ down from the office.* 我年纪够老该退休了.) (*a ~ down transformer* 【电】降压变压器). ***~ forth*** = ***~ forward*** 前进;奋起. ***~ high*** (马)飞跑. ***~ in*** ①走进. ②〔命令〕请进. ③调停,排解;介入,干涉;挤进. ***~ into an estate*** 得到财产. ***~ into sb.'s shoes*** 接替某人,接任某人的位置. ***~ it*** ①跳舞. ②走着去. ③〔口〕赶快. ***~ it with*** 和…齐步. ***~ lively*** 急,赶快. ***~ long*** 大踏步走. ***~ off*** 失策;〔俚〕结婚;〔俚〕死. ***~ on it*** 〔口〕赶快. ***~ on the gas*** 〔美〕加快(汽车)马力;〔口〕赶快. ***~ out*** ①走出屋外. ②下(车). ③放大脚步. ④辞职. ⑤用脚步测量. ⑥〔美口〕去跳舞[玩耍、游荡] (*China has ~ped out on the road to modernization.* 中国已经大踏步地在现代化的道路上前进中. *What I'd do is ~ out for a moment.* 我想出去溜一溜). ***~ out of line*** 采取独立行动. ***~ outside*** 走出,走到外面. ***~ over*** 横越,跨过. ***~ short*** 【军】缩小脚步走. ***~ up*** 走上去;〔美〕促进,加紧;插嘴;提高,【电】升高(电压) (*a ~ up transformer* 升压变压器). ***~ up to*** 接近,走近 (*~ up to a girl* 追求,求婚. *~ up to town* 上城里去). ***~ upstairs*** 上楼去. ***~ well together*** (舞伴)跳得[(马)走得]合拍. — *n.* ①(脚)步. ②梯级,阶磴儿,台阶踏板. ③阶层,等级,升级;〔*pl.*〕梯子,楼梯. ④一步;步调,步伐;发展,阶段. ⑤脚声;足迹. ⑥走路样子,步态. ⑦步骤,手段,措施,办法. ⑧舞步;〔口〕跳舞. ⑨【船】桅座. ⑩【机】轴瓦;级,档. ⑪【乐】音级;度. *He ran down the ~s* 他跑下楼梯来. *Mind your ~.* 小心走路,留神脚底下. *The director will approve such ~s.* 处长会同意这些措施的. *We've made a big ~ forward in our studies.* 我们在学习中前进了一大步. *Your paper marks a forward ~ in the research.* 你的报告标志着研究

工作的向前发展. *Take such ～s as you think best.* 按你认为最好的步骤办吧. *the last [final]* ～(多级火箭的)最末一级. *a* ～ *in the social scale* 社会阶层中的一个阶层. ***break*** ～【军】走乱脚步,用平常脚步. ***fall in*** ～ 顺着(…的)步调走. ***get one's*** ～ 升级. ***give sb. a*** ～ 给(某人)升一级. ***in sb.'s*** ～***s*** 步人后尘. ***in*** ～ 齐步. ***keep*** ～ 整齐步调 *(with)*. ***make a great*** ～ ***forward in*** 在…上有了很大进步[发展]. ***make a*** ～ ***forward [backward]*** 前进[后退]一步. ***miss one's*** ～ 失足. ***out of*** ～ 错了步伐,弄乱步调,不按(…的)步调走. ***pick one's*** ～***s*** 一步一步小心走,步步留心. ***retrace one's*** ～***s*** 走回头路,改变主意,变卦. ***rise a*** ～ ***in sb.'s opinion [estimation]*** 在某人的心目中升高了一步. ～ ***by*** ～ 一步一步;切切实实. ～ ***for*** ～ 用同样步调,并驾齐驱地. ***take a bold*** ～ 采取断然处置. ***take a rash*** ～ 躁急,做错,弄错,失策. ***take*** ～***s*** 设法,采取措施 (*You must take* ～*s to prevent it.* 你得设法防止它). ***tread in the*** ～***s of*** 仿效,跟…的脚步走. ***turn one's*** ～***s to [towards]*** 转向…走去; 改变方向而从事…. ***watch one's*** ～***s*** 小心走路,留心脚底下;小心行动. ～ **bearing**【机】立式止推轴承. ～ **block**【机】级形垫铁. ～**-by** *a.* 逐步的,逐渐的. ～ **cone,** ～ **pulley**【机】级轮, 宝塔轮. ～ **dance** 踢跶舞. ～**-down** *a.* 减缓的,下降的 (～*-down transformer* 降压变压器). ～**-in** ①*a.* (女衣)先把腿伸进去,拉上来而穿上身的. ②*n.* 上述女衣,女内衣. ～ **ladder** 梯子. ～ **motor** 步进电动机. ～**-out**【无】失调, 失步. ～ **rocket** 多级火箭. ～ **turn**【滑雪】侧向换步. ～**-up** *a.* 加速的;增强的;促进的,上升的;【电】增加电压的. *n.* 逐渐增加.

step·broth·er [ˈstepbrʌðə] *n.* 异父兄弟,异母兄弟.

step·child [ˈsteptʃaild] *n.* 夫[妻]和前妻[前夫]所生的子女.

step·dame [ˈstepdeim] *n.* 〔古〕继母,后娘.

step·daugh·ter [ˈstepˌdɔːtə] *n.* 夫[妻]和前妻[前夫]所生的女儿,晚女.

step·fa·ther [ˈstepˌfɑːðə] *n.* 继父,后夫.

step·fa·ther·land [ˈstepˌfɑːðələnd] *n.* 〔美〕归化国.

steph·a·no·tis [ˌstefəˈnəutis] *n.* ①【植】千金子藤花; 千金子藤香. ②〔S-〕千金子藤属.

Ste·phen, Ste·phan [ˈstiːvn] *n.* 斯蒂芬〔男子名〕.

Ste·phens [ˈstiːvnz] *n.* 斯蒂芬斯〔姓氏〕.

Ste·phen·son [ˈstiːvnsn] *n.* ①斯蒂芬森〔姓氏〕. ② **George** ～ 史蒂芬生〔1781—1848, 英国发明家,蒸气机的发明人.〕

step·moth·er [ˈstepˌmʌðə] *n.* 继母,后母,后娘.

step·ney [ˈstepni] *n.* 〔常 S-〕〔英〕(汽车的) 备用轮胎〔又叫 ～-wheel〕.

step·par·ent [ˈstepˌpɛərənt] *n.* 继父,继母.

steppe [step] *n.* ①干草原. ②〔the Steppes〕(尤指东南欧或西伯利亚的)草原地带.

step·per [ˈstepə] *n.* ①步态好的人[马]. ②〔美俚〕舞跳得好的人. ③时间全花在社交上的大学生;【运】跑者.

step·ping stone [ˈstepiŋ-stəun] *n.* ①(跨越浅河)供踏脚的石头. ②上马石; 垫脚石. ③进身的梯阶; (达到目的的)手段,方法. ④中途歇脚处. ***stand on*** ～***s*** 小心翼翼地遵照常规行事,拘泥细节.

step·sis·ter [ˈstepˌsistə] *n.* 异父姊妹,异母姊妹.

step·son [ˈstepsʌn] *n.* 晚子; 妻[夫]和前夫[前妻]所生的儿子.

step·wise [ˈstepwaiz] *a.* ①逐步的,逐渐的,分段的. ②【音】转换音级的. —*ad.* 按阶段地,逐步地.

ster. = stereotype; sterling.

-ster *suf.* ①做…的人. ②与…有关系的人. ③某种样子的人〔常含轻蔑意〕: trick*ster*, gang*ster*, young*ster*.

ste·ra·di·an, ste·rad [stiˈreidiən, ˈsteræd] *n.*【物】球面度〔立体角单位〕.

ster·co·ra·ceous [ˌstɔːkəˈreiʃəs] *a.* 含粪的; 粪状的; 有粪质的.

ster·co·ric·o·lous [ˌstəːkəˈrikələs] *a.*【生】粪栖的〔如某些昆虫〕.

ster·cu·li·a [stəːˈkjuːliə] *a.*【植】梧桐科 *(Sterculiaceae)* 的〔包括可可,柯拉树〕.

stere [stiə] *n.* 立方米 (m^3).

stere- *comb. f.* (用于辅音前) = stereo-.

ster·e·o [ˈstiəriəu] *n., a.* 〔口〕①= stereotype. ②= stereoscopic. ～ *camera.* ③旧闻. ④立体声系统〔装置〕;立体声.

ster·e·o- *comb. f.* ①立体的. ②实体的, 坚固的, 实心的: *stereo*chrome.

ster·e·o·bate [ˈsteriəˌbeit, ˈstiər-] *n.*【建】无柱底基.

ster·e·o·chem·is·try [ˌstiəriəˈkemistri] *n.*【化】立体化学.

ster·e·o·chrome [ˈstiəriəˌkrəum, ˈsteriə-] *n.*【绘画】固色壁画.

ster·e·o·chro·my [ˈstiəriəkrəumi] *n.*【绘画】固色壁画法. **-chro·mic** *a.*

ster·e·o·gram [ˈstiəriəˌɡræm] *n.* ①立体图,体视图,极射(赤面投影)图. ②= stereograph.

ster·e·o·graph [ˈstiəriəɡrɑːf] *n.* 实体画,立体照片; 体视照片. — *vt.* ①摄制成立体照片(体视照片). ②准备(照片)供体视. ③印成盲文.

ster·e·o·graph·ic, -i·cal [stiəriəuˈɡræfik(əl)] *a.* 立体[实体]画法的;立体[体视]摄影术的. *a* ～ *projection* 平射投影. **-cal·ly** *ad.*

ster·e·og·ra·phy [stiəriˈɔɡrəfi] *n.* 立体画法;立体[体视]摄影(术).

ster·e·o·i·so·mer [ˌstiəriəuˈaisəmə] *n.*【化】立体异构体. **-ic** [-ˈmerik] *a.* **-ism** *n.*

ster·e·o·lo·gy [stiəriˈɔlədʒi] *n.* 体视学,立体测量学.

ster·e·om·e·ter [stiəriˈɔmitə] *n.* 体积计;比重计.

ster·e·o·met·ric [ˌstiəriəˈmetrik] *a.* 测体积术的 (= stereometrical).

ster·e·om·e·try [ˌstiəriˈɔmitri] *n.* 测(体)积术,立体几何;比重测定法.

stereo·microscope [ˌstiəriəuˈmaikrəskəup] *n.* 体视显微镜.

ster·e·o·phone [stiərəˈfəun] *n.* 立体声耳机.

ster·e·o·phon·ic [ˌstiəriəuˈfɔnik] *a.* 立体声的. ～ *record* 立体声唱片. **-cal·ly** *ad.* **-oph·o·ny** *n.*

ster·e·o·pho·to·gram·me·try [ˌstiəriəuˌfəutəˈɡræmitri] *n.* 立体摄影测量(术).

ster·e·o·pho·tog·ra·phy [ˌstiəriəufəˈtɔɡrəfi] *n.* 立体摄影术;体视照相摄影术.

ster·e·o·pro·jec·tion [ˌstiəriəuprəˈdʒekʃən] *n.* (投射双像以取体视效应的)立体投影.

ster·e·op·sis [ˌstiəriˈɔpsis] *n.* 立体影象.

ster·e·op·ti·con [stiəriˈɔptikən] *n.* ①(画面可以淡入淡出而叠现的)实体幻灯机. ②投影放大器.

ster·e·op·tics [ˌstiəriˈɔptiks] *n.* 〔可用作 *pl., sing.*〕立体摄影光学,体视光学.

ster·e·o·scope [ˈsteriəskəup] *n.* 实体镜,体视镜;立体照相机. **-scop·ic** [-ˈskɔpik], **-i·cal** *a.* **-i·cal·ly** *ad.*

ster·e·os·co·py [ˌstiəriˈɔskəpi] *n.* ①体视学;体视术,体视法. ②体视.

ster·e·o·sonic [stiəriəuˈsɔnik] *a.* 立体声的.

ster·e·o·tax·is [ˌstiəriəˈtæksis] *n.*【生】向实体运动. **-tac·tic** [-ˈtæktik] *a.*

ster·e·o·tape [stiərəˈteip] *n.* 立体声磁带.

ster·e·o·tel·e·vi·sion [ˌstiəriəuˈteliviʒən] *n.* 立体电视.

ster·e·ot·o·my [ˌstiəriˈɔtəmi] *n.* 分体学[术],切体学[术]〔尤指石头切割术〕.

ster·e·ot·ro·pism [ˌstiəriˈɔtrəpizm] *n.*【生】向实体趋性. **-trop·ic** [-ˈtrɔpik] *a.*

ster·e·o·type [ˈstiəriəutaip] *n.* ①【印】铅版;铅版制版

法,铅版印刷. ②旧框框; 陈规老套, 旧习,成规,定型. ~*-metal* (铸铅字用的)铅. *Party* ~*s* 党八股. — *a.* ①铅版(印刷)的. ②固定不变的,定型的; 陈规旧习的. — *vt.* ①浇成铅版. ②用铅版印刷; 使固定. ③使成陈规旧习,使僵化. *The practice has been* ~*d into a tradition.* 这种作法已经定型成了个传统了. **-typed** *a.* ①浇成铅版的. ②用铅版印刷的. ③固定不变的,陈规旧习的,僵化的 (~*d ways of doing business* 陈规旧习的办事方法). **-typ·ist** *n.* 盲文版印刷工人.

ster·e·o·typ·er [ˈstiərəutaipə] *n.* ①铸版工 (= stereotypist). ②盲文版印制机.

ster·e·o·typ·ic [ˌstiəriəˈtipik, ˌsteriə-] *a.* ①铅版的; 铅版制的. ②浇成铅版的; 用铅版印刷的 (= stereotypical).

ster·e·o·typ·y [ˈstiəriəˌtaipi] *n.* ①铅版印刷,铅版浇铸术,铅版浇铸. ②【医】定型; 刻板症, 反常性重复〔如动作,语词等〕,痴呆〔常见于精神分裂症患者〕.

ster·ic [ˈstiərik, ˈsterik] *a.* 【化】(原子的)空间(排列)的; 位的. ~ **hindrance** 【化】位阻现象. **-cal·ly** *ad.*

ster·i·lant [ˈsterilənt] *n.* 杀菌剂[物],消毒剂.

ster·ile [ˈsterail] *a.* ①不毛的,不肥沃的,收成不好的. ②【动】无生殖力的,不育的 *(of)*. ③【植】不结果实的,中性的; 不发芽的. ④没有思想的,枯燥无味的,缺乏独创性的(诗文等). ⑤无结果的; 无益的,无效果的(交涉等). ⑥无菌的,消过毒的. *a* ~ *woman* 不生育的妇女. ~ *soil* 贫瘠的土地[土壤]. *a* ~ *year* 凶年. ~ *flowers* 中性花. *a* ~ *poem* 乏味的诗. ~ *gloves* 消过毒的手套. ~ *negotiations* 没有结果的谈判. **-ly** *ad.*

ste·ril·i·ty [steˈrility] *n.* ①不毛. ②不育,不孕. ③【植】中性,不稔性; 秕粒; 无菌(状态). ④(思想)贫乏. ⑤无效,无结果.

ster·i·li·za·tion [sterilaiˈzeiʃən] *n.* ①使不毛,使不肥沃. ②绝育. ③消毒,灭菌.

ster·i·lize [ˈsterilaiz] *vt.* ①使(土地)荒瘠. ②使不孕,使绝种. ③使不起作用,使无效果. ④使(思想)贫乏,使(兴味)索然. ⑤杀菌,消毒. ⑥封存(黄金). ⑦拆除(某一地区的)建筑物. *An incompetent teacher* ~*s the young mind.* 一个不称职的教员把青年人的思想弄得贫乏枯竭起来了. *The nurse is* ~*ing the surgical instruments.* 护士在把外科手术器具消毒. ~*d milk* 消毒牛奶. **-r** *n.* 消毒器.

ster·let [ˈstə:lit] *n.* 【动】小体鲟 *(Acipenser ruthenus)* 〔产于里海〕.

Ster·ling [ˈstə:liŋ] *n.* 斯特林〔姓氏,男子名〕.

ster·ling [ˈstə:liŋ] *n.* ①英国货币. ②标准纯银; 〔集合词〕纯银制品. — *a.* ①英国货币的〔写在金额之后, 通常略作 *s.* or *stg.*〕; 英镑的. ②用(纯度为 92.5% 的)标准纯银制成的; 纯粹的, 真正的. ③有价值的(书等); 有权威的,信用过得去的,靠得住的(人等). *five pounds* ~ 英币五镑正〔略 £5 s. 或 £5 stg.〕. *a* ~ *article* 真品. ~ *sense* 可靠的判断力. ~ **area [bloc]** 英镑集团, 用英镑做标准的地区. ~ **balance** 英镑结存. ~ **bonds** 英镑债券,英镑公债. ~ **exchange** 对英汇兑,英汇. ~ **shilling** 英国银币.

stern[1] [stə:n] *a.* ①严格的,严厉的,严峻的,粗暴的,苛刻的. ②坚定的(决心等). *The school is very* ~ *in its discipline.* 学校在纪律方面很严格. *Our teacher is* ~ *to the students.* 我们教员对学生是严厉的. *Only the* ~ *spirits of yours can overcome the difficulties.* 只有你们的坚强的精神才能克服那些困难. *the* ~*er sex* 男性. **-ly** *ad.* **-ness** *n.*

stern[2] [stə:n] *n.* ①船尾,艉. ②臀部. ③(狗等的)尾巴,【徽】狼尾. ④(任何东西的)尾部,后部. *S- all!* = *S- hard!* 【海】向后! ***down by the*** ~ 后部吃水比前部深的. ***from stem to*** ~ 船内到处,全船. ***sit at the*** ~ ***of the state*** 执政. ~ ***foremost*** 船尾朝前,倒退; 笨拙地. ~ ***on*** 船尾向前地. ~ **board** 船的后退. ~ **chase** 跟着船尾追击. ~ **chaser** 【海】舰尾炮; (船赛等的)末艇. ~ **-fast** (line) 船尾缆. ~**foremost** *ad.* = ~ foremost. ~**most** *a.* 在船尾最后部的. ~**post** 船尾柱. ~ **sheets** 〔*pl.*〕小艇尾台. ~**son** 【船】艉曲材〔肘板〕〔也作 ~**son knee,** ~ **knee**〕. ~**ward(s)** *a., ad.* 向船尾(的); 在船尾(的). ~**way** 船的后退,倒驶. ~**-wheel·er** 船尾外轮船.

ster·nal [ˈstə:nl] *a.* 【解】胸骨的; 胸骨部位的; 近胸骨的; (近)腹甲的; (近)腹板的.

Sterne [stə:n] *n.* 斯特恩〔姓氏〕.

stern(o)- *comb. f.* 胸,胸骨,胸骨和(…): *sterno*costal.

ster·no·cos·tal [ˌstə:nəˈkɔstəl] *a.* 胸骨和肋骨的.

ster·num [ˈstə:nəm] *n.* *(pl.* ***-na*** [-nə], ~***s)*** ①【解】胸骨. ②【动】(甲壳类的)腹甲,胸板,(棘皮动物,昆虫的)腹板.

ster·nu·ta·tion [stə:njuˈteiʃən] *n.* 喷嚏,打喷嚏.

ster·nu·ta·tive [stəˈnju:tətiv], **-tory** [-təri] *a.* (催)喷嚏的. — *n.* 催嚏剂. ~ *gas* 喷嚏(性)(毒)气.

ster·nu·ta·tor [ˈstə:njuˌteitə] *n.* 催嚏剂,喷嚏性毒剂.

ster·nu·ta·to·ry [stəˈnju:tətəri] *a.* 催嚏的,喷嚏的. — *n.* 催嚏剂,喷嚏剂,会引起喷嚏的物质.

ster·oid [ˈstiərɔid, ˈsterɔid] *n.* 【生化】甾类化合物,类固醇. **-al** *a.*

ster·tor [ˈstə:tə] *n.* 【医】鼾息; 鼾声.

ster·to·rous [ˈstə:tərəs] *a.* 打呼噜的,鼾声如雷的. **-ly** *ad.*

stet [stet] 〔L.〕不删,保留〔校对用语,略作 st., 在所删字句下打点线, 中国用△表示〕. — *vt.* 【印】不删, 批上'不删'[保留].

steth·o·scope [ˈsteθəskəup] *n.* 【医】听诊器,听筒. — *vt.* 用听诊器诊察.

steth·o·scop·ic, steth·o·scop·i·cal [ˌsteθəˈskɔpik, -ˈskɔpikl] *a.* 【医】听诊(器)的,听筒的; 根据听诊器的. **-cal·ly** *ad.*

steth·os·co·py [steˈθɔskəpi] *n.* 【医】听诊(术).

Stetson [ˈstetsn] 斯特森〔商标名〕. — *n.* 〔常用 s-〕男帽〔尤指美国西部牧童毡帽〕.

Stet·tin [ˈstetin] *n.* = Szczecin.

Stet·tinius [stəˈtinjəs] *n.* 斯特蒂纽斯〔姓氏〕.

Steve [sti:v] *n.* 史蒂夫(男子名)〔Steven 的昵称〕.

stev·e·dore [ˈsti:vidɔ:] *n.* 装货卸货工人,码头工人,搬运工人. — *vt., vi.* ①装[卸]货. ②当码头工人. ~***'s knot*** 装卸工人结.

Ste·ven [ˈsti:vn] *n.* 史蒂文〔男子名〕.

Ste·vens [ˈsti:vnz] *n.* 史蒂文斯〔姓氏〕.

Ste·ven·son [ˈsti:vnsn] *n.* 史蒂文森〔姓氏〕.

Ste·ven·son [ˈsti:vnsn], **Robert Louis** 史蒂文森〔1850—1894,英国小说家〕.

Ste·venson·ian [ˈsti:vnˈsəunjən] *a., n.* 史蒂文森的(研究者).

stew[1] [stju:] *vt.* ①用文火慢慢煨炖. ②〔口〕使焦虑,使着急. — *vi.* ①用文火煨烂,炖烂. ②焦虑,着急. ③(关在房里)闷热得出汗; 发昏; 〔俚〕死用功,用苦功. *S- the pork with sugar.* 把猪肉用糖炖了. *The tea is* ~*ed.* 茶浸泡得过久而太苦[太浓]. ***let sb.*** ~ ***in his own juice [grease]*** 让某人自作自受. ~ ***oneself into an illness*** 愁出病来,急出病来. — *n.* ①炖煮的菜餚〔通常肉类和蔬菜混和在一起〕,混合物. ②〔口〕忧虑,着急. ③〔美俚〕酒鬼. ④〔美俚〕硝化甘油,炸油. ⑤【影】噪声. ⑥〔英俚〕死用功的人. *Would you like some beef* ~? 你喜欢吃点炖牛肉吗? *Everybody went into a terrible* ~ *about it.* 每个人都为它着了一通大急. *Irish* ~ 马铃薯洋葱炖羊肉. ***in a (regular)*** ~ 〔俚〕(因忧虑、愤怒等)心乱如麻,着急,急躁. ~**bum** 〔美〕醉鬼,酒徒. ~**pan** = saucepan. ~**pot** (有盖的)炖锅.

stew[2] [stju:] *n.* 〔英〕鱼塘,养鱼池; 养蠔场.

stew[3] [stju:] *n.* 〔古〕①公共浴室,热浴室. ②妓院; 妓院

区[常作 the ~s].

stew·ard [ˈstjuəd] *n.* *(fem.* **-ess** [-is]*)* ①管事,管家. ②(学校等的)膳务员,财务管理员;(轮船、飞机、旅馆等的)服务员. ③(公会、团体,赛马等的)干事,理事;(舞会等的)招待员. ④[美] 车间[部门,工厂]的工会代表. *the Lord High Steward (of England)* (英国)加冕礼事务大臣;(审判贵族法庭的)审判长. *the Lord Steward of the Household* [英]皇室内务大臣. **-ess** *n.* 女服务员. **-ship** *n.* steward 的职位;管理,经营,处理.

Stew·art [ˈstjuət] *n.* ①斯图尔特[姓氏, 男子名]. ② **Dugald** ~ 斯图尔特[1753—1828,苏格兰哲学家].

stewed [stju:d] *a.* ①用文火煨[燉]的. ②[美俚]喝醉了的. ③焦急不安的 *(up)*. ~ *to the gills* [卑俚]喝得烂醉的.

St. Ex(ch). = Stock Exchange 证券交易所.

stg. = sterling.

St. George's [sntˈdʒɔ:dʒiz] *n.* 圣乔治[格林纳达首府].

St. George's Channel [sntˈdʒɔ:dʒiz] 圣佐治海峡[威尔士与爱尔兰之间].

St. George Town [sntˈdʒɔ:dʒi taun] *n.* 圣乔治[向风群岛首都].

sth. = something.

St. Helena [ˌsentiˈli:nə] 圣赫勒拿岛.

sthe·ni·a [sθiˈnaiə, sˈθi:niə] *n.* ①[医] 有力,强壮. ②(病态)亢进,(过度)兴奋.

sthen·ic [ˈsθenik] *a.* ①[医] 有力的,强壮的(心脏等). ②(病态的)亢进的,兴奋的. ③矮而结实的.

stib·ine [ˈstibi:n, -in] *n.* ①[化]锑化(三)氢.②(…)胇.

stib·i·um [ˈstibiəm] *n.*【化】锑 [Sb].

stib·nite [ˈstibˌnait] *n.*【矿】辉锑矿.

stich [stik] *n.*【诗体学】诗行,一首诗.

stich·o·myth·i·a, sti·chom·y·thy [ˌstikəˈmiθiə, -ˈkɔmθi] *n.* 简短轮流对白[古希腊戏剧中的一种对白]. **-myth·ic** *a.*

stick[1] [stik] *n.* ①棒,棍;手杖,棒状物. ②枝条,枯枝;柴. ③(蔬菜, 草本植物的)茎, 梗. ④条状物 (如炭条等). ⑤【空】手柄,驾驶杆,操纵杆;(汽车等的)变速杆,换档杆. ⑥向同一目标连续投下的炸弹;一批连续投下的伞兵. ⑦【印】排字架,排字盘. ⑧【乐】指挥棒. ⑨[the ~]鞭打;刺戳. ⑩搀在饮料中的酒. ⑪[口]呆子,木头木脑的人;蹩脚演员;⑫【船】桅杆;桁. ⑬一根木料. ⑭[*pl.*] 一件家具, 建筑物的一部分. ⑮【虫】= ~-insect. ⑯[the ~s] [美口]林地,边远的山区,郊区. ⑰[美俚]大麻烟卷. *Father left his hat and ~ in the hall.* 爸爸把帽子和手杖放在过厅里了. *a short ~* 短码尺[1码 = $35^1/_2$英寸]. *a dip ~* 量油尺. *a ~ of candy* 一根糖棒. *the ~ of celery* 水芹的梗. *a joy ~*【火箭】驾驶杆,远距离操纵杆. *He wants the ~.* 他该打. *He is a regular ~.*【剧】他是一个十足的木头人. *~ of bombs* [英] 在轰炸目标上投下的一连串炸弹. *a few ~s of furniture* 几件家具. *big ~ (policy)* [美政]大棒政策,实力政策. ***all on one*** ~ [美, 俚] 都在一起. ***at the ~'s end*** 离开一点儿. ***be on the*** ~ [美俚]警惕的,效率高的. ***beat sb. all to ~s*** [美俚]大败, 使惨败. ***carry the*** ~ [美] 变成街头流浪者; 彷徨. ***cut one's*** ~ [俚] 逃走. ***get [have] hold of the wrong end of the*** ~ 误解, 弄错. ***give sb. the*** ~ 鞭打某人. ***go to ~s and staves*** (捆好的东西等)散开,瓦解,碎掉,变糟,毁掉. ***hold (a) ~(s) with (to)*** 和…旗鼓相当地竞争,和…光明正大地竞争. ***hop the*** ~ 突然离去,死去. ***in a cleft*** ~ 进退两难,为难. ***lean on a*** ~ 拄着拐杖. ~ ***and stone*** 全部,一切都. ~ ***back [forward]***【空】驾驶杆拉后[推前]. — *vt.* ①(用木棍)撑持(植物等). ②【印】把(铅字)排在排字盘里. ③刺,戳,刺死. ④钉住,插牢,放置. ⑤伸出. ⑥迫使偿付 *(up)*, 抢劫. —*vi.* 伸出. *S- the needle into the cloth, Jane.* 珍妮,把针插在布上. *Please ~ the book back on the shelf.* 请把书放回架上. *S- out your tongue.* 伸出你的舌头来. **~ball** 棍球 [儿童在街头玩的类似棒球的球戏]. ~ **force**【机】杆力. **~ful**【印】一排字盘 (排字量). ~ **grenade** 木柄手榴弹. ~ **insect** 竹节虫. ~ **leader** [美棒球]优秀击球员, 带队击球员. **~man** ①(曲棍球的)击球手. ②[美俚](赌场中手执小棒)管骰子摊的人. **~pin** 领带别针. **~seed** [美]【植】鹤虱(属)植物. ~ **shift** [美]手扳变速器. **~tight** [美]【植】①= bur marigold. ②= stickseed. **~weed** [美]【植】北美各种倒刺毛果植物,如豚草,鹤虱.

stick[2] [stik] *(stuck) vi.* ①粘,贴,粘住,粘着,固着,不分离. ②坚持,坚守,忠实,不变心;不离开,留住不动. ③卡住不动;困住,难住,为难;踌躇,犹豫. — *vt.* ①粘住;贴;使固着;安置. ②[俚]忍耐,忍受. ③[口]困住,难住,使为难,使动弹不得,使进退两难,使停顿. *Stamps ~ together.* 邮票互相粘住了. *Better ~ to the programme.* 还是按照原程序较好. *Friends should ~ together.* 朋友要团结互助才好. *S- no bills!* [英] 不许招贴; [美国说 Post no bills!]. *Don't forget to ~ a steamp on the envelope.* 不要忘记在信封上贴邮票. *The ship has been stuck here for three days by bad weather.* 由于天气恶劣船在此被阻已有三天. *James was stuck by the teacher's question in the oral exam.* 在口试中, 詹姆斯被教员的提问难住了. *I simply can't ~ a whole summer in town.* 我决不能整个夏天老呆在城市里. ***be stuck on*** [美俚]爱上,给迷住. ~ ***a button*** [美] 使大学生加入联谊会. ~ ***at a job*** 坚持做一件工作. ~ ***at home*** 守在家里. ~ ***at nothing*** 对什么事都毫不踌躇. ~ ***by*** 忠于, 拥护; 留在手里, 留在记忆里 (*We must ~ by our friends.* 我们必须忠于我们的朋友). ~ ***down*** [口]写下来; 放下; (用浆糊)粘好. (*S- down these idioms in your notebook.* 把这些习语记在你的笔记本上). ~ ***fast*** 牢记,粘牢; 碰钉子, 弄僵 (*Your advice will ~ fast in my mind.* 你的意见会牢记在我心中的). ~ ***in*** 添注,加一笔. ~ ***in one's craw*** [美俚] 令人不快; (食物)味道不好. ~ ***in one's gizzard [throat]*** 难消化; 难下咽; 令人不能接受; 令人难于容忍; 令人讨厌. ~ ***in the mud*** 陷入泥中; 进退两难; 顽固, 保守 (*The car is stuck in the mud.* 汽车陷在泥里了). ~ ***it on*** [俚]乱要价,把帐开高; 夸大地讲. ~ ***it (out)*** [俚] 忍耐,忍受 (*He could not ~ it any longer.* 他不能再忍耐了). ~ ***on*** 贴在…上; (船)搁浅. ~ ***out*** 坚持到底 (*You've only a few pages to go. Stick it out.* 你还有几页书就看完了, 坚持到底吧). [俚] 忍耐,忍受. ~ ***out a mile*** 明明白白,一目了然. ~ ***out for*** 不停地要求,坚持要. ~ ***to*** 粘住,不离,不变,坚持,不放,忠于 (*We must ~ to the principle* 我们必须坚持原则). ~ ***to it*** 忍耐. ~ ***to nothing*** 对任何事都容易生厌,没有恒心. ~ ***to one's colours [guns]*** 坚持(已见); 不改变目的. ~ ***to one's ribs*** [美俚] 吃饱. ~ ***up*** ①突出, 竖立 (*hair ~ing up on end* 头发直竖着). ②[英俚]使为难. ~ ***up for*** 支持,拥护. ~ ***up to*** 不输给, 抵抗; [方]追求 (*~ up to a girl* 追求一个少女). ~ ***with it*** [美] 忍耐. — *n.* 发粘; 卡住不动. **~-at-it** *n.* [口] 坚定的人. **~-in-the-mud** *a., n.* 守旧的(人), 迟钝的(人), 慢手慢脚的 (人) (*Mr. [Mrs.] Stick-in-the-mud* 某某人[夫人][忘记姓名时用]). **~jaw** [俚] (粘牙) 太妃糖 (等). ~ **out** ①*n.* 杰出人物 [才能]. ②*a.* 出色的,显著的. **~-to-it·ive·ness** [美口] *n.* 顽固,坚持. **~-up** *n., a.* 竖领(的); [美俚]强盗, 劫贼; 抢劫(的). **~up man** [俚]拦路抢劫的歹徒.

stick·a·bil·i·ty [ˌstikəˈbiliti] *n.* 耐力; 坚持力; 忍受力. **-able** *a.*

stick·er [ˈstikə] *n.* ①粘贴者; 粘贴物; 固执的人, 坚持不懈的人; 久坐不走的客人; 踌躇不决的人. ③风琴内连结两条杠杆的木棍. ④[美俚] 陈货. ⑤刺戳的人, 杀猪的人; 杀猪用的尖刀. ⑥[口]难题,使人为难的东西. ⑦滞销品. ⑧【板球】再三努力得分仍然不多的击球手. ⑨

〔美〕邮票(等). *Mother says she doesn't want any* ~ *in the house.* 妈妈说她家里不要久坐不走的客人. *Jones proved himself to be a* ~ *in the experiment.* 琼斯在实验中证明他是个坚持不懈的人.

stick·i·ness [ˈstikinis] *n.* 粘结,胶粘,粘着性.

stick·ing [ˈstikiŋ] *a.* 粘的,胶粘的. ~ **place** 搭脚处,螺丝钉转得不能再转进去的地方,顶点 (*screw one's courage to the* ~ *place* 鼓起浑身的勇气). ~ **plaster** 橡皮膏.

stick·le [ˈstikl] *vi.* ①(对于琐事的)争执;拘泥细节,固执己见. ②犹豫,踌躇. ~**-back**【动】刺鱼,棘鱼,丝鱼.

stick·ler [ˈstiklə] *n.* ①争执琐事的人,固执己见的人 (*for*). ②难题,费解的事物. *a* ~ *for quaint ceremonies* 拘泥古怪仪式的人.

stick·um [ˈstikəm] *n.* 〔美口〕粘性物质.

stick·y [ˈstiki] *a.* (*-i·er; -i·est*) ①粘的,胶粘的,粘腻的,粘性的. ②〔口〕闷热的,湿气大的. ③〔口〕顽固的,(无多少道理地)固执的. ④麻烦的,困难的;非常不愉快的,极痛苦的;过分多情善感而令人生厌的. *He'll come to a* ~ *end* 他将来没有好下场. *a* ~*beak* 〔澳〕好管闲事的人. ~ *fingers* 手脚不干净的人,小偷. *a* ~ *end* 〔美〕不好的结果. ~ *wicket*【板球】泥泞的三柱门;〔主英〕困境,尴尬的处境. ~**-back** *n.* (背面涂有胶水的)小相片,小票据. **-i·ly** *ad.* **-i·ness** *n.*

stiff [stif] *a.* ①硬的,挺的. ②(手足等)僵直的,僵硬的;〔俚〕死而僵硬了的,死了的. ③坚牢的,紧绷绷的,绷紧了的(索子). ④不灵便的,不易动的,粘牢了的(活塞);一动就痛的. ⑤偏促的,拘泥的,不自然的,不流畅的,生硬的;顽固的,执拗的,倔强的. ⑥强烈的(酒);狂暴的,猛烈的(风等). ⑦费力的,困难的;严厉的(处罚). ⑧(物价等)昂贵的;(需要)过高的,过多的;高昂的,极高的. ⑨【海】不易倾斜的 (*opp.* crank). ⑩黏的,胶黏的,浓,稠. ⑪〔口语〕极不合理的,严厉的,不能答应的. ⑫〔英方〕结实的,健壮的. *a* ~ *collar* 硬领. *stand straight and* ~ 直挺挺地站着不动. *bore a person* ~ = *scare a person* ~ 吓得某人面孔发青. *a* ~ *bow* 不自然的鞠躬. *a* ~ *gale* 猛烈的风,狂风. *a* ~*'un* (= one) 劲敌〔老练的运动家等〕. *That's a bit* ~. 那太厉害了. *You stood* ~ *in a foolish argument yesterday.* 昨天你倔强地坚持着愚蠢的议论. *Why, they set* ~ *prices on the bikes.* 嗨,他们把自行车定了这般昂贵的价钱. *Take this, Tom. A* ~ *dose.* 喝下这个去,汤姆,一副疗效高的药. ***carry [have, keep] a* ~ *upper lip*** 坚定不移,毅然不动. ***have a* ~ *neck*** 脖子痛得不能转动. ***keep a* ~ *face [lip]*** 板着严肃的面孔;毅然不动. ***keep a* ~ *rein*** 紧紧拉住缰绳. ***take a* ~ *line*** 采取强硬态度. — *n.* 〔俚〕①死尸. ②笨旦,傻瓜;呆板人. ③吝啬鬼;穷光蛋. ④普通工人,流动工人. ⑤〔英〕钞票;私人签发的支票. **-ly** *ad.* **-ness** *n.*【物】劲度.

stiff·en [ˈstifn] *vt.* ①使硬化,使挺,使僵硬. ②加强. ③使绷紧. ④使猛烈. ⑤使生硬呆板. ⑥使浓厚. ⑦使黏腻. — *vi.* ①变硬,变挺,变僵硬. ②变强,加强. ③变猛烈. ④变顽固;变不自然,变生硬. ⑤变黏,变稠,变浓厚. ⑥〔口〕(物价等)上涨,(市面)硬. ⑦变得费劲. *Your job is to* ~ *linen with starch.* 你的活是把亚麻台布浆洗硬了. *He threw the letter on the desk,* ~*ed with astonishment.* 他把信扔在书桌上,吃惊得紧张极了. ~ *one's attitude* 把态度放强硬. *a* ~*ing plale* 加强(铁)板. *a* ~*ing order* (海关发给的)底货装载许可证. *Having talked with the party secretary, our resolution* ~*ed.* 和支书谈了话后,我们的决心加强了. *The tug* ~*ed when we got into the mud.* 我们陷入泥里时,牵拉更费劲了.

stiff·en·er [ˈstifnə] *n.* ①弄硬的人〔物〕. ②硬化剂. ③加固用衬料. ④纸壳的衬心. ⑤补药. ⑥增强(勇气、决心等)的东西. ⑦【建、机】支肋. ⑧【物】加劲杆,加径角. ⑨〔美俚〕打倒的一击.

stiff-necked [ˈstifˈnekt] *a.* 顽固的,倔强的;傲慢的.

sti·fle[1] [ˈstaifl] *vt.* ①使窒息,闷死. ②镇压,阻止(反叛等). ③压灭(火等). ④藏匿,隐蔽,暗中了结 (*up*). ⑤〔美俚〕打垮. — *vi.* ①憋闷;窒息(而死). ②受抑制. *I rushed out of the room because the oppressive air* ~*ed me.* 我急忙地出了那个屋子,因为闷热的空气使我窒息起来. ~ *sobs [yawn]* 压住〔忍住〕哭泣〔呵欠〕. ~ *a rebellion* 镇压叛乱.

sti·fle[2] [ˈstaifl] *n.* (马、狗的)后腿膝关节(病).

sti·fling [ˈstaifliŋ] *a.* 令人窒息的,气闷的;沉闷的. ~**ly** *ad.*

stig·ma [ˈstigmə] *n.* (*pl.* ~*ta* [-tə], ~*s*) ①(*pl.*〔罕〕~*s*) 耻辱,污名. ②〔古〕烙印. ③【植】柱头;眼点. ④【动】气孔,气门;翅痣;(卵的)眼点;点斑 (*pl.* ~*ta*). ⑤【医】(病的)特征;小斑. ⑥(*pl.* ~*ta*)【宗】圣疤. ⑦记号,符号,标记〔例如本词典中的〔美〕〔口〕等〕. *No* ~ *rests on [attaches to] him.* 他清白无疵. *Her behaviour will leave a* ~ *upon her family.* 她的行为会使她家声名有了污点. *He has removed the* ~ *of drug addictions.* 他已经洗去吸毒的污点了.

stig·mas·ter·ol [stigˈmæstəˌrɔːl, -ˌrəul] *n.*【化】豆甾醇.

stig·mat·ic [stigˈmætik] *a.* ①耻辱的,污辱的;丑恶的. ②有烙印的;有记号的. ③【植】(有)柱头的. ④【动】(有)气孔的. ⑤【医】(有)小斑的. ⑦【宗】有圣疤的.

stig·ma·tism [ˈstigmətizm] *n.* 【医】①有小斑. ②【医】正视,折光正常〔焦点集中,无散光现象〕. ③【物】(透镜)无散象现象.

stig·ma·tize [ˈstigmətaiz] *vt.* ①加污名,诬蔑为 (*as*). ②打上烙印;作上记号. ③【宗】使生圣疤;(催眠术等)使生红斑. ~ *sb. as a rogue* 诬蔑(某人)是无赖.

stig·ma·tose [ˈstigmətəus] *a.*【动、植】= stigmatic.

stil·bene [ˈstilbiːn] *n.*【化】芪;反二苯代乙烯.

stil·bes·trol [stilˈbestrɔl] *n.*【生化】己烯雌酚,乙芪酚.

stil·bite [ˈstilbait] *n.*【地】辉沸石.

stile [stail] *n.* ①(牧场围堤上专门供人进出的)梯磴. ②(日晷仪的)晷针. ③横路栅栏,旋转栅门. ④【建】窗(边)梃,门(边)梃;竖框.

sti·let·to [stiˈletəu] *n.* (*pl.* ~*s,* ~*es*) ①短剑. ②(刺绣用的)针眼锥,打眼锥. — *vt.* 用短剑刺(死). ~ **heel** (女鞋的)细高跟.

still[1] [stil] *a.* ①静止的,平静的,静寂的. ②温柔的,低声的. ③沉默寡言的. ④(酒等)不起泡的. ⑤没有活力的,死气沉沉的. *S- waters run deep.* 流静水深;外表沉静者心里的东西〔学识、计谋等〕多. *He is* ~ *of his tongue.* 他沉默寡言. *All sounds are* ~. 万籁俱静. ***as* ~ *as* ~** 静静,非常沉静地. ***in* ~ *meditation*** 在沉思中. — *ad.* ①还,仍,尚,现在还,至今还;但是还. ②〔与比较级连用〕更其,还要,益发. ③〔诗〕常,不断地. *I am tired; (but)* ~ *I will work.* 累是累了,但是还要工作. *Will you* ~ *be here when I return?* 我回来的时候你还在这儿吗? *Take the medicine when it is* ~ *hot.* 趁热把药喝下去. *He is tall enough, but his brother is* ~ *taller.* 他的个子够高了,可是他兄弟还要高. ~ ***and all*** (即使如此)仍然 (*Even though you dislike us,* ~ *and all you should be polite.* 就算你不喜欢我们,你仍然应该对我们客气). ~ ***less*** 〔否定〕何况,更不 (*If you don't know,* ~ *less do I.* 你不知道,我更不知道了. *He is not a scholar,* ~ *less a poet.* 他不是一个学者,更不是一个诗人). ~ ***more*** 〔肯定〕何况,更不用说 (*It is difficult to understand his books,* ~ *more his lectures.* 他写的书很难懂,他的演讲就不用说了). — *n.* ①〔诗〕静止,无声,寂静. ②呆照,普通照片(登在报上或电视节目上的) (*opp.* movies). ③电视室布景;静物摄影照片;〔口〕静物画. ④〔美〕(用电话或口传报的)火灾警报〔又叫 ~ alarm〕. *in the* ~ *of night* 在深更半夜. — *vt., vi.* (使)静止;(使)镇静,遏制(情欲等);止住;(使)安静下来. ~ *one's appetite* 满足食欲. *This will* ~ *the pain of the wound.* 这个药可以止伤口疼. *The wind* ~*s down.* 风

住了. — *conj.* 但是,然而. *He is dull; ~ he tries hard.* 虽然笨, 可是他很刻苦. **~birth** *n.* 死产. **~born** ①死产的, 死胎的, 流产的. ②丝毫不能吸引观众的. **~bugle** 〔英〕 海军军号, 要求全体人员在二次号声前保持原地不动. **~-fish** *vi.* 抛锚停船捕鱼. **~-hunt** *n., vt.* ①偷偷接近的打猎. ②偷袭, 伏击. ③暗中搜寻, 盯梢. ④【政】暗中活动. **~ life** 【美】①(作描画对象的)静物. ②静物画. **~ small voice** 心灵深处的呼声, 良心的私语. **-ness** *n.*

still² [stil] *n.* ①蒸馏器[室],蒸馏锅. ②酿酒场. — *vt.* 〔古〕烧(酒); 蒸馏. **~ room** 〔英〕(酒厂的)蒸馏室; 酒库,酒窖.

stil·lage [ˈstilidʒ] *n.* ①酿酒厂的放桶台. ②釜馏物.

Still(e) [stil] *n.* 斯蒂尔〔姓氏〕.

still·y [ˈstili] *a.* 〔诗〕平静的, 寂静的(夜等). — *ad.* [ˈstilli] 〔罕〕寂静地,平静地.

stilt [stilt] *n.* ①〔常 *pl.*〕高跷;〔美〕腿, 脚. ②【鸟】长脚鹬. ③(水上住宅的)桩柱. ***on ~s*** ①踩着高跷. ②大言不惭地, 骄傲地. ③趾高气扬地, 夸张做作.

stilt·ed, stilt·y [ˈstiltid, ˈstilti] *a.* ①踩着高跷的. ②(文体等)夸张的,浮夸的. ③呆板的,做作的,不自然的. *a ~ arch* 【建】上心拱. *a ~ style* 夸张的文体.

Stil·ton [ˈstiltən] *n.* (英国)斯蒂尔顿干酪.

Stil·well [ˈstilwel] *n.* 史迪威〔姓氏〕.

Stim·son [ˈstimsn] *n.* 斯廷森〔姓氏〕.

stim·u·lant [ˈstimjulənt] *a.* 激励〔鼓励,鼓舞〕…的,刺激(性)的,使兴奋的. — *n.* 刺激物,兴奋剂,酒. *take ~s* 服用兴奋剂;〔尤指〕喝酒.

stim·u·late [ˈstimjuleit] *vt.* ①激励,刺激, 使兴奋, 鼓励. — *vi.* ①起刺激作用. ②〔口〕服兴奋剂,喝酒. *The Party's policies will ~ the masses' enthusiasm for socialist construction.* 党的政策会激发群众社会主义建设的积极性. *Your encouragement will ~ me to further efforts.* 你的鼓励会激发我进一步地努力.

stim·u·la·tion [ˌstimjuˈleiʃən] *n.* 刺激(作用),激励,鼓励; 兴奋(作用).

stim·u·la·tive [ˈstimjulətiv] *a.* 刺激的; 鼓励的,激励的,鼓舞的. — *n.* 刺激物,兴奋剂; 促进因素.

stim·u·la·tor [ˈstimjuleitə] *n.* 鼓励者; 刺激物.

stim·u·lus [ˈstimjuləs] *n.* (*pl.* ***-li*** [-lai]) ①刺激. ②刺激物; 促进因素. ③【电】激源. ④【植】刺毛. ⑤【昆】针,刺. *The country fair trade proves a ~ to agriculture, industry and commerce.* 集市贸易证明是对农工商业的一个促进因素. *basic ~* 衬底色. **~-response** *a.* 【心理】刺激-反应的(过程,关系).

sti·my [ˈstaimi] *n.* ①【高尔夫球】被敌球拦阻. ②〔喻〕阻碍(物). — *vt.* 〔通常用 p.p.〕(敌球)阻碍自己球路.

sting [stiŋ] *vt., vi.* (***stung***[stʌŋ]) ①刺, 螫, 叮. ②刺疼, 使觉得痛; 疼; 使苦闷. ③激励; 刺激(舌等). ④〔主用 *passive*〕〔美俚〕骗, 诓骗; 敲诈; 抢: *be stung by reproaches* 受责(而不快). *be stung with desire* 被欲望所驱使. *I was stung for a fiver.* 我被骗去了五镑. *My tooth ~s* 我的牙齿痛. *a ~ing blow* 痛击,痛打. *a ~ing insult* 奇耻大辱. — *n.* ①(蜂等的)刺,螫,叮; 刺伤. ②苦痛; 刺激; 讽刺. ③【动】针,螫,刺;【植】刺毛,刺. ④【空】支架,探臂支杆. ⑤〔美俚〕皮夹子,钱袋; 赃物,抢劫物. *His words carry a ~.* 他的话中有刺. *feel the ~ of remorse* 觉得悔恨难过. *Your visit will take away the ~ of her sorrow.* 您的来访会消除她的悲伤难过. ***have a ~ in the tail*** 尾上有刺;〔喻〕话中有刺. **~ing hair** 【植】螫毛.

sting·a·ree [ˈstiŋgəriː] *n.* = sting-ray.

sting·er [ˈstiŋə] *n.* ①刺的人; 刺激者; 谈锋锐利的人; 有刺的动物〔植物〕. ②【动】针, 刺, 螫. ③〔口〕痛击, 痛殴; 尖酸刻薄的话. ④薄荷鸡尾酒〔白兰地加薄荷精、冰水调成〕. ⑤〔英俚〕威士忌苏打水.

stin·gi·ly [ˈstindʒili] *ad.* 吝啬地,小气地.

stin·gi·ness [ˈstiŋdʒinis] *n.* 吝啬; 不足.

sting·(ing)-nettle *n.* 【植】荨麻.

stin·go [ˈstiŋgəu] *n.* 〔俚〕烈性啤酒.

sting-ray [ˈstiŋrei] *n.* 【鱼】海鳐鱼,魟,鯆鱼.

stin·gy¹ [ˈstindʒi] *a.* 有刺的; 刺人的; 尖锐的,刺骨的.

stin·gy² [ˈstindʒi] *a.* (***-gi·er; -gi·est***) 吝啬的,小气的 (*in*); 缺乏的,不足的,微小的.

stink [stiŋk] *vi.* (***stank*** [stæŋk], ***stunk*** [stʌŋk] ***;stunk***) ①恶臭. ②名声臭. ③〔美俚〕质量等极坏. ④有大量的 (*of, with*). ⑤有某种气味 (*of*). — *vt.* ①用臭气赶出去 (*out*). ②〔俚〕闻出臭气. *The soup ~s of garlic.* 这汤有大蒜气味. *It's time to ~ out the mosquitoes.* 到了把蚊子熏出去的时候了. ***can ~ it a mile off*** 一英里之外也能闻到这股臭味. ***~ in the nostrils of sb.*** = ***~ in sb.'s nostrils*** 受人讨厌. ***~ of money*** 〔俚〕是著名的有钱人,有铜臭气. ***~ing smut*** 光腥黑穗病; 黑穗病菌. — *n.* ①恶臭,臭气. ②〔*pl.*〕〔英俚〕化学,自然科学. ③〔美俚〕丑事, 丑闻(的张扬). *Don't make a big ~ over such trifles.* 不要为这般的小事大吵大闹. **~ard** = stinker. **~ ball** (过去海战中的)臭弹. **~ bomb** 恶臭炸弹. **~ bug** 【动】臭虫; 臭蜻; 椿象科昆虫. **~coal** 碳氢石. **~horn** 【植】(气味恶臭的)鬼笔(菌). **~ pot** 便器; 讨厌到极点的人,(骂人的)臭话;〔美〕【动】臭龟;〔美俚〕摩托艇. **~stone** 【矿】臭灰岩, 臭石. **~ trap** (阴沟的) 防臭瓣. **~weed** 【植】臭草〔曼陀罗等〕. **~-wood** 【植】臭木(树). **-er** *n.* ①恶臭的人〔动物〕. ②〔俚〕极讨厌的东西〔人、工作、问题 (等)〕. **stink·ing** [ˈstiŋkin] *a.* ①有臭味的, 臭的. ②讨厌的. ③烂醉的. ④〔美俚〕很有钱. — *ad.* 极,非常. **-ly** *ad.*

stink·ard [ˈstiŋkəd] *n.* ①卑鄙的人; 讨厌的人. ②放臭气的动物(如貛等).

stink·o [ˈstiŋkəu] *a.* 〔美俚〕①喝醉了的. ②臭的. ③讨厌的. ④蹩脚的.

stint [stint] *vt., vi.* ①吝惜; 限制,节制(饮食等). ②〔古〕停止. — *n.* ①吝惜; 限制. ②定量,定额 (*of*); 定额的工作. ③【鸟】滨鹬. ***do one's daily ~*** 做每天指定的工作. ***~ oneself in [of] food*** 节制饮食. ***with no ~*** = ***without ~*** 不吝惜地, 无限制地, 慷慨地. **-ing·ly** *ad.* **-less** *a.*

stip. = stipend(iary).

stipe [staip], **sti·pes** [ˈstaipiːz] *n.* ①【植】(羊齿植物的)叶柄; (菌类的)菌柄. ②【虫】茎节; 眼柄. **~d** *a.* 有柄的.

sti·pel [ˈstaipl] *n.* 【植】小托叶.

sti·pend [ˈstaipend] *n.* ①(公务员、教员、牧师等的)俸给, 薪水; 退休金,定期津贴. ②(学生的)助学金,定期津贴.

sti·pen·dia·ry [ˈstaipendjəri] *a.* ①领薪水的. ②有关薪水的. — *n.* ①有薪水的人. ②〔英〕大城市中处理违警案件的有薪水的治安法官〔又叫 ~ magistrate〕.

sti·pes [ˈstaipiːz] (〔*pl.*〕 ***stip·i·tes*** [ˈstipətiːz]) *n.* ① = stipe. ②【动】(昆虫的)茎节.

stip·ple [ˈstipl] *vt.* (雕刻的)点刻; (绘画的)点画,点彩. — *n.* = stip·pling ①点刻(法),点画(法),点彩(法). ②呈点画(或点刻状). **~-graver** *n.* 点刻工具.

stip·u·lar [ˈstipjulə] *a.* 【植】托叶(状)的; 有托叶的.

stip·u·late¹ [ˈstipjuleit] *vt.* ①约定, 订定; 规定, 订明. ②坚持要求以…为协议条件 (*that*). ③保证. *It is ~d in the contract that the workers be paid by the piece.* 合同上规定工人们应领计件工资. *That is not of the ~d quality.* 那不是合同上所约定的品质. *I ~ this only (nothing further).* 我要的条件只这一点(别的不要). — *vi.* ①(作为协议条件而)要求 (*for*). ②规定(*for*). *The contract ~s for the use of seasoned timber.* 合同上订明用干透的木料. **-la·tion** [ˌstipjuˈleiʃən] *n.* 订约,约定; 合同,契约; 约定条件,规定,条款. **-la·tor** [ˈstipjuleitə] *n.* 订约人,立合同人,立约人.

stip·u·late² [ˈstipjuleit] *a.* 【植】有托叶的.

stip·ule [ˈstipjuːl] *n.* 【植】托叶.

stir[1] [stəː] *vt.* ***(stirred,** [ˈstəːd]**; stir•ring** [ˈstəːriŋ]**)*** ①动，摇动；(液体等)移动．②煽动，鼓动；激动；轰动，激起；唤起，惹起(喜、怒、爱、恨等)．③搅动，搅拌．— *vi.* ①动；活动，走动，跑来跑去；〔口〕起床．②兴奋；奋起．③(货币、消息等)流通；传布．~ *the fire* 捅一捅火．*Not a breath ~red the lake.* 湖水纹丝不动．*The audience was deeply ~red.* 听众深为感动〔激动〕．*Nobody in the house is stirring yet.* 那家还没有人起床．*Your presence at the meeting will ~ trouble.* 你出席会议要惹起麻烦．*S- the soup with a spoon, if it's too hot.* 汤要是太热，用匙子搅搅．*He never ~s out of the house.* 他从不外出．*If you ~, I'll shoot.* 你动一动，我就开枪．***not ~ a finger*** 一根指头也不肯动；翻一翻手掌都不肯．***not ~ an eyelid*** 睫毛一根不动；动也不动．***~ one's stumps*** 〔口〕赶快(走)；赶快干．***~ oneself*** 奋起．***~ up*** 搅拌；搅起(火等)；煽动，激励，唤起，惹起．— *n.* ①动；微动；运动，活动；激动，骚动，轰动；混杂，吵闹；刺激，感动．②搅拌，拔，冲，推，挤．*Not a ~ was there [heard].* 全无动静．*The news created (made) a great ~ in the country.* 消息轰动了全国．*Give the fire a ~.* 捅捅火．

stir[2] [stəː] *n.* 〔俚〕监狱．**~-bug** *n.* 〔美俚〕因坐牢而发狂的人．**~-bugs [-cracy, -nuts]** *a.* 因禁闭而发狂的．

stir•a•bout [ˈstəːrəbaut] *n.* 〔英〕麦片粥；忙忙碌碌的人；混乱．— *a.* 吵闹的，忙碌的．

stirk [stəːk] *n.* 〔英方，Scot.〕一两岁的牛犊．

stir•less [ˈstəːlis] *a.* 不动的，平静的；沉静的．

stir•pi•cul•ture [ˈstəːpikʌltʃə] *n.* 【生】优生法，优种繁殖．

stirps [stəːps] *n.* ***(pl. stir•pes** [ˈstəːpiːz]**)*** ①种族，家系．②【法】祖先．③【生】(受精卵内的)决定因子总数．④【动】(相当于总科的)群．⑤【植】种族．

stir•rer [ˈstəːrə] *n.* ①搅动者；搅动器；煽动者，搅乱者．②活动分子．③起得早〔晚〕的人．

stir•ring [ˈstəːriŋ] *a.* ①活跃的，忙碌的；热闹的；吵闹的(城市)．②危险的，动摇民心的．③激动人心的，使人兴奋的，激励的，鼓舞的．*a ~ speech* 激动人心的演说．*a ~ incident* 轰动的意外事件．*the ~ struggle* 惊心动魄的斗争．**-ly** *ad.*

stir•rup [ˈstirəp] *n.* ①马镫；马镫带．②【机】镫形具，支持用铁具．③【建】镫筋，箍筋．④【海】系索，镫索，镫(形铁)链．⑤【解】镫骨．***high up in the ~s*** ＝〔up the ~s〕身分高；富有．***hold the ~s (for)*** (为某人)扶住马镫；服事，奉承．**~ bar** 悬镫铁条；(镫的)横踏板．**~ bone** 【解】镫骨．**~ cup** 〔英〕(古代)马上离别时的饯别酒．**~ iron** 马镫(不连皮带)．**~ leather** 马镫皮带．**~-piece** (木工用的)镫形支架．**~ pump** 〔英〕消防手摇灭火泵．**~ strap** 马镫皮带．

stish•ov•ite [ˈstiʃəˌvait] *n.* 【地】超石英．

stitch [stitʃ] *n.* ①一针；针脚；缝线．②针法，缝法，编法．③〔只 sing.〕(常指肋部)刺痛，剧痛．④碎布；〔口〕一部分，一点儿；少许衣服．⑤〔英方〕畦；(二犁沟间的)窄垄．⑥〔英方〕距离，一段时间．*A ~ in time saves nine.* 及时一针省得以后缝九针；及时处理，事半功倍．***drop a ~*** (编绒线时)织漏一针．***every ~*** 全身(装束)，全付(行头)；风帆的各个部分．***have not a ~ on*** 一丝不挂．***have not a dry ~ on*** 全身湿透．***make small [long] ~es*** 密〔粗〕缝．***feel a ~ in one's side*** 觉得肋部一阵剧痛．***not do a ~ of work*** 一点工作不做．***put a ~ in a garment*** 把衣服缝一缝．***rip out ~es = take out ~es*** 拆缝线．***without a ~ of clothing = have not a ~ on.*** — *vt.* ①缝，缝缀，连缀；缝饰；钉．②(把田地)弄成畦，起垄．— *vi.* 缝纫，拿针缝．**~ up** 缝拢，缝补．**~ing horse** (缝皮料用的)压脚，压板．**~ wheel** (缝皮料用的)穿孔齿锥．**~work** 刺绣，缝纫．**~ wort** *n.* 【植】繁缕(属)；刺草；复活节钟草．

stitch•ery [ˈstitʃəri] *n.* 刺绣术；〔*pl.*〕刺绣品．

stith•y [ˈstiði] *n.* ①〔古，方〕铁砧．②打铁铺；锻冶场．— *vt.* 〔古〕打铁．

sti•ver [ˈstaivə] *n.* ①荷兰旧辅币〔值二十分之一盾〕．②小钱；一点点，不值钱的东西．***do not care a ~*** 毫不介意．***have not a ~*** 一文钱也没有．***not worth a ~*** 一文不值．

stiv•y [ˈstaivi] *a.* ①〔方〕塞满了的．②憋闷的．

St. John [ˌsntˈdʒɔn] *n.* 圣约翰〔姓氏〕．

St. John's [sntˈdʒɔnz] 圣约翰〔安提瓜岛(英)首府〕．

St. Leger [sntˈledʒə] *n.* 圣莱杰〔姓氏〕．

St. Lou•is [sntlwiː] 圣路易斯〔西非塞内加尔 (Senegal) 的首都〕．

St. Lu•ci•a [sntˈluːʃiə] *n.* 圣卢西亚〔拉丁美洲〕．

St. Maur [ˈsntmɔː] *n.* 圣莫尔〔姓氏〕．

stoa [ˈstəuə] *n.* ***(pl. stoae** [ˈstəuiː]**, ~s)*** (古希腊神殿的)拱廊，柱廊．

stoat [stəut] *n.* 【动】(特指夏季被棕色毛的)鼬．

stoc•ca•do, stoc•coa•ta [stəˈkɑːdəu, -ˈkɑːtə] *n.* 〔古〕(用刀、矛等)刺、戮．

sto•chas•tic [stəuˈkæstik] *a.* ①机会的；有可能性的；随便的．②【数】随机的．

stock[1] [stɔk] *n.* 〔G.〕滑雪手杖．

stock[2] [ˈstɔk] *n.* ①(树等的)干，根株，根茎．②【园艺】砧木；苗木；原种．③〔古〕木块，木头．④桩，柱；株．⑤托柄；枪托；刨身；钻柄，把，柄；锚杆．⑥祖先；家系，世系，血统；族；种族，民族．⑦【语】语族，语系．⑧原料，材料，备料；(炖肉等所得的)原汁，汤料．⑨本钱，资本；股份，股票；〔*pl.*〕〔英〕公债．★ 公债美国通常叫 bond；在英国股份叫 share，作买卖对象的股票叫 stock，在美国一律叫 stock．⑩库存品，存货，贮存；买进的货，进货．⑪〔总称〕家畜，牲畜；农具．⑫【生】群体，群落；一群(蜜蜂等)；族类．⑬【动】原种；无性种．⑭(十八世纪男子兼作衣领用的)宽领带．⑮【植】紫罗兰(属)．⑯〔*pl.*〕【船】造船架(枕木)；〔*pl.*〕(兽医等用的)固马架；夹架．⑰〔*pl.*〕【史】足枷；优质砖．⑱【机】台，座；刨台．⑲【地】岩株．⑳估计，估量，信任，相信．㉑(牌局开始时)没发完的牌．㉒〔英〕高级砖．㉓固定在某一剧院上演的剧团或其轮换剧目．*foundation ~ seeds* 原种．*a breeder's ~ farm* 原主种圃．*the ~ of a rifle* 枪托．*He has £50 in the ~s.* 他有五十镑公债票．*a ~ certificate* 〔英〕公债证券；〔美〕股票．*an ordinary ~* ＝〔美〕*a common ~* 普通股．*a preference ~* ＝〔美〕*a preferred ~* 优先股．*take over a farm with the ~* 买下一个连同牲畜农具在内的农场．*dead ~* 农具．*fat ~* 食用家畜．*live ~* 牲畜．*mixed paper- ~* 混合纸料．*a man of Scotish ~* 一个苏格兰血统的男子．*languages of Teutonic ~* 条顿系的语言．*keep a large ~ of dry goods* 存有大量织物货品．*the gold ~* 黄金储备．*put little ~ in sb.* 不大信任某人．*two-ply ~* 夹(层)纸．*malm ~* 白垩砖．***be out of ~*** 没有现货，缺货，卖光．***have [keep] a large ~ of information*** 知识广博．***(have [keep]) in ~*** 有货，办有，备有，持有 (*goods in ~* 现货，存货)．***keep all kinds of goods in ~*** 各货齐备．***lay in a ~ of flour*** 购备面粉．***lock, ~, and barrel*** 枪的全部；全体，一切．***on the ~s*** 【船】建造中；计划中 (*I've got a couple of books on the ~s.* 计划要读的书有两本)．***out of ~*** 售完，脱销，缺货．***take ~*** 清点存货，盘(点存)货；清理，清点；审查，鉴定 *(of)*．***take ~ in*** 买…的股票；和…发生关系，干与；重视；信任．— *vt.* ①给…装托，柄(枪托、钻柄等)．②购备，贮备．③(给农场)购置农具〔家畜〕；(给商店)办货．④播(种) *(with)*；放牧．⑤放养(鱼类)；种上牧草；使(牲畜)受孕．⑥给(罪犯)上枷．— *vi.* ①采办 *(up)*．②长新梢，出新芽，长主茎．*The market is now fully ~ed.* 市场现在货物充足．*Everybody has to ~ his mind with knowledge.* 人人都要使自己的头脑充满着知识．*a well- ~ed library* 藏书充实的图书馆．— *a.* ①库存的，现有的，贮有的；常备的．

②主要的,标准的. ③平凡的,陈腐的;繁殖.④(饲养)家畜的,繁殖用的. ⑤股票[股份]的. ⑥〔英〕公债的. ⑦为某一戏院常年雇用的;常年属于某戏院的. ⑧〔美〕矮胖的. *a ~ actor* 专任演员. *~ sizes in boots* 鞋子常备的标准尺寸. *a ~ play* 保留节目,常演的戏. *a ~ bull* 公的种牛. *a ~ broker* 股票经纪商. ~ **account** 存货帐;股份帐. ~ **beet** 饲用甜菜. ~ **book** 存货簿. ~ **breeder** 畜牧业者. ~ **breeding** 牧畜,畜产,良种繁育. ~ **broker** 股票[证券]经纪人. ~ **brokerage,** ~ **broking** 证券经纪业. ~ **car** ①(火车)家畜车箱. ②常备的普通式样的汽车. ③比赛用汽车. ~ **certificate** 股票. ~ **company** ①股份公司. ②固定在某一剧院上演轮换剧目的剧团. ③〔美〕(非明星制的)演员专任制剧团. ~ **culture** 原种培养,储备培养. ~ **dividend** 以增资股票形式发放的红利;股票息. ~**dove** 【鸟】野鸽. ~**ewe** 传种母羊. ~ **exchange** 证券交易所. ~ **farm** 畜牧场. ~ **farmer** 畜牧业者. ~ **farming** 畜牧业. ~**fish** (未加盐的)鳕鱼干(等). ~-**gang** *n.* (把木料一次锯成木板的)框锯. ~ **holder** ①〔英〕公债持有人. ②〔美〕股东〔英国普通叫做 shareholder〕. ~-**in-trade** ①存货. ②营业用具;必需工具. ③老手段,惯用手段. ~ **jobber** ①〔英蔑〕股票投机商. ②〔美〕股票经纪人. ~ **jobbery,** ~ **jobbing** 证券投机买卖(业). ~ **list** ①〔交易所公布的〕证券行情表. ②存货表. ③〔美〕股份表. ~-**lock** 装牢在门上的锁. ~-**man** ①牧场主. ②〔主澳〕牧场工人,饲养员. ③仓库管理员. ~-**map** 林相图. ~ **market** ①股票市场. ②股票买卖. ③股票行情. ④牲畜市场. ~ **option** 〔美〕(股东的)优先认股权. ~**pile** ①(原料、食品等的)储备;准备急用的备用原料或物资;贮存. ②资源,富源,矿藏量. ③(为战争准备的)核武器. —*vt., vi.* 储备(原料等). ~ **piling** *n.* 贮存,堆存,积存. ~ **plot** 原种圃. ~ **pot** ①炖原汁汤的锅. ②什锦锅. ③杂烩汤. ~ **rail** (转辙器的)本轨. ~ **raising** 畜牧(业),牲畜饲养(业). ~-**rider**〔澳〕骑马牧人. ~**room** ①(物资、商品等的)仓库. ②(旅馆内供旅行推销员用的)商品展出室. ~-**still** 静止的,不动的 (*stand ~-still* 站着不动). ~**taking** ①盘货,清点存货. ②(事业等的)成绩调查[估计]. ③森林调查. ~ **ticker** 证券行情自动记录收报机. ~ **watering** 〔美〕加发股票而未增资. ~ **whip** 牧鞭. ~-**work** ①备售制品. ②【采】网状(矿)脉. ~**yard** (预备屠宰、买卖、装运等用的)牲畜围栏;堆料场.

stock·ade [stɔˈkeid] *n.* ①栅栏,围桩. ②用栅栏围起的一块地方. ③排桩的防波堤. ④〔美军俚〕(军营)监牢;俘虏营. — *vt.* 用栅栏围住;用栅栏防卫.

stock·er [ˈstɔkə] *n.* ①为屠宰而养肥的小公牛. ②枪托制造者. ③(钢铁厂堆料场的)碎料工,装料工. ④【机】储料器;堆料机;加煤机.

Stock·holm [ˈstɔkhəum] *n.* 斯德哥尔摩〔瑞典首都〕. *~ tar* (造船用)松焦油.

stock·i·ly [ˈstɔkili] *ad.* 矮胖地,粗壮地. *a ~ built plumber* 身材矮胖的管子工. -**i·ness** *n.*

stock·i·net(te) [ˌstɔkiˈnet] *n.* ①(内衣等用)松紧织物;弹力织物. ②隔行正反针织法.

stock·ing [ˈstɔkiŋ] *n.* ①〔常 *pl.*〕长袜 (*opp.* sock). ②(毛色和身体其他部分不同的)兽脚. *a pair of ~s* 一双长统袜. *elastic ~s* 【医】(外科用)橡皮袜子. *~ yarn* 针织线. *horse with white ~s* 白脚马. ***in one's ~s [~-feet]*** 光着袜底儿,不穿鞋 (*He is [stands] six feet in his ~s.* 他不穿鞋身长六英尺). ***wear yellow ~s*** 妒忌,吃醋. ~**ed** *a.* 穿袜的. ~ **cap** (冬季戴的有绒球或穗的圆锥形)绒线帽. ~ **frame,** ~ **loom,** ~ **machine** 织袜机.

stock·ish [ˈstɔkiʃ] *a.* 象木头似的;蠢笨的;呆滞的. -**ly** *ad.*

stock·ist [ˈstɔkist] *n.* 存货待售的商人.

stock·y [ˈstɔki] *a.* ***(-i·er; -i·est)*** 矮胖的,结实的. -**i·ly** *ad.* -**i·ness** *n.*

Stod·dard [ˈstɔdəd] *n.* 斯托达德〔姓氏〕.

stodge [stɔdʒ] *vt.* ①暴食,贪婪地吃,使塞饱. ②使充分满足,使感到腻味. ③搅拌,搀和. *be ~d with tea and buns* 塞满茶点. *He often ~s himself with his newspapers.* 他经常遍阅报纸. *It's your treat, but you shouldn't ~ yourself with roast duck and beef stew, John.* 是要款待你,约翰;可是你不要让烤鸭和燉牛肉弄得你吃着发腻呀. — *vi.* ①暴食,狼吞虎咽. ②重步行走,历经艰苦.— *n.* 〔英俚〕①浓厚的、不易消化油腻的食物. ②贪吃的人,暴食者;盛筵. ③枯燥难学的东西,学起来令人生厌的东西.

stodg·y [ˈstɔdʒi] *a.* ***(-i·er; -i·est)*** ①浓厚的(食物),不易消化的,胀肚子的. ②内容枯燥的(书等);乏味的(文体等). ③〔口〕矮胖的,身体笨重的. ④装得满满的. ⑤(人)庸俗的,老派的,守旧的. *I want something to read. These volumes are ~.* 我要一些可读的东西,这些厚本本枯燥乏味. *The gateman was a ~ fellow of 60.* 看门人是个六十岁的矮胖子. -**i·ly** *ad.*

stoep [stuːp] *n.* (南非荷兰式住宅的)屋前游廊;门廊.

sto·gy, sto·gie [ˈstəugi] *n.* 〔美〕笨重的皮靴;细长的(低级)雪茄烟.

Sto·ic [ˈstəuik] *a.* ①斯多噶学派的. ②〔s-〕= stoical. — *n.* 斯多噶学派的人;〔s-〕禁欲(主义)者.

sto·i·cal [ˈstəuikəl] *a.* 斯多噶学派的;禁欲主义的;不以苦乐为意的;能忍受痛苦[不幸]的;淡泊的. -**ly** *ad.*

stoi·ch(e)i·om·et·ry [ˌstɔikiˈɔmitri] *n.* 化学计量学;化学计算法.

Sto·i·cism [ˈstəuisizəm] *n.* 斯多噶哲学;〔s-〕禁欲(主义);淡泊,不以苦乐为意,坚忍.

Stoke [stəuk] *n.* 斯托克〔姓氏〕.

stoke[1] [stəuk] *vt., vi.* ①烧火,加煤,添煤;拨旺火. ②(在车头上等)做司炉. ③〔俚〕狼吞虎咽吃(食物) *(up)*. ~**hold** 【海】生火间,锅炉舱;炉前. ~ **hole** 炉膛口,炉前,生火间.

stoke[2] [stəuk] *n.* 【物】沲〔动力粘度单位〕.

stok·er [ˈstəukə] *n.* ①司炉;烧火工人. ②自动加煤机 (= mechanical ~).

sto·ke·si·a [stəuˈkiːʒiə, ˈstəuksiə] *n.* 〔美〕【植】琉璃菊 *(Stokesia laevis)* 〔产于美国东南部〕.

Stokes mor·tar [ˈstəuks ˈmɔːtə] 斯多克式迫击炮,大口径迫击炮.

STOL = short take off and landing 短距起落(飞机).

stole[1] [stəul] *n.* ①【古罗马】女式长外衣. ②女用长条披肩. ③【宗】(牧师神甫举行仪式时用)圣带,长巾,祭衣.

stole[2] [stəul] *v.* steal 的过去式.

sto·len [ˈstəulən] steal 的过去分词. — *a.* 偷得的;偷走的. *~ goods* 赃物,贼赃.

stol·id [ˈstɔlid] *a.* 呆头呆脑的,感觉迟钝的;不易激动的;顽强的(抵抗). -**lid·i·ty** [stɔˈliditi] *n.* -**ly** *ad.* -**ness** *n.*

stol·len [ˈstəulən] *n.* 〔*G.*〕果子甜面包.

sto·lon [ˈstəulɔn] *n.* 【植】匍匐茎[枝];【动】生殖根. -**ic** *a.*

sto·ma [ˈstəumə] *n.* (*pl.* ~*ta*) 【植】气孔;【动】口;(昆虫的)气门,呼吸孔. -**tal** *a.*

stom·ach [ˈstʌmək] *n.* ①胃. ②〔口〕肚子. ③胃口,食欲;嗜好,欲望;志趣. *She injured her ~ by eating too much.* 她吃得太多伤了胃了. *What a ~ he has got!* 他的肚子多大! *My ~ turns[rises] at it.* 一看到[一想到]这个就发恶心. *It goes against my ~.* 这个不合我的胃口[兴趣]. *a proud [high] ~* 傲慢. *the coat of the ~* 胃黏膜. *coats of the ~* 胃膜,胃的粘膜层. ***have a good ~ for*** 很想吃,渴望. ***have a pain in the ~*** 肚子[胃]痛. ***have no ~ for*** 不想(做某事),(对某事)没有兴趣. ***lie (heavy) on sb.'s ~*** (食物)滞积胃中,不

消化. ***on a full*** ~ 饭后,肚子饱时. ***on an empty*** ~ 空腹时;饿着肚皮,绝食. ***pit of the*** ~ 心窝. ***sour*** ~ 胸口作呕. ***turn sb.'s*** ~ 使人发呕,使人厌恶. — *vt.* ①吃得津津有味;消化. ②忍耐,忍受〔多半与否定词连用〕. ③〔古〕对…发怒. *I cannot* ~ *this insult.* 我不能忍受这种侮辱. ~**-ache** 胃痛,肚子痛. ~ **pump**【医】胃唧筒. ~ **tooth** (幼儿的)下犬齿. ~ **tube**【医】胃管. ~ **warmer**〔英〕热水袋. **-ful** *n.* 一满胃,满腹 (*have a ~ful of grievances* 满腹牢骚). **-less** *a.* 没有胃的;没有胃口[食欲]的.

stom•ach•al [ˈstʌməkəl] *n., a.* = stomachic.

stom•ach•er [ˈstʌməkə] *n.* (17 世纪女用)三角胸衣.

sto•mach•ic, -i•cal [stəˈmækik, -ikəl] *a.* ①胃的. ②健胃的,助消化的. — *n.* 健胃剂.

sto•ma•chy [ˈstʌməki] *a.* ①〔英方〕易怒的,脾气急燥的. ②肚子大的.

sto•ma•ta [ˈstəumətə] *n.* stoma 的复数.

stom•a•tal, sto•mal [ˈstəumətl, -məl] *a.*【动】【植】有气孔的;有气门的.

sto•mate [ˈstəumeit] *a.*【生】stoma(ta) 的. — *n.* = stoma.

sto•mat•ic [stəˈmætik] *a.* ①口的. ②【植】【动】气孔的,呼吸孔的,气门的. — *n.* 口(中用)药.【生】= stomate.

sto•ma•ti•tis [ˌstəuməˈtaitis] *n.*【医】口内炎,口炎.

sto•ma•t(o)- *comb. f.* 表示"口的","象口的": *stomatology.*

sto•ma•to•gas•tric [ˌstəumətəuˈgæstrik] *a.* 口和胃的.

sto•ma•tol•o•gy [ˌstəuməˈtɔlədʒi] *n.*【医】口腔学. **-log•i•cal** [-ˈlɔdʒikl] *a.* **-o•gist** *n.* 口腔学家.

sto•ma•to•pod [ˈstəumətəpɔd, ˈstɔmətə-] *n.*【动】口脚类 (*Stomatopoda*) 动物.

sto•ma•to•scope [stəˈmætəskəup] *n.*【医】口腔镜.

sto•ma•tous [ˈstəumətəs, ˈstɔmə-] *a.* 有孔的,有气孔的.

sto•mo•dae•um, sto•mo•de•um [ˌstəuməˈdiəm, stɔmə-] *n.* (*pl.* ***-dae•a, -de•a*** [-diə])【解】口道,口凹.

stomp[1] [stɔmp] *vt., vi.* = stamp〔尤指踏伤,踩死〕. — *n.*〔美〕①节奏活泼、拍子强烈的爵士乐曲调. ②上述乐曲的舞蹈. ③跺脚,重踩.

stomp[2] [stɔmp] *n., vt.* = stump[2].

S'ton = Southampton.

Stone [stəun] *n.* 斯通〔姓氏〕.

stone [stəun] *n.* ①石,石头,铺石,石料. ②宝石 (= precious ~). ③石碑,界碑,里程碑,纪念碑;墓石. ④磨(刀)石;捣衣石,砧;砑(光)石. ⑤雹,霰. ⑥【医】结石;结石病. ⑦【植】(水果的)硬核. ⑧〔古〕〔常 *pl.*〕睾丸. ⑨【印】整版石台;调墨石台;整纸石台;石印石. ⑩〔英〕(*pl.* ~) 呞〔重量名,照规定是 14 磅(尤以表示体重时常用),但实际上肉类是 8 磅,干酪是 16 磅,麻是 32 磅,玻璃是 5 磅,羊毛是 24 磅;略作 *st.*〕. *Stones will cry out.* (极大的罪恶等)会使石头也叫唤起来. *A rolling ~ gathers no moss.*〔谚〕滚石不生苔,转行不成材. *a ~'s throw [cast] away* 近在咫尺. *blue* ~ 绿礬. *Cornish* ~陶土. *the ~ of Sisyphus* 徒劳. *a heart of* ~ 铁石心肠,残忍. ~ *on the chest*〔美〕肺结核. ***break ~s*** 敲碎(铺路用的)石头;干渺小的差事. ***cast ~s [a ~] at*** 谴责,攻击. ***cast the first*** ~ 向…挑衅. ***get blood from a*** ~ 石中取血;不可能. ***give a ~ and a beating to sb.***〔原赛马〕轻而易举地胜过(某人). ***give sb. a ~ for bread*** 拿石头当面包给;表面帮忙实则愚弄(人). ***leave no ~ unturned*** 挖空心思,用尽一切手段 (*to do*). ***mark with a white*** ~ (古罗马人用白垩在日历上把幸福的日子打上记号,转为)作为喜庆的日子特笔大书. ***set a ~ rolling*** 滚动石头;做劳而无功的事情. ***set ~ out*** 将石块砌成一层比一层稍稍突出状,依次排列. ***swim like a*** ~〔谑〕沉下去. ***throw ~s [a ~] at*** 谴责,攻击. ***throw the first ~ at*** 向…挑衅. ***trip over a*** ~ 被石头绊倒. ***within a ~'s throw of*** 在…的左近;离…不远. — *vt.* ①向…投扔石头(而打死). ②除去石头. ③除去(水果的)核. ④拿石头围住,堆石头;筑石墙,铺石头. ⑤用石头磨刀,磨光(皮革). ~ *a well* 用石头砌一口井. ~ *sb. to death* 用石头甩死(某人). **S- Age** 石器时代. ~ **ax(e)** 石斧. ~**-blind** *a.* ①全瞎的. ②〔美俚〕大醉的. ~ **blue** 灰蓝色. ~**boat**〔美〕运石雪橇. ~**-brash** 砂石[石子]多的土地,砂土. ~**-breaker** *n.* 敲碎石头的工人,碎石机. ~**-broke** *a.*〔俚〕不名一文的,穷困不堪的. ~**-cast** = stone's-cast. ~**chat**【鸟】黑喉石鹏. ~ **coal** 白煤,块状无烟煤. ~**-cold** *a.* 冰冷如石的,冷透的. ~ **composition** 石刻品. ~**crop**【植】景天(轻泻剂). ~ **curlew**【鸟】石鸻. ~ **cut•ter** 石匠,石工;截石机. ~**-dead** *a.* 完全断了气的,完全死了的 (*Stone-dead has no fellow.* 杀人灭口). ~**-deaf** *a.* 完全聋的,一点也听不见的. ~ **fence** 石墙;〔美俚〕混合酒. ~**fly**【动】襀翅类昆虫. ~ **fruit** 有硬核的水果〔如桃、梅等〕. ~**-ground** *a.* 在磨石作坊里研磨的. ~**-horse** *n.*〔方〕种马. ~ **-jug** 石罐;〔俚〕牢监. ~**-leek** 葱. ~ **lily**【植】海百合化石. ~**man** ①石工,石匠. ②(作界标等用)圆锥形石堆. ③【印】装版工人. ~ **martin** ①【动】石貂,榉貂. ②貂皮上衣〔围脖〕. ~**mason** 石匠. ~ **mill** ①碎石机;磨石机. ②石粉工场. ~ **pine**【植】意大利五针松. ~ **pit** 采石场. ~ **powder** 石粉. ~**-race** 边跑边拾石块的一种游戏. ~ **roller**【动】包鳔鱼;裂唇绒口鱼. ~**'s cast** = ~**'s throw** 一投石的距离〔约 50 到 150 码〕. ~**-seed**【植】紫草. ~ **sledge** 石匠鎚. ~**-still** *a.* 非常寂静的,一动也不动的. ~ **wall** ①*n.* 石墙,难以逾越的障碍. ②*vi., vt.*〔主英、口语〕阻碍;阻碍议事进行;【板球】小心地打. ③*a.* 石墙(一样坚固)的;坚定的. ~ **walling** *n.* ①(板球的)慎打. ②〔英〕阻碍议事. ③筑石墙;石墙. ~**ware** 瓩器;粗陶(器). ~**work** ①(建筑物的)砖石部分. ②石方工程;石雕工艺;石制品. ③〔*pl.*〕(作单数用)石制工艺品厂,石场. ~**wort**【植】轮藻纲植物. **-d** *a.* 去核的;喝醉的,沉醉的;(吸毒后)处于麻醉状态的. **-r** *n.* 投石者;铺石块者;去核者.

Stone•henge [ˈstəunhendʒ] *n.* (英国 Salisbury 平原上的)史前巨石群.

stonk [stɔŋk] *vt.* 重炮猛轰;密集炮火猛击. *loose a good ~ on the enemy* 向敌军发射了一阵猛烈的密集炮火.

ston•y [ˈstəuni] *a.* (***-i•er; -i•est***) ①石的,石头的,石质的,象石头(一样硬)的,多石的. ②多核的(水果). ③冷酷的,残忍的(心等);变成石头的;不动的;没有表情的. ④〔俚〕破产的,不名一文的. *The path was ~.* 小道上石头很多. *Her story should soften the stoniest of hearts.* 她的事情会使心肠最冷酷无情的人也为之感动的. *a ~ gaze [stare, look]* 冷眼凝视. ~ *fear* 吓呆了的恐怖. ~**-broke** *a.* = stone-broke. ~ **coral**【动】石珊瑚. ~**-heart•ed** *a.* 铁石心肠的,冷酷的. **-i•ly** *ad.* **-i•ness** *n.*

stood [stud] stand 的过去式及过去分词.

stooge [stu:dʒ] *n.* ①〔口、原美〕(提供笑料、帮腔、作笑谑对象的)丑角的配角. ②〔口语〕善于逗笑的人;陪衬人物;帮闲;奸细,密探. ③傀儡,唯命是从的人,走狗. ④〔英俚〕飞行练习生. ⑤〔美俚〕副驾驶员. — *vi.*〔美俚〕①给丑角帮腔. ②充当帮手[帮闲]. ③〔英空军俚〕盘旋(同一地上) (*over; about; around; etc.*). *I'd play ~ to him in the performance.* 在表演中我来给他当个配角. *the struggle against hegemonism and its ~s* 反对霸权主义及其走狗们的斗争. *The police will have ~s watching every move of the suspected terrorists.* 警察会派密探注意有恐怖分子嫌疑的人的每一活动.

stook [stuk] *n.*〔英〕麦[禾]束堆〔通例是 12 束〕. — *vt., vi.* 堆(麦束).

stook•ie, stook•y [ˈstu:ki] *n.*〔Scot., Ir.〕呆子,傻瓜.

stool [stu:l] *n.* ①凳子;搁脚凳. ②座位,席位. ③便桶;厕所;通便;〔常 *pl.*〕大便;(大便一次的)粪便. ④(园艺压条用的)根株,母株;根生嫩苗. ⑤囮子鸟歇息的树枝;

〔美〕囮鸽 (= ~-pigeon)．⑥【机】垫凳．⑦【建】内窗台．⑧〔美俚〕情报．*a necessary ~* 厕所．*go to ~* 去解大溲．***come to the ground between two ~s = fall (to the ground) between two ~s*** 两头落空．— *vt.* 〔美〕用囮子引诱．— *vi.* ①分蘖．②〔古〕去解大溲．③〔美俚〕替警察局作密探；充当囮子．***~ing stage*** 抽茎，分蘖期．**~ball** (旧时英国的)女子板球．**~ pigeon** 〔美〕①囮鸽．②〔俚〕(诱人赌博等的)囮子．③〔俚〕(警察局的)密探．**~ plate** 【机】垫板．**~ shoot** 根株萌芽．**-ing** *n.* 分蘖力．

stool·ie [ˈstuːli] *n.* = stool pigeon.

stoop[1] [stuːp] *vi.* ①弯身；弯腰 *(down)*．②(树、岩等)倾斜．③屈服，屈从；屈身，忍辱；降低身分，堕落(做下流事等)．④(鹰等)飞袭，飞扑 *(at, on, upon)*．— *vt.* ①屈，弯，曲．②使屈服，屈从，自贬，压倒．③降下(帆、旗等)．*She ~ed down to pick a flower.* 她弯下腰去摘了一朵花．*He ~ed to such meanness.* 他堕落得这般卑鄙．***~ to conquer [win]*** 降低身分而取胜，忍辱取得．***~ to flattery*** 谄媚奉承．— *n.* ①弯腰，屈身，驼背．②屈服，自贬．③(猛禽的)下攫，下扑．*He has a shocking ~.* 他的背驼[弯]得很厉害．**~ labour** 〔美〕需要经常弯腰的作业[劳动]．

stoop[2] [stuːp] 〔美〕*n.* 两侧有可坐的低矮栏干的门前露台；游廊．

stoop[3] [stuːp] *n.* = stoup.

stop [stɔp] *vi.* (**~ped** [-t]，〔诗〕 ***stopt; stop·ping*** [ˈstɔpiŋ]) ①停止；停下来做某事 *(to do sth.)*．②〔口〕逗留，歇宿，(偶然)过访．③踌躇．④被塞住．⑤【乐】压住弦或孔以改变音调．— *vt.* ①止住，堵住，塞住，填塞，盖．②阻止，阻拦；截断，断绝．③停止(工作、吃饭等)；妨碍；停付(支票等)；扣留，扣除；阻止．④止住(伤口)出血；打落(飞鸟等)．⑤【海】系紧(船缆等)．⑥加标点．⑦【乐】压(乐器的弦、孔，以改变音调)．⑧〔美运〕打败(对手)．⑨【海】(用绳子)扎住，扎紧．⑩【园艺】摘心，打顶．*~ to rest* 停下休息．*~ to think* (把某事)停下来，转而进行思考．*~ thinking* 停止思考．*It has stopped raining.* 雨停了．*~ the traffic* 断绝交通．*What is to ~ me from coming?* 我为什么不能来？*S-thief!* 截住强盗！*a badly stopped letter* 标点错乱的信．*~ a bottle with a cork* 用软木塞把瓶子盖上．*The bank ~ped his check.* 银行拒付他的支票了．*We'll ~ at a hotel for the night.* 咱们夜里住旅馆．*I'll ~ at no expense to obtain it.* 我将不惜一切花费来得到它．*I'm ~ping with my uncle.* 我暂时住在叔父家．***~ a bullet [shell]*** 〔俚〕中弹阵亡[受伤]．***~ a cheque*** (通知银行)止付支票．***~ a clock [the clock, the train]*** 〔美俚〕样子不好看[丑陋]．***~ a gap*** 修补；弥补；补空；代理．***~ a packet*** 受重伤；挨臭骂．***~ at*** 住宿(旅店)．***~ at no*** *(sacrifices)* 不惜(一切牺牲)．***~ at nothing*** 什么也做得出，肆无忌惮；勇往直前．***~ at nothing in committing evils*** 无恶不作．***~ away*** 外宿．***~ by*** 〔美〕顺便到(某处)访问 *(He'll ~ by on his way home.* 回家途中他将前来访问)．***~ cold*** 〔美口〕使呆住．***~ dead*** 突然停止．***~ down*** 【摄】把光圈收小．***~ in*** 顺便过访某人．***~ off*** 中途下一下车；用砂填塞(铸模的一部)；〔英口〕进监牢．***~ sb.'s breath*** 闷死人．***~ sb.'s clock*** 〔美〕杀人．***~ one's ears*** 塞住耳朵，不听 *(to; against)*．***~ sb.'s way*** 拦住某人路；反对某人．***~ out*** 遮断(风、日光等)；外宿；扣除(*The cost was stopped out of my salary.* 那一笔费用已经由我的薪水中扣除了)；【摄】置于停影液中．***~ over*** 中途下车；暂留，暂住；住在海外 *(Many motorists were forced to ~ over in that town because of floods.* 由于洪水泛滥，许多汽车驾驶人员不得不在该城镇中途停留)．***~ short*** 猛然停止，停止；使(谈话等)停止；【剑术等】挡住，回击．***~ short of*** 差点儿，险些儿，几乎．***~ the show (cold)*** 〔美剧〕因某一节目演出精采，观众多次要求重演以致耽误继续表演．***~ to look at a fence*** (在障碍前，在困难前)踌躇不前．***~ up*** 醒着，没有睡；熬夜；塞住(洞口)．***~ with a friend*** 住在朋友处．— *n.* ①中止，停止，停车．②停留处，车站，站；飞机场．③逗留，歇宿，停留，停靠，停泊．④终结；终止．⑤〔英〕句号；标点；间断．⑥填塞；妨碍，阻碍．⑦【乐】(以手指压弦、孔)调整音调；〔转义〕说法，语调，调子．⑧【机】制子，制楔，制动器，档；销；断流阀．⑨【乐】风琴的音栓；六弦琴的柱．⑩【语音】闭止音〔t, d, k, b 等〕．⑪【摄】光圈；【物】光阑．⑫【滑雪】遽止．⑬【建】门闩．⑭【海】掣，掣索．⑮【剑术】挡架．*a bus ~* 公共汽车站．*a full ~* 句点．*a field ~* 【物】场阑．*You've four ~s before you get to the station.* 你到火车站以前还有四个公共汽车站．*I told him to put a ~ to the practice.* 我已经告诉他不要搞那个了．*Every sentence should have its proper ~s.* 每句话都应有适当的标点．*It's entirely groundless that you put on the sarcastic ~.* 你发出讽刺的调子是毫无根据的．***bring to a ~*** 使停止，制止．***come to a (full) ~*** (完全)停止．***make a ~*** 停止，休息，停留．***put a ~ to*** 使…停止，使…终止．***put on [pull out, turn on] the pathetic ~*** 用悲伤的语调说．***without a ~*** 不停，不停留，不停车．**~bath** 【摄】停影液．**~block** 止轮楔．**~cock** 【机】管闩，活栓；活塞．**~-collar** 【机】限动环．**~-cylinder press** 自动停滚式印刷机．**~drill** (有凸肩可限制深度的)钻头．**~gap** 塞洞口的东西；填补，充数；权宜之计，敷衍，搪塞．**~ key [knob]** 风琴音钮．**~ light** (交通岗的)红灯，(汽车的)停车灯．**~-loss order** = **~ order** **~-off** 中途停留(地)．**~ order** (要求经纪人在市价达到一定价格时买进或抛售的) 规定价格成交命令；中止命令；止付命令．**~out** *vi.* 中途辍学从事其他活动．**~-out** *n.* 中途缀学从事其他活动的学生．**~over** ①*a.* 中途下车的(票、站等)．②*n.* 〔美〕中途下车(站)；中途下车许可；中途下车票．(*a ~over satellite station* 人造卫星中间站)．**~page** 阻止；阻塞，闭塞，停止；故障；(职工工资的)扣除，扣除额；(争议中的)停工；锁厂，罢工；便秘．**~ plate** 【机】止动片．**~ press** 〔英〕报纸付印时插入的最后消息(栏)．**~ street** 〔美〕停车交通口〔车辆到此必须先停车，得到交通信号才能继续行驶〕．**~valve** 断流阀，停汽阀，节流阀；止阀，闭塞阀．**~ volley** (网球中的)吊短球 (恰好过网使对方无法接住的轻击)．**~ watch** 停表，记秒表．

stope [stoup] *n.* 【矿】回采工作面，梯段开采面；采矿场；矿房．— *vt., vi.* 在回采面开采．

stop·page [ˈstɔpidʒ] *n.* ①(活动)中止，停止．②【军】故障；阻塞，堵塞．③停工，罢工．④停付．⑤扣留，扣除(工资)．

stop·per [ˈstɔpə] *n.* ①填塞者，阻止者，止住者．②阻塞物，塞子．③【机】制动器；限制器；闭锁装置．④【矿】伸缩式凿岩机．⑤(吸烟斗用的)塞烟具．⑥【海】掣(索)．⑦〔美俚〕决定性论断[回答，打击等]．⑧(空袭时用的)耳塞．*put a ~ on* 用塞子塞住；压住，制止．*Papa's stare is a conventional ~ to our requests.* 爸爸的瞪眼是对我们请求事项的习见的决定性的回答．— *vt.* 用塞子塞住；闭塞．

stop·ping [ˈstɔpiŋ] *n.* ①阻止；停止；中止；填塞．②牙齿填塞料．③标点．④【矿】风障，风墙，隔墙．— *a.* 停的，慢车的．**~-place** *n.* 车站．

stop·ple [ˈstɔpl] *n., vt.* (用)塞子(塞住)．

stopt [stɔpt] 【诗】stop 的过去式和过去分词．

stor·a·ble [ˈstɔːrəbl] *a.* 可储藏的，耐贮藏的；可容纳的．—*n.* 〔常 *pl.*〕耐储藏品(如小麦、棉花等)．

stor·age [ˈstɔːridʒ] *n.* ①贮藏(量)，存储(量)；(仓库)保管；库容量．②栈房，仓库，贮藏所．③栈租，栈费．④贮存器．⑤【电】蓄电(瓶)．⑥【自】(计算机的)存储(器)，记忆．*cold ~* 冷藏．*a locker ~* 密闭仓．*a ~ dam* 蓄洪堰．*Pork and mutton should be kept in cold ~.* 猪羊肉应该冷藏．*The reservoir has in ~ about five million cubic* *metres.* 这水库有五百万立方米的储存量. *500 bales of cotton are in ~.* 库内存有五百包棉花. ~ **battery** *n.* 【电】蓄电池(组).

sto·rax [ˈstɔːræks] *n.* ①【药】苏合香. ②药用安息香 *(Styrax officinalis)*. ③安息香属 *(styrax)* 植物. — *a.* 安息香科 *(styracaceae)* 植物的.

store [stɔː, stɔə] *n.* ①〔*sing., pl.*〕贮藏,贮存;准备. ②〔*sing.*〕【自】(计算机的)存储器. ③〔常 *sing.*〕丰富;大量,多量. ④〔英〕栈房,仓库. ⑤〔美〕店铺,商店;〔英〕百货店(通常叫 the -s = 〔美〕department ~). ⑥〔*pl.*〕用品,必需品[粮食、衣服等];补给品,备用品. ⑦【商】原料品,贮存品,存货. ⑧〔常 *pl.*〕= ~ cattle. *a ~ of food* 许多食物. *a great ~ of facts* 许多事实. *a rich ~ of learning* 丰富的知识. *with ~s of experience* 有丰富的经验. *a ~ of strength* 充裕的体力. *a general ~* 百货店. *a book ~* 书店. ***in ~*** 准备着,贮藏着 (*I don't know what the future has in ~ for us.* 不晓得将来究竟怎么样). ***in ~ for*** 就要落到…;替某人准备着 (*I have an hour's talk in ~ for you.* 我有一个钟头的话要跟你谈. *I have a surprise in ~ for you.* 我有一件要使你吃惊的事情). ***keep a ~*** 开一个店. ***lay in ~s for*** 为…准备着. ***set (great) ~ by*** 重视,器重. ***set no great ~ by*** 不重视,轻视. — *a.* ①贮藏的,贮存的;储备的. ②〔美〕现成的. ③畜牧的,畜产的. ~ *bread* 店里烤的面包(区别于家里自做的). *a ~ tooth* 假牙. *a ~ farm* 畜牧农场. — *vt.* ①积蓄,贮藏;储备;存入仓库,交给栈房. ②供应,供给. ③蓄电;容纳. *His head is richly ~d with knowledge.* 他脑子里知识可渊博啦. *Let's ~ the flowers away from frost.* 让我们把盆花入窖过冬. ~ ***away*** 贮藏起来. ~ ***up*** 贮藏 (*~ up a saying in one's heart* 把格言记在心里). ~ **cattle** 为养肥而买进的牛,为出售而养肥的牛. ~**front** 〔美〕①*n.* 商店铺面;沿街的店面房间. ②*a.* 沿街的. ~**house** ①仓库,栈房. ②(知识的)宝库. ~**keeper** ①仓库管理人. ②【海】军需主任. ③〔美〕店主,经理. ④〔美〕滞销货. ⑤【军】军需品管理员. ~**room** 贮藏室商品陈列室. ~ **ship**【军】军需船. ~**(s)man** ①零售店店主. ②仓库工人,仓库管理员. ~**wide** 〔美〕*a.* 百货店全部或大部柜台的,全店的(*a ~wide sale* 全部商品大减价).

sto·rey [ˈstɔːri] *n.* (*pl.* ~*s*) ①〔英〕(房屋的)层. ②排列的层. *a house of one ~* 平房. *a house of three ~s* 三层楼的房子. *the basement ~* 楼底,一楼. *the first ~* 〔英〕二楼. ***the upper ~*** ①楼上. ②脑,头 (*off in his upper ~, wrong in the upper ~* 神经不正常). ③乔木的上部枝桠. *beehives arranged in ~s* 排成一层一层的蜂房. ~**-post**【建】层柱.

-sto·reyed, -sto·ried[1] [-ˈstɔːrid] *a.* 〔构成复合词〕…层楼的;【植】分层的,迭生的. *a five-~ building* 五层的楼房.

sto·ried[2] [ˈstɔrid] *a.* ①传说[故事、历史]上有名的. ②用绘画[雕刻]表现传说[故事、历史]的;用历史画[雕刻]装饰的. *a ~ castle* 传说上著名的城堡. *a ~ wall of the Liao Dynasty* 辽代的历史故事画墙.

sto·ri·ette [ˌstɔːriˈet] *n.* 小故事.

sto·ri·ol·o·gy [ˌstɔːriˈɔlədʒi] *n.* 传说研究,传说学.

stork [stɔːk] *n.*【鸟】鹳. *a common [migratory, white] ~* 白鹳. *a King S-* 〔喻〕暴君. *a visit from the ~* 婴儿诞生〔因旧时骗孩子,说婴儿是鹳鸟送来的〕. ~**'s-bill**【植】老鹳草(属),天竺葵;牻牛儿苗(属).

storm [stɔːm] *n.* ①暴风雨,暴风雪,大雷雨,大冰雹,疯狂天气;狂风暴雨;【海、气】暴风〔风力十一级〕. ②(政治、社会上的)骚动,动乱,风潮. ③(感情上的)激动,爆发. ④【军】冲击,猛攻. *We ought to face the world and brave the ~.* 我们应该经风雨,见世面. *A ~ is gathering [brewing].* 暴风雨快来了[正在酝酿]. *a ~ of applause* 暴风雨似的鼓掌喝采. *a cyclonic ~* 旋风. *a ~ of rain* 大雨. *After a ~ (comes) a calm.* 雨过天青. *revolutionary ~s* 革命风暴. *A ~ of criticism was raised by his new novel.* 他的新小说招致了极其激烈的批评. ~ ***in a tea-cup [puddle]*** 因为一点小事而闹得满城风雨;极小的事情. ***take by ~*** 袭取,强夺;使大吃一惊,使神魂颠倒,使大为感动 (*He took her by ~.* 他使她神魂颠倒). ***the ~ and stress*** 狂飙时期〔尤指十八世纪后半德国文学家反抗古典派而活动的时代〕;大动荡. — *vt.* ①袭击,猛攻. ②大力迅速攻占. — *vi.* ①(天气)起风暴,下暴雨[雪、雹]. ②冲击,冲进. ③暴怒,怒骂 *(at). At dawn, we ~ed the enemy stronghold.* 拂晓时,我们猛攻了敌人的堡垒. *The quack was ~ed with questions.* 江湖骗子受到了猛烈的质问. *It ~ed all night.* 风暴整夜不息. *The boss ~ed into his office.* 老板气冲冲地进了他的办公室. ~**-beaten** *a.* 受暴风雨打击的,饱经风霜的,饱经患难的. ~ **belt** 暴风雨带. ~**bird** = petrel. ~ **boat** 强击登陆艇. ~**bound** *a.* 因暴风雨不能出港(受阻)的. ~**-card** (航行中测绘的)风暴图. ~ **cellar** 〔美〕避风穴. ~ **centre** 暴风雨的中心;骚动的中心人物[问题]. ~ **cloud** 暴风雨前的乌云;动乱的预兆. ~**cock**【鸟】鸫. ~ **cone** 〔英〕(风暴的)警报球. ~ **door** (御风雨、寒气的)外层木板门. ~ **drum** (表示有特大暴风雨的圆柱形的)信号. ~**-finch** 〔英〕= petrel. ~ **glass** 气候变化预测管. ~**ing party** *n.*【军】强击队. ~ **kite** 失事船把索缆送到陆地上的风筝. ~ **lantern,** ~ **lamp** 〔主英〕【海】汽灯,防风灯. ~ **petrel** = stormy petrel. **proof** 耐风暴的,御风暴的. ~ **sail** (风暴时用的)较小而牢的帆. ~ **sash** 外重窗 (= ~ window). ~ **sewer** 雨水管. ~ **signal** 风暴信号. ~ **tide** 暴风潮(因岸向风而产生的). ~**-tossed** *a.* 被暴风乱吹的,被狂风播弄的;心绪极烦乱的. ~ **track** 风暴(中心)路径. ~ **trooper** ①〔S- T-〕纳粹的冲锋队员. ②突击队员. ~ **troops** ①〔S- T-〕纳粹的冲锋队员. ②突击队员,强击部队. ~ **valve**【船】排水口止回阀. ~ **warning** 风暴警报. ~ **wind** 暴风,狂风. ~ **window** (御风雨寒气的)外层木板护窗. ~ **zone** 风暴带,风暴区.

storm·i·ness [ˈstɔːminis] *n.* ①风暴度,猛烈. ②骚乱;吵闹. ③急性子;暴躁,粗暴.

Stor·month [ˈstɔːmʌnθ] *n.* 斯托蒙斯〔姓氏〕.

storm·y [ˈstɔːmi] *a.* ①风暴的. ②暴风雨(似)的;多风波的. ③猛烈的;急性子的,脾气暴躁的,粗暴的. *a man of ~ passion* 性子暴躁的人. *a ~ debate* 激烈的争论. *a ~ life* 颠沛流离的一生. ~ **petrel** 〔美〕【动】海燕;带来麻烦[骚乱,纠纷]的人. **-i·ly** *ad.* **-i·ness** *n.*

Stor·t(h)ing [ˈstɔːtiŋ] *n.* (挪威的)议会.

Sto·ry [ˈstɔːri] *n.* 斯托里〔姓氏〕.

sto·ry[1] [ˈstɔːri] *n.* ①故事,传说,传奇,轶事;小说;历史,沿革. ②传记,履历,来历;阅历,经历. ③对某事的描述,叙述. ④内情,真情,情况. ⑤〔口〕假话,谎话. ⑥(剧等的)情节;电影故事,原作. ⑦〔美新闻〕特写. *the stories of the revolutionary martyrs* 革命烈士的故事. *His ~ is by no means convincing.* 他讲的话丝毫不足令人相信. *All tell the same ~.* 大家异口同声地那么讲. *But that is another ~.* 但那是另外一个问题,那是题外的话. *It is another ~ now.* 现在情形不同了. *I know her ~.* 我知道她的经历. *It's a ~. = 'Tis a ~.* 〔口〕这是假话. *idle stories* 傻话,胡涂话. ***as the ~ goes*** 据传,据说. ***be in a [one, the same] ~*** 众口一词. ***make up the ~*** 虚构,捏造. ***tell one's [its] own ~*** 讲自己的身世〔本身表明,不言而喻〕. ***tell stories*** 编故事;说谎. ***the (same) old ~*** 老一套;陈词滥调;陈规旧习. ***the same ~ over again*** 翻来复去始终不改口的话〔不改变的情况〕. ***The ~ goes [runs] that …*** 据说. ***the whole ~*** 详情,一五一十,始末根由 (*So that's the whole ~.* 原来是这么一回事). ***to make a long ~ short*** 长话短说,总之,简单说来. — *vt.* ①〔古〕讲…的故事[历史];作为故事讲述. ②用故事画装饰. — *vi.* 说假话. *Oh, you ~!* 哦,你说谎! *He storied* *about his academic career and his professional career.* 他编造了他的学历经历. ~ **book** 故事书,小说. ~ **teller** 讲故事的人,说书的;小说作者,小说家;好讲逸话奇闻的人;〔口〕说谎的(人). **~-writer** 故事作者,小说家.

story[2] [ˈstɔri] *n.* = storey.

stoss [stɔs, stɔːs; G. ʃtəus] *a.* 〔美〕【地】(处于)逆冰川运动方向的;迎风面的.

stot [stɔt] *n.* 〔北英、方〕小(公)牛,牛犊.

sto·tin·ka [stɔːˈtiŋkə] *n.* (*pl.* **-tin·ki** [-kiː]) 斯托丁卡〔保加利亚货币名,等于 1/100 列夫〕.

Stough·ton [ˈstɔːtn] *n.* 斯托顿〔姓氏〕.

stound [staund] *n.* ①〔古或方〕短时间. ②〔废或方〕疼痛;震惊. — *vi.* 〔苏格兰、英方〕疼,痛.

stoup [stuːp] *n.* ①【宗】圣水钵. ②〔北英〕大酒杯,酒壶.

stour[1] [stuə] *n.* 〔古英、方〕①战斗,冲突. ②骚动. ③风暴. ④〔苏格兰〕浮尘,灰尘.

stour[2] [stuə] *a.* 〔苏格兰〕①强壮的. ②严厉的,苛刻的.

stout [staut] *a.* ①结实的;坚强的;坚牢的. ②坚定的,坚决的,断然的;勇敢的. ③粗大的,厚的,肥壮的,健壮的;强烈的. ④丰富的(食物等). *Grandma is a ~ old lady.* 祖母是个健壮的老太太. *I want a ~ bike, as the country road is bad.* 我要一辆结实的自行车,因为乡下的路不好走. *a ~ heart* 勇气;勇士. *It's the pay day, for he has brought home a ~ volume from a secondhand bookstore.* 今天发工资,因为他从旧书店里抱来一厚册书. — *n.* ①黑啤酒. ②烈性啤酒. ③特大号衣服. ④身体结实的人. **~-heart·ed** *a.* 勇敢的,无畏的.

stove[1] [stəuv] *n.* ①火炉,电炉,加热器. ②窑. ③干燥室,烘房. ④【园艺】温室. ⑤〔美俚〕烟斗. — *vt.* ①用火炉烤〔烘干〕. ②放入温室内培育. **~pipe** ①火炉烟囱管. ②〔俚〕大礼帽〔又叫 **~-pipe hat**〕; ③〔美俚〕闲谈. ④战壕迫击炮;喷气式战斗机. ⑤〔*pl.*〕〔美〕裤子. **~pipe committee** 〔美俚〕围炉闲谈;在办公室闲谈的人们. ~ **plant** 温室植物.

stove[2] [stəuv] stave 的过去式及过去分词.

sto·ver [ˈstəuvə] *n.* 〔英方〕谷草类干饲料,饲用茎叶.

stow [stəu] *vt.* ①装进 (*away; in; into*);装填,装载;堆垛,堆装. ②收藏,隐藏. ③卷起(帆等). ④使暂留. ⑤〔俚〕〔常用命令式〕不要,别,停止. *Before climbing, we ~ed a little cabin with supplies of mountaineering.* 爬山以前,我们把需要的物品堆放在一间小屋里. *S~ these away from the fire.* 这些东西堆得离火远些. *The doctor says the patient has to be ~ed in the emergency room.* 大夫说病人要暂时留在急诊室里. *S- the chatter!* 别胡扯! ~ ***away*** 收藏,收拾;躲在船里偷渡;〔谑〕吃光,吃得干干净净. ~ ***down*** 装入,装载. ~ ***larks!*** 别开玩笑!别闹着玩! ~ ***the hold with cargo*** 把货物装进舱里.

stow·age [ˈstəuidʒ] *n.* ①装载. ②贮藏;装载〔贮藏〕的处所〔物品、方法、数量、费用〕. ③食量,食欲.

stow·a·way [ˈstəuəwei] *n.* 躲在船里偷渡的人.

Stow(e) [stəu] *n.* 斯托〔姓氏〕.

STP = ①standard temperature and pressure 标准温度与压力. ②standard temperature and pulse 正常体温与脉搏. ③scientifically treated petroleum 放在发动机燃料油中的一种添加剂;一种产生幻觉的药〔性质似墨斯卡林及安非他明〕.

St. Pierre Is. [snt ˈpjɛə] *n.* 圣皮埃尔岛.

STR = submarine thermal reactor 潜水艇用热中子反应堆.

str. = ①steamer. ②strainer. ③strait. ④string(s). ⑤strophe.

stra·bis·mal, stra·bis·mic, -mi·cal [strəˈbizml, -mik(l)] *a.* 【医】斜视的,斜眼的.

stra·bis·mus [strəˈbizməs] *n.* 【医】斜视〔眼〕.

Stra·bo [ˈstreibəu] 斯特雷波 (63? B.C. — A.D.21?), 古希腊地理学家.

stra·bot·o·my [strəˈbɔtəmi] *n.* 【医】斜视纠正手术.

Stra·chey [ˈstreitʃi] *n.* 斯特雷奇〔姓氏〕.

strad·dle [ˈstrædl] *vi.* ①跨立,叉开腿(坐着);叉开腿走. ②不表明态度,骑墙观望. ③【军】为要确定射程而向目标物前后试击,夹叉射击〔轰炸〕. — *vt.* ①跨,骑. ②【军】向(目标)作夹叉射击〔轰炸〕. ③〔美口〕(对政治问题等)采取骑墙观望态度. ④【股】做一手买进一手卖出的交易. ⑤【扑克】加倍. — *n.* ①跨立,叉开两腿. ②大踏步. ③骑墙,观望. ④【军】夹叉射击〔轰炸〕. ⑤【股】一手买进一手卖出的交易. *You shouldn't have ~d when talking with the guests.* 你和客人们谈话的时候,本来不应该叉开腿坐着的. *It's the second time James ~ed. Maybe he'll back out.* 这是詹姆斯第二次不表态了,也许他要打退堂鼓. *George made pots of money by ~ling.* 乔治一手买进一手卖出地赚了一大笔钱. *~-trench* 【军】战地便坑. **-r** *n.*

strafe [strɑːf] *vt.* ①炮击. ②(飞机)扫射,轰炸. ②猛击;惩罚. — *n.* 低空扫射,猛烈轰炸;惩罚. **-r** *n.*

Straf·ford [ˈstræfəd] *n.* 斯特拉福德〔姓氏〕.

strag·gle [ˈstrægl] *vi.* ①迷路;掉队,和大队分离,被丢在后头,落后,落伍;彷徨,流离. ②蔓延,四散;散开,散在;零落,零乱 (*along*). ③(路、河等)纡曲,迤逦,蜿蜒. *The crowd ~d along.* 一大群人七零八落地走过去. *A wisp of hair ~d across her ear.* 一束头发散落在她耳朵上. *Weeds ~ over the garden.* 花园里野草蔓延. *The path ~s out a mile long.* 小路迤逦着一英里长.

strag·gler [ˈstræglə] *n.* ①迷路者;彷徨者;〔美〕荡游者;孤立者. ②【军】掉队者,归队迟到人员,掉队的飞机. ③失群之鸟. ④蔓生的草木. *cut off the ~s* 砍去冗枝. *a ~'s line* 【军】掉队兵收容线.

strag·gling [ˈstrægliŋ] *a.* ①落后的,掉队的. ②散漫的,零乱的,队伍散乱的. ③乱七八糟伸开的,蔓生的;散在的,零零落落的;断续的,稀落的. **-ly** *ad.*

strag·gly [ˈstrægli] *a.* = straggling.

straight [streit] *a.* ①直,一直线的 (*opp.* crooked, bent, curved). ②直挺的;向(目标)直进的. ③直接的,连续的. ④整齐的,规矩的,端正的,有条理的. ⑤正直的,坦率的,有品德的. ⑥〔口〕正确的,可靠的,没有错的(帐等);不加修改的,原样未改的,依次的. ⑦〔俚〕不搀杂的,纯净的;〔美口〕纯粹的. ⑧(发动机)汽缸直排式的. ⑨彻底支持某候选人〔政党〕的. ⑩不论买多少,价钱不变的. *a ~ line* 直线. ~ *hair* 不卷的头发. *a ~ face* (故意装做的)正经面孔. *a ~ accent* 长音符号. *a ~ top* 【机】平顶. *a ~ report* 可靠的报告. *a ~ comedy* 按照原作未加改动的喜剧. *a ~ thinker* 逻辑性强的思想家. *a whisky ~* 纯威士忌酒. *a ~ Republican* 顽固的共和党人. ***(as) ~ as an arrow*** 象箭一样直,笔直. ***be ~ with the world*** 〔美俚〕了清债务. ***get ~*** 〔美〕了解,搞通,办好,弄好. ***in ~ succession*** 连续不断. ***keep ~*** 行为正直,(女子)守贞操. ***make things ~*** 弄直,整顿. ***put [set] things ~*** 整顿〔收拾〕东西. — *ad.* ①直,笔直,垂直. ②正确;老实;率直,坦白;〔俚〕不搀水. ③直接,一直;接续不断地. ④立刻. *He will come ~ from Paris.* 他将直接从巴黎来. ***go ~*** 笔直走;正正经经做人. ***keep ~ on*** 继续快走. ***ride ~*** 骑马跳过障碍一直飞跑. ***run ~*** 笔直跑;正正经经做人,不做坏事. ***shoot [hit] ~*** 瞄准射击,使命中. ~ ***off*** 痛痛快快地,立刻,马上. ~ ***out*** 坦白,露骨 (*tell ~ out* 直讲). — *n.* ①直,直线. ②(赛跑跑道接近终点处的)直线部分. ③(纸牌的)五张牌点数连续的顺子. ④【拳击】直击. ⑤〔俚〕真相. ⑥(赛马)第一名. *They were even as they reached the ~.* 他们快到终点时还不分胜负. *Tell the party secretary the ~ of it.* 把实情告诉支书吧. ***follow the ~ and narrow*** 安分守己;循规蹈距. ***on the ~*** 笔直;老实地,正正经经地. ***out of the ~*** 歪着,弯着. ~ ***A*** 〔美〕成绩极优良的大学生. **~angle** 【数】直角. ~

arch【建】手拱. ~-**arm** (橄榄球)伸直手臂挡住对方. ~ **arrow** *a.* 规距的; 坦率的. ~-**arrow** *n.* 循规蹈距的人; 正直坦率的人. ~**away** 直线跑道; 陆路(或水路上)的直段. ~**chain**【化】直链. ~-**cut** (烟叶)纵切的. ~**edge** *n.* 直尺,标尺. *vt.* 把…一边弄直,用直尺检验. ~-**eight** (汽车)八汽缸直排式,直八式. ~ **eye** 能看出东西是否正或是否直的眼力. ~ **fight** 倾注全力的战斗;【政】两候选人的势均力敌的竞争. ~ **goods**〔美〕确确实实的消息;事实,真相. ~ **jacket** *n., vt.* = straitjacket. ~ **jet** (无螺旋桨的)喷气式飞机. ~ **laced** *a.* = straitlaced. ~ **line** *a.* 直线的,直排式的. ~ **man**〔美运〕被打败的对手;〔美剧〕给喜剧演员作笑料的配角. ~ **paper** 由一个人签发的流通票据. ~ **out** *n.* 对某一政党支持到底的人. *a.* 坦率的,彻底的. ~ **razor** (一般理发馆用的)折迭式剃刀. ~ **shoot**〔美〕直路;最直接的办法. ~ **shooter** 坦白正直的人. ~ **ticket**〔美政〕某一政党的全部候选人名单 (*vote the* ~ *ticket* 把票全投给一个政党的候选人). ~ **time**〔美〕规定工时;规定工时的工资率. ~-**way** *ad.* 直接地,立刻,马上; *a.* 畅通无阻的. **-ly** *ad.* **-ness** *n.*

straight·en [ˈstreitn] *vt.* ①弄直;矫正,纠正. ②整顿,整理. — *vi.* 变直;变正,变挺. *I've made up my mind to* ~ *out a very complicated subject.* 我已经下决心把一个非常复杂的题目搞清楚. *I'm going to* ~ *up my room.* 我马上整顿我的房间去. ~ ***one's face*** (笑过后)恢复正常面孔. ~ ***out*** 弄(得到)澄清;(得到)解决. ~ ***up***〔美〕改善; 正派地过日子. **-er** *n.* 矫正者;改正者;整顿者;【空】整流器.

straight·for·ward [streitˈfɔːwəd] *a.* ①一直向前的;直接的. ②真正的,老实的; 坦率的. ③直截了当的,易懂的. ④明确的. *The explanation was* ~. 解释直截了当. — *ad.* 坦率地. **-ly** *ad.* **-ness** *n.*

straight·for·wards [streitˈfɔːwədz] *ad.* 坦率地.

strain[1] [strein] *vt.* ①用力拉,拉紧,抽紧,扯紧. ②使紧张; 尽量使用(肌肉等). ③强迫,强制;滥用,尽量利用. ④拉伤,用力过度而弄伤,使工作过度;使用过度而弄坏;扭伤. ⑤曲解,牵强附会. ⑥【机】使变形,扭歪. ⑦抱紧. ⑧滤 *(out)*. — *vi.* ①尽力,拼命努力. ②拉,拖 *(at)*. ③扭歪,弯曲,快要折断. ④滤过,渗出. ⑤不肯接受. ~ *one's ears* 竖起耳朵注意听. ~ *one's voice* 拼命呼喊. ~ *one's eyes* 睁大眼睛看. ~ *one's wit* 绞尽脑汁. ~ *oneself* 过劳. ~ *one's authority* 滥用权力. ~ *sb.'s good temper* 利用某人脾气好. *Mary* ~*ed her baby to the breast.* 玛丽把小孩紧抱在怀里. ~ *a rope to the breaking point* 将绳拉紧到快要断的程度. ~*ed relations between officers and men* 搞得不好的官兵关系. ~ *the law* 曲解法律. *a* ~*d interpretation* 歪曲的翻译;牵强的解释. *He is* ~*ing under their pressure.* 他是在他们的压力之下苦撑着. *It's the nature of plants to* ~ *upwards to the light.* 植物的本性是向上挺窜争取阳光. *You, too, will* ~ *at such a demand.* 你也会难以接受这样的要求的. ~ ***a point*** 逾分,过分,任意(曲解). ~ ***after*** 尽力追求,拚命想得到[做到]. ~ ***at*** 为…辛苦[用气力、费神、尽力]. ~ ***at a gnat*** 为小事过分操心. ~ ***at the oar*** 拼命划. ~ ***courtesy*** 太讲礼貌,过分客气. ~ ***every nerve*** 倾全力;全神灌注 *(to do)*. ~ ***under pressure*** 在压迫下拼命挣扎. — *n.* ①拉紧;紧张;尽力,出力. ②过劳,使用过度;滥用,利用. ③扭筋,脱臼. ④【物】变形,歪曲;应力,张力;胁变,应变. ⑤曲解. *put a great* ~ *on sb.'s resources* 使人担负过重的经济负担. *It was a great* ~ *on my resources.* 这在我财力上是一个很大的负担. ***at full [utmost]*** ~ = ***be on the*** ~ 紧张,拼命. ***stand the*** ~ 拼命忍受. ***under the*** ~ 因紧张;因过劳. ~**ing piece [beam]**【建】跨腰梁.

strain[2] [strein] *n.* ①血统,家世;族,种;【生】品系,系;菌株;变种,小种. ②性格,脾气;倾向,气质. ③语气,笔调,文风;作风. ④〔常 *pl.*〕一段音乐,歌曲;诗歌. ⑤一阵子滔滔不绝的言词;一阵子难听的话. *She comes of a peasant* ~. 她出身于世代农家. *The Germany* ~ *in him makes him like philosophy.* 他的德意志民族的血统使得他喜欢研究哲学. *good* ~*s of seed* 良种. *a hybrid* ~ 杂交种. *a meat* ~ 肉用品种. *He has a* ~ *of melancholy in him.* 他有点忧郁. *in the same* ~ 以同样调子[作风]. *It was the commencement day and the head master would talk in a lofty* ~. 那天是始业礼,是校长高谈阔论的日子.

strained [streind] *a.* 紧张的; 勉强的,不自然的(态度等); 牵强附会的(解释等). *Notice the* ~ *manners of George before strangers.* 你注意乔治在陌生人面前的不自然的样子. *Let's straighten out their* ~ *relations.* 咱们把他们之间的紧张关系和解了吧.

strain·er [ˈstreinə] *n.* ①用力拉的人,使劲的人,紧张的人[物]. ②粗滤器,滤网. ③【机】松紧螺旋扣.

strait [streit] *a.*〔古〕①窄,狭,狭隘的,窄小的(地方、衣服等). ②艰难的,窘迫的,穷困的(家境等). ③【圣】严格的,严厉的. *a* ~ *door* 一个狭窄的门. *a* ~ *Catholic sect* 一个严格的天主教教派. — *n.* ①〔常 *pl.* 作单数用〕海峡. ②〔常 *pl.*〕窘迫,穷困,艰难. ③〔罕〕地峡. ④【解】(狭)口. *the Straits* (1) = the straits of Gibraltar. (2) Malacca 海峡. ***in great*** ~***s*** 处境非常困难. ***in*** ~***s for*** 缺乏(某物). ***in increasingly dire*** ~***s*** 处境越来越糟. ~ **jacket** = strait waistcoat. ~-**laced** *a.* 穿着紧身的衣服的;(极端)严谨的,拘谨的,拘泥的;观念狭隘的. ~ **waistcoat** (束缚疯子或狂暴的囚犯用的)紧衣;拘束,束缚. **-ly** *ad.*〔古〕狭,窄;严格. **-ness** *n.*〔古〕窄,狭隘;严厉,严格;困难,艰难,窘迫,缺乏 (*-ness of mind* 思想狭隘,气量小,小心眼儿).

strait·en [ˈstreitn] *vt.* 弄窄;〔古〕限制,收缩,收紧;〔主用 *p.p.*〕折磨,使窘迫. ***be*** ~***ed for*** 缺乏,苦于没有.

strake [streik] *n.* ①轮箍. ②【船】列钣,外钣;船底板. ③(选矿)淘汰盘. ④条纹;狭长(草)地.

stra·mash [strəˈmæʃ, ˈstræməʃ] *n.*〔Scot.〕骚乱;口角,争吵;击碎,撞毁.

stra·mo·ni·um [strəˈməuniəm] *n.*【植】曼陀罗花; 曼陀罗叶〔气喘药〕.

strand[1] [strænd] *n.* ①〔诗〕(海、湖、河等的)滨,岸滩. ②〔the S-〕(伦敦的)河滨马路. — *vt., vi.* ①使(船)触礁;触礁,搁浅. ②(使)处于困境,(使)落后. ***be*** ~***ed*** 搁浅;窘迫,进退两难;因资金匮缺,处于困境(*There were no jobs and most of them were* ~*ed in an alien environment.* 那儿并没有工作可找; 他们中的大多数人都在异国环境里进退两难.) ~ **line** (水退前的)海岸水线.

strand[2] [strænd] *n.* ①(绳子的)股,绞;一股绳子;纤维,绳,线;串. ②【电】导线束;多心裸电缆. ③(思想等的)一个组成部分. — *vt.* ①拆开绳股. ②绞. ③打(绳子). ~*ed wire* 绞合金属线. **-er** 搓绳者,拆绳者;搓绳机.

strandee [strænˈdiː] *n.* (因事故而)中途滞留的旅客.

strange [streindʒ] *a.* ①奇怪的,古怪的,不可思议的. ②不认识的,陌生的;不熟悉的. ③生疏的;没有经验的,生手的,外行的. ④疏远的,冷淡的,不亲热的. ⑤外国的,异乡的,别处的. *He is still* ~ *to the job.* 他还不太习惯这个工作. ~ *fish*〔口〕怪人. *I am quite* ~ *here [to this place].* 我在这里十分人地生疏. *The newcomer is very* ~ *in his manner.* 这新来的人举动上很古怪. *I'm* ~ *at bridge.* 我对桥牌是外行. *Your friends will help you when you're in a* ~ *land.* 你在国外的时候,你的朋友们会帮你的忙的. ***feel*** ~身体有点不对,觉得不舒服; 头晕眼花,发晕;觉得奇怪,觉得不安定. ***make oneself*** ~ 装做生人;装做不知道,装做惊奇的样子. ~ ***as it may sound*** 听[说]起来也许奇怪. ~ ***to say [tell]*** 说也奇怪. **-ly** *ad.* **-ness** *n.*【物】(量子数的)奇异性.

stran·ger [ˈstreindʒə] *n.* ①陌生人,不认识的人;新来的人;客人;异乡人;外国人. ②局外人,门外汉;没有经验的人；不熟悉的人．③【法】第三者，非当事人．④〔美〕先生〔= sir：在乡下对陌生人打招呼用的称呼〕．*the little* ～〔俚〕小孩子．*He is a* ～ *to me.* 我不认识他．*You are quite a* ～.〔口〕好久不见了．*a* ～ *in a strange land* 住在异乡的外国人．*I see [spy]* ～*s*.【英下院】要求禁止旁听，要求旁听者退场．***a*** ～ ***to ...*** 不知道，不懂得；陌生，不习惯于 (*He is a* ～ *to fear.* 他不晓得害怕)．***be shy in the presence of*** ～***s*** 怕生，(小孩子)认生．***make a*** ～ ***of*** 冷淡对待．***make no*** ～ ***of*** 亲热对待．***make oneself a*** ～ 装规矩；拘礼．***no*** ～ ***to*** (*sorrow, poverty*) 饱经(忧患、贫困)．

stran·gle [ˈstræŋgl] *vt.* ①扼死，勒死，绞死．②闷住，塞住呼吸；(硬领等)扼住(脖子)；闭住(呼吸)．③压住；压制．～ *a bill* 压住议案．— *vi.* ①扼(勒，绞)死．②窒息而死．*It is said that he was* ～*ed to death by gas.* 据说他是被煤气熏死的．*When I attended his lecture, I always tried hard to* ～ *yawnings.* 我上他的课时，总是竭力地制止自己打呵欠．～ **hold** *n.* ①【摔角】勒颈；压制．②束缚，压制．

stran·gler [ˈstræŋglə] *n.* ①扼杀者，压制者．②〔英〕【机】阻气门，阻塞门．

stran·gles [ˈstræŋglz] *n.*〔*pl.*〕(作单数用)【兽医】腺疫，传染性卡他．

stran·gu·late [ˈstræŋgjuleit] *vt.* 勒死，绞死；使窒息；【医】绞扼，绞窄(肠子等)．— *vi.*【医】绞扼，绞窄．

stran·gu·la·tion [ˌstræŋgjuˈleiʃən] *n.* 绞窄；窒息．

stran·gu·ry [ˈstræŋgjuri] *n.*【医】痛性尿淋沥．

strap [stræp] *n.* ①带，皮〔布、铁〕带，铁皮条，(电车等的)拉手吊带．②磨刀皮带．③肩章．④搭扣鞋．⑤〔the ～〕鞭打．⑥【机】狭〔带〕条，套带，带圈．⑦【医】橡皮膏．⑧【海】(滑车的)带索．⑨【植】小舌片．⑩〔俚〕信用，赊．⑪【电】捷接，母线．⑫〔爱尔兰〕轻佻女子，娼妓．***on (the)*** ～ 凭信用，赊．— *vt.* ①用带子捆扎；用皮带捆．②用皮带抽打．③用皮带磨．④【医】贴上橡皮膏 (*up; down*)．*The nurse will* ～ *up your wound.* 护士会绑扎你的伤口．*She works with a baby* ～*ped to her back.* 她劳动时把小孩用带子捆扎在背上．～ ***at [to] one's work*** 拼命工作．～ **brake**【机】带闸．～ **hanger** (电车上)拉着吊带站着的乘客．～ **hinge** 束带式铰链；铁板铰．～**-laid** *a.* 用两条三股绳平列缝合的．～**less** 无带的，无肩带的．(～*less bra* 无肩带乳罩)．～**-oil**〔俚〕鞭打．～ **work** 用窄带折迭(或交织)而成的装饰图案．～ **wort**【植】海滨寇秋罗．

strappa·do [strəˈpeidəu] *n.* (*pl.* ～*es*) (从前的)吊坠刑(将犯人用绳吊起然后坠下)．②吊坠刑机器．— *vt.* 处吊坠刑．

strapped [stræpt] *a.* ①用皮带捆住的，勒有皮带的；用皮带装饰的．②〔美俚〕资金短少的，身无分文的．

strap·per [ˈstræpə] *n.* ①用皮带捆绑的人．②用磨刀皮带磨刀的人．③马夫．④〔口〕粗大东西；身材魁梧的人，彪形大汉．

strap·ping [ˈstræpiŋ] *a.* ①〔口〕魁梧的，强壮的，高大而匀称的．— *n.* 皮带材料；橡皮膏；贴膏法．

Stras·bourg, Strass·burg [ˈstræzbəːg] *n.* 斯特拉斯堡〔法国城市〕．

strass [stræs] *n.* 施特拉斯铅玻璃〔一种极闪亮的铅玻璃，用以造假宝石，得名于发明者德国人约瑟夫·施特拉斯〕．

stra·ta [ˈstreitə] stratum 的复数．

strat·a·gem [ˈstrætidʒəm] *n.* 战略，策略；谋略；计策，诡计．

stra·tal [ˈstreitl] *a.*【地】成层的，有层次的；地层的．

stra·te·gic(al) [strəˈtiːdʒik(əl)] *a.* ①战略(上)的；(战略上)重要的．②为战略计划用的．～ *bombardment* 战略轰炸．～ *bombers* 战略轰炸机．～ *materials* 战略物资．～ *points* 战略据点．～ *retreat* 战略退却．

stra·te·gi·cal·ly [strəˈtidʒikəli] *ad.* 战略上，颇为策略地．

stra·te·gics [strəˈtidʒiks] *n.* 战略(学)；兵法．

strat·e·gist [ˈstrætidʒist] *n.* 战略家．*a military* ～ 军事家．

strat·e·gy [ˈstrætidʒi] *n.* ①战略(学)．②策略，作战方针 (*cf.* tactics)．～ *and tactics* 战略与战术．*I know his conception of political* ～. 我晓得他的政治策略的概念．～ *of trading space for time* 用空间换取时间的战略．

Strat·ford-on-Avon [ˈstrætfədɔnˈeivən] *n.* 斯特拉特福〔英国市镇，在埃冯河畔，莎士比亚的故乡〕．

strath [stræθ] *n.*〔Scot.〕老谷底；平底河谷．

strath·spey [stræθˈspei] *n.* (苏格兰)斯特拉斯贝舞〔曲〕．

strat·i [ˈstreitai] stratus 的复数．

strat·i·cu·late [strəˈtikjulit] *a.*【地】薄层的；成薄层的，分层的．**-la·tion** [-ˌtikjuˈleiʃən] *n.*

strat·i·fi·ca·tion [ˌstrætifiˈkeiʃən] *n.* ①【地】层理；分层，层叠形成，成层作用〔现象〕．②【园艺】砂藏．

strat·i·form [ˈstrætiˌfɔːm] *a.* 成层状的；显出层理的；层状的〔如云层〕．

strat·i·fy [ˈstrætifai] *vt.* ①使成层，使分层．②【园艺】层积(保藏)．*stratified alluvium* 成层冲积岩．*stratified rock* 成层岩．*stratified sampling*【统】分层抽样．— *vi.* 成层；分层．

stra·tig·ra·pher [strəˈtigrəfə] *n.* 地层学家．

stra·tig·ra·phic(al) [ˌstrætiˈgræfik(əl)] *a.*【地】地层学的．**-cal·ly** *ad.*

stra·tig·ra·phy [strəˈtigrəfi] *n.* ①地层．②地层学．**-pher** *n.* **-graph·ic** [-ˈgræfik] *a.*

strato- *comb. f.* 表示"层"：*strato*cumulus.

stra·to-cham·ber [ˈstrætəuˌtʃeimbə] *n.* 同温研究室．

stra·to·cir·rus [ˌstrætəuˈsirəs] *n.*【气】低浓层卷云．

stra·toc·ra·cy [strəˈtɔkrəsi] *n.* 军人政治，军阀政治．

stra·to·cruis·er [ˈstreitəukruːzə] *n.* 同温层飞机．

stra·to·cu·mu·lus [ˌstrætəuˈkjuːmjuləs] *n.*【气】层积云．

stra·to-liner [ˈstrætəuˌlainə] *n.* 同温层客机〔班机〕．

stra·to·plane [ˈstrætəuplein] *n.* 同温层飞机．

strat·o·sphere [ˈstrætəusfiə] *n.* ①【气】同温层，平流层．②最上层，最高栏，最高部位．③艰深的学科领域．*a* ～ *Joe*〔美空军口〕高个子，长人．*a* ～ *plane* = stratoplane.

strat·o·spher·ic [ˌstrætəuˈsferik] *a.* 同温层的．

strat·o·vi·sion [ˈstrætəuˌviʒən] *n.*【无】同温层；(通过飞机)转播电视．

stra·tum [ˈstreitəm] *n.* (*pl.* **-ta**) ①地层；层．②阶层．*the field* ～ 地面植被层．*the privileged* ～ 特权阶层．*in all social strata.* 社会各阶层的．

stra·tus [ˈstreitəs] *n.* (*pl.* **-ti** [-tai])【气】层云．

Straus(s) [straus] *n.* 斯特劳斯〔姓氏〕．

stra·vage [strəˈveig] *vi.* (**-vaged; -vag·ing**)〔Scot.〕漫游；游荡 (= stravaig)．

straw [strɔː] *n.* ①稻草，麦秆．②(用稻草，麦秆做成的)东西，(吸冷饮用)麦秆状吸管；草帽〔又叫 ～ hat〕．③不值钱的东西，琐细无聊的事情；一点点．④〔美俚〕头子；帮手，助理．— *a.* ①稻草的，麦秆的．②稻草〔麦秆〕做的．③〔口〕不值钱的，无用的，琐细的．④(作为替身的)稻草人般的；假的〔如作为民意测验的假投票〕；假想的．*A* ～ *shows which way the wind blows.* 草动知风向，观微知著．*They suck soda water through* ～*s (tube).* 他们用麦秆喝汽水．*Cover the heap of* ～ *when it rains.* 下雨时，把草堆盖上．***(a)*** ～***(s) in the wind*** 风向指标，舆论指标，显示大动向的小事．***as a last*** ～ (不断吃亏〔遭殃〕)终于，到了最后．***catch*** (***clutch, grasp***) ***at a*** ～ (落水的人)抓住稻草，抓住靠不住的东西不放．***draw*** ～***s*** 抓(稻草)阄．***gather [pick]*** ～***s*** 想睡．***in the*** ～〔古〕(产妇)做月子．***make bricks without*** ～ 想做不能做的事情．***man of*** ～ 稻草人；没财产的人；靠不住

的人；假想敌。***not care a ～ [two ～s, three ～s]*** 一点儿也不介意。***not worth a ～*** 毫无价值。***One's eyes draw [gather, pick] ～s.*** 昏昏欲睡。***out of the ～*** 分娩之后。***split ～s*** 为一些小事而争吵。***the last ～*** (一系列打击中)终于使人不能忍受的最后一击[最后因素]。***throw ～s against the wind*** 扬草抵风，螳臂挡车。～**bail**〔美〕无资力的保人。～**board** 纸板，马粪纸。～**bond**〔美俚〕假证券。～**boss**〔口〕工头助手。～**colo(u)r** 稻草色，淡黄色。～**dicer**〔美〕麦秸草帽。～**flower** 终年不谢的野花。～**hat theatre** 夏季剧院。～**in the boots**〔美〕财产。～**man** ①稻草人。②无足轻重的人物。③(为了制造取胜的假象而假设的)易于击败的敌对论点。④被用来作挡箭牌的人。～**plait** 草帽缏。～**poll**〔英〕＝～vote. ～**rope** 草绳。～**vote** (考验候选人威望的)测验投票。～**stem** 一种细脚酒杯。～**wine** 稻草葡萄酒〔在酿制前，葡萄先放在稻草垫上晒干，故名〕。～**worm** ①毛翅目昆虫的幼虫(水栖，用为鱼饵)。②膜翅目昆虫的幼虫(有害麦类)。～**yellow** 淡黄色。

straw·ber·ry [ˈstrɔːbəri] *n.*【植】草莓。*a ～ blonde*〔美俚〕红发女郎。～ *leaves*〔英〕公爵的爵位象徵〔因为用草莓叶做冠饰〕；公爵们。*We grow ～ies in our garden.* 我们的园子里种草莓。～**bass**【动】(黑色)北美日鲈。～**bush**【植】美洲卫茅。～**mark** (草莓状)红色胎记，莓状痣。～**roan** 枣红色[红棕色]的马。～**shrub**【植】洋腊梅(属)。～**tomato**【植】酸浆属植物。～**tree**【植】①莓实树。②美洲卫茅。

straw·y [ˈstrɔːi] *a.* ***(-i·er; -i·est)*** 稻草[麦秸]的，稻草[麦秸]做的；稻草[麦秸]形的。

stray [strei] *vi.* ①迷路；走失，失散。②误入歧途，堕落；(议论)离题；(思想)迷失方向。③彷徨，游荡，漂泊。*Be careful not to ～ from [off] the right path of duty.* 注意不要偏离应尽职责的正道。*Don't ～ from the main point of the question.* 不要离开问题的主要之点。—*a.* ①迷了路的，走失了的，离了群的，失散了的。②意外的，零落的，偶然见到的(例子等)；偶然跑来的(客人等)。*a ～ child* 迷路的孩子。*a ～ customer* 偶然的顾客。*a ～ bullet* 流弹。～ *light* 散射光，漫射光。～ *capacity*【电】杂散电容。— *n.* ①迷路者；迷路(离群的)家畜；无家可归的人；迷路的孩子。②〔英〕〔*pl.*〕因无人继承而归公的遗产。③〔*pl.*〕【无】天电，杂电。④【地】(石油钻探中)偶然出现的间层，杂层。**-er** 迷路者；流浪者；不走正路的人。

streak [striːk] *n.* ①纹理，条纹，斑纹，条痕，条层，色条，色线。②【矿】矿脉，矿层；矿物痕[粉]色。③【微】划线，条斑。④倾向；气味(性格上不太显著的)特色。⑤〔口〕一连串，一系列。⑥〔美口〕短时期，暂时。*～s of red light in the east* 东方上空的红光条纹。*He has a ～ of obstinacy in him.* 他有一点儿固执。*a ～ of lightning* 一道闪电。*She has had a long ～ of bad luck.* 她遭遇了一连串的不幸。*I'll hit a ～ someday.* 有一天我会走段好运。***go like a ～***〔美俚〕飞跑。***have a ～ of*** 有…的气味。***(off) like a ～ (of lightning)*** (闪电一样)迅速，风驰电掣地。***the silver～***〔英〕英吉利海峡。— *vt.*〔通例用 *p.p.*〕加纹理，加条纹。—*vi.* 成条纹；〔常作～it〕象闪电一样发光；飞跑。～**camera** 扫描照相机。～**disease**【植】条死病。**-er** *n.* 裸跑者。

streak·ed [striːkt] *a.* 有纹理的，有条纹的；〔美〕狼狈的，慌张的，不安的。**-ly** *ad.*

streak·ing [ˈstriːkiŋ] *n.*〔美〕裸体飞跑。

streak·y [ˈstriːki] *a.* ***(-i·er; -i·est)*** ①有纹理的，有条纹的。②〔口〕不均匀的，混杂的，多变的。③〔俚〕易怒的，脾气坏的。④忧虑的，担心的，不安的。*Wash your dirty ～ face, Johnny.* 洗你那赃的有了泥条的脸去，姜尼。*He is always nervous and ～ about the final exam.* 他对大考总是感到放心不下的。**-i·ly** *ad.* **-i·ness** *n.*

stream [striːm] *n.* ①河流，小河；川，溪。②流出，流注；一连串，(人物等的)辈出。③(事件等的)连续；(财富等的)滚滚而来。④趋势，倾向，潮流。⑤〔英〕(一个年级学生中按智力划分的)班组。*A bridge is being built over the foaming ～.* 正在这条怒流滚滚的河上建造一座桥。*The accident delayed a long ～ of cars, buses and bicycles.* 这事故阻碍住一条汽车、公共汽车和自行车的长流。*a ～ of lava* 熔岩流。*sun ～s* 太阳光线。*the ～ of time [times]* 时代趋势。*the ～ of popular opinion* 舆论趋势。*the ～ of thought* 思潮。***against the ～*** 逆流；违反时势。***down (the) ～*** 顺流，向下游。***go by in a ～*** 一连串陆续通过。***in ～s [a ～]*** 连续，陆续，接连，川流不息地。***in the ～*** 在河的中流。***up (the) ～*** 逆流，向上游。***with the ～***顺流；顺应时势。— *vi.* ①流，流动；(泪等)流出；(光线等)射出。②蜂拥而进，鱼贯而行，川流不息地通过。③(旗等)飘扬，招展；(头发)飘动。— *vt.* ①使流，使流出，倾注。②使飘扬、展开(旗帜等)。③把学生按智力等分班。*Students are now ～ing back to their dormitories.* 现在学生们川流不息地回到宿舍去。*I turned off the light and let the moonlight ～ in through the window-* 我关上电灯，让月光从窗间照射进来。*The red flag is ～ing in the wind.* 红旗在风中飘扬。*a ～ing cold* 流鼻涕淌眼泪的感冒。*a ～ing umbrella* 淌着雨水的伞。*crowd ～ing past* 接连不断走过的群众。*Her eyes ～ed tears.* 她的眼睛流泪。*The honeysuckle was ～ing scent.* 忍冬花放出香气。*The school ～s pupils into three classes.* 学校按智力把学生分成三班。～**line** *n., a., vt.* ①【物】流线。②流线型(的)。③做成流线型；调整机构(使现代化或提高效率)(*a ～lined method* 流水作业法。*a ～lined car* 流线型汽车)。～**liner** 流线型火车〔飞机(等)〕。～**of consciousness** 意识流。～**time** 连续开工时间，工作周期。**-d** *a.* ①＝～line. ②最新式的。

stream·er [ˈstriːmə] *n.* ①飘扬的旗幡(作装饰的)飘带(等)。②测风带。③横幅标语。④〔新闻语〕横贯全版的大标题。⑤【气】光冪；〔*pl.*〕北极光。⑥【电】流光，射光；(电子雪崩产生的)电子流。*a paper ～* 五彩纸带〔开船时送别用(等)〕。

stream·ing [ˈstriːmiŋ] *n.* ①流动。②【生】胞质环流。③〔主英〕学生编班制。

stream·let [ˈstriːmlit] *n.* 小河，细流，小溪。

stream·y [ˈstriːmi] *a.* ①河流多的。②流水般的。③发光的。

street [striːt] *n.* ①街，街道，马路。〔美〕(东西向的)纬路。②车道 *(opp.* sidewalk*)*。③街区；街区居民。④〔the S-〕〔英口〕＝Lombard S-, Fleet S-；〔美口〕＝Wall S-. ⑤〔美俚〕释放出狱，自由。*I met him in* [〔美〕*on*] *the ～.* 我在街上碰见他。*a main [side] ～* 大[背]街。***be dressed for the ～*** 穿着上街的服装。***beat the ～s*** 巡街。***(go) on the ～s*** 漂泊在街上；在街头做妓女。***in the open ～*** 在街上，公然。***in the ～*** 在户外，在屋外。***live in the ～*** 老是在外头，老是不在家。***not in the same ～ with***〔口语〕(能力)不能与…相比。***not the length of a ～*** 相差不远。***take to the ～s*** 睡在街上，走上街头[游行]等。***walk the ～s*** (在街头)作妓女。～**Arab [arab, urchin]** 流浪儿。～**booking office** 市内车票发售处。～**car**〔美〕市内有轨电车。～**cries** (小贩)叫卖声。～**door** 临街大门。～**fighting** 巷战。～**girl** 妓女，～**-map (～-plan)** 街道图。～**market**【交易所】场外市场[交易]。～**orderly**〔英〕街道清扫工。～**paper** 短期支票。～**people** 街头颓废派。～**price** (交易所)场外行情。～**sweeper** ①扫街车，清道机。②街道清洁工。～**walker** 妓女。～**walking** *n.* 卖淫。～**yarn**〔美〕道听途说，无稽之谈。

strem·ma [ˈstremə] *n.*【医】关节脱臼。

strength [streŋkθ] *n.* ①力，力量，实力，体力。②强度，浓度，(要塞等的)抵抗力；长处。③实力；兵力；全体人数，额定人数，编制。④笔力；文势。⑤(证券等)市价坚挺。⑥〔美俚〕(可能的)利润。*have not the ～ to do it* 没有气力做这个。*That will add ～ to your argument.* 那会增加你的辩论的力量的. *Take part in the physical exercises and build up your* ~. 参加体育活动增强体力. *the* ~ *of will* 意志力. *the* ~ *of the alcohol* 这酒精的浓度. *fighting* ~ 战斗力. *mobilized* ~ 战时编制. *effective* ~ 实额,实际人数. *a policy of* ~ 实力政策. *What is your* ~? 你们一共有多少人? *a tower of* ~ 金城铁壁. *the breaking [shock, tensile]* ~ 抗断[抗冲、抗拉]强度. *the working* ~ 资用强度. ~ *of draught* 【机】通风强度. ~ *of material* 材料力学. ~ *of structure* 构造力学. ***be [be taken] on the*** ~【军】编入编制内. ***below*** ~ 不够编制. ***by main*** ~ 奋力. ***in full*** ~ 全体动员. ***in (great)*** ~ 人多势众地, 用巨大力量. ***on the*** ~〔英口语〕在士兵名册上. ***on [upon] the*** ~ ***of*** 依赖, 靠着. ***up to*** ~ 够编制. ***with all one's*** ~ 尽力.

strength·en [ˈstreŋθən] *vt.* ①加强,巩固,使强壮,使坚强有力; 增强实力. ②勉励, 激励. ③增加…的艺术效果. — *vi.* ①实力增强; 变强. ②(价格) 上涨, 坚挺. *The enemy has* ~*ed their defensive position.* 敌人已经加强了他们的防御阵地. *Criticism and self-criticism* ~*s unity.* 批评自我批评巩固了团结. ~ ***sb.'s hand*** 增加某人的资本(实力). ~ ***sb.'s hands*** 使某人得以采取强有力的行动.

stren·u·ous [ˈstrenjuəs] *a.* ①勤奋的,用力的,费劲的,紧张的; 热心的; 热烈的. *a* ~ *job* 一桩费劲的活儿. *a* ~ *examination* 紧张的考试. *make* ~ *efforts* 鼓足干劲, 尽力. **-ly** *ad.* 拼命地. **-ness** *n.*

strep [strep] *n.* streptococcus 的缩略形式.

Streph·on [ˈstrefɔn] *n.* 苦恋的男子〔Sidney 叙事诗中的主人公,牧童〕. ~ **and Chloe** [ˈkləui] 一对恋人.

strep·i·to·so [strepiˈtəusəu] *ad.* 〔It.〕【乐】喧闹地.

strep·to·coc·cus [ˌstreptəuˈkɔkəs] *n.* *(pl.* **-coc·ci** [-ˈkɔkai]*)* 链球菌. **-coc·cic, -coc·cal** *a.*

strep·to·ki·nase [ˌstreptəˈkaineis, -ˈkineis] *n.*【生化】链激酶.

strep·to·my·ces [ˌstreptəˈmaisiːz] *n.* *(pl.* -*ces)*【生】链丝菌属 *(streptomyces)* 菌.

strep·to·my·cin [streptəuˈmaisin] *n.*【药】链霉素.

strep·to·thri·cin [ˈstreptəθraisin] *n.*【生化】链丝菌素,紫放线菌素.

stress [stres] *n.* ①压力,压迫,紧迫,紧张. ②【语音】重音; 重读;【诗】扬音; 语势,着重点. ③重要(性),重点,强调. ④【物】应力; 胁强,重力. *The landlord has imposed a severe* ~ *on the poor tenants.* 房东给贫苦的房客们加了很大的压力. *We must lay* ~ *on self reliance.* 我们必须强调自立更生. *Give* ~ *to the 2nd. syllable.* 重读第二音节. ~ *diagram*【工】应力图. *moisture* ~ 缺水. *tensile* ~【材】抗张应力. ***driven by*** ~ ***of*** = under ~ of. ***in times of*** ~ 在紧张〔繁忙, 困难〕的时候. ***lay [place, put]*** ~ ***on*** 强调, 用力于, 着重于. ***under*** ~ ***of*** 被…逼迫着,在…强制下,由于, 因为. — *vt.* ①着重,强调,加重语气说. ②用重音读. ③加压力[应力], 压, 压迫. **-om·e·ter** [-ˈsɔmitə] *n.*【物】应力计. ~ **mark** 重读符号. **-ful** *a.* **-less** *a.*

stretch [stretʃ] *vt.* ①伸展,伸出; 展开,铺开,扩张; 张,绷,拉直; 拉长,拉扯. ②使(精神, 肌肉等)紧张, 倾注全力; 睁大(两眼等). ③勉强解释,曲解; 充分利用; 乱用,滥用(法律等); 夸大(地讲). ④〔俚〕打倒在地. ⑤〔俚〕吊死; 绞死; 作装殓[埋葬]准备. — *vi.* ①伸展,伸长,扩展; (时间)继续,拖长,延长到; 伸手(脚),伸懒腰; 能伸长; 能扩张. ②夸大地讲,吹牛. ③【海】张帆航行; 前进; 努力. ④做吃饭时的侍应员. ⑤〔俚〕被吊死; 绞死. ~ *a carpet* 铺开地毯. ~ *an umbrella* 撑开洋伞. ~ *out a helping hand* 伸出一只援助的手. *She* ~*ed herself to provide for the family.* 她竭尽全力养家活口. *yawn and* ~ *(oneself)* 打呵欠伸懒腰. *He lay* ~*ed on the lawn.* 他伸开四肢躺在草地上. *The forest* ~*es for miles.* 森林绵延数英里. *His memory* ~*es back to his early childhood.* 他回想起自己的童年. ~ ***a point*** 勉强让步,例外办理[应允]. ~ ***for the impossible*** 勉强去做那些做不到的事情. ~ ***one's credit*** 滥用信用. ~ ***one's powers*** 滥用权力. ~ ***one's legs*** (久坐后)伸腿,散步. ~ ***out*** 伸手; 开始大踏步走. ~ ***to the oar [stroke]*** 用力划. — *n.* ①伸,伸开,伸出,伸长,延亘,连绵. ②紧张; 过度伸张,延伸. ③持续的一段时间,一段路程,一口气;【海】一气航行的距离. ④(赛马场两边的)直线跑道, 最后阶段. ⑤滥用; 越权. ⑥夸张; 夸张话. ⑦〔俚〕徒刑(尤指)一年徒刑. ⑧弹性 *There is a* ~ *of hills near the village.* 在村子附近有一片连绵的小山. *To impose a penalty on smoking in the street is a* ~ *of the law.* 对在街上吸烟罚款是对法律的滥用. *a long* ~ *of time* 一段长时间. *a* ~ *of sea* 一段海滩. *a* ~ *of road [open country, water]* 一段道路[一片原野, 一片汪洋]. ***all the*** ~ ***was gone*** 拉长到不能再拉. ***at a*** ~ 一气儿,不休息地 (*work for six hours at a* ~ 一气工作六个钟头). ***beyond the*** ~ ***of*** 超乎…范围以外. ***bring to the*** ~ 尽力, 紧张. ***by a*** ~ ***of imagination*** 想入非非. ***link up into a single*** ~ 连成一片. ***on a*** ~ = at a ~. ***on [upon] the*** ~ 紧张着. ***put [set] upon the (full)*** ~ 使极度紧张,倾注全力. ***to the utmost [furthest]*** ~ 极度,到极点. ***with a*** ~ ***and a yawn*** 伸着懒腰打着呵欠. — *a.* 弹性的, 有弹力的. ~ *woven fabrics* 弹性织物. ~ *hosiery* 弹力袜.

stretch·a·bil·i·ty [ˌstretʃəˈbiliti] *n.* 伸展,铺开,拉长; 紧张; 曲解,夸大.

stretch·er [ˈstretʃə] *n.* ①伸张者; 拉伸机,延伸器,伸张器; 绷开用具,鞋绷,帽绷,绷画布的框子(等). ②担架. ③【建】顺(砌)砖,顺边砖,横砌石. ④(桌椅腿之间的)横档; 划手的蹬脚板. ⑤(钓鱼用的)蚊钩. ⑥〔俚〕夸张话,谎话. *a pulse* ~ 脉冲展宽器. *a* ~ *bearer* 担架手. *a* ~ *case* 重伤. ~ *bond*【建】顺砖砌合. ~*-party* 担架队.

stretch-out [ˈstretʃaut] *n.*〔美口〕(增加工作量而不加或不按比例增加工资的)加紧劳动强度的工业管理制度; 少花钱多办事的节约措施.

stretch·y [ˈstretʃi] *a.* ①能伸长的,有弹性的; 易伸长的. ②想伸伸懒腰的. ~ nylon 弹性尼龙.

streu·sel [ˈstruːzl, ˈstrɔi-; G. ˈʃtrɔizəl] *n.* (撒在糕点上的)糖粉奶油细末.

strew [struː] *vt.* *(*~*ed;* ~*ed, strewn* [struːn]*)* ①撒(沙、花等)在…上; 播; 散播. ②点缀 *(with)*, 铺盖. *The table is strewn with books.* 桌子铺满了书. *Their custom is to* ~ *flowers over the graves.* 他们的风俗是在坟墓上撒花.

stri·a [ˈstraiə] *n.* *(pl.* **stri·ae** [ˈstraiiː]*)* ①【解、动、植】线条,(条)纹,壳纹; 壳线间隙; (昆虫的)陷线. ②【地】条痕,擦痕. ③【建】柱沟.

stri·ate [ˈstraieit] *vt.* 加条纹,加条痕.

stri·at·e(d) [ˈstraieit(id)] *a.* 有条纹的,有细槽[壳纹]的. **-ly** *ad.*

stri·a·tion, stri·a·ture [straiˈeiʃən, -ˈeitʃə] *n.* (有)条纹,(有)条痕; 擦痕;【物】辉纹.

strick [strik] *n.*【纺】(绢纺的)切丝,(拣麻后的)小麻把.

strick·en [ˈstrikən] *v.* 〔古〕 strike 的过去分词. — *a.* ①被打伤的,受了伤的(鹿); 被侵害的; 受了创伤的; 用斗刮刮平了的. ②〔构成复合词〕受…灾的,患…病的,为…苦恼着的. *a* ~ *deer* 负了伤的鹿. *a* ~ *field* 〔古〕大决战; 战场. *a famine-*~ *area* 受灾地区. *poverty-*~ 为贫困所苦恼着的. ~ ***with*** 被…折磨, 患(…病等). ***well*** ~ ***in years*** 相当上了年纪的, 衰老的. ~ **hour** 整整一小时.

strick·le [ˈstrikl] *n.* ①斗刮. ②【机】元刮板; 刮型器,铸型棍. ③【机】磨石; 油石. ④磨镰刀器.

strict [strikt] *a.* ①严格的; 严厉的. ②精确的,精密的; 严谨的; 严密的. ③【植】笔直的. ④〔古〕紧密的,亲密的. *You seem too* ~ *with your young ones.* 你对小孩子们似乎

太严厉了. *He is very ~ in observing the regulations.* 他在遵守规章方面很严格. *~ discipline* 严格的训练. *a ~ observer of rules* 严守规则的人. ***in ~ confidence*** 十分秘密. ***in the ~ sense of the word*** 严格地讲. ***live in ~ seclusion*** 完全隐居. **-ness** *n.*

stric·tion [ˈstrikʃən] *n.* 收紧;收缩,压缩.

strict·ly [ˈstriktli] *ad.* ①严格地. ②精密地;严密地. ③断然;全然. ④〔美俚〕的确,确实. *He is ~ a honest man.* 他的确是一个老实人. *~ speaking* 严格地讲.

stric·ture [ˈstriktʃə] *n.* ①束紧;束缚,限制. ②【医】狭窄. ③〔常 *pl.*〕酷评,谴责,非难. ***pass ~s on*** 攻击,责难;弹劾.

strid(den) [ˈstrid(n)] stride 的过去分词.

stride [straid] *vi.* ***(strode*** [strəud]***;*** 〔罕〕***strid*** [strid], ***stridden*** [ˈstridn]***)*** ①迈步,大踏步走,迈进. ②跨过*(over)*; 〔罕〕= straddle. — *vt.* ①跨过(水沟等);跨,骑. ②大踏步走过. —*n.* ①大步,阔步. ②一跨(的宽度). ③迈进. ④〔*pl.*〕〔俚〕裤子. *We are striding forward both in English and in mathematics.* 我们的英语和数学都在大踏步地取得进展. *This year we've made a big ~ forward on the road of four modernizations.* 今年我们在四化道路上大大地迈进了一步. ***at [in] a ~*** 一跨,一步(就几尺等). ***get into one's ~*** 开始(顺利,正常,有劲地)进行. ***have a fine ~*** 大踏步悠然自得地走. ***hit one's ~*** =get into one's ~. ***make great [rapid] ~s*** 大有进步,进展迅速,大跃进. ***make tremendous ~s*** 大大跃进. ***strike one's ~*** = get into one's ~. ***take in one's ~*** 一跨而过;轻而易举地解决(困难) (*take obstacles in one's ~* 一跨而过障碍;轻而易举地克服困难). ***with big ~s*** 迈步,大踏步.

stri·dent [ˈstraidnt] *a.* 轧轧叫的,唧唧叫的,扎耳朵的. **-ly** *ad.* **-dence, -cy** *n.*

stri·dor [ˈstraidə] *n.* ①尖锐刺耳的声响. ②【医】喘鸣.

strid·u·late [ˈstridjuleit] *vi.* (蝉、蟋蟀等)唧唧地叫,轧轧地叫;发粗锐声;摩擦发音. **-lant** *a.* **-la·tion** *n.* **-la·to·ry** *a.*

strid·u·lous [ˈstridjuləs] *a.* 发刺耳叫声的. 作唧唧声的 (= stridulant).

strife [straif] *n.* ①竞争,倾轧,吵架,斗争,战争. ②努力奋斗. *internal ~* 内讧. ***at ~*** 不和,相争.

strig·il [ˈstridʒəl] *n.* (古希腊、罗马人浴后,擦去身上水份的)擦身器.

stri·gose [ˈstraigəus], **strigous** [ˈstraigəs] *a.* ①【植】有糙伏毛的,有鳞片的. ②【动】有硬鬃的. ③有细密槽纹的.

strike [straik] *vt.* ***(struck*** [strʌk]***; struck,*** 〔古〕***strick·en*** [ˈstrikn]***)*** ①打,敲,击,殴;碰,撞,攻击,冲击. ②(用尖刀等)刺穿,戳进,咬,抓. ③碰到,到达,发见,找到. ④打制,铸造,打出;擦,压. ⑤拉下,扯下,收起,叠起. ⑥使突然发生,使得病,突然使. ⑦给与印象,使感动,打动,使想起. ⑧采取(态度),装出,摆出. ⑨(钟)敲时间,报时. ⑩商定,决定(市价),结算. ⑪用斗刮刮平. ⑫使植物扎根. ⑬装嘴子(在桶上). ⑭(木匠)打墨线. ⑮罢工; ⑯船(触); (光)照在…上. ⑰勾销,取消. ⑱到达, 进入. ⑲弹奏. ⑳(昆虫)产卵于. ㉑组成陪审团. *~ the table with one's fist* 拿拳头捶桌子. *~ sb. a violent blow* 猛击,痛殴. *~ one's head against the lintel* 把头撞在门楣上. *be struck by lightning* 被雷打. *The ship struck a rock.* 船触礁. *~ sb. with a dagger* 拿尖刀戳某人. *Unfortunately he was struck by a snake.* 很不幸他让蛇咬伤了. *We shall ~ the main road beyond the wood.* 我们过了森林就会找到大路的. *~ oil* 发现石油;〔口〕得到意外收获,发横财. *~ a medal* 冲压而制出纪念章. *~ a match* 擦火柴. *~ a false [right] note* 作出错误[正确]的表示. *~ a sail* 下帆. *~ one's flag* 下旗;〔喻〕投降. *~ a camp* 收帐篷. *~ the tents* 拔营. *~ sb. all of a heap* 〔口〕使吃惊. *be struck dumb* 愣住,目瞪口呆. *~ terror into every heart* 使大家恐怖. *How does his playing ~ you?* 他的演出你觉得怎么样? *~ sb. as ridiculous* 使某人觉得好笑. *An idea has struck me.* 我想起了一个念头. *It ~s me that …* 觉得;想起. *be struck by her beauty* 对她的美丽产生深刻印象. *~ a graceful attitude* 装正经. *It has just struck four.* 刚敲过四点钟. *~ bargains* 做成几笔买卖. *~ a balance* 结帐. *The young pines have struck roots.* 小松树都扎根了. *This item must be struck out.* 这一项必须勾掉. *It is reported that the South Bend firemen will ~ work.* 据报南湾的消防队员要罢工. *Only a few musicians know how to ~ a lyre.* 只有少数的音乐家会弹七弦琴了. — *vi.* ①打,敲,殴,攻击,冲击;碰,撞,触;(船)触礁,搁浅,下帆. ②(蛇兽等)抓咬. ③罢工,罢课,罢市. ④(心脏)搏动,(光)落下,(声)被听到,(蠔)贴附. ⑤(时钟)敲,鸣. ⑥擦(打)火. ⑦刺透,穿透. ⑧打动,给以印象,突然想到. ⑨开始,朝某方向前进. ⑩勾销. ⑪扎根发芽. ⑫降旗. ⑬鱼上钩,拉住钩的鱼. ⑭触发电弧,(雷电)闪击. ⑮努力,力争. *S- while the iron's hot.* 趁热打铁,趁机行事. *The match wouldn't ~.* 火柴擦不着. *~ to the left* 向左走. *Cold ~s into one's marrow.* 冷透骨髓. *The disease struck inwards.* 疾病内攻. *The damp ~s through the walls.* 湿气透入墙壁. *A ship ~s.* 船投降了. *His hour has struck.* 他的死期来到了. *The hour has struck for ….* 应该…的时候到了. *The ship struck on a reef.* 船触礁了. *What ~s at a first reading is its vivid images.* 初读时它给人的印象是形象生动. *The lightning struck again.* 又打闪电了. *The root of the young tree has struck deep into earth.* 小树的根已经深深地扎入土里. *I've struck on a novel means of doing the job.* 我突然想到干这个活的一个新奇的方法. *The workers struck against long hours [for higher wages].* 工人们为反对长工时 [为提高工资] 而罢了工. ***~ a bad patch*** 经历一个倒霉时期. ***~ a blow for …,*** 拼命要得到…. ***~ a line [path]*** 找到门路. ***~ a mine*** 【海】触水雷. ***~ against*** 反对…而罢工. ***~ aside*** 闪开,躲开(刀尖). ***~ at*** 企图打破,袭击,打击,攻打. ***~ at the root of*** 要毁掉…;想根绝…. ***~ back*** 打回来;反射过来. ***~ down*** 打倒,击灭;杀;(将鱼)装桶保藏;(病)侵入(人身),使生(病);(太阳)晒得受不了. ***~ for …*** 要求…而罢工. ***~ hands*** 〔古〕订买卖契约. ***~ home*** 使受致命伤; 击中要害; 取得预期效果 (*His interpretation struck home.* 他的解释得当). ***~ in*** 突然插嘴;干涉;(疾病)内攻 (*Here someone struck in with a question.* 这儿忽然有人提出一个问题来). ***~ into*** 突然, 开始 (*~ into a gallop* 忽然跑起来), (忽然)跑, 逃(进); 打, 扎(进). ***~ it rich*** 〔美口〕发现矿产[油田]; 发横财, 走运. ***~ off*** 斩去; 删去, 涂去; 扣除, 除去(利息等); 印刷 *(~ off a book)*; 当场画[写]; 显眼. ***~ out*** 打去; 打出(火花等) *(of)*; 删去, 涂去; 想出, 创出, 拟出; 使发挥; 使一下子发生(某结果); 用手脚划水游泳; 跳出; 蹶起; (天才等)发挥; 一下子发生;【棒球】使三击不中而出局 (*~ out a plan* 拟出一个计划. *~ the name out* 删去名字. *~ out of a track* 失掉踪迹. *~ out for the midstream* 奋力游向中流). ***~ through*** 删去; 刺穿. ***~ up*** 挡起(敌手、刀剑); (在金属上)浮雕; 开始弹奏, 开始唱; 定(约等); 和人开始…, 结(交) (*~ up an acquaintance* 突然[偶然]做起朋友来). ***~ up with*** 〔美〕偶然碰见(某人). ***~ upon an idea*** 忽然想起一个主意来. — *n.* ①打击, 殴打. ②【军】(集中)攻击; 空袭; 进行一次空袭的一群飞机. ③(钟)报时; 钟声. ④罢工, 罢课(等). ⑤【棒球】(击球员的)击球失败; (投手投出的)正球, 好球 *(opp.* fall*)*; 【滚木球】第一球撞倒全部木柱(的分数). ⑥【地】走向. ⑦〔美俚〕(石油、金矿等的)发见; 大发横财, 走红运; 讹诈, 勒索, 恐吓. ⑧(一次的)铸币额. ⑨(鱼的)上钩. ⑩= strickle. ⑪(酒类的)品级; 烈度. ⑫不利条件; 缺点. ⑬(牧畜的)皮毛蝇蛆病. ⑭【植】植根. *carry out an air ~ against …* 对…进行空袭. *Ten ~s* *from the station clock* 车站的十点钟钟鸣. *a general* ~ 总罢工. ***break up a*** ~ 破坏罢工. ***call a*** ~ 发动罢工. ***call off a*** ~ 停止罢工. ***go on*** ~ 实行罢工. ***have two ~s against one*** 三击中有二击不中;〔美口语〕处境不利,形势不利. ~ **benefit,** ~ **pay** (工会拿出的)罢工津贴. ~**bound** *a.* 因罢工而停业的;罢工所造成的(困难等). ~ **breaker** 破坏罢工的工人,工贼,代替罢工者工作的工人. ~ **breaking** 破坏罢工. ~**-clause** 罢工条件. ~ **fault**【地】走向断层. ~ **fund** 罢工基金. ~ **measure** 斗刮量法. ~ **order** 罢工命令. ~ **out**【棒球】(三击不中)出局. ~ **zone**【棒球】好球区.

strik·er [ˈstraikə] *n.* ①打击者,打手,爱打人的人. ②打铁工匠. ③罢工者. ④(时钟报点的)锤; 报点时钟. ⑤斗刮. ⑥鱼叉. ⑦叉鱼人. ⑧撞针. ⑨〔英〕(网球的)接球人 (*opp.* server). ⑩〔美〕(陆军军官的)勤务兵等.

strik·ing [ˈstraikiŋ] *a.* ①打击的;攻击的,突击的. ②显著的,明显的,触目的,惊人的. ③罢工中的. *a* ~ *force*【军】突击部队. ~ *dockers* 罢工中的码头工人. ~ *suits* 引人注目的成套衣服. ~ *velocity* 弹着速度,命中速度. ~ **distance** 打得到的距离[范围] (*within* ~ *distance of* 在…打得到的距离内). **-ly** *ad.*

string [striŋ] *n.* ①线,带,绳子;〔美〕鞋带〔又叫 shoe-~,〔英〕叫 shoe-lace〕; (穿钱、数珠等的)串线,串绳;穿在线上的东西,一串东西;一连串,一系列. ②一串; 一行,一排, 一列. ③〔集合词〕(训练中的)(常属于一个马主的)一群赛跑的马; 牛群, 马队; 一群. ④(弓)弦;(乐器的)弦;〔the ~s〕弦乐器(演奏者). ⑤纤维;卷须;(豆荚壳等的)筋,腱. ⑥【台球】得分数;计分器. ⑦〔*pl.*〕〔美口〕(附带)条件,限制. ⑧〔美俚〕谎话. ⑨【建】束带层;短梯基. *a piece of* ~ 一根绳子,一条带子. *shoe* ~ 鞋带. *a* ~ *of questions* 一连串问题[质问]. *a* ~ *of buses* 一长列公共汽车. *a* ~ *of houses* 一排房屋. ***a second ~ to one's bow*** 另一种手段,第二套办法. ***by the ~ rather than the bow*** 〔口〕直接了当地. ***harp on one [the same]*** ~ 反复讲同一事件. ***have sb. on a*** ~ 任意操纵某人. ***have two ~s to one's bow*** 备有两手,备有两套办法. ***in a long*** ~ 排成一长串. ***no ~s***〔美运〕时间没有限制. ***no ~s attached*** 没有附带条件. ***on the*** ~〔美〕有希望. ***pull every*** ~ 竭力,拼命. ***pull the ~s*** 在背后拉线,在幕后操纵. ~ ***tied to it*** (个中)条件,缘故. ***the first [second]*** ~ 第一[第二]靠得住的人[物];第一[第二]个办法. ***touch a*** ~〔喻〕触动心弦. ***touch the ~s*** 奏弦乐. — *vt.* (***strung*** [strʌŋ]) ①用绳、线、带子(等)捆、扎、挂. ②〔常用 *p.p.*〕收紧,使紧张,使作好准备;使兴奋. ③用线串起来. ④(在弓上)上弦;调(乐器)弦,抽(豆荚等)筋. ⑤成一串排列起来,排成一列 (*up; out*). ⑥拉直,伸展;扩张,延长;〔口〕引伸. ⑦〔美俚〕欺骗,愚弄,戏弄; — *vi.* ①(人等)排成一串,蜿蜒排列;成线状;列成一行前进;②〔美俚〕欺骗,撒谎,戏弄 ~ *out scouts along the road* 沿路布置警戒. ~ *beans* 掐去菜豆的筋. *He is highly strung for the game.* 他对比赛非常紧张. *I'm strung up to do the job.* 我已经准备好可以干这桩活儿了. ~ ***along with***〔美俚〕陪伴,信任(某人);同意(某事). ~ ***sb. along***〔美俚〕骗人,使人等待,吊人胃口. ~ ***oneself up*** 兴奋紧张;打起精神来想做…. ~ ***out*** (使)节目拖长; 行列长达; (日期)延长到 (*The program was strung out too long.* 节目拖得太长. *The parade strung out for miles.* 游行队伍长达数英里). ~ ***together*** (把事实)连贯起来. ~ ***up***〔口〕勒死;吊,挂起. ~ **bag** 网线袋. ~ **band** 弦乐队. ~ **bark** = stringy bark. ~ **bean**〔美〕菜豆;豆荚. ②〔口〕瘦长条子. ~**-board**【建】楼基盖板. ~ **course**【建】蛇腹层,束带层. ~ **electrometer**【无】弦线静电计. ~ **halt** = spring-halt. ~ **piece**【建】纵梁,楼梯基. ~ **quartet(te)**【乐】弦乐器部合奏(曲). ~ **tie** (蝶形)领结.

stringed [striŋd] *a.* ①有弦(乐器)的. ②有蔓的,有卷须的. *a* ~ *instrument* 弦乐器.

strin·gen·cy [ˈstrindʒənsi] *n.* ①紧急,迫切,逼迫. ②(货币、信用等)紧缩,短缺. ③严格,严重,严厉. ④说服力,魄力. *Bankers say financial* ~ *constitutes a serious threat to the country.* 银行家们说信用紧缩构成了对国家严重的威胁.

strin·gen·do [strinˈdʒendəu] *a., ad.* 〔It.〕【乐】逐步加紧,渐快.

strin·gent [ˈstrindʒənt] *a.* ①紧急的,迫切的;紧迫的. ②(货币等)紧缩的,缺乏的. ③严格的,严重的,严厉的;有说服力的. ~ *necessity* 紧急需要. **-ly** *ad.* **-ness** *n.*

string·er [ˈstriŋə] *n.* ①上弦工人,弦匠. ②【铁路】纵向轨枕. ③【建】纵梁;楼梯基. ④【船】纵材. ⑤【地】脉道. ⑥〔*pl.*〕〔俚〕手铐.

string·y [ˈstriŋi] *a.* (***-i·er; -i·est***) ①线的,带子的;纤维质的,纤维多的, 多筋的(肉等). ②黏性的. ③〔美〕拖遢的. *a* ~ *throat* (瘦得)青筋暴露的喉咙. **-i·ness** *n.*

strip[1] [strip] *vt.* (~ ***ped,***〔罕〕***stript, strip·ping*** [ˈstripiŋ]) ①剥;剥去衣服;剥光;除去,取去 (*of*). ②夺,抢去;剥夺,褫夺 (*of*). ③拆卸,拆除(附属物等);卸去(船上)索具. ④挤干(牛)奶,挤出(鱼卵). ⑤去(烟叶的)梗. ⑥从…中删去不必要的东西. ⑦【矿】剥离(矿层或矿脉上的泥土);使露出;采(锡). ⑧【化】去除(纤维的)颜色,去色;除去挥发性成分. ⑨把…撕成带形,切成细条. ⑩用纸条粘住(书面等). ⑪精洗(原料丝绸). ⑫折断(齿轮的)齿,磨损(螺丝钉的)螺纹;由于膛速过高擦去子弹的皮. — *vi.* ①脱去衣服;表演脱衣舞;剥落. ②(螺丝钉的)螺纹剥落. ③【炮】(炮弹)不旋转地打出去,擦去弹皮; ~ *a tree of its bark* = ~ *the bark from a tree* 剥去树皮. *He* ~*ped off his coat.* 他脱去上衣. ~ *a person of his honours [wealth]* 剥夺人之荣誉[财产]. ~ *the house of everything valuable* 抢去屋内每一件贵重的东西. ~ *sb. naked* 剥光人的衣服. ~ *tobacco* 去烟梗. ~ *for a bath* 脱衣洗澡. ~ ***bare*** 剥光(*winter stripped bare all the trees* 冬天落尽了所有的树叶). ~ ***sb. of*** (*money*) 抢去某人的 (钱). — *n.* 脱衣舞. ~ **act,** ~ **teaser**〔美〕脱衣舞女.

strip[2] [strip] — *n.* ①条带,长条;条板;带状地. ②条状侦察照片;连环漫画. ③支板;插座条. ④【空】跑道;简易机场. ⑤【冶】带钢. ⑥【矿】露天剥采. ⑦捣矿机排矿沉淀槽;脱衣舞. ⑧集邮簿上的一行邮票. ⑨无茎无梗的烟叶. *film ~s* 电影胶卷. *a runway* ~【空】跑道. *leave a* ~〔美俚〕突然停车,急煞车. ~ **cartoon** 连环漫画. ~ **cropping [planting]** (山坡上防止水土流失的)条植法. ~ **leaf** (去茎和梗的) 烟叶. ~**light** (舞台照明的)长条状灯. ~ **log** 片条钻探剖面. ~ **mine** 露天矿. ~ **mining**〔美〕【矿】露天剥采.

stripe [ˈstraip] *n.* ①条纹,条子. ②(人的)类型;类别. ③〔*pl.*〕【军】军服上表示等级的条纹. ④犯人穿的横条囚衣; (一道)鞭痕,鞭伤;鞭打. ⑤条纹衣料,条纹布. ⑥长方形长条洗矿槽. ⑦〔*pl.*〕〔口,马戏团用语〕老虎. ~ *rust* 条锈病. *the Stars and Stripes* 星条旗[美国国旗]. *people of the same* ~ 同一类型的人. *politicians of the Democratic* ~ 民主党一派的政客们. ***get one's ~s*** 升级. ***lose one's ~s*** 降级. ***wear the ~s***〔美〕进监牢. — *vt.* 给加上条纹,使成条纹状. **-r**【军俚】带道道的〔指军官〕. —*vt.* 使…成条纹状,在…上划条纹.

striped [stript] *a.* ①有条纹的. ②喝醉了的. ~**-pants** *a.* (在礼仪,社交活动等方面)过于注重形式的.

strip·ling [ˈstripliŋ] *n.* ①年轻人,小伙子. ②苗木修剪.

strip·per [ˈstripə] *n.* ①剥(烟茎烟梗)的人. ②剥毛梳;刮毛器;剥皮器;折卸器. ③脱光衣服的人;脱衣舞舞女. ④〔俚〕停奶牛. ⑤【化】汽提塔. ⑥【机】冲孔模板. ⑦【油】枯竭井,低产井. ⑧露天矿矿工.

strip·tease [ˈstriptiːz]〔美〕*n.* 脱衣舞. —*vi.* 表演脱衣舞. **-r** *n.*〔俚〕表演脱衣舞的女人.

stripy [ˈstraipi] *a.* 有条纹的;条纹状的 **-i·ness** *n.*

strive [straiv] *vi.* (***strove*** [strəuv]; ***striven*** [ˈstrivn]) ①力

求，努力(*to do*; *for*; *after*)。②竞争，斗争 (*with*)；反抗(*against*)。~ *hard to make greater progress* 力争取得更大的进步。~ *for accuracy* 力争确切。~ *for victory* 争取胜利。~ *with [against] a temptation [difficulty]* 和诱惑[困难]作斗争。**-r** *n.* 努力者；奋斗者；竞争者。

striv·en [ˈstrivn] strive 的过去分词。

strobe [strəub] *n.* 〔缩〕①【物】频闪观测器 (= stroboscope)。②(照相和剧场用的)闪光灯(=strobe light)。③【物】频闪放电管 (= strobotron)。④【无】闸门；选通脉冲。— *a.* = stroboscopic.

stro·bi·la [strəuˈbailə] *n.* (*pl.* **-lae** [-liː])【动】①横裂体；节裂体。②水母叠生体。**-r** *a.* **-la·tion** [-ˈleiʃən] *n.*

stro·bile, strobil [ˈstrəubail, -bil] *n.*【植】球果；球穗花序；孢子叶球。

stro·bi·lus [strəuˈbailəs] *n.* (*pl.* **-li** [-lai]) ①【植】球果，球花。②= strobila.

strob·o·scope [ˈstrəubəskəup] *n.* 圆筒动画镜，万花筒，动态镜；【物】频闪观测器；闪光仪。**-scop·ic, -scop·i·cal** *a.* **-scop·i·cal·ly** *ad.*

strob·o·tron [ˈstrɔbətrɔn] *n.* 频闪放电管。

strode [strəud] stride 的过去式。

stro·ga·noff [ˈstrəugəˌnɔːf, ˈstrɔː-] *a.* 以酸奶油、肉汤、蘑菇等烹调的。

stroke[1] [strəuk] *n.* ①一击，一敲；打，打击；一振，一动；(字的)一笔；一举；一划；(游泳的)一扒；一触；一闪；一刀。②(钟的)鸣声，敲击声；雷打；落雷；(心脏的)跳动，脉搏。③飞来横祸，意外的打击，意外的幸运。④(疾病的)发作；中风。⑤手腕，手法；政策；功劳，成功。⑥(板球等的)打法；游泳方法[方式]；(船的)划法；(坐舵手对面指挥全艇划桨快慢的)尾桨手。⑦笔画。⑧风格。⑨工作量。⑩【机】冲程，行程，动程。*a thick [fine, thin]* ~ 粗[细]笔划。*Little ~s fell great oaks.* 〔谚〕水滴石穿。*a finishing* ~ 最后加工；(决定性的)最后一击；最后一笔。*The clock was on the* ~ *of twelve.* 钟敲十二点。*a* ~ *of apoplexy* 脑溢血。*a great* ~ *of diplomacy* 外交上的大成功。*a* ~ *of genius* 天才的手法。*a fine* ~ 大成功，好成绩。*a* ~ *of state* = coup d'etat. *He has not done a* ~ *of work.* 他一点儿工作也没有做。*back* ~ 仰泳。*breast* ~ 俯泳，蛙式 (游泳)。*over arm* ~ 自由式 (游泳)。*side* ~ 侧泳。~ *of piston* 活塞行程。***a*** ~ ***above*** 〔口〕高出一头，高明一些 (*She was a* ~ *above the other girls.* 她比别的女孩子高明些)。***at a [one]*** ~ 一举；一笔。***be full of ~s from the life*** 充满写实手法[笔调]。***give the*** ~ = set the ~. ***have a*** ~ 中风，脑溢血。***keep*** ~ 整齐一致地划桨。***pull*** ~ 划尾桨 (指挥快慢)。***pull*** ~ ***to another boat*** 和着别船整齐一致地划。***row*** ~ = pull ~. ***set the*** ~ 确定划桨的方法[速度]。~ ***and strife*** 大闹，搅乱。***with a*** ~ ***of the pen*** 大笔一挥 (*You could do it with a* ~ *of the pen.* 你只要大笔一挥[签个字]就能做的)。***with measured ~s*** 有步骤地。— *vt.* (用笔)划线，勾消；担任尾桨划手，划尾桨。~ *an average of 28* 一分钟划二十八下。~ **oar** 尾桨(手)。~ **(oar)sman** 尾桨手。

stroke[2] [strəuk] *vt.* 抚，摩；【裁缝】弄伸绉褶。~ ***sb. down*** 平息某人的怒气。~ ***sb. [sb.'s hair] up (the wrong way)*** 倒撂(动物等的)毛发；逗恼人，触怒某人。— *n.* 抚摩，一抹。**-r** *n.* ①抚摩者。②【印】推纸器。③谄媚者。

stroke[3] [strəuk] *v.* strike 的过去式。

strok·ing·ly [ˈstrəukiŋli] *ad.* 抚摩地；安抚地。

stroll [strəul] *n.* 散步，漫步，溜达；闲逛，游荡；徘徊；流浪；巡回演出。*a ~ing player* 流浪演员。*a ~ing company* 流动剧团。***take [have, go for] a*** ~ 闲逛，散步，漫步。— *vi.* 慢慢儿的走，散步，闲逛，游荡 (*away*; *off*; *over*; *through*; *along*; *about*)；流动演出。— *vt.* 在…上游荡。

stroll·er [ˈstrəulə] *n.* 散步的人，游荡的人；巡回[流动]演员，江湖艺人；流浪者；流氓；〔美〕(折叠式)婴孩车。

stro·ma [ˈstrəumə] *n.* (*pl.* **-ma·ta** [-tə]) ①【解】基质。②【植】基质；子座。**-l, -mat·ic** [-ˈmætik] *a.*

Strong [strɔŋ] *n.* 斯特朗〔姓氏〕。

strong [strɔŋ] *a.* ①强壮的，有力的，有膂力的；强健的；巩固的，坚牢的，坚固的；坚强的(性格等)；强烈的，猛烈的(感情、风等)。②富有的，有财力的，资力雄厚的；有势力的；强大的，优势的；(兵员)总数达…的。③强硬的，热心的；效力强的，烈性的，厉害的，浓烈的(饮料)；刺鼻的。④不易消化的(食物等)；麸质多的；黏土多的；【农】土质肥沃的。⑤【商】坚挺的，上涨的；【语法】强变化的，(*opp.* weak)。⑥能力强的，擅长的。*a* ~ *case* 有力的主张。*a* ~ *man* 强壮的人；果断[有魄力]的人。*the* ~ 强者；健康的人。*the ~er sex* 男性。*How many* ~ *are you?* 你们有多少人？*I have a* ~ *hold over it.* 我紧紧把握着它。*an army 10,000* ~ 一万人的一支军队。*a* ~ *situation* (文艺作品中)动人的情节。~ *language* (咒)骂人的粗话。~ *meat* 难消化的肉。*Markets are* ~. 行情坚挺。*How* ~ *are you?* 〔美〕你有多少钱？***be*** ~ ***against*** 坚决反对。***be*** ~ ***in*** 擅长。***be*** ~ ***under*** 在…下坚定不移。***by the*** ~ ***arm [hand]*** 用极大的力量，靠力量，用暴力。***have a*** ~ ***head*** 酒量大。***many millions*** ~ 千百万。***one's*** ~ ***point*** 一个人的特长，优点。~ ***for*** 〔美俚〕坚决赞成。***take a*** ~ ***root*** 把根扎牢。— *ad.* 坚强地，有力地，大大地，猛烈地。***come it*** ~ = ***go it*** ~ 〔俚〕大干，盲干，拼命干 (*That is coming it rather* ~. 太过分；非分要求)。***go*** ~ 〔口〕健康；旺盛；吃香；强硬。***put it*** ~ 骂，说得刻薄。**-ly** *ad.* **~-arm** ① *vt.* 〔美俚〕殴打，殴打后抢去。② *a.* 用暴力的，狂暴的。③ *n.* 暴力，强硬手段。**~box** 保险箱。~ **boy** (重体量的)拳击选手。~ **breeze** 强风 (六级风)。**~-brown** 坚牢的牛皮纸。~ **drinks** = 〔古〕~ **waters** 烈性酒。~ **gale** 烈风 (九级风)。~ **hold** 要塞；据点，根据地；中心点。**~man,** ~ **man** 大力士；有影响的掌权者，红人；独裁者。~ **measure** 强硬手段。**~-minded** *a.* 意志坚强的，果断的；好胜的，有丈夫气概的(女人等)。~ **room** 〔英〕金库，保险库。~ **sand** 黏合砂。~ **suit** ①(牌戏)张数多而包含大牌的花色。②优点，长处。~ **wheat** 优质小麦。

stron·gyl(e) [ˈstrɔndʒil] *n.*【动】圆线虫属寄生虫。

stron·gy·lid [ˈstrɔndʒilid] *n.*, *a.*【动】圆线科寄生虫(的)。

stron·gy·lo·sis [ˈstrɔndʒiˈləusis] *n.*【医】圆线虫病。

stron·ti·a [ˈstrɔnʃiə, -ʃə, -tiə] *n.*【化】①氧化锶。②氢氧化锶。

stron·ti·an [ˈstrɔnʃiən] *n.* = strontium.

stron·ti·an·ite [ˈstrɔnʃiənˌnait] *n.*【矿】菱锶矿。

stron·tic [ˈstrɔntik] *a.* 锶的。

stron·ti·um [ˈstrɔnʃiəm]【化】锶〔Sr.〕**-tic** *a.*

strook [struk] 〔废〕strike 的过去分词。

strop [strɔp] *n.* (磨剃刀的)皮带；【船】滑车的带索。— *vt.* 在皮带上磨刮使锋利。

stro·phan·thin [strəuˈfænθin] *n.*【医】毒毛旋花子苷〔从毒毛旋花中提取的一种强化剂〕；羊角拗质。

stro·phe [ˈstrəufi] *n.* (古希腊戏剧中歌咏队)向左方舞动唱歌；向左方舞动时唱的歌词；(诗的)节。**-ph·ic, -i·cal** *a.*, **-cal·ly** *ad.*

strove [strəuv] strive 的过去式。

strow [strəu] *vt.* 〔古〕= strew.

stroy [strɔi] *vt.* 〔废〕= destroy.

struck [strʌk] *v.* strike 的过去式，过去分词。— *a.* 〔美〕罢工中的，受罢工影响的。*a* ~ *factory* 因罢工而关闭的工厂。~ **joint**【建】斜刮缝。~ **jury**【法】特选陪审团〔共 12 人〕。~ **measure** 用斗刮刮平的量。

struc·tur·al [ˈstrʌktʃərəl] *a.* 构造上的，结构上的，组织上的。~ *botany* 组织植物学。~ *disease*【医】脏器病。~ *engineering* 建筑工程学；大建筑工程。~ *formula*

【化】结构式. ~ *geology* 地层学. ~ *linguistics*【语】结构语言学. ~ *psychology* 结构心理学. ~ *resistance*【空】前面阻力. ~ *steel* 结构钢,建筑用钢. ~ *weight* 机体重量. **-ly** *ad.*

struc·tur·al·ist [ˈstrʌktʃərəlist] *n.* (社会学、经济学、语言学的)结构论者,结构主义者. — *a.* 结构论者的;结构主义者的,结构论的. **-al·ism** *n.*

struc·tur·al·i·ze [ˈstrʌktʃərəlaiz] *vt.* 使(机能)体现在组织结构中;将…吸引进结构中去. **-za·tion** *n.*

struc·ture [ˈstrʌktʃə] *n.* ①构造,结构;组织;石理,石纹. ②建造物. ③【化】化学结构. ④【心】(直接经验中显现的)结构性,整体性;整体结构. *military* ~*s* 工事. **-d** *a.* **-less** *a.*

stru·del [ˈstruːdl; G. ˈʃtruːdəl] *n.* 果馅奶酪卷.

strug·gle [ˈstrʌgl] *vi.* 挣扎;努力,奋斗;同…斗争 (*against; with; for*);挤过去,想方设法通过 (*along; through; in; on; up*);〔美俚〕跳舞. ~ *against superior numbers* 和优势兵力战斗. ~ ***for breath*** 困难地呼吸. ~ ***on*** 拼命活下去,竭力支持下去;继续努力. ~ ***to one's feet*** 挣扎着站起来. ~ ***with the waves*** 跟波浪搏斗. — *n.* ①奋斗,努力,拼搏. ②格斗;斗争;战争. ③努力奋斗的目标,要认真对待的事,麻烦事. ④【哲】斗争性. *a death bed* [*last-ditch*] ~ 垂死挣扎. *the armed* ~ 武装斗争. *class* ~ 阶级斗争. *line* ~ 路线斗争. *desperate* ~ 垂死挣扎. *It was something of a* ~ *to find the money to pay.* 当时要筹一笔支付款项在某种意义上讲是一件麻烦事. ***put up a last-ditch*** ~ 负隅顽抗. ~ ***for existence*** 生存斗争. ~ **buggy**〔美〕汽车.

strug·gler [ˈstrʌglə] *n.* 挣扎的人;努力者,奋斗者;竞争者,斗争者.

strug·gling·ly [ˈstrʌgliŋli] *ad.* 斗志昂扬地;艰苦奋斗地.

strum [strʌm] *vt.* 拙劣地弹奏,胡乱弹奏. — *vi.* 乱弹(弦乐器),乱奏 (on). — *n.* 胡乱弹的声音. *the* ~ *of typewriters* 打字机的嗒嗒声. **-mer** *n.*

stru·ma [ˈstruːmə] *n.* (*pl.* **-mae** [-miː])【医】腺病;甲状腺肿;【植】瘤状突起,小叶节. **-mose, -mous** [-məus, məs] *a.*

strum·pet [ˈstrʌmpit] *n.*〔古〕妓女.

strung [strʌŋ] string 的过去式,过去分词. ~ **out** 有吸毒瘾(因而虚弱)的.

strut[1] [strʌt] *vi.* 肿胀,鼓起,膨胀;大摇大摆地走,趾高气扬地走;(孔雀等)竖着尾巴走;装模作样地走. — *n.* 高视阔步. ~ ***around*** 招摇过市. ~ ***one's frame***〔美运〕出场比赛. ~ ***one's stuff***〔美俚〕炫耀;自负. **-ling** *a.* 肿胀的,自负的,趾高气扬的.

strut[2] [strʌt] *n.* 支柱,支杆;抗压构件;轨撑.【空】(双翼机的)翼间支柱. — *vt.* (用支柱等)支持,撑住.

stru·thi·ous [ˈstruːθiəs] *a.*【动】鸵鸟目 (*Struthioniformes*) 的.

Strutt [strʌt] *n.* 斯特拉特〔姓氏〕.

strut·ter [ˈstrʌtə] *n.* 高视阔步的人;有翼间支柱的飞机.

stru·vite [ˈstruːvait] *n.*【矿】鸟粪石.

strych·ni·a, strych·nin(e) [ˈstriknia, -niːn] *n.*【化】马钱子碱;士的宁. **-nic** *a.*

strych·nin·ism [ˈstrikninizm] *n.*【医】士的宁中毒,马钱子碱中毒.

Sts. = Saints.

S.T.T.L. =〔L.〕*Sit tibi terra levis*【宗】愿你安眠于地下〔墓碑题铭〕.

Stu. = Stuart.

Stu·art [stjuət] *n.* 斯图尔特〔姓氏〕.

Stuart [stjuət] *n.* ***the*** ~***s*** = ***the House of*** ~ (英国)斯图亚特王朝〔1603—1649,1660—1714〕.

stub [stʌb] *n.* ①树桩;残材. ②短(截)线;(铅笔、雪茄烟等的)剩余部分. ③(坏牙的)根;〔美〕(支票的)存根,票根. — *a.* 粗短的. ~ *pen* 断尖钢笔尖; ~ *nail* 断钉;破损马掌钉. ~ *land* 茬地. ~ *tube* 短管. ~ *tuner*【无】调谐短线. — *vt.* (***stubbed*** [ˈstʌbd], ***stub·bing*** [ˈstʌbiŋ]) 挖去树桩;连根拔除,根除 (*up*);踩熄(烟蒂)(*out*);树桩〔石头等〕绊(脚). ~**bed** *a.* 树桩多的;树桩状的,粗短的. ~ **mortise**【建】短粗榫眼. ~**-tenon**【建】短粗榫.

stub·ble [ˈstʌbl] *n.* ①〔常 *pl.*〕(稻麦的)残茬;〔集合词〕谷茬,麦茬;茬地. ②短发,胡子茬.

stub·bled [stʌbld], **stub·bly** [-bli] *a.* (***-bli·er; -bli·est***) 尽是谷茬〔麦茬〕的,茬多的;茬地的;满脸胡子茬的. ~ **root** 宿根.

stub·born [ˈstʌbən] *a.* 顽固的;倔强的;顽强的;难驾驭的,不听话的;难熔化的(金属等). *a* ~ *resistance* 顽强的抵抗. ~ *facts* 不容抹杀的事实. *a* ~ *illness* 顽疾. ***as*** ~ ***as a mule*** 非常固执的. **-ly** *ad.* **-ness** *n.*

Stubbs [stʌbz] *n.* 斯塔布斯〔姓氏〕.

stub·by [ˈstʌbi] *a.* (***-bi·er; -bi·est***) 多树桩的;树桩似的,粗短的. **-bi·ness** *n.*

stuc·co [ˈstʌkəu] *n.* (*pl.* ~***es***, ~***s***)【建】拉毛水泥,拉毛粉饰,灰墁. — *vt.* 墁上灰泥〔拉毛粉饰〕. ~ **pattern** 拉毛粉饰型板. ~ **work** 毛粉饰(活儿),灰墁,灰泥.

stuck [stʌk] stick 的过去式及过去分词. ~ ***on*** 眷恋;爱上. ~**-up** *a.*〔口〕骄傲的,自高自大的,自以为了不起的;自私的.

stud[1] [stʌd] *n.* 大头钉;饰钉;【机】双头螺栓,柱(头)螺栓 (= ~ bolt);轴;端轴颈;销子,中介轴;(装硬领的)金属扣,(衣袖等的)饰钮;(钟表等的)键钮;【建】壁骨;墙筋;中间柱.〔美〕四明一暗扑克牌戏〔又叫 ~ poker〕. — *vt.* (***stud·ded*** [ˈstʌdid], ***stud·ding*** [ˈstʌdiŋ]) 加饰钉;用饰钮装饰;散饰,散布,点缀;用壁骨支撑. ~***ded with*** 散布着…的,点缀着…的,星罗棋布的.

stud[2] [stʌd] *n.* (专为繁殖、打猎、赛马等饲养的)马,马群;〔美〕种马;种(公)畜;养马场. *a* ~ *farm* 种马农场,配种站. ~**book** (马、犬等的)血统纪录簿. ~**horse** 种马.

stud. = student.

stud·ding [ˈstʌdiŋ] *n.*【建】壁骨(用料);房间净高度. ~**sail**【海】补助帆,翼帆.

stude [stjuːd, stuːd] *n.*〔美俚〕= student.

student [ˈstjuːdənt] *n.* ①(大)学生〔美国也指中学生〕;(大学、研究院的)研究生;(牛津大学 Christ Church 的)公费研究生. ②研究者,学者. *a* ~ *of life* 研究生命问题的学者. ③〔美俚〕初学者,初学吸毒的人. *a law* ~ 法科学生. ~ **assistant** 助教. ~ **government** 学生自治会. ~ **interpreter** 见习翻译员. ~ **lamp**〔美〕(可随意调节高低的)台灯. ~ **teacher**〔美〕实习教员. ~**ship** *n.* 学生的身分;〔英〕奖学金. ~ **union**〔美〕(大学的)学生活动大楼.

stud·ied [ˈstʌdid] *a.* 故意的,有意的,有计划的;深思熟虑的;有知识的,精通的 (*in*). *a* ~ *négligé* 故意不修边幅. *a style which is too* ~ 雕琢太过的文体. **-ly** *ad.* **-ness** *n.*

stu·di·o [ˈstjuːdiəu] *n.* (美术家、照相馆等的)工作室,画室,雕刻室;照相室;〔*pl.*〕电影制片厂;(广播电台的)播音室;【电视】演播室. ~ **apartment**〔美〕以一个房间为单元的公寓. ~ **couch**〔美〕可以作床用的长沙发;三用沙发.

stu·di·ous [ˈstjuːdjəs] *a.* ①好学的,勤勉的,用功的;热心的,专心的;慎重的,谨慎的,小心的. ②有意的,故意的. ***be*** ~ ***of*** 努力,热心,专心. ***be*** ~ ***of doing sth.*** 非常想做某事. ***be*** ~ ***to do sth.*** 热心〔细心〕做某事. ~ ***to please*** 刻意讨好. **-ly** *ad.* **-ness** *n.*

stud·y [ˈstʌdi] *n.* ①用功,勤学;〔常 *pl.*〕学习,研究 (*of*);研究对象,研究项目;值得研究的问题;学问,学业,学科;专题论文;调查. ②书房,书斋;研究室;(个人)工作室. ③〔古〕沉思默想. ④试作;【美】习作;【乐】练习曲. ⑤【剧】背台词,读台词;背台词的演员. *His face was a perfect* ~. 他的面孔真有意思. *To write correctly is my* ~. 我的努力目标是写得正确. *a quick* *[slow]* ~ 台词记得快[慢]的演员. *quit studies* 罢课. ***in a brown*** ~ 呆想,默想,深思. ***make a ~ of*** 研究. — *vt.* ①学习;研究;记诵(台词等),练习. ②用心,考虑,图谋;注意看,仔细端详. — *vi.* 用功,学习,练习;研究;努力,留心;默想. ~ *sb.'s face* 仔细端详某人面貌. ~ *one's own interests* 图谋自己利益. ~ *to avoid disagreeable topics* 努力避免不愉快的话题. ~ *to wrong no man* 留心不误伤别人. ~ ***for the bar*** 为了预备做律师而学习. ~ ***one's part*** 【剧】记诵自己的台词. ~ ***out*** 想出;解(谜等). ~ ***to be wise*** 努力学聪明. ~ ***up*** 用功预备(考试等). ~ ***up on*** 〔口〕认真研究,调查,考查. ~ **hall** 〔美〕自修室;指定在自修室进行的课时. ~**-in** *n.* 〔美〕听课抗议[示威].

stuff [stʌf] *n.* ①材料,原料,资料;〔美剧〕脚本,台词. ②要素;本质,品质. ③织物;〔特指〕毛织品,呢绒. ④所有物,家具;【海】(焦油,松节油等构成,木船防腐用的)混合涂料. ⑤枪弹,炮弹. ⑥〔俚〕〔the ~〕钱,现金;〔美俚〕真材实质,优良特征. ⑦废物,屑;拙劣的作品;梦话;废话. ⑧〔美俚〕毒品,麻醉剂;走私货物,走私威士忌酒,赃物. ⑨〔美空军口〕云;天气. *green [garden]* ~ 蔬菜. *sweet* ~ 糖果,糕点. *doctor's* ~〔口〕药品. ~ *goods* 呢绒. *thick* ~ 四英寸以上的厚木料. *That's the (sort of)* ~ *to give them ['em, the troops].* 〔俚〕对那些家伙处置得正好. 当然了! 不错! *He is made of sterner* ~ *than his father.* 他的性格比他父亲更严厉. *None of your* ~*!* 别说废话! *S- (and nonsense)!* 胡说! 废话! *All* ~*!* 完全是胡说! *This book is good [poor]* ~. 这本书是好[坏]书. ***be great*** ~ 是好家伙[东西]. ***be not afraid of such*** ~ 不怕那一套. ***do [strut] one's*** ~〔美俚〕采取行动;承当难局;拿出自己本领,显出拿手好戏;做自己要做[拿手]的事. ***Do your*** ~*!* 〔美俚〕干你自己的事情! ***little*** ~〔蔑〕小人物. — *vt.* ①填充,塞满;塞入填料;装满;塞住. ②剥制. ③〔美〕(在票箱中)投入大量假选票. ④〔俚〕诓骗. — *vi.* 狼吞虎咽,吃饱. ~ *his fingers into his ears* 拿手指塞住耳朵. ~ *a cushion with feathers* 用羽毛装垫子. ~ *a box with old clothes* 拿旧衣服塞满箱子. ~ *a child with food* 把孩子喂得过饱. *a* ~*ed bird* 剥制的鸟. *a* ~*ed shirt* 〔美俚〕摆架子的人,神气十足的小人;有钱[有地位]的人. ~ ***oneself*** 吃得过饱. ~ ***one's head with*** 满脑袋的…. — *a.* 毛织品做的,呢绒做的. **-er.** ①填充者;填充物;填塞工人. ②(和信件等一同装在信封里的广告之类的附寄物. ③〔俚〕贩卖假货的人.

stuff·ing ['stʌfiŋ] *n.* 填充物,填料〔装进枕头、被子、垫子等的羽毛、棉花等;填在八宝鸡之类里面的配料;(报纸杂志的)补白;剥制. ~ **box** 【机】填充[填料]函.

stuff·y ['stʌfi] *a.* ***(-i·er; -i·est)*** 闷热的,气闷的;鼻子不通气的;沉闷乏味的;古板的,保守的;一本正经的;架子十足的. **-i·ly** *ad.* **-i·ness** *n.*

stug·gy ['stʌgi] *a.* 〔英方〕矮胖的,强壮的.

Stu·ka ['ʃtu:kə, 'stu:kə] *n.* 〔G.〕(德国)俯冲轰炸机.

stull [stʌl] *n.* 【矿】横梁,横撑;支柱.

stul·ti·fi·ca·tion [ˌstʌltifi'keiʃən] *n.* (使)显得愚蠢;愚弄;(使)归于无效;【法】声明精神错乱.

stul·ti·fy ['stʌltifai] *vt.* 使显得愚蠢;愚弄;使自相矛盾;(由于其后的矛盾行为)使归于无效;【法】声明精神错乱. ~ ***oneself*** 显得愚蠢,陷入自相矛盾中,做前后矛盾的事情,取消前言;【法】自己声明精神错乱. **-fi·er** *n.*

stum [stʌm] *n.* 未[半]发酵的葡萄汁. — *vt.* 用防腐剂防止(葡萄酒)过分发酵.

stum·ble ['stʌmbl] *vi.* ①绊倒,踌倒 *(at; over)*; 东歪西倒地走. ②弄错,搞错,犯错误,犯(道德上的)罪过;失足. ③说不出话来,结巴;踌躇. ④偶然碰见 *(on, upon; across)*. — *vt.* 使绊倒,使失足;使为难;使踌躇莫决. ~ *over a stone* 给石头绊倒. ~ *through a speech* 结结巴巴地演说. ~ *over one's words* 结结巴巴地说. ~ *upon a rare book in the library* 在图书馆中偶然发现一本少见的书. ~ ***along*** 东歪西倒地走. ~ ***at a straw*** 动辄为小事发愁. — *n.* 绊倒;失足;差错,失误,过失;失败. ~**-bum** *n.* 〔美俚〕笨手笨脚的人(牲畜);穷醉鬼;喝醉酒的(或蹩脚的)拳击手. **-r** 跌交者;失错者;犯过失者;蹒跚行走者;结结巴巴演说者.

stum·bling block ['stʌmbliŋ blɔk] *n.* 绊脚石;障碍.

stu·mer, stu·mour ['stju:mə] *n.* 〔俚〕假支票,假钱,伪钞;(赛马中预先安排好不会赢的)马;打不出的子弹;大错.

stump[1] [stʌmp] *n.* ①树桩,残株,树茬. ②残肢;牙根;(铅笔、扫帚等的)残部;(吸剩的)烟头. ③(美国竞选时在新开垦地区站在树桩上讲的)树桩演说(场);竞选演说. ④假腿;〔*pl.*〕〔谑〕腿,脚;【板球】柱. ⑤〔美口〕挑衅;挑战,考验. *stir one's* ~*s* 快走;出动. ***go on [take] the*** ~〔开始竞选演说〕. ***on [up] a*** ~〔美口〕为难,不知道怎么办才好. ***on the*** ~ 在进行竞选活动. ***wear to the*** ~***s*** 糟蹋(笔、帚)等;使枯死. ~**-jumper** 〔美〕庄稼汉;树桩演说家. ~ **orator** 树桩演说家. ~ **oratory** 〔美〕树桩演说(术),政治演说(术). ~ **plant** 插条;萌条. ~ **speech** 〔美〕树桩演说,竞选演说. ~ **word** 缩语〔如 bus (< omni*bus*), exam (< *exam*ination)〕. — *vt.* ①砍伐,砍成树桩;掘去树桩. ②(将脚等)碰在石头上;绊,绊倒. ③〔主用 *p.p.*〕妨害,阻碍;使为难. ④〔美口〕挑衅,抵抗;旅行各地进行竞选演说. ⑤【板球】撞倒柱子退场. ⑥当场付款 *(up)*. — *vi.* 用假腿走,迈着沉重步子走 *(across, along, etc.)*; 〔美口〕旅行各地作政治演说. *That* ~*s me.* 那把我难住了. ~ ***it*** 逃走;旅行竞选演说. ~ ***up*** 拔去树桩;〔英俚〕付清(应付款项).

stump[2] [stʌmp] *n.* (画炭画铅笔画时用纸等卷成圆锥形做成的)擦笔. — *vt.* 用擦笔涂出阴影.

stump·age ['stʌmpidʒ] *n.* ①立木,未伐倒的树木. ②立木蓄积,立木价值. ③〔林〕(立木)采伐权.

stump·er ['stʌmpə] *n.* 砍伐树桩者;〔英俚〕= wicket-keeper;〔美口〕= *stump* orator;〔口〕使人为难的事物,难题,困难的工作.

stump·ster ['stʌm*p*stə] *n.* 〔美〕政治演说家.

stump·y ['stʌmpi] *a.* ***(-i·er; -i·est)*** 树桩多的;树桩状的,粗而短的(铅笔、尾巴、人等). — *n.* 矮胖子;〔美俚〕钱. **-i·ly** *ad.* **-i·ness** *n.*

stun [stʌn] *vt.* ①打昏过去. ②(打鼓等)震聋耳朵,闹聋. ③使发愣,使目瞪口呆,使大吃一惊. — *n.* 震惊;晕眩;〔美〕胡桃.

Stund·ism ['stundizm] *n.* 【宗】斯登教〔1860 年农民间信仰新约的一派基督教〕. **-ist** *n.*

stung [stʌŋ] sting 的过去式及过去分词. — *a.* 〔美俚〕受骗上当的.

stunk [stʌŋk] stink 的过去式及过去分词.

stun·ner ['stʌnə] *n.* 打昏人的人[物];把人打昏的一击;〔口〕极好的东西,惊人的东西;〔口〕了不起的人物;极漂亮的人〔尤指女人〕;〔美俚〕第一流的故事.

stun·ning ['stʌniŋ] *a.* 令人晕倒[吃惊]的;震耳欲聋的;〔口〕极好的;极漂亮的;了不起的. **-ly** *ad.*

stun·sail, stun·s'l ['stʌnsl] *n.* = studdingsail.

stunt[1] [stʌnt] *vt.* 阻碍…的发育,使发育不良;阻碍(生长、发育). — *n.* 阻碍发育,发育不全[迟缓];发育不全的,矮小的人[动物、植物]. *a* ~*ed tree* 发育不良的树.

stunt[2] [stʌnt] *n.* ①〔口〕特技,绝技;惊人的技艺;特技飞行 [= ~ flying];惊人的行为;惊人的手段. ②花招,噱头. — *vi., vt.* 作绝技表演;作特技飞行. ~ **man** 【影】特技演员〔专门代替演员作惊险特技动作的〕.

stunt·fest ['stʌntfest] *n.* 〔美〕有种种杂耍做余兴的集会.

stunt·ster ['stʌntstə] *n.* 〔美〕特技表演者.

stu·pa ['stu:pə] *n.* 〔Ind.〕卒塔婆,印度塔,浮屠,舍利塔.

stupe[1] [stju:p] *n.* 【医】热[冷]敷布. — *vt.* 热敷,热罨.

stupe[2] [stju:p] *n.* 〔俚〕傻瓜,笨蛋.

stu·pe·fa·cient [ˌstju:pi'feiʃənt] *a.* 使麻醉的. — *n.* 【医】麻醉剂.

stu•pe•fac•tion [ˌstju:piˈfækʃən] *n.* (使)麻醉；麻木状态；昏迷；恍惚，茫然.

stu•pe•fac•tive, stu•pe•fa•cient [ˌstju:piˈfæktiv, ˌstu:pi-; -feiʃənt] *a.*【医】麻醉的. — *n.* 麻醉药.

stu•pe•fy [ˈstju:pifai] *vt.* 使麻醉；使失去知觉；使茫然，使发呆. **-fi•er** *n.*

stu•pen•dous [stju(:)ˈpendəs] *a.* 惊人的，了不起的；大的. **-ly** *ad.* **-ness** *n.*

stu•pid [ˈstju:pid] *a.* ①愚蠢的；头脑糊涂的. ②无聊的(书)，乏味的. ③感觉迟钝的，麻痺的，昏迷不醒的. — *n.* 〔口〕傻瓜，笨蛋. **-ly** *ad.* **-ness** *n.*

stu•pid•i•ty [stju(:)ˈpiditi] *n.* 愚笨，愚钝，糊涂.

stu•por [ˈstju:pə] *n.* 无感觉，人事不省，麻木，麻痺，昏迷；茫然若失，恍惚. **-ous** *a.*

stur•died [ˈstə:did] *a.* (羊的)晕倒病的.

stur•dy[1] [ˈstə:di] *a.* 健壮的；坚定的；坚强的，不屈的，刚毅的；生长力强的，耐寒的. *a ~ opponent* 顽强的敌手. *~ cloth* 牢的布. *~ knowledge* 真才实学. *~ patriotism* 坚定的爱国精神. **-i•ly** *ad.* **-i•ness** *n.*

stur•dy[2] [ˈstə:di] *n.* (羊的)晕倒病.

stur•geon [ˈstə:dʒən] *n.*【鱼】鲟鱼.

Sturmabteilung [ˈʃturmˌɑptailuŋ] *n.* 〔G.〕(纳粹的) 冲锋队.

Sturm und Drang [ˈʃturm unt ˈdraŋ] *n.* 〔G.〕狂飚时期【运动】(= the Storm and Stress) 动荡不安.

sturt [stə:t] *n.* 激烈的争论；吵架. — *vi.* 争吵. — *vt.* 骚乱，纷扰.

stut•ter [ˈstʌtə] *vt.* 结结巴巴地说出. *~ (out) an apology* 结结巴巴地道歉. — *vi.* 结结巴巴地说话，口吃地说话. — *n.* 结巴，口吃. **-er** *n.* **-ing•ly** *ad.*

Stutt•gart [ˈstutgɑ:t] *n.* 斯图加特〔德意志联邦共和国城市〕.

sty[1] [stai] *n.* 猪圈 (= pig-sty)；猪圈一样 (脏) 的房子[睡处]；藏垢纳污之所；妓院. — *vt., vi.* 关在猪圈.

sty[2], **stye** [stai] *n.*【医】睑腺炎；麦粒肿. *have a ~ in one's eye* 患麦粒肿.

Styg•i•an [ˈstidʒiən] *a.*【希神】冥河 (Styx) 的；阴间的，地狱的；阴暗的，阴郁的；不可违背的，不可摆脱的(誓约). *~ gloom* 漆黑.

sty•lar [ˈstailə] *a.* 笔尖的，象笔尖的，有尖的描划工具的.

style[1] [stail] *n.* ①风格，作风；体裁；式样，型；种类. ②文体；说话的态度，语调. ③模样，仪表，态度，风采；品位，品格. ④时式，时样，时尚. ⑤名种，称呼，尊称. ⑥历法. ⑦(在蜡板上写字用的)铁笔；〔诗〕笔；铅笔；雕刻刀；日晷仪的针；蚀刻针；唱针. ⑧【植】花柱；【动】尾片，节芒，尾须；铗下器；产卵器. ***She has an elegant ~.*** 她具有优雅的风格. *live in (grand) ~* 过豪华的生活. *the ~ of study [writing]* 学[文]风. *a concise ~* 简洁的文体. *democratic ~ of work* 民主作风. *give his full ~* 把他的头衔详细说出. *My ~ is plain John Smith* 我的名字就是约翰·史密斯. *the Old [New] S-* 旧[新]历. ***in ~*** 有样子，很时新. ***in the ~ of*** 仿…式. ***out of ~*** 没有样子，不时新. ***the [that] ~ of thing*** 那样的事，说法，做法，事件 (*I've had quite enough of that ~ of thing.* 那种事我已经受够了). — *vt.* 称，命名；叫做；设计时新样式；使符合流行格式. *~ oneself an old sailor* 自称老海员. *~* **book** *n.* 文字体例样本时装图样；样本.

style[2] [stail] *n.* = stile.

sty•let [ˈstailit] *n.* ①小剑，匕首；②【外】探针；通管丝；管心针；锥刺；【植】小花柱；【虫】螯针，口针.

sty•li [ˈstailai] stylus 的复数.

sty•li•form [ˈstailiˌfɔ:m] *a.* 尖笔状的；尖形的；刺状的；茎状的；针形的.

styl•ish [ˈstailiʃ] *a.* 时髦的，时式的，时样的；漂亮的. **-ly** *ad.* **-ness** *n.*

styl•ish•ner [ˈstailiʃnə] *n.* 〔美〕新样子创造人.

styl•ist [ˈstailist] *n.* 文体家；文体批评家；(家具等的)设计人；动作、风度优美的人〔如运动员〕.

sty•lis•tic(al) [staiˈlistik(əl)] *a.* 文体(家)的；风格上的. **-cal•ly** *ad.* **-s** *n.* 文体论；文体修辞学.

sty•l•ite [ˈstailait] *n.*【宗】(古代住在高柱上的) 柱上苦行者.

styl•i•ze [ˈstailaiz] *vt.* 〔常用 *p.p.*〕使(图画等)具有某种风格；使风格化，使程式化. **-za•tion** [ˌstailaiˈzeiʃən] *n.*

sty•lo [ˈstailəu] *n.* *(pl. ~s)* 〔口〕= stylograph.

stylo- *comb. f.* 柱；尖笔，铁笔: *stylo*bate.

sty•lo•bate [ˈstailəˈbeit] *n.*【建】柱座.

sty•lo•graph [ˈstailəgrɑ:f] *n.* 针尖式自来水笔. **-ic** *a.* 针尖式自来水笔的；铁笔[尖笔]书写(用)的. **-i•cal•ly** *ad.*

sty•log•ra•phy [staiˈlɔgrəfi] *n.* 尖笔书(或画)法.

sty•lo•hy•oid [ˌstailəˈhaiˌɔid] *n.*【解】茎突舌骨.

sty•loid [ˈstailɔid] *a.* 茎状突起的，尖笔形的；【解】柱状的.

sty•lo•lite [ˈstailəˌlait] *n.* 石笔杆〔石灰岩和灰页岩中的小柱状构造〕.

sty•lo•po•di•um [ˌstailəˈpəudiəm] *n.* *(pl. -di•a [-ə])*【植】(花的)柱茎.

sty•lus [ˈstailəs] *n.* *(pl. sty•li* [ˈstailai]) 铁笔，尖笔；(留声机的)唱针；描画针；记录针；日晷指针；【解】笔状突起；花柱；针突；生殖器鞘；产卵管.

sty•mie, sty•my [ˈstaimi] *n., vt.* *(-mied, -mie•ing)* 妨碍(计划等) (= stimy) 阻碍.

sty•mied [ˈstaimi:d] *a.* 〔美〕被袭击的，被侵入的.

styp•sis [ˈstipsis] *n.* 止血剂效用，止血剂的使用.

styp•tic [ˈstiptik] *a., n.*【医】止血的；止血药. *~* **pencil** (用明矾等止血药制成的，用来止住刮脸后出血等小创口的)止血笔.

styp•tic•al [ˈstiptikəl] *a.* = styptic.

styp•tici•ty [stipˈtisiti] *n.* 止血作用，收敛性.

sty•rax [ˈstaiəræks] *n.*【化】苏合香脂.【植】安息香.

sty•rene, sty•rol [ˈstaiəri:n, -rɔl] *n.*【化】苯乙烯.

sty•ro•foam [ˈstairəfəum] *n.*【商标】泡沫 (聚苯乙烯) 塑料.

sty•ron [ˈstairɔn], **sty•rone** [ˈstairəun] *n.*【化】肉桂醇；【商标】斯蒂龙〔一种聚苯乙烯商品〕.

Styx [stiks] *n.*【希神】(围绕地狱的)冥河. *black as the ~* 漆黑. *cross the ~* 死.

SU = strontium unit.

S.U. = set up.

su•a•bil•i•ty [sju(:)əˈbiliti] *n.* 可控告[起诉]，应控告[起诉]. **-a•ble** [ˈsju(:)əbl] *a.* **-a•bly** *ad.*

sua•sion [ˈsweiʒən] *n.* 说服，劝告. *moral ~* 道义上的劝告.

sua•sive [ˈsweisiv] *a.* 劝告性的；有说服力的. **-ly** *ad.* **-ness** *n.*

suave [sweiv] *a.* 温和的，和蔼的；殷勤讨好的(人、态度等)；适口的，平和的(酒、药等). **-ly** *ad.* **-ness** *n.*

sua•vi•lo•quence [ˈswævilәkwәns] *n.*〔美〕谦和的大话.

sua•vi•ter in mo•do, for•ti•ter in re [ˈswævitə in ˈməudəu, ˈfɔ:titə in ˈri:] 〔L.〕态度柔和，行为果断，外柔内刚.

suav•i•ty [ˈswævəti] *n.* 温和，和蔼，谦和；适口，和淡；愉快.

sub[1] [sʌb] *a.* 附属的，辅助的，补充的. *a ~ post office* 邮政支局.

sub[2] [sʌb] *n.* ①代替物，代替者；〔美〕候补队员 (= substitute). — *vi.* 做补充[候补]人员；〔口〕做替工(for). — *vt.* 〔美俚〕替…进行比赛.

sub[3] [sʌb] *n.* 潜水艇.

sub[4] [sʌb] *n.* 〔美俚〕低能者.

sub[5] [sʌb] *n.* 订户 (= subscriber)；订购 (= subscription).

sub[6] [sʌb] *prep.* 〔L.〕在…的下面,…的下面的. ～ ***finem*** [ˈfainəm] 参看本章末〔略 s. f.〕. ～ ***judice*** [ˈdʒu:disi] 审理中的,未决的. ～ ***rosa*** [ˈrəuzei] 秘密地. ～ ***silentio*** [siˈlenʃiəu] 暗中, 偷偷地. ～ ***voce*** [ˈvəusi] 在该词下,参看该词〔略 s. v.〕.

sub. = sabaltern; subject; sublieutenant; submarine boat; subscriber; subscription; substitute; suburb(an); subway.

sub- *pref.* ★ 如在以 c, f, g, m, p, r 等字母为首的从拉丁语来的词之前,则往往因同化作用分别变成 suc-, suf-, sug-, sum-, sup-, 在 c, p, t 等字母前又常变为 sus-. ① 在…之下,在下: *sub*sternal, *sub*way. ②次级的; 局部的; 副; 再,分,子: *sub*prefect, *sub*heading, *sub*species, *sub*divide, *sub*let, *sub*program. ③稍微,接近, 近乎; 次, 亚, 逊: *sub*acid, *sub*alpine, *sub*aquatic, *sub*atom, *sub*tropical, *sub*cylindrical, *sub*delirium, *sub*erect, *sub*human. ④〔附加在倍数形容词前表示该数的倒数〕: *sub*double = 1:2 *[double =2:1]*, *sub*tripe = 1:3 〔triple = 3:1〕.

sub•ac•e•tate [sʌbˈæsiˌteit] *n.* 【化】碱式醋酸盐.

sub•ac•id [ˈsʌbˈæsid] *a.* 带酸味的; (言语等) 有点刺人的; 【化】微酸 (性) 的. **-a•cid•i•ty** [sʌbæˈsiditi] *n.* **-ly** [-ˈæsid-] *ad.* **-ness** [-ˈæsid-] *n.*

sub•a•cute [ˌsʌbəkju:t] *a.* ①稍微尖锐的. ②亚急性的. **-ly** *ad.*

Sub•ad•ult [ˈsʌbˈædʌlt, ˈsʌbəˈdʌlt] *a.* 接近成年的.

sub•aeri•al [sʌbˈεəriəl] *a.* 地面上的,地面上发生的; 接近地面的.

sub•a•gent [ˈsʌbˈeidʒənt] *n.* 副代理人. **-gency** *n.* 分销处.

sub•al•pine [ˌsʌbˈælpain] *a.* ①阿尔卑斯山脉山麓的. ②在山区林线下(四—六千英尺之间)生长的; 亚高山的.

sub•al•tern [ˈsʌbltən] *a.* 下,次,副,部下的,属下的;〔英军〕大尉以下的;【逻】特称的. ～ *opposition*【逻】大小对当. — *n.* 副官,部下,僚属;〔英军〕中〔少〕尉;【逻】特称命题; 特称判断 (= ～ proposition).

sub•al•ter•nate [səbˈɔ:ltənit] *a.* ①循次序的; 连续的. ②【植】近互生的. — *n.*【哲】特称命题. **-ly** *ad.* **-tion** *n.*

sub•ant•arc•tic [ˌsʌbæntˈɑ:ktik] *a.* 环绕南极圈地区的,副南极地区的.

Sub•a•pi•cal [ˈsʌbˈæpikəl] *a.* 在顶点下的; 接近顶点的.

sub•a•quat•ic [ˈsʌbəˈkwætik] *a.* ①【生】半水栖的, 半水生的. ②= subaqueous.

sub•a•que•ous [ˈsʌbˈeikwiəs] *a.* 水下的; 水下发生的; 水下用的.

sub•arc•tic [sʌbˈɑ:ktik] *a.* 近北极的,亚极带的.

sub•ar•ea [ˈsʌbˈεəriə] *n.* 分区.

sub•ar•id [ˈsʌbˈærid] *a.* 亚干燥的. *a* ～ *region* 亚干燥地区.

sub•as•sem•bler [ˈsʌbəˈsembləl] *n.* 部件装配工.

sub•as•sem•bly [sʌbəˈsembli] *n.*【机】局部装配; 配件, 组件,部件.

sub•as•tral [sʌbˈæstrəl] *a.* 星下的,天下的,地上的.

sub•at•mos•pher•ic [ˈsʌbˌætməsˈferik] *a.* 低于大气层的; 低于大气压的.

sub•at•om [sʌbˈætəm] *n.* 逊原子. **-ic** *a.* 逊原子的; 比原子小的; 在原子内的. **-ics** *n.* 逊原子学.

sub•au•di [sʌbˈɔ:dai] *vt., vi.* 〔L.〕〔用于祈使语气〕根据领会补充(所需词语).

sub•au•di•tion [ˈsʌbɔ:diʃən] *n.* 领会言外意义; 言外意义.

sub•au•ric•u•lar [ˈsʌbɔ:ˈrikju:lə] *a.* 【解】位于外耳下的.

sub•av•er•age [ˈsʌbˈævəridʒ] *a.* 低于一般水平的.

sub•base [ˈsʌbˌbeis] *n.*【建】副基层,下基层.

sub•base•ment [ˈsʌbˌbeismənt] *n.*【建】副地下层, 副地下室.

sub•bass [ˈsʌbˈbeis] *n.* 【乐】(管风琴中发出最低音的) 最低音踏瓣[音栓].

sub•bing [ˈsʌbiŋ] *n.* ①做代替人; 做替工. ②地下灌溉. ③【摄】胶层.

sub•branch [ˈsʌbˌbræntʃ] *n.* 小分支; 支店, 次级分店. — *vi.* 分成小分支.

sub•breed [ˈsʌbbri:d] *n.*【生】亚品种.

sub•cabi•net [ˈsʌbˈkæbinit] *n.* (美国总统自选的) 非正式顾问团.

sub•cal•i•ber, subcalibre [sʌbˈkælibə] *a.* ①小口径的〔小于枪炮之口径的〕. ②发射小口径枪子弹的.

sub•car•ti•lag•i•nous [sʌbˈkɑ:tiˈlædʒinəs] *a.*【解】① 在软骨下的. ②半软骨的.

sub•ce•les•tial [ˌsʌbsiˈlestʃəl] *a.* 天下的; 天顶下的; 地球(上)的; 世俗的.

sub•cel•lar [ˈsʌbselə] *n.* 地下室下的地下室,下层地窖.

sub•cen•tral [ˌsʌbˈsentrəl] *a.* 近中心的,在中心之下的. **-ly** *ad.*

sub•cer•e•bral [ˈsʌbˈseribrəl] *a.* 大脑下面的.

sub•chas•er [ˈsʌbtʃeisə] *n.* 〔美〕猎潜舰[艇] (= submarine chaser).

sub•chlo•ride [sʌbˈklɔ:raid] *n.*【化】低氯化物,氯化低价物.

sub•class [ˈsʌbklɑ:s] *n.*【生】亚纲;【数】子集(合).

sub•cla•vi•an [sʌbˈkleiviən]【解】*a.* 在锁骨下的. — *n.* 锁骨下静脉,锁骨下动脉.

sub•clim•ax [sʌbˈklaimæks] *n.*【生态学】亚顶级(植物)群落.

sub•clin•i•cal [sʌbˈklinikl] *a.*【医】无明显临床征候的. **-ly** *ad.*

sub-cloud [ˈsʌbˈklaud] *a.* 云下的. ～ *car n.*【空】云下观测吊舱.

sub•col•le•gi•ate, subcollege [ˈsʌbkəˈli:dʒiit, ˈsʌbˈkɔlidʒ] *a.* 准大学程度的; 为学力不足(或无意入正式大学)的学生设置的.

sub•com•mis•sion•er [ˈsʌbkəˈmiʃənə] *n.* (委员会所属的)小组委员.

sub•com•mit•tee [ˈsʌbkəmiti] *n.* 小组委员(会).

sub•com•pact [ˈsʌbˈkɔmpækt] *n.* (比小型汽车更小的) 超小型汽车.

sub•con•scious [ˈsʌbˈkɔnʃəs] *a.* 下意识的, 潜意识的; 半自觉的. **-ly** *ad.* **-ness** *n.*

sub•con•ti•nent [ˌsʌbˈkɔntinənt] *n.* 次大陆.

sub•con•tract [sʌbˈkɔntrækt] *n., v.* 转订的契约[合同], 转包[分包]合同; 转包工程. **-trac•tor** *n.* 分包者, 转包人.

sub•con•tra•ry [sʌbˈkɔntrəri] *n.* 【逻】小 〔下〕 反对 [对当].

sub•cool [ˈsʌbˈku:l] *vt.* 使过冷,使低温冷却.

sub•cool•ing [sʌbˈku:liŋ] *n.* 低温冷却,局部冷却; 欠火, 加热不足.

sub•cos•tal [sʌbˈkɔstl] *a.*【解】肋下的. — *n.* 肋下肌.

sub•crit•i•cal [sʌbˈkritikl] *a.* ①近乎危急的. ②(原子) 次临界的.

sub•cry•stal•line [ˈsʌbˈkristəlain] *a.* 部分结晶的, 结晶不清楚的.

sub•cul•ture [ˈsʌbˌkʌltʃə] *n.* ①亚文化群〔年龄、地位相当的一伙同道者〕. ②【生】再次培养. **-tur•al** *a.*

sub•cu•ta•ne•ous [ˈsʌbkju(:)ˈteiniəs] *a.* 皮下的. ～ *injection* 皮下注射. **-ly** *ad.*

sub•dea•con [ˈsʌbˈdi:kən] *n.* 【宗】(基督教圣公会、天主教会等的)副助祭; 副执事.

sub•dean [ˈsʌbˈdi:n] *n.* ①(英国教会或天主教的)副教长. ②(大学的)副院长; 副系主任; 副教务长.

sub•deb [sʌbˈdeb] *n., a.* 〔美口〕 = subdebutante.

sub•deb•u•tante [ˈsʌbˈdebju:ˈtɑ̃:nt] *n., a.* 〔美口〕快要进入社交界的年龄不到20岁的姑娘.

sub·de·lir·i·um [ˈsʌbdiˈliriəm] *n.*【医】轻谵妄.
sub·dis·ci·pline [ˈsʌbˈdisiplin] *n.* 学科的分支.
sub·dis·trict [ˈsʌbˌdistrikt] *n.* 分区.
sub·di·vide [ˈsʌbdiˈvaid] *vt., vi.* 再分; 细分. **-rid·able** *a.*
sub·di·vis·i·ble [ˈsʌbdiˈvizəbl] *a.* 可再分[细分]的.
sub·di·vi·sion [ˈsʌbdiviʒən] *n.* 再分,细分; 再分之下的部分; (供出售的)小块土地, 分装的商品;【军】半个师, 半个连. **-al** *a.*
sub·dom·i·nant [ˈsʌbˈdɔminənt] *a., n.* 第二位优势(的);【生】亚优势种(的);【乐】次属音(的).
sub·dou·ble [sʌbˈdʌbl] *a.* 二分之一的.
sub·du·a·ble [səbˈdju:əbl] *a.* 可征服的; 可抑制的.
sub·dual [səbˈdju(:)əl] *n.* 征服,屈服,屈从; 抑制; 缓和.
sub·duce, sub·duct [səbˈdju:s, səbˈdʌkt] *vt.* 减去,取回,扣除.
sub·duc·tion [səbˈdʌkʃən] *n.* 减去,取回, 扣除;【数】减法.
sub·due [səbˈdju:] *vt.* ①使屈从, 打败, 征服(敌国等). ②镇压,压制(情欲), 克制(怒气等); 驯养, 驯伏. ③开辟,开拓(土地); 根除(杂草等). ④放低(声音等),弄低; 弄淡, 减淡(颜色),减弱(光线); 减轻(炎症). ~ *rough land* 开荒. *a ~d voice* 低声. *~d light* 柔(和的)光(线).
sub·dued [səbˈdju:d] *a.* ①被征服的. ②被抑制的. ③缓和的,柔和的.
sub·du·pli·cate [ˈsʌbˈdju:plikit] *a.*【数】用平方根得出的; 用平方根表示的.
sub·ed·it [ˈsʌbˈedit] *vt.* 〔英〕①充任助编,以助编身分进行编辑工作. ②做整理稿件等技术工作; 划版样,批格式.
sub·ed·i·tor [ˈsʌbˈeditə] *n.* 副主笔; 副编辑.
sub·ep·i·der·mal [ˈsʌbˌepiˈdə:məl] *a.*【解】表皮下的.
sub·e·qual [sʌbˈi:kwəl] *a.* 差不多相等的.
sub·er [ˈsju:bə] *n.*【植】木栓(组织); 软木槲; 软木.
sub·e·rect [ˌsʌbiˈrekt] *a.* 几乎直立的,几乎笔直向上生长的.
su·be·re·ous [suˈbiəriəs] *a.*【植】似软木的; 软木质的.
su·ber·ic [sju:ˈberik] *a.* 软木的,木栓的. ~ *acid*【化】辛二酸.
su·ber·in, su·ber·ine [ˈsju:bərin, ˈsu:bərin] *n.*【化】软木脂.
su·ber·i·za·tion [ˌsju:bəraiˈzeiʃən] *n.*【植】栓化(作用).
su·ber·ize [ˈsju:bəˌraiz, ˈsu:-] *vt.*【植】栓化.
su·ber·ose, su·ber·ous [ˈsju:bərəus, -rəs] *a.*【植】木栓状的,软木质的.
sub·ex·change [ˈsʌbikstʃeindʒ] *n.* (电话)支局,分局.
sub·fam·i·ly [ˈsʌbfæmili] *n.*【生】亚科.
sub·floor [ˈsʌbˌflɔ:] *n.* 副地板.
sub·form [ˈsʌbfɔ:m] *n.* 从属形式,派生形式.
sub·for·ma·tion [sʌbfɔ:ˈmeiʃən] *n.* 从属形态;【空】单编队.
sub·freez·ing [ˈsʌbˈfri:ziŋ] *a.* (水的)冰点以下的; 凝固点以下的.
sub·frig·id [sʌbˈfridʒid] *a.* 亚寒带的. ~ *zone* 亚寒带.
sub·fusc [ˈsʌbfʌsk], **sub·fus·cous** [-ˈfʌskəs] *a.* 〔主英〕暗黑的,带黑色的,黑黝黝的.
sub·ge·nus [ˈsʌbˈdʒi:nəs] *n.* (*pl.* ***-genera*** [-dʒenərə], *~es*)【生】亚属.
sub·gla·cial [sʌbˈgleiʃəl] *a.* 冰河底的, 在冰河下的. *a ~ deposit* 冰下沉积. **-ly** *ad.*
sub·grade [ˈsʌbgreid] *n.* 路基; 地基.
sub·group [ˈsʌbgru:p] *n.*【化】(周期表的)族; 副族, B族;【生】亚群,子群;【数】簇,子群.
sub·gum [ˈsʌbˈgʌm] *a.*【烹】(多种蔬菜)什锦的.
sub·heading [ˈsʌbhediŋ] *n.* 小标题; 细目.
sub·hu·man [ˈsʌbˈhju:mən] *a.* ①(发展上)次于人类的; 低于人类的. ②近于人类的.
su·bic [ˈsu:bik] 苏比克〔菲律宾〕.
sub·in·dex [sʌbˈindeks] *n.* (*pl.* ***-di·ces*** [-diˌsi:z]) ①分目(录). ②【数】分指数.
sub·in·feu·da·tion [ˈsʌbinfjuˈdeiʃən] *n.* ①(封建制度的)分赐采邑,分封. ②分封土地所有制. ③封地,采邑.
sub·in·ter·val [ˈsʌbˈintəvəl] *n.*【乐】小音程;【数】子区间.
sub·ir·ri·gate [sʌbˈiriˌgeit] *vt.* 用地下管道灌溉, 地下灌溉. **-ga·tion** *n.*
su·bi·to [ˈsu:biˌtəu] *ad.* 〔意〕【乐】突然地,立刻地.
subj. = ①subject. ②subjective. ③subjunctive.
sub·ja·cen·cy [sʌbˈdʒeisnsi] *n.* ①基座, 基层. ②毗连于下面的部分.
sub·ja·cent [sʌbˈdʒeisənt] *a.* 在下面的; 下层的; 较低处的; 形成基础的.
sub·ject [ˈsʌbdʒikt] *a.* ①受…支配的,附属的, 从属的, 受支配的. ②易受…的,易遭…的, 动不动就…的, 易患…的 *(to)*. ③以…为条件[转移]的,必须得到…的 *(to)*. ④有关本题目的,有关本科目的. *Such conduct is ~ to criticism* 这种行为容易受到批评. *a person ~ to attacks of fever* 容易发寒热的人. *The treaty is ~ to ratification.* 本条约须经批准. *~ to damage* 易遭损害的. *~ to check* 须加核对的. *~ to sale* 以出售为条件的; 供出售的. —*ad.* 在…的条件下,以…为条件,假定 *(to)*. *This can only be done ~ to the consent of the author* 这只有经著者同意才能做. *S- to your consent, I will try again.* 你要是同意,我再试一试. *S- to correction, these are the facts.* 要改请改,事实就是这样. —*n.* ①(君主国的)臣民, 国民. ②主题,问题; 论题,话题; 主因, 原因,起因; 科目, 学科; 主眼,主旨; 主人翁. ③【语法】主语;【哲】主观; 我, 自我, 主体 (*opp.* object);【逻】主位,主辞 (*opp.* attribute);【乐】主题,乐旨,主旋律;【文艺】主题. ④对象; 被催眠者,解剖用尸体; 被实验者,实验材料; 病人,患者; …质的人, …性质的人. *a British ~* 一个英国国籍的人. *the English ~* (集合词)英国国民. *the ~ of a story* 故事的主题. *a serious ~* 重大问题. *a ~ for laughter* 笑柄. *a medical [surgical] ~* 内科[外科]病人. *a good [bad] ~* 有[没有]希望医好的病人. *a hysterical ~* 歇斯底里患者. *a plethoric ~* 多血质的人. — [səbˈdʒekt] *vt.* ①使隶属,使服从,使附属,在…下面 *(to)*. ②使受…,使患…,使遭受…; 加 *(to)*. ③提供,提出, 呈核, 委托, 交给 *(to)*. *~ one's plans to another's consideration* 把计划提交别人斟酌. ***be ~ed to*** 受到,容易受到,遭受,处于; 被…折磨. ***~ oneself to*** 蒙,受. ~ **catalogue** 按学科分类的图书目录. ~ **index** 内容〔主题〕索引. ~ **matter** 题目,论题,话题; 题材; 内容. **-less** *a.* 无题的; 无主题的.
sub·jec·tion [səbˈdʒekʃən] *n.* 征服; 服从, 屈从. ***bring under ~*** 征服; 使服从. ***in ~*** 服从.
sub·jec·tive [sʌbˈdʒektiv] *a.*【哲】主观的 (*opp.* objective);【语法】主格的. —*n.*【语法】主格. **-ly** *ad.*
sub·jec·tive·ness [səbˈdʒektivnis] *n.* 主观,主观性.
sub·jec·tiv·ism [sʌbˈdʒektivizəm] *n.*【哲】主观主义.
sub·jec·ti·vist [səbˈdʒektivist] *a.* 主观主义的. —*n.* 主观主义者. **-tic** *a.*, **-ti·cal·ly** *ad.*
sub·jec·tiv·i·ty [ˌsʌbdʒekˈtiviti] *n.* 主观性; 主观,主观主义. *In studying a problem, we must shun ~.* 研究问题,忌带主观性.
sub·join [ˈsʌbˈdʒɔin] *vt.* 添加,增补,追加.
sub·ju·ga·ble [ˈsʌbdʒəgəbl] *a.* 可征服的,可制服的.
sub·ju·gate [ˈsʌbdʒugeit] *vt.* 征服,制服,使服从; 镇压,压住,抑制(感情等).
sub·ju·ga·tion [ˌsʌbdʒuˈgeiʃən] *n.* 征服; 镇压. *the danger of national ~* 亡国的危险. **-ist** *n.* 亡国论者.
sub·ju·ga·tor [ˈsʌbdʒugeitə] *n.* 征服者; 镇压者.

sub·junc·tive [səbˈdʒʌŋ*k*tiv] *a.*【语法】虚拟的，假设的。— *n.* 虚拟语气；(动词的)虚拟态。*the ~ mood* 虚拟语气。**-ly** *ad.*
sub·king·dom [ˈsʌbˈkiŋdəm] *n.*【生】门。
sub·lap·sar·i·an [ˌsʌblæpˈseriən, -ˈsær-] *n., a.*【宗】= infralapsarian **-ism** *n.*
sub·late [səbˈleit] *vt.* ①【逻，哲】否定；与…相矛盾；扬弃。②消除，勾销。
sub·la·tion [sʌbˈleiʃən] *n.* 否认；消除；【逻】否定；【哲】扬弃。
sub·lease [ˈsʌbˈliːs] *n., vt.* (土地的)转租，分租。**sub·les·see** [ˈsʌbleˈsiː] *n.* 转租入人。**sub·les·sor** [-ˈsɔː] 转租出人。
sub·let [ˈsʌbˈlet] *vt., vi., n.* 转租；分租；转包。
sub·le·thal [sʌbˈliːθəl] *a.* (毒药的量等)不足以致命的。
sub·li·brar·ian [ˈsʌblaiˈbrɛəriən] *n.* 图书馆副馆长[副管理员]。
sub·lieu·ten·ant [ˈsʌbleˈtenənt; 美 ˌsʌbluːˈtenənt] *n.* 〔英海军〕中尉。*an acting ~* 〔英海军〕少尉。
sub·li·mate [ˈsʌblimeit] *vt.*【化】使升华，提纯；提高，使高尚，纯化；理想化。— *vi.* 升华，纯化。— [-mit] *a.* 升华的；纯化的；高尚的。— *n.*【化】升华物；升汞 (= corrosive ~)。
sub·li·ma·tion [ˌsbliˈmeiʃən] *n.*【化】升华，提纯；使高尚，纯化。
sub·lime [səˈblaim] *a.* ①崇高的，庄严的，(地位)高贵的；雄伟的；卓越的，超群的；壮烈的；【化】升华的；〔诗〕崇高的，高蹈的。②傲慢的。③〔谑〕极端的，无比的。④【解】接近表面的，体表的。*a ~ commander* 卓越的指挥员。*~ courage* 英勇出众。*~ impudence* 极端无耻。*~ nerves* 体表神经。*his ~ highness* 〔古〕殿下。— *n.* 〔the ~〕庄严，崇高；壮美；宏伟；至高无上，极点 (of)。*Your answer is the ~ of stupidity.* 你的回答是极端愚妄的。— *vt., vi.* ①提高，使高尚，纯化，理想化。②【化】(使)升华，精练。**-ly** *ad.* **-r** *n.*
sub·lim·i·nal [sʌbˈliminl] *a.*【心】阈下的；潜在的。*the ~ self* 阈下[潜在]自我。**-ly** *ad.*
sub·lim·i·ty [səˈblimiti] *n.* 崇高(性)，雄伟(性)；庄严的东西；崇高的人；极致，极点；精华。
sub·lin·gual [sʌbˈliŋgwəl] *a.*【解】舌下的，舌下腺的。*~* ***gland*** 舌下腺。
sub·lu·na·r, -na·ry [ˈsʌbˈluːnə(ri)] *a.* 月下的；地上的；现世的。
sub·ma·chine·gun [ˈsʌbməˈʃiːngʌn] *n.* 手提机关枪。
sub·man [ˈsʌbmæn] *n.* *(pl.* ***-men****)* 低能者 (*opp.* superman)；人面兽心的人。
sub·mar·gin·al [sʌbˈmɑːdʒinəl] *a.*【生】亚缘的；近边缘的；【植】近叶缘的；【农经】限界以下的，边际以下的，得不偿失的。**-ly** *ad.*
sub·ma·rine [ˈsʌbməriːn] *a.* 水下的，海中的，海底的，海生的。*a ~ armour* 潜水服。*a ~ boat* 潜艇。*a ~ cable* 海底电线。*a ~ volcano* 海底火山。— *n.* 潜艇；海底动物[植物]；〔美〕= hero sandwich；〔*pl.*〕〔美俚〕脚。*an A ~ = an atomic ~* 核潜艇。— *vt.* (用潜艇)击沉，袭击。*~* **sandwich** = hero sandwich. **-r** *n.* 潜艇兵，潜艇人员。
sub·max·il·la [ˌsʌbmækˈsilə] *n.* *(pl.* ***-lae*** [-iː], ***-las****)*【解】下颌；下颌骨。
sub·max·il·lar·y [sʌbˈmæksiˌleri] *a.*【解】颌下的。
sub·me·di·ant [ˌsʌbˈmiːdiənt] *n.*【乐】全音阶的第六度；次中和弦；次中音。
sub·merge [səbˈməːdʒ] *vt.* 浸在水中，放在水中，沉入水中；淹没，使泛滥；使沉溺；使落到贫穷境地。— *vi.* 潜水；沉没，淹没；消失。*The factory is ~d with orders.* 工厂因订单过多而穷于应付。*be ~d* 被水淹没，遭水灾。*~d displacement* 排水量。*~d houses* 被水淹没的房屋。*~d reef* 暗礁。*~d speed* (潜艇的)潜航速度。*the ~d tenth* (占英国人口1/10的贫困不堪的)底层阶级。
sub·mer·gence [sʌbˈməːdʒəns] *n.* 沉没，浸入；淹没，泛滥；潜水，潜航。
sub·mer·gi·ble [sʌbˈməːdʒəbl] *a.* 能沉入水中的；能潜航的。— *n.* 潜艇。
sub·merse [səbˈməːs] *vt.* = submerge.
sub·mersed [sʌbˈməːst] *a.* 没入水中的；生长在水下的。
sub·mers·i·ble [sʌbˈməːsəbl] *a.* = submergible. **-bil·i·ty** *n.* 潜航性能，潜航力。
sub·mer·sion [sʌbˈməːʃən] *n.* = submergence.
sub·mi·cro·scop·ic [ˌsʌbmaikrəˈskɔpik] *a.* 超微观的，普通显微镜下看不见的。
sub·min·i·a·ture [sʌbˈminiətʃə] *a.* (照相机等的)超小型的。*~ camera* 超小型照相机；袖珍照相机。— *n.* 袖珍照相机。
sub·min·i·a·tur·ize [sʌbˈminiətʃərˌaiz] *vt., vi.* 使超小型化。**-za·tion** *n.*
sub·miss [səbˈmis] *a.* 〔古〕恭顺的；卑下的。
sub·mis·sion [səbˈmiʃən] *n.* ①屈服，服从，归顺，投降；谦恭，柔顺。②【法】提交公断；提交物；意见，看法；建议。③提交；呈递。④认过，自白，自白书。*I demand the ~ of the signature to an expert.* 本人要求把签名提交专家鉴定。***be frightened into ~*** 吓倒。***My ~ is that*** … = I submit that … 我的意见是…，我认为…。***with all due ~*** 必恭必敬地。
sub·mis·sive [sʌbˈmisiv] *a.* 服从的；顺从的，柔顺的，谦恭的。**-ly** *ad.* **-ness** *n.*
sub·mit [səbˈmit] *vt.* ①使服从，使顺从；使屈服。②提交，委托；提出，提供；请求判断。③认为 *(that)*。— *vi.* 服从，顺从；屈服，投降；甘受 *(to)*。*All important problems must be ~ted to the committee for discussion.* 一切重要问题均须提交委员会讨论。*I ~ that he is mistaken.* 我认为他是错了。*I ~ that this should be allowed.* 我想这是可以允许的。*I ~ to being parted from you.* 我只好忍痛跟你分别了。*The minority should ~ to the majority.* 少数应服从多数。***~ oneself to*** 甘受，服从。***~ willingly*** 心悦诚服。
sub·mit·tal [səbˈmitəl] *n.* 服从，顺从；屈服。
sub·mon·tane [sʌbˈmɔntein] *a.* 山麓的，山脚下的。
sub·mul·ti·ple [ˈsʌbˈmʌltipl] *n.*【数】因数，约数；次倍量；【电】分谐波。
sub·nar·cotic [ˈsʌbnɑːˈkɔtik] *n.* 轻度麻醉性的。
sub·nor·mal [ˈsʌbˈnɔːməl] *a.* 正常以下的，低能的；逊常的，异常的。— *n.* 低能者；【数】次法矩；次法线。**-ly** *ad.* **-i·ty** [-ˈmæliti] *n.*
sub·o·ce·an·ic [ˌsʌbəuʃiˈænik] *a.*【地】位于[发生于]大洋下的，海洋下的。
sub·oc·u·lar [ˈsʌbˈɔkjulə] *a.*【解】眼下的。
sub·of·fice [ˈsʌbˈɔfis] *n.* 支局，分局，分办事处。
sub·or·bit·al [sʌbˈɔːbitl] *a.* ①【航】(宇宙航行的)小轨迹飞行的。②在眼眶之下的。
sub·or·der [ˈsʌbɔːdə] *n.*【生】亚目。
sub·or·di·nal [sʌbˈɔːdinl] *a.*【生】亚目的。
sub·or·di·nate [səˈbɔːdənit] *a.* 下级的，次级的，副职的；从属的；服从的 *(to)*。*~ clause*【语法】从句。*~ crops* 补播作物。*~ officer* 部属，部下。*~ volcano* 单成火山。— *n.* 部属，部下，下级；从句。— [səˈbɔːdineit] *vt.* 使在次级，放在…下，使从属，使服从；轻视。***be ~d to the state plans*** 被纳入[服从]国家计划。**-ly** *ad.* **-ness** *n.*
sub·or·di·nat·ing [səˈbɔːdineitiŋ] *a.* 从属的。*~ conjunction*【语法】从属[主从]连词 (= subordinate conjunction)。
sub·or·di·na·tion [səˌbɔːdiˈneiʃən] *n.* 放在次级，使从属；次级，次等；服从，附属，从属关系。
sub·or·di·na·tion·ism [səbɔːdiˈneiʃənizm] *n.*【神】(三位一体中的第二位第三位从属于第一位的) 从属说。

sub·or·di·na·tive [səˈbɔːdinətiv] *a.* 从属的,表示从属关系的.

sub·orn [sʌˈbɔːn] *vt.* (用收买办法等)使发假誓,使作假证明;唆使,收买. **-er** *n.*

sub·or·na·tion [ˌsʌbɔːˈneiʃən] *n.* 贿赂人发假誓[做伪证];贿人犯罪;唆使.

sub·or·na·tive [səˈbɔːnətiv] *a.* 发假誓的;使做假证明的;唆使的,收买的,教唆的.

sub·ox·ide [sʌbˈɔksaid] *n.*【化】低氧化物.

sub·pack·age [ˈsʌbˈpækidʒ] *n., vt.* 分装,分包.

sub·phy·lum [sʌbˈfailəm] *n.* *(pl.* **-la** [-lə]*)*【生】亚门.

sub·plot [ˈsʌbplɔt] *n.* (小说、剧本的)次要情节.

sub·p(o)e·na [səbˈpiːnə] *n.*【法】传票. — *vt.* ***(~ed, ~'d)*** 用传票传唤[索取],传讯,传到案.

sub·po·lar [ˈsʌbˈpəulə] *a.* 近(南、北)极的,近极地的;【天】极下的;【气】副极地的.

sub·pre·fect [ˈsʌbˈpriːfekt] *n.* ①副长官(prefect). ②县长;(法国城市的)区长.

sub·pre·fec·ture [sʌbˈpriːfektʃə] *n.* 县;区;县[区]长的职位[权限].

sub·prin·ci·pal [sʌbˈprinsipl] *n.* ①(学校等的)副校长. ②〔木工〕贴近构架主材的椽或系梁. ③【乐】(风琴的)八音的最低音[基本音].

sub·prior [ˈsʌbˈpaiə] *n.* 修道院副院长.

sub·quad·rate [ˈsʌbˈkwɔdrit] *a.* 近正方形的;正方形而有圆角的.

sub·re·gion [ˈsʌbˌridʒən] *n.*【生】亚区;分区.【数】子区域;分压. **-al** *a.*

sub·rep·tion [səbˈrepʃən] *n.* ①用蒙骗手段获取利益〔尤指骗取教会捐赠〕. ②隐瞒真相虚报事实. ③由虚伪事实所引出的推断. **-rep·ti·tious** [-repˈtiʃəs] *a.* **-ly** *ad.*

sub·ro·gate [ˈsʌbrəˌgeit] *vt.* (人员的)取代,接替.【法】取代〔代债务人清偿债务而接替原债权人地位享受其一切权利〕.

sub·ro·ga·tion [sʌbrəˈgeiʃən] *n.*【法】代替;取代;接替.

sub ro·sa [sʌbˈrəuzə] *ad.* 秘密地;私下地;机密地.

sub·rou·tine [ˌsʌbruːˈtiːn] *n.*【电子学】子程序.

subs. = subscription; subsidiary.

sub·sat·el·lite [ˈsʌbˈsætəlait] *n.* 由人造卫星(或飞船)带进轨道后放出的物体.

subs.cap. = subscribed capital 应募资金.

sub·scap·u·lar [sʌbˈskæpjulə] *a.*【解】在肩胛下的.

sub·scribe [səbˈskraib] *vt.* ①捐纳,捐助;认捐,签名(认捐等). ②订购,订阅,预定;征求订户,征求定购者. ③签名,署名. — *vi.* ①认捐,捐助;赞成,同意. ②预约,预定;订阅 *(for, to)*. ③签名,署名 *(to)*. ~ *to a fund* 对某一种基金认捐. ~ *for a book* 订购书籍. *Some one has ~d a motto.* 有人写下了一句座右铭. *The ~d names carry weight.* 签名者的一些姓名起着很大作用.

sub·scrib·er [sʌbsˈkraibə] *n.* ①捐助人,捐款人. ②预约者,订购者;订户. ③〔the ~〕签名人. ④用户. *a telephone ~* 电话用户. *a ~ list* 电话簿.

sub·script [ˈsʌbskript] *a.* 写在下面的 (*opp.* adscript) — *n.* 添标,下标,下角数码〔如 H_2O的2〕.

sub·scrip·tion [səbˈskripʃən] *n.* ①认捐,捐款;预约,预定. ②订费,预约费;(书籍等的)预约,订购;订阅. ③(医生的)(处方下的)调剂附注. ④署名,签名. ***open [close] the ~ lists*** 开始[截止]募捐[预订,认股(等)]. ***solicit ~s*** 募捐. ~ **price** 订费,预约费. ~ **blank**【商】认股单.

subsec. = subsection *(pl. subsecs)*.

sub·sec·tion [ˈsʌbˈsekʃən] *n.* 小节,小组,小区分;细目;(炮兵)分队.

sub·se·quence [ˈsʌbsikwəns] *n.* 接续;紧随…之后;随后发生的事情;后果.

sub·se·quent [ˈsʌbsikwənt] *a.* 其后的,其次的;作为结果而发生的,附随的 *(to)*. ~ *events* 随后发生的事情. ~ *to his death* 在他死后. ~ *upon* 作为…的结果而发生的,接着…发生的. **-ly** *ad.* 其后,其次,接着.

sub·sere [ˈsʌbˌsiə] *n.*【生态】后成演替系列.

sub·serve [səbˈsəːv] *vt.* 帮助,补助;对…有用,对…有帮助;促进.

sub·ser·vi·ent [sʌbˈsəːviənt] *a.* 充当下手的,充当工具(的);从属的;有帮助的,有用的,有贡献的;卑躬屈节的. ***be ~ to*** 追随,屈从. **-ence, -ency** *n.* **-ly** *ad.*

sub·set [ˈsʌbset] *n.* 小集团;【数】子集(合).

sub·sex·tu·ple [sʌbˈsekstjupl] *a.* 六分之一的.

sub·share [ˈsʌbʃɛə] *n.* 利息单,股息券.

sub·shell [ˈsʌbʃel] *n.*【原】支壳层.

sub·shrub [ˈsʌbˌʃrʌb] *n.*【植】半灌木.

sub·side [səbˈsaid] *vi.* ①(船)下沉,沉下去;沉到底,沉淀;(地等)凹下去,下陷. ②(风雨、骚动、冲动等)平静下来,平息;(洪水等)退去,减退;(肿、热度等)消退,退烧. ③〔主、谑〕(象沉下去似的)坐下,跪下,躺下. *Her grief ~d.* 她的悲伤消退了. *The floods have ~d.* 洪水退了.

sub·sid·ence [ˈsʌbsidəns] *n.* 沉淀;沉下,陷下;平静,平息;减退,衰耗.

sub·sider [sʌbˈsaidə] *n.*【化】沉降槽.

sub·sid·ia·ry [səbˈsidjəri] *a.* ①辅助的,帮助的. ②次要的,附属的. ③补足的 *(to)*;(指雇佣兵)为另一国所雇佣的. ~ *coins* 辅币. *a ~ craft* 辅助舰. ~ *payments* 补助金. ~ *business* 业余工作;副业. ~ *foodstuffs* 副食品. *a ~ stream* 支流. *a ~ treaty* 军事援助协定. ~ *troops* 雇佣部队. — *n.* 补给品;附属者,附属品;子公司〔= ~ company〕;【乐】副主题.

sub·si·di·za·tion [ˌsʌbsidiˈzeiʃən] *n.* 补助,津贴,给奖.

sub·si·dize [ˈsʌbsidaiz] *vt.* 给补助金,给津贴,给奖金;用贿赂拉拢,收买.

sub·si·dy [ˈsʌbsidi] *n.* 助学金,补助金,津贴;奖金;(国家间的)财政援助;【英史】(给国王的)特别津贴.

sub·sist [səbˈsist] *vi.* ①生存;活下去,维持生命,维持生活 *(on; upon)*. ②存在;继续存在.【哲】(逻辑上、理论上)存在;抽象地存在. — *vt.* 〔罕〕供给粮食,供养. *We are unable to ~ without air and water.* 没有空气和水我们就活不下去. ~ *by begging* 靠讨饭维持生活.

sub·sist·ence [sʌbˈsistəns] *n.* 生存;存在;生计;生活费;口粮;给养;【哲】存在;存在物,实体. ***gain one's ~*** 活得下去. ***labour for ~*** 做工过日子. ~ **department** 〔美〕粮食部,兵站部. ~ **diet** 维持生命所需要的最小限度食物. ~ **farm [homestead]** 〔美〕(为失业工人办的)自耕自给农场. ~ **money** 生活费. ~ **rates** 〔美〕(船客的)膳费. ~ **stores** 〔美〕粮食,粮饷. ~ **wages** 仅够维持生活的最低工资.

sub·sist·ent [səbˈsistənt] *a.* 生存的;现存的,存在的;生计的;给养的;附著的,固有的.

sub·soil [ˈsʌbsɔil] *n.*【农】下层土,心土,底土;【建】天然地基. — *vt.* 翻起…的底土.

sub·so·lar [sʌbˈsəulə] *a.* 太阳正下面的;赤道的;太阳下的,现世的.

sub·son·ic [ˈsʌbˈsɔnik] *a.* 亚音(速)的;阈限下的.

sub·space [ˈsʌbˌspeis] *n.*【数】子空间.

sub spe·ci·e [sʌbˈspiʃiː] 〔L.〕在…的状态下,以…形式.

sub spe·ci·e ae·ter·ni·ta·tis [sʌbˈspiʃiː aiˌtəːniˈtɑːtis] 〔L.〕在永恒的状态下,以永恒的形式.

sub·spe·cies [ˈsʌbspiːʃiːz] *n.*【生】亚种.

sub·spe·ci·fic [ˌsʌbspiˈsifik] *a.*【生】亚种的.

subst. = substantive; substitute.

sub·stance [ˈsʌbstəns] *n.* ①物质,材料;【哲】实体,本体,本质 *(opp.* appearance*)*. ②实质,内容;(故事等的)要旨,要领,大意,梗概. ③财产,资产,资力. ④【神】灵,(三位一体的)体. ⑤(织品的)质地. *The ~ is usually more important than the form.* 内容总是比形式重要. *I can tell you the ~.* 我可以讲大意给你听. *a porous ~* 多

孔体. *a man of* ~ 资产家,财主. **in** ~ 实质上,本质上;大体上. ***sacrifice the* ~ *for the shadow*** 只图虚名不求实效,舍本逐末. ***waste one's* ~** 浪费财产.

sub·stand·ard [səbˈstændəd] *a.* 标准以下的;〔美〕【法】(食品、药品成分)法定标准以下的;【语】非标准语的;非规范化的.

sub·stan·tial [səbˈstænʃəl] *a.* 实质的,真正的;【哲】实在的,实体的,本体的,本质的. ②有财产的,有资产的;有真价的,有信用的,可靠的. ③富裕的;有实力的. ④有内容的,充实的;有价值的;质地好的,坚固的,坚牢的,结实的. ⑤相当的,多额的,很多的;紧要的. ⑥大体上的,事实上的(一致、成功等). *a* ~ *hope* 可靠的希望. *a* ~ *farmer* 富裕的农民. *a man of* ~ *build* 体格结实的人. *a* ~ *house* 坚固的房子. *a* ~ *concession* 相当大的让步. *a* ~ *improvement* 显著的进步. *a* ~ *point* 重要的地点. **-ism** *n.*【哲】实体论. **-ist** *n.* 实体论者. **-ness** *n.*

sub·stan·tial·i·ty [səbˌstænʃiˈæliti] *n.* (有)实质,(有)内容;(有)实体,(有)形体;坚固.

sub·stan·tial·ize [səbˈstænʃəlaiz] *vt., vi.* (使)实体化,(使)实质化,(使)成为真实.

sub·stan·tial·ly [səbˈstænʃəli] *ad.* ①实体上,本质上,实质上;大体上. ②坚强地,坚固地. ③充分地,丰富地.

sub·stan·tials [səbsˈtænʃəlz] *n.* 〔*pl.*〕实质性部分;重要部分;纲要,要领,大意.

sub·stan·tiate [sʌbsˈtæʃieit] *vt.* 使具体[实体]化;证实,证明某事有根据.

sub·stan·ti·a·tion [səbˌstænʃiˈeiʃən] *n.* 具体化;证实.

sub·stan·ti·a·tive [səbˈstænʃiˌeitiv] *a.* ①表示存在的,表示实在的. ②独立的;有实体的;变为实体的;具体的. ③证实的,确认的.

sub·stan·ti·a·tor [səbˈstænʃieitə] *n.* 证明人,证人.

sub·stan·ti·val [sʌbstənˈtaivəl] *a.*【语法】实词的,名词性的. **-ly** *ad.*

sub·stan·tive [ˈsʌbstəntiv] *a.* ①实体的;真实的. ②独立的,自立的. ③坚固的;实质的;本质的. ④【语法】实词的,名词的;表示存在的. ⑤【法】实体的;规定权利与义务的. — *n.*【语法】实词,名词. ~ *colours* 直接染料. *a* ~ *major* 领正薪的少校. *a* ~ *motion* 正式动议. ~ *enactment* 明文规定. *nexus* ~ 名词性二元语核. *a* ~ *verb* 存在动词〔指 be〕. ~ **right** 基本人权〔指法律规定权利之外的生存权等〕. **-ly** *ad.*

sub·stan·ti·vize [ˈsʌbstəntivaiz] *vt.*【语法】使名词化.

sub·sta·tion [ˈsʌbsteiʃən] *n.* 分站;变压所;支局,分局,派出所. *a power* ~ 变电所.

sub·stit·u·ent [sʌbˈstitjuənt] *n.* 代替者,取代者;【化】取代基.

sub·sti·tute [ˈsʌbstitjuːt] *n.* 代替者[物],代用品;候补员;后补选手;代入(数);【语法】代用词[语];【矿】转接器,短节. *There's no* ~ *for parents.* 父母亲是没有别人可以代替的. — *vt.* 以…代替,用…代替(*for.*);【化】取代. ~ *A for B.* 用 A 代 B. ~ *margarine for butter* 用人造黄油代替黄油. ~ *sb. by [with] another* 用别人接替某人. — *vi.* 作…代理者,〔美〕代替;【化】取代. *John will* ~ *for his father.* 约翰将作为他父亲的代理人.

sub·sti·tu·tion [ˈsʌbstitjuːʃən] *n.* 代,代用,代替,更替,置换;【化】取代;【数】代换;代入;【法】预定继承人;【语法】词的代用. **-al** *a.* **-ary** *a.*

sub·sti·tu·tive [ˈsʌbstitjuːtiv] *a.* 代替的,代用的;取代的;补充的. *a* ~ *tooth* 永久齿.

sub·sti·tu·tor [sʌbsˈtitjuːtə] *n.* 替手;代用品.

sub·strate [ˈsʌbstreit] *n.* ①底层,地层. ②【无】(半导体工艺中的)衬底,基底. ③【生】(生态学中的)基层;【生化】基质;被酶作用物.

sub·strat·o·sphere [sʌbˈstrætəsfiə] *n.*【空】亚[副]平流层;亚同温层.

sub·stra·tum [ˈsʌbˈstrɑːtəm, ˈsʌbˈstreitəm] *n.* (*pl.* **-ta** [-tə]) 下层;基础;【生】(生态学中的)基层;根本;【生化】培养基;基质;【农】下层土;底土,心土;【摄】(胶片片基与乳剂间的)胶层;〔*pl.*〕〔美〕下层社会.

sub·struc·ture, sub·struc·tion [ˈsʌbˈstrʌktʃə, -ʃən] *n.*【建】下部结构,下层建筑,基础工程,地下建筑;基础,根基,根底. **-tur·al** *a.*

sub·sume [sʌbˈsjuːm] *vt.*【逻】包摄,包含.

sub·sump·tion [sʌbˈsʌmpʃən] *n.*【逻】包摄,包含;包容;(三段论法的)小前提.

sub·sur·face [ˈsʌbˈsəːfis] *a.* 表面下的,液面下的;地下的,水面下的. — *n.* 地面下[水面下]的部分〔岩石,土壤,水层等〕.

sub·syn·chron·ous [ˈsʌbˈsiŋkrənəs] *a.*【物】次同步的.

sub·sys·tem [ˈsʌbˌsistim] *n.* (系统的)分部;分体系,支系统.

sub·tan·gent [ˈsʌbˈtændʒənt] *n.*【数】次切线[距].

sub·teen [ˈsʌbˈtiːn] *n.* 〔美〕将近十三岁的儿童.

sub·tem·per·ate [ˈsʌbˈtempərit] *a.* 亚温带的.

sub·ten·an·cy [ˈsʌbˈtenənsi] *n.* (房、地等)转借,转租.

sub·ten·ant [sʌbˈtenənt] *n.* (房屋、土地的)转租租户.

sub·tend [səbˈtend] *vt.*【数】(弦、边)对(弧、角);【植】包在叶腋内.

sub·ten·der [ˈsʌbˈtendə] *n.*【军】潜艇供应船 (= submarine tender).

sub·tense [səbˈtens] *n.*【数】弦,对边. — *a.* 根据所对角度测量的. ~ *method*【测】视测法.

sub·ter- *pref.* 下;在下;少于,次于;私下: *subter*natural.

sub·ter·fuge [ˈsʌbtəfjuːdʒ] *n.* 遁辞,托辞,口实;欺骗,诡计;规避.

sub·ter·human [ˌsʌbtəˈhjuːmən] *a.* 低于人类的.

sub·ter·min·al [ˈsʌbˈtəːminl] *a.* 几乎在末端的.

sub·ter·nat·u·ral [ˌsʌbtəˈnætʃərəl] *a.* 逊于天然的;不十分自然的.

sub·ter·rane [ˈsʌbtərein] *n.* 下层;洞穴,地下室;【地】表层下基岩.

sub·ter·ra·ne·an, -ne·ous [sʌbtəˈreiniən; -niəs] *a.* 地下的,地中的;隐藏的,秘密的. *a* ~ *railroad* 地下铁路. *a* ~ *river* 伏流. *a* ~ *line* 地下线. *a* ~ *dwelling* 地下住所. *a* ~ *pupa* 埋蛹. **-ly** *ad.*

sub·thresh·old [ˈsʌbˈθreʃhəuld] *a.* (药剂量)次于最低限度的,不足以起作用的.

sub·til(e) [ˈsʌtl] *a.* ***(-til·er; -til·est)*** 〔古〕= subtle.

sub·ti·lin [ˈsʌbtilin] *n.*【生化】枯草菌素.

sub·til·ty, sub·til·i·ty [ˈsʌbtəlti, -tiliti] *n.* 〔古〕= subtlety.

sub·til·i·za·tion [ˌsʌtlaiˈzeiʃən] *n.* 稀薄化;纤细化;微妙化;精细化.

sub·til·ize [ˈsʌtilaiz] *vt.* 使稀薄;使纤细;细微区别;使微妙,使精细,精细地讨论;穿凿附会. — *vi.* 趋于精细[微妙];详细讨论;过分精细.

sub·til·ty [ˈsʌtəlti] 〔古〕= subtlety.

sub·ti·lysin [sʌbtiˈlaisin] *n.*【生化】枯草菌溶素.

sub·ti·tle [ˈsʌbtaitl] *n.* (书籍的)副题;小标题;【影】说明字幕;对白字幕. — *vt.* 加副标题;加说明[对白]字幕.

sub·tle [ˈsʌtl] *a.* ***(-tler; -tlest)*** ①精细的;巧妙的,精巧的;敏感的,敏锐的. ②微妙的,难于捉摸的,难解的. ③狡猾的,阴险的(敌人). ④〔古〕稀薄的. ~ *intellect* 睿智. *a* ~ *observer* 敏锐的观察者. ~ *fingers* 灵巧的手指. ~ *power* 神秘不可思议的力量. *a* ~ *perfume* 幽雅的香味. **-ness** *n.*

sub·tle·ty [ˈsʌtlti] *n.* ①精妙;巧妙,纤巧;敏锐,敏感;细微的区别;微妙,难捉摸. ②狡猾,阴险. ③稀薄.

sub·tly [ˈsʌtli] *ad.* 巧妙地;细微地,微妙地;难解地;狡猾地.

sub·ton·ic [sʌbˈtɔnik] *n.*【乐】全音阶的第七个音,下主音.

sub·to·pi·a [sʌbˈtəupjə, -ˈtɔpjə] *n.* 〔英〕〔蔑〕城市化的

乡村地区；城乡一律化丧失自然美景的趋势〔该词由 sub 加 (u)topia 构成〕。**-n** *a.*

sub·to·pic [ˈsʌbˌtɔpik] *n.* (主题的)分题。

sub·to·tal [ˈsʌbˌtəutl] *n.* 部分和,小计。— *vt., vi.* 求部分和,把…小计。

sub·tract [səbˈtrækt] *vt., vi.* 减去，扣除 *(from). That ~s nothing from his merit.* 那丝毫没有减损他的功绩。**-or,** 〔美〕**er,** *n.* 减少者,减去者;【数】减数。

sub·trac·tion [sʌbˈtrækʃən] *n.* 减去，扣除 *(from);* 【数】减法。

sub·trac·tive [sʌbˈtræktiv] *a.* 减少的；【数】(应)减去的,带有减号[负号]的。

sub·tra·hend [ˈsʌbtrəhend] *n.* 【数】减数。

sub·trans·par·ent [ˈsʌbtrænsˈpɛərənt] *a.* 半透明的。

sub·treas·ur·y [sʌbˈtreʒəri] *n.* 〔美〕国[金]库分库。

sub·tribe [ˈsʌbtraib] *n.* 【生】亚族。

sub·trop·ic, -i·cal [ˈsʌbˈtrɔpik(əl)] *a.* 亚热带的。**-ics** *n. pl.* 亚热带。

su·bu·late [ˈsju:bjulit] *a.* 【植】钻状的；锥形的。

sub·um·brel·la [ˌsʌbʌmˈbrelə] *n.* 【动】(水母的)下伞(面)。

sub·urb [ˈsʌbə:b] *n.* ①〔常 *pl.*〕郊区,城郊,市郊,近郊。②〔*pl.*〕附近，周围。***in the ~s*** 在郊区。***the ~s of sorrow*** 悲哀的境遇。

sub·ur·ban [səˈbə:bən] *a.* ①郊区的，住在城郊的。②〔英〕土气的；偏狭的。~ *point of view* 偏狭的观点。— *n.* 〔美〕郊区居民。

sub·ur·ban·ite [səˈbə:bənait] *n.* 郊区居民。

sub·ur·ban·ize [səˈbə:bənaiz] *vt., vi.* 使成市郊，使变为市郊,市郊化。**-i·za·tion** *n.*

sub·ur·bi·a [səˈbə:biə] *n.* 郊区;〔集合词〕郊区居民；郊区居民风习。

sub·ur·bi·car·i·an [səˌbə:biˈkeriən] *a.* 在罗马市郊的;〔尤指〕【天主】教皇的七管区的。

sub·ur·sine [sʌbˈə:sain] *a.* 有点象熊的。

sub·va·ri·e·ty [ˈsʌbvəraiəti] *n.* 【生】亚变种。

sub·vene [səbˈvi:n] *vi.* 〔罕〕进行帮助,来补救,干预。

sub·ven·tion [səbˈvenʃən] *n.* (政府的)补助金；津贴；援助。**-ary** *a.*

sub ver·bo [sʌbˈvə:bəu] 〔L.〕(词典，索引等中)见某词条。

sub·ver·sion [sʌbˈvə:ʃən] *n.* 颠覆(活动)；破坏；覆灭，瓦解。*to protect our country from ~ by external enemies.* 防御国家外部敌人的颠覆活动。**-ary** *a.*

sub·ver·sive [sʌbˈvə:siv] *a.* 颠覆(性)的，破坏(性)的。— *n.* 颠覆分子。**-ly** *ad.* **-ness** *n.*

sub·vert [səbˈvə:t] *vt.* 颠覆,推翻，破坏(国家等)；搅乱(人心),败坏(风化),腐蚀(思想)。**-er** *n.*

sub·vit·re·ous [ˈsʌbvitriəs] *a.* 光泽不及玻璃的；【物】亚琉态的。

sub·vo·cal [ˈsʌbˈvəukəl] *a.* 默读的。**-ize** *vi.* 默读。

sub·way [ˈsʌbwei] *n.* (过马路的)地道(=〔美〕underpass)；〔美〕地下铁道[列车]。

sub·ze·ro [sʌbˈziərəu] *n., a.* 零下(的)；负(的)；严寒的。

suc- *pref.* 〔用于 c 前〕= sub-。

suc·cades [səˈkeidz] *n.* 〔*pl.*〕蜜饯糖果。

suc·ce·da·ne·um [sʌksiˈdeiniəm] *n.* *(pl.* *~s, -nea* [-niə]*)* 代用品〔如牙医代替贵重金属的合金〕；代用药；代理人,替手。**-da·ne·ous** [-ˈdeiniəs] *a.*

suc·ceed [səkˈsi:d] *vt.* 继…之后,继承；接着…发生;〔诗〕使成功。— *vi.* ①成功，完成胜利 *(in);* (计划等)顺利进行。②继承,承受；接连，接着发生 *(to). Summer ~s spring.* 春去夏来。~ *sb. as Premier* 接替某人担任总理。*Nothing ~s like success.* 一事成功事事顺利。~ *in doing sth.* 做某事成功。~ *in examination* 考试及格。*His plans ~ed.* 他的计划成功了。~ ***in life*** 发迹。~ ***oneself*** 〔美〕再度当选；连任，留任。***~ing years*** 接连的几年。

★"继承"意义的 *n., a.* 分别为 succession, successive. "成功"意义的 *n., a.* 分别为 success, successful. **-ent** *a.*

suc·cen·tor [səkˈsentə] *n.* (教堂)唱诗班代理指挥[副指挥]；唱诗班的低音领唱人。

suc·cès de scan·dale [sukˈsei də skɑ̃:nˈdɑl] *n.* 〔F.〕(文艺作品等)因内容丑恶而轰动的臭名声；臭名远扬的作品。

suc·cès d'es·time [sukˈsei desˈti:m] *n.* 〔F.〕(对不大成功的演员、作者的)礼貌上的欢迎[称赞]。

suc·cès fou [sukˈseiˌfu:] *n.* 〔F.〕令人趋之若狂的大成功。

suc·cess [səkˈses] *n.* ①成功,成就；好结果,好成绩；成功者；考试及格者。②〔方、罕〕结果,成绩。*a good ~* 好结果,成功。*an ill [a bad] ~* 坏结果,失败。*have great ~ in life.* 大大发迹了。*He was a great ~ as an actor.* 他的演员生涯是非常成功的。*My holiday in Switzerland was a great ~.* 我在瑞士度过的假期是一次大成功。*The evening was a ~.* 那晚(的宴会)很是热闹愉快。***drink ~ to*** 祝…成功干杯。***make a ~ of ...*** 把…做得很成功。***make (conferences) a ~*** 开好(会议)。***meet with ~*** 成功。~ **worker** 对国家有重大贡献的工人[工作者]。

suc·cess·ful [sʌkˈsesful] *a.* 成功的；结果好的；有成绩[成就]的；及格的；盛大的(会等)；幸运的；出了头的。*a ~ play* 成功的戏剧。*a ~ candidate* 及格者；当选者。*a ~ man* 一帆风顺的人。***be ~ in*** 在…上成功。**-ly** *ad.* **-ness** *n.*

suc·ces·sion [səkˈseʃən] *n.* ①接连发生,继起,接续；继承性；(计算技术的)逐次性。②继承；继承权；继承顺序；继任；后继。③【生】系列；世系,系统；演替；【农】轮栽。*a ~ of disasters* 灾连祸接。*He is not in the ~.* 他没有继承权。***by ~*** 按照继承顺序。***in due ~*** 按自然的次序。***in ~*** 接连,接着。***in ~ to*** 继…之后(担任)。~ **duties** 继承税。

suc·ces·sion·al [sʌkˈseʃənəl] *a.* 相继的,连续的。

suc·ces·sive [sʌkˈsesiv] *a.* 接连的,相继的，连绵的,继续的,连续的；逐次的。~ *inhibition* 相继抑制，后抑制。**-ly** *ad.* 接连,相继,依次。

suc·ces·sor [sʌkˈsesə] *n.* 继承人；继任者,接班人；后继者 *(opp.* predecessor*)*；顶替者 *(to). unworthy ~s* 不肖子孙。*~s to the cause of the revolution* 革命事业的接班人。

suc·ci [ˈsʌkai, ˈsʌksai] *n.* succus 的复数。

suc·ci·nate [ˈsʌksiˌneit] *n.* 【化】琥珀酸盐(或酯),丁二酸盐(或酯)。

suc·cinct [səkˈsiŋkt] *a.* 简洁的,简明的；〔古〕紧束的,紧贴在身上的；卷起的。**-ly** *ad.* **-ness** *n.*

suc·cin·ic [səkˈsinik] *a.* ~ **acid** 琥珀酸,丁二酸。

suc·cin·ite [ˈsʌksinait] *n.* 琥珀(色)。

suc·cor [ˈsʌkə] *n.* 〔美〕= succour.

suc·co·ry [ˈsʌkəri] *n.* 【植】菊苣(= chicory)。

suc·co·tash [ˈsʌkətæʃ] *n.* 〔美〕豆煮玉米〔常加有腊肉〕。

suc·co(u)r [ˈsʌkə] *n.* 援助，救援；援助者，支援物品；〔*pl.*〕〔古〕援军。— *vt.* 帮助,救济,支援。

suc·cu·bus [ˈsʌkjubəs] *n.* *(pl.* **-bi** [-bai]*)* 女妖；妖魔；娼妓。

suc·cu·lence, -cy [ˈsʌkjuləns(i)] *n.* 多汁(性)；青饲料；【植】肉质性。

suc·cu·lent [ˈsʌkjulənt] *a.* 多汁的，多液的；极有兴趣的,津津有味的；有活力的。— *n.* 肉质植物。~ *fodder* 青饲料。**-ly** *ad.*

suc·cumb [səˈkʌm] *vi.* 屈服；死 *(to).* ~ *to curiosity* 被好奇心所驱使。~ *to temptation* 被诱惑所屈服。~ *to one's enemies* 被敌人打败，向敌人屈服。~ *to superior numbers* 被优势压倒。~ *to disease* 病死。

suc·cus [ˈsʌkəs] *n.* 分泌液；液汁；植物液剂。

suc·cuss [səˈkʌs] *vt.* 猛摇(病人)以确定体腔内有无积液。

suc·cus·sa·tory [səˈkʌsətəri] *a.* (地震) 上下振动振幅

小的.

suc·cus·sion [sə'kʌʃən] *n.* 猛摇;【医】振荡(法).

suc·cus·sive [sə'kʌsiv] *a.* 强烈摇动的;〔原尤指〕【医】振荡的〔猛摇(病人)以诊察体腔内有无积液〕.

such 〔常音 sʌtʃ; 弱音 sətʃ〕 *a.*〔无比较级及最高级. 在句中可用作定语、表语;有时为避免形容词的重复出现可作代用词;与 all, any, many, no, one, few, some 一起修饰名词时,放在这些词的后面;引出定语从句修饰名词时,一般放在名词的前面,如放在后面,则含有轻蔑意味;与另一形容词一起修饰单数名词时位于不定冠词 a(n) 之前,如 such a big table〕. ①ⓐ 那样的, 这样的, 那种, 这种. ～ *a man* 那样的人. ～ *men* 那样的人们. *all* ～ *men* 所有那一类人. *any [some]* ～ *man [thing]* 一个这样的人[东西]. *no* ～ *thing* 那种事情不…, 不会不会! ～ *a(n) one* 〔雅〕那样的人;〔古〕某人. *He is not well off, only he seems* ～. 他并不富裕,只是象富裕罢了. *Long may he continue* ～! 希望他永远那样! *You may use my car,* ～ *as it is.* 这样一部汽车,请将就用吧. *S- is life [the world]!* 人生就是这样! *S- master,* ～ *servant.* 有其主必有其仆. ⓑ〔用作关联词, 与 as 相呼应〕象…那样的. ～ *things as iron, silver, and gold* 铁、银、金这一类东西. *I said no* ～ *thing (as that).* 我没说那种事. *Children* ～ *as these will never learn anything.* 这样的孩子终归学不了什么. *I am not* ～ *a fool* (= so foolish) *as to believe that.* 我不是连那种事都相信的笨蛋. *His illness was not (one)* ～ *as to cause anxiety* 他的病不是那种令人着急的病. ⓒ〔用作关联词, 与 that 相呼应〕如此…以致. *She had* ～ *a fright that she fainted.* 她吓得昏倒下去了. *S- was the force of the explosion that all the windows were broken.* 爆炸力大得把所有的窗子都震破了. ②ⓐ〔和形容词连用〕那样,这样;〔口〕非常. *I have never met* ～ *a good man.* 我从来没有碰见过那样好的人. ～ *a big stick* 那样大的手杖. *We had* ～ *a pleasant time* (= so pleasant a time). 〔口〕我们那时候真是开心极了. ⓑ〔不连接形容词,直接连接名词〕那样好的, 漂亮的, 了不得的, 伟大的, 厉害的, 这样坏的. *Did you ever see* ～ *weather?* 你见过这样坏[好]的天气没有? *We had* ～ *sport!* 我们(那时)有趣极了! *We never had* ～ *sport.* 我们从来没有那样快活过. *He cannot come too often, he gives* ～ *pleasure.* 他这样有趣, 可惜他不常来. *Don't be in* ～ *a hurry.* 别这样慌呀. ③〔法律条文或商业文件用语〕上述的, 上开的, 此类的. *Whoever shall make* ～ *return…* 作上述报告者…. ④〔不定意义〕如此这般的,这样的,某某. *We know that on* ～ *a date he lived at number so and so of* ～ *and* ～ *a street.* 我们知道他在这个时期是住在这样一条街的某某号里. *S- and* ～ *results will follow from* ～ *and* ～ *causes.* 有如此这般的原因就有如此这般的结果. — *pro.* ①这样的人[物]〔通常指复数〕. *I dislike* ～. 我不欢喜那种东西. ②…的人们[东西]〔～ *person(s) or thing(s)* 之意〕. ～ *as believe me* 相信我的人们. ③〔卑, 商〕那样的事情, 刚才所说的事情[东西], 那, 这, 他们. *S- can be easily done.* 那容易做. ***all*** ～ 大家,人人,人们 (*So peace to all* ～. 祝大家平安. *all* ～ *as have erred* 有错的人们). ***and*** ～〔口〕等等 (*tools, machines, and* ～ 工具、机器等等). ***another*** ～ 再一个那样的人[物],同样的一个人[物]. ***as*** ～ 本身;以那个资格[身分],名符其实地 (*Wealth, as* ～, *doesn't matter much* 财富本身算不了什么. *In country places strangers are welcome as* ～ 在乡间,外乡人是名符其实作为外乡人受到欢迎的). ～ ***as it is*** 质量不好的,没有什么价值的(东西) (*He won't refuse to give you his help,* ～ *as it is.* 他不会拒绝帮助你的,尽管对你帮助不大).

such-and-such ['sʌtʃənsʌtʃ] *a.* 某某; 这样那样的. *the payment of* ～ *sums to* ～ *persons* 把某些钱付给某些人.

such·like ['sʌtʃlaik] *a.* 这样的, 诸如此类的, 这种. — *pro.* 这样的人[东西],这种人[东西]. *Avoid pork and* ～ *indigestible food.* 忌吃猪肉和这一类不消化的东西.

suck [sʌk] *vt.* ①吮吸,咂(奶头、指头等); 吸进, 吞进, 吃(奶). ②吸收(水分、知识等) *(in)*; 得到(利益等) *(from; out of)*. — *vi.* 吮吸;吃奶;(水泵)抽吸. ～ ***a rich teat*** 〔美〕得到肥缺. ～ ***around***〔美俚〕(为得到好处)老在(某人、某处)四周打转. ～ ***at*** 吸, 抽 (*He sat* ～*ing at his pipe.* 他抽着烟斗坐着). ～ ***in*** 吸进去;吸收(知识);(漩涡等)卷进去. ～ ***in to***〔英学生俚〕拍马屁. ～ ***in your guts***〔美〕别响! ～ ***one's teeth*** 啧啧地不胜羡慕. ～ ***out*** 吸出. ～ ***the blood of*** 吸取…的血;榨取膏血. ～ ***the breast of*** 吃…的奶. ～ ***the monkey***〔俚〕拿瓶子喝. ～ ***up*** 吸,吃(水、奶等)吸收;吸取. ～ ***up (to)***〔英学生俚〕= ～ in to. — *n.* 吮吸,咂,吸入;吃奶;卷入;一口,一杯;〔俚〕(奶瓶等的)奶头;〔俚〕酒;〔英学生俚〕〔*pl.*〕糖果;〔英学生俚〕欺骗;失望,失败. *Sucks!* = *What a* ～! 真是大失所望!〔看见很象有把握的对手失败时说的玩笑话〕. *a child at* ～ 奶娃娃,乳儿. ***be at*** ～ 吃着奶. ***give*** ～ ***to*** 给…吃奶. ***take a*** ～ ***at*** 吸一吸,吸一口. ～**fish** *n.* 鲫鱼. ～**-in** *n.*〔英俚〕失望;失败;欺骗. ～**-up** *n.*〔俚〕拍马屁的人.

suck·er ['sʌkə] *n.* ①吮吸者;吃奶的孩子;(尚未断乳的)仔猪,仔鲸(等). ②吸管;吸皮〔小孩玩具〕;(唧筒的)吸子;〔口〕棒糖 *an ice* ～ 冰棍;【植】徒长枝,腋芽,根出条;(寄生植物的)吸器,吸根;【动】吸盘;【鱼】(有吸盘的)臙脂鱼类. ③〔美俚〕傻瓜,笨旦; 生手; 没有经验的人,初出茅庐,不懂事的人; 容易上当的人; 马戏团看客;〔美俚〕食客,寄生虫;酒量好的人;不正当的经纪人;诈欺取财的人;直译书. *a* ～ *trap*〔美〕骗人的手段[方法]. ***play for a*** ～〔美俚〕骗;骗去别人的钱. ***S- State***〔美〕伊利诺斯 (Illinois) 州的别名. — *vt.* 摘去徒长枝[腋芽];生徒长枝[腋芽]. — *vi.*【植】长出根出条; 成为吸根. ～**fish**【鱼】= remora. ～ **list**〔美俚〕有希望成为顾客或捐献者的人的名单, 容易上当受骗的傻瓜名单.

suck·ing ['sʌkiŋ] *a.* 吮吸的;吃奶的,没有断奶的;〔口〕不熟练的, 不懂事的. *a* ～ *stomach*【动】吸胃. ～**-pig** *n.* (整只烤用的)乳猪.

suck·le ['sʌkl] *vt.* 喂奶, 哺乳; 抚育, 养育; 吮吸, 吸取. **-r** 哺乳动物 (= suckling).

suck·ling ['sʌkliŋ] *n.* 乳儿,乳兽;乳臭未干的小伙子,生手. *babes and* ～*s* 全是娃娃.

su·crase ['su:kreis] *n.*【生化】转化酶; 蔗糖酶 (= invertase).

su·crate ['su:kreit] *n.*【化】蔗糖合物.

Su·cre ['su:krei] *n.* ①苏克雷〔玻利维亚法定首都〕. ② **A. J. de** ～ 苏克雷〔1795—1830, 南美厄瓜多尔和玻利维亚的解放者,玻利维亚第一任大总统〕. ③〔s-〕苏克雷〔厄尔多尔货币单位〕.

su·crose ['sju:krəus] *n.*【化】蔗糖.

suc·tion ['sʌkʃən] *n.* ①吸,吸引, 吸入; 吸力. ②吸气,吸气通风;【物】空吸. ③〔英〕喝酒. ④吸水管. *a* ～ *machine* 吸尘机. ～ *effect* 吸引作用. *a* ～ *head* 吸引高度. *a* ～ *lift* 吸引升力. *a* ～ *filter* 空吸滤器. ～ *pipe* 吸入管, 吸水管. ～ *stroke*【机】吸入(冲)程; 吸气行程. ～ **plate**【机】吸板;【医】吸附假牙床. ～ **pump** 抽水机,真空泵.

suc·to·ri·al [sʌk'tɔ:riəl] *a.*【动】吸的,吸附的; 适于吸的;有吸盘的,吸附生活的;吸血为生的.

Su·dan [su:'dæn] *n.* 苏丹〔非洲北部. 沙哈拉 (Sahara) 沙漠南部、大西洋与红海间辽阔地区的总名称〕. The S- 苏丹(国名). ～ **grass**【植】苏丹草〔一种一年生牧草〕. **-ic** ①*a.* 苏丹的;苏丹语的. ②*n.* 苏丹人.

Su·da·nese [su:də'ni:z] *a.* 苏丹 (Sudan) 的. — *n.* 〔*sing., pl.*〕苏丹人.

su·dar·i·um [sju:'dεəriəm] *n.* *(pl.* ***-ria*** [-riə]*)* ①在上面奇迹地留有耶稣面容的手帕. ②〔泛指〕奇迹一样显现的耶稣像. ③盖过耶稣的头的手巾.

su·da·tion [sju:'deiʃən] *n.* 出汗,发汗.

su·da·to·ri·um [sju:də'tɔ:riəm] *n.* *(pl.* ***-ria*** [-riə]*)*

发汗浴,蒸汽浴;热气浴室.

su·da·to·ry [ˈsjuːdətəri] *a.* 促进发汗的;发汗的. — *n.* 发汗剂;发汗浴;热气浴室 (= sudatorium).

sudd [sʌd] *n.* 〔Ar.〕水面植物堆集.

sud·den [ˈsʌdn] *a.* 突然的,忽然的,意想不到的,急遽的. *a* ~ *load*【工】骤加载荷. *be* ~ *in one's action* 行动唐突. ~ *death* 暴死;(不分胜负时增加的)最后一次决赛时间. — *n.* 突然,忽然. ***(all) of a* ~, *on a [the]* ~, *all on a* ~** 突然,忽然. **-ly** *ad.* **-ness** *n.*

su·dor·if·er·ous [sjuːdəˈrifərəs] *a.* 分泌汗的.

su·dor·if·ic [ˈsjuːdəˈrifik] *a.*, *n.* 发汗的;促进发汗的;发汗药.

Su·dra [ˈsuːdrə] *n.* 首陀罗,首陁〔印度四种姓中的最下等级,即奴隶〕.

suds [sʌdz] *n.* 〔*pl.*〕肥皂液 (= soap-~);肥皂泡;泡沫;〔美俚〕啤酒;钱. ***in the*** ~ 〔俚〕在困难中;穷困;沮丧. **-y** *a.*

sue [sjuː, suː] *vt.* ①控告,控诉,和…打官司. ②请求. ③〔古〕求婚. — *vi.* ①起诉. ~ *at (the) law* 打官司,起诉. ~ *for a breach of promise* 控告违约. ②求. ~ *for peace* 求和. ~ ***and labour clause*** 损害防止条款〔海上保险用语〕. ~ ***out***【法】请求法院而得到(赦免等).

Sue [sjuː, suː] *n.* Susan, Susanna, Susannah (女名)的爱称.

suède [sweid] *n.* (里面经过柔软加工的做手套等用)小山羊皮 (= ~ leather). **-d** *a.* 仿麂皮的.

Suel·len [suːˈelin] *n.* 苏埃琳〔女子名〕.

su·et [ˈsjuit, suit] *n.* (牛羊等腰部的)板油. ~ **pudding** 羊油布丁. **-y** *a.*

Su·ez [ˈsju(ː)iz] *n.* 苏伊士〔埃及港市〕. *the* ~ *Canal* 苏伊士运河〔埃及〕.

suf- *pref.* 〔用于 f 前〕= sub-.

suf. = suffix. **suff.** = suffix; sufficient.

suf·fer [ˈsʌfə] *vt.* ①遭受,蒙受;经受;体验到(痛苦等). ②〔常与否定词连用〕忍受,忍耐,忍住. ③宽恕,原谅;允许,容忍,听任. ~ *a loss* 遭受损失. ~ *death* 死. ~ *punishment* 受罚. *I will not* ~ *such conduct.* 我不能容忍这种行为. *She could not* ~ *criticism.* 她受不了批评. *not* ~ *fools gladly* 看不过糊涂事. *I cannot* ~ *you to be idle.* 我不能让你偷懒. ~ *them to come* 允许他们来. ~ *a great deal* 吃大亏. — *vi.* ①受苦. ②受害,受损失,吃亏. ③(因某事而)受罚 *(for)*. ④患病 *(from)*. *We all have to* ~ *at some time in our lives.* 在我们一生中都免不了有受苦的时候. *Our work will* ~ *greatly if we are careless.* 我们如不小心,工作就会受到很大损失. *He will* ~ *for his folly.* 他会因自己的蠢行而受到惩罚. *The child* ~*s from measles.* 这小孩得了麻疹.

suf·fer·a·ble [ˈsʌfərəbl] *a.* 忍受得了的,忍得下去的;可以容许的. **-ness** *n.* **-bly** *ad.*

suf·fer·ance [ˈsʌfərəns] *n.* ①容许,宽容,默许;忍耐(力),耐性;〔英古〕服从,苦难. ②(海关的)落货许可,起货许可. *a* ~ *wharf [quay]* 公许码头,指定码头. ***be beyond*** ~ 不能忍受. ***on (by, through)*** ~ 经默许;在勉强容忍的情况下.

suf·fer·er [ˈsʌfərə] *n.* 受苦的人,苦恼的人;受难者;遭难者,受害者;病人,患者.

suf·fer·ing [ˈsʌfəriŋ] *n.* 痛苦,苦恼,苦难;〔常 *pl.*〕灾害,损害. *air one's* ~*s* 诉苦. — *a.* 痛苦的,苦恼的,患病的.

suf·fice [səˈfais] *vt.* 满足…的需要,使满足. — *vi.* 足够. *Half-a-dozon* ~*d him.* 半打就使他满足了. *That* ~*s to prove it.* 那足够证明这个了. ***S- it to say that*** … 说…就够了.

suf·fi·cien·cy [səˈfiʃənsi] *n.* 充足,满足;充分的财力;自满,自负;〔古〕能力,资格.

suf·fi·cient [səˈfiʃənt] *a.* ①充分的,足够的. ②〔古〕有能力的,能胜任的,够资格的. ~ *food* 充足的食物. *Not* ~!【银行】存款不足〔略 *N/S*〕. *have not* ~ *courage for it* 没有做这事的充分勇气.【圣】***S- unto the day is the evil thereof*** (= sufficient for the day is its evil). 今天的忧患已够今天打发的(不能再为明天忧虑了). *It is* ~ *to feed a hundred men.* 足够供养一百个人. — *n.* 〔主、卑〕足够(的量). *Have you had* ~? 你(吃)够了吗? **-ly** *ad.*

suf·fic·ing·ly [sʌˈfaisiŋli] *ad.* 足够地.

suf·fix [ˈsʌfiks] *n.* 后缀,词尾;附加器〔物〕;【数】下标;添标,尾标. — [sʌˈfiks] *vt.* (作)后缀;附在后头. *a dummy* ~【物】傀标. **-al** *a.*

suf·fix·a·tion [sʌfikˈseiʃən] *n.* 加后缀,加词尾.

suf·flate [səˈfleit] *vt.* 〔废〕使膨胀,打气 (= inflate). **-fla·tion** *n.*

suf·fo·cate [ˈsʌfəkeit] *vt.* 使窒息,使不能呼吸;闷死,闷坏;闷熄(火等). — *vi.* 呼吸闭塞,窒息;受阻,发展不了. ***be* ~*d by*** 被…闭住呼吸,被…闷死 (*He is* ~*d by grief.* 他悲伤得透不出气来).

suf·fo·cat·ing [ˌsʌfəˈkeitiŋ] *a.* 令人窒息的,憋气的. **-ly** *ad.*

suf·fo·ca·tion [sʌfəˈkeiʃən] *n.* 窒息.

suf·fo·ca·tive [ˈsʌfəkeitiv] *a.* 憋气的,要窒息的. ~ ***catarrh***【医】毛细枝气管炎.

suf·fo·ca·tor [sʌfəˈkeitə] *n.* 令人窒息的东西.

Suf·folk [ˈsʌfək] *n.* ①沙福克〔英国东部一郡〕. ②(无角、黑头黑脚的)英国肉用羊. ③= ~ punch (栗毛短脚的)英国挽马. ④英国小黑猪.

suf·fra·gan [ˈsʌfrəgən] *n.*【宗】副监督,副主教. — *a.* 辅助的;副主教的. *a* ~ *bishop* = *a bishop* ~ 副主教. *a* ~ *see* 副主教辖区. — *n.* = ~ bishop.

suf·frage [ˈsʌfridʒ] *n.*①投票;投票权,选举权,参政权. ②投票赞成;同意,赞成,赞同. ③〔常 *pl.*〕【宗】应祷;代祷. *household* ~ 户主选举权. *manhood (woman)* ~ 成年男子(妇女)选举权. *universal [popular]* ~ 普选(制) ***give one's* ~ *to [for]*** 投…的票〔对…投赞成票〕.

suf·fra·gette [sʌfrəˈdʒet] *n.* 从事妇女参政运动的妇女.

suf·fra·get·tism [ˌsʌfrəˈdʒetizm] *n.* 妇女有选举权的主张,妇女参政主义.

suf·fra·gist [ˈsʌfrədʒist] *n.* 主张扩大参政权者,妇女参政主义者.

suf·fru·ti·cose, suf·fru·tes·cent [sʌˈfruːtiˌkəus, -fruːˈtesnt] *a.*【植】半灌木状的.

suf·fu·mi·gate [səˈfjuːmiˈgeit] *vt.* 从下面熏蒸. **-ga·tion** *n.*

suf·fuse [səˈfjuːz] *vt.* 〔常用 *p.p.*〕(泪、光等)充满,弥漫. *skies* ~*d with amethyst* 一片紫色的天空. ~*d eyes* 泪眼. ***be* ~*d with*** 充满,弥漫.

suf·fu·sion [səˈfjuːʒən] *n.* 充溢,弥漫;(脸等)涨红.

suf·fu·sive [səˈfjuːsiv] *a.* 充满的,洋溢的,弥漫的.

Su·fi [ˈsuːfi] *n.* *(pl.* ~*s)*【伊斯兰教】苏菲派教徒〔一种汎神论神秘主义者〕. **-sm** *n.* 苏菲派.

sug- *pref.* = sub-.

sug [ʃug] *n.* 〔美〕漂亮、可爱的姑娘.

sug·an [ˈsʌgən] *n.* ①〔美俚〕= soogan. ②〔爱尔兰〕手搓的草绳;粗毯子.

sug·ar [ˈʃugə] *n.* ①糖;【化】糖. ②甜言蜜语,阿谀奉承. ③〔俚〕钱,贿金. ④〔美俚〕麻醉品;心爱的人. *block [cube, cut]* ~ 方糖. *confectioner's* ~ 最好白糖. *raw [brown muscovado]* ~ 红糖,黑糖. ~ *of lead* 铅糖,二醋酸铅. ~ *of milk* 乳糖. — *vt.* ①撒糖于,加糖,弄甜;裹上糖衣. ②甜甜蜜蜜地讲,用甜言蜜语哄骗(引诱);〔美俚〕用钱收买. ③〔俚〕〔用被动语态〕该死 (= damn). — *vi.* 糖化;制造枫糖;变成糖状颗粒;〔英俚〕(工人)偷懒. *Liars be* ~*ed!* 你们这些撒谎的家伙真该死! ~ ***off*** 〔美俚〕偷偷跑掉,溜掉. ~ ***the pill*** 把药丸加上糖衣;把

令人痛苦的事情说得婉曲些；把痛苦的事弄成易于接受的．～ **apple**【植】番荔枝．～ **bak·er** 制糖业者．～ **ba·sin**〔英〕(餐桌上的) 糖缸 (= ～ bowl). ～ **beet**【植】甜菜．～ **berry**【植】朴属植物；朴树，朴果．～ **bush**〔美〕糖枫林．～**camp**〔美〕枫糖制造厂．～ **candy**〔英〕冰糖；〔美〕(冰糖做的)上等糖果；甜品；讨人喜欢的人〔物〕．～**-cane**【植】甘蔗．～**coat** *vt.* 使甜蜜；在…上包糖衣．～ **crops** 糖料作物．～**-cured** *a.* 用糖、盐和硝加工过的．～ **daddy**〔美〕老荒唐〔与年轻姑娘厮混〕．～ **diabetes**【医】糖尿病．～ **house** 糖厂；〔英俚〕厕所．～ **loaf** 棒糖,塔糖．～ **maple**【植】糖槭．～ **mill** 糖厂,糖坊．～ **palm** 桄榔．～ **pine**【植】兰伯氏松．～**-plum** 小糖果；甜言蜜语．～ **refinery** 炼糖厂．～ **report**〔美俚〕(尤指寄给士兵的) 情书．～**tit** 糖奶头〔用布包糖成奶头状哄婴孩的〕．～ **tongs**〔*pl.*〕方糖箝子．

sug·ar·er [ˈʃugərə] *n.* 工作偷懒的人．

sug·ar·i·ness [ˈʃugərinis] *n.* ①糖状,糖质,甜味；甜性；甜度．②奉承,甜言蜜语．

sug·ar·y [ˈʃugəri] *a.* 糖状的,含糖的,糖质的,甜的；甜言蜜语的．

sug·gest [səˈdʒest] *vt.* ①暗示,绕着弯儿讲．②建议,提议,提出(计划等)．③使想起,使联想到；表明；提醒,指点,启发．～ *some idea to sb.* 示意某人．*It is ～ed that ...* 有人提议….*Can you ～ any means to do it?* 你能不能给我想个什么办法做这件事？ ***I ～ that ...***,我觉得,我认为．～ ***itself to*** 浮现在…的心中．

sug·gest·i·ble [səˈdʒestibl] *a.* 可暗示的；可提议的；【催眠术】易受暗示的．**-i·bil·i·ty** [səˌdʒestiˈbiliti] *n.*

sug·ges·ti·o fal·si [səˈdʒestiəu ˈfælsai]〔L.〕虚伪的暗示．

sug·ges·tion [səˈdʒestʃən] *n.* ①暗示；指点,启发；联想．②提议,建议,方案,发言．③(猥亵的)挑动．④样子,模样,气味；微量,迹象．*no ～ of provincial accent in sb.'s speech* 听不出某人的话里有任何乡下口音．*blue with a ～ of green* 带绿色的蓝色．***make [offer] a ～*** 提议,建议．***on the ～ of*** 在…的建议下．***～ of the past*** 联想到过去．

sug·ges·tive [səˈdʒestiv] *a.* ①暗示…的,提醒…的,引起对…的联想的 *(of)*．②富于暗示的,可作参考的．③挑动性的,猥亵的．*be ～ of a thief* 使人联想到小偷．～ *medicine* 暗示疗法,催眠疗法．**-ly** *ad.* **-ness** *n.*

sui·cid·al [sjuiˈsaidl] *a.* 自杀(性)的；自灭的．*a ～ policy* 自杀政策．**-ly** *ad.*

sui·cide [ˈsjuisaid] *n.* 自杀；自杀者；自灭(行为)．*commit ～* 自杀,自尽．*a ～ squad* 敢死队．— *vt.*〔～ oneself〕自杀．— *vi.*〔口〕自杀．— *a.* 自杀的；自杀性的．

su·i ge·ne·ris [ˈsju(:)aiˈdʒenəris]〔L.〕独特的；自成一类的；特殊的．

su·i ju·r·is [ˈsjuˈdʒuəris]〔L.〕【法】成年,到法定年龄；有权处理自己的事务．

suil·line [ˈsju:iləin] *a.*【动】属猪科的．

su·int [ˈsju:int, ˈsu:-; swint] *n.* ①羊毛汗,脂汗．②【化】羊毛粗脂．

suisse [swis] *n.* *[fem. suissesse]*〔F.〕〔古〕看门人；门警．

suit [sju:t] *n.* ①申诉,起诉；诉讼,控告；讼案．②请求,恳求；求婚,求爱．③一套房间；一套衣服；一套马具；(纸牌的) 同样花式的一组牌．④〔the ～〕〔美俚〕军装．*a civil [criminal] ～* 民事〔刑事〕诉讼．*a ～ of black* 一套黑衣服〔丧服〕．*a two-piece ～* 由两件组成的一套衣服〔如一件上衣和一条裤子的男服,一件上衣和一条裙子的女服〕．*a business ～*〔美〕一套日常衣服．*a dress ～* 一套夜会服．*a long ～* 同样花式四张以上的一组牌；〔喻〕胜人之处．*one's strong ～* 优点,长处．*a short ～* 同样花式不到四张的牌．*a ～ of dittos* 同一料子的一套衣服．***all of one ～*** 清一色．***bring a ～ against sb.*** 控告某人．***fail in one's ～*** 求婚失败．***follow ～*** 跟牌；仿效别人．***have a ～ to*** 向…有所请求．***in one's birthday ～*** 赤条条地．***institute a ～ against*** 控告某人．***make ～*** 请求,乞求．***out of ～s*** 不和睦．***press [push] one's ～*** 哀求；死乞活赖地求婚．***prosper in one's ～*** 求婚成功．***get [put on] the ～*** 参军．— *vt.* ①适合；相配．②使适合,使适宜 *(to)*；〔英古,美〕供给…一套衣服．③讨好某人．*The date ～s me well.* 这个日子对我很适宜．*The role does not ～ him.* 这个角色不适合他演．*It ～s me to put up with him.* 宽容他正合我的心意．***～ all tastes*** 人人中意(*No book ～s all tastes.* 没有人人中意的书)．***～ sb. down to the ground*** 对…十分合宜．***～ sb.'s book*** 正合某人要求．***～ the action to the word*** 使言行一致,说到做到．*S- yourself.* 随你的便．— *vi.* ①与…相称,对…合适 *(with)*．②合适,适当,可行．*The job ～s with his abilities.* 这工作他做合适．*Red does not ～ with her complexion.* 红色与她的肤色不相称．*Which date ～s best?* 哪个日期最合适？

suit·a·bil·i·ty [sjutəˈbiliti] *n.* 适合,适当,合宜,相配．

suit·able [ˈsju:təbl] *a.* 合适的；适宜的,适当的；相当的 *(to; for)*．*This wine is not ～ to my taste.* 这酒不合我的胃口．*problem ～ for class discussion* 适于作课堂讨论的问题．**-bly** *ad.* **-ness** *n.*

suit·case [ˈsju:tkeis] *n.* 手提箱．

suite [swi:t] *n.* ①随员．②(房间、器具等的)一套,一付；【乐】组曲．*a ～ of rooms* 一套房间．

suit·ing [ˈsju:tiŋ] *n.*【商】〔常 *pl.*〕(上等的,做成套衣服用的)套头料．

suit·or [ˈsju:tə] *n.* *(fem. suitress* [-ris]*)* ①【法】起诉人,原告．②请愿者,请求者．③求婚者,求爱者．

su·key, sukie, suky [ˈsu:ki] *n.*〔方〕开水壶．

suki·yaki [suki:ˈjɑ:ki:] *n.*〔日〕鸡素烧．

Suk·kot, Suk·kos, Suk·koth [suˈkəut, ˈsukəus] *n.* 犹太结茅节〔犹太历1月15—22日〕．

sul·cate, sul·cat·ed [ˈsʌlkeit,-id] *a.*【植,解】有槽的,有沟的,有纵沟的．

sul·cus [ˈsʌlkəs] *n.* *(pl. -ci* [sai]*)* 沟；纵沟；〔尤指〕【解】脑回转间的裂槽．

sul·fa, sul·pha [ˈsʌlfə] *a.* 磺胺的．— *n.*〔*pl.*〕= ～ drugs 磺胺制剂．

sulfa- *comb. f.*〔美〕= sulpha-.

sul·fa·di·a·zine, sul·fa·di·a·zin [ˌsʌlfəˈdaiəzi:n, -zin] *n.*〔美〕【药】磺胺嘧啶．

sul·fa·guan·i·dine; sul·fa·guan·i·din [sʌlfəˈgwænidi:n, -ˈgwɑ:ni-; -din] *n.*〔美〕【药】磺胺胍,肠胃消炎片 (= sulphaguanidin(e)).

sul·fal·de·hyde [sʌlˈfældihaid] *n.*【化】硫醛．

sul·fa·mer·a·zin(e) [ˌsʌlfəˈmerəzi(:)n] *n.*〔美〕【药】磺胺甲基嘧啶 (= sulphamerazin(e)).

sul·fa·me·thoxy·pyri·da·zine [ˌsʌlfəmiˈθɔksipirədæzi:n] *n.*【药】磺胺甲氧嗪〔长效磺胺〕〔略作 SMP〕．

sul·fa·nil·a·mide [ˌsʌlfəˈniləmaid] *n.*〔美〕【药】磺胺,氨苯磺胺,对氨基苯磺酰胺 (= sulphanilamide).

sul·fa·nil·ic acid [ˌsʌlfəˈnilik]【化】磺胺酸,对氨基苯磺酸．

sul·fa·nil·yl·guan·i·dine [ˌsʌlfənililˈgwænidi:n] *n.* = sulfaguanidine.

sul·fa·pyr·a·zin(e) [ˌsʌlfəˈpirəzi(:)n] *n.*〔美〕【药】磺胺吡嗪 (= sulphapyrazine).

sul·fa·pyr·i·din(e) [ˌsʌlfəˈpiridi(:)n] *n.*〔美〕磺胺吡啶 (= sulphapyridine).

sulf·ar·se·nide [sʌlˈfɑ:siˌnaid] *n.*【化】硫砷化物．

sul·fa·sux·i·din(e) [ˌsʌlfəˈsʌksidi(:)n] *n.*〔美〕【药】磺胺杀克啶 (= sulphasuxidine).

sul·fate [ˈsʌlfeit] *n.*〔美〕= sulphate.

sul·fa·thi·a·zole [ˌsʌlfəˈθaiəzəul] *n.*〔美〕= sulphathiazole.

sul·fa·tize [ˈsʌlfətaiz] = sulphatize.

sul·fid·al [ˈsʌlfidl] *n.*【化】胶状硫．

sul•fid(e) [ˈsʌlf(a)id] *n.* 〔美〕 = sulphid(e).
sul•fi•nyl [ˈsʌlfinil] 〔美〕 = sulphinyl.
sul•fi•te [ˈsʌlfait] 〔美〕 = sulphite.
sul•f(o)- *comb. f.* 〔美〕 = sulph(o)-.
sul•fo•acid [ˈsʌlfəuæsid] *n.* 【化】璜酸;硫代酸.
sul•fo•acy•la•tion [ˈsʌlfəuˌæsiˈleiʃən] *n.* 【化】璜基乙酰化作用.
sul•fo•car•bon•ate [sʌlfəuˈkɑːbənit] *n.* 【化】 硫代碳酸盐[酯].
sul•fo•nal [ˈsʌlfənl] *n.* 〔美〕 = sulphonal.
sul•fon•a•mide [ˌsʌlˈfɔnəmid] *n.* 〔美〕磺胺类药物.
sul•fo•nate [ˈsʌlfəˌneit] 〔美〕 = sulphonate.
sul•fone 〔美〕 = sulphone.
sul•fon•ic [sʌlˈfɔnik] 〔美〕 = sulphonic.
sul•fo•ni•um [sʌlˈfəuniəm] 〔美〕= sulphonium.
sul•fon•meth•ane [ˌsʌlfəunˈmeθein] 〔美〕 = sulphonmethane.
sul•fo•nyl [ˈsʌlfənil] 〔美〕 = sulphonyl.
sulf•ox•ide [sʌlˈfɔksaid] 〔美〕 = sulphoxide.
sul•fur [ˈsʌlfə] *n.* 〔美〕 = sulphur.
sul•fu•rate [ˈsʌlfjuˌreit, -fə-] 〔美〕 = sulphurate.
sul•fur-bot•tom [ˈsʌlfəˈbɔtəm] *n.* 【动】白长须鲸 (= blue whale).
sul•fu•reous [sʌlˈfjuriəs] 〔美〕 = sulphureous.
sul•fu•ret [ˈsʌlfjurit; 动词读作 -ˌret] 〔美〕 = sulphuret.
sul•fu•ric [sʌlˈfjurik] 〔美〕 = sulphuric.
sul•fu•rize [ˈsʌlfjuˌraiz, -fə-] 〔美〕 sulphurize.
sul•fu•rous [ˈsʌlfərəs; 第一义常读作 sʌlˈfjurəs] 〔美〕 = sulphurous. **-ly** *ad.* **-ness** *n.*
sul•fur•y [ˈsʌlfəri] *a.* = sulphury.
sul•fur•yl [ˈsʌlfəril, -fjuril] *n.* = sulfonyl.
sulk [sʌlk] *n.* 〔常 *pl.*〕绷脸;愠怒;生气;不高兴;愠怒[生气]的人. ***in a ~, in the ~s*** 生气. ***have the ~s*** 绷着脸,心里不高兴. — *vi.* 生气,绷脸.
sulk•y [ˈsʌlki] *a.* ***(-i•er; -i•est)*** ①含怒的,不高兴的,生气的,绷着脸的. ②阴沉的,阴郁的(天气等);【植】萎缩的,蔫萎的. — *n.* 单座二轮马车. ~ *plough* 双铧犁. **-i•ly** *ad.* **-i•ness** *n.*
sul•lage [ˈsʌlidʒ] *n.* 废物,垃圾;污水;淤泥;【冶】勺内熔化金属的熔渣.
sul•len [ˈsʌlən] *a.* ①不高兴的,愁眉不展的,绷着脸的. ②阴沉的,昏暗的,阴郁的(天气、天空等);悲哀的,悲惨的,伤心的;行动缓慢的,死气沉沉的. — *n.* 〔*pl.*〕〔口〕不高兴,绷脸;忧郁. ***in the ~s*** 在不愉快中,情绪不好. **-ly** *ad.* **-ness** *n.*
Sul•li•van [ˈsʌlivən] *n.* 沙利文〔姓氏,男子名〕.
Sul•ly [ˈsʌli] *n.* 萨利〔姓氏〕.
sul•ly [ˈsʌli] *vt.* 弄脏;玷污,污辱,糟蹋(名誉等),毁损. — *n.* 〔古〕污点,污斑.
sul•pha- [ˈsʌlfə] *comb. f.* 磺胺 (= sulfa-): *sulpha*diazine.
sul•pha•di•a•zine, -a•zin [ˌsʌlfəˈdaiəziːn, -zin] 磺胺嘧啶.
sul•pha•mate [ˈsʌlfəmeit] *n.* 【化】氨基磺酸盐[酯].
sul•pha•meth•yl•thi•a•zole [ˈsʌlfəˌmeθilˈθaiəzəul] *n.* 【药】磺胺甲基噻唑.
sul•pha•pyr•i•dine [ˌsʌlfəˈpiridiːn] *n.* 【药】磺胺吡啶.
sul•pha•quin•ox•a•line [ˌsʌlfəkwiˈnɔksəliːn] *n.* 【药】磺胺喹沙啉.
sul•phate [ˈsʌlfeit] *n.* 【化】硫酸盐;硫酸脂. *ammonium* ~ 硫酸铵. *calcium* ~ 石膏. *copper* ~ 硫酸铜,胆矾. *iron* ~ 硫酸铁,绿矾. *magnesium* ~ 硫酸镁,泻盐. — *vt.* 用硫酸[硫酸盐]处理;使与硫酸(盐)化合;使成硫酸盐;【电】使(蓄电池极板上)硫酸铅化合物沉积. — *vi.* 硫酸盐化;【电】(蓄电池极板)被硫酸铅沉淀覆盖.
sul•pha•thi•a•zole [ˌsʌlfəˈθaiəzəul] *n.* 【药】磺胺噻唑.
sul•pha•ting [ˈsʌlfeitiŋ] *n.* 硫酸垢.
sul•pha•tion [ˈsʌlfeiʃən] *n.* 【电】硫酸化.
sul•pha•tize [ˈsʌlfətaiz] *vt.* 使成硫酸盐.
sul•phide [ˈsʌlfaid] *n.* 【化】硫化物;硫醚. *arsenious* ~ 雄黄,石黄. ~ *dyestuff* 硫化染料. *copper* ~ 硫化铜. *iron* ~ 黄铁矿. *mercury* ~ 辰砂,银朱.
sul•phi•nyl [ˈsʌlfinil] *n.* 【化】亚硫酰荃;亚磺酰.
sul•phite [ˈsʌlfait] *n.* 【化】亚硫酸盐[脂];〔美俚〕(思想、谈话等)有独创性的人.
sul•ph(o)- *comb.f.* 硫代,磺基: *sulpho*nate, *sulpho*nyl.
sul•pho•cyan•ic [ˌsʌlfəusaiˈænik] *a.* ~ **acid**【化】硫氰酸,硫代氰酸. ~ **ester**【化】硫氰酸酯.
sul•pho•nal [ˈsʌlfənl], **sul•phon•meth•ane** [-fəunˈmeθein] *n.*【药】索佛那,二乙眠砜〔催眠药〕;眠砜甲烷.
sul•phon•a•mide [ˌsʌlˈfɔnəmid] *n.*【药】磺胺,磺胺类药物.
sul•pho•nate [ˈsʌlfəˌneit] *n.*【化】磺酸盐. — *vt.* 使磺化.
sul•pho•ne [ˈsʌlfəun] *n.*【化】砜.
sul•phon•ic [sʌlˈfɔnik] *a.* 磺酸的. ~ *acid group*【化】磺(酸)基. ~ *derivatives* 磺基衍生物.
sul•pho•ni•um [sʌlˈfəuniəm] *n.*【化】锍,一价阴性基.
sul•pho•nyl [ˈsʌlfənil] *n.*【化】磺酰,硫酰.
sul•pho•vin•ic [sʌlfəuˈvainik] *a.* ~**acid**【化】烃(换)硫酸;乙(换)硫酸.
sulph•ox•ide [sʌlˈfɔksaid] *n.*【化】亚砜.
sul•phur [ˈsʌlfə] *n.*【化】硫(磺);硫磺色,黄绿色.【动】粉蝶科蝶,缢虫. *flowers of* ~ 硫粉,硫磺华. *milk of* ~ 硫磺乳,白色硫磺华. *roll [stick]* ~ 精制硫磺,棒状硫磺. ~ *and molasses*〔美〕硫磺糖水〔小儿解毒剂〕. — *vt.* 用硫磺熏;用硫磺处理;用亚硫酸盐处理;加硫磺. ~**-bottom (whale)** *n.*【动】长箕鲸. ~ **spring** 硫磺温泉. ~**-weed,** ~**wort** *n.*【植】药用前胡.
sul•phu•rate [ˈsʌlfjureit] *vt.*【化】使硫化;用硫磺处理.
sul•phu•ra•tion [ˌsʌlfjuˈreiʃən] *n.*【化】硫化作用.
sul•phu•ra•tor [ˈsʌlfjureitə] *n.* 硫磺熏蒸器[漂白器].
sul•phu•re•ous [sʌlˈfjuəriəs] *a.* 硫磺(质)的,含硫磺的,硫磺臭的;【植】硫磺色的.
sul•phu•ret [ˈsʌlfjurit] *n.*【化】硫化物,硫醚 (= sul*f*phide). — [-ret] *vt.* 使硫化;用硫处理.
sul•phur•et•ted [ˈsʌlfjuretid] *a.*【化】硫化的,含硫磺的. ~ *hydrogen* 硫化氢.
sul•phu•ric [sʌlˈfjuərik] *a.*【化】(正)硫的. ~ *acid* 硫酸. ~ *anhydride* 三氧化硫,硫(酸)酐.
sul•phu•rize [ˈsʌlfjuəraiz] *vt.* (= sulphurate) 用二氧化硫烟雾处理[漂白、消毒].
sul•phur•ous [ˈsʌlfərəs] *a.* ①【化】亚硫的,有硫磺臭味的;硫磺色的. ②〔喻〕地狱似的,凶恶的;吵闹到极点的;狂热的,紧张的. ~ *acid* 亚硫酸. ~ *anhydride [oxide]* 二氧化硫,亚流酐.
sul•phur•y [ˈsʌlfəri] *a.* (似)硫磺的.
sul•phur•yl [ˈsʌlfəril, -fjuril] *n.*【化】= sulphonyl.
sul•tan [ˈsʌltən] *n.* ①苏丹〔某些伊斯兰国家统治者〕. ②【史】〔S-〕土耳其皇帝. ③土耳其种小白鸡. *the sweet [yellow]* ~【植】紫[黄]矢车菊.
sul•ta•na [sʌlˈtɑːnə] *n.* ①苏丹的妻[女儿、姊妹、母]. ②王妃. ③[səlˈtɑːnə]〔英〕淡黄葡萄干. ④【动】苏丹鸟〔一种小涉禽〕.
sul•tan•ate [ˈsʌltənit] *n.* 苏丹 (sultan)的领地、职位;苏丹统治的国家.
sul•tan•ess [ˈsʌltənis] *n.* = sultana ①.
sul•try [ˈsʌltri] *a.* ***(-tri•er; tri•est)*** 闷热的,酷热的;情绪激动的,狂热的,狂暴的;激烈的(言语等),粗暴的;淫乱的,猥亵的. **-tri•ly** *ad.* **-tri•ness** *n.*
Su•lu [ˈsuːluː] *n.* 苏禄人〔菲律宾的苏禄群岛人,属莫洛部族〕. **-an** *a.*
su•lu [ˈsuːluː] *n.* 苏鲁〔斐济岛人的衣服,象纱龙〕.

SUM = surface-to-underwater missile 舰对水下导弹.

sum [sʌm] *n.* ①总数,总计,总额;【数】和. ②〔the ~〕概略,大要,要点. ③款项,金额. ④算术(题);运算,计算. ⑤【诗】顶点,绝顶,极点. ~, *remainder, product, quotient* 和,差,积,商. *a ~ total* 总计,合计. *the ~ of his opinions* 他的意见的要点. *a good [considerable, round] ~* 一大[整]笔钱. *a large [small] ~ of* 巨[小]额的,大[小]量的. ***be good at ~s*** 算术好. ***do [work, make] a ~(s)*** 计算,做算术题, ***in ~*** 大体上,一言以蔽之,总之. ***the ~ (and substance)*** 要点. ***the ~ of things*** (最高的)公共利益;宇宙. — *vt.* 合计,总计;总结,总括,概括. — *vi.* 总计 (*into, to*); (法官听原告、被告陈述后)概括要点 (*up*). ~ *up* 总计,总结;总起来说. ~ *up experience* 总结经验. ~**up** 〔口〕概括;总结.

sum- *pref.* 〔用于 m 前〕= sub.

su·mac(h) [ˈsuːmæk, ˈʃuː-] *n.* ①【植】漆树属. ②苏模;苏模叶,苏模鞣料. *the Japanese ~* 漆树.

Su·ma·tra [su(ː)ˈmɑːtrə] *n.* 苏门答腊(岛)〔印度尼西亚〕.

Su·ma·tran [suˈmɑːtrən] *a.* 苏门答腊岛(人)的. — *n.* 苏门答腊岛人.

sum·bal,sum·bul [ˈsʌmbæl -bʌl, -bul] *n.* ①五福花阿魏根,麝香根,苏布(根). ②缬草.

Su·mer·i·an [suːˈmiəriən, -ˈmer-] *a.* ①苏美尔的. ②苏美尔人的. — *n.* ①苏美尔人〔古代幼发拉底河下游地区的居民〕. ②苏美尔语.

Su·me·rol·o·gy [ˌsjuːməˈrɔlədʒi] *n.* 苏美尔文史语言研究.

su·mi [ˈsuːmi] *n.* 〔日〕墨,墨汁.

sum·less [ˈsʌmlis] *a.* 无数的,无限的;估计不出的.

sum·ma [ˈsumə] *n.* (*pl.* ***-mae*** [-iː]) ①综合性论文〔中世纪学者所作〕. ②综合性事物.

sum·ma cum lau·de [ˈsʌməˈkʌm ˈlɔːdi] 〔L.〕享有最高荣誉;按最优等级;以最优学业成绩(毕业).

sum·ma·ri·ly [ˈsʌmərili] *ad.* 概括地,扼要地,简单地,立刻,马上.

sum·ma·ri·ness [ˈsʌmərinis] *n.* 摘要,简要,简略,简便,速成,迅速,即刻,速决.

sum·ma·rist [ˈsʌmərist] *n.* 概括者,摘要者.

sum·ma·rize [ˈsʌməraiz] *vt.* 概括,扼要讲;总结;摘要. **-za·tion** *n.* 总结.

sum·ma·ry [ˈsʌməri] *a.* 概括的,扼要的,摘要的;【法】简单(化)的,即决的;当场的,立刻的,马上的. — *n.* 概要,摘要;总结,一览;梗概. ~ *reports* 简报. ~ *jurisdiction* 即决裁判权. ~ *justice* 即决裁判. ~ *punishment* 即刻处罚. ~ *court-martial* 【军】军纪法庭〔只审理一般性小过失〕.

sum·ma sum·ma·rum [ˈsʌmə sʌˈmɛərəm] 〔L.〕总计,合计.

sum·ma·tion [sʌˈmeiʃən] *n.* 总结;总数;【数】加法,求和;【法】(双方论据的)辩论总结. **-al** *a.*

sum·ma·tor [sʌˈmeitə] *n.* 【自】加法器,相加器.

sum·mer[1] [ˈsʌmə] *n.* ①夏季. ②壮年时期;最盛期. ③年岁,年龄〔通常附带数词而用复数〕. *the ~ of life* 壮年时期. *a young woman of some twenty ~s* 二十来岁的年轻女人. *Indian ~* 〔美〕小阳春,风和日暖的天气. *St. Lake's ~* 〔英〕(在十月十八日前后出现的)暖和天气. *St. Martin's ~* 〔英〕(在十一月十一日前后出现的)暖和天气. —*a.*夏季的. ~ *bonnet* 夏季女帽. ~ *vacation [holidays]* 暑假. ~ *resort* 避暑地. ~ *suit* 夏服. — *vi.* 度过夏季,避暑 (*at; in*). — *vt.* 使度过夏季;夏季放牧(家畜). ~ ***over the sugar*** 〔美〕把糖贮存起来度过夏季. ~ **cypress** 【植】地肤. ~ **house** (花园中的)凉亭;〔美〕避暑别墅. ~ **lightning** (距离极远的听不见雷声的)闪电. ~ **school** 暑期学校. ~ **sausage** 夏季香肠〔干硬不易变质的〕. ~ **solstice** 夏至. ~ **squash** 【植】欧洲南瓜,西葫芦. ~**tide,** ~**time** *n.* 夏季. ~ **time** 〔英〕(将钟点拨快一小时的)夏季时间〔略 S.T.; =〔美〕daylight-saving time〕. **S- White House** 〔美〕总统避暑别墅. ~**wood** 晚材,秋材.

sum·mer[2] [ˈsʌmə] *n.* 【建】大梁,檀条;楣;柱顶石.

sum·mer[3] [ˈsʌmə] *n.* 【自】加法器.

Sum·mer [ˈsʌmə] *n.* 萨默〔姓氏〕.

sum·mer·ing [ˈsʌməriŋ] *n.* 夏令牧场〔放牧〕;早熟苹果;暑假;度夏,避暑.

sum·mer·ly, sum·mer·y [ˈsʌməli, -ri] *a.* 夏(天)的,象夏天的.

sum·mer·sault, sum·mer·set [ˈsʌməsɔːlt, -set] *n.* = somersault.

sum·ming-up [ˈsʌmiŋˈʌp] *n.* 总结. *a scientific ~ of the experience of the working class movement.* 工人运动经验的科学总结.

sum·mit [ˈsʌmit] *n.* ①顶,绝顶;最高级级位;最高级会议〔会谈〕;【几】顶点. ②极点,极度. ~ *conference* 最高级会议. **-ry** 最高级会议(外交).

sum·mon [ˈsʌmən] *vt.* ①召唤;传唤(被告等);召集(议会);号召. ②【军】劝降,招降. ③振起,鼓起(勇气等). ~ *a servant* 把仆人叫来. ~ ***up*** 鼓起(勇气等) (*to do; for*). **-er** *n.*

sum·mons [ˈsʌmənz] *n.* (*pl.* ~*es*) 召唤,召集;【法】传唤;传票;【军】招降劝告. *answer sb.'s ~* 应某人之召. *receive a ~* 接到传票,被传. *serve a ~ on [upon] sb.* = *serve sb. with a ~* 把传票送给某人. — *vt.* 〔口〕传到,传唤.

sum·mum bo·num [ˈsʌməmˈbəunəm] 〔L.〕最高善,至善.

Sum·ner [ˈsʌmnə] *n.* 萨姆纳〔姓氏〕.

su·mo (wrestling) [ˈsuːməu] *n.* 〔Jap.〕相扑〔一种摔跤运动〕.

sump [sʌmp] *n.* 唧筒井;水坑;污水坑;油池;盐田;【矿】水仓,水窝,【机】油盘;油柄箱;(汽车的)润滑油壶. ~ **pump** 水仓泵,润滑油泵.

sumph [sʌmf] *n.* 〔英方〕软弱自卑的人;窝囊废.

sump·ter [ˈsʌmptə] *n.* 驮马,驮东西的牲口. ~ **horse** 驮马.

sump·tion [ˈsʌmpʃən] *n.* 【逻】大前提.

sump·tu·a·ry [ˈsʌmptjuəri] *a.* 限定费用的,取缔挥霍浪费的(法令等).

sump·tu·ous [ˈsʌmptjuəs] *a.* 奢侈的,豪华的;高价的. **-ly** *ad.* **-ness** *n.*

sun[1] [sʌn] *n.* ①太阳;阳光. 〔古〕日出,日落. ②(有卫星的)恒星. ③象太阳的东西;中心人物;荣耀;权力. ④〔诗〕日;年. ⑤(旧式用煤气点燃的)簇灯〔= ~-burner〕. ***a place in the ~*** 顺境;显要的地位. ***adore [hail] the rising ~*** 依附新发迹的权势人物. ***against the ~*** 从右向左,反时针方向. ***from ~ to ~*** 从日出到日落,一天到晚. ***have the ~ in one's eyes*** 太阳耀眼睛. ***hold the candle in the ~*** 白费,徒劳. ***in the ~*** 在阳光下;〔美〕喝醉. ***keep out of the ~*** 放在阴处,避晒. ***One's ~ is set.*** 全盛时期已经过去. ***rise with the ~*** 早起. ***see the ~*** 生出,诞生;活着. ***shoot the ~*** 〔俚〕= take the ~. ***take the ~*** ①【海】测量太阳的高度. ②进行日光浴. ***under the ~*** ①在天底下,在地上,在这个世上. ②究竟,到底. ***with the ~*** 从左向右,顺时针方向. — *vt.* 晒,曝,晾. — *vi.* 晒太阳,做日光浴. ~ ***one's moccasins*** 〔美俚〕死. ~ ***oneself*** 晒太阳;受(宠). ~**baked** *a.* 太阳晒干〔晒裂〕的. ~ **bath,** ~ **bathing** 日光浴,日光(浴)疗法. ~**beam** 日光;〔口〕爽朗的孩子(等);〔*pl.*〕〔美俚〕金币. ~**bird** 【动】①太阳鸟. ②= ~**-grebe.** ~ **bittern** 【动】①太阳鹭鸶. ②= ~-grebe. ~ **blind** 〔英〕窗帘,百叶窗. ~**bonnet** 遮阳(女,童)帽. ~**bow** 虹. ~**burn** *vi., n.* 晒黑,晒焦,晒干;晒斑. ~ **burner** 旧式煤气簇灯. ~**burnt** 晒黑的,晒焦的. ~ **burst** (云隙间)入射的阳光;〔美〕(大钻石周围用小钻石镶成光芒状的)旭日形首饰. ~**-cured** *a.* 晒干的,晒制

的(肉、鱼等) (~*-cured tobacco* 晒烟). ~**deck** 日光浴甲板[走廊]. ~**dew**【植】茅膏菜属. ~**dial** 日晷. ~**disk** 日轮[埃及太阳神象征]. ~**dog**【气】幻日;(出现在地平线不高处的)小虹. ~**down** 日落,日没;〔美〕阔边女帽. ~**downer**〔澳〕傍晚时到牧场中借住的无业游民;〔美海俚〕要船员在日落时就回舰的军官. ~**-dried** *a.* 晒干的. ~**drops**【植】日见草属. ~ **fast** *a.* 久晒不变[不褪色]的,耐晒的. ~ **fever** 骨痛热;日射病热. ~**fish**【鱼】翻车鱼. ~**flow•er**【植】向日葵,〔S-〕〔美〕堪萨斯 Kansas 州的别名. ~**glasses** (在阳光下)取火凸镜;〔*pl.*〕太阳眼镜. ~**glow** 朝霞,晚霞;太阳白冕. ~ **god** 日神,太阳神. ~**-grebe**【动】日鹏. ~**helmet** (男子用)硬壳太阳帽. ~**kissed** *a.* ①太阳照到的(山顶). ②太阳晒得透熟的(果实). ~**kist** *a.* 〔美商〕= sunkissed ②. ~ **-lamp** (医疗用)太阳灯;【影】使光线作抛物线反射的大电灯. ~**light** 日光. ~**lit** *a.* 太阳照着的,太阳晒着的. ~**lounge** (=〔美〕~parlor, ~porch) (有长玻璃窗的),日光(浴)室. ~**proof** *a.* 不透日光的;耐光性的,久晒不变的. ~**-pump**【物】日光泵. ~**rays**【医】太阳灯光线. ~**rise** 日出(时);黎明;〔诗〕日出的地方,东方. ~**room** 日光(浴)室. ~**-scald,** ~**-scorch** 晒伤,日灼病. ~**set** 日落,日没;傍晚;晚霞;日落的地方,西方;晚年,末尾,末路;〔S-〕〔美〕亚利桑那(*Arizona*)州的别名. ~**shade** 阳伞;遮阳,天棚;阔边帽;(女帽的)遮阳;【物】物镜遮阳罩. ~**shine** 阳光,日光;太阳晒着的地方;〔美〕黄金;晴天;欢快(*Sunshine State* 〔美〕新墨西哥 (New Mexico) 州的别名). ~**shiny** *a.* 日光一样的;阳光照耀的;愉快的,温暖的,添加活气的. ~**spot** (太阳)黑子;【医】雀斑;【影】光线强烈的大电灯. ~**stone**【矿】日长石;太阳石;猫眼石,金绿石. ~**stroke**【医】日射病,中暑. ~**-struck** *a.* 中暑的. ~**suit** 日光服[由短裤和两根背带组成的童装]. ~**tan** 晒红,晒黑;晒斑. ~**-tanned** *a.* 太阳晒黑的. ~**trap** 阳光异常充足的地方. ~**up**〔美方〕= sunrise. ~**-ward(s)** *a., ad.* 向太阳方面. ~**wise** *ad.* 从左向右;顺时针方向. ~ **worship** 太阳崇拜. **-less** *a.* 没有太阳的,晒不到太阳的,阴暗的;没趣的,寂寞的.

sun², **sunn** [sʌn] *n.* 【植】印度麻, 菽麻;印度麻纤维(= ~ hemp).

Sun. = Sunday.

sun•dae, sun•day [ˈsʌndei] *n.* 〔美〕圣代[冰淇淋加水果奶油等].

Sunda Islands [ˈsʌndə ˈailəndz] 巽他群岛[亚洲].

Sun•da•nese[sʌndəˈniːz] *n.* 〔*sing., pl.*〕巽他人;巽他语.

Sunda Strait (Sumatra 岛与 Java 岛间的)巽他海峡.

Sun•day [ˈsʌndi] *n.* 星期日;(基督教国家的)礼拜日,安息日,主日. *last* ~ = *on* ~ *last* (在)上一个星期日. *next* ~ (在)下一个星期日. *on* ~ 在星期日. *on* ~*s* 每到星期日. *this* ~ (在)本星期日. *Mid-Lent* ~ = *Mothering [Refreshment]* ~. *Show* ~〔牛津大学〕校庆日前的星期日. *Low* ~ 复活节后的星期日. — *a.* 业余的. — *vi.* 过星期日. ***a week [month] of ~s*** 许多时日. ***look two ways to find*** ~ 斜着眼看. ~ **best [clothes]** (节假日穿的)本人最好的衣着. ~ **letter** = dominical letter. ~ **punch**〔美拳〕猛击;〔转义〕(对付敌手的)强有力手段. ~ **run**〔美俚〕长距离. ~ **school** 主日学校(的师生);〔美俚〕扑克牌戏. ~ **school truth** 尽人皆知的道理[事实]. ~ **school words**〔美俚〕漫骂,咀咒;发誓. ~**-go-to-meeting** *a.* 〔俚〕最好的,最上品的,高档的(服装,举止等).

sun•der [ˈsʌndə] *vt., vi.* 分离,分开,切开. ***in*** ~ 分开着.

sun•dries [ˈsʌndriz] *n.* 〔*pl.*〕杂品;杂货;杂事;杂费;【簿】杂项.

sun•dry [ˈsʌndri] *a.* 各种各样的,种种的,杂多的. ***all and*** ~ 全部;所有的人. ***talk of ~ matters*** 谈种种事情. ~ **goods** 杂货.

SUNFED = Special United Nations Fund for Economic Development 联合国经济发展特别基金会.

sung [sʌŋ] sing 的过去式及过去分词.

sunk [sʌŋk] sink 的过去式及过去分词. — *a.* = sunken;〔俚〕败了,完蛋了. *Now we're* ~.〔口〕完了. ~ **fence** 隐篱,伏栅,矮墙. ~ **screw**【机】埋[沉]头螺钉.

sunk•en [ˈsʌŋkən] sink 的过去分词. — *a.* 沉没的,沉下去的;凹下去的;内陷的;水中的,水底的;埋着的,地中的;消瘦的. *a* ~ *battery* 潜伏炮台. ~ *rocks* 暗礁. ~ *cheeks* 下陷[消瘦]的脸颊. ~ *eyes* 凹陷的眼睛.

sun•ket [ˈsʌŋkit, ˈsuŋ-] *n.*〔英方〕食物;美味.

Sun•na, Sun•nah [ˈsunə] *n.* (伊斯兰教)传统教规[以穆罕默德言行为根据的伊斯兰教规;可兰经的附经].

Sun•ni [ˈsuniː] *n.* *(pl.* ***Sun•ni****)* = Sunnite.

Sun•nite [ˈsunˌait] *n.* (伊斯兰教)逊尼派教徒. **Sun•nism** *n.*

sun•ny [ˈsʌni] *a.* *(-ni•er; -ni•est)* 太阳(般)的;阳光照耀的;向阳的,和煦的;愉快的,快乐的,快活的(性情等). ~*days* 大晴天. ~ **side up**〔美俚〕单煎一面蛋黄在上的煎鸡蛋. **the** ~ **side** 向阳的方面;光明面 (*be on the* ~ *side of forty* 没有到四十岁. *look on the* ~ *side of things* 对事情抱乐观态度). **-i•ly** *ad.* **-i•ness** *n.*

sun•ny•a•se(e) [sʌˈnjɑːsi] *n.*〔印〕托钵僧.

sun•shine [ˈsʌnʃain] *n.* ①阳光;阳光所照之处;晴朗的天气;叫人温暖和快乐的人[事物]. ②〔美俚〕金子.

sun•shiny [ˈsʌnʃaini] *a.* 阳光照射的,晴朗的;温暖的;快活的.

Sun•shin•ers [ˈsʌnʃainəz] *n.* 〔美〕新墨西哥 (New Mexico) 州人的别名.

su•o ju•re [ˈsuːəu ˈdʒuri]〔L.〕凭本身的资格,根据本身的权利.

su•o lo•co [ˈləu kəu]〔L.〕处于本身的地位,位置得当.

sup¹ [sʌp] *vt.* ①啜(茶、汤等). ②经验,尝. — *vi.* 啜,用匙喝. ~ *sorrows by the ladleful* 经受大量忧患. *He needs a long spoon that* ~*s with the devil.* 跟恶魔喝汤调羹要长,对坏人必须提防. — *n.* 啜一口. *take neither bit [bite] nor* ~ *of the food* 东西一口也不吃.

sup² [sʌp] *(**supped** [sʌpt], **sup•ping** [ˈsʌpiŋ])* *vi.* 供给晚饭,(使)吃晚饭. ~ ***off***, ~ ***on*** 吃…当晚饭,晚饭吃…. ~ ***out*** 在外面吃晚饭. — *vt.* 晚上喂 *(up)*.

sup. = ①superior. ②superlative. ③supplement; supplementary. ④supply.

sup- *pref.* 〔用于 P 前〕= sub-.

Sup. Ct. = ①Superior Court 上级法院. ②Supreme Court〔美〕联邦最高法院.

supe [suːp] *n.*〔俚〕①〔美〕= supernumerary. ②【空】(发动机的)马力.

su•per [ˈsjuːpə] *n.* ①〔口〕= supernumerary. ②〔口〕= superintendent. ③〔口〕【商】特级品,特大号商品;超级市场;【影】特制影片 = superfilm. ④〔盗贼俚〕表. ⑤【印】(书脊内的)上浆纱布. — *a.* 〔口〕①面积的,平方的. ②超级的,极度的;过分的;超等的,极好的. — *ad.* 非常;过分地. — *vt.* 用上浆纱布装(书脊). — *vi.* 担任跑龙套角色.

su•per- *pref.* 在…之上;从上;再;特别;极,过度;超;总;次,副: ~*-conductor* 超导体.

super. = superintendent; supernumerary.

su•per•a•ble [ˈsjuːpərəbl] *a.* 可胜过的,可凌驾的,可超越的. **-bly** *ad.* **-ness** *n.*

su•per•a•bound [ˌsjuːpəˈbaund] *vi.* 过多,有余;极多.

su•per•a•bun•dance [ˌsjuːpərəˈbʌndəns] *n.* 过度,过多剩余;极丰富,极多.

su•per•a•bun•dant [ˌsjuːpərəˈbʌndənt] *a.* 过多的,多余的;极多的. **-ly** *ad.*

su•per•add [ˈsjuːpərˈæd] *vt.* 外加,再添上,添加;附带说.

su•per•ad•di•tion [ˈsjuːpərəˈdiʃən] *n.* 加加,再添;附加(物),添加(物).

su·per·al·loy [sju:pəˈælɔi] *n.* 超级合金〔防氧化，耐高温及高压的合金〕.
su·per·an·nu·ate [sʲu:pəˈrænjueit] *vt.* 认为过于年老[旧式]而辞退[淘汰]；给养老金使退休；认为年龄太大[成绩太差]而勒令退学.
su·per·an·nu·at·ed [sʲu:pəˈrænjueitid] *a.* 领受养老金而退休的；过了服务年龄的；过时的，废弃了的. *a* ～ *vessel* 老舰，废舰. **-ly** *ad.* **-ness** *n.*
su·per·an·nu·a·tion [ˌsʲu:pərˈænjuˈeiʃən] *n.* 年老退休；淘汰，废弃；退休金.
su·per·a·que·ous [sʲu:pəˈeikwiəs] *a.* 水上的.
su·per·a·tom·ic bomb [ˌsju:pərəˈtɔmik] 超原子弹，氢弹.
su·perb [sʲu:ˈpə:b] *a.* 宏伟的，壮丽的；(色采)美丽的，华美的；〔口〕极好的，超等的，无上的. *a* ～ *binding* 极好的装钉. *a* ～ *view* 壮观，绝景. *a* ～ *courage* 极大的勇气. **-ly** *ad.* **-ness** *n.*
su·per·bi·par·tient [ˈsʲu:pəbaiˈpɑ:ʃiənt] *a.* 三对五的.
su·per·bi·quin·tal [ˌsju:pəbaiˈkwintl] *a.* 五对七的.
su·per·bi·ter·tial [ˌsju:pəbaiˈtə:ʃəl] *a.* 三对五的.
su·per·bomb·er [ˌsju:pəˈbɔmə] *n.* 超级轰炸机.
su·per·cal·en·der [ˌsju:pəˈkæləndə] *n.* 【造纸】超级砑光机. — *vt.* 用超级砑光机砑光.
su·per·cal·en·dered [sʲu:pəˈkælindəd] *a.* 特别光洁的(纸类等).
su·per·car·go [ˈsju:pəkɑ:gəu] *n.* *(pl. ～es, ～s)* (商船) 货物经管员〔代表船主处理一切营业事务〕.
su·per·car·ri·er [ˈsʲu:pəkæriə] *n.* 超级航空母舰.
su·per·charge [ˌsjupəˈtʃɑ:dʒ] *vt., vi.* 增加负荷；【机】增压. **-er** *n.* 增压器.
su·per·cil·i·a·ry [sju:pəˈsiliəri] *a.* 眼睛上面的；眉毛的.
su·per·cil·i·ous [sju:pəˈsiliəs] *a.* 目空一切的，傲慢的，自大的. **-ly** *ad.* **-ness** *n.*
su·per·cit·y [ˈsʲu:pəˌsiti] *n.* = megalopolis.
su·per·class [sju:pəˌklɑ:s,-klæs] *n.* 【生】总纲.
su·per·co·los·sal [ˌsʲu:pəkəˈlɔsl] *a.* 极巨大的.
su·per·co·lum·ni·a·tion [ˌsjupəkəˌlʌmniˈeiʃən] *n.* 【建】重列柱. **-co·lum·nar** [ˌsju:pəkəˈlʌmnə] *a.*
su·per·con·duc·tiv·i·ty [ˌsjupəˌkɔndəkˈtiviti] *n.* 【物】超导电性 (superconduction). **-duct·ing, -duc·tive** *a.* **-duc·tor** *n.*
su·per·con·scious [ˌsʲupə:ˈkɔnʃəs] *a.* 超意识的，知觉异常灵敏的.
su·per·cool [ˌsju:pəˈku:l] *vt.* 使过度冷却〔指冷却到凝固点以下而不凝结〕. — *vi.* 过度冷却.
su·per·cooled [ˌsjupəˈku:ld] *a.* 【化】过冷(的)，(不凝结而)冷却到冰点以下的.
su·per·crat [ˈsju:pəkræt] *n.* 〔美口〕(部长级的)高级官员，大官，大员.
su·per·cres·cent [ˌsju:pəˈkresnt] *a.* 寄生的.
su·per·crim·i·nal [sʲu:pəˈkriminl] *n.* 〔美〕罪魁.
su·per·crit·i·cal [ˌsju:pəˈkritikəl] *a.* 吹毛求疵的.
su·per·dom·i·nant [ˌsju:pəˈdɔminənt] *n.* 【乐】全音阶的第六度；次中和弦，次中音 (= submediant).
su·per·dread·nought [ˌsʲu:pəˈdrednɔ:t] *n.* 超级无畏战舰.
su·per·du·per [ˌsju:pəˈdju:pə] *a., n.* 〔美俚〕极大的，极好的(东西)；了不起的.
su·per·e·go [sʲu:pərˈegəu] *n.* 【心】超我.
su·per·el·e·va·tion [ˌsʲu:pəˌeliˈveiʃən] *n.* 【交】(铁路或公路的)超高.
su·per·emi·nent [ˌsju:pəˈeminənt] *a.* 卓绝的，卓越的，优越的，超群地，异常突出的. **-ence** *n.* **-ly** *ad.*
su·per·em·pir·ic·al [sʲu:pəremˈpirikəl] *a.* 超经验的.
su·per·er·o·ga·tion [ˌsʲu:pərerəˈgeiʃən] *n.* 职责以外的工作，额外工作；【宗】余功.
su·per·er·o·ga·to·ry [ˌsʲu:pəreˈrɔgətəri] *a.* 职责以外的，额外的；【宗】余功的.
su·per·ette [ˈsju:pərit, ˌsju:pəˈret] *n.* 小型自动售货杂货店.
su·per·ex·cel·lence [sʲu:pərˈeksələns] *n.* 极其精美[优良]，卓绝，至高无上.
su·per·ex·cel·lent [sʲu:pəˈreksələnt] *a.* 极其精美的，极其优良的，卓越的；〔口〕极好的，超高级的，无上的.
su·per·ex·ci·ta·tion [ˌsʲu:pəreksiˈteiʃən] *n.* 过度兴奋[刺激].
su·per·ex·ploit [sʲu:pəriksˈplɔit] *vt.* 过度剥削. **-ation** *n.*
su·per·ex·ploit·ed [sʲu:pəriksˈplɔitid] *a.* 遭受过度剥削的.
su·per·fam·i·ly [ˈsju:pəˌfæmili] *n.* *(pl. -lies)* 【生】总科.
su·per·fat·ted [sʲu:pəˈfætid] *a.* (肥皂)含脂过多的.
su·per·fe·cun·da·tion [ˌsju:pəˌfi:kənˈdeiʃən, -ˌfekən-] *n.* 【生】同期复孕.
su·per·fe·ta·tion [ˌsju:pəfi:ˈteiʃən] *n.* 【生】异期复孕.
su·per·fi·cial [sʲu:pəˈfiʃəl] *a.* ①表面的；面积的，平方的. ②肤浅的，浅薄的，一知半解的. ～ *water* 地面水. *a* ～ *wound* 表皮上的伤. ～ *feet* 平方英尺. *a* ～ *writer* 浅薄的作家. **-ly** *ad.*
su·per·fi·ci·al·i·ty [sʲu:pəfiʃiˈæliti] *n.* 肤浅，浅薄；表面性；表面现象.
su·per·fi·ci·a·ry [sʲu:pəˈfiʃiəri] *n.* 【法】有地上权者，租地造屋者.
su·per·fi·ci·es [ˌsʲu:pəˈfiʃii:z] *n.* 〔*sing., pl.*〕表面；面积；表面现象，外观；【法】地上物件；地上权.
su·per·film [ˈsʲu:pəfilm] *n.* 【影】特制影片.
su·per·fine [ˈsʲu:pəˈfain] *a.* 【商】特级的，最好的；过分精细的，特别精细的.
su·per·fix [ˈsju:pəˌfiks] *n.* 【语】语法功能重音〔为了分别词性对同一词标注的不同重音，如 ˈinsert 表示名词，inˈsert 表示动词〕.
su·per·flu·id·i·ty [ˌsju:pəfluˈiditi] *n.* 【物】超流性. **-flu·id** [-ˈflu:id] *n., a.*
su·per·flu·i·ty [ˌsʲu:pəˈfluiti] *n.* 太多，过剩，多余；奢侈(品)；〔常 *pl.*〕不必要的东西，过剩的东西.
su·per·flu·ous [ˌsʲu:ˈpə:fluəs] *a.* 过多的，多余的. *It may be* ～ *to say that* … 说…也许是多余的. **-ly** *ad.* **-ness** *n.*
su·per·for·t(ress) [ˈsʲu:pəˌfɔ:tris] *n.* 〔美〕超级空中堡垒.
su·per·fuse [ˌsju:pəˈfju:z] ①〔罕〕倾注，浇盖. ②= supercool. **-fu·sion** [-ˈfju:ʒən] *n.*
su·per·gi·ant [ˈsju:pəˌdʒaiənt] *n.* 【天】超巨星.
su·per·glob·slop·ti·ous, su·per·gob·o·slop·ti·ous [ˌsʲu:pˈglɔbslɔpʃəs, -ˈgɔbɔ-] *a.* 〔美〕非常漂亮的，非常好的.
su·per·hawk [ˈsju:pəhɔ:k] *n.* 强硬鹰派.
su·per·heat [sʲu:pəˈhi:t] *vt.* 过(度加)热；【化】(使液体不蒸发而)加热到沸点以上. **-er** *n.* 过热器.
su·per·het(e·ro·dyne) [ˈsʲu:pəˈhet(ərədain)] *n.* 【无】超外差式(收音机). — *a.* 超外差的.
su·per·high [ˈsʲu:pəˈhai] *a.* 超高的. ～ frequency 【无】超高频率.
su·per·high·way [ˌsju:pəˈhaiˌwei] *n.* 〔美〕高速公路 (= expressway).
su·per·hu·man [sʲu:pəˈhju:mən] *a.* 超人的；神灵的；超过常人的. **-ly** *ad.*
su·per·im·pose [sʲu:pərimˈpəuz] *vt.* 加在上面；附加，添加 *(on; upon)*. **-si·tion** *n.*
su·per·im·preg·na·tion [ˌsʲu:pərimpregˈneiʃən] *n.* 【生】异期复孕，重孕.
su·per·in·cum·bent [ˌsju:pərinˈkʌmbənt] *a.* ①横在

上面的,搁[架]在上面的;(压力的)自上而下的. ②拱立的, 高悬的, 悬空的. ～bed【地】复层, 叠层. **-cumbence, -cum·ben·cy** *n.* **-ly** *ad.*
su·per·in·duce [ˌsjuːpərinˈdjuːs] *vt.* 再加,添加;另立…为承继人;另娶;(在已有的状态、效果等上)使另有增加[如在某种疾病之上使并发另一疾病].
su·per·in·duc·tion [ˌsjuːpərinˈdʌkʃən] *n.* 添加,附加;影响.
su·per·in·tend [ˌsjuːpərinˈtend] *vt., vi.* 管理, 监督,指挥.
su·per·in·tend·ence, su·per·in·ten·den·cy [sjuːpərinˈtendəns, -dənsi] *n.* 管理;监督(权).
su·per·in·tend·ent [sjuːpərinˈtendənt] *n.* 管理人,监督人,指挥人;(某一部门的)主官,负责人;(陆海军学校等的)校长;厂长,所长.
su·per·in·var [sjuːpərinˈvɑː] *n.* 超殷钢.
Su·pe·ri·or Lake [sju(ː)ˈpiəriə leik] *n.* 苏必利尔湖.
su·pe·ri·or [sjuːˈpiəriə] *a.* *(opp.* inferior) ①在上的,上部的,比…高的;上级的,高级的. ②优良的,上等的,优秀的. ③优势的,比…多的;比…好的,比…强的,胜过…的 *(to; in)*. ④超越…的, 不为…所动的 *(to)*. ⑤傲慢的, 高人一等的. ⑥【植】(萼)在子房上的,(子房)在萼上的,上生的;【印】位于右上角的;较一行中其他铅字略高的. *a ～ person* 有教养的人士;[常谑]自以为了不起的人. *a ～ planet* 外行星. *a ～ figure [letter]* 上角数码或字母[如 X^2 的2]. ***be absolutely ～ in every specific campaign*** 在每一个具体战役上,是绝对的优势. ***be ～ to*** 胜过,强过,比…好;超然于,不为…所动 (*He felt ～ in mathematics to John.* 他觉得自己的数学比约翰强. *be ～ to difficulties* 不屈服于艰难困苦. *be ～ to bribry* 不为贿赂所动). ***rise ～ to*** 超越…,超然于,不为…所影响. (*They were resolved to rise ～ to every obstacle.* 他们决心战胜一切障碍). ***with a ～ air*** 骄傲地. — *n.* 长辈,上级,前辈;优越者;优胜者;[S-]修道院长;【印】上角字码. **～ court** 上级法院. **～ limit** 【数,机】上限, 最大尺寸. **～ numbers** 多数,优势. **-ly** *ad.*
su·pe·ri·or·i·ty [sju(ː)piəriˈɔriti] *n.* 优越(性), 超越,优秀,优势 *(to; over)*; 傲慢 *(to; over)*. *in comparable～ of socialist system over capitalist one* 社会主义制度比之资本主义制度的无比优越性. *～ in strength [ability, intelect]* 实力[能力、智力]方面的优势. *sense of ～* 优越感. *～ to bribery [temptation]* 拒绝贿赂[不受诱惑]的超越精神. ***assume an air of ～*** 摆架子. **～ complex** 优越感【心】,优越情绪.
su·per·ja·cent [ˌsjuːpəˈdʒeisnt] *a.* 压[搁,悬]在上面的.
su·per·jet [ˈsjuːpədʒet] *n.* 超音速喷气机.
su·per·jun·ket [ˈsjuːpədʒʌŋkit] *n.* [美]大宴会.
superl. = superlative.
su·per·la·tive [sjuːˈpəːlətiv] *a.* 最上的,最高的;【语法】最高级的. *the ～ degree*【语法】最高级. — *n.*【语法】最高级;最高级词[形式]. ***full of ～s*** 夸张的(话等). ***speak in ～s*** 夸大地讲. **-ly** *ad.* **-ness** *n.*
su·per·lat·tice [sjuːpəˈlætis] *n.*【物】超点阵,超(结晶)格子.
su·per·lin·er [sjuːpəˈlainə] *n.* 超级客轮[机].
super·lob·gosh·i·ous [sjuːpəˈlɔbgɔʃiəs] *a.* [美]第一流的;吹毛求疵的.
su·per·lu·nar [sjuːpəˈljuːnə] *a.* 月亮上头的,月亮外的,天上的,非现世的 (= superlunary).
su·per·mal·loy [sjuːpəˈmælɔi] *n.* 超透磁合金,超叵姆合金.
su·per·man [ˈsjuːpəmæn] *n.* 超人.
su·per·man·ish [ˈsjuːpəmæniʃ] *a.* [美] 自大的, 骄傲的.
su·per·mar·ket [ˈsjuːpəˌmɑːkit] *n.* 自动售货商店,超级市场,自选商品店.
su·per·mun·dane [sjuːpəˈmʌndein] *a.* 超脱俗界的,超现世的.
su·per·nac·u·lum [sjuːpəˈnækjuləm] *n.* (应该喝得一滴不剩的)美酒. — *ad.* 干杯;(喝得)一滴不剩.
su·per·nal [sjuːˈpəːnl] *a.* 崇高的, 神圣的;[诗]天上的;超凡的. *～ beings* (住在天上的)神仙,天使. **-ly** *ad.*
su·per·na·tant [sjuːpəˈneitənt] *a.* 浮在表层的. — *n.* 浮在表层的东西;【化】上层清液.
su·per·na·tion·al [sjuːpəˈnæʃənl] *a.* 由若干国家组成的;控制几个国家的.
su·per·nat·u·ral [sjuːpəˈnætʃərəl] *a.* 超自然的;不可思议的,怪异的;神乎其神的,神妙的. — *n.* 超自然现象[作用]. **-ism** *n.* 超自然的力[作用,现象];超自然主义. **-ist** *n.* 超自然主义者. **-ly** *ad.* **-ist·ic** *a.*
su·per·nat·u·ral·ize [ˌsjuːpəˈnætʃərəˌlaiz] *vt.* ①使超自然化. ②把…看作超自然的.
su·per·nor·mal [ˈsjuːpəˈnɔːməl] *a.* 超常态的; 异常的.
su·per·no·va [ˌsjuːpəˈnəuvə] *n.* *(pl.* **-vae** [-viː], **-vas***)*【天】超新星.
su·per·nu·mer·ar·y [sjupəˈnjuːmərəri] *a.* 额外的,外加的;补充的,代理的;多余的. — *n.* 额外人员,冗员;临时雇员;跑龙套的小配角;临时演员;杂工;冗物.
su·per·nu·tri·tion [ˌsjuːpənjuːˈtriʃən] *n.* 营养过多.
su·per·or·der [ˈsjuːpəˌɔːdə] *n.*【生】总目.
su·per·or·di·nate [ˌsjuːpəˈɔːdnit, -ˌeit] *a.* 高级的;高官阶的,地位高的.
su·per·or·gan·ic [sjuːpərɔːˈgænik] *a.* 超机体的. *n.* [the ～] 超机体现象.
su·per·or·gan·ism [ˌsjuːpəˈɔːgənizm] *n.* 超有机体[一群相互依赖、共同行为成为一个单位的有机体, 如群居昆虫].
su·per·par·a·site [ˌsjuːpəˈpærəˌsait] *n.*【生】复寄生物. **su·per·par·a·sit·ism** *n.* [*pl.*] 寄生现象.
su·per·pa·tri·ot [ˌsjuːpəˈpeitriət] *n.* 爱国狂. **-ic** *a.* **-ism** *n.*
su·per·phos·phate [sjuːpəˈfɔsfeit] *n.*【化】过磷酸盐,酸性磷酸盐;过磷酸钙[肥料].
su·per·phys·i·cal [ˌsjuːpəˈfizikl] *a.* 超物质的;超出已知物理定律所能解释的.
su·per·plas·tic·i·ty [ˌsjuːpəplæsˈtisiti] *n.* 超塑性, 超黏性. **-plas·tic** *a., n.*
su·per·pol [ˈsjuːpəpɔl] *n.* 政党头面人物.
su·per·pos·a·ble [ˌsjuːpəˈpəuzəbl] *a.* 可置于上面的;【数】可重合的,可迭合的.
su·per·pose [sjuːpəˈpəuz] *vt.* 放在上面, 叠上 *(on; upon)*; 使重合.
su·per·posed [ˌsjuːpəˈpəuzd] *a.*【植】迭生的.
su·per·po·si·tion [ˌsjuːpəpəˈziʃən] *n.* 叠加,重合.
su·per·pow·er [sjuːpəˈpauə] *n.* ①超等的巨大力量;超级大国. ②【电】(一地区的)联合发电总量. ③管强国的国际组织.
su·per·pro·fit [sjuːpəˈprɔfit] *n.* 超额利润.
su·per·pro·ton [sjuːpəˈprəutən] *n.*【物】超子.
super·qua·dri·par·tient [sjuːpəkwɔdriˈpɑːʃiənt] *a.* 九对五的.
su·per·ra·di·ance [sjuːpəˈreidjəns] *n.*【物】超发光.
su·per·ra·di·a·tion [sjuːpəˈreidiˈeiʃən] *n.*【物】超幅射.
su·per·re·al·ism [sjuːpəˈriəlizəm] *n.* = surrealism.
su·per·re·gen·er·a·tion [ˌsjuːpəriˈdʒenəˈreiʃən] *n.* 【无】超再生,超回授. **-a·tive** *a.*
super·rum·dif·fer·ous [ˌsjuːpəˈrʌmdifərəs] *a.* [美] 非常有趣的.
su·per·sat·u·rate [sjuːpəˈsætʃəreit] *vt.*【化】使过饱和. **-ra·tion** *n.* 过饱和.
su·per·scope [ˈsjuːpəskəup] *n.* 超宽银幕.

super·scout [ˈsjuːpəskaut] *n.* 空中侦察.
su·per·scribe [sˈjuːpəˈskraib] *vt.* (将姓名等)写[刻]在上面;(在信封等上)写姓名住址.
su·per·script [ˈsjuːpəskript] *a.* 写在右上角的〔如 a^2 的2〕. — *n.*【数】上标.
su·per·scrip·tion [ˌsjuːpəˈskripʃən] *n.* 写[刻]上;(信封等上的)姓名住址;题名,标题,铭题;(处方上部的)拉丁词 recipe (服用)等字样.
su·per·se·cret [ˌsjuːpəˈsiːkrit] *a.* 绝密的.
su·per·sede [ˌsjuːpəˈsiːd] *vt.* 代替;接替;更替;继任;免职,撤换;废除,废弃. **-sed·ence** *n.* **-r** *n.*
su·per·se·de·as [ˌsjuːpəˈsiːdiæs] *n.*【法】中止[暂缓]执行状.
su·per·se·dure [ˌsjuːpəˈsiːdʒə] *n.* 替代;接替;废弃(= supersedence).
su·per·sen·si·ble [ˌsjuːpəˈsensibl] *a.* 超越感觉的, **-si·bly** *ad.*
su·per·sen·si·tive [ˌsjuːpəˈsensitiv] *a.* 过于敏感的,过敏的.【摄】感光特快的. **-ness, -ti·vi·ty** *n.*
su·per·sen·so·ry [ˌsjuːpəˈsensəri] *a.* = supersensible.
su·per·sen·su·al [ˌsjuːpəˈsenʃuəl] *a.* = ①supersensible. ②= spiritual.
su·per·sen·su·ous [ˌsjuːpəˈsensjuəs] *a.* = supersensual.
super·ses·qui·alter·al [ˌsjuːpəseskwiˈɔːltərəl] *a.* 五对二的.
super·ses·qui·ter·tial [ˌsjuːpəseskwiˈtəːʃəl] *a.* 七对三的.
su·per·ses·sion [ˌsjuːpəˈseʃən] *n.* 代替;接替;更替;撤换;废弃. **-sive** *a.*
super·sleuth [ˈsjuːpəsluːθ] *n.*〔美〕= G-man.
su·per·sol·id [sjuːpəˈsɔlid] *n.* 超立体,多次体.
su·per·son·ic [ˈsjuːpəˈsɔnik] *a.*【物】超声波的;【空】超音速的. — *n.* 超声波[频];〔*pl.*〕超声波学. ~ *waves* 超声波. *a* ~ *aircraft [transport]* 超音速飞机. **-s** *n.* 超声波学.
su·per·sound [ˈsjuːpəsaund] *n.*【物】超声.
su·per·state [ˈsjuːpəˌsteit] *n.* 超级(大)国,"老子"国〔欺压小国的大国〕.
super·stish [ˈsjuːpəstiʃ] *a.*〔美〕迷信的.
su·per·sti·tion [ˌsjuːpəˈstiʃən] *n.* 迷信;迷信习惯[行为];〔古〕邪教,异教,异端. ***break down ~s*** 破除迷信.
su·per·sti·tious [ˌsjuːpəˈstiʃəs] *a.* 迷信(上)的. **-ly** *ad.* **-ness** *n.*
su·per·stra·tum [ˌsjuːpəˈstreitəm, -ˈtrɑː-] *n.* (*pl.* ***-ta*** [-tə]) 上层;覆盖层.
su·per·struc·ture [ˈsjuːpəˌstrʌktʃə] *n.* (对下层基础而言的)上部建筑 (*opp.* substructure),(船舶的)上部构造,(对经济基础而言的)上层建筑. *the reaction of the ~ on the economic base* 上层建筑对于经济基础的反作用. **-tur·al** *a.*
su·per·sub·ma·rine [ˈsjuːpəˈsʌbməriːn] *n.* 超级潜水艇.
su·per·sub·stan·tial [ˌsjuːpəsəbˈstænʃəl] *a.* 超物质的.
su·per·sub·tle [ˌsjuːpəˈsʌtl] *a.* 过分精细的,过分微妙的.
su·per·tank·er [ˈsjuːpəˈtæŋkə] *n.* 超级油船.
su·per·tax [ˈsjuːpətæks] *n.* 附加(累进所得)税;特别附加税.
su·per·ter·ra·ne·an [ˌsjuːpətiˈreiniən] *a.* 地球表面上的.
super·ter·rene [ˌsjuːpətəˈriːn] *a.* = superterrestrial.
su·per·ter·res·tri·al [ˌsjuːpətəˈrestriəl] *a.* 地面上的.
su·per·ton·ic [ˈsjuːpəˈtɔnik] *n.*【乐】(音阶的)第二音,上主音.
super·tri·par·tient [ˌsjuːpətraiˈpɑːʃiənt] *a.* 七对四的.

su·per·va·ca·ne·ous [ˌsjuːpəvəˈkeiniəs] *a.* 多余的,不需要的.
su·per·vene [ˌsjuːpəˈviːn] *vi.* 接着发生,意外发生,附带发生,并发;添加,附加. **-ven·tion** [-ˈvenʃən] *n.* 意外发生,附带发生(事件);附加,添加;续发,并发.
su·per·ven·ient [ˌsjuːpəˈviːnjənt] *a.* 意外发生的,节外生枝的,附加的;接着而来的.
su·per·vise [ˈsjuːpəvaiz] *vt., vi.* 监督;管理.
su·per·vi·sion [ˌsjuːpəˈviʒən] *n.* 监督;管理. ***under the ~ of*** 在…监督下.
su·per·vi·sor [ˈsjuːpəvaizə] *n.* 监督人;管理人;(书的)审订者;〔英〕铁道线路检查员;〔美〕(选举的)镇行政官员;〔美〕督学员. **-ship** *n.* 监督(管理)人的职位.
su·per·vi·so·ry [ˌsjuːpəˈvaizəri, ˈsjuːpəvaizəri] *a.* 监督的,管理的.
su·pi·nate [ˈsjuːpiˌneit] *vt., vi.*【解】旋臂向上(或向外).
su·pi·na·tion [sjuːpiˈneiʃən] *n.* (手脚的)转动(作用),旋后(作用),外转(作用) (*opp.* pronation);仰卧.
su·pi·na·tor [ˈsjuːpiˌneitə] *n.*【解】旋后肌.
su·pine[1] [sjuːˈpain] *a.* ①仰卧的,仰天的;掌心向上[朝外]的. ②懒惰的,因循的,苟安的. **-ly** *ad.* **-ness** *n.*
su·pine[2] [ˈsjuːpain] *n.* ①(拉丁语法中的)动名词. ②(动词不定式的)目的式.
SUPO = superpower water boiler 超功率沸腾式反应堆(水锅炉).
supp., suppl. = supplement; supplementary.
sup·per [ˈsʌpə] *n.* 晚餐;(夜间娱乐后的)宵夜. *have [take] ~* 吃晚饭. *What is there for ~?* 晚饭吃什么? *At what time is ~?* 什么时候开晚饭? *We sat down to a good ~.* 我们坐下来吃了一顿丰盛的晚饭. *the Last S-*【宗】(耶稣被钉死在十字架前夕与十二门徒一同吃的)最后晚餐. *the Lord's S-*【宗】最后晚餐;圣餐(仪式). **~club** 高级夜总会.
sup·plant [səˈplɑːnt] *vt.* (用策略、阴谋手段等)排挤掉;取而代之;代替;移换. **-a·tion** [-ˌlɑːnˈteiʃən] *n.* **-er** *n.*
sup·ple [ˈsʌpl] *a.* (***-pler; -plest***) 柔软的;易弯曲的;(动作)轻快的;柔和的;柔顺的,顺从的,唯唯诺诺的;巴结的,迎合人意的;(思想等)反应灵活的. — *vt.* 使柔软;使柔顺,使顺从;驯(马). — *vi.* 变柔软;变柔和. **~jack** 软韧的藤杖;【植】一些木质藤类植物的通称;〔喻〕〔美〕傀儡. **-ly** *ad.* **-ness** *n.*
sup·ple·ment [ˈsʌplimənt] *n.* 增补;补足,追加;(书报的)补遗,附录;增刊;【数】补角;补码. — [-ment] *vt.* 补足,增补. **-ta·tion** [ˌ-ˈteiʃən] *n.*
sup·ple·men·tal [sʌpliˈmentl] *a.* = supplementary. 补充的,追加的,附加的,增补的;【数】补角的.
sup·ple·men·ta·ry [ˌsʌpliˈmentəri] *a.* 增补的,追加的. — *n.* (***pl. -ries***) 增补者,增补物.
sup·ple·tion [səˈpliːʃən] *n.*【语】异干互补,替补(作用).〔例: *went* 原先是 *wend* 的过去式,现在是 *go* 的过去式的替补形式〕. **-tive** [-tiv] *a.*
sup·ple·to·ry [ˈsʌpliˌtəri, səˈpliːtəri] *a.* = supplementary.
sup·pli·ance [ˈsʌpliəns] *n.* 恳求,哀求.
sup·pli·ant [ˈsʌpliənt] *a., n.* 恳求的[者]. **-ly** *ad.*
sup·pli·cant [ˈsʌplikənt] = suppliant. *a.* 恳请的,祈求的. — *n.* 祈求者,恳请者.
sup·pli·cate [ˈsʌplikeit] *vt.* 恳求,哀求;祈求. — *vi.* 恳求,祈求 (*to sb.; for sth.*). **-cat·ing·ly** *ad.* 死祈百赖地.
sup·pli·ca·tion [sʌpliˈkeiʃən] *n.* 恳求,哀求 (*to; for*);【宗】祈求.
sup·pli·ca·to·ry [ˈsʌplikətəri] *a.* 恳求的,哀求的.
sup·pli·er [səˈplaiə] *n.* 供应者,供给者;补充者;厂商.
sup·ply[1] [səˈplai] *vt.* 供给;供应;配给;补充,填补,弥补(不足、损失等). *Cows ~ us (with) milk.* 母牛供给我们牛奶. *The cow supplies milk.* 这头牛有奶. *~ the market*

供应市场. ～ *a demand* 满足要求. ～ *a want* 弥补不足. ～ *an office* 代理职务. ～ *the place of* 代替. —*n.* ①供给;供应,给养,军需;补充;〔常 *pl.*〕供给物,供应品;生活用品;补给品;存货;贮藏(量);(储备)物资. ②〔废〕代理者,代课教员;代理牧师. ③〔*pl.*〕粮食,口粮;〔*pl.*〕经费,(个人)开支[生活费]. *His father cut off the* ～. 他父亲停止了他的生活费. *a* ～ *and marketing cooperative* 供销合作社. *an inexhaustible* ～ *of coal* 无穷的煤贮藏量. *the Committee of S-* (英国下院的)预算委员会. *economize the household supplies* 节省家用. ***have a good*** ～ ***of*** 备有许多…. ***in short*** ～ 供应不足. ***line of*** ～【军】供应线,补给线. ***short*** ～ 供不应求. ***tension in*** ～ 供应紧张. ***the free*** ～ ***system and the wage system*** 供给制和工资制. ***the*** ～ ***department*** 供应处;军需处. ***the law of*** ～ ***and demand***【经济】供求规律. ～ **base** 兵站,补给基地. ～ **wire** 供电线.

sup·ply[2] [ˈsʌpli] *ad.* = supplely.

sup·port [səˈpɔːt] *vt.* ①支承,支撑;支持;支援,维护. ②援助;拥护,赞助. ③扶养,赡养(家属);资助,维持. ④鼓舞,激励. ⑤忍受,忍耐. ⑥证明,证实. ⑦【剧】扮演(角色);配,担任配角;【乐】伴奏. *S- the government and cherish the people.* 拥政爱民. *He can* ～ *life no longer.* 他的生命维持不下去了. *I can't* ～ *this heat.* 我忍受不了这样的热度. *The speaker was* ～*ed on the platform by the mayor.* 演讲人在讲坛上有市长陪着. ～ *a family* 养家活口. ～ ***oneself*** 自谋生计. —*n.* ①支持,维持;支持者;支柱,支座,支架;桁架. ②扶助,援助;鼓励;拥护;赞成,赞助. ③抚养,赡养;生计,活计,衣食;赡养费. ④【军】支援部队,预备队;【乐】伴奏(部);【剧】助演(者),配角. *a* ～ *of the state* 国家的栋梁. *Price* ～*s* 〔美〕(政府给农民的)补助金. ***enlist the*** ～ ***of*** 争取(某人的)支持. ***give*** ～ ***to*** 支持,支援. ***in*** ～ ***of*** 为了帮助[支援]…,为…辩护而拥护着…. **-less** *a.*

sup·port·a·ble [səˈpɔːtəbl] *a.* 可支持的;可忍受的;可援助的,可拥护的;可赞成的;可抚养的. **-bly** *ad.*

sup·port·er [səˈpɔːtə] *n.* ①支持者;援助者;拥护者,赞成者,赞助者,后盾,后台老板;后援者;〔谑〕腿. ②抚养者,赡养者. ③支持物,支架;托器;【外】缚带,绷带;腹带;护身[运动时保护下体的松紧三角带]. ④【化】载体,担体.

sup·port·ing [səˈpɔːtiŋ] *a.* ①起支持[支撑]作用的. ②协助[配合、支援]的;起配角作用的. ③可提供证据的,证实的. *a* ～ *actor* 男配角. ～ **force** 承力,支力. ～ **angle iron** 角铁托. ～**cast** 助演阵容. ～ **fire**【军】支援射击. ～ **plate** 底板. ～ **resistance**【物】支承阻力.

sup·port·ive [səˈpɔːtiv] *a.* 支持的,支援的,赞许的. ～ **therapy** [treatment] ①【医】谈话疗法. ②辅助疗法.

sup·pos·a·ble [səˈpəuzəbl] *a.* 可设想的,可假设的. **-b·ly** *ad.*

sup·pos·al [səˈpəuzl] *n.* 想象;假定 (= supposition).

sup·pose [səˈpəuz] *vt.* ①设想,推测;猜想某事[某人]如何 *(to do, to be)*. ②假定〔证题时用语,和 given, provided 通用〕. ③意味着;必须先假定,以…为必需条件. ④〔现在分词或祈使语气〕如果…好不好. ⑤〔口〕如果(=if). *I* ～ *you are right.* 我想你说得对. *I should* ～ *him to be about fifty.* 我可也猜他是五十岁左右. *Supposing [suppose] you miss your tiger, he is not likely to miss you.* 你如果打不着老虎,老虎不见得吃不着你. *Purpose* ～*s foresight.* 目的就意味着预见. *S- we try.* 去试试吧. *S- we go to bed.* 咱们去睡吧. ***be*** ～***d to*** *(do)* ①…(在职务上)要,应该 (*You are* ～*d to be here at eight every day.* 你应该每天八点钟到这里). ②〔用于否定句〕〔口〕不许,不准 (*You're not* ～*d to smoke in here.* 不许你在这儿吸烟). —*vi.* 推测,料想. *I* ～ *so.* 我想是的.

sup·posed [səˈpəuzd] *a.* 想象上的,假定的. *the* ～ *prince* 为人所假想的公爵.

sup·pos·ed·ly [səˈpəuzidli] *ad.* 想象上,大概,恐怕. ～ *written by* ..., 被认为是…写的.

sup·po·si·tion [ˌsʌpəˈziʃən] *n.* 想象,推测;假定. ***on the*** ～ ***that*** 假定….

sup·po·si·tion·al [ˌsʌpəˈziʃənəl] *a.* 想象上的;假定的,推测的. **-ly** *ad.*

sup·pos·i·tious [ˌsʌpəˈziʃəs] *a.* = supposititious.

sup·pos·i·ti·tious [səˌpɔziˈtiʃəs] *a.* 顶替的,冒充的,假的;〔罕〕想象的,推测的. *a* ～ *child* 一个冒充的孩子. ～ *writings* 伪书. **-ly** *ad.* **-ness** *n.*

sup·pos·i·tive [səˈpɔzitiv] *a.* 想象的,假定的,推测的. —*n.*【语法】假设连词〔如 *if*, assuming, provided 等〕.

sup·pos·i·to·ry [səˈpɔzitəri] *n.*【医】坐药,栓剂,塞剂.

sup·press [səˈpres] *vt.* ①镇压,压制;扑灭(火等). ②止住,忍住(泪、欲望等);隐瞒(证据等). ③禁止(书等的)发卖,禁止发行;删掉. ～ *a yawn* 忍住呵欠. *with laughter* ～*ed* 忍住笑. **-er** *n.* 〔美〕 = suppersser.

sup·pressed [səˈprest] *a.* ①症状不显明的(病). ②被抑制的,忍住的;删去的. *a* ～ *desire* 〔美〕(瞒着不说的)意中人. *sounds of* ～ *laughter* 抑压住的笑声. *a* ～ *passage* 删去的一节.

sup·press·i·ble [səˈpresibl] *a.* 可镇压的,可禁止的,可制止的.

sup·pres·sion [səˈpreʃən] *n.* ①镇压,扑灭. ②抑制;隐匿;含蓄. ③制止;禁止;删除;【医】闭止;萎缩. ～ *of counterrevolutionaries* 镇压反革命. **zero-**～ *n.*【计】消零.

sup·pres·sio ve·ri [səˈpresiəuˈviərai] 〔L.〕隐瞒事实[真象].

sup·pres·sive [səˈpresiv] *a.* 镇压的;压制的;隐蔽的;抑制的;禁止的;删去的.

sup·pres·sor [səˈpresə] *n.* 镇压者;隐蔽者;禁止者;删除者;抑制因子;【物】消声器,阻尼器;【无】抑制栅极.

sup·pu·rate [ˈsʌpjuəreit] *vi.*【医】酿脓,化脓.

sup·pu·ra·tion [ˌsʌpjuəˈreiʃən] *n.* 化脓;脓.

sup·pu·ra·tive [ˈsʌpjurətiv] *a., n.* 酿脓的,化脓(性)的;化脓剂.

supr. = supreme.

su·pra [ˈsjuːprə] *ad.* 〔L.〕在上,在前 *(opp.* infra*)*. ***vide*** ～ 见上.

su·pra- *pref.* 上,超越,前. *supra*conductivity. ★在解剖学用语中与 super- 同义.

su·pra·con·duc·tiv·i·ty [ˈsjuːprəkɔndʌkˈtiviti] *n.*【物】超导电性.

su·pra·lap·sar·i·an [ˌsjuːprəlæpˈseriən, -ˈsær-] *n.*【宗】堕落前拯救论者「加尔文教派的一个分支,声称上帝在人类堕落前就预定拯救的计划〕. —*a.* 堕落前拯救论者的. **-ism** *n.*

su·pra·lim·i·nal [ˌsjuːprəˈliminl] *a.*【心】阈上的. **-ly** *ad.*

su·pra·mo·lec·u·lar [ˌsjuːprəməˈlekjuləː] *a.*【化】超分子的;许多分子组成的.

su·pra·mun·dane [ˈsjuːprəˈmʌndein] *a.* 超越现世的.

su·pra·na·tion·al [ˌsjuːprəˈnæʃənl] *a.* 超国家的. ～ *authority* 超国家的权威. **-ism** *n.*

su·pra·or·bit·al [ˌsjuːprəˈɔːbitl] *a.*【解】眼上的;眶上的.

su·pra·pol·i·tics [ˈsjuːprəˈpɔlitiks] *a.* 超政治的.

su·pra·pro·test [sjuːprəˈprəutest] *n.*【商,法】参加承兑〔付款人拒绝付款时第三者为维持出票人信誉而出面承兑〕.

su·pra·re·nal [ˌsjuːprəˈriːnl] *a.* 肾上的,肾上腺的. —*n.* 肾上腺 (= ～ gland).

su·pra·spi·nal [ˈsjuːprəˈspainl] *a.*【解】脊棘上的,刺突上的.

su·prem·a·cist [səˈpreməsist, sju-] *n.* (某一)种族优越论者,种族霸权论者. *a white* ～ 白人优越论者[至上主义者].

su·prem·a·cy [sjuˈpreməsi] *n.* 至高;优越性[地位];最高地位;无上权威;霸权. *naval* ~ 制海权;海上霸权. *an oath [act] of* ~〔英〕确认英王对国教有管辖权而否认罗马教皇管辖权的宣誓[法令].

su·preme [sjuːˈpriːm] *a.* 最上的,最高的;极上的,无上的;非常的,极度的;最优秀的,最重要的. *the S- (Being)* 上帝. *the* ~ *Pontiff* 罗马教皇. *a* ~ *measure* 死刑. *the* ~ *end* 最终[最主要的]目的. ***the* ~ *moment [hour]*** 最关紧要的一刹那,生死关头;决定性时刻. ***make the* ~ *sacrifice*** 献出崇高的生命,光荣牺牲. ~ **commander** 最高统帅. **S- Court**〔美〕(全国的或州的)最高法院. **S- Court of Judicature**〔英〕最高法院. ~ **good** 至善. ~ **power** 最高权力. ~ **Soviet** (苏联) 最高苏维埃. ~ **wallop**〔美〕极大的乐趣. **-ness** *n.*

Su·pre·mo [səˈpriməu] *n.* 总裁,首脑.

supt. = ①superintendent. ②support.

sur. = ①surplus. ②surcharged. ③surface.

sur-¹ *pref.*〔用于 r 前〕= sub-.

sur-² *pref.* ①在来自古法语的英语中与 super- 同义: *sur*render, *sur*charge, *sur*face. ②在科学术语中与 super-, supra- 同义: *sur*renal = suprarenal.

su·ra¹ [ˈsuərə] *n.* (伊斯兰教经典的)章;棕榈酒.

su·ra² [ˈsjuərə] *n.*【医】腓肠.

Su·ra·ba·ja, Su·ra·ba·ya [ˌsuːrəˈbɑːjə] *n.* 苏腊巴亚〔即泗水〕〔印度尼西亚港市〕.

su·rah¹ [ˈsuərə] *n.* = sura¹.

su·rah² [ˈsjuərə] *n.* 斜纹软绸 (= ~ silk).

su·ral [ˈsjuərəl] *a.*【解】小腿腹的.

sur·base [ˈsəːbeis] *n.*【建】台基上缘装饰线脚.

sur·based [ˈsəːˌbeist] *a.*【建】①有台基上部线脚的. ②扁拱形的.

sur·cease [səːˈsiːs] *n.*〔古〕停止,终止. — *vt.* 完全停止. — *vi.* 停止.

sur·charge [ˈsəːtʃɑːdʒ] *n.* ①过重,装货过多,超载;装填过多;负荷过重;充电过度. ②过高的要价. ③附加费;(对纳税人的)虚报罚款;(邮票、印花等的)欠资罚款;(邮票上的)改价印记. ④指出对方帐目漏记一笔贷方款项. ⑤【化】总误差. — [səːˈtʃɑːdʒ] *vt.* ①超载,装得过多;(火药)装填过度;使负荷过重;充电过度. ②对…收取附加费;征收虚报罚款;欠资罚款,盖改价印记. ③要价过高. ④指出对方漏记贷方款项.

sur·cin·gle [ˈsəːsiŋgl] *n.* (马的)肚带;(教士长袍上的)腰带. — *vt.* (用肚带)勒紧.

sur·coat [ˈsəːkəut] *n.* 上衣;(中世纪的)女外衣;武士铠甲上穿的外衣.

sur·cu·lose, sur·cu·lous [ˈsəːkjuləus, -ləs] *a.*【植】有根出条[吸根]的.

surd [səːd] *a.*【数】不尽根的,无理数的;【语音】无声的,清音的. — *n.*【数】不尽根,无理数;【语音】无声音,清音〔p, f, s, t, k 等〕.

surd·i·mut·ism [səːdiˈmjuːtizm] *n.* 聋哑.

sur·do·mute [ˈsəːdəmjuːt] *n.* 又聋又哑的人.

sure [ʃuə, ʃɔː] *a.* ①〔*Pred.*〕(主观觉得)确实的;深信,确信;(对…)有信心,有把握 *(of; that)*;肯定(要),一定(会)*(to do; to be)*, ②〔*Attrib.*〕(客观上)无疑问的,真实的,实在的;不可避免的,必然要发生的;(方法、效果等)正确的;可靠的;稳妥的,牢靠的,坚固的;坚定的(立场). *Are you* ~*(of it)?* 你认为确实的吗?真的吗? *I am not so* ~ *of that.* 我不太清楚. *Don't be too* ~. 别太肯定. *Fight no battle you are not* ~ *of winning.* 不打无把握之仗. *I'm not* ~ *if I can do it.* 我不敢肯定我能做. *It's* ~ *to be wet.* 肯定要下雨. *a* ~ *proof* 确凿的证据. *slow and* ~ 稳步地. *a* ~ *draw* 一定可以打出狐狸来的矮树丛;一定可以套出真情来的话. *a* ~ *hand* 可靠的人. *a* ~ *poison*〔美棒球〕优秀投球员. *a* ~ *shot*〔美运〕神枪手,百发百中的射击员. ***be* ~ *of [that]*** 确信,深信 (*He is* ~ *of success.* 他深信他会成功. *You may be* ~ *of his honesty.* 你可以相信他的诚实). ***be [feel]* ~ *of oneself*** 自信. ***be* ~ *to*** *(do)* 必定,一定 (*His work is* ~ *to succeed.* 他的工作必定获得成功. *Be* ~ *to tell me.* 别忘记一定讲给我听). ***feel* ~ *(of, that ...)*** = be ~ (of, that …). ***for* ~** 一定要,必须;必然,当然,毫无疑问 (*Be there by six o'clock for* ~. 你一定要在六点钟以前到那里). ***I am* ~** 的确,真的;一定 (*I'm* ~ *I don't know.* = *I'm* ~ *I can't tell.* 我真的不知道). ***make assurance double [doubly]*** ~ 要稳而又稳,要加倍小心[注意]. ***make* ~** 弄明白,查明白,小心一点;确信 (*I believe the line is from 'Lycidas', but you had better make* ~. 我相信这一句诗是"李西达斯"里面的,然而你最好是查查看. *I make* ~ *it would rain, but it didn't.* 我确信要下雨的,可是没下). ***make* ~ *of*** 将…弄明白,查明白;将…拿到手;叮嘱明白. ***make* ~ *(that)*** 务必;务请 (*Please make* ~ *you understand this point.* 务请你们体谅这一点). ***S- thing!***〔美俚〕真的!当然! *(Shall you be at the dance? — S- thing!)* ***to be* ~.** ①〔让步〕自然,固然. ②〔感叹〕哎呀!真的!一点不假! (*So it is, to be* ~*!* 一点不假!就是那样啦! *Well, to be* ~*!* 哼,好!啊!?) ***Well, I am* ~*!*** = to be sure! — *ad.* 的确,一定;〔美〕当然!好. *Are you coming? — S-!* 你去吗?—当然去! ***as* ~ *as a gun, as* ~ *as eggs is eggs, as* ~ *as death [fate], as* ~ *as nails, as* ~ *as you live*** 〔口〕的的确确. ~ ***enough*** 果真 (*I said it would be, and* ~ *enough it is.* 果然被我说中了). **~-enough** *a.*〔美口〕真正的;确实的. **~-fire** *a.*〔美口〕不错的,确实的(方法),可靠的,必成的. **~-footed** *a.* 脚步稳的(马);踏实的;不会失错的;稳当的,可靠的. **-ness** *n.*

sure·ly [ˈʃuəli] *ad.* 的确,确实,无疑;必定,一定;稳当地,安全地;[回答]当然,好;〔古〕是的,是那样的;不致于,未必. *Should you be willing to try? — S-.* 你愿意试一试吗?—好. *You* ~ *don't mean to be cruel.* 你不致于是打算做残暴的事去. ***as* ~ *as*** = as sure as. ***slowly but*** ~ 稳扎稳打地,确定不移地.

Sure·té [syrte], ***La*** *n.*〔F.〕巴黎警察厅.

sure·ty [ˈʃuəti, ˈʃɔː-] *n.* 保证(人),担保(人);保释金;〔古〕安全,牢靠;确实. ***of a* ~**〔古〕的确,必定. ***stand* ~ *for*** 做…的保证人. **-ship** *n.* 保证人的地位[资格、责任].

surf [səːf] *n.* 拍岸碎浪[涛声],迎头碎浪,海滨浪花. ~**bird**【动】碎浪矶鹬. ~**board** (冲浪运动的)冲浪板. ~**boat**【海】破浪艇. ~**-cast** *vi.* 冲浪捕鱼. ~ **clam**【动】碎浪蛤蜊. ~ **fish**【动】①海鲫鱼科鱼. ②石首鱼科鱼. ~**man** 破浪艇船夫. ~**perch** 海鲫鱼科鱼. ~**-riding** 冲浪运动. ~ **scotor**【动】黑凫;斑头海番鸭. **-er** 冲浪运动员. **-ing** *n.* 冲浪运动.

sur·face [ˈsəːfis] *n.* ①表面;地面;水面;广场,空地. ②外观,外表,皮毛. ③【几】面;切口;【空】翼面; — *a.* 表面的;地面的,水面的;外观的,外表上的;(对高架及地下铁路说的)平地上的; (对矿井内说的)矿井外的. *an adjusting* ~【空】调节板. *a supporting* ~【空】支持面积. *a plane* ~ 平面. ~*s in contact* = *rubbing* ~*s* 摩擦面. *look at the* ~ *only* 只看外表. *One never gets below the* ~ *with him.* 无法看透他的内心. *a* ~ *raider* 海上突击舰. ***look below [beneath] the* ~ *of things*** 看到事物的内部. ***of the* ~** 外观上的,表面的. ***on the* ~** 表面上,外表上. — *vt.* 装面,配面,作表面处理;使成平面;掘开地面;铺(路面);使(潜艇)浮出水面. — *vi.* 地面采掘;井外劳动;浮出水面. ~**-active** *a.*【化】表面活性的. ~**car,**〔美〕地面车辆. ~**colo(u)r** 表面色;凹板印刷用的颜料. ~ **conductance**【电】表面电导. ~ **crystallization** 表面结晶. ~ **displacement**【海】(水上)排水量. ~**-effect ship**〔美〕气垫船. ~**-field**【电】近面电场. ~ **flow** 表流,径流. ~ **force** 地[水]面部队;水面舰艇. ~ **gauge**【机】划平面针

盘. ～ **mail** 普通邮件[与航空邮件相对]. ～ **noise** (唱片上的)杂音. ～**plate** (检验表面平正度的)平板. ～ **printing** 凸版印刷; 凸板印染. ～ **tension**【物】表面张力. ～**-to-air** *a.* 地对空. ～**-to-**～ *a.* 地对地. ～ **transportation** 陆上运输. ～ **water** 地面水,淤水. ～ **wave** (地震的)面波;【电】表面电波, 地表电波. **-man**【矿】井上[地面]工人;【铁道】护路工人.

sur·fac·tant [səːˈfæktənt] *n.*【化】表面活化剂.

sur·fe·it [ˈsəːfit] *n.* (饮食)过度; 过量; 放纵; (饮食过度引起的)不适, 恶心. — *vi.* 吃[喝]得太多 *(of; on; upon)*; 放纵. — *vt.* 给吃[喝]得太多; 使胸中作恶; 使沉溺于 *(with)*.

sur·fi·cial [səːˈfiʃəl] *a.*【地】地表的,地面的.

surf·y [ˈsəːfi] *a.* 多碎浪的,浪花似的.

surg. = surgeon; surgery; surgical.

surge [səːdʒ] *n.* 大浪,波涛; 波涛汹涌的大海; (人群、感情等的)汹涌,洋溢,起伏,高涨; [诗]海;【机】波动,浪涌,喘振;【电】电流急冲,电涌;【海】缆绳滑脱; 急速松缆; (绞盘急速松缆的)锥形部. — *vi.* 起大浪; (人群、感情等), 汹涌,高涨; 蜂拥而来, 迈进;【电】电涌; 振荡;【海】缆绳滑脱; 松缆. — *vt.*【海】急放(锚链,缆索等). *a* ～ *current* 冲激电流. *surging crowds* 蜂拥而来的人群.

sur·geon [ˈsəːdʒən] *n.* 外科医生;【军】军医; 船医. ～ **dentist** 牙医. ～**fish**【动】刺尾鱼科鱼. ～ **general** [美] 军医总监 *(Surgion-General's Department* 军医总监部); [美]公共卫生局医务长官. ～**'s knot**【医】手术结,外科结.

sur·ger·y [ˈsəːdʒəri] *n.* 外科(学); 外科手术; 外科手术[实验]室; [英]医院; 诊所. *clinical* ～ 临床外科. *plastic* ～ 整形外科.

sur·gi·cal [ˈsəːdʒikəl] *a.* 外科的; 外科医术的; 外科用的,外科手术的. *a* ～ *operation* 外科手术. **-ly** *ad.* 用外科手术,在外科上.

surg·y [ˈsəːdʒi] *a.* *(-i·er; -i·est)* 波涛汹涌的.

su·ri·cate [ˈsuriˌkeit] *n.* 貂狸属 *(Suricata)* 的动物 [产于南部非洲].

Su·ri·nam [ˌsuəriˈnæm], **Su·ri·name** [ˌsuəriˈnɑːmə] *n.* 苏里南[拉丁美洲].

sur·lo·in [ˈsəːlɔin] *n.* = sirloin.

sur·ly [ˈsəːli] *a.* *(-li·er; -li·est)* 心眼儿坏的; 凶暴的; 脾气大的; 险恶的(天气等). **-li·ly** *ad.* **-li·ness** *n.*

sur·mis·a·ble [səːˈmaizəbl] *a.* 可推测的.

sur·mise [ˈsəːmaiz] *n., a.* 推测, 猜测; 猜疑. — [səːˈmaiz, ˈsəːmis] *vt.* 推测,猜测.

sur·mount [səːˈmaunt] *vt.* 登上,越过; 克服,打破(困难等); [常用 *p.p.*] 顶上覆盖着, 顶上戴着 *(by; with)*. *a peak* ～*ed with snow* 顶上盖满白雪的峰顶.

sur·mount·a·ble [səːˈmauntəbl] *a.* 可登越的, 可越过的; 可克服的.

sur·mul·let [səːˈmʌlit] *n.*【鱼】一种鲱鲤 (= red mullet).

sur·name [ˈsəːneim] *n.* 姓,氏; 别号, 别名, 绰号. — *vt.* 加上姓[别号],用姓[别号]称呼.

sur·pass [səːˈpɑːs] *vt.* 超过; 优于,胜过. ～ ***oneself*** 干得从来没有的那么好.

sur·pass·ing [səːˈpɑːsiŋ] *a.* 出人头地的,卓越的; 极优越的. **-ly** *ad.*

sur·plice [ˈsəːpləs] *n.*【宗】白色法衣. ～ ***fee*** [英](主持婚丧喜事的)牧师费. **-d** *a.* 穿白色法衣的.

sur·plus [ˈsəːpləs] *n.* 剩余,过剩;【会计】结余;【商】盈余,公积; [美](特指政府为了维持价格而贮存的)剩余农产品. — *a.* 过剩的, 多余的, 剩余的. ～ *food stamps* [美]剩余粮食购买券. ～ *funds* 剩余基金. ～ *labo(u)r* 剩余劳动力. ～ **population** 过剩人口. ～ **value**【经】剩余价值. ～ **valve**【机】溢阀.

sur·plus·age [ˈsəːpləsidʒ] *n.* 剩余, 过剩; 冗词; 废话;【法】(诉状中不必要的或与案情无关的)枝节问题.

sur·plus·itis [səːpləˈsaitis] *n.* [美]生产过剩病.

sur·print [ˈsəːˌprint] *vt., n.*【印】添印,复印.【摄】晒印过度.

sur·pris·al [səˈpraizəl] *n.* [罕] = surprise.

sur·prise [səˈpraiz] *vt.* ①使吃惊; 使惊奇, 使觉得意外. ②出其不意地袭击[捉住]; 突袭占领. ③乘对方不备使其做某事[交待, 承认等], 从其得到某信息. ④当场逮捕; 忽然发现. *The news greatly* ～*d us.* 这消息使我们大为吃惊. *They* ～*d the burglar while he was still trying to open the safe.* 当窃犯还在设法开保险柜的时候,他们出其不意地把他捉住了. ～ *a confession from sb.* 在某人不备时使其供认. ～ *a witness into telling the truth.* 使证人不知不觉中说出真实情况. *I should not be* ～*d if ... [to learn]* 即使…我也不会惊奇. *They* ～*d him in the act.* 他们冷不防地当场抓住了他. — *n.* ①惊奇, 吃惊. ②可惊的事情, 意外事情. ③奇袭, 偷袭. *His arrival was a great* ～. 他的到达真是个意外. *I have a* ～ *for you.* 我有一个意想不到的东西给你看 [消息跟你讲]. *What a* ～*!* 真想不到! ***be taken by*** ～ 冷不防竟被…吓一跳. ***to my great*** ～ 使我非常惊奇的是. —*a.* 出乎意料的; 令人惊奇的. ～ *visit* 事先没有通知的访问. ～ **muster**【军】紧急集合. ～ **packet** [英] 有奖糖果袋. ～ **party** 奇袭队; 令人惊奇的事; [美] 各人自带食品突然到某朋友家里的聚会. ～ **roll-call**【军】紧急点名.

sur·pris·ed·ly [səpˈraizdli] *ad.* 诧奇地,诧异地.

sur·pris·ing [səpˈraiziŋ] *a.* 可惊的,惊人的,意外的,奇怪的,不可思议的. **-ly** *ad.*

sur·prize [səˈpraiz] *vt., n.* = surprise.

sur·qued·ous, -qui- [ˈsəːkwidəs] *a.* 傲慢的.

sur·que·dry, sur·quid·ry [ˈsəːkwidri] [Scot.] *n.* 傲慢.

surr. = surrender(ed); surrogate.

sur·ra [ˈsʌrə, ˈsuːrə] *n.* (牛马等的)恶性贫血症.

sur·re·al [səˈriːl] *a.* 超现实的 (= surrealistic).

sur·re·al·ism [səˈriəlizəm] *n.* 超现实主义.

sur·re·al·ist [səˈriəlist] *n.* 超现实主义者. **-ic** *a.* **-ical-ly** *ad.*

sur·re·but [sʌriˈbʌt] *vi.*【法】(原告)对被告第三次答辩进行驳斥.

sur·re·but·tal [ˌsəːriˈbʌtl] *n.*【法】(原告对被告第三次辩驳)提出证据.

sur·re·but·ter [səriˈbʌtə] *n.*【法】(原告的)第三次驳辩.

sur·re·join [sʌriˈdʒɔin] *vi.*【法】(原告) 驳斥被告的第二次答辩.

sur·re·join·der [sʌriˈdʒɔində] *n.*【法】(原告对被告的)第二次驳斥.

sur·ren·der [səˈrendə] *vt.* (被迫)交出,引渡; 让渡; 放弃; 辞(职); (退回一部分保险费)撤消保险契约; 使…听摆布 [～ oneself]; 按官价供应(产品). ～ ***oneself to*** 向…投降; 沉迷在,沉醉在, 听任…摆布 (～ *oneself to despair* 悲观绝望而不思自拔). ～ ***oneself to justice*** 向法院自首. — *vi.* 屈服,自首, 投降; (要塞)陷落. ～ *and confess ones crimes* 投降认罪. ～ *at discretion* 无条件投降. ～ ***to one's bail*** (犯人) 交保期满后自动归押. — *n.* 让渡,交出; 屈服,投降; 让与; (保险的)解约; (生产单位)额定供应物品. ～ **of a fugitive**【国际法】逃犯的引渡. ～ **value** (被保险人解除保险时) 退保金额; 当做废品处理的价钱.

sur·rep·ti·tious [ˌsʌrəpˈtiʃəs] *a.* 秘密的; 偷偷的. *a* ～ *glance* 偷看. **-ly** *ad.* **-ness** *n.*

Sur·rey [ˈsʌri] *n.* 萨里[姓氏].

sur·rey [ˈsʌri] *n.* [美]双人四轮游览马车[汽车].

sur·ro·gate [ˈsʌrəgit] *n.* ①代理人,代表,委员; [英](宗教法庭上)主教代表. ②[美] 遗嘱检验法庭[法官]. ③代用品,代替,代理 *(for; of)*;【心】代用人物[例如在感情上可代替自己的父母的人〕. — [-geit] *vt.* ①代理. ②【法】代替,代替…的地位.
sur•round [sə'raund] *vt.* 围住,围绕,环绕;【军】包围. ***be ~ed with [by]*** 被…环绕着. — *n.* 外围物;铺在地毯周围的东西;围猎.
sur•round•ing [sə'raundiŋ] *n.* 〔*pl.*〕周围的事物[情形],环境;附近. *picturesque ~s* 画一样的环境. *social ~s* 社会环境. — *a.* 包围着的;周围的. *the ~ country* 附近,近郊.
sur•sum cor•da ['sə:səm'kɔ:də]〔L.〕鼓起勇气来,别气馁.
sur•tax ['sə:tæks] *n., vt.* (征收)附加税,(征收)超额累进所得税.
Sur•tees ['sə:ti:z] *n.* 瑟蒂斯〔姓氏〕.
sur•tout ['sə:tu:, sə:'tu:] *n.* 男用外套;女用有帽斗篷.
surv. = surveying; surveyor.
sur•veil•lance [sə:'veiləns] *n.*【法】监视,管制. ***under ~*** 在管制[监视]下.
sur•veil•lant [sə:'veilənt] *n.* 监视者;密探.
sur•vey [sə:'vei] *vt.* ①眺望,俯瞰,环顾. ②审视;通盘考虑[考察],观察(形势);概括,综合评述. ③测量(土地),勘查,踏勘;检查,调查,鉴定. — *vi.* 测量(土地). — *n.* ['səvei] ①环顾. ②概观;检查,鉴定书. ③调查(表);调查所;测量;测量部;测量图. *a ~ of English literature* 英国文学概观. ***make a ~ of*** 测量;考察;调查,检查.
sur•vey•ing [sə'veiiŋ] *n.* 测量(学、术),勘测. *a ~ reporter* 测量员. *a ~ ship* 测量舰.
sur•vey•or [sə:'veiə] *n.* 测量员,勘测员,测地员;检查员;调查员;〔英〕(度量衡等的)检查官 *(of)*;〔美〕(入口货的)检验官;鉴定人. **~'s level** (矿坑)测量水准器. **~'s measure** 测量长度〔以链计算,一链 = 20.1168米〕.
sur•viv•a•ble [sə'vaivəbl] *a.* 可长存的,可存活的,可残存的. **-a•bil•i•ty** *n.*
sur•viv•al [sə'vaivəl] *n.* 生存;残存;幸存;残存者;成活(植株);残余,残存物,遗物,遗风. *the ~ of the fittest* 适者生存. *philosophy of ~* 保命哲学.
sur•vive [sə'vaiv] *vt.* …之后还活着,比…长命;经受得住;得免,得救;(经历灾难后)还活着. — *vi.* 还活着,活下去,未死;残存. *He ~d his wife.* 他比妻子活得久. *His mental faculties ~d his physical powers.* 身体虽坏精神还好. *The custom still ~s.* 这个风俗还残留着. *~ one's usefulness* 虽已无所作为但还活着. *Only five of the crew ~d the shipwreck* 在这次海船出事沉没中只有五名船员幸免于死. *~ all perils* 历经万险而幸存.
sur•vi•vor [sə'raivə] *n.* 未死的人,生存者,残存者,遗族;残存物,遗物. **-ship** *n.* 未死,尚在,残存;【法】生存者对共有财产中死者所有部分的享有权.
Sus. = Sussex(shire).
sus- *pref.* 〔用于 c, p, t 前〕, = sub-.
Su•sa ['su:sə] *n.* 古代波斯王朝设有夏宫的都市.
Su•san, Su•zan ['su:zn] *n.* 苏珊〔女子名, Susanna(h) 的昵称〕.
Su•san•na(h) [su:'zænə] *n.* 苏珊娜〔女子名〕.
sus•cep•tance [sə'septəns] *n.*【电】电纳.
sus•cep•ti•bil•i•ty [səseptə'biliti] *n.* ①感受性,易感性,敏感性 *(to)*;敏感度,灵敏度;【医】感病性;感药性;〔*pl.*〕敏感之处,感情. ②【物】磁化系数;磁化率. *wound [offend] sb.'s susceptibilities* 伤害某人的感情.
sus•cep•ti•ble [sə'septəbl] *a.* ①易感的,敏感的;易受影响的;易感染的,易害(某病)的 *(to)*;多情善感的. ②〔用作 *Pred.*〕容许…的,能…的 *(of)*. *wood ~ of a high polish* 一擦就光亮的木材. ***be ~ of (proof)***, 能(证明)的. ***be ~ to*** 对…敏感,易感受…,易害…,易被…吸引的 (*be ~ to cold* 容易伤风). **-ti•bly** *ad.* **-ness** *n.*
sus•cep•tive [sə'septiv] *a.* 易感的,敏感的 *(of)*;易于接受(影响)的;许可…的,能…的 *(of)*. **-ness** *n.* **-tiv•i•ty** [ˌsʌsep'tiviti] *n.*
su•shi ['su:ʃi:] *n.* 〔Jap.〕生鱼片冷饭团.
Su•si ['su:si] *n.* (东印度)丝十锦条纹棉布.
Su•sie, Su•sy ['su:zi] *n.* 苏西〔女子名, Susan 的昵称〕.
sus•lik ['sʌslik] *n.*【动】①欧黄鼠 *(Citellus citellus)*〔产于欧亚大陆北部和中部〕. ②欧黄鼠皮.
sus•pect [səs'pekt] *vt.* ①怀疑,觉得可疑,觉得(人、约定等)靠不住. ②猜疑. ③(有点)感觉到,(有点)知道,(有点)发觉(危险、阴谋等). — *vi.* 怀疑事情,怀疑,觉得可疑. *~ sb. of a crime* 猜疑某人犯罪. *a ~ed case* 疑似患者. *I ~ he is ill.* 我感到他是病了. *You, I ~, don't care.* 我想,你不在乎罢[并不喜欢]. — ['sʌspekt] *n.* 嫌疑犯,被怀疑的人. — *a.* 〔用作表语〕可疑的. *The statement of an interested party is naturally ~.* 当事人的陈述是当然可疑的.
sus•pect•a•ble [səs'pektəbl] *a.* 可疑的.
sus•pend [səs'pend] *vt.* ①吊起,悬挂. ②停止;使停职,使停学;除名,开除. ③悬而未决,保留(承诺、判断等). ④中止,暂时停止,暂时作废. ⑤【化】使悬浮(液中). — *vi.* ①暂停,中止;②悬空;悬宕;悬浮. ③【商】无力支付,宣布破产. *~ a bird-cage from the ceiling* 把鸟笼吊在天花板上. *~ payment* 停止支付. *~ a motor licence* 暂时吊销汽车执照. *~ed particles of dust* 悬浮的尘埃微粒. *~ed animation* 不省人事,假死.
sus•pend•er [səs'pendə] *n.* 〔常 *pl.*〕吊杆,吊索;吊材;挂钩;挂篮;〔英〕吊袜带;〔美〕(裤子的)背带【制革】吊鞣池.
sus•pense [səs'pens] *n.* ①悬挂,悬吊. ②中止,暂停,停止. ③悬而未决,含糊不定;悬虑;【法】权利停止. *~ account*【簿】悬帐,暂记帐. *hold one's judgement in ~* 暂时不加判断. ***keep (sb.) in ~*** 不告诉(某人)结果,让(人)悬虑不安.
sus•pense•ful [sə'spensful] *a.* ①犹豫不决的. ②焦急不安的. ③热切的. ④〔罕〕(正当权益的)中止的.
sus•pen•si•ble [səs'pensəbl] *a.* 可吊挂的;可悬浮的;可中止的;可以暂搁的. **-bil•i•ty** *n.*
sus•pen•sion [səs'penʃən] *n.* ①悬吊,悬挂;悬垂;悬架吊架. ②中止,停止;停止支付[宣判,处刑];停职,停学,停权. ③悬置,保留,未决. ④【化】悬浮(液);悬胶(体);【拓】同纬映象;【乐】悬留法;悬留音;【修】悬疑法〔以引起读者的好奇心,关心下文〕;【商】停止[无力]支付. *a ~ switch* (电灯)吊装开关. *~ of arms [hostilities]* 停战. *~ of business* 停业. *~ of publication* 暂停刊行. *~ transport* 悬浮搬运. **~ bridge** 悬桥,吊桥. **~ points, ~periods**【语】省略号[…]. **~ railway** 高架铁路.
sus•pen•si•o per col•lum [səs'pensiəupə:'kɔləm]〔L.〕绞刑〔通常略作 ***sus. per coll.*** ['sʌspə:'kɔl]〕.
sus•pen•sive [səs'pensiv] *a.* 中止的,休止的,暂停的;有停止权的;悬而未决的;悬念的;不安的. *a ~ novel* 情节紧张的小说. **-ly** *ad.*
sus•pen•soid [səs'pensɔid] *n.*【化】悬胶(体).
sus•pen•sor [səs'pensə] *n.*【医】悬带,吊绷带;【植】胚柄,囊柄.
sus•pen•so•ry [səs'pensəri] *a.* 悬吊的,悬挂的;中止的. — *n.* 悬吊物;【医】悬带;吊绷带;【解】悬肌. *a ~ bandage* 悬带. *~ ligament*【解】悬韧带〔尤指眼球水晶体悬韧带〕.
sus. per col(l). ['sʌspə(:)'kɔl] = 〔L.〕*suspensio per collum* (= hanging by the neck).
sus•pi•cion [səs'piʃən] *n.* 怀疑,疑心,猜疑;嫌疑;〔口〕一点儿. *a ~ of arrogance [brandy]* 有点骄傲[白兰地味]. ***above ~*** 无可怀疑. ***have a ~ of*** 具有少许…风味. ***on (the) ~ of*** 因…的嫌疑. ***under ~*** 被怀疑,有嫌疑. ***with ~*** 怀疑,疑心. — *vt.* 〔美俚〕怀疑. **-less** *a.* 不怀疑的.
sus•pi•cious [səs'piʃəs] *a.* ①可疑的. ②多疑的,疑惧

的；对…起疑心 *(of; sth. sb.; that)*. *a ~ character* 可疑的人物. *a ~ nature* 多疑的性质. *There is something ~ about it.* 那有点儿可疑. **-ly** *ad.* **-ness** *n.*

sus·pi·ra·tion [ˌsʌspiˈreiʃən] *n.* 〔罕〕叹息，一声长叹.

sus·pire [səsˈpaiə] *vi.* 〔诗〕叹息.

Sus·sex [ˈsʌsiks] *n.* ①传说中英国古代一王国. ②英国一郡.

sus·tain [səsˈtein] *vt.* ①支撑，支持. ②补养；维持；加强，鼓舞；(精神等)持续；养(家). ③遭受；忍受，忍耐. ④证明，证实；(法庭等)确认，承认，认可；准许. ⑤能胜任；能扮演(角色)，善于表演(性格). ⑥抵挡. *food sufficient to ~ life* 足够维持生活的食物. *~ a defeat* 吃败仗；受挫折. *~ an injury* 负伤. *~ a great loss* 蒙受重大损失. *~ comparison with another* 能和别人相比而无逊色. *~ the objection* 容纳异议. *~ one's rôle* 能扮演所担任的角色. *The sea wall ~s the shock of the waves.* 海堤能抵挡海浪的冲击. **-able** *a.* **-ment** *n.*

sus·tained [səsˈteind] *a.* 持续的；持久(不变)的；被支持的. *make ~ efforts* 再接再厉. *~ efforts* 持续不替的努力. *~ flight.* 稳定持久飞行. 【火箭】巡航飞行. *a ~ note* 【物】持续音[符].

sus·tain·er [səsˈteinə] *n.* 支持者；维持者；持续者；【火箭】主级发动机；〔美〕= sustaining program(me).

sus·tain·ing [səsˈteiniŋ] *a.* 支持的；持续的，持久的；维持着的；补身的，滋补的，增加气力的(食物等)；赞助的. *~ power* 【机】持久力. *~ program(me)* 〔美〕(播音台非营业性的自己的)基本节目，固定节目.

sus·te·nance [ˈsʌstinəns] *n.* 食物，粮食，给养；营养；生计；支持(物)，维持，持久，耐久. *How shall we get ~?* 我们怎样维持生活呢？ *There is no ~ in it.* 这里面没有营养.

sus·ten·tac·u·lum [ˌsʌstenˈtækjuləm] *n.* *(pl.* ***-la*** [-lə]*)* 【解】支持性组织. **-tac·u·lar** *a.*

sus·ten·ta·tion [sʌstenˈteiʃən] *n.* 支持(物)；维持；供养；扶养，生活的维持；粮食，食物. **~fund** (基督教会为接济教士所设的)资助基金.

sus·ten·ta·tive [ˈsʌstenteitiv, səsˈtentətiv] *a.* 支持的；受到支持的；维持的，保存的. — *n.* 支持物，维持物.

sus·ten·tion [səˈstenʃən] *n.* 支撑，被支撑；维持，得到维持.

Su·su [suːˈsuː] *n.* ①*(pl.* ***Su·su(s)****)* 苏苏人〔分布在几内亚等地〕. ②苏苏语.

su·sur·rant [suˈsəːrənt] *a.* 耳语的，喃喃低语的，窸窣作响的 (= susurrous).

su·sur·rate [suˈsəːreit] *vi.* 耳语，喃喃低语，沙沙作响，窸窣作响. **-ra·tion** *n.*

su·sur·rus [suˈsəːrəs] *n.* ①低语声，喃喃低语声，窃窃私语声. ②沙沙声，窸窣声，淙淙，潺潺声.

sut·ler [ˈsʌtlə] *n.* 随军酒食小贩.

Su·tra [ˈsuːtrə] *n.* 〔Sans.〕(婆罗门教，佛教等的)箴言(集)；经文，经典 (= Sutta).

sut·tee [ˈsʌtiː, sʌˈtiː] *n.* 〔Sans.〕殉夫自焚的寡妇；殉节风俗. **-ism** *n.* 殉节风俗.

sut·tle [ˈsʌtl] *n.* 【商】净重.

su·tur·al [ˈsjuːtʃərəl] *a.* 【医】缝合的，位于接缝处的.

su·ture [ˈsjuːtʃə] *n.* 【医】缝合(术)；缝线；【植、动】接缝；【解】缝，骨缝. — *vt.* 缝合，缝拢，连接. **-ral** *a.* **-ration** *n.*

Su·va [ˈsuːvə] *n.* 苏瓦〔斐济首都〕.

Su·zann(e) [suːˈzæn] *n.* 苏珊〔女子名，Susan 的异体〕.

su·ze·rain [ˈsjuːzərein] *n.* 宗主国；【史】封建主，藩王. — *a.* 有宗主权的.

su·ze·rain·ty [ˈsjuːzəreinti] *n.* 宗主权；封建主的权力[地位].

SV = ①〔L.〕*Sancta Virgo* 【基督】圣母(= Holy Virgin). ②sailing vessel 帆船. ③surface vessel 水面舰船. ④stop valve 【机】断流阀，停汽阀，节流阀. ⑤sluice valve 【机】闸水阀. ⑥safety valve 安全阀.

S.V. = ①〔L.〕*Sanctitas Vestra* (= Your Holiness) 陛下(对罗马教皇的尊称). ②*Sons of Veterans* 退伍军人子弟会. ③specific volume 比容.

s.v. = 〔L.〕*sub voce [*或 *sub verbo]* (词典等中表示参看的用语)参看在…词条，在某词下 (= under the word).

Sva·raj [svɑːˈrɑːdʒ] *n.* = swaraj.

svelte [svelt] *a.* 〔F.〕细长的，身材苗条的；文雅的，柔和的；(指美术作品)线条明快的，流畅的.

S.W., SW, s.w. = southwest; southwestern.

swab [swɔb] *n.* (擦洗甲板等用的)拖把，拖帚，墩布；枪炮刷，炮帚；〔俚〕海军军官的肩章；〔海俚〕粗人，蠢货；〔美俚〕(商船上的)水手；【医】(裹有药棉用以擦洗、敷药等的)拭子，药签；用拭子取下的化验标本. — *vt.* 擦抹，揩拭 *(up)*；(拿拖帚等)擦洗 *(down)*；抹药. *~* ***(down) the decks*** 用拖帚擦甲板. *~* ***up*** 用拖帚把水拖干. *~* **down** 擦洗甲板；洗澡.

swab·ber [ˈswɔbə] *n.* 使用墩布拖擦的人；墩布；〔俚〕粗人，蠢材；水手；装管工.

swab·bie, swab·by [ˈswɑːbi] *n.* 〔俚〕水手；〔美俚〕美海军兵士〔常用作称呼〕.

swacked [swækt] *a.* 〔俚〕醉迷糊的，醉熏熏的.

swad·dle [ˈswɔdl] *vt.* ①(尤指用被包、襁褓等)包裹包缠. ②束缚，限制. ***swaddling bands [clothes]*** 被包，襁褓；〔喻〕束缚自由的东西 *(still in [hardly out of] swaddling clothes* 还在襁褓中，还是一个没解包的孩子). —*n.* 襁褓.

Swa·de·shi [swɑːˈdeiʃi] *n.* 〔印〕抵制英[外]货运动.

S. W. Afr. = South-West Africa 西南非洲.

swag [swæg] *n.* 摇晃，倾侧；〔俚〕掠夺来的物品，赃物；用不正当手段得来的东西；〔澳〕(流动工人、流浪者的)背包；悬垂的花枝[花环]；【建】垂花饰；水潭，洼地. — *vi.* 摇晃，倾侧；〔澳〕背着背包旅行；垂下，沉下.

swage [sweidʒ] *n.* 【机】(锻工用)陷型模，铁模. — *vt.* 型锻；(用陷型模)使成形. *~ block* 【机】型砧.

swag·ger [ˈswægə] *vi.* 大摇大摆地走 *(about; in; out)*；摆架子，装模作样；傲慢；吹牛，说大话 *(about)*. — *vt.* 吹牛恫吓. *strut and ~* 装腔作势. *~ sb. into concession* 说大话吓人让步. — *n.* 昂首阔步；摆架子；傲慢态度. — *a.* 〔口〕漂亮的，时髦的(衣服等). *~* **cane** 〔英〕，*~* **stick** (军官用的)短手杖. **-er** *n.* 昂首阔步的人；狂妄自大的人；吹牛者.

swag·ger·ing·ly [ˈswægəriŋli] *ad.* 架子十足地，傲慢地，大摇大摆地.

swag·man [ˈswægmən] *n.* 〔澳口〕无业游民，〔美俚〕收买贼赃的人.

Swa·hi·li [swɑːˈhiːli] *n.* ①*(pl.* ***-lis, -li****)* 斯瓦希里人. ②斯瓦希里语.

swain [swein] *n.* 乡下的年轻人；(牧歌中的)乡下情郎；〔谑〕情人，求婚者；崇拜者.

swain·ish [ˈsweiniʃ] *a.* 〔诗或古〕①乡村少年的. ②乡村情郎的. ③情人的. **-ness** *n.*

S.W.A.K., SWAK, swak = sealed with a kiss 一吻而封〔爱人、小孩等的信封用语〕.

swale [sweil] *vt., vi.* 〔方〕放火烧(树林等)；被烧光；(蜡烛)烧光. — *n.* 〔英方、美〕沼地，洼地；滩槽.

swal·low[1] [ˈswɔləu] *n.* 【鸟】燕子. *One ~ does not make a summer.* 一只燕子不成夏天，不可光凭偶然现象就下断语. *a ~ dive* 燕式跳水. *a ~ coat* 燕尾服. *a ~'s nest* 燕子的窝；燕窝；高处的东西；高地炮兵阵地，高地射击队[便衣队]. **~tail** *n.* ①燕尾；〔口〕燕尾服. ②燕尾旗的末端；【动】凤蝶；燕尾鸢；【木工】燕尾榫，鸽尾榫；【筑城】燕尾外障，(炮台外面的)燕尾形外堡；有倒钩的箭头. **~tailed** *a.* 燕尾形的.

swal·low[2] [ˈswɔləu] *vt.* ①吞，咽 *(down; up; in)*. ②轻信；囫囵吞枣(不加考虑). ③淹没 *(up)*. ④忍耐，忍受(侮辱). ⑤收回(前言). ⑥耗尽，用尽，消尽. —*vi.* 吞，咽. *Such stories are rather hard to ~.* 这种故事很难相

信. ~ *hook, line, and sinker*〔美俚〕轻信. *The expenses ~ up most of profits.* 花费大而利润少. ~ ***a camel*** 吞下骆驼〔隐忍无法无天的事情等〕. ~ ***one's teeth***〔美〕, ~ ***one's words*** 收回前言,认错道歉. ~ ***the anchor*** 永远脱离航海生活;〔美俚〕离开美国海军. ~ ***the bait*** 上钩,上当. ~ ***up*** 吞下去;卷进去;耗尽. — *n.* ①吞咽;一咽,一吞. ②胃管,食道;咽喉,喉咙. ③吸孔. ④【海】(滑车等的)通索孔. ***at one*** ~ 一口就. ***have a small*** ~ 食道狭窄. ***take a*** ~ ***of*** 吞〔喝〕一口. ~**-hole** 石灰坑. **-able** *a.*

swal·low·er [ˈswɔləuə] *n.* 吞咽者;贪吃的人.

swal·low·wort [ˈswɔləuˌwəːt] *n.*【植】①白屈菜. ②牛皮消属植物,药用白前〔如 **black swallowwort** 黑白前 *(Cynanchum nigrum)*, 产于美国东部〕.

swam [swæm] swim 的过去式.

swamp [swɔmp] *n.* 沼泽,沼地,湿地;【矿】煤层聚水洼. — *vt.* 陷入沼泽;淹没,浸在水中;使(小舟)沉没,翻掉;使吃苦头,糟蹋;使陷入困难(不得脱身). —*vi.*满;沉没,翻掉;吃苦头,弄糟蹋掉. ***be*** ~***ed with*** *(invitations)* 陷在(种种应酬)中. ~ **buggy**〔军口〕水陆坦克;水陆两用平底军车;螺旋桨平底快艇. ~ **fever**【医】疟疾. ~ **land** 沼泽地. ~ **seed**〔美俚〕稻米.

swamp·er [ˈswɔːmpə] *n.* ①沼泽地居民. ②帮手,清洁工. ③〔美俚〕卡车司机的帮手;搬运工.

swamp·ish [ˈswɔːmpiʃ] *a.* 沼泽地似的,沼泽似的.

swamp·root [ˈswɔmpraut] *n.*〔美〕威士忌酒.

swamp·y [ˈswɔmpi] *a.* ***(-i·er; -i·est)*** 沼地的;多沼泽的;潮湿的.

swan[1] [swɔn] *n.* ①【鸟】天鹅. ②(杰出的)歌手,诗人;〔S-〕【天】天鹅座. *a black* ~ (澳洲产)黑天鹅;珍品. ~ **dive**〔美〕= swallow dive. ~**herd** 天鹅饲养者. ~**'s-down** 天鹅绒;起毛厚软呢. ~ **shot** 打天鹅等用的巨弹. ~**skin** 天鹅皮;柔毛法兰绒. ~ **song** 传说中天鹅临终时的美妙歌声;最后的诗〔乐曲〕,绝笔,最后的功业. ~**-upping** *n.*〔英〕天鹅嘴上刻标记〔在捕获的小天鹅嘴上刻划记号作为捕获人的标记〕.

swan[2] [ˈswɔn] *vi.* ①闲逛,随意旅行. ②(车辆等)蜿蜒行驶.

swan[3] [swɔn] *vi.*〔方、美俚〕发誓. ***I swan!*** 老天!〔表示吃惊、着急等〕.

swang [swæŋ] *v.*〔古、方〕swing[1] 的过去式.

swank [swæŋk] *n., vi.*〔口〕炫耀(服饰);虚张声势;摆排场;夸嘴,吹牛;优雅;漂亮. — *a.* = swanky.

swank·er [ˈswænkə] *n.*〔主英〕说大话的人;摆排场的人.

swank·y [ˈswænki] *a.* ***(-i·er; -i·est)***〔口〕虚夸的,吹牛的,自大的;爱出风头的;时髦的. **-i·ly** *ad.* **-i·ness** *n.*

swan·ner·y [ˈswɔnəri] *n.* 天鹅饲养所.

Swan·sea [ˈswɔnzi] *n.* 斯旺西〔英国港市〕.

Swan·son [ˈswɔnsn] *n.* 斯旺森〔姓氏〕.

swap [swɔp] *vt., vi.* & *n.* = swop. ~ **credits** 互惠信贷.

swap·er [swɔpə] *n.*〔美〕酒吧间中的侍者.

swap·per [ˈswɔpə] *n.* (物物)交换者;以货易货者;交易者.

swa·raj [swəˈrɑːdʒ] *n.*〔印地〕①自治,独立. ②〔S-〕(英国殖民统治时期争取自治的)印度自治党. **-ist** *n.* 印度自治党人,主张印度自治者.

sward [swɔːd] *n.* 草地;草皮. — *vt., vi.* 铺上草皮.

sware [swɛə]〔古〕swear 的过去式.

swarm[1] [swɔːm] *n.* ①(昆虫的)群;蜂群;【生】浮游单细胞(生物)群,游动孢子. ②大群;大堆. *a* ~ *of sightseers* 大群游客. *a* ~ *of letters* 一大堆信. *the* ~ *theory* (液晶)攒动说. ***in*** ~***s*** = ***in a*** ~ 成群;大批. — *vi.* ①蜂拥成群(而去);(蜜蜂)成群离巢,分群;【生】(细胞等)成群裂出〔浮游〕. ②密集;群集;被挤满;充满. ③攀缘,攀登. *The garden ~s with bees.* 花园里有许多蜜蜂飞来飞去. *The mosquitoes ~ed about us.* 蚊子成群地环绕着我们. *People ~ed into the cinema.* 人们蜂拥而进入电影院. *The swamp ~s with mosquitoes and other insects.* 沼泽地到处都有蚊子和小昆虫. — *vt.* ①攀缘. ②挤满. ~ *(up) a rope* 攀缘绳索. *be ~ed with (rats)* 充满着(老鼠). **-ing**【虫】婚飞;分群;群游.

swarm[2] [swɔːm] *vi., vt.* (抱着)爬(树等).

swarm·er [ˈswɔːmə] *n.* ①【动】蜂涌子,蜂群. ②一大群. ③云集者.

swart [swɔːt] *a.*〔古〕= swarthy.

swarth [swɔːθ] *n.*〔方〕= sward. — *a.* = sworth.

swarth·y [ˈswɔːði] *a.* 黑黝黝的(脸);晒黑了的;黝暗的. **-i·ly** *ad.* **-i·ness** *n.*

swash [swɔʃ] *n.* ①(水的)泼散,激溅,冲刷;奔流声;哗啦哗啦〔水声〕;冲击. ②虚张声势. ③猪饲料. ④湍急的流水;(河口)浅滩;〔美〕为海潮冲刷的沙洲. — *vi.* 泼散(水),(浪)冲激,发出哗啦哗啦的声音;奔流;虚夸;虚张声势;寻衅闹事;恃强凌弱;摆空架子 *(with)*;猛击. — *vt.* 晃动(水等);洗,拨水. *a ~ing blow* 痛击. ~**buckler** *n.* 虚张声势、寻衅滋事的人;暴徒,流氓. ~**-buckling,** ~**bucklering** *n., a.* 虚张声势(的);寻衅滋事(的),恃强凌弱(的). ~ **plate**【机】旋转斜盘.

swas·ti·ka, swas·ti·ca [ˈswæstikə, ˈswɔs-] *n.* ①万字〔卍或卐,古代东方印度等民族象征吉祥的图案;古代印第安人中也流行这一图案,意义不明〕. ②曲十字〔卐为德国纳粹党党徽〕.

swat [swɔt] *n., vt.*〔美口〕拍,打(蝇等);猛击. ~**fest** *n.*〔美俚〕不高明的高尔夫球赛;激烈的拳击比赛;【棒球】击球后上垒次数多的比赛.

swatch [swɔtʃ] *n.* (小块)布样,皮样,样片,样品;一小束,一小簇.

swath [swɔːθ] *n.* *(pl.* ~*s)* 割下的一行草〔麦〕;(一镰刀的)刈幅;(镰刀的)一挥;(刈后的)一条刈迹;一行. ***cut a (wide)*** ~〔美〕夸耀;自以为了不起. ~ **harvesting** 分段收割.

swathe [sweið] *n.* 包带绷带,包布. — *vt.* 绑,缠裹;包围,封住.

swather [ˈswɔːθə] *n.* 割谷机.

swat·ter [ˈswɔtə] *n.* (蝇)拍 (= fly ~);拍打者.

sway [swei] *vi.* ①摇摆,摇动,动摇;歪,倾斜,偏向一边;转向. ②有权力,占支配地位,得势;统治. — *vt.* ①摇,摇动,使动摇;弄歪,使倾斜;使偏向一边. ②支配,操纵,统治. ③挥(剑);【海】扯起(帆桁) *(up)*. *Branches ~ in the wind.* 树枝在风里摇晃. *He is not ~ed by arguments.* 他不为议论所动. ~ *the scepter* 挥舞权杖,掌握大权. ~ *the realm* 统治〔独霸〕一方. — *n.* ①摇动;动摇;倾斜,偏向,偏重;(武器等的)挥舞. ②权势,势力;影响;统治. *one's complete* ~ 独霸. ***hold [bear]*** ~ 掌握全权,有支配…的力量 *(over)*. ***own love's*** ~ 自认被爱情所支配. ***under the*** ~ ***of*** 受着…的支配,在…的支配下. ~**-back** *n.* (马的)特别下凹的背部. ~**-backed** *a.* 背部特凹的(马). **-er** *n.*

Swa·zi [ˈswɑːziː] *n.* *(pl.* ***Swa·zis, Swa·zi)*** ①(非洲东南部)斯威士人. ②斯威士语.

Swa·zi·land [ˈswɑːzilænd] *n.* 斯威士兰〔非洲〕.

SWbS, SW by S = southwest by south 西南偏南.

SWbW, SW by W = southwest by west 西南偏西.

swc = special weapons center〔美〕特种武器中心.

sweal [sweil] *v.* = swale.

swear [swɛə] ***(swore*** [swɔː],〔古〕***sware*** [swɛə]***; sworn*** [swɔːn]*)* *vi.* ①立誓,发誓,宣誓 *(by; on; upon)*;〔口〕断言. ②咒骂,臭骂 *(at)*. — *vt.* 立誓,起誓,发誓;〔口〕郑重申言,断言;使宣誓. ***I'll be*** *sworn.*〔口〕一定的. ***not enough to*** ~ ***by*** 真正一点点. ~ ***a charge [an accusation] against*** 发誓控告〔弹劾〕(某人). ~ ***an oath*** 发誓;大骂. ~ ***at*** 臭骂;〔俚〕(颜色)和…完全不调和. ~ ***before*** = ~ ***by*** 对…发誓;〔口〕非常信赖 *(He ~s by his doctor.* 他极信任他的医生). ~ ***black is white*** 颠倒黑白;强辩. ~ ***by the name of*** 拿…

的名字来发誓。~*for* 保证，担保。~ *in* 使宣誓就职。~ *like a pirate [trooper]* 大骂。~ *off*〔口〕发誓戒(酒等)，发誓不再。~ *on one's sword [the Bible]* 指着刀[把手搁在圣经上]发誓。~ *out*〔美〕通过发誓而获得(对被告的拘捕证)。~ *the peace against sb.* 发誓控告某人要杀害他。~ *(to)* 保证 (*I believe that is true, but I can't ~ (to) it.* 我想那是真的然而我不能绝对肯定)。~ *to oneself* 暗自发誓。— *n.*〔口语〕誓言；发誓，宣誓；咒骂；骂人话。~*word* 咒骂；骂人话；宣誓；怒骂。*hard* ~ 伪证，伪誓。**-er** *n.* **-ing** *n.* 发誓

sweat [swet] *n.* ①汗；出汗。②水气，气汗。③〔口〕吃力的工作；苦差；〔口〕不安，焦急；赶紧；【赛马】赛前练跑；〔俚〕兵。*cold* ~ 冷汗。*night(ly)* ~*s* 盗汗。*They will not take the* ~. 他们是不肯出力的。*Compiling a dictionary is an awful* ~. 编词典是一种吃力的苦工。*an old* ~ 老兵；老手。*all of a* ~ = in a ~. *be running [dripping]* ~ 流着大汗。*by [in] the* ~ *of one's brow [face]* 额上出着汗，靠自己辛勤劳动。*cannot stand the* ~ *of it* 受不了那个辛苦。*in a cold* ~ 捏一把冷汗；提心吊胆地。*no* ~〔美俚〕没有麻烦，没问题；好办。*in a* ~ 流着大汗；担着心，着急地；赶紧。— *(~ed, sweat) vi.* ①出汗；结露水；(烟草等)发酵，发汗。②流着汗工作；努力；累得流汗；被剥削。③不安；焦虑，烦恼。— *vt.* ①使出汗；〔口〕被汗弄脏，弄得尽是汗；使流出，使排出。②(在苛刻的条件下)残酷剥削，吸(人)血汗，榨取(劳力，金钱)。③使(烟叶、皮等)发酵；把汗揩干，把湿气弄干。④(把金银硬币)放在袋里摩擦、收集金银粉末；【冶】加热提炼；热析，熔焊。⑤〔俚〕勒索；〔美俚〕拷问。~ *at night* 出盗汗。*The doctor* ~*s his patient.* 医生使病人发汗。~*ed clothes* 用极低工价制成的衣服。~*ed labo(u)r* 被残酷剥削的劳动，血汗劳动。*He shall* ~ *for it.* 他要后悔的。~ *the game*〔美〕干着急地旁观胜负。~ *away at one's job* 努力工作。~ *down*〔美俚〕大大压缩。~*it* 感到烦恼。~ *it out*〔美〕束手无策地[紧张地、流着汗地]等待或忍受(到最后)。~ *like a trooper*〔美〕汗流得浑身都是，汗流浃背。~ *off* = ~ *out* 发汗祛除〔如医治感冒，减轻体重〕；〔美俚〕辛苦地支持到最后，忍受到最后。~ *with fear* 吓得出冷汗。~*ing system* (残酷剥削的)血汗制度。~**band** (帽子的)防汗衬圈。~ **blood**〔美〕极度紧张的劳动[焦急心情]。~**box** 监狱中的单独牢房，烟叶[生皮]发酵槽；〔美俚〕拷问；〔学生语〕考场。~ **gland** 汗腺。~**pants** 运动长裤。~**shirt** (= T. ~) 短袖圆领紧身汗衫。~**shop** 血汗工厂[残酷剥削工人的工厂]。~**suit** 运动服。

sweat·er [ˈswetə] *n.* ①出汗(过多)的人[物]；发汗剂；发汗[发酵]器。②血汗工人；榨取工人血汗的雇主，包工工头，裁缝包工头。③厚运动衫；圆领绒衣或毛衣。④【化】石蜡发汗室；(烟叶、生皮等的)发汗器。⑤〔美〕在远离牧场办事处的小屋找饭吃的外路人。

sweat·y [ˈsweti] *a.* *(-i·er; -i·est)* ①尽是汗的，汗湿透的；发汗臭的。②汗似的。③流汗的，辛苦的，吃力的。**-i·ly** *ad.* **-i·ness** *n.*

Swed. = Sweden, Swedish.

Swede [swiːd] *n.* ①瑞典人。②[~, s-]〔英〕= rutabaga.【植】芜菁甘蓝，瑞典芜菁，芸苔。

Swe·den [ˈswiːdn] *n.* 瑞典〔欧洲〕。

Swe·den·bor·gi·an [ˌswiːdnˈbɔːdʒiən, -gi-] *n.* 斯韦登博格〔瑞典神秘主义宗教家，自称能与鬼魂交往〕信徒；〔尤指〕新耶路撒冷教会教徒。— *a.* 斯韦登博格的；斯韦登博格教义的；斯韦登博格信徒的。— **-ism -borg·ism** [-ˌbɔːg-] *n.*

Swed·ish [ˈswiːdiʃ] *a.* 瑞典(式)的；瑞典人[语]的。— *n.* 瑞典语；〔the ~〕〔集合词〕瑞典人。~ **massage**【医】瑞典式按摩(疗法)。~ **movements**【医】瑞典式按摩手法。~ **turnip**【植】= rutabaga，芜菁甘蓝，瑞典芜菁，芸苔。

swee·ny [ˈswiːni] *n.*〔美〕(特指马肩的)肌肉萎缩(症)；傲慢。

sweep [swiːp] *vt.* *(swept [swept])* ①扫(房间等)，扫除，打扫；刷，撢(灰尘等)。②(象扫一样)吹去，刮去，冲去 *(along; away; down; off)*；完全消灭，一扫而光，疏浚(河底)；拉(网等)。【军】扫射；扫雷；扫荡；肃清，消灭。③取得全胜。④扫过，擦过，掠过；拖过。〔主诗〕用手指弹(乐器)。⑤四下眺望，周览，环视，扫视；【电视】扫描。⑥描绘…的轮廓。⑦【铸造】刮(模型)。— *vi.* ①用扫帚扫；拿刷子刷；打扫。②掠过，扫过；扫视，飞快地滑过；吹去，刮去；飞去；袭来。③衣裾曳地地走；大摇大摆地通过。④【军】扫荡；扫射；扫雷；(飞机、军舰等)长驱直入；游弋。⑤延伸。⑥(鲸鱼等)摇尾巴。*A new broom* ~*s clean.* 新笤帚扫得干净；新官上任三把火。~ *a constituency* 独占选举区内多数选票(取得全胜)。*be swept along in the crowd* 被人群推动着往前走。*be swept off one's feet* 被(波浪)冲击而站不住脚；被感情所支配不由自主。~ *across the length and breadth of the country* 席卷全国。~ *away* 扫清；迅速消灭，肃清；冲走。~ *everything [the enemy] before (one)* 以破竹之势前进，摧枯拉朽地扫荡敌人。~ *off* 扫清；(疫疠等)杀死(不少人)；吹走。~ *one's audience along with one* (演讲人)紧紧抓牢听众心理。~ *over* 风靡；向…扩展；眺望，环视；袭击；狂刮；将…一扫而光。~ *the board* 扫盘子[赢得全部赌注]；〔喻〕独占鳌头。~ *the deck* (波浪)冲洗甲板；扫射甲板。~ *the seas* 在海上横冲直撞；扫海；扫荡海上敌人。— *n.* ①打扫，扫除。②(风的)刮，吹，扫掠，(水的)冲刷；(波浪的)冲激。【军】扫荡；扫射；扫雷；(飞机，军舰等)游弋；长驱直入；肃清，清除；(手等的)一挥；〔喻〕迅速进步[发展]。③(土地的)延伸，扩张；区域，范围；眺望，环视；天体观测；【电视】扫描。④弯曲；弯路；弯流；偏差。⑤大胜(指选举等)。⑥清扫员，(特指)扫烟囱工人 (= chimney-~)；〔俚〕不干净的人，卑劣的人，讨厌的人。⑦【海】船侧弯曲部；扫海索；长桨；【火箭】后掠翼行，箭形。⑧(桔槔的)称竿。⑨〔*pl.*〕机枪队。⑩〔常 *pl.*〕〔口〕= sweepstakes. ⑪〔常 *pl.*〕扫集物 (= sweepings). *a* ~ *of mountain country* 山国风光一瞥。*as black as a* ~ (象扫烟囱的人一样)漆黑的，脏的。*a regular little* ~ 肮脏的孩子。*You dirty* ~! 你这坏蛋！*at one* ~ 一举[挥，扫]。*beyond the* ~ *of* 达不到的地方，在可达到的范围以外。~ *of* 扫清；完全撤换。*make a* ~ *to the left* 向左拐，向左弯斜。~ **back**【空】后掠形；后掠角；(离心压缩机叶片)后倾，后弯。~ **circuit**【电】扫描电路。~ **(second) hand** (钟表的)长秒针。~ **up** *n.* 大扫除。

sweep·er [ˈswiːpə] *n.* 清扫工人，清扫员；扫除机；扫海船，扫雷艇。

sweep·ing [ˈswiːpiŋ] *a.* ①扫清的；扫荡的；一扫而光的；一网打尽的。②势如破竹的，势不可挡的，厉害的。③包括无遗的；彻底的；概括的，笼统的(陈述等)。④彻底的，大大的。⑤延伸的，弯弯曲曲似的。— *n.* 扫除，扫清，扫荡；扫海；〔*pl.*〕扫集物；一堆垃圾；底层的人们。~ *changes* 大变。~ **brush** 扫帚。~ **[sweep] circuit**【电】扫描电路。~ **[sweep] net** (渔船用的)大拖网；捕虫网。**-ly** *ad.* **-ness** *n.*

sweep·stake(s) [ˈswiːpsteik(s)] *n.*〔*sing.*, *pl.*〕一人或数人赢得赌金的赛马[彩票]，〔泛指〕彩票(赌博)。

Sweet [swiːt] *n.* ①斯威特〔姓氏〕。②**Henry** ~ 斯威特〔1845—1912，英国语音学家，语言学家〕。

sweet [swiːt] *a.* ①甜(蜜)的 *(opp.* bitter, sour*)*；滋味好的；芳香的；醇美的 *(opp.* dry*)*；(音调)甜美的。②〔口〕可爱的；好看的。③愉快的，快乐的；畅快的。④无恶味的；不咸的(水)；新鲜的*(opp.* stale, rancid, sour*)*。⑤温柔的，亲切的。⑥轻快的；轻便的，灵活的；容易驾驶的。⑦【石油】脱硫的，香化的。⑧非酸性的，适于耕作的(土地) *(opp.* sour*)*。~ *chatter* = ~ *line* = ~ *patter*

〔美〕花言巧语. ~ *chow-chow* 糖果蜜饯(等). *a* ~ *man* 〔美〕情郎. ~ *flowers* 香花. ~ *mamma* 【美】甜姐儿. ~ *music* 美妙的音乐. *a* ~ *little dog* 可爱的小狗. *a* ~ *motor* 滑溜无声的发动机. ~ *running* 顺畅的运行. ~ *air* 新鲜空气. *keep the room clean and* ~ 使屋子保持整洁 [宜人,合乎卫生]. *You will have a* ~ *time putting that machine together again.* 〔口〕〔反〕要把那部机器装还原样是很费工夫的. ***at one's own*** ~ ***will*** 任意,随意. ***be*** ~ ***on [upon]*** 〔口〕迷恋; 爱上. ***have a*** ~ ***tooth*** 爱吃甜品. ~ ***and twenty*** 二十岁的美人. ***too*** ~ 〔美〕马上,立刻; 巴不得. — *n.* ①甜味; 好吃的东西; 糖果, 甜食; 餐后的甜点心; 甜酒. ②〔常 *pl.*〕愉快的事; 称心的东西. ③〔主、称呼〕亲爱的人 (= darling). ④〔常 *pl.*〕〔诗〕芳香. ⑤〔美口〕= ~ potato. ⑥〔美音乐俚〕缓慢的旋律优美的跳舞音乐. *the* ~ *and the bitter [the* ~*s and bitters] of life* 人生的苦乐. *the* ~*s of the year* 一年里头的快乐季节. ~ **alyssum** 【植】香雪球. ~ **basil** 【植】紫花罗勒. ~ **bay** 【植】月桂树; 弗吉尼亚木兰. ~**-bough** 〔美〕苹果树. ~ **bread** (小牛、小羊等的)胰脏,脺脏或胸腺〔被认为是一种美味〕. ~ **briar,** ~ **brier** 【植】多花蔷薇. ~ **cherry** 【植】欧洲甜樱桃(树). ~ **clover** 【植】草木犀属植物. ~ **corn** 〔美〕①甜玉米. ②(做菜用的)嫩玉米. ~ **fern** 香蕨木. ~ **flag** 【植】白菖蒲. ~ **gale** 【植】香杨梅. ~ **going** 舒适顺利的愉快旅行. ~ **gum** 【植】枫香属(树脂). 胶皮糖香树(木); 苏合香. ~ **heart** ①*n.* 爱人,情人; 十分讨人欢喜的人[物]. ②*vt., vi.* 〔口〕谈恋爱; 求爱. ~ **heart contract** 黄色工会与资方勾结所订的合同. ~ **John** 【植】狭叶美洲石竹. ~ **majoram** 【植】薄荷属植物〔尤指茉乔栾那, 叶可作烹调香料〕. ~ **meat** 〔常 *pl.*〕糖果,甜食; 蜜饯. ~ **oil** 橄榄油; 菜油. ~ **one** 狠狠一击; 〔称呼〕= darling. ~ **patootie** 甜姐儿. ~ **pea** 【植】香豌豆(花) ~ **pepper** 【植】灯笼椒. ~ **potato** 甘薯. ~ **root** 【植】黄杨叶念珠藤; 菖蒲. ~**-scented** *a.* 香, 香味好的, 有芳香的. ~ **shop** 〔英〕糖果铺. ~ **sixteen** 〔美〕可爱的十六岁小姑娘. ~ **sop** 【植】番荔枝. ~ **sultan** 【植】香芙蓉. ~ **take** 〔美拳击〕售票成绩好. ~**-talk** *vi., vt.* 甜言蜜语奉承巴结. ~**-tempered** *a.* 心地温和的. ~ **toil** 自己乐意干的苦干. ~ **violet** 【植】香堇菜. ~ **water** 淡水, 饮用水. ~ **william [william]** 【植】美洲石竹. ~ **wood** 【植】= ~ bay.

sweet·en [ˈswiːtn] *vt.* ①弄甜,加糖; 弄香,去臭; 使减低酸性; 【石油】脱硫; 〔美俚〕用威士忌酒加浓; 使(声音)美妙,使(音调)好听. ②使愉快. ③使温和, 使温柔; 减轻(悲伤),缓和. ④弄清洁,使新鲜,消毒. ⑤增加(担保品; 扑克赌注). ~ *life* 使生活愉快. ~ *a room* 把房间消毒[搞好房间里的清洁卫生]. — *vi.* 变甜; 变香; 变悦耳; 变得令人愉快; 变清洁; 变美丽; 变清新舒服.

sweet·er·ia, sweeter·y [swiːˈtiəriə, -ˈtiəri] *n.* 〔美〕糖果店.

sweet·ie [ˈswiːti] *n.* ①〔常 *pl.*〕〔儿语〕= sweetmeat. ②〔美口〕情人 = sweetheart. ~**-pie** 情人.

sweet·ing [ˈswiːtiŋ] *n.* 香苹果; 〔古,称呼〕= darling.

sweet·ish [ˈswiːtiʃ] *a.* 有甜味的; 甜甜的; 可爱的. **-ly** *ad.*

sweet·ly [ˈswiːtli] *ad.* 甜(蜜)地, 芬芳地; (音调)美妙; 可爱, 亲切. *reply* ~ 回答得亲切; *speak* ~ 说得亲切〔愉快; 轻快, 温和〕. *The saw cuts* ~. 这把锯子好锯. *The bicycle runs* ~. 这辆自行车好骑.

sweet·ness [ˈswiːtnis] *n.* 甜蜜; 甜味, 美味; 甜度; 新鲜; 芳香; 美音, 佳调; 可爱; 愉快; 温和, 温柔, 亲切.

sweet·ums [ˈswiːtəmz] *n.* 〔美〕甜姐儿.

sweet·y [ˈswiːti] *n.* = sweetmeat.

swell [swel] ***(~ed; swollen*** [ˈswɔːln], 〔古〕***swoln,*** 〔罕〕***~ ed)*** *vi.* ①膨胀; 肿大; 变大, 增大, 增长, 壮大; (土地)隆起. ②(声音等)变高. ③(河水)上涨; 起浪. ④骄傲, 自负, 趾高气扬 *(with)*; (感情)激昂, 紧张, 兴奋. — *vt.* ①使膨胀; 使鼓起; 使肿大; 增大, 增加(支出等); 使高涨; 使增长, 壮大. ②使自负, 使自大, 使趾高气扬, 使得意扬扬. ③【乐】增强. *The injured wrist* ~*ed (up)*. 受伤的手腕肿起来了. *the* ~*ing tide* 正在上涨的潮水. *swollen estimates* 庞大的预算. ~ *a note* 增强乐音. ~ ***the chorus of admiration*** 加入赞美者[崇拜者]之列. ~ ***the ranks of*** 加入, 参加. ~ ***the total*** 使总数增大; 滥竽充数. ~***ed head*** 〔俚〕得意忘形, 自高自大 *(have [suffer from]* ~*ed head* 〔俚〕自以为了不得). ***swollen with indignation*** 怒火填膺. — *n.* ①膨胀; 肿胀, 肿大; 增大, 增加; 加强; 强大; 情绪高涨. ②浪涛汹涌. ③【地】海涌. ④【乐】渐强到渐弱(符号). ⑤(土地的)隆起; (手臂等的)鼓包, 隆起(部分). ⑥〔口〕名人; 名手, 名家; 服装时髦的人; 〔口〕自夸的人, 妄自尊大的人. *a* ~ *in politics* 政界名人. *a* ~ *at tennis* 网球名手. *What a* ~ *you are!* 你多么漂亮啊! — *a.* 〔口〕漂亮的, 极好的(音乐家等); 高级的, 时髦的. *He looks* ~. 他很时髦. *a* ~ *pianist* 了不起的名钢琴家. *a* ~ *dame*〔美〕时髦、漂亮的女子. ~ **box** 【乐】(风琴的)音响调节箱[器]. ~**-differous** 〔美〕有趣的, 舒服的; 优雅的; 华丽的. ~ **doodle** *a.* 〔美〕漂亮的; 可爱的; 时髦的; 优雅的. ~ **fish** 【鱼】圆鲀, 东方鲀. ~ **head** 〔美俚〕自高自大的人. ~ **mob** 〔英〕打扮成绅士的一伙扒手. ~**-mobman** 〔英〕打扮成绅士的扒手. ~ **organ** 有音响调节器的风琴.

swell·dom [ˈsweldəm] *n.* 〔俚〕上流社会, 时髦人物的圈子.

swel·le·gance [ˈsweliːgəns] *n.* 〔美〕非常优雅.

swel·le·gant [ˈsweləgənt] *a.* 〔美〕= swellelegant. 非常优雅的.

swell·el·e·gous [ˈsweləligəs] *a.* 〔美〕优雅的; 漂亮的; 过分华丽的.

swell·ing [ˈsweliŋ] *n.* 肿胀; 增大; 肿瘤; 隆起, 膨胀; 隆起部.

swell·ish [ˈsweliʃ] *a.* 〔俚〕漂亮的, 时髦的.

swelp [swelp] 〔美俚〕= So help (me God). 我敢发誓. — *n.* 可怜的抗议者.

swel·ter [ˈsweltə] *vi., vt.* (使)中暑, (使)热得发昏, (使)热得没气力. — *n.* ①闷热的空气, 酷热, 炎暑. ②满身大汗, 非常紧张的心情. ③混乱.

swel·ter·ing [ˈsweltəriŋ] *a.* 酷热的; 使热得发昏的. **-ly** *ad.*

Swensky [ˈswenski] *n.* 〔美〕瑞典人.

swept [swept] sweep 的过去式及过去分词. ~ **out** *a.* 〔英〕流线形的.

swept·back [ˈsweptˌbæk] *a.* ①有后掠形(箭形)的〔指机翼〕. ②(飞机)有后掠翼的.

swept·wing [ˈsweptˌwiŋ] *a.* 【空】有后掠机翼的, 有箭形机翼的.

swerve [swəːv] *vi.* 转弯; 偏斜; 突然改变方向; 滑出; 闪避; 逸出常轨 *(from)*. — *vt.* 使转弯, 使改变方向; 使滑出; 使离正轨. — *n.* 转向, 偏斜(的程度); 滑出, 逸出; 背离; 【板球】曲球. ~ *from the path of duty* 不守本分; 不负责任. **-less** *a.* 坚定不移的.

swev·en [ˈswevn] *n.* 〔古〕梦; 幻影.

S.W.G., SWG = standard wire ga(u)ge 【电】标准线规.

Swi·a·ge·cats [ˈswiːidʒkæts] *n.* 〔美〕南达科他 (South Dakota) 州和该州居民的别名.

swick·y [ˈswiːki] *n.* 〔美〕威士忌酒.

Swift [swift] *n.* ①斯威夫特〔姓氏〕. ②**Jonathan** ~ 斯威夫特〔1667—1745, 英国讽刺作家, *Gulliver's Travels* 的作者〕.

swift [swift] *a.* ①飞快的, 迅速的, 敏捷的; 即时的, 立刻的(答复等); 突然发生的. ②易…的, 动不动就…的 *(to do)*. ③时间极短的(苦痛等). *a* ~ *wit* 急智. ***as*** ~ ***as***

thought 立刻,马上,一转眼。— *n.*【动】褐雨燕;蝾螈;一种小蜥蜴;鬼蛾;(纺织机等的)大滚筒;纺车,卷线车;急流,急湍;〔口〕快速的排字工人。— *ad.* 迅速地,敏捷地。~**-footed** *a.* 走得快的。~**-handed** *a.* 手快的;行动[操作]敏捷的。~ **fox**【动】(北美的)小狐〔简称 ~〕. ~ **winged** *a.* 飞得快的. **-ly** *ad.* **-ness** *n.*

swift·er [ˈswiftə] *n.*【海】低桅前支索,下前支索;绞盘加固索〔用来连接各绞盘棒末端〕.

swift·y [ˈswifti] *a.* 〔美〕极引人注意的.

swig [swig] *n., vi., vt.* 〔口〕大口喝,痛饮.

swill [swil] *vt.* ①大口喝,痛饮。②冲洗 *(out)*. — *vi.* 大口喝,痛饮。— *n.* ①大喝;痛饮,狂饮;劣酒。②冲涮,洗涤。③泔水,残汤剩菜[猪饲料]。④过度打扮的人. *swell* ~〔美俚〕油水足的残汤剩菜〔意指奢侈的生活〕;奢侈的饮食.

swim [swim] *(swam*[swæm]*; swum*[swʌm]*)* *vi.* ①游水,游泳。②浮游,漂浮,漂流。③充溢,充斥,充满;浸,泡 *(in; with)*. ④浮动,滑动;打转;浮现,恍然出现;眼花,眩晕。—*vt.* 游过;与…比赛游泳;使(狗等)游泳;使(船等)浮起;泡(在水中). *I cannot ~ a stroke.* 我游泳一点也不会. ~ *to the bottom* = ~ *like a stone [tailor's goose]*〔谑〕(不会水)沉下. *swimming eyes* = *eyes that ~ with tears* 眼泪汪汪的眼睛. ~ *a race* 参加游泳比赛. *I will ~ you 100 yards.* 我要跟你赛游100码. ~ *wheat to select seed* 浸麦选种. ***sink or ~*** 好歹试试看,不管是沉是浮. ~ ***against the tide [stream]*** 溯流游泳;违反时势[潮流]. ~ ***between two waters*** 驶行中流;取中庸之道. ~ ***on one's back*** 仰泳. ~ ***with the tide [stream]*** 顺着潮流,顺水推舟. — *n.* ①游泳;浮动,浮现;滑走。②潮流,时势,(事件的)趋势。③眩晕。④深渊. ***be in the ~*** 熟悉内情,顺应潮流,与目前形势一致. ***have [take] a ~*** 游泳. ***out of the ~*** 不明内情,脱离当前形势;不合潮流. ~ **blad·der** (鱼)鳔. ~ **fin**〔美〕(潜水蛙人用的)橡皮脚蹼. ~ **pool** 游泳池. ~ **suit [wear]** 游泳衣.

swi·meet [ˈswimiːt] *n.* 〔美〕游泳比赛.

swim·ma·ble [ˈswiməbl] *a.* ①可游泳的。②游泳活动期的。③游泳距离的.

swim-man-do [swimˈmɑːndəu] *n.*【军】河川突击队.

swim·mer [ˈswimə] *n.* 游泳者;鳔.

swim·mer·et(te) [ˈswimərət] *n.*【动】(甲壳类的)挠肢,游泳足.

swim·ming [ˈswimiŋ] *n.* 游泳;眩晕. *go ~* 去游泳. *I have a ~ in my head.* 我头晕. ~ **bath** (室内)游泳池. ~ **bell**【动】(水母等的)泳钟,游泳体,伞. ~ **bladder** 鱼鳔. ~ **gala** 水上运动会. ~ **hole**〔美〕(河湾等处可供游泳的)游泳水塘. ~ **pool** 游泳池. **-ly** *ad.* (进行)顺利,顺畅.

swim·mist [ˈswimist] *n.* 〔美〕游泳家.

swim·my [ˈswimy] *a.* 有点儿头晕的,引起头晕的;模糊的. **-i·ly** *ad.* **-i·ness** *n.*

Swin·burn(e) [ˈswinbəːn] *n.* 斯温伯恩〔姓氏〕.

swin·dle [ˈswindl] *vt., vi., n.* 诈取,骗取,欺骗,诓骗;伪物. **-r** *n.* 骗子,诈骗犯.

swin·dling·ly [ˈswindliŋli] *ad.* 用诈骗手段.

swine [swain] *n.* 〔*sing., pl.*〕猪;贪鄙下流的家伙. *some sheep and several ~* 几只羊和几只猪. ~ **herd** *n.* 牧猪人,养猪人. ~ **pox**【医】水痘.

swin·er·y [ˈswainəri] *n.* ①猪栏;猪群,②卑鄙下流的行为.

swing [swiŋ] *vi. (swung* [swʌŋ]*, swang* [swæŋ]*; swung)* ①摆动;摇摆,摇动;挥动,摇荡。②(人、马车等)大摇大摆地走*(along; past; by)*,〔摆动着手臂〕轻松地走[跑]。③打秋千。④悬挂着 *(from)*;〔口〕被处绞刑,吊死。⑤回旋;转动,转身;转变方向.【海】(船停泊时因风或潮水)旋转。⑥挥手打击。⑦(指音乐)具有激荡人心的韵调;演奏[唱]摇摆舞音乐。⑧〔美俚〕出风头;赶时髦;非常活跃〔特指追求逸乐〕. — *vt.* ①使摆动,摇摆,摇动;(往复)摇荡;挥舞(棍棒等);回转,转动。②使(一排兵等)转向;使以弧线前进。③吊起,悬挂。④〔美口〕使办成功;经营,办理,处理,支配。⑤演奏[唱](摇摆舞音乐). *Their mind swung as one to home.* 他们不约而同地想念起家乡来. ~ *by one arm from a branch* 用一只胳膊吊在树枝上. *The door swung shut.* 门关上了. *I swung over to the subject of the pictures.* 我转到了有关电影的话题. *He could not ~ the enterprise.*〔口〕他主持不了那个事业. ~ *the door open [shut]* 把门打开[关上]. ~ *a catgut*〔美〕撒网. ***no room to ~ a cat (in)*** 狭窄. ~ ***around*** [〔英〕***round***] ***on one's heel*** 掉转身子. ~ ***(a)round the circle*** 在选区内来回游说. ~ ***at***〔美〕挥拳打,对准…打过去. ~ ***clear of*** (船)掉转方向躲避. ~ ***for it*** 因(…)而被处绞刑. ~ ***in with*** 加入;与…合作. ~ ***into line*** (军队等)转成横队. ~ ***round*** 掉转方向. ~ ***the lead***〔军俚〕假病,逃职. ~ ***to***(门)(砰的一声)关上. — *n.* ①摆动,摇动,摇摆;挥动;摆幅,振幅;摆动量;大摇大摆的步伐。②秋千。③自由活动范围,行动自由。④趋势,倾向;推动力。⑤〔只用 *sing.*〕韵律,音律,旋律。⑥【摄】(暗箱的)转动;【拳击】横击,挥击。⑦【滑雪】旋转;【滑冰】犹豫摆动。⑧〔口〕一阵工作;进行,开展。⑨(巡回)旅行。⑩摇摆舞音乐。⑪【商】行情涨落。⑫〔美〕(态度等的)周期性交替. *a grid ~*【物】栅压荡限. *the ~ of the pendulum* 钟摆的摆动;势力的盛衰交替;党派间的政权交替. *have a ~* 打秋千. *a ~ room*〔美〕(工人等的)吸烟室,休息室. ***get into (the) ~ of one's work*** 工作起劲起来,工作顺利开展. ***give full [free] ~ to it*** 听其自由,放任自流. ***go with a ~*** (音调)流利;(事情)顺利. ***have one's full ~*** 自由行动,自由掌握. ***in full ~*** 正起劲,正在紧张时候,正在积极进行 (*The work is in full ~.* 工作正顺利全速进行). ***let it have its ~*** = give full ~ to it. ***lose on the ~s what you make*** [gain, get back] ***on the roundabouts*** 转木马得来打秋千失去;得东失西,依然如故;失之东隅,收之桑榆. ***take a ~ at***〔美〕= ~ at. ***take one's full ~*** = have one's full ~. ~ **boat** 船形秋千. ~ **bridge** 旋(开)桥. ~**-by**【宇】(利用中间行星或目的行星的引力场调整航向或航轨)借力式航道. ~**(ing)-door** 转门. ~ **ga·teer**〔美〕摇摆音乐家. ~ **jack** 横式起重机. ~ **link**【机】摆杆. ~ **music** 摇摆舞音乐. ~ **room**〔美〕(工厂工人)吸烟室,休息室. ~ **shift**〔美〕(下午四点到半夜的)中班工作,中班工人. ~ **span**〔美〕旋开桥,跳桥. ~ **vote** 决定票. ~**-wing** 后掠翼.

swinge [swindʒ] *vt.* 〔古〕打,猛打;惩戒;把…烧焦.

swing(e)·ing [ˈswiŋdʒiŋ] *a.* 重,凶猛的(打击等);〔口〕极大的,巨大的;了不得的(损失). 极好的,优等的,— *ad.* 极大地,非常地.

swing·er[1] [ˈswiŋə] *n.* ①时髦人物。②〔俚〕浪荡公子.

swing·er[2] [ˈswiŋə] *n.* ①〔废〕彪形大汉。②〔英口〕庞然大物.

swin·ge·roo [ˌswiŋdʒəˈruː] *n.* 〔美〕= swing music.

swing·ing [ˈswiŋiŋ] *a.* ①摆动的,摇摆的。②一挥(摇)而成的。③〔美俚〕活跃的,极时髦的. **-ly** *ad.*

swin·gle [ˈswiŋgl] *n.* 打麻器;打麻棍;(连枷的)打禾棍. — *vt.* 用打麻器打[打制]. ~ **tree** *n.* (兽力车、犁等的)轭,曲木.

swing·ster [ˈswiŋstə] *n.* 〔美〕摇摆舞乐师.

swin·ish [ˈswainiʃ] *a.* 猪的;猪似的;粗鲁的;贪鄙的,下流的. **-ly** *ad.* **-ness** *n.*

swink [swiŋk] *vi. (swank, swonk; swonk·en)* 〔英古〕辛苦,辛辛苦苦地工作. — *n.* 辛苦,苦工.

Swin·ner·ton [ˈswinətən] *n.* 斯温纳顿〔姓氏〕.

swipe [swaip] *n.* 〔口〕柄;握杆;(板球等的)猛打,重击;猛击;摩擦(人、马的)身体;马夫;〔美俚〕贼. — *vt., vi.* ①猛击,猛打;大口喝,牛饮。②〔美俚〕乘机偷. **-r** *n.* ①

猛击者。②酒鬼。③偷窃者。

swipes [swaips] *n.* 〔*pl.*〕〔英〕(低级)啤酒；杯中喝剩的啤酒。

swi·ple, swip·ple [ˈswipl] *n.* 连枷头，连枷上的短棒。

swirl [swəːl] *n.* ①(水、风等的)旋转；漩涡。②卷状的东西；卷曲的形状；(雪的)纷飞。③纷乱。④〔美〕弯曲，围绕。⑤鱼跃。— *vi.* ①打转。②(头)晕。③弯曲盘旋，(雪)纷飞。 **-er** *n.*【空】涡旋式喷嘴，离心式喷嘴。 **-y** *a.* ①成涡旋形的。②〔Scot.〕纠缠的。

swish [swiʃ] *n.* ①(鞭子在空中挥动，衣裙在走动时的)嗖嗖声，沙沙声。②飒飒声。③(鞭棒的)挥动。④漂亮，时髦。⑤〔美俚〕搞同性关系的男子。— *a.* ①漂亮的，时髦的。②〔美俚〕搞同性关系的。 ***in the ~*** 见闻广博，熟悉内情。— *vi.* 嗖嗖地挥动；作沙沙声。— *vt.* 把(鞭子)挥动得嗖嗖地响；刷地甩动(尾巴)；用(棍子)抽断(树枝等)，沙沙地削去 *(off)*；用(鞭子)抽打。 **~-swash** 〔俚〕啤酒。 **-er** *n.* 衣着时髦的人。

swishy [ˈswiʃi] *a.* ***(swish·i·er; swish·i·est)*** ①发嗖嗖声的，作窸窣响的。②〔俚〕搞同性关系的 (= swish)。 **~-~** *a.* 〔美〕三心二意的，靠不住的。

Swiss [swis] *n.* 〔*sing.*, *pl.*〕瑞士 (Switzerland) 人；瑞士语，(特指)瑞士的德国语；(瑞士)卫兵；看门的。— *a.* 瑞士的；瑞士人的。 ~ **chard**【植】= chard, 莙荙菜，牛皮菜。 ~ **guards** (从前法国和现在罗马教皇雇用的)瑞士卫兵。 ~ **roll** (有果酱的)面包卷。

SWISSAIR = Swiss Air Transport Company 瑞士航空公司。

Swit., = Switzerland.

switch [switʃ] *n.* ①(树上折下的)细树枝；软鞭子；鞭打。②假发；(尾巴上的)毛簇。③〔美〕【铁道】道岔扳子，轨闸转辙器；侧线。④【电】开关；电闸；电键；转换器；【电话】接线台。⑤【军】斜行壕。⑥(思想等的)大转变。 *a change-over ~* 转换开关，转向开关。 *a pull ~* 拉线开关。 *a three wire ~* 双联开关。 *a time ~* 定时断路器。 *a clock ~* 定时开关。 *a line ~* (自动电话的)寻线机，预选器；线路开关。 *a ~ room* 配电室，开关室；机键室；(电话)交换室。— *vt.* ①鞭打；摆动；摇(尾)；猛然抢去。②挂断(…的电话)(*~ sb. off*)，关闭(电流)，关(电灯) *(off; out)*。④通(电流)，接通(电话给某人)，开(电灯) *(on)*。⑤改变，转变(思想、谈话等)；【铁道】给扳道岔；调配(车厢)。— *vi.* 鞭打；【铁道】扳道岔；调车；挂断电话 *(off)*；转换，转变。 *~ an electric light on [off]* 开[关]灯。 *~ off to another line of thought* 改变想法[思路]。 *Let's ~.* 〔美〕走吧；开动吧。 ***I'll be ~ed*** 〔美口〕〔表示否定、惊讶〕(*I'll be ~ed if you do.* 你要是能的话我把头砍掉)。 ~ ***off [on to]*** 不收听[收听](某一广播)。 ~ ***over*** 换位置，转换，改换 (*~ over to garrison duty* 转而担任守卫)。 ~ ***through*** 【电信】转接。 **~back** (游乐园里乘着玩的)惊险小铁路；【铁路】之字形爬山铁路；【影】倒叙往事的镜头。 **~-blade knife** (按纽后会自动打开的)弹簧折刀。 ~ **board**【电】配电盘；(电信、电话)交换机，交换台；配电盘。 ~ **cane**【植】软条青篱竹。 ~ **gear** 开关齿轮。 **~-hitter** 左右手都能击球的棒球运动员。〔美俚〕多才多艺的人。 ~ **man** 扳道工人；调车助手。 ~ **mugger** 〔美〕电话接线生。 **~over** 大转变。 ~ **signal** 转辙信号。 **~-tower** 〔美〕信号房。 ~ **yard** (铁路的)调车场；编组站。

switche·roo [ˌswitʃəˈruː] *n.* 〔俚〕突然变化，可怕的巨变。

swith [ˈswiθ] *ad.* 〔方〕立即，迅速地。

swith·er [ˈswiðə] *vi.*, *n.* 〔Scot.〕疑惑；踌躇，拿不定主意。

Switz. = Switzerland.

Switz·er [ˈswitsə] *n.* 〔古〕瑞士人；瑞士雇佣兵；(罗马教皇的)瑞士卫兵。

Switz·er·land [ˈswitsələnd] *n.* 瑞士〔欧洲〕。

swiv·el [swivl] *n.*【机】转环，转节；旋转接头；旋轴；活节；回旋炮；旋桥；(旋椅的)底座。 *a ~ dude* 坏蛋。 *a ~ loom* 绣花机。 *~ plough.* 双向犁。— *vi.*, *vt.* ***(-ll-)*** 旋转，回转；用转节固定[支住]。 ~ **chair,** 转椅 (*a ~-chair man* 〔美〕高级职员)。 ~ **eye** 斜视。 ~ **gun** 回旋炮。 ~ **hook** 转动钩。 **~-led** *a.* 装了转环[活节]的。 ~ **table**【机】转台。 ~ **weaving**【纺】挖花织造。

swiv·et [ˈswivət] *n.* 〔方，口〕烦躁不安，极度激动；不安。

swiz(z) [swiz] *n.* ***(pl. swizzes)*** 〔方〕欺骗，诈取。

swiz·zle [ˈswizl] *n.* 〔口〕碎冰鸡尾酒。— *vt.* 用搅酒棒搅和。— *vi.* (过量地)喝酒。 ~ **stick,** 搅和混合用的玻璃棒。

swob [swɔb] *n.*, *vt.* = swab.

swob·ble [ˈswɔbl] *vt.*, *vi.* 〔美俚〕大口大口地吞；急急忙忙地吃。

swol·len [ˈswəulən] swell 的过去分词。— *a.* 肿起的；膨胀的；涨了水的；浮夸的；骄傲的。 **~-headed** *a.* 骄傲的，自高自大的。 ~ **cranium** 〔美〕自负；自我主义。

swoon [swuːn] *n.* 昏厥，晕倒；神魂颠倒。 ***fall into a ~*** 晕过去，昏倒。— *vi.* ①晕过去，昏倒；神魂颠倒。②(乐声等)渐渐微弱，渐渐消失。

swoop [swuːp] *vi.* (鹰)飞下猛扑；突然袭击 *(down; on; upon)*。 *~ down upon an enemy* 突袭敌人。— *vt.* 攫去；〔口〕抢去 *(up)*。— *n.* 飞扑；从上攫取；抢夺；【空】下扑。 ***at a single ~*** 一下子，一举。 ***at one fell ~*** (灾难的)迅速而恐怖地袭来；一下子。 ***make a ~ at*** 突袭，飞扑。 ***with a ~*** 一抓；一下子。

swoosh [swuːʃ, swuʃ] *vi.*, *vt.* 哗哗地流；嗖嗖地动[发射]。—*n.* 哗哗声，嗖嗖声。

swop [swɔp] *n.* 〔俚〕交换。 *Shall we try a ~?* 咱们交换交换好吗？ *take a ~* 〔商俚〕交易未成被顾客骂一顿。— *vt.*, *vi.* 〔俚〕交换，互换。 *Never ~ horses while crossing the stream.* 过河莫换马〔困难局面中不可随便采取人事等变动〕。

sword [sɔːd] *n.* ①剑，刀；〔军俚〕刺刀。②〔the ~〕武力；兵权；权力；杀戮，战争。 *the ~ and the purse* 武力和财力。 *the ~ of justice* 司法权。 *the ~ of the Spirit* 上帝的话。 *the fire and ~* (侵略军的)烧杀；强暴的军事手段。 *~ of State [honour]* 国剑〔大节日在英王前所捧的宝剑〕。 ***at the point of the ~*** 被迫，在威胁下。 ***be at ~'s points (with each other)*** (彼此)不和。 ***cross ~s*** 交锋，决斗；争论 *(with)*。 ***draw the ~*** 拔剑；发动战争。 ***measure ~s*** (决斗前)检查剑长；决斗，战斗 *(with)*。 ***put to the ~*** 杀死。 ***put up [sheathe] the ~*** 收剑，把剑插进鞘里；停止战争，讲和。 ***throw one's ~ into the scale*** 采取使用武力的办法。 ***wear the ~*** 当兵。 ~ **arm** 右臂。 ~ **bayonet** (枪上的)刺刀。 ~ **bean** 刀豆。 ~ **bearer** 捧剑侍从〔帝王、武士的侍从〕。 ~ **belt** 剑带，刀带。 ~ **bill**【动】长嘴蜂雀。 ~ **cane** 藏有刀剑的手杖。 ~ **craft** 剑术；〔现罕〕军事力量[技巧]。 ~ **cut** 刀伤。 ~ **dance** 舞剑；剑舞。 ~ **fish**【鱼】箭鱼；〔S-〕【天】旗鱼座；剑鱼座；〔S-〕〔英〕双翼海上飞机。 ~ **flag**【植】黄菖蒲。 ~ **grass**【植】刀状或齿状叶草。 ~ **guard** (刀剑的)护手。 ~ **hand** 右手。 ~ **knot** 剑柄带结。 ~ **law** 强权政治；军事管制，戒严令。 ~ **lily**【植】唐菖蒲，水仙菖蒲。 **~play** 剑术；舞剑；激烈的争论；唇枪舌剑。 **~proof** 刀剑不入的。 **~smith** 刀剑匠。 **~stick** = sword cane. ~ **tail**【动】剑尾鱼。

swords·man [ˈsɔːdzmən] *n.* 剑客；〔古〕军人，武士。 **~-ship** *n.* 剑术。

swore [swɔː, swɔə] swear 的过去。

sworn [swɔːn] swear 的过去分词。— *a.* 盟誓的。 *~ brothers* 结拜弟兄；死党。 *~ friends* 莫逆(朋友)。 *~ enemies [foes]* 死敌，不共戴天之仇。 *~ evidence* 经过发誓的证据[证言]。

swot[1] [swɔt] *vt.* 〔英学生俚〕下苦功学；临时(抱佛脚地)攻读(功课) *(up)*。— *vi.* 死用功，用功学习。 ***~ at a subject = ~ (a subject) up*** 匆匆忙忙用功学习(某一

功课)．— *n.* (尤指数学的)刻苦用功；辛苦；吃力的工作；用功的人．*What a ～!* 真吃力！好苦！〔美〕猛击．
swot[2] [swɔt] *vt., n.* = swat.
swound [swaund] *vi., n.*〔古〕= swoon.
'swounds [zwaundz] *int.*〔古〕畜类！该死的家伙！〔为 God's wounds 的缩简形式，= zounds〕.
swtz. = Switzerland.
swum [swʌm] swim 的过去分词．
swung [swʌŋ] swing 的过去式及过去分词．～ **dash** 代字号〔～〕.
swuz·zy [ˈswʌzi] *a.*〔美〕可爱的，有吸引力的；有趣的．
swy flat·ter [ˈswaiˌflætə] *n.*〔美〕蝇拍．
S.Y. = steam yacht 蒸汽机快艇(游艇).
SY = square yard 平方码．
sy-, *pref.*〔用于 s ＋ 辅音之前或 z 前，为 syn- 的变体〕: *sy*stem, *sy*zygy.
Syb·a·rite [ˈsibərait] *n.* 息巴利 (Sybaris)〔意大利一古都〕人；〔or s-〕爱奢侈享乐的人，纵情逸乐的人．— *a.* =Sybaritic.
Syb·a·rit·ic -rit·i·cal [sibəˈritik, -əl] *a.* 息巴利人的；纵情逸乐的．**-i·cal·ly** *ad.*
syb·a·rit·ism [ˈsibəraitizəm] *n.* 奢侈享乐；骄奢淫逸．
Syb·il [ˈsibil] *n.* 西比尔〔女子名〕.
syb·il [ˈsibil] *n.* sybyl 的变体．
syc·a·mine [ˈsikəm(a)in] *n.*【圣】黑子桑．
syc·a·more [ˈsikəmɔː, -mɔə] *n.*【植】埃及榕；美国梧桐；假挪威槭．
syce [sais] *n.*〔印〕马夫．
sycee [saiˈsiː] *n.* (旧时中国使用的)银锭 (= ～ silver).
sy·chno·carp·ous [ˌsiknəˈkɑːpəs] *a.*【植】多年生的，多次结果的．
sy·co·ni·um [saiˈkəuniəm] *n.* *(pl. -ni·a* [-ə]*)*【植】隐头花序．
syc·o·phan·cy [ˈsikəfənsi] *n.* 谄媚，拍马．
syc·o·phant [ˈsikəfənt] *n.* 谄媚者．— *a.* 谄媚的．**-ly** *ad.* **-ism** = sycophancy.
syc·o·phan·tic, syc·o·phan·tish [sikəˈfæntik -ˈfæntiʃ] *a.* 谄媚的．
sy·co·sis [saiˈkəusis] *n.*【医】须疮．
Syd·ney [ˈsidni] *n.* 悉尼〔澳大利亚港市〕.
sy·e·nite [ˈsaiənait] *n.*【地】正长岩．**-nit·ic** [-ˈnitik] *a.*
Sykes [saiks] *n.* 赛克斯〔姓氏〕.
syl- *pref.*〔用于 l 前〕= syn: *syl*logism.
syll = syllable(s).
syl·la·bar·i·um [ˌsiləˈbæriəm] *r.*〔L.〕 *(pl. syl·la·bar·a* [-riə]*)* (= syllabary).
syl·la·ba·ry [ˈsiləbəri] *n.* 音节表；字音表．*the Japanese* ～ 日本语五十音图，假名表．
syl·la·bi [ˈsiləbai] *n.* syllabus 的复数．
syl·lab·ic [siˈlæbik] *a.* 音节的，拼音的；表示音节的；构成音节的；音节分明的；按音节的；(诗体)以音节数为格律的．— *n.* 构成音节的声音，浊音；有声字；〔*pl.*〕以音节数为格律的诗．**-i·cal·ly** *ad.*
syl·lab·i·cate [siˈlæbkeit] *vt.* 分成〔构成〕音节．
syl·lab·i(fi)·ca·tion [ˈsilˌæbi(fi)ˈkeiʃən] *n.* 构成音节，区分音节．
syl·lab·i·cit·y [silæˈbisiti] *n.* 成音节，可构成音节．
syl·lab·i·fy, syl·la·bize [siˈlæbifai, ˈsiləbaiz] *vt.* = syllabicate.
syl·la·bism [ˈsiləbizm] *n.* ①音节文字．②分成音节．
syl·la·ble [ˈsiləbl] *n.* ①音节．②一言半字．*Not a ～!* 半个字也不说！— *vt.* 分成音节；分成音节发音〔读出，说出〕;〔诗〕说出(名字、话)，讲．～**d**〔构成复合词〕有…音节的．*a three ～d word* 三音节的词．
syl·la·bub [ˈsiləbʌb] *n.* = sillabub.
syl·la·bus [ˈsiləbəs] *n.* *(pl. -bi* [-bai], *～es)* (讲义等的)摘要，提纲；课程提纲，教学大纲；【法】(判例前的)判决要旨．
syl·lep·sis [siˈlepsis] *n.* *(pl. -ses* [-siːz]*)*【语法，修】共轭法，一笔双叙法．〔如 *either they or I am wrong*, 谓语 am wrong 一肩双挑 they 和 I 两个主语．〕**-lep·tic·(al)** *a.*
syl·lo·gism [ˈsilədʒizəm] *n.* ①【逻】推论式，三段论(法)．②演绎法．③巧妙的推论；诡辩．
syl·lo·gis·tic, -ti·cal [siləˈdʒistik, -tikl] *a.* 三段论法的；演绎的．**-ti·cal·ly** *ad.* 用三段论法；演绎地．
syl·lo·gize [ˈsilədʒaiz] *vi., vt.* 用三段论法推论．
sylph [silf], *n.* ①(十五至十六世纪德国医学家 Paracelsus 学说中生存在空气里没有灵魂但有生死的)“气精”．②身材苗条的妇女．③【鸟】长尾蜂鸟．～**like** [-laik] *a.* 窈窕的．
sylph·id [ˈsilfid] *n.* ①小“气精”〔*cf.* sylph 条〕．②身材苗条的女孩．**-id·ine** [-din, -ˌdain] *a.*
syl·va [ˈsilvə] *n.* *(pl. ～s, -vae* [-viː]*)* 森林；林木；林木志．
syl·van [ˈsilvən] *a.* 森林(多)的；林栖的．— *n.* 森林女妖；林中居民，林栖鸟兽．
syl·van·ite [ˈsilvəˌnait] *n.*【矿】针碲金矿．
syl·vat·ic [silˈveitik] *a.* 森林的，森林中的；伤害森林动物的．～ *plague* 森林瘟疫〔南北美洲西部森林中伤害野生动物的一种瘟疫，啮齿动物及其跳蚤是病菌的媒介〕.
Syl·ves·ter [silˈvestə] *n.* 西尔威斯特〔男子名〕.
Syl·vi·a [ˈsilviə] *n.* 西尔维娅〔女子名〕.
syl·vi·cul·ture [ˈsilvikəltʃə] *n.* 造林(学).
syl·vite [ˈsilvait], **syl·vin(e)** [ˈsilvin] *n.*【化】钾盐．
sym- *pref.*〔用于 b, p, m 前〕=syn-.
sym. = symbol, symbolic【化】symmetrical; symphony.
sym·bi·ont [ˈsimbaiɔnt] *n.* ①共栖生物．②共生者；〔体〕共生成分．**-tic** *a.*
sym·bi·o·sis [simbaiˈəusis] *n.*【生】共生(现象)，共栖．*antagonistic ～* 拮抗性共生(藓苔等).
sym·bi·ot·i·cal [ˌsimbaiˈɔtikl] *a.*【生】共生的．**-cal·ly** *ad.*
sym·bol [ˈsimbəl] *n.* ①记号，符号．②象征，表征．③【宗】信条．*a chemical ～* 化学符号．*White is the ～ of purity.* 白是纯洁的象征．— *vt., vi.*〔罕〕= symbolize.
sym·bol·ic, -i·cal [simˈbɔlik, -ikl] *a.* 记号的，符号的；象征的．～ *logic* 符号逻辑．
sym·bol·ics [simˈbɔliks] *n.*【宗】信条神学；【人类学】古代宗教仪式学；符号象征学．
sym·bol·ism [ˈsimbəlizəm] *n.* ①记号表示，符号使用；象征的表现；象征意义，象征性；【语】表象；【哲】符号论．②(特指文艺方面的)象征主义．③【宗】符号象征〔如以十字架象征基督受难〕.
sym·bol·ist [ˈsimbəlist] *n.* (象征)符号使用者；象征派诗人〔画家〕，象征主义者；符号论者；符号象征学学者．**-is·tic** [ˌsimbəˈlistik] *a.*
sym·bol·ize [ˈsimbəlaiz] *vt.* 用符号表示，是…的符号；象征，代表．**-i·za·tion** [ˌsimbəlaiˈzeiʃən] *n.*
sym·bol·o·gy [simˈbɔlədʒi] *n.* 符号表示法；表号学，象征学；符号论．
Sy·ming·ton [ˈsaimiŋtən] *n.* 赛明顿〔姓氏〕.
sym·met·al·lism [simˈmetəlizəm] *n.*【经】金银混合本位．
sym·met·ric, -ri·cal [siˈmetrik; -rikəl] *a.* 对称的，匀称的，相称的，平衡的．**-ri·cal·ly** *ad.*
sym·me·trize [ˈsimitraiz] *vt.* 使对称；使匀称，使相称，使平衡．**-tri·za·tion** [ˌsimitraiˈzeiʃən] *n.*
sym·me·try [ˈsimitri] *n.* 对称；匀称；调和；匀称美．*bilateral ～* 左右对称．*radial ～* 放射对称．
Sym·onds [ˈsaiməndz, ˈsiməndz] *n.* 西蒙兹〔姓氏〕.
Sy·mons [ˈsaimənz, ˈsimənz] *n.* 西蒙斯〔姓氏〕.
sym·pa·thec·to·my [ˌsimpəˈθektəmi] *n.* *(pl. -mies)*【医】交感神经切除术．

sym•pa•thet•ic [simpəˈθetik] *a.* ①同情的,有同情心的,表示同情的. ②相投合的; 称心的, 满意的. ③〔口〕抱好感的; 抱同感的. ④【生理】交感(神经)的. ⑤【物】共鸣的, 共振的. *a ~ strike* 同情罢工. *~ ink*【化】(起初无色后来经过某种作用才现色的)隐显墨水. *~ nerve*【解】交感神经. *~ vibrations*【物】共振. — *n.* 交感神经系; (对催眠术等)易感受的人. **-i•cal•ly** *ad.*

sym•pa•thin [ˈsimpəθin] *n.*【生化】交感(神经)素.

sym•pa•thize [ˈsimpəθaiz] *vi.* 表示同情; 相怜; 同感; 共鸣; 同意, 赞成; 一致, 调和 *(with)*; 吊慰, 安慰. *~ with sb. in his grief* 对某人的悲痛表示同情.

sym•pa•thiz•er [ˈsimpəθaizə] *n.* 同情者; 同感者; 支持者, 赞助者.

sym•pa•tho•lyt•ic [ˌsimpəθəuˈlitik] *a.* 有减少交感神经系统活动作用的〔指药品, 化学品等〕.

sym•pa•tho•mi•met•ic [ˌsimpəθəumiˈmetik] *n.* 模仿交感神经作用的〔指药品, 化学品等〕.

sym•pa•thy [ˈsimpəθi] *n.* ①同情(心); 怜悯. ②同感, 同意, 赞成: 一致, 协调. ③慰问, 吊慰;【物】共振, 共鸣;【生理】交感; 感应; 引力. *You have my sympathies.* 你得到我的同情. ***express ~ for*** 慰问. ***feel ~ for, have ~ for*** 同情. ***in ~ with*** 同情; 赞成; 跟着, 和…一致 (*Prices are low in ~ with the general depression.* 物价是随着市面的普遍萧条而低落的). ***out of ~*** 出于同情. ***out of ~ with*** 对…不同情; 不赞成, 对…没有同感; 和…不一致. ***~ strike*** 同情罢工. ***win ~ of*** 博得…的同情.

sym•pat•ric [simˈpætrik] *a.*【生, 生态】分布区重叠的. **-pat•ri•cal•ly** *ad.* **-pat•ry** *n.*

sym•pet•al•ous [simˈpetləs] *a.*【植】合瓣的 (=gamopetalous).

sym•phon•ic [simˈfɔnik] *a.*【乐】交响乐(式)的; 谐音的, 调和的 *~ poem*【乐】交响诗. **-i•cal•ly** *ad.*

sym•pho•ni•ous [simˈfəuniəs] *a.* 谐音的, 调和的. **-ly** *ad.*

sym•pho•nist [ˌsimfənist] *n.* 交响乐作曲家.

sym•pho•ny [ˈsimfəni] *n.*【乐】交响乐, 交响曲. 〔口〕交响音乐会. 〔古〕和音, 谐音, 协音; (色彩等的)调和. ***~ or-chestra*** 交响乐团[队].

sym•phyl•lous [ˈsimfiləs] *a.*【植】联生叶的.

sym•phys•ial [ˌsimˈfiziəl] *a.* ①【解, 动】联合的. ②【植】拼生的 (= symphyseal).

sym•phy•sis [ˈsimfisis] *n.* (*pl.* ***-ses*** [-si:z])【解】(骨的)联合(线);【虫】膜连;【植】合生, 拼生.

sym•po•di•um [simˈpəudiəm] *n.* (*pl.* ***-di•a*** [-ə])【植】合轴. **-di•al** *a.*

sym•po•si•ac [simˈpəuziˌæk] *a.* ①(古希腊)酒会的, 宴会的. ②座谈会的: 讨论会的. ③专题文集的.

sym•po•si•arch [simˈpəuziɑ:k] *n.* 宴会[酒会]的主人: (宴席上的)中心人物; 专题讨论会上的主席.

sym•po•si•ast [simˈpəuziˌæst] *n.* 座谈会, 酒会等的参加者.

sym•po•si•um [simˈpəuziəm, -ˈpɔ-] *n.* (*pl.* ***-sia*** [-ziə]) ①(古代希腊的)酒会, 宴会. ②专题讨论会, 座谈会, 学术报告会. ③专题论集, 论丛.

symp•tom [ˈsim*p*təm] *n.* 症状, 征候; 征兆. *an objective [a subjective] ~* 客观[主观]症状; 医生所能看出的外征〔病人感到的内征〕. **-less** *a.*

symp•tom•at•ic, -i•cal [simptəˈmætik, -ikəl] *a.* 有症状的, 有症候的; 有征兆的; 根据症状的; 表征的. **-cal•ly** *ad.*

symp•tom•a•tize [ˈsimptəməˌtaiz] *vt.* 表现出…的症状, 表征 (= symptomize).

symp•tom•a•tol•o•gy [simptəməˈtɔlədʒi] *n.*【医】症状学, 征候学; (一种病的)总症状, 全部症状; 症候群.

syn. = synonym; synonymous; synonymy.

syn- *pref.* 〔在 l 前作 syl-, 在 b, m, p 前作 sym-, 在 r 前作 syr-, 在 s 前作 sys- 或 sy-〕共, 合, 同, 与, 连, 类.

syn•aer•e•sis syn•er•e•sis [siˈniərisis] *n.*【语音】(二)元音溶合, 元音缩合;【生】凝线;【化】胶体脱水收缩(作用); 凝块, 凝胶.

syn•aes•the•si•a, syn•es•the•sia [sinəsˈθi:ziə] *n.*【生理】伴生感觉, 联觉. **-thet•ic** *a.*

syn•a•gog(ue) [ˈsinəgɔg] *n.* 犹太教会堂: 犹太教徒的集会. **-gog•al, gog•ic, gog•i•cal** *a.*

syn•a•loe•pha, syn•a•le•pha [ˌsinəˈli:fə] *n.* 元音溶合, 溶合音节〔两个相邻元音通常是通过省略而溶合为一个音节. 如: *th' eagle for the eagle, the eagle* 溶合成 *th' eagle*〕.

syn•an•thous [siˈnænθəs] *a.*【植】花和叶同时出现的.

syn•apse [siˈnæps] *n.*【解】突触, (神经元的)触处.

syn•ap•sis [sinˈæpsis] *n.* (*pl.* -ses [-si:z])【生】染色体结合; 联会;【解】突触: (神经元的)触处. **-ap•tic** *a.*

syn•ar•thro•di•al [ˌsinɑ:ˈθrəudiəl] *a.*【解】不动关节的.

syn•ar•thro•sis [sinɑ:ˈθrəusis] *n.* (*pl.* ***-ses*** [-si:z])【解】不动关节.

sync, synch [siŋk] *vt., vi.* synchronize 的缩略词. — *n.* synchronization 的缩略词.

syn•caine [siŋˈkein] *n.*【化】顺卡因(即普鲁卡因).

syn•carp [ˈsinkɑ:p] *n.* ①【植】复果, 聚花果 (= multiple fruit). ②合心皮果.

syn•car•pous [sinˈkɑ:pəs] *a.*【植】①合心皮的. ②合心皮果的. **-car•py** *n.*

syn•chon•dro•sis [ˌsiŋkənˈdrəusis] (*pl.* -ses [-si:z]) *n.*【解】软骨结合.

syn•chro [ˈsiŋkrəu] *n.*【电】(自动)同步机. —*a.* 同步的.

syn•chro- *comb. f.* 表示"同步": *synchromesh, synchronous.*

syn•chro-cy•clo•tron [ˈsiŋkrəuˈsaiklətrɔn] *n.*【原】稳相[同步回旋]加速器.

syn•chro•flash [ˈsiŋkrəuflæʃ] *a.*【摄】用闪光和快门同步装置的.

syn•c(h)ro•mesh [ˈsiŋkrəmeʃ] *n., a.*【机】同步啮合(的). *~ gear* 同步齿轮.

syn•chro•nal [ˈsiŋkrənəl] *a.* = synchronous.

syn•chron•ic, -i•cal [siŋˈkrɔnik, -ikəl] *a.* ① = synchronous. ②只涉及某一特定时期(而不考虑历史演变)的,【语言】共时性的. ~ **linguistics** 共时语言学.

syn•chro•nism [ˈsiŋkrənizəm] *n.* ①【物】同步(性); 并发, 同时性,【电】同期. ②(历史事件的)同时处理, 综合对照表示, 对照历史年表;【绘画】异时事迹的同幅表现;【影】同步画面与声音.

syn•chro•nis•tic [siŋkrəˈnistik] *a.* = synchronous.

syn•chro•ni•za•tion [ˌsiŋkrənaiˈzeiʃən] *n.* 同时; 同时性;【物】同步, 同期;【影】同期[步]录音, 配音译制.

syn•chro•nize [ˈsiŋkrənaiz] *vi.* 同时化, 同时发生[举行] *(with)*; (几个钟表)指示同一时刻;【物】同步, 整步;【影】声、象同步化, 同步录音. — *vt.* ①使同时;【物】使同[整]步. ②校准, 对准(钟表). ③同时处理, 综合对照表示(历史事件);【影、电视】使声象一致; 作同时[步]录音处理.

syn•chro•niz•er [ˈsiŋkrənaizə] *n.*【电】同步器; 整步器; 协调器. ~ **gear** 同步齿轮.

syn•chro•nous [ˈsiŋkrənəs] *a.* 同时的, 同期的;【物】同步的. ~ **discharger**【电】同步放电器. ~ **machine**【电】同步电动机, 同步变流机. ~ **motor**【电】同步电动机. ~ **vibration**【物】同步振动. **-ly** *ad.*

syn•chro•ny [ˈsiŋkrəni] *n.*【物】同步; 同步性.

syn•chro•scope [ˈsiŋkrəˌskəup] *n.*【电】同步指示仪, 同步示波器.

syn•chro•tron [ˈsiŋkrətrɔn] *n.*【原】同步加速器.

syn•clas•tic [sinˈklæstik] *a.*【数】【物】(曲面)同方向

的. ~ **surface** 同向曲面. ~ **curvature** 同向曲率.
syn·cli·nal [siŋˈklainl] *a.*【地】向斜的. — *n.* 向斜. ~ **axis** 向斜轴. ~ **valley** 向斜谷.
syn·cline [ˈsiŋklain] *n.*【地】向斜.
syn·cli·no·ri·um [ˌsiŋkləˈnɔːriəm] *n.* *(pl.* -ri·a [-ə]*)*【地】复向斜.
syn·con [ˈsiŋkɔn] *n.* 电话会议,电视会议.
syn·co·pal [ˈsiŋkəpl] *a.* ①【语】词中略去字母或音节的,如 *Gloucester* 略成 *Gloster*. ②假死的;昏厥的.
syn·co·pate [ˈsiŋkəpeit] *vt.*【语】词中省略,中略〔省去中间字母或音节;如将 never 省略成 ne'er〕;【乐】切分. **-pa·tion** [ˌsiŋkəˈpeiʃən] *n.*
syn·co·pe [ˈsiŋkəpi] *n.*【语】词中省略,中略(语);【乐】切分;【医】昏厥.
syn·cre·tize [ˈsiŋkrəˌtaiz] *vt., vi.* (使)混合, (使)溶合, (使)调合.
syn·cretism [ˈsiŋkritizəm] *n.* (哲学上、宗教上的)诸说混合;【语】不同变化形式的合并. **-tic** *a.* **-ist** *n., a.* (宗教)信仰诸说混合论者(的).
syn·crom·esh *n., a.* = synchromesh.
syn·cy·ti·um [sinˈsiʃiəm], *n.* *(pl.* **-ti-a** [-ə]*)*【动】多核体;合胞体. **-cy·ti·al** [-əl] *a.*
synd. = syndicate.
syn·dac·tyl(e) [sinˈdæktl] *a.* 并趾的,并指的. — *n.* 并趾哺乳动物(或鸟). **-ism** *n.*
syn·de·sis [ˈsindisis] *n.* *(pl.* **-ses** [ˌ-siːz]*)* ①捆扎, 联结. ②【遗】染色体结合 (= synapsis).
syn·des·mo·sis [ˌsindesˈməusis] *n.* *(pl.* **-ses** [-siːz]*)*【解】韧带联合. **-mot·ic** [-ˈmɔtik] *a.*
syndet = synthetic detergent 合成洗涤剂.
syn·det·ic [sinˈdetik] *a.*【语法】连结的, (用连接词)连接的. **-i·cal·ly** *ad.*
syn·dic [ˈsindik] *n.* ①地方行政长官. ②【法】经理, 理事. ③(特指剑桥 (Cambridge) 大学委员会的)委员. ④〔美〕破产管财人.
syn·di·cal [ˈsindikl] *a.* 市政官的;大学理事的;商业代理人(或经理)的;工团主义的.
syn·di·cal·ism [ˈsindikəlizəm] *n.* 工团〔工联〕主义. **-cal·ist** *n.* 工团主义者,工联派. ~ **is·tic** *a.*
syn·di·cat [sɛ̃ːndiˈkɑː] *n.* 〔F.〕工会.
syn·di·cate [ˈsindikit] *n.* ①大学委员会的职务;理事会;(特指剑桥大学的)委员会. ②辛迪加〔企业的联合组织〕. ③〔美〕报业辛迪加〔向各报刊同时出售稿件,供同时发表的企业〕. ④罪犯辛迪加,操纵犯罪集团的组织. — [-keit] *vt., vi.* 组织辛迪加;由辛迪加承办;通过报业〔杂志业〕辛迪加在多家报刊上同时发表. **-ca·tion** [ˌsiŋdiˈkeiʃən] *n.*
syn·di·ca·tor [ˈsindiˌkeitə] *n.* 辛迪加组织者〔经营者,参加者〕.
syn·drome [ˈsindrəum] *n.* ①【医】综合症,症候群. ②(某一事物的)全部特征;特征群;(具有某种共同性的不同事物的)集合.
syn·drom·ic [sinˈdrəumik, -ˈdrɔmik] *a.* 综合病症的;症候群的.
syne [sain] *ad., prep., conj.* 〔Scot.〕= since; 曾经,以前. *auld lang* ~ 已往,从前.
syn·ec·do·che [siˈnekdəki] *n.*【修】提喻法,举隅法〔以局部代表全部和以全部喻指部分,例如用 roof 表示整个 house, 用 the army 表示某一个 soldier〕. **-chic, -chic·al** *a.* **-cal·ly** *ad.*
syn·ec·tics [siˈnektiks] *n.* 群体〔环境〕生态.
syn·e·col·o·gy [ˌsiniˈkɔlədʒi] *n.*【生】群落生态学.
syn·e·phrine [siˈnefriːn] *n.*【化】交感醇.
syn·er·e·sis [siˈniərəsis] *n.* ① = synaeresis. ② = synizesis.
syn·er·get·ic [ˌsinəˈdʒetik] *a.* 合作的,协作的. **-cal·ly** *ad.*
syn·er·gid [siˈnəːdʒid, ˈsinə-] *n.*【生】助细胞.
syn·er·gism [ˈsinədʒizm] *n.* ①配合作用〔尤指药物〕. ②(人体各器官各部位如肌肉的)协同作用. **-gis·tic** *a.* **-gis·ti·cal·ly** *ad.*
syn·er·gist [ˈsinədʒist] *n.* ①【生理】协同器官;【药】配合剂,增强剂,增效剂,佐药. ②【宗】神人协力论者.
syn·er·gy [ˈsinədʒi], *n.* 协同, 配合 (= synergism). **-gic** [siˈnədʒik] *a.*
syn·e·sis [ˈsinisis] *n.*【语法】意义明确而不合语法的结构〔如 Neither of them are present〕.
syn·es·the·si·a [ˌsinisˈθiːʒə, -ʒiə] *n.* ①【生理】反射性反应. ②【心】联感〔如某种颜色引起某种嗅感〕. **-thet·ic** [-ˈθetik] *a.*
syn·ga·my [ˈsiŋgəmi] *n.*【生】配子配合;两性生殖. **-mic, -mous** *a.*
Synge [siŋ] *n.* 辛〔姓氏〕.
syn·gen·e·sis [sinˈdʒenisis] *n.*【生】有性生殖;群落发生;群落演替. **-ge·net·ic** [-ˈdʒenitik] *a.*
syng·na·thous [ˈsiŋnəθəs] *a.* (鱼)颚部向外伸成管状吻部的.
syn·i·ze·sis [ˌsiniˈziːsis] *n.* ①【语音】元音缩〔溶〕合〔两相邻元音缩合而成一音节,但不构成双元音〕. ②【生】凝线.
syn·kar·y·on [sinˈkæriˌɔn, -ən] *n.*【生】合子核;结合核.
syn·od [ˈsinəd] *n.*【宗】宗教会议;〔转义〕讨论会,会议;【天】会合. **-al** *a.*
syn·od·ic, -i·cal [siˈnɔdik(əl)] *a.* ① = synodal. ②【天】会合的,相合的. ***a*** ~ ***month*** 朔望月. **-ly** *ad.*
syn·oe·cious [siˈniːʃəs] *a.*【植】①雌雄混生同苞的. ②精子器与颈卵器同簇的. **-ly** *ad.*
syn·oi·cous [siˈnɔikəs] *a.* = synoecious.
syn·o·nym [ˈsinənim] *n.* 同义语,类语 *(opp.* antonym*)*;〔口〕类似物;【生物】(不正确的)异名. **-i·ty** [sinəˈnimiti] *n.* 同意义. **-ic** *a.*
syn·o·nym·ist [siˈnɔnimist] *n.* 同义词研究者.
syn·on·y·mize [siˈnɔniˌmaiz] *vt.* 举出…的各同义词,分析…的同义词.
syn·on·y·mous [siˈnɔniməs] *a.* 同义语的,类语的;同义的 *(with)*. **-ly** *ad.*
syn·on·y·my [siˈnɔnimi] *n.* 同义(语);同义语研究;(为加强意义)同义语叠用.
synop. = synopsis.
syn·op·sis [siˈnɔpsis] *n.* *(pl.* **-ses** [-siːz]*)* 提要,提纲,梗概,大意;对照表,一览;说明书.
syn·op·size [siˈnɔpsaiz] *vt.* 作…的提要,总结,摘要.
syn·op·tic, -ti·cal [siˈnɔptik, -tikəl] *n.* 〔常 S-〕以共同观点叙述的福音书(作者). 〔指新约的前三部福音书及其作者〕. — *a.* 提要的,大意的;以共同观点叙述的(福音书的). *a* *synoptic chart* 天气概要图. **-cal·ly** *ad.*
syn·op·tist [siˈnɔptist] *n.* 以共同观点叙述的福音书作者.
syn·os·te·ol·o·gy [sinɔstiˈɔlədʒi] *n.* 关节学.
syn·os·te·o·sis [ˌsinəstiˈəusis], **syn·os·to·sis** [ˌsinəˈstəusis] *n.*【解】骨性结合. **syn·os·to·tic** [ˌsinəˈstɔtik] *a.*
syn·o·vi·a [siˈnəuviə] *n.*【解】滑液,滑膜.
syn·o·vi·al [siˈnəuviəl] *a.* 滑液的;滑膜的.
syn·o·vi·tis [sinəˈvaitis] *n.*【医】滑膜炎.
syn·sep·al·ous [sinˈsepləs] *a.*【植】合萼的 (= gamosepalous).
syn·tac·tic, -ti·cal [sinˈtæktik, -tikəl] *a.* 句法的. **-ti·cal·ly** *ad.* **-tac·tics** *n.* 〔*pl.*〕【语】句法学;【数】错列组合论;【逻】句法学;符号关系学,符号组合学.
syn·tax [ˈsintæks] *n.*【语法】①句法;句子结构学. ②措辞法,字句排列法.
syn·the·sis [ˈsinθisis] *n.* *(pl.* **-ses** [-siːz]*)* 综合;【化】

合成;【逻】综合(法);【语】综合(性);语词的合成;【医】接合;【物】合成综合.
syn·the·sist [ˈsinθisist] *n.* 综合者;合成法使用者.
syn·the·size [ˈsinθisaiz] *vt.* 综合;用综合法处理;人工合成. — *vi.* 综合;合成.
syn·the·siz·er [ˈsinθiˌsaizə] *n.* 合成者,合成物;〔尤指〕【电】合成器,综合器.
syn·thet·ic, -i·cal [sinˈθetik, -ikəl] *a.* 综合的;合成的,人造的(橡胶等);代用的;摹拟的,假想的;虚构的;【语】综合(性)的. ~ *detergent* 合成洗涤剂. ~ *fertilizer* 人造肥料. ~ *gasoline* 人造汽油,合成汽油. ~ *resin* 【化】合成[人造]树脂. ~ *rubber*【化】合成橡胶. ~ *steel* 合成钢. — *n.* 化学合成物;合成纤维(织物);合成剂[品]. **-cal·ly** *ad.* **-thet·ics** *n.* 〔*pl.*〕合成品.
syn·the·tize [ˈsiŋθitaiz] *vt.* = synthesize.
syn·thon [ˈsinθɔn] *n.* 合成纤维.
syn·to·my·cin, syn·tho·my·cin [sintɔˈmaisin, -θɔ-] *n.*【药】合霉素.
syn·ton·ic [sinˈtɔnik] *a.*【无】谐振[调]的;【心】情绪平静的,与环境相适应的. ~ **circuit** 谐振电路. **-i·cal·ly** *ad.*
syn·to·ni·za·tion [ˌsintənaiˌzeiʃən] *n.*【无】谐振法;同步,同期.
syn·to·nize [ˈsintənaiz] *vt.*【无】使调谐,使谐振. **-r** *n.*【无】共振器.
syn·to·nous [ˈsintənəs] *a.*【无】谐振的.
syn·to·ny [ˈsintəni] *n.*【无】谐振,共振,调谐.
syph·i·lis [ˈsifilis] *n.*【医】梅毒. *primary [secondary, tertiary]* ~ 第一[二、三]期梅毒. ~ *insontium* 先天性梅毒.
syph·i·lise, syph·i·lize [ˈsifilaiz] *vt.* 使感染梅毒. **-li·sa·tion** *n.*
syph·i·lit·ic [sifiˈlitik] *a.* 梅毒的,梅毒性的,患梅毒的. —*n.* 梅毒病患者.
syph·i·loid [ˈsifiˌlɔid] *a.*【医】类梅毒的.
syph·i·lol·o·gy [ˌsifiˈlɔlədʒi] *n.*【医】梅毒学. **-o·gist** *n.*
syph·i·lo·ma [ˌsifiˈləumə] *n.* 〔医〕梅毒瘤.
sy·phon [ˈsaifən] *n., vt., vi.* = siphon.
syr. = syrup.
Syr·a·cuse [ˈsaiərəkju:z] *n.* ①叙拉古〔西西里岛东部一港口〕. ②锡拉丘兹〔美国纽约州中部城市〕.
sy·ren [ˈsaiərən] *n.* = siren.
Syr·ette [siˈret] *n.* 〔美〕西来皮下注射针管〔商标名〕.
Syr·i·a [ˈsiriə] *n.* 叙利亚〔亚洲〕.
Syr·i·ac [ˈsiriæk] *a.* 叙利亚的;古叙利亚语的;〔罕〕叙利亚的. — *n.* 古叙利亚语.
Syr·i·a·cism [ˈsiriəsizəm] *n.* 叙利亚语风.
Syr·i·an [ˈsiriən] *a.* (现代或古代)叙利亚的;叙利亚人的. — *n.* 叙利亚人.
Sy·rin·ga [siˈriŋɡə] *n.*【植】①丁香花(属). ②〔s-〕山梅花;紫丁香花.
syr·inge [ˈsirindʒ] *n.* 注射器;水枪,注水器;注油器;洗涤器;灌肠器. *a hypodermic* ~ 皮下注射器. — *vt.* 注射;(用注水器)灌溉,浇(草木等);洗涤.
sy·rin·ge·al [siˈrindʒiəl] *a.*【动】(鸟的)鸣管的.
sy·rin·go·my·e·li·a [siˌriŋɡəumaiˈi:liə] *n.*【医】脊髓空洞症,脊髓神经胶瘤病.
syr·inx [ˈsiriŋks] *n. (pl. ~es, sy·rin·ges* [siˈrindʒi:z]*)* ①牧神排管芦笛. ②(鸟的)鸣管. ③【解】耳咽管;欧氏管. ④【医】瘘管,瘘. ⑤【考古】(古埃及金字塔中通往墓穴的)曲折起伏隧道.
syr·phus fly [ˈsə:fəs]【动】食蚜虻科 *(Syrphidae)* 昆虫(= syrphid).
syr·tis [ˈsə:tis] *n.* (非洲北海岸的)流沙,浮沙.
syr·up [ˈsirəp] *n.* ①糖浆. ②甜蜜的情感. ③〔俚〕金钱. *cough* ~ 咳嗽糖浆. *golden* ~【商】(餐桌用高级的)金黄糖浆.
syr·up·y [ˈsirəpi] *a.* 糖浆状的;(音乐等)甜蜜的.
sys- *pref.* 〔用于 s 前〕= syn-.
sys(t). = system.
sys·sar·co·sis [ˌsisɑ:ˈkəusis] *n.*【解】肌性结合,肌性联合.
sys·tal·tic [sisˈtæltik] *a.*【医】(心脏等)收缩舒张交替的.
sys·tem [ˈsistim] *n.* ①体系,系统;分类法;组织;设备,装置. ②方式;方法;作业方法. ③制度;主义. ④次序,规律. ⑤世界,宇宙. ⑥〔the ~〕身体,全身;机体. ⑦【天】系;说. ⑧【乐】总谱表. *ideological* ~ 思想体系. *a* ~ *of philosophy* 哲学体系. *a refrigerating* ~ 致冷装置. *the water regulating* ~ 分水闸. *a* ~ *of management* 一整套管理方法. *a clear cutting* ~【林】皆伐作业. *a* ~ *of rating* 定额法. *the sales* ~ 销货法. *What* ~ *do you go upon [on]?* 你用什么方法进行呢? *social* ~*s* 社会制度. *primitive communal* ~ 原始公社制度. *the feudal* ~ 封建制度. *the great* ~ 宇宙. *the Ptolemaic* ~ 托勒密天动说. *the solar* ~ 太阳系. *Too much tea is bad for the* ~. 喝茶过多有害身体. ***have one's*** ~ ***out of order*** 身体不好. ~**s analysis**【信息】系统分析法. ~**s engineering**【信息】系统工程学. **-less** *a.*
sys·tem·at·ic [sistiˈmætik] *a.* ①有系统的,成体系的;有组织的;有条不紊的,有步骤的. ②【博】分类(学)的. ③存心的,蓄意的;一贯的,惯常的. *a* ~ *worker* 有条不紊地工作[有一套办法]的工人. ~ *botany [zoology]* 植物[动物]分类学. *a* ~ *liar* 一贯撒谎的人. ~ *intrigues* 有计划有组织的阴谋. **-i·cal** *a.* **-i·cal·ly** *ad.*
sys·tem·at·ics [ˌsistiˈmætiks] *n.* 〔动词用单数〕分类学,分类(法) (=taxonomy).
sys·tem·a·tism [ˈsistimətizm] *n.* 分门别类;制度化;体系化.
sys·tem·a·tist [ˈsistimətist] *n.* ①照章办事者,按照系统行事者,履行制度者. ②分类学者.
sys·tem·a·ti·za·tion [ˈsistimətaiˈzeiʃən] *n.* 组织化;系统化,体系化;分类.
sys·tem·a·tize [ˈsistimətaiz] *vt.* 组织起来,组织化,体系化,定次序,使有系统;分类.
sys·tem·a·ti·zer [ˈsistimətaizə] *n.* 使系统化者;组织者;分类者;【商】组织业者,承包业者.
sys·tem·a·tol·o·gy [ˌsistiməˈtɔlədʒi] *n.* 体系学[论],系统学[论].
sys·tem·ic [sisˈtemik] *a.* 系统的,体系的;【生理医】全身的;【生】内吸收的;【农药】散发的,内吸的. ~ *circulation* 全身循环. ~ *insecticide* 内吸杀虫剂. **-i·cal·ly** *ad.*
sys·tem·ize [ˈsistimaiz] *vt.* = systematize. **-i·za·tion** [ˌsistimətaiˈzeiʃən] *n.*
sys·to·le [ˈsistəli] *n.*【生理】心脏收缩;(希腊、拉丁语诗律)长音节的缩短. **-tol·ic** [sisˈtɔlik] *a.*
sys·tyle [ˈsistail] *a.*【建】相邻二柱间距离等于柱直径之二倍的,柱间较狭的.
sys;ty·lous [ˈsistiləs] *a.* 〔植〕花柱联着的.
sy·zy·gi·al [siˈzidʒiəl] *a.*【天】朔望的.
syz·y·gy [ˈsizidʒi] *n.* 〔常 *pl.*〕【天】对点[合点,望点];朔望. **-y·gal, syz·y·get·ic, sy·zyg·i·al** [ˈsizəɡəl, ˈsizidʒiəl, -ˈdʒetik] *a.*
Szcze·cin [波 ʃtʃeˈtsin] *n.* 什切青〔波兰省、省会〕.
Sze·ged [ˈseɡed] *n.* 塞格德〔匈牙利城市〕.

T

T, t [tiː] *(pl.* **T's, t's** [tiːz]*)* ①英语字母表第二十字母. ②T 字形物, 丁字物. *a T bandage* 丁字形绷带. ***be marked with a T*** 〔英〕(犯人拇指上)被盖上T字烙印; 是有名的盗贼. ***cross one's [the] t's*** 不忘给字母t划上短横; 点横不漏; 细致入微; 着重[细讲]某点〔*cf.* i's〕. ***to a T*** 〔口〕精确, 恰好, 正好(*You hit it off to a T.* 你猜得恰好). **T-shirt** 短袖圆领男汗衫. **T square** 丁字尺.

T [tiː] 中世纪罗马数字的160. $\bar{T}$ = 160,000.

t' [t] ①〔古〕〔在动词原形前〕= to: *t'attempt* = *to attempt.* ②〔方〕〔在名词前〕= the: *t' bottle.*

't [t] ①〔诗〕= it: *'tis* = *it is.* *do't* = do it. *on't* = on it. ②〔口〕= not: *can't* = cannot.

T., t. = ①tenor. ②territory; territorial. ③〔L.〕*tomus* (= volume). ④ton(s). ⑤tablespoon(s). ⑥Testament. ⑦Tuesday. ⑧Turkish. ⑨tare. ⑩target. ⑪teaspoon(s). ⑫telephone. ⑬temperature. ⑭〔It.〕*tempo.* ⑮tome. ⑯town(ship). ⑰transit. ⑱transitive. ⑲troy.

T.A. = ①teaching assistant 助教. ②telegraphic address 电报挂号. ③Territorial Army〔英〕本土军.

Ta =【化】tantalum.

ta [tɑː]〔俚、儿〕谢谢. *You must say* ~. 你要说声谢谢. *Ta muchly.* 多谢.

TAA = Technical Assistance Administration (UN) (联合国)技术援助局.

Taal, t- [tɑːl] *n.* 塔尔语(南非荷兰语).

TAB = ①Technical Assistance Board (of the United Nations) (联合国)技术援助委员会. ②*Technical Abstract Bulletin* (US Dept. of Defense Publication) «科技简报»〔美国国防部刊物〕.

Tab [tæb] *n.* 〔英俚〕〔Cantab(rigian) 之略〕剑桥大学学生[毕业生].

tab[1] [tæb] *n.* ①(附属在衣服等上的)垂片, 荷叶边; (附属在物件上用来拉动、悬挂的)拉手, 耳片, 扣环, 带子; (帽子的)护耳; 鞋带, 鞋带头包铁; (卡片、纸张边上供写标签、编号用的)凸出部. ②【火箭】调整片, 薄片, 阻力板. ③〔口〕帐单; 全部费用. ④【军】参谋的领章. ⑤〔美〕小报; 【剧】短剧 (= tabloid). 药片(= tablet). ⑥表格; 制表人(= tabulator). ⑦平板; 【机】工作台. ***go*** ~〔美〕把戏剧缩短. ***keep (a)*** ~ ***[~s] on***〔美〕看守, 检查, 监督(*He is keeping ~s on the boys.* 他看守着孩子们). — *vt.* 〔口〕①做上耳片等. ②选择, 选取. ③制…的一览表; 记录. ~ **show**〔美〕傻瓜.

tab·a·nid [ˈtæbənid] *n.* 【动】虻科 *(Tabanidae)* 动物〔包括马虻和鹿虻〕.

tab·ard [ˈtæbəd] *n.* (中世纪武士穿在铠甲外面绣有纹章的)战袍; 侍从武官制服; (中世纪农民穿的)粗呢宽外衣.

ta·bar·dil·lo [tɑːbɑːˈdiːljəu] *n.* 〔Sp.〕墨西哥斑疹伤寒.

tab·a·ret [ˈtæbərit] *n.* 【纺】塔巴勒绸〔异色波纹和缎纹条子间隔排列〕.

Ta·bas·co, t- [təˈbæskəu] *n.* 塔巴斯哥(墨西哥地名)辣酱油.

taba·sheer, taba·chir [ˈtæbəʃiə] *n.* 竹黄〔印度人用以治疗痔疮等病的药材〕.

tab·bi·net, tab·by·net [ˈtæbinet] *n.*【纺】波纹塔夫绸〔毛葛〕.

tab·by [ˈtæbi] *n.* ①【纺】平纹绸 〔织物〕. ②斑猫(= ~ cat); 雌猫; 斑蛾 (= ~ moth). ③〔主英〕老处女; 爱搬弄是非的妇女. ④【建】(沙土及碎石混合的)土质混凝土, 灰砂. — *a.* 斑纹的; 有平纹的. — *vt.* 加上平纹.

tab·e·fac·tion [ˌtæbiˈfækʃən] *n.* 【医】病瘦, 憔悴, 衰弱.

tab·er·na·cle [ˈtæbə(ː)nækl] *n.* ①临时住房; 帐篷. ②〔T-〕圣幕〔古犹太的移动式神堂〕; 犹太神堂. ③(非国教徒的)礼拜堂, 教堂, 会堂; 〔T-〕〔美〕(摩门教) Mormon 大会堂. ④【宗】(安置圣徒像等的)圣龛; 圣室; 圣柜. ⑤(作为灵魂的临时住所的)躯壳. ⑥【海】(木船的)桅座. — *vi.* 暂时栖身, 灵魂附体. — *vt.* 使居住…, 置于圣龛中. **-nac·u·lar** *a.*

ta·bes [ˈteibiːz] *n.* 【医】①消瘦, 消耗, 痨症. ②脊髓痨(= *dorsal* ~ 或 ~ *dorsalis*).

ta·bes·cent [təˈbesnt] *a.* 造成浪费的, 消耗性的, 摧毁性的. **-cence** *n.*

tabes dor·sa·lis [ˈteibiːz dɔːˈseilis, -sælis] 【医】脊髓痨, 运动性运动失调.

ta·bet [ˈteibit] *n.* 〔Scot.〕感觉, 感触.

ta·bet·ic [təˈbetik], **tab·id** [ˈtæbid] *a.* 【医】脊髓痨的; 脊髓梅毒性的. —*n.* 脊髓痨患者; 脊髓梅毒病患者.

tab·i·net [ˈtæbinit] *n.* = tabbinet.

tab·la [ˈtɑːblɑː] *n.* 【乐】(音高可以调整的)对鼓〔尤指印度的手鼓〕.

tab·la·ture [ˈtæblətʃə] *n.* 桌状面; 【乐】(弦乐器用的)弦线标谱(法); 〔古〕想象中的景象, 生动的描述; 【考古】载有题铭、绘画、图案的平面[版片]; 碑版.

ta·ble [ˈteibl] *n.* ①桌子; 饭桌, 餐台. ②手术台; 工作台; 游戏台; 赌台; 写字台. ③(饭桌上的)食物, 酒菜, 伙食; 一桌人〔指进餐者、玩牌者〕. ④平面; 平板, 平盘; 书板, 画板; 板画; 碑版. ⑤表, 目录; 〔*pl.*〕(古代刻有法典的)铜表; 法典. ⑥【地】高原, 台地. ⑦(手相)掌, 手掌; 【乐】共鸣板; 【解】(头盖的)骨板. ⑧【建】上楣, 花檐; 装饰板; 镶板; 束带层. *the pleasures of the* ~ 饮食之乐. ~ *manners* 餐桌[吃饭]礼仪. *a humble [poor]* ~ 简陋的饭食. *a liberal [bountiful]* ~ 丰盛的饮食. *the high* ~ (英大学)校长餐桌. *a* ~ *finisher*〔美〕食量大的人. *a green* ~ (铺着绿呢桌布的)赌台, 棋桌. *an operating* ~ 手术台. *the logarithmic* ~ 对数表. *the multiplication* ~ 乘法表. *a* ~ *of contents* 目次. *water* ~ 潜水面, 地下水面[水位]. ***at*** ~ 在吃饭. ***(be) upon the*** ~ 尽人皆知, 公开讨论的. ***keep a good*** ~ 经常吃得好. ***keep an open*** ~ (摆饭桌)欢迎客人. ***lay*** *(a measure)* ***on the*** ~ 将(议案)延期讨论. ***lay [set, spread] the*** ~ 摆饭桌. ***learn one's ~s*** 学会乘法表. ***lie on the*** ~ (议案等)搁置. ***on the*** ~公开地; 摆在桌面上. ***put sb. under the*** ~〔美〕打败(人); 灌醉, 使醉. ***set the*** ~ ***in a roar*** 使满座的人哄笑起来. ***sit(down) at (the)*** ~ 入席, 就座用膳. ***turn the ~s*** 扭转形势; 转败为胜(*The ~s are turned.* 形势[局面]扭转过来了). ***under the*** ~ ①昏头昏脑; 酒醉. ②作为贿赂, 私下, 走后门(*put sb. under the* ~ 使人头昏脑胀. *drink sb. under the* ~ 灌醉某人. *give money under the table to get a position* 为谋求职位花钱贿赂). ***upon the*** ~ 尽人皆知.〔英〕***wait at*** ~ =〔美〕***wait on*** ~ 伺候进餐. — *vt.* 放在桌子上; 提交讨论[考虑]; 〔美〕搁置(议案); 支付; 嵌接(木材); 制表, 记入表内; 缝上宽边加强(风帆). ~ **bell** 桌铃. ~ **book** 数学计算表手册〔如对数表等〕; 桌上摆设书本

〔通常为画册〕. ~**cloth** 桌布,台布. ~**-cut** *a.* (宝石)顶面磨平了的. ~ **flap** (折叠式桌面的)折板. ~**-glass** (餐桌上的)玻璃器皿. ~**-hop** *vi.* (在餐馆、舞场中)周旋于餐桌之间. ~**-inking**【印】调墨板. ~ **knife** 餐刀. ~**-land**【地】高原,台地. ~ **linen** 餐桌用布类.(桌布,餐巾等). ~ **money** 俱乐部的餐费;(贴补高级军官的)交际津贴; ~ **mount** 平顶海底山; 桌状山 (= guyot). ~ **planing machine** 龙门刨床. ~ **salt** (精制)食盐. ~**-service** 成套餐具. ~ **shore** 平低岸. ~**spoon** 汤匙,大调羹. ~ **talk** 餐桌谈话; 座谈, 茶话. ~ **talker** 吃饭时能说会道的人. ~ **tennis** 乒乓球. **The T-s of the Law** (基督教)摩西十诫. ~**-topped** *a.* 顶上平的. ~**-ware** 餐具. ~ **water** 餐用矿泉水. ~ **wine** 开胃酒〔含酒精 8—13%〕.

tab·leau [ˈtæbləu] *n.* *(pl.* ~**x** [-z], ~**s)** ①动人的场面,景色. ②舞台造型〔由活人扮演的动人场面〕; 戏剧性场面. ***Tableau!*** 想象一下这种情景!〔电影舞台倒叙等用语〕(= Curtain!) ~ ***vivant*** [ˈvi:vɑ̃:ŋ] 活画.

table d'hôte [ˈtɑ:blˈdəut] *(pl. tables d'hote)*〔F.〕(规定价格和菜餚供应的)客饭,份饭;(旅馆等的)公共餐桌.

tab·let [ˈtæblit] *n.* ①(木、石等的)平板; 牌子; 匾额; 门牌. ②书板〔古代人在上写字的木质、象牙、金属薄板〕; 〔常 *pl.*〕便条簿,信纸簿,图画纸簿(等). ③(开火车时交司机的)开车牌,开车证;【医】药片,片剂;(糖、肥皂等的)小块,片;【建】笠石,顶层. *a memorial* ~ 纪念碑.

ta·bling [ˈteibliŋ] *n.* ①桌布, 餐巾. ②制表; 造册. ③【建】盖顶; 墙帽; 束带层. ④(木工)嵌合. ⑤【海】(帆的加固)阔边.

tab·loid [ˈtæblɔid] *n.* ①〔T-〕药片. ②(文简图多的)小报. ③文摘. — *a.* 摘要的, 缩编的. *a* ~ *journalism [newspaper]* 小报. *a* ~ *play* 短剧. ***in*** ~ ***form*** 以扼要压缩形式.

tab·loid·ish [ˈtæblɔidiʃ] *a.* 〔美〕小报的; 简约的; 非正式的.

ta·boo [təˈbu:] *n.* ①【宗】禁忌; 戒律. ②视为禁忌的习俗; 禁止接近〔使用,交际〕. ③【语】禁忌语. ***put the*** ~ ***on sth., put sth. under*** ~ 严禁. — *vt.* 列为禁忌; 禁止.

tabo(u)r [ˈteibə, -bɔ:] *n.* 手鼓. — *vi.* 敲手鼓.

tab·o(u)·ret [ˈtæbərit] *n.* 矮凳; 绣框,绣架;(小)手鼓.

tab·o·rin [ˈtæbərin] *n.*【乐】(用一根鼓棒打的) 小鼓 (= taborine).

Ta·briz [tɑ:ˈbri:z] *n.* 大不里士〔伊朗城市〕.

ta·bu [təˈbu:] *n., vt.* = taboo.

tab·u·la [ˈtæbjulə] *n.*〔L.〕*(pl.* ***-læ*** [-li:])〔L.〕牌子,平板; 书板;【解】骨板;【动】(腔肠动物的)横隔板;【古生】横板. ~ ***rasa*** [ˈreisə], 干净(无字)的书板; 白纸状态,白纸一样纯洁的心.

tab·u·lar [ˈtæbjulə] *a.* ①板(状)的; 扁平的; 薄板做成的; 薄层的. ②表(格)的,按表格计算的. ~ *spar*【矿】硅灰石. *arrange in* ~ *form* 排列成表格(形式). *a* ~ *cash-book* 多桁[表格]式现金出纳簿. *the* ~ *standard* 按物价指数计算的币值标准表. **-ly** *ad.*

tab·u·late [ˈtæbjuleit] *vt.* ①使成板[片]状, 使成平面. ②制成表格,制…的一览表. *the* ~*d quotation* 行情表. — [-it] *a.* 平面的,板状的;【动】有横隔板的.

tab·u·la·tion [ˌtæbjuˈleiʃən] *n.* 制表,造册; 表格.

tab·u·la·tor [ˈtæbjuleitə] *n.* 制表人; (打字机的)制表键; 制表机.

TAC = ①Technical Assistance Committee (of the Economic and Social Council of the United Nations) (联合国经济及社会理事会)技术援助委员会. ②Tactical Air Command 〔美〕战术空军司令部. ③Thai Airways Company 泰国航空公司.

tac·a·ma·hac [ˈtækəməˌhæk] *n.*【植】①大叶钻天杨树脂. ②大叶钻天杨 *(Populus balsamifera)* (= tacamahaca, tacmahack).

tac·au·tac [ˈtækəuˈtæk] *n.*【剑】格刺; 快速连续的挡架和攻击.

ta·ce [ˈteisi:] *vi.* 〔L.〕别说话! *T- is Latin for a candle.* 〔谑〕别漏嘴! 别开口!

ta·cet [ˈteiset, ˈtæ-] *n., vi.* 〔L.〕【乐】静默,休止.

tach(e) [tætʃ] *n.* 〔古〕钩,环,扣.

tache [tɑ:ʃ, tæʃ] *n.* ①【医】斑点; 雀斑,痣. ②〔Scot.〕瑕疵,缺点.

tach·isme [ˈtæʃizəm, F. tɑ:ˈʃism] *n.*【绘】(把颜料泼于画布上的)泼色画法. **-iste** *a.*

tachisto-, tacho-, tachy- *comb. f.* 〔Gr.〕急,速: *tachy*metry.

ta·chis·to·scope [təˈkistəˌskəup] *n.* 速示器. **-scop·ic** [-ˈskɔpik] *a.*

ta·chom·e·ter [tæˈkɔmitə] *n.* 转速计,旋速计;(飞机等的)速度计; 流速计;【生理】血流计.

ta·chom·e·try [tæˈkɔmitri] *n.* 转速测定法.

tach·o·scope [ˈtækəuskəup] *n.* 转速表.

tachy- *comb. f.* 急,速.

tach·y·car·di·a [ˌtækiˈkɑ:diə] *n.*【医】心搏[动]过速.

tach·y·graph [ˈtækiˌgrɑ:f, -ˌgræf] *n.* ①速记. ②速记者.

ta·chyg·ra·pher [tæˈkigrəfə, tə-] *n.* 速记者.

tach·y·graph·ic, -i·cal [ˌtækiˈgræfik(ə)l] *a.* 速记术的.

ta·chyg·ra·phy [ˌtækiˈgræfi] *n.* 速记术. **-phist** *n.*

tach·y·la·li·a [ˌtækiˈleiliə] *n.*【语】语言急速; 速语癖.

tach·y·lyte, -lite [ˈtækilait] *n.*【矿】玄武玻璃.

ta·chym·e·ter [tæˈkimitə] *n.*【测】(供快速测定距离、方位等用的)速测仪,准距计.

ta·chym·e·try [tæˈkimitri] *n.* 准距快速测定术,速测法.

tach·y·on [ˈtæki:ɔn] *n.* 速子.

ta·chys·ter·ol [tæˈkistəˌrəul, tə-] *n.*【化】速甾醇.

tac·it [ˈtæsit] *a.* ①缄默的,不发表意见的; 心照不宣的; 暗中的. *a* ~ *agreement [understanding]* 默契. ~ *approval* 默许. ~ *consent* 默认[许]. ②【法】因法律的执行而引起的. ~ *declaration*【法】默示. *the* ~ *law* 习惯法. **-ly** *ad.* **-ness** *n.*

tac·i·turn [ˈtæsitə:n] *a.* 无言的, 沉默寡言的. **-tur·ni·ty** [ˌtæsiˈtə:niti] *n.*

tack[1] [tæk] *n.* ①平头钉; 图钉. ②(裁缝)暂缝,粗缝,假缝. ③(英议会随财政法案提出的)附带条款. ④【海】纵帆当风面的上下角索; 横帆当风面的上下角;(视帆向而定的)航向; 同一航向的一个航程; 逆风换抢,抢风行驶;〔转义〕曲折前进. ⑤方针; 方法; 策略. ⑥〔Scot.〕贷借契约,借地契约; 租得的牧地. ⑦(半干油漆等的)粘着性. *a thumb* ~ 图钉. *try another* ~ 改变方针. ***be on the right [wrong]*** ~ 航向正确[错误], 方针对头[错误]. ***be on the*** ~ 〔口〕戒酒. ***come [get] down to (brass)*** ~***s*** 〔美〕直截了当地说, 谈实际问题. ***sail on the port [starboard]*** ~【海】左舷[右舷]抢风航行. ~ ***and*** ~【海】接二连三地抢风调向. — *vt.* ①(用平头钉)钉 *(down)*. ②附加,添 *(to; on to)*. ③暂时缝上,假缝,粗缝 *(together; to)*. ④(英议会在财政法案上)附加没有关系的条款. ⑤【海】使抢风掉向. — *vi.*【海】抢风掉向; 改变方针[政策].

tack[2] [tæk] *n.*【海】食物. *hard* ~ (航海用的) 硬面包; 粗劣的食品. *soft* ~软面包; 较精美的食品. ~ **room**(牲口棚旁的)饲料间.

tack·i·fy [ˈtækifai] *vt.* 使发粘了. **-ier** *n.*【化】增粘剂.

tack·le [ˈtækl] *n.* ①〔复〕滑车. 【海】[ˈteikl] 帆的滑车索具. ②用具, 装备. ③【橄榄球】抱住 (对方抱[带]球奔跑的球员). — *vt.* ①用滑车拉上; 用滑车固定. ②(给马)配上马具. ③抓住,捉住,扭住,【橄榄球】抱住(对方抱[带]球奔跑的球员). ④就某事向某人交涉[争论] *(sb. on sth.)* ⑤应付,处理(工作等). — *vi.* 认真开始 *(to)*. *I* ~*d him on this question.* 我跟他在这个问题上展开争论. ~**-fall** *n.* 复滑车的通索. **-r** *n.*

tack·ling [ˈtækliŋ] *n.* 扭住; 复滑车装置; 〔古〕(船的)索具.
tack·y[1] [ˈtæki] *a.* 发粘的,胶粘的.
tack·y[2] [ˈtæki] *a.* 〔美口〕①邋遢的; 褴褛的,破旧不堪的. ②俗气的,不雅观的,寒酸的.
TACMAR [ˈtækmɑː] (= tactical multifunction array radar)战术多性能排列雷达.
ta·co [ˈtɑːkəu] *n.* *(pl.* ***-cos)*** (墨西哥)炸玉米卷〔夹有肉末和莴苣丝〕.
Ta·co·ma [təˈkəumə] *n.* 塔科马〔美国港市〕.
tac·on·ite [ˈtækəˌnait] *n.* 【矿】铁燧石.
tact [tækt] *n.* 机智,机敏; 得体; 老练, 圆滑; 【乐】拍子; 〔罕〕触觉.
tact·ful [ˈtæktful] *a.* 机智的,机敏的; 得体的; 老练的,圆滑的. **-ly** *ad.* **-ness** *n.*
tac·tic [ˈtæktik] *n.* = tactics. — *a.* ①顺序的,依次排列的. ②【化】有规结构的;【生】(有)趋性的.
tac·ti·cal [ˈtæktikəl] *a.* 战术(上)的; 策略(高明)的, 善于机变的. *a* ~ *diameter*【海】廻转直径. *a* ~ *flagship*【美海】作战旗舰. *a* ~ *march* 战备行军. ~ *obstacles* 战斗障碍物. ~ *situation* 战况. **-ly** *ad.*
tac·ti·cian [tækˈtiʃən] *n.* 战术家; 战略家; 策略家.
tac·tics [ˈtæktiks] *n.* ①战术 (*cf.* strategy); 策略; *grand [minor]* ~ 高等[小]战术. *the two* ~ 两种策略; 两手. *customary* ~ 惯用的伎俩. ②【语】法素学; 序素学.
tact·ile [ˈtæktail] *a.* 触觉的,有触觉的, 能触知的;【绘】表现[具有]实体感觉的. ~ *hairs*【生】触毛. *a* ~ *organ* 触觉器官. ~ *values* 触觉值. ~ *corpuscle* 触觉小体.
tac·til·i·ty [tækˈtiliti] *n.* 感触性.
tac·tion [ˈtækʃən] *n.* 〔罕〕接触.
tact·less [ˈtæktlis] *a.* 无机智的,不机敏的; 不圆滑的, 笨拙的.
tac·tom·e·ter [ˈtæktɔmitə] *n.* 触觉计.
tac·tu·al [ˈtæktjuəl] *a.* 触觉的,触觉器官的. **-ly** *ad.* 用触觉.
tad[1] [tæd] *n.* 〔美俚〕小(男)孩.
tad[2] [tæd] *n.* 少量.
tad·pole [ˈtædpəul] *n.* 【动】蝌蚪;〔*pl.*〕〔美谑〕*Mississippi* 人的别名;〔美〕法国小孩. ***~'s shimmy***〔美〕适当的东西.
Ta·dzhik·i·stan [tɑːˌdʒikiˈstɑːn] *n.* 塔吉克〔苏联加盟共和国名〕.
taedi·um vi·tae [ˈtiːdiəmˈvaitiː] 〔L.〕厌世观.
tael [teil, ˈteiəl] *n.* 两〔中国从前的衡量和货币单位; 印度、印度支那等的重量单位,约 = $1\frac{1}{3}$ 盎斯〕.
ta'en [tein] 〔方、诗〕= taken.
tae·ni·a [ˈtiːniə] *n.* *(pl.* ***-niæ*** [-niiː]*)* (古希腊、罗马的)头带;【解】带状结构;【建】(多利斯建筑的) 束带饰;【动】绦虫. **~cide**【医】杀绦虫剂. **~cidal** *a.* 杀绦虫的. **-sis**【医】绦虫病.
tae·ni·oid [ˈtiːniɔid] *a.* 带状的; (象)绦虫的.
TAF = Tactical Air Force〔美〕战术空军.
taf·fer·el, taff·rail [ˈtæfərəl, ˈtæfreil] *n.* 【船】船尾上部; 船尾栏杆.
taf·fe·ta, taf·fe·ty [ˈtæfitə, ˈtæfiti] *n.* 塔夫绸,平纹绸,府绸.
taf·fy [ˈtæfi] *n.* ①= toffee 太妃糖. ②〔美俚〕拍马屁,奉承. ~ **pull**〔美〕拍马奉承的交际集会.
taf·ia, taf·fi·a [ˈtæfiə] *n.* 塔非亚酒 〔西印度群岛用甘蔗制的一种甜酒〕.
Taft [tæft, tɑːft] *n.* 塔夫脱〔姓氏〕.
tag[1] [tæg] *n.* ①(衣服上的)垂下物, 附属物; 带端的金属箍〔包头〕. ②标签; 附笺,贴纸. ③(动物的)尾; (衣服等的)边,饰缝; (电缆等的)终端. ④(文章、演说终了时的)结束语; 陈套语,(诗歌末尾的)叠句; (戏剧的)收场白. ⑤卑劣人物; 下层平民. ⑥卷发,卷毛; (羊的)缠结纷乱的毛. ⑦(花体字的)拖长的尾巴. ⑧〔美俚〕诨名. *a parts* ~ 零件牌. *a price* ~ 价目标签. ***~ and rag*** = ~, ***rag and bobtail*** = tagrag 下层社会. — *vt.* ①装金属箍(在带端); 标记; 加标签; 加上(附加物),添加 *(to; on to)*; 接连 *(together)*; 押韵. ②剪(羊的)缠结难分的乱毛. ③〔口〕尾随. ④〔口〕给…起诨名,把…叫做. ⑤〔原〕(用同位素)作标记,示踪. ⑥〔美口〕(对车辆)放上一张停车票; (对开车者)给一张犯规通知. — *vi.* 〔口〕紧跟在后头,钉在后头, 追随, 尾随 *(at sb.'s heels, after sb.)*. *tagged atom* 示踪原子, 标记原子. **~board** 作货运标签等用的硬纸. ~ **day** 〔美〕慈善事业街头募捐日(对捐款者赠以小标签). ~ **end** 末端; 残余. **~-line**〔美俚〕(高潮下的)结尾语. ~ **question**【语法】附加疑问〔例: You're ready, *aren't you?*〕 **~rag** 跟在后面瞎哄乱嚷的人们; 下层社会; (破烂衣服上垂挂着的) 破布, 褴褛. ~ **sale** 标签出售. **~-tail**〔美〕食客; 帮闲. ~ **up**【棒球】返垒.
tag[2] [tæg] *n.* 捉迷藏. — *vt.* (玩捉迷藏时)捉住.
Ta·ga·log [tɑːˈgɑːlɔg, ˈtægəlɔg] *n.* ①*(pl.* ***-logs, -log)*** 他加禄人〔菲律宾岛上的马来亚人〕. ②他加禄语〔1962年定为菲律宾国语〕.
tag·ger [ˈtægə] *n.* ①垂下物; 附随者. ②装(金属箍等)的人; 加贴标签的人. ③剪乱羊毛的器具. ④〔*pl.*〕极薄的铁片. ⑤(捉迷藏中的)捉人者.
tag·meme [ˈtægmiːm] *n.* 【语】法位〔语法单位〕, 序位; 语法功能段. **-me·mic** [-ˈmiːmik] *a.*
tag·me·mics [tægˈmiːmiks] *n. pl.* 〔动词用单数〕【语】法位学,序位学.
Ta·hi·ti [tɑːˈhiːti] *n.* 塔希提岛〔南太平洋〕.
Ta·hi·ti·an [təˈhiːʃən, tɑː-; -hiːtiən] *a.* 塔希提岛的, 塔希提人的,塔希提语的. — *n.* ①塔希提人〔尤指塔希提岛的波利尼西亚人〕. ②塔希提语〔指波利尼西亚语〕.
TAI = 〔F.〕*Transports Aêriens Intercontinentaux*〔法〕洲际航空运输公司.
tai·ga [ˈtaigə] *n.* (北部亚寒带的)针叶林带; 泰加群落〔森林〕; 针叶树大森林.
tail[1] [teil] *n.* ①尾巴. ②尾状物,垂下物; (西服的)垂尾, 燕尾;〔*pl.*〕燕尾服. ③辫子; 风筝尾巴. ④末端; 结尾, 后部;〔俚〕屁股. ⑤随员, 扈从;【军】军属队伍; 属员, 跟在后面的人, 晚辈;〔美俚〕尾随的侦探; (等候购物等)排成一行的人们, 长蛇阵. ⑥钱币的反面. ⑦【建】(瓦、石板等露出的)下部;【乐】符尾;【空】尾翼, 尾面;【天】彗星尾;【印】(书页的)地脚. ⑧〔*pl.*〕渣滓,(剩下的)尾脚. *the* ~ *of the eye* 外眼角. *She wears her hair in a* ~. 她梳着辫子. *a* ~ *gate* 下闸门. *a* ~ *wind* 由后面吹来的风. *a* ~ *fin* 尾鳍. ***at the*** ~ ***of*** 在末尾, 在最后. ***cannot make head or*** ~ ***of*** 不知道是什么事情. ***close on sb.'s*** ~ 迫近某人后头, 就在某人后头. ***get one's*** ~ ***down*** 畏缩, 害怕, 丧失勇气. ***get [keep] one's*** ~ ***up*** 情绪很高,振奋,有勇气, 有精神. ***go into ~s*** 穿燕尾服(等). ***have one's*** ~ ***up [down]*** 情绪好〔不好〕. ***keep the*** ~ ***in waters***〔口〕兴隆,走运. ***out of the*** ~ ***of the eye*** 斜睐. ***play (at) heads and ~s*** 扔钱猜正面还是反面. ***~s up*** (人)精神好;〔喻〕跃跃欲试. ***turn*** ~ 退走,掉头, 逃走. ***twist the*** ~ ***of*** 做出使…讨厌的事情; 触犯…. ***with the*** ~ ***between the legs*** 夹着尾巴;〔喻〕惊恐,垂头丧气,畏缩. ***with the*** ~ ***of the eye*** 斜睐. — *vt.* 装上(风筝)尾巴; 添上, 接上, 连结上 *(on; on to)*; 跟踪,尾随;〔口〕切去尾巴, 切去末端; (狗等)拖着尾巴;【建】(把材料的一端)嵌入 *(in; into; on)*. — *vi.* 尾巴似地垂下,拖着尾巴; 尾巴似的[分散地] 拖在后面; 跟在后头,排成队; 船尾搁浅(在暗礁上); (停泊时)把船尾掉向顺风[顺流]方面; (鱼)把尾巴露出水面. ~ ***after*** 尾随, 排在…的后头 (*Some fifteen boys* ~*ed after the parade.* 十五六个男孩尾随在游行队伍之后). ~ ***away [off]*** 零零落落地落在后头,弄得零零落落; 渐渐变细, 渐渐减少, 渐渐消失 (*The path* ~*s off into the woods.* 小径逐渐消失在树林中). ~ ***out***〔美〕逃走; 走. ~ ***to the***

tide = ~ ***up and down the stream*** (停泊的船)使船尾顺着潮流[河流]. ~ **up**〔美〕使病牛站起. ~**back**【橄榄球】(置于发球线后方的)尾卫. ~**board**(卡车,装货马车等的)后箱板.~ **bone** 尾骶骨.~ **coat** 燕尾服. ~ **covert**【动】尾部复羽. ~ **dive**【空】尾坠. ~**-down** *ad.*, *a.*【空】机尾朝下(的). ~ **drop**【空】尾坠. ~ **end** 尾端;末尾;〔*pl.*〕(谷类的)屑.~**fan**【动】扇尾鳍.~ **fin** *n.* 尾鳍;【空】直尾翼;垂直安定面. ~**gate** ①= ~board. ②*vi.*, *vt.* 紧跟前车行驶.~**-heavy** *a.*【空】尾部重的;后头重的. ~**-light** (= ~ **lamp**) (汽车等的)尾灯. ~ **margin**【印】(书页的)地脚. ~**piece** 尾片;附属物;【建】半端梁;【机】尾端件;【印】补白图案;(提琴等的)系弦板. ~**pipe** (汽车等的)排气尾管;(烟斗的)吸管. ~ **plane**【空】横尾翼,水平安定面. ~**race** (水车的)泄水道. ~ **skid**【空】尾橇. ~**slide**【空】尾滑. ~ **spin**【空】尾旋,螺旋;〔转义〕失去控制;混乱. ~**stock**【机】尾座[架];顶针[尖]座.(= foot stock). ~**-turret**【空】机尾炮塔. ~**-wagging** (滑雪中)高速转身;【空】摆尾〔一种特技飞行〕. ~ **wind** 顺风. **-ee** *n.* 被钉梢的人. **-ing** *n.* 装尾巴;【建】嵌入墙壁内的砖石凸出部;屑,糟,渣滓,矿渣. **-ism** *n.* 尾巴主义.

tail[2] [teil] *n.* ①【法】限定继嗣;限定继承权;限嗣继承财产. ②【印】(书籍页面的)地脚;底边空白. *an estate in* ~ 限嗣继承财产. *an heir in* ~ 限定继承人. — *a.* 限定继承的.

tail·end·er [ˈteilendə] *n.* 占倒数第一名者.

tail·gate[1] [ˈteilˌgeit] *n.* ①(车辆后部的)尾板,后档板. ②(运河的)下闸门.— *vt.*,*vi.* 紧跟前面的车辆之后行驶.

tail·gate[2] [ˈteilgeit] *n.*〔美〕狂热的爵士音乐演奏. **-r** *n.*

taille [teil; F. tɑːj] *n.* ①(法国国王或领主征收的)封建税〔指人头税或代役税〕. ②〔罕〕妇女胸部的形状,或妇女背心的式样.

tai·lor [ˈteilə] *n.* (*fem.* ~*ess* [-ris]) 裁缝,缝工,成衣工;【军】缝纫兵. *The* ~ *makes the man.*〔谚〕佛靠金装人靠衣裳. ~*'s clippings* 衣料样本. ***ride like a*** ~ 不善骑马. ***sit*** ~ ***fashion*** 盘腿坐. — *vi.* 开服装店;做裁缝,做衣服. — *vt.* 缝制(衣服);供应服装. *He is well* ~*ed.* 他的衣服做得好. ~**bird** 长尾缝叶莺. ~**-made** *a.* ①缝制得讲究的;服装讲究、大方的. ②定做的. ②香烟机卷的〔自卷之对〕.

tai·lor·ed [ˈteiləd] *a.* ①(女式服装)线条简单、腰身合体的. ②〔美〕简单明瞭的,干净利落的.

tai·lor·ing [ˈteiləriŋ] *n.* ①裁缝业,成衣业. ②裁缝法,缝工.

tain [tein] *n.* 薄锡板,锡箔.

Taine [tein], **H.A.** 泰纳〔1828—1893, 法国的批评家、历史家〕.

Tai·no [ˈtainəu] *n.* ①(*pl.* **-nos, -no**) 泰诺人〔西印度群岛的一支已绝种的印第安人〕. ②泰诺语〔属阿拉瓦语〕.

taint [teint] *vt.* 弄脏,污染;使感染(病毒等);毒化(思想,感情等);使腐败;使堕落. — *vi.* 沾染;感染;腐败,堕落. *His character is* ~*ed by selfseeking.* 他的性格带有利己的缺点. ~*ed family* 有遗传病的家族. ~*ed goods* 非工会会员制造或经手的商品,来历不明的商品. ~*ed meat* 腐肉. ~*ed money* 肮脏钱. *Meat will readily* ~ *in close weather.* 肉在闷热天气容易腐败. — *n.* ①污点;污名. ②传染;腐败. ③〔废〕气味,痕迹.

'taint [teint]〔方、卑〕= it isn't, it hasn't.

taj [tɑːdʒ] *n.* (伊斯兰教徒的)圆锥形高帽. **T- Mahal** [məˈhɑːl] (印度 Agra 的)泰姬陵.

Ta·jik [ˈtɑːdʒik] *n.* ①(*pl.* **-jiks, -jik**) 塔吉克人[族]. ②= Tajiki.

Ta·jik·i [ˈtɑːdʒiki, tɑːˈdʒiːki] *n.* 塔吉克语〔塔吉克人说的波斯方言〕.

take [teik] *vt.* (***took*** [tuk]; ***taken*** [ˈteikən]) ①(用手)拿,取,抓,握;捕,捉,逮捕;俘虏;攻取,占领;【牌】吃掉,胜过. ~ *(sb.) in the act* 当场逮捕. ~ *sb. in one's arms [heart, breast]* 抱住某人,拥抱某人;爱上某人. ~ *sb. by the nose* 捏住某人鼻子.~ *a fortress by storm* 用猛攻夺下要塞.~ *sth. up with one's fingers* 用手指拿起某物. ~ *sth. on one's shoulder* 掮起某物.②取得;获得,拿到;(从某处)得到,取出;发源于. ~ *a degree* 取得学位. *He* ~*s 100 dollars a month.* 他拿一百块钱的月薪. *What will you* ~ *for this bicycle?* 这部自行车你要(卖)多少钱? *I will not* ~ *a cent less.* 一分钱也不能少. ~ *a name from the inventor* 得名于它的发明者. *The river* ~*s its rise from a lake.* 这条河发源于一个湖. ③携带;带去;带领参观;搬移. ~ *sb. about a town* 领人参观城市. ~ *sb. through a book* 指导某人读一本书. *Will this road* ~ *me to the station?* 这条路能到车站吗? ~ *the dog out for a walk* 带领狗出去散散步. ④买;预定(座位等);订阅;租借(房子). *I'll* ~ *the book for two yuan.* 这书要是卖两元我就买了. *Which newspapers do you* ~? 你订阅哪几份报纸? ~ *a cottage at the seaside for the Summer* 在海边租一所小房子过夏. ⑤接受(礼物等);娶(妻);收(房客等);采用,选取;接纳(新会员等). ~ *things as they come* 来什么接受什么. ~ *medical advice* 受医生诊断. ~ *a wife* 娶妻. ~ *a woman to wife* 娶一个女人做妻子. ~ *lodgers* 收房客. ⑥理解,领悟(言语、行动的意义);认为,想象,当做. *I* ~ *it that* …我以为…. *Do you* ~ *me?* 你懂我的意思吗? *How would you* ~ *this passage?* 这一节你怎么解释? ~ *something well [in good part]* 往好的方面解释某事,把…当做好意. ~ *something ill [amiss, in ill part]* 往坏的方面解释某事,把…当做恶意. *Must not* ~ *ill of him.* 不要怪他. ⑦听从(忠告);甘受,忍受(侮辱等);担负(责任);答应(请求等);担任(职位);执行(任务等). *T- my word for it* = *You may* ~ *it from me.* 你相信我的话好了. 你可以相信那是真的. ~ *the blame* 担负过失的责任. ~ *orders* 接受命令[任命]. ~ *the throne [crown]* 接受王位;即位. ⑧耗费(时间等);需要(多少时间等). *These things* ~ *time.* 这些事情需要花费时间. *It* ~*s an hour to go there.* 到那里需要一个钟头. ⑨搭乘,骑;进去,隐藏;越过,渡过. ~ *a train* 坐火车. ~ *ship* 坐船. ~ *a hurdle* 跳过栏去. ~ *a bus to town* 乘公共汽车进城. ⑩拿走,取走,消除;减去. ~ *sb.'s life* 杀死. ~ *3 from 5* 五减三. ⑪记录,记下;描画;拍摄;量(尺寸等). ~ *notes* 做记录. ~ *a speech* (听报告)做笔记. ~ *measurements* 量尺寸. ~ *sb.'s measure* 量某人身长;〔喻〕看穿某人. ~ *sb.'s temperature* 量某人的体温. ⑫采取(某一行动);发生(某种感情等),经验. ~ *action* 采取行动. ~ *comfort* 得到安慰. ~ *delight (in)* 对…感觉愉快[快乐],欢喜…. ~ *a trip* 旅行. ~ *a walk* 散步. ~ *a rest* 休息. *A disease* ~*s its course.* 病加重. ⑬吃;喝;吸入;服用. ~ *a cup of tea* 喝一杯茶. ~ *a meal* 吃饭. ~ *a deep breath* 行深呼吸. ~ *too much* 吃得[喝得]太多. *die by taking poison* 服毒死亡. ⑭(病)侵袭;(火)着起来,烧到;吸收(染料等). *be taken ill [bad]* 生病. ~ *fire* 着火;发怒,生气. ⑮打中,击中;出其不意地袭击;吸引,迷住;欺骗;〔美俚〕打败,打垮. ~ *sb. by surprise* 突然袭击某人. *be much taken with [by] a girl* 深深地爱上一个姑娘. ~ *sb.'s fancy* 占有某人的心. ~ *a fancy to sb.* 爱上某人. *He took his readers with him.* 他把他的读者吸引住. *I was badly taken.* 我大大受骗了. ⑯采取(形状、态度、意见、主义等);发(誓). ~ *an oath* 发誓. ⑰【乐】奏,弹,唱. — *vi.* ①拿,取,获得;获得财产. ②拿去,除去;减去;损失(价值等);扣除. ③(鱼鸟等)被捕,被捉. *Fish always* ~ *best after rain.* 雨后鱼最好钓. ④(药)奏效;(牛痘等)发;〔罕〕烧着;【化】凝结,凝固;(墨水在纸上)吃得牢,不容易褪色. *Dry fuel* ~*s readily.* 干燥的燃料极易着火. ⑤欢喜,爱好 *(to)*;开始 *(to)*. ⑥受欢迎,博得喝采. ⑦(相)照得(好或不好). *She* ~*s better standing.* 她的相是站着照较好. ⑧去,前进,赴,到 *(across* fields, *to* the wood*)*. ~ *down the mountain on a run* 一气儿跑下山. ⑨〔口〕得(病),(病)传染. ~ *ill*

〔口、方〕= be taken ill. ⑩生根；发芽. ⑪〔美〕(立刻)采取行动而…〔用 ~ *and* ... 的形式，差不多没有增加什么意义〕. *If you do so I will ~ and tell father.* 你要是这样做我就告诉父亲. ***be taken in one's prime*** 夭亡，短命而死. ***be taken prisoner*** 被俘，成俘虏. ***be taking a beating*** 挨打. ~ ***a back seat***〔美俚〕让别人领头，谦逊. ~ ***a bow***〔美俚〕鞠躬答谢喝采；〔美〕值得赞美. ~ ***a brief***【法】受理案件. ~ ***a brodie***〔美俚〕得不到喝采；跌倒；(演出)失败；(名誉等)迅速败坏. ~ ***a bush*** 逃进树丛里. ~ ***a challenge lying down***〔美俚〕拒绝挑战，不参加比赛. ~ ***a chance***〔美〕冒险，做做看. ~ ***a corner*** 拐弯. ~ ***a cottage course***〔美〕(大学生)在毕业前结婚. ~ ***a fall***〔美俚〕跌倒；(被)打败；受挫折. ~ ***a flier*** 做投机买卖. ~ ***a gander at***〔美口语〕看，瞧，仔细检查. ~ ***a hot squat***〔美俚〕被执行死刑. ~ ***a knock***〔美〕被监禁. ~ ***a licking***〔美俚〕失败；弄糟；赔本. ~ ***a poke at***〔美俚〕打，殴，正面攻击人；讽刺人. ~ ***a pot shot***〔美俚〕乱打(枪)；瞎猜. ~ ***a program***〔美俚〕顺从，照办. ~ ***a punch at***〔美俚〕打算. ~ ***a risk***【商】承受保险. ~ ***a (run-out) powder***〔美俚〕逃掉，跑掉. ~ ***a shot at***〔美俚〕抓牢机会；努力，试. ~ ***a slope*** 上坡. ~ ***a swap [swop]*** 售物者挨顾客一顿骂. ~ ***a turn (on the beach)*** (在岸上)散步. ~ ***a whirl at***〔美俚〕企图. ~ ***after*** 尾随；仿效；象. ~ ***an account of stock***【商】清点存货，盘货. ~ ***an opponent over the sticks***【美体】打败对手. ~ ***away*** 拿走；剥夺；减；收拾饭桌. ~ ***back*** 拿回，收回；取消(约定等)，承认说了错话. ~ ***coolly*** 泰然处之. ~ ***cover*** 躲避，躲藏. ~ ***down*** 拿下，扯下，降下，卸下；卷起；记下；卸下；拆，拆毁(房子)，拆散(头发)，分开；挫其骄气；吞下去，咽下去. ~ ***down one's (back) hair*** [~ one's (back) hair down]〔美俚〕坦白地说；推心置腹. ~ ***earth*** (狐)逃进洞里；隐藏. ~ ***for*** 认为，以为；当做；误认，弄错 (*I was taken for my sister.* 人家把我错认做我的姐妹了. *What do you ~ me for?* 你把我当作什么人？你以为我是做什么的？) ~ ***for a ride***〔美匪俚〕绑去杀死；欺骗. ~ ***from*** 减少(…的重量、价值等) (*~ from the pleasure* 减少兴趣. *The size of her hat ~s from her height.* 因为帽子大她的身段就显得矮了). ~ ***in*** ①收进；收容，留宿；装入(货物)；带进(房间等). ②接收(钱)；在自己家里承接(洗衣、缝纫等)；〔英〕订阅(报纸等). ③包括，包容，加以考虑；〔美〕访问，参观. ④缩小，弄窄(衣服等)；卷(帆)，收帆. ⑤理会，了解. ⑥欺骗 (*I was nicely taken in.* 我上了大当). ~ ***(a boy) in charge*** 收养(孩子). ~ ***in tow***【海】牵船；牵航. ~ ***in your washing!***【海】收护舷物；收索端！ ~ ***into account [consideration]*** 考虑到. ~ ***into camp sb.*** 骗过，瞒过；使某人上当. ~ ***into (one's) confidence*** 信任. ~ ***into one's head [mind]*** 忽然想起[想到]. ~ ***it*** 相信；〔口〕受罚；〔美俚〕甘心受批评[奚落]；勇敢地忍受不幸(等). ~ ***it and like it***〔美俚〕不大甘心地忍受批评[嘲笑、不幸(等)]. ~ ***it away***〔美俚〕去干吧. ~ ***it easy*** 轻松. ~ ***it hard*** 关心，担心；悲伤. ~ ***it on the chin***〔美俚〕赛输；考不上，失败. ~ ***it on the lam***〔美俚〕仓皇逃走. ~ ***it out of*** 向…报仇[泄恨]；使失势；使疲乏；虐待，剥削，榨取…的血汗.〔俚〕~ ***it out on (sb.)*** 拿(别人)出气. (*They were taking it out on one another because of their hopeless dissatisfaction.* 他们由于没有希望获得满足而彼此以恶言相敬来出气). ~ ***it that*** 相信，信以为，认为. ~ ***it (up) on one(self)*** (*to* do) = ~ upon one(self). ~ ***off*** ①*vt.* 取出，拿走；脱去(帽子、衣服等)，剥；放(手等)；移，移送；带走，带去；免除 (*~ off a heavy tax* 免除重税)；杀死，弄死 (*be taken off by cholera* 患霍乱丧命)；免职；减(价)；喝干；抄写，印；学(人家的样)，学样取笑. ②*vi.* 动身，起程；走掉；退职；跳出；【空】起飞；(潮)退落；(风)停息. ~ ***on*** ①*vt.* 承接，担任(工作等)；较量 (*~ sb. on at golf* 和某人比赛高尔夫球)；装(某种样子)；呈现(形势)；长(肉)；雇用，给加入，给入伙；〔美〕打败人. ②*vi.*〔口〕愤激，激昂，悲伤欲狂 (*Don't ~ on so!* 别这样悲伤)；受欢迎，得人心. ~ ***on a cargo of this***〔美〕请细心听这件事吧. ~ ***one's life in one's hand*** 冒极大危险. ~ ***one's life upon a thing*** 拼着性命去做某事. ~ ***oneself away [off]*** 走掉，离开. ~ ***out*** 取出；带到，带出(散步等)；拔(牙等)，除去(污点等)；取得(专卖权等)，拿到(执照等)；借出(书籍等)；摘出(要点)；(桥牌)表示不同意伙伴所叫的花色而改叫. ~ ***out of*** 取出，除去；要赔偿；报仇 (*That ~s all the fun out of it.* 那扫兴极了. *~ a leaf out of sb.'s book* 仿效某人). ~ ***over*** 接收，接手；接办，接管；继承. ~ ***sb. by the hand*** 握住[牵着]某人的手. ~ ***sb. for all in all*** 无论从哪一点来看，各方面都. ~ ***sth. lying down*** 甘心容忍[屈服] (*He doesn't ~ such an insult lying down.* 他不能忍受这样的侮辱). ~ ***the air*** 升空，飞行. ~ ***the cake***〔美俚〕赢得奖赏；胜过别人，出人头地；获得成功. ~ ***the count***〔美俚〕被打昏过去，死掉. ~ ***the field*** 出征. ~ ***the measure of sb.'s foot*** 看出某人弱点. ~ ***the rap***〔美俚〕挨骂，受罚，被打败，失败. *(You must)* ~ ***the rough with the smooth*** (你必须)了解有快乐就有痛苦. ~ ***the water*** 跳入水中(逃走). ~ ***to*** 爱，喜欢，嗜好；开始，开始做；参加；逃入；沉迷在；…起来 (*~ to smoking* 抽起烟来. *He took to studying English* 他开始学习英语. *~ to the air with* 开始播送). ~ ***to be*** = ~ for. ~ ***to the boat*** 改乘小船. ~ ***to the timber***〔美〕躲起来. ~ ***to the woods***【美政】逃避责任；弃权. ~ ***up*** ①拿起；举起；拾起；给搭(火车等)，(汽车等)接纳(乘客)；(船)承装(货物)；收做(徒弟等)；保护. ②逮捕. ③吸收(水分等)；耗费(时间)，占(地位)；吸引(注意等). ④打断人家的话，打岔；责备. ⑤开始，动手(工作等)，从事；提出，处理(问题)；继续(中断的话)，接下去讲. ⑥承接(定货)；接受(挑战、打赌)，应征；承兑(期票)，支付. ⑦定居(住处). ~ ***up the chant*** 人云亦云. ~ ***up with*** 甘受；忍受(虐待等)；采用；遵奉(某说)，信奉(学说)；和…亲近；与…同居；向…求婚. ~ ***upon one(self)*** ①负担，承担(责任等). ②毅然，大胆 (*~ (it) upon one(self) to say sth.* 毅然说出某事). —*n.* 捕获；收获；捕获量，收获量；〔俚〕利益，盈益；(入场券的)售得金额；【印】(排字工人)一次所排的原稿；【影】(一次拍摄的)镜头. *a great ~ of salmon* 鲑鱼的大量捕获. *make a large ~* 大量猎获. **~away** *a.*〔英〕(饭菜)外卖的，买回去的. **~down** *a.*, *n.* 可拆散的(机器)；可拆下的部分；〔口〕叫人受气的人[事]，欺人的人[事]. **~-home pay**〔美〕(扣去捐税等后的)净薪. **~-in**〔口〕欺骗. **~-it-or-leave-it** *a.* 要求作出断然抉择的，不容讨价还价，模棱两可或觅取妥协办法的. **~-off** 缺点；(滑稽的)摹仿；讽刺画；起点；起跳点；【空】起飞(点)，离水(点) (*~-off run* 起飞滑行距离). **~out** ①*n.* 取出，拿出；〔美〕(餐馆)外卖菜. ②*a.* 卖外卖菜的(餐馆)；【桥牌】暗示改叫花色的加倍. **~over** 接收，接管(政权等). **~up** 提升，拉紧，绷紧；拉紧装置；(缝纫机上提针线上升的)提升装置；【影】卷片装置；纠正.

taken [ˈteikən] take 的过去分词. ~ ***altogether*** 总括起来说；总之.

tak·er [ˈteikə] *n.* 取者；捕获者；接受者；收取者；购买者；打赌者. *a ticket ~* 收票员.

tak·er-in [ˈteikəin] *n.*【纺】(梳棉机的)刺毛辊〔亦作 licker-in〕.

takin [ˈtɑːkin, ˈtei-] *n.*【动】扭角羚 *(Budorcas taxicolor)*〔栖于喜马拉雅山的森林中〕.

tak·ing [ˈteikiŋ] *a.* ①迷人的，可爱的. ②会传染的. —*n.* ①捕获；捕获物；捕获总量. ②〔*pl.*〕售得金额，所得，收入. ③〔口〕激动，兴奋；烦恼. ***in a ~*** ①在激动中. ②在困难中 (*in a great ~* 心烦意乱). **~-off** 除去；【空】起飞. **-ly** *ad.* **-ness** *n.*

tak·y [ˈteiki] *a.*〔口〕=taking.

T

tal·a·poin [ˈtæləpɔin] *n.* (斯里兰卡及泰国等地的)和尚;【动】小长尾猴[产于西非].

ta·lar·i·a [təˈlɛəriə] *n.* [*pl.*] [L.]【希神、罗神】(Mercury, Iris 等的)脚翼;翼靴.

talc [tælk] *n.*【矿】滑石;云母. — *vt.* ***(talc(k)ed, talced; talc(k)·ing, talc·ing)*** 用滑石处理. ~ *powder* 滑石粉,爽身粉. ~ *spar* 菱镁矿.

tal·cite [ˈtælsait] *n.*【地】①滑块石. ②变白云母.

talck·y [ˈtælki] *a.* = talcose.

talc·ose, talc·ous [ˈtælkəus, -kəs] *a.* (含)滑石的.

talcum [ˈtælkəm] *n.* ①= talc. ②滑石粉,爽身粉 (= ~ powder).

tale [teil] *n.* ①故事,传说. ②坏话;谣言;谎话. ③[古]计算;总计. *a fairy* ~ 神仙故事,童话. *traveler's ~s* 大话,牛皮. *old wives' ~s* 荒唐故事. *a ~ of a tub* 无稽之谈. *a ~ of nought* [废]无聊琐事. *a ~ of a roasted horse* 弥天大谎. *Thereby hangs a ~.* 这里头有来由. *The shepherd tells his ~.* [古]牧羊人清点他的羊数. *The ~ is complete.* [古]数目不错,并无短缺. *His ~ is told [has been told].* 他已经完了[运数尽了]. ***a ~ that is told*** 废话;陈腐话. ***bring ~s = carry ~s*** = tell ~s. ***if all ~s be true*** 据说. ***in a [the same] ~*** 同一,一致. ***jump in one ~*** 一致. ***one and the same ~*** 同一事件. ***tell its own ~*** 自白来历;不说自明. ***tell one's ~*** 自述;说本人要[应]说的话;(使者)陈述所负使命. ***tell ~s (out of school)*** 讲坏话,说小话,搬弄是非. **~-bearer** 说人隐私的人;搬弄是非的人. **~-bearing** 搬弄是非. **~teller** 说人隐私的人;搬弄是非的人;讲故事的人.

tal·ent [ˈtælənt] *n.* ①天资;才能,才干,本事. ②[集合词]人材. ③[俚][集合词]【赛马】老赌手;【商】内行. ④古希腊[希伯莱]的重量及货币名. ***hide one's ~s in a napkin*** 埋没自己的才能,不好好利用自己的才能. ~ **scout** 物色人材者.

tal·ent·ed [ˈtæləntid] *a.* 有才能的;能干的.

tal·ent·less [ˈtæləntlis] *a.* 没有天资的;无能的.

ta·ler [ˈtɑːlə] *n.* *(pl.* ***ta·ler)*** 泰勒[德国旧时一种银币].

ta·les [ˈteiliːz] *n.* [L.]【法】候补陪审员(名册);候补陪审员召集令. **~man** *n.* 候补陪审员.

tali [ˈteilai] *n.* talus¹ 的复数.

Tal·i·a·cotian [tæliəˈkəuʃən] *n.* 隆鼻术,美鼻术.

tal·i·on [ˈtæliən]【法】同态惩罚(法);同态报复(法);以牙还牙;反坐.

tal·i·ped [ˈtæliˌped] *a.* 畸形足的,拐脚的. — *n.* 拐脚的人,拐脚的动物.

tal·i·pes [ˈtæliˌpiːz] *n.*【医】畸形足 (= clubfoot).

tali·pot [ˈtælipɔt] *n.* ①【植】扇形棕榈. ②从扇形棕榈提炼的淀粉.

tal·is·man [ˈtælizmən] *n.* *(pl.* *~s)* 护符,辟邪物;法宝. *a protective* ~ 护身符. ***cherish as a ~*** 奉为至宝. **-ic(al)** *a.* 护符的;有神奇魔力的.

talk [tɔːk] *vi.* 谈话;商谈;(用动作等)表示意思;(用无线电)通信;饶舌,唠叨;空谈;(开水壶)嚷叫,发响. — *vt.* 讲,谈;谈着消磨(光阴);谈论;讲着话使… *(into; out of)*. *Let's sit down and ~.* 让我们坐下来谈谈. *~ in English* 用英语讲. *~ English* 讲英语. *~ politics* 谈政治. *~ a child to sleep* 用话哄孩子睡. *(He would) ~ a horse's [a donkey's] hind leg off.* = *~ the bark off a tree.* [美]讲个不停,滔滔不绝地讲. *~ oneself hoarse (out of breath)* 讲得声音嘶哑(喘不过气来). *~ in one's sleep* 说梦话. *People will ~.* 人家会说闲话的,人言可畏. ***Money ~s.*** 金钱万能. ***~ a leg off = ~ an arm off*** [美]说个不停,刺刺不休. ***~ about*** 讲(某事),谈论 (*What are you talking about?* 你们在谈论什么? *I do not want to be ~ed about.* 我不愿意人谈论我). *The accused begins to ~.* 被告开始交代了. ***~ against time*** 说话消磨时间. ***~ at*** 暗指着…说,影射某人. ***~ away*** 说着话消磨(时间);靠讲话来忘记(恐怖等). ***~ baby*** 用对小孩子讲话的口气说 *(to)*. ***~ back*** 反唇相讥,回嘴. ***~ big [tall]*** [俚]夸口,吹牛. ***~ business*** 谈正经事. ***~ (cold) turkey*** [美]照实说,老老实实说;正正经经讨论,讨论基本问题. ***~ down*** 驳倒;放低嗓子说;放大声音盖过其他声音;【空】(用无线电)引导着陆. ***~ from the point*** 离题,说得不着边际. ***~ (sb.) into [out of]*** 说服(某人)做[停止做]…. ***~ of*** 讲,谈论;说要 (*T- of the devil, and he will appear* 说到曹操,曹操就到. *He is ~ing of going abroad.* 他说要出国去. *Talking of ...* 说到,讲到). ***~ one's head off*** [美] = ***~ a leg off.*** 说个没完. ***~ out*** 尽量谈;彻底说,说完;[英]将(议案的)讨论拖到闭会而悬置不决. ***~ out of turn*** [美俚]弄错;干涉,阻碍. ***~ over*** ①*vi.* 商谈,商量. ②*vt.* 说服. ***~ round*** ①*vi.* 转弯抹角地讲. ②*vt.* 说服;说得使回心转意. ***~ shop*** 讲自己的本行话[事情]. ***~ through one's hat = ~ through (the back of) one's neck*** [口]夸张,吹牛,乱说. ***~ to*** 向…谈;[口]申斥,劝谏 (*I'll ~ to him.* 要说他一顿了). ***~ to hear one's teeth rattle*** [美]胡说. ***~ to oneself*** 自言自语. ***~ together*** 商量,谈判. ***~ United States*** [美]说明美国公民的意见;讲英语;讲美国话. ***~ up*** 大声讲,明白地讲,[美]讨论. — *n.* 谈话;商谈,商议,谈判;讲演;谣传;话题,话柄;空话;隐语,黑话;方言;语调,口气. *big* ~ [美口]大话. *an idle* ~ 无聊话,闲扯,山海经. *small* ~ 闲谈. *tall* ~ 大话. *I heard it in ~.* 我是听人传说的. *He is all ~.* 他只会说(不会做). *It will end in ~.* 这不过是空话[传闻]罢了. *That's the ~.* [美]好,洗耳恭听. ***all ~ and no cider*** 议而不决,空谈而无结果. ***make a ~*** 造成口实,使人议论. ***make ~*** 一味空谈;闲聊. **~-in** 演讲示威;座谈;讨论. ~ **show** (广播中的)答问节目.

talk·a·thon [ˈtɔːkəθɔn] *n.* [美](议会中为拖延时间而进行的)冗长的讨论;冗长的演说;候选人的长篇广播[电视]竞选答问.

talk·a·tive [ˈtɔːkətiv] *a.* 喜欢说话的,多嘴的,健谈的 *(opp.* taciturn*)*. **-ly** *ad.* **-ness** *n.*

talk·ee-talk·ee [ˈtɔːkiˈtɔːki] *n.* ①闲话;唠叨话. ②(黑人等的)蹩脚英语. ③[美]爱说话的人.

talk·er [ˈtɔːkə] *n.* ①谈话人. ②饶舌者. ③空谈家. ④[美]有声电影. *a good* ~ 健谈的人.

talk·ie [ˈtɔːki] *n.* 有声电影.

talk·i·ness [ˈtɔːkinis] *n.* ①喜欢说话;多嘴. ②对话多.

talk·ing [ˈtɔːkiŋ] *a.* (会)说话的;多嘴的;富于表情的(眼睛等). *a ~ doll* 会叫的洋娃娃. *a ~ iron* [美俚]手枪. ~ **book** (盲人用)书刊录音唱片[带]. **~-down system**【空】无线电导航(着陆)装置. ~ **machine** 留声机. ~ **point** 论点. **~-to** [口]责备,责斥.

talk·y [ˈtɔːki] *a.* = talkative. ***talky-talky*** [口]对话(过)多的.

tall [tɔːl] *a.* ①身材高的,高大的. ②[美口](数量)大的. ③[俚]过分的,夸张的. *a ~ chimney* 高烟囱. *He is 6 feet ~.* 身高六英尺. *a ~ price* 高价. *a ~ dinner* 丰盛的饭菜[宴席]. *a ~ story* 大谎话. *~ talk* 大话. *a ~ order* 苛刻的要求,难办的差使. *~ grass country* [美]西部草原地带. *~ hat* 大礼帽. *~ timber [uncut]* [美]深山野地. *~ water man [sailor]* 远洋海员. — *ad.* [口]夸大地;趾高气扬地. **-ness** *n.*

tal·lage [ˈtælidʒ] *n.* [古英](封建领主向佃户征收的)地租.

tall·boy [ˈtɔːlbɔi] *n.* ①[英]高脚橱柜. ②(烟囱顶部的)通风管. ③高脚杯.

Tal·lin(n) [ˈtælin] *n.* 塔林[苏联城市].

tal·lit, tal·lith [tɑːˈliːt, ˈtɑːlis] *n.* 祈祷披肩[犹太教徒晨祷时所穿].

tal·low·y [ˈtæləui] *a.* 兽脂质的;牛脂似的;油腻的;苍白的.

tal·ly [ˈtæli] *n.* ①符木,符节,符契;计数的签筹,货签,筹

码;(符契上的)刻记;符合物，对中之一;一模一样的东西. ②〔罕〕帐;计算;得分;(货物计算上的)单位数〔如一打,一百等,交点货物如说 8,10,tally 时,这 tally 就指12或一打;如说96,98,tally 时,这 tally 就指一百〕. ③【海】理货,点数. ④木牌,铜牌;标签. *a hand* ~ 计数器. *a* ~ *card* 〔美〕计数卡片. *(sell goods)* ***by the*** ~ 按打[按捆](出售货物). ***live (on)*** ~ = ***live*** ~ ***with*** *(a woman)* 〔俚〕姘居. ***make [earn] a*** ~ ***in a game*** 在比赛中得分. ***strike*** ~ 符合;行动一致. — *vt.* 刻在符木上;计算,总结 *(up)*;记录;使符合;(上货卸货时)点数;【海】(向船尾方向)拉(帆脚索). — *vi.* 符合,吻合 *(with)*. *The two stories do not* ~. 两种说法对不上. *It tallies with the facts.* 合乎事实. ~ **clerk** ①(选举的)检票员. ②= tallyman ②. ~**man** ①分期付款赊卖人;拿样品卖货的人. ②(船上的)理货员,司签员. ③〔俚〕姘夫. ~**-register** 计数器. ~ **sheet** 帐单;〔美〕(选举的)票数记录纸. ~ **shop** 〔英〕分期付款赊卖店. ~ **system,** ~ **trade** 〔英〕分期付款赊销法. ~**-woman** 姘妇.

tal·low [ˈtæləu] *n.* 牛[羊]脂,兽脂. ~ *candle* (牛)脂烛. —*vt.* 涂兽脂;把(牲畜)养肥. **beef [mutton]** ~ 牛[羊]脂. ~**-chandler** (牛)脂烛制造人,卖脂烛的商人. ~**-faced** *a.* 脸色苍白的.

tal·ly·ho [tæliˈhəu, ˈtælihəu] *int.* 嗬嗬〔猎人嗾狗声〕. — *n. (pl.* ~*s)* ①"嗬"声. ②〔美〕四马马车[雪橇] — *vi.* 发出"嗬"声. — *vt.* 嗬嗬地嗾(狗).

tal·ma [ˈtælmə] *n.* (19世纪前半期的)塔尔马式披肩.

tal·mi·gold [ˈtælmigəuld] *n.* 镀金黄铜.

Tal·mud [ˈtælmud] *n.* 犹太圣法经传. **-ic** [tælˈmʌdik], **-i·cal** *a.* **-ist** *n.*

tal·on [ˈtælən] *n.* 〔常 *pl.*〕(猛禽,猛兽的)爪;爪形手;魔爪;【建】爪饰;【牌】分剩的牌;锁键上受到钥匙推压的部分;剑柄的根部;(债券、股票等上的)息票.

tal·qual =〔L.〕*talis qualis* (= just as they come; average quality)普通的,平常的.

ta·lus[1] [ˈteiləs] *n. (pl.* ***-li)*** 【解】距骨;踝.

talus[2] [ˈteiləs] *n.* 斜面;斜坡;(城墙的)斜面;【地】(断崖下的)塌磊,山麓堆积.

Tam. = Tamil.

tam [tæm] *n.* = tam-o'-shanter.

tam·a·bil·i·ty [ˌteiməˈbiliti] *n.* 可驯养性.

tam·a·ble [ˈteiməbl] *a.* 可驯养的.

ta·mal, ta·ma·le [təˈmɑːli] *n.* (墨西哥的)玉米面包卷的辣味肉饼子〔蒸或烤的〕.

ta·man·dua [ˌtɑːmɑːnˈdwɑː] *n.* 【动】小食蚁兽*(Tamandua tetradactyla)*〔产于热带美洲〕.

Ta·ma·ra [təˈmærə] *n.* 塔玛拉〔女子名〕.

tam·a·rack [ˈtæmərӕk] *n.* 【植】①美洲落叶松. ②美洲落叶松木材.

tam·a·rin [ˈtæmərin] *n.* 【动】绢毛猴〔南美洲产〕.

tam·a·rind [ˈtæmərind] *n.* 【植】罗望子树〔豆科常绿乔木〕;罗望子果,酸荚〔做清凉饮料等用〕. *bastard* ~ 合欢.

tam·a·risk [ˈtæmərisk] *n.* 【植】柽柳属植物.

ta·ma·sha [təˈmɑːʃə] *n.* (印度的)展览;演出,娱乐节目;典礼.

Ta·ma·tave [ˌtæməˈtɑːv] *n.* 塔马塔夫〔马达加斯加省省会〕.

tam·bac [ˈtæmbæk] *n.* 【植】沉香.

tam·bour [ˈtæmbuə] *n.* (低音)鼓;(圆形)绣花绷架;绷架上做的绣品;(筑城)(出入口前的)圆堡;【建】鼓形柱. — *vt., vi.* (用绷架)绣;装饰.

tam·bour·a, tam·bur·a [tɑːmˈburə] *n.* 【乐】塔姆布拉〔类似吉他的印度古老乐器,在东方流行〕.

tam·bou·rine [tæmbəˈriːn] *n.* (周围有发声金属片的)手鼓;铃鼓;(法国南部的)手鼓舞(曲);【动】一种非洲野鸽.

tam·bu·rit·za [tæmˈburitsə] *n.* 【乐】塔姆布里扎流特琴一类的古老乐器,在斯拉夫地区南部流行〕.

tame [teim] *a.* ①驯养了的 *(opp.* wild*)*. ②栽培的(植物);开垦的(土地). ③驯服的,温顺的;没有骨气的. ④单调的,平淡的,沉闷的(景色等). ⑤没有精神的,无精打采的,不活泼的. *a* ~ *cat* 家猫;食客. *a* ~ *description* 单调的描写. — *vt.* ①驯养(禽兽). ②驯服,制服. ③使没精神,抑制(热情等). ④把(色彩等)弄柔和.

tame·a·ble [ˈteiməbl] *a.* = tamable.

tame·less [ˈteimlis] *a.* 难驯养的;野性的,暴烈的.

tame·ly [teimli] *ad.* 驯熟地;柔顺地;乖乖地,没有骨气地.

tame·ness [ˈteimnis] *n.* 驯熟;温柔,无气力;平凡,沉闷.

tam·er [ˈteimə] *n.* 驯(养)…的人. *a* ~ *of lion* = *a lion* ~ 驯狮人.

Tam·er·lane [ˈtæmə(ː)lein] *n.* 〔Timour 或 Timur 的别名,意为"跛帖木儿"〕帖木儿〔1336—1405〕.

Tam·il [ˈtæmil] *n.* (南亚的)泰米尔人;泰米尔语.

Tam·ma·ny [ˈtæməni] *n.* 〔美〕坦慕尼协会〔= ~-Society, 纽约市民主党组织〕. — *a.* 坦慕尼协会成员的;坦慕尼协会式的. ~ **Hall** 坦慕尼厅. **-ism** *n.* **-ny-ite** *n.*

tam·my [ˈtæmi] *n.* = tam-o'-shanter.

tam-o'-shan·ter [tæməˈʃæntə] *n.* (苏格兰人的)宽顶无沿圆帽.

tamp [tæmp] *vt.* ①用粘土等填塞(装有炸药的洞口). ②捣固,砸牢(路基等). *a* ~*ing bar* 【铁道】砸道棒.

tam·pal·a [tæmˈpælə] *n.* 【植】雁来红 *(Amaranthus gangeticus)*.

tam·per[1] [ˈtæmpə] *vi.* 干扰,损害,削弱;窜改(遗嘱、稿件等);贿赂. ~ *with an illness* (医生)故意瞎医使病拖长. ~ *with voters* 收买投票人.

tamper[2] [ˈtæmpə] *n.* ①(爆破孔)填塞人;捣固者. ②夯,夯具. ③(中子)反射器;(中子)反射剂.

Tam·pe·re [ˈtɑːmpere] *n.* 坦佩雷〔芬兰城市〕.

Tam·pi·co [tæmˈpiːkəu] *n.* 坦皮科〔墨西哥港市〕.

tam·pi·on [ˈtæmpiən] *n.* 塞子;炮口塞;【乐】风琴管上端的塞子.

tam·pon [ˈtæmpən] *n.* ①【医】(塞伤口用的)棉塞,止血塞. ②(塞在头发里的)假发. — *vt.* 用棉塞塞住(伤口).

tam·pon·ade [ˈtæmpənid], **tam·pon·age** [-idʒ], **tam·pon·ment** [-mənt] *n.* 棉塞填入法;填塞(法).

tam-tam [ˈtʌmtʌm] *n.* ①锣. ②= tom-tom.

tan[1] [tæn] *vt.* ①鞣(革),硝(皮);上栲油(在网等上). ②晒红,晒黑(皮肤等). ③〔俚〕鞭打. — *vi.* 变柔软;晒红,晒黑. ~ ***sb.'s hide*** 〔美俚〕鞭打(某人). — *n.* ①鞣料树皮;(鞣皮后的)鞣料渣〔又叫 *spent* ~, 铺路等用〕. ②黄褐色,棕黄色,晒黑的皮色;〔*pl.*〕棕黄色皮鞋〔衣著〕. *kiss the* ~〔俚〕从马上掉下来. *the* ~〔俚〕马戏团. — *a.* 黄褐色的,棕黄色的. ~**bark** 鞣料树皮. ~**yard** 制革厂.

tan[2] [tæn] *n.* = tangent.

ta·na [ˈtɑːnə] *n.* = thana.

tan·a·ger [ˈtænədʒə] *n.* 【鸟】(中南美)莺类.

Ta·na·na·rive [F. tananariːv] *n.* 塔那那利佛〔马达加斯加首都〕.

tan·dem [ˈtændəm] *a., ad.* (两匹马)前后纵列;串联,串列 *(opp.* abreast*)*. *a* ~ *bus* [trolleybus] 联挂公共汽车[无轨电车]. *a* ~ *bicycle* 双人自行车. *a* ~ *sender* 转接记发器. *drive* ~ 将马前后串联着驾驶. — *n.* 两匹[数匹]前后串联在马车上的马;双马串联马车;双人自行车;串翼型飞机.

tang[1] [tæŋ] *n.* ①(刀剑等插入柄中的)柄脚. ②强烈的气味[臭味]. ③气息,意味;风味. *wine with a* ~ *of the cask* 带有桶味的酒. *be seasoned with the* ~ *of humour* 带有幽默的意味. — *vt.* 使其有…气味.

tang[2] [tæŋ] *n.* 响亮而有余音的声音;哨的一声. — *vt.,*

vi. (敲金属物等)使铛铛地响,使鸣响.
tang³ [tæŋ] *n.*【海】墨角藻;海产草本植物通称.
Tan·ga [ˈtæŋgə] *n.* 坦噶〔坦桑尼亚港市〕.
Tan·gan·yi·ka [ˌtæŋgəˈnji:kə] *n.* 坦噶尼喀〔坦桑尼亚-地区〕.
tan·gen·cy [ˈtændʒənsi] *n.* 接触.
tan·gent [ˈtændʒənt] *a.* ①接触的. ②【数】切线的,相切的;正切的. ③离题的. — *n.*【数】切线;切面;正切(线);正切尺,瞄准表尺;〔美口〕(铁路的)直线区间离题的行为;与目的无关的路线[方向]. ~ *elevation* 瞄准角. *a* ~ *scale [sight]* 正切尺,瞄准表尺. ***fly [go] off at [in, on, upon] a*** ~ (思想)忽然转变;突然越出本题,突然改变话题[做法]. *fly off at a* ~ *into outside matters* 突然离开本题说些不相干的题外话.
tan·gen·tal [tænˈdʒentl], **-tial** [tænˈdʒenʃəl] *a.* ①【数】切线的;切的;正切的. ②稍微有点关系的;肤浅的,离开本题的;突然越出常态的. *a* ~ *angle* 切角. ~ *coordinates* 切线座标. ~ *movement* 水平运动,切向运动. **-tial·ly** *ad.*
Tan·ge·rine [ˈtændʒəˈri:n] ①*a.* (Morocco 国)丹吉尔. ②丹吉尔人.
tan·ge·rine *n.* ①(欧洲)红桔,柑桔. ②桔红色.
tan·gi·ble [ˈtændʒəbl] *a.* 可触知的,有实质的,实在的;确实的;【法】有形的. ~ *material benefits* 看得见的物质利益. ~ *assets* 有形财产. **-ness** *n.* **-bly** *ad.* **-bili·ty** *n.*
Tan·gier [tænˈdʒiə] *n.* 丹吉尔〔摩洛哥港市〕.
tan·gle [ˈtæŋgl] *vt., vi.* (使)缠结;弄乱,(使)纷乱,(使)纠缠;笼络,诱陷;(使)受牵累;〔美俚〕吵闹,打架;竞争 *(with)*. — *n.* ①缠结;纠缠;纠纷;混乱. ②〔美俚〕吵闹,打架;拳赛. ③海底动植物采集器;海带(类). *His thoughts were in a* ~. 他的思想陷于紊乱. ~**foot** 粘虫胶;〔美俚〕威士忌酒. ~**some** *a.* 紊乱的;复杂的. **-r** *n.*
tan·gly [ˈtæŋgli] *a.* 缠结的,紊乱的.
tan·go [ˈtæŋgəu] *n. (pl. ~s)* 探戈舞(曲). — *vi.* 跳探戈舞. *a* ~ *tea* 探戈舞茶会.
tan·gram [ˈtæŋgrəm] *n.* (中国的)七巧板.
tangy [ˈtæŋi] *a.* *(-i·er; -i·est)* 有浓烈气味[滋味]的;怪臭的. **-i·ness** *n.*
tan·ist [ˈtænist, ˈθɔ:n-] *n.* (古爱尔兰)选妥的(凯尔特酋长)继承人〔当酋长活着时便在亲属中选出〕.
tank [tæŋk] *n.* ①罐,槽;箱;柜〔盛液体或气体的大容器〕;(火车头的)水柜;(船上的)液体舱;〔美、英方〕水堰,贮水池;游泳池;【船】模型试航池;【电】储能电路. ②【军】战车,坦克. ③〔美俚〕小镇市,小村庄;酒量大的人;(拘禁新犯人)的牢房. —*vt.* 装满槽[柜];贮存在槽[柜]里. *an air* ~【火箭】压缩空气瓶. *a heavy [light]* ~ = *a male [female]* ~ 重[轻]坦克. *a* ~ *crew* 坦克手. *a* ~ *circuit* 储能电路. ~ *farming* 无土[槽式]栽培法. ~ **buster** 防坦克飞机. ~ **car** 运油[水]汽车[车厢],油[水]槽车. ~ **ship** 油船. ~ **station** 给水站. **-man** 坦克手. ~ **top** 〔美〕背心装. ~ **town** (尤指火车停车加煤水的)小镇. **-er** 油船;【空】加油车;油罐.
tan·ka [ˈtɑ:ŋkə] *n.* 〔Jap.〕短歌〔三十一音节字的日本诗体〕.
tank·age [ˈtæŋkidʒ] *n.* (油等的)罐贮过程[措施];罐贮费用;罐容量;罐贮量;(用碎肉、内脏等脱脂后制成的)桶装下脚〔肥田用〕. *animal* ~ 骨肉粉.
tank·ard [ˈtæŋkəd] *n.* (有柄)大(啤酒)杯;一大杯. *cool* ~ 冷饮,清凉饮料.
tankette [tæŋˈket] *n.* 小坦克.
tank·ful [ˈtæŋkfəl] *n.* *(pl. -fuls)* 一罐之量.
tan·na = thana.
tan·na·ble [ˈtænəbl] *a.* 可鞣的,可硝制的.
tan·nage [ˈtænidʒ] *n.* 鞣皮;制革(法).
tan·nate [ˈtænit] *n.*【化】鞣酸盐,单宁酸盐.
tan·ner¹ [ˈtænə] *n.* 制革工人,鞣皮工人.
tanner² [ˈtænə] *n.* 〔英俚〕六辨士(旧)硬币.
tan·ner·y [ˈtænəri] *n.* 制革[鞣皮]厂;〔罕〕鞣皮法.
tan·nic [ˈtænik] *a.* 鞣质的,丹宁的;由鞣酸皮得到的. ~ *acid*【化】鞣酸,单宁酸.
tan·nin [ˈtænin] *n.* 鞣质,单宁,单宁酸.
tan·ning [ˈtæniŋ] *n.* 鞣皮(法),制革(法);(皮肤)晒黑;〔俚〕鞭打,责打. ~ **agent** 鞣剂.
Ta·no·an [ˈtɑ:nəuən] *n.* 塔努安语〔北美种印第安语语系,包括基奥瓦语和目前新墨西哥一些村庄中说的三种语言〕.
tanrec [ˈtænrək] *n.* = tenrec.
tan·sy [ˈtænzi] *n.*【植】艾菊.
tan·ta·late [ˈtæntəˌleit] *n.*【化】钽酸盐.
tan·tal·ic [tænˈtælik] *a.*【化】含钽的;五价钽的;正钽的.
tan·ta·lite [ˈtæntəˌlait] *n.*【化】钽铁矿.
tan·ta·li·za·tion [ˌtæntəlaiˈzeiʃən] *n.* 令人着急;逗人.
tan·ta·lize [ˈtæntəlaiz] *vt.* 使看到拿不到而焦急[难受],要给不给地逗弄,逗惹,愚弄. *The sight is most tantalizing.* 这光景真惹人着急. **-liz·ing** *a.* **-liz·ing·ly** *ad.*… 得令人着急.
tan·ta·lous [ˈtæntələs] *a.*【化】亚钽的,三价钽的.
tan·ta·lum [ˈtæntələm] *n.*【化】钽〔Ta〕.
tan·ta·lus [ˈtæntələs] *n.* 〔英〕(初看似可随意取用、实则有暗锁的)玻璃酒柜.
tan·ta·mount [ˈtæntəmaunt] *a.* 同等价值[效力]的,与…相等的 *(to)*. *Such an explanation is* ~ *to a confession.* 这样一种解释等于一篇自白.
tan·ta·ra [tænˈtɑ:rə] *n.* 喇叭声,角笛声.
tan·tiv·y [tænˈtivi] *n.* 〔古〕疾驰;快跑;【猎】催促赶快向前的叫声. — *ad.* 快,迅速,疾驱. — *a.* 快的,突进的,猛冲的.
tan·to [ˈtæntəu] *ad.* 〔It.〕【乐】太;甚. *allegro non* ~ 急速但不太快地.
tan·trum [ˈtæntrəm] *n.* 〔口〕发脾气. ***be in one's ~s*** 在发脾气. ***fly [get, go] into one's ~(s)*** 发脾气.
Ta·nya [ˈtænjə] *n.* 塔尼娅(女子名)〔Tatiana 的昵称〕.
Tan·za·ni·a [ˌtænzəˈni:ə] *n.* 坦桑尼亚〔非洲〕.
Tao [tɑ:əu, tau] *n.* 〔汉〕道〔道家学说〕;〔t-〕(儒家的)道.
Ta·o·ism [ˈtɑ:əuizəm] *n.* (中国的)道教;道家学说.
Ta·o·ist [ˈtɑ:əuist, ˈtauist] *n., a.* 道家(的);道教徒(的),道士(的). **-ic** *a.*
tap¹ [tæp] *vt.* ①轻打[拍,敲]. ②补鞋底,打鞋掌;打(着做)出〔如用发报机打出电讯〕. ③选举,选择. — *vi.* ①轻敲,轻打 *(at; on)*. ~ *the door with a stick* = ~ *a stick against the door* 用手杖轻轻叩门. ~ *at [on] the door* 敲门. — *n.* 轻打,轻敲;轻敲声;(装在踢跶舞鞋底尖上的)铁片;(补鞋底的)掌子;〔*pl.*〕〔英军〕吃饭号(声);〔美军〕熄灯号(声). *I hear a* ~ *at [on] the door.* 我听见门上敲了一下. ~**-dance** [跳]踢跶舞. ~**-danc·er** 跳踢跶舞的人,踢跶舞家.
tap² [tæp] *n.* (酒桶等的)流出口,嘴子;(水管的)分支,支管;〔英〕旋塞,龙头,活嘴;【电】分接头,抽头;〔英〕酒吧间;【机】螺丝攻,阴螺模;(电话线上)搭线窃听;(各种流出口的)流出物. *liquor of the same* ~ 同样品质的酒. ***in [on]*** ~ 随时能取用的(酒);随时能买到的(债券等);〔美俚〕手边的,随时可得到的,现成的. ~**bolt**【机】带头螺栓. ~**hole** 放液口. ~ **water** 自来水. ***turn the ~ on [off]*** 放开[关上]龙头. — *vt.* ①装嘴子;从嘴子里放酒(等),出来,开桶;(在树等上)作切口采取树液;【医】(腹部等开洞)放出液体. ②开辟,开发(矿山等). ③【电】分接(电流);分接头;(从总管)分接(自来水等);搭线窃听(电话等). ④〔喻〕提倡(新学说等),开拓(新领域). ⑤〔俚〕求取,借取(捐款、小帐等). ⑥【机】(用螺丝攻)刻螺母. ~ *the admiral*【海俚】偷桶里的酒. *a* ~*-ped coil* 多(接)头线圈. ~ **bond** 〔美〕国库债券. ~ **borer** 开塞锥;【机】螺孔钻. ~**-house**〔英〕小酒馆;酒吧;小旅店. ~**-room** 酒吧间,酒室. ~**root**【植】直根,主根.

T

tapa, tappa [ˈtɑːpə] *n.* 塔帕〔太平洋某些岛上居民用来做衣服的构树皮〕(又叫 ～ cloth).

tape [teip] *n.* 狭带,棉线带;卷尺,带尺;电报收报纸带;磁带,录音带;【电】绝缘胶布.【运】决胜线上的细绳;【机】传动带;【动】绦虫;〔俚〕烈酒;〔美俚〕舌头. *red* ～ (扎公文文件的)红带;官样文章,文牍主义; [Red T-] 威士忌酒商标. *breast the* ～ 赛跑得第一名. — *vt.* 用带捆扎;钉上带子;用胶带粘住;【装钉】穿线钉(书);用卷尺测量;用磁带录音;〔俚〕估量,判断(某人). *a* ～*d window* 贴上纸条的玻璃窗. *I have (got) him* ～*d.* 我看出他是个什么人了. ～ **deck** 〔美俚〕简化的磁带录音放音盘. ～**grass** 【植】苦草. ～**line,** ～ **measure** 卷尺,带尺. ～ **machine** (股票行市)自动收报机;磁带录音机. ～**recorder** 磁带录音机. ～**transport** (录音机的)磁带传送系统. ～**worm** 【动】绦虫.

ta·per [ˈteipə] *n.* ①细小的蜡烛;蜡烛心. ②〔诗〕微光;(形体、力量)逐渐缩减,逐渐缩减. ③尖塔形;锥形;锥度,斜度; ④【机】拔梢. — *a.* ①渐细的,锥形的;斜的. ②依次递减的. — *vi.* 渐细,变尖 *(away; off; down)*;渐少,递减. — *vt.* ①使渐细,使尖. ②依次递减,逐渐减少. **-ed** *a.* **-ing** *a.* **-ing·ly** *ad.*

tap·es·try [ˈtæpistri] *n.* 墙毯,挂毯;家具的绣[织]花罩毯. — *vt.* 用墙毯装饰;罩上绣[织]花罩毯.

ta·pe·tum [təˈpiːtəm] *n.* *(pl.* **-pe·ta** [-ə]*)* ①【解、动】毯〔尤指照膜;反光组织;反光色素层;纤维毯〕. ②【植】绒毡层. **-pe·tal** *a.*

tap·i·o·ca [ˌtæpiˈəukə] *n.* (用 cassava 根制成的)木薯淀粉,珍珠粉.

ta·pir [ˈteipə] *n.* 【动】貘.

tap·is [ˈtæpi(ː)] *n.*织花帷幕,挂毯,(尤指议事桌上的)桌毯. ***on [upon] the*** ～ 在审议中,在商讨中.

ta·pote·ment [təˈpəutmənt] *n.* 【医】叩抚法,轻叩按摩法.

tap·per [ˈtæpə] *n.* 轻敲者;〔方〕啄木鸟;轻击锤;(发报机的)电键;散屑器;树液采集器.

tap·pet [ˈtæpit] *n.* 【机】挺杆.

TAPPI = Technical Association of the Pulp and Paper Industry〔美〕纸浆与造纸工业技术协会.

tap·ping¹ [ˈtæpiŋ] *n.* 轻敲(声).

tap·ping² [ˈtæpiŋ] *n.* ①(开孔) 导出液体. ②【医】穿刺抽液;放腹水. ③【冶】出钢;出铁; 出渣. ④【电】抽头,分支,分流. ⑤【机】攻螺丝.

tap·ster [ˈtæpstə] *n.* 酒吧间招待员.

tapu [təˈpuː] *n.* = tabu, taboo.

tar¹ [tɑː] *n.* ①焦油;柏油,焦油沥青. ②〔美俚〕黑咖啡. —*vt.* **(-red, -ring)** 涂柏油;〔喻〕弄污. ～ *boilers [heels]* 〔美〕北卡罗来纳 (North Carolina) 州人的别名. *He was* ～*red with profiteering brush.* 他因谋取不正当的利益而声名狼藉. ***be tarred with the same brush [stick]*** 都有同样的缺点;都做着同样的坏事,一丘之貉. ～ ***and feather*** 将人浑身涂满柏油再粘上羽毛〔一种私刑〕; 严加惩罚 *(be* ～*red and featherd for what one has done* 因所作所为而受到严惩). ～**brush** 柏油刷 *(a knight of the* ～*brush* 水手). ～**macadam** 柏油碎石(路面).

tar² [tɑː] *n.* 〔口〕水手,水兵. *a Jack T-* 水手. *an old* ～ 老水手.

tar·a·did·dle [ˈtærədidl] *n.* 〔口〕谎话.

tar·an·tara [ˌtærənˈtɑːrə] *n.* 喇叭声,角笛声.

ta·ran·tass [ˌtærənˈtæs] *n.* (俄国)四轮马车.

tar·an·tel·la [ˌtærənˈtelə], **-telle** [-ˈtel] *n.* 塔兰台拉舞〔曲〕〔意大利那不勒斯 (Naples) 地区的一种轻快的民间舞(曲)〕.

tar·ant·ism [ˈtærəntizəm] *n.* 【医】塔兰图拉毒蛛病,跳舞病〔一种臆病,过去认为系受塔兰图拉毒蜘蛛所致,可以跳舞来医治〕. ★易与 chorea 混同.

Ta·ran·to [təˈræntəu] *n.* 塔兰托〔意大利的海军基地〕

ta·ran·tu·la [təˈræntjulə] *n.* *(pl.* ～*s,* **-lae** [-liː]*)* 【虫】(南欧的)多毛毒蜘蛛,塔兰图拉毒蛛.

tar·a·tan·ta·ra [ˈtærətænˈtɑːrə] *n.* 喇叭声,角笛声.

Ta·ra·wa [tɑːˈrɑːwɑː] *n.* 塔拉瓦〔吉尔伯特群岛首府〕.

ta·rax·a·cum [təˈræksəkəm] *n.* 【植】蒲公英(属);蒲公英(制剂).

tar·boosh [tɑːˈbuːʃ] *n.* 〔Ar.〕土耳其帽〔通常带有红色穗子〕.

tar·da·men·te [ˌtɑːdəˈmente] *ad.* 〔It.〕【乐】缓慢地.

tardi·grade [ˈtɑːdigreid] *a., n.* 迟钝(的);【动】缓步类(动物).

tar·di·ly [ˈtɑːdili] *ad.* 缓慢地; 迟缓地; 不愿意地; 拖拉地.

tar·di·ness [ˈtɑːdinis] *n.* 缓慢;迟缓;拖拉.

tar·do [ˈtɑːdəu] *a., ad.* 〔It.〕【乐】徐缓的[地].

tar·dy [ˈtɑːdi] *a.* ***(-di·er; -di·est)*** 缓慢的;迟延的,迟到的 *(in)*; 磨蹭的,拖拉的. *make a* ～ *appearance* 迟到. *a* ～ *reform [amendment]* 为时已晚的改革[补救]. *a* ～ *consent* 勉强的答应.

tare¹ [tɛə] *n.* ①【植】巢菜〔救荒野豌豆〕;小巢菜〔硬毛果野豌豆〕. ②稗子,莠草. ③坏影响,不良成分.

tare² [tɛə] *n.* ①(货物的)皮重. ②车身自重〔燃料等除外〕. ③【化】容器的重量;配衡体. ～ ***and tret*** 皮重估定法. — *vt.* 量皮重;【物】校准.

tar·fu(bar) [ˈtɑːfjuː(bɑː)] 〔美海俚〕= *t*hings *a*re *r*eally *f*ouled *u*p (*b*eyond *a*ll *r*ecognition) 搞得面目全非.

targe [tɑːdʒ] *n.* 〔古〕小圆盾.

tar·get [ˈtɑːgit] *n.* 靶子,标的; 目标; (嘲笑等的)对象;笑柄 *(for)*; (储蓄,贸易等的)定额,指标; 小羊的颈胸肉;【物】(X射线管中的)对阴极;【测】标杆,标板;【铁路】圆板信号机;〔古〕小圆盾. *a* ～ *area* 轰炸目标地区. *a* ～ *ship* 靶舰. *a* ～ *buster* 〔美俚〕打飞靶的人. ～ *practice* 打靶,射击演习. ***hit a*** ～ 达到定额[指标]. ***one's*** ～ ***for tonight*** 〔英军俚〕女友. ～ **card** (打靶用的)记分卡. ～**date** 预定日期. ～**language** 归宿语言 (*opp.* source language 始发语言).

Tar·gum [ˈtɑːgəm] *n.* *(pl.* ～*s;* ～*im)* 阿拉米亚 (Aramaic)语译的旧约圣经. **-ist** *n.* Targum 的译者,研究者.

Tar·heel [ˈtɑːˌhiːl] *n.* 〔美口〕北卡罗来纳州人〔因北卡罗来纳州曾称为 *Tarheel*州〕.

tar·iff [ˈtærif] *n.* ①关税(表),税率(表),税则. ②〔英〕(旅馆、铁路等的)价目表,收费表;(电话等的)计价,收费. *conventional [statutory]* ～*s* 协定[国定]税率. *preferential [retaliatory]* ～*s* 特惠[报复]税率. ～*rates* 税率,(保险等的)协定率. *a* ～ *scale* 税率表;工资等级表;运费[收费]表. — *vt.* 征收关税;定税率;定收费标准. ～ **wall** 关税壁垒.

tar·la·tan [ˈtɑːlətən], **tar·letan** [-le-] *n.* 【纺】塔拉丹〔达尔拉顿〕薄纱.

Tarmac, t- [ˈtɑːmæk] *n.* ①铺路柏油. ②〔英〕= tarmacadam.

tarn¹ [tɑːn] *n.* 【地】冰斗湖,山中的池;【鸟】= tern¹.

tarn² [tɑːn] *n.* = tern¹.

tar·nal [ˈtɑːnəl] *a., ad.* 〔美俚〕真正(的),十足(的);极度(的)〔eternal 的别字,用来加强语气〕. **-ly** *ad.*

tar·na·tion [tɑːˈneiʃən] *n.* 〔美俚〕诅咒,咒骂 (= damnation). — *int.* 〔方,俚〕该死! 讨厌! — *a.* 该死的,讨厌的. *Why are you in such a* ～ *hurry?* 你为什么这样瞎忙?

tar·nish [ˈtɑːniʃ] *vt.* ①使晦暗,使丧失光泽. ②使生锈,使变色. ③玷污,败坏(名誉等). — *vi.* 变晦暗,(丧)失(光)泽,生锈,变色. — *n.* 晦暗,锈;表面变色; 污点 **-a·ble** *a.*

ta·ro [ˈtɑːrəu] *n.* *(pl.* ～*s)* 【植】(野)芋;芋头.

tar·ot [ˈtærəuət, tæˈrəu-] *n.* 〔常用 T-〕(算命用的)有图纸牌.

tarp [tɑːp] *n.* 〔口〕 tarpaulin.

tar·pan [ˈtɑːpæn] *n.* (苏联草原地带产)草原野马.

tar·pau·lin [tɑːˈpɔːlin] *n.* ①(防水)柏油〔焦油〕帆布; 盖舱板的油布. ②(船员用的)雨衣,雨帽. ③〔古、口〕水手,船员. — *a.* 油布做的.

tar·pon [ˈtɑːpɔn] *n.* 【动】(美国南海岸及西印度群岛一带产)大海鲢.

tarra·did·dle [ˈtærədidl] *n.* = taradiddle.

tar·ra·gon [ˈtærəgən] *n.* 【植】(西伯利亚的)龙蒿,(作调味作料用的)龙蒿叶,茵陈蒿.

tar·ra·go·na [ˌtærəˈgəunə] *n.* (西班牙)塔拉贡纳甜酒.

tarred [tɑːd] *a.* 涂有柏油的. ~ *cloth* 黑油布. ~ *roofing felt* 油毛毡,沥青纸板.

tar·ri·ance [ˈtæriəns] *n.* 〔古〕①耽搁; 迟延. ②旅居,逗留.

tar·ri·er [ˈtæriə] *n.* 拖延者,逗留者.

tar·ri·ness [ˈtɑːrinis] *n.* 涂柏油,柏油(质).

Tar·ring [ˈtæriŋ] *n.* 塔灵〔姓氏〕.

tar·ry[1] [ˈtæri] *vi.* ①逗留,暂住,旅居. ②〔美口〕迟延,耽搁,踌躇,犹豫; 等待. ~ *a few day in Shanghai* 在上海逗留几天. ~ *on the way* 在路上耽搁. ~ *for sb.* 等待某人. *Why do you* ~ *so long?* 你干什么耽搁这么久? — *vt.* 〔古〕等待. ~ *a reply* 等待答复. — *n.* 〔美〕逗留. *during his* ~ 在他逗留期间.

tarry[2] [ˈtɑːri] *a.* 柏油(质)的; 涂柏油的; 给柏油弄脏的.

tar·sal [ˈtɑːsəl] *a.* 【解】跗骨的,跗节的; 睑板的. — *n.* 跗骨(关节).

tar·si·a [ˈtɑːsiə] *n.* (15 世纪意大利流行的)嵌木制品.

tar·si·er [ˈtɑːsiə] *n.* 【动】(东印度)眼镜猴.

tar·so·met·a·tar·sus [ˌtɑːsəuˌmetəˈtɑːsəs] *n.* 【动】跗蹠骨.

Tar·sus [ˈtɑːsəs] *n.* 塔瑟斯〔古城名,在今土耳其南部,为圣保罗之故乡〕.

tar·sus [ˈtɑːsəs] *n.* (*pl.* *-si* [-sai]) 【解】跗骨; 睑板; 鸟胫骨; (昆虫的)跗节; 蹠节.

tart[1] [tɑːt] *a.* ①酸的,辛辣的. ②尖酸刻薄的; 严厉的. *a* ~ *flavour* 酸味. *a* ~ *reply to our letter* 对我们函件尖刻的答复. **-ly** *ad.* **-ness** *n.*

tart [tɑːt] *n.* ①〔英〕(果)馅饼;〔美〕上有牛奶蛋糊或果酱的馅饼. ②(原系表示亲爱的用词,现在通常用指(轻佻的)少女,女人; 妓女. ~ **up** *vi.* 〔主英俚〕打扮得花哨〔尤指用价廉的服饰〕.

tar·tan[1] [ˈtɑːtən] *n.* ①格子花呢(服). ②(穿格子花呢衣服的)苏格兰高地人〔苏格兰高地联队的士兵〕. — *a.* 格子花呢的.

tartan[2] [ˈtɑːtən] *n.* (航行于地中海沿岸的)独桅三角帆船.

Tar·tar [ˈtɑːtə] *n.* ①鞑靼人,鞑靼语; 塔塔尔族,塔塔尔人. ②〔常作 t-〕剽悍的人,强暴的人,难对付的人. ③悍妇. — *a.* 鞑靼(人)的. *catch a* ~ 碰到劲敌; 骑虎难下. *a young* ~ 强横的孩子.

tar·tar(e) [ˈtɑːtə] *n.* ①【化】酒石; 酒石酸氢钾. ②【医】牙垢; 牙石. *cream of* ~ 酒石(英). ~ *emetic* 催吐酒石,酒石酸氧锑钾. ~ *sauce* (也作 tartare sauce) 酸泡菜调味酱〔由蛋黄酱、碎酸泡菜、油橄榄、香葱搅和制成,食海味时用〕.

Tar·tar·e·an [tɑːˈtɛəriən] *a.* 地狱(般)的.

Tar·tar·i·an [tɑːˈteriən] *a.* 鞑靼的,鞑靼人的.

tar·tar·ic [tɑːˈtærik] *a.* 酒石(酸)的,含酒石(酸)的. ~ *acid* 酒石酸.

tar·tar·ize [ˈtɑːtəraiz] *vt.* 酒石化; 用酒石处理. **-i·za·tion** *n.*

tar·tar·ous [ˈtɑːtərəs] *a.* 酒石的,酒石性的,象酒石的,含酒石的.

Tar·ta·rus [ˈtɑːtərəs] *n.* ①【希神】大恶人死后受罪罚之处的极深层地狱. ②冥府,地狱.

Tar·ta·ry [ˈtɑːtəri] *n.* 鞑靼(地方).

tart·let [ˈtɑːtlit] *n.* 小(果)馅饼.

tar·trate [ˈtɑːtreit] *n.* 【化】酒石酸盐. ~**d** 从酒石中提取的,含酒石(酸盐)的.

Tar·tuffe [tɑːˈtuf] *n.* ①答尔丢夫〔法国十七世纪喜剧作家莫里哀所作同名喜剧的主人公〕. ②〔t-〕伪君子,伪善人,假信徒.

tas·e·om·e·ter [ˌtæsiˈɔmitə] *n.* 应力计.

Tash·kent [tæʃˈkent] *n.* 塔什干〔苏联城市〕.

ta·sim·e·ter [təˈsimitə] *n.* 微压计. **-e·try** *n.* 微压测定. **-met·ric** *a.*

task [tɑːsk] *n.* ①(派定的)工作,任务,功课. ②艰苦的工作,苦差使. ③〔废〕租税,税款. *set (sb.) a* ~ 派(某人)一个任务. *be at one's* ~ 在做着工作. *It's quite a task to figure out 10 problems in an hour.* 一小时内算出十道习题可是个艰苦的工作. ***bring [call, take] sb. to*** ~ *(for doing sth.)* (为…)责备(某人). ***take a*** ~ ***upon oneself*** 接受任务. — *vt.* ①派给工作. ②虐待,使作苦工. ③〔废〕课税. ~ *one's energies* 尽全力. ~ **force** 【军】特混(特遣)部队或舰队;〔转义〕专门工作组. ~ **master** (*fem.* **-mistress**) 工头; 监工; 虐待者,严厉的主人. ~ **wages** 包工工资. ~ **work** 派定的工作,包工; 吃重的工作.

Tas·man [ˈtæzmən] 塔斯曼〔1602? —1959, 荷兰航海家,大洋洲的塔斯马尼亚岛及新西兰的发现者〕.

Tas·ma·nia [tæzˈmeinjə] *n.* 〔略 Tasm.〕(大洋洲东南的)塔斯马尼亚岛. **Tas·ma·nian** [tæzˈmeinjən] *a.*, *n.* (大洋洲东南)塔斯马尼亚的(人). ~ **devil** 袋熊. ~ **wolf** 袋狼.

Tass, TASS [tæs] = 〔Russ.〕 *Telegrafnoye Agenstvo Sobyetskovo Soyuza* 〔苏联〕塔斯社 (= Telegraph Agency of the Soviet Union).

tass [tɑːs, tæs] *n.* 〔Scot.〕①小酒杯或有足无柄的小杯. ②一杯的量,一口的量.

tasse [tæs] *n.* 盔甲的腿甲,腿罩.

tasse [təs] *n.* 〔F.〕杯子.

tas·sel[1] [ˈtæsl] *n.* ①缨,绶,流苏. ②垂花,穗状花序. ③丝带书签. ④〔美〕玉米的穗状雄花. ⑤【建】承梁木. — *vt.* (〔英〕 ***-ll-***) ①装上缨绶〔流苏〕. ②使抽穗; (为了使作物茁长)摘去穗状雄花. — *vi.* 抽穗,(玉米)长穗须. *a golden-~ed silk banner* 金穗锦旗.

tas·sel[2] [ˈtæsl] *n.* 〔废〕 = tercel.

tast·a·ble [ˈteistəbl] *a.* = tasteable 可尝的; 可口的,滋味好的.

taste [teist] *vt.* ①尝,尝味,品(尝)味道; 吃出…的味道; 〔通例用于否定句〕饮食,吃. ②经验,享受; 体会(双关语等); 〔古〕爱好. — *vi.* ①尝味,辨味. ②有…的味道,有…的滋味 (*of*); 有…的气味 (*of*). ③〔古〕吃一口,喝一口; 〔古〕尝,经验 (*of*). ~ *tea* 品茶. *The wounded soldier has not ~d food for two days.* 这伤员两天来什么也没吃. *He has ~d the sweets and bitters of life.* 他尝遍了人生的酸甜苦辣. *It ~s sour* 这东西有酸味. *It ~s of mint.* 这东西有薄荷味. *Good medicine ~s bitter to the mouth.* 良药苦口. *The valiant never ~s of death but once.* 勇士舍生取义只经历一次死的痛苦. — *n.* ①滋味; 味觉. ②尝味; (贫穷等的)滋味,经验. ③一口; 一点点,些微. ④爱好,兴趣; 审美力,鉴别力,欣赏力. ⑤风味; 风格. *It is bitter to the* ~. 这个味苦. *A cold dulls sb.'s* ~. 伤风使某人吃东西没味道〔使失去辨别滋味的能力〕. *Tastes differ [vary].* 口味人各不同. *English* ~ 英国人的爱好〔口味〕. ***a bad*** ~ ***in the mouth*** 令人不快的余味; 坏印象. ***a matter of*** ~ 爱好〔口味〕问题. ***be in bad*** ~ 很俗气,样子不好,不雅致. ***be in good [excellent, admirable]*** ~ 很有风味,很雅致. ***be out of*** ~ 没有审美力,粗俗; 没眼光. ***give (sb.) a*** ~ ***of*** 给尝,使经验. ***have a (small)*** ~ ***of*** 尝一口…看看. ***have a*** ~ ***for*** 爱好; 对…具有兴趣. ***man of*** ~ 有欣赏力的人. ***to sb.'s*** ~ 合乎某人的口味. ***to*** ~ 酌量,…到适合口味

(add pepper to ~*). to the king's [queen's]* ~ 很好，毫无问题，很有水平. ~ **bud**【生理】味蕾. ~**maker** 时髦风尚的带头人.

taste·ful [ˈteistf*u*l] *a.* ①有鉴赏力的，有欣赏力的. ②雅致大方的. ③美观的. ④美味的. **-ly** *ad.* **-ness** *n.*

taste·less [ˈteistlis] *a.* ①没有味道的，不好吃的. ②没有趣味的，乏味的. ③不雅致的，粗俗的，煞风景的；无鉴别力[欣赏力]的. ~*s beer* 淡而无味的啤酒. *a* ~ *melodrama* 一出索然无味的情节剧. *a set of* ~ *furniture* 一套俗气的家具.

tast·er [ˈteistə] *n.* ①以尝味来鉴定质量为职业的试味员. ②【史】封建帝王贵族为防下毒而设的试食员. ③尝味器〔长柄匙，小杯等〕. ④【化】吸移管，吸量管，吸管. ⑤【动】触须，触肢. ⑥(出版社的)审稿员. ⑦〔口〕碟装冰淇淋. *a wine* ~ 品酒人.

tast·y [ˈteisti] *a.* *(-i·er; -i·est)* ①〔口〕美味的，可口的，好吃的. ②〔口〕有风味的，雅致的，大方的(服装等). *a* ~ *hors d'œuvre* 美味的餐前小吃. **-i·ly** *ad.* **-i·ness** *n.*

tat[1] [tæt] *n.* ①轻打. ②〔口〕(只有 4，5，6 三数的)骰子. *tit for* ~ 一报还一报地，针锋相对地.

tat[2] [tæt] *vi., vt.* *(tatted, tat·ting)* 梭织；用梭织法编织.

tat[3] [tɑːt] *n.* 粗麻布.

tat[4] [tɑːt] *n.* (印度英语)矮种马，小马.

ta-ta [ˈtæˈtɑː] *int.* 〔口、儿〕再会；*n.* 〔美俚〕机关枪.

ta·ta·mi [təˈtɑːmi] *n.* *(pl. -mi, -mis)* 〔Jap.〕(日本人铺在房屋地板上的)草垫，草席.

Ta·tar [ˈtɑːtə] *n., a.* = Tartar. **Ta·tari·an, Ta·taric** *a.*

Ta·ta·ry [ˈtɑːtəri] = Tartary.

Tate [teit] *n.* 泰特〔姓氏〕.

Tate Gal·ler·y [ˈteitˈgæləri] 泰特绘画陈列馆〔英国美术馆的俗称，得名于最初捐赠所藏美术品的泰特〕.

ta·ter [ˈteitə] *n.* 〔口〕= potato 土豆.

Ta·tia·na [ˌtætiˈɑːnə] *n.* 塔蒂亚娜〔女子名〕.

ta·tou·(ay) [ˈtɑːtuː(-ai)] *n.*【动】犰狳 = armadillo.

tat·ter[1] [ˈtætə] *n.* 〔常 *pl.*〕破布条，碎布，碎纸片，破衣服. *in (rags and)* ~*s* 破烂，褴褛. *tear to* ~*s* 扯得稀烂，扯碎；驳得体无完肤，痛驳. — *vt.* 扯碎，撕碎.

tatter[2] [ˈtætə] *n.* 梭编者.

tat·ter·de·ma·lion [ˌtætədəˈmeiljən] *n.* 衣服褴褛的人.

tat·tered [ˈtætəd] *a.* (衣服等)破碎的，破烂的；衣服褴褛的.

tat·ter·sall [ˈtætəˌsɔːl] *n.* 浅色衬底上的深色方格图案. — *a.* 有浅色衬纸上的深色方格图案的.

Tat·ter·sall's [ˈtætəsɔːlz] *n.* (伦敦)塔特赛尔马市场. *He knows his* ~ *better than his Greek Testament.* 〔英〕他不爱功课专爱赛马.

tat·ter·y [ˈtætəri] *a.* (衣服等)破烂的；褴褛的.

tat·ting [ˈtætiŋ] *n.* ①梭编法. ②用梭编法编的花边.

tat·tle [ˈtætl] *n.* ①闲谈，空话. ②饶舌. ③谈论别人的隐私. *a* ~ *basket* = ~ *box*〔美〕搬弄是非的人；传闻. — *vi., vt.* ①闲谈，空谈. ②饶舌. ③乱讲(别人的私事等) *(about)* 泄露秘密. ~ *about the squabbles of the family next door* 乱讲隔壁那户人家的口角. — *a.* 饶舌的，乱搬弄是非的. ~**tale** 乱讲别人私事的人，乱搬弄是非的人.

tat·tler [ˈtætlə] *n.* ①爱说闲话的人. ②喜欢谈论别人隐私的人. ③【鸟】鹬类.

tat·too[1] [təˈtuː, tæˈt-] *n.* *(pl. ~s)* ①【军】归营信号(号声或鼓声. ②门规. ③冬冬连敲声. ④〔英〕(配有军乐作为娱乐的)归营行军. *beat the devil's* ~(焦躁或沉思等时候)用手指得得得地敲桌子，脚跟着地脚尖敲出嗒嗒声. — *vi.* ①吹归营号. ②得得地敲.

tat·too[2] [təˈtuː] *n., vt.* 文身，刺花，黥墨. **-er** 文身师，黥墨师. **-ist** 文身的人.

tat·too·ing [tæˈtuːiŋ] *n.* ①刺字，文身. ②皮肤所刺的花纹.

tat·ty[1] [ˈtæti] *n.* (印度用于阻挡户外热气或防臭的)湿香帘.

tat·ty[2] [ˈtæti] *a.* 〔英口〕①衣衫褴褛的，破旧的，不整洁的. ②低劣的. ③不调合的. **-ti·ly** *ad.* **-i·ness** *n.*

Ta·tum [ˈteitəm] *n.* 泰特姆〔姓氏〕.

tau [tɔː, tau] *n.* ①希腊字母第十九字〔T. τ 相当于拉丁字母的 t〕. ②T 字形. ③T 字形物. ~ *cross* T 字形十字架.

Tauch·nitz [ˈtauknits] *n.* 陶赫尼次版〔德国 Tauchnitz 书店翻印的廉价本英语书籍〕.

taught [tɔːt] teach 的过去式及过去分词.

taunt[1] [tɔːnt] *n.* ①辱骂，奚落，嘲弄. ②反激. ③嘲弄的对象，笑柄. ~ *sb. with his conduct* 责骂某人的行为. *endure the* ~*s of one's classmates* 忍受同班学生的嘲弄. — *vt.* ①辱骂，嘲弄. ~ *Little Tom with being a newcomer* 嘲弄小汤姆是个新手. ②用嘲笑刺激. **-er** *n.* **-ing·ly** *ad.*

taunt[2] [tɔːnt] *a.*【海】很高的(桅等). — *ad.* 扯满风帆.

taupe [təup] *n.* 灰褐色.

tau·rine [ˈtɔːr(ː)n, -rain] *a.* ①象公牛的. ②牛类的. ③【天】金牛座的. — *n.*【化】牛磺酸，氨基乙磺酸，牛胆碱.

tau·ro·cho·lic acid [ˌtɔːrəˈkəulik]【化】牛磺胆酸.

tau·rom·a·chy [tɔːˈrɔməki] *n.* 斗牛戏.

Tau·rus [ˈtɔːrəs] *n.*【天】金牛座；金牛宫.

Taus·sig [ˈtausig] *n.* 陶西格〔姓氏〕.

taut [tɔːt] *a.* ①【海】(绳子等)拉紧的，绷紧的. ②(筋肉、神经)紧张的. ③(服装、器具等)整齐的，整洁的；秩序井然的. ④纪律严明的，严格的，严峻的. *a* ~ *hand*【海】严格的军官. *a* ~ *helm* 船逆风开驶时的舵. **-ly** *ad.* **-ness** *n.*

taut·en [ˈtɔːtn] *vt., vi.* 拉紧，绷紧.

tauto- *comb. f.* 相同：*tauto*logical.

tau·to·chrone [ˈtɔːtəkrəun] *n.*【物】等时降落轨迹.

tau·to·chro·nism [tɔːˈtɔkrənizəm] *n.*【物】等时性.

tau·tog [tɔːˈtɔg] *n.*【动】(美国大西洋岸的)蠓隆头鱼 *(Tautogaonitis)*.

tau·to·log·i·c(al) [ˌtɔːtəˈlɔdʒik(əl)] *a.* ①同义反复的，重言式的，类语叠用的. ②重复的，赘述的. **-ly** *ad.*

tau·tol·o·gism [tɔːˈtɔlədʒizm] *n.* 重言式，同义反复，赘述.

tau·tol·o·gist [tɔːˈtɔlədʒist] *n.* 爱叠用类语的人；说话罗唆的人.

tau·tol·o·gize [tɔːˈtɔlədʒaiz] *vi.* 叠用类语，同义反复.

tau·tol·o·gous [tɔːˈtɔləgəs] *a.* ① = tautological. ②分解的，分析的. **-ly** *ad.*

tau·tol·o·gy [tɔːˈtɔlədʒi] *n.* ①重言(式)，同义反复，类语叠用〔如：in sorrowful grief〕. ②重复，赘述.

tau·to·mer [ˈtɔːtəmə] *n.*【化】互变(异构)体.

tau·tom·eri·sm [tɔːˈtɔmərizəm] *n.*【化】互变(异构)现象[体].

tau·to·nym [ˈtɔːtəˌnim] *n.*【生】重名；属种同名. **-ic** *a.* [-ˈtɔnimik] **-y** [-ˈtɔnimi] *n.*

tau·toph·o·ny [tɔːˈtɔfəni] *n.* 同音反复.

tav [tɑːf, tɔːv] *n.* 希伯来语第二十三个字母 (= taw).

tav·ern [ˈtævə(ː)n] *n.* ①酒馆，酒店. ②小旅馆，客栈. **-er** 酒店主.

taw[1] [tɔː] *vt.* ①(不用单宁而用明矾和盐的溶液)鞣制(生皮)，硝(皮). ②〔方〕鞭打.

taw[2] [tɔː] *n.* ①弹石游戏. ②弹石. ③弹石游戏的基线. *come [bring] to* ~【运】(使)站在起步线上，(使到)预定的位置.

taw·dry [ˈtɔːdri] *a.* *(-dri·er; -dri·est)* 价廉而花哨的，俗气的. ~ *clothing* 价廉而花哨俗气的衣服. — *n.* 价廉而花哨的东西. **-i·ly** *ad.* **-i·ness** *n.*

taw·ny [ˈtɔːni] *n., a.* 黄褐色(的)，茶色(的).

taws(e) [tɔːz] *n.* 〔*sing., pl.*〕〔Scot.〕(抽打纺锤使旋转的，打孩子用的)细小皮鞭. — *vt.* 鞭打.

tax [tæks] *n.* ①税，租税，租款 *(on; upon)*. ②〔美〕会费.

③负担. ④*(pl. -es)*〔英口〕收税官. *an additional* ~ 附加税. *a business* ~ 营业税. *a housing and land* ~ 房地产税. *an income* ~ 所得税. *an import (export)* ~ 进(出)口税. *a poll (capitation)* ~ 人头税. *free of* ~ 免税. ~*-free imports* 免税进口货. ~ *in kind* 用实物缴纳的税. *a heavy* ~ *upon one's health* 有害健康的繁重负担. — *vt.* ①对…抽税,征税. ②使负重担,虐待;绞(脑汁);竭(力等). ③责备,谴责,非难. ④〔美〕讨(价);要人支付. ⑤【法】评定(损失赔偿金, 诉讼费等). ~ *one's ingenuity* 用尽心机. ~ *sb. with a fault* 责备某人的过失. *How much did they* ~ *you for that hat?* 〔美〕那顶帽子他们要你多少钱? ~ **bearer** 纳税人. ~ **[~ed] cart** 〔英〕(免税的)农[商]用二轮单马运货车. ~ **collector** 〔古〕, ~**-gatherer** 收税官. ~**-deductible** *a.* 计算所得税时可扣除的. ~ **duplicate** ①不动产估税证书. ②(按估税证书开票的)核税根据单. ~ **dodger** 偷税人. ~**-exempt** *a.* 免税的. ~ **farmer** 包税人. ~**-free** *a.* 免税的,无税的; 上过税的. ~**-payer** 纳税人. ~ **stamp** 纳税印花. ~ **title**【法】〔美〕(购买公开拍卖的不动产的不纳税的)买主所有权.

tax·a [ˈtæksə] *n.* taxon 的复数.

tax·a·ble [ˈtæksəbl] *a.* ①应征税的,有税的. ②【法】当然可要求的. **-ness** *n.* **-bil·i·ty** [ˌtæksəˈbiliti] *n.* **-bly** *ad.*

tax·a·tion [tækˈseiʃən] *n.* ①征税,抽税. ②税制. ③税额(款). ④税收(额). ⑤清算诉讼费用. *a* ~ *bureau [office]* 税务局[署]. *progressive* ~ 累进税率. ***be subject to*** ~ 应纳税. ***be exempt from*** ~ 免税.

tax·eme [ˈtæksi:m] *n.*【语言】语法元素; 语法元素分类标志. **-e·mic** [tækˈsi:mik] *a.*

tax·i [ˈtæksi] *n.* ①出租汽车 (= ~-cab). ② = taximeter. ③ = taxiplane. — *vi.* ***(~'d, ~ed; tax·i·ing, tax·y·ing)*** ①〔口〕搭乘出租汽车. ②【空】滑行. —*vt.* ①用出租汽车接送. ②使(飞机)滑行. ~**cab** = taxi. ~**-coach**〔罕〕大型出租汽车. ~ **dancer**舞女. ~**-flying**【空】滑走飞行. ~**meter** (乘出租汽车等的)车费计算表, 计程器; ~**plane** 出租飞机. **-man** 出租汽车司机. ~ **rank (~ stand)** 出租汽车站[停车处]. ~**-way**【空】滑行道.

tax·i·der·mal, tax·i·der·mic [ˌtæksiˈdə:məl, -mik] *a.* 动物标本剥制(术)的.

tax·i·der·mist [ˈtæksidə:mist] *n.* (动物标本) 剥制师.

tax·i·der·my [ˈtæksidə:mi] *n.* (动物标本)剥制术.

tax·ing [ˈtæksiŋ] *a.* 繁重的,费力的,使疲劳的.

tax·is[1] [ˈtæksis] *n.* ①【语法】排列,次序. 【医】②(脱肠等的)整复(术). ③【动】分类(法). ④【生】移性, 趋(向)性. ⑤〔古希腊〕(军队的)队,分队.

tax·is[2] [ˈtæksis] *n.* taxi 的复数.

-taxis *comb. f.* 排列: parataxis.

tax·ite [ˈtækˌsait] *n.*【地】斑杂岩. **-it·ic** [-ˈsitik] *a.*

tax·ol·o·gy [tækˈsɔlədʒi] = taxonomy.

tax·on [ˈtæksɔn] *n.* *(pl. tax·a* [-sə]*)* 分类单位[类别, 项目].

tax·o·nom·ic(al) [ˌtæksəˈnɔmik(əl)] *a.* 分类学的, 分类的.

tax·on·o·mist [tækˈsɔnəmist] *n.* 分类学者.

tax·on·o·my [tækˈsɔnəmi] *n.* ①(尤指动植物) 分类. ②分类学,分类法.

tax·us [ˈtæksəs] *n.* *(pl. tax·us)*【植】紫杉属*(Taxus)*植物.

tax·y·ing [ˈtæksiiŋ] taxi 的现在分词. *The airliner was* ~ *for a takeoff.* 班机正在滑行准备起飞.

Tay·lor [ˈteilə] *n.* 泰勒〔姓氏〕.

TAZARA = Tanzania-Zambia Railway 坦赞铁路.

taz·za [ˈtɑ:tsə] *n.* 浅杯,扁花瓶〔常带垫座,作装饰用〕.

TB, T.B. = ①torpedo boat 鱼雷(快)艇. ②tubercle bacillus 结核杆菌. ③tuberculosis 肺结核.

T/B = trial balance (会计)试算表.

Tb =【化】terbium.

T/BA = Tables of Basic Allowance【军】基准津贴表.

T-bar [ˈti:ˌbɑ:] *n.* T 形滑杆〔挂在用电来带动的很长的钢缆上,拉两个滑雪者上山〕.

TBD, T.B.D. = torpedo-boat destroyer 舰队, 驱逐舰〔旧称〕.

Tbi·li·si [ˈtpilisi] *n.* 第比利斯〔苏联城市〕.

TBM = tactical ballistic missile 战术弹道导弹.

T-bone steak [ˈti:bəun] 带 T 形骨的腰部嫩肉片.

tbs., tbsp. = tablespoon; tablespoonful.

TC = Trusteeship Council (UN) (联合国)托管理事会.

T.C. = ①Tank Corps 〔英〕坦克部队. ②temporary constable 临时警察. ③Town Councillor〔英〕镇议员.

Tc【化】= (technetium).

TCA = Trans-Canada Airlines 全加拿大航空公司.

TCBM = transcontinental ballistic missile 洲际弹道导弹.

T.C.D. = Trinity College, Dublin 〔爱〕都伯林圣三一学院.

tchick [tʃik] *n.* 乞!〔赶马的声音〕. — *vi.* (赶马时)发乞乞声.

TD = ①tank destroyer 自行防坦克炮. ② = tractor-drawn 牵引车牵引.

T.D. = ① Telegraph Department 电报局[处]. ②〔L.〕*ter die* (= three times a day)【处方】每日三次. ③ Territorial Decoration. 〔英〕本土军服役勋章.

T.D.N., t.d.n. = total digestible nutrients 完全可以消化的养分.

T.E. = Topographical Engineer 测绘工程师.

Te =【化】tellurium.

tea [ti:] *n.* ①茶; 茶叶. ②茶树. ③茶水; 茶汤. ④〔英〕午后茶点,午后小吃; 茶会. ⑤〔美俚〕大麻(叶),大麻香烟. *black* ~ 红茶. *green* ~ 绿茶. *brick [tile]* ~ 砖茶. *strong [weak]* ~ 浓[淡]茶. *cold* ~ 冷茶;〔口〕酒. *the first infusion (of)* ~ 刚泡出的茶, 头遍茶. *early* ~ 早茶. *afternoon* ~ = *five o'clock* ~ 午后茶点. *high* ~ = *meat* ~ 茶点便餐〔比一般午后茶点晚一点有肉食冷盆的正式茶点〕. ***come [go] to*** ~ ***with*** 和…吃茶点去. ***make***~ 泡茶. ***take*** ~ ***with sb.*** 与某人打交道; 与某人发生冲突. — *vi.* 吃午后茶点; 拿出午后茶点. *We* ~ *at 4.* 我们在四点钟吃茶点. — *vt.* ~ *a guest* 请客人喝茶. ~ **bag** 袋装茶叶〔沏茶时连袋泡在水里〕. ~ **ball** 滤茶器. ~**-berry**【植】平铺白珠树(果实),冬青油, 冬绿油. ~ **biscuit** 茶点. ~ **board** 茶盘. ~ **boat**〔美俚〕一杯茶. ~ **bread** (吃茶点时的)软面包. ~ **caddy** 茶叶罐. ~ **cake** 〔英〕午后吃茶时的点心. ~ **canister**〔美俚〕头. ~**cart** = ~ **wag(g)on.** ~ **chest** 茶叶箱. ~ **cloth** *(pl.* ~**-cloths** 吃茶点用的小台布; (茶器等的)擦布. ~ **cosy** 茶壶保温罩. ~ **cult (ceremony)** 日本的茶道, 品茗会. ~ **cup** 茶杯,一茶杯的量 (*storm in a cup* 茶杯里的风波; 因小事而争吵). ~ **cupful** 一茶杯的量. ~**-dance** 有茶点的傍晚舞会. ~ **dealer** 茶商. ~ **fight** 〔口〕= *tea party*. ~ **garden** 茶园, 茶圃, 有茶室的花园. ~ **gossip** 茶话. ~ **gown** (女人的)茶会服, 访问服. ~ **grounds** 茶渣. ~ **grove** 茶山. ~ **house** (中国、日本等的)茶馆, 茶室. ~ **jar** 茶叶瓶, 茶叶缸. ~ **kettle** 开水壶. ~ **leaf** 茶叶, *(pl.)* 茶渣. ~ **of heaven** 甜茶. ~ **oil** 茶子油. ~ **party** 茶会, 茶话会. ~ **plant** 茶树. ~ **plantation** 茶园. ~ **pot** 茶壶. ~ **poy** (三脚)茶几. ~ **room** 茶馆. ~ **rose** 香水月季. ~ **service** = ~ **set** 一套茶具. ~ **shop** 茶馆,〔英〕便餐馆. ~ **spoon** 茶匙. ~ **stall** 茶摊, 茶馆. ~ **stirrer** 搅茶器. ~ **table** 茶桌. ~**-table** *a.* 象在茶桌前喝茶似的. ~ **taster** (鉴别茶叶质量的)品茶员. ~**-things** = tea set. ~ **time** 喝茶(吃茶点)的时候. ~ **tray** 茶盘. ~ **tree** 茶树. ~ **urn** 开水壶. ~ **wag(g)on** (有轮的)茶具台.

teach [ti:tʃ] ***(taught*** **[tɔ:t]*)*** *vt.* ①(向某人)教、讲授(某课程);使某人学会做某事 *(to do sth.)*. ②(以某事或某经验教训)教育、教导某人 *(that)*. ③〔口〕(如对方做某事则予以)教训;告诫某人别做某事. ④使…学习;做…的教师. ~ *a child to read* 教孩子识字〔阅读〕. ~ *physics to the students* 教学生物理. *I taught him how to swim.* 我曾教他游泳. *T- your granny to suck eggs!* = *T- a dog to bark!* 〔谚〕班门弄斧. *This will ~ you to speak the truth.* 再撒谎就是这样〔责骂孩子等说谎〕. *The practice of science ~es us that knowledge is power.* 科学的实践使我们认识到知识就是力量. ~ *oneself* 自学. ~ *school* 当教员. — *vi.* ①(进行)教书、教学、讲授(活动). ②(学科)被讲授;(课程)教起来(如何如何). *She ~es at a primary school.* 她在小学教书. *I've been ~ing four periods this morning.* 今天上午我已教了四节课. *a course that ~es easily* 一门容易教的课. *I will ~ you to meddle in my affairs.* 你再管我的事我就要教训你了.

teach·a·ble [ˈti:tʃəbl] *a.* ①可教的;受教的,肯听教训(学)的,驯顺的. ②适合教学的,便于讲授的.

teach·er [ˈti:tʃə] *n.* ①教师,教员,老师,先生. ②【空】教练机. *a bomb* ~ 轰炸预习机. ***be one's own*** ~ 自学. *a ~ of Mathematics in a secondary school* 中学的数学教员. *a lady [woman] teacher* 女教师. *a ~'s college* 师范学院. ~ ***by negative example*** 反面教员.

teach·er·age [ˈti:tʃəridʒ] *n.* 〔美西部〕教员住宅(区).

teach-in [ˈti:tʃˌin] *n.* (大学师生对引起争论的问题进行讨论或辩论的)宣讲会〔尤指为反对某一政策而举办的宣讲会〕.

teach·ing [ˈti:tʃiŋ] *n.* ①教学,讲授. ②〔常 *pl.*〕教导,教训,教义,学说. *methods of* ~ 教学方法. *the ~ of Lenin on democratic centralism* 列宁关于民主集中制的教导. ~ **fellow** 兼任教职的研究生. ~ **machine** (装有电子计算机自动配合学生学习进度的)电子教学机.

Teague [ti:g] *n.* 〔蔑〕爱尔兰人〔因爱尔兰人爱用 Tadhg [te:g, ti:g, taig] 这个字做名字〕.

teak [ti:k] *n.* 【植】柚树(木) (= ~-wood).

teal [ti:l] *n. (pl.* ~*s,* 〔集合词〕~*)* 【鸟】短颈野鸭;小凫;水鸭. *mandarin* ~ 鸳鸯. ~ *blue* 青凫.

team [ti:m] *n.* ①(运动比赛的)队,团;工作队,工作组,作业班;一班〔一组〕工人. ②(一起拖车子的)一队牲口,联畜,联兽. ③(野鸭等的)群;同胎仔,一窝的雏. ④牲口和所拉的车. *a basket-ball* ~ 篮球队. *a ~ race* 团体赛跑. *a ~ event* 团体赛. *a production* ~ 生产队. *an inspection* ~ 视察小组. — *vi.* 协同工作;赶联畜;驾驶卡车. — *vt.* 把(牛马等)联套在车上;用联畜运;〔美〕(将工作)交给承包人;使转包工作. ~ ***up with*** 〔美〕和…协作. ~ **mate** 同队队员. ~ **teaching** 小组教学〔若干教师分任专题,共同完成一项教学任务〕. ~**wise** *ad.* 象联畜一样成组〔成一行〕. ~**work** 合作,协同工作.

team·ster [ˈti:mstə] *n.* ①〔美〕联畜驾驭者. ②联畜中的一匹〔一只〕. ③〔美〕卡车司机.

tear[1] [tiə] *n.* ①泪. ②滴,水珠,露珠,玻璃珠,树脂珠(等). ③〔*pl.*〕〔美俚〕珍珠. ~*s of Eos* 朝露. ~*s of joy* 快乐的眼泪. ~*s of strong wine* 烈酒气化而结在杯边上的酒珠. *Job's ~s* 薏苡. ***draw ~s from*** 引出眼泪. ***drop a ~ over*** 哀悼. ***in ~s*** 流着泪,含泪,哭着. ***laugh away one's ~s*** 笑着把眼泪掩饰过去. ***laugh till the ~s come*** 笑到淌眼泪. ***move sb. to ~s*** 使感动得流泪 (*He is easily moved to ~s.* 他爱淌眼泪). ***shed ~s*** 流泪. ***squeeze out a ~*** 勉强淌一点眼泪. ***with ~s*** 哭着,含泪 (*Her eyes swim with ~s.* 她眼泪汪汪). ***without ~s*** 轻松地;不必(因受苦而)流泪. ~ **bomb** 催泪弹. ~ **drop** ①*n.* 泪(珠). ②*a.* 泪珠状的. ~ **duct** 泪腺〔管〕. ~ **gas** *n., vt.* (用)催泪毒气(袭击). ~ **jerker** 〔美俚〕使人流泪的戏剧〔电影〕. ~ **shell** = ~ bomb. ~ **smoke** 催泪毒气. ~**-stained** *a.* 有泪痕的.

tear[2] [tɛə] *vt.* ***(tore*** **[tɔ:]*;*** ***torn*** **[tɔ:n]*)*** ①撕,撕开,撕裂 *(in two; to pieces; apart; asunder)*. ②扯(头发等);刺破,刺伤,划破,抓破(皮肤等). ③抢去,夺去,扯掉 *(away; down; from; off; out; up)*. ④使分裂(国家等). ⑤使烦恼〔激动〕,使精神不安. ~ *down a poster* 扯下一张招贴画. *A nail tore a hole in her overcoat.* 钉子把她的大衣戳了个洞. ~ *a child from sb.'s arms* 把某人抱着的孩子夺过去. ~ *a leaf from a calendar* 从日历牌上撕下一页. ~ *up a tree by the root* 把一棵树连根拔起. ~ *off several pages* 扯掉好几页. *The club is torn by factions.* 俱乐部因派系而分裂. *Her heart is born by conflicting emotions.* 矛盾的感情使她心胸极为烦闷. ~*'em out of their chairs* 〔美剧〕引起观众热烈喝采. — *vi.* 撕,扯 *(at)*;裂开,拉破;猛冲,飞跑,狂奔 *(about; along)*. *This brown paper ~s easily.* 这牛皮纸一撕就破. *The cover of the parcel won't ~.* 这包裹的封皮撕不开. ~ *at the cover of a postal parcel* 扯邮包的封皮. *children ~ing about in the courtyard* 在院子里飞跑的孩子. ~ *up the staircase two steps at a time* 两级一步地飞跑奔上楼梯. ***be torn with grief*** 悲伤得要死. ***feel torn between two choices*** 左右为难. ~ ***away*** 撕掉;扯开;飞跑. ~ ***down*** 扯下;拆毁;猛冲 (~ *down a hill* 飞跑下山). ~ ***in pieces*** 撕得粉碎. ~ ***it*** 〔口〕打破计划〔希望等〕(*That's torn it.* 那就糟了,那就完蛋了). ~ ***into*** 跑进. ~ ***off*** 扯掉,扯开;飞跑;〔美俚〕急急忙忙做成某事(*He tore ~ off some sleep.* 他匆匆忙忙睡一忽). ~ ***oneself away from*** 忍痛离开…而去,和…忍痛分离;挣开,甩开(讨厌的人). ~ ***one's hair*** (因悲哀或发怒)扯头发. ~ ***one's way*** 猛进. ~ ***out*** 撕下,扯下. ~ ***out of*** 跑出. ~ ***out one's hairs*** = ~ one's hairs. ~ ***round [around]*** 〔美〕到处奔忙;过放纵生活. ~ ***through*** 飞快地穿过〔横贯〕. ~ ***to pieces*** 撕碎,扯碎;摧毁,彻底揭发,驳得体无完肤. ~ ***up*** 撕碎,扯碎;拔出,连根拔起;使离散,扰乱;跑上. ~ ***up jack*** 引起骚动. — *n.* 裂缝,绽线的地方;撕裂;狂奔,激怒;〔美〕狂闹,闹饮. ***stand wear and*** ~ 耐穿耐用. ~ **and wear** 磨损;损伤;损失. ~ **sheet** 报刊中某部分的单印页〔特指交给广告投登人的广告样张〕. ~ **strip** 拉开包装用的狭带.

tear·ful [ˈtiəful] *a.* ①流泪的,含泪的,泪汪汪的. ②使人流泪的,悲痛的(消息等). *grandpa's ~ face* 祖父的老泪纵横的脸. ~ *voice* 哭声. ~ *news* 悲痛的消息. **-ly** *ad.* **-ness** *n.*

tear·ing [ˈtɛəriŋ] *a.* ①撕裂的. ②把心撕裂似的,令人痛苦的. ③〔口〕激烈的(宣传). ④猛烈的(风);狂奔的,狂冲的. ⑤〔主英〕了不起的. *a ~ toothache* 剧烈的牙痛. *proceed at a ~ pace* 疾步前进. *a ~ wind* 极其猛烈的风. *a ~ success* 了不起的成就.

tear·less [ˈtiəlis] *a.* 没有泪的.

tear·y [ˈtiəri] *a.* ***(-i·er; -i·est)*** = tearful.

Teas·dale [ˈti:zdeil] *n.* 蒂斯代尔〔姓氏〕.

tease [ti:z] *vt.* ①逗弄;取笑,戏弄. ②强求,勒索. ③梳理(羊毛等);起(呢绒的)毛,起绒,拉绒. ~ *a boy about his curly hair* 戏弄一个小男孩长的打卷的头发. ~ *grandma for money* 缠着祖母要钱. ~ *sb. with jest* 和某人开玩笑逗弄他. — *n.* 逗惹,戏弄;〔口〕爱戏弄人的人.

tea·sel [ˈti:zl] *n.* ①【植】川续断(属),起绒草. ②【纺】起绒刺果;起毛机. *full's* ~ 【植】起绒草. — *vt.* (〔英〕*-ll-*) (用起绒刺果)使(布)起毛. **-er** 【纺】起绒机;拉毛工人.

teas·er [ˈti:zə] *n.* ①(爱)惹恼人的人;②强求者,勒索者. ③〔口〕令人烦恼的事物;难题. ④〔商口〕含蓄而容易引起人好奇心的广告. *It doesn't pay to invite a ~ like that.* 犯不上招引那样的头痛的事儿.

teat [ti:t] *n.* 乳头;乳房;橡皮奶头;(机械上的)小突.

teazel, teazle [ˈti:zl] *n., vt.* = teasel.

Te·bet, Te·vet [ˈteiˈveit, ˈteivəs] *n.* 〔Heb.〕犹太历的

第四月。

tec [tek] *n.* 〔俚〕 = detective.

tech. = technical; technology.

tec(h) [tek] *n.* 〔俚〕技术学校。

teched [tetʃt] *a.* 神经不正常的。

tech·i·ly [ˈtetʃili] *ad.* 恼怒地;情绪不佳地。

tech(n). = technical(ly); technology.

tech·net·i·des [ˈtekniˈtaidis] *n.* 〔*pl.*〕【化】锝系元素。

tech·ne·ti·um [tekˈniːʃiəm] *n.* 【化】锝 (Tc) 〔旧名 masurium 钨〕。

tech·ne·tron·ic [ˌtekniˈtrɔnik] 〔美〕 *a.* 使用电子技术(解决各种问题为特征)的。 *a ~ society* 使用电子技术的社会。

tech·nic [ˈteknik] *n.* ①专门术语;专门技术。②〔常 *pl.*〕技巧。③ = technics. — *a.* = technical.

tech·ni·cal [ˈteknikl] *a.* ①技术(性)的,工艺的;学术(上)的;专门(技术)的。②【法】根据法律的,法律上的。③【商】人造的;用工业方法制造的,由市场内部因素(如投机等)引起的。④〔美俚〕外表的,表面上的,浅薄的。 *~ skill* 专门技能,技术水平。 *a ~ expert* 技术专家。 *a ~ adviser* 技术顾问。 *a ~ book* 专门性的书。*a ~ difficulty* 技术[法律、手续]上的困难。~ **analysis** 技术[工艺]分析。 ~ **assault** (根据法律而成立的)人身攻击。~ **school** 技术学校。 ~ **sergeant** 〔美军〕(空军或海军陆战队的)技术军士;陆军上士的旧称[现称 sergeant first class]。 ~ **terms** 术语,专门名词。

tech·ni·cal·i·ty [ˌtekniˈkæliti] *n.* 技术性,专门性,学术性;学术性事项,专门事项;专门术语。

tech·ni·cal·ly [ˈteknikəli] *ad.* 技术上,学术上,专业上;用术语。

tech·ni·cian [tekˈniʃən], **tech·ni·cist** [ˈteknisit] *n.* 技术员,技师;专家。

tech·ni·col·our [ˈteknikʌlə] *n.* 【影】彩色印片法;彩色电影[电视]。 — *a.* 彩色(印片法)的;色彩鲜艳的。

teck·ni·con [ˈteknikɔn] *n.* 【乐】弹奏技巧练习器。

tech·nics [ˈtekniks] *n.* 〔*pl.*〕 ①(专门)技术;工艺;技巧,手法。②术语,专门用语。③学术上[专业性]的事项。

tech·ni·phone [ˈteknifəun] *n.* (练习指法用的)无声钢琴。

tech·nique [tekˈniːk] *n.* ①(专门)技术;(艺术上的)技巧,技能。②手法[如画法,演奏法等]。③方法。 *advanced cinematic ~* 高级电影技巧。 *a newly-developed ~* 一项新发展的技能。 *a statistic ~* 一种统计方法。

techno- *comb. f.* 技术,工艺;技巧。

tech·noc·ra·cy [tekˈnɔkrəsi] *n.* 专家政治(论),技术统治(论)〔主张一切工作,从生产到国家行政,全部由专家管理的学说〕。 **techno·crat** *n.* 技术统治论者,专家治国论者;(高级)技术人员。

tech·no·crat [ˈteknəkræt] *n.* 专家政治论者;专家治国论者。

tech·nog·ra·phy [tekˈnɔgrəfi] *n.* 技术发展史。

technol. = technology; technological.

tech·no·la·try [tekˈnɔlətri] *n.* 技术崇拜。

tech·no·log·ic, tech·no·log·i·cal [ˌteknəˈlɔdʒik,-kəl] ①*a.* 技术[工程](上)的,技术学的。②因工业技术高度发展而引起的。 *a ~ school* 技术学校。 *~ unemployment* 技术失业,因技术高度发展所造成的失业。

tech·nol·o·gist [tekˈnɔlədʒist] *n.* 技术员,工艺师,(工程技术)专家。

tech·nol·o·gy [tekˈnɔlədʒi] *n.* ①技术,工程,工艺。②制造学,工艺学。③术语(汇编)。 *science and ~* 科学和技术。 *the ~ of sugar* 制糖法。

tech·nop·o·lis [tekˈnɔpəlis] *n.* 专家政治,专家体制。

tech·no·struc·ture [ˌteknəˈstrʌktʃə] *n.* 技术专家体制;〔集合词〕技术专家。

techy [ˈtetʃi] *a.* = tetchy.

teck [tek] *n.* 〔美俚〕 = detetive.

tec·nol·o·gy [tekˈnɔlədʒi] *n.* 儿童学 (= pedology[2]).

tec·to·gene [ˈtektədʒiːn] *n.* 【地】深地槽,海渊。

tec·tol·o·gy [tekˈtɔlədʒi] *n.* 【生】组织形态学。

tec·ton·ic [tekˈtɔnik] *a.* ①构造的;建筑的。②【生】构造的。③【地】地壳构造上的,起因于地壳运动的。

tec·ton·ics [tekˈtɔniks] *n.* ①【建】筑造学,构造学。②【地】构造地质学,大地构造学。

tec·ton·ism [ˈtektənizm] *n.* 【地】地壳运动 (= diastrophism).

tec·to·rial [tekˈtɔːriəl] *a.* 构成覆盖物的。 *~ membrane* 【解】耳蜗覆膜。

tec·trix [ˈtektriks] *n.* (*pl.* ***-tri·ces***[-trəˌsiːz])【动】复羽。

tec·tum [ˈtektəm] *n.* (*pl.* ***tec·ta*** [-tə]) 【解、动】①盖。②致密层。 **-tal** *a.*

Ted [ted]*n.* 特德〔男子名,Edward 或 Theodore的昵称〕。

ted [ted] *vt.* **(ted·ded,ted·ding)**摊晒(干草等);撒,散开。

Ted·der [ˈtedə] *n.* 特德〔姓氏〕。

ted·der [ˈtedə] *n.* 摊晒干草的人,干草撒散机。

Ted·dy [ˈtedi] *n.* 特迪〔男子名〕〔Edward 或 Theodore 的昵称〕。 ~ *Football* 〔美〕〔拟人语〕足球先生。 ~ **bear** 玩具熊。 ~ **boy** (英国六十年代的)无赖青年。~ ~ **girl** 无赖女青年。

ted·dy [ˈtedi] *n.* (常用 *pl.* ***-dies***)〔美〕妇女连衫衬裤〔尤指二十世纪二十年代流行的一种内衣〕。

Te De·um [teiˈdeium, tiːˈdiːəm] 〔L.〕感恩赞美诗;感恩赞美诗的音乐。

te·di·ous [ˈtiːdiəs] *a.* 单调沉闷的,令人生厌的,冗长乏味的。 *a ~ speech* 一个冗长乏味的讲演。 *Too many abstract statements made his paper very ~ to me.* 他的读书报告抽象的讲法太多使我生厌。 **-ly** *ad.* **-ness** *n.*

te·di·um [ˈtiːdiəm, -djəm] *n.* 沉闷,单调,冗长乏味。

tee[1] [tiː] *n.* ①英语字母 T. ②T 字[丁字]形物;T(形)管,三通;丁字铁。 *a ~-piece* 丁字接头。 ***to a ~*** 恰好地,丝毫不差地。 ~ **shirt** 圆领短袖汗衫。

tee[2] [tiː] *n.* ①(高尔夫球发球时放球的)球座;②发球点〔美式足球开球时的发球点〕。③(套圈等游戏中的)目标。 *dead from the ~* 发球时未打中球。 *a ~ topnotcher* 〔美〕高尔夫球名手。 — *vt., vi.* ①放(球)在球座上。②准备。 *Joe ~ed the ball up for the final hole.* 乔把高尔夫球放在球座上准备打向最后的球穴。 ~ ***off*** 从球座发球;开始;〔美俚〕严厉责备,痛骂*(on)*;触怒,使不快。

tee[3] [tiː] *n.* (塔顶的)笠状顶饰。

tee-hee [ˈtiːˈhiː] *int., n.* — *vi.* = tehee 嘿〔窃笑(或傻笑)声〕。

teel [tiːl] *n.* ① = sesame. ②麻油。

teem[1] [tiːm] *vi.* ①充满;富于,有很多 *(with)*。②〔古〕产崽仔,结实。 *That book ~s with blunders.* 那本书错误不少。 *Fish ~ in Chinese waters.* = *Chinese waters ~ with fish.* 中国近海鱼产丰富。 — *vt.* 〔古〕产,生。

teem[2] [tiːm] *vt.* ①〔古〕把…倒空;倒出。②【冶】把(钢水等)…注入模具。 — *vi.* (雨水等)倾注。

teem·ing [ˈtiːmiŋ] *a.* 多产的;充满的,丰富;很多的。 *a ~ brain* (思想)丰富的头脑。

teen[1] [tiːn] *n.* ①〔古、方〕悲哀,痛苦。②不幸。③损害,伤害。 ④〔苏格兰〕愤怒。

teen[2] [tiːn] *n.* ① = teen-ager 13—19岁。②13—19 世纪。 — *a.* 十几岁的;13—19 岁的。

-teen *suf.* 十〔基数词 13—19 的后缀〕: sixteen.

teen-age [ˈtiːnidʒ] *n., a.* (~d) 少年[13—19岁] 时代(的)。

teen-ag·er [ˈtiːnidʒə] *n.* (13—19 岁的)少年,少女。

teener [ˈtiːnə] *n.* = teen-ager.

teens [tiːnz] *n.* 〔*pl.*〕 十多岁[13—19岁]。 ***enter one's ~*** 刚 13 岁。 ***in one's ~*** 十多岁时,在少年时代。 ***out of one's ~*** = ***pass one's ~*** (刚)过了少年时代。

teen·ster [ˈtiːnstə] *n.* 〔美〕 = teen-ager.

teen·sy [ˈtiːnsi] *a.* 〔口〕 = tiny.

tee·ny [ˈtiːni] *a.* ***(-ni·er; ni·est)***〔方、口;主儿〕tiny 的变体. ～ ***weeny***〔口〕小小的;小额的.
teen·y-bop·per [ˈtiːniˌbɔpə] *n.*〔美俚〕摹嬉士〔二十世纪六十年代学嬉皮士那一套的青少年;尤指女子〕.
tee·pee [ˈtiːpi] *n.* (北美印第安人的)圆锥形帐篷.
tee·ter [ˈtiːtə] *vi., vt.*〔美口〕①(使)蹒跚. ②颠簸. ③摇摆. ④跷跷板. *Look! There's a drunken man ～ing at the head of the stairs.* 看,有个醉汉在楼梯顶那里摇摇欲坠呢. —*n.* ①蹒跚. ②颠簸. ③摇摆. ④跷跷板. ～**board** 跷跷板. ～**-totter** 跷跷板.
teeth [tiːθ] tooth 的复数.
teethe [tiːð] *vi.* 出乳牙,生牙.
teeth·ing [ˈtiːðiŋ] *n.* 出乳牙,出牙期. ～ *ring* (供出牙期婴儿咬的)橡皮环. ～ *troubles* 生牙期的疼痛;〔喻〕事情开始期的暂时困难.
teeth·ridge [ˈtiːθˌridʒ] *n.*【医】上齿龈前部的内壁;牙嵴.
tee·to·tal [tiːˈtəutl] *a.* 主张戒酒的,绝对戒酒的;〔口〕完全的,绝对的,彻底的. ～ *drink* 不含酒精的饮料. *His Majesty's* ～ *hotel*〔俚〕监狱. **-ism** *n.* 绝对戒酒主义. **-er**〔英〕**-tal·ler** *n.* 绝对戒酒(主义)者.
tee·to·tum [tiːˈtəutəm] *n.* (用手指捻转的)四方〔六方〕陀螺,捻转儿. *like a* ～ 旋转着.
tef·lon [ˈteflɔn]【化】(商标名)特氟纶,聚四氟乙烯.
TEG, teg, t.e.g. = top edge(s) gilt 顶端烫金〔指书籍〕.
teg(g) [teg] *n.* 两岁的羊.
teg·men [ˈtegmən] *n.* *(pl.* ***teg·mi·na*** [ˈtegminə]*)* ①外皮,被覆;壳. ②【植】内种皮. ③【动】(昆虫的)复翅;阳(茎)基. **-mi·nal** [-minəl] *a.*
Te·gu·ci·gal·pa [teˌguːsiˈgælpə] *n.* 特古西加尔巴〔洪都拉斯首都〕.
tegu·lar [ˈtegjulə] *a.* 瓦的,象瓦的,瓦状(排列)的.
teg·u·ment [ˈtegjumənt] *n.*【动、植】皮,外皮,被膜;壳.
te·hee [tiːˈhiː] *int., n.* 嘻! 窃笑(声),傻笑(声). — *vi.* 窃笑,嗤嗤地(傻)笑.
Teh·ran, Te·he·ran [tiəˈrɑːn, ˌtehəˈrɑːn] *n.* 德黑兰〔伊朗首都〕.
Te·huel·che [teˈweltʃi] *n.* *(pl.* ***-ches, -che****)* 德卫尔彻人〔南美巴塔哥尼亚的主要土著民族,以身躯高大著称〕.
te·ig·i·tur [teiˈidʒiˌtuə] *n.*【天主】"因此你…"〔弥撒主祷文的开始二词〕.
teil (-tree) [tiːl] *n.*【植】(欧洲)菩提树.
tek·tite [ˈtekˌtait] *n.*【矿】熔融石,玻殒石,雷公墨.
tel. = telegram; telegraph(ic); telephone.
tel, tell [tel] *n.*【考古】(层层覆盖古代遗址的)人工丘阜.
te·laes·the·sia [ˌtelisˈθiːziə] *n.* = teles the sia.
tel[1]**-** *comb. f.* = tele[1]-.
tel[2]**-** *comb. f.* = tete[2]-.
tel·a·mon [ˈteləmən] *n.* *(pl.* ***telamones*** [teləˈməuniːz]*)*【建】男像柱.
tel·an·gi·ec·ta·sis, tel·an·gi·ec·ta·sia [telˌændʒi-ˈektəsis, -ˈteiʒiə] *n.* *(pl.* ***-ses*** [-ˌsiːz]*)*【医】毛细管扩张. **-tat·ic** [-ˈtætik] *a.*
tel·au·to·gram [teˈlɔːtəgræm] *n.* 传真电报.
tel·au·to·graph [teˈlɔtəgrɑːf] *n.* 传真电报(机).
tel·au·tog·ra·phy [ˌtelɔːˈtɔgrəfi] *n.* 传真电报学〔术〕.
tel·au·to·mat·ics [teˈlɔtəmətiks] *n.* ①【无、自】自动遥控机械学. ②【力学】自动遥控装置.
Tel A·viv [ˌteləˈviːv] 特拉维夫〔以色列港市〕.
tele[1]**-** *comb. f.* 远,远距离,遥空;电视;电信;电传: *tele*meter; *tele*vision.
tele[2]**-** *comb. f.* 目的,末端: *tele*ology.
tel·e [ˈteli] *n.* 电视 (= television).
tel·e·arch·ics [teˈliɑːkiks] *n.* 无线电飞机操纵术.
tel·e·ba·rom·e·ter [telibəˈrɔmitə] *n.* 远距气压计.
tel·e·bit [teliˈbiːt] *n.* 二进制遥测系统.
tel·e·came·ra [teliˈkæmərə] *n.* 电视摄象机.
tel·e·cast [ˈtelikɑːst] *n.*〔口〕①电视广播. ②电视节目. — *vt., vi.* ***(～, ～ed)*** 用电视广播,作电视广播. **-er** *n.* 电视广播员.
tel·e·cen·tric [ˈteliˌsentrik] *a.*【物】焦阑的,远心的.
tel·e·cin·e [ˈteliˈsiniː] *n.* ①电视(传送)电影. ②电视电影演播室. ③电视电影传送装置.
tel·e·com·mu·ni·ca·tion [ˈtelikəmjuːniˈkeiʃən] *n.* ①电信. ②〔*pl.*〕电信学.
tel·e·con [ˈtelikɔn] *n.* 电话会议 (= teleconference).
tel·e·con·fer·ence [teliˈkɔnfərəns] *n.* (用电传打字电报机)电报会议;电话会议;远距离通讯会议.
tel·e·con·trol [ˈtelikənˈtrəul] *n.* 遥控. — *vt.* **-trol·led** 遥控. — *a.* 遥控的.
tel·e·course [ˈteliˌkɔːs] *n.* 电视讲座,电视(传授的)课程.
te·le·diag·no·sis [ˈteliˌdaiəgˈnəusis] *n.* (医生与病人通过电视进行的)电视诊断.
tel·e·du [ˈteliduː] *n.*【动】马来貛.
tel·e·fac·sim·i·le [ˈtelifæksimili] *n.* 电报传真.
tel·e·film [ˈtelifilm] *n.* 电视影片. — *vt.* 把…摄成电视影片.
teleg. = telegram; telegraph(y).
te·le·ga [teˈlegɑː] *n.* 苏联运货马车.
tel·e·gauge [teliˈgeidʒ] *n.* 遥测仪.
tel·e·gen·ic [teliˈdʒenik] *a.* 适于拍摄电视的.
telego·ni·o·meter [ˈteligəuniˈɔmitə] *n.* 方向计,遥远测角计,无线电测向仪.
te·leg·o·ny [tiˈlegəni] *n.*【生】感应遗传,前父遗传〔认为与某一母兽交配过的公兽的特性能经由这一母兽而遗传给与其他公兽所生的后代〕. **tel·e·gon·ic** [ˌteliˈgɔnik] *a.*
tel·e·gram [ˈteligræm] *n.* 电报. *a* ～ *in cipher [plain] language* 密码〔明码〕电报. *a* ～ *in code language* 号码〔密码〕电报. *a* ～ *form* [〔美〕*blank*] 电报纸. *by* ～ 用电报. *milk [tap] a* ～ 偷电报. *send a* ～ 拍发电报.
tel·e·graph [ˈteligrɑːf] *n.* ①电报机. ②电报. ③信号机. ④(船上驾驶台与轮机之间的)传令钟. ⑤(运动比赛等的)报分牌 (= ～-board). ⑥电讯〔报纸名,如 *The Daily T-*〕. *a* ～ *office [station]* 电报局. *a* ～ *slip* 电报纸. *a* ～ *restante* 留局待领电报. *by* ～ 用电报. *submarine* ～ 海底电报. — *vt.* ①打电报,用电报通知〔传送信息〕,电告. ②电汇. ③在揭示板上示出(比分等). ④无意中流露. ～ *sb. a message* 给某人打电报. ～ *sb. the score of the game* 把球赛比分电告某人. *a smile that* ～*ed consent* 流露出同意的微笑. — *vi.* 打电报. *Shall I* ～*?* 我可以打电报吗? ～ *to her at once.* 立刻给她打电报. ～ *for sb. [to sb. to come]* 电邀某人. ～**board** (运动比赛时得分)揭示板. ～ **cable** 电报电缆. ～ **code** 电码. ～ **key** 电报发报键,电钥. ～**line** 电报线路. ～ **operator** 报务员. ～ **plant**【植】午萩〔印度豆科灌木〕. ～ **pole [post]** 电线杆. ～ **receiver** 收报机. ～ **register** 收报机. ～ **repeater** 电报帮电机,电报转发机〔中继机〕. ～ **transmitter** 发报机. ～**wire** 电报电线.
te·leg·ra·pher [tiˈlegrəfə] *n.* 报务员.
tel·e·graph·ese [ˈteligrɑːfiːz] *n., a.* 电报体裁(的).
tel·e·graph·ic, tel·e·graph·i·cal [ˌteliˈgræfik(əl)] *a.* ①电报的,电信的. ②电报机的. ③电送的. ④电报体裁的,简洁的. *a* ～ *message* 电报. *a* ～ *money order* 电汇. *a* ～ *picture* 电传图片. **-cal·ly** *ad.*
te·leg·ra·phist [tiˈlegrəfist] *n.*〔英〕电信技术员;〔英军〕通信兵;电信技术家.
te·leg·ra·phone [tiˈlegrəfəun] *n.* 录音电话机.
te·leg·ra·phy [tiˈlegrəfi] *n.* 电信技术〔工程〕;电报学;电报. *electric wave* ～ = *Hertzian [wireless]* ～ 无线电报(术). *line* ～ 有线电报(术). *facsimile (picture)*

T

～ 传真电报(术). *submarine* ～ 海底电报(术).

tel·e·ki·ne·sis [ˌteliki'ni:sis] *n.* 【心灵学】心灵遥感(现象). **-net·ic** [-'netik] *a.*

tel·e·lec·ture ['teliˈlektʃə] *n.* ①电话扬声器. ②电话讲课,电话讲演.

tel·e·mark ['telimɑ:k] *n.* 【滑雪】屈膝旋转法, 旋转停止法.

tel·e·me·chanics ['telimiˈkæniks] *n.* 遥控机械学; 遥控力学.

tel·e·me·ter ['telimi:tə, ti'lemitə] *n.* ①遥测计[仪], 遥测发射器. ②测远仪,测深仪, 测距仪. — *vt., vi.* 遥测;用遥测发射器传送. *data* ～*ed from a spaceship* 从宇宙飞船传来的数据.

tel·e·me·ter·ing ['telimi:təriŋ] *n.* 遥测; 沿无线电遥测线路传送(信息).

te·lem·e·try [ti'lemitri] *n.* 遥测学; 遥测术, 测距术. **-met·ric** *a.* **-ri·cal·ly** *ad.*

tel·e·mi·cro·scope [teli'maikrəskəup] *n.* 望远显微镜.

tel·e·mo·tion [teli'məuʃən] *n.* 无线电操纵, 遥控(操纵).

te·le·mo·tor ['teliməutə] *n.* ①(使用电力、水力或机力等的)动力遥控装置. ②【电】遥控电动机. ③【船】油压操舵器.

tel·en·ceph·a·lon [ˌtelen'sefəlɔn] *n.* *(pl.* **-la** [-lə]*)* 【解】端脑〔前脑的最前部〕. **-ce·phal·ic** [-si'fælik] *a.*

teleo- *comb. f.* 目的,末端 (= tele²-).

tel·e·ol·o·gy [ˌteli'ɔlədʒi] *n.* 【哲】目的论. **-log·ic** **-log·i·cal** *a.* **-ol·gist** *n.* 目的论者.

Tel·e·o·sau·rus [ˌteliə'sɔ:rəs] *n.* 【古生】完龙.

tel·e·ost; tel·e·os·te·an ['teliˌɔst, 'ti:li-; -'ɔstiən] *n.* 【动】新鳍类 *(Neopterygii)* 或真骨类 *(Teleostei)* 鱼. — *a.* 新鳍类或真骨类鱼的.

te·le·pa·per ['teliˌpeipə] *n.* 电视传真报纸(或文件).

tel·e·path·ic [ˌteli'pæθik] *a.* 心灵感应的,以心传心的.

te·lep·a·thy [ti'lepəθi] *n.* 心灵感应(术),传心术.

teleph. = telephone; telephony.

tel·e·phone ['telifəun] *n.* 电话(机). *a dial* ～ 自动电话. *a public* ～ 公用电话. *a* ～ *booth [box]* (公用)电话间. *a* ～ *directory [book]* 电话用户号码簿. *a* ～ *operator* 话务员. *a* ～ *receiver* (电话)听筒. *a* ～ *set* 电话机. *a* ～ *subscriber* 电话用户. *a* ～ *transmitter* (电话)话筒. *speak to sb. over the* ～ 和某人通电话. *You are wanted on the* ～. 请你去接电话. ***by*** ～ 用电话. ***call (sb.) on the*** ～ 给(某人)打电话. ***call sb. to the*** ～ 叫某人听电话. ***talk on [over] the*** ～ 打电话, 通电话. — *vt.* 打电话给某人,把某事用电话通知某人. — *vi.* 给某人打电话 *(to)*. ～ *the secretary* 打电话给秘书. ～ *a message to sb.* 打电话给某人告诉他一项消息. *He* ～*ed that he would come in the afternoon.* 他打电话来说他下午来.

tel·e·phon·ee [ˌtelifəu'ni:] *n.* 受电话的人.

tel·e·phon·er ['telifəunə] *n.* 打电话的人.

tel·e·phon·ic [ˌteli'fɔnik] *a.* 电话的,用电话传送的,电话机的. **-i·cal·ly** *ad.*

te·leph·o·nist [ti'lefənist] *n.* 〔主英〕话务员; 电话接线员.

tele·pho·no·graph [ˌteli'fəunəgrɑ:f] *n.* 电话录音机.

te·leph·o·ny [ti'lefəni] *n.* 电话技术. *rural* ～ 乡村电话. *secret* ～ 保密电话. *toll* ～ 长途电话(技术). *wireless* ～ 无线电话(术).

tel·e·phote ['telifəut] *n.* ①传真电报机. ②远距照相机.

tel·e·pho·to ['teli'fəutəu] *a.* ①远距照相的, ②传真照相的. *a* ～ *camera* 远距照相机. *a* ～ *lens* 远距照相镜头,摄远镜头. — *n.* ①远距照相(术), 远距摄影(术). ②传真电报,传真照片. ③摄远镜头 (=～ lens).

tel·e·pho·to·graph ['teli'fəutəgrɑ:f] *n.* 远距摄影照片; 电传照片. —*vt., vi.* 用远摄镜头拍摄;用电传照片发送. **-ic** *a.* **-i·cal·ly** *ad.*

tel·e·pho·tog·ra·phy ['telifə'tɔgrəfi] *n.* 远距摄影(术);电报传真术.

tele·pho·to·me·ter [ˌtelifəu'tɔmitə] *n.* 远距光度计.

tel·e·play ['teliˌplei] *n.* 电视广播剧.

tel·e·por ['telipɔ:] *vt.* 远距传物〔将物质转变为能, 传送到目的地后重新转变为物质〕. **-ta·tion** [-'teiʃən] *n.*

tel·e·print·er ['teliprintə] *n.* 电传打字电报机.

tel·e·promp·ter ['teliˌprɔmptə] *n.* (在电视演说者面前将讲稿逐行现出的)讲词提示器〔原商标名〕.

tel·e·ran ['teliræn] *n.* 电视雷达导航仪. (*tele*vision, *ra*dar, *a*ir 和 *n*avigation 的缩合词).

tel·e·re·ceiv·er [ˌteliri'si:və] *n.* 〔美〕电视(接收)机.

tel·e·re·cord ['teliriˌkɔ:d] *vt.* 将为…摄制为电视片,录象. **-ing** *n.* 电视录象,电视片摄制;电视片放映,电视片.

tel·er·gy ['telədʒi] *n.* ①透视力,视觉特异功能. ②【心】远隔精神作用.

tel·e·sat ['telisæt] *n.* 通信卫星〔系 telecommunications satellite 的缩合词〕.

tel·e·scope ['teliskəup] *n.* ①望远镜. ②【天】远镜座. *an astronomical* ～ 天文望远镜. *a binocular* ～ 双筒望远镜. *an equatorial* ～ 赤道仪. *a radio* ～ 射电望远镜. *a reflecting* ～ 反射式望远镜. *a relief* ～ 体视望远镜. *a sighting* ～ 瞄准望远镜. — *vi.* 嵌进,套叠;(列车等)相碰撞而嵌在一起. *The two cars collided and* ～*d.* 两节车相撞嵌在一起了. — *vt.* 嵌进,(使)套入,(使)(依次)叠进;(使)缩短. ～ **bag** (旅行用)伸缩皮包. ～ **fish** 鼓眼金鱼. ～ **level** 水准仪.

tel·e·scop·ic [ˌtelis'kɔpik] *a.* ①望远镜的; 用望远镜看的,只能用望远镜看见的. ②能看见远处的,远视的. ③套筒的,套管的; 伸缩自如的. *a* ～ *chimney* 伸缩烟囱. ～ *joint* 套叠接合. *a* ～ *object* 只有用望远镜才能看到的物体. *a* ～ *screw* 套叠螺旋. *a* ～ *sight* (大炮上的)望远瞄准器. *a* ～ *tube* 套叠管. **-i·cal·ly** *ad.*

tel·e·scop·i·form [ˌtelis'kɔpifɔ:m] *a.* 望远镜形的;套叠的;可伸缩的.

tel·e·sco·pist [ti'leskəpist] *n.* (善于)使用望远镜的人.

te·les·co·py [ti'leskəpi] *n.* 望远镜使用法; 望远镜制造法.

tel·e·script ['teliskript] *n.* ①电视广播稿. ②电视剧本.

tel·e·scrip·tor [ˌtelis'kriptə] *n.* = teletypewriter.

tel·e·seism ['telisaizəm] *n.* 远地地震,远震.

tel·e·seme ['telisi:m] *n.* (旅馆等的)电铃; 信号机.

tel·e·set ['teliset] *n.* 电视(接收)机.

tel·e·sis ['telisis] 〔美〕 *n.* (自然和社会力量)有目的使用;有计划的发展.

tel·e·spec·tro·scope [ˌteli'spektrəˌskəup] *n.* 远距分光镜.

tel·e·ster·e·o·scope [ˌtelis'teriəskəup] *n.* 体视望远镜.

tel·es·the·si·a [ˌtelis'θi:ʒə, -ziə] *n.* 【心】超阈限感觉. **-thet·ic** [-'θetik] *a.*

te·les·tic, te·les·tich ['te'listik, ti'le-] *n.* 各行最后一字母可以拼成一[几]个词的诗.

tel·e·switch ['teliswitʃ] *n.* 遥控键,遥控开关.

tel·e·ther·mom·e·ter [ˌteliθə'mɔmitə] *n.* 【物】遥测温度计.

tel·e·thon ['teliθɔn] *n.* 〔美〕 (马拉松式)长时间电视节目.

tel·e·type ['teliˌtaip] *n.* 〔美〕 ①电传打字电报机. ②电传打字电报. ③电传打字电报术. — *vt., vi.* ***(-typed, -typ·ing)*** 用电传打字机发送(电报). **-typ·ist** *n.* 电传打字电报员.

tel·e·type·set·ter [ˌteli'taipˌsetə] *n.* 〔美〕电传排字机.

tel·e·type·writ·er ['teli'taipraitə] *n.* 〔美〕电传打字电报机.

te·leu·to·spore [tə'lu:təˌspɔ:] *n.* 【生】冬孢子 (=

teliospore). **-spor·ic** *a.*

tel·e·view [ˈtelivjuː] *vt., vi.* 用电视机收看;看电视. **-er** *n.* 看电视的人.

tel·e·vise [ˈtelivaiz] *vt.* ①电视播送,实况播送. ②摄制成电视节目;(用电视机)收看. *The tennis final will be ~d live.* 网球决赛实况将由电视转播. *a ~d panel discussion* 由电视广播的问题公开讨论会.

tel·e·vi·sion [ˈteliˌviʒən] *n.* 电视. *black-and-white ~* 黑白电视. *closed-circuit [industrial] ~* 内部闭路[工业]电视. *colour ~* 彩色电视. *combat ~* 指挥作战用的电视. *commercial [sponsored] ~* 商业电视. *the two-way ~* 双向电视. *I won't allow Little Mary to watch ~ till midnight* 我不会让小玛丽看电视到午夜的. *That's the third time the varsity team appeared on ~ this season.* 那是我们校队本季第三次在电视上出现. **-al, -ary** *a.*

tel·e·vi·sor [ˈtelivaizə] *n.* 电视播送[接收]机;电视播送者;电视机观看者.

tel·e·vis·u·al [ˌteliˈvizjuel, ˌteliˈviʒuəl] *a.* ①电视的. ②适于上电视镜头的. *a ~ scene* 一个适于拍电视的场面.

tel·e·vox [ˈtelivɔks] *n.* (由声音操纵的)机器人.

tel·e·writ·er [ˌteliˈraitə] *n.* 电传打字机.

tel·ex [ˈteleks] *n.* ①(与电话线路接通的)电报用户直通电路. ②用户直通电报. — *vt.* 发用户直通电报.

tel·fer *n.* 〔美〕= telpher.

telg. = telegram.

tel·har·mo·ni·um [ˌtelhɑːˈməuniəm] *n.* 音乐电传机.

te·li·al [ˈtiːliə, ˈteliəl] *a.* 【生】①冬孢子堆的. ②后期锈菌的.

te·lic [ˈtiːlik, ˈtelik] *a.* 抱有某种目的的,有目的的. *~ movements* 有目的的行动.

te·li·o·spore [ˈtiːliəˌspɔː, ˈteliə-] *n.* 【生】冬孢子. **-spor·ic** [-ˈspɔrik] *a.*

te·li·um [ˈtiːliəm, ˈteliəm] *n.* *(pl. -li·a [-ə])* 【生】冬孢子堆.

tell [tel] *vt.* *(told [tould])* ①讲;说. ②告诉,吩咐,命令(某人做某事) *(to do sth.)*; 指示 *(where; that; how; what)*. ③泄漏(秘密等),明白说出,吐露. ④断定说,保证. ⑤辨别,区别 *(from)*; 决定;知道,明白,了解. ⑥点数. *I'm ~ing you.* 〔美俚〕注意听我说(这是很重要的). *T- (sb.) good-bye.* 〔美〕道别. *Let me ~ the good news to everybody.* 让我把好消息告诉大家. *The old peasant told us of (about) his sufferings before liberation.* 老农民给我们讲述他在解放前受的苦. *I told him to go on.* 我吩咐他继续下去. *T- us how you fixed up the machine.* 告诉我们你是怎样修好这架机器的. *His face told (that) he was satisfied with the speech.* 他脸上显示出他对演讲感到满意. *It is very important that one should be able to ~ the true friends from the false ones.* 能辨别真假朋友是非常重要的. *I can ~ you that it's not easy.* 我敢断定地告诉你这事不易. *Let's ~ the noses and call it a day.* 咱们计算一下人数收工吧. *I can ~ you. = I ~ you. = Let me ~ you.* 的确,真的. *No, I ~ you.* 真的不可以. *I'll ~ you what.* 讲给你听,告诉给你,有话跟你讲. *Never ~ me = Don't ~ me.* 不至于罢;不见得罢;我不信〔表示惊讶,不快或恐惧等〕. *You're ~ing me!* 〔美俚〕这事不用你说,我全知道了. — *vi.* ①讲,报告 *(about; of)*; 〔口〕搬弄是非,说坏话;〔儿〕告发;〔英方〕嚼舌头 *(on; of)*. ②奏效,产生效果;影响;命中,打中,击中. ③证明;(颜色、声音等)显明,表明. ④〔古〕计数;数票,检票. *I told you so! = Did I not ~ you so?* 我不是跟你讲过了吗? *The story ~s of the life of a famous poet.* 这故事讲的是一个著名诗人的生平. *Tom is the man who ~s on sb. where there's sth. wrong.* 汤姆是个一出毛病就告发别人的家伙. *Smoking will ~ on you when you're getting old.* 你上年纪时就会感受到吸烟的影响了. *How can I tell?* 我怎么说得上来呢? *Who (can) ~?* 谁知道? 谁也不知道. *You can never ~.* 谁也不知道. *It is the man behind the gun that ~s.* 重要的不是枪而是打枪的人,胜败在人不在武器. *Every shot told.* 百发百中. *The colour of the ink ~s of the fraud.* 墨水的颜色说明是作弊. ***do ~*** 不见得罢,不至于罢. ***~ a tale*** 讲故事;泄露内中原因. ***~ against the motion*** 宣布提案(因只有少数票)不能成立. ***~ all*** 〔美俚〕自白,说出秘密,说出真话. ***~ apart*** 辨别,识别(*~ things apart* 辨明情况). ***~ away*** 念咒文驱除(病痛等). ***~ down*** *(money)* 〔口〕数(钱)付帐. ***~ it to sweeney [the marines]*** 〔美〕没有那样的事. ***~ noses*** 〔口〕点人数. ***~ off*** 数清;分派(工作);【军】编号;谴责. ***~ on [upon]*** 告密,告发;对…有效,影响到. ***~ one's prayers*** 祈祷. ***~ out*** ①数钱付帐. ② = *~ away*. ***~ over one's hoard*** 数积蓄的钱. ***~ the tale*** 〔俚〕编造假话;讲述可怜的遭遇博取同情. ***~ the world*** 〔美〕公开讲,扬言. ***~ (so many) years*** 〔口〕显出有(几)岁了〔一般指显老〕. — *n.* 〔方〕话,传闻. *I've a ~ for you.* 我有一句话要跟你说. *according to their ~* 〔美卑〕据说.

Tel·ler [ˈtelə] *n.* 特勒〔姓氏〕.

tell·er [ˈtelə] *n.* ①讲述者,讲故事的人. ②(银行的)出纳员. ③计算者,(投票的)点票员. ④【军】防空情报报告员. *a frequency ~* 频率指示器. *a deposit ~* 存款员. *a paying (receiving) ~* 付(收)款员. **-ship** *n.* teller 的职位.

tell·ing [ˈteliŋ] *a.* ①有效的,有力的. ②生动的;透露真情的,说明问题的. ***with ~ effect*** 有显著效验. *a ~ blow* 有效的打击. *a ~ stanza in the poem* 那首诗中生动的一节. *That's ~. = That would be ~.* 〔口〕说这种话就要露马脚了. — *n.* 讲,可讲的事. *There is no ~.* 难说;不知道. *take a ~* 〔口〕听劝告. **-ly** *ad.*

tell·tale [ˈtelteil] *n.* ①告密的人,搬弄是非的人. ②泄露内情的事物,证据. ③【机】指示器;登记机;(指示油罐充油程度等的)警告器. ④【海】舵位指示器;挂罗针仪. ⑤(考勤卡上记录职工上下班时间的)考勤钟. — *a.* 告密的,搬弄是非的;泄露内情的;起警告作用的. *a ~ blush* 泄露隐情的脸红. *a ~ signal* 【电】警告讯号.

tel·lu·ral [teˈljuərəl] *a.* 地球的,地上的;地球居民的.

tel·lu·rate [ˈteljureit] *n.* 【化】碲酸盐;碲酸酯.

tel·lu·ri·an¹ [teˈljuriən] *a.* 地球的,地上的;住在地球上的; — *n.* 地球居民.

tel·luri·an² [teˈljuriən] *n.* = tellurion.

tel·lu·ric¹ [teˈljuərik] *a.* 地球的,生自土地的,陆生的.

tel·luric² [teˈljuərik] *n.* 【化】(正)碲的. *~ acid* 碲酸.

tellu·ride [ˈteljuraid] *n.* 【化】碲化物,碲醚,碲根.

tel·lu·ri·on [teˈljuəriɔn] *n.* (表示地球公转、自转的)地球仪.

tel·lu·rite [ˈteljuˌrait] *n.* ①【化】亚碲酸盐. ②【矿】黄碲矿.

tel·lu·ri·um [teˈljuəriəm] *n.* 【化】碲 (Te).

tel·lu·rize [ˈteljuˌraiz] *vt.* *(-rized; -riz·ing)* 【化】使碲化,使与碲结合,使含碲.

tel·lu·rous [ˈteljurəs, teˈlurəs] *a.* 【化】亚碲(的).

Tel·lus [ˈteləs] *n.* 【罗神】地的女神;〔拟人语〕地,地球.

tel·ly [ˈteli] *n.* 〔英口〕电视;电视机.

telo¹- *comb. f.* = tele¹-.

telo²- *comb. f.* = tele²-.

tel·o·dy·namic [ˌtelədaiˈnæmik] *a.* 远程传送动力的. *~ transmission* 远程传送[输电].

te·lome [ˈtiːləum] *n.* 【植】顶枝.

tel·o·mer [ˈteləmə] *n.* 【化】调聚物.

te·lome·ter [tiˈlɔmitə] *n.* = telemeter.

tel·o·phase [ˈteləfeiz] *n.* 【生】(细胞分裂的)末期.

tel·o·type [ˈtelətaip] *n.* ①电传打字电报机. ②(一份)电传打字电报.

tel·pher [ˈtelfə] *n., a.* 电动缆车(的);高架电动索道(的). *a ~ railway* 高架索道. — *vt.* 用电动缆车(电动索道)

运输. ~**age** [-ridʒ] *n.* 索道,高架[电动缆车]运输.

tel·son [telsn] *n.*【动】尾节.

Tel·star, tel·star [ˈtelˌstɑː] *n.*〔美〕通信卫星〔商标名〕.

Tel·u·gu [ˈteləˌguː] *n.* ①泰卢固语〔印度东部德拉维人语言〕. ②*(pl.* ***-gus, -gu)*** (印度)泰卢固人. — *a.* 泰卢固语的;泰卢固人的 (= Telegu).

tem·blor [temˈblɔː] *n. (pl.* ***-s, -blor·es*** [-ˈblɔːreis]*)*〔美〕地震.

tem·er·ar·i·ous [ˌteməˈrɛəriəs] *a.* 不顾前后的, 鲁莽的, 轻率的, 蛮勇的. *a ~ crossing of the Pacific by a small sailing boat.* 乘一支小帆船轻率的横渡太平洋. **-ly** *ad.*

te·mer·i·ty [tiˈmeriti] *n.* 鲁莽,轻率,蛮勇.

temp. =①temperature. ②temporal. ③temporary. ④〔L.〕*tempore* (= in the time of).

Tem·pe [ˈtempi] *n.* ①潭蓓谷〔(古希腊)提萨里 (Thessaly) 地方的溪谷. ②〔转义〕风光明媚的溪谷.

Tem·pe·an [temˈpiːən] *a.* 潭蓓谷的; 风光明媚的.

Tem·pel·hof [ˈtempəlhəuf] *n.* 柏林郊外的国际飞机场.

tem·per [ˈtempə] *n.* ①气质; 性情,脾气. ②情绪,心情; 激动的情绪,激愤,暴躁. ③特征, 倾向. ④(粘土的)粘度; (灰泥的)稠度; (钢等的)锻炼; 淬硬,回火; 淬火度; 含碳量; 硬度; 韧度. ⑤中和剂; 调合物; 增效剂. ⑥〔古〕适中,中庸,中和. *an equal [even, a calm] ~* 性情平和. *a hot [quick, short, fiery] ~* 急躁的脾气. ***(be) in a ~ (bad ~)*** 发着脾气,生着气. ***(be) in a good ~*** 心情好. ***get [go, fly] into [in] a ~*** 发怒,发脾气. ***(get) out of ~*** 动气,发怒. ***in a fit of ~*** 在发怒中. ***in a good [bad] ~*** 在平静[不快]的心情中. ***keep [control] one's ~*** 忍气. ***lose one's ~*** 发脾气, 动怒. ***lost ~*** 退火[减低硬度]. ***put sb. out of ~*** 惹怒某人. ***show ~*** = get out of ~. *the ~ of modern Chinese painting* 近代中国绘画的倾向. — *vt.* ①调和,使缓和, 调节; 减轻; 镇定. ②揉和(粘土等);【冶】使回火; 硬化(玻璃);〔转〕锻炼;【乐】(按平均律)调音. *~ justice with mercy* 恩威并施. *~ed [~ing] steel* 回火钢. *a well-~ed sword* 锻造得极好的剑. — *vi.* 变柔软; (金属)经回火后具有适当韧度.

tem·pe·ra [ˈtempərə] *n.* (用蛋黄调和颜料的)蛋黄彩画(法); 蛋黄颜料; 招贴画颜料.

tem·per·a·ble [ˈtempərəbl] *a.* ①可回火的; 可锻炼的. ②(灰泥等)可调和的,可揉和的.

tem·per·a·ment [ˈtempərəmənt] *n.* ①气质, 性情, 脾气. ②(中世纪生理学中的)质〔分为多血、粘液、胆汁、忧郁等四质〕. ③(性情)暴躁, 喜怒无常,易激动. ④【乐】平均律. *a nervous ~* 神经质. *be excitable [placid] by ~* 性情易激动[冷静]. *a scale of equal ~* 等程音阶.

tem·per·a·men·tal [ˌtempərəˈmentl] *a.* 气质的,性情的; 性情暴躁[浮躁]的; 神经质的; 多变的, 变幻无常的. *a ~ dislike for music* 对音乐方面生性不喜欢. *a ~ weather* 变幻无常的天气. **-ly** *ad.*

tem·per·ance [ˈtempərəns] *n.* ①节制,节欲; 适中, 稳健;〔古〕自制,克己. ②节酒, 戒酒. *practise ~ in diet* 节制饮食. *a ~ hotel* 不卖酒的旅馆. *~ drinks* 无酒精的饮料.

tem·per·ate [ˈtempərit] *a.* ①有节制的,节欲的; 适中的, 不过分的,稳健的. ②节酒的,戒酒的. ③(气候等)温和的. *a man of ~ habits* 有节制的人. *a ~ statement* 稳健的说明. *the north ~ zone* 北温带. **-ly** *ad.* **-ness** *n.*

tem·per·a·ture [ˈtempəritʃə] *n.* ①温度, 气温. ②体温. ③〔口〕发烧, 高烧. ***have [run] a ~*** 〔口〕(体温)比常高,发烧. ***take one's ~*** 量体温. ~ **curve** (病人的)体温曲线; 温度曲线. ~ **gauge** 温度计. ~ **gradient** 气温(变化)陡度〔尤指高度增加下的变化〕.

tem·pered [ˈtempəd] *a.* ①回火的, 经过锻炼的. ②调合的; 温和的. ③性情…的, 脾气…的. ④【乐】调正的〔尤指调成平均律的〕. *~ steel* 回火钢. *bad ~* 脾气坏的.

tem·pest [ˈtempist] *n.* ①大风暴,暴风雨,暴风雪. ②骚动,动乱,风潮,暴动. *The wind grew to a ~.* 风势加剧成了风暴. *a ~ of applause* 暴风雨般的掌声. *a ~ in a barrel (bucket, teapot)* 小事引起的大风波. — *vt., vi.* 使骚动; 狂暴. ~**-beaten** *a.* 受暴风雨袭击的. ~**-swept** *a.* 为暴风雨席卷的. ~ **tossed** (-tost) *a.* (受暴风雨振荡)飘摇不定的.

tem·pes·tu·ous [temˈpestjuəs] *a.* 大风暴的, 暴风雨[雪]的; 骚动的, 动乱的. *a ~ state* 动乱状态. **-ly** *ad.*

tempi [ˈtempiː] tempo 的复数.

Tem·plar [ˈtemplə] *n.* ①〔基督教〕圣殿骑士, 圣殿骑士团团员. ②[T- or t-] (属于伦敦 Inner Temple 或 Middle Temple 法学协会的)律师, 法学家. ③〔美〕圣殿骑士互济会会员. *Knights ~s* 1118 年为保护耶路撒冷耶稣墓及朝拜基督教圣地而在该城组织的基督教信徒. *Good ~s* 戒酒会.

tem·plate [ˈtemplit] *n.* = templet.

Tem·ple [ˈtempl] *n.* 坦普尔〔姓氏〕.

tem·ple[1] [ˈtempl] *n.* ①庙,寺, 圣堂, 神殿. ②(基督教的)教堂; 礼拜堂, 大厦. ③某些老人互助会的地方分会. ④〔美〕专供某种活动之用的场所. ⑤〔美卑〕厕所, 化妆室,电影院. 〔the T-〕伦敦圣殿骑士团的圣殿〔现为法学协会 (Inns of Court) 的两个会所, 即 Inner Temple 和 Middle Temple〕. *a ~ of luxury and beauty.* 玉殿金阙.

temple[2] [ˈtempl] *n.* ①太阳穴, 鬓角, 颞. ②【虫】后颊. ③(眼镜的)柄脚.

temple[3] [ˈtempl] *n.*【纺】(织机的)边撑, 伸幅器.

tem·plet [ˈtemplit] *n.* ①(切金属、石、木等时用的)样板, 模板. ②(供描摹用的)透明图样. ③【建】垫石[木]; (墙中的)承梁. ④【船】船架的楔.

tem·po [ˈtempəu] *n. (pl.* ***~s, tempi*** [ˈtempiː]*)* 〔It.〕①【乐】速度, 拍子. ②〔喻〕(局势等的)发展速度, 步调. ③(下棋的)一着,一步. *slow ~* 缓缓的拍子. *We won't let any unreasonable delay upset the ~ of production.* 我们决不容许任何毫无道理的迟延捣乱了生产的发展速度.

tem·po·ral[1] [ˈtempərəl] *a.* ①暂时的,片时的, 转瞬间的 *(opp.* eternal). ②此世的, 现世的; 世俗的 *(opp.* spiritual). ③时的, 时间的 *(opp.* spatial*)*;【语法】表示时间的, 时态的. — *n.* ①一时的事物[权力等]; 俗事, 世事. ②世俗的权力〔多指教会的财产和收入〕. *a ~ death* 假死. *~ aims* 世俗的目标. *~ conjunctions* 时间连接词 (如 when, while 等). *~ matters* 世俗的事物. *~ peers = lords ~* 不居僧职的上院议员. **-ly** *ad.*

tem·po·ral[2] [ˈtempərəl] *n.* 太阳穴, 颞部; 颞骨[肌, 动脉等]. — *a.* 颞的. *the ~ bone* 颞骨.

tem·po·ral·i·ty [ˌtempəˈræliti] *n.* ①一时,暂时, 无常. ②世事, 俗利, 俗人; 俗界. ③〔*pl.*〕宗教团体的财产[收入].

tem·po·ra·ry [ˈtempərəri] *a.* ①一时的, 暂时的, 临时的 *(opp.* lasting*)*. ②昙花一现的, 无常的 *(opp.* permanent*)*. *a ~ receipt* 临时收据. *~ needs* 临时需要. *~ planting* 假植. *~ punishment* 有期徒刑. *~ workers* 临时工. — *n.* 临时工 (= ~ worker) **-i·ly** *ad.* **-i·ness** *n.*

tem·po·rize [ˈtempəraiz] *vi.* ①顺应时势,迎合潮流; 两面讨好, 骑墙. ②采取权宜手段. ③因循, 拖延. ④妥协,姑息. *temporizing measures* 权宜手段,临时办法. *~ between the section chief and the head clerk* 为组长和管理员之间谋求妥协. **-za·tion** [ˌtempəraiˈzeiʃən] *n.*

tem·po·riz·er [ˈtempəraizə] *n.* 顺应时势的人, 迎合潮流的人,两面讨好的人,骑墙主义者; 因循姑息的人,一味临时应付的人.

tem·po·riz·ing·ly [ˈtempəraiziŋli] *ad.* 姑息地, 因循地,暂时应付地.

tempt [tem*p*t] *vt.* ①诱惑,教唆; 引起(食欲等); 引诱; 怂

恿。②诱导；使发生兴趣。③冒…的风险。④〔古〕试探，尝试，试验；〔古〕蔑视；激怒。～ *sb. to sin* 诱人犯罪。*I am ～ed to have a look at it.* 总想去看一看。*Can't I ～ you to have another helping?* 再吃一点好吗？～ *the storm* 冒着暴风雨的危险。 **-able** *a.* 易被引诱的，可诱惑的。 **-a·bil·i·ty** *n.* 可诱惑性。

temp·ta·tion [temp'teiʃən] *n.* 诱惑；诱惑物；魔道；〔古〕考验。*resist* ～抵制诱惑。***fall into [give way to, yield to]*** ～ 受诱惑。***lead*** *(sb.)* ***into*** ～ 使人入迷。

temp·ta·tious [temp'teiʃəs] *a.* 〔美〕诱惑性的。

tempt·er ['temptə] *n.* (*fem.* **temptress** [-ris]) 诱惑者，诱惑物；〔the T-〕魔鬼。

tempt·ing ['temptiŋ] *a.* 诱惑的，迷人的。*This orange looks very* ～. 这个橘看来很吸引人。*a* ～ *market* 吸引人的市面。 **-ly** *ad.*

tempt·ress ['temptris] *n.* 引诱人的女人，妖妇。

tem·pu·ra ['tempuˌrɑː, tem'purə] *n.* 干炸鱼虾〔一种日本菜，将鱼、虾及蔬菜等蘸上鸡蛋、牛奶面糊炸熟〕。

tem·pus fu·git ['tempəs'fjuːdʒit] 〔L.〕光阴似箭。

ten [ten] *num.* (基数)十，十个；第十(页、章等)。— *n.* ①十个人。②十件东西。③十的记号。④十元纸币。⑤(早晨或晚上的)十点钟。⑥十岁。*the second paragraph on page* ～ 第十页第二段。*Please give me five* ～*s and* ～ *fives for this hundred.* 这张百元券请兑换给我五张十元券和十张五元券。**～*s of thousands*** 好几万。***the upper*** ～ ***(thousand)*** 贵族阶层，上流社会。★ ten 和 twenty, hundred, thousand 等一样，常用以泛指'多'义。例：*He is* ～ *times the man you are.* 他比你高明得多。*I'd* ～ *times rather stay here.* 我极愿呆在这里。～ times as easy 容易得多。～ **gallon hat** 〔美俚〕宽边高顶帽。～**-minute man** 〔美〕精力充沛的人。～**-percenter**〔美俚〕演员、作家、职业运动员等的代理人(抽百分之十佣金的人)。～**-space hitch**〔美俚〕十年徒刑。～**-spot** ①十元一张的纸币。②〔美俚〕十年的刑期。～ **strike** 〔美〕〔十柱戏〕十柱全倒；大量，侥幸的意外；大胜利，大成功；优异成绩。～ **to one** 什九，十之八九 (*T- to one it'll clear up in an hour or so.* 一个小时左右后，天准会放晴)。～**-twenty-thirty** 〔美俚〕只会演老套戏的小剧团或剧场；微不足道的(剧团)。～ **yards** 〔美俚〕一千元。

ten. = tenement; tenor; 〔It.〕*tenuto.*

ten·a·ble ['tenəbl, 'tiːn-] *a.* ①守得住的(城市、阵地、堡垒等)，可防守的。②站得住的(意见等)。③有条理的(学说等)。④能保持[继续]的。*a* ～ *analysis of* 站得住的分析。*a* ～ *scholarship at a university for a period of three years* 可保持三年的大学奖学金。 **-bil·i·ty** [ˌtenə'biliti] *n.* **-ness** *n.*

ten·ace ['teneis] *n.* 【桥牌】同花但不完全连续的几张大牌〔如 A, Q 间无 K〕。

te·na·cious [ti'neiʃəs] *a.* ①固执的，顽固的，执拗的。②抓牢不放的；强韧的，牢靠的(记忆等)。③粘(性)的，粘着力强的。*be* ～ *in defense* 坚守。*be* ～ *of life* 生命力强的〔指动物〕。*be* ～ *of one's opinion* 固持己见。*have a* ～ *memory for dates* 对年月日记忆力强。～ **clay** 粘土。 **-iy** *ad.*

te·nac·i·ty [ti'næsiti] *n.* ①固执，坚持，顽强，不屈不挠，顽固。②紧握。③坚韧，(记忆力)强。④粘性。⑤【物】韧性，韧度。*adhere to the principle with an unremitting* ～ 不屈不挠地坚持原则。～ *of purpose* 不屈不挠的志愿。

te·nac·u·lum [tə'nækjuləm] *n.* (*pl.* **-la** [-lə]) 【医】(外科手术用的)持钩，挟钩。

te·naille, te·nail [tə'neil] *n.*【筑城】钳堡，凹角堡。

ten·an·cy ['tenənsi] *n.* ①(土地、房屋的)租佃，租用。②租借权。③租期。④(职位、处所等的)占据，据有。*His* ～ *of the office has not very long to run.* 他的办公室的租期即将届满。

ten·ant ['tenənt] *n.* ①租地人，佃户；租屋人，房客；凭借人，租户。②居住者，住户，占用者。②【法】(不动产诉讼的)被告；不动产占有人。～*s of the woods [trees]* 林间居民〔指鸟类〕。*a* ～ *by courtesy* 【法】继承亡妻遗产的男人。*a* ～ *in dower* 【法】继承亡夫遗产的女人。*the* ～ *of the grave* 死人。— *vt.* 租借；租用(房子，土地)。— *vi.* 居住。～ **farmer** (-peasent) 佃户，佃农。～ **farming** 佃耕。～ **right** 租地权，佃耕权。 **-able** *a.* 可租的，可借的，可住的。 **-less** *a.* 没有人借的；没有人住的，空(地)。 **-ry** *n.* 〔集合词〕租地人，佃户，房客，租户。

tench [tentʃ] *n.* (*pl.* ～**es**, 〔集合词〕～) 【鱼】欧洲鲤，丁鲹鱼。

tend[1] [tend] *vt.* ①看管(牛羊等)，照料，照管，管理(植物等)。②护理。③【海】守望，照料(船身随潮水转动时锚索不绕乱)。～ *a flock of sheep* 看一群羊。*James* ～*s a drug store for his uncle.* 詹姆士替他叔父照料着一家药店。～ *the wounded* 护理伤员。— *vi.* ①服侍，招待 (*on; upon*)。②注意，照看；办理 (*to*)。～ *on (upon) the distinguished guests* 招待贵宾。～ *to one's affairs* 办理(某人自己的)事务。 **-ing** *n.* 田间管理。

tend[2] [tend] *vi.* ①趋向(于)，倾向(于)〔后接介词 *to, towards*〕。②对…有帮助，有助于〔后接不定式 *to* …〕。③有…倾向〔后接不定式 *to* …〕。*It* ～*s to the same conclusion.* 趋向于同一结论。*His religious philosophy* ～*s towards pantheism.* 他的宗教思想倾向于泛神论。*Prices are* ～*ing upward.* 物价趋涨。*measures* ～*ing to increase the annual output.* 有助于提高年产量的种种设施。*She* ～*s to be sad.* 她动不动就有伤感。

tend·ance ['tendəns] *n.* 服侍，照料，看护；关心，注意；〔古，集合词〕侍从人员。

ten·dencious, -tious [ten'denʃəs] *a.* 有倾向性的。～ *novel* 倾向性小说〔提出并阐述某一鲜明主题的小说，即 thesis novel〕。 **-ly** *ad.*, **-ness** *n.*

tend·en·cy ['tendənsi] *n.* ①倾向，趋势。②性情，偏好 (*to; toward*)。③(话或作品等的)旨趣，意向，倾向性。*right opportunist tendencies* 右的机会主义倾向。***have a*** ～ ***to [towards]*** 有…的倾向，渐趋。*show a* ～ *to fall behind with his studies* (他)显示出功课跟不上的倾向。

tan·der[1] ['tendə] *a.* ①嫩，软 (*opp.* tough)。②幼弱的，柔弱的。③敏感的，易受损伤的；易受感动的；容易疼痛的。④温柔的；慈悲的；亲切的。⑤未成熟的，不懂世故的。⑥柔和的(色、光等)。⑦需要慎重对待的，微妙的，难处理的(问题等)。⑧胆小的，对…顾虑多的，小心的，慎重对待…的 (*of; for*)。⑨【海】易倾侧的，稳度小的。～ *green* 嫩绿。*a* ～ *beefsteak* 嫩牛排。*He is* ～ *to weakness.* 他和善到柔弱的地步。*a* ～ *conscience* 慈悲的心肠。*a* ～ *plant* 幼树，难培育的树；难对付的人。*a* ～ *shoot* 嫩芽。*a* ～ *spot* 痛处，弱点。***be*** ～ ***for sb.'s honour*** 顾虑某人面子。***be*** ～ ***of hurting sb.'s feelings*** 生怕伤害人家感情。***grow*** ～ ***of sb.*** 爱上，钟情于。***of*** ～ ***age*** 年纪还小。～ **foot** *n.* (*pl.* **-foots; -feet**) 〔美俚〕新来的人，生手；(童子军的)新团员。～**-hearted** *a.* 心地温和的，慈善的。～ **loin** 〔美〕里肌肉，脊肉；〔T- *or* t-〕(纽约等大城市内)罪恶活动区，警察人员便于榨取贿赂的油水肥厚区。 **-ly** *ad.* **-ness** *n.*

tend·er[2] ['tendə] *n.* ①照看者；看管者。②附属船，供应船，联络船。③【铁路】煤水车；(附属在墩布等上的)小给水器。

ten·der[3] ['tendə] *vt.* ①(正式)提出，提供。②【法】清偿，偿付，赔出(赔偿费)。③〔美〕给与(接见等)。— *vi.* 估价，投标 (*for*)。～ *one's resignation* 提出辞呈。～ *one's thanks* 致谢。～ *(him) a reception* 给予接见；给予欢迎〔开欢迎会〕。～ *for the construction of three new dormitories* 投标承建三所新宿舍。— *n.* ①提出，提供。②【法】清偿，偿付，赔交；赔偿费；提供物；投标；估价单，投标书。③法定货币 (= legal ～)。*call for* ～*s for a building* 建造新楼投标。*put in [make, send in] a* ～ *for sth.* 参加对…的投标。～ ***bidding*** 投标。～ ***offer*** 招标。

ten·der·ome·ter [ˌtendəˈrɔmitə] 【植】成熟度测定装置.
ten·di·ni·tis [ˈtendiˈnaitis] *n.* 【医】腱炎.
ten·di·nous [ˈtendinəs] *a.* 【解】腱的;腱质[状]的.
ten·don [ˈtendən] *n.* 【解】腱.
ten·drac [ˈtendræk] *n.* = tenrec.
ten·dril [ˈtendril] *n.* 【植】卷须. *a* ~ *of hair* 卷发.
tend·some [ˈtendsəm] *a.* 【医】需要看护的.
ten·e·brif·ic [ˌteniˈbrifik] *a.* 产生黑暗的;阴暗的.
ten·e·brifi·cate [ˌteniˈbrifikɑːt] *vt.* 使阴暗[阴郁]的.
ten·e·brous [ˈtenibrəs] *a.* 〔古〕黑暗的, 阴暗的, 阴沉的,阴郁的;难解的,晦涩的. *a* ~ *chamber* 一个阴暗的房间. *a* ~ *saying* 晦涩的话.
ten-eight·y, 1080 [ˈtenˈeiti] *n.* 〔美〕1080 灭鼠药.
ten·e·ment [ˈtenimənt] *n.* ①占有[保有, 享有]物(土地、房屋、爵位等);租用地;租住的房子.②房屋,住房,公寓;(公寓中的)一套房间;(几户合住的低级)公共住宅(= -house). ~ *of clay* = *the soul's* ~〔诗〕肉体. **-al, -a·ry,** *a.*
te·nesmus [təˈnezməs] *n.* 【医】里急后重;下坠,后坠.
te·net [ˈtiːnet, ˈtenit] *n.* 教义,教条,信条; 原则. *I hold to the* ~ *that theory should be united with practice.* 我坚持理论和实践必须相结合的原则.
ten·fold [ˈtenfəuld] *a.* 十倍的,十重的. — *ad.*
Tenn. = Tennessee.
ten·ner [ˈtenə] *n.* 〔英〕十镑纸币;〔美〕十元纸币.
Ten·nes·se·an [ˌtenəˈsiən] *n., a.* (美国)田纳西州的;田纳西州人.
Ten·nes·see [ˌteneˈsiː, -nə-] *n.* 〔美〕田纳西州. *the* ~ *Valley Authority* 田纳西流域(水利工程)管理局〔略TVA〕.
ten·nis [ˈtenis] *n.* 网球. *a* ~ *ball [court]* 网球用球[场]. ~ *sets* 网球用具.
ten·nist [ˈtenist] *n.* 〔美〕网球运动员.
Ten·ny·son [ˈtenisn] *n.* 坦尼森〔姓氏〕.
ten·on [ˈtenən] *n.* 【木工】雄榫,榫舌, 凸榫. — *vt.* 接榫;造榫. **-er** *n.* 接榫者,制榫机.
ten·or¹ [ˈtenə] *n.* ①(生活等的)进程,方向, 趋向. ②要旨,大意; 性质. ③【法】(法律文件的)正确文本;謄本. ④(支票的)限期. ⑤【矿】(矿石的)金属含量,品位. *the* ~ *of a lecture* 演讲的大意. *the even* ~ *of one's life* 平凡的生平经历.
tenor² [ˈtenə] *n.* ①男高音,男高音歌手. ②次中音部;次中音乐器. ③〔乐曲〕(一组钟里的)最低音钟. — *a.* ①男高音的. ②次中音部的. ③(一组钟里)最低音的. ~ *clef* 次中音谱号.
ten·o·rite [ˈtenəˌrait] *n.* 【矿】黑铜矿.
te·nor·rha·phy [təˈnɔːrəfi, -ˈnɔ-] *n.* *(pl.* **-phies***)* 【医】腱缝术.
te·not·o·my [tiˈnɔtəmi] *n.* 【医】腱切断术.
ten·pen·ny [ˈtenpəni] *a.* (价格)十辨士的. — *n.* (每百根十辨士的)3寸大钉(或其长度).
ten·pin [ˈtenpin] *n.* 〔美〕(十柱戏的)柱子.
ten·pins [ˈtenpinz] *n.* 〔美〕①〔作单数用〕十柱戏.②〔作复数用〕十柱戏的十根木柱.
ten-pounder [ˈtenˈpaundə] *n.* ①十磅重的东西;十磅炮弹. ②价值十镑的东西,十镑纸币. ③【英史】一年支付租金十镑而享有选举权的市民. ④【动】海鲢.
ten·rec, ten·drac [ˈtenrek, -dræk] *n.* 【动】无尾猬〔非洲马达加斯加岛产〕.
tense¹ [tens] *n.* ①【语法】时, 时态. ②〔L.〕〔古〕时间. *the perfect* ~ 完成时. *the progressive [continuous]* ~ 进行时. *at prime* ~ 最初,起初;立即.
tense² [tens] *a.* ①拉紧的,抽紧的(绳子) *(opp.* lax, loose*)*. ②紧张的. ③【语音】紧的. *a* ~ *atmosphere* 紧张的气氛. *a* ~ *vowel* 紧元音. ~ *muscles* 绷紧的肌肉. ~ *nerves* 紧张的神经. *He read the letter with a* ~ *anxiety.* 他紧张焦虑地看那封信. — *vt., vi.* (使)绷紧, (使)紧张. **-ly** *ad.* **-ness** *n.*
ten·si·ble [ˈtensibl] *a.* 能拉长的, 能伸展的. **-bil·i·ty** [ˌtensiˈbiliti] *n.* 可伸长性. **-ly** *ad.*
ten·sile [ˈtensail] *a.* 张力[拉力]的; 抗张的; 能伸长的. ~ *force* 【物】张力. ~ *strain* 【物】张应变. ~ *strength* 【物】抗张强度,拉力. ~ *stress* 【物】张胁强,张应力. *a* ~ *test* 拉力试验. **-sil·i·ty** [-ˈsiliti] *n.*
ten·sime·ter [tenˈsimitə] *n.* (气体)张力计.
ten·si·om·e·ter [ˌtensiˈɔmitə] *n.* 张力计,表面张力计.
ten·sion [ˈtenʃən] *n.* ①拉紧;伸张. ②(精神、局势等)紧张. ③【物】张力,拉力,牵力;(弹性体的)应力;(蒸气等的)膨胀力,压力. ④【电】电压, 拉伸力;拉紧[绷紧]装置, 绷子. *create [ease, reduce] the international* ~ 制造[缓和]国际紧张局势. *reduce [relieve] the* ~ *of the market* 缓和市场紧张情况. *T- runs high.* 形势极为紧张. *surface* ~ 表面张力. *vapor* ~ 蒸气压. *a high* ~ *current* 高压电流. ~ *failure* 伸张破坏. — *vt.* 张紧,使紧张. **-al** *a.*
ten·si·ty [ˈtensiti] *n.* 紧张(度);张力.
ten·son [tənˈsəun] *n.* 〔古,罕〕顶嘴诗,对吟争论诗 (= tenzon).
ten·sor [ˈtensə] *n.* ①【解】张肌. ②【数】张量.
ten-spot [ˈtenspɔt] *n.* 〔美俚〕十点(纸牌).
ten-strike [ˈtenstraik] *n.* ①【十柱戏】十柱全倒. ②〔美口〕大成功.
tent¹ [tent] *n.* ①帐篷;帐篷状东西.②寓所,住处. ③【摄】携带暗室 (= dark ~). ④【医】(防止气体散发用的)帷罩. *pitch a* ~ 搭帐棚. *strike a* ~ 拆帐棚. — *vt.* ①用帐篷遮盖. ②(使)住在帐篷里. — *vi.* ①住帐篷;宿营. ②暂居. *We're going to* ~ *in the Western Hills for a week.* 我们将在西山宿营一周. ~ **bed** (能调节温度、湿度的)帐篷式卧床;行军床. ~ **fly** 帐棚盖. ~ **guy** 帐棚支索. ~ **peg** 帐棚桩子. ~ **pegging** 跑马拔桩戏. ~ **show** 帐篷下的户外演出. ~ **stitch** (刺绣)斜向平行针脚.
tent² [tent] *n.* 【医】塞条. — *vt.* 将塞条嵌进伤口, 插入塞条.
tent³ [tent] *n.* (西班牙产)深红葡萄酒.
tent⁴ [tent] 〔Scot.〕*n., vt.* ①注意. ②看护, 照料. ③观察.
ten·ta·cle [ˈtentəkl] *n.* ①【动】触器,触手,触须,触角;【植】触丝,触毛. ②〔喻〕象触手的东西. *cut off the* ~*s of the aggressors* 斩断侵略者的魔爪. ~**d** *a.* 有触器的.
ten·tac·u·lar [tenˈtækjulə] *a.* 触手(状)的. ~ **cirri** 触须.
ten·tac·u·late [tenˈtækjuleit] *a.* ①【动】具触手(触角,触须)的. ②【植】具触毛的. ~**d** *a.* 具触手[触角, 触须,触毛]的.
ten·tac·u·li·ferous [tenˌtækjuˈlifərəs] *a.* 具触手的.
ten·tac·u·li·form [tenˈtækjulifɔːm] *a.* 触手状的.
ten·tage [ˈtentidʒ] *n.* 〔总称〕帐篷,宿营装备.
ten·ta·tive [ˈtentətiv] *a.* ①试验(性质)的;尝试的;暂时的. ②踌躇(莫决)的,不确定的;无把握的. *a* ~ *suggestion* 试探性建议. *a* ~ *agenda* 暂定议程. — *n.* ①试验;试验性提案,假说. ②【法】未遂罪. **-ly** *ad.* **-ness** *n.*
tente d'abri [tant dabri] *n.* 〔F.〕轻帐篷.
ten·ter¹ [ˈtentə] *n.* ①【纺】拉幅机,绷布机,绷布架. ②〔古〕拉幅钩,张布钩. — *vt., vi.* 用绷布机绷(布), (把)布绷紧. *be on (the)* ~*s* 〔古〕=be on ~hooks. 提心吊胆,焦虑不安. ~ **frame** 【纺】拉幅机;张布架. ~**hook** 拉幅钩,张布钩.
tent·er² [ˈtentə] *n.* 〔英〕(尤指工厂看机器的)看守人,看管人.
tenth [tenθ] *num.* 第十(的); 十分之一(的). — *n.* 〔the ~〕①(月中的)十日,十号. ②十分之一. ③【乐】第十音;十度音程. ④【空】(妨碍视线的)云层〔由于厚度分为十级〕. ⑤【史】什一税. *a ~ part* 十分之一. *There was ten ~s cloud at that time.* 当时云层厚度是十度. *~-rate* 最劣等的. **-ly** *ad.*

ten·ty [ˈtenti] *a.* 〔Scot.〕注意的,提防的.

ten·u·is [ˈtenjuis] *n.* *(pl.* ***tenues*** [-iːz]*)*【语】清爆破音 ([k], [t], [p]).

te·nu·i·ty [təˈnju(ː)iti] *n.* ①细, 薄. ②(空气、流体等的)稀薄, 稀薄度. ③(光声等)微弱,无力. ④薄弱; 无力;贫乏. *the ~ of one's style of writing* 文体平淡.

ten·u·ous [ˈtenjuəs] *a.* ①〔罕〕细的, 薄的. ②稀薄的. ③微细的,精细的, 烦琐的. ④贫乏的; 空洞无力的. *a ~ fog* 薄雾. *~ wires* 细电线. *ideas too ~ to be adopted* 太空洞不值得采纳的想法.

ten·ure [ˈtenjuə] *n.* ①(财产、职位等的)占有,保有,享有. ②占有期间. ③占有条件. ④(土地的)使用(权,期),所有权. *collective land ~* 土地的集体所有权. *during his ~ of office* 他在职的期间. *one's ~ of life* 寿命. *He holds his life on a precarious ~.* 他过着朝不保夕的生活. *On what ~ does he hold the house.* 他占用这所房子凭着什么条件?

ten·u·ri·al [teˈnjuəriəl] *a.* 土地占有[使用]的; 依赖于保有权的;任职期的. *This~ revolution never degenerated into a scrabble for land.* 这个土地革命从未沦为土地的抢夺. **-ly** *ad.*

te·nu·to [teˈnuːtəu] *a.* 〔It.〕【乐】持续,保持原有时值或音量〔在音符上写 ten. 或画横线表示〕. — *n.* *(pl. ~s, -ti* [-tiː]*)* 持续号,保持号.

tenzon [ˈtenzn] *n.* 对吟争论诗,顶嘴诗〔十一至十三世纪法国南部及意大利北部的抒情浪漫诗人对吟的一问一答抒情诗〕.

te·o·cal·li [ˌtiəˈkæli; Sp. teəuˈkɑːji] *n.* *(pl.* ***-cal·lis*** [-iːz; Sp. -jiːz]*)* (中美洲等地的)古代神庙.

te·o·sin·te [ˌtiəˈsinti] *n.*【植】墨西哥类蜀黍 *(Euchlaena mexicana)*.

te·pee [ˈtiːpiː] *n.* = teepee.

tep·e·fac·tion [ˌtepiˈfækʃən] *n.* 微温;温热.

tep·e·fy [ˈtepifai] *vt.* 使微热,使温. — *vi.* 变微热, 变温.

te·phi·gram [ˈtiːfigræm] *n.*【气】温熵图.

teph·ra [ˈtefrə] *n. pl.* 〔动词用单数或复数〕【地】火山灰,火山碎屑.

teph·rite [ˈtefrait] *n.*【地】碱玄岩. **-rit·ic** [-ˈritik] *a.*

tep·id [ˈtepid] *a.* ①不冷不热的,微热的, 温热的. ②不大热心的(招待、赞扬等). ③〔美剧〕(收入)平常的. *~ tea* 温热的茶. *a ~ evening* 不冷不热的晚上. *a ~ reception* 不大热情的招待. **-ly** *ad.* **-i·ty, -ness** *n.*

tep·i·dar·i·um [ˌtepiˈdɛəriəm] *n.* *(pl.* ***-dari·a*** [-riə]*)* (古罗马澡堂的)温水浴室.

te·poy [ˈtiːpɔi] *n.* = teapoy.

te·qui·la [təˈkiːlə] *n.* 〔美〕①龙舌兰酒. ②【植】墨西哥龙舌兰.

ter [təː] *ad.* 〔It.〕①【音】三度. ②【医】三次.

ter. = terrace; territory.

ter- *comb. f.* 三度,三次,三倍: ternate.

tera- *comb. f.* 垓,万亿,兆兆 (= 10^{12}).

te·rai [təˈrai] *n.* (在亚热带戴的)阔边毡帽.

ter·aph [ˈterəf] *n.* *(pl.* ***teraphim*** [ˈterəfim]*)* (古希伯莱的)家神像.

ter·a·tism [ˈterətizm] *n.* ①【生,医】畸形胎; 异形, 畸形. ②恶魔崇拜. ③好奇癖.

terato- *comb. f.* 畸形,怪物.

ter·a·to·gen [ˈterətədʒən] *n.*【医】畸形因素〔如化学原因或疾病等〕. **-geny** [-dʒəni] *n.*【医】畸形发生, 畸胎形成. **-gen·ic** [-ˈdʒenik] *a.*

tera·toid [ˈterətɔid] *a.*【生】奇形怪状的,畸形的.

ter·a·tol·o·gy [ˌterəˈtɔlədʒi] *n.* ①【生】畸形学; 畸胎学. ②怪物研究,怪物故事讲述, 怪物故事集. **-log·i·c** [-rətəˈlɔdʒik], **-log·i·cal** *a.*

ter·bi·a [ˈtəːbiə] *n.*【化】氧化铽.

ter·bi·um [ˈtəːbiəm] *n.*【化】铽〔Tb〕. *~ metals* 稀土族金属.

terce [təːs] *n.* = tierce.

ter·cel [ˈtəːsl], **tercelet** [ˈtəːslit] *n.* (鹰猎用的) 雄鹰, 雄隼.

ter·cen·te·na·ry, ter·cen·ten·ni·al [ˌtəːsenˈtiːnəri, -ˈtenjəl] *n., a.* 三百年(间)(的); 三百年纪念日(的),三百年纪念日的庆祝(的).

ter·cet [ˈtəːsit] *n.* ①【乐】(二拍中的连奏)三连音符. ②三拍子;【韵】同押一韵的连续三行诗.

ter·e·bene [terəˈbiːn, ˈterəb-] *n.*【化】萜, 特惹萜, 芸香烯.

ter·e·bic [teˈrebik] *n.*【化】芸香酸 (= ~ acid).

ter·e·binth [ˈterəbinθ] *n.*【植】笃耨香 (树). *oil of ~* 松节油.

ter·e·bin·thine [ˌterəˈbinθain] *a.* 笃耨香的,萜(质)的.

te·re·do [təˈriːdəu] *n.* *(pl. ~s,* ***-di·nes*** [-diniːz]*)*【动】凿船虫(属),船蛆.

Ter·ence, Ter·rance, Ter·rence [ˈterəns] *n.* 特伦斯〔男子名〕.

te·reph·thalic [ˈteˌrefˈθælik] *a.*【化】对苯二酸,对酞酸 (= ~ acid).

Te·re·sa [təˈriːzə] *n.* 特丽萨〔女子名, Theresa 的异体〕.

te·rete [təˈriːt, ˈteriːt] *a.*【生】圆柱状的,圆筒形的.

ter·gal [ˈtəːgəl] *a.*【解】背的,背板的.

ter·gem·i·nate [təːˈdʒeminit] *a.*【植】三次双生的.

ter·gi·ver·sate [ˈtəːdʒivəseit] *vi.* ①变节,背叛. ②(以言词)支吾, 搪塞, 有意改变或曲解词义. **-sa·tion** [ˌtəː-dʒirəˈseiʃən] *n.* **-sator** *n.*

ter·gum [ˈtəːgəm] *n.* *(pl.* ***-ga*** [-gə]*)* 〔L.〕【动】背甲; (昆虫的)背板.

ter·i·ya·ki [ˌteriˈjɑːki] *n.* 〔Jap.〕沾糖色烤〔日本式烤肉或鱼,将肉或鱼在酱油里腌泡过或蘸过后烤熟〕.

term [təːm] *n.* ①期限,期间. ②学期,任期; (支付)结算期;【法】开庭期, (权利的)有效期间; 定期租借(地产). ③字眼,词语; 术语,专门名词; 〔*pl.*〕措词,说法. ④【数,物】项; 条;【逻】项; 名词. ⑤〔*pl.*〕交谊,关系,地位. ⑥〔*pl.*〕(契约、谈判等的)条件,条款,约定,协定; 要求额, 价钱; 费用. ⑦界石,界标; 界限,极限,尽头,终点. ⑧【海】船尾栏杆两端的装饰. ⑨【建】胸象柱. ⑩(正常的) 分娩期. *accept [reject] sb.'s ~s* 接受[拒绝]某人条件. *a derogatory ~* 贬义词. *a long [short] ~* 长 [短] 期. *the major [middle, minor] ~*【逻】大 [中、小]项. *technical [scientific] ~s* 专门[科学]术语. *Terms cash.* 条件为现金支付. *Terms two dollars a week.* 学费每周两元. *~s for peace* 媾和条件. ***be born at full ~s*** (小孩)足月生. ***be in ~s*** 在谈判 [交涉、商量]中. ***bring (sb.) to ~s*** 使某人接受条件, 使某人就范[投降]. ***come to ~s*** 达成协议,谈判成功; 投降,让步. ***during one's ~ of office*** 在任期内. ***extreme ~*** (数) 外项. ***for a ~ of five years*** 限期五年. ***force sb. to come to ~s*** 迫使…就范. ***in any ~*** 无论如何,在任何条件下. ***in black and white ~s*** 白纸黑字, 毫不含糊. ***in (good) set ~s*** 明确地. ***in high ~s*** 极力称赞. ***in plain ~s*** 简单说. ***in ~s of*** 依…,据…; 从…方面; 用…特有的字眼 *(in ~s of approval [reproach]* 赞成[谴责]*)*. ***keep a ~*** 上一个学期的课. ***keep on good [friendly] ~s*** 保持良好[友好]关系. ***keep ~s with*** 和…继续谈判 [交涉]. ***make ~s with*** 和…谈妥[妥协]. ***not (up)on any ~s*** 决不. ***not on borrowing ~s*** 不友好,无交情. ***on bad ~s*** 不和,不睦 *(with)*. ***on easy ~*** 以宽大的条件. ***on equal ~s*** 处于平等的地位. ***on even ~s*** (和…) 不相上下 *(with)*. ***on one's own ~s*** 按照自己的条件(价钱). ***on speaking ~s*** 谈谈话的关系,泛泛之交 *(with)*. ***on visiting [familiar, first-name, intimate, writing] ~s with***

和…有往来[很熟、通信]的朋友关系. ***sales ~s*** 售货条起. ***set a ~ to*** 对…加以限制，给…规定期限. ***set ~s*** 定条件. ***upon no ~s*** 决不. — *vt.* 把…叫做，把…称为. *He ~ed this gas argon.* 他把这种气体叫做氩气. *He has no right to ~ himself an expert.* 他没有权力自封为专家. *I would ~ it a case of treason.* 我想称之为一起叛国案. ~ **day** 支付日，租金等[苏格兰]法定季度结帐日;【律】开庭日，科学工作的观察日. ~ **deposit** 定期存款. ~ **insurance** 定期人寿保险. ~ **of public summons**【法】公告期间. ~ **of redemption**【法】偿还期限. ~ **of validity**【法】有效期间. ~ **paper** 学期论文. ~ **policy** 定期人寿保险契约(保单). ~**s of reference** 权限;受权调查范围.

term. = terminal; termination.

ter·ma·gan·cy [ˈtəːməgənsi] *n.* (女人的)凶悍，暴躁.

ter·ma·gant [ˈtəːməgənt] *a.* 好骂人的，好争吵的，凶悍的，暴躁的. — *n.* 好争吵[骂人]的女人，悍妇，泼妇.

term·er [ˈtəːmə] *n.* 服徒刑的罪犯. *a life ~* 服无期徒刑的罪犯.

ter·mi·na·ble [ˈtəːminəbl] *a.* 可终止的，有限期的. **-bil·i·ty** *n.* 限期性. **-ness** *n.* **-bly** *ad.*

ter·mi·nal [ˈtəːminl] *a.* ①终端的，终点的，结尾的；极限的. ②定期的，每期[季]的；每学期的，学期中[末]的. ③期终的；末期的；【植】顶生的；【解、动】末梢的；分界处的，端的. ④【逻】名辞的. *a ~ landmark* 界标. *the ~ stage* 末期. *the ~ station* 终点站. —*n.* ①末尾，末端. ②【语言】词尾〔最后的音节，字母，音素，音节等，结尾的词〕. ③【电】电极，(电池的)端；接头，端子；线端. ④〔美〕终点(站). ⑤〔*pl.*〕卸货(等)车站用费. ⑥【建】端饰；胸像柱. ⑦学期考试，大考. ~ **charges** 上货[卸货]费. ~ **check valve**【机】管端止回阀. ~ **juncture**【语言】停顿时刻. ~ **leave**〔美〕(老兵退役前的)末次假期. ~ **market** (农产品)集散的中心市场. ~ **nose-dive**【空】极限垂直俯冲. ~ **parenchyma**【植】轮界薄壁组织. ~ **velocity**【物】收尾速度.

ter·mi·nal·ly [ˈtəːminəli] *ad.* 在末端，在终点；每期，每季；在学期末尾.

ter·mi·nate [ˈtəːmineit] *vt.* ①使结束，使停止，使终止. ②解除(契约等)；结束. ③限定，定界. — *vi.* 终止，结束，归于，以…告终 *(in)*；达到尽头；满期. — [ˈtəːminit] *a.* 终止的；有限的(小数等). *It is said that the General Motors is going to ~ your contract.* 据说通用汽车公司要解除和你订的契约. *What's the meaning of the word that ~s the sentence?* 那句话结尾的词意思是什么? *Her appeal has ~d favourably.* 她的上诉胜诉了. *Murphy's unhappy married life ~d in divorce.* 墨菲的不幸的婚姻以离婚告终.

ter·mi·na·tion [ˌtəːmiˈneiʃən] *n.* ①末端，终点；终止，终结；结局，结束. ②限定，界限，限度. ③【语法】词尾. *the ~ of an agreement* 契约满期日. *the ~ of our trip* 我们旅行的终点. *a ~ slip*〔美〕解雇通知书. ***bring to a ~*** 使了结，结束. ***put a ~ to sth.*** 结束某事. **-al** *a.*

ter·mi·na·tive [ˈtəːminətiv] *a.* ①结尾的，终止的；限定的. ②【语】结尾的，(动词等)表示动作完成的. — *n.*【语】词尾. **-ly** *ad.*

ter·mi·na·tor [ˈtəːmineitə] *n.* ①限定者[物]；终止者[物]. ②【化】(链的)终止剂. ③【天】(月、星表面上的)明暗界线.

termi·ner [ˈtəminə] *n.*【法】判决 *(cf.* oyer*)*.

termi·ni [ˈtəːminai] *n.* terminus 的复数.

ter·mi·nism [ˈtəːminizəm] *n.*【神】忏悔期限论；【哲】= nominalism.

ter·mi·no·log·i·cal [ˌtəːminəˈlɔdʒikəl] *a.* 术语的，用语上的；术语学(上)的. **a ~ inexactitude** 谎言，假话.

ter·mi·nol·o·gy [ˌtəːmiˈnɔlədʒi] *n.* ①〔集合词〕专门名词，术语. ②术语学；名词学. **-gist** *n.* 术语学家.

ter·mi·nus [ˈtəːminəs] *n.* *(pl. ~es, -ni)* ①(铁路，汽车，航路等的)终点. ②〔英〕终点站〔美国叫 terminal〕. ③界限，极限. ④〔T-〕(古罗马的)守界神. ⑤界桩，界标，界柱.

ter·mi·nus ad quem [ˈtəːminəs ædˈkwem]〔L.〕(辩论等的)归结点，目标；结论；(契约的)终止期.

terminus a quo [ˈtəːminəs eiˈkwəu]〔L.〕(辩论等的)出发点；(契约的)开始期.

ter·mi·tar·i·um [təːmiˈtɛəriəm] *n.* *(pl.* ***termitaria*)**,

ter·mi·ta·ry [ˈtəːmitəri] 螱窠；人工白蚁巢，白蚁养殖器.

ter·mite [ˈtəːmait] *n.*【虫】白蚁. *a ~ hill [heap]* 白蚁的窠.

term·less [ˈtəːmlis] *a.* 无限的，无期限的；无条件的；〔诗，古〕难于形容的.

term·ly [ˈtəːmli] *a., ad.* (指事物发生、款项支付等)定期的(地).

term·or [ˈtəːmə] *n.*【法】定期租户，终身租户.

tern[1] [təːn] *n.*【鸟】燕鸥.

tern[2] [təːn] *n.* ①三个一套，三个一组，三重. ②〔美〕三桅帆船(= ~ schooner)；中彩的三个号码；中彩三个号码的奖. — *a.* = ternate.

ter·na·ry [ˈtəːnəri] *a.* ①三个的，三个组成的，三重的. ②第三的. ③【化】三元[成分]的；【数】三元的，三变数的，三进位的. ~ **alloy(s)** 三元合金. ~ **scale** 三进记数法. ~ **set**【数】三分点集.

ter·nate [ˈtəːneit] *a.* ①三个的. ②【植】三出的. *a ~ leaf* 三裂叶. **-ly** *ad.*

terne, terne·plate [ˈtəːn, -pleit] *n.* (镀铅锡)薄钢板，白铁板.

ter·ni·on [ˈtəːniən] *n.* ①〔现罕〕三个一套；三合一；三人(事物或思想等)的组合. ②三价原子，三价基. ③【乐】三和弦.

ter·pene [ˈtəːpiːn] *n.*【化】萜烯，萜(烃).

ter·pin·e·ol [təˈpiniˌəul, -ˌɔːl] *n.*【化】萜品醇.

Terp·sich·o·re [təːpˈsikəri] *n.*【希神】特普丝歌利〔司歌舞的女神〕.

Terp·si·cho·re·an [ˌtəːpsikəˈri(ː)ən] *a.* ①特普丝歌利的. ②〔t-〕舞蹈的. — *n.*〔t-〕〔谑〕跳舞的人；舞蹈家.

ter(r). = terrace; territory.

ter·ra [ˈterɑː] *n.*〔L.〕①地；土. ②〔T-〕土地(神). ~ **alba** 管土，白土〔如石膏粉，瓷土，镁氧〕. ~ **cariosa** 矽藻土. **terrae filius** *(pl.* ***terrae filii*)** 小百姓. ~ **firma** 大地，陆地；稳固的地位. ~ **incognita** [inˈkɔgnitə] *(pl.* ***terrae incognitae*** [ˈteriːinˈkɔgnitiː]*)* 未知的土地；未知的领域. ~ **Japonica** = gambier. ~ **nera** [ˈneirə] (古代画家做颜料用的)黑土. ~ **rossa** (钙质)红土. ~ **verde** [ˈvɛədei] = ~ **verte** [vɛrt] 绿土；绿土颜料.

ter·race [ˈterəs] *n.* ①台地，阶地，梯田；坛，坪；有花坛(等)的庭园. ②(房屋前面的)平台；露台，阳台. ③柱廊，(东方式)平屋顶. ④〔美〕(马路中央的)小公园. ⑤高台街〔高于街道的一排房屋，有这样房屋的街道〕. ⑥【地】(海岸等的)阶丘. — *vt.* 使成台地，使成坛，筑坛建造成平顶. *a ~d roof* 平的屋顶. *~d fields* 梯田.

ter·ra·cot·ta [ˈterəˈkɔtə] *n.* ①制陶赤土，赤土陶器. ②赤褐色. ③空心砖，琉璃砖. ④一种褐色的柑子.

ter·rain [ˈterein] *n.* ①地面；地带；地区. ②(知识的)领域，范围. ③【军】地形，地势. ④【地】岩层，岩群，地体；地质建造. *a difficult ~ for a counterattack* 不利于反攻的地形. *the whole ~ of home economics* 家政学的整个领域.

ter·ra·ma·re [ˌterəˈmɑːri] *n.*〔*pl.*〕*(sing.* ***ter·ra·ma·ra*** [ˌterəˈmɑːrə]*)* 土性沉积物；(南欧)史前沉积.

ter·ra·mycin [terəˈmaisin] *n.* 土霉素，土链丝菌素，氧四环素〔旧名地霉素〕.

ter·rane [təˈrein, ˈterein] *n.*【地】= terrain.

ter·ran·eous [teˈreiniəs] *a.*【植】地上生长的，陆生的.

ter·ra·pin [ˈterəpin] *n.*【动】龟鳖类爬行动物〔如泥龟，

甲鱼〕.

ter·ra·que·ous [teˈreikwiəs] *a.* 由水陆形成的,水陆的.

ter·rar·i·um [teˈrɛəriəm] *n.* *(pl. ~s, -raria* [-ˈrɛːriə]*)* 陆地动物饲养场.

ter·raz·zo [təˈræzəu, təˈrɑːtsəu, te-] *n.* 〔It.〕【建】水磨石(地板).

Ter·rell [ˈterəl] *n.* 特雷尔〔姓氏,男子名〕.

ter·rene [ˈteriːn] *a.* ①土质的;陆地的,地球的. ②尘世的,世俗的. — *n.* ①地球,陆地. ②【地】地表.

ter·re·plein [ˈtɛəplein] *n.* 【军】垒道〔炮台上安炮处〕.

ter·res·tri·al [tiˈrestriəl] *a.* ①地球(上)的. ②地上的(生活等),人间的 *(opp.* celestial*)*,现世的. ③陆地的,陆生的,陆栖的(动植物). — *n.* ①地球居民. ②〔*pl.*〕陆生动〔植〕物,陆栖动物. ③〔罕〕地球. *the [this] ~ globe [ball]* 地球. *a ~ globe* 地球仪. *a ~ journey* 陆地旅行. *~ aims [interests]* 名利心.

terret [ˈterit] *n.* (笼头上套住韁绳的)铁环;(系链条,皮带等的)扣环.

terre-verte [ˈtɛəˌvɛt] *n.* 【地】绿色土.

ter·ri·ble [ˈterəbl, -ribl] *a.* ①可怕的,骇人的. ②〔口〕非常的,厉害的,极度的. ③〔口〕极坏的. *a ~ accident* 一桩可怕的意外事件. *a ~ winter* 极冷的冬天. *in a ~ hurry* 慌慌忙忙地. *a ~ performance* 极坏的演出. *It's ~!* 糟得很! — *ad.* 〔口〕非常,很,极. *The weather was ~* (= terribly) *hot.* 天气热极了. — *n.* 〔主 *pl.*〕可怕的人〔东西〕. **-ness** *n.*

ter·ri·bly [ˈteribli] *ad.* ①可怕地. ②〔口〕厉害,很,极. *He speaks Chinese ~ well.* 他的汉语讲得非常好. *It's ~ late.* 太晚了.

ter·ric·o·lous [teˈrikələs] *a.* 【生】陆栖的,陆生的.

ter·ri·er[1] [ˈteriə] *n.* ①㹴〔灵敏的小猎狗〕. ②〔英俚〕本土军士兵. *a bull [fox] ~* 短毛㹴. *an Irish [Scotch, Skye, Yorkshire] ~* 长毛㹴. *a Maltese [toy] ~* 玩赏㹴.

ter·ri·er[2] [ˈteriə] *n.* 【法】地产册,地籍簿.

ter·rif·ic [təˈrifik] *a.* ①可怕的,凄惨的. ②〔口〕极大的,非常的,猛烈的. ③〔美俚〕了不起的,极好的. *drive at a ~ speed* 以极高的速度开车. *think oneself ~* 自以为了不起. *He weathered a ~ storm.* 他度过了一场可怕的暴风雨. **-rif·i·cal·ly** *ad.*

ter·ri·fy [ˈterifai] *vt.* 使恐怖,吓唬,威胁. *You ~ me!* 吓我一跳! ***be terrified at [by, of, with]*** 给…吓一跳. ***be terrified out of one's senses (wits)*** 吓得魂不附体. *~ (sb.)* ***into doing*** 威胁(某人)做某事.

ter·rig·e·nous [teˈridʒinəs] *a.* 【地】①陆源(沉积)的. ②陆生的.

Ter·rill [ˈteril] *n.* 特里尔〔姓氏,男子名〕.

ter·rine [teˈriːn] *n.* 〔F.〕(连同内装食品卖的)陶罐.

ter·ri·to·ri·al [ˌteriˈtɔːriəl] *a.* ①领土的. ②土地的. ③区域的,地方的. ④〔T-〕〔美〕准州的,领土(或领地)的. — *n.* ①〔T-〕〔英〕本土军士兵. ②地方部队的士兵. *~ air [sky, waters, seas]* 领空〔海〕. *~ ambitions* 领土野心. *~ expansion* 领土扩张. *~ industry* 地方工业. *~ integrity* 领土完整. *T- laws* 美国领地的法律. *~ limit* 国界. *~ sovereignty* 领土主权. **-ly** *ad.*

ter·ri·to·ri·al·ism [ˌteriˈtɔːriəlizəm] *n.* ①地主阶级统治制. ②地方政府权力高于教会的制度. ③〔常 T.〕犹太人居住地自治主义〔运动〕. ④【史】(神圣罗马帝国的)领地居民信奉当地宗教的规定.

ter·ri·to·ri·al·ist [ˌteriˈtɔːriəlist] *n.* (地方)政府权力高于教会制度的鼓吹者,主张地方政府权力高于教会制度的人.

ter·ri·to·ri·al·i·ty [ˌteriˌtɔːriˈæliti] *n.* ①地区性. ②【人性学】(动物的)地盘性,地区性.

ter·ri·to·ri·al·ize, -ise [ˌteriˈtɔːriəˌlaiz] *vt.* ①扩张领土. ②(通过扩张)使成为领土;(通过扩张)使成为领地. ③按地区分配. **-al·i·za·tion** *n.*

ter·ri·to·ry [ˈteritəri] *n.* ①领土,版图,领地. ②地区. ③(科学知识、行动等的)领域,范围. ④【商】势力范围. ⑤(野鸟的)生活范围. ⑥〔T-〕〔美〕(美国、加拿大的)准州(地区). *a leased ~* 租借地. *in the ~ [sphere, field, domain] of physics* 在物理学的领域内. ***take in too much ~*** 走极端;说得过分;牵涉过多.

ter·ror [ˈterə] *n.* ①恐怖. ②恐怖的原因. ③可怕的人〔物〕. ④〔口〕极可憎的人. ⑤〔the T-〕= the Reign of T-. *a holy ~* 难对付的家伙. *a perfect ~* 讨厌到极点的家伙. ***be a ~*** 〔口〕做使人为难的事情,捣蛋的人. ***be a ~ to*** 对…是一个恐怖,使…畏惧〔害怕〕. ***be in ~ of*** 害怕…. ***have a ~ of sth.*** 对某事害怕. ***flee in ~*** 非常惊慌地逃跑. ***strike ~ into sb.'s heart*** 使某人恐怖,吓坏. ***the king of ~s*** 死. ***the Reign of T- = the (Red) T-*** 【法史】恐怖时代〔指法国革命中1793年5月到翌年7月一段时期〕. ***the White T-*** 白色恐怖〔特指1795年保王党员对革命党的残酷报复〕.

ter·ror·ism [ˈterərizəm] *n.* ①恐怖主义〔手段,政治〕. ②威吓,胁迫.

ter·ror·ist [ˈterərist] *n.* 恐怖主义者,恐怖分子.

ter·ror·ize [ˈterəraiz] *vt., vi.* ①(使)恐怖;采取恐怖手段,胁迫. ②实行恐怖统治. **-i·za·tion** *n.*

ter·ror·i·zer [ˈterəraizə] *n.* ①采取恐怖手段的人. ②〔美〕【影】恐怖片.

ter·ror-strick·en, -struck [ˈterəstrikən, -strʌk] *a.* 受了惊吓的,吓破了胆的.

Ter·ry [ˈteri] *n.* ①特里〔姓氏,男子名,Terence 的昵称〕. ②特丽〔女子名, Theresa 的昵称〕.

ter·ry [ˈteri] *n.* ①【纺】起毛毛圈;毛圈织物. ②〔俚〕无线电(雷达自动)测高计.

terse [təːs] *a.* (言谈,文笔等)简练的,简洁的,简短的. *a ~ and vigorous style* 简洁有力的文体. *a ~ note of dismissal with no explanation* 一封没有说明理由的简短的辞退信. **-ly** *ad.* **-ness** *n.*

ter·tial [ˈtəːʃəl] *a.* 第三列的〔指鸟翼基部关节上所生的拔风羽〕. — *n.* ①第三列拔风羽,臂翼. ②【语法】状语词,第三级成分.

ter·tian [ˈtəːʃən] *a.* 隔一天发生的,间日的. — *n.* 【医】间日热,三日热. *~ malaria* 间日疟.

ter·ti·a·ry [ˈtəːʃəri, -ʃiə-] *a.* ①第三的,第三位的,第三级的. ②【化】特,叔,三代的. ③【医】第三期的. ④〔T-〕【地】第三纪的;第三系的. *the T- period [system]* 【地】第三纪〔系〕. *~ alcohol* 叔醇. *~ phosphate* 三代磷酸盐. — *n.* ①〔T-〕【地】第三纪,第三系,第三纪层. ②【宗】第三级教士. ③【动】第三列拔风羽,臂翼. ④【医】〔*pl.*〕第三期梅毒的症状. ⑤【语】三级语级〔叶斯帕森用语,指句中用作状语成分的语词或结构〕.

ter·tio [ˈtəːʃiəu] *ad.* 〔L.〕第三.

ter·ti·um quid [ˈtəːʃiəm ˈkwid] 〔L.〕①(模棱两可,地位暧昧的)第三者. ②中间物. ③〔谑〕三角关系中的第三者.

ter·tius [ˈtəːʃjəs, -ʃiəs] *a.* 〔L.〕第三的,(三者中)年纪〔年级〕最小的. *Jones ~* 三个琼斯中年纪〔年级〕最小的(那个). *~* ***gaudens*** [ˈgɔːdənz] 得渔翁之利的第三者.

ter·va·lent [təˈveilənt] *a.* ①【化】三价的. ②【生】三价染色体 (= trivalent).

ter·y·lene [ˈteriˌliːn] *n.* 【纺】涤纶〔原商标名〕.

ter·za ri·ma [ˈtəːtsə ˈriːmə] *(pl. terze rime* [ˈteːtsei ˈriːmei]*)* 〔It.〕(象但丁《神曲》中所用的)三行诗隔句押韵法〔韵律为 aba, bcb, cdc ...〕.

ter·zet·to [təːˈtsetəu] *n.* 〔It.〕【乐】三重奏〔唱〕;三声中部.

Tes·la [ˈteslə], **Nikola** 泰斯拉〔1857—1943, 美国电机工程师〕. *~* **coil** 泰斯拉(空心)变压器.

tes·la [ˈteslə] *n.* 【电】泰斯拉〔磁束密度 MKS 单位〕.

TESOL [ˈtiːsəl] (= teaching English to speakers of other languages) 对说外国语人的英语教学.

tes·sel·lar [ˈtesələ] *a.* ①似小(长)方形镶嵌物的. ②用

小(长)方形镶嵌物嵌成的.

tes·sel·late [ˈtesileit] *vt.* (把路面等)镶嵌作花纹状. — *a.* = ~d; **-d** *a.* ①嵌成花纹的, 镶嵌细工的. ②【植】具方格斑纹的;【动】棋盘格形的. *a ~d pavement* 嵌装图案的人行道.

tes·sel·la·tion [ˌtesəˈleiʃən] *n.* 嵌石装饰, 棋盘形布置〔嵌石装饰〕.

tes·se·ra [ˈtesərə] *n.* (*pl.* **-rae** [-riː]) ①镶嵌物〔玻璃、象牙、大理石等作成的小方块〕. ②【古罗马】(骨、象牙、木头等做的)入场券[证]; 骰子; 标记.

tes·se·ral [ˈtesərəl] *a.* ①镶嵌物(似)的. ②【物】等轴(晶系)的.

tes·si·tura [ˌtesiˈtjuərə] *n.* 〔It.〕【乐】(应用)声域, 音域.

Test. = Testament.

test[1] [test] *n.* ①检验, 检查; 考查; 测验, 考试; 考验. ②检验用品; 试金石;【化】试药; (判断的)标准. ③【化】化验; (用试剂检查出来的)检查结果;【冶】(分析用)灰皿, 烤钵, 提银盘. ④〔口〕= ~match. ⑤【英史】宣誓. *an acceptance* ~ 验收. *an achievement* ~ 成绩测验. *a blood* ~ 血液检查. *a live* ~【火箭】载人试验. *a performance* ~ 性能试验. *a service* ~ 运行试验, 使用试验. *a strength* ~ 强度试验. *a ~ in physics* 物理测验(考试). *a ~ object* (显微镜的) 检验物. *a ~ pilot* (新飞机的) 试飞员. *the supreme* ~ 最高标准. *the ~ of practice* 实践的检验. ***put to the ~*** 试验, 检验. ***stand [bear, pass] the ~*** 试验合格. ***take the ~*** 就职宣誓. — *vt.* ①考查, 测验, 试验, 检验, 考验. ②【化】(用试药)检验, 化验. ③【冶】精炼(金银). *A game like that ~ed our strength.* 象那样的一场球赛考验了我们的力量. ***I'll have my blood ~ed.*** 我要检查一下血. ~ *ore for gold* 检验矿砂的含金成分. —*vi.* ①受试验, 受测验. ②测得结果. ③(为鉴定而)进行测验 (*for*). *Let's use another method to ~ for its pulling force.* 让我们用另外一种方法来测验它的拉力. ~ **ban** 禁止核试验协定. ~**-bed** 试验台, 试验机器用的支架. ~ **field** 试验场地. ~ **match** (国际)板球决赛. ~ **mixer** 试验混合器. ~ **paper** ①试纸. ②测验题目纸〔试卷〕. ③〔美〕鉴定笔迹用的文件. ~ **pattern**【电视】测试图. ~ **pilot** 试飞员. ~ **tube** 试管. ~ **types**〔*pl.*〕试力鉴定表. ~**-working** (机器的)试车, 试开. **the ~ act** ①宣誓书. ②〔T- A-〕〔英史〕审查条例. **-a·ble** *a.* ①可试验的. ②【法】有资格作证〔立遗嘱〕的, 可根据遗嘱处理的. **-ed** *a.* 经过考验的.

test[2] [test] *n.*【动】(软体类的)介壳, 甲壳;【植】(外)种皮.

testa [ˈtestə] *n.* (*pl.* **-tae** [-tiː])【植】(外)种皮.

tes·ta·cean [tesˈteiʃən] *a.*【动】介壳类的, 有介壳的根足虫类的. — *n.* 介壳类动物.

tes·ta·ce·o·lo·gy [ˈtesˌteisiˈɔlədʒi] *n.* 贝类学; 介类学.

tes·ta·ceous [tesˈteiʃəs] *a.* ①介壳的; 有介壳的; 介壳质的. ②【生】红砖色的, 黄褐色的.

tes·ta·cy [ˈtestəsi] *n.*【法】留有遗嘱.

tes·ta·ment [ˈtestəmənt] *n.* ①契约; 誓约. ②〔T-〕【宗】(基督教)圣约书, 旧约全书或新约全书. ③〔口〕一部新约全书. ④【法】遗言, 遗嘱. ⑤确实的证明. ⑥信仰的宣告、声明. *the New [Old] T-* 新〔旧〕约全书. *one's last will and ~*【法】(处理身后财产的)遗嘱. *make one's ~* 立遗嘱. *a military* ~ 军人遗嘱; 口头遗嘱. **-tal** (根据) 遗嘱的.

tes·ta·men·ta·ry [ˌtestəˈmentəri] *a.* (根据)遗嘱的; 遗嘱中写明的.

tes·ta·mur [tesˈteimə] *n.* (英国大学的)试验及格证.

tes·tate [ˈtestit] *a.* 留有遗嘱的. —*n.*【法】留有遗嘱而死的人; 立遗嘱人.

tes·ta·tor [tesˈteitə] *n.* (*fem.* ***-trix*** [-triks] *pl.* ***-tri·ces*** [-trisiːz]) 立有〔留有〕遗嘱的人.

test·ee [tesˈtiː] *n.* 受测验者, 测验对象.

test·er[1] [ˈtestə] *n.* ①试验者, 检验者, 化验者. ②检验器, 化验装置. ③(试验用的)对照物. *a ~ strain*【生】测交品系. *a carpet* ~〔俚〕射频脉冲发生器.

tester[2] [ˈtestə] *n.* (床、布道坛等上的)天盖, 华盖.

tester[3] [ˈtestə] *n.* (一面有头像的) 古银币;〔古、谑〕六辨士.

testes [ˈtestiːz] *n.* testis 的复数.

tes·ti·cle [ˈtestikl] *n.*【解】睾丸; 精巢. **-tic·u·lar** *a.* 睾丸的, 睾丸状的.

tes·tic·u·late [tesˈtikjuleit] *n.*【植】①睾丸状的. ②双丸状的.

tes·ti·fy [ˈtestifai] *vi.* 证明; 证实 (*to*); 证言, 作证 (*to*). — *vt.* 证明, 证言; (事物)成为证据, 证实; 表明, 声明. ~ *against sb.* 作不利于某人的证言. ~ *to sb.'s honesty* 证明某人诚实. ~ *one's regret* 表示歉意, 说对不起. ~ *under oath that* 发誓证明(声明). **-fi·ca·tion** [ˌtestifikeiʃən] *n.* 证明; 证言; 证据. **-fi·er** *n.* 证明人.

tes·ti·mo·ni·al [ˌtestiˈməunjəl, -niəl] *n.* ①(人品、能力、资格等的)证明书; 鉴定书, 推荐书. ②奖状, 奖品, 感谢信, 表扬信, 纪念品. —*a.* ①有关证明(鉴定)书的. ②褒奖的, 表扬的. **-ize** [**-ise**] *vt.* ①给…开证明书. ②赠送…奖品.

tes·ti·mo·ny [ˈtestiməni] *n.* ①证据; 证明, 证言. ②声明, 宣言. ③表示, 表明. ④〔the ~〕〔古〕(基督教) 十诫;〔*pl.*〕神的箴言. ⑤〔古〕抗议 (*against*). *give ~ as to ...* 关于…作证. *give false* ~ 作假证明. *His smile was ~ of his consent.* 他的微笑表明他同意了. *I can bear ~ to his good character.* 我可以证明他的品德良好. ~ *of witness*【法】人证. ***call sb. in ~*** 传某人作证. ***produce ~ to [of]*** 提出…的证据.

tes·ti·ness [ˈtestinis] *n.* 易怒, 暴躁.

tes·tis [ˈtestis] *n.* (*pl.* ***testes*** [-tiːz])【解】= testicle.

tes·ti·tis [tesˈtaitis] *n.*【医】睾丸炎.

tes·ton, tes·toon [ˈtestən, -ˈtuːn] *n.* 头像银币〔正面有人头的欧洲古银币, 尤指 a) 十六世纪法国的一种银币; b) 铸有亨利八世头像的英国硬币〕.

tes·tos·ter·one [tesˈtɔstərəun]【生化】睾丸激素〔甾酮〕.

test-tube [ˈtesˈtjuːb, ˈtesˈtuːb] *a.* ①在试管中培养(或生长)的. ②由人工授精而生产的. ③化学合成的. *a ~ body* 试管婴儿, 人工受胎婴儿, 人工受精儿.

tes·tu·di·nal [tesˈtjuːdinəl, -tuːd-] *a.* 龟的; 龟甲的, 如龟的.

tes·tu·di·nar·i·ous [ˌtestjuːdiˈnɛəriəs] *a.* 玳瑁形的.

tes·tu·di·nate [tesˈtjuːdineit] *a.* ①龟甲形的. ②龟的. —*n.* 龟.

tes·tu·di·neous [ˌtestjuːˈdiniəs] *a.* 如龟甲形的.

tes·tu·do [tesˈtjuːdəu] *n.* (*pl.* ~***s, -dines*** [-diniːz]) ①【古罗马】攻城用龟甲形掩蔽物. ②〔T-〕【动】陆龟(属).

tes·ty [ˈtesti] *a.* (***-ti·er; -ti·est***) ①性急的, 易怒的, 暴躁的. ②(话等)气恼的, 烦躁的. *grow more and more ~ with age* 随着年纪大而变得越来越性急. *the ~ manager* 暴躁的经理. *one's ~ remarks* 某人的气话. **-ti·ly** *ad.*

Tet [tet] *n.* (越南的)春节.

te·tan·ic [tiˈtænik] *a.*【医】破伤风性的, 强直性痉挛的. — *n.*【药】痉挛诱起剂; 强直剂.

tet·a·nize [ˈtetənaiz] *vt.* (***-nized, -niz·ing***)【医】引起强直性痉挛, 使强直. **-za·tion** [ˌtetənaiˈzeiʃən] *n.*

tet·a·nus [ˈtetənəs] *n.*【医】①破伤风; 破伤风菌. ②强直(性痉挛), 强直.

tet·a·ny [ˈtetəni] *n.*【医】手足搐搦; 强直.

te·tar·to·he·dral [tiˌtɑːtəuˈhiːdrəl] *a.*【物】四半面的〔一种晶形, 它仅显出晶系的对称所需完面数的四分之一的〕.

tetched [tetʃt] *a.* ①被触动的, 受触犯的. ②精神有点失常的.

te(t)ch·y [ˈtetʃi] *a.* 易怒的, 脾气乖戾的. **-i·ly** *ad.* **-i·ness** *n.*

tête-à-tête [ˈteitɑːˈteit] *ad.* 〔F.〕 仅仅两人地, 面对面地, 两人私下地. — *n.* 促膝谈心; 对谈, 相对密谈; (两人之

间谈的)心腹话;对坐的两人;面对面式的双人椅 〔沙发〕. — *a.* 仅两人的,面对面的,两人私下的. *have a ~ (talk) with sb.* 和某人密谈. *dine ~ with sb.* (单独或私下)同某人一起进餐.

tête-bêche [ˈtetˈbeʃ] *a.* (两张邮票)图案一正一反的.

teth, tet [tet] *n.* 希伯来文的第九个字母.

teth·er [ˈteðə] *n.* ①(拴牛马等的)系绳,系链. ②(知识、力量、权限等的)限度,范围. ***at the end of one's ~*** 智穷才尽,用尽方法,穷途末路;忍无可忍地. ***beyond one's ~*** 为某人力所不及;在某人权限外. — *vt.* ①(用绳、铁链)拴系. ②拘束,束缚. *a horse ~ed to a tree* 一匹拴在树上的马.

teth·er·ball [ˈteðəˌbɔːl] *n.* ①绳球(游戏)〔用绳将一小球系在木杆上,两人用手或木棒反向击球,看谁先将绳完全绕在木杆上〕. ②(绳球游戏用的)小球.

Te·ton [ˈtiːtən] *n.* ①*(pl. -tons, -ton)* 提顿族人〔美国达科他的印第安人〕. ②提顿语.

tetr- *comb. f.* 〔用于元音前〕四: *tetrode.*

tetra- *comb. f.* 〔用于辅音前〕四: *tetragon.*

tet·ra [ˈtetrə] *n.* 【动】脂鲤〔一种热带鱼〕.

tet·ra·bas·ic [ˌtetrəˈbeisik] *a.* 【化】四碱价的;四元的;四代的.

tet·ra·brach [ˈtetrəˌbræk] *n.* 【韵、诗】有四个短音节的词或音步.

tet·ra·bran·chi·ate [ˌtetrəˈbræŋkiˌeit, -it] *a.* 【动】四鳃类 *(Tetrabranchia)* 动物〔包括鹦鹉螺;魟鱼〕.

tet·ra·chlo·ride [ˌtetrəˈklɔːraid] *n.* 【化】四氯化物.

tet·ra·chord [ˈtetrəkɔːd] *n.* 【乐】①四度音阶. ②(古代的)四弦乐器. **-al** *a.*

te·trac·id [teˈtræsid] *n.* 【化】①四酸. ②具有四个氢氧基的醇类.

tet·ra·cyclic [ˌtetrəˈsiklik] *a.* 【植】四轮列的,四轮花的.

tet·ra·cy·cline [ˌtetrəˈsaiklin, -lain] *n.* 【药】四环素.

tet·rad [ˈtetræd] *n.* ①四个;四个一组的东西. ②【生】四合子,四分体. ③【化】四价元素. ④【儿】拼四小组. **-ic** *a.*

tet·ra·dac·tyl(e) [ˌtetrəˈdæktil] *a., n.* 四趾的(动物). **-tyl·ous** *a.*

te·trad·y·mite [ˌteˈtrædiˌmait] *n.* 【矿】辉碲铋矿.

tet·ra·eth·yl lead [ˌtetrəˈeθl] 【化】四乙铅.

tet·ra·gon [ˈtetrəgən] *n.* ①【几】四角〔边〕形. ②【物】四重轴.

tet·ra·gon·al [teˈtrægənl] *a.* ①四角〔边〕形的. ②【物】正方晶的. *~ prism* 正方柱.

tet·ra·gram [ˈtetrəgræm] *n.* 由四个字母组成的词,四文字符号.

tet·ra·hed·ral [ˌtetrəˈhedrəl] *a.* ①有四面的. ②【几】四面(体)的;【植】四分同裂的. *~ complex* 四面线丛.

tet·ra·he·drite [ˌtetrəˈhiːdrait] *n.* 【矿】黝铜矿.

tet·ra·hed·ron [ˌtetrəˈhedrən] *n.* *(pl. ~s, -dra* [-drə]*)* ①【几】四面体. ②【植】四分体形. **-dral** *a.*

tet·ra·hy·dro·can·na·bi·nol [ˌtetrəˌhaidrəuˈkænəbiˌnɔl] *n.* 【药】四氢大麻酚.

tet·ral·o·gy [teˈtrælədʒi] *n.* ①(戏剧、歌剧、小说等的)四部曲. ②【古希腊】四部剧〔由三部悲剧一部喜剧组成〕.

te·tram·er·ous [teˈtræmərəs] *a.* 【生】四附节的;(花的部分,如花轮)四个一组的;四复的,四重的 (= 4-merous).

tet·ram·e·ter [teˈtræmitə] *n.* 四音步句〔诗〕.

tet·ra·pet·a·lous [ˌtetrəˈpetələs] *a.* 【植】四花瓣的.

tet·ra·phyl·lous [ˌtetrəˈfiləs] *a.* 【植】四叶的.

tetra·ploid [ˈtetrəplɔid] *n., a.* 【生】四倍体(的). **-y** *n.*

tet·ra·pod [ˈtetrəpɔd] *n., a.* ①【动】四脚动物(的). ②四脚体〔四脚从一个中心以放射状伸出,互成 120° 角;三脚支在一个平面上站立时,一脚向上〕.

tet·rapo·dy [teˈtræpɔdi] *n.* = tetrameter.

te·trap·ter·ous [teˈtræptərəs] *a.* ①【动】四翅的,四翼的. ②【植】四翅(状)的.

te·trarch [ˈtiːtrɑːk, ˈte-] *n.* ①四分之一统治者;四分之一长官〔古罗马行省的四分之一的地区长官〕. ②从属小君主,小诸侯等权力较小的统治者. ③共同掌权的四人(四个官吏). ④〔古希腊军队〕方阵的小队长. ⑤【植】四原型.

te·trarch·ate, te·trach·y [ˈtiːtrɑːkeit, -ki] *n.* ①(罗马帝国行省)四分之一地区的长官职位;四分之一辖区或职权. ②四头统治,四头统治集团.

tet·ra·spo·ran·gi·um [ˌtetrəspɔːˈrændʒiəm] *n.* *(pl. -gia* [-ə]*)* 【植】四分孢子囊.

tet·ra·spore [ˈtetrəˌspɔː] *n.* 【植】四分孢子.

tet·ra·stich [ˈtetrəˌstik] *n.* 四行一节的诗,四行诗. **-ic** *a.*

te·tras·ti·chous [teˈtræstikəs] *a.* 【植】四列的.

tet·ra·syl·lab·ic [ˈtetrəsiˈlæbik] *a.* 四音节的.

tet·ra·syl·la·ble [ˈtetrəsiləbl] *n.* 四音节词.

tet·ra·tom·ic [ˌtetrəˈtɔmik] *a.* 【化】①四原子的. ②四羟基的.

tet·ra·va·lent [ˌtetrəˈveilənt] *a.* 【化】①四价的. ②有四种原子价的 (= quadrivalent).

tet·rode [ˈtetrəud] *n.* 【电】四极管.

tet·ro·do·tox·in [ˌtetrədəuˈtɔksin] *n.* 河豚毒.

te·trox·ide [teˈtrɔksaid] *n.* 【化】四氧化物.

tet·ryl [ˈtetril] *n.* 【化】特屈儿,三硝基苯(替)甲硝胺.

tet·ter [ˈtetə] *n.* 【医】水泡疹,皮疹,湿疹. *moist ~* = *humid ~* 湿疹. *scaly ~* 鳞屑癣.

Teut. = Teuton; teutonic.

Teu·to·ma·ni·a [tjuːtəˈmeiniə] *n.* 亲条顿狂;亲德.

Teu·to·ma·ni·ac [tjuːtəˈmeiniæk] *n.* 亲条顿狂者;亲德者〔派〕.

Teu·ton [ˈtjuːtən] *n.* 条顿人〔指: ①古代条顿族的成员. ②现代条顿系民族的成员,尤指德国人;又称日尔曼人〕. — *a.* = Teutonic.

Teu·to·nes [ˈtjuːtnˌiːz, ˈtuːtnˌiːz] *n. pl.* 条顿族〔居住在易北河北的一个古代民族〕.

Teu·ton·ic [tjuˈtɔnik] *a.* ①条顿民族的,北欧民族的;德国民族的. ②条顿〔日耳曼〕语的. — *n.* 条顿语,日耳曼语. ~ **Order** 条顿骑士团〔中世纪十字军中的一个组织〕.

Teu·ton·i·cism, Teu·ton·ism [tjuːˈtɔnisizəm, ˈtjuːtənizəm] *n.* ①条顿(语)风,条顿腔. ②外国语中的德语成分. ③条顿(或德国)文化. ④条顿〔日耳曼〕主义. ⑤条顿〔日耳曼〕民族优越论.

Teu·ton·ist [ˈtjuːtnist, ˈtuː-] *n.* ①条顿民族优越论者〔尤指日耳曼民族优越论者〕. ②赞同条顿〔日耳曼〕风俗(生活等)者. ③条顿或日耳曼(语)学家.

Teu·ton·i·za·tion [ˌtjuːtənaiˈzeiʃən] *n.* 条顿化,日耳曼化.

Teu·ton·ize [ˈtjuːtənaiz] *vt.* 条顿化〔日耳曼化〕.

Teu·to·phile [ˈtjuːtəufail] *a., n.* 亲条顿人的(人),亲德的(人).

Teu·to·pho·be [ˈtjuːtəfəub] *n., a.* 恐惧条顿人(者,的);恐惧日耳曼人(者,的). **-bia** *n.* 对条顿人〔日耳曼人〕的恐惧.

TEW = tactical early warning 战术预先警报,战术远程警戒.

Te·wa [ˈteiwə] *n.* ①*(pl. -was, -wa)* 特瓦人〔居住在新墨西哥印第安人村庄的六个印第安种部族中任何一族的成员〕. ②特瓦语.

Tex. = Texan; Texas.

tex [teks] *n.* 【纱】特克斯支数制〔每千米克数〕.

Tex·an [ˈteksən] *a., n.* 〔美〕得克萨斯州的(人).

Tex·as [ˈteksəs] *n.* ①得克萨斯〔美国州名〕. ②〔美〕(内河轮船的)最高甲板舱. ~ **fever** 〔美〕得克萨斯牛瘟. ~ **Rangers** 〔美〕得克萨斯州骑警队. ~ **tower** 〔美〕海上雷达站〔在海上建起平台,上设雷达,用于监视来自空中的袭击〕.

texas [ˈteksəs] *n.* 〔美〕(内河轮船的)最高甲板舱.

text [tekst] *n.* ①原文,本文,正文. ②课文,课本,教科书. ③基督教圣经经文,经句〔常引作说教题目〕. ④主题,论题. ⑤(歌谱的)歌词. ⑥版本. ⑦= ~hand. *a full ~* 全文,正文. *a ~ book example* 极好的例子. *a ~ in physics* 物理课本. ***stick to one's ~*** (谈话)不离本题. **~book** 教科书,课本. **~bookish, booky** *a.* 〔口〕教科书式的,象教科书一样呆板无味的. **~ edition** 供教学用的版本. **~ hand** 粗体正楷字. **~ letter** 黑体字.

tex•tile [ˈtekstail] *n.* 〔常 *pl.*〕纺织品;纺织原料. — *a.* 纺织(品)的. ~ *fabrics* 纺织品,纺织物. ~ *fibres* 纺织纤维. ~ *glass* 纺织玻璃纤维. **~ machinery** 纺织机器.

tex•to•lite [ˈtekstəlait] *n.* 层压胶布板,织物酚醛塑胶,夹布胶木.

text. rec. = 〔L.〕*textus receptus* (= the received *or* accepted text) 通用文本.

tex•tu•al [ˈtekstjuəl] *a.* 原文的,本文的;按照原文的,原原本本的;教科书的. **~ criticism** (古籍的)校勘. **-ism** 严守原文〔尤指基督教圣经经文〕;校勘学. **-ist** *n.* 墨守(或精通)原文的人〔尤指基督教圣经经文〕. **-ly** *ad.*

tex•tu•ar•y [ˈtekstjuəri] *a.* = textual. — *n.* *(pl. -aries)* = textualist.

tex•tur•al [ˈtekstʃərəl] *a.* 织物的;组织上的.

tex•ture [ˈtekstʃə] *n.* ①(织物的)组织,结构,质地,织法. ②织品,织物. ③(皮肤的)肌理;(岩石、木材等的)纹理. ④【生】组织. ⑤(文艺作品等的)结构,组织. ⑥气质,性格,本质,实质,特征. *cloth of (a) coarse [(an) open] ~* 粗纹织物. *cloth of (with) (a) close ~* 密纹织物. *the ~ of the culture of the Tang Dynasty* 唐代文化的特征. — *vt.* 使具有某种结构或特征. **-less** *a.* 无明显结构的,无定形的.

T.F. = ①task force 特遣部队. ②Territorial Force 〔英〕本土军部队. ③time factor 时间因数.

Tg = type genus【生】标准属(分类).

tg = ①telegram. ②telegraph.

T-group [ˈti-gruːp] *n.* 训练小组〔现代美国的一种所谓精神治疗法,受治疗者在专门训练员的指导下,在小组内不受约束地用言语表达内心感情〕.

TGSM = terminally guided sub-missile【军】终点制导子导弹.

Th. = ①【化】thorium. ②Theodore. ③Thomas. ④Thursday.

th. = thermal.

-th[1] *suf.* ①作 four 以上序数词的后缀: four*th*, sixtie*th*. ②表示分母: three-fif*th* 五分之三.

-th[2] *suf.* 由形容词、动词构成抽象名词: tru*th*, grow*th*.

-th[3] *suf.* 〔古〕构成动词陈述语气现在第三人称单数〔相当于现在的 -s, -es〕: do*th* (= does), ha*th* (= has).

Thack•er•ay [ˈθækəri] *n.* 撒克里〔姓氏〕.

Thad [θæd] *n.* 撒德〔男子名, Thaddeus 的昵称〕.

Thad•deus [θæˈdi(ː)əs] *n.* 撒迪厄斯〔男子名〕.

Tha•i [ˈtɑːi(ː)] *n., a.* 泰国语〔人〕(的).

Thai•land [ˈtailænd] *n.* 泰国〔亚洲〕. **-er** *n.* 泰国人.

thal•a•men•ceph•a•lon [ˌθæləmenˈsefəˌlɔn] *n.* *(pl. -la* [-lə]*)*【医】间脑 (= diencephalon). **-ce•phal•ic** [-siˈfælik] *a.*

tha•lam•ic [θəˈlæmik] *a.*【解】丘脑的;【植】花托的.

thal•a•mus [ˈθæləməs] *n.* (*pl. -mi* [-mai]) ①【解】丘脑;室,床. ②【植】(柱状)花托. ③(古希腊的)闺房,内室. *optic thalami*【解】视神经床,视丘.

tha•las•sic [θəˈlæsik] *a.* ①(关于)海洋的,深海的. ②(关于)海湾的,内海的.

thal•as•soc•ra•cy [ˌθælɑˈsɔkrəsi] *n.* 制海权. **-las•soc•rat** [-læsəkræt] *n.* 拥有制海权者.

thal•as•sog•ra•phy [ˌθæləˈsɔgrəfi] *n.* 海洋学. **-pher** *n.*

t(h)a•ler [ˈtɑːlə] *n. sing. pl.* 德国旧银币名.

Tha•les [ˈθeiliːz] *n.* 泰勒斯〔640?—546? B.C., 希腊哲学家〕.

Tha•li•a [θəˈlaiə] *n.*【希神】①萨拉亚〔司喜剧、田园诗的女神〕. ②(赐人美丽和欢乐的)三女神 (the Graces) 之一. **-li•an** *a.*

tha•lid•o•mide [θəˈlidəˌmaid] *n.*【药】擦里多米德〔镇静药,会引起婴儿畸形〕.

thal•lic [ˈθælik] *a.*【化】(正)铊的;三价铊的;含(正)铊的.

thal•li•um [ˈθæliəm] *n.*【化】铊〔Tl〕.

thal•loid [ˈθælɔid] *a.*【植】似叶状体的.

thallo•phyte [ˈθæləfait] *n.*【植】菌藻植物. **-phyt•ic** *a.*

thal•lous [ˈθæləs] *a.*【化】亚铊的;一价铊的.

thal•lus [ˈθæləs] *n.* *(pl. thal•luses* [-ləsiz], *thalli* [-lai]*)*【植】叶状体;菌体.

thal•weg [ˈtɑːlweg] *n.*【地】河流谷底线.

Thames [temz] *n.* (英国)泰晤士河. ***set the ~ on fire*** 惊人之举;成为杰出的人物;大显身手.

than [强 ðæn; 弱 ðən, ðn] *conj.* ①〔用于形容词、副词比较级之后〕比,比较. *Health is better ~ money.* 健康胜于金钱. *He is taller ~ I (am).* 他比我高〔现在口语常作 ~ *me*〕. *You love him more ~ I.* 你爱他胜过我爱他. *That morning I got up later ~ usual.* 那天早上我比平常起床晚些. *You love him more ~ me.* 你爱他胜过爱我. *He is more of a teacher ~ a scholar.* 他是一位教师,不是什么学者. *Something is better ~ nothing.* 聊胜于无. ②〔用于 *rather, sooner* 等之后〕与其…(毋宁、宁愿、不如、索性). *I would rather [sooner] die ~ disgrace myself.* 与其受辱不如死了好. ③〔接用于 hardly, scarely, barely 之后〕(刚刚…)就 (= when). *Hardly had she heard the news ~ she began to cry.* 她一听到那个消息就开始大哭. *We barely arrived ~ it was time to leave.* 我们刚刚到达,就到了应该离开的时间了. ④〔接用于 *other, else, anywhere, different* 等之后〕除…(以外), 除…(以外的). *He has no other friend ~ you.* 他除你以外没有朋友. *He is otherwise ~ I thought.* 他不是我所想象的那样人. *You won't find such friendship anywhere ~ in this country.* 除了在这个国家,你在别处是得不到这种友谊的. *It was none other ~ the principal.* 不是别人,是校长本人. *He did nothing else ~ watching television all the day.* 他整天除了看电视外什么也没有干. — *prep.* 比〔用于 ~ whom, ~ which〕. *Here is my new teacher, ~ whom a better does not exist.* 这就是我的新教员,谁也比不上他. ***no more ~*** 仅仅,只是. (*It's no more ~ a misunderstanding.* 这只是个误会). ***no other ~*** ①只有. ②正是,就是 (*It is no other ~ his mother.* 那就是他母亲).

tha•na [ˈtɑːnə] *n.* ①〔印英〕警察局. ②军事基地.

than•age [ˈθeinidʒ] *n.*【英史】大乡绅 (thane) 的身分〔地位、领地〕.

thanat(o)- *comb. f.* 死: *thanato*logy.

than•a•toid [ˈθænətɔid] *a.* ①象死的,死一般的. ②致死的,致命的.

than•a•to•lo•gy [θænəˈtɔlədʒi] *n.* 死亡学,死因学.

than•a•to•phi•di•a [ˌθænətəˈfidiə] *n.* 〔*pl.*〕毒蛇.

than•a•to•pho•bi•a [ˌθænətəˈfəubiə] *n.* 死亡恐怖〔畏惧〕;(病态的)畏死.

than•a•top•sis [ˌθænəˈtɔpsis] *n.* 对于死的见解〔思考〕.

thane [θein] *n.* ①【英史】(因服兵役而领有封地的)大乡绅,相当于后来的骑士、男爵等. ②【苏格兰史】(有封地的)氏族长. **-dom** *n.* = thanage. **-hood** *n.* ①〔总称〕大乡绅,领主. ②大乡绅的地位〔职权〕. **-ship** *n.* = thanage.

thank [θæŋk] *vt.* ①感谢,道谢. ②劳驾. ~ *sb. for a thing* 为某事感谢人. *T- you!* 谢谢〔偶然也说 *I ~ you!*〕. *T- you for that ball!* 劳您驾拿那个球给我! *No more, ~*

you. 够了,谢谢你。*No, ~ you.* 不,谢谢(你)〔表示拒绝时说的客气话〕。*T- God [Heaven]!* 谢天谢地! *T- you for nothing!* (表示蔑视的拒绝)算了,别瞎起劲,别管闲事! *Thanking you in anticipation.* (承蒙…)谨先致谢〔请托信中套语〕。***have (only) oneself to ~ for = ~ oneself for*** 〔谑〕真是活该,真是自作自受,只能怪自己(*You have only yourself to ~ for that. = You may ~ yourself for that.* 你真是活该,你真是自作自受)。***I will ~ you to** (do).* 请你,劳驾;〔反、谑〕(还是请)…好 (*I will ~ you to shut the door.* 劳驾把门关上。*I will ~ you to be a little more polite.* 还是文明礼貌点儿好)。— *n.* 〔*pl.*〕谢意,谢忱,感谢,谢辞,谢礼。*express one's ~s* 道谢。*Thanks!* 谢谢! (=Thank you!) *No, ~s.* 不,谢谢。*Thanks for your kindness.* 谢谢你的好意! *A thousand ~s. = (Many,* 〔古〕*Much) ~s. = (Please accept) my best ~s.* 多谢多谢。*Small* [〔谑〕*Much*] *~s I got for it.* 人家并不领情[感谢]! 〔谑〕感谢得很〔其实不感谢〕! **bow one's ~s** 鞠躬致谢。**give [return] ~s to** 感谢。**No ~s!** 别管闲事! (*No ~s to him though.* 可是请他别管闲事吧)。**~s a million** 〔美俚〕= ~ you. **~s to** 幸亏,由于 (*~s to my foresight* 幸亏我有先见之明)。**~ offering** 【宗】感恩的供品,谢恩的奉献。**-er** *n.* 感谢者。**-ee, -y, -ye** [ˈθæŋkjiː] *int.* 谢谢。

thank·ful [ˈθæŋkfəl] *a.* ①感谢的,感激的,感恩不尽的 *(to* sb.; *for* a thing*)*。②感到欣慰,非常高兴 *(that)*。*We are ~ to you for all your assistance.* 我们感谢您们的一切协助。*You should be ~ that your son has won the scholarship.* 你应该为你的儿子获得奖学金感到高兴。**-ly** *ad.* **-ness** *n.*

thank·less [ˈθæŋklis] *a.* ①不感激的,忘恩负义的。②不受人感谢的,不受人注意的;不讨好的,不合算的,徒劳的,无利的(工作等)。*a ~ task* 一项徒劳无益的任务。**-ly** *ad.* **-ness** *n.*

thanks·giv·ing [θæŋksˈɡiviŋ] *n.* ①感谢,感恩,谢恩;谢恩祈祷。②〔T-〕(基督教)感恩节〔在美国是十一月的最后一个星期四,在加拿大是十月的第二个星期一〕。③谢恩供品。

thank·worth·y [ˈθæŋkwəːði] *a.* 〔古〕应该感谢的,可感谢的。

thank-you-ma'am, -mam, -marm [ˈθæŋkjumɑːm] *n.* 〔美俚〕(使车子震动的)横贯路中的小沟;道路的凹凸不平处。

thar [tɑː] *n.* 【动】(尼泊尔产)一种羚羊。

tharm *n.* 〔Scot.〕肠;〔美〕肚子;(做琴弦用的)肠线。

that[1] [ðæt] *pro.* (*pl.* **those** [ðəuz]) ①〔指示代名词〕(a)〔指眼前的、说过的事物或人,又指比较 this 稍微远一点的〕那;那个东西;那件事情;那个人。*What is ~?* 那是什么? *T- is what I want to know.* 那就是我想知道的事情。*Who is ~ in the parlour?* 客厅里的那个人是谁? *Which will you have, this or ~?* 你要哪个,这个还是那个? (b)〔用作关系代名词的先行词,该关系代名词为宾格时常省略〕(…的)事物;(…的)人。*Those may try it who choose.* 想试的人可以试一下。*All those (~) I saw were inadequate.* 我所看见的都不行。(c)〔用来代替前面已提到的名词,以免重复〕*The area of Shanghai is larger than ~ of Soochow.* 上海的面积比苏州的(面积)大。*After ~ we had a quiz.* 随后我们考了个小测验。(d)〔指前述二物中的〕前者 (*opp.* this 后者)。②〔关系代名词〕[ðət] (a)〔引出修饰先行词的定语从句,口语中宾格的 that 常省去〕…的。*those ~ love us* 爱我们的人们。*those (~) we love* 我们所爱的人们。*His article contains much ~ is useful.* 他的文章里有很多有用的东西。*Is this the book (~) you were looking for?* 你要找的书是这本吗? (b)〔用作关系副词承接表示时间等的名词〕…的(时候、样子、方法等,常省略)。*the last time ~ I saw you* 上次见你的时候。*the way ~ he did it* 他做这事的方法。(c)(在从句中用于不加冠词的,表示某种特性的词后,作表语)*Newcomer ~ he is, he knows what's the right thing to do.* 尽管他是个新手,他却知道应该做些什么。**and all ~** 以及这类的东西[事情];…等、**and ~** 而且 (*He makes mistakes, and ~ very often.* 他犯了错误,而且是常常犯)。**and at ~** ①虽然如此还是;〔口〕而且 (*The price of the tea was five dollars, and not a very good tea at ~.* 茶叶要五块钱一斤,而且不是很好的茶。*It was a dull play but at ~ Jack enjoyed it.* 那是出枯燥无味的戏,可是贾克还真喜欢它)。②〔美俚〕真正,实在。**Come out of ~!** 〔俚〕走开,出去;滚蛋! **for all ~** 然而仍旧。**like ~** 那样地。**only ~** 就只那么多。**So ~'s ~ = That's ~** 完了,就是这样〔发言完毕时的话〕(*I won't go and ~'s ~.* 说不去就不去)。**~ being so** 因为那个原故,因此。**~ is (to say)** 这就是说,即。**That's it.** 对啦,正是如此。**That's so! = That's right!** 好;是的;〔美〕赞成! **T- [those] will do.** 那正好[正合适],行了。**upon ~** 于是,于是马上。**with ~** 于是;这样说着。— *a.* 〔指示形容词,后接复数名词时用 these〕[ðæt] ①那,那个。(a)〔指面前看得见的〕:*Can you see those trees?* 你看得见那些树吗? *~ man there* (看)那个人。(b)〔指不详细说也知道的东西〕: *What was ~ noise?* 那声音是什么? (c)〔用指远处的一切东西或过去的时候〕: *from ~ day on* 从那天起。*in ~ country* 在那个国家。*in those days* 在那时候。*~ day* 那一天。*~ once* 那一次。(d)〔和 *this* 搭配应用〕: *He went to this doctor and ~.* 他看过好些医生〔这个和那个等等医生〕。②那,那个,那种。*~ sonorous voice which we know so well* 我们所熟悉的那种洪亮的声音。*~ horse of yours* 你那匹马。*~ courage which you boast of* 你所夸耀的那种勇气。③〔和连词 *that* 同用〕那样的。*He has ~ confidence in his theory that he would put it into practice tomorrow.* 他对自己理论抱有那样的自信简直明天就要拿去实行一样。*He was angry to ~ degree that he foamed at the mouth.* 他气得嘴边沫子直冒。**~ kind** 〔美俚〕那种(没价值),不愉快的〔东西、人〕。—〔强 ðæt; 弱 ðət〕*conj.* ①〔引导名词从句,本身无词汇意义,常可省去〕。*I know (~) it was so.* 我知道当时是那样的。*It is certain ~ he was there.* 他当时在那里,这是确实的。*He said (~) he was there.* 他说当时他在那里。②〔引导包含 may, might, should 等情态动词的状语从句,表示目的〕为…。*We eat ~ we may live.* 我们是为了活下去而吃饭的。③〔在 so, such 之后引出表示结果的状语从句〕。*I am so tired (~) I cannot stand.* 我累得站不住。④〔引出表示理由或原因的状语从句〕因为。*I am glad ~ he came.* (因为)他来了我很高兴。*Not ~ I'm unwilling to do the job, but I'm unequal to it.* 不是因为我不愿意干这个工作,而是我干不了。⑤〔引出表示判断的标准的状语从句〕*Are you mad ~ you speak so wild?* 你疯了吗? 那样乱讲! ⑥〔引导表示愿望、惊愕、愤恨等的从句,主语常可省略〕要是…多好;想不到…;希望。*T- [Would ~] I had never been born!* 我要是没有生下来那多好。*T- it should ever come to this!* 想不到会到这个地步。*O [Would] ~ it might be the last.* 希望这是最后一次〔希望不要再有这种事〕。**in ~** 〔古、书面语〕以…的理由,因为 (*in ~ they are men* 因为他们是男人)。**not ~** (...之事)并非如此 (*not ~ I know of* 据我所知并非如此)。**now ~** 既然,由于 (*Now ~ you mention it, I do remember.* 你这样一说,我想起来了)。**seeing ~** 因为。— [ðæt] *ad.* 〔口〕那样,那么。*He wasn't ~ angry.* 他没有那么生气。*He knows only ~ much.* 他就知道那么多。*Can she walk ~ far?* 她能走得那么远吗? *I stayed in your house for a week when you were ~ high.* 你才那么高的时候,我在你家住过一个星期。

thatch [θætʃ] *n.* ①盖屋顶的材料〔稻草、茅草、棕榈〕。②草屋顶。③〔口、谑〕(长在头上的)头发。④(作物下的地面上的)杂草。— *vt.* (用稻草等)盖(屋顶);象用茅草盖屋顶般复盖。**-er** *n.* 盖屋顶者。**-y** *a.*

thatch·ing [ˈθætʃiŋ] *n.* ①葺屋顶,盖屋顶。②葺屋顶的

材料,葺屋稻草[茅草].

thau·ma·tol·o·gy [ˌθɔːməˈtɔlədʒi] *n.* (研究神奇事物的)神奇学.

thau·ma·trope [ˈθɔːmətrəup] *n.* 幻影转盘〔一种玩具,圆盘的一面画鸟笼,另一面画鸟,旋转时好象鸟在笼中〕.

thau·ma·turge [ˈθɔːmətəːdʒ] *n.* 奇术师;魔术师,术士. **-tur·gic, -tur·gi·cal** *a.*

thau·ma·tur·gist [ˈθɔːmətəːdʒist] *n.* = thaumaturge.

thau·ma·tur·gy [ˈθɔːmətəːdʒi] *n.* 魔术;奇术;幻术.

thaw [θɔː] *vi.* ①(冰、雪等)解冻,融化. ②〔口〕(冰冷的身体)渐渐温暖起来. ③(态度、感情等)缓和起来. *It ~s.* = *It is ~ing.* 解冻了. *The ground has ~ed out.* 雪已经融化了. *After the talk, he began to ~.* 谈话之后,他的态度开始缓和下来. — *vt.* 使融化;使暖和. *~ out the frozen assets* 解除对资产的冻结. *~ (out) the guests* 使客人们不再拘束. — *n.* ①融雪,融霜;解冻. ②缓和. ③融雪[融霜]的温暖气候. *a silver ~* 树冰,雾冰. *A ~ has set in.* 融雪的气候[解冻的时节]到了. *a ~ point* 露点. **-less** *a.* (永)不融化的.

thaw·y [ˈθɔːi] *a.* 融雪的,融霜的;解冻的.

ThB = thorium B 钍 B [铅的同位素 Pb^{212}].

Thc = thorium C 钍 C [铋的同位素 Bi^{212}].

THD = thread.

ThD = thorium D 钍 D [铅的同位素 Pb^{208}].

the [强 ðiː; (元音之前) 弱 ði, (辅音之前) 弱 ðə, ð] *art.* 〔定冠词〕.

I. 〔特定用法〕这(个),那(个);这种,那种;这一类,那一类的〔限定意义很轻,通常不必译出〕. ①〔指只说出名称对方就知道是什么的事物〕.(a)〔表示已被确认、提到,遇到,正在谈到,熟悉的实际存在的人或事物,意义相当于"这(些)","那(些)",以区别于 a, an "一个","某个"〕: *~ mountain* 这(个)山〔区别于 a mountain〕. *Shut ~ door, please.* 请关上门. *We keep a horse and are all fond of ~ horse.* 我们养着一匹马,我们大家都喜欢那匹马. (b)〔独特的、独一无二的东西〕: *~ sun* 太阳. *~ earth* 地球. *~ world* 世界. *~ universe* 宇宙. *~ House (of Commons)* 英国的下议院. *~ Channel* 英吉利海峡. (c)〔季节、自然现象方位等(特别当这些名词前不用形容词时)〕: *(~) spring* 〔春夏秋冬前不用冠词也行〕. *~ day* 白天. *~ night* 黑夜. *~ wind* 风. *~ cold* 冷(空气等). *~ east* 东方. (d)〔病名(现除口语及俚语中古复数形式的名词前尚保留外,其余通常省略)〕: *(~) smallpox* 天花. *(~) measles* 麻疹. *(~) gout* 痛风. *~ blues* 忧郁. *~ drink* 〔俚〕酒癖. (e)〔指身体的一部分,为物主代词的代用语〕: *I took him by ~ hand.* 我牵住他的手 (*cf.* I took his hand.) (f)〔用于乐器名称前〕: *play ~ violin* 拉小提琴. ②〔用于专有名词前〕(a)〔复数形式的山(脉),地区,国家〕: *~ Alps* 阿尔卑斯山(脉). *~ Balkans* 巴尔干的国家. *~ United States* 美利坚合众国. (b)〔河流、运河、半岛、沙漠名〕: *~ Thames* 泰晤士河. *~ Panama (Canal)* 巴拿马运河. *~ Crimea* 克里米亚半岛. *~ Sahara* 撒哈拉沙漠. (c)〔习惯上使用定冠词的某些场所、街道、城市、国家等〕: *~ Oxford Road* 牛津路. *~ Congo* 刚果. *~ Argentine* 阿根廷. *T- Hague* 海牙. (d)〔船名、飞机名、铁路名〕: *~ Queen Mary* 〔常作 *S.S. Queen Mary*〕玛丽女王号. *~ Stockton and Darlington Railway* 斯达克敦—达灵敦铁路. (e)〔某些旅馆,剧院等建筑物〕: *~ Imperial Hotel* 帝国旅馆. *~ Capital* 首都剧院. (f)〔语言名〕: *~ English.* (g)〔某些书报杂志名〕: *~ Times*《时报》. *~ Beijing Review*《北京周报》. ★用人名做书名时不加 the: Robinson Crusoe. (h)〔称号、爵位等之前〕: *~ Duke of Wellington* 威灵顿公爵. *~ Right Honourable ...* *Dr. Wang* 王博士阁下, *Alfred ~ Great* 艾尔弗雷德大帝. 〔其后接姓名时不用 the: King George〕. (i)〔爱尔兰、苏格兰等族长姓氏前〕: *~ Macnab, ~ Fitz-Gerald.* ③〔表示一定前后关系〕.(a)〔用于被限制性的名词或定语从句修饰的名词前〕: *~ pencil in my hand* 我手中的(那)支笔. *~ book you lost* 你丢失的那本书. (b)〔附加在形容词最高级或序数词前〕: *~ greatest possible victory* 最大最大的胜利. *~ hundredth time* 第一百次. *~ last but not ~ least* 最后的但并不是最不重要的. (c)〔普通名词前 = such [such a]; 抽象名词前 = such = so = enough〕: *He is not ~ man to betray a friend.* 他不是出卖朋友的人 (= ... not such a man as will betray ...). *He had ~ kindness to show me the way.* 承他好意给我指路. *T- impudence of the fellow!* 那家伙真无耻! ④〔加强语气的用法〕出色的,典型的,无双的(等). *Caesar was ~ general of Rome.* 凯撒是罗马唯一的将军. *Do you mean ~ Gorky?* 你是说(大文豪)高尔基吗?〔通常用斜体字表现,发音 [ˈðiː]〕. ⑤〔英〕〔计量单位名词前〕: *at one dollar ~ pound [yard]* 每磅[码]一元钱. *hire by ~ week* 按周雇用. *so much by ~ day* 一日若干钱. *8 minutes to ~ mile* 八分钟跑一英里.

II. 〔代表用法〕…那样的东西,…那种东西. ①〔用单数普通名词代表它的一类时(所谓代表的单数)〕. (a)〔表示动植物等的种类、种属〕: *T- horse is useful to man.* ★ man 和 woman 除与 child, boy, girl 等对照应用外,代表单数不用 the: Man has tamed the horse. (b)〔the + 单数普通名词,则指出其功能,属性等使具抽象性〕: *pleasant to ~ eye* (= sight) 看着舒服. *keep ~ wolf from the door* 免于饥饿. *The pen is mightier than ~ sword.* 文的比武的力量大. (c)〔the + 形容词 = 抽象名词或具体名词〕: *~ sublime = sublimity* 崇高(的事物). *~ beautiful = beauty* (美). *~ unexpected* 意料不到的事. *~ old and ~ young* 老年和青年. ②〔复数名词前〕〔用在人民、阶级、人群或家族姓名等的名词前,表示集体或全体〕: *~ Clives* 克来弗一家(的人们). *those renowned among ~ Chinese* 中国人中的有名的人们. *a plant not yet known to ~ botanists* 植物学家们还不知道的一种植物. — [ðə, ði] *ad.* ①〔加在形容词、副词比较级前,用作指示副词〕更,越发;反而. *He worked ~ harder, because he had been encouraged.* 他因为受了鼓励,工作越发努力了. *I like him all ~ better for his criticism on me.* 他批评了我,我反而更喜欢他. ②〔加在形容词副词前作关联副词用〕愈…愈. *T- sooner, ~ better.* 愈早愈好. ★(1)前头的 the 是关联副词,后头的 the 是指示副词. (2)关联副词从句也可以放在后面: One wants, ~ more one has. = T- more one has, ~ more one wants. 越有越贪. ***so much ~ better [worse]*** 那样更好[坏].

the·an·dric [θiˈændrik] *a.* 神人两性的;神人的.

the·an·throp·ic, -throp·i·cal [θiːænˈθrɔpik, -kəl] *a.* 具有神人两性的;把神性体现在人身上的,神人同形的.

the·an·thro·pism [θiˈænθrəpizm] *n.* ①神人一体. ②神人一体说〔尤指耶稣基督〕. **-pist** *n.*

the·ar·chy [ˈθiːɑːki] *n.* 神的统治;神治国;神权政治;(统治的)神们.

theat(r) = theatre; theatrical(ly).

the·a·tre, 〔美〕**the·a·ter** [ˈθiətə] *n.* ①剧场,戏院. ②〔the ~〕戏,戏剧;〔集合词〕(某一国、某一作家的)戏剧作品,戏剧文学. ③戏剧效果;表现手法. ④(阶梯式)讲堂,会场;手术教室. ⑤活动场所,(发生重要事件的)场所;【军】战区;战场. *a patent ~* 〔英〕钦许剧场. *a picture ~* 电影院. *do a ~ = go to the ~* 看戏去. *the modern ~* 近代剧. *the ~ of Lao She* 〔总称〕老舍的剧作. *the ~ of the absurd* 荒诞派戏剧. *the ~ of war* 战场. *The opera was good ~.* 这出歌剧的舞台效果好. **~goer** 经常(或爱)看戏的人. **~going** 看戏. **~-in-the-round** (表演场地设于中心,观众围着观看的)圆形剧场. **the living ~** 舞台剧(与电影及电视剧相对而言).

the·at·ric [θiˈætrik] *a.* = theatrical.

the·at·ri·cal [θiˈætrikəl] *a.* ① 剧场的,戏院的. ②戏剧(式)的,戏剧性的;做戏似的,夸张的. *~ effect* 戏剧效果. *~ scenery* 剧景. *~ way of speaking* 做戏似的讲

话方式. — *n.* ①〔*pl.*〕戏剧(表演)〔尤指业余演出〕. ②〔*pl.*〕戏剧表演艺术; 做戏似的动作. ③戏剧演员. *private [amateur] ~s* 业余戏剧〔演出〕. **-ism** *n.* 戏剧演出法, 戏剧行为〔派头〕, 夸张作风. **-i·ty** [θiˌætriˈkæliti] *n.* 戏剧性〔行为、派头、作风〕. **-ly** *ad.* 用戏剧; 做戏似地.

the·at·ri·cal·ize [θiˈætrikəˌlaiz] *vt.* ①使适合于演出. ②把…戏剧化, 夸张. **-i·za·tion** *n.*

the·at·rics [θiˈætriks] *n. pl.* 〔用作 sing.〕戏剧演出(法); 舞台表演艺术; 戏剧〔舞台〕效果; 戏剧化的言行.

the·ba·ine [ˈθiːbəˌiːn, θiˈbeiin] *n.* 【化】蒂巴因.

Thebes [θiːbz] *n.* ①底比斯〔埃及尼罗河畔的古城〕. ②底比斯〔希腊古城〕. **-ban** [ˈθiːbən] *a.*

the·ca [ˈθiːkə] *n.* *(pl.* **-cae** [-siː]*)* ①【植】药室; 孢蒴. ②【动,解】鞘; 壳; 囊; 膜; (珊瑚的)外壁. **-l** *a.*

the·cate [ˈθiːkit] *a.* 有膜的, 有鞘的.

thé dan·sant [ˈtei dɑ̃ːnsɑ̃ŋ] 〔F.〕 *(pl.* ***thés dan·sants*** [dɑ̃ːsɑ̃ŋ]*)* (午后茶点时间的)茶舞 (= tea dance).

thee [ðiː; 弱 ði] *pro.* 〔thou 的宾格〕你. *Get ~ gone!* 走开! ★教友会教徒作 thou 用, 并且接第三人称形式的动词: Thee does (= You do) not understand. 你不懂.

thee·lin [ˈθiːlin] *n.* 〔废〕【医】= estrone.

thee·lol [ˈθiːlɔːl, -ləul] *n.* 〔废〕【医】= estriol.

theft [θeft] *n.* ①偷窃(罪), 盗窃(罪). ②被盗, 失窃. ③〔罕〕赃物. *commit a ~* 做盗窃案. *~s from a musium* 从博物馆盗窃的赃品. **~less** 非盗窃的; 不会失窃的. **~proof** 防盗的.

thegn [θein] *n.* 〔古〕= thane.

the·ic [ˈθiːik] *n.* 喝茶过多的人, 嗜茶成癖的人.

the·in(e) [ˈθiːi(ː)n] *n.* 【化】茶碱, 咖啡因.

their [ðɛə; (元音之前)弱 ðər] *pro.* ①〔they 的所有格〕他们的. ②〔泛指, 用以代替不确定的单数先行词〕他的, 她的 (= his, her). *Our thanks to any one who will support us after their deliberation.* 对经过深思熟虑愿意支持我们的任何人表示感谢. *I don't think the house is ~ own.* 我想那房子不是他们自己的.

theirn [ðɛən] *pro.* 〔方〕= theirs; their own.

theirs [ðɛəz] *pro.* 〔they 的物主代词, 既可指代上文提过的东西, 也可指代下文提到的事物〕①他们的东西, 他〔她〕们的亲属〔或有关的人〕. ②〔泛指用以代替不确定的单数先行词〕他(她)的 = his, hers. *These books are ~.* 这些书是他们的. *That's not the custom of ~.* 那不是他们的习俗. *T- is the largest house on the blcck.* 他们的住宅是该街区最大的住宅. *Are you a friend of ~?* 你是他的朋友吗? *I have my book, does each student have ~?* 我已有书本了, 是不是每位同志都有了? *I will do my part if everybody else will do ~.* 要是大家都干那我也干.

the·ism[1] [ˈθiːizəm] *n.* 有神论 *(opp.* atheism*)*; 一神论. **the·ist** *n.* **-is·tic, -is·ti·cal** *a.*

the·ism[2] [ˈθiːizəm] *n.* 【医】茶(碱)中毒.

Thel·ma [ˈθelmə] *n.* 塞尔玛〔女子名〕.

them [强 ðem; 弱 ðəm] *pro.* ①〔they 的宾格, 用作宾语, 口语中也用作表语〕他们, 她们, 它们. *The books are new; take care of ~.* 这些书是新的, 对它们当心些. *It was very kind of ~.* 他们太客气了. *That's ~.* 就是他们. — *a.* 〔非标准用法〕〔= those〕*He doesn't want ~ books.* 他不要那些书.

the·mat·ic, -mat·i·cal [θiːˈmætik(əl)] *a.* ①主题〔论题〕的. ②【语言】词干的, 构干的. ③【乐】主旋律的. *a ~ vowel* 构干元音. **-i·cal·ly** *ad.*

theme [θiːm] *n.* ①(文章, 讨论的)主题; 论题; 话题. ②(学生的)作文, 论文, 作文题. ③【语言】词干;【乐】主题, 主旋律. ④【无】= signature;【无】信号曲〔调〕. ⑤(某人的)口头禅; 爱谈的话题. *a favourite ~ for poetry (of, with) (the poets)* 诗里(诗人们)喜欢用的主题. *~ song* 主题歌.

The·mis [ˈθiːmis, ˈθemis] *n.* 【希神】特弥斯〔司法律、正义的女神〕;〔人格化〕法律, 正义.

them·selves [ðəmˈselvz] *pro.* 〔*pl.*〕①〔强义〕他〔她、它〕们亲自〔自己〕. ②〔反身〕他〔她、它〕们自己. ③〔泛指〕用以代替不确定的单数先行词他(她)自己 = himself 或 herself. *They did it ~.* 那是他们自己做的. *They are deceiving ~.* 他们在欺骗自己.

then [ðen] *ad., conj.* ①〔指过去或未来的一个特定时间〕那时, 当时. ②〔表示顺序〕. (a)〔时间〕然后; 其次. (b)〔序列〕此外, 加上, 加之, 而且. (c)〔推理〕既然这样, 那么; 因此. *Things were different ~.* 那时一切都和现在不同. *First comes spring, ~ summer.* 先到的是春天, 然后是夏天. *And ~ she had such a fine head of hair.* 而且她有一头非常美丽的头发. *T- it is useless to go on.* 那么继续下去也没用. *Let's begin, then.* 那么, 咱们就开始吧. **but ~** 但是; 但是另一方面. **now … ~ …** 有时…有时…. **now ~**〔抗议、警告〕可是, 喂! *(Now ~, a little less noise there.* 喂喂, 静一点! *Now ~, what are you doing?* 慢着, 你在干什么呢? *Now ~, don't hit me in the eye!* 当心, 别打着我的眼睛). **~ and not till ~** 那时候才开始. **~ and there = there and ~** 当时, 当场, 即时. **well ~** 既然这样. **what ~ [~ what]** (下一步)怎么办, 又怎么样呢. — *a.* 当时的. *the ~ conditions* 当时的情况. *the ~ ruler* 当时的统治者. — *n.* 那时. *before ~* 那时以前. *by ~* 到那时, 那时. *from ~ on* 从那时起. *since ~* 那时以来, 以后. *till ~* 到那时, 那时以前. **every now and ~** 时时.

the·nar [ˈθiːnɑː] *n.* ①手掌; 足底. ②鱼际〔大拇指根部掌上突出的肌肉〕. — *a.* 手掌的; 足底的; 鱼际的.

thence [ðens] *ad.* 因此;〔古〕从那里;〔罕〕从那时起(自那以后). *It ~ appears that* 由此看来显然是. *T- it follows that* 所以就…了. *I would suggest that we (should) go to the Summer Palace and ~ to Xiangshan.* 我建议去颐和园, 然后从那里去香山. **~ forth, ~ forward** *ad.* 从那时, 其后; 从那里.

the·o- *comb. f.* 神: *theology, theophany.*

The·o·bald [ˈθiəbɔːld] *n.* 西奥博尔德〔男子名〕.

the·o·bro·mine [ˌθiəˈbrəumiːn, -min] *n.* 【化】可可碱.

the·o·cen·tric [ˌθiəˈsentrik] *a.* 【神】以神为中心的. **-cal·ly** *ad.* **-i·ty** [-ˈtrisiti] *n.* **-tri·sm** [-trizm] *n.*

the·oc·ra·cy[1] [θiˈɔkrəsi] *n.* ①神权政治, (尤指古犹太的)僧侣〔祭司〕政治. ②神权国家. ③占统治地位的(掌握政权的)僧侣集团.

the·oc·ra·cy[2] [θiˈɔkrəsi] *n.* ①泛神崇拜〔如既信奉基督教又拜佛像〕. ②通过冥想使心灵与上帝贯通融合.

the·o·crat [ˈθiːəkræt] *n.* 神权主义者, 神权政治中的统治者.

the·od·o·lite [θiˈɔdəlait] *n.* 【测】经纬仪. **-ic** *a.*

The·o·dore [ˈθiədɔː] *n.* 西奥多〔男子名〕.

the·og·o·ny [θiˈɔgəni] *n.* 神谱; 叙述神统的史诗; 神统系谱学. **-nic** *a.*

theol. = theologian; theological; theology.

the·o·lo·gi·an [θiəˈləudʒjən] *n.* 神学家, 神学研究者.

the·o·log·i·cal [θiəˈlɔdʒikəl] *a.* 神学(上)的; 神学性质的; 根据圣经的, 作为神言来看的. **-gist** *n.* **-ly** *ad.*

the·ol·o·giz·e [θiˈɔləˌdʒaiz] — *vt.* 使神学化. — *vi.* 作神学理论上的阐述. **-r** *n.* 神学理论的阐述者.

the·o·log(ue) [ˈθiːəlɔg] *n.* 〔美口〕神学院学生, 神学家.

the·ol·o·gy [θiˈɔlədʒi] *n.* 神学.

the·om·a·chy [θiˈɔməki] *n.* 诸神间的战争; 对诸神的战争.

the·o·mor·phic [ˌθiəˈmɔːfik] *a.* 神形的, 有神的形象的. **-phism** *n.*

the·on·o·mous [θiˈɔnəməs] *a.* 神统治的, 神控制的. **-ly** *ad.* **-o·my** *n.*

the·op·a·thy [θiˈɔpəθi] *n.* *(pl.* ***-thies****)* (宗教信仰的)虔诚.

the·oph·a·ny [θiˈɔfəni] *n.* 神的显现.

The·o·phras·tus [θi(:)əˈfræstəs] *n.* 西奥弗拉斯塔〔372?—287 B.C., 希腊的哲学家〕.
the·o·phyl·line [ˌθiəˈfili:n, -in] *n.*【化】茶碱.
theor. = theorem.
the·or·bo [θiˈɔ:bəu] *n.* *(pl. ~s)* (17世纪琵琶状) 双首琴.
the·o·rem [ˈθiərəm] *n.* ①(能证明的)一般原理, 公理, 定律,法则. ②【数】定理. **-mat·ic** [-ˈmætik], **-mat·i·cal** *a.* **-i·cal·ly** *ad.*
the·o·ret·ic [θiəˈretik] *a.* = theoretical.
the·o·ret·i·cal [θiəˈretikəl] *a.* ①理论(上)的,学理上的 *(opp.* applied*)*. ②假设(性)的;纯理论的,推理的. ③空论的*(opp.* practical*)*. ~ *physics* 理论物理学. ~ *prepossession* 脱离实际预先形成的印象. **-ly** *ad.*
the·o·re·ti·cian [ˌθiərəˈtiʃən] *n.* 理论家.
the·o·ret·ics [θiəˈretiks] *n.* 〔*pl.* 用作单数〕(某一学科的)理论(内容).
the·o·rist [ˈθiərist] *n.* 理论家;学说创立人;空论家.
the·o·rize [ˈθiəraiz] *vi.* ①创立学说. ②建立理论,理论化. ③作理论上讨论,推理. **-riz·er** *n.*
the·o·ry [ˈθiəri] *n.* ①理论, 学理, 原理. ②学说, 论说 *(opp.* hypothesis*)*. ③推测,揣度. ④〔口〕见解,意见. *the ~ of two points* 两点论. *the ~ of class struggle* 阶级斗争学说[理论]. *Darwin's ~ of evolution* 达尔文的进化论. *the atomic ~* 原子说. *Our scheme is good both in ~ and in practice.* 我们的方案在理论上和实施上都是好的. *combine [separate] ~ with [from] practice*理论结合 [脱离]实际. *My ~ is that we must bring new blood into the Institute through appointment of younger men to important positions.* 我的意见是我们学院应该通过重用年轻一些的人来注入新的血液. *~ of games* 博弈论,对策论,权衡利弊得失的形势分析.
the·o·soph[θiəˈsɔf], **the·os·o·pher** [θiˈɔsəfə], **-phist** [-fist] *n.* 通神论者;接神论者.
the·os·o·phy [θiˈɔsəfi] *n.* ①【宗】神知学, 通神论. ②〔常 T-〕(万物轮回, 人可以通过修持获得神性的)接神论.
ther·a·p. = therapeutics.
ther·a·peu·tic, -ti·cal [θerəˈpju:tik, -tikəl] *a.* 治疗(学)的,疗法(上)的. **-ti·cal·ly** *ad.*
ther·a·peu·tics [ˌθerəˈpju:tiks] *n.*【医】治疗学; 疗法论.
ther·a·peu·tist [ˌθerəˈpjutist], **thera·pist** [ˈθerəpist] *n.* 治疗学家;临床医生.
ther·a·pist [ˈθeərəpist] *n.*【医】治疗学家 (= therapeutist).
ther·a·py [ˈθerəpi] *n.*【医】疗法;疗效. *new acupuncture ~* 新针疗法, *radio ~* 放射疗法.
-therapy *suf.* 治疗,疗法: radio*therapy*.
ther·blig [ˈθə:blig] *n.* (工业生产中) 操作动作的基本单位(记号).
there [ðɛə] *ad.* ①在那里,到那里,在那个地方. ②在那一点上. ③[强 ðɛə; 弱 ðə]〔无场所观念,用于 be, come, go 等动词之前. 主语除人称代词外应置于后面,以加强语气引起注意; 与 be 连用时表示"有"的意思〕. ④与 seem, appear 等动词连用. *I see a bird ~.* 我看见一只鸟在那里. *I am now on my way ~.* 我正在往那里去. *You are right ~.* 在那一点上你说得对. *T- you go again.* 你又来这一套了. *Is ~ a telephone in your house?* 你家有电话吗? *T- is no one there.* 那里一个人也没有. *T- comes the bus at last.* 公共汽车可来啦. *T- seems (to be) something wrong about the teletype.* 电传打字电报机好象有点毛病. *T- goes the bell.* 钟响了. *T- he goes!* 看,他做[说]那样的事! *T- it goes!* 嗳呀, 掉下来了[坏了,不见了,等等]. ***Are you ~?*** 〔电话用语〕喂喂? ***...as ~ is*** 如果说有…. ***be all ~***〔口〕(能力、精神)很正常, 一切很好 (*He is all ~ as a teacher.* 他当教员很好). ***get ~*** 〔俚〕达到目的,成功. ***have been ~ before***〔口〕到过那里(所以很熟习). ***here and ~*** 这里那里. ***neither here nor ~*** 不得要领;不相干;没有关系. ***then and ~*** 在当时当地. ***there is no ...ing*** 很难…,无法…, 不能… (*T- is no telling when he will arrive.* 很难说他什么时候会来). ***T- it is!*** 就在那里. ***~ or thereabouts*** 〔场所、价格、数目或时间等〕大约,大致那样. ***There's a good boy.*** 真是乖孩子〔哄孩子时说的话〕. ***T- you are!*** 原来你在这儿! 你这才来! 就是这个,就在这儿; 就是这样嘛; 这就是你要的,拿去吧! 完了,就是这些,目的达到了. ***You have me ~.*** 这就输给你了; 这一下让你抓住了. — *pro.* 〔用于介词之后〕那里. ***from ~*** 从那里. ***(live) near ~*** (住) 在那附近. ***up to ~*** 到那里. — *int.* 那! 唷! 哎呀! 你瞧! 好啦! 〔表示确信、胜利、失望、鼓励、安慰、挑衅、嗾使等, 引起注意, 加强语气〕. *T-! ~! Never mind.* 好啦! 好啦! 不要紧的. *T- now!* 你瞧! 你看多好! *You ~!* 喂. *I think I've a say in the matter, so ~!* 我认为我有发言权,就是这样.
there·a·bout(s) [ˈðɛərəbaut(s), ˌðɛərəˈb-] *ad.* ①(表示地点)附近. ②(表示数量,时间,程度等)左右; 大约, 上下. *from the year 1963 or ~* 从1963年前后. *in three years or ~* 三年左右.
there·aft·er [ðɛərˈɑ:ftə] *ad.* ①〔书面语〕此后. ②〔罕〕据此.
there·a·gainst [ˌðɛərəˈgeinst] *ad.* 相反,反对;对立地.
there·a·nent [ˌðɛərəˈnent] *ad.* 〔Scot.〕关于那.
there·at [ðɛərˈæt] *ad.* 〔古〕在那里[那时]; 因此; 据此.
there·by [ˈðɛəˈbai] *ad.* ①因此, 所以. ②〔古〕在那附近 = thereabout(s). *T- hangs a tale.* 其中有点蹊跷〔必有原因〕.
there·for [ðɛəˈfɔ:] *ad.* 〔古〕因此; 为此; 由于这样.
there·fore [ˈðɛəfɔ:, -fɔə] *ad., conj.* 因此, 为此, 所以. *We are communists and ~ we will practice criticism and self-criticism.* 我们是共产党员,所以我们要进行批评和自我批评. *It rained; ~ the track and field meet was put off.* 天下雨,因此运动会延期.
there·from [ðɛəˈfrɔm] *ad.* 〔古〕从那里.
there·in [ðɛərˈin] 〔古〕*ad.* 其中; 在那里; 在那点上.
there·in·aft·er [ˌðɛərinˈɑ:ftə] *ad.*【法】在下(文).
there·in·be·fore [ˌðɛərinbiˈfɔ:, -biˈfɔə] *ad.* ①【法】在上(文). ②(文章或讲话等)在前的一部分中,在上文中.
there·in·to [ðɛərˈintu(:)] *ad.* 〔古〕往那里面,往其中.
ther·e·min [ˈθerəmin] *n.* 铁耳明式电子乐器.
there·of [ðɛərˈɔv, -ˈɔf] *ad.*〔古、谑〕(把)它; 将它; 它的; 由此. *Do not eat ~.* 不要吃它. *an evil and the remedy ~* 一项弊端及其匡正办法. *Excess in drinking is the evil ~.* 饮酒过度由此而生祸害.
there·on [ðɛəˈɔn] *ad.* 〔古〕①在其上, 在那上面. ②= thereupon. *the latest news and our commentary ~* 最新消息以及我们关于它的述评.
there·out [ðɛəˈaut] *ad.* 〔古〕从那(里面); 在…外面.
there's [强 ðɛəz; 弱 ðəz] = there is [has]. ★ There is (尤其是 There's) 之后常有复数主语.
The·re·sa [tiˈri:zə, təˈri:zə] *n.* 特丽萨〔女子名〕.
there·to [ðɛəˈtu:] *ad.* 〔古〕到那里;〔古、诗〕此外,又.
there·to·fore [ˌðɛətəˈfɔ:] *ad.* 那时以前,直到那时.
there·under [ðɛərˈʌndə] *ad.* 在其下; 在那一项目〔条款〕下. *a word and the excmples given ~* 一个词及其下面所举的例句.
there·un·to [ðɛərˈʌntu:] *ad.* 〔古〕= thereto.
there·up·on [ˌðɛərəˈpɔn] *ad.* 于是,因此; 于是立刻;〔古〕在那上面.
there·with [ðɛəˈwiθ, -ˈwið] 〔古〕*ad.* 以那,以这; 于是; 立刻, 同时. *every person connected ~* 每一个与之有关的人.
there·with·al [ˌðɛəwiˈðɔ:l] 〔古〕*ad.* 于是; 此外, 又, 同时.

the•ri•ac [ˈθiəriæk] *n.* ①糖浆. ②(蛇毒的)解毒剂. ③万灵药.
the•ri•an•throp•ic [ˌθiəriænˈθrɔpik] *a.* 半人半兽的.
the•ri•o•mor•phic [ˌθiəriəˈmɔːfik] *a.* 兽形的〔指某些神而言〕.
therm. = thermometer.
therm- *comb. f.* = 热;热电 (= therm-).
therm(e) [θəːm] *n.* ①【物】克卡〔即小卡 = 4.2 × 10^7 erg〕. ②大卡, 千卡. ③煤气热量单位〔在英国 = 100,000 B. T. U.; 在美国 = 1,000千卡〕.
thermae [ˈθəːmiː] *n.*〔*pl.*〕〔L.〕【古希腊、罗马】温泉;公共浴室,大澡堂.
ther•mal [ˈθəːməl] *a.* ①热的,热量的,温热的,由热造成的. ②温泉的. ~ *barrier*【空】热障. ~ *capacity* 热容量. ~ *conductivity*【物】导热性;导热系数. *a* ~ *power station* 热电站, 火力发电站. *a* ~ *unit* 热量单位. ~ *springs* 温泉. — *n.*【空】上升暖气流. **-ly** *ad.*
therm•al•loy [ˈθəːməlɔi] *n.*【冶】热合金, 耐热耐蚀合金,镍铜合金.
therm•an•(a)es•the•si•a [ˌθəːmænəsˈθiːʒə, -ʒiə, -ziə] *n.* 无冷热感觉(力);冷热感麻木.
ther•mate [ˈθəːmeit] *n.*【军】混合燃烧剂〔燃烧弹及榴弹中所用的混合剂,由铝热剂及其他物质混合制成〕.
ther•mel [ˈθəːmel] *n.* (装有热电偶的)热电温度计.
therm•(a)es•the•si•a [ˌθəːmesˈθiːʒə, -ʒiə, -ziə] *n.* 冷热敏感性,冷热感觉(力).
ther•mic [ˈθəːmik] *a.* 热的,由于热的. ~ *rays* 热线. ~ *fever* 日射病.
Ther•mi•dor [E. ˈθəːmiˌdɔː, F. tɛrmiˈdɔːr] *n.* 热月〔法国资产阶级革命时期共和历的第十一月, 相当于公历七月十九日到八月十七日〕. **-ean, -ian** *a.* 热月的;热月政变式的,热月党人的.
therm•i•on [ˈθəːmaiən] *n.*【物】热离子.
therm•i•on•ic [ˌθəːmiˈɔnik] *a.*【物】热离子的. *a* ~ *tube [valve]* 热离子管. ~ *current* 热电子〔离子〕电流. ~ *emission* 热电子放射. **-s** *n.* 热离子学.
ther•mistor [θəːˈmistə] *n.*【电】热敏电阻;热控管;热变电阻器.
ther•mit [ˈθəːmit], **-mite** [-mait] *n.*【冶、化】铝粉焊接剂;铝热剂. ~ *bomb* 铝热剂燃烧弹. ~ *iron* 铝热还原铁. ~ *method* (或 process) 铝热(剂)法. ~ *welding* 火焊.
thermo- *comb. f.*〔用于辅音前〕热;热电: *thermo*nuclear, *thermo*phone.
ther•mo•am•me•ter [ˈθəːməuˈæmitə, -ˈæmmiːtə] *n.*【电】热[温差]电(偶)安培计,热电流表.
ther•mo•ba•rom•e•ter [ˌθəːməubəˈrɔmitə] *n.* ①温度气压计. ②虹吸气压表.
ther•mo•bat•ter•y [ˌθəːməuˈbætəri] *n.*【电】温差电池组.
ther•mo•chem•i•cal [ˌθəːməˈkemikl] *a.* 热化学的.
ther•mo•chem•is•try [ˈθəːməuˈkemistri] *n.*【化】热化学.
ther•mo•cline [ˈθəːməˌklain] *n.* 温水层〔较热的水面区与较冷的深水区之间的水层〕.
ther•mo•colo(u)r [ˈθəːməuˌkʌlə] *n.* 热敏油漆, 示温涂料,色温标示.
ther•mo•cou•ple [ˈθəːməukʌpl] *n.*【电】热[温差]电偶 (= thermoelectric couple).
ther•mo•cut•out [ˌθəːməuˈkʌtaut] *n.* 热保险装置, 热断流器.
ther•mo•duric [θəːməuˈdjuərik] *a.*【菌】耐热的, 不能用巴氏灭菌法杀灭的.
ther•mo•dy•nam•ic [ˈθəːməudaiˈnæmik] *a.* 热力的. *a* ~ *cycle* 热力循环. **-s** *n.* 热力学.
ther•mo•e•lec•tric(al) [θəːməuiˈlektrik(l)] *a.*【电】热[温差]电的. *a* ~ *current* 温差电流,热电流. *a* ~ *pyrometer* 热电(偶)高温计. ~ *couple* 温差电偶,热电偶. *a* ~ *thermometer* 温差电温度计.
ther•mo•e•lec•tric•i•ty [ˈθəːməuiˌlekˈtrisiti] *n.*【电】温差电(学),热电(学).
ther•mo•e•lec•trom•e•ter [ˌθəːməuiˌlekˈtrɔmitə] *n.*【电】电热计.
ther•mo•e•lec•tro•mo•tive [ˌθəməuiˌlektrəˈməutiv] *a.*【电】热电动的,温差电的.
ther•mo•e•lec•tron [ˌθəːməuiˈlektrɔn] *n.*【物】热电子.
ther•mo•el•e•ment [ˌθəːməuˈelimənt] *n.*【电】温差电偶,热电偶.
ther•mo•gen•e•sis [θəːməuˈdʒenisis] *n.*【生理】生热(作用). **-ge•net•ic** *a.* 生热的,生热作用的. **-gen•ic** *a.* 生热的,产热的.
ther•mo•gram [ˈθəːməgræm] *n.* 自记温度图(曲线);温谱图.
ther•mo•graph [ˈθəːməgrɑːf, -græf] *n.* 温度记录;记录温度计.
ther•mog•ra•phy [θəːˈmɔgrəfi] *n.* ①温度记录,发热记录;自记温度. ②热写法;炙出写法.
ther•mo•labile [ˌθəːməuˈleibil] *a.*【生化】感热的, 非耐热性的 (*opp.* thermostable).
ther•mol•o•gy [θəːˈmɔlədʒi] *n.* 热学.
ther•mo•lu•mi•nes•cence [ˌθəːməuˌluːmiˈnesns] *n.* 热发光(现象). **-nes•cent** *a.*
ther•mol•y•sis [θəˈmɔlisis] *n.*【化】热(分)解(作用);【生理】散热(作用). **-lyt•ic** *a.*
ther•mo•mag•net•ic [ˌθəːməumægˈnetik] *a.*【物】热磁的. ~ *effect* 热磁效应.
ther•mom•e•tre,〔美〕**-ter** [θəˈmɔmitə] *n.* 寒暑表,温度计;体温表 (= clinical ~). *a combination* ~ (三氏)对照寒暑表. *a maximum [minimum]* ~ 最高[最低]温度表. ***a centigrade [Celsius]*** ~ 摄氏温度计〔略 C〕. ***a Fahrenheit*** ~ 华氏温度计〔略 F〕. ***a Réaumur*** ~ 列氏温度计〔略 R〕.
ther•mo•met•ric, -ri•cal [ˌθəːməˈmetrik, -rikəl] *a.* 温度计的,寒暑表的,测温的,据温度计测得的. **-al** *a.*
ther•mom•e•try [θəːˈmɔmitri] *n.* ①检温, 温度测量. ②检温学,温度测量法.
ther•mom•o•dule [ˌθəːməuˈmɔdjul] *n.*【物】热电微型组件.
ther•mo•mo•tor [ˌθəːməˈməutə] *n.* 热力机〔尤指蒸汽机〕.
ther•mo•nu•cle•ar [ˌθəːməuˈnjuːkliə] *a.*【原】热核(反应)的. *a* ~ *bomb* 热核炸弹. *a* ~ *reaction* 热核反应. *a* ~ *weapon* 热核子武器. *a* ~ *war* 热核战争.
ther•mo•nu•cle•o•nics [ˌθəːməuˈnjuːkliˈɔniks] *n.*【原】热核子学;热核技术.
ther•mo•nuke [ˈθəːmənjuːk]【物】〔美口〕核子武器.
ther•mo•paint [ˈθəːməupeint] *n.* 示温涂料; 彩色温标示漆,测温漆.
ther•mo•pen•e•tra•tion [ˈθəːməuˌpeniˈtreiʃən] *n.*【医】内科透热法.
ther•mo•pe•ri•od•ism [ˌθəːməuˌpiəriˈɔdizəm] *n.*【生】温周期现象. **-pe•ri•o•dic•i•ty** *n.*
ther•mo•phase [ˈθəːməufeis] *n.*【植】温期.
ther•mo•phile [ˈθəːməˌfail] *n.*【医】嗜热性.
ther•moph•i•lic [ˌθəːməˈfilik] *a.*【生】嗜热性的,适温的,喜温的. ~ *bacteria* 适温细菌.
ther•mo•phone [ˈθəːməfəun] *n.* ①【讯】热线式受话器,热致发声器. ②传声温度计(或器).
ther•mo•phore [ˈθəːməufɔː, -fɔə] *n.* 畜热器.
ther•mo•pile [ˈθəːməpail] *n.*【物】温差电堆,热电堆.
ther•mo•plas•tic [ˌθəːməˈplæstik] *n.* 热塑塑料; 热塑性物质. — *a.* 热塑性的 (*opp.* thermosetting). **-i•ty** *n.* 热塑性.

ther·mo·reg·u·la·tion [ˌθə:məuˌregjuˈleiʃən] *n.* ①温度调节. ②【生理】体温调节.
ther·mo·reg·u·la·tor [ˌθə:məˈregjuleitə] *n.* 温度调节器.
ther·mo·run·away [ˈθə:məuˈrʌnəwei] *n.* 【物】热致击穿,热致破坏.
ther·mos (bottle [flask]) [ˈθə:mɔs] *n.* 热水瓶,暖瓶.
ther·mo·scope [ˈθə:məskəup] *n.* 验温器,测温器[锥]. **-scop·i·c(al)** *a.*
ther·mo·set [ˈθə:məset] *n.*【化】热固性,热硬性. — *a.* 热固(硬)性的,热变定的.
ther·mo·set·ting [ˌθə:məuˈsetiŋ] *a.*, *n.*【化】热固(的),热硬性(的),热后就坚硬化(的) (*opp.* thermoplastic).
ther·mo·si·phon [θə:məuˈsaifən] *n.* 热虹吸管; 温差环流系统.
ther·mo·stable [θə:məuˈsteibl] *a.* 【生化】耐热性的 (*opp.* thermolabile).
ther·mo·stage [ˈθə:məusteidʒ] *n.*【植】春化阶段; 温期阶段.
ther·mo·stat [ˈθə:məstæt] *n.* ①恒温器. ②(灭火设备等)温变自动启闭装置. *a* ~ *blade* 温变断流器. **-ic** *a.* **-i·cal·ly** *ad.*
thermo·statics [ˌθə:məˈstætiks] *n.*【物】静热力学.
ther·mo·tax·is [ˌθə:məˈtæksis] *n.* ①【生】向热性,趋温性. ②【生理】体温调节. **-tax·ic, -tac·tic** [-tik] *a.*
ther·mo·ten·sile [ˌθə:məˈtensl] *a.* 有热抗张强度的.
ther·mo·ther·a·py [ˌθə:məuˈθerəpi] *n.* 【医】热疗(法).
ther·mot·ro·pism [θə(:)ˈmɔtrəpizəm] *n.* 【生】向热[温]性, 趋热性. *negative* ~ 背热性,负向热性. *positive* ~ 向热性,正向热性. **ther·mo·trop·ic** *a.*
the·roid [ˈθiərɔid] *a.* 野兽似的,兽性的.
the·rol·o·gy [θiəˈrɔlədʒi] *n.*【动】哺乳动物学.
The·ron [ˈθirən] *n.* 西伦〔男子名〕.
the·ro·pod [ˈθiərəˌpɔd] *n.*【古生】兽脚亚目 (*Theropoda*) 动物〔如恐龙〕.
ther·sit·i·cal [θəˈsitikl] *a.* 大声的,辱骂的,庸俗下流的,满口下流话的.
the·sau·rus [θi(:)ˈsɔ:rəs] *n.* (*pl.* ~*es* [-iz], -*ri* [-rai]) ①宝库; 知识的宝库. ②(尤指同义词等的)词典,百科全书; (分类)词汇集,(词语、资料等的)汇编,文选.
these [ði:z] *pro., a.* 〔*this* 的复数〕这些. *in* ~ *days* 近来. ~ *days* 近来. ~ *times* 现时. *We have been working the case* ~ *ten days.* 近十天来我们一直搞这个案子. ***one of* ~ *days*** 两三天内. ★ ***one of*** ~〔常带轻蔑意〕一个这种人: *He's one of* ~ *artist chaps.* 他是一个不三不四的艺术家.
these [ˈte:zə] *n.* 〔G.〕纲领; 提纲.
The·seus [ˈθi:siəs, ˈθisju:s]【希神】提修斯〔雅典王子,曾除灭盗贼立功,并进入克里特岛迷宫斩妖除怪〕.
the·sis [ˈθi:sis] *n.* (*pl.* ***theses*** [ˈθi:si:z]) ①论点,论题;【逻】命题,假设. ②作文; 毕业论文,学位论文. ③ [ˈθesis]【韵】(现代诗韵中的)抑音节,弱音节 (*opp.* arsis); (古希腊、罗马诗中的)扬音节;【乐】强声部. *sb.'s principal theses* 某人的主要论点. *scientific theses* 科学论断. ~ *novel* (= tendentious novel) 阐明某一鲜明主题的主题小说.
Thes·pi·an [ˈθespiən, -pjən] *a.* ①(古希腊诗人)狄斯比斯 (Thespis) 的. ②悲剧(性)的; 戏剧的〔尤指悲剧的〕. — *n.* 演员; 悲剧演员. *the* ~ *art* 戏剧.
Thes·sa·lo·ni·an [ˌθesəˈləunian] *a.* (Thessalonica) 萨洛尼卡的,萨洛尼卡人的. — *n.* 萨洛尼卡人.
the·ta [ˈθi:tə] *n.* 希腊字母表的第八字母〔Θ、θ, 相当于英语的 th〕.
thet·ic, thet·i·cal [ˈθetik(ə)l] *a.* ①武断的,规定的. ②【诗】以抑音节开始的; 以抑音节组成的. **-i·cal·ly** *ad.*
the·ur·gy [ˈθi:ə:dʒi] *n.* 妖术; 法术; 神通. **-gic, -gi·cal** [θiˈə:dʒik(ə)l] *a.* **-gist** *n.* 术士,施妖术者,法师.
thew [θju:] *n.* 〔常用 *pl.*〕①肌肉. ②筋力,体力,膂力,活力. ③〔古〕精神[道德]的素质.
thew·less [ˈθju:lis] *a.* 〔主苏格兰〕①无活力的,无精神的. ②肌肉不发达的,体力虚弱的.
thew·y [ˈθju:i] *a.* (***thew·i·er; thew·i·est***) 肌肉发达的,强壮有力的,精力充沛的.
they [常音 ðei; 弱 ðe] *pro.* 〔*pl.*〕〔人称代词、第三人称、复数、主格; 所有格 their, 宾格 them, 物主代词 theirs〕①他们,她们,它们. ②众人,人们. *T- say that* 据说.
they'd [ðeid] ①= they had. ②= they would.
they'll [ðeil] (= they will; they shall).
they're [ðeiə] (= they are).
they've [ðeiv] (= they have).
thi- *comb. f.* 〔用于元音前〕硫: *thi*azine *thi*azole.
thi·a·min(e) [ˈθaiəmi(:)n] *n.*【生化,药】硫胺〔即维生素 B_1〕.
thi·a·za·mide [θaiˈæzəmaid] *n.*【药】磺硋噻唑.
thi·a·zine [ˈθaiəˌzi:n, -zin] *n.*【化】噻嗪,硫氮杂苯.
thi·a·zole [ˈθaiəˌzəul] *n.*【化】①噻唑,间氮硫茂. ②噻嗪染料.
Thi·bet [tiˈbet] *n.* = Tibet.
thick [θik] *a.* ①(*opp.* thin)厚的; 粗大的(树枝). ②浓厚的,粘稠的; 混浊的,不透明的; 不清楚的,不清晰的(声音沙哑,口齿不清等); 阴霾的,有浓雾的. ③茂密的(树林等); (毛发)浓密的; 密集的,挤满人的,充满…的. ④频数的,接连不停的(雨,雪等). ⑤混杂的(*with*); 众多的; 丰富的 (*with*). ⑥迟钝的(器官,头脑). ⑦〔口〕亲密的,知己的,友好的 (*with*). ⑧〔英俚〕太过分的. ⑨显著的. *The ice is 3 inches* ~. 冰厚3英尺. *spread the butter* ~ 奶油涂得厚. *a* ~ *mist [fog]* 浓雾. ~ *clouds* 密云. ~ *of hearing* 听觉不灵. ~ *speech* 口齿不清的讲话. ~ *syrup* 粘稠的糖浆. *trees* ~ *with leaves* 叶子茂密的树. *the air* ~ *with snow* 大雪密集的天空. *The car is* ~ *with people.* 车子挤满了人. *The conditions are a bit too* ~. 条件太过分了. *The river looks* ~ *after the rain.* 雨后河水浑浊. ***as*** ~ ***as thieves*** 非常亲密. ***rather [a little too, a bit]*** ~〔英俚〕(行为、要求等)太过分,太不要脸,受不了. ***get a*** ~ ***ear*** 〔英俚〕被打肿了耳朵. ***give (sb.) a*** ~ ***ear***〔英俚〕把(某人)打肿耳朵. — *n.* ①最厚[粗]的部分,最浓部分,最活跃的部分,密茂处,(战争等的)最激烈处,正当中,正起劲的时候. ②〔口〕笨蛋,傻子. ③〔俚〕可可粉. ***in the*** ~ ***of*** 在…的正当中,在…正起劲时. ***through*** ~ ***and thin*** 在任何情形下,不顾艰难困苦; 不避艰险,赴汤蹈火. ***go into the*** ~ ***of practical struggles*** 深入实际斗争. — *ad.* ①厚; 浓; 密; 深. ②频数,时常. ③(声音)浊; 不清晰地. ④〔口〕太过分,过度. *The heart beats* ~. 心跳得厉害. ***lay it on*** ~ 乱恭维. ~ **and fast** 纷至沓来,频数,密集地. **~-and-thin** *a.* 不辞水火的,始终不变的,忠实的. **~-brained** *a.* 头脑迟钝的,低能的. **~head** 笨人,呆子. **~-leafed** *a.* 树叶密的; 叶厚的. ~ **set** ① *a.* 矮胖的,粗而短的; 繁茂的; 浓密的; 质地厚实的. ② *n.* 丛林; 密篱; 厚灯芯绒. **~-skinned** *a.* 厚皮的; 脸皮厚的; 感觉迟钝的. **~-skulled, ~-witted** *a.* 愚钝的.
thick·en [ˈθikən] *vt.* ①使厚; 使粗大; 使浓; 使浊; 稠化. ②使繁茂,使密. ③使深; 加多; 加强,加牢. — *vi.* ①变厚,变粗大,变浓,变浊. ②变模糊,变暗. ③变厉害,增多,变复杂. ④变坚牢,变结实. *Night* ~*s.* 夜渐深. *If you want to* ~ *the soup, add some flour.* 如果你想使汤浓些,加一点面粉. *Use the paper to* ~ *your notebook.* 用这些纸加厚你的笔记本. *The plot* ~*s.* 情节复杂起来. *The soup* ~*s by boiling.* 汤煮开就变稠了. **-er** 增稠器[剂]. **-ing** *n.* ①增浓(粗、密、厚),稠化,增浓过程,稠化过程. ②增稠剂. ③被加厚[加浓等]的东西[部分].
thicket [ˈθikit] *n.* ①灌木丛. ②丛状物,密集的东西. ③【植】植丛,乱丛棵子,薮. ④【物】障.

thick·et·ed [ˈθikitid] *a.* 灌木丛的,成丛状的,密集的.

thick·ly [ˈθikli] *ad.* = thick.

thick·ness [ˈθiknis] *n.* ①厚;粗;厚度;粗大. ②浓度;浓厚,粘稠. ③密度;稠密. ④模糊不清;多烟雾,混浊. ⑤愚笨;迟钝. ⑥最厚[粗,密,浓]处. ⑦(有一定厚度的东西的)一张,一层. ⑧亲密. *coal seams of less ~ than five feet* 厚度不及五英尺的煤层. *the ~ of population in Shanghai* 上海的人口密度. *wood of different ~* 厚度不同的木头. *five ~es of cardboard* 五层纸板.

thick'un [ˈθikən] *n.* 〔英俚〕一镑金币;五先令银币.

thief [θiːf] *n.* (*pl.* ***thieves*** [θiːvz]) ①贼,小偷. ②〔口〕(使蜡外流的)蜡烛心结的烛花. *Beware of thieves* 谨防小偷. *to arrest, catch, chase, take up a ~* 捉(追)贼. ***thieves' Latin*** 盗贼黑话. ~ **knot** 平结.

thieve [θiːv] *vt., vi.* 偷;行窃. — *n.* 小偷.

thiev·er·y [ˈθiːvəri] *n.* 偷窃;贼赃.

thiev·ish [ˈθiːviʃ] *a.* 爱偷窃的;贼(似)的,偷偷摸摸的;不正当的. **-ly** *ad.* **-ness** *n.*

thigh [θai] *n.* 【解】大腿,大腿骨;【虫】股节. **~bone** *n.* 大腿骨,股骨.

thig·mo·tax·is [ˌθigməˈtæksis] *n.* 【医】向实体运动 (= stereotaxis). **-tac·tic** *a.*

thig·mot·ro·pism [ˈθigˈmɔtrəpizm] *n.* 【医】向实体趋性 (= stereotropism). **-trop·ic** [-ˈtrɔpik] *a.*

thill [θil] *n.* (车的)杠,辕. **-er** *n.* 驾辕马 (= ~ horse).

thim·ble [ˈθimbl] *n.* ①(缝纫用)顶针. ②隐豆戏法用杯子(参阅 thimblerig 条). ③= thimbleful. ④〔盗贼俚〕手錶. ⑤【机】套筒,套管,外接头,联轴器;离合器;封底管道,盲管道. *a ~ knight* 〔美〕裁缝. ~ **berry** 【植】糙莓 (= black raspberry). ~ **coupling [joint]** 套筒联轴节. ~ **weed** 【植】①银莲花(属)〔如长果银莲花,河岸银莲花,弗吉尼亚银莲花等〕. ②金光菊(属);黄雏菊.

thim·ble·ful [ˈθimblˌful] *n.* (酒等的)少量. *a ~ of whiskey* 少量的威士忌酒. *He has just a ~ of insight into human behaviour.* 他对人们的行为只有一点点见识.

thim·ble·rig [ˈθimblrig] *n.* 隐豆戏法〔用三只杯子和一粒豆表演的快手戏法〕. — *vi.* 表演隐豆戏法;变戏法,欺骗. **-ger** *n.* 骗子.

Thim·bu [ˈθimbuː], **Thim·phu, Thim·pu** *n.* 廷布〔不丹首都〕.

thi·mer·o·sal [θaiˈmerəˌsæl, -ˈməː-] *n.* 【药】噻汞撒.

thin [θin] *a.* (***~ner; ~nest***) ①薄的 (*opp.* thick);瘦的 (*opp.* fat, stout);细小的;【印】细体的. ②稀少的,稀疏的 (*opp.* dense). ③稀薄的,淡薄的(液体、气体等) (*opp.* thick);浅薄的,空洞的,没有什么内容的,不充实的. ④显而易见的,易看破的. ⑤〔美口〕手头缺钱的;简陋的,微少的(供给等). ⑥〔美俚〕无聊的,不舒服的,不愉快的. ⑦〔美俚〕将要垮掉的,守不住的. ⑧【摄】(照片、底版)衬度弱的. *a ~ board* 薄板. *a ~ house* 观众稀少的戏院. *a ~ meeting* 来人稀少的集会. *a ~ slice of bolony* 〔美〕极夸大的要求;傻话;露骨的虚伪;瞎说乱讲的人. *a ~ soup* 淡而无味的汤. *a ~ story* 内容空洞的故事. *~ green* 淡绿. *~ hair* 稀疏的头发. *~ one* 〔美〕十分银币. *That's (a lot) too ~.* 〔口〕太露骨,太显而易见. ***be ~ in the face*** 脸瘦. ***have a ~ time (of it)*** 碰到不愉快事. ***look ~ after illness*** 病后显得清瘦. — *ad.* 〔诗〕稀薄,淡,细,疏,稀疏,微. — *n.* 细小部分,稀薄部分. — *vt.* 使薄,使细,使稀薄,使淡,使稀疏;【农】间苗;使瘦. — *vi.* 变薄;变细;变稀薄,变淡;变稀疏;变瘦. *Famine and war had thinned the population.* 灾荒和战争使人口减少了. *When the crowd ~ned, we left the square.* 人群散开的时候,我们离开了广场. ***~ down*** 弄细;变细. ***~ out*** 间(苗),疏(果);(听众)减少;变薄. **-ly** *ad.* **-ness** *n.*

thine [ðain] *pro.* 〔古、诗〕①〔thou 的物主代词〕你[您]的东西. ②〔作为 thou 的所有格,用于首字母是元音或 h 音的名词前〕= thy: *~ eyes, heart, etc.*

thing[1] [θiŋ] *n.* ①(有形或无形的)东西,物;事物. ②事,事件,局面,消息;〔*pl.*〕情形,形势,事态. ③〔*pl.*〕个人所有物,衣饰,服装,随身物品;用具,家具,财产. ④【法】〔*pl.*〕动产(或不动产). ⑤题目,主题. ⑥细节,要点. ⑦(带感情色彩)家伙,东西〔指人或动物,表示轻蔑,爱情,怜悯〕. ⑧事业,行为,成就,成果. ⑨举动,行动,目标. ⑩(艺术的)作品;歌曲. ⑪〔the ~〕正适合(需要)的东西[事情];最流行的东西. ⑫〔*pl.*〕文物〔后接形容词〕. *all ~s* 万物,宇宙. *a living ~* 生物. *dumb ~s* 牲畜. *a pretty young ~* 〔俚〕漂亮的小姑娘〔也有说作 a P.Y.T. 的〕. *You stupid ~!* 你这蠢东西! *He takes ~s too seriously.* 他把事情看得太认真了. *Things have changed greatly.* 情形大大不同了. *~s Chinese* 中国的文物. *tea ~s* 茶具. *a little ~ of mine* 拙作. *That is just the ~ for me.* 那正合我的心意,那对我正好. *I am not quite the ~ this morning.* 今早身体不大舒服. *It is not (quite) the ~.* 有点不对,有点不好的地方. *How are ~s going at the Institute?* 学院里的情况怎么样? *Take your ~s upstairs.* 把你的衣物拿到楼上去. *I've a lot of ~s to do this morning.* 我今天上午有许多事要做. *He spoke of many ~s at the meeting.* 他在会上讲了好多的问题. *In designing the machine, not a ~ is to be overlooked.* 在设计这架机器时一点细节也不要忽略. *This is just the ~ I want.* 这正是我所要的. *At fifty, he would be a man to accomplish great ~s.* 他到五十岁时会有很大的成就. *The ~ now is to see the party secretary at once.* 现在要做的是立刻去见党支书. ***among other ~s*** 其中;尤其,格外. ***... and ~s*** 〔口语〕…等. ***as ~s are [stand]*** 据目前形势[情形]. ***do the handsome ~ by*** 宽大对待. ***for another ~*** 二则,其次. ***for one ~ ... (, for another ...)*** 一方面…(,另一方面);一则…(,再则…);首先…(,其次…). ***get ~s done*** 完成工作任务. ***in all ~s*** 无论在什么问题上. ***know [be up to] a ~ or two*** 〔口〕机敏,精明,不落空. ***learn a ~ or two*** 学得一点东西. ***make a good ~ of*** (因)…赚到钱[获利]. ***no such ~*** 哪里会,没有这样的事. ***of all ~s*** 偏偏(有这种事). ***one ~ ... another*** 一样一样,各方面;…是一回事…又是一回事,…和…是不同的(*taking one ~ with another* 一样一样[前前后后]想一想. *A man of talent is one ~, and a pedant another.* 有才能的人和卖弄学问的人是不一样的). ***Poor ~!*** 可怜! ***see ~s*** 发生幻觉,见神见鬼. ***take ~s as they are*** 随遇而安,对一切事情都处之泰然. ***the latest ~ in (hats)*** (帽子的)最新式样,最时髦的(帽子). ***The ~ is ...*** 目前的问题是,目前最要紧的是. ***~ in itself*** 【哲】自在之物,物自体. ***~ of naught [nothing]*** 不足道的东西[事情]. ***~s have long been in a bad way (for sb.)*** 某人的日子很不好过,情况很坏. **~s mortgaged** 【法】抵押品. **~s personal [real]** 【法】动产[不动产].

thing[2] [θiŋ] *n.* (斯堪的纳维亚各国的)议会[司法机构] (= ting).

thing·a·my, thing·a·ma·bob [ˈθiŋəmi, -əˈmɑːbɔb]; **thing·um·a·jig** [-əmidʒig], **thingum·bob** [-əmbɔb]. **thingum·my** [-əmi] *n.* 〔口〕①(对叫不出名字或暂时忘记的人或物的代称)那么个东西[人]. ②机件装置;零件.

thing·y [ˈθiŋi] *a.* 物(体)的,物质的;实际的.

think [θiŋk] *vt.* (***thought*** [θɔːt]) ①想,思索,构思;考虑. ②想出,想起. ③认为,以为. ④猜想,想象. ⑤想要,打算. ⑥使想. ⑦感到. *I ~ I shall meet him today.* 我想[认为]今天会遇见他. *I don't ~ it's five o'clock yet.* 我看还不到五点. *I ~ him (to be) honest.* 我认为他(是)老实(的). *I'll ~ the matter over.* 这事我得细细考虑考虑. *We should always use our brains and ~ everything over carefully.* 凡事应该用脑筋好好想一想. *I can't ~ how she could figure out all the problems in an hour.* 我想不出她怎么在一个小时之内算出所有的习题的. *Let's go and have* *a walk in the garden. You will ~ yourself silly.* 咱们出去在花园里散散步，你要把自己想得傻了. *I thought to finish these letters before ten o'clock.* 我原来打算十点钟以前把这些封信都写好了. *I thought to find you in the library.* 我原来猜想会在图书馆里找到你. *Who would have thought that they could win the game.* 谁会想到他们竟能赢得那场球呢. *I ~ no harm in pay a visit to the Jones.* 我感到拜访琼斯家没有害处. — *vi.* ①想. ②想象，思索，思考，考虑 *(over; about; of; on).* ③想出，想起 *(of;on).* ④企图，想要，打算*(of).* ⑤料想. *Only ~!* 嗳，你想想看! *~ evil* 想干坏事. *Please ~ again.* 请再想想. *A university student should learn to ~.* 一个大学生应该学会思考. *I don't ~ so.* 我认为不是那样. *I'm thinking about the plan we're going to lay out.* 我在考虑我们要提出的计划. *T- over what I've said.* 把我所讲的话细细地想想. *What do you ~ of the idea?* 你认为这个想法怎么样? *That's a useful book to people who ~ of literary life.* 那是一本对想要从事文学生活的人有用的书. *I've thought deeply on our difficulties and the ways to get out of them.* 我深思了我们的困难及其解决办法. ***I don't ~.*** 〔俚〕我倒有点不相信〔添加在反话，讥刺话等后面〕*(You are a pattern of tact, I don't ~.* 你的手腕了不起，我倒有点不相信). ***I ~*** 是…罢〔插句或句尾〕. ***I ~ not.*** 我以为不是那样. ***~ and ~*** 想了又想，细想. ***~ aloud*** 自言自语，边想边说. ***~ away*** 想开了(如不信神了); 想得忘了(如牙齿痛). ***~ better of ...*** 改变…的念头; 对某人有较高的评价. ***~ fit [good, proper, right] to*** *(do)* 认为…适当 *(I ~ fit to refuse.* 我以为拒绝的好). ***~ harm to*** 想害…，企图加害. ***~ highly [no end, well] of*** 看重某人(某事)，评价极高. ***~ little [nothing] of*** 看不起，轻视; 满不在乎 *(~ nothing of walking 30 miles a day* 一天 30 英里也满不在乎). ***~ much of*** 重视，看重; 赞美，夸奖. ***~ of*** ①想起; 想出 *(I cannot ~ of the right word).* ②想，企图*(He is ~ing of ...).*③细想 *(T- of what I told you).* ***~ oneself into a dilemma*** 想得无所适从. ***~ oneself into a fever*** 想得头脑发热〔兴奋不已〕. ***~ out*** 想透; 想出. ***~ out loud*** 〔美〕= ~ aloud. ***~ sense*** 通情达理地设想. ***~ shame*** 以为耻辱，羞愧. ***~ through*** = ~ out. ***~ to oneself*** 暗暗地自言自语; 在心中想〔打算，思量〕. ***~ twice*** 踌躇. ***~ up*** 〔美〕想出，想起;〔口〕发明. ***~ well [ill] of*** 认为好〔坏〕. ***~ with*** 和…意见相同. — *n.* 〔方、口〕思考; 想法，念头. *Give it another ~.* 再想想吧. *Let's exchange ~s.* 咱们交换交换想法. ***have a hard ~*** 苦思冥想 — *a.* 思想(方面)的; 供思考的. *a ~ teleplay* 引人思索的电视剧. ~ **piece** 〔美新闻语〕署名的评论文章〔背景资料等〕. ~ **centre [tank, factory]** 智囊团〔班子〕，智囊〔谋划〕中心. ~**-tanker** 智囊(人物).

think·a·ble [ˈθiŋkəbl] *a.* 可想象的; 可能的. *I'm sorry to say her idea is hardly ~.* 对不起，她的想法是几乎不可想象的. **-ness** *n.* **-a·bly** *ad.*

think·er [ˈθiŋkə] *n.* 思想家; 思考者. *a deep ~* 深刻的思想家.

think·ing [ˈθiŋkiŋ] *n.* ①思考，思索，考虑. ②思想，观点，见解，想法. *plain living and high ~* 朴素的生活与崇高的思想. *It is man's social being that determines his ~.* 人们的社会存在，决定人们的思想. *There is nothing either good or bad but ~ makes it so.* 无所谓好坏，只是有那种想法才弄成这样子. *He is of my way of ~.* 他和我意见〔想法〕相同. ***to my ~*** 我以为. — *a.* 思想的; 有思想的; 通情达理的; 深思熟虑的. *a ~ part* (戏剧里)不说话的脚色. ***all ~ men*** 凡是有头脑的人都(这样说等). ***put on one's ~ cap*** 深思. ~**-machine** 电子计算机. **the ~ public** 思想界. **-ly** *ad.* **-ness** *n.*

think·so [ˈθiŋksəu] *n.* 〔口〕单纯的初步意见.

thin·ner [ˈθinə] *n.* 稀释剂，冲淡剂，稀料; 对…进行稀释(或冲淡)的人.

thinning [ˈθiniŋ] *n.* 【农，园艺】间苗; 蔬花，蔬果.

thin·nish [ˈθiniʃ] *a.* 有点薄(细，瘦，稀疏)的. *His new novel is tinged with ~ humour.* 他的新小说略带诙谐.

thin-skinned [ˈθinˈskind] *a.* 薄皮的; 敏感的，神经过敏的; 易怒的.

thi(o)- *comb. f.* 硫，硫代: *thion*timonate.

thi·o [ˈθaiəu] *a.* 【化】硫的，含硫的. ~ **acid** 硫代酸.

thi·o·al·de·hyde [ˌθaiəuˈældəhaid] *n.* 【化】硫醛; 乙硫醛.

thi·o·an·ti·mo·nate, -mo·ni·ate [ˌθaiəuˈæntiməˌneit, -ˈməuniˌeit] 【化】硫代锑酸盐，全硫锑酸盐.

thi·o·an·ti·mo·ni·te [ˌθaiəuˈæntiməˌnait] *n.* 【化】硫代亚锑酸盐.

thi·o·ar·se·nate [ˌθaiəuˈɑːsiˌneit, -snit] *n.* 【化】硫代砷酸盐.

thi·o·ar·se·nite [ˌθaiəuˈɑːsiˌnait] *n.* 【化】硫砷酸盐.

thi·o·bac·te·ri·a [ˌθaiəubækˈtiəriə] *n. pl.* *(sing.* ***-rium*** [-əm]*)*【化】硫细菌.

thi·o·car·ba·mide [ˌθaiəuˈkɑːbəˌmaid] *n.* 【化】硫脲 (= thiourea).

thi·o·cy·a·nate [ˌθaiəuˈsaiəˌneit] *n.* 【化】硫(代)氰酸盐(或酯).

thi·o·gly·col·(l)ic [ˌθaiəuglaiˈkɔlik] *a.* 【化】~ *acid* 巯(基)醋酸，硫代乙醇酸.

thi·o·kol [ˈθaiəkəul] *n.* 聚硫橡胶，乙硫橡胶〔商标名〕.

thi·ol [ˈθaiəul, -ɔːl] *n.* 【化】硫醇(类) = mercaptan.

thi·o·nate [ˈθaiəˌneit] *n.* 【化】连(若干)硫酸盐.

thi·onic [θaiˈɔnik] *a.* 【化】硫黄的; 含硫的. ~ *acid* 连(若干)硫酸.

thi·o·nine [ˈθaiəˌniːn, -nin] *n.* 【化】硫堇; 劳氏紫.

thi·o·nyl [ˈθaiənil] *n.* 【化】亚硫酰.

thi·o·pen·tal(sodium) [ˌθaiəˈpentæl, -tɔːl, -tl] 【药】喷妥撒钠〔麻醉，安眠剂〕.

thi·o·phene [ˈθaiəˌfiːn] *n.* 【化】噻吩，硫(杂)茂.

thi·o·phos [θaiˈɔfəus] *n.* = parathion.

thi·o·phos·phate [ˌθaiəuˈfɔsfeit] *n.* 【化】硫代磷酸盐.

thi·o·sin·am·ine [ˌθaiəusinˈæmiːn, -ˌsinəˈmiːn] *n.* 【化】硫代芥子胺; 硫代烯丙氨腈.

thi·o·sul·fate [ˌθaiəuˈsʌlfeit] *n.* 【化】硫代硫酸盐(或酯).

thi·o·u·ra·cil [ˌθaiəuˈjurəsil] *n.* 【化】硫尿嘧啶，硫尿间氮苯.

thi·o·u·re·a [ˌθiəujuəˈriə] *n.* 【化】硫脲.

thi·ram [ˈθairæm] *n.* 【化】秋兰姆，(某)氨硫羰(基)〔一种加硫促进剂的简称〕.

third [θəːd] *num.* ①第三〔略 3rd〕. ②三分之一(的). — *n.* ①〔the ~〕第三. ②第三者〔指人〕. ③(时间或角度的)一秒的六十分之一. ④〔the ~〕(某月的)三日. ⑤〔*pl.*〕【法】归遗孀所有的亡夫遗产的三分之一. ⑥【乐】第三音; 三度音程; 三度和音. ⑦(汽车的)第三档(速度). *one ~ of the total* 全体的三分之一. *two ~s* 三分之二. *No ~ ever joined our conferences.* 没有第三者曾参加我们的会议. *a major ~* 【乐】大三度. *a ~ sex* 不男不女的人; 搞同性关系的人; 阉人. ~ **base** (= the ~). 【体】(棒球)第三垒. ~ **class** *a.* ①三等，三级，三等品，三等舱. ②〔美〕三类邮件(书，广告信等). —*ad.* 坐三等车(舱). ~ **contact** 【天】生光. ~ **degree** 〔美〕逼供，疲劳讯问，拷问. ~**-degree burn** 【医】三级烧伤. ~ **dimension warfare** 立体战. ~**-dimensional** *a.* 第三维的，有深(厚)度的，栩栩如生的. ~ **ear** 〔美俚〕告密者. ~ **estate** (法国革命前的)第三阶级，平民阶级. ~ **eyelid** 【解】瞬膜. ~ **floor** 〔英〕四楼，〔美〕三楼. ~ **force** 第三种力量; 起平衡作用的力量. ~ **house** 〔美俚〕(国会的)第三院〔院外活动集团〕. **T- International** 第三国际. ~ **market** 第三市场，证券市场. ~ **party** 【法】第三党. ~ **person** 第三者;【语法】第三人称. ~ **rail** 电动机车的输电轨;〔美俚〕酒. ~ **rate** *a.*

三等的,第三流的,低劣的,下等的. ~ **rater** *n.* 低等(下等)的人物. **T- Reich** 第三帝国〔1933—45 年间希特勒统治下的德国〕. **T- Republic** 法兰西第三共和国(1870—1940). **T- Sea Lord**〔英〕海军部第三把手副部长,海军军需长. ~ **service** 航空. ~ **stream**【乐】第三乐派〔将爵士音乐即兴技术与古典音乐技术结合起来的乐派〕. ~ **ventricle**【解】第三脑室. ~ **world** 第三世界.

third·ly [ˈθəːdli] *ad.* 第三.

thirl [θəːl] *vt., vi.*〔英方〕①钻孔,穿孔. ②= thrill.

thirst [θəːst] *n.* ①渴. ②渴望,热望 *(after; for; of)*. ③(土地等的)干燥,干旱. ④〔口〕酒瘾,想喝酒. *have a ~*〔口〕想喝一杯. *feel (quench, relieve, slake) ~* 感觉(止)渴. *awaken one's ~ for further study* 唤起某人作进一步研究的热望. — *vi.* 渴望 *(after; for)*;〔古〕渴. *All the students of our class ~ after knowledge [to learn].* 我们班的所有的同学都渴望知识〔学习〕.

thirst·i·ly [ˈθəːstili] *ad.* 口渴地;渴望着.

thirst·i·ness [ˈθəːstinis] *n.* 渴;渴望;干旱.

thirst·y [ˈθəːsti] *a.* *(-i·er; -i·est)* ①口渴的. ②爱喝酒的. ③渴望 *(for)*. ④干燥的,干旱的. ⑤使人口渴的(工作等). *Young man should be ~ for knowledge.* 青年人应该渴望知识. *a ~ soul* 爱喝酒的人,酒徒.

thir·teen [ˈθəːˈtiːn] *num., n.* (基数)十三,十三个;十三个人〔东西〕;十三岁;十三的记号. *the ~ superstition* 以十三为不吉的迷信.

thir·teenth [ˈθəːˈtiːnθ] *num., n.* 第十三;十三分之一(的);(月的)十三日. *a ~ juryman*〔美俚〕不公正的法官. **-ly** *ad.*

thir·ti·eth [ˈθəːtiiθ] *num., n.* 第三十;三十分之一(的);(月的)三十日.

thir·tish [ˈθəːtiʃ] *a.* 三十岁的,三十岁左右的.

thir·ty [ˈθəːti] *num.* (基数)三十,三十个(的) — *n.* 三十的记号;【网球】得两分时的称呼;〔*pl.*〕〔the ~〕三十多岁,〔*pl.*〕三十年代;〔美新闻语〕完,终〔原稿末页记上"30",表示"完"〕;死. ***in the nineteen thirties*** 在 20 世纪 30 年代〔略 in 1930's〕. ***in nineteen ~*** 在 1930 年. ***in the thirties*** (年龄)三十多岁(的);在(某一世纪的)三十年代(的);(温度表)三十多度(的). ~ **cents**〔美〕不良的;劣质的. ~**fold** *a., ad.* 三十倍的;成三十倍. ~-**second note**【乐】三十二分音符(= demisemiquaver). ~-**twomo** *n.* *(pl. -mos)*【印】三十二开本〔略 32 mo〕;三十二开纸.

this [ðis] *(pl. these)* *pro.*〔指示代词〕①这,这个,这事,这人. ②这时;这里. ③下面所说的事,刚才(以上)所说的事. ④(前述二物中的)后者 (*opp.* that 前者). *What is all ~?* 这是怎么回事? *T- is speaking Mr. Wang.* 我是小王〔打电话用语〕. *T- is Mr. Smith.* 这位是史密斯先生. *It was Miss Mary ~ and Miss Mary that.* 这也是玛丽小姐那也是玛丽小姐〔风头十足〕. *Get out of ~!* (从这里)滚出去! *The reason is ~.* 理由是这样. *Of the two plans, ~ is perhaps more practical.* 两个计划中,后者比前者也许更切合实际一些. *T- is the latest news from the front.* 下面是前线报导的最新消息. ***at ~*** 这里. ***by ~*** 这时. ***for all ~*** 尽管如此. ***like ~*** 这样的;象这样. ***put ~ and that together*** 把二者综合起来(一想). ***~ here ['ere]***〔俚、方〕= this. ***~, that, and the other*** 一切东西,种种东西〔人〕. ***with ~*** 一面这样说(一面就…),说完这个(就…). — *a.* ①这,这个. ②今…,本…. ③〔与表示时间的词组连用〕刚过去的,即将来到的. *~ fountain pen of yours* 你的这支自来水笔. *~ year* 今年. *~ month* 本月. *~ day month* 上一个月〔下一个月〕的今天. *~ morning* 今晨. *~ day* 今天. *~ time* 这次;这时候. ***for ~ once = for ~ time*** 只这一次. ***to ~ day*** 到今天. — *ad.* 就是这样,这样地. *~ early* 这样早. *~ high* (就)只这样高,到这样的高度. *~ much* 就只这些,到此为止.

thisa and thata [ˈðisə ænd ðætə]〔美俚〕各种有趣的玩意儿.

this·ness [ˈðisnis] *n.*【哲】"此"性;现实性.

this·tle [ˈθisl] *n.* ①【植】蓟. ②〔英〕〔the T-〕蓟花勋位〔勋章〕. ***grasp the ~ firmly*** 毅然解决棘手局面. ~ **digger**〔美〕土头土脑的人. ~ **down** 蓟的种子〔冠毛〕;轻物. ~ **finch** 金翅雀.

this·tly [ˈθisly] *a.* 多蓟的,蓟繁茂的;象蓟的;有刺的,会刺的.

thith·er [ˈðiðə] *ad.*〔古〕到那里,到那边. — *a.* 对过的,对岸的,那边的. *the ~ side of the stream* 河对岸. *on the ~ side of forty* 四十(岁)开外. ***hither and ~*** 到处,向各处,忽此忽彼. ~ **to** *ad.* 直到那时. ~**ward(s)** *ad.* 到那里,到那边.

thix·ot·ro·py [θikˈsɔtrəpi] *n.*【医】触变性;摇溶(现象). **-trop·ic** [-ˈtrɔpik] *a.*

tho, tho' [ðəu; 弱 ðo] *ad., conj* = though.

Tho. = Thomas.

thole[1] [θəul] *vt.*〔英方,苏格兰〕①忍受,遭受(苦痛等). ②接受;允许.

thole[2] [θəul] *n.* 桨座,桨架,桨脚;镰柄(= tholepin).

Thom·as [ˈtɔməs] *n.* 托马斯〔姓氏,男子名〕.

Tho·mism [ˈtəumizəm, ˈθəu-] *n.*【宗,哲】托马斯主义〔指托马斯阿奎那神学及其现代流派〕. **-mist** *n., a.* 托马斯主义者〔的〕;托马斯神学的. **-mis·tic** *a.*

Thomp·son [ˈtɔmpsn] *n.* 汤普森〔姓氏〕.

Thom·son [ˈtɔmsn] *n.* 汤姆森〔姓氏〕.

thong [θɔŋ] *n.* 皮带,皮条,皮鞭,鞭梢. — *vt.* 装皮带;用皮带系结;用皮带(鞭)打.

Thon·ga [ˈθɔŋgə] *n.* ①*(pl. -gas, -ga)* 桑格人〔指莫桑比克农民〕. ②桑格语〔属班图语〕.

Thor [θɔː] *n.*【北欧神】雷神〔司雷雨、战争、农业〕.

tho·rac·ic [θɔ(ː)ˈræsik] *a.*【解】胸(廓)的,胸部的. ~ *cavity* 胸腔. ~ *duct* 胸导管.

thoracico-,thorac(o)- *comb. f.*【医】胸,胸廓: *thoracoplasty.*

tho·ra·co·lum·bar [ˌθɔːrəkəuˈlʌmbə] *a.*【解】①胸腰部的. ②交感神经的.

tho·ra·co·plas·ty [ˈθɔːrəkəuˌplæsti] *n.* *(pl. -ties)*【医】胸廓成形术.

tho·ra·cot·o·my [ˌθɔːrəˈkɔtəmi] *n.* *(pl. -mies)*【医】胸廓切开术.

tho·rax [ˈθɔːræks] *n.* *(pl. ~es, thoraces* [θɔːˈreisiːz]*)* ①【解】胸,胸腔,胸廓,胸部(昆虫体三部分的中间部分). ②【古希腊】胸甲,胸板.

Tho·ra·zine [ˈθɔːrəˌziːn]【药】氯普鲁马嗪〔chlorpromazine 的商标名〕.

Thor·eau [ˈθɔːrəu] *n.* 索罗〔姓氏〕.

tho·ri·a [ˈθɔːriə] *n.*【化】氧化钍.

thori·a·nite [ˈθɔːriənait] *n.*【矿】方钍石〔含放射能〕.

tho·rite [ˈθɔːrait] *n.*【矿】硅酸钍,钍石.

tho·ri·um [ˈθɔːriəm] *n.*【化】钍.

thorn [θɔːn] *n.* ①刺;荆棘. ②【动】壳针. ③苦恼,忧虑的原因. ④古代英语字母的 p (= th). *Roses have ~s.* 玫瑰多刺,有快乐就有苦恼. *a ~ in one's side [flesh]* 不断使人苦恼的东西. ***be [sit, stand, walk] (up)on ~s*** 如坐针毡,焦虑不安. ~ **forest** 热带旱生林. ~ **apple**【植】①白花蔓陀罗. ②山楂果. ~**back**【鱼】鲉鱼. ~**bush** 有刺灌木;刺丛. **-less** *a.* 无刺的. **-like** *a.* 象刺一样的.

Thorn·dike [ˈθɔːndaik] *n.* 桑代克〔姓氏〕.

Thorn·ton [ˈθɔːntən] *n.* 桑顿〔姓氏〕.

thorn·y [ˈθɔːni] *a.* *(-i·er; -i·est)* ①多刺的,有针的;象刺的. ②刺丛繁茂的. ③棘手的,困难多的;痛苦的. *a ~ path* 荆棘丛生的小路,难走的道路. *a ~ subject* 争论多的题目,难题. **-i·ly** *ad.*

thoro [ˈθʌrə] *a., ad., prep., n.*〔废〕= thorough.

thoron [ˈθɔːrɔn] *n.* 【化】钍射气(略 Tn)〔射气同位素, Em^{220}〕.

thor·ough [ˈθʌrə] *a.* ①彻底的,全面的,充分的,彻头彻尾的,根本的,详尽的,严密的. ②绝对的,完善的. ③非常精确的,(对细节)不厌其烦的. *a ~ reform* 彻底的改革. *~ investigation* 周密的调查. *a ~ rest* 绝对的安静. *a ~ description of the game* 对该球赛的详尽的描述. *be ~ in one's work* 工作严谨认真. *a ~ person* 一丝不苟的人. *a ~ insulator* 套管绝缘子. — *prep., ad.*〔古〕= through. — *n.*〔T-〕【英史】(如英王查理一世实行的)专横政策 (= a policy of ~). ~ **bass**【乐】通奏低音(记谱法);和声法;和声学. ~ **brace** 张在马车下起弹簧作用的皮带. ~ **bred** ① *a.* 纯种的(动物);〔T-, t-〕纯种的(马犬等),精神奕奕的(人),受过严格训练的,优美的,第一流的,高尚的. ②*n.* 纯种动物;〔T-〕纯种马. ③有教养的人,受过严格训练的人. ④最好的车子(等). ~ **fare** 通道,大街,大路 *(opp. cul-de-sac,* private road*)*;水路;通行 (*No ~ fare!* 禁止通行!) ~ **going** *a.* 完全的,彻底的,十足的. ~**paced** *a.* 训练得十分好的(马等);完全的,彻底的,彻头彻尾的(坏蛋等). ~**pin** (马的) 跗关节肿胀. ~**wort**【植】贯叶泽兰(= boneset).

thorp(e) [θɔːp] *n.*〔古〕村庄. ★现仅用于英国北部地名.

Thos. = Thomas.

those [ðouz] *pro.*〔*that* 的复数〕那些东西[人];人们. *There are ~ who say ...* 也有说…的人们. — *a.* 那些. *in ~ days* 那时,当时.

Thoth [θouθ, tout] *n.* 古埃及的智慧和魔术的神〔鹭头人身〕.

thou[1] [ðau] *pro. (pl. ye)*〔人称代名词、第二人称、单数、主格;所有格为 thy 或 thine, 宾格为 thee, 物主代词为 thine〕〔古〕你,汝. ★ 现仅用于祈祷、诗、方言(基督教公谊会教徒 (Quakers) 常用以代 you 但有时也用 thee 代). —*vi., vt.* (不说 you 而)用 thou 称呼.

thou[2] [θau] *n.*〔俚〕〔thousand 的缩语〕一千,〔英〕一千镑;〔美〕一千元.

though [ðou; 弱 ðə] *ad.* 可是,但是,然而,不过还是;话虽这样说. *The grapes, ~, may be sour.* 可是,葡萄也许是酸的. *I wish you had told me, ~.* 话虽这样说,你告诉我就好了. *He said he would write to her. He didn't, ~.* 他说他要写信给她,可是,他没有写. *I've a bit of headache. It's nothing much, ~.* 我有一点头痛,不过并不厉害. — *conj.* 虽然,虽则,尽管,即使,纵然. *T- it was late, we decided to set out.* 虽然已经晚了,我们还是决定动身了. *T- he was a professor [Professor ~ he was], he took an active part in politics.* 虽然他是个大学教授,他在政治上很活跃. ***as ~ ...*** 恰如,好象. ***even ~*** 即使,纵然. ***What ~ ...?*** 即使…有什么要紧[关系]? 怕什么?

thought[1] [θɔːt] *n.* ①思想. ②思维;思考;推理能力,思想活动. ③思潮,思想方式. ④〔除否定外常 *pl.*〕(想做某事的)想法,意图,观念,意向,打算. ⑤关心,顾虑,挂念,忧虑,顾虑. ⑥〔与不定冠词 a 连用作状语〕一点,些许,稍微. *Marxism-Leninism-Mao Zedong Thought* 马列主义毛泽东思想. *What is the central ~ of this article?* 这篇文章的中心思想是什么? *Keep quiet. Father is deep in ~.* 安静些,爸爸在沉思. *Professor Wang is going to open a course in modern literary ~.* 王教授将开一门现代文艺思潮的课. *Don't keep your ~s to yourself.* 不要把你的想法闷在心里. *He never gives a ~ to his studies.* 他从来不把功课放在心上. *You are much in my ~s.* 我常常想念你. *Please be a ~ more straightforward.* 请稍许坦率一点. *I have ~s of singing.* 我想唱歌. *That's a happy [striking] ~* 那是个好主意[好想法]. ***after much [serious] ~*** 仔细考虑后. ***as quick as ~*** 立刻,马上. ***at the ~ of*** 一想到. ***be lost [sunk, absorbed, buried] in ~*** 在呆呆地默想. ***bestow a ~ on = give a ~ to*** 考虑一下,想一想. ***beyond ~*** 意想不到的. ***in ~*** 左思右想. ***on second ~s*** 再次考虑后,重新考虑后. ***take ~*** 担忧,担心 (*Take no ~ for the future.* 不要担心将来). ***two schools of ~***〔美俚〕两个意见,两种可能. ***upon [with] a ~*** 立刻,马上. ***without a moment's ~*** 立刻,当场. ***without ~*** 不加考虑就…,贸然. ~**-out** *a.* 思虑周到的;经过仔细考虑的. ~**-provoking** *a.* 令人深思的,发人深省的. ~**-reader** 读心术者;善于揣摩别人思想的人. ~**-reading**【心】测心术. ~ **transference**【心】思想传授. ~**way** 思想方法.

thought[2] [θɔːt] think 的过去式及过去分词.

thought·ful [ˈθɔːtful] *a.* ①认真思考的,不轻率的;细心的,沉思的,若有所思的. ②体贴人的,亲切的;对…关心的;对…忧虑的 *(of)*. ③思想丰富的,富有思想的,经过认真考虑的,有创见的. *For about ten minutes, he didn't say anything and was ~.* 有十分钟的功夫,他没有讲话,在沉思着. *How ~ of you!* 考虑得真周到! ***be ~ of one's safety*** 关心[注意]自已的安全. ***be ~ of others*** 考虑到[关心]别人. **-ly** *ad.* **-ness** *n.*

thought·less [ˈθɔːtlis] *a.* ①无思想的. ②轻率的;粗心的,缺乏考虑的. ③不体贴人的,自私的. *Maybe it's ~ of me.* 也许是我粗心了. *It's quite natural that a boy of nine is ~ of future.* 九岁的小孩子当然不会考虑到将来的事. **-ly** *ad.* **-ness** *n.*

thou·sand [ˈθauzənd] *a.* ①千,千个的. ②无数的,很多的. *a ~ times* 几千次;好多次,屡次. *a ~ times easier* 容易得多(一千倍). *A ~ thanks [pardons, apologies].* 万分感谢[对不起]. ***(a) ~ and one*** 无数的,很多很多的. ***different in a ~ and one ways*** 千差万别. ***for the ~ and first time*** 无数次,三番五次. ***in the upper ten ~***〔古、口〕属于上层贵族阶级. — *n., num.* ①千,一千个[人,东西];千的记号. ②〔*pl.*〕无数,许多. *a ~ = one ~* 一千. *three ~* 三千. *a hundred ~* 十万. *~s of people* 数千人. ***a ~ to one*** =〔口语〕***a ~ nuts to an orange pip*** 千对一,几乎绝对的. ***by the ~*** 论千,按千(出售等). ***by ~s*** 好几千. ***one in a ~*** 千里挑一的人物,罕有[杰出]人物;例外. ***tens of ~s of men*** 几万人. ***~s and tens of ~s*** 千千万万.

thou·sand·fold [ˈθauzəndfould] *a.* 千倍的. — *ad.* 成千倍.

thou·sandth [ˈθauzənθ] *n. (pl. ~s), a.* 第一千(的);千分之一(的);微小的.

THQ = Theatre Headquarters 战区司令部.

thr = through.

Thra·cian [ˈθreiʃən] *a.* 色雷斯〔巴尔干半岛东半部〕的,色雷斯人的. — *n.* ①色雷斯人. ②色雷斯语〔现已灭绝,属印欧语系〕.

thral(l)·dom [ˈθrɔːldəm] *n.* 奴隶的身分[地位,状态];奴役;束缚.

thrall [θrɔːl] *n.* 奴隶 *(of; to)*;奴役;奴隶状态[地位];束缚,被束缚的身体. — *a.*〔古〕被奴役的,被束缚的;拘泥于…的;变成奴隶的 *(to)*. ***in ~*** 受奴役. ***in ~ to*** 被…束缚着;拘泥于…. *We wouldn't allow you to make yourself a ~ to such an evil person as James.* 我们不会听任你给象詹姆士那样的坏人当奴隶的. *At the concert, I was held in ~ by the music.* 在音乐会上,我让音乐给迷住了. — *vt.* 使成奴隶;迷惑住,使神魂颠倒 *(to)*. **-dom** *n.* = thral(l)dom.

thrash [θræʃ] *vt.* ①打(谷),使脱粒. ②(用棍、鞭等)痛打;猛烈摆动. ③〔美口,运〕击败,胜过. ④反复进行;千锤百炼;仔细研讨,搞清楚*(out)*. ⑤【海】使(船)逆风破浪前进. *Let's ~ the matter over before putting it on the agenda.* 这件事我们要反复研究之后再把它列入议事日程. *It's time to ~ out all the problems.* 是把所有的问题都搞得一清二楚的时候了. — *vi.* ①打谷,打禾,脱粒;打,击. ②翻来复去;东撞西碰;(腿脚)乱跌;(手臂)乱挥. ③逆风前进. *The patient ~ed about with pain.*

病人痛得直翻腾．— *n.* 打击；击败；【泳】(自由式用脚、手)打水．

thrash·er [ˈθræʃə] *n.* ①打谷者；打谷机，脱粒机．②【鱼】长尾鲨鱼．③〔美〕美洲一种鸫属鸣禽．*brown* ~ 【动】褐噪鸫．

thrash·ing [ˈθræʃiŋ] *n.* 脱粒，打谷；鞭打，笞打．~ **floor** 打谷场．~ **machine** 打谷机．

thra·son·i·cal [θrəˈsɔnikəl] *a.* 自负的，夸口的．

thrawn [θrɔːn] *a.* 〔Scot.〕①弯曲的，扭弯的．②倔强的，邪恶的，不法的，不正当的，违反常情的，任性的．

thread [θred] *n.* ①线；细丝；〔英〕麻纱，〔美〕棉纱；纤维．②细线，细流，细矿脉．③(议论等的)思路，条理，线索，情节．④螺齿，螺丝．⑤〔*pl.*〕〔美〕衣服．*a piece of* ~ 一根线．*a* ~ *of light* 细细的一线亮光．*the* ~ *of one's argument* 争辩的头绪．***be worn to a*** ~ (衣服由于长久地穿着)磨得快要破烂．***cut one's mortal*** ~ 割断命脉，自杀．***gather up the*** ~***s*** 综合(分别处理的问题、部分等)．***hang by [(up)on] a*** ~ 朝不保夕；千钧一发．***have not a dry*** ~ ***on one*** 浑身湿透．***resume [pick up, take up] the*** ~ ***of a story*** (回到正题)言归正传．~ ***and thrum*** (好好歹歹)扫数，尽都，全都．~ ***of life*** 生命线，命脉，生命．— *vt.* ①穿线(入针眼等)；拿线穿(珠粒等)．②为照相机装胶片．③穿过，挤过．④车螺纹．~ *a camera* 为照相机装胶片．~ *a needle* 穿针．~ *one's way through the crowd* 穿过人丛．*a* ~*ed mandrel* 【机】螺纹心轴．— *vi.* ①通过，穿透过．②(糖浆等)滴下成丝状．*They* ~*ed carefully along the narrow pass.* 他们沿着狭窄的小路小心翼翼地鱼贯而行．~ **bare** *a.* (衣服由于长久穿着而)露出底子的织线的；破旧的；陈腐的，陈旧的(议论等)．~ **fin**【动】马鲅科的鱼．~ **lace** 织线花边．~**like** 细长的．~ **mark** (纸币纸上的)彩色丝纹．~**-needle** 穿线游戏〔大家拉手排成一行，由一头的人挨次穿过另一头的两人间〕．~ **paper** ①裹线束的纸条．②瘦子，细长的人．~**worm**【动】蛲虫 (= pinworm)．

thread·y [ˈθredi] *a.* ①线(做)的，纤维(或丝状物)构成的．②线状的，丝状的．③纤细的；微弱的(脉搏)．④能形成一丝一丝的．**-i·ness** *n.*

threap [θriːp] *vt.* ①责骂，吵架．②顽固地坚持，执拗．

threat [θret] *n.* ①恐吓，威吓，威胁．②凶兆，(…的)样子，(…的)危险．*There is a* ~ *of rain.* 象要下雨．*The* ~ *of flood has been relieved.* 洪水的威胁解除了．*I won't be intimidated by a* ~ *against my life.* 对生命的威胁是吓不倒我的．— *vt., vi.* 〔古、方〕= threaten.

threat·en [ˈθretn] *vt.* ①恐吓，恫吓，威胁．②预示凶兆，有…的危险．— *vi.* 象要发生；快要来临．*It will greatly* ~ *the security of this country.* 它将会极大地威胁本国的安全．~ *him with death* 用死威胁他．*The company is* ~*ed with bankruptcy.* 这家公司有破产的危险．*Do you mean to* ~? 你是想恫吓吗？*It* ~*s to rain.* 好象就要下雨了．★ 用于"威胁某人"的含义，threaten 主要意在通过威胁达到威胁者的目的；menace 除有书面语的意味外，侧重威胁者是怀有敌意的．**-er** *n.*

threat·en·ing [ˈθretəniŋ] *a.* 恐吓的，威胁的；危险的，险恶的．**-ly** *ad.*

three [θriː] *num.* (基数)三，三个；第三(章、页等)．~ *days of grace*【法】三天内付款的宽限期．~ *foot three* 三英尺三英寸．*the* ~ *C's*〔美〕三大产物〔Copper, Corn 及 Cotton〕．*the* ~ *K's*〔英〕国王、宪法、教会．*the* ~ *L's*【海】了望、测铅、纬度 (= Look-out, Lead and Latitude)．*a* ~ *Op. packet*【海】有三名无线电通讯员的客船．~ *parts* 四分之三；大部分；八九成，几乎．~ *quarters* 四分之三；九个月〔一年的四分之三〕．~ *services* 三军〔海陆空军〕．*give sb.* ~ *cheers [~ times ~]* 对某人欢呼三次〔九次〕．— *n.* ①三个人〔东西〕．②三岁，三时．③【板球】3 字型．~ *and six*〔英〕三先令六辨士〔3s. 6d.〕．~ *ten*〔英〕三镑十先令〔£ 3 10s.〕．***a child of*** ~ 三岁的孩子．*the One in T-* = *the T- in One*【宗】(上帝的)三位一体．***by [in]*** ~***s*** = ~ ***by*** ~ 每三个(人)；三个三个地．~**-bagger**〔棒球俚〕三垒打〔= three-base hit〕．~**-bottle** *a.* 能一次喝三瓶葡萄酒的，酒量大的．~**-colo(u)r** *a.* 三色的 (~*-colour process* 三(原)色版印刷〔照相〕术．~*-colour printing* 三色版)．~**-corner** *a.* 三棱的．~**cornered** *a.* 三角的；由三个竞争者形成的 (~*-corner relation* 三角关系)．~**-D** (= ~ dimensions) *n., a.* 三维(的)，三度空间(的)；【影】立体的．~**-decker** (从前的)三层甲板都装有炮的军舰；三层楼房；三卷本小说(或书)，三层夹心面包．~**fold** ①*a.* 三倍的，三重的．②*ad.* 成三倍，成三重．~**halfpence**，~**-ha'pence** 一辨士半[$1^1/_2$ d.]．~**-handed** *a.* 三只手的；(游戏)三人玩的．~ **handkerchief**〔美俚〕(引人落泪不止的)伤感剧．~ **in-one** ①三结合．②【宗】(上帝的)三位一体．~**-legged** *a.* 三脚的 (~*-legged race* 二人三脚竞走)．~**-master** 三桅船；〔特指〕三桅纵帆船．~**-mile limit**【法】(沿岸三海里内的)领海．~**-monthly** *a., n.* 三个月出版一次的；季刊．~**-pair**〔英〕四层楼上的房间；住在四楼的人．~**pence** [ˈθrepəns, ˈθrip-] 三辨士硬币；三辨士(金额)．~**penny** [ˈθrepəni, ˈθrip-] *a.* 三辨士的；不足道的，廉价的 (*a* ~*-penny bit [piece]* 三辨士硬币)．~**-percents** ①*a.* 百分之三的；利息三厘的．②*n.* 〔*pl.*〕〔英〕三厘公债．~**-phase** *a.* 【电】三相的．~**-piece** *a.* 三件一套的(西服)．~**-pile** *a., n.* 有三层绒毛的(毛毡)，特级毛毡．~**-ply** ①*a.* 三重的，三股头的(线等)．②*n.* 三夹板，三合板．~**-pointer**〔军俚〕①= ~-point landing．②绝对正确的事物．~**-point landing**【空】主轮尾轮三轮同时着陆法．~**-quarter**，~**-quarters** ①*a.* 四分之三的；【摄】大半身的；脸的四分之三的〔正面与侧面之间〕．②*n.* 四分之三；【橄榄球】(half-back 和 full-back 之间的) 中后卫〔threequarter back 之略〕．~**-ring circus** 三个场地可同时表演的大马戏场；热闹的场面〔演出〕(*Their family reunions are always* ~*-ring circuses.* 他们全家团聚的场面，热闹非凡)．~ **R's** ①读，写，算．②基本功，基础知识；要害．~**score** *n., a.* 六十(的)，六十岁(的)．~**-seater** 三人座(的飞机、汽车等)．~**some**【高尔夫球】三人比赛；〔美俚〕三个一组，三个一队．~**-square** *a.* 截面成等边三角形的．~**-star** *a.* (美军将官)三星级的 (a ~ star general 中将)．~**-thirty**〔美军俚〕限制活动三个月并罚款三十元的惩罚．~**-two**〔美俚〕啤酒．~**-way** *a.* 三向的；三路的．~**-wheeler** 三轮汽车〔摩托车〕．

threm·ma·tol·o·gy [ˌθreməˈtɔlədʒi] *n.* 动植物养育学，饲育学．*plant* ~ 育种学．

thre·net·ic, -i·cal [θriˈnetik, -ikəl] *a.* 悲哀的，哀悼的，哀歌的．

thre·no·de, thre·no·dy [ˈθriːnəud, -nədi] *n.* ①悲歌，哀歌；挽歌．②悲哀，哀悼．**-nod·ic, -i·cal** *a.* **-ist** *n.*

thre·o·nine [ˈθriːəni(ː)n] *n.*【生化】苏〔羟丁〕氨酸．

threp·sol·o·gy [θrepˈsɔlədʒi] *n.* 营养学．

thresh [θreʃ] *vt., vi.* = thrash. — *n.* 脱粒．~***ing floor*** 打谷场，脱粒场．~***ing machine*** 打谷机，脱粒机．**-er** *n.* ①打谷机，脱粒机，打谷者．②【动】长尾鲨．

thresh·old [ˈθreʃ*h*əuld] *n.* ①门槛；入口，门口．②【心】阈限．③界限，限度．④【物】临界值，阈．⑤入门，开始，开端．*Seniors of the* ~ *of the diplomatic career are expected to take this course.* 希望即将从事外交工作的四年级生选修本课程．***at the*** ~ ***of*** 在…的开始，就要开始的时候．***cross sb.'s*** ~ 走进某人家里．***cross the*** ~ 跨进门内．***on the*** ~ 在门口．***on the*** ~ ***of*** 在…的开头，就要…．~ **of consciousness**【心】识阈．

threw [θruː] throw 的过去式．

thrice [θrais] *ad.* ①三次，三度；三倍．②屡次，再三；十分，非常．~ *blessed [happy, -favo(u)red]* 极幸福的．

thrid [θrid] *vt.* 〔古、方〕= thread；〔特指〕穿过．

thrift [θrift] *n.* ①俭约,节俭. ②兴旺,繁荣;健壮. ③〔Scot.〕繁荣的手段,工作,劳动,(植物的)繁茂,有利可图的职业. ④【植】海石竹. *To practice ~ is a virtue.* 节俭是美德. ~ **shop** 节俭商店〔出售人们丢弃的旧衣著什物,尤指将出售所得用于慈善目的的〕.

thrift·less [ˈθriftlis] *a.* ①不节俭的,浪费的. ②不兴旺的. ③不健壮的,不繁茂的. ④无价值的. **-ly** *ad.* **-ness** *n.*

thrift·y [ˈθrifti] *a.* *(-i·er; -i·est)* ①节约的,俭省的. ②兴旺的,繁茂的,健壮的,繁荣的. *We will bring in a measure to be ~ with raw materials.* 我们要提出一项节约原材料的措施. **-i·ly** *ad.* **-i·ness** *n.*

thrill [θril] *n.* ①一阵毛骨悚然的感觉,一阵激动的感觉;(由于恐怖或快感的)紧张感. ②战慄,发抖,震颤,颤动. ③心跳,脉搏;【医】(心脏的)震颤(音). ④(电影,电视剧,小说的)刺激性,紧张感. ⑤惊险小说 (= thriller). *We got (felt, experienced) a ~ of surprised pleasure out of the mountain-climbing.* 在那次爬山中我们感觉到一种意想不到的快乐. *The news sent a ~ of joy to my heart.* 这消息使我心中感到一阵激动的欢乐. — *vt.* ①使毛骨悚然,使紧张,使激动,使心里怦怦地跳;使热血沸腾. ②使颤动,使发抖,使震颤. —*vi.* ①受激动,心里怦怦地跳. ②颤动,发抖 (*with*). ③(感情等)闪过 *(along; through; over) Little Tom was so ~ed at going to the movie.* 小汤姆去看电影是那么地激动. *His voice ~s with terror.* 他恐怖得声音发抖. *Fear ~ed through my veins.* 我毛骨悚然地感到一阵害怕.

thrill·er [ˈθrilə] *n.* 〔口〕使人激动的东西〔人物〕;使毛骨悚然〔战慄〕的东西;〔特指〕惊险小说〔电影,戏剧〕.

thrill·ing [ˈθriliŋ] *a.* ①毛骨悚然的;惊心动魄的,动人的,使人激动的. ②颤动的,抖动的. ③刺骨的. *"How ~!", he cried.* 他大声说道,"多么令人激动啊!" *Put on your overcoat. The wind's ~.* 穿上你的大衣,寒风刺骨. **-ly** *ad.*

thrips [θrips] *n.* 【虫】蓟马〔谷类害虫〕.

thrive [θraiv] *vi.* *(throve* [θrəuv],〔罕〕*thrived* [θrivd]; *thriven* [ˈθrivən] 〔罕〕*thrived)* ①兴旺,繁荣;成功;致富. ②茁壮成长,(动物)上膘,发胖,(植物)繁茂,蔓延. *Seeing that the domestic markets are ~ing, the bankers here know that their capital can be safely invested.* 看到国内市场繁荣,这里的银行家们晓得他们的资本可以稳妥地投资. *Tropical plants ~ in a green house.* 热带植物在温室里茁壮生长.

thriv·en [ˈθrivən] thrive 的过去分词.

thro', thro [θruː] *prep., ad., a.* 〔美〕= through.

throat [θrəut] *n.* ①【解】咽喉,喉咙;喉头;颈前. ②嗓子,嗓音. ③(器物的)咽喉状部分;窄路,出入口. ④【火箭】(喷管的)临界截面. ~ *latch* 〔美俚〕喉(头);会厌. (马笼头上的)喉勒. *a sore ~* 咽喉炎〔痛〕. *a clergyman's sore ~* 慢性喉炎. *a ~ of brass* 尖锐的嗓音. ***at the top of one's ~*** 尽量放大嗓子. ***clear one's ~*** (说话前) 清嗓子. ***cut one another's ~s*** 采取两败俱伤的政策,相互残杀. ***cut one's (own) ~*** 抹脖子,自刎;自招灭亡. ***cut the ~ of*** 杀死;使灭亡. ***fly at sb.'s ~*** ①(狗等)扑向某人. ②攻击,袭击. ***full (up) to the ~*** 吃得很饱. ***give sb. the lie in his ~*** 面责某人说谎,揭破谎话. ***have a bone in one's ~*** 难于启齿. ***jump down sb.'s ~*** 〔美俚〕突然反唇回击,打断某人讲话,使某人无话可说,突然猛烈攻击〔批评〕. ***lie in one's ~*** 扯大谎. ***pour [send] down the ~*** 把(金钱等)花在饮食上;喝酒. ***stick in one's ~*** 骨梗在喉;(话)要说说不出. ***take [catch, have, hold, seize] by the ~*** 扼住喉咙. ***thrust [cram, force, push, ram] sth. down sb.'s ~*** 逼人接受〔向人强行灌输〕(意见等). — *vt.* ①用喉音说唱,沙哑地说唱. ②掘(沟);开槽.

throat·y [ˈθrəuti] *a.* *(-i·er; -i·est)* ①(声音)喉部发出的. ②喉音的,嗄声的,沙哑的. **-i·ly** *ad.* **-i·ness** *n.* 嗓音沙哑;粗声粗气.

throb [θrɔb] *n.* ①(心等的)跳动,悸动;搏动. ②(有规律的)颤动. — *vi.* ***(throbbed; throb·bing)*** (心脏,脉搏等的)跳动,悸动,抽动,(有规律地)颤动;激动;(轮船)噗噗地颤动. *My heart is ~bing violently.* 我的心在剧烈地跳动着. *A rural district 15 years ago, the city is now ~bing with the pulse of modern industry.* 这个城十五年前还是个农业地区,现在有了现代工业顺利地活跃着. **~bing** *a.* 跳动的;抽动的;震动的. **~bing·ly** *ad.*

throe [θrəu] *n.* ①〔常 *pl.*〕剧痛,痛苦,苦闷;死亡前的挣扎. ②〔*pl.*〕(分娩时的)产痛,阵痛;(新事物等)产生前的斗争〔困难〕. *the ~ of composition* 创作的阵痛〔构思的艰苦〕. ***in the ~s of ...*** 在产生…之前的斗争中. —*vi.* 非常受痛苦,苦闷.

Throg·mor·ton Street [θrɔgˈmɔːtən-] *n.* 盔街〔伦敦商业中心〕;伦敦股票交易所;〔集合词〕伦敦股票交易(经纪人);股票市场.

throm·bin [ˈθrɔmbin] *n.* 【生化】凝血酶.

throm·bo·cyte [ˈθrɔmbəˌsait] *n.* 【医】血小板,凝血细胞 (= plateler). **-cyt·ic** [-ˈsitik] *a.*

throm·bo·em·bo·lism [ˌθrɔmbəuˈembəlizm] *n.* 【医】血栓栓塞.

throm·bo·gen [ˈθrɔmbədʒən, -ˌdʒen] *n.* 【医】凝血酶原 (= prothrombin).

throm·bo·ki·nase [ˌθrɔmbəuˈkaineis, -ˈkineis] *n.* 【医】凝血(酶)致活酶 (= thromboplastin).

throm·bo·pe·ni·a [ˌθrɔmbəuˈpiːniə] *n.* 【医】凝血酶减少症.

throm·bo·phle·bi·tis [ˌθrɔmbəufliˈbaitis] *n.* 【医】血栓(性)静脉炎.

throm·bo·plastic [ˌθrɔmbəuˈplæstik] *a.* ①血栓形成的. ②凝血的. **-cal·ly** *ad.*

throm·bo·plas·tin [ˌθrɔmbəuˈplæstin] *n.* 凝血激酶;【药】(止血的)凝血质.

throm·bo·sis [ˌθrɔmˈbəusis] *n.* 【医】血栓形成.

throm·bot·ic [θrɔmˈbɔtik] *a.* 血栓形成的.

thrombus [ˈθrɔmbʌs] *n.* 【医】血栓.

throne [θrəun] *n.* ①(帝王的)宝座;王〔帝〕位;王权. ②国王,皇帝. ③教皇座,主教座;教皇〔主教〕的地位. ④【宗】〔T-〕〔*pl.*〕九级天使中的第三级. ***come to [mount] the ~*** 即位. — *vt.* 〔诗〕使即王位,使登极. ~ **room** (设有宝座的)正式觐见室;权势的所在地方〔中枢〕.

throng [θrɔŋ] *n.* ①大群;人群,一大群人. ②事务纷集〔紧迫〕. ③众多,大量. *a ~ of people* 一大群人. *He was ~ed by the multitude.* 他被一大群人所包围. *On the square there was a wildly cheering ~.* 广场上有一大群欢呼雷动的人群. — *vi., vt.* 群集,拥塞,挤满 *(about; round)*;蜂拥而到. *These thoughts ~ed on my mind.* 这些想法纷然地杂集在我的心头之上;(我)浮想联翩.

thros·tle [ˈθrɔsl] *n.* ①【鸟】画眉= song thrush. ②【纺】翼锭精纺机〔又叫 ~-frame〕.

throt·tle [ˈθrɔtl] *n.* ①〔方〕喉咙,气管. ②【机】风门,节气阀,节流阀〔又叫 ~ valve〕;风门杆,节流杆〔又叫 ~ lever〕. ③【无】扼流圈. ***at full ~ = with the ~ against the stop*** 全速地,开足马力. — *vt.* ①掐喉咙,扼杀,缢死,使窒息. ②压制,抑压,抑制(讨论、贸易等). ③【机】(用节汽阀等)调节;使节流;使减速. — *vi.* ①窒息. ②【机】节流,减速. *High tariffs ~ trade between nations.* 高的关税抑制着国与国之间的贸易. ~ **hold** 扼杀;压制,抑制.

through [θruː] *prep.* ①通过,穿过,贯穿. ②从(洞孔等)中间,透过. ③〔时间〕从…的开始到末了,从头到尾;〔场所〕到处,全面. ④〔指方法、手段等〕经由,通过,以…. ⑤〔指原因、理由〕由于,因为;多亏. ⑥做完,用尽. *The river flows ~ the city.* 这条河贯穿这个城. *May I ~ you ask the delegate of ... to ...* 可否通过你代为请求某代表…. *The sun breaks ~ the clouds.* 日光从云缝中穿漏出

来. ~ *the winter* 整个冬天,一冬. ~ *life* 一生中,毕生. ~ *long years* 长年间. *be famous* ~ *the world* 闻名全世界. *go* ~ *an operation* 做完手术. *go* ~ *college* 修完大学课程. *pass* ~ *crisis [tribulation]* 度过危机[历尽千辛万苦]. ~ *carelessness* 由于疏忽. *to fulfil the task* ~ *your help* 完成任务多亏你帮忙. *build up the production team* ~ *diligence and thrift* 勤俭建队. ***be on display* ~ *April 30*** 展览至四月三十日截止. ***be* ~ *one's task*** 做完工作[课题]. ***see* ~ *a brick wall [a millstone]*** 能透过一道砖墙看见;[转义]眼光敏锐 (*One can't see* ~ *a brick wall.* 不可能的事情就是不可能). ~ ***all ages*** 永远. ~ ***the cabin window*** (海军军官)靠人情升官. ~ ***the hawse-pipe*** 水兵升成军官. ~ ***thick and thin*** 遍历艰苦. ***unity* ~ *struggle*** 以斗争求团结. — *ad.* 穿过,通过,经历;从头到尾,完全,全部;到最后,到底,彻底;透;完毕. ④出来. *pierce a thing* ~ 刺穿一件东西. *come* ~ 〔美俚〕取得成功;取胜. *all the night* ~ 通宵,彻夜. *read the book* ~ 将书看完. *This train goes* ~ *to Beijing.* 这一列车直达北京. *Is he* ~? 〔口〕他(考试)及格了吗? *I am* ~ *now.* 〔口〕我已经做好了. *The enemy is trying to break* ~. 敌人企图突围. ***all* ~** 一直,从来就. ***be* ~ *with*** 〔口〕做好(工作等);和…绝交;和…分手 (*I am* ~ *with that fellow.* 我和那个家伙断绝关系了.) ~ ***and*** ~ 完完全全;彻头彻尾 (*wet* ~ *and* ~ 浑身湿透). — *a.* ①直通的,直达的. ②(道路)可以通行的. ③穿过的,有洞的. ④〔英〕(电话)接通;〔美〕通话完毕. *a* ~ *street* 直通街道,干道. ~ *transport by land and water* 水陆联运. *a* ~ *ticket* 联运票,全程票. *a* ~ *train* 直达车. *Jack's trousers are* ~ *at the knees.* 贾克的裤子膝盖处破了洞了. *You are* ~. 你要的电话接通了. *He is almost* ~. 他的电话快打完了. ~ **bolt** 【机】贯穿螺栓. ~ **cock** 【机】直旋塞. ~**-put** 生产量[能力],生产率;通过量;容许能力. ~**-station** 中间站. ~ **stone** 【建】系石. ~**way** 〔美〕(= expressway) ①高速公路. ②直通街道.

through·ly [ˈθruːli] *ad.* 〔古、圣〕= thoroughly.

through·out [θru(ː)ˈaut] *prep.* 从一头贯通到另一头;从头贯穿到底;完完全全;从头到尾;自始至终;到处,全面,彻头彻尾. ~ *the day* 终日,整天. ~ *one's life* 毕生,整个一生中. ~ *the country* 全国. — *ad.* 任何部分,任何地方,到处;全部;彻头彻尾;自始至终. *The house is well built* ~. 这房子整个儿都造得好. *be of one piece* ~ 完全一样.

throve [θrəuv] thrive 的过去式.

throw [θrəu] *vt.* (***threw*** [θruːn]; ***thrown*** [θrəun]) ①扔,抛,投,摔,掷,丢. ②摔倒,使翻倒;(将船等)冲上(暗礁等);(马)把…摔下来. ③匆匆穿上或披上(大衣等) (*on; over*);匆匆脱掉(*off*);(蛇)蜕(皮). ④伸(四肢),挺(胸)仰(首),挥(拳). ⑤使挨(骂等). ⑥丢弃,放弃;摆脱;发出,射出(光线等);发射(炮弹等). ⑦出(纸牌),掷(骰子). ⑧(家畜)产仔. ⑨捻(生丝);【窯】旋制陶坯. ⑩突然变动(身体的一部分姿势);转动,推动,打开,关闭(离合器等机件). ⑪推(入某状态),使陷于,使…化. ⑫〔美〕故意输掉(比赛等). ⑬〔俚〕开办,举行(舞会等). —*vi.* 扔,摔,投,掷 (*at*);投球,扔球;掷骰子. *Who threw a stone over the fence?* 是谁把块石头扔过篱笆的? *At last I threw Tony to the ground.* 我终于把汤尼摔倒在地上. *Knowing it was late, he threw on his overcoat and went to school.* 他晓得晚了,匆忙地穿上大衣上学去了. *Take care! Fish is able to* ~ *the hook.* 当心! 鱼儿是能挣脱鱼钩的. *The engineer's advice threw light on the scheme.* 工程师的意见有助于我们对计划的理解. *You'll have to* ~ *your chests out when marching in parade.* 在游行时要挺起胸来. *The door was thrown open.* 门突然大开. *The country has been thrown into an upheaval.* 这个国家已经陷入动乱之中. *don't* ~ *off your own responsibility* 不要把你的职责摔掉了. *This kind of watch has been thrown out of the market.* 这路表已被排挤出市场上了. *The ship was thrown on the coast.* 那只船被(浪)打到岸上去了. ***be thrown into confusion*** 陷入混乱. ~ ***a fit*** 〔美〕狂怒. ~ ***a monkey wrench into the transmission*** 〔美俚〕妨碍;干涉;破坏. ~ ***a party*** 〔美口〕举行舞会. ~ ***sb. into the shade*** 使相形见绌. ~ ***a scare into*** 〔美〕威胁;吓坏. ~ ***a veil over*** 掩蔽,遮蔽,隐藏. ~ ***a vote*** 投票. ~ ***about*** 到处抛扔;挥舞(手臂);使…回转 (~ *money about* 挥金如土. ~ *one's arms about* 挥舞手臂). ~ ***away*** 抛弃;白费,浪费 (*upon*);拒绝(劝告);失去(机会) (*Kindness is thrown away upon him.* 对他好是白费). ~ ***back*** ①使后退,拒绝. ②反射. ③拉回,阻止. ④【遗传】呈返祖现象. ~ ***by*** 废弃,抛弃. ~ ***cold water on*** 拨冷水,打击别人的热情. ~ ***down*** ①摔倒,打倒,推翻,拆毁. ②扔下,贬;使沉淀;〔俚〕拒绝 (~ *down one's arms* 放下武器,投降,屈服. ~ *down one's brief* (律师)拒绝接受案件. ~ *down one's tools* 丢下工具罢工). ~ ***for large stakes*** 下大注. ~ ***good money after bad*** 想捞回损失而损失更大. ~ ***in*** ①投入,扔进. ②发边界球. ③注入;插入;使(齿轮等)咬合,接合;【电】接通;添加 (~ *in a word* 插嘴). ~ ***in one's hand*** 丢弃(不要的牌);(从争执中)抽身. ~ ***into*** 使热烈从事,使投身于,使专门从事. ~ ***into shape*** 使具雏形;整理. ~ ***into the bargain*** 添加,再加. ~ ***it with*** 〔美〕和某人合伙干. ~ ***light on*** (*a matter*) 说明,弄明白. ~ ***off*** ①抛弃,丢弃. ②脱掉(衣服). ③摆脱(习惯、拘束等). ④切断(电路等). ⑤推翻. ⑥一气写成,即席作成(诗等). ⑦甩掉,脱离(追踪者等). ⑧开始,(猎狗)开始出猎,跳出,咬起来. ~ ***sb. off his guard*** 使(某人)不留心. ~ ***oneself at the head of*** 公然表示亲热〔指女性对男性〕;(不得体地)竭力讨好. ~ ***oneself down*** 躺下. ~ ***oneself into*** 开始热心做(某事),起劲地投身于某事(*You must* ~ *yourself eagerly into the work.* 你必须热诚地、竭力地投入工作). ~ ***oneself into the arms of*** 投入…怀抱;成为…的妻子. ~ ***oneself (up)on*** 依靠;求助于;完全依赖于;猛扑,突袭. ~ ***one's hat into the ring*** 〔美俚〕加入比赛,参加竞争. ~ ***open*** 推开;猛然打开;开放 (*to*) (~ *open the door to* 使…成为可能,打开…的门路). ~ ***out*** ①投出,扔出. ②派出. ③突出. ④增建(侧房). ⑤发出(热、光等). ⑥萌(芽等). ⑦逐出,撵出. ⑧显示. ⑨转弯抹角地说. ⑩拒绝;否决(议案). ⑪跑过(人). ⑫【棒球】使出局. ⑬使(离合器等)分离,脱开. ~ ***out of work*** 使失业. ~ ***over*** ①抛弃(难友等);放弃,毁弃(合同等). ②转换,变换. ~ ***together*** (*artificially*) (勉强)凑成,(勉强或偶然)凑集. ~ ***up*** ①抛上,举起,抬起,推上(窗). ②急造. ③丢弃,辞(职等). ④呕吐. ⑤使显眼. (~ *up one's arms* 举起双手;投降. ~ *one's eyes up* 抬起眼睛;因恐怖或惊呆睁大眼睛). ~ ***up one's toenails*** 〔美〕剧烈[大量]呕吐. —*n.* ①扔,丢,摔,投,掷,抛. ②投距,射程. ③(银幕,扩音器等的)距离. ④投球. ⑤(摔跤中)将对方摔倒(的方法). ⑥掷骰;掷出的点数. ⑦冒险. ⑧(女用)围巾. ⑨(沙发,卧床等的)罩单. ⑩(钓鱼)投钓丝. ⑪【机】冲程;行程;摆度. ⑫(陶工的)车床,镟床. ⑬【地】断层垂直位移,落差. ⑭【测】冲掷(幅). *a good* ~ 好球. ***at a stone's* ~** 在一投石之遥,在近处. ~ ***of money*** 资产;很多钱. ~**away** ① *n.* 〔俚〕广告传单. ②*a.* 可扔掉的. ~**back** 后退;阻止;返祖遗传(现象). ~**off** (打猎、赛跑的)起步,出发,机会 (*at the first* ~*off* 在刚开始时; *one's last* ~*off* 最后的机会). ~**out** 被抛弃的人[东西];废品,次货. ~ **rug** 小块地毯 (= scatter rug). ~ **weight** (导弹的)有效载荷. **-er** *n.* 喷射器.

thrown [θrəun] throw 的过去分词. — *a.* 捻了的. ~ *silk* 捻丝.

throw·ster [ˈθrəustə] *n.* ①掷骰子的人. ②捻丝人,捻丝工.

thru [θru:]〔美〕= through. ~**way** *n.*〔美〕高速公路.

thrum[1] [θrʌm] *n.* ①【纺】织边,绒边;机头. ②〔*pl.,sing.*〕粗乱纱头,线头;乱丝头,接头纱. ③碎屑;【海】〔*pl.*〕绳屑. ④缨子,缌子. ⑤【植】雄蕊;花丝,花药. ***not to care a*** ~一点也不介意. ***thread and*** ~ 好好歹歹.

thrum[2] [θrʌm] *vi.,vt.* ①单调地[拙劣地]弹拨,随便地弹拨(弦乐器). ②用指头敲(桌子等). ③单调乏味地讲述. ~ *a guitar out of tune* 弹吉他弹得不搭调. — *n.* 弹拨(声);得得声,轧轧声.

thru·out [θru:ˈaut] *ad., prep.*〔美〕= throughout.

thrush[1] [θrʌʃ] *n.*【鸟】鸫属的鸟;画眉. *the song* ~ (欧洲)画眉鸟.

thrush[2] [θrʌʃ] *n.*【医】鹅口疮;真菌性口炎;【兽医】蹄叉腐疽.

thrust [θrʌst] *vt.* ***(thrust)*** ①猛推,冲;猛掷,冲入,插入,推入(出),突出,伸出,塞,刺,戳,戳穿. ②逼迫,把[将]…强加于…*(into)*. ③突然提出,不恰当地插进(插嘴等). — *vi.* ①推,冲;强行推入,冲入;强行推进,突进;冲过去. ②挺伸,延伸. ~ *one's hand into one's pocket* 将手插进口袋里. ~ *one's way through a crowd* 冲过人群. *It's not time for you to* ~ *in a question now.* 现在轮不到你插嘴提问题. *It was John who* ~ *a person aside.* 是约翰把一个人猛推在一旁的. *Unexpected events* ~ *themselves continually athwart our path.* 在我们工作的进程中,出乎意料的事层出不穷. *When he invented the new drilling machine, honours were* ~ *upon him.* 他发明了新的钻机之后,许多荣耀都加在他的身上了. *He showed great reluctance to accept the responsibility* ~ *upon him.* 是否接受强加给他的责任他显得十分迟疑. ~ *at sb. with a dagger* 以匕首戳人. ~ *on one's gloves* 急忙带上手套. ~ *through* 挤过. ***be*** ~ ***into fame*** 突然出名. ~ ***a hand in*** 插手,干与. ~ ***aside*** 推开. ~ ***home*** 把(短刀等)深深刺入. ~ ***(sth.) (up)on (sb.)*** (将东西)推给(某人);强卖给(某人). ~ ***oneself forward*** = ~ ***oneself in*** = ~ ***one's nose in*** 探听;插嘴;出头,干涉. ~ ***one's way*** 向前推进,勉强挤过. ~ ***out*** 推出;逐出,赶出;挤出,排出;发射. ~ **hoe** 推锄. ~ **point**【军】推力点;突破战术. ~ **stage** ①三面对着观众的舞台. ②戏场内向前伸出很远的舞台前台. — *n.* ①推,冲;刺. ②攻击;苛评,讥刺. ③【军】突入,突击,冲锋;【机】推力,侧向压力;【地】冲断层;逆断层;【矿】煤柱压裂. *a reactive* ~ 反冲力. *make a* ~ *with a dagger* 用匕首冲刺. *the* ~ *and parry of A and B* 甲乙两人间唇枪舌剑的激烈辩论[攻击].

thruster [ˈθrʌstə] *n.* ①冲的人;戳的人. ②向上钻营者. ③〔口语〕插嘴的人. ④推冲器,起飞加速器.

thrust·ing [ˈθrʌstiŋ] *a.* 自作主张的,盛气凌人的,无情的. **-ly** *ad.*

thruway [ˈθru:wei] *n.*〔美〕= throughway.

thud [θʌd] *n.* ①砰的一声,啪嚓一声[重物坠落,重声等声音]. ②砰然一击. *The tree fell to the ground with a* ~. 树轰隆一声倒在地上. — *vt., vi.* 砰的一声重击;砰的一声落下(倒下);发出轰的一声. *a thudding fist* 强有力的拳头.

thug [θʌg] *n.* ①〔常 T-〕谋杀教团团员[印度旧时,因崇拜破坏女神,以杀人抢劫为业的宗教组织成员]. ②凶手,暴徒.

thug·gee [ˈθʌgi:], **thug·ger·y** [ˈθʌgəri], **thug·gism** [ˈθʌgizm] *n.* 谋杀,谋财害命. **-gish** *a.*

thuja [ˈθju:dʒə]【植】侧柏,金钟柏(= arborvitae ①).

Thu·le [ˈθju:li(:)] *n.* ①(古代航海家所谓的)北极. ②神秘地区;世界尽头. ③〔t-〕遥远的目标. *the ultima* ~ 世界的尽头;天涯海角;最远点;绝顶,极点;最终目的.

thu·li·a [ˈθu:liə] *n.*【化】氧化铥.

thu·li·um [ˈθju:liəm] *n.*【化】铥 (Tm 或 Tu).

thumb [θʌm] *n.* ①拇指. ②【建】馒形饰. *Put your* ~*s up!*〔俚〕使劲! ~*s down!* 差劲儿! *Thumbs up!*〔俚〕好! 顶好! *a golden* ~ = *a* ~ *of gold* = *a miller's* ~ 摇钱树. *a* ~ *nail*〔美〕一块钱. *a* ~ *pusher*〔美〕在路上要求搭乘别人汽车的人. —*vt.* ①翻阅,用拇指翻脏[翻坏](书页等);反覆读. ②笨手笨脚地做;拙劣地弹(钢琴等). ③〔美口〕翘起拇指要求搭乘. *He* ~*ed his way to Boston.* 他搭乘别人顺路的车去波士顿. ***be all*** ~***s*** 手笨 (*His fingers are all* ~*s.* 他手笨脚笨). ***bite the*** ~***s at*** 蔑视. ***by rule of*** ~ 单凭不多的经验,根据粗浅的常识. ***count one's*** ~***s*** 消磨时间. ***turn up [down] the*** ~ 表示赞成[反对],表示称赞[贬低],表示满意[不满]. ***turn*** ~***s down to*** 反对 (*We turned* ~*s down to that suggestion.* 我们反对这个建议). ***turn*** ~***s up[on]***赞成. ***twiddle*** (或 ***twirl***) ***one's*** ~***s*** 抚弄大拇指,无聊. ***under sb.'s*** ~ 受人支配,仰人鼻息. ~***ed pic***〔美〕禁止上演的影片. ~ ***it*** (要求)搭乘顺路的车. ~ ***one's nose at***〔美〕嗤之以鼻. ~ ***the nose at***〔美运〕打败敌手. ~ ***through*** 翻查一过. ~**s-down** *n.* 责备,不赞成. ~ **index [notch]** (书边)指标索引. ~**mark** (尤指留在书页上的)拇指痕. ~**nail** ① *n.* 拇指甲;极小的东西,简短的文字,简明的提要[略图]. ② *a.* 极小的,微型的;简短的(论文等). ~ **nut** 蝶形螺母. ~ **pin**〔美〕图钉. ~**-print** 拇指印纹;〔美俚〕个人性格特征. ~**-screw**【机】指拧螺旋;蝶形螺钉;(古时的)拇指夹刑具. ~**stall** 拇指套. ~**tack**〔美〕= ~ pin.

thumb·er [ˈθʌmə] *n.* (要求)搭坐顺路汽车旅行的人.

thump [θʌmp] *n.* 砰,咚[用拳头、棍子等重击的声音]. ②重击. ③(电话中的)电报噪音. ④【无】键击[低音]噪音. *He threw the box on the table with a* ~. 他砰的一声把匣子扔在桌子上. — *vt.* (砰地)重击;(用拳头等)捶打. — *vi.* 重击,捶击 *(at, on)*, 咚咚地走,脚步沉重地走;(心脏等)卜卜地跳,悸动. *Getting very angry, the boss* ~*ed the desk with his fist.* 老板生气了,用拳头重捶桌子. *There is a man thumping at the door.* 有个人捶门哪. *On hearing the news, my heart* ~*ed with excitement.* 听到这消息,我兴奋得心砰砰地跳. ~ ***the [a] cushion*** (牧师讲道时)敲着讲坛垫子用力地讲.

thump·er [ˈθʌmpə] *n.* ①敲打的人[物]. ②〔口〕巨大的人[物]. ③极大的谎话.

thump·ing [ˈθʌmpiŋ] *a.* ①〔口〕非常的,巨大的;极好的;极大的(谎话等). ②尺码大的. ③极好的. *She gave birth to a* ~ *ten-catty baby last night.* 昨天夜里,她生了个好大的十斤重的小孩. — *ad.* 非常地.

thun·der [ˈθʌndə] *n.* ①雷,雷声. ②轰响. ③〔*pl.*〕怒喝,谴责,威吓,恐吓,弹劾. ④〔古〕霹雳. ⑤〔在惊恐、愤怒、强调时加强语气〕究竟,倒底. ~*s[a* ~*s] of applause* 雷鸣般的喝采声[掌声]. *the* ~ *of the People's Daily* 人民日报上的激烈抨击. *What in* ~ *[What the* ~*] is that?* 那究竟是怎么件事情? *Where in* ~ *did he lose the money?* 他的款倒底是在什么地方丢的? — *vi.* ①打雷. ②轰响. ③大声叫. ④怒喝,骂,谴责 *(against)*. — *vt.* ①象打雷一样地讲[谴责,恫吓,发射等]. ②大声说出,吼叫. *It* ~*s.* 打雷,雷鸣. ~ *at the door* 象打雷一样地敲门. *Guns* ~*ed a salute.* 轰地放了阵礼炮. ~ *into the stretch*〔美〕开始赛马. ***By*** ~***!*** 哎! 真的! 岂有此理! ***run away with sb.'s*** ~ = ***steel sb.'s*** ~ 先声夺人,抢先讲某人要讲的话;窃取某人的方案[发明等]抢先发表[利用]. ~**-and-lightning** ①*n.* 雷电,谴责,攻击. ②由截然相反的色彩配在一起,彩色夺目的. ~ **bird** (北美印第安人神话中)引起雷雨的巨鸟. ~**bolt** 雷电,霹雳,落雷;恐吓,怒喝;意外的事情,意外打击;闪电熔岩;【古生】箭石 (*This information was a* ~*bolt to her.* 这消息对她真是一个晴天霹雳. *with the power of a* ~*-bolt* 以雷霆万钧之势). ~**clap** *n.* 霹雳;晴天霹雳(似的消息[事件]). ~**cloud** 雷云. ~**gust** 伴有大风的暴雷雨. ~**head**【气】(雷雨前的)雷雨[雷暴]云砧. ~**peal** = ~clap. ~**shower** 雷阵雨. ~ **squll** 雷飑. ~**stone** (旧时以为是雷电发射下来的)飞来石

〔实际为化石，古代石器等〕. **~storm** *n.* 雷雨. **~strick·en, ~struck** *a.* 被雷霹的；吓坏了的，大吃一惊的.

thun·der·a·tion [ˈθʌndəˈreiʃən] *n.* 雷电；霹雳；意外的事件，晴天霹雳.

thun·der·er [ˈθʌndərə] *n.* 怒喝的人，咆哮如雷的人. *the T-* ①=【罗神】朱庇特 (Jupiter). ②〔英谑〕伦敦泰晤士报 *(The Times)* 的外号.

thun·der·ing [ˈθʌndəriŋ] *a.* ①雷鸣的，打雷的；雷一样响亮的. ②〔口〕非常的，极大的(谎话、错误、坏蛋等). *a ~ great fellow* 非常高大的家伙. *a ~ error* 极大的错误. — *ad.* 〔口〕非常，异常. **-ly** *ad.*

thun·der·ous [ˈθʌndərəs] *a.* 雷的；雷鸣似的，轰隆轰隆响的. ②多雷的，形成雷的. ③可怕的.

thun·der·y [ˈθʌndəri] *a.* 打雷似的；将要打雷似的；形势不稳的.

Thur. = Thursday.

Thur·ber [ˈθəːbə] *n.* 瑟伯〔姓氏〕.

thu·ri·ble [ˈθjuəribl] *n.*【天主教】香炉.

thu·ri·fer [ˈθjurifə, ˈθur-] *n.*【天主教】祭坛侍僧〔僧童〕〔祭坛上捧香炉的侍僧或僧童〕.

thu·ri·fi·ca·tion [ˌθjuərifiˈkeiʃən] *n.* 焚香.

thu·ri·fy [ˈθjurifai] *vt.* 在…前〔附近〕烧香；用香熏.

Thur·man [ˈθəːmən] *n.* 瑟曼〔姓氏，男子名〕.

Thur(s). = Thursday.

Thurs·day [ˈθəːzdi] *n.* 星期四〔略 Thur., Thurs.〕. *Holy ~* (基督教)①升天节(复活节后四十天的星期四). ②复活节前三天的星期四 (= Maundy [ˈmɔːn-di] ~). **-s** *ad.* 〔美〕每星期四，在任何星期四.

Thurs·ton [ˈθəːstən] *n.* 瑟斯顿〔男子名〕.

thus [ðʌs] *ad.* ①如此，这样，象这样，例如. ②到这程度，到这地步，这么. ③如下. ④于是，因此. *T- it goes on.* 如此继续下去. ***It ~ appears that*** … 因此看起来好象…. ***~ and so*** 〔美〕= so. ***~ and*** 云云，这样这样，如此这般. ***~ far*** 至今，迄今，到现在为止，至此，到这里为止. ***~ much*** 这么多，到这里为止 (*T- much at least is clear.* 至少这一些是明白的). **-ly** *ad.* = thus.

thus·ness [ˈðʌsnis] *n.* 〔谑〕这个样子. *Why this ~?* 为什么会这样?

thwack [θwæk] *n., vt., vi.* 〔拟声词〕拍地一声打；重击 (= whack).

thwaite [θweit] *n.* 〔英〕新开地，开垦地.

thwart [θwɔːt] *vt.* ①反对；阻挠，挫败(对方意图等). ②〔古〕横过，穿过. — *a.* 横着的，穿过的；不利的. — *ad., prep.* 横跨，横过. — [θɔːt] *n.* (横贯小艇的)坐板. *I don't think that will ~ our purposes.* 我认为那不会使我们的目的受到挫折. *It's only too natural that he will be ~ed in his ambitions.* 他的图谋遭到挫败是很自然的事. **~ship** *a.* 横贯船身的. **~ships** *ad.*

T.H.W.M. = Trinity House high water mark〔英〕海务局高潮水位标志.

ThX (= thorium X) 钍 X〔即 Ra^{224} 镭^{224}〕.

thy [ðai] *pro.* 〔古〕〔thou 的物主格〕你的.

Thy·es·te·an [θaiˈestiən] *a.* 吃人肉的〔希腊神话，Thyestes 与其弟妹 Atrens 通奸，遭怨恨，食间，后者杀前者儿子供餐，前者不知食之，故有此意〕.

thy·la·cine [ˈθailəˌsain,-sin] *n.*【动】袋狼 (= tasmanian wolf).

thyme [taim] *n.*【植】百里香(属)，麝香草.

thy·mic¹ [ˈθaimik] *a.*【解】胸腺的.

thy·mic² [ˈθaimik] *a.*【植】百里香的；麝香草的.

thy·mi·dine [ˈθaimiˌdiːn,-ˌdin] *n.*【药】胸腺嘧啶脱氧核苷.

thy·mine [ˈθaimiːn, -min] *n.*【药】胸腺嘧啶.

thy·mol [ˈθaimɔl] *n.*【化】百里(香)酚，麝香草酚.

thy·mus [ˈθaiməs] *n.* ①【解】胸腺. ②麝香草. **~ gland** 胸腺.

thym·y [ˈtaimi] *a.* 多百里香的，有麝香草香的.

thy·ra·tron [ˈθairətrɔn] *n.*【无】闸流管.

thy·ris·tor [θaiˈristə] *n.*【无】闸流晶体管；半导体开关元件；半导体电子.

thy·rite [ˈθairait] *n.* ①几利〔砂砾陶，一种非线性电阻〕. ②泰利〔电阻值随所加电压而变的一种材料〕.

thy·rode [ˈθairəud] *n.* ①泰罗〔一种计数器用电子管〕. ②硅可控整流器.

thy·roid [ˈθaiərɔid] *a.* ①盾状的. ②【解】甲状(软骨)的；甲状腺的. *~ cartilage* 甲状软骨. *~ gland [body]* 甲状腺. — *n.* ①【解】甲状腺；甲状软骨. ②【药】甲状腺剂.

thy·ro·ad·e·ni·tis [ˈθairəuˌædˈnaitis]【医】= thyroiditis.

thy·roid·ec·to·my [ˌθairɔiˈdektəmi] *n.* *(pl. -mies)*【医】甲状腺切除术.

thy·roid·i·tis [ˌθairɔiˈdaitis] *n.*【医】甲状腺炎.

thy·ro·tox·i·co·sis [ˌθairəuˌtɔksiˈkəusis] *n.*【医】甲状腺机能亢进，甲状腺毒症 (= hyperthyroidism).

thy·rot·ro·phin, -ro·pin [θaiˈrɔtrəfin, -pin] *n.*【医】促甲状腺激素.

thy·rox·in(e) [θaiˈrɔksi(ː)n] *n.*【生化】甲状腺素.

thyr·soid, -soi·dal [ˈθəːsɔid, -ˈsɔidl] *a.*【植】聚伞圆锥花序的.

thyr·sus [ˈθəːsəs] *n.* *(pl. -si* [-sai]*)* ①【希神】酒神杖〔酒神 (Bacchus) 所执的顶端为松果形的手杖〕. ②【植】聚伞圆锥花序.

thy·sa·nu·ran [ˌθaiseˈnjurən, ˌθise; -ˈnur-] *n.*【动】缨尾目 *(Thysanura)* 动物〔包括衣鱼〕. **-nu·rous** *a.*

thy·self [ðaiˈself] *pro.* ①你自己〔thou 的反身代词〕. ②〔加强语气用〕你本人，你亲自.

Ti =【化】titanium.

ti¹ [tiː] *n.*【乐】长音阶七唱名的第七音 (= si).

ti² [tiː] *n.*【植】铁树 *(Cordyline terminalis)*〔产于波利尼西亚和澳大利亚〕.

tia·mat [ˈtaiəmæt] *n.* 〔美空军〕试验用的无人驾驶火箭飞机.

ti·a·ra [tiˈɑːrə] *n.* ①古波斯人的头巾；古波斯王的王冕. ②罗马教皇的三重冕〔象征现世、灵界、地狱三者〕. ③罗马教皇的职权. ④女式冕状头饰.

Tib·bett [ˈtibit] *n.* 蒂贝特〔姓氏〕.

Ti·ber [ˈtaibə] *n.* 第伯尔河〔横贯罗马市的河名〕.

Ti·be·ri·us [taiˈbiəriəs] *n.* 台比留〔42B.C. — AD37，全名为 ~ Claudius Nero Caesar，公元一世纪14—37年间为罗马皇帝〕.

Ti·bet [tiˈbet] *n.* 西藏.

Ti·bet·an [tiˈbetən] *a., n.* 西藏的(人)；西藏语.

Ti·bet·o-Bur·man [tiˌbetəuˈbəːmən] *n.* 藏缅语〔汉藏语系的一支，包括藏语和缅语〕. — *a.* 藏缅语的.

tib·i·a [ˈtibiə] *n.* *(pl. -ae* [ˈtibiiː]*)* ①【解】胫骨；【动】(昆虫的)胫节；鸡脚的下节. ②(原由动物胫骨制成的)胫笛. **-l** *a.*

Tibione [ˈtiːˈbiːwʌn] *n.*【医】替比昂〔抑制结核杆菌和麻风杆菌药，即 TB_1〕.

tic [tik] *n.*【医】①(颜面)痉挛，痉挛性颜面神经痛. ②(局部肌肉小)抽搐. *~ douloureux* 三叉神经痛 (= trigeminal neuralgia).

tic·ca [ˈtikə] *a.* 〔印〕(车等)出租的. *a ~ gharry* 出租马车.

ti·cal [tiˈkɑːl, -ˈkɔːl] *n.* ①泰国旧货币单位〔现为 *baht* 铢〕. ②泰国旧重量单位.

tick¹ [tik] *vi.* ①(钟表)滴嗒滴嗒响〔走〕. ②一步一步推移；〔口〕(象钟表般地)持续活动. *Don't worry. After the operation, he'll ~ along fine.* 不用担心，手术后他会活得很好. *What makes it ~?* 什么使它这样地动作? — *vt.* ①打点，作记号 *(off)*. ②滴嗒滴嗒记录时间〔发出信息〕*(out)*；把时间滴滴嗒嗒地打发掉. *The teletype is*

~*ing out messages*. 电传打字电报机滴嗒滴嗒地打出电报来. (*the clock*) ~ ***away [off] the time*** (*of*) 随着滴嗒的钟声，…的时间过去了. ~ ***off*** ①打上记号. ②〔英俚〕斥责，责骂. ③〔口〕证明是同一东西;核实无误. ④〔俚〕激怒. ⑤简略地描述. ~ **out** (电报机)发出(消息). ~ **over** (内燃机等)慢车转动着，松开传动装置;〔喻〕接近停滞,踌躇,吞吞吐吐. ***what makes a person [a thing]*** ~ 使人[事]持续活动的动力 (*That's what makes the world* ~. 使世界持续活动的动力,就在于此). — *n*. ①滴嗒(声). ②一点,一划,查讫号[√]. ③【物】标记(器);【无】无线电信号. ④〔英口〕一会儿，一刹那间. *I'll be with you in half a* ~. 稍等片刻,我就来陪你. *come in a* ~ 马上就来. *radio* ~ 无线电报时信号. *time* ~ 计时器. **to [on] the** ~ 极为准时地 (*get there at five on the* ~ 五时正到达那里).

tick² [tik] *n*. ①褥套, 枕套〔指中间填塞羽毛等物的内套〕; (做褥套等用的)条纹棉布或麻布; 褥面. ②(弹簧椅等的)面子. **tight as a** ~ 〔美俚〕喝得烂醉的.

tick³ [tik] *n*. 【动】扁虱,蜱,壁虱. ~ *fever* 【医】蜱热.

tick⁴ [tik] *n*. 〔口〕①信用,赊欠,放债. ②赊(销). — *vi*. 赊销; 赊购. — *vt*. 赊销(购)(货物);赊给(某人). ***buy [get] sth. on*** ~ 赊购. ***give tick*** 赊销. ***go (on)*** ~ = ***run on*** ~ 赊购;借款.

tick·er [ˈtikə] *n*. ①滴嗒滴嗒响的东西. ②蜂音器,振动子. ③(钟表的)摆. ④〔美俚〕挂表,座钟. ⑤〔美俚〕心脏. ⑥(电报的)收报机; 股票行市自动收录机. ⑦【无】断续装置; 断续器. ~ **tape** ①(收报机等用的)纸带. ②(庆祝，欢迎,送行等抛扔用的)彩色纸带. ~**-tape** *a*. 抛彩带的, 热烈的 (*get a* ~*-tape reception [welcome, parade]* 受到抛彩带的盛大欢迎).

tick·et [ˈtikit] *n*. ①票,入场券,车票,票证. ②标签,标价牌,价目签. ③当票; 招租帖. ④(给违反交通规则者等的)传票. ⑤〔英军俚〕解除军职命令. ⑥〔美〕候选人名单;列有候选人名单的选举票;〔喻〕(政党的)政见,政纲;计划,规划. ⑦(资格)证明书;许可证;(飞行员等)执照. ⑧〔the ~〕〔口〕适当[所需]的东西;当然的事情,正好的事情;计划,方针. *a platform* ~ 月台票. *a season* ~ 月[季]票. *a single [return]* ~ 单程[来回]票. *a price* ~ 价目标签. *cash* ~*s* 门市发票. *vote a straight* ~〔美〕所有票数均投选某一政党的候选人. *split a* ~ = *vote a split* ~〔美〕兼投另一政党候选人的票. *The whole* ~ *was returned*. 候选人全部当选. *the Democratic* ~〔美〕民主党的政纲. *That's the* ~. 〔口〕那正好,那才对. *What's the* ~? 〔口〕怎样才好? 结果怎样? — *vt*. ①加标签,附上标价牌. ②〔美〕卖票. ***admit by*** ~ ***alone*** 凭券入场. ***carry a*** ~〔美〕使本党候选人全部当选. ***cut a*** ~〔美口〕涂掉选票上候选人的名字, 投反对票. ***get one's*** ~【军】被解除军职. ***given a*** ~〔美剧〕被辞退. ***not quite the*** ~ 有点不适合[不对头]. ***vote the split*** ~〔美〕兼投一党以上的候选人的票. ***vote the straight*** ~〔美〕只投某一政党全部候选人的票. ***work one's*** ~〔军口〕(装病等)退役. ***write one's own*** ~ 自行计划,自行决定. ~ **agent**〔美〕售票员. ~ **chopper** 剪票员. ~ **day** (交易所的)决算日. ~ **inspector** 查票员. ~ **night** 演员照各自推销票数分配得款的演出日. ~ **of leave** *n*. 假释许可证. ~**-of-leave** *a*. 假释的(~*-of-leave man* 假释犯). ~ **office**〔美〕售票处, 票房. ~**-porter**〔英〕(车站内的)搬运员. ~ **punch** 轧票钳. ~ **scalper**〔美俚〕(套卖戏票的)黄牛党.

tick·et·y-boo [ˈtikitiˌbuː] *a*. 〔英俚〕很好,没问题,行.

tick·ing¹ [ˈtikiŋ] *n*. 滴嗒声.

tick·ing² [ˈtikiŋ] *n*. 褥套料〔做褥套等用的厚底棉布〕. *an art* ~ 印花[织花]褥套料.

tick·le [ˈtikl] *vt*. ①搔触(使觉得痒),呵(痒); 撩拨. ②逗笑;使高兴,使快乐; 使满足. ③用手抓住(鳝鱼等). — *vi*. 觉得痒,(东西)使人发痒. *He* ~*d me in the ribs*. 他搔触我的肋骨. *I was greatly* ~*d at the joke*. 想起这个笑话感到有趣得了不得. *My ear* ~*s*. 我耳朵痒. *The rough sheets* ~. 粗床单使人发痒. ~ ***sb.'s palm*** 给某人赏钱[贿赂]. ~ ***sb.'s vanity*** 满足某人的虚荣心. ~ ***the fancy*** 迎合所好. ~ ***the ivories***〔美〕弹的琴. ~ ***to death*** 使笑破肚皮 (*I was* ~*d to death at the joke*. 听了那笑话,我的肚皮都笑破了). — *n*. ①搔痒. ②使人发痒[高兴]的东西[事物]. ③愉快的情绪. ~***d pink*** *a*. 〔美俚〕非常开心,高兴 (*He was* ~*d pink that somebody had remembered his birthday*. 他非常高兴，因为还有人记得他的生日).

tick·ler [ˈtiklə] *n*. ①使感到痒[高兴]的人[物]. ②〔口〕难事,难题. ③〔美〕记事本,备忘录. ④〔美口〕小瓶;(威士忌酒等的)一杯. ⑤【无】屏极回授线圈;【机】初给器. *He's meeting the* ~ *successfully*. 他在顺利地处理着这难题.

tick·lish [ˈtikliʃ] *a*. ①怕痒的. ②易变的. ③摇晃不稳的; 棘手的,难对付的(人、物). ④易怒的. *a* ~ *situation* 难对付的形势. *The news is quite* ~ *to the ear*. 这消息听起来使人觉得有些难办.

tick·seed [ˈtikˌsiːd] *n*. 【植】①金鸡菊 (= coreopsis). ②鬼针草属植物〔bur marigold 的俗称〕.

tic(k)·tac(k), tic(k)·tic(k), tick·tock [ˈtikˈtæk, -tik, -ˈtɔk] *n*. ①滴嗒滴嗒〔钟表声〕. ②〔儿语〕钟. ③卜卜〔心脏的鼓动等〕, 悸动. ④(儿童恶作剧用的)遥控敲门装置. ⑤〔英俚〕给赛马赌博者提供情报的人 (= ~ man); 提供这种情报时打的手势.

tick-tack-toe [ˌtiktækˈtəu], **-too** [-ˈtuː] *n*. 三连棋. ②(儿童)使用遥控敲门装置的恶作剧.

tick·y tack·y, ticky-tacky [ˈtiki ˈtæki] *a*. 单调的,一模一样的〔如房屋〕.

t.i.d., TID =〔L.〕*ter in die* 每日三次〔药剂处方用语〕(= three times a day).

tid·al [ˈtaidl] *a*. ①潮汐的; 潮水(似)的. ②由于潮水作用的, 定时涨落的; 开船时间视潮汐而变动的 (客船班次). *His speech caused a* ~ *wave of indignation throughout the country*. 他的演说在全国掀起了怒潮. ~ **air** = ~ **breath** 每一呼吸进出肺部的空气. ~ **boat** 开航时间视潮汐而变动的客船. ~ **current** 潮流. ~ **forest** 潮湿林. ~ **harbour** 潮汐港. ~ **river** 潮汐河. ~ **train** 临港列车. ~ **wave** ①潮浪, 潮汐波. ②海啸. ③(喻)(情绪上的)大波动,(人事上的)大变动.

tid·bit [ˈtidbit] *n*. 〔美〕= titbit.

tiddl(e)y [ˈtidli] *n*. 〔主英俚〕酒. — *a*. ①喝醉的,步履不稳的. ②〔口〕很小的,微不足道的.

tid·dl(e)y·wink [ˈtidliwiŋk] *n*. ①〔英俚〕没有执照的酒吧[当铺], 下等酒吧. ②〔美〕〔*pl*.〕投圆形小筹码进入桌中央杯碟中的游戏.

tide [taid] *n*. ①潮,潮汐,涨潮时. ②消长,盛衰. ③潮流,趋势,倾向,形势,时机,机运. ④【矿山】班,十二个钟头. ⑤时期, 季节. ⑥(宗教上的) 节期〔通例用作复合词〕. *Christmas* ~ 圣诞节节期. *at high [low]* ~ 处于高[低]潮. *ebb [flood]* ~ 落[涨]潮. *the flowing [rising]* ~ 涨潮. *the ebbing [falling]* ~ 退潮. *spring [neap]* ~ 大[小]潮. *The* ~ *is in [out* or *down* 或 *coming in, going out]* 现在是涨潮[落潮]. *The* ~ *is making [ebbing]*. 潮正在涨[落]. ***attempt to go against the*** ~ ***of history*** 倒行逆施. ***catch the*** ~ 抓住时机, 趁机. ***full*** ~ ***of pleasure*** 欢乐的绝顶. ***go with the*** ~ 随大流,赶潮流,顺从时势. ***roll back the*** ~ ***of war*** 击退侵略. ***save the*** ~ 趁涨潮进出港口. ***swim with the*** ~ 随大流,随波逐流. ***tail to the*** ~ (船只停泊中)随潮起伏. ***take fortune at the*** ~ = ***take the*** ~ ***at the flood*** 及时利用时机,因利乘便. ***The*** ~ ***turns***. 形势经常在变化 (*The* ~ *turned to [against] him*. 形势变得对他有利[不利]). ***work double*** ~***s*** 昼夜工作,日夜苦干. — *vi*. ①顺应潮水航行. ②象潮水般汹涌(高涨,奔流). —*vt*. ①使随潮水漂行. ②克服. *The General Meigs* *is ~tiding into(out of) the harbor.* 梅格斯将军号在趁潮进港(出港). *The money is enough to ~ him over the difficulties.* 这笔钱足够他渡过困难了. ~ **gauge** 测潮计. ~ **land** (随潮水涨落而出没的)潮淹区;〔*pl.*〕沿岸线水地带. ~ **lock** 潮闸. ~**-mark** 潮标. ~ **rip** 潮流冲激成的大浪. ~**rock** 随潮水起落出没的礁石. ~ **table** 潮汐表. ~**waiter** ①海关水上稽查员. ②机会主义者,观潮派. ~**water**〔美〕①潮水. ②受潮水涨落影响的水区和地区. ~**way** ①潮路;潮流. ②(河流的)受潮汐影响的部分.

ti·dings [ˈtaidiŋz] *n.* 〔*pl.*〕 消息,音信〔动词单复数通用〕. *glad ~* 喜讯. *good [evil] ~* 好[坏]消息. *That's the best ~ for the future.* 那对前途说来是最好的消息. *When the sad ~ of his death were (was) received, we all wept.* 听到他去世的噩耗时,我们都哭了.

ti·dy [ˈtaidi] *a.* ***(-di·er; -di·est)*** ①整洁的,整齐的,爱整洁的. ②〔口〕相当好的,相当大的(款项). ③〔口〕健康的. — *n.* ①沙发,椅背,扶手等的罩布. ②装零碎东西的容器[袋子、筐子等]. *a ~ room* 整洁的房间. *a street ~* 街道上的废物箱. — *vt.* 弄整洁,整理,收拾 *(up). It's your turn to ~ the room.* 这回该你收拾房间了. *Wait a minute. I have to ~ myself (up) a bit.* 等一会儿,我梳理一下. **-i·ly** *ad.* **-i·ness** *n.*

tie [tai] *vt.* ①(用绳带等)扎,系,绑;用带子束紧(帽、鞋等);打(结、领结等);束缚,绑住. ②约束,限制. ③连接;〔口〕使结为夫妇. ④【乐】用连接符连接;【铁路】固定铁轨;铺设枕木. ⑤【运】与…打成平局. *~ one's tie* 打领结. *~ one's shoes* 结鞋带. *My tongue is ~d.* 我不能说. *Never fear! The dog is ~d up.* 不要怕;狗拴着呢. *I am much ~d.* 我被工作拖住,一点闲空没有. *See that the boat is securely ~d.* 注意要把小船拴牢了. *a ~d house* (专供本企业职工租用的)企业宿舍;(专销某家酒的)特约酒店. — *vi.* ①结合,连接,结住. ②打结. ③打成平局,不分胜负;势均力敌. *~ with one's competitor* 跟对手不分胜负. *This ~s up with what I've told you.* 这和我对你讲过的有关. — *n.* ①结扎,结子,结儿. ②带子,绳子,领带;毛皮的颈饰;鞋带;〔美〕〔*pl.*〕= Oxford shoes. ③联系,关系,缘分. ④束缚,牵累. ⑤【运】平局,不分胜负,淘汰赛,平局后决胜负的决赛. ⑥【建】连系材. ⑦【乐】连接线[符号]. ⑧〔美〕铁路枕木. ⑨【统】相持. *draw close the ~s between the Party and the masses* 密切党群关系. *It tends to a stronger ~ of friendship between us.* 这有助加强我们之间的朋友关系. *Children are a great ~.* 小孩子们是很大的拖累. ***be ~d to time*** 被时间束缚着,必须在一定时间内做好. ***get ~d up*** 结婚. ***hit the ~s*** 〔美俚〕顺铁路徒步旅行. ***play [run, shoot] off the ~*** 平局后再举行决胜负的决赛. ***ride and ~*** 两人轮流骑一马旅行. ***~ off*** (为了止血)缚住血管. ***~ one down*** 使不能起立地绑住某人;束缚,牵制. ***~ sb.'s tongue*** 使某人缄默,堵住某人的嘴. ***~ the knot***〔美〕结婚. ***~ to***〔美俚〕信赖,倚靠;迷恋. ***~ up*** ①绑;系;包扎,包装. ②(船只)系泊. ③(使)拮据[穷困]. ④(罢工中)使交通停顿 (*The accident ~d up traffic the entire day.* 那个意外事件使交通整天停止). ⑤冻结(遗产、资本). ⑥〔美〕联合行动;合伙. ***~ up with*** 和…有(密切)关系. ***~d to a tree***〔美〕被打败. ~ **back** 拴窗帘、帷幕的绳带;〔常 *pl.*〕带有系带的帘幕. ~ **bar [clasp, clip]** 领带夹. ~ **beam**【建】系梁,小屋梁. ~**-dye** *n., vt.* 扎染(法);扎染的布. ~**-in** *n., a.* 搭配在一起出售的[货品];关系,联系. ~ **line**【电】联络线(路);直接接连线;拉线;直接通信线路. ~ **peeler,** ~ **whacker** 〔美〕(森林中)解制枕木的工人. ~**pin** = stickpin. ~ **rod** 系杆;拉杆. ~ **tack** 领带别针. ~**-up** 关系,牵连;〔美〕(交通工作等)断绝,停顿;(船的)系泊处;〔美方〕拴系牲畜的地方.

tie·mann·ite [ˈtiːməˌnait] *n.*【矿】硒汞矿.

tier· = tierce.

tier[1] [tiə] *n.* ①(阶式看台等的)(一)排,(一)行,(一)层. ②(衣服等上的)一行褶裥. ③【电】定向天线. ④等级. *seats arranged in ~s* 排成一层一层的座位. *the highest ~ of society* 社会的最上层. — *vt., vi.* 成层堆积[排列];层层上升. ~ *building* 多层房屋. ~ *table* 宝塔桌(有两张或更多的相互重叠的圆桌面小桌).

tier[2] [ˈtaiə] *n.* ①捆扎者(或工具),包扎工. ②〔美方〕(儿用)围涎,胸围.

tierce [tiəs] *n.* ①(装 42 个美国加仑的)中号酒桶;42 加仑的量. ②【乐】(音阶的)第三音. ③【天主】白天的第三时〔午前九时〕,第三课(第三时作的祈祷). ④【剑术】第三姿势. ⑤[təːs] 【牌戏】三张同花顺. ~ *and quarts* 剑术.

tier·cel [ˈtiəsl] *n.* 雄鹰 (= tercel).

Tier·ra del Fuego [ˈtjerrɑˌdelˈfwegəu] *n.* (南美南端的)火地岛.

tiers é·tat [ˈtjeəzeiˈtɑː]〔F.〕(区别于贵族和教士阶级的)第三等级,平民阶级.

tiff [tif] *n.* ①(一杯)酒,(一口)酒. ②小争执,小口角. *a labour ~* 劳资纠纷. — *vt.*〔英〕喝一杯. — *vi.* ①生气,动怒. ②口角,争吵. ③〔印〕吃午饭. *have a ~ with one's classmate* 和同班同学发生小口角.

tif·fa·ny [ˈtifəni] *n.* ①丝纱罗. ②上浆亚麻薄布.

tif·fin [ˈtifin]〔印〕*n.* 午饭. — *vi.* 吃午饭.

Tiflis, Tbilisi [ˈtiflis, tˈbilis] *n.* 第比利斯〔苏联格鲁吉亚共和国的首都〕.

tig[1] [tig] *n., vt.* 触摸;捉迷藏;〔口〕吵架.

tig[2] [tig] *n.* 一种旧式带把酒杯.

ti·ger [ˈtaigə] *n.* ①【动】虎. ②凶汉,凶性,残性,暴徒. ③(穿着制服的)少年马夫. ④〔英口〕(网球等比赛的)劲敌 *(opp.* rabbit*).* ⑤〔美〕(欢呼三声后)加喊的欢呼〔喝彩声〕,喝彩尾声 *(three cheers and a ~). a red ~* = cougar. *an American ~* 美洲豹 (= jaguar). *the (Tammany) T-* 〔美〕= Tammany Hall. ***work like a ~*** 生龙活虎地工作. ~ **beetle**【虫】斑蝥. ~ **cat**【动】豹猫;薮猫. ~**eye,** ~**'s-eye**【矿】虎眼石. ~**flower**【植】虎斑草. ~**grass**【植】棕叶芦. ~ **lily**【植】卷丹. ~**man**〔美〕摔跤选手. ~ **moth**【虫】灯蛾. ~ **solamander**【动】虎纹钝口螈. ~ **sweat**〔美俚〕威士忌酒. **-ish** *a.* 虎一般凶猛残忍的,虎纹的. **-ism** *n.* 狞猛,残忍凶暴.

tight [tait] *a.* ①坚实的;坚固的,坚牢的,紧的,不松动的. ②紧密的;密封的,气密的;不漏的. ③紧张的,绷紧的 *(opp.* slack, loose*).* ④严格的,严厉的. ⑤紧贴的,正合身的(衣服等);装紧的,密集的. ⑥麻烦的,棘手的,困难的;危险的. ⑦整洁的(少女等). ⑧〔美口〕吝啬的,啬刻的. ⑨【商】供应紧张的. ⑩(比赛等)势均力敌的. ⑪(文字,作品等)紧凑的,精炼的,排得紧的. ⑫〔俚〕醉醺醺的. *The stopper is too ~ that it can't be withdrawn.* 瓶塞太紧拔不出来了. *These shoes are painfully ~.* 这双鞋紧得难受. *Fill the cases so that they are ~.* 把这些匣子装得满满的. *I know you're in a ~ place again.* 我晓得你又处于困境了. *An armyman must be under ~ discipline.* 军人应守严格纪律. *Money is ~.* 银根紧. *a ~ squeeze* 紧紧的握手;〔口〕下不得台的情形;〔美〕九死一生;难分胜负的战斗. — *n.*〔*pl.*〕紧身衣. — *ad.* 紧,紧紧地. *sit ~* 坐稳,固执,坚持. ***be in a ~ place*** 处境困难[窘迫]. ***get ~*** 〔俚〕大醉. ***keep a ~ rein [hand] on*** 严厉控制,抓紧. ***perform on the ~ rope*** 走钢丝. ***~ as a mink*** 〔美〕喝得烂醉的. ***~ corner [spot]*** 穷境. ~**-fisted** *a.* 吝啬的. ~**-fitting** *a.* 紧身的. ~ **knit** *a.* 紧密编结的,紧凑的. ~**-laced** *a.* 穿着紧腰衣的;严格的. ~**-lipped** *a.* 闭紧嘴的,嘴紧的,话少的. ~ **money market** 银根紧的金融市场. ~ **riveting**【机】紧密铆合. ~**rope** (杂技中走索用的)紧绷索. ~**wad**〔美俚〕吝啬鬼. **-ly** *ad.* **-ness** *n.*

tight·en [ˈtaitn] *vt., vi.* 收紧,拉紧,抽紧;绷紧;固定.

~ one's belt 〔谑〕束紧裤带；节省支出.

ti·glon [ˈtaiglən], **ti·gon** [ˈtaigən] *n.* 虎狮〔公虎与母狮杂交后代〕.

ti·gress [ˈtaigris] *n.* 【动】母老虎；凶恶泼辣的女人.

ti·grine [ˈtaigrain] *a.* 虎(似)的，虎纹的.

Ti·gri·nya [tiˈgri:njə] *n.* 现代埃塞俄比亚语.

Ti·gris [ˈtaigris] *n.* 〔the〕底格里斯河〔亚洲〕.

tigrish [ˈtaigriʃ] *a.* = *tiger*ish.

T. I. H. = Their Imperial Highnesses 〔英〕殿下们.

tike, tyke [taik] *n.* ①野狗，杂种狗；小孩子. ②〔口〕顽皮的孩子. ③〔Scot.〕乡下佬. *a Yorkshire ~* 约克佬〔无轻蔑意〕.

tik·ker [ˈtikə] *n.* 【无】= ticker.

til [til, ti:l] *n.* = teel.

til·ak [ˈtilək] *n.* (印度人)用红化装油点在前额上的圆点.

til·bu·ry [ˈtilbəri] *n.* 双人坐的二轮轻便马车.

tilde [tild, ˈtildi] *n.* ①〔Sp.〕颚化符号(即西班牙字母 *n* 上加的发音符号〔señor 的 '~'〕). ②代字号〔~〕(又叫 swung dash). ③【数，逻】否定号〔~〕.

Til·den [ˈtildin, ˈtidən] *n.* 蒂尔登〔姓氏〕.

tile [tail] *n.* ①瓦；【建】瓷砖，花砖，(软木，橡胶等制的)弹性地砖，贴砖，铺瓦，瓦片，瓦面，瓦管. ②〔口语〕礼帽，高顶帽. ③(中国麻将牌的)牌. *a Dutch ~* 彩砖，花砖，画砖. *~ floor* 砖地. *~ roofing* 瓦屋顶. — *vt.* ①用瓦盖，铺瓦，砌瓷砖. ②(秘密结社集会时)派人守望，使发誓守秘密，严守秘密. ***be (out) on the ~s*** 〔俚〕寻欢作乐，花天酒地. ***fly a ~*** 〔俚〕把帽子打掉. ***have a ~ loose*** 〔俚〕有点疯，神志有点错乱. *~* **stone**【建】石瓦，石板. *~* **tea** 茶砖.

til·er [ˈtailə] *n.* 制瓦工人；瓦匠；秘密结社守望人.

til·er·y [ˈtailəri] *n.* ①瓦厂. ②装饰性砖瓦铺贴术.

til·ing [ˈtailiŋ] *n.* ①盖瓦；铺瓷砖. ②〔集合词〕(屋)瓦，瓦类，瓷砖，花砖. ③瓦屋顶，瓦面，砖面，砖瓦结构.

till[1] [til] *prep.* 〔基本上与 until 相同，但句首一般不用 till，而用 until〕①直到…为止. ②〔在否定句中〕直到…才…；在…前(不…). *Wait ~ tomorrow.* 等到明天. *serve the people ~ death* 为人民服务到死为止〔一生〕. *He did not return ~ ten.* 他到十点钟才回. *It was not ~ evening that I knew the fact.* 到黄昏时我才知道那件事. — *conj.* ①直到…为止. ②〔在否定句后〕在…之前，直到…的时候才…. *We lived in Beijing till I was twenty.* 我们住在北京住到我二十岁的时候. *People do not know the value of health ~ they lose it.* 失去健康时，人们才知道健康的价值. *~* ***all's blue*** 到极点. ***"T- Called For"***【铁路】留站(待领)；【邮局】留局(待领). *~* ***the cows come home*** 〔美〕将长时期地；永久地.

till[2] [til] *n.* ①(帐桌中)放钱的抽斗，抽屉. ②(橱柜中)放贵重物的格子或抽屉. ③钱柜，钱箱. *~ money* 备用现金.

till[3] [til] *n.* 【地】冰碛(物).

till[4] [til] *vt., vi.* 耕种，翻耕，耕作. *We've five tractors to ~ the land.* 我们有五架拖拉机耕地. *~ed crops* 中耕作物.

till·a·ble [ˈtiləbl] *a.* 适于耕种的.

till·age [ˈtilidʒ] *n.* ①耕种，耕作，整地. ②耕作(地)；耕地上的作物.

til·land·si·a [tiˈlændziə] *n.* 【植】铁兰属 (*Tillandsia*) 植物〔尤指铁兰〕.

till·er[1] [ˈtilə] *n.* 耕作者，农夫. *land to the ~* 耕者有其田.

till·er[2] [ˈtilə] *n.* 【船】舵柄. **~-chain** *n.* 转舵链. **~-rope** *n.* 转舵索.

till·er[3] [ˈtilə] *n.* 【植】分蘖，(树桩上长出的)萌蘖. — *vi.* 萌蘖，生新芽，长嫩苗.

till·ite [ˈtilait] *n.* 【地】冰碛岩.

tilt[1] [tilt] *vi.* ①倾斜(侧)，歪斜；翘起. ②(在马上)拿枪扎；马上刺枪比赛；〔喻〕抨击，攻击 *(at; against)*；战斗. — *vt.* ①使倾侧；使歪斜，使翘起. ②(拿枪)扎，戳，戳过去；〔喻〕攻击；驳，抨击. ③用跳动鎚锻打. *He likes to ~ his head forward.* 他喜欢把头往前倾. *Don't ~ your hat sideways.* 不要歪戴帽子. *In the class meeting, Jack ~ed at John.* 班会上，贾克猛烈地抨击了约翰. *The table ~ed (over) and the thermos slid off it to the ground.* 桌子歪了，热水瓶从上面滑到地上. — *n.* ①偏倾，歪斜，倾侧；斜坡，坡度. ②马上刺枪比赛；〔喻〕激烈的竞争，争论. ③〔美〕比赛；拳赛；竞争；争论. ④跳动锤，落鎚. ⑤跷跷板. ***(at) full ~*** 开足速力，用全速力；猛冲，拼命(冲过去等). ***give a ~*** 使倾斜. ***have a ~ at*** ①偏向，向…歪. ②攻击，驳斥. ***on the ~*** 倾斜着，歪着. *~* ***of wave front***【物】波前倾斜. **~ham·mer** *n.* 跳动锤 (= clinometer). **~meter** 测斜器. **~-top** 可调节桌面〔顶板〕倾斜度的. **~yard** *n.* (中世纪的)马上冲刺比赛场. **-ed** *a.* 倾斜的，翘起的.

tilt[2] [tilt] *n.* (小舟、车辆、地摊等的)帐篷，遮阳；车盖. — *vt.* 用帐篷遮盖，搭帐篷.

tilth [tilθ] *n.* ①耕种，耕作(深度)，翻耕. ②耕作地，已耕地〔土层〕；整地.

Tim [tim] *n.* 蒂姆〔男子名，Timothy 的昵称〕.

Tim. = Timothy.

tim·bal, tim·bul [ˈtimbəl] *n.* ①铜鼓 (= kettledrum). ②【动】(蝉等的)鼓膜，鼓室，鸣腔.

tim·bale [tæmˈbɑ:l, ˈtimbəl; *F.* tɛ̃bal] *n.* ①香烤三味〔用鸡、虾、鱼，加大量作料，于鼓形容器内烘烤〕. ②炸(烤)馅饼(= timbale case).

tim·ber [ˈtimbə] *n.* ①原木，木材，木料. ②(可作木材的)树木；森林；〔美〕森林地，林场. ③横木，栋木；【船】船骨，肋材. ④品质；素质；〔美〕才能，才干. ⑤〔英〕【猎】木造障碍物〔围栏等〕，(猎狐时用的)木栅栏，木门. ⑥〔板球俚〕三柱门. *cut down (fell) ~* 伐木. *We must safeguard forest ~.* 我们必须保护林木. *Fire destroyed thousand acres of ~.* 火焚毁了千亩林木. *He is a statesman of the highest ~.* 他是个高尚的政治家. *My ~s! = Shiver [Dash] my ~s!* 〔海俚〕混蛋！可恶！讨厌！〔水手最普通的骂人话.〕—*int.* (伐木工在木倒时喊)倒啦！— *vt.* 备以木材；用木料支撑. *~* **beast**〔美〕森林工人，伐木工人. *~* **cart** 运木车. *~* **connector** 木结构. *~* **dealer** 木材商. *~* **headed** *a.* 〔俚〕笨的. *~* **hitch** (套吊圆材的) 绳结，8 字结. *~* **jack** 〔美〕伐木人. *~* **land** 〔美〕林场，森林. *~* **line** 树木线. *~* **rattlesnake**【动】林响蛇. *~* **skipper** = *~ topper* 〔美〕跳栏运动员. *~* **stand improvement**【林】疎伐. *~* **toes** 〔口〕装有木头假脚的人. *~* **wolf** 大灰狼；〔俚〕伐木人. **~work** 木结构，木材料，木料工厂. **~yard** 〔英〕木材堆置场；〔板球俚〕打球员方面的三柱门.

tim·bered [ˈtimbəd] *a.* ①木制的. ②森林的，多树木的. ③露出栋木的〔如墙〕.

tim·ber·ing [ˈtimbəriŋ] *n.* ①〔集合词〕木材. ②结构材，木结构.

tim·bre [tɛ̃:mbr, ˈtæmbə] *n.* 〔F.〕【乐】音色，音质.

tim·brel [ˈtimbrəl] *n.* = tambourine.

Tim·buk·tu, Tim·buc·too [ˌtimbʌkˈtu:] *n.* 廷巴克图〔马里城市〕.

time [taim] *n.* ①时，时间，时日，岁月. ②时候，时刻；期间；时节，季节；〔常 *pl.*〕时期，年代，时代；〔the ~〕当代，现代. ③怀孕期，分娩期；修业期，服役期，学徒期间；(规定的)工作时间，占用时间，所需时间；〔口〕刑期；死期，临终；一生；闲暇，余暇. ④时机，机会；时局，形势. ⑤次，度，回；倍. ⑥【运】开始！停！〔裁判员的口令〕. ⑦【乐】拍子，进行速度，节奏. ⑧【军】步伐. ⑨【地】纪. *T- flies.* 光阴似箭. *The new scheme will save both ~ and labour.* 新方案既省时间又省劳力. *Have you ~ to help us with the job?* 你有时间帮我们干干活儿吗？*nap ~* 〔美〕睡觉时间. *dead ~* 【火箭】滞后时间，迟滞. *What ~ is it?* 现在几点钟？*Have you the ~?* 现在几点? *ancient* ~*s* 古代. *men of the* ~ 现代的人. *We have to remould our world outlook, since* ~*s are different.* 我们必须改造世界观,因为时代不同了. *hard* [*bad*] ~*s* 萧条,不景气. *What a* ~ *you have been!* 相当费工夫了吧! *Now is your* ~! 现在正是你的好机会! *Mary is near her* ~. 玛丽快要分娩了. *I learned much while sewing my* ~. 我当学徒时,学了不少的东西. *We were pressed for* ~. 我们时间很紧迫. *Each* ~ *I spelt the word, I made the same mistake.* 我每次拼写这个词,总是犯同样的错误. *Six* ~*s five is thirty.* 五乘六得三十. *beat* ~ 打拍子. *Time and tide wait for no man.* 岁月不等人. ~ *of effect*【商】有效期间. ~ *of grace*〔法〕禁猎期. — *vt.* 为…选择时机; 安排…时间; 测定(赛跑等的)时间; 校准(钟表); 使合拍. — *vi.* 合拍; 一致, 调和;【剑术】乘隙进攻. ~ *the speed* 计算速度. ~ *a watch* 对表. *The remark was not well* ~*d.* 这话说得不是时候. *The plane is* ~*d to take off at 5 a.m.* 飞机定于上午五时起飞. *There's no hurry. One must* ~ *one's blows.* 不要忙, 我们要伺机予以打击. ***abreast of the*** ~***s*** 赶上时代,不落后于时代; 最新式的; 熟悉现况的. ***against*** ~ 尽快地,分秒必争地,力争及时完成地. ***ahead of*** ~ 提早,比原定提前地. ***all in good*** ~ 时机一到. ***all the*** ~ 始终;〔美〕老是. ***and about*** ~ ***too!*** 正是时候,正合时机. ***as*** ~ ***goes on*** 随着时代的推移. ***as*** ~***s go*** 在现在这个时势,在现在这个时节. ***at a set*** ~ 在约定的时候. ***at a*** ~ 一次(多少); 同时; 曾经; 连续 (*Take two pills at a* ~. 一次吃两粒(药). *for weeks at a* ~ 连续好几个星期). ***at all*** ~***s*** 不论什么时候; 老是. ***at no*** ~ 在任何时候都不,从来没有,决不. ***at one and the same*** ~ 在同时,一面…一面又. ***at one*** ~ 同时; 有一个时期,曾经. ***at other*** ~***s*** 往常, 平素. ***at the same*** ~ 同时; 但还是. ***at this time of (the) day*** 这个时候,到这个时候,这样早[迟]. ***at this*** ~ ***of the year*** 在这个时节. ***at*** ~***s*** 时时. ***be behind [ahead of] the [one's]*** ~***(s)*** 落后[先进]. ***be doing*** ~ ***at*** … 在…服徒刑中. ***be pressed for*** ~ 忙,没工夫. ***before one's*** ~ ①提前,不足月(而生). ②在某人出世前. ③早衰,夭折. ***before the [one's]*** ~***s*** (跑)在时代前头. ***behind*** ~ 迟(到). ***between*** ~***s*** 时时,偶尔,间或. ***bid one's*** ~ 等待时机. ***buy*** ~ 拖延时间,赢得时间. ***by the*** ~ 到…的时候. ***by this*** ~ 在这个时候以前; 快到这个时候. ***call*** ~ (裁判员)宣布时间已到. ***can see the*** ~ 可指日以待. ***can tell the*** ~ 会看钟; 知道现在是几点钟. ***come to*** ~ 履行义务. ***do*** ~ 服徒刑. ***down*** ~【计算机】停机时间. ***find*** ~ 有工夫,有空. ***for a*** ~ 暂时 (*It will last for a* ~. 暂时还经得住). ***for the*** ~ ***being*** 暂时,在目前. ***from one*** ~ ***to the next*** 每一次. ***from*** ~ ***to*** ~ 时时. ***give sb. the*** ~ ***of his life*** 见 ~ of one's life. ***give (sb.)*** ~ 宽限时间, 给与考虑的时间. ***half the*** ~ ①一半时间 (*We fulfilled the quota in half the* ~. 我们只用一半时间就完成了定额). ②(几乎)经常. ***has done [served] its*** ~ (物品)已经用得不能再用了. ***have a good [royal]*** ~ ***(of it)*** 很愉快 (*I have had a good [bad]* ~ *of it.* (今天)愉快[倒霉]极了). ***have a hard*** ~ = ***have a tough*** (rough) ~ ***of it*** 日子不好过. ***have the*** ~ ***of one's life*** 快活[痛苦]已极. ***Have I*** ~ ***(to …)?*** 有…的工夫吗? 赶得上…吗? ***have no*** ~ ***to spare*** 没有空,忙得很. ***have oneself a*** ~ 过得快乐. ***have*** ~ ***to burn*** 有用不完的时间. ***in a week's*** ~ 一星期后. ***in good [bad]*** ~ 按[误]时,及[不及]时. ***in jig*** ~〔口〕极快地. ***in (less than) no*** ~〔口〕立刻. ***in one's own good*** ~ 在有便的时候. ***in one's own*** ~ 在有空的时候. ***in one's*** ~ 在…年轻的时候. ***in slow [true]*** ~ 用缓慢的[正常的]节拍. ***in (the) course of*** ~ 最后,经过一段时间. ***in the mean*** ~ 在那个时间中; 同时. ***in the nick of*** ~ 正是时候,正在关键时刻. ***in*** ~ ①在恰好的时候,及时,赶上. ②经过一段时间以后; 早晚,总有一天. ③和…合拍 (*with*). ***keep good [bad]*** ~ (钟)准[不准]. ***keep*** ~ 使(脚)合拍子 (*with*). ***kill*** ~ 消磨时间. ***know the*** ~ ***of day*** ①消息灵通,有经验. ②处事机警, 能见机行事. ***lose no*** ~ ***in*** … 赶紧…,立刻…. ***lose*** ~ (钟表)慢; 耽搁. ***make*** ~ ①腾出时间做(某事) (*Could you make* ~ *to type this out?* 你能腾出时间把这个打出来吗?) ②(以某种速度) 进行. ***many a*** ~ ***[***或 ***many*** ~***s]*** 多次, 常常. ***many a*** ~ ***and of*** (或 ***many and many*** ~) 〔诗〕许多次. ***mark*** ~ ①【军】原地踏步. ②(转义)停滞不前, 没有进展. ***near one's*** ~ 快死; (产妇)快生. ***of the*** ~ 当时的〔尤指当今的, 现在的〕. ***on*** ~ 按时, 准时. ***on full*** ~ 全日制的, 专任的. ***on one's own*** ~ 在规定工作时间以外. ***on short*** ~ 开工时间不足, 以部分时间开工. ***once upon a*** ~ 从前〔故事开头用语〕. ***one*** ~ ***with another*** 先后合起来 (*He was president one* ~ *with another for ten years.* 他先后一共当了十年主席). ***out of*** ~ 过迟; 不合时宜; 不合拍的. ***pass the*** ~ ***of day (with sb.)*** (与某人)打招呼(如说"你早"之类). ***play for*** ~ 拖延着以争取时间. ***serve one's*** ~ 做满学徒期间. ***some*** ~ ***or other*** 早晚,迟早. ***take a long*** ~ 费时间. ***So that's the*** ~ ***of day!*** 〔俚〕情况原来如此! (或原来是你耍的花招!) ***straight*** ~ 正规的工作时间(不包括请假或加班等时间). ***take all one's*** ~ 相当麻烦. ***take one's*** ~ ***(in)*** 从容, 慢慢干, 不急. ***take*** ~ 需要时日,费时间. ***talk against*** ~ ①在规定时间内尽快讲完. ②用谈话(讨论)消磨时间(以阻挠议案通过等). ***the good old*** ~***s*** 往昔. ***There are*** ~***s when*** … 有时常会…. ***There is a*** ~ ***for everything.*** 做事要当其时. ***Those were (fine)*** ~***s!*** 好快活的岁月呀! ~ ***about*** 〔Scot.〕轮流. ~ ***after*** ~ = ~ ***and (***~***) again*** 反复,再三再四. ~ ***and a half*** 超过原工资标准一半的加班工资. ~ ***and tide*** 时候. ~ ***enough*** 有充分时间. ***Time hangs heavily on sb.'s hands.*** 某人感到时间过得沉闷. ***Time is money.*** 〔谚〕一寸光阴一寸金. ~ ***is up*** 时间已到. ***(the)*** ~ ***of day*** ①时刻 (*at this* ~ *of day* 这个时候). ②情况, 形势, 事态 (*He knows the* ~ *of day.* 他知道情况). ***(the)*** ~ ***of one's life*** 〔俚〕(不)快活的时候 (*give sb. the* ~ *of his life* 使人快活[痛苦]已极. *have the* ~ *of one's life* 快活 [痛苦] 已极). ~ ***out of mind [***~ ***immemorial]*** 自从很早很早以来; 很久以前. ~ ***to run***【商】扣除日; 经过日数. ~ ***to spare*** 余暇. ~***s out of*** (或 ***without) number*** 数不清的再三再四, 无数次. ***Times Square*** ①(纽约市 Broadway 与 42 号街交叉处的) 纽约时报广场. ②〔美〕纽约方言. ***T- was when*** …. 事情发生在从前…的时候. ***to*** ~〔英〕=〔美〕on ~. ***up to*** ~ 准时. ***watch one's*** ~ 伺机. ***work against*** ~ 以最大的速度工作. ***with*** ~ 随着时间的经过. ~ **alarm** 定时警报. ~ **ball** 报时球. ~ **bargain**【商】期货交易. ~ **base** ①时间坐标;【无】时基, 时轴. ②扫描. ~ **bill** ①〔英〕(火车的)时间表. ②【商】(定)期(付现支)票. ~ **bomb** ①定时炸弹. ②潜在的爆炸性局势. ~ **book** ①出勤记录簿. ②= ~ table. ~**-card** 出勤[工作]时间记录卡片. ~ **capsule** 当代文物史料储放器〔埋藏起来供后人了解当时情况〕. ~ **clock** 生产[出勤]纪录钟;【无】时钟脉冲. ~**-consuming** *a.* 花费大量时间的. ~ **deposit** 定期存款. ~ **difference** 时差. ~ **discount**【商】贴现. ~ **draft**【商】期票. ~**-expired** *a.*【军】满服役期的. ~ **exposure**【摄】时间曝光〔半秒钟以上〕; 时间曝光相片. ~ **fuse** 定时信管 (~-*fuse bomb* 定时炸弹). ~ **gun** 午炮. ~**-honoured** *a.* 自古以来的, 历史悠久的; 久享盛名的. ~ **immemorial** *a.* ①太古的; 久远的. ②【英法】有史以前的〔法令规定为 1189 年, 理查一世统治时为界〕. ~**-interval** 时间(间隔). ~**keeper** 钟表; 工作时间记录员; (运动比赛等

的)计时员 *(a good [bad] ~keeper* 时间准确[不准确]的钟表[人]). ~ **killer** ①消磨时间的人. ②消遣物. ~**lag** (一事和另一事之间的)时间间隔;【物】时滞. ~**-lapse** *a.*【影】微速摄影的[以低速摄影，用正当速度放映,用来显示植物的缓慢生长过程]. ~ **limit** 期限,限期. ~ **loan (money)** 定期贷款. ~ **lock** 定时锁. ~**-out** 休息时间;不算在工作时间内的时间;【运】暂停时间. ~**piece** ①= chronometer. ②钟表. ~**rate** 计时工资制. ~**saving** *a.* 节约时间的. ~**server** 趋炎附势的人. ~**serving** *n., a.* 随波逐流(的),骑墙(的),趋炎附势(的);无节操(的). ~ **sharing**【自】分时,时间分割[划分]. ~ **sheet** = ~-card 作业时间预定表. ~**-shell**【军】曳火弹,空炸炮弹. ~ **signal** 报记录卡片. ~ **signature**【乐】拍子记号. ~ **space** 时空,四维空间. ~ **spirit** 时代精神. ~**table** 时间表. ~**-tested** *a.* 经过时间检验的;为时间所证明了的. ~ **unit** 时间单位;准时器,测时计. ~**work** 计时工作. ~**worn** *a.* 陈旧的. ~ **zone**【天】时区.

time·less [ˈtaimlis] *a.* ①超时间的,无限的,永久的,长期有效的,不定期的,不定时的. ②不是时候的,不合时宜的. **-ly** *ad.*

time·li·ness [ˈtaimlinis] *n.* 合乎时机,适时,及时.

time·ly [ˈtaimli] *a.* **(-li·er; -li·est)** 及时的,适时的,合时的,正好的. ~ *help* 及时的帮助. *a* ~ *joke* 正合时机的笑话.

tim·er [ˈtaimə] *n.* ①时计,跑表. ②记时员. ③定时继电器;程序调节器,定时(延迟)调节器,定时装置,自动定时仪. ④(内燃机的)发火定时器. ⑤(汽车的)时速表. ⑥按时计酬的工人. *a first ~ in the office* 初次到职工作的人. *a half ~* 〔英〕半工半读的学龄儿童. *an old ~* 〔美〕老资格,老手;守旧的人.

time·ous [ˈtaiməs] *a.* 〔Scot.〕= timely.

Times [taimz], ***The*** (英国)泰晤士报. *write to The ~* 给泰晤士报投稿;向报社写信.

tim·id [ˈtimid] *a.* ①胆小的,羞怯的,提心吊胆的. ②〔用作表语〕对…害怕 *(of)*; (对生人)难为情 *(with)*; (对事)缩手缩脚 *(about)*. *Jane is ~ of the bull dog.* 简害怕那条叭喇狗. ***as ~ as a hare*** 胆子极小的. **-ly** *ad.* **-ness** *n.*

ti·mid·i·ty [tiˈmiditi] *n.* 胆小,羞怯. *Wang shows an almost childlike ~ in talking with strangers.* 王和生人谈话简直象小孩子般地羞怯.

tim·ing [ˈtaimiŋ] *n.* ①时间选择. ②定时,校时,计时;调速. ③【自】同步;时限. *The ~ of our statement is very opportune.* 我们发表声明选择的时机很恰当. *pulse ~* 脉冲同步,脉冲计时. *a ~ dial* (收音机的)电眼. *a ~ generator* 定时信号发生器. *~ devices* 定时装置.

ti·moc·ra·cy [taiˈmɔkrəsi] *n.* ①(柏拉图〔Plato〕著作中)荣誉政治. ②(亚里士多德〔Aristotle〕著作中)财权政治. **-crat·ic** [-ˈkrætik] *a.*

Ti·mon [ˈtaimən] *n.* ①泰门〔希腊哲学家〕. ②〔t-〕愤世嫉俗的人.

Timor [ˈtiːmɔː] *n.* 帝汶岛〔马来群岛之一〕.

tim·or·ous [ˈtimərəs] *a.* = timid. *Don't think I'm a ~ teacher who can't control the children.* 不要认为我是个胆子小不敢管小学生的老师. **-ness** *n.*

Tim·o·thy [ˈtiməθi] *n.* 蒂莫西〔男子名〕.

tim·o·thy [ˈtiməθi] *n.*【植】梯牧草,猫尾草.

Ti·m(o)ur [tiˈmuə] *n.* 帖木儿 (= Tamerlane).

tim·pa·no [ˈtimpənəu] *n.* *(pl.* ***-ni*** [-niː]*)*【乐】定音鼓. **-pa·nist** *n.* 鼓手.

tim·pan·ol·o·gy [ˌtimpæˈnɔlədʒi] *n.*【乐】打鼓学.

tin [tin] *n.* ①锡. ②镀锡薄钢板,马口铁,白铁. ③锡器;罐头;(容量)〔英〕一罐[听] (=〔美〕can). ④〔美俚〕警察的徽章;警察. ⑤〔俚〕钱. *stream ~* 砂锡. *wood ~* 纤锡矿,木锡石. *a ~ of biscuits* 一听饼干. — *a.* ①锡制的;马口铁制的. ②无价值的,蹩脚的;假冒的. *a ~ beard* 假胡须. *a little ~ god* 自以为了不起的小人物;小爬虫. — *vt.* ①镀锡,包锡,包白铁. ②〔美〕做成罐头食品. ***not on your ~ type*** 〔美俚〕决不. ***put the ~ hat on*** 结束,制止. ~ **can** ①锡杯,锡罐. ②罐头;洋铁罐. ③〔美俚〕老式汽车. ④〔美海军俚〕小驱逐舰,潜艇,深水炸弹. ~ **hat** 〔军俚〕钢盔;兵. ~**clad** *n.* 〔谑〕装甲舰. ~ **cow** 〔美俚〕罐头牛奶. ~ **ear** 〔美俚〕①聋耳朵;受伤后畸形的耳朵;重听. ②不懂音乐的人,听音乐感. ~ **fish** 〔美俚〕鱼雷. ~ **foil** *n.* ①锡箔,锡纸. ② *vt.* 包上锡箔,用锡纸包. ~ **hat** 钢盔;〔*pl.*〕【海俚】醉鬼. ~**horn** *a., n.* 〔美俚〕不值钱的,吹牛的;无聊人物,浅薄的花花公子,赌金少的赌徒. ~**-lined pipe**【机】衬锡管. ~ **liquor**【化】二氯化锡液. ~ **lizzie** 〔或 L-〕老式汽车;价钱便宜的汽车〔飞机〕. ~**man** *n.* = tinsmith. ~ **opener** 开罐头的刀. ~**pants** 〔美俚〕(石蜡处理过的)防水帆布裤. ~**plate** 马口铁,镀锡铁皮. ~ **pot** ①锡罐,锡壶,马口铁罐. ②镀锡时用的鎔锡器皿. ~**-pot** *a.* 低劣的,微不足道的. ~**smith** 白铁匠. ~ **solder** 锡焊,软焊锡,软焊料. ~**star** 〔美俚〕私家侦探. ~**stone**【矿】锡石. ~**ware** 白铁工艺品 *(hand out the ~ware* 〔美〕道贺;奖赏;褒奖). ~**work** 锡器,白铁制品;〔*pl.*〕锡器厂,白铁制品厂.

Ti·na [ˈtiːnə] *n.* 蒂娜〔女子名〕.

tin·a·mou [ˈtinəmuː] *n.*【鸟】(南美产的)一种鹑科鸟.

tin·cal, tin·kal [ˈtiŋkəl] *n.*【矿】原[粗]硼砂.

tinct. = tincture.

tinct [tiŋkt] *n.* 颜色;色调;染料. — *a.* 着色的,染色的.

tinc·tion [ˈtiŋkʃən] *n.* 着色,染色.

tinc·to·ri·al [tiŋkˈtɔːriəl] *a.* 颜色的,生色的,着色的,染色的. *a ~ pattern* 色样.

tinc·ture [ˈtiŋktʃə] *n.* ①色,色彩;色泽,色调. ②染料,颜料. ③(染上的)色;迹象,气息;气味,特征. ④【徽】(金属、彩色、毛皮等的)颜色. ⑤【医】酊剂,药酒. *a ~ of red* 红的色调. *a ~ of French manners* 法国人的气味. *I'd say he is a man who has the least ~ of learning.* 我认为他是个最没有学术气味的人. *~ of iodine* 碘酒. — *vt.* ①着色,染. ②使有某种风味;使带某种气味[色彩]. *be ~d with prejudice* 带有偏见. *Your cigar ~s the room with an awful smell.* 你吸雪茄烟弄得满屋子都是臭味.

tin·der [ˈtində] *n.* ①火绒,火种,引火物. ②导火线. *burn like ~* 易燃. ~**box** ①火绒箱. ②易燃的物品(建筑,场所). ③脾气暴躁的人. ~ **ore** 羽毛矿.

tin·der·y [ˈtindəri] *a.* 火绒似的,易燃烧的.

tine [tain] *n.* (叉、鹿角等的)尖齿,叉. ~ **test**【医】结核菌素穿刺试验.

tin·e·a [ˈtiniə] *n.*【医】癣.

tined [taind] *a.* 有齿的,有叉的. *a three-~ fork* 三齿叉.

tin·e·id [ˈtiniːid] *n.*【动】谷蛾科 *(Tineidae)* 动物〔包括衣蛾 *(Tinea Pellionella)*〕. — *a.* 谷蛾科的.

ting[1] [tiŋ] *n.* 玎玲声,铃声. — *vt., vi.* (使)玎玲玎玲响.

ting[2] [tiŋ] *n.* = thing[2].

ting-a-ling [ˈtiŋəliŋ] *n., ad.* 铃声;玎玲玎玲地(响).

tinge [tindʒ] *n.* ①(较淡的)色彩,色调. ②迹象,味道,气味. ③微量;少许. —*vt.* ***(ting(e)·ing)*** ①染,着色于. ②使具有某种气味. *This dish has a strong ~ of Chinese cuisine.* 这道菜很有些中国菜的风味. *have a ~ of hypocrisy* 有点伪善气. *There is a slight ~ of humour in it.* 这里边有点幽默气味. *These are words ~d with cynicism.* 这是些有挑毛病气味的字眼. *Now the maple leaves are ~d with autumn red.* 现在枫叶染上了秋天的红色了.

tin·gle [ˈtiŋgl] *n.* ①刺痛;(耳等的)鸣响. ②震颤. ③激动,兴奋. — *vi.* ①(身体因寒冷、打击等)刺痛. ②(耳等)鸣叫. ③震颤,激动,兴奋. *Don't make such a harsh noise. My ears are ~ing.* 别这样刺耳地吵,我都震聋了.

ti·ni·ness [ˈtaininis] *n.* 极小,微小.

tin·kal [ˈtiŋkəl] *n.* = tincal.

tink·er [ˈtiŋkə] *n.* ①〔英〕小炉匠；补锅匠；修补匠；补锅；修补。②拙劣的工人；粗劣的修补。③〔美〕杂活工人，打杂工。④〔苏，爱〕吉卜赛；流浪工人；流浪者；乞丐。⑤小臼炮。⑥〔美〕小鲐鱼。— *vi., vt.* 做补锅匠；拙劣地修补。***have a ~ at …*** 笨拙地设法修理。***not care a ~'s damn [curse, cuss]*** 一点不在乎。***not worth a ~'s cuss (curse, damn)*** 毫无价值。**T- toy** 〔美〕(原商标名)结构玩具〔一套各种形状的零件，儿童可用螺栓等接合零件自由地结合成房屋，车辆等结构〕。**-ly** *a.* 补锅匠似的；粗笨的，拙劣的。

tin·kle [ˈtiŋkl] *n.* ①玎玲(声)。②〔俚〕电话。*give sb. a ~* 给某人打电话。— *vi., vt.* ①(使)玎玲玎玲响。②〔美，儿〕撒尿。*~ a bell* 摇铃。

tin·kler [ˈtiŋklə] *n.* ①玎玲玎玲响的东西〔人〕。②〔俚〕铃铛。**-kling** *a.* 玎玲玎玲响的。

tinned [tind] *a.* ①镀锡的，包锡〔包白铁〕的。②〔英〕罐头的 (=〔美〕canned)。*~ iron [plate]* 白铁皮，马口铁。*~ air* 【海】人工通风。*~ salmon* 罐头鲑鱼。

tin·ner [ˈtinə] *n.* ①白铁匠。②〔英〕罐头商；罐头食品工人。③锡矿矿工。

tin·ner·y [ˈtinəri] *n.* 白铁厂；锡厂；罐头食品厂。

tin·ni·ness [ˈtininis] *n.* ①含锡成分，似锡。②光亮而不值钱；(声音)细弱无力；(文章等)空洞无味。

tinning [ˈtiniŋ] *n.* 锡器〔白铁器皿〕制造(业)；罐头。

tin·ni·tus [tiˈnaitəs] *n.* 【医】耳鸣。

tin·ny [ˈtini] *a.* ***(-ni·er; -ni·est)*** ①锡的，多锡的，含锡的，产锡的。②象锡的；(声音)不响亮的；不耐久的，光亮不值钱的，细弱无力的，空洞无内容的。

tin-pan, tin-pan·ny [tinˈpæn, -i] *a.* 象敲白铁罐那样的，噪音的，嘈杂的。***Tin-Pan Alley*** 〔美俚〕流行歌曲作家和发行人的集中地；〔总称〕流行歌曲作家和发行人；流行歌曲。

tin·sel [ˈtinsəl] *n.* ①(做节日衣饰等、闪闪发光的)金属箔，金属丝；闪亮的装饰。②金银丝织品。③华丽而不值钱的东西，俗丽的东西。— *a.* ①金银丝(箔)制的，闪亮的。②华丽而不值钱的，俗丽的，虚饰的。— *vt.* 用金属箔丝等装饰；装饰得灿烂华丽。**-ly** *a.*

tint [tint] *n.* ①色彩，色调，色泽，色度；着色。②气息，迹象，痕迹。③【物】色辉。④【镌版】线晕〔用平行线表现的阴影〕。⑤【印】淡色，(支票等上用网线构成的)底色。*autumnal ~s* 秋色，金黄色，红叶。*in all ~s of red* 用种种浓淡不同的红色。*red of [with] a blue ~* 带蓝的红色。*crossed [ruled] ~* 网线〔花纹〕版。**flat ~** 制服。— *vt.* 给…着(染)色；作线晕。**~ block** 【印】(印底色用的)底色版。**~less** *a.* 无色的。**~ tool** 刻线刀。**~er** *n.* ①着(染)色者，着(染)色器。②(作衬底的)素色幻灯片。

tin·tin·nab·u·lar, -ula·ry [ˌtintiˈnæbjulə, -ləri] *a.* 玎玲玎玲响的(铃等)，铃似的。**-la·tion** *n.* 玎玲声。

tin·tin·nab·u·lous [ˌtintiˈnæbjuləs] *a.* 玎玲玎玲响的。

tin·tin·nabu·lum [ˌtiŋtiˈnæbjuləm] *n.* ***(pl. -la*** [-lə]***)*** ①铃，(小金属所构成的)响器。②铃声。

tin·tom·e·ter [tinˈtɔmitə] *n.* 【物】色辉计，比色计。

ti·ny [ˈtaini] *a.* ***(-ni·er; -ni·est)*** 极小的。— *n.* ①小孩子。②【医】癣。*little ~* = *~ little* 〔口〕怪小的，小得可怜的。

-tion 〔来自动词的名词后缀〕动作，状态，结果〔*cf.* -ation, -cion, -ion, -sion, -xion〕: addi*tion*, tempta*tion*.

-tious 〔来自 -tion 型名词的形容词后缀〕…的，有…的: ambi*tious*, ficti*tious*.

tip¹ [tip] *n.* ①(塔、手指、尾巴等的)尖，尖端，顶端，末端，梢。②装在末端的东西，加固末端的金属环〔箍〕；鞋尖。③香烟的过滤嘴。④镀金用毛刷。⑤(鸟或飞机的)翼尖(梢)。*a mountain ~* 山顶。— *vt.* ①装尖头。②(用金属箍等)包上尖头。③割去顶梢。④剪(发)。***from ~ to ~*** (张开的翼的)从这一翼尖到那一翼尖。***from ~ to toe*** 彻头彻尾，完完全全。***have at the ~s of one's fingers*** 精通；(在手头)随时可以使用。***on [at] the ~ of one's tongue*** (想说的话)已到舌尖，险些要说出。***~ in*** (装订时)插入图片页。***to the ~s of one's fingers*** 彻底，彻头彻尾。***walk on the ~s of one's toes*** 踮着脚走。

tip² [tip] *vt.* ***(tipped*** [tipt]; ***tip·ping*** [ˈtipiŋ]***)*** ①使倾；翻倒，使倾覆；扔出；推倒(人)。②倒出，倒光，倒掉(沙砾、垃圾等)。③脱(帽)打招呼。— *vi.* 倾斜；翻倒；翻转。*~ the scale(s)* 使天平倾斜；起决定作用，举足轻重；扭转局势；占优势。*He got so angry that he ~ped the table up.* 他气得把桌子推翻了。*Don't ~ your tea into the saucer.* 不要把茶倒进茶碟里。*The ship ~ped over at 10 a.m.* 船是上午十时翻的。—*n.* ①倾斜。②(垃圾等的)弃置场。*The lamp post has a slight ~ to the west.* 灯杆稍微有点向西歪。**~ off** 倒出；〔俚、方〕死；杀死。**~ out** 倒光；翻倒；(被)扔出；〔俚、方〕死。**~ over** ①翻倒。②〔美俚〕死。③〔美俚〕抢劫，搜查。**~ over the perch** 〔美俚〕死。**~ up** 倾，歪，翻倒。**~-box** 倾卸箱。**~car, ~cart, ~lorry** 自动卸货车，倾倒车。

tip³ [tip] *vi.* ①给小费。②〔口〕(赌博等)暗通消息。— *vt.* ①轻触，轻击。②给(小费)，赏(酒钱)。③〔口〕暗中通知，秘密报知，提醒。*Don't ~ freely.* 不要乱给小费。*T- us a signal, if you can.* 有可能时，给我们个信号。*T- us a song.*〔口〕唱一个歌给我们听听吧。*~ fives* 〔美〕握手。*~ grand* 〔美〕跑；溜掉。*~ one* 〔美〕干一杯(酒)。*~ one's mitt* 〔美〕握手；泄漏自己的计划。— *n.* ①轻击；【棒球】擦球(立即往垒上跑)。②赏钱，酒钱，小费。③暗示；(行情等的)秘密消息，特别消息，预测。④妙法，秘诀；警告。*the straight ~* 可靠的秘密消息。*Take my ~.* 照我的话去做。*the ~ for extracting grease-spots* 去油迹的秘诀。***get the ~ to*** 接到关于怎样做某事的秘密通知。***give the ~ to*** 暗中关照去做某事。***miss one's ~*** 〔口〕打错主意，失策。**~ off** 〔俚〕忠告，警告，提醒，给…递点子。**~ sb. the wink** (向某人)使眼色。**~-and-ran** ①*n.* 【棒球】碰球立即前跑。②*a.* 碰球立即前跑的，打了就跑的 (*a ~-and-run raid* 打了就跑)。**~ sheet** (股票等的)内情通报。

tip-off [ˈtipɔ(:)f] *n.* ①警告。②预先告诉的消息，暗示。③(篮球赛开始时的)跳球。

tip·pet [ˈtipit] *n.* ①(女用)斗篷；披肩。②(法官、教士的)无袖罩裳。

tip·ple¹ [ˈtipl] *vt.* 一点点地喝(烈酒)，品(酒)。— *vi.* 饮烈酒，酗酒。— *n.* 酒，〔尤指致醉的〕烈酒。**-pler** *n.* 饮烈酒者；酒徒。

tipple² [ˈtipl] *n.* ①〔美〕倒煤场，筛煤场(等)。②翻斗机；自动倾卸装置；翻锭机。

tip·py¹ [ˈtipi] *a.* ①毛尖多的(茶)。②〔美口〕易歪向一边的，易倾斜的，摇晃的。

tip·py² [ˈtipi] *a.* 易倾斜的，倾斜的；摇摇晃晃的。

tip·py-toe, tip·py·toe [ˈtipiˌtəu] *n., vi., a., ad.* 〔口〕= tiptoe.

tip·si·fy [ˈtipsifai] *vt.* 使喝醉。

tip·staff [ˈtipstɑ:f] *n.* ***(pl. -staves*** [-teivz], ***~s)*** ①铁头杖。②随身携带铁头杖行走的人〔巡警等〕。

tip·ster [ˈtipstə] *n.* 〔口〕提供(赛马等)消息〔内情、行情〕的人。*a ~ sheet* 〔美〕由华尔街透露出来的秘密消息。

tip·sy [ˈtipsi] *a.* ***(-si·er; -si·est)*** ①喝醉了的；微醉的。②摇摇晃晃的，步履不稳的。③东歪西倒的。*a ~ lurch* 摇摇晃晃的步伐。*On my day off, I'll fix the ~ fence.* 我歇班那天就修理歪了的篱笆。**~ cake** (浸葡萄酒的)醉蛋糕，醉饼。**-i·ly** *ad.* **-i·ness** *n.*

tip·toe [ˈtiptəu] *n.* 脚尖。*Your cap is on the table, Tom. Stand on ~ and get it.* 你的帽子在桌子上，汤姆，踮起脚来够它吧。*Don't make any noise. Steal a ~ to the door.* 别作声，踮着脚儿走到门口那儿。***be on the ~ of expectation*** 伸长脖子〔殷切〕等待，翘首而望。***be on ~ of excitement*** 非常兴奋。***on ~*** 踮着脚(站立、走路等)；小心地，蹑手蹑脚地；悄悄地；伸长脖子。— *a.* 踮着脚走〔站着〕的；殷切

期待的;偷偷摸摸的,蹑手蹑脚的. — *ad.* 踮着脚;翘首盼望着;蹑手蹑脚地;悄悄,偷偷. — *vi.* 踮着脚(走),蹑手蹑脚地行进.

tip·top [ˈtipˈtɔp] *n.* ①绝顶. ②〔口〕极上,最上,极盛. — *a.* ①绝顶的. ②〔口〕极上的,极好的,头等的. ③有趣的. — *ad.* 非常,极,至高无上.

ti·rade [taiˈreid, tiˈrɑːd] *n.* ①长篇议论[攻击](等),激烈言论,激烈演说. ②长文,长诗. ③【乐】全音阶的插入音.

ti·rail·leur [ˌtiraiˈləː] *n.* 〔F.〕【军】散兵;狙击兵.

Ti·ra·na, Ti·ra·në [tiˈrɑːnə] *n.* 地拉那[阿尔巴尼亚首都].

tire[1] [ˈtaiə] *vi.* 疲倦,累 *(with)*; 厌倦 *(of)*. — *vt.* 使疲倦;使厌倦. *Walking soon ~s me.* 我一走路就累. *She never ~s of speaking English.* 她讲起英语来从不厌倦. ~ **down** 把…追赶到跑不动;使疲备到精疲力尽;逐渐微弱. ~ **out** = ~ **to death** 使疲倦到极度 (*I am ~d out.* 我累得要死,十分疲倦).

tire[2], **tyre** [ˈtaiə] *n.* 轮箍;轮胎. *a pneumatic* ~ 橡皮轮胎. ~ *chain* 轮胎防滑链. — *vt.* 装轮胎.

tire[3] [taiə] *n.* ①〔古〕(女用)头装,头饰. ②衣装. ③〔美〕围裙. —*vt.* 〔古〕打扮,装饰. ②梳头.

tired [ˈtaiəd] *a.* ①疲乏,累 *(with)*; (对…感到)厌倦 *(of)*. ②〔口语〕生气. ③破旧的,陈腐的. *be [get] ~ with walking [reading]* 走路[读书]累了. *be ~ out.* 累得要死,累极了. ***I'll take turns with you at the wheel, when you get ~.*** 你要是累了,我来替你换着开车. *be ~ of the same food every day* 每天吃同样的东西吃腻味了. *get ~ from long overwork* 长期过分劳动后感到疲倦. ~ ***as a dog*** 〔美〕累极了. **T- Tim = T- Timothy** 懒鬼,懒虫. **-ness** *n.*

tire·less[1] [ˈtaiəlis] *a.* 不疲倦的;不累的;孜孜不倦的;不屈不挠的,坚忍的. **-ly** *ad.*

tire·less[2] [ˈtaiəlis] *a.* 无轮箍[轮胎]的.

Ti·re·si·as [taiəˈriːsiæs] *n.* 【希神】蒂利希阿斯[因看智慧女神洗澡而致双目失明的、懂鸟语的底庇斯卜卦者].

tire·some [ˈtaiəsəm] *a.* 令人厌倦[生厌]的,沉闷的,没趣的;麻烦的,讨厌的. *How ~! I have left my watch behind.* 真讨厌! 我忘了带表了. *Nobody likes to attend the ~ lecture.* 谁也不愿意上那个令人生倦的课.

tire·wom·an [ˈtaiəwumən] *n.* 〔古〕伺候穿衣的侍女;(剧场的)女服装员.

tir·ing [ˈtaiəriŋ] *a.* 使人疲倦[厌倦]的; 麻烦的. ~ **house** (剧院的)化装间. ~ **room** (戏院的)剧装室,化妆室.

tiro [ˈtaiərəu] *n.* *(pl. ~s)* = tyro.

ti·ro·cin·ium [ˌtaiərəuˈsiniəm] *n.* *(pl.* ***ti·ro·cin·i·a*** [ˌtaiərəuˈsiniə]*)* ①学徒期限,学徒身分. ②技艺入门.

TIROS = television infrared observation satellite 电视红外线观察卫星.

Ti·ros [ˈtairəus] *n.* 电视红外线观测卫星,泰罗斯卫星 (= television infrared observation satellite).

tir·ra·lir·ra [ˈtirəˌlirə] *n., ad.* 云雀叫声;快活地.

T.I.S. = Technical Information Service 〔美〕技术情报服务处.

'tis [tiz] 〔诗、方〕 = it is.

ti·sane [tiˈzæn; *F.* tiˈzan] *n.* = ptisan.

Tish·ah b'Ab [tiːˈʃɑːbəˈɑːv, ˈtiʃəˌbɔːv] (为纪念犹太圣殿被毁的)犹太斋戒日[即犹太历五月九日].

Tish·ri [tiʃˈriː, ˈtiʃriː] *n.* 〔Heb.〕(犹太历)元月.

tis·sue [ˈtisjuː] *n.* ①薄绢,薄纱罗(等织物). ②薄纸,棉纸 = ~-paper. ③(编造的谎话等的)一套,一连串. ④【摄】碳素印象纸. ⑤【生】组织. *toilet* ~ 手纸,卫生纸. *the muscular* ~ 肌肉组织. *the nervous* ~ 神经组织. ~ **culture**【医】组织培养;培养出来的组织. ~ **paper** 薄绉纸,纱纸.

tit[1] [tit] *n.* ①【鸟】山雀. ②〔古〕小马,瘦马. ③〔古、蔑〕小丫头.

tit[2] [tit] *n.* 奶头.

tit[3] [tit] *n.* 轻打. ~ ***for tat*** 一报还一报;用同一方式报复;针锋相对. *give [pay] ~ for fat* 针锋相对. *a ~-for-tat struggle* 针锋相对的斗争.

tit. = title.

Ti·tan [ˈtaitən] *n.* *(fem.* ***-ess*** [taitənis]*)* ①【希神】泰坦巨人族〔*Uranus* (= heaven) 和 *Gaea* (= earth) 的子女们〕之一;〔~ or t-〕巨人. ②力大无比的人;(学界、政界等的)巨头. ③【军】大力神导弹. ④〔诗〕日神. *a ~ crane* (自动)巨型起重机. *the weary ~* 老大帝国〔如英国〕.

ti·tan·ate [ˈtaitəneit] *n.* 【化】钛酸盐,钛酸脂.

Ti·tan·ic [taiˈtænik] *a.* ①【希神】泰坦巨人族的. ②〔常作 t-〕巨大的,力大无比的;伟大的.

ti·tanic [taiˈtænik] *n.* 【化】钛的,得自钛的.

ti·tan·if·er·ous [ˌtaitnˈifərəs] *a.* 含钛的.

Ti·tan·ism [ˈtaitnizəm] *n.* 〔也作 t-〕泰坦精神;(对社会习俗等方面的)造反精神.

ti·ta·nite [ˈtaitˌnait] *n.* 【化】木屑石 (= sphene).

ti·ta·ni·um [taiˈteinjəm, ti-] *n.* 【化】钛 (Ti). ~ *dioxide [white]* 二氧化钛 (= titanic oxide).

titan·o·saur [ˈtaitənəsɔː], **Ti·tan·o·sau·rus** [ˌtaitənəˈsɔːrəs] *n.* 【古生】(南美白垩纪的)雷龙.

ti·tan·ous [taiˈtænəs, ti-; ˈtaitnəs] *a.* 【化】三价钛的,亚钛的.

tit·bit [ˈtitbit] *n.* (好吃的东西的)一口,少量;有趣的新闻,珍闻.

ti·ter [ˈtaitə] *n.* ①【化】滴定量;滴定(浓)度,滴定率;效价;脂酸冻点(测定). ②【纺】纤度.

tith·a·ble [ˈtaiðəbl] *a.* 可征收什一税的;应缴什一税的.

tithe [taið] *n.* ①(以产品缴纳的)什一税;〔常 *pl.*〕十分之一的教区税. ②十分之一;小部分;一点点. *great [coarse, large] ~* 主要收获的什一税〔小麦、干草、柴、水果等〕. *mixed ~s* 农产物的什一税〔乳酪、牛奶、小家畜等的十分之一〕. *personal [predial] ~s* 个人劳动所得〔土地收益〕的什一税. *I don't know a ~ of it.* 我一点儿不知道. — *vt.* 向…征收[缴纳]什一税. — *vi.* 缴纳什一税. ~ **barn** 储放什一税农产品的仓库. ~ **pig** 作为什一税缴纳的猪.

tith·er [ˈtaiθə] *n.* (= tithe).

tith·ing [ˈtaiðiŋ] *n.* ①(征收)什一税. ②【英古法】(负联保责任的)十户,十人. ③(英国部分地区仍保持的行政单位)十户区.

Ti·tho·nus [tiˈθəunəs] *n.* 【希神】蒂索诺斯[为特洛伊王子,受曙光女神之宠,并许以永远不死,但事被女神遗忘,终于日见衰老,最后化为蝉].

ti·ti [tiˈtiː] *n.* 【动】①狨(绢毛猴) *(callithrix jacchus)* 〔产于巴西和玻利维亚〕. ②伶猴属 *(Callicebus)* 动物〔产于南美〕.

ti·tian [ˈtiʃiən, ˈtiʃən] *n.* (妇女头发的)金黄色,赤黄色;〔美〕红发女.

tit·il·late [ˈtitileit] *vt.* ①呵痒. ②使高兴,使兴奋,使兴趣、想象等活跃. *Scientific stories ~ the fancy of the school boys.* 科学故事使小学生们的想象力活跃起来. *The news ~d the curiosity of the public.* 这桩新闻引起了群众的好奇心. **-la·tion** [ˌtitiˈleiʃən] *n.* **-tive** *a.* **-r** *n.*

tit·(t)i·vate [ˈtitiveit] *vt., vi.* 〔口〕打扮,妆饰. **-tion** [ˌtitiˈveiʃən] *n.*

tit·lark [ˈtitlɑːk] *n.* 【鸟】鹨(属)〔如水鹨,草地鹨等〕.

ti·tle [ˈtaitl] *n.* ①(书籍、诗歌、乐曲等的)标题,题目,题;篇名,书名. ②(书的)标题页,扉页. ③【影】字幕. ④称号;尊称,头衔,爵位,学位. ⑤权利,资格. ⑥【法】土地财产所有权;地契. ⑦【运】冠军,锦标. ⑧(用 carat 表示的)金子的纯度[成色]. ⑨【宗】圣职就任资格;(天主教的)教区及该教区内的教堂. *a man of ~* 有头衔的人,贵族. *The Party Committee conferred the ~ of Advanced*

Worker on Comrade Wang. 党委授予王同志以先进工作者的称号。*Li said he would give a good ~ to his new book.* 李说他要给他的新书起个好书名。*His services give him a ~ to our gratitude.* 他工作勤恳,有资格受到我们的感谢。*He has many ~s to distinction.* 他有好多资格使他知名。*quiet ~*【法】判决产权属谁。*regal ~* 王的称号。*Has Jones any ~ to the land?* 琼斯有这块土地的产权吗? — *vt.* ①加标题于;【影】附加字幕。②授头衔〔爵位等〕。③用头衔〔尊称〕称呼。~ **deed**【法】地契。**~-holder** 选手权保持者,(冠军)称号保持者。~ **match** 锦标赛。~ **page** 书名页,扉页,里封面。**~-part** = ~ **rôle**【剧】(名字作为剧名的)剧名角色,片名角色。**-d** *a.* 有爵位的,有贵族头衔的。

ti·tler [ˈtaitlə] *n.*【影】字幕编写员。

tit·ling[1] [ˈtitliŋ] *n.* = titlark; = titmouse ①.

ti·tling[2] [ˈtaitliŋ] *n.* 书脊烫金;烫在书脊上的标题;烫金工序。

ti·tlist [ˈtaitlist] *n.* 冠军称号保持者。

tit·mouse [ˈtitmaus] *n.* *(pl. **-mice** [-mais])* ①【鸟】山雀(属);银喉长尾山雀;花雀。②小气鬼。③小东西;小男孩,小女孩。*tufted ~* 黑额冠山雀。

titrant [ˈtaitrænt] *n.*【化】滴定剂,滴定标准液。

ti·trate [ˈtaitreit] *vt.*【化】滴定(法)。

ti·tra·tion [ˈtaitreiʃən] *n.*【化】滴定(法)。

titre [ˈtaitə] *n.* = titer.

tit-tat-toe [ˌtittætˈtəu] *n.* = tick-tack-toe.

tit·ter [ˈtitə] *n.* ①嗤嗤地笑,傻笑;窃笑。②〔美〕(不懂事的)小姑娘。— *vi.* 噗哧一笑,吃吃地窃笑。

tit·tie [ˈtiti:] *n.* 〔苏格兰〕姐妹(= titty).

titti·vate [ˈtitiveit] *v.* = titivate.

tit·tle [ˈtitl] *n.* ①一点点。②文字上的小点,小符号。*I don't care one jot or one ~ of what he says.* 他所说的我一点也不在乎。***to a ~*** 准确地,一笔不苟地,丝毫不差地。— *vi.* 闲谈,杂谈;讲闲话。**~-tattle** *n.* 荒唐话,无聊闲谈,杂谈。

tit·tup [ˈtitʌp] *n.* ①活泼的动作〔举止〕。②轻佻的行为。③(马等的)慢跑。④(船等的)摇摆;不稳重。— *vi.* ①举动活泼;跳跳蹦蹦 *(along)*。②(马)缓跑,小跑。③(船等)摇摆。④【海俚】掷钱赌酒。*The children ~ed all day on the beach.* 小孩子们在海滩上跳跳蹦蹦了一整天。

tit·tup·py [ˈtitəpi] *a.* 愉快的,活泼的;轻佻的;摇摆的。

tit·ty [ˈtiti] *n.* *(pl. **-ties**)* 〔废,俚〕奶头,乳房。

tit·u·ba·tion [ˌtitjuˈbeiʃən] *n.* 摇摇晃晃, 蹒跚(步行)。

tit·u·lar [ˈtitjulə] *a.* ①享有所有权的,有正当权利的,有资格的。②名义上的,挂名的,有名无实的。③(有)头衔〔称号、尊称〕的。④标题的,被用做题名的。*O'Connor gave up his ~ possessions and conducted business in America.* 欧康纳放弃了他有权得到的财产而去美国经商。*a ~ distinction* 头衔显赫。*a ~ rank* 爵位。*a ~ character* (名字作为作品题名的)主题人物。— *n.* ①有头衔〔官阶、称号〕的人。②只有名义的人,挂名的人。③= ~ saint (以其名为教堂名的)教堂的主保圣徒。**-ly** *ad.* 名义上,有名无实地;头衔上,标题上。

titu·la·ry [ˈtitjuləri] *a., n.* = titular.

Ti·tus [ˈtaitəs] *n.* 泰特斯〔男子名〕。

Tiu [ˈti:u:] *n.* 蒂尤〔日耳曼神话中司天空与战争的神〕。

T.I.V. = thermal-insulating value 绝热值,热隔绝值。

tiz·zy [ˈtizi] *n.* ①〔英俚〕六辨士。②〔俚〕战栗;极度兴奋狂乱的心境〔尤指对于小事〕。

T.J. = turbo jet 涡轮喷气发动机。

TK = tank.

TKO = technical knockout (拳击中的)技术性击倒〔被击倒〕。

Tl =【化】thallium.

tlac [tla:k] 〔美俚〕钱。

Tlin·git [ˈtliŋgit] *n.* ①*(pl. **Tlin·gits, Tlin·git**)* 特里吉特人〔阿拉斯加南部和英属哥仑比亚北部沿海地区以航海为职业的美洲印第安人〕。②特里吉特语。

T.L.O., TLO. = total loss only【商】(保险业)仅负完全损失之责。

TM = ①trademark 商标。②tactical missile 战术导弹。③training manual 〔美〕训练手册。④trench mortar 迫击炮。

T.M. = twist multiplier【纺】粘(度)系数。

Tm =【化】thulium.

T-man [ˈti:mæn] *n.* *(pl. **-men**)* 〔口〕美国财政部特派员。

tme·sis [ˈtmi:sis] *n.*【语法】分割法,(为要插入他一词时)复合词分割法: whatsoever → *what* place *soever;* absolutely → *abso*-blooming-*lutely;* Yourselves → *your* good *selves.*

T.M.O. = telegraph money order 电汇。

TMV = tobacco mosaic virus 烟草花叶病毒。

T.N. = true north.

Tn =【化】thoron; train.

tn = ton.

tns = tons.

TNT, T.N.T. [ˈti:enˈti:] *n.* ①【军】梯恩梯,茶褐药: *TNT* equivalence 梯恩梯当量。②trinitrotoluene 梯恩梯炸药。

T.O. = ①technical order 技术说明。②Telegraph Office 电报局。③Transport Officer 运输军官。④turn over 见背面。

T/O = Tables of Organization 〔美〕编制表。

to 〔在句的末尾强 tu:; 元音前弱 tu; 辅音前弱 tə〕 *prep.* ①〔运动的方向〕向,到,去 *(opp.* from*)*. *turn ~ the left* 向左转。*from east ~ west* 由东到西。*get ~ London* 到达伦敦。*have been ~ ...* 去过,到过,到…回来。*To arms!* 取武器! *To horse!* 上马! ②〔状态的变化〕向,到。*change [go, turn] from bad ~ worse* 日益恶化。*reclaim a lost child ~ virtue* 挽救一个误入歧途的儿童回到正道上来。*stand ~ attention* 采取立正姿势。*put ~ death* 处死。③〔范围、程度〕到,达到;…到,…得。*from six ~ nine* 六到九。*This apple is rotten ~ the core.* 这个苹果烂透心了。*an Englishman ~ the core* 一个道地的英国人。*The room was hot ~ suffocation.* 房间热得闷人。*~ the best of my ability* 尽我可能。*~ his name be it said* (虽说是敌人然而)真是名不虚传。*~ a certain degree [extent]* 在某种程度上。④〔时间〕到;缺(…分)。*~ this day* 到今天。*from six ~ nine* 六点到九点。*a quarter ~ nine* 九点差一刻。⑤〔目的〕为。*~ that end* 为那个目的。*come ~ the rescue* 来援救。*He was brought up ~ joinery.* 被训练成细木工。*drink ~ sb.'s health* 为某人的健康干杯。⑥〔比较〕和…比较,和…比起来;比;对;每,一。*This is nothing ~ that.* 和那个比起来这不算什么。*The score was 4 ~ 1.* 比分是四比一。*ten ~ one* 十对一;什九。*He is far superior ~ me* 他比我高明得多。*four shillings ~ the pound* 四先令一镑。⑦依后面名词和前面动词而表示: (a)〔结果〕…的结果…,…的是。*He was flattered ~ his ruin.* 他由于受人吹捧,结果是一败涂地。*~ no purpose* 徒然,白白。(b)〔对立〕对。*face ~ face* 面对面。*fight hand ~ hand* 肉搏。(c)〔适合、协调〕按,应,合。*boots made ~ any foot* 做得谁都合穿的靴子。*quite ~ my taste* 很合我的脾胃。(d)〔随伴〕跟着;配合。*sing ~ the piano* 跟着钢琴唱。(e)〔接触〕在。*hold ~ one's heart* 抱在怀里。(f)〔附加〕在,加在。*add ~ ...* 加在。*That's all there is ~ it.* 那件事情不过如此罢了。*There's nothing ~ him.* 他不过是那样一个人罢了。*Wisdom he has, and ~ his wisdom, courage.* 他聪明,不但聪明,而且勇敢。(g)〔所属〕的。*porch ~ the house* 那房子的门廊。(h)〔古〕作为 (= as). *He took her ~ wife* 他娶她为妻。*call ~ witness* 传来作证人。(i)〔在 confess, swear, testify, witness 等动词的后面时〕是…,承认。*confess ~ crime* 承认犯罪。*He* *swore* ~ *the miracle* 他发誓说这是奇迹. (j)〔选择〕而不. *prefer death* ~ *surrender* 宁死不降. ⑧〔表示接受动作的人或物〕: *Give this book* ~ *him.* 把这本书给他. *do harm* ~ *sb.* 损害某人. *drink* ~ *him* 给他干杯, 敬他一杯. *keep [have, get] the room* ~ *oneself* 独用房间. ⑨〔构成动词不定式〕: *To err is human.* 过失为人之常〔用作名词〕. *a house* ~ *let* 出租的房子〔用作定语〕. *I have come* ~ *see you.* 我来看你〔用作状语〕. ★ 在知觉动词 (see, hear, feel 等), 使役动词 (let, make, have) 及 please, help 等后不定式 to 常略去(美语即使在其他动词后的 to 也常略去), 但在被动结构中则不略去: *She helped me (~) compile the dictionary. I saw him run. He was seen* ~ *run.* ⑩〔方、美〕= at. *You can get this article* ~ *Brown's.* 这个东西可以在布朗商店买到. ⑪ *T- you.*〔古〕知道了. ⑫作为不定式的代用词: *We didn't want to go but we had* ~. 我们不想去, 但我们不得不去〔此处 to 代替 to go〕. — [tu:] *ad.* 到某种状态;〔特指〕到停止状态; 关闭. ★ 也常和动词结合, 略去其后宾语, 而构成成语: *The door is* ~. 门关着. *push [shut] the door* ~ 把门关上. ***bring sb.*** ~ 使苏醒. ***bring** (a ship)* ~ 命令(停船). ***come*** ~ *(oneself)* 苏醒. ***fall*** ~ 开始; 开始吃; 开始攻击敌人. ***go*** ~〔古〕喂喂; 别胡说! ***heave*** ~ 停船.

toad [təud] *n.* ①【动】蟾蜍, 癞蛤蟆. ②讨厌的家伙;〔古、谑〕家伙, 小家伙〔常作小孩的爱称〕. ***eat sb.'s ~s*** 拍某人的马屁. ***the biggest ~ in the puddle*** (在政治方面或其他集团中)众所公认的头子, 要人. ~ ***under a harrow*** 受压迫〔迫害〕的人. ~ **eater** 谄媚者, 拍马者. ~ **eating** 谄媚, 奉承, 拍马屁. ~ **fish**【鱼】蟾鱼科的鱼; 河豚. ~ **flax**【植】柳穿鱼(属). **~-in-the-hole** (裹有湿面的)烤牛排. ~ **skin**〔美〕钞票. ~ **spit,** ~ **spittle** = cuckoospit. ~ **stabber, ~-sticker**〔美〕小刀. ~ **stone**【地】蟾蜍岩; 玄武斑岩. ~ **stool**【植】伞菌科菌, 牛肝菌科菌; (尤指)毒菌.

toad·y [ˈtəudi] *n.* 拍马屁的人. — *vt., vi.* 奉承, 拍马屁. **-ism** 谄媚, 奉承, 拍马屁.

to-and-fro [ˈtu(:)-ənd-ˈfrəu] *a.* 往复的, 走来走去的; 来回的; 动摇的. — *n. (pl. tos-and-fros)* 走来走去, 来回, 往复; 交互运动, 波动, 动摇. — *ad.* 往复地, 来回.

toast¹ [təust] *n.* 烤面包片. *buttered [dry]* ~ 涂有〔不涂〕奶油的烤面包. ~ *and water* = ~-water. ***as warm as a*** ~〔口〕暖烘烘, 很暖. — *vt., vi.* ①烘烤(面包片等). ②〔口〕烤暖(脚等), 烤火. ~ *oneself (before the fire)* 烤火. ~ **rack** (餐桌上可放几片烤面包片的)面包架. ~ **water** 泡过烤面包片的水〔病人喝的清凉饮料〕. **~-wich**〔美〕夹肉烤面包片.

toast² [təust] *n.* ①祝酒, 干杯; 祝酒词. ②被举杯祝贺的人〔物; 女人〕. ③有名的人. *The* ~ *was duly drunk.* 宾主照例祝酒干杯. ***have sb. on*** ~〔俚〕自由摆布某人, 欺骗某人, 愚弄某人. ***propose a*** ~ 建议举杯祝酒. ***propose the*** ~ ***of*** 建议为…干杯. — *vt., vi.* 祝(…健康)干杯, 敬…一杯. ~ *the poet* 敬诗人一杯. ~ **list** 祝酒名单. ~ **master** (宴会上)讲祝酒词的人, 宴会的主持人. ~ **mistress** 宴会的女主持人. **~ee** *n.* 被祝酒的人.

toaster¹ [ˈtəustə] *n.* 烤面包片器〔小电炉〕.

toaster² [ˈtəustə] *n.* 祝酒者; 致祝酒词的人; 奉承女人的人.

toast·y [ˈtəusti] *a.* ***(toast·i·er, toast·iest)*** ①祝酒的. ②温暖, 舒畅, 舒适的.

Tob. = Tobias; Tobit.

to·bac·co [təˈbækəu] *n.* ***(pl.*** *~s,* ***~es)***【植】烟草; 烟叶; 烟丝, 卷烟, 纸烟, 嚼烟. *flue-cured* ~ 烤烟. *sun-cured* ~ 晒烟. *smoking* ~ 板丝烟. ***T- Road***〔美〕南部种植烟草的地区. ~ **cutter** 切烟机, 切烟人. ~ **heart**【医】烟毒性心脏(病). ~ **pipe** 烟斗, 烟管. ~ **plant**【植】烟草. ~ **pouch** 烟丝袋. ~ **worm, moth**【动】烟草天蛾. **-nize** *vt., vi.* 用烟叶熏; 抽烟卷.

to·bac·co·nist [təˈbækənist] 烟草商(店); 香烟〔烟丝〕制造人;〔废〕抽烟的人.

to-be [təˈbi:] *a.*〔常用在名词后面〕未来的. *His father-in-law* ~ 他的未来的岳父. — *n.*〔the-〕*Some people only think of the* ~. 有些人总是为未来的事设想.

To·bi·as [təˈbaiəs] *n.* 托拜厄斯〔男子名〕.

to·bin [ˈtəubin] *n.* 托宾式室内通风机***(= ~'s tube, ~'s ventilator).***

To·bit [ˈtəubit]【宗】托比特书〔《旧约》外经之一〕.

to·bog·gan [təˈbɔgən] *n.* 平底雪橇; 突然下降〔跌价〕. — *vi.* 坐平底雪橇滑下山坡; (股票等)突然跌价, 猛跌. ~ **shoot,** ~ **slide** 平底雪橇滑行场. **-er, -ist** 坐平底雪橇的人.

To·bruk' Tu·bruq [ˈtəubruk] *n.* 图卜鲁格〔利比亚港市〕.

To·by [ˈtəubi] *n.* 托比〔男子名, 女子名, Tobias 的昵称〕.

T-jug = toby①.

to·by [ˈtəubi] *n.* ①胖老人形啤酒杯 (= Toby jug). ②〔美卑〕下等雪茄烟. ~ **collar** 有褶宽领.

toc·ca·ta [təˈkɑ:tə] *n.* 〔It.〕【乐】托卡塔曲〔表现键盘乐器演奏者技巧的即兴曲〕.

To·char·i·an, To·khar·i·an [təuˈkɛəriən, -ˈkær-, -ˈkɑ:r-] *n.* ①吐火罗人〔约在公元1000年前住在中亚〕. ②吐火罗语〔现已绝灭的一种印欧语, 包括两大方言, 最早的记载见纪元前七世纪的文件中〕. — *a.* 吐火罗的, 吐火罗语的.

toch·er [ˈtɔxə] *n.*〔Scot.〕嫁妆.

tochka [ˈtɔtʃkɑ:] *n.*〔Russ.〕小地堡, 火力点.

to·co, to·ko [ˈtəukəu] *n.*〔英俚〕责打, 惩罚; 痛苦. *catch [get]* ~ 挨打, 受罚.

to·col·o·gist [təuˈkɔlədʒist] *n.*【医】产科学者, 产科医师.

to·col·o·gy [təuˈkɔlədʒi] *n.*【医】产科学.

to·copher·ol [təuˈkɔfərəul] *n.*【生化】生育酚; 抗不育维生素, 维生素 E.

toc·sin [ˈtɔksin] *n.* 警钟; 警报, 警戒信号.

tod [tɔd] *n.* ①〔Scot.〕狐; 狡猾的人. ②〔古〕树丛, 薮; (尤指常春藤叶的)繁茂处. ③【纺】托德〔羊毛重量单位, 通常为 28 磅〕.

to·day, to-day [təˈdei, tuˈdei] — *n.* 今日, 今天; 现代, 现今, 当代. *science of* ~ 现代科学. *the writers of* ~ 现代作家. *~s and yesterdays* 现在和过去. — *ad.* 在今天; 现代, 现今, 当代. *a week ago* ~ 上一个星期的今天. ~ *week [a week* ~*]*. 下星期的今天.

Todd [tɔd] *n.* 托德〔姓氏, 男子名〕.

tod·dle [ˈtɔdl] *vi.* (刚学走的小孩子等)蹒跚;〔谑〕散步; 闲荡;〔美〕跳舞. — *n.* 晃晃荡荡的步子;〔口〕一瘸一瘸走路的小孩; 散步. *We must be toddling.* 我们要走了.

dot·dler [ˈtɔdlə] *n.* 晃晃荡荡走路的人, 晃晃荡荡走路的小孩;〔谑〕散步的人.

tod·dy [ˈtɔdi] *n.* 棕榈汁〔酒〕; 威士忌〔白兰地等〕; 热饮料〔加柠檬、砂糖用开水调成的甜酒〕.

to-do [təˈdu:, tuˈdu:] *n.* ***(pl.*** *~s****)***〔口〕吵闹, 骚扰; 混乱. *make a terrible* ~ *about losing sb.'s luggage* 因某人丢了行李而闹得天翻地覆.

to·dy [ˈtəudi] *n.*【鸟】(西印度)翡翠.

toe [təu] *n.* 脚趾, 脚尖;〔口〕脚; (鞋、袜等的)尖; 蹄尖; 蹄铁尖; 工具的尖端;【高尔夫球】球棒尖; (铁轨的)轨端;【建】坡脚; (木工的)斜钉;【机】轴踵. *the big [great]* ~ (脚的)拇趾. *the little* ~ (脚的)小趾. *the light fantastic* ~〔谑〕跳舞. ***on one's ~s***〔喻〕精神振作, 活跃; 机警; 热心; 在活动(*This job kept John on his ~s.* 这工作使约翰忙个不停). ***toast one's ~s***〔口〕烘脚.〔美〕~ ***and heel (it)*** 跳舞. ***~s up***〔俚〕死. ~ ***to*** ~〔美拳〕旗鼓相当地. ***tread [step] on sb.'s ~s*** 踩某人的脚尖; 得罪某人. ***turn one's ~s in [out]*** 脚尖朝内〔外〕

走路. ***turn up one's ~s*** 〔俚〕死. — *vt.* 用脚趾踩,用脚趾钩;装[修补]鞋尖[袜尖等];用脚尖踢;【高尔夫球】用棒尖打(球);【木工】斜钉(钉子). — *vi.* 动脚尖;脚尖朝…(方面). ~ *sb. out of the room* 将某人踢出房外. ***~ in [out]*** 脚尖朝内[外]走路. ~ ***the line [mark, scratch]*** (赛跑等时)将脚尖抵在起步线上站着;服从规定[政纲],服从命令. ~ ***the line of*** 和…一鼻孔出气,追随. ~ **cap** 鞋尖装饰,鞋尖饰皮. ~ **crack** (马的)蹄裂病. ~ **dance** = **~-dancing** 脚尖舞. **~hold** 立足点,基础;实力. **~-in** 前轮内倾;车轮内向. **~nail** 脚趾甲. ~ **shoe, ~slipper** 芭蕾舞鞋. ~ **smithing** 〔美〕跳舞.

toed [təud] *a.* ①有(若干)趾的. ②斜钉的,以斜钉固定的.

toff [tɔf] *n.* 〔英俚〕*n.* (自以为的)上流社会人物;花花公子,爱打扮的人. *He came out no end of a ~.* 他打扮得怪漂亮地出来了. *the ~s* 上层社会.

tof·fee, tof·fy [ˈtɔfi] *n.* 奶油太妃糖. ***can't shoot for ~*** 〔俚〕怎么打[射击]也打不好,枪法不高明. ***not for ~*** 〔俚〕绝对不,决不….

T. of Opns. = Theatre of Operations 战区.

toft [tɔft] 〔英方〕*n.*【法】宅地,屋基;小丘. ~ *and croft* 宅地和宅旁耕地(全部).

tog [tɔg] *n.* 上衣;〔常 *pl.*〕〔口〕(一套)衣服. *long ~s*【海、俚】上岸穿的外衣. — *vt.* 给穿上,打扮 *(out; up)*. *togged out in full uniform* 穿着礼服[正式制服].

to·ga [ˈtəugə] *n.* *(pl. ~s, togæ* [ˈtəudʒiː]*)* (古罗马市民穿的)宽大长袍〔= ~ virilis [viˈrailis]〕;(法官,议员等的)长袍,制服;〔美〕参议员的职位.

to·gat·ed [ˈtəugeitid] *n.* ①和平景色的. ②威严的,神气的;穿外袍的.

to·geth·er [təˈgeðə] *ad.* ①一同,共同;并合,合起来;混合;互相. ②同时,一齐;连续,不停地. *go ~* 一块儿去. *rent a house ~* 合租房子. *compare ~* 放在一起互相比较. *fight ~* 互打. *Both ~ exclaimed.* 两人同时叫了起来. *for hours ~* 连续好几个钟头. ***belong ~*** 合成一体. ***get ~*** 集合;编纂,汇齐. ***hang ~*** ①结合[纠结]在一起. ②符合. ***put two and two ~*** 综合起来考虑. ***taken [taking] ~*** 合起来看. ~ ***with*** 和…一起[合起来]. — *a.* 〔美俚〕头脑清楚的;稳当可靠的.

to·geth·er·ness [təˈgeðənis] *n.* 家庭聚会〔家庭亲属间经常进行社交或来往以增进和稳定亲属关系〕.

tog·ger·y [ˈtɔgəri] *n.* 〔口〕〔集合词〕衣服;(特种)服装.

tog·gle [ˈtɔgl] *n.*【海】挂索栓,绳针,套索钉;【机】肘节〔=~ joint〕套环;肘环套接;【无】反复电路. — *vt.* 用绳针系紧,拴牢;配备套环[肘节];打开肘节开关(投弹). ~ **flip-flop** 反转触发器. ~ **iron** (刃部可移动的)捕鲸标枪. ~ **press**【机】肘杆式冲床[压力机]. ~ **switch**【电】肘节开关.

To·go [ˈtəugəu] *n.* 多哥〔非洲〕.

toil[1] [tɔil] *n.* 苦工,苦役;难事;劳苦,辛苦. — *vi.* 辛苦工作,劳动 *(at; for)*;辛苦行进 (*up; through; along* 等).

toil[2] [tɔil] *n.* 〔常 *pl.*〕圈套,罗网,网;魔力,迷惑力;阴谋. ***be taken in the ~s*** 落网;上圈套,被迷住.

toile [twɑːl] *n.* 〔F.〕薄亚麻织物;麻布.

toil·er [ˈtɔilə] *n.* 辛苦工作的人.

toi·let [ˈtɔilit] *n.* 梳洗,打扮,化妆;化妆用具;梳妆台;妆饰,服装;厕所,浴室,盥洗室;【医】(手术前后的)洗涤. — *vt.* 给…穿衣[打扮];照料小孩上厕所. — *vi.* 梳妆,打扮;上厕所,上盥洗室. ***go down the ~*** 全功尽弃,一败涂地. ***make one's ~*** 打扮. ~ **bowl** 抽水马桶. ~ **tissue cover** 梳妆台布. ~ **cream** 雪花膏. ~ **paper,** ~ **tissue** 手纸,草纸;桑皮纸. ~ **powder** 扑粉. ~ **roll** 卫生卷纸. ~ **room** 化妆室;厕所,盥洗室. ~ **set** (一套)化妆用具. ~ **soap** 香皂. ~ **table** 梳妆台. ~ **training** 训练小孩大小便. ~ **vinegar** 加在洗手水里的香料. ~ **water** 花露水.

toi·let·ry [ˈtɔilitri] *n.* (一套)化妆用具;〔美〕化妆品.

toi·lette [twɑːˈlet] *n.* (女人的)化妆,梳妆;服装,装束;礼服,盛装.

toil·ful [ˈtɔilfəl] *a.* 辛苦的,劳苦的.

toil·less [ˈtɔilis] *a.* 不费力的,容易的.

toil·some [ˈtɔilsəm] *a.* 辛苦的,劳累的. **-ly** *ad.*

toil·worn [ˈtɔilwɔːn] *a.* 工作疲乏的,做累了的.

To·jo [ˈtəudʒəu],**Hideki** 东条(英机)〔1885—1948,日本军人,政治家,以侵略中国战犯罪被判处绞刑〕.

To·kay [təuˈkei] *n.* 妥凯白[紫]葡萄;妥凯葡萄酒〔匈牙利妥凯 (Tokay) 地方产的〕.

toke [təuk] *n.* 〔英俚〕食物,(尤指)干面包;〔美俚〕吸香烟〔尤指大麻香烟〕一口. — *vt.* 〔美俚〕吸一口(烟).

Toke·lau Is. [təukəˈlau ˈailənd] *n.* 托克劳群岛.

to·ken [ˈtəukən] *n.* 象征,记号,标记;表示物,证物;纪念品;代币,代价券;【语】语言符号;【英史】私铸货币;【圣】前兆;暗号. — *a.* 作为标志的;象征性的. *a ~ of love* 爱的象征. ***as a ~ of*** = in ~ of. ***by (the same)*** ~ 据此看来;而且,还有;更加,越发. ***by this [that]*** ~ 照这个〔那个〕看来. ***in ~ of*** 作为…的标志〔表示,证物,象征,纪念品〕. ***more by ~*** 〔古〕= by the same ~. ***reduce … down to ~ contingents*** 把…裁减[缩减]到象征性的限额. ~ **forces** 有名无实[象征性]的部队. ~ **import**【贸易】(为将来正式输入开路的、小额的)试样输入. ~ **money** 〔英史〕(商店发行的)代币. ~ **payment** 部分偿付. ~ **raid [resistance]** 象征性空袭[抵抗]. ~ **vote** 〔英〕(会议)原则同意的象征拨款决议〔实际金额总数不须再行讨论〕.

To·ken·house Yard [ˈtəukənhaus ˈjɑːd] *n.* (伦敦)土地拍卖市场〔因所在地命名〕.

to·ken·ism [ˈtəuknizm] *n.* 装门面;表面文章.

to·ko [ˈtəukəu] = toco.

to·kus [ˈtʌkəs] *n.* 〔俚〕屁股.

To·ky·o [ˈtəukjəu] *n.* 东京〔日本首都〕. ~ *Bay* 东京湾〔日本〕.

to·la [ˈtəulə] *n.* 托拉〔印度金银重量单位,1 金托拉 = 180 grain 或 11.664 gram.〕.

to·lan [ˈtəulæn] *n.*【化】二苯(基)乙炔.

To·land [ˈtəulənd] *n.* 托兰〔姓氏〕.

tol·booth [ˈtəulˌbuːθ] *n.* 〔Scot.〕牢狱.

tol·bu·ta·mide [təlˈbjuːtəˌmaid] *n.*【药】氨磺酰.

told [təuld] tell 的过去式及过去分词.

tole[1] [təul] *vt.* 〔古、方〕引诱,诱惑,诱使,怂恿.

tole[2] [təul] *n.* 金属薄片,镀锡铁皮.

To·le·do *n.* ①[təˈliːdəu] 托利多〔美国港市〕. ②[təˈleidəu] 托莱多〔西班牙城市〕. ③[təˈleidəu] 托莱多宝剑〔西班牙托莱多城精炼的好剑〕.

tol·er·a·bil·i·ty [ˌtɔlərəˈbiliti] *n.* 可忍受度;勉强,凑和;(健康)尚可.

tol·er·a·ble [ˈtɔlərəbl] *a.* 可忍受的;可容忍的;可原谅的;过得去的;〔口〕可算得健康的. **-a·bly** *ad.*

tol·er·ance [ˈtɔlərəns] *n.* 忍受;容忍;宽容;耐性;【物】容限;【医】耐受[药]性,耐(药)力;耐(药)量;【植】耐阴性;耐量;【造币、机】公差,容许量. ~ *deviation* 容许偏差. ~ *on fit* 配合公差. ~ *unit* 公差单位.

tol·er·ant [ˈtɔlərənt] *a.* ①忍受的;容忍的,原谅的,宽大的. ②有耐药性[力]的. ***be ~ of [toward]*** 对…能容忍. ~ ***and understanding with each other*** 互相宽容并互相谅解.

tol·er·ate [ˈtɔləreit] *vt.* 忍受;容忍;宽容,默认,容许;有耐药性[力]. *to ~ only praise and no criticism* 只让人表扬,不让人批评. ***cannot supinely ~*** 不能置之不理. **-er** *n.*

tol·er·a·tion [ˌtɔləˈreiʃən] *n.* 忍受;宽容,默认,默许;信仰自由;容忍异端[教]. **-tive** *a.*

tol·i·dine [ˈtɔliˌdiːn, -din] *n.*【化】联甲苯胺.

toll[1] [təul] *n.* ①税,通行税,过境税;过桥费,渡河费. ②租费,港口税;市场税,摊税;运费;(用所磨谷类一部分作酬的)磨费;长途电话(费). ③(各种使用费的)收费权. ④(常用单数)代价;牺牲,死伤人数. *a death* ~ 死亡人数. *a heavy* ~ *of lives* 死伤惨重. ***take*** ~ ***of*** 扣去…的一部分;夺去;使…遭受伤亡. —*vt., vi.* 缴纳[征收]通行税[欠费]. ~ **bar** (通行税征收处的)关木,关闸. ~ **board** 【电话】长途交换台. ~ **broadcasting** 〔美〕收费的无线电广播. ~ **bridge** 收费桥. ~ **cable** 长途电话电缆. ~ **call** 长途电话. ~ **central office** 长途电话总局. ~ **gate** 通行税征收卡. ~ **house** (过桥费等的)征收所. ~ **in gate**【法】入城税. ~ **keeper** 收税[费]人. ~**-man** 收税[费]人. ~ **road** 收费道路. ~ **thorough**【法】通行税,过桥税. ~ **traverse**【法】私有地通行费. ~ **turn** 〔英〕【法】牲畜市场税,征收所. **-age** *n.* 捐税,税收;纳税[费],收税[费]. **-er** *n.* 收税员,收费员.

toll[2] [təul] *vt.* 鸣(钟);(鸣钟)宣告[召唤];(鸣钟)报丧. — *vi.* 鸣钟;(钟)响,鸣. *For whom the bell ~s?* 丧钟为谁而鸣? — *n.* 钟声. ~ *the hour* 鸣钟报时. ~ *in the people* 敲钟召集群众.

tol-lol, tol-lol•ish [tɔlˈlɔl, -iʃ] *a.* 〔俚〕相当的,中等的,过得去的.

tol•ly [ˈtɔli] 〔英俚〕 *n.* 蜡烛;棍,杖;塔尖. — *vi.* (在熄灯后)点蜡烛.

Tol•tec [ˈtɔltek] *n.* (古代居住于墨西哥,受马雅文化影响的一支印第安人)托尔铁克人.

Tol•tec•an [ˈtɔltekn, ˈtəu-] *a.* 托尔铁克人的,托尔铁克文化的.

tol•u(balsam) [tɔˈljuː] *n.* (南美)妥卢香脂[胶] *(=* ~ *balsam).* ~ **tree**【植】妥卢胶树.

tol•u•ate [ˈtɔljuˌeit] *n.*【化】甲苯(甲)酸盐[或酯].

tol•u•ene, tol•u•ol [ˈtɔljuiːn, ˈtɔljuɔl] *n.*【化】甲苯.

tol•u•ide, to•lu•i•dide [ˈtɔljuˌwaid, -ˈluːˌdaid] *n.*【化】酰替甲苯胺.

tol•u•yl [ˈtɔljuwil] *n.*【化】甲(基)苯甲酰.

tolyl [ˈtɔlil] *n.*【化】甲苯基.

Tom [tɔm] *n.* 汤姆[男子名, Thomas 的昵称].

tom [tɔm] *n.* ①[T-] Thomas 的爱称;大钟;〔俚〕= tomato. ②雄性动物;(特指)雄猫 (= ~-cat). ③大傻瓜 (= T- Fool). ④【矿】倾斜粗洗淘金槽;【海】主炮. — *vi.* 〔T-〕 ***(Tommed; Tom•ming)*** 〔美口〕(象汤姆叔一样)逆来顺受. *Blind T-* 捉迷藏. *Old T-* 强烈的杜松子酒. **T- and Jerry** 〔美〕吃喝玩乐的浪荡子;奶蛋热甜酒. **T- Bowling**【海】海员. ~**boy** 爱玩爱吵的姑娘. **T- Collins** 〔美〕冰冻柠檬糖汁汽水杜松子酒. **T-, Dick, and Harry** 〔口〕普通人. **T- Farthing [Fool]** 傻子,笨蛋 (*There's more [More people] knows T- Fool than T- Fool knows.* 臭名声并不光彩[蠢人的蠢事别人都看在眼里]). **T- Long** 老长个子;讲话冗长的人. ~**nobody** 笨人,傻子. **T- O' Bedlam** 狂人,疯子. **T- Thumb** (英国童话里的小人儿)大拇哥;矮小的人[东西]. **T- Tiddler's ground** 宝山,金山;[儿童游戏]占金山. **T- Tyler [Tiler]** 怕老婆的人 .

tom•a•hawk [ˈtɔməhɔːk] *n.* (北美印第安人的)战斧,钺;〔澳〕斧子;〔T-〕(美国)战斧式驱逐机. ***bury [lay aside] the*** ~ 停战讲和. ***dig up [raise, take up] the*** ~ 宣战. — *vt.* 用战斧斩[杀];激烈批评[抨击].

tom•al•ley [ˈtɔmˌæli] *n.* 龙虾肝.

to•man [ˈtəuˈmɑːn] *n.* 托曼[伊朗金币,值十里亚尔];【史】蒙古军队的一师[10,000 人].

to•mat•in [təˈmeitin] *n.*【生化】番茄素.

to•ma•to [təˈmɑːtəu] *n.* ***(pl. -toes)*** ①【植】番茄,西红柿. ②〔美俚〕姑娘;男人;脸. ③不行的拳击师;棒球用球. ~ *worm moth* 番茄天蛾.

tomb [tuːm] *n.* 坟墓;墓穴;墓碑;〔the ~〕死. — *vt.* 埋葬. ***The Tombs*** 〔美〕纽约市监狱. ~ **stone** *n.* 墓石,墓碑;〔*pl.*〕〔美俚〕牙齿.

tom•bac, tom•bak [ˈtɔmbæk] *n.* 顿巴黄铜,人造金,德国黄铜[铜与锌的合金].

tom•bo•lo [ˈtɔmbəˌləu] *n.* ***(pl. -los)*** 【地】沙颈岬,陆连岛,连岛沙洲.

tom•boy•ish [ˈtɔmˌbɔiiʃ] *a.* 男孩子气的女孩的,顽皮的女孩的. **-ly** *ad.* **-ness** *n.*

tom-cat [ˈtɔmkæt] *n.* 公猫.

tom•cod [ˈtɔmˌkɔd] *n.*【动】①大西洋霜鳕 *(Microgadus tomcod).* ②太平洋霜鳕 *(Microgadus proximus).*

tome [təum] *n.* (书的)一卷,一册;(一本)大书,大部头的书,一本巨著.

-tome, -tomo, -tomy *comb. f.* ①一节,一段. ②【医】切割器,切开: micro*tome*, thyro*tome*; hepatec*tomy*.

to•men•tose [təuˈmentəus] *a.*【动、植】被有棉毛[绒毛]的.

to•men•tum [təuˈmentəm] *n.* ***(pl. -ta*** [-tə]***)***【动】棉毛;【植】绒毛;【解】软脑膜的毛状膜里.

tom•fool•er•y [ˈtɔmfuləri] *n.* 愚蠢举动[言语];小丑姿态;恶俗的妆饰;愚蠢而无聊的玩笑.

Tom•lin•son [ˈtɔmlinsn] *n.* 汤姆林森[姓氏].

Tom•my, Tom•mie [ˈtɔmi] *n.* 汤米[男子名, Thomas 的昵称].

tom•my [ˈtɔmi] *n.* ①(尤指抵作工资的)面包或食物;实物工资制;〔英〕工人带着上班的食物. ②〔常 T-〕〔俚〕英国兵;〔集合词〕英国军队. ③【机】螺丝旋棒[杆]. (= ~-bar). *soft* ~ 软面包. **T- Atkins** 英国兵. **T- cooker** 轻便火油炉. **T- Gee** 〔美俚〕机关枪手;犯罪恶汉. ~ **gun** 〔美口〕冲锋枪. ~ **rot** 〔俚〕荒唐事,蠢事;大话. ~ **screw**【机】贯头螺丝. ~ **shop** 实行实物工资制的工厂;厂内使用工资代价券的商店;面包店.

tomo•gram [ˈtəuməgræm] *n.* 〔*pl.*〕【医】层面X线相片. **-graphy** 层面 X 线照相术.

to•mor•row, to-mor•row [təˈmɔrəu, tuˈm-] — *n.* 明日,明天;来日,未来. ~ *week* 下星期的明天(八天后). *the day after* ~ 后天. *He will start* ~ *morning.* 他明天早上动身. *T- never comes.* 切莫依赖明天. *Never put off till* ~ *what you can do today.* 今天能做的事不要拖到明天;今日事今日毕. *the world's* ~ 世界的未来. — *ad.* 在明天;未来某一时候. *See you* ~. 明天见. *People* ~ *will have different ideas about this.* 将来的人们对此会有不同的想法. **-er** *n.* 做事拖延的人.

tom•pi•on [ˈtɔmpiən] *n.* = tampion.

Tomp•kins [ˈtɔmpkinz] *n.* 汤普金斯[姓氏].

tom•tit [ˈtɔmˈtit] *n.* 〔英〕【鸟】山雀科小鸟;山雀,青山雀.

tom-tom [ˈtɔmtɔm] *n.* (印度等地用手拍击的)长筒鼓(鼓声);锣. — *vi.* 拍击长筒鼓.

-tomy *n. suf.*【医】切割,切开,切除: ana*tomy*.

ton [tʌn] *n.* ①吨[(a)重量单位,英吨 = 2,240 磅(=long ~ = gross ~), 美吨 = 2,000 磅 (= short ~), 中国通用的公吨 = 1,000 公斤 (= metric ~). (b)商船注册的容积单位 = 100 立方英尺 (= register ~ = net ~). (c)特定货物装载单位: 木材(等) = 40 立方英尺,石料 =16 立方英尺,煤 = 49 bushels, 小麦 = 20 bushels, 盐 = 42 bushels, 葡萄酒 = 252 wine gallons 等.(d)船舰排水单位[排水吨] (= 海水 35 立方英尺 = displacement ~). (e)一般货物装载单位 (尺码吨或水脚吨) (= 40 立方英尺, = freight ~ = shipping ~)]. ②〔*pl.*〕〔口〕沉重的重量;许多,大量;〔俚〕每小时一百英里的速度. *five* ~*(s) of coal* 五吨煤. *a deadweight* ~ 【海】重量吨,英吨. *This box of yours weighs a* ~. 你这只箱子真沉重. *a* ~ *of books* 许多书. ~*s of times* 屡次,许多次. *That is* ~*s better.* 〔口〕那个好得多. ~ ***for*** ~ ***and man for man*** 【海】把捕获奖金公平分给友船. ***hit like a*** ~ ***of bricks*** 〔美

俚〕让人吓呆. ~-**mile** *n.* 吨英里〔吨数与英里数之积; 铁路、飞机运输量单位〕.
ton [tɔ̃:ŋ] *n.* 〔F.〕时兴,时髦,流行. ***in the*** ~ 合乎时髦式样.
-ton *suf.* 都市,城市: Hampton.
ton·al [ˈtəunəl] *a.* 音调的,调子的,音色的,声音的;【乐】调性的;【绘画】色调的. ~ **density** 色调密度; 音品密度. ~ **paper** 扩音纸.
to·nal·i·ty [təuˈnæliti] *n.* ①音调,(音乐的)调性,音色. ②【绘画】色调.
to·name [ˈtu:neim] *n.* 〔方〕(区别同姓同名用的)别名,外号;姓.
ton·dino [tənˈdi:nəu] *n.* 圆盘形图画〔浮雕〕;【建】半圆形装饰.
ton·do [ˈtɔndəu] *n.* *(pl. tondi* [ˈtɔndi]*)* 圆形意大利瓷盘;圆盘形图画〔浮雕〕.
Tone [təun] *n.* 托恩〔姓氏〕.
tone [təun] *n.* ①调子,音调;音色;音乐. ②语调,语气;(报刊等的)论调. ③格调,风格;风气,气氛,情调;常态;情况;行情;思想状态. ④【乐】乐音 *(opp.* noise*)*; 全音,全音程;【无】可听音;【医】(正常的)健康状态;【语音】声调,语调;音的高低,抑扬;【绘画】色调,色泽,明暗. *a* ~ *of command* 命令的口气. *in an angry* ~ 用发怒的口气. *raise the* ~ *of the school [army]* 提高校风〔军纪〕. *the* ~ *of a market* 市场情况,市况. *He tock a high* ~. 他语气很傲慢. *recover* ~ 恢复健康. *the four* ~*s* (汉语的)四声. *the oblique [deflected]* ~ 仄声. *the upper [lower, even]* ~ 上〔下,平〕声. ***in a*** ~ 一致. — *vt.* 抑扬顿挫地说,用一种声调说;装腔作势地说;加上调子,调整(乐器的)调子;柔和色调;【摄】调色; 使有…的风格. — *vi.* 具有某种色调;(颜色)调和 *(with)*; *a red hat with a coat to* ~ 红帽子和一件色调相配的外衣. ~ ***down*** 使柔和;变柔和. ~ ***(in) with*** (使)调和. ~ ***up*** 提高,加强;变强 (*Exercise* ~*s up the muscles.* 运动能使肌肉发达). ~ **arm** 留声机的拾音臂. ~ **cluster**【乐】音群. ~ **colour** 音色;【文艺】风格. ~ **control** 音调控制,音色调节. ~-**deaf** *a.* 不善于辨别音高的. ~ **language**【语言】声调语言. ~ **poem**【乐】音诗〔不拘泥形式的旧乐曲〕. ~ **quality** 音品,音色. ~ **row [series]**【乐】= 音体系. ~ **wheel** 音轮.
toned [ˈtəund] *a.* ①(语言)有声调的. ②有…音质的〔常构成复合词〕. ③年久变色的〔指纸张等〕.
tone·less [ˈtəunlis] *a.* 单调的,平板的; 无声调〔色调〕的.
ton·er [ˈtəunə] *n.* 调色剂,增色剂;上色剂.
to·net·ic [təˈnetik] *a.* 声调语言的,与声调语音有关的. **-i·cal·ly** *ad.*
to·net·ics [təˈnetiks] *n.* 声调学.
tong [tɔŋ] *n.* 〔使用 *pl.*〕 夹子,钳子. *fire* ~*s* 火钳. *a pair of* ~*s* = *a* ~*s* 一把钳子. ***would not touch with a pair of*** ~***s*** 碰也不想碰,实在讨厌. — *vt., vi.* 用钳子(夹).
ton·ga [ˈtɔŋgə] *n.* (印度的)双轮小马车.
Ton·ga [ˈtɔŋgə] *n.* 汤加〔西太平洋〕.
tongue [tʌŋ] *n.* ①舌;口条〔食用的牛舌等〕. ②口才,说法;语言;国语;方言;国民. ③舌状物;(环扣的)针; 岬,湾;火舌;(皮鞋钮扣下面的)舌皮;铃舌;【建,机】雄榫,榫舌;舌饰;【电】衔铁,舌簧; (继电器的)舌片;【铁路】尖轨; 留在舌上的余味〔多指不愉快的余味〕. ④〔美俚〕律师. *a coated [dirty, furred]* ~【医】长了舌苔的舌头. *Good brandy leaves no* ~ *in the morning.* 好白兰地不会使人第二天感到嘴里不舒服. *one's mother* ~ 家乡话,本国话. *the Chinese* ~ 中国话. ***all*** ~***s*** 所有国民. ***bite the*** ~ 保持沉默. ***find one's*** ~ (张口结舌等之后)能说话了,能开口了. ***give*** ~ (猎狗发现猎获物)咬,吠;(人)叫喊. ***have a bitter [spiteful]*** ~ 嘴毒,说话刻薄. ***have a ready [fluent]*** ~ 口齿伶俐,口才好. ***have a rough*** ~ 说话粗鲁. ***hold one's*** ~ 保持沉默. ***keep a civil*** ~ ***in one's head*** 措辞谨慎. ***lose one's*** ~ (因害臊等)说不出话来. ***oil one's*** ~ 说恭维话. ***on the tip of one's*** ~ 险些讲出. ***on the*** ~***s of men*** 被人谈论. ***put out one's*** ~ 伸舌头;〔转义〕(表示某种情绪)做鬼脸. ***stick [put, thrust] one's*** ~ ***in one's cheek*** 用舌头顶起脸颊〔侮蔑相〕. ***throw*** ~ = give ~. ***wag one's*** ~ 不断地唠叨. ***with one's*** ~ ***in one's cheek*** 不老实地,讽刺地, 挖苦地 (*speak with one's* ~ *in cheek about peace* 空谈和平). — *vt., vi.* 用舌头控制着吹奏;吹奏时使用舌头;舐;做舌榫(在板上);(将板等)做成雌雄榫〔企口接缝,舌槽〕接上〔= ~ and groove〕;〔诗〕讲,说;〔口〕申斥,谴责. ~-**and-groove joint** 企口接缝,舌槽榫,雌雄榫. ~ **bit** 有阻舌片的马嚼子. ~-**lashing**〔口〕辱骂;训斥. ~**let** 小舌,舌状突起. ~-**shy** 羞得说不出话来. ~-**tie** ①*n.* 短舌. ②*vt.* 使说不出话. ~-**tied** 舌头短的;张口结舌的. ~ **twister** 绕口令〔如: Peter Piper picked a peck of pickled pepper〕. **-less** *a.* 没有舌头的; 缄默的;哑的.
To·ni [ˈtəuni] *n.* 托妮〔女子名, Antonia 的昵称〕.
ton·ic [ˈtɔnik] *a.* 滋补的,强身的; 增强的,使精神振作的,鼓励的;【医】强直的,僵硬性的;【乐】主音的;【语音】声调的;主重音的;声调语言的. — *n.* 补药,强壮剂;增强剂;兴奋剂;鼓舞物;【乐】主音;【语音】浊音;主重音音节. *hair-*~ 生发油〔水〕. ~ *medicine* 补药. ~ *action* 紧张动作. ~ *spasm*【医】强直性痉挛. *a* ~ *chord*【乐】主和音. ~ **sol-fa** (用唱名 do, re, mi, fa, sol, la, ti 表示的)唱名记谱法〔教唱法〕.
to·nic·i·ty [təˈnisiti] *n.* 强壮;(肌肉组织的)紧张力,强壮度;(溶液的)张性;(体液的)浸透压.
to·night, to-night [təˈnait, tu-] *n.* 今夜,今晚. — *ad.* 在今晚.
to·nite [ˈtəunait] *n.*【化】徒那特〔一种猛烈的棉火药〕.
tonk [tɔŋk] *vt.* 〔英俚〕猛打;彻底击败;【高尔夫球】把球击得飞起.
ton·ka bean [ˈtɔŋkəbi:n]【植】零陵香豆.
tonkin [ˈtɔnkiŋ] *n.* (越南产)硬竹〔作钓竿等用〕. *a* ~ *cane* 青篱竹.
tonn. = tonnage.
ton·nage [ˈtʌnidʒ] *n.* 吨数;(船的)装载吨数,吨位〔每吨按 100 立方英尺计算〕;(特指一国、一个港口的商船的)总吨数;(船、货的)吨税. *gross* ~ 总吨数;〔按吨计算的〕运费. *net [registered]* ~ 登记吨数〔位〕. *displacement* ~ (军舰的)排水量〔吨数〕. ~ *(and poundage)*【英史】港税.
tonne [tʌŋ] *n.* 公吨 (= metric ton).
ton·neau [ˈtɔnəu] *n.* *(pl.* ~*s,* ~*x* [-z]*)* 〔F.〕(旧式汽车的)后部座席;(这种旧式汽车的)车身;(法国)二轮轻马车.
-ton·ner [ˈtʌnə] *n. suf.* …吨的船. *a ten-*~ 十吨的船.
to·nom·e·ter [təuˈnɔmitə] *n.*【物】音调计; 准音器;【物,化】汽压计;【医】眼压计;张力计;血压计. **-e·tric** [ˌtɔnəˈmetrik] *a.*
to·nom·e·try [təuˈnɔmitri] *n.* ①音调测量学. ②张力测定法.
ton·o·scope [ˈtɔnəskəup] *n.*【物】音高镜.
tono·tron [ˈtɔnətrɔn] *n.*【无】雷达显示管.
ton·sil [ˈtɔnsil] *n.*【解】扁桃体〔腺〕. ~ *bath* 〔美俚〕酒,一杯酒.
ton·sil·lar [ˈtɔnsilə] *a.* 扁桃体〔腺〕的.
ton·sil·lec·to·my [ˌtɔnsiˈlektəmi] *n.* *(pl.* **-mies)**【医】扁桃体切除术.
ton·sil·li·tis [tɔnsiˈlaitis] *n.*【医】扁桃体〔腺〕炎.
ton·sil·lot·o·my [ˌtɔnsiˈlɔtəmi] *n.* *(pl.* **-mies)**【医】扁桃体切开术.
ton·so·ri·al [tɔnˈsɔ:riəl] *a.* 〔谑〕理发师的; 理发的. *a* ~ *artist [parlour]* 〔谑〕理发师〔店〕. **-ist** *n.* 〔美谑〕理

发师.

ton·sure [ˈtɔnʃə] *n.* 削发(仪式);剃光的圆顶,剃去头发的部分;出家;僧职. — *vt.* 剃(头);为…举行剃发式.

ton·tine [tɔnˈtiːn] *n.* (17世纪意大利银行家 Tonti 氏倡导的)聚金养老法;〔集合词〕聚金养老会会员;聚金养老会的基金会员所得的养老金.

to·nus [ˈtəunəs] *n.* 【医】紧张〔正常肌肉处于休息状态时的轻微收缩〕.

To·ny [ˈtəuni] *n.* ①托尼〔男子名, Ant(h)ony 的昵称〕. ②〔美俚〕(有关戏剧艺术的任何一种)年度奖金.

ton·y [ˈtəuni] *a.* 〔美俚〕漂亮的,时髦的,豪华的〔常含讥讽意思〕.

too [tuː] *ad.* ①太. ②很,非常,极. ③也,还,同样;又,而且,而又,加之. ④〔口〕(不)还是,真的. *This house is ~ large for me.* 这房子我住太大了. *We cannot be ~ careful.* 无论怎么小心也不算太过;愈小心愈好;不怕过分小心. *I'm going, ~.* 我也去. *She is wise, and active ~.* 她又聪明,又活泼. *I mean to do it ~.* (不单是说)是真要干的. *You are not going.—Yes, I am, ~.* 你不去啦.——不,还是要去的. ★③④意之 too 美语有用在句首的: *Too, there were rumours of his resignation.* 〔美〕又有他辞职的谣传了. ***all ~*** 太 (*The holidays ended all ~ soon.* 假期过得太快了). ***but ~ (true)*** 不幸(是事实). ***none ~ (pleasant)*** 一点也不(快乐). ***only ~*** ①= but ~. ②非常,极,很 (*I am only ~ pleased.* 那我是高兴极了). ***quite ~*** = too too (*This is quite ~.* 简直太好了). ***~ bad*** 〔美〕真不幸,真抱歉. ***~ (bloody) Irish [right]!*** 〔军俚〕当然! ***~ ... for*** 太…不合〔不配〕. ***~ little*** 不够. ***(...) ~ many*** 多…个 (*You have given me two ~ many.* 你多给了我两个). ***one ~ many for sb.*** 胜过(某人),比(某人)聪明 (*She is one ~ many for me.* 她比我强). ***~ much for sb.*** 比(某人)强;对…来说太困难了 (*This task is ~ much for him.* 这任务对他来说太难了). ***~ much (of a good thing)*** 令人受不了,太那个 (*This was ~ much for him.* 这个他受不了). ***~ previous*** 〔美〕慌忙. ***~ ... to*** 太…以致不能 (*I went ~ late to see him.* 我去得太迟,没有见到他). ***~ ~*** 非常,很;极好 (*~ ~ apparent* 很明白. *This is ~ ~.* 好极了〔后略去 delightful 等形容词,表示假意感激或十二分感激的口气〕). ***very nice ~*** 非常赞成.

toodle-oo [tuːdlˈuː] *int.* 〔谑〕再会〔模仿汽车喇叭声的拟声词〕.

took [tuk] take 的过去式.

tool [tuːl] *n.* ①工具,用具,器具;【机】刀具;工具母机(= machine ~). ②爪牙,傀儡,走狗;〔美俚〕扒手. ③【装订】压印机. ④〔*pl.*〕〔美俚〕刀叉(等). *Books are the ~s of a scholar.* 书籍是学者的工具. *~ steel* 工具钢. *a broad ~* (石工的)宽刃凿. *an edge(d) ~* 刀. *literary ~s* 文具. *a poor ~* 不行的工人. ***throw down one's ~s = down ~s*** 罢工. — *vt., vi.* ①用工具加工,用工具制造,用凿刀修整(石头);【装订】压印. ②〔英口〕开车;乘车;〔美俚〕闲逛,闲荡. *Let me ~ you down to the station.* 我用车送你上车站吧. *blind ~ing* 【印】(硬封面上的)本色压印.

tool·er [ˈtuːlə] *n.* 石工用的宽凿.

tool·ing [ˈtuːliŋ] *n.* ①凿出的装饰. ②(工厂投入生产前的)机床安装. ③书籍封面上烫压成的装饰.

tool·mak·er [ˈtuːlˌmeikə] *n.* 制造,维修,校准机床的机工. **-mak·ing** *n.*

toom [tuːm] *a.* 〔Scot.〕空虚的. *A ~ purse makes an oblate merchant.* 口袋一文不名,会使商人烦闷. —*vt.* 喝干.

toon [tuːn] *n.* 【植】印度桃花心木.

toot[1] [tuːt] *n.* 嘟嘟〔喇叭、笛子等的声音〕;〔美〕闹饮;庆祝. — *vt.* 吹(喇叭、笛子等),使嘟嘟叫. — *vi.* 吹喇叭〔笛子〕嘟嘟地叫;(松鸡等)叫. *Don't ~.* 勿揿喇叭. ***~ one's own horn*** 〔美口〕自夸,自傲. ***~ the ringer [ding-dong]*** 〔美口〕按门铃.

toot[2] [tuːt] *n.* 酒宴;痛饮.

toot·er [ˈtuːtə] *n.* 〔美〕宣传员,广告员.

tooth [tuːθ] *n.* (*pl.* ***teeth***) ①牙齿. ②齿状突出,轮齿,锯齿,耙齿(等). ③嗜好. ④〔常 *pl.*〕(象牙齿那样能咬人的)威力,猛力,(正面)迎击. ⑤〔海口〕〔*pl.*〕船上的大炮. *a canine ~* 犬齿. *a false (artificial) ~* 假牙. *a milk ~* 乳牙. *a molar ~* 臼齿. *a wisdom ~* 智牙. *I have a sweet ~.* 我欢喜吃甜东西. *the ~ of the wind* 风的威力. ***armed to the teeth*** 武装到牙齿,全副武装. ***between the teeth*** 低声地. ***cast [throw] sth. in sb.'s teeth*** (引用某事)谴责某人. ***clench one's teeth*** = set one's teeth. ***cut a ~*** 出牙齿. ***cut one's wisdom teeth (eyeteeth)*** 开始懂事. ***draw (pull) sb.'s teeth*** 消除某人不平〔烦恼〕的根由;拔除某人的爪牙(使无能为害). ***escape by (with) the skin of one's teeth*** 〔口〕幸免于难. ***from one's teeth = from the teeth outwards [forwards]*** 怀恨在心地,无诚意的. ***grind one's teeth*** 咬牙切齿;生闷气. ***have a great ~ for (fruit)*** 很爱吃(水果). ***in spite of sb.'s teeth*** 不顾某人反对. ***in the teeth*** 反抗;公然. ***in the teeth of*** 不管,不顾;冒着…;正面受着…. ***long in the ~*** 年纪大 (*She is a bit long in the ~ to play the part of a young girl.* 她扮演少女的角色年龄太大了一点). ***lose a handful of teeth*** 〔美拳击〕下巴受猛击. ***put teeth in [into] a new law*** 给与新法律的强制性威力. ***set one's teeth*** 咬紧牙关,拼命忍耐. ***set sb.'s ~ on edge*** 使牙齿发酥〔发涩〕,使腻烦〔恼怒〕. ***show one's teeth*** 张牙露齿,怒视,威吓. ***to sb.'s teeth*** 当面,大胆地. ***~ and nail*** 拚命 (战斗、反对等) (*They fought ~ and nail but lost.* 他们竭尽全力拼搏,结果还是输了). — *vt.* 使具齿状;给…装牙齿;刻齿,锉齿(在锯条上等);(用牙齿)咬(住). — *vi.* (齿轮等)咬合. **~ache** 牙痛. **~brush** 牙刷. **~ carpenter** 〔美俚〕牙医. **~comb** 细(齿)梳. **~let** 小齿(状突起). **~ outline = ~profile** 【机】齿廓,齿形. **~ paste** 牙膏. **~pick** 牙签;〔军俚〕刺刀. **~ powder** 牙粉. **~ shell** 【动】掘足纲动物. **~some** *a.* 美味可口的. **~-wash** 刷牙水. **~wort** 【植】石芥花(属). **-ful** *n.* 〔俚〕(白兰地酒等的)一滴,一点点,一小口. **-less** *a.* 没有牙齿的;无力的.

toothed [tuːθt, tuːðd] *a.* (装)有牙齿的;锯齿状的. *a ~ wheel* 齿轮. *~ whale* 齿鲸亚目动物.

tooth·ful [ˈtuːθful] *n.* (酒等)少量,一小口.

tooth·y [ˈtuːθi] *a.* 露出牙齿的,有凸牙的.

toot·in', toot·ing [ˈtuːtin, -tiŋ] *a.* 〔美俚〕说得中肯的,说得有道理的;夸口的,吹牛的. *You're darn ~.* 你的话的确很对.

too·tle [ˈtuːtl] *vi.* 轻轻吹,反复吹(笛子等);(鸟)嘟嘟叫;(鸡)喔喔叫;空谈,讲废话,写无聊文章. — *n.* 吹笛声;空谈,废话;无聊文章.

too-too[1] [ˈtuːtuː] *ad.* 极,非常,很. — *a.* ①过度的,过分的;矫揉造作的. ②〔英〕极好的. *The movie was simply ~.* 这个电影矫揉造作.

too-too[2] [tuːˈtuː] *vi.* 嘟嘟地作声〔指吹笛子,哼唱歌等〕.

toots [tuːts] *n.* 〔美俚〕宝贝儿,亲亲〔对女孩等的亲热称呼〕.

toot·sy, toot·sie [ˈtuːtsi] *n.* (尤指儿童或妇女的)脚;〔俚〕= toots;少女,女人. **~-wootsy** = toots.

Top. = topographic.

top[1] [tɔp] *n.* (*opp.* bottom, foot) ①顶,顶部,顶端. ②头,头顶;尖端;树梢,树顶;(事物的)上层部分. ③最高位,首席;艇首的第一号划手. ④极致,绝顶;最好的部分. ⑤〔常 *pl.*〕(根菜类的)叶子 (*opp.* bottom); 顶芽. ⑥(地、桌子等的)上面,上边;(书页等的)上栏;书顶. ⑦盖;车盖,车顶;顶篷;壕沟胸壁的顶. ⑧〔汽车、俚〕高速;剧院最高票价;【机】末档齿轮 (= ~ gear);(香水瓶等的)塞子. ⑨【纺】束〔= 一磅半;毛条,纤维等的计量单位〕；毛条；化纤束。⑩【海】桅楼。⑪〔*pl.*〕仅仅表面镀金的钮扣；(长筒靴的)筒子；〔*pl.*〕长筒靴，马靴。⑫〔美俚〕(尤指马戏团的)大帐篷。⑬【化，油】蒸馏出来的轻馏份，蒸馏时的最初挥发成分。⑭〔*pl.*〕〔英俚〕上流社会；贵族。⑮【桥牌】最大的牌。*the gilt* ～ (书的)天头金边。*the fighting [military]* ～ 战斗桅楼。*big* ～〔美口〕马戏团的大帐篷。***at the*** ～ ***of*** 在…最高地位；用最高[最大]的(速度、声音等)。***come out (at the)*** ～ 得头名，占首位。***come out on*** ～ 赛赢，比赛得头名；获得大成就，出人头地，取得很高的社会地位。***come to the*** ～ 得到名誉；出人头地。***from*** ～ ***to bottom [toe, tail]*** 从头到脚，完全；全部；结果，事实上；绝对。***(go) over the*** ～ 跳出壕沟进攻；采取最后手段，采取断然处置；〔美〕赛赢。***on (the)*** ～ ***of*** 在…之上，在…的上面；逼近；胜任(工作等)；掌握(情况等)。***on*** ～ 在上；〔英〕在(双层公共车辆的)顶座；成功；占优势。***on (the)*** ～〔英〕〔汽车〕开足马力。***on*** ～ ***of the world***〔口〕满意到极点。***on*** ～ ***of that*** 到了最后，最后终于。***take the*** ～ ***of the table*** 坐上座；做主人；做主席。***talk off the*** ～ ***of one's head*** 即席谈话；假充内行谈外行话。***the*** ～ ***of the milk*** 最好[最精采的]部分；精华。***the*** ～ ***of the tide*** 满潮；情况最好的时候，正当高潮时候。***the*** ～ ***of the tree [ladder]*** 最高地位，(某一范围的)最上层，顶儿尖儿。***to the*** ～ ***of one's bent*** 极力。～ ***and tail*** 全体，全部；结果，事实上；彻头彻尾。～ ***heavy***〔美〕喝得烂醉的。***the*** ～ ***of the morning (to you)***〔方〕早，你早。～ ***or tail***〔否定式中〕全然(*I could not make* ～ *or tail of it.* 我完全弄不懂)。～ ***to bottom*** 倒，逆；从头到脚，完全。— *a.* 最高的，主要的，第一名的。*the* ～ *layer* 最上层。～ *honours* 极大的荣誉。～ *quality* 最好品质。***at*** ～ ***speed*** 用最高速度。***come out*** ～ ***dog*** 占上风；取胜。***the*** ～ ***notch of***〔美〕最高(度)。***(the)*** ～***s***〔俚〕最好的；最精干的；最受欢迎的。— *vt.* ①戴上，盖上；装顶部。②到…的顶上；高过，比…高；胜过，超过；得头名。③高过；高度为(多少)。④面施，铺施(肥料在地面上)；去(树)梢，打顶，摘心；剪(蜡烛的)芯；【染】末染；【高尔夫球】打球顶；【海】使(桅桁等)倾斜。⑤〔美俚〕绞死。— *vi.* 完成；结束 (off, out, up)；取胜；拔尖。～ *a fence* 跳过篱笆。*He* ～*s six feet.* 他身高六英尺。*He* ～*s his father by half a head.* 他比他父亲高出半个头。*a deer that topped 300 pounds* 三百多磅重的一只鹿。～ ***off*** 完成；结束；〔美〕暗杀 (～ *off one's dinner with liqueur* 用酒结束晚餐)。～ ***one's part***【剧】出色地完成…演出任务。～ ***the standing***〔美拳〕占第一位。～ ***up*** 装满，加满。***T- your boom!*** 别闹！滚出去！～ **banana** 主要演员，喜剧主角；主要人物。～ **billing**〔美剧〕主角。～ **boots**〔*pl.*〕马靴。～ **bracket**〔美俚〕主要角色。～ **brass** 要员，高级官员[军官]。～ **coat** 大衣，外套。～ **cross**【生】顶交。～ **dog**〔俚〕优胜者；〔美俚〕团体的领袖，老板。～ **drawer** *a.* 最重要的，第一位的。～**-dress** *vt.* 施顶肥，铺肥。～ **end** 顶端，(较细一头的)尖儿 (*opp.* butt end)。～ **flight** *a.*〔口〕高级的，最好的。～ **gear**【机】高速(档)；末档齿轮；【海】缆索和帆桁等。～**hamper** 大树树干上部；【海】中桅以上的帆、索具(等)；甲板上的重物〔炮塔、救生艇等，多余的笨重东西〕。～ **hand**〔美〕精通牧场工作的牧童。～ **hat** 大礼帽。～**-heavy** *a.* 头重脚轻的；不稳定的，不平衡的；资本过大的。～**-hole** ①*a.*〔英俚〕极好的，头等的。②*n.*【冶】出钢口。～ **horse**〔美〕最好的马。～ **kick**〔美俚〕上士。～**knot** 鸟的冠毛；鸟冠；顶髻；蝴蝶结〔十七世纪妇女的头饰〕；〔口〕头；【鱼】比目鱼类。～ **lantern** = ～ **light**【海】桅头灯。～ **level** *a.* 尖[顶]端的 (～*-level stuff* 尖端材料)；最高级(人士，官员)的。～ **line** 报纸标题。～**-line**，～**line** *a.*①可上头条新闻的；最重要的 (～*-line news* 头条新闻)。②第一流的，最优秀的 (～*line hotel* 第一流的旅馆)。～ **liner**〔英口〕主要的人[物]；主要演员。～ **line jobs** 最重要的工作。～ **lofty** *a.* 骄傲的，傲慢的。～**man** = ～*-sawyer*，～*sman*。～**mast**【海】中桅。～**most** *a.* 最上的，最高的，绝顶的。～ **news** 时事新闻。～ **notch** *a.*〔口〕最高的，第一流的。～ **price(s)** 高价。～ **removal** 摘心，打顶。～**sail**【海】中桅帆。～ **sawyer** (锯木坑的) 上锯人；〔古〕在上的人，上司。～ **secret** 绝密。～ **sergeant**【军】司务长；军士长。～**side** ①〔美〕二楼，楼上；〔常 *pl.*〕(水线以上的)船舷；(军舰的)上甲板。②*ad.* 上面，上边〔多指船上甲板上〕。～**sman**【海】桅楼员。～**soil** 表土；耕作层土壤。～ **talks** 最高级会谈。**-full** *a.* 满满的。**-less** *a.* 无顶的；(衣服)无上身的〔袒胸露臂的〕；高得看不见顶的。

top[2] [tɔp] *n.* 陀螺。*The* ～ *sleeps.* 陀螺飞速旋转得好象定住一样。***an old*** ～〔俚〕老朋友。***sleep like a*** ～ 睡熟。

top- *comb. f.*〔用于元音前〕= topo-.

to·paz [ˈtəupæz] *n.*【矿】黄玉；【动】南美蜂鸟。*false [common]* ～ 黄水晶。

to·paz·o·lite [təuˈpæzəˌlait] *n.*【矿】黄榴石。

tope[1] [təup] *n.* 座佛状圆顶塔，塔婆，浮屠；印度塔；庙，陵。

tope[2] [təup] *n.* (印度的)芒果林，树林，灌木林；园林。

tope[3] [təup] *n.* (欧洲沿岸的)星鲨，角鲛。

tope[4] [təup] *n.*【海】中国小木船。

tope[5] [təup] *vi.*, *vt.* 狂欢，纵酒。

to·pec·to·my [təˈpektəmi] *n.*【医】脑皮质的部分切除。

top·er [ˈtəupə] *n.* 酒徒，酒鬼；醉汉。

top·gal·lant [tɔpˈgælənt] *n.*【海】上桅(帆)。— *a.* 上桅(帆)的；最高[上]的。

To·phet, Topheth [ˈtəufet] *n.* (耶路撒冷的)垃圾焚化场〔从前是犹太人供凶神 Moloch 的地方〕；(灼热)地狱。

to·phus [ˈtəufəs] *n.* *(pl.* *tophi* [ˈtəufai]*)*【医】痛风石。

to·pi·a·ry [ˈtəupiəri, -pjə-] *a.* 修剪成装饰性质的(篱树等)，修剪得美观的。— *n.* 装饰性树木修剪法。～ **art** 林木修剪术。～ **work** 树木整形[修剪]。

top·ic [ˈtɔpik] *n.* ①论题，题目；话题；标题，细目。②(节、段的)主题。③原理，原则；【逻、修】总论，概论。④【医】局部药。*a* ～ *sentence* 段落主题提示句。*current* ～*s* 今天的话题。— *a.*【医】局部的。

top·i·cal [ˈtɔpikəl] *a.* ①题目的，论题的；条分缕析的。②有关时事的。③地方的。④【医】局部的。⑤原理的，原则的。*in* ～ *form* 分列标题，有提纲细目地。*a* ～ *caricature* 时事漫画。*a* ～ *anaesthetic* 局部麻醉剂。**-ly** *ad.*

top·i·cal·i·ty [ˌtɔpiˈkæliti] *n.* 地区性，主题性，时事性，【医】局部性。

top·min·now [ˈtɔpˌminəu] *n.*【动】①花鳉科 *(Poeciliidae)* 鱼〔如食蚊鱼 *(Gambusia offinis)*〕。②鳉科 *(Cyprinodontidae)* 鱼。

topo- *comb. f.* 场所；地方：*topo*graphy, *topo*logy.

to·pog. = topographical; topography.

to·pog·ra·pher [təˈpɔgrəfə], **-phist** [-fist] *n.* 地志作者，地志学者；地形测量员。

to·po·graph·ic, -i·cal [ˌtɔpəˈgræfik, -ikəl] *a.* 地志的，地形(学上)的；地形测量的。*a* ～ *drawing* 地形图。*a* ～ ***machine***【空】歪斜矫正机。

to·pog·ra·phy [təˈpɔgrəfi] *n.* 地志；地形(测量)学；地形，地势；地势图；(物产的)分布状况；【解】局部解剖学。

to·pol·o·gy [təˈpɔlədʒi] *n.* 地志学；【数】拓扑学；拓扑(结构)；【解】局部解剖学。**-i·cal** *a.*

to·pon·o·my [təˈpɔnəmi], **to·pon·y·my** [-nimi] *n.* 地名志；地名研究；【解】局部[部位]命名法。

top·o·nym [ˈtɔpəˌnim] *n.* ①地名。②表明起源、地点的名称〔如在动物词汇手册中〕。

top·per [ˈtɔpə] *n.* 上层的东西；【商】(水果等商品的)盖面货；高档货，尖儿货；高浪；〔俚〕高顶大礼帽；〔英俚〕第一流人物；女式宽大短外衣。

top·ping [ˈtɔpiŋ] *a.* 高耸的，屹然的；〔美〕傲慢的；〔罕〕

第一流的;上等的;愉快的,健康的. — *n.* 顶部,上层;〔*pl.*〕剪下来的小枝;【油】拔顶;〔美俚〕〔*pl.*〕饭后的点心. *a* ~ *axe* 修枝斧. ~ *cove*〔俚〕刽子手. ~ *lift*【海】千斤索,吊扣索.

top·ple [ˈtɔpl] *vi., vt.* (高的东西)摇摆,摇摇欲坠,倒塌;摇动,推倒,推翻. ~ *old idols* 破除古老的偏见[迷信]. ~ **down** (使)垮下来. ~ **over** 推倒,摇倒.

tops [tɔps] *a.* 〔用作表语〕(能力、技巧、智力、品质等)极好,最好,首屈一指,无与伦比,呱呱叫;最高级的,第一流的,高档的. *His work is* ~. 他的作品是第一流的. *That car is* ~. 那辆车质量最高. — *n.*〔俚〕〔常作 the ~,为 top¹ 的复数形式〕第一流人物,最佳产品. *He's the* ~. 他是第一流人物.

top·sy·tur·vy [ˈtɔpsiˈtə:vi] *ad., a.* 颠倒地[的];乱七八糟地[的]. — *n.* 颠倒;混乱. — *vt.* 弄颠倒;弄得乱七八糟. **-dom** *n.* 〔谑〕颠倒[混乱]状态.

toque [təuk] *n.* 无檐女帽;【动】头巾猿 = tuque.

tor [tɔ:] *n.* 多岩石小山;【地】(特指英国 Dartmoor 的)突岩.

to·rah, to·ra [ˈtɔ:rə] *n.* ***(pl. -roth*** [-rəuθ]***)*** 〔H.〕【犹太教】①经学,律法,教导. ② = pentateuch. ③旧约全书. ④全部经典〔包括旧约和圣法经传〕.

torc [tɔ:k] *n.* = torque①.

torch [tɔ:tʃ] *n.* 火炬,火把;【机】气炬,喷灯;〔英〕手电筒;知识的光[源泉];〔美俚〕手枪. *the* ~ *of Hymen* 恋情. *the inverted* ~ 倒火炬,死的象征. *an electric* ~ 手电筒. ***carry a [the]* ~ *for*** 迷恋,单恋;热烈赞助. ***hand on the*** ~ 把知识[文化]的火把传给后代. ~ **bearer** 执火炬者;传授文化[知识]者;某一运动的首倡者[领导者]. ~ **fishing** 灯光捉鱼法. ~ **light** 火炬(的光) (*a* ~ *light procession [parade]* 火炬游行). ~ **race**【古希腊】火炬接力赛跑. ~ **song**〔美俚〕单恋之歌. ~ **welding**【机】气炬焊接. ~ **wood** (多树脂的)火炬木.

torch·ier, torch·iere [tɔ:ˈtʃiə] *n.* (可在地上移动的)落地灯,脚灯〔没有灯罩而有一个反射盘,使光线向上射,形成间接照明〕.

tor·chon [ˈtɔ:ʃən] *n.* 〔F.〕拭布〔擦拭器皿和家具等用〕. ~ **lace** 镶边花边,饰带花边. ~ **paper** 粗面水彩画纸.

torch·y [ˈtɔ:tʃi] *a.* 伤感恋歌式的.

tore¹ [tɔ:] *n.* 【建】座盘饰;【几】环形圆纹曲面;管环,环面.

tore² [tɔ:, tɔə] tear 的过去式.

tor·e·a·dor [ˈtɔriədɔ:] *n.* 〔Sp.〕(骑马)斗牛士. ~ *pants* 紧身半长女运动裤.

to·re·ro [təuˈreərəu] *n.* 〔Sp.〕徒步的斗牛士.

to·reu·tic [təuˈru:tik] *a.* 雕金术,(金属)浮雕术. ~**s** 〔*pl.*〕〔用作单〕金属浮雕工艺.

to·ri [ˈtɔ:rai] *n.* torus 的复数.

tor·ic [ˈtɔ:rik] *a.* 花托的,花托状的;座盘饰的;环形圆纹曲面的.

To·ri·no [tɔˈri:nɔ] *n.* 托里诺〔意大利城市,即都灵 Turin〕.

tor·ment [ˈtɔ:ment] *n.* 苦痛,苦恼;苛责,拷问;讨厌[麻烦]的东西;〔古〕拷问台. *The child is a positive* ~. 〔口〕这孩子讨厌极啦. — [tɔ:ˈment] *vt.* 使苦恼,使痛苦,折磨;使混乱;欺负,虐待;拷问. **-er** *n.*

tor·men·t·il [ˈtɔ:mentil] *n.* 【植】直立委陵菜〔根部可用于硝皮或作染料〕.

tor·men·tor, tor·menter [tɔ:ˈmentə] *n.* ***(fem. -tress)*** 使苦痛的人[物],折磨者;【农】轮耙;【海】长肉叉;舞台两侧的固定幕布;(摄声片时的)回声防止幕;【法】死刑执行人.

tormi·na [ˈtɔ:minə] *n.* 〔*pl.*〕【医】肠绞痛;剧烈腹痛.

torn [tɔ:n] tear 的过去分词.

tor·na·do [tɔ:ˈneidəu] *n.* ***(pl. ~es, ~s)*** ①【气】陆龙卷,大旋风,龙卷风. ②〔喻〕(喝彩、责骂声、子弹等的)爆发,大批袭来. ~ **cellar**〔美〕避难所. **-dic** [tɔˈnædik] *a.*

to·roid [ˈtɔ:rɔid] *n.* ①【电】环,环形线. ②【几】超环面. **-al** *a.*

To·ron·to [təˈrɔntəu] *n.* 多伦多〔加拿大港市〕.

to·rose [ˈtɔ:rəus, tɔ:ˈrəus] *a.* ①膨胀的,鼓起的. ②【植】节状的 (= torous).

tor·pe·do [tɔ:ˈpi:dəu] *n.* ***(pl. ~es)*** 鱼雷,水雷;(油井)爆破筒;【铁路】(警报用)信号雷管;掼炮;鱼雷形汽车;【鱼】电鲼,鳐;〔美俚〕(被雇用的)刺客. *a guided* ~ 制导鱼雷. *an aerial* ~ 空雷;遥控滑翔导弹. *a* ~ *battery* 鱼[水]雷炮台. *a diving* ~ 深水炸弹. *a ground* ~ 海底水雷. *a* ~ *shop* 鱼雷工厂. — *vt., vi.* 用鱼雷[空雷]袭击;发射鱼雷;敷设水雷;(在油井内)装置爆破筒;破坏(政策、制度、计划等);使失却(活动能力等). ~ **boat** 鱼雷艇 *(a* ~ *boat catcher* = *a* ~ *boat destroyer* 舰队驱逐舰〔略作 t. b. d., 正式名叫 destroyer〕*).* ~ **bomber** 鱼雷轰炸机. ~ **catcher** 水雷捕捉网,鱼雷艇捕捉舰. ~ **gunboat** 水雷炮舰〔正式名称叫 *torpedo-boat*〕. ~ **net,** ~ **netting** 鱼雷防御网. ~ **plane**【空】鱼雷轰炸机. ~ **planter**【海】水敷雷舰. ~ **station** 鱼雷艇根据地. ~ **tube** 鱼雷发射管.

Torpex [ˈtɔ:peks] *n.* 【海军】(爆炸能力为 TNT 1.5 倍的)铝蜡炸药.

tor·pid [ˈtɔ:pid] *a.* 麻痹的;不活泼的;迟钝的;(动物)冬眠的. —〔英〕*n.* ①〔*pl.*〕(牛津大学)四旬节艇赛. ②四旬节艇赛选手[用艇]. **-ly** *ad.* **-ness** *n.*

tor·pid·i·ty [tɔ:ˈpiditi] *n.* 麻痹,迟钝;冬眠,蛰伏.

tor·pi·fy [ˈtɔ:pifai] *vt.* 使麻痹,使失去知觉;使迟钝.

tor·por [ˈtɔ:pə] *n.* 麻痹;迟钝;冬眠.

tor·por·if·ic [ˌtɔ:pəˈrifik] *a.* 使麻痹的,有麻痹性的,使迟钝的.

torps [tɔ:ps] *n.*〔海军俚〕水雷军官.

tor·quate [ˈtɔ:kweit] *a.* ①(动物颈部)有异色毛圈的. ②有颈圈的,戴项链的;具环的.

torque [tɔ:k] *n.* ①(古代条顿人、高卢人戴的)金丝项圈. ②【物】扭(力)矩,转(力)矩. ~ **converter** 转矩变换器,液力变扭器. ~**-meter** 扭力表,转矩计. ~ **switch**【空】(陀螺仪)校正马达开关. ~**s** 【动】(动物颈部等的)异色毛皮[羽毛]圈. ~ **wrench**【机】转矩扳手.

torr [ˈtɔ:] *n.* 【电】毛〔真空单位〕.

tor·re·fac·tion [ˌtɔriˈfækʃən] *n.* 烘,烤,焙;干炒.

tor·re·fy [ˈtɔrifai] *vt.* 烘,烤,焙;干炒.

tor·ren·ize [ˈtɔ:rəˌnaiz, ˈtɔ-] *vt.* 按托伦斯法登记(财产).

Tor·rens law [ˈtɔ:rənz lɔ:, ˈtɔr-] 托伦斯法〔在政府登记土地所有权,由政府发给所有证的各种法令〕.

tor·rent [ˈtɔrənt] *n.* 急流,湍流,洪流;(质问等的)连发,(感情等的)爆发,迸发. *a* ~ *of lava* 熔岩的奔流. *a* ~ *of abuse* 连珠炮一样的谩骂. *It rains in* ~*s*. 大雨倾盆. ~*s of rain* 倾盆大雨. ~*s of water* 奔流. ***stem the*** ~ 抵制;阻止. ~**-regulation** *n.* 防洪工事,防砂工事.

tor·ren·tial [tɔˈrenʃəl] *a.* 奔流的,急流的;汹涌的,猛烈的,奔放的. *a* ~ *rain* 倾盆大雨.

Tor·ri·cel·li [ˌtɔriˈtʃeli], **E.** 托里切利〔1608—1647, 意大利数学家、物理学家、晴雨表创制者〕.

tor·rid [ˈtɔrid] *a.* 晒热的;酷热的,灼热的;热烈的. ~ *heat* 炎热. *the T- Zone* 热带. **-i·ty** *n.*

torri·fy [ˈtɔrifai] *vt.* = torrefy.

tor·sade [tɔ:ˈseid] *n.* ①带条. ②饰带.

tor·sel [ˈtɔ:səl] *n.* 【建】承梁木;漩涡饰.

tor·si·bil·i·ty [ˌtɔ:siˈbiliti] *n.* 耐扭力,抗扭力.

tor·sion [ˈtɔ:ʃən] *n.* 扭转;扭(转)力;【物】扭(力)矩,转(力)矩;【医】捩转. ~ *pairing* 扭曲配对. ~ **balance** 扭秤. ~ **bar** 扭条,捻杆. ~ **meter** 扭力计.

tor·sion·al [ˈtɔ:ʃənəl] *a.* 扭的,扭转的. ~ **moment**【物】扭(力)矩. ~ **pendulum** 扭摆. ~ **strength** 抗扭强度.

torsk [tɔːsk] *n.* *(pl. torsk, torsks)*【动】鳕科 *(Gadidae)* 鱼.

tor·so [ˈtɔːsəu] *n.* *(pl. ~s, -si* [-siː]*)*〔It.〕(人体的)躯干;【雕刻】(断头缺肢的)躯干;雕像;残破不完整的东西;未完成的作品. **~-tosser** *n.*〔美俚〕舞女〔尤指滑稽戏中的〕.

tort [tɔːt] *n.*【法】民事侵权行为[罪]〔不包括违背契约〕.

torte [tɔːt; G. ˈtəutə] *n.* *(pl. tortes,* G. *tor·ten* [ˌtəutən]*)* 圆形(果仁)大蛋糕.

tort-fea·sor [ˈtɔːtˈfiːzə] *n.*【法】有民事侵权行为的人,犯民事侵权罪的人.

tor·ti·col·lis [ˌtɔːtiˈkɔlis] *n.*【医】斜颈,捩颈,歪头.

tor·tile [ˈtɔːtail, -til] *a.* 扭转的,扭弯的;卷曲的;【植】扭卷的.

tor·til·la [tɔːˈtilə, -ˈtiːljə] *n.*〔Sp.〕(墨西哥的)玉米面饼[面包].

tor·tious [ˈtɔːʃəs] *a.*【法】民事侵权行为的.

tor·toise [ˈtɔːtəs] *n.* 龟(= testudo);迟钝的人[东西]. **~ beetle** 龟甲虫〔龟状小甲虫的通称〕. **~-eater**〔英空军俚〕(能从空中打坦克的)飞行大炮. **~ shell** 龟甲,鳖甲. **~-shell** *a.* 玳瑁(色)的 (*a ~-shell cat* 玳瑁色的猫. *a ~-shell turtle*【动】玳瑁).

tor·to·ni [tɔːˈtəuni] *n.* 意大利式冰淇淋〔加有樱桃,杏仁等配料〕.

tor·tri·cid [ˈtɔːtrisid] *n.*【动】卷蛾.

tor·tu·os·i·ty [ˌtɔːtjuˈɔsiti] *n.* ①弯扭,曲折. ②不正当. ③委婉.

tor·tu·ous [ˈtɔːtjuəs] *a.* ①弯扭的,曲折的(路、河等),盘旋的. ②不正派的,不正当的,骗人的(政策等). ③委婉的(话). **-ly** *ad.* **-ness** *n.*

tor·ture [ˈtɔːtʃə] *n.* ①拷问,拷打. ②〔常 *pl.*〕折磨;痛苦,苦恼. ***put sb. to (the) ~*** 拷问. ***~ of animals***【法】动物虐待. — *vt.* 拷问,拷打;折磨;使痛苦;曲解(法律条文等) *(out of; into)*;扭弯,扭折.

tor·u·la [ˈtɔːrulə] *n.* *(pl. -lae,* [-liː], *-las)* 酿母,串状酿母菌属,串菌属.

toru·lin [ˈtɔrjulin] *n.*【化】维生素 B_1.

to·rus [ˈtɔːrəs] *n.* *(pl. -ri* [-rai]*)*【植】花托;【解】隆凸[起],圆凸;【建】座盘饰;【几】环形曲面(体).

To·ry [ˈtɔːri] *n.*【英史】托利党党员;【美史】(独立战争时的)亲英派,保王派;〔主 t-〕保守党党员,保守派. — *a.* 托利党(党员)的;〔主 t-〕保守党(党员)的,保守派的. **-ism** *n.* 保王主义[行为];〔主 t-〕保守主义;保守行为.

-tory *suf.* = -ory.

tosh[1] [tɔʃ] *n.*〔主英俚〕胡说,废话;【板球、网球】(容易接的)慢球.

tosh[2] [tɔʃ] *a., ad.*〔Scot.〕整齐,漂亮;舒服;友善,亲切. — *vt.* 弄整齐,收拾打扮,装饰.

tosh·er [ˈtɔʃə] *n.*〔英俚〕(综合大学中)不隶属任何学院的学生.

toss [tɔs] (〔诗〕*tost*) *vt.* ①(轻)扔,(轻)投,抛;(轻)拌;【网球】把(球)打高;(马)摔落(骑手) *(off)*;(公牛用角)将(人等)挑上去;忽然抬起(头等). ②(风、浪等)使动荡,使摇摆,使颠簸;给与精神上的动摇. ③掷钱(等)决定事情. ④打扰;扰乱;使不安. ⑤【矿】摇选(锡矿等). — *vi.* 颠簸,摇摆;翻来翻去;摇动;掷钱;【美剧】停止. *The ship was ~ed by the waves.* 船被浪打得东摇西晃. *~ a pancake* (拿着锅把里面的饼抛起)翻煎饼. *a ~ing sea* 波涛汹涌的海. ***~ a dinner***〔美俚〕举行宴会;请客. ***~ about all night*** 整夜翻来复去. ***~ aside*** 扔弃;搁置不管. ***~ cold water on***〔美运〕照规则禁止. ***~ down*** (倾杯)一口喝下. ***~ hay about*** 翻(晒)干草. ***~ oars*** 举桨(致敬). ***~ off*** 一口喝干(酒);敏捷地做好. ***~ one's head*** 把头往后一扬〔摆架子或有点不耐烦时的动作〕. ***~ the platter***〔美运〕掷铁饼. ***~ to and fro*** 辗转反侧. ***~ up*** 一下子做好[烧好](菜等);掷钱 (*Let us ~ up for first choice.* 让我们掷钱决定谁先取吧). — *n.* ①抛,扔;②掷钱[猜正反面];掷钱决定;双方各有一半的机会. ③落马;(头等的)猛抬. ④动摇,兴奋. ⑤投掷距离. *the ~ of a ball* 投球. *It is quite a ~ [~-up] whether he comes or not.* 他来不来的可能性各占一半. ***take a ~***〔俚〕从马上摔下来. ***win [lose] the ~*** 掷钱猜赢[猜输];顺利[不顺利]. ***within the ~ of a ball*** 在球所能投到的距离内. **~ pot** 酒徒. **~up, ~-up** 用掷钱看正反的办法决定;双方[是否]各有一半的机会;碰运气的事 (*At ten o'clock this morning it was still a ~-up whether we should be able to get here.* 今天早上十点钟的时候还很难说我们是否能够到达这里).

tost [tɔst]〔诗〕toss 的过去式及过去分词.

tos·ta·da, tos·ta·do [təusˈtɑːdə, -dəu] *n.*〔美〕脆玉米饼.

tot[1] [tɔt] *n.*〔口〕〔爱称〕小娃娃,小宝宝;小东西;小杯子;(酒等的)一杯,一口;少量.

tot[2] [tɔt] *n.*〔口〕合计;总数,总和. *long ~s* 巨大数目的计算. — *vt., vi.* 加起来*(up)*;共总… *(up)*.

to't [tut]〔方、俚〕= to it.

to·tal [ˈtəutl] *a.* 总计的(金额等);全部的;完全的(失明等),绝对的(禁酒等). *a ~ war* 全面战争. *~ defence* 全面防御. *the sum ~* 总额. *~ output* 总产量. *~ weight* 总重(量). *~ color blindness* 全色盲. *~ abstinence* 绝对禁酒. *~ recall*〔美〕完整的回忆(能力). — *n.* 总数,全体;合计,总计〔常叫 grand ~〕. — *vt.* (〔英〕*-ll-*) ①总计达,计算…的总数. ②〔美俚〕完全摧毁;向…清算,向…报复. *The visitors ~led 151.* 来访者共计 151 人. **-ly** *ad.* — *vi.* 合计;计算总数;总数达到[计有] *(to, up to)*. *His debts had ~led to $5,000.* 当时他的债务总数达到 5,000 美元.

to·tal·i·sa·tor [ˈtəutəlaizeitə] *n.* = totalizator.

to·tal·is·tic, to·tal·ist [ˌtəutˈlistik, ˈtəutlist] *a.* = totalitarian. **-tal·ism,** *n.*

to·tal·i·tar·i·an [ˌtəutæliˈtɛəriən] *a., n.* 极权主义的;极权主义者. *a ~ state* 极权国家〔如纳粹统治下的德国〕. **-ism** *n.* 极权主义.

to·tal·i·ty [təuˈtæliti] *n.* 完全,完备;全体,总数;【天】全蚀(时间). ***without viewing things in their ~*** 不看事情的全体.

to·tal·i·za·tor [ˈtəutəlaizeitə] *n.* 总额计算机;(赛马等赌博的)赌金计算机.

to·tal·ize [ˈtəutəlaiz] *vt.* 加起来,总计. — *vi.* 用计算机计算总数. *a ~d war* 总体战.

to·tal·iz·er [ˈtəutəlaizə] *n.* 计算总数的人,加法计算器〔尤指赌金计算器〕.

to·ta·quine [ˈtəutəˌkwiːn, -kwin] *n.*【药】金鸡纳全碱,金奎宁.

tote[1] [təut] *vt.*〔美口〕携带;运,搬,运输;抱,背;〔美俚〕以…武装,带(枪). — *n.* 装运物. **~ bag** (布制或草编的)大手提包.

tote[2] [təut] *n.*〔英口〕= totalizator;〔方〕总额;〔方〕绝对戒酒的人. — *vt.* 计算(总数);总数为…. **~ board** 赌金结算揭示牌.

to·tem [ˈtəutəm] *n.* ①图腾〔原始民族崇奉为自己祖先的某种天然物,如鹿、狼、龟等〕. ②图腾像. ③〔喻〕崇拜对象. **~ post [pole]** (刻有图腾像的)图腾柱. **-ic, -is·tic** [ˌtəutəˈmistik] *a.*

to·tem·ism [ˈtəutəmizəm] *n.* 图腾崇拜,图腾制度.

to·tem·ist [ˈtəutəmist] *n.* 图腾制种族成员;图腾制研究者.

t'oth·er, toth·er [ˈtʌðə] *pro., a.*〔方、口、俚〕另一个,别的. ***tell ~ from which***〔谑〕= ***tell one from ~*** 把一个同另一个区别开来.

to·ti·dem ver·bis [ˈtɔtidem ˈvəːbis]〔L.〕(原文)就是这几个词.

tot·i·es quot·i·es [ˈtɔtiiːz ˈkwɔtiiːz]〔L.〕每次.

to•ti•pal•mate [ˌtəutiˈpælmeit] *a.* 【动】全蹼的〔如鸭; 鹈等〕. **-ma•tion** *n.*

to•tip•o•tent [təuˈtipətənt] *a.*【动】能由(分)裂球变成胚胎的. **-ten•cy** [-tənsi] *n.*

to•to cae•lo [ˈtəutəu ˈsiːləu] 〔L.〕天那样大; 极度; 完全. ***differ toto caelo*** 有天壤之别.

Totten•ham pudding [ˈtɔtənəm] 〔俚〕(用厨房废料做成的)猪饲料.

tot•ter [ˈtɔtə] *vi.* 蹒跚,摇摆,趔趔趄趄地走; 摇动; 摇摇欲坠. — *n.* 蹒跚; 摇摆,动摇. *a ~ing government* 动摇不稳的政府.

tot•ter•ing•ly [ˈtɔtəriŋli] *ad.* 蹒跚地; 摇摇欲坠地.

tot•ter•y [ˈtɔtəri] *a.* 蹒跚的; 动摇的,摇摇欲坠的.

tou•can [ˈtuːkæn] *n.* 【鸟】鵎鵼,巨嘴鸟; 〔T-〕【天】巨嘴鸟座.

touch [tʌtʃ] *vt.* ①触,碰,摩,摸; 触知;【医】触诊;【宗】摸治(瘰疬); 用试金石试. ②接触; 邻接,毗邻;【几】(直线)切(圆等). ③使(二物)接触. ④感动; 触犯,触怒. ⑤(在物质上)给与影响; 害,伤; (精神上)伤害; 〔用 p.p.〕使发疯,使发狂; 触痛隐私. ⑥到,及,达; 〔用于否定句〕(能力等)匹敌,相等. ⑦按,揿(铃等); 弹,奏(乐器). ⑧画,写; 添画,修改; 略加颜色; 完成,修整. ⑨〔用于否定句〕吃,喝; 插手,发生关系; 涉及. ⑩提到,谈到,论及. ⑪〔俚〕告借(钱),讨(钱); (用不正当手段)弄(钱); 偷; 侵占. — *vi.* ①触,碰; 接触; 【几】切. ②(触到时)有…的感觉. ③【医】触诊; 【宗】摸治(有瘰疬的)病人. ④接近; 将近,将达 *(at; to; on; upon)*. ⑤(兵士)密集. ⑥提及,论及,同…有关 *(on; upon)*. ⑦(船)停靠 *(at)*. *The sad story ~ed his heart.* 那个悲惨的故事触动了他的心弦. *He is a little ~ed.* 他有点儿感动. *You ~ me there.* 你的话我受不了[扎耳朵]. *The plants were ~ed with frost.* 这植物被霜冻伤了. *He ~ed his 20.* 他已经到二十岁了. *I couldn't ~ the algebra paper.* 我啃不动[做不出]代数问题. *Nothing will ~ these stains.* 没有什么东西能消除这些斑点. *The abuse does not ~ me.* 那种话骂不着我. *I never ~ a drop.* 我一滴酒都不沾. *clouds ~ed with rose* 带玫瑰色的云彩. *The law can't ~ him.* 法律干涉不了他. *There is nothing to ~ mountain air for giving you an appetite.* 没有任何东西能比得上山间的空气更能促进你的食欲. ***as ~ing*** 关于. ***~ at*** 停靠(某一港埠); 接近. ***~ down*** = ~-down. ***~ elbows*** 紧接; 亲密. ***~ (sb.) for (a fiver)*** 〔俚〕(向某人)借[讨](五块钱). ***~ (sb.) home [to the quick]*** 触怒,触犯; 触及痛处. ***~ in*** 增改,添画(细微部分). ***~ it off to the nines*** 好好干. ***~ (sb.) nearly*** (与某人)有密切关系. ***~ (sb.) off*** 超过(某人). ***~ off*** 正确地表现; 草草写; 添画; 发射; 使(炸药)爆发; 使开始; 挂断电话. ***~ on*** 说到,接近 (*~ on the matter lightly* 轻描淡写地说一说). ***~ one's hat to ...*** 用手触帽行礼. ***~ out*** 【棒球】触杀; 〔俚〕碰到好运气,弄得好. ***~ pitch*** 参加干坏事; 接近坏人. ***~ success*** 终于成功. ***~ the spot*** 〔口〕奏效. ***~ the wind*** 【海】开足马力. ***~ up*** 润色; 完成; 用鞭等轻轻打(马); 轻轻打痛; 唤起(回忆等). ***~ upon*** = ~ on. — *n.* ①触,碰; 摸,摩; 接触; 联系. ②触感,触觉. ③一触,一碰; 修饰,添画,润色; 一笔; 笔触; 技巧,手腕. ④精神接触,感动; 同情,同感; 一致. ⑤痕迹,微量,一点点; 小毛病. ⑥特性,性质; 气质,风味. ⑦论到,提到,说到; 暗示. ⑧(金银的)纯度; (纯度)检验戳记; 验证; 标准; 试验; 试金石; 【物】接触磁化; 【乐】弹奏(法); 【医】触诊; 【橄榄球】触地; (边线与球门线间的)可触地得分的地区. ⑨〔儿戏〕捉迷藏. ⑩〔俚〕告借; 侵吞; 偷. *~ of nature* 自然的感情; 人情味. *~ of the sun* 轻微的中暑[日射病]. *finishing ~es* (绘画等时)最后修饰的几笔; 完成. *a characteristic ~* (话等的)特色. *a shilling ~* 〔口〕一先令上下. *the Nelson ~* (对付难局的)奈尔逊式的果断手腕. *a ~ of irony* 一点讽刺意味. *want a ~ of salt* 咸味不够; 不够味. *This piano is wanting in ~.* 这架钢琴键盘不好[声音不好]. ***a near ~*** 九死一生. ***at a ~*** 稍微一触就,一碰就 (*at a ~ he yielded.* 才一接触他就让步了). ***bring to the ~*** 试验. ***have a ~ of the tar-brush*** 〔卑〕带有一点儿黑人的血统. ***in ~ of*** 在…能达到的地方, 在…的附近. ***in ~ with*** 取得[保持]联系; 同情, 一致. ***keep [lose] ~ with*** 同…保持[失去]联系; 知道[不知道]…的情况. ***out of ~ with*** 和…没有通信, 和…失去联系, 不表同情; 和…不一致. ***put to the ~*** 试验. ***true as ~*** 的的确确,一点没错. ***within ~ of*** 在…的附近. **~-and-go** *n., a.* (稍微接触就跑掉的)快速(行动); 轻率(的), 简略(的); 一触即发的(不稳局面). **~ body, ~ corpuscle** 【解】触觉体. **~-down**【橄榄球】触地得分;【空】着陆; 着陆过程中的一部分; 着陆时间. **~hole** (旧式炮的)火门. **~-last** 捉迷藏. **~line** 【足球】边线. **~-me-not**【植】凤仙花(属); 苍白凤仙花; 喷瓜;【医】狼疮; 碰不得的人[事物]. **~ paper** 导火纸. **~stone** 试金石; 〔喻〕检验标准. **~ system** 打字的指法. **~-type** *vi.* 按固定指法打字. **~wood** 火绒; 易着火的东西; 暴躁的人; (一碰到树就不能捉的)捉猫游戏.

touch•a•ble [ˈtʌtʃəbl] *a.* 可触知的; 可食用的. **-a•bil•i•ty** *n.*

tou•ché [tuːˈʃei] *int.* 〔击剑〕击中〔对方击中得分〕; 〔转喻〕言中! 〔承认争论中对方论点正中要害〕.

touched [tʌtʃt] *a.* ①激动的,感动的. ②有点发痴的,精神轻微失常的 (= touched in the head).

touch•er [ˈtʌtʃə] *n.* 触摸的人[物]; 神枪手; 〔俚〕一触即发[千钧一发]的危急状况. ***as near as a ~*** 〔俚〕差一点,快要,险些儿.

touch•ing [ˈtʌtʃiŋ] *a.* 动人的; 令人感动的. — *prep.* 关于,提到 (= as ~).

touch•y [ˈtʌtʃi] *a.* *(-i•er; -i•est)* 易怒的,暴躁的; 麻烦的,棘手的,难办的(工作等); 过分敏感的; 易燃烧的. **-i•ly** *ad.* **-i•ness** *n.*

tough [tʌf] *a.* ①强韧的, 弯折不断的; 胶粘的. ②硬,嚼不动的(肉等); 强健的; 〔口〕强硬的(政策等). ③不屈不挠的,坚强的; 顽固的,固执的. ④〔美〕无法无天的,暴戾的,凶恶的. ⑤难办的,费力的,棘手的(工作等); 〔口〕困苦的(命运等). ⑥〔美俚〕极好的. — *n.* 〔美俚〕恶棍,无赖. *a ~ customer* 〔口〕粗卤的家伙. *a ~ guy* 〔美〕无赖. *Things are ~.* 生活艰难. *a ~ story* 难以相信的故事. ***Tough!*** 〔俚〕不见得吧! ***get ~*** 〔美俚〕凶恶起来; 行动勇敢. ***have a ~ time of it*** 日子不好过. ***~ luck*** 〔美俚〕时运不佳; 不幸. ***~ on the suckers*** 〔美〕笨人需要花很多钱才能得到的经验. — *vi.* 〔美俚〕忍耐困难. *~ it out* 忍耐过去. **~-break** 〔美俚〕小小的不幸. **~-minded** *a.* (态度, 思想)现实的,讲究实际的; 意志坚强的, 顽强的. **~ racket** 〔美〕困难的工作. **~rubber** 硬橡皮. **~ wood** 韧木. **-ness** 韧度,韧性.

tough•en [ˈtʌfn] *vt., vi.* 使[变]强韧; 使[变]硬; 使[变]强健; 使[变]坚强; 使[变]顽固; 使[变]困难.

tough•ie, tough•y [ˈtʌfi] *n.* *(pl. -ies)* 〔口〕①暴徒, 流氓,恶棍. ②难题; 困境.

Tou•lon [tuːlɔ̃ːŋ] *n.* 土伦〔法国港市〕.

tou•pee, tou•pet [ˈtuːpei] *n.* 〔F.〕(尤指头顶上的)一缕头发; (遮住秃顶的)男用假发.

tour [tuə] *n.* 漫游,游览,周游; 旅行; (剧团的)巡回演出; 巡回医疗; 【军】(在海外基地为时 2—3 年的)服役期 (= ~ of duty); (轮值的)班. *a ~ of inspection* 视察旅行,巡视. *a ~ of the country* = *a provincial ~* 外地巡回演出. ***go on a ~*** 漫游,巡回,周游. ***make a ~ of the world*** 周游世界. ***on ~*** 漫游中,周游中,巡回中. ***the grand ~*** 【史】(旧时英国大学生毕业前的)大陆旅行. — *vi., vt.* 周游,游览,旅行; 参观(画展等); (使)巡回演出[医疗]; (车)慢慢开行. *~ France and Italy* 周游法国和意大利. **~ing car** (一般指能坐 5—6 人的)游览(汽)车. **~ing company** 巡回剧团.

tou·ra·co [tu:rəˈkəu] *n.* 【鸟】(非洲)大杜鹃.
tour·bil·lion [tuəˈbiljən] *n.* ①旋风，旋风涡. ②回旋烟火.
tour de force [ˈtuədəˈfɔ:s] 〔F.〕壮举，绝技；(艺术上的)力作.
tour·er [ˈtuərə] *n.* 旅游者，游客；游览车[飞机].
tourism [ˈtuərizəm] *n.* ①旅游，游览旅行. ②= tourist industry.
tour·ist [ˈtuərist] *n.* 漫游者；旅游者，观光者，游客；〔美〕冬季到南部做工的流动工人. ~ **agency** 旅行社. ~ **attraction** 旅游胜地；吸引游客的事物. ~ **bureau** 旅行社；旅游招待所. ~ **class** 〔美〕(轮船的)经济舱，(火车，飞机的)经济座[舱]. ~ **court** = motel. ~ **industry** 旅游事业. ~ **home** 有房间租给旅客的私人住宅. ~ **party** 游览参观团. ~ **sleeper** 〔美〕(软席)卧车[客舱]. ~ **ticket** 旅游经济票. ~ **trap** 敲竹杠的旅馆、饭店、商店等.
tour·ma·lin(e) [ˈtuəməli:n] *n.* 【矿】电气石，碧珊.
tour·na·ment [ˈtuənəmənt] *n.* (中世纪武士的)马上比武大会；比赛，锦标赛. *a chess* ~ 象棋比赛. *a league* ~ 联赛.
tournay [ˈtuəˈnei] *n.* (家具装饰用)陶奈印花细呢.
tour·ne·dos [tuəniˈdəu] *n.* ***(pl. -dos*** [-ˈdəu]***)*** 酱汁嫩牛排.
tour·ney [ˈtuəni] *n.* = tournament. — *vi.* 参加马上比武；参加比赛.
tour·ni·quet [ˈtuəniket] *n.* 【医】止血带，压脉器.
tour·nure [ˈtuənjuə] *n.* 〔F.〕轮廓；身材；(张裙)腰架；(女服的)臀部.
Tours [tuəz] *n.* 图尔斯〔姓氏〕.
tou·sle, tou·zle [ˈtauzl] *vt.* 〔口〕搅乱，弄乱(头发等)；搞乱. — *n.* 乱发；蓬头散发；纷乱状态.
tou·sy [ˈtauzi] *a.* ①蓬头散发的，乱套的. ②简陋的，不讲究的.
Tout [taut] *n.* 陶特〔姓氏〕.
tout [taut] *vi.* 招徕，兜售；死乞白赖地劝诱；〔美〕拉选票 *(for)*；秘密打听(赛马)情报 *(round)*. — *vt.* ①竭力称许[推荐]；招徕，兜售. ②打听有关…的消息；暗通. ③提供赛马情报；〔美〕供给(赛马)情报；做(赛马)情报员. — *n.* 劝诱；招揽；招揽员；(赛马)情报员，暗通消息的人；〔口〕替盗贼把风的人.
tout à fait [ˌtu:təˈfei] 〔F.〕完全，全然.
tout court [tu:ˈkuə] 〔F.〕简单地，简短地. *He called me Jones tout court.* 他简单地叫我琼斯.
tout en·sem·ble [ˌtu:tɑ̃:nˈsɑ̃:mbl] 〔F.〕整体；概观；整体效果.
tout le monde [tu lə mɔ̃d] 〔F.〕全世界；所有的人.
tou·zle [ˈtauzl] *n., vt.* = tousle.
to·va·risch [təuˈvɑ:riʃ] *n.* 〔Russ.〕同志；苏联人.
To·vey [ˈtəuvi, ˈtʌvi] *n.* 托维〔姓氏〕.
TOW = ①tube-launched optically-tracked wire-guided (anti-tank missile) "陶"式反坦克导弹〔一种用纯管式发射器发射的光学跟踪有线制导反坦克导弹〕. ②takeoff weight 起飞全重.
tow¹ [təu] *vt.* (人、马等沿岸)拉(纤等)；(一船用绳子)拖(其他的船)；用绳子牵(牛等)；拖着走，拉着(孩子)走；在水面上拉(标本采集网). *a ~ed target* 拖靶. *a ~ing airplane* 拖靶飞机. — *n.* 用绳拖曳；拖绳；拖船；拖车. *a number of admirers in* ~ 身后跟着一大群赞赏[崇拜]他的人[影迷、戏迷等]. ***have in ~ = take in ~*** 拉纤，拖航；指导，照顾；拖带，身后跟着. ~**boat** 拖轮，拖驳. ~ **line** 拖缆，纤. ~**net** (采集用)拖网. ~**path** 纤路. ~ **rope** 拖缆，拖索. ~ **truck** 拖曳车[用来拖走抛锚或停放在禁止停放地点的车辆].
tow² [tau] *n.* ①【纺】落纤；短麻屑；亚麻短纤维；丝束，纤维束. ②亚麻色头发. ~ *cloth* 粗麻布. ~**head** 亚麻色头发；头发淡黄的人.
tow·age [ˈtəuidʒ] *n.* 牵引；拖船；拖船费.
to·ward, to·wards [təˈwɔ:d, -wɔ:dz] *prep.* ①〔运动、方向、位置〕朝，向；走向. *set out* ~ *the town* 向镇上出发. *a tendency* ~ *co-operation* (走向)合作的趋势. *The house looks* ~ *the sea.* 房子朝着海. *get* ~ 靠近 (*cf. get* to). *I look* ~ *you.* 〔谑〕= *Here's* ~ (普通 *to*) *you.* 敬您一杯. ②〔时间〕近…，左右. ~*s evening* 天快黑时. ~ *five o'clock* 五点钟模样. ~ *sixty years of age* 快近60岁. ③〔数〕近，约. *There were* ~ *a thousand of them.* 来了[约有]一千人左右. ④〔目的〕为，有助于，可用于. *I saved something* ~ *his education.* 我为了他的教育储蓄了一些钱. *This money goes* ~ *the debts.* 这钱预备用来还债. *go far* ~ 大有助于. ⑤〔关系〕对…. *I felt kindly* ~ *him.* 我对他产生了好感. *their attitude* ~ *the new republic* 他们对新共和国的态度. — [ˈtəuəd] *a.* ①〔古〕〔用作 *pred.*〕迫近的，就要发生[举行]的. ②前途有望的(青年等). ③〔英古〕温顺的，听话的 *(opp.* froward*)*. ④正在进行中. *There is some work* ~. 有的工作正在进行中. **-ly** *ad.*
tow·el [ˈtauəl, taul] *n.* 毛巾；〔美〕擦脸[手]纸 (= paper ~). ***a lead*** ~ 〔俚〕子弹. ***an oaken*** ~ 〔古、俚〕棍棒. ***throw [toss] in the*** ~ 【拳击】承认打败；认输，投降. — *vt., vi.* (〔英〕***-ll-***) 用毛巾擦；〔俚〕殴打. ~ *away at one's face* 拿毛巾擦脸. ~ *oneself* 拿毛巾擦身体. ~ **gourd** 丝瓜. ~ **horse,** ~ **rack** 毛巾架. ~ **rail** (钉在墙上的)毛巾架.
towel·ling, 〔美〕 **tow·el·ing** [ˈtauəliŋ] *n.* 毛巾布[料]；用毛巾擦；〔俚〕殴打.
tow·er [ˈtauə] *n.* 塔，楼塔；城堡，碉堡；要害地；〔罕〕(负伤鸟的)笔直向上飞；〔美〕铁路信号所. *a bell* ~ 钟楼. *a keep* ~ 城楼. *a martello* ~ 【史】海岸圆炮塔. *a watch* ~ 望楼. *a water* ~ 给水塔；(水库泄水口的)水塔. *the T- (of London)* 伦敦塔. ~ *and town* 〔诗〕有人家的地方. ~ *of ivory* 象牙塔. ~ *of strength* 非常可靠的人；干城，柱石. — *vi.* 高耸 *(above)*；胜过；(鹰等)翱翔；(负伤的鸟)笔直飞上去. ~ **clock** 屋顶钟，楼钟. ~ **house** 中世纪的城堡. ~ **man,** ~**-operator** 〔美〕信号员，守望员.
tow·ered [ˈtauəd] *a.* 高耸云霄的；有塔的.
tow·er·ing [ˈtauəriŋ] *a.* 高耸的，屹立的；突出的；高傲的；激烈的. ~*ing crimes* 滔天罪行.
Tow·er(s) [ˈtauə(z)] *n.* 托尔(斯)〔姓氏〕.
tow·er·y [ˈtauəri] *a.* 有塔的；高耸的.
tow·head [ˈtəuˌhed] *n.* ①浅黄头发. ②浅黄头发的人. **-ed** *a.*
tow·hee [ˈtauhi:, ˈtəu-] *n.* 〔美〕【动】(北美)雀科的鸟.
town [taun] *n.* ①镇，市镇，城镇〔狭义：大于 village (村)而非 city(市)的地方. 广义：和 country (乡村)相对而言时，不独 city 和 borough (自治市)，连 urban district 市(区)亦可称为 ~. 有 market 或 fair (市集)的小于 urban district 的村落，亦称为 ~. 美国 New England 各州把相当于 city，无行政机关，仅有 ~ meeting 的自治市称为 ~；其他各州的 ~ 则相当于 ~ship 的 ②义〕. ②〔the ~〕城镇居民；全体居民. ③〔不用冠词〕城市；市区，商业中心区. ④〔Scot.〕小农场内的房屋；〔方〕村，小村庄；土拨鼠的窠. *a county* ~ 县城. *the* ~ (附近的)市镇；镇民，市民. *The whole* ~ *knows of it.* 镇上的人没有一个不知道. *woman of the* ~ 妓女. ***a man about*** ~ (尤指伦敦的)在俱乐部、剧场等处闲混日子的人，高等游民. ***carry a*** ~ 洗劫市镇. ***come to*** ~ 到京里[城里]来；出现，登场；入伙；发迹，成功. ***come upon the*** ~ 变成都市里的高等游民；变成娼妓[盗贼]. ***go down*** ~ 〔美〕到商业区去，买东西去；〔俚〕成功. ***go to*** ~ ①进京，上省，进城. ②〔美〕去市区买东西；过浮华生活；会活动；有声望. ***hit*** ~ 到达. ***in*** ~ 在京里，在省上[城里]，〔英〕在伦敦. ***jump the*** ~ 逃亡. ***on*** [= upon] ***the*** ~ 过着高等游民的生活；过着娼妓[盗贼]的生活;〔美〕受城里慈善机构的救济. ***out of*** ～ 已离京[城市],〔英〕不在伦敦;已到乡下. ～ **and gown**(英国牛津和剑桥的)市民和大学里的人. ～ **clerk** 镇公所秘书长. ～ **council** 镇议会. ～ **councillor** 镇议会议员. ～ **crier** 到处宣述新颁规则等的镇公务员;〔美俚〕声音特别大的电台歌手. ～ **dweller** = townsman. ～ **farm**〔美〕养老院. ～ **girl** 城镇女郎;妓女. ～ **hall** 市政厅,镇公所. ～ **house**〔英〕①市内住宅,英国贵族的伦敦住宅(*opp*. country seat, country house). ② = ～ hall. ～**let** 小城市. ～ **mains** 城市(煤气)总管道. **T- Major**【军】(市镇)驻军军官. ～ **marshal**〔美〕市警察局长. ～ **meeting**〔美〕市民大会;市政会议〔尤指新英格兰市镇中有选举权者计议市政的集会〕. ～ **planning** 都市计划. ～**ship** ①【英史】=parish. ②〔美〕区〔县下的行政区划〕(New England 的)自治市. ③〔澳〕(计划中的)市区. ～**sman** 市民;镇民代表. ～ **talk** 街谈巷议. ～ **woman** 城市女居民;妓女.

Town(e) [taun] *n.* 汤〔姓氏〕.

town·ee, town·ie [tauˈniː] *n.* 城市[市镇]居民.

Townes [taunz] *n.* 汤斯〔姓氏〕.

towns·folk, towns·people [ˈtaunzfəuk, -piːpl] *n.*〔*pl.*〕都市[城镇]居民.

towns·man [ˈtaunzmən] *n.* 市民,镇民;同市镇的人. *a fellow* ～ 同乡.

tow·ser [ˈtauzə] *n.* ①大狗. ②〔口〕高大粗犷的男人;精明强悍的人. *He is a* ～ *for work and perfect for job*. 他工作扎扎实实,对业务精益求精.

tow·y [ˈtəui] *a.* 麻屑(色一样)的;淡黄头发的.

tox. = toxic.

tox·al·bu·min [ˌtɔksælˈbjuːmin] *n.*【化】毒清蛋白.

toxa·phene [ˈtɔksəfin] *n.*【化】毒杀芬,氯化莰〔有机氯杀虫剂〕.

tox·(a)e·mi·a [tɔkˈsiːmiə] *n.*【医】毒血症.

tox·e·mic [tɔkˈsimik] *a.*【医】毒血症的.

tox·ic [ˈtɔksik] *a.* 有毒的;中毒的. ～ *smoke [gases]* 毒烟,毒气. ～ *value* 毒效. ～ *anaemia* 中毒性贫血. ～ *symptoms* 中毒症状. **-i·cal·ly** *ad.*

tox·i·cant [ˈtɔksikənt] *a.* 有毒性的. — *n.* 毒;毒物,毒药;毒素.

tox·i·cation [ˌtɔksiˈkeiʃən] *n.* 中毒.

toxico- *comb. f.* 表示"有毒,中毒": *toxico*genic, *toxico*logy.

tox·i·co·gen·ic [ˌtɔksikəuˈdʒenik] *a.* 产生有毒物质的.

tox·i·co·log·ic, -log·i·cal [ˌtɔksikəˈlɔdʒik, -lɔdʒikəl] *a.* 毒物学的.

tox·i·col·o·gy [ˌtɔksiˈkɔlədʒi] *n.* 毒理学,毒物学. **-o·gist** *n.* 毒物学家.

tox·i·co·sis [ˌtɔksiˈkəusis] *n.*【医】中毒.

tox·in(e) [ˈtɔksin] *n.* 毒素,毒质.

tox·in·an·ti·tox·in [ˈtɔksinˌæntiˈtɔksin] *n.*【药】毒素抗毒素合剂.

tox·oid [ˈtɔksɔid] *n.* 类毒素.

tox·o·ly·sin [ˈtɔksəlaisin] *n.* 解毒素.

tox·oph·i·lite [tɔkˈsɔfilait] *n.* 箭术研究家,爱好箭术的人. **-lit·ic** *a.*

tox·y [ˈtɔksi] *a.*〔Scot.〕〔俚〕喝醉了的.

toy [tɔi] *n.* 玩具;玩物;儿戏一样的事情;游戏;消遣;象玩具一样的小东西;矮小的人;小动物;无实用价值的东西;小装饰品;〔古〕废话;滑稽文章,无聊文章;双关话,诙谐,戏谑;〔美〕怪人. — *a.* 玩具的,模型的;玩具一样的. *a* ～ *dog* 养着玩的小狗. *a* ～ *soldier* (铅制的)玩具兵. *a* ～ *drama* 木偶戏剧本. ***make a*** ～ ***of*** 当做玩具[消遣],玩弄,不认真做;(小孩子)做…玩. — *vi.* 玩耍;玩弄,当做玩具;玩弄,调戏,戏弄 *(with)*. ～ **box** 玩具箱;〔海俚〕船上的轮机室. ～**shop** 玩具店. ～ **theatre** 木偶戏剧场;小剧场.

To·ya·ma [təuˈjaːmə] *n.* 富山〔日本城市〕.

toy·man [ˈtɔimən] *n.* 玩具商;玩具制作者.

Toyn·bee [ˈtɔinbi] *n.* 托因比〔姓氏〕.

to·yon [ˈtaujən] *n.*【植】柳叶石楠 *(Heteromeles arbutifolia)*〔产于加利福尼亚州〕.

tp. = telephone; township; troop.

t.p. = title page.

t.p.i. = twists per inch【纺】每英寸拈数.

TPN = Triphospho-pyridine nucleotide【生化】三磷酸吡啶核甙酸.

tpr. = trooper.

TPR = temperature, pulse, respiration【医】体温、脉搏、呼吸.

tps. = townships.

TR = Training Regulations 操典.

Tr. =①Treasurer. ②Troop. ③Trust. ④Trustee.

tr = ①tare. ②tower. ③trace. ④train. ⑤transactions. ⑥transition. ⑦transitive. ⑧translated. ⑨translator. ⑩transport(ation). ⑪treasurer. ⑫tributary. ⑬trill. ⑭trust(ee).

Tr(s) = troops.

tra- *pref.* = trans-.

tra·be·at·ed [ˈtreibiˌeitid] *a.* 有横梁的. **tra·be·a·tion** [ˌtreibiˈeiʃən] *n.*【建】横梁式结构;柱顶盘.

tra·bec·u·la [trəˈbekjulə] *n.* *(pl. -lae,* [-ˌliː] *-las)* ①【解、动】(昆虫的)蕈体柄;梁,桁,柱;(古生物的)羽榍. ②【植】横条;横隔片. **-r, -te** *a.*

trace[1] [treis] *n.* ①迹,足迹;踪迹,去向. ②痕迹;证迹,线索,结果;【心】记忆痕;【植】(脉)迹. ③微量,【化】痕量;一点点. ④迹线,图形,图样;【筑城】示意图,略图;(自记仪器的)记录图象;(示波器上的)扫描(行程),扫迹. ⑤【几】交点,交线;接触线;描迹;描绘;【军】经始线;【气象】小到不能计量的雨量〔略作 T〕. *a* ～ *of fear* 微微有点害怕. ***(hot) on the*** ～***s of*** 追踪,追近. — *vt.* ①跟踪,追踪;侦探,探索,查找. ②顺着去,跟着…去;追溯由来,追究. ③描绘,画轮廓,打图样;【军】画出(军事设施的)经始线;(用心)写;〔喻〕计画. ④描摹,映描;复写. ⑤【建】用花窗格装饰. ～ **back** 追溯 (*The report has been* ～*d back to you*. 这个谣言追究到你这里来了). ～ **beans**〔美俚〕非常好奇. ～ **out** 探寻踪迹;描摹,映写;计画 (～ *(out) a plan* 映绘平面图. ～ *(out) a policy* 草拟一项政策). — *vi.* ①沿路走;沿路线走. ②追溯到 *(to)*. ～ **element** 痕量[微量元素].

trace[2] [treis] *n.* (马车等的)挽绳,挽车的皮带;【机】连动杆;【植】(脉)迹. ***in the*** ～***s*** 上着挽绳;负担日常工作. ***jump the*** ～***s*** 挣脱挽绳;〔喻〕摆脱束缚. ***kick over the*** ～***s*** (马)踢脱挽绳;〔喻〕不受驾驭,反抗.

trace·a·ble [ˈtreisəbl] *a.* 可追踪的;可追溯的;起源于…的;证迹明白的;可映摹的;可描画的,可摹写的. **-bly** *ad.* **-ness, -bil·i·ty** *n.*

trace·less [ˈtreislis] *a.* 无痕迹的. **-ly** *ad.*

trac·er [ˈtreisə] *n.* 追踪者;追踪物,示踪物;描摹者;描图员;描记器;画线笔,尖笔;航迹自画器;失物追查员;失单;【物】示踪物;曳光剂;【军】曳光弹;【医】探针. *a* ～ *atom* 示踪原子. ～ **bullet** [～ **shell**]【军】曳光弹.

trac·er·y [ˈtreisəri] *n.* ①【建】(哥德式建筑的)花窗格 ②(刺绣、雕刻等的)网眼工艺.

tra·che·a [trəˈkiːə] *n.* *(pl.* ～*s, -che·ae* [-kiiː]*)*【解】气管;【植】导管;(昆虫的)呼吸管.

tra·che·ate [ˈtreikiˌeit] *a.*【动】通过气管(呼吸管)呼吸的.

tra·che·id [ˈtreikiːid] *n.*【植】管胞. **-al** *a.*

trach·e·i·tis [trækiˈaitis] *n.*【医】气管炎.

tracheo- *comb. f.* 气管,导管: *tracheo*tomy, *tracheo*phyte.

tra·che·o·bron·chi·al [ˌtreikiəuˈbrɔŋkiəl] *a.*【解】气管支气管的.

tra·che·ole [ˈtreikiˌəul] *n.*【动】(昆虫的)小气管.

tra·che·o·phyte [ˈtreikiəuˌfit] *n.*【植】导管植物.

trach·e·ot·o·my [ˌtrækiˈɔtəmi] *n.*【医】气管切开术.

tra·cho·ma [trəˈkəumə] *n.*【医】颗粒性结膜炎，沙眼．**-tous** *a.*
tra·chyte [ˈtreikait, ˈtrækait] *n.*【地】粗面岩．
tra·chyt·ic [trəˈkitik] *a.* 粗面的．
trac·ing [ˈtreisiŋ] *n.* 追踪，追溯，追查；描摹，映写，复写；摹图；映写图，透写物；示踪，显迹；【物】线路图寻迹；自动仪表的记录图象．～ **cloth** = ～ **linen** 描图布．～ **paper** 透明描图纸．
track[1] [træk] *vt.* 用纤拉船．— *vi.* 拉纤行驶．～ **road** 纤道．**-age** *n.* 拉纤．**-er** *n.* 拉纤的人．
track[2] [træk] *n.* ①轨迹，轮迹，航迹，痕迹；〔*pl.*〕足迹．②小路，小径；【物】径迹；历程，路程；行程；行动路线；思路．③(阴谋等的)形迹，线索；跟踪目标；导向装置．④【运】跑道；径赛[田径]运动；〔美〕铁道路线，轨道；(录音磁带的)音轨．【机】履带，环带；跨距；(两轮间的)轮距；【地】开合脉．*the beaten* ～ 踏出来的路；常规，惯例．*a single [double]* ～ 单[双]轨．***clear the*** ～ 让路；〔命令〕走开！让开！***cover (up) one's ～s*** 隐匿行踪；隐藏自己的企图[计划等]．***in one's ～s***〔俚〕就在那里，就那样；〔美〕当场；立刻．***in the ～ of*** 仿…的例，学…的样；在…的中途，正在…．***jump [leave] the*** ～〔美〕出轨．***keep ～ of*** 追踪；记录；保持联系；密切注意…的动向．***lay ～s*** 铺轨．***lose ～ of***〔喻〕忘记，失去联系．***make ～s*** 走开；跑掉，逃走；追 *(for)*．***off the*** ～ 出轨；出岔子；(话)离题；(猎狗)失去嗅迹，失去(犯人的)线索．***on the ～ of*** 跟踪追赶，尾追；没有出轨；未出岔子；话未离题；得到…的线索．***put sb. on the ～ of*** 使追踪．***throw off the*** ～ 摆脱(追踪者)．— *vt.* 跟踪 追赶 *(down)*；踏成(道路)；践踏，踏脏，踏平(等)；通过(荒漠)；铺设铁路[铁轨]；顺着走(旧辙)；探索 *(out)*；拖(船)．— *vi.* 追踪；留下行迹；铺设铁路[铁轨]；(车)顺着一定线路走；(车轮)具有一定轮距；〔美口〕走小路，前进；(船)被拖着走．～ *mud through a house* 踏得一屋子泥．～ **athletics [events]**【运】径赛．～ **clearer** (机车、雪车等前方的)排障器；(机车的)排雪装置．～ **gauge** 轨距；轨距规．～**ing station** 雷达跟踪站．～ **layer**〔美〕铺轨工人．～ **laying** 铺轨．～ **line** 架空线．～**man**〔美〕铁路护路员，田径运动员．～**master**【铁路】护路员．～**meet**〔美〕田径运动会．～ **record** 成绩纪录．～ **road** 纤道．～ **system** 按学生测验成绩编班制．～ **walker**〔美〕护路员．～ **way** 轨道．**-age** 拖船；〔集合词〕轨道；铁道路线；铁道路线全长里数；铁道使用权[使用费]．**-er** 追踪者；【无】跟踪系统；跟踪器；【军】跟踪标定仪；搜索者；纤夫．**-ing** 跟踪，跟踪目标；【影】跟踪摄影 (*aided [automatic] tracking* 半自动[自动]跟踪)．
track·less [ˈtræklis] *a.* 没有足迹的；人迹未到的；没有路的；不留痕迹的；没有轨道的 (*trackless trams [trolley]* 无轨电车)．
tract[1] [trækt] *n.* ①广阔的地面；(一大段)土地[森林]，地带；地域；广阔海面[天空]．②〔古〕一段时间，长时间．③【解】管，道，系统；(神经纤维的)束．*a wooded* ～ 一大片森林．*digestive* ～ 消化道．*the optic* ～ 视(神经)束．*the motor* ～ 运动神经索．
tract[2] [trækt] *n.* (政治、宗教的)短论；小册子；传单；【天主】续唱．
tract·a·ble [ˈtræktəbl] *a.* 温顺的，驯良的，易驾驭的；易处理的，易加工的．**-bly** *ad.* **-bil·i·ty** *n.*
Trac·tar·i·an [trækˈtɛəriən] *a.* (十九世纪三十年代鼓吹复兴天主教的)牛津运动的．— *n.* 牛津运动者；牛津运动论文作者．**-ism** [-izm] *n.* = Oxford movement.
trac·tate [ˈtrækteit] *n.* (专题)论文；小册子．
tractile [ˈtræktail] *a.* 可拉长的；可牵引的．
trac·tion [ˈtrækʃən] *n.* 拖曳，拖拉，牵引；牵引力；〔喻〕吸力，魅力；【医】(对于肌肉等的)牵引(术)；〔美〕市内铁路，有轨电车．*force of* ～ 拖力．*animal* ～ 畜力．*motor [steam]* ～ 汽车[铁路]运输．～ **engine** 牵引机．～ **wheel** (火车头的)动轨．**-al** *a.*
trac·tive [ˈtræktiv] *a.* 拖的，牵引的．～ *effort [force, power]* 牵引力．～ *resistance* 牵引阻力．
trac·tor [ˈtræktə] *n.* 拖拉机；牵引车；〔空〕牵引式飞机 *(opp.* pusher*)*；【医】牵引器．*a farm* ～ 农用拖拉机．～**-trailer** 拖拉机拖车．
trac·to·rette [ˌtræktəˈret] *n.*〔美〕拖拉机女驾驶员．
Tracy [ˈtreisi] *n.* 特蕾西〔姓氏，女子名〕．
trade [treid] *n.* ①贸易；商业，交易；零售商．②职业；行业；(铁匠、木匠等的)手艺．③〔the ～〕〔集合词〕同业，同行；〔口〕酒品制造商人，酒商；〔美〕〔集合词〕顾客，主顾．④〔美〕(政党间的)妥协，政治交易．⑤〔the ～s〕【气象】贸易风；〔英军俚〕潜艇部队．⑥〔方〕碎屑；〔方〕路；常习．*domestic [home]* ～ 国内贸易．*foreign [international]* ～ 对外[国际]贸易．*fair* ～ 互惠贸易；*free* ～ 自由贸易；〔古〕走私．*balance of* ～ 贸易差额．*the* ～ *of war* 军人的职业．*a* ～ *test* 技能考试，技术考试．*service* ～*s* 服务(性)行业．*every man for his own* ～ *[every one to his* ～*]* 各专其业．***be in*** ～ 是零售商，做小买卖．***by*** ～ 职业是．***drive [do, make] a roaring*** ～ 生意兴隆．— *vi.* ①贸易，做买卖．②买东西 *(at)*．③对换；做正当或不正当交易 *(in; with; for)*．～ *in salt* 做盐生意．～ *at a store* 在商店买东西．— *vt.* ①从事(证券等)交易．②以某物换取他物 *(sth. for sth. else)*；同某人交换某物 *(sth. with sb.)*．～ ***away*** 卖掉．～ ***in*** 用交换方式购入．～ ***off*** 卖出．～ ***(up)on*** *(sb.'s reputation)* 利用(某人的)名声．～ **acceptance** 商业承兑汇票．～ **agreement** (职业等的)雇佣合同．～ **association** 同业公会．～ **board** 劳资协商会议．～ **book [edition]** 普及版．～ **books** 商业帐簿．～ **circular** 传单；回单；报单．～ **cycle**【商】(景气的)周期性．～ **discount** 同行折扣．～ **guild [organization]** 同业公会．～ **hall** 工会会所．～**-in** ① *n.* 折价物；作价提交的货品；夹有折价物的交易；折价价格．② *a.* 作价提交的．～ **journal** 行业杂志[公报]．～**-last** 交换的好消息〔希望换取对方把听到赞扬自己的话告诉自己，而告诉对方的自己所听到的赞扬对方的话〕(*I have a* ～*-last for you.* 我听到有人称赞你啦)．～**-mark** ① *n.* 商标．② *vt.* 贴上商标；登记…的商标．～**s' man** (小)商人，零售商人；〔方〕工匠，熟练工人．～ **name** 商号；商品的业内名称．～**-off** 交易．～**s' people** 商人们；〔集合词〕零售商贩；零售商贩的家属．～ **première**【影】(内部)试映．～ **price** 批发价，同行价．～ **route** 商人路线，商船航线．～ **school** 中等职业学校．～ **secret** 厂商的制造秘密．～ **show**【影】预映．～**s' union**〔主英〕= trade union〔美国叫 labor union〕．～**s' woman** 女零售商人．～ **union** 工会．～ **unionism** 工会主义．～ **unionist** 工会会员；工会主义者．～ **waste** 工业废液．～ **wind**【气象】信风，贸易风．
trad·er [ˈtreidə] *n.* ①商人．②〔美〕证券交易所中以自己做买卖为主的经纪人．③商船．
trad·es·can·ti·a [ˌtrædisˈkænʃiə] *n.*【植】紫露草属植物 (= spiderwort).
trading [ˈtreidiŋ] *a.* 从事商业的．～ **estate** (计划性的)商业区．～ **post** (欧美贸易商在非洲等处内地设立的与当地人交易的)贸易站．～ **stamp**〔美〕赠品兑换券．
tra·di·tion [trəˈdiʃən] *n.* ①传说，口碑．②传统；惯例．③【宗】经外传说．④【法】移交，引渡．*break* ～ 打破惯例．*stage* ～ 舞台惯例．***by*** ～ 照传统；据口传．***handed down by*** ～ 口头相传．***T- says [runs] that*** ... 据历代传说．***true to*** ～ 名不虚传地．
tra·di·tion·al, tra·di·tion·a·ry [trəˈdiʃənəl, -ʃənəri] *a.* 口头传说的；传统的，惯例的，因袭的．～ *Chinese medicine* 中药．
tra·di·tion·al·ism [trəˈdiʃənəlizəm] *n.* 传统主义；因袭[墨守]惯例．
tra·di·tion·al·ist [trəˈdiʃənlist] *n.* 传统主义者，因循守旧者．**-is·tic** *a.*

tra·di·tion·al·ly, tra·di·tion·ar·i·ly [trəˈdiʃənəli, -ʃənərili] *ad.* 传说上;传统上,照惯例.
tra·di·tion·ist [trəˈdiʃənist] *n.* ①传统拥护者. ②研究(纪录、传播)传统习惯的人.
trad·i·tive [ˈtræditiv] 〔罕〕 = traditional.
trad·i·tor [ˈtræditə] *n.* *(pl.* ***trad·i·to·res*** [-tɔ:ri:z]*)* 【史】(在受到罗马人迫害时)基督徒中的叛变者.
tra·duce [trəˈdju:s] *vt.* 诽谤,中伤,诋毁. **-ment** *n.* 诽谤,诋毁.
tra·duc·er [trəˈdju:sə] *n.* 诽谤者.
tra·du·cian·ism [trəˈdju:ʃənizəm, -ˈdu:-] *n.*【神】灵魂遗传论〔认为灵魂和肉体一样,也是父母传下来的〕. **-cian·ist** *n.*
traf·fic [ˈtræfik] *n.* ①交通,(人、车、船、飞机的)来往;交通量;运输;运输量;运输业;旅客,货物. ②交易,贸易 *(in)*;交往;交流. ③电信(业务),通信量,通话量. ~ *in rice* 大米交易. *ships of* ~ 商船. *little* ~ 交通[行人]稀小. *heavy* ~ 交通[行人]拥挤. *the* ~ *department [section]*【铁路】运输科[局]. — *vt.* *(-ficked; -fick·ing)* 在…上通行;以…作交易;出卖[牺牲](名誉等). —*vi.* 交易,买卖;做肮脏生意 *(in; with; for, away)*. ***be open to [for]*** ~ 开放;通车. ~ **circle** (十字路的)环状交叉口. ~ **constable** = ~ **cop** 〔美〕交通警察. ~ **island** 交通岛,安全岛. ~ **jam** 交通拥挤. ~ **load** 交通载荷. ~ **manager** 运输经理,运输科长. ~ **pattern** 【空】起落航线. ~ **policeman** 交通警察. ~ **regulation** 交通规则. ~ **returns** 运输(统计)报告. ~ **ship**【军】联络舰. ~ **signal [light]** 交通信号(灯). ~ **volume** 交通量.
traf·fi·ca·tor [ˈtræfikeitə] *n.* (汽车的)方向指示器.
traf·fick·er [ˈtræfikə] *n.* 奸商 *(in)*;出卖(秘密等)的人.
trag·a·canth [ˈtrægəkænθ] *n.*【植】胶黄蓍;【化】黄蓍胶.
tra·ge·di·an [trəˈdʒi:diən, -djən] *n.* 悲剧演员;悲剧作者.
tra·ge·di·enne [trəʒi:diˈen] *n.*〔F.〕悲剧女演员.
trag·e·dy [ˈtrædʒidi] *n.* 悲剧 *(opp.* comedy*)*;惨剧,悲惨事件. *a* ~ *king [queen]* 著名悲剧演员[女演员]. *The* ~ *of it!* 真是悲剧!
trag·ic [ˈtrædʒik] *a.* 悲剧的;悲剧性的,悲惨的. *a* ~ *tale (scene)* 悲惨的故事(景色). ~ *drama* 悲剧. ~ *flaw* (悲剧主角性格中的)悲剧性缺点. *the* ~ *lesson* 惨痛教训. *the* ~ *stage* 悲剧. *the* ~ (人生、文学中的)悲剧性,悲惨因素.
trag·i·cal [ˈtrædʒikəl] *a.*〔罕〕= tragic. **-ly** *ad.* **-ness** *n.*
trag·i·com·e·dy [trædʒiˈkɔmidi] *n.* 悲喜剧;又悲又喜的事情[场合]. **-com·ic, -com·i·cal** *a.*
trag·o·pan [ˈtrægəpæn] *n.*【鸟】(亚洲)角雉(属);红胸角雉.
tra·gus [ˈtreigəs] *n.* *(pl.* ***-gi*** [-dʒai]*)*【解】耳屏.
trail [treil] *vt.* ①拖曳(衣脚等),拖着走;拖带着;提(枪). ②跟踪追赶;〔美俚〕落后于. ③拉长声音讲(话). ④〔美〕踏出路来,开辟道路. — *vi.* ①拖曳;(发等)拖着;(植物)爬在地上;(蛇)慢慢爬行;拖着尾巴;(云霞、烟雾等)飘. ②拖着脚走*(along)*;落在(队伍)后面;(队伍)四散. ③(道路)伸展;(议论)离题. ④(猎犬等)追踪猎物. ⑤减低、变弱 *(away, off)*. ~ *an oar* 拖着桨. ~ *mud into the house* 把污泥带进屋内. ~ *a stranger to see a friend* 带着一个陌生人去看朋友. ~ *the grass* 在草地上踩出一条路. *T- arms!* 提枪! ~*ing antenna*【无】拖尾天线. ~ *off* (声音)逐渐消失. ~ *cn* 拖延下去. ~ *with* 〔美俚〕老和…作伴;和…合作. — *n.* ①痕迹;足迹;踏成的路,小路;长长地拖垂后头的东西;(流星等的)尾;衣裾;(云霞等的)尾迹;(炮架的)架尾,车尾. ②线索,形迹;猎兽的臭迹;(暴风雨等的)余波. ③【军】提枪(的姿势). ④〔美俚〕邋遢人,〔尤指〕邋遢女人. ***at the*** ~ 【军】取提枪姿势. ***be hot on sb.'s*** ~ 紧追某人. ***blaze a*** ~ 开路;带头. ***hit the*** ~ 出发;立即走开. ***off the*** ~ 失去臭迹[线索];迷失. ***on the*** ~ 找到臭迹[线索]. ***on the*** ~ ***of*** 跟踪追赶. ~ ***after*** 追随. ~ ***one's coat [coat-tails]*** 故意挑衅. ~ **bike** 爬山车. ~ **stake** 盘费,路费.
trail·er [treilə] *n.* 拖曳者;拉车牲口;追踪者,追猎者;拖车;拖挂的车辆;蔓草;【影】预告片;〔美口〕〔*pl.*〕跟着马戏班(等)跑的闲人们;〔美〕拖车式活动房屋 (图书编目的)篇身片,片尾. ~ **bus** 带拖车的公共汽车. ~ **card** (图书编目的)缩微卡片篇身片. ~ **net** 拖网. ~ **park [camp, court]** 拖车式活动房屋集中地. ~ **pump** 装在拖车上的消防泵.
trail·er·ite [treilərait] *n.*〔美〕住拖车式活动房屋的人.
train [trein] *vt.* ①训练;培养,养成;锻炼(身体);【园艺】使向一定方向生长,整形,整枝 *(up; over)*. ②瞄准,对准(炮等) *(on; upon)*. ③〔罕〕拖,曳. ④〔古〕引诱,吸引 *(away; from)*. — *vi.* ①接受训练;练习;锻炼身体*(for)*. ②〔口〕坐火车旅行;〔美俚〕交际,来往;〔美俚〕跳来跳去. *At school we should* ~ *young children (how) to be good citizens.* 我们在初等学校应当训练青少年(如何)当好优秀公民. *half-*~*ed* 训练[锻炼]不够的. *over-*~*ed* 训练[锻炼]过度的. *under-*~*ed* 训练[锻炼]差的. ~ *fine* 严格训练[锻炼]. *He* ~*ed to be a doctor but decided to become an actor instead.* 他接受的是医生的训练,可是后来却决定做演员了.' *Every morning he spends two hours* ~*ing for race.* 他每天早晨花两个小时锻炼赛跑. ~ ***down*** (选手)练轻体重. 〔口〕~ ***it*** 坐火车去. ~ ***off*** 用锻炼减轻[减肥];(子弹)打歪,没打中. ~ ***on*** 练好. ~ ***with*** 〔美〕交往;合作[联合]. — *n.* ①列车,火车. ②队伍;一行,排,列;系列;〔集合词〕随从,随员. ③链,(思想等的)连续;一连串(事件);接着发生的事件,后事,结果. ④次序;状态. ⑤拖在后头的东西;衣裾;【军】辎重队;后勤部队;(炮架的)架尾;彗星的尾;鸟尾;导火线;(重而长的)大雪橇. ⑥【机】(传动的)轮列,轮系;齿轮组. *a down [an up]* ~ 下行[上行]列车. *a funeral* ~ 送丧的队伍. *a long* ~ *of sightseers* 一大批游客. *an accommodation [express]* ~ 普通[特快]列车. *a through* ~ 直达列车. *All is now in (good)* ~. 完全停当了,全好了. *Everything fell into its old* ~ *again.* 一切又恢复原状了. ~ *of mechanism*【机】机构系. ~ *of powder* 【军】导火线. ***by*** ~ 坐火车. ***catch [make] one's*** ~ 正赶上火车. ***in (good)*** ~ 准备妥当. ***in the*** ~ ***of*** 接着,继…之后. ***miss one's*** ~ 没赶上火车. ***put on a special*** ~ 挂临时加车. ***put things in*** ~ 安排妥贴. ***ride the gravy*** ~ 获得赚钱好机会;干不费劲的活儿. ***take*** ~ ***to ...*** 坐火车去…. ~ ***de luxe*** 花车. ~**band** 【史】民团. ~**bearer** (举行婚礼时替新娘等)拉长衣裾的人. ~**butcher**〔美〕火车里卖东西的人. ~**crew** (列车的)全体乘务员;司炉. ~ **dispatcher** 〔美〕列车调度员. ~ **ferry** 列车渡船. ~ **man**〔美〕列车乘务员;(尤指)制动手. ~ **master** 货运列车车长;铁路段段长. ~**-mile** 列车英里. ~ **oil** 鲸油. ~**sick** *a.* 晕车的. ~ **sickness** 晕车.
trai·nee [treiˈni:] *n.* 受训练的人[动物]. ~**ship** (受)训练,(受)军训.
train·er [ˈtreinə] *n.* 训练者,教员;教练(员);调马师;〔美海军〕(炮的)瞄准手;〔英空军〕教练机;教练设备;【园艺】枝架.
train·ing [ˈtreiniŋ] *n.* 训练,教练,练习;锻炼;(马等的)调驯;(枪炮、摄影机等的)瞄准,对准;【园艺】整枝法. ***be in [out of]*** ~ 练习得好[不好]. ***go into*** ~ 开始练习. ~ **bit** (烈马用的)马衔. ~ **college** 〔英〕师范学院. ~ **school** ①〔英〕= ~-college. ②〔美〕养成所 *(a* ~ *school for nurses* 护士养成所). ~ **ship** 练习舰[船]. ~ **table** 体育锻炼人员的膳食[食堂].
traipse [treips] *n.* 〔方、口〕= trapes.
trait [treit] *n.* ①特色,特点,特征;性格;脾气;容貌. ②—

触,一笔,一画. ③〔罕〕一点点, 少许*(of)*. *a new* ~ 新品质[特点]. *marked Japanese* ~*s* 日本人的显著特点. *national* ~*s* 国民性. *a bad* ~ 不好的特点. *a* ~ *of humour* 有点幽默感.

trai·tor [ˈtreitə] *(fem.* **-tress** [-tris]*)* *n.* 卖国贼;叛徒*(of)*. *a hidden* ~ 内奸. ~ *and spy* 奸细. *turn* ~ *to one's country* 变成叛国分子.

trai·tor·ous [ˈtreitərəs] *a.* 反叛的;叛逆罪的;出卖朋友的;不忠的. *a* ~ *action* 反叛行为. *a* ~ *scheme* 奸计. ~ *clique* 卖国[叛徒]集团. **-ly** *ad.* **-ness** *n.*

trai·tress [ˈtreitris] *n.* 女叛徒;女叛逆者;女卖国贼.

tra·ject [trəˈdʒekt] *vt.* 〔现罕〕传导,传达, 输送, 运送. **-jec·tion** *n.*

traj·ec·to·ry [ˈtrædʒiktəri, trəˈdʒektəri] *n.* (抛射体的)轨道,弹道;流轨;【几】轨线. *a curved [direct-fire, flat, highangle fire, low]* ~ 曲射[直射、平射、高射、低射]弹道.

tra·la [trɑːˈlɑː], **tra·la·la** [-lɑːˈlɑː] *int.* 脱啦(啦)〔模拟吹奏乐器,表示欢快的呼声〕.

tram[1] [træm] *n.* ①〔英〕(有轨)电车;有轨电车轨道;〔*pl.*〕电车路线. ②= tramcar; tramroad; tramway. ③煤车, 矿车. ④(索道的)吊兜, 吊车. *by* ~ 坐电车. — *vt.* 用电车(等)运. — *vi.* 坐[开]电车. ~**car** 电车;煤车. ~**line** =~way;〔*pl.*〕〔口〕网球场周围的铁丝. ~**rail** 轨条;〔*pl.*〕电车轨道;索道. ~ **road** (电[矿]车)轨道;货车[手摇车]轨道. ~ **service** (有轨)电车交通. ~ **stop** 电车站. ~**way** ①=~road. ②电车轨道;电车. ③〔美〕索道.

tram[2], **trame** [træm] *n.* (丝织品的)纬线.

tram[3] [træm] *n.* ① = trammel. ② 正确的调整;正确的位置. — *vt.*, *vi.* (用调整装置或椭圆规)调整.

tram·mel [ˈtræməl] *n.* ①马梏. ②〔常 *pl.*〕(习惯、礼仪等的)拘束,束缚,妨害. ③(捕鸟、鱼等的) 细网 (= ~ net). ④〔*pl.*〕椭圆规,长径规,梁规. ⑤【机】横木规. ⑥锅钩. ~*s of examinations* 考试的束缚. — *vt.* (〔英〕**-ll-**) 拘束,束缚,妨害;用网捕(鱼等). *a cross-trammelled horse* 对角两脚有白斑的马.

tra·mon·tane [trəˈmɔntein] *a.* (从意大利方面说)(阿尔卑斯)山外边的;外国的; 野蛮的. — *n.* 山外边的人;外国人,野蛮人.

tramp [træmp] *vi.* 踩,践踏 *(on; upon)*; 用沉重的脚步走;慢慢走,徒步旅行[尤指长途];漂泊,流浪;(货船)不定期航行. — *vt.* 步行,徒步走; 踩洗(衣服等); 使(货船)不定期航行. ~ ***down*** 踏坏,踩碎. ~ ***under one's foot [feet]*** 践踏;蹂躏. — *n.* 坚苦的长途徒步旅行;徒步旅行者;流动工匠;流浪者;妓女,淫妇;候鸟;(军队行进等的)脚步声;(保护鞋底的)底铁;(在冰上防滑的)鞋底钉;不定期货船;【机】吹火器. *an ocean* ~ 远洋不定期货船. *a* ~ *[steamer]* 不定期货船. ***go on a*** ~ 乘不定期货船去. ***on the*** ~ 到处流浪. ***take a long*** ~ ***to*** 长途跋涉到. **-er** 流浪者;流动工匠;不定期货船.

tram·ple [ˈtræmpl] *vt.*, *vi.* 踩(烂、碎);踏(坏、倒);蹂躏,摧残;蔑视, 轻视, 看不起*(on; upon)*. ~ ***down [under foot]*** 践踏;蹂躏,摧残. — *n.* 践踏;践踏声.

tram·po·line [ˈtræmpəˌliːn, -lin; ˌtræmpəˈliːn] *n.* 蹦床〔杂技表演中翻筋斗用〕. **-lin·er, -lin·ist** *n.*

tran *pref.* 〔用于 s 前〕= trans-.

trance [trɑːns] *n.* 出神;恍惚;【医】迷睡;神志昏迷,昏睡状态;催眠状态. ***fall into a*** ~ 精神恍惚;出神. — *vt.* = entrance.

tran·quil [ˈtræŋkwil] *a.* *(~er; ~est;* 〔英〕 *~ler; ~lest)* 平静的;安静的,镇静的; 稳定的. **-ly** *ad.* **-ness** *n.*

tran·quil·(l)i·ty [træŋˈkwiliti] *n.* 平静,镇定;稳定.

tran·quil·(l)ize [ˈtræŋkwilaiz] *vt.*, *vi.* (变)镇定,(变)安定. **-(l)ization** *n.*

tran·quil·iz·er [ˈtræŋkwilaizə] *n.* ①使镇定的人[物]. ②镇静剂;镇定剂;止痛药.

trans. = transaction(s); transfer(red); transitive; translated; translation; transportation; transpose.

trans- *pref.* ①横断,横过: *trans*atlantic. ②贯通,穿通;彻底, 完全: *trans*fix. ③超越: *trans*cend. ④变化; 移转: *trans*form; *trans*late. ⑤外,在[到]那一边: *trans*alpine.

trans·act [trænˈzækt, -ˈsækt] *vt.* 办理;处理,执行(事务等),进行(谈判等). — *vi.* 办事,处理事务;交易,谈判;协议. **-or** *n.*

trans·ac·tion [trænˈzækʃən] *n.* 办理,处理;交易;业务,事务;【法】和解;〔*pl.*〕(学会等的)会议记录;学报. *cash* ~*s* 现金交易. ~ *for account* 记帐交易. ~ *for money* 现金交易. ~ *on credit* 赊帐交易. *the* ~*s tax* 营业税. **-al** *a.* **-al analysis** 人与人关系的心理分析.

trans·al·pine [ˈtrænzˈælpain] *a.*, *n.* (从意大利那边说)阿尔卑斯山外[北]边的(人).

trans·am·i·nase [trænˈsæmineis, -zæmineiz] *n.* 【生化】氨基移转酶;转氨(基)酶.

trans·am·i·na·tion [trænˌsæmiˈneiʃən, -ˈzæmi-] *n.* 【生化】氨基转移作用.

trans·at·lan·tic [ˈtrænzətˈlæntik] *a.* 大西洋彼岸的,隔着大西洋的;〔英〕美洲的;美国的;横渡大西洋的(轮船、航线等). ~ *humour* 〔英〕(使人大笑多于微笑的)美国式幽默. — *n.* 大西洋那边的人[物];美国[洲]人;横渡大西洋的轮船.

trans·ca·lent [trænsˈkeilənt] *a.* 透热的,传热的. **-len·cy** *n.*

Trans·cau·ca·si·a [trænsəkɔːˈkeiziə] *n.* 外高加索〔包括Armenia, Azerbaijan 及 Georgia〕. **-n** *a.*, *n.* 外高加索的[人].

trans·ceiv·er [trænˈsiːvə] *n.* 【无】收发两用机.

tran·scend [trænˈsend] *vt.*, *vi.* 超出,超过(经验、理性、信念、理解力等);【哲、宗】超越(宇宙、物质世界等);胜过,凌驾. ~ *description* 没法形容.

tran·scend·ence, -en·cy [trænˈsendəns, -si] *n.* 超越,超绝,卓绝;【神】超然存在,先在.

tran·scend·ent [trænˈsendənt] *a.* 出类拔萃的,卓越的,超群的;〔经院哲学〕超越亚里士多德的范畴的;【康德哲学】超验的;【神】超越宇宙的. — *n.* 卓越的人,尤物;【康德哲学】超越认识的事物.

tran·scen·den·tal [trænsenˈdentl] *a.* 卓越的;〔口〕暧昧的,玄妙的,空幻的;【康德哲学】超验的,直觉的,由直觉得到的(知识等);【数】超越的. — *n.* 【数】超越数;〔*pl.*〕〔经院哲学〕超越物〔真、美、善等〕;抽象的普遍概念. ~ *curve* 超越曲线. ~ *function* 超越函数. **-ly** *ad.* **-ism** *n.*【哲】超验论,超验哲学;超越主义;(Emerson 的)超越论. **-ist** *n.*

trans·con·duct·ance [ˌtrænskənˈdʌktəns] *n.* 【电子】互导,跨导.

trans·con·ti·nen·tal [ˈtrænzkɔntiˈnentəl] *a.* 横贯大陆的;大陆那边[另一端]的. — *n.* 〔*pl.*〕〔美〕横贯大陆中西部通到太平洋岸的铁路.

tran·scribe [trænsˈkraib] *vt.* 誊写, 抄录; 记录(演说词等);转写,翻译;(将速记符号等)改写成文字;【乐】改作,改编;【无】转录; 播送录音. — *vi.* 播放录音. **-er** *n.* 誊写者; 抄录器;读数器;信息转换器.

tran·script [ˈtrænskript] *n.* 誊本,抄本,缮本; 副本; 记录;正式文本;肄业证书;(以另一种形式)转述,改写本.

tran·scrip·tion [trænsˈkripʃən] *n.* 誊写,抄写;转录;抄本,缮本,副本;转写,翻译;【乐】乐曲改作;【无】录音;录音广播;(广播用)唱片[磁带等]. *phonetic* ~*s* 音标;用音标写成的文字. ~ **machine** 录音机. **-al** *a.*

tran·scrip·tive [trænsˈkriptive] *a.* 誊写的,抄写的;爱抄写的;好模仿的. **-ly** *ad.*

trans·cur·rent [trænsˈkʌrənt] *a.* 横贯的;横延的.

trans·cu·ta·ne·ous [ˌtrænskju(ː)ˈteinjəs] *n.*【医】经皮的,由皮的.

trans·duc·er [trænzˈdjuːsə] *n.*【无】转换器;换流器;变

频器；换能器；转换装置；发送器；传感器.

trans·duc·tion [træns'dʌkʃən] *n.* ①换能，转换，变频. ②【生】转导.

tran·sect [træn'sekt] *vt.* 横切，横断. — *n.*【林】样条. *a belt* ～ 样带.

tran·sec·tion [træn'sekʃən] *n.* 横切；横断面.

tran·sept ['trænsept] *n.*【建】(教堂的)交叉甬道，十字(形)耳堂. **-al** *a.*

transf. = transferred.

transfer[1] ['trænsfəː] *n.* ①移送，转送；调职；调任[转学]证书；变换. ②(财产、权利等的)转让，让与(证书)，移转，授受；(股票等的)过户凭单. ③〔美〕划拨，汇划，汇兑；换算. ④(用船载列车乘客的)渡轮码头；(车辆、火车等的)渡轮. ④转车车票 (= ～ ticket). ⑤(供)转印的图画[图案]. ⑥【军】转队兵；转学生；【医】(病物的)迁移. *a* ～ *company* 转运公司. *a* ～ *line* 输送管，传递线. *a telegraphic* ～ 电汇. *a* ～ *slip* 划款条，拨款单. ～ **book** 过户总帐. ～ **day**〔英〕(公债等的)过户日〔星期1—5〕. ～ **ink**【印】转写墨. ～ **paper** 复写用纸；(制图、美术等用)转写用纸；【印】复制图片等用的纸基. ～ **payments**〔美〕(失业救济等的)开支.

trans·fer[2] [træns'fəː] *vt.* *(trans·ferred* ['trænsfəːd]; *trans·fer·ring* [-fəriŋ]*)* ①转移；传递；转送；调动，调任，转学；移置；移栽. ②改变，变换. ③交付，转让，让与(财产等). ④转印；(壁画等的)临摹. — *vi.* ①转移；调职，转学 *(to)*. ②换车[船]，转车.

trans·fer·(r)a·ble [træns'fəːrəbl, -fərəbl] *a.* 能转移[传送，调任]的. **-bil·i·ty** [træns͵fəːrə'biliti] *n.*

trans·fer·ase ['trænsfə͵reis, -͵eiz] *n.*【生化】转移酶.

trans·fer·ee ['trænsfəː'riː] *n.* 买者，承买人；受让人；被调动的人.

trans·fer·ence ['trænsfərəns] *n.* 转移，移动；职务调动；搬运，转送，(财产等的)转卖，让与，交付；权利转移；【心】移情(作用)；【电】输电. **-fer·en·tial** *a.*

trans·fer·or, trans·fer·rer [træns'fəːrə] *n.* 移交人，转让[让与]人；转印者.

trans·fer·rin [træns'ferin] *n.*【生化】铁传递蛋白.

trans·fig·u·ra·tion [͵trænsfigjuə'reiʃən] *n.* 变形；改观；美化；〔T-〕(耶稣的)变容，变容节.

trans·fig·ure [træns'figə] *vt.* 改变…的形状[容貌]，使变形；使改观；美化，理想化，神圣化.

trans·fi·nite [͵træns'fainait] *a.* ①无限的. ②【数】超穷的，超限的. ～ *cardinal (number)* 超穷基数. ～ *ordinal (number)* 超穷序数.

trans·fix [træns'fiks] *vt.* 戳穿，刺穿；钉住；〔喻〕(恐怖等)把(人)吓得不能动弹；使大吃一惊. ～ *sb.'s heart with a spear* 拿标枪戳穿某人心脏. *He was* ～*ed at its sight.* 他看见这个光景就吓呆了.

trans·fix·ion [træns'fikʃən] *n.* 刺穿；钉住；【医】贯穿固定(术).

trans·form [træns'fɔːm] *vt.* (使)变形；(使)变化[转化，转变]；变态，改变(性质、机能等)，改造，改革；【数】变换；【电】变换；转换；变压. — *vi.* 变形，变化，转化；变态. *A caterpillar is* ～*ed into a butterfly.* 毛虫变成蝴蝶. — *n.*【数】变换式；【化】反式. **-able** *a.*

trans·for·ma·tion [͵trænsfə'meiʃən] *n.* 转变，变化；变形；【生】(尤指昆虫的)转化，变态；改造，改革；变质；【数】变换；【电】变压；【化】(原子结构等)蜕变；〔商店用语〕(女用)假发. *socialist* ～ 社会主义改造. **-ist** *n.* = transformist.

trans·for·ma·tion·al [͵trænsfə'meiʃənl] *a.* ①变形的，变态的. ②〔现罕〕(女人用的)假发的. ③【语法】转换(生成)的，转换(派生)的. ④【数】变换的. **-ist** *n.* 转换语法学家.

trans·form·a·tive [træns'fɔːmətiv] *a.* 有改革能力的；起改造作用的.

trans·for·ma·tor [træns'fɔːmeitə], **trans·form·er** [træns'fɔːmə] *n.* 使变化的人[东西]；【电】变压器；变换器；互感器. *polarity of* ～ 变压器绕线方向.

trans·form·ism [træns'fɔːmizəm, trɑːns-] *n.*【生】变种说，物种演变(论)；进化论；进化. **-ist** *n.* 变种论者；进化论者.

trans·fron·tier [træns'frʌntjə, trɑːns-] *a.* 国境外的.

trans·fuse [træns'fjuːz] *vt.* 移注(液体)；注入；转输；渗入，渗透，灌输；【医】输血；输液，注射(食盐水等). *He* ～*d his own courage into his men.* 他用自己的勇气鼓舞了部下.

trans·fu·sion [træns'fjuːʒən] *n.* 移注；渗入，渗透；灌输；【医】输血(法)；输液(法).

trans·gress [træns'gres] *vt.* 侵越；超过(界限等)；违犯(法律等). — *vi.* 侵越，越界；犯法，犯规，违法乱纪. **-gres·sion** *n.* 侵越；违犯；超过；【地】海侵，海进. **-ive** *a.* **-or** *n.* 犯法者；违背者；(宗教、道德上的)罪人.

tran·ship [træn'ʃip] *vt.* = trans-ship.

trans·hu·mance [træns'hjuːməns] *n.* 季节性迁移放牧〔牧民和牲畜随季节在山地和洼地之间的迁移放牧〕. **-hu·mant** *a.*

tran·si·ence, -sien·cy ['trænziəns(i)] *n.* 短暂，暂时性，无常. *the* ～ *of human life* 人生朝露.

tran·si·ent ['trænziənt] *a.* 短暂的，一时的；过渡的；匆匆而过的；易逝的；虚幻的，无常的 *(opp.* lasting, permanent*)*；【物】瞬变的；〔美口〕过路的，留一会儿就走的(客人等). ～ *guest* 暂住的客人. ～ *current* 瞬变电流. ～ *pleasures* 片刻的快乐. *snatch a* ～ *glance of* 匆匆瞅了一眼. *a* ～ *note*【乐】经过音. — *n.* 暂时性的东西[人]；候鸟；过渡状态；【物】暂态值，瞬变值；【无】瞬变现象[过程]，瞬态；过渡现象；〔美〕过客，短期住客. **-ly** *ad.* **-ness** *n.*

tran·si·gent ['trænsidʒənt] *n.* 妥协者. — *a.* 动摇的，犹豫不决的；妥协的.

transili·ent [træn'siliənt] *a.* (飞快地)跳跃而过的；跳动不居的，跳动地改变的.

trans·il·lu·mi·nate [͵trænsi'luːmi͵neit, ͵trænz-] *vt.*【医】透照.

trans·il·lu·mi·na·tion ['trænsi͵ljuːmi'neiʃən] *n.*【医】透照(法).

tran·si·re [træn'zaiəri] *n.* 〔L.〕【商】(海关发给船主的)货物通行单.

tran·sis·tance [træn'sistəns] *n.*【电】晶体管作用；晶体管效应.

tran·sistor [træn'zistə] *n.*【无】晶体(三极)管；晶体管[半导体]收音机. *a* ～ *radio* 晶体管[半导体]收音机.

tran·sis·tor·ize [træn'zistə͵raiz] *vt.* 装晶体管于，使晶体管化.

tran·sit ['trænsit] *n.* 通过，通行；渡越，飞越；运输；通路，运输线；转变，变迁；【天】中天；凌日；中星仪；经纬仪. — *vt.* 通过；运送过；【天】(天体)经过. — *vi.* 通过. ***in*** ～ 运输中. ～ **circle**【天】子午仪. ～ **company** 运输公司. ～ **dues,** ～ **duties**〔*pl.*〕(货物的)过境税，通行税. ～ **instrument**【天】中星仪；【测】经纬仪. ～**passengers** 过客. ～ **shed** 临时堆栈. ～ **theodolite**【测】转镜经纬仪. ～ **time**【电子管】飞越时间.

tran·si·tion [træn'siʒən,-'ziʃən] *n.* 转变，演变，变迁，变化；飞越；过渡期；【乐】变调，转调；【修】语次转变；【语法】转换.【物】跃迁；【地】转移层；【建】(式样、时期等的)过渡. *forced* ～【物】受迫跃迁. *a* ～ *period [stage]* 过渡时期[阶段]. *an age of* ～ 过渡期. *Early T- English* (古代英语到中世英语的)早期过渡期英语. *Late T- English* (中世英语到近代英语的)后期过渡期英语. ～ **element**【化】过渡元素. ～ **energy** 转变能，跃迁能. **-al, -ar·y** *a.* **-al·ly** *ad.*

tran·si·tive ['trɑːnsitiv, 'træn-] *a.* 传递的，可转移的；【语法】及物的；【物】过渡的. — *n.* 及物动词 *(opp.* intransitive*)*. ～ **covenant**【法】连署契约. ～ **law**

【法】经过法. **-ly** *ad.* **-ness** *n.*

tran·si·to·ry [ˈtrænsitəri] *a.* 暂时的,瞬间的,昙花一现的;无常的,空幻的.

transl. = translated; translation.

trans·lat·a·ble [trænsˈleitəbl] *a.* 可翻译的;能译的.

trans·late [trɑːnsˈleit, træns-, trænz-] *vt.* ①翻译[指笔译]. ②解释(动作等);说明. ③把…改作,把…改成,把…表现成;使转化; 使变成; 把…落实到 *(into)*. ④〔口〕(用旧衣等)改做,翻改. ⑤使转移;调动;【宗】调任; 移葬; 使升天. ⑥【讯】自动转拍;【机】使平移[作直线运动];【医】(把病菌)转移(到别处). ⑦〔罕〕使狂喜;〔古〕使变形. — *vi.* 翻译;能翻译. ~ *English into Chinese* 把英语翻译成汉语. *This I* ~ *as a protest.* 我把这个解释作抗议. *Kindly* ~. 请解释明白罢. ~ *emotion into action* 把感情化为行为. ~ *schemes into actions* 使计划变成行动.

trans·la·tion [trænsˈleiʃən] *n.* ①翻译;译文;译本;解释,说明. ②改变,转化;换置,调换;【医】移置,移位. ③〔口〕(旧衣等的)翻改,翻新. ④转移;调动;【宗】肉身升天;(主教的)调任. ⑤【机】直线运动;【物】平动,平移;【讯】自动转拍;【无】转播,传送. ⑥【法】财产让渡. *a free [literal]* ~ 意[直]译. **-al** *a.*

trans·la·tive [trænsˈleitiv] *a.* ①【法】〔指权利〕转让的,让渡的. ②翻译的. ③转移的,移动的.

trans·la·tor [trænsˈleitə] *n.* 翻译者;【无】译码机; 帮电机;变换器;传送器;转发器;转播器; 翻译机; (衣服的)翻改者;〔*pl.*〕翻新过的衣服;【植】载粉器.

trans·lit·er·ate [trænzˈlitəreit] *vt.* (按字母)直译; 音译; 用字母[音标]拼写. **-er·a·tion** [ˌtrænzlitəˈreiʃən] *n.* **-er·a·tor** *n.* 直译者;音译者.

trans·lo·cate [trænsˈləukeit] *vt.* 改变…的位置, 移位; 移置,转移.

trans·lo·ca·tion [ˌtrænsləuˈkeiʃən] *n.* ①改变位置. ②【植】转移(作用);运输(作用). ③【遗】易位.

trans·lu·cence, -cen·cy [trænzˈlju:səns, -sənsi] *n.* 半透明(性,度).

trans·lu·cent [trænzˈlju:snt] *a.* 半透明的. **-ly** *ad.*

trans·lu·cid [trænsˈlu:sid] *n.* 半透明的,透明的.

trans·lu·na·r(y) [trænsˈlju:nə(ri)] *a.* 越过月球的; 月球外侧的;理想的,空想的.

trans·ma·rine [ˌtrænzməˈri:n] *a.* 海外的,海那边的;横渡海洋的.

trans·mi·grant [ˈtrænzmaigrənt] *a.* 移居的, 移民的,迁徙的;【宗】轮回的,转生的. — *n.* 移居者,移民;【宗】转生者.

trans·mi·grate [ˈtrænzmaigreit] *vi.* 移居,迁徙; 【宗】(轮回)转生.— *vt.* 使投生[转生]. **-gra·tion, -gra·tor** *n.* **-gra·to·ry** *a.*

trans·mis·si·bil·i·ty [trænzˌmisəˈbiliti] *n.* 可传送[递]性;遗传性;可透性;可传染性.

trans·mis·si·ble [trænzˈmisəbl] *a.* 可递送的;可传动的,可传导的;可发送[射]的;【医】可遗传的,可传染的. *a* ~ *disease* 传染病.

trans·mis·sion [trænzˈmiʃən] *n.* 递送;传递;传达;传染;移转;【机】传动;传递;变速器;联动机件;【无】传送; 发射;播送;通话; 传输;【物】发射,发送;透射;传导;【生,医】遗传;传染. *beam* ~ 定向发射,束射发送. *directive* ~ 定向发射. ~ *oil* 润滑油. **-mis·sive** *a.*

trans·mis·sive [trænzˈmisiv] *a.* ①能传送的, 能传达的. ②能传导的,可传动的;能透射的. ③可播送的,可发射的. ④遗传的,传染的.

trans·mit [trænzˈmit] *vt.* ①传送,寄,送(信、货等). ②送达,传达(命令、话等);透射(光), 传导(热等), 传声.【无】发报. ③留传(财产、称号等). ④遗传,传染(疾病等). *I'll* ~ *the money by special messenger.* 我将派专人前来送交该款. *Metals* ~ *electricity.* 金属传电. *Parents* ~ *some of their characteristics to their children.* 父母把一些特殊气质遗传给儿女. — *vi.* 发射信号;发报. *Glass* ~*s light.* 玻璃透光.

trans·mit·tal [trænzˈmitl, træns-] *n.* = transmission.

trans·mit·tance [ˌtrænsˈmitns] *n.* ①透射作用,透射过程. ②【物】透射比.

trans·mit·tan·cy [trænsˈmitnsi] *n.* ①透光度. ② = transmittance.

trans·mit·ter [trænzˈmitə] *n.* 传送者;传达者;寄交者;传导物;遗传者;【无】发送机;发射机;发报机;送话机,话筒;【火箭】发射机. *hit the* ~〔美〕播送. *an inset* ~ 送话器盒, 炭精盒. *a light-beam* ~ 光束扫描发射机. *television* ~ 电视发射机.

trans·mog·ri·fy [trænzˈmɔgrifai, træns-] *vt.* 〔口,谑〕使完全改观,使改变形貌.

trans·mon·tane [trænsˈmɔ:ntein] *a.* = tramontane.

trans·mun·dane [trænsˈmʌndein] *a.* 世界以外的,超人世间的.

trans·mut·a·ble [trænzˈmju:təbl] *a.* 能变形的, 能变质的,能变化的;【化】可嬗变[蜕变]的. **-bly** *ad.*

trans·mu·ta·tion [ˌtrænzmju:ˈteiʃən] *n.* 变形,变质,变化;(中世纪炼金术所幻想的)炼制[变贱金属为贵金属];【物,化】嬗变,蜕变;【生】演变, 衍变;【法】所有权的让与[转移]. ~ *glaze* 虹色釉药. ~*s of fortune* 盛衰荣枯;运气的多变. **-al** *a.*

trans·mut·a·tive [trænzˈmju:tətiv] *a.* 有变化力的,变形的, 变质的.

trans·mute [trænsˈmju:t, trænz-] *vt.* 使变形[变质],使变化;【化】使嬗变. — *vi.* 变化,变形,变质.

trans·na·tion·al [trænsˈnæʃənl] *a.* 超越国界的, 跨国的. *a* ~ *company* 跨国公司.

trans·nat·u·ral [trænsˈnætʃərəl] *a.* 超自然的.

trans·nor·mal [trænzˈnɔ:məl] *a.* 超常规的;异常的.

trans·o·ce·an·ic [ˈtrænzəuʃiˈænik] *a.* 大洋那边的; 横渡大洋的. ~ *operations* 渡洋作战.

tran·som [ˈtrænsəm] *n.* (车辆等的)横梁; 船尾肋板;【建】(门、窗的)横档;〔美〕气窗,楣窗 (= ~ window);【军】(炮车尾部)横梁.

tran·son·ic [trænˈsɔnik] *a.* = transsonic.

trans·pa·cif·ic [ˈtrænspəˈsifik] *a.* 横渡太平洋的; 太平洋那边的.

trans·pa·dane [ˈtrænspəˈdein] *a.* (从罗马那边说) 波河(Po R.)对岸[北岸]的.

trans·par·ence [trænsˈpɛərəns] *n.* 透明(性);透明度.

trans·par·en·cy [trænsˈpɛərənsi] *n.* 透明(性);透明度;明了,明澈,透明物体;透明装饰[图片];(瓷器的)透明花样;幻灯片. *his [your etc.] T-* 〔谑〕阁下.

trans·par·ent [trænsˈpɛərənt] *a.* 透明的;可为(X光等)透射的;明了的;明白的(文体等);透彻的;坦率的, 开朗的(性格等); 显而易见的(托辞等). *Yellow T-* 黄魁(品种)苹果.~ *colours*【绘画】透明颜料. ~ *honesty* 坦白率直. ~ *soap* 半透明肥皂. **-ly** *ad.* **-ness** *n.*

trans·per·son·al [trænsˈpə:sənl] *a.* 超越个人的,非个人的.

tran·spic·u·ous [trænˈspikjuəs] *a.* 透明的, 易懂的. **-ly** *ad.*

trans·pierce [trænsˈpiəs] *vt.* 刺穿,刺透.

tran·spi·ra·tion [ˌtrænspiˈreiʃən] *n.* 蒸发(作用); 发散;泄露秘密;透露;【植】叶面蒸发;【物】流逸;【植】蒸腾(作用);【医】不自觉性出汗.

tran·spire [trænsˈpaiə] *vi.* 蒸发,发散;【医】发汗;排出;(秘密)被泄漏,透露;(事情)发生. — *vt.* 使蒸发, 发散(气体); 排出(液体). *the event which* ~*d yesterday* 昨天发生的事情.

trans·plant [trænsˈplɑ:nt] *vt.* ①移植,移种,移栽;移接;【医】移植(皮肤等). ②移民;迁移.— *vi.* 宜于移栽[移植];移居. ~ *one's family to* 把家迁往某处. *Poppies do not* ~ *well.* 罂粟经不起移植. — *n.* 移栽,移植,移植多

次的苗木;移植体;移居者. **-er** *n.* 移植者,移植机 (*rice* ～ 插秧机).

trans·plan·ta·tion [ˌtrænsplɑːnˈteiʃən] *n.* 移植,移种,移栽;移接;移民,殖民;【医】移植(法).

tran·spon·der [trænˈspɔndə] *n.*【无】脉冲转发器,发射机应答器,询问机.

trans·pon·tine [ˈtrænzˈpɔntain] *a.* 桥那边的;泰晤士(Thames)河南岸的;受群众欢迎的. *a* ～ *drama* 大众化戏剧. *a* ～ *hero* 大众化戏剧中的主人公.

trans·port [trænsˈpɔːt] *vt.* ①运输,运送,输送. ②【史】处流刑,流放.③杀死. ④〔常用被动语态〕使心情极度激动,使欣喜若狂. 使心旷神怡. ～ *wheat from the farms to the mills* 把小麦从农场运至面粉厂. *be* ～*ed with joy [grief, rage]* 快乐[悲哀、愤怒]得了不得. —[ˈtrænspɔːt] *n.* ①运输,运送;转运;运输机关;运输船;运输机. ②心荡神移,欣喜若狂. ③流放犯. ～ *ship* 运输船. *He was in* ～*s.* 他高兴极了. ***in a*** ～ ***of*** *(rage)* 一怒之下. **T-Command** 〔英空军〕运输部. **T- House**〔英〕工党本部;工党干部. ～ **tales** 马上就传遍的传说. **T- Workers** 交通工会.

trans·port·a·ble [trænsˈpɔːtəbl] *a.* 可输送的;该流放的. **-bil·i·ty** [trænsˌpɔːtəˈbiliti] *n.*

trans·por·ta·tion [ˌtrænspɔːˈteiʃən] *n.* 运输,输送;转运,搬运;迁移;〔美〕运输机关;运输工具;运输票;运费;【史】流放. **-al** *a.*

trans·port·er [trænsˈpɔːtə] *n.* 运输者;运输装置;运输机.

trans·pos·a·ble [trænsˈpəuzəbl] *a.* 可换位的;有换位可能的. **-a·bil·i·ty** *n.*

trans·pos·al [trænsˈpəuzl] *n.* = transposition.

trans·pose [trænsˈpəuz] *vt.* 换位,改变次序,调换,颠倒;【数】移项;【语法】改变词序;【乐】变调;【电】使(电路)换位.

trans·po·si·tion [ˌtrænspəˈziʃən] *n.* 换位,调换;【数】移项,易位,对换;【语法】词序改变;【乐】变调(曲);(电路)导线交叉.

trans·pos·i·tive [trænsˈpɔzitiv] *a.* ①互换位置的,换位的,转换的. ②【数】移项的.【音】变调的.

trans·rhenane [ˈtrænsriːnein] *a.* 莱茵河那边的;德国(式)的.

trans·sex·u·al [trænˈsekʃuəl, træns-] *n.* ①性欲倒错者. ②性别改变者〔进行外科手术或荷尔蒙注射后改变性别的人〕. **-ism** *n.*

trans-ship [trænsˈʃip] *vt., vi.* (使)换船[换车]. **-ment** *n.*

trans·son·ic [ˈtrænsˈsɔnik] *a.* 超声速的,跨声速的,近声速的〔每小时700—780英里〕.

tran·stage [ˈtrænˌsteidʒ] *n.* 第三级火箭.

tran·sub·stan·ti·ate [ˌtrænsəbˈstænʃieit] *vt.* 使变质;【宗】使化体〔指圣餐面包和酒化为耶稣的肉和血〕. **-ti·a·tion** *n.*

tran·su·date [ˈtrænsjuˌdeit] *n.* 渗出液.

tran·su·da·tion [ˌtrænsjuˈdeiʃən] *n.* 渗漏,渗出(物).

tran·sude [trænˈsjuːd] *vi.* 渗出.

trans·u·ranic [trænsjuˈrænik] *a.*【化】超铀的,铀后的. ～ *elements* 铀后元素.

transuranium [trænsjuˈreiniəm] *n., a.*【化】超铀的(元素),铀后的(元素).

Trans·vaal [ˈtrænzvɑːl] *n.*〔the ～〕德兰士瓦〔南非(阿扎尼亚)省名〕.

trans·val·ue [trænsˈvæljuː] *vt.* 重新估价,按新原则估价. **-u·a·tion** *n.*

trans·ver·sal [trænzˈvəːsəl] *a.* 横向的,横切的,横断的,截断的;截线的. — *n.*【数】截线,贯线;【解】横肌,横行组织.

trans·verse [ˈtrænzvəːs] *n.* 横向,横截;横轴;横骨;横墙;【解】横肌 (= ～ muscle). — *a.* 横向的,横切的,横断的;向横活动的. ～ *artery*【解】横动脉. ～ *colon*【解】横结肠. ～ *process*【解】横突. ～ *section* 横断面. ～ *wave* 横波. ～ *illumination* 横向照明[照度]. ～ *strain*【工】弯曲应变. ～ *strength* 抗弯强度. **-ly** *ad.*

trans·vest [trænzˈvest] *vt.* 使穿别人的衣服,使穿异性服装.

trans·ves·tite [trænsˈvestait] *n.* 易装癖者;异性模仿欲. **-ves·(ti·)tism** *n.*

tran·ter [ˈtræntə] *n.*〔英方〕搬运工;小贩〔拥有自己的马和大车〕.

trap[1] [træp] *n.* ①(捕动物的)捕兽机,夹子,陷阱;圈套,诡计. ②靶鸽发射器;射球戏;(射球戏用的)鞋形射球器. ③【机】防臭瓣,凝气瓣;汽水阀;(下水道的)存水弯;放泄弯管. ④【宇】(固体火箭发动机的)火药柱挡板;吸尘罩;陷波电路. ⑤〔英〕二轮轻便马车;〔澳俚〕警察;〔美俚〕嘴;〔美俚〕(车船中)私货藏置处;〔俚〕造伪币的模子. ⑥= trap-door. ⑦〔常 *pl.*〕(爵士音乐的)打击乐器. *a box* ～ 陷笼. *a wave* ～【物】陷波器[电路]. ***be caught in a*** ～ = ***fall into a*** ～ 落入陷阱,落入圈套. ***be up to*** ～ 不好欺负;精明;狡猾. ***land in sb.'s deadly*** ～ 中某人毒计. ***lay [set] a*** ～ ***for*** 安捕机捕捉;设计诱陷. ***understand*** ～ 懂得自己的利益,精明. — *vt.* 安捕兽机捕捉,设陷阱捕捉,诱捕;设圈套诱陷,设计诱陷;安防臭瓣,安凝汽瓣;发射(泥鸽);设地板门(在舞台上);【棒球】假捉. — *vi.* 装捕兽机,设陷阱 *(for)*;充当(矿坑)通风口的值班. ～**ball** *n.* 射球戏. ～**circuit**【电】陷扰电路. ～ **crop** 诱虫作物. ～ **door** (舞台等的)地板门,活板门,坠门,(房顶的)天窗;【采】通气门;(衣服等的)钩破缝 (*a* ～ *door spider*【动】蝗蛄). ～**lamp** 诱虫灯. ～ **log** = ～ **tree** 饵木,诱虫树. ～**shoot·ing** 靶鸽[飞靶]射击.

trap[2] [træp] *n.*〔*pl.*〕〔口〕随身物品[行李]. — *vt.* 给(马)穿马衣[配上装饰品].

trap[3] [træp] *n.*〔*pl.*〕梯子.

trap[4] [træp] *n.*【矿】暗色(火成)岩. ～ **rock** 离群石,暗色岩.

tra·pan [trəˈpæn] *n., vt.*〔古〕= trepan.

trapes [treips] *n.* ①邋遢[懒]女人. ②闲荡;跋涉;无目的地步行. — *vi.* (尤指女人)闲荡;跋涉;无目的地长时间步行.

tra·peze [trəˈpiːz] *n.* ①【几何】= trapezium. ②(杂技及体操用的)吊架,高秋千. *a* ～ *acrobat* (杂技)空中飞人. *a* ～ *bar*【机】吊架;吊杆.

tra·pezi·form [trəˈpiːzifɔːm] *a.* 不规则四边形的.

tra·pe·zi·um [trəˈpiːzjəm, -ziəm] *n.* ***(pl.*** ～***s, -zia*** [-zjə, -ziə]***)***【数】不规则四边形;梯形;【解】大多角骨.

trap·e·zo·he·dron [ˌtræpizəuˈhiːdrən] *n.*【数】梯面体;偏方二十四面体.

trap·e·zoid [ˈtræpizɔid] *n., a.* ①〔英〕不规则四边形(的). ②〔美〕梯形(的);【解】小多角骨. **-al** *a.* (*trapezoidal thread*【机】梯形螺蚊).

trap·per [ˈtræpə] *n.* (特指为取得毛皮)用捕兽机捕兽的人;【电】陷波器;【矿】(矿坑)通风口值班工人.

trap·pings [ˈtræpiŋz] *n.*〔*pl.*〕装饰;礼服;马饰,(装饰性的)马具.

Trap·pist [ˈtræpist] *n.* (严肃沉默的)特拉比斯特派修道士.

Trappist·ine [ˈtræpistin, -tain] *n.* ①特拉比斯特派修道女. ②〔t-〕(法国)特拉比斯特甜酒.

trap·py [ˈtræpi] *a.* ***(-pi·er; -pi·est)***〔口〕有圈套的,危险的;欺骗性的.

trap·rock [ˈtræpˌrɔk] *n.*【地】暗色岩〔圆柱形的黑色火成岩〕.

traps [træps]〔*pl.*〕*n.* ①随身携带物;行李. ②家具. ③什物.

trapt [træpt]〔古〕trap 的过去式和过去分词.

tra·pun·to [trəˈpuntəu] *n.* ***(pl. -tos)*** 贴绣品.

trash [træʃ] *n.* 废料;垃圾;碎屑,修剪下来的枝叶;落叶;玉米稭(等);废烟叶;渣滓;不值钱的东西;劣货;粗制滥造的作品,无聊作品;废话;流氓无赖,社会渣滓. *the white* ~〔美〕南部的贫穷白种人. — *vt.* 摘(甘蔗的)叶;除去废料;〔美西部〕擦去;(表示反抗或反叛)捣毁,杀死,消灭. ~ **can** 垃圾筒. ~ **ice** (混杂着水的)碎冰. **-y** *a.* **-er** *n.* 捣毁者.

trash·er·y [ˈtræʃəri] *n.* 废物,垃圾,残屑.

trash·y [ˈtræʃi] *a.* 垃圾似的;无价值的.

trass [træs] *n.*【地】火山土;粗面凝灰岩.

trat·to·ria [ˌtrætəˈriːə] *n.*〔It.〕(意大利的)饮食店,饭馆.

trau·ma [ˈtrɔːmə] *n.* ***(pl.*** ***~ta, ~s)***【医】外伤,损伤,创伤;外伤症状[原因];【心】(精神)创伤.

trau·mat·ic [trɔːˈmætik] *a.* 外伤的,损伤的,创伤的;治外伤的. — *n.* 外伤药.

trau·mat·ism [ˈtrɔːmətizəm] *n.*【医】损伤(病),创伤(病);重外伤.

trau·ma·tize [ˈtraumәˌtaiz] *vt.* ①【医】使受外伤. ②【心】使受精神创伤.

trau·ma·tol·o·gy [ˌtrɔːməˈtɔlədʒi] *n.*【医】外伤学.

trav. = travel; traveller.

trav·ail [ˈtræveil] *n.* ①辛苦,劳苦;苦工;劳动,工作. ②分娩;阵痛. ***in*** ~ 在阵痛中. — *vi.* 辛苦工作;发生[感到]阵痛.

trave [treiv] *n.*〔现罕〕①横木,横梁;天花板格. ②挂掌架,钉蹄铁架〔给牲畜钉铁掌用〕.

trav·el [ˈtrævl] *vi.* (〔英〕***-ll-***) ①旅行〔尤指到外国或远地〕. ②到外地推销. ③(火车等)行驶;行进;(声、光)传播;(机件等)走动,移动;依次看去,依次想去. ④与…交往[常在一起]. ⑤(牲口)一面吃草一面向前走;〔美口〕飞快地走,飞跑;【篮球】带球走. — *vt.* 旅行;赶(畜群等),使移动. ~ *second [third] class* 乘软[硬]席车旅行. ~ *for a firm* 代表商行到外地去推销[出差]. *Light ~s faster than sound.* 光比声音传播得快. *We have ~led far from those days.* 从那时候到现在已经过了很多日子. *The car is ~ling.* 汽车飞快地跑着. *Her mind ~led over recent events.* 她反复想着最近发生的事情. *Keep ~ling!*〔美口〕去! ~ ***along***〔口〕(快步)走. ~ ***it*** 步行,(徒步)旅行. ~ ***on steel runners*** 乘雪橇旅行. ~ ***out of the record*** 谈到题外(枝节问题). ~ ***through the air*** 乘飞机旅行. — *n.* ①〔常 *pl.*〕(特指远程的)旅行;旅行记,游记. ②往来,交通. ③【机】行程,动程,冲程;(彗星、光、音等的)进行,移动,传播. *space ~s* 宇宙飞行[航行]. *go on a* ~ 旅行. ~ *of valve*【机】阀行程. *~s in the blue* 沉思冥想. ~ **agency** [~ **bureau**] 旅行社. ~**-stained** [~ **-soiled**] *a.* 旅行中弄脏的,仆仆风尘的. ~**-worn** *a.* 满面风尘的;旅行中用旧的.

travel(l)ed [ˈtrævld] *a.* 旅行过许多地方的,旅行经验多的,见闻广的;旅客多的;【地】漂积的.

travel·(l)er [ˈtrævlə] *n.* ①旅行者,旅客. ②旅行推销员(= commercial ~). ③【机】移动式起重机;【船】(铁杆或缆索上的)活环;带有活环的铁杆. ④〔前用形容词修饰〕走得…的马[车(等)]. *This horse is a fast* ~. 这匹马是一匹走得快的马. ***play the*** ~ ***upon (sb.)*** = ***tip (sb.) the*** ~ 骗(某人). ~**'s cheque** 旅行支票. ~**'s joy**【植】葡萄叶铁线莲. ~**'s tale** 旅行见闻谈;无稽之谈. ~**'s-tree** 旅人蕉〔马达加斯加 (Madagascar) 产叶柄基部所贮汁水可供旅行者解渴〕.

travel·(l)ing [ˈtrævliŋ] *a.* 旅行的,游历的;流动的,移动的. — *n.* 旅行,游历;流动(剧团);移动;滑走. ~ *expenses* 旅费,盘费. ~ **allowance** 旅行津贴. ~ **companion** 旅伴. ~ **crane** 横动起重机. ~ **dress** 旅装. ~ **library**〔美〕流动图书馆. ~ **stock**【铁路】车辆;〔澳〕赶送中的畜群. ~ **trolley** [**crab**]【机】滑车. ~**-wave tube**【无】行波管.

trav·e·log(ue) [ˈtrævəlɔg] *n.* (同时放映幻灯、电影的)旅行报告(会);旅行记录片.

trav·ers·a·ble [ˈtrævəːsəbl] *a.* 能横过的,能越过的;可拒绝的;【法】可否认[反驳]的.

trav·ers·al [træˈvəːsl] *n.* ①横过,横越,横断物,(横向)往返移动. ②(城墙,壕沟的)护墙,障碍物;【登山】Z 字形攀登.

trav·erse [ˈtrævəːs] *vt.* ①横越,横切,横贯;通过;横卧,横放. ②〔罕〕(用东西)阻住,遮断(道路). ③跋涉,游历;经历. ④〔喻〕详细考察,详论(问题);测定. ⑤【木工】横刨,横削;【法】否认,反驳;【炮】转动(炮口). — *vi.* 横越,横切,横断;转动,摆动;(马等)走离正道;【爬山】作 Z 字形爬登;【测】导线测量. — *n.* 横越(旅行);横断物;横木,隔板;阻碍,障碍(物);【建】横梁;(两建筑物之间的)通廊;【筑城】(有盖通路的)横墙;避弹障;【海】Z 字形航行;【爬山】Z 字形爬登(处);【数】横截线;【机】横动;【计算机】穿程;【法】否认,反驳,抗辩;【炮】炮口的转动. — *a.* 横断的,横越的,横贯的. ~ *sailing* Z 字形航行.

trav·ers·er [ˈtrævəsə] *n.* 横越者,横过物;【法】否认者,反驳者,抗辩者;【铁路】转盘,转[移]车台.

trav·erse·table [ˈtrævəsteibl] *n.*【铁路】转盘,转[移]车台;【海】经纬表,方位表.

trav·er·tin(e) [ˈtrævətin] *n.*【矿】拟灰石,石灰华,钙华.

trav·es·ty [ˈtrævisti] *n.* 滑稽模仿;谐摹诗[文];拙劣的做法[演出];牵强附会,曲解. — *vt.* 滑稽化;拙劣地表演. ~ *sb.'s manner* 滑稽地摹仿某人的举止.

Tra·vis [ˈtrævis] *n.* 特拉维斯(姓氏,男子名).

tra·vois [trəˈvɔiz] *n.* ***(pl.*** ***-vois, -vois·es)*** 马拉雪橇;狗拉雪橇;〔北美印第安人所用的一种雪橇〕(= travoise).

trawl [trɔːl] *n.* 拖网;〔美〕(主绳特长而分钩众多的)排钩(钓丝)(= ~-line). — *vi.*, *vt.* 拖网;用拖网捕鱼,从事拖网渔业. ~**boat** 拖网渔船. ~**net** 拖网.

trawl·er [ˈtrɔːlə] *n.* 拖网渔船;拖网渔夫.

tray [trei] *n.* 盘子,托盘;(博物标本等用的)浅盘,浅箱;(书桌上的)公文格;(皮箱内的)隔底匣;【无】发射箱[架];【火箭】发射架;〔美俚〕三;〔澳俚〕三便士硬币. *a developing* ~【摄】显影盘. *a tea* ~ 茶盘. *an ash* ~ 烟灰碟. *a pen* ~ 钢笔盒. ~ **bone**〔美俚〕好极了的;极亲切的. ~ **agriculture** = hydroponics.

tray·ful [ˈtreiful] *n.* 满盘,一盘子.

T.R.C. = Thames Rowing Club〔英〕泰晤士河划船俱乐部.

Tr.Co = Trust Company〔美〕信托公司.

treach·er·ous [ˈtretʃərəs] *a.* 叛逆的,背叛的,不忠的 *(to)*;奸诈的,靠不住的. *a* ~ *act* 叛逆行为. ~ *weather* 靠不住的天气. ~ *ice* (看起来坚固而)踏上去会破裂的冰. *a* ~ *horse* 外表好看的劣马. *a* ~ *smile* 奸笑. ~ *memory* 不可靠的记忆. **-ly** *ad.* **-ness** *n.*

treach·er·y [ˈtretʃəri] *n.* 叛逆,谋反,反叛,变节,不忠,背信.

trea·cle [ˈtriːkl] *n.* 糖浆,糖蜜(=〔美〕molasses);解毒剂;妙药.

trea·cly [ˈtriːkli] *a.* 糖蜜似的;糖蜜般甜的;甜蜜的.

tread[1] [tred] *vi.* ***(trod*** [trɔd],〔古〕***trode; trodden*** [ˈtrɔdn], ***trod)*** ①踩,踏;走. ②踩碎,踏扁;踩躏 *(on; upon)*. ③(雄鸟)交尾 *(with)*. — *vt.* ①踩,踏;在…上走;踩实,踩出(道路等);践踏,踩躏. ②(雄鸟)交尾. ③跳. ~ *grapes* 踩葡萄(榨汁). ~ *wine* 踩取葡萄汁做酒. ~ *a measure* (合着音乐)跳一个舞. ~ ***away*** 弄错,失败. ~ ***down*** 踩结实;踩碎,践踏;压制(感情等);压服. ~ ***in*** 用脚把…踩入(地里). ~ ***in sb.'s steps*** 仿效某人;跟某人跑. ~ ***lightly [warily]*** 轻轻走;小心处理. ~ ***on sb.'s corns [toes]*** 踩痛某人脚趾;〔喻〕伤人感情;得罪某人. ~ ***on air*** 欢天喜地. ~ ***(as) on eggs*** 如履薄冰. ~ ***on sb.'s heels of*** 踩着某人鞋后跟;跟着某人到来. ~ ***on one's own tail*** 踩自己尾巴;〔喻〕想打人反而打伤自己. ~ ***on the gas*** 踏动汽车的加速器;加速,赶紧. ~ ***on the heels of*** (人)接踵而至,(事件)接连发生. ~ ***on the***

neck of 骑在…头上；蹂躏，压迫．～ ***one's shoe away*** (妇女)失去节操，堕落．～ ***out*** 踩灭(火等)；扑灭(叛乱等)；踩榨(葡萄汁等)；踩出(麦等的)谷粒．～ ***shoe leather*** ＝ ～ ***this earth*** 活着．～ ***the boards [stage]*** 登上舞台，做演员．～ ***the deck*** 上船，做水手．～ ***the ground*** 走路，散步．～ ***the paths of exile*** 亡命．～ ***under foot*** 践踏，蹂躏．～ ***water*** 踩水，立泳．— *n.* ①踩，踏，踏行，步行；步态；脚步声；(雄鸟)交尾．②【建】(楼梯的)踏板，梯级；级宽；【筑城】(踏垛的)垛顶；【机】轮距〔左右轮距离〕；轮(触轨)面，轮底；轨顶〔轨条接触轮底的部分〕；(车胎的)花纹．③(鞋、雪车滑行部的)底．④自行车两踏板间的距离；【兽医】(蹄的)践伤；【生】卵的胚点，卵黄系带．*approach with cautious* ～ 轻轻走近．～**-board** (楼梯的)踏板．～**mill** (从前罚囚犯踩踏的)踏车；单调的工作．～**wheel** 踏车．

trea•dle [ˈtredl] *n.* (纺车等的)踏板 (＝ ～ pedal)．— *vi., vt.* 踩踏板，踏动踏板；踩踏板开动(缝纫机等)．

Treas. ＝ Treasurer; Treasury.

trea•son [ˈtriːzn] *n.* 谋反，叛逆(罪)，叛国罪；不忠，背信 *(to)*．～ **felony**〔英〕【法】叛逆罪．

trea•son•a•ble, trea•son•ous [ˈtriːznəbl, -əs] *a.* 谋反的，叛逆的，卖国的，不忠的．

treas•ure [ˈtreʒə] *n.* ①财富，金银财宝，珍宝；珍藏，宝藏．②最亲爱的人，爱儿，宝贝；宝贵的人材．*a* ～ *day*〔剧俚〕发薪日．*buried* ～ 地财．*a* ～ *room* (船等的)贵重物品保管室．*T- State*〔美〕*Montana* 州的别名．～*s of art* ＝ *art* ～*s* 珍贵美术品〔名画、名雕刻等〕．*My* ～．〔尤指呼唤孩子〕宝贝，心肝儿．***spend blood and*** ～ 牺牲生命财产．— *vt.* 当做珍宝保存，珍藏；珍重；爱护，爱惜；热爱；铭记 *(up)*．～ *up stamps* 集邮．～ **house** 宝库，宝藏．～ **hunt** 寻找藏物游戏．～**-trove**【法】地财〔窖藏金银等〕．

trea•sur•er [ˈtreʒərə] *n.* 司库，财务员，出纳员；(美)财政部出纳局长．*Lord High T-* (英国从前的)财政大臣．*T- of the Household* 英国皇室财务主管．**-ship** *n.* 财务员、财政部出纳局长等的职位．

treas•ur•y [ˈtreʒəri] *n.* ①宝库，宝藏．②金库；〔the T-〕英国财政部；国库；国库券，公债券．③贮藏所，库房．④宝典，宝鉴；知识宝库〔指人或书籍〕．⑤〔剧、俚〕剧团团员的周薪．**T- Bench** (英国下院议长右边的)内阁阁员席．～ **bill**〔英〕财政部证券．**T- Board** ＝ ***Lords (Commissioners) of the T-***〔英〕财政委员会．～ **bond** (美国财政部发行的)证券．～ **certificate** (美国财政部发行的)中期有息证券．**T- Department**〔美〕财政部．～ **note**〔英〕代替一镑(或十先令)金币的纸币；〔美〕财政部证券．～ **solicitor**【法】无遗嘱遗产管理人．～ **stock**【商】未发行股份．**T- warrant** 国库支付命令书．

treat [triːt] *vt.* ①对待，待遇；处置，处理．②款待，请(客) *(to)*；招待．③探讨，论述．④【化，医】处理(药品等)；涂(药等)；医治，治疗．— *vi.* 款待，请客；商议，谈判，交涉，协商 *(with)*；讨论 *(of; upon)*．*I'll* ～ *you to a bottle of beer.* 我请你喝一瓶啤酒．～ *a disease* 治病．*a* ～*ing plant* 净化(处理)设备．*The book* ～*s of this question.* 这本书是讨论这个问题的．*Whose turn is it to* ～ *next?* 下次该谁请客？～ ***oneself to*** 舍得(吃、穿等)．— *n.* 款待，请客；轮到请客的人；〔口〕愉快的事情，快乐的事情；(为学生举办的)娱乐〔集会，远足等〕．*It is my* ～ *now.* 这次轮到我请客了．***get on a fair*** ～〔英俚〕进步很快．〔口〕***stand*** ～ 负担请客的费用，请客．**-er** *n.* 谈判者；用化学药品处理物品者；【化】处理器，提纯器，精制器．

trea•tise [ˈtriːtiz, -tis] *n.* 论文 *(on)*．

treat•ment [ˈtriːtmənt] *n.* 待遇；作业；处理，处置；讨论，论述；【医】治疗，疗法；(种子的)消毒(处理)．*preferential* ～ 优待．*hard* ～ 虐待．*heat* ～ 热处理．*mechanical* ～ 机械加工．*water* ～ 水的净化．***under medical*** ～ 治疗中．

trea•ty [ˈtriːti] *n.* (国家间的)条约，协定；(个人间的)约定；协商，谈判，交涉．***in*** ～ ***with*** 和…交涉中．～ **port** (条约规定的)通商口岸．～ **powers** 缔约各国．

tre•ble [ˈtrebl] *a., n.* 三倍(的)，三重(的)；【乐】最高音部(的)；尖锐刺耳(的)；高音(的)．— *vt., vi.* (使)成为三倍，增加两倍．～ **clef**【乐】高音符号；高音部．

tre•bly [ˈtrebli] *ad.* 三倍地，三重地．

treb•u•chet [ˈtrebjuʃei, -ʃet] *n.* 抛石机〔中古兵器〕；分析天平；(捕小鸟等的)捕机，活套儿．

treb•uck•et [ˈtrebjukit] *n.* ＝ trebuchet.

tre•cen•tist [treiˈtʃentist] *n.* 十四世纪的意大利文学家〔美术家〕；十四世纪意大利文艺模仿者〔研究者〕．

tre•cen•to [treiˈtʃentəu] *n.* 〔It.〕(意大利文艺的)十四世纪．

tre•chom•e•tre [treˈkɔmitə] *n.* 车程计，轮转计．

Tree [triː] *n.* 特里〔姓氏〕．

tree [triː] *n.* ①树〔主要指乔木，也可指较大的灌木〕．★玫瑰可以称为 bush，也可以称为 tree．②木料，木材；木构件；〔古〕绞首台；〔the ～〕(钉死耶稣的)十字架；鞋楦．③树形(物)；世系图，家系 (＝ family ～)；【数】树(形)；【化】树状晶体．*a banana* ～ 香蕉树．*an axle-*～ 心棒，轴料．*a boot-*～ 靴楦〔型〕．*a saddle-*～ 鞍架．***at the top of the*** ～ 在最高地位．～ ***of Buddha*** 菩提树．～ ***of heaven*** 臭椿．～ ***of knowledge (of good and evil)***【圣】知道善恶的树，智慧之树．～ ***of life*** 生命之树，生命力的源泉；【植】金钟柏．***up a*** ～〔口〕进退两难，不知所措．— *vt.* 赶(猎兽等)上树躲避；〔口〕使处于困境；穷追；把鞋型〔楦〕插入(鞋内)．～ **agate**【矿】苔纹玛瑙．～ **calf** (做书面用的)木纹小牛皮．～ **creeper**【鸟】旋木雀．～ **fern**【植】灰白水龙骨．～ **frog**【动】雨蛙．～ **heath**【植】欧石南．～ **hopper**【动】角蝉．～ **house** 造在树上的小屋．～ **lawn** 街心绿化带．～**less** *a.*无树的．～ **line** 树木线．～ **milk** 树乳〔可饮用〕．～**nail** 木钉〔栓〕．～ **peony**【植】牡丹．～ **percent** 成苗率．～ **ring** 年轮，～ **shears** 修枝剪．～ **shrew**【动】树鼩．～ **squirrel**【动】松鼠(属)．～ **surgery** 树外科学．～ **toad**【动】雨蛙．～**top** 树顶，树梢．

treed [triːd] *a.* 育林的，植树的．

tref [treif] *a.*【犹太教】(根据饮食律法)不干净的，不可食的．

tre•foil [ˈtrefɔil, ˈtriːf-] *n.*【植】三叶草，车轴草；三叶植物；【建】三叶形〔饰〕．*yellow* ～【植】天兰．～ *knot* 三叶结．

tre•ha•lose [ˈtriːhələus, triˈhɑːləus] *n.*【化】海藻糖．

treil•lage [ˈtreilidʒ, treˈjɑːʒ] *n.* 葡萄架；【建】格构．

trek [trek] *vi.*〔南非英语〕(坐牛车)旅行，(坐牛车)(集体)迁移；(牛)拉货车；〔口〕旅行〔尤指艰苦步行〕．— *vt.* (牛)拉(车)．— *n.*〔南非英语〕牛车旅行；集体迁移；牛车一段旅程；〔口〕旅行，跋涉，步行．**-ker** *n.*

trel•lis [ˈtrelis] *n.* 格子；格子墙〔篱〕；格子凉亭；(葡萄等的)棚架；【建】格(子结)构．— *vt.* 装格子(在窗上)；用棚架支撑．～**work** 格子；格子结构．

trem•a•tode [ˈtreməˌtəud, ˈtriːmə-] *n.*【动】吸虫纲 *(Trematoda)* 动物．— *a.* 吸虫纲的．

trem•ble [ˈtrembl] *vi.* ①发抖，打颤；(地等)震动；(树叶等)摇晃；(声音)震颤．②(因恐怖、忧虑等)战慄，焦虑，担心 *(at; for)*．— *vt.* 使发抖，使战慄，使震动．*I* ～ *at the thought.* 我一想到这个就发抖．*I* ～ *for his safety.* 我非常担心他的安全．*Hear and* ～! 听了别害怕(现在要讲啦)！好，你记着(我会报复你的)！～ ***in one's shoes*** 害怕得发抖．～ ***in the balance*** 处于危急〔紧要〕关头．～ ***out*** 颤抖着说．— *n.* 发抖，震颤，战慄；〔*pl.*〕(牛马的)中毒性震颤病；(人饮用震颤病牛的乳而起的)乳毒病．***(all) in a*** ～ ＝ ***all of a*** ～ ＝ ***on the*** ～〔口〕浑身颤抖着．

trem•bler [ˈtremblə] *n.* 发抖的人，震颤的东西；【电】自动震动器；电铃；继续器，蜂鸣器．

trem•bling [ˈtrembliŋ] *n.* 发抖，震颤，战慄；【医】羊虱毒

病. ***in fear and*** ～ 浑身颤抖着. — *a.* 发抖的，震颤的，战慄的；颤抖的. ～ **poplar**【植】欧洲山杨. **-ly** *ad.*

trem·bly [ˈtrembli] *a.* 〔口〕震颤的，颤抖的.

tre·men·dous [triˈmendəs] *a.* 可怕的，惊人的；〔口〕巨大的；〔俚〕极好的，非常巧妙的(手段等). *It means a ～ lot to him.* 那对他非常重要. — *ad.* 〔俚〕极，非常. *a ～ long way* 一段非常远的路程. **-ly** *ad.* **-ness** *n.*

trem·o·lan·do [treməˈlændəu] *ad.* 〔It.〕【乐】用颤音，用碎音.

trem·o·lite [ˈtreməˌlait] *n.*【矿】透闪石.

trem·o·lo [ˈtreməlau] *n.* 〔It.〕【乐】碎音，颤声；风琴的颤音装置.

trem·or [ˈtremə] *n.* 震颤；战慄，发抖；惊恐；颤音；震动，地震. **-ous** *a.*

trem·u·lant [ˈtremjulənt] *a.* = tremulous.

trem·u·lous [ˈtremjuləs] *a.* 发抖的，颤抖的；吓得打颤的，胆小的；好象发抖一样的(快乐等)；颤抖着写的；神经过敏的. **-ly** *ad.* **-ness** *n.*

tre·nail [ˈtri:neil, ˈtrenl] *n.* = treenail.

Trench [trentʃ] *n.* 特伦奇〔姓氏〕.

trench [trentʃ] *vt.* 掘沟，开畦沟；掘翻(田地)，深耕；【军】掘壕沟，用战壕防守；【木工】作沟槽；切断，切开. — *vi.*【军】挖战壕，掘壕前进 *(down; along)*；切断；侵犯，侵占(权利、土地等) *(on; upon)*；接近 *(on; upon)*. — *n.* 沟，渠；【军】战壕，壕沟；【林】防火线. *a cover ～* 掩蔽壕. *a fire ～* 散兵壕. ***mount the ～es*** 进战壕布防. ***open the ～es*** 掘战壕，开沟. ***relieve the ～es*** 和战壕里的兵换班. ***search the ～es*** (用开花弹等)攻击战壕. ～ **back**【医】战壕背痛. ～ **cart** 战壕手推车. ～ **cavalier**【筑城】斜堤上造的高胸墙. ～ **coat** 战壕雨衣. ～ **digger** 开沟机. ～**fever**【医】战壕热. ～**foot** 战壕足痛. ～ **gun [mortar]** 迫击炮. ～ **knife**【军】(白刃战用)双刃短刀. ～ **mouth**【医】战壕口炎. ～ **warfare** 阵地战.

trench·ant [ˈtrentʃənt] *a.* ①〔古诗〕锐利的，犀利的，锋利的. ②(话等)尖锐的，有力的；严厉的，激烈的. ③清晰的，鲜明的(轮廓等). **-ly** *ad.* **-chan·cy** *n.*

trench·er [ˈtrentʃə] *n.* ①掘沟人；挖战壕的士兵；开沟机. ②〔古〕木盘，木碟；(餐桌上切面包用的)垫板；〔古、喻〕食物；饮食，饮食之乐. ～ *companions* 酒肉朋友. ～**cap** (大学的)方帽. ～**-fed** *a.* (猎人自己家里)亲自饲养的(猎狗). ～**man** 吃的人 (*a good [poor] ～ man* 食量大[小]的人)；食客，寄食者.

trend [trend] *n.* (路、河、海岸、山脉等的)走向；方向，方位；倾向，趋势，动向. *the ～ of events* 形势. — *vi.* 走向，伸向，转向，侧向；倾向，趋向 *(towards)*. **-y** *a.* 最流行[时髦]的；合乎潮流的.

Trent [trent] *n.* 特伦特〔姓氏，男子名〕.

tren·tal [ˈtrentl] *n.*【天主】(给死者做的)三十日连续弥撒.

tre·pan[1] [triˈpæn] *n.*【医】环钻，环锯〔新式的叫 trephine〕；凿井器，【矿】钻(矿)机. — *vt.*【医】用环锯[钻](在颅骨上)穿孔；开孔，(在毛刷把上)打眼；(从金属板等上)切出圆盘形物；钻出(岩心).

tre·pan[2] [triˈpæn] *vt.* ***(tre·panned; tre·pan·ning)*** 诱捕；诱入圈套，设计诱陷，引诱 *(into; from)*.

trep·a·na·tion [ˌtrepəˈneiʃən] *n.*【医】环钻术，环锯术.

tre·pang [triˈpæŋ] *n.*【动】海参.

treph·i·na·tion [ˌtrefiˈneiʃən] *n.*【医】环钻术，环锯法.

tre·phine [triˈfi:n, -ˈfain] *n.*【医】环钻，环锯. — *vt.* 用环钻(在颅骨上)施手术[开圆孔].

trep·i·da·tion [trepiˈdeiʃən] *n.* (手足的)发抖，颤抖，痉挛；黄道的震动；战慄，恐怖；(心的)动摇.

trep·o·ne·ma [ˌtrepəˈni:mə] *n.* ***(pl. -mas, -ma·ta*** [-mətə]***)***【微】回线属，密旋体属. **-l, -tous** [-mətəs] *a.*

tres·pass [ˈtrespəs] *n.* 侵入；【法】非法侵入[犯]；侵入(私人)房屋[土地]；侵害诉讼；(宗教道德上的)干犯，罪过；叨扰，打扰 *(on; upon)*. *One ～ more I must make on your patience.* 还有一件事要叨扰. *timber ～* 木材盗伐. — *vi.* ①侵占，侵入(土地等)；侵犯，侵害(权利等) *(on; upon)*；〔古〕干犯天理[道]；违犯，犯罪 *(against)*. ②〔客气话〕叨扰，打扰，妨碍 *(on; upon)*. ③〔古〕罪. — *vt.* 违犯；破坏. *I shall ～ on your hospitality.* 我要来叨扰你了. *May I ～ on you for that book?* 请你拿[借]那本书给我好吗? **-er** *n.* trespass 的人 (*Trespassers will be prosecuted.* (告白)侵入者扭交法办).

tress [tres] *n.* (女人的)一束长发，卷发；辫子；〔*pl.*〕〔诗谑〕(女人的)松散的长发；〔罕〕花束. — *vt.* 〔常用 *p.p.*〕卷(头发)，梳成一束，打成辫子.

-tress *comb. f.* 表示阴性的名词词尾.

tressed [trest] *a.* 梳[结]成发髻的，梳[结]成辫子的.

tressel [ˈtresl] *n.* = trestle.

tressy [ˈtresi] *a.* ***(-i·er; -i·est)*** 头发松散的.

tres·tle [ˈtresl] *n.* 支架；台架；【建】高架桥，栈桥〔又叫 ～ bridge〕；栈架. ～**-core**【机】转心架. ～**table** 搁板桌. ～**tree**【船】桅顶纵桁. ～**work** 栈架结构；栈桥.

tret [tret] *n.*【商】(为弥补运输时损耗而给买主每百磅加四磅的)饶头，添头.

Tre·vel·yan [triˈviljən, triˈveljən] *n.* 特里维廉〔姓氏〕.

trevet *n.* = trivet.

trews [tru:z] *n.* 〔*pl.*〕〔Scot.〕紧身格子呢裤.

trey [trei] *n.* (牌、骰子上的)三点；三点的纸[骨]牌；〔美运〕三；〔美俚〕三块钱.

T.R.H., TRH = Their Royal Highnesses (对王族的尊称)殿下〔间接提及一人以上时用〕.

tri-, *comb. f.* 三，三重，三倍.

tri·a·ble [ˈtraiəbl] *a.* 可试的，可试验的；【法】应审问的，应审判的. **-ness** *n.*

tri·ac [ˈtraiæk] *n.*【电子学】三端双向可控硅开关元件.

tri·ac·e·tate [traiˈæsiˌteit] *n.*【化】三醋酸酯，甘油三醋酸酯.

tri·ac·id [traiˈæsid] *a.*【化】①三(酸)价的. ②三元酸.

tri·ad [ˈtraiəd] *n.* 三人一组，三个一组，三种事物[思想]的组合，三合一；【乐】三和弦；【植】三分体，三分细胞；【化】三价原子，三价基；(古 Wales 诗形的)三组配合. **-ic** *a.*

tri·age [triˈɑ:ʒ] *n.*【医】治疗类选法〔根据紧迫性和救活的可能性等在战场上决定那些人优先治疗的方法〕.

tri·al[1] [ˈtraiəl] *n.* ①(好坏、性能等的)试验；(人或物的)试用；试车. ②【运】选拔赛，预赛. ③考验，磨难，困难，患难；讨厌的人[东西]；【法】审问；审判. *a firing ～*【火箭】起动试验，发射试验. *a ～ and error method* 反复试验法. *a ～ balloon* 风向试探气球；舆论[人心]的试探. *a ～ match*【运】预赛. *～s of life* 生活的磨炼. *a criminal ～* 刑事审判. *the first ～* 初审. *a new ～* 复审. *an open ～ = a public ～* 公审. ***bring (sb.) to ～*** 告发，检举；交付审问. ***by way of ～*** 试试. ***give a ～*** 试用. ***make (a) ～ of*** 试，试验. ***make the ～*** 试一试，费一点工夫；努力. ***on ～*** 试验性质，暂时；试验后，看试验的结果(采用等)；在受审 (*take [have, employ] sb. [sth.] on ～* 试用某人[物]). ***put (sb.) to ～*** = bring (sb.) to ～. ***run a ～*** 试开. ***stand one's ～ = take [undergo] one's ～*** 受审. ～ ***of the pyx*** 硬币样品检查. ～ **balance**【会计】试算表. ～ **boring** 试钻；【机】钻验. ～ **cruise** 试航. ～ **eights** 赛艇预选选手. ～ **flight** 试飞. ～ **horse** 同强手对阵的练习对手. ～ **jury**【法】小陪审团 (= petit jury). ～ **run [trip]** 试运转，试车[航]. ～ **test** 探索性试验.

trial[2] [ˈtraiəl] *a.* = trinal.

tri·an·gle [ˈtraiæŋgl] *n.*【几】三角形；三角形的东西；三角板；【乐】三角铁；〔T-〕【天】三角座；〔常 *pl.*〕【军】(英国从前的)三戟刑具；【船】三圆材起重机；三角关系. *an equilateral [isosceles] ～* 等边[等腰]三角形. *obtuse*

～ 钝角三角形. *scalene* ～ 不规则三角形.

tri·an·gu·lar [trai'æŋgjulə] *a.* 三角(形)的; 由三个部分构成的,三重的; 三方面的(斗争等); 三国间的(条约等). ～ *compasses* 三脚规. ～ *numbers* 【数】三角数. ～ *organization* 【军】三三制. *a* ～ *situation* 三角关系. *a* ～ *treaty* 三国条约.

tri·an·gu·late [trai'æŋgjuleit] *vt.* 使成[分成]三角形; 作三角测量; 弄成三角(形). — [-lit] *a.* 三角形的; 由三角形形成的,有三角形花样的.

tri·an·gu·la·tion [trai,æŋgju'leiʃən] *n.* 三角测量; 三角剖分. *a net of* ～ 三角网.

tri·arch·y ['traiɑːki] *n.* 三头政治[国家].

Tri·as ['traiəs] *n., a.* 【地】三叠纪[系](的).

Tri·as·sic [trai'æsik] *a.* 【地】三叠纪[系]的. — *n.* 三叠纪[系] (= ～ Period [system]).

tri·at·ic [trai'ætik] *a.* 由三部形成的. ～ *stay* 【海】(两桅头间的)水平支索,桅间索.

tri·a·tom·ic [traiə'tɔmik] *a.* 【化】含三原子的; 三代的; 三羟(基)的. ～ *acid* 三价酸. ～ *alcohol* 三元醇. ～ *molecule* 三原子分子.

tri·ax·i·al [trai'æksiəl] *n.* 有三轴的.

tri·a·zine ['traiə,ziːn, -zin; trai'æziːn, -in] *n.* 【化】三嗪三氮杂萘.

tri·a·zole ['traiə,zəul, trai'æzəul] *n.* 【化】三唑.

trib·a·dism ['tribədizəm, 'trai-] *n.* 女子同性爱.

trib·al ['traibəl] *a.* 部落的,部族的.

trib·al·ism ['traibəlizəm] *n.* ①部族制; 部族文化, 部族组织[生活]. ②对宗族[党派]的忠诚. **-ist** *a.*

tri·bas·ic [trai'beisik] *a.* 【化】三碱(价)的, 三元的, 三代的.

tribe [traib] *n.* 部落,部族; 种族; 〔蔑〕一帮, 一伙; 家族; 【古罗马】三部族(后为三十五部族)之一; 【生】族; 群,一群; 〔*pl.*〕许多; 〔美俚〕棒球队. *the dog* ～ 犬族. *Mongol* ～*s* 蒙古各部族. *the scribbling* ～ 〔口〕文士们. *the whole* ～ *of alarmists* 那批大惊小怪的家伙.

tribes·man ['traibzmən] *n.* 部族(男)成员; 同族人.

tribes·wom·an ['traibz,wumən] 部族女成员.

trib·let ['triblit] *n.* 【机】心轴,心棒(制管、环、螺帽等用).

tri·bo·e·lec·tric·i·ty [,traibəui,lek'trisiti] *n.* 【物】摩擦电. **-elec·tric** *a.*

tri·bol·o·gy [trai'bɔlədʒi] *n.* 摩损学.

tri·bo·lu·mi·nes·cence [,traibəu,lumi'nesns] *n.* 摩擦发光. **-mi·nes·cent** *a.*

tri·bom·e·ter [trai'bɔmitə, tri-] *n.* 【物】摩擦计.

tri·bo·phys·ic [,traibəu'fiziks] 〔*pl.*〕 *n.* 〔单复数同〕摩擦物理学.

trib·rach ['tribræk] *n.* 【韵】三短节音步(◡◡◡).

tri·bro·mide [trai'brəumaid] *n.* 【化】三溴化合物.

tri·bro·mo·eth·a·nol [trai,brəuməu'eθə'nəul, -,nɔːl] *n.* 【化】三溴乙醇.

trib·u·la·tion [,tribju'leiʃən] *n.* 苦难,磨难,灾难; 艰辛,困苦.

tri·bu·nal [tri'bjuːnl, trai-] *n.* ①审判员席,法官席; 法庭. ②制裁,裁判; 〔英〕(第一次大战中的)兵役免除审查局. *a military* ～ 军事法庭. *the Hague T-* 海牙国际法庭. *before the* ～ *of public opinion* 在舆论制裁下.

trib·u·na·r·y ['tribjunəri] *a.* (古罗马)护民官的.

trib·u·nate ['tribjunit] *n.* (古罗马)护民官的职位.

trib·une¹ ['tribjuːn] *n.* ①【古罗马】护民官〔由平民中选出,原为二名,后增至十名〕; 军团司令官〔共六名,一年中每名轮流指挥两个月〕. ②民众领袖; 人民的保护人. **-ship** *n.* 护民官职位[任期].

trib·une² ['tribjuːn] *n.* 讲坛; 论坛; 〔T-〕〔作报刊名称用〕《论坛报》; (大教堂中的)主教席; (古罗马公会堂的)执政官席位; (赛马场的)看台.

trib·u·ta·ry ['tribjutəri] *a.* 纳贡的; 从属的, 附庸的(国等); 补助的,进贡的; 支流的. — *n.* 纳贡者; 属国, 附庸国; 支流. ～ *states* 属国. ～ *tears at the tomb* 在坟墓前流下来的眼泪. *a* ～ *river* 支流.

trib·ute ['tribjuːt] *n.* 贡物[金],贡品; 纳贡义务[地位]; 勒索款; 赠品,礼物; 赞辞,颂辞; 〔英〕【采】(给矿工的)份子. *a silent* ～ 默哀. *floral* ～*s* 献花; (丧礼的) 供花. *a* ～ *of praise* 赞辞. ～ *silk* (中国的)贡缎. ***lay a* ～ *on ... = lay ... under* ～** 使进贡. ***pay (a) (high)*～ *to*** 赞颂. ***pay the last* ～ *to*** 向…最后告别. ***pay warm* ～ *to*** 热烈赞扬. ***the* ～ *of a tear*** 一把同情的眼泪. ～ ***to sb.'s memory*** 悼辞. ***work on* ～ = *work the* ～ *system*** 按照交纳一定贡物的办法工作.

tri·car ['traikɑː] *n.* 三轮摩托车.

tri·car·box·yl·ic [trai,kɑːbɔk'silik] *a.* 【生化】三羧基(的).

tri·car·pel·lar·y [trai'kɑːpiləri] *a.* 【植】三心皮的; 三果爿的.

trice¹ [trais] *vt.* 【海】(用绳索或绞辘)吊起; 拉起并捆住 *(up)*.

trice² [trais] *n.* 瞬间,顷刻. ***in a* ～** 转瞬间.

tricel ['trisl] *n.* 【纺】特列赛尔〔三醋酯纤维织物, 商标名〕.

tri·cen·te·na·ry [traisen'tiːnəri] *a., n.* = tercentenary.

tri·cen·ten·ni·al [,traisen'teniəl] *a.* ①三百年才出现一次的. ②延续三百年的. — *n.* 三百周年纪念日,三百周年的庆祝活动.

tri·ceps ['traiseps] *n.* 【解】三头肌.

tri·cer·a·tops [trai'serə,tɔps] *n.* 【古生】三觭龙.

-trices -trix 的复数.

trich- *comb. f.* = tricho-.

trich·i ['tritʃi] *n.* 〔口〕 = trichinopoli.

tri·chi·a·sis [tri'kaiəsis] *n.* 【医】倒睫; 倒生毛.

tri·chi·na [tri'kainə] *n.* *(pl.* ***-nae*** [-niː]*)* 【动】毛线虫,旋毛形线虫.

trich·i·nize ['triki,naiz] *vt.* 【医】使患旋毛虫(毛线虫)病.

trich·i·nop·o·li, -ly [,tritʃi'nɔpəli] *n.* 印度平头雪茄烟〔略 trichi〕.

trich·i·no·sis [triki'nəusis] *n.* 【医】毛线虫病, 旋毛虫病.

trich·i·nous ['trikinəs, tri'kainəs] *a.* 【医】①旋毛虫感染病的. ②有旋毛虫病的,旋毛虫病的.

trich·ite ['trikait] *n.* 【地】岁雏晶,晶岁.

tri·chlo·ride [trai'klɔːraid] *n.* 【化】三氯化物.

tri·chlo·ro·eth·yl·ene [trai,klɔːrəu'eθi,liːn] *n.* 【化】三氯乙烯.

tricho- *comb. f.* 头发.

trich·o·cyst ['trikə,sist] *n.* 【动】(刺)丝胞. **-ic** *a.*

trichogen ['trikədʒen] *n.* 【药】生发药.

trich·o·gyne ['trikə,dʒain, -dʒin] *n.* 【生】受精丝. **-gyn·i·al** [-dʒiniəl], **-gyn·ic** *a.*

tri·choid ['trikɔid] *a.* 毛状的,发状的.

tri·chol·o·gy [tri'kɔlədʒi] *n.* 毛发学. **-o·gist** *n.* 毛发学家; 〔美俚〕〔广告用语〕理发专家[名手].

tri·chome ['traikəum, 'trikəum] *n.* ①【植】(表皮)毛状体. ②藻丝. **-chom·ic** [-'kɔmik, -'kəumik] *a.*

trich·o·mon·ad [,trikə'mɔnæd, -'məunæd] *n.* 【动】毛滴虫属 *(Trichomonas)* 动物.

trich·o·mo·ni·a·sis [,trikəmə'naiəsis] *n.* 【医】毛滴虫病; 〔尤指〕阴道毛滴虫病; 引起母牛消瘦和流产的滴虫病.

trichomycin [,trikə'maisin] *n.* 【药】抗滴虫霉素.

trichopathy [tri'kɔpəθi] *n.* 【医】(毛)发病; (毛)发病治疗.

tri·chord ['traikɔːd] *n.* 三弦乐器, 三弦琴. — *a.* 三弦的.

tri·cho·sis [tri'kəusis] *n.* 【医】(毛)发病.

tri·chot·o·mize [traiˈkɔtəˌmaiz] *vt.* 分成三部分，分成三类，成分三组.

tri·chot·o·my [traiˈkɔtəmi] *n.* 三分(法)；【逻】三断法；【神】(把人分为肉体、精神、灵魂)三相法.

tri·chro·ism [ˈtraikrəuizm] *n.* 三色性. **-chro·ic** *a.*

tri·chro·mat [ˈtraikrəuˌmæt] *n.* 有三色视觉的人.

tri·chro·mat·ic [traikrəuˈmætik], **tri·chromic** [-mik] *a.* 三(原)色的；三色版的；能正常辨别三原色的. ～ *photography* 天然色照相(术). ～ *printing* 三色版印刷.

trick [trik] *n.* ①奸计，诡计，骗术；欺骗. ②戏法；快手把戏，幻术；【影】特技(表现法)；(狗等的)把戏；〔常贬〕秘诀，诀窍，手法，手腕；手艺. ③恶作剧，鬼把戏，卑鄙手段. ④(态度、讲话等的)习惯，怪癖. ⑤〔美〕无聊的装饰；玩具；〔*pl.*〕杂货. ⑥舵手的一班(通常二小时)，值班时间，班. ⑦【桥牌戏】一墩. ⑧〔口〕漂亮的姑娘〔小孩〕. ⑨〔美俚〕犯罪. *conjurer's* ～*s* 戏法. *(the)* ～*s of fortune* 意外的侥幸，命运的恶作剧. *a dirty [nasty, shabby, dog's]* ～ 卑鄙手段. *None of your* ～*s with me!* 不上你的鬼当！ *He is at his* ～*s again.* 他又在玩鬼把戏了. *the night* ～ 夜班. ***do the*** ～〔俚〕达到目的，顺遂. ***in*** ～【徽】用线画，线画的. ***know a*** ～ ***or two*** 相当精明，相当有办法. ***know a*** ～ ***worth two of that*** 知道比那好得多的方法. ***play a*** ～ ***on*** = ***play [serve] sb. a*** ～ 跟(某人)开玩笑；欺骗. ***the whole bag of*** ～***s*** 全部，统统. ～ ***flying [riding]*** 特技飞行〔马术〕. ～ ***of senses*** = ～ ***of the imagination*** 错觉. ～***s of the memory*** 记错. ***turn the*** ～〔俚〕= do the ～. — *vt.* 骗，诈欺；装饰，打扮 *(off, out; up)*. ～ *sb. out of his money* 诈骗某人的钱财. *be* ～*ed into buying a poor car.* 受骗买一部次品汽车. *be* ～*ed out in jewels* 打扮得珠光宝气. — *vi.* 骗人；变戏法；玩鬼把戏，开玩笑 *(with)*. — *a.* ①有诀窍的；特技的. ②弄虚作假的，欺诈的. ③漂亮的，能干的. ④靠不住的；(关节等)突然撑不住的. ～ ***or treat!*** 不请客就捣乱〔万圣节前夕孩子们挨户要礼物时用语〕. ～ ***sb. into [out of]*** 骗人去…〔骗取…〕. ～ **cycling** 车技. ～ **photography** 特技摄影. ～ **scene** 旋转舞台. ～ **shot**【影】特技镜头. ～**-track** 俄国双六戏.

trick·er [ˈtrikə] *n.* 耍诡计者；骗子.

trick·er·y [ˈtrikəri] *n.* 欺骗，诈欺；奸计，诡计，手段，圈套.

trick·i·ly [ˈtrikili] *ad.* 用欺骗手法，用诡计.

trick·i·ness [ˈtrikinis] *n.* 欺骗；(工作、问题等的)繁难，复杂.

trick·ish [ˈtrikiʃ] *a.* 欺骗的；狡猾的；诡计多端的.

trick·le [ˈtrikl] *vi.* 滴下，淋下，滴滴嗒嗒流〔落〕*(down; out; along)*；稀稀落落地来〔去，前进〕；(秘密等)慢慢泄漏 *(out)*. — *vt.* 使滴下；使淌下，使一滴一滴地流. *Tears* ～*d down her cheeks.* 泪水从她的面颊一滴一滴地流下. *The brook* ～*d through the valley.* 小溪在峡谷间潺湲流过去. *He* ～*d the water into the container.* 他将水徐徐注入容器中. — *n.* 滴，滴下；细流，涓流；稀稀落落地〔去，前进〕的人. *a* ～ *of visitors* 稀稀落落的访客〔参观者〕. ～ **charger**【电】涓流充电器. ～**-down** *a.* 〔美〕积极投资的. ～**-down theory**【经】利益扩散理论.

trickly [ˈtrikli] *a.* 滴滴嗒嗒滴〔流，落〕的.

trick·ster [ˈtrikstə] *n.* 骗子；耍诡计的人；狡猾的人.

trick·sy [ˈtriksi] *a.* *(-si·er; -si·est)* 欺骗的，狡猾的；恶作剧的，顽皮的；漂亮的；(工作、问题等)繁难的. **-si·ness** *n.*

trick·track [ˈtriktræk] = trictrac.

trick·y [ˈtriki] *a.* *(-i·er; -i·est)* 狡猾的；机智的；巧妙的；不易处理的，需要技巧的(工作等)，错综复杂的.

tri·clin·ic [traiˈklinik] *a.*【物】三斜的，三斜晶系的.

tri·clin·i·um [traiˈklinjəm, tri-] *n.* *(pl. -nia [-njə])*【古罗马】(围在餐桌三面的)躺椅；设有躺椅餐桌的餐厅.

tri·co·line [ˈtrikəlin] *n.* 特里可绫〔丝光棉府绸的一种〕.

tri·col·our [ˈtraikələ] *a.* 〔美〕三色的. — *n.* 三色旗〔特指法国国旗〕. **T- Banner** 法国国旗. ～ **camera** 三色照相机.

tri·con [ˈtraikɔːn] *n.*【空】有三个地面台的雷达导航系统.

tri·corn(e) [ˈtraikɔːn] *a., n.* 有三个角的；三角帽.

tri·cos·tate [traiˈkɔsteit] *a.*【植、动】有三中脉的；有三肋的.

tri·cot [ˈtrikəu] *n.* 〔F.〕【纺】绒线织品；经编针织物；(芭蕾舞用的)紧身衣；大纹仿毛织品. *a* ～ *machine* 经编机.

tric·o·tine [trikəˈtiːn] *n.*【纺】巧克丁；针织细绸；急斜纹精纺细毛哔叽；条子细棉府绸.

tri·cro [ˈtrikrɔ] *n.* 万亿〔10^{12}〕.

tri·crot·ic [traiˈkrɔtik] *a.*【生理】三重搏的. **-cro·tism** *n.*

tric·trac [ˈtrikˌtræk] *n.* 十五子游戏〔一种双方各有十五枚棋子，掷骰子决定行棋格数的游戏，尤指既用木签又用棋子的那一种〕.

tri·cus·pid [traiˈkʌspid] *a.* 三尖的；【解】三尖瓣的. *a* ～ *tooth* 三尖齿. — *n.*【解】三尖瓣 (= ～ valve)；三尖牙.

tri·cus·pi·date [traiˈkʌspiˌdeit] *a.* 有三个尖头的.

tri·cy·cle [ˈtraisikl] *n.* 三轮(脚踏)车；〔美车夫语〕三轮摩托车. — *vi.* 骑三轮(脚踏)车.

tri·cy·clic [traiˈsaiklik, -ˈsiklik] *a.*【化】三环的.

tri·dac·tyl, tri·dac·tyl·ous [traiˈdæktil, -əs] *a.* 三指的，三趾的.

tri·dent [ˈtraidənt] *n.* ①(海神 Neptune 的)三叉戟. ②三齿鱼叉. ③制海权. ④【几】三叉曲线. ⑤〔T-〕三叉戟(式)飞机. — *a.* 三齿的.

tri·den·tate [traiˈdenteit] *a.* 三齿的，三尖的，有三叉的.

Tri·den·tine [traiˈdentain] *a.* 意大利北部特伦托(Trent)的；特伦托宗教会议的；遵守特伦托宗教会议所规定的教义的. — *n.* 天主教徒.

tri·di·men·sion·al [ˌtraidiˈmenʃənl] *a.* (长、宽、高)三度的，立体的.

tried [traid] *v.* try 的过去式及过去分词. — *a.* 试验过的；经过考验的；确实的，可靠的(朋友等). ～ *recipe* 验方. ***old and*** ～ 完全可靠的.

tri·en·ni·al [traiˈenjəl, -niəl] *a.* 继续三年的；每三年的，三年一次的；【植】三年生的. — *n.* 每三年举行一次的纪念节(等)；【植】三年生植物. **-ly** *ad.*

tri·enni·um [traiˈeniəm] *n.* *(pl.* ～*s* ***-enni·a*** *[-ˈeniə])* 三年(期间).

Trier [triə] *n.* 特里尔〔德意志联邦共和国城市〕.

tri·er [ˈtraiə] *n.* ①试验者；试验物，试料；试验机. ②试图者，尽力尝试者. ③审问者，法官；审查员.

tri·er·arch [ˈtraiəˌrɑːk] *n.* ①(古希腊)三层桨(座)战船之司令官. ②雅典三层桨(座)战船的修造人.

tri·er·arch·y [ˈtraiəˌrɑːki] *n.* *(pl. -arch·ies)* ①(古希腊)三层桨(座)战船司令官的职务. ②三层桨(座)战船司令官之统称. ③为国家建造、维修三层桨(座)战船的制度.

tri·eth·yl [traiˈeθl] *a.*【化】三乙(烷)基.

tri·fa·cial [traiˈfeiʃəl] *a., n.* = trigem

tri·fid [ˈtraifid] *a.*【植】三(尖)裂的

tri·fle [ˈtraifl] *n.* ①小事，琐事；

量，些许；零钱. ③葡萄酒蛋糕

He doesn't stick at ～*s.* 他

～ 稍微，有点，一点 (*H*

生气). ***stand upon***

儿，闹着玩儿地讲

做无聊事，讲无

～ *with you*

meal 吃一

笑的样

益智

tri·fler ['traiflə] *n.* 闹玩儿的人,开玩笑的人,轻浮的人;做无聊事的人,讲无聊话的人;吊儿郎当的人.

tri·fling ['traifliŋ] *a.* 少许的,不足道的,琐碎的;无聊的;轻浮的,轻薄的;吊儿郎当混日子的. *a ~ gift* 薄礼. *of ~ value* 价值很小的. *~ talk* 无聊的谈话. **-ly** *ad.*

tri·fo·cal [trai'fəukl] *a.*【物】三焦距的. — ['trai,fəukl] *n.* ①三焦距透镜. ②〔*pl.*〕有三焦距的眼镜.

tri·fo·li·ate [trai'fəuliit] *a.*【植】有三叶的.

tri·fo·li·o·late [trai'fəuliəleit] *a.*【植】有三小叶的. ~ **orange**【植】臭桔.

tri·fo·li·um [trai'fəuliəm] *n.*【植】车轴草属〔三叶草属〕植物;红车轴草;白车轴草[白三叶草] (= clover).

tri·fo·ri·um [trai'fɔ:riəm] *n.* *(pl. -ria* [-riə]*)*【建】教堂拱门上面的拱廊.

tri·form(ed) ['traifɔ:m(d)] *a.* (有)三种形态[式]的;由三部形成的.

tri·fur·cate [trai'fə:keit] *a.* 三叉的. **-d** *a.* **-ca·tion** *n.*

trig[1] [trig] *n.* 〔英〕(放在车轮下的)制轮棒[石]. — *vt.* 煞住,制住(车轮) *(up)*.

trig[2] [trig] *a.* 漂亮的,潇洒的,整洁的;精确的;坚牢的;健全的;诚实的. — *vt.* 〔英〕使整洁,修饰,打扮 *(out; up)*.

trig[3] [trig] *n.* 〔学生话〕三角.

trig. = trigonometric; trigonometry.

trig·a·mist ['trigəmist] *n.* 结过三次婚的人;有三妻[三夫]的人.

trig·a·mous ['trigəməs] *a.* 结过三次婚的;有三夫[三妻]的;【植】有雄、雌、雌雄三种花的.

trig·a·my ['trigəmi] *n.* 三次结婚;一妻三夫,一夫三妻.

tri·gem·i·nal [trai'dʒeminl] *a.* 【解】三叉神经的. — *n.* 三叉神经.

trig·ger ['trigə] *n.* (枪上的)扳机;【机】扳柄;闸柄;制轮(机),制滑器;【物】触发器,引爆器;【化】(连锁反应)引起物;〔转〕触发物.【电】起动线路;起动装置. ***pull [press] the ~*** 扳扳机,射击. ***quick on the ~*** 打得快的;〔口〕动不动就开枪的;敏速的;〔美俚〕性急的;三心两意的. — *vt.* 扳动扳机射击;触发,激起 *(off)*. — *vi.* 松开扳柄. **~-crazy** 杀人不眨眼的. **~ finger** 右手的食指. **~ fish**【动】(热带)鳞鲀. **~-happy** 动辄开枪的,好乱开枪的;好战的,轻易发动战争的.

tri·glot ['traiglɔt] *a.* 用三种语文写的[对照的].

tri·glyc·er·ide [trai'glisə,raid] *n.*【化】甘油三酸酯.

tri·glyph ['traiglif] *n.*【建】(陶立克柱式的)三陇板,三角槽排档. **~ic** *a.*

tri·gon ['traigən] *n.*【几】三角形;三角日晷;【古希腊】三角琴;三人球戏;【占星】(十二宫中)互隔 120 度的三宫;三分一对座〔二行星相隔120度时的天象,被视为吉兆〕.

trigon. = trigonometric; trigonometry.

trig·o·nal ['trigənl] *a.* 三角(形)的. ~ **system**【物】三角晶系.

trig·o·nom·e·ter [,trigə'nɔmitə] *n.* 直角三角计;三角学家;三角测量者.

trig·o·no·met·ric, -i·cal [tri'gənə'metrik, -ikəl] *a.*【数】三角学的;(用)三角法的. ~ **function** 三角函数.

trig·o·nom·e·try [,trigə'nɔmitri] *n.*【数】三角法,三角学;关于三角学的论文[教科书].

trig·o·nous ['trigənəs] *a.* 三角形的,有三个角的.

tri·graph ['traigrɑ:f] *n.*【语言】三字母一音.

tri·hed·ral [trai'hedrəl] *a.* 有三面的,三面体的;三面角的. — *n.* 三面体.

tri·hed·ron [trai'hedrən] *n.* *(pl. ~s, -dra* [drə]*)*【数】三面体.

tri·hy·drate [trai'haidreit] *n.*【化】三水合物. **-d** *a.*

tri·hy·drox·y [,traihai'drɔksi] *a.*【化】三羟(基)的.

...o·do·thy·ro·nine [trai,aiədəu'θairə,nin] *n.*【化】...腺氨酸.

...] *a.* 由三个喷气发动机发动的.

...s ['traidʒugeit, -gəs] *a.*【植】

有三对小叶的.

trike [traik] *n., v.* 〔口〕(乘)三轮(脚踏)车 = tricycle.

tri·lat·er·al [trai'lætərəl] *a.*【几】三边的. — *n.* 三边形,三角形. **-ism** *n.* 三边主义[作法]. **-ly** *ad.*

tril·by ['trilbi] *n.* 〔英口〕特里比式软毡帽〔又叫 T-hat〕.

tri·lin·e·ar [trai'liniə] *a.*【数】三线的.

tri·lin·gual [trai'liŋgwəl] *a.* (懂得)三国语言的.

tri·lit·er·al [trai'litərəl] *a., n.* 三(辅音) 字母的;三字母词(根). ~ *languages* 三字母词根语言〔词根用三个辅音字母组成的闪族语等〕. **~ism** 三个(辅音)字母组成的词.

tri·lith, tri·li·thon ['trailiθ, -ɔn] *n.*【考古】(在二直立巨石上搭一块巨石的)三巨石结构.

trill [tril] *n.* 抖动声,颤声;【乐】颤音;【语音】(r 的)卷舌音;(鸟的)啼啭. — *vt., vi.* 用颤音发声[歌唱];(字母 r)发卷舌音;(鸟)啼啭. **-er** *n.*

tril·ling ['triliŋ] *n.* 三胞胎中一个;【结晶】三连晶.

tril·lion ['triljən] *n., a.* 〔美、法〕万亿,兆〔百万的二乘方〕;〔英、德〕百亿亿,百万兆〔百万的三乘方〕;大量. **-th** ①*a.* (第)万亿[百亿亿]的. ②*n.* 万亿[百亿亿]分之一.

tril·li·um ['triliəm] *n.* *(pl. ~s)*【植】延龄草(属).

tri·lo·bate [trai'ləubeit] *a.*【植】三裂(片)的 (= trilobated, tribobed).

tri·lo·bite ['trailəbait] *n.*【古生】三叶虫.

tri·lo·bit·ic [,trailə'bitik] *a.*【古生】三叶虫纲*(Trilobita)*的.

tri·loc·u·lar [trai'lɔkjulə] *a.*【生】有三室[房、腔]的.

tril·o·gy ['trilədʒi] *n.* (古希腊)连演的三部悲剧;三部曲.

trim [trim] *a.* *(~mer; ~mest)* 整齐的,整洁的,漂亮的. — *ad.* 整齐[整洁]地. — *n.* ①调整,整顿,整齐(状态);准备,预备;服装;装饰;(轮船、汽车的)内部装修;(健康等的)情形,状态. ②修剪;修剪下来的东西. ③【空】配平;【无】微调,垫整;【军】潜艇的浮力;【海】吃水差;(船的)平衡;(风帆的)受风状况;【建】贴面. *a ~ stone* 镶边石. ***in fighting ~*** (军舰等)在备战状态中. ***in (good, proper) ~*** 准备好;整齐;情形好;【海】很平衡匀称. ***in hunting ~*** 穿着猎装. ***in sailing ~*** 做好开船准备. ***into ~*** 成适宜的状态. ***out of ~*** 未准备妥当,情形不好,有毛病;不整齐;(船)一边过重. ***~ by the bow [stern]***【空】头[尾]重. — *vt.* ①调整,整理,整顿,收拾;使整洁,使洁净;布置,装饰 *(with)*. ②修剪(头发、指甲等);剪断,剪掉 *(away; off)*;剪(灯心);刨平,刨去(木料的角). ③【海】装备,(整理舱货等)使(船身)平衡;(将货物等)装进船舱;卸货时搬到舱口;搬匀(船舱内的煤炭);【空】使(飞机)配平. ④(鱼群)游近(海岸). ⑤〔口〕责备,谴责;鞭打,打. ⑥〔卑〕骗取;〔美俚〕欺骗,打垮,打败. *~ one's nails* 剪指甲. *~ off the edges of a photograph* 切齐相片(四边). — *vi.* ①(政客等)两面讨好,随风转舵,骑墙 *(between)*. ②(船)平衡;调整帆篷. ③整理,整顿;修剪. ***~ by [on] a wind*** 尽可能扯着帆顺风开行. ***~ in*** 把(木板等)刨整齐嵌入[镶入]. ***~ one's course*** (船)顺风扯帆前进;顺着大势前进. ***~ one's sail*** 见风使舵,随机应变. ***~ oneself up*** 打扮. ***~ sb.'s jacket*** 〔俚〕殴打某人. **~ size** 实际尺寸. **-ly** *ad.*

trim. = trimetric. 斜方(晶)的.

tri·ma·ran ['traimə,ræn] *n.* 三体艇.

tri·mer ['traimə] *n.* 【化】①一种三分子的缩合物. ②三聚物. **-ic** *a.*

trim·er·ous ['trimərəs] *a.* ①【植】(花)三基数的(=3-merous). ②【动】(昆虫)三跗节的.

tri·mes·ter [trai'mestə] *n.* (约)三个月;(一年三学期制的)学期.

trim·e·ter ['trimitə] *n., a.*【韵】三音格的(诗句),三音步(的).

tri·meth·a·di·one [trai,meθə'daiəun] *n.*【药】三甲环二酮.

tri·met·ric [traiˈmetrik] *a.* ①三音格[步]的. ②【结晶】斜方晶系的 (= orthorhombic). ~ **projection** 三度投影 (= trimetrical).

tri·met·ro·gon [traiˈmetrəˌgɔn] *n.*【测】三镜空中摄影法;【军】垂直倾斜混合空中照相; ~ **mapping** 垂直倾斜混合空中照相制图.

trim·mer [ˈtrimə] *n.* ①调整者,整顿者, 整理者; 装饰者; 修剪人, 修理人. ②【机】修剪器; (船上的)堆煤机;【空】调整器;配平器;【无】微调电容器.【建】托梁, 承接梁; 修木器,修整器,剪切具[灯心铗、剪刀等]. ③两面讨好的人,随风转舵的人,机会主义者. ④[口]责备者, 殴打者; 装货工人. ~ **arch** (壁)炉前拱.

trim·ming [ˈtrimiŋ] *n.* ①整顿,整理; 调整, 平衡. ②修剪,修理; [*pl.*] 切屑,碎料. ③[*pl.*] 装饰(品); 婉转的措词. ④[*pl.*] [口]配料,配药; [美]加入茶中的糖和牛乳. ⑤[口]申斥; 殴打; 败,输; 诈骗. ⑥两面讨好,骑墙,随风转舵. ~ **condenser**【无】微调电容器.

tri·mo·lec·u·lar [ˌtraiməˈlekjulə] *a.*【化】三分子的.

tri·month·ly [traiˈmʌnθli] *a.* 每三个月一次的.

tri·morph [ˈtraimɔːf] *n.*【矿】三异晶体同质矿物[可结成三种不同晶体的矿物].

tri·mor·phism [traiˈmɔːfizəm] *n.* ①【结晶学】三晶现象. ②【植】三形的. ③【动】三态性. **-phic, -phous** *a.*

tri·mo·tor [ˈtraiˌməutə] *a.* 三引擎(发动的)飞机.

Tri·mur·ti [triˈmuəti] 印度教之三神 (*Brahma, Vishnu* 和 *Siva*)一体[创造者, 维持者, 破坏者与再造者的合称].

tri·nal, tri·na·ry [ˈtrainl, -nəri] *a.* 三倍的,三重的,三层的; 由三个部分形成的.

Trin·co·ma·lee, Trin·co·ma·li [ˈtriŋkəuməˈliː] *n.* 亭可马里[斯里兰卡港市].

trine [train] *a.* 三倍的,三重的,三层的, 三部分组成的;【占星】三分一对座的. — *n.* 三个一组;【占星】三分一对座[两行星相距120度的天象, 被视为吉兆]; [the T-] 三位一体.

trin·gle [ˈtriŋgl] *n.* ①帐杆[包括挂帘子和悬帷帐等的横木]. ②【建】狭直条饰, 方角花边. ③(炮座端的)制冲棒[缓和后座力].

Trinidad and Tobago [ˈtrinidæd ənd təˈbeigəu] 特立尼达和多巴哥[拉丁美洲].

trin·i·scope [ˈtrainiskəup] *n.* (彩色电视用的)阴极射线管.

Trin·i·tar·i·an [triniˈtɛəriən] *a.*, *n.*【宗】三位一体(说)的; 信三位一体的(人); [t-]有三个部分的; 三倍的. **-ism** *n.* 三位一体说[信仰].

tri·ni·tro·cre·sol [traiˌnaitrəuˈkrisəul, -sɔːl] *n.*【化】三硝基甲酚[24].

tri·ni·tro·glyc·er·in [traiˌnaitrəuˈglisərin] *n.*【化】硝化甘油,甘油三硝酸脂 (= nitroglycerin).

tri·ni·tro·tol·u·ene, tri·ni·tro·tol·u·ol [traiˈnaitrəuˈtɔljuiːn, -ˈtɔljuəul] *n.*【化,军】三硝基甲苯[猛烈茶褐炸药,略 TNT].

trin·i·ty [ˈtriniti] *n.* ①[the T-]【宗】三位一体; 三位一体的象征. ②三人一组,三个一套的东西; [俚](烟斗等)三件烟具. ③= T- Sunday. **T- Brethren** Trinity House 的会员. **T- House** [英]领港公会[掌管领港员的考试、灯台的建设等]; 海务局. **T- sittings** 高等法院第四期开庭期. **T- Sunday** 三一节, 复活主日 [Whitsunday 的下个礼拜天]. **T- term** ①=T- sittings. ②(英国牛津大学)紧接 Easter term 之后的学期.

trin·ket [ˈtriŋkit] *n.* (戒指等)小装饰品, 零碎小物件. **-ry** *n.* [集合名词]小装饰品,小物件.

tri·no·mi·al [traiˈnəumjəl, -miəl] *a.*【数】三项(式)的;【动、植】三名法的. — *n.*【数】三项式;【动、植】(属名、种名与亚种名)三名(法). **-ism** *n.* 三名法.

tri·nomi·nal [traiˈnɔminl] *a.*【动、植】= trinomial.

tri·o [ˈtriːəu] *n.* (*pl.* ~*s*) 三人(一组), 三人演出小组, 三个一套;【几】拼三小组;【乐】三重奏[唱]; 三部合奏[唱]曲; 进行曲的中央乐部; (piquet 牌戏) king, queen, jack, ace 各三张的一付牌. *the scenic* ~ *of Beijing* 北京三景.

tri·ode [ˈtraiəud] *n.*, *a.*【无】三极管(的).

tri·oe·cious [traiˈiːʃəs] *a.*【植】雌花雄花两性花异株的,单全异株的.

tri·ol [ˈtraiɔːl, -əul] *n.*【化】三醇.

tri·ole [ˈtriəul] *n.*【乐】三连音符.

tri·o·let [ˈtri(ː)əulet, ˈtrai-] *n.*【韵】二韵脚八句诗.

Tri·o·nes [traiˈəuniːz] *n.* [*pl.*]【天】北斗七星.

tri·or [ˈtraiə] *n.*【法】= trier.

tri·ose [ˈtraiəus] *n.*【化】丙糖.

tri·ox·ide [traiˈɔksaid] *n.*【化】三氧化物.

trip [trip] *n.* ①(短程)旅行,短程行程,航行. ②摔倒,绊倒; 失足, 失脚; 过失; 失言, 说错. ③【机、电】解扣; 跳闸. ④轻快的步子. ⑤[俚](服麻醉品者的) 迷幻感觉; 迷幻麻醉品. ⑥出渔一次的捕获量(或其利益). *a round* ~往返的行程; 周游. — *vi.* (***tripped*** [tript]; ***trip·ping*** [ˈtripiŋ]) ①轻快地跑[走]; 轻轻跳跃. ②绊倒,失脚 *(on; over)*; 弄错,做错; 犯过失; 失言, 讲错; 说不出话. ③【机】(擒纵机件的)走动. ④旅行. — *vt.* ①绊倒, 使失脚; 勾脚摔倒 *(up)*. ②找错, 挑错 *(up)*; 使犯错误, 使失败. ③【海】卷起(锚); 竖直(帆桁). ④【机】解扣, 松开棘爪而开动. ⑤产生迷幻感觉. *Such people are bound to* ~ *and fall.* 这样的人是没有不跌交子的. ***be ~ped by a difficult question*** 被一个困难问题难倒. ***catch sb. ~ping in sb.'s*** ... 挑某人…的错处. ***go ~ping*** 顺利进行. ~ ***it*** 跳舞. ~ ***off*** 跳开. ~ ***over the root of a tree [on a stone]*** 绊倒在树根上[石头上]. ~ ***the light fantastic*** [美]跳舞. ~ **circuit**【电】解扣电路. ~ **dog**【机】跳档. ~ **flare** 绊索照明弹. ~ **gear** 跳动装置. ~**-hammer**【机】杵锤. ~ **pass** 旅行免费车票. ~ **wire** 绊网; 地雷拉发线.

TRIP = transformation-induced plasticity【冶】高强度及高延性.

tri·pal·mi·tin [traiˈpælmitin] *n.* 三棕榈精; 甘油三个棕榈酸脂.

tri·par·tite [ˈtraiˈpɑːtait] *a.* 分成三部的; 三个一组的, 三个一付的; 一式三份的;【法】三者间的;【植】(叶)三深裂的. *a* ~ *indenture* 三方契约, 三联合同. *a* ~ *treaty* 三国条约. **-ti·tion** *n.*

tripe [traip] *n.* ①【烹】(反刍动物的)肚子. ②[*pl.*] [古、卑]内脏,肚腹. ③[英俚]没有价值的[可厌的]东西; 废话. ~*s and keister* [美俗](路边小贩的)三脚架和手提包.

tri·per·son·al [traiˈpəːsnəl] *a.*【神】三人的, 三人组成的[指上帝、圣子、圣灵三位一体而言].

tri·pet·al·ous [traiˈpetləs] *a.*【植】三花瓣的.

trip·ham·mer [ˈtripˌhæmə] *n.* 杵锤 (= trip hammer).

tri·phase [ˈtraifeiz] *a.*【电】三相的.

tri·phen·yl·meth·ane [traiˌfenlˈmeθein, -finl-] *n.*【化】三苯甲烷.

tri·phib·i·an [traiˈfibiən] *n.* ①水陆空三用飞机. ②海陆空联合作战指挥官. — *a.* ①海陆空联合作战的. ②海陆空三栖的. ③能在 [从] 陆上、水上、雪地或冰上开动[起飞]的.

tri·phib·i·ous [traiˈfibiəs] *a.* = triphibian *(a.)*.

triph·thong [ˈtrifθɔŋ] *n.*【语言】三合元音. **-al** *a.*

triph·y·lite [ˈtrifiˌlait] *n.*【矿】磷酸锂铁矿.

tri·pin·nate [traiˈpineit] *a.*【植】三回羽状的. **-ly** *ad.*

Tri·pi·takas [traipiˈtɑːkəs] *n.*【宗】(佛教的)三藏经.

tri·plane [ˈtraiplein] *n.*【空】三翼(飞)机.

tri·ple [ˈtripl] *a.* 三倍的,三重的,三层的,三部分的;【法】三者间的. — *n.* 三倍的数[量]; 三个一组;【棒球】三垒打. ~ **bond**【化】三键. ~ **écran**【影】三倍大的银幕.

~ **jump** 三级跳远. ~ **measure** =~ time. ~**-nerved**【植】离基三出脉的. ~**-space** *vt.* 空两行打印. ~ **tail**【动】松鲷. ~ **thread**【机】三线螺蚊. ~ **threat** 三面手〔有三种特长的足球运动员〕. ~ **time**【乐】三拍子. — *vi.* 增至三倍.

trip·let [ˈtriplit] *n.* 三个一组,三个一付;三份;【韵】押韵的三句;【乐】三连音符;【物】三重线;三合(透)镜;〔口〕三胞胎中的一个;〔*pl.*〕三胞胎,三人脚踏车;【船】三链环.

trip·lex [ˈtripleks] *a.* 三部分的;三倍的;三重的;三层的;生三种效果的. — *n.* 由三部分组成的东西;【音】三拍子;三部合奏[唱]曲. *a* ~ *building* 三套住房成一单元的房屋. ~ **glass** 夹层玻璃.

trip·li·cate [ˈtriplikit] *a.* 三倍的,三重的;三乘的;三个一付的;三份的,一式三份的. *a* ~ *agreement* 一式三份的协定书. — *n.* 三个一付中之一;三份中之一;三个一付;三份. *be drawn up in* ~ 作成三份(的文件等). — [-keit] *vt.* 使成三倍;作成三份. ~**ratio**【数】三乘比.

trip·li·ca·tion [ˌtripliˈkeiʃən] *n.* 三倍;增加成三倍的东西;作三份.

Tri·pli·ce [ˈtriplitʃei] *n.* 〔It.〕(1882—83年德、奥、意)三国同盟.

trip·lic·i·ty [tripˈlisiti] *n.* 三倍,三重;三个一付;三位一体;【占星】十二宫中相距各120度的三宫.

trip·lite [ˈtriplait] *n.*【矿】磷铁锰矿.

trip·lo·blas·tic [ˌtripləuˈblæstik] *a.*【动】三胚层的.

trip·loid [ˈtriplɔid] *a.*【生】三倍体的. — *n.* 三倍体. **-y** *n.*

tri·ply [ˈtripli] *ad.* 三倍,三重,三层.

tri·pod [ˈtraipɔd] *n.* 三脚台;三脚桌子[凳子];三脚架;(三足)鼎,三脚香炉;【古希腊】Delphi 的青铜三脚祭坛;Delphi 祭坛模型. ~ *of life* = *vital* ~ 心脏、肺脏和脑髓. ~ **landing gear**【空】三轮起落架. **-al, -ic** *a.*

trip·o·dy [ˈtripədi] *n.* *(pl.* ***-dies)*** 三音步诗,三音诗句.

Trip·o·li [ˈtripəli] *n.* ①的黎波里〔利比亚首都〕. ②的黎波里〔黎巴嫩港市〕.

trip·o·li [ˈtripəli] *n.*【矿】风化硅石,硅藻土. ~ *earth* 板状硅藻土.

trip·o·lite [ˈtripəˌlait] *n.*【矿】硅藻土.

tri·pos [ˈtraipɔs] *n.* (剑桥大学的)荣誉学位考试.

trip·per [ˈtripə] *n.* ①轻快地走[跳]的人. ②〔英口〕(当日来回的)游客. ③(使)绊倒者;勾脚使绊倒者;【机】钩杆,自动解扣装置;倾卸装置;(铁路上)信号发送装置.

trip·pet [ˈtripit] *n.*【机】(有规律地撞击他物的)凸轮(或其他机械部件).

trip·ping [ˈtripiŋ] *a.* ①轻快地走路的,脚步轻快的. ②〔古〕犯过失的;失足犯罪的. — *n.* 轻快的跳舞. ~ **bar**【机】钩杆,跳动杆. ~ **bracket**【海】防颠肘板. ~ **device**【机】解装置. **-ly** *ad.* 轻快地;流畅地(讲话等).

trip·tane [ˈtriptein] *n.*【化】2,2,3-三甲基丁烷.

trip·ter·ous [ˈtriptərəs] *a.*【植】三翅的.

trip·tych [ˈtriptik] *n.* 三幅一联的图画,三件一组的雕刻;三折写字板.

trip·wire [ˈtripˌwaiə] *n.* 绊网.

tri·que·trous [traiˈkwi:trəs, -ˈkwetrəs] *a.* ①三角形的,三面形的. ②具有三角形横断面的. ③【植】三棱的. **-ly** *ad.*

tri·ra·di·ate [traiˈreidi:it, -ˌeit] *a.* 三射的,有三辐射线的. **-ly** *ad.*

trir·eme [ˈtrairi:m] *n.*【古希腊】三层桨战船.

tri·sac·cha·ride [traiˈsækəˌraid] *n.*【化】三糖.

tri·sect [traiˈsekt] *vt.* 三分,三截;【数】三等分.

tri·sec·tion [traiˈsekʃən] *n.* 三分;【数】三等分.

tri·sec·tor [traiˈsektə] *n.* 三分,三截;【几】三等分.

tri·sep·tate [traiˈsepteit] *a.*【生】具三隔膜的.

tri·shaw, tri·sha [ˈtraiˌʃɔ:] *n.* 三轮车 (= pedicab).

tris·kai·dek·a·pho·bi·a [ˌtriskaiˌdekəˈfəubiə] *n.* 对数字13的迷信忌讳,对13的憎恶.

tris·kel·i·on [trisˈkeliɔn, traiˈskel-] *n.* *(pl.* ***-i·a*** [ə]*)* 三枝(腿,臂)所成的幅射状图形 (= triskele).

tris·mic [ˈtrizmik, ˈtris-] *a.* 牙关紧闭的.

tris·mus [ˈtrizməs] *n.*【医】牙关紧闭.

tris·oc·ta·he·dron [trisˌɔktəˈhi:drən] *n.* 三八〔二十四〕面体. *trigonal* ~ 三方八面体,三角面二十四面体. *tetragonal* ~ 偏方三八面体 (= trapezohedron). **-he·dral** *a.*

tri·so·di·um [traiˈsəudiəm] *a.*【化】三钠(化的).

tri·some [ˈtraisəum] *n.*【生】三体生物细胞.

tri·so·mic [traiˈsəumik] *a.*【生】三体生物的. — *n.* 三体生物细胞,三体生物机体. **-so·my** [ˈtraisəumi] *n.*

triste [tri:st] *a.* 〔F.〕悲哀的,悲惨的,忧愁的,沉闷的.

tris·tesse [tri:sˈtes] *n.* 〔F.〕悲伤,忧郁.

trist·ful [ˈtristful] *a.* 〔古〕悲哀的,阴郁的.

tris·tich [ˈtristik] *n.*【诗】(押韵的)三行诗.

tris·tich·ous [ˈtristikəs] *a.* 成三行的,三列的〔尤指成三纵列的植物叶〕.

tri·sub·sti·tut·ed [traiˈsʌbstiˌtju:tid, -ˌtu:tid] *a.*【化】三代的,三元取代的.

tri·sul·fide [traiˈsʌlfaid] *n.*【化】三硫化合物.

tri·syl·lab·ic [ˈtraisiˈlæbik] *a.* 三音节的.

tris·yl·la·ble [ˈtraiˈsiləbl] *n.* 三音节词.

tri·tag·o·nist [traiˈtægənist, tritˈægəunist] *n.*【古希腊剧】第三演员.

trite [trait] *a.* 用旧了的;陈腐的(字句、观念等). **-ly** *ad.* **-ness** *n.*

tri·the·ism [ˈtraiθi:izəm] *n.*【宗】三位异体说,三神论. **-the·ist** *n.* 三神论者.

tri·ti·at·ed [ˈtritiˌeitid, ˈtriʃ-] *a.*【化】含氚的;氚化了的.

trit·i·um [ˈtritiəm] *n.*【化】氚,超重氢〔H^3 或 T〕.

trit·o·ma [ˈtritəmə] *n.*【植】剑叶兰属 *(Kniphofia)* 植物〔产于非洲〕.

Tri·ton [ˈtraitn] *n.*【希神】半人半鱼的海神;〔t-〕【动】蝾螈;梭尾螺(壳). *a T- among* [*of*] *the minnows* 鹤立鸡群.

triton [ˈtraitn, ˈtraitɔn] *n.*【化、物】氚核.

tri·tone [ˈtraiˌtəun] *n.*【乐】三全音音程.

tri·to·ri·um [traiˈtɔ:riəm] *n.* 分液器.

trit·u·rate [ˈtritjureit] *vt.* ①研成粉,磨碎,捣碎. ②【生理】咀嚼. — *n.*【药】研制剂.

trit·u·ra·tion [ˌtritjuˈreiʃən] *n.* 研碎,磨碎,【药】研制(法),研磨(法);研制剂〔尤指和有乳糖的〕.

trit·u·ra·tor [ˌtritjuˈreitə] *n.* 捣〔研〕碎的人,磨粉人;捣碎器,研钵.

tri·umph [ˈtraiəmf] *n.* ①【古罗马】凯旋式. ②凯旋;胜利,征服 *(over)*;大成功,功绩;胜利[成功]的喜悦,得意洋洋的样子;最好的例子. *His life was a* ~ *over ill health.* 他的一生是克服疾病的一个最好范例. *a* ~ *of architecture* 建筑术上的大成功. *the* ~ *of ugliness* 丑恶无比. **in** ~ 耀武扬威地,扬扬得意地. ***with ill-dissembled*** ~ 带着无可隐藏的得意样子. — *vi.* 欢庆胜利,得胜而狂欢;得胜,战胜,打败,成功 *(over)*;【古罗马】举行凯旋式. *The forces representing the advanced ideas are bound to* ~ *sooner or later.* 代表先进思想的势力总有一天会要成功的.

tri·um·phal [traiˈʌmfəl] *a.* 凯旋(式)的;祝捷的,庆祝胜利的;胜利的(歌曲等). *a* ~ *arch* 凯旋门. *a* ~ *car*【古罗马】凯旋车. *a* ~ *entry* 凯旋入城式. *a* ~ *feast* 庆功宴. *a* ~ *progress* 胜利游行. *a* ~ *return* 凯旋.

tri·um·phant [traiˈʌmfənt] *a.* 得到胜利的,战胜的;成功的;耀武扬威的,得意洋洋的. **-ly** *ad.*

tri·um·vir [traiˈʌmvə:] *n.* *(pl.* ***~s, -vi·ri*** [-virai]*)*【古罗马】三执政之一.

tri•um•vi•ral [traiˈʌmvərəl] *a.* (古罗马) 三执政之一的,三头政治中的执政者之一的;三执政的,三头政治的,三人一组的.
tri•um•vi•rate [traiˈʌmvirit] *n.* ①【古罗马】三头政治;三执政官的职位. ②三人组,三人同盟. *a ~ of friends* (常在一起的)三个朋友.
tri•une [ˈtraiju:n] *a.* 三位一体的. — *n.* 三人一组,三个一套;【宗】〔the T-〕三位一体.
tri•uni•ty [traiˈju:niti] *n.* = trinity.
tri•va•lence [traiˈveiləns, ˈtrivə-] *n.* 【化】三价 (= trivalency).
tri•va•lent [traiˈveilənt] *a.* 【化】三价的.
tri•valve [ˈtraivælv] *a.* 【动,植】三瓣的,三活瓣的;三裂爿(指果)的.
triv•et [ˈtrivit] *n.* 三脚架;(火炉上的)三脚铁架. ***as right as a ~*** 〔罕〕正好,十分正确,完全顺利, 非常健康. ***~ table*** 三脚桌.
triv•i•a [ˈtriviə] *n.* 〔*pl.*〕〔动词常用单数〕平凡的事情;琐碎的事情;琐事.
triv•i•al [ˈtriviəl] *a.* 琐细的,轻微的;浅薄的, 无价值的;平常的, 平凡的; 通俗的(名称);【生】种的 *(opp.* generic*)*; *~ matters* 琐事. *T- formalities have been done away with.* 废除烦琐的礼节. *a ~ man* 轻薄的人. *the ~ round of daily life* 平凡的日常生活. *a ~ name* 俗名. *a ~ term* 【生】种名. **-ism** *n.* = triviality. **-ly** *ad.* **-ness** *n.*
triv•i•al•i•ty [triviˈæliti] *n.* 小事,琐事;不足道的东西;(人的)浅薄,轻浮;寻常,平凡;一点儿.
triv•i•al•ize [ˈtriviəlaiz] *vt.* 使琐碎;平凡化;使浅薄〔轻浮〕;轻视. **-i•za•tion** *n.*
triv•i•um [ˈtriviəm] *n.* *(pl.* ***-i•a*** [-iə]*)* (中世纪学校的)三学科〔语法、逻辑、修辞〕;【动】三道体区.
tri•week•ly [ˈtraiˈwi:kli] *a., ad.* 三星期一次(的);一星期三次(的). — *n.* 三周刊;一星期三次的出版物.
-trix *suf.* -(t)or 的女性后缀: avia*trix*; 【数】表示"点";"线";"面": genera*trix*.
Trk = truck.
troat [traut] *vi., n.* (公鹿等)叫春(声).
tro•car [ˈtrəukɑ:] *n.* 【医】套(管)针.
tro•cha•ic [trəuˈkeiik] *a.* 【韵】扬抑〔长短, 强弱〕格的. — *n.* = trochee.
tro•chal [ˈtrəukl] *a.* 【动】轮状的.
tro•chan•ter [trə*u*ˈkæntə] *n.* 【解】(股骨的)转子,粗隆;(昆虫腿上的)转节.
tro•char [ˈtrəukɑ:] *n.* 【医】(外科用)套针.
troche [trəuʃ, ˈtrəuki] *n.* 【药】片剂,锭剂;糖锭.
tro•chee [ˈtrəuki:] *n.* 【韵】长短格,强弱格,扬抑格.
troch•el•minth [ˈtroklˌminθ] *n.* 【动】担轮动物门 *(Trochelminthes)* 动物〔包括腹毛纲〕.
troch•i•lus [ˈtrɔkiləs] *n.* *(pl.* ***-ili*** [-ilai]*)* (传说中的)鳄鸟;【鸟】蜂鸟.
troch•le•a [ˈtrɔkliə] *n.* *(pl.* ***-leae*** [-lii:]*)* 【解】滑车;(蜂的)翅厚基;【植】滑车形的.
troch•le•ar [ˈtrɔkliə] *a.* 【解】滑车状的;【植】滑车形的.
tro•choid [ˈtrəukɔid] *n.* 【数】长短辐旋轮线,次摆线,余摆线;转迹线;【解】滑车〔枢轴〕关节;【贝】蝾螺类. — *a.* 轮子一样动的,用轴旋转的;滑车形的,陀螺形的,圆锥形的(贝). **~wave** 【物】摆动波. **-al** *a.*
tro•chom•e•ter [trəuˈkɔmitə] *n.* = trechometer.
troch•o•phore [ˈtrɔkəˌfɔ:] *n.* 【动】担轮幼虫.
trochotron [ˈtrəukətrɔn] *n.* 【电】电子转换器; 摆线管;余摆管;磁旋管.
trod [trɔd] tread 的过去式及过去分词.
trod•den [ˈtrɔdn] tread 的过去分词.
trode [trəud] *v.* 〔古〕 tread 的过去式.
trof•fer [ˈtrɔfə] *n.* 〔美〕天花板凹槽〔供装荧光灯用〕.
trog•lo•dyte [ˈtrɔglədait] *n.* (史前的)穴居人; 隐居者;不喜欢与人交往的人; 粗野堕落的人;【动】类人猿;鹪鹩. **-dyt•ic, dyt•i•cal** *a.*
tro•gon [ˈtrəugɔn] *n.* 【动】咬鹃〔产于热带〕.
troi•ka [ˈtrɔikə] *n.* 〔俄〕①三驾马车〔雪橇〕;并驾拉车的三匹马. ②紧密结合在一起的三个人〔三件东西〕; 三巨头,三人执政.
trois-temps [ˈtrwɑ:tɑ̃:ŋ] *n.* 〔F.〕三拍子华尔兹舞(= ~ waltz).
Tro•jan [ˈtrəudʒən] *a.* 特洛伊 (Troy) 城〔人〕的. — *n.* 特洛伊人;〔口〕勤勉的人; 拳击家,勇士;〔口〕愉快的人,有趣的人,酒友. ***like a ~*** 勇敢地,坚强地,辛苦地. **~ horse** 【神话】特洛伊木马〔特洛伊战争时希腊人把战士藏在里面混进特洛伊城〕; 〔喻〕内部的破坏集团. **~ War** (古希腊传说中的)特洛伊战争, 荷马史诗《伊利亚特》*(Iliad)* 即以此战争为中心内容.
troll[1] [trəul] *n.* ①轮唱;轮唱歌曲;反复. ②钓丝的卷车;拟饵钩. — *vt., vi.* ①轮唱;(一面工作一面)用愉快的声音唱〔说〕. ②(用拟饵钩)拖钓. ③〔古〕传递(酒等). **-er** *n.* 轮唱者.
troll[2] [trəul] *n.* 【北欧神】洞窟巨人,爱恶作剧而态度友好的侏儒.
trol•ley, trol•ly [ˈtrɔli] *n.* ①手推车;〔英〕(装有脚轮,用来送食物的)小台. ②(铁路上的)手摇车; 空中吊运车. ③(电车上的)触轮;〔英〕无轨电车 (= trackless ~ bus);〔美〕(有轨)电车. *a bow ~* (电车上的)弓形滑接线. ***off one's ~*** 〔美俚〕神经失常,发疯. — *vi., vt.* 搭乘(电车, 手摇车等);用电车,手推车等运载. **~ bus** 〔英〕无轨电车. **~ car** 〔美〕电车. **~ line** (无轨)电车路线. **~ pilot** 〔美〕电车司机. **~ pole** 触轮杆. **~ wheel** 触轮. **~ wire** (电车的)触轮线,架空线. **-man** 电车司机〔售票员〕.
trol•lop [ˈtrɔləp] *n.* 邋遢女人,懒妇;堕落的女人;妓女. **-ish** *a.*
Trol•lope [ˈtrɔləp] *n.* 特罗洛普〔姓氏〕.
trol•ly [ˈtrɔli] *n., vi., vt.* = trolley.
trom•ba [ˈtrɔmbə] *n.* 〔It.〕【乐】小号.
trom•bi•di•a•sis [ˌtrɔmbiˈdaiəsis] *n.* 【医】恙螨病 (= trombidiosis).
trom•bone [trɔmˈbəun] *n.* 【乐】长号,拉管.
trom•bon•ist [trɔmˈbəunist] *n.* 长号吹奏者.
trom•mel [ˈtrɔməl] *n.* 【矿】滚筒筛;洗矿筒.
tro•mom•e•ter [trɔˈmɔmitə] *n.* (地震)微震计.
tromp [trɔmp] *vt., vi.* = tramp.
trompe [trɔmp] *n.* (熔矿炉的)水风筒.
-tron *suf.* 表示"工具","仪器","装置"等(尤指真空管,逊原子操纵装置等设备,如 magnetron 磁控电子管, cyclotron 回旋加速器等).
tro•na [ˈtrəunə] *n.* 【化】天然碱.
Trond•heim [ˈtrɔnheim] *n.* 特隆赫姆〔挪威港市〕.
troop [tru:p] *n.* ①〔*pl.*〕 军队;部队. ②(在行动中的) 大群(人);(动物等的)群; 一队, 一组;(戏剧演员等的)一团. ③【军】骑兵连. ④进军鼓. *a ~ of boys* 一队儿童. *regular ~s* 常备军. *shock ~s* 突击队. *the ~s* 〔军口〕我们部队〔I 或 me 的代用语〕. *~ disposition* 军队部署. ***despatch ~s*** 出兵,派兵. ***get one's ~*** 升任骑兵连长. ***withdraw ~s*** 撤兵. — *vi.* ①集合,聚拢,群集 *(up; together)*. ②成群结队地走,排着队前进 *(along; in; out; to)*. ③若干人匆匆走掉 *(off; away)*. — *vt.* ①编成(队伍, 骑兵连). ②运输(军队). *They came ~ing in.* 他们成群结队地进来了. *~ the colour(s)* 行军旗敬礼分列式;举行军旗授与典礼. **~ carrier** 部队运送机(车、船). **~horse** 战马. **~ ship** 军队运输船.
troop•er [ˈtru:pə] *n.* ①骑兵,伞兵;骑警;战马. ②运兵船. ③〔美口〕州警察. ***swear like a ~*** 大骂,痛骂.
troost•ite [ˈtru:stait] *n.* 【矿】锰硅锌矿.
trop. = tropic(al).
trop [trəu] *ad.* 〔F.〕太,太多,过分,非常,很.

tro·pae·o·lin, tro·pae·o·line [trəˈpiəlin] *n.*【染】金莲橙 (= tropeolin, tropeoline).
tro·pae·o·lum [trəuˈpi:ələm] *n.*【植】旱金莲属植物.
trope [trəup] *n.* ①【修】转义;比喻. ②【数】奇异切面.
troph·al·lax·is [ˌtrɔfəˈlæksis] *n.* *(pl. -lax·es* [-si:z]*)*【动】交哺现象. **troph·al·lac·tic** [-ˈlæktik] *a.*
troph·ic [ˈtrɔfik] *a.* (司)营养的;口器的. ~ **behaviour** 趋食行为. ~ **disturbance** 营养失调.
tro·phied [ˈtrəufid] *a.* 用战利品装饰的.
troph·o·blast [ˈtrɔfəˌblæst] *n.*【生】滋养层. **-ic** *a.*
tro·phol·o·gy [trɔˈfɔlədʒi] *n.* 营养学.
troph·o·neu·ro·sis [ˌtrɔfəunjuəˈrəusis] *n.*【医】神经性营养不良.
troph·o·plasm [ˈtrɔfəplæzm] *n.*【生】滋养质.
troph·o·thera·py [trɔfəˈθerəpi] *n.*【医】营养疗法.
troph·o·zo·ite [ˌtrɔfəˈzəuit] *n.*【生】滋养体.
tro·phy [ˈtrəufi] *n.* ①战利品;战胜纪念物;战利品装饰[图案];奖品[银杯等]纪念品. ②(古希腊、罗马的)战胜纪念碑. *a* ~ *belt*〔美运〕优胜纪录.
-trophy *suf.* 营养: hyper*trophy*.
trop·ic[1] [ˈtrɔpik] *n.* ①【天】回归线. ②〔the ~s〕热带(地区). — *a.* 热带(地区)的. *T- of Cancer [Capricorn]* 北[南]回归线,夏[冬]至线.
trop·ic[2] [ˈtrɔpik] *a.*【生】向性的. ~ **behaviour** 向性行为. ~ **hormone** 促激素.
trop·i·cal [ˈtrɔpikl] *a.* ①热带(地区)的,回归线下的. ②非常热的;热情的,热烈的,激烈的. ③〔罕〕比喻的;转义的. ~ **cyclone** 热带气旋. ~ **fish** 热带鱼. ~ **suiting** 夏季衣料. ~ **year**【天】太阳年,回归年. ~ **zone** 热带.
tro·pine [ˈtrəupi:n] *n.*【化】托品,莨菪碱.
trop·ism [ˈtrəupizəm] *n.*【生】向性.
tro·pist [ˈtrəupist] *n.* 作比喻者,用比喻者.
tro·pis·tic [trəuˈpistik] *a.*【生】向性的.
trop·o·log·i·cal [ˌtrɔpəˈlɔdʒikl] *a.* 比喻的. **-ly** *ad.*
tro·pol·o·gy [trəuˈpɔlədʒi] *n.* ①比喻的使用. ②(圣经中的)比喻的解释. ③比喻语言的论文;比喻语的编纂.
trop·o·pause [ˈtrɔpəupɔ:z] *n.*【气】对流层顶.
tro·poph·i·lous [trəuˈpɔfiləs] *a.*【植】湿旱生的.
trop·o·phyte [ˈtrɔpəufait, ˈtrəupəu-] *n.*【植】湿旱生植物. **trop·o·phyt·ic** [-ˈfitik] *a.*
trop·o·scat·ter [ˈtrɔpəuskætə] *n.*【气】对流层散射 (= tropospheric scatter).
trop·o·sphere [ˈtrɔpəusfiə] *n.*【气】对流层.
trop·o·spher·ic [ˌtrɔpəuˈsferik, -ˈsfiər-] *a.*【气】对流层的.
trop·po [ˈtrɔpəu] *ad.* 〔It.〕【乐】过度, 过甚. *allegro ma non* ~ 轻快但不过甚. *andante ma non* ~ 温和而适度地.
trot [trɔt] *vi.* *(trot·ted* [ˈtrɔtid]; *trot·ting* [ˈtrɔtiŋ]*)* ①(马)小跑;(人)小跑着走,急匆匆地走. ②〔谑〕走着去. — *vt.* ①使(马)小跑;快步走过;搁在膝上颠(小孩等). ②〔口〕带着走,领着走 *(round; to)*. ③〔美俚〕使用现成的译本(做课外作业). ④〔美〕跳舞. *The child ~ted along after his mother.* 小孩跟在母亲后面很快地往前走. ~ *the hills and valleys* 翻山越谷. ***~ a child on the knee*** 使小孩子骑在膝头上颠. ***~ sb. off his legs*** 叫人走得脚软腿酸. ***~ along*** 〔口〕快点去. ***~ away from the pole*** 〔美〕话离题. ***~ in double harness*** 〔美〕已结婚. ***~ out*** 牵马出来得意扬扬地给人看步伐;〔口〕给人看, 供人展览; 讲(笑话);〔俚〕带着女(人)走路;愚弄. ***~ round*** 〔口〕领着到处串 *(I will ~ you round Shanghai.* 我要领着你逛上海). — *n.* ①(马交互举起前右脚与后左脚或前左脚与后右脚而快走的)小跑;驾车赛马. ②(人的)慢跑;散步. ③〔英口〕摇摇摆摆走路的[刚学走的]小孩. ④(为工作的)奔走. ⑤〔美俚〕(做课外作业时用来作弊的)现成译本. ⑥〔蔑〕老太婆. ⑦〔俚〕〔*pl.*〕腹泻. ⑧= trotline. ***(always) on the ~*** 一刻不停,席不暇暖,忙忙碌碌. ***go for a ~*** 去散步. ***keep (sb.) on the ~*** 使一刻不停地忙碌奔波.
troth [trəuθ, trɔθ] *n.* 〔古〕①忠诚. ②真实. ③誓言;婚约. ***by [upon] my ~*** 发誓,一定. ***(in) ~*** 〔古〕实在,的确. ***plight one's ~*** 盟誓,(尤指订婚)山盟海誓. ~ **plight** 〔古〕订婚.
trot·line [ˈtrɔtˌlain] *n.* (钓鱼用的)滚钓线.
Trot·sky·ist [ˈtrɔtskiist], **Trot·sky·ite** [-ait] *n., a.* 托(洛茨基)派(分子)(的).
trot·ter [ˈtrɔtə] *n.* ①小跑的马;走得快的人,工作机敏的人. ②〔*pl.*〕【烹】猪(等的)脚,猪爪;〔口、谑〕(尤指孩子、少女的)脚.
trot·toir [ˈtrɔtwɑ:] *n.* 〔F.〕人行道,步行道.
tro·tyl [ˈtrəutil] *n.*【化】三硝基甲苯 (= trinitrotoluene).
trou [trau] *n.* 〔美俚〕裤子 (= trousers).
trou·ba·dour [ˈtru:bəduə] *n.* ①(11—13 世纪法国南部及意大利北部等地的)抒情诗人,行吟诗人. ②〔转〕民谣歌手,民谣曲乐师.
trou·ble [ˈtrʌbl] *n.* ①苦恼,烦恼;麻烦;困难,艰难;灾难. ②苦恼的原因;使烦恼的人,麻烦家伙;疾病;生产,怀孕. ③(政局等的)风潮,纠纷,骚动,纷扰. ④故障,事故,干扰. ⑤【矿】断层. *Thank you for your ~.* 麻烦您了,多谢多谢. *It is too much ~.* 麻烦死了. *What is the ~?* 怎么不好啦? 那里不舒服? *The ~ is that ...,* 麻烦的是…. *digestive ~(s)* 胃弱. *heart ~* 心脏病. *engine ~* 机器上的毛病. *labour ~(s)* 劳资纠纷. *political ~* 政治风潮. *a ~ man = a ~ shooter* (电路、煤气管等的)检修员. ***ask for ~*** 〔口〕自讨苦吃. ***be a ~ to*** 对…是一个麻烦. ***be at the ~ of doing*** 特意…. ***be in ~(s) with*** 和…闹纠纷. ***get into ~*** 招致麻烦,卷入纠纷;受责备;未结婚而怀孕. ***get sb. into ~*** 给某人造成麻烦. ***get sb. out of ~*** 帮助某人解除困难. ***get out of ~*** 摆脱麻烦事;免罚. ***give sb. ~*** 麻烦人,打扰人. ***go to the ~ of ...ing*** 特意…;不辞劳苦…. ***have a ~ with*** 和…闹纠纷[搅不清]. ***have ~ to (do)*** 做…很费事. ***in ~*** 为难,窘困;被捕;未婚怀孕. ***look for ~*** = ask for ~. ***make ~*** 捣乱,吵闹. ***make ~ for sb.*** 给某人制造麻烦. ***put sb. to ~*** 麻烦人,使人受累. ***save sb. ~*** 免去某人麻烦,不必某人费事[操心]. ***spare sb. ~*** 不打搅[不麻烦]某人 (*You may spare yourself the ~.* 你不必费神[费事]). ***stir up ~*** 兴风作浪,惹是生非. ***take the ~ to (do)*** 不怕麻烦去…,不辞…之劳. ***take ~*** 不辞劳苦,费力,忍苦耐劳 (*He dislikes to take ~.* 他怕麻烦). — *vt.* ①扰乱;搅浑. ②使烦恼,使困苦,使为难,使受累;麻烦,烦扰;请求 *(for)*;(病等)折磨. — *vi.* 费力,费神;担心,忧虑;激动. ***be ~d about [with] money matters*** 为钱操心. ***I will ~ you to (do)*** 我要麻烦你去…. ***May I ~ you for [to (do)]*** 麻烦你…好吗? ***Pray don't ~.*** 请不要费事. ***~ sb. for money*** 问…要钱. ***~ oneself about*** 担心,害怕. ***~ oneself to (do)*** 不辞劳苦地(做)…,特意…. ~ **clerk** 故障记录员. **~-free** *a.* 可靠的,无故障的. ~ **lamp** 故障探查灯. ~ **maker** 惹是生非的人;闹事者,捣乱者. ~ **making** 制造麻烦,闹事. **~-shooter** 故障检修员;排解纠纷者.
trou·bled [ˈtrʌbld] *a.* 为难的,不安的,困惑的;骚乱的,不宁的. ~ ***times*** 乱世. ~ ***waters*** 波涛汹涌的海;混乱状态 (*to fish in ~ waters*〔喻〕浑水摸鱼,趁火打劫).
trou·ble·some [ˈtrʌblsəm] *a.* 讨厌的;麻烦的,困难的;(孩子等)难管的,吵闹的. **-ly** *ad.* **-ness** *n.*
trou·blous [ˈtrʌbləs] *a.* 〔古〕①动乱的,骚乱的. ②= troublesome. ~ *times* 乱世.
trou-de-loup [tru:dəˈlu:] *n.* *(pl. trous-* [tru:-]*)* 〔F.〕【军】(阻敌进攻的)狼穿.
trough [trɔf, trɔ:f] *n.* ①木盆;马槽,猪槽;承溜;水笕;洗矿槽. ②[trau] (面包店的)揉面盆,面钵. ③【海】(深

6000 米以上的)深海漕;【电】电槽(= ~ battery);【物】波谷;【数】凹点;【气】槽形低气压. ④〔美剧〕脚光. *a pneumatic ~* 集气槽. *a ~ truck* 油槽车.

trounce [trauns] *vt.* ①痛打;严责,痛骂. ②〔口〕打败(对手).

troupe [tru:p] *n.* ①剧团,戏班子;马戏团. ②一团,一班,一伙. — *vi.* (参加戏班子)巡回演出.

troup·er [ˈtru:pə] *n.* (剧团、马戏团等的)演员,团员;〔口〕有经验的演员.

troup·i·al [ˈtru:piəl] *n.*【动】拟椋鸟.

trou·ser [ˈtrauzə] *n.*〔*pl.*〕裤子. *a pair [three pairs] of ~s* 一条[三条]裤子. ★〔口〕〔用单数〕: Here is a smart ~. 这是一条漂亮的裤子. ***wear the trousers*** (女人)欺压丈夫. — *a.* 裤子的. ~**(s) pocket** 裤兜. ~ **stretcher** 撑裤器〔使保持挺拔〕. ~ **suit**〔英〕(上衣与裤子相配的)女衫裤套装(= pantsuit).

trou·sered [ˈtrauzəd] *a.* 穿着裤子的;〔喻〕男的.

trou·ser·ing [ˈtrauzəriŋ] *n.* 裤料.

trous·seau [ˈtru:səu] *n.* *(pl. ~s, ~x [-z])* 嫁妆.

trout [traut] *n.* *(pl. ~s,* 〔集合词〕 *~)*【鱼】鲑鱼(属);红点鲑鱼(属);真鳟. — *vi.* 钓[捕]鳟鱼. **~-coloured** *a.* (马)白毛黑花的. ~ **lily**【植】美洲赤莲,犬齿赤莲. **~-perch**【动】鲑鲈.

trout·let, trout·ling [ˈtrautlit, -liŋ] *n.* 小鳟鱼.

trout·y [ˈtrauti] *a.* 多鳟鱼的;象鳟鱼的.

trou·vaille [ˈtru:vail] *n.*〔F.〕意外的收获,挖到的地财.

trou·vère [tru:ˈvɛə] *n.*〔F.〕(11—14 世纪间活跃于法国北部的)行吟诗人.

trove [trəuv] *n.* = treasure-trove.

tro·ver [ˈtrəuvə] *n.* ①【法】要求赔偿被侵占所受损失的诉讼. ②(不由购买而由发见的)取得.

trow [trəu] *vi., vt.*〔古〕想;〔附在疑问句后用〕不知道…. *What ails him, (I) ~?* 不知道他什么不舒服?

trow·el [ˈtrauəl] *n.* (泥水匠等的)泥刀,泥铲儿,抹子;【园艺】移植手铲. ***lay it on with a ~*** 用泥铲儿涂抹;大事渲染;竭力阿谀. — *vt.* 用泥铲儿涂抹.

Troy[1] [trɔi] *n.* 特罗伊〔姓氏,男子名〕.

Troy[2] [trɔi] *n.* 特洛伊〔小亚细亚的古城〕.

troy (weight) [trɔi] *n.* 金衡〔金、银、宝石的衡制〕.

trs = trustees.

trs. = transpose.

tru·an·cy [ˈtru:ənsi] *n.* 玩忽职守;(尤指学生的)旷课,逃学.

tru·ant [ˈtru:ənt] *n.* 玩忽职守者,偷懒者;无故旷课者,逃学者. — *a.* 偷懒的,无故缺席的,逃学的;混日子的. ***play ~*** 逃学,赖学. — *vi.* 玩忽职守;偷懒;无故旷课,赖学,逃学. ~ **officer** 训导主任. ~ **school**〔英史〕流浪儿学校. **-ry** *n.* 玩忽职守,偷懒;逃学.

Truben·ize [ˈtru:binaiz] *vt.*【纺】〔商标〕托律本硬挺整理.

truce [tru:s] *n.* ①休战,停战(协定). ②暂停,休止,中止. *a flag of ~* 停战旗. *a general [special] ~* 全面[局部]停战. *an industrial ~* 劳资和解. *A ~ to [with] jesting!* 别再开玩笑了! *A ~ to nonsense!* 别讲废话! **tru·cial** *a.*

truck[1] [trʌk] *n.* ①〔美〕运货汽车,卡车;货车(=〔英〕lorry). ②(铁路上的)手摇车;手推车,(车站上的)电动搬运车;〔英〕无盖货车;转向车;(铁路车辆等的)车架. ③桅杆帽,旗杆帽(等). ④【机】转向架. ⑤〔罕〕小车轮. *an air ~* 运货飞机. *a sound ~* 广播车. — *vt.* 把…装上卡车(等);用卡车(等)运. — *vi.* 用卡车运输;充当卡车司机. ~ **driver,** ~ **man** 卡车司机;卡车运输业者. ~ **load** 一卡车的装载量;一卡车的运费. ~ **spring** 车架弹簧. ~ **tractor** 货运拖曳汽车. ~ **trailer** 货运拖挂车.

truck[2] [trʌk] *n.* ①交易,物物交换;买卖. ②交易品;零星货物. ③实物工资(制). ④〔美〕(作商品出卖的)菜蔬;〔口〕垃圾,废物;废话. ***have no ~ with*** 不和…交易,不和…来往. ***stand no ~*** 不要妥协(等);不能讲废话. ~ **crops** 蔬菜作物. ~ **farm [farmer]**〔美〕菜圃[农]. ~ **garden**〔美〕菜[果]园. ~ **system** 实物工资制. — *vt., vi.* ①物物交换. ②沿街叫卖. ③交易,打交道.

truck·age [ˈtrʌkidʒ] *n.* 货车运费;货车租费;卡车运输.

trucker[1] [ˈtrʌkə] *n.* 卡车司机,手车搬运员;卡车运输业者.

trucker[2] [ˈtrʌkə] *n.* ①物物交易者. ②小贩. ③〔美〕菜农.

truck·le[1] [ˈtrʌkl] *n.* ①小轮;滑车(轮). ②有脚轮的矮脚卧床〔不用时可以推入其他床下,又叫 ~-bed〕. ③〔英方〕小圆筒形乳酪.

truckle[2] [ˈtrʌkl] *vi.* 屈从,谄媚 *(to; for)*.

truc·u·lence, -len·cy [ˈtrʌkjuləns, -lənsi] *n.* 残暴,野蛮,横蛮无理. **truc·u·lent** *a.* 残暴的,凶恶的,横蛮无理的,嚣张的.

Trud·dy [ˈtru:di] *n.* 特鲁迪〔女子名, Gertrude 的昵称〕.

trudge [trʌdʒ] *vi., vt.* 沉重地跋涉,艰苦疲累地走 *(along)*. — *n.* ①徒步跋涉. ②沉重的脚步;沉重疲累地走着的人. **-er** 跋涉[步行]者.

trudg·en,〔别字〕**trudg·eon** [ˈtrʌdʒən] *n.*【泳】特拉真式游泳法〔头面向下两手交拍向前,又叫 ~ stroke〕.

true [tru:] *a.* ①真实的,真正的 *(opp.* false*)*; 正当的. ②(朋友等)忠实的,诚实的. ③正确的,没有错的;丝毫不差的,逼真的. ④纯正的,(动植物等)纯种的. ⑤(声音等)音调正确的. ⑥(车轮等)位置正确的. *a ~ story* 真实情况[叙述]. *~ gold* 真金. *the ~ time* 正确的时间. ***as ~ as steel [flint, touch]*** 绝对忠实可靠的. ***come ~*** (预言等)成事实;实现;(作物)不变种地发芽生长. ***good men and ~*** 正直人士;陪审员. ***hold ~*** 有效;适用. ***(It is) ~, but …*** 果然不错,但是…. ***out of (the) ~*** 不准确,(机械的一部分等)有毛病. ***the ~*** 真理,真实. ***~ as I stand here*** 绝对真实,一点不假. ***~ to life*** 逼真,和原物一模一样,维妙维肖. ***~ to nature*** 逼真. ***~ to one's colours*** 忠于自己的信念[主义(等)]. ***~ to one's name*** 名副其实. ***~ to oneself*** 安分守己的,忠实的,老实的. ***~ to the original*** 忠于原文的(翻译等). ***~ to type*** 典型的. ***~ value of seeds*** 种子利用率. — *ad.* ①真正地,确实地. ②正当地. ③正确地. *Tell me ~* 老老实实跟我说吧. *aim ~* 瞄得准. *breed ~ to type* (优良杂种)育成定型纯种. — *vt.* 配准,配齐(工具、车轮等);校准;整形. *truing up* 校准. ~ **absorption**【物】真吸收. ~ **bill**【法】陪审员的罪证审定背签;受理起诉状;真实的叙述 (*bring in a ~ bill* 认为有罪而予以起诉). ~ **blue** ① 不褪色的蓝. ②(对主义等)绝对忠诚坚定的人. ③(十七世纪苏格兰的)长老会教徒. **~-blue** ① *a.* (对党派)非常忠诚的. ② *n.* 忠实的人. **~born** *a.* 嫡出的;道地的,真正的. **~bred** *a.* 纯种的;受过良好教育的 (*a ~-breeding hybrid* 不分离杂种). ~ **fly** 苍蝇. ~ **fruit**【植】真果. **~-hearted** *a.* 诚实的,忠实的. ~ **length** 实长. ~ **level** 真水平,标准水平. **~love** ①意中人,情人. ②撞羽草 (*~love [~lover's] knot* 同心结〔象征爱情的蝴蝶结〕). **~penny** ① *n.*〔古〕老实人. ② *a.*〔口〕真正的,纯粹的. ~ **ribs**【解】真肋. **~-to-life** *a.* 写实的;反映真实情况的. ~ **weight** 实重. **-ness** *n.* 真实;纯粹,纯正;忠实,诚实;认真;正确.

truf·fle [ˈtrʌfl] *n.*【植】块菌(属)〔味鲜美,调味用〕. **-d** *a.* 加有块菌的,用块菌调味的.

trug [trʌg] *n.*〔方〕①浅底牛奶桶. ②(装水果等用的)浅底篮. ③= trull.

tru·ism [ˈtru:izəm] *n.* ①自明之理;明明白白的事情,起码的常识. ②陈词滥调,老套语.

tru·is·tic [ˈtru:istik] *a.* ①自明之理的;平凡的. ②陈词滥调的.

trull [trʌl] *n.* 〔古〕妓女.

tru·ly [ˈtru:li] *ad.* ①真正;确实. ②精确地,正确地. ③忠实地,诚实地;老实说. ④正当地,合法地. *Why, ~, I cannot say.* 嗯,老实说,我不能告诉你. *Yours ~ [Truly yours]* 忠实于您的人〔信末签名前的客套话〕;〔谑〕本人,鄙人(= myself).

Tru·man [ˈtru:mən] *n.* 杜鲁门〔姓氏,男子名〕.

trump[1] [trʌmp] *n.* ①王牌;有效办法,最后的手段. ②〔口〕老实人,好人. *All his cards are ~s.* 〔口〕有利条件都在他一边;他事事顺遂. ***hold some ~s*** 手里还有王牌;胸有成竹,有必胜把握. ***play a ~*** 拿出王牌;做出惊人之举. ***put sb. to his ~s*** 使人打出王牌,逼得人使出最后办法. ***turn up ~s*** 〔口〕意外顺遂;碰上好运. — *vt.* ①出王牌吃掉(对手的牌). ②胜过. — *vi.* 出王牌;拿出有效办法[最后手段]. ~ **card** 王牌;有利条件,最后手段 (*play one's ~ card* 打出王牌;使出绝招).

trump[2] [trʌmp] *vt.* 捏造. ~ *up a charge against sb.* 冤枉[诬陷]某人. ~**ed-up** *a.* 捏造的,诬告的,虚构的;欺诈的.

trump[3] [trʌmp] *n.* 〔古,诗〕喇叭;喇叭声,号声. — *vi., vt.* 吹喇叭(宣告). ***the last ~*** 【宗】最后审判日的喇叭声.

trump·er·y [ˈtrʌmpəri] *n.* ①中看不中用的东西;废物,废料. ②无聊话,胡话. — *a.* 中看不中用的;不足取的;肤浅的.

trump·et [ˈtrʌmpit] *n.* ①喇叭;【乐】小号;喇叭声,小号声;喇叭般的声音〔如象的吼声等〕. ②【乐】(风琴的)小号音栓. ③喇叭形物;【解】喇叭管;【机】漏斗状筒;传声筒;【贝】法螺贝. ④〔古〕号手;自夸自赞的人. *blow one's own ~* 自夸,自负,自吹自擂. *the Feast of Trumpets* 犹太人的新年. — *vt.* ①吹喇叭通知. ②到处宣扬;鼓吹,极力吹嘘[称赞]. — *vi.* ①吹喇叭. ②(象等)发出喇叭似的声音. ~ **call** 集合号;要求,命令;激励. ~ **conch,** ~ **creeper**【植】美洲凌霄花;中国凌霄花;紫葳. ~ **flower** 喇叭花〔美洲凌霄花等喇叭形花〕. ~ **honeysucker**【植】贯叶忍冬. ~ **major** (骑兵团的)号兵长. ~ **shelly**【动】海螺(壳). ~ **vine**【植】美洲凌霄花. ~**weed**【植】泽兰(属);贯叶泽兰;斑茎泽兰;粉绿茎泽兰.

trump·et·er [ˈtrʌmpitə] *n.* ①喇叭手,号手,号兵. ②吹鼓手,吹嘘者;自夸自赞的人. ③高声鸣禽〔如鹤、白天鹅等〕. *be one's own ~* 自夸,自吹自赞. ***Your ~'s dead!*** 〔口〕这倒吹得活象!

trun·cal [ˈtrʌŋkəl] *a.* 树干的;躯干的.

trun·cate [ˈtrʌŋkeit] *vt.* ①截去(圆锥等的)尖端,修剪(树等). ②删简(冗长的引语等). ③【结晶】截(棱)成平面. ④【数】舍位,舍项. — *a.* ①截平的,平头的. ②删简了的,断章取义的. ③【动,植】(羽,叶)截平的,平头的.

trun·cated [ˈtrʌŋkeitid] *a.* ①截短的;截平的,平头的;截成平面的;【几】截去尖端的. ②删简了的,不完全的,断章取义的.

trun·ca·tion [trʌŋˈkeiʃən] *n.* ①切断,剪断,截去. ②【植】切干萌芽.

trun·cheon [ˈtrʌntʃən] *n.* ①短棍;〔英〕警棍. ②(作权威标记拿着的)权杖,元帅杖,指挥棍. — *vt.* 拿短棒打.

trun·dle [ˈtrʌndl] *n.* ①小轮,矮轮;(床等的)脚轮. ②【机】灯笼式小齿轮,转轴颈. ③滚动(声). ④〔罕〕手推车. ⑤= ~-bed. — *vi.* ①靠矮轮动;滚动,旋转. ②走开. ③【板球】扔球. — *vt.* ①用矮轮推动;推(手推车);转动,滚动(球等). ②撵走,打发走. ③【板球】扔(球). ~ **bed** (可推入大床下的)带脚轮矮床.

trunk [trʌŋk] *n.* ①树干 (*opp.* branch);躯干,身躯. ②本体,主要部分;(河的)主流;(铁道等的)干线;大血管,大神经(等);【计算机】信息通路;【建】柱身. ③象的长鼻;(鸟虫的)长喙. ④(旅行用)大衣箱;汽车后部的行李箱. ⑤槽,【矿】洗矿槽;总管,筒;筒形唧子;【机】管杆. ⑥【讯】中继(线);〔*pl.*〕〔英〕长途电话. ⑦【船】半显舱室;凸起舱口;围壁洞道. ⑧〔*pl.*〕男用运动裤;〔美〕游泳裤. ⑨= ~ hose. ⑩〔美俚〕行李. *the clear ~*【林】(树干的)枝下高. ***live in one's ~s*** 老穿着旅行服装. — *vt.* 【矿】(铅矿等)在槽中洗选. ~ **airline** 航空干线. — *a.* 躯干的;主要的;干线的;箱形的;有筒管的. ~ **call** 〔英〕长途电话(呼叫) (=〔美〕long distance call). ~ **drawers**【商】短裤. ~ **engine**【机】筒状活塞发动机. ~ **exchange** 长途电话局. ~**fish**【动】箱鲀. ~ **hose** ① *n.* (16—17 世纪时的)大脚短裤. ② *a.* 古式的. ~ **line** (铁路的)干线;(电话的)干线,中继线,长途线. ~ **main**【电】中继干线. ~ **nail** (皮箱等用的)饰钉. ~ **piston**【机】筒状活塞. ~ **relay**【自】中继线替续器. ~ **road** 干道,大路;〔美〕(铁路)干线.

trun·nel [ˈtrʌnl] *n.* 定缝销钉,木钉 (= treenail).

trun·nion [ˈtrʌnjən, -niən] *n.* 【炮】炮耳;【机】耳轴;空枢. **-ed** *a.* 有炮耳的;有耳轴的.

truss [trʌs] *n.* ①(干草等的)捆,把,束,一束干草〔老干草 56 磅,新干草 60 磅,稻草 36 磅〕. ②【医】疝带. ③【植】伞形花,穗状花;花束;果穗. ④【船】维系帆桁中段在桅杆上的铁具[绳索]. ⑤【工】构架,桁架,钢梁. *a ~ dam* 草包堤. *a bridge ~* 桥的构架. — *vt.* ①【烹】将(鸡、鸭的)翅膀[脚]扎在身上;将(人的)两手绑在身体上. ②用桁架支持(屋顶、桥等). ③〔古〕扎紧,捆牢(衣服等). ④把…处绞刑 (*up*). ~ **bridge** 桁架桥,钢梁桥. **-ing** *n.* ①桁架;梁,桁条. ②用桁架支撑[加固];捆紧,扎紧.

trust [trʌst] *n.* ①信任,信赖 (*in*). ②责任,义务. ③确信,希望;所倚靠的人[物]. ④委托;保管;委托物;【法】信托;信托财产;【商】赊帐,赊卖. ⑤【经】托辣斯,企业联合. ***fulfil one's ~*** 尽责. ***have [put, repose] ~ in sb.*** 信任某人. ***hold [be in] a position of ~*** 居于负责地位. ***investment ~*** 投资信托公司. ***leave in ~*** 委托. ***on ~*** 信任着,不看证据地;赊帐. ***take a ~ on oneself*** 负起责任. ***take everything on ~*** 轻信. — *vt.* ①信任,信用,信赖. ②委任,委托,信托,托付,交 (*to; with*);说出(秘密) (*with*). ③赊卖 (*for*). ④确信,希望,期待 (*that; to do*). *~ sb. with a charge* 把任务委托某人. *~ sb. with a secret* 对某人说出秘密,把秘密告诉某人. *~ sb. for wheat* 赊卖小麦给某人. *I ~ that he will come.* 我相信他会来的. — *vi.* ①相信 (*in*);信赖 (*on*);信赖而托付,恃,靠 (*to*);期待 (*for*). ②赊卖. *~ to chance* 交给命运,碰运气. ~ **account** 托管财产;信托帐户. ~ **buster** 〔美〕反托拉斯官员. ~ **company** 信托公司. ~ **deed** 【商】委托书. ~ **fund** 托管基金. ~ **money** 委托[托管]金. ~ **territory** 托管地,托管领土. ~**worthiness** 可信赖,可靠,确实. ~**worthy** *a.* 可靠的. **-less** *a.* 不可信托的;不相信别人的.

trus·tee [trʌsˈti:] *n.* 受信托人,受托人;保管人;受托管国;保管委员;(大学等的)评议员,理事. — *vt.* ①移交(财产)给受托[保管]人. ②〔美〕【法】扣押. **-ship** *n.* 受托人的职责[地位];(受托管国对被托管地的)托管(制度);托管状态.

trust·ful [ˈtrʌstfəl] *a.* 信任的,深信不疑的. **-ly** *ad.* **-ness** *n.*

trust·i·fy [trʌsˈtifai] *vt.* 组成托辣斯.

trust·ing [ˈtrʌstiŋ] *a.* 信任的,相信的. **-ly** *ad.*

trust·wor·thy [ˈtrʌstˌwə:ði] *a.* 值得信任的,可靠的,确实. **-i·ness** *n.*

trust·y [ˈtrʌsti] *a.* ***(-i·er; -i·est)*** 应相信的,可信赖的,可靠的,忠实的. — *n.* 可[受]信任的人[物];〔美〕(得到信任的)受优待囚犯. **-i·ly** *ad.* **-i·ness** *n.*

truth [tru:θ] *n.* (*pl.* ~*s* [tru:ðz, tru:θs]) ①真理;真实;真相,事实 (*opp.* lie). ②真实性. ③诚实,老实. ④(机械的)精确度. *To seek ~ from facts.* 实事求是. *There is no ~ in him.* 那家伙一点也不老实. *T- is [lies] at the bottom of a well.* 真理潜伏在井底〔极难发

现〕. *home ~s* 关于自己的逆耳之言. ~ ***to life [nature]*** 逼真. ***in ~*** = 〔古〕***of a ~*** 真正,实在;说实在话,老实说. ***out of ~*** (机器)安装得有毛病. ***The ~ is that*** ... 实际是…. ***tell [speak] the ~*** 说实话. ***to tell the ~ = ~ to tell*** 实际是,说实在话. ~ **drug [serum]** (使人吐露真情的)诱供麻醉药.

truth·ful [ˈtruːθful] *a.* (人等)诚实的,老实的;真实的,真正的. **-ly** *ad.* **-ness** *n.*

truth·less [ˈtruːθlis] *a.* 不诚实的; 不真实的, 虚伪的. **-ness** *n.*

try [trai] *vt.* ①试,尝试,试行;努力. ②试验,考验;试用,试穿. ③【法】审问,审判. ④(问题等)解决. ⑤折磨;使过劳,过度使用. ⑥精制,精炼*(out)*;炼(油);榨(油);最后刨光*(up)*. ~ *one's best to win success* 努力争取胜利. ~ *each car before selling it* 每辆车试验过后再出售. ~ *a new pen* 试用新笔. ~ *a jump* 跳跳看. *Do ~ more* 再吃〔喝〕一点. *He has been sorely tried.* 他受尽了折磨〔考验〕. *This malady tries me so much.* 这个病使我非常痛苦. *The lard was tried in a big kettle.* 这猪油是在大锅里炼出的. — *vi.* ①尝试;试验;努力. ②〔同 and 和另一个动词原形结构连用〕.争取,尽力. *T- again.* 再试一遍. ~ *at a somersault* 试翻筋斗. ~ *for the first prize* 争取得头奖. *He is ~ing to solve the problem.* 他正在努力解决这个问题. *It's hard, but I will try.* 这不容易办,但我要试试看. *T- and finish the work in three days.* 要力争在三天之内把这工作搞完. ~ ***a fall with*** 〔美运〕测验技能. ~ ***and (do*** 或 ***be)*** ...〔口〕尽量,竭力… (*Try and [Try to] be punctual.* 竭力遵守时间). ~ ***back*** ①(回来)再试一试. ②【海】放松(绳索等). ~***ing by hook or by crook*** 千方百计. ~ ***for*** 求;企图达到;立志要. ~ ***hard*** 拼命试试看 (~ *hard to dupe the public opinion* 竭尽混淆视听之能事). ~ ***it on*** ①(老着面皮) 试试看. ②摆架子. ~ ***it on the dog*** 〔口〕拿食物给狗吃吃看;〔美口〕新戏先在乡下演出以试探效果. ~ ***on*** 试穿 (衣服); 试试看. ~ ***one's best [hardest]*** 尽全力. ~ ***one's hand at*** 试行,做来看看. ~ ***one's luck*** 碰碰运气试一试. ~ ***one's weight*** 量体重. ~ ***out*** (采用前)严密试验;筛矿;量(金属的)纯度. ~ ***over*** 试演(戏剧等). ~ ***sb. for [on] murder*** 以杀人罪审判某人. ~ ***sb. for his life*** 判决某人死罪. ~ ***sb.'s patience*** (使)某人生气〔着急〕(*This boy tries my patience.* 这个孩子真急人). — *n.* ①试, 尝试, 试验. ②【橄榄球】触球;(因触球获得的)向球门踢球的权利. ***have a ~ at it [for it]*** 试试看. ~**-on** 〔口〕尝试, 试验;(特指)诈骗;(假缝服装等的)试穿. ~**-out** 〔俚〕试验,尝试;【剧】试演;〔美口〕选拔赛,选拔表演(*give the play a ~ at Paris* 给这出戏在巴黎来一次试探演出). ~ **sail** 【海】斜桁纵帆〔风暴时用〕. ~ **square** 曲尺,验方角尺.

try·ing [ˈtraiiŋ] *a.* ①令人难于忍受的;难堪的;艰难的;令人气愤的. ②试验的. *How very ~ this is!* 这就叫人为难了!— *n.* 【裁缝】假缝. ~ **plane** (木工的)长刨. ~ **square** = try square.

tryp·a·no·some [ˈtripənəsəum], **-so·ma** [-ˈsəumə] *n.* 【动】锥体虫.

tryp·a·no·so·mi·a·sis [ˌtripəˌnəusəuˈmaiəsis] *n.* 【医】锥体虫病.

tryp·ars·a·mide [tripˈɑːsəmaid] *n.* 【药】锥虫胂胺.

tryp·sin [ˈtripsin] *n.* 【生化】胰朊酶,胰蛋白酶.

tryp·sin·o·gen [tripˈsinədʒən] *n.* 胰蛋白酶原.

tryp·tic [ˈtriptik] *a.* 【生化】胰蛋白酶的.

tryp·to·phan(e) [ˈtriptəfæn] *n.* 【生化】色氨酸.

tryst [traist, trist] 〔古〕*n.* 约会,幽会;约会处, 幽会处 (= ~ing place). *a lover's ~* 情人的幽会. ***keep [break] ~*** 遵守〔不遵守〕约会. — *vt.* 和(人)约会;定(约会时间或地点);与…订婚. *the ~ing place* 约会地点. —*vi.* 约会;赴约.

TS = tensile strength 抗拉强度.

tsa·di [ˈtsɑːdi] *n.* 希伯来语第十八个字母.

tsat. = temperature of saturation 饱和温度.

Tsar [zɑː, tsɑː], **Tsa·ri·na, tsarism** 等 *n.* = Czar, Czarina, czarism 等.

tset·se, tset·se-fly [ˈtsetsi] *n.* 【虫】舌蝇,采采蝇.

T/Sgt., T·Sgt. = Technical Sergeant〔美〕空军〔海军陆战队〕技术军士.

T.S.H. = Their Serene Highness 尊贵的殿下.

Tshi [tʃwiː] *n.* = Twi.

Tshi·lu·ba [tʃiˈluːbə] *n.* 齐鲁巴语〔属班图语系,为刚果广大地区的一种混合语〕.

T-shirt [ˈtiːˌʃəːt] *n.*〔美〕①针织圆领衫. ②圆领运动服.

tsim·mes [ˈtsiməs] *n.* 骚乱,暴动;大惊小怪;嚷闹,骚扰.

tsk [tisk] *int., n.* 咂咂声〔表示不同意、同情或假同情等所发的声音〕. — *vt.* 发咂咂声.

T.S.O. = Town Suboffice〔英〕市镇支行(支局,分局).

tsor·is [ˈtsɔːris, ˈtsuər-] *n.* 烦恼,麻烦,苦恼,悲哀 (= tsores, tsorriss, tsooris).

tsp. = teaspoon.

T-strap [ˈtiːˌstræp] *n.*〔美〕①丁字形鞋面. ②(妇女或女孩穿的)丁字鞋.

Tsu·ga·ru [ˈtsuːgəruː] *n.* 津轻海峡〔日本北海道与本州岛之间〕(= ~ Strait).

tsu·na·mi [tsjuːˈnɑːmi] *n.*〔日〕海啸,海震. **-c** *a.*

Tsu·shi·ma [ˈtsuːʃimə, tsu(ː)ˈʃiːmə] *n.* 对马(岛)〔日本〕. ~ **Strait** 对马海峡.

TT = telegraphic transfer 电汇.

T.T. = ①teetotaller 绝对戒酒(主义)者. ②tourist trophy 旅游者纪念品. ③tuberculintested (牛奶)已作结核菌素检验.

T-time [ˈtiːˈtaim] *n.* (火箭、导弹等的)试验发射时间 (= time for test-firing).

TTL = to take leave 告别.

TTR =①target-tracking radar 目标跟踪雷达. ②thermal test reactor 热中子试验反应堆.

TU = ①trade union 工会. ②training unit 训练单位.

Tu = 【化】①thulium. ② tungsten.

Tu. = Tuesday.

tu·an [tuːˈɑːn] *n.*〔马来亚敬称〕先生,老板.

Tua·reg [ˈtwɑːreg] *n.* *(pl. ~(s))* 西撒哈拉和中撒哈拉的柏柏尔人;柏柏尔语.

tu·a·ta·ra [ˌtuːəˈtɑːrə] *n.* 【动】斑点楔齿蜥 *(Sphenodon punctatum)*〔新西兰产〕.

tub [tʌb] *n.* ①桶,木盆;满桶;一桶(的分量). ②澡盆,浴盆;〔口谑〕洗澡. ③〔蔑〕(说教、讲道的)讲坛. ④〔蔑〕木盆一样的小船;练习用赛艇. ⑤【矿】矿车;(运矿)吊桶;(矿井的)桶框. ⑥〔美俚〕(行进速度迟慢的)旧船. ***a big ~*** 〔美俚〕低音大鼓. ***Every ~ must [Let every ~] stand on its own bottom*** 人须自立,人贵自助. ***a tale of a ~*** 无稽之谈. ***in the ~*** 〔美俚〕破产. ***take a cold ~*** 洗冷水澡. ***throw out a ~ to the whale*** 转移对方的注意力(以便乘机脱险). ~ ***of guts***〔美〕肥胖笨拙的人;庸俗的人;不足取的人. — *vt.* ①使入浴;(在浴缸里)为…洗澡. ②使…用练赛艇练习. ③把…种在木盆里;把…装进桶里. ④【矿】用铁板等在矿井内作侧壁. — *vi.* ①洗盆浴. ②(衣服等)被放在桶里洗. ~ **eight** 八人坐的练习用赛艇. ~ **pair** 两人坐的练习赛艇. ~ **thumper** 慷慨激昂的讲道师〔演讲者〕. ~**-thumping** ① *n.* 慷慨激昂的演讲(姿势);〔美〕【无】大吹大擂的广播广告. ②*a.* 慷慨激昂的;大吹大擂的.

tu·ba [ˈtjuːbə] *n.* *(pl. -s, -bae [-biː])* ①【乐】大号,低音大喇叭;(风琴的)低音大号音栓. ②(古罗马的)喇叭.

tub·al [ˈtjuːbl, ˈtuːbl] *a.* 管的〔尤指输卵管的〕. *a ~ pregnancy* 管孕,输卵管妊孕.

tu·bate [ˈtjuːbeit, ˈtuː-] *a.* 有管的;成管的;管的,管形的.

tub·ba·ble [ˈtʌbəbl] *a.* 可放在桶里洗的;可沐浴的.

tub·ber [ˈtʌbə] *n.* 沐浴者.

tub·bing [ˈtʌbiŋ] *n.* ①制桶;制桶材料. ②【矿】丘宾洞,井壁.

tub·bish [ˈtʌbiʃ] *a.* ①桶状的. ②肥胖(象木桶似)的.

tub·by [ˈtʌbi] *a.* ***(-bi·er; -bi·est)*** 桶状的;空桶敲击声似的,(乐器等)钝音的;(人等)矮胖的.

tube [tjuːb] *n.* ①管,筒;颜料管. ②管状地下隧道;〔口〕(伦敦的)地下铁道. ③【炮】炮身;【汽锅】锅管;【解】管;管乐器;轮胎内胎. ④〔美〕真空管,电子管;电视显象管;电视(机). *an optic* ~ 望远镜. *a wheel [an inner]* ~ 内轮胎. *a photoelectric* ~ 光电管. *a display* ~ (雷达)显示管;(电视)显象管. *a pick-up [picture]* ~ 摄象[显象]管. *a pilot* ~ 指示灯. ***go by*** ~〔口〕坐(伦敦)地下铁道车去. — *vt.* ①把…装上管;把…弄成管状. ②使通过管子;〔英〕坐地下铁道车去. ~ **colo(u)rs** 〔*pl.*〕管装颜料. ~ **culture** (细菌的)试管培养. ~ **foot** 【动】(棘皮动物的)管足. ~ **like** *a.* 管状的. ~ **well** 管井.

tu·ber [ˈtjuːbə] *n.* ①【植】块茎,球根. ②【解】结节. ③〔T-〕【植】块菌属. ~ **crops** 【植】块茎作物.

tu·ber·cle [ˈtjuːbəːkl] *n.* ①【植】小块茎;根瘤;小突. ②【解,医】结节,小结;结核(节). ~ **bacillus** 结核菌〔略 T.B.〕.

tu·ber·cled, tu·ber·cu·late, tu·ber·cu·lated [ˈtjuː-bəːkld, -kjulit, -kjuleitid] *a.* ①(有)根瘤[小突等]的. ②结核菌[病]的.

tu·ber·cu·la [tju(ː)ˈbəːkjulə] *n.* (*pl.*) tuberculum 的复数.

tu·ber·cu·lar [tju(ː)ˈbəːkjulə] *a.* = tuberculous. — *n.* 结核病病人. **-ize, -ise** *vt.* = tuberculize.

tu·ber·cu·late [tju(ː)ˈbəːkjulit], **tu·ber·cu·lat·ed** [-leitid] *a.* ①有结节的,有小瘤的. ②结核性的,结核病的. **tuberculation** *n.*

tu·ber·cule [ˈtjuːbəːkjuːl] *n.* = tubercle.

tu·ber·cu·lin [tju(ː)ˈbəːkjulin] *n.* 结核菌素,结核菌苗.

tu·ber·cu·lize [tju(ː)ˈbəːkjulaiz] *vt.* 使生瘤;使生结核(病).

tu·ber·cu·loid [tjuˈbəːkjuˌlɔid] *a.* 结核节状的;结核病状的.

tu·ber·cu·lo·sis [tjuːˌbəːkjuˈləusis] *n.* 【医】结核病;〔特指〕肺结核,〔略 TB, t.b.〕. *pulmonary* ~ 肺结核.

tu·ber·cu·lous [tju(ː)ˈbəːkjuləs] *a.* ①结节(状)的. ②结核(性)的;结核病的.

tu·ber·cu·lum [tjuˈbəːkjuləm] *n.* ***(pl. tubercula*** [-lə]***)*** 【解】结节,小结.

tu·ber·ose [ˈtjuːbərəus] *a.* = tuberous. — *n.* 【植】晚香玉.

tu·ber·os·i·ty [tjúːbəˈrɔsiti] *n.* ①有块茎(状态);块茎状;结节状[性]. ②【解】粗隆;(骨的)结节.

tu·ber·ous [ˈtjuːbərəs] *a.* 有块茎的;结节性的. ~ **root** 块根.

tubi- *comb. f.* 表示"管子","管道","管状".

tu·bi·fex [ˈtjuːbəˌfeks, ˈtuː-] *n.* ***(pl. -fex·es, -fex)*** 【动】颤蚓.

tu·bi·form [ˈtjuːbifɔːm] *a.* 管状的.

tub·ing [ˈtjuːbiŋ] *n.* ①装管,配管,制管. ②管道(系统);管料. ③管的一部分. ④〔集合词〕管类.

tu·boid [ˈtjuːbɔid] *a.* 似管的,管状的.

tu·bu·lar [ˈtjuːbjulə] *a.* ①管系组织的;管状的. ②管子做的;有管的. ③发吹管般声音的. *a* ~ *frame* 管架. ~ *furniture* 钢管家具[铁床等]. **-i·ty** *n.*

tu·bu·late [ˈtjuːbjuˌlit] *a.* = tubular. — *vt.* **-la·tion** *n.*

tu·bule [ˈtjuːbjuːl] *n.* 小管;【解】细管.

tu·bu·li·flo·rous [ˌtjuːbjuliˈflɔːrəs, tuː-] *a.* 【植】管状小花的.

tu·bu·lose [ˈtjuːbjuləus], **tu·bu·lous** [-ləs] *a.* ①管状的;有小管的. ②【植】有管筒状花的. *a tubulous boiler* 管式锅炉.

tu·bu·lure [ˈtjuːbjuˌluə, ˈtuː-] *n.* (曲颈瓶,蒸馏器的)短管口.

TUC = Trades Union Congress〔英〕职工大会.

tuck[1] [tʌk] *n.* ①(袖子等上的)缝褶,横褶,横裥;折起[折进]部分. ②(伸到大网中取鱼用的)网兜儿. ③【海】船尾突出部下方[两侧外板接合处]. ④〔英俚〕食品,糕点,酒席. ⑤【运动】折叠式姿势[两手抱住小腿,膝部贴住前胸]. — *vt.* ①在(袖等上)打横褶,打裥;翻折,卷[折]起(袖子等) *(up)*. ②包起,裹起,卷紧. ③把…挤进[塞进],(收)藏起 *(in; into; away)*. ④〔英俚〕吃,喝,拼命吃 *(in; away)*. ⑤用网兜儿从大网中把(鱼)捞出. ⑥〔俚〕勒死 *(up)*. — *vi.* ①打横褶;缩拢. ②〔俚〕狼吞虎咽地吃,拼命吃 *(in; away)*. ~ ***away*** 藏起 (*The village is* ~*ed away in a quiet valley.* 村子隐藏在一个幽静的山谷中). ~ ***in*** 把一端折进[塞进];〔口〕耙进;尽量吃 *(at* food*)*. ~ ***into*** 藏进;〔口〕把(食物)塞进肚子里. ~ ***on*** 〔俚〕乱讨价,瞎要(价钱). ~ ***oneself up in bed*** 裹在被窝里. ~ ***up*** 折起一头,卷起;包;〔口〕绞死(犯人) (~ *up one's sleeves* 卷起袖子). ~**-in,** ~**-out** 〔俚〕饱吃. ~ **net,** ~ **seine** 网兜儿. ~ **shop** 〔英学生语〕糖果食品店.

tuck[2] [tʌk] *n.* 〔Scot.〕鼓声;〔古〕喇叭声.

tuck[3] [tʌk] *n.* 活力,精力.

tuck[4] [tʌk] *n.* 〔古〕一种细长的剑.

tuck[5] [tʌk] *n.* tuxedo 的缩略词.

tuck·a·hoe [ˈtʌkəˌhəu] *n.* ①【植】茯苓 *(Poria cocos)*. ②茯苓根和块茎.

tuck·er [ˈtʌkə] *n.* ①打横褶的人,作褶裥的人;缝褶机;(装上去的)衣领;(17、18 世纪时的女用)领布. ②〔澳俚〕食物. ③〔美口〕疲倦. ***make [earn] one's*** ~ 勉强糊口. ***one's best bib and*** ~ (个人所有的衣服中)最好的一件[套]. — *vt.* 〔美口〕使疲倦,使精疲力尽*(out)*.

tuck·et [ˈtʌkit] *n.* 〔古〕响亮的喇叭声.

Tuc·son [tuːˈsɔn] *n.* 图森[美国城市].

-tude *suf.* 与形容词、过去分词构成表示性质、状态的抽象名词: alti*tude*, magni*tude*, soli*tude*.

Tu·dor [ˈtjuːdə] *a., n.* 英国都铎王室[朝]的(人);【建】都铎朝式样(的). *the* ~*s* = *the House of* ~ 都铎王室. ~ **arch** 四心拱. ~ **flower** 都铎式花样. ~ **rose** 都铎王室蔷薇徽.

Tues. = Tuesday.

Tues·day [ˈtjuːzdi] *n.* 星期二. **-s** *ad.* 每星期二.

tufa [ˈtjuːfə] *n.* 【地】华;石灰华,泉华. **-ceous** *a.*

tuff[1] [tʌf] *n.* 【地】凝灰岩. **-aceous** [tʌˈfeiʃəs] *a.*

tuff[2] [tʌf] *a.* 〔俚〕极佳的.

tuf·fet [ˈtʌfit] *n.* ①草丛. ②矮凳.

tuft [tʌft] *n.* ①(头发、羽毛等的)簇,丛,束. ②树林;乱丛棵子. ③【织】毛撮,毛绒束;〔美俚〕(下巴上的)山羊胡子. ④【解】丛脉;(细血管)丛. ⑤(坐垫等边上的)饰缕;帽缕;有帽缕的贵族人物. — *vt.* ①给…饰上饰缕,用饰缕装饰. ②使成簇[丛,球];簇生,丛生. ~**hunter** 〔古〕拍权贵马屁的人. **-ed** *a.* 簇状的;有一簇毛发的 (*a* ~*ed duck* 冠凫,凤头鸭).

tuft·y [ˈtʌfti] *a.* 成簇[丛]的;多簇[丛]的;簇生的,丛生的.

tug [tʌg] *vt.* ***(tugged*** [tʌgd]; ***tug·ging*** [ˈtʌgiŋ]***)*** (吃力地)拉,拖(船);用拖船拖曳. — *vi.* ①用力拖 *(at)*. ②尽力,努力,挣扎. ~ *a boat onto shore* 把船拖到岸上. ~ ***at the [an] oar*** 拼命划船;拼命苦干. ~ ***in a subject*** 勉强穿插上一段情节. — *n.* ①拖,拉,曳引. ②尽力,努力,挣扎,奋斗;激战,搏斗. ③拖轮;(曳引用的)绳索,链条;(马具的)曳革;【矿】装有滑车的铁钩. ④〔俚〕(英国 Eton 学校的)公费生. *We felt a great* ~ *at parting.* 离别时真难受. ~ **boat** 拖船. ~**-o'-war** = ~**-of-war** 拔河(游戏);激战.

tu·grik [ˈtuːgrik] *n.* 图格里克〔蒙古人民共和国的货币单位〕.

tu·i [ˈtuːi] *n.* 【动】(新西兰)蜜雀 *(Prosthemadera novaeseelandiae).*

tuille [twiːl] *n.* (铠甲的)腿裙,腰甲.

tu·i·tion [tjuːˈiʃən] *n.* ①教诲. ②学费. **-al** *a.* ①教诲的. ②学费的.

tu·la·r(a)e·mi·a [ˌtuːləˈriːmiə] *n.* 〔美〕【医】兔热病,土拉(伦斯)菌病. **-re·mic** *a.*

tu·le [ˈtjuːli] *n.* 〔美〕【植】锐藨草 *(Scirpus acutus)*; 软茎藨草 *(Scirpus validus)* 〔美国西南部产〕.

tu·lip [ˈtjuːlip] *n.* ①【植】郁金香(属); 山慈姑. ②【炮】炮口带. ~ **tree [poplar]** *n.* 【植】鹅掌楸属; 美国鹅掌楸. ~**wood** 鹅掌楸木.

tulle [tjuːl] *n.* 面纱; 薄纱, 绢网.

tul·li·bee [ˈtʌliˌbiː] *n.* 【动】湖白鲑.

tum·ble [ˈtʌmbl] *vi.* ①跌倒,摔倒; 倒塌; 滚下. ②打滚,翻滚. ③翻觔斗. ④〔口〕跌跌撞撞地来[去],慌慌张张地来[去] *(to; up; down)*; 滚进 *(into)*; 一翻身跳出 *(out of)*. ⑤(市价)猛跌. ⑥无意中遇到, 碰见 *(into; on)*. ⑦〔俚〕(突然)察觉,恍然大悟 *(to)*. ⑧〔俚〕同意 *(to)*. — *vt.* ①摔翻, 摔倒 *(down)*; 使倒摔下来. ②扔出, 扔散 (衣服等); 弄乱, 搅乱. ③把…放入磨箱里磨光. ④打中(鸟兽等). ~ *down (up) the stairs* 东倒西歪地下(上)楼梯. ~ *off a horse* 摔下马来. ~ *over a stone* 在石头上绊倒. *It was a long time before she tumbled (to what I mean).* 好长时间她才(对我的意思)恍然大悟. *I ~d on him there.* 我在那里无意中遇见了他. ~ **and toss** 乱翻乱滚,遍地打滚 *(He ~d and tossed from pain.* 他痛得打滚). ~ **down the sink** 〔美〕牛饮. ~ **home** 【海】(舷侧上部)向内弯曲. ~ **in** 【木工】嵌进;〔俚〕(上床倒下就)睡;【海】= ~ home. — *n.* 跌倒; 滚落; 翻滚; 混乱,乱七八糟. **all in a** ~ 混乱到极点. **give [get] a** ~〔口〕给予[得到]好评. **have a slight [nasty]** ~ 跌了轻轻一交[一大交]. ~**bug** 【虫】金龟子(科甲虫),蜣螂. ~**-down** *a.* (房子等)摇摇欲坠的,破烂的. ~ **weed** 【植】风滚草; 丝石竹; 苋属,广布苋.

tum·bler [ˈtʌmblə] *n.* ①(平底)玻璃酒杯. ②摔倒的人,打滚的人; 翻觔斗的人; 杂技演员; 不倒翁; (会在空中翻觔斗的) 翻飞鸽. ③衣服干燥机. ④(机枪的)机心; (锁里的)制动栓. ⑤【机】转臂; 转筒; 摆动换向齿轮, 转向轮. ⑥〔英方〕运肥[粪]车. ~ **gears** 【机】三星牙. ~ **switch** 倒扳[起倒]开关. **-ful** *n.* 一平底玻璃杯之量.

tumbling barrel [box] 研磨滚筒.

tum·brel, tum·bril [ˈtʌmbrəl, -bril] *n.* ①〔英〕粪车,肥料车. ②【军】二轮弹药车. ③(法国革命时代的)死刑犯押送车.

tu·me·fa·cient [ˌtjuːmiˈfeiʃənt, tuː-] *a.* 【医】引起肿胀的; 肿胀的.

tu·me·fac·tion [tjuːmiˈfækʃən] *n.* 【医】肿大,肿胀; 疙瘩,疮.

tu·me·fy [ˈtjuːmifai] *vt., vi.* (使)肿起,(使)肿胀,(使)胀大.

tu·mes·cence [tjuˈmesns, tuː-] *n.* ①肿胀,肿大. ②肿胀部分.

tu·mes·cent [tjuːˈmesnt] *a.* 肿大的,肿胀的.

tu·mid [ˈtjuːmid] *a.* 肿胀的; 涨满的; (文风等)浮夸的,夸张的.

tu·mid·i·ty [tjuːˈmiditi] *n.* 肿大,肿起; 浮夸,夸张.

tum·my [ˈtʌmi] *n.* 〔儿〕肚子. ~**ache** 肚子痛.

tumo(u)r, [ˈtjuːmə] *n.* 【医】肿瘤, 癌, 疙瘩, 赘疣. *a benign [malignant] ~* 良[恶]性肿瘤. **-ous** *a.* 肿瘤的; 夸张的 *(tumourous growth* 【农】陡长).

tump [tʌmp] *n.* 〔英方〕①小岗,小丘. ②丛〔如草丛〕.

tump·line [ˈtʌmplain] *n.* 〔美〕背物带〔经过前额后转到肩后,使重物正好背在背上〕.

tu·mu·lar [ˈtjuːmjulə, ˈtuː-] *a.* 土墩的; 坟堆的.

tu·mu·li [ˈtjuːmjuli, -lai] *n.* 〔*pl.*〕 tumulus 的复数.

tu·mu·lose [ˈtjuːmjuˌləus, ˈtuː-] *a.* 丘陵地的 (= tumulous).

tu·mult [ˈtjuːmʌlt] *n.* 骚动; 暴动; 吵闹,喧嚣; 激动,烦乱. *His mind was in a ~.* 他心烦意乱.

tu·mul·tu·a·ry [tjuːˈmʌltjuəri] *a.* ①吵闹的,喧嚣的; 激动的; 不稳的, 混乱的. ②(军队等) 没有纪律的, 乌合之众的.

tu·mul·tu·ous [tjuˈmʌltjuəs] *a.* 吵闹的,喧嚣的; 动乱的,纷乱的; 激动的. *a roaring and ~ river* 汹涌澎湃的河流. **-ly** *ad.* **-ness** *n.*

tu·mu·lus [ˈtjuːmjuləs] *n.* *(pl. **-es, -li** [-lai])* 冢,古坟.

tun [tʌn] *n.* ①大(酒)桶,(酿造用)发酵桶. ②桶〔252 加仑的液量〕. — *vt.* 把(酒)装入大桶.

tu·na [ˈtjuːnə] *n.* 〔美〕【鱼】金枪鱼(科) (= tunny); 金枪鱼罐头. ~ **clipper** 金枪鱼捕捞船.

tun·a·ble [ˈtjuːnəbl] *a.* ①可调音的. ②能合调的; 能发出和声的; 和谐的, 音调优美的; 悦耳的. ③【无】可调谐的.

tun·dra [ˈtʌndrə] *n.* 【地】苔原,冻原,冻土带,寒漠.

tune [tjuːn] *n.* ①曲调,调子; 语调; 态度. ②和谐,调谐,调和. ③情绪; 正常状态. ④程度; 数量. *the ~ the (old) cat [cow] died of* 〔口〕刺耳的音乐〔歌唱〕. *I am not in ~ for talk.* 我不想说话. **call one's own ~ = call the ~** 点戏,点唱; 任意指挥,发号施令. **change one's ~ = sing another (= a different) ~** 改变调子; 改变态度. **in ~** 合调; 和谐,和睦 *(with)*. *His ideas are in ~ with the times.* 他的思想适合时代潮流. **keep... in ~** 使…保持正常状态. **out of ~** 不合调; 失调. *The piano is out of ~.* 钢琴走调; 不和谐, 不和睦 *(with)*. **to the ~ of (£5)**, 达(5 镑)之多. — *vt.* ①校准(乐器的)音调,调准. ②调整,使调和, 使一致 *(to)*. ③〔诗〕唱,奏. ④【无】调谐; 调整(频率); 收听. — *vi.* ①协调 *(with)*. ②【无】调谐,调好频率; 收听. ~ **in** 【无】调谐,调准; 收听;〔美〕开始 (~ *in to Radio Beijing* 收听北京电台广播). ~ **off** 【无】中途断绝. ~ **out** 【无】①调准收音机使无(杂音); 解谐,失谐. ②〔美〕无视,注意到别处. ~ **up** ①开始演奏,开始唱; 调音,调谐;〔谑〕(孩子)哭起来; (猎狗) 咬起来; 使发挥全部能力;〔美〕练习(运动比赛). ②用化学溶剂清除发动机中沉积物. ~**d amplifier** 【无】调谐放大器. ~**smith** (流行歌曲的)作曲者. ~**up,** ~**-up** ①调正,调节,调谐. ②(运动前的)准备动作.

tune·a·ble [ˈtjuːnəbl] *a.* = tunable.

tune·ful [ˈtjuːnfəl] *a.* 和谐的, 音调优美的. **-ly** *ad.* **-ness** *n.*

tune·less [ˈtjuːnlis] *a.* ①不合调子的, 不和谐的; 无韵律的,非乐音的. ②(乐器)无声的. **-ness** *n.*

tun·er [ˈtjuːnə] *n.* 调音的人,调音师; 调音器;【无】调谐器.

tung [tʌŋ] *n.* 〔Chi.〕桐. ~ **oil** 桐油; ~ **tree** 【植】油桐树.

tung·ar [ˈtʌŋgə] *n.* 【无】(二极)钨氩(整流)管.

tung·state [ˈtʌŋstit] *n.* 【化】钨酸盐.

tung·sten [ˈtʌŋstən] *n.* 【化】钨〔w〕. ~ **filament** 钨丝. ~ **steel** 【冶】钨钢. **-ic** [tʌnsˈtenik] *a.*

tung·stic [tʌŋˈstik] *a.* 【化】六价钨的,(正)钨的; 五价钨的. ~ **ocher** 【矿】= tungstite.

tung·stite [ˈtʌŋstait] *n.* 【矿】钨华 (= tungstic ocher).

Tun·gus [tunˈguz] *n.* ①*(pl. **-gus·es, -gus**)* 通古斯人. ②通古斯语. — *a.* 通古斯人的; 通古斯语的; 通古斯文化的 (= Tunguz).

Tun·gus·ic [tunˈguzik] *n.* 通古斯语〔属于阿尔泰语系的一语族,为亚洲中部和东北部人说的,包括通古斯语和满语]. — *a.* ①通古斯人的. ②通古斯语的.

tu·nic [ˈtju:nik] *n.* ①(古罗马、古希腊人的)长达膝盖的外衣；古时穿在铠甲上的战袍. ②(现代妇女运动、舞蹈用的)束腰外衣；[英]平常军[警]服[制服]上衣. ③【植】种皮；鳞茎皮；膜被；原套；【动】膜；被囊；【解，动】膜；层. ④【天主】= tunicle.

tu·ni·ca [ˈtju:nikə, ˈtu:-] *n.* *(pl.* **-cae** [-si:]*)* 【解，动】膜；被囊.

tu·ni·cate [ˈtju:nikeit] *a.* 【植】具外皮[鳞茎皮]的；具膜被的；【动】叠套的；被囊类的. — *n.* 【动】被囊类动物.

tu·ni·cle [ˈtju:nikl] *n.* ①【天主】助祭(穿的)祭服；[*pl.*] 主教穿的轻绸衣[身长袖宽]. ②【动、植】薄被膜.

tun·ing [ˈtju:niŋ] *n.* ①【乐】调音[弦]. ②【无】调谐；收听. ~ **crook** 调音曲管. ~ **fork** 【乐】音叉. ~ **hammer** 调音锤. ~ **key** 调音键. ~ **peg,** ~ **pin** (弦乐器的)弦轴，弦栓.

Tu·nis [ˈtju:nis] *n.* 突尼斯[突尼斯首都].

Tu·ni·sia [tju(:)ˈniziə] *n.* 突尼斯[非洲]. ~**n** *n. a.* 突尼斯人[的].

tunnage [ˈtʌnidʒ] *n.* = tonnage.

tun·nel [ˈtʌnl] *n.* 隧道；地道；坑道；管道，烟道，风洞；【矿】石巷，平峒. ~ *warfare* 地道战. — *vt.* ([英]**-ll-**) ①在…凿隧道[掘坑道]. ②凿隧道通过. ~ *one's way (through; into)* 挖隧道[巷道](穿过；进到). — *vi.* ①凿隧道[掘坑道]. ②通过坑道 *(through)*; 进隧道 *(into)*. ~ **borer** 隧道挖凿机. ~ **net** (捕鱼用的)袋网. ~ **diode** 【无】隧道二极管. ~ **disease** 【医】隧道病，潜函病. ~ **vision** 【军】坑道视界；目光短浅. **-er, -ler** 隧道(掘进)工；隧道掘进机.

tun·ny [ˈtʌni] *n.* 【鱼】金枪鱼(类).

tu·no·scope [ˈtu:nəuskəup] *n.* (无线电收音机上调谐用的)电眼，调谐指示器.

tun·y [ˈtju:ni] *a.* 音调和谐的，音调优美的；【乐】曲调明朗的；易唱的.

tup [tʌp] *n.* ①[英方]公羊. ②【机】冲锤；动力锤的头部；冲面.

tupe·lo [ˈtu:pələu] *n.* 【植】(多花)紫树 (= black gum)；紫树木料.

Tu·pi [tu:ˈpi:, ˈtu:pi] *n.* ①*(pl.* ***Tu·pis Tu·pi)*** 图皮族[南美印第安人的一种，居住在巴西和巴拉圭的某些地区]. ②图皮语[图皮族人说的图皮-拉瓜尼语的方言，以前为亚马孙地区说的一种混合方言]. ③南美印第安语系[包括图皮-拉瓜尼语和南美广大地区所说的其它三十多种语言].

Tu·pi-Gua·ra·ni [tu:ˈpi:ˌgwa:ra:ˈni:, ˈtu:pi-] *n.* ①图皮-拉瓜尼语. ②= tupi.

tup·pence [ˈtʌpəns] *n.* [英口] = twopence.

tuque [tju:k] *n.* (有鸭舌帽檐的)绒线帽.

tu quo·que [ˈtju:ˈkwəukwi] [L.] ('你也一样'式的)反驳；(彼此彼此式的)应酬话. *a tu quoque reply* 旗鼓相当的回答；照样回敬一句.

tu·ra·cou, tu·ra·ko [ˈtuərəkəu] *n.* = touraco.

Tu·ra·ni·an [tjuəˈreinjən, -niən] *a.* 都兰语族的，乌拉尔阿尔泰 (Ural-Altai) 语族的. — *n.* 都兰语族；说都兰语族语言的人.

tur·ban [ˈtə:bən] *n.* ①(穆斯林的)缠头巾. ②缠头巾式女帽. ③(卷贝的)涡纹，螺旋. **-ed** *a.* 缠缠头巾的；戴缠头巾式女帽的.

tur·ba·ry [ˈtə:bəri] *n.* *(pl.* **-ries***)* ①泥炭采掘场. ②【英法】(在他人土地上的)泥炭采掘权.

tur·bel·lar·i·an [ˌtə:biˈlɛəriən] *n.* 【动】涡虫纲 (*Turbellaria*) 动物. — *a.* 涡虫纲的.

tur·bid [ˈtə:bid] *a.* 浑浊的；烟雾浓密的，不透明的；混乱的，一团糟的. **-ly** *ad.* **-ness** *n.*

tur·bi·dim·e·ter [tə:biˈdimitə] *n.* 浊度计. **tur·bi·di·met·ric** [ˌtə:bidiˈmetrik] *a.* **tur·bi·dim·e·try** *n.* 浊度.

tur·bi·dite [ˈtə:biˌdait] *n.* 【地】浊流岩.

tur·bid·i·ty [tə:ˈbiditi] *n.* 浑浊，浊度；不透明；混乱. ~ **current** 【地】浊流.

tur·bid·ness [ˈtə:bidnis] *n.* ①混浊；多泥. ②浊；(云，烟的)浓密；暗黑. ③混乱.

tur·bi·nal [ˈtə:binl] *a.* = turbinate. — *n.* 【解】鼻甲(骨).

tur·bi·nate [ˈtə:binit] *a.* ①陀螺似[形]的；倒圆锥形的. ②【解】鼻甲(骨)的. ③象陀螺般转的；螺旋状的. — *n.* 螺旋贝壳；【解】鼻甲骨.

tur·bi·nat·ed [ˈtə:biˌneitid, -nitid] *a.* ①陀螺状的，倒锥状的. ②【解，动】鼻甲的.

tur·bi·na·tion [tə:biˈneiʃən] *n.* 倒圆锥形；陀螺状旋转[螺旋].

tur·bine [ˈtə:bin, -bain] *n.* 【机】(涡)轮机，叶轮机，汽轮机，透平机. *a hydraulic [water]* ~ 水轮机. *a steam* ~ 气轮机. *a* ~ *steamer* 涡轮汽船.

tur·bit [ˈtə:bit] *n.* 【动】(冠毛卷如螺贝的)浮羽鸽.

tur·bo [ˈtə:bəu] *n.* ①透平机，涡轮机. ②= turbosupercharger.

tur·bo- *comb. f.* 意为"涡轮".

tur·bo·car [ˈtə:bəuka:] *n.* 涡轮汽车.

tur·bo·cop·ter [ˈtə:bəukɔptə] *n.* 涡轮直升飞机.

tur·bo-ex·haus·ter [ˌtə:bəuigˈzɔ:stə] *n.* 涡轮排气机.

tur·bo·fan [ˈtə:bəuˌfæn] *n.* ①涡轮通风器 (= turbofan engine). ②涡轮风扇.

tur·bo·gen·er·a·tor [ˈtə:bəuˈdʒenəreitə] *n.* 涡轮发电机，透平发电机.

tur·bo·jet [ˈtə:bəudʒet] 【空】涡轮喷气发动机 (= turbojet engine)；涡轮喷气飞机.

tur·bo·prop [ˈtə:bəuprɔp] *n.* ①涡轮螺桨发动机 (= turboprop engine). ②涡轮螺桨飞机.

tur·bo-pro·pel·ler en·gine [ˈtə:bəuprəˈpelə] 涡轮螺桨发动机.

tur·bo-ram-jet [ˈtə:bəuˈræmdʒet] 【空】带加力燃烧室的涡轮喷气发动机[飞机].

tur·bo·su·per·charg·er [tə:bəusju:pəˈtʃa:dʒə] *n.* 【空】涡轮增压器.

tur·bot [ˈtə:bət] *n.* *(pl.* **~s,** [集合词] **~***)* 【动】大菱鲆；鳞鲀.

tur·bo·train [ˈtə:bəutrein] *n.* 涡轮火车[时速可达 170 英里].

tur·bu·lence, -len·cy [ˈtə:bjuləns, -lənsi] *n.* ①(风等的)狂暴；激流(现象). ②骚乱，动乱；强横. ③【气】湍流. *a* ~ *amplifier* 紊流型放大器.

tur·bu·lent [ˈtə:bjulənt] *a.* ①激流的；湍流的. ②骚乱的；强横的. ~ **flow** 【物】涡流.

Turco- *comb. f.* = Turkish: *Turco*phil 爱好土耳其(风俗、习惯)的人. *Turco*phobia 憎恶土耳其(风俗、习惯)的人.

Tur·co·man [ˈtə:kəmən] *n.* = Turkoman.

turd [tə:d] *n.* [俗]粪块.

tu·reen [təˈri:n] *n.* (盛汤用)有盖的陶磁大盘.

turf [tə:f] *n.* *(pl.* **-s;** [罕] ***turves*** [tə:vz]*)* ①草皮，草根土；草地. ②[美、Scot.] 泥煤. ③[the ~] 赛马场；赛马. ④[美俚](流氓集团的)地盘，势力范围. ***on the*** **~** ①以赛马为生. ②卖淫. ③穷得身无分文. — *vt.* ①把(地面)铺上草皮. ②赶出，驱逐. ~ ***it*** [美]徒步旅行. ~ ***out*** [俚]抛出(东西)，赶出(人). **~-bound** *a.* 铺有草皮的. ~ **court** 草地网球场. ~ **peat** 泥煤.

turf·ite, turf·man [ˈtə:fait, ˈtə:fmən] *n.* 欢喜赛马的人，赛马迷[尤指自己养马或驯马的].

turf·y [ˈtə:fi] *a.* ①草地的，铺着草皮的；草地似的. ②赛马场的，赛马的. ③泥煤的. ~ **soil** 生草土.

tur·gent [ˈtə:dʒənt] *a.* [现罕]肿的，肿胀的.

tur·ges·cence, -cen·cy [tə:ˈdʒesns, -snsi] *n.* ①肿，肿胀. ②【植物生理】紧涨，膨压. ③夸张. **-cent** *a.*

tur·gid [ˈtə:dʒid] *a.* ①肿胀的. ②浮夸的，夸张的.

-ness *n.*

tur•gid•i•ty [tə:ˈdʒiditi] *n.* ①肿胀,肿大. ②【植物生理】紧涨度. ③浮夸,夸张.

tur•gite [ˈtə:dʒait] *n.*【矿】水赤铁矿.

tur•gor [ˈtə:gə] *n.* ①肿胀,胀大. ②紧涨(现象),膨压.

Tu•rin [tjuˈrin] *n.* 都灵〔即 Torino 托里诺〕〔意大利城市〕.

tu•ri•on [ˈtjuəriən] *n.*【植】有鳞芽的根出条. **-i•fer•ous** [-ˈnifərəs] *a.*

Turk [tə:k] *n.* ①土耳其人;突厥人;(尤指)土耳其的穆斯林. ②土耳其马. ③强暴的人,残忍的人. ④淘气鬼,顽童. ⑤〔美〕爱尔兰人. *the Grand [Great]* ~【史】土耳其皇帝. *the Young* ~ 青年土耳其党. *a young [little]* ~ 淘气鬼,顽童. **~'s cap** *n.*【植】①舟形乌头. ②= ~'s head ①. **~'s-cap lily**【植】缠头巾状百合. **~'s-head** *n.* ①【植】仙人球. ②= pepe's-head 长柄撣箒. ③= ~'s-head pan (中部有烟筒的)烤锅. ④【海】(索端的)缠头巾状饰结.

Turk. = Turkey; Turkish.

Turk- *comb. f.* 表示: ①突厥(人)的,突厥语的. ②土耳其(人,语)的.

Tur•ke•stan [tə:kisˈtæn,-ˈtɑ:n] *n.* 〔苏联〕土耳其斯坦.

Tur•key [ˈtə:ki] *n.* 土耳其〔亚洲〕.

tur•key [ˈtə:ki] *n.* ①【鸟】火鸡,吐绶鸡. ②〔美俚〕劣等货品〔作品〕; 演出失败,失败的广播节目. ③〔美俚〕(装模作样)摆臭架子的人. ④〔美俚〕五角银币;随身携带的卧具;装器具的帆布袋. ⑤〔美俚〕懦夫 *boned* ~【烹】(美国西部的)兔肉. ***have a ~ on one's back*** 〔美俚〕酒醉;吸毒成瘾. ***say ~ to one and buzzard to another.*** 〔美俚〕厚此薄彼. ***talk (cold)*** ~ 〔美口〕照实说,直说. ~ **buzzard**【动】(南美)兀鹰. **~cock** 雄火鸡;摆臭架子的人 (*as red as a ~-cock* (因生气等)面孔通红). ~ **trot** 火鸡舞. ~ **vulture** = ~ buzzard.

Tur•ki [ˈtuəki:, ˈtə:-] *n.* ①中亚突厥语〔尤指现代维吾尔语〕. ②突厥人. — *a.* 中亚突厥语的,中亚突厥人的.

Tur•kic [ˈtə:kik] *a.* ①突厥语族的〔属阿尔泰语系,包括土耳其语,阿塞尔拜疆语,鞑靼语,维吾尔语,乌兹别克语和土库曼语〕. ②突厥语民族的. — *n.* 突厥语族.

Turk•ish [ˈtə:kiʃ] *a.* 土耳其(人)的;土耳其式的;土耳其语的. — *n.* 土耳其语; 土耳其卷烟; 土耳其糖果. ~ *bath* 土耳其浴,蒸汽浴;〔*pl.*〕土耳其〔蒸汽〕浴室. *a* ~ *delight* 橡皮糖. *a* ~ *pound* 土耳其镑〔通常写作£T〕. *a* ~ *towel* 土尔耳毛巾〔浴巾〕.

Turk•ism [ˈtə:kizəm] *n.* 土耳其文化;土耳其风俗;土耳其的宗教信仰等.

Tur•ki•stan [tə:kiˈstæn] *n.* = Turkestan.

Turk•man [ˈtə:kmən] *n.* (*pl.* ***-men***) 土库曼共和国人. ~ **carpet** 土库曼地毯.

Turk•men [ˈtə:kmən] *n.* 土库曼语. — *a.* 土库曼的. ~ **Soviet Socialist Republic** 土库曼苏维埃社会主义共和国.

Tur•kmen•i•stan [ˌtə:kmeniˈstɑ:n] *n.* 土库曼〔苏联加盟共和国名〕.

Turko•man [ˈtə:kəmən] *n.* (*pl.* ***~s***) 土库曼人,土库曼语.

Turks and Caicoc Islands 特克斯和凯科斯群岛〔美洲〕.

Tur•ku [ˈtuəku] *n.* 图尔库〔芬兰港市〕.

turma•lin(e) [ˈtə:məlin] *n.* = tourmalin(e).

tur•mer•ic [ˈtə:mərik] *n.* ①【植】薑黄(属);郁金. ②郁金根粉〔用作染料、刺激剂、调味料等〕. **~-paper**【化】薑黄(试)纸.

tur•moil [ˈtə:mɔil] *n.* 骚动,喧嚷,混乱. *His mind was in a ~.* 他心里七上八下.

turn [tə:n] *vt.* ①转,转动,旋转,使转弯;移动,拨动,触动. ~ *a wheel* 转动轮子. ~ *the tap* 拧塞子,旋龙头. *He will not ~ a finger to help* 他不会略费力气帮一点忙. ②转过去,绕过去;【军】迂回(敌人侧面). ~ *the corner* 转弯,拐弯儿. ③翻转过来做(衣服等);翻(书页);折(边等);弄卷(刀口);挖翻(土地);倒转,翻倒,倒置,颠倒;【印】倒植. ~ *an old garment* 翻做旧衣. ~ *things upside down* 颠倒是非,混淆黑白. ④转向,朝向,指向;〔喻〕集中(注意、努力等); 用于,抵充(用途),利用;改变路线. *T- your face this way.* 请把脸转到这边. ~ *one's attention to business* 把注意力集中到事务上. ~ *the conversation to something else* 把话岔到别的事情上. ⑤使变化,改变;使变成(…的状态);(货币的)兑换; 翻译; 使变质,使变坏; 使(脑子)错乱; 使恶心. ~ *English into Chinese* 把英语译成汉语. *Hot weather ~s milk.* 天热会使牛奶变坏. *His head is ~ed.* 他神经错乱了. *Success has ~ed his head.* 成功冲昏了他的头脑. ~ *sb.'s stomach* 使人作呕. ⑥用镞床镞;〔喻〕做得好看(美观、圆满),弄得象样;表现得好. ~ *wooden vessels* 用镞床做木碗(等). *He was perfectly well ~ed for trade* 他做生意最适宜. ~ *a period well* 圆满地构造长句. *well-~ed sentences* 构造得精致的句子. ⑦越过, 超过 (年龄、时刻等). *He has just ~ed 50.* 他刚过五十(岁). *He is ~ed of boy.* 他已经不是小孩子了. *It's just ~ed 3 o'clock.* 刚过三点. ⑧赶走. ~ *sb. out (from one's door)* 把某人赶出去. — *vi.* ①转,旋转;打滚,折腾,翻腾;翻倒. *A wheel ~s on its axis.* 轮子在轴上旋转. ~ *in bed [in one's sleep]* 睡眠中翻身. ②转向;回头;转弯;弯曲;(刀刃)卷口;倾斜;注意. *T- to the left.* 向左转(弯). *It is time to ~ now.* 现在该折回了. ③变;改变;(形势)倒转;变成…;变质;转(业);(头)晕;发恶心,想呕. *The milk has ~ed (sour).* 牛奶变酸了. *My stomach ~s.* 我直恶心. ④(镞床工艺)被镞,做成. ⑤转过身来作出反应;反抗. *A worm will ~.* 虫也会反抗的. ***as it ~ed out*** 偶尔(是…),碰巧(是…). ~ ***about*** 回头; 转向, 调向. ~ ***against*** 背叛,反抗;使对抗;厌恶. ~ ***and rend sb.*** 突然袭击〔辱骂〕某人. ***~ and ~ about*** 轮流地. ~ ***aside*** ①*vt.* 架开,避开. ②*vi.* 脱出,迷失;背过脸去,把脸避开. ~ ***away*** ①*vt.* (把脸)转(过去);避开;驱逐,轰出;防止(灾祸等); 解雇. ②*vi.* 转过脸去; 表示轻蔑〔不赞成〕. ③*n.*〔美〕拥挤在场外的群众. ~ ***back*** ①*vi.* 折回,回来. ②*vt.* 逐回,赶回去;拨慢(钟表);折起(衣服). ~ ***down*** 翻下(衣领等), 折(纸); 扭小(灯火等) (*T-that radio down at once!* 马上把收音机开得小一些); 拒绝考虑,否决,推翻(提案等);拒绝(某人). *He asked Jane to marry him but she ~ed him down.* 他向珍妮求婚但她拒绝了他. ~ ***in*** ①*vi.* 向里(弯曲);转身进去;(把杂草、肥料等)翻入地内;〔美〕带进,拿进;走近. ②*vt.* 折进;使向里;上交,递入 (*T- in everything captured.* 一切缴获要归公). 〔口〕上床睡觉. ~ ***in all standing*** 和衣躺下睡觉. ~ ***(sth.) inside out*** 把…翻到外面来. ~ *one's pockets inside out* 把口袋里子翻出来. ~ ***loose*** 释放,解放 (~ *loose upon the world* 使…自由生活). ~ ***off*** ①*vt.* 解雇,逐出; 叉开, 引开(不愉快的话题等);完成,制成,生产; 关掉(自来水、收音机、电灯等); 使失掉兴趣 (*Popular music really ~s me off.* 流行音乐确实使我厌烦);〔俚〕处绞刑;〔俚〕举行婚礼. ②*vi.* (人)走入旁路 (*We ~ed off into a side street.* 我们拐入一条横街); (路)分歧. ~ ***on*** ①转向, 对准; 对…进行突击 (*The dog ~ed on me and bit me in the leg.* 那条狗向我扑上来,在我腿上咬了一口);反抗; 要看…而定, 关键就在(*The question ~s on this point.* 问题关键就在这一点上). ②开(电灯、收音机、自来水);【电】接通(电路);〔口〕使人开始(某事) (*to do*); 朝向;(突然或自然而然地)显示 (~ *on the power* (突然)显示出力量). ~ ***one's hand to*** 试,试试看. ~ ***out*** ①*vi.* 向外弯曲,向外; 罢工;【电】切断;〔口〕起床;(消防队、军队等)出动;结果变成;结果弄清楚是…,原来是… (*The rumour has ~ed out (to be) false.* 谣言原来是假的). ②*vt.* 驱逐, 逐出, 撵出 (~ *sb. out of the room*); 欢送(毕业生);(把牛、羊等)放出牧场;

倒出,翻出(容器、房间里的东西);翻转,翻过来;暴露;制出,造出;培养;打扮;关断(煤气等),熄(灯等). ~ ***over*** ①*vi.* 翻滚,打滚;翻身. ②*vt.* 使翻倒,倾覆;交付,移交;翻(书页);耕翻(土地);使生活一新;处理;做(多少钱的)买卖,卖得…;〔喻〕熟思,再三考虑 (~ *the matter over in one's mind* 心里再三考虑这件事. ~ *over £ 500 a week* 每星期卖得五百镑). ~ ***over a new leaf*** 翻开新的一页,重新开始[做人],洗心革面. ~ ***ridicule on*** 嘲笑. ~ ***round*** ①*vi.* 旋转;回头;调向,转向;变计;叛变;反对,反抗;【海】停靠(某港) (*He ~s round to oppress the common people.* 他反过来压迫老百姓). ②*vt.* 使旋转;朝向;改变 (政策); 使叛变. ~ ***sb. round one's (little) finger*** 任意驱使[玩弄]某人. ~ ***the corner*** 渡过危机;情形好转. ~ ***the edge of*** 钝…锐气,弄钝…的锋芒. ~ ***the hands to*** 【海】使全体船员各就岗位. ~ ***the hands up*** 【海】把全体船员集中在甲板上. ~ ***the point of*** = ~ the edge of. ~ ***the route*** (特指赛马)跑一定距离. ~ ***the trick*** 〔美运〕赛赢. ~ ***to*** 变成;请求 (~ *to sb. for help* 求人帮助);着手工作,使着手工作. ~ ... ***to account*** 利用. ~ ***up*** ①*vi.* 向上;朝天;出来,来到;出现,出席;被找到,突然发生 (*be ready to ~ up for interrogation whenever they are wanted* 随叫随到,接受讯问). 证明是(= ~ out to be). ② *vt.* 扭大(灯火等);向上弯曲;朝向上面;翻开(牌);掘起;找出;〔口〕使作呕 (~ *up one's nose at* 轻视…). ~ ***up one's toes*** 〔口〕死亡. ~ ***up the sleeves*** 卷起衣袖;〔喻〕准备行动[工作]. ***wait for something to ~ up*** 期待发生变化;抱观望[骑墙]态度. ~ ***upon*** = ~ on ①. — *n.* ①旋转(运动);转身;(杠上运动的)小翻滚;(溜冰的)曲线转折;改变方向,调转方向;转向,转弯;【军】迂回. ②弯曲;转角,转弯处,屈折部. ③变化,变动;机会;转折点,关键. ④倾向,性情,癖性;气质;特殊才能. ⑤一个回合;走一圈,散步;(恶意或善意的)行为. ⑥〔英〕(杂技)演员. ⑦说法,口吻. ⑧轮流,轮班. ⑨形状,样子. ⑩一卷,一圈;线匝;圈数,匝数. ⑪吃惊,意外. ⑫〔*pl.*〕月经. ⑬【乐】回音;【印】(无本字时暂用的)倒头铅字;【机】车床;(转动把手而开关的)门扣. ⑭〔美俚〕(杂耍、广播等的)一个节目. ⑮〔古〕必要,需要. *the ~ [a ~] of the tide* 潮汐的转变;形势的转变. *Right [Left] ~!* 向右[左]转! *a shallow ~* 慢转弯,大转弯. *a sharp [steep] ~* 急转弯,小转弯. *Matters have taken a bad ~.* 事情恶化了. *He is of a humo(u)rous ~.* 他性情幽默. *take a ~ round the garden* 在园子里走一圈(散步). *a beautiful ~ of words* 漂亮的说法. *It is your ~ to sing.* 这次轮到你唱了. *The news gave me a ~.* 这消息使我吃了一惊. ***at every ~*** 在每一个关键时刻;在每一个角落;到处;老是,常常. ***by ~s*** 轮流. ***come to a critical ~*** 到危险关头,到关键时刻. ***do sb. a good [an ill] ~*** 对…做好事[坏事],待人好[不好]. ***give a new ~ to*** 对…给与新的变化[看法]. ***in one's ~*** 接替,值班. ***in the ~ of a hand*** 反掌之间,立刻. ***in ~*** 挨次,依次. ***on the ~*** 正在变化,就要转变;(牛奶)快要变酸. ***make a ~ for the better [worse]*** 使好转[恶化]. ***out of ~*** 次序混乱;在倒霉的时候;不合时宜;〔口〕狂妄自大 (*talk out of one's ~* 说冒昧话). ***serve one's ~*** 合用,有用. ***take a ~***(轮流)干一阵子 (*take a ~ at the oars* 划一阵桨, *take a ~ of work* 做一阵工作). ***take a favo(u)rable ~*** 好转. ***take a ~ for the better [worse]*** 好转[变坏]. ***take ~s*** 替换,换班. ***take one's ~ (to*** do) 轮流接替. ***the ~ of life*** 绝经期,更年期. ***to a ~*** 〔尤指食物〕(煮得)恰到好处. ~ ***of speed*** 速力. ~ ***of the market*** 买卖差价. ~ **about** 转身;立场改变;叛变;叛徒;急进主义者;〔美〕旋转木马. ~**-about-face** 改变立场. ~**-and-bank [~-and-slip] indicator**【空】转弯倾斜仪,侧滑指示器. ~**around** ①车辆掉头处;(思想、立场的)转变. ②回航[卸货、加油、检修、上货]所需时日;来回. ③小修,预防修理. ~ **bridge** 旋开桥. ~ **buckle** 【机】松紧螺丝扣;【空】紧线器 (*a ~buckle screw* 松紧螺套). ~**cap** (烟囱的)旋转帽. ~**coat** 叛徒. ~**cock** 水龙头开关管理员. ~**down** ①*a.* 翻下的(衣领等);折叠式的(卧铺). ②*n.* 翻领;〔俚〕拒绝. ~ **indicator** 【海】转向指示计. ~**key** (监狱的)看守. ~ **off** 岔开,避开;岔道;产品;成品. ~**-on** 刺激(因素). ~**out** ①走出屋外的人群;(集会的)出席者,到会者;外貌;服装;装备. ②生产(量). ③〔英〕罢工(者). ④临时召集;〔口〕起床(时间). ⑤马车的全套配备和人员. ⑥【铁路】让车岔道. ~**over** ①(车等的)翻倒;翻折;翻折的东西;半圆煎饼;转换;转让;转页新闻. ②(一定期间内的)补充工人数;补充工人对工人总平均数的比率;(转给另一厂主的)转雇学徒;(一期间的)营业额,周转(额);临时投资额;工程维持费. ~**pike** 【史】征收通行税的路;通行税征收所,收税栅;通行大路;〔美〕收税高速公路. ~**plate** 〔英〕= turntable. ~**-round** (轮船的)停泊[船的入港、卸货、装货和离港]. ~**screw** 螺丝钻,改锥. ~**sole** 【植】向日葵. ~**spit** (旧时训练好会用踏车转动烤肉叉的)转叉狗;旋转烤肉叉的人;旋转式烤肉叉. ~**stile** (能统计出入人数的)旋转栅门. ~**stone** 【鸟】翻石鹬(属). ~**table** 转盘式餐桌;(转换机车方向的)转车台,旋车盘;(唱机上的)转盘;(广播用)录音转播机. ~**up** ①〔口〕突然出现的人;突发事件;骚动. ②斗殴,打架;拳击比赛. ③卷起的部分;(裤脚的)卷边.

Tur·ner [ˈtəːnə] *n.* 特纳[姓氏].

turn·er[1] [ˈtəːnə] *n.* ①镟(床)工(人),车工. ②〔英〕翻飞鸽.

turn·er[2] [ˈtəːnə] *n.* 〔美〕翻觔斗的杂技演员,体育运动员;体育俱乐部会员.

turn·er·y [ˈtəːnəri] *n.* 镟制[镟磨]工艺;镟制[镟磨]法;镟制[镟磨]品;车削车间.

turn·ing [ˈtəːniŋ] *n.* 旋转,转动;转向;弯曲;转弯处;镟制[车削]工艺;镟坯;〔*pl.*〕镟屑;制作. *take the first ~ to the right* 由第一个转角处向右拐. *the ~ of verses* 作诗. ~ **point** 转折点;关键时刻 (*the ~ point of a disease* 病势的转折点). ~**-saw** = compass saw.

tur·nip [ˈtəːnip] *n.* ①【植】芜菁,萝卜. ②〔俚〕大怀表. ***get blood from a ~*** 从大头菜中榨血,做不可能的事. ~ **radish** (圆)萝卜. ~ **tops** 〔*pl.*〕芜菁叶.

Turn·ver·ein [ˈtunfɛəˌain; F. ˈtəːnfəˌrain]〔G.〕*n.* 体育[体操运动员]协会.

tur·pen·tine [ˈtəːpəntain] *n.* 松脂(精);松节油 [= oil of ~]. — *vt.* 涂松节油;制松节油;采松脂. **T- State** 〔美〕北卡罗来纳州[别名]. **-ti·nous** *a.*

tur·pi·tude [ˈtəːpitjuːd] *n.* 奸恶,卑鄙,卑劣(行为).

turps [təːps] *n.* 〔俚〕松节油.

tur·quoise [ˈtəːkwaːz, -kwɔiz] *n.* ①【矿】绿松石. ②青绿色,天蓝色. ~ *blue* 湖蓝,翠蓝.

tur·ret [ˈtʌrit] ①【建】塔楼,角塔. ②【古军】(攻城用)移动塔楼. ③【军】(飞机、坦克、军舰的)炮塔;转塔. ④【机】= ~-head. *a ~ lathe* 六角车床. ~ **captain** 〔美〕炮塔长. ~ **gun** 炮塔炮. ~**head** 【机】六角转头;转台. ~ **ship** 旋转炮塔舰.

tur·ric·u·late [təˈrikjuˌleit, -lit] *a.* 有小角塔的,形似小角塔的 (= turriculated).

tur·tle[1] [ˈtəːtl] *n.* 【动】龟;(特指)青蠵龟,海龟,海鳖;海龟汤〔= ~-soup, 美国的 ~-soup 多指甲鱼 (terrapin) 汤〕. *a green ~* 海龟. *a snapping [mud] ~* 鳖,甲鱼. *a hawk's-bill ~* 玳瑁. ***turn ~*** 把海龟翻转身来加以捕捉;〔海口语〕(把船等)翻掉;(使)无活动能力. — *vi.* 捉海龟为业. ~**back** 【船】鲸背甲板. ~**head** 【植】龟头花(属);白龟头花, ~**neck** 圆翻领(服装).

tur·tle[2] [ˈtəːtl] *n.* 〔古〕= turtledove. ~**dove** *n.* 斑鸠 (*a pair of ~doves* 一对情人).

turves [təːvs] 〔古〕turf 的复数.

Tus·can [ˈtʌskən] *a.* 托斯卡纳 (Tuscany〔意大利中西部地名〕)的;(帽子等)托斯卡纳秆的;【建】托斯卡纳式

的.— *n.* 托斯卡纳人[语].

Tus·ca·ro·ra [ˌtʌskəˈrɔːrə] *n.* ①*(pl. -ras, -ra)* 塔斯卡洛拉族人〔印第安的一个部落,原居于美国弗吉尼亚和北卡罗来纳州,1722年参加了易洛魁联盟后移居在纽约和安大略州〕. ②塔斯卡洛拉语〔易洛魁语的一种方言〕.

tush[1] [tʌʃ] *int., n.* 〔古〕啐!〔表示申斥、轻蔑等〕. — *vi.* 说一声啐.

tush[2] [tʌʃ] *n.* (马等的)犬齿;(象、猪等的)长牙.

tush·er·y [ˈtʌʃəri] *n.* 爱用啐声骂人的习惯[人,文章].

tusk [tʌsk] *n.* ①(象、猪等的)长牙. ②〔谑〕(人的)犬牙,獠牙,暴牙. ③獠牙似的东西,尖物,(犁等的)尖头. — *vt.* 用长牙齿掘[刺,咬]. **~like** 獠牙[长牙]状的. **-ed** *a.* 有长牙[獠牙]的.

tusk·er [ˈtʌskə] *n.* 有长牙的动物;象,野猪(等).

tus·sah, tus·seh, tus·ser [ˈtʌsə] *n.* ①【动】柞蚕. ②柞蚕丝;柞绸. **~-silk** *n.* 柞蚕丝;柞绸.

Tus·saud [ˈtuːsəu] *n.* 图索[姓氏].

Tus·saud's [təˈsəuz] (伦敦的)特索氏蜡人馆.

tus·sis [ˈtʌsis] *n.*【医】咳,咳嗽. **tus·sive** [-iv] *a.*

tus·sle [ˈtʌsl] *n., vi.* ①扭打. ②争论;奋斗 *(with)*;〔美运〕比赛;争胜.

tus·sock [ˈtʌsək] *n.* ①草丛; 沼泽上的草丛丘阜. ②〔罕〕丛,簇. ③【植】= ~ ***grass*** 生草丛,高丛早熟禾草. ~ **moth**【动】毒蛾. **-y** *a.*

tus·sor(e) [ˈtʌsɔː], **tus·sur** [ˈtʌsə] *n.* = tussah.

tut[1] [tʌt] *int., n.* 嘘! 啧!〔表示不耐烦、轻蔑、指责〕. — *vi.* '啧!'〔表示轻蔑等〕(= tut-tut).

tut[2] [tʌt] *n., vi.*【矿】计件制(工作).

tu·tee [tjuːˈtiː, tuː-] *n.* 〔美〕受监护者;受教导者,受指导者.

tu·te·lage [ˈtjuːtilidʒ] *n.* ①保护,监护;教育,教导,指导. ②受保护. ③导师或监护人的职责.

tu·te·lar, tu·te·la·ry [ˈtjuːtələ, -ri] *a.* 保护(人)的,监护(人)的.

tu·te·nag [ˈtjuːtinæg] *n.* 中国白铜;生锌;锌铜镍合金.

tu·tor [ˈtjuːtə] *n.* ①私人教师,家庭教师;师傅;〔英大学〕导师;〔美〕助教;(考试)辅导员. ②【法】监护人. — *vt., vi.* ①做私人[家庭]教师(教);辅导(学生);教练;训斥. ②监护. ③抑制(感情等). ④〔美〕接受单独训练.

tu·tor·age [ˈtjuːtəridʒ] *n.* ①家庭教师[监护人]的地位[职务];辅导. ②(家庭教师的)酬金.

tu·tor·ess [ˈtjuːtəris] *n.* tutor 的女性.

tu·to·ri·al [tjuːˈtɔːriəl] *a.* (大学)导师的;家庭教师的;辅导的;监护人的. —*n.* 个人辅导时间;受大学教育时间. *the ~ system* 导师制.

tu·tor·ship [ˈtjuːtəʃip] *n.* tutor 的职务[身份].

tu·toy·er [ˌtuːtwaˈjei; F. tytwaˈje] *vt.* 以亲切而随便的口吻交谈〔如在法语中用"你"(tu或toi)而不用"您"(vous)〕.

tu·tress [ˈtjuːtris] *n.* = tutoress.

tut·ti [ˈtutiː] *a.*〔It.〕【乐】全体的. — *n.* 合奏;齐唱;(独奏者以外的)全体演奏者.

tut·ti·frut·ti [ˈtuːtiˈfruti] *n.* 〔美〕①加有糖渍水果的冰淇淋(或糖果). ②具有多种水果味的香料.

Tut·tle [ˈtʌtl] *n.* 塔特尔[姓氏].

tut-tut [ˈtʌtˈtʌt] *int., n.* 嘘嘘! 啧啧!〔表示不耐烦、轻蔑、责难〕.

tut·ty [ˈtʌti] *n.* 不纯锌华[氧化锌].

tu·tu [ˈtuːtuː] *n.*〔F.〕(芭蕾舞的)短裙.

Tu·tu·i·la [ˌtuːtuˈiːlɑː] *n.* 土土伊拉岛〔萨摩亚(Samoa)群岛中最大岛〕.

tu·um [ˈtjuːəm] *pron.* 〔L.〕你的(东西,财产等)〔拉丁语物名代名词单数第二人称的中性,常指所有物,所有权〕.

Tuvalu [ˈtuːvəlu] *n.* 图瓦卢[大洋洲].

tu-whit, tu-whoo [tuˈhwit, tuˈ*h*wuː] *vi.* (猫头鹰)嗬嗬地叫. —*n.*嗬嗬的叫声.

tux [tʌks] *n.* 〔美口〕= tuxedo.

tux·e·do [tʌkˈsiːdəu] *n. (pl. ~s)* 〔美〕夜会便服,无尾夜礼服〕小夜礼服〔略 tux〕;〔美俚〕(精神病患者穿的)紧身衣.

tu·y·ère [ˈtwiːjɛə] *n.* 〔F.〕【冶】(熔矿炉的)吹风管嘴;风口.

TV, T.V. = television. **TV dinner** 盒装便餐〔一种速冻餐,吃前稍热即可〕.

TVA = Tennessee Valley Authority〔美〕田纳西流域管理局.

TWA = Trans World Airlines〔美〕环球航空公司.

twa [twɑː] *a., n.* 〔Scot.〕two 的变体.

twad·dell [ˈtwɔdl] *n.* 托窝德尔比重计〔用以测量比水重的液体〕.

twad·dle [ˈtwɔdl] *n.* 闲聊;无聊的废话,讲[写]蠢话. *ignorant ~* 无知妄说. —*vi.* 聊天. **-r** *n.* 爱说[写]废话的人.

twain [twein] *n., a.* 〔古〕二,两,双,一对. *cut in ~* 切成两个,一分为二.

twang[1] [twæŋ] *n.* ①(拨)弦声. ②鼻音;带鼻音的(方言)口音. ③(突然的一阵)痛苦. — *vt., vi.* ①(使)嘡地响;嘡地一声从弓弦上射出. ②〔罕〕用鼻音讲. **-y** *a.* ①似弦声的. ②带鼻音的.

twang[2] [twæŋ] *n.* ①长久不散的气味,强烈的气味. ②遗迹,痕迹,迹象;含意.

twan·gle [twæŋgl] *vt.* ①〔罕〕使发拨弦声. ②带鼻音讲. ③(使)嘡地(射)出去.

twan·kay [ˈtwæŋkei] *n.* 〔中〕屯溪茶〔一种绿茶〕.

'twas [强 twɔz; 弱 twəz]〔古〕= it was.

twat·tle [ˈtwɑːtl] *n., vi., vt.* = twaddle.

tway·blade [ˈtweiˌbleid] *n.*【植】羊耳蒜属 *(Liparis)* 植物;双叶兰 *(Listera cordata)*.

tweak [twiːk] *n.* ①拧,捏,扭;力扯. ②〔俚〕好办法,妙计. — *vt.* 拧(面颊,耳鼻等),扭,抓住拉;用力拉.

twee [twiː] *a.* 〔英口〕装成聪明(优雅)的样子的;装出讨人喜欢的样子的.

Tweed [twiːd] *n.* 特威德[姓氏].

tweed [twiːd] *n.* (粗)花呢;〔*pl.*〕花呢衣服. **-y** *a.* ①(粗)花呢的;常常穿着漂亮花呢衣服的. ②爱好户外生活[运动]的;好游乐的.

twee·dle [ˈtwiːdl] *n.* ①(乐器等的)尖锐声. — *vt., vi.* (吹奏,歌唱)(使)发出尖细的声音. ②= wheedle.

twee·dle·dum and twee·dle·dee [ˈtwiːdlˈdʌmənd-ˈtwiːdlˈdiː] 难以区别的[极相似的]两个人[物].

Tweeds·muir [ˈtwiːdzmjuə] *n.* 特威兹缪尔[姓氏].

'tween [twiːn] *prep.* 〔诗〕= between. ~ **deck**【海】(主甲板下的任何一层)中甲板.

tween·y [ˈtwiːni] *n.* ①〔古〕(帮助烧饭和做杂务的)年轻女仆 (= betweenmaid). ② 小雪茄烟.

tweet [twiːt] *vi.* (小鸟)吱吱地叫,啾鸣. — *n.* 小鸟叫声,啾啾声. **-er**【无】高频扬声器;高音重发器.

tweeze [twiːz] *vt.* 〔口〕用镊子拔(毛等).

tweez·er [ˈtwiːzə] *n.* 镊子,小钳〔用复数,常作 *a pair of ~s*〕. — *vt.* 用镊子钳[拔](毛等).

Twelfth-cake *n.* 主显节的糕饼.

twelfth [twelfθ] *num.* ①第十二,第十二号. ②十二分之一(的). — *n.* ①(某月的)十二日. ②【乐】第十二音,十二分音,十二度音程. *the ~* 〔英〕八月十二日〔松鸡猎期开始日〕. **Twelfth-day**【宗】主显节〔圣诞节后第十二日, = Epiphany〕. **Twelfth-night** 主显节的前夜;主显节的夜晚.

twelve [twelv] *num.* (基数)十二;〔用于章、节、行、页等词后〕第十二. — *n.* ①十二,十二个. ②十二个东西[人];十二的记号;十二点钟;十二岁;十二英寸炮. ③十三世纪. ④〔the T-〕【宗】= the T- Apostles. *in ~s*【印】十二开本. *strike ~ the first time [all at once]* 一开头就显出全副本领〔获得大成功〕. ***~mo***

[-məu] *a.*, *n.* *(pl.* **-mos***)* = duodecimo〔略 12 mo〕. ~**month**〔英〕十二个月,一年 (*this day ~-month* 明年[去年]的今天). ~**penny** *a.*〔英〕十二便士的;价廉的. ~**tone** *a.*【乐】十二音体系的.

twen·ti·eth [ˈtwentiiθ] *num.* ①第二十,第二十号. ②二十分之一. — *n.* (某月的)二十日. *a ~ part* 二十分之一.

twen·ty [ˈtwenti] *num.* (基数)二十;〔用于名词后表示顺序〕第二十. ~ ***times*** 二十次;屡次,再三,多次. ~ ***and*** ~ 许许多多,不计其数. — *n.* ①二十,二十个. ②二十个东西[人];二十的记号. ③许多,大量. ④〔*pl.*〕二十年代〔略'20s〕. ⑤〔*pl.*〕二十多岁. *And ~ of these puny lies I'll tell.* 这种毫无价值的瞎话要多少我都可以造出来. ***in nineteen ~*** 在1920年. ***in the nineteen twenties*** 在二十世纪二十年代〔略1920's〕. ***in the twenties*** 二十多岁(的);在二十年代(的);二十多度(的). ~**-five**【橄榄球、曲棒球】距(球门)25码界限(以内). ~**fold** *a.* 二十倍的. ~**four**【印】〔*pl.*〕24开(本). ~**fourmo** *(pl. -s)* 24开本(的书)〔略24 mo〕. ~**-twenty** *a.*【眼科】20/20的,视力正常的〔或写作20/20〕.

'twere [强 twəː; 弱 twə]〔古〕= it were.

twerp [twəːp] *n.*〔俚〕无足轻重的人;可鄙可笑的人.

TWI, T.W.I. = Training within Industry 企业内(不脱产)训练.

twi- *pref.* 二,双重,两倍,两次: twibill, twifold, twi-forked, twi-formed.

Twi [tʃwiː] *n.* ①契维语〔属于克瓦(kwa)语支,主要在加纳通用〕. ②*(pl.* ***Twis, Twi****)*说契维语的人.

twi·bil(l) [ˈtwaibil] *n.* 双刃战斧;阔刀;双刃丁字锄〔一刃与柄平行,一刃与柄垂直〕;镰刀.

twice [twais] *ad.* 两次;两倍. *It is ~ as good.* 加倍地好. ~ *as much* 两倍(的份量). *He is ~ the man he was.* = *He has ~ the strength he had.* = *He is ~ as strong as he was.* 他比从前加倍强壮了. *T- two is four.* 二二得四. ***in ~***〔口〕分两次. ***once or ~*** 一两次. ***think ~*** 重行考虑,仔细考虑 (*do not think ~ about* 不再考虑,断然…;不再想起,忘掉,忽视). ~ ***or thrice*** 两三次. ~**-laid** *a.* 再生的〔用旧绳搓成的绳,用旧料做的东西〕. ~**-told** *a.* 讲过两次[好几次]的;(话等)陈腐的. **-r** 再度做某事的人,做某事两次的人〔如做两次礼拜〕;兼做两件事的人〔如排字兼印刷工人〕;双倍的结果;〔主英〕骗子.

twid·dle [ˈtwidl] *vt.* 捻弄. — *vi.* ①玩弄 *(with)*. ②花式弹奏. ③〔英方〕忙于琐事. — *n.* ①捻. ②波状线,波纹. ~ ***[twirl] one's thumbs,*** 见 twirl 条. **twiddly** *a.*

twig[1] [twig] *n.* ①桠枝,细枝. ②深矿杖. ③卜杖. ④【解】(血管等的)枝脉;【电】枝线. ***hop the ~*** 逃掉,躲开;突然离去;突然死去. — *vt.*【美俚】用细枝打. **-gy** *a.*

twig[2] [twig]〔英口〕*vt., vi.* 懂得,明白,了解;注目,注意,认出,看出,发现.

twi·light [ˈtwailait] *n.* ①黎明;薄暮,黄昏;微明;朦胧;【天】晨昏蒙影,曙暮光. ②懵懂;(意义的)模糊. ③衰退没落阶级[状态]. ④〔美俗〕厕所,盥洗室. — *a.* 微明的,幽暗的,朦胧的,有微光的. — *vt.* 使微明,朦胧地照亮. ~ **sleep**【医】(无痛分娩法的)半麻醉. ~ **zone**【无】半阴影区.

twi·lit [ˈtwailit] *a.* 沉浸在柔和的微光中的.

twill [twil] *n.* 斜纹织物[组织,图案] (= ~ weave). *artillery ~* 斜纹马裤呢. — *vt.* 把…织成斜纹.

'twill [twil]〔诗〕= it will.

twin [twin] *a.* ①孪生的. ②成对的,酷似的. ③【植】双生[对生]的. *a ~ amplifier* 孪放大器. ~ *brothers* 孪生兄弟. ~ *crystal*【物】孪晶. ~ *elements*【化】孪元素. *a ~ engine* 双发动机. ~ *triode*【无】双三极管. *a ~ volume* 两卷一部的书籍中的一册. *a ~ vase* 一对花瓶的一个. — *n.* ①孪生儿之一;〔*pl.*〕孪生儿,双胎,联胎. ②相象的人[物],一对中的一方;〔*pl.*〕对. ③【结晶】孪[双]晶. ④〔T-〕〔*pl.*〕【天】双子座;双子宫. ***Siamese ~s***【医】暹罗双胎,剑突联胎〔身体相联的双胎〕. — *vt., vi.* ①(使)生孪生儿. ②(同…)成对 *(with)*. ③【物】(使)成双晶. ~**berry**【植】总苞忍冬;蔓虎刺(树,果). ~ **bill** ①放映两部影片的一场电影. ②(同一对球队)一天两场的比赛. ~**born** *a.* 孪生的. ~**-engined**【空】双发动机的. ~**flower**【植】林奈花(属). ~**-screw**【船】双轴的.

twine [twain] *n.* ①二股(以上的)线,捻线,细绳;麻线[绳]. ②搓捻;盘绕;缠绕;纠缠. — *vt., vi.* ①捻,搓;织,编. ②使缠绕,绕住;缠住;缠绕,卷. ③蜿蜒. ~ *one's arms round* 两臂抱着前胸. **-r** ①捻[织、编等]的人;捻[搓、编]成物,缠绕物. ②缠绕植物〔如扁豆藤〕.

twinge [twindʒ] *n.* ①刺痛,阵痛,剧痛. ②痛心,内疚. — *vt., vi.* (使)刺疼,(使)一阵一阵地疼.

twi-night, twi·night [ˈtwaiˌnait] *a.*【美棒球】一天连赛两场〔通常指同对球队〕.

twin·kle [ˈtwiŋkl] *vi.* ①(星等)闪烁. ②眨眼;(眼睛)闪亮. ③(舞蹈者的腿等)轻快有节奏地一闪一闪摆动. — *vt.* 使闪烁,使闪亮;眨(眼). — *n.* ①闪烁,闪光. ②眨眼;瞬间,霎时间,一刹那. ③一闪一闪有节奏的活动. ***in a ~ = in the ~ of an eye*** 一眨眼工夫. **-r** *n.* 闪闪发光体[物]. **-rs**〔美〕眼睛.

twin·kling [ˈtwiŋkliŋ] *a.* 闪烁的,闪亮的,(星等)闪闪发光的. — *n.* ①闪烁. ②眨眼;瞬间,转眼间. ***in a ~ = in the ~ of an eye = in the ~ of a bed post*** 一眨眼工夫,转瞬间.

twirl [twəːl] *vt.* ①使滴溜溜地旋转. ②挥转(手杖等). ③捻;捻转. ④【美棒球】扔(球). ~ *[twiddle] one's thumbs* 闲极无聊中两手的拇指互相捻弄;无所事事,无事可做. ~ *one's moustache* 捻胡子. — *vi.* ①滴溜溜地旋转. ②【美棒球】扔球,投球. — *n.* ①旋转;回旋. ②捻弄. ③(花体字的)拉长的笔道. ④〔美俚〕万能钥匙.

twirp [twəːp] *n.* = twerp.

twist [twist] *vt.* ①拧,扭,绞. ②捻,搓;编,织,作,造. ③缠绕,卷. ④扭弯,扭歪;扭伤. ⑤曲解,牵强附会;抢夺;折磨;扰乱. ⑥弯弯曲曲地通过 *(through; along)*, ⑦使(球)旋转,拧转(球). ~ *threads into a string* 把几根线拧成一条绳. ~ *a towel* 绞毛巾. ~ *a garland* 编花圈. ~ *a fine story* 编造一个巧妙的故事. *He ~ed it out of my hand.* 他从我手中抢去了. ~ *one's way through the crowd* 弯弯曲曲地在人群中穿过去. — *vi.* ①挠曲,扭转;转身;扭伤. ②捻上,搓上;缠上,卷住;盘绕;编花圈. ③成旋涡形;成螺旋形;(球)旋转着前进. ④曲曲弯弯地穿过去. ⑤跳扭摆舞. ***turn, ~ and wind sb.*** = ~ ***sb. round one's (little) finger*** 任意驱使[摆弄]某人. ~ ***off*** 拧断,扭断,拧开. ~ ***one's features*** (痛得)皱眉蹙脸. ~ ***the tail***〔美〕使汽车开动. ~ ***up*** 捻,搓;卷. — *n.* ①一拧,一扭,一捻,一搓;捻转,扭转,扭歪;缠绕,绕乱. ②怪癖;别扭. ③曲解,牵强. ④捻合线,绳子. ⑤绞花面包;捻卷烟;混合酒. ⑥〔口〕食欲,胃口. ⑦弯拐,曲折;螺旋状;【纺】经纱;捻度;【炮】膛线的缠绕度;拧球,旋球;扭摆舞;【造船】转线. ⑧〔美俚〕(轻浮的)姑娘;妇人. *gin ~* 白兰地杜松子(混合)酒. *a ~ drill* 麻花钻. ***a ~ in one's nature*** 怪癖,拗脾气. ***a ~ in one's tongue*** 发音[口齿]不清. ***a ~ of the wrist***〔喻〕熟练,诀窍. ~***s and turns*** 迂回曲折;〔喻〕曲折复杂的情况.

twist·a·ble [ˈtwistəbl] *a.* 可拧扭[搓捻,缠绕,旋转等]的. **-a·bil·i·ty** [ˌtwistəˈbiliti] *n.*

twist·er [ˈtwistə] *n.* ①扭转的人. ②绞扭器. ③【纺】捻接工人;捻线机. ④【气象】旋风,陆[水]龙卷;沙柱;尘旋. ⑤【运】旋球. ⑥〔口〕歪曲事实的人,说谎的人;不正派的人,谎话. ⑦难事,难题;拗口令 (= tongue ~). ⑧(杂技中的)空中扭身筋斗.

twist·y [ˈtwisti] *a.* ①弯弯曲曲的,扭曲的. ②不正直的. **-i·ly** *ad.* **-i·ness** *n.*
twit[1] [twit] *vt., n.* ①责备. ②挖苦,嘲笑.
twit[2] [twit] *n.* 〔英俚〕傻瓜;可鄙的人.
twit[3] [twit] *n.* 颤搐〔一种神经激动的状态〕.
twitch [twitʃ] *vt., vi.* ①急抽,猛拉;抢去 *(off)*. ②抽动;(使)痉挛, 抽搐. ③(使)发生剧痛. — *n.* ①猛拉, 猛抽. ②痉挛,抽筋,抽搐. ③【兽医】捻鼻器.
twite [twait] *n.* 【鸟】黄嘴朱顶雀〔= ~-finch〕.
twit·ter [ˈtwitə] *vi.* ①(燕子等)喊喊喳喳地叫. ②(激动得)打颤; 吃吃地笑. — *vt.* ①〔口〕(人) 喊喊喳喳地讲. ②抖动. — *n.* ①啭鸣, 喊喊喳喳的鸣叫声〔说话声〕,吃吃笑声. ②兴奋,抖颤. ③〔方〕忍笑,偷笑. ***in a ~*** 激动中,抖颤着. **-y** *a.*
'twixt [twikst] *prep.* 〔诗、方〕 = betwixt.
two [tuː] *num.* ①〔基数〕二;〔从数量上限定表示事物或人的名词〕两个;〔用于表示章节等词之后〕第二. — *n. (pl. ~s)* ①两人; 两个东西,一对. ②二的记号. ③两点钟. ④两岁. *a total of* ~总数两个. *one or* ~ 一两个,少数. *Two heads are better than one.* 三个臭皮匠胜过诸葛亮. ~ *bits* 〔美俚〕 两角五分. *T- of a trade seldom agree.* 同行是冤家. *Two's company, three's none.* 两好三别扭. *That's a game that ~ can play.* = *T- can play at that game.* 互不相让;一个能打一个能还;一报还一报. ***a day or ~*** 一两日. ***at ~*** 在两点钟. ***by ~s and threes*** 三三两两,零星地. ***in ~*** 为两. ***in ~ ~s*** 〔口〕立刻,一转眼 (*The business was over in ~ ~s.* 工作一转眼之间就好了). ***put ~ and ~ together*** 根据情况推论. ***~ and ~*** = ***~ by ~*** 两个两个. ***~ by four*** = ~-by-four. ***~-fifty grand*** 〔美〕二十五万元. ***~ party line*** 【电】两户合用线. ***~-to-one shop*** 当铺. ***~ whoop and a holler*** 〔美〕不远的地方,很短的距离. **~-and-one-half-striper** 〔美俚〕海军少校. **~-base hit**, 〔俚〕**~-bagger** 【美棒球】二垒打〔击球者能安全进入二垒的〕. **~-bit** *a.* 〔美口〕二角五分的;〔俚〕不值钱的;劣等的, 不足道的. **~-by-four** *a., n.* 厚 2 英寸宽 4 英寸的(木料);〔美俚〕极微末的, 不足道的. **~-cleft** *a.* 【植】二裂的. **~-cycle** 【机】 二程循环的. **~decker** 有两层甲板的船, 二层战舰; 双层电车〔公共汽车〕. **~-edged** *a.* 双刃的; 有两种作用的; 暧昧的. **~-faced** *a.* = double-faced. **~-fer** 〔美口〕〔常 *pl.*〕买一送一的货品〔尤指戏票〕. **~-fisted** *a.* 〔美口〕双拳并用的; 强壮有力的. **~fold** ① *a.* 两个部分的,两件事的; 两倍的, 两重的. ② *ad.* 成两个部分; 成两倍,成两重. **~-four** *a.* 【乐】四分之二拍子的. **2,4-D** 【化】 2.4- 二氯苯氧醋酸 〔一种除草剂〕. **2,4,5-T** 【化】 三氯苯氧基醋酸〔一种除草剂〕. **~-handed** *a.* 有两只手的; 双手拿的 (剑等); 双手都能操作的; 两人操作的; 两人玩的. **~-input** *a.* 【自】有两个输入的 *(a ~-input adder* 半加法器). **~-legged** *a.* 两条腿的. **~-line** 【印】两行宽的,比普通型号大一倍的(铅字). **~-name** *a.* (出票人及背书人)两重署名的. **~pence** [ˈtʌpəns] 〔英〕两便士; 两便士银币 (*not care ~pence* 一点也不在乎. *~pence coloured* 价廉物美的). **~penny** [ˈtʌpni] 〔英〕① *a.* 两便士的; 不值钱的,低廉的. ② *n.* 两便士铜币; (1 quart 卖两便士的)廉价啤酒; 少量, 一点儿. **~penny-halfpenny** *a.* 〔英〕不足道的,低廉的. **~-phase** *a.* 【电】二相的. **~-piece** *a.* 两件一套的. **~-ply** *a.* 织成两层的; 双重的; 双股的(线). **~-seater** 双人坐的飞机〔汽车〕. **~-sided** *a.* 有两面的, 两面派的, 怀贰心的. **~-some** 两人玩的游戏〔舞蹈〕(等);【高尔夫球】双人比赛;〔美俚〕一对,一双. **~-speed** *a.* 【机】双速的. **~-star** *a.* 【美军】二星(少将级)的. **~-step** 二拍子圆舞(曲);〔美俚〕小鸡. **~-time** *vt., vi.* 〔美俚〕背叛,欺骗,出卖. **~-time loser** 两次坐牢者; 两次失败者; 两次离婚者; 两度破产者. **~-timer** 〔美俚〕叛徒; 骗人〔出卖人〕的人. **~-tongued** *a.* 说假话的; 骗人的. **~-twenty** *n., a.* 〔美〕二百二十(的). **~-way** *a.* 双向的; 两路的 (*a ~-way cock* 【机】双通〔双向〕龙头. *a ~-way radio* 收发两用无线电设备. *a ~-way repeater* 【电】双向转发器,双向增音器. *a ~-way traffic* 双向交通. *a ~-way switch* 双向〔路〕开关); 正反两用的. **-ness** *n.*
'twould [强 twud; 弱 twəd, təd] 〔诗〕 = it would.
T.W.U. = Transport Workers' Union 〔美〕运输工人联合会.
twy- *pref.* = twi-.
twyer [ˈtwaiə] *n.* = tuyère.
tx. = tax(es).
Ty. = Territory.
-ty[1] *suf.* 十: twen*ty*.
-ty[2] *suf.* 表示性质、状态的名词后缀: loyal*ty*, safe*ty*.
Ty·burn [ˈtaibəːn] *n.* 【史】伦敦死刑场. *a ~ tippet* 〔英〕绞索. *the ~ tree* 〔英〕绞刑架.
T.Y.C. = Thames Yacht Club 〔英〕泰晤士河游艇俱乐部.
Tyche [ˈtaiki] *n.* 【希神】=【罗神】Fortuna.
ty·coon [taiˈkuːn] *n.* 〔Jap.〕 ①【史】大君,将军〔日本德川幕府时代的将军〕. ②〔美口〕(实业界,政界的)巨头.
ty·ing [ˈtaiiŋ] *n.* 结子,结儿; 系结.
tyke [taik] *n.* ①野狗,杂种狗. ②〔Scot.〕 乡下人; 粗野的人. ③小孩;〔口〕顽皮孩子. *a Yorkshire ~* 约克郡乡下人.
Ty·ler [ˈtailə] *n.* 泰勒〔姓氏〕.
tyl·er [ˈtailə] *n.* 共济会秘密会所守门人.
ty·lo·pod [ˈtailəpɔd] *a., n.* 【动】有肉趾的(动物); 骆驼类〔附目〕动物. **-ous** *a.*
ty·lo·sis [taiˈləusis] *n.* ①【医】胼胝症. ②【植】(导管内的)侵填体.
tym·bal [ˈtimbl] *n.* = timbal.
tym·pan [ˈtimpən] *n.* ①鼓. ②(印刷机的)压纸格; 衬垫. ③鼓膜(状物). ④【解、建】 = tympanum.
tym·pa·na [ˈtimpənɑ, -nə] *n.* tympanum 的复数.
tym·pa·ni [ˈtimpənai] *n.*〔*pl.*〕【乐】定音鼓.
tym·pan·ic [timˈpænik] *a.* ①鼓皮似的,有鼓皮一样作用的. ②【解】鼓膜的; 鼓室的,中耳的. ~ **bone** 【解,动】鼓骨. ~ **membrane** 【解】鼓膜.
tym·pa·nist [ˈtimpənist] *n.* 【乐】鼓手.
tym·pa·ni·tes [timpəˈnaitiːz] *n.* 【医】(腹部) 臌胀,气臌.
tym·pa·ni·tis [timpəˈnaitis] *n.* 【医】中耳炎,鼓室炎.
tym·pa·num [ˈtimpənəm] *n. (pl. ~s, -na* [-nə]*)* ①鼓. ②【解】耳膜,鼓膜; 鼓室, 中耳; (电话机的)振动膜;【动】颈侧气囊,鸣腔. ③【建】山墙的三角面部分, 门楣中心. ④【机】溜槽水车,鼓形水车.
tym·pa·ny [ˈtimpəni] *n. (pl. -nies)* 【医】①气鼓,鼓胀; 鼓响. ②夸张,浮夸,自负.
Tyn·dale [ˈtindl] *n.* 廷代尔〔姓氏〕.
Tyndall [ˈtindl] *n.* ①廷德尔〔姓氏〕. ②**J.** ~ 丁铎尔〔1820—1893,英国的物理学家〕. **T- effect** 【物】丁铎尔效应.
Tyn·wald [ˈtinwɔld] *n.* 马恩岛 (Isle of Man) 的议会.
typ. = ①typographer. ②typographical. ③typography.
typ·al [ˈtaipl] *a.* ①标本的,模型的. ②典型的,模范的,代表性的.
typ·a·ble, type·a·ble [ˈtaipəbl] *a.* 可(用打字机)打字的.
type [taip] *n.* ①型,类型,(工业产品的)品种; 风格,型式. ②典型,榜样,样本,样板,模范,范本; 典型人物; 具有某种显著特性的人〔物、事件〕. ③记号, 符号; 表征,象征. ④【宗】预示. ⑤【化】(典)型,类型;【生】型,类型,模式标本. ⑥【印】铅字, 活字〔也可作集合词〕; 印刷文字, 字体. ★ ①书籍杂志正文所用铅字通常有三种: roman (罗马体)〔正体〕, italic (斜体), bold (黑体). 每种均有 capital (大写), 小大写 (small capital) 和 lower-case

[small] letter 小写。②字体主要有 Gothic 哥特体(美国叫 Text 或 Black Letter), Old Style 旧体, Modern 新体, Egyptian 埃及体(美国叫 Antique 古体), Sans-serif 滑体(美国叫 Gothic), Script 手写体,草体等。③按宽度可分为: Condensed 狭身, Standard 常身, Extended 阔身。④按笔划粗细可分为 Lightface 细长体, Medium [Standard] 正常体, Boldface 粗黑体。⑤按铅字大小可分为: 3 点 (excelsior), 3.5点 (brilliant), 4.5 点 (diamond), 5 点 (pearl), 5.5 点(〔英〕 ruby, or 〔美〕 agate), 6 点 (nonpareil), 6.5 点 (emerald), 7 点 (minion), 8 点 (brevier), 9 点 (bourgeois), 10 点 (long primer), 11 点 (small pica), 12 点 (pica), 14 点 (English), 16 点(columbian), 18 点 (gzeat primer), 48 点 (canon) 等〔点即 point, 有音译为磅的〕. *blood* ～血型. *a woman of a certain* ～ 〔婉〕某一类型的女人[妓女]. *the* ～ *genus* 【植】(一科中的)代表属. *wooden* ～ 印刷木版. ***appear in*** ～ 出版. ***in*** ～ 用铅字排成(的). ***set*** ～ 排字. ***true to*** ～ 典型的. — *vt.* ①代表,成为…的典型;(是…的)象征. ②付排,用打字机打. ③【医】鉴定(血型). ④使归属为某一类型; 分配 (演员)演不同类型的角色. ⑤浇铸(铅字). — *vi.* 打字 (= typewrite). ～ **bar** 铸成一条的一行铅字. ～**cast** *vt.* 按类型分配角色; 分配给 (演员) 非常合适的角色. ～**-cast** *vt., vi.* 铸字,浇字. ～ **cutter** 刻铜模的工人. ～**-face** 铅字面,铅字印出的字样. ～ **founder** 铸字厂老板; 铸字工人. ～ **foundry** 铸字厂. ～ **genus** 【生】模式属. ～**-high** *a.* (木刻板)(厚度)跟铅字高度一样的. ～ **metal** 铅字合金. ～**script** 用打字机打的原稿[文件], 打印本. ～**set** *vt.* 排字, 排版. ～**setter** 排字工人; 排字机. ～**setting** 排字. ～ **species** 【生】原种. ～ **specimen** 【生】模式标本. ～ **wheel** (某些打字机、电报机上的)活字轮.

-type *suf.* = type: proto*type*, ferro*type*.

typ·er [ˈtaipə] *n.* ①〔口〕= typist. ②〔美俚〕机关枪.

type·write [ˈtaiprait] *vt.* ***(-wrote*** [-rəut]; ***-writ·ten*** [-writn]) (用打字机)打印.

type·writ·er [ˈtaipraitə] *n.* ①打字机. ②〔罕〕= typist. ③〔美俚〕机关枪.

type·writ·ten [ˈtaipritn] *a.* 用打字机打印的.

typh·lit·ic [tifˈlitik] *a.* 【医】阑尾炎的.

typh·li·tis [tifˈlaitis] *n.* 【医】阑尾炎.

Ty·pho·eus [taiˈfəujuːs] *n.* 【希神】百头巨怪.

ty·pho·gen·ic [ˌtaifəuˈdʒenik] *a.* 【医】引起(斑疹)伤寒的; 引起肠热病的.

ty·phoid [ˈtaifɔid] *a.* 【医】伤寒性的. — *n.* 【医】伤寒 (= ～fever). **T- Mary** 伤寒病患者[带菌者]; 传染病患者. **-al** *a.*

ty·pho·ma·ni·a [ˌtaifəuˈmeinjə] *n.* 【医】伤寒性谵妄(症候).

Ty·phon [ˈtaifɔn] *n.* 【希神】①= Typhoeus. ②Typhoeus 之子.

ty·phon·ic [taiˈfɔnik] *a.* 飓风(似)的.

ty·phoon [taiˈfuːn] *n.* 飓风.

ty·phous [ˈtaifəs] *a.* 【医】斑疹伤寒(性)的.

ty·phus [ˈtaifəs] *n.* 【医】斑疹伤寒 (= ～ fever). *malignant [simple]* ～ 恶性[轻]斑疹伤寒.

typic [ˈtipik] *a.* ①典型的,定型的,有代表性的. ②正常的,正规的.

typ·i·cal [ˈtipikl] *a.* ①代表的,典型的. ②模范的,成为标本的. ③特有的,独特的. ④象征的. ***be*** ～ ***of*** ... 代表; 象征. **-ly** *ad.* **-ness, -ty** *n.*

typ·i·fy [ˈtipifai] *vt.* ①成为…的典型; 象征; 代表; 具有…的特质. ②【宗】预示. **-fi·er** *n.* 典型代表者, 有代表性的事物. **-fi·ca·tion** *n.* 典型化.

typ·ing [ˈtaipiŋ] *n.* ①打字; 打字术; 打字机使用法. ②打印本,打印稿,打印文件.

typ·ist [taipist] *n.* 打字员,打字者.

ty·po [ˈtaipəu] *n.* *(pl. -s)* ①〔口〕印刷工人; 排字工人. ②〔美口〕排印错误,打字错误.

typo- *comb. f.* = type 〔元音前用 typ-〕.

typo(g). = typ.

ty·pog·ra·pher [tiˈpɔgrəfə] *n.* ①印刷工人. ②印刷术专家. ③印刷业者.

ty·po·graph·ic, -i·cal [ˌtaipəˈgræfik,-ikəl] *a.* 印刷(术)上的. *a* ～ *error* 排印上的错误. **-cal·ly** *ad.*

ty·pog·ra·phy [taiˈpɔgrəfi] *n.* ①印刷(术). ②印刷品. ③排字式样,印刷体裁. *The* ～ *is clear.* 印刷清晰.

ty·pol·o·gy [taiˈpɔlədʒi] *n.* ①【宗】预示论, 象征论. ②预兆. ③【哲,语言,生】类型学. **-log·i·cal** [-ˈlɔdʒikəl] *a.*

ty·po·nym [ˈtaipənim] *n.* 【生】①类型名称,模式名称〔按类型、模式命名的名称〕. ②同模式异名. **-al, -ic** *a.*

ty·po·script [ˈtaipəskript] *n.* = typescript.

ty·poth·e·tae [taiˈpɔθiˌtiː] *n.* 〔*pl.*〕①〔动词用单数〕印刷业公会. ②印刷商.

typo·tron [ˈtaipətrɔn] *n.* (高速)字标管,显字管.

TYPP, t.y.p.p. = 【纺】thousands of yards per pound. 千码/磅.

typ·tol·o·gy [tipˈtɔlədʒi] *n.* 敲击显灵招魂术〔一种江湖骗术,说是鬼魂会用敲击办法与人交通〕.

Tyr [tiə] *n.* 【北欧神话】战神蒂尔.

ty·ra·mine [ˈtairəˌmiːn, -min] *n.* 【化】酪胺.

ty·rannic, -ni·cal [tiˈrænik, -nikəl] *a.* 暴君的; 专制的; 暴虐的. **ty·ran·ni·cal·ly** *ad.*

ty·ran·ni·cide [tiˈrænisaid] *n.* 诛戮暴君(者). **-ci·dal** [-ˈsaidl] *a.*

tyr·an·nize [ˈtirənaiz] *vi., vt.* (对…)施行暴政,压制,强横霸道 *(over)*.

ty·ran·no·saur [tiˈrænəˌsɔː, tai-] *n.* 【动】恐龙 (= tyrannosaurus).

tyr·an·nous [ˈtirənəs] *a.* 暴政的,暴虐的, 专横的. **-ly** *ad.*

tyr·an·ny [ˈtirəni] *n.* ①暴政; 专制政治, 高压政治. ②暴虐,残暴,专横. ③【希腊史】僭主政治.

ty·rant [ˈtaiərənt] *n.* ①暴君; 专制君主. ②暴虐专横的人. ③【希腊史】僭主, 霸主. *a local* ～ 恶霸, 土豪. *scholar* ～*s* 学阀.

Tyre [ˈtaiə] *n.* 提尔〔古代腓尼基(Phoenicia) 的有名港口,现属黎巴嫩〕.

tyre[1] [ˈtaiə] *n., vt.* 〔英〕= tire[2].

tyre[2] [ˈtaiə] *n.* 〔印度英语〕凝乳.

Tyr·i·an [ˈtiriən] *a., n.* 提尔(Tyre)的(人). ～ **purple** 提尔红紫〔染料或染织品〕.

ty·ro [ˈtaiərəu] *n.* *(pl. ～s)* 初学者,生手,新手(= tiro).

ty·ro·ci·dine [ˌtairəˈsaidn, -saidiːn] *n.* 【化】短杆菌酪素.

Tyr·o·lese [tirəˈliːz] *n.* 〔*sing., pl.*〕(奥地利) 蒂罗尔 (Tyrol) 人. — *a.* 蒂罗尔 (人)的.

Ty·ro·lienne [tirəuliˈen] *n.* 〔F.〕蒂罗尔民间舞(曲).

Ty·rone [tiˈrəun] *n.* 蒂龙〔男子名〕.

tyro·sin(e) [ˈtirəsiːn] *n.* 【生化】酪氨酸; 3- 对羟苯基丙氨酸.

ty·ro·si·nase [ˈtairəsineis, taiˈrɔsiˌneis] *n.* 【化】酪氨酸酶.

ty·ro·thri·cin [ˌtairəˈθraisin, -ˈθrisin] *n.*【化】短杆菌素.

tyr·o·tox·i·con [ˌtaiərəˈtɔksikɔn] *n.* 【生化】干酪毒.

Tyr·rhene, Tyr·rhe·ni·an [ˈtiriːn, tiˈriːniən, -njən] *a., n.* = Etruscan. **Turrhenian Sea** (意大利西面的)第勒尼安海.

Ty·rwhitt [ˈtirit] *n.* 蒂里特〔姓氏〕.

tythe [taið] *n., v.* 〔英〕= tithe.

Tyu·men [tjuːˈmen] *n.* 秋明〔苏联城市〕.

tyu·ya·mu·nite [ˌtjujəˈmuːnait] *n.* 【矿】钙钒铀矿.

Tzar, Tza·ri·na 等 [zɑː, zɑːˈriːnə] *n.* = Czar, Cza-

rina 等.
T-ze•ro [ˈtiˈziərəu] *n.*【宇】(人造卫星等的)发射时间.
tzet•ze [ˈtsetsi] *n.* = tsetse.
tzi•gane [tsiˈgɑːn], **-ga•ny** [-ni] *n., a.* 茨冈人(的), 吉普赛人(的).

U

U, u [juː] *(pl. U's, u's* [juːz]*)* ①英语字母表第二十一字母. ②U 字形的东西. ③铀的符号 (=uranium). *U-bolt* U 形[马蹄]螺栓. *U-tube* U字管. — *a.* 〔U〕〔口〕上流社会的,上层阶级的.
U.,u. = ①Uncle. ②Union. ③University. ④unit. ⑤upper. ⑥uranium. ⑦you. ⑧universal. ⑨uncle.
U./a. u.a. = underwriting account 保险帐户［帐目］.
UAAC = Un-American Activities Committee〔美〕非美活动调查委员会.
U.A.B. = Unemployment Assistance Board〔英〕失业救济委员会.
UAE = United Arab Emirates 阿拉伯联合酋长国〔亚洲〕.
UAM = underwater-to-air missile 水下对空导弹.
UAT =〔F.〕*Union Aéromaritime de Transport*〔法〕联合海空运输公司.
UAW = United Auto, Aircraft and Agricultural Implements Workers of America 美国汽车、飞机、农业机械工人联合会.
UBA = Union of Burma Airways 缅甸联邦航空公司.
U-bahn [ˈjuːbɑːn] *n.*〔G.〕地下铁道.
Ub•be•lohde [ˈʌbələud] *n.* 厄布洛德〔姓氏〕.
Ü•ber•mensch [ˈjuːbəˌmenʃ] *n. (pl. -mensch•en* [-ən]*)*〔G.〕①超人. ②具有超过常人力量的人.
u•bi•e•ty [juːˈbaiəti] *n.*【哲】在一定的场所; 所在; 位置,位置关系.
u•bi in•fra [ˈjuːbi ˈinfrə]〔L.〕在下面提及之处, 见下.
u•biq•ui•tous [juːˈbikwitəs] *a.* 无所不在的, 遍在的; 〔谑〕(人)到处看见其踪影的. *The struggle between opposites is* ~. 对立面的斗争无所不在. **-ly** *ad.* **-ness** *n.*
u•biq•ui•ty [ju(ː)ˈbikwiti] *n.* (同时)无所不在(性), 遍在(性).
u•bi su•pra [ˈuːbiˈsuːprə, ˈjuː-]〔L.〕在上面提及之处, 见上.
U-boat [ˈjuːbəut] *n.* (德国)潜水艇.
U-bomb [ˈjuːbɔm] *n.* 铀原子弹.
U.C. = ①University College〔英〕大学学院. ②Upper Canada 上加拿大(现称安大略省).
U/C = ①undercharge 装料不足. ②unclassified 不保密的.
u.c. = ①〔It.〕*una corda*【乐】(钢琴)用弱音踏板(的). ②upper case【印】大写字母(盘).
U.C.L. = University College, London.〔英〕伦敦大学学院.
U.D. = the Underground (Railway London) 伦敦地铁.
U•dall [ˈjuːdəl] *n.* 尤德尔〔姓氏〕.
U.D.C. = ①Union of Democratic Control〔美〕民主管理协会. ②Urban District Council〔英〕城镇(区)议会.
ud•der [ˈʌdə] *n.* (牛、羊等的)乳房,乳腺.
ud•dered [ˈʌdəd] *a.*〔多用以构成复合词〕乳房…的,有(…的)乳房的. *heavy-~ cows* 乳房沉甸甸的母牛.
ud•dre•less [ˈʌdlis] *a.* 没有乳房的; 没有母乳的; (小羊等)没有母羊的.
u•do [ˈuːdəu] *n. (pl. ~s)*〔Jap.〕【植】土当归.
u•dom•e•ter [ju(ː)ˈdɔmitə] *n.* 雨量计.
UE, UEW = United Electrical, Radio and Machine Workers of America 美国电气、无线电和机器工人联合会.
UEA = Universal Esperanto Association 国际世界语协会.
UFO [ˈjuːfəu, ˌjuːefˈəu] *n. (pl. UFOs, UFO's)* = *unidentified flying object* 不明飞行物,飞碟,真象未明的太空飞行物〔尤指1947年以来看到的在太空不同高度以不同速度飞行的东西〕.
u•fol•o•gist [juːˈfɔlədʒist] *n.* "飞碟"研究者,爱好研究真象未明的太空飞行物者.
u•fol•o•gy [juːˈfɔlədʒi] *n.* "飞碟"学,不明飞行物研究.
U•gan•da [ju(ː)ˈgændə, uːˈgændə] *n.* 乌干达〔非洲〕. **-n** ① *n.* 乌干达人. ② *a.* 乌干达的.
U•ga•rit•ic [ˌjuːgəˈritik, ˈuː-] *n.* 乌嘎利特语〔很接近古希伯来语的一种已消亡的闪语〕. —*a.* 乌嘎利特语的; 乌嘎利特人的.
ugh [ūːx, ʌx, uh] *int.* 嘿; 呸; 啊;〔表示憎厌、恐怖等〕.
ug•li•fi•ca•tion [ˌʌglifiˈkeiʃən] *n.* 丑化 *(opp.* beautification*)*.
ug•li•fi•er [ˈʌglifaiə] *n.* 破坏美观者,使丑化的人[物].
ug•li•fy [ˈʌglifai] *vt.*〔口〕弄丑,丑化,使丑陋; 糟蹋(美等).
ug•ly [ˈʌgli] *a. (-li•er; -li•est)* ①丑的, 丑陋的, 难看的. ②(道德上)丑恶的,邪恶的; 丢脸的, (传说等)难听的; 不愉快的,(工作等)讨厌的. ③〔口〕爱吵架的,性情别扭的; 险恶的; (天气等)象要刮风下雨的. *an ~ deed* 丑行. *an ~ word* 难听的话. *an ~ task* 讨厌的工作. *The sky has an ~ look.* 天气靠不住[阴沉]. ***as ~ as sin*** 极丑,极难看; 极恶劣. ***cut up ~*** 发脾气,发怒. ***~ as a mud fence***〔美〕非常粗野的. ***~ customer***〔口〕讨厌的人,难对付的家伙. ***~ duckling*** 丑小鸭;〔喻〕小时家里人看不起[不好看]大来变得出人头地[变美]的孩子. — *n.* 〔口〕①丑陋的人[东西]. ②(十九世纪流行的)女帽(上的丝质)遮阳. **-li•ness** *n.*
U•gri•an [ˈjuːgriən, ˈuː-] *a.* ①(西伯利亚以西的或匈牙利(包括马扎尔)的) 芬兰-乌戈尔族人的. ②乌戈尔语支〔包括匈牙利语(马扎尔语),佛古尔语和奥斯提雅克语在内的芬兰-乌戈尔语族的一个语支〕. — *n.* ①乌戈尔族人. ②乌戈尔语.
U•gric [ˈjuːgrik, ˈuː-] *n., a.* = Ugrian.
U.G.R.R. = Underground Railroad〔英〕地下铁道.
UGT, ugt = urgent〔美〕〔电报用语〕急电.
uh [ʌ, ʌn] *int.* ①= huh. ②嗯〔讲话时思索一个词儿或凝思时所发出的声音〕.
UHF, uhf = ultrahigh frequency【无】超高频.
uh-huh [ˈʌhʌ] *int.* ①嗯嗯 (= yes). ②〔读时带重鼻音〕嗯(= no). — *vi.*〔美俚〕求爱.
uh•lan [ˈuːlɑːn] *n.*【德史】枪骑兵.
u•hu•ru [uːˈhuruː] *n., int.*〔Swahili〕乌呼噜,自由.

U

u.i. =〔L.〕*ut infra* 如下所述，如下所示 (= as below).
Ui·g(h)ur [ˈwiːɡuə] *n., a.* *(pl. ~(s))* ①维吾尔(族)人(的). ②维吾尔语(的).
u·in·ta·ite, u·in·tah·ite [juˈintəait] *n.* 【矿】〔美〕硬沥青.
uit [ɔit] *prep.* 〔Afrik.〕外的 (= out).
uit·land·er [ˈɔitlændə]〔或作 U-〕*n.* 〔Afrik.〕外国人，外侨〔尤指布尔战争前居住在(南非)德兰士瓦省非荷兰血统的外国人〕.
U.J.D. =〔L.〕*Utriusque Juris Doctor* (= Doctor of both, 即 Civil & Canon Laws) 民法及教会法规博士.
UK, U.K. = United Kingdom 联合王国.
UKAEA = United Kingdom Atomic Energy Authority 联合王国原子能委员会.
u·kase [juːˈkeiz] *n.* 〔Russ.〕①(沙皇的)圣旨；(沙皇政府的)敕令. ②专横的(官方)命令[布告、通令].
uki·yo·(y)e [uˈkiːjəujei] *n.* 〔Jap.〕浮世绘.
Ukr. = Ukraine.
U·kraine [ju(ː)ˈkrein] *n.* 乌克兰〔苏联一加盟共和国〕.
U·krain·i·an [ju(ː)ˈkreinjən] *n.* ①乌克兰人. ②乌克兰语. — *a.* ①乌克兰的. ②乌克兰人的. ③乌克兰语的.
u·ku·le·le [juːkəˈleili] *n.* 【乐】尤克里里〔夏威夷的四弦乐器,象小型的吉他〕.
u·la·ma [ˈuːləmɑː, ˌuːləˈmɑː] *n. pl.* = ulema.
u·lan [ˈjuːlən, ˈuːlɑːn] *n.* = uhlan.
U·lan Ba·tor [ˈuːlɑːn ˈbɑːtɔː] 乌兰巴托〔蒙古人民共和国首都〕.
-ular *suf.* 构成形容词,表示"…的","似…的": crevicular.
ul·cer [ˈʌlsə] *n.* 【医】溃疡;〔喻〕积弊,病,症结. *a gastric ~* 胃溃疡. *a ~ gulch* 〔美俚〕下等餐馆.
ul·cer·ate [ˈʌlsəreit] *vi., vt.* 〔作 *vt.* 时主用被动语态〕(使)生溃疡;(使)溃烂;(使)(道德上)腐败,败坏.
ul·cer·a·tion [ˌʌlsəˈreiʃən] *n.* 溃烂;糜烂;腐败.
ul·cer·a·tive [ˈʌlsərətiv] *a.* 使生溃疡的;使腐败的.
ul·cer·ous [ˈʌlsərəs] *a.* 溃疡(性)的;生溃疡的,溃烂的. *an ~ hatred* 痛恨. **-ly** *ad.*
-ule *suf.*, 用以构成名词,表示"小": globule, pustule.
u·le·ma [ˈuːlimɑː] *n. pl.* ①乌力马〔穆斯林的学者或宗教、法律的权威,尤指在土耳其的〕. ②〔动词用单数〕乌力马委员会[学会];乌力马学会的成员.
ULF, ulf = ultra-low frequency【无】超低频.
ul·lage [ˈʌlidʒ] *n.* ①(容器的)缺量;(桶装液体等的)漏损(量);折耗,损耗. ②(桶内)油品体积的测定. ③〔*pl.*〕〔英俚〕杯中剩酒;残渣. *estimate 2% for ~* 折耗估计百分之二. *on ~* 并非满满的. *~* **rule** (不浸入油内的)测油尺.
ul·min [ˈʌlmin] *n.* 【化】棕腐质;赤榆树脂. **ul·mic, ul·min·ic** [ʌlˈminik] *a.* 棕腐质的 *(ulmic acid*【化】赤榆酸,棕腐酸).
ULMS = underwater long-range missile system 水下远程导弹系统.
ul·na [ˈʌlnə] *n.* *(pl. -nae* [-niː]*)* 【解】尺骨. **-r** *a.*
-ulose *suf.* 〔构成名词〕【化】含有酮基的…糖: levulose.
u·lot·ri·chous [juˈlɔtrikəs] *a.* 毛发卷缩(紧)的.
-ulous *suf.* 〔构成形容词〕有…倾向的,充满…特点的: populous.
Ul·ster [ˈʌlstə] *n.* ①厄尔斯特〔昔时为爱尔兰一地区,今为北爱尔兰及爱尔兰共和国分割〕. ②(爱尔兰共和国的)北爱尔兰省. ③〔口〕北爱尔兰. ④〔u-〕一种有带的粗呢宽大衣.
ult. = ultimate(ly).
ult. = 〔L.〕*ultimo.*
ul·te·ri·or [ʌlˈtiəriə] *a.* ①那一边的. ②(计划等)以后的,将来的. ③藏在背后的;不可告人的;心里的. *the ~ consequences of one's act* 某人行为的后果. *a man with ~ motives* 别有用心的人. *for the sake of ~ ends* 别有用心. *have an ~ object in view* 心里有鬼,别有用心. *the ~ region* 边远地区. **-ly** *ad.*
ul·ti·ma [ˈʌltimə] *a.* 〔L.〕终末的,末尾的,最后的;最远的. — *n.* 【语音】末音节. *~* ***ratio*** 最后的争辩[制裁,手段]. *~* ***ratio regum*** (路易十四刻在大炮上的铭文)王者的最后论据[最后手段],武力,战争. *~* ***Thule*** [ˈθjuːliː] 天涯海角,极限;最后目的.
ul·ti·mate [ˈʌltimit] *a.* ①最后的,最终的,极限的,结局的. ②根本的,首要的,基本的. ③最远的;终极的;【力学】最大的. *the ~ end of life* 人生的终极目的. *to the ~ ends of the world* 到天涯海角. — *n.* 终极;顶点;最后结果;基本事实,基本原理. ***in the ~*** 到最后,终于. *~* **analysis**【化】元素分析,最终分析. *~* **cause** 终极原因. *~* **constituent**【语】最终成分,(基本)构成要素. *~* **element** 元素. *~* **particle**【物】基本粒子. *~* **production** 总产量. *~* **stage**【林】安定期. *~* **strength**【工】极限强度. *~* **stress** 极限应力,极限胁强. *~* **yield** (加工后产品的)最终收率. **-ly** *ad.* **-ness** *n.*
ul·ti·ma·tum [ˌʌltiˈmeitəm] *n.* *(pl. ~s, -ta* [-tə]*)* ①最后要求[陈述],最后通牒,哀的美敦书;最后条件. ②最后结论,基本意义[原理].
ul·ti·mo [ˈʌltiməu] *a.* 〔L.〕上月的〔常略作 ult, ulto.〕. *the 10th ult.* 上月十日.
ul·ti·mo·gen·i·ture [ʌltiməuˈdʒenitʃə] *n.*【法】幼子继承(制).
ulto. = *ultimo.*
ul·tra [ˈʌltrə] *a.* 过度的,过激的,极端的. — *n.* 过激论者,极端分子,急进分子,激烈分子. **-ism** *n.* 过激论;极端主义. **-ist** *n., a.* 极端主义者(的).
ultra- *comb. f.* 极端,超: *ultra*-right; *ultra*micro.
ul·tra-a·cous·tics [ˈʌltrə-əˈkuːstiks] *n. pl.* 〔动词用 *sing.* 或 *pl.*〕.【物】超声学.
ul·tra-audion [ˈʌltrəˈɔdiən]【无】超三极管.
ul·tra·ba·sic [ˈʌltrəˈbeisik] *a.* 【化】超碱的,超基性的. *~* **rock** 超碱岩,超基性岩.
ul·tra·cen·tri·fuge [ˌʌltrəˈsentrəfjuːdʒ] ①*n.* 超速离心机. ②*vt.* 用超速离心机分离.
ul·tra·con·ser·va·tive [ˈʌltrəkənˈsəːvətiv] *a.* 极端保守(主义)的. **-ser·va·tism** *n.*
ul·tra-de·moc·ra·cy [ˈʌltrədiˈmɔkrəsi] *n.* 极端民主化.
ul·tra·fash·ion·a·ble [ˈʌltrəˈfæʃənəbl] *a.* 极端时髦的,极其流行的.
ul·tra·fax [ˈʌltrəfæks]【无】电视传真电报.
ul·tra·fiche [ˈʌltrəfiːʃ] *n.* 超微缩胶片.
ul·tra·high [ˈʌltrəhai] *a.*【无】超高的. *~* **frequency** 超高频.
ul·tra·is·tic [ˌʌltrəˈistik] *a.* 过激论的,极端主义的.
ul·tra-left [ˈʌltrəˈleft] *a.* 极"左"的. **-ist** *n.* 极"左"分子.
ul·tra·ma·rine[1] [ˌʌltrəməˈriːn] *a.* 海外的,海那边的. *~ trade* 海外贸易.
ul·tra·ma·rine[2] [ˌʌltrəməˈriːn] *n., a.* 佛青色(的),群青色(的);深蓝色(的).
ul·tra·mi·cro [ˌʌltrəˈmaikrəu] *a.* 超微的,小于百万分之一的.
ul·tra·mi·cro·chem·is·try [ˈʌltrəˌmaikrəuˈkemistri] *n.*【化】超微(量)化学.
ul·tra·mi·cro·fiche [ˈʌltrəˈmaikrəufiʃ] *n.* 超微缩照片.
ul·tra·mi·crom·e·ter [ˈʌltrəmaiˈkrɔmitə] *n.* 超测微计.
ul·tra·mi·cro·scope [ˌʌltrəˈmaikrəskəup] *n.* 超度显微镜,超倍显微镜.
ul·tra·mi·cro·scop·ic [ˌʌltrəˌmaikrəˈskɔpik] *a.* ①超出普通显微镜可见度范围的. ②超度显微镜的,超倍显微镜的.
ul·tra·mi·cros·co·py [ˌʌltrəmaiˈkrɔskəupi] *n.* 超显微术,超度[倍]显微镜的应用.
ul·tra·mod·ern [ˈʌltrəˈmɔdən] *a.* 超[过于]现代化的;

最新式的.

ul•tra•mon•tane [ˌʌltrəˈmɔntein] *a., n.* ①山那边的(人);阿尔卑斯山以南的(人). ②〔U-〕【史】信奉教皇至上主义的(人).

ul•tra•mon•ta•nism [ˌʌltrəˈmɔntinizəm] *n.* 【史】教皇至上主义. **-ta•nist** *n.* 信奉教皇至上主义者.

ul•tra•mun•dane [ˈʌltrəˈmʌndein] *a.* 世界之外的, 太阳系外的;超俗世的,超世间的.

ul•tra•nation•al•ism [ˈʌltrəˈnæʃənəlizəm] *n.* 极端民族主义. **-ist** *n., a.* 狭隘民族主义者(的).

ul•tra•pho•tom•e•ter [ˈʌltrəfəˈtɔmitə] *n.* 【物】超光度计.

ul•tra•ra•pid [ˈʌltrəˈræpid] *a.* (电影拍摄中胶片运行)超速的. ~ **picture** (用超速摄影法拍成的)慢动作影片.

ul•tra•ray [ˈʌltrərei] *n.* 宇宙线.

ul•tra-re•ac•tion•ar•y [ˈʌltrəriˈækʃənəri] *a.* 极端反动的.

ul•tra•red [ˈʌltrəˈred] *a.* 【物】红外线的.

ul•tra-right [ˈʌltrəˈrait] *a.* 极右的. **-ist** *n.* 极右分子.

ul•tra•short [ˈʌltrəˈʃɔːt] *a.* 【物】超短波的.

ul•tra•son•ic [ˈʌltrəˈsɔnik] *a.* 超声的, 超音速的. ~ *wave* 超声波. — *n.* 超声波.

ul•tra•son•ics [ˌʌltrəˈsɔniks] *n. pl.* 〔动词用单数〕【物】超声波学.

ul•tra•son•o•graph [ˈʌltrəsəˈnɔgrəfi] *n.* 【医】超声波探病仪.

ul•tra•sound [ˈʌltrəˈsaund] *n.* 超声波〔用于医学上诊断、治疗和外科手术等方面〕.

ul•tra•struc•ture [ˈʌltrəˈstrʌktʃə] *n.* 超(显)微结构,亚显微结构. **-struc•tur•al** *a.*

ul•tra•vi•o•let [ˈʌltrəˈvaiəlit] *a.* 【物】紫外的;紫外线的;产生〔应用〕紫外线的. — *n.* 紫外线辐射. ~ **light [rays]** 紫外线.

ul•tra vi•res [ˈʌltrə ˈvaiəriːz] 〔L.〕超出(个人、公司等的)法定权限.

ul•tra•vi•rus [ˈʌltrəˈvairəs] *n.* 【医】过滤性病毒;超显微病毒.

u•lu [ˈuːlu] *n.* (爱斯基摩妇女用的)圆叶刀.

ul•u•lant [ˈjuːljulənt] *a.* 嗥嗥叫的, 啸啸地叫的; 哀鸣的.

u•lu•late [ˈjuːljuleit] *vi.* ①(狗、狼等)嗥吠,吼; (猫头鹰等)啸啸地叫. ②哀鸣;悲泣. **-la•tion** [-ˈleiʃən] *n.*

Ul•ya•novsk [uːˈljɑːnɔfsk] *n.* 乌里扬诺夫斯克〔旧称 Simbirsk (辛比尔斯克),苏联城市〕.

U•lys•ses [ju(ː)ˈlisiːz] *n.* ①尤利塞斯〔男子名〕. ②【罗神】尤利西斯〔即希腊神话中的奥德修斯 (Odyssus), 曾参加围攻特洛伊 (Troy) 城,智勇双全,亦为荷马史诗《奥德赛》(Odyssey) 的主人公〕.

um. = unmarried.

u.m. = under-mentioned.

um•bel [ˈʌmbəl] *n.* 【植】伞形花(序).

um•bel•lar, um•bel•late [ˈʌmbələ, ˈʌmbəleit] *a.* 【植】伞形花(序)的.

um•bel•lat•ed [ˈʌmbəlitid -ˌeit-] *a.* 【植】伞形的.

um•bel•lif•er•ous [ˌʌmbeˈlifərəs] *a.* 【植】有伞形花(序)的; 伞形科的.

um•bel•lule [ˈʌmblˌjuːl, əmˈbeljuːl] *n.* 【植】小伞(形花序). **-lu•late** *a.*

um•ber [ˈʌmbə] *n.* 【化】赭土, 棕土, 焦茶色, 暗褐色. *burnt* ~ 煅赭土〔颜料〕. *raw* ~生赭土〔颜料〕. — *a.* 赭色的,焦茶色的. — *vt.* 把…涂〔染〕成赭色.

um•bili•cal [ˌʌmbiˈlaikəl] *a.* ①肚脐的;脐侧的;脐状的. ②〔古〕中心的. ③似以脐带联系的, (关系)密切的. 〔罕〕母系的, 女系的. ~ **ancestor** 母系祖先. ~ **cord** ①【解】脐带.【动】卵黄囊蒂;【植】珠柄. ②【军】(导弹发射前检验内部装置的)操纵缆; 【宇】(与舱外工作宇宙员联系并提供氧气等的)空间生命线. ~ **hernia** 【医】脐疝.

um•bil•i•cate [ʌmˈbilikit] *a.* ①肚脐状的,中凹的. ②有肚脐的.

um•bil•i•cat•ed [ʌmˈbilikitid, -ˌkeitid] = umbilicate.

um•bil•i•ca•tion [ʌmˌbiliˈkeiʃən] *n.* ①脐状. ②脐形涡〔如小脓疱〕.

um•bil•ic•u•lar [ˌʌmbiˈlikjulə] *a.*脐(状)的. ~ *contemplation* (佛教徒)(意守脐下的)坐禅.

um•bil•i•cus [ʌmˈbilikəs] *n.* (*pl.* ~*es* [-isai]) ①【解】脐;【植】种脐;【动】(单瓣贝的)涡孔;【数】脐点. ②〔转〕中心,核心.

um•bil•i•form [ʌmˈbilifɔːm] *a.* 脐形的.

um•bo [ˈʌmbəu] *n.* (*pl.* ~*s, um•bo•nes* [ʌmˈbəuniːz]) ①盾心浮雕. ②【动】(两瓣贝的)壳顶; 盾顶; 【解】(中央)凸;鼓膜凸;【植】(菌盖的)中心突起.

um•bo•nal, -bo•nate, -bon•ic [ˈʌmbənl, -neit, -ˈbɔnik] *a.* 具鳞脐的;具脐状突起的;具凸结的.

um•bra [ˈʌmbrə] *n.* (*pl.* **-brae** [-briː]) ①阴影;【天】本影;暗影;(太阳黑子的)中央暗黑部. ②(古罗马)随客来的不速之客;〔罕〕幽灵. **-l** *a.*

um•brage [ˈʌmbridʒ] *n.* ①树荫;叶丛;〔诗〕荫处,荫影. ②不快;愤怒;悔恨, 遗憾. ③〔罕〕痕迹;痕量,微少. ④怀疑,疑念. ***give ~ (to)*** 使不愉快,惹怒. ***take ~ (at)*** 对(…)感觉不快,见怪;生气.

um•bra•geous [ʌmˈbreidʒəs] *a.* ①成荫的,多荫的. ②〔罕〕多疑的,易怒的. **-ly** *ad.* **-ness** *n.*

um•brel•la [ʌmˈbrelə] *n.* ①伞,雨伞;〔罕〕(遮)阳伞〔通常称 sunshade 或 parasol〕. ②〔喻〕保护, 保护伞. ③【军】(由战斗机构成的)空中掩护幕; (防止敌机的)掩护火力网 (= ~ barrage). ④【动】水母〔海蜇〕的伞膜;伞具 (= ~-shell). ⑤【船】烟囱顶罩. — *a.* ①伞状的,似伞的. ②包罗众多的,机构庞大的. —*vt.* ①用伞遮覆. ②以战斗机队保护伞保护; 掩护. *an air* ~ 【军】空中掩护幕. ~ **antenna** 【无】伞形天线. ~ **arch** 【建】道护拱. ~ **bird** 〔南美〕伞鸟. ~ **grass** 【植】澳洲稷. ~ **leaf** 【植】山荷叶. ~**man** 摊贩. ~ **pine** 【植】金松. ~ **plant [palm]** 【植】细弱伞莎草. ~ **stand** 伞架. ~ **tree** 【植】(北美)木兰树;〔口〕伞形树.

um•brette [ʌmˈbret] *n.* 【鸟】(非洲)短颈鹭.

Um•bri•an [ˈʌmbriən] *a.* (意大利中部)翁布里亚(地区)的;翁布里亚人的. — *n.* ①翁布里亚人. ②已消亡的奥斯肯-翁布里亚语.

um•brif•er•ous [ʌmˈbrifərəs] *a.* 成荫的, 有阴影的. **-ly** *ad.*

u•mi•ak [ˈuːmiæk] *n.* (爱斯基摩女子划的) 木框皮艇.

um•laut [ˈumlaut] *n.* 〔G.〕【语音】①曲音, 元音变化〔如德语的 mann,复数变为 männer; 英语的 man, 复数变为 men, foot 变为 feet〕. ②变音的元音. ③(加在 a, o, u 上的)变音符号(¨). — *vt.* ①使(元音)变音. ②在(元音字母上)加变音符号.

UMP = 【化】uridine monophosphate 一磷酸尿苷, 尿苷酸 (= uridylic acid).

ump [ʌmp] *n.* 裁判员 — *vi.* 当裁判,当裁判〔umpire 的缩略词〕.

umph[1] [əm(f), mh] *int.* = humph.

umph[2] [uːmf] *n.* 〔美俚〕= oomph.

um•pir•age [ˈʌmpaiəridʒ] *n.* ①公断人〔仲裁人, 裁判员〕的地位〔职务〕; 公断权. ②公断人的裁决.

um•pire [ˈʌmpaiə] *n.* ①公断人,仲裁人; (运动的)裁判员;【军】演习讲评教官;【法】裁定人. ②决定性的事物. — *vt.* 公断, 仲裁, 裁判, 裁定. — *vi.* 任公断人, 当裁判. ~**ship** *n.* = umpirage.

um•(ps)teen [ˈʌm(ps)tiːn] *a.* 〔俚〕许多的,大量的; 无数的. **-th** *a.* 〔俚〕(经过无数次后)又一次的.

ump•ty [ˈʌmpti] *a.* 〔俚〕几十的〔20,30…90〕; 若干的.

umpty-umpth [ˈʌmptiˈʌmpθ] *n., a.* ①〔俚〕很多(的), 几十几(的) 〔20,21…99〕. ②〔美〕又一个〔次〕(的). ***for***

U

the ~ time 几十次.
UMT = Universal Military Training〔美〕普遍军训.
um·teen [ˈʌmtiːn] = umpteen.
UMW = United Mine Workers of America 美国联合矿工工会.
UN, U.N. = United Nations 联合国.
un, 'un [ən] *pro.*〔俚〕家伙,人;东西(= one). *a little ~* 小家伙,小孩子. *He's a tough 'un.* 他是个厉害家伙. *That's a good 'un.* 妙极〔指双关语、谎话等〕. *you [we] 'uns*〔美南部〕你们〔我们〕全体. *a red 'un*〔俚〕金币,金挂表. ***a stiff 'un***〔俚〕①老运动员. ②(赛马中)一定要输的马. ③尸体. ***a wrong 'un***〔俚〕①坏人. ②伪币.
un- [ʌn] *pref.* ①构成动词表示下列意义: 相反动作; 如 *un*bend, *un*coil; 使丧失,夺去,废止,如 *un*sex, *un*man; 由…解放出,由…取出,如 *un*earth, *un*horse; 彻底,如 *un*loose, *un*rip. ②加在形容词、副词、名词前表示: 不,无,非,未; 如 *un*happy, *un*happily, *un*happiness, *un*rest.
U·na [ˈjuːnə] *n.* 尤纳〔女子名〕(亦作 **Ona, OOna, Oonagh**).
un·a·bashed [ˈʌnəˈbæʃt] *a.* 不脸红的,不害臊的,不怕难为情的,脸厚的,满不在乎的; 沉着的.
un·a·bat·ed [ˈʌnəˈbeitid] *a.* 不减少的; 不减退的.
un·ab·bre·vi·at·ed [ˈʌnəˈbriːvieitid] *a.* 不省略的; 不删节的; 未经压缩的; 全文拼写的.
un·a·ble [ˈʌnˈeibl] *a.* 不能,不会;〔罕、诗〕弱,无力的. *I am ~ to walk.* 我不能走路.
unabr. = unabridged.
un·a·bridged [ˈʌnəˈbridʒd] *a.* 没有省略的, 没有删节的,完全的. *an ~ edition* 足本.
un·ac·cent·ed [ˈʌnækˈsentid] *a.*【语音】非重音的. *an ~ part*【乐】弱音部. *an ~ syllable* 不发重音的音节.
un·ac·cept·a·ble [ˈʌnəkˈseptəbl] *a.* 不能接受的; 难以承认的,难答应的; 不受欢迎的; 不称心的,不中意的.
un·ac·com·mo·dat·ed [ˈʌnəˈkɔməˌdeitid] *a.* ①不适应的,不适合的. ②缺乏必需品的; 无(膳宿等)设备的.
un·ac·com·mo·dat·ing [ˈʌnəˈkɔmədeitiŋ] *a.* ①不应允的,不与人方便的, 不肯通融的. ②不亲切的,不随和的; 没人情的.
un·ac·com·pa·nied [ˈʌnəˈkʌmpənid] *a.* ①没有伴的; 无人伴随的 *(by; with)*. ②【乐】无伴奏的.
un·ac·com·plished [ˈʌnəˈkɔmpliʃt] *a.* ①未完成的,无成就的. ②无技术的,无能的. *an ~ offence*【法】未遂罪行.
un·ac·count·a·bil·i·ty [ˈʌnəˌkauntəˈbiliti] *n.* ①无法解释; 莫名其妙; 奇怪. ②没有责任; 不负责任(= unaccountableness).
un·ac·count·a·ble [ˈʌnəˈkauntəbl] *a.* ①无法解释的; 莫名其妙的. ②没有责任的,不负责的 *(for)*. **-bly** *ad.*
un·ac·count·ed(-for) [ˈʌnəˈkauntid(fɔː)] *a.* 未予说明的,未予解释清楚的.
un·ac·cus·tomed [ˈʌnəˈkʌstəmd] *a.* ①不习惯…的 *(to)*. ②不平常的; 没有看惯的; 珍奇的, 奇异的. *I am ~ to public speaking.* 我不习惯在公众面前讲话.
un·ac·knowl·edged [ˈʌnəkˈnɔlidʒd] *a.* ①(地位等)不被人承认的. ②(错误等)未公开承认的. ③(信件等)未得答复的. ④(致意等)未得回敬的.
una cor·da [ˈuːnəˈkɔːdə]〔It.〕【乐】用柔音踏板(的); 用独弦(的). **una corda pedal** (钢琴的)弱音踏板.
un·ac·quaint·ed [ˈʌnəˈkweintid] *a.* ①不知道的, 不懂的,不熟悉的 *(with)*. ②不认识的,不熟识的,陌生的; 不接近的 *(with)*.
un·act·a·ble [ˈʌnˈæktəbl] *a.* 不能上演的, 不适合于演出的.
un·act·ed [ˈʌnˈæktid] *a.* ①未演出的. ②未付诸行动的. ③未受影响的.
un·ac·tu·at·ed [ˈʌnˈæktjueitid] *a.* ①(机器等)未开动的. ②未推动的,未经激励的,不受驱使的.
un·a·dapt·a·ble [ˈʌnəˈdæptəbl] *a.* ①不能适应的. ②不能改编的.
un·a·dapt·ed [ˈʌnəˈdæptid] *a.* ①不适应的; 不适合的. ②未经改编的.
un·ad·dressed [ˈʌnəˈdrest] *a.* (信件)无地址的.
un·ad·mit·ted [ˈʌnədˈmitid] *a.* ①不让进入的. ②未被承认的.
un·a·dopt·ed [ˈʌnəˈdɔptid] *a.*〔英〕未被采用的; (尤指新设道路)未为地方当局接手维持的.
un·a·dorned [ˈʌnəˈdɔːnd] *a.* 没有装饰的; 不加渲染的; 原来的,自然的,朴素的.
un·a·dul·ter·at·ed [ˌʌnəˈdʌltəreited] *a.* 没有搀杂的,纯粹的; 真正的,地道的. **-ly** *ad.*
un·ad·vis·a·ble [ˈʌnədˈvaizəbl] *a.* ①不能推许的,不适宜的,不智的; 不好的,没有好处的. ②不接受劝告的.
un·ad·vised [ˈʌnədˈvaizd] *a.* 未作过商量〔咨询〕的; 愚蠢的,轻率的,鲁莽的; 未接受忠告的. **-ly** [ˌʌnədˈvaizidli] *ad.*
UNAEC = United Nations Atomic Energy Commission 联合国原子能委员会.
un·af·fect·ed [ˌʌnəˈfektid] *a.* ①不矫揉造作的, 自然的; 不装扮的,无装饰的,不虚伪的; 真心的, 真实的. ② [ˈʌnəˈfektid] 未受影响的, 未被感动的; 未变动的. **-ly** *ad.* **-ness** *n.*
un·a·fraid [ˈʌnəˈfreid] *a.* 不怕的,不畏惧的.
un·aid·ed [ˈʌnˈeidid] *a.* 未受〔无人〕帮助的; 独力的. *observe with an ~ eye* 以肉眼观察.
un·aired [ˈʌnˈɛəd] *a.* 不通风的; 潮湿的.
un·a·ligned [ˈʌnəˈlaind] *a.* 不结盟的. *~ countries [nations]* 不结盟国家.
unal·lied [ˈʌnəˈlaid] *a.* ①非同盟的. ②无关系的, 无所属的. *~ species* 互不相种.
un·al·low·a·ble [ˈʌnəˈlauəbl] *a.* 不能允许的,禁止的; 不能承认的.
un·al·loyed [ˈʌnəˈlɔid] *a.* ①非合金的. ②没有杂物的, (金属)纯粹的; (幸福)完全的,真正的.
un·al·ter·a·ble [ʌnˈɔːltərəbl] *a.* 不能变更的,不可改变的,不变的.
un·al·tered [ˈʌnˈɔːltəd] *a.* 不变的,依然如故的.
un·am·big·u·ous [ˈʌnæmˈbigjuəs] *a.* 不含糊的,显明的,明确的.
un·am·bi·tious [ˈʌnæmˈbiʃəs] *a.* 无奢望的,没有野心的; 谨小慎微的; 不显眼的,朴实的. **-ly** *ad.*
un-A·mer·i·can [ˈʌnəˈmerikən] *a.* ①不合美国派头的,(风俗、习惯等)非美国式的. ②反美的, 非美的. *~ activities* 非美活动(指所谓违反美国利益的活动).
un·a·mi·a·ble [ˈʌnˈeimjəbl] *a.* 不和蔼的,难亲近的,不友好的. **-a·bly** *ad.*
un·an·chor [ˈʌnˈæŋkə] *vt.* 使不安定,使不安.
un·a·neled [ˈʌnəˈniːld] *a.*【宗】〔古〕不涂油的; 未受临终涂油礼的.
u·na·nimi·ter [ˌjuːnəˈnimitə] *ad.*〔L.〕【法】= unanimously.
u·na·nim·i·ty [ˌjuːnəˈnimiti] *n.* 无异议; 全体一致. *the ~ of the Cabinet* 全体阁员意见一致. *the ~ of the applause* 全场拍掌叫好.
u·nan·i·mous [ju(ː)ˈnæniməs] *a.* 一致同意的; 无异议的,全体一致的. *be ~ in protesting* 齐声抗议. *be greeted with ~ applause* 受全场拍掌欢迎.
un·an·nealed [ˈʌnəˈniːld] *a.* ①【冶】未退火的. ②〔喻〕未经锻炼的.
un·an·nounced [ˈʌnəˈnaunst] *a.* 未经宣布的; 未经通报姓名的.
un·an·swer·a·ble [ʌnˈɑːnsərəbl] *a.* 不能回答的, (议论等)不能辩驳的; 没有责任的 *(for)*. **-a·bly** *ad.*
un·an·swered [ʌnˈɑːnsəd] *a.* 无回答的; 无反响的. *~ love* 单恋.

un·ap·peal·a·ble [ˈʌnəˈpiːləbl] *a.*【法】(判决等)不可上诉的.
un·ap·peal·ing [ˈʌnəˈpiːliŋ] *a.* 无吸引力的,不能打动人的.
un·ap·peas·a·ble [ˈʌnəˈpiːzəbl] *a.* 无法平息的,(愤怒)压制不住的,(饥饿)忍受不住的;不能满足的.
un·ap·pe·tiz·ing [ˈʌnˈæpitaiziŋ] *a.* 引不起食欲[兴趣]的.
un·ap·pre·ci·at·ed [ˈʌnəˈpriːʃieitid] *a.* 未受赏识的;不被领情的.
un·ap·pre·hend·ed [ˈʌnˌæpriˈhendid] ①未被理解的. ②未被逮捕的.
un·ap·pre·hen·sive [ˈʌnˌæpriˈhensiv] *a.* ①理解力差的. ②不怀疑的;不忧惧的.
un·ap·proach·a·ble [ˌʌnəˈprəutʃəbl] *a.* ①难接近的. ②无可匹敌的;难企及的. ~ *eloquence* 无比的口才. **-a·bly** *ad.* **-ness, -a·bil·i·ty** *n.*
un·ap·pro·pri·at·ed [ˌʌnəˈprəuprieitid] *a.* 未占用的,(尤指)不属于或未分配给任何人的;非专用的.
un·ap·proved [ˈʌnəˈpruːvd] *a.* 未经承认的,未经允许的,未准的.
un·apt [ˈʌnˈæpt] *a.* ①不相称的,不适当的. ②迟钝的,笨拙的*(to do; at)*. ②不易于…的,没有…倾向的;不惯于…的 *(to do)*. **-ly** *ad.*
un·ar·gu·a·ble [ˈʌnˈɑːgjuəbl] *a.* ①不可论证的. ②无可争辩的.
un·arm [ˈʌnˈɑːm] *vt.* 解除…的武装;缴…的械,夺去…的武器;使无害. —*vi.* 抛弃武器;放下武器.
un·armed [ˈʌnˈɑːmd] *a.* ①没有武装的,徒手的. ②【动、植】没有(角、刺等)防御器官的.
un·ar·mo(u)red [ˈʌnˈɑːməd] *a.* 不穿铠甲的;(舰船等)非装甲的.
un·ar·ti·fi·cial [ˈʌnɑːtiˈfiʃəl] *a.* 非人工的;非人为的;自然的,单纯的.
un·a·shamed [ˈʌnəˈʃeimd] *a.* ①不知羞耻的,无耻的,恬不知耻的. ②问心无愧的.
un·asked [ˈʌnˈɑːskt] *a.* 未受请托的;未受请求的,未经要求的;主动提出的. *He came* ~. 他不请自来.
un·as·sail·a·ble [ʌnəˈseiləbl] *a.* ①攻不破的,防守坚固的. ②没有争论[批评]余地的,无懈可击的. **-a·bly** *ad.*
un·as·ser·tive [ˈʌnəˈsəːtiv] *a.* 不武断的;不过分自信的;谦逊的.
un·as·sist·ed [ˈʌnəˈsistid] *a.* = unaided.
un·as·sum·ing [ˈʌnəˈsjuːmiŋ] *a.* 不摆架子的,谦逊的. **-ly** *ad.*
un·as·sured [ˈʌnəˈʃuəd] *a.* ①不确定的,无把握的;无自信的. ②未得保证的,不安全的. ③【商】未经保险的;无保险单的.
un·at·tached [ˈʌnəˈtætʃt] *a.* ①无所属的;自由的;中立的. ②尚未订婚[结婚]的. ③【军】待分配的. ④〔英〕(大学中有学籍而)不专属于某一学院的. ⑤【法】未被逮捕的,未被扣押的. *an* ~ *young lady* 〔口〕还没有订婚的年轻女人. *place sb. on the* ~ *list* 使等待分配.
un·at·tain·a·ble [ˈʌnəˈteinəbl] *a.* 难得到的;难达到的,难完成的.
un·at·tend·ed [ˈʌnəˈtendid] *a.* ①没有随从的,没有人伴随的. ②没人照顾的,没人管的. ③(伤口)没有扎绷带的. ④(会议等)无人出席的.
un·at·trac·tive [ˌʌnəˈtræktiv] *a.* ①不引人注意的,无吸引力的;枯燥乏味的. ②不美的. **-ly** *ad.* **-ness** *n.*
u·nau [juˈnɔː, uˈnau] *n.*【动】(南美洲)两趾树懒.
un·au·then·tic [ˈʌnɔːˈθentik] *a.* 来路不明的,无根据的,难信的,不可靠的;不是真品的.
un·au·thor·ized [ˈʌnˈɔːθəraizd] *a.* 未被授权的;越权的;未经许可的,未经批准的;没有根据的. *make an* ~ *change* 擅自更改[修改].
un·a·vail·a·ble [ˈʌnəˈveiləbl] *a.* ①不可得到的. ②没用的,没有效果的;不能利用的. *Your manuscript is* ~. 〔美〕尊稿不拟采用. ~ **energy**【物】无用能. ~ **water** 无效水(分).
un·a·vail·ing [ˈʌnəˈveiliŋ] *a.* 无益的,无用的,无效的. **-ly** *ad.*
un·a·void·a·ble [ʌnəˈvɔidəbl] *a.* ①不能避免的,不得已的. ②不能废除的,不能取消的. **-a·bly** *ad.*
un·a·ware [ˈʌnəˈweə] *a.* 〔用作表语〕没有觉察[注意]到,不知道 *(of; that)*. *be* ~ *of the danger* 未察觉危险. *I am not* ~ *that* ..., 我不是不知道…. — *ad., n.* = unawares. **at** ~ = at unawares. *They may involve themselves* ~. 他们可能不知不觉地使自己卷了进去. **-ness** *n.*
un·a·wares [ˈʌnəˈweəz] *ad.* 没想到,不料,忽然,突然,无意中,不知不觉间,一个不留神. ***be taken* ~ *by sb.'s question*** 冷不防被人质问. ***at* ~** 忽然,突然,出其不意. ***catch sb.* ~ = *take sb.* ~** 冷不防地捉住某人,出其不意地袭击.
un·backed [ˈʌnˈbækt] *a.* ①(马)无人骑过的,没有驯服的. ②无支援人的,无后援的. ③(赛跑的马)无人买票[下赌注]的.
unbaked [ˈʌnˈbeikt] *a.* (面包)没有烤过的;未熟的,生硬的.
un·bal·ance [ˈʌnˈbæləns] *vt.* *(-anced, -anc·ing)* ①使…失去平衡[均衡]. ②扰乱了…的机能;使(心情)紊乱. ~ *sb's mind* 使某人心情紊乱. ~ *the budget* 使预算失去平衡. — *n.* ①(精神、心情的)紊乱状态. ②失去平衡;不对称.
un·bal·anced [ˈʌnˈbælənst] *a.* ①失去平衡的;不稳定的. ②(心等)紊乱的. ③【商】未决算的. *His reason is* ~. 他理智紊乱了. *an* ~ *type of character* 不稳定的性格. ~ *books* 未决算帐簿.
un·bal·last·ed [ˈʌnˈbæləstid] *a.* ①(船)没有压舱物的,卸去底货的. ②(路基)未铺沙石的. ③未经不稳定化的.
un·bar [ˈʌnˈbɑː] *vt.* ①卸除…的横木;拔掉…的门闩;开放. ②清除…的障碍. ③挖毁(堤防).
un·barbed [ˈʌnˈbɑːbd] *a.* 拆除了有刺铁丝网的.
un·bat·ed [ʌnˈbeitid] *a.* ①〔诗〕未减轻的,未减少的. ②〔古〕不钝的.
un·bear·a·ble [ʌnˈbeərəbl] *a.* 难堪的,难受的,不能忍受的,不能容忍的;承受不住的. **-a·bly** *ad.*
un·beat·a·ble [ˈʌnˈbiːtəbl] *a.* 打不垮的,不可摧毁的.
un·beat·en [ˈʌnˈbiːtn] *a.* ①未被打过的,未捣碎的. ②未踩过的;未走过的. ③未被击败的;未被超越的. ~ *paths* 人迹未至的小径. ~ *records* 未被打破的记录.
un·be·com·ing [ˈʌnbiˈkʌmiŋ] *a.* ①不相称的,不适当的 *(to; for)*. ②不体面的,不好看的,不象样子的;不谨慎的,失礼的,(演说等)岂有此理的. ②(衣服等)不相配的,不合身的. **-ly** *ad.* **-ness** *n.*
un·be·fit·ting [ˈʌnbiˈfitiŋ] *a.* 不适合的,不相配的,不合式的;不相称的.
un·be·known [ˈʌnbiˈnəun] *a.* 〔口〕未知的,不得而知的 *(to)*. — *ad.* 瞒着. *He did it* ~ *to me.* 他瞒着我干那件事.
un·be·knownst [ˈʌnbiˈnəunst] *a., ad.* 〔方〕= unbeknown.
un·be·lief [ˈʌnbiˈliːf] *n.* 怀疑;不信;无(宗教)信仰.
un·be·liev·a·ble [ˈʌnbiˈliːvəbl] *a.* 不可信的.
un·be·liev·er [ˈʌnbiˈliːvə] *n.* ①不信教的人,异教徒. ②怀疑(论)者.
un·be·liev·ing [ˈʌnbiˈliːviŋ] *a.* ①多疑的;怀疑的;没有信心的. ③不信教的. **-ly** *ad.*
un·belt [ˈʌnˈbelt] *vt.* ①解下…的带子. ②解开带子拔出(刀剑等).
un·bend [ˈʌnˈbend] *vt.* ***(un·bent*** [ˈʌnˈbent], ***~ed)*** ①弄

直,伸直(弯曲的东西). ②放松,弄宽舒,宽解, 使休息. ③【海】解下,卸下(帆篷),放松(绳索等),解开(结子等). ～ *a bow* (解下弓弦)使弓松弛. — *vi.* 伸直; 松弛; 宽舒,舒畅. *He only ～s in the family circle.* 他只在家庭中才舒服.

un·bend·ing [ˈʌnˈbendiŋ] *a.* ①不弯曲的,坚硬的; 不屈不挠的,(精神等)坚定的; 固执的,顽固的. ②〔罕〕松弛的,不拘束的.

un·bent [ˈʌnˈbent] *v.* *unbend* 的过去式及过去分词. — *a.* ①不弯的; (弓等)松弛的. ②不屈服的.

un·be·ru·fen [ˈunbəˈru:fən] *a.* 〔G.〕罪过! 恕我多嘴! 〔一种迷信习惯,在说了自夸或过分自信的话之后, 以为这样说一声可免受恶报〕.

un·be·seem·ing [ˈʌnbiˈsi:miŋ] *a.* = unbecoming.

un·be·spoken [ˈʌnbiˈspəukən] *a.* 不预定的,不接受预约的.

un·bi·as(s)ed [ˈʌnˈbaiəst] *a.* 没有偏见的, 不偏不倚的, 公平的.

un·bid [ʌnˈbid] *a.* = unbidden.

un·bid·den [ˈʌnˈbidn] *a.* ①没有受命令的, 没有被指使的,自愿的,自动的,自发的. ②(客人等)未受邀请的.

un·bind [ˈʌnˈbaind] *vt.* (***un·bound*** [ˈʌnˈbaund]) 解开(结子等); 为…解开束缚,解放,释放.

un·bit·ted [ʌnˈbitid] *a.* ①(马)无嚼子的,无韁的. ②不受约束的; 不受控制的; 无管理的.

un·blank·ing [ˈʌnˈblæŋkiŋ] *n.* ①【无】增辉. ②(信号)开启; 开锁.

un·bleached [ˈʌnˈbli:tʃt] *a.* 没有漂白过的; 原色的. ～ *wax* 生蜡.

un·blem·ished [ʌnˈblemiʃt] *a.* 无疵的,没有缺点的; 清白无瑕的.

un·blessed, un·blest [ʌnˈblest] *a.*【宗】①未得神佑的. ②未受祝福的. ③被咀咒的; 邪恶的. ④可怜的; 不幸的. ⑤缺少某种好处的. *a hut ～ with electricity* 没有电力供应的简陋小屋.

un·blood·ed [ʌnˈblʌdid] *a.* ①非纯种的. ②尚未入门的〔指打猎等〕.

un·blush·ing [ʌnˈblʌʃiŋ] *a.* 不脸红的,不害臊的, 厚颜无耻的. **-ly** *ad.*

un·bod·ied [ˈʌnˈbɔdid] *a.* ①无实体或体形的; 非物质的; 无定形的. ②脱离开肉体的; 脱离现实的.

un·bolt [ˈʌnˈbəult] *vt.* 拔开(门上的)闩; 拔出(窗户等的)插梢,打开.

un·bolt·ed[1] [ˈʌnˈbəultid] *a.* 未上栓的,未栓上的.

un·bolt·ed[2] [ˈʌnˈbəultid] *a.* 粗的,未筛过的〔如面粉〕.

un·bon·net [ˈʌnˈbɔnit] *vi.* 脱帽,摘去头巾. — *vt.* 从…上取下帽子. **-ed** *a.*

un·bon·ny [ˈʌnˈbɔni] *a.* 〔Scot.〕丑的,不健康的.

un·born [ˈʌnˈbɔ:n] *a.* ①未出生的; 后代的, 未来的. ②无开始的, 原来就存在的. *an ～ child* 未出生的孩子. ～ *generations* 未来的人们.

un·bos·om [ˈʌnˈbuzəm] *vt.* 吐露 (心事),说出 (秘密), 剖明(心迹). ～ *oneself (to)* (对…)吐露心事, 表明心迹.

unbound[1] [ˈʌnˈbaund] *v.* unbind 的过去式及过去分词. — *a.* 解除绑缚的, 得到了自由的. *Prometheus U-* 被解放了的普罗美修士.

un·bound[2] [ˈʌnˈbaund] *a.* ①未装订(成书)的. ②【化】非结合的. ～ **water**【化】非结合水.

un·bound·ed [ˈʌnˈbaundid] *a.* ①无边的,无涯的, 无限制的. ②无限的,无节制的,不受控制的. *the ～ ocean* 无边无际的海洋. *be received with ～ enthusiasm* 获得极热烈的欢迎. **-ly** *ad.*

un·bowed [ˈʌnˈbaud] *a.* ①不躬身的,不弯腰的. ②不屈服的; 未被征服的.

un·brace [ˈʌnˈbreis] *vt.* ①放松,解开. ②使松懈; 减弱.

un·bred [ˈʌnˈbred] *a.* ①没有教育的,粗鲁的, 不知礼仪的. ②未受训练的. ③(牲畜)未交配过的.

un·bridge·a·ble [ˈʌnˈbridʒəbl] *a.* 不能架桥的; 不可逾越的.

un·bri·dled [ʌnˈbraidld] *a.* 没有韁绳的; 没有拘束的; 肆无忌惮的,放肆的; 猖獗的; 激烈的,猛烈的.

un·bro·ken [ˈʌnˈbrəukən] *a.* ①没有破损的,完好的,完整的; 未受挫折的,不沮丧的. ②未受阻碍的, 继续不断的. ③(马等)未驯服的. ④未开垦的. ⑤(条约等)没有受到破坏的; (纪录等)没有被打破的; (队伍)没有受到扰乱的,未涣散的,整齐的.

un·buck·le [ˈʌnˈbʌkl] *vt.* 解开(鞋扣等); 把(剑等)从带子上解下. — *vi.* ①解开带扣. ②变得不拘束.

un·build [ˈʌnˈbild] *vt.* ①拆毁,摧毁; 夷平. ②【物】减低(磁性).

un·built [ˈʌnˈbilt] *a.* ①未建造的,建筑前的. ②无建筑物的.

un·bundle [ˈʌnˈbʌndl] *vt.* 把(不同产品、服务等的价目)作分门别类的处理.

un·bur·den [ʌnˈbə:dn] *vt.* 使卸除负荷, 使放下担子; 〔喻〕倾诉(压在心里的话). ～ *a mule* 卸下骡子的负荷. ～ *oneself to sb.* 对别人倾吐自己的心事.

un·bur·ied [ˈʌnˈberid] *a.* ①尚未埋葬的, 没有埋葬的. ②被(从坟里)掘出的.

un·but·ton [ˈʌnˈbʌtn] *vt.* ①解开…的钮扣; 使舒畅, 使松弛. ②打开(装甲车等的)顶盖.

un·but·toned [ʌnˈbʌtnd] *a.* ①钮扣解开的. ②随便的; 漫不经心的; 不拘礼节的; 无拘束的.

unc [ʌŋk] 〔俚〕unconscious 的缩略字.

un·cage [ˈʌnˈkeidʒ] *vt.* 把(鸟等)从笼里释放,放出.

un·cal·cu·lat·ed [ˈʌnˈkælkjuleitid] *a.* 未经事先筹划〔考虑〕的.

un·called [ˈʌnˈkɔ:ld] *a.* 没有被召唤的, 未受邀请的; 未被请求的, 未被要求的 *(for)*. *come ～* 不请自来. ～ **capital**【商】未缴资金,未缴股款. ～**-for** *a.* 多余的,不必要的; 唐突的,多此一举的; 不适当的, 没有理由的,无缘无故的 (*His exhibition of temper was quite ～-for.* 他发脾气实在没理由).

un·can·ni·ness [ʌnˈkæninis] *n.* ①神秘〔尤指可怕, 离奇〕. ②不可思议. ③〔Scot.〕危险; 严重.

un·can·ny [ʌnˈkæni] *a.* (***-ni·er; -ni·est***) ①可怕的,令人毛骨悚然的; 不可思议的, 神秘的. ②〔Scot.〕危险的; 厉害的,严重的.

un·cap [ˈʌnˈkæp] *vt., vi.* ①脱(帽); 打开(覆盖物). ②透露,揭示.

un·cared-for [ˈʌnˈkɛədfɔ:] *a.* 没人照顾的,没人理睬的, 被遗忘的; 被厌弃的.

un·cart [ˈʌnˈkɑ:t] *vt.* 从车上卸下.

un·case [ˈʌnˈkeis] *vt.* 从(匣子等中)拿出; 使公开; 使露出,显示. ～ *the colours* 挂出军旗.

un·cast [ˈʌnˈkɑ:st] *a.* 演员未选定的,未定角的.

un·cat·a·logued [ˈʌnˈkætəlɔgd] *a.* 未列入目录的.

un·caused [ʌnˈkɔ:zd] *a.* 无前因的; 非创造的; 自存的. *a first great cause which is itself ～* 【哲】 本身无前因的始初巨因.

UNCDF = United Nations Capital Development Fund 联合国资本开发基金会.

un·ceas·ing [ʌnˈsi:siŋ] *a.* 不断的,不绝的, 不停的. **-ly** *ad.*

un·cen·sored [ˈʌnˈsensəd] *a.* ①(书刊等) 未经审查的; (书信)未经检查的. ②(新闻等)不受限制的; 不拘束的.

un·cer·e·mo·ni·ous [ˈʌnˌseriˈməunjəs, -niəs] *a.* ①不拘仪式〔形式〕的,随便的. ②没礼貌的. **-ly** *ad.* **-ness** *n.*

un·cer·tain [ʌnˈsə:tn] *a.* ①(行动)不定的, 含糊的; 不确定的,易变的; 不可靠的. ②不能断定的,不明的,未定的. ③忽明忽暗的, 闪烁不定的. *walk with ～ steps* 脚步不稳地走. *be ～ of the facts* 不确实知道事实. *a lady of ～ age* 年龄难于估计的中年女人. *the ～ flicker of a* *candle* 烛光摇曳. ～ **region**【物】不可辨区. **-ly** *ad.*

un·cer·tain·ty [ʌnˈsəːtnti] *n.* ①不确定,不确实,易变;不可靠;含糊. ②不确实知道,半信半疑. ③【物】测不准性. *the ～ of life* 人生的无常. ***void for ～***【法】(遗嘱、证书等)因辞句含糊而无效. ～ **principle**【物】测不准原理.

un·chain [ˈʌnˈtʃein] *vt.* 给…解除锁链;解放,释放.

un·chal·lenged [ˈʌnˈtʃælindʒd] *a.* 不成为问题的,(问题等)没有引起争论的;无异议的;无人挑战的. *go ～* (陈述等)无问题通过.

un·chanc·y [ˈʌnˈtʃɑːnsi] *a.* 〔Scot.〕不走运的;危险的.

un·change·a·ble [ʌnˈtʃeindʒəbl] *a.* 不可改变的. *～ of purpose* 意志坚定的. **-ness** *n.*

un·changed [ˈʌnˈtʃeindʒd] *a.* 不变的,没有变化的,依然如故的.

un·chang·ing [ʌnˈtʃeindʒiŋ] *a.* 不变的.

un·charge [ˈʌnˈtʃɑːdʒ] *v.* 〔罕〕= unload.

un·charged [ˈʌnˈtʃɑːdʒd] *a.* ①没有负荷的. ②未装弹药的. ③不付费用的. ④未被正式控告的. ⑤【电】无电荷的,不带电荷的.

un·char·i·ta·ble [ʌnˈtʃæritəbl] *a.* 没有慈悲心的;不宽恕的;严厉的;无情的. **-ta·bly** *ad.* **-ness** *n.*

un·chart·ed [ˈʌnˈtʃɑːtid] *a.* ①(岛屿等)海洋图上没有(标记)的;(区域)未经测绘的. ②未知的.

un·chaste [ˈʌnˈtʃeist] *a.* 不贞节的,不正经的;淫荡的;(嗜好等)下流的.

un·chas·ti·ty [ˈʌnˈtʃæstiti] *n.* 不贞节;不正经;淫荡;下流.

UNCHE = United Nations Conference on the Human Environment 联合国人类环境会议.

un·checked [ˈʌnˈtʃekt] *a.* ①未受抑制的. ②未经检查的.

un·chris·tian [ˈʌnˈkristjən, ˈʌnˈkristʃən] *a.* ①不信奉基督教的. ②违反基督教教义的. ③与基督教教徒不相称的. ④〔口〕令人不能容忍的;糟透的.

un·church [ˈʌnˈtʃəːtʃ] *vt.* ①把(某人)逐出教会. ②把(某教派)开除出教会;剥夺(某教派)教会资格[权利].

un·churched [ˈʌnˈtʃəːtʃt] *a.* ①不属于任何教会的;与任何教会无关的;不到任何教堂去的.②被逐出教会的. *the vast masses of ～ people* 不属于任何教会的广大群众.

un·ci·al [ˈʌnsiəl, ˈʌnʃəl] *n.* 安色尔字体〔古代用于抄本的一种圆体字〕;用安色尔字体写的抄本. — *a.* 安色尔字体的.

un·ci·form [ˈʌnsifɔːm] *a.* 钩形的;【解】钩骨的. — *n.*【解】钩骨.

un·ci·na·ri·a·sis [ˌʌnsinəˈraiəsis] *n.*【医】钩虫病 (= hookworm disease).

un·ci·nate [ˈʌnsinit] *a.* 钩状的;钩曲的.

U.N.C.I.O. = United Nations Conference on International Organization 联合国国际组织会议.

un·cir·cum·cised [ˈʌnˈsəːkəmsaizd] *a.*【宗】未受割礼的;不是犹太人的;【圣】异邦人的;异端的;精神上不获重生的.

un·cir·cum·ci·sion [ˈʌnˌsəːkʌmˈsiʒən] *n.* ①【宗】无割礼. ②【圣】[the ～]〔集合词〕不受割礼的人,非犹太人,异教徒.

un·cir·cum·stan·tial [ˈʌnˌsəːkəmˈstænʃəl] *a.* 不详尽的;非细节的.

un·civ·il [ˈʌnˈsivil] *a.* 不文明的,没礼貌的;粗野的;〔古〕野蛮的,未开化的. **-ness** *n.*

un·civ·i·lized [ˈʌnˈsivilaizd] *a.* 未开化的,野蛮的.

un·clad [ʌnˈklæd] unclothe 的过去式及过去分词的另一种写法. — *a.* 不穿衣的;赤身裸体的,一丝不挂的.

un·claimed [ˈʌnˈkleimd] *a.* 无人认领的,没人来取的. *an ～ baggage*〔美〕没人来取的行李. *an ～ balance* 不来提取的存款余额. *～ goods* 无人提取(认领)的货物.

un·clasp [ˈʌnˈklɑːsp] *vt.* 解开…的扣子;放开(抓住的手). — *vi.* 放开;松开.

un·classed [ˈʌnˈklɑːst] *a.* ①未归类的. ②(比赛等)未进入前三名的.

un·clas·si·cal [ˈʌnˈklæsikəl] *a.* ①非古典的,反古典的. ②【物】(定律等)不能用牛顿物理学来说明的.

un·clas·si·fied [ʌnˈklæsifaid] *a.* ①未分类〔分级〕的. ②非保密的.

un·cle [ˈʌŋkl] *n.* ①叔伯;舅父;姑父,姨父. ②〔口〕〔对年长者的客气,亲切称呼〕大叔,大伯. ③援助者,支持者;忠告者. ④〔俚〕开当铺者. ⑤〔自称〕老子. *U- Three-balls* 当铺. ***at (one's) ～'s*** 在当铺里典押中. ***cry [say] ～***〔美俚〕投降;承认失败. ***talk like a Dutch ～*** 严厉训诫(人),见 *Dutch* 条. ***U- Benny***〔美口〕当铺(老板). ***U- Dudley***〔美口〕= your ～. ***～ on maternal side*** 舅父. ***～ on paternal side*** 叔父,伯父. ***U- Sam*** 山姆大叔〔美国政府;美国人的绰号〕. ***U- Tom*** 汤姆叔叔〔美国女作家斯陀所著长篇小说 U- Tom's Cabin 中的主角〕;〔有时作 u- Tom〕逆来顺受的人. *U- Tomism* (黑人的)逆来顺受主义. ***Your ～ (Dudley)***〔谑〕我老子〔自称〕.

un·clean [ˈʌnˈkliːn] *a.* 不清洁的,污秽的;行为不正的,不贞洁的;下流的. *～ spirit* 邪鬼(尤指人心中的邪念). **-ly** *ad.*

un·clear [ˈʌnˈkliə] *a.* 不清楚的;难懂的;不明白的.

un·clench [ˈʌnˈklentʃ], **un·clinch** [ˈʌnˈklintʃ] *vt.* 使松开,弄开,撬开. — *vi.* 松开.

un·cloak [ˈʌnkləuk] *vt.* 脱去(外套);揭开(伪装),暴露. — *vi.* 脱去外套.

un·close [ˈʌnˈkləuz] *vt., vi.* 打开;(使)露出.

un·closed [ˈʌnˈkləuzd] *a.* ①(门)开着的;(眼界)开阔的. ②没有结束的,未完的.

un·clothe [ˈʌnˈkləuð] *vt.* (*-d,*〔古〕**un·clad** [ˈʌnˈklæd]) 抢去[剥去]…的衣服;剥光;暴露,揭露.

un·cloud·ed [ˈʌnˈklaudid] *a.* 没有云的,晴朗的;开朗的;(思路)清晰的.

un·club·ba·ble, un·club·a·ble [ˈʌnˈklʌbəbl] *a.* 不善于[不爱]交际的.

un·co, un·co' [ˈʌŋkəu] *a.* 〔Scot.〕①不熟知的,陌生的. ②奇怪的,可怕的. ③值得注意的,显著的. *an ～ sigh* 奇异的景象. ***the ～ guid*** 自命清高的人,过份古板的教徒. — *n.* ①稀奇的人[物]. ②〔*pl.*〕特讯,新闻. — *ad.* 很,极,非常.

un·coil [ˈʌnˈkɔil] *vt., vi.* (使)(卷着的东西)展开. *The snake slowly ～ed.* 蛇慢慢伸开(盘着的)身体.

un·col·oured, 〔美〕 **un·col·ored** [ˈʌnˈkʌləd] *a.* 无色的;未染色[着色]的,本色的;没有修饰的,原样的,(话等)不夸张的.

un·combed [ˈʌnˈkəumd] *a.* (头发等)没有梳过的;蓬乱的.

un·com·bined [ˈʌn-kəmˈbaind] *a.* ①没有结合的;未联合的. ②【化】未化合的;分离的.

un·come-at-a·ble [ˈʌnkʌmˈætəbl] *a.*〔口〕①难得到的. ②难接近的.

un·come·ly [ˈʌnˈkʌmli] *a.* ①不优美的,不漂亮的,丑陋的. ②不体面的;没礼貌的;不恰当的.

un·com·fort·a·ble [ʌnˈkʌmfətəbl] *a.* 不舒适的,不安的,不自在的. *be in an ～ predicament* 处境困难. **-a·bly** *ad.* **-ness** *n.*

un·com·mer·cial [ˈʌnkəˈməːʃəl] *a.* ①非商业(性质)的;非营利的. ②违反商业道德的.

un·com·mit·ted [ˈʌnkəˈmitid] *a.* ①(犯罪等)未遂的. ②不承担义务的,不受(诺言)约束的. ③尚未提交委员会的. ④未监禁的;未送入疯人院的. ⑤未被授权的,未受委托的. *an ～ crime* 未遂罪. *the ～ unit*【军】未投入战斗的部队.

un•com•mon [ʌn'kɔmən] *a.* 不平常的,不常见的;难得的,非常的,非凡的,珍奇的。— *ad.*〔卑口〕= uncommonly.

un•com•mon•ly [ʌn'kɔmənli] *ad.* 难得;非常,极其。~ *cold* 极冷。

un•com•mu•ni•ca•tive ['ʌnkə'mju:nikətiv] *a.* 不爱说话的,沉默寡言的,拘谨的。**-ness** *n.*

un•com•pan•ion•a•ble ['ʌn-kəm'pænjənəbl] *a.* 难相处的;不爱交际的。

un•com•plain•ing ['ʌnkəm'pleiniŋ] *a.* 没有怨言的,不诉苦的,不发牢骚的;坚忍的,有耐心的。**-ly** *ad.*

un•com•pli•men•ta•ry ['ʌnˌkɔmpli'metəri] *a.* 非赞美性的,贬抑的。

un•com•pro•mis•ing ['ʌn'kɔmprəmaiziŋ] *a.* 不让步的,不妥协的,不肯通融的;强硬的;坚决的;不屈的;严厉的。**-ly** *ad.*

un•con•cern ['ʌnkən'sə:n] *n.* 漫不经心,不关心,冷淡,不在乎,不介意。*with complete* ~ 十分冷淡,满不在乎。

un•con•cerned ['ʌnkən'sə:nd] *a.* ①漫不经心的,不关心的,冷淡的,满不在乎的 *(about)*。②与…没有关系的 *(in, with)*。③无私心的。**-ly** *ad.* **-ness** *n.*

un•con•di•tion•al ['ʌnkən'diʃənəl] *a.* 无条件的;无限制的;无保留的;绝对的。*an* ~ *surrender* 无条件投降。**-ly** *ad.*

un•con•di•tioned ['ʌnkən'diʃənd] *a.* ①无条件的,无限制的,绝对的。②无条件入学的。***the U-***【哲】绝对者。~ **reflex**【生】无条件反射。

un•con•fessed ['ʌn-kən'fest] *a.* 未认罪忏悔的;未供认的。

un•con•fined ['ʌn-kən'faind] *a.* ①无拘束的;自由的;无限制的。②(头发等)松散的。

un•con•firmed ['ʌn-kən'fə:md] *a.* ①未最后确定的。②未证实的;未确证的;未经认可的。③【宗】未受坚信礼的。

un•con•form•a•ble ['ʌn-kən'fɔ:məbl] *a.* ①不顺从的,不服从的。②不适合的;不一致的。③【地】不整合的。**-a•bly** *ad.*

un•con•form•i•ty ['ʌn-kən'fɔ:miti] *n.* ***(pl. -ties)*** ①不相符;不一致;不相称;不顺从。②【地】不整合;不整合面。

un•con•nect•ed ['ʌn-kə'nektid] *a.* ①不连结的;分开的。②不相关联的;不连贯的。③无亲属关系的。

un•con•quer•a•ble [ʌn'kɔŋkərəbl] *a.* 不可克服[征服]的;难压制的,遏制不了的。

un•con•scion•a•ble [ʌn'kɔnʃənəbl] *a.* ①不受良心控制的;肆无忌惮的。②无节制的,过度的。③不合理的,不公平的,【法】不正当的。*an* ~ *bargain*【法】不正当的契约。**-a•bly** *ad.*

un•con•scious [ʌn'kɔnʃəs] *a.* ①无意识的;失去知觉的,不省人事的。②不知道的,未发觉的 *(of)*。③无意的,不自觉的。*He was blissfully* ~ *of it all.* 他本人幸亏一点不晓得。— *n.*【心】无意识〔人不自觉的思想、欲望、行动等〕。**-ly** *ad.* 无意识地,无意中,不知不觉,不留神。**-ness** *n.*

un•con•sid•ered ['ʌn-kən'sidəd] *a.* ①不考虑的;未加考虑的。②轻率的;未经深思熟虑的。*a hasty,* ~ *remark* 脱口而出的莽撞话。

un•con•stant ['ʌn'kɔnstənt] *a.* = inconstant.

un•con•sti•tu•tion•al ['ʌnkɔnsti'tju:ʃənəl] *a.* 违反宪法的。**-ly** *ad.* **-i•ty** ['ʌnˌkɔnstiˌtju:ʃə'næliti] *n.* 违(反)宪(法)。

un•con•strained ['ʌn-kən'streind] *a.* ①不受强制的,自由的。②非强迫的,自发的,自动的。③(态度)不勉强的,从容的。**-ly** ['ʌn-kən'streinidli] *ad.*

un•con•straint ['ʌn-kən'streint] *n.* 无拘束,不受强制,自由,自愿。

un•con•tam•i•nat•ed ['ʌn-kən'tæmineitid] *a.* 没有被污染的;未沾染的。

un•con•tem•plat•ed ['ʌn'kontempleitid] *a.* ①未料想到的,意外的。②未经思考的。

un•con•test•ed ['ʌnkən'testid] *a.* ①无竞争者的,无竞争的。②无异议的;明白的,无议论余地的。

un•con•trol•la•ble [ˌʌn-kən'trəuləbl] *a.* 不能控制的,(孩子)无法管束的。

un•con•trolled ['ʌn-kən'trəuld] *a.* 未受控制的,无人管束的,自由的,无拘束的。**-ly** *ad.*

un•con•ven•tion•al ['ʌn-kən'venʃənəl] *a.* 非常规的;不按照习惯[惯例]的;不落陈套的。**-ly** *ad.* **-i•ty** ['ʌn-kənˌvenʃə'næliti] *n.*

un•con•vert•ed ['ʌn-kən'və:tid] *a.* ①(形态、作用等)无变化的。②未改变信仰的〔尤指未改信基督教的〕。

un•con•vert•i•ble ['ʌn-kən'və:təbl] *a.* 不能改变的,难变换的;不能兑换[兑现]的。**-bly** *ad.*

un•cooked ['ʌn'kukt] *a.* 未煮过的,生的。*eat* ~ 生吃。

un•cool ['ʌn'ku:l] *a.*〔俚〕①极易激动的。②打扰人的,使人不愉快的,粗野的。

un•co•op•er•a•tive ['ʌn-kəu'ɔpərətiv] *a.* 不合作的;不配合的。

un•co•or•di•nat•ed ['ʌn-kəu'ɔ:dineitid] *a.* ①不协调的。②不同等的;不对等的。

un•cord ['ʌn'kɔ:d] *vt.* 解开…的绳索;拆下(弓上的)弦。

un•cork ['ʌn'kɔ:k] *vt.* 拔去…的塞子[瓶塞];〔口〕吐露,说出(感情等)。**-ed** *a.*

un•cor•rect•able ['ʌn-kə'rektəbl] *a.* 不可挽回的,不可弥补的。

un•cor•rect•ed ['ʌn-kə'rektid] *a.* ①未经改正的;未修改的。②未加管教的,未受谴责的。③未调整的。

un•cor•rupt ['ʌn-kə'rʌpt] *a.* = uncorrupted.

un•cor•rupt•ed ['ʌnkə'rʌptid] *a.* 未腐败的;未堕落的;收买不动的,廉洁的。

un•cor•rupt•i•ble ['ʌn-kə'rʌptəbl] *a.* 不会腐败的;不能收买的 (= incorruptible).

un•count•a•ble ['ʌn'kauntəbl] *a.* ①不可数的。②数不清的;无法估量的。③无数的。— *n.*【语法】不可数名词。

un•count•ed ['ʌn'kauntid] *a.* ①没有数过的。②无数的。*a stack of* ~ *bills* 一叠没有数过的钞票。

un•coup•le ['ʌn'kʌpl] *vt.* 解开(车辆等的)连结挂钩;解开(把狗系在一起的)皮条;拆散,分离开。~ *railway trucks* 使车皮脱钩分开。*an* ~*d axle*【机】不联轴。*an* ~*d wheel* 活轮。— *vi.* 分开,脱开。*The glider* ~*d from the tow plane.* 滑翔机与拖机脱开。

un•cour•te•ous ['ʌn'kə:tiəs] *a.* 没礼貌的,粗野的。

un•couth [ʌn'ku:θ] *a.* ①笨拙的,粗野的,粗鲁的,不文明的。②〔古〕陌生的,没有见惯的;〔书〕(地方等)荒凉的;古怪的,怪异的。**-ly** *ad.* **-ness** *n.*

un•cov•e•nant•ed [ʌn'kʌvənəntid] *a.* ①无契约许可[保证、承认]的。②无契约条款约束[规定]的。

un•cov•er [ʌn'kʌvə] *vt.* ①去除…的遮盖物,打开…的盖子。②拿下(头上)戴的东西,脱(帽)。③使露出,揭露;使知道;【军】暴露;除去…的掩护。④将(狐)赶出。~ *the head* = ~ *oneself* 脱帽表示敬意。~ *one's heart to sb.* 对某人吐露心事。— *vi.* ①揭去盖子,拿掉覆盖物,掀开盖子。②脱帽致敬。

un•cov•ered [ʌn'kʌvəd] *a.* ①无遮盖的;暴露的;无掩护的。②未经保险的;无附加担保的。③不戴帽的。④不包括在服务范围之内的。*an* ~ *shed* 无遮盖的小棚。~ *legs* 裸露的腿。

un•cracked [ʌn'krækt] *a.* 未裂开的;无裂缝的。~ *asphalt* 未裂化沥青。

un•krate ['ʌn'kreit] *vt.* 拆箱取出(货物)。

un•cre•at•ed ['ʌnkri'eitid] *a.* ①尚未创造出来的;不存在的。②【神学】永生的,永存的;自存的。

un•crit•i•cal ['ʌn'kritikəl] *a.* ①无批判力的;批评不当

的. ②不加批判的;不加鉴别的.

un·cropped [ˈʌnˈkrɔpt] *a.* ①未收割的; 未采摘的. ②(头发、毛等)未修剪的; 未剪短的. ③(土地)未种植的; 无收获的.

un·cross [ʌnˈkrɔːs] *vt.* 使不交叉. ~ *one's leg* 把交叉的腿分开. **-ed** ①未遇妨碍的,未受挫折的. ②〔英〕(支票)未划线的. ③未被划掉[取消]的.

un·crown [ˈʌnˈkraun] *vt.* = dethrone.

un·crush·a·ble [ˈʌnˈkrʌʃəbl] *a.* ①压不碎的; 压不住的. ②揉不皱的.

UNCTAD = United Nations Conference on Trade and Development 联合国贸易和发展会议.

unc·tion [ˈʌŋkʃən] *n.* ①【宗】涂油礼;【医】药膏涂布. ②涂油礼用的油;油膏;〔喻〕安慰物,甜言蜜语. ③(宗教性的)热情,感激. ④(做作出来的)感动,同情. ⑤热心;兴趣. *Lay not that flattering* ~ *to your soul.* 不要在你的灵魂上涂抹那种使你感到自慰的香膏吧. *give the dying man extreme* ~ (神父)给临终的人行涂油礼.

unc·tu·os·i·ty [ˌʌŋktjuˈɔsiti] *n.* ①油性, 油滑. ②(某些矿石给予触觉的)油滑感. ③(土壤的)松软肥沃. ④可塑性. ⑤油腔滑调.

unc·tu·ous [ˈʌŋktjuəs] *a.* ①油性的,油质的;油腻的;滑溜的;(土壤)松软的. ②塑性的. ③甜言蜜语的;(装作)虔诚的,热忱的,假殷勤的,假情假义的. **-ly** *ad.* **-ness** *n.*

un·cul·ti·vat·ed [ˈʌnˈkʌltiveitid] *a.* ①未经耕作的,未开垦的. ②未经磨炼的;没有教养的,粗野的,未开化的.

un·curl [ˈʌnˈkəːl] *vt.* 把(卷发等)弄直;展开. ~*ed hair* 不卷曲的头发. *lie* ~*ed on the bed* 直挺挺地躺在床上. — *vi.* 变直,伸直;伸开,展开.

un·cus [ˈʌŋkəs] *n.* (*pl.* **un·ci** [-sai])【解】(昆虫的)爪形突.

un·cut [ˈʌnˈkʌt] *a.* ①未切割[修剪]的. ②(宝石等)未琢磨的. ③(书)尚未切边的,毛边的. ④未删削的.

un·cy·ber·nat·ed [ˈʌnˌsaibəˈneitid] *a.* 非电子化的.

un·damped [ˈʌnˈdæmpt] *a.* ①不潮湿的; 不沮丧的; 不气馁的. ②【电】无衰减的,无阻尼的,等幅的.

un·dat·ed [ˈʌnˈdeitid] *a.* ①没有注明日期的. ②日期[期限]不一定的. ③(一生)无突出事件的.

un·daunt·ed [ʌnˈdɔːntid] *a.* 无畏的, 勇敢的; 刚毅的. **-ly** *ad.* **-ness** *n.*

UNDC United Nations Disarmament Commission 联合国裁军委员会.

un·dé, un·dée [ˈʌndei] *a.*【纹】波状的.

un·dec·a·gon [ʌnˈdekəˈgɔn] *n.* 十一边形; 十一角形.

un·de·ceive [ˈʌndiˈsiːv] *vt.* 使不再受骗,使醒悟,打破…的迷梦. ~ *sb. of his mistakes* 使某人明白自己的错误. **be** ~**d** 醒悟过来;不再抱幻想.

un·de·cid·ed [ˈʌndiˈsaidid] *a.* ①未决的, 未定的. ②(天气等)不稳定的. ③优柔寡断的. ④(形状等)不明确的,模糊的. **-ness** *n.*

un·de·clared [ˈʌndiˈkleəd] *a.* ①未经宣布的. ②不公开的. ③未向海关申报的.

un·dec·y·le·nic [ˌʌndesiˈliːnik, -ˈlenik] **acid**【化】十一碳烯酸.

un·de·fend·ed [ˈʌndiˈfendid] *a.* ①未设防的. ②无充分论据[理由]的. ③无人为之辩护的; 无辩护的. *an* ~ *city* 不设防城市.

un·de·filed [ˈʌndiˈfaild] *a.* 没有弄脏的,未玷污的;纯洁的;纯粹的.

un·de·fined [ˈʌndiˈfaind] *a.* ①未下定义的, 不用定义解释的. ②不明确规定的;模糊的.

un·dem·o·crat·ic [ˈʌndeməˈkrætik] *a.* 不[非]民主的.

un·de·mon·stra·ble [ˈʌnˈdemənstrəbl] *a.* 无法表明的;不可论证的.

un·de·mon·stra·tive [ˈʌndiˈmɔnstrətiv] *a.* 不露声色的,克制的,谨慎的. **-ly** *ad.* **-ness** *n.*

un·de·ni·a·ble [ʌndiˈnaiəbl] *a.* ①不可否认的,无法抵赖的,无可争辩的;不可否定的. ②无可疵议的,优秀的. **-a·bly** *ad.*

un·de·nom·i·na·tion·al [ˈʌndiˌnɔmiˈneiʃənəl] *a.* 不属于任何宗派[教派]的;无宗派[教派]拘束的;非宗派的.

un·der [ˈʌndə] *prep.* ①〔位置〕在…下;在表面之下,在…内部;被…遮蔽着;在…脚下,在…底下. ~ *a tree* 在树下. ~ *the skin* 在皮下. ~ *cover* 在掩蔽之下. *a field* ~ *grass* 长满了草的田地. ~ *water* 在水下. ~ *a hill* 在山脚下. ~ *the sun* 在阳光下;天下,在世界上. ②〔从属关系〕(a) 隶属[从属, 指导]之下. ~ *the British government* 隶属在英国政府之下. *study* ~ *Dr. Eliot* 在埃利奥特博士指导下研究. (b) 附属…之下, 归属于. *come* ~ *this head* 包含在本项目中. ~ *Article 43* 在第四十三条下. ③处在某种作用、条件、状态等下或某一期间、过程中. *groan* ~ *tyranny* 在残暴压制下呻吟. ~ *medical treatment* 在治疗中. *land* ~ *the plough* = *land* ~ *cultivation* 耕地. ~ *the influence of drink* 酒醉. *He tottered* ~ *a heavy load.* 他在重担下摇摇晃晃地走. *It is forbidden* ~ *pain of death.* 违犯者处死. *I am* ~ *an engagement to go.* 我有约会要去. ④〔程度、量值、等级〕(地位)低于…,比…低级的;(年龄、时间、价格、数量等)在…以下(的),未满…(的), 不足…(的). ~ *cooling* 过冷. ~ *the hour* 在该时间内. *No one* ~ *a captain can hold the post.* 海军上校以下不能担任此职. *children* ~ *twelve years old* 未满十二岁的儿童. ⑤在某种名义、口实下;以…为代表. ~ *a false name* 用假名. ~ *the mask of friendship* 借友谊为名,在友谊的伪装下. ~ *a new name* 换用新名字. ⑥根据, 依据, 按照. ~ *the law* 根据法律. ~ ***age*** 未成年(未满二十一岁). ~ ***sb.'s hand and seal*** 经某人签名盖章. ~ ***arms*** 武装着,手执武器. ~ ***avow*** 发过誓,在誓言下. ~ ***favour*** 如果允许(这样说)的话〔多作插入句〕. ~ ***fire*** 在弹雨下,冒着炮火 (*land* ~ *fire* 在炮火下登陆). ~ ***foot*** 地上 (*It was wet* ~ *foot* 地上潮湿); 在脚下(踩着). ~ ***night*** 〔Scot.〕在夜间. ~ ***one's breath*** 小声,低声. ~ ***sb.'s (very) eye*** 在某人眼皮底下,显而易见. ~ ***the line***【海】在赤道下. ***with a good meal*** ~ ***one's belt*** 饱餐一顿. — *ad.* ①在下,从属着,服从着. *bring* ~, *get* ~, *keep* ~ 等, 参看各该动词条. *The ship went* ~. 船下沉了. ②在下文中. *See* ~ *for further information.* 更详尽资料见下文. ③少于,低于. *five dollars or* ~ 五美元或五美元以下. — *a.* ①下面的,下部的 (*opp.* upper);附属的,从属的. ②较次的; 低劣的. ③过少的,过小的,不足的. *the* ~ *lip* 下唇. ~ *servants* 仆役的下手. ~ *grazing* 轻度放牧.

under- *comb. f.* 表示: ①"在以下","下面[下方]的": *under*ground. ②"次于","低于": *under*secretary, *under*graduate. ③"不足","不够","不充分": *under*act, *under*develop.

un·der·a·chieve [ˈʌndərəˈtʃiːv] *vi.* (**-chiev·ed; -chiev·ing**) 学校学习成绩低于智力测验所得的分数. **-ment** *n.* **-r** *n.* 学校学习成绩低于智力商数的学生.

un·der·act [ˈʌndərˈækt] *vt., vi.* 表演(角色)不足[不充分],表演得含蓄.

un·der·ad·ver·tis·ing [ˈʌndəˈrædvətaiziŋ] *n.* 宣传不够,广告做得不够.

un·der·age[1] [ˈʌndəˈeidʒ] *a.* ①未成年的. ②未到法定年龄的.

un·der·age[2] [ˈʌndəridʒ] *n.* 短少;不足.

un·der·arm [ˈʌndərɑːm] *ad.*【板球、网球】用低手,手在肩下部动作 (= underhand). — *a.* ①手臂下的, 腋下的. ②【板球,网球】低手击出[扔出]的.

un·der·armed [ˈʌndəˈɑːmd] *a.* 武器装备不足的; 武装得不充分的.

un·der·bel·ly [ˈʌndəbeli] *n.* ①下腹部. ②〔喻〕薄弱部位;易受攻击的区域.

un·der·bid [ˈʌndəˈbid] *vt.* ***(~; un·der·bid·den*** [ˈʌndəˈbidn],~***)*** ①(投标时)出价低于(他人). ②【牌】以低于可能的得分叫牌. ③愿以较低报酬做(某事); 以低价售出. — *vi.* ①(投标时)出价不足; 出价过低. ②【桥牌】叫牌过低.

un·der·bod·y [ˈʌndəˌbɔdi] *n.* ①动物下体. ②车身底板. ③船体水下部分.

un·der·bought [ˈʌndəˈbɔːt] underbuy 的过去式和过去分词.

un·der·bred [ˈʌndəˈbred] *a.* ①缺乏教养的, 没有礼貌的,粗野不文的. ②(马)不是纯种的.

un·der·brush, un·der·bush [ˈʌndəbrʌʃ, -buʃ] *n.* (树林内的)下层林丛,矮树丛,乱丛棵子.

un·der·buy [ˈʌndəˈbai] ***(-bought*** [-bɔːt]***)*** *vt.* 买得比市价[别人]便宜.

un·der·cap·i·tal·ize [ˈʌndəˈkæpitəlaiz] *vt., vi.* ***(-iz·ed; -iz·ing)*** (对…)投资不足. **-tal·i·za·tion** *n.*

un·der·car·riage [ˈʌndəkæridʒ] *n.* ①(车辆, 重武器的)下部构造,底架,下架,底盘. ②飞机脚架,起落架.

un·der·charge [ˈʌndəˈtʃɑːdʒ] *vt.* ①对(买方)少要[少算]价钱. ②给…充电不足; 给…少填火药.

un·der·class·man [ˌʌndəˈklɑːsmən] *n.* ***(pl. -men)*** (大学的)低年级生〔一、二年级〕.

un·der·clay [ˈʌndə-klei] *n.* 【矿】底粘土, 煤层底粘土层.

un·der·clerk [ˈʌndəˈklɑːk] *n.* 下级职员[办事员],助理办事员.

un·der·cliff [ˈʌndə-klif] *n.*【地】(因滑坡或坍塌而形成的)副崖,阶地.

un·der·clothed [ˈʌndəkləuðd] *a.* 穿得单薄的.

un·der·clothes [ˈʌndəkləuðz, -kləuz] *n. pl.* 内衣裤,衬衣裤; 汗衫,贴身衣. ★可用 many 修饰,但不可与数字连用.

un·der·clothing [ˈʌndəkləuðiŋ] *n.* = underclothes.

un·der·coat [ˈʌndəkəut] *n.* ①大衣内的上衣. ②〔口〕(女用)衬裙. ③(动物长毛下面的)浓密的绒毛. ④(涂在车辆底部的)底部防锈层; (上漆之前的)内涂层. — *vt.* 给…加内涂层.

un·der·cool [ˈʌndəˈkuːl] *vt., vi.* (使)过度冷却 (= supercool).

under·cover [ˌʌndəˈkʌvə, ˈʌndəˌkʌvə] *a.* 秘密的,暗中进行的,隐蔽的,掩蔽下的. *an ~ scheme* 密谋.

un·der·croft [ˈʌndə-krɔft] *n.* 地下室, 地穴〔尤指教堂的墓穴〕.

un·der·cur·rent [ˈʌndəˌkʌrənt] *n.* ①(水流等的)底流, 潜流. ②(时势等的)暗流, 潜在倾向, 潜伏的情绪. ③【电】电流不足. ④【矿】(宽平的)分支洗金槽.

un·der·cut [ˈʌndəkʌt] *n.* ①〔英〕(牛、猪的)里脊肉. ②〔美〕(伐木的)砍伐切口; 伐采不足量. ③【焊】咬边; 下陷. ④(网球等)下旋球;【高尔夫球】逆削打法;【拳击】由下上击. — [ˈʌndəˈkʌt] *vt., vi.* ***(-cut)*** ①从下切割[斫伐]; 切去(…的)下部; 砍进,挖. ②(网球等)用下旋手法击(球); 【高尔夫】用逆削法打(球); 【商】削低(商品)价格; 削价与(竞争者等)抢生意; 愿领较低报酬和(他人)抢做某工作. — *a.* 下部被削去[切去、挖掉、凿去]的.

un·der·de·vel·op [ˈʌndədiˈveləp] *vt., vi.* ①(使)发展不充分. ②【摄】(使)显影不足.

un·der·de·vel·oped [ˈʌndədiˈveləpt] *a.* ①发展不充分的,不发达的〔尤指经济和工业不够发达, 以致生活水平相对低下的〕. ②【摄】显影不足的. *~ nations* 不发达国家.

un·der·do [ˈʌndəˈduː] *vt., vi.* ***(-did*** [-ˈdid]***; -done*** [-ˈdʌn]***)*** ①嫩煮,嫩烤(肉等). ②不尽全力地做, 少做; (使)做得不够.

un·der·dog [ˈʌndədɔg] *n.* ①斗输了的狗; 失败者; 打败了的选手. ②退居下风的人; 〔美〕地位低的人, 受压迫的人.

un·der·done [ˈʌndəˈdʌn] *a.* 〔英〕烤[煮]得嫩的; 半生不熟的.

un·der·dose [ˈʌndədəus] *vt.* 使服少量 [低于通常剂量] 的药. — *n.* 小药量,不足的剂量.

un·der·drain [ˈʌndədrein] *n.* 阴沟,暗渠,地下沟道. — [ˈʌndəˈdrein] *vt.* 用暗渠排去 (…处)的水. **-age** *n.* 地下排水.

un·der·draw [ˈʌndəˈdrɔː] *vt.* ***(-drew*** [-ˈdruː]***; -drawn*** [-ˈdrɔːn]***)*** ①描画[描写]不充分. ②在…下划线. **-ing** *n.* 底稿.

un·der·draw·ers [ˈʌndədrɔːəz] *n. pl.* 衬裤.

un·der·dress [ˈʌndəˈdrəs] *vt., vi.* (使)穿着得不够郑重, (使)穿过分朴素的服装; (使)穿单薄的衣服. — [ˈʌndədres] *n.* = underclothes.

un·der·em·ployed [ˌʌndəimˈplɔid] *a.* ①未充分就业的〔尤指非全日性雇佣, 以致生活水平低下的〕. ②未按专长雇佣的〔本是技工,干的是技术性很低的工作, 故工资低微〕.

un·der·em·ploy·ment [ˌʌndəimˈplɔimənt] *n.* ①未充分就业. ②未按专长就业.

un·der·es·ti·mate [ˈʌndərˈestimeit] *vt.* 估低; 把…的价值估计过低; 看轻; 估计不足. — *n.* 过低估价,过低评价; 轻视; 估计不足(= underestimation).

un·der·ex·pose [ˈʌndərikˈspəuz] *vt.* ***(-posed; -pos·ing)*** 【摄】使(底片等)曝光不足. **-ex·po·sure** [-ˈspəuʒə] *n.*

un·der·fed [ˈʌndəˈfed] underfeed 的过去式和过去分词. — *a.* 没有喂饱[吃饱]的; 营养不良的.

un·der·feed [ˈʌndəˈfiːd] *vt.* ***(-fed*** [-ˈfed]***)*** ①不给…充分的食物, 不喂饱. ②不供给…充分的燃料. ③从下部给…进料. —*vi.* 减食,吃得不够.

un·der·fired[1] [ˌʌndəˈfaiəd] *a.* (陶器)烧得不够的.

un·der·fired[2] [ˈʌndəˌfaiəd] *a.* (锅炉等的)从下生火[加热]的.

un·der·flow [ˈʌndəfləu] *n.* = undercurrent.

un·der·foot [ˌʌndəˈfut] *ad.* ①在脚下; 践踏,蹂躏; 贱视. ②〔美口〕挡道,妨碍人, 碍手碍脚. — *a.* ①在脚下的, 在地上的. ②〔美口〕碍事的.

un·der·fur [ˈʌndəfəː] *n.* (河狸、海豹等长毛下面的)细软绒毛.

un·der·gar·ment [ˈʌndəgɑːmənt] *n.* 衬衣,内衣.

un·der·gird [ˈʌndəˈgəːd] *vt.* ***(-gird·ed*** [-ˈgəːdid], ***-girt*** [-ˈgəːt]***; -girding)*** ①(用绳索等) 从底层捆牢[加固]. ②对…给予支持[提供雄厚基础].

un·der·glaze [ˈʌndəgleiz] *a.*【制陶】(陶瓷的花样、色彩等)上釉之前画[着色]的, 釉底的. — *n.* 釉下画; 釉底色彩.

un·der·go [ʌndəˈgəu] *vt.* ***(-went*** [-ˈwent]***; -gone*** [-ˈgɔn]***)*** 经受(检阅、考验等); 经验, 经历(变迁等); 遭受(苦难等).

un·der·grad [ˌʌndəˈgræd] *n.* 〔口〕*n., a.* = undergraduate.

un·der·grad·u·ate [ˌʌndəˈgrædjuit] *n., a.* (肄业中的)大学生(的).

un·der·grad·u·ette [ʌndəgrædjuˈet] *n.* 〔谑〕大学女生.

un·der·ground [ˈʌndəgraund] *a.* ①地(面)下的. ②隐蔽的,秘密的. ③(电影,报刊等)标新立异的,试刊的,试验性而非正式的. ④反传统的, 反现存体制的, 激进的,(艺术等)先锋派的. — *n.* 地面下层; 地下空间, 地道; 〔英〕地下铁道 (=〔美〕subway); 〔the ~〕地下活动,地下组织. *an ~ cellar* 地下室,地窖. *~ water* 地下水. *~ intrigues* 阴谋. *~ movement* 地下活动. *~ party* 地下团体,秘密组织. — [ˈʌndəˈgraund] *ad.* 在地下; 秘密地, 偷偷地. *go ~* 潜入地下. *~* **railway** [〔美〕 ~ **railroad, subway**] 地下铁道;【美史】〔常作 U- R-〕(反蓄奴组织帮助黑人逃亡到非蓄奴州或加拿大去的) 地下渠道[组织]. ~ **savages** 〔海俚〕轮机室工作人员.

un·der·grown [ˈʌndəˈgrəun] *a.* 发育不全的,未长足的.

un·der·growth [ˈʌndəgrəuθ] *n.* ①林下植物，下层林丛，矮树丛，乱丛棵子．②(兽毛下的) 绒毛．③发育不全．

un·der·hand [ˈʌndəhænd] *a., ad.* ①【板球、网球】低位手的[地]〔手的位置在肩或肘的水平线下〕；低手扔[打]的[地]；(射箭)瞄准时目标见于左手下方的[地]．②秘密的[地]；不光明正大的[地]，阴险的[地]，卑鄙的[地]．

un·der·hand·ed [ˈʌndəhændid] *a.* ①秘密的，暗中的，不光明正大的．②人手不足的．**-ly** *ad.* **-ness** *n.*

un·der·hung [ˈʌndəˈhʌŋ] *a.* ①下颚突出的．②【木工】自下承接的；(拉门)靠轮子拉动的；在轨道上滑动的．*an ~ spring* 悬簧．

un·der·kill [ˈʌndəkil] *n.* 核杀伤力不足；不足以达到特定目的的活动．

un·der·laid [ˈʌndəˈleid] *a.* ①放置于下的；【矿】向下延伸的．②有垫层的，有底基层的，有下支撑物的．

un·der·lap [ˌʌndəˈlæp] *vt.* ***(-lap·ped; -lap·ping)*** 使(某物)局部置于[延伸于](另一物)之下；(伸展时)使部分重叠．

un·der·lay [ˌʌndəˈlei] ***(-laid*** [-ˈleid]***)*** *vt.* (以某物)铺在…的下面；【印】衬垫．— *vi.*【矿】(矿脉等)向下延伸．— [ˈʌndəlei] *n.* ①【印】下衬．②(垫在地毯下的)油纸、油布(等)．③【矿】向下延伸矿体．

un·der·lease [ˈʌndəliːs]*n.*【法】转租，转借．

un·der·let [ˈʌndəˈlet] *vt.* ***(~)*** 廉价租出；转租，转借．

un·der·lie [ˌʌndəˈlai] *vt.* ***(-lay*** [-ˈlei]***; -lain*** [-ˈlein]***; -lying)*** ①位处在…下面；成为…的基础．②【经】拥有优先于…的权利，作为优先于…的担保[抵押品]．③【语】成为(派生语的)语根．

un·der·line[1] [ˌʌndəˈlain] *vt.* ①划线于…下面，给…划字下线；加强，强调；使突出．②在(戏单下面)预告下期节目．— [ˈʌndəlain] *n.* ①字下线．②(戏单下面的)下期预告．③图下说明文字．

un·der·line[2] [ˌʌndəˈlain] *vt.* 作…的衬里；衬在…下面．

un·der·lin·en [ˈʌndəlinin] *n.* (麻布)衬衣，内衣．

un·der·ling [ˈʌndəliŋ] *n.*〔蔑〕下属，下手．

un·der·lin·ing [ˌʌndəˈlainiŋ] *n.* (衣服的)里子，衬料．

un·der·lip [ˈʌndəˈlip] *n.* 下唇．

un·der·ly·ing [ˈʌndəˈlaiiŋ] *a.* ①在下的，下层的．②基础的．③隐晦的；潜在的．④【法】(债券)优先的；【经】第一的，(担保、权利等)主要的．*the ~ mortgage* 第一担保[抵押]．

un·der·man [ˈʌndəˈmæn] *vt.* 给(船只等)配备人员过少．

un·der·manned [ˈʌndəˈmænd] *a.* 人员[手]不足的．

un·der·men·tion·ed [ˈʌndəˈmenʃənd] *a.* 下述的．

un·der·mine [ˌʌndəˈmain] *vt.* 掘…的下面，在…下面掘地道，暗掘；冲蚀；削弱…的基础；用阴险手段毁损，暗中破坏(名声等)；伤害(健康等)．*~ a fortress* 挖地道破坏堡垒．**-r** *n.*

un·der·most [ˈʌndəməust] *a.,ad.* 最下(位)的[地]，最低的[地]．

un·der·neath [ˈʌndəˈniːθ] *ad.* ①在下面[底下]．②在下部[下层]．*Someone was pushing up from ~.* 有人在下面往上推．*wear wool ~* (外衣)里面穿着毛线衫．*a house rotten ~* 底部已经坍坏的房屋．*He got ~ the skin of his audience* 他深入了听众的内心．— *prep.* ①在…的下面[下部]．②在…的支配下，隶属于…．③〔古〕在…的形式下，在…的幌子下．*the river flowing ~ the bridge* 在桥下流过的河．*sit ~ a tree* 坐在树下．*~ the yoke of ...* 在…的枷锁下．— *a.* ①下面的；底层的；较低的．②潜在的，字里行间的．*~ meanings* 字里行间的意义，弦外之音．— *n.* 下部，下面．

un·der·nour·ish [ˈʌndəˈnʌriʃ] *vt.* 使营养不足；使吃不饱．**-ed** *a.* 营养不足的．**-ment** *n.* 营养不足．

un·der·pants [ˈʌndəˌpænts] *n. pl.* 衬裤．

un·der·part [ˈʌndəpɑːt] *n.* ①(动物的)下体；(飞机机身的)腹部．②附属地位；次要角色．

un·der·pass [ˈʌndəpɑːs] *n.*〔美〕(在铁路等下面通过的)地道；下穿交叉道；高架桥下通道．

un·der·pay [ˈʌndəˈpei] *vt.* ***(-paid*** [-peid]***)*** ①付得太少，付得不足．②少付…工资，扣付…工资．**-ment** *n.*

un·der·pin [ˌʌndəˈpin] *vt.* 从下方支持，用东西支撑(建筑物等)；加固，使坚固；支援，支持．**-pin·ning** *n.* ①加支柱；支柱，支持物；支承结构，支承基础，墙基；支援．②〔口〕〔常作 *pl.*〕腿．

un·der·play [ˈʌndəˈplei] *vt., vi.* ①表演得不充分；故意地不作充分表演．②【牌戏】扣着(大牌)不出而出小牌；未充分发挥(手中大牌)的威力．— [ˈʌndəplei] *n.* 含蓄克制的表演；暗中活动；出小牌．

un·der·plot [ˈʌndəplɔt] *n.* ①(小说、戏剧等的) 次要情节，穿插．②阴谋诡计．

un·der·priv·i·leged [ˈʌndəˈprivilidʒd] *n.*〔the ~〕〔总称〕部分基本权利被剥夺的阶层；〔婉〕社会地位低下的阶层．— *a.* 享受不到正当权利的；贫困的；社会地位低下的，在社会下层的．

un·der·pro·duc·tion [ˈʌndə-prəˈdʌkʃən] *n.* 生产不足(以满足需求)．

under·proof(ed) [ˌʌndəˈpruːf(d)] *a.* 含酒精成分在标准强度以下的．*~ spirit* 纯度低于标准的酒精．

un·der·prop [ˌʌndəˈprɔp] *vt.* ***(-propped; prop·ping)*** 支撑于下；支撑；支持．

un·der·quote [ˈʌndəˈkwəut] *vt.* ***(-quot·ed; -quot·ing)*** ①对(货物)报价过低；报价低于(别的价格)；报价低于(市场价格)．②报价低于(其他售者)．

un·der·rate [ˌʌndəˈreit] *vt.* 估低，贬低；看轻，轻视．

un·der·run [ˈʌndəˈrʌn] *vt.* ***(-ran*** [-ˈræn]***; ~)*** ①在…下通过[跑过，穿过，伸展]．②【海】拉起(缆绳等)从头到尾检查，乘小船沿(缆绳)下方检查．*The boat underran the bridge.* 那只船从桥下驶过．— *n.* ①在下通过的东西；暗流．②低于估计的产量．

un·der·score [ˌʌndəˈskɔː] *vt.* 在…下面划线；强调．— *n.* [ˈʌndəskɔː] 字下线．

un·der·sea [ˌʌndəˈsiː] *a., ad.* 海面以下，海底的[地]．*ad.* 也作 **un·der·seas**.

un·der·sec·re·ta·ry [ˈʌndəˈsekritəri] *n.* 副部长，次长．*Under-Secretary of State*〔美〕副国务卿．

un·der·sell [ˈʌndəˈsel] *vt.* ***(-sold*** [-ˈsəuld]***)*** 以低于别人的价格出售；廉价出售．

un·der·set[1] [ˈʌndəˈset] *vt.* ***(~)*** ①支撑；支持；放在…下面．②〔英〕转租，转借．

un·der·set[2] [ˈʌndəset] *n.* (和海面流向或风向相反的)底流；【矿】下部矿脉．

un·der·sexed [ˈʌndəˈsekst] *a.* 性欲不强的，性欲冷淡的．

un·der·sher·iff [ˈʌndəˌʃerif] *n.* 副郡长，县副警长．

un·der·shirt [ˈʌndəʃəːt] *n.* (衬衫里面的)汗衫，贴身内衣．

un·der·shoot [ˌʌndəˈʃuːt] *vt.* ***(-shot*** [-ˈʃɔt]***; -shoot·ing)*** ①(发射炮弹、射箭等)因角度太低而脱(靶)，因射程太短而未达(目标)．②(飞机因失速等) 降落未达(跑道，着陆场)．— *vi.* 脱靶，未达目标．

un·der·shorts [ˈʌndəˌʃɔːts] *n. pl.* (男人和儿童穿的)裤衩．

un·der·shot [ˈʌndəʃɔt] *a.* 下射的，(水轮)下击的；下部[下半部]突出的．

un·der·shrub [ˈʌndəʃrʌb] *n.* 小灌木(丛)．

un·der·side [ˈʌndəsaid] *n.* 下面；内面；下腹．

un·der·sign [ˌʌndəˈsain] *vt.* 在(文件、信等)的下面[后面]签名．***the ~ed*** [ˈʌndəsaind] 在下面签名者〔用作单或复〕．

un·der·size(d) [ˈʌndəˈsaiz(d)] *a.* ①比普通小的，小型的；个子小的；不够大的．②(矿砂等)经过一定规格筛孔中筛下的．

un·der·skirt [ˈʌndəˈskəːt] *n.* 衬裙．

un·der·slung [ˈʌndəˈslʌŋ] *a.* ①(汽车底盘)装附于车轴弹簧上的。②重心在底部的，下大上小的。③(嘴合拢后)下齿突出于上齿外的,突下颌的。

un·der·soil [ˈʌndəsɔil] *n.* 心土,底土,地面下的土壤。

un·der·song [ˈʌndəˌsɔŋ] *n.* 【乐】(歌曲的)伴唱附歌；〔喻〕言外之意。

un·der·staffed [ˈʌndəˈstɑːft, -ˈstæft] *a.* 人员过少的；人手不足的。

un·der·stand [ˌʌndəˈstænd] *vt.* ***(-stood** [-ˈstud], 〔古〕**-ed, -standing)*** ①懂得；了解,明白,理解,领悟,领会(真意等)；熟悉,通晓(学问等)；知道，晓得对付(孩子、马等)。②听说,获悉。③推测,推定,以为；以为当然。④〔常用被动语态〕隐含，不言而喻地省略(话等)。*Do you ~ me?* 你懂我的意思吗？*He ~s French.* 他懂法语。*I fail to ~ the reason.* 我不了解那个理由。*Am I to ~ that you refuse?* 你是说不愿意吗？*Please ~ me, I absolutely refuse.* 请你不要弄错,我是绝对拒绝的。*I ~ him to say that ...* 我以为他是说…。*Do I ~ (you to say) that ...?* 那么你是说…吗？*In this case the verb may be understood.* 这种情形动词可以省掉。— *vi.* ①懂得,了解,明白，理解；有理解力。②谅解。③听说。*When you speak Japanese she cannot ~.* 你讲日语她不懂。*Do animals ~?* 动物有理解力吗？*He is ill, I ~.* 我听说他生病了。***a tongue not ~ed of the people*** 异邦之言，外国语。***give sb. to ~ that*** 通知某人…,告诉某人…；使某人领会…(*He gave me to ~ that ...* 他说…)。***It is understood that*** 当然…；不用说…。***It must be understood that ...*** 话得说明白…。***make oneself understood*** 使自己的意思为人了解,说明自己的意思(*Can you make yourself understood in English?* 你能用英语说明你的意思吗？)。***Now, ~ me!*** 喂,听着！〔常表示惊恐或警告〕。***~ one another*** 互相了解,互相谅解,互相同情(而要好起来)。**-a·ble** *a.* 可懂的,可理解的。

un·der·stand·ing [ˌʌndəˈstændiŋ] *n.* ①认识,了解,理解,领悟,理会。②悟性,理解力,智力；【哲】知性 〔*opp.* reason〕。③谅解；同情；默契；协议；约定,条件。④〔*pl.*〕〔英俚、谑〕鞋；脚。*It is a matter of ~.* 那是认识问题。*a man of ~* 头脑清楚的人。*a man without ~* 头脑不清楚的人。*a tacit ~* 默契。***arrive at [come to] an ~ with*** 和…取得谅解,和…达成(非正式的)协议。***have [keep] a good ~ with*** 和…意见一致。***on the ~ that ...*** 以…为条件。***on this ~ = with this ~*** 以这条件，在这一谅解之下。— *a.* ①能体谅别人的,通情达理的。②明智的,聪明的,颖悟的。*an ~ man* 通情达理的人。

un·der·state [ˈʌndəˈsteit] *vt.* ①打着折扣说，有意识地轻描淡写；少报(损失等),少说(能力、要求等) (*opp.* exaggerate)。**-ment** *n.* 保守的说法，谨慎的陈述；压低估计；少报。

un·der·stock[1] [ˈʌndəˈstɔk] *vt.* ①不充分供应,使存货不充足。②不充分供应(农场等)牲畜。— [ˈʌndəstɔk] *n.* 存货不足。

un·der·stock[2] [ˈʌndəstɔk] *n.* 【植】①(嫁接用的)砧木。

un·der·stood [ˌʌndəˈstud] understand 的过去式及过去分词。— *a.* ①得到充分理解的。②取得同意的。③不言自明的。

un·der·strap·per [ˈʌndəstræpə] *n.* 〔口〕= underling.

un·der·stra·tum [ˈʌndəˈstreitəm] *n.* *(pl.* ***~s, -ta*** [-tə]*)* = substratum.

un·der·strength [ˈʌndəˈstreŋθ] *a.* ①力量不足的,强度不够的。②兵员不足的。

un·der·struc·ture [ˈʌndəˌstrʌktʃə] *n.* 基础,下层结构。

un·der·stud·y [ˈʌndəstʌdi] *vt.* ①【剧】练习做(临时替角)；临时代替(某演员)演出。②实地研习，实习(某工作)。— *n.* ①垫角,临时替角,候补演员；〔美运〕候补队员。②候补人员；生力军。

un·der·sur·face [ˈʌndəˈsəːfis] *n.* 底面。— *a.* 水面下的；表面下的。*an ~ craft* 潜水艇。

un·der·take [ˌʌndəˈteik] *vt.* ***(-took*** [-ˈtuk]***; -ta·ken*** [-ˈteikən]*)* ①承担；承办；答应,约定 (*to do sth.*)。②担保,保证(*that*)。③断言(*that*)。④着手,从事。⑤〔古〕向…挑战。*He undertook to be here at ten o'clock.* 他答应十点钟到这儿来。*~ a dangerous task* 承担一件危险任务。— *vi.* ①〔古〕担保,保证,负责,做证人(*for*)；应承,约定。②[ˈʌndəteik]〔口〕承办丧事。*He undertook for her security.* 他保证她的安全。

un·der·tak·er [ˌʌndəˈteikə] *n.* ①承担人,承办人；计划者,营业者。②[ˈʌndəteikə] 殡仪事业经营人。

un·der·tak·ing [ˌʌndəˈteikiŋ] *n.* ①计划,企图；承办(承包)；事业,企业；工作。②担保，保证，应承，约定。③[ˈʌndəteikiŋ] 殡仪事业。*welfare ~s* 生活福利事业。

un·der·ten·ant [ˈʌndəˈtenənt] *n.* 转租的承租人。

under-the-counter [ˈʌndəðəˈkauntə] *a.* 〔口〕①秘密(出售)的；走后门的；非法的。②稀罕的,贵重的。

under-the-table [ˈʌndəðəˈteibl] *a.* 秘密的,暗中进行的。

un·der·things [ˈʌndəθiŋz] *n. pl.* (女用)内衣裤。

un·der·tint [ˈʌndətint] *n.* 淡色；浅色；柔和的颜色。

un·der·tone [ˈʌndətəun] *n.* ①低音；小声。②潜在性质〔成分,意义〕；(市场的)潜在趋势。③浅色,淡色；底色。

un·der·took [ˌʌndəˈtuk] undertake 的过去式。

un·der·tow [ˈʌndətəu] *n.* ①从岸边退回去的浪，退浪。②【地】底流,下层逆流。

un·der·trick [ˈʌndətrik] *n.* 【桥牌】未完成定约的任一墩。

un·der·val·u·a·tion [ˈʌndəˌvæljuˈeiʃən] *n.* 低估价值,过低评价；轻视。

un·der·val·ue [ˌʌndəˈvæljuː] *vt.* ①把…的价值估低〔评价过低〕；看轻,小看,轻视。②降低…的价值。

un·der·vest [ˈʌndəˈvest] *n.* 〔英〕汗衫，贴身衣 (=〔美〕undershirt)。

un·der·waist [ˈʌndəweist] *n.* 〔美〕穿在罩衫下的内衫；小孩的内衣。

un·der·wa·ter [ˈʌndəˈwɔːtə] *a.* ①在水下的，水中的。②用于水下的。③【船】吃水线以下的。*an ~ boat* 潜水艇。— *ad.* ①在水下。②【船】在吃水线以下。— *n.* (海洋等)水面下的水；水下,水底。

un·der·way [ˈʌndəˈwei] *a.* ①【海】在航行中的。②在旅途〔行进〕中(发生、进行、使用)的；正在进行〔工作〕中的。— *ad.* 进行中 (= under way)。

un·der·wear [ˈʌndəwɛə] *n.* 〔集合词〕衬衣,内衣。

un·der·weight [ˈʌndəˈweit；形容词读作 ˌʌndəˈweit] *n., a.* 重量不足(的)。

un·der·went [ˌʌndəˈwent] undergo 的过去式。

un·der·wing [ˈʌndəwiŋ] *n.* (昆虫的)后翅。

Un·der·wood [ˈʌndəwud] *n.* 安德伍德〔姓氏〕。

un·der·wood [ˈʌndəwud] *n.* = undergrowth.

un·der·work [ˈʌndəˈwəːk] *vt.* ***(-worked;*** 〔古〕***-wrought*** [-ˈrɔːt]*)* ①对…支付的劳力不够；对…未尽力工作；未完成。②未充分使用；不使(牛马等)尽力劳动。③拿低于…的工资工作。— *vi.* 不尽力劳动〔工作〕，劳动〔工作〕得不够。—[ˈʌndəwəːk] *n.* ①附属工作,杂务。②松松散散的工作。③【建】支持结构,下层结构,根基。

un·der·world [ˈʌndəwəːld] *n.* ①下界,地狱，阴间。②(地球另一面的)对跖点。③下层社会,社会的底层〔尤指从事卖淫，盗窃等罪恶活动的社会集团〕。④〔古〕地上；地球。

un·der·write [ˈʌndərait] *vt.* ***(-wrote*** [-rəut]***; -writ·ten*** [-ˌritn]*)* ①〔除过去分词外不常用〕写在下面，署名。②签名承认〔担保〕,签名接受(保险)；签名承受,认购，认捐；赞同。*the underwritten signatures [names]* 签名人。— *vi.* 经营(海上)保险业。

un·der·writ·er [ˈʌndəraitə] *n.* ①保险商；(特指)水险商。②(股份、公债等的)承购人。③承诺支付者。

un·der·writ·ing [ˈʌndəraitiŋ] *n.* ①保险业;水险业。②(股份等的)签名承受。*an U- Member* 〔英〕伦敦劳埃德*(Lloyd)*船舶协会的正式会员。

un·der·wrought [ˈʌndəˈrɔːt] underwork 的过去式及过去分词。

un·de·scrib·a·ble [ˈʌndisˈkraibəbl] *a.* 无法描写的,难用笔墨形容的。

un·de·served [ˈʌndiˈzəːvd] *a.* ①不该受的,不应得的,不当的。②冤枉的。**-ly** [-ˈsəːvidli] *ad.*

un·de·serv·ing [ˈʌndiˈzəːviŋ] *a.* 不配…的,不值得…的*(of)*。*Such trifles are ~ of attention.* 这类鸡毛蒜皮的小事不值得注意。

un·de·signed [ˈʌndiˈzaind] *a.* 不是故意的,非预谋的;无意中做的,偶然的。**-ly** *ad.* 无意中,偶然。

un·de·sign·ing [ˈʌndiˈzainiŋ] *a.* 无欺的;直爽的;诚实的;不狡诈的;不卑劣的。

un·de·sir·a·bil·i·ty [ˈʌndiˌzaiərəˈbiliti] *n.* 不受欢迎,讨厌,不愉快;不合需要。

un·de·sir·a·ble [ˈʌndiˈzaiərəbl] *a.* 不合要求的,不受欢迎的,不良的,讨厌的,不愉快的,不方便的。*~ aliens* 不受欢迎的外国人。*at a most ~ moment* 在最不巧的时候。— *n.* ①不受欢迎的人[东西]。②不良分子。**-a·bly** *ad.*

un·de·tect·ed [ˈʌndiˈtektid] *a.* 没有被发现的,没有被识破的。

un·de·ter·mined [ˈʌndiˈtəːmind] *a.* ①未确定的,尚待确定的。②优柔寡断的,没有决断力的。

un·de·vel·oped [ˈʌndiˈveləpt] *a.* 不发达的,未发展的;(土地等)未开发的。

un·de·vi·at·ing [ʌnˈdiːvieitiŋ] *a.* 未离正道的,没有迷失正路[方向]的。**-ly** *ad.*

un·de·vout [ˈʌndiˈvaut] *a.* 没有敬神念头的,不虔诚的。**-ly** *ad.*

un·did [ˈʌnˈdid] undo 的过去式。

un·dies [ˈʌndiz] *n. pl.* 〔俚〕女用内衣。

un·dif·fer·en·ti·at·ed [ˈʌnˌdifəˈrenʃieitid] *a.* 无差别的;一致的。

un·dig·ni·fied [ʌnˈdignifaid] *a.* 不尊严的,不庄重的;有损尊严的,不体面的,不象样的。

un·di·lut·ed [ˈʌndaiˈljuːtid] *a.* 没有冲淡的,没有搀杂的,未稀释的;纯粹的。

un·di·min·ished [ˈʌndiˈminiʃt] *a.* 没有减少的,没有衰落的,没有降低的。

un·dine[1] [ˈʌndiːn][1] *n.* 女水仙,水中精灵〔据说须和凡人结婚后才能具有灵魂和生孩子〕。

un·dine[2] [ˈʌndain] *n.*【医】洗鼻器;洗眼壶。

un·di·rect·ed [ˈʌndiˈrektid] *a.* ①未受指导的;不受指引的。②(信等)未写姓名住址的,无通讯处的。

un·dis·cern·ing [ˈʌndiˈsəːniŋ, -ˈzəː-] *a.* 没有识别力的;感觉迟钝的。

un·dis·charged [ˈʌndisˈtʃɑːdʒd] *a.* ①(货等)未卸下的。②(水等)未放[排]出的(炮弹等)未引发的,未射出的。③(人员等)未遣散的。④(职责等)未履行的;(债务等)未偿清的。

un·dis·ci·plined [ʌnˈdisiplind] *a.* ①没有训练的,训练不足的。②没有修养的;散漫的,(军队等)无纪律的。

un·dis·closed [ˈʌndisˈkləuzd] *a.* ①未让人知的,未泄露的。②没有指名的;身分不明的。

un·dis·cov·ered [ˈʌndisˈkʌvəd] *a.* 未被发现的;未知的;隐藏的。

un·dis·crim·i·nat·ing [ˈʌndisˈkrimineitiŋ] *a.* ①不加区别的;不分青红皂白的;一视同仁的。②无鉴别力的。

un·dis·guised [ˈʌndisˈgaizd] *a.* 没有伪装的;不掩饰的;露骨的,公然的,赤裸裸的。**-ly** *ad.*

un·dis·mayed [ˈʌndisˈmeid] *a.* 不沮丧的,不气馁的;镇定自若的,不害怕的。*be ~ by failure* 不为失败所吓倒。

un·dis·posed [ˈʌndisˈpəuzd] *a.* ①未处理的,未卖出的。②(身体)不适的,不爽的。③不乐意的,不想的 *(to do sth.)*

un·dis·put·ed [ˈʌndisˈpjuːtid] *a.* 无争议的,无疑的,确实的,当然的。

un·dis·so·ci·at·ed [ˈʌndiˈsəuʃieitid] *a.*【化】未离解的。

un·dis·tin·guish·a·ble [ˈʌndisˈtiŋgwiʃəbl] *a.* 不能区别的,分别不清的;紊乱的。

un·dis·tin·guished [ˈʌndisˈtiŋgwiʃt] *a.* ①未区别开的,不加分别的。②听[看]不清楚的。③不特别显眼的;不著名的,平凡的。

un·dis·turbed [ˈʌndisˈtəːbd] *a.* 没有受到搅乱[干扰、妨碍]的;镇静的;泰然自若的。

un·di·ver·si·fied [ˈʌndaiˈvəːsifaid] *a.* 没有变化的,千篇一律的;单一的。

un·di·vid·ed [ˈʌndiˈvaidid] *a.* ①没有分开的;(利润等)未分配的。②连绵不断的;完整的。③专心的,专一的。*~ attention* 专心。

un·do [ˈʌnˈduː] *vt.* ***(-did*** [-ˈdid]; ***-done*** [-ˈdʌn]*)* ①使恢复原状,使复旧;取消,废除。②脱去,拆去,解开,打开,放松。③〔古〕说明,解释,解(谜等)。④破坏;毁灭;糟蹋,败坏;使落魄,使破落。⑤勾引,诱奸。*What's done cannot be undone.* 覆水难收。*It is better for the doer to ~ what he has done.* 解铃还需系铃人。*~ a match* 解除婚约。*~ a parcel* 打开包裹。*~ a knot* 解开结子。

un·dock [ˈʌnˈdɔk] *vt., vi.* ①【海】(使)(船)驶出船坞[驶离码头]。②【宇】(使)(会合后的宇宙飞船)在宇宙空间中相脱离。

un·do·er [ˈʌnˈduːə] *n.* ①取消者。②解开…的人。③败坏者,毁掉(别人)的人,诱惑者。

un·do·ing [ˈʌnˈduːiŋ] *n.* ①使复旧,取消。②解开。③毁灭,败坏,破落;祸根。*Drink will be his ~.* 喝酒将使他毁灭。

un·do·mes·ti·cated [ˈʌndəˈmestikeitid] *a.* ①不适于[不惯于]家庭生活的(人)。②(动物)未驯服的。

un·done[1] [ˈʌnˈdʌn] undo 的过去分词。— *a.* ①脱去的,解开的,放松的。②毁灭的,败坏的,破落的。*The package came ~.* 行李解开了。*I am ~.* 我已经不行啦[完啦]!

undone[2] [ˈʌndʌn] *a.* 没有做的,未做完的。*leave (things) ~* (把事情)放着不做,搁起来。*remain ~* 未做。

un·dou·ble [ʌnˈdʌbl] *vt.* ***(-bled; -bling)*** ①使之不再成倍。②展开,摊开,使挺直。

un·doubt·ed [ˈʌnˈdautid] *a.* 没有疑问的,肯定的,确实的,真正的。**-ly** *ad.*

un·doubt·ing [ˈʌnˈdautiŋ] *a.* 不怀疑的;信任的。

UNDP = United Nations Development Program(me) 联合国发展方案〔或译联合国发展计划署,系联合国管理援助或支援发展中国家的各种基金的一个机构〕。

un·dra·mat·ic [ˈʌndrəˈmætik] *a.* ①缺乏戏剧性的,平淡无奇的,非戏化的。②不适合于戏剧[舞台]的。

un·drape [ˈʌnˈdreip] *vt.* ①使脱去衣服。②揭开,打开。**-d** *a.* ①没有用布盖着的。②没有穿衣服的,裸体的。

un·draw [ˈʌndrɔː] *vt., vi.* ***(-drew*** [-ˈdruː]; ***-drawn*** [-ˈdrɔːn]*)* 拉回来,拉向旁边,拉开(帐幕等)。

un·dreamed-of, un·dreamt-of [ʌnˈdremtɔv] *a.* 梦想不到的,意外的。

un·dress [ˈʌnˈdres] *vt.* ①使脱去[脱光]衣服。②使卸下装饰。③暴露,剥除…的伪装。④【医】解掉…的绷带。*~ oneself* 脱衣服。— *vi.* 脱衣服。— *n.* (家常)便服;【军】军便服。

un·dressed[1] [ˈʌnˈdrest] *a.* ①没有穿衣服的,裸体的。②穿着家常便服的;未穿与当时情况所要求的服装的。

un·dressed[2] [ˈʌndrest] *a.* ①没有扎绷带的。②没有加调料、配料的;未加工的;没有整理好的;(皮等)未鞣的。*~ meat* 未加调味品的肉。*~ leather* 生皮。*~ ore* 原矿。

un·due [ˈʌnˈdjuː] *a.* ①过度的,过分的,不相称的。②非常的。③不正当的,非法的。④【商】(期票等)未到期的。*Don't treat the matter with ~ haste.* 不要过急地处理那个问题。~ ***influence***【法】不当压迫,威胁手段。

un·du·lant [ˈʌndjulənt] *a.* 波状的,波动的。~ **fever**【医】波状热,布鲁氏杆菌病。

un·du·late [ˈʌndjuleit] *vi.* (水面、风中的麦田等)波动,起浪;(土地等)起伏。— *vt.* 使波动,使起伏。— [ˈʌndjulit] *a.* 波状的;波动起伏的(= undulated)。**-lat·ing** *a.* **-lat·ing·ly** *ad.*

un·du·la·tion [ˌʌndjuˈleiʃən] *n.* 波动;波状起伏;【物】波动,振动;【医】悸动,心跳。

un·du·la·to·ry [ˈʌndjulətəri] *a.* 波动的;起伏的;波浪形的。*the ~ theory (of light)*【物】(光的)波动说。

un·du·ly [ˈʌnˈdjuːli] *ad.* 不相称地;不适[正]当地;过度。

un·du·ti·ful [ˈʌnˈdjuːtifəl] *a.* 不顺从的,不忠的;不尽责的。**-ly** *ad.*

un·dy·ing [ʌnˈdaiiŋ] *a.* 不死的,不朽的,永恒的;不绝的,无休止的。**-ly** *ad.*

un·earned [ˈʌnˈəːnd] *a.* (收入等)不劳而获的;分外的。~ *income* 不劳所得(如房租、利息等)。~ *increment* (土地的)自然增价。

un·earth [ˈʌnˈəːθ] *vt.* ①(从地中)掘出;从洞中赶出(狐等)。②发现;揭露,揭发(阴谋等)。

un·earth·ly [ʌnˈəːθli] *a.* ①不是这个世界的,非尘世的,超自然的。②神秘的;可怕的,令人毛骨悚然的,奇怪的。③〔口〕荒谬的。*Why call me at this ~ hour?* 怎么在这个时候叫醒我?**-li·ness** *n.*

un·eas·y [ʌnˈiːzi] *a.* ①不安的;忧虑的,担心的。②不舒服的,不自在的,不适意的,拘束的。③〔罕〕不容易的,困难的。*feel ~ about the result* 对将来结果忧虑不安。*feel ~ in tight clothes* 衣服紧,觉得不舒服。~ *manners* 不自然的态度。**-i·ly** *ad.* **-i·ness** *n.*

un·e·co·nom·ic, -i·cal [ˈʌnˌiːkəˈnɔmik, -əl] *a.* 不经济的;浪费的。

UNEDA = United Nations Economic Development Administration 联合国经济开发署。

un·ed·i·fy·ing [ˈʌnˈedifaiiŋ] *a.* ①不起启发[开导]作用的。②(道德上)不体面的,不光彩的。

un·ed·it·ed [ˈʌnˈeditid] *a.* ①未作过编辑加工的。②未刊行的。③(新闻等)未经审查的;【影】未剪辑的。

un·ed·u·cat·ed [ˈʌnˈedjukeitid] *a.* 没受教育的,失学的,没有知识的。

UNEF = United Nations Emergency Force 联合国紧急部队。

un·e·mo·tion·al [ˈʌniˈməuʃənl] *a.* 不易激动的;缺乏感情的;冷漠的。

un·em·ploy·a·ble [ˈʌnimˈplɔiəbl] *a.* 不适于[不能被]雇用的。— *n.* 不能被雇用的人。

un·em·ployed [ˈʌnimˈplɔid] *a.* ①没有受雇用的,失业的。②不用的,未加利用的,闲置的;空闲的。— *n.* 〔the ~〕〔集合词〕失业者。~ **capital**【商】游资。

un·em·ploy·ment [ˈʌnimˈplɔimənt] *n.* 失业;失业状况。~ **benefit [compensation]** 失业救济。~ **dole** 失业津贴。~ **insurance** 失业保险。~ **pay** 失业补贴。

un·en·closed [ˈʌninˈkləuzd] *a.* ①没有(用墙、篱等)围起来的;公共的。②(修道院等)没有被围墙与世隔绝的;(修女等)不住在修道院内的。

un·en·cum·bered [ˈʌninˈkʌmbəd] *a.* 不受妨碍的;没有(债务,子女等)负担的。

un·end·ing [ʌnˈendiŋ] *a.* ①无尽的,不停的,不断的。②无穷的,永久的。

un·en·dur·a·ble [ˈʌninˈdjuərəbl] *a.* 不可容忍的,难忍受的。

un·en·gaged [ˈʌninˈgeidʒd] *a.* ①没有约定的;未定婚的。②没有占用的;有空的,闲着无事的。

un-Eng·lish [ˈʌnˈiŋgliʃ] *a.* 非英国式的;不象英国人的;不符合英语习惯的。

un·en·light·ened [ˈʌninˈlaitnd] *a.* ①〔古〕未照亮的。②落后的;无知的,未经启蒙的。

un·en·tan·gle [ˈʌninˈtæŋgl] *vt.* 解开(结等);排解(纠纷等)。

un·en·ter·pris·ing [ˈʌnˈentəpraiziŋ] *a.* ①无事业心的;没有冒险精神的。②疲沓的;保守的。

un·en·vi·a·ble [ˈʌnˈenviəbl] *a.* 不值得羡慕的。**-a·bly** *ad.*

un·en·vi·ous [ˈʌnˈenviəs] *a.* ①不妒忌的;无恶意的。②不吝惜的。

un·eq·ua·ble [ˈʌnˈekwəbl] *a.* ①(气候等)不调匀的,不温和的。②不稳定的;无规律的。③易怒的。

un·e·qual [ˈʌnˈiːkwəl] *a.* (大小、轻重、长短等)不等的。②不齐的,不平均的;不平等的;不对称的。③(品质、价格)不一样的、不同的,不均一的。④不适合的,不胜任的,不充分的 *(to)*。~ *treaties* 不平等条约。*an ~ contest* 双方实力不相等的比赛。~ *pulsations* 跳动不均匀的脉搏。*be ~ to the duty* 不能胜任。~ **stops**【机】不对称触止。**-ly** *ad.*

un·e·qualled, 〔美〕 **un·e·qualed** [ˈʌnˈiːkwəld] *a.* ①不等同的。②无敌的,无比的,无双的;极好的。

un·e·quiv·o·cal [ˈʌniˈkwivəkəl] *a.* 不含糊的,明确的;直率的,坦白的。**-ly** *ad.*

un·err·ing [ˈʌnˈəːriŋ] *a.* 没有错的,没有过失的;准确的,正确的。

UNESCO, U·nes·co [ju(ː)ˈneskəu] = United Nations Educational, Scientific and Cultural Organization 联合国教育科学及文化组织。

un·es·cort·ed [ˈʌnesˈkɔːtid] *a.* 无人伴送的,无护送的;无护航的。

un·es·sen·tial [ˈʌniˈsenʃəl] *a.* 非本质的;不是主要的;不必要的。— *n.* 不必要之物。

un·e·ven [ˈʌnˈiːvən] *a.* ①不平坦的,凹凸不平的。②不一律的,参差不齐的;品质不匀的。③不势均力敌的,不平衡的。④【数】奇数的。*of ~ temper* 喜怒无常的,三心两意的。*an ~ contest* 力量悬殊的竞争。~ *numbers* 奇数。**-ly** *ad.*

un·e·vent·ful [ˌʌniˈventful] *a.* 无重大事故的;过程平凡的;平淡无事的。**-ly** *ad.*

un·ex·am·pled [ˌʌnigˈzɑːmpld] *a.* 无先例的,前所未有的,空前的,无比的;例外的。

un·ex·cep·tion·a·ble [ˌʌnikˈsepʃənəbl] *a.* 无懈可击的,无从指摘的,极好的,完美的。**-a·bly** *ad.*

un·ex·cep·tion·al [ˌʌnikˈsepʃənl] *a.* ①非例外的;平常的。②不许有例外的。

un·ex·e·cut·ed [ˈʌnˈeksikjuːtid] *a.* 没有实行的,未执行的;未根据条款履行的。

un·ex·haust·ed [ˈʌnigˈzɔːstid] *a.* ①未(用)尽的。②取用不完的。③(对问题的研究等)尚不彻底的;研究不完的。④不会疲倦的。⑤(罐中煤气等)未完全排出的。

un·ex·pect·ed [ˈʌniksˈpektid] *a.* 想不到的,料不到的,意外的,忽然的,突然的。**-ly** *ad.* **-ness** *n.*

un·ex·posed [ˈʌniksˈpəuzd] *a.* ①未曝光的。②未揭露的;未公开的。

un·ex·pressed [ˈʌniksˈprest] *a.* 不明说的;未表达的。

un·ex·press·ive [ˈʌnikˈspresiv] *a.* ①未能表达原意的。②无表情的;沉默的。③〔废〕无法表达的;不可表达的。

un·ex·pur·gat·ed [ˈʌnˈekspəːgeitid] *a.* 未删节的〔指淫秽处未加删除的书籍〕。

un·fad·ing [ʌnˈfeidiŋ] *a.* 不褪色的;不凋萎的;不衰的,不朽的。~ *glory* 不朽的荣誉。**-ly** *ad.*

un·fail·ing [ʌnˈfeiliŋ] *a.* ①无尽的,无穷的。②可靠的,不会失错的,确实的。**-ly** *ad.*

un·fair [ˈʌnˈfɛə] *a.* 不公平的,不公正的,有偏私的;不光明正大的,不正直的。~ *means* 卑劣手段。**-ly** *ad.* **-ness**

n.

un•faith•ful [ˈʌnˈfeiθful] *a.* ①不忠实的；不正直的；不贞洁的。②(翻译等)不可靠的,不正确的。**-ly** *ad.* **-ness** *n.*

un•fal•ter•ing [ʌnˈfɔːltəriŋ] *a.* 坚定的；不犹豫的。

un•fa•mil•iar [ˈʌnfəˈmiljə] *a.* ①不熟知的；不熟悉的，生疏的；没有经验的 *(with; to)*。②新奇的，陌生的。*I am ~ with the Greek language.* 我对希腊语不怎么熟悉。**-ly** *ad.*

UNFAO = United Nations Food and Agriculture Organization 联合国粮食及农业组织。

un•fash•ion•a•ble [ˈʌnˈfæʃənəbl] *a.* 不流行的，不时髦的,过时的,旧式的。**-a•bly** *ad.*

un•fash•ioned [ˈʌnˈfæʃənd] *a.* 未成形的；未加工的。

un•fast•en [ˈʌnˈfɑːsn] *vt., vi.* 放松；解开；松开。

un•fa•thered [ˈʌnˈfɑːðəd] *a.* ①〔诗〕无父的；〔喻〕不认识父亲的,私生的。②原著者[学说创立者(等)]不明的，出处不明的。

un•fa•ther•ly [ˈʌnˈfɑːðəli] *a.* 不象父亲的；无慈父之情的。

un•fath•om•a•ble [ʌnˈfæðəməbl] *a.* ①深不可测的，无底的。②深奥的，难解的。

un•fath•omed [ˈʌnˈfæðəmd] *a.* ①(深度)还没有探测清楚的。②(事件、性格等)难理解的。③(刑事案件等)尚未侦破的,没有得到解决的。

un•fa•vour•a•ble, 〔美〕**-vor-** [ˈʌnˈfeivərəbl] *a.* ①不适宜的，不顺利的，不利的。②〔古〕(容貌)丑陋的。③不吉的，不祥的。④否定的，相反的。⑤令人不快的。*the ~ balance of trade* 贸易逆差，入超。***make allowance for ~ occurrences*** 留有余地以备出现不利情况。**-a•bly** *ad.* **-ness** *n.*

un•fea•si•ble [ˈʌnˈfiːzəbl] *a.* 不能实行[实施]的。

un•fed [ˈʌnˈfed] *a.* ①得不到食物的，饥饿的。②没有加燃料的。③没有得到支持的。

un•feed [ˈʌnˈfiːd] *a.* 未得到工资[小费]的；无报酬的。

un•feel•ing [ʌnˈfiːliŋ] *a.* ①没有感觉的。②无情的，残酷的，冷酷的。**-ly** *ad.*

un•feigned [ʌnˈfeind] *a.* 不是伪装的，真实的，诚实的。**-ly** [ʌnˈfeinidli] *ad.*

un•felt [ˈʌnˈfelt] *a.* 未感觉到的。

un•fem•i•nine [ˈʌnˈfeminin] *a.* 不适合女性的；不象女性的；不温柔的。

un•fenced [ˈʌnˈfenst] *a.* 没有篱笆[土墙、木栅]的；没有防御的。

un•fer•ti•lized [ˈʌnˈfəːtilaizd] *a.* ①(土地)不肥沃的。②【生】未受精的。

un•fet•ter [ˈʌnˈfetə] *vt.* 打开…的脚镣；释放，使自由。

un•fet•tered [ˈʌnˈfetəd] *a.* 解去脚镣的；没有受到拘束的，自由的。*the ~ press* 自由出版(权)。

un•fil•i•al [ˈʌnˈfiliəl] *a.* 不象儿子的，不孝的。

un•filled [ˈʌnˈfild] *a.* ①未填充的，空的。②(定货等)未供应的。

un•fil•ter•a•ble [ˈʌnˈfiltərəbl] *a.* 【生】(病原菌)非滤过性的。

un•fin•ished [ˈʌnˈfiniʃt] *a.* ①未完成的，没有做好的。②未加琢磨的，没有完成最后加工的[如抛光，修整等]。③【纺】未整理过的；未漂白[染色]的。

un•fit [ˈʌnˈfit] *a.* ①不适当的，不适宜的，不适任的。②(身体、精神)不健全的人。*a house ~ for human habitation* 不适宜人住的房子。— [ʌnˈfit] *vt.* 使不适当，使不适宜 *(for)*；未供应某种装备。*houses unfitted with baths* 无浴室设备的房子。— *n.* 〔the ~〕①不适宜[不称职]的人们。②(身体、精神)不健全的人。**-ness** *n.*

un•fix [ˈʌnˈfiks] *vt.* ①解下，拆下，摘下，拔去；放松。②使(人心等)动摇；使不固定，使不稳定。*U- bayonets!* 【军】〔口令〕下刺刀!

un•fixed [ˈʌnˈfikst] *a.* ①被解下的，被摘下的，被拔下的；被放松的。②不固定的，动摇的；未确定的。

un•flag•ging [ʌnˈflægiŋ] *a.* 不减弱[松懈]的；不垂头丧气的，不倦的。**-ly** *ad.*

un•flap•pa•ble [ˈʌnˈflæpəbl] *a.* 〔口〕不易激动的；不易手足失措的；镇定自若的。**-pa•bil•i•ty** [ʌnˌflæpəˈbiliti] *n.*

un•fledged [ˈʌnˈfledʒd] *a.* 未生羽毛的，羽毛未丰的；未十分发达的，未成熟的，乳臭未干的。

un•flinch•ing [ʌnˈflintʃiŋ] *a.* 不畏缩的，不退缩的；果敢的。**-ly** *ad.*

un•fold[1] [ʌnˈfəuld] *vt.*, ①打开，张开，摊开，铺开(折叠的东西等)。②展开；开展，发展。③逐渐表露；说明。*~ a newspaper* 打开报纸。*~ one's intentions* (逐渐)表露意图。— *vi.* ①(运动等)展开。②显露；呈现。③(蓓蕾等)张开。*Buds ~ into flowers.* 蓓蕾开成花朵。

un•fold[2] [ˈʌnˈfəuld] *vt.* 将(羊等)放出栏外。

un•forced [ˈʌnˈfɔːst] *a.* ①非强迫的，自愿的。②不勉强的，自然的，不费力的。

un•fore•seen [ˈʌnfɔːˈsiːn] *a.* 未预见到的，意外的；偶然的。*the ~* 未预见到的事情，意外的事情。

un•for•get•ta•ble [ˈʌnfəˈgetəbl] *a.* 难忘的；铭刻肺腑的。**-ta•bly** *ad.*

un•for•giv•a•ble [ˈʌn-fəˈgivəbl] *a.* 不可原谅[饶恕]的。

un•for•giv•ing [ˈʌnfəˈgiviŋ] *a.* 不宽恕的，不原谅人的；爱记仇的；无情的。

un•formed [ʌnˈfɔːmd] *a.* ①无定形的；不成形的。②未形成的；未发展起来的。③未作成的；未创造出来的。

un•for•ti•fied [ˈʌnˈfɔːtifaid] *a.* ①(城市等)未设防的。②〔转义〕未加强的。③信念不足的；不稳定的。

un•for•tu•nate [ʌnˈfɔːtʃənit] *a.* ①不幸的；运气不好的，倒霉的。②不成功的，不恰好的，效果不好的。③使人遗憾的；可叹的。— *n.* 不幸的人；被社会遗弃的人。**-ly** *ad.* **-ness** *n.*

un•found•ed [ˈʌnˈfaundid] *a.* ①没有根据[理由]的，(谣言等)无稽的。②没有创立的。*~ hopes* 虚幻的希望。**-ly** *ad.* **-ness** *n.*

un•freeze [ˈʌnˈfriːz] *vt.* ***(-froze*** [-ˈfrəuz]; ***-froz•en*** [-ˈfrəuzn], ***-freez•ing)*** ①使融化。②解除(对价格、物资等控制的)冻结。

un•fre•quent [ʌnˈfriːkwənt] *a.* 不常出现的；难得的，珍奇的。

un•fre•quent•ed [ˈʌnfriˈkwentid] *a.* 人迹罕到的，行人稀少的，冷落的。

un•friend•ed [ʌnˈfrendid] *a.* 没有朋友[伙伴]的；孤立无援的。

un•friend•ly [ˈʌnˈfrendli] *a.* ①不友好的，有敌意的。②(气候)不宜人的，不利的，不顺利的 *(to; for)*。

un•frock [ˈʌnˈfrɔk] *vt.* ①脱去…法衣，免去…的圣职。②剥夺…的职权；开除，罢黜，把…除名。

un•froze [ˈʌnˈfrəuz] unfreeze 的过去式。

un•fro•zen [ˈʌnˈfrəuzn] unfreeze 的过去分词。— *a.* 不冻的，不冷的；未凝结的。

un•fruit•ful [ˈʌnˈfruːtful] *a.* ①不结果实的；不毛的，贫瘠的；(动物等)不产子的。②没有结果的，无效的，(努力等)徒然的。

un•fund•ed [ˈʌnˈfʌndid] *a.* ①未备基金的，没有经费的。②暂时借入的，(公债)短期的。*the ~ debt* 暂借款。

un•fun•ny [ˈʌnˈfʌni] *a.* 不滑稽的。

un•furl [ʌnˈfəːl] *vt., vi.* 展开(旗、帆等)；打开(雨伞等)；展示，揭示，公开。

un•fur•nished [ˈʌnˈfəːniʃt] *a.* 无装备的，无供应的；(房间等)没有家具等设备的。

UNGA = United Nations General Assembly 联合国大会。

un•gain•ly [ʌnˈgeinli] *a., ad.* ①笨拙的[地]。②难看的[地]；粗俗的[地]。③拙劣的[地]。**-i•ness** *n.*

un•gar•bled [ˈʌnˈgɑːbld] *a.* ①〔古〕未经拣选的；未经筛

分的. ②不歪曲的; 没窜改的. ③清楚的; 明白的, 率直的.

un·gat·ed [ʌnˈgeitid] *a.* 无(大)门的; 闭塞的. ～ *level crossing* 无道口拦木的公路与铁路交叉.

un·gear [ˈʌnˈgiə] *vt.* ①把(齿轮等)脱开. ②使脱节. ③卸下(马具等).

un·gen·er·ous [ˈʌnˈdʒenərəs] *a.* 不慷慨的, 不大度的; 胸襟狭窄的, 小气的; 吝啬的.

un·gen·tle·man·ly [ʌnˈdʒentlmənli] *a.* 没有绅士风度的; 缺乏教养的; 粗鄙的.

un·get-at·able [ˈʌngetˈætəbl] *a.* 不容易到达[接近]的.

un·gift·ed [ˈʌnˈgiftid] *a.* ①缺乏才能的. ②〔古〕空手的, 无所获的.

un·gird [ˈʌnˈgəːd] *vt.* *(-girded, -girt* [-ˈgəːt]*)* 解开…的带.

un·girt [ˈʌnˈgəːt] ungird 的过去式和过去分词. — *a.* ①不缚带的; 带子松的. ②缺乏纪律的; 松弛的.

un·glazed [ˈʌnˈgleizd] *a.* ①(陶瓷器等)没有上釉的, 素烧的. ②(纸张)无光的; 没有上矾水的. ③没有镶玻璃的, 没有玻璃窗的.

un·gloved [ˈʌnˈglʌvd] *a.* 没有带手套的.

un·glued [ˈʌnˈgluːd] *a.* 脱粘的, 脱开的; 拆开的. *a stamp* ～ *from an envelope* 从信封上揭下的邮票. ***come*** ～〔俚〕情急心躁.

un·god·ly [ʌnˈgɔdli] *a.* ①不信神的, 不怕神的. ②邪恶的, 罪孽深重的; 无法无天的. ③〔口〕荒唐的; 不可容忍的. **-li·ness** *n.*

un·gov·ern·a·ble [ʌnˈgʌvənəbl] *a.* ①难治理的, 难控制的. ②放肆的; 激烈的.

un·grace·ful [ˈʌnˈgreisful] *a.* 不优美的, 不雅致的; 粗鄙的, 没礼貌的; 难看的, 没样子的. **-ly** *ad.* **-ness** *n.*

un·gra·cious [ˈʌnˈgreiʃəs] *a.* ①不亲切的, 冷淡的. ②没礼貌的, 粗野的. ③令人不快的, 讨厌的. **-ly** *ad.* **-ness** *n.*

un·gram·mat·i·cal [ˈʌngrəˈmætikəl] *a.* 不合[违反]语法的; (文字)不通的.

un·grate·ful [ʌnˈgreitful] *a.* ①不感恩的, 忘恩负义的. ②徒劳的, 白费气力的. ③讨厌的, 不愉快的. *an* ～ *food* 令人厌恶的食物. **-ly** *ad.* **-ness** *n.*

un·ground·ed [ˈʌnˈgraundid] *a.* ①没有根据[理由]的, 不从事实出发的. ②不真实的, 捏造的. ③【无】非接地的.

un·grudg·ing [ˈʌnˈgrʌdʒiŋ] *a.* ①不吝惜的, 慷慨的. ②自愿的. *give sb.* ～ *praise* 满口称赞某人. **-ly** *ad.* 慷慨; 欣然.

un·gual [ˈʌŋgwəl] *a.* 爪[距、蹄](似)的; 有爪[距、蹄]的.

un·guard·ed [ˈʌnˈgɑːdid] *a.* ①不留神的, 不谨慎的. ②没有防备的. ***in an*** ～ ***moment*** 一个不留神, 一不小心. **-ly** *ad.*

un·guent [ˈʌŋgwənt] *n.* ①药膏. ②(机器的)润滑油. **-ary** *a.*

un·gui·bus et ros·tro [ore] [ˈʌŋgwibəs et ˈrɔstrəu, ˈɔre] 〔L.〕用爪和嘴; 用全力; 拼命.

un·guic·u·late [ʌŋˈgwikjuleit] *a.*【动】有爪的;【植】花瓣有爪状底部的. — *n.* 有爪动物. 亦作 **-d.**

un·gui·form [ˈʌngwifɔːm] *a.* 爪[蹄]状的.

un·guis [ˈʌŋgwis] *n.* *(pl. un·gues* [-gwiːz]*)*【动】爪, 距, 蹄;【植】(某些花的花瓣的)爪状底部.

un·gu·la [ˈʌŋgjulə] *n.* *(pl. -lae* [-liː]*)* ①【几】蹄状体. ②【植】(某些花的花瓣的)爪状底部.

un·gu·lar [ˈʌngjulə] *a.* = ungual.

un·gu·late [ˈʌŋgjuleit] *a.* 蹄状的; 有蹄的; 有蹄类的. — *n.* 有蹄动物.

un·hack·neyed [ʌnˈhæknid] *a.* ①未陈旧的; 不陈腐的; 还新鲜的; 崭新的; 有创造性的. ②〔古〕不熟练的; 没有经验的.

un·hair [ˈʌnˈhɛə] *vt., vi.* 拔除…的毛[发]. 使无毛〔如革鞣制前〕.

un·hal·low [ʌnˈhæləu] *vt.* 亵渎, 污渎. **-ed** *a.* 亵渎神明的.

un·hand [ʌnˈhænd] *vt.* 把手从…放开; 放掉.

un·han·dled [ˈʌnˈhændld] *a.* ①未经手触过的; 未经处理过的; 未讨论过的. ②未经驯服的.

un·hand·some [ˈʌnˈhænsəm] *a.* ①不美丽的, 不漂亮的, 难看的. ②没礼貌的. ③吝啬的, 小气的. **-ly** *ad.*

un·hand·y [ˈʌnˈhændi] *a.* ①笨拙的. ②难处理[使用]的, 不便的. ③不在手边的. **-i·ly** *ad.* **-i·ness** *n.*

un·hap·pi·ly [ʌnˈhæpili] *ad.* ①不幸福地; 悲惨地, 愁苦地, 不快乐地. ②不幸, 偏巧, 可惜. ③不适当地, 拙劣地.

un·hap·py [ʌnˈhæpi] *a.* ①不幸的; 悲惨的, 不快乐的; 不吉利的. ②不凑巧的. ③(讲法等)不恰当的. **-i·ness** *n.*

un·harmed [ˈʌnˈhɑːmd] *a.* 没有受损害的, 没有受伤的; 平安无事的, 无恙的.

un·harm·ful [ˈʌnˈhɑːmful] *a.* 无害的. **-ly** *ad.*

un·harm·ing [ˈʌnˈhɑːmiŋ] *a.* 不伤人的; 无害的.

un·har·ness [ˈʌnˈhɑːnis] *vt.* ①解下(马等的)马具. ②解下…的铠甲. **-ed** *a.* 解下了马具的; (瀑布、风等)不能利用作动力的.

un·hat [ʌnˈhæt] *vi.* 〔古〕脱帽致敬.

un·hatched [ˈʌnˈhætʃt] *a.* ①未孵化的; 未充分孵化的. ②未准备就绪的; 没实现的.

UNHCR = United Nations High Commissioner for Refugees 联合国难民事务高级专员办事处.

un·health·ful [ˈʌnˈhelθful] *a.* 有害身体的, 不卫生的; 不健康的. **-ly** *ad.*

un·health·y [ʌnˈhelθi] *a.* ①不健康的, 病弱的. ②有害健康的, (风土等)有害的. ③(精神上)不健全的, 不良的. **-i·ly** *ad.* **-i·ness** *n.*

un·heard [ˈʌnˈhəːd] *a.* ①未被听到的. ②不被倾听的; (案件等)未予审问的; 未被给予申述机会的. ③〔古〕前所未闻的.

un·heard-of [ʌnˈhəːdɔv] *a.* 从未听见过的, 前所未闻的, 空前的. *on an* ～ *scale* 以空前的规模.

un·heed·ed [ʌnˈhiːdid] *a.* 没有受到注意的, 没人理睬的, 没人注意的.

un·heed·ing [ˈʌnˈhiːdiŋ] *a.* 不注意的, 不留心的; 疏忽的. **-ly** *ad.*

un·help·ful [ˈʌnˈhelpful] *a.* ①无用的, 无益的. ②不予帮助的, 不予合作的.

un·hemmed [ˈʌnˈhemd] *a.* 没有褶边[卷边]的.

un·hes·i·tat·ing [ʌnˈheziteitiŋ] *a.* 不踌躇[犹豫]的; 即时的, 迅速的. **-ly** *ad.*

un·hewn [ˈʌnˈhjuːn] *a.* 未经刀斧斫削成形的; 粗糙的; 粗野的.

un·hinge [ʌnˈhindʒ] *vt.* ①取下…的铰链; 把…从铰链上摘下. ②使分开, 使裂开. ③使(精神等)发狂, 动摇, 搅乱, 扰乱. ～ *a door* 摘下一扇门. *Her mind was* ～*d.* 她精神失常了.

un·hip [ˈʌnˈhip] *a.* 〔美口〕无时代感的; 不流行的.

un·his·tor·ic, -tor·i·cal [ˈʌnhisˈtɔːrik, -ˈtɔrikəl] *a.* ①非历史的; 仅属传说的, 未真正发生过的; 〔尤指〕【语】无历史根据的. ②不熟悉历史的. ③偶然的, 例外的.

un·hitch [ˈʌnˈhitʃ] *vt.* 解下(拴着的马等), 解开.

un·ho·ly [ʌnˈhəuli] *a.* *(-li·er; -li·est)* ①不神圣的, 不洁净的. ②不信神的, 不虔敬的. ③邪恶的. ④〔口〕厉害的, 可怕的. ⑤〔口〕不合理的. *They were kicking up an* ～ *row.* 他们正引起一场大闹. **-li·ly** *ad.* **-li·ness** *n.*

un·hon·oured, 〔美〕**-ho·nored** [ˈʌnˈɔnəd] *a.* ①没有受到尊敬的. ②(支票)被拒绝接受[支付]的.

un·hook [ˈʌnˈhuk] *vt.* ①把…从钩上取下. ②解开(衣服等的)搭钩.

un·hoped(-for) [ʌnˈhəupt(fɔː)] *a.* 意外的, 没想到的. *get unhoped success* 得到意外的成功.

un·horse [ˈʌnˈhɔːs] *vt.* ①把…拉下马来，使摔下马来. ②赶…下台；推翻. ③卸去(驾车的)马.
un·house [ʌnˈhauz] *vt.* ①把…撵出去，把…赶出屋外，使无家可归[无处居住]. ②【商】由仓库中提出.
un·hu·man [ʌnˈhjuːmən] *a.* ①非人类的. ②超人类的，非人间的. ③〔罕〕残酷的，不近人情的.
un·hung [ˈʌnˈhʌŋ] unhang 的过去式和过去分词.
un·hur·ried [ʌnˈhʌrid] *a.* 不匆忙的；从容不迫的；悠闲的.
un·hurt [ˈʌnˈhəːt] *a.* 没有受伤的；未受损害的.
un·hus·band·ed [ʌnˈhʌzbəndid] *a.* ①无丈夫的，未嫁的. ②(土地)未耕耘的.
un·husk [ʌnˈhʌsk] *vt.* 剥去(稻谷等的)外壳；〔喻〕揭露.
un·hy·phen·at·ed [ʌnˈhaifəneitid] *a.* ①未附加连字号的. ②(人种)纯粹的.
u·ni- *comb. f.* 一，单；一个；一边，一方: *uni*florous, *uni*lateral.
U·ni·ate, U·ni·at [ˈjuːniət, -ˌeit] *n., a.* 合并教派的(教徒)〔主张与罗马天主教会合并的东正教教徒〕.
u·ni·ax·i·al [ˈjuːniˈæksiəl] *a.* 单轴的. ～ **crystal**【物】单轴结晶体.
u·ni·cam·er·al [ˈjuːniˈkæmərəl] *a.* (议会)一院制的.
UNICEF [ˈjuːnisef] = United Nations International Children's Emergency Fund 现名 United Nations Children's Fund 联合国儿童基金会.
u·ni·cel·lu·lar [ˈjuːniˈseljulə] *a.*【生】单(细)胞的. ～ *animals* 单细胞动物.
u·ni·corn [ˈjuːnikɔːn] *n.* ①独角兽〔传说中身体似马、头中央有一螺蛳状独角的怪兽〕；【圣】独角野牛. ②【动】独角鲸；独角甲虫；有角状棘的贝类. ③〔the U-〕【天】麒麟座. ④三马马车；三马马车的一套马. *a Chinese* ～ 麒麟.
u·ni·cos·tate [ˌjuːniˈkɔsteit] *a.* 单肋的；【植】单叶肋的，中脉显明的〔指叶〕.
u·ni·cy·cle [ˈjuːnisaikl] *n.* (杂技表演用)独轮自行车.
un·i·de·a'd, -de·aed [ˈʌnaiˈdiəd] *a.* 无思想的；无头脑的，愚钝的.
un·i·de·al [ˈʌnaiˈdiəl] *a.* ①非唯心的. ②非理想的；非想象的. ③不理想的；不完美的；平淡无味的.
un·i·den·ti·fied [ˈʌnaiˈdentifaid] *a.* 不能辨认的，来路[身分]不明的. *an* ～ *plane* 国籍不明的飞机. *an* ～ *flying object* 飞碟，不明飞行物.
u·ni·di·men·sion·al [ˈjuːnidiˈmenʃənl] *a.* 一维的，一度的；线性的.
u·ni·di·rec·tion·al [ˈjuːnidiˈrekʃənl] *a.* 单向的.
UNIDO = United Nations Industrial Development Organization 联合国工业发展组织.
u·ni·fi·a·ble [ˈjuːnifaiəbl] *a.* 可统一的；可联合的；能一致的.
u·ni·fi·ca·tion [ˌjuːnifiˈkeiʃən] *n.* 统一，合一，联合；一致.
u·ni·fi·er [ˈjuːnifaiə] *n.* 统一物；联合者；使一致的人[物].
u·ni·fi·lar [ˈjuːniˈfailə] *a.* 单线的，仅有一条线的，单丝的.
u·ni·flo·rous [ˈjuːniˈflɔːrəs] *a.*【植】单花的.
u·ni·fo·li·ate [ˈjuːniˈfəuliit] *a.*【植】①单叶的. ② = unifoliolate.
u·ni·fo·li·o·late [ˈjuːniˈfəuliəleit, -lit] *a.* (复叶)具一小叶的.
u·ni·form [ˈjuːnifɔːm] *a.* ①(形状、性质等)一样的，同一的，一致的；相同的. ②一贯不变的；始终如一的. ③规格一致的，均匀的，齐一的. *be* ～ *in size [shape]* 大小[形状]一律. — *n.* ①制服；军服；〔the ～〕军人. ②通讯中用以代表字母 u 的词. *an undress* ～ 军便服. *a full-dress* ～ 军礼服. ***in full*** ～ 全副军装. ***out of*** ～ (未穿制服而)穿着便服. — *vt.* 使规格一律，使均一；使穿制服. ～ **acceleration** 匀加速(度). ～ **crop**【林】同龄林. ～ **function**【数】单值函数. ～ **motion**【机】匀速运动. ～ **system**【林】伞伐作业. **-ly** *ad.*
u·ni·formed [ˈjuːnifɔːmd] *a.* 穿军服的；穿制服的.
u·ni·form·i·tar·i·an [ˌjuːniˌfɔːmiˈtɛəriən] *a.* ①【地】均变说的；持均变说的. ②坚持某种均等一致说的. — *n.*【地】均变论者；坚持某种均等一致说者.
u·ni·form·i·tar·i·an·ism [ˌjuːniˌfɔːməˈtɛəriənizəm] *n.*【地】均变说〔认为地质纪元中一切地质变化都可用浸蚀、沉积、火山作用等现有物理和化学作用来解释〕.
u·ni·form·i·ty [ˌjuːniˈfɔːmiti] *n.* ①一样，一律，一式，划一，一致. ②均匀；无变化，单调.
u·ni·fy [ˈjuːnifai] *vt.* 使成一体，合一；统一，使一致，使一元化.
u·nij·u·gate [juˈnidʒəgeit; ˌjuːniˈdʒuːgit] *a.*【植】具一对(小叶)的.
u·ni·lat·er·al [ˈjuːniˈlætərəl] *a.* ①一方的，一侧的，单边的，单方的，片面的. ②单系的〔指父系或母系一方〕. ③【植】单侧的. ④【语音】单边音的. ～ **conduction**【电】单向导电. ～ **contract**【法】单方(承担义务)契约. ～ **relative** 单侧亲缘. ～ **winding**【电】单向绕法，单向绕组. **-ly** *ad.*
u·ni·lat·er·al·ism [ˈjuːniˈlætərəlizəm] *n.* 单方，单向，片面，单系(现象)；【植】单侧(状态).
u·ni·lay·er [ˈjuːniˈleiə] *n.*【物】单分子层.
u·ni·lin·e·ar [ˈjuːniˈliniə] *a.* ①始终遵循一条发展(或前进)道路的；一条路线贯穿始终的；单线的. ②分阶段发展的.
u·ni·loc·u·lar [ˈjuːniˈlɔkjulə] *a.*【生】单室的；单房的.
un·i·mag·in·a·ble [ˌʌniˈmædʒinəbl] *a.* 不能想象的；想不到的；无法理解的. **-a·bly** *ad.*
u·ni·mod·al [ˈjuːniˈməudl] *a.*【统计】(曲线)单峰的.
u·ni·mod·u·lar [ˈjuːniˈmɔdjulə] *a.*【数】单位模的.
un·im·paired [ˈʌnimˈpɛəd] *a.* 未受损伤的；未削弱的；没有减少的.
un·im·pas·sioned [ˈʌnimˈpæʃənd] *a.* 没有热情的；不动感情的. **-ly** *ad.*
un·im·peach·a·ble [ˌʌnimˈpiːtʃəbl] *a.* 无可怀疑的；无可指摘的；无懈可击的；无过失的，无罪的. **-a·bly** *ad.*
un·im·por·tant [ˈʌnimˈpɔːtənt] *a.* 不重要的；琐细的，平凡的.
un·im·pos·ing [ˈʌnimˈpəuziŋ] *a.* ①给人印象不深刻的，不引人注目的；没有威严的. ②(工作等)不是非做不可的.
un·im·pressed [ˈʌnimˈprest] *a.* 无印记的；没有印象的；未受感动的.
un·im·pres·sive [ˈʌnimˈpresiv] *a.* 给人印象不深的；不令人信服的.
un·im·proved [ˈʌnimˈpruːvd] *a.* ①没有改善[改良]的；没有得到增进的. ②(土地)没有耕作的. ③(机会等)没有充分利用的. ④(牛羊等)未经选种的. ⑤(道路)没有坚实路面的.
un·in·cor·po·rat·ed [ˈʌninˈkɔːpəreitid] *a.* ①未组成社团的. ②未被承认为自治组织的；未包含[合并]在内的. *an* ～ *village* 非自治村落.
un·in·flu·enced [ˈʌnˈinfluənst] *a.* 不为他人所动的，不受影响的，不受感化的；没有偏见的，公平的.
un·in·flu·en·tial [ˈʌninfluˈenʃəl] *a.* 不发生影响的；没有左右别人的力量的.
un·in·form·a·tive [ˈʌninˈfɔːmətiv] *a.* 不提供情报的.
un·in·formed [ˈʌninˈfɔːmd] *a.* ①没有得到通知[情报]的. ②无知识的；蒙昧的.
un·in·hab·it·a·ble [ˈʌninˈhæbitəbl] *a.* 不适于居住的.
un·in·hab·it·ed [ˈʌninˈhæbitid] *a.* 没有人住的，(岛等)无人的.
un·in·hib·it·ed [ˈʌninˈhibitid] *a.* 放纵不羁的，不受抑制的〔尤指言行等不受通常的社会制约或心理上的约

U

束〕.

un·in·jured [ˈʌnˈindʒəd] *a.* 没有受损伤的.

un·in·spired [ˈʌninˈspaiəd] *a.* 未受鼓舞的，思想感情不活跃的；无独创性的；庸庸碌碌的.

un·in·tel·li·gent [ˈʌninˈtelidʒənt] *a.* 无知的；缺乏智力的，愚蠢的. **-gence** *n.* **-ly** *ad.*

un·in·tel·li·gi·ble [ˈʌninˈtelidʒəbl] *a.* 难理解的，莫名其妙的. **-bly** *ad.* **-bil·i·ty** [ˈʌninˌtelidʒəˈbiliti] *n.*

un·in·tend·ed [ˈʌninˈtendid] *a.* 非故意的，不是存心的.

un·in·ten·tion·al [ˈʌninˈtenʃənəl] *a.* 不是故意的，无意的，无心的. **-ly** *ad.*

un·in·ter·est·ed [ˈʌnˈintristid] *a.* ①没有(利害)关系的；公平的. ②不感觉兴趣的，不注意的，漠不关心的，冷淡的.

un·in·ter·est·ing [ˈʌnˈintristiŋ] *a.* 无趣的，乏味的，令人厌倦的. **-ly** *ad.*

un·in·ter·rupt·ed [ˈʌnintəˈrʌptid] *a.* ①不停的，不断的，连续的. ②未受干扰的. **-ly** *ad.* **-ness** *n.*

u·ni·nu·cle·ate [ˈju:niˈnju:kliit] *a.* 【原】单核的.

un·in·vit·ed [ˈʌninˈvaitid] *a.* 没有被邀请的；多此一举的，多余的；冒昧的.

un·in·vit·ing [ˈʌninˈvaitiŋ] *a.* 不吸引人的，无吸引力的. **-ly** *ad.*

U·ni·o [ˈju:niəu] *n.* ①【动】珠蚌(属). ②〔u-〕蛤蜊；蠔.

u·nion [ˈju:njən] *n.* ①联合，结合，合并；团结，融洽，一致. ②同盟，联盟. ③公会，协会；工会；〔U-〕大学生俱乐部. ④结婚，婚姻. ⑤〔the U-〕联邦. ⑥〔英〕联合教会. ⑦〔英〕教区间的救济工作联合会；联合救济院. ⑧联邦旗，(特指)英国国旗. ⑨【纺】(棉和麻等的)混纺织物；交织织物. ⑩【机】联接，管接，管套接. ⑪【数】并集；逻辑和. ⑫【医】愈合. *peasants'* ～ 农会. *U- is strength.* 团结就是力量. *a three-way* ～ 三通管接头. ***fly a flag*** ～ ***down***【海】挂倒旗〔遭难信号〕. ***in*** ～ 共同，一同. ***the Union*** ①1707 年英吉利和苏格兰的合并；1801 年大不列颠和爱尔兰的合并. ②美利坚合众国. ***the Soviet U-*** 苏联. ***the U- flag*** = ***the U- Jack*** 英国国旗. ***the U- of Soviet Socialist Republics*** 〔略 U.S.S.R.〕苏维埃社会主义共和国联盟，苏联. ～ ***by (the) first intention***【医】第一期愈合. ～ ***by (the) second intention***【医】第二期愈合〔化脓后愈合〕. ～**-busting** *n., a.* 打击工会(的). ～ **card** 工会会员证. ～ **catalogue** 联合图书目录. ～ **colour** 统一染料，万用染料. ～ **hours** 〔美棒球〕九回. **U- House** = ～ **workhouse** 〔英〕联合救济院. ～ **jack** (国旗上)象征联合的部分；联合象征旗. ～ **link**【机】联环. ～ **man** (= ～ **member**) 〔美〕工会会员. ～ **nut** 接合螺母. ～ **shop** 须按资方与工会协定条件雇用工人的工厂. ～ **suit** 〔美〕连衫裤. ～ **three-way cock**【机】三通旋塞. ～ **wages** 工会规定的工资率.

u·nion·ism [ˈju:njənizəm] *n.* ①联合主义，联合原则. ②工会主义；工联主义. ③【美史】〔the U-〕(南北战争时反对南北分裂的)联邦主义.

u·nion·ist [ˈju:njənist] *n.* ①联合主义者. ②〔U-〕【美史】(南北战争时的)联邦主义者；【英史】(反对爱尔兰自治案的)统一党党员. ③工会会员；工会〔工联〕主义者. **-ic** [ˌju:njəˈnistik] *a.*

u·nion·i·za·tion [ˌju:njənaiˈzeiʃən] *n.* ①组织成工会. ②使符合工会会章.

u·nion·ize [ˈju:njənaiz] *vt.* ①联合. ②使成为工会；使加入工会；使遵守工会规章. — *vi.* ①联合. ②加入工会；加入联合组织.

un·i·on·ized [ʌnˈaiənaizd] *a.* 【物，化】未电离的.

u·nip·a·rous [juˈnipərəs] *a.* ①【植】每一分枝只生一茎轴的，单梗的〔如聚伞花序〕. ②【动】每次产一个卵的；每胎生一子的；只生过一子的.

u·ni·par·tite [ˌju:niˈpɑ:tait] *a.* 未分裂的；不能分割的.

u·ni·ped [ˈju:niped] *a.* 单足的，独脚的.

u·ni·per·son·al [ˌju:niˈpə:snəl] *a.* ①仅作为个人存在的；仅包含一个人的；仅以个人形式表现出来的. ②【语法】(动词)仅用于单一人称的〔尤指第三人称单数〕.

u·ni·pet·al·ous [ˌju:niˈpetləs] *a.* 【植】单(花)瓣的，仅有一花瓣的.

u·ni·pla·nar [ˌju:niˈpleinə] *a.* 单面延展的；在同一平面的.

u·ni·pod [ˈju:nipɔd] *n.* 独脚(支撑)架.

u·ni·po·lar [ˈju:niˈpəulə] *a.* 【电】单极的；【生】单尾的，(细胞等)单极的.

u·ni·po·lar·i·ty [ˌju:nipəuˈlæriti] *n.* ①【电】单极性. ②【动】单极体.

u·nip·o·tent [ju(:)ˈnipətənt] *a.* ①只能向一个方向发展的，只有一个结果的. ②【生】偏能的.

u·nique [ju:ˈni:k] *a.* ①唯一的；无双的；无比的；独特的. ②〔口〕珍奇的，极好的. ③【数，物】单价的；单值的. — *n.* 独一无二的人〔物、事实〕. **-ly** *ad.* **-ness** *n.*

u·ni·ra·mous [ˌju:niˈreiməs] *a.* 有单枝的.

u·ni·sex [ˈju:niseks] *a.* 〔口〕(服装，发式等)不分男女的.

u·ni·sex·u·al [ˈju:niˈseksjuəl] *a.* ①【生】单性的；雌雄异体的. ②限于一种性别的，非男女同校的. **-i·ty** [ˈju:niˌsekjuˈæliti] *n.*

u·ni·son [ˈju:nizn, -sn] *n.* ①调和，一致. ②【乐】同音，同度；齐唱，齐奏. ***in*** ～ 一齐(唱等)；一致(行动等). **-al** *a.*

u·ni·so·nant [ˈju:niˈsaunənt] *a.* 一致的；【乐】同音的，同度的.

u·ni·so·nous [ˈju:niˈsaunəs] *a.* = unisonant.

u·nit [ˈju:nit] *n.* ①个体，一个，一人. ②(计值、组织、机构)单位；单元；小组，分部；【军】部队；分队. ③【机】机组，装置；元件，部件，附件；一组用具〔设备〕. ④【数】单位数；最小整数；基数. *the guerrilla* ～*s* 游击队. *army* ～*s* 陆军部队. *international electrical* ～*s* 国际电力单位〔volt, ohm 等〕. *the C.G.S. system of* ～*s* 厘米、克、秒单位制. *a line* ～【电】接线盒. *the remote control* ～ 遥控装置. *the drive* ～ 传动装置. *a point* ～ 质点. *a missile-borne* ～ 导弹附件. *an infrared detection* ～【火箭】热探头. ***be a*** ～ 〔美〕一致 (*We were a* ～ *on the question.* 我们在这个问题上是一致的). ～ **area** 单位面积. ～ **cell**【物，无】(单位)晶胞；单位粒子. ～ **character**【遗】单位性状. ～ **factor**【生】单一因子. ～ **holder** 联合托拉斯股票持有人. ～ **(magnetic) pole**【物】单位磁极. ～ **price** 单价. ～ **rule** 〔美〕单位投票制〔一个代表团可不顾其中少数人的意见，作为一个单位投票〕. ～ **school**【军】随营学校. ～ **train** 专列货车. ～ **trust** 联合托拉斯〔共同投资的企业、互惠基金等〕.

u·nit·age [ˈju:nitidʒ] *n.* 计量单位(的规定).

UNITAR = United Nations Institute for Training and Research 联合国训练研究所.

U·ni·ta·ri·an [ju:niˈtɛəriən] *n.* ①【宗】(基督教的)唯一神教派教徒. ②〔u-〕一神论者；一元论者；单一政府主义者，中央集权主义者. — *a.*【宗】唯一神教派的；〔u-〕单一的，一元的. **-ism** 唯一神教派.

u·ni·ta·ry [ˈju:nitəri] *a.* ①一个的，单一的，单元的. ②整体的，一致的. ③中央集权主义的. ④【数】单式的，酉的；幺正的. ⑤【哲】一元论的. *a* ～ *operator* 幺正算符. ～ *space* 单式空间.

u·nite[1] [ju(:)ˈnait] *vt.* ①使合成一体，结合；接合；使联合，合并. ②使混合，粘合. ③使结婚. ④兼备(种种性质). ～ *one with another* 合并〔结合〕甲和乙. ～ *bricks with cement* 用水泥砌砖. — *vi.* 成为一体，合一，联合，团结；混合，一致，协力. *Working men of all countries* ～*!* 全世界无产者，联合起来！

u·nite² [ˈju:nait, juˈnait] *n.* 由奈特〔英国詹姆斯一世时的金币,等于二十先令〕.

u·nit·ed [juˈnaitid] *a.* ①联合起来的;合并在一起的,统一的. ②一体同心的,团结一致的,协力的. ③【植】连生的. *a ~ front* 统一战线. *a ~ action* 一致行动. *U- we stand, divided we fall.* 团结顶得住,分裂必垮台. *break into a ~ laugh* 一齐哄笑起来. *in one ~ body* 成一体. ***the U- Arab Emirates*** [eˈmiərits] 阿拉伯联合酋长国. ***the U- Kingdom*** (大不列颠和北爱尔兰的)联合王国〔略 U.K.〕. ***the U- States (of America)*** 美利坚合众国〔略 U.S. (A.)〕. **U- Nations** 联合国〔略 UN.〕. **U- Nations Organization** 〔略 UNO〕联合国组织. **U- Nations Security Council** 联合国安全理事会. **U- Press (International)** (美国)合众(国际)社. **-ly** *ad.* 联合,一致,协力.

u·ni·tive [ˈju:nitiv] *a.* ①统一的. ②趋于统一的.

u·nit·ize [ˈju:nitaiz] *vt.* ***(-iz·ed, -iz·ing)*** 使成为一单位或一整体. **-i·za·tion** [ˌju:nitaiˈzeiʃən] *n.*

u·ni·ty [ˈju:niti] *n.* ①单一,唯一;个体,整体,统一体. ②团结,一致,和睦,调和. ③同质,同式,同样;不变性,一贯性. ④统一;合一. ⑤【数】一,单位元素. ⑥【法】共同租地权,共有. *~ and multiplicity* 一和多. *the dramatic unities = the unities of time, place, and action* 戏剧上时间、场所、情节的一致,三一律. *family ~* 家庭融洽. *national ~* 全国一致. ***live at [in] ~*** 融洽过日子,和睦相处 *(with)*. ~ **coupling** 【机】完整耦合.

Univ. = Universalist;〔英〕University.

univ. = ①universal(ly). ②university.

UNIVAC = universal automatic computer 通用电子计算机.

u·ni·va·lence [ˌju:niˈveiləns], **-len·cy** [-lənsi] *n.* 【生】单价;【化】一价,独价.

u·ni·va·lent [ˌju:niˈveilənt, juˈnivələnt], *a.* ①【生】(染色体)单价的,单独的. ②【化】一价的〔指一种元素只有一种价〕;独价的.

u·ni·valve [ˈju:nivælv] *n.* 【动】单壳(软体动物)〔如蜗牛〕. —*a.* ①单壳(的). ②(介壳虫的)单盖瓣(的). **-d** *a.*

u·ni·ver·sal [ˌju:niˈvə:səl] *a.* ①宇宙的,万有的,万物的;完全的,绝对的;全世界的. ②人类全体的,万人的;全面的,普及的,普通的. ③一般的,普遍的;【机】通用的,万能的;【逻】全称的. ④万般的;多方面的;多才多艺的. *a ~ peace* 世界和平. *a ~ language* 世界通用语言. *~ brotherhood* 四海同胞. *a ~ maid* 打杂女用工. *a ~ agent* 总代理人,全权代理人. ~ **algebra** 泛代数(学). —*n.*【逻】全称命题;【哲】一般(性),普遍(性);共相. ~ **arithmetic** 一般算术,代数学. ~ **boiler graphite** 【机】洗锅用铅粉. ~ **chuck** 【机】自动卡盘. ~ **constant** 【数】普适常数〔恒量〕. ~ **coupling** 【机】万向(联轴)节,万向接头. = ~ joint. ~ **gravitation** 【物】万有引力. ~ **instrument** 【天】万能仪. ~ **joint** 【机】万向接头. ~ **joint knuckle** 【解】自由关节. ~ **mill** 【机】万能铣床. ~ **suffage** 普选(权). ~ **time** 【天】世界时. ~ **validity** 【哲】普遍有效〔正确〕性. **-ly** *ad.*

u·ni·ver·sal·ism [ˌju:niˈvə:səlizəm] *n.* ①〔U-〕【宗】宇宙神教;普济主义. ② = universality.

U·ni·ver·sal·ist [ˌju:niˈvə:səlist] *n.* 宇宙神教徒. —*a.* = universalistic.

u·ni·ver·sal·is·tic [ˌju:niˌvə:səˈlistik] *a.* ①〔U-〕【宗】宇宙神教(徒)的. ②普遍的,一般的.

u·ni·ver·sal·i·ty [ˌju:nivəˈsæliti] *n.* 一般性,普遍性,无所不包性. *the ~ of contradiction* 矛盾的普遍性.

u·ni·ver·sal·i·za·tion [ˌju:niˌvə:səlaiˈzeiʃən] *n.* 一般化,普遍化,普及.

u·ni·ver·sal·ize [ˌju:niˈvə:səlaiz] *vt.* 使一般化,使普遍化.

u·ni·ver·sal·ness [ˌju:niˈvə:səlnis] *n.* ①宇宙性,万有. ②普遍性. ③整体,全体. ④全面;多面. ⑤通用. ⑥广用. ⑦【逻】全称性.

u·ni·verse [ˈju:nivə:s] *n.* ①宇宙;万有,天地万物,森罗万象;全世界;全人类. ②全领域;【统】全域;【逻】整体. ③【天】银河系;恒星与星辰系. *the fundamental law of the ~* 宇宙的根本规律. ***~ of discourse*** 【逻】论域.

u·ni·ver·si·ade [ˌju:niˈvə:siæd] *n.* 〔口〕世界大学生运动会 (=the World University Games).

u·ni·ver·si·ty [ˌju:niˈvə:si:ti] *n.* ①(综合)大学. ②大学当局. ③〔集合词〕大学人员. ④〔口〕【体】大学选手,大学队. *The ~ carried the day* 大学队得胜了. ~ **extention** 大学教育普及运动〔如成人业余教育,夜大学等〕. ~ **man** 大学生;受过大学教育的人.

u·niv·o·cal [ˌju:niˈvəukəl] *a.* 一义的,单意的;不含糊的.

un·joint [ʌnˈdʒɔint] *vt.* ①使分开,使脱节. ②把(关节)拆离.

un·just [ˈʌnˈdʒʌst] *a.* ①不义的,不正当的,不法的. ②不公平的,不公道的. *~ enrichment* 不正利得,横财. *the ~* 不正当的人们. **-ly** *ad.*

un·jus·ti·fi·a·ble [ʌnˈdʒʌstifaiəbl] *a.* 不能认为合理的,不能认为正当的,不能为之辩护的,无理的. **-a·bly** *ad.*

un·kempt [ˈʌnˈkempt] *a.* ①不整洁的,乱七八糟的;(服装等)邋遢的. ②(头发)未梳的,蓬乱的. ③(言语等)粗野的,生硬的. **-ness** *n.*

un·kenned [ʌnˈkend] *a.* 〔scot.〕不知道的;奇异的.

un·ken·nel [ʌnˈkenl], *vt.* ***(-neled, -nelled; -nel·ing)*** ①把(狐等)从洞穴中逐出;放(犬)出窝. ②暴露;揭开;揭发. — *vi.* (狐等)出洞;(犬)出窝.

un·key [ˈʌŋki] *n.* 〔美俚〕黑人老头子.

un·kind [ʌnˈkaind] *a.* 不和善的;不亲切的;冷酷的. **-ness** *n.*

un·kind·ly [ʌnˈkaindli] *a.* = unkind. — *ad.* 不和善地,不亲切地;冷酷地.

un·knit [ʌnˈnit] *vt.* ***(~, un·knit·ted*** [ʌnˈnitid]***)*** 拆(编织物);解(结);平整(皱褶);〔喻〕展开(皱起的眉头).

un·knot [ʌnˈnɔt] *vt.* ***(un·knot·ted*** [ʌnˈnɔtid]; ***-knot·ting)*** ①解(结). ②解决(难题〔困难〕).

un·know·a·ble [ˈʌnˈnəuəbl] *a.* 不可知道的;【哲】不可知的. — *n.* 〔the U-〕【哲】不可知物.

un·know·ing [ʌnˈnəuiŋ] *a.* ①不知道的,没察觉…的 *(of)*. ②无知的. *~ aid to enemy* 无知的〔自己不知道的〕利敌行为. **-ly** *ad.*

un·known [ˈʌnˈnəun] *a.* ①未知的,未详的;未被发觉的. ②数不清的,无数的. *a man ~ to me* 我不知道〔认识〕的人. *~ wealth* 巨富. ~ ***to ...*** 所不知道的;〔作副词用〕没有给…知道,不给…晓得*(He did it ~ to me.* 他没有让我知道就做了那件事了). —*n.* 未〔不〕认识的人〔物〕;【数】未知数〔量,元〕. ***the Great U-*** 伟大的匿名作家〔Sir Walter Scott 的历史小说《威弗利》匿名出版时,人们对该书作者的尊称〕. ***the U- Warrior [〔美〕Soldier]*** 无名战士〔其遗体被选出作为阵亡将士的代表接受国葬〕. ***venture into the ~*** 闯进未知世界中,大胆地探索未知的世界.

un·la·boured [ˈʌnˈleibəd] *a.* ①未经耕作的. ②(似乎)不费力的. ③自然的,流利的.

un·lace [ˈʌnˈleis] *vt.* ①解开(鞋等的)带子. ②【猎】把(打到的野兽)切成块.

un·lade [ˈʌnˈleid] *vt.* 给…卸货;卸(货). — *vi.* 卸货.

un·laid [ˈʌnˈleid] unlay 的过去式和过去分词.

un·la·ment·ed [ˈʌnləˈmentid] *a.* 没有人悲悼的,没有人叹息的,没有人惋惜的.

un·lash [ʌnˈlæʃ] *vt.* 解开(绑着的东西).

un·latch [ˈʌnˈlætʃ] *vt.* 拉开(门窗的)闩;开(门上的)暗锁;解开(鞋)扣.

un·law·ful [ˈʌnˈlɔːful] *a.* ①不法的,违法的,非法的,不正当的. ②私生的. *an ~ assembly* 非法集会. **-ly** *ad.* **-ness** *n.*

un·lax [ʌnˈlæks] *vi., vt.*〔美〕= relax.

un·lay [ˈʌnˈlei] *vt.* **(-laid** [-ˈleid]**)**【海】退缠(缠绕着的绳缆等),拧散(绳线的股).

un·lead·ed [ʌnˈledid] *a.* ①没有用铅包的,未用铅来增加重量的. ②【印】在间隔中未插铅条的.

un·learn [ˈʌnˈləːn] *vt., vi.* **(~ed, -learnt** [-ˈləːnt]**)**(使)忘掉(学过的东西);(使)抛弃(谬见、坏习惯等).

un·learn·ed¹ [ʌnˈləːnid] *a.* 无学识的;无文化的;未受教育的. — *n.*〔the ~〕蒙昧无知的人们. **-ly** *ad.*

un·learned² [ʌnˈləːnt, -ləːnd] *a.* ①不是学来的,不学就知道的. ②未学过的,未学会的.

un·learnt [ʌnˈləːnt] unlearn 的过去式和过去分词. — *a.* = unlearned².

un·leash [ˈʌnˈliːʃ] *vt.* ①解开…的皮带[链索]. ②〔喻〕解放,使自由;放纵;发动. *~ one's desire* 纵欲. *~ a war* 发动战争.

un·leav·ened [ˈʌnˈlevnd] *a.* ①不含酵素的,未予发酵的. ②没有受到影响[感化]的.

un·less [ənˈles, ʌnˈles] *conj.* 如果不,要是不,除非. *We shall go ~ it rains.* 如果不下雨我们就去. *U- you work harder you will not pass the examination* 如果不加劲用功,你就不能通过考试. *U- absolutely compelled, I shall not go.* 除非万不得已,我是不去的. *~* ***and until*** = until〔~ and 是冗语〕. — *prep.* 除…之外. *U- a miracle, he'll not be back in time.* 除非发生奇迹,他不会及时赶回来. ★此种用法隐含着一个动词被省略,即相当于 U- a miracle (happens) ....

un·let·tered [ˈʌnˈletəd] *a.* ①不是用文字写成的;无字的;没有字母等记号的. ②没有学识的;目不识丁的.

un·li·censed [ˈʌnˈlaisənst] *a.* ①没有执照[许可证]的. ②无节制的,放纵的. *an ~ physician* 没有执照的医生,未经许可的医生.

un·licked [ˈʌnˈlikt] *a.* ①(仔兽)没有经过母兽舐干净的. ②不象样的;撒野的,没礼貌的. *an ~ cub* 撒野的小兽;撒野的小伙子[小姑娘].

un·like [ˈʌnˈlaik] *a.* 不同的,不相似的,相异的. *~ signs* 不同的符号. — *prep.* 不象…,和…不同. *The picture is quite ~ him.* 这张照片完全不象他. *How ~ you to forget your dinner!* 你怎么也会忘记吃饭!

un·like·ly [ʌnˈlaikli] *a.* ①未必有的,不象是真的,不一定有希望的. ②〔后接不定式,可用作表语〕未必可能的,不大可能的,不一定有把握的. *What he tells us is an ~ tale.* 他告诉我们的,不象是真事. *A victory is ~ but not impossible.* 胜利不一定有希望但也不一定不可能. *He is ~ to come.* 他未必会来. *It is not ~ that a huge wave has overturned his boat.* 一阵大浪把他的船打翻了,这种情况不是不可能的. ***in the ~ event of*** 万一. **-i·hood, -i·ness** *n.*

un·lim·ber¹ [ʌnˈlimbə] *a.* 不易弯屈的;僵硬的. — *vt., vi.* (使)变得柔软;(使)柔软.

un·lim·ber² [ʌnˈlimbə] *vt., vi.* 卸下(炮的)牵引车准备(开炮);(使)准备行动.

un·lim·it·ed [ʌnˈlimitid] *a.* ①无边的,无限的;没有限制的;没有限定的,不定的. ②极大的;过多的,过度的. *~ liability* 无限责任. *an ~ company* 无限公司. *~ exposure* 长时间露光. *drink ~ coffee* 喝过多的咖啡. **-ly** *ad.*

un·link [ˈʌnˈliŋk] *vt., vi.* 解开(链环);拆散.

un·liq·ui·dat·ed [ˈʌnˈlikwideitid] *a.* 未清算的,未决算的;未偿还的,未付的.

un·list·ed [ʌnˈlistid] *a.* ①未登上名册的. ②非公开登记的;内部安排的. ③(证券)未上证券市场的.

un·lit [ˈʌnˈlit] *a.* 未点燃的;未点亮的.

un·liv·a·ble [ˈʌnˈlivəbl] *a.* 不宜居住的;不舒适的〔指居住条件〕.

un·live [ˈʌnˈliv] *vt.* 抹除[忘却](过去的生活经历);(以新的生活)消除(过去经历的后果). *History cannot be ~d* 历史是不能抹掉[忘却]的. *He wishes to ~ the crimes he has committed* 他希望(以新的生活)消解他所犯的罪行.

un·load [ˈʌnˈləud] *vt.* ①从…卸下货载;卸下(货载). ②解除…的负担;摆脱(身上的负担);倾吐(压在心里的思想). ③退出(枪膛里的)子弹. ④【商】抛售(证券). — *vi.* ①卸货,起货. ②退出枪弹. **-er** *n.* 卸货人;卸载机.

un·lock [ˈʌnˈlɔk] *vt.* ①开(门、箱等的)锁. ②使张开;使开启. ③表白(心迹). ④揭露(秘密);破译;解读. ⑤释放出. —*vi.* 开启着,被解开;不受羁绊.

un·looked-for [ʌnˈluktfɔː] *a.* 未予寻求过的;没有预料到的,想不到的,意外的.

un·loose [ˈʌnˈluːs], **un·loos·en** [-n] *vt.* 解开,放松;释放. **-loos·a·ble** *a.*

un·love·ly [ˈʌnˈlʌvli] *a.* 不可爱的,不美的;可厌的.

un·lov·ing [ˈʌnˈlʌviŋ] *a.* 无爱意的,无情的,冷酷的.

un·luck·i·ly [ʌnˈlʌkili] *ad.* 不幸;偏巧,偏偏.

un·luck·y [ʌnˈlʌki] *a.* **(-i·er; -i·est)** ①不幸的,倒霉的. ②不凑巧的;令人遗憾的. ③不顺利的,不成功的. ④不吉利的,不祥的. ***in an ~ hour*** 偏偏,偏巧. **-i·ly** *ad.*

unm. = unmarried.

un·make [ˈʌnˈmeik] *vt.* **(-made** [-ˈmeid]**)** ①破坏,毁坏;使消失. ②使变形,使变质. ③废除(国王等). ④改变(决定等).

un·man [ˈʌnˈmæn] *vt.* ①使失去男子汉气概,使落魄[沮丧]. ②阉割,给…去势. ③撤去…的人员[船员].

un·man·age·a·ble [ʌnˈmænidʒəbl] *a.* 无法处理的,难办理的,难收拾的;难管理的,难应付的,难弄的;(孩子)不听话的. *the ~ situation* 难收拾的局势. *an ~ horse* 劣马. **-a·bly** *ad.*

un·man·ly [ˈʌnˈmænli] *a.* **(-li·er; -li·est)** 不象男子汉的;娇气的;没胆量的,懦弱的.

un·manned [ʌnˈmænd] *a.* ①无人驾驶[操纵]的,遥控的. ②无人居住的,荒废的. ③失去男子气概的. ④被阉割过的.

un·man·ner·ly [ʌnˈmænəli] *a., ad.* 没礼貌的[地],粗野的[地].

un·marked [ˈʌnˈmɑːkt] *a.* ①未做记号的. ②没被注意到的.

un·marred [ˈʌnˈmɑːd] *a.* 未玷污的;未损伤的,未损坏的.

un·mar·ried [ˈʌnˈmærid] *a.* 未婚的;独身的.

un·mask [ˈʌnˈmɑːsk] *vi.* 脱去假面具,现出本来面目. — *vt.* 撕下…的假面具;暴露;揭露;【军】(开炮佯射)使(敌方炮位)暴露.

un·match·a·ble [ˈʌnˈmætʃəbl] *a.* ①难匹敌的,无可比拟的,不能对抗的. ②不能相配的.

un·matched [ˈʌnˈmætʃt] *a.* ①无敌的,无比的. ②(颜色等)不相配[衬]的.

un·mean·ing [ʌnˈmiːniŋ] *a.* ①没有意义的. ②(面孔等)呆板的,没表情的. **-ly** *ad.*

un·meant [ʌnˈment] *a.* 不是故意的.

un·meas·ured [ʌnˈmeʒəd] *a.* ①不可测量的. ②无边无际的;没有界限的. ③【韵】不按照韵律的.

un·meet [ʌnˈmiːt] *a.* = unfit.

un·men·tion·a·ble [ʌnˈmenʃənəbl] *a.* 说不出口的,难于出口的. — *n.*〔*pl.*〕①难于说出口的事物. ②〔谑〕裤子;内衣.

un·mer·ci·ful [ʌnˈməːsiful] *a.* ①无慈悲心的,无情的,残忍的. ②过分的,过大的. **-ly** *ad.*

un·mer·it·ed [ˈʌnˈmeritid] *a.* 无功而得的,不该得的;不配的,(赏罚)不当的.

un·me·thod·i·cal [ˈʌnmiˈθɔdikəl] *a.* 没有什么方法的,不讲究方式的;没有组织的,没有条理的;胡乱的.

-ly *ad.*
un·met·ri·cal [ˈʌnˈmetrikəl] *a.* 不按照音律的.
un·mil·i·ta·ry [ˈʌnˈmilitəri] *a.* ①非军事的. ②违反军队训练[规则]的. ③不象军人的.
un·mind·ful [ʌnˈmaindful] *a.* 不注意的,漫不经心的;易忘的 *(of; that)*. **-ly** *ad.*
un·mis·tak·a·ble [ˈʌnmisˈteikəbl] *a.* 不会弄错的, 不可能发生误解的, 明白的. *The slogans are* ~. 口号明确. **-a·bly** *ad.*
un·mit·i·gat·ed [ʌnˈmitigeitid] *a.* ①没有和缓的, 没有减轻的. ②十足的,纯粹的. *an* ~ *lie* 纯粹的骗人话. *an* ~ *ass* 大傻瓜. **-ly** *ad.*
un·mixed, -mixt [ˈʌnˈmikst] *a.* 没有搀杂的; 纯粹的. *not an* ~ *blessing* 不是纯粹的幸福.
un·mo·lested [ˈʌnməuˈlestid] *a.* 未受到烦扰的; 平静的.
un·moor [ˈʌnˈmuə] *vt., vi.*【海】①(使)拔锚, (使)解缆. ②(使)改泊单锚.
un·mor·al [ˈʌnˈmɔrəl] *a.* ①非道德的; 和道德无关的, 不涉及道德的. ②没有道德观念的; 不道德的. **-ly** *ad.*
un·mount·ed [ˈʌnˈmauntid] *a.* ①(图画、照片等)没有镶边框的. ②未上炮架的. ③不骑马的.
un·moved [ˈʌnˈmu:vd] *a.* ①(决心等)坚定的. ②不动心的,冷静的,镇定的.
un·muf·fle [ʌnˈmʌfl] *vt.* ***(-fled; fling)*** ①揭去(脸上, 头上等的)遮盖物. ②脱去(桨、鼓等的)套子. — *vi.* 脱去覆盖物.
un·mur·mur·ing [ˈʌnˈmə:məriŋ] *a.* 不嘟囔的; 不发牢骚的. **-ly** *ad.*
un·mu·si·cal [ˈʌnˈmju:zikəl] *a.* ①非音乐的; 不悦耳的,不合调子的,难听的. ②不懂音乐的, 没有音乐修养的;对音乐没有兴趣的;没有音乐技巧的.
un·muz·zle [ˈʌnˈmʌzl] *vt.* ①拿下(狗等的)口罩. ②〔喻〕对…解除束缚言论自由的法令.
un·nam(e)·a·ble [ˈʌnˈneiməbl] *a.* 叫不出名字来的; (恐怖等)不可名状的.
un·named [ˈʌnˈneimd] *a.* 没有名称的; 未指名的; 没有明确指定[说明]的.
un·nat·u·ral [ʌnˈnætʃərəl] *a.* ①不合自然规律的,不应有的. ②不自然的; 做作的, 勉强的. ③不合人情[人道]的; 变态的; 残忍的. ④奇异的, 奇怪的. *die an* ~ *death* 横死, 死于非命. *an* ~ *smile* 假笑. ~ **crime [vice, act]** 鸡奸. **-ly** *ad.* **-ness** *n.*
un·nec·es·sa·ri·ly [ʌnˈnesisərili] *ad.* 不必要地, 多余地,无用地,徒然,无谓.
un·nec·es·sa·ry [ʌnˈnesisəri] *a.* 不必要的, 多余的,无用的,无益的. *with* ~ *care* 怀着不必要的顾虑. — *n.* 〔罕〕〔常 *pl.*〕不必要[多余]的东西.
un·neigh·bour·ly, 〔美〕 **-bor·ly** [ˈʌnˈneibəli] *a.* 不象邻人的,没有邻舍情谊的; 不懂交际的, 不友好的; 不亲切的.
un·nerve [ˈʌnˈnə:v] *vt.* 使失去意志力, 使丧失勇气; 使身心交疲.
un·no·ticed [ˈʌnˈnəutist] *a.* 不受人注意的; 没有受到注意的; 不触目的; 没人理睬的. *pass* ~ 被忽略过去; 被遗漏.
un·num·bered [ˈʌnˈnʌmbəd] *a.* ①没有数的. ②数不清的, 无数的. ③未编号的.
UNO [ˈju:nəu] = United Nations Organization 联合国组织.
uno ani·mo [ˈjunəu ˈæniməu] 〔L.〕一致地,无异议地.
un·ob·jec·tion·a·ble [ˈʌnəbˈdʒekʃənəbl] *a.* ①难反对的, 不能指摘的, 无可非议的. ②不致引起反感的; 婉转的.
un·ob·serv·ant [ˈʌnəbˈzə:vənt] *a.* ①不注意[留心]的; 没有观察力的. ②不遵守(规章等)的 *(of)*.
un·ob·served [ˈʌnəbˈsə:vd] *a.* ①没有观察到的,没有受到注意的. ②(规章等)未受人遵守的.
un·ob·tru·sive [ˈʌnəbˈtru:siv] *a.* 不突出的,不触目的; 不冒昧的,谦逊的. **-ly** *ad.*
un·oc·cu·pied [ˈʌnˈɔkjupaid] *a.* ①(房子等)没人住的, 空着的. ②【军】未被占领的; 无人占领的. ③空闲的, 无事的.
un·of·fend·ed [ˈʌnəˈfendid] *a.* 没被冒犯的, 没被得罪的; 不生气的.
un·of·fend·ing [ˈʌnəˈfendiŋ] *a.* ①不侵犯人的,不冲撞人的. ②无害的,无罪的.
un·of·fi·cial [ˈʌnəˈfiʃəl] *a.* 非官方的, 非正式的; 非法定的. *an* ~ *candidate* 非正式候补人. **-ly** *ad.*
un·o·pened [ˈʌnˈəupənd] *a.* ①没有打开过的; 没有拆开的, 封着的. ②(书页)未裁开的. ③(港口等)不开放的.
un·or·gan·ized [ˈʌnˈɔ:gənaizd] *a.* ①未加组织的; 未编成的; 无组织的. ②【生】无细胞结构的. ③〔美〕没有加入工会组织的. ~ **ferment** 非生(物)酶,抗热酶,非机体酵素.
un·o·rig·i·nal [ˈʌnəˈridʒənəl] *a.* ①无独创性的. ②非原先的.
un·or·tho·dox [ˈʌnˈɔ:θədɔks] *a.* 非正统的; 异端的. **-ly** *ad.*
un·os·ten·ta·tious [ˈʌnˌɔstenˈteiʃəs] *a.* 不虚饰门面的; 不自大的,不傲慢的; 朴素的. **-ly** *ad.*
un·pack [ˈʌnˈpæk] *vt.* 打开(包裹等),解开; 从(包裹等)中拿出; 从(车、马上)卸下货物. — *vi.* 打开包裹[行李(等)].
un·paged [ʌnˈpeidʒd] *a.* (书等)未标页码的.
un·paid [ˈʌnˈpeid] *a.* ①未付的,(债等)未还的,未缴纳的. ②不受酬的,名誉上的; 没薪水的,无报酬的. *letters posted* ~ 欠资信件. ***the (great)*** ~ 〔主英〕无薪法官.
un·paired [ˈʌnˈpeəd] *a.* ①未配对的; 无配偶的. ②(鱼)奇(鳍)的.
un·pal·at·a·ble [ʌnˈpælətəbl] *a.* 味道不好的, 不好吃的; 没味的; 可厌的. **-a·bly** *ad.*
un·par·al·leled [ʌnˈpærəleld] *a.* 无比的,无双的; 空前的. *an* ~ *victory* 空前大胜. ~ *in history* 史无前例的.
un·par·don·a·ble [ʌnˈpɑ:dnəbl] *a.* 不能宽恕的, 不能原谅的. **-a·bly** *ad.*
un·par·lia·men·ta·ry [ˈʌnˌpɑ:ləˈmentəri] *a.* 违反议会法[议会惯例]的; 议会内所不许的. ~ *language* 不谨慎的话,气愤话. **-i·ly** *ad.*
un·pat·ent·ed [ˈʌnˈpeitəntid] *a.* 未获得专利权的, 非专利的.
un·pa·tri·ot·ic [ˈʌnpætriˈɔtik] *a.* 不爱国的, 没有爱国心的. **-i·cal·ly** *ad.*
un·paved [ˈʌnˈpeivd] *a.* 没有铺砌的; 没有铺路的.
un·peg [ʌnˈpeg] *vt.* ***(pegged; -peg·ging)*** ①从…拔去木栓. ②拔去[除去]木栓以松开. ③使(证券等)解冻.
un·peo·ple [ˈʌnˈpi:pl] *vt.* 消灭(某地)的居民,把(某地)弄成无人居住之地. **-d** *a.* 无居民的,无人的.
un·per·ceived [ˈʌnpəˈsi:vd] *a.* 未被发觉的, 没有给人看见[被人注意]的.
un·per·fect [ˈʌnˈpə:fikt] *a.* = imperfect.
un·per·son [ˈʌnˈpə:sn] *n.* 退出一切公开场合的人, 被完全忘却[象不存在一样]的人,没落人物〔指失去影响的政治家、知名人士等〕. — *vt.* 使变成没落人物.
un·per·suad·a·ble [ˈʌnpəˈsweidəbl] *a.* 不能说服的; 坚定不移的,固执的.
un·per·turbed [ˈʌnpəˈtə:bd] *a.* 没有受到搅乱的; 平静的,镇定的.
un·pick [ˈʌnˈpik] *vt.* ①拔开,割开. ②拆开(针脚); 拆开(衣服等的)针脚.
un·picked¹ [ˈʌnˈpikt] *a.* 拆开针脚的,拆缝的.
un·picked² [ˈʌnˈpikt] *a.* ①未经挑选的,未拣过的. ②(花等)未摘的.

un·pin [ʌnˈpin] *vt.* (从衣服等上)拔去别针; 拔去别针拆开; 拔掉(门)闩,拔去(插销).
un·pit·ied [ˈʌnˈpitid] *a.* 没人怜悯的,没人同情的.
un·placed [ˈʌnˈpleist] *a.* ①未得到安置的; 没有固定位置[职位]的. ②【赛马】未获得前三名的.
un·planned [ˈʌnˈplænd] *a.* ①无计划的; 未经筹划的. ②意外的.
un·play·a·ble [ˈʌnˈpleiəbl] *a.* ①无法用乐器演奏的. ②(高尔夫球等)无法击出的.
un·pleas·ant [ʌnˈpleznt] *a.* 令人不愉快的, 不舒服的, 可厌的. **-ly** *ad.*
un·pleas·ant·ness [ʌnˈplezntnis] *n.* ①不愉快,不快,煞风景,无趣. ②不和, 倾轧. ***have a slight ~ with sb.*** 和某人有点不痛快. ***the late [recent] ~*** 〔美谑〕南北战争〔又指南北战争后的美西战争、世界大战等〕.
un·pleas·ing [ˈʌnˈpli:ziŋ] *a.* 令人不愉快的;可厌的; 没趣的.
un·plug [ˈʌnˈplʌg] *vt.* ***(-ged; -ging)*** 拔去…的塞子[插头];去掉…的障碍物.
un·plumbed [ʌnˈplʌmd] *a.* ①未用铅锤线测量过垂直度的. ②未查明的; 不完全懂的. ③无煤气、水管、下水道等设备的. ④未加铅封的.
un·pol·ished [ˈʌnˈpɔliʃt] *a.* ①没有磨光的, 没有擦亮的,没有光泽的. ②未经润饰的. ③不文雅的, 粗鲁的, 没礼貌的.
un·po·lit·i·cal [ˈʌnpəˈlitikəl] *a.* ①无政治意义的;非政治的. ②不关心政治的.
un·polled [ʌnˈpəuld] *a.* ①未记名的; (选票)未登记的, 未投票的,未点票的. ②未作过民意测验[意见调查]的.
un·pop·u·lar [ˈʌnˈpɔpjulə] *a.* 无人望的, 不受欢迎的; 不流行的. *become more and more ~* 越来越不得人心.
un·pop·u·lar·i·ty [ˈʌnˌpɔpjuˈlæriti] *n.* 无人望, 不受欢迎;不流行.
un·prac·ti·cal [ˈʌnˈpræktikəl] *a.* 没有实践的, 不切实际的;不实用的.
un·prac·tised, 〔美〕 **-ticed** [ʌnˈpræktist] *a.* ①练习不足的;不熟练的; 缺少经验的. ②未实行的; 未实际应用的,未使用的.
un·prec·e·dent·ed [ʌnˈpresidəntid] *a.* ①没有前例的, 空前的;无比的. ②新奇的; 崭新的. *an ~ success* 空前的成功. **-ly** *ad.*
un·pre·dict·a·ble [ˈʌn-priˈdiktəbl] *a.* 无法预言的. **-a·bly** *ad.*
un·prej·u·diced [ʌnˈpredʒudist] *a.* ①没有偏见[成见]的,公平的. ②(权利等)没有受到损害的.
un·pre·med·i·tat·ed [ˈʌnpriˈmediteitid] *a.* 非预谋的,不是故意的; 没有预先考虑过的. *~ homicide* 非预谋杀人. **-ly** *ad.*
un·pre·pared [ˈʌnpriˈpɛəd] *a.* ①没有预备[准备]的; 临时的, (演说)即席的. ②还没有决心[准备好]的 *(for)*. *Fight no battle ~.* 不打无准备之仗. *You caught me ~.* 你钻了我的空子. **-ly** *ad.*
un·pre·pos·sess·ing [ˈʌnˌpri:pəˈzesiŋ] *a.* 不讨人喜欢的,不吸引人的.
un·pre·sent·a·ble [ˈʌn-priˈzentəbl] *a.* 见不得人的;不象样的,拿不出去的.
un·pre·tend·ing [ˈʌnpriˈtendiŋ], **un·pre·ten·tious** [-tenʃəs] *a.* 不装腔作势的,不骄傲的,谦逊的. **-ly** *ad.*
un·prin·ci·pled [ʌnˈprinsəpld] *a.* 无原则的, 无节操的,无耻的,无道德的;蛮横无理的.
un·print·a·ble [ʌnˈprintəbl] *a.* (因淫猥等)不能付印的,不适于付印的.
un·priv·i·leged [ˈʌnˈprivilidʒd] *a.* 没有特权的,享受不到特权的; 〔美〕 处在社会下层的.
un·pro·duc·tive [ˈʌnprəˈdʌktiv] *a.* ①没有出产物的, 不毛的;没有收益的. ②非生产性的. ③没有效果的,徒然的. **-ly** *ad.*
un·pro·fessed [ˈʌn-prəˈfest] *a.* 不公开宣称的.
un·pro·fes·sion·al [ˈʌnprəˈfeʃənəl] *a.* ①不是专家的; 不是本行的; 不在行的. ②违反职业上习惯[道德、行规]的. ③非职业性的,业余的. ④与专门职业无关的. **-ly** *ad.*
un·prof·it·a·ble [ʌnˈprɔfitəbl] *a.* 没有利润的, 赚不到钱的;无益的,无效的,没用的. **-a·bly** *ad.*
un·prom·is·ing [ˈʌnˈprɔmisiŋ] *a.* 没有希望的,前途无望的;结果未必良好的.
un·prompt·ed [ˈʌnˈprɔmptid] *a.* 未经提示的; 未经敦促的,自发的.
un·pro·nounce·a·ble [ˈʌnprəˈnaunsəbl] *a.* 不能发音的;难发音的.
un·pro·pi·tious [ˈʌnprəˈpiʃəs] *a.* 不吉利的,不祥的,背时的,倒霉的. **-ly** *ad.*
un·pro·tect·ed [ˈʌnprəˈtektid] *a.* ①没有防卫的, 不设防的. ②无装甲的. ③没有得到关税保护的. ④无保护(人)的.
un·proved [ˈʌnˈpru:vd] *a.* 未被证明的;未经检验的.
un·pro·vid·ed [ˈʌn-prəˈvaidid] *a.* ①无供给的, 无生活来源的. ②未作准备的.
un·pro·voked [ˈʌn-prəˈvəukt] *a.* 无缘无故的, 非因触犯而发生的.
un·pub·lished [ˈʌnˈpʌbliʃt] *a.* 未发表过的; 未公开出版的.
un·pun·ished [ˈʌnˈpʌniʃt] *a.* 未受处罚的,得免刑罚的; 逍遥法外的.
un·pu·ri·fied [ˈʌnˈpjuərifaid] *a.* 未纯化的,未精制的.
un·qual·i·fied [ˈʌnˈkwɔlifaid] *a.* ①不够格的, 没有资格的;不适任[适当]的. ②[ʌnˈkwɔlifaid] 无条件[限制]的,绝对的; 〔口〕十足的, 彻底的. *an ~ fool* 大傻瓜. **-ly** *ad.*
un·quench·a·ble [ʌnˈkwentʃəbl] *a.* 不能熄灭的; (热情)压制不住的;止不住的. **-a·bly** *ad.*
un·ques·tion·a·ble [ʌnˈkwestʃənəbl] *a.* 无疑问的, 不成问题的; 无可非议的; 确实的, 当然的, 明确的. **-a·bly** *ad.*
un·ques·tioned [ʌnˈkwestʃənd] *a.* ①不成为问题的. ②未受调查[审问]的. ③无人争辩[怀疑]的,无异议的.
un·ques·tion·ing [ʌnˈkwesʃəniŋ] *a.* 不提问题[质问]的,没有疑问的;毫不迟疑[踌躇]的;无条件的,绝对的.
un·qui·et [ˈʌnˈkwaiət] *a.* ①不平静的; 动摇的,不稳的. ②不安的. — *n.* ①动荡. ②焦虑,不安. **-ly** *ad.* **-ness** *n.*
un·quot·a·ble [ˈʌnˈkwəutəbl] *a.* 不能引用的, 无引用价值的.
un·quote [ˈʌnˈkwəut] *int.* 〔美〕〔口授用语〕引语结束!
un·rav·el [ʌnˈrævəl] *vt.* ①解开,拆散,拆开(毛线、绳索等). ②解明,阐明,解决. — *vi.* 散开,松线.
un·read [ˈʌnˈred] *a.* ①(书等)未读的; 尚未审阅的. ②不读书的,无教育的;无学识的.
un·read·a·ble [ʌnˈri:dəbl] *a.* ①不能读的; 不能辨认的. ②难读的;不值得读的.
un·read·y [ˈʌnˈredi] *a.* ①没有预备[准备]的. ②不敏捷的. ③〔古、方〕拖遢的, 衣着不讲究的. **-i·ly** *ad.* **-i·ness** *n.*
un·re·al [ˈʌnˈriəl, ˈʌnˈri:əl] *a.* 不实在的;非现实的; 不真实的. **-ly** *ad.*
un·re·al·is·tic [ˈʌnriəˈlistik] *a.* 不现实的; 不实际的; 空想的. **-cal·ly** *ad.*
un·re·al·i·ty [ˈʌnriˈæliti] *n.* ***(pl. -ties)*** ①不真实, 不实在. ②幻想. ③虚构;不切实际.
un·rea·son [ˈʌnˈri:zn] *n.* 无理,缺乏理性;不合理;背理.
un·rea·son·a·ble [ʌnˈri:znəbl] *a.* ①无理性的,不懂道理的,不讲理的. ②不合理的,荒唐的;过度的,(价格等)过高的,(收费等)不当的. **-a·bly** *ad.*
un·rea·soned [ʌnˈri:znd] *a.* 不合理的,无理的.

un·reason·ing [ʌnˈriːzniŋ] *a.* 无理性的；不加考虑的；不懂[不讲]道理的. **-ly** *ad.*
un·re·claimed [ˈʌnriˈkleimd] *a.* ①(人)未改造好的，未改邪归正的. ②(土地)未开垦的. ③(物品)未收回的.
un·rec·og·nized [ˈʌnˈrekəgnaizd] *a.* ①未被认识的，未认出的，没人认识的. ②未被承认的.
un·re·con·struct·ed [ˈʌnˌriːkənˈstrʌktid] *a.* 〔美〕①未重建的，未改造的. ②坚持早已过时的做法或观点的〔尤指反对美国南北战争后南部各州改组〕.
un·reel [ˈʌnˈriːl] *vt., vi.* = unwind.
un·reeve [ˈʌnˈriːv] ***[-rove*** [-ˈrəuv], ***-reeved]*** *vt.* 从(滑车等)拉回(绳子).
un·re·fined [ˈʌnriˈfaind] *a.* ①未精炼的，非精制的. ②粗俗的，下流的.
un·re·flect·ing [ˈʌnriˈflektiŋ] *a.* ①不反省的，不顾前后的，轻率的. ②不反射的. **-ly** *ad.*
un·re·gard·ed [ʌnriˈgɑːdid] *a.* 不受注意的，无人理睬的，被轻视的，被疏忽的.
un·re·gen·er·ate, -ated [ˈʌnriˈdʒenərit, -itid] *a.*【宗】灵魂不得再生的〔尤指改变信仰使精神上得到再生的〕；不改过自新的；不改悔的；罪孽深重的.
un·re·lent·ing [ˈʌnriˈlentiŋ] *a.* ①不宽恕的，铁面无私的，冷酷无情的. ②坚定的；毫不松懈的，不屈不挠的. **-ly** *ad.*
un·re·li·a·ble [ˈʌnriˈlaiəbl] *a.* 不能信任的；不可靠的. **-a·bly** *ad.* **-bil·i·ty** [ˈʌnˌrilaiəˈbiliti] *n.*
un·re·lieved [ˈʌnriˈliːvd] *a.* ①未得缓和的；(病痛、疾苦等)未经解除的；(贫民)未受救济的. ②无变化的；单调的.
un·re·li·gious [ˈʌnriˈlidʒəs] *a.* ①无宗教的，无宗教信仰的；漠视[反对]宗教的；违反宗教原则的，亵渎的，不虔诚的. ②与宗教无牵连的；非宗教的.
un·re·mark·a·ble [ˈʌnriˈmɑːkəbl] *a.* 不值得注意的；不显著的；平凡的.
un·re·mit·ting [ˌʌnriˈmitiŋ] *a.* 不断的，不停的；坚持不懈的，坚忍的. *an* ~ *struggle* 坚持不懈的斗争. **-ly** *ad.*
un·re·mu·ner·a·tive [ˈʌnriˈmjuːnərətiv] *a.* 不合算的，无利可获的，无报酬的.
un·re·pent·ant [ˈʌnriˈpentənt] *a.* ①不改悔的. ②顽固不化的.
un·re·quit·ed [ˈʌnriˈkwaitid] *a.* ①无报答的；(工作)得不到报酬的. ②有仇未报复的. ~ *love [affection]* 单恋.
un·re·serve [ˈʌnriˈzəːv] *n.* 不保留，坦率.
un·re·served [ˈʌnriˈzəːvd] *a.* ①无保留的，坦白的，无隐瞒的，率直的. ②不加克制的. ③无限制的，无条件的，完全的. ④(座位等)没有人预定的. **-ly** *ad.* **-ness** *n.*
un·re·solved [ˈʌnriˈzɔlvd] *a.* ①不坚决的，无决心的. ②未解决的；未议决的；未澄清的. ③未分解的，未加分析的.
un·res·pon·sive [ˈʌnrisˈpɔnsiv] *a.* 无反应[答复]的，迟钝的；冷淡的. **-ly** *ad.*
un·rest [ˈʌnˈrest] *n.* 不稳；不安；骚乱.
un·re·strained [ˈʌnriˈstreind] *a.* 无限制的，不受约束的；自由的. **-ly** *ad.*
un·re·straint [ˈʌnriˈstreint] *n.* 无限制；无拘束，放纵，放肆，猖獗.
un·re·strict·ed [ˈʌnrisˈtriktid] *a.* 不受限制的；不受约束的；无管制的；自由的.
un·rid·dle [ˈʌnˈridl] *vt.* 解(谜)；说明.
un·rig [ˈʌnˈrig] *vt.* 【海】解去(船的)索具；拆去…的装备；〔口〕剥去…的衣服.
un·right·eous [ʌnˈraitʃəs] *a.* 不公正的，不正当的；不义的，罪恶的. *the* ~ 歹徒. **-ly** *ad.* **-ness** *n.*
un·rip [ʌnˈrip] *vt.* ***(-rip·ped; -rip·ping)*** ①割开，扯开；劈开；剖开. ②〔现罕〕使…知道，揭示.
un·ripe [ˈʌnˈraip] *a.* 未(成)熟的；时机未熟[未到]的，过早的；年轻的.
un·ri·valled, 〔美〕 **-valed** [ʌnˈraivəld] *a.* 无敌的，没有竞争对手的，无比的，无双的.
un·robe [ˈʌnˈrəub] *vt., vi.* (使)脱去长袍，(使)脱去衣服.
un·roll [ˈʌnˈrəul] *vt., vi.* 解开(卷物)，打开，铺开；展开，(使)现出.
un·roof [ˈʌnˈruːf] *vt.* 拆去…的屋顶[覆盖].
un·root [ˈʌnˈruːt] *vt.* = uproot.
un·round [ʌnˈraund] *vt.* 【语音】①不圆唇发出(某元音). ②使(唇)保持不圆形〔如发 *she* 的元音〕. **-ed** *a.*
un·rove [ʌnˈrəuv] unreeve 的过去式及过去分词.
UNRRA, U.N.R.R.A. [ˈʌnrɑː] = United Nations Relief and Rehabilitation Administration 联合国善后救济总署，联总.
un·ruf·fled [ˈʌnˈrʌfld] *a.* ①不骚动的，不混乱的；稳定的，沉着的，平静的. ②不起皱的.
un·ruled [ˈʌnˈruːld] *a.* ①不受支配[统治]的，调皮捣蛋的. ②(纸)没有画格子的.
un·ru·ly [ʌnˈruːli] *a.* ***(-li·er; -li·est)*** 不受拘束的；不守规矩的；难驾驭的，横蛮的，任性的. *to be* ~ *in word or deed* 乱说乱动. ***an*** ~ ***member*** 舌头. **-li·ness** *n.*
UNRWA = United Nations Relief and Works Agency 联合国难民救济及工程局.
un·sad·dle [ˈʌnˈsædl] *vt.* ①卸下(马等的)鞍. ②使从鞍上摔下来，使坠马. — *vi.* 卸鞍.
un·safe [ˈʌnˈseif] *a.* 不安全的，不安稳的，危险的.
un·said [ˈʌnˈsed] unsay 的过去式及过去分词. — *a.* 未说出口的. *leave it* ~ 搁置不提.
un·sal(e)·a·ble [ˈʌnˈseiləbl] *a.* 不能出卖的；卖不掉的；没有销路的.
un·sal·a·ried [ˈʌnˈsælərid] *a.* 不拿薪金的；没有报酬的.
un·sanc·tioned [ˈʌnˈsæŋkʃənd] *a.* 未经认可的，未批准的；不可接受的.
un·san·i·ta·ry [ˈʌnˈsænitəri] *a.* 不卫生的，有碍健康的.
un·sat·is·fac·to·ry [ˈʌnsætisˈfæktəri] *a.* 不能令人满意的；不合要求的；不充分的.
un·sat·is·fied [ˈʌnˈsætisfaid] 未满足的；不满意的.
un·sat·u·rat·ed [ˈʌnˈsætʃəreitid] *a.* 未饱和的；不饱和的. ~ *compounds* 不饱和化合物. ~ *steam* 未饱和蒸汽.
un·sa·vour·y, -vor·y [ˈʌnˈseivəri] *a.* ①不好吃的，味道不好的. ②可厌的；令人不快的；(名誉等)不好的. **-i·ly** *ad.* **-i·ness** *n.*
un·say [ˈʌnˈsei] *vt.* ***(-said*** [-ˈsed]***)*** 取消，收回，撤回(前言).
UNSC = ①United Nations Security Council 联合国安全理事会. ②United Nations Social Commission 联合国社会委员会.
un·scal·a·ble [ˈʌnˈskeiləbl] *a.* 爬不上的，无法攀登的.
un·scared [ˈʌnˈskɛəd] *a.* 未吓倒的，不害怕的.
un·scathed [ˈʌnˈskeiðd] *a.* (身、心等)没有受损伤的.
UNSCCUR = United Nations Scientific Conference on the Conservation and Utilization of Resources 联合国保存与运用资源科学会议.
un·schol·ar·ly [ˈʌnˈskɔləli] *a.* 没有学问的，没有学识的；不象学者的.
un·schooled [ˈʌnˈskuːld] *a.* ①没有受过学校教育的，没有受过训练的；没有经验的. ②非后天的，未受教育影响的；天赋的. ③(某地)没有学校的.
un·sci·en·tif·ic [ˈʌnsaiənˈtifik] *a.* ①非科学的；非学术的；不科学的. ②不按照科学方法的. ③无科学知识的. **-i·cal·ly** *ad.*
UNSCOP = United Nations Special Commission on Palestine 联合国巴勒斯坦特别调查委员会〔曾于1947年9月成立过的一个联合国机构〕.
un·scram·ble [ʌnˈskræmbl] *vt.* ***(-bled; -bling)*** 〔口〕①使不再混乱；整理，清理. ②分解(集成物)使恢复原

状。③使(收音机排除杂音干扰而)收听清晰;使(电视等)图象变清楚;破解(密码)。~ *an omelet* 想把鸡蛋卷重新摊开复原,想做办不到的事。

un·screw [ˈʌnˈskruː] *vt., vi.* 起[扭松](…的)螺丝;取下(螺丝)。

un·scru·pu·lous [ʌnˈskruːpjuləs] *a.* 毫无顾忌的;不择手段的;无所不为的;肆无忌惮的;没有节操的,无耻的。~ *and vicious* 穷凶极恶的。**-ly** *ad.* **-ness** *n.*

un·seal [ˈʌnˈsiːl] *vt.* ①打开…的封印,拆封。②使解除束缚;打开(某种象封住似的情况)。

un·seam [ˈʌnˈsiːm] *vt.* 拆(缝);使开缝;使裂开。

un·search·a·ble [ʌnˈsəːtʃəbl] *a.* 不能探寻的;神秘的;不可测的。**-a·bly** *ad.*

un·sea·son·a·ble [ʌnˈsiːznəbl] *a.* ①不合时令的,季候不顺的,(气候等)反常的。②过时的,不合时宜的。③不适于某种场合的,不得当的。**-a·bly** *ad.* **-ness** *n.*

un·sea·soned [ˈʌnˈsiːznd] *a.* ①没有调味的,未加佐料的。②未成熟的;没有经验的。③未干的。④不习惯于某地风土[气候]的,不服水土的。~ *timbers* 还没有干的木料。~ *wood* 新砍倒的木材。

un·seat [ˈʌnˈsiːt] *vt.* ①使从座位上摔下,把…拉下马来。②使失去座位;夺去(议员的)议席,使失去资格;使离职。

un·sea·wor·thy [ˈʌnˈsiːwəːði] *a.* 经不住海上风浪的,(船)不适于航海的。

un·se·cured [ˈʌnsiˈkjuəd] *a.* ①不安全的,不稳当的;未固定的。②无保证的,无担保的。*an* ~ *loan* 没有担保的贷款。

un·seem·ly [ˈʌnˈsiːmli] *a., ad.* 不体面,不好看;不相称;不适当。**-i·ness** *n.*

un·seen [ˈʌnˈsiːn] *a.* ①看不见的。②未被看到的。③未见过的。④未事先过目的,不用参考材料的,即席的。⑤毋需事先研究就能看懂的。— *n.* 即席翻译;即席翻译的章节。*the* ~ 看不见的东西;灵魂世界。*an* ~ *(translation)* 即席翻译(一段章节)。*an* ~ *passage* 考试时让考生即席翻译[讲解]的一段文字。

un·seg·re·gat·ed [ˈʌnˈsegrigeitid] *a.* 打成一片的;未实行种族隔离的。

un·sel·dom [ˈʌnˈseldəm] *ad.* 屡见不鲜;常常。*not* ~ 〔误用〕= unseldom.

un·self·ish [ˈʌnˈselfiʃ] *a.* 不利已的,大公无私,没私心的,无我的。**-ly** *ad.* **-ness** *n.*

un·sell [ˈʌnˈsel] *vt.* ***(un·sold*** [ˈʌnˈsəuld]) 劝(某人)打消(某种念头),动摇(某人)对(某事的支持等)。~ *the public on its faith in sth.* 劝说公众不要对某事表示信心。~ *sb. on the idea of doing sth.* 劝说某人放弃做某事。

un·serv·ice·a·ble [ˈʌnˈsəːvisəbl] *a.* 无用的,不能(再)使用的;不能胜任[作战]的。

un·set [ˈʌnˈset] *a.* ①未安装上的,未镶上的。②(水泥、沥青等)尚未凝固的。③(太阳)尚未落山的。

un·set·tle [ˈʌnˈsetl] *vt.* 搅乱,动摇;使不安定;使不能稳定。— *vi.* 动乱不定;离开固定位置。**-ment** *n.*

un·set·tled [ˈʌnˈsetld] *a.* ①易变的,(天气等)不稳定的;(意见等)动摇的;不安定的,(状态等)动乱的。②未付清的,未清算的。③未定的;(问题等)未决的。④未定居的;(岛等)无居民的。*an* ~ *market* 动荡的市面。

un·set·tling [ˈʌnˈsetliŋ] *a.* 使人不安的;(消息)混乱的。

un·sex [ˈʌnˈseks] *vt.* ①使失去性的特征(尤指女性特征);使男性化。②使失去性功能。

un·shack·le [ˈʌnˈʃækl] *vt.* 解去…的枷锁;释放。

un·shack·led [ˈʌnˈʃækld] *a.* 被解去枷锁的;不受束缚的。

un·shad·ed [ˈʌnˈʃeidid] *a.* ①(光线)未被遮住的,(窗等)无遮蔽的。②(图画)未画阴影的;(照片)无光度差别的。③(声调)无变化的。

un·shad·owed [ˈʌnˈʃædəud] *a.* 无暗影的;没被阴影笼罩的。

un·shak·a·ble [ʌnˈʃeikəbl] *a.* 不可动摇的;坚定不移的。

un·shak·en [ˈʌnˈʃeikən] *a.* 不动摇的;坚定的。

un·shaped [ˈʌnˈʃeipt] *a.* ①未成形的。②畸形的,难看的,不成样子的。③粗制的;粗糙的。

un·shape·ly [ˈʌnˈʃeipli] *a.* 不好看的,样子不好的;不匀称的;畸形的。

un·shap·en [ʌnˈʃeipən] *a.* ①无[未]定型的;不成形的。②畸形的;破相的;丑陋的(= unshaped).

un·shav·en [ˈʌnˈʃeivn] *a.* 未剃须的,未修面的。

un·sheathe [ˈʌnˈʃiːð] *vt.* ①拔(剑等)出鞘。②揭开覆盖物;脱去(衣服)。~ *the sword* 拔剑;宣战,开战。

un·shel·tered [ˈʌnˈʃeltəd] *a.* 无遮蔽的,暴露的;无保护的。

un·ship [ˈʌnˈʃip] *vt., vi.* ①从船中起出(货),卸(货);使(船客等)下船。②【海】解下(桨、船具等)。③〔口〕取去,除去。

un·shod [ˈʌnˈʃɔd] *a.* ①没有穿鞋的,赤脚的。②(马)没有钉蹄铁的,蹄铁脱落的。③没有轮缘的;没有轮胎[外胎]的。④(杖等)无铁包头的。

un·shrink·a·ble [ˈʌnˈʃriŋkəbl] *a.* 不会收缩[缩小]的;防缩的。

un·shrink·ing [ʌnˈʃriŋkiŋ] *a.* 不退缩的,不畏缩的,不踌躇的。

un·sift·ed [ˈʌnˈsiftid] *a.* ①没有筛过的。②未经仔细审察过的。

un·sight·ed [ˈʌnˈsaitid] *a.* ①未看见的;看不见的。②未经检查的,未审视的。③无瞄准器的;不用瞄准器的。***buy sth.*** **~, *unseen*** 看也不看就买下某物。**-ly** *ad.*

un·sight·ly [ʌnˈsaitli] *a.* ***(-li·er; -li·est)*** 不好看的;不美观的,难看的。**-li·ness** *n.*

un·skil·ful un·skill·ful [ˈʌnˈskilful] *a.* 不熟练的;不灵活自如的。**-ly** *ad.* **-ness** *n.*

un·skilled [ˈʌnˈskild] *a.* ①不熟练的;笨劣的 *(in)*。②不需要熟练技能的。~ *labour* 粗活。*the* ~ 生手工人。

un·sling [ˈʌnˈsliŋ] *vt.* ***(-slung*** [-ˈslʌŋ]; ***-sling·ing)*** ①把挂着的(步枪等)取下来。②【海】取下…的吊索;自吊索上放下。

un·snap [ʌnˈsnæp] *vt.* ***(-snap·ped, -snap·ping)*** ①(犬等)松(咬)。②解开(衣服上的)钮扣,拉开(皮包等的)揿钮。

un·snarl [ʌnˈsnɑːl] *vt.* 解开…的纠缠;解决(纠纷)。

un·so·cia·ble [ʌnˈsəuʃəbl] *a.* ①不爱[善]交际的;孤僻的。②简慢的,不和气的;不亲切的。③不能并存的,水火不相容的。**-bly** *ad.* **-ness, -bil·i·ty** [ˈʌnˌsəuʃəˈbiliti] *n.*

un·so·cial [ˈʌnˈsəuʃəl] *a.* ①非社会的。②不合群的;不爱[善]交际的;孤僻的。③反社会的。**-ly** *ad.*

un·soiled [ˈʌnˈsɔild] *a.* ①没有弄脏的;洁净的。②未玷污的;清白的。

un·sold·er [ˈʌnˈsɔldə] *vt.* ①拆焊,拆开(焊接物)。②使分开,分离。

un·so·lic·it·ed [ˈʌn-səˈlisitid] *a.* 未经请求[恳求]的;主动提供的;自发的;无缘无故的,没来由的;多余的。~ *testimonials* (未经请求)顾客主动寄来的表扬信。

un·solv·a·ble [ˈʌnˈsɔlvəbl] *a.* ①无法解释[解答,解决]的。②不能溶解的。③【数】不可解的。

un·solved [ˈʌnˈsɔlvd] *a.* 未解释的;未解决的。

un·son·sy [ʌnˈsɔnsi] *a.* 〔scot.〕带来厄运的,显出厄运的;不祥的。

un·so·phis·ti·cat·ed [ˈʌnsəˈfistikeitid] *a.* ①不老练的;单纯的,思想不复杂的,天真烂漫的。②简单易懂的。③不掺假的,真正的,纯正的。**-ly** *ad.* **-ness** *n.*

un·sort·ed [ˈʌnˈsɔːtid] *a.* 未分级的,未分选的。~ *coal* 原煤。

un·sought [ˈʌnˈsɔːt] *a.* 未经谋求(而得到)的;意外获得的。

un·sound [ˈʌnˈsaund] *a.* ①不健全的,有病的。②腐烂

了的,(商品等)已坏的. ③根据不足的; 理由不充分的. ④不安全的,不坚固的; 没有信用的,(商店等)不可靠的. ⑤(睡眠)不沉的,不酣的. *a person of ~ mind* 精神不健全的人. *~ slumber* 不深的微睡. **-ly** *ad.* **-ness** *n.*

un•sound•ed[1] [ˈʌnˈsaundid] *a.* 未经探测的, 深度未明的.

un•sound•ed[2] [ˈʌnˈsaundid] *a.* ①未说出的. ②(字母等)不发音的.

un•spar•ing [ʌnˈspɛəriŋ] *a.* ①大方的,不吝惜的,慷慨的. ②不宽恕的, 不客气的, (批评)严厉的. *be ~ in one's efforts* 拼命努力. *be ~ of [in] praise* 竭力表扬. *give with ~ hand* 慷慨给与. **-ly** *ad.*

un•speak [ʌnˈspiːk] *vt.* ***(-spoke*** [-ˈspəuk]; ***-spok•en*** [-ˈspəukən]) 〔废〕取消(前言).

un•speak•a•ble [ʌnˈspiːkəbl] *a.* ①说不出的,形容不出的. ②恶劣透顶的, 坏不堪言的. ③不能说的, 不可说的,怕说的,一说就讨厌[恐惧]的;〔美〕不愿说的. *His manners are ~.* 〔口〕他的举动是说不出的令人讨厌. **-a•bly** *ad.*

un•spe•cial•ized, -ised [ˈʌnˈspeʃəlaizd] *a.* ①非专门化的. ②【生】(机体)非特(殊)化的; 无特定功能的.

un•spec•i•fied [ˈʌnˈspesifaid] *a.* ①未指定的; 未加规定的. ②未特别指定[规定]的; 未详细说明的.

un•spent [ˈʌnˈspent] *a.* 没有用完的,未耗尽的.

un•sphere [ʌnˈsfiə] *vt.* ***(-spher•ed, -spher•ing)*** 〔古〕使(星辰等)离开某一范围; 使失势.

un•spo•ken [ˈʌnˈspəukən] unspeak 的过去分词. — *a.* ①不说出口的, 未说的. ②无言的. ③无人与之交谈的 *(to).* ④不言而喻的,意在不言中的.

un•sports•man•like [ˈʌnˈspɔːtsmənlaik] *a.* ①不象运动员[猎人]的,违反[缺少]运动员精神的. ②不公正[光明正大]的.

un•spot•ted [ˈʌnˈspɔtid] *a.* 没有斑点[污点、瑕疵]的; 纯洁的,清白的. ***~ from the world*** 没有染上社会恶习的.

un•sprung [ˈʌnˈsprʌŋ] *a.* (车、椅等)没有装弹簧的.

un•sta•ble [ˈʌnˈsteibl] *a.* ①不稳定的,不牢固的. ②不坚定的,动摇的,易变的,反复无常的.

un•stained [ˈʌnˈsteind] *a.* 没有被染污的; 清白的, 没有瑕疵的. *~ friendship* 纯洁的友谊.

un•state [ˈʌnˈsteit] *vt.* 〔古〕使失去尊严[地位].

un•stead•y [ˈʌnˈstedi] *a.* ①不稳固的. ②不坚定的; 动摇的; 易变的,反复无常的,不可靠的. ③行为古怪的; 品行不好的. ***be ~ of purpose*** 拿不定主意. — *vt.* 使不稳定,使动荡. **-i•ly** *ad.* **-i•ness** *n.*

un•steel [ˈʌnˈstiːl] *vt.* ①使失去坚硬性. ②解除…的武装. ③使软下来; 使回心转意[改变决定].

un•step [ˈʌnˈstep] *vt.*【海】把桅杆(从桅座上)取下来.

un•stick [ˈʌnˈstik] *vt.* ***(un•stuck*** [ˈʌnˈstʌk]) ①使不粘着,使脱胶; 扯开(粘着的东西). ②〔口〕使(飞机)离地. ***come unstuck*** 〔俚〕弄糟,失败.

un•stint•ing [ˈʌnˈstintiŋ] *a.* 没有限制的; 慷慨的. **-ly** *ad.*

un•stop [ˈʌnˈstɔp] *vt.* ①拔去…的塞子; 打开(风琴的)音栓. ②排除(管道等的)障碍[阻塞].

un•sto•red [ˈʌnˈstɔːrid] *a.* 未载入史册的; 未记进故事的.

un•strap [ˈʌnˈstræp] *vt.* 解开…的皮带.

un•stressed [ˈʌnˈstrest] *a.* ①不强调的,不着重说的; 放松了的; 不加强语势的. ②【语音】不重读的; 非重音的. ③【物】无应力的,无应变的.

un•string [ˈʌnˈstriŋ] *vt.* ***(un•strung*** [ˈʌnˈstrʌŋ]) ①把(弦)解下[放松]; 解开(绳索[带子]); 从线上退下(珠子等). ②〔常用被动语态〕使(神经等)衰弱[混乱]; 使不安.

un•struc•tured [ʌnˈstrʌktʃəd] *a.* 非正式[有系统地]组织起来的; 松散的; 自由的; 开放的.

un•strung [ʌnˈstrʌŋ] unstring 的过去式和过去分词. — *a.* ①神经质的, 精神失常的; 不安的; 丧失勇气的. ②(弓)弦松的,(球拍等)网绳松的.

un•stuck [ʌnˈstʌk] unstick 的过去式和过去分词. — *a.* ①松开的; (附着的东西)脱开的; 未粘住的. ②紊乱的; 失灵的,受到挫折的.

un•stud•ied [ʌnˈstʌdid] *a.* ①非学到的, 非由自觉努力而获得的. ②自发的; 自然的; 不装腔作势的. ③未曾学习过的; 不熟习的; 不精通的 *(in).* ④随便的, 即席作成的.

un•sub•dued [ˈʌnsəbˈdjuːd] *a.* ①没有被征服的. ②未能克制的. ③未减轻的; 未缓和的.

un•sub•si•dized [ˈʌnˈsʌbsidaizd] *a.* 没有补助的; 不受津贴[资助]的.

un•sub•stan•tial [ˈʌnsəbˈstænʃəl] *a.* ①无实质的,无实体的; (房屋等)不结实的; 单薄的,(饭菜等)不丰盛的,内容不充实的. ②非现实的, 空想的. **-ly** *ad.* **-ti•al•i•ty** [ˈʌnsəbˌstænʃiˈæliti] *n.*

un•sub•stan•ti•at•ed [ˈʌnsəbˈstænʃieitid] *a.* 无确实根据[证据]的.

un•suc•cess•ful [ˈʌnsəkˈsesful] *a.* 不成功的, 失败的. **-ly** *ad.* **-ness** *n.*

un•suit•a•ble [ˈʌnˈsjuːtəbl] *a.* 不合适的,不适宜的; 不相适应的,不相称的. **-a•bly** *ad.* **-bil•i•ty** *n.*

un•suit•ed [ˈʌnˈsjuːtid] *a.* 不适宜的; 不适当的,不合适的 *(for; to)*; 不相称的,不相容的.

un•sul•lied [ˈʌnˈsʌlid] *a.* ①没弄赃的. ②没有污点的,洁白的; 清白的.

un•sung [ˈʌnˈsʌŋ] *a.* ①(歌)未唱出的. ②未被诗人礼赞的,未被诗歌中歌颂的.

un•sunned [ˈʌnˈsʌnd] *a.* ①晒不到太阳的; 未受日晒的; 未晒黑的. ②没有公开的. ③阴郁的,闷闷不乐的.

un•sup•port•ed [ˈʌnsəˈpɔːtid] *a.* ①没有支撑的. ②没有受到支持[支援,证实]的.

un•sure [ˈʌnˈʃuə] *a.* ①缺乏信心的; 没有把握的. ②不确知的. ③不稳定的; 不安全的. ④不可靠的.

un•sur•passed [ˈʌnsə(ː)ˈpɑːst] *a.* 未为人胜过的; 无比的,卓绝的,(同类中)最优的.

un•sus•pect•ed [ˈʌn-səsˈpektid] *a.* ①无嫌疑的; 不受怀疑的. ②不知其存在的; 意外的. *an ~ danger* 未曾料想到的危险.

un•sus•pect•ing [ˈʌnsəsˈpektiŋ] *a.* ①不怀疑的; 不猜疑的; 相信的. ②没有料想到…的 *(of)*. **-ly** *ad.*

un•sus•pi•cious [ˈʌnsəsˈpiʃəs] *a.* 不怀疑[猜疑]的. **-ly** *ad.* **-ness** *n.*

un•swathe [ˈʌnˈsweið] *vt.* 解开…的裹布[绷带等].

un•swayed [ˈʌnˈsweid] *a.* 不为所动的; 不受影响的.

un•swear [ˈʌnˈswɛə] *vt.* ***(un•swore*** [ˈʌnˈswɔː], ***un-sworn*** [ˈʌnˈswɔːn]) (发新誓) 取消 (前誓); 违背(誓言). — *vi.* 违背誓言; 食言.

un•sweet [ˈʌnˈswiːt] *a.* ①不甜的; 不可口的. ②难闻的,臭的. ③难听的. ④令人不快的,令人厌恶的.

un•swept [ˈʌnˈswept] *a.* 未扫(清)的.

un•swerv•ing [ʌnˈswəːviŋ] *a.* ①没有(走)歪的; 不偏离的. ②〔喻〕忠贞的,坚定的. **-ly** *ad.* **-ness** *n.*

un•swore [ˈʌnˈswɔː] unswear 的过去式.

un•sworn [ˈʌnˈswɔːn] unswear 的过去分词.

un•sym•met•ri•cal [ˈʌnsiˈmetrikəl] *a.* 不对称的, 不匀称的. **-ly** *ad.*

un•sym•pa•thet•ic [ˈʌnsimpəˈθetik] *a.* ①不同情的; 无同情心的,无情的,冷淡的. ②不抱好感的,抱有反感的. **-i•cal•ly** *ad.*

un•sys•tem•at•ic [ˈʌnsistiˈmætik] *a.* 无系统的, 不规则的; 无组织的. **-i•cal•ly** *ad.*

UNTAA = United Nations Technical Assistance Administration 联合国技术援助局.

un•taint•ed [ˈʌnˈteintid] *a.* 未染服的; (品德)没有污点的,清白的.

un•tamed [ˈʌnˈteimd] *a.* ①未驯养的, 野性的. ②未受抑制[控制]的; 奔放不羁的.

un•tan•gle [ˈʌnˈtæŋgl] *vt.* ①解开(乱结). ②清理;解决(纠纷等).
un•tanned [ˈʌnˈtænd] *a.* ①(皮革)未鞣的. ②(皮肤)没有晒黑的.
un•taught [ˈʌnˈtɔːt] unteach 的过去式及过去分词. — *a.*① 无教育的,无知识的. ②不教自会的;没有人教过的,非习得的;天生的,自然的. ~ *modesty* 天生的谦逊.
un•taxed [ˈʌnˈtækst] *a.* 免税的;未完税的;负担不过重的.
un•teach [ˈʌnˈtiːtʃ] *vt.* ①使忘记[抛弃](学过的东西);使不相信. ②进行与…相反的教育,使改变想法.
un•teach•a•ble [ˈʌnˈtiːtʃəbl] *a.* ①不可教的,难教导的;不听话的. ②无法传授的.
un•tem•pered [ˈʌnˈtempəd] *a.* ①【冶】未回火的;〔喻〕未经锻炼的. ②(石灰等)未拌和[调和]的. ③未减轻[缓和]的;不加节制的.
un•ten•a•ble [ˈʌnˈtenəbl, -ˈtiːn-] *a.* ①维持[支持]不住的;(论点等)站不住的. ②守不住的. ③不能租赁[占用]的. **-a•bly** *ad.*
un•tend•ed [ˈʌnˈtendid] *a.* 被忽略了的;未受到照顾的.
un•thank•ful [ˈʌnˈθæŋkful] *a.* ①不感谢的 *(to, for)*;忘恩负义的. ②不令人感谢的;没有什么好处的;令人不快的. *She was ~ to her boy friend for his gift.* 她并不感谢男朋友送东西给她. *an ~ task* 吃力不讨好的工作. **-ly** *ad.* **-ness** *n.*
un•think [ˈʌnˈθiŋk] *vt.* ***(un•thought*** [ˈʌnˈθɔːt]***)*** 打消(某个念头);不再想…;对…改变想法. — *vi.* 放弃想法,停止思考.
un•think•a•ble [ˈʌnˈθiŋkəbl] *a.* ①不能想象的,想象不出的. ②〔口〕绝不可能的;荒谬不经的,不可相信的. ③不能考虑的;不必加以考虑的.
un•think•ing [ˈʌnˈθiŋkiŋ] *a.* ①无思想的;无思考能力的. ②不经心的,轻率的. ③未作思考的. **-ly** *ad.*
un•thought-of [ʌnˈθɔːtɔv] *a.* 没有想到的;意外的.
un•thread [ˈʌnˈθred] *vt.* ①从(针上等)把线抽下. ②摆脱(缠缚). ③曲折地走出(迷宫等);解(谜).
un•thrift•y [ˈʌnˈθrifti] *a.* ①不俭省的,浪费的,奢侈的. ②不经济的;无利可图的. ③不繁茂的;不兴隆的.
un•throne [ʌnˈθrəun] *vt.* 废去…的王位(= dethrone). **-ment** *n.*
un•ti•dy [ʌnˈtaidi] *a.* ①不整齐的,邋遢的;杂乱的,乱七八糟的. ②不合适的,不适宜的. ③不干净利落的,不简练的. — *vt.* 使不整洁,使杂乱无章. **-di•ly** *ad.* **-di•ness** *n.*
un•tie [ˈʌnˈtai] *vt.* ①解开. ②使解去束缚,使解除约束,解放. ③解决(困难等). — *vi.* 解开,松开.
un•til [ənˈtil, ʌnˈtil] *prep.* 〔时间〕①直到…为止;到. ②在…以前;不到…(不)〔用在否定句中〕. *Wait ~ four o'clock.* 等到四点钟. *It was not ~ yesterday that I learned it.* 到昨天我才知道. — *conj.* ①直到…为止;到(…的时候). ②在…以前;不到…(不)〔用在否定句中〕. *Wait here ~ I come.* 在这儿一直等到我来. *He didn't come back ~ the sun had set.* 他直到太阳落山以后才回来. ★ till 与 until 同义,但在主句之前的从句或短语中,通常用 until: Until he returns, nothing can be done. 他不回来什么也不能做. ***unless and ~*** = until.
un•time•ly [ʌnˈtaimli] *a.* ①不到时候的,不合时令的;过早的,未熟的. ②不凑巧的,不合时宜的. — *ad.* ①不合时令地;过早地. ②不凑巧. **-li•ness** *n.*
un•time•ous [ʌnˈtaiməs] *a.* 〔Scot.〕= untimely.
un•tir•ing [ʌnˈtaiəriŋ] *a.* 不(知)疲倦的,不屈不挠的. **-ly** *ad.*
un•ti•tled [ˈʌnˈtaitld] *a.* ①没有称号[头衔]的. ②没有标题的. ③没有权利[资格]的.
un•to [元音前 ˈʌntu, 辅音前 ˈʌntə, 句尾、孤立时 ˈʌntuː] *prep.* 〔古〕①到;对. ★ 与 to 同,但不能用作不定式的符号. ②直到;到…时为止 (=until). *The soldier was faithful ~ death.* 战士至死忠贞不渝.
un•told [ˈʌnˈtəuld] *a.* ①未叙述的,没有说到的,没有泄漏的,没有传出去的. ②说不尽的;数不清的,无数的;极大的,(痛苦等)说不出的. ~ *wealth* 不知其数的财富.
un•tomb [ˈʌnˈtuːm] *vt.* 从(墓中)掘出;发掘.
un•touch•a•ble [ʌnˈtʌtʃəbl] *a.* ①不可触摸的,碰不得的. ②碰不到的,不可及的. ③不可捉摸的,无形的. ④(因肮脏、使人厌恶等)不可接触的. — *n.* ①不可接触者,贱民〔印度的最低社会阶层〕. ②被遗弃的人. ③棘手的事. ④无可疵议的人.
un•touched [ˈʌnˈtʌtʃt] *a.* ①没有碰过的,没有动过的;原原本本的. ②不受感动的,不动心的. ③没有谈论到的,没有提到的. *The subject remains ~ upon.* 这个题目仍然没有触及.
un•to•ward [ʌnˈtəuəd] *a.* ①〔古〕不听话的,倔强的. ②不顺利的;麻烦的;(境遇等)不幸的. ③不适当的;不合宜的. *an ~ event* 麻烦事. ~ *circumstances* 逆境. **-ly** *ad.* **-ness** *n.*
un•trace•a•ble [ˈʌnˈtreisəbl] *a.* ①难摹写的. ②难追查的;难寻觅的.
un•tram•melled, 〔美〕**-meled** [ˈʌnˈtræməld] *a.* 没有上脚镣[手铐]的;没有受到阻碍[束缚]的;自由的.
un•trans•fer•a•ble [ˈʌn-træsˈfəːrəbl] *a.* 不可转移的;不可让与的.
un•trans•lat•a•ble [ˈʌntrænsˈleitəbl] *a.* 不可翻译的;不宜译的.
un•trav•elled, un•trav•eled [ʌnˈtrævld] *a.* ①不见人迹的〔指道路等〕. ②不大旅行的〔尤指远行〕.
un•tread [ˈʌnˈtred] *vt.* ***(un•trod*** [ˈʌnˈtrɔd], ***un•trod-den*** [ˈʌnˈtrɔdn], ***un•trod)*** 折回(原路),返回(=retrace).
un•treat•ed [ˈʌnˈtriːtid] *a.* 未处理的;未加工的,未浸渍的. ~ *rubber* 生橡胶.
un•tried [ˈʌnˈtraid] *a.* ①未试过的.未试验过的,还没实验过的;未试用过的;没有经验的. ②【法】尚未审问的. *leave nothing [no means] ~* 没有一种办法未试过,用尽手段.
un•trod(den) [ˈʌnˈtrɔd(n)] untread 的过去分词. — *a.* 未受践踏的;人迹未到的.
un•trou•bled [ˈʌnˈtrʌbld] *a.* ①未受烦扰的,没有忧虑的. ②(湖面)平静的.
un•true [ˈʌnˈtruː] *a.* ①不真实的,虚伪的,假的. ②不忠实的;不贞洁的;不诚实的. ③不合标准[型号、尺寸]的;不正的,不准的. ④不正当的. **-tru•ly** *ad.*
un•truss [ʌnˈtrʌs] *vt.* ①解掉…的束缚. ②〔废〕使脱衣.
un•trust•wor•thy [ˈʌnˈtrʌstwəːði] *a.* 不能信任[信赖]的,靠不住的.
un•truth [ˈʌnˈtruːθ] *n.* ***(pl. ~s*** [-ðz, -θs]***)*** ①不真实;虚假;虚伪;虚妄. ②谎话.
un•truth•ful [ˈʌnˈtruːθful] *a.* ①不真实的,虚伪的;不正确的. ②不诚实的,说谎的. **-ly** *ad.* **-ness** *n.*
un•tuck [ˈʌnˈtʌk] *vt.* 拆散(褶子等);展开. ~ *the rug* 展平地毯. ~ *one's legs* 把腿分开.
un•turned [ˈʌnˈtəːnd] *a.* 没有翻转的,没有颠倒的;没有掘翻的. ***leave no stone ~*** 用尽一切手段,千方百计.
un•tu•tored [ˈʌnˈtjuːtəd] *a.* ①没有教育的;粗野的;无知的. ②单纯的,纯朴的,天真的.
un•twine [ˈʌnˈtwain] *vt., vi.* 解开(缠绕的东西),拆开,解开. ~ *two climbers* 把缠绕在一起的两根蔓藤分开.
un•twist [ˈʌnˈtwist] *vt., vi.* 拆开,解开(搓合的绳、线等).
un•used [ˈʌnˈjuːzd] *a.* ①未用过的;不用的,空着的;未消耗的. ②[ˈʌnˈjuːst] 不习惯的,无经验的 *(to)*. *hands ~ to toil* 不习惯劳动的手.
un•u•su•al [ʌnˈjuːʒuəl] *a.* ①不常见的,不普通的,难得的. ②例外的;奇异的. **-ly** *ad.* **-ness** *n.*
un•ut•ter•a•ble [ʌnˈʌtərəbl] *a.* ①(快乐、苦痛等)说不出的;形容不出的. ②十足的,彻底的,极端的. ③【语

音】无法发音的. — *n.*〔*pl.*〕〔谑〕裤子. **-a•bly** *ad.*
un•val•ued [ˈʌnˈvæljuːd] *a.* ①不受重视的，没有价值的. ②价值未经估定的,未估价的. *an ~ policy* 未估价的保险单.
un•va•ried [ʌnˈvɛərid] *a.* ①经常一贯的,不变的. ②单调乏味的,千篇一律的.
un•var•nished [ˈʌnˈvɑːniʃt] *a.* ①没有涂(清)漆的. ②[ʌnˈvɑːniʃt]〔喻〕未加装饰的,未加修饰的；原样的,直率的.
un•var•y•ing [ʌnˈvɛəriiŋ] *a.* 无变化的；不改变的；恒定的. **-ly** *ad.*
un•veil [ʌnˈveil] *vt.* ①除去…的面纱；除去…的覆盖物；(举行揭幕礼时)揭开…的幕；〔美剧〕使(戏)开幕. ②使现出本来面目；揭露(秘密等). *~ a statue* 举行雕象揭幕礼. — *vi.* ①除去面纱[幕布]. ②显露. **-ing** *n.* 揭幕式.
un•ver•i•fi•able [ˈʌnˈverifai-əbl] *a.* 不能证实的；无可考证的；无法检验的.
un•versed [ˈʌnˈvəːst] *a.* 不精通的；不熟练的；无知的；没有经验的.
un•voice [ʌnˈvɔis] *vt.*【语音】把(某浊辅音)读作(其对应的)清辅音,把…发成清辅音.
un•voiced [ˈʌnˈvɔist] *a.* ①未表示的；未说的；未说出的. ②【语音】读成清辅音的；发清辅音的,无声的.
un•want•ed [ˈʌnˈwɔntid] *a.* ①不需要的；无用的；多余的. ②讨厌的；有缺点的.
un•war•like [ˈʌnˈwɔːlaik] *a.* 不好战的.
un•warned [ˈʌnˈwɔːnd] *a.* 没有受警告[告诫]的；没有预先通知的,出其不意的.
un•war•rant•a•ble [ʌnˈwɔrəntəbl] *a.* ①难保证的；不能承认的；难允许的. ②无法辩护的；不可原谅的；不应当的. **-a•bly** *ad.*
un•war•rant•ed [ˈʌnˈwɔrəntid] *a.* ①没有保证的. ②[ʌnˈw-] 未经授权的；不能承认的；不许可的；没有根据的；不应当的. *an ~ action* 不许可的行为.
un•war•y [ˈʌnˈwɛəri] *a.* 不注意的,不审慎的,疏忽的；轻率的. **-i•ly** *ad.* **-i•ness** *n.*
un•washed [ˈʌnˈwɔʃt] *a.* ①没有洗的，不清洁的. ②不是沿海[沿河]的. ③无知的,地位卑下的,群氓的. — *n.*〔the ~〕〔集合词〕无知和地位卑下的大众，低下的社会阶层,群氓. ***the great ~*** 群氓.
un•wa•ver•ing [ʌnˈweivəriŋ] *a.* 不动摇的；不犹豫的,坚定的,毅然的. **-ly** *ad.*
un•wea•ried [ʌnˈwiərid] *a.* 不疲劳的；不倦的；不屈不挠的. **-ly** *ad.*
un•wea•ry•ing [ʌnˈwiəriiŋ] *a.* ①不会疲倦的；坚持不懈的. ②不使人疲倦的；不令人厌烦的.
un•weave [ˈʌnˈwiːv] *vt.* ***(un•wove*** [ˈʌnˈwəuv], **un•wo•ven** [ˈʌnˈwəuvən]**)** 拆散(织物).
un•wel•come [ʌnˈwelkəm] *a.* (客人等)不受欢迎的(= unwelcomed). ②(消息等)不愉快的,讨厌的. — *n.* 冷淡. — *vt.* 冷淡地对待[接受]. **-ly** *ad.* **-ness** *n.*
un•well [ˈʌnˈwel] *a.* ①不舒服的，病弱的；有病的. ②〔婉〕月经期中.
un•wept [ˈʌnˈwept] *a.* ①不被人哀悼的. ②(泪)不流下的.
un•whole•some [ˈʌnˈhəulsəm] *a.* ①不卫生的，有碍健康的；对身心有害的；腐败的. ②(象)有病的. ③(气味、滋味等)令人不快的,讨厌的. **-ly** *ad.* **-ness** *n.*
un•wield•y [ʌnˈwiːldi] *a.* ①使用不便的,不便利的. ②笨重的. ③笨拙的. **-i•ly** *ad.* **-i•ness** *n.*
un•will [ʌnˈwil] *vt.* 打消(原有意图)；改变(主意,意图,期望).
un•willed [ˈʌnˈwild] *a.* 不是故意的；无意识的.
un•will•ing [ˈʌnˈwiliŋ] *a.* ①不愿意的,不情愿的；厌恶的. ②勉强做[说、给]的. *be ~ to do* 不愿意做. *~ admiration* 勉强的赞美. **-ly** *ad.* **-ness** *n.*

un•wind [ˈʌnˈwaind] *vt., vi.* ***(un•wound*** [ˈʌnˈwaund]**)** ①解开,展开(卷绕的东西). ②放松；伸直.
un•wis•dom [ˈʌnˈwizdəm] *n.* 愚蠢(行为)；蠢话.
un•wise [ˈʌnˈwaiz] *a.* 不聪明的,不明智的,愚蠢的；不适当的. **-ly** *ad.*
un•wish [ʌnˈwiʃ] *vt.* ①放弃(希望),不再希望. ②〔废〕祈愿除去.
un•wished-for [ʌnˈwiʃtfɔː] *a.* 非所希望的,不欢迎的.
un•wit•nessed [ˈʌnˈwitnist] *a.* ①未被觉察到的. ②无证人签署的.
un•wit•ting [ʌnˈwitiŋ] *a.* 不知不觉的,无意的,无心的. **-ly** *ad.*
un•wom•an•ly [ʌnˈwumənli] *a.* 不象女人的；女人不应有的.
un•wont•ed [ʌnˈwəuntid] *a.* ①不常有的,罕有的,异常的. ②〔罕〕不习惯的,不熟悉的 *(to)*. **-ly** *ad.* **-ness** *n.*
un•work•a•ble [ˈʌnˈwəːkəbl] *a.* 无法工作[使用、开动、处理、实行(等)]的.
un•worked [ˈʌnˈwəːkt] *a.* ①未制成形的；粗糙的. ②未使用的.
un•world•ly [ˈʌnˈwəːldli] *a.* ①非尘世的；非世俗的,超脱名利之外的；精神世界的,出世的. ②没有社会经验的. *the ~ (-minded) people* 无俗念[名利心]的人们. **-li•ness** *n.*
un•worn [ˈʌnˈwɔːn] *a.* ①没有磨损的,没有擦破的. ②没有用旧的；没有穿旧的；不常穿的. ③〔喻〕(精神、感觉等)没有受损伤的；清新的.
un•wor•thi•ness [ʌnˈwəːðinis] *n.* 无价值,不相称；卑鄙.
un•wor•thy [ʌnˈwəːði] *a.* ①没有价值[优点]的；不足取的,卑劣的. ②不值得,不配,辜负 *(of)*；…所不应有的 *(of)*. *an ~ son* 不肖之子. *~ of praise* 不配受表扬. *a conduct ~ of an artist* 艺术家所不应有的行为. **-thi•ness** *n.*
un•wound [ˈʌnˈwaund] unwind 的过去式和过去分词. — *a.* ①(钟、表等)没有上发条的. ②(从卷绕状态)松散的.
un•wound•ed [ˈʌnˈwuːndid] *a.* 未受伤的；完好无损的.
un•wove [ˈʌnˈwəuv] unweave 的过去式.
un•wo•ven [ˈʌnˈwəuvən] unweave 的过去分词.
un•wrap [ˈʌnˈræp] *vt.* 打开，解开(包扎等). — *vi.* 散开.
un•writ•ten [ˈʌnˈritn] *a.* ①没有写下的,没有记录的. ②口头的,口传的；未成文的. ③白纸一张的,没有写着字的. *~* **constitution**【法】不成文宪法. *~* **law**【法】不成文法,习惯法.
un•wrought [ˈʌnˈrɔːt] *a.* ①没有制造的；未最后成形的；没有做成功的. ②没有加工的；未开发的；(矿山等)没有开采的. *~ materials* 原料.
un•yield•ing [ʌnˈjiːldiŋ] *a.* ①不屈服的；顽强的,坚强的. ②坚硬的,弯曲不了的. **-ly** *ad.* **-ness** *n.*
un•yoke [ˈʌnˈjəuk] *vt.* 解(轭)；解除(束缚)；解开,分开. — *vi.* 卸去轭；〔喻〕停止工作.
un•zip [ʌnˈzip] *vt., vi.* ①拉开(拉链). ②拉开(…的)拉链(以敞开衣襟等).
un•zoned [ˈʌnˈzəund] *a.* 没有划分区域的；不受限制的.
up [ʌp] (*opp.* down) *ad.* ***(superl. up•per•most*** [ˈʌpəməust]**)** ①向[在]上,向[在]上面；向[在]被认为处于上方的地方或方面〔如河流的源头,首都,上级机构,北方等〕. *go ~ to the top of a hill* 走上山顶. *Come ~ here.* 上这儿来；到上边来. *I'm going ~ to Beijing.* 我上北京去. ②(站)起,(坐)起,(从床上)起身. *She was already ~.* 她已经起床了. *be [stay] ~ all night* 通夜未睡. ③〔数量等〕以上；〔时间等〕以后,…以来. *from $ 50 ~* 五十美元以上,从 50 美元起. *from my youth ~* 我青年时代以后〔以来〕. ④上涨,升高；上升；高声；猛然；奋起；激昂；(开始活动)起来；发迹. *Prices have gone ~.* 物价全涨

了。*sing* ～ 高声唱。*The country was* ～. 全国人民发动起来了。*All the town is* ～. 全市生气蓬勃。*The hunt is* ～. 围猎正在开始。*The beer is very much* ～. 这啤酒泡沫很多〔比较: *Beer is* ～. 啤酒正在涨价〕。*His temper is* ～. 他正在发脾气。*He has gone* ～ *in my opinion.* 他在我的心目中的地位已经上升。*start* ～ *the engine* 把机器开动起来。⑤(问题)提起,出现;(事情)发生。*The question came* ～ *in conversation.* 这个问题在谈话中提出了。*Is anything* ～? 有什么事情发生吗? *What's* ～ *(with you)?* (你)怎么啦? (你)出了什么事? ⑥(全部)完毕。*eat* ～ *everything* 吃得干干净净。*The time is* ～. 时间到了;时间没有了。*The game is* ～. 一切完了。*The House is* ～. 议会闭会了。*It is all* ～ (=〔俚〕*It is all U. P.* [ˈjuːˈpiː]) *with him.* 那个人已经没有希望了。*Your chance is* ～. 你的机会已经完了。⑦赶上,跟上;胜过。*She worked hard to catch* ～ *with the rest of the class.* 她努力用功以求赶上班上其余的人。*Never fall behind, keep* ～! 不要落后,要跟上(时代)! ⑧(收藏)起来;(收集)起来;(加)起来;(扎)起来。*save* ～ *money* 把钱贮存起来。*add* ～ *these figures* 把这些数目加起来。*tie* ～ *the package* 把这包东西扎起来。⑨〔省略动词〕…起来,…上来。*Up with it!* 竖起来! 抬起来! *Up with you!* 站起来! 上来! *Up!* 起来! 上来! ⑩【海】迎风,向风。*Up helm!* 【海】迎风转舵! ⑪【棒球】任打击手,处于进攻一方;【高尔夫球】以(若干穴数)胜过;【网球】以(若干分)超过;【体】〔美、加〕双方各得(…分),平。*The golfer was two strokes* ～ *on his opponent.* 该高尔夫球选手胜对手两穴。*She was two* ～ *on her opponent.* 她胜过对手两分。*The score is 10.* 比分为十平。⑫〔构成动词短语,大致有三种情况〕: 1)改变原动词的意义,构成新义,如 *look* ～ 寻找; *turn* ～ 出现。2) 加强原动词的语气,如 *dress* ～; *clean* ～. 3)并不增加任何意义,这常在口语中出现,如 *write* ～ *a story.* ***be not*** ～ ***to much*** 不是怎样了不起的(好)东西。***be not*** ～ ***to one's job*** 承当[干]不了…的工作。～ ***against*** 〔口〕面临;遭遇(障碍等)。～ ***against it*** 〔美俚〕面临(经济)困难,处境困难。***be*** ～ ***and about*** (病人)已经起床走动了。***be*** ～ ***and doing*** 工作积极;非常活跃。***be*** ～ ***for*** *(an examination)* 正在(考试)。***be*** ～ ***in [on]*** *(art)* 擅长(艺术)。～ ***and at*** 〔美〕攻击;承受。～ ***and down*** ①上上下下,忽上忽下。②升降浮沉。③各处,到处;来来去去 (*run* ～ *and down* 跑来跑去)。～ ***in arms*** 武装起义;采取敌对态度。～ ***in the air*** 〔美〕狼狈的,惊慌的;激昂的。～ ***on one's toes*** 〔美〕机敏热心的。～ ***there*** 在那里;〔美俚〕天堂。～ ***to*** ①到,一直到 (*from a pauper* ～ *to a prince* 从乞丐一直到王子。～ *to the present day* 直到现在)。②〔口〕做(着),干(着),计划(着) (*What are you* ～ *to now?* 你现在在做什么? *He is* ～ *to no good.* 他净干坏事)。③胜任,适于 (*be* ～ *to the needs of an emergency* 紧急时可用)。④〔原美〕…的责任,轮到…;靠(*It is* ～ *to me to* …,…是我的责任[义务]。*It is* ～ *to us to organize the people.* 人民靠我们去组织)。～ ***to [with]*** ①和…并排 (*I could not get [catch]* ～ *to him* 我追不上他。*Slow down a bit and let me come* ～ *with you.* 跑慢一点让我赶上吧)。②(功绩、成功等)不相上下,可以相比,相近 (*He is* ～ *to his father as a scholar.* 他是一个和他父亲不相上下的学者)。～ ***to snuff*** 见 snuff. ～ ***to the gills*** 〔美俚〕烂醉的。～ ***to the handle*** 〔美俚〕完全。***well*** ～ ***in*** *(mathematics)* 精通,长于(数学)。— *prep.* ①(从低处、低位置等)向[在]高处,向[在]…的上面,向[在]上面。②向[在](河的)上游,溯(流)。③顺着(路等)。④(离海)向[在](内地);向内部。*live* ～ *a mountain* 住在山上。*work one's way* ～ *a form* 向上一级升进。*travel* ～ *(the) country* 向内地旅行[进行]。～ ***a tree*** 〔美俚〕进退两难。～ ***hill and down dale*** 翻山越谷;不顾一切,彻底。～ ***one's alley*** 〔美俚〕适合某人的才能[能力、素养]。～ ***the pole*** ①进退两难。②醉醺醺;发着疯。～ ***the river*** 〔美俚〕在坐牢,吃着官司。— *a.* (***up·per*** [ˈʌpə]; ***up·most*** [ˈʌpməust], ***up·per·most*** [ˈʌpəməust]) 上面的,向上面的,向上头的;【海】(舵)转向上风头的。*an* ～ *train* 上行车;〔英〕(到伦敦去的)上行车。*the* ～ *line* 【铁路】上行线;【电讯】上行线路。*an* ～ *platform* 上行线月台。*an* ～ *stroke* 往上写的笔画。— *n.* ①上面,上头;高处,高地;上坡路。②繁荣,兴盛。③正在逐步上升的人,有名望的人。④上行车。⑤〔美俚〕〔*pl.*〕刺激性毒品。***on the*** ～ ***and*** ～ 〔美俚〕光明正大地,正直地。～***s and downs*** (人生等的)盛衰,浮沉;(土地等的)高低,起伏 (*a house full of* ～*s and downs* 楼梯多的房子。*He has had his* ～*s and downs in life.* 他现在已体验到生活中的酸甜苦辣了)。— *vt.* 〔口、方〕举起,拿起 *(with)*;抬高,提高(价格),增加(产量)。*try to* ～ *output* 设法提高产量。*an upped sail* 扬起的风帆。— *vi.* ①〔口,方〕举起,拿起 *(with)*. ②〔口、卑〕站起来,起来,突然跳起来,突然开口,突然做某事。*He* ～*ped with his fist [stick].* 他举起了他的拳头[拿起了他的手杖]。*He* ～*s and says.* 他突然开口说。*He* ～ *[upped] and struck me.* 他突然跳起来打我。

up- *comb. f.* = up. ①带有副词的意义,加用于动词(主要为被动语态)及动名词前: *up*lifted, *up*bringing. ②带有前置词的意义,构成副词、形容词及名词: *up*hill, *up*country. ③添加形容词的意义: *up*land, *up*stroke.

U.P., UP = United Press 〔美〕合众国际社。

u.p. = under proof (酒精含量)低于标准,在标准以下。

U.P. [ˈjuːˈpiː] *ad.* 〔口〕完了 (= up). *All is U.P. with her.* 她一切全完了,她完蛋了。

up. = ①upper. ②underproof.

up·a·long [ˌʌpəˈlɔŋ] *ad.* 〔方〕向上,朝上;向东方,从西部。

up-and-about [ˈʌpəndəˈbɔt] *a.* ①(病人)已起床走动。②非常活跃的。

up-and-coming [ˈʌpəndˈkʌmiŋ] *a.* 〔美〕精力饱满的,奋发有为的,进取的,积极努力的;新起的。

up-and-down [ˈʌpənˈdaun] *a.* ①〔俚〕一上一下的,(运动)往复的;(道路)起伏不平的。②(命运等)盛衰无定的。③〔美〕(答复等)直率的;断然的;(谎话等)十足的。*an* ～ *life* 命运多变的生活。*an* ～, *cheerful girl* 直爽快活的姑娘。～ **dial** 附有显示发条松紧程度指示针的钟表面。

up-and-up [ˈʌpəndˈʌp] *n.* ①〔美俚〕日益向上[进步]。②诚实,光明磊落。*on the* ～ 进行顺利,繁荣;诚实地,公平地。

U·pani·shad [uːˈpæniʃəd] *n.* 《奥义书》〔印度《吠陀》圣典的最后部分〕。

u·pas [ˈjuːpəs] *n.* ①【植】见血封喉树〔一种毒树〕。②见血封喉树的毒液。③(道德上的)有害影响,毒害。

up·beat [ˈʌpbiːt] *n.* ①向上的趋势;向上摆动。②【乐】弱拍;(指挥棒)向上挥舞(以示弱拍)。— *a.* 活泼的;愉快的,高兴的,乐观的。

up·blaze [ʌpˈbleiz] *vi.* 燃烧起来。

up·borne [ʌpˈbɔːn] *a.* ①被高举的,被抬高的,升高了的。②被支持着的。

up·bow [ˈʌpˌbəu] *n.* (小提琴、大提琴等的)上弓,全弓奏〔记号是∨〕。

up·braid [ʌpˈbreid] *vt.* 责备,谴责。～ *sb. with his ingratitude [for being ungrateful]* 责备某人忘恩负义。**-er** *n.* 责备者。**-ing** *n., a.* 责备(的)。

up·bring·ing [ˈʌpbriŋiŋ] *n.* 抚养,养育;教育,培养。*training and* ～ *of successors to the revolutionary cause.* 训练和培养革命事业接班人。

up·build [ʌpˈbild] *vt.* (***up·built*** [ʌpˈbilt], ***up·build·ing*** [ʌpˈbildiŋ]) 建立;组织;振兴。**-er** *n.* 建立者;组织者;振兴者。

up·cast [ˈʌpkɑːst] *a.* 向上扔的,向上投掷的;向上的,朝上的。— *n.* 上投,上抛;向上扔的东西;【矿】上风井,上风口. — *vt.* 把…向上抛.

up·chuck [ˈʌptʃʌk] *vi., vt., n.* 〔美俚〕呕吐.

up·com·ing [ˈʌpˌkʌmiŋ] *a.* 即将到来的.

up·coun·try [ˈʌpˈkʌntri] *n.* (远离海岸线的)内地. — *a.* ①〔蔑〕乡下的; 内地的. ②单纯的, 纯朴的. — [ʌpˈk-] *ad.* 〔口〕向内地, 在内地. *travel* ~ 在内地旅行.

up·date [ʌpˈdeit] *vt.* 〔美〕(通过修订、增补)使(书等)成为最新式的[现代化的], 使(书等)与(当前条件)相适应. — *n.*【自】(供电子计算机使用的)最新情报.

up·draft [ˈʌpdrɑːft] *n.*【气】上曳气流, 上升气流. — *a.* 向上通风的.

up·end [ʌpˈend] *vt., vi.* (使)颠倒, (使)倒竖. 倒置, 倒转.

up·grade [ˈʌpgreid] *n., a.* 〔美〕上坡(的); 上升(的). — *ad.* 往山上, 上坡. — *vt.* 提升(…级别); 提高(重要性、质量等); 使升级.

up·growth [ˈʌpgrəuθ] *n.* ①成长, 发育, 发展. ②发展的结果, 成长物.

up·heav·al [ʌpˈhiːvəl] *n.* ①鼓起, 举起, 抬起;【地】隆起. ②骚扰, 动乱; 激变, 剧变.

up·heave [ʌpˈhiːv] *vt., vi.* ***(up·heaved, up·hove*** [ʌpˈhəuv]***)*** 鼓起; 举起, 顶起, 抬起; (因火山、地震等)(使)隆起.

up·held [ʌpˈheld] uphold 的过去式和过去分词.

up·hill [ˈʌpˈhil] *a.* ①上坡的; 上升的. ②费力的, 辛苦的, 艰难的. ③高处的. *It is an ~ road all the way.* 这条路一直是上坡路. *an ~ work* 费力的工作. — *ad.* 上山; 上坡; 艰难地. — *n.* 向上的斜坡.

up·hold [ʌpˈhəuld] *vt.* ***(up·held*** [ʌpˈheld]***)*** ①抬高, 举起. ②支持, 支援; 鼓励. ③赞同, 拥护;【法】确认, 批准(判决等). ④〔英〕= upholster. ~ *justice* 伸张正义. **-er** *n.* 抬高者, 举起者; 支持者; 确认者.

up·hol·ster [ʌpˈhəulstə] *vt.* ①(用家具)布置, (用地毯、帷帘等)装饰. ②给(沙发等)做软垫[布面等]. *an ~ed chair* 装有软垫[皮面垫子]的椅子.

up·hol·ster·ed [ʌpˈhəulstəd] *a.* ①(房间)经过布置的. ②(沙发等)装软垫的. ③〔美俚〕肥胖的; 稳重的. ~ **mittens** 〔美俚〕拳击用皮手套.

up·hol·ster·er [ʌpˈhəulstərə] *n.* 室内装饰商, 家具商.

up·hol·ster·y [upˈhəulstəri] *n.* ①室内装饰品[帷帘、地毯等]. ②室内装饰业, 家具业.

up·hove [ʌpˈhəuv] *v.* upheave 的过去式及过去分词.

UPI = United Press International 〔美〕合众国际社 (= UP).

up·keep [ˈʌpkiːp] *n.* ①维修, 保养. ②维修费, 保养费.

up·land [ˈʌplənd] *n.* 〔*sing., pl.*〕高地, 山地, 台地; 〔*pl.*〕高地地区, 旱地. — *a.* 高地的, 山地的. ~ **cotton** (短纤维)陆地棉. ~ **rice** 旱地稻. ~ **plover**【动】高原鸻.

up·lift [ʌpˈlift] *vt.* ①举起, 提起. ②打起(精神); 发扬(优良品德), 鼓起(干劲). ③提高(社会地位). ④【地】使(地面)隆起. — [ˈʌplift] *n.* ①举起, 抬起. ②【地】隆起. ③〔美〕(优良品德的)发扬, (精神的)高涨, (感情的)激发; 进步. ④〔口〕(使胸部鼓起的)乳罩 (= ~ brassiere). *an ~ worker* 热心社会工作的人. **-r** *n.*

up·man·ship [ˈʌpmənˌʃip] *n.* one-upmanship (胜人一筹的本事)的缩略词.

up·most [ˈʌpməust] *a., ad.* = uppermost.

up·on [强 əˈpɔn; 弱 əpən] *prep.* = on *(prep.)* ★ upon 和 on 意义相同, 一般可互相调换; 但①日期前只用 on. ②口语中多用 on. ③upon 语气较强, 与动词连用或在句末, 多用 upon, 如: *I have not enough to live ~.* 我收入不够生活. ④在某些习语中, on 与 upon 不能互换, 如: *once upon a time* 等习语用 upon, 而 *on no account* 则必须用 on. ~ ***my word*** 一定, 的确, 决无虚言. ~ ***this*** 于是.

up·per [ˈʌpə] *a.* ①(更)上面的, 上方的, 上部的; 较高的; 上级的; (议会)上院的; (衣服)穿在外面的. ②上流的; 高原地带的; 内地的. ③【地】地表层的; 〔常 **U-**〕后期的. *the ~ seats [circle]* (戏院的)楼座, 花楼. *the ~ lip* 上唇. ***get [have] the ~ hand of*** 胜过, 占上风〔优势〕. — *n.* ①〔常 *pl.*〕鞋面皮, 鞋帮; 〔*pl.*〕布绑腿; 〔口〕(车船卧铺的)上铺. ②〔美俚〕兴奋剂, 刺激性药物〔尤指安非他明〕. ***(down) on one's ~s*** 鞋底完全磨平; 非常贫穷. **U- Bench**【英史】高等法院. ~ **Benjamin** 〔美〕外套. ~ **bound**【数】上界. **U- Cambrian**【地】后期寒武纪. ~ **case**【印】大写字母(盘). **~-case** ① *a.* 大写字母(盘)的. ②*vt.* 用大写字母排印. ~ **course** 上游. ~ **crust** 〔美俚〕上层阶级; 头, 脑袋. ~ **cut**【机】二次割削. ~ **dead center**【机】上静点. **U- Germany** 上德意志[德国南部]. **U- House** 上院, 参议院. ~ **keyboard**【乐】键盘的右方. ~ **leather** 鞋面皮. ~ **story** 二楼; 〔俚〕头, 头脑. ~ **ten (thousand)** 上层阶级. ~ **works**【船】水线以上的船体; 〔口〕头, 脑袋; 智力.

up·per-class [ˈʌpəˈklɑːs] *a.* 上层阶级(特有)的.

up·per·class·man [ˈʌpəˈklɑːsmən] *n.* ***(pl. -men)*** 〔美〕(高等学校的)高班生[三、四年级学生].

up·per-crust [ˈʌpəˈkrʌst] *n., a.* ①(馅饼、面包等的)上外皮(的). ②〔美口〕上层阶级(的). ③〔俚〕头(的).

up·per·cut [ˈʌpəkʌt] *vt., vi., n.*【拳击】上击.

up·per·most [ˈʌpəməust] *a.* ①最上的, 最高的. ②最主要的, 首先浮现在心头的. *one's ~ thoughts* 首先发生的念头. — *ad.* ①最上, 最高. ②首先, 最初.

Upper Volta [ˈʌpə ˈvɔltə] 上沃尔特〔非洲〕. **Upper Voltaic** [vɔlˈteiik] 上沃尔特人.

up·pish [ˈʌpiʃ] *a.* ①〔口〕骄傲的, 傲慢的. ②〔主英〕稍微朝上的. **-ly** *ad.* **-ness** *n.*

up·pi·ty [ˈʌpiti] *a.* 〔口〕= uppish.

up·raise [ʌpˈreiz] *vt.* 〔常用被动语态〕举起, 抬起; 提高. *hands ~d in prayer* 高举双手祷告.

up·rear [ʌpˈriə] *vt.* ①举起, 竖起. ②养育. ③赞扬; 支持. ~ *a monument in marble* 建造大理石纪念碑. ~ *children* 养儿育女. ~ *one's head* 抬起头.

up·right [ˈʌpˈrait] *a.* ①笔直的, 直立的, 竖立的. ② [ˈʌprait] 正直的. *set things ~* 把东西竖直. *an ~ piano* 竖钢琴. *an ~ man* 正直的人. — *ad.* 笔直, 竖立着. — [ˈʌprait] *n.* ①笔直的东西,【建】柱. ②【乐】竖钢琴. ③〔*pl.*〕【足球】球门柱 (= goal posts). ***bolt ~*** 笔直. **-ly** *ad.* **-ness** *n.*

up·rise [ʌpˈraiz] *vi.* ***(up·rose*** [ʌpˈrəuz]; ***up·ris·en*** [ʌpˈrizn]***)*** ①上升, 升起; 立起, 站起来. ②起身, 起床. ③爬上; 登上. ④起坡, 成坡; 高起, 高涨; 起浪. ⑤起义, 暴动; 行动起来. ⑥出现. — *n.* = uprising.

up·ris·ing [ʌpˈraiziŋ] *n.* ①升起; 立起; 起床. ②起义, 暴动. ③(逐渐升高的)斜坡. *armed ~* 武装起义.

up·riv·er [ˈʌpˈrivə] *a.* 上游的, 源头的. — *ad.* 向上游.

up·roar [ˈʌprɔː, -rɔə] *n.* 喧闹, 鼓噪, 骚嚷, 人声鼎沸, 轰鸣[响].

up·roar·i·ous [ʌpˈrɔːriəs] *a.* 喧闹的. ~ *laughter* 哄然大笑. **-ly** *ad.* **-ness** *n.*

up·root [ʌpˈruːt] *vt.* ①连根拔[掘起]; 根绝, 绝灭. ②把(某人)赶出住所[家园等]. *the ~ed* 被逐出家乡的人们. ~ *poverty* 彻底消除贫困. — *vi.* ①被连根拔起. ②成为无家可归.

up·rose [ʌpˈrəuz] uprise 的过去式.

up·rouse [ʌpˈrauz] *vt.* 唤起, 唤醒; 激起.

up·sa·dai·sy [ˈʌpsəˈdeizi] *int.* = upsy-daisy.

up·set [ʌpˈset] *vt.* ***(up·set)*** ①推翻, 颠覆; 弄翻, 打翻. ②搅乱, 打破(计划); (体育比赛、政党竞选等中)意外地击败(被认为强悍的对手). ③使狼狈, 使烦乱; 使(胸口、肚子等)不舒服. ④【机】缩锻, 顿锻; 顿粗; 压缩(车轮内径). ~ *a glass of wine* 弄翻一杯酒. *A boat was ~.* 一条船(被风)吹翻了. ~ *sb.'s plan* 打乱某人的计划. ~ *a room* 把房间弄乱. — *vi.* 翻倒, 颠覆. ~ ***sb.'s apple cart*** 打乱某人的计划. ~ ***the dope*** 〔美俚〕(形势大变)

使预测[打算]落空. — *n.* ①倾覆,翻倒;颠覆. ②心乱,烦乱,混乱. ③不和,吵架. ④意外的失败. ⑤【机】缩锻; 缩锻过的金属棒的粗大部分; 缩锻用陷型模. — [ˈʌpset] *a.* ①被推翻[弄翻]了的;混乱的;被挫败的. ②心绪烦乱的. ③固定的,一定的. ~ **price** (拍卖开始时的)最低价格;开拍价格.

up·shift [ˈʌpʃift] *vi.* (汽车驾驶)换高一档;加速.

up·shot [ˈʌpʃɔt] *n.* ①结果,结局; 终点. ②结论; 要点. ***be brought [come] to the ~*** 得出结论. ***in the ~*** 最后,终于. ***when it comes to the ~*** 如果细细推究起来.

up·side [ˈʌpsaid] *n.* ①上边, 上面, 上部, 上段. ②【铁路】上行线月台.

up·side-down [ˈʌpsaidˈdaun] *ad.* 颠倒; 混乱, 乱七八糟. *He turned the room ~ to hunt for the lost key.* 他把屋子翻得乱七八糟,寻找遗失的钥匙. — *a.* 颠倒的, 混乱的,乱七八糟的. ~ **cake** 把水果放在下层烤的蛋糕[食用时翻转来则水果在上].

up·sides [ʌpˈsaidz] *ad.* 〔Scot. 方〕各半, 不相上下地. ***be ~ with*** 与…不相上下. ***get ~ with*** 〔方〕同样回敬;报复.

up·si·lon [juːpˈsailən] *n.* 希腊语字母表第二十字〔Υ, *υ* 相当于英语的 u〕.

up·spring [ʌpˈspriŋ] *vi.* ***(up·sprang*** [ʌpˈspræŋ], ***up-sprung*** [ʌpˈsprʌŋ]***)*** 向上弹, 跃起. — *n.* 向上弹(跳).

up·stage [ˈʌpˈsteidʒ] *a.* ①在[向]舞台后方的. ②〔口〕傲慢的, 狂妄自大的. — *ad.* 在舞台后方; 朝着舞台后方. — *vt.* ①(在演出中占据舞台后方)逼使(另一演员)背向观众, 抢(别人的)戏. ②傲慢地对待. *n.* ①后台. ②舞台上较后的位置.

up·stair [ˈʌpˈstɛə] *a.* = upstairs*(a.)*.

up·stairs [ˈʌpˈstɛəz] *ad.* ①在楼上; 往楼上. ②〔口〕在较高地位上; 〔空军口〕在高空. ④〔美俚〕在头脑里. ***kick ~*** 〔口〕把…明升暗降. — *a.* ①楼上的. ②【空】在高空的. ③上层的. — *n.* 楼上;楼上房间.

up·stand·ing [ʌpˈstændiŋ] *a.* ①直立的; 挺拔的. ②正直的,诚实的. **-ness** *n.*

up·start [ˈʌpstɑːt] *n.* ①暴发户; 新贵, 突然获得地位的人. ②傲慢无礼的人. — *a.* 暴发的, 突然出现[显赫]的. *the ~s pushing into society* 这些正在挤进上流社会的新贵. — [ʌpˈstɑːt] *vt., vi.* (使)突然跳起[出];(使)暴发,(使)一步高升.

up·state [ˈʌpˈsteit] *a.* 〔美〕(一州内) 远离大都市[海边]的,北边的. — *n.* 内地,(特指)纽约州北部地区. **-r** *n.* 〔美〕内地人;纽约州北部的人.

up·stream [ˈʌpˈstriːm] *ad.* 向上游,溯流. — *a.* 溯流而上的.

up·stretched [ʌpˈstretʃt] *a.* 向上伸张,向上伸延的.

up·stroke [ˈʌpstrəuk] *n.* 向上的一笔[一击].

up·surge [ʌpˈsəːdʒ] *vi.* ①高涨,上涌. ②增长. — [ˈʌp-ˌsəːdʒ] *n.* 高涨; 高潮 (*opp.* ebb). *the tempestuous ~ of the national-liberation movement* 风起云涌的民族解放运动. **up·sur·gence** [-əns] *n.*

up·sweep [ˈʌpswiːp] *n.* ①向上倾斜,向上卷曲. ②头发在头顶上卷起的发型. — [ʌpˈswiːp] *vt., vi.* ***(up·swept*** [ˈʌpˌswept]***)***(使)向上斜,(使)向上弯曲.

up·swell [ʌpˈswel] *vi.* ***(up·swell·ed; up·swell·ed, up-swol·len*** [ʌpˈswəulən]***)*** 膨胀,增加,壮大.

up·swept [ˈʌpˌswept] upsweep 的过去式和过去分词. — *a.* 向上卷曲的,向上倾斜的; (一种发型)头发在头顶上卷起的.

up·swing [ˈʌpswiŋ] *n.* ①向上的摆动; 向上趋势; 向上的运动; 〔尤指〕(生意的)兴隆. ②进步,改进,提高. — [ʌpˈswiŋ] *vi.* ***(up·swung*** [ʌpˈswʌŋ]***)***①向上摆动;上进. ②提高;改进.

up·sy-dai·sy [ˈʌpsəˈdeizi, ˈʌpsi-] *int.* 举高高儿〔举高小孩时的戏耍语〕.

up·take [ˈʌpteik] *n.* ①举起, 拿起. ②了解, 领会. ③【物,生】吸收;【机】(把烟尘等抽吸到屋外的)升烟道,上升通风管;扬水管;【矿】上风井,上风口. *quick [slow] in the ~.* 领会得快[慢].

up·throw [ˈʌpˌθrəu] *n.* ①向上的一投. ②【地】上投(地貌),隆起.

up·thrust [ˈʌpˌθrʌst] *n.* ①向上的一推[一冲]. ②【地】上冲断层.

up·tick [ˈʌptik] *n.*【商】(股票)报升〔比上一盘交易高的成交价格〕.

up·time [ˈʌptaim] *n.* (电子计算机等的)正常运行时间.

up·tight, up·tight [ˈʌpˈtait] *a.* 〔俚〕①非常紧张的,非常神经质的; 非常焦急的. ②极端保守的; 过于严格的. ③(经济情况)很糟糕的 (= up tight).

up·tilt [ʌpˈtilt] *vt.* ①使倾斜. ②(拿枪)向上斜刺,上击.

up-to-date [ˈʌptəˈdeit] *a.* ①直到最近的. ②最新(式)的; 现代化的,尖端的. **-ly** *ad.* **-ness** *n.*

Up·ton [ˈʌptən] *n.* 厄普顿〔姓氏〕.

up·town [ˈʌpˈtaun] *ad.* 〔美〕远离商业区; 在[向]非商业区;在住宅区. — *n., a.* (住在) 远离商业区的市区(的),住宅区(的).

up·turn [ʌpˈtəːn] *vt., vi.* ①(使)朝上翻;翻起,掘翻. ②(使)向上,(使)好转. — [ˈʌptəːn] *n.* ①上升;升迁. ②好转, 改善. **-ed** [ˈʌpˈtəːnd] *a.* ①朝上(翘)的. ②翻转的.

UPU = Universal Postal Union 万国邮政联盟(联合国).

up·ward [ˈʌpwəd] *a.* 向上的, 朝上的; 上涨的. *an ~ glance* 抬眼一看. *Prices show an ~ tendency.* 物价趋涨. — *ad.* = upwards. ~ **mobility** 社会地位和经济地位上升的流动性〔指努力提高自己经济与社会地位的能力和倾向〕. **-ly** *ad.*

up·wards [ˈʌpwədz] *ad.* ①在上面, 向上头. ②向水源[震源地]方面; 向内地. ③上涨, 腾贵. ④从…起以后; 以上. *look ~* 仰望. *Prices tend ~.* 物价趋涨. *from her school days ~* 从她学生时代以后. *children of six years and ~* 六岁及六岁以上的孩子. ***~ of …*** 以上(*~ of ten years* 十年以上).

up·wind [ˈʌpˈwind] *ad., a.* 迎风向地[的],逆风向地[的]. — *n.* 逆风.

ur [ʌ(ː), ə(ː)] *int.* 呃,嗯[表示踌躇].

UR 〔美空俚〕= unsatisfactory report.

Ur. = 【化】元素 uranium 的符号.

ur-[1] *pref.* 〔G.〕原始的,原来的,最初的.

ur-[2] *pref.* uro- 的异体.

u·ra·cil [ˈjurəsil] *n.*【化】尿嘧啶,尿间二氮苯.

u·rae·mi·a [juəˈriːmiə] *n.*【医】尿毒症. **-mic** *a.* (患)尿毒症的.

u·rae·us [juˈriəs] *n.* (*pl.* ***u·rae·i*** [juˈriai]) (古埃及神像及帝王头饰上的)毒蛇形标记.

u·ra·gogue [ˈjuərəgɔg] *n.*【药】一种利尿剂.

U·ral [ˈjuərəl] *n.* 乌拉尔〔苏联一地区〕.

U·ral-Al·ta·ic [ˈjuərəlælˈteiik] *a.* 乌拉尔阿尔泰 (Ural-Altai) 地方(居民)的;乌拉尔阿尔泰语族的. — *n.* 乌拉尔阿尔泰语族〔芬兰语、土耳其语、蒙古语等〕.

U·ral·ic [juˈrælik], **U·ra·li·an** [juˈreiliən] 乌拉尔语系的〔包括芬兰-乌戈尔语和萨摩耶德语族〕. — *n.* 乌拉尔语系.

u·ral·ite [ˈjuərəlait] *n.*【地】纤闪石. **-ic** [juəˈrælik] *a.*

u·ra·nal·y·sis, u·ri·nal·y·sis [ˌjuərəˈnælisis] *n.*【医】尿分析.

U·ra·ni·a [juəˈreiniə] *n.* ①【希神】掌管天文的缪斯 (Muse) 女神. ②爱情与美之女神 (Aphrodite) 的别名.

U·ra·ni·an[1] [juəˈreiniən] *a.* 缪斯女神的.

U·ra·ni·an[2] [juəˈreiniən] *a.*【天】天王星的.

u·ran·ic[1] [juəˈrænik] *a.* 天的;天文学的.

u·ran·ic[2] [juəˈrænik] *a.*【化】六价铀的,(正)铀的,含铀的. ~ *acid*【化】铀酸.

u·ra·nide [ˈjuərənaid] *n.*【化】铀系;超铀元素.

u·ran·i·nite [juəˈræninait] *n.* 【矿】晶质铀矿, 沥青铀矿; 天然氧化铀.

u·ra·nite [ˈjuərənait] *n.* 【矿】铀矿类; 云母铀.

u·ra·ni·um [juəˈreiniəm] *n.* 【化】铀 (U). *fertile* ~ 铀 238. ~ **dioxide** 【化】二氧化铀. ~ **fission** 铀核裂变. ~ **product** 铀变物. ~ **trioxide** 【化】三氧化铀.

urano- *pref.* 表示"天": *urano*metry.

u·ra·nog·ra·phy [ˌjuərəˈnɔgrəfi] *n.* 【天】星图学. **-ra·pher** *n.* 星图学家. **-graph·ic,** [ˌjuərənəuˈgræfik] **-graph·i·cal** *a.*

u·ra·nol·o·gy [ˌjuərəˈnɔlədʒi] *n.* 天体学; 天文学〔旧称〕.

u·ra·nom·e·try [ˌjuərəˈnɔmitri] *n.* ①(古代)天体志〔图〕; 星座志. ②天体测量(术).

u·ra·nous [ˈjuərənəs, juəˈrei-] *a.* 【化】铀的, 含铀的〔尤指含低价铀〕.

Ura·nus [ˈjuərənəs] *n.* ①【希神】优拉纳斯神〔大地女神 Gaca 的儿子〕. ②【天】天王星.

u·ra·nyl [ˈjuərənil] *n.* 【化】铀酰, 氧铀.

u·rate [ˈjuəreit] *n.* 【化】脲酸盐〔酯〕.

ur·ban [ˈəːbən] *a.* ①城市的, 在城市里的, 住在城市中的, 城市居民的. ②习惯于〔喜爱〕城市生活的. *the* ~ *population* 城市人口. ~**-centered** *a.* 以城市为中心的. ~ **critic** 城市问题评论家. ~ **district** 〔英〕准自治市. ~ **guerrilla** 城市游击队(员). ~ **renewal** 城市环境更新, 城市改造. ~ **sprawl** (无限制的)城市扩张. ~ **town [township]** 〔美〕城镇〔人口 25,000 以上或人口密度至少为 1500 人/平方英里〕.

ur·bane [əːˈbein] *a.* ①都〔城〕市气派的. ②有礼貌的, 文雅的(*opp.* rustic). **-ly** *ad.* **-ness** *n.*

ur·ban·ism [ˈəːbənizəm] *n.* ①城市生活的特点; 城市生活(组织、问题等); 对城市生活等的研究. ②人口流入城市; 人口集中于城市; 城市化. **ur·ban·ist** *n.* 城市规划专家. **ur·ban·is·itic** *a.*

ur·ban·ite [ˈəːbənait] *n.* 城市居民.

ur·ban·i·ty [əːˈbæniti] *n.* ①有礼; 文雅, 优雅. ②〔*pl.*〕文雅的举止.

ur·ban·i·za·tion [ˌəːbənaiˈzeiʃən] *n.* 城市化; 使具有城市特点.

ur·ban·ize [ˈəːbənaiz] *vt.* ①使都〔城〕市化. ②使文雅, 使有礼貌, 使优雅.

ur·ban·oid [ˈəːbənɔid] *a.* 具有大城市特点的.

ur·ban·ol·o·gist [ˌəːbəˈnɔlədʒist] *n.* 都市学专家, 城市问题学者〔专家〕.

ur·ba·nol·o·gy [ˌəːbəˈnɔlədʒi] *n.* 城市学, 都市学.

ur·bi·a [ˈəːbiə] *n.* 〔集合词〕市区〔以区别于郊区 *(suburbia)* 和远郊 *(exurbia)*〕.

ur·bi·ci·dal [ˌəːbiˈsaidl] *a.* 毁灭城市的, 对城市起毁灭作用的.

ur·bi·cul·ture [ˈəːbiˌkʌltʃə] *n.* 城市(生活)特有的习俗〔社会问题等〕.

ur·bi et or·bi [ˈuəbi et ˈɔːbiː] 〔L.〕(降福于)城市〔指罗马〕和世界〔教皇祝福用语〕.

URBM = ultimate range ballistic missile 最远程弹道导弹.

ur·ce·o·late [ˈəːsiəlit] *a.* 瓶形的, 瓮形的, 缸状的.

ur·chin [ˈəːtʃin] *n.* ①顽童; 儿童, 少年. ②【动】海胆〔通常称 sca-urchin〕. ③〔方〕刺猬.

urd [əːd] *n.* 〔Hind.〕【植】黑绿豆 *(Phaseolus mungo)*.

Ur·du [ˈuəduː, Hind. wrdu] 乌尔都语〔用阿拉伯字母写的一种印地语; 巴基斯坦的正式语言〕.

-ure *suf.* 由动词构成名词的后缀, 表示: 动作(例: cens*ure*); 结果(例: creat*ure*); 集合体(例: legislat*ure*)等.

u·re·a [ˈjuəriə] *n.* 【化】脲, 尿素. **-l, u·re·ic** [ˌjuəˈriːik] *a.*

u·re·a-form·al·de·hyde [juriəfɔːˈmældihaid] **re·sins** 【化】脲醛树脂, 尿素甲醛树脂.

u·re·ase [ˈjuərieis, -eiz] *n.* 【化】尿素酶.

u·re·din·i·um, u·re·di·um [ˌjuəriˈdiniəm, -ˈdiəm] *n.* *(pl.* **-i·a** [-ə]*)* 【植】夏孢子堆. **-din·i·al** *a.*

u·re·do [juˈriːdəu] *n.* 【医】= urticaria.

u·re·do·spore, u·re·di·o·spore [juˈriːdəspɔː, -diəspɔː] *n.* 【植】夏孢子.

u·re·do·stage [juˈriːdəsteidʒ] *n.* 【植】夏孢子期.

u·re·ide [ˈjuəriaid, -id] *n.* 【化】酰脲.

u·remi·a [juˈriːmiə] *n.* = uraemia. **u·remic** [juˈriːmik] *a.* = uraemic.

u·re·ter [juəˈriːtə], *n.* 【解】输尿管. **-al, -ic** [ˌjuəriˈterik] *a.*

u·re·ter·i·tis [juˌriːtəˈraitis] *n.* 【医】输尿管炎.

u·re·ter·os·to·my [juˌriːtəˈrɔstəmi] *n.* *(pl.* ***-mies)*** 【医】输尿管造口术.

u·re·thane, [ˈjuəriθein], **u·re·than** [ˈjuəriθæn] *n.* 【化】尿烷, 氨基甲酸乙酯.

u·re·thra [juəˈriːθrə] *n.* *(pl.* ***-thrae*** [-θriː], ***~s)*** 【解】尿道. **-l** *a.*

u·re·thri·tis [ˌjuəriˈθraitis] *n.* 【医】尿道炎.

u·re·thro·scope [juˈriːθrəskəup] *n.* 【医】尿道镜. **-scop·ic** [juˌriːθrəˈskɔpik] *a.*

u·ret·ic [juəˈretik] *a.* 【医】尿的; 利尿的. — *n.* 利尿剂.

U·rey [ˈjuəri] *n.* 尤里〔姓氏〕.

urge [əːdʒ] *vt.* ①推进, 驱策, 赶(马等). ②催促, 强迫; 促进, 奖励, 鼓励, 劝告, 怂恿; 号召. ③极力主张, 强调. ④苦练, 勤苦地使用. ~ *a horse on* [*onward*] 赶马前跑. ~ *sb. to take steps in the matter* 催人处理事件. ~ *upon sb. the necessity of doing so* 向某人强调有这样做的必要. ~ *a programme* 提出一个纲领. — *vi.* 极力主张; 强烈要求. — *n.* ①推动力. ②〔常用 *sing.*〕刺激, 冲动, 迫切要求. *the sex* ~ 性的冲动.

ur·gen·cy [ˈəːdʒənsi] *n.* ①迫切, 紧急; 【政】紧急决议. ②催促, 硬要, 强调. *a matter of great* ~ 非常紧急的事. *an* ~ *signal* 紧急信号.

ur·gent [ˈəːdʒənt] *a.* ①紧急的, 迫切的. ②催促的, 硬要的, 极力主张的, 纠缠不休的. *an* ~ *telegram* 急电. *be in* ~ *need of (help)* 急需(援助). *on* ~ *business* 因急务. *an* ~ *motion* 紧急动议. *He was* ~ *with me for* [*to disclose*] *further particulars.* 他硬要我说得更详细点. **-ly** *ad.*

urg·er [ˈəːdʒə] *n.* 推进者, 催促者, 劝告者, 极力主张者.

-urgy *comb. f.* 构成名词, 表示: 制作技术; 加工: chem*urgy*, metall*urgy*.

-uria *comb. f.* 表示"因含某种物质而使尿呈病态: *glycosuria*, albumin*uria*.

U·riah [juəˈraiə] *n.* 尤那依〔姓氏〕. ~ **Heep** 尤那依·希普〔阴险虚伪的小职员典型, 狄更斯小说《大卫·科柏菲》中的人物〕.

u·ric [ˈjuərik] *a.* 【化】尿的. ~ *acid* 尿酸.

u·ri·cos·u·ric [ˌjuərikəuˈsjuərik] *a.* 【医】增加〔促进〕尿酸排泄的.

u·ri·dine [ˈjuəridiːn] *n.* 【化】尿核甙; 尿定.

u·ri·nal [ˈjuərinl] *n.* 尿壶; 小便处〔池〕.

u·ri·nal·y·sis [ˌjuəriˈnælisis] *n.* *(pl.* ***-ses*** [-siːz]*)* 【医】尿分析(法).

u·ri·na·ry [ˈjuərinəri] *a.* 尿的, 泌尿(器)的. — *n.* 〔*pl.*〕①小便处. ②尿池. ~ **bladder** 膀胱. ~ **calculus** 尿结石. ~ **diseases** 泌尿系统疾病. ~ **tubule** 尿细管.

u·ri·nate [ˈjuərineit] *vt., vi.* (使)小便, (使)排尿.

u·ri·na·tion [ˌjuəriˈneiʃən] *n.* 小便, 排尿.

u·rine [ˈjuərin] *n.* 尿. *pass* [*discharge*] *(one's)* ~ 小便, 排尿.

u·ri·nif·er·ous [ˌjuəriˈnifərəs] *a.* 【医】导尿的.

u·ri·no·gen·i·tal [ˌjuərinəuˈdʒenitl] *a.* = urogenital.

u·ri·nom·e·ter [ˌjuəriˈnɔmitə] *n.* 尿比重计, 量尿器.

u·ri·nous [ˈjuərinəs], **u·ri·nose** [-nəus] *a.* 尿(似)的,

含尿的.

urn [əːn] *n.* ①瓮,缸,坛. ②骨灰瓮; 坟墓. ③水壶; 咖啡壶. ④【植】蒴壶. — *vt.* 〔罕〕把(遗骨等)装进瓮里. **-ing** *n.* 〔卑〕(男子)同性恋.

uro- *pref.* ①表示"尿": *uro*chrome. ②表示"尾": *uro*dele.

u·ro·chrome [ˈjuərəukrəum] *n.* 【生化】尿色素,尿色肽.

u·ro·dele [ˈjuərəudiːl] *n.* 【动】有尾目 *(Caudata)* 动物.

u·ro·gen·i·tal [ˌjuərəuˈdʒenitl] *a.* 尿(生)殖的,泄殖的.

u·rog·e·nous [juˈrɔdʒinəs] *a.* ①生尿的. ②尿中含有的; 出自尿中的.

u·ro·ki·nase [ˌjuərəuˈkaineis, -ˈkineis] *n.* 【生化】尿激酶,尿致活酶.

u·ro·lith [ˈjuərəliθ] *n.* 【医】 = urinary calculus. **-ic** *a.*

u·ro·log·ic [ˌjuərəuˈlɔdʒik] *a.* 泌尿学的(= urological).

u·rol·o·gy [juəˈrɔlədʒi] *n.* 【医】泌尿学. **-log·i·cal** [ˌjuərəuˈlɔdʒikəl] *a.*

u·ro·pod [ˈjuərəpɔd] *n.* 【动】尾足; 腹足.

u·ro·pyg·i·um [ˌjuərəuˈpidʒiəm] *n.* *(pl.* **-i·a** [-ə], *~s)* (鸟的)尾臀. **-pyg·i·al** *a.*

u·ro·scop·ic [ˌjuərəuˈskɔpik] *a.* 检尿(法)的.

u·ros·co·py [juəˈrɔskəpi] *n.* 【医】尿检,尿检视法.

Ur·quhart [ˈəːkət] *n.* 厄克特〔姓氏〕.

Ur·sa [ˈəːsə] *n.* 〔L.〕 =bear. ~ ***Major [Minor]*** 【天】大[小]熊座.

ur·si·form [ˈəːsifɔːm] *a.* 熊状的.

ur·sine [ˈəːsain] *a.* ①熊的,熊类的; 似熊的. ②(毛虫等)长满硬毛的.

Ur·spra·che [ˈuːəˌʃpraːkhə] *n.* 〔G.〕 原始语〔一种由推论而重新构定的母语,如原始日耳曼语〕.

Ur·su·la [ˈəːsjulə] *n.* 厄休拉〔女子名〕.

Ur·ti·cant [ˈəːtikənt] *a.* 产生痒[痛]的; (毛虫)能刺人使生痒肿块的.

ur·ti·car·i·a [ˌəːtiˈkɛəriə] *n.* 【医】荨麻疹,风疹. **-al** *a.*

ur·ti·cate [ˈəːtikeit] *vt.* ①用荨麻拍打(麻痹的肢体等)使恢复感觉. ②刺痛,用荨麻刺. — *vi.* 诱发荨麻症.

ur·ti·ca·tion [ˌəːtiˈkeiʃən] *n.* 【医】①用荨麻拍打. ②刺痒的感觉. ③生风疹块,生荨麻疹.

Uru. = Uruguay.

Uru·guay [ˈurugwai] *n.* 乌拉圭〔拉丁美洲〕.

Uru·guay·an [ˌuruˈgwai-ən] *n.* 乌拉圭人. — *a.* 乌拉圭(人)的; 乌拉圭文化的.

U·rum·chi, U·rum·tsi [uˈrumtʃi] *n.* 乌鲁木齐〔中国新疆维吾尔自治区首府〕.

u·rus [ˈjuərəs] *n.* 原牛 *(Bos primigenius)* 〔一种已绝种的野牛,过去在欧洲常见,被认为是现今家牛的祖先〕.

u·ru·shi·ol [ˈuːruːʃiˌɔːl, uˈruː-; -əul] *n.* 【化】漆醇.

us [强 ʌs; 弱 əs] *pron.* ①〔we 的宾格〕我们. ②〔诗、古〕朕= (ourselves). ③〔口〕〔用作表语〕我们 (= we). ④〔方、口〕我 (= me, to me). *Let* ~ [ˈletəs] *go.* = *Let's* [lets] *go.* 我们走吧. *Let* ~ [let ʌs] *go.* 让我们走吧,放我们走吧. *Who are you?* 谁呀? *It's* ~. 是我们. *Give* ~ *a penny.* 〔口〕给我一个子儿吧.

U. S., US = ①United States (of America) 美国,美利坚合众国. ②Uncle Sam 〔口〕山姆大叔〔美国、美国政府或美国人的绰号〕.

US ① = U. S. ②如果后面附有一个阿拉伯数码, 则意为"美国某号公路"如 US 40, 即美国第 40 号公路.

u.s. = 〔L.〕 ①*ubi supra* 〔书籍等中的参照用语〕在上面提及之处. ②*ut supra* 如上所述,如上所示.

U.S.A., USA = ①United States of America 美利坚合众国. ②United States Army 美国陆军.

us·a·bil·i·ty [ˌjuːzəˈbiliti] *n.* ①可用; 有用. ②适用,便于使用(= usableness).

us·a·ble [ˈjuːzəbl] *a.* ①可用的,能使用的. ②便于使用的. **-ness** *n.*

USAEC = United States Atomic Energy Commission 美国原子能委员会.

USAF = ①United States Air Force 美国空军. ②United States Army Forces 美国陆军部队.

USAFE = United States Air Force in Europe 美国驻欧空军.

USAFI = United States Armed Forces Institute 美国武装部队业余进修学院.

us·age [ˈjuːzidʒ] *n.* ①使用; 用法; 对待. ②习惯,惯例,习俗. ③【语法】惯用法;【法】习惯(法). ④【机】用损,损蚀; 使用度. *an old man who met with harsh* ~ 一个受到虐待的老人. *a car damaged by harsh* ~ 一辆因使用不经心而被损坏的汽车. *modern English* ~ 现代英语惯用法. *keep an old* ~ *alive* 保持旧习俗. ***according to*** ~ 依照惯例. ***by*** ~ 习惯上; 视为惯例.

us·ance [ˈjuːzəns] *n.* ①【商】支付汇票的习惯期限, 支付期票的期限. ②【经】利得; (高利贷的)利息. ③〔古〕使用; 惯例,习惯. ***at*** ~ 在(习惯)期限内支付.

USAREUR = United States Army in Europe 美国驻欧陆军.

U.S.C. = ①United States of Colombia 〔旧〕哥伦比亚合众国. ②United States Code《美国法典》.

USCG = United States Coast Guard 美国海岸警卫队.

use [juːs] *n.* ①使用,利用,应用; 使用的机会[需要]. ②使用的能力. ③使用的自由, 使用权. ④使用法. ⑤用途; 效用,用处,利益. ⑥习惯,惯例; 惯常的作法[仪式]. ⑦【法】(托管土地等的)收益权. *Will there be any further* ~ *for big battleship in the future war?* 在未来的战争中还有使用大型战舰的必要[机会]吗? *He has lost the* ~ *of an arm.* 他的一只胳膊残废了. *What is the* ~ *of talking?* 说有什么用呢? *put the* ~ *of one's house at sb's disposal* 让某人自由使用自己的房子. *a computer with many* ~*s* 一种多用途的电子计算机. *according to an ancient* ~ 按照一种古老的习俗. *Use is (a) second nature.* 习惯是第二天性. *Use makes perfect.* 熟能生巧. *Once a* ~*, for ever a custom.* 习惯成自然. ***be of (great)*** ~ (非常)有益. ***be out of*** ~ 没有人用, 不时行, 现在不用, 作废. ***bring sth. into*** ~ 开始使用(某物). ***come into*** ~ (某物)开始被使用. ***for the*** ~ ***of*** *(students)* 供(学生)使用. ***get [go, fall] out of*** ~ 开始不用, 渐废. ***have no*** ~ ***for*** ①不需要, 用不着. ②〔口〕不愿再与之打交道, 不喜欢, 厌腻. ***in*** ~ 正在用; 通行. ***make*** ~ ***of*** 利用, 使用. ***no*** ~ 〔口〕没(有)用(处) *(It is no* ~ *talking [to talk].* 说也没用). ***of no*** ~ = no ~. ***of*** ~ 有用 *(It is of great* ~. 这非常有用). ***put to*** ~ 用,利用 (*put to a good* ~ 善用). ~ ***and wont*** 习惯, 惯例. ***with*** ~经常在用 (*The carpet has got worn with* ~. 这块地毯由于经常使用,已经磨坏了). — [juːz] *vt.* ①用,使用,利用,应用; 服用,食用. ②消费,耗费. ③对待(人). ④行使,动用. ⑤使习惯〔此义现在只将过去分词形 used 用如形容词,参看 used¹〕. ~ *one's revolver upon sb.* 对某人使用手枪. ~ *tobacco* 抽烟. ~ *five tons of coal a week* 每周耗煤5吨. ~ *sb. well [ill]* 待人好[不好]. ~ *one's brains* 用脑筋, 想. ~ *care* 小心,注意. ~ *diligence* 努力. ~ *economy* 节省. ~ *one's ears [eyes]* 听[看]. *U- your discretion.* 请考虑考虑吧. *U- your pleasure.* 请自便, 请随意. *How is the world using you?* 〔俚〕近来好吗? — *vi.* 常, 惯常〔此义现在只用过去形, 参看 used²〕. ~ ***oneself*** 处身. ***U- others as you would have them*** ~ ***you.*** 你愿意别人怎样待你,你就应该怎样待人. ~ ***up*** ①用完, 用光. ②〔口〕使筋疲力尽. **-a·ble** *a.* = usable.

used¹ [juːst, 〔在 to 前〕 juːs*t*] *a.* ①习惯于〔作表语用〕. ②[juːzd] 〔美〕用过的,用旧了的,半旧的; 精疲力尽的. ~ *books* 〔美〕旧书. ~ *heat* 废热, 余热. ***be*** ~ ***to*** 惯于. *(be* ~ *to getting up early* 习惯早起. *be* ~ *to hard work* 惯于吃苦耐劳). ***get [become]*** ~ ***to*** 变得习惯于. ~ ***up***①〔美〕筋疲力尽的, 疲劳不堪的. ②用完了的; 〔美〕被杀死了的,已阵亡的.

used² [〔带 to 时〕 ju:st, 〔不带 to 时〕 ju:st] *vi.* 〔用法同助动词，其后的不定式表示过去多次发生的动作〕常常，经常，往往。*I ~ to go there.* 我(以前)常到那里。*He does not come as often as he ~ (to).* 他不象从前那样常来了。*What ~ he to say? — He ~ not to answer.* 他向来怎么讲？——他向来不回答。*It ~ to be said that ...* 过去(人家)常说…。*There ~ to be a house here.* 原来这里是有一所房子的。*Used there to be swallows here?* 这里是否一向都有燕子？★口语或美国用法说作 Did there use to ....

used-to-be [ˈju:stəbi] *n.* 〔美口〕时代落伍者，过时人物。

use·ful [ˈju:sful] *a.* ①有用的，有益的，有效的，有帮助的。②〔俚〕值得称赞的，精通…的 *(at).* ***make oneself generally*** ~ 事事有用，事事帮得来忙 (*He must make himself generally ~.* 他可事事都干得来)。*a pretty ~ performance* 相当精采的演出。*His wife is very ~ at cooking.* 他的妻子很会做菜。~ **area** 有效面积，可用面积。~ **life** 有效期限，使用寿命。~ **load**【空】实用负载。**-ly** *ad.* **-ness** *n.*

use·less [ˈju:slis] *a.* ①没用的，无益的，无效的。②〔俚〕身体不舒服的，没精神的。*I am feeling ~.* 我觉得精神不行了〔不舒服〕。**-ly** *ad.* **-ness** *n.*

us·er¹ [ˈju:zə] *n.* ①使用者，用户。②吸毒成瘾者。

user² [ˈju:zə] *n.*【法】(财产等的)使用(权)，行使(权)，享受(权)，享有(权)。

USES = United States Employment Service 美国就业局。

USEUCOM = United States European Command 美军驻欧司令部。

ush [ʌʃ] *n., vt., vi.* 〔俚〕 = usher.

ush·er [ˈʌʃə] *n.* (*fem.* ***-ette*** [ˈʌʃəˈret]) ①看门人，门房；传达；〔美〕(戏院的)引座员，领票(员)，(婚礼中的)迎宾(员)；〔英〕皇室礼宾官。②〔英〕〔谑〕助理教员，助教。— *vt.* ①引导，领引，招待。②宣告，展示 *(in).* *The waiter ~ed the guests into the dining room.* 服务员把客人领进宴会厅。*She ~ed me to my seat.* 她把我领到坐位上。~ *in a new era of revolution* 宣告一个革命新世纪的到来。— *vi.* 作招待员；担任前导。~ ***in*** 迎接(来客)；传报，预报，告诉(来临等)。~ ***out [forth]*** 送出。

USIA = United States Information Agency 美国新闻署。

USIB = United States Intelligence Board 美国情报局。

USIS = United States Information Service 美国新闻处。

USL = United States Legation 美国公使馆。

USM = ①underwater-to-surface missile 水下对地导弹。②United States Mail 美国邮政。③United States Marine(s) 美国海军陆战队。④United States Mint 美国造币厂。

USMA = United States Military Academy 美国陆军军官学校〔即西点军校〕。

USMC = United States Marine Corps 美国海军陆战队。

USN = United States Navy 美国海军。

USNA = ①United States National Army 美国国民军。②United States Naval Academy 美国海军军官学校。

USNG = United States National Guard 美国国民警卫队。

USNR = United States Naval Reserve 美国海军后备队。

USO = United Services Organizations. 〔英旧〕劳军联合组织，美军慰问协会。

USOM = United States Operations Mission 美国援外使团。

USP, U.S.P. = ①United States Patent 美国专利。② = U. S. Pharm.

U. S. Pharm. = United States Pharmacopoeia 美国药典(规格)。

USPO ① = United States Patent Office 美国专利局。②=United States Post Office 美国邮政局。

us·que·baugh [ˈʌskwibɔ:] *n.* 〔Scot., Ir.〕 = whisky.

USS = ①United States Senate 美国参议院。②United States Ship [Steamer, Steamship] 美国船。③United States Standard 美国(工业)规格，美国(工业)标准。

USSC = United States Supreme Court 美国最高法院。

USSR, U.S.S.R. = Union of Soviet Socialist Republics 〔苏联〕苏维埃社会主义共和国联盟。

U·ssu·ri [uˈsu:ri] *n.* 乌苏里江〔黑龙江支流〕(= Wusuli River).

us·tu·late [ˈʌstjuleit, -lit] *a.* (烧焦而)变色的，变黑的。

us·tu·la·tion [ˌʌstjuˈleiʃən] *n.* 燃烧，烧焦，烧灼。

usu. = usual; usually.

u·su·al [ˈju:ʒuəl] *a.* 通常的，常有的，常见的；平常的，普通的；平时的，平日的；一向的，老是那一套的。*He came earlier than ~.* 他比平时来得早。*She came early as was ~ with her.* 她象平日那样来得很早。*the ~ (thing)* 老一套，老调。*He said all the ~ things.* 他讲的全是老一套。***as per*** ~〔谑〕= as ~. ***as*** ~ 照例，照常，仍然。(*He was late, as ~.* 他照例迟到了)。**-ly** *ad.* **-ness** *n.*

u·su·ca·pion [ju:zjuˈkeipiən], **u·su·cap·tion** [ˌju:zjuˈkæpʃən] *n.*【法】时效所有权〔在法定时间内始终占有而取得的所有权〕。

u·su·fruct [ˈju:sju(:)frʌkt] *n.*【法】收益享用，用益权。— *vt.* 根据用益权占有。

u·su·fruc·tu·ar·y [ˌju:sjuˈfrʌktjuəri] *n.*【法】有用益权者。— *a.* (有)用益权的。

u·su·rer [ˈju:ʒərə] *n.* 高利贷者，吃重利的人，重利盘剥者。

u·su·ri·ous [ju:ˈʒuəriəs] *a.* 高利贷(者)的，高利的；重利盘剥的；掠夺性的。**-ly** *ad.* **-ness** *n.*

u·surp [ju:ˈzə:p] *vt.* 篡夺，侵占，盗用；强夺。~ *state (government) power* 篡政。~ *the throne* 篡夺王位。~ *the name of ...* 盗用…的名义。*a ~ed beard* 假胡须。— *vi.* 〔罕〕篡夺，篡位；侵占，侵犯，侵害 *(up; upon).* **-er** *n.* 篡夺者；篡位者，侵占者。

u·sur·pa·tion [ˌju:zə:ˈpeiʃən] 篡夺，侵占，强夺；【法】冒认。

u·sur·pa·to·ry [ju(:)ˈzə:pətəri] *a.* 篡夺的；侵占的；夺取的。

u·surp·ing·ly [ju(:)ˈzə:piŋli] *ad.* 篡夺地；侵占地；夺取地。

u·su·ry [ˈju:ʒuri, -ʒəri] *n.* ①高利贷；高利。②〔喻〕利益。

usus loquendi [ˈju:səs ləuˈkwendai] 〔L.〕习惯说法；语言习惯，文风。

USV = United States Volunteers 美国志愿兵。

U.S.W., u.s.w. = ultrashort wave 超短波。

u.s.w. = 〔G.〕 *und so weiter* (= and so forth)诸如此类。

USWB = United States Weather Bureau 美国气象局。

UT, U.T., u.t. = universal time 世界时，格林威治时。

ut [ʌt] *conj.* 〔L.〕 如。~ ***dictum*** [ˈdiktəm]【处方】照(医生)所嘱，如医嘱，照指示。~ ***infra*** [ˈinfrə] 如下(所述)。~ ***supra*** [ˈsju:prə] 如上(所述)。

ut [ʌt, u:t] *n.*【乐】音阶的第一音， 七个唱名的第一个，Do 音。

ut. = utilities.

UTA = 〔F.〕 *Union Transports Aériens* 〔法〕联合航空运输公司。

U·tah [ˈju:tɑ:; 美 ˈju:tɔ:] *n.* 犹他〔美国州名〕。

U.T.C. = Uncle Tom's Cabin 〔美国作家斯陀夫人所作反蓄奴制小说《汤姆叔叔的小屋》〕。

ut dict. = 〔L.〕 *ut dictum* 〔见 *ut* 条〕。

Ute [ju:t, ˈju:ti] *n.* ①*(pl.* ~*(s))* 犹特人〔以游牧为生的肖松尼印第安人一个部落，曾居住在美国科罗拉多州，犹他州，后到新墨西哥州和亚利桑那州〕。②犹特语〔属肖松尼语〕。

u·ten·sil [ju(:)ˈtensil] *n.* 器具,用具;家庭厨房用具. *farming* ~*s* 农具. *kitchen* ~*s* 厨房用具. ~*s of war* 武器. *writing* ~*s* 文具.

u·ter·ine [ˈjuːtərain] *a.* ①【解】子宫的. ②同母异父的. ~ *diseases* 子宫病. ~ *brothers* 异父兄弟. ~ *descent* 母系. ~ **cake** 胎盘.

u·ter·i·tis [ˌjuːtəˈraitis] *n.*【医】子宫炎.

u·te·rus [ˈjuːtərəs] *n.* (*pl.* **-ri** [-rai])【解】子宫.

u·ti·le dul·ci [ˈjuːtili ˈdʌlsi]〔L.〕愉快而有益的东西.

u·ti·lise [ˈjuːtlˌaiz] *vt.* = utilize.

u·til·i·tar·ian [ˌjuːtiliˈtɛəriən] *a.* ①功利的;实利的. ②功利主义的,实利主义的. — *n.* 功利主义者,实利主义者. **-ism** *n.*【哲】功利主义,实利主义.

u·til·i·ty [juːˈtiliti] *n.* ①有用,有益;实用,【经】效用;功利;〔常 *pl.*〕有用的东西. ②【哲】功利主义. ③【剧】跑龙套的[演配角的]演员. ③〔美〕公用事业 (= public ~);〔*pl.*〕公用事业股票. *marginal* ~【经】边际效用,限界效用. ***of no*** ~ 没用的,无益的. — *a.* ①多用途的,各种工作都会做的,通用性的. ②实用的,经济实惠的. ③(牲畜)为谋利而饲养的〔不是为了玩赏的〕. ④公用事业的,公用事业公司股票价格的. ~ **aircraft** 运输机. ~ **factor** (设备)使用率. ~ **man** 跑龙套的演员;打杂人员;【棒球】万能候补队员. ~ **room** 家庭用具存放室. ~ **service** 公用服务事业. ~ **vehicle** 多用途运载工具.

u·ti·li·za·tion [ˌjuːtilaiˈzeiʃən] *n.* 利用;效用.

u·ti·lize [ˈjuːtilaiz] *vt.* 利用. **-liz·a·ble** *a.* 可利用的.

ut inf. =〔L.〕*ut infra*〔见 *ut* 条〕.

u·ti pos·si·de·tis [ˈjuːti pɔsiˈdiːtis]〔L.〕【国际法】占领地保有原则〔指交战国各方可在战后占有实际占领的地区〕;【罗马法】保护现在占有者权利的法律.

ut·most [ˈʌtməust] *a.* ①极度的,极端的. ②最远的,尽头处的. *a state of the* ~ *confusion* 极端的混乱状态. *the* ~ *limits* 极限. *to the* ~ *ends of the earth* 到世界的尽头,到天涯海角. — *n.* 极限,极度,极端,最大限度. ***at the*** ~ 至多. ***do one's*** ~ 尽所有力量,竭力. ***make the*** ~ ***of*** … 充分利用. ***to the*** ~ 尽力,极力,极度 (*enjoy oneself to the* ~ 尽情享受一番). ***to the*** ~ ***of one's power*** 竭力.

U·to-Az·tec·an [ˈjuːtəuˈæztekən] *a.* 犹特—阿兹特卡语系的〔美国西部、墨西哥和中美洲一个大的美洲印第安语系〕. — *n.* 犹特—阿兹特卡语〔包括肖松语、尤蒂-阿茨蒂克语、比马语、霍皮语、犹特语等〕.

U·to·pi·a [juːˈtəupjə, -piə] *n.* 乌托邦;〔常 u-〕理想的国土[社会等]空想的社会改良计划〔源出英国空想社会主义者托·摩尔所作«乌托邦»一书〕.

U·to·pian [juːˈtəupjən] *a.*〔有时作 u-〕乌托邦(似)的;理想的,空想的. — *n.* ①乌托邦[理想国]的居民. ②空想社会主义者,理想家. ~ **socialism** 空想社会主义.

u·to·pi·an·ism [juˈtəupiənizəm] *n.* 乌托邦思想(理论);不切实际的社会改革方案.

UTP =【化】Uridine triphosphate 三磷酸尿苷.

U·trecht [ˈjuːtrekt] *n.* 乌得勒支〔荷兰城市〕.

u·tri·cle [ˈjuːtrikl] *n.* ①小囊,小胞. ②【植】胞果;胞囊. ③【解】椭圆囊;前列腺囊.

u·tric·u·lar [juːˈtrikjulə] *a.* 小囊(状)的,(具)胞果的.

ut sup. =〔L.〕*ut supra*〔见 *ut* 条〕.

ut·ter[1] [ˈʌtə] *a.* (*superl.* **~most**) ①完全的,十足的. ②无条件的,绝对的,断然的. ③外边的〔现在除 ~ bar (【法】外席)及 ~ barrister (【法】外席律师)二例外罕用〕. *an* ~ *stranger* 完全不认识的人. ~ *darkness* 漆黑. *an* ~ *fool* 大傻瓜. *an* ~ *refusal* 断然的拒绝. ***be at an*** ~ ***loss what to do*** 完全不晓得怎样才好. **-ly** *ad.*

utter[2] [ˈʌtə] *vt.* ①发出(声音等);讲,说;说出,说明,表明,吐露(心事等);公开申言. ②使用,行使,流通(伪钞等). ③发射;喷射. ~ *a groan* 发出呻吟声. ~ *the truth* [*a lie*] 说真话[说谎话]. ~ *false coin* 使用伪造的钱币. **-a·ble** *a.*

ut·ter·ance[1] [ˈʌtərəns] *n.* ①发声;发言;发言能力. ②〔仅用 *sing.*〕口才;语调,发音. ②(说出的)话;言辞. ③〔罕〕表达,发表. ④〔罕〕使用,行使,流通. *his public* ~*s* 他的公开言论. *a clear* ~ 清楚的语调[发音]. *a man of good* ~ 口才好的人. *a defective* ~ 有缺陷的发音. ***give*** ~ ***to*** (*one's rage*) 说出,讲出,表明(愤怒).

ut·ter·ance[2] [ˈʌtərəns] *n.*〔英、古〕最后,死〔现仅用于 ***to the*** ~ 到最后,到死〕.

utter·most [ˈʌtəməust, -məst] *a.* 最远的;最大限度的. — *n.* 最大限度. *to the* ~ *of one's power* [*capacity*]. 竭力,尽(可能).

U-turn [ˈjuːtəːn] *n.* ①(车辆等的)作U形转弯〔尤指车辆在街道上作180°调头〕. ②似U形转弯的东西;〔喻〕方向的大改变. — *vi.* 作180度大转弯.

UUM = underwater-to-underwater missile 水下对水下导弹.

UV = ultraviolet.

u·van·ite [ˈjuvænait] *n.*【矿】钒铀矿.

u·va·rov·ite [uːˈvɑːrəvait] *n.*【矿】钙铬榴石.

u·ve·a [ˈjuːviə] *n.*【解】眼色素层;葡萄膜.

u·ve·i·tis [ˌjuːviˈaitis] *n.*【医】眼色素层炎,眼葡萄膜炎.

u·vi·ol(glass) [ˈjuviəul(glɑːs)] *n.* 紫外玻璃.

u·vu·la [ˈjuːvjulə] *n.* (*pl.* **~s, -lae** [-liː])【解】①悬雍垂,小舌. ②小脑悬雍垂,蚓垂.

u·vu·lar [ˈjuːvjulə] *a.* ①【解】悬雍垂[小舌]的. ②【语音】软口盖的. — *n.*【语言】软口盖音.

UW = under water 水下.

U/w(s), U/WS = underwriters.

UX_1 = uranium X_1〔即 Th (钍)[234]〕.

UX_2 = uranium X_2〔即 Pa (钋)[234]〕.

Ux. =〔L.〕*uxor* (=wife).

ux·or·i·cide [ʌkˈsɔːrisaid] *n.* 杀妻(罪);杀妻者.

ux·o·ri·ous [ʌkˈsɔːriəs] *a.* 溺爱妻子的;怕老婆的. **-ly** *ad.* **-ness** *n.*

UY = uranium Y〔即 Th (钍)[231]〕.

UZ = uranium Z〔即 Pa (钋)[234]〕.

Uz·beg, Uz·bek [ˈʌzbeg] *n.* ①乌兹别克人. ②乌兹别克语. — *a.* ①乌兹别克的. ②乌兹别克人[语]的.

Uz·bek·i·stan [ˌuzbekiˈstɑːn] *n.* 乌兹别克〔苏联加盟共和国名〕.

V

V, v [viː] (*pl.* **V's, v's** [viːz]) ①英语字母表第二十二字母. ②V 字形;V 形物. ③〔V〕(罗马数码)五;〔美俚〕票面额为五元的钞票;五年徒刑;保险箱. ④〔V〕【化】元素钒 (vanadium) 的符号. *a V-belt*【机】三角皮带. *a V sign* 胜利手势〔向上伸出食指和中指的手势〕(V = Victory). *a V spot*〔美〕一张五元钞票. IV = 4.

VI = 6. XV = 15. VL = 45. LV = 55. $\overline{V}$ = 5,000.

V., v. = ①Venerable. ②Vicar. ③Viscount. ④valve. ⑤verb. ⑥version. ⑦versus. ⑧very. ⑨vice. ⑩〔L.〕 *vide.* ⑪village. ⑫vise. ⑬vocative. ⑭voice. ⑮voltage. ⑯volume. ⑰〔G.〕 *von.* ⑱vowel.

V-1 [ˈvi(:)ˈwʌn] *n.* "报复"武器第一号,V-1火箭〔第二次世界大战末期德国的火箭,用以轰炸英国〕.

V-2 [ˈvi(:)ˈtu(:)] *n.* "报复"武器第二号,V-2火箭〔*cf.* V-1条〕.

V-8 [ˈviːˈeit, ˈviˈet] *n.* = V-8 engine.

V-8 engine (汽车的)V型8汽缸引擎.

VA = ①Veterans' Administration 〔美〕退伍军人管理局. ②vicar apostolic【天主】名誉主教. ③vice admiral 海军中将. ④volt-ampere【电】伏安,伏特安培. ⑤value analysis【社会学】价值分析.

Va. = Virginia 弗吉尼亚〔美国州名〕.

va [vɑː] 〔It.〕【乐】继续下去,继续…〔指挥用语〕. ~ ***piano*** 继续弱.

v.a. = ①verb active. ②verbal adjective.

vac. = ①vacant. ②〔口〕 vacation. ③vacuum.

va·can·cy [ˈveikənsi] *n.* ①空虚,空;空间,空隙,空处;空地,空房(等).②精神空虚,心不在焉,没精神,出神,茫然若失. ③空位,空额. ④闲暇;无所事事. *gaze into [at, on] ~* 凝视空中. *fill a ~ in one's knowledge* 填补知识空白. *fill (up) the ~ (by election)* (用选举办法)补充空额. *when a ~ occurs* 有空额的时候.

va·cant [ˈveikənt] *a.* ①空无所有的, 空虚的. ②(房子等)空着的,没人住的;(位置等)空缺的. ③精神空虚的;茫然的,出神的,无精打采的;无意义的,无聊的;不感兴趣的. ④空闲的;无所事事的;没职业的. ⑤【法】无人利用的;无主的;遗弃的;无继承人的. *The house is still ~.* 这房子还空着. *a ~ lot* 一块空地. *a ~ possession* 〔出租广告用语〕空房. *a ~ succession*【法】继承人不明的遗产. *situation ~ columns* (报纸的)召聘(广告)栏. *a ~ look* 发呆的样子. *~ frivolities* 无聊的举动. *~ hours* 暇时,闲暇时光. **-ly** *ad.* ①发呆地,茫然;无所事事地. ②〔美俚〕离开,走掉.

va·cate [vəˈkeit, veiˈk-; Am. ˈveikeit] *vt.* ①使空无所有,使空虚;腾出,搬出,退出(房间、市镇等). ②解除[辞去](职位),空出(地位)[席位]. ③【军】使撤退;【法】使作废,取消(契约等). — *vi.* ①空出,退出,腾出. ②〔美〕休假,度假;辞职.

va·ca·tion [vəˈkeiʃən] *n.* ①假期;休假;(法庭等的)休庭期.②搬出,迁出,退出;辞职. ③(职位的)空缺(期间). *the long [summer] ~* 暑假;(法院的)暑期休庭. *~ subscriptions* 〔美〕(报纸)星期增刊的订阅. **be on ~** 在度假,放假期间. — *vi.* 〔美〕放假,休假;度假. *go ~ing* 去休假旅行. **~land** 旅游胜地,休假地. **~ school** 暑期中的讲习会,暑期学校. **-er, ~ist** *n.* 〔美〕度假者,放假休息的人,休假旅行的人.

vac·ci·nal [ˈvæksinl] *a.*【医】疫苗的;接种的,种痘的.

vac·ci·nate [ˈvæksineit] *vt., vi.* (给…)接种(疫苗);(给…)种痘;(给…)打预防接种针.

vac·ci·na·tion [ˌvæksiˈneiʃən] *n.*【医】接种(疫苗);种痘;预防注射. **-ist** *n.* 主张(强迫)接种疫苗[种痘,预防注射]的人.

vac·ci·na·tor [ˈvæksineitə] *n.* ①接种[种痘]员. ②种痘刀[器],接种针.

vac·cine [ˈvæksiːn] *a.* 牛痘的;预防疫苗的;种痘的. — *n.* 疫苗;牛痘苗;菌苗. **~ lymph [virus]** 痘苗. **~ farm** 疫苗培养所. **~ point** 接种针.

vac·cin·ee [ˌvæksiˈniː] *n.* 已接种牛痘[疫苗]者.

vac·cin·i·a [vækˈsiniə] *n.*【医】牛痘. **-l** *a.*

vac·il·lant [ˈvæsilənt] *a.* 游移的,踌躇的,摇摆不定的.

vac·il·late [ˈvæsileit] *vi.* ①摆动,波动,振荡. ②动摇不定,踌躇莫决. *~ between different opinions* 在种种不同意见间摇摆. *a vacillating person* 三心二意的人.

vac·il·la·tion [ˌvæsiˈleiʃən] *n.* ①摇摆,波动,振荡. ②犹豫不决,踌躇,优柔寡断.

vac·u·a [ˈvækjuə] *n.* vacuum 的复数.

vac·u·i·ty [væˈkju(:)iti, və-] *n.* ①空,空虚;真空;空间,空处. ②精神空虚,出神,茫然若失,发呆. ③无聊,无所事事. ④〔常 *pl.*〕无聊事,无聊话. *the ~ of expression* 没有表情.

vac·u·o [ˈvækjuəu] *n.* 〔L.〕 真空.

vac·u·o·late, -lated [ˈvækjuəleit, -leitid] *a.*【生】有液泡的.

vac·u·o·la·tion [ˌvækjuəˈleiʃən] *n.*【生】空泡形成.

vac·u·ole [ˈvækjuəul] *n.*【生】空泡;液泡.

vac·u·om·e·ter [ˌvækjuˈɔmitə] *n.* 真空计;低压计.

vac·u·ous [ˈvækjuəs] *a.* ①空虚的;空洞的. ②精神空虚的;发呆的, 茫然若失的,出神的. ③无所事事的. ④无思考力的. ⑤(生活)没意义的. **-ly** *ad.* **-ness** *n.*

vac·u·um [ˈvækjuəm] *n.* ***(pl. ~s, vac·u·a*** [ˈvækjuə]***)*** ①真空;空处,空虚,空白. ②〔美口〕吸尘器 (= ~ cleaner). *a low [partial] ~* 低度[未尽]真空. ***feel a ~ in the lower regions*** 〔谑〕觉得饿. — *vi., vt.* 〔美口〕①用吸尘器扫除. ②用真空干燥机干燥. — *a.* ①真空的. ②用以产生真空的. ③利用真空的. *~ canning* 真空装罐(法). **~ bottle** 热水瓶. **~ brake** 真空制动器,低压煞车. **~ cleaner** 吸尘器. **~ flask** = ~ bottle. **~ gauge** 真空计. **~-packed** *a.* 真空包装的〔包装前抽去大量空气的〕. **~ pump** 真空泵,真空抽机. **~ tube** 〔美〕=~ valve. **~ valve** 〔主英〕【无】电子管,真空管. **-ize** *vt.* ①在…内造成真空. ②用真空装置打扫[干燥]. ③真空包装.

V.A.D. = Voluntary Aid Detachment 志愿辅助勤务队.

va·de me·cum [ˈveidi ˈmiːkəm] *n.* 〔L.〕手册,便览;随身物件.

V.-Adm. = Vice-Admiral.

va·dose [ˈveidəus] *a.*【地】渗流.

Va·duz [fɑːˈduːts] *n.* 瓦杜兹〔列支敦士登首都〕.

vae vic·tis [viːˈviktis] 〔L.〕被征服者惨矣;战败者活该遭殃!

vag *n.* 〔美〕 = vagrant.

vag·a·bond [ˈvægəbɔnd, -ˌbɔnd] *n.* 流浪者, 漂泊无定的人;〔口〕流氓,无赖,浪荡子. — *a.* 流浪(性)的,漂泊不定的;懒散的,无赖(一样)的. *a ~ life* 流浪生活. — *vi.* 〔口〕流浪, 漂泊. **-age** [-ij] *n.* 流浪(生活、习惯) *(live in [take to] ~age* 过[开始]流浪生活);〔集合词〕流浪者. **-ism** *n.* = vagabondage. **-ize** *vi.* 〔常作 ~ it〕过流浪生活,流浪.

va·gal [ˈveigl] *a.*【解】交感神经的,迷走神经的.

va·ga·ry [vəˈgɛəri, ˈveigəri] *n.* 狂妄古怪的行为,异想天开;怪想,妄想,幻想;变幻莫测. *a ~ of fashion* 古怪的时髦风气[时装式样]. **-gar·i·ous** *a.*

vag·ile [ˈvædʒail, ˈvædʒil] *a.* 漫游的.

va·gi·na [vəˈdʒainə] *n.* ***(pl. ~s, -nae*** [-niː]***)***【动】鞘;【解】阴道;【植】稃,叶鞘. **-l** *a.*

vag·i·nate [ˈvædʒinit], **vag·i·nat·ed** [ˈvædʒineitid] *a.*【动】①有鞘的. ②鞘状的.

vag·i·ni·tis [ˌvædʒiˈnaitis] *n.*【医】阴道炎.

va·gi·tus [vəˈdʒaitəs] *n.*【医】婴儿哭声.

va·go·de·pres·sor [ˌveigəudiˈpresə] *a.*【医】抑制迷走神经的. — *n.* 迷走神经抑制剂.

va·got·o·my [veiˈgɔtəmi] *n.* ***(pl. -mies)***【医】迷走神经切断术.

va·go·to·ni·a [ˌveigəuˈtəuniə] *n.*【医】迷走神经过敏,副交感神经过敏. **-ton·ic** [-ˈtɔnik] *a.*

va·go·trop·ic [ˌveigəuˈtrɔpik] *a.* 影响迷走神经[交感神经]的,作用于迷走神经[交感神经]的.

va·gran·cy [ˈveigrənsi] *n.* ①漂泊,流浪(生活). ②变幻无常,游移不定. ③【法】流浪罪. ④〔集合词〕流浪者.

V

va·grant [ˈveigrənt] *a.* ①流离失所的,漂流浪荡的;流浪(性)的. ②多变的,不定的,见异思迁的,(心、思想等)变化无常的. ~ *habits* 流浪习性. ~ *clouds* 浮云. — *n.* 流浪者,漂流浪荡的人,无定居的人;游民;无赖,流氓. **-ly** *ad.* **-ness** *n.*

vague [veig] *a.* ①含糊的,笼统的,暧昧的;不说明的. ②无表情的;发呆的,出神的. *a* ~ *answer* 含糊的回答. *I haven't the vaguest notion what to do.* 我一点儿也不晓得怎样办才好. — *n.* 模糊不定状态. *My plans are still in the* ~. 我的计划还没有确定呢. **-ly** *ad.* **-ness** *n.*

va·gus [ˈveigəs] *n.* *(pl.* ***va·gi*** [-dʒai]*)*【解】迷走神经,交感神经 (= ~ nerve).

va·hi·ne [vaːˈhiːnei] *n.* (大洋洲东部塔希提岛上的)波利尼西亚女人;妻〔当地居民的土语〕.

vail[1] [veil] *vt.* 〔古〕脱(帽等表示投降或敬意); 低下. — *vi.* 脱帽(等),低头.

vail[2] [veil] *vt., vi.* 〔古〕有用(于),有利(于),有助(于). — *n.* 〔古〕〔常 *pl.*〕赠与,赏钱;贿赂.

vail[3] [veil] *n., vt.* 〔古〕= veil.

vain [vein] *a.* ①徒然的,无益的,没效果的;愚蠢的;不足道的. ②空的,空虚的;虚有其表的,表面好看的,虚饰的. ③自夸的,自负的;爱虚荣的. ~ *efforts* 徒劳. ~ *titles* 空名,虚衔. *a* ~ *attempt* 妄想. *a* ~ *man* 虚荣心强的人. **be** ~ **of** 自夸,自以为…了不起 (*She is* ~ *of her voice.* 她自以为她的嗓音了不起). ***in vain*** ①无益地,徒然 (*We protested in* ~. 我们白白抗议了. *pass one's life in* ~ 虚度一生). ②轻忽地,轻慢地,亵渎地 (*take sb.'s name in* ~ 轻慢地提到某人的名字 (尤指轻慢地谈到上帝)).

vain·glo·ri·ous [veinˈglɔːriəs] *a.* 过于自负的, 狂妄自大的;虚荣心很强的.

vain·glo·ry [veinˈglɔːri] *n.* 自负;虚荣心.

vain·ly [ˈveinli] *ad.* 虚妄地,无益地; 自负地. ***be*** ~ ***proud of*** 以…而目空一切. ~ ***hope for*** 妄想.

vain·ness [ˈveinnis] *n.* 无益;〔罕〕自负,自夸,虚荣.

vair [vɛə] *n.* 〔古〕(中世高级阶层作服饰的) 灰鼠毛皮;【徽】毛皮纹.

Vaish·na·va [ˈvaiʃnəvə] *n.* 〔印度教〕信奉毗湿奴 (Vishnu, 印度教三大神之一)的人.

Vais·ya [ˈvaiʃiə] *n.* 〔Sansk.〕吠舍,毗舍〔印度四种姓的第三等级,即商人和农民〕.

Val [væl] *n.* 瓦尔〔男子名, Valentine 的昵称〕.

Val. = ①valentine. ②valuation. ③value.

val·ance [ˈvæləns] *n.* ①(窗帘顶部的) 挂布式框架. ②床沿挂布;桌帷.

vale [veil] *n.* 谷,峪;槽,沟. *the White Horse V-* 白马峪. *the earthly* ~ = *this* ~ *of tears* 现世. *the* ~ *of years* 老年.

va·le [ˈveiliː, ˈwaːlei] *int.* 〔L.〕再见;〔道别语,原意为"愿你健康"〕. — *n.* 离别;告别.

val·e·dic·tion [ˌvæliˈdikʃən] *n.* 告别;告别词.

val·e·dic·to·ri·an [ˌvælidikˈtɔːriən] *n.* 〔美〕作告别演说者;(代表毕业生)致告别词的学生.

val·e·dic·to·ry [ˌvæliˈdiktəri] *a.* 告别的. — *n.* 告别演说,告别词;〔美〕毕业生代表的告别词.

va·lence[1] [ˈveiləns] *n.*【化】(化合)价; (原子)价;【生】效价. ~ **electrons**【物】价电子.

val·ence[2] [ˈvæləns] *n.* = valance.

Va·len·ci·a [vəˈlenʃiə] *n.* ①巴伦西亚〔西班牙港市〕. ②巴伦西亚〔委内瑞拉城市〕.

va·len·ci·a [vəˈlenʃiə] *n.* ①〔常 *pl.*〕(英国)华冷西亚斜纹薄呢;凸纹背心料. ②〔*pl.*〕(西班牙)(巴伦西亚 出产的)巴旦杏〔干葡萄〕.

Va·len·ci·ennes [ˌvælənsiˈen] (法国)华冷西恩花边.

valen·cy [ˈveilənsi] *n.*【化】= valence[1].

-valent *comb. f.*【化】原子〔化合〕价的,…价的〔常作复合词用〕: mono*valent*.

Val·en·tine [ˈvæləntain, ˈvæləntin] *n.* ①[ˈvæləntin] 瓦伦丁〔姓氏〕. ②[ˈvæləntain] **St.** ~ 圣瓦伦丁〔公元三世纪的基督教殉道者〕. **~'s day** 圣瓦伦丁节(2月14日).

val·en·tine [ˈvæləntain] *n.* ①在圣瓦伦丁节寄给异性的卡片〔书信,礼物〕. ②(圣瓦伦丁节时作为自己选中对象而赠与礼品的)对象;情人. ③〔喻〕任何表示想念的事物. *His essay is a* ~ *to London.* 他那篇散文是为怀念伦敦而写的.

va·ler·ate [ˈvæləreit] *n.*【化】戊酸盐,戊酸酯.

va·le·ri·an [vəˈliəriən] *n.*【植】缬草(属);拔地麻.

val·et [ˈvælit, ˈvæli, F. vals] *n.* ①(专司看管衣物及替主人穿衣的)男子的男仆,随从. ②(旅馆,客船中)照料旅客衣服烫洗等事的服务员. ③衣架. ④驯马用刺针. — *vt.* 做…的男侍仆;侍候. ~ ***de pied*** 〔F.〕= footman. ~ ***de place*** 〔F.〕(尤指法国的) 导游者. ~ ***de chambre*** 〔F.〕= valet.

val·e·tu·di·nar·i·an [ˌvæliˌtjuːdiˈnɛəriən] *a., n.* 多病〔虚弱〕的(人); 过分关心个人健康的(人). **-ism** *n.* 病弱. **-na·ry** [ˌvæliˈtjuːdinəri] *a.,n.* = valetudinarian.

val·gus [ˈvælgəs] *n.*【医】①外翻足. ②外偏手(膝、臀、拇趾等). — *a.* ①外翻的. ②内翻的,膝内弯的.

Val·hal·la [vælˈhælə] *n.*【北欧神】①(Odin) 神招待阵亡英灵的殿堂. ②烈士纪念堂,忠烈祠.

val·iant [ˈvæljənt] *a.* ①勇敢的, 英勇的, 英雄的. ②〔方〕(身体)强健的. *the* ~ *record* 英勇事迹. — *n.* 勇敢的人. **-ly** *ad.*

val·id [ˈvælid] *a.* ①(理由、证据等) 有确实根据的,确凿的;正确的;健全的,站得住的. ②【法】(契约、选举等)经过正式手续的,有效的(*opp.* void). ②〔罕〕强健的;有力的. ③【逻】含有暗示之结论的前提的. ~ *ballot papers* 有效选票. **-ly** *ad.*

val·i·date [ˈvælideit] *vt.* ①证实,确证;证明正确. ②使(在法律上)有效,使生效, 使合法化 (*opp.* invalidate);批准,确认. **-da·tion** [ˌvæliˈdeiʃən] *n.*

va·lid·i·ty [vəˈliditi] *n.* ①正确,正当,妥当,确实性. ②【法】有效,真确,合法性. ③【哲】效准. *the term of* ~ 有效期间.

valin(e) [ˈvæliːn] *n.*【生化】缬氨酸.

va·lise [vəˈliːz, -liːs] *n.* 〔主、美〕旅行手提包〔箱〕;旅行袋;【军】背包.

val·la·tion [væˈleiʃən] *n.* ①壁垒,堡垒. ②筑城术.

val·lec·u·la [vəˈlekjulə] *n.* *(pl.* ***-lae*** [-liː]*)* ①【植】(线)沟. ②【解】谷,窝,溪. **-r** *a.*

Val·let·ta [vəˈletə] *n.* 瓦莱塔〔马耳他首都〕.

val·ley [ˈvæli] *n.* ①谷,峪,河谷;凹处. ②流域. ③【建】屋谷,屋面天沟. *the* ~ *of the shadow of death* 死荫的幽谷〔源出《圣经》《诗篇》〕;临死的(痛苦)时候.

val·lum [ˈvæləm] *n.* *(pl.* ***-la*** [-lə]*)* ①【古罗马】壁垒,阵营. ②【解】眉毛,睫毛.

va·lo·ni·a [vəˈləuniə] *n.* (欧洲、亚洲的)大鳞栎斗〔含单宁酸的橡树果实壳,可作染料〕.

val·or [ˈvælə] *n.* 〔美〕= valour.

val·o·rize [ˈvæləraiz] *vt.* (政府) 以给予各种补助的形式稳定〔维持〕(商品)价格. **-ri·za·tion** [ˌvæləraiˈzeiʃən] *n.*

val·or·ous [ˈvælərəs] *a.* 勇敢的, 英勇的, 大胆的;气概豪迈的. **-ly** *ad.*

val·o(u)r [ˈvælə] *n.* ①勇猛, 英勇; 豪迈气概. ②〔罕〕勇士.

Val·pa·rai·so [ˌvælpəˈraizəu], **Val·pa·ra·i·so** 〔Sp.〕[ˌbalparaˈiso] *n.* 瓦尔帕莱索〔智利港市〕.

Val·sal·va [vælˈsælvə] **maneuver** 佛萨瓦氏 *(Valsalva)* 压力均衡法〔在飞机升降时, 紧紧地捏鼻, 闭嘴, 使劲鼓气〕.

valse [vaːls] *n., vi.* 〔F.〕= waltz.

val·u·a·ble [ˈvæljuəbl] *a.* ①有价值的. ②贵重的,宝贵

的. ③可评价〔估价〕的. — *n.*〔常 *pl.*〕贵重物品. ~ *papers* 有价证券. ~ **consideration** 与受益价值相等的报酬. **-a·bly** *ad.* **-ness** *n.*

val·u·ate [ˈvæljueit] *vt.* *(-at·ed; -at·ing)* 评价,估价;鉴定,品定. **-a·tor** *n.* 评价者,估价者;鉴定者.

val·u·a·tion [væljuˈeiʃən] *n.* 估价, 评价; 估定价格;价值;【数】赋值. ***be disposed of at a low ~*** 廉价售出〔处理〕. ***put [set] too high a ~ on*** …把…估计得〔看得〕太高.

val·u·a·tor [ˈvæljueitə] *n.* 评价者;估价者; 核价员; 价格核定人.

val·ue [ˈvælju:, -ju] *n.* ①价值;重要性;益处. ②估价, 评价. ③价格, 所值; 交换力. ④(邮票的)面值. ⑤等值;值得花的代价. ⑥(字等的)真义, 意义. ⑦【数】值;【语言】音值;【生】(分类上的)等级;【乐】音的长短;【绘画】明暗配合. ⑧〔*pl.*〕生活的理想, 道德价值; 社会准则. *rated* ~ 额定值. *proper* ~【物】本征值. *commercial [economic]* ~ 经济价值. *exchange(able)* ~ (= ~ in exchange) 交换价值. ~ *in use* 使用价值. *surplus* ~ 剩余价值. *face* ~ 票面价格. *market* ~ 市价. *pay full* ~ *for sth.* 对某物付足代价. *the* ~ *of the dollar* 美元的购买力. *the* ~ *of a symbol* 某符号的意义. ***be of [no]*** ~ 有〔无〕价值. ***(for)*** ~ ***received***〔支票用语〕货款…正. ***of*** ~ 有价值的 (*news of* ~ 重要消息). ***out of*** ~ (绘画等) 明暗不调和. ***place a*** ~ ***on*** 估价,评价. ***put [set] a high [much]*** ~ ***(up)on*** 高估;重视,看重. — *vt.* ①给…估价,定…的价. ②对…作出评价; 尊重, 看重. (*Troops are* ~*d for quality rather than for number.* 兵贵精不贵多). ~ ***oneself for*** *(what one does, etc.)* 夸耀(自己事业等). ~ ***oneself (up)on*** 自夸(*sth.*) (~ *up (on) one's knowledge* 夸耀自己的知识). ~ **engineering** 价值工程学〔研究如何以最低成本提高产品价值的科学〕. ~ **judg(e)ment** 评头品足;多管闲事的议论;对人〔事物〕的价值、善恶等所作的主观论断.

val·ued [ˈvælju:d] *a.* ①贵重的; 被尊重的,重要的. ②估定了价格的;有(一定)价值的. ~ ***favour***〔美〕①定货. ②【商】信;通信.

val·ue·less [ˈvæljulis] *a.* 没有价值的,不足道的,没有用处的.

val·u·er [ˈvæljuə] *n.* 估价者,评价者.

va·lu·ta [vəˈlu:tə] *n.* ①币值〔尤指欧洲某些国家的货币,汇率〕. ②可使用的外汇总额.

val·val [ˈvælvəl] *a.* = valvular.

val·vate [ˈvælveit] *a.* ①具阀的,有阀门的. ②【植】镊合状〔指花被卷迭式〕;瓣裂的〔指雄蕊,果实〕.

valve [vælv] *n.* ①【机】阀,活门,舌门;汽门. ②【解、动】瓣,瓣膜;(贝)壳瓣;【植】荚片;(藻的)瓣;(果实的)裂片. ③【建】门的一扇. ④〔英〕【无】电子管,真空管. *a change* ~ 三通阀. *an exhaust* ~ 排气阀. *a pulmonary* ~【解】肺动脉瓣. *a safety* ~ 安全活门,保险阀. **-d** *a.* 有阀〔瓣等〕的. **-less** *a.* 无阀〔瓣等〕的. **-let** *n.* 小阀〔瓣等〕.

val·vu·la [ˈvælvjulə] *n.* *(pl. -lae* [-li:]*)* = valvule.

val·vu·lar [ˈvælvjulə] *a.* ①阀的,瓣的;活门的; 瓣膜的. ②【植】由瓣形成的. ~ *disease (of the heart)*【医】心脏瓣膜病. ~ *insufficiency* 心瓣闭锁不全.

val·vule [ˈvælvju:l] *n.*【解、植】小瓣,瓣膜;(昆虫的)产卵瓣.

val·vu·li·tis [ˌvælvjuˈlaitis] *n.*【医】心脏瓣膜炎.

vam·brace [ˈvæmbreis] *n.* 下臂护甲.

va·moos(e) [vəˈmu:s] **va·mos(e)** [vəˈməus] *vi.*, *vt.* 〔美俚〕(从某处)突然〔匆匆〕离开,跑掉,逃亡. ★常用命令式.

vamp[1] [væmp] *n.* ①鞋面,靴面;鞋面皮. ②补块,补靪;旧物上蒙的新面;任何补缀物. ③【乐】即席伴奏. — *vt.* ①给(鞋、靴等)换面. ②修补,翻新*(up)*. ③拼凑;拼拢来做*(up)*. ④捏造. ⑤【乐】为(独唱等)作即席伴奏. — *vi.*【乐】即席伴奏. ~ ***up*** ①把(旧物)翻新. ②拼凑. ③捏造(谣言等).

vamp[2] [væmp] *n.*〔美俚〕(诱引男子的)妖妇. — *vt.*, *vi.* 用媚术诱惑(男人)借以勒索金钱.

vamp·er [ˈvæmpə] *n.* 补鞋工人;修补者;即席伴奏者.

vam·pire [ˈvæmpaiə] *n.* ①吸血鬼; 吸人膏血的人. ②〔美〕= vamp[2]. ③演妖妇角色的演员;勾引男子的女人. ④【动】吸血蝠, 魑蝠 (= ~ bat). ⑤【剧】(舞台的)机关活门〔活盖〕.

vam·pir·ic [væmˈpirik] *a.* (象)吸血鬼的.

vam·pir·ism [ˈvæmpaiərizm] *n.* ①吸血鬼迷信. ②(民间传说中的) 吸血鬼行为;〔尤指〕吸血. ③吮人膏血;勒索钱财.

Van [væn] *n.* 范〔男子名〕.

van[1] [væn] *n.* ①(有盖的)载货大马车,搬运车;【铁路】行李车,有盖货车. ②(吉卜赛人所住的)大篷车; 囚车. *a luggage* ~行李车. *a radio diffusion*~ 广播车. *a television reporting* ~流动电视车. — *vt.* 用车搬运(货物). ~ **line**〔美〕长途搬运公司.

van[2] *n.* ①【军】先锋, 前锋部队〔舰队〕. ②先驱, 前驱;领袖,领导人(= vanguard). ***in the*** ~ ***of*** 在…的前列,作为先驱,领导着. ***lead the*** ~ ***of*** 担任…的先驱.

van[3] [væn] *n.* ①〔古、方〕簸扬器〔机〕. ②〔古、诗〕翼. ③〔矿〕洗矿铲. — *vt.* 选(矿).

van[4] [væn] *prep.*〔Du.〕= of, from〔出现于荷兰人姓名中,表示出生地,亦作 Van〕.

van·a·date [ˈvænədeit] *n.*【化】钒酸盐,钒酸酯.

va·nad·ic [vəˈnædik] *a.*【化】钒的〔指含有三价钒或五价钒的化合物的〕. ~ **acid** 钒酸.

va·nad·i·nite [vəˈnædinait] *n.*【矿】钒铅矿.

va·na·di·um [vəˈneidiəm, -djəm] *n.*【化】钒〔符号为 V〕. ~ **steel**【冶】钒钢.

van·a·dous [ˈvænədəs] *a.*【化】亚钒的〔指含有二价钒或三价钒的化合物的〕.

Van Al·len [vænˈælin] *n.* 范阿伦〔姓氏〕.

Van·brugh [ˈvænbrə] *n.* 范布勒〔姓氏〕.

Van·bu·ren [vænˈbjuərən] *n.* 范布伦〔姓氏〕.

Vance [væns] *n.* 万斯〔姓氏,男子名〕.

van·co·my·cin [ˌvænkəˈmaisin] *n.*【药】万古霉素.

Van·cou·ver [vænˈku:və] *n.* ①范库弗〔姓氏〕. ②温哥华〔加拿大西南角一港口〕.

van·da [ˈvændə] *n.*【植】万带兰属 *(Vanda)* 植物.

Van·dal [ˈvændəl] *n.* ①汪达尔人〔四、五世纪时侵入罗马帝国的日耳曼民族〕. ②〔常 v-〕文化、艺术的摧残者. — *a.* 凡达尔人的;〔有时作 v-〕摧残文化艺术的,野蛮的. **-ic** [vænˈdælik] *a.*

Van·dal·ism [ˈvændəlizəm] *n.* ①汪达尔人的行为. ②〔v-〕(对公私财物,尤指文化、艺术品的)恶意破坏; 野蛮行为.

van·dal·ize [ˈvændlaiz] *vt.* *(-iz·ed; -iz·ing)* 破坏(公私财物,尤指文化艺术品).

Van·de·grift [ˈvændəgrift] *n.* 范德格里夫特〔姓氏〕.

Van·den·berg [ˈvændənbə:g] *n.* 范登堡〔姓氏〕.

Van·der·bilt [ˈvændəbilt] *n.* 范德比尔特〔姓氏〕.

V. and M. = Virgin and Martyr.

Van Do·ren [vænˈdɔ:rən] *n.* 范多伦〔姓氏〕.

van·drag·ger [ˈvænˈdrægə] *n.*〔英俚〕打劫货车的强盗.

Van·dyke[1] [vænˈdaik] *n.* ①范戴克(姓氏). ②**Sir Anthony** ~ 安·范戴克〔1599—1641,出生于英国的弗兰德斯画家〕.

Van·dyke[2] [vænˈdaik] *n.* ①范戴克(风格)的画. ②锯齿饰边领. (= ~ collar [cape]). ③【纺】人字形穿综法;锯齿形饰边. ④(下巴上的) 尖髯 (= ~ beard). — [ˈvændaik] *a.* ①画家范戴克(创作、风格)的. ②锯齿形饰边的. ~ **brown** 深褐色(颜料);【化】铁棕.

Vane [vein] *n.* 文恩〔姓氏〕.

vane [vein] *n.* ①【气】风向标, 风信旗; 〔喻〕随风倒的

V

人. ②(风车、推进机等的)翼,(导向)叶片,叶轮. ③【测】瞄准板;(罗盘等的)视准器. ④【鸟】羽片;(翮上的)短毛,翈. *a guide* ~ 导流片. *an air* ~ 【火箭】空气舵.
Van Fleet [væn'fli:t] *n.* 范佛里特〔姓氏〕.
vang [væŋ] *n.*【海】斜桁支索.
van·guard ['vængɑ:d] *n.* ①【军】先锋,前卫,(列成战斗队形的舰队的)先头舰只. ②先进分子,先驱,前导者. *the Communist Party — the* ~ *of the working class* 共产党——工人阶级的先锋队.
va·nil·la [və'nilə] *n.* ①〔V-〕【植】香子兰属. ②【植】香子兰;香草子;(做香料用的)香草香精.
va·nil·lic [və'nilik] *a.*【化】香子兰的;香草醛的.
va·nil·lin [və'nilin, 'vænilin] *n.*【化】香草醛〔精〕;香兰素.
van·ish ['væniʃ] *vi.* ①消失不见;消灭,消散 *(from)*. ②【数】成零. ~ *into smoke* 烟消云散. ~ *into thin air* 消失. — *n.*【语音】弱化音〔*ei, ou* 的 *i, u* 等〕. **~ing cream** 雪花膏. **~ing point** (透视画的)消灭点;没影点;〔口〕快消灭的最后一点. **~ing target**【军】隐显目标.
van·i·ty ['væniti] *n.* ①空虚;无用,无益〔无聊〕的事物〔行为等〕. ②虚荣,浮华;虚荣心,自负,自大,浮夸. ③(妇女装随身化妆品的)小手提包 (= ~ bag〔box, case〕). ④梳妆台. *the pomps and* ~ 浮华与虚荣. **V- Fair** ①(英国作家班扬在宗教小说《天路历程》中所写的)浮华市场. ②《名利场》〔英国作家萨克雷所著小说名〕;浮华虚荣的社会. ~ **press [publisher]** 专为著者自费印制书籍的出版社. ~ **surgery** 整容外科.
van·quish ['væŋkwiʃ] *vt.* 征服,战胜,击败;克服,抑制(感情等). *the* ~*ed* 被征服者. — *vi.* 得到胜利,成为胜利者. **-er** *n.* 征服者,胜利者.
Van·sit·tart ['vænsitət] *n.* 范西塔特〔姓氏〕.
van·tage ['vɑ:ntidʒ] *n.* ①优势;优越的地位. ②【网球】平分(deuce) 后得到的一分〔发球手 (server) 得到的叫 ~-in, 接球手 (receiver) 得到的叫 ~-out〕. ③〔罕〕= advantage. ④〔古〕利益,获利. ***a point of*** ~ = ***a coign(e) of*** ~ = ~-ground. ***for the*** ~ 何况,加之. ***have [take] (sb.) at*** ~ 比(某人)处于有利的地位,占(某人)上风. ***to the*** ~ = for the ~. **~-ground, ~-point** 有利的地位;上风.
van·ward ['vænwəd] *a.* 在前的,先头的,(部队)先锋的. — *ad.* 向前.
vap·id ['væpid] *a.* ①(食物等)没味道的,(啤酒等)走了味的. ②无趣味的,没有生气的,没有趣味的. ③不尖锐的,不痛快的. *run* ~ 走气. **-ly** *ad.* **-ness** *n.*
va·pid·i·ty [və'piditi] *n.* ①无味,乏味;走味,走气. ②没生气,没精神;没趣味.
va·por ['veipə] *n.*〔美〕= vapour.
va·po·ret·to [ˌvɑ:pəu'retəu;〔Eng.〕ˌvæpə'retəu] *n.* *(pl.* ***-ret·ti*** [-ti:], ~*s)*〔It.〕(威尼斯运河上的)公共汽艇.
va·por·if·ic [ˌveipə'rifik] *a.* 发生蒸汽的.
va·por·im·e·ter [ˌveipə'rimitə] *n.*【化】挥发度计.
va·por·i·sa·tion, -za·tion [ˌveipərai'zeiʃən] *n.* 蒸发〔挥发〕(作用),汽化.
va·por·ise, -ize ['veipəraiz] *vt., vi.* (使)蒸发〔挥发〕,(使)汽化.
va·por·is·er ['veipəraizə] *n.* 蒸发器,汽化器;喷雾器.
va·por·ous ['veipərəs] *a.* ①汽状的;蒸气状的,雾气弥漫的. ②朦胧的. ③无实质的,空幻的;幻想的. ④夸夸其谈的,浮夸的. ⑤〔古〕忧郁性的.
vapour ['veipə] *n.* ①汽,蒸汽,水蒸气;烟雾,雾,霭;【物】汽化液体,汽化固体. ②没有实质的东西;幻想,空想,妄想;〔古〕狂妄,自大. ③〔*pl.*〕郁闷,忧郁病. ④【医】吸入剂. — *vt.* ①使蒸发,使汽化. ②〔古〕使患忧郁症. — *vi.* ①蒸发,挥发 *(away)*. ②自夸,吹牛. ~ *forth high-flown fancies* 大吹牛皮. ~ **bath** 蒸汽浴. ~ **lock**【机】汽塞现象. ~ **trail**【空】雾化尾迹 (= contrail).
va·pour·ing ['veipəriŋ] *a.* 自负的,傲慢的,自夸的,夸张的. — *n.* 夸口的言谈,放肆的言谈;傲慢的态度,无节制的举动.
va·pour·ish ['veipəriʃ] *a.* ①蒸汽状的,多蒸汽的. ②忧郁的. **-ness** *n.*
va·pour·y ['veipəri] *a.* = vaporous.
va·que·ro [væ'keərəu] *n.*〔Sp.〕*(pl.* ~*s)* (墨西哥、美国西南部的)牧放牲畜者,牧童.
VAR = visual-aural (radio) range【无】可见可听式无线电航向信标,声影显示无线电航向信标.
var = volt-ampere reactive【电】乏,无功伏安.
var. = ①variable. ②variant. ③variation. ④variety. ⑤various.
va·ra ['vɑ:rɑ:] *n.* ①西班牙及拉丁美洲的尺度名,约合31至33英寸. ②西班牙及拉丁美洲的面积单位,即31(33)平方英寸.
va·rac·tor [və'ræktə] *n.*【电子学】变容二极管;可变电抗器.
var·ec(h) ['værek] *n.* ①【植】海草;巨藻,浮游海草. ②海藻灰.
vari- *comb. f.* = vario.
var·i·a ['vɛəriə] *n.*〔*pl.*〕①杂物. ②杂录,杂文集.
var·i·a·bil·i·ty [ˌvɛəriə'biliti] *n.* 易变,变化性;【生】变异性.
var·i·a·ble ['vɛəriəbl] *a.* ①易变的,变化无常的,无定的 (*opp.* constant, steady). ②可变的,能变的;变换的. ③【数】变量的;【天】变光的;【生】变异的. *Prices are* ~ *according to the exchanges.* 物价跟着汇率变动. *a man of* ~ *character* 反复无常的人. *a rod of* ~ *length* (伸缩)如意棒. *a word of* ~ *construction* 可以作种种解释的词. ~ *capital* 可变资本. *a* ~ *budget* 临时预算. — *n.* ①易变的东西. ②【数】变量,变数,变项,变元 (*opp.* constant);【天】变星 (= ~ star);【海】(方向不定的)变风,不定风 (*opp.* trade wind);〔*pl.*〕(贸易风带中的) 变风带. **V- Zone**【地理】温带. **-a·bly** *ad.* **-ness** *n.*
va·ri·a lec·ti·o ['vɛəriə'lekʃiəu]〔L.〕***(pl. vari·ae lec·tio·nes*** ['vɛərii 'lekʃiəul]*)* (不同版本间的)异文,异读.
va·ri·ance ['vɛəriəns] *n.* ①变化,变动,变更;变度,变量;【统计】(平)方(偏)差. ②(意见等的)相异;不和,冲突,争论. ③【法】诉状和供词的不符. ***at*** ~ ***with*** 和…不和;和…不符 (*at* ~ *with the facts* 不符事实. *His conduct is at* ~ *with his words.* 他言行不符). ***set at*** ~ 使不睦,离间.
va·ri·ant ['vɛəriənt] *a.* ①相异的,不同的,不一致的. ②各种各样的. ③易变的,不定的. *a* ~ *reading (in some MSS.)* (某抄本的)异文. *40* ~ *types of pigeons* 鸽子的四十种变种. — *n.* ①变体,变形;变量. ②(字音的)转讹;(字的)异体. ③【统】变式;【生】变种,变异体.
var·i·ate ['vɛəriit] *n.*【数】变量. — ['vɛərieit] *vt.* 使变化,使变异.
var·i·a·tion [ˌvɛəri'eiʃən] *n.* ①变化,变动. ②变量,变度,偏差. ③【语言】语尾变化;变体,异体;【数】变分,协变;顺列;【生】变异,演变,变种;【乐】变奏曲;【天】变差;(月的)二均差;【物】磁差. *a principle without* ~ 不变的方针〔原则〕. *be capable of* ~ 可能变化. *be liable to* ~ 容易变化. *These prices are subject to* ~. 上列价格可能变更. **-al** *a.*
var·i·a·tor ['vɛərieitə] *n.* ①【机】(伸)胀缝,伸缩(接)缝. ②【机】变速器;变化器. ③【无】聚束栅.
var·i·cel·la [ˌværi'selə] *n.*【医】水痘.
var·i·cel·late [ˌværi'selit, -ait] *a.* (某些贝壳)有细明脊纹的.
var·i·ces ['væriˌsi:z] *n.* varix 的复数.
varico- *comb. f.* 表示"静脉曲张": *varicocele.*
var·i·co·cele ['værikəusi:l] *n.*【医】精索静脉曲张.
var·i·col·o(u)red ['vɛərikʌləd] *a.* 杂色的,多色的,五色缤纷的;各种各样的.

var·i·cose [ˈværikəus] *a.* (治疗)静脉曲张的.
var·i·co·sis [ˌværiˈkəusis], **var·i·cos·i·ty** [-ˈkɔsəti] *n.* 【医】静脉曲张.
var·i·cot·o·my [ˌværiˈkɔtəmi] *n.* *(pl. -mies)* 【医】曲张静脉切开术.
var·ied [ˈvɛərid] *a.* ①各种各样的. ②改变了的,有变化的. ③杂色的,斑驳的. *birds of the most ~ kinds* 变种最多的鸟. *a ~ life* 变动多的生活. **-ly** *ad.*
var·ie·gate [ˈvɛərigeit] *vt.* ①使成杂色,使斑驳. ②使丰富多彩;使多样化.
va·r·ie·gat·ed [ˈvɛərigeitid] *a.* ①杂色的,斑驳的. ②(经验等)富于变化的;变化多端的;多样化的. *~ copper ore* 斑铜矿.
var·ie·ga·tion [ˌvɛəriˈgeiʃən] *n.* 杂色,花斑,彩斑.
var·i·er [ˈvɛəriə,ˈvær-] *n.* ①性喜变异的人. ②串种的植物.
va·ri·e·tal [vəˈraiətl] *a.* ①有变异的,变种的. ②(具有某种特性的)品种的. **-ly** *ad.*
va·ri·e·ty [vəˈraiəti] *n.* ①变化,多样性 (*opp.* monotony, uniformity). ②(各种东西的)杂凑. ③异种;种类;项目;【生】品种;变种;【语】异体. ④〔主英〕杂耍表演 (= ~ show). *an improved ~* 育成[改良]品种. ***every ~ of form*** 各种形式. ***for a ~ of reasons*** 因种种理由. ***for ~'s sake*** 为了不单调起见. ***full of ~*** 富于变化的,丰富多采的. ***have a great ~ to choose from*** 有很多种类可供选择. ***in a ~ of ways*** 用种种方法. ~ **entertainment** 杂耍演出. ~ **house [theater]** 〔英〕杂耍剧场. ~ **shop** [〔美〕**store**] 杂货铺,百货店. ~ **show** 杂耍演出.
var·i·form [ˈvɛərifɔ:m] *a.* 有种种形态的.
var·i·o·coup·ler [ˌvɛəriəuˈkʌplə, ˌvær-] *n.* 【无】可变耦合器.
va·ri·o·la [vəˈraiələ] *n.*【医】天花,痘疮 (= smallpox).
va·ri·o·lar [vəˈraiələ] *a.* 天花的;有痘痕的,脸麻的.
var·i·ole [ˈvɛəriəul] *n.* ①【动】小凹陷,痘斑. ②【地】(球颗玄武岩中的)球颗.
va·ri·o·mat·ic [ˌvɛəriəuˈmætik] *a.* 【自】可变自动程序的.
var·i·o·lite [ˈvɛəriəlait] *n.* 【地】球颗玄武岩.
var·i·o·loid [ˈvɛəriələid] *a.* 类似[轻型]天花的,变形痘的. — *n.* 【医】变形痘,轻型天花.
va·ri·o·lous [vəˈraiələs] *a.* 【医】天花的,痘症的;有痘痕的,脸麻的.
var·i·om·e·ter [ˌvɛəriˈɔmitə] *n.* 【电】磁力比较器,磁偏计;【无】(可)变(电)感器,【空】气压测量器;变压表;升降速度表.
var·i·o·rum [ˌvɛəriˈɔ:rəm] *a.* ①(古典作品)有诸家注解的,集注的. ②(例证等)引自不同来源[版本]的. — *n.* ①(古典作品的)集注版. ②附有异文的校刊本.
va·ri·ous [ˈvɛəriəs] *a.* ①不同的,各种各样的. ②多样的,多方面的;富于变化的;〔古〕多才多艺的. ③好几个的,许多的;许多种类的. ④各个的,个别的. ⑤〔用作代词〕〔口〕好几个人,许多人. *~ opinions* 种种意见. *riots in ~ places* 各地的暴动. *too ~ to form a group* 种类杂多难成一类. *V- have assured me.* 许多人已向我保证. ***for ~ reasons*** 因种种理由. **-ly** *ad.* **-ness** *n.*
va·ri·sized [ˈvɛərisaizd] *a.* 各种大小的,不同尺寸的.
va·ris·tor [vəˈristə] *n.* 【电子学】变阻器,非线性电阻,可变电阻.
var·i·tron [ˈvɛəritrɔn] *n.* 【原】变换子.
var·ix [ˈvɛəriks] *n.* *(pl. var·i·ces* [ˈværisi:z, ˈvɛər-]*)* ①【医】静脉曲张. ②【动】(卷贝的)螺层.
var. lect. = *varia lectio.*
var·let [ˈvɑ:lit] *n.* ①【史】侍童,跟班;仆人. ②〔古〕无赖,歹徒.
var·let·ry [ˈvɑ:litri] *n.* ①〔古〕仆从,走卒. ②〔蔑〕乱民;群氓,乌合之众.
var·mint [ˈvɑ:mint] *n.* ①〔俚、方〕顽童,淘气鬼;歹徒. ②有害动物. *the ~* 〔猎俚〕狐〔vermin 的别字〕.
Var·na [ˈvɑ:nə] *n.* 瓦尔纳〔保加利亚港市〕.
var·na [ˈvə:nə] *n.* (印度的)种姓 (= caste).
var·nish [ˈvɑ:niʃ] *n.* ①清漆,罩光漆,凡立水;釉子. ②(天然的)光泽面;表面光泽,外饰;(坏事等的)粉饰,掩饰. ③〔英〕指甲油. ④〔*pl.*〕〔美俚〕旅客列车. ***put a ~ on ...*** 文饰,掩饰. — *vt.* ①给…上清漆. ②使表面光泽;美化,文饰,掩饰 *(up; over)*. ~ **paint** (清)漆. ~ **tree** 清漆树. **-er** *n.*
var·nish·ing-day [ˈvɑ:niʃiŋdei] *n.* ①画展之前作者修饰作品的一天. ②艺术展览会开幕日.
va·room [vəˈru:m] *n., vi.* = vroom.
vars·al [ˈvə:səl] *a.* 〔口、方〕= universal.
var·si·ty [ˈvɑ:siti] *n.* ①〔英口〕= university. ②〔美运〕大学代表队. — *a.* 大学代表队的.
Var·u·na [ˈvərunə, ˈvær-, ˈvɑ:r-] 〔Sans.〕(印度教的)宇宙神.
var·us [ˈvɛərəs, ˈvær-] *n.* 【医】内翻,内偏〔尤指足向内翻的残疾〕. — *a.* 内翻的,内偏的〔指臀部、膝盖或足〕.
varve [vɑ:v] *n.* 【地】纹泥,季候泥.
va·ry [ˈvɛəri] *vt.* ①改变,变更,修改. ②使变化,使多样化. ③【乐】变奏;使变调. *~ one's plans* 改变计划. — *vi.* ①变化;多样化;不同,相异. ②违背,逸出 *(from)*. ③【生】变异;【数】(随着另一个值的改变)变化. *Opinions ~ on this point.* 在这一点上意见各不相同. *~ from a rule* 违背规则. ***~ (directly) as*** 和…成正比例而变化. ***~ inversely as*** 和…成反比例而变化. ***~ with*** 照…变化,跟着…变化.
vas [væs] *n.* *(pl. va·sa* [ˈveisə]*)* 〔L.〕【解,生】管,血〔脉〕管;导管. *~ deferens* [ˈdefərenz] 输精管. **vas·al** *a.*
vas·cu·lar [ˈvæskjulə] *a.* 【解、生】脉管的,由脉管形成的;血管的. ~ **bundle**【植】维管束. ~ **cylinder**【植】维管柱 (= stele). ~ **plant**【植】导管植物 (= tracheophyte). ~ **ray**【植】髓射线 (= medullary ray). ~ **system** 导管[血管、淋巴管等]系统. ~ **tissue**【植】导管组织;【动】脉管组织. **-ly** *ad.* **-i·ty** *n.*
vas·cu·lum [ˈvæskjuləm] *n.* *(pl.* **la** [-lə], *~s)* ①植物标本采集箱. ②【植】瓶状体. ③【解】小(脉)管;阴茎.
vase [vɑ:z; Am. veis] *n.* ①(花)瓶;水瓮. ②希腊瓶. ③【建、家具】瓶饰.
vas·ec·to·my [væˈsektəmi] *n.*【医】输精管切除(术).
vas·e·line [ˈvæzili:n] *n.* ①【化】凡士林,石油冻,矿脂. ②〔美俚〕奶油.
vas·o·con·stric·tor [ˌvæsəukənˈstriktə, ˌveiz-] *a.*【医】血管收缩的. — *n.* 血管收缩神经;血管收缩药. **-striction** *n.* 血管收缩.
vas·o·di·la·tor [ˌvæsəuˈdaileitə, ˌveiz-] *a.*【医】血管舒张的. — *n.* 血管舒张神经;血管舒张药. **-dil·a·ta·tion** [-ˌdiləˈteiʃən], **-di·la·tion** [-daiˈleiʃən] *n.*
vas·o·in·hib·i·tor [ˌvæsəuinˈhibitə, ˌveiz-] *n.*【医】血管抑制药,血管抑制剂. **-y** *a.*
vas·o·li·ga·tion [ˌvæsəuliˈgeiʃən, ˌveiz-] 【医】输精管结扎术.
vas·o·mo·tor [ˌvæsəuˈməutə, ˌveiz-] *a.* 【生理】血管舒缩的.
vas·o·pres·sin [ˌvæsəuˈpresn, ˌveiz-] *n.*【生化、医】后叶加(血)压素,加压素.
vas·o·pres·sor [ˌvæsəuˈpresə, ˌveiz-] *a.* 【医】血管加压的. — *n.* 血管加压神经,血管加压素.
vas·o·spasm [ˈvæsəuˌspæzm, ˈveiz-] *n.* 【医】血管痉挛.
vas·ot·o·my [væsˈɔtəmi, veiz-] *n.* *(pl. -mies)* 【医】输精管切断术.
vas·o·va·gal [ˌvæsəuˈveigl, ˈveiz-] *a.* 【医】交感神经作用于(血管)循环系统(引起)的〔如晕厥〕.
vas·sal [ˈvæsəl] *n.* ①(封建时代的)诸侯,陪臣. ②附庸;

V

部属;奴隶. —*a.* ①陪臣的,臣属的. ②隶属的;效忠的;奴隶的. *a ~ state* 仆从国. *a ~ court* 陪臣的小朝廷.
vas·sal·age [ˈvæsəlidʒ] *n.* ①陪臣身分;附庸[臣属]地位. ②效忠,臣属. ③领地,采地.
vast [vɑːst] *a.* ①广大的,辽阔的,(海、平原等)茫茫的,浩瀚的. ②许许多多的,(数、量等)巨大的. ③〔口〕非常的,很大的. *a ~ expanse of desert [ocean]* 茫茫沙漠[大海]. *a ~ scheme = a scheme of ~ scope* 庞大的计划. *a ~ calamity* 大灾祸. *a ~ difference*〔口〕天渊之别. *a ~ sum of money* 一笔巨款. *a ~ multitude* 一大群人. *of ~ importance* 非常重要的. — *n.*〔诗〕广大无边的空间;大海. *the [a] ~ of ocean [water]* 汪洋大海. **-ly** *ad.* **-ness** *n.* **-y** *a.*〔诗〕= vast.
vas·ti·tude [ˈvɑːstitjuːd, ˈvæstituːd] *n.* ①广度. ②广阔境界[空间].
vat [væt] *n.* ①(酿造、制革等用的)大桶,大缸. ②比利时和荷兰的液量名. ③【染】还原染缸[染剂]. — *vt.* 把…装入大桶;在大桶里处理. ~ **dyes** 还原性染料,瓮染料. ~**-dyed** *a.* 用还原染料染的.
VAT = Value-Added Tax 增值税.
Vat. = Vatican.
vat·ic [ˈvætik] *a.* 预言的,先知的.
Vat·i·can [ˈvætikən] *n.* ①梵蒂冈〔欧洲〕〔罗马教廷所在地〕. ②〔the ~〕罗马教廷. **V- City** 梵蒂冈城. **-ism** *n.* 教皇绝对权主义. **-ist** *n.* 教皇绝对权主义的支持者.
vat·ic·i·nal [væˈtisinl] *a.* 预言的.
vat·ic·i·nate [væˈtisineit] *vt., vi.* 预言,预告. **-na·tor**, **-na·tion** *n.*
vaude [ˈvɔud] *n.*〔美〕杂耍.
vau·de·ville [ˈvɔudəvil, -viːl] *n.* ①〔英〕轻松歌舞剧,轻松喜剧. ②〔美〕杂耍. ③(法国的)讽刺民歌. ~ **house**〔美〕杂耍场(=〔英〕music hall). ~ **performance**〔美〕杂耍表演.
vaude·vil·lian [ˌvɔudəˈviljən] *n.* 轻歌舞演员;杂耍演员. — *a.* 杂耍的.
Vau·din [ˈvɔudin] *n.* 沃丁〔姓氏〕.
Vaughan [vɔːn] *n.* 沃恩〔姓氏,男子名〕.
vault[1] [vɔːlt] *n.* ①【建】拱顶,穹窿. ②穹窿状覆盖物;天空,苍穹. ③圆顶房间[地下室];〔美〕地窖;地下保险库;安放骨灰的地下灵堂;地牢;洞窟. ④【解】腔拱,穹窿. *the blue ~ of heaven* 苍穹. — *vt.* 给…盖圆顶;使造成穹窿形. — *vi.* 成穹状.
vault[2] [vɔːlt] *vi.* (用棒或手撑着)跳,跳跃;进行撑竿跳. — *vt.* (以手撑物或撑竿)跳过. ~ *from [into] the saddle* 跳下[跳上]马鞍. ~ *on (to) [upon] a horse* 跳上马. ~ *over a ditch* 跳过沟. — *n.* 跳过,跳跃;撑竿跳〔又称 pole-~〕.
vault·ed [ˈvɔːltid] *a.* 有拱顶的;圆顶的,穹窿形的,拱状的.
vault·ing[1] [ˈvɔːltiŋ] *n.*【建】拱顶工程;〔集合词〕拱顶.
vault·ing[2] [ˈvɔːltiŋ] *n.* = vault[2]. — *a.* ①支撑着跳的;跳跃用的. ②夸大的;过度的. ~ *ambition* 狂妄的野心. *a ~ imagination* 大胆[腾空]的想象. ~ **horse**【运】鞍马.
vaunt [vɔːnt] *vi., vt.* 夸张,自夸;宣扬(优点);称扬. — *n.* 自夸,自负. ***make a ~ of*** 夸扬. ~**-courier** ①先遣者,先驱. ②〔古〕先锋队的一员(= avant-courier). **-y** *a.*
vaunt·er [ˈvɔːntə] *n.* 自负[自夸]的人,爱说大话的人.
vaunt·ing·ly [ˈvɔːntiŋli] *ad.* 自夸着,自负地,骄傲地.
Vaux [vɔːz, vɔks] *n.* 沃克斯〔姓氏〕.
v. aux. = verb auxiliary【语法】助动词.
vav [vɔv, vɔːv] *n.* 希伯来字母表的第六个字母.
vav·a·sor, vav·a·sour [ˈvævəˌsɔː, -ˌsuə] *n.* 中世纪低于男爵的小诸侯;陪臣. **-y** *n.* 小诸侯的土地[租地权].

va·ward [ˈvɑːwɔːd] *n.*〔古〕= vanguard.
vb. = verb; verbal.
V-belt [ˈviːˈbelt] *n.*【机】三角皮带.
vb. n. = verbal noun.【语法】动名词.
VC = ①veterinary corps 陆军兽医队. ②vice-chairman 副主席,副议长. ③vice-chancellor 大学副校长,副大法官. ④vice-consul 副领事. ⑤Victoria Cross〔英〕维多利亚十字勋章. ⑥Vietcong. ⑦volunteer corps 志愿军[队].
VCR = ①video cassette recording 盒式磁带录像. ②video cassette recorder 盒式录像机.
VD = vapour density 蒸气密度.
V.D. = ①venereal disease 性病,花柳病. ②Volunteer (officer's) Decoration〔英〕志愿军官勋带.
Vd =【化】vanadium.
v. d. = various dates 不同日期.
V-Day [ˈviːdei] *n.* (第二次世界大战的)胜利日,胜利节.
v.dep. = verb deponent 字形被动词义主动的动词.
V.D.H. = valvular disease of the heart 心脏瓣膜病.
VE = value engineering 价值工程学.
've [v] *v.*〔口〕= have. ★(1)英语仅用于I, we, you, they 及 who 之后: I've = I have. (2)美俚语亦用于 would, might 等之后: might've [would've] been.
Ve·a·dar [ˌveiɑːˈdɑː, ˈviːɑːdɑː] *n.* 犹太历的闰月.
veal [viːl] *n.* ①(食用)小牛肉. ②小牛 (= vealer).
veal·er [ˈviːlə] *n.* 小牛,犊.
veal·y [ˈviːli] *a.*〔口〕小牛一样的;幼稚的.
Veb·len [ˈveblən] *n.* 维布伦〔姓氏〕.
vec·to·graph [ˈvektəgrɑːf] *n.* ①(用偏光眼睛看的)立体电影[照片等]. ②【数】矢量图,向量图. **-ic** [ˌvektəˈgræfik] *a.*
vec·tor [ˈvektə] *n.* ①【数】向量,矢量,动径. ②【空】飞机航线;航向指示. ③【天】幅,矢径. ④【生】带菌者[体],传病媒介. — *vt.*【空】对(飞行中的飞机)指示航向. — *vi.*【空】电(磁)波导航. ~ **analysis** 向量解析. ~ **diagram** 向量图. ~ **product**【数】矢积. ~ **quantity** 有向量. ~ **sum**【数】矢和.
Ve·da [ˈveidə, ˈviːdə] *n.*〔Sans.〕吠陀〔印度婆罗门教四部古经的总称,或指其中之一〕. **-ic** *a.* = Vedic.
ve·da·li·a [viˈdeiliə, -ˈdeiljə] *n.*【动】澳洲瓢虫 *(Rodolia cardinalis)*〔现已引进世界各地以治介壳虫〕.
Ve·dan·ta [viˈdɑːntə, -ˈdæn-], *n.*【哲】吠檀多〔以吠陀经最后一部分即《奥义书》为基础的印度哲学〕. **Ve·dan·tic** *a.* **Ve·dan·tism** *n.*
V-E Day〔美〕(第二次世界大战中的)欧洲胜利日〔1945年5月8日,即德国投降日〕.
Ved·da(h) [ˈvedə] *n.* 维达人〔斯里兰卡的原住民〕.
ve·dette [viˈdet, vəˈd-] *n.*【军】骑哨;舰载水雷艇,哨艇.
Ve·dic [ˈveidik, ˈviːdik] *a.*〔Sans.〕吠陀的. — *n.* 吠陀梵语,早期梵语.
vee [viː] *n.* ①英语字母 V, v. ②v 形的东西. ③〔美口〕五元票面的钞票. — *a.* v 形的.
vee·no [ˈviːnəu] *n.*〔美俚〕酒;葡萄酒.
Veep [viːp] *n.*〔美口〕①(美国的)副总统 (= vice-president). ②〔v-〕〔*pl.*〕要人们.
veer [viə] *vi.* ①(风)转变方向;【气】风向(按时针方向)顺转;【海】掉转船尾向着风;顺风换抢. ②(意见、感情等)转变,改变*(round)*. — *vt.* 使转变方向;【海】把(船尾)转向风;使处顺风方位. ②放松(锚、缆等)*(away; out)*. ~ ***and haul*** (把绳等)一会儿放松一会儿拉紧;(风向)改变. — *n.* 方向的改变. **-ing·ly** *ad.*
vee·ry [ˈviəri] *n.* *(pl.* ***veer·ies)***〔美〕【动】韦氏鸫〔产于美国〕.
vee·tol [ˈviːtɔːl] *n.* (飞机的)垂直起落(=VTOL).
veg [vedʒ] *n.*〔口〕=①vegetable. ②vegetarian (restaurant).

Ve·ga [ˈviːɡə] *n.*【天】织女一,天琴座α星.

ve·ga [ˈveiɡə] *n.*〔Sp.〕(南美的)低湿平原[草地];(古巴的)烟草种植地.

veg·e·ta·ble [ˈvedʒitəbl] *n.* ①植物. ②蔬菜〔俗指豆类、芜青、青菜等,有时不指马铃薯〕. ③(生理上或精神上)象植物一样没有生气的人. *green* ~*s* 青菜; 蔬菜. ***become a mere*** ~ 变得象植物一样呆板, 呆板单调地过日子. — *a.* ①植物(性)的; 得自植物的; 关于植物的. ②蔬菜的. ~ *fibers* 植物纤维. ~ *oil* 植物油. ~ *crops* 蔬菜. *a* ~ *dish* 一盘蔬菜. ~ *soup* 蔬菜汤. ~ **anatomy** 植物解剖学. ~ **butter** 素黄油,(食用)植物脂. ~ **charcoal** 木炭. ~ **earth [mould]** 腐殖土. ~ **ivory** 植物象牙. ~ **down** 木棉. ~ **kingdom** 植物界. ~ **life** 植物. ~ **marrow**〔主英〕菜瓜[南瓜之类], 食用葫芦; 菜瓜瓤. ~ **medicine** 草药. ~ **oyster**〔美〕【植】波罗门参(= salsify). ~ **parchment** 充羊皮纸. ~ **silk** 植物丝. ~ **sponge** 丝瓜筋, 丝瓜瓤. ~ **tallow** 植物脂.

veg·e·tal [ˈvedʒitl] *a.* ①植物(性)的. ② = vegetative. — *n.* 植物; 青菜, 蔬菜.

veg·e·tant [ˈvedʒitənt] *a.* 使生长旺盛的,促进生长的,促使强壮的; 植物性的.

veg·e·tar·i·an [ˌvedʒiˈtɛəriən] *a.* ①素食主义(者)的. ②只有蔬菜的, 素菜的. *a* ~ *diet* 素食. ~ *principles* 素食主义. *a* ~ *restaurant* 素菜馆. — *n.* 蔬食主义者, 吃蔬的人;〔美〕怕吃荤腥肉类的人. **-ism** *n.* 素食主义; 素食.

veg·e·tate [ˈvedʒiteit] *vi.* ①(植物)生长; 象植物一样发育. ②坐吃,过呆板的闲静生活,过单调的生活. ③【医】(赘疣等)生长,长大; 增殖.

veg·e·ta·tion [ˌvedʒiˈteiʃən] *n.* ①【植】营养体生长, 发育;〔集合词〕植物, 植被, 植生, 草木. ②无所作为的生活,单调的生活. ③【医】赘生物,增殖体. *natural* ~ 自然植被. *tropical* ~ 热带植物. *the luxuriant* ~ 茂盛的草木. **-al** *a.*

veg·e·ta·tive [ˈvedʒitətiv] *a.* ①植物的; 蔬菜的. ②会生长的,有生长力的; 发育生长的(*opp.* reproductive); 无性繁殖的; 能使植物生长的; 植物生长和营养的, (土地)肥沃的. ③植物似的; 生活单调的, 无所作为的, 闲混日子的. ④【医】生长性的,植物性的. *during the* ~ *stage* 在生长过程中. *a* ~ *hybrid* 营养杂种, 无性杂种. ~ *propagation* 营养繁殖, 无性繁殖. *a* ~ *little* 营养性小菌落. ~ *functions* 营养机能. ~ *mass* 营养体. *a placid and* ~ *sort of character* 静如草木的性格. *the philosophy of mere* ~ *existence* 苟且偷生的哲学. **-ly** *ad.*

Veh Dep〔英〕= Vehicle Depot 停车处.

ve·he·mence [ˈviːimǝns] *n.* 激烈; 猛烈; 热烈.

ve·he·men·cy [ˈviːimənsi] *n.*〔罕〕=vehemence.

ve·he·ment [ˈviːimənt] *a.* ①激烈的; 猛烈的. ②激情的, 热烈的. **-ly** *ad.*

ve·hi·cle [ˈviːikl, ˈviəkl] *n.* ①车辆; 载运工具; 飞行器; 运行工具. ②媒介物,媒质. ③【药】赋形剂. ④【绘画、化】展色料,载色剂. *a space* ~ 宇宙飞船. *an escape* ~ 宇宙飞行器. *a rocket* ~ 火箭. *a staged* ~ 多级火箭. *a seeking* ~ 自动寻找目标的火箭. *an airborne* ~ 飞机载运导弹. *the greater [lesser]* ~【佛教】大[小]乘. *Language is the* ~ *of thought.* 语言是表达思想的工具.

ve·hic·u·lar,〔罕〕**-lar·y** [viˈhikjulə, -ləri] *a.* ①车辆的; 车辆交通的; 运载的. ②作为媒介的.

V-8 [ˈviːˈeit] *a.*【机】〔美〕V 形八汽缸式. — *n.* ①V 形八汽缸式发动机. ②装有 V 形八汽缸式发动机的汽车.

veil [veil] *n.* ①面纱, 面罩. ②(修女的)头巾;〔喻〕修女生活. ③幔,帐, 幕; 遮布; 遮蔽物. ④口实, 假托. ⑤【解、动、植】= velum. ⑥声音不响亮. ***beyond the*** ~ 在来世,在死后的无知境界. ***draw a [the]*** ~ ***over*** 遮掩,掩藏; 避不说明. ***drop a*** ~ 放下面罩. ***pass the*** ~ 死去. ***raise a*** ~ 揭开面罩. ***take the*** ~ (带上面纱)做修女. ***under the*** ~ ***of*** 躲在…的背后, 假托…. ***within the*** ~ 在天国. *be* ~*ed in mystery* 隐藏在神秘中. ~*ed threats* 暗示性的恫吓. *a* ~*ed voice* 不清楚的声音, 微哑的声音. — *vt.* 使盖上面纱; 遮盖; 隐匿. — *vi.* 蒙上面纱.

veil·ing [ˈveiliŋ] *n.* 用面纱遮掩; 面纱(料); 帐幔(料). ~ **luminance**【物】光度耗散.

vein [vein] *n.* ①【解】静脉;〔口〕血管. ②【植】叶脉;【动】翅脉;【地】矿脉,岩脉; 水脉. ③裂痕,裂缝,罅隙. ④脉,筋; 纹理. ⑤气质,倾向; 性情,性格,风格; 心境,情绪. *systemic* ~*s* 大静脉. *a* ~ *of ore* 矿脉. *a* ~ *of humour* 幽默气质. *I am not in (the)* ~ *just now.* 我现在没有兴致. *in a humorous* ~ 带着诙谐的情绪. *in the giving* ~ 在慷慨的情绪下. ***in the*** ~ ***for*** 想…,有心…. — *vt.*〔常用被动语态〕使有筋脉[纹理], 使显出静脉. ~*ed crape* 花纹绉绸.

vein·er [ˈveinə] *n.* (木刻用的) V 形小凿.

vein·let [ˈveinlit] *n.*【解】小静脉;【动】小翅脉;【植】细叶脉,支叶脉.

vein·ous [ˈveinəs], **vein·y** [-i] *a.* ***(-i·er; -i·est)*** 静脉[叶脉、翅脉、纹理]的; (手等)筋脉多的.

vein·stone [ˈveinstəun] *n.* 脉石、矿石中杂质 (= gangue).

vein·ule [ˈveinjuːl] *n.* = venule.

vel. = ①vellum. ②velocity.

ve·la [ˈviːlə] *n.* velum 的复数.

Ve·la [ˈviːlə] *n.*【天】船帆座〔南天星座名〕. ~**-Hotel**〔美〕"船帆座旅馆"〔监视宇宙空间核爆炸的人造卫星系统〕.

ve·la·men [viˈleimən] *n.* ***(pl. -lam·i·na*** [-ˈlæminə]***)*** ①【解】帆,膜,被膜. ②【植】根被.

ve·lar [ˈviːlə] *a.* ①【解】帆的, 膜的. ②【语音】(辅音等)软腭音的. — *n.*【语音】软腭音.

ve·lar·i·um [viˈlɛəriəm] *n.* ***(pl. -ria*** [-riə]***)*** (古罗马)露天剧场的遮阳(帐篷),天幕. ②【动】拟缘膜.

ve·lar·ize [ˈviːləraiz], *vt.* ***(-iz·ed; -iz·ing)***【语音】使软腭化. **-i·za·tion** [ˌviːləraiˈzeiʃən] *n.*

ve·late [ˈviːleit, -lit] *a.*【解,生】有帆的,有软腭的; 有膜的; 有缘膜的; 有菌幕的.

Vel·cro [ˈvelkrəu] *n.*〔美〕尼龙拉带(原商标名).

veld(t) [velt] *n.* (南非)无林[疏林]草原.

vel·i·ta·tion [ˌveliˈteiʃən] *n.*〔古〕小争斗, 小争执, 争论.

ve·li·tes [ˈviːlitiːz] *n. pl.* (古罗马的)轻步兵.

vel·le·i·ty [veˈliːiti] *n.* 极微弱的意欲; 无行动的单纯愿欲;【哲】不完全意欲.

vel·li·cate [ˈvelikeit] *vt., vi.* 扯; (使)跳动,(使)抽动[痉挛]; 掐.

vel·li·ca·tion [ˌveliˈkeiʃən] *n.* 痉挛; 抽动.

vel·lum [ˈveləm] *n.* ①精制犊[羔]皮纸, 上等皮纸. ②皮纸文件[抄本]. ~ **paper** 仿羔皮纸. **-y** *a.*

Vel·ma [ˈvelmə] *n.* 维尔玛〔女子名〕.

ve·lo·ce [viˈləutʃi] *ad.*〔It.〕【乐】快速地,敏捷地.

vel·o·cim·e·ter [ˌveləˈsimitə] *n.* 速度计; 测速仪.

ve·loc·i·pede [viˈlɔsipiːd] *n.* ①旧式自行车;〔谑〕自行车. ②〔英俚〕儿童三轮脚踏车. ③【铁路】轻便手压车(= handcar).

ve·loc·i·ty [viˈlɔsiti] *n.* ①迅速, 快速. ②速度; 速率. ③周转率. *at a* ~ *of 100 miles per hour* 用每小时一百英里的速度. *dart off with the* ~ *of a bird* 象鸟一样迅速飞跑过去. *drag-free* ~ 无阻力飞速,真空飞速. *escape* ~ (克服地球引力的) 第二宇宙速度, 逃逸速度. *final* ~ (发射物的) 终速. *initial [muzzle]* ~ (发射物的) 初速[腔口速度]. *uniform [variable]* ~ 匀[变]速. ~ **microphone**【无】振速传声器.

ve·lo·drome [ˈviːləudrəum] *n.* (自行车等的) 倾斜赛

车场.
ve·lom·e·ter [vi'lɔmitə] *n.* 速度计;【海】(轮船用)调速器;【空】升力系数指示器.
ve·lour, ve·lours [və'luə] *n.* ①丝绒;天鹅绒;棉绒. ②绒皮帽 (=~ hat). ③(制皮帽用的兔、海狸等的)毛皮.
ve·lou·té [vilu:'tei] *n.* 〔F.〕奶油,鲜肉[鱼]调味汁〔肉汁或鱼汁中加面粉和黄油调浓而成〕(= valouté sauce).
ve·lou·tine [vəlu'ti:n] *n.* 〔F.〕绒面呢.
vel·skoen ['vel,skju:n, 'fel-] *n.* 〔*pl.*〕南非粗皮鞋〔非洲南部人穿用的未经鞣制的皮鞋〕(= veldskoen).
ve·lum ['vi:ləm] *n.* ***(pl. ve·la*** ['vi:lə]***)*** ①【解,动】帆;软腭;膜,缘膜;(水母类的)边膜,游泳盘;膜突. ②【植、生】(唇形花的)小唇,菌幕.
vel·ure [və'ljuə] *n.* ①天鹅绒;似天鹅绒的织物. ②绒垫子. — *vt.* 用丝绒装饰[擦](帽子).
ve·lu·ti·nous [və'lju:tinəs] *a.* 【植、动】有短绒毛的;天鹅绒似的 (= velvety).
vel·ver·et ['velvərit] *n.* 粗天鹅绒.
vel·vet ['velvit] *n.* ①丝绒,天鹅绒,天鹅绒一样的东西[表面];天鹅绒海绵 (= ~ sponge). ②鹿角上的绒毛状嫩皮,鹿茸的嫩皮. ③〔俚〕(赌博中)赢得的钱;盈利,赚头. ④〔口〕舒适愉悦的景况. *cotton* ~ 棉天鹅绒. *silk* ~ (反面是棉的)丝(天鹅)绒. *cut* ~ 修剪过的天鹅绒. *pile [terry]* ~ 没有剪毛的天鹅绒. ~ *pile* 天鹅绒一样的织品. ***be on ~ = stand on ~*** 在有利地位上,(现在主指投机)在必赚地位上. ***to the ~***【商】给贷方. — *a.* 天鹅绒制的;天鹅绒似的,柔软的;(脚声等)轻软的. ***a [the] ~ glove*** 丝绒手套 (*an iron hand in a ~ glove* 外柔内刚. *handle with a ~ glove* 用外柔内刚的手段处理). ***a ~ paw*** 猫脚;隐藏的[外貌和善的]残忍. ~ **ant**【动】蚁蜂. ~ **bean**【植】绒毛黧豆.
vel·vet·een ['velvi'ti:n] *n.* ①棉(天鹅)绒,假天鹅绒,平绒. ②〔*pl.*〕棉(天鹅)绒裤. ③〔*pl.*〕猎场看守(人).
vel·vet·ing ['velvitiŋ] *n.* ①天鹅绒的绒毛. ②〔*pl.*〕〔集合词〕天鹅绒制品.
vel·vet·y ['velviti] *a.* ①天鹅绒似的;柔软的. ②(酒等)温和的,可口的.
Ven. = ①Venerable. ②Venice.
ve·na ['vi:nə] *n.* ***(pl. ve·nae*** [-ni:]***)*** 〔L.〕静脉. ~ **cava**【解】大静脉,腔静脉.
ve·nal ['vi:nl] *a.* ①(地位、选票等)可用金钱得来的,能收买的. ②(人等)贪财的,贪污的,腐败的. **~ly** *ad.*
ve·nal·i·ty [vi(:)'næliti] *n.* 贪财,见利忘义;贪污,受贿.
ve·nat·ic, -al [vi'nætik, -l] *a.* 〔罕〕狩猎的,狩猎用的.
ve·na·tion [vi:'neiʃən] *n.* 脉络,纹理;【植】脉理,脉序;【昆】脉相;〔集合词〕叶脉,翅脉.
vend [vend] *vt., vi.* ①卖,出售〔主要为法律用语〕. ②贩卖,叫卖(小商品). ③发表(意见,言论).
ven·dace ['vendeis,'vendis] *n.* ***(pl. ~, -dac·es)*** 英白鲑 *(Coregonus vandesius)*〔产于英格兰和苏格兰的少数湖中〕.
Ven·dée [vɑ:n'dei] (法国西部的)旺代省;(1793—96年间的)旺代保皇党的叛乱. **Ven·de·an** [ven'diən] ① *a.* 旺代省(人)的. ②*n.* 旺代省人,旺代保皇党成员.
ven·dee [ven'di:] *n.*【法】买主,买受人.
vend·er ['vendə] *n.*【法】出卖人;叫卖商,负贩.
ven·det·ta [ven'detə] *n.* (特指意大利某些地区和 Corsica 岛的)族间世仇;族间仇杀;长期争斗. **-tist** *n.*
vend·i·ble ['vendəbl] *a.* 可以出卖的;有销路的. — *n.* 〔主 *pl.*〕可卖物品. **-bil·i·ty** [,vædə'biliti] *n.* **-bly** *ad.*
ven·di·tion [ven'diʃən] *n.* 卖,出售.
ven·dor ['vendɔ:] *n.* ①= vender. ②自动售货机 (= vending machine). *street ~s* 摊贩.
ven·due [ven'dju:] *n.* 〔美〕公开拍卖.
ve·neer [və'niə] *n.* ①镶面板,表层饰板;镶饰表面的东西,表面镶饰;饰面,护面. ②外饰,虚饰. *a thin ~ of respectability* 薄薄的一层表面尊严. *barbarians with a ~ of culture* 披着文化外皮的野蛮人. — *vt.* ①在…盖镶片,在…盖镶板,(用象牙、大理石、珍珠等)镶盖(木、石等);虚饰,粉饰. ~ **sheet** 层板,胶合板.
ve·neer·ing [və'niəriŋ] *n.* ①镶盖术,镶木术,镶面. ②胶合薄片料,镶木,镶盖板.
ven·e·nate ['venineit] *vt.* 使中毒. — *vi.* (虫等在吮血时)放出毒液. — *a.* ①中毒的. ②有毒的.
ven·e·na·tion [,veni'neiʃən] *n.*【医】中毒.
ven·en·ous ['veninəs] *a.* 有毒的.
ven·e·punc·ture ['veni,pʌŋktʃə, ,vi:ni-] *n.*【医】静脉穿刺术 (=venipuncture).
ven·er·a·ble ['venərəbl] *a.* ①可尊敬的;〔特指〕年高而值得尊敬的,年高德劭的. ②森严的,(神殿)神圣的,古老的;历史悠久的,有来历的. ③基督教会一种尊称〔英国国教中对副主教;天主教对最低一级圣徒,略作 Ven.〕. *your ~ father* 令尊. ~ *age* 高龄. ~ *antiquity* 太古. *a ~ commander* 老司令官. *a ~ building* 古建筑物. ~ *relic* 古代文物. *a ~ oak* 古槲. **-a·bil·i·ty** *n.* **-a·bly** *ad.*
ven·er·ate ['venəreit] *vt.* 尊敬;尊崇.
ven·er·a·tion [,venə'reiʃən] *n.* 尊敬;尊崇.
ven·er·a·tor ['venəreitə] *n.* 尊敬者,崇拜者.
ve·ne·re·al [vi'niəriəl] *a.* ①性交的;因性交发生的. ②性病的. ③(药)治性病的. ④引起性欲的. ~ *desire* 性欲. *a ~ disease* 性病〔略 V.D.〕.
ve·ne·re·ol·o·gy [vi,niəri'ɔlədʒi] *n.*【医】性病学. **-gist** *n.* 性病学专家.
ven·er·y[1] ['venəri] *n.* 〔古〕性欲;性交;纵欲.
ven·er·y[2] ['venəri] *n.* 〔古〕狩猎.
ven·e·sec·tion [,veni'sekʃən] *n.*【医】静脉切开(放血)术.
Ve·ne·tian [vi'ni:ʃən] *a.* 威尼斯(式)的. — *n.* ①威尼斯 (Venice) 人. ②〔或作 v-〕= ~ blind. ③〔v-〕直贡呢;威尼斯缩绒呢. ~ **blind**【建】威尼斯式软百叶帘,板帘. ~ **carpet** (铺走廊等的)威尼斯地毯. ~ **chalk**【裁缝】(划线用的)滑石. ~ **glass** 威尼斯玻璃器皿[料器]. ~ **mast** (装饰街市的)彩色饰柱. ~ **pearl** 人造珍珠. ~ **red** 威尼斯红;褐红色. ~ **school** (意大利文艺复兴时期的)威尼斯画派. ~ **window**【建】三尊窗.
Ve·net·ic [vi'netik] *n.* 维尼提亚语〔一种灭绝了的意大利语言,留存于大约 200 篇短碑文中〕.
Ven·e·zue·la [,vene'zweilə] *n.* 委内瑞拉〔拉丁美洲〕. **-n** ①*a.* 委内瑞拉的;委内瑞拉人的;委内瑞拉文化的. ②委内瑞拉人.
venge·ance ['vendʒəns] *n.* 报仇,复仇,报复. ***exact a ~ from sb. for ...,*** 对某人报…的仇. ***inflict [take] ~ (up)on*** 对…报仇[雪恨]. ***with a ~*** 〔口〕猛烈地,厉害地;彻底地;过度地. (*It rains with a ~.* 雨下得很凶.) ***wreak ~ (up)on*** = inflict ~ (up)on.
venge·ful ['vendʒful] *a.* 报仇心重的;报复性的;利于报复的. **-ly** *ad.*
V-en·gine ['vi:'endʒin] *n.* (双汽缸排成 V 形的)内燃机,V 型发动机.
ve·ni·al ['vi:niəl, -njəl] *a.* 可原谅的;(罪过)不大的,轻微的 (*opp.* deadly; mortal). **-i·ty** [vi(:)'næniti] *n.* **-ly** *ad.* **-ness** *n.*
Ven·ice ['venis] *n.* 威尼斯〔意大利港市〕. *Gulf of ~* 威尼斯湾〔Adriatic Sea 的别名〕. ~ **glass** = Venetian glass.
Ve·nik ['vi:nik] *n.* (苏联的)金星探测器.
ven·in ['venin] *n.* 动物毒液中所含的毒素.
ven·i·punc·ture [,veni'pʌŋktʃə, ,vini-] *n.*【医】静脉穿刺术.
ve·ni·re (fa·ci·as) [vi'naiəri('feiʃiæs)]〔L.〕【法】陪审员召集令.
ve·ni·re·man [vi'naiərimən] *n.* ***(pl. -men)***【法】候召陪审员.

ven·i·son [ˈvenizn] *n.* ①鹿肉. ②野味.
ve·ni, vi·di, vi·ci [ˈveiniˈviːdiːˈviːtʃiː; ˈweiniːˈwiːdiːˈwiːki; ˈviːnaiˈvaidaiˈvaisai]〔L.〕我来了,我见到了,我胜利了〔朱利乌斯·恺撒(Julius Caesar)向元老院报告胜利的文字〕.
ve·ni·te [viˈnaiti] *n.*【地】脉混合岩.
ven·om [ˈvenəm] *n.* ①(毒蛇、蜘蛛等的)毒液;毒,毒物. ②恶意,恶毒;怨恨;恶意行为;诽谤. *a ~ duct [fang, gland]* 毒管[牙,腺]. *a look of ~* 恶意的样子. — *vt.* 放毒.
ven·om·ous [ˈvenəməs] *a.* ①有毒的,分泌毒液的,有毒腺的. ②恶意的,怀恨的. *~ snakes* 毒蛇. *a ~ attack* 恶毒的攻击. **-ly** *ad.* **-ness** *n.*
ve·nose [ˈviːnəus] *a.*【生】具脉的,翅脉的.
ve·nos·i·ty [viˈnɔsiti] *n.*【生】具脉性,翅脉性.
ve·nous [ˈviːnəs] *a.* 静脉的;静脉中的. *~ blood* 静脉血. **-ly** *ad.*
vent [vent] *n.* ①孔,口,漏口,喷口,裂口;通风孔;(烟囱的)烟道;出气孔,喷气孔;排气孔[道]. ②(管乐器的)指孔. ③炮眼,火门. ④【动】(鸟、虫、鱼的)肛门. ⑤(感情等的)发泄;吐露. ***find [make] a ~ in*** 在…上找到发泄处;出现在;发泄在. ***find (a) ~ for*** 找到…的出气口. ***give ~ to*** 发出,发泄,吐出(*give ~ to one's flames of anger* 发泄怒火,出气). ***take ~*** 泄漏于世;传播,被大家知道. — *vt.* ①给…一个出口,在…上开孔. ②放出,发出,发泄,吐露(感情). *He ~ed himself in grief.* 他借发泄悲痛获得自慰. ***~ one's disgust on*** 向…发泄忿恨. ***~ itself*** 出来,出现;表现(*His anger ~ed itself in curses.* 他用咒骂来出气[发泄愤怒]). —*vi.*〔英〕(水獭)露头呼吸. ~ **gutter** 通风道. ~ **hole** 通风孔;排气孔. ~ **peg** (桶等的)气孔塞. ~ **pipe** 排气[通风]管. ~ **plug** ①通气孔塞. ②(枪炮的)火门塞.
vent. = ventilation.
vent·age [ˈventidʒ] *n.* ①小孔;出口;排气[排水(等)]口. ②(感情的)发泄. ③(笛的)指孔. *give ~ to anger* 发怒.
ven·tail [ˈventeil] *n.* (可移动,用以通气的)盔弁,盔的护面.
ven·ter [ˈventə] *n.* ①【解】腹部;(鸟的)下腹;【虫】腹部,腹面. ②【法】母,胎. *a son by another ~ = the son of another ~* 异母子. *brothers of same ~* 同母[同产]兄弟.
ven·ti·duct [ˈventidʌkt] *n.*【建】(地下)通风管[道].
ven·ti·fact [ˈventifækt] *n.*【地】风棱石,风磨石.
ven·ti·late [ˈventileit] *vt.* ①使通风,使换气;给…装置通风设备;在…上开气孔;使通气. ②【医】使(血液)吸取氧气;用新鲜空气净化(血液). ③发泄(感情),发表(意见);公开讨论;让舆论来决定(问题等). *~ a room by opening windows* 开窗使室内透气. *The lungs ~ the blood.* 肺以新鲜空气使血液静化. **ventilating shaft**【采】通气井.
ven·ti·la·tion [ˌventiˈleiʃən] *n.* ①通风,换气(法);通风装置. ②发泄,发表;(问题的)公开讨论;诉诸舆论.
ven·ti·la·tive [ˈventileitiv] *a.* 通风的,换气的.
vent·i·la·tor [ˈventileitə] *n.* 通风设备,换气装置;通风机;风箱;通风孔,通风管,气窗;(帽子等的)气孔.
ven·ti·la·to·ry [ˈventilətəri] *a.* ①通风的,有通风孔的;换气的,有换气孔的. ②【医】(给血液)充氧的.
ven·tral [ˈventrəl] *a.*【解、动】腹(部、面)的;【空】机身的;【植】腹面的,前面的,下面的. — *n.*【鱼】腹鳍. *~ fin* 腹鳍. *~ massage* 腹部按摩. **-ly** *ad.*
ven·tre à terre [ˈvɑ̃ːtrɑːˈtɛə]〔F.〕用全速,全速地.
ven·tri- *pref.* 腹: *ventri*cose.
ven·tri·cle [ˈventrikl] *n.*【解】室;心室.
ven·tri·cose [ˈventrikəus], **ven·tri·cous** [-kəs] *a.*【动、植】一面膨的,半边膨起的;大腹便便的.
ven·tric·u·lar [venˈtrikjulə] *a.* ①【解】(心)室的. ②膨胀的.
ven·tric·u·lus [venˈtrikjuləs] *n.* *(pl.* ***-u·li*** *[-kjulai])* ①= ventricle. ②(昆虫的)胃;(鸟类的)砂囊.
ven·tri·lo·qui·al [ˌventriˈləukwiəl] *a.* 口技的,腹语的. **-ly** *ad.*
ven·tril·o·quism, ven·tril·o·quy [venˈtriləkwizəm, -kwi] *n.* 口技;腹语;腹语术.
ven·tril·o·quist [venˈtriləkwist] *n.* 口技表演者,腹语(术)者.
ven·tril·o·quize [venˈtriləkwaiz] *vt., vi.* 用口技发(声),用腹语术讲(话).
ven·tro·dor·sal [ˌventrəˈdɔːsl] *a.* 腹背面的.
ven·tro·lat·er·al [ˌventrəˈlætərəl] *a.* 腹侧的.
ven·ture [ˈventʃə] *n.* ①冒险(行动),冒险事业;(商业)投机. ②投机物[船、船货、商品等];代销货;赌注. ③〔古、罕〕幸运,偶然,侥幸. *joint ~* 合资经营. ***at a ~*** 冒险,碰运气. ***ready for any ~*** 不辞任何危险. — *vi.* 冒险,孤注一掷地试一试(*on; upon*);大胆…,胆敢…;冒着危险去;〔与不定式连用,缺乏自信时的谨慎说法〕奋勇,鼓勇,十分冒昧. *I shall ~ on a mild protest.* 我要冒昧提一个温和的抗议. *Will you ~ on another glass of wine?* 再喝一杯葡萄酒怎么样? *I ~ to differ from you.* 对不起,我不同意你的意见. *I hardly ~ to say it, but ...* 我不敢跟你说,可是…. *May I ~ to ask your opinion?* 请问您的意见怎么样? *I ~ to say.* 我要大胆[冒昧]地说. — *vt.* ①冒险,敢…,大胆干,下决心干,(冒着危险把意见等)说说看,提出来看看. ②拿(生命、财产等)冒险. *I won't ~ a step farther.* 我没勇气[不想]再上前一步了. *~ one's life for a cause* 为主义[事业]冒生命的危险. ***Nothing ~, nothing have.*** 不入虎穴,焉得虎子. ~ **capital**〔美〕投机[冒险]资本. **-r** [ˈventʃərə] *n.* 冒险者;投机者.
ven·ture·some [ventʃəsəm] *a.* ①冒险的,鲁莽的,大胆的,投机的. ②(有)危险的. **-ly** *ad.* **-ness** *n.*
ven·tu·ri (tube) [venˈtuəri]【物、机】文氏管,汾丘里流量计.
ven·tur·ous [ˈventʃərəs] *a.* (爱)冒险的,大胆的,鲁莽的;危险性的. **-ly** *ad.* **-ness** *n.*
ven·ue [ˈvenjuː] *n.* ①【法】犯罪地点;现场;审判管辖区,审判地点;起诉书上对审判地点的指示. ②〔俚〕(指定的)集合地点;立场,根据. *change the ~* 变更审判地点. *lay [fix, place] a ~* 指定审判地点.
ven·ule [ˈvenjuːl] *n.* ①【解】小静脉. ②【生】(叶的)细脉;(昆虫的)支脉. **ven·u·lar** [-julə] *a.* **ven·u·lose** [-juˌləus] *a.*
Ve·nus [ˈviːnəs] *n.* ①【罗神】维纳斯〔司爱和美的女神〕;维纳斯雕像[画像]. ②美女,美人. ③性爱,色情. ④【天】金星,太白星. ⑤【贝】帘介属. ~**berg** 维纳斯山〔中世纪传说,维纳斯在此设有宫殿,引诱旅客〕. **~'s hair**【植】掌叶铁线蕨. **~'s flower-basket**【动】偕老同穴(海绵). **~'s fly-trap**【植】捕蝇草. **~'s-slipper** *n.* = lady's-slipper.
Ve·nus·i·an [ˈviːnəsiən] *a.* 金星的. — *n.* (科学幻想小说中的)金星人.
ver. = verse(s).
Ver·a[1] [ˈviərə] *n.* 维拉〔女子名〕.
Vera[2] [ˈviːrə] *n.*【无】(录放电视图象和声音的)电子录像机(= vision electronic recording apparatus).
ve·ra·cious [vəˈreiʃəs] *a.* ①说真话的,诚实的,老实的. ②真实的. **-ly** *ad.*
ve·rac·i·ty [vəˈræsiti] *n.* ①诚实. ②确实;真实(性),正确(度),精确率.
Ver·a·cruz [ˈverəˈkruːz] *n.* ①韦拉克鲁斯〔墨西哥港市〕. ②韦拉克鲁斯〔墨西哥州名〕.
ve·ran·da(h) [vəˈrændə] *n.* 游廊;走廊;阳台.
ve·rat·ri·dine [vəˈrætridiːn] *n.*【化】藜芦定.
ver·a·trin(e) [ˈvɛərəˌtriːn, -trin] *n.*【化】①藜芦碱. ②= veratridine.

ve·ra·trum [vəˈreitrəm] *n.* ①藜芦属植物〔包括蒜藜芦 *(V. album)* 和绿藜芦 *(U viride)*〕. ②藜芦碱.

verb [vəːb] *n.*【语法】动词. *strong [weak] ～s* 强[弱]变化动词. *substantive [copulative] ～s* 存在[连系]动词.

ver·bal [ˈvəːbəl] *a.* ①话的,言语(上)的;文字的;字句的,用字上的;口头的 *(opp.* written*)*. ②(翻译等)逐字的. ③【语法】(出自)动词的. *a ～ picture of a scene* 某一场面的文字描述. *a ～ note* 便条,字条;【外交】不署名备忘录,口头照会. *a purely ～ criticism* 纯言语上的批评. *a ～ agreement [contract]* 口头协议[约定]. *a ～ dispute.* 口头争论,舌战. *～ evidence* 口头证据. *a ～ message* 口信. *a ～ translation* 逐字翻译,直译. — *n.*【语法】①非限定动词〔gerund, infinitive, participle〕. ②〔罕〕= ～ noun. ③〔美口〕口供. ～ **nouns** 动名词〔infinitive 和 gerund 以及动词派生的名词〕. **-ism** *n.* 言语表现,措词;咬文嚼字;赘语;措词啰嗦[冗长]. **-ist** *n.* 善于措词用句的人;咬文嚼字的人;措词啰嗦的人. **-ize** ① *vt.*把…变成动词;用言语表现. ②*vi.* 措词冗长. **-ly** *ad.* ①口头(上);用语言文字. ②逐字地. ③作为动词.

ver·ba·tim [vəːˈbeitim] *ad., a.* 逐字(的),一字不变地[的]. — *n.* 逐字报告.

ver·ba·tim et lit·e·ra·tim [vəːˈbeitim et ˌlitəˈreitim] 〔L.〕一字不改,完全照字面;逐字逐句.

ver·be·na [vəːˈbiːnə] *n.*【植】美人樱,(戟叶)马鞭草.

ver·bi·age [ˈvəːbiidʒ] *n.* ①(措词)啰嗦,冗长. ②〔蔑〕措辞. ***to indulge in ～*** 夸夸其谈.

ver·bid [ˈvəːbid] *n.*【语法】动词性词,非限定动词〔指动名词、不定式和分词等非谓语形式〕.

verb·i·fy [ˈvəːbifai] *vt.* 使动词化;把…用作动词.

ver·bose [vəːˈbəus] *a.* (措词)啰嗦的,(说话)唠叨的;冗长的. **-ly** *ad.*

ver·bos·i·ty [vəːˈbɔsiti] *n.* 啰嗦,唠叨,冗长.

ver·bo·ten [fɛəˈbəutən] *a.* 〔G.〕被禁止的.

verb. (sat) sap. = verbum (sat) sapienti [ˈvəːbəm-(ˈsæt)ˌsæpiˈentai] 〔L.〕对聪明人说一个字就够了(= A word is enough for the wise.);举一反三,不必多言.

verbi gratia [ˈvəːbi greiʃə] 〔L.〕例如 (= for example) 〔略 v.g.〕.

ver·dan·cy [ˈvəːdənsi] *n.* ①翠绿,新绿. ②不成熟,无知,单纯,幼稚.

ver·dant [ˈvəːdənt] *a.* ①青葱的,绿叶繁茂的. ②年轻不懂事的,没有经验的,幼稚的. ～ **green** 浅绿,嫩绿(*Mr. V- green* 〔口〕幼稚的人). **-ly** *ad.*

verd an·tique [ˈvəːdænˈtiːk] ①(古铜器上的)铜绿. ②(古罗马作室内装饰用的)绿斑蛇纹石. ③【矿】古绿石,美斑石.

ver·der·er, ver·der·or [ˈvəːdərə] *n.*【英史】王室护林官.

ver·dict [ˈvəːdikt] *n.* ①【法】(陪审团的)评决,裁决. ②判断,意见,决定. *the popular ～* 公众的意见. *a ～ for the plaintiff* 原告胜诉的评决. *What is your ～ on the coffee?* 你觉得这咖啡怎么样? ***an open ～*** 存疑裁决〔指判定某行为有罪而不确知犯人,或指死因未详的裁决〕. ***a partial ～*** 部分裁判〔只判定行为的一部分有罪〕. ***a privy [sealed] ～*** 密封裁决书〔陪审员在法官休庭后交给法院书吏的初步书面裁决〕. ***a special ～*** 特别裁决〔陪审团只提供已证明的事实,交由法庭进行判决〕. ***bring in [deliver, give, return] a ～ of 'not guilty'*** (陪审团)评决无罪. ***pass one's ～ upon*** 对…下判断. ***to reverse the ～*** 翻案.

ver·di·gris [ˈvəːdigris] *n.* ①铜绿. ②【化】碱性碳[醋]酸铜.

ver·din [ˈvəːdin] *n.*【动】黄头山雀 *(Auriparus flaviceps)* 〔产于美国西南部和墨西哥北部〕.

ver·di·ter [ˈvəːditə] *n.* 铜盐颜料,碳酸铜. ～ **blue** (蓝铜矿研制的)蓝色铜盐颜料. ～ **green** (孔雀石研制的)绿色铜盐颜料.

Ver·dun *n.* ①[ˈvɛədʌn] 凡尔登〔法国城市〕. ②[vəː-ˈdʌn] 凡尔登〔加拿大城市〕.

ver·dure [ˈvəːdʒə, -djə] *n.* ①青绿,新绿;青青的草木;新绿的嫩叶. ②新鲜,生气;繁盛. ③风景挂毯.

ver·dur·ous [ˈvəːdʒərəs] *a.* 〔诗〕青青的,翠绿的;草木葱茏的.

Ver·ein [fəˈriːn, -ˈrain] *n.* 〔G.〕同盟,联盟,公会,协会,社,组.

verge[1] [vəːdʒ] *n.* ①边缘;(长草的)路边;(花坛的)镶边;界限,范围,境界. ②权杖,节杖. ③【建】饰柱;蟒羽〔凸出簷边的屋瓦〕. ④(钟表等的)轴. ***bring sb. to the ～ of…*** 使某人濒于… ***on the ～ of*** 将近(几岁);即将…,快要… *(He was on the ～ of betraying his secret.* 他险些儿[差点]泄露了秘密). — *vi.* 接近,逼近,濒临. *～ on madness* 濒于疯狂.

verge[2] [vəːdʒ] *vi.* 向…倾斜,斜向;倾向,趋向. *～ to a close* 将近末了. *～ towards old age* 渐渐趋于老年.

ver·ger [ˈvəːdʒə] *n.* ①〔英〕(为主教、大学副校长等在举行仪式的行列中)执权标的人. ②教堂管理人.

ver·glas [vɛəˈglɑː] *n.* 地上薄冰,(薄)冰面.

ve·rid·ic, -i·cal [vəˈridik, -ikəl] *a.* 〔常谑〕不骗人的,不说谎的,诚实的;真实的. **-ly** *ad.*

ver·i·est [ˈveriist] *a.* 〔*very* 的最高级〕极端的,彻底的,十足的. *the ～ rascal* 不可救药的恶棍. *The ～ baby could do it.* 最小的小孩也做得到. ***a ～ tyro*** 〔美运〕十足的生手.

ver·i·fi·a·ble [ˈverifaiəbl] *a.* 可证实的;可检验的;可考证的. **-bil·i·ty** [-ˈbiliti] *n.*

ver·i·fi·ca·tion [ˌverifiˈkeiʃən] *n.* ①证实,证明,确定;核验,验证,核对;检验,校验. ②【法】诉状[答辩书]结尾的举证说明. *～ of machines* 机器的校准[检定].

ver·i·fi·er [ˈverifaiə] *n.* ①证实者,确定者;核验者;证明者. ②煤气计量器. ③检验器;(计算数据的)核对器,核对员.

ver·i·fy [ˈverifai] *vt.* ①证实;证明,核验,核实,验证;校准. ②【法】(用证据或宣誓)证实;在(诉状或答辩书结尾)提供举证说明. *verified statistics* 核实的(统计)数字.

ver·i·ly [ˈverili] *ad.* 〔古〕真正地;肯定地;忠实地;真实地.

ver·i·sim·i·lar [ˌveriˈsimilə] *a.* 好象真(实)的;可能的. **-ly** *ad.*

ver·i·si·mil·i·tude [ˌverisiˈmilitjuːd] *n.* ①貌似真实;逼真;可能性. ②逼真的事物.

ver·ism [ˈviərizəm, ˈvɛərizəm] *n.* 写实主义〔尤指在歌剧艺术中优先采用日常生活题材的主张〕. **ver·ist** ① *a.* 写实主义的. ②*n.* 写实主义者. **ve·ris·tic** [viˈristik] *a.*

ver·is·mo [veiˈriːzməu] *n.* 〔It.〕= verism.

ver·it·a·ble [ˈveritəbl] *a.* 真实的,的的确确的,真正的. **-a·bly** *ad.*

ve·ri·tas [ˈveritæs] *n.* 〔L.〕①真理. ②= ***bureau veritas*** 法国船舶协会.

ver·i·ty [ˈveriti] *n.* 真实(性);事实,真理. *the eternal verities* 永久不变的真理. ***in all ～*** 确实〔发誓用〕. ***in ～*** 真正,的确. ***of a ～*** 〔古〕真正,的确.

ver·juice [ˈvəːdʒuːs] *n.* ①酸果汁. ②(脾气的)乖戾;(脸色的)阴沉;(情况的)别扭.

ver·meil [ˈvəːmeil] *n.* ①〔诗〕朱红色;【矿】硃砂. ②镀金的银[青铜、铜]. ③亮漆,清漆 (= transparent varnish). — *a.* 朱红色的,(嘴唇)鲜红的.

Ver·mes [ˈvəːmiːz] *n. pl.*【动】蠕形动物,蠕虫类.

ver·mi- *comb. f.* 蠕虫: *vermian.*

ver·mi·an [ˈvəːmiən] *a.* 蠕虫类的,蠕虫一样的.

ver·mi·cel·li [ˌvəːmiˈseli, -ˈtʃeli] *n.* 〔It.〕(用通心粉做的)细面条,挂面.

ver·mi·cide [ˈvəːmisaid] *n.* 杀蠕虫剂;(特指)杀肠虫药;打虫药. **-ci·dal** *a.*

ver·mic·u·lar [vəːˈmikjulə] *a.* ①蠕虫(状)的;蠕动的.

②虫蛀形的，虫迹形的. ～ *motion* (肠子的)蠕动(作用). ～ **appendix [process]**【解】阑尾. ～ **work** 虫迹形镶工，虫蛀形雕刻.

ver·mic·u·late [vəːˈmikjulit] *a.* ①蠕虫状的；虫蛀(形)的，虫迹形的. ②蠕虫多的. ③〔罕〕转弯抹角的，婉转的，暗指的. — [-leit] *vt.* 使成虫蛀状；给…作虫迹形装饰. — *vi.* 变成虫蛀形.

ver·mic·u·la·tion [vəˌmikjuˈleiʃən] *n.* ①成蠕虫状，成虫迹状. ②蛀迹，虫迹. ③蠕动.

ver·mic·u·lite [vəːˈmikjulait] *n.*【矿】蛭石.

ver·mi·form [ˈvəːmifɔːm] *a.* 蠕虫形状的. ～ **appendix**【解】阑尾. ～ **process**【解】①脑中叶. ②阑尾.

ver·mi·fuge [ˈvəːmifjuːdʒ] *n.*【医】驱虫药，打虫药. **-fu·gal** [-fjuːgəl] *a.*

ver·mi·grade [ˈvəːmigreid] *a.* 蠕动的，蜿蜒前进的.

ver·mil·(l)ion [vəˈmiljən] *n.* 银硃，朱砂；朱红色. — *a.* (涂)朱红色的. — *vt.* 染[涂]朱红色于. ～ **paint** 朱红涂料.

ver·min [ˈvəːmin] *n.* 〔*sing.,pl.*〕①害虫；寄生虫；害兽，害鸟. ②(社会的)害人虫；歹徒，坏蛋.

ver·mi·nate [ˈvəːmineit] *vi.* 生(肠)虫；生害虫；生寄生虫.

ver·mi·na·tion [ˌvəːmiˈneiʃən] *n.* ①生害虫. ②寄生虫病，肠虫病.

ver·mi·no·sis [ˌvəːmiˈnəusis] *n.* 蠕虫病；肠虫病；蠕虫[肠虫]病的蔓延.

ver·min·ous [ˈvəːminəs] *a.* ①生虫的；害虫丛生的；蚤[虱等]多的；因害虫而引起的. ②虫一般的，卑劣的，讨厌的.

ver·miv·o·rous [vəːˈmivərəs] *a.* (鸟等)吃虫的.

Ver·mont [vəːˈmɔnt] *n.* 佛蒙特〔美国州名〕. **-er** 佛蒙特州人. **-ese** [-tiːz] ①*a.* 佛蒙特州(人)的. ②*n.* 佛蒙特州人.

ver·m(o)uth [ˈvəːməθ, ˈvəːmuːθ; 老式读法 ˈvəːmuːt] *n.* 苦艾酒.

ver·nac·u·lar [vəˈnækjulə] *n.* ①本国语，本地话，土话；口语，日常语；方言. ②行话；俗话；下流话. ③【动、植】俗名. *He addressed me forcibly in the* ～. 他用下流话对我不客气地说话. — *a.* ①本国的，(语言等)本乡的；日常语的，口语的；地方(特有)的；用地方语(土话)写的，用土话的；民间的. ②【动、植】俗名的. ～ *papers* 当地语报纸. ～ *language* = *the* ～ *tongue* 土话，口语，俗话 (*opp.* literary [learned] language). *the* ～ *Chinese* 中国白话文. *a* ～ *disease*【医】地方病. **-ism** *n.* 当地语(表达法)；俗话(表达法)；方言(表达法)；土腔，土调. **-ize** *vt.* ①把…说成当地语. ②使口语化. ③用俗话说. **-ly** *ad.*

ver·nal [ˈvəːnl] *a.* ①春的，春天似的；春天发生的；(花等)春天开的. ②有生气的，朝气蓬勃的；青春的，青年的，妙龄的. ～ *breezes* 春风. ～ *flowers* 春天开的花. *the* ～ *spirits of youth* 青年人的朝气. ～ **equinox [point]** 春分(点). **-ly** *ad.*

ver·nal·ize [ˈvəːnəlaiz] *vt.*【植】催进发育；使春化，用春化处理. **ver·nal·i·za·tion** [ˌvəːnəlaiˈzeiʃən] *n.* 春化作用；春化处理.

ver·na·tion [vəːˈneiʃən] *n.*【植】①芽型. ②多叶卷叠式；幼叶卷叠式.

Vern(e) [vəːn] *n.* 弗恩(男子名).

Ver·ner [ˈvəːnə] *n.* 弗纳(姓氏).

ver·ni·er(scale) [ˈvəːniə] *n.*【机】游标(尺)，微分尺，千分尺. ～ **cal(l)iper** 游标卡尺. ～ **condenser**【电】微变电容器. ～ **depth gauge**【机】精密测深尺. ～ **dial** 游标刻度盘. ～ **rocket** 微调火箭发动机.

ver·nin [ˈvəːnin] *n.*【化】维尔宁，蚕豆嘌呤核甙.

ver·nis·sage [ˌvεəniˈsɑːʒ] *n.* (*pl.* **-sages** [-ˈsɑːʒ]) 美术展览会首日；预展〔正式开幕的前一日〕.

Ver·non [ˈvəːnən] *n.* 弗农〔姓氏，男子名〕.

Ve·ro·na [viˈrəunə] *n.* 维罗纳〔意大利城市〕.

Ve·ro·nal [ˈverənl] *n.*【药】佛罗拉〔巴比妥 (barbital) 的商品名，一种安眠药〕.

Ve·ro·ne·se [verəˈniːz] *n.* 〔*sing.,pl.*〕意大利维罗纳(Verona)人. — *a.* 维罗纳的.

ve·ron·i·ca [vəˈrɔnikə] *n.* ①【植】婆婆纳(属)水苦荬(属). ②= sudarium. ③〔V-〕维罗妮卡(女子名).

ver·ru·ca [veˈruːkə] *n.* (*pl.* **-cae** [-siː])【医】疣，瘊子；【动】肉赘；毛瘤.

ver·ru·ci·form [veˈruːsifɔːm] *a.* 疣状的.

ver·ru·cose [veˈruːkəus] *a.* 多疣的.

ver·ru·cous [ˈverukəs] *a.* 疣的；疣状的.

vers [vəːs] *n.*【数】= versed sine.

Ver·sailles [vεəˈsai, vəːˈseilz] *n.* ①凡尔赛〔法国城市〕. ②凡尔赛宫. ～ **Treaty** 凡尔赛和约〔1919年6月签订，结束第一次世界大战〕.

ver·sant[1] [ˈvəːsənt] *a.* ①熟悉…的，精通…的. ②专心从事…的，关心…的.

ver·sant[2] [ˈvəːsənt] *n.* (山或山脉的)斜面；倾斜；山坡，山侧；坡度；(一个地区的)总倾斜度.

ver·sa·tile [ˈvəːsətail] *a.* ①多面手的，多才多艺的. ②通用的，万能的. ②〔罕〕易变的，多变的，反复无常的，三心两意的. ③【动】(足趾等)可向前或向后转动的. ④【植】丁字形的. *a* ～ *man* 多面手. *a* ～ *writer* 多才多艺的作家. **-ly** *ad.*

ver·sa·til·i·ty [ˌvəːsəˈtiliti] *n.* ①多面性；多才多艺. ②易变性；反复无常. ③可转性.

vers de so·cié·té [vεr də sɔsjete]〔F.〕社交诗，诙谐俏皮的酬应诗(=society verse).

verse [vəːs] *n.* ①诗句，诗行. ②诗篇；诗节. ③韵文 (*opp.* prose)；诗，诗歌. ④(圣经的)节〔略 v.〕. ⑤【宗】=versicle. ⑥【乐】(赞美诗等的)独唱部. *blank* ～ 无韵诗. *elegiac* ～ 哀歌，挽歌. *free* ～ 自由诗. ***give chapter and*** ～ ***for*** 注明(引用文句等的)章节[确切出处]. ***in*** ～ 用诗写的，韵文的. ***put [turn] into*** ～***s*** 把…写成诗. ***set Greek [Latin]*** ～ 叫(学生)翻译希腊[拉丁]诗. — *vt.* ①用诗表现. ②(把…)写成诗. — *vi.* 作诗. ～**monger** 打油诗人，拙劣的诗人，作劣诗者.

versed[1] [vəːst] *a.* 熟练的，精通的 (*in*). *be (well)* ～ *in* 通晓，精通，对…有造诣.

versed[2] [vəːst] *a.*【数】反，反转的. ～ **cosine**【数】余矢. ～ **sine**【数】正矢.

vers·et [ˈvəːset, ˈvəːsit] *n.* ①短诗〔尤指宗教经典中的〕. ②(为管风琴谱写的)短插曲[序曲].

ver·si·cle [ˈvəːsikl] *n.* 短诗；【宗】(牧师领唱或领读的)短句.

ver·si·co·lo(u)r [ˈvəːsikʌlə] *a.* ①杂色的，多色的. ②(因光的不同)颜色多变化的，变色的，虹色的.

ver·si·fi·ca·tion [ˌvəːsifiˈkeiʃən] *n.* ①作诗(法)；诗律. ②韵文化.

ver·si·fi·er [ˈvəːsifaiə] *n.* ①诗人；改写散文成诗的人. ②打油诗人.

ver·si·fy [ˈvəːsifai] *vi.* 作诗. — *vt.* ①把(散文)改成韵文；改(散文)成诗. ②用诗表达.

ver·sion [ˈvəːʃən] *n.* ①翻译；译本，译文. ②(个人对某事的)说法，不同看法[意见]. ③版本；形式，型；变形，变体. ④改写本；经过改编的乐曲. ⑤〔常 V-〕基督教《圣经》的译本. ⑥表演. ⑦【医】胎位倒转(术)；子宫倾侧. *the Authorized V-* (詹姆斯王)钦定《圣经》英译本〔略 A.V.〕. *the Revised V-* 《圣经》英译修订本〔略 R.V.〕. *the dramatic* ～ *of a novel* 一部小说的戏剧改编本. *What is your* ～ *of the affair?* 你对于这件事的看法怎么样?

vers li·bre [vεə ˈliːbr]〔F.〕自由体诗.

vers li·brist(e) [vεə ˈliːbrist] *n.*〔F.〕自由诗作者.

ver·so [ˈvəːsəu] *n.* (*pl.* ～**s**) ①(书的)左页，反页 (*opp.* recto)；封四，封底. ②(货币、金牌等的)反面，背面

(opp. obverse*)*.
verst [vəːst] *n.* 俄里〔= 1.067 公里〕.
ver·sus [ˈvəːsəs] *prep.* 〔L.〕 ①(诉讼、运动等中的)对(= against). ②与…相对[相比]〔略作 v. 或 vs.〕. *Shanghai v. Beijing* 【运】上海对北京. *traveling by plane ~ traveling by train* 乘飞机与坐火车旅行的比较.
Vert. = Vertebrata.
vert[1] [vəːt] *n.* ①【英国山林法】林中草木(采伐权). ②【纹】绿色.
vert[2] [vəːt] *vi.* 〔英口〕改宗, 改变信仰. — *n.* 改宗者; 变节者;〔美〕改邪归正的人.
ver·te·bra [ˈvəːtibrə] *n. (pl. **-brae** [-briː])* 【解】椎骨; 脊椎.
ver·te·bral [ˈvəːtibrəl] *a.* 椎骨的,脊椎的,由脊骨形成的. *the ~ column* 脊椎.
Ver·te·bra·ta [ˌvəːtiˈbreitə, -ˈbrɑː-] *n.* 〔*pl.*〕【动】脊椎动物门.
ver·te·brate [ˈvəːtibrit] *n.* 【动】脊椎动物. — *a.* ①有脊骨[脊椎]的; 脊椎动物的. ②(作品等)结构严密的. **-d** *a.*
ver·te·bra·tion [ˌvəːtiˈbreiʃən] *n.* ①脊椎形成,椎骨形成. ②结构的严密性.
ver·tex [ˈvəːteks] *n. (pl. ~s, **-ti·ces** [-tisiːz])* ①顶(点),绝顶. ②【解】颅顶,头顶;【天】天顶;【几】顶(点). *~ of a cone* 锥点. *~ of an angle* 角的顶点.
ver·ti·cal [ˈvəːtikəl] *a.* ①垂直的,直立的,竖立的,纵的 *(opp.* horizontal*)*. ②顶上的,顶点的,绝顶的. ③【解】头顶的. ④【植】纵长的,直上的. *a ~ line* 垂直线, 纵线. *a ~ section* 纵断面. *a ~ motion* 上下运动. *a ~ angle* 对顶角; 顶角. *~ extent* 深度. *~ range* 纵度. — *n.* ①垂直线; 垂直面; 垂直圈. ②竖立位置. ③【建】竖杆. ~ **axis** 【数】(直)立轴. ~ **circle** 【天】平经圈,高度圈. ~ **combination** 【经】垂直统一管理〔指从生产一直到销售〕. ~ **drill** 竖式钻床. ~ **envelopment** 【军】(伞兵配合地上部队所成的)垂直包围. ~ **erosion** 【地】向下浸蚀. ~ **file** ①直立式档案箱. ②可供迅速查阅的资料. ~ **fins** ①【鱼】竖鳍. ②(飞机的)垂直尾翼. ~ **fire** 【军】高角射击. ~ **integration** =~ combination. ~ **plane** 垂直面,铅垂面. ~ **rudder** 【空】纵舵, 方向舵. ~ **thinking** 按常识进行的思考. ~ **turn** 【空】垂直旋转. ~ **union** 同一工业部门内跨行业的工会 (= industrial union). **-ly** *ad.* **-i·ty** *n.*
ver·ti·ces [ˈvəːtisiːz] *n.* vertex的复数.
ver·ti·cil, -cel [ˈvəːtisil] *n.* 【植、动】轮; 环; 轮生体; 环生体; (昆虫的)触角毛轮.
ver·ti·cil·las·ter [ˌvəːtisiˈlæstə] *n.* 【植】①轮状聚伞花序. ②轮伞.
ver·tic·il·late [vəˈtislit; ˌvəːtiˈsileit] *a.* 【植】轮生的(= verticillated). **-la·tion** *n.*
ver·tig·i·nes [vəːˈtidʒiniːz] *n.* vertigo 的复数.
ver·tig·i·nous [vəːˈtidʒinəs] *a.* ①滴溜溜转的,旋转的. ②眩晕的,发晕的,眼花的; (高度等)使人眼花的. ③迅速变动的; 不稳定的. *a ~ wind* 旋风. **-ly** *ad.*
ver·ti·go [ˈvəːtigəu] *n. (pl. ~es, **-tig·i·nes** [vəːˈtidʒiniːz])* 【医】眩晕, 眼花;【兽医】(马羊等的)晕倒症.
ver·tim·e·ter [vəːˈtimitə] *n.* 【空】升降速度表.
ver·ti·port [ˈvəːtipɔːt] *n.* 垂直升降机机场.
ver·tu [vəːˈtuː] *n.* = virtu.
ver·vain [ˈvəːvein] *n.* 【植】马鞭草.
verve [vɛəv, vəːv] *n.* ①(艺术品等的)气韵,神韵. ②活力,热情,生气. ③〔古〕才能.
ver·vet [ˈvəːvit] *n.* 【动】(非洲产)长尾黑颚猴.
ver·y [ˈveri] *ad.* ①〔用于修饰形容词副词或分词〕很,甚,颇,极,非常. ②〔与否定词结合〕(不)怎样, (不)大. ③〔在形容词最高级前以加强语气〕充分,完全,真,实在,正. *a ~ cold day* 很冷的一天. *I like it ~ much.* 我很喜欢它. *I am not ~ keen on going there.* 我不大想到那里去. *not of ~ much use* 不怎么有用. *It is the ~ last thing I expected.* 这完全出乎我意料之外. *my ~ own* 绝对是[完全是、实在是]我自己的(东西). *Keep it for your ~ own.* 你替你自己收下来. *I will do my ~ best.* 我要尽我的力量. *in the ~ same place* 就是在这同一个地方. *Very fine!* 〔常作反语用〕好极了! *Very good [well].* 好的〔表示同意、承认,但 Very well 常作反语用,如: Oh, ~ well! if you insist. 你要是坚持,那就这样吧! (没有办法)〕. — *a. (**ver·i·er; -i·est**)* ①真的,实在的,真正的; 十足的. ②〔加强语气,和 the, this, that 或 my, your, his 等连用〕那个,同一个,就是那个,正是那个; 甚至于,连. ③〔修饰作名词用的 many, few, little 等〕很,非常. *a ~ knave* 真正的恶棍. *A verier humbug would be hard to meet.* 比这个更坏的骗子恐怕没有了. *The veriest coward would fight.* 就是最懦弱的人也会起来反抗的. *He is the ~ man I saw yesterday.* 他就是我昨天看见的那个人. *He is the ~ picture of his father.* 他活象他父亲. *For ~ pity's sake have mercy.* 千万请饶了我吧. *That's the ~ thing!* 正是那个! *in the ~ act* 当场(被捕等). *His ~ children despise him.* 连他的孩子也看不起他. *The ~ stones cry out.* 连石头也叫起来了. *V- few believe in it.* 很少人相信. ~ **high frequency** 【电信】甚高频〔略 V.H.F., v.h.f.〕. ~ **low frequency** 【电信】甚低频〔略 V.L.F., v.l.f.〕.
Ver·y [ˈveri] *n.* 维利〔姓氏〕. ~ **light** 【海军】(用信号手枪射出的)维利式色光信号(弹). ~ **pistol** 【海军】维利式信号手枪.
ves·i·ca [veˈsaikə] *n. (pl. **-cae** [-siː])* 【解】囊; 膀胱; 胆囊; (鱼的)鳔;【植】(孢粉的)气囊,小泡; 泡囊. ~ **piscis** (哥特式建筑、绘画的)双圆光轮. ~ **urinaria** 【解】膀胱.
ves·i·cal [ˈvesikəl] *a.* 【解】膀胱的. ~ **calculus** 【医】膀胱(结)石.
ves·i·cant [ˈvesikənt] *n.* 【医】发疱膏,糜烂剂. — *a.* 发疱的,(使)起疱的,糜烂性的.
ves·i·cate [ˈvesikeit] *vt., vi.* 【医】(使)起疱,(使)发疱,(使)糜烂.
ves·i·ca·tion [ˌvesiˈkeiʃən] *n.* 【医】发疱,糜烂.
ves·i·ca·to·ry [ˈvesikətəri] *n., a.* = vesicant.
ves·i·cle [ˈvesikl] *n.* 囊,泡;【医】小水疱;【植、解】小泡; 气泡囊;【地】气孔. *the seminal ~s* 精囊.
ve·sic·u·lar [viˈsikjulə], **ve·sic·u·late** [-leit] *a.* (有)小泡的,多泡(状)的,起泡的; 多孔(状)的, 小囊(状)的. ~ **emphysema** 【医】肺气肿. ~ **murmur** 【医】肺泡呼吸音. ~ **tissue** 泡沫组织.
ves·per [ˈvespə] *n.* ①〔V-〕金星,太白星,长庚星;〔诗〕傍晚,黄昏. ②【宗】晚祷钟 (= ~ bell);〔*pl.*〕〔有时作 V-〕晚祷; 晚祷时间; 晚祷曲[词]. ***Sicilian Vespers*** 西西里晚祷事件〔1282年复活节翌日在西西里岛 Palermo 地方以晚祷钟声为信号驱杀法国人的事件〕.— *a.* ①夜晚的. ②晚祷的. ~ **sparrow** 【动】夜鸣鹀. ~ **tide** 晚祷时间; 晚上,黄昏.
ves·per·al [ˈvespərəl] *a.* 〔罕〕傍晚的,黄昏的,晚祷的. — *n.* 【宗】①晚祷书. ②祭坛罩布.
ves·per·til·i·o·nid [ˌvespəˈtiliənid] *n.* 【动】蝙蝠科 *(Vespertilioniloe)* 动物.
ves·per·tine [ˈvespətain], **ves·per·ti·nal** [ˌvespəˈtainəl] *a.* ①傍晚的,黄昏的. ②【植】傍晚开花的;【动】傍晚出来(找吃)的. ③【天】日没时没落的(星).
ves·pi·a·ry [ˈvespiəri] *n.* 黄蜂窠[群].
ves·pid [ˈvespid] *n.* 【动】黄蜂科 *(Vespidoe)* 动物. — *a.* 黄蜂(科)的.
ves·pine [ˈvespain] *a.* 黄蜂(似)的.
Ves·puc·ci [vesˈpuːtʃi], **Amerigo** *(Americus Vespucius)* 维斯普奇〔1451—1512, 意大利商人、冒险家、航海家,一说 'America' 就是由他得名的〕.
ves·sel [ˈvesl] *n.* ①容器,器皿〔桶、钵、碗等〕. ②船,舰; 飞船. ③〔喻、谑〕人. ④【解、动】管,脉管,血管;【植】导

管. *a coasting* ～ 沿海商船. *a composite* ～ 铁骨木船. *a sailing* ～ 帆船. *a war* ～ 战舰. *a* ～ *drawing twenty feet of water* 吃水二十英尺的船. *a* ～ *under way* 航行中的船. *a weak* ～ 不牢靠的器皿;不能依靠的人. *the weaker* ～ 女人,女性. *the lymphatic* ～ 淋巴管. ***the ～s of wrath*** 遭天罚的人〔宗教说法,喻人为接受某种影响的容器〕.

vest [vest] *n.* ①〔美〕背心;马甲. ②〔英〕汗衫. ③内衣,衬衣〔美国只指女人和孩子的〕. ④女服胸前V形饰布. ⑤〔古〕衣服;外衣,上衣;法衣;礼服. ***play (it) close to the*** ～ 把…保守秘密;避免不必要的危险. ***pull down one's*** ～〔美俚〕从容不迫;不乱说乱动(不多管闲事);保持安静. — *vt.* ①授与,给与,赋与;【法】授与所有[行使]权. ②使穿衣服,给穿上(法衣、祭服等). ③在(祭坛上)挂布. *be ～ed power to do sth.* 被授予做某事的权力. ～ *sb. with authority [rights]* 授予某人权柄[权益]. — *vi.* ①(权利、财产等)属于,归属 *(in)*. ②穿衣服,穿祭服. *Upon the death of the father, the ～ed in [upon] his son.* 父死后财产归属其子. **～-pocket** *n., a.* 背心口袋;袖珍的,小型的(照片,书等).

Ves·ta [ˈvestə] *n.* ①【罗神】女灶神. ②【天】四号小行星,灶神星. ③【商】〔v-〕〔英〕一种涂蜡的短火柴,蜡火柴(= wax ～).

ves·tal [ˈvestl] *a.* ①女灶神的;献身给女灶神的;修女的. ②处女的,贞洁的. — *n.* ①灶神守护祭司〔四名守护女灶神神殿里永远点燃圣火的处女祭司之一,后减为一人,亦作 ～ virgin〕. ②处女,贞洁的女子. ③修女,尼姑.

vest·ed [ˈvestid] *a.* ①【法】既定的,既得的. ②穿着祭服的. ～ **interest** ①既得利益[权利]. ②〔*pl.*〕既得利益集团. ～ **rights** 既得权利(尤指职工在达到退休年龄以前离职仍应获得的权利).

vest·ee [vesˈtiː] *n.* ①女式小背心,假背心. ②女服胸前V形饰布.

ves·ti·bule [ˈvestibjuːl] *n.* ①门道,门厅. ②〔美〕连廊,通廊〔客车车厢两头出入处〕. ③【解】前庭;(昆虫的)外生殖腔. — *vt.* ①给…设门廊. ②用通廊连接(两节车厢等). ～ **car**=～ train. ～ **door** 避风门. ～ **school** (工厂训练新来工人的)工人训练所. ～ **train**〔美〕(各车相通的)连廊列车 (=〔英〕corridor train). **ves·tib·u·lar** *a.*

ves·tige [ˈvestidʒ] *n.* ①痕迹,遗迹;证据. ②〔罕、诗〕足迹. ③【生】(退化器官的)残迹. ④一点儿,丝毫〔通常带否定词〕. *without a* ～ *of clothing* 一丝不挂. *He has not a* ～ *of evidence for this assertion.* 他没有丝毫证据证明这个论断. **ves·tig·i·al** [vesˈtidʒiəl] *a.* ①尚留有痕迹的. ②(器官)发育不全的,萎缩的,退化的.

ves·ti·ment [ˈvestimənt] *n.* = vestment.

vest·ing [ˈvestiŋ] *n.* ①背心料子. ②(雇工)保留退休金的权利.

vest·ment [ˈvestmənt] *n.* ①衣服;外衣;制服. ②礼服;法衣,弥撒祭服. ③祭坛布.

ves·try [ˈvestri] *n.* ①祭服室,祭具室. ②(教堂的)小礼拜室〔也用作事务室、星期学校教室等〕. ③教区纳税人(代表);教区会(会议室). **～man** 教区代表,教区委员.

ves·ture [ˈvestʃə] *n.* ①罩衣;笼罩着的东西;〔诗〕衣服. ②【法】地面生长物〔树林除外〕. *a* ～ *of mist* 雾幕. *a* ～ *of verdure* 绿色的覆盖〔指原野上青翠的草木〕. — *vt.* 使穿衣服;(雾等)笼罩;覆盖.

Ve·su·vi·an [viˈsuːviən, -vjən] *a.* ①维苏威 (Vesuvius) 火山的;火山(性)的. ②突然暴发的. — *n.* 〔v-〕①(抽烟用的)耐风火柴. ②【矿】符山石〔又叫 vesuvianite〕.

vet[1] [vet] *n.*〔口〕= veterinarian. — *vt.*〔口〕诊疗,治疗(马、狗等);〔口〕检查. — *vi.* 当兽医.

vet[2] [vet] *n.*〔美口〕= veteran.

vet., veter. = veteran; veterinarian; veterinary surgeon.

vetch [vetʃ] *n.* 【植】巢菜(属);箭筈豌豆,大巢菜,苕子. *common* ～ 苕子. *hairy* ～ 毛苕子. *Chinese milk* ～ 紫云英.

vetch·ling [ˈvetʃliŋ] *n.* 【植】山黧豆(属);牧地香豌豆.

vet·er·an [ˈvetərən] *n.* ①老手,老练的人;老练的兵,老兵;有战斗经验的军人. ②〔美〕复员军人,退役军人. ③老树〔尤指胸径二英尺以上的〕. ***put on the airs of ～s*** 摆老资格. ***Veterans of Foreign Wars of the United States*** 美国海外退伍军人协会〔曾在海外作战的美国退伍军人组织,略作 V. F. W.〕. — *a.* ①(尤指军事方面)老练的,经验丰富的;资格老的. ②由老兵组织成的. ～ *troops* 战斗经验丰富的军队. ～ *skill* 熟练. ～ *service* 多年的服务资历,老资格. *a* ～ *worker* 经验丰富的工人;老工人. **Veterans' Administration**〔美〕退伍军人管理局. **Veterans' Day**〔美〕退伍军人节(11月11日). ***～s' preference***〔美〕对退伍军人的优待〔尤指文职官员选拔考试时的优先录取〕.

vet·er·i·nar·i·an [ˌvetəriˈnɛəriən] *n.* 兽医. — *a.* = veterinary.

vet·er·i·na·ry [ˈvetərinəri] *a.* 兽医(学)的. — *n.* 兽医〔略 Vet., vet.〕(=～ surgeon).

vet·i·ver [ˈveitivə] *n.* 【植】①(东印度)香根草(岩兰草) *(Vetiveria zizanioides)*. ②香根草根.

ve·to [ˈviːtəu] *n.* ***(pl.*** ***～es)*** ①否决;禁止. ②否决权,禁止权. ③(行政机构反对立法机构所通过的法案时申述的)否决理由 (=～ message). *exercise one's* ～ 行使否决权. *a pocket* ～〔美〕(总统的)不签署议案. ***put a [one's]*** ～ ***(up)on*** 否决,不批准. ～ ***in detail***【法】部分否决(权). — *vt.* 否决(议案等);不批准;禁止. **-er, -ist** *n.* 否决者. **-less** *a.* 无否决权的;不否决的.

ve·ttu·ra [veˈtuːrə] *n.* ***(pl.*** ***-re*** [-rei]***)***〔It.〕(意大利式)四轮马车.

VEWS = very early warning system 极早期预警系统,超远程预警系统.

vex [veks] *vt.* ①使烦恼,使苦恼;使焦急;使为难;使悲伤. ②使恼怒,使生气〔主用被动语态〕. ③〔诗〕使激荡,使汹涌. ④纷纷议论;长期争论. *I shall be ～ed if you* ...假若你…我就要生气了. *winds that* ～ *the sea* 使海洋汹涌澎湃的风. *a ～ed question* 为人长期争论的问题. ***be ～ed at*** 对…生气;为…懊恼;因…为难. ***be ～ed with sb. for*** 因某人…而发怒. ***feel ～ed*** 生气;着急. ***How ～ing!*** 真令人着急[生气]! ～ ***oneself*** 生气;不耐烦.

vex·a·tion [vekˈseiʃən] *n.* ①苦恼,懊恼;烦恼;着急;生气. ②苦恼[烦恼]的原因;使人生气的事情. *Much to my* ～ *I just missed a chance of visiting* .... 错过一个参观…的机会,真气人.

vex·a·tious [vekˈseiʃəs] *a.* ①令人烦恼[着急]的,气人的;令人困恼的. ②混乱的,麻烦的. ③【法】(诉讼)无确实根据的,旨在使被告困恼的. *How* ～ *to miss one's train!* 没赶上火车真气人! ～ **suit**【法】缠讼〔旨在困扰对方的诉讼〕. **-ly** *ad.* **-ness** *n.*

vex·il·la [vekˈsilə] vexillum 的复数.

vex·il·lar [ˈveksilə] *a.* ①(古罗马的)军旗的,旗帜的. ②【植】旗瓣的;【动】羽瓣的.

vex·il·la·ry [ˈveksiləri] *a.* = vexillar. — *n.* ①【古罗马】(编属某面军旗下的)旗兵. ②持旗者;旗手.

vex·il·late [ˈveksilit] *a.* ①有(古罗马骑兵的)军旗的;(在同一面军旗下服役的)一队士兵的. ②【植】有旗瓣的;【动】有羽片的,有翈的.

vex·il·lum [vekˈsiləm] *n.* ***(pl.*** ***-la*** [-lə]***)*** ①【古罗马】军旗;统属同一军旗下的部队. ②【宗】牧杖上的小旗;行列旒旗;行列十字架. ③【植】旗瓣;【动】翈,羽片;膨大跗端.

VF = ①very fair, very fine 很好〔作业批语〕. ②video frequency【无】(电视)视频. ③visual field 视野. ④fighter plane【美海军】战斗机.

VFR = visual flight rules【空】目视飞航规则.

VFR flight【空】目视飞航.

V

VFW, V.F.W. = Veterans of Foreign Wars〔美〕参加过国外战争的退伍军人.

v.g. = ①very good 很好. ②〔L.〕*verbi gratia* 例如(= for example).

VHF, vhf = very high frequency【无】甚高频.

VI =①viscosity index【油】粘度指数. ②volume indicator【无】音量计,音量指示器. ③Virgin Islands 维尔京群岛〔拉丁美洲〕.

Vi【化】元素 virginium (钫)的符号.

v.i. = ①verb intransitive【语法】不及物动词. ②〔L.〕*vide infra* 见下,参看下文 (= see below).

vi·a [ˈvaiə, ˈviːə] *n.* 道路. — *prep.* ①经过,经由,取道. ②凭借,以…为谋介,通过(某种手段). ~ *Shanghai* 经由上海. ~ *airmail* 航空(邮递).

vi·a [ˈvaiə] *n.*〔L.〕①道; 路. ②【医】管道. ~ **crucis** [ˈkruːsis] 十字架之路,苦难之路. ***V- Lactea*** [ˈlæktiə] 银河. ~ ***media*** [ˈmiːdiə] 中间道路,中间路线.

vi·a·bil·i·ty [ˌvaiəˈbiliti] *n.* (尤指胎儿或婴儿的)生存能力,生活力,成活力.

vi·a·ble [ˈvaiəbl] *a.* ①能养活的,能成活的;能生存的;有生活力的;能生长的. ②可行的. ~ **count** 活菌计数.

vi·a·duct [ˈvaiədʌkt] *n.* ①(山谷中的)高架桥,跨线桥,旱桥. ②高架铁路[公路];栈道. ③【美拳】鼻.

vi·al [ˈvaiəl] *n.* (小)玻璃瓶; 药水瓶; 管(状)瓶. ***pour out the ~s of (one's) wrath (up)on*** 向…报仇;〔口〕找…发泄怒气.

vi·am·e·ter [vaiˈæmitə] *n.* 路程计(= hodometer).

vi·and [ˈvaiənd] *n.* ①(一件)食品. ②〔*pl.*〕菜餚,佳餚;食物.

vi·at·ic [vaiˈætik] *a.* 道路的;旅行的,旅途的.

vi·at·i·cum [vaiˈætikəm] *n.* ①【古罗马】(官员出差的)旅费[供应品]. ②旅行的用费[用品]. ③〔常 V-〕【天主】临终的圣餐. ④【天主】活动祭坛〔常置于临终者床侧〕.

vi·a·tor [vaiˈeitə] *n.* ***(pl. -tor·es*** [ˌvaiəˈtɔːriːz]***)*** 旅行者,走路的人,徒步旅行者.

vibes [ˈvaibz] *n. pl.* ①〔美口〕= vibraphone. ②〔美俚〕= vibration.

vib·ist [ˈvaibist] *n.* = vibraphonist.

vi·brac·u·lum [vaiˈbrækjuləm] *n.* ***(pl. -la*** [-lə]***)***【动】振鞭体;鞭器. **-u·lar** *a.*

vi·bra·harp [ˈvaibrəˈhɑːp] = vibraphone.

vi·brance, vi·bran·cy [ˈvaibrəns, -si] *n.* 振动;颤动;响亮;活跃.

vi·brant [ˈvaibrənt] *a.* ①振动的,颤动的. ②振响的;响亮的. ③精神振奋的,生气勃勃的. ④【语音】振动声带发出的,有声音的. *cities ~ with life and energy* 生气勃勃的城市. — *n.*【语音】有声音 (*opp.* surd). **-ly** *ad.*

vi·bra·phone [ˈvaibrəfəun] *n.*【乐】电颤琴〔型似木琴,共鸣器有电动阀门产生颤音〕. **-phon·ist** *n.* 电颤琴演奏者.

vi·brate [vaiˈbreit] *vi.* ①摇动,振动;颤动. ②心中打颤,胸口卜卜地跳;精神振奋. ③振响,反响. ④(象钟摆一样地)摆动;〔罕〕动摇, 犹豫. — *vt.* ①使摇动;使振动;使颤动;使摆动. ②振动着发出(声音,光);摆动着表示. *a ~ing type regulator*【机】摆动式调节器.

vi·bra·tile [ˈvaibrətail] *a.* 能振动的; 颤动性的. ~ *cilia* 颤动纤毛. **-til·i·ty** [ˌvaibrəˈtiliti] *n.* 振动性, 颤动性.

vi·bra·tion [vaiˈbreiʃən] *n.* ①振动,颤动;摆动;【物】振动. ②(心的)震颤. ③(思想情绪的)激动. ④犹豫. *the amplitude of ~*【物】振幅. *the ~ period = the period of ~* 振动周期. **~-proof** *a.* 耐振的,防振的. **-al** *a.*

vi·bra·tive [vaiˈbreitiv] *a.* = vibratory.

vi·bra·to [viˈbrɑːtəu] *n.* ***(pl. ~s)***〔It.〕【乐】(演奏[演唱]时的)颤动效果;轻微颤音.

vi·bra·tor [vaiˈbreitə] *n.* ①(使)振动的人[物]. ②【电】振子. ③振动器[装置];【建】(混凝土) 振捣器. ④【医】颤振按摩器. ⑤【印】振动滚筒. ⑥【乐】(风琴等的)簧.

vi·bra·to·ry [ˈvaibrətəri] *a.* (使)振动的;振动(性)的. ~ *motion* 振动.

vib·ri·o [ˈvibriəu] *n.* ***(pl. ~s)***【生】弧菌属细菌〔如霍乱弧菌 ***(Vibrio comma)***〕.

vi·bris·sa [vaiˈbrisə] *n.* ***(pl. -sae*** [-siː]***)*** ①鼻毛. ②触毛,触须. ③(鸟的)羽须.

vi·bro·graph [ˈvaibrəgrɑːf] *n.*【物】示振器;震动计.

vi·broll [ˈvaibrəul] *n.* 震动压路机.

vi·bron·ic [vaiˈbrɔnik] *a.* 电子振动的.

vi·bro·pack [ˈvaibrəpæk] *n.*【电】振动子整流器[换流器].

vi·bro·scope [ˈvaibrəskəup] *n.* 振动计,示振仪.

vi·bro·shock [ˈvaibrəʃɔk] *n.* 减振器,缓冲器.

vi·bro·tron [ˈvaibrətrɔn] *n.*【电】振敏管.

vi·bur·num [vaiˈbəːnəm] *n.*【植】荚蒾(属). ~ *sargenti*【药】鸡树条.

vic [vik] *n.* ①〔美俚〕犯人(=convict). ②〔英空俚〕V 字队形〔因信号兵把 V 读作 vik〕.

Vic. = ①Vicar. ②Victor. ③Victoria(n).

vic·ar [ˈvikə] *n.* ①教区牧师;〔美〕教堂牧师. ②【天主】教皇. ③教皇[主教]代理. ④〔诗〕代理人. *a ~ of Bray* 随风转舵的人, 两面派. *the V- of Christ*【天主】教皇. ~ **apostolic**【天主】(在传教地区代表教皇的) 名誉主教. **~-general** ①(英国国教在诉讼事务等方面协助大主教或主教的)代理监督. ②【天主】教区代理主教.

vic·a·rage [ˈvikəridʒ] *n.* 教区牧师的薪俸[住宅、职位].

vi·car·i·al [vaiˈkɛəriəl, vi-] *a.* ①教区牧师的. ②执行教区牧师职务的. ③代理的.

vi·car·i·ate [vaiˈkɛərit, -ˌeit] *n.* ①教区牧师的职权. ②教区牧师管辖的教区.

vi·car·i·ous [vaiˈkɛəriəs] *a.* ①代理(人)的. ②替代(别人)的; 做替身的;(想象别人的苦乐而) 产生同感[共鸣]的. ③【医】替代性的. ~ *authority* 代理职权. ~ *haemorrhage*【医】替代性出血. **-ly** *ad.* **-ness** *n.*

vice[1] [vais] *n.* ①罪恶,不道德;缺德行为; 恶习, 坏习惯;(马等的)恶癖. ②(人格、文体等的)缺点, 瑕疵, 毛病. ③(肉体的)缺陷,疾病. ④〔the V-〕(英国劝善剧中)道德败坏的丑角. *virtue and ~* 善与恶,德行与邪恶. ~ *of intemperance* 嗜酒. ~ **squad**〔美〕风化纠察队〔取缔卖淫、赌博的警察〕. **-less** *a.*

vice[2] [vais] *n.*【机】老虎钳,轧钳. *a grip like a ~*象老虎钳一般的紧握. — *vt.* 用老虎钳夹紧;钳制.

vice[3] [vais] *n.* 〔口〕= vice-chancellor, vice-president 等.

vice[4] [ˈvaisi] *prep.* 代,代替. *He was gazetted as captain ~ Captain Jones promoted.* 公报上刊载他被任为上尉以代替迁升的琼斯上尉.

vice- [vais-] *pref.* 〔用于表示职位的名词前〕副,代理,次. **~-admiral** 海军中将. **~-chairman** 副主席,副会长,副委员长,副议长. **~-chancellor** 大学副校长;副大法官. **~-consul** 副领事. **~-governor** 副州长,副总督. **~-king** = viceroy. **~-minister** 副部长,次长. **~-president** 副总统; 副会长; 副社长; (大学) 副校长. **~-principal** 副校长. **~-regent** *n.*, *a.* 副摄政(的).

vice·ge·ren·cy [ˌvaisˈdʒiərinsi] *n.* ***(pl. -cies)*** 摄政,代理职,代理权.

vice·ger·ent [ˈvaisˈdʒerənt] *a.* 代理的. — *n.* 代理人;摄政官;代理官. *God's ~* 教皇.

vic·e·nar·y [ˈvisinəri] *a.* ①二十的. ②以二十记数的.

vi·cen·ni·al [vaiˈsenjəl] *a.* 二十周年的;二十年(一次)的;连续二十年的. *a ~ celebration* 二十周年纪念.

Vice-Pres. = Vice-President.

vice·re·gal [ˈvaisˈriːgəl] *a.* ①副王的;代表王权的. ②总督的.

vice·reine [ˈvaisˈrein] *n.* 总督夫人;女总督.

vice·roy [ˈvaisrɔi] *n.* ①副王;总督. ②【动】副王蝶〔美洲产一种红黑色蝴蝶〕*(Limenitis archippus)*.

vi·ce ver·sa [ˈvaisi ˈvəːsə] 〔L.〕反过来;反过来也是一样,反之亦然. *He distrusts her, and vice versa* (= *She* distrusts *him*). 他不信任她,她也不信任他.

Vi·chy [ˈviːʃiː] *n.* ①维希〔法国城市〕. ②维希矿泉水(= ~ water). ③与维希矿泉水相似的人造〔天然〕水.

Vi·chy·ite [ˈviːʃiait] *n.* 维希分子〔第二次世界大战期间拥护设在维希的贝当傀儡政权的法国投降派〕.

vi·chy·ssoise [ˌviʃiˈswɔz] *n.* 维希奶油浓汤〔用土豆、洋葱配制的浓奶油汤,常供冷食〕.

vic·i·nage [ˈvisinidʒ] *n.* ①附近(地区),邻近. ②邻近居民;邻舍.

vic·i·nal [ˈvisinəl] *a.* ①附近的. ②地方性的;本地区的. ③【矿】邻晶的;【化】连位的. *a ~ way* 本地的路;支路〔*cf.* highway〕.

vic·in·i·ty [viˈsiniti] *n.* ①附近(地区),邻近;近傍;近邻. ②〔罕〕近亲. ***in the ~ of*** ①在…附近;靠近…的,…左近的. ②在…上下;在…左右. *in the ~ of 50* 五十上下〔左右〕.

vi·cious [ˈviʃəs] *a.* ①罪恶的,恶劣的;不道德的 *(opp.* virtuous*)*;品行坏的, 习惯坏的. ②有错误的, 有缺陷的,不完全的. ③脾气坏的; (马等)难骑的. ④恶毒的;凶恶的;恶意的. ⑤恶性的; (空气、水等)污浊的. *~ companions* 坏朋友. *a ~ headache* 剧烈的头痛. *a ~ pronunciation* 不正确的发音. *a ~ text* 错误百出的文本〔课本〕. *a ~ remark* 刻毒话. ~ **circle** ①恶性循环. ②【逻】循环论法. **-ly** *ad.* **-ness** *n.*

vi·cis·si·tude [viˈsisitjuːd] *n.* ①变动,变迁. ②荣枯,盛衰. ③(昼夜、四季的)推移. ④〔古、诗〕代谢,交替. *a life marked by ~s* 多变的生活. *the ~ of night and day* 昼夜的推移. **-tu·di·nous** [viˌsisiˈtjuːdinəs], **-tu·di·na·ry** [-ˈtjuːdinəri] *a.*

Vicki, Vicky, Vickie [ˈviki] *n.* 维基(女子名)〔Victoria 的昵称〕.

vi·comte [viˈkɔ̃t] *n.* 〔F.〕子爵. ***vi·com·tesse*** [-tes] *n.* 〔F.〕子爵夫人.

Vict. = Victoria(n).

vic·tim [ˈviktim] *n.* ①牺牲(品). ②牺牲者,受害者,遭难者 *(of)*;受骗者. *~s of war = war ~s* 战争受害者. *a ~ of disease* 病人. ***become the ~ of = fall a ~ to*** 成为…的牺牲品.

vic·tim·ize [ˈviktimaiz] *vt.* ①屠杀(牲畜等)供作牺牲. ②使牺牲〔受损害〕;迫害. ③欺骗. **-i·za·tion** [ˌviktimaiˈzeiʃən], **-r** *n.*

vic·tim·o·lo·gist [ˌviktiˈmɔlədʒist] *n.* 受害者研究专家.

vic·tim·o·lo·gy [ˌviktiˈmɔlədʒi] *n.* 受害者研究〔研究受害者在罪案中的作用〕.

Vic·tor [ˈviktə] *n.* ①维克托(男子名). ②通讯中用以代表字母 v 的词.

vic·tor [ˈviktə] *n.* 胜利者,战胜者. — *a.* 胜利(者)的.

Vic·to·ri·a [vikˈtɔːriə] *n.* ①维多利亚〔塞舌尔首都〕. ②维多利亚〔澳大利亚州名〕. ③维多利亚〔加拿大港市〕. ④维多利亚(女子名). ⑤胜利女神像. ⑥维多利亚女王〔英国女王,1819—1901, 在位期为1837—1901〕. ~ **Cross** (英国)维多利亚十字勋章〔最高军功章, 略作 VC〕.

vic·tori·a [vikˈtɔːriə] *n.* ①双人四轮折篷马车;折篷汽车. ②【植】(南美)睡莲. (=~ (water) lily).

Vic·to·ri·an [vikˈtɔːriən] *a.* 维多利亚 *(Victoria)* 女王(时代、式)的;旧式的. — *n.* 维多利亚女王时代的人〔文学家、名士、文物〕. **-ism** *n.* 维多利亚女王时代的风格〔风气〕.

vic·to·rine [ˌviktəˈriːn] *n.* (女用)毛皮围脖.

vic·to·ri·ous [vikˈtɔːriəs] *a.* 得胜的;胜利的,战胜的;象征胜利的. *the ~ team* 优胜队. **-ly** *ad.*

vic·to·ry [ˈviktəri] *n.* ①胜利,战胜;征服,克服. ②〔V-〕【罗神】胜利女神(像). *a decisive ~* 决定性的胜利. ***~ over oneself [one's lower self]*** 克制自己. ***win a [the] ~ over*** 战胜,击败. ***win ~*** 得到胜利. ~ **garden** 〔美〕(二次大战中为增加食物用庭园改作的)战时菜园.

vic·tress [ˈviktris] *n.* 〔罕〕女胜利者.

vic·tro·la [vikˈtrəulə] *n.* (旧式的)胜利牌留声机;留声机的旧称.

vict·ual [ˈvitl] *n.* 〔*pl.*〕〔主口、方〕食物, 粮食;〔美〕剩饭. — *vt.* (〔英〕*-ll-*) 给…供应食物; 给…储备粮食. — *vi.* ①〔罕〕吃饭;(牛、羊)吃草. ②(船等)装贮食物.

vict·ual(l)·er [ˈvitlə] *n.* ①食物供应者. ②〔英〕(有卖酒执照的)饮食店主,餐馆老板, 旅馆老板. (= licensed ~). ③食物补给船.

vict·ual(l)·ing [ˈvitliŋ] *n.* 储备〔供给〕粮食〔食物〕. ~ **bill** 〔英〕船用食品装载申报单. ~ **house** 餐馆. ~ **note** 〔英海军〕(给新兵持交炊事管理员的)准餐通知书. ~ **yard** 〔英海军〕后勤(给养)仓库.

vi·cu·gna, vi·cu·ña [viˈkjuːnjə] *n.* 〔Sp.〕【动】①(南美)骆马. ②骆马绒(软呢).

vid. = 〔L.〕*vide.*

Vi·da [ˈviːdə] *n.* 维达(女子名).

vi·de [ˈvaidi] *v.* 〔L.〕见,参看〔略 *v., vid.*〕. ***quod*** [kwɔd] ~ 参看该条,见该项. ~ ***ante*** [ˈænti] 见前. ~ ***infra*** [ˈinfrə] 见下. ~ ***p. 30 = v.p. 30*** 见第 30 页. ~ ***post*** 见后. ~ ***supra*** [ˈsjuːprə] 见上. ~ ***the press passim*** [ˈpæsim] 见各报刊. ~ ***ut supra*** 见上所述, 见前所述,参见上述.

vi·de·li·cet [viˈdiːliset, vai-] *ad.* 〔L.〕即,就是说. ★略作 viz, 通常读作 namely.

vid·e·o [ˈvidiəu] *n.* 电视;视频;影象. — *a.* 电视(用)的,视频的;录像的. ~**disc** 录像盘,开卷式录像带. ~ **frequency** 【视】视频(率). ~ **cartridge [cassette]** 录像带盒. ~**cast** 电视广播. ~**phone** 电视电话. ~**-player** 录像带放映机, 放像电视机. ~ **signal** 视频信号. ~ **tape** 录像(磁)带. ~**tape** *vt.* 给…录像. ~ **(tape) recorder** (磁带)录像机.

vi·dette [viˈdet] *n.* = vedette.

vid·i·con [ˈvidikɔn] *n.* 【无】光导摄像管.

vi·di·mus [ˈvaidiməs] *n.* *(pl. ~es)* 〔L.〕①(帐目等的)检查. ②(文件等的)摘要.

vie [vai] *vi.* *(~d; vying)* 竞争. ~ *with another for sth. [in doing sth.]* 和人争夺某物〔竞争某事〕. —*vt.* ①〔罕〕下(赌注);冒…危险. ②〔古〕使竞争.

Vi·en·na [viˈenə] *n.* 维也纳〔奥地利首都〕.

Vi·en·nese [vieˈniːz] *a.* ①维也纳(式)的. ②维也纳人的. — *n.* 〔*sing., pl.*〕维也纳人.

Vien·tiane [vjenˈtjæn] *n.* 万象〔老挝首都〕.

Vi·et [vjet] *n.* 〔口〕①= Viet Nam. ②*n., a.* = Vietnamese.

vi et ar·mis [ˈvaiet ˈɑːmis] 〔L.〕【法】用武力,用暴力.

Vi·et·cong [ˈvjetˈkɔŋ] *n.* 越共;越共成员〔西方报刊用语〕.

Vi·et·minh [ˈviətˈmin, ˈvjet-] *n.* ①越盟〔西方报刊用语〕. ②〔动词用复数〕越盟成员. — *a.* 越盟的.

Vi·et Nam, Vi·et·nam [ˈvjetˈnæm] *n.* 越南〔亚洲〕.

Vi·et·nam·ese [ˌvjetnəˈmiːz] *a.* 越南的;越南人的;越南语的. — *n.* 〔*sing., pl.*〕①越南人. ②越南语.

view [vjuː] *n.* ①看,望;眺望,展望;观察,考察. ②视力;视域,视野,眼界. ③看见的东西,风景,情景,景色;风景画;风景照片;【工】(视)图. ④看法,意见,见解. ⑤目的,意向,意图;期待. ⑥【法】查验,检查;验尸. *a house with a ~ of the sea* 能望见海的房子. *a field of ~* 视界,视野. *a back [front] ~* 背视〔正视〕图. *an end ~* 侧视图. *a difference of ~* 意见的不同. *a point of ~* 观点. *do some ~s of ...* 画…的风景. *be lost to ~* 看不见了. *be exposed to ~* 看得见, 暴露. *fall in with sb.'s ~s* 和某人意见一致. *from a clear ~ of the situation*

V

根据对形势的清楚估量. ***give a ~ of*** 大致说一说. ***have ... in ~*** ①= keep ... in ~. ②订(计划), 筹画; 企图. ***have ~s upon*** (眼睛)盯牢, 注视. ***in my ~*** 照我看来. ***in ~*** ①看见, 望见. ②放在心里, 作为目的; 考虑中的 (*a project in ~* 考虑中的计划). ***in ~ of*** ①在看得见…的地方, 在…能看见的地方, …看得见了 (*come in ~ of* 来到看得见…的地方, …能看见了. *stand in full ~ of the crowd* 站在人群能清楚看见的地方). ②鉴于, 由…看来 (*in ~ of the fact that ...* 由…这一事实看来, 考虑到…这个事实). ③估计[预料]到才. ④〔俚〕认为. ⑤为要, 为了. ***keep (something) in ~*** 眼睛盯牢; 放在看得见的地方; 记在心里, 记住. ***leave sth. out of ~*** 不加以考虑, 不当做问题. ***meet sb.'s ~*** 附和某人意见. ***on (the) ~ of*** 一见…就; 观察着. ***on ~*** 供人观看; 陈列着. ***take a ~ of*** 观察, 视察, 检查 (*take a dark ~ of* 对…抱悲观态度. *take a general ~ of* 综观, 概观. *take a grave ~ of* 很重视). ***take long [short] ~s*** 作[不作]长期打算; 眼光远大[短浅]; 有[没有]先见之明. ***to the ~*** 公开, 公然. ***upon the ~ of*** = on (the) ~ of. ***with a ~ to*** ①以…为目的; 希望…而 (*doing*). ②为…起见; 抱着…的目的. ③〔俚〕= in ~ of. ***with no ~ of*** 无…的希望. ***with the [〔俚〕a] ~ of*** = *with a ~ to* ①②. ***with this [that] ~*** 因为这个[那个]目的; 因为这个[那个]. — *vt.* ①看, 望, 眺望. ②观察; 视察. ③【法】查验, 检查. ④揣度, 估料; 看做, 认为. ⑤〔口〕用电视机观看(演出节目等)(= teleview). ⑥(猎狐时)见到(狐). *an order to ~*【法】检查许可(证). *~ the body* 验尸. *I ~ the matter in a different light.* 我的看法不同. *I ~ his conduct in the gravest light.* 我以极严重的态度看待他的行为. ~ **finder**【摄】取景器;【物】探视器. ~ **halloa [hallo(o)]** 狐狸出来啦! 〔猎狐时看见猎物时的喊声〕. ~**phone** 电视电话 (= videophone). ~**point** *n.*〔口〕观点; 看法, 见解;【物】视点. **-er** *n.* ①观看者, 观众; 电视观众. ②观察者; 检查者,【法】查验员, 视察员. ③【物】视察器. **-less** *a.*〔诗〕①看不见的; 瞎的, 盲的. ②没有意见的.

view·y [ˈvjuːi] *a.*〔口〕①空想的, 胡思乱想的; 好奇的. ②外表漂亮的, 引人注目的, 炫耀的. **-i·ness** *n.*

vi·ga [ˈviːgə] *n.* (西班牙老式房屋建筑中用的)椽, 木角.

vi·ges·i·mal [vaiˈdʒesiməl] *a.* ①(第)二十的; 二十分之一的. ②以二十为基础的;【数】二十进位(法)的.

vig·il [ˈvidʒil] *n.* ①守夜; 熬夜. ②〔常 *pl.*〕节日[戒斋]前夜的守夜[祝祷仪式]. *keep ~* 守夜; 熬夜. *sick-room ~s* 病房的值夜.

vig·i·lance [ˈvidʒiləns] *n.* ①守夜, 警戒. ②警惕(性). ③【医】警醒(症); 失眠症. *relax ~* 放松警惕. *sharpen one's ~* 提高警惕. ~ **committee**〔美〕自警团〔市民不通过司法机关维持治安的自治组织〕. ~ **man** 自警团团员.

vig·i·lant [ˈvidʒilənt] *a.* 不睡的, 时时警惕着的, 警戒着的; 极留神的; 警醒的. **-ly** *ad.*

vig·i·lan·te [ˌvidʒiˈlænti] *n.*〔美〕自警团团员. ~ **corps**〔美〕自警团.

vig·i·lan·tism [ˌvidʒiˈlæntizəm] *n.*〔美〕自警团的政策[制度, 做法].

vig·na [ˈvignə] *n.*【植】豇豆.

vi·gnette [viˈnjet] *n.* ①【建】(葡萄藤)蔓叶花样. ②起头字母的蔓叶花饰; 书籍章头章尾的小花饰 [小插图]. ③(晕影)半身照片[画像]. ④(简短优美的)描述; 简介; 小品文. — *vt.* ①用蔓草花样装饰. ②使(画或照片的背景)晕映. ③简洁地描述. *a ~ing effect* 晕影效应.

vig·or [ˈvigə] *n.*〔美〕= vigour.

vig·or·ish [ˈvigəriʃ] *n.*〔美俚〕①(赌博中的)抽头. ②(高利贷者索取的)超额利息.

vi·go·ro·so [ˌvigəˈrəusəu] *a., ad.*〔It.〕【乐】有力的[地]; 精力充沛的[地].

vig·or·ous [ˈvigərəs] *a.* ①精力旺盛的, 强健的; 精神饱满的, 活泼的. ②有力的, 有魄力的. *a ~ mass movement* 轰轰烈烈的群众运动. *a ~ style* 富有活力的文体. *~ development of ...* …的蓬勃发展. *~ expansion of production* 大力发展生产. *~ in spirit* 精神振奋. **-ly** *ad.*

vig·our [ˈvigə] *n.* ①精力, 活力. ②气力, 精神; 生气; 体力; 强壮; 气魄, 魄力. ③有力行动;【生】优势. ***be in full ~*** 精力旺盛. ***in ~*** 仍然有效的. ***with ~*** 有力地, 精神饱满地. **-less** *a.* 没有精力的; 没有精神的.

Vi·king [ˈvaikiŋ] *n.* ①(8—10 世纪的)北欧海盗. ②〔v-〕海盗. ③〔口〕斯堪的纳维亚人.

vil. = village.

vile [vail] *a.* ①卑劣的, 恶劣的; 粗鄙的, 恶俗的. ②〔口〕极坏的, 讨厌的. ③〔罕、古〕不足道的, 无价值的. *resort to ~ means* 采取卑劣手段. *What a ~ pen!* 这个笔尖坏透了! *~ weather* 恶劣的天气. **-ly** *ad.*

vil·i·fi·ca·tion [ˌvilifiˈkeiʃən] *n.* 诽谤.

vil·i·fier [ˈvilifaiə] *n.* 诽谤者, 诬蔑者, 中伤者.

vil·i·fy [ˈvilifai] *vt.* ①说…的坏话, 诬蔑, 诽谤; 辱骂. ②贬低. ③〔罕〕使卑劣, 使堕落.

vil·i·pend [ˈvilipend] *vt.* ①诬蔑, 诋毁. ②轻视; 贬低.

vil·la [ˈvilə] *n.* ①别墅. ②〔英〕郊区住宅.

vil·la·dom [ˈvilədəm] *n.*〔英〕〔集合词〕①市郊住宅(区). ②居住市郊住宅区的人们〔常指有闲阶级〕.

Vil·la·fran·chi·an [ˌviləˈfræŋkiən] *a.*【地】第一冰蚀期以前的下更新世的.

vil·lage [ˈvilidʒ] *n.* ①村庄, 农村, 乡村〔小于 *town*, 大于 *hamlet*〕. ②〔集合词〕村民. ③(动物的)群落. *~ industry* 农村工业. ~ **community**【经济史】农村公社; 村社.

vil·lag·er [ˈvilidʒə] *n.* 村民; 乡村居民, 乡下人.

vil·lain [ˈvilən] *n.* ①坏人, 坏蛋; (戏剧等的)反派角色; 〔口〕淘气孩子. ②〔古〕村夫, 庄稼汉. ③【英史】〔有时作 -lin〕隶农, 半自由的农奴(= villein). *play the ~* 演反派角色. *You little ~!* 你这小淘气!

vil·la(i)n·age [ˈvilinidʒ] *n.* = villeinage.

vil·lain·ous [ˈvilənəs] *a.* ①坏人(似)的; 极恶的, 凶恶的; 卑劣的; 腐化堕落的. ②〔口〕(旅馆、衣服、饭菜等)极坏的, 讨厌的. *a ~ character* 反面人物. **-ly** *ad.* **-ness** *n.*

vil·lain·y [ˈviləni] *n.* ①卑劣, 凶恶; 腐化堕落. ②〔*pl.*〕坏事, 恶劣行为, 罪恶.

vil·la·nel·la [ˌviləˈnelə; It. ˌviːlaːˈnelaː] *n.* ***(pl. -le*** [-iː; It. -li]***)***【乐】①农村舞曲, 农村舞蹈; 维拉涅拉歌舞〔意大利古代农村的一种歌舞〕. ②那不勒斯民歌〔意大利十六世纪时的一种无伴奏的歌曲, 如牧歌〕.

Vil·lard [viˈlaːd] *n.* 维拉德(姓氏).

vil·lat·ic [viˈlætik] *a.* 别墅的; 农场的; 田园的, 乡村的, 农家的. *~ fowl* 家禽.

vil·lein [ˈvilin] *n.*【英史】隶农〔对于领主说是农奴, 对于外人说是自由民〕. — *a.* 隶农的.

vil·le(i)n·age [ˈvilinidʒ] *n.* 隶农制; 隶农租地(条件); 隶农身份; 〔集合词〕隶农.

ville Lumière [vil lymjɛir] *n.*〔F.〕巴黎的别名〔意为光明的城市〕.

vil·li [ˈvilai] *n.* villus 的复数.

vil·li·form [ˈvilifɔːm] *a.* ①绒毛 (或长柔毛)状的. ②绒毛开的, 绒毛齿的.

vil·lose [ˈviləus], **vil·lous** [ˈviləs] *a.*【解】(被复)绒毛的;【植】有长柔软毛的.

vil·los·i·ty [viˈlɔsiti] *n.* ①长柔毛性, 毛茸. ②绒毛. ③长柔毛覆盖.

vil·lus [ˈviləs] *n.* ***(pl. -li*** [-lai]***)***【解】绒毛; 〔*pl.*〕【植】长柔毛.

Vil·na [ˈvilnə] *n.* = Vilnius.

Vil·ni·us, Vil·ny·us [ˈvilniəs] *n.* 维尔纽斯〔苏联城市〕.

vim [vim] *n.*〔口〕力气, 精力, 活力.

vi·men [ˈvaimen] *n.* ***(pl. vim·i·na*** [ˈviminə]***)***【植】枝

V

条,柔韧枝条;苗.
vim·i·nal [ˈviminəl] *a.* 【植】(发)小枝的.
vi·min·e·ous [vaiˈminiəs] *a.* ①枝条(编制)的. ②【植】(生有)柔韧的枝条的.
v. imp. = verb impersonal 非人称动词.
vin [vɛ̃] *n.* 〔F.〕 酒;葡萄酒.
vi·na [ˈviːnə] *n.* (印度的)七弦琴.
vi·na·ceous [vaiˈneiʃəs] *a.* 葡萄(似)的;(红)葡萄酒色的.
vin·ai·grette [ˌvineiˈgret] *n.* ①(提神的)香醋盒〔瓶〕;嗅瓶. ②调味酸酱油.
vi·nal[1] [ˈvainl] *a.* = vinous.
vi·nal[2] [ˈvainl] *n.* 【纺】维纳尔,聚乙烯醇纤维.
Vin·cent [ˈvinsənt] *n.* 文森特(男子名).
Vin·ci [ˈvintʃi(ː)], ***Leonardo da*** 达·芬奇〔1452—1519, 意大利的画家、雕刻家、建筑家、科学家〕.
vin·ci·ble [ˈvinsibl] *a.* 〔罕〕可战胜的,可征服的. **-bil·i·ty** [ˌvinsiˈbiliti], **-ness** *n.*
vin·cris·tine [vinˈkristiːn, -tin] *n.* 【化】长春新碱〔治白血症的抗肿瘤药〕.
vin·cu·lum [ˈviŋkjuləm] *n.* ***(pl. -la*** [-lə]***)*** ①联结,纽带,结合(物). ②【数】插线,线括号. ③【解】纽,系带.
vin·di·ca·ble [ˈvindikəbl] *a.* 可辩护的;可维护的;可证明为正当的. **-bil·i·ty** [ˌvindikəˈbiliti] *n.*
vin·di·cate [ˈvindikeit] *vt.* ①维护. ②为…辩护;为…辩明, 剖白. ③证明…的正当. ④〔古〕为…报仇. ～ *one's rights* 为权利申辩. ～ *oneself* 维护自己权利;为自己辩护. ～ *oneself a permanent place in history* 保持永久不变的历史地位. *Subsequent events* ～*d their policy.* 以后的结果证明他们的政策是正确的.
vin·di·ca·tion [ˌvindiˈkeiʃən] *n.* 维护; 辩解,辩白,证明.
vin·dic·a·tive [ˈvindikətiv] *a.* ①起维护〔辩护〕作用的. ②〔古〕报复的;惩罚的. **-ly** *ad.* **-ness** *n.*
vin·di·ca·tor [ˈvindikeitə] *n.* ①维护者. ②辩白者;证明者. ③〔古〕报仇者,复仇者.
vin·di·ca·to·ry [ˈvindikətəri] *a.* ①维护的. ②辩明的;证明的. ③【法】惩罚的;报复性的;复仇的.
vin·dic·tive [vinˈdiktiv] *a.* ①复仇的,报复的. ②仇恨深的. ③〔古〕惩罚的. ～*[exemplary] damages* 惩罚性赔偿损失.
vine [vain] *n.* ①葡萄树(=〔美〕grape-vine). ②有蔓植物,蔓草,藤. *love* ～【植】菟丝子. *rose* ～*s*〔美〕【植】蔓蔷薇. ***a clinging*** ～ 依赖男子的孤苦妇女. ***die on the*** ～ (计划)夭折. ***dwell under one's*** ～ ***and fig tree*** 在自己家里过安闲日子. ～**dresser** 修剪葡萄枝的人. ～**yard** ①葡萄园. ②工作场所,苦心经营的地方.
vin·e·gar [ˈvinigə] *n.* ①醋. ②乖戾;尖酸刻薄〔常作表语用〕. ③〔口〕充沛的精力. *aromatic* ～ 香醋. *a* ～ *countenance* 乖戾〔不快〕的神色. — *vt.* 加醋于. ～ **blink** 〔美〕白葡萄酒. ～ **eel [worm]**【动】醋线虫. **-ish** 不愉快的;乖戾的.
vin·e·gar·y [ˈvinigəri] *a.* ①醋似的,有酸味的,酸的. ②(性情,情绪)乖戾的. *a* ～ *spinster* 乖张的老处女. *a* ～ *smile* 苦笑.
vin·er·y [ˈvainəri] *n.* ①葡萄温室;葡萄园;藤本植物温室〔园圃〕. ②〔集合词〕葡萄丛.
vingt-et-un [ˈvæntei ˈəːŋ] *n.* 〔F.〕二十一点〔牌戏〕.
vini- *comb. f.* 葡萄酒.
vi·nic [ˈvainik, ˈvinik] *a.* 葡萄酒的,在葡萄酒中的,从葡萄酒(提取)的.
vin·i·cul·ture [ˈviniˌkʌltʃə] *n.* (酿酒)葡萄栽培. **-tur·al** *a.* **-tur·ist** *n.*
vi·nif·er·ous [vaiˈnifərəs] *a.* 生产〔酿造〕葡萄酒(用)的.
vin·i·fy [ˈvinifai] *vt.* 发酵(葡萄等的)果汁酿酒.
vi·no [ˈviːnəu] *n.* 〔It., Sp.〕 葡萄酒;果酒.
vi·nom·e·ter [vaiˈnɔmitə] *n.* 酒精比重计.
vin or·di·naire [ˈvænɔːdiˈnɛə] 〔F.〕 普通葡萄酒,廉价葡萄酒.
vi·nos·i·ty [vaiˈnɔsiti] *n.* ①葡萄酒性,酒质. ②嗜好葡萄酒.
vi·nous [ˈvainəs] *a.* ①葡萄酒的;具有葡萄酒性质的;有葡萄酒味的; 葡萄酒色的. ②用(葡萄)酒提神的; 爱喝(葡萄)酒的;有酒意的. *in a somewhat* ～ *condition* 有点儿醉.
vin ro·sé [vɛ̃ rəuˈze] 〔F.〕 = rose 玫瑰色葡萄酒.
vins de liqueur [vɛ̃dəlikøːr] 〔F.〕 甜葡萄酒.
Vin·son [ˈvinsn] *n.* 文森(姓氏).
vint [vint] *vt.* (用水果)酿造(酒).
vin·tage [ˈvintidʒ] *n.* ①葡萄收获;葡萄收获期. ②葡萄收获量;(当年)葡萄酒产量. ③酒;(特指某年某地所产的)佳酿酒,美酒 (= vintage wine). ④(同年代的)一批产品. ⑤制造的时期. *a hat of last year's* ～ 去年制成的帽子. *He is of the Yale* ～. 他是耶鲁大学毕业生. — *a.* ①酒的;酿造的. ②属于某一时期制造的. ③最佳的. ④古老的;过时的. — *vt.* 为酿酒而收(葡萄). — *vi.* 收葡萄. ～ **wine** (陈年)佳酿. ～ **year** 佳酿酒酿成的年分.
vin·tag·er [ˈvintidʒə] *n.* 葡萄采收人.
vint·ner [ˈvintnə] *n.* 〔主英〕(葡萄)酒商.
vin·y [ˈvaini] *a.* (象)葡萄树的;多葡萄树〔蔓藤〕的.
vi·nyl [ˈvainil, ˈvinil] *n.* 【化】乙烯基. ～ **alcohol** 乙烯醇. ～ **chloride** 乙烯基氯,氯乙烯. ～ **idene** 亚乙烯基. ～ **plastic** 乙烯基塑料. ～ **resin** 乙烯基树脂.
vi·nyl·on [ˈvainilɔn] *n.* 【织】维尼纶〔聚乙烯醇缩纤维的总称〕.
vi·ol [ˈvaiəl, ˈviəl] *n.* 中世纪六弦提琴. *a bass* ～ = violoncello.
Vi·o·la[1] [ˈvaiələ, ˈviələ] *n.* 怀奥拉(女子名).
Vi·o·la[2] [ˈvaiələ] *n.* 【植】堇菜(属).
vi·o·la [viˈəulə, ˈviələ] *n.* 【乐】中提琴;【史】= viol. ～ **da braccio** (旧式)次中音提琴. ～ **da gamba** (旧式)低音提琴,膝琴. ～ **clef** 中音谱号 (= alto clef). ～ **d'amore** 一种古提琴.
vi·o·la·ble [ˈvaiələbl] *a.* 可违犯的,可破坏的;可亵渎的;易受侵犯的.
vi·o·la·ceous [ˌvaiəˈleiʃəs] *a.* 紫罗兰色的.
vi·o·late [ˈvaiəleit] *vt.* ①违犯,违反, 破坏. ②亵渎(神圣);污辱. ③妨碍,妨害;侵犯,侵害, 侵入. ④强奸, 蹂躏(妇女). ～ *the law* 犯法. ～ *sleep* 妨碍睡眠. ～ *sb.'s privacy* 侵扰某人(的安静);闯入私室. **vi·o·la·tor** *n.* 违犯者;侵扰者;亵渎者;强奸者.
vi·o·la·tion [ˌvaiəˈleiʃən] *n.* ①违犯,违背. ②妨害;侵害,侵犯. ③亵渎;污辱. ④强奸. ⑤【体】违例,犯规. ***in*** ～ ***of*** 违反,违背.
vi·o·lence [ˈvaiələns] *n.* ①猛烈,激烈,热烈;【炸药】猛度. ②暴力,强暴,暴虐. ③冒渎,不敬. ④歪曲(事实),曲解(意义);窜改(语句). ⑤【法】强奸. ***do*** ～ ***to*** 对…行凶;侵害,伤害;违犯;歪曲(事实等);亵渎. ***offer*** ～ ***to*** 袭击. ***resort to*** ～ 用暴力,动武. ***use*** ～ 用暴力.
vi·o·lent [ˈvaiələnt] *a.* ①(风、爆炸等)猛烈的,狂暴的. ②(话等)热烈的,激烈的. ③厉害的,极端的;(病等)剧烈的. ④强暴的,暴虐的. ⑤(死等)暴力(造成)的;非自然的. *a* ～ *wind* 暴风. *a* ～ *attack* 猛击, 猛攻. ～ *contrast* 极端的不同. ～ *assumption* 瞎猜,乱推测. ***lay*** ～ ***hands on*** 对…行凶,对…下毒手. ***resort to*** ～ ***means*** 用强暴手段. ～ *death* 横死. ～ **presumption**【法】根据几乎已具决定性的证据所作的推断. **-ly** *ad.*
vi·o·les·cent [ˌvaiəˈlesnt] *a.* (带)紫罗兰色的.
Vi·o·let [ˈvaiəlit] *n.* 怀奥莱特(女子名).
vi·o·let [ˈvaiəlit] *n.* 【植】堇菜(属);紫罗兰;紫罗兰色,兰光紫. — *a.* 紫罗兰色的. *the March* ～ = *the English* ～ = *the sweet* ～ 香堇菜(花). ～ **rays**【物】①紫射

线,紫光。②〔误用〕紫外线(= ultraviolet rays)。
vi·o·lin [ˌvaiəˈlin] *n.* 【乐】小提琴;小提琴手。*the first [second]* ~ 第一[第二]小提琴(手)。***play first*** ~ 奏第一小提琴;担任主要职位,当第一把手。
vi·o·lin·ist [ˌvaiəˈlinist] *n.* 小提琴手。
vi·ol·ist [ˈvaiəlist] *n.* 中提琴手。
vi·o·lon·cel·lo [ˌvaiələnˈtʃeləu] *n.* ***(pl. -s)*** 【乐】= 大提琴(cello)。**-cel·list** *n.* 大提琴手(= cellist)。
vi·o·lone [ˈvaiələun] *n.* ①低音提琴。②(风琴的)低音提琴音音栓。
vi·o·my·cin [ˌvaiəˈmaisin] *n.* 【药】紫霉素。
vi·os·ter·ol [vaiˈɔstərɔ:l] *n.* 【化】= calciferol.
VIP, V.I.P. = very important person 要人;大人物。
vi·per [ˈvaipə] *n.* ①【动】蝰蛇;毒蛇。②毒蛇般的坏人。③〔美俚〕毒品贩子。***cherish [nourish] a ~ in one's bosom*** 厚待忘恩负义的人,姑息养奸。**~'s bugloss** 【植】蓝蓟(= blue weed)。
vi·per·ine [ˈvaipərin] *a.* 毒蛇(般)的;有毒的。
vi·per·ish [ˈvaipəriʃ], **vi·per·ous** [-rəs] *a.* 毒蛇般的,有毒的;阴险的,恶毒的。
VIPs *n.* VIP 的复数。
vi·ra·go [viˈreigəu] *n.* ***(pl. ~(e)s)*** ①泼妇,悍妇。②〔英古〕男子气的健壮女人。
vi·ral [ˈvairəl] *a.* 病毒(的),含病毒的,病毒所致的。
vir·e·o [ˈviriəu] *n.* ***(pl. ~s)*** 【动】(美洲)维丽俄鸟〔绿色小鸣禽,又称 greenlet〕。
vi·res [ˈvaiəri:z] *n.* 〔L.〕 vis 的复数。
vi·res·cent [vaiəˈresnt] *a.* 淡绿〔嫩绿〕的,带绿的;开始转绿的;【植】变绿的,绿化的。**-cence** *n.*
Virg. = Virginia 弗吉尼亚〔美国州名〕。
vir·ga [ˈvə:gə] *n.* 【气】幡状(云),雨幡。
vir·gate[1] [ˈvə:git, -geit] *n.* 威尔格〔英国旧地积单位,无一定算法,通常约合 30 英亩〕。
vir·gate[2] [ˈvə:git] *a.* 棒状的;【植】直细枝(多)的;帚状的。
Vir·gil [ˈvə:dʒil] *n.* ①弗吉尔〔男子名〕。②维吉尔〔公元前70—19,古罗马诗人,其主要作品为史诗《埃涅伊德》〕。
Vir·gil·i·an [və:ˈdʒiliən] *a.* 诗人维吉尔(风格)的。
vir·gin [ˈvə:dʒin] *n.* ①处女,未婚少女;【宗】童贞修女。②〔the V-〕圣母马利亚。③〔罕〕童贞男子。④【动】单性生殖雌虫;未交配雌虫。⑤【天】〔V-〕室女座,室女宫(= Virgo)。~ *paper* 白纸。~ *whiteness* 纯白。*a* ~ *forest* 处女林,原生林。*a* ~ *blade* 还没有用过的刀。— *a.* ①处女的。②处女特有的,象处女的,易害羞的。③没有玷污的,纯洁的,新鲜的。④没有搅乱的,没有搀杂的;还没有用过的;没有耕过的;原来的;【化】直馏的;(植物油)初榨的;【冶】由矿石直接提炼的。⑤首次的,创始的。~ **clay** (没有烧过的)生粘土。~ **birth [generation]** 【生】单性生殖。~ **fortress** 从未陷落过的要塞。~ **gold** 纯金。~ **honey** 未产过卵的蜂箱中取出的蜂蜜;蜂房中自然流出的蜂蜜。**V- Islands** 维尔京群岛〔西印度群岛中一小群岛〕。~ **kerosene** 直馏煤油。**V- Mother** 【宗】圣母马利亚。~ **queen** 还没有受孕的蜂王;〔**the V- Q**〕伊丽莎白 Elizabeth 女王一世的别名。**~s-bower** 【植】弗吉尼亚铁线莲。~ **soil** 处女地,生荒地。~ **stand** 原始林。
vir·gin·al [ˈvə:dʒinl] *a.* 处女的,象处女的,纯洁的;【动】未受精的。~ *bloom* 纯洁而美好的少女(时代)。~ **generation** 【生】单性生殖。~ **membrane** 【解】处女膜。
Vir·gin·i·a [və(:)ˈdʒinjə] *n.* ①弗吉尼亚(女子名)。②(美国)弗吉尼亚州。③美国弗吉尼亚烟叶。~ **creeper** 【植】五叶地锦。~ **cowslip [bluebell]** 【植】弗吉尼亚风铃草。~ **(rail) fence** 犬牙形篱笆。
vir·gin·i·bus pu·er·is·que [və:ˈdʒinibəs pjuəˈriskwi:] 〔L.〕为少年男女(的),适合少年男女(的)。
vir·gin·i·ty [və:ˈdʒiniti] *n.* 童贞;纯洁;新鲜。
vir·gin·i·um [və:ˈdʒiniəm] *n.* 【化】钫 (Vi)。
Vir·go [ˈvə:gəu] *n.* 【天】室女座;室女宫。~ ***intacta*** 【法】未与人交接过的处女。
vir·gu·late [ˈvə:gjulit] *a.* 细枝状的,小帚状的。
vir·gule [ˈvə:gju:l] *n.* 【印】斜线号(/)。*A* and/or *B*. 甲与乙或甲或乙。
vi·ri·cide [ˈvaiərisaid] *n.* 杀病毒剂。**-ci·dal** *a.*
vir·i·des·cence [ˌviriˈdesns] *n.* ①嫩绿;淡绿。②新鲜,生气,活气。
vir·i·des·cent [ˌviriˈdesnt] *a.* 淡绿色的,带绿色的;变成绿色的。
vi·rid·i·an [viˈridiən] *n.* 铬绿〔水合氧化铬的一种蓝绿色颜料〕。
vi·rid·i·ty [viˈriditi] *n.* ①新绿,鲜绿。②新鲜,生气。③纯洁,天真,无经验。
vir·ile [ˈvirail] *a.* ①成年男子的,壮年的,年富力强的;有生殖力的。②男性的,有男子气概的,刚强有力的,强壮的。*a* ~ *government* 强有力的政府。
vir·i·les·cent [ˌviriˈlesnt] *a.* (年老的雌性动物的)雄性化;(女性的)男性化。**-cence** *n.*
vir·i·lism [ˈvirilizəm] *n.* 【医】(妇女的)男性现象,男性化;(妇女)发生男性第二性征。
vi·ril·i·ty [viˈriliti] *n.* ①(男子的)成人,成年;年富力强;生殖力。②男子气,丈夫气;气魄,雄劲,雄浑。
vi·ri·on [ˈvairiˌɔn] *n.* 【医】病毒颗粒。
vi·rol·o·gy [ˌvaiəˈrɔlədʒi] *n.* 病毒学 (= viruology)。**-gist** *n.* 病毒学家。
vi·rose [ˈvaiərəus], **vi·rous** [ˈvaiərəs] *a.* 有(病)毒的;【植】有恶臭的。
vi·ro·sis [ˌvaiəˈrəusis] *n.* 【医】病毒病〔症〕。
v. irr. = verb irregular 不规则动词。
vir·tu [və:ˈtu] *n.* ①艺术品的嗜好;古玩癖。②〔集合词〕艺术品,古玩。*articles [objects] of* ~ 古玩,古董。*a piece of* ~ 一件古董。
vir·tu·al [ˈvə:tjuəl, -tʃuəl] *a.* ①实际上的,实质上的,事实上的。②【物】虚的。③【物】有效的。④〔古〕具有可产生某种效果之内在力的。*a* ~ *ruler* 事实上的统治者。~ **ampere [value]** 【电】有效安培[值]。~ **displacement [work]** 【物】虚位移[功]。~ **height** 【物】有效高度。~ **image** 【物】虚像。
vir·tu·al·ly [ˈvə:tjuəli] *ad.* 实际上,实质上,事实上。
vir·tue [ˈvə:tju:] *n.* ①德,品德;德行,善行 *(opp.* vice) 美德;节操,贞操。②价值,长处,优点。③力,效能,效力,功效。④【宗】〔*pl.*〕第七级天使。*paint sb. utterly without a single* ~. 把某人说得一无是处。*a man of* ~ 有品德的人。*a woman of* ~ 贞淑的女人。*a lady of easy* ~ 行为不检的女人。*drugs of great* ~ 效力大的药。***by*** ~ ***of*** = ***in*** ~ ***of*** 靠,因,靠…的力量 (*He was promoted in* ~ *of his abilities.* 他是靠他的才能被提升的)。***make a*** ~ ***of necessity,*** 见 necessity 条。
vir·tue·less [ˈvə:tju:lis] *a.* 无道德的;无长处[优点]的;没有效力的。
vir·tu·os·i·ty [ˌvə:tjuˈɔsiti] *n.* ①艺术鉴别力。②艺术(尤其是音乐)上的熟练技巧。③〔集合词〕艺术鉴赏界。④〔罕〕(浅尝的)艺术趣味。
vir·tu·o·so [və:tjuˈəuzəu, -səu] *n.* ***(pl. -s, -si*** [-zi:]***)*** ①艺术鉴赏家[爱好者]。②(艺术的)大师,名家;〔尤指〕音乐演奏名手。**-ship** *n.* = virtuosity.
vir·tu·ous [ˈvə:tjuəs] *a.* ①有道德的,有德行的,善良的。②贞洁的。③〔古〕有效力的;勇敢的。**-ly** *ad.* **-ness** *n.*
vi·ru·cide [ˈvaiərəsaid] *n.* = viricide. **-ci·dal** *a.*
vir·u·lence [ˈvirulәns] *n.* ①有毒,毒力,毒性。②刻毒,恶毒,恶意。③【医】病毒性;致病力。
vir·u·lent [ˈvirulənt] *a.* ①有剧毒的,致死的,有毒害的。②病毒的,致病性强的;恶性的。③有恶意的,恶毒的。*a* ~ *(bacterio) phage* 病毒噬菌体。*a* ~ *poison* 剧毒。**-ly**

V

ad.

vi·ruol·o·gy [ˌvaiəˈrɔlədʒi] n. 病毒学.

vi·rus [ˈvaiərəs] n. ①【医】病毒；滤过性病原体. ②毒素；毒害. ③恶意，恶毒.

vis. = visual.

Vis. = Viscount(ess).

vis [vis] n. (pl. **vi·res** [ˈvaiəri:z]) 〔L.〕力. ～ ***a fronte*** [-əˈfrɔnte] 前面来的力. ～ ***a tergo*** [-əˈtə:gəu] 后面来的力. ～ ***animi*** [ˈænimi] 勇气. ～ ***elastica*** [eˈlæstikə] 弹力. ～ ***inertiae*** [iˈnə:ʃii:] 惰性，惯性力. ～ ***major*** [ˈmeidʒə] 【法】不可抗力. ～ ***medicatrix naturae*** [mediˈkeitriks neiˈtju:ri:] 【医】自然治愈力，自愈力. ～ ***mortua*** [ˈmɔ:tjuə] 【物】死势，致动力. ～ ***motiva*** [məuˈtaivə] 原动力. ～ ***vitae*** [ˈvaiti] = ～ ***vitalis*** [ˈvaitəlis] 活力；生命力. ～ ***viva*** [ˈvaivə] 【物】活劲，活势；工作能力.

vi·sa [ˈvi:zə] n., vt. (*-ed, -d; -ing*) = visé.

vis·age [ˈvizidʒ] n. 脸，面貌，容貌；外表.

vis·ard [ˈvizəd, ˈvaizəd] n. = visor.

vis-à-vis [ˈvi:zɑ:vi:] n. ①相对[面对面]的人[物]；对等人物；对方，对谈者，对舞者. ②面对面的谈话；密谈. ③两人[四人]对坐马车；两人对坐的 S 形长椅. — a. 相对[面对面]的，相向的. — ad. 相对着，面对面，对坐着 *(to; with)*. — *prep.* 在…的对过，对着.

Vi·sa·yan [viˈsɑ:jən] n. ①(菲律宾的)米沙鄢人. ②米沙鄢语. — a. 米沙鄢人的；米沙鄢语的.

Vi·sa·yan Is·lands, Visayas [vi:ˈsɑ:jɑ:z] (菲律宾的)米沙鄢群岛.

Visc. = Viscount(ess).

vis·ca·cha [visˈkɑ:tʃə] n.【动】鼷 *(Lagostomus trichodactylus)* 〔产于南美大草原〕.

vis·cer·a [ˈvisərə] n. 〔pl.〕(*sing.* ***vis·cus***) ①内脏，脏腑. ②内容；内部的东西.

vis·cer·al [ˈvisərəl] a. ①内脏的. ②内心的. ③本能的；食欲的；粗鄙的. *the ～ cavity* 腹腔，体腔. ～ **cleft** 【生】鳃裂.

vis·cer·ate [ˈvisəreit] vt. 挖出…的内脏.

vis·cer·o·gen·ic [ˌvisərəˈdʒenik] a. 发自体内的.

vis·cid [ˈvisid] a. ①粘的，胶粘的，粘质的. ②半流体的. **-ly** ad. **-i·ty** [viˈsiditi] n. 粘(着)性.

vis·co·e·las·tic [ˌviskəuiˈlæstik] a. 粘弹性的.

vis·coid [ˈviskɔid], **vis·coi·dal** [visˈkɔidəl] a. 粘丝体的.

vis·com·e·ter [visˈkɔmitə] n. = viscosimeter.

vis·cose [ˈviskəus] n.【化】粘胶液，粘胶(纤维). — a. ①粘胶(制)的. ②粘滞的；粘性的.

vis·co·sim·e·ter [ˌviskəuˈsimitə] n.【物】粘度计，粘滞计.

vis·cos·i·ty [visˈkɔsiti] n. 粘性；粘(滞)度；【物】粘滞性.

vis·count [ˈvaikaunt] n. 子爵. **-cy, -y, -ship** n. 子爵的地位[头衔、身份]. **-ess** n. 子爵夫人；女子爵.

vis·cous [ˈviskəs] a. ①粘的，胶粘的；【物】粘性的. ②【植】具有粘质的. ～ **fluid** 粘滞流体. **-ly** ad.

Visc(t). = Viscount(ess).

vis·cus [ˈviskəs] n. 〔L.〕〔罕〕内脏.

vise [vais] n., vt. 〔美〕 = vice².

vi·sé [ˈvi:zei] n. (护照等的)背签，签证. *an entry [exit]* ～ 入境[出境]签证. — vt. (*-ed, -d; -ing*) 在…上背签，签准.

Vish·nu [ˈviʃnu:] n.【宗】毘湿奴〔印度教三大神之一，保持之神〕.

vis·i·bil·i·ty [ˌviziˈbiliti] n. ①能见性[度]；可见物；可见度；可见性. ②可见距离；视界. ③显著，明显(度)，明白.

vis·i·ble [ˈvizəbl] a. ①可见的，看得见的，肉眼能见的. ②显著的，显明的，明白的. ③能会见的. ④(资料等)显露式的，露出部分内容以便易于查找的. *the ～ phenomena* 可视现象. *with ～ impatience* 带着显然不耐烦的样子. *When will he be ～?* 什么时候可以会见他呢? *Is he ～?* 能会见他吗? ～ *distance* 可见距离. —n. ①看得见的事物；直观教具. ②〔the ～〕物质世界，现实世界 *(opp.* the invisible). ～ **exports [imports]**【商】有形进[出]口，商品进[出]口. ～ **horizon** 可见地平线. ～ **means** 有形财产. ～ **ray** 【物】可见光. ～ **signal** 可见信号. ～ **sound** (收音机的)示波器，电眼. ～ **spectrum**【物】可见光谱(段). ～ **speech**【语】可见语言；视觉信号传话法；(教聋人说话用的)发音部位分解图. ～ **supply** 有形供应量，商品粮总量 *(opp.* invisible supply).

vis·i·bly [ˈvizəbli] ad. 看得见地；显然，明明白白.

Vis·i·goth [ˈvizigɔθ, -gɔ:θ] n. 西哥特人〔公元四世纪入侵罗马帝国并在法国和西班牙建立王国的条顿族人〕. **-ic** [ˌvisiˈgɔθik] a.

vi·sion [ˈviʒən] n. ①视力，视觉. ②〔不用冠词〕先见，洞察；想象力. ③景象，光景；姿态；美景；极美的人(尤指妇女)；绝妙的东西. ④幻影，幻象；【宗】显圣；【医】幻视. ⑤【修】想象描述；【影】回忆场面；幻想场面. ⑥电视〔与收听广播相对〕. *the field of ～* 视野. *a man of broad ～* 见界广阔的人. *The bride was a lovely ～.* 新娘子模样儿很可爱. *a poet's ～* 诗人的想象力. *～s of youth* 青春的梦想. ***beyond one's ～*** 看不见的. — vt. 在梦(幻)中看见；想象，想见. ～**-mix**【影】溶合(镜头).

vi·sion·al [ˈviʒənəl] a. 梦幻的，在梦幻中看见的，幻影的，幻象的；幻想的，梦想的，空想的. **-ly** ad.

vi·sion·a·ry [ˈviʒənəri] a. ①幻影的；幻想的，梦想的，空想的，非现实的，(计划等)不能实行的. ②专爱空想的. *a ～ image* 幻影. —n. 幻想家，梦想者，空想家.

vis·it [ˈvizit] vt. ①拜访，访问，探望，问候；(作客)暂住；去…游览，参观；常常去，常常出入. ②视察，调查，巡视；去(某处)检查；出诊. ③(疾病、灾害等)侵袭；降临. ④惩罚(罪人)；施加(报复，报应). ⑤〔古〕降福于. ～ *a friend* 拜访朋友. ～ *Rome* 去罗马游览. ～ *public houses* 出入小酒馆. *The plague ～ed London in 1665.* 瘟疫在 1665 年侵袭过伦敦. —vi. ①访问，拜访，拜望，探望；参观，游览；视察，巡视；逗留. ②〔美〕叙谈，闲谈 *(with)*. ～ *at strange houses* 客居在陌生人家. ～ *with one's friend* 留住在朋友那里. ～ *with a return in kind* 用同样东西报答. *We don't ～.* 我们互不往来. ～ *a friend on the telephone* 在电话里与朋友交谈. — n. ①访问；往来；参观，游览. ②(作客)逗留. ③巡视，视察；出诊. *a farewell ～* 辞行. *a domiciliary ～*【法】住所搜查. ***give [make, pay] sb. a ～*** 访问(某人). ***make [pay] a ～ to some place*** 参观(某地). ***on a ～ to ...*** ①去看某人；住在…家里. ②在访问…，在参观…. ***pay ... a long ～*** 在…家住一个很长时期. ***receive a ～ from sb.*** 受(某人)访问. ***return a ～*** 回拜，答访. ***the right of ～*** = the right of *visitation*. ～ ***of ceremony*** 正式访问. ～ ***of civility [courtesy, respect]*** 拜谒.

vis·it·a·ble [ˈvizitəbl] a. ①可拜访的. ②适于访问的，值得访问的. ③会受到检查[访问，视察等]的.

vis·it·ant [ˈvizitənt] n. ①(特指身分高的)来访者；贵宾. ②(神话中所说)下凡的神仙. ③【鸟】候鸟. ④〔V-〕圣母访问会的修道女. — a. 访问的，来访的.

vis·it·a·tion [ˌviziˈteiʃən] n. ①访问，游览，参观. ②巡视，视察，检查；船舶检查. ③天罚，祸；天惠，福；(良心的)制裁，报应. ④〔V-〕【宗】圣母访问节〔7 月 2 日〕. ⑤〔口〕久坐(不走). ⑥(候鸟的)群集. *the right of ～*【国际法】(船舶的)检查权.

vis·it·a·to·ri·al [ˌvizitəˈtɔ:riəl] a. 访问的；巡视的，视察的；(有权)检查的.

vis·it·ing [ˈvizitiŋ] a., n. 访问(的)；视察(的). *a ～ committee* 视察委员会. ***be on ～ terms with*** = ***have a ～ acquaintance with*** 和…常互相访问，和…关系密切. ～ **book** 来宾留名簿. ～ **card** 名片. ～ **day** 会客日，接见来客日. ～ ***fireman*** 〔美俚〕游客.

V

vis·i·tor [ˈvizitə] *n.* *(fem.* ***vis·i·tress*** [-tris]*)* ①访问者,来客,来宾;留住客,住客;游客,来游者,参观者。②〔*pl.*〕【运】客队,来访队。③〔常 V-〕巡视员,视察员,检查员;(大学的)监察员。*Visitors not admitted.* 谢绝参观。~**'s book** (旅馆等的)旅客登记簿;来客留名簿。

vis·i·to·ri·al [ˌviziˈtɔːriəl] *a.* = visitatorial.

vi·sor [ˈvaizə〔美又〕ˈvi-] *n.* ①【史】(盔的)面罩,脸甲。②〔美〕帽舌,遮阳。③【机】护目镜,防眩罩;遮阳板。

VISTA [ˈvistə] = Volunteers in Service to America 美国志愿服务队〔1964年美国政府制定一项计划,派遣志愿队员去美国及其属地以及波多黎各等地的贫困区服务〕。

vis·ta [ˈvistə] *n.* ①展望;林荫路景,峡谷风光〔从两排树木或房屋之间一直望过去的景色〕。②瞻望前途;追溯往事。*look back through the ~ of the past* 追溯一件件往事。

vis·u·al [ˈvizjuəl] *a.* ①视觉的,观看的;视力的。②看得见的。③光学的。④形象化的。~ **acuity**【医】视敏度。~ **aids** 直观教具。~ **binary [double]**【天】幻视双星〔肉眼看为一单星,望远镜中看才能看出为双星〕。~ **display unit** 可视显示单位。~ **field** 视野。~ **instrument** 电子视觉琴。~ **literacy** 直观力。~ **nerve** 视神经。~ **organ** 视官。~ **pollution** (市内广告牌等造成破坏自然景观的)视觉污染。~ **resolution** 视力分辨率。~ **sensations** 视觉。**-ly** *ad.*

vis·u·al·i·sa·tion, 〔美〕**-za·tion** [ˌvizjuəlaiˈzeiʃən] *n.* 显现;形象;想像;形象化。

vis·u·al·ize, -ise [ˈvizjuəlaiz] *vt., vi.* (使)显现;想象;(使)形象化,(使)具体化。

vi·ta [ˈvaitə; ˈviːtə, ˈwitə] *n.* *(pl.* ***-tae*** [ˈvaiti; ˈviːtai, ˈwiː-]*)* ①传记,自传〔通常指传略或小传〕。②履历书(= curriculum vitae)。

Vi·ta·glass [ˈvaitəglɑːs] (能透过紫外线的)维他玻璃〔商品名〕。

vi·tal [ˈvaitl] *a.* ①生命的;维持生命所必需的;有生命的;充满活力的,生气勃勃的,生动的。②生死攸关的,致命的;重大的,紧要的;不可缺少的。~ *energies [power]* 生命力,活力。~ *functions* 生活机能。~ *phenomena* 生命现象。~ *warmth* 体温。*a ~ wound* 致命伤。~ *interests* 切身利益。*Perseverance is ~ to success.* 坚忍是成功的重要条件。*of ~ importance* 极重要的。~ **capacity** 肺活量。~ **centre**【生理】生命中枢。~ **hardiness** 生活抵抗力,抗性。~ **measuring** 机能测量〔指体温,脉搏等〕。~ **part** (身体的)要害处,命门。~ **signs** 生命特征〔指脉搏、呼吸、体温和血压〕。~ **staining** 活体染色(法)。~ **statistics** ①人口动态统计。②〔谑〕(女性的)身材尺寸〔指胸围、腰围和臀围〕。**-ly** *ad.* **-ness** *n.*

vi·tal·ism [ˈvaitəlizəm] *n.*【哲】活力论,生机说〔论〕*(opp.* mechanism*)*.

vi·tal·ist [ˈvaitəlist] *n.* 活力论者;生机论者。

vi·tal·is·tic [ˌvaitəˈlistik] *a.* 活力论的;生机论的。

vi·tal·i·ty [vaiˈtæliti] *n.* ①生命力,(生)活力;生命强度,茂盛度;体力;(植物的)发芽力。②活气,生气;生动性。③(文艺作品等的)持久力,持久性,(物件的)使用寿命。

vi·tal·ize, -ise [ˈvaitəlaiz] *vt.* 赋与…生命,给与…活力〔生气〕;使生动活泼;激发,鼓舞。**-i·za·tion** [ˌvaitəlaiˈzeiʃən] *n.*

vi·tal·li·um [vaiˈtæliəm] 维他良〔一种抗腐蚀的钴铬钼合金的商品名称,用于牙科、骨科、整形术、铸造等〕。

vi·tals [ˈvaitlz] *n. pl.* 要害器官〔心、肺、脑〕;要害,紧要处,核心。*tear the ~ out of a subject* 抓住问题的要害。

vi·ta·min(e) [ˈvaitəmin, ˈvi-] *n.* 维生素,维他命。**-ic** [ˌvaitəˈminik] *a.* 维生素(性)的。

vi·ta·min·i·za·tion [ˌvaitəminaiˈzeiʃən] *n.* 加入维他命;增加生气。

vi·ta·phone [ˈvaitəfəun] *n.* 维太风〔腊盘配音的有声电影〕。

vi·ta·scope [ˈvaitəskəup] *n.* 一种早期电影放映机。

vi·tel·lin [viˈtelin] *n.*【生化】卵黄磷朊〔蛋白〕;卵黄素。

vi·tel·line [viˈtelin] *a.* 卵黄的。— *n.* 卵黄。

vi·tel·lus [viˈteləs] *n.* 卵黄;【植】胚乳。

viti- *comb. f.* 葡萄: *viti*culture.

vi·ti·a·ble [ˈviʃiəbl] *a.* ①可损害的,可弄坏的。②可腐蚀的;可使道德败坏的,堕落的。③可使(合同等)失去法律作用的;可使变无效的。

vi·ti·ate [ˈviʃieit] *vt.* ①损害,弄坏;弄脏,弄污,使腐败。②使失效〔无效〕。③使道德败坏。*~d air* 污浊的空气。*~ a contract* 使契约失效。**-a·tion** [ˌviʃiˈeiʃən], **-a·tor** [ˈviʃieitə] *n.*

vit·i·cul·ture [ˈvitikʌltʃə, ˈvait-] *n.* 葡萄栽培(学)。**-tur·al** [ˌvitiˈkʌltʃərəl] *a.*

vit·i·li·go [ˌvitiˈlaigəu] *n.*【医】白斑(病),白癜疯。

vit·rain [ˈvitrein] *n.*【矿】镜煤,闪炭。

vit·re·ous [ˈvitriəs] *a.* 玻璃的;玻璃质〔状〕的;透明的。~ *china* 玻璃瓷。~ *luster* 玻璃光泽。~ **body** (眼睛的)玻璃体。~ **copper**【矿】辉铜矿。~ **electricity** 玻璃电〔磨擦玻璃发生的阳电〕。~ **humour** (眼睛的)玻璃液。~ **layer** 角膜层。~ **silver**【矿】熔凝〔透明〕石英(= fused quartz)。**-ly** *ad.* **-ness** *n.*

vi·tres·cence [viˈtresns] *n.* 玻(璃)态,玻(璃)状。

vi·tres·cent [viˈtresnt] *a.* 会变成玻璃质的,能化为玻璃质的。

vitri- *comb. f.* 玻璃: *vitri*form.

vit·ric [ˈvitrik] *a.* 玻璃的;有玻璃特性的;玻璃状的。

vit·rics [ˈvitriks] *n. pl.* ①〔动词用单数〕玻璃制品工艺学,玻璃器皿制作术。②玻璃制品,玻璃器皿。

vit·ri·fac·tion [ˌvitriˈfækʃən] *n.* 玻璃化,透明化。

vit·ri·fi·a·ble [ˈvitrifaiəbl] *a.* 能玻璃化的。

vit·ri·fi·ca·tion [ˌvitrifiˈkeiʃən] *n.* = vitrifaction.

vit·ri·form [ˈvitrifɔːm] *a.* 玻璃状的。

vit·ri·fy [ˈvitrifai] *vt., vi.* (使)玻璃化。*a vitrified pipe* 陶管。

vit·rine [viˈtriːn] *n.* 玻璃柜〔置放艺术陈列品或古玩等用〕。

vit·ri·ol [ˈvitriəl] *n.* ①【化】硫酸(盐);矾。②刻薄话;尖酸刻薄的讽刺。*black ~* 粗制胆矾。*blue [copper] ~* 胆矾,硫酸铜。*green [iron] ~* 绿矾。*nickel ~ = ~ sulfate* 翠矾。*oil of ~* 浓硫酸。*red [cobalt] ~* 红矾,硫酸钴。*white [zinc] ~* 皓矾,硫酸锌。***dip one's pen in ~*** 写尖酸刻薄的文章。***throw ~ over [at]*** *(sb.'s face)* (在某人脸上)泼硫酸(以毁损其容貌)。— *vt.* (〔英〕***-ll-***) 用硫酸烧伤;浸在稀硫酸内,用硫酸处理。~**-throwing** 以硫酸浇人面部毁其容貌的行为。

vit·ri·ol·ic [ˌvitriˈɔlik] *a.* ①硫酸(盐)的,由硫酸制成的。②(批评等)尖酸刻薄的,辛辣的。*a ~ plant* 硫酸厂。

vit·ri·ol·ize [ˈvitriəlaiz] *vt.* 用硫酸烧;用硫酸(盐)处理。

vit·ta [ˈvitə] *n.* *(pl.* ***vit·tae*** [ˈvitiː]*)* ①(古罗马人的)头带。②【植】(伞形科果实的)油道,油管。③【动,植】色带,色条。

vit·tle [ˈvitl] *n., v.* 〔废、方〕= victual.

vit·u·line [ˈvitjulain] *a.* (象)小牛(肉)的。

vi·tu·per·ate [viˈtjuːpəreit, vaiˈt-] *vt.* 骂,责骂,辱骂。**-a·tion** [-ˈreiʃən] *n.* **-a·tive** [-reitiv] *a.* **-a·tor** [-reitə] *n.* 辱骂者。

vi·va [ˈviːvə] *int.* 〔It.〕万岁! — *n.* 万岁声;〔*pl.*〕欢声,欢呼声。

vi·va·ce [viˈvɑːtʃi] *ad.* 〔It.〕【乐】活泼地〔速度极快〕。

vi·va·cious [viˈveiʃəs, vai-] *a.* ①快活的,活泼的;生气勃勃的。②〔古〕长生的,长寿的;难杀死的。③【植】多年生的。**-ly** *ad.*

vi·vac·i·ty [viˈvæsiti, vai-] *n.* 活泼;快活;愉快。

V

vi·van·dière [vivɑ̃:ndiˈɛə] *n.* 〔F.〕(特指法国军队中卖烟酒等的)女随军商贩.
vi·var·i·um [vaiˈvɛəriəm] *n.* *(pl. ~s, -var·i·a*[-riə]*)* (由人工造成、环境与动植物所处自然条件相似的)生态动物园,生态饲养场[室,箱].
vi·vat [ˈvaivæt] *int.* 〔L.〕万岁! *V- regina* 女王[王后]万岁! *V- rex* 国王万岁! — *n.* 万岁声,欢呼声.
vi·va vo·ce [ˈvaivə ˈvəusi] *ad.* 〔L.〕①大声地;口头地. ②口试 *be voted viva voce* 口头表决. **viva-voce** *a.* 口头的 (*a viva-voce vote* 口头的表决).
vive [vi:v] *int.* 〔F.〕万岁! *V- le roi!* 国王万岁!
vi·ver·rine [vaiˈverin] *a.* 【动】灵猫科 *(Viver-ridae)* 的. — *n.* 灵猫科动物.
vi·vers [ˈvaivəz] *n. pl.* 〔Scot.〕食物,粮食.
vives [vaivz] *n.* 【兽医】(马的)颔下腺炎.
vivi- *comb. f.* 表示"活的": *vivify.*
Viv·i·an [ˈviviən] *n.* 维维安〔男子名,女子名〕.
viv·i·an·ite [ˈviviənait] *n.* 【矿】蓝铁矿.
viv·id [ˈvivid] *a.* ①活泼的,生气横溢的. ②(光、色)鲜明的,鲜艳的,闪亮的. ③如在眼前的,生动的,栩栩如生的,逼真的,清楚的. *a ~ imagination* 活跃的想象力. *a ~ description* 生动的描写. *~ in one's memory* 记得清清楚楚. **-ly** *ad.* **-ness** *n.*
viv·i·fy [ˈvivifai] *vt.* ①给与生气;使活泼,使生动. ②使复生. **-fi·ca·tion** [ˌvivifiˈkeiʃən] *n.* **-fi·er** [-ə] *n.*
vi·vip·a·ra [viˈvipərə, vai-] *n.* 〔*pl.*〕【动】胎生动物.
viv·i·par·i·ty [ˌviviˈpæriti] *n.* ①【动】胎生. ②【植】(种子在母株上发芽的)胎萌,株上萌发.
vi·vip·a·rous [viˈvipərəs, vai-] *a.* ①.【动】胎生的. ②【植】(种子)在母株上发芽的,株上萌芽的.
viv·i·sect [ˌviviˈsekt, ˈvivisekt] *vt., vi.* 活体解剖(动物).
viv·i·sec·tion [ˌviviˈsekʃən] *n.* 活体解剖. **-al** *a.* **-ist** *n.* 活体解剖(论)者.
viv·i·sec·tor [ˌviviˈsektə] *n.* 活体解剖者.
vi·vo [ˈvi:vəu] *ad.* 〔It.〕【乐】= vivace.
vix·en [ˈviksn] *n.* ①雌狐. ②泼妇,悍妇.
vix·en·ish [ˈviksəniʃ] *a.* 泼辣的;爱吵架[骂人]的;狠毒的.
Vi·yel·la [vaiˈjelə, vi-] *n.* 维也拉(法兰绒)〔一种英国制毛棉混纺物商品名称〕.
viz(.) = 〔L.〕*videlicet.* ★ viz. 通常都读作 namely.
viz·ard [ˈvizəd] *n.* = visor.
vi·zi(e)r [viˈziə, ˈviziə] *n.* (伊斯兰教国家的)大臣. *the grand ~* (土耳其等国的)内阁总理,首相. **-ate** *n.* 伊斯兰教国家大臣的职位[职权].
vi·zor [ˈvaizə] *n.* = visor.
VJ (Day) = Victory over Japan (Day). (第二次世界大战)对日作战[抗日战争]胜利(日).
VL = Vulgar Latin 通俗拉丁语.
v.l. = 〔L.〕*varia lectio* (稿本的)异文 (= variant reading).
Vla·di·vos·tok [ˌvlædiˈvɔstɔk] *n.* 符拉迪沃斯托克〔即海参崴〕〔苏联港市〕.
v.l.c.c. = very large crude carrier 超级油轮〔载重超过二十万吨的原油运输船〕.
VLF, vlf = very low frequency 【无】甚低频.
Vlo·ra, Vlo·rë [ˈvlɔurə] *n.* 发罗拉〔阿尔巴尼亚港市〕.
v.m. = voltmeter.
v/m = volts per metre 每米的伏特数.
V-mail [ˈvi:meil] *n.* 〔美〕(用微型胶片缩制的)缩印邮件〔寄达目的地后再放大〕.
VMD, V.M.D. = 〔L.〕*Veterinariae Medicinae Doctor* 兽医学博士 (= Doctor of Veterinary Midicine).
vn, v.n. = verb neuter 不及物动词.
V-neck [ˈvi:nek] *n.* V 形领口.
V.O. = Victorian Order, Royal 〔英〕皇家维多利亚勋章.
vo. = verso.
vo = verbal orders 口头命令.
VOA = Voice of America 美国之音(电台).
Voc. = ①vocational. ②vocative.
vocab. = vocabulary.
vo·ca·ble [ˈvəukəbl] *n.* (特指不作为意义单位、只作为语音单位的)词,单词.
vo·cab·u·la·ry [vəˈkæbjuləri] *n.* ①词汇,单词集. ②(某作家、某一阶层人们的)用词数,用词范围. *the ~ of a dictionary* 词典的词汇. *His ~ is limited.* 他的词汇很有限. *exhaust one's ~* 用尽自己知道的词汇. **~ control** 词汇控制. **~ entry** (词典中的)词条,词目.
vo·cal [ˈvəukəl] *a.* ①声的,(关于)声音的. ②发为声的;口头的;表现为言语的;(用言语)把意见表达出来的. ③〔诗〕(流水等)响,鸣,作声. ④【语音】有声音的,元音(性)的;浊音的;【乐】声乐的,歌唱的. *a ~ communication* 口头传达. *a ~ performer* 歌手. *Public opinion has at last become ~.* 舆论终于喧嚷起来了. — *n.* ①【语音】元音. ②【乐】声乐作品;声乐表演. ③【天主】有投票权的人. **~ bands [c(h)ords, ligaments]** 【解】声带. **~ music** 【乐】声乐. **~ print** 声纹 (= voice print). **~ solo** 【乐】独唱. **-ly** *ad.* 用声音,口头.
vo·cal·ic [vəuˈkælik] *a.* 【语音】元音的;由元音构成的;含元音的;多元音的. — *n.* (构成音节中最响亮部分的)元音[复合元音].
vo·cal·ise [ˌvəuklˈi:z] *n.* 【乐】(不用歌词而用唱名或元音来练唱)练声;练声练习曲.
vo·cal·ism [ˈvəukəlizəm] *n.* ①发声;元音发音;元音系统. ②【乐】声乐(技巧);歌唱.
vo·cal·ist [ˈvəukəlist] *n.* 【乐】声乐家,歌唱家[者].
vo·cal·i·za·tion [ˌvəukəlaiˈzeiʃən] *n.* ①发声(法);有声化;发声法.②【乐】练唱,练声〔特指用元音的练唱法〕.
vo·cal·ize [ˈvəukəlaiz] *vt.* ①发为声,清晰地发音;使成有声音,有声化. ②在(字母)上加元音符号(如在希伯莱字母上等). ③使发成元音[浊音]. —*vi.* ①(声音)被发成元音,元音化. ②【乐】元音练唱,练声. ③〔谑〕讲谈,叫,喊,唱,哼.
vo·ca·tion [vəuˈkeiʃən] *n.* ①天命;天职,使命. ②(对于某种职业的)适合性,才能. ③职业,行业. *He felt no ~ for the ministry.* 他不以为做牧师是自己的天职. *He has little [no] ~ to [for] literature.* 他不大[完全不]适合搞文学. *mistake one's ~* 选错职业. *take up the ~ of engineering* 选择工程技术作专业.
vo·ca·tion·al [vəuˈkeiʃənəl] *a.* 职业(上)的;天职的;有助于职业的. *~ education* 职业教育. *a ~ school* 职业学校. *~ diseases* 职业病. *~ studies* 业务学习. *one's ~ level* 业务水平. **-ism** *n.* 强调职业教育的主张,职业教育论. **-ly** *ad.*
voc·a·tive [ˈvɔkətiv] *a., n.* 【语法】呼格(的);呼唤的. *the ~ case* 呼格. — *n.* 呼唤语;呼格.
vo·ces [ˈvəusi:z] *n.* *vox* 的复数.
vo·cif·er·ance [vəuˈsifərənst] *n.* 大声嚷叫[吵闹].
vo·cif·er·ant [vəuˈsifərənt] *a., n.* 大声嚷叫[吵闹]的人.
vo·cif·er·ate [vəuˈsifəreit] *vt.* (大声)叫喊着说. *He ~d "Sit down!"* 他大声叫喊'坐下来!' — *vi.*叫嚣,喧嚷,吵闹. **-ation** [-ˌsifəˈreiʃən] *n.* **-ator** [-ə] *n.* 叫喊者.
vo·cif·er·ous [vəuˈsifərəs] *a.* 大声嚷叫的;喧嚷的,吵闹的,叫嚣的. **-ly** *ad.*
vo·cod·er [ˈvəuˌkəudə] *n.* 〔美〕语音编码机.
vo·der [ˈvəudə] *n.* 语音合成器〔由 *voice* operation *de*monstrator 缩略而成〕.
vod·ka [ˈvɔdkə] *n.* 〔Russ.〕伏特加酒.
voe [vəu] *n.* 小湾;小海湾.
Vogt [vəukt] *n.* 沃格特(姓氏).
vogue [vəug] *n.* ①时髦,时样,风气,时尚;流行. ②时髦

的事物[人物]，流行物. *a mere passing* ～ 仅仅是一时风尚. *It is now the* ～. 这是现在流行的东西[风气]. *His lectures had a great* ～. 他的演讲大受欢迎. ***all the*** ～最新流行品. ***be in (full)*** ～ (十分)流行. ***be out of*** ～ 已不流行. ***bring into*** ～使流行,使时兴. ***come into*** ～ 开始流行. ***give*** ～ ***to*** 使流行. ***have a great [short]*** ～ 大[不很]流行. — *a.* 时髦的，流行的. *a* ～ *word* 时髦的词,流行字眼.

vogue la galère [vəug lɑ gɑleːr] 〔F.〕划船呀! 不管怎样坚持下去吧! (= Row the galley! Keep on, come what may!).

vo·guish [ˈvəugiʃ] *a.* ①时髦的，漂亮的. ②一度流行的,流行时期短暂的.

Vo·gul [ˈvəugul] *n.* ①(西伯利亚西部的)芬兰一乌戈尔人. ②芬兰一乌戈尔语.

voice [vɔis] *n.* ①语声; 嗓音; 鸣声;〔喻〕呼声. ②发声力,语言(力); 想说话的欲望. ③(学说，主义等的)代言人,表述者,喉舌. ④(尤指投票时的)愿望,意见,选择;发言权,投票权,参与权. ⑤【语法】语态. ⑥【语音】有声音;声带振动; 浊音(特性). ⑦【乐】声部;歌唱才能,歌喉,嗓子;歌声;歌手. ⑧【电】口声. *a chest* ～ 胸音. *a head* ～ 头音. *a deep* ～ 深沉有力的嗓音. *a veiled* ～ 嗄哑的语声. *the* ～ *of the tempter* 诱惑. *Indignation gave me* ～. 气得我开了口. *My* ～ *is against [for]* .... 我的意见是反对[赞成]…. *a chorus of 100* ～*s* 一百人的大合唱. ***at the top of one's*** ～ 用最大的嗓门. ***be in*** ～ 嗓子好. ***find one's*** ～ 开口说,发出声音. ***find*** ～ ***in song*** 借歌发泄[表露]. ***give one's*** ～ ***for*** 赞成. ***give*** ～ ***to*** 说出,吐露,表现(*The dog gave* ～ *to his joy.* 狗高兴得汪汪地叫). ***have a [no]*** ～ ***in*** 对…有[没有]发言权. ***in a hushed*** ～ 低声私语地. ***in a loud*** ～ 用高声,大声. ***in bad*** ～ 嗓子不好. ***in good*** ～ 用嘹亮的声音,嗓子好. ***lift up one's*** ～ 提高嗓门说话,喧嚷;抗议,诉苦. ***lose one's*** ～ 嗓子哑了,(尤指)倒了嗓子,说不出话来. ***not in*** ～ = ***out of*** ～ 嗓子不好. ***recover one's*** ～ 开口说起话来. ***speak under one's*** ～ 低声说. ***with one*** ～ 异口同声,全场一致 (*He was chosen with one* ～. 全场一致选了他. — *vt.* ①把…发为声音,把…发为言语,用话把…说出来,讲出. ②【乐】调准(风琴管);【语音】把…发成有声音，使发成浊音. ～ *opinions* 发表意见. ～ *one's discontent* 发牢骚，鸣不平. ～**-over** (电视等的)画面外的语声,画外音〔评论员的说明等〕. ～**print** 〔美〕(用特殊设备记录下来,像指纹一样因人而异的)声纹,语音特征波纹. ～**printing** 声纹鉴别法.

voiced [vɔist] *a.* ①发为声音的,…声的〔用以构成复合词〕. ②【语音】有声的，浊音的. *rough-*～ 粗声的. ～ *consonants* 浊辅音.

voice·less [ˈvɔislis] *a.* ①无声的;沉默无言的,哑的. ②无发言[投票]权的. ③【语音】清音的. ～ *consonants* 清辅音. **-ly** *ad.*

voic·er [ˈvɔisə] *n.* ①(风琴音栓的)调准者. ②表示意见者;投票者.

void [vɔid] *a.* 空的,空虚的,没人住的;(职位)空缺着的. ②没有的，缺乏的 *(of)*. ③〔诗〕无益的;【法】无效的. *a* ～ *space* 空无所有的空间. *a* ～ *dwelling-house* 空房. *The office is* ～ *[fell* ～*].* 这个职位空着. *a proposal wholly* ～ *of sense* 一个完全缺乏考虑的建议. ***null and*** ～【法】无效(的). ～ ***and voidable*** 【法】无效且可作废的. — *n.* ①空虚;空处,空隙,空穴;空席，空位; 真空. ②空虚的感觉，寂寞的心情. ③【桥牌】缺门. *emerging out of the* ～ 凭空出现. — *vt.* ①排泄,放出. ②使[宣告]无效,把…作废，取消. ③〔古〕退出，搬出(房子等),出空. ～ **volume**【物】孔隙率. **-ness** *n.*

void·a·ble [ˈvɔidəbl] *a.* 可以宣告无效的,可以作废[取消]的.

void·ance [ˈvɔidəns] *n.* ①排泄,放出;放弃,退出,脱出. ②(职位等)出缺.

void·ed [ˈvɔidid] *a.* ①空的,成空的;成无用,无效的;空虚的. ②【纹】中空的.

voi·là [vwaˈla] *int.* 〔F.〕那就是! 瞧! 可不是!

voile [vwɑːl, vɔil] *n.* 〔F.〕【纺】巴里纱〔一种透明薄纱〕.

voir dire [ˌvwɑːˈdiə] 〔F.〕 ①【法】一切照实陈述〔见证人或陪审员在接受审核时的誓语〕. ②对见证人、陪审员的审查.

voi·ture [vwaˈtyr] *n.* 〔F.〕轻便马车;轻便敞篷汽车.

voi·tur·ette [vwɑːtjuəˈret] *n.* 〔F.〕小型汽车.

voix cé·leste [vwɑː seiˈlest] 〔F.〕【乐】音质柔颤如弦的风琴音节栓.

VOKS = 〔Russ.〕 *Vsesoiuznoe Obshchestvo Kul'turnoi Sviazi s Zagranitsei* 苏联对外文化协会 (= All-Union Society for Cultural Relations with Foreign Countries).

vol. = ①volcano; volcanic. ②volume. ③volunteer.

vo·la [ˈvəulə] *n.* 〔L.〕手掌,脚掌.

vo·lant [ˈvəulənt] *a.* 〔F.〕①【动】会飞的,能飞的,飞行的. ②【纹】飞翔态的. ③迅速的,敏捷的.

Vol·a·pük, Vol·a·puk [ˈvɔləpuk] *n.* 一种世界语〔德国人施莱尔 (Johann Martin Schleyer) 于 1879 年创制〕.

VOLAR = volunteer army 志愿军.

vo·lar [ˈvəulə] *a.*【解】手掌的; 脚掌的.

vol·a·tile [ˈvɔlətail] *a.* ①挥发(性)的,飞散(性)的. ②快活的，轻快的. ③易变的，反复无常的，轻浮的. ～ *camphor oil* 白(樟脑)油. ～ *matter* 挥发性物质. ～ *oil* 挥发油,精油.

vol·a·til·i·ty [ˌvɔləˈtiliti] *n.* ①挥发性; 挥发度. ②轻快,快活. ③变动不止,反复无常;轻浮.

vol·at·il·i·za·tion [vɔˌlætilaiˈzeiʃən] *n.* 挥发(作用).

vol·at·il·ize, -ise [vɔˈlætilaiz] *vt., vi.* (使)挥发.

vol-au-vent [ˈvɔləuˈvɑ̃ːŋ] *n.* 〔F.〕肉馅油酥合.

vol·can·ic [vɔlˈkænik] *a.* ①火山(性)的;火山作用形成的,火成的. ②有火山的，火山多的. ③暴发性的，猛烈的,激烈的. ～ *ash(es)* 火山灰. *a* ～ *character* 暴烈的性格. ～ **glass**【矿】火山玻璃,黑耀石. ～**rocks**【矿】火山岩. **-i·cal·ly** *ad.*

vol·can·ic·i·ty [ˌvɔlkəˈnisiti] *n.* 火山性; 火山活动〔作用、现象〕.

vol·can·ism [ˈvɔlkənizəm] *n.* = volcanicity.

vol·can·ist [ˈvɔlkənist] *n.* 火山学家;火成论者.

vol·can·ize [ˈvɔlkənaiz] *vt.* *(-iz·ed, -iz·ing)* 【地】使受火山热，因火山热而变化，受火山影响. **-i·za·tion** [ˌvɔlkənaiˈzeiʃən] *n.*

vol·ca·no [vɔlˈkeinəu] *n.* *(pl.* ～*(e)s)* 火山. *an active [extinct]* ～ 活[死]火山. *a submarine* ～ 海底火山.

vol·ca·no·gen·ic [vɔlˌkeinəuˈdʒenik] *a.* 火山(生成)的.

vol·can·ol·o·gist [ˌvɔlkəˈnɔlədʒist] *n.* 火山学家

vol·can·ol·o·gy [ˌvɔlkəˈnɔlədʒi] *n.* 火山学.

vole[1] [vəul] *n.*【动】鼷,田鼠.

vole[2] [vəul] *n.*【牌戏】全赢. ***go the*** ～ 孤注一掷. — *vi.*【牌戏】全胜,大满贯.

Vol·ga [ˈvɔlgə] *n.* 伏尔加河〔苏联〕.

Vol·go·grad [ˈvɔlgəgrɑːd] *n.* 伏尔加格勒〔原称斯大林格勒〕〔苏联城市〕.

vol·i·tant [ˈvɔlitənt] *a.*【动】(能)飞翔的.

vol·i·ta·tion [ˌvɔliˈteiʃən] *n.* ①飞行,飞翔. ②飞行本领,飞翔能力.

vo·li·tion [vəuˈliʃən] *n.* 意志(力),决心;意志作用,愿欲. ***of one's own*** ～ 出于本人自己的意志.

vo·li·tion·al, -a·ry [vəuˈliʃənl, -əri] *a.* 意志的. ～ *power* 意志力.

vol·i·tive [ˈvɔlitiv] *a.* ①意志的,愿欲的. ②【语法】表示意愿的. ～ *faculty* 意志力.

Volks·kammer [ˈfɔlkskɑːmə] *n.* 〔G.〕(德意志民主共

和国的)人民议会。

Volks·lied [ˈfəulksliːt] *n.* 〔G.〕 ***(pl. ~s, ~er*** [-ə]***)*** 民歌,民谣。

vol·ley [ˈvɔli] *n.* ①(箭、子弹等的)齐射;排枪[排炮]发射。②(质问、咒骂等的)迸发,连发。③【网球、足球】(不待球着地)挡击,飞击,飞踢。*a ~ of laughter* 一阵哄笑。*a ~ of oaths* 齐声咒骂。*a ~ of applause* 齐声喝采。***by ~(s)*** 一齐。— *vt.* ①齐射(子弹等); 迸发(咒骂等)。②【网球、足球】飞击,飞踢。— *vi.* ①一齐射击; (枪炮等)齐响。②【网球、足球】飞击,飞踢。**~ball**【运】排球。**~baller** 排球运动员。

vol·om·e·ter [ˈvəuloˌmiːtə] *n.*【电】伏安表;万能电表。

vo·lost [ˈvəulɔst] *n.* 〔Russ.〕①(沙俄时代的)乡。②(苏联的)乡苏维埃。

vol·plane [ˈvɔlˈplein] *n., vi.*【空】(向地面)滑翔。

vols. = volumes.

Vol·sci [ˈvɔlsai] *n. pl.* 〔L.〕沃尔斯奇民族〔古代拉齐奥人,公元前四世纪被罗马人征服〕。

Vol·scian [ˈvɔlʃən] *a.* 沃尔斯奇人的,沃尔斯奇语的。— *n.* ①沃尔斯奇人。②沃尔斯奇语。

Vol·stead Act [ˈvɔlsted-]〔美〕禁酒法〔由议员 Volstead 提出〕。

Vol·stead·ism [ˈvɔlstedizəm] *n.* 〔美〕禁酒主义。

volt[1] [vault, vɔlt] *n.* ①【马术】环骑,环行成圈的步伐;环行的场地。②【剑术】闪避。

volt[2] [vəult] *n.*【电】伏(特)。*the heater ~* 灯丝电压。*the legal ~* 法定[国际]伏特。**~-ampere** 伏(特)安(培)。

Vol·ta [ˈvɔltə], **A.** 伏打(1745—1827),意大利物理学家。

vol·ta [ˈvɔltə] *n.* ***(pl. -te*** [-ti]***)*** 〔It.〕【乐】次,回。*prima [seconda] ~* 第一[二]回。*una [due] ~* 一[二]次,一[二]回。

volt·age [ˈvəultidʒ, ˈvɔl-] *n.*【电】电压,电压量,伏特数。*the working ~* (贮电器的)耐压限度。**~ amplifier** 电压放大器。**~ divider** 分压器。**~ regulator** 电压调整器。**~ sensitivity** 电压灵敏度。

Vol·ta·ic [vɔlˈteiik] *a.* ①上沃尔特的;上沃尔特人的;属于上沃尔特的;属于上沃尔特人的。②沃尔特语支的;属于沃尔特语支的。— *n.* 沃尔特语支〔属尼日尔—刚果语族〕。

vol·ta·ic [vɔlˈteiik] *a.* 电流的;动电的;伏打(式)的。**~ battery** 伏打电池组。**~ cell** 伏打[一次]电池。**~ pile** 伏打电堆。**~ wire** 导线。

Vol·taire [ˈvɔlteə], **F.M.A. de** 伏尔泰〔1694—1778,法国作家、哲学家、启蒙思想家〕。

vol·ta·ism [ˈvɔltəizəm] *n.*【电】流电;流电学 (= galvanism).

vol·tam·e·ter [vɔlˈtæmitə] *n.*【电】库仑计[表],电量计。*a gas [water] ~* 气解[水解]电量计。

volt·am·me·ter [ˈvəulˈtæmmiːtə] *n.*【电】伏(特)安(培)计,电压电流两用表。

volt-am·pere [ˈvəultˈæmpiə] *n.*【电】伏安〔伏特安培〕。

vol·te [vɔlt] *n.* = volt[1].

vol·te [ˈvɔlti] volta 的复数。

volte-face [ˈvɔltfɑːs] *n.* 〔F.〕转向;(意见、议论等的)逆转,变卦,180 度转变。

volt·me·ter [ˈvɔltmiːtə] *n.*【电】电压表,伏特计。

vol·to·lize [ˈvɔltəlaiz] *vt.* 对…作无声放电处理,对…作高电压处理。**-li·za·tion** [-laiˈzeiʃən] *n.* 无声放电处理(法);高电压处理(法)。

vol·u·bil·ate [vəˈljuːbilit], **vol·u·bile** [ˈvɔljubil] *a.*【植】缠绕的。

vol·u·bil·i·ty [ˌvɔljuˈbiliti] *n.* ①(口才、文章的)流畅,流利;有口才,善辩。②旋转性。*with ~* 流利地,滔滔不绝地。

vol·u·ble [ˈvɔljubl] *a.* ①流利的,流畅的,口若悬河的,善辩的。②易旋转的,旋转性的。③【植】会缠绕的。*~ excuses* 流利的辩解。

vol·u·bly [ˈvɔljubli] *ad.* 流畅地,滔滔不绝地。

vol·ume [ˈvɔljum] *n.* ①卷,册;书籍;【史】书卷,卷轴。②〔常 *pl.*〕大块,大量,许多。③体积;容积;分量,额;【物、乐】音量;强度,响度。*a novel in three ~s* 一部总共有三卷的小说。*~s of vapour* 大量的水蒸汽,蒸汽弥漫。*atomic ~* 原子量。*the ~ of retail sales* 商品零售额。***express ~s*** 说得意义很充实[很有内容]。***gather ~*** (程度)增大 (*Her anger was gathering ~.* 她的愤怒更大了)。***pour out ~s of abuse*** 破口大骂。***speak ~s*** = express ~s. ***speak ~s for*** 足够证明,有力地说明。***tell ~s*** = express ~s. ~ **expansion**【物】体积膨胀。~ **indicator** 容积指示器,体积指示器;强[响]度指示器。~ **level**【物】强[响]度级。**~-produce** *vt.* ①大量生产。②【林】材积收获。~ **unit** 响度[音量]单位。

vol·umed [ˈvɔljumd, -jəmd] *a.* ①〔现罕〕包括数卷的。②【诗】大量的。

vol·u·me·nom·e·ter [ˌvɔljumiˈnɔmitə] *n.*【物】排水容积计,体积计;视密度计。

vo·lu·me·ter [vəˈljuːmitə] *n.*【物】体积计,容积计。

vol·u·met·ric [ˌvɔljuˈmetrik] *a.* 测量容积[体积]的;容积的,容量的,体积的。~ *analysis* 容量[体积]分析(法)。*a ~ flask* 量瓶。

vo·lu·mi·nous [vəˈljuːminəs] *a.* ①卷数多的,大部头的;著作多的。②很多的;容积[体积]大的,广大的;(衣服)宽大的。*a ~ work* 大部头的著作。*a ~ writer* 多产作家。**-ly** *ad.* **-ness** *n.* **vo·lu·mi·nos·i·ty** [vəˌljuːmiˈnɔsiti]*n.*

vol·un·tar·i·ly [ˈvɔləntərili] *ad.* 自愿地,志愿地,自动地。

vol·un·tar·i·ness [ˈvɔləntərinis] *n.* 自愿,自动。

vol·un·tar·ism [ˈvɔləntərizəm] *n.*【哲】唯意志论 (= voluntaryism).

vol·un·ta·ry [ˈvɔləntəri] *a.* ①自愿的,自发的,自动的 *(opp.* compulsory*)*;志愿的。②靠自愿捐助的。③故意的,有意的。④【生理】随意的。⑤【法】无偿的;自愿的。*a ~ confession* 自动供认。*a ~ army* 志愿[义勇]军。*~ murder* 蓄意谋杀。*~ conveyance* 无偿让与。*a ~ grantee* 无偿受让人。*a ~ escape* (得监视人同意的)同意逃走。— *n.* ①自愿捐助者;自动行为;自愿地做的工作。②【乐】(教堂礼拜仪式中的)风琴独奏;即兴演奏,自选节目。~ **bankruptcy**【法】自动破产申请。~ **muscle**【解】随意肌。~ **school**〔英〕靠自由捐助维持的学校。~ **service** 志愿服役。~ **waste** (对他人不动产的)故意损害。

vol·un·ta·ry·ism [ˈvɔləntəriizəm] *n.* 自愿捐助制度[办法,主义];募兵制。

vol·un·teer [ˌvɔlənˈtiə] *n.* ①自愿者,志愿者。②【军】义勇军,志愿兵。③【法】自愿行为者;无偿让渡让受人。④【植】自生植物;【林】先锋树种。⑤〔V-〕〔美〕田纳西州的别名;〔Volunteers〕田纳西州人的别名。— *a.* ①自愿的,志愿的;志愿兵的;自动的。②【植】自生的。*a ~ corps* 义勇军团。*the Chinese People's Volunteers* 中国人民志愿军。— *vt.* 自愿去做,自动请求去做。*~ a difficult duty* 自愿担任困难任务。— *vi.* ①志愿;当志愿兵[义勇军]。②【植】自生自长。*~ for service* 自动参军。~ **growth**【林】前生树。~ **plants**【植】自生植物。

vo·lup·tu·a·ry [vəˈlʌptjuəri] *a., n.* 纵欲的(人),纵情官能享乐的(人),淫逸的(人),迷恋酒色的(人)。

vo·lup·tu·ous [vəˈlʌptjuəs] *a.* ①淫逸的,贪恋酒色的。②肉欲的;色情的,妖娆的。*~ beauty* 妖艳。*~ music* 色情音乐。**-ly** *ad.* **-ness** *n.*

vo·lute [vəˈljuːt] *n.* ①涡旋形(物)。②【建】(Ionic 和 Corinthian 式柱头的)盘蜗(饰)。③【空】集气环;【化】涡囊。④【贝】涡螺;(壳上的)螺环。— *a.* 涡旋形的,盘蜗形的,螺旋形的。*a ~ spring*【机】涡形螺簧。**-d** *a.* = volute*(a.)*.

vol·u·tin [ˈvɔljutin] *n.*【微】异染粒。

vo·lu·tion [vəˈljuːʃən] *n.* 涡旋,(贝壳的)涡卷,螺环;【解】旋转.
vol·va [ˈvɔlvə] *n.*【植】菌托. **-te** [-ˌveit, -vit] *a.*
vol·vox [ˈvɔlvɔks] *n.*【植】团藻属 *(Volvox)* 植物.
vol·vu·lus [ˈvɔlvjuləs] *n.*【医】肠扭转.
vo·mer [ˈvəumə] *n.*【解】(鼻的)犁骨. **-ine** [-rin] *a.*
vom·it [ˈvɔmit] *vi., vt.* 呕吐;吐出,喷出(烟、脏话等). — *n.* 吐出物;吐剂;脏话. *black* ~ 【医】= vomito (negro). **-er** *n.* 呕吐者.
vom·i·tive [ˈvɔmitiv] *a.* 令人作呕的,催吐的. — *n.* ①催吐剂. ②(古罗马圆形剧场等的)大门.
vom·i·to (negro) [ˈvɔmitəu (ˈniːgrəu)] *n.*【医】(黄热病人的)黑色吐出物;黄热病.
vom·i·to·ry [ˈvɔmitəri] *a.* = vomitive.
vom·i·tu·ri·tion [ˌvɔmitjuəˈriʃən] *n.*【医】干呕;作呕.
vom·i·tus [ˈvɔmitəs] *n.* 呕吐物.
von [fɔn] *prep.* 〔G.〕= of; from. ★ 在德国人人名中,最初用于地名前表示出生地,领地,后来也用于贵族的姓氏前: Fürst (= Prince) ~ Bismarck 俾斯麦公爵.
V-one, V-l [ˈviːˈwʌn] *n.* V-l 型火箭〔第二次大战末期德方的一种火箭炸弹, *cf.* V-1条〕.
voo·doo [ˈvuːduː] *n.* ①〔美〕伏都教〔西印度群岛和美国南部等地某些黑人中流行的巫术信仰〕. ②伏都教徒;黑人巫师. — *a.* 伏都教的. — *vt.* 〔美〕对…施行(伏都教)巫术. **-ism** *n.* = voodoo ①.
Vo·po [ˈvəupəu] *n.* 〔G.〕(德意志民主共和国的)民警.
vo·ra·cious [vəˈreiʃəs] *a.* ①狼吞虎咽的,贪吃的. ②贪婪的,贪心的,难满足的. *a* ~ *reader* 饥不择食的读者. *a* ~ *whirlpool* 什么都要卷进去的旋涡. **-ly** *ad.* **-ness** *n.*
vo·rac·i·ty [vɔ(ː)ˈræsiti] *n.* 贪食;暴食;贪婪.
-vorous *comb. f.* 吃…的: carni*vorous*, gramini*vorous*, omni*vorous*.
vor·tex [ˈvɔːteks] *n.* *(pl.* ~*es* [-iz], *-ti·ces* [-tisiːz]*)* ①旋涡;旋风;旋卷行云. ②【物】涡旋;【空】涡流;【动】〔V-〕单肠涡虫的一属. *the* ~ *of war* 战乱. *the* ~ *of revolution* 革命的旋涡. ***be drawn into the*** ~ ***of*** 被卷入…的旋涡中. ~ **street**【物】涡列. ~ **theory** 原子涡动说. ~**ring** (喷烟所成的)涡环.
vor·ti·cal [ˈvɔːtikəl] *a.* 旋涡(似)的;卷成旋涡的;旋转的. **-ly** *ad.*
vor·ti·cel·la [ˌvɔːtiˈselə] *n.* *(pl. -cel·lae* [-iː]*)*【动】钟虫 *(Vorticella)* 属动物.
vor·ti·ces [ˈvɔːtisiːz] vortex 的复数.
vor·tic·ism [ˈvɔːtisizəm] *n.*【绘画】旋涡画派〔未来派的一种〕. **-tic·ist** *n.* 旋涡派画家.
vor·ti·cose [ˈvɔːtikəus] *a.* 旋涡的,回旋的.
vor·tig·i·nous [vɔːˈtidʒinəs] *a.* 〔古〕①旋转的. ②在旋涡中转动的;旋涡似的.
vot·a·ble [ˈvəutəbl] *a.* 可提交表决的,可选举的;付诸表决的.
vo·ta·ry [ˈvəutəri], **vo·ta·rist** [-st] *n.* *(fem.* **vo·ta·ress** [ˈvəutəris]*)* ①皈依者,信仰者,信徒. ②热心者,崇拜者;爱好者;提倡者. *a* ~ *of science* 献身科学的人. *a* ~ *of sports* 运动爱好者.
vote [vəut] *n.* ①投票(过程,手续);表决. ②投票权,选举权;投票人,选举人;(属于同一派别的)一群投票者. ③投票纸;(选)票;投票数,得票数. ④议决,议决事项,议决(金)额. ⑤〔英〕〔V-〕下院会议记录. *an open [a secret]* ~ 记名[无记名]投票. *chosen by* ~ 投票选出的. ~ *by rising [a show of hands]* 起立[举手]表决. *pass a* ~ 通过议案;议决. *The motion was carried by fourteen* ~*s.* 该项动议以十四票获得通过. *At what age should women have a* ~*?* 妇女要到几岁才有选举权? *a casting* ~ (主席的)决定性投票. *The candidate polled two thousand* ~*s.* 这个候选人得了两千票. *a*~ *of $ 1000 for a new building* 建筑费一千元的拨款决议. ***cast a*** ~ ***for [against]*** 投票拥护[反对]. ***come to the*** ~ = go to the ~. ***get out a [the]*** ~ 〔美〕获得预期的投票者[支持者]. ***give [record] one's*** ~ ***to [for]*** 投…的票. ***go back upon a*** ~ 重新表决. ***go to the*** ~ (议案等)被提交表决. ***put to the*** ~ 付表决. ***take a*** ~ ***on*** *(a question)* (对某问题)进行表决. ~ ***of account*** 〔英〕(议会拨与政府使用的)预算金额. ~***(s) of credit*** 〔英〕(议会给予政府的)预算外可借用金额. — *vi.* 投票 *(for; against)*, 选举;提议. — *vt.* ①投票给…,投…的票;投票决定,表决. ②〔口〕由舆论[公议]决定,(舆论)公认. ③〔口〕提议. *The measure was* ~*d a failure.* 大家都说这个办法是要失败的. *I* ~ *that we go to the theatre tonight.* 我提议今晚看戏去. ***be*** ~***d*** 〔美〕被公认为. ~ ***(a measure) through*** 使(议案)表决通过. ~ ***a split ticket*** 〔美〕兼投两党候选人的票. ~ ***by ballot*** 不记名投票. ~ ***by "yes" and "no"*** 口头表决. ~ ***down*** 否决. ~ ***for*** ①投票赞成,赞成,选举(某人). ②〔口〕建议,提议 (*I* ~ *for stopping.* 我提议停止). ~ ***... in*** 选出,选举. ~ ***... out [out of]*** 投票驱逐,对…投反对票;(公议)停止. ~**-winner** 争取选票的手段. **-able** = votable.
vot·er [ˈvəutə] *n.* 投票者;选举人. *a casting* ~ 决定性投票者[主席].
vot·ing [ˈvəutiŋ] *n., a.* 投票(的),选举(的). ~ **district** 选举区. ~ **machine** 票数计算机. ~ **paper** 〔英〕投票纸;选票.
vo·tive [ˈvəutiv] *a.* 奉献的,还愿的;诚心祈求的,许愿的. **-ly** *ad.*
vo·tress [ˈvəutris] *n.* = votaress.
vou. = voucher.
vouch [vautʃ] *vi.* 保证,担保,作证. ~ *for sb.'s honesty* 保证某人诚实. — *vt.* ①担保,保证. ②确定;断言. *I can't* ~ *that ...* 我不能断定….
vouch·er [ˈvautʃə] *n.* ①保证人,证明人. ②证件;证书;收据,收条;(付款)凭单.
vouch·safe [vautʃˈseif] *vt.* 给,赐;允诺 *(to do)*. *V- me a visit.* 请赐予光临. *He did not* ~ *a reply.* 他一句回话也不给.
vous·soir [ˈvuːswɑː] *n.*【建】楔形拱石.
vow [vau] *n.* ①誓言,誓约;誓愿. ②誓约内容,誓约行为(等). ***be bound by a*** ~ = ***be under a*** ~ *(to do)*, 已立誓…;在誓言约束下 (*I am under a* ~ *to drink no wine.* 我已立誓不喝酒). ***make [take] the*** ~***s*** 立誓,发誓. ***take*** ~***s*** 立誓出家当修士[修女].— *vt.* ①起誓,许愿;誓约;申言誓必…. ②〔古〕断言. ~ *vengeance against the oppressor* 发誓要对压迫者复仇. — *vi.* 发誓;许愿. ~ ***and declare*** 〔古、俚〕指天发誓地说.
vow·el [ˈvauəl] *n.* 【语音】元音(字母) *(opp.* consonant*)*.— *a.* 元音的. — *vt.* 加元音(符号)于. ~ **mark,** ~ **point** 元音符号. ~ **system** 元音系统.
vow·el·ize, -ise [ˈvauəlaiz] *vt.* 【语音】加元音符号于(希伯来语、阿拉伯语等的字母)之上. **-i·za·tion** [ˌvauəlaiˈzeiʃən] *n.*
vox [vɔks] *n.* 〔L.〕*(pl.* ***vo·ces*** [ˈvəusiz]*)* 语声,声音;语言,呼声. ~ ***humana*** [hjuːˈmɑːnə] (风琴的)肉声音栓. ~ ***pop*** 〔美〕①〔英俚〕街头民意〔行人被临时采访时发表的政见等〕. = 〔L.〕~ *populi*. ~ ***populi*** [ˈpɔpjulai] 人民的呼声,舆论 (~ *populi,* ~ *Dei* [ˈdiːai] 〔L.〕民声即天声). ~ ***angelica***【乐】= voix celeste.
voy·age [vɔidʒ, ˈvɔiidʒ] *n.* 航海,航行;旅行;航程. *a* ~ *round the world* 环球航行. *a rough* ~ 艰难的航程. ***a broken*** ~【捕鲸】没有渔获的一次航行. ***go on a*** ~ 航海去. ***on the*** ~ 航行中. — *vi.* 航行,航海. — *vt.* 渡过;飞过. ~ **charter**【海】航次租赁. ~ **policy**【海】航次保险.
voy·age·a·ble [ˈvɔidʒəbl] *a.* 能[可]航行[航海]的.
voy·ag·er [ˈvɔiədʒə, ˈvɔiidʒə] *n.* 航行者,(特指冒险的)航海者;旅行者.

vo·ya·geur [vwɑːjɑːˈʒəː] *n.* 〔F.〕(从前在加拿大水道上为毛皮公司运送货物人员的)包运船户;(僻远地区的)木材流放者,船夫.
vo·yeur [vwɑˈjœː] *n.* 〔F.〕【医,心】观淫癖患者〔从观看性器官或性行为中得到变态的性满足〕. **-ism** *n.* 观淫癖. **-is·tic** *a.*
V.P., VP = ①vice-president 副总统,大学副校长. ②vapour pressure 蒸汽压力.
VPA = Vietnam People's Army 越南人民军.
VPM, vpm = ①vibrations per minute 每分钟的振动数. ②volts per mil 每密耳的伏特数.
V.R. = ①〔L.〕*Victoria Regina* (= Queen Victoria)〔英〕维多利亚女王. ②Volunteer Reserve 〔英〕(皇家空军)志愿后备队.
v.r. = verb reflexive 反身动词.
vrai·sem·blance [vreisɑ̃ːmˈblɑ̃ːns] *n.* 〔F.〕逼真;神似;似真的情况.
V.R.C. = Volunteer Rifle Corps 〔英〕志愿步枪队.
v.refl. = verb reflexive 反身动词.
V.Rev. = Very Reverend 最尊敬的〔对教长的尊称〕.
vroom [vruːm] *n.* 〔拟声〕弗鲁〔汽车加速时发出的声音〕. — *vi.* 〔口〕发弗鲁声,弗鲁声中开动.
VS, V.S. = veterinary surgeon 〔主英〕兽医.
vs. = ①verse. ②versus.
v.s. = 〔L.〕*vide supra* 见上 (= see above).
V-shaped [ˈviːˌʃeipt] *a.* V 字形的.
V/STOL = vertical/short takeoff and landing 垂直短距离起落(飞机).
VT, V.T. =①vacuum tube 真空管,电子管. ②〔L.〕*Vetus Testamentum* 《旧约全书》.
Vt. = Vermont.
v.t. = verb transitive【语法】及物动词.
V.T.C.=Volunteer Training Corps〔英〕志愿人员训练团.
Vte. = 〔F.〕*Vicomte* 子爵.
VT fuze= variable timing fuze 无线电引信,变时引信.
VTOL=vertical takeoff and landing 垂直起落(飞机).
VTR = ①video tape recorder 视频信号磁带记录器,磁带录像器. ②= video tape recording (磁带)录像.
V-two, V-2 [ˈviːˈtuː] *n.* V-2 型火箭〔第二次大战末期德方的一种火箭炸弹〕.
vug, vugg, vugh [vʌg, vuːg] *n.*【地】晶簇. **vug·gy** *a.*
Vul·can [ˈvʌlkən] *n.* ①【罗神】火与锻冶之神. ②【天】祝融星. ③〔v-〕锻冶者;铁匠.
Vul·ca·ni·an [vʌlˈkeiniən], **Vul·can·ic** [-ˈkænik] *a.* ①火与锻冶之神的. ②〔v-〕锻冶的,铁工的;【地】火山的,火山作用的;火成的.
vul·can·ism [ˈvʌlkənizəm] *n.*【地】= volcanism.
vul·can·ist [ˈvʌlkənist] *n.* ①【地】火成论者;火山学家. ②热月学家〔认为月球内部有热能和火山活动的科学家,亦作 hot mooner〕.
vul·can·ite [ˈvʌlkənait] *n.* 硬橡皮.
vul·can·i·zate [ˈvʌlkənizeit] *n.* 硫化物〔产品,橡胶〕;橡皮.
vul·can·i·za·tion [ˌvʌlkənaiˈzeiʃən] *n.* 硫化(作用);(橡胶)硬化(作用).
vul·can·ize, -ise [ˈvʌlkənaiz] *vt.* 使硫化,在…中加硫;使硬化. — *vi.* (橡胶等)硫化;硬化.
vul·can·ol·o·gy [ˌvʌlkəˈnɔlədʒi] *n.* = volcanology. **-o·gist** *n.*= volcanologist.
Vulg. = Vulgate.
vulg. ①vulgar. ②vulgarly.
vul·gar [ˈvʌlgə] *a.* ①平民的,民众的. ②庸俗的,俚俗的,粗俗的,下流的. ③通俗的;世俗的;一般大众的,老百姓的. ~ *manners* 粗俗的态度. ~ *words* 粗俗话. ~ *errors* 世俗谬见〔误解〕. ~ *superstitions* 世俗〔民间〕迷信. ***the*** ~ ***tongue*** (尤指从前对拉丁语说的)本国话. ~ **fraction** 普通分数(= common fraction). **V- Latin**【语言】俗拉丁文,民间拉丁文. **-ly** *ad.*
vul·ga·ri·an [vʌlˈgeəriən] *n.* 粗俗的人,〔特指〕庸俗的暴发户.
vul·gar·ism [ˈvʌlgərizəm] *n.* ①粗俗,庸俗,粗鄙. ②【语言】粗俗话〔词语〕;词语的非规范用法.
vul·gar·i·ty [vʌlˈgæriti] *n.* ①粗俗,庸俗,下流. ②粗俗语;粗俗行为.
vul·gar·i·za·tion [ˌvʌlgəraiˈzeiʃən] *n.* 庸俗化,粗俗化;〔罕〕世俗化;大众化.
vul·gar·ize, -ise [ˈvʌlgəˌraiz] *vt.* 使庸俗,使粗俗;〔罕〕使通俗化,使大众化.
Vul·gate [ˈvʌlgit] *n.* ①拉丁文圣经〔公元四世纪译出,为天主教所承认的唯一文本〕. ②〔v-〕定本,通行本. ③白话,口语,土话,俗话. — *a.* ①拉丁文圣经的. ②〔v-〕公认的,通行的.
vul·gus [ˈvʌlgəs] *n.* ①〔英学俚〕拉丁〔希腊〕文短诗翻译作业. ②平民,老百姓.
vul·ner·a·ble [ˈvʌlnərəbl] *a.* ①易受伤的,脆弱的;易受责难〔攻击、损坏〕的,有弱点的. ②【桥牌】有局的. *a* ~ *point* (易受伤的)弱点. *be* ~ *to criticism* 易受抨击. **-bil·i·ty** [ˌvʌlnərəˈbiliti] *n.* **-a·bly** *ad.*
vul·ner·a·ry [ˈvʌlnərəri] *a.* 医治创伤的,敷创伤的. — *n.* 创伤愈合剂.
Vul·pec·u·la [vʌlˈpekjulə] *n.*【天】狐狸座.
vul·pine [ˈvʌlpain] *a.* 狐(狸)的;狐狸似的;狡猾的.
vul·ture [ˈvʌltʃə] *n.*【鸟】兀鹰;秃鹫;贪得无厌者,劫掠者. **-tur·ine** [-tʃurain] *a.*
vul·tur·ish [ˈvʌltʃuriʃ], **vul·tur·ous** [-rəs] *a.* 兀鹰似的;贪得无厌的,掠夺性的.
vul·va [ˈvʌlvə] *n.* (*pl.* ***-vae*** [-viː], ~***s***)【解】女阴,外阴,阴户,阴门;【动】孔. **-l, -r** *a.*
vul·vate [ˈvʌlveit] *a.* 阴门(状)的.
vul·vi·form [ˈvʌlviˌfɔːm] *a.*【解】似阴门(的).
vul·vi·tis [vʌlˈvaitis] *n.*【医】外阴炎.
vul·vo·vag·i·ni·tis [ˌvʌlvəuˌvædʒiˈnaitis] *n.*【医】外阴阴道炎.
vum [vʌm] *vi.* 〔美方〕发誓,赌咒.
vv. = ①verses. ②violins.
v.v. = 〔L.〕vice versa.
vv.ll. = 〔L.〕*variae lectiones* (稿本的)异文 (= variant readings).
vy = very.
vy·cor [ˈvaikɔ] *n.* 石英玻璃;硼硅酸耐热玻璃.
vy·ing [ˈvaiiŋ] vie 的现在分词. — *a.* 竞争的.

W

W,w [ˈdʌblju(ː)] (*pl.* **W's, w's** [ˈdʌblju(ː)z]) ①英语字母表第二十三字母. ②W 字形物. ③〔W〕【化】元素钨(wolfram) 的符号. ④【印】W 铅字.
W,w = ①warden. ②warehouse. ③watt(s). ④weight.

⑤west; western. ⑥width. ⑦【物】work. ⑧〔W〕Wales; Welsh. ⑨〔W〕Washington. ⑩week(s). ⑪wide. ⑫wife. ⑬with. ⑭won.

WA = ①West Africa 西非. ②Western Australia 西澳大利亚. ③with average【商】水渍险(承保单独海损).

wa' [wɔː, wɑː] *n.* 〔Scot.〕wall 的缩略词.

Waadt [vɑːt] = Vaud 沃州〔瑞士西部〕.

wab·ble [ˈwɔbl] *vi.* (陀螺、人等)摇摆,摆动,摇晃;(声音)震颤;(政策、人心等)动摇. — *vt.* 使摇摆〔颤动, 动摇〕. — *n.* 摇摆,摇晃;摆动;动摇 (= wobble). **-r** *n.* ①摇动者;摇摆者,迟疑不决的人. ②【机】(能旋转的)削截器. ③〔英方〕煮过的羊腿. **-bling** *a.*

WAC = Women's Army Corps〔美〕陆军妇女队.

Wac [wæk] *n.* 〔美〕陆军妇女队成员.

wack [wæk] *n.* 〔美俚〕怪人.

wack·e [ˈwækə] *n.* 【地】玄(武)土.

wack·y [ˈwæki] *a.* 〔美俚〕古怪的,反常的,疯癫的.

WACS, Wacs [wæks] *n.* 〔美〕Wac 的复数.

wad¹ [wɔd] *n.* ①(棉絮等软物的)一团,一撮. ②〔口〕(纸币的)一叠;(布的)一块;一捆. ③填料,填絮;【军】炮塞,弹塞. ④〔常 *pl.*〕〔俚〕钞票,钱;一大笔(钱). *plug one's ears with ~s of cotton* 用棉絮团塞住耳朵. *a ~ of bills*〔美〕一叠钞票. ***shoot one's ~***〔美俚〕①说出想说的话. ②表示反对,诉怨. ③用尽最后手段; 把钱花完. ④自夸; 刺刺不休. — *vt.* ①把…弄成一团; 〔美俚〕把(纸)卷成一卷. ②填塞;填棉花(入衣服); 装填弹塞(入枪). *be well wadded with conceit* 十分自负〔自满〕;得意洋洋.

wad² [wɔd] *n.* 【矿】锰土,沼锰矿.

wad·a·ble [ˈweidəbl] *a.* 可涉水而过的.

wad·ding [ˈwɔdiŋ] *n.* 填料, 填絮; 填弹塞原料; 填塞物;填塞.

wad·dle [ˈwɔdl] *vi.* (鸭、矮胖子等)摇摇摆摆地走,趔趔趄趄地走. — *n.* 摇摆的步子. **-dling·ly** *ad.*

wad·dy¹ [ˈwɔdi] *n.* ①〔澳〕(土著居民战斗用)棍棒. ②手杖. — *vt.* 用棍棒打.

wad·dy² [ˈwɔdi] *n.* 〔澳、美西部〕牧童,骑马牧童,牛仔.

Wade [weid] *n.* 韦德〔姓氏,男子名〕.

wade [weid] *vi., vt.* ①蹚,蹚过. ②费力前进, 好容易通过. — *n.* 跋涉, 蹚水; (可以蹚过的)浅水. *the wading bird*【动】涉水禽鸟. *a wading pool* (公园中的)儿童玩水池. *~ through a book* 很吃力地读完一本书. ***~ in*** ①入浅水;参加,干涉. ②猛烈地攻击对方. ③〔美口〕精神勃勃地开始〔动手〕. ***~ into*** 猛烈攻击; 〔美口〕精神勃勃地开始. ***~ through slaughter [blood] to*** *(a throne)* 踏着杀戮的鲜血取得 (王位), 用屠杀办法达到〔取得〕. — *n.* ①跋涉, 蹚水. ②(可以蹚过的) 浅水. **-able** *a.* = wadable.

wad·er [ˈweidə] *n.* ①蹚水的人,涉渡者;【鸟】涉水禽鸟. ②〔*pl.*〕(钓鱼用)涉水长靴.

wad·i, wad·y [ˈwɔdi] *n.* ①(仅雨季有水的) 干涸河床,旱河;【地】旱谷. ②流经干涸河床的水流. ③(沙漠中的)绿洲(= oasis).

wad·na [ˈwɑːdnə]〔Scot.〕= would not.

wae [wei] *n.* 〔Scot.〕悲哀,苦恼,忧伤 (= woe).

wae·sucks [ˈweisʌks] *int.* 〔Scot.〕唉(=alas).

WAF = Women in the Air Force〔美〕空军妇女队.

Waf [wæf] *n.* 〔美〕空军妇女队成员.

w.a.f. = with all faults 一经售出,概不退换.

wa·fer [ˈweifə] *n.* ①薄脆饼;薄饼一样的东西;【物、无】圆片;薄片;晶片;【医】糯米纸〔包药用的干糊片〕. ②(封信用的)胶纸. ③【宗】圣饼〔一种供圣餐用的未发酵圆面包皮〕. *thin as a ~* 非常薄的. — *vt.* 用胶纸封. **-er** *n.* 压片机,切片机.

wa·fer·y [ˈweifəri] *a.* 薄脆饼似的;极薄的.

waff¹ [wɑːf, wæf] *n.* ①(作为信号的)挥动. ②噗的一吹(喷);阵风. ③一瞥. ④鬼,幽灵.

waff² [wɑːf, wæf] *a.* 〔Scot.〕没有价值的,不足取的,不足道的.

waf·fle [ˈwɔfl] *n.* 奶蛋格子饼,华夫饼. **~ iron** 烤奶蛋格子饼的夹板铁模.

WAFS, Wafs [wæfs] *n.* 〔美〕Waf 的复数.

waft [wɑːft, wɔft] *vt.* 吹送,飘送;使浮动,使漂荡. *~ a kiss* 丢吻. *a fragrance ~ed from the meadow* 牧场上吹来的香气. — *vi.* 浮动,漂荡. — *n.* ①浮动,漂荡,飘浮. ②一吹;一阵风. ③(鸟翅膀的)一搧. ④飘香. ⑤【海】信号旗;(遇险)信号. *a ~ of bells* 风中传来的钟〔铃〕声. *a ~ of joy* 一阵短暂的欢乐. **-er** *n.* 转盘风扇.

waft·age [ˈwɑːftidʒ] *n.* 〔古〕①吹送; 飘浮; 飘荡. ②运送;传达;传播.

waf·ture [ˈwɑːftʃə, ˈwæf-] *n.* ①浮动,飘荡,波动;飘送,浮运. ②飘动物〔如因微风飘动的东西〕.

wag. = wagon.

wag¹ [wæg] *vt.* 摇,摆动(特指尾巴等). *A dog ~s its tail.* 狗摇尾巴. — *vi.* ①摇动;摆动. ②(舌头)不停地动;喋喋不休. ③〔古〕(时势等)推移,变迁. ④摇摇摆摆地走. ⑤〔俚〕动身,出发,走掉. *How ~s the world (with you)?* (你)情形怎么样? *So the world ~s.* 人世变迁就是这样,这就是人世. *The beards [chins, jaws, tongues] are wagging.* 大家不停地谈着. *Your tongue ~s too freely.* 你的嘴太随便了. ***~ one's finger at*** 向…摇指头〔表责难、轻视〕. ***The tail ~s the dog.*** 上下颠倒;小人物掌权. — *n.* 摇动,摆动.

wag² [wæg] *n.* ①滑稽角色,爱说笑的人. ②〔英俚〕逃学,偷懒. ***play (the) ~***〔英俚〕逃学,偷懒. — *vi.* 〔英俚〕逃学. ***~ it***〔英俚〕赖学,逃学.

wage¹ [weidʒ] *n.* 〔常 *pl.*〕①工资. ②报应. ★ *pl.* 常作 *sing.* 用. *time ~s* 计时工资. *~s by the piece* 计件工资. ***at a ~ [at ~s] of $*** *... a month* 每月工资…美元. ***get good ~s*** 拿高薪. **~ day** 发工资日. **~ earner** 工资劳动者,工资生活者; 雇佣劳动者. **~ freeze**〔英〕工资冻结. **~ hike** 加薪. **~ packet**〔英〕工资袋. **~ pattern** 标准工资等级. **~ scale** 工资等级. **~worker**〔美〕= wage earner.

wage² [weidʒ] *vt.* ①实行,进行,作(战等) *(on; against)*. ②〔方〕雇佣. ③〔古〕打赌;抵押;担保.

wa·ger [ˈweidʒə] *n.* 赌金,赌注;打赌. — *vt.* 打赌; 担保,保证. *~ five dollars on the white horse* 在那匹白马身上下五美元赌注. *I ~ that it shall be so.* 我保证(它)会这样.

wag·ger·y [ˈwægəri] *n.* 诙谐;恶作剧,开玩笑.

wag·gish [ˈwægiʃ] *a.* 玩笑的;诙谐的; 淘气的, 恶作剧的. **-ly** *ad.*

wag·gle [ˈwægl] *vi., vt., n.* = wag¹.

wag·gly [ˈwægli] *a.* 摇摇晃晃的.

wag·(g)on [ˈwægən] *n.* ①(二马以上的四轮) 运货马车. ②〔英〕(铁路的)无盖货车. ③手推车. ④【采】矿车. ⑤〔美〕面包车〔小型多座汽车〕. ⑥巡逻警车. ⑦〔美俚〕婴孩车. ⑧〔the ~〕囚车. ⑨〔the W-〕【天】北斗七星. ⑩〔美俚〕左轮(手枪). ***hitch one's ~ to a star*** 妄想登天; 追求力所不及的东西. ***on [off] the ~***〔美俚〕在〔不〕戒酒. — *vt.* 用运货马车〔货车、手推车等〕运送. **~ boss**〔美〕抓犯人的警察长. **~ drift** 工资浮动. **~ box** 车箱中载客〔装货〕部分. **~-headed** *a.* (建筑)拱形的. **~ load** 一车货载. **~ stop**〔英〕工资限额法〔规定失业津贴不得多于工作时的工资〕. **~-stop** *vt.* 对(失业者)采取工资限额法. **~ top**【机】斜顶. **~ train** 车队;护送车队;辎重车队;【美史】向西部移民车队.

wag·(g)on·age [ˈwægənidʒ] *n.* ①运货马车运输. ②运货马车运费. ③〔集合词〕运货(马)车.

wag·(g)on·er [ˈwægənə] *n.* ①(运货马车的)御者;【采】矿车工. ②〔the W-〕【天】御夫座.

wag·(g)on·ette [wægəˈnet] *n.* (坐六人或八人的)四轮

敞(篷)马车.

Wag·ner [ˈwægnə] *n.* ①瓦格纳〔姓氏〕. ②**Richard** ～ 李·瓦格纳〔1813—1883,德国歌剧家〕.

Wag·ne·ri·an [vɑːgˈniəriən] *a.* ①(德国歌剧家)瓦格纳的;瓦格纳音乐论的;瓦格纳音乐手法〔风格〕的. ②瓦格纳歌剧专业歌唱家的 *a* ～ *soprano* 瓦格纳歌剧女高音. — *n.* 瓦格纳音乐的崇拜者〔门徒〕;瓦格纳音乐论的崇拜者〔门徒〕.

wa·gon-lit [ˈvægɔ̃ːnliː, ˈwæg-] *n.* 〔F.〕铁路卧车.

wa·hi·ne [wɑːˈhiːnei] *n.* 〔美〕(大洋洲东部)玻里尼西亚 *(Polynesian)* 女人〔尤指夏威夷女人〕.

wa·hoo[1] [wɑːˈhuː] *n.* 〔美〕【植】火树 (*Euonymus* 属);翅榆 *(Ulmus alata)*.

wa·hoo[2] [ˈwɑːhuː, wɑːˈhuː] *n.* ***(pl. -hoo, -hoos)***【动】刺鲅鱼 *(Acanthocybium solanderi)*〔产于暖水海洋〕.

wa·hoo[3] [wɑːˈhuː, ˈwɑːhuː] *int.* 啊哈!〔开心或兴奋时的喊叫声〕.

waif [weif] *n.* ①流浪者,无家可归的人;〔特指〕流浪儿童;无主〔迷途〕动物. ②无主物品,拾得物品;漂流物;盗贼丢弃的赃物. ③【海】信号(旗). ***～s and strays*** ①无家可归的人们,流浪儿童们. ②零碎东西.

wail [weil] *vi.* ①痛哭,大哭. ②悲叹;哀悼;(风)哀鸣,悲号. ③〔美俚〕(爵士乐)表演得特别好. ④〔美俚〕用音乐或语言表现情感. — *vt.* ①〔古〕哀悼,为…恸哭. ②哀号着说. — *n.* 痛哭,恸哭;(风的)哀鸣声. **Wailing Wall** 饮泣墙〔耶路撒冷犹太会堂的残壁,犹太人凭吊故国的地方〕;〔喻〕安慰物,慰藉. **-er** *n.* 哀悼者,恸哭者. **-ful** *a.* **-ing·ly** *ad.*

wain [wein] *n.* ①〔主、诗〕= wagon, cart;〔古〕战车. ②〔the W-〕【天】= the Wagon.

wain·scot [ˈweinskət] *n.*【建】护壁板;腰板;室内墙壁有装饰的下部;护壁材料. — *vt.* ***(〔英〕-tt-)***【建】在…装护壁板.

wain·scot(t)·ing [ˈweinskətiŋ] *n.* ①护壁材料. ②〔集合词〕装有护壁板的墙壁.

wain·wright [ˈweinrait] *n.* (四轮)运货马车制造人.

waist [weist] *n.* ①腰;腰部;(衣服的)腰身. ②〔美〕(女人、小孩子的)背心. ③【海】中部上甲板;船腰;(帆船的)主桅与前桅之间部分;【空】机身中部〔腰部〕. ④【动】蜂腰. *She has no* ～. 她胖得腰身也看不出了. ～**band**, ～**belt** 腰带,裤带. ～**cloth** 围腰布. ～**coat** 〔英〕背心. ～-**deep** *ad., a.* 深到腰(的). ～-**down** *a.* 下半身的. ～-**high** *ad., a.* 深〔高〕齐腰(的). ～**line**【裁缝】腰围.

waist·ing [ˈweistiŋ] *n.* 〔美〕背心料子.

wait [weit] *vi.* ①等,等候,等待 *(for)*. ②服侍,伺候. *This can* ～. 这个不急. — *vt.* 等待;〔口〕耽搁,拖延. *Don't* ～ *dinner for me.* 晚饭不要等我. *W- a moment* 等一等. ***be kept ～ing*** 一直等着. ***keep sb. ～ing*** = ***make sb.*** ～ 叫人等着. ～ ***at [〔美〕on] table*** 侍候(用膳). ～ ***for*** 等;等待. ***W- for it.*** 〔英〕等一等,听着!〔要听者注意下面要讲的令人惊奇的事〕. ～ ***(up)on*** ①服侍,侍奉;伺候. ②拜访,进谒(上面的人). ③跟随〔追随〕着…而来(*May good luck* ～ *upon you.* 祝你幸福). ④〔古〕护卫,侍从. ～ ***out*** 一直等到…完毕. ～ ***(the) table*** 〔Scot.〕=～ at table. — *n.* ①等,等待;等候(的时间);埋伏. ②〔the ～s〕(特别是圣诞节期晚上为募集慈善捐赠在街头或挨户演唱的)募捐合唱队. ***lay [lie in]*** ～ ***for*** 埋伏着等候. ～**-a-bit** 荆棘,有刺植物. ～**-and-see** *a.* 观望的 (*adopt a* ～*-and-see attitude* 采取观望态度). ～**-list** *vt.* 把…登入申请人名单 (*～-list them for the afternoon flight* 把他们列入下午班机的等候名单中).

wait·er [ˈweitə] *n.* ①侍者,侍应员,服务员;盆,托盘. ②等候(时机)的人. ③轻便食品台;运送食物升降机 (= dumbwaiter).

wait·ing [ˈweitiŋ] *n.* 等,等候,等待;侍候,服侍. ***in*** ～ 侍奉(王室)的 (*a lady-in-*～ 侍从女官. *a lord in* ～ 侍从). ～ **game** 待机而动的策略. ～ **maid** 侍女,丫头. ～ **list** 候补〔申请〕人名单. ～ **room** 候车室,候诊室(等). ～ **woman**=～ maid.

wait·ress [ˈweitris] *n.* 女侍应员;〔美〕(家庭的)侍女.

waive [weiv] *vt.* ①放弃(权利、要求等),丢弃(赃物等),撤回;停止,不继续(坚持等). ②暂时搁置,推延. ③省免;撇开,不予考虑. ～ *formalities* 省免正式手续.

waiv·er [ˈweivə] *n.*【法】①放弃,弃权. ②弃权声明书.

Wake [weik] *n.* 威克岛〔北太平洋〕(= ～ Island).

wake[1] [weik] *vi.* ***(woke*** [wəuk], ***waked; waked, woken*** [ˈwəukən]***)*** ①醒,醒来;醒着. ②警觉,醒悟. ③苏醒,复活,活过来. — *vt.* ①弄醒,叫醒 *(up)*;使觉醒,使醒悟,使振作,使发奋*(up)*;激发(感情等);引起(反响等). ③使苏醒,使复活. ④〔古、方〕为…守夜,为…守灵. ***a waking dream*** 白日梦,空想. ***in one's waking hours*** 在醒着的时候. ***kept sb. waking*** 使…一直睡不着. ～ ***the echoes*** 引起回响. ～ ***to*** 发觉,意识到 (～ *to the gravity of the situation* 意识到事态的严重性). ～ ***up*** ①叫醒. ②醒来;振作起来. ***waking or sleeping*** 无论睡着或醒着. — *n.* ①通宵礼拜〔仪式〕;(葬礼前通宵)守灵;通宵宴会. ②〔常 *pl.*〕(Lancashire, Yorkshire 等英国北部工业都市工人的)一年一次的假日.

wake[2] [weik] *n.* (船航过时的)尾波,航迹;【空】尾流;余迹;踪迹;(气流中的)涡区,扰流. ***in the*** ～ ***of*** 在…后接踵而来;在后追随,仿效. ～ **surfing** 滑水〔以机动船拖动的乘浪滑行运动〕.

Wake·field [ˈweikfiːld] *n.* 韦克菲尔德〔姓氏〕.

wake·ful [ˈweikful] *a.* 睡不着的,醒着的;不眠的;警醒的,不睡地警戒着的,警惕性高的. **-ly** *ad.* **-ness** *n.*

wak·en [ˈweikən] *vi.* 醒来;醒着. — *vt.* 弄醒,唤醒;使觉醒,振起,鼓励.

wake·rife [ˈweikraif] *a.* 〔Scot. 英方〕= wakeful.

wake-rob·in [ˈweik-rɔbin] *n.*【植】①〔英〕海芋(属)〔= cuckoopint〕. ②〔美〕延龄草(属);天南星.

wake-up [ˈweikˌʌp] *n.* 〔美口〕北美金翼啄木鸟 (= flicker).

Waks·man [ˈwæksmən] *n.* 瓦克斯曼〔姓氏〕.

Wal·ach [ˈwɔlək] *n.* = Wallach.

Wa·la·chi·a [wɑˈleikiə] *n.* = Wallachia.

Wa·la·chi·an [wɑˈleikiən] *a.* = Wallachian.

Wal·do [ˈwɔːldəu] *n.* 沃尔多〔姓氏,男子名〕.

wale [weil] *n.* ①(肿起的)鞭痕,血痕. ②(织物上隆起的)条纹,棱线;(筐篮上编得特粗而隆起的)箍;(木船船舷上)加固的木条或腰板. — *vt.* ①把…抽出血痕;鞭打. ②在…上织出隆起条纹,为…编上筐箍.

Wal·er [ˈweilə] *n.* 新南威尔士(New South Wales)产的马;澳洲马.

Wales [weilz] *n.* 威尔士〔英国〕.

Wa·ley [ˈweili] *n.* 韦利〔姓氏〕.

Wal·hal·la [vælˈhælə] *n.* = Valhalla.

walk [wɔːk] *vi.* ①走,步行;【篮球】带球走步;(马)用常步走. ②走着去;散步. ③(鬼等)出来. ④〔喻〕处世,处身,生活. — *vt.* ①在…走;踩,踏. ②使行走;使(马)用常步走. ③带着走,领着走. ④〔口〕把(笨重箱子等)一步一步移走. ⑤与…竞走. ③步测;用步行执行. ～ *the floor* 在屋子里走来走去. *I'll* ～ *you ten miles any day you like.* 随便哪一天我跟你竞走十英里吧. ～ ***about*** 闲步;散步. ～ ***after [in] the flesh*** 过(放纵的)肉欲生活. ～ ***around*** 〔美俚〕跳舞. ～ ***... away*** 带走. ～ ***away from*** ①从…走开;从…脱身. ②毫不费力地就超过〔胜过〕. ～ ***away with*** 拐逃,偷走,抢走,夺走. ～ ***by faith*** 过宗教生活. ～ ***chalk mark*** = ～ the chalk. ～ ***one's chalks*** 〔俚〕不告而去,不辞而行. ～ ***in darkness*** 过罪孽生活. ～ ***in sb.'s shoe*** 仿效(某人). ～ ***in the light*** 在光亮中行走,过光明正大的生活. ～ ***into*** ①走进. ②〔俚〕打骂(仆人等). ③〔俚〕大吃. ～ ***off*** ①离开;用走路来消散. ②带走,拉去(犯人等). ～ ***(sb.) off his***

legs 使某人走得脚软腿酸. ~ ***off with*** 拐逃,偷走,抢走(奖品). ~ ***on air*** (因成功)高兴得飘飘然. ~ ***out*** 出去,离开;〔美〕罢工;(丢开人)走掉 *(on.)* ~ ***out with*** 和(异性朋友)出去玩. ~ ***over*** (无竞争者时)独自走完(跑场);轻易击败(对方). ~ ***one's round (s)*** 巡回. ~ ***the boards*** 做演员. ~ ***the chalk*** 顺着车道白线笔直地走〔向警察证明自己没有喝醉〕. ~ ***the earth*** (鬼)出现. ~ ***the hospitals [wards]*** 在医院里实习. ~ ***the plank*** ①被海盗强迫从跳板上坠海. ②被迫辞职;被迫放弃. ~ ***the streets*** ①走马路. ②卖淫. ~ ***through*** 〔美影〕排练(= to rehearse). ~ ***through a part*** 【剧】毫无兴趣地扮演所担任的角色;走过场. ~ ***through life [the world]*** 度日,涉世. ~ ***up*** 使猎犬将(鸟等)惊飞. ***W- up!*** 请进来!〔戏院管门人的呼声〕. ~ ***up to*** 走近. — *n.* ①行走,步行;徒步;散步. ②步法;步态;(马的)慢步. ③步行距离,步程,走路时间;【运】竞走. ④步道,人行道;散步场. ⑤牧羊场; 养禽场,鸡舍; (小狗等的)饲养所;(某种作物的)种植场. ⑥〔英〕负责地区,管区;【林】巡视地区;〔古〕(负贩等)常去的地区. ⑦制绳所(= ropewalk). ⑧生活态度,处世;行为. *a mile* ~ 一英里路程. *I know him by his* ~. 我从步态上就知道是他. ***a cock of the*** ~ 自命不凡的人. ***an upright*** ~ 老老实实的生活态度. ***at a*** ~ 用常步,用普通步子. ***fall into a*** ~ (跑着的马)改成常步行走. ***go at a*** ~ (马)用慢步走;散步. ***in a*** ~ 〔美〕容易地. ~ ***in life*** = ~ ***of life*** 职业;身分;阶级,阶层. **-able** *a.* 适于步行的,可以步行的.

walk·away [ˈwɔːkəwei] *n.* 〔美〕轻易得到的胜利;轻而易举的工作.

walk·down [ˈwɔːkdaun] *n.* 地下室;地下商店.

walk·er [ˈwɔːkə] *n.* ①步行者;散步者. ②〔美〕(供幼孩学步或病残者用)助步车. ③【鸟】走禽. ④〔*pl.*〕走路用的短裤〔鞋〕. ***be much of a*** ~ 爱散步〔步行〕.

Walk·er[1] [ˈwɔːkə] *n.* 沃克〔姓氏〕.

Walk·er[2] [ˈwɔːkə] *int.* 〔俚〕(表示不相信)不会吧!

walk·ie-look·ie [ˈwɔːlkiˈluki] *n.* 手提式电视摄影机.

walk·ie-talk·ie [ˈwɔːkiˈtɔːki] *n.* 〔美〕(背负式)步话机;袖珍无线电话机.

walk-in [ˈwɔːkˌin] *a.* 〔美〕①宽敞得可在里面步行的. ②(不经门廊)直接进入的. — *n.* ①(人进得去的)大壁橱; 大房间. ②容易取得的胜利. ③简易门诊所. ④未经预约而来的人,不请自来的人.

walk·ing [ˈwɔːkiŋ] *n.* ①步行;步法,步态. ②道路状态. — *a.* ①步行(用)的. ②(能)行走的. ③解雇的,被免职的. *a* ~ *plow* (牛马拉的)步犁. *The* ~ *is slippery.* 路滑. ~ **chair** 婴儿学步用的有轮小车(= go cart). ~ **delegate** (工会的)工厂巡视员. ~ **dictionary** 活字典. ~ **dress** 散步服装,出去穿的衣服. ~ **fern** 〔美〕【植】根叶过山蕨菜. ~ **gentleman [lady]** 跑龙套的男〔女〕配角. ~ **leaf** ①【动】蛸. ②【植】根叶过山蕨(= ~ fern). ~ **papers** 〔*pl.*〕〔美口〕解雇(通知). ~ **shorts** 百慕大(齐膝)短裤. ~ **stick** ①〔英〕手杖. ②【动】直翅目昆虫(= stick-insect). ~ **ticket** = ~ papers. ~ **tour** 徒步旅行. ~ **tractor** 手扶拖拉机.

Walk·ley [ˈwɔːkli] *n.* 沃克利〔姓氏〕.

walk-on [ˈwɔːˌkɔn] *n.* 次要演员,跑龙套演员. — *a.* 出现于舞台上的.

walk·out [ˈwɔːkˈaut] *n.* ①〔美〕罢工(者);罢课(者). ②退席(以示抗议). ③告别仪式.

walk·over [ˈwɔːkˈəuvə] *n.* 〔口〕【赛马】只有一匹马参加的比赛,单骑走完跑道;一帆风顺,轻易得胜,轻易得到. *have a* ~ 轻易得胜.

walk-through [ˈwɔːkθruː] *n.* ①(戏剧等的)初排;(电视)不拍摄的排练;草率的表演. ②地下步行道.

walk-up [ˈwɔːkʌp] *n.* 〔美口〕无电梯设备的公寓(房间). — *a.* ①(公寓)无电梯设备的; (房间)在无电梯的楼上的. ②(服务设施等)临街的〔不用走进房子就可得到服务〕.

walk·way [ˈwɔːkˌwei] *n.* 走道,通道,人行道〔尤指其上有遮蔽者〕.

walk·y-talk·y [ˈwɔːkiˈtɔːki] *n.* *(pl.* ***-talk·ies)*** 〔美〕= walkie-talkie.

wall[1] [wɔːl] *n.* ①墙壁;(石、砖等的)围墙;城墙. ②(形状、用途)象墙壁的东西,障壁;土堤,堤防. ③(矿井、容器的)内壁,壁面. ④(路的)靠墙部分,沿墙. *a blank* ~ 没有装饰的墙壁;没有门、窗的墙壁. *the* ~ *of the chest* 【生理】胸壁. *the cell* ~ 【生】细胞壁. ***(can) see through [into] a brick*** ~ 怪有眼光,怪精明〔常作反语用〕. ***drive [push, thrust] (sb.) to the*** ~ 把(某人)逼至绝境. ***give sb. the*** ~ 把靠墙的路让给某人〔表示好感等〕. ***go over the*** ~ 〔美俚〕越狱. ***go to the*** ~ 陷入绝境;(事业)失败;被遗忘. ***hang by the*** ~ 被遗忘. ***jump over the*** ~ 舍弃教会〔教职〕. ***run one's head against a*** ~ 拿头去撞墙;一心要蛮干. ***take the*** ~ ***of sb.*** 不给某人让路;抢着出风头,抢先. ***the Great W- of China*** 万里长城. ***the W-*** ①(把东、西柏林分开的)柏林墙. ②= Wailing W-. ***with one's back to the*** ~ 陷入绝境;以寡敌众;负隅(顽抗). ***within four*** ~***s*** 在房屋内. — *vt.* 筑墙〔城〕围住,筑城防御;筑墙堵塞(孔、口等) *(up).* *a* ~*ed-in garden* 有围墙的花园. *a* ~*ed city* 〔美俚〕监狱. ~**board** 墙板;建筑纸板. ~ **creeper** 【动】旋壁雀. ~**eye** ①(马的)白星眼;(鱼等的)大而闪亮的眼睛. ②大眼鱼. ③【医】角膜白斑;分开性斜视. ~**eyed** *a.* ①白星眼的;眼睛大而闪亮的. ②【医】患角膜白斑〔分开性斜视〕的. ③〔美俚〕喝醉了的. ~**eyed pike** 【动】大眼鲕鲈. ~**eyed pollack** 【动】狭鳕,明太鱼. ~**eye surfperch** 【动】鼓眼鱼,鼓眼浪鲈. ~ **fern** 【植】水龙骨〔一种攀缘植物〕. ~**flower** ①【植】桂竹香. ②〔口〕(舞会中没有舞伴的人,尤指女子)墙花. ~ **painting** 壁画. ~ **paper** 糊墙纸. ~**-paper** *vt.* 在…上糊以壁纸. ~**-piece** (旧时) 装于墙边或船边的小炮. ~ **plate** 【建】承梁板. ~ **rock** 【地,矿】围岩,母岩. ~ **rocket** 【植】芸苔(属). ~ **rue** 【植】墙生铁角蕨. ~ **(telephone) set** 【电话】墙机,挂机. ~**-to-**~ *a.* (地毯)铺满地板的. **-less** *a.* 没有围墙〔城墙〕的.

wall[2] [wɔl] *vt., vi.* 演戏般转动(眼睛).

wal·la [ˈwɑːlə] *n.* = wallah.

wal·la·by [ˈwɔləbi] *n.* *(pl.* ***-bies)*** ★ 也作集合词用. ①【动】鷬;小(种)袋鼠;〔美俚〕(马戏团里的)袋鼠. ②〔俚〕澳洲人. ***on the*** ~ ***(track)*** 〔澳俚〕流浪中;失业.

Wal·lace [ˈwɔlis] *n.* 华莱士〔姓氏,男子名〕.

Wal·lach [ˈwɔlək] *n.* 瓦拉几亚人.

Wal·la·chi·a [wɔˈleikiə] *n.* 瓦拉几亚〔从前欧洲东南部一王国;1861 年与摩尔多瓦合并作罗马尼亚的一部分〕.

Wal·la·chi·an [wɔˈleikiən] *a.* 瓦拉几亚的;瓦拉几亚人〔语〕的. — *n.* 瓦拉几亚人〔语〕.

wal·lah [ˈwɑːlə] *n.* 〔印英〕①干某种事的人,执行某种任务的人〔作后缀用〕. ②〔口〕人. *a punka-*~ 拉布风扇的仆人.

wal·la·roo [wɔləˈruː] *n.* 【动】大袋鼠〔尤指岩大袋鼠(属)〕.

walled [wɔːld] *a.* ①有墙的, 有围墙的. ②设(防御)工事的. ③(如墙似)围着的,用篱笆围着的,设了障碍的.

Wal·ler [ˈwɔlə] *n.* 沃勒〔姓氏〕.

wal·let [ˈwɔlit] *n.* ①钱包, 皮夹子. ②(皮制)零星工具袋. ③〔古〕(旅行者等的)行囊. ~ **curve** 【数】钱囊线.

Wal·lis [ˈwɔlis] *n.* 沃利斯〔姓氏〕.

Wal·loon [wɔˈluːn] *n.* (比利时南部的)窝龙人; 窝龙语〔法语的一种方言〕.

wal·lop [ˈwɔləp] *vt.* 〔口〕猛击;击溃,打垮;【棒球】猛打. — *vi.* 〔方、口〕①窜过去,冲过去;笨拙沉重地走,摇摇晃晃地走;(动物)在泥中打滚; (车等)颠簸. ②沸腾作声. ③〔古、方〕= gallop. — *n.* ①〔方、口〕笨拙的动作. ②〔口〕猛击,痛打;冲击力;〔喻〕作用力,效力. ③〔美口〕强烈快感. ④〔英俚〕啤酒. — *ad.* 〔仅用于下列习语〕: ***go (down)*** ～ 唏哩哗啦地落下.

wal·lop·er [ˈwɔləpə] *n.* ①〔口〕猛击者, 痛殴者. ②〔英方〕特大物, 异常的东西, 怪物, 怪事.

wal·lop·ing [ˈwɔləpiŋ] 〔口〕 *n.* 猛打; 溃败. — *a.* 巨大的; 极好的.

wal·low [ˈwɔləu] *vi.* ①(猪等在泥、水中)翻滚, 打滚; 〔喻〕沉迷(在酒、色等中)*(in)*. ②起浪. ③(烟、水等)迸出, 涌出, 喷出. ～ ***in money*** 非常有钱. — *n.* (水牛等)打滚(的泥潭); 动物打滚形成的凹坑.

wall·pa·per·ize [ˈwɔːlpeipəraiz] *vt.* 使成废币, 使(纸币)无价值.

Wall Street [ˈwɔːl striːt] 华尔街〔美国纽约市的一条街道, 是美国大垄断组织和金融机构的集中地〕. **Wall Streeter** 华尔街大老板.

wall·y [ˈweili] *a.* 〔Scot.〕①好的, 第一流的; 漂亮的. ②魁伟的, 强大的, 健壮的. ③令人愉快的. — *n.* 装饰品, 玩具; 〔*pl.*〕漂亮的服饰.

wal·ly·drag [ˈweilidræg] *n.* 〔Scot.〕 ①孱弱而发育不良的动物. ②懒散的人; 〔尤指〕懒婆娘 (= wally-draigle).

Walms·ley [ˈwɔːmzli] *n.* 沃姆斯利〔姓氏〕.

wal·nut [ˈwɔːlnət] *n.* 【植】胡桃; 胡桃树; 胡桃木. *an English [a Persian]* ～ 薄壳核桃. ***over the ～s and the wine*** 在饭后闲谈中, 在餐后吃水果等的时候.

Wal·pole [ˈwɔːlpəul] *n.* 沃波尔〔姓氏〕.

Wal·pur·gis [vælˈpuəgis, vɑːl-] **Night** *n.* 华尔普吉斯之夜〔四月三十日夜, 民间传说是夜女巫在德国布罗肯山聚会, 进行狂欢酒宴〕.

wal·rus [ˈwɔːlrəs] *n.* 【动】海象; 〔美俚〕矮胖子.

Walsh [wɔːlʃ] *n.* 沃尔什〔姓氏〕.

Wal·ter [ˈwɔːltə] *n.* ①沃尔特〔姓氏, 男子名〕. ②〔w-〕飞机应急雷达发射机.

Wal·ton [ˈwɔːltən] *n.* 沃尔顿〔姓氏, 男子名〕.

waltz [wɔːls] *n.* 华尔兹舞(曲), 圆舞(曲); 〔喻〕轻松愉快的工作. *a deux-temps [trois-temps]* ～ 二拍子[三拍子]华尔兹. — *vi.* ①跳华尔兹舞; 〔口〕轻快顺利地走动; 旋转. ②轻易地进行 *(through)*. ～ *across the streets* 蹦蹦跳跳[轻快地]走过街去. ～ *off on the ear* 〔美〕急匆匆做. ～ *through an exam* 轻而易举地通过考试. — *vt.* ①与…跳华尔兹舞. ②(象跳华尔兹舞一样)轻快地引领(他人). **-er** *n.* 跳华尔兹舞的人.

wam·ble [ˈwɑːmbl, ˈwæmbl] *vi.* 〔主方〕①晕转. ②摇摆, 摇幌, 眼花. ③〔废〕嗯心; (胃产生)嗯心感. — *n.* 〔主方〕①晕, 昏转; 摇摆, 摇幌. ②嗯心感. **-bly** *a.*

wame [weim] *n.* 〔Scot. 英方〕肚子, 腹.

wam·pa·no·ag [ˌwɑːmpəˈnəuæg] *n.* ***(pl.*** ～***(s))*** 瓦帕浓人〔北美印第安人阿尔衮琴族一部落, 后移居美国马萨诸塞州东南部〕.

wam·pum [ˈwɔmpəm] *n.* ①(以前印地安人作货币或饰品的)贝壳串珠. ②〔美俚〕钱.

wan[1] [wɔn] *a.* ①苍白的; 没有血色的. ②病弱的, 软弱无力的. ③〔古〕暗淡的, 阴暗的.

wan[2] [wɑːn, wɔːn] 〔废〕 win 的过去式.

Wan·a·ma·ker [ˈwɔnəmeikə] *n.* 沃纳梅克〔姓氏〕.

wand [wɔnd] *n.* ①(柳树等的)嫩枝, 细枝. ②(魔术师的)短杖; 权杖; 【乐】指挥棒. ③〔英〕(做箭靶的)细枝条; 〔美〕(做箭靶的)狭长木板.

Wan·da [ˈwɔndə] *n.* 旺达〔女子名〕.

wan·der [ˈwɔndə] *vi.* ①(无目的地)漫步, 漫游; 徘徊, 彷徨; 流浪, 漂移. ②迷路; 走岔, 离开. ③(河)曲曲折折地流; (山脉)蜿蜒错列. ④(思想等)离开正道; 错乱; 离题乱说. ⑤【医】游走. ～ *from the subject* (谈话)离开本题. *He is* ～*ing.* = *His mind is* ～*ing.* 他正(烧热得)发昏. *His wits are* ～*ing.* 他有点疯了. — *vt.* 〔诗〕漫游. ～ ***about*** 徘徊, 彷徨, 流浪. — *n.* 徘徊, 彷徨, 流浪. **-er** *n.* ①漫游者, 流浪汉. ②仿徨者; 迷路的动物.

wan·der·ing [ˈwɔndəriŋ] *a.* ①漫游的; 徘徊的. ②流离失所的; 迷途的. ③(河流)曲折的. ④错乱的; 胡说乱讲的. ⑤【植】攀绕的; 有卷须的. ⑥【医】游走的. — *n.* 〔常 *pl.*〕①徘徊; 流浪; 漫游; 漂移, 偏移. ②错乱, 胡话. ③【地】迁[漂]移. *the* ～*s of a madman* 狂人的胡话. ～ **albatross** 【动】阿房鸟. ～ **cell** 【生】游走细胞. **W- Jew** ①〔the W- J-〕流浪的犹太人〔中古传说中一个名叫 Joannes Buttadeus 的犹太人, 因其嘲弄被钉上十字架的耶稣, 遭天谴永远流浪〕; 流浪者. ②〔w-Jew, W-jew〕【植】攀绕植物. ～ **nursery** 移动苗圃.

Wan·der·jahr [ˈvɑːndəjɑː] *n.* ***(pl. -jah·re*** [-jɑːrə]***)*** 〔G.〕漫游时代〔原为欧洲中世纪习俗, 学徒满师后就业前到各地漫游一年〕.

Wan·der·lust [ˈvɑːndəlust] *n.* 〔G.〕旅行热; 流浪癖.

wan·der·oo [ˌwɔndəˈruː] *n.* 【动】龄猴, 大黑猿.

W and W = Wash and Wear 【织】洗了就可穿; 免烫.

wane [wein] *vi.* (月)缺损, 亏; *(opp.* wax*)*; (光、势力等)衰落, 衰微; 减少. ～ ***to the close*** 接近末了. ***wax and*** ～ 盈亏; 盛衰. — *n.* ①月亏(期). ②衰退(期). ③(木材的)缺损. ***on [in] the*** ～ (月)正在亏缺中; 衰落中, 减少中.

wane·y [ˈweini] *a.* ***(wan·i·er; wan·i·est)*** ①衰落的; 减少的; 没落的. ②常缺损的; 不整齐的〔尤指锯解的木料还带树皮的〕.

wan·gle [ˈwæŋgl] *vt.* 〔口〕①用计谋办到, 巧妙地取得. ②(从人群中)扭身挤出; 从(困境中)脱身. ③哄骗; 掩饰, 捏造; 伪造. ～ *an extra week's holiday* 巧妙地弄到一周额外的休假. ～ *business records* 伪造业务记录. ～ *a book out of sb.* 从某人手上骗得一本书. — *vi.* ①扭身挤出, 脱身. ②玩弄诡计; 花言巧语. — *n.* ①诡计; 哄骗; 骗得的东西. ②虚饰, 伪造.

wan·i·gan, wan·ni·gan [ˈwɑːnigən] *n.* 〔美〕①(伐木场的食物等)贮藏柜. ②小寝室; 炊事棚车.

wan·ion [ˈwɑːnjən, ˈwɔːn-] *n.* 〔古〕不幸, 倒霉; 灾祸; 天灾, 灾害.

wan·na [ˈwɔnə] 〔美俚〕 = want to.

wan·nish [ˈwɔniʃ] *a.* 有点苍白的.

want [wɔnt] *vt.* ①(想)要, 想望; 想得到. ②需要, 必要; 必须. ③征求; 征聘; 通缉. ④缺少, 没有; 不够, 差欠. *I* ～ *you to come.* (=〔俚〕*I* ～ *for you to come.* 或 *I* ～ *(that) you should come*). 我希望你来. *What do you* ～ *with me?* 你找我有什么事? *You're* ～*ed.* 有人找你. *You won't be* ～*ed this afternoon.* 今天下午没事需要你做. *the* ～*ed man* 被通缉的人. *You don't* ～ *to be rude.* 你不必粗暴. *Wanted a typist* 征聘打字员. *Situation* ～*ed by a typist* 打字员求职. *It* ～*s 3 inches of 6 feet.* 六英尺差三英寸. *It* ～*s something of perfection* 还有一点不完满的地方. — *vi.* ①缺少, 没有; 不够, 差 *(in)*. ②生活困难, 穷困. ～ *in stature* 身长不够. *Let him* ～ *for nothing.* 不要让他短缺什么东西〔生活上有什么匮乏〕. ～ ***in [out, off]*** 〔口、方〕想要进来[出去] (*The cat* ～*s in.* 那只猫想进来). ～ ***to*** 〔口〕应该(*You* ～ *to eat a balanced diet.* 你应该吃营养均衡的食物). — *n.* ①缺乏, 不足; 需要. ②匮乏, 穷困, 贫穷. ③欲求; 〔主 *pl.*〕 想要的东西, 必需品. *know the bitterness of* ～ 知道贫穷的苦处. *a man of few* ～*s* 欲求少的人. ***for*** ～ ***of*** 因缺少…. ***in*** ～ 贫穷. ***in*** ～ ***of*** 需要…(的); 缺少…(的). ～ **ad.** (报刊上的)征聘[征求, 求职]广告. ～ **column** (报纸上的)征聘[求职]栏. ～ **list** (收藏家或博物馆等向商人发出的)需购艺术品货单. **-able** *a.* 称心的, 有吸引力的. **-age** *n.* 缺少(量). **-er** *n.* ①缺乏者; 贫乏者. ②〔方〕求偶者. **-less** *a.* 无欲求的.

want·ing [ˈwɔntiŋ] *a.* ①短缺的, 缺失的; 不足的; 不够的 *(in)*. ②〔方〕智力不足的, 低能的. *He is* ～ *in honesty.* 他不老实. *be a bit* ～ 有点笨. — *prep.* 缺, 短少. *a year* ～ *three days* 一年差三天. *W- courage, victory is*

impossible. 没有勇气就无法取得胜利。
wan·ton [ˈwɔntən] *a.* ①放肆的,放纵的;任性的;反复不定的,变化无常的;卤莽的,粗暴的;荒唐的,没有理由的,胡作非为的。②行为不检的,淫荡的。③淘气的,顽皮的;嬉闹的。④〔诗〕(花草)繁茂的。*a ~ breeze* 变化无常的微风。*~ rivers* 奔流的江河。*~ profusion* 浪费。*~ mischief* 瞎胡闹。*a ~ woman* 荡妇。*a ~ child* 顽童。— *n.* 水性杨花的人,荡妇;〔罕〕任性的孩子。— *vi.* ①任性,反复无常;放肆。②挥霍;胡闹,嬉戏。③繁茂。— *vt.* 挥霍,浪费。**-ly** *ad.* **-ness** *n.*
wan·y [ˈweini] *a.* ***(wan·i·er; wan·i·est)*** = waney.
wap [wɔp] *vt.* ①〔方〕打;打败,击败。②〔古〕= whop.
wap·en·take [ˈwɔpənteik] *n.* 【英史】百户村 (= hundred).
wap·i·ti [ˈwɔpiti] *n.* ***(pl. ~s,*** 〔集合词〕***~)*** 【动】(北美)马鹿。
Wap·pen·s(c)haw [ˈwɑːpənʃɔː] *n.*〔Scot.〕①【史】武装检阅。②来复枪射击比赛。
wap·per-jawed [ˈwɔpədʒɔːd] *a.* 〔英方〕歪下巴的;〔美口〕突下巴的。
war[1] [wɔː, wɔə] *n.* ①战争;军事。②兵学,战术。③武器,兵器。④斗争;敌意,不和。*an aggressive ~* 侵略战争。*a people's ~* 人民战争。*the civil ~* 国内战争。*conventional ~* 常规战争。*guerrilla ~* 游击战。*nuclear ~* 核战争。*People's W- of Liberation* 人民解放战争。*revolutionary ~* 革命战争。*the W- of American Independence* 〔英〕= *the W- of Independence* 〔美〕(美国)独立战争。*the seat [theater] of ~* 战场。*a ~ criminal* 战犯。*a prisoner of ~* 战俘。*the ~ of the pen* 笔战。*a ~ of words* 舌战。*a ~ of annihilation* 歼灭战。*a ~ of attrition* 消耗战。*a ~ of propaganda* 宣传战。*art of ~* 战术,兵法。*the Secretary (of State) for W- = the W- Secretary* 〔英〕陆军大臣。*the W- Department* 〔美〕陆军部〔国防部中的一部〕。*the W- Office* 〔英〕陆军部。*~ expenditure* 军费。*~ industries* 军事工业。***at ~ with*** 和…交战;和…不和。***declare ~*** *(against; on, upon)* (对…)宣战。***drift into ~*** 逐渐卷入〔陷入〕战争。***go to the ~(s)*** 去参军;〔古〕出征。***go to ~*** *(against)* (和…)进行战争。***have been in the ~s*** 打过仗,受过伤;〔谑〕经历过忧患,吃过苦头。***levy [make, wage] ~*** *(on, upon, against)* (和…)开战,作战。— *a.* 战争的,军事的。— *vi.* 打仗,作战;斗争,竞争 *(with; against)*。— *vt.* 〔Scot.〕击败。*~* **baby** ①战时诞生的孩子;士兵的私生子。②因战争需要而大为发展的工业。*~***bird** 〔美俚〕作战飞机。*~* **bonnet** (印第安人的)战帽。*~* **chest** 战争基金;竞选基金。*~* **cloud** 战云。*~* **colour** 卡其色,保护色。*~* **correspondent** 随军记者。*~* **crime** 战争罪。*~* **cry** 战斗呐喊;政党的(战斗)口号〔标语〕。*~* **fatigue** 厌战(情绪)。*~* **footing** 战时编制;战时体制。*~* **game** 募拟演习 (= kriegspiel)。*~***head** 弹头 (*a nuclear ~-head* 核弹头)。*~* **horse** 〔古、诗〕军马,战马;〔口语〕老兵;〔口〕老练的人;〔美俚〕男子气概的女人。*~***lock** 〔古〕魔术师;骗子。*~***lord** 军阀。*~*-**monger** 战争贩子。*~* **paint** 印第安人打仗前身上涂抹的颜料;〔美俚〕盛装,正式宴会打扮;化妆(品)。*~* **party** 主战派。*~***path** (美洲印第安人的)征途;〔转义〕敌对行动〔情绪〕。*~***plane** 军用飞机。*~* **scape** 战争〔战场〕景色(图片,画幅)。*~***ship** 军舰。*~* **song** 军歌。*~***time** 战时。*~***vessel** 军舰。*~*-**weariness** 厌战情绪。*~*-**weary** *a.* 厌战的。*~***worn** *a.* 久经战阵的;被战争弄得筋疲力尽的;被战火破坏的,饱经战祸的。
war[2] [wɔː] *a., ad.* 〔Scot.〕= worse.
War. = Warwickshire.
war·ble[1] [ˈwɔːbl] *vi., vt.* ①(鸟)啼啭;(人)象鸟啭似地唱,用颤音唱。②〔美〕=yodel. — *n.* 啼啭;颤音;颤音歌唱(法);唱歌。
war·ble[2] [ˈwɔːbl] *n.* ①(马背的)鞍瘤;(马背的)虻肿。②牛蝇(的幼虫)。*~ fly* 【动】皮蝇。
war·bler [ˈwɔːblə] *n.* ①鸣禽;(颤音)歌手。②【动】莺莺。③【物】颤音器;【电】电抗管调制器;频率摆动器。
war·craft [ˈwɔːkrɑːft] *n.* 〔*sing., pl.*〕①军舰;军用飞机。②战略;战术,谋略。
Ward [wɔːd] *n.* 沃德〔姓氏,男子名〕。
ward [wɔːd] *n.* ①监视,监督,监护,守护;监禁;防卫。②【法】受监护人*(opp.* guardian*)*。③(行政)区,选举区。④病房,病室;(监狱的)监房;(济贫院的)收容室;(城堡内的)旷场。⑤〔古〕看守人;守卫队。⑥(锁内的)齿凸;(钥匙的)齿凹。⑦(剑术等的)防卫姿势。*an isolation [a maternity] ~* 隔离〔产科〕病房。*a condemned ~* 死刑犯监房。*a casual ~* 临时收容室。***be in ~ to*** 在…的监护下(*To whom is this patient in ~?* 这病人由谁监护?)。***be under ~*** 被监禁着。***keep watch and ~*** 日夜监视。***put sb. in ~*** 对某人加以保护;监禁(某人)。— *vt.* ①〔古〕保护,守护。②收容。③挡住,架住,击退,防止 *(off)*。*~ off an attack* 挡开对手的攻击。*~* **boss** 〔美〕选区政客。*~* **heeler** 〔美俚〕〔贬〕选区政客的走卒;为政党拉选票的小角色。
-ward(s) *suf.* 向…: south*wards*.
ward·ed [ˈwɔːdid] *a.* 有看守的,有监守的,有防护的〔如用锁或钥匙锁上的〕。
Ward·en [ˈwɔːdn] *n.* 〔有时用 w-〕华登冬梨〔供煮食〕。
ward·en [ˈwɔːdn] *n.* ①〔古〕看门人,看守人;保管人;监察人;〔美〕典狱长;【史】摄政者。②〔英〕校长;(同业公会)会长;院长;某些主管官员的称号;【史】州长,县长,区长(等);教区委员;〔美 Connecticut 州〕市长。③民间防空员〔消防员〕。**-cy, -ship** *n.* 看守人〔保管人等〕的职位〔职权〕。
ward·er [ˈwɔːdə] *n.* ①(监狱)看守;保管员;守望员;卫兵。②(王或司令官的)权杖。
Ward·our [ˈwɔːdə-] **Street** 沃德街〔伦敦古董(店)街〕。***Wardour-street English*** 古腔古调的英语。
ward·ress [ˈwɔːdris] *n.* 〔英〕监狱女看守员。
ward·robe [ˈwɔːdrəub] *n.* ①衣橱。②藏衣室。③(个人、剧团的)全部服装。*a ~ dealer* 旧衣商。*a ~ trunk* 衣橱式衣箱。*a ~ mistress* 服装女保管员。
ward-room [ˈwɔːdrum] *n.* 【海】①(舰长以外军官休息及进餐用的)军官室。②〔集合词〕(舰长以外)全部军官。
ward·ship [ˈwɔːdʃip] *n.* ①监护。②(封建主对佃户的子女和财产的)监护权。
ware[1] [wɛə] *n.* ①〔用作复合词〕制品,成品,器皿,物件〔如 hardware, ironware 等〕;〔常冠以产地地名〕陶器。②〔*pl.*〕商品,货品;(演员等的)看家本领。*glass ~s* 料器。*toilet ~s* 化妆品。*small ~s* 小百货〔带子、钮扣等〕。*praise one's own ~s* 自夸自赞。
ware[2] [wɛə] *a.* ①〔古,诗〕谨慎的,小心的。②有知觉的,意识〔注意〕到的。
ware[3] [wɛə] *vt.* ①小心,留心,注意。②避免。*W- the dog!* 小心狗! *W- your money.* 不要浪费银钱。*W- the bottle!* 请节制喝酒。
ware·house [ˈwɛəhaus] *n.* ①仓库,货栈。②批发庄;大零售店。— [-hauz] *vt.* 把…存入仓库,使落栈;把…存入保税仓库。**-man** *n.* 仓库业者;仓库管理员;批发商。
ware·room [ˈwɛəruːm] *n.* 商品贮藏室;商品陈列室。
war·fare [ˈwɔːfɛə] *n.* 战争,战争状态〔行为〕,斗争;冲突;军事行动。*the science of ~* 战争科学,战术(学)。*chemical ~* 化学战。*To learn ~ through ~.* 从战争学习战争。
war·fa·rin [ˈwɔːfərin] *n.* ①杀鼠灵,华法令。②【医】华法令阻凝剂〔用华法令与氢氧化钠中和的一种阻凝剂〕。
war·gasm [ˈwɔːgæzəm] *n.* 〔美〕全面战争突然爆发;全面战争危机。
war·i·ly [ˈwɛərili] *ad.* 注意地,谨慎地,小心地。
war·i·ness [ˈwɛərinis] *n.* 注意,谨慎,小心。

war·like [ˈwɔːlaik] *a.* ①战争的,军事的;好战的;尚武的。②有战争迹象的。～ *preparations* 备战。～ *spirit* 尚武精神。～ *times* 乱世。

warm [wɔːm] *a.* ①暖和的,温暖的;保暖的。②热情的,热心的,热烈的;多情的。③易怒的;兴奋的;激烈的,激昂的。④亲热的;亲密的。⑤(颜色等)有温暖感觉的,暖色的;浓艳的;挑拨性的,色情的;【猎】(臭迹等)新鲜的,强烈的。⑥〔俚〕富裕的,宽裕的。⑦〔口〕费力的,困难的;不愉快的,呆不下去的。⑧〔口〕差一点就要找到〔猜中〕的。⑨(官员等)职位稳固的。*a* ～ *heart* 热情的心。*a* ～ *water port* 不冻港。*a* ～ *welcome* 热烈的欢迎。*a* ～ *temper* 急性子。*a* ～ *friend* 亲密的朋友。～ *descriptions* 色情描写。*The place became too* ～ *for him.* 那里他已经呆不下去了。***be getting*** ～ (隐藏者、待猜事物)差一点就要被找到〔猜中〕;〔喻〕接近真实。***get*** ～ 暖起来;激昂起来,兴奋起来。***grow*** ～ 激昂,热烈。***have*** ～ ***work in doing it*** 那件事做起来有困难。***in*** ～ ***blood*** 生气,激忿。***keep a place*** ～ (代某人)暂时占据某地。***keep it*** ～ 〔美〕继续讨论某一问题〔不使冷却〕。***make things*** ～ ***for sb.*** 烦扰〔攻击〕某人,使某人不愉快。～ ***with*** 加开水和糖的白兰地酒 (*cf.* cold without)。～ ***words*** 〔美俚〕骂上帝(的话)。～ ***work*** 吃力的〔危险的〕工作;激战,苦斗。— *vt.* ①暖,使暖,使加温;使热心,激发,鼓励,使兴奋。②〔口〕占(坐位)。③〔口〕鞭打,责打。～ *oneself at the fire* 烤火取暖。— *vi.* 暖,变暖;热中;兴奋;同情 (*to; towards*)。～ ***sb.'s jacket*** 〔口〕打某人。～ ***up*** 加热,热一热(汤);变暖;热中〔热心〕起来,兴奋起来;【运】作准备动作;(机件等)预热。— *n.* 〔口〕暖一暖。～ **blood** ①温血〔指哺乳动物及禽类体温,在 98°—112°F. 之间〕。**～-blooded** *a.* 温血的;热血的;热烈的;热情的。～ **corner** 〔口〕激战地区;不愉快的处境。～ **front** 【气】暖锋。**～-hearted** *a.* 热情的,恳切的,亲切的。**～-heartedness** 热忱。～ **sector** 【气】暖区。～ **spring** 水温低于 98° F. 的温泉。

warmed-over [ˈwɔːmdˈəuvə] *a.* ①再热的,回锅的。②老一套的,"炒冷饭"的,旧事重提的。～ *ideas* 重弹的老调。～ *hash* 回锅肉丁,回锅肉丝。

warm·er [ˈwɔːmə] *n.* 取暖器,加温器;使热的人〔东西〕。*a foot-*～ 脚炉。

warm·ing-pan [ˈwɔːmiŋpæn] *n.* ①暖床器;火盆;焊炉。②(本人就职前的)代理人。

warm·ing-up [ˈwɔːmiŋˈʌp] *a.* 【运】(比赛前的)准备动作的;热身的。

warm·ly [ˈwɔːmli] *ad.* 暖和地,温暖地;热心地;亲热地。

warmth [wɔːmθ] *n.* ①暖和,温暖。②热心,热情;兴奋;忿激;亲切,诚恳。

warm-up [ˈwɔːmˈʌp] *n.* ①加温;使暖,变暖。②【运】(比赛前的)准备动作,热身;(引擎,马达,收音机等)预热。

warn [wɔːn] *vt.* ①警戒,警告;训诫,告诫。②预先通知,预告。～ *(sb.) against (another)* 告诫(某人)提防(别人)。～ *(sb.) of (danger)* 警告(某人)有危险。

War·ner [ˈwɔːnə] *n.* 沃纳〔姓氏,男子名〕。

warn·er [ˈwɔːnə] *n.* 警告者;通知者,告知者。

warn·ing [ˈwɔːniŋ] *n.* ①警告,警报;警戒;训诫。②预告,通知。③号召,召唤。④殷鉴;前兆。*Don't blame the speaker but take his words as a* ～. 言者无罪,闻者足戒。*a beacon lighted as a* ～ 报警的烽火。*a* ～ *network* 警报网。*a* ～ *order* 准备命令。***at a minute's [moment's]*** ～ (不预先通知地)突然之间。***give*** *(sb. a month's* ～*)* 前一个月通知(解雇)。***give*** ～ 警告;告诫,预告。***take*** ～ ***by*** *(me)*. 拿(我)做前车之鉴吧。～ **coloration** 【动】警戒色。～ **track** 【棒球】警告跑道〔用以警告接球的外场队员已接近看台等〕。

warp [wɔːp] *vt.* ①使卷曲,翘曲,弯曲;挠曲,扭歪。②歪曲,使偏倾。③【海】用绞船索牵曳。④(为利用河泥等沉积物肥田而)引水淹没(土地)。⑤【纺织】整经。*timber* ～*ed by heat* 因受热而翘曲的木材。*judgement* ～*ed by self-interest* 被私利所歪曲了的判断。— *vi.* 卷曲,翘曲;歪曲;歪,偏。— *n.* ①翘曲;歪曲,歪斜;偏倾;乖戾。②(织物的)经 (*opp.* woof)。③【海】绞船索。④【农】沉泥。～ **beam** 【纺】经轴。**-er** *n.* 【纺】整经工;整经机。

war·rant [ˈwɔrənt] *n.* ①正当理由;根据;(被授予的)权力。②保证;证明文件;许可证,执照;收据;认股证书;栈单;委任状;授权证书;【法】搜查证,拘票(等)。③【商】付款通知单;(仓库给货主的)栈单。④【军】准尉委任状。*Diligence is a sure* ～ *of success.* 勤勉是成功的可靠保证。***search*** ～ (住宅)搜查证。～ ***for [of] arrest*** 拘票。～ ***of attorney*** 诉讼代理委托状。***with the*** ～ ***of a good conscience*** 问心无愧地。***without a*** ～ 没有正当理由地。— *vt.* ①证明…正当,证明…具有充分根据。②授权,批准。③保证,保用(…年)。④〔口〕断定。*Coffee* ～*ed pure.* 咖啡保证纯净。*Nothing can* ～ *such rudeness.* 这样无礼是不行的。*This* ～*s our attention.* 这是值得我们注意的。***I [I'll]*** ～ ***(you)*** 〔插入句〕的确,真的。**～-officer** 〔英美陆海空军〕准尉 (*a chief* ～*-officer* 〔美陆空军〕一级准尉。*a commissioned* ～*-officer* 〔美海军〕一级准尉)。

war·rant·a·ble [ˈwɔrəntəbl] *a.* ①可保证的。②可承认〔批准〕的;可以认为是正当的。③(公鹿)已达可猎年龄的〔五、六岁〕。**-a·bly** *ad.*

war·ran·tee [ˌwɔrənˈtiː] *n.* 【法】被保证人。

war·rant·er [ˈwɔrəntə], **war·ran·tor** [-tɔː] *n.* 保证人,担保人。

war·ran·ty [ˈwɔrənti] *n.* ①保证(书)。②根据,理由。③授权(证)。④【法】(商品等的)保单。～ **deed** 【法】(房地产)担保契约。

War·ren [ˈwɔrin] *n.* 沃伦〔姓氏,男子名〕。

war·ren [ˈwɔrin] *n.* ①养兔场;〔英〕【法】野生鸟兽育猎特许地〔特权〕。②大杂院,住户拥挤的公寓〔地区〕。**-er** 养兔场主,养兔场看管人。

war·ring [ˈwɔːriŋ] *a.* 进行战争的,交战的;斗争的;敌对的;势不两立的。

war·ri·or [ˈwɔriə] *n.* 勇士,战士,武士,军人。*the Unknown W- [Soldier]* (遗体被选出代表阵亡将士接受国葬的)无名战士。*a* ～ *nation* 勇武的民族。

War·saw [ˈwɔːsɔː], **War·sza·wa** [vɑːˈʃɑːvə] *n.* 华沙〔波兰首都〕。

war·saw [ˈwɔːsɔː] *n.* 〔美〕【动】黑石斑鱼 (*Epinephelus nigritus*) 〔产于西印度洋和美国佛罗里达州的暖水海洋中〕。

wart [wɔːt] *n.* ①【医】疣,肉赘,瘊子。②【植】树瘤。③〔美俚〕讨厌的人,不重要的人。***paint (sb.) with his*** ～***s*** 把(某人)一切如实地描绘出来。～ **hog** 【动】(非洲野生)疣猪。

War·ton [ˈwɔːtn] *n.* 沃顿〔姓氏〕。

wart·y [ˈwɔːti] *a.* ***(-i·er; -i·est)*** 疣似的;有瘊子的;(有)树瘤的。

War·wick [ˈwɔrik] *n.* 沃里克〔姓氏〕。

War·wick·shire [ˈwɔrikʃiə] *n.* 沃里克郡〔英格兰中南部〕。

war·y [ˈweəri] *a.* ***(-i·er; -i·est)*** 小心的,留神的;谨慎的。**-i·ly** *ad.*

was [强 wɔz; 弱 wəz] be 的过去式,第一人称及第三人称单数。

Wash [wɔʃ], **the** 沃希湾〔英国东部 Norfolk 与 Lincolnshire 两郡之间的海湾〕。

Wash. = Washington 华盛顿〔美国州名〕。

wash [wɔʃ] *vt.* ①洗,洗涤。②洗掉,洗去 (*off; out*);洗净,洗清;【矿】洗(矿),冲洗,冲选。③(雨露)滋润;(浪)冲击。④〔主用被动语态〕冲走,冲垮 (*away; off, along; up; down*);冲刷,冲蚀。⑤薄薄着色于;薄薄镀(金等)于。*The rose is* ～*ed with dew.* 蔷薇有露水滋润。*a district* ～*ed by the sea* 沿海地区。*The bridge was* ～*ed*

W

away. 桥被冲走了. *the walls ~ed with blue* 淡淡地刷上蓝色的墙壁. *a gold ~ed cup* 镀金杯子. — *vi.* ①洗(脸、手等),洗身体,洗澡. ②洗衣服(等). ③可洗, 经洗. ④〔口〕(话等)可靠,过硬,经得住考验. ⑤冲洗, 哗啦哗啦地冲击. ~ *before dinner* 吃饭前洗手. *This cloth ~ well [won't ~].* 这布经洗[不经洗]. *That story won't ~.* 那段话靠不住. ***(be) ~ed out*** 退了色的; 筋疲力尽的; 失败了的; 形容憔悴的; 被冲蚀的. ***be ~ed up*** 〔美俚〕筋疲力竭的,失败了的; 终止了的,断绝了的. ***W- and Use [Wear]*** 〔商业用语〕洗后不烫即平,免烫 (= ~-wear). ~ ***against*** 洗,洗刷, 冲洗. ~ ***down*** 洗掉; 冲进,冲下. ~ ***for a living*** 做洗衣生意. ~ ***one's dirty linen at home [in public]*** 〔美〕掩藏[暴露]家丑. ~ ***one's hands*** ①洗手;〔婉〕上厕所. ②洗手不干, 断绝…的关系 *(of).* ~ ***oneself*** 洗澡. ~ ***out*** ① *vt.* 漱(口);〔美〕(洪水)冲走;〔美俚〕淘汰,剔除, 排斥, 丢掉. ② *vi.* 颜色被洗掉,洗去;(铁路等)被冲走. ~ ***up*** ①洗(手、碗碟). ②〔美口〕洗手不干, 不再过问. — *n.* ①洗濯, 洗涤;【矿】洗矿, 冲选; 〔the ~〕〔集合词〕洗濯物. ②〔the ~〕奔流;(浪的)冲洗,冲击; 波浪声;(船、飞机驶过后的) 尾流; 涡流; 〔美〕浅水湾; (常受涝害的) 低湿地;〔美西部〕干河床. ③冲积物,冲积土,污泥. ④(厨房的)泔水〔猪的食料〕; 稀薄的食物. ⑤洗涤剂; 化妆水; (涂墙面的)水泥浆. ⑥淡彩,淡涂; 金属涂覆, (金等的)薄镀. ⑦无聊话, 废话. *This soup is mere ~.* 这汤淡得没味儿. ***come out in the ~*** 〔俚〕暴露, 真相大白. ***get a ~*** 洗. ***hang out the ~*** 〔美俚〕降落伞兵. ***send to the ~*** 送去洗. ***stand ~*** 经洗. ~ **basin** 脸盆. ~ **basket** 洗衣篓. ~**board** 洗衣板;【建】壁脚板;【船】防波板. ~**bowl** 〔美〕脸盆. ~**cloth** 毛巾. ~**day** 〔美〕洗衣日〔普通是星期一〕. ~ **drawing** (透明色) 水彩画; 淡墨画. ~ **goods** 耐洗纺物[衣服]. ~**-hand basin** 脸盆. ~**-hand stand** 脸盆架. ~**house** 洗衣所; 洗衣作. ~ **leather** 麂皮,软皮; 充软皮. ~**out** 〔美〕①(道路、桥梁的)冲溃,冲溃的土地. ②〔俚〕大失败. ③失败者; 无用的人,靠不住的人. ~**rag** 〔美〕毛巾. ~**-room** 〔美〕厕所,盥洗室. ~ **sale [trade]** 〔美〕(股票的)虚抛,虚卖. ~**stand** 脸盆架. ~**tub** 洗衣盆; 洗涤槽. ~**-up** 【矿】①冲洗出来的矿沙量. ②洗涤(处所). ~**-woman** 〔美〕= washer-woman. **-able** *a.* 经洗的.

wash·er [ˈwɔʃə] *n.* ①洗涤者. ②洗衣机; 洗涤器[机]. ③【矿】洗矿机; 洗煤机. ④【机】垫圈. ~**-drier** 附有脱水机的洗衣机. ~**man** 洗衣工. ~**woman** ①洗衣女工. ②【鸟】〔英方〕斑羽鹡鸰.

wash·ing [ˈwɔʃiŋ] *n.* ①洗涤; 〔集合词〕需要洗涤的衣物. ②洗出物. ③镀金. ④= washsale. ⑤〔*pl.*〕洗涤剂. — *a.* 洗濯用的; 经洗的. ~ **machine** 洗涤机. ~ **soda** 洗用碱,晶碱. ~ **stand** 洗脸架, 脸盆架.

Wash·ing·ton[1] [ˈwɔʃiŋtən] *n.* ①华盛顿〔姓氏〕. ② **George** ~ 华盛顿〔1732—1799, 美国第一任总统(1789—1797)〕. ~**'s Birthday** (美国首任总统)华盛顿诞辰〔二月二十二日,美国大多数州的法定假日〕.

Wash·ing·ton[2] [ˈwɔʃiŋtən] *n.* ①华盛顿(市)〔美国首都〕; 美国政府. ~, ***D.C.*** (或 ~, District of Columbia) 哥伦比亚特区华盛顿〔即美国首都华盛顿〕. ②华盛顿〔美国州名〕(= ~ State). ~ **pie** 〔美〕夹心(多层)蛋糕.

Wash·ing·to·ni·an [ˌwɔʃiŋˈtəunien] *a.* 华盛顿市[州]的(人的). — *n.* 华盛顿市[州]的人.

wash·y [ˈwɔʃi] *a.* *(-i·er; -i·est)* ①水分多的,淡的;(颜色等)浅的. ②(文章等)无力的, 贫乏的. **-wash·i·ness** *n.*

wasn't [ˈwɔznt] 〔口〕 = was not.

Wasp, WASP [wɔsp] *n.* 祖先是英国新教徒的美国人; 美国社会中享有特权的白人 (= White Anglo-Saxon Protestant). **Waspy, Waspish** *a.*

wasp [wɔsp] *n.* ①黄蜂. ②暴躁的人, 脾气不好的人. ~ **waist** (束紧的)细腰. **-y** *a.*

wasp·ish [ˈwɔspiʃ] *a.* ①黄蜂似的; 腰细的. ②易怒的; 刻毒的. **-ly** *ad.* **-ness** *n.*

was·sail [ˈwɔseil] *n.* 〔古〕宴会,欢宴; 宴会的祝酒. — *vi.* 干杯; 祝酒; 欢宴; 痛饮. — *vt.* 为…干杯,向…祝酒.

Was·ser·mann [ˈvɑːsəmɑːn], **A·von** 瓦塞尔曼〔1866—1952,德国细菌学家〕. ~ **test [reaction]** (梅毒的)瓦塞尔曼氏检查[反应].

wast [强 wɔst; 弱 wəst] 〔古〕 be 的过去式, 第二人称单数〔主词为 thou 时〕.

wast·age [ˈweistidʒ] *n.* 浪费; 损耗(量); 废料.

waste [weist] *a.* ①荒芜的,不毛的,荒废了的; 未开垦的; 荒凉的. ②废弃的,无用的; 多余的; 身体内排泄的. ~ *land(s)* 荒地. ~ *paper* 废纸. ~ *heat* 废热, 余热. ~ *products* (工厂出品中的)废品. ~ *product* (身体组织中的)废料. ***lay ~*** 糟蹋,毁坏,蹂躏; 劫掠. ***lie ~*** (土地)荒芜,未开垦. ***the ~ periods of history*** 历史上单调平凡[荒芜]的时期. — *vt.* ①糟蹋,浪费. ②毁坏, 破坏, 蹂躏,使荒芜. ③消耗,使衰弱;【法】(因使用不当而)损坏(房屋等);【石工】把(石头)解成适当的大小. ④〔美俚〕毒打; 消灭; 凶杀. ~ *an opportunity* 浪费机会. *Kind words are ~d (up)on him.* 跟他说好话是白说了. — *vi.* ①消耗; 消瘦,衰弱. ②浪费. ③(时间)过去, 消逝. *Day [Night] ~s.* 太阳下山[天快亮]了. ~**d work** 【机】耗功. ~ ***away*** 消瘦. ***W- not, want not.*** 不浪费,不愁穷. ~ ***one's words [breath]*** 徒费口舌. — *n.* ①浪费. ②〔常*pl.*〕荒地,荒野,未开垦地; 沙漠; 荒芜. ③消耗(量),损耗; 衰弱; 渐损;【法】毁损, 损坏. ④废料, 废品,废物; 剩余物,废屑; 破布. ⑤【机】碎纱, 纱头〔机器工人擦手用〕. ⑥【地】风化物; (被水流冲蚀的) 岩屑. ⑦垃圾; 污水;〔*pl.*〕粪便. ~ *of time* 浪费时间. *(a) ~ of speech* 浪费唇舌. *a ~ of waters* 茫茫大海. ***run [go] to ~*** 糟蹋掉;(钱财等)被浪费掉. ~ ***and repair*** 消耗和补充. ~ ***recovering*** 废料回收. ~ **basket** 〔美〕字纸篓. ~ **book** 【簿】流水帐. ~**bin** 废物箱, 垃圾桶. ~**-butt** ①客栈[酒馆]老板. ②〔谑〕小饭店. ~**land** 荒地,荒野,荒漠. ~**lot** 〔加〕(长满野草或堆满垃圾的)荒地. ~**paper** 废纸. ~**paper basket** = ~ basket. ~ **pipe** 废水[污水]管. ~ **waste** 下等马口铁.

waste·ful [ˈweistful] *a.* 浪费的; 糟蹋的,不经济的; 破坏性的;〔诗〕荒芜的. *be ~ of resources* 浪费资源. *a ~ man* 挥霍无度的人. **-ly** *ad.*

wast·er [ˈweistə] *n.* ①浪费者; 挥霍者. ②〔口〕无用的人. ③破坏者. ④废物,废品. ⑤【医】瘦弱的婴儿.

wast·ing [ˈweistiŋ] *a.* 消耗性的,渐减的; 使荒废的; 破坏性的. — *n.* 浪费; 糟蹋; 消耗,【医】虚痨. *a ~ disease* 消耗性疾病〔如结核病〕; 痨病.

wast·rel [ˈweistrəl] *n.* ①流浪儿童. ②无用的人,饭桶. ③浪费者. ④废物; 废品.

wat [wɑːt] *n.* (泰国等的)佛寺,寺院.

watch [wɔtʃ] *n.* ①表; 船钟. ②值夜,值班; 守夜; 看守人; 哨兵. ③看守, 监视; 注意; 警戒. ④【海】(每 4 小时轮换的)值班(时间);〔集合词〕值班人员, 一班. ⑤〔古〕更〔犹太人把一夜分作 *first* ~ 首更, *middle* ~ 中更, *morning* ~ 末更; 罗马人分为 *first [evening]* ~ 头更, *second [midnight]* ~ 二更, *third [cock crowing]* ~三更, *fourth [morning]* ~ 四更〕. ***be on [off] ~*** 值班[不值班]. ***be on the ~ for*** 看守着, 监视着, 提防着; 守候着. ***call the ~*** 召集值班人. ***in the night ~es*** = ***in the ~es of the night*** 在睡不着的夜里. ***keep (a) ~*** 看守; 值班. ***keep ~ over*** 守护; 密切注意. ***pass as [like] a ~ in the night*** 立刻被忘记掉. ***through the silent ~es of the night*** 更深夜静的时候. ~ ***and ward*** 昼夜警戒. ~ ***and ~*** 【海】四小时轮流值班, 半舷值班. — *vt.* ①注视; 注意,留心观察. ②看守, 监视. ③守候(机会等) *(for)* — *vi.* ①注视, 看着; 密切注意. ②警戒,守卫,监视. ③守候,期待 *(for).* ④〔古〕守夜; 通夜看

W

护;【宗】守夜[作通宵祈祷]. ~ *and say nothing* 静观不语. ~ *all night at the bedside of a patient* 在病人床边通宵侍候. — *vt.* ①观看,注视. ②看守,守卫;照管,守护;监视. ③守候,等待. ***A ~ed pot never boils.*** 见pot条. ***be closely ~ed*** 被严密监视. ***if you don't ~ it*** 〔俚〕你要是不小心. ~ ***one's time*** 等待时机. ~ ***out*** ①〔美俚〕监视,警戒. ②密切注视 *(for)* (*W- out for cars.* 当心车辆). ~ ***over*** 监视;留心,注视;看护,照顾. **~-and-wait policy** 观望政策. **~band** 表带. ~ **cap** 水手冬帽. **~case** 表壳. ~ **chain** 表链. **W- Committee** 〔英〕市镇治安委员会. **~dog** 看门狗;监视者〔也指一个集体〕. ~ **file** 钟表锉. ~ **fire** 营火. ~ **glass** 表玻璃. ~ **guard** 表链,表带(等). **~house** 哨房,班房,岗房;拘留所. ~ **maker** 钟表匠. **-man** 更夫;看守人;夜班警卫员. ~ **meeting**【宗】除夜礼拜. ~ **night**【宗】除夜(礼拜);圣诞节前夜礼拜. ~ **oil** 机器油. **~-out** 监视,警戒. ~ **pocket** (背心上的)表袋. ~ **spring** 表的发条. ~ **tower** 望楼. **~word** 暗号;(回答步哨的)口令;标语,口号. **-able** *a.* 值得注意[注视]的.

watch·er [ˈwɔtʃə] *n.* 注视者;看守人;值班员;守夜人;看护人;哨兵;〔美〕(投票所)监票员.

watch·ful [ˈwɔtʃful] *a.* ①注意的,注视的,留心的,小心提防的,警戒的 *(of; against)*. ②〔古〕不眠的. ~ *waiting* 待机,观察,警戒.

wa·ter [ˈwɔːtə] *n.* ①水;雨水;露;〔常作 *pl.*〕矿泉,温泉;药水. ②〔常 *pl.*〕水体;水域;水道;海;湖;河;海域;领海. ③水深,水位,水面. ④分泌液,体液[如尿、汗、口水、泪等];(船的)漏水. ⑤水色〔宝石的光泽透明度〕,品质. ⑤(织品的)波纹,光泽. ⑥〔*pl.*〕积水;洪水. ⑦【商】(超过实际资产的)虚值;虚[清水]股. *fresh [sweet]* ~ 淡水. *piped* ~ 自来水. *brandy and* ~ 白兰地加水[特别调制的饮料]. *He is taking the ~s at Karlsbad.* 他正在卡斯巴托作矿泉疗养. ~ *of hydration*【化】化合水. *the distant [near] ~s* 远[近]海. *the blue* ~ 苍海. *cross the ~s* 渡过大海. *an ornamental* ~ (人工修造的)装饰用水池. *high [low]* ~ 高[低]潮. *high* ~ *season* 汛期. *dead* ~ (静止的)死水;船尾涡流;(最低)小潮. *The boat is making* ~. 船漏水了. ***above*** ~ 摆脱(经济)困难. ***back*** ~ ①倒划桨. ②〔美〕立场倒退,退缩. ***bring the ~ to sb.'s mouth*** 使垂涎. ***by*** ~ 经由水道,用船运. ***cast one's bread upon the*** ~ 只做好事不求报酬;积阴德. ***cast ~ into the Thames*** 白费气力. ***draw ~ to one's mill*** 牟取私利. ~ ***water with a sieve*** 竹篮打水一场空. ***drink the ~s*** 喝矿泉;作矿泉疗养. ***fish in troubled*** ~ 浑水摸鱼. ***get into hot*** ~ 陷入困境. ***go over the*** ~ 越过河流[湖海];流亡;被流放. ***hold*** ~ ①不漏水;无漏洞,无疵罅,(理由)站得住;完好. ②(用桨)弯住,制住. ***in deep ~(s)*** 遭遇艰难,在水深火热中,陷入困境. ***in hot*** ~ 处于困境. ***in low*** ~〔俚〕不如意,经济不宽裕. ***in smooth ~(s)*** 平稳地,顺利地. ***in rough [toubled]*** ~ 处境很困难. ***keep one's head above*** ~ 避免破产,设法保住地位[应付困境]. ***like*** ~ (用钱)如水;(流血)如注. ***make*** ~ ①小便. ②【海】(船只)漏水. ***Much ~ runs by the mill that the miller knows not of*** 世上有许多事是我们所不知道的. ***of the first*** ~ 品质最好的;第一流的 (*a diamond of the first* ~ 第一等的钻石. *a blunder of the first* ~ 无比的疏忽). ***on the*** ~ ①漂在水上. ②在船上. ***pass*** ~ = make ~. ***pour oil on the ~s*** 调停[平息]纠纷. ***take (the)*** ~ (船)下水;举行下水礼;下水游泳;乘船. ***take the ~s*** = drink the ~s. ***take (to) the*** ~【空】在水上降落. ***take the ~s*** 作矿泉疗养. ***take*** ~〔美俚〕沮丧,退却;投降. ***throw cold ~ on*** 泼冷水[打击别人的热情]. ***tread*** ~ 踩水,立游. ***turn on [off] the*** ~ 扭开[关上]水龙头. ***under*** ~ 在水中;浸水. ~ ***and soil conservation*** 水土保持. ~ ***bewitched*** 淡茶;搀水的酒. ~ ***of life*** 生命之水;起死回生[长生不老]的神水;白兰地酒. ***Still ~s run deep.*** 静水流深;大智若愚. ***strong ~s*** 〔古〕烈酒. ***written in*** ~ 昙花一现的,转眼即逝的. — *vt.* ①注水于,灌水于;把…浸在水中;给浇水;灌溉. ②给…水喝,给水. ③在(织物上)加波纹. ④在…中搀水,冲淡. ⑤【商】名义增(资),发行(虚股);不增加资本而虚增(股额等). ~ *the milk* 在牛奶中搀水. ~ *cattle* 给家畜饮水. — *vi.* ①(动物)饮水;被供给水,加水. ②淌眼泪;垂涎;渴望. ***make sb.'s eyes*** ~ 使淌眼泪. ***make sb.'s mouth*** ~ 使垂涎;使渴望. ~ ***down*** 冲淡,打折扣. **~age**〔英〕水道运输(运费). **~-ash** *n.*【植】加罗林梣. ~ **back** 炉后热水箱. ~ **bag** 水袋;(胎儿的)衣胞. ~ **bailiff** 船舶检查员. ~ **barrow** 撒水车. ~ **bed** 电热温水褥[病人用装水橡皮褥]. ~ **beetle**【虫】(龙虱等)水虫. ~ **biscuit** 薄脆饼干. ~ **blister**【医】水疱. ~ **boatman** 水虫(科). **~-borne** *a.* ①水道运输的;漂流着的. ②(传染病)由饮用水媒介的(*-borne trade* 海外贸易). ~ **brash**【医】反酸;胃灼热. ~ **brain** (羊的)回旋病 (= gid). **~buck**【动】(南非)大羚羊. ~ **buffalo** ①【动】水牛. ②〔军俚〕登陆牵引车. ~ **bug**【动】①水生蝽. ②茶婆虫. ~ **butt** 承雨水桶. ~ **can** 浇水壶. ~ **cannon** 水炮. ~ **capacity** 持水量. ~ **carriage** 水上运输[交通](工具);〔英方〕排水道. ~ **carrier** ①从事水上运输的人;运水的人,卖水的人. ②【天】〔W-〕【天】宝瓶宫. ~ **cart** 运水车;洒水车. ~ **chestnut**【植】①荸荠. ②欧菱. ~ **chinquapin**【植】美洲黄花莲;黄花莲果. ~ **chute** (乘小船从高斜处滑入水中的)滑水运动(滑槽). ~ **circulation**【机】冷水环流. ~ **circulator**【机】环流器. ~ **clock** 水钟,滴漏. ~ **closet** (有卫生设备的)厕所,抽水马桶. ~ **cock** ①自来水龙头. ②【动】鸟翁. **~-colo(u)r**【绘画】水彩(画);水彩颜料. **~-colo(u)rist** 水彩画家. ~ **content** 含水量. ~ **control** 治水. **~-convovulus**【植】蕹菜. **~-cool** *vt.* 以水冷却. **~-cooled** *a.*【机】水冷式的. ~ **cooler**【机】水冷器. **~-cooling**【机】水冷法. ~ **course** 水流,河,运河;水道;河床. **~craft** ①驾船技艺;水上运动技艺. ②船只. ~ **crane**【机】水鹤;水压起重机. ~ **cress**【植】水田芹. ~ **croop** 吸水管. ~ **cure**【医】水疗法;(热)水处治;(热)水熟化;(热)水硫化;〔美俚〕灌水逼供的刑罚. ~ **cushion**【机】水垫. ~ **cycle** 踏行船. ~ **dog** ①会游水的狗;〔俚〕老练的水手;熟习水性的人. ②【动】(美洲)大螈蝾. ~ **diviner** = ~ finder. **~-drinker** 喜喝矿泉水的人;绝对戒酒者. ~ **electrode**【电】水(成)电极. ~ **equivalent**【化】水当量. **~fall** 瀑布;〔美俚〕下垂的长卷发. ~ **faucet** 水龙头. **~-feed(er)**【机】给水器. **~finder** 找地下水脉的人;试水器. ~ **flea**【动】水蚤. **~-flood** *vt.* 注水入(油井). ~ **front** ①水边,滨湖[河等]地,湖滨[沿河]马路. ②装在火炉前部的热水缸. ~ **gap**〔美〕水峡. ~ **gas**【化】水煤气. ~ **gate** 水门,水闸. ~ **gauge** 水位尺,测水表. ~ **glass** ①计时玻璃水漏. ②【化】水玻璃;硅酸钠. ③(玻璃)水标尺;水底观察镜;水杯. ~ **gruel** 薄粥,米汤. ~ **guard** 水上警察;海关水上巡察员. **~-hardening**【冶】水淬硬化. ~ **head** ①水源;水位差. ②【医】脑积水. ~ **hemlock**【植】毒芹(属). ~ **hen**【鸟】鷭. ~ **hole** (干河床上的)水坑. ~ **hyacinth**【植】凤眼兰. ~ **ice** 水冰,人造冰;〔英〕= sherbet. **~-inch** 在最小压力下口径一英寸管子24小时放水量〔约500立方英尺〕. **~ing call**【军】饮马号. **~ing can** 喷壶,浇水器. **~ing cart** = water cart. **~ing place** (牛马的)饮水处;温泉地,水疗场;海水浴场. **~ing pot** ①= watering-can. ②【贝】喷壶介. ~ **inlet**【机】入水口. ~ **jacket**【机】水套;(机枪的)冷水套筒. ~ **jet** 水注. ~ **jump** (越野赛马中的)水沟. ~ **leaf**【植】田茎麻科植物. **~less** *a.* 无水的;干的;不需水的. ~ **lettuce**【植】大薸. ~ **level** 水平面;【地】汗水面,地下水位;水准器;(船的)吃水线. ~ **lily**【植】睡莲. ~ **line, ~line** (吃)水线;(印在纸里的)水印横

W

格线. ~**-locks** 水闸. ~ **locust**【植】水生皂荚. ~**-logged** *a.*(船)因进水而航行困难的;(木材等)浸饱水的;水涝的(~*-logged farmland* 水涝地). ~ **main** 自来水总管. ~**manship** 桨手本领;划船术,水上职业;熟习水性. ~**mark** ①*n.* (压印在纸里的)水印. ② *vt.* 印水印(在纸上). ~ **mass**【海洋】(同温度、同化学成分的)水团. ~**melon**【植】西瓜. ~ **meter** 水量计,水表. ~ **milfoil**【植】狐尾藻(属). ~ **mill** 水车; 水磨. ~ **mocassin**(北美)水栖蝮蛇;水蛇. ~ **monkey** (冷开水用的)长颈水缸. ~ **motor** 水力发动机. ~**nymph** 水精. ~ **oak**【植】黑栎. ~ **outlet**【机】出水口. ~ **ouzel**【动】河鸟. ~ **parting** 分水岭. ~ **pepper**【植】蓼; 美洲线叶苹. ~ **pimpernel**【植】①水茴草. ②水绿. ~ **pipe** 水管,给水管,自来水管; 水烟筒. ~ **plane** ①【海】(船的)水线平面. ②【空】水上飞机. ~ **plantain**【植】泽泻(属). ~ **polo**【运】水球. ~ **power** 水力. ~ **press**【机】水压机. ~**proof** ①*a.* 不透水的,防水的. ②*n.* 防水物,防水材料;防水布, 油布; 防水服, 雨衣. ③*vt.* 使(布等)作防水处理,给(布)上胶. ~**-quenching**【冶】水淬火. ~ **ram** 水力夯锤. ~**-raising engine**【机】扬水机. ~ **rat**【动】河鼠;〔美〕麝香鼠;〔美俚〕徘徊江边的小偷〔无业游民〕. ~ **rate** 自来水费;【机】耗汽率, 耗水率. ~**-repellent** *a.* 拒水的. ~**-resistant** *a.* 抗水的. ~ **right**【法】取水权,用水权. ~ **sapphire**【矿】蓝堇青石. ~ **scape** 水上〔海洋〕风景(画). ~ **scorpion**【动】红娘华科昆虫. ~ **seal**【机】水封闭. ~ **seasoning** 树液抽出干燥法. ~**shed**〔英〕分水岭;〔口〕流域. ~ **shield**【植】莼菜. ~**shoot** 排水管 = ~ chute. ~**side** 水边. ~ **ski**【运】(用汽艇拖的)滑水橇. ~**skin** 运水用皮袋. ~ **snake**【动】水蛇; 游蛇(属). ~ **softener**【化】软水剂;软水槽. ~ **soldier**【植】水兵草. ~**-soluble** *a.*【化】水溶性的,可溶于水的. ~**-souchet**, ~**-souchy** 原汁炆鱼. ~**spout** 水落管; 水龙卷; 暴雨. ~ **sprout**【植】速发枝条. ~**-strainer**【机】滤水器. ~ **supply** 供水(设备); 给水(量). ~ **system** 水系; 供水(系统). ~ **table** ①【建】承雨线脚; 泻水台. ②【地】潜水面,地下水位. ~ **tank** 水箱. ~ **thrush**【动】鹡鸰. ~**tight** *a.* 不漏水的,不透水的,防水的;(讨论等)无懈可击的. ~ **toothpick** 水柱洁齿器〔利用压力水柱清洁牙齿或牙缝的设备〕. ~ **tower** 水塔; 灭火用喷水塔. ~ **vapor** 水蒸气,水汽. ~**-vascular system** (棘皮动物的)水管系统. ~ **vole** = water rat. ~ **wag(g)on** 洒水车,运水车 (*on the ~ waggon* 戒酒). ~**-wave** 水烫卷发. ~**-waving**【理发】水烫. ~**-way** 水路,航路;【船】水口, 排水沟. ~**weed**【植】菲藻(属); 加拿大菲藻. ~ **wheel** 水车; 扬水车. ~**-white** *a.* 无色的, 清澈的. ~ **wings** (学游泳的)浮袋. ~**work** 水道设备; 给水装置; 自来水厂; 喷水装置; 〔俚〕眼泪 (*turn on the ~works*〔俚〕哭起来). ~**worn** *a.* 水蚀的. **-ing**【纺】波纹,云纹.

wa·tered [ˈwɔːtəd] *a.* ①搀水的. ②灌溉过的. ③有波纹的; 有波光的. ④【经】虚增的, 空头发行的. ~ *silk* 波纹绸. ~ *capital* 虚增资本. *a ~ stock*【商】虚股.

Wa·ter·gate [ˈwɔːtəgeit] *n.* ①水门事件〔美国政治丑闻,共和党总统竞选连任委员会于 1972 年6月 17 日派人潜入水门大厦民主党总部安装窃听器, 此事暴露后导致尼克松总统辞职〕. ②(类似水门事件的)政治丑闻.

wa·ter·i·ness [ˈwɔːtərinis] *n.* ①多水, 象有雨的光景. ②清淡; 稀薄;(食物)淡薄,无味.

Wa·ter·loo [ˌwɔːtəˈluː] *n.* ①滑铁卢〔比利时城镇〕(一八一五年拿破仑军队战败处). ②〔喻〕惨败. *meet one's ~* 遭遇惨败.

Wa·ter·man [ˈwɔːtəmən] *n.* 沃特曼〔姓氏〕.

Wa·ters [ˈwɔːtəz] *n.* 沃特斯〔姓氏〕.

wa·ter·y [ˈwɔːtəri] *a.* ①水的; 水汪汪的, 水分多的. ②含泪的. ③水一般的,搀水(过多)的; 无味的; 淡, 浅(色等). ④软弱无力的,(文章等)缺乏内容的. ⑤潮湿的,象要下雨的. *a ~ grave* 水葬. ~ *clouds* 雨云. ~ *sky* 象要下雨的天空.

Wat·son [ˈwɔt-sn] *n.* 沃森〔姓氏〕.

Watt [wɔt] *n.* ①瓦特〔姓氏〕. ②**James** ~ 詹·瓦特〔1736—1819,苏格兰发明家,蒸气机发明人〕.

watt [wɔt] *n.*【电】瓦特〔电力单位〕. ~**-hour** *n.* 瓦(特)小时. ~**-hour meter** 瓦时计,电(度)表〔俗名 wattmeter〕.

watt·age [ˈwɔtidʒ] *n.*【电】瓦(特)数.

Wat·teau [vɑˈtəu; F. wɑːˈtəu] *a.* 华托式的〔一种女服式样, 因常见于法国画家让·安东尼·华托 (*Jean Antone Watteau*)的绘画中而得名〕.

Wat·ter·son [ˈwɔtəsn] *n.* 沃特森〔姓氏〕.

watt-hr. = watt-hour.

wat·tle [ˈwɔtl] *n.* ①枝条,篱笆条,篱笆. ②(火鸡等的)垂肉. ③(鱼的)触须. ④【植】金合欢属. ~ *and daub*【建】夹条墙,泥笆墙. — *vt.* 用枝条编制(篱笆、篮等). ~ **bird**【动】(澳洲的)食蜜鸟.

wat·tled [ˈwɔtld] *a.* ①用枝条编〔做〕的. ②有垂肉的.

watt·me·ter [ˈwɔtmiːtə] *n.* 瓦特计,电表.

Watts [wɔts] *n.* 瓦茨〔姓氏〕.

Wa·tu·si [wɑːˈtuːsi] *n.* (*pl.* ~*(s)*) 瓦图西〔非洲布隆迪和卢旺达的隆迪人中的牧主阶级〕(= Watutsi).

Waugh [wɔː] *n.* 沃〔姓氏〕.

waul [wɔːl] *vi.* 象猫一样叫唤; 哇哇地哭.

WAVE, Wave [weiv] *n.* 〔美海军〕女志愿军人〔见 WAVES 条〕.

wave [weiv] *n.* ①波浪; 碎浪; 〔the ~(s)〕〔诗〕海. ②波动; 波状起伏; 波浪形;【军】(攻击)波; 批; (绸缎的)波纹; 波线. ③波动, 风潮; 高潮. ④(用手等的)挥动(信号);【火箭】振动,射流;【物】波;【气象】浪. *attack in ~s*【军】波状进攻. *They defy difficulties and advance ~ upon ~.* 他们不怕困难, 前赴后继. *a ~ of prosperity [depression]* 一阵子的繁荣〔萧条〕. *permanent ~s* 电烫(头发). *a ~ of buying* 一阵子的抢购浪潮. *a ~ of revolution* 革命高潮. *a tidal ~* 海啸. *long [short] ~s* 长〔短〕波. *ultra-short ~s* 超短波. *a cold ~* 寒潮. *a heat ~* 热浪. ***attack in ~s***【军】作波状攻击. ***make ~s*** 兴风作浪; 打乱正常的进程〔惯例等〕. — *vi.* ①起波,波动; 摇摆, 招展, 飘扬. ②(头发等)作波浪形, 起伏. ③挥手〔招手〕示意. *Her hair ~s.* 她的头发呈波浪形. — *vt.* ①摇, 挥; 使招展. ②摇〔挥〕动表示. ③使起浪; 将(头发)弄成波浪形; 加波纹. ~ *a farewell* = ~ *sb. adieu* 挥手告别. ~ *sb. nearer* 招手叫某人走近一点. ~ ***aside*** 挥手使站开; 挥手拒绝〔排斥〕. ~ ***away [off]*** 挥手使去; 拒绝. ~ ***the bloody shirt***〔美〕唤起复仇心, 挑拨敌对情绪. ~ **band**【无】波段. ~ **base** 波底〔静水中水面波动扬不起沉淀物的深度〕. ~ **cloud**【气】波状云. ~ **detector**【无】检波器. ~ **equation**【数】波动方程式. ~ **front**【物】波阵面,波前. ~ **function**【数】波函数. ~ **guide**【电】波导(管). ~**-hopping**【空】掠水飞行. ~ **length**【无】波长. ~**let** 小浪;【物】子波,弱波,小波,基元波,成分波. ~ **mechanics**【物】波动力学. ~**meter**【电】波频计, 波长计. ~ **motion** 波状运动. ~ **propagation**【物】波的传播. ~ **train**【物】波列. ~ **velocity**【无】波速. **-d** *a.* ①波浪形的,起伏的; (织物等)有波纹的. ②飘动的. **-less** *a.* 没有浪的,不起浪的,平静的.

wa·vell·ite [ˈweivilait] *n.*【地】银星石.

wa·ver[1] [ˈweivə] *n.* ①挥动者, 摇动者; 波动的东西. ②做卷发的理发师〔美容师〕; 卷发器. ③【无】波段开关; 波形转换器.

wa·ver[2] [ˈweivə] *vi.* ①摇摆;(火焰等)颤动. ②(军队等)动摇;(声音等)震颤. ③犹豫不决, 拿不定主意. ~ *in determination* 犹豫不定, 踌躇不决. — *n.* 犹豫. *be upon ~* 犹豫不决. **-er** 动摇〔摇摆〕者, 犹豫不决的人. **-ing** *a.* 摇摆的,动摇的,犹豫不决的.

WAVES = Women Accepted for Volunteer Emergency Service〔美旧〕(海军)妇女预备队.

wav·y [ˈweivi] *a.* ***(-i·er; -i·est)*** ①波状的,起伏的. ②动摇的,摇摆的. ③波涛汹涌的. *a ~ terrain* 起伏不平的地形. **-i·ly** *ad.* **-i·ness** *n.*

wawl [wɔːl] *vi.* = waul.

wax[1] [wæks] *n.* ①(蜂)蜡;蜡状物. ②耳垢. ③(鞋匠用的)擦线蜡 (=cobbler's ~);石蜡;树蜡;火漆,封蜡. ④〔美〕(糖枫制的)糖蜜. ⑤〔美俚〕蓄音蜡盘,唱片. *vegetable [Japan] ~* 植物蜡. *a ~ candle* 蜡烛. ***be mo(u)lded like ~*** (象蜡一样柔软)任人摆布;毫无抵抗能力. — *a.* 蜡制的. — *vt.* 涂蜡于,上蜡于,用蜡擦;灌(唱片). — *vi.* 录音在唱片上,灌唱片. ~ **bean**【植】扁豆. ~**berry**【植】①= snowberry. ② = bayberry. ~ **bill**【动】梅花雀. ~ **cloth** 蜡布. ~ **doll** 蜡人;美貌而没表情的女人,蜡美人. ~ **end** (鞋匠上过蜡的)底线. ~ **insect**【动】水蜡虫. ~ **myrtle**【植】= bayberry;南部杨梅. ~ **palm**【植】蜡棕榈;巴西蜡棕. ~ **paper** 蜡纸. ~ **tree** 野漆树.

wax[2] [wæks] *vi.* ①大起来,变大,增大;(月)渐渐变大,变圆 *(opp.* wane*)*. ②渐渐变化. *~ and wane* (月)盈亏,盈虚;盛衰. *~ old* 渐渐变老. *~ angry* 生起气来. *~ facetious* 变得好笑. *~ indignant* 变忿慨. *~ fat* 胖起来.

wax[3] [wæks] *n.*〔英口〕生气,发怒. ***get into ~*** 发怒,动气. ***in a ~*** 气忿;生气. ***put (sb.) in a ~*** 使(人)发怒.

wax·en[1] [ˈwæksən] *a.* ①蜡制的;上过蜡的. ②象蜡的,蜡质的;苍白的;蜡黄的. ③柔软的;柔顺的.

wax·en[2] [ˈwæksn]〔古〕wax 的过去分词.

wax·i·ness [ˈwæksinis] *n.* 蜡质,柔软;柔顺.

wax·wing [ˈwækswiŋ] *n.*【鸟】连雀.

wax·work [ˈwækswəːk] *n.* ①蜡制品. ②〔*pl.* 作单数用〕蜡人(馆);蜡制品展览馆.

wax·y[1] [ˈwæksi] *a.* ***(-i·er; -i·est)*** ①蜡(似)的,蜡制的,上过蜡的;蜡质的. ②柔顺的. ③【医】蜡样变性的. *~ crude*【油】含蜡[多蜡]原油.

wax·y[2] [ˈwæksi] *a.*〔俚〕生气的,动气的,忿怒的.

way[1] [wei] *n.* ①路,道路,通路. ②路程;距离. ③(要走的)路线;途中,路上;进行,前进;【法】通行权. ④方向,方面. ⑤方法,手段. ⑥方式,式样,样子. ⑦习惯,风气;〔常 *pl.*〕一贯作风. ⑧方针,决心;自己的意向. ⑨…点,事项. ⑩(职业、行动等的)范围;规模;〔口〕行业,专业. ⑪〔口〕状况,情况;〔英口〕激动状况. ⑫【海】航行;〔*pl.*〕(新船的)下水台;【机】(车床等的)导轨. ⑬〔口〕近邻,附近;地区. ⑭〔the W-〕【宗】(基督教的)教义. *ask the ~* 问路. *the ~ to the station* 到车站去的路. *The furthest [longest] ~ about is the nearest [shortest] ~ home.* 按步就班反而先到;欲速则不达. *The plan is making good ~.* 计划正在顺利进行中. *Look this ~.* 看这边. *That was always her ~.* 那是她的一贯作风. *~ of production* 生产方式. *a statement false in two ~s* 有两点错误的声明. *He is in a grocery ~.* 他在做杂货生意. *live somewhere Beijing ~* 住在北京附近的一个地方. ***a little [long] ~(s)*** 在…的不远处[很远处];不长一段[老远一段]路. ***a little [great, long] ~ off*** 在不远处[很远处];离得近[远]. ***affect foreign ~s*** 模仿外国方式. ***all the ~*** ①一路上,路上一直;远远,老远. ②〔美〕(从…到…)逐一,逐步 (*It is estimated all the ~ from 50 to 100 dollars* 据估计为 50 元到 100 元). ***all the ~ up to*** 直至. ***be in a bad ~*** 情况不好. ***be in a (great) ~*** 正在(非常)生气[激动]. ***both ~*** = this ~ and that. ***by the ~*** ①在路旁;在路上. ②〔插入语〕顺便说;附带说说. ***by ~ of*** ①当做,作为;作出…的样子. ②经由. ③〔英〕正逐步,在…中. ④以便,为了 (*a stick by ~ of weapon* 当做武器的棍子. *by ~ of apology* 作为辩解,作为道歉. *She is by ~ of becoming a fine pianist.* 她正在逐步成长为一个优秀钢琴家). ***come one's ~*** ①临头,发生于某人身上. ②到…处. ③〔俚〕进行;(事情)进行顺利. ***cut both ~s*** 模棱两可. ***each ~*** 单程. ***face two ~*** 碰到叉路站住. ***find one's ~ into*** 进入…;进入…的境遇 (*It found its ~ into the papers.* 这事上了报了). ***find one's [the] ~ to*** 到达(目的地). ***find one's ~ out of*** 设法走出,脱出. ***force one's ~ (out)*** 挤(出去),冲(出去). ***gather ~*** 加大速度,快起来. ***get in the ~*** 妨碍. ***get out of the ~*** ①*vi.* 避开,让开. ②*vt.* 除去;处分. ***get under ~*** 开始进行,开始;开船. ***give ~*** ①崩溃,倒塌;失败,屈服,让步 *(to)*;支持不住,忍不住…了出来[起来]. ②划起来,用力划. ③(价格)跌落. ***go a good [long] ~ with*** 非常有用,非常有效. ***go a little ~*** 有一点点用处[效果]. ***go little ~*** 不怎么有用[有效],不够. ***go one's ~(s)*** 动身,出发,走掉. ***go out of one's ~*** ①绕弯儿走;不怕麻烦. ②特地;故意 (*go out of the [one's] ~ to be rude* 故意蛮干). ***go some ~*** =go a little ~. ***go the ~ of all the earth [of all flesh, of nature]*** 死. ***have a ~ of (do)ing*** 有…的毛病[习惯]. ***have (everything) one's own ~.*** 为所欲为,一意孤行. ***have ~ on*** (船)正在开行. ***hold one ~*** = keep one's ~. ***in a bad ~*** 情形不见好;(病人)情形不好. ***in a big [great] ~*** 大规模地;豪华地 (*go in for industry in a big ~* 大办工业). ***in a hundred and one ~s*** 千方百计地. ***in a small ~*** 小,小规模地,简朴地 (*an author in a small ~* 一个小小的作家. *live in a small ~* 生活简朴). ***in a [one] ~*** 有几分,有点,稍微;在某一点上,在某种意义下. ***in an all-round ~*** 全面. ***in no ~*** 决不,无论如何不. ***in one's (own) ~*** 本来,原来;有特色的 (*He is a poet in his own ~* 他是一个有特色的诗人). ***(in) one's own ~*** 照…自己的办法[想法]. (*Do it your own ~.* 照你自己的办法去做吧). ***(in) one ~ or another [the other]*** (好歹)设法. ***in the family ~*** 怀孕. ***in the ~*** ①在路上,在途中. ②妨碍. ***in the ~ of*** ①妨碍. ②在…方面,关于. ③使能于,使能遇见…,在便于做[得到]…的地位. ***keep one's ~*** 继续前进. ***keep out of the ~*** 避开. ***lose the [one's] ~*** 迷路. ***lose ~*** 慢起来. ***make much [little] ~*** 走得快[慢];进步[不进步]. ***make one's (own) ~*** ①走向,前往. ②繁荣,兴隆,发迹 (*make one's ~ home* 回家去. *make one's ~ in the world* 发迹,成功). ***make the best of one's ~*** 尽量快去. ***make ~*** 开路,让路 *(for)*;前进,进步 (*cannot make any ~* 一点也不能前进). ***mend one's ~*** 改变习惯. ***no ~***〔美方〕无论如何不,决不,一点也不(*no ~ inferior* 一点也不次). ***nothing out of the ~*** 没有什么特别的地方,平凡. ***on one's ~ to*** 到…去的途中. ***on the ~*** 在路上;在旅行中. ***once in a ~*** 时或,偶然. ***one ~ or another [the other]*** 以某种方式;想方设法. ***out of the ~*** ①向傍边,使不妨碍;让开,离开,避开. ②迷失;误;异常. ③特意,不顾困难地. ***pay one's ~*** 不借债过日子 (*pay one's ~ through college* 刻苦自持地上完大学). ***put sb. in the ~ of doing*** 给(某人)…的机会. ***see one's ~ (clear) to (do or doing)*** (清楚)知道怎么做;能做到. ***stand in the ~ of*** 妨碍,阻住…的路. ***take one's own ~*** = go one's own ~. ***take one's ~ to [towards]*** 上…去,向…出发. ***that ~***〔美俚〕在恋爱中. ***that ~ about*** 爱着. ***the easy [hard] ~*** 用巧[笨]法. ***that good old ~s*** 自古以来的习惯. ***the other [wrong] ~ about [round, around]*** 相反(地),以相反方式[方向]. ***the parting of the ~s*** 岔路;必须抉择其一的重要关头. ***the right of ~*** 通行权;得到通行权的地带;〔美〕铁路路线. ***the right ~*** ①正道. ②最正确的方法. ③方向正确地〔作状语〕. ***the specific ~s and means of*** … 的具体方式和方法. ***the ~*** ①(做…)的方式[办法]. ②〔美口〕= as. ***the ~ I see it*** …照我看来. ***the ~ of the world*** (世上的)一般

习惯,常情. ***this ~ and that*** 忽左忽右;下不了决心. ***to sb.'s ~ of thinking*** 据某人的想法. ***to put it (in) another ~*** 换言之. ***under ~*** 进行着;【海】航行中. ***W- enough!*** 【海】停划! ***~ in [out]*** 入[出]口. ***~s and means*** 方式方法;财源 (*the Committee on* [英] *of* Ways and Means 岁入调查委员会).

way[2], **way** [wei] *ad.* ①= away. ②〔美口〕…得多,远为. ★与 above, ahead, behind, below, down, off, out, over, up 等副词、介词连用,以加强语气. *~ back* 老早以前; *~ down upon the river Thames* 在老远老远的泰晤士河边; *~ up* 还在上面;好得多. *~ out of balance* 逆差很大很大.

way·bill [ˈweibil] *n.* 乘客单;(铁路等的)运货单.

way·board [ˈweibɔːd] *n.* (两厚层之间的)薄隔板.

way·far·er [ˈweifɛərə] *n.* 赶路的人,旅客,徒步旅行者.

way·far·ing [ˈweifɛəriŋ] *a.* (徒步)旅行的,旅行中的. — *n.* (徒步)旅行. **~-tree** *n.* 【植】绵毛荚蒾.

way·go·ing [ˈweigəuiŋ] *a.* 出发的,离开的. — *n.* 出发;告别,离别.

Way·land [ˈweilənd] *n.* 韦兰〔日耳曼和英国民间传说中的隐身铁匠〕(= Wayland (the) Smith).

way·lay [ˈweiˈlei] *(-laid* [-ˈleid]*)* *vt.* 埋伏等候,伏击. *He was waylaid by thieves.* 他在路上被抢了.

way·leave [ˈweiliːv] *n.* 〔英〕通行权.

Wayne [wein] *n.* 韦恩〔姓氏,男子名〕.

way-out [ˈweiˈaut] *a.* 〔美口〕极不寻常的;超出常规的;标新立异的. — *n.* 观点激进的人.

-ways *suf.* 表示:方向,位置;方式,状态: al*ways*; length*ways*; side*ways*.

way·side [ˈweisaid] *n., a.* 路边(的).

way·sta·tion [ˈweisteiʃən] 〔美〕(快车不停的)小站.

way·train [ˈweitrein] 【美、铁路】逢站必停的普通客车.

way·ward [ˈweiwəd] *a.* ①任性的,恣意妄为的;刚愎自用的,固执的;不听话的. ②反复无常的;(方针、方向等)动摇的,不定的. ③意料不到的;违背愿望的;不利的. **-ly** *ad.* **-ness** *n.*

way·wise [ˈweiwaiz] *a.* ①〔美〕熟悉路途[地理]的. ②〔方〕富有经验的.

way·worn [ˈweiwɔːn] *a.* 在旅途中劳累[疲乏,削瘦]了的.

wayz·gooze [ˈweizguːs] *n.* 对印刷工人的一年一次夏季招待宴会或野餐.

WB = ①World Bank 世界银行(联合国). ②= W/B.

W/B = waybill 运货单;乘客单.

w.b. = ①warehouse book 【商】仓库帐簿. ②westbound. ③water ballast 【海】压舱水.

WBC = ①Westinghouse Broadcasting Company 〔美〕威斯汀豪斯广播公司. ②white blood cell 【解】白血球,白(血)细胞.

WbN, W by N = west by north 西偏北.

WbS, W by S = west by south 西偏南.

w.c. = ①water closet 盥洗室,厕所;抽水马桶. ②without charge 免费.

W.C.A. = Women's Christian Association 基督教妇女协会.

WCC = World Council of Churches 世界基督教协进会.

W.D. = ①War Department 〔美旧〕陆军部. ②Works Department 工程部.

wd = ①would. ②wiring diagram 电路图,接线圈.

we [wiː, 弱 wi] *pro. pl.* ①〔人称代词第一人称的复数、主格;所有格是 our, 宾格是 us, 物主代词是 ours〕我们. ②〔I 的代用〕(帝王君主的自称)朕;(报纸社论中代表编辑部的)我们. ③〔用作不定代词〕大家,人们. ④ = you 〔表示亲切〕. *We are not naturally bad.* 人不是生来坏的. *We had* (= There was) *much rain in last year.* 去年雨水不少. *How are ~ this morning, Child?* 孩子,咱们今儿早晨好吧?

weak [wiːk] *a.* ①柔弱的;虚弱的,有病的. ②无力的,软弱的;(根据等)薄弱的,不充分的. ③不中用的;愚钝的;脆弱的,易坏的. ④有弱点的. ⑤淡薄的;麸质少的 (*opp.* strong). ⑥(文章等)松懈的,无力的. ⑦【语法】弱变化的,按规则变化的. ⑧【商】疲软的,低落的. *one's ~ point [side]* 弱点. *the ~er sex [vessel]* 女性. *a ~ vessel* 不可靠[不中用]的人. *The ~est goes to the wall.* 优胜劣败. *~ evidence* 不充分的证据. *a ~ mind* 低能. *~ surrender* 不光彩的投降. *a ~ book* 没有什么价值的书. *He is ~ in mathematics.* 他数学不行. *~ tea* 淡茶. *~ brandy and water* 搀水冲淡的白兰地酒. **~fish** 【动】犬牙石首鱼(属). ~ **force** 【物】(控制中微子相互作用的)弱力. **~-headed** *a.* 脑筋钝的,笨,低能的. ~ **interaction** 【物】(粒子的)弱相互作用. **~-kneed** *a.* 膝盖骨软的;没有骨气的;优柔寡断的. **~-minded** *a.* = weak-headed. **~-sighted** *a.* 眼力差的. ~ **sister** 〔美俚〕懦夫,不可靠[不中用]的人;能力低劣者.

weak·en [ˈwiːkən] *vt.* ①使弱,削弱;使衰减. ②冲淡,弄稀薄. — *vi.* ①变(软)弱;衰减. ②变得拿不定主意,变得优柔寡断.

weak·ling [ˈwiːkliŋ] *a., n.* 虚弱的(人);柔弱的(人);低能的(人).

weak·ly [ˈwiːkli] *a.* *(-li·er; -li·est)* 软弱的;虚弱的. — *ad.* 软弱地;虚弱地;懦弱地;优柔寡断地.

weak·ness [ˈwiːknis] *n.* ①弱;衰弱,虚弱. ②柔弱;薄弱;懦弱,怯懦;优柔寡断. ③弱点,缺点. ④〔口〕偏爱,癖好,嗜好*(for)*. *have a ~ for the bottle* 非常喜欢喝酒. 有爱喝酒的毛病.

weal[1] [wiːl] *n.* 〔古〕福利,幸福. *the common ~* 公共福利. *the general [public] ~* 社会[公共]福利. ***in ~ or [and] woe*** 无论是祸是福. ***share ~ and woe with the people*** 和群众同甘共苦.

weal[2] [wiːl] *n., vt.* = wale.

weald [wiːld] *n.* 森林地带;(未开垦)旷野.

wealth [welθ] *n.* ①财富;财产;〔集合词〕富豪(阶级). ②富裕. ③丰富,丰饶,大量. ④〔古〕幸福,福利,繁荣. *a man of ~* 富人. *a ~ of learning* 丰富的学识. *W- of words is not eloquence.* 多言非雄辩. ~ **tax** 财产税.

Wealth·y [ˈwelθi] *n.* 〔美〕一种红色的、中等大小的秋苹果.

wealth·y [ˈwelθi] *a.* *(-i·er; -i·est)* 财产多的,富有的;丰富的,充分的;大量的. **-i·ly** *ad.* **-i·ness** *n.*

wean[1] [wiːn] *vt.* ①使断奶. ②使从…中脱离出来,使疏远 *(from)*;使隔离开,拉开;使断绝 *(from)*. *He had ~ed (away) himself from tobacco.* 他戒了烟了.

wean[2] [wiːn] *n.* 〔Scot.〕婴儿;小儿.

wean·er [ˈwiːnə] *n.* 断了奶的幼畜;断奶器.

wean·ling [ˈwiːnliŋ] *a., n.* 刚断奶的(婴孩或幼畜).

weap·on [ˈwepən] *n.* 武器,兵器;斗争工具[手段]. *absolute ~s* 〔美〕原子武器,氢武器. *massive ~s* (大规模杀伤的)原子武器,热核武器;核弹头导弹. *~s of mass destruction* 大规模毁灭性武器. *supersonic ~s* 超音速导弹. — *vt.* 武装. **-eer** *n.* 武器专家(尤指核武器专家). **-ry** ①武器设计和制造. ②武器库;〔集合词〕武器.

wear[1] [wɛə] ***(wore*** [wɔː]; ***worn*** [wɔːn]***)*** *vt.* ①穿着,戴着,挂着,佩着,带着. ②留着(胡须等);有着(记忆等). ③带着(某种表情,气味等);表现出,呈现着. ④磨损,用旧. ⑤使疲乏,使软弱无力. ⑥磨成,消蚀成(洞、沟等). ⑦消磨(时间). ⑧(船)升(旗). *~ eyeglasses* 戴着眼镜. *~ one's hair long* 留长头发. *~ a smile* 带着微笑. *He ~s her in his heart [memory].* 他心里记着她. *She is worn to a shadow with care.* 她忧愁得象瘦鬼一样了. *much worn clothes* 非常流行的衣服;穿得很旧的衣服. *~ a hole in* 在…上磨成一个洞. — *vi.* ①经用,耐用. ②损耗,磨破,变旧 *(away; out; off)*. ③疲乏,衰弱. ④(时间、季节等)慢慢过去,消逝. *It won't ~.* 这个东西不经

久. *The metal is ~ing.* 金属慢慢在磨损. ~ ***away*** ①*vi.* 渐渐度过;渐渐消耗,磨损. ②*vt.* 消磨(时间); 慢慢地磨灭. ~ ***down*** ①使衰弱;挫败;慢慢破坏;消蚀. ②坚韧不拔地克服(困难等). ~ ***off*** ①*vi.* 磨损,磨灭,消灭,渐渐消逝. ②*vt.* 磨损,磨灭,消耗. ~ ***on*** ①(时间)消逝,过去. ②使恼火;骚扰. ~ ***one's years well*** 不显老,显得年轻. ~ ***out*** ①*vt.* 穿坏,穿旧;耗尽,用尽;使疲乏不堪〔也用作比喻〕;消磨(时间、一生等)(~ *out sb.'s welcome* (因为访问次数太多等)使人觉得讨厌. *His patience was worn out at last.* 他终于忍耐不下去了). ②*vi.* 疲乏不堪;耗尽. ~ ***through the day*** 好容易挨过一天. ~ ***well*** 经用;经老,显得年轻 (*He is ~ing best.* 他比任何人都不显老). — *n.* ①穿著,佩戴. ②穿戴的东西;衣类,服装. ③流行物;时装. ④磨损,磨坏,穿旧,穿坏. ⑤经用,耐用. *everyday* ~ 便服. *There is still much ~ in these shoes.* 这双鞋子还能穿不少时候. *There is no ~ in it.* 这个不经久[快要破]了. *It is the only ~.* 这就是现在非常流行的东西. ***be in*** ~ 被人穿着;流行着. ***be the worse for*** ~ 被穿破,被用坏. ***have in*** ~ (经常)穿着. ~ ***and tear*** 消磨,消耗,磨损;衰竭;伐采. ~ **iron [plate]** 耐磨铁板. ~**proof,** ~**-resistant** *a.* 不磨损的.

wear² [wɛə] ***(wore*** [wɔː], ***worn*** [wɔːn]***)*** *vt., vi.* 【海】(把)(船头)转向下风.

wear³ [wiə] *n.* = weir.

wear·a·ble [ˈwɛərəbl] *a.* 可穿著的,可佩戴的,适于穿着[佩戴]的. — *n.* 〔*pl.*〕衣服.

wear·er [ˈwɛərə] *n.* ①穿着者,佩戴者. ②磨损物,消耗物.

wea·ri·ful [ˈwiəriful] *a.* 讨厌的; 令人疲倦的. **-ly** *ad.* **-ness** *n.*

wea·ri·less [ˈwiərilis] *a.* 不疲倦的; 不厌烦的. **-ly** *ad.* **-ness** *n.*

wear·ing [ˈwɛəriŋ] *a.* ①穿着的,服用的. ②消耗(性)的. ③使疲倦的. ~ **apparel** 衣服;服装. **-ly** *ad.*

wea·ri·some [ˈwiərisəm] *a.* 令人疲倦的; 叫人厌倦[生厌]的;乏味的.

wea·ry [ˈwiəri] *a.* ***(-ri·er; -ri·est)*** ①疲倦的,困乏的. ②感到厌倦的 *(of)*. ③令人厌倦[生厌,发腻]的;乏味的. *a ~ journey* 令人厌倦的旅程. *be ~ of life* 对生活感到厌烦[厌倦]. — *vt.* 使疲倦,使疲乏;使厌倦,使生厌,使发腻;烦扰,为难. *He is wearied of patience.* 他忍无可忍了. — *vi.* ①疲倦,疲乏;厌倦,厌烦 *(of)*. ②〔美,Scot.〕渴望,切望*(for)*. ~ ***out*** ①使疲累不堪;使腻烦不堪. ②厌烦地消磨时日. **-ri·ly** *ad.* **-ri·ness** *n.*

wea·sand [ˈwiːznd] *n.* 【解】①食管;喉. ②〔古〕气管.

wea·sel [ˈwiːzl] *n.* ①【动】鼬鼠. ②〔美口〕鬼鬼祟祟的人;卑劣的人. ③〔美口〕模棱两可的话,含糊的话 (= ~ word). ④〔*pl.*〕〔美〕南卡罗来纳 *(South Carolina)* 州人的绰号. ***catch a ~ asleep*** 瞒[骗]过精明的人;乘人不备. — *vi.* ①避免;躲避;逐渐放弃(义务);逐渐背弃(以前声明);〔美〕支吾,躲闪. ②〔美俚〕告密.

weath·er [ˈweðə] *n.* ①天气,气候;暴风雨(天气). ②(某种)时候;处境;状况. *broken* ~ 不正常的天气. *dirty [rough]* ~ 狂风暴雨的天气. *seasonable* ~ 良好的天气. *merry* ~ 快乐的时候. *a fair ~ friend* 酒肉朋友. ***April*** ~ 乍晴乍雨的四月天气;一会哭一会笑. ***dance and sing all ~s*** 随风转舵,顺应时势. ***in all ~s*** 不论晴雨. ***in fair ~ or foul*** 不论天气好坏. ***keep the*** ~ 【海】战胜[度过]暴风雨;控制局势. ***make bad*** ~【海】遇到暴风雨[恶劣天气]. ***make fair*** ~ 谄媚,拍马屁. ***make good*** ~ 【海】遇到好天气;操纵自如. ***make heavy*** ~ 遇到暴风雨[恶劣天气];难于操纵;感到难于应付. ***make heavy ~ of*** 碰到…的灾难. ***under stress of*** ~ 因暴风雨,碰到恶劣天气. ***under the*** ~ 〔俚〕①有病,不舒服. ②经济困难. ③喝醉了酒. ~ ***permitting*** 天气良好时. — *vt.* ①使暴露在风雨中;通风;晾干,吹干. ②【地】〔常用被动语态〕使风化. ③使(屋顶等)成泻水斜面. ④【海】战胜[度过]暴风雨;〔喻〕冲过,渡过,捱过,熬过. ~ *a point*【海】向风行驶. ~ *a storm* 战胜暴风雨;渡过难关. ~ *storms together* 同舟共济;共同克服困难[度过难关]. ~ *a financial crisis* 度过经济危机. — *vi.* ①因天气受损伤,因天气发生变化,风化. ②经受风雨 *(out)*. ~ ***in*** (飞机)因天气恶劣而停航;(机场)因天气恶劣而关闭. ~ ***out*** ①因天气坏而未能进入(某处). ②因天气坏而取消(飞行等). ~**-beaten** *a.* 受过风吹雨打的;满脸风霜的;饱经世故的(*a ~-beaten sailor* 航海经验丰富的水手). ~ **board** ①*n.*【建】檐板;【海】上风舷;炮门的挡雨板;防浪板. ②*vt.* 在…装檐板. ~**-bound** *a.* 被恶劣天气所阻的. ~ **breeder** 风雨的预兆〔将有风雨的晴天等〕. ~ **bureau** 〔美〕气象局. ~ **chart** 气象图. ~ **cock** 风信鸡,向标;易变心的人,随风倒的人. ~ **deck**【海】露天甲板. ~**-driven** *a.* 被暴风吹着跑的. ~ **eye** ①气候观察眼;注意天气. ②留神 (*keep one's ~-eye awake [open]* 时时警惕着). ~ **forecast** 天气预报. ~ **ga(u)ge**【海】上风位置;比别的船[别人]有利的地位 (*have [get] the ~ gauge of* 比…占有利地位). ~ **glass** 晴雨表;湿度表. ~**-man**〔口〕气象学家;测候员,天气预报员;〔美〕气象局职员. ~ **map** 气象图. ~ **mo(u)lding**【建】泻水线条,滴水(石). ~**ometer** 老化试验器;(测试塑料性能的)大气腐蚀计. ~**-proof** *a.* 抗风蚀的,不受天气影响的,经得起风雨的. ~ **prophet** 天气预测家;天气预报器;能预报天气的东西〔鸟、虫等〕. ~ **report** 气象通报;天气预报. ~ **service** 气象服务(站). ~ **stained** *a.* (墙壁等)被风雨弄退了色的. ~ **station** 气象台. ~ **strip**【建】(塞在窗门缝里)挡风雨的木条[橡皮条]. ~ **vane** = weathercock. ~**-wise** *a.* 很会预测天气的;对舆论敏感的;善于体会别人感情[意见]的,善于见风使舵的. ~**worn** *a.* 被风雨剥蚀了的. **-ing** ①【地】风化. ②【建】泻水(斜面) (*weathering test* 耐候性试验,老化试验). **-ly** *a.*【海】能驶向上风的.

weave [wiːv] ***(wove*** [wəuv], 〔罕〕***~d; wo·ven*** [ˈwəuvən], 【商】***wove)*** *vt.* ①织;编制;织结;编拢,编进. ②〔喻〕构成,作成,编成,设计. ③使曲曲弯弯行进. ~ *facts into a story* 把事实编成故事. — *vi.* 织布,编织;纠缠;〔英空俚〕闪避,迂回躲避. *a weaving mill* 织造厂. ~ ***all pieces on the same loom*** 用千篇一律的笔调写. ~ ***one's way through [out of] a crowd*** 弯弯曲曲穿过[走出]人群. — *n.* 织,织法,编法.

weav·er [ˈwiːvə] *n.* ①织者,织工;编制者. ②【鸟】鹲,织巢鸟 ***(= ~-bird)***;【虫】豉豆;织网蜘蛛. ~**'s hitch [knot]** 单索花绳结.

wea·zen [ˈwiːzn] *a.* = wizen.

web [web] *n.* ①蜘蛛网;蛛网状东西,网状组织;【纺】棉[毛]网. ②(一匹)布,织物. ③编织品,捏造的东西;做成的圈套. ④(水鸟的)蹼,掌皮;羽瓣. ⑤一大捲[筒]印刷用纸. ⑥【机】连结板;金属薄片[薄条];【建】工字梁腹(部);圆拱;【解】膜. *a ~ of railroads* 铁路网. *a ~ of lies* 一大片编造的谎话. *a ~ of life [destiny]* 命运. *the ~ of a saw* 锯身. *the ~ of a sword* 刀身. *a twist* ~【机】麻花钻心. — *vt.* ①在…上织网;丝网般密布在…上. ②用丝网网住;使入圈套. — *vi.* ①形成网状. ②织丝网. ~ **eye** 眼翳病. ~**-fingered** *a.* 指间有蹼的,有蹼指的. ~**foot** 蹼足[鸟];〔美〕〔谑〕俄勒冈 (Oregon) 州人的别名[因该州多湿地]. ~**-footed** *a.* 有蹼的,蹼足的. ~**footers** 〔*pl.*〕〔美〕 = webfoot. ~ **spinner**【动】仿足目昆虫. ~**-toed** *a.* = ~-footed. ~**-worm**【动】结网蠕虫.

Webb(e) [web] *n.* 韦布〔姓氏〕.

webbed [webd] *a.* 有蹼的.

web·bing [ˈwebiŋ] *n.* ①(作马腹带、车上吊带等用的)带子;(垫子等的)厚边,边带. ②【动】蹼.

web·by [ˈwebi] *a.* ***(web·bi·er, web·bi·est)*** ①丝网

W

(性,状)的. ②由丝网组成的.

We·ber [ˈwiːbə] *n.* ①韦伯〔姓氏〕. ②**Wilhelm Edward** ～ 威廉·韦伯〔1804—1891,德国物理学家〕.

we·ber [ˈweibə, ˈwiː-; ˈwebə] *n.* 【电】韦(伯)〔磁通单位,等于 10^8 麦克斯韦〕.

Web·ster [ˈwebstə] *n.* ①韦伯斯特〔姓氏〕. ②**Noah** ～ 韦伯斯特〔1758—1843,美国词典编辑家〕.

web·ster [ˈwebstə] *n.* 〔废〕织者,织工.

WEC, WECO = Westinghouse Electric Corporation 〔美〕威斯汀豪斯电气公司.

wed [wed] *vt.* ***(～ded; ～ded,*** 〔罕〕 ***wed)*** ①与…结婚. ②娶;嫁;使结婚. ③使结合. ～ *one's daughter to sb.* 把女儿嫁给某人家. — *vi.* 结婚. ～ ***over the mixen*** 和附近的人结婚. ～ ***over the moor*** 和远地人结婚. ～ ***with a rush ring*** 勉强结婚. **～-in** 集体婚礼.

Wed. = Wednesday.

we'd [wiːd; 弱 wid] = we had; we would; we should.

wed·ded [ˈwedid] *a.* ①结了婚的. ②固执的;拘泥的,死守. *the* ～ *pair* 夫妇. *a* ～ *life* 结婚生活. ～ *love* 婚后的爱情. ～ *to one's habits* 墨守旧习. *He is* ～ *to his pipe.* 他烟斗从不离嘴.

wed·ding [ˈwediŋ] *n.* ①婚礼;婚宴;结婚(纪念). ②结合. *a penny* ～〔英〕由亲友凑集资金及家用物品的婚礼. *the paper [wooden, tin, crystal, china, silver, golden, diamond]* ～ 纸[木、锡、水晶、玻璃、瓷、银、金、钻石]婚,结婚 1 〔5,10,15,20,25, 50, 60〕周年纪念. ～ **bell** (教堂的)报婚钟 (*All went merry as a* ～ *bell.* 事事愉快). ～ **breakfast** (结婚仪式后举行的)婚宴. ～ **cake** 婚礼大蛋糕. ～ **chest** 新娘的妆奁箱子. ～ **day** 婚礼日;结婚纪念日. ～ **garment** 结婚礼服. ～ **march** 结婚进行曲. ～ **ring** 结婚戒指.

we·del [ˈveidəl] *vi.* 作短回旋花式滑雪.

we·deln [ˈveidəln] *n.* 短回旋花式滑雪.

WEDF = Women's International Democratic Fedaration 国际民主妇女联合会.

wedge [wedʒ] *n.* ①楔,尖劈,楔形物;【几】楔形. ②【冶】高压顶点. ③〔喻〕可以逐渐扩大作用的开端. *a* ～ *of cake* 切成楔形的一块蛋糕. *retardation* ～【物】减速光劈. ***drive in [get in, insert] the thin end of the*** ～ 打进楔子尖;微微突破一点(以便慢慢扩大作用). ***knock out the ～s*** 〔俚〕使人陷入困境而冷眼旁观. — *vt.* 用楔子楔牢 (*up*);用楔子劈开;挤进. — *vi.* 楔入,挤进. ～ ***away*** 推开. ～ ***off*** 分开, 推开. ～ ***oneself in*** 挤入. ～ ***brake***【机】楔轫. ～ ***formation***【空】楔形编队. ～ ***ring***【机】劈形环. **～-shaped** *a.* 楔形的. **～wise** *ad.* 成楔形,以楔子状.

wedg·ies [ˈwedʒiz] *n.* 〔*pl.*〕〔美〕一种镶有楔形后跟的女式平底鞋〔源自商标名〕(= cobbies).

Wedg·wood [ˈwedʒwud] *n.* ①韦奇伍德〔姓氏〕. ②**J.** ～ 韦奇伍德〔1730—1795,英国陶瓷工艺家〕.

wedg·y [ˈwedʒi] *a.* ***(wedg·i·er, wedg·i·est)*** 似楔的,楔形的,可作楔用的.

wed·lock [ˈwedlɔk] *n.* 婚姻;结婚状态〔生活〕. ***born in lawful*** ～ 婚生的. ***born out of*** ～ 非婚生的,私生的.

Wednes·day [ˈwenzdi] *n.* 星期三.

wee [wiː] *a.* ***(we·er*** [ˈwiːə]; ***we·est*** [ˈwiːist]***)*** 〔Scot. 儿〕小小的,极小的. *a* ～ *bit* 一丁点. *a* ～ *folk* 小仙人,小鬼(等). — *n.* 〔Scot. 方〕一会儿. *bide a* ～ 等一会儿. ～ **hours** 凌晨.

weed[1] [wiːd] *n.* ①杂[莠]草. ②〔the ～〕〔口〕烟草;雪茄烟;纸烟;〔美俚〕大麻烟(=marijuana). ③废物,没出息的人;没用的东西〔牲畜〕,不值钱的东西. ④瘦长的人,瘦弱的马. ⑤〔*pl.*〕〔美〕无业游民〔失业工人,流浪工人〕聚居处. *the soothing [fragrant, Indian]* ～ = *the* ～ 烟草. *Ill ～s grow apace.* 莠草长得快. ～ *killer* 除莠剂. — *vt.* 除去(某处的)草,除去(害物、多余物等);清除;清理;淘汰;扫清(*out*). ～ *a garden* 除去园中杂草. — *vi.* 拔草,除草. ～ ***out*** ①清除,肃清. ②〔美〕恣意多取(自己不该分取的利益等).

weed[2] [wiːd] *n.* ①丧章;〔*pl.*〕(寡妇的)丧服. ②〔古〕衣服.

weed·er [ˈwiːdə] *n.* 除草人;除草机.

weed·y [ˈwiːdi] *a.* ①杂草多的,尽是杂草的;象杂草一样蔓生(长得快)的;(谣言)散播得极快的. ②不中用的,没用的,没价值的. ③细瘦的;瘦弱的.

week [wiːk] *n.* ①星期,周;七天(的期间). ②星期日以外的六天,工作日. *What day of the* ～ *is it?*=*What is the day of the* ～*?* 今天是星期几? *this* ～ 这个星期. *last [next]* ～ 上[下]一个星期. *this day week* 上[下]星期的这天〔如这天是星期三即指上星期或下星期的星期三〕. *tomorrow week* 上[下]星期的这天的次日. *yesterday* ～ 上[下]星期的这天的前一天. *Friday* ～ 上[下]星期的星期五. *～s ago* 好几个星期以前,很久以前. ***(a)*** ～ ***about*** 每隔一星期. ***a*** ～ ***ago today*** 上星期的今天. ***a*** ～ ***of Sundays*** = ***a*** ～ ***of ～s*** 〔口〕七个星期;老过不完的漫长时期;永远. ***knock [send] (sb.) into the middle of next*** ～〔俚〕撵跑;杀死(某人). ～ ***in,*** ～ ***out*** 一星期又一星期地〔指连续几个星期〕. **～day** 平日 (*opp.* Sunday). **～days** *ad.* 在平日. ～ **end** 周末;周末休假. **～-end** ①*a.* 周末的. ②*vi.* 过周末,作周末旅行. **～-ended** *a.* 度过了周末的. **～-ender** *n.* 周末旅行的人. **～ends** *ad.* (常)在周末,每逢周末. **～-night** 周日的晚上〔指星期一至星期五的晚上〕.

Week·ley [ˈwiːkli] *n.* 威克利〔姓氏〕.

week·ly [ˈwiːkli] *a.* 一星期(一次)的,每周的,周刊的. — *ad.* 一星期一次,每周. — *n.* 周刊,周报.

Weeks [wiːks] *n.* 威克斯〔姓氏〕.

Weems [wiːmz] *n.* 威姆斯〔姓氏〕.

ween [wiːn] *vt.* 〔古、诗〕①想,相信,认为,以为,设想,想象. ★ 常作 I ～, 用作插入成分. ②期待, 预期 (*to do*).

ween·ie [ˈwiːni] *n.* 〔美口〕= wiener.

ween·y [ˈwiːni] *a.* 〔美口〕很小的.

weep [wiːp] *vi.* ***(wept*** [wept]***)*** ①哭泣;悲叹,叹息 (*for; over*). ②流泪; 滴下. ③(枝)垂下, 低垂. — *vt.* ①流(泪);为…流泪. ②悲叹;哀悼. ③(岩石、植物等)渗出(水汽),分泌出,滴(水滴). ～ ***away*** 在哭泣中度过 (～ *away a whole day* 整整哭了一天). ～ ***for [with] joy*** 快乐得流泪. ～ ***Irish*** 假哭. ～ ***one's life away*** 在悲伤叹息中过日子. ～ ***oneself out*** 尽情痛哭. ～ ***oneself to sleep*** 哭得渐渐睡着了. ～ ***out*** 边哭边说. — *n.* ①〔俚〕哭泣,流泪. ②(水等的)渗出. ***the ～s*** 一阵痛哭;(妇女)痛哭的时间. ～ **hole** (护壁等上)滴水的洞孔.

weep·er [ˈwiːpə] *n.* ①哭泣者;悲叹者;爱哭泣的人. ②(旧时丧礼中雇用的)号哭者. ③丧章. ④寡妇用的黑面纱;〔*pl.*〕寡妇用的白袖边.

weep·ing [ˈwiːpiŋ] *a.* ①流泪的,哭泣的. ②渗出的;滴下的. ③下雨的. ④垂枝的. *a* ～ *pipe* 排水管. ～ **eczema**【医】渗出性湿疹. ～ **willow** 垂柳.

weep·y [ˈwiːpi] *a.* ***(weep·i·er; weep·i·est)*** ①要哭的;泪汪汪的;流液的,渗液的. ②哭泣的;易使人哭的. **-i·ness** *n.*

wee·ver [ˈwiːvə] *n.* 【鱼】鲈鱼.

wee·vil [ˈwiːvil] *n.* 【虫】象鼻虫,姑蠹. *the pea* ～【虫】豌豆象. **-y, -ly** *a.* = weevilled.

wee·vill·ed [ˈwiːvild] *a.* 有象鼻虫(蛀害)的.

wee-wee [ˈwiːˈwiː] *vt.* ***(-weed, -wee·ing)*** 〔儿〕嘘嘘(撒尿). — *n.* 小便,撒尿.

weft[1] [weft] *n.* 纬线,纬纱;〔诗〕织物.

weft[2] [weft] *n.* 【海】(表示风向、遇险等的)信号旗;(用旗等表示的)信号,求救信号.

we-group [ˈwiːgruːp] *n.* 我们的集团,圈内(=in-group).

Wehr·macht [ˈveːrmaxt] *n.* 〔G.〕(德国)国防军〔指二次

世界大战时及以前的德国军队〕.

wei·ge·la [waiˈdʒilə, -ˈgiː-] *n.*【植】锦带花属 *(Weigela)* 植物;〔尤指〕锦带花 *(Weigela florida)* (= weigelia).

weigh[1] [wei] *vt.* ①称,量;(用手)掂估. ②衡量,估量(…的)优劣,比较考察. ③(用重量)压,压下. ④折磨,使吃重,使垂头丧气. ⑤【海】起(锚). *She is ~ed down with many troubles.* 她被许多麻烦事压得透不过气来. *~ anchor* 起锚(开船). — *vi.* ①量体重;重…,有…重. ②可重视,重要. ③重压,压迫,吃重. ④衡量,估计. ⑤【海】起锚,开船. *When did you ~ last?* 你上次什么时候称过体重? *She ~s 85 pounds.* 她体重85磅. ***~ down*** 使负重担;压迫,压下,压倒. ***~ in*** 骑师〔拳师等〕在比赛前受体重检查. ***~ in with*** ①有相当把握地提出(议论、事实等). ②额外提出,另加;插言. ***~ light*** (称起来)分量轻;不重要. ***~ little*** 没有多少分量;没啥了不起,无关紧要. ***~ nothing*** 没什么,一点儿也不重要. ***~ on [upon] one's mind*** 使人烦恼,使人心情沉重. ***~ one's words*** 斟酌语句,仔细考虑着讲. ***~ out*** ①(从全部中)称量出(若干分量). ②骑师〔拳师等〕在比赛后受体重检查. ***~ the pros and cons*** 权衡利弊. ***~ the thumb*** 〔美〕骗称头〔克扣分量〕. ***~ up*** ①称量,估量. ②称出. ③重得使另一头翘起来. ***~ with*** 被…重视;和…有重大关系 (*the point that ~s with me* 对我来说是重要的地方). — *n.* 称量,衡量,过秤. **~ beam** 秤杆儿. **~ bridge** (称车马重量的)台称,桥秤. **~house** 过磅处,过秤处. **~-in** *n.* (拳师等)赛前量体重. **~-lock** 衡闸〔运河中称船重的水闸〕. **~man** 过磅员,过秤员. **~master** 管理公共磅秤的人;(厂矿中)称量产品重量者. **~shaft** 【机】摇臂钻.

weigh[2] [wei] *n.* 【海】 = way 〔仅用于下列习语中〕: ***under ~*** 在进行中 (under way).

weigh·er [ˈweiə] *n.* ①过磅员,验秤员. ②衡器,台称,称(物)机.

weigh·ing-ma·chine [ˈweiiŋməʃiːn] 称(物)机,衡器,台秤.

weight [weit] *n.* ①重量;体重;求心力,重力,(地心)引力. ②斤两,分量,衡,计重单位. ③(压东西的)重物. ④砝码,秤锤,秤砣. ⑤重担,重压;负担,重任. ⑥重要性;影响力,势力. ⑦【统计】权,加重值,权重,重要度. ⑧(合于季节的衣料的)重量,厚薄. ⑨拉弓所需的力. ⑩【赛马】马应负载的重量〔包括马鞍、骑师等〕. ⑪(拳师、摔跤手等的)体重级别. *a paper ~* 镇纸. *a pound ~* 一磅重的秤砣〔砝码〕. *a man of ~* 重要人物,有势力的人. *a suit of summer ~* 夏服一套. ***by ~*** 论重量(卖等). ***carry great [no] ~*** 极〔不〕重要,极受〔不受〕重视. ***gain [lose] ~*** 体重增加〔减少〕. ***give short ~*** 骗称头,克扣分量. ***have ~ with*** *(sb.)* 对(某人)有影响. ***pull one's ~*** 尽自己的本分,见 pull 条. ***put on ~*** 体重增加,发胖. ***throw one's ~ about*** 大摆架子;作威作福,仗势欺人. ***under the ~ of*** 在…的重压下,迫于…. ***~ empty*** 空重,皮重;空载. ***~s and measures*** 度量衡. — *vt.* ①在…上加重量,把重量放在…上. ②使负担,装载;使负重担,装载过重;折磨,压迫. ③在(织品、丝等内)搀重晶石(等)以增加分量. ④【统计】使加权,附加加重值于. ⑤视…为重要,强调. ***~ed with*** 因…加重;因…烦恼. **~ lifting**【运】举重. **~ throw** 【体】链球运动. **~ watcher** 减肥者,节食者. **-less** *a.* 无重的;失重的. **-lessness** *n.* 失重.

weight·y [ˈweiti] *a.* *(-i·er; -i·est)* ①重的,有分量的;有权势的. ②重要的,重大的,严重的;有影响的. ③沉重的,承受不了的. **-i·ly** *ad.* **-i·ness** *n.*

Wei·mar [ˈvaimɑː] *n.* 魏玛〔德意志民主共和国城市,过去为一公国〕. **~ Constitution** 魏玛宪法〔1919年在魏玛召开的国民议会制定的德意志共和国宪法〕. **~ Republic** 魏玛共和国〔1918年德皇退位后到1933年第三帝国成立间的德国〕.

Wei·ma·ra·ner [ˈvaimərɔnə, ˈwai-] *n.* 【动】魏玛伦纳猎狗.

Weir [wiə] *n.* 韦尔〔姓氏〕.

weir [wiə] *n.* ①〔英〕堰,(导流)坝. ②水口. ③鱼梁.

weird [wiəd] *a.* ①〔古〕命运(三女神)的. ②超自然的,不可思议的,令人不愉快的,叫人毛骨悚然的;神怪的. ③〔口〕离奇的,古怪的. — *n.* 〔Scot. 古〕命运,预言;前兆;〔W-〕命运三女神之一. ***the W- Sisters*** 命运三女神;(莎士比亚所作《麦克佩斯》一剧中的)三女巫.

weis·en·heim·er [ˈwaizenhaimə] *n.* 〔美俚〕自作聪明的人,自以为什么都知道〔了不起〕的人.

Weis·mann·ism [ˈvaismənizəm] *n.* 【生】魏斯曼学说〔德国生物学家魏斯曼(1834—1914)的学说,认为种质可世代相传,但后天获得性不能遗传〕.

we·ka [ˈweikɑː, ˈwiːkə] *n.* 【动】新西兰黑秧鸡.

Welch [welʃ, weltʃ] *n.* 韦尔奇〔姓氏〕.

welch [welʃ] *v.* 〔俚〕 = welsh. **-er** *n.* = welsher.

wel·come [ˈwelkəm] *a.* *(-com·er; -com·est)* ①受欢迎的,吃香的. ②很好的;可喜的,叫人快乐的,可感谢的. ③〔只用作表语〕可随便使用,能自由使用;不必感谢的;〔谑〕随便…罢. *Welcome = You are [You're] ~.* 欢迎欢迎;别客气,不用谢. *a ~ guest* 受欢迎的客人. *~ news* 好消息,喜信. *You are ~ to (use) any book here.* 你可随意使用这里的书. *Sympathy is ~ to the unfortunate.* 不幸的人容易得到同情. ***and ~*** 而且是受欢迎的;尽可随意 (*You may have it, and ~.* 你尽管用好啦). ***be ~ to*** 可以自由〔随意〕… (*You are ~ to my purse.* 我这钱请你随意用吧. *He is ~ to say what he pleases.* 让他随便说罢). ***make (sb.) ~*** 款待(某人). — *int.* 欢迎! *W- home, to New China!* 欢迎你回来,回到新中国! — *n.* ①欢迎,款待;欢迎辞. ②自由使用〔享受〕的特权. ***bid (sb.) ~ = say ~ to (sb.)*** 向某人表示欢迎. ***give (sb.) a warm ~*** 热烈〔竭诚〕欢迎某人;〔反〕猛烈迎击. ***outstay [wear out] sb.'s ~*** 因呆得太久〔去得太频繁〕而不再受欢迎. — *vt.* 欢迎. *~ candid criticism* 欢迎直率批评. *~ in the new year* 欢欢喜喜迎来新年. **~ mat** 欢迎垫〔门前的擦鞋棕垫〕(*put out the ~ mat* 热忱接待). **~ waggon** ①(带给新迁入户有关迁进地区的消息、土特产等的)欢迎礼品车. ②〔常作 W- W-〕作上述服务的人们. **-er** *n.* 欢迎者. **-ly** *ad.* **-ness** *n.*

weld[1] [weld] *n.* 焊接(点),熔接点. — *vt.* 焊〔熔〕接;使密切接合,结合. *a ~ed joint* 【机】熔接头. — *vi.* 被焊接〔熔接〕. *~ing powder* 焊粉. *a ~ing rod* 焊条. *gas ~ing* 气焊. *resistance ~* 电焊. *a ~less pipe* 无缝管. **-er** *n.* ①焊工. ②焊接机. **-ing** 焊接 (*-ing torch* 熔焊炬).

weld[2] [weld] *n.* 【植】淡黄木樨草;(由淡黄木樨草采取的)黄色染料.

Wel·don [ˈweldən] *n.* 韦尔登〔姓氏,男子名〕.

wel·fare [ˈwelfɛə] *n.* 福利(事业);繁荣,兴隆. *Advisory Committee for Child W-* 儿童福利促进会. *public ~ funds* 公共福利基金. *the national ~ and the people's livelihood* 国计民生. **~ centre** 福利中心〔设施,机构〕. **~ fund** 福利基金. **~ mother** 〔美〕领福利救济的母亲〔指有孩子而无丈夫、需接受社会福利救济的妇女〕. **~ state** 福利国家. **~ stater** 福利国家论者,鼓吹福利国家主义的人. **~ statism** 福利国家论〔主义〕. **~ work** 福利事业〔工作〕.

wel·far·ism [welˈfɛərizm] *n.* ①福利主义. ②福利事业. **-far·ist** *n., a.*

wel·kin [ˈwelkin] *n.* 〔诗〕苍穹,天空. ***make the ~ ring*** 响彻云霄.

well[1] [wel] *n.* ①井. ②泉水;源头,来源. ③坑,穴,凹处;【矿】矿井,竖坑;【军】(地雷的)井坑;【建】井孔;通风竖井;楼梯井,升降机井道. ④【机】(插仪表的)插孔,(油轴承中的)室. ⑤(渔船的)养鱼舱;(书桌上的)墨水池. ⑥(阶式教室的)讲坛;(法庭的)律师席. *an artesian ~* 自流井,喷水井. *an oil ~* 油井. *a landing gear ~* 【空】

起落架舱. — *vi.* 涌出，喷出 (*up; out; forth*). — *vt.* 使涌出，使喷出，使流出. *eyes ~ing tears of joy* 涌出欢乐泪水的眼睛. *a fountain ~ing pure waters* 喷射清水的喷泉. ~ ***over*** 溢满. ~**head** 源头，水源；井栏. ~**sinker** 凿井工人. ~**spring** 源泉，水源. ~ **tube** (钻井)套管.

well² [wel] *ad.* ***(bet·ter*** [ˈbetə]; ***best*** [best]***)*** ①好. ②适当，恰当，合适，正好. ③足够；完全；充分. ④很，相当. ⑤大概；很可能. ⑥有理. ⑦关心地，优待；赞扬. *That is ~ said.* 说得好. *W- done!* 好！做得好！*It was ~ done of you to come.* 你来得正好. *live ~* 生活得优越. *It may ~ be true.* 这大概是真的. *You may ~ say that.* 你那么说也有理. *be treated ~* 受优待，得到照顾. ***as ~*** 又，也；同样 (*He is a scientist, but he is a poet as ~.* 他是科学家又是诗人). ***as ~ as*** (除…之外)又…，既…又…；和…一样；…不用说 (*He gave me clothes as ~ as food.* 他给我食物又给我衣服. *As ~ be hung for a sheep as a lamb.* 一不做二不休，要干索性大干). ***be ~ on [advanced] in life*** 年纪很大. ***be ~ past*** *(forty)* 远远超过(四十岁). ***be ~ up in the list*** 列在最前面几个当中. ***do oneself ~*** 日子过得很好[富裕]. ***may as ~*** 还是…的好. (*You may as ~ go at once.* 你还是马上去的好). ***may (as) ~*** 也不坏，也有好处(*We might ~ make the experiment.* 我们做做实验也不坏). ***might as ~*** 等于，不如 (*You might as ~ throw your money into the sea as lend it to him.* 你借钱给他等于丢在海里). ***stand ~ with …*** 中…的意，受…欢迎. ***W-met!*** 幸会，幸会！ ***~ off = ~ to do*** 经济宽裕，富裕. ***~ over*** *(a hundred)* 远远超过 (一百). — *a.* ***(better; best)*** ①健康(的)，痊愈(的)，健全(的). ②适当(的)，得当(的). ③正好(的)，好；满意(的). *a ~ man*〔美〕健康的人. *Quite ~, thank you.* 我很好，谢谢你. *It is ~ you came along.* 你来得正好 [恰好]. ***be as ~ …*** 也好 (*It may be as ~ to explain.* 说明说明也好). ***It is all very ~, but …*** 这好倒是很好，可是…. ***very ~*** 非常好；非常健康；好. ***Well and good.*** (既然…，那就)好吧，没法了；那也好. ~ ***enough*** 相当好. — *n.* 好，满意. *I wish him ~.* 我希望他幸福. ***Let ~ alone.*** 那样很好，别去管它；不要画蛇添足；不要多事. — *int.*〔表示吃惊、安心、让步、谈话的重新开始、期待、断念等的意思〕①哎呀，唷；怎么！②好啦. ③好，那么，那么说的时候. ④喔，这个；可是，且说，至于. ⑤后来. ⑥算啦. *W-, to be sure! = W-, I never! = W- now!* 唷，这倒奇怪！*W-, here we are at last.* 好啦，好容易到了. *W-, do as you please.* 那么[好吧]，随你的便罢. *W- then, say no more about it.* 那么这事情就这样算啦. *W-, who was it?* 可是，那是谁呢？*W- then?* 后来怎样啦？*W-, it cannot be helped.* 算了，没办法. ~**-advised** *a.* 细想过的，慎重的，考虑周密的；有见识的，聪明的. ~**-appointed** *a.* 已准备 [装备] 齐全的；设备完善的. ~**-assembled** *a.* 〔美〕身材美的 (姑娘). ~**-balanced** *a.* 正常的；有常识的；匀称的，端整的. ~**-behaved** *a.* 行动正派的，举动得当的，有礼貌的. ~**-being** 生活平安，安宁，幸福，福利. ~**-beloved** *a.* ①很受人爱的；受人尊敬的. ②*n.* 亲爱的人. ~**-born** *a.* 身家清白的；出生名门的. ~**-bred** *a.* ①教养得好的，有教育的；有礼貌的；优雅的. ②(马等)良种的. ~**-chosen** *a.* 精选的；恰当的. ~**-connected** *a.* 有很好的社会关系[亲戚朋友]的. ~**-content** *a.* 十分满意[足]的. ~**-disposed** *a.* 具有好意的，好心的；性情[情绪]好的. ~**-doer** *n.* 做好事的人. ~**-doing** *n.* 善行，德行. ~**-done** *a.* ①干得出色的. ②煮得很熟的，煮透的. ~**-dressed** *a.* 穿得好的. ~**-drilled** *a.* 训练[练习]得好的. ~**-earned** *a.* 凭自己力量[工作]得来的，正当的 (*~-earned rest* 应得的休息；*~-earned punishment.* 自作自受的惩罚). ~**-favo(u)red** *a.* 漂亮的，标致的. ~**-fed** *a.* 营养充足的，吃[饲养]得好的. ~**-fixed** *a.*〔美〕①兴旺的；相当富有的. ②喝醉了的. ~**-formed** *a.* 符合语法规则的；合适的. ~**-found** *a.* = well-appointed. ~**-founded** *a.* 有根据的，有理由的. ~**-groomed** *a.* 喂养得很好的，修整得很好的；衣着整洁的. ~**-grounded** *a.* ①受过基本教育［训练］的. ②=well-founded. ③理由充足的. ~**-handled** *a.* 处理［经营管理]得很好的. ~**-heeled** *a.*〔美俚〕有充足武装的；富有的. ~**-informed** *a.* 消息灵通的，见闻广博的. ~**-intentioned** *a.* 善意的，好心(做)的. ~**-judged** *a.* 判断正确的，适宜的，恰当的. ~**-knit** *a.* 结实的；缜密的. ~**-known** *a.* 众所周知的，著名的；熟知的. ~**-liking** *a.* 〔古〕茂盛的；丰满的；健康的；状况良好的. ~**-looking** *a.* 漂亮的，美丽的. ~**-made** *a.* 做得好的；样子好的，匀称的. ~**-mannered** *a.* 有礼貌的；举动得当的；态度好的. ~**-marked** *a.* 明确的. ~**-meaning** *a.* 善意的，好心的. ~**-meant** *a.* = well-intentioned. ~**-measured** *a.* 恰如其分的. ~**-off** *a.* ①顺利的；处于优越地位的；幸运的，运气好的；手头宽裕的，有钱的，富有的. ②得到充分供应的，丰富的. ~**-oiled** *a.* ①甜言蜜语的，甘言奉承的. ②光滑的；顺利的；运行良好的. ③〔美俚〕有点醉意的. ~**-ordered** *a.* 秩序井然的；【化】良序的. ~**-paid** *a.* 工资高的. ~**-pleasing** *a.* 满意的. ~**-preserved** *a.* 保存［保养］得良好的. ~**-proportioned** *a.* 很均匀的，很匀称的. ~**-read** *a.* 书读得多的；博学的. ~**-regulated** *a.* 整理得好的，有规则的，井井有条的. ~**-remembered** *a.* 清楚记得的. ~**-reputed** *a.* 名气好的，有名气的. ~**-rounded** *a.* 面面俱到的；全面的；多才多艺的；圆满无缺的；丰满的. ~**-seeming** *a.* 满意似的. ~**-seen** *a.* 〔古〕熟练的；明显的. ~**-set (up)** *a.* 牢固的；妥贴的；(骨骼等)结实的. ~**-spent** *a.* (时间等)充分利用[使用得当]的. ~**-spoken** *a.* 说话漂亮[得当]的；说得巧妙的. ~**-thought-of** *a.* 名声好的. ~**-timbered** *a.* ①用木材撑牢的. ②强状的. ③林木繁茂的. ~**-timed** *a.* 时机正好的，正合时的；合拍的. ~**-to-do** 经济宽裕的，富裕的 (*the ~-to-do* 富裕阶级) (*opp.* the needy). ~**-tried** *a.* 经过多次试验的. ~**-trod(den)** *a.* 踏得很平的；〔喻〕有人弄过的，有人做过的. ~**-turned** *a.* ①【机】车得[切削得]极好的. ②措词巧妙的，说得得体的. ~**-up** *ad.* 靠近顶部[最前列]. ~**-weighed** *a.* 经过斟酌的. ~**-wired** *a.* 消息灵通的. ~**-wisher** 表示良好祝愿的人，具有善意的人. ~**-worn** *a.* 用旧了的；陈腐的，平常的.

we'll [wiːl; 弱 wil] (= we shall; we will.)

well·a·day [ˈweləˈdei] *int.*〔古、谑〕呜呼！哀哉！哎唷！

well·a·way [ˈweləˈwei] *int.* = welladay.

Wel·ler [ˈwelə] *n.* 韦勒〔姓氏〕.

Welles [welz] *n.* 韦尔斯〔姓氏〕.

Welles·ley [ˈwelzli] *n.* 韦尔斯利〔姓氏〕.

Wel·ling·ton [ˈweliŋtən] *n.* ①惠灵顿〔姓氏〕. ②**A.W.** ~ 惠灵顿〔1769—1852，在滑铁卢击败拿破仑的英国将军〕. ③惠灵顿〔新西兰首都〕. ④〔*pl.*〕惠灵顿长靴 (= ~ boots). — *a.* ①新西兰首都惠灵顿的；惠灵顿流行的式样的. ②新西兰惠灵顿省区的；惠灵顿省区流行的式样的.

well·nigh [ˈwelnai] *ad.* 〔古〕几乎.

Wells [welz] *n.* ①韦尔斯〔姓氏〕. ②**H. G.** ~ 威尔斯〔1866—1946，英国作家〕.

Welsh [welʃ] *a.* 威尔士(人)的；威尔士语的. — *n.* 威尔士语；〔集合名词〕〔the ~〕威尔士人. ~ **Corgi** [ˈkɔːgi] (威尔士) 狐头矮脚狗. ~**man** 威尔士人. ~ **mutton** (威尔士山中产的)小白羊的肉. ~ **rabbit**〔常误作 ~ rarebit〕(用来抹面包或苏打饼干的)熔化干酪；涂有熔化干酪的烤面包. **-woman** *n.* 威尔士女人. ~ **terrier**【动】威尔士㹴.

welsh [welʃ]〔口〕*vi.* (赛马赌输) 不付赌金溜掉；赖债溜走；逃避义务. **-er** *n.*

welt [welt] *n.* ①(鞋底和鞋帮间的)窄条接缝皮；滚边，贴边，贴缝. ②鞭痕；〔口〕鞭打. — *vt.* ①给…滚边，上接缝皮(在鞋上). ②把…打出鞭痕;〔口〕鞭打.

Welt [velt] *n.* 〔G.〕世界.

Welt·an·schau·ung [ˈveltænˈʃauuʌŋ] *n.* 〔G.〕世界观.

Welt·an·sicht [ˈveltɑ:nziçt] *n.* 〔G.〕世界观.

wel·ter[1] [weltə] *vi.* ①翻滚,(猪在泥潭中)打滚; 挣扎;(浪)起伏,翻腾. ②浸;染污;沉迷 *(in)*. ③混乱;〔方〕摇摆. — *n.* ①滚转,打滚;(波浪的)起伏,翻腾; 动摇. ②混乱,纷扰.

wel·ter[2] [ˈweltə] *n.* ①重量级骑师(= ~weight). ②次重量级的摔交手〔拳师〕. — *a.* 负重赛马的. **~-race** 负重赛马. **~-weight** ①重量级骑师. ②(跳栏赛马时)加在马身上的特别重量. ③【拳击】次中量级(拳师)〔体重 135—147 磅〕.

Welt·schmerz [ˈveltʃmeəts] *n.* 〔G.〕厌世,悲观.

We·myss [wi:mz] *n.* 威姆斯〔姓氏〕.

wen[1] [wen] *n.* ①【医】皮脂腺囊瘤,粉瘤. ②(人口众多成为赘物的)大城市. ***the great ~*** 伦敦市.

wen[2] [wen] *n.* 古英语字母"ƀ"〔十一世纪起用 w 取代〕.

wench [wentʃ] *n.* ①少女; 女儿; 少妇; 乡下姑娘; 女工; 女仆; 〔美俚〕下层阶级女子〔尤指女仆〕. ②〔古〕妓女; 荡妇. — *vi.* 私通;(尤指经常地)嫖妓;与荡妇发生关系.

wend [wend] *vt., vi.* ***(~ed** or* 〔古〕 ***went*** [went]*)* 〔古〕走往;去. ★ went 是古英语 wend 的过去式,现沿用作 go 的过去式. ~ ***one's way*** *(to)* 去,赴.

Wend [wend] *n.* (德国东北部)温德族. **-ic, -ish** *a.*

Wen·dell [ˈwendl] *n.* 温德尔〔姓氏,男子名〕.

Wen·dy [ˈwendi] *n.* ①温迪〔女子名〕. ②~ **house**〔英〕温迪之家〔供一个儿童玩耍的游戏室〕.

Wens·ley·dale [ˈwenzlideil] *n.* (英国 Yorkshire 产的)温斯利代干酪.

went [went] *v.* ①go 的过去式. ②〔古〕 wend 的过去式.

wen·tle·trap [ˈwentlˌtræp]【动】*n.* 海蛳(属).

wept [wept] weep 的过去式及过去分词.

were [强 wə:, weə; 弱 wə] be 的过去式, 陈述语气用于复数,虚拟语气用于单数及复数. *I wish it ~ so.* 我巴不得这样. ***as it ~*** 如同,好似,仿佛. ***~ it not for*** 要是没有…的话;要不是….

we're [wiə] = we are.

weren't [wə:nt, weənt] = were not.

wer(e)·wolf [ˈwə:wulf] *n. (pl.* ***-wolves)*** ①【神】变成狼的人,狼人. ②大而残忍的狼;凶狠残酷的人.

wer·geld [ˈwə:geld, weə-] *n.*【法】赎杀金, 抚恤金〔盎格鲁萨克逊和日耳曼人法律, 杀人者家属赔偿被杀者家属的一笔钱,以免受报复〕(亦作 weregild, wergild).

Wer·ner [ˈwə:nə] *n.* 沃纳〔男子名〕.

wer·ner·ite [ˈwə:nərait] *n.*【地】柱石.

wert [强 wə:t; 弱 wət] *vi.* 〔古〕(主词是 thou 时的) be 的第二人称、单数、过去、陈述语气及虚拟语气.

Wer·ther·ism [ˈveətərizəm, ˈwə:θə-] *n.* 维特情绪, 病态的感伤性〔维特原为德国大作家哥德的小说《少年维特之烦恼》中因失恋而自杀的主人公〕.

wes·kit [ˈweskit] *n.* 〔美〕= vest.

Wes·ley [ˈwezli, ˈwesli] *n.* ①韦斯利〔姓氏,男子名〕. ② **John** ~约翰·韦斯利〔1703—1791, 英国传教士,美以美教派的创始人〕.

Wes·ley·an [ˈwezliən] *a.* (美以美教派 (Methodism) 创始人)约翰·韦斯利(派)的. — *n.* 〔主英〕美以美教派信徒(= Methodist).

West [west] *n.* 韦斯特〔姓氏〕.

west [west] *n.* ①〔常作 the ~〕西,西方,西部(地方). ②〔the W-〕西洋;西欧;〔有时作 W-〕〔美〕西部. ③西风. — *a.* 西的,西部〔方〕的;在西的; 向西的; (风等)从西面来的. — *ad.* 在西,在西方;向西方. ***due ~*** 向正西方. ***go ~*** 向西去;〔俚〕上西天,死. ~ ***of*** 在…的西面. **~bound** *a.* 西行的,向西的. ~ **by north [south]** 西偏北〔南〕. **~-northwest** 西西北. **~-southwest** 西西南. ~ **country**〔英〕西部地方. **W- End** 伦敦西区. **W-Germany** 西德. **W- Point**〔美〕西点陆军军官学校.

West·cott [ˈwestkət] *n.* 韦斯科特〔姓氏〕.

west·er [ˈwestə] *vi.* 向西, 西行. — *n.* 西风〔尤指带来暴风雨的西风〕.

west·er·ing [ˈwestəriŋ] *a.* 偏西的,西下的.

west·er·ly [ˈwestəli] *a.* 西(方)的;向西的; 从西面来的(风). — *ad.* 在西,向西面.

west·ern [ˈwestən] *a.* ①西的,西方的;在西的; 向西的; 从西方来的. ②〔W-〕西洋的, 西欧的. ③日落西山的, 衰颓的. — *n.* ①西部人;西欧人. ②〔美影〕西部片; 西部小说〔多以骑马牧童的生活为题材〕. *the W- [Latin] Church* 拉丁教会,罗马天主教. **W- Hemisphere** 西半球. **~-most** *a.* 最西的,极西的. **W- Ocean**〔古〕大西洋. **W- Sider** ①(纽约曼哈坦的)西城区居民. ②约旦河西岸的居民. **W- States** 〔美〕西部诸州. **W- Wall** = Wailing Wall. **-er** (美国)西部人;西欧人. **-ize** *vt.* 使西方化.

west·ern·ism [ˈwestənizm] *n.* 西方特有的语言、文化和风格〔尤指美国西部特有的词语或方言〕.

Western Sahara [ˈwestən səˈhɑ:rə] 西撒哈拉〔非洲〕.

Western Samoa [ˈwestən səˈməuə] 西撒摩亚〔南太平洋〕.

West·fa·len [vestˈfɑ:lən] = Westphalia.

West-In·dian [ˈwestˈindjən] *a., n.* 西印度的〔人〕.

West Indies [ˈwest ˈindiz] 西印度群岛〔拉丁美洲〕.

west·ing [ˈwestiŋ] *n.* ①【海】西距,西行距离; 西航. ②(风)从西方吹来.

West·ing·house [ˈwestiŋhaus], **G.** 威斯丁豪斯〔1846—1914,美国发明家〕.

Westm. = Westminster.

West·min·ster [ˈwestminstə] *n.* ①威斯敏斯特〔伦敦市的一个行政区,英国议会所在地〕; 议会; 议会政治. ② =~ Abbey. ***at ~*** 在议会. ~ **Abbey** (伦敦)威斯敏斯特教堂〔举行国葬之处〕; 〔喻〕(可享受国葬礼遇的)光荣逝世. ~ **School** 威斯敏斯特公学.

West·pha·li·a [westˈfeiliə, -ˈfeiljə] 威斯特伐利亚〔德意志联邦共和国地名〕. *peace of ~* 威斯特伐利亚和约〔于 1648 年签订,以此结束三十年战争〕. **-n** *a., n.*

West Virginia [ˈwest və(:)ˈdʒinjə] 西弗吉尼亚〔美国州名〕.

west·ward [ˈwestwəd] *ad.* 向西方. — *a.* 向西的. — *n.* 西方,西部. **-ly** *a., ad.* 向西,靠近〔坐落〕西部; 从西部吹来的(风).

west·wards [ˈwestwədz] *ad.* = westward.

wet [wet] *a. (opp.* dry*)* ①湿, 潮湿的, 有湿气的. ②雨的,下雨的,多雨的. ③〔美俚〕允许卖〔制〕酒的, 不禁酒的;反对禁酒的. ④湿性的;【化】湿式的. ⑤〔俚〕喝醉了的;(人、物等)讨厌的;愚笨的;动不动流泪的;伤感的. *W- paint.*【告白】油漆未干 (=〔英〕Fresh paint). *a ~ day* 下雨天. *a ~ bargain* 喝酒时做成的交易. *He is all ~.* 他真是发疯了;他完全搞错了. ~ ***behind the ears*** 没有经验的; 不成熟的. — *n.* ①湿气, 水分; 液体, 水. ②雨, 雨天. ③〔俚〕酒, 饮酒;〔美〕反对禁酒的人. ④〔俚〕笨蛋. — *vt.* ①把…弄湿. ②喝酒庆祝〔进行〕. ~ *the bed* 尿床, 撒尿在床上. ~ *a bargain* 喝着酒做交易. ~ *sb.'s commission [stripes]*〔军俚〕喝酒庆祝升任军官. ~ *one's whistle*〔美〕喝酒. — *vi.* 湿;〔方〕下雨. **~back**〔美〕(非法入境或被带进美国的)墨西哥流动农业工人. ~ **bar** 有自来水的酒吧或柜台. ~ **blanket [smack]**〔美俚〕讨厌的人,扫人兴的人〔事物〕. **~-blanket** *vt.* 用湿毡压灭(火); 〔喻〕使扫兴. ~ **bob** (*Eton* 校内)爱划艇的学生. **~-bulb thermometer**【气】湿球温度计. ~ **cell** 湿电池. ~ **clutch**【机】湿式离合器. ~ **dream** 梦遗. ~ **fly** (钓鱼用)水下假蝇暗钩. ~ **goods**〔美俚〕酒. ~ **hen**〔美〕讨厌的伙伴. ~ **lab**

W

增压降压舱〔海底实验室中工作人员由此进出的一个舱〕. ~**land**〔常 *pl.*〕沼泽地;〔美〕野兽保护沼地. ~**look**【染】光面〔在纤维表面涂上尿浣后产生的光泽效果〕. ~-**nurse** ①*n.* 乳母〔*cf.* dry-nurse 保姆〕. ②*vt.* 为…当乳母,奶(小孩). ~ **pack**【医】湿裹法. ~ **suit** 保温潜水服. ~ **treatment**【矿】湿处理,湿选. ~ **wash** ①洗后未熨的湿衣服. ②湿洗〔洗后不擦干的洗车法〕.

weth·er [ˈweðə] *n.* 阉羊.

wet·ness [ˈwetnis] *n.* 湿润;雨水,雨天;湿的东西.

wet·ta·bil·i·ty [ˌwetəˈbiliti] *n.* ①可湿性. ②【化、物】可湿度.

wet·ta·ble [ˈwetəbl] *a.* ①可湿的. ②【化、物】易粘的,可附着的,可吸收的.

wet·ter [ˈwetə] *n.* ①(在各种操作中)使物件湿润的工人. ②润湿剂.

wet·tish [ˈwetiʃ] *a.* 有点潮湿的;有点湿润的.

WEU = Western European Union (NATO) (北大西洋公约组织)西欧联盟.

we've [wiːv; 弱 wiv] (= we have).

wey [wei] *n.*〔英〕会,英担〔货物重量单位,约 2—3 cwt,因物而异,羊毛是 182 磅〕.

WF = withdrawn failing 不及格退学〔教师给学生评定的成绩等级,该生以成绩不及格退出某课程〕.

w.f., wf = wrong fount【印】异体铅字.

WFB = World Fellowship of Buddhists 世界佛教徒联谊会.

WFD = World Federation of the Deaf 世界聋人联合会.

WFDY = World Federation of Democratic Youth 世界民主青年联盟.

W.F.L. = Women's Freedom League 妇女自由联盟.

WFP = World Food Program(me) (UN) 世界粮食方案(世界粮食计划组织)(联合国).

WFSW = World Federation of Scientific Workers 世界科学工作者协会.

WFTU = World Federation of Trade Unions 世界工会联合会,世界工联.

WFUNA = World Federation of United Nations Associations 联合国协会世界联合会.

W.G. = Westminster Gazette〔英〕《威斯敏斯特公报》.

w.g = wire gauge 线规.

W.Gmc. = West Germanic 西部日耳曼语(族).

wh. = ①watt-hour. ②which. ③white.

whack [*h*wæk] *vt., vi.* ①〔口〕用力抽打. ②〔俚〕一份一份地分开,分配(*up*). — *n.* ①〔口〕殴打(声),重打. ②〔俚〕分配,份. ③〔美俚〕试,尝试;情况;条件,机会. *I have had my* ~ *of pleasure.* 我也得到了我们一份愉快〔分享到愉快〕. ***He is in fine*** ~. 他很健康. ***That's [It's] a*** ~. 就这样一言为定. ***get [have, take] one's*** ~ 得到自己的一份. ***have [take] a*** ~ ***at***〔俚〕试试.

whack·er [*h*wækə] *n.* ①〔方〕用力抽打的人〔如赶车的〕. ②〔口〕(同类中)挺大的人〔东西〕. ③大谎.

whack·ing [*h*wækiŋ] *n.* 殴打. — *a.*〔口〕挺大的,巨大的,非常的. — *ad.*〔口〕极,非常.

whack·y [ˈ*h*wæki] *a.* = wacky.

whale[1] [*h*weil] *n.*【动】鲸;庞然大物;〔W-〕【天】鲸鱼座. *a bull [cow]* ~ 雄〔雌〕鲸. *the head [right]* ~ 脊美鲸. *the grey* ~ 小鲸. ***a*** ~ ***of***〔美〕大量的;大得了不得的;了不起的 (*a* ~ *of a mathematician* 了不起的数学家). ***a*** ~ ***on [at, for]*** 非常会…的,…极好的,热衷于…的. ***very like a*** ~ 的确,真的〔用讥讽口气赞同悖理话的反语〕. — *vi.* 捕鲸. ~**back** 鲸背状物;〔美〕龟甲甲板船. ~**boat** 捕鲸船;捕鲸船形的船. ~**bone** 鲸须〔骨〕;鲸须〔骨〕制品. ~ **calf** 仔鲸. ~**fin**【商】鲸须. ~**fishery** 捕鲸业;捕鲸场. ~**line [rope]** (捕鲸用)叉索. ~**man** 捕鲸者;捕鲸船员. ~ **oil** 鲸油. ~ **shark**【动】鲸鲨.

whale[2] [*h*weil] *vt.*〔美口〕殴打;猛击;使遭惨败. *They* ~*d their rivals 22 to 0.* 他们以 22 比 0 大败对方. — *vi.* 猛烈攻击.

whal·er [*h*weilə] *n.* 捕鲸者;捕鲸船.

whal·ing [ˈ*h*weiliŋ] *n.* 捕鲸. ~ **gun** 捕鲸炮.

wham [*h*wæm] *vi., vt.*〔美俚〕使劲打,重击. — *n.* 重击;重击声.

wham·my [ˈwæmi, ˈhwæ-] *n.* ***(pl. -mies)***〔美俚〕不祥之物;咀咒;狠毒的眼光. ***put a [the]*** ~ ***on*** 使…倒霉〔失败〕.

whang [*h*wæŋ] *vt.*〔口〕重击,使劲打. — *vi.*〔口〕(鼓等)咚咚地响. — *n.* ①〔方〕重击(声). ②〔Scot.〕(面包等的)大片,大块;皮带,皮鞭.

whap [wɑːp, hwɑːp] *vi.* ***(whapped; whap·ping)*** = whop.

whap·per [ˈwɑːpə, ˈhwɑː-] *n.*〔口〕= whopper.

wharf [*h*wɔːf] *n.* ***(pl. wharves,*** ~***s)*** 码头. *a* ~ *rat*〔美俚〕码头贼. — *vt.* 把(船)靠码头;把(货)卸上码头.

wharf·age [ˈ*h*wɔːfidʒ] *n.* 码头费;码头(设备);码头业务〔货物装卸,进入仓库等〕.

wharf·in·ger [ˈ*h*wɔːfindʒə] *n.* 码头所有人;码头管理员.

Whar·ton [ˈ*h*wɔːtn] *n.* 沃顿〔姓氏〕.

wharve [*h*wɔːv] *n.*【纺】锭盘;【机】小飞轮.

wharves [*h*wɔːvz] *n.* wharf 的复数.

what [*h*wɔt] *a.* ①〔疑问〕什么;多少. *W- books have you read?* 你读过什么书? *W- matter?* 什么事? 怎么啦? *W- news?* 什么新闻? *W- money have you got?* 你手头有多少钱? ②〔感叹〕多! 多么! 真! *W- a fool you are!* 你多笨! *What a genius he is!* 他真是个天才! ③〔关系形容词〕*Give me* ~ *paper you don't use.* 把你不用的纸给我. *Little did he foresee* ~ *a difference this would make.* 他做梦也未曾想到这件事会有这么大的影响. ~ ***countryman*** 哪国人 (*W- countryman is she?* 她是哪国人?) ~ ***price*** 什么价钱 (*W- price gold?* 黄金何价?) ~ ***time*** 在…的时候 (= when, while). (*W- time I am afraid, I will trust in thee.* 我感到害怕时将求助于你). ~ ***way*** 如何(= how)(*W- way was she drowned?* 她是怎样淹死的?). — *pro.* ①〔疑问〕什么,什么东西〔事情〕;怎样的东西〔事情〕;怎样的人;做什么的人,什么人;多少. *W- is he?* 他是什么人〔问职业、身分、籍贯等〕. *W- like is he?*〔方〕= *W- is he like?* 他是怎样一个人? *W- of him?* 他怎么啦? *W- is the fare?* 车〔船〕费是多少? *W- is your name?* 你叫什么名字? *W-?* 什么? *W- of it?* 怎么了? 有什么问题? *What's eating you?*〔美俚〕你有什么麻烦事? *Come* ~ *will [may], I am prepared for it.* 不管发生什么事,我已经下定决心了. *I know* ~. 我有一个主意. *I'll tell you* ~. 我告诉你该怎么办吧;我来告诉你是怎么回事吧. ②〔感叹〕*W-! are you late again?* 什么,你又晚啦? *W- ho!* 啊! 喂! ③〔关系〕(所)…的 (= that [those] which, the thing(s) which, anything that). *W- I say is true.* 我(所)说的是真话. *Do* ~ *you please.* 做你喜欢做的吧. ④〔关系〕〔引导插入句〕 *He said it, and,* ~ *is more surprising, he did it.* 他那样说了,更意外的是,他还做了. ⑤〔表示另有下文或其他可能性等〕*Shall we go or* ~*?* 我们是去呢还是…? ⑥〔英〕〔征求意见〕好不好?是不是? *Come tomorrow,* ~*?* 明天来,好不好? *An unusual chap,* ~*?* 一个了不起的家伙,是不是?★此种用法中的 what 为一虚字,无实际意义,且均置于句末. ***and*** ~ ***not*** 诸如此类,等等 (*He called me fool and* ~ *not.* 他骂我是傻瓜还骂我这一类的许多话). ***but*** ~〔用于否定句〕①不 (*Not a day but* ~ *it rains.* 没有一天不下雨. *Not a man but* ~ *likes him.* 没有一个人不欢喜他). ②除非;不…的 (*Use no arguments but* ~ *you believe in yourself.* 不要用你自己不相信的论证). ★ but what 与 but, but that, that ... not 等意义相同,但较不常用. ***for*** ~ ***they are*** 本来面目.

not but ～ 见 not 条. ***So*** ～? 〔口〕那又怎么样呢?〔表示不高兴不重视等〕. ～ ***about*** ...? 〔征求意见、询问消息等〕①…好不好?②…怎么样了?(*W- about bed?* 睡觉去,好不好? *W- about the boys?* 那些小伙子怎么样?) ～ ***for*** ①为什么,为何种目的 (*W- for?* 为的是什么?为什么?)②〔方〕哪一种 (*W- for tobacco are you smoking?* 你抽哪一种烟). ③〔俚〕=～-for. ***(or)*** ～ ***have you*** 〔美俚〕等等. ～ ***is called*** 所谓. ～ ***is more*** 加之,而且〔插入语〕. ～ ***it takes*** 〔美俚〕成功的必要条件. **～'s** ～〔口〕事物的真象,事物的道理 (*know* ～*'s* ～ 很懂事;有鉴别力). — *ad.* 怎样,多少. *W- does it benefit you?* 它是怎样使你受益的? *W- he has suffered!* 他吃了多少苦头啊! ～ ***between ... and (～ between)*** = ～ ***with ... and (～ with),*** 见 with 条. — *conj.* = as much as. *He helps me* ～ *he can.* 他尽所能地帮助我.

what-d'ye-call-him [-her, -it, 'em] [*h*wɔtdjiˈkɔːl*h*im, -*h*ə, -it, -əm] *n.* 那个不知叫什么的人〔女人、东西(等)〕;某某.

what·ev·er, 〔诗〕**what·e'er** [*h*wɔtˈevə, -ˈɛə] *pro.* ①〔关系代词〕什么都,…的都. ②〔连接代词〕无论,不管. ③〔俚〕〔强调时的疑问词〕究竟…什么. *W- it says, goes.* 说得出,做得到. *W- is done has to be done by human beings.* 一切事情都是要人去做的. *Do* ～ *you like.* 你爱干什么就干什么. *W- I have is yours.* 我所有的全是你的. *Do it,* ～ *happens.* 无论怎样都这样做. *W- do you mean?* 你究竟是什么意思? ★ whatever 也可分写作 what ever 二词. — *a.* ①〔关系形容词〕无论什么…都,任何…都. ②〔疑问形容词〕无论怎样…都. ③〔用于否定句、疑问句中名词、代词之后〕任何…也,一点儿…也. *Take* ～ *measures are considered best.* 凡是被认为最优良的措施都请采用吧. *W- excuses he may make, we do not believe him.* 不管他怎样分辩,我们都不相信他. *W- results follow, I will go.* 无论结果如何,我都要去. *I cannot see anyone* ～. 一个人我也没看见. *No one* ～ *would accept.* 谁也不会答应. *Is there any chance* ～? 还有任何一点儿希望吗?

what·for [ˈ*h*wɔtfɔː] *n.* 〔口〕①理由. ②处罚;严厉的责骂. *give an unruly boy* ～ 把一个不守规矩的男孩子加以处罚.

What·man (Paper) [ˈ*h*wɔtmən] *n.* 瓦特曼(绘图)纸.

what-not [ˈ*h*wɔtnɔt] *n.* ①陈列各种收藏物的玻璃柜,古董架,书架(等). ②〔口〕喜爱的东西,各种各样的物品;难于描述的人〔东西〕.

what's [*h*wɔts] 〔口〕=what is; what has; what does.

whats·is [ˈ*h*wɔtsiz], **whats·it** [-it] *n.* 不知道叫什么的人〔东西〕.

what·so [ˈ*h*wɔtsəu] *pro., a.* 〔古〕= whatever.

what·so·ev·er, what·so·e'er [*h*wɔtsəuˈevə, -ˈɛə] *pro.* = whatever.

what·you·may·call·it [ˈ*h*wɔtjuːmeikɔːlit] *n.* 〔美〕= whatsis.

whaup [wɔːp, hwɔːp] *n.* 〔Scot.〕麻鹬 (= curlew).

wheal[1] [*h*wiːl] *n.* 〔英方〕(锡)矿山.

wheal[2] [*h*wiːl] *n.* ①条痕;鞭痕. ②【医】(荨麻疹等的)风团,风疹块;疱疹,水疱.

wheat [*h*wiːt] *n.* ①【植】小麦. ②〔美俚〕生手;老实人〔青年〕;乡下人. *bread* ～ 普通小麦. *English [rivel]* ～ 圆锥小麦. *bearded [unbearded]* ～ 有芒〔无芒〕小麦. *spring* ～ 春小麦. *winter [fall]* ～ 冬小麦. *durum [flint]* ～ 硬粒小麦. *Indian* ～ 荞麦. ***as good as*** ～ 非常好. ～ **belt** 产麦区. ～**cake** 面粉烤饼. ～ **germs** 〔美〕麦芽精. ～**land** ①小麦产地. ②适于种小麦的地方. ～**less** *a.* 不产小麦的. ～ **rust** 小麦锈病(菌).

wheat·ear [ˈ*h*wiːtiə] *n.* ①麦穗. ②【鸟】麦鹟.

wheat·en [ˈ*h*wiːtn] *a.* 小麦(制)的;小麦色的.

wheat·grass [ˈ*h*wiːtgrɑːs] *n.* 【植】冰草(属); 匍匐冰草.

Wheat·ley [ˈ*h*wiːtli] *n.* 惠特利〔姓氏〕.

Wheat·stone bridge [ˈ*h*wiːtstən-] *n.*【电】惠斯登电桥,单臂电桥.

whee [wiː, hwiː] *int.* 嘻嘻!〔表示愉快、快感和欣喜等〕.

whee·dle [ˈ*h*wiːdl] *vt., vi.* 哄,骗;用甜言蜜语引诱 *(into)*;用甜言蜜语骗取. ～ *sth. out of sb.* 用甜言蜜语骗去某人的某物. ～ ***one's way*** 以谄媚手段达到目的. **-dler** *n.* 行骗者. **-dling·ly** *ad.*

wheel [*h*wiːl] *n.* ①轮,车轮;轮状物. ②〔口〕自行车;【船】舵轮;(汽车的)方向盘,驾驶盘;(制陶)转盘;纺车;轮转焰火;【史】车磔的刑车;〔美俚〕〔*pl.*〕汽车. ③旋转;【军】迂回(运动). ④〔常 *pl.*〕原动力;机构. ⑤大人物,红人. ⑥〔美俚〕银元;〔*pl.*〕重要匪徒;〔*pl.*〕腿. ⑦〔美剧〕巡回演出,联营剧场. *the Fortune's* ～ 命运. *the* ～ *of birds* 一群鸟的旋回飞翔. *the* ～*s of government* 政府机构. *the* ～*s of life* 人体的机能. ***a*** ～ ***within*** ～***s [a*** ～***]*** = ～s within ～s. ***at the next turn of the*** ～ 下次遇机会时,下次运气有所改变时. ***at the*** ～ 掌着舵的;掌握着大权的,担任着领导[管理]工作的. ***break a butterfly [fly] on the*** ～ 杀鸡用牛刀,小题大作. ***break sb. on the*** ～ 处车磔刑. ***go on*** ～***s*** 顺利进行. ***keep the cart on the*** ～***s*** 孜孜不倦地进行工作. ***on*** ～***s*** ①用车. ②轮子动着;顺利,顺畅. ***put a spoke in sb.'s*** ～ 妨碍某人. ***run on*** ～***s*** = go on ～s. ***the fifth*** ～ ***of a coach [waggon 等]*** 多余的东西,蛇足. ***the turn of the*** ～ 命运的转变. ～ ***of life*** ①【宗】轮回. ②万花筒. ***have*** ～***s in the head*** 〔美〕发疯,有神经病. ～***s within*** ～***s*** 复杂的机构;复杂的事情;神秘复杂的原因〔过程〕. — *vt.* ①推动,拉动,开动(车子);用车子运;装车轮于. ②旋转,转动;使转变方向. — *vi.* ①轮转,旋转;转变方向. ②〔口〕骑自行车(等). ～ *out the table* 把(有脚轮的)桌子推出来. ～ *round* 转身. *Right [Left]* ～! 【军】右〔左〕转弯走! ～ ***and deal*** 〔美俚〕不受一切束缚地独断独行;牢牢地控制,掌握支配权. ～ **animalcule** 【动】轮虫纲动物. ～**barrow** 独轮手(推)车. ～**base** 【机】轴距;(机车的)轮组定距. ～**boss [nave]** 轮毂. ～ **box** 【机】轮箱;齿轮箱,变速箱. ～ **brake** 轮轫. ～ **bug** 【动】冠毛猎蝽. ～ **casing [cover]** 轮罩,轮箱. ～ **chair** (病人用)轮椅. ～ **horse** ①马车的后马,辕马. ②坚苦勤奋的人,勤勤恳恳工作的人. ③〔美俚〕只会做人尾巴的人,应声虫〔尤指政治上〕. ～**house** 【船】①舵手室. ②外轮罩壳,轮箱. ～ **lock** 轮枪机;带轮枪机的枪. ～**man** ①舵手. ②〔美〕骑自行车的人;汽车驾驶人. ～**reversing gear** 【机】齿轮换向机构. ～**s man** = ～man ①. ～ **watch** 守舵值班. ～ **window** 轮窗. ～**work** 【机】传动齿轮组;(齿轮)转动装置. ～**wright** 车轮制造人,轮匠.

Wheel·er [ˈ*h*wiːlə] *n.* 惠勒〔姓氏〕.

wheel·er [ˈ*h*wiːlə] *n.* ①推车者;〔英〕车轮制造人. ②(马车的)后马. ③〔构成复合词〕有(若干个)轮子的东西. ④〔美〕骑摩托车的警察. ～**-dealer** 【美俚】手腕泼辣的事业家〔投机商人、政客等〕. ～**-dealing** 精明的交易〔计划等〕.

wheel·ing [ˈ*h*wiːliŋ] *n.* ①车运;骑自行车. ②旋转. ③道路的好坏,行车情况〔行车鉴定〕. *It is a good* ～. 这条路好走.

wheen [wiːn, hwiːn] *n.* 〔Scot.〕少量,几个;相当的数量.

wheeze [*h*wiːz] *vi.* 喘息;(因喘息等)喝哧喝哧地出声. — *vt.* 喝哧喝哧地喘着气说 *(out)*. — *n.* ①喝哧喝哧喘息声. ②〔剧俚〕演员自己插入的台词〔俏皮话、笑话等〕. ③(一般)笑话,俏皮话;巧妙的主意〔办法〕.

wheez·y [ˈ*h*wiːzi] *a.* ***(-i·er; -i·est)*** 喝哧喝哧叫的,喘鸣的. **-i·ly** *ad.*

whelk[1] [welk] *n.* 【贝】油螺;峨螺.

whelk[2] [welk] *n.* ①条痕;鞭痕. ②【医】丘疹;小脓疱;面疱.

W

whelm [*h*welm] *vt.* ①〔英方〕用…覆盖. ②淹没，使沉没；(在感情等方面)压倒. *She was ~ed in sorrow.* 她沉浸在忧愁中. — *vi.* 淹没.

whelp [*h*welp] *n.* ①小狗；(狮、虎、狼等的)仔. ②〔蔑〕孩子，小鬼. ③【机】(链轮的)扣链齿；(绞盘等的)辐杆. ④〔W-〕〔*pl.*〕〔美〕田纳西 (Tennessee) 州人的别名. — *vi., vt.* (兽)生(仔)；〔蔑〕(妇女)生(孩子). ②计划，盘算(奸计等).

when [*h*wen] *ad.* ①〔疑问〕什么时候，几时. *W- did you see him?* (这以前)你几时见他的？②〔关系，引导定语从句〕当…的时候. *He came at a time ~ I least expected him.* 他在我最想不到的时候来了. ③从前境况差时. **brag of having known sb. ~** 夸耀自己是某人过去的患难之交[布衣之交]. — *conj.* ①当…的时候. ②(刚)…就…. ③如果. ④然后. ⑤既然. ⑥可是，却. *Come ~ you please.* 你高兴的时候来好啦. *I was just going to speak, ~ the bell rang.* 我刚要讲，钟就响了. *Why use wood ~ you can use plastic?* 既然能用塑料，何必非用木料？*Please ring me up ~ she comes.* 如果她来了，请打电话给我. *I stayed till noon, ~ I went home.* 我留到中午，然后就回家了. *We have only three books ~ we need five.* 我们要五本书，可是只有三本. *He walks ~ he might ride.* 可以坐车，他却走路. **~ all comes to all** 结果. **~ due** 到期时. **~ (he was) king** 做国王时. **~ in position** 恢复原位后. — *pro.* ①〔疑问〕什么时候. *Till ~ can you stay?* 你可以待到什么时候？②〔关系〕那时. *They left on Monday, since ~ we have heard nothing.* 他们星期一动身，以后就没有消息了. — *n.* 时候，时间，日期，场合. *the ~ and the where* 时间和地点.

when·as [ˈ*h*wenˈæz] *conj.* 〔古〕① = when. ② = while, whereas. ③ = as.

whence [*h*wens]〔古〕★现在通常说作 from where, where ... from, from which. — *ad.* ①〔疑问〕从哪里；为什么. *W- are you?* 你从哪儿来？ *W- comes it?* 为什么这样了？ ②〔关系〕…的；(到)…的地方. *the source ~ these evils spring* 这些祸害(从之)发生的根源. *Let him return ~ he came.* 让他回到他来的那个地方. — *pro.* ①〔疑问〕哪里，什么地方. *From ~ is he?* 他是哪里人？②〔关系〕…的那里. *the source from ~ it springs* 这个发生的根源. — *n.* 来源，来处；根源. *We know neither our ~ nor our whither.* 我们不知道从哪里来到哪里去.

whence·so·ev·er [ˌ*h*wenssəuˈevə] *ad.* 无论从什么地方；无论由于什么原因.

when·ev·er [*h*wenˈevə]，〔诗〕**when·e'er** [-ˈεə]，**when·so·ev·er** [-səuˈevə] *conj.* 无论什么时候，随时；每次…总是，…的时候一定；一…就. *I'll see him ~ he likes to come.* 他高兴什么时候来我什么时候见他. *~ he comes* 他每次来总…. — *ad.*〔表示强调〕究竟什么时候. *W- did she tell you that?* 她究竟什么时候告诉你的？★ whensoever 的语气比 whenever 强.

where [*h*wεə] *ad.* ①〔疑问〕在哪里，向哪里；哪里；在哪一点上. *W- is my hat?* 我的帽子在哪里？ *W- are yon looking?* 你在看哪里？ *W- does it concern us?* 这在哪一点上和我们有关系？ *W- is the sense of it?* 这有什么意义？(= There is no sense in it). ②〔关系，有先行词〕*the place ~ they sing* 他们唱歌的地方. *I came to London, ~ I found him.* 我来到了伦敦，那儿我就见到他了. ③〔关系，无先行词〕*This is ~ I live.* 这就是我住的地方. *That's ~ it is.* 〔口〕那就是真正的理由. *That's just ~ you are wrong.* 那正是你错误的地方. **~ it's at**〔美俚〕(重要活动、发展等的)中心点；事情[形势]的核心所在. **~ sb. is at** 某人的本质所在. — *conj.* 在[去]…的地方. *Go ~ you like.* 你爱到哪里就到哪里. *W- there's a will, there's a way.* 有志气就有办法，有志者事竟成. — *pro.* 哪里，什么地方. *W- do you come from?* 你是什么地方的人？*W- have you come from?* 你刚从什么地方来？*W- are you going (to)?* 你去哪里？**W- from?** 〔口〕打哪儿来？**W- to?**〔口〕到哪儿去？— *n.* 地点，场所. *The ~s and whens are important.* 地点和时间是重要的.

where- *comb. f.* ① = 疑问代名词的 what 或关系代名词的 which: *where*by, *where*in, *where*with. ★ 这一类复合词除公文、诗、谚语、及无教育者的言语中外，普通少用. ②= 疑问副词的 where: *where*abouts.

where·a·bout [ˈ*h*wεərəˈbaut] *ad., n.* 〔罕〕= whereabouts.

where·a·bouts [ˈ*h*wεərəˈbauts] *ad.* 〔疑问〕在哪一带，在什么附近；〔关系〕…的地方. *W- did you put it?* 你把它放在哪里了？— [ˈ*h*wεərəbauts] *n.* 〔用作 *sing.* 或 *pl.*〕下落，踪迹，所在. *His present ~ is unknown.* 他现在下落不明[不知道在什么地方].

where·as [*h*wεərˈæz] *conj.* ①〔公文用语〕有鉴于. ②而，却，倒；其实，反过来. *W- the peoples of the colonies have been grieved and burdened with taxes ...* 鉴于各殖民地民众备受重税负担之苦…. *I hate, ~ you merely dislike, him.* 你不过不喜欢他，我却恨他.

where·at [*h*wεərˈæt] *ad.* ①〔关系〕对于…，所…的；在这里. ②〔古〕〔疑问〕为什么. *W- are you angry?* 你为什么生气？*I know the things ~ you are displeased.* 我知道你所不高兴的是什么.

where·by [*h*wεəˈbai] *ad.* ①〔古〕〔疑问〕凭什么，依什么，怎样，怎么. ②〔关系〕由那个，凭那个；由此. *W- shall we know him?* 我们凭什么知道是他呢？ *W- I saw that he was angry.* 由那一点我看出他生气了. *a plan ~ to escape* 逃走的办法.

where'er [*h*wεərˈεə] *ad.* 〔诗，古〕= wherever.

where·fore [ˈ*h*wεəfɔː, -fɔə] *ad.* ①〔疑问〕为什么，因什么理由，何以. ②〔关系〕因此，所以. *I know not ~ it befell.* 我不知道为什么变成这个样子. *He was angry, ~ I was afraid.* 他在发脾气，所以我害怕. — *n.* 原因，理由. *We must always go into the whys and ~s of anything.* 我们对任何事情都要问一个为什么.

where·from [wεəˈfrɔm, hwεə-] *ad., conj.* 由此，自此处，所由.

where·in [*h*wεərˈin] *ad.* ①〔疑问〕在哪一点上，在什么地方. ②〔关系〕在那里，在那一点上，在那时候. *W- does the difference lie?* 分歧在什么地方？ *There are the points ~ we differ.* 这些就是我们意见不同的地方.

where·of [*h*wεərˈɔv] *ad.* ①〔疑问〕谁的，什么的，哪个的，关于什么的. ②〔关系〕那个人的，那个，所…的. *the matter ~ we spoke* 我们所讲的问题.

where·on [*h*wεərˈɔn] *ad.* ①〔疑问〕在什么上面，在什么，在谁身上. ②〔关系〕在那上面 = whereupon. *W- is your trust?* 你指望的是谁？ *the rock ~ the house is built* 上面建有房子的岩石.

where·so·ev·er, where·so·e'er [ˌ*h*wεəsəuˈevə, -ˈεə] *ad.* = wherever.

where·through [wεəˈθruː, hwεə-] *conj.* 〔古〕经此，由此.

where·to [*h*wεəˈtuː] *ad.* ①〔疑问〕向哪里，到哪里；为什么. ②〔关系〕…去的(地方)；对之. *W- he thus replied.* 他对之作如是回答. *the point ~ they hasten* 他们急急忙忙去的那个地方.

where·un·to [ˌ*h*wεərʌnˈtuː]〔古〕= whereto.

where·up·on [ˌ*h*wεərəˈpɔn] *ad.* ①〔疑问〕= whereon. ②〔关系〕于是；因此. *W- he rose to speak.* 于是他站起来说话了.

wher·ev·er [*h*wεərˈevə] *conj.* 无论哪里，无论什么地方；无论(…)到什么地方. *W- there is struggle there is sacrifice.* 要奋斗就会有牺牲. *The enemy was vanquished ~ his pen pointed.* 笔锋指处，所向披靡. *Sit ~ you like.* 请随便坐. — *ad.*〔表示强调〕究竟在[到]哪里. *W- are you going?* 你究竟到哪里去？

where·with [*h*wεəˈwiθ] *ad.* ①〔疑问〕用什么. ②〔关系〕

用以. *W- shall they be fed?* 给他们吃什么好呢? *the means ~ to pay for the trip* 用以支付旅费的钱.

where·with·al [ˌ*h*wɛəwiːˈðɔːl] *ad.* 〔古〕= wherewith. — [ˈ*h*wɛəwiðɔːl] *n.* 〔the ~〕资金,资力,手段. *the ~ to buy bread* 买面包的钱.

wher·ry [ˈ*h*weri] *n.* 摆渡船; 单人小船; 〔英〕(河上交通运输用)平底大船.

whet [*h*wet] *vt.* ***(whet·ted)*** ①磨,磨快. ②刺激,加强,助长(食欲、好奇心等). *~ a sword* 磨刀剑. *~ one's appetite* 开胃,刺激食欲. *~ one's curiosity* 激起好奇心. — *n.* ①研磨. ②开胃物,一杯酒; 刺激物,激励. ③〔方〕一段(短)时间(的工作).

wheth·er [ˈ*h*weðə] *conj.* ①〔接间接疑问的名词从句〕是…呢还是…呢,(是)不(是)…,…还是…. ②〔接让步的副词从句〕不管,无论. *I don't know ~ he will be here.* 我不晓得他来不来. *I wonder ~ it is true.* 我不晓得真不真. *He does not know ~ to go or not.* 他不知道去还是不去. *W- sick or well, she is always cheerful.* 她不管有病没病总是快快活活的. *~* ***or no*** 无论如何,总之; 必定 (*We must stick to it ~ or no.* 无论如何我们必须坚持). — *pro.* 〔古〕(在…之中)哪一个. *W- of them is the worse?* 他们当中哪一个更坏? — *n.* 可能的选择. *~ all the whys and ~s of the matter* 考虑事情的所有原因和可能作的选择.

whet·stone [ˈ*h*wetstəun] *n.* ①磨(刀)石;【机】油石. ②刺激品; 激励者,激励物.

whew [hw(j)uː] *int.* 哎呀! 啃! 〔表示惊愕等〕. — *n.* "哎呀"声.

whey [*h*wei] *n.* 乳清. ***a ~ belly*** 〔美〕废马,不中用的马. **~face** 苍白的脸; 脸色苍白的人. **~-faced** *a.* 脸色苍白的; 失色的. **-ey** [ˈ*h*weii] *a.* 似乳清的; 含乳清的.

whf. = wharf.

which [*h*witʃ] *a.* ①〔疑问〕哪一个,哪个; 哪一些. *W- boy won the prize?* 哪一个孩子得了奖? ②〔关系〕这个〔这些个〕,那个〔那些个〕. *He was a great liar, ~ fact was not know at first.* 他是一个撒谎大王,但这个事实起初没人晓得. ③〔连接〕无论哪个〔些〕〔一般多用 whichever〕. ***W- end up?*** 〔美〕那究竟是怎么一回事情? — *pro.* ①〔疑问〕哪个,哪一个(人); 哪一些. *W- is the largest?* 哪一个最大? *I don't know ~ is ~.* 我不知道哪一个是哪一个. *W- to reject and ~ to accept?* 何去何从? ②〔关系〕这(个),那(个)〔有先行词〕*the house in ~ I once lived* 我从前住过的房子. *I lost my way, ~ delayed me considerably.* 我迷了路,这使我耽搁了很久. ③〔关系〕这(个),那(个)〔无先行词〕*Choose ~ you like best.* 拣你最喜欢的吧. ***the*** ~〔古〕= which.

which·ev·er, which·so·ev·er [*h*witʃˈevə, -səuˈevə] *a.* ①〔关系〕无论哪一个,随便哪一个. ②〔强势疑问〕究竟哪一个…. *I will take ~ book you reject.* 随便哪一本书拿你不要的给我. *Pray take ~ suits you best.* 请随便挑选你最中意的一个吧. *W- hat do you like?* 你究竟喜欢哪一种帽子? — *pro.* ①〔关系〕无论哪一个. ②〔强势疑问〕究竟哪一个. *I will take ~ you reject.* 随便哪一种,拿你不要的给我. *W- are you going to choose?* 你究竟要挑选哪一个?

whick·er [ˈwikə, ˈhwikə] *vi.* 〔拟声〕①压住声地笑; 吃吃地笑,偷笑. ②(马)嘶,嘶叫.

whid [wid, whid] *vi.* ***(whid·ded, whid·ding)*** 〔Scot.〕灵活地活动; 敏捷地行动.

whid·ah(-bird), whid·ah(-finch) [ˈ*h*widə (-bəːd, -fintʃ)] *n.* 【动】(非洲)长尾莺.

whiff[1] [*h*wif] *n.* ①(风、烟等的)一吹,一喷,一冒; (香烟的)一口; 一阵香气. ②【商】小雪茄烟. ③【捧球,高尔夫】击球不中〔失败〕. ④〔英〕泰晤士 (Thames) 河上的一种轻艇. *I want a ~ of fresh air.* 我要吸一口新鲜空气. ***take a ~ or two*** 抽一两口(香烟). — *vt., vi.* ①轻轻地吹; 吹送; 喷送; 发出一阵(香气); 抽吸. ②【棒球,高尔夫】(使)击球失败.

whiff[2] [*h*wif] *n.* 【鱼】一种比目鱼.

whiff[3] [*h*wif] *vi.* 垂饵于水面钓鱼.

whif·fet [ˈ*h*wifit] *n.* ①〔美口〕小狗; 藐小的人〔物〕. ②轻轻一吹.

whif·fle [ˈ*h*wifl] *vi.* ①(风)轻轻一吹; 不规则地吹. ②动摇不定; 变卦; 变方向. — *vt.* 吹散; 使动摇. **~ball** (儿童作为棒球玩的)一种塑料空心球. **~ tree** (两端连接拖索,中心连接车子的)车前横木,犁槩(= whippletree).

whif·fler[1] [ˈwiflə, ˈhwi-] *n.* ①易改变主意者,无定见者. ②(在辩论中)使用遁辞的人,躲闪诡辩者.

whif·fler[2] [ˈ*h*wiflə] *n.* 〔英〕(游行队伍前的)开道者.

whif·fy [ˈ*h*wifi] *a.* 发出阵阵臭气的.

Whig [*h*wig] *n.* ①【英史】(自由党前身的)辉格党党员. ②【美史】(共和党前身的)自由党党员. ③辉格党〔自由党〕的支持者. **Whig·ger·y, Whig·gism** *n.* 辉格党的纲领〔行动〕; 自由主义. **Whig·gish** *a.* 辉格党的,自由主义的.

whig·ma·lee·rie, whig·ma·lee·ry [ˌwigməˈliəri, ˌhwig-] *n.* ***(pl. -ries)*** 〔主 Scot.〕①幻想,怪想. ②奇异古怪的小玩艺儿.

while [*h*wail] *n.* 一段时间; 一会儿; (所需、所费的)功夫. *rest a ~* 休息一会儿. *a long [good] ~* 长久. ***after a ~*** 过了一会儿. ***all the ~*** 始终,一直. ***at ~s*** 有时,时常. ***between ~s*** 时常,不时地. ***every little ~*** = at ~s. ***for a [one] ~*** 暂时,一时. ***in a little ~*** 不久,没一会儿,立刻. ***make it worth sb.'s ~*** 酬劳; 行贿. ***once in a ~*** 时常,有时. ***the ~ [whilst]*** ①当时; 其间,在那中间; 同时. ②〔诗〕…当中〔此义常用 *whilst*〕. ***worth (sb.'s) ~*** 有…的价值,值得; 有利益的 (*It is worth ~ to see the museum.* 参观博物馆是有益的). — *conj.* ①当…的时候; 和…同时. ②而,但是,可是,倒,却,但另一方面,反过来; 虽则. *He was drowned ~ swimming.* 他游泳时淹死了. *W- I like the colour of the hat, I do not like its shape.* 我倒喜欢这顶帽子的颜色,但不喜欢那个式样. *One lost a leg, another an arm, ~ a third was killed outright.* 一个人折了一只腿,一个人丢了一只胳膊,另一个人呢,当场死了. ***at a time when ... ~ ...*** 一面…一面又…. — *vt.* 消磨,闲混(时间) *(away)*. — *prep.* 〔古〕直至(某时). *W- then, God be with you.* 直至彼时,上天将保佑汝.

whiles [*h*wailz] 〔古〕*conj.* = while. — *ad.* 有时,偶尔. — *n.* 〔the ~〕= the while.

whi·lom [ˈ*h*wailəm] 〔古〕*ad.* 以前,从前,曾经. — *a.* 以前的,从前的.

whilst [*h*wailst] *conj.* 〔英〕= while. — *n.* 〔古〕〔the ~〕= the while.

whim [*h*wim] *n.* ①忽起的念头,一时的兴致; 奇想,怪想; 任性. ②【矿】采矿辘轳; 绞盘; 绞车. ***full of ~s (and fancies)*** 异想天开的; 狂热的; 任性的. ***take [have] a ~ for reading*** 一时兴起读起书来. ***while the ~ lasts*** 在有兴致的时候; 兴之所至. **~-wham** 古怪的装饰品,奇装异服; 怪想; 〔*pl.*〕精神失常.

whim·brel [ˈ*h*wimbrəl] *n.* 【鸟】杓鹬.

whim·per [ˈ*h*wimpə] *vi.* 抽噎,啜泣,呜咽; (狗等)悲嗥. — *vt.* 抽噎地诉说. — *n.* 啜泣,呜咽; 悲嗥声; 怨声. **-er** *n.* 啜泣者; 抱怨者. **-ing·ly** *ad.*

whim·sey [ˈ*h*wimzi] *n.* = whimsy.

whim·si·cal [ˈ*h*wimzikəl] *a.* ①异想天开的. ②古怪的; 奇形怪状的. ③反复无常的. **-ly** *ad.* **-i·ty** *n.*

whim·sy [ˈ*h*wimzi] *n.* ①异想天开,奇想. ②奇怪行为; 反复无常. **~-wham·sy** [-ˌ*h*wæmzi] 奇想,怪念头.

whin[1] [*h*win] *n.* 【植】荆豆(花); 芒柄花.

whin[2] [*h*win] *n.* 【地】暗色岩,粗玄岩.

whin·chat [ˈ*h*wintʃæt] *n.* 【鸟】欧洲石鵰,野鶲.

whine [*h*wain] *vi.* ①(狗等)悲嗥; 啜泣; 哀诉,诉怨. ②发

牢骚*(about)*. — *vt.* 哀诉；嘀咕地说 *(out)*. — *n.* (狗等的)悲嗥声；啜泣声；哀诉，怨诉；牢骚. **whin·er** *n.* 啜泣者；悲嗥者；哀诉者. **whin·ing·ly** *ad.*

whing·ding [ˈwiŋˌdiŋ, ˈhwiŋ-] *n.* = wingding.

whing·er [ˈhwiŋə] *n.* [方]短剑，短刀；匕首.

whin·ny[1] [ˈhwini] *n.* (表示高兴的) 马嘶；嘶声. — *vi.* 嘶，响鼻子. — *vt.* 嘶声地说；慨然表示(答应等).

whin·ny[2] [ˈwini, ˈhwini] *a.* *(-ni·er; -ni·est)* 盖满金雀花的.

whin·stone [ˈhwinstəun] *n.* 暗色岩〔玄武岩、燧石等的俗名〕.

whin·y [ˈwaini, ˈhwaini] *a.* *(whin·i·er; whin·i·est)* 哀鸣的，呜咽的. *a ~ child* 呜咽的小孩. **-i·ness** *n.*

whip [hwip] *vt.* ①鞭打，抽打；鞭挞，攻击，责打；鞭策，驱使；激励，督促. ②纠集，使列队 *(up)*. ③对…采取迅速行动；猛然抓住[抢去、抽出、打出(等)] *(away; off)*. ④打(谷)；搅打，把(蛋、奶油等)打到起泡沫. ⑤[口]击败，打败，打胜，超过，凌驾. ⑥缠，把…绕(在棒上). ⑦交叉着缝，锁(缝眼). ⑧【海】用滑车拉起. ⑨用钓竿抽钓 *(for)*. — *vi.* ①责打，抽打；(旗在风中)拍拍作声. ②迅速地突然动作；逃走；跳出[入] *(away; out; in)*. ③(蛋等)被搅打. ④抽钓. *They whipped away [off] to France.* 他们一下子远走高飞到法国去了. *~ a fault out of* 鞭打…矫正缺点. *~ creation* 打败所有敌人. *~ in* 用鞭子召集(猎狗)；召集(议员). *~ off* ①猛然脱落；突然拿去；突然带走. ②用鞭子驱散(猎狗). ③突然走开. *~ out* 猛然抽出[跳出]；突然叫喊. *~ round* 回头. *~ together* 用鞭子召集猎狗；(在议会里)团结友党；拼凑. *~ up* ①鞭(马等)飞跑；督促；集合(听众等). ②抓住. — *n.* ①鞭. ②(四马的)马车夫；猎犬指挥员. ③[英](政党内督促议员勿缺席的)议院督导员，(某党)议员领袖〔又称 party ~；美国称 floor leader〕；[英](政党发给本党议员的)出席[表态]命令. ④小滑车；振动发条. ⑤打蛋器，搅打器；(搅奶油之类)搅打成的食品. ⑥【无】鞭状天线. *a loaded ~* (灌铅的)铅心棍棒. *a good ~* 好车夫. *a ministerial [government] ~* 执政党的议院督导员[组织秘书]. *a three-line ~* (画着三条线的)紧急出席命令. *send a ~ round* (议院督导员向本党议员)送发出席命令. *~ and spur* 赶紧，快马加鞭地. **~ crane** 动臂起重机. **~ cord** ①鞭绳；肠线. ②马裤呢. **~cord** *a.* 绷紧的；坚强的；肌肉发达的. **~ hand** 执鞭的手，右手；优势 *(get [have] the ~ hand of* 操纵，控制；占优势). **~lash** ①(鞭子头上的)鞭头绳. ②鞭打. ③(坐汽车引起的)头部受伤. **~ped cream** (打成泡沫状的)搅奶油. **~ ray**【动】魟. **~-round** [英口]劝募(传单). **~ scorpion**【动】鞭蝎. **~ snake**【动】鞭蛇(属). **~stitch** *vt., n.* 锁缝. **~stock** 鞭柄. **~-tail**【动】长尾鳕. **~worm**【动】鞭虫(属).

whip·per [ˈhwipə] *n.* ①鞭打的人；(用滑车给船)上货的人. ②[英议会] = ~-in ②. **~-in** ①猎犬指挥员. ②[英]议院中政党的督导员[组织秘书]. ③【赛马】跑末名的马. **~snapper** 无足轻重的人；妄自尊大的小伙子.

whip·pet [ˈhwipit] *n.* ①极灵巧的杂种小猎狗[赛跑狗]. ②【军】快速轻坦克.

whip·ping [ˈhwipiŋ] *n.* ①鞭打，笞刑；惩罚. ②用来缚扎[抽打]的绳索. ③[口] 打败；赛输. ④抽钓. ⑤搅打. **~ boy**【史】(陪王子读书，代受鞭责的)受鞭伴读；替罪羊. **~ cream** 脂肪含量高可打成泡沫状的奶油. **~ post** (缚受鞭刑者的) 鞭挞柱. **~ top** (用鞭子抽的)陀螺.

Whip·ple [ˈhwipl] *n.* 惠普尔〔姓氏〕.

whip·ple·tree [ˈhwipl-] *n.* = whiffletree.

whip·poor·will [ˈhwippuəwil] *n.*【鸟】北美蚊母鸟.

whip·py [ˈhwipi] *a.* ①鞭子一样的. ②富有弹性的. **-piness** *n.*

whip·saw [ˈhwipsɔː] *n.* 狭边(钩齿)粗木锯；双人横切锯. — *vt.* ①用狭边钩齿粗木锯(或双人横切锯)锯. ②使受双重损害〔指受骗或因急欲补偿损失而低价抛出证券等所致〕；(两个人)串同对…欺骗；(牌戏)一次赢得(某人)两项赌注[一局中赢两次]. ③使两方相争而坐收渔利.

Whip·snade [ˈhwipsneid] **Park** *n.* (英国 Bedfordshire 的)自然动物园.

whip·stall [ˈhwipˌstɔːl] *n.* [美]【空】(由于垂直上升太快操纵杆后拉过多形成完全失速而引起的) 机头急坠失速.

whip·ster [ˈhwipstə] *n.* = whipper-snapper.

whir(r) [hwəː] *n.* 呼呼地飞或旋转的声音. — *vi., vt.* (使)呼呼地飞[旋转].

whirl [hwəːl] *vi.* ①旋转；卷成旋涡；旋转着前进. ②眼花，眩晕. ③(车或人坐车)飞跑，急行. ④(思想、事件等)迅速接连发生，相继涌起；混成一团. — *vt.* 使旋转；使卷成旋涡；旋转着扔(石子等)；迅速卷走[带走]；用车运. *~ aloft [up]* (风)卷起(枯叶等)；盘旋而上. *~ away* 卷走；带走；溜掉. *~ing motion* 涡动，旋动. — *n.* ①旋转；使人眼光撩乱的变迁；旋风，旋涡；涡流；混乱. ②【植、动】轮，环. *in a ~* 在旋转中；在混乱中 *(My thoughts are in a ~.* 我思想一片混乱). *the ~ of society* 社交界的忙碌. **~about** *n.* 旋转，盘旋.

whirl·i·gig [ˈhwəːligig] *n.* ①陀螺. ②旋转木马. ③旋转运动. ④循环；变迁. ⑤【虫】鼓虫，科甲虫 (= ~ beetle). *the ~ of life [time]* 人世[时代]的变迁.

whirl·pool [ˈhwəːlpuːl] *n.* ①旋涡. ②混乱，纷乱. **~ bath**【医】旋流温水浴疗法.

whirl·wind [ˈhwəːlwind] *n.* ①旋风；旋流；涡动. ②猛烈的势力. *a ~ visit* 旋风似的[突然的]访问. *ride the ~* (天使)驾御旋风；叱咤风云. *sow the wind and reap the ~* (种下)一恶收(到)十(倍的恶)报；恶有恶报，害人反害己.

whirl·y·bird [ˈhwəːliˌbəːd, ˈhwəː-] *n.* [口]直升飞机 (= helicopter).

whirr [ˈhwəː] *v., n.* = whir.

whir·ry [ˈhwəːri] *vi.* *(-ried; -ry·ing)* [Scot.] 急去，急转，赶紧，加快. — *vt.* 急送.

whir·y·pig [ˈhwəːripig] *n.* [美俚]警用直升飞机.

whish [hwiʃ] *vi.* 飕飕地迅速移动；作飕飕声. — *n.* 飕飕声.

whisht [hwiʃt] *int.* = whist.

whisk [hwisk] *vt.* ①撢，拂，扫 *(away; off)*. ②打，搅拌(蛋等). ③突然带走；突然拿走 *(away; off)*. ④(狗等) 摇(尾巴)，挥动. *The dog came ~ing its tail.* 狗摇着尾巴来了. *The mouse ~ed into its hole.* 老鼠(迅速地)溜进洞里去了. — *vi.* 急急地去，飞跑，突然不见，突然跑掉. — *n.* ①(撢子、尾巴等的)扫，拂，撢；急过，急行. ②小帚，撢帚，刷帚；(蛋、奶油等的)搅拌器. *a tea ~* 搅茶器. **~ broom [brush]** 刷帚.

whisk·er [ˈhwiskə] *n.* ①[*pl.*] 连鬓胡子，络腮胡子；(猫等的)胡须；触须；鸟嘴周围的羽毛. ②细须[丝]；晶须；须触线；触簧. ③[*pl.*] [美俚] 腮帮子，下巴颏儿；上了年纪的人. ④【海】斜墙三角帆支杆. ⑤[*pl.*]【化】须晶〔一种单晶合成物，用以增加塑料强度〕. *lose by a ~* [美运]以极少的差数输掉. *(Mr.) Whiskers* [美俚]联邦政府；联邦法律执行官.

whis·key [ˈhwiski] *n.* ①= whisky. ②[W-]通讯中用以代表字母 w 的词.

whis·ky[1] [ˈhwiski] *n.* 威士忌酒. ★在美国 whiskey 是指本地制品，whisky 是指进口货. **~ cold [hot]** 加冷水[热水]的威士忌酒. **~ neat** 纯威士忌酒. **~ sour** 柠檬威士忌酒. **~ straight** [美]纯威士忌酒.

whis·ky[2] [ˈhwiski] *n.* 二轮轻马车.

whis·ky-jack [ˈhwiskidʒæk] *n.* 【动】加拿大噪鸦 (= Canada jay).

whis·per [ˈhwispə] *vi.* ①低语；耳语. ②密谈；告密，背后指责，背后(发)议论；密谋坏事. ③(风，流水等)沙沙地响，飒飒地响. ～ *in sb.' ear* 跟某人交头接耳地说. — *vt.* 低声地讲；私下说. *It is ～ed that* 有人私下说…，听说. — *n.* ①低语，耳语；密谈；私话，小话；传闻. ②沙沙声；【医】嗫音. *give the ～* 给暗示，悄悄嘱咐. *in a ～ = in ～s* 悄声，悄悄地，低声地.

whis·per·er [ˈ*h*wispərə] *n.* 低声说话的人；耳语的人；搬弄是非的人，说小话的人，告密者；〔美剧〕提词人.

whis·per·ing [ˈ*h*wispəriŋ] *a.* 耳语的，私语的 (= whispery). — *n.* ①窃窃私语. ②流言蜚语，耳语声. ～ **campaign** 有组织地散布流言蜚语（以达到政治目的）. **-ly** *ad.*

whis·per·ing-gal·ler·y, -dome [ˈ*h*wispəriŋˈgæləri, -dəum] *n.* (能把声音远远传去的)低语廊，传声廊，回音圆廊.

whist[1] [*h*wist] *int.* 肃静！嘘！ — *a.* 无声的，静寂的. — *n.* 静(默). *Hold your ～!* 静！别响！嘘！ — *vt., vi.* (使)肃静.

whist[2] [*h*wist] *n.* 惠斯特〔四人玩的一种牌戏，桥牌的前身〕. *long [short] ～* 十点[五点]赢牌.

whis·tle [ˈ*h*wisl] *vi.* ①吹口哨. ②放汽笛；〔美俚〕吹笛. ③吹口哨通知；放汽笛通知. ④(风等)嘘嘘地叫，(子弹)嘘地打出，呼啸. ⑤密告，告诉. — *vt.* ①用口哨吹(歌曲). ②吹口哨叫(狗)，吹口哨通知[召集]，放汽笛通知. ③嘘地放. ***bid [let] sb. go ～*** 不顾某人的意愿. ***～ down the wind*** ①〔由鹰猎比喻〕放，放走；放弃；听其自由. ②散布流言，诽谤，中伤. ***～ for*** ①吹口哨子叫(狗等). ②徒然想望. — *n.* 口哨；汽笛；警笛；哨子；啸声，嘘声；〔口〕喉咙；〔美俚〕笛. *a penny [tin] ～* (六孔)锡笛. ***as clear [clean] as a ～*** 干净利落；十分安全. ***not worth the ～*** 毫无价值. ***pay (dear) for one's ～*** 付出高昂代价（买贱东西）；因一时高兴而吃苦头. ***wet one's ～*** 喝杯(酒). **～-blower** 〔主美俚〕告密者，揭发者. **～-blowing** 告密，揭发.

Whis·tler [ˈ*h*wislə] *n.* 惠斯勒〔姓氏〕.

whis·tler [ˈ*h*wislə] *n.* ①吹口哨的人；发啸声的东西. ②【动】(北美)大土拨鼠；【鸟】白颊凫. ③【兽医】患喘鸣症的马. ④【无】啸声干扰.

whis·tle-stop [ˈ*h*wisl-stɔp] *n.* ①〔美口〕快车不停的小站；小镇. ②〔美〕(竞选旅行中车站上的)短暂逗留. — *vt., vi.* (在…)作竞选活动.

whis·tling [ˈ*h*wisliŋ] *n.* ①吹笛，吹口哨；发哨声，啸声. ②(患喘鸣症的马所发的)喘鸣.

whit [*h*wit] *n.* 一点点；丝毫. ***be not one ～ inferior to*** 比…毫无逊色. ***never [not] a ～ = no ～*** 一点儿也不….

Whit·a·ker's [ˈ*h*witikəz] **Almanac** *n.* (1868年 *Joseph Whitaker* 创始的)英国韦提克年鉴.

White [*h*wait] *n.* 怀特〔姓氏〕.

white [*h*wait] *a.* ①白(色)的，雪白的；白晰的，带白色的；苍白的. ②白种人的. ③银制的；白衣的；白发的. ④洁白的，清白的，纯洁的；善良的；〔口〕高尚的，公正的；无恶意的. ⑤幸福的. ⑥无色的，透明的；（葡萄酒）浅色的；〔英〕(咖啡)加牛奶的 *(opp.* black*)*. ⑦保守的；反革命的 *(opp.* red*)*. *a ～ Christmas* 有雪的圣诞节. *a ～ day* 吉日. *a ～ night* 不眠的一夜. ***as ～ as a sheet*** （面色）刷白. ***be in ～ terror*** 吓得脸色发白. ***bleed ～*** (使)流尽鲜血；(使)榨尽血汗；(使)耗尽国力[财产]. ***days marked with a ～ stone*** 幸福的日子. ***mark one's name ～ again*** 洗清污名，雪耻. ***mark with a ～ stone*** 特笔大书. ***stand in a ～ sheet*** 忏悔. ***turn ～*** 变苍白，发白. — *n.* ①白色，洁白. ②白种人〔尤指高加索人种〕. ③眼白. ④蛋白. ⑤白面包；白葡萄酒；白色颜料，白色染料；白衣；白布制品. ⑥白马，白(种)猪；白毛动物. ⑦〔常作 W-〕反革命分子，反动分子. ⑧〔*pl.*〕【医】白带. ⑨(书写、印刷等留下的)空白. ⑩【虫】白蝶类. ⑪【英史】白色舰队. *the ～ of an egg* 鸡蛋白. *nurses in ～* 白衣护士. ***in the ～*** 尚未完工. ～ **admiral** 白纹蛱蝶 *(Limenitis arthemis)*. ～ **alkali**【化】白苏打. ～ **alloy [metal]** 假银. ～ **ant** 白蚁. ～ **arsenic**【化】砒霜，白砒，三氧化二砷. ～**bait**【鱼】银鱼. ～**beard** 白须翁. ～ **birch** ①纸皮桦（= parer birch). ②欧洲白桦 *(Betula pendula)*. ～ **blacklash** 美国白人对黑人运动的对抗. ～ **blood cell** 白血球，白血细胞（= ～ blood corpuscle). ～**book**（有关政府政治、外交问题的）白皮书. ～ **bread** 白面包. ～ **cap** ①白帽人. ②〔常 *pl.*〕白浪. ～ **cedar**【植】①白扁柏〔产于美国东部沼泽地〕；白扁柏林. ②金钟柏〔产于美国东北部〕；金钟柏木. ～ **city**（设有旋转木马、打靶场等的）游乐场. ～ **clover**【植】白车轴草，白三叶〔一种饲料草〕. ～ **coal** 白煤〔指作为能源的水力〕. ～ **coffee** ①牛奶咖啡. ②〔美俚〕威士忌酒；烈酒；私酒. ～ **coffer**〔美俚〕酒. ～**-collar** *a.*〔美〕白领的，脑力工作者的，靠薪水生活的. ～**corpuscle** 白血球；淋巴液. ～ **crappie**【动】环纹北美白鲈. ～ **crops**（小麦、玉米等成熟后变白的）白谷. ～ **damp**（在煤矿里发生的）一氧化碳. ～ **dwarf**【天】白矮星. ～ **elephant** 白象；〔美俚〕累赘的东西；赘疣. ～ **ensign** 英国海军旗. ～**eye**【动】绣眼儿〔产于亚洲东部，非洲南部及澳洲等地〕. ～**face**〔美俚〕(马戏团的) 丑角. ～**-faced** *a.* 脸色苍白的；脸上有白斑的. ～ **feather** 害怕的脸色，怯懦的表现.（*find a ～ feather in sb.'s tail* 看出某人怯懦. *show the ～ feather* 露出害怕的神色). ～ **finger(s)**【医】白指症. ～ **fish**【动】白鲑；洋方头鱼；白鲸. ～**fly** *(pl. -flies)*【动】粉虱科昆虫. ～**flag** 白旗；降旗；休战旗. ～ **fox**【动】北极狐. **W- Frair** 白袍僧【天主】加尔默罗会的托钵僧. ～ **gasoline [gas]** 没有四乙铅添加剂的汽油. ～ **gloves**〔英〕(送给闲职法官的)白手套. ～ **gold**（镍、锌与白金合成的）充白金. ～ **goods** ①家用的漂白织物〔如被里子、枕套、毛巾等〕. ②家庭大型用具〔如电冰箱、火炉等〕. **Whitehall** 白厅〔伦敦中央政府机关集中的街道〕；英国政府(的政策). ～**-handed** *a.* ①两手雪白的；不劳动的. ②廉洁的，正直的. ～**hands** ①(不劳动的) 雪白的手. ②〔喻〕纯洁，廉洁. ～**-haired** *a.* ①有白发(的)，有浅色发的. ②〔口〕得宠的（= fair-haired). ～**head** ①【动】白头鸟. ②〔口〕粟粒疹(= milium). ～ **heat**【物】白热；极端激动的情绪（*～ heat of love [wrath]* 热爱［震怒］. *study at a ～ heat* 拼命用功). ～ **hope**〔美〕白种拳击选手. ～ **horse(s)** 白浪. ～**-hot** *a.* 白热的. **W- House**〔美〕白宫；〔口〕美国总统的职权[意见(等)]. ～ **iron** 白铁，马口铁. ～ **knight** 白衣骑士〔指政治改革家或事业上的得胜者〕. ～**knuckled** *a.* 令人极度紧张的，使人捏一把汗的. ～ **lead**【化】①铅白，碱式碳酸铅. ②白铅，铅粉，白粉〔各种含铅的白色涂料〕. ～ **leather** 白革，矾鞣革. ～ **lie** 小谎，圆场谎〔为了不使人难堪而说的谎话〕. ～ **light** ①【物】白光. ②公正无私的裁判. ～ **lightning**〔美俚〕家酿白干〔尤指谷类制成的无色烈性威士忌酒〕. ～ **light district**〔美〕(纽约的) 不夜区. ～ **line** ①(印刷页面的) 空行. ②马蹄的白色角质层. ③〔美俚〕威士忌酒；便宜酒；酒精. ～**-livered** *a.* 胆小的，怯懦的. ～ **lupine**【植】白羽扁豆〔产于地中海〕. ～ **matter**【解】白质. ～ **meat** 白肉〔尤指鸡鸭等胸部的肉〕. ～ **metal** 白色金属；白合金〔指各种浅色的合金〕；以锡铅或锑为基的合金〔如白镴或锡蜡〕. ～ **mixture** 缓泻药. ～ **money** 银币. ～ **mule**〔美俚〕私酒. ～ **mustard**【植】白芥. ～ **noise**【声】白噪声. ～ **oak**【植】白栎（= American ～ oak). ②白栎木. ～**out** ①【气】乳白天空；南北极地区内由刺目的白色反光造成的方向不明. ②由南北极地区白色反光造成的暂时失明. ～ **paper** 白纸；〔英〕白皮书. ～ **pepper** 白胡椒. ～ **perch**【动】①白石鮨〔产于美国沿海与河流中〕. ②淡水石首鱼. ③ = silver perch. ④= ～ crapple. ～ **pine**【植】美洲五针松；美洲五针松木. ～ **plague** 结核；肺结核. ～ **poplar**【植】①美国银白杨. ②美国鹅掌楸（= tulip tree)；美国鹅掌楸木(= tulipwood). ～ **potato** =potato. ～ **primary** 白人预选〔指美国最高法院于1944

年以不成文法宣布的在美国南部某些州剥夺黑人投票权的直接预选〕. ~ **race** 白色人种. ~ **rage** (面色发白的)震怒. ~ **rent** ①锡矿矿工税. ②用银币支付的租金. ~ **room** 绝尘室〔温度湿度和气压均受控制的房间,用于安装和修理精密机械仪表〕. **W- Russia** 白俄罗斯〔苏联一加盟共和国〕. ~**sale** 白布贩卖. ~ **sapphire**【矿】刚玉. ~ **sauce** 奶油调味白汁〔一种用于蔬菜、肉、鱼等的卤,用脂肪、奶油、面粉、牛奶或汤料,以及调料做成〕. **White-Slave Act**〔口〕(宣布迫诱妇女为娼系犯罪行为的)麦恩法案 (= Mann Act). ~ **slaver** 迫诱良女为娼的人. ~ **slavery** 拐卖妇女业. ~**smith** 洋铁匠,锡匠,银匠;镀银匠. ~ **smog** 白雾〔指猛烈阳光与空气中悬浮的汽车排泄物作用而产生的光化学烟雾〕. ~ **supremacy** 白人至上论,白种优越论〔白种人自认为优越种族的谬论〕. ~ **supremacist** 白人至上论者. ~**tail**【动】白尾动物〔如弗吉尼亚鹿〕. ~**-tailed deer** 弗吉尼亚鹿. **W- Terror** 白色恐怖. ~**-thorn**【植】山楂(= hawthorn). ~ **throat**【鸟】白喉雀;白喉蜂雀. ~**-throated sparrow**【动】白喉带鹀〔产于北美〕. ~ **tie** ①白(蝴蝶)领结〔通常与燕尾服相配〕. ②整套燕尾服〔包括燕尾服及其附带穿戴的服饰〕,燕尾服. ~ **trash**〔集合词,贬〕穷苦白人. ~ **vitriol**【化】皓矾,硫酸锌(= zinc sulfate). ~ **war** 不流血战争,经济战. ~**wall** ① *a.* 外侧有白圈的 (亦作 ~**-wall**). ② *n.* 外侧有白圈的汽车胎. ~ **walnut**【植】灰胡桃(树) (= butternut). ~**-wash** ① *n.* 石灰水;水粉;粉饰,掩饰;〔口〕【运】零分惨败;白葡萄酒. ② *vt.* 在…上涂石灰水;粉饰,掩饰;开脱(罪责);〔英〕免除(破产人的)债务负担;〔口〕使吃零分. ~ **water** ①水花流;泡沫水流〔如浪头、湍流等激起者〕. ②(浅水区的)清流. ~ **wax** 白蜡. ~ **weed**【植】法国菊. **W- Week** = Whitesuntide. ~ **whale**【动】白鲸 (= belnga).

White·field [ˈ*h*waitfiːld] *n.* 怀特菲尔德〔姓氏〕.

White·head [ˈ*h*waithed] *n.* 怀特海〔姓氏〕.

whit·en [ˈ*h*waitn] *vt.* 使白,涂白;漂白. — *vi.* 变白.

whit·en·er [ˈwaitnə] *n.* 涂白者;漂白者,漂布者;漂白剂. ~ **wine** 白葡萄酒. ~**wing** ①〔美〕清道夫. ②〔诗〕帆. ~**wood**【植】郁金香树(的木材);椴木属的俗名. ~ **X-rays** 连续X射线.

whit·en·ing [ˈ*h*waitniŋ] *n.* ①使白;变白. ②白垩;加白胶泥水.

white·y [ˈ*h*waiti] *n.*〔俚、贬〕白人;白种人;白人社会. — *a.* = whity.

whith·er [ˈ*h*wiðə] *ad.*〔古〕①〔疑问〕到哪里,在什么地方. *W- did he go?* 他到哪里去了? *I see ~ your question tends.* 我明白你发问的意图了. ②〔关系〕向何处 (= to which place). *the village ~ I went* 我去的那个村子. ③〔不带前行词〕(到)随便什么地方. *Go ~ you please.* 随便你到什么地方去. ④〔用于报刊等文章标题〕走向何处去? *W- France?* 法国向何处去? — *n.* 去处,目的地. *our whence and our ~* 我们的来处和去处. **no ~**〔古〕没有去处,不到任何地方.

whith·er·so·ev·er [*h*wiðəsəuˈevə] *ad.*〔古〕无论到哪里;…的地方都….

whith·er·ward [ˈ*h*wiðəwəd] *ad., conj.*〔古、诗〕向何方,向何处,在何方向.

whit·ing[1] [ˈ*h*waitiŋ] *n.*【鱼】(欧洲)小鳕鱼,牙鳕;鳕.

whit·ing[2] [ˈ*h*waitiŋ] *n.* 白垩粉,白粉,铅粉.

whit·ish [ˈ*h*waitiʃ] *a.* 带白色的,带苍白的,微白的.

whit·leath·er [ˈ*h*witleðə] *n.* 白鞣皮;【解】(颈部的)项韧带 (= white leather).

Whit·ley [ˈ*h*witliː] *n.* 惠特利〔姓氏〕. ~ **Council**〔英〕劳资问题协商会议. **-ism** *n.* 劳资协商制.

whit·low [ˈ*h*witləu] *n.*【医】瘭疽,指〔趾〕头脓炎,甲沟炎.【兽医】(羊的)蹄冠炎.

Whit·man [ˈ*h*witmən] *n.* ①惠特曼〔姓氏〕. ②**Walt** ~ 惠特曼〔1819—1892,美国诗人〕.

Whit·mon·day [ˈ*h*witˈmʌndi, -dei] *n.* 降灵节的后一日〔英国银行假日〕.

Whit·ney [ˈ*h*witni] *n.* ①惠特尼〔姓氏〕. ②**E.** ~ 惠特尼〔1765—1825,美国发明家,轧棉机的发明者〕. ③**W.D.** ~ 惠特尼〔1827—1894,美国比较语言学家、词典编辑家〕.

Whit·sun [ˈ*h*witsʌn] *a.*【宗】圣灵降临节的.

Whit·sun·day [ˈ*h*witˈsʌndi] *n.*【宗】圣灵降临节〔复活节后的第七个星期日〕.

Whit·sun·tide [ˈ*h*witsntaid] *n.* 圣灵降临节节期,圣灵降临周〔圣灵降临节后的一周,尤指头三天〕.

Whit·tier [ˈ*h*witiə] *n.* 惠蒂尔〔姓氏〕.

whit·tle [ˈ*h*witl] *vt., vi.* 切;削;削减,减少;削瘦,损害. *(down; away).* — *n.*〔古、英方〕切肉用大刀;屠刀.

Whit·worth [ˈ*h*witwɔːθ] **thread**【机】惠氏螺纹.

whit·y [ˈ*h*waiti] *a.* 带白色的 (= whitish). ★常与其他色名结合: ~-brown 发白的褐色.

whiz,[1] **whizz** [*h*wiz] *n.* 嘘,飕. — *vi.* (箭、子弹等)飕飕作声,发呼啸声.

whiz[2] [*h*wiz] *n.*〔美俚〕①扒手. ②伶俐的人;优秀的学生;能手,专家. ③有吸引力的东西. ④同意,达成交易. — *vt., vi.*〔美俚〕扒窃. ~ **kid**〔美〕神童.

whiz[3] [*h*wiz] *n.*〔口〕短期旅行. *take a ~ to the shore* 到海滨小玩几天.

whiz-bang [ˈhwizbæŋ] *n.* ①【军俚】小口径超高速炮弹. ②一种爆竹. ③〔美俚〕=whiz[2] 义项②. — *a.*〔美俚〕极好的;极伶俐的,极有用的.

whiz·zer [ˈ*h*wizə] *n.* ①飕飕作声的东西. ②离心干燥机. ③〔俚〕品质特别好的东西〔人〕;能手,专家. — *vi.* 脱水,去水,甩水.

WHO = World Health Organization 世界卫生组织(联合国).

who [huː] *pro.* (宾格 ***whom;*** 所有格 ***whose***) ①〔疑问〕谁,什么人;怎样的人. *Who told you?* 谁跟你讲的? *Who goes there?* 谁?是哪个? *Whom* [〔口〕 *Who*] *do you mean?* 你说的是谁? *Whose son is he?* 他是谁的儿子? ② [huː, hu, u(ː)]〔关系,有先行词〕. *Anyone ~ chooses can apply.* 有意者均可申请. *a man (whom) one can trust* 可靠的人. *I know the man whom you mean.* 我知道你说的那个人. ③〔古〕〔关系,无先行词〕*Who is not for us is against us.* 不赞成我们的都是反对我们的. *W- breaks pays.* 损坏者需作赔偿. ④〔口〕哪位先生〔小姐、太太等〕〔置于 Mr., Miss 等称谓之后,用于问清楚某人姓名之情况下〕. *"A Mr. Amherst rang you up this morning."*——*"Mr. ~?"* "今天早上有位阿姆赫斯特先生打电话给您."——"哪位先生?" ***as ~ should say***〔古〕正象人所说的那样;所谓. ***~'s milking this cow***〔美俚〕别来管闲事. ***~'s ~*** ①名人的身分,特色. ②〔W-'s W〕名人录;人名词典;〔集合词〕著名人物,重要人物.

whoa [wəu] *int.* ①遏!〔叫马停住〕. ②〔谑〕停止.

who·dun·(n)it [huːˈdʌnit] *n.*〔美俚〕侦探小说〔戏剧、影片等〕.

who·ever [huːˈevə]〔诗〕**who·e'er** [huːˈεə] *pro.* (宾格 ***whomever;*** 所有格 ***whosever***) ①任何人(都);谁(都),什么人(都),凡是…的人(都). ②不管谁…,无论什么人…. ③〔俚〕究竟是谁 *W- comes is welcome.* 来的人都受欢迎. *W- [Whomever] I quote, you retain your opinion.* 我无论引用什么人的话,你都不改变你的意见. *Whoever's [Whosever] it was, it is now mine.* 不管从前是谁的,现在是我的. *W- said so?* 究竟是谁那样说的.

whole [həul] *a.* ①全部的,整个的;所有的,一切的,全…. ②完全的,完整的;没有缺漏的;无疵的,没有破损的,原样未动的,无恙的. ③整整的,刚好的;【数】整数的,不含分数的. ④〔古〕健康的,壮健的;(伤)已治愈,(病)已复原. *the ~ body* 全身. *a ~ day* 整天. *the ~ world* 全世界. *the ~ truth* 一丝不差的〔全部〕真相,原原本本. *the ~ sum* 总数. ~ *milk* 全脂奶. *swallow a raisin ~* 囫囵吞下一粒葡萄干. *escape with a ~ skin* 安然逃脱. *a ~ year* 整整一年. *They that be ~ need not a physician.* 健康的人不需要医生. **a lie of ~ cloth**〔美口〕十足的谎话. **a ~ lot of**〔口〕很多的[整整一批]…. **be the ~ show** 演独脚戏. **out of ~ cloth**〔美口〕瞎编的,全无根据的. **a ~ shooting match**〔美俚〕整个团体,全体群众. ~ **smear**〔美俚〕全体〔指团体、群众或搜集物〕. — *n.* 整个;全部,全体,完全的东西;统一体;总体. *Breaking up the ~ into parts, assembling the parts into a ~.* 化整为零,化零为整. *Nature is a ~.* 自然是一个统一体. **as a ~** (作为一个)整体,(由)全体[全部、全局](*the war situation as a ~* 战争的全局. *in the world as a ~* 在全世界范围内). **(up)on the ~** 从全体来看;大体上,总之. ~ **blood** ①全血〔供输血用,没有抽出任何成份〕. ②(同父母)嫡亲关系;纯种. ~ **brothers [sisters]** 同胞[同父同母]弟兄[姐妹]. ~ **cheese**〔美俚〕自我中心的人;主观强的人. **~-colo(u)red** *a.* 纯色的. **~-hearted** *a.* **~-heartedly** *ad.* 全心全意的[地]. ~ **gale**【气】狂风〔十级风旧称〕. ~ **hog** *n., a.*〔俚〕全部(的),完全(的),彻底(的)(*accept the ~-hog* 全部接受. *go the ~-hog*〔口〕干到底;走极端). **~-hogger** 极端派;〔特指〕极端保护贸易派. **~-hoofed** *a.* 单蹄的. **~-length** ① *a.* 全长的,全身的. ② *n.* 全身像. **~-meal** *n., a.* (没有去麸的)粗面粉(的)(*~-meal bread* 粗面粉面包). ~ **note**【乐】全音符. ~ **number**【数】整数. **~-souled** *a.* 全心全意的. ~ **step [tone]**【乐】全音(步). **~-wheat** *a.* = whole-meal.

whole·ness [ˈhəulnis] *n.* 全体;一切;完全.

whole·sale [ˈhəulseil] *a.* ①批发的,趸卖的. ②大规模的,大批的;全部的. *~ prices* 批发价格. *a ~ slaughter* 大屠杀. *make ~ arrests of* 把…一网打尽. — *n.* 批发,趸卖. **by ~**=〔美〕**at ~** 照批发,整批;大规模地;大批,完全. — *ad.* ①照批发,整批. ②大规模地;大批大批地,完全. —*vt.* 批发,趸卖. — *vi.* ①经营批发业. ②整批售货.

whole·sal·er [ˈhəulseilə] *n.* 批发商.

whole·some [ˈhəulsəm] *a.* ①适合卫生的,有益健康的. ②(身体)健全的,有生气的. ③对身心有益的. ④安全的. *~ air* 新鲜空气. *a ~ food* 卫生食品. *~ advice [reading]* 有益劝告[读物]. *It wouldn't be ~ for you to go there.* 你去那儿恐怕不安全. **-ly** *ad.*

who·lism [ˈhəulizm] *n.* = holism.

who'll [hu:l] = who will [shall].

whol·ly [ˈhəulli] *ad.* 完全地,全部;十足,统统;专门,净. *I don't ~ agree.* 我不完全赞成.

whom [hu:m, hum] *pro.* who 的宾格〔但在口语中常用 who 代替之〕.

whom·ev·er, whom·so·ev·er [hu:mˈevə, hu:msəuˈevə] *pro.* whoever, whosoever 的宾格.

whomp [hwɔmp] *vt.* ①打,击,敲. ②决定性地击败,击溃. *~ up* ①迅速准备. ②激起,引起. ③草率做成. — *n.* 打,击,敲;击打声,敲打声.

whoop [hu:p] *int.* 喝!嗬!〔欢喜声、兴奋声〕. — *n.* ①高呼;呐喊. ②嗬嗬的叫声;(百日咳特有的)高音吼声;哮喘声;猫头鹰的叫声. ③〔口〕〔用于否定句〕叫一声嗬的价值,极微小的价值;些微. ④【鸟】戴胜〔产于欧、亚及北非,一种羽毛美丽的鸟〕. **be not worth a ~** 毫无价值. **not care a ~**〔美〕一点也不在乎. **~s and jingles**〔美俚〕酒疯,醉后谵语;神经极度紧张. — *vi.* ①高声喊叫[说话]. ②大叫大嚷地走过. ③嗬嗬地叫. ④发哮喘声;(百日咳病人一面咳一面)吓吓地说. — *vt.* ①高声说. ②呐喊着追赶. ③引起(兴趣等);哄抬(价钱)(*up*). **~ it up** = **~ things up**〔美俚〕= make whoopee. **~ it up for**〔美俚〕喝采,叫万岁.

whoop-de-do, whoop-do-doo [ˈhu:p diˈdu:, ˈhwu:p-] *n.*〔口〕①起哄;嚷闹. ②激烈的公开辩论.

whoop·ee [ˈhwu:pi:] *int.*〔美口〕喝!嗬!〔表示高兴、快乐等感情〕. — *n.* 狂欢,喝酒欢闹. **make ~**〔美俚〕狂欢,喝酒欢闹. ~ **period** (市面)繁荣时期. ~ **water** 酒.

whoop·er [ˈhu:pə] *n.* 高呼者;狂欢的人;作呼呼叫声的鸟类;〔特指〕美洲鹤. **~up**〔美俚〕= make whoopee.

whoop·ing [ˈhu:piŋ] *a.* 发嗬嗬声的;发咳声的. **~-cough**【医】百日咳(= hooping-cough). ~ **crane**【动】北美咳声鹤(*Grus americana*).

whoop·la [ˈhu:plɑ:, ˈhwu:p-, ˈhup-] *n.*〔美口〕狂欢;嬉闹;大吹大擂的宣传;痛饮作乐(= hoopla).

whoosh [*h*wuʃ] *vi.* ①(物件在空气中飞速移动)发出嘶嘶声[嘘嘘声]. ②发嘶嘶声飞过,嘘地飞过. *Rockets ~ed by.* 火箭嘶声飞过. — *vt.* 使发嘶嘶声[嘘嘘声],使嘶声飞过. — *n.* 嘶声,嘶声飞过. — *int.* 嘶!嘘!〔表示惊讶、疲乏等〕.

whoo·sis [ˈhu:zis] *n.*〔美俚〕= whosis.

whop [*h*wɔp] *vt.*〔口〕(鞭)打;打败,打垮. — *n.*〔口〕重打(声).

whop·per [ˈ*h*wɔpə] *n.*〔口〕①庞然大物. ②弥天大谎.

whop·ping [ˈ*h*wɔpiŋ] *n.*〔口〕(重)打;打败. — *a.*〔口〕非常大的;非常的,极大的,(谎话等)荒唐的. — *ad.* 非常,极(大等).

whore [hɔ:, hɔə] *n.* ①妓女. ②出卖信仰[才能]者. — *vi.* ①卖淫;嫖. ②邪神[偶像]崇拜. **~house** 妓院. **~master, ~monger** 嫖客;给妓女拉纤的人. **~son** ① *n.* 私生子;无赖恶棍. ② *a.* 卑劣无耻的,无赖的. **-dom** *n.* ①卖淫;妓院. ②邪神崇拜.

who're [ˈhu:ə] (= who are).

whor·ish [ˈhɔ:riʃ] *a.* 妓女似的;淫乱的.

whorl [*h*wə:l] *n.* ①【植】轮(= verticil). ②【动】(螺蛳等的)壳阶,螺层,螺环;螺旋部;(昆虫等的)毛轮. ③手指的螺纹. ④【纺】锭盘. **-ed** *a.* ①【植】轮生的. ②有螺纹[螺环]的.

whor·tle·ber·ry [hwə:tlberi] *n.*【植】越桔(树).

who's [hu:z] ①who is. ②who has.

whose [hu:z] *pro.* who, which 的所有格. ①〔疑问〕谁的. ②〔关系〕那个人的,那些人的;他[她]的,他们[她们]的;它(们)的. *W- book is this?* 这是谁的书? *a river ~ banks are covered with trees* 两岸长着树的河. **~ever, ~soever,** *pro.* whoever 等的所有格.

who·sis [ˈhu:ziz] *n.*〔美俚〕忘了叫什么的一个人[一种东西];那人;那东西.

who·sit [ˈhuzzit] *n.*〔美俚〕某某人(=who's it).

who·so [ˈhu:səu],〔古〕**who·so·e'er** [-səuˈɛə], **who·so·ev·er** [-səuˈevə] *pro.* = whoever〔语气比 whoever 强〕.

whr. = watt-hour.

whump [hwʌmp] *n., vt., vi.*〔口〕= thump.

whup [hwʌp] *vt.*〔美俚〕大胜.

why [*h*wai] *ad.* ①〔疑问〕为什么. *W- do you think so?* 你为什么这样想? *You are late —— W-?* 你晚了——为什么? *He does not know ~ he failed.* 他不知道他为什么失败. *W-? = W- so?* 为什么(那样)? *W- not?* 为什么不好[不行]. ②〔关系〕…的原因[理由]. *The reason ~ he failed was his laziness.* 他失败的原因就是他懒惰. *That is ~ he came here.* 那就是他到这儿来的原因[理由]. ★ 后一例句是省去先行词的用法. — *n. (pl. ~s)* ①原因,理由,(理由的)说明. ②难解的问题. *the ~s and wherefores* 理由和原因. *all the great ~s of life* 一切难解的人生问题. — [wai] *int.*〔发觉、承认〕哎呀!唷!当然!;〔问题太容易时〕什么?;〔在思考过程中〕唔,是呀;〔抗议、反对〕什么!什么话!;〔后接从句〕那么. *W-, of course.* 唔,当然. *"Is it true?" — "W-, yes, I think so."* '那是真的吗?' —— '唔,是呀,我是那样想'. *"What is twice two?" — "W-, four."* '二的

两倍是多少？''什么？四呀'. *If silver will not do,* ～, *we must try gold.* 倘若银子不行，那么，我们应该用金子试一试.
whyd·ah (bird) [ˈhwidə(bəːd)]【动】非洲凤凰雀.
why-for [hwaiˈfɔː] *ad.* 〔美俚〕 = why.
Whyte [hwait] *n.* 怀特〔姓氏〕.
W.I. = ①West Indies 西印度群岛. ②West India(n) 西印度群岛(的).
Wic·ca [ˈwikə] *n.* 巫术迷信.
wick[1] [wik] *n.* ①灯芯；蜡烛芯. ②【机】虹吸油芯，吸油绳. ③【外】塞伤口的纱布. ④【电】电极芯；导火线.
wick[2] [wik] *n.* ①镇，村〔常构成地名或复合词，如 Hampton Wick, bailiwick〕. ②农场(建筑物)；〔特指〕奶牛场，奶牛棚.
wick·ed [ˈwikid] *a.* ①邪恶的；不道德的；恶劣的. ②恶意的；顽皮的，淘气的. ③〔美俚〕显示高超技艺的. *a* ～ *urchin* 顽童. *a* ～ *look* 邪恶的样子. *play a* ～ *game of tennis* 打得一手好网球. **-ly** *ad.*
wick·er [ˈwikə] *n.* (编制筐篓的)枝条；柳条(编制品). — *a.* 枝条［柳条］编的. *a* ～ *basket* 柳条篮子. *a* ～ *chair* 柳条椅子. ～**work** 柳条编结构造；柳条制品.
wick·er·ed [ˈwikəd] *a.* 柳条编的.
wick·et [ˈwikit] *n.* ①(大门上的)便门；边门 (= ～-door, ～-gate). ②旋转栅门. ③(银行等的)营业窗口；售票窗口. ④(马房等分上下两半而只下半常开的)半门；(运河的)闸门. ⑤【板球】三柱门；投球场的情况；投法；【槌球戏】铁丝小门. *be on a good [sticky]* ～ 处于有利［不利］地位. *keep one's* ～ *up* (击球员)没有被打出局；〔喻〕保持自己的地位. *take a* ～ 使一个击球员出局. *win by ten [two]* ～*s* 无人被打出局［有二人留存］而赢. ～**keeper**【板球】守门员.
wick·ing [ˈwikiŋ] *n.* 灯芯(绳)，烛芯(绳).
wick·i·up [ˈwikiʌp] *n.* ①〔美〕(印第安人的)椭圆形茅棚. ②简陋的临时住处.
wic·o·py [ˈwikəpi] *n.*【植】①沼泽革木 (= leatherwood). ②椴属植物 (= basswood). ③柳属植物〔如柳兰〕.
wid·(d)er·shins [ˈwidəʃinz] *ad.* = withershins.
wide [waid] *a.* (*opp.* narrow) ①宽阔的. ②广阔的，广大的，宽敞的. ③广博的；范围广大的；广泛的. ④远离的；(偏)差得远的，错得厉害的. ⑤开口大的，张开的，分得很开的. ⑥【语音】(元音)开的，松的. ⑦【农】(饲料)蛋白质少的. ⑧〔英俚〕精明的；机警的. *10 feet* ～ 宽十英尺. *a* ～ *cloth* 门面宽的布. ～ *intervals* 宽阔的间隔. ～ *reading* 广泛阅读. *a* ～ *difference* 巨大的差异. *a guess* ～ *of the truth* 与实况相差很远的猜测. *be of* ～ *distribution* 分布宽广. *be* ～ *of the mark* 离目标很远；满不对头. *give a* ～ *berth to* 离开，(远远)避开. *hazard a* ～ *guess* 随便乱猜. *take* ～ *views* 采取开通的观点. ～ *place [spot] in the road* 〔美俚〕小市镇. *with* ～ *eyes* 睁大了眼睛. — *ad.* ①广阔地. ②张得很大. ③远远；歪，不中，弄错. *He is* ～ *awake.* 他很精明［机警］. *The shot went* ～. 子弹打歪了. *speak* ～ *of the mark* 讲得不得要领. *far and* ～ 到处，普遍. *have one's eyes* ～ *open* 眼睛睁得很大；警觉；精明，机警. *open one's mouth too* ～ 野心太大. ～ *open* 开得很大；〔美〕(城市)对卖酒、卖淫等取缔不严的；〔新闻〕有充分登载新闻余地的. — *n.* ①〔the ～〕广大的世界. ②【板球】歪球 (=～ ball). *broke to the* ～〔俚〕①一个铜子也没有. ②完全失掉信用. *(be) done [whacked] to the* ～〔军俚〕累透. ～ **ball**【板球】(送一分给击球员的)投向远离击球员方面的歪球. ～**-angle** *a.*【摄，影】广角的〔指镜头，拍摄场面，放映角度等〕 ～**-eyed** *a.* 睁大眼睛的〔指惊讶，恐惧，好奇等〕. ～ **screen** 宽银幕. ～**-screen** *a.* 宽银幕的. ～**spreading** *a.* 广泛传播［流行］的. **-ly** *ad.*
wide-a·wake [ˈwaidəˈweik] *a.* 完全清醒的；精明的，机警的. — [ˈwaidəweik] *n.* (阔边)呢帽.
wid·en [ˈwaidn] *vt.* 弄阔，放宽；使张开. — *vi.* 变阔，变宽；扩大.
wide-spread [ˈwaidspred] *a.* 广布的；蔓延的；流传宽广的，普及的，普遍的.
WIDF = Women's International Democratic Federation 国际民主妇女联合会.
widg·eon [ˈwidʒən] *n.*【鸟】某几种野鸭的通称；赤颈凫，鹡鸰，水鸷.
wid·get [ˈwidʒit] *n.* ①〔口〕小机械，小器具〔尤指设想中的新装置〕. ②〔美俚〕装饰物.
wid·ish [ˈwaidiʃ] *a.* 有点阔的，稍宽的，宽宽的.
wid·ow [ˈwidəu] *n.* ①寡妇. ②【牌戏】放在一边的几张牌〔如打百分中扣着的牌〕. ③【印】(上页多出移转下页的)半行，短行，一个单词. ④〔美口〕丈夫老是不在身边的妇人〔多用以构成复合词，如 a golf ～ 丈夫老是去打高尔夫球而常被丢在家里的妇人〕. **grass** ～ 离婚或与丈夫分居的妇女. — *vt.* ①〔常用被动语态〕使成寡妇；使成鳏夫；使失去丈夫［妻子］. ②〔诗〕夺去，分离 *(of)*. *The trees are* ～*ed of their fruits.* 〔诗〕果实摘光树空留. ～ **bewitch** = grass ～. ～ **bird**【动】凤凰雀 (= whydah bird). ～ **lady** 寡妇. ～**'s cruse** 见 *cruse* 条. ～**'s men** (薪额移作寡妇基金的)空额水兵. ～**'s mite** 寡妇的少量捐款〔少而可贵〕. ～**'s peak** 脑门上的V形发尖. ～**'s third [tierce]** 寡妇所得的遗产〔亡夫财产的三分之一〕. ～**'s walk** 望夫台〔用以眺望归帆的屋顶平台〕. ～**'s weeds** 寡妇的丧服.
wid·ow·er [ˈwidəuə] *n.* 鳏夫.
wid·ow·hood [ˈwidəuhud] *n.* 寡妇的身份；孀居.
width [widθ] *n.* 广阔；宽度；幅度；(布匹的)门面；幅员；广博. *12 feet in* ～ 阔12英尺. ～ *in the clear*【林】除皮直径. ～ **aspect** 宽边比. ～**wise,** ～**ways** *a., ad.* 横向的［地］，纬向的［地］.
wield [wiːld] *vt.* ①挥(剑等). ②用，使用. ③支配，统治，掌握. ～ *a facile pen* 运笔轻快. ～ *power* 行使权力. ～ *influence* 施加影响. ～ *the sceptre* 掌握大权；行使权力.
wield·y [wiːldi] *a.* 易使用的，易挥动的；易于处理的.
Wien [viːn] *n.* 〔G.〕 = Vienna.
wie·ner [ˈwiːnə], **wie·nerwurst** [-wəːst], **wie·nie** [ˈwiːni] *n.* 〔美〕维也纳香肠，小红肠.
Wies·ba·den [ˈviːsbɑːdn] *n.* 威斯巴登〔德意志联邦共和国城市〕.
wife [waif] *n.* (*pl.* **wives** [waivz]) ①妻. ②〔古〕女人，乡下妇人. ③〔美俚〕脚镣；〔军俚〕同房伙伴. *wedded [lawful]* ～ 正妻，元配. *plural wives* 妻妾. *man [husband] and* ～ 夫妇. **an old** ～ ①(多嘴的)老太婆. ②〔俚〕烟囱帽，烟罩. **give sb. to** ～ 嫁. **have a** ～ 已娶妻. **take [have] sb. to** ～ 娶某人为妻. **-ly** *a.* = wifelike.
wife·less [ˈwaiflis] *a.* 无妻的.
wife·like [ˈwaiflaik] *a.* 妻子的，象妻的.
wig [wig] *n.* ①假发. ②〔口〕法官〔因旧时法官戴假发〕. ③〔谑、口〕头发；头；头脑. ④〔美俚〕知识分子. ⑤【动】海狗. *You had better brush your untidy* ～. 你最好想想清楚吧. ～*s on the green* 打架；激烈的论争. — *vt.* ①给…装假发. ②〔口〕痛骂，严责. ③〔美俚〕使激动；使发狂. — *vi.* 〔美俚〕激动；发狂. ～ *out* 〔美俚〕①(因服麻醉品)感到飘飘然. ②极端兴奋.
wig·an [ˈwigən] *n.* 一种平纹厚棉布〔原产地为英国西北部的 Wigan〕.
wi·geon [ˈwidʒən] *n.* = widgeon.
wigged [wigd] *a.* 戴假发的.
wig·ger·y [ˈwigəri] *n.* 〔罕〕①〔集合词〕假发. ②用假发装饰，戴假发.
wig·ging [ˈwigiŋ] *n.* 〔英口〕责骂，叱责.
wig·gle [ˈwigl] *vt.* ①〔口、方〕摇摆，扭动. ②(在船尾)划

(船). — *vi.* 摆动,扭动. — *n.* ①快速摆动，扭动. ②弯曲线. ③奶油青豆烧鱼[虾、蛤蜊等]. *Get a ~ on you!* 〔美俚〕赶快！快点！

wig·gler [ˈwiglə] *n.* ①扭动［摆动］的人［物]. ②【动】孑孓.

wig·gly [ˈwigli] *a.* ***(-gli·er; -gli·est)*** ①摆动的；扭动的；蠕动的；蜿蜒的. ②有波形的,起伏的.

wight[1] [wait] *n.* ①〔废〕活物，动物. ②〔古〕人. ③〔古〕妖精,鬼怪.

wight[2] [wait] *a.* 〔古、方〕快速的；轻捷的，活泼的；勇敢的.

wig·let [ˈwiglit] *n.* 小型假发，局部假发；〔尤指〕女用假发.

wig·wag [ˈwigwæg] *vt., vi.* ①摆动，摇动. ②(用手旗，灯光等)打(信号、暗号). — *n.* 发信号；旗语信号.

wig·wam [ˈwigwæm] *n.* ①(印第安人的) 棚屋. ②〔美俚〕(政治性集会等用的) 临时大会场. ③〔the W-〕=〔美〕Tammany Hall.

wik·i·up [ˈwikiʌp] *n.* = wickiup.

Wil·ber [ˈwilbə] *n.* 威尔伯〔姓氏,男子名〕.

Wil·ber·force [ˈwilbəfɔːs] *n.* 威尔伯福斯〔姓氏〕.

Wil·bert [ˈwilbət] *n.* 威尔伯特〔姓氏,男子名〕.

Wil·bur [ˈwilbə] *n.* 威尔伯〔姓氏,男子名〕.

Wil·burn [ˈwilbəːn] *n.* 威尔伯恩〔姓氏,男子名〕.

wil·co [ˈwilkəu] *int.* 行！可以！照办！〔无线电话通话中用语；为 will comply 的缩略形式〕.

Wil·cox [ˈwilkɔks] *n.* 威尔科克斯〔姓氏〕.

wild [waild] *a.* ①野生的 *(opp.* domestic; cultivated*)*；野性的,未驯养的. ②未耕作的,荒野的；没人住的,无人烟的,完全自然的. ③未开化的,野蛮的. ④狂暴的,狂乱的；任性的. ⑤猛烈的,波涛汹涌的,狂风暴雨的. ⑥疯狂(似)的,热狂的；疯狂地想…. ⑦鲁莽的，莽撞的；荒唐的；古怪的；不着边际的. ⑧散乱的,邋遢的. ⑨【牌】百搭的. *a ~ beast* 野兽. *a ~ bird* 野鸟. *a ~ boar* 野猪. *a ~ flower* 野花. *a ~ park* 天然公园. *~ fancies* 狂想,妄想. *~ fluctuations* (行市的)狂涨暴跌. *~ living* 放荡的生活. *He settled down after a ~ youth.* 他少年时候放荡后来老实了. *a ~ night* 暴风雨之夜. *a ~ sea* 波涛汹涌的大海. *~ with joy* 狂喜. *~ rage* 暴怒. *a ~ blow* 乱打. *a ~ pitch* 乱投. *a ~ shot* 乱射. *~ times* 乱世. ***be ~ about*** ①热中于,给…迷住. ②因某事狂怒. ***be ~ with excitement*** 兴奋若狂. ***drive sb. ~*** 激怒某人. ***go ~*** 兴奋；高兴. ***grow ~*** 野生，自然生长. ***make sb. ~*** 使某人生气. ***run ~*** 变野蛮；变粗暴；放肆起来；(植物)乱长. ***~ and woolly*** 〔美〕粗野的；莽撞的；(美国) 西部的. ***~ cats*** 〔美俚〕水兵. ***~ willie west*** 〔美〕供人参观的西部牧场. ***~ work*** 粗暴的动作. — *ad.* 狂暴地；猛烈地；胡乱地. *shoot ~* 乱射. *talk ~* 瞎讲. — *n.* 〔常 *pl.*〕荒地，荒野；未开化的地方. ~ **allspice**【植】黄果山胡椒 (= spicebush). ~ **brier** 野玫瑰或野蔷薇,〔尤指〕多花蔷薇或犬蔷薇. ~ **carrot**【植】(野生)胡萝卜. ~**cat** ① *n.* 野猫,山猫；【动】猞猁；〔喻〕性子暴躁的人；〔美〕盲目的、不可靠的事业[投机]；瞎拟的计划；〔美口〕瞎掘的油[气]井；〔美口〕(调车用)小型机车；【船】锚链滚筒；持链滚筒；锚机. ② *a.* 莽撞的,狂乱的；盲目的；骗人的，(股票等)投机性质的；〔美〕(列车等)不按规定时间行驶的，乱开行的 (*a ~cat strike* 未经工会批准或违反合同的野猫罢工). ③*vi., vt.* 〔美俚〕做危险的投机；未得许可私自预售座位；瞎掘 (油井). ~**catter** 〔美俚〕瞎掘油井的人；做冒险[投机]事业的人. ~ **duck** 野鸭. ~**-eyed** *a.* ①显得暴怒的，狂暴的. ②激进的 (*~ ideas* 激进的思想，激进的意识形态). ~ **fig** = caprifig. ~ **fowl** 猎鸟. ~ **goose**【鸟】雁 (*~-goose chase* 无益[无望]的追求). ~ **hog** ①野猪 (= wild boar). ②西貒 (= peccary). **W- Hunt** (欧洲民间传说的)鬼猎人夜游〔鬼猎人夜间在乡间或天空奔驰〕. **W- Huntsman** 鬼猎人. ~ **hyacinth**【植】①大西洋卡马夏. ②蓝绵枣儿 (= wood hyacinth). ~ **indigo**【植】赝靛属植物 (= baptisia). ~**lettuce**【植】野莴苣〔尤指加拿大莴苣〕. ~**-life**〔集合词〕野禽，野生动物. ~**lifer** 野生生物保护者；自然环境保护论者. ~ **mustard**【植】十字花科〔尤指田芥菜〕. ~ **oat(s)**【植】①小颚花〔产于北美〕. ②燕麦属植物〔尤指野燕麦,乌麦〕(*sow one's ~* 男人青年期未婚前的放荡). ~ **olive** 类齐墩果属植物〔如沙枣〕. ~ **pansy**【植】三色堇. ~ **parsnip**【植】欧洲防风草. ~ **pink**【植】麦瓶草属植物〔尤指加罗林雪轮〕. ~ **rice**【植】①菰〔产于美国和加拿大的湖河的沼泽区〕. ②菰米. ~ **rose**【植】野玫瑰，野蔷薇〔如多花蔷薇〕. ~ **rye**【植】野麦属植物〔产于北美洲〕. ~**-track** *a.*【影】(画外)配音的. ~ **turkey**【动】野吐绶鸡. ~ **type**【生】野生型. **W- West** 〔或作 **w- W-**〕〔美〕蛮荒的西部〔在早先拓荒时代的美国西部地区，该地当时无法律〕. ~ **West show**〔美〕由牛仔、印第安人等演出的)骑术表演. ~**-wood** 自然[原始]林.

Wil·da [ˈwildə] *n.* 威尔达〔女子名,Willa 的昵称〕.

Wilde [waild] *n.* ①怀尔德〔姓氏〕. ②**Oscar** ~ 奥斯卡・王尔德〔1854—1900,英国诗人,唯美主义者. **-an** *a.* 王尔德(作品)的.

wil·de·beest [ˈwiːldəbiːst] *n.*【动】角马.

Wil·der [ˈwaildə] *n.* 怀尔德〔姓氏〕.

wil·der [ˈwildə] *vt., vi.* 〔古〕(使)迷途；(使)迷惑，(使)困惑.

wil·der·ness [ˈwildənis] *n.* ①荒地,荒野,旷野；荒芜[荒凉]的地方. ②无数,一大堆；许多. *a ~ of waters = a ~ of sea = a watery ~* 茫茫大海. *a ~ of streets* 纵横交错的许多街道. ***a voice in the ~*** 旷野里的呼声，无人理睬的改革家的呼声.

wild·fire [ˈwaildfaiə] *n.* ①(从前海战中用以焚烧敌船的)难灭燃烧剂. ②磷火；鬼火. ③闪电. ***spread [run] like ~*** 象燎原的火一样(迅速)蔓延.

wild·ing [ˈwaildiŋ] *n.* ①野生植物(的果实)；野生苹果. ②野兽. — *a.* 〔诗〕野生的.

wild·ish [ˈwaildiʃ] *a.* 有点狂暴[狂乱]的,疯狂似的.

wile [wail] *n.* 〔常 *pl.*〕诡计,奸计；欺骗. — *vt.* ①诱骗. *(away; from; into; out of)*. ②消磨(时间) *(away)* 〔系 while 一词的误用〕. *~ sb. into [out of]* 把某人骗进[骗出]….

Wi·ley, Wy·lie [ˈwaili] *n.* 怀利〔姓氏,男子名〕.

Wil·ford [ˈwilfəd] *n.* 威尔福德〔姓氏,男子名〕.

Wil·fred [ˈwilfrid] *n.* 威尔弗雷德〔男子名〕.

wil·ful [ˈwilfəl] *a.* ①任性的；固执的. ②故意的. *~ ignorance* 顽固不化. **-ly** *ad.* **-ness** *n.*

Wil·helms·ha·ven [ˈvilhelmshɑːfən] *n.* 德国北部港口.

Wilkes [wilks] *n.* 威尔克斯〔姓氏〕.

Wil·kin·son [ˈwilkinsn] *n.* 威尔金森〔姓氏〕.

Will [wil] *n.* 威尔〔男子名，William 的昵称〕.

will[1] [强 wil; 弱 l, wəl] *v. aux.* **(**现在形 ***will*** or ***'ll,***〔古〕主语为 thou 时 ***wilt*** 或 ***'lt;*** 过去形 ***would*** 或 ***'d,***〔古〕thou ***would(e)*** 或 ***'dst;*** 否定省略形 ***won't*** = will not; ***wouldn't*** 或 ***d'not*** = would not**)** ①〔表示现在的意志、愿望等〕要,希望. *I ~ go, rain or shine.* 无论下雨天晴，我都要去. *What would they?* 他们要什么？*the haven where I would be* 我所希望的栖身之所. *It shall be as you ~.* 这个随你的意思. *Would that he were come.* 要是他来了多好. *Would [I would] I were a bird!* 真希望我是一只鸟！*They had to obey, whether they would or not.* 不管他们愿不愿,他们必须服从. ②〔表示坚持、固执、拒绝等〕总是,无论如何(不). *You ~ have your (own) way.* 你总是照你的意思做. *He ~ not go any further.* 他无论如何不肯再往前走. *This door ~ not open [shut].* 这扇门就是开不开［关不上]. *Boys ~ be boys* 孩子究竟是孩子. *Accidents ~* 〔重读作 [wil]〕*happen.* 事故难免. ③〔表示习惯、习性等〕时常,经常,往往. *He ~ often sit up all night.* 他时常通夜不睡. *An ostrich ~ stand from ten to* *twelve feet.* 鸵鸟身高十到十二英尺. ④〔尚待实现的意志,主语为第一人称时表示约定、答应与否、主张、选择等〕要,会. *I* ~ *invite you to it.* 我要请你参加. *I'll be a good boy for the future.* 我以后要做一个好孩子. *I* ~ *let you know.* 我会让你知道的. *I* ~ *not be caught again.* 我不会再给捉住了. ⑤〔尚待实现的意志,在主语为第二人称的疑问句、命令句中表示温和的请求〕请…;…可以吗? *W- [Would] you pass me the salt?* = *Pass me the salt,* ~ *you?* 把盐递给我好吗? *You* ~ *please do so.* 请你那样做吧. ⑥〔用于主语为第二人称的条件句〕要是肯,如果愿意. *I shall be glad [pleased] to go, if you* ~ *accompany me.* 你要是肯陪我去,我才高兴去. ⑦〔纯粹未来,表示预想、预言、猜测等(第二人称及第三人称)〕将…,会〔第一人称用 shall〕. *He* ~ *die.* 他会死的. *W- he come tomorrow?* 他明天会来吗? *W- [Would] you [they] be able to hear at such a distance?* 你离得这样远听得见吗? *I don't know who it would be.* 我不知道是谁. *This'll be our train, I fancy.* 我想这就是我们搭的火车了. ⑧〔用于间接叙述法中〕*She says she* ~ *do her best.* 她说她要尽她所有的力量 (= *She says, "I* ~ *do my best"*). ★若是过去式的间接叙述法,则用 would: *You promised you would not be caught again.* 你说过你是不会再被捕了 (= *You said, "I* ~ *not be caught again"*).

will[2] [wil] *n.* ①意志;意志力. ②决心. ③愿望,希望,目的,志愿,志向. ④(对待人的)心意,心地. ⑤【法】遗嘱. *freedom of the* ~ 意志的自由. *free* ~ 自由意志. *have a strong* ~ 意志坚强. *the* ~ *to live* 求生的愿望. *Where there is a* ~ *there is a way.* 有志者事竟成. *(a man of) iron* ~ 铁石心肠(的人). *What is your* ~*?* 你要怎样呢? 你希望什么呢? *(show) good [ill]* ~ (表示)好[恶]意. *make [draw up] a* ~ 立遗嘱. ***against one's*** ~ 违背本意,不得已. ***at one's own*** ~ 照自己的意志;任意. ***at*** ~ = ***at one's*** ~ = ***at one's own sweet*** ~ 随意. ***do the*** ~ ***of sb.*** 服从某人,照某人的意愿做. ***have one's*** ~ 坚持到底,照自己的意思去做;遂愿. ***of one's own free*** ~ 自动,自愿. ***take the*** ~ ***(for the deed)*** 体会(那个行为的)意思;心领. ***with a*** ~ 热心,努力. ***work one's*** ~ ***(upon)*** 按自己的意思去行事. ~**power** 意志力. **-less** *a.* ①无意志力的. ②非自愿的,勉强的. ③未立遗嘱的.

will[3] [wil] *(~s,*〔古〕*~est; ~ed,*〔古〕*~edst) vt.* ①决心要,立志要. ②凭意志的力量使…. ③立遗嘱表示,遗赠. *He who ~s success is half way to it.* 决心要成功的人已经成功了一半. ~ *oneself into contentment* 勉强满足. ~ *one's money to a hospital* 遗赠金钱给医院. — *vi.* 行使意志力. *have no power to* ~ 无力行使意志.

Wil·la [ˈwilə] *n.* 威拉〔女子名〕.

will·a·ble [ˈwiləbl] *a.* 可求的,可希望的,可下决心的,可立志的.

will-call [ˈwil ˈkɔːl] *n., a.* (大商店为顾客保存已付款之货物待以后领取的)预售寄存部(的).

Wil·lard [ˈwilɑːd] *n.* 威拉德〔姓氏,男子名〕.

Will·cocks, Wil·lcox [ˈwilkɔks] *n.* 威尔科克斯〔姓氏〕.

-willed [-wild] *a.* 意志…的〔用以组成复合词〕. *ill-~* 恶意的. *strong-~* 意志坚强的.

wil·lem·ite [ˈwilimait] *n.*【矿】硅锌矿.

Wil·lem·stad [ˈwiləmˌstɑːt] *n.* 威廉城〔安的列斯群岛(荷属部分)首府〕.

wil·let [ˈwilit] *n.*【鸟】(北美)鹬类.

will·ful [ˈwilful] *a.*〔美〕= wilful.

Wil·liam [ˈwiljəm] *n.* 威廉〔男子名〕.

Wil·liams [ˈwiljəmz] *n.* 威廉斯〔姓氏〕.

Wil·liam·son [ˈwiljəmsn] *n.* 威廉森〔姓氏〕.

Wil·lie [ˈwili] *n.* ①威利 〔男子名, William 的昵称〕. ②威莉〔女子名〕.

wil·lie [ˈwili] *n.*〔*pl.*〕〔美俚〕神经紧张;害怕,发抖. *It gives me the ~s.* 这使我汗毛都竖起来了. *get the ~s* 吓得发抖.

will·ing [ˈwiliŋ] *a.* ①情愿的,乐意的,欣然的. ②自愿的,自动的,(援助等)诚心的;很听话的,(马等)温驯的;〔喻〕正好的,(风)顺利的. ***be*** ~ ***to (do)*** 乐意进行,欣然从事.

Wil·lis [ˈwilis] *n.* 威利斯〔姓氏,男子名〕.

Will·kie [ˈwilki] *n.* 威尔基〔姓氏〕.

will-o'-the-wisp [ˈwiləðwisp] *n.* ①鬼火,磷火. ②幻影,幻象;使人迷惑的人〔东西〕;不可捉摸的东西. ③行踪不定的人.

wil·low[1] [ˈwiləu] *n.* ①柳(属). ②柳木制品,(尤指棒球、板球的)球棒. *a weeping* ~ 垂柳. ***sing*** ~ = ***wear (the)*** ~ = ***wear the*** ~ ***garland*** = ***wear the green*** ~ ①服丧,戴孝. ②失恋. ③悼念爱人的死〔因从前戴柳叶花圈表示哀思〕;失去所爱的人. ~ **herb**【植】①柳叶菜(属). ②千屈菜. ~ **oak**【植】(北美)柳栎. ~ **pattern** 柳树图案〔1780 年源出英国的瓷器图案,由河流,宝塔,柳树构成〕. ~**ware**〔美〕绘有柳树图案的瓷器.

willow[2] [ˈwiləu] *n.*【纺】威罗机. — *vt.* (用威罗机)清理(棉花)纤维.

wil·low·y [ˈwiləui] *a.* ①多柳树的. ②柳条似的;柔软的,苗条的.

wil·ly [ˈwili] = willow[2].

wil·ly-nil·ly [ˈwili ˈnili] *ad.* 有背意愿地,无可奈何地,勉强地,不管愿意与否. — *a.* ①不管愿不愿意的. ②〔误用〕犹豫不决的,拖延的.

wil·ly-wil·ly [ˈwili ˌwili] *n.* (澳大利亚的)大旋风,气旋,陆龙卷,畏来风.

Wil·ma [ˈwilmə] *n.* 威尔玛〔女子名〕.

Wil·mer [ˈwilmə] *n.* 威尔默〔姓氏,男子名〕.

Wil·mot(t) [ˈwilmɔt] *n.* 威尔莫特〔姓氏〕.

Wil·son [ˈwilsn] *n.* 威尔逊〔姓氏,男子名〕.

Wil·son (cloud) chamber【物】(威尔逊)云室 (= cloud chamber).

Wil·son·i·an [wilˈsəuniən] *a.* (美国第二十八届总统)威尔逊的;威尔逊的政见的,威尔逊的政策的.

wilt[1] [wilt] *v. aux.*〔古〕will 的第二人称单数〔主语为 thou 时〕.

wilt[2] [wilt] *vi.* (草木)枯萎,萎蔫,凋谢;憔悴;〔喻〕颓丧. — *vt.* 使凋谢,使枯萎;使衰弱;使颓丧. — *n.*【植】萎蔫病,(棉花)枯萎病. *verticillium [fusarium]* ~ (棉花)黄萎[枯萎]病.

Wil·ton [ˈwiltən] *n.* 威尔顿〔姓氏,男子名〕. ~ **carpet** (英国)威尔顿机织地毯.

Wilts. = Wiltshire.

Wilt·shire [ˈwiltʃə] *n.* ①威尔特郡〔英格兰〕. ②威尔特羊〔原产于英国的一种纯白绵羊,长头长弯角〕.

wil·y [ˈwaili] *a.* *(-i·er; -i·est)* 诡计多端的;足智多谋的;狡猾的,诡谲的. **-i·ly** *ad.*

wim·ble [ˈwimbl] *n.* ①锥,(螺旋)钻. ②【矿】钻孔清除器. — *vt.*〔古〕钻.

Wim·ble·don [ˈwimbldən] *n.* (伦敦郊区)温布尔顿(网球场);(在该处举行的)英国全国网球锦标赛.

wimp [wimp] *n.* 软弱无能的人. **-y** *a.* 软弱无能的.

wim·ple [ˈwimpl] *n.* ①修女头巾〔从前普通女人也戴〕. ②折裥,折缝;(道路等的)弯曲;微波,涟漪. — *vt.* ①用修女头巾包起来;〔喻〕覆盖,遮饰. ②使起波浪(如麦浪). — *vi.* 成褶子;〔主 Scot.〕(小河)弯弯曲曲;起涟漪,起波纹;摇动.

WIN = Whip Inflation Now "立即制止通货膨胀运动"〔美国总统福特于 1975 年提出的一项计划〕.

win[1] [win] *vt.* ***(won)***①胜,赢. ②打下(要塞等),夺得(奖品等);争取;赚得,挣得(生活费等). ③博得,赢得(爱情、名誉等). ④达到,到达(山顶等). ⑤说服;诱惑. ⑥【矿】采掘到;提炼到;准备好(矿井等). ~ *a battle* 打一个胜仗. ~ *a victory* 得胜. ~ *national liberation* 争取[取得]民族解放. *The book won him fame.* 那本书使他

出了名. *You have won me.* 你算是把我说服了. ~ *sb. to consent* 说服[赢得]某人同意. — *vi.* ①得胜,赢. ②达到目的,成功. ③争取,影响,吸引 (*on; upon*). ④到达 ~ *in a contest* 比赛得胜. ~ *by two lengths* 以两艇之长的距离得胜. *a theory that ~s upon sb.* 影响某人的一种理论. ~ ***a lady's hand*** 赢得某一个女人许婚. ~ ***back*** 〔口〕努力收复(失地). ~ ***by a whisker*** 〔美运〕以少许之差得胜. ~ ***free [clear, loose]*** 挣脱; 好容易渡过. ~ ***one's bread*** 挣得生活之资. ~ ***one's cap [letter]*** 〔美运〕大显本领. ~ ***one's way*** 排除障碍前进; 刻苦成功. ~ ***out [through]*** 〔口〕摆脱, 克服 (~ *through all difficulties* 排除万难). ~ ***over*** 争取过来, 拉过来 (*Win over all who can be won over.* 争取一切可能争取的人. ~ *over sb. to a policy* 争取某人赞同某一政策). ~ ***the day [the field]*** 得胜; 成功. ~ ***round*** 争取过来. ~ ***up*** 起立; 上马; 登上. — *n.* 〔口〕胜利, 成功. *celebrate a* ~ 庆祝胜利. *three ~s and no defeats* 三胜无败.

win² [win] *vt.* 〔英方〕把(草等)吹干[烘干].

wince¹ [wins] *n., vi.* (由于疼痛、吃惊等)畏缩,退缩.

wince² [wins] *n.* 【染】(洗染布时用的)绞车,六角绞盘.

win·cey [ˈwinsi] *n.* 【纺】(英国)棉毛绒布, 棉毛法兰绒. (= winsey).

win·cey·ette [ˌwinsiˈet] *n.* 【纺】(英国)色织薄绒布.

winch [wintʃ] *n.* 绞盘,绞车; 曲柄. — *vt.* 用绞车拖吊.

Win·ches·ter [ˈwintʃistə] *n.* ①温彻斯特〔英格兰南部城市〕. ②〔美〕温彻斯特式连发枪(= ~ rifle).

wind¹ [wind, 〔诗中有时读〕 waind] *n.* ①风; 大风, 暴风; 气流; 【机】压缩空气. ②【海】上风; 风向; 〔古〕〔*pl.*〕方向. ③气息, 呼吸. ④(腹中的)肠气, 屁. ⑤空谈, 空话. ⑥吹来的气味; 臭迹; 风声, 传说. ⑦风气; 趋势; 时势; 影响. ⑧【兽医】羊的鼓胀症. ⑨〔the ~, ~s〕吹奏乐器, 管乐器; 吹奏乐器演奏者. ⑩〔俚〕心窝. ⑪【军】惊吓. *a gust of* ~ 一阵风. *an adverse* ~ 逆风. *a constant* ~ 恒风. *fair [contrary] ~s* 顺[逆风]. *a hard* ~ 顶头风. *a high* ~ 强风. *The ~ rises [falls].* 风吹起来了[停了]; 风加强[减弱]. *be troubled with* ~ 肠里老是产生气体而不舒服. *His speech was mere ~.* 他的演说只是一些空话. ***against the*** ~ 顶着风. ***all in the*** ~ 船头吃风. ***before [down] the*** ~ 顺风. ***between ~ and water*** 在(船的)水线处; 在要害处; 易受损伤之处. ***break*** ~ 放屁. ***broken*** ~ (尤指马的) 喘气. ***by the*** ~ 顶风, 抢风. ***cast [fling, scatter, throw] ... to the (four) ~s*** 把…抛到九霄云外; 不再考虑, 弃置不顾. ***find out how the ~ blows [lies]*** 识风向; 看清形势. ***from the four ~s*** 从四面八方. ***gain [get] the ~ of*** = take the ~ of. ***get one's*** ~ 喘(一口)气, 歇一会儿. ***get the ~ up*** 〔军俚〕吃惊, 吓一跳, 愣一愣. ***get*** ~ 为人所知, 传播出去. ***get ~ of*** 听到…的风声. ***go like the*** ~ 飞跑. ***have a free*** ~ 顺风前进. ***have a good [bad]*** ~ 呼吸长[短]. ***have one's ~ taken*** 被打中心窝晕倒. ***have the ~ of*** = take the ~ of. ***have the ~ up*** = get the ~ up. ***in the teeth [eye] of the ~=in the ~'s eye*** 逆风. ***in the*** ~ ①将要发生, (秘密地)在进行; 将要成问题 (*There is something in the ~.* 好象要发生什么问题了). ②未决定. ③【海】喝醉. ***It is an ill ~ that blows nobody good.*** 〔谚〕除非是恶风才会对一切人都不利[任何事都对有些人不利, 对有些人有利]. ***know [see] how [where] the ~ blows [lies, sits]*** 知道风向; 知道(舆论)动向. ***lose one's*** ~ 断气, 接不上气. ***off the*** ~ 【海】顺风航行. ***on a [the]*** ~ 【海】逆风, 顶风. ***put the ~ up*** ①〔军俚〕使…吓一跳. ②〔美俚〕说骂人话. ***raise the*** ~ 〔俚〕筹款. ***recover one's*** ~ = get one's ~. ***run before the*** ~ 【海】顺风行驶. ***sail against the*** ~ ①近于顶风航行. ②在困难情况下做事. ***sail before the*** ~ ①顺风航行. ②成功, 发迹. ***sail near [close to] the*** ~ ①迎风航行. ②几乎犯法; 几乎出事. ***sail with every [shift of]*** ~ 在任何环境中都能取得好处. ***take the ~ of*** 占(他船)的上风, 较…占有利地位. ***take the ~ out of one's sails*** 先发制人; 抢先说[做]. ***take ~*** = get ~. ***under the*** ~ 在下风. ***up the*** ~ 向风中, 迎着风. ~ ***abaft [ahead]*** 【海】正后 [正前]风. ***with the*** ~ 跟着风, 随风. — [wind] *vt.* (***wind·ed*** [-id]) ①刮(风); 放(声), 发出(叫声). ②透风, 通风; 使风干. ③嗅出; 察觉, 发觉(阴谋等). ④使喘气, 使接不上气; 使歇一歇. *I am quite ~ed by the climb.* 爬山爬得喘不过气来. ~ *the horse* 让马歇一会儿. — *vi.* ①嗅到猎物的气味. ②喘口气歇一歇. ~ ***down*** (使)逐步收缩; (使)降级; (使)逐步结束. **~-bag** 气囊; 风箱; 〔谑〕胸; 肺; 〔俚〕饶舌者; 满口空话的人. **~blast** ①阵风. ②爆炸气浪〔从高速飞机中弹出的驾驶员所遇到的一种致命的空气摩擦〕. **~-blown** *a.* 〔美〕(树等)终年当风的; (头发)风飘式的. **~-borne** *a.* (花粉等)靠风传播的. **~-bound** *a.* 【海】为风所困的, 因逆风[大风]不能航行的. ~ **box** 气室; 风箱. **~break** ①防风林; 防风设备, 防风墙. ②(树木的)风折. **~breaker** 防风(皮)外衣. **~-broken** *a.* 呼吸器受伤的, (马)喘气的. **~cheater** 〔英〕防风上衣 (= parka). **~chill (factor)** 【气】风冷因素〔风速作为决定流动空气对物体致冷效应的一个因素〕. ~ **cone** 圆锥风标, 风向袋. **~-down** 逐步收缩[结束]; 降级. **~-driven dynamo [generator]** 风动发电机. ~ **egg** 软壳蛋; 无精卵. **~fall** ①被风吹落的果实; 被风吹折的树(枝); (森林中的)树木倒折地区. ②横财, 意外的收入. **~flaw** 阵风, 一阵狂风. **~flower** 【植】五叶银莲花. ~ **furnace** 【冶】风炉. **~gall** 【兽医】(马脚踝)关节软瘤. ~ **gap** 【气】风隙. ~ **gauge** 风力计, 风速计; (风琴的)风压计; (枪炮的)风力调节表. **~hover** 〔英〕【动】茶隼(= kestrel). ~ **instrument** 【乐】管乐器, 吹奏乐器 (*brass ~-instruments* 铜管乐器〔喇叭类〕. *wood ~-instruments* 木管乐器[笛类]). **~jammer** 〔口〕①帆船; 帆船水手. ②〔军俚〕号兵; 〔俚〕吹牛的人; 〔美俚〕(尤指马戏团中的)音乐师. ~ **loading** 风载荷〔风力施加在建筑物上的应力〕. **~mill** 风车 (*fight [tilt at] ~mills* 和假想〔不存在〕的敌人战斗. *fling [throw] one's cap over the ~mills* 蛮干, 不守常规). **~pipe** 【解】气管. **~-pollinated** *a.* 【植】风媒传播的. ~ **pressure** 风压. **~proof** *a.* 不透(怕)风的, 防风的. ~ **resistance** 风(对运动)的阻力(= air resistance). ~ **rose** 风(向)图, 风玫瑰. **~row** 摆成一行的风干谷束[草束(等)]; (甘蔗的)播种沟. **~sail** 风车翼; 【船】(通至船底的)帆布通风筒. ~ **scale** 【气】风级. ~ **screen [shield]** (汽车的)挡风玻璃. ~ **shake** (树木的)轮裂. ~ **sleeve,** ~ **sock** 风向袋, 套筒风标. **~stick** 〔军俚〕(飞机的) 螺旋桨. **~storm** 风暴. **~-sucking** (马匹啃槽等时大声吸气)吭气 (声). **~-swept** *a.* 当风的, 被风乱吹的. ~ **tee** 【气】风向齿〔航用齿形风向器〕. **~throw** 【林】风倒〔大风将树木连根拔起〕. **~tight** *a.* 不透风的, 不通风的. ~ **tunnel** 风洞〔飞机等检查风压的气室〕. ~ **vane** 风向标. **-less** *a.* 无风的, 平静的.

wind² [waind] *vt.* (*~ed, **wound*** [waund]) 吹(角笛、喇叭等). ~ *a call* 吹哨子(召唤). — *vi.* 吹响号角.

wind³ [waind] *vt.* (***wound*** [waund], *~ed* [-id]) ①卷绕, 缠绕. ②上(发条) (*up*); 摇转, 转. ③(用绞车等) 绞起. ④【海】使(船) 掉转方向. ⑤蜿蜒前进〔通常用 ~ its way〕. *The brook ~s its way.* 这条小河弯弯曲曲地流着. ~ *oneself [one's way] into (sb.'s) affections* 转弯抹角地巴结(人), 转弯抹角地讨(人)欢喜. ~ *round a pole* (藤等)缠住支柱. — *vi.* ①卷起, 缠绕; (木板)翘曲. ②(河、路等)弯曲, 纡曲. ~ ***off*** 卷开, 缠开(卷着的东西). ~ ***sb. round one's (little) fingers*** 任意操纵(某人), 完全笼络住. ~ ***up*** ①卷紧, 卷拢; 绕紧; 绞起, 吊起(矿石等); 上(发条). ②使振作精神, 使紧张. ③解散(公司等); 终止, 结束(谈话等). ④【棒球】投球前挥转胳臂

(*He was wound up to a high pitch of excitement.* 他极度兴奋. *The company has wound up.* 这个公司倒闭了). — *n.* ①卷绕(动作); 卷绕物的一圈. ②蜿蜒,弯曲,曲折.

W. Ind. = West Indies 西印度群岛.

wind·age [ˈwindidʒ] *n.* ①【炮】游隙〔炮筒内径和炮弹间的空隙〕. ②(子弹飞过而引起的)气流; (子弹因风而生的)偏差; 风力影响; 风力修正量. ③【海】(船体的)对风面. ~ *of tank* 油罐通风. ~ **loss**【物】风阻损失.

wind·ed [ˈwindid] *a.* ①喘不过气来的. ②〔构成复合词〕(以某种方式)呼吸的. *long-~* 呼吸长的; 冗长的.

wind·er[1] [ˈwaində] *n.* ①卷绕者; 缠绕植物; 卷纸机; 缠绕器, 线板儿; 绞车. ②〔纺〕络纱工; 络纱[筒]机. ③【建】螺旋形梯级. ④上发条的钥匙.

wind·er[2] [ˈwində] *n.* 〔美俚〕①(肚子上的)猛击. ②激烈的(健身)运动[跑步等].

Wind·hoek [ˈvinthuk] *n.* 温得和克〔纳米比亚(西南非洲)首府〕.

wind·i·ness [ˈwindinis] *n.* ①有风, 多风. ②(多)肠气. ③大话, 夸口; 多嘴; 空谈.

wind·ing [ˈwaindiŋ] *a.* ①卷绕的; 绕线的, 绕组的. ②纡回曲折的, 蜿蜒的. *a ~ path* 弯弯曲曲的小路. *a ~ staircase* 螺旋楼梯. — *n.* ①卷绕起来的一盘(绳索等); 卷绕动作; 络纱. ②弯曲, 纡曲; 不正行为. ③【采】卷扬, 提升;【电】绕组, 绕法; 线圈. *banked ~*【电】简单绕组; 重叠绕法. *series ~*【电】串激绕组. *in ~* (木板)翘曲. *out of ~* 不翘, 不弯曲. ~ **engine** 卷扬机, 吊桶机. ~ **sheet** 包尸布; 寿衣. ~**-up** (公司)解散; 关闭; 清算; 了结.

wind·lass [ˈwindləs] *n.* 绞车, 卷扬机, 起锚机. — *vt.* 用绞车吊起.

win·dle·straw [ˈwindlstrɔː] *n.* 〔Scot.〕①枯草茎. ②纤弱的人; 细长而脆弱的东西.

win·dow [ˈwindəu] *n.* ①窗; 窗口, 窗户; 窗扉, 窗框; 窗玻璃; (商店的)橱窗. ②【无】(反雷达)金属干扰带; 偶极子干扰; 反射干扰; 触发脉冲. ③【宇】(火箭等的)最佳发射时限(= launch ~). ④大气窗〔电磁波谱的一区, 其辐射不被地球大气层吸收而能抵达地球〕; (飞船返航时的)大气层边缘通过区. ⑤〔*pl.*〕〔美俚〕眼镜. *a French ~* (通阳台的) 双扇落地玻璃门. *a blank [blind, dead, false] ~* 假窗. *The eyes are the ~s of the mind.* 眼睛是心灵的窗子. *come in by the ~* 越窗潜入. ***have all one's goods in the ~*** 肤浅, 内容空虚. ***in the ~*** (广告等)贴在窗口; (商品等)摆在橱窗里. ***look out (of) the ~*** 从窗里看外面. ***throw the house out at (the) ~*** 使陷入大混乱. ~ ***of tube*** 萤光屏. — *vt.* 在…安窗子; 开窗孔于. ~ **bar** 窗闩. ~ **box**【建】窗锤箱; 窗台上的花盆箱. ~ **bolt** 窗插梢. ~ **curtain** 窗帘. ~ **dressing** 橱窗装饰(法); 〔喻〕修饰外表; 炫耀自己; (银行、公司等的)假帐. ~ **envelope** (使信纸上收信人姓名住址露出的)开窗信封. ~ **frame** 窗框, 窗架. ~ **glass** 窗玻璃. ~**pane** 窗玻璃, 玻璃板. ~**-rattler**〔美〕打鼾的人. ~ **regulator** 窗开关. ~ **sash** (上下开关的)窗扇. ~ **seat** 窗下座位; (飞机等上的) 靠窗座位. ~ **shade** 窗口遮阳篷. ~**-shop** *vi.* 观看橱窗 (而不买). ~**-shopper** 只看橱窗不买货的人. ~ **sill**【建】窗槛, 窗台. ~ **ventilator** 气窗.

Wind·sor[1] [ˈwinzə] *n.* ①温泽〔姓氏〕. ②温莎〔英国城市〕. ③温泽〔加拿大城市〕.

Wind·sor[2] [ˈwinzə] *n.* 温莎〔当代英国王室的名称〕. *the House of ~* 温莎王室. ~ **Castle** (英国王室的) 温莎宫. ~ **chair** 一种细骨靠椅. ~ **knot** 双活结〔绳结的一种〕. ~ **tie** 温莎领结〔领结式样, 一个松散的蝴蝶结〕.

wind·up [ˈwaindʌp] *n.* ①终结, 完结, 结局. ②〔美〕【棒球】投球前摆动手臂的准备动作.

wind·ward [ˈwindwəd] *n., a., ad.* 上风(的); 向风(的), 迎风(的), 逆风 (的). ***cast [lay] an anchor to ~*** 在上风抛锚; 未雨绸缪. ***get to (the) ~ of*** 驶到(他船)的上风; (为躲避臭气)转到…的上风; 占有比…有利的地位, 占上风, 超出. ***keep to (the) ~ of*** 对…保持上风; 避开(某人).

Wind·ward Is. [ˈwindwəd] *n.* 向风群岛〔西印度群岛的一部分〕.

wind·y [ˈwindi] *a.* ***(-i·er; -i·est)*** ①有风的; 当风的, 受风的, 多风的, 起风的. ②狂风的, 风大的. ③生肠气的, 腹胀的. ④吹牛的, 只会空谈的; 空洞无内容的; 空虚的. ⑤〔俚〕受了惊的. 吓坏了的. ⑥〔古〕= windward. ⑦〔方〕轻率的; 轻佻的; 〔俚〕神经质的; 易激动[生气]的. *a ~ tempest* 大风暴. *It is ~ today.* 今天风大. ~ *dishes* 胀肚子的食品. ~ *expression* 空话. ~ *joy* 空喜欢. ***on the ~ side of*** 在(法律)达不到的地方, 在…的范围外. **W- City** 风城〔美国 Chicago 市的别号〕. **-i·ly** *ad.*

wine [wain] *n.* ①葡萄酒; 酒. ②果酒. ③〔英〕(大学生晚餐后的) 酒会. ④【医】葡萄酒溶剂. ⑤葡萄酒色, 暗红色. *Adam's ~* 〔谑〕水. *green ~* (酿造后一年的)新酒. *still ~* 非发泡性葡萄酒. ***have a ~ in one's room*** 〔英大学〕在房间里开酒会. ***in ~*** 喝醉. ***new ~ in old bottles*** 旧瓶装新酒, 旧形式里的新内容. ***take ~ with*** 和…举杯互祝健康. — *vt., vi.* 用葡萄酒招待; (请…)喝酒. ~ **acid**【化】酒石酸. ~**bag** 装酒的皮囊; 〔俚〕酒量大的人; 酒鬼. ~**berry** 〔美〕= bilberry; raspberry; 〔美口〕葡萄. ~**bibber** 酒徒. ~**bibbing** *n., a.* 酒量大(的). ~**bottle** ①(葡萄)酒瓶. ②皮酒囊. ~**bowl** 大酒杯; 酒癖 (*drown care in the ~bowl* 喝酒解愁). ~ **cell**【生】绛色细胞. ~ **cellar** 酒窖. ~**-coloured** *a.* (葡萄)酒色, 暗红[紫]色的. ~ **cooler** 冰酒器. ~**cup** = winebowl. ~**fat** *n.* 〔古〕= winepress. ~ **gallon** 酒加仑 (= 231立方英寸). ~**glass** 葡萄酒杯; 酒杯; 一酒杯(= 4汤匙). ~**glassful** 一酒杯(的分量). ~**grower** 〔美〕葡萄园主人; 葡萄酒酿造人. ~ **growing** *n., a.* 〔美〕葡萄园经营业(的). ~ **palm** (制造棕榈酒用的)棕榈. ~ **press** 葡萄榨汁器. ~**sap** 〔美〕醇露 (品种)苹果. ~**skin** (整个羊的皮做成的) 皮酒囊; 〔俚〕酒鬼. ~**stone**【化】(粗) 酒石; 葡萄子. ~**vault** = winecellar.

win·er·y [ˈwainəri] *n.* (葡萄)酒厂, 酿酒厂.

Win·field [ˈwinfiːld] *n.* 温菲尔德〔姓氏, 男子名〕.

Win·fred [ˈwinfrid] *n.* 温弗雷德〔男子名〕.

wing [wiŋ] *n.* ①翼, 翅膀; 鸟; 鸟群; 飞行, 飞翔. ②(飞机)机翼; 翼状物; (汽车的)挡泥板; 〔诗常 *pl.*〕船帆. ③〔谑〕(四足兽的)前足; 〔谑〕(人的)胳臂. ④【植】翼瓣;【动】翼状突起;【军】(侧)翼. ⑤空军部队; 〔英〕空军大队; 〔美〕空军联队; 〔*pl.*〕空军徽章. ⑥(足球等运动中的)翼, 边锋. ⑦【筑城】翼面; 侧面;【建】侧厅; (主楼左右两侧的) 侧楼;【船】翼舱; 舞台边厢. ⑧电子管阳极. ⑨(政党等内部的)派系, (左、右) 翼. *a ~ of sparrows* 一群麻雀. *a touch in the ~* 〔谑〕胳臂负伤. *the left [right] ~ (of an army)* (军队的)左[右]翼. ***a gray goose ~*** 箭. ***add [lend] ~s to*** 加快, 促进 (*Fear lent him ~s.* 吓得他一溜烟地跑掉). ***get the [one's] ~s*** 得到空军资格. ***on the ~*** 飞着, 飞行中, 动着; 旅行中; 振翅欲飞(的), 即将出发(的). ***on the ~s of the wind*** 飞也似地, 非常快地. ***on ~s*** (高兴得)飘飘欲仙. ***take ... under one's ~*** 庇护. ***take ~*** (鸟) 飞起来; 〔喻〕逃走, 逃亡. ***take ~s to itself*** (钱等) 不翼而飞; 迅速消失. ***under sb.'s ~ = under the ~ of*** 在…的保护下. ~ ***and ~***【海】两面都扯上风帆. — *vt.* ①给…装翅膀; 给(箭杆末梢) 装羽毛. ②放 (箭等). ③飞过. ④空运. ⑤使飞, 使加速. ⑥弄伤(鸟的)翅膀; 弄伤 (人的) 胳臂; 〔口〕击落飞机. ⑦用羽毛帚扫. ⑧【建】附建侧厅 [楼] 于. ~ ***it*** 〔美俚〕临时准备; 临时凑成. — *vi.* ①飞翔, 飞行. ②飞快行进; 飞跑; 飞行. ~ *an arrow at the mark* 对准靶子射箭. ~ *its way* (鸟)飞去. ~ *the air [sky]* 飞翔空中. *Fear ~ed his steps.* 吓得他加快了脚步. ~-

bar【空】翼杆. ~ bow【动】翅角. ~ case [cover] (昆虫的)鞘翅. ~ chair (便于靠头休息的)高背沙发. ~ commander〔英〕空军中校. ~ covert (鸟)覆羽,羽茎小毛. ~footed *a.*〔诗〕脚上有翼的;健步如飞的. ~ former【空】翼梢保形条. ~ gun【空】机翼固定机枪. ~let 小翼. ~ loading【空】机翼(单位)负荷. ~man【空】僚机(驾驶员). ~manship 飞行技术. ~ nut【机】蝶形螺母. ~over【空】横转,翻转. ~ rail【工】翼轨. ~ screw 翼形螺钉. ~ sheath = ~ case. ~ shell【贝】莺贝. ~ ship〔美空军〕(飞在领队飞机后的)右翼[左翼]飞机. ~ shot 飞鸟射击,打飞靶;飞射能手. ~span【空】翼展. ~-spread【空】翼距,翼展. ~ tank【空】机翼油箱. ~ tip【空】翼梢. -less *a.* 无翼的;不能飞的.

wing·ding [ˈwiŋdiŋ] *n.*〔俚〕①狂欢的宴会,社交活动. ②激动人心的事物,惊人的事物. ③狂怒,癫狂.

winged [wiŋd, ˈwiŋid] *a.* ①有翼的,有翅膀的. ②〔诗〕群飞的,飞鸟成群的. ③飞快的,迅速的. ④翅膀受了伤的;胳臂受了伤的. ⑤(话)恰当的,高超的,(思想等)崇高的. ~ *seeds* 能飞散的种子. ~ *sentiments* 高尚的情操. ***the ~ air***〔诗〕飞鸟成群的天空. ***(the) ~ horse*** ①【神话】飞马. ②诗歌. ③〔W- H-〕【天】天马座. ***the ~ spindle tree***【植】卫茅. ***~ words*** 正中要害的话,意味深长的;中肯话.

winger [ˈwiŋə] *n.*〔主英〕【运】翼(运动员). *left [right]* ~ 左[右]翼(运动员).

Wi·ni·fred [ˈwinifrid] *n.* 威妮弗雷德〔女子名〕.

wink [wiŋk] *vi.* ①眨眼. ②使眼色. ③假装没有见,宽恕,默许,纵容 *(at)*. ④(光、星等)闪烁,闪亮. ⑤突然终止;结束;熄灭*(out)*. ⑥(用灯光)打信号. — *vt.* 眨(眼);使(眼色). ***~ at*** 对…使眼色;假装没有见,放过(缺点等). ***~ away [back]*** 眨掉(眼泪). — *n.* ①眨眼;使眼色. ②一眨眼功夫,瞬间,瞬息;〔*pl.*〕小睡. ③(光、星等的)闪烁,一闪. ***forty ~s***〔口〕小睡;〔美俚〕一会儿. ***give a ~*** 瞟了一眼. ***in a ~*** 转瞬间,一眨眼功夫. ***not sleep a ~ = not get a ~ of sleep*** 一睡也没睡. ***tip (sb.) the ~***〔俚〕丢眼色给(某人).

wink·er [ˈwiŋkə] *n.* ①〔罕〕眨眼[使眼色]的人. ②〔口〕眼睫毛;眼睛;(马的)遮眼罩. ③(汽车的)明灭式方向指示灯.

wink·ing [ˈwiŋkiŋ] *n.* 眨眼. ***as easy as ~*** 极容易(的). ***like ~***〔俚〕转瞬间;很快地;出乎意外地;有力地.

win·kle[1] [ˈwiŋkl] *n.*【动】食用峨螺;玉黍螺;滨螺.

win·kle[2] *vt.*〔口〕挑出,剔出,抽出 *(out)*;揭出(秘密等);逐出.

win·kle-pick·er [ˈwiŋklˌpikə] *n.*〔俚〕尖头鞋,尖头靴,火箭鞋.

Win·ne·ba·go [ˌwinəˈbeigəu] *n.* ①*(pl.* ~, *~(e)s)* 温尼贝戈人〔居于东威斯康星等地的北美洲印第安人〕. ②温尼贝戈语.

win·ner [ˈwinə] *n.* 胜利者;胜马;得奖者. **~'s circle** (赛马场附设供拍照、领奖等活动的)优胜者(与人会见的)小(圆)场地.

win·ning [ˈwiniŋ] *n.* ①赢得(物);缴获;占领;胜利,成功. ②〔*pl.*〕奖金,奖品. ③【矿】开采;备采煤区. — *a.* ①使得到胜利的,决胜的. ②(马等)得胜的. ③得人欢心的;迷人的,可爱的. ~ **post** (赛马场的)决胜终点. **-ly** *ad.* 可爱地.

Win·ni·peg [ˈwinipeg] *n.* 温尼伯〔加拿大城市〕.

win·now [ˈwinəu] *vt.* ①扬(场),簸(谷),筛掉(米糠等) *(away; out; from)*. ②辨别(真假等);甄别,挑选,选择 *(out)*;除去 *(away)*. ③〔诗〕吹散,吹乱(头发等);鼓(翼). *a ~ing fan [basket]* 簸箕. ~ *the false from the true* = ~ *truth from falsehood* 去伪存真,辨别真假. — *vi.* 扬谷,簸谷. **-ing** *n.* 扬场.

win·now·er [ˈwinəuə] *n.* ①簸扬者. ②簸谷机,风选机,扇车,风车.

win·o [ˈwainəu] *n.* *(pl.* ~*s)*〔美俚〕酒鬼,醉汉〔尤指只喝劣酒者〕.

win·some [ˈwinsəm] *a.* ①赢得人注意的;迷人的;可爱的;使人愉快的. ②活泼的;快活的. **-ly** *ad.* **-ness** *n.*

Win·ston [ˈwinstən] *n.* 温斯顿〔姓氏,男子名〕.

win·ter [ˈwintə] *n.* ①冬,冬天,冬季. ②〔诗〕年,岁;冷季. ③衰落期,萧条期. *a hard* ~ 严冬. *a mild [soft]* ~ 暖和的冬天. *a man of sixty ~s* 六十岁的人. — *a.* 冬天的,冬季的;越冬的;冬播的. *a ~ crop* 越冬作物. — *vt.* ①冬季饲养(家畜),冬季贮藏(植物). ②使受冻,使萎缩. — *vi.* 过冬,越冬. ~ **aconite**【植】菟葵. ~ **barley** 冬大麦. **~-beaten** *a.* 冻伤了的,冷得难过的. **~berry**【植】冬青(属);夹檀木,光滑冬果冬青. **~-bourne** 冬流小河,冬溪. **~feed** *vt.* 冬饲. ~ **flounder**【动】北美黄盖鲽. ~ **garden** (供人游览的)玻璃花房. **~green** ①【植】(北美)白珠树;〔英〕鹿蹄草. ②【化】(由白珠树的叶提炼的)冬青油;冬青油的香味. ~ **hardiness** 耐冬性,耐寒性;越冬性,冬性定型. **~kill** *vt., vi.*〔美〕(越冬)冻死. **~killing** 冻害,越冬冻死. **~-lodge**【植】冬芽. ~ **melon**【植】甜瓜(=casaba). **~phobia**〔美〕怕冷,畏冬病. ~ **quarters**〔*pl.*〕【军】冬营地. ~ **sleep** 冬眠. ~ **solstice** 冬至. ~ **squash**【植】南瓜;筒瓜. ~ **tide**〔诗〕, **~time** 冬天,冬季.

win·ter·ize [ˈwintəraiz] *vt.* 给(汽车等)作过冬准备;给…加防寒设备,使防冻.

win·ter·ly [ˈwintəli] *a.* ①冬(天)的;象冬天的. ②寒冷的. ③冷漠的. ④闷闷不乐的.

win·ter·y [ˈwintəri] *a.* = wintry.

Win·ton [ˈwintən] *n.* 温顿〔姓氏,男子名〕.

Winton. = Wintoniensis (〔L.〕 = of Winchester).

win·try [ˈwintri] *a.* *(-tri·er; -tri·est)* ①冬(天)的;冬天似的,寒冷的;荒凉的. ②(态度等)冷冰冰的,冷淡的. **-tri·ness** *n.*

win·y [ˈwaini] *a.* *(-i·er; -i·est)* ①有(葡萄)酒味的,(葡萄)酒似的;(葡萄)酒喝醉了的. ②(空气)清新的.

winze [ˈwinz] *n.*【矿】(上坑道通向下坑道,垂直或倾斜的)下通小暗井.

wipe [waip] *vt., vi.* ①擦,拭,揩;擦去,消除 *(away; off; up)*;〔喻〕雪(耻). ②【机】拭接(铅管). ③〔俚〕(拿刀、棍等)打 *(at)*;〔美俚〕杀死,暗杀 (= ~ out). *W- (away) your tears.* 把眼泪擦掉. *a ~ing cloth* 一块抹布. ***W- it off!***〔美口〕别笑了!别开玩笑了! ***~ off one's chin***〔美俚〕喝一杯(酒). ***~ one's boots on*** 对…进行侮辱. ***~ sb.'s eye*** *(for him)*〔俚〕抢在别人前面,先发制人. ***~ one's eyes = ~ one's tears away*** 擦眼泪. ***~ one's hands of*** 洗手不干,和…断绝关系. ***~ out*** 擦去(污点等),还清(债款等);雪(耻),报仇;歼灭,消灭,扫除;抹煞;〔美俚〕杀死,暗杀. ***~ the clock***〔美俚〕停止工作. ***~ the floor [earth, ground] with***〔俚〕使完全屈服;彻底击败,使…惨败. — *n.* ①擦,拭. ②〔口、方〕打;〔喻〕拒绝. ③〔俚〕手巾,手绢儿. ④= wiper ③. *He fetched me a* ~. 他打了我一下. **~-out** ①擦去. ②【无】遮蔽;遮蔽地域;【电视】划出. ③〔美俚〕(从冲浪板等上)被波浪扫下去;(从滑橇等上)跌下;完全失败. ④全部消灭.

wip·er [ˈwaipə] *n.* ①擦的人[物]. ②毛巾,手巾,手绢儿;揩布,擦布;(汽车风挡上的)乱水器;擦具;涂油工具. ③【机】(凸轮式的)起杆,凸齿. ④【无】弧刷,接触电刷,接帚;天电强烈信号的破溃声;【电】电位计游标. ⑤〔美俚〕暗杀者,凶手.

wire [ˈwaiə] *n.* ①金属线,铜丝,铁丝,钢丝;【电】导线;线路;金属丝网;【造纸】抄网. ②电信;〔口〕电报. ③〔*pl.*〕(木偶的)牵线,操纵绳;背后操纵的势力;秘密引线;秘密策略. ④〔卑〕扒手;〔美俚〕对囚犯好的看守. ⑤〔美赛马〕终点线. *an aerial* ~ 天线. *an open* ~ 裸线. *barbed* ~ 带刺铁丝. *a sounding* ~ 测深索. *a fuse [safety]* ~ 保险丝. *a party* ~【电话】合用(电话)线.

a private ~ 专用(电话)线. *He sent me a* ~. 他打了个电报给我. ***a live*** ~ 通电电线;〔喻〕生龙活虎的人. ***be (all) on*** ~***s*** 兴奋,紧张,焦急. ***by*** ~ 用电信;用电报. ***lay*** ~***s for*** 为…作好准备. ***pull the*** ~***s*** 在背后操纵. ***under the*** ~〔美俚〕完了的,结束了的. ~***s crossed***〔美俚〕混乱的;错乱的;疯狂的. — *vt., vi.* ①用金属丝卷[绑住]. ②(在…)安电线;用金属线穿(珠子). ③用铁丝网捉(鸟). ④电送;〔口〕(给…)打电报. *I* ~*d to him.* 我已打电报给他. ~ *a house for electric light* 给房屋装电灯线. ~ ***collect*** 打由收电人付款的电报. ~ ***for*** (打)电(报)召唤. ~ ***in*** [〔罕〕***away***] ①用铁丝网圈起来. ②〔俚〕拼命努力,拼命苦干. ~ ***into***〔俚〕开始(狼吞虎咽地)吃;开始拼命进行工作. ~ **clip** 钢丝剪. ~ **cloth** 钢丝布,漉网. ~ **cutter** 钢丝钳,铁丝网剪刀. ~**dancer** 走钢丝杂技演员. ~**dancing** 走钢丝. ~**draw** ***(-drew; -drawn)*** *vt.* ①把(金属)拉成金属丝. ②(过分)拉长,拖长;条分缕析;过分琐细而牵强附会. ~**drawing** *n.* ①拉(铁)丝;【机】抽丝现象. ②(议论等的)过分拉长[琐细]. ~**drawn** ① *v.* wiredraw 的过去分词. ② *a.* (议论、区别等)过于细微的. ~ **edge** (刀刃磨得过分时的)卷口. ~ **entanglement** 铁丝网. ~ **gauge**【机】(量金属丝粗细的)金属丝量规. ~ **gauze** 铁纱,(金属)线网. ~ **glass** 络网[铁丝网]玻璃. ~ **grass**【植】扁蓄,狗尾草. ~**hair** 猎狐刚毛狗. ~**-haired** *a.* (狗)刚毛的. ~**man** ①报务员. ②线路工,架线工. ~**nail [tack]** (圆)铁钉. ~ **netting**【机】烟囱篦;铁丝网. ~**photo** 有线传真设备[相片]. ~**pull** *vi., vt.* 在幕后操纵. ~**puller** (木偶等的)牵线人;幕后操纵者. ~**pulling** 幕后操纵. ~ **recorder** 钢丝录音机. ~ **rope** 钢丝索. ~**-stitched** *a.* 用金属丝装订的. ~**tap** ① *n.* 窃听装置,窃听器. ②*vt.* 用窃听器监听;在…装窃听器. ~ **tapper**〔美〕窃听电话[电报]的人. ~ **tapping**〔美〕(有线)窃听(电话等). ~**work** 金属丝网[制品]. ~**-works** 金属丝制造厂. ~**worm**【虫】铁线虫,切根虫;马蚿. ~**-wove** *a.* (信纸等)上等的;铁纱的.

wired [ˈwaiəd] *a.* 使用金属线的;有线的. ~ **radio** 有线载波通信.

wire·less [ˈwaiəlis] *a.* 无线的;无线电报的,无线电的;无线电话的. *a* ~ *enthusiast [fan]* 无线电迷. *a* ~ *operator* 无线电报务员. *a* ~ *set* 无线电信机;〔英〕无线电收音机. *a* ~ *station* 无线电台. *a* ~ *telegram* 无线电报. ~ *telegraph(y)* 无线电报(术). ~ *telephony* 无线电话(术). — *n.* 无线电;无线电话;无线电报;无线电收音机. ***by*** ~ 用无线电. ***over the*** ~ 用无线电(收听等). — *vi., vt.* 用无线电发送[联系].

wir·er [ˈwaiərə] *n.* ①用金属线缠结的人. ②电线安装工. ③发(电)报人. ④〔古〕(用铁丝网)诱捕(鸟兽)者.

wir·ing [ˈwaiəriŋ] *n.* ①【电】线路;配线;接线;布线;架线. ②【医】(骨折的)金属镍缝合术. *concealed [exposed]* ~ 暗[明]线.

wir·ra [ˈwiərə] *int.*〔Ir.〕呜呼!哎呀!〔表示忧伤或悲哀等〕.

wir·y [ˈwaiəri] *a.* ①金属线的. ②铁丝似的;坚硬的;韧的. ③铁丝(等)制的. ④削瘦而结实的. ⑤(声音)金属弦(发出)的.

wis [wis] *vi.*〔古〕知道.

Wis., Wisc. = Wisconsin.

Wis·con·sin [wisˈkɔnsin] *n.* 威斯康星〔美国州名〕. **-ite** *n.* 威斯康星州人.

wis·dom [ˈwizdəm] *n.* ①智慧,聪明,才智. ②〔古〕学问,知识,学识. ③〔罕〕格言,名言. ④〔集合词〕贤哲. ⑤〔W-〕= Wisdom of Solomon. *Much thinking yields* ~. 多想出智慧. *pour forth* ~ 说出一连串聪明话. *the wit and* ~ *of the place* 当地的能人贤士. ***W- of Solomon*** 《所罗门的智慧》[《圣经》旧约伪经中的一卷]. ~**-tooth** 智齿 (*cut one's* ~*-tooth* 生智齿;开始懂事).

Wise [waiz] *n.* 怀斯[姓氏].

wise[1] [waiz] *a.* ①有智慧的;聪明的,贤明的 *(opp.* foolish*)*;〔美俚〕狡猾的,精明的. ②博学的,博识的. ③象聪明的,象智者的. ④明白的,了解的. ⑤〔俚〕自作聪明的;自高自大的. ⑥〔古〕通妖术的. ***as*** ~ ***as before*** 依然如故(没有进步),依旧啥也不懂. ***be*** ~ ***in*** *(physics)* 精通(物理学). ***be*** ~ ***on [to]*** = ***get*** ~ ***to*** 懂得…. ***He was as*** ~ ***as he went.*** 他和从前一样啥也不懂. ***none the wiser*** = as ~ as before. ***put*** *(sb.)* ~ ***to***〔美俚〕使(某人)弄通,启发(某人)懂得. ***Who will be the wiser?*** 谁会知道?谁也不会知道. ~ ***after the event*** 事后聪明. ***with a*** ~ ***shake of the head*** 活象懂得似地摇摇头. —*vt., vi.*〔俚〕(使)知道,(使)懂得. ~ ***up***〔美俚〕知道;使知道,告诉. ~ **baby**〔美俚〕狡猾[精明]的人. ~ **guy**〔美俚〕自以为聪明的人. ~ **man** 聪明人;贤哲;〔古〕术士,男巫. ~ **money**〔美俚〕= smart money. ~ **old bird**〔美俚〕狡猾的人,滑头. ~ **saw** 金言,格言. ~ **woman** 聪明的女人;〔古〕女巫;收生婆,接生妇.

wise[2] [waiz] *n.*〔古〕方式,方法;程度. ***in any*** ~ 无论如何. ***in like*** ~ 以同样方式;同样地. ***(in) no*** ~ 绝不,一点儿也不. ***in some*** ~ 有点,总. ***on this*** ~ 这样,如此.

wise[3] [waiz] *vt.*〔Scot.〕①指点;引导;劝导. ②迫使;遣送.

-wise *suf.* 方法,方式;方向: any*wise*, clock*wise*.

wise·a·cre [ˈwaizeikə] *n.* 自作聪明的(蠢)人.

wise·crack [ˈwaizkræk] *n.*〔美俚〕俏皮话,妙语. — *vi.* 说俏皮话.

wise·ly [waizli] *ad.* 明智地,聪明地,精明地.

Wise·man [ˈwaizmən] *n.* 怀斯曼[姓氏].

wis·en·heim·er, wise·heim·er [ˈwaizənhaimə] *n.*〔美俚〕= wiseacre.

wi·sent [ˈviːzənt] *n.*【动】欧洲野牛 *(Bison bonasus)*.

wish [wiʃ] *vt.* ①希望,但愿〔以略去 that 的从句作宾语〕. *I* ~ *(that) it would rain.* 我希望会下雨(就好了). *I* ~ *I were a bird!* 我要是一只鸟那多好. *I* ~ *you would come and help us.* 你能来帮助我们就好了. *I* ~ *it may not prove a failure.* 这事不要失败才好〔反面有 I am afraid it will 的意思〕. *I* ~ *I may live to see it.* 但愿我能活着看到它(就好了). *It is to be* ~*ed that* …希望…. ②切望,盼望.〔下接宾语和表语〕. ~ *sb. away* 盼望某人走掉. ~ *sb. happy* 切望某人幸福. ~ *sb. further [at the devil]*〔俚〕希望某人快快滚蛋. ~ *oneself at home* 心想还是呆在家里的好[出来后后悔]. ②想,要〔后接不定式 to do〕. *I* ~ *to go.* 我想去. *I* ~ *to see you.* 我想见到你. ③希望看到…;希望别人做到…. *I* ~ *you to do it.* 希望你做这件事. *What do you* ~ *me to do?* 你要我怎么做呢? *I* ~*it (to be) finished.* 希望把它做完. *Don't tell her anything you* ~ *(to be) forgotten.* 你希望忘记掉的事情不可以告诉她. ④〔罕〕需要〔下接单一宾语(尤其是代词)〕 *Which do you* ~*?* 你要哪一个? ⑤祝,祝愿〔下接两个宾语〕 *I heartily* ~ *you success.* 我衷心祝您成功. *I* ~ *you a happy New Year.* 恭贺新禧. *I* ~ *you joy.* 愿你快乐. *I* ~ *him joy of it.*〔反话〕我祝那家伙走运〔那家伙是不会有好下场的〕. *He* ~*es me well.* 他希望我好. *He* ~*es nobody ill.* 他不希望任何人有什么不好. ⑥向…致(问候等)〔下接两个宾语〕. *He* ~*ed me goodbye [farewell].* 他向我告别了. *I'll* ~ *you good morning.* 再会,明儿见. ⑦把(负担、不愉快的事情等)强加给 *(on).* ~ *a hard job on sb.* 把一项吃力的工作强加给某人. — *vi.* 希望,想要 *(for; after). How I* ~ *for a pair of wings!* 我要是有一对翅膀多好. *The weather is all one could* ~ *for.* 天气再好没有了. *He* ~*es well to all men.* 他希望一切人都好. — *n.* ①愿望;祝愿;请求. ②希求的事情[东西] *The* ~ *is father to the thought.* 有志者事竟成. *I have got my* ~. 我达到愿望了. *Please accept my best* ~*es for your happiness.* 请接受我最诚恳的良好祝愿;祝您幸福. ***attend to [carry out] sb.'s*** ~***es*** 实

现某人愿望. *to one's* ~ 照自己的愿望. ***with best ~es, with every good*** ~ 抱着由衷的祝愿. ~ **fulfillment** 愿欲的实现;【心】愿望满足.

wish·bone [ˈwiʃbəun] *n.* (鸟胸的)叉骨,如愿骨〔二人同扯吃剩的叉骨,得长段者据说能达到愿望〕.

wish·ful [ˈwiʃful] *a.* ①想望,渴望 *(to do)*; 怀着渴望的. ②基于愿望(而非基于事实)的. ~ *eyes* 充满渴望的眼光. *be* ~ *to do sth.* 想做某事. *be* ~ *for sth.* 想获得某物. ~ *dreams of an easy peace* 幻想轻易得到和平的愿望. ***a*** ~ ***thinking*** 根据愿望(不根据事实)的想法,如意算盘;痴心妄想. **-ly** *ad.* 希望着,渴望着. **-ness** *n.*

wish·ing [ˈwiʃiŋ] *n.* 愿望. ~ **bone** = wishbone. ~ **cap** 如愿帽〔据说带了便能事事如愿〕.

wish-think [ˈwiʃθiŋk] *vt.* 一厢情愿地想,打如意算盘地想.

wish-wash [ˈwiʃwɔʃ] *n.* 〔蔑〕淡而无味的饮料;空洞无聊的话〔文字〕.

wish·y-wash·y [ˈwiʃiˌwɔʃi] *a.* ①(茶等)淡而无味的,(话等)空洞无聊的,没意思的. ②优柔寡断的.

wisp [wisp] *n.* ①(稻草等的)小捆,把;(头发等的)束,股. ②(帚状)毛刷. ③(鸟的)一群. ④鬼火. ⑤瘦小纤细的东西〔人〕. *a* ~ *of smoke* 一股烟. *a mere* ~ *of an old man* 瘦得只剩皮包骨头的老人.

wisp·y [wispi] *a.* ***(-i·er; -i·est)*** ①小捆〔小束〕状的. ②细微的. ③飘渺的.

wist [wist] wit² 的过去式和过去分词.

wis·ta·ri·a [wisˈtɛəriə], **wis·te·ri·a** [wisˈtiəriə] *n.* 【植】紫藤(属). *Chinese* ~ 紫藤.

Wis·ter [ˈwistə] *n.* 威斯特〔姓氏〕.

wist·ful [ˈwistful] *a.* ①渴望的,不满足似的. ②沉思的,默想的;愁闷的. ③引起怀念的. **-ly** *ad.* **-ness** *n.*

wit¹ [wit] *n.* ①智慧;理智,理解. ②〔常 *pl.*〕机智,才智;妙语,打趣的话;(健全的)头脑. ③头脑敏捷〔清楚〕的人,富有机智的人. ④〔古〕圣贤. *conversation full of* ~ 充满机智的谈话. *Brevity is the soul of* ~. 简洁是智慧的灵魂. *a nimble* ~ 一个机敏的才子. *the university* ~*s* 〔英〕大学派〔伊丽莎白时代大学出身的一派戏剧作家〕. ***at one's ~'s [~s'] end*** 智穷才尽;毫无办法,不知所措. ***have not the ~(s) to*** 没有…的才能. ***have [keep] one's ~s about one*** 头脑冷静;保持警惕. ***have quick [slow] ~s*** 机敏〔迟钝〕. ***in (one's right) ~s*** 神志清醒. ***live by one's ~s*** 靠小聪明东拼西凑地过日子. ***out of one's ~s*** 神经错乱. ***the five ~s*** 〔古〕五官. **~ster** *n.* 妙语连珠的人.

wit² [wit] *vi., vt.* (***wist*** **[wist]**) 〔古〕知道. ***to*** ~ 即,也就是说(= namely, that is to say).

wit·an [ˈwitn] *n. pl.* 【英史】(盎格鲁撒克逊时代的)谘议院谘议.

witch [witʃ] *n.* ①(据说会行妖术,与魔鬼来往的)妖巫;女巫,巫婆. ②妖妇,迷人的女人. ③刁钻刻毒的女人;丑婆子;〔美俚〕丑姑娘. ④〔英方〕【动】灰鲽. ⑤【数】箕舌(曲)线. — *vt.* 对…施行巫术;迷惑,蛊惑. ***a white*** ~ 做善事的女巫. ~ **ball** (悬挂在舞厅天花板上、旋转时反射出两点般光线的)反光球;一种有彩饰的玻璃球. **~craft** 妖〔巫〕术;魅力. ~ **doctor** 巫医. **~es'-broom** 【植】扫帚病,丛枝病. **~es' cauldron** 可怕的混乱状态. **~es' Sabbath** (一年一度的)女巫狂欢聚会. ~ **grass** 【植】毛线稷. ~ **hazel** 【植】(北美)金缕梅;金缕梅皮止痛水. ~ **hunt**, ~ **hunting** ①对巫师的搜捕. ②以莫须有罪名进行的政治迫害. ~ **moth** 【动】魔女蛾.

witch- *pref.* = wych-.

witch·er·y [ˈwitʃəri] *n.* 巫术;魔法,妖术;魔力,魅力,诱惑力. ~ *of the blue sky* 碧空如洗,使人心醉.

witch·ing [witʃiŋ] *n.* 施妖〔巫〕术;妖法;魅力. — *a.* 有魔力的,迷人的,蛊惑的. ***the ~ time of night*** 夜半.

wite [wait] *n., vt.* (***wit·ed; wit·ing***) 〔Scot.〕谴责,非难,申斥,归咎.

wit·en·a·ge·mot [ˈwitinəgiˈməut] *n.* 【英史】(盎格鲁撒克逊时代国王的)谘议院.

with [wið, 在无声音前常作 wiθ] *prep.* ①和…一起,和…一块儿,和…同时. *Go* ~ *him.* 跟他一块儿去. *live* ~ *a friend* 和朋友一块儿生活〔住在朋友家里〕. *have dealings* ~ 和…有交易关系. *be in touch [contact]* ~ 和…经常接触. *meet [fall in]* ~ 遇见,碰见. *coeval [contemporary]* ~ 和…同时代的. *rise* ~ *the sun* 和太阳一块儿起来,早起. *W- that he went away.* 说完了这些话他便走了. *accord* ~ 和…一致. *combine* ~ 和…结合,联合. *compare* ~ 和…比较(对照). *mingle [blend]* ~ 和…混合. ②和,跟. *quarrel [argue]* ~ *sb.* 跟某人吵架〔拌嘴〕. *compete* ~ *a friend* 和朋友竞争. ③用. *cut it* ~ *a knife* 用小刀切. *have no pen to write* ~ = *have no pen* ~ *which to write* 没有笔写. *be adorned* ~ *frescoes* 用壁画装饰着. ④伴随着;带着;具有. *I have no money* ~ *me.* 我没带钱. *An old man was lying there,* ~ *his eyes open* 一位老人睁着两只眼睛躺在那里. *walk* ~ *a stick in one's hand* 拿着手杖走. *He went out* ~ *no hat on.* 他不戴帽子出去了. *What a lonely world it will be* ~ *you away!* 没有了你,这个世界将多么寂寞. ⑤和…一致;赞成. *He that is not* ~ *me is against me.* 不赞成我的人便是反对我的. *sympathize* ~ *sb.* 同情某人. *vote* ~ *the Socialists* 投社会党的票. ⑥存给,交给…手里;归…的手. *Leave the parcel* ~ *the porter* 这包裹交给搬运员. *It rests* ~ *you to decide.* 决定的权力在你手里. ⑦由于,因. *tremble* ~ *fear* 吓得发抖. *bent* ~ *age* 由于年老弯腰驼背. *excite* ~... 因…兴奋. *die* ~ *hunger.* 饿死. ⑧〔行动的方式、样子〕…地,…着. ~ *calmness* 沉着地. *behave* ~ *courage* 勇敢地行动. ~ *ease* 轻易地. *He greeted me* ~ *smiles* 他笑着招呼我. ⑨关于;对于;在…,由…看来,就…来说. *How shall we proceed* ~ *our industrialization?* 我们的工业化怎样搞呢? *Such is the case* ~ *me.* 我的情形就是这样. *be angry* ~ 对…生气. *be patient* ~ *him* 对他要忍耐. *to be frank* ~ *you* 坦白对你说. *What do you want* ~ *me?* 你要我做什么? *What is the matter* ~ *you?* 你怎么啦? *It is usual [the custom]* ~ *the French.* 这在法国人是普通的〔是习惯〕. *How are you getting along* ~ *your work?* (关于)你的工作怎么样了? ⑩虽有,虽. *W- all her merits, she was not proud.* 她虽有那么多的优点,但并不骄傲. ⑪〔与副词连用,表示命令、愿望等,构成祈使句〕. *Off* ~ *your clothes!* 把衣服脱下来. *Away* ~ *him!* 把他带走! *Down with imperialism!* 打倒帝国主义. ***be in*** ~ 和…很熟,和…友善. ***be one*** ~ 和…是一体,和…成一体,和…合并. ***be*** ~ 和…意见相同. ***be ~ it*** 〔美俚〕①消息灵通. ②对某事颇感兴趣. ***go*** ~ 和…调和,相配 (*Blue does not go* ~ *green.* 蓝和绿不调和). ***have done*** ~ = ***have nothing to do*** ~ 和…断绝关系. ***keep in*** ~... 和…保持友好关系. ***what ~ ..., (and) what ~ ...*** 一则因…一则因…;一方面因…一方面因…;因…和…. ~ ***child*** 有孕. ~ ***that*** 接着,于是(= thereupon). ~ ***the chickens*** 〔美〕早 (*get up [go to bed]* ~ *the chickens* 早起〔早睡〕). ~ ***this*** 这样做了以后,说了这话以后(=saying this, doing this) (*With this, she shut the book and left the room.* 说了这话以后,她便合上书走出房间了). ~ ***young*** (兽类)有孕. ~ ***your leave*** 〔口〕请原谅(= by your leave).

with- *comb.f.* 向后,往回〔返回〕;对抗,相对. *with*draw; *with*hold; *with*stand.

with·al [wiˈðɔːl] *ad.* 而且,又,加之;同样;同时;然而. — *prep.* 〔古〕用,以 (= with)〔常用在句末或片语后〕. *What shall he fill his belly* ~? 他该用什么来充饥呢?

with·draw [wiðˈdrɔː] *vt.* ***(-drew*** **[-ˈdruː]*; -drawn*** **[-ˈdrɔːn])** ①缩回(手等). ②抽回,收回,领回,使退出. ③回收(通货等);提取(存款). ④撤退(军队等). ⑤撤销;褫夺(特权). ⑥取消,撤回(申请、诉讼等). ~ *a* *boy from school* 把孩子从学校里领回[退学]. ～ *troops from a place* 把部队撤离某处. — *vi.* ①退去,缩回. ②退出,脱离(集团等);(军队)撤退. ③取消,撤回. *After dinner the ladies withdrew.* 饭后妇女们退出〔到卧室去安息〕. ～**ing room**〔古〕客厅(=drawing room).

with·draw·al [wiðˈdrɔːəl] *n.* ①缩回;引退;退出. ②收回. ③撤退,撤兵. ④取消,撤回;撤销;褫夺. ⑤【商】提款;退股.

with·drawn [wiðˈdrɔːn] withdraw 的过去分词. — *a.* ①孤独的,离群的. ②偏僻的. **-ness** *n.*

with·drew [wiðˈdruː] withdraw 的过去式.

withe [wiθ, wið] *n.* *(pl.* ～*s* [-θs, -ðz]) (捆柴等的)枝条,柳条. — *vt.* 用枝条捆扎.

with·er [ˈwiðə] *vi.* ①凋残,萎谢,枯萎 *(up)*; 衰弱. ②(希望等)破灭,消衰 *(away)*. — *vt.* ①使凋残,使萎谢,使枯萎 *(up)*. ②使衰弱;使消衰,减弱;使畏缩[局促];损坏(名誉). *Age cannot* ～ *her* 岁月并未使她的容颜减色. ～ *sb. with a look* 一瞪眼使某人手足失措.

with·ered [ˈwiðəd] *a.* 凋败了的;枯萎的;衰弱的,干瘪的,(手等)尽是皱纹的;(希望等)所剩不多的.

with·er·ing [ˈwiðəriŋ] *a.* ①使枯萎的;毁灭性的;摧毁的. ②(茶叶等)用以干燥他物的. **-ly** *ad.*

with·er·ite [ˈwiðəˌrait] *n.*【矿】毒重石.

With·ers [ˈwiðəz] *n.* 威瑟斯[姓氏].

with·ers [ˈwiðəz] *n. pl.* ①马肩隆〔马肩骨间隆起部〕. ②〔古〕情绪,感情. ***My*** ～ ***are unwrung.*** 那样的非难很不中肯,我满不在乎,一点也不感到难受.

with·er·shins [ˈwiðəʃinz] *ad.* 〔Scot.〕①和太阳运行方向相反地,倒过来,反时针方向. ②不吉的.

with·held [wiðˈheld] withhold 的过去式及过去分词.

with·hold [wiðˈhəuld] *vt.* *(-held* [-ˈheld]) ①压住,制住,抑制. ②不给,扣住,勒扣,不(答应). — *vi.* 抑制;忍住.

with·in [wiðˈin] *prep.* ①在…内,在…里面. ②不超过,在…的范围内;在…能达到的地方. ～ *doors* 在户内,在屋内;向屋内. ～ *reach of* 在…附近. ～ *call* 在一叫就听得见的地方. ～ *a week* 在一个星期内. *It is true* ～ *limits.* 在某些范围内那是真实[正确]的. ***keep (it)*** ～ ***bounds*** 保持在限制范围内,不越出范围. ～ ***an ace of*** ...差一点…. ～ ***oneself*** 在心里;从容不迫地 *(run well* ～ *oneself* 从从容容地跑). — *ad.* ①在内,在里头;在户内,在屋内. ②在心中,心里是. *go* ～ 走进屋里. *Is Comrade Chang* ～? 张同志在家吗? *be pure* ～ 心地纯洁. *beauty without and foulness* ～ 外貌美丽内心丑恶. — *n.* 内部,里面. *The door opens from* ～. 这扇门从里面开.

with·in·doors [wiðˈindɔːz] *ad.* 在户内 (= indoors).

with-it [wiˈðit] *a.*〔美俚〕打扮入时的;时髦的,赶上潮流的. ～**-ness** *n.*

with·out [wiðˈaut] *prep.* ①在…(范围)外. ②没有;不. ～ *the gates* 在门外. *things* ～ *us* 外界事物. ～ *the pale of* 在…的范围外. ～ *regard for* 不顾. ～ *taking leave* 假也不请(就…). ～ *saying a word* 不说一句话就. *all* ～ *exception* 没有例外地都. ～ *day* 没有日期,无限期. ～ *end* 无限地,永远地;无止境地. ～ *reserve* 不客气地. *It goes* ～ *saying that* ..., …那是不用说的[当然的]. — *ad.* ①在外部;在户外;在屋外,在外面. ②外面是,外表是. ③在没有(某种不言而喻的东西)的情况下. *stand* ～ 站在屋外. *listen to the wind* ～ 倾听户外风声. *The apple is red* ～ *and white within.* 苹果皮红肉白. *Never mind, I can manage* ～. 没关系我没有(那东西)也能凑合. — *n.* 外部,外面. *as seen from* ～ 从外面来看. — *conj.*〔古、卑〕除非,如果不. *He never goes out* ～ *he loses his umbrella.* 他出门没有一次不丢伞的.

with·out·doors [ˈwiðˈautˌdɔːz] *ad.*〔古〕在户外 (= outdoors).

with·out-it [wiðˈautit] *a.* 不时髦的,老式的,守旧的.

with·stand [wiðˈstænd] *vt.* *(-stood* [-ˈstud]) 抵挡;挡住,顶住;反抗,反对;经得起,耐得住. ～ *the enemy* 挡住敌人. ～ *temptation* 经得起诱惑. ～ *fire* 耐火. *They have withstood all tests.* 他们经受[通过]了一切考验. — *vi.*〔诗〕反抗.

with·y [ˈwiði] *n.* ①【植】柳;杞柳. ②柳条;韧枝 (= withe). — *a.* ①坚韧的. ②(人)瘦长而结实的.

wit·less [ˈwitlis] *a.* 无才智的,没脑筋的,没思想的;轻率的;愚笨的. **-ly** *ad.*

wit·ling [ˈwitliŋ] *n.* 玩弄小聪明的人,假作聪明的人.

wit·ness [ˈwitnis] *n.* ①证据;证实,证明. ②证人,亲眼看见的人,目击者. ③〔常省略定冠词〕【法】证人;连署人. ***be a*** ～ ***to*** 是…的目击者. ***bear sb.*** ～ 为某人作证;证明(某人)所说的话. ***bear*** ～ ***to [of]*** 作…的证人〔证据〕,证明. ***call ... to*** ～ 请…证明,叫…做证人. ***challenge*** ～ 要求证人回避. ***give*** ～ ***on behalf of*** 替…作证. ***hear [examine] the*** ～ 询问证人. ***in*** ～ ***of*** 作为…的证据. ***in*** ～ ***thereof...*** 此证〔证件上惯用语〕. ***take ... to*** ～ = call ... to ～. ***with a*** ～〔古〕明明白白,无疑地,确实,(这)正是. ***W- Heaven!***〔古〕让老天爷作证吧! — *vt.* ①亲眼看见,目击,目睹. ②【法】(签名)作证. ③〔古〕证,证明. ④表示,表明. — *vi.* 证实,证明 *(against; for; to)*. ～ **box**〔英〕(法庭的)证人席. ～ **mark** (土地的)界标,(测量的)标竿(等). ～ **stand**〔美〕=～ box *(take the* ～ *stand* 作证).

wit·ted [ˈwitid] *a.* 有(某种)智力的〔常用以构成复合词〕. *slow-*～ 智力迟钝的.

wit·ti·cism [ˈwitisizəm] *n.* 名言;妙语,俏皮话.

witting [ˈwitiŋ] *a.* ①〔多用作表语〕明明知道的,自觉的. ②〔常作 ～ and willing〕故意的. — *n.*〔英方〕知道;理解. **-ly** *ad.* 故意,有意.

wit·tol [ˈwitl] *n.*〔古〕知道妻子不贞而予以容忍的丈夫.

wit·ty [ˈwiti] *a.* *(-ti·er; -ti·est)* ①机智的;会说俏皮话的;诙谐的. ②〔英方、Scot.〕聪明的. **-ti·ly** *ad.*

wive [waiv]〔古〕*vt., vi.* 娶(妻);给(某人)娶妻.

wi·vern [ˈwaivəːn] *n.*【徽】两脚飞龙.

wives [waivz] wife 的复数.

wiz [wiz] *n.*〔美口〕奇才 (wizard 的缩略).

wiz·ard [ˈwizəd] *n.* ①术士,男巫;变戏法的人. ②〔美口〕奇才. — *a.* ①有魔力的. ②巫术的;着魔的. ③〔主英俚〕(人)聪明的,巧妙的,巧(具),妙(品);漂亮的;稀奇的. *a cue* ～ 台球名手. ***the Welsh W-*** 威尔士奇才〔英国首相劳合·乔治(Lloyd George)的别名〕. ***the W- of the North*** 北方奇才〔英国作家司各特(Sir Walter Scott)的别名〕. **-ly** *a.*

wiz·ard·ry [ˈwizədri] *n.* 法术,妖术.

wiz·en(ed) [ˈwizn(d)] *a.* 凋败的,枯萎的.

wk. = ①week. ②weak. ③work.

wks. = ①weeks. ②works.

WL., W. L. = water line (船的)吃水线,水平面线.

W/L, w.l. = wave length 波长.

W.L.A. = Women's Land Army〔英〕陆军妇女队.

W. long. = west longitude 西经.

Wm. = William.

WMC = War Manpower Commission〔美〕战时人力委员会.

wmk. = watermark 水位标记.

WMO = World Meteorological Organization 世界气象组织(联合国).

W.N.L.F. = Women's National Liberal Federation.〔英〕全国女自由党人联合会.

W.N.W., WNW,w.n.w. = west-northwest.

WO, W.O. = ①War Office〔英旧〕陆军部. ②Warrant Officer 准尉.

W/O = ①water in oil 油中水,水混油. ②weight percent 重量百分比.

wo [wəu] *int.* = ①whoa. ②woe.

woad [wəud] *n.* ①【植】菘蓝. ②菘蓝(靛青)染料. ～

waxen【植】染料木.
wo•back [ˈwəu-bæk] *int.* 〔命令马〕退!
wob•ble [ˈwɔbl] *v., n.* = wabble. **-bler** *n.* = wabbler. **-bling** *a.* =wabbling. ~ **pump**【空】(紧急情况下用)手摇燃料泵.
wob•bly[1] [ˈwɔbli] *a.* 颤动的; 摇摆的, 动摇的; 无定见的.
wob•bly[2] [ˈwɔbli] *n.* 〔美俚〕世界产业工会 (IWW) 会员.
wo•be•gone [ˈwəubigɔn] *a.* = woebegone.
Wode•house [ˈwudhaus] *n.* 沃德豪斯〔姓氏〕.
wodge [wɔdʒ] *n.* 〔英口〕一大块, 一团.
woe [wəu] *n.* ①悲哀, 悲痛; 苦恼. ②祸, 灾难, 灾殃 *(opp.* weal*)*. *W- is me!* = *W- to me!* 我真伤心〔倒霉〕呀! (= Alas!) *W- worth the day!* 见 *worth*[2] 条. ***in weal and*** ~ 无论祸福. ***W- (be) to sb.!*** = ***W- betide sb.!*** 愿某人受难! 愿某人吃苦头! — *int.* 〔表示悲伤、不幸、懊悔〕咳! 哎! 呀!
woe•be•gone [ˈwəubigɔn] *a.* ①悲哀的, 忧愁的; 苦恼不堪的. ②愁容满面的.
woe•ful [ˈwəuful] *a.* ①悲伤的, 悲惨的, 悲哀的; 不吉利的. ②可悲的; 不幸的; 糟糕透顶的. *a* ~ *day* 不吉利的日子. *a* ~ *cry* 悲哀的叫声. **-ly** *ad.*
wog [wɔg] *n.* 〔俚、蔑〕东方〔中东〕佬, 外国佬.
wok [wɔk] *n.* 〔Chin.〕镬, 铁锅〔源自广东话〕.
woke [wəuk] wake 的过去式及过去分词.
wok•en [ˈwəukn] *v.* 〔英、美方〕wake 的过去分词.
Wol•cot(t) [ˈwulkət] *n.* 沃尔科特〔姓氏〕.
wold[1] [wəuld] *n.* ①荒瘠不毛的高原, 荒原. ②〔废〕森林.
wold[2] [wəuld] *n.*【植】= weld[2].
wolf [wulf] *n.* *(pl.* ***wolves*** [wulvz]*)* ①狼. ②残忍的人; 贪婪的人; 〔美俚〕色鬼, 追逐女人的饿狼一样的男人. ③极端的贫困; 饥饿. ④严重危害谷仓的各种害虫(的幼虫). ⑤【医】狼疮. ⑥【乐】调弦不谐协; 不谐协弦所产生的不协调音; 粗厉音; (弓弦乐器的) 颤音粗厉. *a* ~ *in sheep's clothing* 披着羊皮的豺狼; 伪君子; 伪装友善的敌人. ***cry*** ~ 喊"狼来了"骗人, 发假警报. ***have [hold] a*** ~ ***by the ears*** 骑虎难下, 窘迫到极点, 进退两难. ***have a*** ~ ***in the stomach*** 饿到极点. ***have seen a*** ~ = see a ~. ***keep the*** ~ ***from the door*** 勉强摆脱困境; 免于饥饿. ***see a*** ~ 说不出话来, 目瞪口呆. ***ugly enough to tree a (barking [curly, gray, white])*** ~ 〔美俚〕丑陋已极; 不中用到极点. ***wake a sleeping*** ~ 打草惊蛇; 自找麻烦. — *vt.* 〔俚〕狼吞虎咽地大吃 *(down)*. — *vi.* 打狼, 猎狼. ~**berry**【植】西方雪果. ~**-call** 〔美俚〕(流氓调戏妇女的)怪叫[口哨等]. ~ **cub** 小狼; 〔英〕(8—11岁的)幼童军. ~ **dog** 猎狼狗; 狼狗. ~ **fish**【鱼】狼鳚. ~**hound** 猎狼狗; 狼狗. ~ **pack** ①【军】群狼袭击队〔二次大战中, 德方用大批潜水艇或战斗机袭击敌方劣势部队的战术单位〕. ②饿狼帮〔以追逐妇女为事的流氓集团〕. ~**-soup** 〔美俚〕(候选人的)夸张而不可靠的诺言. ~ **spider**【动】狼蛛〔一种不结网的多毛大蜘蛛〕. ~ **whistle** 色鬼调戏妇女时所发的怪声口哨. **-er** *n.* 猎狼者.
Wolfe [wulf] *n.* 沃尔夫〔姓氏〕.
Wolf•gang [ˈwulfgæŋ] *n.* 沃尔夫冈〔姓氏〕.
wolf•ish [ˈwulfiʃ] *a.* 狼的; 狼似的; 残忍的; 贪婪的. **-ly** *ad.*
wolf•ram [ˈwulfrəm] *n.* ①= wolframite. ②【化】钨 (=tungsten) 〔略号 W〕.
wolf•ram•ite [ˈwulfrəmait] *n.*【矿】黑钨矿, 钨锰铁矿.
wolf•ra•mi•um [wulfˈreimiəm] *n.* 〔废〕【化】= wolfram②.
wolf's-bane, wolfs'-bane [ˈwulfsbein] *n.*【植】乌头(属); 附子草; 黄花乌头, 狼毒乌头.
wolf's-claws [ˈwulfsklɔ:z], **wolf's-foot** [ˈwulfsfut] *n.*【植】石松; 卷柏.
Wol•las•ton [ˈwuləstən] *n.* 沃拉斯顿〔姓氏〕.
wol•las•ton•ite [ˈwuləstənait] *n.*【矿】硅灰石.
Wo•lof [ˈwəulɔ:f] *n.* ①*(pl.* ~*(s))* 沃洛夫人〔塞内加尔和冈比亚人〕. ②沃洛夫语.
Wolse•ley [ˈwulzli] *n.* 沃尔斯利〔姓氏〕.
Wol•sey [ˈwulzi] *n.* 沃尔西〔姓氏〕.
wol•ver [ˈwulvə] *n.* = wolfer.
wol•ver•ene, -ine [ˈwulvəri:n] *n.* ①黑獾类; 狼獾. ②〔W-〕〔美〕密执安 (Michigan) 州人的绰号. **W- State** 〔美〕密执安 州的别名.
wolves [wulvz] wolf 的复数.
woman [ˈwumən] *n.* *(pl.* ***wo•men*** [ˈwimin]*)* ①女人, 妇人; 成年女人; 〔不加冠词〕〔集合词〕妇女, 女性. ②〔英口〕打杂女工; 〔古〕侍女, 婢. ③女人似的男人. ④〔the ~〕女人性格, 女人本能, 女人的感情. ⑤情人; 情妇; 〔方〕妻子. *an old* ~ 老妇人; 老太婆似的软弱无能的男人. *all the old women of both sexes* 老太婆般的男男女女, 婆婆妈妈的人们. *the old women in the Cabinet* 软弱无能的阁员们. *He is a* ~ *in tenderness.* 他温柔得象女人一样. *All the* ~ *in her rose in rebellion.* 她的女人本能全部暴发出来进行反抗. ***a little*** ~ 女孩; 象大人样子的小女孩. ***a*** ~ ***of the streets*** 娼妓. ***a*** ~ ***of the world*** 善于交际应酬的女人, 精通世故的女人. ***a*** ~ ***with a past*** (过去)行为不太清白的女人. ***born of*** ~ 女人生的, 凡人的. ***make an honest*** ~ ***of*** 跟(发生过不正当关系的女人)正式结婚. ***(my) little*** ~ 〔对小女孩的亲切, 打趣的称呼〕大姑娘. ***my good*** ~ 喂喂〔对女人打招呼用语〕. ***play the*** ~ 表现出女人的态度〔如哭、害怕等〕. — *a.* 妇女的; 女性的. *a* ~ *doctor* 女医生. — *vt.* 使做出女人的行为〔泣哭等〕; 使软弱无能; 对(女人)打招呼〔用 my good ~ 打招呼〕. ~**aut** 女宇航员, 女太空人. ~**-hater** 厌恶妇女的人. ~**jawed** *a.* 〔美〕歪斜. ~**hood** ①(女子的)成年身分; (女子) 成年期. ②女性, 女人脾气. ③〔集合词〕妇女, 女人. ~**kind** 妇女, 女子, 女人, 〔集合词〕女性 (*sb.'s womankind [womenkind]* 女眷, 家属中的女性成员). ~**'s rights** 妇女权利; 女权运动. ~ **suffrage** 妇女选举权 [参政权]. **-like** = womanly. **-ish** *a.* 女人气的, 女性特有的; 〔常蔑〕柔弱的, 懦弱的. **-ize, -ise** ①*vt.* 把…弄得象女人; 使柔弱, 使懦弱. ② *vi.* 变柔弱; 玩弄女人, 追逐女色, 与女子发生不正当关系. **-li•ness** *n.* **-ly** *a.* 女子气的, 象女人的, 温柔的; 宜于妇女的.
womb [wu:m] *n.* 子宫; 胎; 〔喻〕内部; 发源地, 孕育处. *the* ~ *of a ship* 船体内部. ***from the*** ~ ***to the tomb*** 从生到死, 一生中. ***in the*** ~ ***of time*** (在)将来. ***the fruit of the*** ~ 子女.
wom•bat [ˈwɔmbət] *n.*【动】(澳洲)袋熊.
women [wimin] woman 的复数. ~ **folk(s)** 〔*pl.*〕〔集合词〕妇女. ~**kind** = womankind. **Women's Lib** 妇女解放运动 (=Women's Liberation). **Women's Libber** 妇女解放运动的组织成员〔主张者, 追随者〕(= Women Liberationist). ~**'s room** 女厕所.
wom•er•a [ˈwɔmərə] *n.* (澳大利亚土著所用的)投矛机.
womp [wɔmp] *n.* ①(由光学系统内部反射产生的) 图像亮区. ②【电视】(亮度突增的)闪光, 白闪.
won[1] [wʌn] win 的过去式及过去分词.
won[2] [wɔn] *n.* *(sing., pl.)* 〔Kor.〕(朝鲜)圆〔南北朝鲜的货币单位〕.
won•der [ˈwʌndə] *n.* ①惊奇, 惊异, 惊叹. ②不可思议, 奇异, 奇妙; 奇异的事情〔东西〕, 奇迹; 奇观; 奇才. *No* ~*!* 难怪! 并不奇怪! *The child is a* ~. 这孩子是个神童. ***a nine day's*** ~ 昙花一现的新鲜事. ***and no*** ~ 难怪, 当然. ***do*** ~***s*** 行奇迹, 做奇事; 做出惊人成就. ***for a*** ~ 说也奇怪; 意想不到的. ***in silent*** ~ 惊奇得哑口无言. ***in the name of*** ~ 究竟. ***in*** ~ 在惊奇中, 由于惊奇. ***It is a*** ~ ***that …*** = ***The*** ~ ***is that …*** 奇怪的是…. ***(It is) no [small]*** ~ ***that …*** = ***What*** ~ ***that …?*** 〔常省去 *that*〕… 并不奇怪, 难怪…. ***perform*** ~***s*** = do ~s. ***to a*** ~ …得叫人惊异. ***work*** ~***s*** =do ~s.

— *vt., vi.* 惊奇,惊讶,诧异,(对…)觉得奇怪 *(that)*;(对…)感到怀疑;惊叹,佩服. *I ~ (that) he did it at last.* 真奇怪,他终于做了那件事了. *I ~ (if, what, who, why* 等), 不晓得,不知道 (*I ~ if he can.* 不晓得他能不能. *I ~ what the time is.* 不知道现在是几点钟了. *I ~ whether I might ask you a question.* 不知道可不可以问你一个问题). *~ **about** = ~ **as to*** 怀疑. *~ **at*** 看见[听见]…而惊奇,惊叹,惊服; 惊讶,诧异 (*I ~ at you.* 你怎么搞的; 你真奇怪). ~**monger** 好说奇闻异事的人; 好用新奇物品的人.

won·der·ful [ˈwʌndəful] *a.* ①令人惊奇的,可惊叹的,奇异的. ②〔口〕极好的,精采的. *a man of ~ patience* 耐性极好的人. **-ly** *ad.*

won·der·ing [ˈwʌndəriŋ] *a.* 觉得[表示]惊奇的 (表情等). **-ly** *ad.*

won·der·land [ˈwʌndəlænd] *n.* (童话里的)奇境,仙境. *a scenic ~* 风景优美的地方.

won·der·ment [ˈwʌndəmənt] *n.* ①惊奇, 惊愕, 惊叹. ②奇迹,奇观. ③好奇心.

wonder-struck [ˈwʌndəstrʌk], **-strick·en** [-strikən] *a.* 大吃一惊的,感到非常惊奇的.

won·der·work [ˈwʌndəwəːk] *n.* 〔美〕使人惊叹的行为[技艺(等)]; 奇迹. **-er** *n.* 做出惊人事情的人; 创造奇迹的人; 魔术师. **-ing** *a.* 创造奇迹的; 巧妙的, 巧夺天工的.

won·drous [ˈwʌndrəs] *a.* 〔诗、古〕令人惊奇的, 奇异的, 奇妙的. — *ad.* 〔修饰形容词〕惊人地, 令人惊叹地, 非常. *~ kind* 亲切得出奇的. **-ly** *ad.* **-ness** *n.*

wonk [wɔŋk] *n.* 〔俚〕蛀书虫,书呆子,死用功的学生. — *vi.* 〔俚〕啃书本,死读书.

wonk·y [ˈwɔŋki] 〔英俚〕*a.* 脚步不稳的,摇摇晃晃的; 靠不住的; 身体虚弱的; 优柔寡断的.

Won·san [ˈwænsɑn] *n.* 元山〔朝鲜民主主义人民共和国港市〕.

wont [wəunt] *a.* 〔用作表语〕惯常, 习以为常 *(to* do). *as he was ~ to say* 象他常常说的. *sitting as I am ~* 象平常那样坐着. — *n.* 习惯. *It is his ~ to get up early.* 早起是他的习惯. ***use and ~*** 通常习惯. — *vi., vt.* 〔古〕(使)习惯于.

won't [wəunt] = will not.

wont·ed [ˈwəuntid] *a.* 〔仅作定语用〕习惯的, 平常的, 照常的. *with his ~ courtesy* 象他平常那样谦恭地. *return at one's ~ hour* 在惯常的时刻回来.

won ton [ˈwɔn ˌtɔn] 〔Chin.〕馄饨.

woo [wuː] *vt.* ①向…求婚,求爱. ②追求(名誉、幸福等). ③招致, 惹出(祸等). ④死乞白赖地请求; 劝说, 拉拢(人)(做某事,投入某项行动等). *~ one's own destruction* 自取灭亡. *~ sb. to do sth.* 缠着某人要他做某事. *~ sb. to an action* 死乞白赖地要某人投入某项行动. — *vi.* ①求婚,求爱. ②恳求. *~ the Muses* 从事[研究]艺术. **-er** *n.*

Wood [wud] *n.* 伍德〔姓氏〕.

wood[1] [wud] *n.* ①〔常 *pl.*〕树林, 森林. ②木质. ③木材; 木板; 木柴; 木球; (高尔夫球)木棍. ④〔the ~〕(装酒的) 木桶. ⑤〔the ~〕【乐】木管乐器 (= ~-wind); 〔集合词〕木管乐器部(演奏者). *black ~* 黑檀. *three-ply [multi-ply] ~*三合板. *wine in the ~* 桶装酒. *beer from the ~* 桶中倒出的啤酒. ***be out of the ~s*** [〔英〕~] 走出森林; 摆脱危险, 渡过难关, 到达安全地点. ***cannot see the ~ for the trees*** 见树不见林; 见局部而不见整体; 见小不见大. ***get out of the ~s*** = be out of the ~s. ***in the green ~*** 处境顺利,景况优裕. ***saw ~*** 〔美俚〕①埋头工作, 不管闲事; (在政治上)采取消极态度. ②打鼾; 睡觉. ***take to the ~s*** 〔美俚〕逃进树林; 回避责任,弃权,逃脱. ***the ~s*** 乐团中吹奏木管乐器的全体团员. — *vt.* ①在…植树造林. ②供木材给…. ③用木头垫住[支住]. — *vi.* ①收集木材. ②得到木材的供应. ~ **alcohol**【化】甲醇, 木醇. ~ **anemone**【植】白头翁类. ~**-beetle**【虫】木蠹蛾. ~ **betony**【植】马先蒿属植物 (= Louse wort). ~**bin** 装木柴的大箱. ~**bind,** ~**bine** ①= honeysuckle. ②〔美〕= Virginia creeper. ③(欧战时兵士抽的) 廉价卷烟. ④〔美俚〕英国兵. ~ **block** ①= ~cut. ②(铺马路的) 铺木, 木块. ~ **buffer**【机】木缓冲器. ~ **carving** 木刻(法). ~**chat**【动】鹏伯劳. ~**chopper** 伐木者; 〔美俚〕木琴师. ~**chuck**〔美〕【动】土拨鼠类. ~ **coal** 木炭; 褐煤. ~**cock**【鸟】丘鹬, 山鹬. ~**craft** 林中作业技能; 木材加工(技术); 森林学; 木刻(术). ~**craftsman** 木刻家. ~**cut** 木刻; 版画. ~**cutter** 伐木工人; 樵夫; 木刻家. ~ **duck**【动】北美鸳鸯. ~**enware** 木制器具. ~ **engraver** 木刻家;【虫】钻心虫. ~ **engraving** 木刻(术); 木刻画,木版画. ~ **fibre**【造纸】木质纤维. ~ **file** 木锉. ~**-head**〔美〕木头人, 笨人. ~**hen**【动】①(= woodcock) 丘鹬, 山鹬. ②(= weka) 新西兰里秧鸡. ~**house** 木材贮藏所; 柴屋. ~ **hyacinth**【植】欧洲蓝绵枣儿. ~ **ibis**【鸟】林鹳,林鹭. ~**land** ① *n.* 森林地[地带]; 木本群落. ② *a.* 林地的,树林的; 林栖的. ~**lander** 林中居民. ~ **lark**【动】欧洲林百灵. ~ **leopard**【虫】豹蛾 (= leopard moth). ~ **lot** 造林地; (农场中的)一小片树林. ~ **louse** *(pl. ~ lice)*【虫】土鳖,地鳖. ~**man** 伐木工人; 樵夫; 〔英〕林务管理员; 林中居民. ~**sman** 林中居民; 熟悉山林情况的人; 〔美〕=lumberman. ~ **notes**〔*pl.*〕林间鸟兽的鸣叫; 林鸟一样的歌唱; 朴质自然的诗歌. ~ **nymph** ①森林妖精. ②(南美的) *Thalurania* 属鸣禽; *Euthisanotia* 属蛾. ~ **oil** 木油; 桐油. ~ **paper** 木造纸. ~ **pavement** 木砖路, 铺木路. ~**pecker**【鸟】啄木鸟. ~ **pewee**【动】林鹟. ~ **pigeon**【鸟】斑鸠; 斑尾林鸽; (北美)野鸽. ~**pile** ①柴堆. ②〔美俚〕= xylophone. ~ **plane** 木刨. ~ **pulp** 木(纸)浆. ~ **pussy**〔方〕臭鼬 (= skunk). ~**ranger**〔美〕森林巡视员. ~ **rat**【动】林鼠属动物 (= pack rat). ~ **ray** 木射线 (= xylem ray). ~**roof,** ~**row,** ~**ruff** *n.*【植】香车叶草. ~ **rush**【植】地杨梅. ~ **screw** 木螺丝. ~**shed** 堆木柴的棚屋. ~ **sorrel**【植】酢浆草. ~ **spirit** 甲醇, 木精. ~ **sugar** 木糖 (= xylose). ~ **tar** 木焦油. ~ **thrush**【鸟】林鸫 (= ~ robin). ~ **turning**【木工】木车削. ~ **vinegar**【化】木醋酸, 焦木酸(= pyrol-gneous acid). ~ **warbler** = warbler. ~**-waxen** = woad-waxen. ~**wind** 木管乐器. ~**-wool** 纤细的绒状刨花, 木丝. ~**work** 木制品; 木建部分, 木结构; 木工活. ~**working** *n., a.* 木器制造(的), 木工技艺(的). ~**worm** 钻[蛀]木虫. ~**yard** 堆木场.

wood[2] [wud] *a.* 〔古〕 ①失去理智的, 精神错乱的. ②大怒, 暴怒; 愤怒, 激愤.

wood·ed [ˈwudid] *a.* ①树木繁茂的, 多树林的. ②〔常用以在构成复合语〕木质…的. *a hard-~ tree* 一种木质坚硬的树.

wood·en [ˈwudn] *a.* ①木(制)的. ②木然的,没表情的, 木头人似的; 没有活气[精神]的; 笨拙不灵的. *~ manners.* 笨拙的举止. *~ wits* 愚钝的头脑. ~**head** 笨人, 蠢货; 愚钝的头脑. ~**headed** *a.* 笨的, 愚钝的. **W- Horse** (或 w- h-)【希史】特洛伊木马; 〔喻〕钻进内部的破坏集团(=Trojan Horse). ~ **Indian** ①木雕美洲印第安人(立像)〔烟草店作招徕用〕. ②〔口〕愚钝的人; 无精打采的人; 口齿不清的人. **W- Nutmeg State** 〔美〕 Connecticut 州的别名. ~ **overcoat**〔美俚〕棺材. ~ **walls** 〔旧〕木城〔指军舰, 因旧时军舰为木制, 军舰的保卫国家功用同于城墙〕. ~**ware**〔集合词〕木器.

Wood·row [ˈwudrəu] *n.* 伍德罗〔姓氏〕.

wood·si·a [ˈwudziə] *n.*【植】岩蕨属 *(Woodsia)* 植物.

woods·y [ˈwudzi] *a.* 〔美〕森林(一样)的.

wood·y [ˈwudi] *a.* ①树林繁茂的, 多树木的. ②木本的, 木质的. ③木头般的. ④〔罕〕森林的. *~ parts of a plant* 植物的木质部分. *a ~ plant* 木本植物. ~ **night-**

shade 【植】白英.

woof[1] [wu:f] *n.* ①纬线 (*cf.* warp). ②织物. ③(织物的)组织,质地. ④基本元素;基本材料.

woof[2] [wu:f] *n.* ①(象狗等发出的) 低吠声. ②(扬声器等发出的)低音;低调. — *vi.* 发出低吠声[低调].

woof·er [ˈwufə] *n.* 低音扬声器. **~-and-tweeter** 高低音两用喇叭;〔喻〕忠实的发言人.

wool [wul] *n.* ①羊毛. ②绒线;毛织品; 呢绒; 呢衣. ③羊毛状物;棉花;绒毛,软毛. ④象绒毛似的卷发;〔谑〕头发. ⑤蒙蔽真象的事物. *carding [short]* ~ 粗梳毛, 短毛. *combing [long]* ~ 精梳毛,长毛. *glass* ~ 玻璃绒. *rock* ~ 石绒. ***all cry and no*** ~ = more cry than ~. ***all*** ~ 纯粹地. ***all ~ and a yard wide*** 〔美〕真正的;极好的;货真价实的. ***dyed in the*** ~ 生染的; 彻底的. ***go for ~ and come home shorn*** 偷鸡不着蚀把米. ***lose one's*** ~ 激动,生气,发脾气. ***more cry than ~ = much cry and little*** ~ 空叫嚷而不做实事; 为琐事大叫大嚷. ***pull the ~ over sb.'s eyes*** 蒙蔽某人,骗某人. **~-bear** 【虫】虎蛾(的幼虫),灯蛾. ~ **clip** 羊毛(年)产量. ~ **comber** 梳羊毛的人. ~ **fat [grease, oil]** 羊毛脂. **~fell** 羊毛皮. **~gathering** ① *n.* 采集(挂在草丛上的)羊毛;琐碎无聊的工作;出神;茫然空想. ② *a.* 出神的, 呆呆的 (*His wits have gone [run] ~ gathering.* 他在出神). **~-grower** (毛用羊) 牧羊业者. **~man** 羊毛商. **~pack** ①〔英〕(240磅重的) 羊毛捆. ②羊毛打包布. ③【气】卷毛云. **~sack** ①羊毛袋. ②〔英〕(衬有羊毛的) (上院)议长座位; 〔the ~〕上院议长[大法官]的职位 (*reach the ~sack* 任大法官 [上院议长]. *take seat on the ~-sack* 〔英〕举行上院会议). **~shed** 剪毛和打包工棚. **~sorters' disease** 【医】毛工病, 炭疽 (= anthrax). ~ **staple** 羊毛, 羊毛的品质[长度];羊毛市场. ~ **stapler** 分理羊毛的人; 羊毛商. **~work** 绒线刺绣.

wool·len, 〔美〕 **wool·en** [ˈwulin] *a.* 羊毛的,羊毛制的,毛织的;呢绒的. ~ *cloth* 呢绒. — *n.* 毛线,绒线;毛织品,呢绒;〔常 *pl.*〕 呢绒衣服.

Woolf [wulf] *n.* 伍尔夫〔姓氏〕.

Wool·ley [ˈwuli] *n.* 伍利〔姓氏〕.

wool·ly [ˈwuli] *a.* ***(-li·er; -li·est)*** ①羊毛的,羊毛制的;毛茸茸的;【植】生满绒毛的. ②朦胧的;【绘画】模糊的,不鲜明的; (声音)嘶哑的. ③〔美〕(象从前西部生活那样)粗野不文的. — *n.* 〔口〕①毛线衣; 〔特指〕运动上衣. ②〔*pl.*〕 羊毛内衣. ③〔美方,澳〕羊. *the ~ flock* 羊群. ~ **aphid** 【动】绵蚜. ~ **bear** 【动】灯蛾科昆虫的幼虫. **~-headed, ~-minded** *a.* 头脑不清楚的,思想混乱的,糊涂的. **-li·ness** *n.*

Wool·worth [ˈwulwə:θ] *n.* 伍尔沃斯〔姓氏〕.

Wool·worth's best [ˈwulwəθs best] *n.* 〔美俚〕 廉价零碎商品店的(售价低廉)货品.

wooly [ˈwuli] *a.* = woolly. **-i·ness** *n.*

woo·mer·a [ˈwu:mərə] *n.* = womera.

woops [wu:ps, wups] *vi., vt.* 〔口〕 呕吐,吐出;喷出.

woo·ra·li, woo·ra·ra [wu:ˈrɑ:li, -rə] *n.* = curare.

woosh [wuʃ] *vi., vt., n., int.* = whoosh.

wootz [wu:ts] *n.* (用印度古代原始方法锻制的)印度钢.

wooz·y [ˈwu:zi] *a.* 〔美俚〕头昏眼花的, 眩晕的; 糊里糊涂的;喝醉了的.

Wop [wɔp] *n.* 〔美俚〕〔贬〕(移住北美的) 意大利人,南[中]欧人.

Worces·ter [ˈwustə] *n.* ①伍斯特〔姓氏〕. ②伍斯特〔英国城市〕. ~ **china** 伍斯特磁器.

Worces·ter·shire [ˈwustəʃə] 伍斯特郡. ~ **sauce** (伍斯特郡)辣酱油.

Worcs. = Worcestershire.

word [wə:d] *n.* ①单词;〔*pl.*〕歌词,台词. ②〔常 *pl.*〕谈话,话,言语. ③〔不加冠词〕音信,消息,传言, 口信;【自】代码,字码. ④命令;口令,口号,暗号. ⑤〔*pl.*〕口角,争论. ⑥〔the W-〕【宗】道 (=Logos); 圣经 (=W- of God 或 God's W-). 福音,基督的教义. ⑦格言,标语. ⑧誓言;诺言. *notional [form] ~s* 实义[虚]词. *hard ~s* 难字;坏话,谩骂. *A truer ~ was never spoken.* 一字不差,字字为实. *fair ~s* 恭维话. *high [hot, sharp, warm] ~s* 争吵,争论. *a man of few ~s* 沉默寡言的人. *a man of his ~* 守信用的人. ***a ~ and a blow*** 一句话不对就动手打;急躁;说干就干. ***a ~ in sb.'s ear*** 秘密话, 耳语. ***a ~ in [out of] season*** 合[不合]时宜的话. ***a ~ to the wise*** 聪明的人一句话就够. ***A ~ with you.*** 想跟你讲一句话. ***as good as one's*** ~ 守信,履约,言行一致. ***at one [a]*** ~ 说了就, 马上, 立刻. ***be the ~ for it*** 是恰当的话[批评]. ***break one's*** ~ 失信;食言;失约,毁约. ***bring*** ~ 带话,通知,告知,告诉. ***by ~ of mouth*** 口头地. ***come to (high) ~s*** 声音大起来;争论起来. ***eat one's ~s*** 承认说错话;收回前言. ***give one's*** ~ 答应,约定,保证. ***give the*** ~ 说出口令. ***give the ~ to [for] ...*** 下令. ***go back on one's*** ~ 食言, 背弃诺言. ***hang on sb.'s ~s*** 专心听某人讲话, 倾听. ***have a ~ to say*** 有句话要说. ***have a ~ with*** 和…说一句话. ***have no ~s for it*** 这个难用言语形容,这没有恰当的话来表达. ***have ~s with*** 和…争论. ***in a few ~s = in a [one]*** ~ 一言以蔽之,要之,总而言之. ***in other ~s*** 换言之, 换句话说. ***in so many ~s*** 要言不繁地; 直截了当地. ***in ~ and deed*** 言行都…;真正. ***keep one's*** ~ 守约. ***leave*** ~ 留下话, 留下口信[字条]. ***my ~!*** 〔插入语〕 真是! 真没想到! ***my ~ upon it*** 的的确确. ***of many ~s*** 爱说话的,多嘴的. ***on the*** ~ 这样说着, 这样说完就, 立刻. ***pass one's ~*** = give one's ~. ***play upon ~s*** 玩弄字眼,说俏皮话. ***proceed from ~s to blows*** 由争论变成打架. ***put in a*** ~ 插嘴. ***say a good ~ for*** 为某人说好话,推举,推荐. ***send*** ~ 带口信, 带信, 传话 (*to*). ***suit the action to the*** ~ 说到做到. ***take sb. at sb.'s*** ~ 相信某人的话. ***take the ~s out of sb.'s mouth*** 抢先说出某人要说的话. ***take (up) the*** ~ (接着或代替某人)谈,论,讲;相信, 当做真. ***the last*** ~ 定论; 最新成就;最新型式[品种]. ***the last ~s*** 临终遗言. ***upon my*** ~ ①发誓,一定, 必定. ②=my ~. ***with the*** ~ = on the ~. ~ ***for*** ~ 逐词, 一字不变地. ~ ***of honour*** 以名誉担保的诺言 [声明]. ~ ***with the bark on it*** 〔美〕简单明了的话[说明];最后通牒. — *vt.* 用话表达,措辞,说. ~ ***it*** 〔罕〕争论. **~-blind** *a.* 【医】字盲症的, 失去阅读能力的. ~ **bomb** 纸弹 [空中撒下的传单]. **~book** 词汇集; 词典. **~-deaf** *a.* 【医】语聋症的,失去听懂言语能力的. **~-for-~** *a.* 逐字的; 一字不改的. **~-of-mouth** *a.* 口头表达的, 口传的. ~ **order** 【语言】词序. ~ **painting** 栩栩如生的描述. **~-perfect** *a.* 一字不错地熟记的;(演员)台词记得完全的. ~ **picture** 生动的文章[叙述]. **~play** 字句的争论; 巧妙的对话;双关话, 俏皮话. **~-sign** 文字记号. **~-smith** 〔美〕耍笔杆的人,作家. ~ **splitting** 过分烦琐地区分词义. **~-square** 缀词方阵[纵横都能拼成单词,见下图].

H E A R T
E M B E R
A B U S E
R E S I N
T R E N D

-less *a.* 无言的,沉默的.

word·age [ˈwə:didʒ] *n.* ①措词,用字. ②〔美〕〔集合词〕词汇(量);(书等的)字数. ③啰嗦,冗长. *This writer has the fault at excess ~.* 这个作家有过分啰嗦的缺点.

word·ing [wə:diŋ] *n.* 措词,用字.

Words·worth [ˈwə:dzwə(:)θ] *n.* ①沃兹沃斯〔姓氏〕. ② **William** ~ 威廉·沃兹沃斯〔1770—1850,英国诗人〕.

word·y [ˈwə:di] *a.* ***(-i·er; -i·est)*** ①(用) 言语的,口头

的. ②话多的,啰嗦的. ~ *warfare* 争论;舌战;笔战,笔墨官司. *a* ~ *conflict* 吵嘴. *a* ~ *speaker* 说话啰嗦的人. **-i•ly** *ad.* **-i•ness** *n.*

wore [wɔː, wɔə] wear 的过去式.

work [wəːk] *n.* ①工作,操作,劳动,作业;工件;功课;努力;行为,作用. ②(待办的)事务,业务;职业. ③〔前有形容词〕行为,事业,做法,手腕. ④针线活,缝补,刺绣;工序,加工制造;工艺品,制造品,制件,产品. ⑤著作;(艺术)作品;〔*pl.*〕著作集. ⑥〔俚、谑〕内脏. ⑦〔常 *pl.*〕土木工程;【军】〔常 *pl.*〕(防御)工事. ⑧〔*pl.*,常作单数用〕工厂. ⑨〔*pl.*〕机器,机构. ⑩【物、机】功. ⑪【宗】德行,功德. *All* ~ *and no play makes Jack a dull boy.* 整天工作不玩耍,孩子变成大呆瓜. *W- is struggle.* 工作就是斗争. *a man of all* ~ 多面手. *the* ~ *of poison* 毒的作用. *mighty* ~*s* 奇迹. *a great* ~ 伟业;杰作. *good* ~ 好事. *It was sharp* ~. 手腕精明. *a frame* ~ 框架,框;地板,面板,底板. *Selected Works of Mao Tsetung*《毛泽东选集》. *the Ministry of Works*〔英〕建筑工程部. *advance* ~*(s)* 前哨工事. *hot* ~ 热加工. *(a) glass* ~*s* 玻璃厂. *the* ~*s of a watch* 表的机构. *effective* ~【物】有效功. *idle* ~【物】虚功. *a* ~ *distance*【物】运用距离;工作距离. ~ *of art* 艺术品,工艺美术品. ***a nasty piece of*** ~〔俚〕讨厌的家伙,下流东西;下流〔卑鄙〕行为. ***all in the day's*** ~ 日常的事情,不稀奇. ***at*** ~在做活,在工作;起着作用;运转中. ***be in regular*** ~ 有固定的职业. ***do its*** ~ 有效,起作用. ***get the*** ~***s***〔美俚〕遭虐待,吃苦头;被判死刑,被杀. ***give (sb.) the*** ~***s***〔美俚〕宣判某人死刑,杀死;痛打;虐待;给某人吃苦头. ***have one's*** ~ ***cut out for one*** 有排定的繁忙工作. ***in*** ~ 有工作,有职业;(某事)正在进行中. ***look for*** ~ 找事,找职业. ***make light*** ~ ***with [of]*** 轻而易举地做[打发掉]. ***make sad*** ~ ***of it*** 做坏,弄得一团糟. ***make short*** ~ ***of*** 很快地完成,很快地处理;杀死. ***make*** ~ ①使混乱,搅乱,大闹. ②派工作;做(…的)工作. ***out of*** ~ 失业;(机器等)有毛病. ***set to*** ~ ① *vt.* 使开始工作,指派工作. ② *vi.* 开始工作. ***to each according to his*** ~ 按劳分配. ***upper*** ~***s***【海】干舷〔船身水上部分〕. — *vi.* ***(worked,*** 〔古〕 ***wrought*** [rɔːt]***)*** ①做活,工作*(at, in)*. ②做…活*(in)*;做针线活;绣花. ③(器官、机器等)工作,运转;(车轮等)旋转*(on)*. ④进行顺利,成功;有效,作用. ⑤进行,穿过,通过,行动*(in; into; past; through)*. ⑥发酵;发芽. ⑦经营,做工,做事,有职业. ⑧(心、脸等)跳动,抽动;(浪)激荡;(船因风浪)航行困难;(机器)运转不顺畅. *We must* ~ *hard.* 我们一定要发奋图强. *It would not have* ~*ed in practice.* 那在事实上是不行的. *The wind has* ~*ed round.* 风向变了. — *vt.* ①使工作;使用(牛马等). ②使用(打字机等);驾驶(船、车等). ③经营(事业、农场等). ④开采(矿藏等). ⑤拟订,研究,执行(计划等). ⑥计算;解决(问题). ⑦〔过去式和过去分词常用 wrought〕研制,制造;加工;做好,完成. ⑧〔过去式和过去分词常用 wrought〕使发生,引起(变化、影响等);打动,诱使;激发. ⑨费力地通过;努力得到. ⑩缝上;绣. ⑪炼(铁);揉(面). ⑫〔俚〕利用;处理;除去. ⑬使发酵;使发芽. ⑭〔美口〕骗,瞒;毒打,殴打. ⑮耕耘(土地). ~ *a stream* 在河里打鱼. *a vase cunningly wrought* 做得很精致的花瓶. *Can you* ~ *buttonholes?* 你能锁钮扣眼吗? ~ *a mine* 开采矿山. ~ *the soil* 耕耘土地. ***won't*** ~ 不行 (*To try to convince them by force simply won't* ~. 以力服人是不行的). ~ ***against a cause*** 反对某一事业. ~ ***against time*** 拼命赶时间(以便如期完成). ~ ***at*** 从事;在…方面用功,用功读. ~ ***away*** 继续工作,不断地工作. ~ ***double tides*** 昼夜苦干,拼命努力. ~ ***for*** 为(人)工作,被…雇用着;为(主义等)尽力;参加. ~ ***hand in glove with*** 与…狼狈为奸. ~ ***in*** 插入;加入;镂;突入;合;混和;调和. ~ ***it***〔俚〕做好,弄好;完成. ~ ***its way into [out]*** 钻进[出]. ~ ***loose*** 松弛. ~ ***off*** ① *vt.* 慢慢除去;卖出;解掉(毒、闷气等);做完;发泄;制造;改进;印,印刷;塞给(假钱等);〔口〕杀死,勒死. ② *vi.* 脱出,溜出;肠等排泄;(毒)解掉. ~ ***on*** ①= ~ away. ②对…有效[有作用];动(人、感情等);发动,向…做工作;左右;使兴奋. ~ ***one's passage*** 在船中作工代付船费. ~ ***one's way*** 一面做事一面旅行;勤苦读完(大学);设法通过 (~ *one's way through a crowd* 挤过人丛). ~ ***one's will upon*** 随意处理[操纵]. ~ ***oneself into a lather***〔美运〕兴奋;忿怒. ~ ***oneself into favour with*** 巴结. ~ ***out*** ① *vt.* 努力做好,刻苦完成;详细拟定(计划等);算出(总数);解,解决(问题等);掘尽,采完(矿山等);做工偿还(债务);〔美〕做工抵补. ② *vi.* 算出,合计是,结果是 *(at)*. ~ ***over*** ①重新做,改作. ②仔细检查,认真研究. ③〔口〕粗暴对待,痛打,殴打. ~ ***up*** ①渐渐做成,刻苦完成. ②刺激,使兴奋;煽动,激起. ③展开(故事的情节). ④混合,捏合,揉合. ~ ***with*** 打动,发动,感动. ~**bag** 针线袋. ~**basket** 缝纫工具筐. ~**bench**【机】工作台. ~**book** (学生用的)作业课本;工作手册;工程手册;实验手册;(机器等)说明书,操作手册. ~**box** 工具箱;缝具箱,针线箱. ~ **camp** ①犯人劳动所. ②志愿劳动营〔如为宗教团体而开设者〕. ~ **council**〔英〕劳资协议会. ~**day** *n.* 工作日;平日 *(opp.* holiday*)* (〔美〕= working day). ~ **ethic** 工作道德. ~**fare** 劳动福利计划〔要求接受福利的待业者参加公益服务或技工训练的一种政府救济计划〕. ~ **farm** 罪犯农场,劳动教养农场. ~**-folk(s)**〔集合词〕〔现罕〕劳动人民,劳动者〔尤指农业劳动者〕. ~ **force**【经】(一个国家、地区或工厂等的)劳动力,劳动大军. ~ **function**【理】功函数. ~**-horse** ①耕马;驮马. ②踏实地干重活的人. ③结实耐用的机器〔车辆等〕. ~ **house** 救贫院,贫民习艺所;〔美〕感化院,劳动教养院. ~**-in** 到职罢工;到校罢课〔照常上班或上课,但不按正常规章或秩序工作或学习〕. ~ **load** 工作负荷(量),劳动负荷(量)〔在一定时间内分配[指定]完成的工作量或劳动量〕. ~**mate** 工作伙伴,同事. ~**-out** 体育锻练;紧张的锻练,紧张的工作;【运】选拔赛;测试,试验. ~**-out** *a.*【经】疲软的(市场). ~ **people**〔*pl.*〕〔主英〕工人们,劳工们〔尤指产业工人〕. ~**piece** 工作件. ~**place** 工作场所;车间;工厂. ~**room** 工作室;工场间. ~ **sheet** ①(工厂的)工作单,工票,记工单. ②(学生的)作业单. ③操作单〔注明注意事项、初步方案等〕. ~**s council**〔英〕(资方组织的)劳资协议会. ~**-shop** ①工场;作坊;车间. ②(学术专题)讨论会. ③(写作等的)实习班;实验班. ④(文艺)创作室;创作法. ~**-shy** ①*a.* 厌恶工作的,逃避劳动的. ②*n.* 懒汉. ~ **song** 劳动号子. ~**table** 工作台;(附有抽屉的)裁缝台. ~**-to-rule** *n.*〔英〕按章怠工〔上班按章工作但故意怠慢时间的一种怠工方式〕. ~**-up** ①【印】(印刷物表面的)印痕,污迹. ②病情的检查. ~**week** 工作周,一周的总工时. **-less** *a.* 没有工作的(*the workless*〔集合词〕失业者).

work•a•ble [ˈwəːkəbl] *a.* 可应用的;可开动的,可运转的;可采掘的;可实行的;可加工的;可耕种的. **-a•bly** *ad.*

work•a•day [ˈwəːkədei] *a.* ①工作日的,平常日子的. ②普通的;平凡的. ③枯燥无味的,使人厌倦的. *in this* ~ *world* 在这个平凡庸碌的世界里.

work•a•hol•ic [ˌwəːkəˈhɔlik] *n.*〔口〕(为免遭辞退)废寝忘食工作的人. **-hol•ism** *n.* (为免遭辞退而)废寝忘食工作.

work•er [ˈwəːkə] *n.* ①工作者;工人,劳动者,职工,工作人员;技工. ②【虫】工蜂(= ~-bee);工蚁(= ~-ant). ③【印】电铸版. *a brain* ~ 脑力劳动者. *farm* ~ 雇农,农业工人. *a shock* ~ 突击手. ***lay up*** ~***s*** 窝工.

work•ing [ˈwəːkiŋ] *a.* ①工作的,从事劳动的. ②操作的,作业的. ③工人的. ④(用于)实际工作的,任事的;使用(中)的,运转(中)的;经营的,营业的,流动的. ⑤完成的,(可)实行的;有效的. ~ *hours* 工作时间. ~ *expenses* 经营费用. ~ *cost* 生产费. — *n.* ①作用;劳动;

工作;作业;操作;加工;维护;运转,驾驶;(数学的)运算,计算。②〔常 *pl.*〕(矿山、采石场等的)作业现场;发酵作用. *cool* ~ 冷却. *old* ~*s*【矿】废井. ~ **capital** 流动资本. ~ **class** 工人阶级. ~ **clothes** 工作服. ~ **day** 工作日;(一天的)工作时间. ~**-day** *a.* = workaday. ~ **drawing** 图纸,施工图纸. ~ **mean** 假定平均数. ~ **mile** (铁路等的)营业里数. ~ **order** (机器等)正常运转状态,良好状态. ~**-out** 工程计划;计算;【乐】展开. ~ **paper**【会计】核算工作底稿. ~ **papers** (未成年人或外籍工人) 雇用证书. ~ **partner** 劳力股股东. ~ **people** 劳动人民. ~ **plan** 作业计划. ~ **stress**【物】资用应力,工作应力;【林】安全应力. ~ **substance** (开动发动机活塞等所需的)资用物质,工质〔如各种气体,液体〕. ~ **title** 〔美〕(影片摄制时)暂定名称.

work·man [ˈwəːkmən] *n.* ***(pl. -men)*** 工人,劳动者;工作者,工作人员. *a good [skilled]* ~ 优良工人,熟练工人. *a master* ~ 名工;〔美〕工会会长. *a* ~*'s train* (清早开行票价特低的)工人专车. ~**like** *a.* 象职工的;精巧的,有本领的. ~**'s compensation** (对工伤,职业病的)劳动补偿金. **-ship** 手艺,技巧,本领,本事;(制造的)巧拙;作品,制品,制件.

work·woman [ˈwəːkˌwumən] *n.* ***(pl. -wo·men)*** 女工;(女性的)工作者;女裁缝.

world [wəːld] *n.* ①世界;地球. ②万物;天地,宇宙;天体. ③全世界的人,人类. ④世间,世上,现世. ⑤世事,人事. ⑥世态,世故,世俗. ⑦世人. ⑧上层社会,社交界(的人们). ⑨…界,…社会. ⑩广大;大量 *(of)*. *the third* ~ *[the Third W-]* 第三世界. *How goes the* ~ *with you?* = *How is the* ~ *using you?* 近来怎么样?近来好吗? *All's right with the* ~. 天下太平. *a universe of* ~*s* 全宇宙. *the great* ~ = *the fashionable* ~ (旧社会中的)上流社会. *the literary* ~ = *the* ~ *of letters* 文学界. *the scientific* ~ 科学界. *the vegetable [animal]* ~ 植物[动物]界. ***a man [woman] of the*** ~ 饱经世故的人[女人]. ***a*** ~ ***of*** 许许多多的,无数的 (*a* ~ *of troubles* 无数的麻烦. *a* ~ *of faults* 无数的缺点). ***a*** ~ ***too (many [much])*** 太多,过多. ***against the*** ~ 和全世界作对,抗拒时势. ***all the*** ~ 全世界,举世;世界上的一切(财富);最重要的东西. ***all the*** ~ ***and his wife*** 〔谑〕无论谁都,所有的人都. ***all the*** ~ ***over*** = ***all over the*** ~ 在全世界,世界到处. ***as long as the [this]*** ~ ***lasts*** 永远,永久. ***as the*** ~ ***goes*** 照一般的人讲. ***be a*** ~ ***too wide*** 太广大. ***be all the*** ~ ***to sb.*** 对于某人说来的最重要的事;无价之宝. ***begin the*** ~ 开始在社会上立身〔谋生〕. ***begin the*** ~ ***anew*** 重新做人. ***bring into the*** ~ 生孩子;产生. ***come into [to] the*** ~ 出世,出生;出版. ***depart out of this*** ~ 死去. ***end of the*** ~ 世界末日. ***for (all) the*** ~ 无论怎样看〔怎样说〕都,完全(*for all the* ~ *like [as if] a monkey* 活象猴子一样). ***give*** ~***s [the*** ~***] to (do)*** 愿出任何代价(去做某事),渴求(做某事). ***go out into the*** ~ = begin the ~. ***go out of this*** ~, ***go to the better*** ~ 死. ***have the*** ~ ***against one*** 四面楚歌,举世与之为敌. ***have the*** ~ ***before one*** 有(远大)前途. ***in the*** ~ ①在世界上. ②〔加强 *what, who, how* 等的意义〕究竟(*What in the* ~ *was it?* 这究竟是什么?). ***know the*** ~ 通达世事. ***make a noise in the*** ~ 见 noise 条. ***not for the*** ~ = ***not for anything in the*** ~ 决不,绝对不. ***nothing in the*** ~ 什么也没有. ***on the top of the*** ~ 〔美俚〕顶好,最好;得意扬扬. ***out of this [the]*** ~ 〔美俚〕特别好的,举世无双的. ***see the*** ~ 懂世故. ***set the*** ~ ***on fire*** 作惊人举动,哄动一时. ***take the*** ~ ***as it is [as one finds it]*** 随遇而安;顺应时势. ***the lower [nether]*** ~ 地狱. ***the other*** ~ = ***the next*** ~ = ***the*** ~ ***to come [to be]*** 阴间;来世. ***the*** ~***, the flesh, and the devil*** 种种诱惑〔名利、肉欲、邪念〕. ***to the*** ~ 〔俚〕完全;极度(*I am tired to the* ~. 我累透了). ***to the*** ~***'s end*** 到天涯海角,永远. ~ ***without end*** 永远,永久. **World Bank** 世界银行〔联合国的一个机构,正式名称为 International Bank for Reconstruction and Development (国际复兴开发银行)〕. **W- Banker** 世界银行总裁. ~**beater** 〔口〕超众非凡的人(或物),出类拔萃的人物. ~**-class** *a.* 国际水平的. **World Council of Churches** 基督教世界会议. **World Court** 国际法庭〔全名为 Permanent Court of International Justice 前国际联盟为了处理国家间争端而建立〕. ~**-famous** *a.* 世界闻名的. ~**-issue** *n.* 世界问题;世界性的大纠纷. ~ **line**【物】世界线〔基本粒子在时空上经过的路线〕. ~**-old** *a.* 极其古老的. ~ **outlook** 世界观. ~**-power** 世界强国. ~**-shaking** *a.* 震撼世界的. **World Series** 〔也作 w- s-〕(美国两大棒球协会中胜队之间的)年度冠军棒球联赛. **W- War I** 第一次世界大战,欧(洲大)战(1914—1918). **W- War II** 第二次世界大战 (1939—1945). ~**-weary** *a.* 厌世的. ~**-wide** *a.* 全世界(范围)的;(名声等)传遍世界的,世界性的. **-ling** (追逐名利的)俗人;凡人.

world·ly [ˈwəːldli] *a.* ***(-li·er; -li·est)*** ①世间的,世上的. ②世俗的. ③追逐名利的,鄙俗的. *He is of the world* ~. 他是俗人中的俗人. ~ *affairs* 俗事. ~ *goods* 财物,财产. ~ *wisdom* 处世的才能;世故. ~**-minded** *a.* 世俗的,一心追逐名利的. ~**-wise** *a.* 精明老练的,精通世故的. **-li·ness** *n.* 名利心;烦恼.

worm [wəːm] *n.* ①蠕虫;虫,蛆;〔*pl.*〕(小孩等的)肠虫,寄生虫病. ②虫一般的人,小人物. ③(内心的)痛苦,苦恼. ④【机】螺线;螺丝杆,蜗杆,无限螺旋;(蒸馏器的)螺旋管. *A* ~ *[Even a* ~*] will turn.* 虫也会反抗(何况于人). *I am a* ~ *today.* 我今天不舒服〔没有精神〕. *the* ~ *of conscience* 良心的谴责;折磨人的内疚. — *vi.* 虫一般地爬,爬似地慢慢前进 *(through; into; out of)*. — *vt.* ①使(虫一般)慢慢向前;慢慢地爬过. ②〔喻〕慢慢巴结〔钻营〕*(oneself into)*. ③慢慢探听出,骗出(秘密等). ④驱除肠虫;驱除(花坛等的)害虫. ~ ***oneself [one's way]*** 慢慢前进,慢慢进行. ~ ***(a secret) out of (sb.)*** 从(某人处)骗出一项秘密. ~ **cast** 蚯蚓粪. ~**-eaten** *a.* 虫蚀的,虫蛀的,蛀孔多的;陈旧的,过时的,落伍的. ~ **fence** 〔美〕曲折栅栏. ~ **fishing** 用蚯蚓钓鱼,虫饵钓. ~ **gear**【机】蜗轮. ~ **gearing**【机】蜗轮传动装置. ~**hole** (树木等的)虫孔,蛀洞. ~ **lizard**【动】蚓蜥科动物. ~ **snake**【动】盲蛇科或蠕蛇科动物. ~ **tablet** 驱虫药. ~ **wheel** = worm-gear.

worm·seed [ˈwəːmsiːd] *n.*【植】美洲(驱虫)土荆芥,山道年. ~ **goosefoot**【植】土荆芥.

worm·wood [ˈwəːmwud] *n.* ①【植】蒿(属);苦艾;茵蔯. ②苦恼(的原因),奇耻大辱.

worm·y [ˈwəːmi] *a.* ***(-i·er; -i·est)*** ①虫蛀的;虫多的. ②虫似的;卑劣的. **-i·ness** *n.*

worn [wɔːn] wear 的过去分词. — *a.* ①用旧了的,磨破了的. ②陈腐的. ③形容憔悴的;筋疲力尽的.

worn-out [wɔːn-ˈaut] *a.* ①磨损了的,用坏了的,穿旧了的. ②筋疲力尽的,衰弱的. ③陈腐的. *a* ~ *age* 风烛残年. ~ *tune* 陈词滥调.

wor·ried [ˈwʌrid] *a.* 困恼的,为难的.

wor·ri·er [ˈwʌriə] *n.* ①使人烦恼的人[事物],折磨者. ②自找烦恼的人.

wor·ri·less [ˈwʌrilis] *a.* 没有苦恼的,无忧无虑的.

wor·ri·ment [ˈwʌrimənt] *n.*〔主美口〕苦恼,烦闷,烦恼,忧虑.

wor·ri·some [ˈwʌrisəm] *a.* ①困难的,麻烦的;使人烦恼的. ②易于烦恼的. **-ly** *ad.*

wor·rit [ˈwʌrit] *v., n.*〔英方〕= worry.

wor·ry [ˈwʌri] *vt.* ①(狗等)咬着(鼠、羊等)折磨;把…衔在口里摇;反复触动. ②使烦恼,使苦恼,使为难,使窘困;使担心,使忧虑,使着急. — *vi.* 焦虑,忧虑,操心,烦恼,发愁 *(about)*. *I should* ~ 〔美口〕我才不在乎;那倒很好．***be much worried*** 非常着急（担心）．***~ about personal gain*** 计较个人得失．***~ along [through]*** 在艰难困苦中凑合着过下去．***~ down*** 〔谑〕好容易吞下去；〔美〕急忙喝下一杯(酒)．***~ oneself*** 着急，担心，发愁．***~ (a problem) out*** 绞尽脑汁解决掉(问题)．— *n.* ①猎狗咬住[折磨]猎获物．②苦恼，愁闷，操心．③〔常 *pl.*〕苦恼[困苦]的根源；麻烦．**~ beads** 解忧珠〔供松弛神经或娱乐用的手数串线小珠，原流行于中东国家〕．**~wart** 〔美口〕终日因微末小事而烦恼的人．

wor·ry·ing [ˈwʌriiŋ] *a.* 烦闷的，发愁的，着急的；麻烦的，令人烦恼的．*I had a ~ time.* 我发愁极了．**-ly** *ad.*

worse [wəːs] *a.* 〔bad, ill 的比较级〕(*opp.* better) 更坏，还要坏；病情(更重)．*He is ~ today.* 他今天病况更坏了．*a change for the ~* 变坏，趋向坏的方面的变化．*grow rapidly ~* 越来越坏．*He is none the ~ for it.* 虽然这样他倒一点也不在乎[没有什么]．***(and) what is ~ = ~ than all = to make the matter ~*** 更坏的是．***be the ~ for drink*** 喝醉．***be the ~ for wear*** (衣服)穿旧，破旧．***be ~ off*** 经济情况更不好，更拮据．***be ~ than one's word*** 不守约．***one's ~ half*** 〔谑〕丈夫[妻子叫 *better half*]．— *ad.* 〔badly, ill 的比较级〕更坏，较坏，还要坏；更厉害，更猛烈．*behave ~ than ever* 行为日愈恶劣．***go farther and fare ~*** 每下愈况．***none the ~*** 并不更差；还是，仍旧 (*I like him none the ~ for being outspoken.* 他说话虽然不客气但我仍然喜欢他)．***think none the ~ of*** 还是尊重，仍然尊敬．— *n.* 更坏的事情[情况]；〔the ~〕更坏的方面，损失，失败，不利．*There is ~ to tell.* 还有更坏的事情．***do ~*** 做更坏[更荒唐]的事情．***for better (or) for ~*** 祸福与共；不论变好变坏．***for the ~*** 向坏的方面，更坏，恶化．***go from bad to ~*** 越发变坏，越发恶化，变本加厉．***have the ~*** 失败，输．***put (sb.) to the ~*** 打败，击败．***turn for the ~*** 恶化．

wors·en [ˈwəːsn] *vt.* 使更坏；损坏．— *vi.* 变得更坏，恶化．

wors·er [ˈwəːsə] *a., ad.* 〔口、方〕= worse.

wor·ship [ˈwəːʃip] *n.* ①【宗】礼拜；礼拜仪式．②崇拜，敬仰，仰慕．③〔古〕名誉，尊严，威严．④〔英〕〔前接所有格人称代词〕阁下〔有时是反语〕．*a house of ~* 礼拜堂．*a man of ~* 有身份的人．*Your [His] W-* 阁下 (*His W- the Mayor of ....* …市长阁下)．— *vt.* 〔英〕***(-pp-)*** ①【宗】礼拜，参拜．②崇拜，敬仰，仰慕；敬爱，恋慕(女人等)．— *vi.* 做礼拜．〔英〕**-per** 〔美〕**-er.** 礼拜[崇拜、爱慕]者．

wor·ship·ful [ˈwəːʃipful] *a.* ①可贵的，可尊敬的〔用于对治安法官等的称呼〕．②有价值的．③虔敬的．*the Most [Right] ~* 阁下．**-ly** *ad.*

worst [wəːst] *a.* 〔bad, ill 的最高级〕(*opp.* best) 最坏的，最恶劣的；最厉害的，最猛烈的．— *n.* 最坏的事情[人、东西]，最坏的情形．*The ~ has happened.* 最坏的情形发生了．*be prepared for the ~* 准备万一〔最坏的可能出现〕．***at (the) ~*** ①无论怎样坏．②= at one's ~．***at one's ~*** 在…情况最坏的时候．***do one's ~*** 拼命瞎干，蛮干 (*Do your ~.* 〔挑战语〕你尽管瞎干好啦)．***get [have] the ~ of it*** 大败．***If [When] the ~ comes to the ~*** 万一发生最坏的情况．***make the ~ of it*** ①极端夸大地说．②作最坏的想法[考虑]．***put (sb.) to the ~*** 打败[击败]某人．***The ~ of it is that*** …最坏的是，最糟的是．— *ad.* 〔badly, ill 的最高级〕最坏，极坏；〔俗〕极度．— *vt.* 击败，打败；赶过，驾凌．*be [get] ~ed* 〔古〕被打败，被击败．

wor·sted [ˈwustid] *n.* 精纺绒[毛]线．— *a.* 绒线做的．*~ socks* 绒线袜子．

wort [wəːt] *n.* (作为啤酒原料，发酵前的)麦芽汁．

wort [wəːt] *comb.f.* 用来构成某些植物名称，特别是草本植物，如：spleen*wort*.

worth[1] [wəːθ] *a.* 〔用作表语〕①有…的价值，值…．②值得…．③有…的财产．*It is not ~ a penny.* 不值一文．*It is as much as my place is ~ to let you see it.* 给你看了，我的地位就保不住啦．*Whatever is ~ doing at all is ~ doing well.* 凡是值得做的事情都值得好好地做．*It's ~ hearing [seeing].* 这值得听[看]．*It's ~ nothing.* 这毫无价值．*He is ~ a million.* 他是个百万富翁．***be little ~*** 〔诗〕= ***be ~ little*** 几乎没有价值．***for all one is ~*** 〔俚〕拼命，尽力，用全力．***for what it is ~*** (真伪未明但)不妨暂时这样(说[听、看]) (*take the story for what it is ~* 姑妄听之)．***not ~ a damn [fig, pin 等]*** 毫无意思[价值]．***not ~ one's salt*** 值不了那么多的薪水，没用，无能．***~ it*** = ~ while. ***~ (sb.'s) while*** 有…的价值，值得；有益，见 *while* 条．— *n.* ①价值；真价．②值(多少钱的东西)．*of great ~* 非常有价值的，很好的．*of little ~* 价值少的，不足道的．*Give me a dolllar's ~ of this sugar.* 给我一块钱的这种糖．

worth[2] [wəːθ] *vt.* 〔古〕= befall. *Woe ~ the day!* 今天真是个坏日子！

worth·less [ˈwəːθlis] *a.* 没有价值的，不足取的，不足道的．

worth·while [ˈwəːθˈhwail] *a.* 值得出力的，值得做的；很好的．

wor·thy [ˈwəːði] *a.* ***(-thi·er; -thi·est)*** ①有价值的，可尊敬的，很好的，有道德的．②〔口〕〔仅用作表语〕值得…的，足以…的，该…的．*a ~ man* 高尚的人．*a man ~ of praise [~ to be praised]* 值得称赞的人．*His enthusiasm is ~ of a better cause.* 象他那样的热情用在那种事情上太可惜了．*a poet ~ of the name* 名副其实的诗人．*in words ~ of the occasion* 正合时宜的话．★现在很少在 worthy 后不用 of 的：He is not ~ (of) my steel. 与他作敌有辱我刀．— *n.* ①(一国、一个时代等的)名人，杰出人物．②〔谑〕大人物；人．*Who is the ~ over there?* 那边是哪一位？**-thi·ly** *ad.* **-thi·ness** *n.*

-worthy *comb.f.* ①应…的，值得…的：blame*worthy*．②【空、海】耐…的，适于…的：air*worthy*, sea*worthy*.

wot[1] [wɔt] wit 的第一人称或第三人称单数现在式．

wot[2] [wɔt] *a.* 〔美俚〕= what. *W- a life!* 这种生活！

would [强 wud; 弱 wəd, əd] *auxil. v.* will 的过去式．①〔在间接叙述法中表示单纯未来或意志未来〕会，打算．*He said he ~ succeed.* 他说他会成功．*I determined that I ~ go to sea.* 我决心去做海员．②〔在以 if 开头的条件句中表现某种假设的意志〕只要有…的意志；愿意．*I could do so, if I ~.* 我要是想做，我是做得到的（但不想做）．③〔条件句，在主句中用法如 will〕(如果…)是愿意…的，是会…的．*I ~ do so, if I could.* 我要是能做，我是要做的(但不能做)．*If I were you, I ~ never do it.* 我要是你，我是决不做的．*One ~ have thought that.* 谁都会那样想的．④〔表示推测〕大概，或许，似乎．*That plan ~ be carried out in 1987.* 该项计划可能在 1987 年实现．⑤〔过去的习惯〕常，有…的习惯．*He ~ often call on me.* 他常来看我．⑥〔表示一般的意志〕乐意于，肯，愿意．*He ~ eat nothing.* 他不肯吃东西．*I ~ fain do…* 我很高兴…．*I ~ rather [sooner] not do it.* 这个我还是宁愿不做[我不想做]．⑦〔表示请求或个人的想法、看法等，语气婉转〕．*W- you mind showing me the way?* 请你带带路好吗？*I ~ like to speak a few words.* 我想讲几句话．*It ~ seem that ...* 看来…．⑧〔祈使句，表示假想的愿望〕但愿…就好了．*W- that ... = W- to God that...* 希望，愿…．*W- that I were young again.* 要是能再年轻一次多好．***~ rather [sooner]*** 宁愿，宁可…也不…(*~ rather die than surrender* 宁死不降)．

would-be [ˈwudbiː] *a.* 自称的，冒充的，所谓；想…的．*a ~ poet* 自命的诗人．*a ~ suicide* 未遂的自杀．— *n.* 想要成为某种人物的人．

wouldn't [ˈwudnt] = would not. *I ~ know* 〔美俚〕= I don't know.

wouldst [wudst] 〔古、诗〕will[1] 的第二人称单数过去时

(= wouldest.)
wound[1] [wu:nd] *n.* 伤,负伤,创伤;损害,损伤;屈辱;苦痛;〔诗〕恋爱的苦痛. *a mortal* ~ 致命伤. *an open* ~ 有伤口的伤;显露的耻辱. *a severe [slight]* ~ 重[轻]伤. *receive a* ~ 受伤. — *vt.* 伤,伤害(人、感情等). *the* ~*ed* 受伤的(人),伤员. ~ *sb.'s pride* 损伤某人的自尊心. — *vi.* 打伤;伤害. *willing to* ~ 怀有恶意的.
wound[2] [waund] wind[2,3] 的过去式及过去分词.
wove [wəuv] weave 的过去式. ~ **paper** 网目纸.
wov·en [ˈwəuvən] weave 的过去分词.
wow[1] [wau] *int.* 哎唷!〔表示惊叹、快乐、痛苦等〕. — *n.* 〔美俚〕(戏剧等的)大成功. — *vt.* 〔美俚〕使大为赞赏,使惊叹,使佩服,使产生热烈反应. ~ *'em* 大受赞赏;大败对方.
wow[2] [wau] *n.* 在复制录音时因速度变化引起的失真;录声和放声中的颤动而生的频率偏差.
WOWS = Women Ordnance Workers 妇女军械服务队.
wow·ser [ˈwauzə] *n.* 〔主澳俚〕老古板(太拘谨、苛刻的人,拘泥于清教规则的人);虔诚的清教徒.
WP = withdrawn passing 及格退学〔教师评定的学生成绩等级,该生以及格成绩退出某课程〕.
WPA = ①with particular average 单独海损赔偿,担保单独海损,水渍险. ②Works Progress Administration 〔美〕公共事业振兴署.
WPB=①waste paper basket 字纸篓. ②War Production Board 〔美旧〕军工生产委员会.
WPC = World Peace Council 世界和平理事会.
WPD = War Plans Division 〔美旧〕作战计划处.
W.R. = ①West Riding 西赖丁〔英国约克郡的一个行政区〕. ②war reserve (police) 战时(警察)后备队.
W.R.A.C. = Women's Royal Army Corps 〔英〕皇家陆军妇女队.
wrack[1] [ræk] *n.* ①波浪打到岸上的海草;漂来的东西. ②失事船,失事船的残骸[剩余物]. ③箱板材. ④〔古〕毁灭,破坏,灭亡. ⑤〔方〕杂草. *go to* ~ *and ruin* 毁灭,灭亡. — *vt.,vi.* 摧毁,毁坏;(使)破灭.
wrack[2] [ræk] *n.* 一片飞云;水气,雾气(= rack).
W.R.A.F. = Women's Royal Air Force 〔英〕皇家空军妇女队.
wraith [reiθ] *n.* ①(迷信传说的)阴魂;鬼魂;鬼. ②幻影. ③一股稀薄的烟雾.
wran·gle [ˈræŋgl] *n.* 口角,争吵,拌嘴;争论. — *vi.* 争吵. — *vt.* ①通过争辩使某人… *(into; out of)*. ②〔美西部〕放牧,看守(马群).
wran·gler [ˈræŋglə] *n.* ①争吵者. ②〔英古〕(Cambridge 大学)数学学位甲等及格者. ③〔美西部〕牧童,牧人〔尤指牧放乘用马的工人〕.
wrap [ræp] *vt.* ***(wrapped, wrapt*** [ræpt], ***wrap·ping)*** ①卷,缠(绕),包裹. ②隐蔽(意义、真理等) *(up)*. ③折叠. *The mountain is wrapped in mist.* 山隐在雾里. ~ *up the meaning in an allegory* 把意义隐含在一个譬喻里. —*vi.* ①缠绕;互叠. ②穿起来 *(up)*. ③包起来 *(up)*. *Mind you* ~ *up well if you go out.* 出门时注意穿好衣服(不要受凉). ~*ping machine* 包装机. ~*ping paper* 包装纸. ***be wrapped up in*** 包在…里,被…掩蔽;埋头在;和…发生密切关联[牵连在一起]. ~ ***over*** 叠起. — *n.* 〔常 *pl.*〕①膝毯;披肩;围巾,围脖;头巾;罩衫;外套,大衣. ②包装纸. ③〔*pl.*〕〔俚〕机密. *a new weapon under* ~*s* 一种秘密的新武器. ~**around** *a.* 包着的,围着的;包括一切的. ~**-up** ① *a.* 包装东西的;结论性的,总结性的. ② *n.* 〔美口〕结局;结论,总结说明;〔美俚〕爽快的销售;爽快的买主.
wrap·page [ˈræpidʒ] *n.* 包装材料;包裹物;包袱布;包皮,封套.
wrap·per [ˈræpə] *n.* ①包装者. ②包装纸;封套;〔英〕(书的)护封(纸). ③膝毯;披肩;包袱(布). ④(室内用)晨衣,化妆衣. ⑤(雪茄烟的)外卷烟叶.
wrap·ping [ˈræpiŋ] *n.* 〔常用 *pl.*〕包装材料.
wrasse [ræs] *n.* 【鱼】隆头鱼科的鱼;濑鱼,厚唇鱼,伸口鱼.
wras·tle [ˈræsl] *n., vi., vt.* ***(-tled; -tling)*** 〔方或口〕= wrestle (= wrassle).
wrath [rɔːθ] *n.* ①愤怒,激怒. ②报仇雪耻;惩罚;【宗】神谴,天罚. *nurse one's* ~ 怀恨在心. *slow to* ~ 不容易发怒的.
wrath·ful [ˈrɔːθful] *a.* ①忿怒的,激怒的. ②表现愤怒的;愤怒造成的. **-ly** *ad.*
wrath·y [ˈrɔːθi] *a.* ***(-i·er; -i·est)*** 〔旧口〕= wrathful
wreak [riːk] *vt.* ①泄(怒);雪(恨). ②惩罚,处罚;〔古〕报仇. ~ *vengeance upon an enemy* 对敌人报仇雪恨. ~ *one's thought upon expression* 畅所欲言.
wreath [riːθ] *n.* *(pl.* ~*s* [riːðz, -θs]*)* ①花环,花冠,花圈. ②(烟、云等的)圈,环;〔诗〕(旁观者等的)圈,一圈. ③〔the W-〕【天】南冕座. *place [lay] a* ~ *at [on] the tomb of the Unknown Soldier.* 在无名战士墓上献花圈.
wreathe [riːð] *vt.* ①把(花等)编成花圈;编扎(花圈);用花圈装饰[戴上]. ②盘缠;缠住,缠绕. ③拧,扭歪(脸等). *be* ~*d in each other's arms* 互相拥抱. *a face* ~*d in smiles* 满是笑容的脸. — *vi.* (树木)围住;(烟等)滚滚上升,缭绕.
wreck [rek] *n.* ①(船只等的)失事,遭难;破坏;破灭;毁坏. ②失事船,遭难船;失事船物件;破毁物;残骸;落魄者;被社会遗弃的底层人物;残废(者). ③【法】漂流物,(失事船只中)漂到岸上的货物. *save a ship from* ~ 营救失事船. *the shore strewn with* ~*s* 满布失事船残骸物件的海岸. *make a* ~ *of sb.'s life* 毁掉某人的一生. ***be a [the]*** ~ ***of one's former self*** 身体坏得不成样子. ***go to*** ~ ***(and ruin)*** 毁灭,灭亡. — *vt.* ①使(船只)遇险[失事]. ②破坏;摧毁;毁坏;折毁. ③使倒闭,使破产. ④使瓦解;挫败. — *vi.* ①(船只)失事,遇险破坏. ②毁灭,败落,落魄. ③找拾失事船物件;援救失事船.
wreck·age [ˈrekidʒ] *n.* (船只等的)失事,遭难;破坏;破灭;毁坏;破片;难船残余货物,漂流物;残骸.
wreck·er [ˈrekə] *n.* ①使船只失事的人;劫掠失事船货物者;破坏者. ②营救失事船者[人、船等],抢救失事船货物者;营救[打捞]船;救险车. ③包拆废屋[废船]的人.
wreck·ing [ˈrekiŋ] *n.* ①(船只的)失事,遭难. ②营救(失事船)工作. ③破坏,毁坏;〔美〕拆毁废屋. — *a.* 使失事的;破坏性的. *a* ~ *amendment* (前议案的)大修正案. *a* ~ *car* 救险(列)车. *a* ~ *company [crew]* 营救公司[队];救险公司[队]. *a* ~ *train* 救险列车. ~ **bar** 撬棍,铁撬.
wreck-master [ˈrekmɑːstə] *n.* 失事船货物指定管理人.
Wren [ren] *n.* 雷恩〔姓氏〕.
wren [ren] *n.* ①【鸟】鹪鹩. ②〔美俚〕女人,女子;女大学生.
wrench [rentʃ] *vt.* ①(用力)拧,扭转;拧去,扭去,夺去 *(off; away)*. ②扭伤. ③歪曲,曲解(意义、事实等). — *vi.* 扭转,扭动;扭转身子. — *n.* ①(用力)拧,扭转. ②扭伤. ③〔美〕扳钳,扳手(=〔英〕spanner). ④【物】偶单力组. ⑤突然的悲痛[伤心],伤别. *an adjustable (end)* ~ 活动扳手. *a pipe [Stillson]* ~ 圆管扳钳.
wrest [rest] *vt.* ①(用力)拧,扭;扭夺,夺取,抢去(武器等) *(from)*. ②歪曲(事实等),曲解. ③探出(秘密),逼迫(承认等) *(from)*. ④费力取得,勉强取得. ~ *a living from the barren ground* 在不毛的土地上勉强生活. — *n.* ①拧,扭. ②【乐】(调校琴弦的)校音钥.
wres·tle [ˈresl] *n.* ①【运】摔交,角力. ②搏斗;力战,奋斗. — *vi.* ①摔交,角力;格斗 *(with)*;〔美西部〕扭倒要打烙印的牲畜. ②战斗,苦斗 *(with; against)*;(为工作、问题等)拼命;深思,斟酌. ~ *with [against] temptation* 和诱惑斗争,抵抗诱惑. ~ *with a task* 拼命设法完成一件任务. — *vt.* ①摔(交). ②与…搏斗. ③(用力)移动,搬动. ④〔美西部〕为打烙印而把(小牛等)摔倒.

~ *a bout* 摔一个回合. ~ *a match* 作一次摔交比赛. ~ *a leopard* 与豹搏斗. ~ *a car along gravelly roads* 在碎石路上困难地行车. ~ ***down*** 把…摔倒. ~ ***one's hash***〔美俚〕吃. ~ ***with God*** = ~ ***in prayer*** 诚心祷告. ~ ***out*** 拼命干, 奋力完成.

wres·tler [ˈreslə] *n.* 摔交运动员; 搏斗者.

wres·tling [ˈresliŋ] *n.* 摔交; 扭斗, 搏斗.

wretch [retʃ] *n.* ①不幸的人, 苦命的人; 倒霉的人. ②卑劣的人, 无耻的人, 坏人. ③〔谑〕(可爱的)家伙. *a ~ of a child* 可怜的孩子. *You ~!* 你这个卑鄙家伙!

wretch·ed [ˈretʃid] *a.* ①不幸的; 悲惨的; 可怜的. ②卑劣的; 恶劣的, 实在不行的; 十分讨厌的. *a ~ life* 悲惨的生活. *a ~ horse* 不成样子的瘦马. *a ~ inn* 糟糕不堪的旅馆. *a ~ joke* 令人作呕的玩笑(话). **-ly** *ad.*

W.R.I. =①War Risks Insurance 战时保险. ②Women's Rural Institute〔英〕妇女农村讲习所.

wrick [rik] *vt.* 轻微扭伤(颈、脊骨等). —*n.* 扭筋. *give sb.'s back a ~* 扭伤某人背脊. *have a ~ in one's neck* 脖子扭筋.

wrig·gle [ˈrigl] *vi.* ①蠕动; 扭动 *(about)*. ②蠕动着前进 *(along; through; out; in)*. ③用计逃脱, 设法赖掉. *Keep still, and don't ~.* 沉住气, 别乱动[慌]. ~ *out of a difficulty* 从困难中挣扎出来. ~ *out of a bargain* 支支吾吾地想赖约. — *vt.* 使扭动(身体、手、尾巴等); 挣. ~ *itself out at a small hole* (蚯蚓等)蠕动着钻出小洞外. ~ *one's way* 扭动着前进. ~ *oneself into (sb.'s) favour* 想方设法巴结(某人). — *n.* 扭动, 蠕动; 蠢动. **-gly** *a.*

wrig·gler [ˈriglə] *n.* ①扭动的人[东西]. ②【动】孑孓. ③善于钻营的人.

Wright [rait] *n.* 赖特〔姓氏〕.

wright [rait] *n.* 工人, 制作者, …工, …匠〔现在主要用于复合词: play*wright*, ship*wright*, wheel*wright*〕.

wring [riŋ] *vt.* ***(wrung*** [rʌŋ]) ①绞, 拧, 扭. ②扭干, 绞出, 榨出(水等); 榨取, 敲诈, 勒索(金钱等); 强力取得, 强求(别人承认等) *(from; out of)*. ③折磨, 使苦恼. ④歪曲(言语的意义), 曲解. ~ ***off*** 扭断, 扭掉. ~ ***sb.'s hand*** (热烈地)紧握某人的手. ~ ***one's hands*** (悲痛得)双手使劲互相绞扭. ~ ***out*** 绞出, 扭出; 榨取, 勒索, 逼出(钱等); 强力取得(承认等). ~***ing wet*** 湿得可以拧出水来〔口语略去 wet〕. — *n.* 绞, 扭, 拧; 紧紧握手; 痂痛, 剧痛. *Give those clothes a ~.* 把那衣服拧一把. **~-wet** *a.* 湿淋淋的, 湿得能拧出水来的.

wring·er [ˈriŋə] *n.* ①绞扭的人; 绞扭机. ②强夺者, 勒索者, 敲诈者. ③造成痛苦、艰难的事件.

wrin·kle[1] [ˈriŋkl] *n.* ①(皮肤的)皱褶, 皱纹, ②(布等的)皱纹, 褶子. — *vt., vi.* (使)皱起; (使)起皱. ~ *(up) one's forehead* 皱起额头. ~ *with age* 老得皮肤皱起.

wrin·kle[2] [ˈriŋkl] *n.* ①好主意, 妙计; 新招. ②方法; 技巧; (技术等的)革新. *Give me [Put me up to] a ~ or two.* 帮我出一个主意. ***be full of ~s*** 妙计多. ***up to a ~*** 打着好主意.

wrin·kly [ˈriŋkli] *a.* 有皱纹的; 易皱的.

wrist [rist] *n.* ①腕; (衣袖等的)腕部;【解】腕关节;【机】肘节; 肘杆; 轴; 枢轴; 耳轴; 销轴. ②腕部能力[技巧], 腕力; 〔喻〕手腕. ***kick in the ~***〔美俚〕喝酒. — *vt.* 用腕力移动[送出、抛掷等]. **~band** (衬衫等的)袖口. ~ **drop**【医】腕垂病. ~ **exercise**〔美剧〕鼓掌喝采. ~ **joint**【解】腕关节. ~ **pin**【机】活塞销; 肘节销. **~watch** 手表. **~work** 腕部动作.

wrist·let [ˈristlit] *n.* ①腕套; (防寒用)腕筒. ②手镯; 腕饰; 手表带; 〔俚〕手铐. *a ~ watch* 手表.

writ[1] [rit] *n.* ①〔古〕文书, 文件. ②【法】公文; 命令, 票. ③〔the W-〕【宗】《圣经》. *serve a ~ on sb.* 对某人照命令执行, 把传票送达某人. ~ ***of attachment***【法】拘票. ~ ***of certiorari***【法】(上级法院发往下级法院的)诉状移送令 (= certiorari). ~ ***of error***【法】再审令. ~ ***of prohibition***【法】(推翻错误原判的)停审令. ~ ***of right***【英法】权利令状. ***the Holy [Sacred] ~*** (基督教的)《圣经》.

writ[2] [rit]〔古〕*write* 的过去式及过去分词. ~ ***large*** (弊害等)变大, 反而厉害起来; 大书特书; 用大字写着, 明显地表现出; 大大地, 大规模地.

write [rait] *vt.* ***(wrote*** [rəut], 〔古〕***writ*** [rit]; ***writ·ten*** [ˈritn], 〔古〕***writ)*** ①写, 记, 录, 抄, 誊; 填写; 签发; 签订; 签署. ②写作, 著作. ③铭记(心中), 留印象于;【计算机】写入, 存入; 写印〔从记忆系统中发出或印出数据〕. ④写信给; 把…函告. ⑤把…写入[写成为]; 通过写作使…成为某种状态. ~ *a check* 开支票. ~ *a letter* 写信. ~ *to a friend* 写信给朋友. ~ *it in your hat*〔美〕绝对确实, 真真实实. *He ~s himself "General".* 他自称'将军'. *He has "coast" written all over him.* 他浑身上下是海滨气息[他是海边长大的]. — *vi.* ①写字. ②写文章; 著作; 作曲. ③写信, 寄信, 通信. ④做书记, 做抄写员. ⑤(笔被使用时)有某种表现; 好写. *This pen ~s (well).* 这支笔好写[好使]. ~ *cleverly* 文章写得好. ~ ***a good [bad] hand*** 字写得好[坏]. ~ ***down*** ①写下来, 记下来. ②用文字攻击, 贬低, 批评 (~ *him down a fool* 在文章里说他是傻瓜). ③减低帐面价值. ④把…拨作公积金, 摊提资产. ~ ***for*** ①替(报纸等)撰稿, 投稿; 为(生活)写文章. ②写信订购. ~ ***in*** 写进去, 插入(文件中). ~ ***in [for] the paper*** 投稿给(报纸). ~ ***off*** ①勾消, 注消(债款等); 报废. ②流畅地写, 当场写, 提笔就写(文章等). ③减低资产帐面额. ~ ***out*** ①写出; 誊清, 缮写. ②(作家等)写得写不出, 写枯了脑筋. ~ ***over*** ①改写, 重写. ②写满. ~ ***up*** ①写在高处, 揭示; 用文字赞扬, 书面表扬. ②一直写到最近事情; 详细写. ③提高帐面价值; 评价过高. ④〔美〕开传票传唤.

write-in [ˈraitin] *n.* ①投票人另提名候选人的投票. ②候选人名单外被写进选票的人. — *a.* 投票人可在选票上另提候选人的选举.

writ·er [ˈraitə] *n.* ①书写者; 书记, 抄写员, 录事; 笔记者. ②作者, 著作, 作家. ③打字机; 记录器. ④(特指外语的)作文指导书, 作文范本. ⑤〔Scot.〕律师. *the ~ (of this [hereof])* = *the present ~* (本文)作者, 笔者. *a musical ~* 音乐批评家. ~ ***to the signet***〔Scot.〕律师〔略 W.S.〕. **~'s *cramp [palsy, spasm]***【医】指痉挛, 书写痉挛. **-ship** *n.* 书记的职务[工作].

write-up [ˈraitˈʌp] *n.* 〔口〕①(尤指报纸上的)捧场文章, 捧场报告. ②〔美〕资产帐面价格的非法增加. ③补写到现在.

writhe [raið] *vt.* ***(~d; ~d,*** 〔诗〕***writh·en*** [ˈraiðən]**)** 扭, 扭歪, 翻腾(身体等). — *vi.* ①蠕动, 蜿蜒移动. ②(痛苦等时)折腾, (耍赖)打滚, 翻来翻去 *(at; under)*. ③痛苦, 苦恼. — *n.* 扭动; 翻滚.

writ·ing [ˈraitiŋ] *n.* ①写, 写作, 执笔; 习字, 书法. ②文件, 契据; 铭. ③〔*pl.*〕著作, 作品. ④笔迹, 手迹. *at this ~* 写这个的时候. *be busy with one's ~* 忙于写作. ***in ~*** 写, 用书面. ***put … in ~*** 把…写成文字. ~ ***on the wall*** 危机紧迫的征兆, 参见 wall 条. ~ **book** 习字本. ~ **brush** 毛笔. ~ **case** 文具盒. ~ **desk** 写字台, 书桌. ~ **ink** 墨水. ~ **machine** 打字机. ~ **master** 书法教员. ~ **materials** 文具. ~ **paper** 书写用纸; 信纸, 信笺. ~ **set** (一套)文具. ~ **table** 写字台, 书桌. ~ **telegraph** 打字电报机; 书写电报.

writ·ten [ˈritn] write 的过去分词. — *a.* 写成的, 书面的; 笔记的, 成文的. *a ~ application* 书面申请; 申请书. *a ~ contract* 书面契约, 章程. *a ~ examination* 笔试. ~ *language* 书写语言, 书面语. ~ *law* 成文法. *a ~ will* 遗嘱.

W.R.N.S. = Women's Royal Naval Service.〔英〕皇家海军妇女勤务队.

wrnt. = warrant.

wrong [rɔŋ] *a.* *(opp.* right) ①(道义上)不好的, 不公正的. ②错误的, 不正确的. ③反对的, 相反的, 颠倒的, 背

面的，里面的。④不适当的。⑤〔用作表语〕有毛病的，失常的；无聊的；不舒服的。*a ~ 'un [one]* 坏蛋。*Lying is ~.* 撒谎是不好[错误]的。*the ~ move* 走错棋子；有欠考虑的[不好的]措施。*the ~ end* 相反的一头。*the ~ side of the cloth* 布的反面。*the ~ side out* 把里子翻朝外面，翻转过来。*The watch is ~.* 这表有毛病。*What is ~ with it?* 〔俚〕这怎么啦？这样不好吗？***get [have] hold of the ~ end of the stick*** 弄错，搞错，误解，颠倒(理论、立场等)。***get out of bed on the ~ side*** 情绪不佳。***go the ~ way*** (食物)误入气管。***in the ~ box*** 处于为难的境地，着慌；不得其所。***on the ~ side of*** ①已过…岁。②亏欠，变成负债 (*She is on the ~ side of fifty.* 她已经五十多岁了)。***Something is ~ with (sb., sth.)***. (某人，某物)出毛病。***take the ~ way*** 走错路。***~ fo(u)nt***【校对】铅字(字体或大小)不对〔略 *w. f.*〕。— *ad.* ①不好，不公正。②不对，错误，失当。③逆，颠倒，翻转。④有毛病，不舒服。*do a sum ~* 算错。★ wrong, right 等可作为后置副词；用于动词之前须作 wrongly, rightly 等：*He guessed wrong [right]. He wrongly [rightly] guessed.* 他猜错〔对〕了。***get (sb.) in ~ = get in ~ with (sb.)*** 〔美口〕受某人讨厌；惹某人生气，得罪某人。***get it ~*** 算错；误解。***go ~*** (人)走错路；搞不好，格格不入，龃龉；堕落；失败；(女人)失身；(机器等)发生故障。***right or ~*** 不管好坏。— *n.* ①不正，邪恶；坏事，罪。②过失，错误；不得当的处置；冤枉，不公正的对待；【法】侵犯(权利)；损害；虐待。***do sb. ~ = do ~ to sb.*** 害某人，虐待某人，对某人处置失当，对待某人不得当[公正]，误解某人(的动机)；强迫某人 (*You do me ~.* 你误解我了)。***do ~*** 干坏事；犯罪，犯法。***in the ~*** 不对，错误；不正当。***know the right from the ~*** 知道好歹。***put (sb.) in the ~*** 冤枉[委屈]某人，诬害某人。***suffer ~*** 受害，受虐待；受非法[不公正]对待。— *vt.* ①(损)害；使受害；不正当[公正]地对待，虐待；侮辱，诬害。②冤枉，误解。③玷污(女子)。④【海】追过，超过。**~ number** (电话)错号；因错号而找错的人；〔俚〕不适用的人[物]；不是所找的人[物]；不对头的人[物]；不可信赖的人[物]。**-ly** *ad.* **-ness** *n.* ①谬误，不当。②不公正；不正直。

wrong·do·er [ˈrɔŋˈduːə] *n.* 做坏事的人；罪犯；加害者。

wrong·do·ing [ˈrɔŋˈduːiŋ] *n.* 不正当行为；坏事，犯罪。

wrong·ful [ˈrɔŋful] *a.* 不正当的，非法的；有害的，不好的。**-ly** *ad.*

wrong-head·ed [ˈrɔŋˈhedid] *a.* 思想错误的；固执的，顽固的。**-ly** *ad.*

wrote [rəut] write 的过去式。

wroth [rəuθ] *a.* ①〔诗、谑〕〔用作表语〕勃然大怒，怒气冲天。②〔诗〕(大海等)汹涌的。*be ~ with sb.* 大生某人的气。*the ~ sea* 波涛汹涌的大海。

wrought [rɔːt] 〔古、诗、方〕work 的过去式及过去分词。— *a.* ①制造的；精制的；精炼的，锻炼的。②装饰的，刺绣的。*a highly ~ article* 精致的工艺品。**~ iron** 锻铁，熟铁。**~ silver** 银制工艺品。**~ steel** 焊接钢。

wrought-up [ˈrɔːt-ˈʌp] *a.* 兴奋的，激动的，勃然大怒的。

W.R.S.S.R. = White Russian Soviet Socialist Republic 白俄罗斯苏维埃社会主义共和国。

wrung [rʌŋ] wring 的过去式及过去分词。— *a.* 心中有烦恼的。**~-out** *a.*【海】(帆)张成蝴蝶形的。

wry [rai] *a.* ***(wri·er, ~er; wri·est, ~est)*** ①扭歪的，歪曲的，歪斜的；搞错了的；错误的，处置不当的；牵强附会的；彆扭的。②讽刺的，讥嘲的。*a ~ mouth [nose]* 歪嘴[鼻子]。*a ~ smile* 苦笑。*make a ~ face* 皱起面孔，做苦脸。**~-faced** *a.* 脸歪的。**~-mouthed** *a.* ①嘴歪的。②用滑稽口气说奉承话的。**~neck** ①【医】歪头颈，斜颈。②【鸟】蚁鴷。**~-necked** *a.* 斜颈的，脖子歪的。**-ly** *ad.* **-ness** *n.*

WS = Weather Station 气象站。

W.S. = ①war strength 战斗力。②West Saxon 西撒克逊人。③wet spinning 湿纺。④wireless set〔英〕无线电收音机。⑤writer to the signet〔英〕苏格兰律师。

WSA = War Shipping Administration〔美旧〕战时航运管理局。

WSCF = World's Student Christian Federation 世界基督教学生同盟。

WSJ = *Wall Street Journal*〔美〕《华尔街日报》。

W.S.P.V. = Women's Social and Political Union 妇女社会政治同盟。

W.Sup = water supply 供水，给水。

W.S.W.,WSW, w.s.w. = west-southwest.

W.T. = ①watertight. ②wireless telegraphy [telephony]

W/T = wireless telegraphy 无线电报。

wt. = ①weight. ②watt. ③warrant.

WTK = water tank 水箱，水舱。

Wt. Stn = Weather Station 气象站。

wun·der·bar [ˈvundəbɑː] *a., int.* 〔G.〕可惊异的；神奇的；绝美的，极好的。

Wun·der·kind [ˈvundəkint] *n.* ***(pl. -kin·der)*** 〔G.〕神童。

Wundt [vunt], **Wilhelm** 冯特〔1832—1920，德国心理学家、哲学家〕。

wurst [wəːst, wuəst; G. vuəʃt] *n.* 香肠，红腊肠〔常用在复合词中，如：*bratwurst* 烤香肠，炙红肠，*knackwurst* 大熏腊肠〕。

wuz·zle [ˈwʌzl] *vt.* 〔美、方〕混合；混淆；使混杂。

wuz·zy [ˈwʌzi] *a.* = woozy.

W.Va. = West Virginia 西弗吉尼亚〔美国州名〕。

W.V.S., WVS = Women's Voluntary Service〔英旧〕妇女志愿服务队。

WW = ①warehouse warrant 货栈证券。②water-white 透明的。③waterworks 自来水厂。

WW I = World War I 第一次世界大战。

WW II = World War II 第二次世界大战。

WWW = World Weather Watch 世界天气监视网。

Wy. = Wyoming.

Wy·an·dot [ˈwaiəndɔt] *n.* 怀安多特族〔北美印第安人休伦联盟中的一族〕；怀安多特语〔休伦语中一种方言〕。

Wy·an·dotte [ˈwaiəndɔt] *n.* 怀恩多特鸡〔美国卵肉兼用品种鸡〕。

Wy·at(t) [ˈwaiət] *n.* 怀亚特〔姓氏，男子名〕。

wych-elm [ˈwitʃˈelm] *n.*【植】无毛榆；榆木。

Wych·er·ley [ˈwitʃəli] *n.* 威彻利〔姓氏〕。

wych-ha·zel [ˈwitʃˈheizl] *n.* ①【植】= wych-elm. ②〔美〕= witch-hazel.

Wyc·lif(fe) [ˈwiklif] *n.* 威克利夫〔姓氏〕。

wye [wai] *n.* 字母 Y；Y 形物。

Wyke·ham·ist [ˈwikəmist] *a., n.* (英国)温彻斯特学院 (Winchester College) 的(学生或毕业生)。

Wyld(e) [waild] *n.* ①怀尔德〔姓氏〕。②**H.C.** ~ 怀尔德〔1870—1945，英国语言学家〕。

wynd [waind] *n.* 〔Scot.〕小路，巷，胡同。

Wyo. = Wyoming.

Wy·o·ming [waiˈəumiŋ] *n.* 怀俄明〔美国州名〕。

wy·vern [ˈwaivəːn] *n.* = wivern.

X

X^{1},x [eks] *(pl.* **X's, x's** [ˈeksiz]*)* ①英语字母表第二十四个字母．②X形状的东西．③〔x-〕【数】第一个未知数；横坐标；〔喻〕未知的人或物；难预测的事物〔情况，力量〕．④【无】空中障碍．⑤〔美俚〕十美元(钞票)．⑥〔美学俚〕考试；厕所．⑦〔X-〕〔美〕= X-rated．⑧〔X〕文盲用以代替签名的记号．⑨〔X〕接吻的符号〔写在情书末端〕．⑩〔X〕(连接两个数字时的)乘法符号．***double X*** 烈啤酒符号〔写在酒桶上作XX〕．***treble*** X最烈啤酒符号〔XXX〕．**X chromosome**【生】X 染色体．**X particle** = meson．**x punch**【计】11 行穿孔．**X-radiation** x 辐射．**X ray** ①〔*pl.*〕x 光线．② x 光照相．**x wool** 64 支羊毛．

X^{2} = (罗马字码) 10．XX = 20．IX= 9．XV= 15．XL= 40．LX = 60．XC =90．DXL = 540．MX= 1010．

X^{3} = ①【化】xenon．②Christ(ian)．③experimental．④【电】reactance．

x^{1} = box(es)．

x^{2} [eks] *vt.* ***(x-ed, x'd*** [ekst]; ***x-ing, x'ing)*** ①用x符号标出(自己对候选人、试题答案等的选择)*(in)*．②用单个〔连续几个〕"x" 符号划去；用"x"符号表示删去 *(out)*．*He x-ed his ballot clearly.* 他在选票上清清楚楚地勾下了选择的记号．*She x-ed out most of what she had written.* 她用x记号划掉了已经写出的大部分文字．

xanth- = xantho-．

xan•thate [ˈzænθeit] *n.*【化】黄原酸盐〔酯〕．

xan•the•in(e) [ˈzænθiin] *n.*【化】花黄素，胞液黄素．

xan•thene [ˈzænθiːn] *n.*【化】呫吨，(夹)氧杂蒽．～ **dye** 呫吨染料．

xan•thic [ˈzænθik] *a.* ①黄色的，带黄色的；花黄素的；黄质的．②【化】黄嘌呤的．～ *flowers* 黄花．～ *acid*【化】黄原酸；氧荒酸．

xan•thin [ˈzænθin] *n.* ①【化】(不溶性)黄质；叶黄素；茜草色素．②= xanthine．

xan•thine [ˈzænθiːn, -θin] *n.*【化】黄质；黄嘌呤，羟基嘌呤．

Xan•thip•pe [zænˈθipi, -ˈtipi] *n.* ①粘西比〔古希腊哲学家苏格拉底 (Socrates) 的凶悍泼辣的妻子〕．②〔喻〕泼妇，悍妇．

xantho- *comb. f.* 黄，黄色：*xantho*phyll．

Xan•thoch•ro•i [zænˈθɔkrəuai] *n.*〔*pl.*〕金发白肤人种〔高加索人种〕．**-chro•ic** *a.*

xan•tho•chroid [ˈzænθəukrɔid] *a.*〔罕〕金发白肤的．— *n.*〔罕〕金发白肤的人．

xan•tho•ma [zænˈθəumə] *n.* ***(pl.*** ～***s, -ma•ta*** [-mətə]***)*** 黄瘤，脂瘤性纤维瘤．**-tous** *a.*

xan•tho•my•cin [zænθəuˈmaisin] *n.*【化】链霉黄素．

xan•thone [ˈzænθəun] *n.*【化】呫吨酮．

xan•tho•phyl(l) [ˈzænθəfil] *n.*【植】黄色素，叶黄素．

xan•thop•si•a [zænˈθɔpsiə] *n.*【医】黄视症，黄幻视，视物显黄症．

xan•thous [ˈzænθəs] *a.* ①黄色的，带黄色的．②黄色人种的；蒙古人种的．③头发浅黄色〔棕色、红色〕的人种的．

Xan•tip•pe [zænˈtipi] *n.* = Xanthippe．

xas•er [ˈzæzə] *n.*【物】X 射线激射(器)．

xat [zɑːt] *n.* (北美印第安人立于屋前的)雕花图腾柱．

X-axis [ˈeks-ˌæksis] *n.*【数】X 轴，横坐标轴．

x.c., x.-c., x.-cp. = ex coupon 无利息券的(= without coupon)．

xd. x-d., X-div. = ex dividend 无红利的 (= without dividend)．

Xe =【化】元素氙(xenon) 的符号．

xe•bec [ˈziːbek] *n.* (地中海沿岸的)三桅帆船．

xe•ni•a [ˈziːniə] *n.*【植】种子直感，(胚乳)异粉性．

xe•ni•al [ˈziːniəl] *a.* 招待客人的，主客关系的．

xen•o- [ˈzenəu-] *comb. f.* 异乡的；异国的；外来的：*xeno*gamy, *xeno*phobia．

xen•o•bi•ol•o•gy [ˌzenəubaiˈɔlədʒi] *n.* 外(层)空(间)生物学．

xen•o•di•ag•no•sis [ˌzenəuˌdʒaiəgˈnəusis] *n.*【医】异体接种诊断法，病媒接种诊断法．

xe•nog•a•my [ziːˈnɔgəmi] *n.*【植】异株异花授粉〔受精〕；【动】杂交配合．

xen•o•gen•e•sis [ˌzenəuˈdʒenisis] *n.*【生】①自然发生(= heterogenesis)．②异种生殖．③无生源说〔认为有生物发生于无生物〕．**-gen•ic, -ge•net•ic** *a.*

xe•nog•e•nous [zeˈnɔdʒinəs] *a.* 由体外原因发生的．

xen•o•graft [ˈzenəgrɑːft] *n.* 异种皮移植．

xen•o•lith [ˈzenəliθ] *n.*【矿】捕虏体〔岩〕．

xen•o•mor•phic [ˌzenəuˈmɔːfik] *a.*【矿】他形的．

xen•on [ˈzenɔn] *n.*【化】氙 (Xe)．～ **hexafluoride** 六氟化氙．～ **tetrafluoride** 四氟化氙．

xen•o•phobe [ˈzenəfəub] 畏惧或憎恨外国人〔事物〕的人．

xen•o•pho•bi•a [ˌzenəˈfəubiə] *n.* 畏惧和憎恶外国(族)；仇外．

Xen•o•phon [ˈzenəfən] 色诺芬〔434?—355? B.C.，希腊将军，历史家，著有《长征记》*(Anabasis)* 一书〕．

xen•o•time [ˈzenətaim] *n.*【矿】磷钇矿．

xe•ran•sis [ziəˈrænsis] *n.*【医】干燥，除湿．

xe•ran•the•mum [ziəˈrænθiməm] *n.* ①(干后形状和色彩不变的)干鲜花卉．②【植】年枯草；鼠麴草；灰毛菊(属)．

xe•rarch [ˈziərɑːk] *a.*【生态】旱生演替的，(生态演替)在旱地发展的．

xe•ra•si•a [ziəˈreiziə] *n.*【医】毛发干燥病．

xe•ric [ˈziːrik] *a.* ①旱生(植物)的；耐旱的．②干旱的，沙漠般的．

xe•ro- *comb. f.* 干旱，干燥．

xe•ro•der•ma [ˌziərəuˈdəːmə] *n.*【医】鳞癣；干皮病(= ichthyosis)．

xe•ro•form [ˈziərəfɔːm] *n.*【药】干仿，塞罗仿，三溴酚铋．

xe•ro•gram [ˈziərəgræm] *n.* 静电复印副本；干式影印副本．

xe•rog•ra•phy [ziˈrɔgrəfi] *n.*【印】静电复印术．**xe•ro•graph•ic** [ˌziərəuˈgræfik] *a.*

xe•ro•mor•phy [ˈziərəˌmɔːfi] *n.*【植】旱性形态．

xe•roph•i•lous [ziəˈrɔfiləs] *a.* ①【植】喜旱的，适旱的．②【动】旱栖的．

xe•roph•o•bous [ziəˈrɔfəbəs] *a.*【植】【动】避旱的，嫌旱的．

xe•roph•thal•mi•a [ˌziərɔfˈθælmiə] *n.*【医】结膜干燥

症,干眼病.

xe·ro·phyte [ˈziərəfait] *n.* 【植】旱生植物. **xe·ro·phyt·ic** [ˌziərəuˈfitik] *a.*

xe·ro·ra·di·og·ra·phy [ˌziərəureidiˈɔgrəfi] *n.* 干放射性照相术.

xe·ro·sere [ˈziərəsiə] *n.* 【生态】旱生演替系列.

xe·ro·sis [ziˈrəusis] *n.* 【医】(皮肤或结膜)干燥(病).

xe·ro·ther·mic [ˌziərəˈθə:mik] *a.* ①【地】干热期(指后冰河干热期)的. ②(动植物等)适应于干热环境的.

Xe·rox [ˈziərɔks] *n.* 静电印刷品[复制品]〔原商标名〕. — *vt.*, *vi.* 用静电印刷复制.

X-eyed [ˈeksˈaid] *a.* 斜视的.

X-film [ˈeks-film] *n.* 〔英〕限制性电影〔指16岁以下儿童不许看的电影〕.

Xho·sa [ˈkəusɑ:, -zɑ:] *n.* ① ***(pl.*** **~*(s))*** 科萨人〔住在南非开普省的牧民〕. ②科萨语(南非开普省牧民的班图语)(=Xosa). 也作 **Xo·sa.**

xi [sai, zai Gr. ksi:] *n.* 希腊字母表第十四个字母[Ξ,ξ].

X. i., x-i, x-int. = ex interest 无利息.

-xion *suf.* 表示动作、状态等的名词词尾: conne*xion*, cruci*fixion*.

xiph·(i)-, xiph·o [ˈzif(i)-, ˈzifəu-] *comb. f.* 剑: *xiph*oid.

xiph·i·ster·num [ˌzifiˈstə:nəm] *n.* ***(pl.*** ***-na*** [-nə]***)*** 【解、动】剑胸骨. **-ster·nal** *a.*

xiph·oid [ˈzifɔid] *n.* 【解】剑突. — *a.* 【解】剑突的; 剑状的.

xiph·o·su·ran [ˌzifəuˈsjurən, -ˈsur-] *n.*, *a.* 【动】剑尾目 *(Xiphosura)* 动物(的).

XL = extra large 特大号.

Xm., Xmas. [ˈkrisməs] = Christmas (基督教)圣诞节.

Xn. = Christian.

x.n. = ex new 无新股票权.

Xnty. = Christianity.

X partical [ˈeksˈpɑ:tikl] 【原】X 粒子,介子.

xpln = explanation.

x.q. = cross-questioning 盘问.

xr = ex rights 无权认购新股.

X-ra·di·a·tion [ˈeksˌreidiˈeiʃən] *n.* 【物】X 射线; X 射线辐射.

X-rat·ed [ˈeksˈreitid] *a.* 〔美〕(电影限制范围)禁止十六岁以下儿童观看的,(影片) X 级的.

X-ray [ˈeksrei] *n.* X (射)线,伦琴射线; X 光; X 光照片. — *a.* X (射)线的,伦琴线的. *an ~ examination* X 线检查. — [ˈeksˈrei] *vt.* 用 X 线检查[摄影、处理、治疗]. ~ **astronomy** X 射线天文学. ~ **nova** 【天】X 射线新星. ~ **pulsar** 【天】X 射线脉冲星. ~ **star [source]** 【天】X 射线星[X 射线源]. ~ **telescope** 【天】X 射线望远镜. ~ **therapy** 【医】X 光线疗法. ~ **tube** X 线管.

Xrds, X roads = cross-roads 交叉道.

X-rts = ex rights 无权认购新股.

X.S. = extra strong 特强的.

XTAL, X-tal = crystal.

Xtian.,Xt. = Christian.

xtra = extra.

xtry = extraordinary.

Xty. = Christianity.

XU = X-unit X单位(一种波长单位).

X-u·nit [ˈeksˈju:nit] *n.* 【物】〔略作 X.U.〕 X 单位〔X 射线波长单位〕.

XW = ex warrants 无令状[委任状、批准令等].

X Wt = experimental weight 实验重量.

XX 〔英〕劣等纸或微疵纸包皮上的标记(=〔美〕R) 〔*cf.* retree〕.

XX ①= double X 〔啤酒强度标记〕. ②【生】同配子型〔雌性〕.

X.X.H., X.X.h. = double extra heavy 特超重的.

X.X.S., X.X.s. = double extra strong 特超强的.

XXX = triple X 〔啤酒强度标记〕.

xyl(o)- *comb. f.* 木: *xyl*an.

xy·lan [ˈzailæn] *n.* 【化】木糖胶,木聚糖.

xy·lem [ˈzailem] *n.* 【植】木质部. ~ *ray* 木射线.

xy·lene [ˈzaili:n] *n.* 【化】二甲苯.

xy·lic [ˈzailik] *a.* ~ **acid** 【化】二甲基苯甲酸.

xy·li·dine [ˈzailidi:n], **xy·li·din** [ˈzailidin] *n.* 【化】二甲基苯胺〔指二甲基苯甲酸的六种异构体的任一种或上述六种异构体的混合物〕.

xylo- = xyl-.

xy·lo·carp [ˈzailəkɑ:p] *n.* 【植】硬木质果(树).

xy·lo·car·pous [ˌzailəuˈkɑ:pəs] *a.* 【植】有硬木质果的,硬木质果的.

xy·lo·gen [ˈzailədʒen] *n.* 【植】木质.

xy·lo·graph [ˈzailəgrɑ:f] *n.* 木版[木雕]印刷物; 木版印画; 木纹图案[装饰]. **-er** *n.* 木版[木雕]工. **-ic(al)** *a.*

xy·log·raphy [zaiˈlɔgrəfi] *n.* 木版[木雕]印刷术; 木刻术,木版印画法.

xy·loid [ˈzailɔid] *a.* 木质的,似木的.

xylol [ˈzailəul] *n.* 【化】(混合)二甲苯.

xy·lon·ite [ˈzailənait] *n.* 【化】假象牙; 赛璐珞 (=celluloid).

xy·loph·a·gous [zaiˈlɔfəgəs] *a.* (昆虫等)蚀木的, 蛀木的,在木上穿孔的.

xy·lo·phone [ˈzailəfəun] *n.* 【乐】木琴.

xy·lose [ˈzailəus] *n.* 【化】木糖.

xy·lot·o·mous [zaiˈlɔtəməs] *a.* (昆虫)能蛀[钻]木的.

xy·lot·o·my [zaiˈlɔtəmi] *n.* 木材解剖(术); 木材切片术(供显微镜用).

xy·lot·o·mist [zaiˈlɔtəmist] *n.* 木材解剖[切片]员.

xy·lyl [ˈzailil] *n.* 【化】二甲苯基; 甲苄基.

xy·lyl·ene [ˈzailili:n] *n.* 【化】苯(撑)二甲基.

xyst [zist] *n.* = xystus.

xys·ter [ˈzistə] *n.* 【医】刮骨刀.

xys·tus [ˈzistəs] *n.* ***(pl.*** ***-ti*** [-tai]***)*** (古代希腊、罗马的)室内运动场; 柱廊; (古罗马)园内林荫道.

Y

Y,y [wai] ***(pl.*** **Y's, y's** [waiz]***)*** ①英语字母表第二十五字母. ② *Y* 字形物. ③【数】第二个未知数. ④中世纪罗马数字150. ⑤〔Y〕【化】元素钇 (yttrium) 的符号. ⑥〔y〕【数】纵坐标. *a Y-branch* 叉状管. *a Y-cross* Y 字形十字架. *a Y-gun* Y 形双筒炮. *a Y-joint* Y 字形关节. *a Y-level* Y字形水平仪. *Y-track* Y 形轨道〔机车调换方向用〕.

Y.,y. = ①Young Men's Christian Association 基督教青年会. ②〔y.〕 yard(s). ③〔y.〕 year(s).

y- *pref.* 保留在某些古语中的古英语前缀, 表示过去分词、集合名词: *y*clad (= clad), *y*clept (= called), *y*wis (= surely) 等.

-y[1] *suf.* ①抽象名词后缀: fur*y*, glor*y*, histor*y*, -log*y* 等. ②形容词后缀: peremptor*y*, primar*y*.

-y[2] *suf.* ①表示"小、亲密、亲爱"等意义的名词后缀: dogg*y* 小狗; pigg*y* 小猪; doll*y* 小洋娃娃 (*cf.* nurse, dogg*ie*, ladd*ie*); Johnn*y* 约翰哥儿; nurs*y* 奶奶. ②加在形容词后构成名词: dark*y* 黑人; fatt*y* 胖子. ★(1)语尾为 -y 的名词有时反比其原语更为通用: baby (<babe). (2)在苏格兰语中 -ie 较普通. (3)在现代口语中,常用来替代多音节名词、形容词第一音节外的部分: hank*y* (=handkerchief), night*y* (= night-dress), comf*y* (= comfortable). ③加在名词后, 表示"行业"、"营业场所"或"全体": laundr*y*, chandler*y*, soldier*y*. ④加在动词后构成名词,表示"动作"、"行为"等: inquir*y*, entreat*y*.

-y[3] *suf.* 〔法语过去分词形名词后缀,即 -é, -ée〕被…者: deput*y*, arm*y*, treat*y*, etc.

yab·ber [ˈjæbə] *n.*, *vi.* 〔澳〕①饶舌; 闲谈, 聊天. ②急促、不清楚地说话.

yacht [jɔt] *n.* 快艇,游艇. *a racing* ~ 竞赛用快艇. — *vi.* 乘快艇, 驾驶快艇, 乘游艇旅游. **~-club** 游艇俱乐部. **~-race, ~-racing** 快艇比赛.

yacht·ing [ˈjɔtiŋ] *n.* 快〔游〕艇驾驶(法); 乘游艇旅游. *go* ~ 坐快〔游〕艇去. *a* ~ *man* 快艇艇员. *a* ~ *race [match]* 快艇竞赛.

yachts·man [ˈjɔtsmən] *n.* *(pl. -men)* 快艇驾驶人; 游艇主人. **-ship** 快艇驾驶法.

yack [jæk], **yack·e·ty-yack** [ˈjækitiˈjæk] *n.*, *vi.* = yak[2].

YAF = Young Americans for Freedom 美国青年争取自由组织.

yaf·fle(r), yaf·fil [ˈjæfl(ə), ˈjæfil] *n.* 〔英方〕【鸟】红冠绿身啄木鸟.

YAG = yttrium aluminum garnet 钇铝柘榴石〔用于产生激光束的氧化铝合成晶石〕.

ya·ger [ˈjeigə] *n.* ①猎人; (过去德、奥的)狙击兵, 步兵 (=〔G.〕Jäger). ②(过去美国用的) 短枪管大口径步枪.

ya·gi (antenna) [ˈjɑːgiː, jæˈgiː] 【无】八木天线, 波道式天线.

yah[1] [jɑː] *int.* 嗳呀! 嗬! 〔表示厌恶、嘲笑等〕.

yah[2] [jɑː] *ad.* 〔英方、美俚〕= yes. *a ~-man* 〔美〕老好人,怎么说怎么好的人 (= yes-man).

Ya·hoo [jəˈhuː, jɑː-] *n.* ①雅虎〔《格列佛游记》*(Gulliver's Travels)*中的人形兽〕. ②〔y-〕人面兽心的人; 〔美〕粗汉.

yahr·zeit [ˈjɑːtsait, ˈjɔː-] *n.* 〔Yid.〕【犹太教】周年忌辰(仪式)〔犹太人的双亲或直系亲属死后一周年忌辰(按犹太历) 的纪念仪式; 点二十四小时蜡烛 (*yahrzeit candle* 忌辰烛)和念颂神词等〕.

Yah·veh, -vei [ˈjɑːvei], **yah·weh** [ˈjɑːwei] *n.* = Jehovah.

Yah·wism [ˈjɑːwizm] *n.* ①耶和华教; 耶和华崇拜; 耶和华教义. ②称上帝为"耶和华".

Yah·wist [ˈjɑːwist] *n.* 称"上帝"为"耶和华"的旧约作者〔在旧约圣经中, 提到"上帝"时称 Yahweh (耶和华)而不称 Elohim (艾洛辛)的佚名作者〕. **-ic** *a.*

yak[1] [jæk] *n.* 【动】牦牛.

yak[2] [jæk] *vi.* *(yakked* [jækt], *yak·king* [ˈjækiŋ]) 【拟声词】〔美俚〕谈个没完没了, 闲扯. — *n.* 〔美俚〕①闲扯谈. ②噱头,哄堂大笑.

Yak·i·ma [ˈjækimə] *n.* ① *(pl. ~(s))* 雅吉瓦人〔住在美国华盛顿州的萨哈泼丁印第安部族人〕. ②雅吉瓦语.

Ya·kut [jɑːˈkut] *(pl. ~(s))* *n.* 雅库特人〔住在西伯利亚东部〕; 雅库特(地区); 雅库特语.

Ya·kutsk [jɑːˈkutsk] *n.* ①(苏联)雅库茨克(地区)〔即雅库特地区〕. ②(苏联)雅库茨克(城).

Yalding [ˈjældiŋ] *n.* 耶尔丁〔姓氏〕.

Yale [jeil] *n.* ①耶鲁大学〔在美国 Connecticut 州 *New Haven*〕. ②耶尔〔姓氏,男子名〕. ③〔y〕弹簧锁,撞锁 (= ~ lock). **~man** 耶鲁大学毕业生.

y'all = 〔美南部〕you-all.

yal·ler [ˈjælə] *a.* 〔美俚〕= yellow. *a ~ dog* 卑鄙龌龊的人; 告密者; 叛徒.

Yal·ta [ˈjæltə] *n.* 雅尔塔〔苏联港市〕. ~ **conference** 雅尔塔会议〔1945年斯大林, 罗斯福, 丘吉尔在雅尔塔举行的, 讨论战后问题的会议〕.

yam [jæm] *n.* 【植】薯蓣属植物; 〔Scot.〕马铃薯; 〔美南部〕甘薯. *Chinese [Japanese]* ~ 【植】薯蓣,山药.

Ya·ma [ˈjɑːmə] *n.* 〔Sans.〕阎魔,阎罗王.

ya·mal·ka, ya·mul·ka [ˈjɑːməlkə] *n.* = yarmulke.

Ya·ma·to [ˈjɑːmədəu] *n.* 〔Jap.〕大和民族(的一员). — *a.* 大和民族的.

Ya·men, ya·mun [ˈjɑːmən] *n.* 〔Chin.〕衙门.

yam·mer [ˈjæmə] *n.*, *vi.* 〔口、方〕啼哭; 啜泣; 哭诉; 诉苦; 大叫; 叫嚷; (鸟)叫. — *vt.* 〔口、方〕抱怨地说出, 大声说出.

Y. and L. R. = York and Lancaster Regiment 〔英〕约克一兰开斯特团.

yang ko [ˈjɑːŋˈkəu] *n.* 〔Chin.〕秧歌.

yank [jæŋk] *vt.*, *vi.*, *n.* 〔美口〕猛拉, 使劲拉.

Yank [jæŋk] *n.* 〔俚〕= Yankee.

Yan·kee [ˈjæŋki] *n.* ①杨基佬〔尤指老式作风的新英格兰人〕. ②〔美南部〕(南北战争时的)北军; 北部人, 北方佬. ③〔英口〕美国佬; 〔*pl.*〕【商】美国铁路股份. — *a.* ①美国北方人的. ②美国佬式的. **~dom** ①= ~land. ②〔集合词〕= ~s. ~ **Doodle** 〔美〕(独立战争时期流行的) 美国歌曲. **~-Doodle** 美国人. ~ **land** ①美国. ②新英格兰. ③(美国)北部. ~ **market** (英国交易所内的) 美国证券交易市场. ~ **notions** 美国式用具〔设备等〕. ~ **rails** 〔英俚〕美国铁路股票. ~ **State** 俄亥俄州的别名. ~ **trick** 〔美〕卑劣行为. **-ism** 美国佬脾气; 美国式; 美国语风, 美国腔.

Yan·kee·fied [ˈjæŋkifaid] *a.* 美国化的; 美国式的.

Yan·kee·fy [ˈjænkifai] *vt.* 使美国化.

Yanks [jæŋks] 〔美俚〕= New York Yankees 纽约扬基棒球队.

Yan·qui [ˈjɑːŋkiː] 〔Sp.〕美国人〔区别于拉丁美洲人〕.

Ya·oun·de [ˌjɑːunˈdei] *n.* 雅温得〔喀麦隆首都〕.

Ya·ourt [ˈjɑːuət] *n.* = yogust.

yap [jæp] *vi.* ①(小狗)狂吠, 大声咬. ②大声骂; 〔俚〕瞎嚷嚷. ③〔美俚〕发牢骚, 找碴儿, 高声叫嚷. — *n.* ①(狗的)乱咬声. ②〔美俚〕嘴. ③〔美俚〕讨厌的人; 年轻无赖; 歹徒; 蠢汉. ④〔美俚〕发牢骚, 叫嚷. **~head** 〔美俚〕蠢汉, 夜郎自大的人.

ya·pok, ya·pock [jəˈpɔk] *n.* 【动】蹼足负鼠 (*Chironectes minimus*) 〔产于中南美洲〕.

yapp [jæp] *n.* (留有护边的)宽边皮面装钉. **-ed** *a.*

Ya·qui [ˈjɑːkiː] *n.* 雅基人〔墨西哥皮曼 (Piman) 族印第安人〕.

yar·bor·ough [ˈjɑːbərə] *n.* (桥牌或 whist 牌戏) 没有九点以上的一手牌.

yard[1] [jɑːd] *n.* ①围场, 院子; (学校的)运动场. ②场地; 工场, 厂, 制造场, 工作场, 停留处, 堆置场. ③【铁路】(站内)车场; 调车场, 编组场. ④〔the Y-〕伦敦警察厅(刑事部) (= Scotland Yard). *a front [back]* ~ 前〔后〕院. *a brick-*~ 砖厂. *a cab-*~ 出租马车停留处. *a builder's* ~ 营造场. *a hump* ~【铁路】驼峰编组场. ~ ***birds*** 〔美俚〕新兵; 受处罚只准在一个地方劳动的兵士; 犯人. — *vt.* 把(家畜) 赶进栏里. **~man** 【铁路】站内车场员工, 调车员(等). **~master** 站内车场主任.

yard[2] [jɑːd] *n.* ①码〔合三英尺, 约 91.4 cm〕. ②一码长的东西. ③【海】帆桁. ④〔美俚〕百元(钞票); 千元(钞票). *5 ~s of cloth* 5 码布. ***man the ~s*** 举行登舷礼. ***~s apeak*** 把帆桁作×状挂着〔报丧等〕. **~arm** 【船】

(帆)桁端. ~ **goods** 匹头,(作为商品的)布匹,织物. ~**land** 雅兰[英国旧地亩单位,约合30英亩(=virgate)]. ~ **measure** 码尺. ~ **rope**【船】(帆)桁索. ~**stick**, ~**wand** 码尺; 尺度,衡量[检验,评判]标准.

yard·age[1] [ˈjɑːdidʒ] *n.* (立方)码数; 按码计算.

yard·age[2] [ˈjɑːdidʒ] *n.* (铁路上运家畜时)站内留养场的使用(权)[使用费].

yare [jɛə] *a.* 〔古、方〕准备好了的; 敏捷的; 迅速的; 活泼的; 容易操纵的. — *ad.* 快; 敏捷地.

Yar·mouth [ˈjɑːməθ] *n.* ①雅茅斯〔加拿大一城市〕. ②大雅茅斯〔英国英格兰东海岸渔业中心 = Great Yarmouth〕.

yar·mul·ke [ˈjɑːrməlkə] *n.* 犹太人的室内便帽.

yarn [jɑːn] *n.* ①纱,纱线,毛线; 人造丝; 塑料丝,金属丝; 绳子. ②(航海者等的)故事; 旅行谈; 奇谈. ③谎话,捏造的话,谣言. *a cable* ~ 油麻绳. *a sportsman's* ~ (不可靠的)猎人的故事,奇谈. *Spin us a* ~. 讲一个故事给我们听. — *vi.* 〔俚〕讲故事. ~ **beam** = ~ roll. ~**-dyed**【纺】原纱染色的, 色织的. ~ **number [size]**【纺】纱线支数. ~ **roll**【纺】经线卷轴. ~ **sizing** 纱线上浆.

yar·o·vize [ˈjɑːrəvaiz] *vt.* = jarovize.

yar·row [ˈjærəu] *n.*【植】欧[西洋]蓍草.

yash·mak [ˈjæʃmæk] *n.* (伊斯兰教国家妇女在公共场所戴的,只露出眼睛的)面纱.

yat·a·ghan [ˈjætəgən] *n.* (土耳其人的)无锷弯刀.

ya-ta-ta [ˈjɑːtətɑː] *n.* 〔美俚〕瞎聊,空谈.

yat·ter [ˈjætə] *vi.* 〔俚〕闲扯,瞎聊. — *n.* 闲谈. *Among the* ~ *there are these sentences of wisdom.* 闲谈中夹有充满明智的话句.

yat·tit·y-yat·tit·y [ˈjætitiˈjætiti] *n.* 〔美俚〕瞎聊.

yaud [jɔːd, jɔd] *n.* 〔Scot.〕老而无用的(母)马.

yauld [jɔːd, jɔd, jɔːld] *a.* 〔Scot.〕活跃的, 敏捷的,精力充沛的.

yaup [jɔːp, jɑːp] *vi.*, *n.* 〔口、方〕= yawp.

yau·pon [ˈjɔːpən] *n.*【植】(美国南部)代茶冬青.

yaw [jɔː] *n.*【海、空】偏航(角); 侧滑(角). —*vi.*【海、空】偏航,左右摇转; 摇摇晃晃地前进; 盘旋. — *vt.* 使偏航; 使左右摇转; 使摇摇晃晃地前进. ~ **guy [line]** 系塔索. ~**meter** 偏航计,偏流计. **-er** *n.*【空】偏航控制器; 方向舵.

yawl[1] [jɔːl] *n.* 船载小艇,舰载杂用船; 二桅帆船; 小渔船; 水雷艇.

yawl[2] [jɔːl] *vi.*, *n.* 〔方〕= yowl.

yawn [jɔːn] *vi.* ①打呵欠. ②张开口. ③(深渊、裂缝等)张着大口. *make (sb.)* ~ 使想睡, 使困倦. *"What is the use?" he* ~*ed.* "有什么用?"他打着呵欠说. *The hell* ~*s for him.* 地狱张着大口等他. — *vt.* 打着呵欠说. *He* ~*ed out a good-night.* 他打着呵欠说明儿见. —*n.* ①呵欠; 张开大口. ②裂缝, 裂口. ③讨厌的人; 乏味的事物. **with a** ~ 打着呵欠.

yawn·ing [ˈjɔːniŋ] *a.* 打着呵欠的,张开大口的. — *n.* 打呵欠. **-ly** *ad.* 打着呵欠.

yawp [jɔːp, jɑːp] *vi.* 〔口、方〕大声叫嚷; 〔俚〕大声讲话; 愚蠢地讲话; 大声打呵欠. — *n.* 怪叫,叫嚷; 大声的说话,粗鲁的语言; 蠢话.

yaws [jɔːz] *n. pl.*【医】雅司病〔一种热带慢性痘疹状皮肤传染病〕.

y-ax·is [ˈwai,æksis] *n.*【数】y 轴,纵座标轴.

YB, Y.B., Yb = year-book.

Yb =【化】ytterbium.

y·clept, y·cleped [iˈklept] *a.* 〔古、谑〕名叫…的.

yd. = yard(s).

yds. = yards.

ye[1] [jiː, ji] *pro.* 〔*pl.*〕〔古、诗、方〕thou 的复数. ★现在有下列几种用例: (1)〔诗、谑〕〔呼唤〕Ye gods (and little fishes)! 天呀! [唷,吓了一跳!; 不是,没这回事! (等)]. Ye zephyrs gay. 快活的西风呀. Go it, ~ cripples! 去呀,喂瘸子! (2)〔俚、方〕= you. How d' ~ do? [haudiˈduː]〔俚〕你好? Thank ~ [ˈθæŋki].〔俚〕谢谢你. (3)〔古、方〕〔用于命令句〕Hark ~ [ˈhɑːki]. 听着. Look ~ [ˈluki]. 看呀.

ye[2] [ðiː; 弱 ðə, ði 或 jiː 等]〔定冠词〕〔古〕= the.

yea [jei] *ad.* 〔古〕①是,不错 (*opp.* nay); 真, 的确. ②而且,而又,何况,加之. ~ ***and*** 而且,而又. — *n.* 肯定,赞成; 投票赞成(者). *Let your* ~ *be* ~. 赞成就说赞成好了; 请爽快表示. ~***s and nays*** 赞成和反对(的票数).

yeah [jɑː] *ad.* 〔美、口〕= yes.

yean [jiːn] *vt.*, *vi.* (羊等)产(仔).

yean·ling [ˈjiːnliŋ] *n.* 小羊,小山羊. — *a.* 刚生的; 幼小的.

year [jəː, jiə] *n.* ①年,岁; 一年. ②年度,学年. ③〔*pl.*〕年纪,年龄,岁数; 〔*pl.*〕老年. ★在表示岁数时, years 常略去不说,如: He is five. ④〔*pl.*〕多年,数年; 几年; 一生中的某一时期; 时代. ⑤〔美俚〕= here. *this [last, next]* ~ 今[去,明]年. *the next* ~ 次年,第二年,翌年. *every* ~ 每年. *every other* ~ 每隔一年,每二年. *Years bring wisdom.* 年岁年岁增智增慧. *an astronomical [a solar, a natural, a tropical]* ~ 太阳年. *the common* ~ 平年. *the [a] leap* ~ 闰年. *the* ~ *of grace [Christ, our Lord]* 公元,耶稣纪元. *the fiscal* ~ 会计年度. *the academic [school]* ~ 学年. *old in* ~*s but young in vigour* 年纪老但精力不老. *He is young [old] for his* ~*s.* 比年龄显得年轻[显得老]. *We had not met for* ~*s.* 我们好几年没见面了. ***a* ~ *and a day***【法】满一年,一整年;〔谑〕长期间. ***all the* ~ *round*** 一年到头. ***for* ~*s*** 好几年. ***from* ~ *to* ~** = ~ by ~. ***in a* ~*'s time*** 经过一年. ***in the* ~ *one*** 在公历元年; 很久以前. ***in* ~*s*** 上了年纪,年纪老; 〔美〕好几年. ***of late* ~*s*** 近年. ***over the* ~*s*** 长年累月. ***the* ~ *round*** 〔美〕= all the ~ round. ~ ***after*** ~ 一年一年地. ~ ***by*** ~ 年年; 逐年. ~ ***in***, ~ ***out*** 年年; 不断地,始终,老是.

year-book [ˈjəːbuk, ˈjiə-] *n.* 年鉴,年刊,年报.

year·ling [ˈjəːliŋ, ˈjiə-] *n.* ①一岁仔,一岁的孩子[动物]; 一年生植物[树苗];【赛马】一岁的马. ②〔美俚〕(西点军校的)二年级生. — *a.* 一岁的; 经过了一年的. *a* ~ *bride* 结婚满一年的新娘子.

year·long [ˈjəːlɔŋ] *a.* 整整一年的; 继续一年的.

year·ly [ˈjəːli] *a.* 一年一次的; 每年的; 一年间的. *a* ~ *income* 岁入. *a* ~ *plant* 一年生植物. — *ad.* 年年; 一年一次; 在那一年间. — *n.* 年刊.

yearn [jəːn] *vi.* ①想念,怀念,向往,留恋,恋慕 (*for [after]* sth.; *to [towards]* sb.). ②热望,渴望,切望,极想 (*to* do). ~ *for home* 想家. ~ *after rest* 渴望休息. ~ *to see one's old friends* 想见到老朋友,思念故交.

yearn·ing [ˈjəːniŋ] *n.* 思慕,怀念; 热望,渴望 (*for*). — *a.* 思慕的,想念的; 渴望的. **-ly** *ad.* 想念着,怀念着,依恋着; 渴望着 (*as he so yearningly calculates* 按照他的如意算盘).

year-round [ˈjiəˈraund] *a.* (开放、使用或运转等)一年到头的,经历全年的.

yea·say·er [ˈjei,seiə] *n.* (对生活或事物)肯定者.

yeast [jiːst] *n.* ①酵母(菌). ②发酵粉; 酵母饼,酵母片. ③泡,泡沫. ④动乱,激动. *Chinese* ~ 酒药. ~ **cake** ①(发面用的)酵母饼. ②发酵的糕. ~ **cell [-plant]** 酵母,酵母菌. ~ **powder** 发酵粉.

yeast·y [ˈjiːsti] *a.* ①酵母的,会发酵的; 起泡的. ②动荡的,不安定的. ③无实质的,空虚的; 浅薄的. **-i·ness** *n.*

Yeats [jeits] *n.* ①耶茨〔姓氏〕. ②**William Butler** ~ 叶芝〔1865—1939,爱尔兰诗人及剧作家〕.

yegg, yegg·man [jeg, -mən] *n.* 〔美俚〕盗贼〔尤指开保险箱[库]的〕; 凶手.

yeld [jeld] *a.* 〔Scot.〕①不妊的,不育的. ②不产生乳汁的.

Y

yelk [jelk] *n.*〔古、方〕= yolk.

yell [jel] *vi.* 叫喊，大嚷；喊加油；(突然)大笑. ~ *with pain* 痛得叫喊. — *vt.* ①喊出；大声叫. ②向…喊. ~ *a command* 大声叫口令. *They ~ed their good-bys as the bus left.* 汽车开动时，他们大喊再见再见. ~ ***out an oath*** 破口咒骂. — *n.* 大声叫喊声；〔美〕(拉拉队鼓动运动员的)呼喊声. ~ **leader** 拉拉队长.

yellow [ˈjeləu] *a.* ①黄(色)的. ②皮肤黄的；蒙古〔黄色〕人种的. ③忧郁的；妒忌的，猜忌的. ④〔卑〕胆小的，没骨气的；卑劣的. ⑤(新闻等)耸人听闻的. ***the sere, the ~ leaf*** (枝叶枯黄的)老年. — *n.* ①黄色. ②黄色物；蛋黄. ③黄色颜料. ④黄色的鸟〔蝶，蛾〕. ⑤黄色报刊. ⑥〔the ~s〕【医】黄疸；【植】黄化病；〔古〕忌妒. ⑦〔俚〕胆小，懦弱. — *vt.* 把…弄成黄色，染成黄色. ~ **alert** (空袭)预备警报. ~ **ammer** = ~-hammer. ~ **arsenic** 雌黄. ~ **back** 黄皮小说〔十九世纪流行的通俗廉价小说〕. ~**bill** 黑凫. ~**bird**【动】〔英〕金莺；〔美〕金翅雀. **Y-Book** 黄皮书〔法国政府的报告书〕. ~ **boy**〔卑〕金币；〔美〕黑白杂种. ~**cartilage**【解】(构成动脉壁等的)黄色软骨. ~ **daisy**〔美口〕【植】金光菊属植物 (= black-eyed susan). ~ **dog** 野狗；〔美〕卑劣的人. ~**-dog contract** 以不加入工会为条件的雇佣契约. ~**-dog fund** 收买基金. ~ **enzyme**【生化】黄酶，黄朊. ~ **fever**【医】黄热病. **Y-flag** (轮船入港时挂的)检疫旗，黄旗. ~**-green algae**【植】黄藻纲. ~ **gum** ①【医】初生儿黄疸. ②【植】(澳洲)桉树. ~ **hammer**【鸟】鹀鸭；〔美〕金翼啄木鸟；〔美〕俄亥俄人的别名. ~ **Jack**〔〔美〕**jack**〕①【医】= ~ fever. ②〔美〕= Y-flag. ③〔美〕【动】(Florida 州的)金银鱼. ~ **jacket** ①(中国清代的)黄马褂. ②〔美俚〕黄色胡蜂. ~ **jasmine**【植】常绿钩吻〔原产于美国东南部〕. ~ **jaudice** 黄疸. ~ **journalism** 黄色报刊作风〔指不择手段吸引读者〕. ~ **legs**【动】(北美)黄脚鹬. ~**-livered** *a.* 〔美〕胆小的. ~ **looks** 阴沉〔多疑〕的神色. ~ **men [race]** 黄种人. ~ **oak**【植】栎树. ~ **ocher**【化】黄铁华〔氧化铁与粘土的混合物，用作黄色颜料、涂料〕. ~ **paint** 黄铅油；黄色油漆. ~ **pages** (电话)黄页查号簿〔美国电话本中按行业、职业分类的部分；常用黄纸印刷〕. ~ **peril** 黄祸〔指所谓黄种人对西方构成的威胁〕. ~ **pine**【植】黄松，黄松木. ~ **poplar**【植】美国鹅掌楸(= tulip tree)(美鹅掌楸木). ~ **press** 黄色报刊. **Y- River** 黄河. ~ **rust**【植】(= strip rust) 条锈病. **Y- Sea** 黄海. ~**-shafted flicker**【动】赤耳金翅啄木鸟 (=woodpecker). ~ **spot**【解】黄斑. **Y- stone National Park** (美国)黄石公园. ~ **straw pulp** 稻草纸浆. ~ **streak** 胆小；卑怯. ~**tail** ①【鱼】鰤. ②【虫】金毛虫蛾. ~**throat**〔动〕(美洲)黄喉地莺. ~**-throated warbler**【动】黄喉森莺. ~ **wax** 黄蜡. ~**wood**【植】美洲香槐.

yel·low-bel·lied [ˈjeləubelid] ①胆小的；懦怯的. ②腹部黄色的. ~ **sapsucker**【动】黄腹吸汁啄木鸟.

yel·low·bel·ly [ˈjeləuˌbeli] *n.* *(pl. -lies).* ①黄腹鱼. ②可卑的胆小鬼.

yel·low·ish [ˈjeləuiʃ] *a.* 淡黄色的.

yel·low·y *a.* [ˈjeləui] 带黄色的，淡黄色的.

yelp [jelp] *vi.* (狗)汪汪地叫，吠；叫喊. — *vt.* 叫喊着说. — *n.* 狗吠声；叫喊声.

Yem·en [ˈjemən] *n.* 也门. *the ~ Arab Republic* 阿拉伯也门共和国〔亚洲〕. *the People's Democratic Republic of ~* 也门民主人民共和国〔亚洲〕.

Yem·en·i [ˈjeməni] *n., a.* 也门人(的).

Y

yen[1] [jen] *n.*〔*sing., pl.*〕圆，日元〔日本货币单位，略¥〕. ~**bond** (日本政府或企业发行的)日元公债.

yen[2] [jen] *n.* 〔俚〕(汉语中的) 瘾；热望，渴想. *a ~ for knowledge* 求知识的热望. *a ~ to write* 写作的热情. *have a ~ on* 渴想. — *vi.* 热望 *(for)*.

Ye·ni·se·i [jeniˈsei] *n.* (苏联)叶尼塞河.

yen·ta, yen·te [ˈjentə] *n.* 〔Yid.〕 长舌妇，好管闲事的女人.

yentz [jents] *vi.*〔美俚〕欺骗. **-er** *n.* 欺骗者.

yeo [jəu] *int.* = yo.

yeo(m). = yeomanry.

yeo·man [ˈjəumən] *n.* ①【英史】自由民. ②小地主，自耕农. ③(自由民子弟组成的) 义勇骑兵. ④【英史】(皇室、贵族的)侍者，随从；卫士. ⑤〔美〕【海军】做事务工作的军士〔仓库管理员，信号员等〕. ***a Y- of the Guard*** (英国国王的)亲卫兵. ***to do ~ service for*** 为…效忠〔效劳〕. ***~('s) service*** (一旦有事时的) 切实援助〔效劳〕. **-ly** *a.* (象) yeoman 的.

yeo·man·ry [ˈjəumənri] *n.* ①〔集合词〕自由民；小地主们，自耕农. ②义勇骑兵.

yep [jep] *ad.*〔美俚〕= yes.

-yer *suf.*〔常接在 -w 之后〕从事…者: bow*yer*, law*yer*, saw*yer*.

yer *pro.*〔美俚〕= your.

yer·ba [ˈjəːbə] *n.* (冬青叶制成的)巴拉圭茶. ~ **buena**〔美〕【植】加州小薄荷.

Ye·re·van [ˌjereˈvɑːn] *n.* 埃里温〔苏联城市〕.

yerk [jəːk] *vt., n.*〔方〕猛地一拉、一扭、一推 (= jerk).

Yer·kes [ˈjəːkiːz] *n.* 耶基斯〔姓氏〕.

yes [jes, jɛːs, jəːs, jəh] *ad.* ①〔肯定、同意的回答〕(a)〔回答问话、招呼等〕是. *"Were you there?"* — *"Y-."* (当时)你在那里吗？——是的(在那里). *"Isn't it raining?"* — *"Y-, it is."* 在下雨吗？——是，正在下. ★不管问话的方式怎样，如果回答的事实是肯定的，就须用~. (b)〔表示同意对方的话〕是的，对的，不错. *"This is an excellent book."* — *"Y- [jɛːs], it is."* 这是一本好书. ——不错. ②(a)〔怀疑或促人往下讲〕真的吗？啊？不会吧？原来如此，那么呢？〔向不声不响地等着的人〕你有什么事？(= What is it?). *"I was always good at drawing."* — *"Y-?"* 我画图一向总是拿手. ——啊？〔是吗？〕. *"I have come to the conclusion that ..."* — *"Y-?"* 我得到了这样的结论(那就是…)——哦，那么怎么样？(b)〔接在自己的话之后〕知道了吗？晓得了吧？: *"We first go two miles west, then bear to the north and continue in a straight line for several miles* — *~?* 我们先向西走两英里，然后朝北笔直走五、六英里——晓得了吧？ ③〔加强语气〕〔常作 ~, and; ~, or〕而且. *"He will insult you, ~, and cheat you as well."* 他会侮辱你，而且也会骗你. — *n.* *(pl. ~'es* [ˈjesiz]) "是"，"行"，同意，答应，肯定(的回答)；赞成(票). *To say ~ and mean no.* 口是心非. *say ~* 说'行'；答应.

ye·shi·va [jəˈʃiːvə; Heb. jeʃiːˈvɑː] *n.* *(pl. vas;* Heb. *-ˈvot* [-ˈvəut]) ①(犹太教)法典研究院；〔尤指〕神学院. ②(宗教研究与世俗学科相结合的)犹太学校.

yes'm [ˈjesm]〔俚〕= yes, ma'am [madam].

yes·man [ˈjesmæn] *n.*〔美俚〕随声附和的人；唯唯诺诺的人；应声虫.

yes·ter- [ˈjestə-] *comb. f.* 〔构成名词、副词〕: *yester*night 昨夜； *yester*eve 昨晚； *yester*week 上星期； *yester*year 去年.

yes·ter·day [ˈjestədi] *n.* ①昨日，昨天. ②〔*pl.*〕过去(的日子). ③近来，最近. ~ *morning [evening]* 昨天早晨〔傍晚〕. *~'s newspaper* 昨天的报纸. *all ~* 昨天一(整)天. *(a thing) of ~* 最近的(事情). *on ~*〔美〕(在)昨天. *the day before ~* 前天. — *ad.* (在)昨天；最近. *He went away ~.* 他昨天走了. *I was not born ~.* 我又不是昨天刚生的娃娃.

yes·ter·eve [ˈjestəˈriːv]〔诗〕, **yes·ter·e·ven** [-ˈiːvən], **yes·ter·e'en** [-iːn] 〔古、方〕, **yes·ter·eve·ning** [-ˈiːvniŋ]〔古〕*n., ad.* 昨天傍晚，昨晚.

yes·ter·morn〔诗〕, **yes·ter·morn·ing** [ˈjestəˈmɔːn, -ˈmɔːniŋ]〔古、方〕*n., ad.* 昨天早晨.

yes·ter·night [ˈjestəˈnait] *n., ad.*〔古、诗〕昨夜.

yes·ter·year [ˈjestəˈjəː] *n., ad.*〔诗〕去年；近年来；过去

不久.

yes·treen [jesˈtriːn] *n.*, *ad.* 〔Scot. 诗〕昨晚.

yet [jet] *ad.* ①还,现在还是,依然,仍旧; 到目前为止. ②还(不…),还(没有…),暂时还. ③现在,已经. ④又,再,更,此外还. ⑤回头,早晚,不久. ⑥〔和 *nor* 同用〕何况(不是…); 连,甚至于. ⑦〔和比较级同用〕更. ⑧虽…可是,但是. *Is he ~ alive?* 他还活着吗? *the largest ~ found* 迄今为止发见之中的最大的. *~ unfinished task* 还没有完的工作. *I have never ~ lied.* 我从未撒过谎. *Need you go ~?* 你还是要走吗? ★若在疑问句中用 already 代替 yet, 则是表示惊异、疑惑: Need you go already? 你非得就要走吗? [暂时不走不好吗?] *I'll do it ~!* 我迟早要做的! *He will not accept help nor ~ advice.* 他,不要说帮助,连劝告也不会接受的. *Not finished nor ~ begun.* 不要说完成甚至于还没有开始. *a ~ more difficult task* 更难的工作. *poor, ~ honest* 虽穷然而是诚实的. ***and ~*** 虽然…但是 (*strange and ~ true* 虽然奇怪但却真实的). ***another and ~ another*** 一个又一个,陆陆续续. ***as ~*** 迄今,到目前为止还; 到那时为止还(*It has worked well as ~.* 到目前为止还没有出毛病). ***but ~*** 但还是,可是还 (*It seems proved, but ~ I doubt.* 这好象证实了,但我还是怀疑). ***just ~*** 恰好现在; (不会)马上就 (*It will not happen just ~.* 这不会马上就发生的. *I can't come just ~.* 我现在还不能马上去). ***more and ~ more*** 愈来愈多; 愈来愈; 更…. ***~ again = ~ once (more)*** 再,再一次. — *conj.* 虽然…但是,可是. *He is old, ~ active.* 他年纪虽老但精神很好. *though deep, ~ clear = deep ~ clear* (水)深而清.

ye·ti [ˈjeti] *n.* 〔西藏语〕〔常作 Y-〕(据传生活于喜马拉雅山的)雪人 (= abominable snowman).

yew [juː] *n.* 【植】紫杉属; 短叶紫杉, 浆果紫杉; 紫杉木; 紫杉(木制的)弓.

Yg(g)·dra·sil [ˈigdrəsil] *n.* 【北欧神】 宇宙生命大桉树〔象征天上、人间、地狱和宇宙间的一切有生命物〕.

Y-gun [ˈwaigʌn] *n.* 【军】Y 字形防潜深水炸弹发射管.

Y.H.A. = Youth Hostels Association 〔英〕青年招待所协会.

Yid [jid] *n.* 〔俚〕犹太人.

Yid·dish [ˈjidiʃ] *n.* 依地语,意第绪语〔德语、希伯莱语和斯拉夫语的混合语,犹太人使用的国际语〕. — *a.* ①依地语的. ②〔俚〕犹太人的.

yield [jiːld] *vt.* ①生出,产生(作物、报酬、利益等). ②给与,让与; 让渡; 放弃(权利、地位等); 交出. ③承认. ④让步; 投降. *This land ~s heavy crops.* 这块地的产量非常高. *Cows ~ milk.* 奶牛产奶. *Sin ~s bitter fruit.* 罪恶招祸患,恶因生恶果. *~ a fortress to the enemy* 放弃要塞让敌人占领. — *vi.* ①(土地等)生产作物,生产,有收获. ②屈服,服从; 让步; 听从,应允,答应 *(to)*. ③(因压力)弯曲,凹进 *(to)*. ④(疾病因医疗或药物而)好转. *The land ~s well [poorly].* 这个土地产量高[低]. *~ to persuasion [despair, temptation]* 在劝说[失望,诱惑]下失去抵抗力. *The frost has ~ed to the sun.* 霜在太阳底下开始融化了. ***~ consent*** 答应. ***~ oneself prisoner*** 投降做俘虏. ***~ possession*** 让出所有权. ***~ precedence (to another)*** 让(别人)占先. ***~ submission*** 屈服,服从. ***~ the palm to*** 把胜利[荣誉]让给. ***~ the [a] point*** 在讨论的[某一]问题上让步. ***~ to conditions*** 答应条件. ***~ to none*** 不让给谁; 不落人后. ***~ up the ghost [life, soul, breath, spirit]*** 死去. — *n.* ①出产; 产品. ②产额,产量. ③收获(量),收成; 回收(率). ④收益,利益. ⑤屈服; 击穿; 极限. ⑥二次放射系数. *a large ~* 丰收; 巨大产量. ***~ of counter*** 计算器效率. ***~ of radiation*** 辐射强度. **~ point**【物】软化点,屈服点;【橡胶】流动点. **~ sharing forest** 共有林.

yield·ing [ˈjiːldiŋ] *a.* ①有出产的. ②易受影响 [感化] 的; 易说服的,柔顺的; 易屈服的,易让步的. ③易弯的,会变形的.

YIG = yttrium iron garnet 钇铁石榴石〔一种具有多项磁特性的氧化铁合成晶体,常用于调节激光〕.

yill [jil] *n.* 〔Scot.〕= ale.

yin [jin] *a.*, *pron.*, *n.* 〔Scot.〕 = one.

yip [jip] *n.* 〔口〕①小狗叫声; 叫喊(声); 怨言. ②小狗. — *vi.* ①(小狗)吠叫; 叫喊. ②发怨言; 找碴儿.

yipe [jaip] *int.* 哎哟! 〔表示疼痛、悲痛、沮丧、惊慌等〕.

yip·pee [ˈjipiː] *int.* 好哇! 妙! 〔表示快乐、愉快等〕.

Yip·pie [ˈjipiː] *n.* 〔美俚〕易比士, 易比派的一员〔亦可写作 Yip, 源出反对侵越战争的组织 YIP, 即 Youth International Party 青年国际党〕.

yird [jəːd] *n.* 〔Scot.〕= earth.

yit *ad.* 〔美俚〕 = yet.

Yl = yellow.

-yl *suf.*【化】根,基: meth*yl*, eth*yl*.

yld = ①yield. ②your letter dated.

Y.L.I. =Yorkshire Light Infantry 〔英〕约克郡轻步兵团.

y·lem [ˈailəm] *n.* 【哲】以仑, 基质〔在某些宇宙进化论中所假设的最原始物质,一切元素都由此衍生〕.

Y lev·el [ˈwaiˈlevl] *n.* 【测】Y 式水准仪,回转水准仪.

YMCA = Young Men's Christian Association 基督教青年会.

Y.M.H.A. = Young Men's Hebrew Association. 犹太人青年会.

yo [jəu] *int.* ①唷! 〔表示鼓励、警告〕. ②= yoho. — *ad.* 〔美俚〕 = yes.

Y.O. = yearly output 年产量.

y.o. = year-old 满一年的.

YOB = year of birth 出生年.

yob [jɔb] *n.* 〔英俚〕小家伙; 小坏蛋; 笨蛋 (= yobbo).

yock [jɔk] *n.* 〔美俚〕大笑; 大笑料.

yod, yodh [jɔːd, jud] *n.* 希伯来文的第十个字母.

yo·del, yo·dle [ˈjəudl] *n.* 岳得尔调〔瑞士 Tyrol 山间居民用常声和假声轮替的歌曲调子〕. — *vt.*, *vi.* (用岳得尔调)唱[呼喊].

yo·ga [ˈjəugə] *n.*【印度教】瑜伽; 瑜伽派; 瑜伽苦行,瑜伽修行法.

yo·ghort, yo·g(h)urt [ˈjəuguət] *n.* 〔Turk.〕酸乳酪,酸乳饼.

yo·gi [ˈjəugi] *n.* 【印度教】瑜伽信奉者; 瑜伽论者; 实行瑜伽修行方法者.

yo-heave-ho [ˈjəuhiːvˈhəu], **yo-ho** [jəuˈhəu] *int.*【海】唷嗬! 〔水手劳动时的呼声〕.

yo·him·bine [jəuˈhimbiːn] *n.*【化】育亨宾,壮阳碱.

yoick [jɔik] *vi.*, *vt.* 发出"唷唷"声促使(猎犬)上前 *(on)*.

yoicks [jɔiks] *int.* 唷! 〔催促猎犬的叫唤声〕.

yoke [jəuk] *n.* ①轭; 〔*sing.*, *pl.*〕(同一轭上牛的)一对牲口. ②〔英古〕一对牛[牲口]一日所耕的土地; 一气[一趟]农活; (一日中的)一段工作时间. ③轭状物; 轭状扁担; 吊钟的横木. ④(上衣、衬衫等的)抵肩; 裙子的腰. ⑤【物】轭铁;【无】轭,架,座; 偏转线圈. ⑥【船】横舵柄;【空】飞机操纵杆;【铁路】护轨夹;【机】系铁,横铁子;【建】窗头板. ⑦【动】翅轭. ⑧【罗马史】轭门〔用轭或架起三支枪作成,战俘在下俯首通过,象征屈服〕; 奴役,羁绊,束缚; (外族的)统治. ⑨〔喻〕〔罕〕夫妇关系. *a ~ [two ~] of oxen* 一对[两对]牛. *the heavy ~ of opinion* 舆论的严厉制裁. ***pass [come] under the ~*** 屈服. ***send under the ~*** 使屈服. ***shake [throw] off the ~*** 摆脱束缚. ***submit to sb.'s ~*** 受某人的束缚. — *vt.* ①给…上轭,用轭连起; 把(牛、马)套在(车上). ②结合 *(to)*. ③〔多用被动语态〕使成配偶. *be ~d in marriage* 被婚姻结合在一块. — *vi.* 结合; 连合; 配合; 同事 *(together; with)*. **~bone**【解】颧骨. **~fellow, ~mate** (一同工作的)伙伴; 同事; 配偶. **~lines, ~ropes** 〔*pl.*〕【船】操舵索,横舵柄索.

yo·kel [ˈjəukəl] *n.* 庄稼汉, 乡下佬. **~-colour** 〔谑〕 = local colour.

Yo·ko·ha·ma [ˌjəukəˈhɑːmə] *n.* 横滨〔日本港市〕.
Yo·ko·su·ka [ˌjəukəˈsuːkə] *n.* 横须贺〔日本港市〕.
yolk [jəuk] *n.* ①蛋黄,卵黄. ②羊毛油脂. ③【生】(胚囊内的)胚乳;〔喻〕真髓;核心. *hen egg ~ powder* 蛋黄粉. **~-bag, ~-sac**【生】卵黄囊. **~ stalk**【动】卵黄(囊)蒂.
yolk·y [ˈjəuki] *a.* *(-i·er; -i·est)* ①蛋黄(质)的. ②有羊毛脂的. ③油腻的.
yom [jəum,〔口〕jɔm] *n.*〔Heb.〕日. ***Y- Kip·pur*** [ˈkipə]【犹太教】赎罪日〔为犹太历的七月十日〕.
yon [jɔn] *a., ad.*〔古、诗、方〕= yonder. — *pro.*〔古、方〕那里的东西[人].
yond [jɔnd] *a., ad.*〔古、方〕= yonder.
yon·der [ˈjɔndə] *ad., a.* 那里(的),那边(的),远处(的). *Y- stands an oak.* 那里有一棵栎树. *He lives in ~ cottage.* 他住在那边的小屋里. ★ 此字是指示形容词,所以不用冠词. — *pron.* 那边,远处;那边[远处]的东西. *from here to ~* 从这边到那边.
yo·ni [ˈjəuni] *n.*【印度教】女阴像〔作为女性生殖力的象征来礼拜〕.
yoo-hoo [ˈjuːˌhuː] *int., n.* 喂,唷嗬〔用以吸引别人注意的喊声或招呼〕.
yore [jɔː, jɔə] *n.*〔废〕昔,往昔〔现仅用于 of ~〕. ***in days of ~*** 在从前. ***of ~*** 从前(的);往昔.
York [jɔːk] *n.* ①〔英〕约克郡 (= Yorkshire). ②【英史】约克王朝(1461—1485). **~ rite** (共济会中一个派别所遵奉的)约克郡仪式. **-ist** *n., a.*【英史】约克王朝成员(的);约克王朝支持者(的).
york [jɔːk] *vt.*【板球】扔出恰在击球棒下面落下的球使(击球者)退场. **-er** *n.* 扔得恰在击球棒下面落下的球.
York(e) [jɔːk] *n.* 约克〔姓氏〕.
Yorks [jɔːks], **Yorks.** = **York·shire** [ˈjɔːkʃiə] *n.* (英格兰的)约克郡. ***come ~ over [on] sb.* = *put ~ on sb.*** 骗某人,叫某人上当. **~ grit** (磨大理石用的)约克郡磨石. **~ pudding** 约克郡布丁. **~ terrier** 约克郡矮脚长体丝毛狗.
York·shire [ˈjɔːkʃə] *n.* ①约克郡〔英国郡名〕. ②英国约克夏种的白猪.
Yo·ru·ba [ˈjɑːrubə, jɔruˈbɑː] *n.* ① *(pl. -bas; -ba)* (西非)约鲁巴人〔尼日利亚西南部和达荷美东南部的大种族集团〕. ②约鲁巴语. **-n** *a.*
Yo·sem·i·te [jəuˈsemiti] **(National Park)** *n.* (美国)约塞米提国立公园. **Y- Falls** 约塞米提瀑布.
Yost [jəust] *n.* 约斯特〔姓氏〕.
you [juː; 弱 ju] *pro.* 〔*sing., pl.*〕①〔人称代词第二人称、主格及宾格;所有格 your, 所有格代词 yours〕你,您;你们,诸位,各位. ②〔在呼唤、感叹句等中〕喂. ③〔不定代词〕(一般)人,谁都,谁也. ④〔古〕= yourself. *~ and I [me]* 你和我. *You're another.* 〔卑〕你也一样〔被骂时的回答话〕. *Don't ~ go away.* 〔命令〕别走. *Y- begin.* = *Begin ~.* 你开始. *Y- liar, ~!* 你这个撒谎的! *Y- often find that just when ~ want something ~ haven't got it by ~.* 想要一样东西的时候那东西偏偏不在手头,这是谁也常常经验到的事情. *~ fellows [people, chaps]* 你们. *Are ~ there?* 〔打电话〕喂,喂! *Y- there, what is your name?* 喂,你叫什么名字? *There's a rogue for ~!* 那才是个恶棍! *Y- never can tell.* 谁也不能预断. *You're telling me!* 〔美俚〕这件事我很清楚〔不必你说,我老早知道了〕. *Get ~ gone.* 滚! ***all of ~*** 你们全体. ***Y- ain't seen nothin' yet.*** 〔美俚〕精彩[厉害]的还在后面呢. ***~ all*** ①= all of ~. ②= you-all. ***Y- and me both.*** 〔美俚〕我十分同意你的话,我的情形和你一样. ***Y- and what army.* = *Y- and who else.*** 〔美俚〕〔对威胁的强硬回答〕你一个人还不行. ***Y- and your ...!*** 你又…了,你这个…又来了(等). ***Y- bet!* = *Y- betcha!*** [ˈbetʃə] 〔美俚〕当然啰;一定是那. ***Y- said it.*** 〔美俚〕知道了. ***Y- tell 'em.*** 〔美俚〕我也不反对. ***You're on.*** 〔美俚〕我同意了,这事就这样决定了. ***You're sick.*** 〔美俚〕你错了. ***You're the doctor.*** 把你的意见讲给我听听;请你出个主意.
you-all [ˈjuːɔːl, ˈjuːl] *pro.* 〔美南部〕你们;〔美南部卑〕你.
you'd [juːd; 弱 jud] = ①you had. ②you would.
you'll [juːl; 弱 jul] = you will; you shall.
You·mans [ˈjuːmənz] *n.* 尤曼斯〔姓氏〕.
Young [jʌŋ] *n.* 扬〔姓氏〕.
young [jʌŋ] *a.* *(-er* [ˈjʌŋgə]; *-est* [-gist]*)* ①年轻的,幼小的,幼嫩的 *(opp.* old*)*. ②少年气盛的,生气勃勃的,精力充沛的. ③没有经验的,未成熟的 *(in; at)*. ④(时日、季节的)早;新兴的,初期的,摇篮期的. ⑤(区别同名的人以及父子兄弟时)年纪小的. ⑥青春时代的,青年(特有)的. ⑦进步派的;青年党的. ⑧【地】幼年的,受侵蚀尚少的. *a ~ child* 年幼的孩子. *a ~ plant* 幼苗. *a ~ family* 家属中年纪小的几个. *Look here, ~ man!* 喂,小伙子! *a ~ lady* 年轻女人[姑娘];〔俚〕情人. *his ~ woman* 他的情妇. *her ~ man* 她的情人. *~ people* 青年(男女),年轻人;(特指已到结婚年龄的)小伙子. *~ things* 年轻人们. *you ~ rascal* 喂,小家伙. *a ~ dreadful boy* 淘气的小孩子. *a ~ hopeful* 大有希望的孩子. *I was but ~ at the work.* 我对那工作真是没经验. *the ~er Pitt = Pitt the Younger* 小皮特〔皮特的儿子〕. *a ~er brother [sister]* 弟弟[妹妹]. *the ~est son* 最小的儿子. *The night is yet ~.* 夜还不深[夜未央]. *a ~ country* 新兴国家. ***be ~ for his age*** 显得年轻. ***in one's ~ days*** 年轻的时候. ***~ and old*** 无论老少. ***~ volume*** 〔美俚〕小册子,学生写的长篇论文. — *n.*〔集合词〕(动物的)仔. ***be with ~*** (动物)怀着孕,在怀胎. **~ berry** 〔美〕浓紫色大粒黑莓,杨氏黑莓. **~ blood**〔集合词〕青年;青春活力,青年人的思想或行动;新鲜血液,新接纳的成员;〔集合词〕时髦人. **~ers** 年幼的人们;孩子们. **~-eyed** *a.* 具有(青少年的)亮晶晶眼睛的;朝气蓬勃的,有生气的;热情的,乐观的. **~ish** *a.* 相当年轻的,还年轻的,幼小的. **~ lady** 小姐. **~ling** ① *n.* 幼小者;幼儿;年轻人;幼兽;幼树(等);(没有经验的)新手. ② *a.* 年轻的;幼小的. **~ man** 青年;男朋友[情人](*~ man in a hurry* 急进分子). **~ one(s)** 小孩子们;小鸡. **~ timer** 〔美〕年轻人;没有经验的人. **~ster** ①年轻人;小孩子;(活泼的)少年. ③【英海军】(服役未满四年的)海军少尉候补生;【美海军】海军学校二年级生. ④幼兽〔特指幼驹〕. **Y- Turk**【史】青年土耳其党人;(一个集团中的)少壮派. **~'un** 〔俚〕年轻人,小伙子;〔招呼〕喂,年轻人!
Young·hus·band [ˈjʌŋˌhʌzbənd] *n.* 扬哈斯本〔姓氏〕.
youn·ker [ˈjʌŋkə] *n.* ①= youngster. ②〔古〕贵族青年.
your [jɔː, juə; 弱 jə] *pro.* 〔you 的所有格〕①你(们)的. ②〔口、古〕所谓,大家都很知道的〔常含轻蔑意〕. *Y- good sense must tell you that ....* 聪明的诸位一定会知道…. *~ and my father* 你和我的父亲 (*cf.* ~ and my fathers = ~ father and mine 你的父亲和我的父亲). *~ dismissal of him* 你把他解雇这件事情 (*cf.* ~ dismissal by him 你被他解雇这件事情). *No one is so fallible as ~ expert.* 再没有象所谓内行人那样容易错的了.
you're [juə, jɔə] = you are.
yours [jɔːz, juəz] *pro.* 〔you 的物主代词〕①你(们)的东西. ②你的家属. ③来信,尊函. ④你的责任[义务]. *those hands of ~* 你那双手. *you and ~* 你和你的家属. *Y- is to hand.* 接读来信. *It is ~ to help him.* 帮助他是你的责任. *What's ~?* 〔口〕你要喝什么? — *a.* ①你(们)的(东西). ②〔信末署名前用语〕*ever ~ = ~ truly [faithfully, affectionately] = ~ to command* 等. =〔美〕*~ sincerely [cordially 等]* (相当于中国旧式书信署名后的)谨上(等). ***~ truly*** 〔口、谑〕鄙人,我(= I, me) (*But ~ truly will not be there.* 但鄙人不打算到那里去).

Y

your·self [jɔːˈself, juə-, 弱 jə-] *pro.* *(pl.* **-selves** [-ˈselvz]*)* 你自己. *You ~ said so.* = *You said so ~.* 你自己这样说的. *You are not quite ~ tonight.* 你今晚有点儿不大正常. *Have you hurt ~?* 有没有受伤? *Help ~ to some more meat.* 请再吃一点肉吧. ***all by ~*** = by ~. ***Be ~.*** 〔美口〕你打起精神来. ***by ~*** 独个儿,独自;独力. ***for ~*** 独力. ***How's ~?*** 〔俚〕你也好吗? 〔被问 How are you? 的回答话〕.

youth [juːθ] *n.* *(pl.* **~s** [juːðz]*)* ①少年,少小时候,少年[青年]时代,青春时期;初期. ②年轻,精神;轻快,明朗. ③年轻人;男青年;小伙子. ④〔集合词〕青年(男女)们. *the secret of perpetual ~ [of keeping one's ~]* 永葆青春的秘诀. *the ~ of nations* 民族[国家]的初期. *the ~ of the world* 世界的青春时代;古代,上古. *a ~ of twenty* 一个二十岁的青年. *a bevy of ~s and maidens* 一群青年男女. *the ~ of the country* 这个国家的青年. ***China's Y- Day*** 中国五四青年节. ***Communist Y- League of China*** 中国共产主义青年团. ***from ~ onwards*** 从青年时代起. ***in one's hot [raw, vigorous] ~*** 在某人血气方刚的时代. ***in (the days of) one's ~*** 在…青年时代. **~-and-old-age** *n.* 【植】百日草. **~ culture** 青年文化〔多指三十岁以下的一代人倾向于接受的道德观念等〕. **~quake** 〔美〕青年动乱〔指六十年代与七十年代间由学生闹事引起的动荡不安〕.

youth·ful [ˈjuːθful] *a.* ①青年(特有)的;年轻的,富有朝气的;年轻气盛的. ②早期的,初期的;【地】= young. *the ~ season of the year* 春季. **-ly** *ad.* **-ness** *n.*

you've [juːv, 弱 juv] = you have.

yow(e) [jəu] *n.* 〔Scot.〕母羊 (= ewe).

yowl [jaul] *n.*, *vi.* (长声)悲号;长吼,狂啸.

yow·man [ˈjəumən] *int.* 〔美俚〕= yes; yes, ma'am.

yow·sah [ˈjəuzɑː] *int.* 〔美俚〕= yes; yes, sir.

yo-yo [ˈjəujəu] *n.* 【商标】约约〔一种用线扯动使忽上忽下的轮形木制玩具〕;〔美俚〕迟钝愚蠢的人. — *vi.* 玩约约;忽上忽下.

YP = yield point 屈服点.

Y.P. = young people 青年.

y·per·ite [ˈiːpərait] *n.* 【化】芥子气,双氯乙基硫.

Y·quem [iːˈkem] *n.* 易其姆白葡萄酒〔法国易其姆堡所产的一种优质白葡萄酒〕.

yr. = ①year. ②younger. ③your.

Yr. B. = year book.

yrs. = ①years. ②yours.

YS = yield strength 屈服强度.

Yt = 【化】yttrium.

Y.T. = Yukon Territory 育空地区.

yt·ter·bi·a [iˈtəːbiə] *n.* 【化】镱氧,氧化镱.

yt·ter·bic [iˈtəːbik] *a.* 【化】镱的,含镱的.

yt·ter·bi·um [iˈtəːbiəm] *n.* 【化】镱 (Yb).

yt·tri·a [ˈitriə] *n.* 【化】钇氧,氧化钇.

yt·tric, yt·tri·ous [ˈitrik, ˈitriəs] *a.* 【化】钇的,含钇的.

yt·trif·er·ous [iˈtrifərəs] *a.* 【化】含钇的.

yt·tri·um [ˈitriəm] *n.* 【化】钇 (Y). **~ garnet** 【矿】钇榴石. **~ metals** 【化】钇属金属.

yt·tro·tan·ta·lite [ˌitrəˈtæntəlait] *n.* 【矿】钇钽矿.

yu·an [juːˈɑːn] *n.* 〔*sing.*, *pl.*〕元〔中国的货币单位〕.

Yuc. = Yucatan.

Yu·ca·tan [juːkəˈtɑːn, -ˈtæn] *n.* ①(中美)尤卡坦半岛. ②(墨西哥)尤卡坦州.

Yu·ca·tec [ˈjuːkəˌtek] *n.* ①*(pl.* **~(s)***)* 尤卡特克人〔墨西哥尤卡坦半岛上的美洲印第安部族人〕. ②尤卡特克语. **-an** *a.*

yuc·ca [ˈjʌkə] *n.* 【植】丝兰(花). **Y- country** 丝兰之乡〔美国西南部的别名〕.

yuck [jʌk] *n.*, *vi.* = yuk.

Yu·go·slav [ˈjuːgəuˌslɑːv] *a.*, *n.* 南斯拉夫人(的). (= Jugoslav). **-sla·vi·an** ①*n.* 南斯拉夫人. ②*a.* 南斯拉夫(人)的. **-slav·ic** [ˌjuːgəuˈslɑːvik] *a.* 南斯拉夫(人)的.

Yu·go·sla·vi·a [ˈjuːgəuˈslɑːvjə] *n.* 南斯拉夫〔欧洲〕.

yuk [jʌk] *n.* 〔拟声〕〔美俚〕咯咯大笑;引起咯咯大笑的趣事. — *vi.* *(***yuk·ked; yuk·king***)* 大笑.

yu·ka·ta [juːˈkɑːtɑː] *n.* 〔Jap.〕(日本男子)夏季穿的单衣;浴衣.

Yu·kon [ˈjuːkɔn] *n.* ①育空〔加拿大西北一地区〕. ②育空河〔北美洲〕. **~ Standard Time** (加拿大)育空标准时间〔较格林威治标准时间晚 9 小时〕.

yule [juːl] *n.* 〔常作 Y-〕【基督教】圣诞节;圣诞节期.

yule·tide, yule·time [ˈjuːltaid, -taim] *n.* 〔常作 Y-〕圣诞节(期).

Yu·ma [ˈjuːmə] *n.* ①*(pl.* **~(s)***)* 尤马族人〔亚利桑那与加利福尼亚州科罗拉多河下游的北美印第安人〕. ②尤马语方言.

Yu·man [ˈjuːmən] *a.* ①尤马族的,尤马族人的;尤马语的;尤马语系的某方言的. — *n.* 尤马语系.

yum·my [ˈjʌmi] *n.* *(***-mi·er; -mi·est***)* 〔口〕好吃的;美味的;挺好的,挺美的.

yum·yum [ˈjʌmjʌm] *int.* 〔美儿〕真好吃!

yup [jʌp] *ad.* 〔美俚〕是的;对啊,不错.

yurt [juət], **yurta** [ˈjuətə] *n.* (兽皮或毛毡)圆顶帐篷. *a Mongolian ~* 蒙古包.

Y·vette [iˈvet] *n.* 伊维特〔女子名〕.

Y·vonne [iˈvɔn] *n.* 伊冯〔女子名〕.

YWCA = Young Women's Christian Association 基督教女青年会.

Y.W.H.A. = Young Women's Hebrew Association 犹太人女青年会.

y·wis [iˈwis] *ad.* 〔古〕= iwis.

Z

Z, z [zed; 〔古〕izəd] *n.* *(pl.* **Z's, z's** [zedz; Am. ziːz]*)* ①英语字母表第二十六个字母. ②【数】第三个未知数; (中世罗马数字的)2,000. ③Z 字形物. ***from A to Z*** 从头到尾,自始至终. **Z Day** 会议闭幕日.

Z., z. = ①zone. ②Zenith distance 【天】天顶距. ③atomic number 【化】原子序(数). ④【化】zirconium. ⑤zero.

za·ba·glio·ne [ˌzæbəˈljəuniː, It. ˌdzɑːbɑːˈljəune] *n.* 消食甜酒〔一种易消化的甜食,将鸡蛋、糖和马尔萨拉白葡萄酒调[打]好冲入开水而成〕.

za·ca·ton [ˈsɑːkɑːˈtəun] 【植】①萨卡通草〔生长于美国西南部和墨西哥,可制刷和扫帚、纸张〕. ②赖特氏鼠尾粟(= sacaton).

zaf·fre, zaf·fer [ˈzæfə] *n.* 【化】钴蓝釉.

zaf·tig [ˈzɑːftig] *a.* 〔俚〕(妇女)身材丰满俊俏的.

Za·greb [ˈzɑːgreb] *n.* 萨格勒布〔南斯拉夫城市〕.

zai·ba·tsu, -tzu [zaiˈbɑːtsuː] *n.* 〔*sing., pl.*〕〔Jap.〕财阀.

Za·ire [zəˈiːrə] *n.* ①扎伊尔〔非洲〕. ②〔the ~〕扎伊尔河〔即刚果河〕〔非洲〕. ③〔z-〕扎伊尔〔扎伊尔货币单位〕. **-an, -se** [-riːz] ①*n.* 扎伊尔人. ②*a.* 扎伊尔的.

Zal·o·phus [ˈzæləufəs] *n.*【动】海驴属.

Zam·bi·a [ˈzæmbiə] *n.* 赞比亚〔非洲〕. **-n** ①*n.* 赞比亚人. ②*a.* 赞比亚的.

zam·bo [ˈzæmbəu] *n.* 黑人和印第安人混血儿〔特指父为黑人,母为印第安人的子女〕.

Zam·bo·an·ga [sɑːmbəuˈɑːŋgɑː] *n.* 三宝颜〔菲律宾民答那峨 (Mindanao) 岛港口〕.

Za·men·hof [ˈzɑːmenhɔf], **L.L.** 柴门霍夫〔1859—1917,波兰眼科医生,世界语创始人〕.

za·mi·a [ˈzeimiə] *n.*【植】泽米(属).

za·min·dar [zəˈmindɑː] *n.* = zemindar.

Zane [zein] *n.* 赞恩〔姓氏,男子名〕.

Zang·will [ˈzæŋgwil] *n.* 赞格威尔〔姓氏〕.

za·ny [ˈzeini] *n.* ①【史】摹仿主要丑角动作的小丑;丑角. ②傻瓜,笨人. — *a.* (象丑角那样)荒唐可笑的; 愚蠢笨拙的.

Zan·zi·bar [ˌzænziˈbɑː] *n.* ①桑给巴尔(岛)〔坦桑尼亚一地区〕. ②桑给巴尔〔坦桑尼亚港市〕.

Zan·zi·ba·ri [ˌzænziˈbɑːri] *a., n.* 桑给巴尔的(人).

zap [zæp] *vt., vi.* ***(zapped; zap·ping)*** 〔美俚〕(嗞地一下)打败,攻击,弄死. — *n.* 〔美俚〕①精力,活力. ②攻击;急促的嘘声. — *int.* 嚓! ~ **rays** 死光.

zap'em-up [ˈzæpəm-ʌp] *a.* (电影场面)以太空枪摧毁一切敌人的,科学幻想式的.

Za·po·tec [ˈzɑːpəˌtek] *n.* ①***(pl. -tecs, -tec)*** 萨巴特克人〔墨西哥的印第安人〕. ②萨巴特克语. **~an** 萨巴特克语〔墨西哥印第安人说的任何一种语言〕.

za·ra·tite [ˈzɑːrəˌtait] *n.*【矿】翠镍矿.

za·re·ba, za·ree·ba, za·ri·ba [zəˈriːbə] *n.* (非洲苏丹地方保护村庄的)防护木栅(等); 有防护木栅的村庄.

zarf [zɑːf] *n.* (地中海东部沿岸喝热咖啡用的)金属杯.

zar·zue·la [zɑːˈzweilə] *n.* ①查瑞拉小轻歌剧〔西班牙的一种传统的对话形式与乐曲相结合的抒情小歌剧,得名于首次上演地点查瑞拉宫〕. ②西班牙式燉海鲜.

zax [zæks] *n.* 修整(屋顶)石板用的凿刀.

z-ax·is [ˈzedˌæksis] *n.*【数】z 轴(线).

za·yin [ˈzɑːjin] *n.* 希伯来文的第七个字母.

z.B. = 〔G.〕*zum Beispiel* 例如 (= for example).

zeal [ziːl] *n.* 热心,热诚,热情; 奋发, 奋起 *(for). feel ~ for* 为…而奋发.

Zea·land [ˈziːlənd] *n.* (丹麦)西兰岛.

zeal·ot [ˈzelət] *n.* 热心者; 狂热者; 〔Z-〕【史】(公元 60—70 年间反抗罗马帝国迫害的) 富于战斗性的犹太教信徒. **-ry** *n.* 热情; 狂热行为.

zeal·ous [ˈzeləs] *a.* 热心的,热诚的. ***be ~ in one's ...*** 热心从事….

ze·a·xan·thin [ziəˈzænθin] *n.*【生化】玉米黄质.

ze·bec(k) [ˈziːbek] *n.* = xebec.

ze·bra [ˈziːbrə] *n.*【动】斑马; (北美)斑蝶. — *a.* 有斑马般斑纹的; 有条纹的. ~ **crossing** 斑马线〔指马路上涂有黑白相间颜色的人行横道〕. ~ **danio**【动】斑马担尼鱼. ~ **finch**【动】灰头文鸟. ~ **fish** (热带)条纹鱼, 斑马鱼〔一种胎生观赏鱼〕. **~wood** (制家具用的)条纹木料.

ze·brass [ˈziːbræs] *n.* 雄斑马和母驴的杂种.

ze·bra·wood [ˈziːbrəwud] *n.* 斑木; 斑木树.

ze·brine [ˈziːbrain], **ze·broid** [-brɔid] *a.* (象)斑马的.

ze·bru·la [ˈziːbrulə], **ze·brule** [ˈziːbruːl] *n.* 雄斑马与雌马的杂种.

ze·bu [ˈziːbuː] *n.*【动】(印度)瘤牛,封牛.

zech·in [ˈzekin] *n.* = sequin.

zed [zed] *n.* ①〔英〕字母 Z. ②Z 形铁条.

zed·o·a·ry [ˈzedəuəri] *n.*【植】蓬莪术〔印度等处产薑科植物的根茎,作药及香料用〕.

zee [ziː] *n.* 〔美〕= zed.

Zee·man effect [ˈzeimən]【物】塞曼效应. *normal [anomalous]* ~ 正规[非正规]塞曼效应.

ze·in [ˈziːin] *n.* ①【生化】玉米朊. ②玉米朊纤维.

Zeiss [zais] *n.* (德国)蔡斯 (厂) 透镜.

Zeit·ge·ber, z- [ˈtsaitgeibər] *n.* 〔G.〕【生】环境钟〔指能够影响生物对时间之感应的任何一种时间指示因素,如光、黑暗、温度等〕.

zeit·geist [ˈtsaitgaist] *n.* 〔G.〕时代精神.

Ze·la·ni·an [ziˈleiniən] *a.* 新西兰 (*New Zealand*) 的.

Zel·da [ˈzeldə] *n.* 泽尔达〔女子名〕.

ze·lo·so [ziˈləusəu] *a., ad.* 〔It.〕【乐】热衷的[地].

ze·min·dar [ˈzimindɑː] *n.*【史】(印度的)地主; 地税包收者.

zem·stvo [ˈzemstvəu] *n.* (帝俄的)地方自治会,州会.

Zen [zen] *n.* (佛教的)禅(宗). ~ **gesture** 双手合十(的手势). **-ist** *n.* 禅宗信徒.

ze·na·i·da (dove) [ziˈneidə, -nai-]【动】哀鸽〔产于美洲〕.

ze·na·na [zeˈnɑːnə] *n.* ①(印度富家的) 闺房; (闺房中的)妇女. ②女用薄衣料 (= ~ cloth).

Zend [zend] *n.* ①(祆教经典)《亚吠陀》古波斯语译解. ②(八世纪时)古波斯语. **-ic** *a.* **~-Avesta** *n.* 《亚吠陀》经解合刊.

Ze·ner, ze·ner [ˈziːnə] *n.*【无】齐纳. ~ **breakdown**【无】齐纳击穿. ~ **current**【无】齐纳电流. ~ **diode**【无】齐纳二极管, 稳压二极管. ~ **effect**【无】齐纳效应. ~ **voltage**【无】齐纳电压.

Zeng·er [ˈzeŋə] *n.* 曾格〔男子名〕.

zen·ith [ˈzeniθ] *n.* ①【天】天顶 *(opp.* nadir*)*. ②顶点,极点,绝顶,全盛. ***at the ~ of*** 达到…的绝顶, 在…的绝顶的. ***one's ~*** 某人的全盛时期. ~ **distance**【天】天顶距. ~ **telescope**【天】天顶仪.

ze·nith·al [ˈzeniθəl] *a.* 天顶的; 顶点的,绝顶的.

Ze·no [ˈziːnəu] *n.* 芝诺① ~ **of Citium** 季蒂昂的芝诺〔340?—265? B.C., 希腊哲学家, 斯多葛派创始人〕. ② ~ **of Elea** 埃利亚的芝诺〔公元前五世纪希腊埃利亚学派哲学家〕.

ze·o·lite [ˈziːəlait] *n.*【矿】泡沸石.

zeph·yr [ˈzefə] *n.* ①〔Z-〕〔拟人语〕西风(老人). ②〔诗〕和风, 微风. ③轻软毛织物 (= ~ cloth); 轻软的衣著; (刺绣用)细绒线 (= ~ yarn [worsted]).

ze·ro [ˈziərəu] *n.* ***(pl. ~s, ~es)*** ①【数】零; 零号. ②零位; 零点,起点; (温度表的)零度, 冰点; 座标原点; 无. ③最低点;【天】天底;【空】零高度. ④没价值的人[物]. ⑤【军】= ~ hour. *the absolute* ~【物】绝对零度〔-273.7°C〕. *the air* ~ 原子弹空中爆炸中心. ***fly at ~*** 超低空 (1000 英尺高度以下的) 飞行. — *vt.* ①把(调节器等) 调整到零位. ②把…减少到零位. ~ ***in*** ①调整(枪炮的)射距, 把(枪炮等的照尺)调整到标准无风部位瞄准. ②把 (火力) 对准目标 *(on)*. ~ **capacity**【电】起点电容. ~ **gravity**【物】零重力; 失重. ~ **hour**【军】预定行动开始时刻; 严格考验的起点; 能率的最低点. ~ **meridian** 本初子午线. ~ **method** 衡消法. ~ **reading** 起点读数. ~ **point**【生】致死临界温度. ~ **population growth** 零度人口增长〔即无增长〕. ~ **thrust pitch**【机】无推力螺距. ~ **water** 蒸馏水. — *a.* ①零(度)的. ②【气】 云幕低于 50 英尺, 能见度小于 165 英尺的. **~-zero** ①*n., a.*【气, 空】云幕和能见度极低(的). ② *vt.* 把…减到零; 把…调整到零位.

ze·ro·ra·di·o·graphy [ˌziərəreidiˈɔgrəfi] *n.* 干放射线照相术.

zest [zest] *n.* ①(酒里的)风味,香味; 富于刺激性的作料,香料. ②风趣; 有刺激力的成分[性质]. ③兴趣, 热心, 热情. ④热功率热核反应装置. ***add [give] (a) ~ to*** 给…增加兴趣[风趣]. ***with ~*** 津津有味地,热烈地,热

情地 (*enter into a piece of work with* ~ 热情地开始工作). **-ful** *a.* **-ful•ly** *ad.*
ze•ta [ˈziːtə] *n.* 希腊语第六个字母 [Z,ζ].
ze•tet•ic [ziˈtetik] *a., n.* 追究着进行(的),探究(性的).
zeug•ma [ˈzjuːgmə] *n.*【语法】共轭支配〔指以一个形容词或动词勉强修饰或支配两个名词的方法,如将 kill the boys and destroy the luggage 说作 kill the boys and the luggage〕. **-mat•ic** *a.*
Zeus[1] [zjuːs] *n.*【希神】宙斯〔相当于罗马神话中的朱庇特 (Jupiter)〕.
Zeus[2] = Zero Energy Uranium System〔英〕零功率铀装置(系统).
Z/F = zone of fire 射界.
Z.G. = ①zinc gauge 锌规格. ②Zoological Garden 动物园.
Z-hour, z.hr. = zero hour 零时.
ZI = zone of interior 后方地带;美国本土.
zib•el(l)•ine [ˈzibəlain] *a.* 黑[紫]貂的;黑[紫]貂皮做的. — *n.* 黑[紫]貂皮;充黑貂皮的有光长绒呢,黑貂绒.
zib•et, zib•eth [ˈzibit] *n.*【动】灵猫,香猫,印度麝猫.
Zie•gler [ˈziːglə] *n.* 齐格勒〔男子名〕.
zig [zig] *n.* ① Z [之]字形路线的一个转折. ②(方向的)转变,急转. —*vi.* ***(zigged; zig•ging)*** 作 Z [之]字形转弯,急转.
zig•gu•rat [ˈziguræt] *n.* 亚述古庙塔〔古时亚述人和巴比伦人所筑的庙塔〕.
zig•zag [ˈzigzæg] *a.* 乙字形的,之字形的,锯齿形的,曲折的. — *n.* 乙字形图案〔线条、道路、壕沟(等)〕;【建】曲折的线条;锯齿状. ~ *reflection* 多次反射. ~ *riveting*【机】错纵铆. — *ad.* 作 Z 字形,曲折地. — *vt.* 把…作成 Z 字形;使成锯齿形. — *vi.* 作 Z 字形进行,成 Z 字形;取之字形前进. **-er** 锁边机.
zik•ku•rat, zik•u•rat [ˈzikuræt] *n.* = ziggurat.
zilch [ziltʃ] *n.* ①〔美俚〕无,乌有,零. ②〔Z-〕某人;普通人,一般人,小人物.
zil•lah [ˈzilə] *n.* 齐拉〔印度在英国统治时期的一种行政单位,相当于县,州,郡〕.
zil•lion [ˈziljən] *n.*〔美口〕千千万〔一个很大的,不定的数字〕.
zil•lion•aire [ˌziljəˈnɛə] *n.* 亿万富翁,大富翁.
Zim•ba•bwe [zimˈbɑːbwei] *n.* 津巴布韦〔非洲〕.
Zim•mer•man [ˈziməmən] *n.* 齐默曼〔姓氏〕.
Zim•mern [ˈzimən] *n.* 齐默恩〔姓氏〕.
zinc [ziŋk] *n.*【化】锌 (Zn.) — *vt.* ***(~ed, zincked)*** 用锌包,在…上镀锌. *flowers of* ~ = ~ *oxide* 锌华,氧化锌. ~ **blende**【矿】闪锌矿. ~ **galvanizing** 镀锌. ~ **ointment** (氧化)锌油膏. ~ **plate [sheet]** 锌片;【印】锌版. ~ **sulphate** 硫酸锌. ~ **white** 锌白,氧化锌.
zinc•ate [ˈziŋkeit] *n.*【化】锌酸盐〔两可性氢氧化锌的盐〕.
zinc•ic [ˈziŋkik] *a.* 锌的;从锌得来的;含锌的. ~ *acid*【化】锌酸.
zinc•if•er•ous [ziŋˈkifərəs] *a.* 含锌的;产锌的.
zinc•i•fi•ca•tion [ˌziŋkifiˈkeiʃən] *n.* 镀锌(法),包锌(法);加锌;锌饱和.
zinc•i•fy [ˈziŋkifai] *vt.* 在…上镀锌;在…上包锌;在…中加锌;使呈锌饱和.
zinc•ite [ˈziŋkait] *n.*【矿】红锌矿.
zinck•y [ˈziŋki] *a.* = zinky.
zin•co [ˈziŋkəu] *n., vt.* = zincograph.
zin•co•graph [ˈziŋkəgrɑːf] *n.*【印】锌版;锌版印刷[复制]物. — *v.* 用锌版复制;制锌版.
zin•cog•ra•phy [ziŋˈkɔgrəfi] *n.* 制锌版术. **-graph•ic** [ˌzinkəuˈgræfik], **-graph•i•cal** *a.*
zinc•oid [ˈziŋkɔid] *a.* 锌的;象锌的.
zin•co•type [ˈziŋkəutaip] *n.* = zincograph.
zinc•ous [ˈziŋkəs] *a.* (含)锌的;(电池)阳极的.
zin•eb [ˈzineb] *n.*〔美〕【化】乙撑两个氨荒酸锌〔一种用于植物和果实的杀虫剂和杀菌剂〕.
zin•fan•del [ˈzinfənˌdel] *n.* 馨芳葡萄酒;制这种酒用的紫红色葡萄.
zing [ziŋ] *n.* ①〔拟声语〕〔俚〕尖啸声. ②热情;活力;兴致;风趣,趣味. — *vi.* 发出尖啸声(迅速飞过等); — *vt.* (投掷,迅速拉动等)使发尖啸声. ~ ***up***〔美俚〕使充满活力. **-y** *a.*
Zin•ga•ra [ˈziŋgərə] *n.*〔It.〕(*pl.* ***-re*** [-re]) 吉普赛女人.
Zin•ga•ro [ˈziŋgərəu] *n.*〔It.〕***(pl. -ri*** [-riː]) 吉普赛人 = Gypsy.
zing•er [ˈziŋə] *n.*〔美俚〕① 有力的言语[行动];有力的反驳. ②精神抖擞的人.
zin•gi•ber [ˈzindʒibə] *n.*【植】①姜. ②[Z-] 姜属.
zin•gi•ber•a•ceous [ˌzindʒəbəˈreiʃəs] *a.*【植】属于姜科的.
zin•ken•ite [ˈziŋkiˌnait] *n.*【矿】辉锑铅矿.
zink•y [ˈziŋki] *a.* 锌制的,含锌的,似锌的.
zin•ni•a [ˈzinjə, ˈziniə] *n.*【植】百日草(属).
Zins•ser [ˈzinsə] *n.* 津泽〔姓氏〕.
Zi•on [ˈzaiən] *n.* ①锡安山〔亦译作郇山,在耶路撒冷,犹太民族文化中心的象征〕. ②耶路撒冷市. ③(古犹太人理想的)神治,神权统治. ④〔集合词〕神的选民,犹太人. ⑤天国,天堂. ⑥基督教会;英国非国教派教堂. **-ism** *n.* 犹太复国主义. **-ist** *n., a.* 犹太复国主义者(的). **-ward(s)** *ad.* 向天国.
ZIP, zip [zip] *n.* = zip code.
zip [zip] *n.* ①尖啸声,嘘,咻〔子弹等飞射声或撕布声〕. ②精神;精力;活力. ③〔英〕拉链,拉锁. ④〔俚〕零分. *have lots of* ~ *and go* 精神十足. — *vi.* 嘘地响,嘘地飞;突进,直冲. — *vt.* ①将…嘘的一下送出去. ②用拉链扣上;拉开(拉链). ③〔口〕使增加活力 [风味] *(up)*. ④〔美俚〕逮捕. ~ ***across the horizon***〔美口〕忽然有起名来. ~ ***up*** 加油,打气. ~**-fastener** = zipper. ~**-top** *a.* (罐头等)拉边开盖的〔指拉开罐顶边缘的窄条即可把盖打开〕.
ZIP code [ˈzipˈkəud] (美国)邮区编号制〔以五位号码代表邮区的制度,以加速邮递〕;划分美国邮区的五位号码.
zip gun [ˈzip ˈgʌn]〔美〕(由玩具枪、猎枪等改装成的)自制小手枪.
zip•per [ˈzipə] *n.*〔美〕① 嘘地飞过的东西;动作迅速的人. ② 拉链,拉锁;〔Z-〕【商标】拉链胶皮靴. — *vt.* 拉开[拉上](拉链).
zip•py [ˈzipi] *a.* ***(-pi•er; -pi•est)*** 活泼的,精神饱满的.
zi•ram [ˈzaiəræm] *n.*【化】二甲氨荒酸锌.
zir•cite [ˈzəːkait] *n.*【化】氧化锆.
zir•cal(l)•oy [ˈzəːkəlɔi] *n.* 锆合金〔具有耐热、耐腐蚀等特性,常在原子反应堆中用以分隔燃料和冷却剂〕.
zir•con [ˈzəːkɔn] *n.*【矿】锆石.
zir•co•nate [ˈzəːkəneit] *n.*【化】锆酸盐.
zir•co•ni•a [zəːˈkəuniə, -njə] *n.*【化】氧化锆.
zir•con•ic [zəːˈkɔnik] *a.*【化】锆的,象锆的;含锆的. ~ *acid* 锆酸.
zir•co•ni•um [zəːˈkəuniəm] *n.*【化】锆 (Zr). ~ *oxide* 氧化锆.
zirk•ite [ˈzəːkait] *n.* = zircite.
zith•er [ˈziθə] *n.*【乐】齐特拉琴〔一种古代拨弦乐器,有五根旋律弦和 30—40 根和声弦〕. **-ist** *n.*
zith•ern [ˈziθən] *n.* ① = cittern. ② = zither.
zit•tern [ˈzitən] *n.* = cittern.
zi•zit, zi•zith [tsiˈtsiːt, ˈtsitsis] *n.*〔*pl.*〕〔Heb.〕旧派犹太教徒祈祷披肩上的流苏.
zizz [ziz] *n.*〔英俚〕打盹,打瞌睡.
zlot•y [ˈzlɔti] *n.* *(pl.* ~*s,*〔集合词〕~*)* 兹罗提〔波兰货币单位〕.

Z

Zn = 【化】zinc.
zo·a [ˈzəuə] zoon 的复数.
-zoa *suf*. 表示"动物": Protozoa.
zo·an·tha·rian [ˌzəuænˈθeəriən] *n*. 【动】六放珊瑚类(*Zoantharia*)动物〔包括珊瑚; 海葵〕. — *a*. 六放珊瑚类的.
zo·an·thro·py [zəuˈænθrəpi] *n*. 【医】变兽妄想.
zo·di·ac [ˈzəudiæk, -djæk] *n*. 【天】黄道带; 黄道十二宫图; 〔罕〕一圈. *the signs of the* ~【天】黄道十二宫.
zo·di·a·cal [zəuˈdaiəkəl] *a*. 黄道带的.
Zoe [ˈzəui] *n*. 佐伊〔女子名〕.
zo·e·a [zəuˈi:ə] *n*. *(pl*. ***zo·e·ae***, [-i:], ***zo·e·as)*** 【动】海蟹幼虫. **-l** *a*.
zo·e mou, sas a·ga·po [ˈzəui mu: sɑ:s ɑ:gɑ:ˈpəu] 〔Gr.〕我的生命呀,我爱你 (= My life, I love thee).
zo·e·trope [ˈzəuitrəup] *n*. 活动连环画转筒〔把画有连续动作的图像贴在转筒内壁下段,转筒上段刻有隙缝,转筒回旋时从隙缝中看连续图像,就象图像在活动一样〕.
Z. of A. = zone of action 作战地带.
zof·tig [ˈzɔftig] *a*. = zaftig.
Zo·har [ˈzəuhɑ:] *n*. 《光明篇》〔犹太教神秘主义对摩西五书的注疏〕.
zo·ic [ˈzəuik] *a*. ①动物的; 动物生活的. ②有生命物的. ③【地】含动植物遗骸的. *sapro* ~ 食腐的. *Archaeo* ~ 太古代的. *Meso* ~ 中生代的.
zois·ite [ˈzɔisait] *n*. 【矿】黝簾石.
Zo·la [ˈzəulə], **Emile** 左拉〔1840—1902,法国小说家〕.
Zo·la·esque [ˌzəuləˈesk] *a*. (法国文豪)左拉风格的.
Zo·la·ism [ˈzəuləiizəm] *n*. 左拉主义〔作风〕; (贬义的)自然主义. **-ist** *n*. 左拉主义者.
Zoll·ver·ein [ˈtsɔl-fərain] *n*. 〔G.〕关税同盟.
zom·bi, zom·bie [ˈzɔmbi:] *n*. *(pl*. *~s)* ①(西非民族及西印度、美国南部伏都教的)蛇神(崇拜). ②(伏都教信仰中的)起死回生巫术. ③还魂尸; 僵尸. ④行动僵直不灵的人; 〔俚〕傻瓜,笨蛋; 怪人. ⑤兰姆酒等加果汁的混合酒.
zo·mo·ther·a·py [ˌzəuməuˈθerəpi] *n*. 生肉食疗法〔旧时用吃生牛肉的办法医治结核病〕.
zon·al [ˈzəunl] *a*. ①成带的,带状的. ②区域〔地区〕性的. ~ *structure*【矿】带状构造,环带构造.
zon·a·ry [ˈzəunəri] *a*. 带(状)的,成带的.
zon·ate [ˈzəunit] *a*. 【动、植】有环带的,有轮层带的.
zo·na·tion [zəuˈneiʃən] *n*. 分带〔如颜色〕; 【生】成带(现象).
zone [zəun] *n*. ①【地理】(地)带. ②区域,范围,界. ③〔古、诗〕(腰)带. ④圈,环带. ⑤【数】(球面)带; 【物】晶带; 晶层. ⑥〔美〕(为计算邮包寄费而划分的)邮包区 (= parcel post zone). ⑦【自】(穿孔卡片顶部的)三行区. *the frigid* [*temperate*, *torrid*] ~ 寒〔温、热〕带. *a fortified* ~ 要塞地带. *the* ~ *of action* 作战区域. *a school* [*business*, *residence*] ~ 学校〔商业、住宅〕区. *the* ~ *of influence* 势力范围. *soil* ~ 土层. ***loose the maiden* ~ *of*** 破坏…的处女童贞. — *vt*. ①用带圈绕. ②把…分成地带. ~ **defence** 区域联防. ~ **time** 地方时〔*Greenwich* 标准时之对〕.
zone-plate [ˈzəunpleit] *n*. 【光】同心圆绕射板,波带片,波域片.
zon·ing [ˈzəuniŋ] *n*. ①〔美〕分区制,分区布局; (邮包)区域制. ②分区取样. ~ **commission** 城市规划委员会.
zonked [zɔŋkt] *a*. 〔美俚〕烂醉如泥的; (被麻醉品)麻醉了的.
zon·ta club [ˈzɔntə] *n*. 〔美〕(各行业的)女经理人互助福利俱乐部.
zon·ule [ˈzəunju:l] *n*. 【解】小带. **zon·u·lar** *a*.
zoo [zu:] *n*. ①〔口〕动物园〔*zoological garden* 的缩写〕; 〔the Z-〕伦敦动物园. ②〔美俚〕(铁路货车的最后一节)守车.
zoo- *comb. f*. 动物(生活); 游动; *zoo*blast, *zoo*gamete.
zo·o·blast [ˈzəuəublæst] *n*. 【生】动物细胞.
zo·o·chem·is·try [ˌzəuəuˈkemistri] *n*. 动物化学.
zo·o·dy·nam·ics [ˌzəuəudaiˈnæmiks] *n*. 动物动力学.
zo·oe·ci·um [ˈzəui:siəm] *n*. 【动】(苔藓虫的) 虫室,虫胞.
zo·o·gam·ete [ˌzəuəˈgæmi:t, -gəˈmi:t] *n*. 【生】游动配子.
zo·og·a·my [zəuˈɔgəmi] *n*. 【生】有性生殖.
zo·o·gen·ic [ˌzəuəˈdʒenik] *a*. 原于动物的,由动物感染的,从动物蔓延的〔如疾病〕(= zoogenous).
zo·og·e·ny [zəuˈɔdʒini] *n*. 动物发生论.
zo·o·ge·og·ra·phy [zəuədʒiˈɔgrəfi] *n*. 动物(分布)地理学. **-ra·pher** *n*. **-graph·ic** [ˌzəuədʒiəˈgræfik], **-graph·i·cal** *a*.
zo·o·gloe·a [ˌzəuəˈgli:ə] *n*. *(pl*. ***-ae*** *[-i:])* 【生】菌胶团,粘液聚落. **-l**, **-gloe·ic** *a*.
zo·og·o·ny [zəuˈɔgəni] *n*. ① = zoogeny. ②胎生.
zo·o·graft [ˈzəuəugrɑ:ft] *n*. 【医】动物质的人体移植. **~ing** *n*. 动物移植术.
zo·og·ra·pher [zəuˈɔgrəfə], **zo·og·raph·ist** [-fist] *n*. 动物志学家.
zo·o·graph·ic [zəuəˈgræfik] *a*. 动物志的.
zo·og·ra·phy [zəuˈɔgrəfi] *n*. 动物志学.
zo·oid [ˈzəuɔid], **zo·oi·dal** [zəuˈɔidl] *a*. 动物性的,象动物的. — *n*. 【动】(分裂增殖后生成的)独立个体; 【生】(构成群体的)个体; 游动孢子.
zool. = ①zoological. ②zoology.
zo·ol·a·ter [zəuˈɔlətə] *n*. 动物崇拜者.
zo·ol·a·try [zəuˈɔlətri] *n*. 动物崇拜.
zo·o·lite [ˈzəuəlait] *n*. 化石动物; 动物化石.
zo·o·log·i·cal [ˌzəuəˈlɔdʒikəl] *a*. 动物学(上)的. ~ ***garden(s)*** 动物园. **-ly** *ad*.
zo·ol·o·gist [zəuˈɔlədʒist] *n*. 动物学家.
zo·ol·o·gy [zəuˈɔlədʒi] *n*. ①动物学. ②(某一地区的)全部动物; (某种动物的)动物特性〔特征〕.
zoom [zu:m] *vi*., *vt*. ①(使)作嗡嗡声; 嗡嗡地活动. ②【空】(使)陡直上升; (使)迅速上升; 激增; 〔俚〕(使)大受欢迎,大成功; (使)价格直线上涨. ③【电视】用可变焦距镜头迅速将摄像机对准〔移离〕(目标). — *n*. ①直线上升; 激增. ②嗡嗡声. ③【摄】可变焦距镜头 (= ~ lens). **-er** 可变焦距镜头. **-y** *a*. 使用可变焦距镜头拍摄的.
zo·o·mag·net·ism [zəuəuˈmægnitizəm] *n*. 动物磁(现象).
zoo·man [ˈzu:mən] *n*. 〔美〕动物园动物饲养员.
zo·o·me·chan·ics [ˌzəuəumiˈkæniks] *n*. = zoodynamics.
zo·om·e·ter [zəuˈɔmitə] *n*. 动物数计.
zo·om·e·try [zəuˈɔmitri] *n*. 动物躯体测定学. **zo·o·met·ric** [ˌzəuəˈmetrik] *a*.
zo·o·mor·phic [ˌzəuəuˈmɔ:fik] *a*. 动物形的; 兽形的.
zo·o·mor·phism [ˌzəuəuˈmɔ:fizm] *n*. ①(崇拜对象〔神〕的)动物形态〔特征〕. ②动物图案(法).
zoon [ˈzəuɔn] *n*. *(pl*. ***zoa*** *[ˈzəuə])*, 动物; 群生动物中的个体.
-zoon *suf*. = zoon.
zo·on·ic [zəuˈɔnik] *a*. 动物的; 动物质的.
zo·on·o·my [zəuˈɔnəmi] *n*. 动物生理学.
zo·on·o·sis [zəuˈɔnəsis, ˌzəuəˈnəusis] *n*. *(pl*. ***-on·o·ses*** *[-ˈɔnəˌsi:z, -əˈnəusi:z])* 【医】(可由脊椎动物传染的)传人动物病. **-not·ic** [-ˈnɔtik] *a*.
zo·o·par·a·site [ˌzəuəuˈpærəsait] *n*. 寄生动物. **-sit·ic** [-ˈsitik] *a*.
zo·o·pa·thol·o·gy [zəuəupəˈθɔlədʒi] *n*. 动物病理学.
zo·oph·a·ga [zəuˈɔfəgə] *n*. 〔*pl*.〕【动】食肉动物.
zo·oph·a·gan [zəuˈɔfəgən] *n*. 【动】食肉动物.

zo•oph•a•gous [zəuˈɔfəgəs] *a.* 食肉(动物)的.
zo•o•phile [ˈzəuəfail] *n.* ①【植】以动物为媒介传播的植物. ②动物爱护者. **zo•o•phil•ic** [ˈzəuəfilik] *a.* 爱护动物的.
zo•oph•i•lism [zəuˈɔfilizm] *n.* 【心,医】动物喜爱癖〔尤指具有性变态心理的〕(= zoophily, zoophilia). **-phil•ic** *a.*
zo•oph•i•list [zəuˈɔfilist] *n.* 动物爱护者; 有动物喜爱癖者.
zo•oph•i•lous [zəuˈɔfiləs] *a.* ①动物喜爱癖的. ②【植】以动物为媒(授粉)的.
zo•oph•i•ly [zəˈɔfili] *n.* = zoophilism.
zo•o•pho•bi•a [ˌzəuəuˈfəubjə] *n.* 【心, 医】动物恐怖(症); 对动物的恐惧.
zo•o•phys•ics [zəuəuˈfiziks] *n.* 动物构造学; 比较动物解剖学.
zo•o•phyte [ˈzəuəfait] *n.* *(pl. zoophyta)* 【动】植物形动物〔海盘车、珊瑚虫等〕. **-phyt•ic** *a.*
zo•o•phy•tol•o•gy [zəuəfaiˈtɔlədʒi] *n.* 植物形动物学. **-gist** *n.*
zo•o•plank•ton [ˌzəuəˈplæŋktən] *n.* 【动】浮游动物. **-ic** [-ˈtɔnik] *a.*
zo•o•plas•ty [ˈzəuəuˈplæsti] *n.* 【医】动物组织人体移植术. **-tic** *a.*
zo•o•psy•chol•o•gy [zəuəusaiˈkɔlədʒi] *n.* 动物心理学.
zo•o•sperm [ˈzəuəspəːm] *n.* 【动】游动精子;【植】游动孢子.
zo•o•spo•ran•gi•um [ˌzəuəspəˈrændʒiəm] *n.* *(pl. -gia [-ə])* 【植】游动孢子囊. **-ran•gi•al** [-əl] *a.*
zo•o•spore [ˈzəuəspɔː] *n.* 【植】游动孢子.
zo•os•ter•ol [zəuˈɔstəˌrɔːl, -ˌrəul] *n.* 【生化】动物甾醇.
zo•o•tax•y [ˈzəuətæksi] *n.* 动物分类学, 动物系统学.
zo•o•tech•ny [ˈzəuəˌtekni] *n.* 畜牧学.
zo•o•the•ism [ˈzəuəθiːizəm] *n.* 动物神崇拜.
zo•ot•o•mist [zəuˈɔtəmist] *n.* 动物解剖学家.
zo•ot•o•my [zəuˈɔtəmi] *n.* 动物解剖(学).
zo•o•to•xin [ˈzəuətɔksin] *n.* 动物(性)毒素.
zoot suit [zuːt ˈsjuːt] *n.*〔美〕阻特装〔四十年代流行于爵士音乐迷等类人中的上衣达膝、裤子狭窄的一种服装〕. **zoot-suit** *a.* **zoot-suiter** *n.* 穿阻特装的人.
zo•ri [ˈzəuri] *n.* *(pl. zo•ris, zo•ri)* 〔Jap.〕(草)屐.
zor•il [ˈzɔril] *n.* 【动】南非臭猫.
Zor•o•as•tri•an [zɔrəuˈæstriən] *a.* 拜火教的, 祆教的. — *n.* 拜火教徒, 祆教徒. **-ism** *n.* 拜火教, 祆教.
zos•ter [ˈzɔstə] *n.* (古希腊男子用的)腰带; 【医】带状疱疹.
Zos•ter•ops [ˈzɔstərɔps] *n.* 【鸟】绣眼儿属; 〔z-〕 绣眼儿属的鸟.
zou•ave [zuːˈɑːv] *n.* ①〔or Z-〕(穿阿拉伯式制服的)法国轻步兵; (美国南北战争时穿阿拉伯式制服的)义勇兵. ②女用绣花短上衣〔又称 ~ jacket〕.
zounds [zaundz] *int.* 〔英〕〔古〕咄!〔诅咒语, 表示愤怒或惊奇〕.
zo•wie [ˈzaui] *int.* 〔美俚〕好! 要得! 啧!〔表示赞成, 称赞, 兴奋等〕.
zoy•si•a [ˈzɔisiə] *n.* 【植】结缕草属 *(Zoysia)* 植物〔如结缕草 *(Z. japonica)*, 沟叶结缕草 *(Z. matrella)* 等〕.
ZPG = zero population growth 零人口增长率.
ZPI = zone position indicator 分区位置指示器.
Zr = 【化】zirconium.
Z.S. = Zoological Society 〔英〕动物学会.
Z.S.T. = Zone Standard Time 标准区时.
ZT = ①zone time 区时. ②zero time 零时.
Zu [zuː] *n.* (古巴比伦的)风雨神.
zuc•chet•to [tsuˈketəu] *n.* 【天主】(神职人员所戴, 以不同颜色区别教阶的)圆形小帽.
zuc•chi•ni [zuːˈkiːniː] *n.* *(pl. -ni, -nis)* 〔美〕【植】绿皮西葫芦.
Zu•lu [ˈzuːluː] *n., a.* ①(非洲东南部班图族的一支)祖鲁人(的); 祖鲁语(的). ②通讯中用以代表字母 z 的词.
Zu•ñi [ˈzuːnji, ˈsuː-] *n.* (居住于美国 New Mexico 西部印第安村落的)祖尼族〔人〕. **-an** *n., a.* 祖尼人(的).
zwie•back [ˈzwiːbæk] *n.* 〔G.〕 面包干.
zwit•ter•i•on [ˈtsvitəraiən] *n.* 【化】两性离子〔Zwitter〔G.〕 = hybrid〕.
zyg•a•poph•y•sis [ˌzigəˈpɔfisis, ˌzaigə-] *n.* *(pl. -ses [-ˌsiːz])* 【动、解】脊椎关节突. **-ophys•e•al** *a.*
zy•go- *comb. f.* 轭状的, 成对的.
zy•go•dac•tyl(e) [ˌzaigəuˈdæktil] *a.* 【鸟】前后各有一双趾的. — *n.* 对趾鸟, 攀禽. **-tyl•ic, -ty•lous** *a.* **zy•go•dac•tyl•ism** [-izəm] *n.* (前后各有一双趾) 对趾形态.
zy•go•gen•e•sis [ˌzaigəuˈdʒenisis] *n.* 【生】合子形成. **-ge•net•ic** *a.*
zy•goid [ˈzaigɔid] *a.* 【生】合子的, 受精卵的.
zy•go•ma [zaiˈgəumə] *n.* *(pl. ~ta [-tə])* 【解】颧骨; 颧弓. **-mat•ic** *a.* (*zygomatic arch* 颧弓. *zygomatic bone* 颧骨. *zygomatic process* 颧突).
zy•go•mor•phic [ˌzaigəuˈmɔːfik] *a.* 【生】两侧对称的, (生物、器官等的)从中轴可等分的 (= zygomorphous). **-mor•phism, -mor•phy** *n.*
zy•go•my•cete [ˌzaigəuˈmaisiːt] *n.* 【微】接合菌.
zy•go•phyl•la•ceae [ˌzaigəufiˈleisiiː, ˌzigə-] *n.* 〔*pl.*〕【植】蒺藜科. **-ceous** *a.*
Zy•go•phyl•lum [ˌzaigəufiləm] *n.* 【植】霸王属.
zy•go•phyte [ˈzaigəufait] *n.* 【植】合子植物, 接合植物.
zy•go•sis [zaiˈgəusis] *n.* 【生】结合.
zy•go•sperm, zy•go•spore [ˈzaigəuspəːm, -spɔː] *n.* 【生】接合孢子, 合子.
zy•gote [ˈzaigəut] *n.* 【生】合子, 接合孢子; 接合体; 受精卵.
zy•go•tene [ˈzaigəˌtiːn, ˈzigə-] *n.* 【生】偶线(期).
zy•mase [ˈzaimeis] *n.* 【生化】酒化酶, 酿酶.
zyme [zaim] *n.* 【生化】酶.
zy•m(o)- [ˈzaiməu-] *comb. f.* 酶, 酵母; 发酵: *zymogene.*
zy•mo•gen(e) [ˈzaimədʒen] *n.* 【化】酶原.
zy•mo•gen•e•sis [ˌzaiməˈdʒenisis] *n.* 【生化】激酶作用, 产酶作用.
zy•mo•gen•ic [ˌzaiməuˈdʒenik] *a.* 【生化】酶原的(= zymogenous).
zy•mol•o•gy [zaiˈmɔlədʒi] *n.* 【生化】 酶〔发酵〕学. **zy•mol•o•gist** [-ˈmɔlədʒist] *n.* 【生化】酶〔发酵〕学家.
zy•mol•y•sis [zaiˈmɔlisis] *n.* 【生化】发酵; 酶解(作用). **-lyt•ic** *a.*
zy•mom•e•ter [zaiˈmɔmitə], **zy•mo•sim•e•ter** [zaiməuˈsimitə] *n.* 发酵计, 验酿器, 发酵检验器.
zy•mo•plas•tic [ˌzaiməuˈplæstik] *a.* 形成酵素的; 凝血的.
zy•mo•scope [ˈzaiməuskəup] *n.* 发酵力计.
zy•mo•sis [zaiˈməusis] *n.* 发酵; 【医】发酵病, 传染病.
zy•mos•ter•ol [ˌzaiˈmɔstərəl] *n.* 【化】酵母甾醇.
zy•mo•tech•nics [ˌzaiməuˈtekniks] *n.* 发酵法, 酿造法.
zy• mot•ic [zaiˈmɔtik] *a.* 发酵(作用)的; 发酵引起的.
zy•mur•gy [ˈzaiməːdʒi] *n.* 酿造学.
zy•thum [ˈzaiθəm] *n.* 古埃及的啤酒.
ZZZ ①〔拟声〕打鼾声. ②= zigzag.